MORRIS AUTOMATED INFORMATION NETWORK
0 1029 0687386 8

D1238451

About Peterson's

Peterson's®, a Nelnet company, has been your trusted educational publisher for over 50 years. It's a milestone we're quite proud of, as we continue to offer the most accurate, dependable, high-quality education content in the field, providing you with everything you need to succeed. No matter where you are on your academic or professional path, you can rely on Peterson's for its books, online information, expert test-prep tools, the most up-to-date education exploration data, and the highest quality career success resources—everything you need to achieve your educational goals For our complete line of products, visit **www.petersons.com.**

For more information, contact Peterson's, 3 Columbia Circle, Suite 205, Albany, NY 12203-5158; 800-338-3282 Ext. 54229; or find us online at **www.petersons.com.**

ISSN 1093-8443
ISBN: 978-0-7689-4170-8

Printed in the United States of America

10 9 8 7 6 5 4 3 2 1 20 19 18

Fifty-second Edition

PETERSON'S®
GRADUATE PROGRAMS IN BUSINESS, EDUCATION, INFORMATION STUDIES, LAW & SOCIAL WORK

2018

CONTENTS

ACADEMIC AND PROFESSIONAL PROGRAMS IN EDUCATION

A Note from the Peterson's Editors

The six volumes of Peterson's *Graduate and Professional Programs*, the only annually updated reference work of its kind, provide wide-ranging information on the graduate and professional programs offered by accredited colleges and universities in the United States, U.S. territories, and Canada and by those institutions outside the United States that are accredited by U.S. accrediting bodies. More than 44,000 individual academic and professional programs at approximately 2,200 institutions are listed. Peterson's *Graduate and Professional Programs* have been used for more than fifty years by prospective graduate and professional students, placement counselors, faculty advisers, and all others interested in postbaccalaureate education.

Graduate & Professional Programs: An Overview contains information on institutions as a whole, while the other books in the series are devoted to specific academic and professional fields:

- ***Graduate Programs in the Biological/Biomedical Sciences & Health-Related Medical Professions***
- ***Graduate Programs in Business, Education, Information Studies, Law & Social Work***
- ***Graduate Programs in Engineering & Applied Sciences***
- ***Graduate Programs in the Humanities, Arts & Social Sciences***
- ***Graduate Programs in the Physical Sciences, Mathematics, Agricultural Sciences, the Environment & Natural Resources***

The books may be used individually or as a set. For example, if you have chosen a field of study but do not know what institution you want to attend or if you have a college or university in mind but have not chosen an academic field of study, it is best to begin with the Overview guide.

Graduate & Professional Programs: An Overview presents several directories to help you identify programs of study that might interest you; you can then research those programs further in the other books in the series by using the Directory of Graduate and Professional Programs by Field, which lists 500 fields and gives the names of those institutions that offer graduate degree programs in each.

For geographical or financial reasons, you may be interested in attending a particular institution and will want to know what it has to offer. You should turn to the Directory of Institutions and Their Offerings, which lists the degree programs available at each institution. As in the Directory of Graduate and Professional Programs by Field, the level of degrees offered is also indicated.

All books in the series include advice on graduate education, including topics such as admissions tests, financial aid, and accreditation. **The Graduate Adviser** includes two essays and information about accreditation. The first essay, "The Admissions Process," discusses general admission requirements, admission tests, factors to consider when selecting a graduate school or program, when and how to apply, and how admission decisions are made. Special information for international students and tips for minority students are also included. The second essay, "Financial Support," is an overview of the broad range of support available at the graduate level. Fellowships, scholarships, and grants; assistantships and internships; federal and private loan programs, as well as Federal Work-Study; and the GI bill are detailed. This essay concludes with advice on applying for need-based financial aid. "Accreditation and Accrediting Agencies" gives information on accreditation and its purpose and lists institutional accrediting agencies first and then specialized accrediting agencies relevant to each volume's specific fields of study.

With information on more than 40,000 graduate programs in more than 500 disciplines, Peterson's *Graduate and Professional Programs* give you all the information you need about the programs that are of interest to you in three formats: **Profiles** (capsule summaries of basic information), **Displays** (information that an institution or program wants to emphasize), and **Close-Ups** (written by administrators, with more expansive information than the **Profiles**, emphasizing different aspects of the programs). By using these various formats of program information, coupled with **Appendixes** and **Indexes** covering directories and subject areas for all six books, you will find that these guides provide the most comprehensive, accurate, and up-to-date graduate study information available.

Peterson's publishes a full line of resources with information you need to guide you through the graduate admissions process. Peterson's publications can be found at college libraries and career centers and your local bookstore or library—or visit us on the Web at www.petersons.com.

Colleges and universities will be pleased to know that Peterson's helped you in your selection. Admissions staff members are more than happy to answer questions, address specific problems, and help in any way they can. The editors at Peterson's wish you great success in your graduate program search!

THE GRADUATE ADVISER

The Admissions Process

Generalizations about graduate admissions practices are not always helpful because each institution has its own set of guidelines and procedures. Nevertheless, some broad statements can be made about the admissions process that may help you plan your strategy.

Factors Involved in Selecting a Graduate School or Program

Selecting a graduate school and a specific program of study is a complex matter. Quality of the faculty; program and course offerings; the nature, size, and location of the institution; admission requirements; cost; and the availability of financial assistance are among the many factors that affect one's choice of institution. Other considerations are job placement and achievements of the program's graduates and the institution's resources, such as libraries, laboratories, and computer facilities. If you are to make the best possible choice, you need to learn as much as you can about the schools and programs you are considering before you apply.

The following steps may help you narrow your choices.

- Talk to alumni of the programs or institutions you are considering to get their impressions of how well they were prepared for work in their fields of study.
- Remember that graduate school requirements change, so be sure to get the most up-to-date information possible.
- Talk to department faculty members and the graduate adviser at your undergraduate institution. They often have information about programs of study at other institutions.
- Visit the websites of the graduate schools in which you are interested to request a graduate catalog. Contact the department chair in your chosen field of study for additional information about the department and the field.
- Visit as many campuses as possible. Call ahead for an appointment with the graduate adviser in your field of interest and be sure to check out the facilities and talk to students.

General Requirements

Graduate schools and departments have requirements that applicants for admission must meet. Typically, these requirements include undergraduate transcripts (which provide information about undergraduate grade point average and course work applied toward a major), admission test scores, and letters of recommendation. Most graduate programs also ask for an essay or personal statement that describes your personal reasons for seeking graduate study. In some fields, such as art and music, portfolios or auditions may be required in addition to other evidence of talent. Some institutions require that the applicant have an undergraduate degree in the same subject as the intended graduate major.

Most institutions evaluate each applicant on the basis of the applicant's total record, and the weight accorded any given factor varies widely from institution to institution and from program to program.

The Application Process

You should begin the application process at least one year before you expect to begin your graduate study. Find out the application deadline for each institution (many are provided in the **Profile** section of this guide). Go to the institution's website and find out if you can apply online. If not, request a paper application form. Fill out this form thoroughly and neatly. Assume that the school needs all the information it is requesting and that the admissions officer will be sensitive to the neatness and overall quality of what you submit. Do not supply more information than the school requires.

The institution may ask at least one question that will require a three- or four-paragraph answer. Compose your response on the assumption that the admissions officer is interested in both what you think and how you express yourself. Keep your statement brief and to the point, but, at the same time, include all pertinent information about your past experiences and your educational goals. Individual statements vary greatly in style and content, which helps admissions officers differentiate among applicants. Many graduate departments give considerable weight to the statement in making their admissions decisions, so be sure to take the time to prepare a thoughtful and concise statement.

If recommendations are a part of the admissions requirements, carefully choose the individuals you ask to write them. It is generally best to ask current or former professors to write the recommendations, provided they are able to attest to your intellectual ability and motivation for doing the work required of a graduate student. It is advisable to provide stamped, preaddressed envelopes to people being asked to submit recommendations on your behalf.

Completed applications, including references, transcripts, and admission test scores, should be received at the institution by the specified date.

Be advised that institutions do not usually make admissions decisions until all materials have been received. Enclose a self-addressed postcard with your application, requesting confirmation of receipt. Allow at least ten days for the return of the postcard before making further inquiries.

If you plan to apply for financial support, it is imperative that you file your application early.

ADMISSION TESTS

The major testing program used in graduate admissions is the Graduate Record Examinations (GRE®) testing program, sponsored by the GRE Board and administered by Educational Testing Service, Princeton, New Jersey.

The Graduate Record Examinations testing program consists of a General Test and eight Subject Tests. The General Test measures critical thinking, verbal reasoning, quantitative reasoning, and analytical writing skills. It is offered as an Internet-based test (iBT) in the United States, Canada, and many other countries.

The GRE® General Test's questions were designed to reflect the kind of thinking that students need to do in graduate or business school and demonstrate that students are indeed ready for graduate-level work.

- **Verbal Reasoning**—Measures ability to analyze and evaluate written material and synthesize information obtained from it, analyze relationships among component parts of sentences, and recognize relationships among words and concepts.
- **Quantitative Reasoning**—Measures problem-solving ability, focusing on basic concepts of arithmetic, algebra, geometry, and data analysis.
- **Analytical Writing**—Measures critical thinking and analytical writing skills, specifically the ability to articulate and support complex ideas clearly and effectively.

The computer-based GRE® General Test is offered year-round at Prometric™ test centers and on specific dates at testing locations outside of the Prometric test center network. Appointments are scheduled on a first-come, first-served basis. The GRE® General Test is also offered as a paper-based test three times a year in areas where computer-based testing is not available.

You can take the computer-based GRE® General Test once every twenty-one days, up to five times within any continuous rolling twelve-month period (365 days)—even if you canceled your scores on a previously taken test. You may take the paper-based GRE® General Test as often as it is offered.

Three scores are reported on the revised General Test:

1. A **Verbal Reasoning score** is reported on a 130–170 score scale, in 1-point increments.
2. A **Quantitative Reasoning score** is reported on a 130–170 score scale, in 1-point increments.
3. An **Analytical Writing score** is reported on a 0–6 score level, in half-point increments.

The GRE® Subject Tests measure achievement and assume undergraduate majors or extensive background in the following eight disciplines:

- Biochemistry, Cell and Molecular Biology
- Biology
- Chemistry
- Computer Science
- Literature in English
- Mathematics
- Physics
- Psychology

The Subject Tests are available three times per year as paper-based administrations around the world. Testing time is approximately 2 hours and 50 minutes. You can obtain more information about the GRE® by visiting the ETS website at www.ets.org or consulting the *GRE® Information and Registration Bulletin.* The *Bulletin* can be obtained at many undergraduate colleges. You can also download it from the ETS website or obtain it by contacting Graduate Record Examinations, Educational Testing Service, P.O. Box 6000, Princeton, NJ 08541-6000; phone: 609-771-7670.

If you expect to apply for admission to a program that requires any of the GRE® tests, you should select a test date well in advance of the application deadline. Scores on the computer-based General Test are reported within ten to fifteen days; scores on the paper-based Subject Tests are reported within six weeks.

Another testing program, the Miller Analogies Test® (MAT®), is administered at more than 500 Controlled Testing Centers, licensed by Pearson, in the United States, Canada, and other countries. The MAT® computer-based test is now available. Testing time is 60 minutes. The test consists of 120 partial analogies. You can obtain the *Candidate Information Booklet,* which contains a list of test centers and instructions for taking the test, from http://www.milleranalogies.com or by calling 800-328-5999 (toll-free).

Check the specific requirements of the programs to which you are applying.

How Admission Decisions Are Made

The program you apply to is directly involved in the admissions process. Although the final decision is usually made by the graduate dean (or an associate) or the faculty admissions committee, recommendations from faculty members in your intended field are important. At some institutions, an interview is incorporated into the decision process.

A Special Note for International Students

In addition to the steps already described, there are some special considerations for international students who intend to apply for graduate study in the United States. All graduate schools require an indication of competence in English. The purpose of the Test of English as a Foreign Language (TOEFL®) is to evaluate the English proficiency of people who are nonnative speakers of English and want to study at colleges and universities where English is the language of instruction. The TOEFL® is administered by Educational Testing Service (ETS) under the general direction of a policy board established by the College Board and the Graduate Record Examinations Board.

The TOEFL® iBT assesses the four basic language skills: listening, reading, writing, and speaking. It was administered for the first time in September 2005, and ETS continues to introduce the TOEFL® iBT in selected cities. The Internet-based test is administered at secure, official test centers. The testing time is approximately 4 hours. Because the TOEFL® iBT includes a speaking section, the Test of Spoken English (TSE) is no longer needed.

The TOEFL® is also offered in the paper-based format in areas of the world where Internet-based testing is not available. The paper-based TOEFL® consists of three sections—listening comprehension, structure and written expression, and reading comprehension.

The TOEFL® paper-based test (TOEFL® PBT) began being phased out in mid-2012. For those who may have taken the TOEFL® PBT, scores remain valid for two years after the test date. The Test of Written English (TWE®) is also given. The TWE® is a 30-minute essay that measures the examinee's ability to compose in English. Examinees receive a TWE® score separate from their TOEFL® score. The *Information Bulletin* contains information on local fees and registration procedures.

Additional information and registration materials are available from TOEFL® Services, Educational Testing Service, P.O. Box 6151, Princeton, New Jersey 08541-6151. Phone: 609-771-7100. Website: www.toefl.org.

International students should apply especially early because of the number of steps required to complete the admissions process. Furthermore, many United States graduate schools have a limited number of spaces for international students, and many more students apply than the schools can accommodate.

International students may find financial assistance from institutions very limited. The U.S. government requires international applicants to submit a certification of support, which is a statement attesting to the applicant's financial resources. In addition, international students *must* have health insurance coverage.

Tips for Minority Students

Indicators of a university's values in terms of diversity are found both in its recruitment programs and its resources directed to student success. Important questions: Does the institution vigorously recruit minorities for its graduate programs? Is there funding available to help with the costs associated with visiting the school? Are minorities represented in the institution's brochures or website or on their faculty rolls? What campus-based resources or services (including assistance in locating housing or career counseling and placement) are available? Is funding available to members of underrepresented groups?

At the program level, it is particularly important for minority students to investigate the "climate" of a program under consideration. How many minority students are enrolled and how many have graduated? What opportunities are there to work with diverse faculty and mentors whose research interests match yours? How are conflicts resolved or concerns addressed? How interested are faculty in building strong and supportive relations with students? "Climate" concerns should be addressed by posing questions to various individuals, including faculty members, current students, and alumni.

Information is also available through various organizations, such as the Hispanic Association of Colleges & Universities (HACU), and publications such as *Diverse Issues in Higher Education* and *Hispanic Outlook* magazine. There are also books devoted to this topic, such as *The Multicultural Student's Guide to Colleges* by Robert Mitchell.

Financial Support

The range of financial support at the graduate level is very broad. The following descriptions will give you a general idea of what you might expect and what will be expected of you as a financial support recipient.

Fellowships, Scholarships, and Grants

These are usually outright awards of a few hundred to many thousands of dollars with no service to the institution required in return. Fellowships and scholarships are usually awarded on the basis of merit and are highly competitive. Grants are made on the basis of financial need or special talent in a field of study. Many fellowships, scholarships, and grants not only cover tuition, fees, and supplies but also include stipends for living expenses with allowances for dependents. However, the terms of each should be examined because some do not permit recipients to supplement their income with outside work. Fellowships, scholarships, and grants may vary in the number of years for which they are awarded.

In addition to the availability of these funds at the university or program level, many excellent fellowship programs are available at the national level and may be applied for before and during enrollment in a graduate program. A listing of many of these programs can be found at the Council of Graduate Schools' website: http://www.cgsnet.org. There is a wealth of information in the "Programs" and "Awards" sections.

Assistantships and Internships

Many graduate students receive financial support through assistantships, particularly involving teaching or research duties. It is important to recognize that such appointments should not be viewed simply as employment relationships but rather should constitute an integral and important part of a student's graduate education. As such, the appointments should be accompanied by strong faculty mentoring and increasingly responsible apprenticeship experiences. The specific nature of these appointments in a given program should be considered in selecting that graduate program.

TEACHING ASSISTANTSHIPS

These usually provide a salary and full or partial tuition remission and may also provide health benefits. Unlike fellowships, scholarships, and grants, which require no service to the institution, teaching assistantships require recipients to provide the institution with a specific amount of undergraduate teaching, ideally related to the student's field of study. Some teaching assistants are limited to grading papers, compiling bibliographies, taking notes, or monitoring laboratories. At some graduate schools, teaching assistants must carry lighter course loads than regular full-time students.

RESEARCH ASSISTANTSHIPS

These are very similar to teaching assistantships in the manner in which financial assistance is provided. The difference is that recipients are given basic research assignments in their disciplines rather than teaching responsibilities. The work required is normally related to the student's field of study; in most instances, the assistantship supports the student's thesis or dissertation research.

ADMINISTRATIVE INTERNSHIPS

These are similar to assistantships in application of financial assistance funds, but the student is given an assignment on a part-time basis, usually as a special assistant with one of the university's administrative offices. The assignment may not necessarily be directly related to the recipient's discipline.

RESIDENCE HALL AND COUNSELING ASSISTANTSHIPS

These assistantships are frequently assigned to graduate students in psychology, counseling, and social work, but they may be offered to students in other disciplines, especially if the student has worked in this capacity during his or her undergraduate years. Duties can vary from being available in a dean's office for a specific number of hours for consultation with undergraduates to living in campus residences and being responsible for both counseling and administrative tasks or advising student activity groups. Residence hall assistantships often include a room and board allowance and, in some cases, tuition assistance and stipends. Contact the Housing and Student Life Office for more information.

Health Insurance

The availability and affordability of health insurance is an important issue and one that should be considered in an applicant's choice of institution and program. While often included with assistantships and fellowships, this is not always the case and, even if provided, the benefits may be limited. It is important to note that the U.S. government requires international students to have health insurance.

The GI Bill

This provides financial assistance for students who are veterans of the United States armed forces. If you are a veteran, contact your local Veterans Administration office to determine your eligibility and to get full details about benefits. There are a number of programs that offer educational benefits to current military enlistees. Some states have tuition assistance programs for members of the National Guard. Contact the VA office at the college for more information.

Federal Work-Study Program (FWS)

Employment is another way some students finance their graduate studies. The federally funded Federal Work-Study Program provides eligible students with employment opportunities, usually in public and private nonprofit organizations. Federal funds pay up to 75 percent of the wages, with the remainder paid by the employing agency. FWS is available to graduate students who demonstrate financial need. Not all schools have these funds, and some only award them to undergraduates. Each school sets its application deadline and workstudy earnings limits. Wages vary and are related to the type of work done. You must file the Free Application for Federal Student Aid (FAFSA) to be eligible for this program.

Loans

Many graduate students borrow to finance their graduate programs when other sources of assistance (which do not have to be repaid) prove insufficient. You should always read and understand the terms of any loan program before submitting your application.

FEDERAL DIRECT LOANS

Federal Direct Loans. The Federal Direct Loan Program offers a variable-fixed interest rate loan to graduate students with the Department of Education acting as the lender. Students receive a new rate with each new loan, but that rate is fixed for the life of the loan. Beginning with loans made on or after July 1, 2013, the interest rate for loans made each July 1st to June 30th period are determined based on the last 10-year Treasury note auction prior to June 1st of that year, plus an added percentage. The interest rate can be no higher than 9.5%.

Beginning July 1, 2012, the Federal Direct Loan for graduate students is an unsubsidized loan. Under the *unsubsidized* program, the grad borrower pays the interest on the loan from the day proceeds are issued and is responsible for paying interest during all periods. If the borrower chooses not to pay the interest while in school, or during the grace periods, deferment, or forbearance, the interest accrues and will be capitalized.

Graduate students may borrow up to $20,500 per year through the Direct Loan Program, up to a cumulative maximum of $138,500, including undergraduate borrowing. No more than $65,500 of the $138,500 can be from subsidized loans, including loans the grad borrower may have received for periods of enrollment that began before July 1, 2012, or for prior undergraduate borrowing. You may borrow up to the cost of attendance at the school in which you are enrolled or will attend, minus estimated financial assistance from other federal, state, and private sources, up to a maximum of $20,500. Grad borrowers who reach the aggregate loan limit over the course of their education cannot receive additional loans; however, if they repay some of their loans to bring the outstanding balance below the aggregate limit, they could be eligible to borrow again, up to that limit.

For Unsubsidized loans first disbursed on or after July 1, 2016, and before July 1, 2017, the interest rate was 5.31%. For those first disbursed on or after July 1, 2017, and before July 1, 2018, the interest rate is 6%.

A fee is deducted from the loan proceeds upon disbursement. Loans with a first disbursement on or after July 1, 2010 but before July 1, 2012, have a borrower origination fee of 1 percent. For loans disbursed after July 1, 2012, these fee deductions no longer apply. The Budget Control Act of 2011, signed into law on August 2, 2011, eliminated Direct Subsidized Loan eligibility for graduate and professional students for periods of enrollment beginning on or after July 1, 2012, and terminated the authority of the Department of Education to offer most repayment incentives to Direct Loan borrowers for loans disbursed on or after July 1, 2012.

Under the *subsidized* Federal Direct Loan Program, repayment begins six months after your last date of enrollment on at least a half-time basis. Under the *unsubsidized* program, repayment of interest begins within thirty days from disbursement of the loan proceeds, and repayment of the principal begins six months after your last enrollment on at least a half-time basis. Some borrowers may choose to defer interest payments while they are in school. The accrued interest is added to the loan balance when the borrower begins repayment. There are several repayment options.

Federal Perkins Loans. The Federal Perkins Loan is available to students demonstrating financial need and is administered directly by the school. Not all schools have these funds, and some may award them to undergraduates only. Eligibility is determined from the information you provide on the FAFSA. The school will notify you of your eligibility.

Eligible graduate students may borrow up to $8,000 per year, up to a maximum of $60,000, including undergraduate borrowing (even if your previous Perkins Loans have been repaid). The interest rate for Federal Perkins Loans is 5 percent, and no interest accrues while you remain in school at least half-time. Students who are attending less than half-time need to check with their school to determine the length of their grace period. There are no guarantee, loan, or disbursement fees. Repayment begins nine months after your last date of enrollment on at least a half-time basis and may extend over a maximum of ten years with no prepayment penalty.

Federal Direct Graduate PLUS Loans. Effective July 1, 2006, graduate and professional students are eligible for Graduate PLUS loans. This program allows students to borrow up to the cost of attendance, less any other aid received. These loans have a fixed interest rate (7.0% for the 2017–2018 academic year), and interest begins to accrue at the time of disbursement. Beginning with loans made on or after July 1, 2013, the interest rate for loans made each July 1st to June 30th period are determined based on the last 10-year Treasury note auction prior to June 1st of that year. The interest rate can be no higher than 10.5%. The PLUS loans do involve a credit check; a PLUS borrower may obtain a loan with a cosigner if his or her credit is not good enough. Grad PLUS loans may be deferred while a student is in school and for the six months following a drop below half-time enrollment. For more information, you should contact a representative in your college's financial aid office.

Deferring Your Federal Loan Repayments. If you borrowed under the Federal Direct Loan Program, Federal Direct PLUS Loan Program, or the Federal Perkins Loan Program for previous undergraduate or graduate study, your payments may be deferred when you return to graduate school, depending on when you borrowed and under which program.

There are other deferment options available if you are temporarily unable to repay your loan. Information about these deferments is provided at your entrance and exit interviews. If you believe you are eligible for a deferment of your loan payments, you must contact your lender or loan servicer to request a deferment. The deferment must be filed prior to the time your payment is due, and it must be re-filed when it expires if you remain eligible for deferment at that time.

SUPPLEMENTAL (PRIVATE) LOANS

Many lending institutions offer supplemental loan programs and other financing plans, such as the ones described here, to students seeking additional assistance in meeting their education expenses. Some loan programs target all types of graduate students; others are designed specifically for business, law, or medical students. In addition, you can use private loans not specifically designed for education to help finance your graduate degree.

If you are considering borrowing through a supplemental or private loan program, you should carefully consider the terms and be sure to read the fine print. Check with the program sponsor for the most current terms that will be applicable to the amounts you intend to borrow for graduate study. Most supplemental loan programs for graduate study offer unsubsidized, credit-based loans. In general, a credit-ready borrower is one who has a satisfactory credit history or no credit history at all. A creditworthy borrower generally must pass a credit test to be eligible to borrow or act as a cosigner for the loan funds.

Many supplemental loan programs have minimum and maximum annual loan limits. Some offer amounts equal to the cost of attendance minus any other aid you will receive for graduate study. If you are planning to borrow for several years of graduate study, consider whether there is a cumulative or aggregate limit on the amount you may borrow. Often this cumulative or aggregate limit will include any amounts you borrowed and have not repaid for undergraduate or previous graduate study.

The combination of the annual interest rate, loan fees, and the repayment terms you choose will determine how much you will repay over time. Compare these features in combination before you decide which loan program to use. Some loans offer interest rates that are adjusted monthly, quarterly, or annually. Some offer interest rates that are lower during the in-school, grace, and deferment periods and then increase when you begin repayment. Some programs include a loan origination fee, which is usually deducted from the principal amount you receive when the loan is disbursed and must be repaid along with the interest and other principal when you graduate, withdraw from school, or drop below half-time study. Sometimes the loan fees are reduced if you borrow with a qualified cosigner. Some programs allow you to defer interest and/or principal payments while you are enrolled in graduate school. Many programs allow you to capitalize your interest payments; the interest due on your loan is added to the outstanding balance of your loan, so you don't have to repay immediately, but this increases the amount you owe. Other programs allow you to pay the interest as you go, which reduces the amount you later have to repay. The private loan market is very competitive, and your financial aid office can help you evaluate these programs.

Applying for Need-Based Financial Aid

Schools that award federal and institutional financial assistance based on need will require you to complete the FAFSA and, in some cases, an institutional financial aid application.

If you are applying for federal student assistance, you **must** complete the FAFSA. A service of the U.S. Department of Education, the FAFSA is free to all applicants. Most applicants apply online at www.fafsa.ed.gov. Paper applications are available at the financial aid office of your local college.

After your FAFSA information has been processed, you will receive a Student Aid Report (SAR). If you provided an e-mail address on the FAFSA, this will be sent to you electronically; otherwise, it will be mailed to your home address.

Follow the instructions on the SAR if you need to correct information reported on your original application. If your situation changes after you file your FAFSA, contact your financial aid officer to discuss amending your information. You can also appeal your financial aid award if you have extenuating circumstances.

If you would like more information on federal student financial aid, visit the FAFSA website or download the most recent version of *Funding Education Beyond High School: The Guide to Federal Student Aid* at http://studentaid.ed.gov/students/publications/student_guide/index.html. This guide is also available in Spanish.

The U.S. Department of Education also has a toll-free number for questions concerning federal student aid programs. The number is 1-800-4-FED AID (1-800-433-3243). If you are hearing impaired, call toll-free, 1-800-730-8913.

Summary

Remember that these are generalized statements about financial assistance at the graduate level. Because each institution allots its aid differently, you should communicate directly with the school and the specific department of interest to you. It is not unusual, for example, to find that an endowment vested within a specific department supports one or more fellowships. You may fit its requirements and specifications precisely.

Accreditation and Accrediting Agencies

Colleges and universities in the United States, and their individual academic and professional programs, are accredited by nongovernmental agencies concerned with monitoring the quality of education in this country. Agencies with both regional and national jurisdictions grant accreditation to institutions as a whole, while specialized bodies acting on a nationwide basis—often national professional associations—grant accreditation to departments and programs in specific fields.

Institutional and specialized accrediting agencies share the same basic concerns: the purpose an academic unit—whether university or program—has set for itself and how well it fulfills that purpose, the adequacy of its financial and other resources, the quality of its academic offerings, and the level of services it provides. Agencies that grant institutional accreditation take a broader view, of course, and examine university-wide or college-wide services with which a specialized agency may not concern itself.

Both types of agencies follow the same general procedures when considering an application for accreditation. The academic unit prepares a self-evaluation, focusing on the concerns mentioned above and usually including an assessment of both its strengths and weaknesses; a team of representatives of the accrediting body reviews this evaluation, visits the campus, and makes its own report; and finally, the accrediting body makes a decision on the application. Often, even when accreditation is granted, the agency makes a recommendation regarding how the institution or program can improve. All institutions and programs are also reviewed every few years to determine whether they continue to meet established standards; if they do not, they may lose their accreditation.

Accrediting agencies themselves are reviewed and evaluated periodically by the U.S. Department of Education and the Council for Higher Education Accreditation (CHEA). Recognized agencies adhere to certain standards and practices, and their authority in matters of accreditation is widely accepted in the educational community.

This does not mean, however, that accreditation is a simple matter, either for schools wishing to become accredited or for students deciding where to apply. Indeed, in certain fields the very meaning and methods of accreditation are the subject of a good deal of debate. For their part, those applying to graduate school should be aware of the safeguards provided by regional accreditation, especially in terms of degree acceptance and institutional longevity. Beyond this, applicants should understand the role that specialized accreditation plays in their field, as this varies considerably from one discipline to another. In certain professional fields, it is necessary to have graduated from a program that is accredited in order to be eligible for a license to practice, and in some fields the federal government also makes this a hiring requirement. In other disciplines, however, accreditation is not as essential, and there can be excellent programs that are not accredited. In fact, some programs choose not to seek accreditation, although most do.

Institutions and programs that present themselves for accreditation are sometimes granted the status of candidate for accreditation, or what is known as "preaccreditation." This may happen, for example, when an academic unit is too new to have met all the requirements for accreditation. Such status signifies initial recognition and indicates that the school or program in question is working to fulfill all requirements; it does not, however, guarantee that accreditation will be granted.

Institutional Accrediting Agencies—Regional

MIDDLE STATES ASSOCIATION OF COLLEGES AND SCHOOLS

Accredits institutions in Delaware, District of Columbia, Maryland, New Jersey, New York, Pennsylvania, Puerto Rico, and the Virgin Islands.

Dr. Elizabeth Sibolski, President
Middle States Commission on Higher Education
3624 Market Street, Second Floor West
Philadelphia, Pennsylvania 19104
Phone: 267-284-5000
Fax: 215-662-5501
E-mail: info@msche.org
Website: www.msche.org

NEW ENGLAND ASSOCIATION OF SCHOOLS AND COLLEGES

Accredits institutions in Connecticut, Maine, Massachusetts, New Hampshire, Rhode Island, and Vermont.

Dr. Barbara E. Brittingham, President/Director
Commission on Institutions of Higher Education
3 Burlington Woods Drive, Suite 100
Burlington, Massachusetts 01803-4531
Phone: 855-886-3272 or 781-425-7714
Fax: 781-425-1001
E-mail: cihe@neasc.org
Website: http://cihe.neasc.org

THE HIGHER LEARNING COMMISSION

Accredits institutions in Arizona, Arkansas, Colorado, Illinois, Indiana, Iowa, Kansas, Michigan, Minnesota, Missouri, Nebraska, New Mexico, North Dakota, Ohio, Oklahoma, South Dakota, West Virginia, Wisconsin, and Wyoming.

Dr. Barbara Gellman-Danley, President
The Higher Learning Commission
230 South LaSalle Street, Suite 7-500
Chicago, Illinois 60604-1413
Phone: 800-621-7440 or 312-263-0456
Fax: 312-263-7462
E-mail: info@hlcommission.org
Website: www.hlcommission.org

NORTHWEST COMMISSION ON COLLEGES AND UNIVERSITIES

Accredits institutions in Alaska, Idaho, Montana, Nevada, Oregon, Utah, and Washington.

Dr. Sandra E. Elman, President
8060 165th Avenue, NE, Suite 100
Redmond, Washington 98052
Phone: 425-558-4224
Fax: 425-376-0596
E-mail: selman@nwccu.org
Website: www.nwccu.org

SOUTHERN ASSOCIATION OF COLLEGES AND SCHOOLS

Accredits institutions in Alabama, Florida, Georgia, Kentucky, Louisiana, Mississippi, North Carolina, South Carolina, Tennessee, Texas, and Virginia.

Dr. Belle S. Wheelan, President
Commission on Colleges
1866 Southern Lane
Decatur, Georgia 30033-4097
Phone: 404-679-4500 Ext. 4504
Fax: 404-679-4558
E-mail: questions@sacscoc.org
Website: www.sacscoc.org

WESTERN ASSOCIATION OF SCHOOLS AND COLLEGES

Accredits institutions in California, Guam, and Hawaii.

Dr. Mary Ellen Petrisko, President
Accrediting Commission for Senior Colleges and Universities
985 Atlantic Avenue, Suite 100
Alameda, California 94501
Phone: 510-748-9001
Fax: 510-748-9797
E-mail: wasc@wascsenior.org
Website: http://www.wascsenior.org/

Institutional Accrediting Agencies—Other

ACCREDITING COUNCIL FOR INDEPENDENT COLLEGES AND SCHOOLS
Anthony S. Bieda, Executive in Charge
750 First Street, NE, Suite 980
Washington, DC 20002-4241
Phone: 202-336-6780
Fax: 202-842-2593
E-mail: info@acics.org
Website: www.acics.org

DISTANCE EDUCATION AND ACCREDITING COMMISSION (DEAC)
Accrediting Commission
Leah Matthews, Executive Director
1101 17th Street, NW, Suite 808
Washington, DC 20036-4704
Phone: 202-234-5100
Fax: 202-332-1386
E-mail: info@deac.org
Website: www.deac.org

Specialized Accrediting Agencies

ACUPUNCTURE AND ORIENTAL MEDICINE
Mark S. McKenzie, LAc MsOM DiplOM, Executive Director
Accreditation Commission for Acupuncture and Oriental Medicine
8941 Aztec Drive
Eden Prairie, Minnesota 55347
Phone: 952-212-2434
Fax: 301-313-0912
E-mail: coordinator@acaom.org
Website: www.acaom.org

ALLIED HEALTH
Kathleen Megivern, Executive Director
Commission on Accreditation of Allied Health Education Programs (CAAHEP)
25400 US Hwy 19 North, Suite 158
Clearwater, Florida 33763
Phone: 727-210-2350
Fax: 727-210-2354
E-mail: mail@caahep.org
Website: www.caahep.org

ART AND DESIGN
Karen P. Moynahan, Executive Director
National Association of Schools of Art and Design (NASAD)
Commission on Accreditation
11250 Roger Bacon Drive, Suite 21
Reston, Virginia 20190-5248
Phone: 703-437-0700
Fax: 703-437-6312
E-mail: info@arts-accredit.org
Website: http://nasad.arts-accredit.org

ATHLETIC TRAINING EDUCATION
Micki Cuppett, Executive Director
Commission on Accreditation of Athletic Training Education (CAATE)
6850 Austin Center Blvd., Suite 100
Austin, Texas 78731-3184
Phone: 512-733-9700
E-mail: micki@caate.net
Website: www.caate.net

AUDIOLOGY EDUCATION
Doris Gordon, Executive Director
Accreditation Commission for Audiology Education (ACAE)
11480 Commerce Park Drive, Suite 220
Reston, Virginia 20191
Phone: 202-986-9550
Fax: 202-986-9500
E-mail: info@acaeaccred.org
Website: www.acaeaccred.org

AVIATION
Dr. Gary J. Northam, Executive Director
Aviation Accreditation Board International (AABI)
3410 Skyway Drive
Auburn, Alabama 36830
Phone: 334-844-2431
Fax: 334-844-2432
E-mail: bayenva@auburn.edu
Website: www.aabi.aero

BUSINESS
Robert D. Reid, Executive Vice President and Chief Accreditation Officer
AACSB International—The Association to Advance Collegiate Schools of Business
777 South Harbour Island Boulevard, Suite 750
Tampa, Florida 33602
Phone: 813-769-6500
Fax: 813-769-6559
E-mail: bob@aacsb.edu
Website: www.aacsb.edu

BUSINESS EDUCATION
Dennis N. Gash, President and Chief Executive Officer
International Assembly for Collegiate Business Education (IACBE)
11257 Strang Line Road
Lenexa, Kansas 66215
Phone: 913-631-3009
Fax: 913-631-9154
E-mail:iacbe@iacbe.org
Website: www.iacbe.org

CHIROPRACTIC
Craig S. Little, President
Council on Chiropractic Education (CCE)
Commission on Accreditation
8049 North 85th Way
Scottsdale, Arizona 85258-4321
Phone: 480-443-8877 or 888-443-3506
Fax: 480-483-7333
E-mail: cce@cce-usa.org
Website: www.cce-usa.org

CLINICAL LABORATORY SCIENCES
Dianne M. Cearlock, Ph.D., Chief Executive Officer
National Accrediting Agency for Clinical Laboratory Sciences
5600 North River Road, Suite 720
Rosemont, Illinois 60018-5119
Phone: 773-714-8880 or 847-939-3597
Fax: 773-714-8886
E-mail: info@naacls.org
Website: www.naacls.org

CLINICAL PASTORAL EDUCATION
Trace Haythorn, Executive Director
Association for Clinical Pastoral Education, Inc.
1549 Clairmont Road, Suite 103
Decatur, Georgia 30033-4611
Phone: 404-320-1472
Fax: 404-320-0849
E-mail: acpe@acpe.edu
Website: www.acpe.edu

DANCE
Karen P. Moynahan, Executive Director
National Association of Schools of Dance (NASD)
Commission on Accreditation
11250 Roger Bacon Drive, Suite 21
Reston, Virginia 20190-5248
Phone: 703-437-0700
Fax: 703-437-6312
E-mail: info@arts-accredit.org
Website: http://nasd.arts-accredit.org

DENTISTRY
Dr. Sherin Tooks, Director
Commission on Dental Accreditation
American Dental Association
211 East Chicago Avenue, Suite 1900
Chicago, Illinois 60611
Phone: 312-440-4643 or 800-621-8099
E-mail: accreditation@ada.org
Website: www.ada.org

DIETETICS AND NUTRITION
Mary B. Gregoire, Ph.D., Executive Director; RD, FADA, FAND
Academy of Nutrition and Dietetics
Accreditation Council for Education in Nutrition and Dietetics (ACEND)
120 South Riverside Plaza, Suite 2000
Chicago, Illinois 60606-6995
Phone: 800-877-1600 Ext. 5400 or 312-899-0040
Fax: 312-899-4817
E-mail: acend@eatright.org
Website: www.eatright.org/ACEND

EDUCATION PREPARATION
Christopher Koch, President
Council for the Accreditation of Education Preparation (CAEP)
1140 19th Street NW, Suite 400
Washington, DC 20036
Phone: 202-223-0077
Fax: 202-296-6620
E-mail: caep@caepnet.org
Website: www.caepnet.org

ENGINEERING
Michael Milligan, Ph.D., PE, Executive Director
Accreditation Board for Engineering and Technology, Inc. (ABET)
415 North Charles Street
Baltimore, Maryland 21201
Phone: 410-347-7700
E-mail: accreditation@abet.org
Website: www.abet.org

FORENSIC SCIENCES
Nancy J. Jackson, Director of Development and Accreditation
American Academy of Forensic Sciences (AAFS)
Forensic Science Education Program Accreditation Commission (FEPAC)
410 North 21st Street
Colorado Springs, Colorado 80904
Phone: 719-636-1100
Fax: 719-636-1993
E-mail: njackson@aafs.org
Website: www.fepac-edu.org

FORESTRY
Carol L. Redelsheimer
Director of Science and Education
Society of American Foresters
5400 Grosvenor Lane
Bethesda, Maryland 20814-2198
Phone: 301-897-8720 or 866-897-8720
Fax: 301-897-3690
E-mail: redelsheimerc@safnet.org
Website: www.safnet.org

HEALTHCARE MANAGEMENT
Commission on Accreditation of Healthcare Management Education (CAHME)
Anthony Stanowski, President and CEO
1700 Rockville Pike
Suite 400
Rockville, Maryland 20852
Phone: 301-998-6101
E-mail: info@cahme.org
Website: www.cahme.org

HEALTH INFORMATICS AND HEALTH MANAGEMENT
Claire Dixon-Lee, Executive Director
Commission on Accreditation for Health Informatics and Information Management Education (CAHIIM)
233 North Michigan Avenue, 21st Floor
Chicago, Illinois 60601-5800
Phone: 312-233-1100
Fax: 312-233-1948
E-mail:E-mail: claire.dixon-lee@cahiim.org
Website: www.cahiim.org

HUMAN SERVICE EDUCATION
Dr. Elaine Green, President
Council for Standards in Human Service Education (CSHSE)
3337 Duke Street
Alexandria, Virginia 22314
Phone: 571-257-3959
E-mail: info@cshse.org
Web: http://www.cshse.org

INTERIOR DESIGN
Holly Mattson, Executive Director
Council for Interior Design Accreditation
206 Grandview Avenue, Suite 350
Grand Rapids, Michigan 49503-4014
Phone: 616-458-0400
Fax: 616-458-0460
E-mail: info@accredit-id.org
Website: www.accredit-id.org

JOURNALISM AND MASS COMMUNICATIONS
Susanne Shaw, Executive Director
Accrediting Council on Education in Journalism and Mass Communications (ACEJMC)
School of Journalism
Stauffer-Flint Hall
University of Kansas
1435 Jayhawk Boulevard
Lawrence, Kansas 66045-7575
Phone: 785-864-3973
Fax: 785-864-5225
E-mail: sshaw@ku.edu
Website: http://www2.ku.edu/~acejmc/

LANDSCAPE ARCHITECTURE
Kristopher D. Pritchard, Executive Director
Landscape Architectural Accreditation Board (LAAB)
American Society of Landscape Architects (ASLA)
636 Eye Street, NW
Washington, DC 20001-3736
Phone: 202-216-2359
Fax: 202-898-1185
E-mail: info@asla.org
Website: www.asla.org

LAW
Barry Currier, Managing Director of Accreditation & Legal Education
American Bar Association
321 North Clark Street, 21st Floor
Chicago, Illinois 60654
Phone: 312-988-6738
Fax: 312-988-5681
E-mail: legaled@americanbar.org
Website: http://www.americanbar.org/groups/legal_education/resources/accreditation.html

LIBRARY
Karen O'Brien, Director
Office for Accreditation
American Library Association
50 East Huron Street
Chicago, Illinois 60611-2795
Phone: 312-280-2432
Fax: 312-280-2433
E-mail: accred@ala.org
Website: www.ala.org/accreditation/

MARRIAGE AND FAMILY THERAPY
Tanya A. Tamarkin, Director of Educational Affairs
Commission on Accreditation for Marriage and Family Therapy Education (COAMFTE)
American Association for Marriage and Family Therapy
112 South Alfred Street
Alexandria, Virginia 22314-3061
Phone: 703-838-9808
Fax: 703-838-9805
E-mail: coa@aamft.org
Website: www.aamft.org

MEDICAL ILLUSTRATION
Kathleen Megivern, Executive Director
Commission on Accreditation of Allied Health Education Programs (CAAHEP)
1361 Park Street
Clearwater, Florida 33756
Phone: 727-210-2350
Fax: 727-210-2354
E-mail: mail@caahep.org
Website: www.caahep.org

MEDICINE
Liaison Committee on Medical Education (LCME)
Robert B. Hash, M.D., LCME Secretary
American Medical Association
Council on Medical Education
330 North Wabash Avenue, Suite 39300
Chicago, Illinois 60611-5885
Phone: 312-464-4933
E-mail: lcme@aamc.org
Website: www.ama-assn.org

Liaison Committee on Medical Education (LCME)
Heather Lent, M.A., Director
Accreditation Services
Association of American Medical Colleges
655 K Street, NW
Washington, DC 20001-2399
Phone: 202-828-0596
E-mail: lcme@aamc.org
Website: www.lcme.org

MUSIC
Karen P. Moynahan, Executive Director
National Association of Schools of Music (NASM)
Commission on Accreditation
11250 Roger Bacon Drive, Suite 21
Reston, Virginia 20190-5248
Phone: 703-437-0700
Fax: 703-437-6312
E-mail: info@arts-accredit.org
Website: http://nasm.arts-accredit.org/

NATUROPATHIC MEDICINE
Daniel Seitz, J.D., Ed.D., Executive Director
Council on Naturopathic Medical Education
P.O. Box 178
Great Barrington, Massachusetts 01230
Phone: 413-528-8877
E-mail: www.cnme.org/contact.html
Website: www.cnme.org

NURSE ANESTHESIA
Francis R.Gerbasi, Ph.D., CRNA, COA Executive Director
Council on Accreditation of Nurse Anesthesia Educational Programs (CoA-NAEP)
American Association of Nurse Anesthetists
222 South Prospect Avenue, Suite 304
Park Ridge, Illinois 60068-4010
Phone: 847-655-1160
Fax: 847-692-7137
E-mail: accreditation@coa.us.com
Website: http://home.coa.us.com

NURSE EDUCATION
Jennifer L. Butlin, Executive Director
Commission on Collegiate Nursing Education (CCNE)
One Dupont Circle, NW, Suite 530
Washington, DC 20036-1120
Phone: 202-887-6791
Fax: 202-887-8476
E-mail: jbutlin@aacn.nche.edu
Website: www.aacn.nche.edu/accreditation

Marsal P. Stoll, Chief Executive Officer
Accreditation Commission for Education in Nursing (ACEN)
3343 Peachtree Road, NE, Suite 850
Atlanta, Georgia 30326
Phone: 404-975-5000
Fax: 404-975-5020
E-mail: mstoll@acenursing.org
Website: www.acenursing.org

NURSE MIDWIFERY
Heather L. Maurer, M.A., Executive Director
Accreditation Commission for Midwifery Education (ACME)
American College of Nurse-Midwives
8403 Colesville Road, Suite 1550
Silver Spring, Maryland 20910
Phone: 240-485-1800
Fax: 240-485-1818
E-mail: info@acnm.org
Website: www.midwife.org/Program-Accreditation

NURSE PRACTITIONER
Gay Johnson, CEO
National Association of Nurse Practitioners in Women's Health
Council on Accreditation
505 C Street, NE
Washington, DC 20002
Phone: 202-543-9693 Ext. 1
Fax: 202-543-9858
E-mail: info@npwh.org
Website: www.npwh.org

NURSING
Marsal P. Stoll, Chief Executive Director
Accreditation Commission for Education in Nursing (ACEN)
3343 Peachtree Road, NE, Suite 850
Atlanta, Georgia 30326
Phone: 404-975-5000
Fax: 404-975-5020
E-mail: info@acenursing.org
Website: www.acenursing.org

OCCUPATIONAL THERAPY
Heather Stagliano, DHSc, OTR/L, Executive Director
The American Occupational Therapy Association, Inc.
4720 Montgomery Lane, Suite 200
Bethesda, Maryland 20814-3449
Phone: 301-652-6611 Ext. 2682
TDD: 800-377-8555
Fax: 240-762-5150
E-mail: accred@aota.org
Website: www.aoteonline.org

OPTOMETRY
Joyce L. Urbeck, Administrative Director
Accreditation Council on Optometric Education (ACOE)
American Optometric Association
243 North Lindbergh Boulevard
St. Louis, Missouri 63141-7881
Phone: 314-991-4100, Ext. 4246
Fax: 314-991-4101
E-mail: accredit@aoa.org
Website: www.theacoe.org

OSTEOPATHIC MEDICINE
Director, Department of Accreditation
Commission on Osteopathic College Accreditation (COCA)
American Osteopathic Association
142 East Ontario Street
Chicago, Illinois 60611
Phone: 312-202-8048
Fax: 312-202-8202
E-mail: predoc@osteopathic.org
Website: www.aoacoca.org

PHARMACY
Peter H. Vlasses, PharmD, Executive Director
Accreditation Council for Pharmacy Education
135 South LaSalle Street, Suite 4100
Chicago, Illinois 60603-4810
Phone: 312-664-3575
Fax: 312-664-4652
E-mail: csinfo@acpe-accredit.org
Website: www.acpe-accredit.org

PHYSICAL THERAPY
Sandra Wise, Senior Director
Commission on Accreditation in Physical Therapy Education (CAPTE)
American Physical Therapy Association (APTA)
1111 North Fairfax Street
Alexandria, Virginia 22314-1488
Phone: 703-706-3245
Fax: 703-706-3387
E-mail: accreditation@apta.org
Website: www.capteonline.org

PHYSICIAN ASSISTANT STUDIES
Sharon L. Luke, Executive Director
Accredittion Review Commission on Education for the Physician Assistant, Inc. (ARC-PA)
12000 Findley Road, Suite 150
Johns Creek, Georgia 30097
Phone: 770-476-1224
Fax: 770-476-1738
E-mail: arc-pa@arc-pa.org
Website: www.arc-pa.org

PLANNING
Ms. Shonagh Merits, Executive Director
American Institute of Certified Planners/Association of Collegiate Schools of Planning/American Planning Association
Planning Accreditation Board (PAB)
2334 West Lawrence Avenue, Suite 209
Chicago, Illinois 60625
Phone: 773-334-7200
E-mail: smerits@planningaccreditationboard.org
Website: www.planningaccreditationboard.org

PODIATRIC MEDICINE
Alan R. Tinkleman, M.P.A., Executive Director
Council on Podiatric Medical Education (CPME)
American Podiatric Medical Association (APMA)
9312 Old Georgetown Road
Bethesda, Maryland 20814-1621
Phone: 301-581-9200
Fax: 301-571-4903
Website: www.cpme.org

PSYCHOLOGY AND COUNSELING
Jacqueline Remondet Wall, CEO of the Accrediting Unit,
Office of Program Consultation and Accreditation
American Psychological Association
750 First Street, NE
Washington, DC 20002-4202
Phone: 202-336-5979 or 800-374-2721
TDD/TTY: 202-336-6123
Fax: 202-336-5978
E-mail: apaaccred@apa.org
Website: www.apa.org/ed/accreditation

Carol L. Bobby, Ph.D., Executive Director
Council for Accreditation of Counseling and Related Educational Programs (CACREP)
1001 North Fairfax Street, Suite 510
Alexandria, Virginia 22314
Phone: 703-535-5990
Fax: 703-739-6209
E-mail: cacrep@cacrep.org
Website: www.cacrep.org

Richard M. McFall, Executive Director
Psychological Clinical Science Accreditation System (PCSAS)
1101 East Tenth Street
IU Psychology Building
Bloomington, Indiana 47405-7007
Phone: 812-856-2570
Fax: 812-322-5545
E-mail: rmmcfall@pcsas.org
Website: www.pcsas.org

PUBLIC HEALTH
Laura Rasar King, M.P.H., MCHES, Executive Director
Council on Education for Public Health
1010 Wayne Avenue, Suite 220
Silver Spring, Maryland 20910
Phone: 202-789-1050
Fax: 202-789-1895
E-mail: Lking@ceph.org
Website: www.ceph.org

PUBLIC POLICY, AFFAIRS AND ADMINISTRATION
Crystal Calarusse, Chief Accreditation Officer
Commission on Peer Review and Accreditation
Network of Schools of Public Policy, Affairs, and Administration (NASPAA-COPRA)
1029 Vermont Avenue, NW, Suite 1100
Washington, DC 20005
Phone: 202-628-8965
Fax: 202-626-4978
E-mail: copra@naspaa.org
Website: www.naspaa.org

RADIOLOGIC TECHNOLOGY
Leslie Winter, Chief Executive Officer Joint Review Committee on Education in Radiologic Technology (JRCERT)
20 North Wacker Drive, Suite 2850
Chicago, Illinois 60606-3182
Phone: 312-704-5300
Fax: 312-704-5304
E-mail: mail@jrcert.org
Web: www.jrcert.org

REHABILITATION EDUCATION
Frank Lane, Ph.D., Executive Director
Council on Rehabilitation Education (CORE)
Commission on Standards and Accreditation
1699 Woodfield Road, Suite 300
Schaumburg, Illinois 60173
Phone: 847-944-1345
Fax: 847-944-1346
E-mail: flane@core-rehab.org
Website: www.core-rehab.org

RESPIRATORY CARE
Thomas Smalling, Executive Director
Commission on Accreditation for Respiratory Care (CoARC)
1248 Harwood Road
Bedford, Texas 76021-4244
Phone: 817-283-2835
Fax: 817-354-8519
E-mail: tom@coarc.com
Website: www.coarc.com

SOCIAL WORK
Dr. Stacey Borasky, Director of Accreditation
Office of Social Work Accreditation
Council on Social Work Education
1701 Duke Street, Suite 200
Alexandria, Virginia 22314
Phone: 703-683-8080
Fax: 703-519-2078
E-mail: info@cswe.org
Website: www.cswe.org

SPEECH-LANGUAGE PATHOLOGY AND AUDIOLOGY
Patrima L. Tice, Accreditation Executive Director
American Speech-Language-Hearing Association
Council on Academic Accreditation in Audiology and Speech-Language Pathology
2200 Research Boulevard #310
Rockville, Maryland 20850-3289
Phone: 301-296-5700
Fax: 301-296-8750
E-mail: accreditation@asha.org
Website: http://caa.asha.org

TEACHER EDUCATION
Christopher A. Koch, President
National Council for Accreditation of Teacher Education (NCATE)
Teacher Education Accreditation Council (TEAC)
1140 19th Street, Suite 400
Washington, DC 20036
Phone: 202-223-0077
Fax: 202-296-6620
E-mail: caep@caepnet.org
Website: www.ncate.org

TECHNOLOGY
Michale S. McComis, Ed.D., Executive Director
Accrediting Commission of Career Schools and Colleges
2101 Wilson Boulevard, Suite 302
Arlington, Virginia 22201
Phone: 703-247-4212
Fax: 703-247-4533
E-mail: mccomis@accsc.org
Website: www.accsc.org

TECHNOLOGY, MANAGEMENT, AND APPLIED ENGINEERING
Kelly Schild, Director of Accreditation
The Association of Technology, Management, and Applied Engineering (ATMAE)
275 N. York Street, Suite 401
Elmhurst, Illinois 60126
Phone: 630-433-4514
Fax: 630-563-9181
E-mail: Kelly@atmae.org
Website: www.atmae.org

THEATER
Karen P. Moynahan, Executive Director
National Association of Schools of Theatre Commission on Accreditation
11250 Roger Bacon Drive, Suite 21
Reston, Virginia 20190
Phone: 703-437-0700
Fax: 703-437-6312
E-mail: info@arts-accredit.org
Website: http://nast.arts-accredit.org/

THEOLOGY
Dr. Bernard Fryshman, Executive VP
Emeritus and Interim Executive Director
Association of Advanced Rabbinical and Talmudic Schools (AARTS)
Accreditation Commission
11 Broadway, Suite 405
New York, New York 10004
Phone: 212-363-1991
Fax: 212-533-5335
E-mail: office@aarts-schools.org

Daniel O. Aleshire, Executive Director
Association of Theological Schools in the United States and Canada (ATS)
Commission on Accrediting
10 Summit Park Drive
Pittsburgh, Pennsylvania 15275
Phone: 412-788-6505
Fax: 412-788-6510
E-mail: ats@ats.edu
Website: www.ats.edu

Dr. Timothy Eaton, Interim President
Transnational Association of Christian Colleges and Schools (TRACS)
Accreditation Commission
15935 Forest Road
Forest, Virginia 24551
Phone: 434-525-9539
Fax: 434-525-9538
E-mail: info@tracs.org
Website: www.tracs.org

VETERINARY MEDICINE
Dr. Karen Brandt, Director of Education and Research
American Veterinary Medical Association (AVMA)
Council on Education
1931 North Meacham Road, Suite 100
Schaumburg, Illinois 60173-4360
Phone: 847-925-8070 Ext. 6674
Fax: 847-285-5732
E-mail: info@avma.org
Website: www.avma.org

How to Use These Guides

As you identify the particular programs and institutions that interest you, you can use both the ***Graduate & Professional Programs: An Overview*** volume and the specialized volumes in the series to obtain detailed information.

- ***Graduate Programs in the Biological/Biomedical Sciences & Health-Related Professions***
- ***Graduate Programs in Business, Education, Information Studies, Law & Social Work***
- ***Graduate Programs in Engineering & Applied Sciences***
- ***Graduate Programs the Humanities, Arts & Social Sciences***
- ***Graduate Programs in the Physical Sciences, Mathematics, Agricultural Sciences, the Environment & Natural Resources***

Each of the specialized volumes in the series is divided into sections that contain one or more directories devoted to programs in a particular field. If you do not find a directory devoted to your field of interest in a specific volume, consult "Directories and Subject Areas" (located at the end of each volume). After you have identified the correct volume, consult the "Directories and Subject Areas in This Book" index, which shows (as does the more general directory) what directories cover subjects not specifically named in a directory or section title.

Each of the specialized volumes in the series has a number of general directories. These directories have entries for the largest unit at an institution granting graduate degrees in that field. For example, the general Engineering and Applied Sciences directory in the ***Graduate Programs in Engineering & Applied Sciences*** volume consists of **Profiles** for colleges, schools, and departments of engineering and applied sciences.

General directories are followed by other directories, or sections, that give more detailed information about programs in particular areas of the general field that has been covered. The general Engineering and Applied Sciences directory, in the previous example, is followed by nineteen sections with directories in specific areas of engineering, such as Chemical Engineering, Industrial/Management Engineering, and Mechanical Engineering.

Because of the broad nature of many fields, any system of organization is bound to involve a certain amount of overlap. Environmental studies, for example, is a field whose various aspects are studied in several types of departments and schools. Readers interested in such studies will find information on relevant programs in the ***Graduate Programs in the Biological/Biomedical Sciences & Health-Related Professions*** volume under Ecology and Environmental Biology and Environmental and Occupational Health; in the ***Graduate Programs in the Physical Sciences, Mathematics, Agricultural Sciences, the Environment & Natural Resources*** volume under Environmental Management and Policy and Natural Resources; and in the ***Graduate Programs in Engineering & Applied Sciences*** volume under Energy Management and Policy and Environmental Engineering. To help you find all of the programs of interest to you, the introduction to each section within the specialized volumes includes, if applicable, a paragraph suggesting other sections and directories with information on related areas of study.

Directory of Institutions with Programs in Business, Education, Information Studies, Law & Social Work

This directory lists institutions in alphabetical order and includes beneath each name the academic fields in which each institution offers graduate programs. The degree level in each field is also indicated, provided that the institution has supplied that information in response to Peterson's Annual Survey of Graduate and Professional Institutions.

An M indicates that a master's degree program is offered; a D indicates that a doctoral degree program is offered; an O signifies that other advanced degrees (e.g., certificates or specialist degrees) are offered; and an * (asterisk) indicates that a **Close-Up** and/or **Display** is located in this volume. See the index, "Close-Ups and Displays," for the specific page number.

Profiles of Academic and Professional Programs in the Specialized Volumes

Each section of **Profiles** has a table of contents that lists the Program Directories, **Displays**, and **Close-Ups.** Program Directories consist of the **Profiles** of programs in the relevant fields, with **Displays** following if programs have chosen to include them. **Close-Ups,** which are more individualized statements, are also listed for those graduate schools or programs that have chosen to submit them.

The **Profiles** found in the 500 directories in the specialized volumes provide basic data about the graduate units in capsule form for quick reference. To make these directories as useful as possible, **Profiles** are generally listed for an institution's smallest academic unit within a subject area. In other words, if an institution has a College of Liberal Arts that administers many related programs, the **Profile** for the individual program (e.g., Program in History), not the entire College, appears in the directory.

There are some programs that do not fit into any current directory and are not given individual **Profiles**. The directory structure is reviewed annually in order to keep this number to a minimum and to accommodate major trends in graduate education.

The following outline describes the **Profile** information found in the guides and explains how best to use that information. Any item that does not apply to or was not provided by a graduate unit is omitted from its listing. The format of the **Profiles** is constant, making it easy to compare one institution with another and one program with another.

A ★ graphic next to the school's name indicates the institution has additional detailed information in a "Premium Profile" on Petersons.com. After reading their information here, you can learn more about the school by visiting www.petersons.com and searching for that particular college or university's graduate program.

Identifying Information. The institution's name, in boldface type, is followed by a complete listing of the administrative structure for that field of study. (For example, University of Akron, Buchtel College of Arts and Sciences, Department of Theoretical and Applied Mathematics, Program in Mathematics.) The last unit listed is the one to which all information in the **Profile** pertains. The institution's city, state, and zip code follow.

Offerings. Each field of study offered by the unit is listed with all postbaccalaureate degrees awarded. Degrees that are not preceded by a specific concentration are awarded in the general field listed in the unit name. Frequently, fields of study are broken down into subspecializations, and those appear following the degrees awarded; for example, "Offerings in secondary education (M.Ed.), including English education, mathematics education, science education." Students enrolled in the M.Ed. program would be able to specialize in any of the three fields mentioned.

Professional Accreditation. Some **Profiles** indicate whether a program is professionally accredited. Because it is possible for a program to receive or lose professional accreditation at any time, students entering fields in which accreditation is important to a career should verify the status of programs by contacting either the chairperson or the appropriate accrediting association.

Jointly Offered Degrees. Explanatory statements concerning programs that are offered in cooperation with other institutions are included in the list of degrees offered. This occurs most commonly on a regional basis (for example, two state universities offering a cooperative

Ph.D. in special education) or where the specialized nature of the institutions encourages joint efforts (a J.D./M.B.A. offered by a law school at an institution with no formal business programs and an institution with a business school but lacking a law school). Only programs that are truly cooperative are listed; those involving only limited course work at another institution are not. Interested students should contact the heads of such units for further information.

Program Availability. This may include the following: part-time, evening/weekend, online only, 100% online, blended/hybrid learning, and/or minimal on-campus study. When information regarding the availability of part-time or evening/weekend study appears in the **Profile**, it means that students are able to earn a degree exclusively through such study. Blended/hybrid learning describe those courses in which some traditional in-class time has been replaced by online learning activities. Hybrid courses take advantage of the best features of both face-to-face and online learning.

Postbaccalaureate Distance Learning Degrees. A post-baccalaureate distance learning degree program signifies that course requirements can be fulfilled with minimal or no on-campus study.

Faculty. Figures on the number of faculty members actively involved with graduate students through teaching or research are separated into full- and part-time as well as men and women whenever the information has been supplied.

Students. Figures for the number of students enrolled in graduate and professional programs pertain to the semester of highest enrollment from the 2016–17 academic year. These figures are broken down into full- and part-time and men and women whenever the data have been supplied. Information on the number of matriculated students enrolled in the unit who are members of a minority group or are international students appears here. The average age of the matriculated students is followed by the number of applicants, the percentage accepted, and the number enrolled for fall 2016.

Degrees Awarded. The number of degrees awarded in the calendar year is listed. Many doctoral programs offer a terminal master's degree if students leave the program after completing only part of the requirements for a doctoral degree; that is indicated here. All degrees are classified into one of four types: master's, doctoral, first professional, and other advanced degrees. A unit may award one or several degrees at a given level; however, the data are only collected by type and may therefore represent several different degree programs.

Degree Requirements. The information in this section is also broken down by type of degree, and all information for a degree level pertains to all degrees of that type unless otherwise specified. Degree requirements are collected in a simplified form to provide some very basic information on the nature of the program and on foreign language, thesis or dissertation, comprehensive exam, and registration requirements. Many units also provide a short list of additional requirements, such as fieldwork or an internship. For complete information on graduation requirements, contact the graduate school or program directly.

Entrance Requirements. Entrance requirements are broken down into the four degree levels of master's, doctoral, first professional, and other advanced degrees. Within each level, information may be provided in two basic categories: entrance exams and other requirements. The entrance exams are identified by the standard acronyms used by the testing agencies, unless they are not well known. Other entrance requirements are quite varied, but they often contain an undergraduate or graduate grade point average (GPA). Unless otherwise stated, the GPA is calculated on a 4.0 scale and is listed as a minimum required for admission. Additional exam requirements/recommendations for international students may be listed here. Application deadlines for domestic and international students, the application fee, and whether electronic applications are accepted may be listed here. Note that the deadline should be used for reference only; these dates are subject to change, and students interested in applying should always contact the graduate unit directly about application procedures and deadlines.

Expenses. The typical cost of study for the 2017–2018 academic year (2016–17 if 2017–18 figures were not available) is given in two basic categories: tuition and fees. Cost of study may be quite complex at a graduate institution. There are often sliding scales for part-time study, a different cost for first-year students, and other variables that make it impossible to completely cover the cost of study for each graduate program. To provide the most usable information, figures are given for full-time study for a full year where available and for part-time study in terms of a per-unit rate (per credit, per semester hour, etc.). Occasionally, variances may be noted in tuition and fees for reasons such as the type of program, whether courses are taken during the day or evening, whether courses are at the master's or doctoral level, or other institution-specific reasons. Respondents were also given the opportunity to provide more specific and detailed tuition and fees information at the unit level. When provided, this information will appear in place of any typical costs entered elsewhere on the university-level survey. Expenses are usually subject to change; for exact costs at any given time, contact your chosen schools and programs directly. Keep in mind that the tuition of Canadian institutions is usually given in Canadian dollars.

Financial Support. This section contains data on the number of awards administered by the institution and given to graduate students during the 2015–16 academic year. The first figure given represents the total number of students receiving financial support enrolled in that unit. If the unit has provided information on graduate appointments, these are broken down into three major categories: fellowships give money to graduate students to cover the cost of study and living expenses and are not based on a work obligation or research commitment, research assistantships provide stipends to graduate students for assistance in a formal research project with a faculty member, and teaching assistantships provide stipends to graduate students for teaching or for assisting faculty members in teaching undergraduate classes. Within each category, figures are given for the total number of awards, the average yearly amount per award, and whether full or partial tuition reimbursements are awarded. In addition to graduate appointments, the availability of several other financial aid sources is covered in this section. Tuition waivers are routinely part of a graduate appointment, but units sometimes waive part or all of a student's tuition even if a graduate appointment is not available. Federal WorkStudy is made available to students who demonstrate need and meet the federal guidelines; this form of aid normally includes 10 or more hours of work per week in an office of the institution. Institutionally sponsored loans are low-interest loans available to graduate students to cover both educational and living expenses. Career-related internships or fieldwork offer money to students who are participating in a formal off-campus research project or practicum. Grants, scholarships, traineeships, unspecified assistantships, and other awards may also be noted. The availability of financial support to part-time students is also indicated here.

Some programs list the financial aid application deadline and the forms that need to be completed for students to be eligible for financial awards. There are two forms: FAFSA, the Free Application for Federal Student Aid, which is required for federal aid, and the CSS PROFILE®.

Faculty Research. Each unit has the opportunity to list several keyword phrases describing the current research involving faculty members and graduate students. Space limitations prevent the unit from listing complete information on all research programs. The total expenditure for funded research from the previous academic year may also be included.

Unit Head and Application Contact. The head of the graduate program for each unit may be listed with academic title, phone and fax numbers, and e-mail address. In addition to the unit head's contact information, many graduate programs also list a separate contact for application and admission information, followed by the graduate school, program, or department's website. If no unit head or application contact is given, you should contact the overall institution for information on graduate admissions.

Displays and Close-Ups

The **Displays** and **Close-Ups** are supplementary insertions submitted by deans, chairs, and other administrators who wish to offer an additional, more individualized statement to readers. A number of graduate school and program administrators have attached a **Display** ad near the **Profile** listing. Here you will find information that an institution or program wants to emphasize. The **Close-Ups** are by their very nature more expansive and flexible than the **Profiles**, and the administrators who have written them may emphasize different aspects of their programs. All of the **Close-Ups** are organized in the same way (with the exception of a few that describe research and training opportunities instead of degree programs), and in each one you will find information on the same basic topics, such as programs of study, research facilities, tuition and fees, financial aid, and application procedures. If an institution or program has submitted a **Close-Up**, a boldface cross-reference appears below its **Profile**. As with the **Displays**, all of the **Close-Ups** in the guides have been submitted by choice; the absence of a **Display** or **Close-Up** does not reflect any type of editorial judgment on the part of Peterson's, and their presence in the guides should not be taken as an indication of status, quality, or approval. Statements regarding a university's objectives and accomplishments are a reflection of its own beliefs and are not the opinions of the Peterson's editors.

Appendixes

This section contains two appendixes. The first, "Institutional Changes Since the 2017 Edition," lists institutions that have closed, merged, or changed their name or status since the last edition of the guides. The second, "Abbreviations Used in the Guides," gives abbreviations of degree names, along with what those abbreviations stand for. These appendixes are identical in all six volumes of ***Peterson's Graduate and Professional Programs***.

Indexes

There are three indexes presented here. The first index, "Close-Ups and Displays," gives page references for all programs that have chosen to place **Close-Ups** and **Displays** in this volume. It is arranged alphabetically by institution; within institutions, the arrangement is alphabetical by subject area. It is not an index to all programs in the book's directories of **Profiles**; readers must refer to the directories themselves for **Profile** information on programs that have not submitted the additional, more individualized statements. The second index, "Directories and Subject Areas in Other Books in This Series", gives book references for the directories in the specialized volumes and also includes cross-references for subject area names not used in the directory structure, for example, "Computing Technology (see Computer Science)." The third index, "Directories and Subject Areas in This Book," gives page references for the directories in this volume and cross-references for subject area names not used in this volume's directory structure.

Data Collection Procedures

The information published in the directories and Profiles of all the books is collected through Peterson's Annual Survey of Graduate and Professional Institutions. The survey is sent each spring to nearly 2,300 institutions offering postbaccalaureate degree programs, including accredited institutions in the United States, U.S. territories, and Canada and those institutions outside the United States that are accredited by U.S. accrediting bodies. Deans and other administrators complete these surveys, providing information on programs in the 500 academic and professional fields covered in the guides as well as overall institutional information. While every effort has been made to ensure the accuracy and completeness of the data, information is sometimes unavailable or changes occur after publication deadlines. All usable information received in time for publication has been included. The omission of any particular item from a directory or Profile signifies either that the item is not applicable to the institution or program or that information was not available. Profiles of programs scheduled to begin during the 2017–18 academic year cannot, obviously, include statistics on enrollment or, in many cases, the number of faculty members. If no usable data were submitted by an institution, its name, address, and program name appear in order to indicate the availability of graduate work.

Criteria for Inclusion in This Guide

To be included in this guide, an institution must have full accreditation or be a candidate for accreditation (preaccreditation) status by an institutional or specialized accrediting body recognized by the U.S. Department of Education or the Council for Higher Education Accreditation (CHEA). Institutional accrediting bodies, which review each institution as a whole, include the six regional associations of schools and colleges (Middle States, New England, North Central, Northwest, Southern, and Western), each of which is responsible for a specified portion of the United States and its territories. Other institutional accrediting bodies are national in scope and accredit specific kinds of institutions (e.g., Bible colleges, independent colleges, and rabbinical and Talmudic schools). Program registration by the New York State Board of Regents is considered to be the equivalent of institutional accreditation, since the board requires that all programs offered by an institution meet its standards before recognition is granted. A Canadian institution must be chartered and authorized to grant degrees by the provincial government, affiliated with a chartered institution, or accredited by a recognized U.S. accrediting body. This guide also includes institutions outside the United States that are accredited by these U.S. accrediting bodies. There are recognized specialized or professional accrediting bodies in more than fifty different fields, each of which is authorized to accredit institutions or specific programs in its particular field. For specialized institutions that offer programs in one field only, we designate this to be the equivalent of institutional accreditation. A full explanation of the accrediting process and complete information on recognized institutional (regional and national) and specialized accrediting bodies can be found online at www.chea.org or at www.ed.gov/admins/finaid/accred/index.html.

DIRECTORY OF INSTITUTIONS AND THEIR OFFERINGS

ABILENE CHRISTIAN UNIVERSITY
- Accounting M
- Business Administration and Management—General M
- Education—General M,O
- Educational Leadership and Administration M,D,O
- Educational Media/Instructional Technology M,O
- Higher Education M
- Human Resources Development M
- Human Services M,O
- Social Work M

ACACIA UNIVERSITY
- Education—General M
- Educational Leadership and Administration M
- Elementary Education M
- English as a Second Language M
- Secondary Education M
- Special Education M

ACADEMY OF ART UNIVERSITY
- Advertising and Public Relations M
- Art Education M

ACADIA UNIVERSITY
- Counselor Education M
- Curriculum and Instruction M
- Education—General M,D
- Educational Leadership and Administration M
- Educational Media/Instructional Technology M
- Mathematics Education M
- Recreation and Park Management M
- Science Education M
- Social Sciences Education M
- Special Education M

ADAMS STATE UNIVERSITY
- Counselor Education M
- Education—General M
- Physical Education M
- Special Education M

ADELPHI UNIVERSITY
- Accounting M
- Art Education M
- Business Administration and Management—General M
- Education—General M,D,O
- Educational Leadership and Administration M,O
- Educational Media/Instructional Technology M
- Elementary Education M
- English as a Second Language M,O
- Finance and Banking M
- Health Education M,O
- Human Resources Management M,O
- Management Information Systems M
- Marketing M
- Physical Education M,O
- Reading Education M
- Secondary Education M
- Social Work M,D
- Special Education M,O
- Sports Management M
- Supply Chain Management M

ADLER GRADUATE SCHOOL
- Counselor Education M

ADLER UNIVERSITY
- Counselor Education M,D,O
- Nonprofit Management M,D,O

ADRIAN COLLEGE
- Accounting M
- Athletic Training and Sports Medicine M

AIR FORCE INSTITUTE OF TECHNOLOGY
- Logistics M,D
- Management Information Systems M

ALABAMA AGRICULTURAL AND MECHANICAL UNIVERSITY
- Art Education M
- Business Education M,O
- Counselor Education M,O
- Early Childhood Education M,D,O
- Education—General M,D,O
- Educational Media/Instructional Technology M,O
- Elementary Education M,D,O
- English Education M,O
- Home Economics Education M,O
- Hospitality Management M
- Kinesiology and Movement Studies M
- Mathematics Education M,O
- Music Education M
- Physical Education M
- Reading Education M,D,O
- Science Education M,O
- Secondary Education M,O
- Social Sciences Education M,O
- Social Work M,O
- Special Education M,D,O

ALABAMA STATE UNIVERSITY
- Accounting M
- Business Administration and Management—General M
- Counselor Education M,D,O
- Early Childhood Education M,O
- Education—General M,D,O
- Educational Leadership and Administration M,D,O
- Educational Media/Instructional Technology M,D,O
- Educational Policy M,D,O
- Elementary Education M,O
- English Education M,O
- Health Education M
- Mathematics Education M,O
- Music Education M,O
- Physical Education M
- Reading Education M,O
- Science Education M,O
- Secondary Education M,O
- Social Sciences Education M,O
- Social Work M
- Special Education M,O

ALASKA PACIFIC UNIVERSITY
- Business Administration and Management—General M
- Education—General M
- Elementary Education M
- Environmental Education M
- Investment Management M,O
- Middle School Education M

ALBANY LAW SCHOOL
- Law M,D

ALBANY STATE UNIVERSITY
- Accounting M
- Business Administration and Management—General M
- Counselor Education M,O
- Early Childhood Education M,O
- Education—General M,O
- Educational Leadership and Administration M,O
- English Education M
- Health Education M,O
- Human Resources Management M
- Logistics M
- Middle School Education M,O
- Physical Education M,O
- Social Work M
- Special Education M,O
- Supply Chain Management M

ALBERTUS MAGNUS COLLEGE
- Accounting M
- Business Administration and Management—General M
- Education—General M
- Human Services M
- Organizational Management M

ALBRIGHT COLLEGE
- Early Childhood Education M
- Education—General M
- Elementary Education M
- English as a Second Language M
- Special Education M

ALCORN STATE UNIVERSITY
- Agricultural Education M,O
- Business Administration and Management—General M
- Counselor Education M,O
- Education—General M,O
- Elementary Education M,O
- Health Education M,O
- Physical Education M,O
- Secondary Education M,O
- Special Education M,O
- Vocational and Technical Education M,O

ALFRED UNIVERSITY
- Accounting M
- Business Administration and Management—General M
- Counselor Education M,D,O
- Education—General M
- Reading Education M
- Student Affairs M

ALLEN COLLEGE
- Health Education M,D

ALLIANT INTERNATIONAL UNIVERSITY–IRVINE
- Educational Psychology M,D,O

ALLIANT INTERNATIONAL UNIVERSITY–LOS ANGELES
- Business Administration and Management—General D
- Education—General M,O
- Educational Psychology M,D,O
- Student Affairs M,D,O

ALLIANT INTERNATIONAL UNIVERSITY–SACRAMENTO
- Education—General M,O

ALLIANT INTERNATIONAL UNIVERSITY–SAN DIEGO
- Business Administration and Management—General M
- Education—General M,O
- Educational Leadership and Administration M,D,O
- Educational Psychology M,D,O
- English as a Second Language M,D,O
- Higher Education M,D,O
- Student Affairs M,D,O

ALLIANT INTERNATIONAL UNIVERSITY–SAN FRANCISCO
- Counselor Education M
- Education—General M,O
- Educational Leadership and Administration M,D,O
- Educational Psychology M,D,O
- English as a Second Language M,O
- Higher Education M,D,O
- Law D
- Multilingual and Multicultural Education M,O
- Special Education M,O

ALVERNIA UNIVERSITY
- Business Administration and Management—General M
- Education—General M
- Organizational Management D
- Urban Education M

ALVERNO COLLEGE
- Adult Education M
- Business Administration and Management—General M
- Education—General M
- Educational Leadership and Administration M
- Educational Media/Instructional Technology M
- Reading Education M
- Science Education M
- Special Education M

AMBERTON UNIVERSITY
- Business Administration and Management—General M
- Human Resources Development M
- Human Resources Management M
- Management Strategy and Policy M
- Project Management M

AMERICAN BUSINESS & TECHNOLOGY UNIVERSITY
- Accounting M
- Business Administration and Management—General M
- Finance and Banking M
- International Business M
- Management Information Systems M
- Marketing M
- Project Management M

AMERICAN COLLEGE OF EDUCATION
- Curriculum and Instruction M
- Education—General M
- Educational Leadership and Administration M
- Educational Media/Instructional Technology M
- English as a Second Language M
- Multilingual and Multicultural Education M

THE AMERICAN COLLEGE OF FINANCIAL SERVICES
- Business Administration and Management—General M
- Finance and Banking M
- Organizational Management M

AMERICAN COLLEGE OF THESSALONIKI
- Business Administration and Management—General M,O
- Entrepreneurship M,O
- Finance and Banking M,O
- Marketing M,O

AMERICAN GRADUATE UNIVERSITY
- Business Administration and Management—General M,O
- Supply Chain Management M,O

AMERICAN INTERCONTINENTAL UNIVERSITY ATLANTA
- International Business M
- Management Information Systems M

AMERICAN INTERCONTINENTAL UNIVERSITY HOUSTON
- Business Administration and Management—General M

AMERICAN INTERCONTINENTAL UNIVERSITY ONLINE
- Accounting M
- Business Administration and Management—General M
- Curriculum and Instruction M
- Education—General M
- Educational Leadership and Administration M
- Educational Measurement and Evaluation M
- Educational Media/Instructional Technology M
- Finance and Banking M
- Human Resources Management M
- Industrial and Manufacturing Management M
- International Business M
- Marketing M
- Project Management M

AMERICAN INTERNATIONAL COLLEGE
- Accounting M,D,O
- Business Administration and Management—General M,D,O
- Counselor Education M,O
- Early Childhood Education M,O
- Education—General M,D,O
- Educational Leadership and Administration M,D,O
- Educational Psychology M,D,O
- Elementary Education M,O
- Exercise and Sports Science M,D
- Hospitality Management M,D,O
- Middle School Education M,O
- Reading Education M,O
- Secondary Education M,O
- Special Education M,O
- Taxation M,D,O

AMERICAN JEWISH UNIVERSITY
- Business Administration and Management—General M
- Education—General M
- Nonprofit Management M
- Social Work M

AMERICAN NATIONAL UNIVERSITY
- Business Administration and Management—General M

AMERICAN PUBLIC UNIVERSITY SYSTEM
- Accounting M
- Business Administration and Management—General M
- Curriculum and Instruction M
- Distance Education Development M
- Educational Leadership and Administration M
- Elementary Education M
- English as a Second Language M
- Entrepreneurship M
- Exercise and Sports Science M
- Finance and Banking M
- Human Resources Management M
- Legal and Justice Studies M
- Logistics M
- Management Information Systems M
- Management Strategy and Policy M
- Marketing M
- Nonprofit Management M
- Organizational Management M
- Project Management M
- Reading Education M
- Secondary Education M
- Social Sciences Education M
- Special Education M
- Sports Management M
- Transportation Management M

AMERICAN SENTINEL UNIVERSITY
- Business Administration and Management—General M
- Management Information Systems M

AMERICAN UNIVERSITY
- Accounting M,O
- Education—General M,O
- Educational Measurement and Evaluation M,O
- Educational Policy M,O
- English as a Second Language M,O
- Entrepreneurship M,D,O
- Finance and Banking M
- Health Education M,O
- Human Resources Management M,O
- International and Comparative Education M
- Management Information Systems M,D,O
- Marketing M
- Multilingual and Multicultural Education M,O
- Nonprofit Management M,D,O
- Organizational Management M,O
- Project Management M,O
- Real Estate M,O
- Special Education M
- Sports Management M,O
- Sustainability Management M
- Taxation M,O

THE AMERICAN UNIVERSITY IN CAIRO
- Business Administration and Management—General M,O
- Education—General M
- Educational Leadership and Administration M
- English as a Second Language M,O
- Finance and Banking M,O
- International and Comparative Education M
- Law M,O

THE AMERICAN UNIVERSITY IN DUBAI
- Business Administration and Management—General M
- Education—General M
- Finance and Banking M
- International Business M
- Marketing M

AMERICAN UNIVERSITY OF ARMENIA
- Business Administration and Management—General M
- English as a Second Language M
- Law M
- Management Information Systems M

AMERICAN UNIVERSITY OF BEIRUT
- Business Administration and Management—General M
- Education—General M,D
- Finance and Banking M,D
- Human Resources Management M

THE AMERICAN UNIVERSITY OF PARIS
- Business Administration and Management—General M
- International Business M
- Law M

AMERICAN UNIVERSITY OF PUERTO RICO
- Art Education M
- Education—General M
- Elementary Education M
- Physical Education M
- Science Education M
- Special Education M

AMERICAN UNIVERSITY OF SHARJAH
- Accounting M
- Business Administration and Management—General M
- English as a Second Language M

AMRIDGE UNIVERSITY
- Counselor Education M,D
- Human Services M,D

ANAHEIM UNIVERSITY
- Business Administration and Management—General M,D,O
- English as a Second Language M,D,O
- Entrepreneurship M,D,O
- International Business M,D,O
- Sustainability Management M,D,O

ANDERSON UNIVERSITY (IN)
- Accounting M,D

Business Administration and Management—General M,D
Education—General M

ANDERSON UNIVERSITY (SC)
Business Administration and Management—General M
Education—General M
Educational Leadership and Administration M
Elementary Education M
Human Resources Management M
Marketing M
Supply Chain Management M

ANDREWS UNIVERSITY
Accounting M
Curriculum and Instruction M,D,O
Education—General M,D,O
Educational Leadership and Administration M,D,O
Educational Psychology M,D
Elementary Education M,D,O
English as a Second Language M,D,O
English Education M,D,O
Finance and Banking M
Foreign Languages Education M,D,O
Higher Education M,D,O
International and Comparative Education M
Religious Education M,D,O
Science Education M,D,O
Secondary Education M,D,O
Social Sciences Education M,D,O
Social Work M
Special Education M

ANGELO STATE UNIVERSITY
Accounting M
Business Administration and Management—General M
Counselor Education M
Curriculum and Instruction M
Educational Leadership and Administration M
English as a Second Language M
Higher Education M
Science Education M
Sports Management M

ANNA MARIA COLLEGE
Business Administration and Management—General M,O
Early Childhood Education M,O
Education—General M,O
Elementary Education M,O
English Education M,O
Social Work M

ANTIOCH UNIVERSITY LOS ANGELES
Business Administration and Management—General M
Education—General M
Human Resources Development M
Nonprofit Management M
Organizational Management M

ANTIOCH UNIVERSITY MIDWEST
Business Administration and Management—General M
Early Childhood Education M
Education—General M
Educational Leadership and Administration M
Management Strategy and Policy M
Middle School Education M
Special Education M

ANTIOCH UNIVERSITY NEW ENGLAND
Business Administration and Management—General M
Early Childhood Education M
Education—General M,O
Educational Leadership and Administration M,O
Educational Media/Instructional Technology M,O
Elementary Education M,O
Environmental Education M
Foundations and Philosophy of Education M,O
Science Education M
Special Education M,O
Sustainability Management M

ANTIOCH UNIVERSITY SANTA BARBARA
Business Administration and Management—General M
Education—General M
Management Strategy and Policy M
Nonprofit Management M

ANTIOCH UNIVERSITY SEATTLE
Adult Education M
Education—General M

APPALACHIAN SCHOOL OF LAW
Law D

APPALACHIAN STATE UNIVERSITY
Accounting M
Business Administration and Management—General M
Counselor Education M
Curriculum and Instruction M
Educational Leadership and Administration M,O
Educational Media/Instructional Technology M,O
Elementary Education M
English Education M
Exercise and Sports Science M
Foreign Languages Education M
Higher Education M,O
Library Science M,O
Mathematics Education M
Middle School Education M
Reading Education M
Science Education M
Social Sciences Education M
Social Work M
Special Education M
Student Affairs M
Taxation M
Vocational and Technical Education M

AQUINAS COLLEGE (MI)
Business Administration and Management—General M
Education—General M
Marketing M
Organizational Management M
Sustainability Management M

AQUINAS COLLEGE (TN)
Education—General M
Elementary Education M
Secondary Education M

ARCADIA UNIVERSITY
Advertising and Public Relations M
Art Education M,D,O
Business Administration and Management—General M
Computer Education M,D,O
Curriculum and Instruction M,D,O
Early Childhood Education M,D,O
Education—General M,D,O
Educational Leadership and Administration M,D,O
Educational Media/Instructional Technology M,D,O
Elementary Education M,D,O
English Education M,D,O
Environmental Education M,D,O
Health Education M
Mathematics Education M,D,O
Music Education M,D,O
Reading Education M,D,O
Science Education M,D,O
Secondary Education M,D,O
Special Education M,D,O

ARGOSY UNIVERSITY, ATLANTA
Accounting M,D
Business Administration and Management—General M,D
Counselor Education M,D,O
Education—General M,D,O
Educational Leadership and Administration M,D,O
Educational Media/Instructional Technology M,D,O
Elementary Education M,D,O
Finance and Banking M,D
Higher Education M,D,O
International Business M,D
Management Information Systems M,D
Marketing M,D
Secondary Education M,D,O

ARGOSY UNIVERSITY, CHICAGO
Accounting M,D
Adult Education M,D,O
Business Administration and Management—General M,D
Community College Education M,D,O
Counselor Education D
Education—General M,D,O
Educational Leadership and Administration M,D,O
Elementary Education M,D,O
Finance and Banking M,D
Higher Education M,D,O
International Business M,D
Management Information Systems M,D
Marketing M,D
Organizational Behavior D
Organizational Management D
Secondary Education M,D,O
Sustainability Management M,D

ARGOSY UNIVERSITY, DALLAS
Accounting M,D,O
Business Administration and Management—General M,D,O
Counselor Education D
Education—General M,D
Educational Leadership and Administration M,D
Finance and Banking M,D,O
Higher Education M,D
International Business M,D,O
Management Information Systems M,D,O
Marketing M,D,O
Sustainability Management M,D,O

ARGOSY UNIVERSITY, DENVER
Accounting M,D
Business Administration and Management—General M,D
Community College Education M,D
Counselor Education M,D
Education—General M,D
Educational Leadership and Administration M,D
Educational Media/Instructional Technology M,D
Elementary Education M,D
Finance and Banking M,D
Higher Education M,D
International Business M,D
Management Information Systems M,D
Marketing M,D
Organizational Management M,D
Sustainability Management M,D

ARGOSY UNIVERSITY, HAWAI'I
Accounting M,D,O
Adult Education M,D
Business Administration and Management—General M,D,O
Education—General M,D
Educational Leadership and Administration M,D
Elementary Education M,D
Finance and Banking M,D,O
Higher Education M,D
International Business M,D,O
Management Information Systems M,D,O
Marketing M,D,O
Organizational Management D
Secondary Education M,D
Sustainability Management M,D,O

ARGOSY UNIVERSITY, INLAND EMPIRE
Accounting M,D
Business Administration and Management—General M,D
Community College Education M,D
Education—General M,D
Educational Leadership and Administration M,D
Elementary Education M,D
Finance and Banking M,D
Higher Education M,D
International Business M,D
Management Information Systems M,D
Marketing M,D
Organizational Management M,D
Secondary Education M,D
Sustainability Management M,D

ARGOSY UNIVERSITY, LOS ANGELES
Accounting M,D
Business Administration and Management—General M,D
Community College Education M,D
Education—General M,D
Educational Leadership and Administration M,D
Elementary Education M,D
Finance and Banking M,D
Higher Education M,D
International Business M,D
Management Information Systems M,D
Marketing M,D
Organizational Management M,D
Secondary Education M,D
Sustainability Management M,D

ARGOSY UNIVERSITY, NASHVILLE
Accounting M,D
Business Administration and Management—General M,D
Counselor Education D
Education—General M,D,O
Educational Leadership and Administration M,D,O
Educational Media/Instructional Technology M,D,O
Elementary Education M,D,O
Finance and Banking M,D
Higher Education M,D,O
International Business M,D
Management Information Systems M,D
Marketing M,D
Secondary Education M,D,O

ARGOSY UNIVERSITY, NORTHERN VIRGINIA
Accounting M,D,O
Business Administration and Management—General M,D,O
Community College Education M,D,O
Counselor Education M,D
Education—General M,D,O
Educational Leadership and Administration M,D,O
Elementary Education M,D,O
Finance and Banking M,D,O
Higher Education M,D,O
International Business M,D,O
Management Information Systems M,D,O
Marketing M,D,O
Organizational Management M,D,O
Secondary Education M,D,O
Sustainability Management M,D,O

ARGOSY UNIVERSITY, ORANGE COUNTY
Accounting M,D,O
Business Administration and Management—General M,D,O
Community College Education M,D,O
Education—General M,D
Educational Leadership and Administration M,D
Educational Media/Instructional Technology M,D
Elementary Education M,D
Finance and Banking M,D,O
Higher Education M,D
International Business M,D,O
Management Information Systems M,D,O
Marketing M,D,O
Organizational Management D
Secondary Education M,D
Sustainability Management M,D,O

ARGOSY UNIVERSITY, PHOENIX
Accounting M,D
Adult Education M,D,O
Business Administration and Management—General M,D
Community College Education M,D,O
Education—General M,D,O
Educational Leadership and Administration M,D,O
Educational Media/Instructional Technology M,D,O
Elementary Education M,D,O
Finance and Banking M,D
Higher Education M,D,O
International Business M,D
Management Information Systems M,D
Marketing M,D
Secondary Education M,D,O
Sustainability Management M,D

ARGOSY UNIVERSITY, SALT LAKE CITY
Accounting M,D
Business Administration and Management—General M,D
Counselor Education M,D
Education—General M,D
Educational Leadership and Administration M,D
Finance and Banking M,D
International Business M,D
Management Information Systems M,D
Marketing M,D
Sustainability Management M,D

ARGOSY UNIVERSITY, SAN DIEGO
Accounting M,D
Business Administration and Management—General M,D
Community College Education M,D
Education—General M,D
Educational Leadership and Administration M,D
Elementary Education M,D
Finance and Banking M,D
Higher Education M,D
International Business M,D
Management Information Systems M,D
Marketing M,D
Organizational Management M,D
Secondary Education M,D

ARGOSY UNIVERSITY, SAN FRANCISCO BAY AREA
Accounting M,D
Business Administration and Management—General M,D
Community College Education M,D
Education—General M,D
Educational Leadership and Administration M,D
Educational Media/Instructional Technology M,D
Elementary Education M,D
Finance and Banking M,D
Higher Education M,D
International Business M,D
Management Information Systems M,D
Marketing M,D
Organizational Management M,D
Secondary Education M,D
Sustainability Management M,D

ARGOSY UNIVERSITY, SARASOTA
Accounting M,D,O
Business Administration and Management—General M,D,O
Counselor Education M,D,O
Education—General M,D,O
Educational Leadership and Administration M,D,O
Educational Media/Instructional Technology M,D,O
Elementary Education M,D,O
Finance and Banking M,D,O
Higher Education M,D,O
International Business M,D,O
Management Information Systems M,D,O
Marketing M,D,O
Organizational Management M,D,O
Secondary Education M,D,O
Sustainability Management M,D,O

ARGOSY UNIVERSITY, SCHAUMBURG
Accounting M,D,O
Business Administration and Management—General M,D,O
Finance and Banking M,D,O
Human Resources Management M,D,O
International Business M,D,O
Management Information Systems M,D,O
Marketing M,D,O
Organizational Management M,D,O
Sustainability Management M,D,O

ARGOSY UNIVERSITY, SEATTLE
Accounting M,D
Adult Education M,D
Business Administration and Management—General M,D
Community College Education M,D
Education—General M,D
Educational Leadership and Administration M,D
Educational Media/Instructional Technology M,D
Elementary Education M,D
Finance and Banking M,D
Higher Education M,D
International Business M,D
Management Information Systems M,D
Marketing M,D
Organizational Management M,D
Secondary Education M,D
Sustainability Management M,D

ARGOSY UNIVERSITY, TAMPA
Accounting M,D
Business Administration and Management—General M,D
Community College Education M,D,O
Counselor Education M,D,O
Education—General M,D,O

*M—masters degree; D—doctorate; O—other advanced degree; *—Close-Up and/or Display*

Educational Leadership and Administration M,D,O
Elementary Education M,D,O
Finance and Banking M,D
Higher Education M,D,O
International Business M,D
Management Information Systems M,D
Marketing M,D
Organizational Management M,D
Secondary Education M,D,O
Sustainability Management M,D

ARGOSY UNIVERSITY, TWIN CITIES
Accounting M,D
Business Administration and Management—General M,D
Education—General M,D,O
Educational Leadership and Administration M,D,O
Educational Media/Instructional Technology M,D,O
Elementary Education M,D,O
Finance and Banking M,D
Higher Education M,D,O
International Business M,D
Management Information Systems M,D
Marketing M,D
Organizational Management M,D
Secondary Education M,D,O
Sustainability Management M,D

ARIZONA STATE UNIVERSITY AT THE TEMPE CAMPUS
Accounting M,D
Art Education M,D
Aviation Management M
Business Administration and Management—General M,D
Counselor Education M
Curriculum and Instruction M
Education—General M,D,O
Educational Leadership and Administration M,D
Educational Measurement and Evaluation D
Educational Media/Instructional Technology M,O
Educational Policy D
Elementary Education M
English as a Second Language M,D,O
Entrepreneurship M,D
Exercise and Sports Science M,D
Finance and Banking M,D
Foreign Languages Education M,D
Health Education D
Higher Education M
International Business M,D
Law M,D
Legal and Justice Studies M,D,O
Management Information Systems M,D
Management Strategy and Policy M,D
Marketing M,D
Mathematics Education M,D,O
Music Education M,D
Nonprofit Management M,D,O
Organizational Behavior M,D
Physical Education M
Real Estate M,D
Secondary Education M
Social Work M,D,O
Special Education M,O
Supply Chain Management M,D
Travel and Tourism M,D,O

ARIZONA SUMMIT LAW SCHOOL
Law D

ARKANSAS STATE UNIVERSITY
Accounting M
Agricultural Education M,O
Business Administration and Management—General M
Business Education O
Community College Education M,D,O
Counselor Education M,D,O
Early Childhood Education M,D,O
Education of the Gifted M,D,O
Education—General M,D,O
Educational Leadership and Administration M,D,O
Elementary Education M,D,O
English Education M,O
Exercise and Sports Science M,O
Foundations and Philosophy of Education M,D,O
Health Education M,D,O
Management Information Systems O
Mathematics Education M
Middle School Education M,D,O
Music Education M,O
Physical Education M,O
Reading Education M,D,O
Science Education M,O
Social Sciences Education M,D,O
Social Work M,O
Special Education M,D,O
Sports Management M,O
Student Affairs M,O

ARKANSAS TECH UNIVERSITY
Business Administration and Management—General M
Counselor Education M,D,O
Curriculum and Instruction M,D,O
Education—General M,D,O
Educational Leadership and Administration M,D,O
Educational Media/Instructional Technology M,D,O
Elementary Education M,D,O
English as a Second Language M
English Education M
Student Affairs M,D,O

ARLINGTON BAPTIST COLLEGE
Curriculum and Instruction M
Education—General M
Educational Leadership and Administration M

ARMSTRONG STATE UNIVERSITY
Adult Education M,O
Athletic Training and Sports Medicine M,O
Business Administration and Management—General M,O
Curriculum and Instruction M,O
Early Childhood Education M,O
Education—General M,O
Exercise and Sports Science M,O
Physical Education M,O
Reading Education M,O
Secondary Education M,O
Special Education M,O

ART ACADEMY OF CINCINNATI
Art Education M

ASBURY THEOLOGICAL SEMINARY
Religious Education M,D,O

ASBURY UNIVERSITY
Educational Leadership and Administration M
English as a Second Language M
Mathematics Education M
Reading Education M
Science Education M
Social Sciences Education M
Social Work M
Special Education M

ASHLAND THEOLOGICAL SEMINARY
Counselor Education M,D

ASHLAND UNIVERSITY
Business Administration and Management—General M
Education of the Gifted M
Education—General M,D
Educational Leadership and Administration M,D
Educational Media/Instructional Technology M
Exercise and Sports Science M
Foundations and Philosophy of Education M
Reading Education M
Special Education M

ASHWORTH COLLEGE
Business Administration and Management—General M
Human Resources Management M
International Business M
Marketing M

ASPEN UNIVERSITY
Business Administration and Management—General M,O
Finance and Banking M,O
Management Information Systems M,O
Project Management M,O

ASSUMPTION COLLEGE
Accounting M,O
Business Administration and Management—General M,O
Finance and Banking M,O
Human Resources Management M,O
International Business M,O
Marketing M,O
Nonprofit Management M,O
Special Education M,O

ATHABASCA UNIVERSITY
Adult Education M,O
Business Administration and Management—General M,D,O
Counselor Education M,O
Distance Education Development M,D,O
Education—General M,D,O
Organizational Management M,O
Project Management M,D,O
Science Education M,O

ATLANTA'S JOHN MARSHALL LAW SCHOOL
Law M,D

A.T. STILL UNIVERSITY
Athletic Training and Sports Medicine M,D,O
Kinesiology and Movement Studies M,D,O
Organizational Behavior M,D,O

AUBURN UNIVERSITY
Accounting M
Adult Education M,D,O
Business Administration and Management—General M,D
Curriculum and Instruction M,D,O
Education—General M,D,O
Educational Leadership and Administration M,D,O
Educational Media/Instructional Technology M,D,O
Elementary Education M,D,O
Exercise and Sports Science M,D,O
Finance and Banking M
Health Education M,D,O
Higher Education M,D,O
Physical Education M,D,O
Real Estate M
Special Education M,D

AUBURN UNIVERSITY AT MONTGOMERY
Accounting M
Business Administration and Management—General M
Counselor Education M,O
Early Childhood Education M,O
Education—General M,O
Educational Leadership and Administration M,O
Educational Media/Instructional Technology M,O
Elementary Education M,O
Exercise and Sports Science M,O
Legal and Justice Studies M
Management Information Systems M
Organizational Management M
Physical Education M,O
Secondary Education M,O
Special Education M,O
Sports Management M,O

AUGSBURG COLLEGE
Business Administration and Management—General M
Education—General M
Organizational Management M
Social Work M

AUGUSTANA UNIVERSITY
Education—General M
Educational Media/Instructional Technology M
Reading Education M
Science Education M
Special Education M
Sports Management M

AUGUSTA UNIVERSITY
Business Administration and Management—General M
Counselor Education M,O
Curriculum and Instruction M,O
Educational Leadership and Administration M,O
Educational Media/Instructional Technology D
Elementary Education M,O
Foreign Languages Education M,O
Middle School Education M,O
Music Education M,O
Secondary Education M,O
Special Education M,O

AURORA UNIVERSITY
Accounting M
Adult Education M,D
Business Administration and Management—General M
Curriculum and Instruction M,D
Education—General M,D
Educational Leadership and Administration M,D
Educational Media/Instructional Technology M,D
English as a Second Language M,D
Higher Education M,D
Reading Education M,D
Social Work M,D
Special Education M,D

AUSTIN COLLEGE
Education—General M

AUSTIN PEAY STATE UNIVERSITY
Business Administration and Management—General M
Counselor Education M,O
Curriculum and Instruction M,O
Developmental Education M
Education—General M,O
Educational Leadership and Administration M,O
Elementary Education M,O
Exercise and Sports Science M
Health Education M
Human Resources Management M
Management Strategy and Policy M
Music Education M
Reading Education M,O
Secondary Education M,O
Social Work M
Special Education M
Sports Management M

AVE MARIA SCHOOL OF LAW
Law D

AVERETT UNIVERSITY
Accounting M
Business Administration and Management—General M
Curriculum and Instruction M
Education—General M
Educational Leadership and Administration M
Human Resources Management M
Marketing M
Special Education M

AVILA UNIVERSITY
Accounting M
Business Administration and Management—General M
Education—General M,O
Educational Media/Instructional Technology M
English as a Second Language M,O
Finance and Banking M
Human Resources Management M
International and Comparative Education M,O
International Business M
Management Information Systems M
Marketing M
Organizational Management M
Project Management M
Reading Education M,O

AZUSA PACIFIC UNIVERSITY
Athletic Training and Sports Medicine M
Business Administration and Management—General M
Counselor Education M
Curriculum and Instruction M
Education—General M,D,O
Educational Leadership and Administration M,D
Educational Media/Instructional Technology M
English as a Second Language M
Entrepreneurship M
Finance and Banking M
Foundations and Philosophy of Education M
Higher Education M,D
Human Resources Development M
Human Resources Management M
International Business M
Library Science M,O
Management Strategy and Policy M
Marketing M
Multilingual and Multicultural Education M
Music Education M
Nonprofit Management M
Organizational Management M
Physical Education M
Religious Education M
Social Work M
Special Education M
Student Affairs M

BABSON COLLEGE
Accounting M,O
Business Administration and Management—General M,O
Entrepreneurship M,O

BAKER COLLEGE CENTER FOR GRADUATE STUDIES–ONLINE
Accounting M,D
Business Administration and Management—General M,D
Finance and Banking M,D
Human Resources Management M,D
Management Information Systems M,D
Marketing M,D

BAKER UNIVERSITY
Business Administration and Management—General M
Education—General M,D
Organizational Management M

BAKKE GRADUATE UNIVERSITY
Business Administration and Management—General M,D
Entrepreneurship M,D
Urban Education M,D

BALDWIN WALLACE UNIVERSITY
Accounting M
Business Administration and Management—General M
Education—General M
Educational Leadership and Administration M
Educational Media/Instructional Technology M
Entrepreneurship M
Health Education M
Human Resources Management M
International Business M
Management Strategy and Policy M
Marketing Research M
Reading Education M
Special Education M
Sustainability Management M

BALL STATE UNIVERSITY
Accounting M
Actuarial Science M
Adult Education M,D
Advertising and Public Relations M
Business Administration and Management—General M,O
Business Education M,O
Computer Education M,D,O
Counselor Education M,D
Curriculum and Instruction M,D
Education of the Gifted M,D,O
Education—General M,D,O
Educational Leadership and Administration M,D,O
Educational Measurement and Evaluation M,D,O
Educational Media/Instructional Technology M,D
Educational Policy D
Educational Psychology M,D
Elementary Education M,D,O
English as a Second Language M
Environmental Education M,O
Exercise and Sports Science M,D
Foundations and Philosophy of Education D
Higher Education M,D
Kinesiology and Movement Studies M,D,O
Management Information Systems M,O
Mathematics Education M
Middle School Education M
Music Education M,D,O
Physical Education M
Quantitative Analysis M
Reading Education M,D,O
Secondary Education M
Special Education M,D,O
Sports Management M

BANK STREET COLLEGE OF EDUCATION
Early Childhood Education M
Education—General M
Educational Leadership and Administration M
Elementary Education M
Foundations and Philosophy of Education M
Mathematics Education M

Multilingual and Multicultural Education M
Museum Education M
Reading Education M
Special Education M

BAPTIST THEOLOGICAL SEMINARY AT RICHMOND
Religious Education M,D,O

BARD COLLEGE
Education—General M
Mathematics Education M
Science Education M
Secondary Education M
Sustainability Management M,O

BARRY UNIVERSITY
Accounting M
Athletic Training and Sports Medicine M
Business Administration and Management—General M,O
Counselor Education M,D,O
Curriculum and Instruction D,O
Distance Education Development O
Early Childhood Education M,D,O
Education of the Gifted M,D,O
Education—General M,D,O
Educational Leadership and Administration M,D,O
Educational Media/Instructional Technology M,D,O
Elementary Education M,D,O
English as a Second Language M,D,O
Exercise and Sports Science M
Finance and Banking O
Higher Education M,D
Human Resources Development M,D
Human Resources Management O
International Business O
Kinesiology and Movement Studies M
Law D
Management Information Systems O
Marketing O
Reading Education M,D,O
Social Work M,D
Special Education M,D,O
Sports Management M

BARTON COLLEGE
Elementary Education M

BARUCH COLLEGE OF THE CITY UNIVERSITY OF NEW YORK
Accounting M,D
Business Administration and Management—General M,D,O
Educational Leadership and Administration M,O
Entrepreneurship M,D
Finance and Banking M,D
Higher Education M
Human Resources Management M,D
Industrial and Manufacturing Management M,D
International Business M,D
Management Information Systems M,D
Marketing M,D
Nonprofit Management M
Organizational Behavior M,D
Quantitative Analysis M
Real Estate M
Sustainability Management M,D
Taxation M

BAYAMÓN CENTRAL UNIVERSITY
Accounting M
Business Administration and Management—General M
Counselor Education M,O
Early Childhood Education M,O
Education—General M,O
Educational Leadership and Administration M,O
Elementary Education M,O
Finance and Banking M
Marketing M
Special Education M,O

BAYLOR UNIVERSITY
Accounting M
Business Administration and Management—General M
Curriculum and Instruction M,D
Education—General M,D,O
Educational Leadership and Administration M,O
Educational Measurement and Evaluation M,D,O
Educational Psychology M,D,O
Entrepreneurship D
Health Education M,D
Law D
Management Information Systems M,D
Physical Education M,D
Social Work M,D
Special Education M,D,O

BAY PATH UNIVERSITY
Accounting M
Curriculum and Instruction M
Educational Leadership and Administration M
Educational Media/Instructional Technology M
Entrepreneurship M
Higher Education M
Management Information Systems M
Management Strategy and Policy M
Nonprofit Management M
Special Education M

BECKER COLLEGE
Counselor Education M

BELHAVEN UNIVERSITY (MS)
Business Administration and Management—General M
Education—General M
Educational Media/Instructional Technology M
Elementary Education M
Human Resources Management M
Multilingual and Multicultural Education M
Reading Education M
Secondary Education M
Sports Management M

BELLARMINE UNIVERSITY
Business Administration and Management—General M
Education—General M,D,O
Educational Leadership and Administration M,D,O
Elementary Education M,D,O
Higher Education M,D,O
Management Strategy and Policy M,D,O
Middle School Education M,D,O
Reading Education M,D,O
Secondary Education M,D,O
Special Education M,D,O

BELLEVUE UNIVERSITY
Business Administration and Management—General M,D
Counselor Education M
Educational Media/Instructional Technology M
Finance and Banking M,D
Human Resources Management M,D
Human Services M
Management Information Systems M
Organizational Management M
Project Management M

BELMONT UNIVERSITY
Accounting M
Business Administration and Management—General M
Law D

BEMIDJI STATE UNIVERSITY
Education—General M
Mathematics Education M
Special Education M

BENEDICTINE COLLEGE
Business Administration and Management—General M
Education—General M
Educational Leadership and Administration M

BENEDICTINE UNIVERSITY
Accounting M
Business Administration and Management—General M,D
Curriculum and Instruction M
Education—General M
Educational Leadership and Administration M,D
Elementary Education M
Entrepreneurship M
Exercise and Sports Science M
Finance and Banking M
Health Education M
Higher Education D
Human Resources Management M
International Business M
Logistics M
Management Information Systems M
Marketing M
Organizational Behavior M,D
Organizational Management M,D
Reading Education M
Science Education M
Secondary Education M
Special Education M

BENTLEY UNIVERSITY
Accounting M,D
Business Administration and Management—General M,D,O
Finance and Banking M
Management Strategy and Policy O
Marketing M
Taxation M

BERKELEY COLLEGE–WOODLAND PARK CAMPUS
Business Administration and Management—General M

BERKLEE COLLEGE OF MUSIC
Entertainment Management M

BERRY COLLEGE
Business Administration and Management—General M
Curriculum and Instruction M,O
Early Childhood Education M
Education—General M,O
Educational Leadership and Administration O
Middle School Education M
Reading Education M
Secondary Education M

BETHANY COLLEGE
Education—General M

BETHEL COLLEGE
Business Administration and Management—General M
Education—General M

BETHEL UNIVERSITY (MN)
Business Administration and Management—General M,D,O
Education—General M,D,O
Educational Leadership and Administration M,D,O
Elementary Education M,D,O
Organizational Management M,D,O
Secondary Education M,D,O
Special Education M,D,O

BETHEL UNIVERSITY (TN)
Business Administration and Management—General M
Educational Leadership and Administration M

BINGHAMTON UNIVERSITY, STATE UNIVERSITY OF NEW YORK
Accounting M
Business Administration and Management—General M,D
Early Childhood Education M
Education—General M,D,O
Educational Leadership and Administration M,D,O
English as a Second Language M
English Education M
Foreign Languages Education M
Foundations and Philosophy of Education M,D,O
Legal and Justice Studies M,D
Mathematics Education M
Reading Education M
Science Education M
Secondary Education M
Social Sciences Education M
Social Work M
Special Education M
Student Affairs M

BIOLA UNIVERSITY
Business Administration and Management—General M
Curriculum and Instruction M,O
Early Childhood Education M,O
Education—General M,O
English as a Second Language M,D,O
Religious Education M,D,O
Science Education M,O
Special Education M,O

BISHOP'S UNIVERSITY
Education—General M,O
English as a Second Language M,O

BLACK HILLS STATE UNIVERSITY
Business Administration and Management—General M
Curriculum and Instruction M
Management Strategy and Policy M

BLOOMFIELD COLLEGE
Accounting M

BLOOMSBURG UNIVERSITY OF PENNSYLVANIA
Accounting M
Athletic Training and Sports Medicine M
Business Administration and Management—General M,O
Business Education M
Counselor Education M
Curriculum and Instruction M,O
Early Childhood Education M
Education—General M,O
Educational Leadership and Administration M
Educational Media/Instructional Technology M,O
English Education M
Exercise and Sports Science M
Mathematics Education M
Middle School Education M
Reading Education M
Science Education M
Social Sciences Education M
Special Education M,O
Student Affairs M

BLUEFIELD COLLEGE
Education—General M

BLUE MOUNTAIN COLLEGE
Elementary Education M
Reading Education M

BLUFFTON UNIVERSITY
Accounting M
Business Administration and Management—General M
Curriculum and Instruction M
Education—General M
Finance and Banking M
Industrial and Manufacturing Management M
Organizational Management M
Reading Education M
Special Education M

BOB JONES UNIVERSITY
Accounting M,D,O
Business Administration and Management—General M,D,O
Counselor Education M,D,O
Curriculum and Instruction M,D,O
Educational Leadership and Administration M,D,O
Elementary Education M,D,O
English Education M,D,O
Mathematics Education M,D,O
Music Education M,D,O
Secondary Education M,D,O
Social Sciences Education M,D,O
Special Education M,D,O
Student Affairs M,D,O

BOISE STATE UNIVERSITY
Accounting M
Art Education M
Business Administration and Management—General M
Counselor Education M,O
Curriculum and Instruction M,D,O
Distance Education Development M,D,O
Early Childhood Education M
Education—General M,D,O
Educational Leadership and Administration M,D,O
Educational Media/Instructional Technology M,D,O
English as a Second Language M
English Education M
Kinesiology and Movement Studies M
Mathematics Education M
Multilingual and Multicultural Education M
Music Education M
Organizational Management M,O
Reading Education M
Science Education M,D
Social Work M
Special Education M
Sports Management M
Taxation M

BORICUA COLLEGE
English as a Second Language M
Human Services M

BOSTON COLLEGE
Accounting M
Business Administration and Management—General M
Curriculum and Instruction M,D,O
Education—General M,D,O
Educational Leadership and Administration M,D,O
Educational Measurement and Evaluation M,D
Educational Psychology M,D
Elementary Education M
Finance and Banking M,D
Higher Education M,D
International and Comparative Education M
Law D
Organizational Behavior D
Organizational Management D
Reading Education M,O
Religious Education M,D,O
Science Education M,D
Secondary Education M
Social Work M,D
Special Education M,O

BOSTON UNIVERSITY
Actuarial Science M
Advertising and Public Relations M
Art Education M
Athletic Training and Sports Medicine D
Business Administration and Management—General M,D
Education—General M,D,O
Finance and Banking M
International Business M
Law M,D
Management Information Systems M,O
Management Strategy and Policy M,O
Music Education M,D
Organizational Management M
Project Management M,O
Religious Education M,D
Social Work M,D
Supply Chain Management M
Travel and Tourism M

BOWIE STATE UNIVERSITY
Business Administration and Management—General M
Counselor Education M
Education—General M
Educational Leadership and Administration M,D
Elementary Education M
Human Resources Development M
Management Information Systems M,O
Reading Education M
Secondary Education M
Special Education M

BOWLING GREEN STATE UNIVERSITY
Accounting M
Art Education M
Business Administration and Management—General M
Business Education M
Counselor Education M
Curriculum and Instruction M
Educational Leadership and Administration M,D,O
Educational Media/Instructional Technology M
Higher Education D
International and Comparative Education M
Kinesiology and Movement Studies M
Leisure Studies M
Mathematics Education M,D
Music Education M,D
Organizational Management M
Reading Education M,O
Recreation and Park Management M
Science Education M
Special Education M

*M—masters degree; D—doctorate; O—other advanced degree; *—Close-Up and/or Display*

Sports Management M
Student Affairs M
Vocational and Technical Education M

BRADLEY UNIVERSITY
Accounting M
Business Administration and Management—General M
Counselor Education M
Curriculum and Instruction M
Education—General M,D,O
Educational Leadership and Administration M
Nonprofit Management M

BRANDEIS UNIVERSITY
Business Administration and Management—General M
Distance Education Development M
Educational Leadership and Administration M,O
Educational Measurement and Evaluation O
Elementary Education M,O
Entrepreneurship M
Finance and Banking M,D
Health Education D
Human Services M
International Business M,D
Management Information Systems M
Management Strategy and Policy M
Marketing M
Nonprofit Management M
Project Management M
Real Estate M
Religious Education M,O
Secondary Education M,O

BRANDMAN UNIVERSITY
Accounting M
Business Administration and Management—General M
Counselor Education M,D
Education—General M,D
Educational Leadership and Administration M,D
Elementary Education M,D
Entrepreneurship M
Finance and Banking M
Human Resources Management M
International Business M
Marketing M
Organizational Management M
Secondary Education M,D
Special Education M,D

BRANDON UNIVERSITY
Counselor Education M,O
Curriculum and Instruction M,O
Education—General M,O
Educational Leadership and Administration M,O
Music Education M
Special Education M,O

BRENAU UNIVERSITY
Accounting M
Business Administration and Management—General M
Early Childhood Education M,O
Education—General M,O
Middle School Education M,O
Organizational Management M
Project Management M
Secondary Education M,O
Special Education M,O

BRESCIA UNIVERSITY
Business Administration and Management—General M
Curriculum and Instruction M
Social Work M

BRIDGEWATER COLLEGE
Athletic Training and Sports Medicine M

BRIDGEWATER STATE UNIVERSITY
Accounting M
Art Education M
Business Administration and Management—General M
Counselor Education M,O
Early Childhood Education M
Education—General M,O
Educational Leadership and Administration M,O
Educational Media/Instructional Technology M
Elementary Education M
Finance and Banking M
Mathematics Education M
Physical Education M
Reading Education M,O
Science Education M
Secondary Education M
Social Sciences Education M
Social Work M
Special Education M

BRIERCREST SEMINARY
Business Administration and Management—General M
Organizational Management M

BRIGHAM YOUNG UNIVERSITY
Art Education M
Athletic Training and Sports Medicine M,D
Business Administration and Management—General M
Education—General M,D,O
Educational Leadership and Administration M,D
Educational Measurement and Evaluation D
Educational Media/Instructional Technology M,D
Educational Policy M,D
Educational Psychology M,D
English as a Second Language M
Entrepreneurship M
Exercise and Sports Science M,D
Finance and Banking M
Foreign Languages Education M
Foundations and Philosophy of Education M,D
Human Resources Management M
Law M,D
Marketing M
Mathematics Education M
Music Education M
Nonprofit Management M
Physical Education M
Reading Education M
Religious Education M
Science Education M,D
Social Work M
Special Education M,D,O
Supply Chain Management M

BRISTOL UNIVERSITY
Business Administration and Management—General M
International Business M
Marketing M
Sports Management M

BROADVIEW UNIVERSITY–WEST JORDAN
Business Administration and Management—General M
Management Information Systems M

BROCK UNIVERSITY
Accounting M
Business Administration and Management—General M
Education—General M,D
English as a Second Language M
Legal and Justice Studies M

BROOKLYN COLLEGE OF THE CITY UNIVERSITY OF NEW YORK
Accounting M
Art Education M
Business Administration and Management—General M
Counselor Education M
Early Childhood Education M,O
Education—General M,O
Educational Leadership and Administration M
Elementary Education M,O
English Education M
Environmental Education M
Exercise and Sports Science M
Finance and Banking M
Foreign Languages Education M
International Business M
Kinesiology and Movement Studies M
Mathematics Education M
Middle School Education M,O
Multilingual and Multicultural Education M
Music Education M
Organizational Behavior M,D
Physical Education M
Science Education M
Secondary Education M
Social Sciences Education M
Special Education M,O
Sports Management M

BROOKLYN LAW SCHOOL
Law M,D

BROWN UNIVERSITY
Education—General M
Elementary Education M
English as a Second Language M,D
English Education M
Multilingual and Multicultural Education M,D
Science Education M
Secondary Education M
Social Sciences Education M
Urban Education M

BRYAN COLLEGE
Business Administration and Management—General M

BRYANT UNIVERSITY
Accounting M,O
Business Administration and Management—General M,O
Finance and Banking M,O
International Business M,O
Management Strategy and Policy M,O
Supply Chain Management M,O
Taxation M,O

BRYAN UNIVERSITY
Business Administration and Management—General M

BRYN MAWR COLLEGE
Social Work M,D

BUCKNELL UNIVERSITY
Education—General M
Student Affairs M

BUENA VISTA UNIVERSITY
Counselor Education M
Curriculum and Instruction M
Education—General M
English as a Second Language M

BUFFALO STATE COLLEGE, STATE UNIVERSITY OF NEW YORK
Adult Education M,O
Art Education M
Business Education M
Early Childhood Education M
Educational Leadership and Administration O
Educational Media/Instructional Technology M
Elementary Education M
English Education M
Human Resources Management M,O
Mathematics Education M
Multilingual and Multicultural Education M
Reading Education M
Science Education M
Social Sciences Education M
Special Education M
Student Affairs M
Vocational and Technical Education M

BUTLER UNIVERSITY
Accounting M
Business Administration and Management—General M
Counselor Education M,O
Education—General M,O
Educational Leadership and Administration M,O
Finance and Banking M
International Business M
Marketing M
Music Education M
Special Education M,O

CABRINI UNIVERSITY
Accounting M
Education—General M
Organizational Management M

CAIRN UNIVERSITY
Accounting M,O
Business Administration and Management—General M,O
Education—General M,O
Educational Leadership and Administration M,O
Entrepreneurship M,O
Nonprofit Management M,O
Organizational Management M,O

CALDWELL UNIVERSITY
Accounting M
Business Administration and Management—General M
Counselor Education M,O
Curriculum and Instruction M,D,O
Education—General M,D,O
Educational Leadership and Administration M,D,O
Reading Education M,D,O
Special Education M,D,O

CALIFORNIA BAPTIST UNIVERSITY
Accounting M
Adult Education M
Advertising and Public Relations M
Athletic Training and Sports Medicine M
Business Administration and Management—General M
Counselor Education M
Curriculum and Instruction M
Distance Education Development M
Education—General M
Educational Leadership and Administration M
Educational Media/Instructional Technology M
English as a Second Language M
English Education M
Entrepreneurship M
Exercise and Sports Science M
Health Education M
Higher Education M
International and Comparative Education M
Music Education M
Nonprofit Management M
Organizational Management M
Physical Education M
Reading Education M
Science Education M
Social Work M
Special Education M
Sports Management M
Vocational and Technical Education M

CALIFORNIA COAST UNIVERSITY
Business Administration and Management—General M
Curriculum and Instruction M,D
Education—General M,D
Educational Leadership and Administration M,D
Educational Psychology M,D
Human Resources Management M
Marketing M
Organizational Management M,D

CALIFORNIA COLLEGE OF THE ARTS
Finance and Banking M
Organizational Management M

CALIFORNIA INSTITUTE OF INTEGRAL STUDIES
Health Education M,D

CALIFORNIA INTERCONTINENTAL UNIVERSITY
Business Administration and Management—General M,D
Entertainment Management M,D
Entrepreneurship M,D
Finance and Banking M,D
Human Resources Management M,D
International Business M,D
Management Information Systems M,D
Marketing M,D
Organizational Management M,D
Project Management M,D
Quality Management M,D

CALIFORNIA INTERNATIONAL BUSINESS UNIVERSITY
Business Administration and Management—General M,D

CALIFORNIA LUTHERAN UNIVERSITY
Business Administration and Management—General M,O
Counselor Education M,D
Education—General M,D
Educational Leadership and Administration M,D
Elementary Education M,D
Entrepreneurship M,O
Finance and Banking M,O
Higher Education M,D
International Business M,O
Management Information Systems M,O
Marketing M,O
Middle School Education M,D
Nonprofit Management M,O
Organizational Behavior M,O
Special Education M,D

CALIFORNIA MIRAMAR UNIVERSITY
Business Administration and Management—General M
Management Strategy and Policy M
Taxation M

CALIFORNIA POLYTECHNIC STATE UNIVERSITY, SAN LUIS OBISPO
Accounting M
Agricultural Education M
Business Administration and Management—General M
Education—General M
Kinesiology and Movement Studies M
Taxation M

CALIFORNIA STATE POLYTECHNIC UNIVERSITY, POMONA
Accounting M
Business Administration and Management—General M
Curriculum and Instruction M
Educational Leadership and Administration D
Hospitality Management M
Kinesiology and Movement Studies M
Management Information Systems M
Reading Education M

CALIFORNIA STATE UNIVERSITY, BAKERSFIELD
Business Administration and Management—General M
Counselor Education M
Educational Leadership and Administration M,D
Mathematics Education M
Middle School Education M
Science Education M
Secondary Education M
Social Work M
Special Education M
Student Affairs M

CALIFORNIA STATE UNIVERSITY CHANNEL ISLANDS
Business Administration and Management—General M

CALIFORNIA STATE UNIVERSITY, CHICO
Agricultural Education M
Business Administration and Management—General M
Curriculum and Instruction M
Kinesiology and Movement Studies M
Mathematics Education M
Recreation and Park Management M
Social Work M
Special Education M
Travel and Tourism M

CALIFORNIA STATE UNIVERSITY, DOMINGUEZ HILLS
Business Administration and Management—General M
Counselor Education M
Curriculum and Instruction M
Early Childhood Education M
Education—General M
Educational Leadership and Administration M
English as a Second Language M,O
International and Comparative Education M
Mathematics Education M
Physical Education M
Quality Management M
Science Education M
Social Work M
Special Education M

CALIFORNIA STATE UNIVERSITY, EAST BAY
Accounting M
Actuarial Science M
Business Administration and Management—General M
Counselor Education M
Early Childhood Education M
Education—General M
Educational Leadership and Administration M,D
Educational Media/Instructional Technology M
English as a Second Language M
Entrepreneurship M
Finance and Banking M
Human Resources Management M
Industrial and Manufacturing Management M

International Business M
Management Information Systems M
Management Strategy and Policy M
Marketing M
Mathematics Education M
Organizational Management M
Physical Education M
Reading Education M
Recreation and Park Management M
Social Sciences Education M
Social Work M
Special Education M
Supply Chain Management M
Travel and Tourism M

CALIFORNIA STATE UNIVERSITY, FRESNO
Counselor Education M
Curriculum and Instruction M
Early Childhood Education M
Education—General M,D
Educational Leadership and Administration M,D
English as a Second Language M
Exercise and Sports Science M
Kinesiology and Movement Studies M
Mathematics Education M
Music Education M
Reading Education M
Social Sciences Education M
Social Work M
Special Education M
Sports Management M
Student Affairs M

CALIFORNIA STATE UNIVERSITY, FULLERTON
Accounting M
Business Administration and Management—General M
Counselor Education M
Educational Leadership and Administration M,D
Educational Media/Instructional Technology M
Electronic Commerce M
Elementary Education M
Entrepreneurship M
Finance and Banking M
International Business M
Management Information Systems M
Management Strategy and Policy M
Marketing M
Mathematics Education M
Multilingual and Multicultural Education M
Music Education M
Organizational Management M
Physical Education M
Science Education M
Secondary Education M
Social Work M
Special Education M
Taxation M
Travel and Tourism M

CALIFORNIA STATE UNIVERSITY, LONG BEACH
Art Education M
Athletic Training and Sports Medicine M
Business Administration and Management—General M
Counselor Education M,D
Education—General M,D
Educational Leadership and Administration M,D
Educational Psychology M,D
Elementary Education M
English as a Second Language M,O
Exercise and Sports Science M
Health Education M
Higher Education M,D
Kinesiology and Movement Studies M
Leisure Studies M
Mathematics Education M
Physical Education M
Recreation and Park Management M
Science Education M
Secondary Education M
Social Work M
Special Education M,D
Sports Management M
Student Affairs M,D

CALIFORNIA STATE UNIVERSITY, LOS ANGELES
Accounting M
Art Education M
Business Administration and Management—General M,O
Counselor Education M,D
Curriculum and Instruction M
Education—General M,D,O
Elementary Education M
Finance and Banking M
International Business M
Kinesiology and Movement Studies M,O
Management Information Systems M
Marketing M
Music Education M
Physical Education M,O
Social Work M
Special Education M,D

CALIFORNIA STATE UNIVERSITY MARITIME ACADEMY
Transportation Management M

CALIFORNIA STATE UNIVERSITY, MONTEREY BAY
Business Administration and Management—General M
Education—General M
Management Information Systems M
Social Work M

CALIFORNIA STATE UNIVERSITY, NORTHRIDGE
Art Education M
Business Administration and Management—General M
Counselor Education M
Curriculum and Instruction M
Early Childhood Education M
Education—General M,D
Educational Leadership and Administration M,D
Educational Media/Instructional Technology M
Educational Psychology M
Elementary Education M
English Education M
Entertainment Management M,O
Health Education M,O
Hospitality Management M,O
Kinesiology and Movement Studies M
Mathematics Education M
Multilingual and Multicultural Education M
Music Education M
Nonprofit Management O
Reading Education M
Recreation and Park Management M,O
Science Education M
Secondary Education M
Social Work M,O*
Special Education M
Taxation M,O
Travel and Tourism M

CALIFORNIA STATE UNIVERSITY, SACRAMENTO
Accounting M
Business Administration and Management—General M
Counselor Education M,D
Curriculum and Instruction M,D
Education—General M,D
Educational Leadership and Administration M,D
Educational Media/Instructional Technology M,D
Educational Policy M,D
English as a Second Language M
Foreign Languages Education M
Higher Education M,D
Human Resources Development M
Human Resources Management M
Human Services M
Multilingual and Multicultural Education M,D
Physical Education M
Reading Education M,D
Real Estate M
Recreation and Park Management M
Social Work M
Special Education M,D

CALIFORNIA STATE UNIVERSITY, SAN BERNARDINO
Accounting M
Business Administration and Management—General M
Community College Education M
Counselor Education M
Education—General M
Educational Leadership and Administration M,D
Entrepreneurship M
Finance and Banking M
International Business M
Management Information Systems M
Marketing M
Mathematics Education M
Social Work M
Supply Chain Management M

CALIFORNIA STATE UNIVERSITY, SAN MARCOS
Business Administration and Management—General M
Education—General M,D
Educational Leadership and Administration M,D
Health Education M
Reading Education M,D
Social Work M
Special Education M,D

CALIFORNIA STATE UNIVERSITY, STANISLAUS
Business Administration and Management—General M
Community College Education D
Counselor Education M
Curriculum and Instruction M
Education—General M,D,O
Educational Leadership and Administration M,D
Educational Media/Instructional Technology M
Elementary Education M
English as a Second Language M,O
Multilingual and Multicultural Education M
Physical Education M
Reading Education M
Secondary Education M
Social Work M
Special Education M

CALIFORNIA UNIVERSITY OF MANAGEMENT AND SCIENCES
Business Administration and Management—General M,D
International Business M,D
Management Information Systems M,D
Sports Management M,D

CALIFORNIA UNIVERSITY OF PENNSYLVANIA
Athletic Training and Sports Medicine M
Business Administration and Management—General M
Counselor Education M
Education—General M
Educational Leadership and Administration M
Elementary Education M
Entrepreneurship M
Exercise and Sports Science M
Legal and Justice Studies M
Management Strategy and Policy M
Reading Education M
Secondary Education M
Social Work M
Special Education M
Sports Management M
Vocational and Technical Education M

CALIFORNIA WESTERN SCHOOL OF LAW
Accounting M,D
Law M,D

CALUMET COLLEGE OF SAINT JOSEPH
Educational Leadership and Administration M
Quality Management M

CALVARY UNIVERSITY
Curriculum and Instruction M
Education—General M
Educational Leadership and Administration M
Elementary Education M
Organizational Management M
Religious Education M

CALVIN COLLEGE
Curriculum and Instruction M
Education—General M

CALVIN THEOLOGICAL SEMINARY
Religious Education M,D

CAMBRIDGE COLLEGE
Business Administration and Management—General M
Counselor Education M,D,O
Curriculum and Instruction M,D,O
Early Childhood Education M,D,O
Education—General M,D,O
Educational Leadership and Administration M,D,O
Educational Measurement and Evaluation M,D,O
Educational Media/Instructional Technology M,D,O
Elementary Education M,D,O
English as a Second Language M,D,O
Entrepreneurship M
Health Education M,D,O
Home Economics Education M,D,O
Mathematics Education M,D,O
Middle School Education M,D,O
Nonprofit Management M
Organizational Management M
Reading Education M,D,O
Science Education M,D,O
Social Sciences Education M,D,O
Special Education M,D,O

CAMERON UNIVERSITY
Business Administration and Management—General M
Education—General M
Educational Leadership and Administration M
Entrepreneurship M

CAMPBELLSVILLE UNIVERSITY
Business Administration and Management—General M
Education—General M
Music Education M
Social Work M
Special Education M

CAMPBELL UNIVERSITY
Business Administration and Management—General M
Counselor Education M
Education—General M
Educational Leadership and Administration M
Elementary Education M
Law D
Middle School Education M
Physical Education M
Secondary Education M

CANISIUS COLLEGE
Accounting M
Business Administration and Management—General M
Business Education M,O
Counselor Education M
Early Childhood Education M
Education of the Gifted M,O
Education—General M,O
Educational Leadership and Administration M,O
Educational Media/Instructional Technology M,O
Elementary Education M,O
English as a Second Language M,O
International Business M
Kinesiology and Movement Studies M
Middle School Education M
Physical Education M,O
Reading Education M,O
Secondary Education M,O
Special Education M,O
Sports Management M
Student Affairs M,O

CAPE BRETON UNIVERSITY
Business Administration and Management—General M

CAPELLA UNIVERSITY
Accounting M,D
Adult Education M,D
Business Administration and Management—General M,D
Business Education D
Counselor Education M,D
Curriculum and Instruction M,D
Distance Education Development M,D
Early Childhood Education M
Education—General M,D
Educational Leadership and Administration M,D
Educational Media/Instructional Technology M,D
Educational Psychology M,D
Elementary Education M,D
Entrepreneurship M,D
Finance and Banking M,D
Higher Education M,D
Human Resources Management M,D
Human Services M,D
Management Information Systems M,D
Management Strategy and Policy M,D
Marketing M,D
Middle School Education M,D
Nonprofit Management D
Organizational Management M,D
Project Management M,D
Reading Education M,D
Social Work D
Special Education M,D
Supply Chain Management M,D
Vocational and Technical Education D

CAPITAL UNIVERSITY
Business Administration and Management—General M
Law M,D
Legal and Justice Studies M
Music Education M
Taxation M

CAPITOL TECHNOLOGY UNIVERSITY
Business Administration and Management—General M
Management Information Systems M

CARDINAL STRITCH UNIVERSITY
Business Administration and Management—General M
Education—General M,D
Educational Leadership and Administration M,D
Higher Education M,D
Reading Education M,D
Special Education M,D
Sports Management M
Student Affairs M,D
Urban Education M,D

CARIBBEAN UNIVERSITY
Curriculum and Instruction M,D
Early Childhood Education M,D
Education—General M,D
Educational Leadership and Administration M,D
Educational Media/Instructional Technology M,D
Elementary Education M,D
English Education M,D
Foreign Languages Education M,D
Human Resources Management M,D
Mathematics Education M,D
Physical Education M,D
Science Education M,D
Social Sciences Education M,D
Special Education M,D

CARLETON UNIVERSITY
Business Administration and Management—General M,D
Legal and Justice Studies M,O
Social Work M

CARLOS ALBIZU UNIVERSITY, MIAMI CAMPUS
Business Administration and Management—General M,D
Education of the Gifted M,D
English as a Second Language M,D
Entrepreneurship M,D
Human Services M,D
Nonprofit Management M,D
Organizational Management M,D
Special Education M,D

CARLOW UNIVERSITY
Business Administration and Management—General M
Counselor Education M,O
Early Childhood Education M
Education—General M,O
Educational Leadership and Administration M
Human Resources Management M

*M—masters degree; D—doctorate; O—other advanced degree; *—Close-Up and/or Display*

Organizational Management M,D,O
Project Management M
Special Education M

CARNEGIE MELLON UNIVERSITY
Accounting D
Business Administration and Management—General M,D
Entertainment Management M
Entrepreneurship D
Finance and Banking D
Industrial and Manufacturing Management M,D
Management Information Systems M,D
Marketing D
Music Education M
Organizational Behavior D

CAROLINA CHRISTIAN COLLEGE
Religious Education M

CARROLL UNIVERSITY
Adult Education M
Business Administration and Management—General M
Early Childhood Education M
Education—General M
Educational Leadership and Administration M
Elementary Education M
Secondary Education M

CARSON-NEWMAN UNIVERSITY
Business Administration and Management—General M
Counselor Education M
Curriculum and Instruction M
Education—General M
Educational Leadership and Administration M
Elementary Education M
English as a Second Language M
Organizational Management M
Secondary Education M

CARTHAGE COLLEGE
Art Education M,O
Counselor Education M,O
Education of the Gifted M,O
Education—General M,O
Educational Leadership and Administration M,O
English Education M,O
Reading Education M,O
Science Education M,O
Social Sciences Education M,O

CASE WESTERN RESERVE UNIVERSITY
Accounting M,D
Art Education M
Business Administration and Management—General M,D
Finance and Banking M
Health Law M,D
Industrial and Manufacturing Management M,D
Intellectual Property Law M,D
Law M,D
Legal and Justice Studies M,D
Logistics M,D
Music Education M,D
Nonprofit Management M,D,O
Organizational Behavior M,D
Social Work M,D
Supply Chain Management M,D
Sustainability Management D

CASTLETON UNIVERSITY
Curriculum and Instruction M
Education—General M,O
Educational Leadership and Administration M,O
Reading Education M,O
Special Education M,O

CATAWBA COLLEGE
Elementary Education M
Science Education M

THE CATHOLIC UNIVERSITY OF AMERICA
Accounting M
Business Administration and Management—General M
Early Childhood Education M,O
Education—General M,O
Educational Leadership and Administration M,O
Human Resources Management M
Information Studies M,O
Law M,D
Legal and Justice Studies M,D,O
Library Science M,O
Management Information Systems M,O
Music Education M,D,O
Project Management M,O
Secondary Education M,O
Social Work M,D
Special Education M,O

CEDAR CREST COLLEGE
Business Administration and Management—General M
Education—General M

CEDARVILLE UNIVERSITY
Business Administration and Management—General M,D
Curriculum and Instruction M,D
Education—General M,D
Educational Leadership and Administration M,D

CENTENARY COLLEGE OF LOUISIANA
Business Administration and Management—General M
Education—General M
Elementary Education M
Secondary Education M

CENTENARY UNIVERSITY
Accounting M
Business Administration and Management—General M
Education—General M,D
Educational Leadership and Administration M,D
Reading Education M,D
Special Education M,D

CENTRAL CONNECTICUT STATE UNIVERSITY
Accounting M
Actuarial Science M,O
Art Education M,O
Business Administration and Management—General M
Counselor Education M,O
Early Childhood Education M,O
Education—General M,D,O
Educational Leadership and Administration M,D,O
Elementary Education M,O
Exercise and Sports Science M,O
Foreign Languages Education M,O
Industrial and Manufacturing Management M,O
Information Studies M
Logistics M,O
Music Education M,O
Physical Education M,O
Reading Education M,O
Science Education M
Secondary Education M,O
Special Education M,O
Supply Chain Management M,O
Vocational and Technical Education M

CENTRAL EUROPEAN UNIVERSITY
Business Administration and Management—General M,D
Finance and Banking M,D
International Business M,D
Law M,D
Legal and Justice Studies M,D
Management Information Systems M,D

CENTRAL METHODIST UNIVERSITY
Counselor Education M
Education—General M
Music Education M

CENTRAL MICHIGAN UNIVERSITY
Accounting M,O
Business Administration and Management—General M,O
Community College Education M,D,O
Counselor Education M
Curriculum and Instruction M,D,O
Early Childhood Education M,O
Education—General M,D,O
Educational Leadership and Administration M,D,O
Educational Media/Instructional Technology M,D,O
Elementary Education M,D,O
English as a Second Language M
Exercise and Sports Science M,D
Finance and Banking M
Higher Education M,D,O
Human Resources Management M,O
Industrial and Manufacturing Management M
International Business M,O
Logistics M,O
Management Information Systems M,O
Marketing M,O
Mathematics Education M,D
Music Education M
Nonprofit Management M,O
Reading Education M,D,O
Recreation and Park Management M,O
Science Education M
Secondary Education M,D,O
Special Education M,O
Sports Management M,O
Student Affairs M,D,O

CENTRAL PENN COLLEGE
Management Information Systems M
Organizational Management M

CENTRAL WASHINGTON UNIVERSITY
Accounting M
Counselor Education M
Curriculum and Instruction M
Education—General M
Educational Leadership and Administration M
English as a Second Language M
Exercise and Sports Science M
Foundations and Philosophy of Education M
Health Education M
Home Economics Education M
Physical Education M
Reading Education M
Special Education M
Sports Management M
Vocational and Technical Education M

CHADRON STATE COLLEGE
Business Administration and Management—General M
Business Education M,O
Counselor Education M,O
Education—General M,O
Educational Leadership and Administration M,O
Elementary Education M,O
English Education M,O
Secondary Education M,O
Social Sciences Education M,O

CHAMINADE UNIVERSITY OF HONOLULU
Accounting M
Business Administration and Management—General M
Early Childhood Education M
Education—General M
Educational Leadership and Administration M
Elementary Education M
Nonprofit Management M
Secondary Education M
Special Education M

CHAMPLAIN COLLEGE
Business Administration and Management—General M
Early Childhood Education M
Law M

CHAPMAN UNIVERSITY
Accounting M
Athletic Training and Sports Medicine M
Business Administration and Management—General M
Counselor Education M,D,O
Curriculum and Instruction M,D,O
Education—General M,D,O
Educational Leadership and Administration M,D,O
Educational Psychology M,D,O
Elementary Education M,D,O
Environmental Law M,D
Law M,D
Secondary Education M,D,O
Special Education M,D,O
Taxation M,D

CHARLESTON SCHOOL OF LAW
Law M,D

CHARLESTON SOUTHERN UNIVERSITY
Accounting M
Business Administration and Management—General M
Education—General M
Educational Leadership and Administration M
Elementary Education M
Finance and Banking M
Human Resources Management M
Management Information Systems M
Organizational Management M

CHATHAM UNIVERSITY
Accounting M
Art Education M
Business Administration and Management—General M
Early Childhood Education M
Education—General M
Elementary Education M
English Education M
Environmental Education M
Mathematics Education M
Science Education M
Secondary Education M
Social Sciences Education M
Special Education M
Sustainability Management M

CHESTNUT HILL COLLEGE
Early Childhood Education M
Education—General M
Educational Leadership and Administration M
Educational Media/Instructional Technology M,O
Elementary Education M
Human Services M,O
Middle School Education M
Reading Education M
Secondary Education M
Special Education M,O

CHEYNEY UNIVERSITY OF PENNSYLVANIA
Education—General M,O
Educational Leadership and Administration M,O
Elementary Education M
Special Education M
Urban Education M

THE CHICAGO SCHOOL OF PROFESSIONAL PSYCHOLOGY
Organizational Management M,D

CHICAGO STATE UNIVERSITY
Counselor Education M
Early Childhood Education M
Education—General M,D
Educational Leadership and Administration M,D
Educational Media/Instructional Technology M
Elementary Education M
Foundations and Philosophy of Education M
Higher Education M,D
Library Science M
Middle School Education M
Multilingual and Multicultural Education M
Physical Education M
Reading Education M
Secondary Education M
Social Work M
Special Education M
Vocational and Technical Education M

CHOWAN UNIVERSITY
Education—General M

CHRISTIAN BROTHERS UNIVERSITY
Accounting M,O
Business Administration and Management—General M,O
Education—General M
Educational Leadership and Administration M
International Business M,O
Project Management M,O

CHRISTOPHER NEWPORT UNIVERSITY
Education—General M

THE CITADEL, THE MILITARY COLLEGE OF SOUTH CAROLINA
Business Administration and Management—General M
Counselor Education M,O
Early Childhood Education M,O
Education—General M,O
Educational Leadership and Administration M,O
English Education M,O
Health Education M,O
Mathematics Education M,O
Middle School Education M,O
Physical Education M,O
Project Management M,O
Reading Education M,O
Science Education M,O
Secondary Education M,O
Social Sciences Education M,O
Sports Management M,O
Student Affairs M,O

CITY COLLEGE OF THE CITY UNIVERSITY OF NEW YORK
Business Administration and Management—General M
Early Childhood Education M
Education—General M,O
Educational Leadership and Administration M,O
English as a Second Language M
English Education M,O
Foreign Languages Education M
Management Information Systems M,D
Marketing M
Mathematics Education M,O
Middle School Education M,O
Multilingual and Multicultural Education M
Reading Education M
Science Education M
Secondary Education M,O
Social Sciences Education M,O
Special Education M,O

CITY UNIVERSITY OF NEW YORK SCHOOL OF LAW
Law D

CITY UNIVERSITY OF SEATTLE
Accounting M,O
Business Administration and Management—General M,O
Counselor Education M,O
Curriculum and Instruction M,O
Education—General M,O
Educational Leadership and Administration M,D,O
Elementary Education M,O
Finance and Banking M,O
Human Resources Management M,O
International Business M,O
Management Information Systems M,O
Marketing M,O
Organizational Management M,O
Project Management M,O
Reading Education M,O
Special Education M,O
Sustainability Management M,O

CITY VISION UNIVERSITY
Entrepreneurship M

CLAFLIN UNIVERSITY
Business Administration and Management—General M

CLAREMONT GRADUATE UNIVERSITY
Archives/Archival Administration M,D,O
Business Administration and Management—General M,D,O
Education—General M,D,O
Educational Leadership and Administration M,D,O
Educational Measurement and Evaluation M,D,O
Electronic Commerce M,D,O
Higher Education M,D,O
Human Resources Development M,D,O
Human Resources Management M
Management Information Systems M,D,O
Management Strategy and Policy M,D,O
Special Education M,D,O
Student Affairs M,D,O
Urban Education M,D,O

CLAREMONT MCKENNA COLLEGE
Finance and Banking M

CLAREMONT SCHOOL OF THEOLOGY
Religious Education M,D

CLARION UNIVERSITY OF PENNSYLVANIA
Accounting M
Advertising and Public Relations O
Business Administration and Management—General M
Curriculum and Instruction M
Early Childhood Education M
Education—General M
Entrepreneurship M
Finance and Banking M
Library Science M,O
Mathematics Education M
Reading Education M
Science Education M

Special Education M
Vocational and Technical Education M

CLARK ATLANTA UNIVERSITY
Accounting M
Business Administration and Management—General M
Counselor Education M
Curriculum and Instruction M
Education—General M,D,O
Educational Leadership and Administration M,D,O
Educational Psychology M
Mathematics Education M
Science Education M
Social Work M,D
Special Education M

CLARKE UNIVERSITY
Business Administration and Management—General M
Education—General M
Educational Leadership and Administration M
Social Work M

CLARKSON UNIVERSITY
Business Administration and Management—General M,O
Early Childhood Education M
Education—General M
Human Resources Management M,O
International Business M,O
Middle School Education M
Secondary Education M
Supply Chain Management M,O
Vocational and Technical Education M

CLARKS SUMMIT UNIVERSITY
Counselor Education M
Curriculum and Instruction M
Educational Leadership and Administration M
English as a Second Language M
Organizational Management M,D
Reading Education M
Religious Education M,D

CLARK UNIVERSITY
Accounting M
Business Administration and Management—General M
Education—General M
Finance and Banking M
Health Education M
Management Information Systems M
Marketing M
Sustainability Management M

CLAYTON STATE UNIVERSITY
Accounting M
Archives/Archival Administration M
Business Administration and Management—General M
Education—General M
English Education M
Human Resources Management M
International Business M
Mathematics Education M
Sports Management M
Supply Chain Management M

CLEARY UNIVERSITY
Business Administration and Management—General M,O
Educational Media/Instructional Technology M,O
Finance and Banking M,O
Management Strategy and Policy M,O

CLEMSON UNIVERSITY
Accounting M
Agricultural Education M
Business Administration and Management—General M,D
Business Education M,D
Counselor Education M,O
Curriculum and Instruction D
Distance Education Development M,D,O
Early Childhood Education M,O
Education—General M,D,O
Educational Leadership and Administration M,D,O
Educational Measurement and Evaluation D
Entrepreneurship M
Higher Education D
Human Resources Development M,D,O
Human Resources Management M,D,O
Management Information Systems M,D
Management Strategy and Policy M
Mathematics Education M,O
Middle School Education M,D,O
Nonprofit Management M,O
Organizational Management M,D,O
Physical Education M
Reading Education M,D
Real Estate M
Recreation and Park Management M,D,O
Science Education M,D,O
Secondary Education M
Special Education M,D
Sports Management M,D,O
Student Affairs M,D,O
Supply Chain Management M,D
Travel and Tourism M,D,O

CLEVELAND STATE UNIVERSITY
Accounting M
Adult Education M,D,O
Art Education M
Business Administration and Management—General M,D
Counselor Education M,D,O
Early Childhood Education M
Education of Students with Severe/Multiple Disabilities M
Education—General M,D,O
Educational Leadership and Administration M,D,O
Educational Media/Instructional Technology D
Educational Policy D
English as a Second Language M
Foreign Languages Education M
Health Education M
Higher Education D
Human Resources Management M
Law M,D,O
Management Information Systems D
Marketing D
Mathematics Education M
Music Education M
Nonprofit Management M,O
Physical Education M
Science Education M
Social Work M
Special Education M
Urban Education D

COASTAL CAROLINA UNIVERSITY
Accounting M,O
Business Administration and Management—General M,O
Distance Education Development M,O
Education—General M,O
Educational Leadership and Administration M,O
Educational Media/Instructional Technology M,O
English as a Second Language M,O
Management Information Systems M,D,O
Special Education M,O
Sports Management M,D,O

COGSWELL POLYTECHNICAL COLLEGE
Entrepreneurship M

COKER COLLEGE
Reading Education M
Sports Management M

COLGATE UNIVERSITY
Secondary Education M

THE COLLEGE AT BROCKPORT, STATE UNIVERSITY OF NEW YORK
Accounting M,O
Counselor Education M,O
Curriculum and Instruction M
Early Childhood Education M
Education—General M,O
Educational Leadership and Administration M,O
English Education M,O
Health Education M
Mathematics Education M,O
Middle School Education M
Multilingual and Multicultural Education M,O
Nonprofit Management M,O
Physical Education M,O
Reading Education M
Science Education M,O
Social Sciences Education M,O
Social Work M,O
Sports Management M,O

COLLEGE FOR FINANCIAL PLANNING
Finance and Banking M

COLLEGE OF CHARLESTON
Accounting M
Business Administration and Management—General M
Early Childhood Education M
Education—General M,O
Elementary Education M
English as a Second Language O
Foreign Languages Education M
Management Information Systems M
Mathematics Education M
Music Education M
Science Education M
Special Education M

THE COLLEGE OF IDAHO
Curriculum and Instruction M
Education—General M

COLLEGE OF MOUNT SAINT VINCENT
Education—General M,O
Educational Media/Instructional Technology M,O
English as a Second Language M,O
Middle School Education M,O
Multilingual and Multicultural Education M,O
Urban Education M,O

THE COLLEGE OF NEW JERSEY
Counselor Education M
Early Childhood Education M
Education—General M,O
Educational Leadership and Administration M,O
Elementary Education M
English as a Second Language M,O
Health Education M
International and Comparative Education M,O
Physical Education M
Reading Education M,O
Secondary Education M
Special Education M,O

THE COLLEGE OF NEW ROCHELLE
Art Education M
Early Childhood Education M
Education of the Gifted O
Education—General M,O
Educational Leadership and Administration M,O
Elementary Education M
English as a Second Language M,O
Human Resources Development M,O
Multilingual and Multicultural Education M,O
Reading Education M
Special Education M

COLLEGE OF SAINT ELIZABETH
Business Administration and Management—General M
Education—General M,D,O
Educational Leadership and Administration M,D,O
Educational Media/Instructional Technology M,D,O
Exercise and Sports Science M,O
Higher Education M,D,O
Human Resources Management M
Organizational Management M
Student Affairs M,D,O

COLLEGE OF ST. JOSEPH
Business Administration and Management—General M
Counselor Education M
Education—General M
Elementary Education M
English Education M
Reading Education M
Secondary Education M
Social Sciences Education M
Special Education M

COLLEGE OF SAINT MARY
Education—General M
Educational Leadership and Administration M
Educational Measurement and Evaluation M
English as a Second Language M
Health Education D
Organizational Management M

THE COLLEGE OF SAINT ROSE
Accounting M
Business Administration and Management—General M
Counselor Education M,O
Curriculum and Instruction M,O
Early Childhood Education M,O
Education—General M,O
Educational Leadership and Administration M,O
Educational Psychology M,O
Finance and Banking O
Higher Education M,O
Management Strategy and Policy M,O
Middle School Education M,O
Organizational Management O
Reading Education M,O
Secondary Education M,O
Social Work M
Special Education M,O
Student Affairs M

THE COLLEGE OF ST. SCHOLASTICA
Athletic Training and Sports Medicine M
Business Administration and Management—General M,O
Education—General M,O
Exercise and Sports Science M
Management Information Systems M,O
Social Work M

COLLEGE OF STATEN ISLAND OF THE CITY UNIVERSITY OF NEW YORK
Accounting M
Business Administration and Management—General M
Education—General M,O
Educational Leadership and Administration O
Elementary Education M
English as a Second Language M,O
English Education M
Foundations and Philosophy of Education M
Mathematics Education M
Music Education M
Reading Education M
Science Education M
Secondary Education M
Social Sciences Education M
Social Work M
Special Education M,O

THE COLLEGE OF WILLIAM AND MARY
Accounting M
Business Administration and Management—General M
Counselor Education M,D
Curriculum and Instruction M,D
Education of the Gifted M
Education—General M,D,O*
Educational Leadership and Administration M,D
Educational Media/Instructional Technology M,D
Educational Policy M,D
Elementary Education M
Foreign Languages Education M
Law M,D
Mathematics Education M
Reading Education M
Science Education M
Secondary Education M
Special Education M

COLORADO CHRISTIAN UNIVERSITY
Business Administration and Management—General M
Business Education M
Curriculum and Instruction M
Distance Education Development M
Early Childhood Education M
Education—General M
Educational Media/Instructional Technology M
Elementary Education M
Project Management M
Special Education M

THE COLORADO COLLEGE
Art Education M
Education—General M
Elementary Education M
English Education M
Foreign Languages Education M
Mathematics Education M
Music Education M
Science Education M
Secondary Education M
Social Sciences Education M

COLORADO MESA UNIVERSITY
Business Administration and Management—General M
Education of the Gifted M,O
Education—General M,O
Educational Leadership and Administration M,O
English as a Second Language M,O
Special Education M,O

COLORADO STATE UNIVERSITY
Accounting M
Adult Education M,D
Advertising and Public Relations M,D
Business Administration and Management—General M
Counselor Education M,D
Education—General M,D
Educational Leadership and Administration M,D
English as a Second Language M
Exercise and Sports Science M,D
Finance and Banking M
Higher Education M,D
Management Information Systems M
Music Education M
Recreation and Park Management M,D
Social Work M,D
Student Affairs M,D
Sustainability Management M
Taxation M
Travel and Tourism M,D

COLORADO STATE UNIVERSITY–GLOBAL CAMPUS
Accounting M
Business Administration and Management—General M
Education—General M
Educational Leadership and Administration M
Finance and Banking M
Human Resources Management M
International Business M
Management Information Systems M
Organizational Management M
Project Management M

COLORADO STATE UNIVERSITY–PUEBLO
Art Education M
Business Administration and Management—General M
Education—General M
Educational Media/Instructional Technology M
Foreign Languages Education M
Health Education M
Music Education M
Physical Education M
Special Education M

COLORADO TECHNICAL UNIVERSITY AURORA
Accounting M
Business Administration and Management—General M
Finance and Banking M
Human Resources Management M
Industrial and Manufacturing Management M
Marketing M
Project Management M

COLORADO TECHNICAL UNIVERSITY COLORADO SPRINGS
Accounting M,D
Business Administration and Management—General M,D
Finance and Banking M,D
Human Resources Management M,D
Industrial and Manufacturing Management M,D
Logistics M,D
Marketing M,D
Project Management M,D

COLUMBIA COLLEGE (MO)
Accounting M
Business Administration and Management—General M
Education—General M
Educational Leadership and Administration M

*M—masters degree; D—doctorate; O—other advanced degree; *—Close-Up and/or Display*

Human Resources Management M

COLUMBIA COLLEGE (SC)
Education—General M
Educational Leadership and Administration M
Elementary Education M
Higher Education M

COLUMBIA COLLEGE CHICAGO
Entertainment Management M

COLUMBIA INTERNATIONAL UNIVERSITY
Counselor Education M,D,O
Curriculum and Instruction M,D,O
Early Childhood Education M,D,O
Education—General M,D,O
Educational Leadership and Administration M,D,O
Elementary Education M,D,O
English as a Second Language M,D,O
Multilingual and Multicultural Education M,D,O
Religious Education M,D,O

COLUMBIA SOUTHERN UNIVERSITY
Business Administration and Management—General M,D
Finance and Banking M
Human Resources Management M
Marketing M
Organizational Management M

COLUMBIA UNIVERSITY
Accounting M,D
Actuarial Science M
Archives/Archival Administration M
Business Administration and Management—General M,D
Entrepreneurship M
Finance and Banking M,D
Foreign Languages Education M,D
Foundations and Philosophy of Education M,D
Human Resources Management M
Information Studies M
International Business M
Kinesiology and Movement Studies M,D
Law M,D
Legal and Justice Studies M,D
Marketing M,D
Nonprofit Management M
Quantitative Analysis M,D
Real Estate M
Science Education M,D,O
Social Work M,D
Sports Management M
Sustainability Management M

COLUMBUS STATE UNIVERSITY
Art Education M
Business Administration and Management—General M,O
Counselor Education M,D,O
Curriculum and Instruction M,D,O
Early Childhood Education M,O
Education—General M,D,O
Educational Leadership and Administration M,D,O
English as a Second Language O
English Education M,O
Exercise and Sports Science M
Health Education M
Higher Education M,D,O
Human Resources Management M,O
Mathematics Education M,O
Middle School Education M,O
Music Education M,O
Organizational Management M,O
Physical Education M
Science Education M,O
Secondary Education M,O
Social Sciences Education M,O
Special Education M,O

CONCORDIA COLLEGE
Education—General M
Foreign Languages Education M

CONCORDIA COLLEGE–NEW YORK
Organizational Management M
Special Education M

CONCORDIA UNIVERSITY (CANADA)
Adult Education M,O
Art Education M,D
Business Administration and Management—General M,D,O
Education—General M,O
Educational Media/Instructional Technology M,O
English as a Second Language M,O
Exercise and Sports Science M
Finance and Banking M,D,O
Marketing M,D,O
Mathematics Education M,D
Organizational Management M,O
Supply Chain Management M,D,O

CONCORDIA UNIVERSITY (UNITED STATES)
Business Administration and Management—General M
Curriculum and Instruction M,D
Early Childhood Education M,D
Education—General M,D
Educational Leadership and Administration M,D
Educational Media/Instructional Technology M,D
Elementary Education M,D
English as a Second Language M,D
Environmental Education M,D
Mathematics Education M,D
Reading Education M,D
Science Education M,D
Secondary Education M,D
Special Education M,D
Vocational and Technical Education M,D

CONCORDIA UNIVERSITY ANN ARBOR
Curriculum and Instruction M
Educational Leadership and Administration M
Organizational Management M

CONCORDIA UNIVERSITY CHICAGO
Business Administration and Management—General M
Counselor Education M,O
Curriculum and Instruction M
Early Childhood Education M,D
Education—General M
Educational Leadership and Administration M,D,O
Educational Media/Instructional Technology M
Elementary Education M
Exercise and Sports Science M
Human Services M
Reading Education M
Religious Education M
Secondary Education M

CONCORDIA UNIVERSITY IRVINE
Business Administration and Management—General M
Counselor Education M
Curriculum and Instruction M
Education—General M
Educational Leadership and Administration M
Educational Media/Instructional Technology M
Physical Education M
Sports Management M

CONCORDIA UNIVERSITY, NEBRASKA
Early Childhood Education M
Education—General M
Educational Leadership and Administration M
Elementary Education M
Reading Education M
Religious Education M
Secondary Education M

CONCORDIA UNIVERSITY, ST. PAUL
Business Administration and Management—General M
Curriculum and Instruction M,D,O
Education—General M,D,O
Educational Leadership and Administration M,D,O
Educational Media/Instructional Technology M,D,O
Exercise and Sports Science M,D
Human Resources Management M
Human Services M,D
Organizational Management M
Reading Education M,D,O
Special Education M,D,O
Sports Management M,D

CONCORDIA UNIVERSITY TEXAS
Education—General M

CONCORDIA UNIVERSITY WISCONSIN
Art Education M
Business Administration and Management—General M
Counselor Education M
Early Childhood Education M
Education—General M
Educational Leadership and Administration M
Environmental Education M
Finance and Banking M
Health Education M,D
Human Resources Management M
International Business M
Management Information Systems M
Marketing M
Organizational Management M
Reading Education M
Special Education M

CONCORD LAW SCHOOL
Law D

CONCORD UNIVERSITY
Education—General M
Educational Leadership and Administration M
Reading Education M
Social Work M
Special Education M

CONSERVATORIO DE MUSICA DE PUERTO RICO
Music Education M

CONVERSE COLLEGE
Art Education M
Education of the Gifted M
Education—General M,O
Educational Leadership and Administration M,O
Elementary Education M
English Education M
Mathematics Education M
Middle School Education M
Music Education M
Reading Education O
Science Education M
Secondary Education M
Social Sciences Education M
Special Education M

COPENHAGEN BUSINESS SCHOOL
Business Administration and Management—General M,D
International Business M,D
Logistics M,D
Management Information Systems M,D

COPPIN STATE UNIVERSITY
Adult Education M
Curriculum and Instruction M
Education—General M
Human Services M
Reading Education M
Special Education M

CORBAN UNIVERSITY
Business Administration and Management—General M
Education—General M
Nonprofit Management M

CORNELL UNIVERSITY
Accounting M,D
Adult Education M,D
Agricultural Education M,D
Business Administration and Management—General M,D
Curriculum and Instruction M,D
Education—General M,D
Educational Policy M,D
Facilities Management M
Finance and Banking D
Foreign Languages Education M,D
Hospitality Management M,D
Human Resources Management M,D
Information Studies D
Law M,D
Marketing D
Mathematics Education M,D
Organizational Behavior M,D
Quantitative Analysis M,D
Real Estate M
Secondary Education M,D
Social Work M,D

CORNERSTONE UNIVERSITY
Business Administration and Management—General M,O
Education—General M,O
English as a Second Language M,O

COVENANT COLLEGE
Education—General M

CRANDALL UNIVERSITY
Education—General M
Organizational Management M
Reading Education M

CREIGHTON UNIVERSITY
Accounting M
Business Administration and Management—General M
Counselor Education M
Education—General M
Educational Leadership and Administration M,D
Elementary Education M
Finance and Banking M
Law M,D,O
Organizational Management M
Secondary Education M

CULVER-STOCKTON COLLEGE
Accounting M
Business Administration and Management—General M
Finance and Banking M

CUMBERLAND UNIVERSITY
Business Administration and Management—General M
Education—General M

CURRY COLLEGE
Business Administration and Management—General M,O
Education—General M,O
Elementary Education M,O
Finance and Banking M,O
Foundations and Philosophy of Education M,O
Reading Education M,O
Special Education M,O

DAEMEN COLLEGE
Accounting M
Business Administration and Management—General M
Early Childhood Education M
Education—General M
Health Education M
International Business M
Management Information Systems M
Marketing M
Middle School Education M
Nonprofit Management M
Social Work M
Special Education M

DAKOTA STATE UNIVERSITY
Business Administration and Management—General M,D,O
Education—General M
Educational Media/Instructional Technology M
Management Information Systems M,D,O
Management Strategy and Policy M,D,O

DAKOTA WESLEYAN UNIVERSITY
Curriculum and Instruction M
Education—General M
Educational Leadership and Administration M
Secondary Education M

DALHOUSIE UNIVERSITY
Business Administration and Management—General M,O
Electronic Commerce M,D
Finance and Banking M
Health Education M
Information Studies M
Kinesiology and Movement Studies M
Law M,D
Leisure Studies M
Library Science M
Management Information Systems M
Social Work M

DALLAS BAPTIST UNIVERSITY
Accounting M
Business Administration and Management—General M,D
Counselor Education M,O
Curriculum and Instruction M
Distance Education Development M
Early Childhood Education M,D
Education—General M
Educational Leadership and Administration M,D
Educational Media/Instructional Technology M
Elementary Education M
English as a Second Language M
Entrepreneurship M
Finance and Banking M
Higher Education M,D
Human Resources Management M
International Business M
Kinesiology and Movement Studies M
Management Information Systems M
Marketing M
Multilingual and Multicultural Education M
Nonprofit Management M
Organizational Management M,D
Project Management M
Reading Education M
Religious Education M
Secondary Education M
Special Education M
Sports Management M
Student Affairs M

DALLAS THEOLOGICAL SEMINARY
Adult Education M,D,O
Educational Leadership and Administration M,D,O
Religious Education M,D,O

DARTMOUTH COLLEGE
Business Administration and Management—General M
Entrepreneurship D

DAVENPORT UNIVERSITY
Accounting M
Business Administration and Management—General M
Finance and Banking M
Human Resources Management M
Management Strategy and Policy M

DEFIANCE COLLEGE
Business Administration and Management—General M
Education—General M
Management Strategy and Policy M

DELAWARE STATE UNIVERSITY
Adult Education M
Art Education M
Business Administration and Management—General M
Curriculum and Instruction M
Education—General M,D
Educational Leadership and Administration M,D
Exercise and Sports Science M
Foreign Languages Education M
Mathematics Education M
Reading Education M
Science Education M,D
Social Work M
Special Education M

DELAWARE VALLEY UNIVERSITY
Accounting M
Business Administration and Management—General M
Curriculum and Instruction M
Educational Leadership and Administration M
Educational Media/Instructional Technology M
Entrepreneurship M
Finance and Banking M
Human Resources Management M
International Business M
Supply Chain Management M

DELTA STATE UNIVERSITY
Accounting M
Aviation Management M
Business Administration and Management—General M
Counselor Education M,D,O
Education—General M,D,O
Educational Leadership and Administration M,D,O
Elementary Education M,D,O
English Education M
Exercise and Sports Science M
Health Education M
Higher Education D
Physical Education M
Recreation and Park Management M
Secondary Education M,D,O
Social Sciences Education M
Special Education M

DEPAUL UNIVERSITY
Accounting M
Adult Education M,D
Advertising and Public Relations M
Business Administration and Management—General M
Counselor Education M,D
Curriculum and Instruction M,D
Early Childhood Education M,D

Education—General M,D
Educational Leadership and Administration M,D
Electronic Commerce M,D
Elementary Education M,D
Entrepreneurship M
Finance and Banking M
Foreign Languages Education M,D
Foundations and Philosophy of Education M,D
Health Law M,D
Hospitality Management M
Human Resources Management M
Industrial and Manufacturing Management M
Intellectual Property Law M,D
Investment Management M
Law M,D
Management Information Systems M,D
Management Strategy and Policy M
Marketing M
Mathematics Education M,D
Multilingual and Multicultural Education M,D
Music Education M,O
Nonprofit Management M
Organizational Management M
Reading Education M,D
Real Estate M
Science Education M,D
Secondary Education M,D
Social Work M
Special Education M,D
Sports Management M
Student Affairs M,D
Sustainability Management M
Taxation M,D

DEREE - THE AMERICAN COLLEGE OF GREECE
Marketing M

DESALES UNIVERSITY
Accounting M
Business Administration and Management—General M
Education—General M,O
Educational Media/Instructional Technology M,O
English as a Second Language M,O
Finance and Banking M
Human Resources Management M
Management Information Systems M,O
Marketing M
Project Management M,O
Secondary Education M,O
Special Education M,O
Supply Chain Management M

DEVRY COLLEGE OF NEW YORK–MIDTOWN MANHATTAN CAMPUS
Business Administration and Management—General M

DEVRY COLLEGE OF NEW YORK
Business Administration and Management—General M

DEVRY UNIVERSITY
Business Administration and Management—General M,O

DEVRY UNIVERSITY
Accounting M
Business Administration and Management—General M
Education—General M
Educational Media/Instructional Technology M
Finance and Banking M
Human Resources Management M
Management Information Systems M
Project Management M

DEVRY UNIVERSITY ONLINE
Business Administration and Management—General M

DOANE UNIVERSITY
Business Administration and Management—General M
Counselor Education M
Curriculum and Instruction M
Education—General M
Educational Leadership and Administration M

DOMINICAN COLLEGE
Accounting M
Business Administration and Management—General M
Education—General M
Elementary Education M
Special Education M

DOMINICAN UNIVERSITY
Accounting M
Business Administration and Management—General M
Early Childhood Education M
Education—General M
Elementary Education M
English as a Second Language M
Information Studies M,D,O
Management Information Systems M,D,O
Reading Education M
Social Work M
Special Education M

DOMINICAN UNIVERSITY OF CALIFORNIA
Business Administration and Management—General M
Education—General M
International Business M
Management Strategy and Policy M
Special Education M
Sustainability Management M

DORDT COLLEGE
Education—General M

DRAKE UNIVERSITY
Business Administration and Management—General M
Education—General M,D,O
Law M,D

DREW UNIVERSITY
Community College Education M,D,O
Elementary Education M,D,O
Health Education M,D,O
Secondary Education M,D,O
Special Education M,D,O

DREXEL UNIVERSITY
Accounting M,D,O
Archives/Archival Administration M
Business Administration and Management—General M,D,O
Curriculum and Instruction M,D
Education—General M,D*
Educational Leadership and Administration M,D
Educational Media/Instructional Technology M,D
Entrepreneurship M
Finance and Banking M,D,O
Higher Education M,D
Hospitality Management M
Human Resources Development M,D
International and Comparative Education M,D
Library Science M,D,O
Management Information Systems M,D,O
Management Strategy and Policy M,D,O
Marketing M,D,O
Organizational Behavior M,D,O
Project Management M
Quantitative Analysis M,D,O
Real Estate M
Special Education M,D
Sports Management M

DRURY UNIVERSITY
Business Administration and Management—General M
Curriculum and Instruction M
Distance Education Development M
Education of the Gifted M
Education—General M
Educational Leadership and Administration M
Educational Media/Instructional Technology M
Elementary Education M
Middle School Education M
Nonprofit Management M
Organizational Management M
Reading Education M
Secondary Education M
Special Education M

DUKE UNIVERSITY
Accounting D
Business Administration and Management—General M,D,O
Education—General M
Entrepreneurship M,O
Finance and Banking M,D,O
Industrial and Manufacturing Management M,D,O
International Business M,O
Law M,D
Management Strategy and Policy M,D,O
Marketing M,D,O
Organizational Management M,D,O
Quantitative Analysis M,D,O

DUNLAP-STONE UNIVERSITY
Law M

DUQUESNE UNIVERSITY
Accounting M
Business Administration and Management—General M
Counselor Education M,D,O
Curriculum and Instruction M,O
Early Childhood Education M,D,O
Education—General M,D,O
Educational Leadership and Administration M,D,O
Educational Measurement and Evaluation M
Educational Media/Instructional Technology M,D,O
Elementary Education M
English as a Second Language M
English Education M
Finance and Banking M
Foreign Languages Education M
Foundations and Philosophy of Education M
Law M,D
Management Information Systems M
Marketing M
Mathematics Education M
Middle School Education M
Music Education M,O
Organizational Management M
Reading Education M
Science Education M
Secondary Education M
Social Sciences Education M
Special Education M,D
Sports Management M
Sustainability Management M

D'YOUVILLE COLLEGE
Business Administration and Management—General M
Education—General M,D
Educational Leadership and Administration M,D
Elementary Education M,D
International Business M
Secondary Education M,D
Special Education M,D

EARLHAM COLLEGE
Education—General M

EAST CAROLINA UNIVERSITY
Accounting M
Adult Education M
Art Education M
Business Administration and Management—General M,D,O
Business Education M
Community College Education M,D,O
Counselor Education M,D,O
Curriculum and Instruction M,O
Early Childhood Education M,D,O
Education—General M,D,O
Educational Leadership and Administration M,D,O
Educational Media/Instructional Technology M,O
Elementary Education M,O
English as a Second Language M,D,O
English Education M,D,O
Exercise and Sports Science M,D,O
Foreign Languages Education M,O
Health Education M
Hospitality Management M,O
Industrial and Manufacturing Management M,D,O
Kinesiology and Movement Studies M,D,O
Leisure Studies M,O
Library Science M
Logistics M,D,O
Management Information Systems M,D,O
Mathematics Education M,O
Middle School Education M
Music Education M,O
Physical Education M,D,O
Quality Management M,D,O
Reading Education M
Recreation and Park Management M,O
Science Education M,O
Social Sciences Education M
Social Work M,O
Special Education M,O
Sports Management M,D,O
Vocational and Technical Education M

EAST CENTRAL UNIVERSITY
Counselor Education M
Education—General M
Human Resources Management M
Human Services M

EASTERN CONNECTICUT STATE UNIVERSITY
Accounting M
Early Childhood Education M
Education—General M
Educational Media/Instructional Technology M
Elementary Education M
Organizational Management M
Reading Education M
Secondary Education M

EASTERN ILLINOIS UNIVERSITY
Accounting M
Art Education M
Business Administration and Management—General M
Community College Education M
Counselor Education M
Early Childhood Education M
Education—General M,O
Educational Leadership and Administration M,O
Elementary Education M
Exercise and Sports Science M
Kinesiology and Movement Studies M
Mathematics Education M
Middle School Education M
Special Education M
Student Affairs M

EASTERN KENTUCKY UNIVERSITY
Agricultural Education M
Art Education M
Business Administration and Management—General M
Business Education M
Counselor Education M
Curriculum and Instruction M
Education—General M
Educational Leadership and Administration M
Elementary Education M
English Education M
Health Education M
Higher Education M
Home Economics Education M
Library Science M
Mathematics Education M
Music Education M
Physical Education M
Recreation and Park Management M
Science Education M
Secondary Education M
Social Sciences Education M
Special Education M
Sports Management M
Vocational and Technical Education M

EASTERN MENNONITE UNIVERSITY
Business Administration and Management—General M
Counselor Education M
Education—General M
Nonprofit Management M
Organizational Management M

EASTERN MICHIGAN UNIVERSITY
Accounting M
Art Education M
Athletic Training and Sports Medicine M,O
Business Administration and Management—General M,O
Community College Education M,D,O
Counselor Education M,O
Curriculum and Instruction M,O
Distance Education Development M,O
Early Childhood Education M
Education—General M,D,O
Educational Leadership and Administration M,D,O
Educational Measurement and Evaluation M,O
Educational Media/Instructional Technology M,O
Educational Policy M,O
Educational Psychology M,O
Electronic Commerce M,O
English as a Second Language M,O
English Education M
Entrepreneurship M,O
Exercise and Sports Science M
Finance and Banking M,O
Foreign Languages Education M,O
Foundations and Philosophy of Education M
Health Education M,O
Higher Education M,D,O
Hospitality Management M,O
Human Resources Management M,O
Human Services O
International Business M,O
Kinesiology and Movement Studies M
Management Information Systems M,O
Marketing M,O
Middle School Education M
Museum Education O
Nonprofit Management M,O
Organizational Management M,O
Physical Education M
Quality Management M,O
Reading Education M,O
Science Education M
Secondary Education M
Social Work M
Special Education M,O
Sports Management M
Student Affairs M,D,O
Supply Chain Management M,O
Urban Education M,O

EASTERN NAZARENE COLLEGE
Business Administration and Management—General M
Early Childhood Education M,O
Education—General M,O
Educational Leadership and Administration M,O
Elementary Education M,O
English as a Second Language M,O
Middle School Education M,O
Reading Education M,O
Secondary Education M,O
Special Education M,O

EASTERN NEW MEXICO UNIVERSITY
Business Administration and Management—General M
Counselor Education M
Curriculum and Instruction M
Early Childhood Education M
Education—General M
Educational Leadership and Administration M
Educational Media/Instructional Technology M
Elementary Education M
English as a Second Language M
Exercise and Sports Science M
Human Services M
Multilingual and Multicultural Education M
Physical Education M
Reading Education M
Secondary Education M
Special Education M
Sports Management M
Vocational and Technical Education M

EASTERN OREGON UNIVERSITY
Business Administration and Management—General M
Education—General M
Elementary Education M
Secondary Education M

EASTERN UNIVERSITY
Business Administration and Management—General M,D
Counselor Education M,O
Early Childhood Education M,D,O
Education—General M,D,O
Educational Leadership and Administration M,D,O
Elementary Education M,D,O
English as a Second Language M,D,O
English Education M,D,O
Foreign Languages Education M,D,O
Health Education M,D,O
Mathematics Education M,D,O

*M—masters degree; D—doctorate; O—other advanced degree; *—Close-Up and/or Display*

Middle School Education M,D,O
Multilingual and Multicultural Education M,D,O
Nonprofit Management M,D
Organizational Management M,D
Physical Education M,D,O
Reading Education M,D,O
Science Education M,D,O
Secondary Education M,D,O
Social Sciences Education M,D,O
Special Education M,D,O

EASTERN WASHINGTON UNIVERSITY
Adult Education M
Business Administration and Management—General M
Computer Education M
Counselor Education M
Curriculum and Instruction M
Early Childhood Education M
Education—General M
Elementary Education M
English as a Second Language M
Exercise and Sports Science M
Foundations and Philosophy of Education M
Music Education M
Physical Education M
Reading Education M
Recreation and Park Management M
Secondary Education M
Social Work M
Sports Management M

EAST STROUDSBURG UNIVERSITY OF PENNSYLVANIA
Athletic Training and Sports Medicine M
Early Childhood Education M
Education—General M,D
Educational Media/Instructional Technology M
Elementary Education M
Health Education M
Physical Education M
Reading Education M
Secondary Education M,D
Special Education M
Sports Management M

EAST TENNESSEE STATE UNIVERSITY
Accounting M
Business Administration and Management—General M,O
Counselor Education M
Curriculum and Instruction M,O
Early Childhood Education M,D,O
Education—General M,D,O
Educational Leadership and Administration M,D,O
Educational Media/Instructional Technology M,O
Elementary Education M,O
Entrepreneurship M,O
Exercise and Sports Science M,D
Finance and Banking M,O
Kinesiology and Movement Studies M,O
Library Science M,O
Marketing M,O
Middle School Education M,O
Nonprofit Management M,O
Reading Education M,O
Secondary Education M,O
Social Work M
Special Education M,D,O
Sports Management M,O

EAST TEXAS BAPTIST UNIVERSITY
Business Administration and Management—General M
Curriculum and Instruction M
Education—General M
Educational Leadership and Administration M
Entrepreneurship M
Kinesiology and Movement Studies M
Physical Education M

ECOLE HÔTELIÈRE DE LAUSANNE
Hospitality Management M

EDGEWOOD COLLEGE
Accounting M
Adult Education M,D,O
Business Administration and Management—General M
Education—General M,D,O
Educational Leadership and Administration M,D,O
Special Education M,D,O
Sustainability Management M

EDINBORO UNIVERSITY OF PENNSYLVANIA
Art Education M
Counselor Education M,O
Early Childhood Education M,O
Educational Leadership and Administration M
Educational Psychology M,O
Middle School Education M
Reading Education M,O
Secondary Education M
Social Work M
Special Education M,O

ELIZABETH CITY STATE UNIVERSITY
Community College Education M
Education—General M
Educational Leadership and Administration M
Elementary Education M
Mathematics Education M
Science Education M

ELMHURST COLLEGE
Business Administration and Management—General M
Educational Leadership and Administration M
Management Information Systems M
Project Management M
Special Education M
Supply Chain Management M

ELMS COLLEGE
Accounting M
Business Administration and Management—General M
Early Childhood Education M,O
Education—General M,O
Elementary Education M,O
English as a Second Language M,O
English Education M,O
Finance and Banking M
Foreign Languages Education M,O
Reading Education M,O
Science Education M,O
Secondary Education M,O
Special Education M,O

ELON UNIVERSITY
Business Administration and Management—General M
Education of the Gifted M
Education—General M
Elementary Education M
Law D
Special Education M

EMBRY-RIDDLE AERONAUTICAL UNIVERSITY–DAYTONA
Aviation Management M*
Business Administration and Management—General M
Finance and Banking M
Supply Chain Management M

EMBRY-RIDDLE AERONAUTICAL UNIVERSITY–WORLDWIDE
Aviation Management M
Business Administration and Management—General M
Education—General M
Finance and Banking M
Human Resources Management M
Industrial and Manufacturing Management M
International Business M
Logistics M
Management Information Systems M
Management Strategy and Policy M
Organizational Management M
Project Management M
Supply Chain Management M

EMERSON COLLEGE
Advertising and Public Relations M
International Business M
Marketing M

EMMANUEL COLLEGE (UNITED STATES)
Business Administration and Management—General M,O
Education—General M,O
Human Resources Management M,O

EMORY & HENRY COLLEGE
Education—General M
Organizational Management M
Reading Education M

EMORY UNIVERSITY
Accounting M,D
Business Administration and Management—General M,D
Education—General M,D
Entrepreneurship M
Finance and Banking M,D
Health Education M,D
Industrial and Manufacturing Management M
International Business M
Law M,D,O
Management Information Systems M,D
Marketing M,D
Middle School Education M,D
Organizational Management M,D
Real Estate M
Secondary Education M,D

EMPIRE COLLEGE
Law M,D

EMPORIA STATE UNIVERSITY
Accounting M
Business Administration and Management—General M
Business Education M
Counselor Education M
Curriculum and Instruction M
Early Childhood Education M
Education of the Gifted M
Education—General M
Educational Leadership and Administration M
Educational Media/Instructional Technology M
Elementary Education M
English as a Second Language M
Information Studies M
Library Science M,D,O
Physical Education M
Reading Education M
Special Education M

ENDICOTT COLLEGE
Business Administration and Management—General M
Distance Education Development M
Early Childhood Education M
Educational Leadership and Administration M,D
Elementary Education M
Management Information Systems M
Organizational Management M
Reading Education M
Secondary Education M
Special Education M,D
Sports Management M

ERIKSON INSTITUTE
Early Childhood Education M,D
English as a Second Language M,O

ESSEC BUSINESS SCHOOL
Business Administration and Management—General M,D
Hospitality Management M,D
International Business M,D

EVANGEL UNIVERSITY
Counselor Education M
Curriculum and Instruction M,D
Education—General M
Educational Leadership and Administration M,D
Organizational Management M
Reading Education M
Secondary Education M

EVEREST UNIVERSITY
Accounting M
Business Administration and Management—General M
Human Resources Management M
International Business M

EVERGLADES UNIVERSITY
Accounting M
Business Administration and Management—General M
Entrepreneurship M
Human Resources Management M
Industrial and Manufacturing Management M
Project Management M

THE EVERGREEN STATE COLLEGE
Education—General M

EXCELSIOR COLLEGE
Business Administration and Management—General M,O
Health Education M,O
Human Resources Management M,O
Organizational Management M,O

FAIRFIELD UNIVERSITY
Accounting M,O
Business Administration and Management—General M,O
Counselor Education M,O
Education—General M,O
Educational Media/Instructional Technology M,O
Elementary Education M,O
English as a Second Language M,O
Entrepreneurship M,O
Finance and Banking M,O
Foundations and Philosophy of Education M,O
Health Education M,O
Human Resources Management M,O
International Business M,O
Management Information Systems M,O
Management Strategy and Policy M,O
Marketing M,O
Multilingual and Multicultural Education M,O
Secondary Education M,O
Special Education M,O
Taxation M,O

FAIRLEIGH DICKINSON UNIVERSITY, COLLEGE AT FLORHAM
Accounting M
Business Administration and Management—General M,O
Early Childhood Education M,O
Education—General M,O
Educational Leadership and Administration M
Educational Media/Instructional Technology M,O
Entrepreneurship M,O
Finance and Banking M,O
Hospitality Management M
Human Resources Management M,O
International Business M,O
Marketing M,O
Organizational Behavior M,O
Organizational Management M,O
Reading Education M,O
Sports Management M
Supply Chain Management M
Sustainability Management O
Taxation M,O

FAIRLEIGH DICKINSON UNIVERSITY, METROPOLITAN CAMPUS
Accounting M,O
Business Administration and Management—General M,O
Curriculum and Instruction M,O
Early Childhood Education M
Education—General M,O
Educational Leadership and Administration M
Educational Media/Instructional Technology M,O
Electronic Commerce M
Entrepreneurship M,O
Finance and Banking M,O
Foundations and Philosophy of Education M
Hospitality Management M
Human Resources Management M,O
International Business M
Management Information Systems M,O
Marketing M,O
Multilingual and Multicultural Education M
Nonprofit Management M,O
Reading Education M,O
Science Education M
Special Education M
Sports Management M
Taxation M

FAIRMONT STATE UNIVERSITY
Business Administration and Management—General M
Education—General M
Educational Media/Instructional Technology M
Exercise and Sports Science M
Reading Education M
Special Education M

FASHION INSTITUTE OF TECHNOLOGY
Business Administration and Management—General M*
Marketing M*

FAULKNER UNIVERSITY
Business Administration and Management—General M
Counselor Education M
Education—General M
Law D

FAYETTEVILLE STATE UNIVERSITY
Business Administration and Management—General M
Educational Leadership and Administration M,D
Elementary Education M
Middle School Education M
Secondary Education M
Social Sciences Education M
Social Work M

FELICIAN UNIVERSITY
Business Administration and Management—General M,D
Education—General M,O
Educational Leadership and Administration M,O
Entrepreneurship M,D
Religious Education M,O

FERRIS STATE UNIVERSITY
Art Education M
Business Administration and Management—General M
Community College Education D
Curriculum and Instruction M
Developmental Education M
Education—General M
Educational Leadership and Administration M,D
Human Services M
Management Information Systems M
Project Management M
Special Education M
Supply Chain Management M

FIELDING GRADUATE UNIVERSITY
Education—General M,D,O
Educational Leadership and Administration M,D,O
Nonprofit Management M,D,O
Organizational Management O

FISHER COLLEGE
Business Administration and Management—General M
Management Strategy and Policy M

FITCHBURG STATE UNIVERSITY
Accounting M
Art Education M,O
Business Administration and Management—General M
Counselor Education M,O
Curriculum and Instruction M
Early Childhood Education M
Educational Leadership and Administration M,O
Elementary Education M
English Education M,O
Human Resources Management M
Middle School Education M
Reading Education O
Science Education M,O
Social Sciences Education M,O
Special Education M
Vocational and Technical Education M

FIVE TOWNS COLLEGE
Early Childhood Education M,D
Music Education M,D

FLORIDA AGRICULTURAL AND MECHANICAL UNIVERSITY
Accounting M
Adult Education M,D
Business Administration and Management—General M
Business Education M
Counselor Education M,D
Education—General M,D
Educational Leadership and Administration M,D
Elementary Education M
English Education M
Finance and Banking M
Law D
Management Information Systems M
Marketing M
Mathematics Education M
Physical Education M
Science Education M
Secondary Education M
Social Sciences Education M

Social Work M
Sports Management M
Vocational and Technical Education M

FLORIDA ATLANTIC UNIVERSITY
Accounting M
Adult Education M,D,O
Art Education M
Business Administration and Management—General M
Counselor Education M,D
Curriculum and Instruction M,D,O
Early Childhood Education M,D,O
Education—General M,D,O
Educational Leadership and Administration M,D,O
Educational Media/Instructional Technology M
Educational Psychology M
Elementary Education M
English as a Second Language M,D,O
English Education M
Environmental Education M
Exercise and Sports Science M
Finance and Banking M
Foundations and Philosophy of Education M
Higher Education M,D,O
Management Information Systems M
Marketing M
Mathematics Education M
Multilingual and Multicultural Education M,D,O
Music Education M
Nonprofit Management M,D
Reading Education M,D
Science Education M,D
Social Sciences Education M,D
Social Work M,D
Special Education M,D

FLORIDA COASTAL SCHOOL OF LAW
Law D

FLORIDA GULF COAST UNIVERSITY
Accounting M
Business Administration and Management—General M
Curriculum and Instruction M
Education of the Gifted M
Education—General M
Educational Leadership and Administration M
Elementary Education M
English Education M
Mathematics Education M
Middle School Education M
Science Education M
Social Sciences Education M
Social Work M
Special Education M
Taxation M

FLORIDA INSTITUTE OF TECHNOLOGY
Aviation Management M
Business Administration and Management—General M,D
Computer Education M
Education—General M
Educational Media/Instructional Technology M
Electronic Commerce M,D
Elementary Education M
Entrepreneurship M
Environmental Education M
Human Resources Management M,D
Logistics M,D
Management Information Systems M,D
Mathematics Education M,D,O
Organizational Behavior M
Organizational Management M
Project Management M,D
Quality Management M,D
Science Education M,D,O
Supply Chain Management M,D
Transportation Management M,D

FLORIDA INTERNATIONAL UNIVERSITY
Accounting M
Adult Education M,D,O
Art Education M,D,O
Athletic Training and Sports Medicine M
Counselor Education M,D,O
Curriculum and Instruction M,D,O
Early Childhood Education M,D,O
Educational Leadership and Administration M,D,O
Educational Media/Instructional Technology M,D,O
Elementary Education M,D,O
English as a Second Language M,D,O
English Education M,D,O
Finance and Banking M
Foreign Languages Education M,D,O
Higher Education M,D,O
Hospitality Management M
Human Resources Development M,D,O
Human Resources Management M,D
International and Comparative Education M,D,O
International Business M,D
Law M,D
Management Information Systems M,D
Marketing M
Mathematics Education M,D,O
Multilingual and Multicultural Education M,D,O
Music Education M
Physical Education M,D,O
Reading Education M,D,O
Real Estate M
Recreation and Park Management M,D,O
Science Education M,D,O
Social Sciences Education M,D,O
Social Work M,D
Special Education M,D,O
Sports Management M,D,O
Urban Education M,D,O

FLORIDA MEMORIAL UNIVERSITY
Business Administration and Management—General M
Education—General M
Elementary Education M
Reading Education M
Special Education M

FLORIDA NATIONAL UNIVERSITY
Business Administration and Management—General M
Finance and Banking M
Marketing M

FLORIDA SOUTHERN COLLEGE
Accounting M
Business Administration and Management—General M
Education—General M,D
Educational Leadership and Administration M,D

FLORIDA STATE UNIVERSITY
Accounting M,D
Actuarial Science M,D
Art Education M,D
Business Administration and Management—General M,D
Community College Education M
Curriculum and Instruction M,D,O
Early Childhood Education M,D,O
Education—General M,D,O
Educational Leadership and Administration M,D,O
Educational Measurement and Evaluation M,D,O
Educational Media/Instructional Technology M,D,O
Educational Policy M,D,O
Educational Psychology M,D
Elementary Education M,D,O
English Education M,D,O
Environmental Law M,D
Exercise and Sports Science M,D
Finance and Banking M,D
Foreign Languages Education M,D,O
Foundations and Philosophy of Education M,D
Health Education M,D
Higher Education M,D
Human Resources Management M,D
Information Studies M,D,O
Insurance M,D
International and Comparative Education M,D
International Business M,D
Law M,D
Library Science M,D,O
Management Information Systems M,D,O
Management Strategy and Policy M,D
Marketing M,D
Mathematics Education M,D,O
Organizational Behavior M,D
Reading Education M,D,O
Science Education M,D,O
Social Sciences Education M,D,O
Social Work M,D
Special Education M,D,O
Sports Management M,D,O
Taxation M,D

FONTBONNE UNIVERSITY
Accounting M
Art Education M
Business Administration and Management—General M
Curriculum and Instruction M
Early Childhood Education M
Education—General M
Educational Media/Instructional Technology M
Elementary Education M
Middle School Education M
Reading Education M
Secondary Education M
Special Education M
Supply Chain Management M

FORDHAM UNIVERSITY
Accounting M
Business Administration and Management—General M
Counselor Education M,D
Curriculum and Instruction M,O
Early Childhood Education M,O
Education—General M,D,O
Educational Leadership and Administration M,D,O
Educational Psychology M,D
Electronic Commerce M
Elementary Education M,O
English as a Second Language M,O
Entrepreneurship M
Finance and Banking M
Intellectual Property Law M,D
Investment Management M
Law M,D
Management Information Systems M
Management Strategy and Policy M
Marketing M
Nonprofit Management M,D
Quantitative Analysis M
Religious Education M,D,O
Social Work M,D
Special Education M,O
Taxation M

FORT HAYS STATE UNIVERSITY
Business Administration and Management—General M
Counselor Education M
Education—General M,O
Educational Leadership and Administration M,O
Educational Media/Instructional Technology M
Health Education M
Physical Education M
Special Education M

FORT LEWIS COLLEGE
Educational Leadership and Administration M,O

FORT VALLEY STATE UNIVERSITY
Counselor Education M,O

FRAMINGHAM STATE UNIVERSITY
Business Administration and Management—General M
Curriculum and Instruction M
Early Childhood Education M
Educational Leadership and Administration M
Educational Media/Instructional Technology M
Elementary Education M
English as a Second Language M
English Education M
Foreign Languages Education M
Health Education M
Human Resources Management M
Mathematics Education M
Reading Education M
Social Sciences Education M
Special Education M

FRANCISCAN UNIVERSITY OF STEUBENVILLE
Business Administration and Management—General M
Curriculum and Instruction M
Education—General M
Educational Leadership and Administration M

FRANCIS MARION UNIVERSITY
Business Administration and Management—General M
Education—General M
Special Education M

FRANKLIN COLLEGE
Athletic Training and Sports Medicine M

FRANKLIN PIERCE UNIVERSITY
Business Administration and Management—General M,D,O
Curriculum and Instruction M,D,O
Elementary Education M,D,O
Human Resources Management M,D,O
Management Information Systems M,D,O
Special Education M,D,O
Sports Management M,D,O
Sustainability Management M,D,O

FRANKLIN UNIVERSITY
Accounting M
Business Administration and Management—General M
Educational Media/Instructional Technology M
Marketing M

FRANKLIN UNIVERSITY SWITZERLAND
International Business M

FREED-HARDEMAN UNIVERSITY
Accounting M
Business Administration and Management—General M
Counselor Education M,O
Curriculum and Instruction M,O
Education—General M,O
Educational Leadership and Administration M,O
Management Strategy and Policy M
Special Education M,O

FRESNO PACIFIC UNIVERSITY
Business Administration and Management—General M
Counselor Education M
Curriculum and Instruction M
Education—General M,O
Educational Leadership and Administration M
Educational Media/Instructional Technology M
English as a Second Language M,O
Kinesiology and Movement Studies M
Mathematics Education M
Reading Education M,O
Science Education M
Special Education M
Student Affairs M,O

FRIENDS UNIVERSITY
Accounting M
Law M
Logistics M
Management Information Systems M
Management Strategy and Policy M
Supply Chain Management M

FROSTBURG STATE UNIVERSITY
Business Administration and Management—General M
Counselor Education M
Curriculum and Instruction M
Education—General M
Educational Leadership and Administration M
Educational Media/Instructional Technology M
Elementary Education M
Reading Education M
Recreation and Park Management M
Secondary Education M
Special Education M

FULL SAIL UNIVERSITY
Business Administration and Management—General M
Educational Media/Instructional Technology M
Entertainment Management M
Marketing M

FURMAN UNIVERSITY
Curriculum and Instruction M,O
Early Childhood Education M,O
Education—General M,O
Educational Leadership and Administration M,O
English as a Second Language M,O
Reading Education M,O
Special Education M,O

GALLAUDET UNIVERSITY
Counselor Education M,D,O
Early Childhood Education M,D,O
Education—General M,D,O
Elementary Education M,D,O
International and Comparative Education M,D,O
Multilingual and Multicultural Education M,D,O
Secondary Education M,D,O
Social Work M,D,O
Special Education M,D,O

GANNON UNIVERSITY
Athletic Training and Sports Medicine M
Business Administration and Management—General M
Curriculum and Instruction M,O
Education—General M,O
Educational Leadership and Administration D,O
English as a Second Language O
Exercise and Sports Science M
Finance and Banking M
Human Resources Management M
Marketing M
Organizational Management D
Reading Education M,O

GARDNER-WEBB UNIVERSITY
Business Administration and Management—General M
Curriculum and Instruction D
Education—General M,D,O
Educational Leadership and Administration M,D,O
English Education M
Exercise and Sports Science M
Organizational Management D
Physical Education M
Religious Education M,D

GARRETT-EVANGELICAL THEOLOGICAL SEMINARY
Religious Education M,D

GATEWAY SEMINARY
Early Childhood Education M,D,O
Educational Leadership and Administration M,D,O

GENEVA COLLEGE
Business Administration and Management—General M
Counselor Education M
Education—General M
Educational Leadership and Administration M
Finance and Banking M
Higher Education M
Marketing M
Nonprofit Management M
Organizational Management M
Project Management M

GEORGE FOX UNIVERSITY
Accounting M,D
Business Administration and Management—General M,D
Counselor Education M,O
Education—General M,D,O
Educational Leadership and Administration M,D,O
Educational Media/Instructional Technology M,O
English as a Second Language M,O
Finance and Banking M,D
Human Resources Management M,D
Marketing M,D
Organizational Management M,D
Reading Education M,O
Social Work M
Special Education M,O

GEORGE MASON UNIVERSITY
Accounting M,O
Art Education M
Business Administration and Management—General M
Community College Education M,D,O
Counselor Education M
Curriculum and Instruction M
Early Childhood Education M
Education of the Gifted M

*M—masters degree; D—doctorate; O—other advanced degree; *—Close-Up and/or Display*

Education—General M,D,O
Educational Leadership and Administration M,O
Educational Media/Instructional Technology M
Educational Psychology M,O
Elementary Education M
English as a Second Language M
English Education M
Exercise and Sports Science M,O
Foreign Languages Education M
Higher Education D,O
Human Resources Management M
International and Comparative Education M
International Business M
Law M,D
Logistics M,O
Management Information Systems M
Mathematics Education M
Multilingual and Multicultural Education M
Music Education M
Organizational Management M
Physical Education M
Project Management M,D
Reading Education M
Science Education M
Secondary Education M
Social Sciences Education M
Social Work M
Special Education M,D,O
Transportation Management M,O

GEORGETOWN COLLEGE
Education—General M
Reading Education M
Special Education M

GEORGETOWN UNIVERSITY
Advertising and Public Relations M
Business Administration and Management—General M
Environmental Law M,D
Finance and Banking M,D
Health Law M,D
Hospitality Management M,D
Human Resources Management M,D
Industrial and Manufacturing Management D
International Business M,D
Law M,D
Real Estate M,D
Sports Management M,D
Taxation M,D

THE GEORGE WASHINGTON UNIVERSITY
Accounting M
Adult Education O
Art Education M
Business Administration and Management—General M,D,O
Counselor Education M,D,O
Curriculum and Instruction M,D,O
Distance Education Development O
Early Childhood Education M
Education—General M,D,O
Educational Leadership and Administration M,D,O
Educational Media/Instructional Technology M,O
Educational Policy M,D,O
Elementary Education M
Exercise and Sports Science M
Finance and Banking M,D
Foreign Languages Education M
Higher Education M,D,O
Hospitality Management M,O
Human Resources Development M,D,O
Human Resources Management M,O
International and Comparative Education M,D,O
International Business M,D
Investment Management M,D
Law M,D
Legal and Justice Studies M,D,O
Management Information Systems M,D
Management Strategy and Policy M,D,O
Marketing M,D
Mathematics Education M
Multilingual and Multicultural Education M,D,O
Museum Education M
Nonprofit Management M,O
Organizational Management M,O
Project Management M,D,O
Real Estate O
Science Education M
Secondary Education M
Special Education M,D,O
Sports Management M,O
Student Affairs M,D,O
Travel and Tourism M,O
Vocational and Technical Education O

GEORGIA CHRISTIAN UNIVERSITY
Business Administration and Management—General M

GEORGIA COLLEGE & STATE UNIVERSITY
Accounting M
Business Administration and Management—General M
Early Childhood Education M
Education—General M,O
Educational Leadership and Administration O
Educational Media/Instructional Technology M
Exercise and Sports Science M
Health Education M
Kinesiology and Movement Studies M
Logistics M
Management Information Systems M
Music Education M
Physical Education M
Reading Education M
Secondary Education M
Special Education M,O

GEORGIA INSTITUTE OF TECHNOLOGY
Business Administration and Management—General M,D
International Business M
Logistics M
Management Information Systems M

GEORGIAN COURT UNIVERSITY
Business Administration and Management—General M,O
Counselor Education M,O
Education—General M,O
Educational Leadership and Administration M,O
Educational Media/Instructional Technology M,O
Nonprofit Management M,O
Special Education M,O

GEORGIA SOUTHERN UNIVERSITY
Accounting M
Business Administration and Management—General M
Counselor Education M,O
Curriculum and Instruction M,D
Early Childhood Education M,O
Education—General M,D,O
Educational Leadership and Administration M,D,O
Educational Measurement and Evaluation M,D,O
Educational Media/Instructional Technology M,O
English Education M
Foreign Languages Education M
Health Education M,D
Higher Education M
Kinesiology and Movement Studies M
Logistics D
Management Information Systems M,O
Middle School Education M,O
Multilingual and Multicultural Education D
Music Education M
Nonprofit Management O
Reading Education M,O
Secondary Education M,O
Special Education M,O
Sports Management M
Supply Chain Management D
Taxation M

GEORGIA SOUTHWESTERN STATE UNIVERSITY
Business Administration and Management—General M
Early Childhood Education M,O
Education—General M,O
English Education M,O
Management Information Systems M,O
Mathematics Education M,O
Middle School Education M,O
Special Education M,O

GEORGIA STATE UNIVERSITY
Accounting M
Actuarial Science M
Art Education M
Athletic Training and Sports Medicine M
Business Administration and Management—General M,D
Counselor Education M,D
Curriculum and Instruction M,D
Early Childhood Education M,D,O
Education of Students with Severe/Multiple Disabilities M
Education—General M,D,O
Educational Leadership and Administration M,D,O
Educational Measurement and Evaluation M,D
Educational Media/Instructional Technology M,D
Educational Policy M,D,O
Educational Psychology M,D
Elementary Education M,D,O
English Education M,D
Entrepreneurship M,D
Exercise and Sports Science M
Finance and Banking M,D,O
Foreign Languages Education M,O
Foundations and Philosophy of Education M,D
Health Education M,D
Human Resources Management M,D
Human Services M,O
Insurance M,D,O
International Business M
Kinesiology and Movement Studies D
Law D
Management Information Systems M,D,O
Management Strategy and Policy M,D
Marketing M,D
Mathematics Education M,D,O
Middle School Education M,D
Music Education M,D,O
Nonprofit Management M,D,O
Organizational Management M,D
Physical Education M
Reading Education M,D
Real Estate M,D,O
Science Education M,D
Secondary Education M,D
Social Sciences Education M,D
Social Work M,O
Special Education M,D
Sports Management M
Taxation M

Urban Education M,D,O

GLION INSTITUTE OF HIGHER EDUCATION
Hospitality Management M

GLOBAL UNIVERSITY
Religious Education M,D

GODDARD COLLEGE
Business Administration and Management—General M
Education—General M
Sustainability Management M

GOLDEN GATE UNIVERSITY
Accounting M,D,O
Advertising and Public Relations M,D,O
Business Administration and Management—General M,D,O
Environmental Law M,D
Finance and Banking M,D,O
Human Resources Management M,D,O
Intellectual Property Law M,D
International Business M,D,O
Law M,D
Legal and Justice Studies M,D
Management Information Systems M,D,O
Management Strategy and Policy M,D,O
Marketing M,D,O
Supply Chain Management M,D,O
Taxation M,D,O

GOLDEY-BEACOM COLLEGE
Business Administration and Management—General M
Finance and Banking M
Human Resources Management M
International Business M
Management Information Systems M
Marketing M
Taxation M

GONZAGA UNIVERSITY
Accounting M
Business Administration and Management—General M
Education—General M
Elementary Education M
English as a Second Language M
Law D
Organizational Management M,D
Secondary Education M
Special Education M
Sports Management M
Taxation M

GORDON COLLEGE
Early Childhood Education M,O
Education—General M,O
Educational Leadership and Administration M,O
Elementary Education M,O
English as a Second Language M,O
Mathematics Education M,O
Middle School Education M,O
Music Education M
Reading Education M,O
Secondary Education M,O
Special Education M,O

GOSHEN COLLEGE
Environmental Education M

GOUCHER COLLEGE
Business Administration and Management—General M
Education—General M,O
Educational Leadership and Administration M,O
Educational Media/Instructional Technology M,O
Elementary Education M,O
Middle School Education M,O
Physical Education M,O
Reading Education M,O
Secondary Education M,O
Special Education M,O

GOVERNORS STATE UNIVERSITY
Accounting M
Business Administration and Management—General M
Early Childhood Education M
Education—General M
Educational Leadership and Administration M,D
Human Services M,D
Legal and Justice Studies M
Management Information Systems M
Reading Education M
Social Work M
Special Education M

GRACELAND UNIVERSITY (IA)
Curriculum and Instruction M
Education—General M
Educational Leadership and Administration M
Educational Media/Instructional Technology M
Organizational Management M,D,O
Reading Education M
Special Education M

THE GRADUATE CENTER, CITY UNIVERSITY OF NEW YORK
Accounting D
Business Administration and Management—General D
Educational Psychology D
Finance and Banking D
Management Information Systems D
Organizational Behavior D
Social Work D
Urban Education D

GRADUATE INSTITUTE OF APPLIED LINGUISTICS
Multilingual and Multicultural Education M,O

GRAMBLING STATE UNIVERSITY
Counselor Education M,D,O
Curriculum and Instruction M,D,O
Developmental Education M,D,O
Education—General M,D,O
Educational Leadership and Administration M,D,O
Educational Media/Instructional Technology M,D,O
Higher Education M,D,O
Human Resources Management M
Mathematics Education M,D,O
Reading Education M,D,O
Science Education M,D,O
Social Sciences Education M
Social Work M
Special Education M
Sports Management M
Student Affairs M,D,O

GRAND CANYON UNIVERSITY
Accounting M
Business Administration and Management—General M,D
Curriculum and Instruction M,D,O
Early Childhood Education M,D,O
Education of the Gifted M,D,O
Education—General M,D,O
Educational Leadership and Administration M,D,O
Educational Media/Instructional Technology M,D,O
Elementary Education M,D,O
English as a Second Language M,D,O
Entrepreneurship M
Finance and Banking M
Human Resources Management M
Marketing M,D
Organizational Management M,D
Project Management M
Reading Education M,D,O
Science Education M,D,O
Secondary Education M,D,O
Special Education M,D,O
Sports Management M

GRAND RAPIDS THEOLOGICAL SEMINARY OF CORNERSTONE UNIVERSITY
Religious Education M

GRAND VALLEY STATE UNIVERSITY
Accounting M
Adult Education M
Business Administration and Management—General M
Curriculum and Instruction M
Early Childhood Education M
Education—General M
Educational Leadership and Administration M,O
Educational Media/Instructional Technology M
Elementary Education M
English as a Second Language M
English Education M
Higher Education M
Management Information Systems M
Middle School Education M
Nonprofit Management M
Reading Education M
Secondary Education M
Social Work M
Special Education M
Taxation M

GRAND VIEW UNIVERSITY
Athletic Training and Sports Medicine M,O
Educational Leadership and Administration M,O
Organizational Management M,O
Sports Management M,O
Urban Education M,O

GRANITE STATE COLLEGE
Business Administration and Management—General M
Organizational Management M
Project Management M

GRANTHAM UNIVERSITY
Business Administration and Management—General M,O
Human Resources Development M,O
Human Resources Management M,O
Management Information Systems M,O
Management Strategy and Policy M,O
Project Management M,O

GRATZ COLLEGE
Education—General M
Educational Leadership and Administration M,D
Nonprofit Management M
Religious Education M,D
Social Work M,O

GREEN MOUNTAIN COLLEGE
Business Administration and Management—General M

GREENSBORO COLLEGE
Education—General M
Elementary Education M
English as a Second Language M
Special Education M

GREENVILLE COLLEGE
Education—General M
Elementary Education M
Secondary Education M

GWYNEDD MERCY UNIVERSITY
Business Administration and Management—General M
Counselor Education M
Education—General M
Educational Leadership and Administration M
Management Strategy and Policy M
Special Education M

HALLMARK UNIVERSITY
Business Administration and Management—General M
International Business M

HAMLINE UNIVERSITY
Business Administration and Management—General M,D
Education—General M,D
English as a Second Language M,D
Environmental Education M,D
Nonprofit Management M,D
Reading Education M,D
Science Education M,D

HAMPTON UNIVERSITY
Business Administration and Management—General M,D
Counselor Education M,D,O
Education—General M,D,O
Educational Leadership and Administration M,D
Elementary Education M
Music Education M
Secondary Education M
Sports Management M
Student Affairs M,D,O

HANNIBAL-LAGRANGE UNIVERSITY
Education—General M
Reading Education M

HARDING UNIVERSITY
Art Education M,O
Business Administration and Management—General M
Counselor Education M,O
Early Childhood Education M,O
Education—General M,O
Educational Leadership and Administration M,O
Elementary Education M,O
English as a Second Language M,O
English Education M,O
Foreign Languages Education M,O
Health Education M,O
International Business M
Mathematics Education M,O
Organizational Management M
Reading Education M,O
Secondary Education M,O
Social Sciences Education M,O
Special Education M,O

HARDIN-SIMMONS UNIVERSITY
Business Administration and Management—General M
Counselor Education M
Education of the Gifted M
Education—General M,D
Educational Leadership and Administration D
Kinesiology and Movement Studies M
Music Education M
Reading Education M
Recreation and Park Management M
Science Education M,D
Sports Management M

HARRISBURG UNIVERSITY OF SCIENCE AND TECHNOLOGY
Educational Media/Instructional Technology M
Entrepreneurship M
Management Information Systems M
Management Strategy and Policy M
Project Management M

HARRISON MIDDLETON UNIVERSITY
Education—General M,D
Legal and Justice Studies M,D
Science Education M,D

HARVARD UNIVERSITY
Accounting D
Art Education M
Business Administration and Management—General M,D,O
Curriculum and Instruction M
Education—General M,D
Educational Leadership and Administration M,D
Educational Media/Instructional Technology M,O
Educational Policy M
Educational Psychology M
Foundations and Philosophy of Education M,O
Industrial and Manufacturing Management D
International and Comparative Education M
Law M,D
Legal and Justice Studies D
Management Strategy and Policy D
Marketing D
Mathematics Education M,O
Organizational Behavior D
Reading Education M

HASTINGS COLLEGE
Education—General M

HAWAI'I PACIFIC UNIVERSITY
Accounting M
Business Administration and Management—General M
Elementary Education M
English as a Second Language M
Finance and Banking M
Hospitality Management M
Human Resources Management M
International Business M
Management Information Systems M
Marketing M
Organizational Management M
Secondary Education M
Social Work M

HEBREW COLLEGE
Early Childhood Education M,O
Education—General M,O
Middle School Education M,O
Music Education M,O
Religious Education M,O
Special Education M,O

HEBREW UNION COLLEGE–JEWISH INSTITUTE OF RELIGION (NY)
Education—General M
Nonprofit Management M
Religious Education M

HEC MONTREAL
Accounting M,O
Business Administration and Management—General M,D,O
Electronic Commerce M,O
Finance and Banking M,O
Human Resources Management M
Industrial and Manufacturing Management M
International Business M
Logistics M
Management Information Systems M
Management Strategy and Policy M
Marketing M
Organizational Management M
Supply Chain Management M,O
Taxation M,O

HEIDELBERG UNIVERSITY
Business Administration and Management—General M
Education—General M
Music Education M

HENDERSON STATE UNIVERSITY
Business Administration and Management—General M
Counselor Education M,O
Curriculum and Instruction M,O
Early Childhood Education M,O
Education—General M,O
Educational Leadership and Administration M,O
English as a Second Language M,O
Middle School Education M,O
Physical Education M
Special Education M,O
Sports Management M

HENDRIX COLLEGE
Accounting M

HERITAGE UNIVERSITY
Counselor Education M
Education—General M
Educational Leadership and Administration M
English as a Second Language M
Multilingual and Multicultural Education M
Reading Education M
Science Education M
Special Education M

HERZING UNIVERSITY ONLINE
Accounting M
Business Administration and Management—General M
Human Resources Management M
Marketing M
Project Management M

HIGH POINT UNIVERSITY
Business Administration and Management—General M
Education—General M
Educational Leadership and Administration M
Elementary Education M
Mathematics Education M
Nonprofit Management M
Secondary Education M
Special Education M

HODGES UNIVERSITY
Accounting M
Business Administration and Management—General M
Legal and Justice Studies M
Management Information Systems M

HOFSTRA UNIVERSITY
Accounting M,O
Advertising and Public Relations M
Art Education M,D,O
Business Administration and Management—General M,O
Business Education M,D,O
Counselor Education M,O
Early Childhood Education M,D,O
Education of the Gifted M,D,O
Education—General M,D,O
Educational Leadership and Administration M,D,O
Educational Media/Instructional Technology M,D,O
Elementary Education M,D,O
English as a Second Language M,D,O
English Education M,D,O
Entertainment Management M,O
Finance and Banking M,O
Foreign Languages Education M,D,O
Health Education M,D,O
Health Law M,D
Human Resources Management M,O
International Business M,O
Investment Management M,O
Law M,D
Legal and Justice Studies M,D
Management Information Systems M,O
Management Strategy and Policy M,O
Marketing Research M,O
Marketing M,O
Mathematics Education M,D,O
Middle School Education M,D,O
Multilingual and Multicultural Education M,D,O
Music Education M,D,O
Physical Education M,D,O
Quality Management M,O
Quantitative Analysis M,O
Reading Education M,D,O
Science Education M,D,O
Secondary Education M,D,O
Social Sciences Education M,D,O
Special Education M,D,O
Sports Management M,D,O
Taxation M,O

HOLLINS UNIVERSITY
Education—General M

HOLY FAMILY UNIVERSITY
Accounting M,D
Business Administration and Management—General M
Early Childhood Education M
Education—General M,D
Educational Leadership and Administration M,D
Elementary Education M
English as a Second Language M
Finance and Banking M
Human Resources Management M
Management Information Systems M
Reading Education M
Special Education M

HOLY NAMES UNIVERSITY
Business Administration and Management—General M
Education—General M,O
Educational Psychology M,O
Finance and Banking M
Marketing M
Music Education M,O
Special Education M,O
Urban Education M,O

HOOD COLLEGE
Accounting M
Business Administration and Management—General M
Curriculum and Instruction M,O
Education—General M,O
Educational Leadership and Administration M,O
Elementary Education M,O
Finance and Banking M
Human Resources Management M
Management Information Systems M
Marketing M
Mathematics Education M,O
Organizational Management D
Reading Education M,O
Science Education M,O
Secondary Education M,O
Special Education M,O

HOPE INTERNATIONAL UNIVERSITY
Education—General M
Educational Leadership and Administration M
Elementary Education M
International Business M
Marketing M
Nonprofit Management M
Secondary Education M

HOUSTON BAPTIST UNIVERSITY
Business Administration and Management—General M
Counselor Education M,D
Curriculum and Instruction M,D
Education—General M,D
Educational Leadership and Administration M,D
Educational Measurement and Evaluation M,D
English as a Second Language M,D
English Education M
Human Resources Management M
International Business M
Reading Education M,D

HOWARD PAYNE UNIVERSITY
Business Administration and Management—General M
Educational Leadership and Administration M
Sports Management M

HOWARD UNIVERSITY
Accounting M
Business Administration and Management—General M
Counselor Education M
Education—General M,D,O
Educational Leadership and Administration M,D,O
Educational Policy M,D,O
Educational Psychology D
Elementary Education M
Exercise and Sports Science M
Finance and Banking M
Health Education M
Human Resources Management M
International Business M
Law M,D
Leisure Studies M
Management Information Systems M
Marketing M
Multilingual and Multicultural Education M,D
Music Education M
Physical Education M
Secondary Education M
Social Work M,D
Special Education M
Sports Management M
Supply Chain Management M

HULT INTERNATIONAL BUSINESS SCHOOL (UNITED STATES)
Business Administration and Management—General M
Entrepreneurship M
Finance and Banking M
International Business M
Management Strategy and Policy M
Marketing M
Project Management M

HUMBOLDT STATE UNIVERSITY
Business Administration and Management—General M
Education—General M
English as a Second Language M
Kinesiology and Movement Studies M
Social Work M

HUMPHREYS UNIVERSITY
Law D

HUNTER COLLEGE OF THE CITY UNIVERSITY OF NEW YORK
Accounting M
Counselor Education M
Early Childhood Education M,D,O
Education of Students with Severe/Multiple Disabilities M
Education—General M,D,O
Educational Leadership and Administration D,O
Elementary Education M
English as a Second Language M
English Education M
Foreign Languages Education M
Mathematics Education M
Multilingual and Multicultural Education M
Music Education M
Science Education M
Secondary Education M
Social Sciences Education M
Social Work M
Special Education M

HUNTINGTON UNIVERSITY
Education—General M,D
English as a Second Language M,D
Middle School Education M,D

HUSSON UNIVERSITY
Business Administration and Management—General M
Counselor Education M
Hospitality Management M
Organizational Management M
Sports Management M

HUSTON-TILLOTSON UNIVERSITY
Educational Leadership and Administration M

IDAHO STATE UNIVERSITY
Business Administration and Management—General M,O
Counselor Education M,D,O
Curriculum and Instruction M,O
Education—General M,D,O
Educational Leadership and Administration M,D,O
Educational Media/Instructional Technology M,D,O
Elementary Education M,O
English as a Second Language M,D,O
Health Education M
Management Information Systems M,O
Mathematics Education M,D
Physical Education M
Reading Education M,O
Secondary Education M,O
Special Education M,D,O
Vocational and Technical Education M

IGLOBAL UNIVERSITY
Accounting M
Business Administration and Management—General M
Entrepreneurship M
Finance and Banking M
Hospitality Management M
Human Resources Management M
International Business M
Management Information Systems M
Project Management M
Travel and Tourism M

ILLINOIS COLLEGE
Education—General M

*M—masters degree; D—doctorate; O—other advanced degree; *—Close-Up and/or Display*

ILLINOIS INSTITUTE OF TECHNOLOGY
Business Administration and Management—General M,D
Computer Education M,D
Entrepreneurship M
Finance and Banking M,D
Human Resources Development M,D
Industrial and Manufacturing Management M
Law M,D
Legal and Justice Studies M,D
Management Information Systems M,D
Marketing M
Mathematics Education M,D
Science Education M,D
Sustainability Management M
Taxation M,D

ILLINOIS STATE UNIVERSITY
Accounting M
Business Administration and Management—General M
Curriculum and Instruction M,D
Education—General M,D,O
Educational Leadership and Administration M,D
Educational Policy M,D
Health Education M
Higher Education M,D
Management Information Systems M
Mathematics Education M,D
Physical Education M
Reading Education M
Social Work M
Special Education M,D,O
Student Affairs M

IMCA–INTERNATIONAL MANAGEMENT CENTRES ASSOCIATION
Business Administration and Management—General M

IMMACULATA UNIVERSITY
Educational Leadership and Administration M,D,O
Educational Psychology M,D,O
English as a Second Language M
Multilingual and Multicultural Education M
Organizational Management M
Secondary Education M,D,O
Special Education M,D,O

INDEPENDENCE UNIVERSITY
Business Administration and Management—General M

INDIANA STATE UNIVERSITY
Athletic Training and Sports Medicine M,D
Business Administration and Management—General M
Counselor Education M,D,O
Curriculum and Instruction M,D
Education—General M,D,O
Educational Leadership and Administration M,D,O
Educational Media/Instructional Technology M,D
English as a Second Language M,D,O
Foreign Languages Education M,D,O
Health Education M,D
Higher Education M,D,O
Human Resources Development M
Multilingual and Multicultural Education M,D,O
Music Education M
Physical Education M,D
Recreation and Park Management M,D
Science Education M,D
Social Work M
Sports Management M,D
Student Affairs M,D,O
Vocational and Technical Education M

INDIANA TECH
Accounting M
Business Administration and Management—General M
Human Resources Development M
Human Resources Management M
International Business D
Marketing M
Organizational Management M

INDIANA UNIVERSITY BLOOMINGTON
Art Education M,D,O
Athletic Training and Sports Medicine M,D
Business Administration and Management—General M,D
Counselor Education M,D,O
Curriculum and Instruction M,D,O
Education—General M,D,O
Educational Leadership and Administration M,D,O
Educational Measurement and Evaluation M,D,O
Educational Media/Instructional Technology M,D
Educational Policy M,D,O
Educational Psychology M,D,O
Elementary Education M,D,O
English as a Second Language M,D
Exercise and Sports Science M,D
Finance and Banking M,D,O
Foreign Languages Education M,D
Foundations and Philosophy of Education M,D,O
Health Education M,D
Higher Education M,D,O
International and Comparative Education M,D,O
Kinesiology and Movement Studies M,D
Law M,D,O
Leisure Studies M,D
Library Science M,D,O
Management Information Systems M,D,O
Mathematics Education M,D,O
Multilingual and Multicultural Education M,D
Nonprofit Management M,D,O
Organizational Management M,D,O
Physical Education M,D
Reading Education M,D,O
Recreation and Park Management M,D
Science Education M,D,O
Secondary Education M,D,O
Social Sciences Education M,D,O
Special Education M,D,O
Sports Management M,D
Student Affairs M,D,O
Sustainability Management M,D,O
Travel and Tourism M,D

INDIANA UNIVERSITY EAST
Education—General M
Social Work M

INDIANA UNIVERSITY KOKOMO
Accounting M,O
Business Administration and Management—General M,O

INDIANA UNIVERSITY NORTHWEST
Accounting M,O
Business Administration and Management—General M,O
Education—General M,O
Educational Leadership and Administration M,O
Elementary Education M,O
Management Information Systems M,O
Nonprofit Management M,O
Secondary Education M,O
Social Work M

INDIANA UNIVERSITY OF PENNSYLVANIA
Adult Education M
Business Administration and Management—General M
Business Education M
Counselor Education M
Curriculum and Instruction D
Education—General M,D,O
Educational Leadership and Administration D,O
Educational Media/Instructional Technology M,D
Educational Psychology M,O
English as a Second Language M,D
English Education M,D
Exercise and Sports Science M
Foreign Languages Education M
Health Education M
Higher Education M
Human Resources Development M
Mathematics Education M
Music Education M
Nonprofit Management D
Physical Education M
Reading Education M,O
Special Education M
Sports Management M
Student Affairs M
Vocational and Technical Education M

INDIANA UNIVERSITY–PURDUE UNIVERSITY FORT WAYNE
Business Administration and Management—General M
Counselor Education M,O
Education—General M,O
Educational Leadership and Administration M,O
Elementary Education M
English as a Second Language M,O
English Education M,O
Facilities Management M
Mathematics Education M,O
Organizational Management M,O
Secondary Education M
Special Education M,O

INDIANA UNIVERSITY–PURDUE UNIVERSITY INDIANAPOLIS
Accounting M
Business Administration and Management—General M
Counselor Education M,O
Curriculum and Instruction M,O
Early Childhood Education M,O
Education—General M,O
Educational Leadership and Administration M,O
English as a Second Language M,O
Entrepreneurship M
Finance and Banking M
Foreign Languages Education M,O
Health Education M,D
Health Law M,D,O
Intellectual Property Law M,D,O
Kinesiology and Movement Studies M,O
Law M,D,O
Library Science M,O
Marketing M
Mathematics Education M,D
Nonprofit Management M,O
Organizational Management M,O
Physical Education M,O
Reading Education M,O
Social Work M,D,O
Special Education M,O
Supply Chain Management M

INDIANA UNIVERSITY SOUTH BEND
Accounting M,O
Business Administration and Management—General M,O
Counselor Education M,O
Education—General M,O
Educational Leadership and Administration M,O
Educational Media/Instructional Technology M,O
Elementary Education M,O
Finance and Banking M,O
Human Resources Management M,O
Legal and Justice Studies M,O
Marketing M,O
Nonprofit Management M,O
Secondary Education M,O
Social Work M
Special Education M,O

INDIANA UNIVERSITY SOUTHEAST
Business Administration and Management—General M
Counselor Education M
Education—General M
Elementary Education M
Finance and Banking M
Secondary Education M

INDIANA WESLEYAN UNIVERSITY
Accounting M,O
Business Administration and Management—General M,O
Counselor Education M
Educational Leadership and Administration M,O
Higher Education M
Human Resources Management M,O
Organizational Management M,D,O

INSTITUTE FOR CHRISTIAN STUDIES
Education—General M,D

INSTITUTE FOR CLINICAL SOCIAL WORK
Social Work D

INSTITUTO CENTROAMERICANO DE ADMINISTRACIÓN DE EMPRESAS
Business Administration and Management—General M
Finance and Banking M
Real Estate M

INSTITUTO TECNOLOGICO DE SANTO DOMINGO
Accounting M,O
Adult Education M,O
Business Administration and Management—General M,O
Education—General M,O
Educational Leadership and Administration M,O
Educational Psychology M,O
Environmental Education M,D,O
Finance and Banking M,O
Human Resources Management M,O
Industrial and Manufacturing Management M,O
International Business M,O
Marketing M,O
Organizational Management M,O
Quality Management M,O
Quantitative Analysis M,O
Secondary Education M,O
Social Sciences Education M,O
Taxation M,O
Transportation Management M,O

INSTITUTO TECNOLÓGICO Y DE ESTUDIOS SUPERIORES DE MONTERREY, CAMPUS CENTRAL DE VERACRUZ
Business Administration and Management—General M
Education—General M
Educational Leadership and Administration M
Educational Media/Instructional Technology M
Electronic Commerce M
Finance and Banking M
International Business M
Management Information Systems M
Marketing M

INSTITUTO TECNOLÓGICO Y DE ESTUDIOS SUPERIORES DE MONTERREY, CAMPUS CHIHUAHUA
International Business M,O

INSTITUTO TECNOLÓGICO Y DE ESTUDIOS SUPERIORES DE MONTERREY, CAMPUS CIUDAD DE MÉXICO
Business Administration and Management—General M,D
Education—General M,D
Educational Media/Instructional Technology M,D
Finance and Banking M,D
International Business M,D
Law O
Management Information Systems M,D
Quality Management M,D

INSTITUTO TECNOLÓGICO Y DE ESTUDIOS SUPERIORES DE MONTERREY, CAMPUS CIUDAD JUÁREZ
Business Administration and Management—General M
Education—General M
Educational Leadership and Administration M
Educational Media/Instructional Technology M,D
Electronic Commerce M
Management Information Systems M
Quality Management M

INSTITUTO TECNOLÓGICO Y DE ESTUDIOS SUPERIORES DE MONTERREY, CAMPUS CIUDAD OBREGÓN
Business Administration and Management—General M
Developmental Education M
Education—General M
Finance and Banking M
Management Information Systems M
Marketing M
Mathematics Education M

INSTITUTO TECNOLÓGICO Y DE ESTUDIOS SUPERIORES DE MONTERREY, CAMPUS CUERNAVACA
Business Administration and Management—General M
Finance and Banking M
Human Resources Management M
International Business M
Marketing M

INSTITUTO TECNOLÓGICO Y DE ESTUDIOS SUPERIORES DE MONTERREY, CAMPUS ESTADO DE MÉXICO
Business Administration and Management—General M,D
Education—General M,D
Educational Leadership and Administration M,D
Educational Media/Instructional Technology M,D
Electronic Commerce M,D
Finance and Banking M,D
Industrial and Manufacturing Management M,D
Management Information Systems M,D
Marketing M,D
Quality Management M,D

INSTITUTO TECNOLÓGICO Y DE ESTUDIOS SUPERIORES DE MONTERREY, CAMPUS GUADALAJARA
Business Administration and Management—General M
Finance and Banking M

INSTITUTO TECNOLÓGICO Y DE ESTUDIOS SUPERIORES DE MONTERREY, CAMPUS IRAPUATO
Business Administration and Management—General M,D
Education—General M,D
Educational Leadership and Administration M,D
Educational Media/Instructional Technology M,D
Electronic Commerce M,D
Finance and Banking M,D
Industrial and Manufacturing Management M,D
International Business M,D
Library Science M,D
Management Information Systems M,D
Marketing Research M,D
Quality Management M,D

INSTITUTO TECNOLÓGICO Y DE ESTUDIOS SUPERIORES DE MONTERREY, CAMPUS LAGUNA
Business Administration and Management—General M
Management Information Systems M

INSTITUTO TECNOLÓGICO Y DE ESTUDIOS SUPERIORES DE MONTERREY, CAMPUS LEÓN
Business Administration and Management—General M

INSTITUTO TECNOLÓGICO Y DE ESTUDIOS SUPERIORES DE MONTERREY, CAMPUS MONTERREY
Business Administration and Management—General M,D
Finance and Banking M
International Business M
Marketing M
Science Education M,D

INSTITUTO TECNOLÓGICO Y DE ESTUDIOS SUPERIORES DE MONTERREY, CAMPUS QUERÉTARO
Business Administration and Management—General M

INSTITUTO TECNOLÓGICO Y DE ESTUDIOS SUPERIORES DE MONTERREY, CAMPUS SONORA NORTE
Business Administration and Management—General M
Education—General M

INSTITUTO TECNOLÓGICO Y DE ESTUDIOS SUPERIORES DE MONTERREY, CAMPUS TOLUCA
Business Administration and Management—General M

INTER AMERICAN UNIVERSITY OF PUERTO RICO, AGUADILLA CAMPUS
Accounting M
Business Administration and Management—General M
Educational Leadership and Administration M
Elementary Education M
Finance and Banking M
Human Resources Management M
Management Information Systems M
Marketing M

INTER AMERICAN UNIVERSITY OF PUERTO RICO, ARECIBO CAMPUS
Accounting M
Business Administration and Management—General M
Counselor Education M
Curriculum and Instruction M
Education—General M
Educational Leadership and Administration M
Elementary Education M
English as a Second Language M
Finance and Banking M
Foreign Languages Education M
Human Resources Management M
Mathematics Education M
Science Education M
Social Sciences Education M

INTER AMERICAN UNIVERSITY OF PUERTO RICO, BARRANQUITAS CAMPUS
Accounting M
Business Administration and Management—General M
Curriculum and Instruction M
Education—General M
Educational Leadership and Administration M
Elementary Education M
English as a Second Language M
Finance and Banking M
Foreign Languages Education M
Library Science M
Mathematics Education M
Science Education M
Social Sciences Education M
Special Education M

INTER AMERICAN UNIVERSITY OF PUERTO RICO, BAYAMÓN CAMPUS
Human Resources Management M

INTER AMERICAN UNIVERSITY OF PUERTO RICO, FAJARDO CAMPUS
Business Administration and Management—General M
Educational Leadership and Administration M
Elementary Education M
Management Information Systems M
Marketing M
Special Education M

INTER AMERICAN UNIVERSITY OF PUERTO RICO, GUAYAMA CAMPUS
Business Administration and Management—General M
Early Childhood Education M
Elementary Education M
Marketing M

INTER AMERICAN UNIVERSITY OF PUERTO RICO, METROPOLITAN CAMPUS
Accounting M
Athletic Training and Sports Medicine M
Business Administration and Management—General M
Business Education M
Counselor Education M,D
Curriculum and Instruction M,D
Education—General M,D
Educational Leadership and Administration M,D
Educational Media/Instructional Technology M
Elementary Education M
English as a Second Language M
Exercise and Sports Science M
Finance and Banking M
Foreign Languages Education M
Health Education M
Higher Education M
Human Resources Development M
Human Resources Management M
Industrial and Manufacturing Management M
International Business M,D
Management Information Systems M
Marketing M
Mathematics Education M
Music Education M
Physical Education M
Religious Education D
Science Education M
Social Sciences Education M
Social Work M
Special Education M
Vocational and Technical Education M

INTER AMERICAN UNIVERSITY OF PUERTO RICO, PONCE CAMPUS
Accounting M
Elementary Education M
English as a Second Language M
Finance and Banking M
Human Resources Management M
Marketing M
Mathematics Education M
Science Education M
Social Sciences Education M

INTER AMERICAN UNIVERSITY OF PUERTO RICO, SAN GERMÁN CAMPUS
Accounting M,D
Business Administration and Management—General M,D
Business Education M
Counselor Education M,D
Curriculum and Instruction D
Elementary Education M
English as a Second Language M
Finance and Banking M,D
Health Education M
Human Resources Development M,D
Human Resources Management M,D
Industrial and Manufacturing Management M,D
International Business M,D
Kinesiology and Movement Studies M
Library Science M
Management Information Systems M,D
Marketing M,D
Mathematics Education M
Music Education M
Physical Education M
Science Education M
Special Education M

INTER AMERICAN UNIVERSITY OF PUERTO RICO SCHOOL OF LAW
Law D

INTERDENOMINATIONAL THEOLOGICAL CENTER
Religious Education M,D

INTERNATIONAL BAPTIST COLLEGE AND SEMINARY
Education—General M

INTERNATIONAL COLLEGE OF THE CAYMAN ISLANDS
Business Administration and Management—General M
Business Education M
Human Resources Management M

INTERNATIONAL INSTITUTE FOR RESTORATIVE PRACTICES
Organizational Behavior M,O

INTERNATIONAL TECHNOLOGICAL UNIVERSITY
Business Administration and Management—General M,D

INTERNATIONAL UNIVERSITY IN GENEVA
Business Administration and Management—General M,D
Entrepreneurship M,D
International Business M,D
Marketing M,D

THE INTERNATIONAL UNIVERSITY OF MONACO
Business Administration and Management—General M
Entrepreneurship M
Finance and Banking M
International Business M
Marketing M

IONA COLLEGE
Accounting M,O
Advertising and Public Relations M,O
Business Administration and Management—General M,O
Early Childhood Education M
Education—General M
Educational Leadership and Administration M
English Education M
Finance and Banking M,O
Foreign Languages Education M
Human Resources Management M,O
International Business M,O
Marketing M,O
Mathematics Education M
Nonprofit Management M,O
Project Management M,O
Recreation and Park Management M,O
Science Education M
Social Sciences Education M
Special Education M
Sports Management M,O

IOWA STATE UNIVERSITY OF SCIENCE AND TECHNOLOGY
Accounting M
Agricultural Education M,D
Business Administration and Management—General M
Counselor Education M,D
Curriculum and Instruction M,D
Education—General M,D
Educational Leadership and Administration M,D
Educational Measurement and Evaluation M,D
Educational Media/Instructional Technology M,D
Elementary Education M,D
English as a Second Language M
Exercise and Sports Science M
Finance and Banking M
Foundations and Philosophy of Education M,D
Higher Education M,D
Human Resources Development M,D
Kinesiology and Movement Studies M,D
Management Information Systems M,D
Mathematics Education M,D
Science Education M
Special Education M,D
Student Affairs M,D
Transportation Management M
Vocational and Technical Education M,D

ITHACA COLLEGE
Accounting M
Agricultural Education M
Business Administration and Management—General M
Elementary Education M
English Education M
Exercise and Sports Science M
Foreign Languages Education M
Health Education M
Mathematics Education M
Music Education M
Physical Education M
Secondary Education M
Social Sciences Education M
Sports Management M

JACKSON STATE UNIVERSITY
Accounting M
Business Administration and Management—General M,D
Counselor Education M
Early Childhood Education M,D,O
Education—General M,D,O
Educational Leadership and Administration M,D,O
Elementary Education M,D,O
English Education M
Health Education M
Higher Education M,D,O
Mathematics Education M
Music Education M
Physical Education M
Reading Education M,D,O
Science Education M
Social Work M,D
Special Education M,O
Sports Management M
Vocational and Technical Education M,D

JACKSONVILLE STATE UNIVERSITY
Business Administration and Management—General M
Counselor Education M
Early Childhood Education M
Education—General M,O
Educational Leadership and Administration M,O
Educational Media/Instructional Technology M
Elementary Education M
Physical Education M,O
Reading Education M
Secondary Education M
Special Education M

JACKSONVILLE UNIVERSITY
Accounting M
Business Administration and Management—General M,D*
Educational Leadership and Administration M
Finance and Banking M
Kinesiology and Movement Studies M
Marketing M
Organizational Management M
Sports Management M

JAMES MADISON UNIVERSITY
Accounting M
Art Education M
Business Administration and Management—General M
Early Childhood Education M
Education of the Gifted M
Educational Leadership and Administration M
Educational Measurement and Evaluation M,D
Educational Media/Instructional Technology M
Elementary Education M
English as a Second Language M
Entrepreneurship M
Exercise and Sports Science M
Foreign Languages Education M
Health Education M
Higher Education M
Human Resources Management M
Kinesiology and Movement Studies M
Management Information Systems M
Management Strategy and Policy D
Mathematics Education M
Middle School Education M
Multilingual and Multicultural Education M
Music Education M
Nonprofit Management M,D
Organizational Management D
Physical Education M
Reading Education M
Secondary Education M
Special Education M
Sustainability Management M
Taxation M
Vocational and Technical Education M

THE JEWISH THEOLOGICAL SEMINARY
Religious Education M,D

JOHN BROWN UNIVERSITY
Business Administration and Management—General M
Counselor Education M,O
Curriculum and Instruction M
Education—General M
International Business M
Secondary Education M

JOHN CARROLL UNIVERSITY
Accounting M
Business Administration and Management—General M
Counselor Education M,O
Educational Psychology M,O
Nonprofit Management M
Secondary Education M

JOHN F. KENNEDY UNIVERSITY
Business Administration and Management—General M,O
Education—General M
Health Education M
Human Resources Development M,O
Law D
Organizational Management M,O

JOHN JAY COLLEGE OF CRIMINAL JUSTICE OF THE CITY UNIVERSITY OF NEW YORK
Legal and Justice Studies M,D
Organizational Behavior M,D

THE JOHN MARSHALL LAW SCHOOL
Law M,D

JOHNS HOPKINS UNIVERSITY
Business Administration and Management—General M,O
Counselor Education M,O
Early Childhood Education M
Education of the Gifted M,O
Education—General M,D,O
Educational Leadership and Administration M,D,O
Educational Media/Instructional Technology M
Educational Policy D
Elementary Education M
Finance and Banking M,D,O
Health Education M,D
Investment Management M,O
Management Information Systems M,O
Marketing M
Nonprofit Management M,O
Organizational Management M
Reading Education M
Real Estate M
Secondary Education M
Social Sciences Education M
Special Education M,O
Urban Education O

JOHNSON & WALES UNIVERSITY
Accounting M
Business Administration and Management—General M
Business Education M
Education—General M
Educational Leadership and Administration D
Elementary Education M
Finance and Banking M
Hospitality Management M
Human Resources Management M
Management Information Systems M
Nonprofit Management M
Secondary Education M
Special Education M
Supply Chain Management M

JOHNSON C. SMITH UNIVERSITY
Social Work M

JOHNSON STATE COLLEGE
Counselor Education M
Curriculum and Instruction M
Education—General M
Foundations and Philosophy of Education M
Special Education M

JOHNSON UNIVERSITY
Counselor Education M,D,O
Education—General M,D,O
Educational Media/Instructional Technology M,D,O
Higher Education M,D,O
Nonprofit Management M,D,O

JOHN WESLEY UNIVERSITY
Organizational Management M,D

JOSE MARIA VARGAS UNIVERSITY
Early Childhood Education M

THE JUDGE ADVOCATE GENERAL'S SCHOOL, U.S. ARMY
Law M

JUDSON UNIVERSITY
Business Administration and Management—General M
Human Services M
Organizational Management M
Reading Education M,D

JUNIATA COLLEGE
Accounting M

KANSAS STATE UNIVERSITY
Accounting M
Adult Education M,D,O
Advertising and Public Relations M
Agricultural Education M
Business Administration and Management—General M,O
Counselor Education M,D,O
Curriculum and Instruction M,D,O
Distance Education Development M,D,O
Early Childhood Education M,D,O
Education—General M,D,O
Educational Leadership and Administration M,D,O
Educational Media/Instructional Technology M,D,O
Elementary Education M,D,O
English as a Second Language M,D,O
English Education M,D,O
Entrepreneurship M,O
Finance and Banking M,D,O

*M—masters degree; D—doctorate; O—other advanced degree; *—Close-Up and/or Display*

Health Education M,D
Hospitality Management M,D
Human Services M,D,O
Kinesiology and Movement Studies M,D
Marketing M,O
Middle School Education M,D,O
Reading Education M,D,O
Special Education M,D,O
Student Affairs M,D,O

KANSAS WESLEYAN UNIVERSITY
Business Administration and Management—General M
Sports Management M

KAPLAN UNIVERSITY, DAVENPORT CAMPUS
Business Administration and Management—General M
Education—General M
Educational Leadership and Administration M
Educational Media/Instructional Technology M
Entrepreneurship M
Finance and Banking M
Higher Education M
Human Resources Management M
International Business M
Law M
Legal and Justice Studies M,O
Logistics M
Management Information Systems M
Marketing M
Mathematics Education M
Organizational Management M
Project Management M
Reading Education M
Science Education M
Secondary Education M
Special Education M
Student Affairs M
Supply Chain Management M

KEAN UNIVERSITY
Accounting M
Art Education M
Business Administration and Management—General M
Counselor Education M
Curriculum and Instruction M
Early Childhood Education M
Education—General M
Educational Leadership and Administration M,D
English as a Second Language M
Exercise and Sports Science M
Foreign Languages Education M
International Business M
Management Information Systems M
Multilingual and Multicultural Education M
Nonprofit Management M
Reading Education M
Social Work M
Special Education M

KEENE STATE COLLEGE
Counselor Education M,O
Curriculum and Instruction M,O
Education—General M,O
Educational Leadership and Administration M,O
Special Education M,O

KEISER UNIVERSITY
Accounting M
Business Administration and Management—General M,D
Distance Education Development M
Education—General M
Educational Leadership and Administration M,D,O
Educational Media/Instructional Technology D,O
Health Education M
International Business M,D
Management Information Systems M
Marketing M,D
Organizational Management D

KENNESAW STATE UNIVERSITY
Accounting M
Art Education M
Business Administration and Management—General M,D
Early Childhood Education M
Education—General M,D,O
Educational Leadership and Administration M,D,O
Educational Media/Instructional Technology M
Elementary Education M
English as a Second Language M
English Education M
Exercise and Sports Science M
Foreign Languages Education M
Mathematics Education M
Middle School Education M
Reading Education M
Secondary Education M
Social Work M
Special Education M

KENT STATE UNIVERSITY
Accounting M,D
Advertising and Public Relations M
Art Education M
Athletic Training and Sports Medicine M,D
Business Administration and Management—General M
Computer Education M,D
Counselor Education M,D,O
Curriculum and Instruction M,D,O
Early Childhood Education M,D,O
Education of the Gifted M,D,O
Education—General M,D,O
Educational Leadership and Administration M,D,O
Educational Measurement and Evaluation M,D
Educational Media/Instructional Technology M,D
Educational Psychology M
English as a Second Language M,D
English Education M,D
Exercise and Sports Science M,D
Finance and Banking D
Foundations and Philosophy of Education M,D
Health Education M,D
Higher Education M,D,O
Hospitality Management M
Human Services M,D,O
Library Science M
Management Information Systems M,D
Marketing D
Mathematics Education M,D
Middle School Education M
Music Education M,D
Reading Education M
Recreation and Park Management M
Secondary Education M,D
Social Sciences Education M,D
Special Education M,D,O
Sports Management M
Student Affairs M
Travel and Tourism M
Vocational and Technical Education M

KENT STATE UNIVERSITY AT STARK
Business Administration and Management—General M
Curriculum and Instruction M
Education—General M

KENTUCKY STATE UNIVERSITY
Business Administration and Management—General M
Human Resources Development M,D
Special Education M,D

KETTERING UNIVERSITY
Business Administration and Management—General M

KEUKA COLLEGE
Business Administration and Management—General M
Early Childhood Education M
Elementary Education M
Secondary Education M
Social Work M

KEYSTONE COLLEGE
Accounting M
Early Childhood Education M
Educational Leadership and Administration M
Sports Management M

KING'S COLLEGE
Education—General M

KING UNIVERSITY
Accounting M
Business Administration and Management—General M
Finance and Banking M
Human Resources Management M
Marketing M
Project Management M

KUTZTOWN UNIVERSITY OF PENNSYLVANIA
Art Education M
Business Administration and Management—General M
Counselor Education M
Curriculum and Instruction M
Education—General M
Educational Leadership and Administration M
Educational Media/Instructional Technology M
Elementary Education M
English Education M
Library Science M
Middle School Education M
Reading Education M
Secondary Education M
Social Sciences Education M
Social Work M,D

LAGRANGE COLLEGE
Curriculum and Instruction M,O
Education—General M,O
Middle School Education M,O
Organizational Management M
Secondary Education M,O

LAKE ERIE COLLEGE
Business Administration and Management—General M
Education—General M
Management Information Systems M

LAKE ERIE COLLEGE OF OSTEOPATHIC MEDICINE
Health Education M,D,O

LAKE FOREST COLLEGE
Art Education M
Education—General M
Elementary Education M
English Education M
Mathematics Education M
Music Education M
Science Education M
Secondary Education M
Social Sciences Education M

LAKE FOREST GRADUATE SCHOOL OF MANAGEMENT
Business Administration and Management—General M
Finance and Banking M
International Business M
Marketing M
Organizational Behavior M

LAKEHEAD UNIVERSITY
Education—General M,D
Exercise and Sports Science M
Kinesiology and Movement Studies M
Social Work M

LAKELAND UNIVERSITY
Accounting M
Business Administration and Management—General M
Counselor Education M
Education—General M
Finance and Banking M
Project Management M

LAMAR UNIVERSITY
Accounting M
Business Administration and Management—General M
Counselor Education M
Education—General M,D,O
Educational Leadership and Administration M,D
Educational Media/Instructional Technology M,D
Entrepreneurship M
Foreign Languages Education M
Kinesiology and Movement Studies M
Special Education M,D

LANCASTER BIBLE COLLEGE
Counselor Education M,D
Elementary Education M,D
Secondary Education M,D
Special Education M,D

LANCASTER THEOLOGICAL SEMINARY
Religious Education M,D,O

LANDER UNIVERSITY
Early Childhood Education M
Education—General M

LANGSTON UNIVERSITY
Education—General M
Elementary Education M
English as a Second Language M
Multilingual and Multicultural Education M
Urban Education M

LA ROCHE COLLEGE
Accounting M
Human Resources Management M,O

LA SALLE UNIVERSITY
Accounting M,O
Advertising and Public Relations M,O
Business Administration and Management—General M,O
Early Childhood Education M,O
Education—General M,O
Educational Leadership and Administration M,O
Educational Media/Instructional Technology M,O
English as a Second Language M,O
Finance and Banking M,O
Human Resources Development M,O
Human Resources Management M,O
International Business M,O
Marketing M,O
Middle School Education M,O
Multilingual and Multicultural Education M,O
Nonprofit Management M
Quantitative Analysis M,O
Reading Education M,O
Secondary Education M,O
Social Sciences Education M,O
Special Education M,O

LASELL COLLEGE
Advertising and Public Relations M,O
Business Administration and Management—General M,O
Education—General M
Elementary Education M
Hospitality Management M,O
Human Resources Management M,O
Marketing M,O
Nonprofit Management M,O
Project Management M,O
Special Education M
Sports Management M,O
Travel and Tourism M,O

LA SIERRA UNIVERSITY
Accounting M,O
Advertising and Public Relations M
Business Administration and Management—General M,O
Counselor Education M,O
Curriculum and Instruction M,D,O
Education—General M,D,O
Educational Leadership and Administration M,D,O
Educational Psychology M,O
Finance and Banking M,O
Human Resources Management M,O
Marketing M,O
Religious Education M

LAURENTIAN UNIVERSITY
Business Administration and Management—General M
Science Education O
Social Work M

LAWRENCE TECHNOLOGICAL UNIVERSITY
Business Administration and Management—General M,O
Educational Media/Instructional Technology M,O
Finance and Banking M,O
Human Resources Development M,O
Industrial and Manufacturing Management M,D
Management Strategy and Policy M,O
Marketing M,O
Project Management M,O

LEBANESE AMERICAN UNIVERSITY
Business Administration and Management—General M

LEBANON VALLEY COLLEGE
Athletic Training and Sports Medicine M
Business Administration and Management—General M
Mathematics Education M,O
Music Education M
Science Education M,O
Social Sciences Education M,O

LEE UNIVERSITY
Business Administration and Management—General M
Counselor Education M
Curriculum and Instruction M,O
Early Childhood Education M,O
Education—General M,O
Educational Leadership and Administration M,O
Elementary Education M,O
English as a Second Language M,O
Higher Education M,O
Mathematics Education M,O
Middle School Education M,O
Music Education M
Secondary Education M,O
Social Sciences Education M,O
Special Education M,O

LEHIGH UNIVERSITY
Accounting M
Business Administration and Management—General M
Counselor Education M,D,O
Education—General M,D,O
Educational Leadership and Administration M,D,O
Educational Media/Instructional Technology M,D,O
Elementary Education M,D,O
Entrepreneurship M
Environmental Law M,O
Finance and Banking M
Human Services M,D,O
International and Comparative Education M,D,O
Project Management M
Quantitative Analysis M
Special Education M,D

LEHMAN COLLEGE OF THE CITY UNIVERSITY OF NEW YORK
Accounting M
Business Education M
Counselor Education M
Early Childhood Education M
Education—General M
Elementary Education M
English as a Second Language M
English Education M
Health Education M
Mathematics Education M
Multilingual and Multicultural Education M
Music Education M
Reading Education M
Recreation and Park Management M
Science Education M
Social Sciences Education M
Special Education M

LE MOYNE COLLEGE
Business Administration and Management—General M
Early Childhood Education M,O
Education—General M,O
Educational Leadership and Administration M,O
Elementary Education M,O
English as a Second Language M,O
English Education M,O
Foreign Languages Education M,O
Management Information Systems M
Middle School Education M,O
Reading Education M,O
Secondary Education M,O
Social Sciences Education M,O
Special Education M,O

LENOIR-RHYNE UNIVERSITY
Accounting M
Athletic Training and Sports Medicine M
Business Administration and Management—General M
Community College Education M
Counselor Education M
Distance Education Development M
Education—General M
Educational Leadership and Administration M
Educational Media/Instructional Technology M
Entrepreneurship M
Human Services M
International Business M
Management Information Systems M
Management Strategy and Policy M

- Organizational Management M
- Secondary Education M

LESLEY UNIVERSITY
- Adult Education M,D,O
- Art Education M,D,O
- Computer Education M,D,O
- Curriculum and Instruction M,D,O
- Distance Education Development M,D,O
- Early Childhood Education M,D,O
- Education—General M,D,O
- Educational Leadership and Administration M,D,O
- Educational Media/Instructional Technology M,D,O
- Elementary Education M,D,O
- English as a Second Language M,D,O
- Mathematics Education M,D,O
- Middle School Education M,D,O
- Reading Education M,D,O
- Science Education M,D,O
- Secondary Education M,D,O
- Special Education M,D,O

LES ROCHES INTERNATIONAL SCHOOL OF HOTEL MANAGEMENT
- Hospitality Management M

LETOURNEAU UNIVERSITY
- Business Administration and Management—General M
- Curriculum and Instruction M
- Educational Leadership and Administration M
- Management Strategy and Policy M

LEWIS & CLARK COLLEGE
- Curriculum and Instruction M
- Educational Leadership and Administration M,D,O
- Elementary Education M
- Environmental Law M,D
- Law M,D
- Secondary Education M
- Special Education M
- Student Affairs M,D,O

LEWIS UNIVERSITY
- Accounting M
- Aviation Management M
- Business Administration and Management—General M
- Counselor Education M
- Education—General M,D
- Educational Leadership and Administration M,D
- Educational Media/Instructional Technology M
- Electronic Commerce M
- Elementary Education M
- English as a Second Language M
- English Education M
- Finance and Banking M
- Higher Education M
- Human Resources Management M
- International Business M
- Management Information Systems M
- Marketing M
- Mathematics Education M
- Nonprofit Management M
- Organizational Management M
- Project Management M
- Reading Education M
- Science Education M
- Secondary Education M
- Social Sciences Education M
- Special Education M
- Sports Management M
- Student Affairs M

LIBERTY UNIVERSITY
- Accounting M,D,O
- Advertising and Public Relations M,D,O
- Business Administration and Management—General M,D,O
- Counselor Education M,D,O
- Education of the Gifted M,D,O
- Education—General M,D,O
- Educational Leadership and Administration M,D,O
- Human Services M,D,O
- International Business M,D,O
- Law D
- Management Information Systems M,D,O
- Marketing M,D,O
- Mathematics Education M,D,O
- Middle School Education M,D,O
- Music Education M,D
- Project Management M,D,O
- Reading Education M,D,O
- Recreation and Park Management M,D,O
- Religious Education M,D,O
- Secondary Education M,D,O
- Sports Management M,D,O
- Travel and Tourism M,D,O

LIFE UNIVERSITY
- Athletic Training and Sports Medicine M
- Exercise and Sports Science M

LIM COLLEGE
- Business Administration and Management—General M
- Entrepreneurship M
- Marketing M

LIMESTONE COLLEGE
- Business Administration and Management—General M

LINCOLN CHRISTIAN SEMINARY
- Religious Education M,D

LINCOLN CHRISTIAN UNIVERSITY
- Organizational Management M

LINCOLN MEMORIAL UNIVERSITY
- Business Administration and Management—General M
- Counselor Education M,D,O
- Curriculum and Instruction M,D,O
- Education—General M,D,O
- Educational Leadership and Administration M,D,O
- English Education M,D,O
- Higher Education M,D,O
- Human Resources Development M,D,O
- Law D

LINCOLN UNIVERSITY (CA)
- Business Administration and Management—General M,D
- Finance and Banking M,D
- Human Resources Management M,D
- International Business M,D
- Investment Management M,D
- Management Information Systems M,D

LINCOLN UNIVERSITY (MO)
- Accounting M
- Business Administration and Management—General M
- Counselor Education M
- Elementary Education M
- Higher Education M
- Management Information Systems M
- Middle School Education M
- Secondary Education M

LINCOLN UNIVERSITY (PA)
- Early Childhood Education M
- Educational Leadership and Administration M
- Finance and Banking M
- Human Resources Management M
- Human Services M
- Special Education M

LINDENWOOD UNIVERSITY
- Accounting M
- Business Administration and Management—General M,O
- Education of the Gifted M,D,O
- Education—General M,D,O
- Educational Leadership and Administration M,D,O
- Educational Media/Instructional Technology M,D,O
- English as a Second Language M,D,O
- Entrepreneurship M
- Finance and Banking M
- Human Resources Management M,O
- International Business M
- Management Information Systems M,O
- Marketing M,O
- Nonprofit Management M
- Project Management M,O
- Sports Management M
- Supply Chain Management M

LINDENWOOD UNIVERSITY–BELLEVILLE
- Business Administration and Management—General M
- Counselor Education M
- Education—General M
- Educational Leadership and Administration M
- Human Resources Management M

LINDSEY WILSON COLLEGE
- Counselor Education M,D
- Educational Leadership and Administration M

LIPSCOMB UNIVERSITY
- Accounting M,O
- Business Administration and Management—General M,O
- Education—General M,D,O
- Educational Leadership and Administration M,D,O
- Educational Media/Instructional Technology M,D,O
- English Education M,D,O
- Exercise and Sports Science M
- Finance and Banking M,O
- Human Resources Management M,O
- Management Information Systems M
- Nonprofit Management M,O
- Organizational Management M
- Reading Education M,D,O
- Special Education M,D,O
- Sports Management M,O
- Sustainability Management M,O

LOCK HAVEN UNIVERSITY OF PENNSYLVANIA
- Actuarial Science M
- Athletic Training and Sports Medicine M
- Business Education M
- Education—General M
- Educational Leadership and Administration M
- Elementary Education M
- Health Education M
- Human Services M
- Information Studies M
- Sports Management M

LOGAN UNIVERSITY
- Exercise and Sports Science M,D
- Health Education M,D

LOMA LINDA UNIVERSITY
- Counselor Education M,D,O
- Health Education M,D
- Social Work M,D

LONDON METROPOLITAN UNIVERSITY
- Athletic Training and Sports Medicine M,D
- Early Childhood Education M,D
- Education—General M,D
- English Education M,D
- Foreign Languages Education M,D
- Higher Education M,D
- Human Resources Management M,D
- Law M,D
- Management Information Systems M,D
- Social Work M,D
- Special Education M,D

LONG ISLAND UNIVERSITY–BRENTWOOD CAMPUS
- Counselor Education M,O
- Early Childhood Education M,O
- Elementary Education M,O
- Reading Education M,O
- Special Education M,O

LONG ISLAND UNIVERSITY–HUDSON
- Business Administration and Management—General M,O
- Counselor Education M,O
- Early Childhood Education M,O
- Educational Leadership and Administration M,O
- Elementary Education M,O
- English as a Second Language M,O
- Finance and Banking M,O
- Middle School Education M,O
- Multilingual and Multicultural Education M,O
- Reading Education M,O
- Special Education M,O

LONG ISLAND UNIVERSITY–LIU BROOKLYN
- Accounting M,O
- Athletic Training and Sports Medicine M,D,O
- Business Administration and Management—General M,O
- Counselor Education M,O
- Early Childhood Education M,O
- Education—General M,O
- Educational Leadership and Administration M,O
- English as a Second Language M,O
- Exercise and Sports Science M,D,O
- Human Resources Management M,O
- Multilingual and Multicultural Education M,O
- Nonprofit Management M,O
- Social Sciences Education M,D,O
- Social Work M,D,O
- Special Education M,O
- Taxation M,O
- Urban Education M,O

LONG ISLAND UNIVERSITY–LIU POST
- Accounting M
- Art Education M,D,O
- Business Administration and Management—General M
- Early Childhood Education M,D,O
- Education—General M,D,O
- Educational Leadership and Administration M,D,O
- Educational Media/Instructional Technology M,D,O
- English as a Second Language M,D,O
- Finance and Banking M
- International Business M
- Management Information Systems M
- Marketing M
- Middle School Education M,D,O
- Music Education M,D,O
- Nonprofit Management M,O
- Reading Education M,D,O
- Secondary Education M,D,O
- Social Work M,O
- Special Education M,D,O
- Taxation M

LONG ISLAND UNIVERSITY–RIVERHEAD
- Early Childhood Education M,O
- Elementary Education M,O
- English as a Second Language M,O
- Middle School Education M,O
- Reading Education M,O
- Secondary Education M,O
- Special Education M,O

LONGWOOD UNIVERSITY
- Business Administration and Management—General M
- Counselor Education M
- Education—General M
- Educational Media/Instructional Technology M
- Elementary Education M
- Health Education M
- Mathematics Education M
- Middle School Education M
- Physical Education M
- Reading Education M
- Real Estate M
- Special Education M

LORAS COLLEGE
- Educational Leadership and Administration M
- Special Education M

LOUISIANA COLLEGE
- Education—General M

LOUISIANA STATE UNIVERSITY AND AGRICULTURAL & MECHANICAL COLLEGE
- Accounting M,D
- Agricultural Education M,D
- Business Administration and Management—General M,D
- Business Education M,D
- Counselor Education M,D,O
- Education—General M,D,O
- Educational Leadership and Administration M,D,O
- Educational Measurement and Evaluation M,D,O
- Educational Media/Instructional Technology M,D,O
- Elementary Education M,D,O
- Finance and Banking M,D
- Higher Education M,D,O
- Home Economics Education M,D
- Human Resources Development M,D
- Information Studies M
- International and Comparative Education M,D
- Kinesiology and Movement Studies M,D
- Law M,D
- Library Science M
- Management Information Systems M,D
- Music Education M,D
- Secondary Education M,D,O
- Social Work M,D
- Vocational and Technical Education M,D

LOUISIANA STATE UNIVERSITY IN SHREVEPORT
- Business Administration and Management—General M
- Counselor Education M
- Curriculum and Instruction M
- Education—General M
- Educational Leadership and Administration M,D
- Nonprofit Management M

LOUISIANA TECH UNIVERSITY
- Accounting M,D
- Business Administration and Management—General M,D
- Counselor Education M,D
- Curriculum and Instruction M,D
- Early Childhood Education M,D
- Education—General M,D
- Educational Leadership and Administration M,D
- Exercise and Sports Science M
- Finance and Banking M,D
- Higher Education M,D
- Middle School Education M,D
- Physical Education M

LOURDES UNIVERSITY
- Business Administration and Management—General M
- Curriculum and Instruction M
- Educational Leadership and Administration M
- Organizational Management M
- Reading Education M

LOYOLA MARYMOUNT UNIVERSITY
- Accounting M
- Business Administration and Management—General M
- Counselor Education M
- Education—General M,D
- Educational Leadership and Administration M,D
- Elementary Education M
- Higher Education M
- Law M,D
- Mathematics Education M
- Multilingual and Multicultural Education M
- Reading Education M
- Recreation and Park Management M
- Religious Education M
- Secondary Education M
- Special Education M
- Urban Education M

LOYOLA UNIVERSITY CHICAGO
- Accounting M
- Business Administration and Management—General M,O
- Counselor Education M,O
- Curriculum and Instruction M,D
- Education—General M,D,O
- Educational Leadership and Administration M,D,O
- Educational Measurement and Evaluation M,D
- Educational Policy M,D
- Elementary Education M,O
- Entrepreneurship M
- Finance and Banking M
- Higher Education M,D
- Human Resources Management M
- Information Studies M,O
- International Business M
- Law M,D
- Legal and Justice Studies M,O
- Marketing M
- Religious Education M,O
- Secondary Education M,O
- Social Work M,D,O
- Special Education M,O
- Supply Chain Management M,O

LOYOLA UNIVERSITY MARYLAND
- Accounting M
- Business Administration and Management—General M

*M—masters degree; D—doctorate; O—other advanced degree; *—Close-Up and/or Display*

Counselor Education M,O
Curriculum and Instruction M
Early Childhood Education M,O
Education—General M,O
Educational Leadership and Administration M,O
Educational Media/Instructional Technology M
Elementary Education M,O
Finance and Banking M
Management Information Systems M
Music Education M
Reading Education M
Secondary Education M

LOYOLA UNIVERSITY NEW ORLEANS
Business Administration and Management—General M
Education—General M
Entrepreneurship M
Law M,D
Marketing M
Organizational Management M
Secondary Education M

LYNCHBURG COLLEGE
Business Administration and Management—General M
Counselor Education M
Curriculum and Instruction M
Educational Leadership and Administration M,D
Higher Education M
Reading Education M
Science Education M
Special Education M

LYNDON STATE COLLEGE
Counselor Education M
Curriculum and Instruction M
Education—General M
Reading Education M
Science Education M
Special Education M

LYNN UNIVERSITY
Aviation Management M
Business Administration and Management—General M
Early Childhood Education M,D
Education of the Gifted M,D
Education—General M,D
Educational Leadership and Administration M,D
Hospitality Management M
Human Resources Management M
International Business M
Investment Management M
Marketing M
Middle School Education M,D
Special Education M,D
Sports Management M

MAASTRICHT SCHOOL OF MANAGEMENT
Business Administration and Management—General M,D
Facilities Management M,D
Sustainability Management M,D

MADONNA UNIVERSITY
Business Administration and Management—General M
Education—General M
Educational Leadership and Administration M
English as a Second Language M
International Business M
Quality Management M
Reading Education M
Special Education M

MAHARISHI UNIVERSITY OF MANAGEMENT
Accounting M,D
Business Administration and Management—General M,D
Sustainability Management M,D

MAINE MARITIME ACADEMY
International Business M
Supply Chain Management M
Transportation Management M

MALONE UNIVERSITY
Business Administration and Management—General M
Counselor Education M
Curriculum and Instruction M
Education—General M
Educational Leadership and Administration M
Organizational Management M
Special Education M

MANCHESTER UNIVERSITY
Athletic Training and Sports Medicine M

MANHATTAN COLLEGE
Business Administration and Management—General M
Counselor Education M,O
Early Childhood Education M,O
Education—General M,O
Educational Leadership and Administration M,O
Educational Media/Instructional Technology M
Elementary Education M,O
Multilingual and Multicultural Education M,O
Organizational Management M
Special Education M,O
Student Affairs M,O

MANHATTANVILLE COLLEGE
Accounting M
Art Education M
Business Education M
Early Childhood Education M,O
Education—General M,D,O*
Educational Leadership and Administration M,D,O
Elementary Education M,O
English as a Second Language M,O
English Education M
Entrepreneurship M
Exercise and Sports Science M,O
Finance and Banking M
Foreign Languages Education M
Human Resources Management M
International Business M
Investment Management M
Management Strategy and Policy M
Marketing M
Mathematics Education M
Middle School Education M
Music Education M
Organizational Management M
Reading Education M
Science Education M
Secondary Education M,O
Social Sciences Education M
Special Education M,O
Sports Management M
Urban Education M,O

MANSFIELD UNIVERSITY OF PENNSYLVANIA
Art Education M
Education—General M
Elementary Education M
Information Studies M
Library Science M
Organizational Management M
Secondary Education M
Special Education M

MAPLE SPRINGS BAPTIST BIBLE COLLEGE AND SEMINARY
Religious Education M,D,O

MARANATHA BAPTIST UNIVERSITY
Education—General M

MARCONI INTERNATIONAL UNIVERSITY
Business Administration and Management—General M,D
Educational Leadership and Administration M,D
Educational Media/Instructional Technology M,D
International Business M,D

MARIAN UNIVERSITY (WI)
Business Administration and Management—General M
Curriculum and Instruction M,D
Education—General M,D
Educational Leadership and Administration M,D
Educational Media/Instructional Technology M,D
Organizational Management M
Special Education M,D

MARIST COLLEGE
Business Administration and Management—General M,O
Education—General M,O
Management Information Systems M,O
Marketing M

MARLBORO COLLEGE
Business Administration and Management—General M
Computer Education M,O
Education—General M,O
Educational Media/Instructional Technology M,O
English as a Second Language M
Entrepreneurship M
Legal and Justice Studies M
Organizational Management M
Project Management M

MARQUETTE UNIVERSITY
Accounting M
Advertising and Public Relations M,O
Business Administration and Management—General M,O
Counselor Education M,D
Curriculum and Instruction M,D,O
Education—General M,D,O
Educational Leadership and Administration M,D,O
Educational Policy M,D,O
Elementary Education M,D,O
Entrepreneurship M,O
Finance and Banking M,O
Foreign Languages Education M
Foundations and Philosophy of Education M,D,O
Human Resources Development M
Human Resources Management M,O
Industrial and Manufacturing Management M,O
International Business M,O
Law D
Management Information Systems M,O
Marketing Research M
Marketing M,D
Mathematics Education M,D
Reading Education M,D,O
Real Estate M
Secondary Education M,D,O
Sports Management M
Student Affairs M,D,O
Supply Chain Management M,O

MARSHALL UNIVERSITY
Accounting M
Adult Education M
Advertising and Public Relations M
Athletic Training and Sports Medicine M
Business Administration and Management—General M
Counselor Education M,O
Early Childhood Education M
Education—General M,D,O
Educational Leadership and Administration M,D,O
Elementary Education M,O
Exercise and Sports Science M
Health Education M
Human Resources Management M
Reading Education M,O
Secondary Education M
Social Work M
Special Education M
Sports Management M
Vocational and Technical Education M

MARS HILL UNIVERSITY
Elementary Education M

MARTIN LUTHER COLLEGE
Curriculum and Instruction M
Early Childhood Education M
Education—General M
Educational Leadership and Administration M
Educational Media/Instructional Technology M
Special Education M

MARY BALDWIN UNIVERSITY
Education—General M
Elementary Education M
Middle School Education M

MARYGROVE COLLEGE
Education—General M
Educational Leadership and Administration M
Educational Media/Instructional Technology M
Elementary Education M
Human Resources Management M
Legal and Justice Studies M
Reading Education M
Secondary Education M
Urban Education M

MARYLAND INSTITUTE COLLEGE OF ART
Art Education M
Business Administration and Management—General M

MARYLHURST UNIVERSITY
Business Administration and Management—General M
Education—General M
Elementary Education M
Hospitality Management M
Real Estate M

MARYMOUNT CALIFORNIA UNIVERSITY
Business Administration and Management—General M

MARYMOUNT UNIVERSITY
Business Administration and Management—General M,O
Community College Education M,O
Counselor Education M
Education—General M
Elementary Education M
English as a Second Language M
English Education M,O
Health Education M
Human Resources Management M,O
Management Information Systems M,O
Nonprofit Management M,O
Project Management M,O
Secondary Education M
Special Education M

MARYVILLE UNIVERSITY OF SAINT LOUIS
Accounting M,O
Actuarial Science M
Business Administration and Management—General M,O
Business Education M,O
Early Childhood Education M,D
Education of the Gifted M,D
Education—General M,D
Educational Leadership and Administration M,D
Elementary Education M,D
Finance and Banking M,O
Higher Education M,D
Human Resources Management M,O
Logistics M,O
Marketing M,O
Middle School Education M,D
Organizational Management M
Project Management M,O
Reading Education M,D
Secondary Education M,D
Sports Management M,O
Supply Chain Management M,O

MARYWOOD UNIVERSITY
Art Education M
Business Administration and Management—General M
Counselor Education M
Early Childhood Education M
Education—General M
Educational Leadership and Administration M,D
Elementary Education M
Exercise and Sports Science M
Finance and Banking M
Health Education D
Higher Education M,D
Investment Management M
Management Information Systems M
Music Education M
Reading Education M
Secondary Education M
Social Work M,D
Special Education M

MASSACHUSETTS COLLEGE OF ART AND DESIGN
Art Education M,O

MASSACHUSETTS COLLEGE OF LIBERAL ARTS
Business Administration and Management—General M,O
Curriculum and Instruction M,O
Education—General M,O
Educational Leadership and Administration M,O
Educational Media/Instructional Technology M,O
Health Education M,O
Physical Education M,O
Reading Education M,O
Special Education M,O

MASSACHUSETTS INSTITUTE OF TECHNOLOGY
Business Administration and Management—General M,D
Logistics M
Real Estate M

MASSACHUSETTS MARITIME ACADEMY
Facilities Management M

MASSACHUSETTS SCHOOL OF LAW AT ANDOVER
Law D

MCDANIEL COLLEGE
Counselor Education M
Curriculum and Instruction M
Educational Leadership and Administration M
Educational Media/Instructional Technology M
Elementary Education M,O
English as a Second Language M
Exercise and Sports Science M
Human Resources Development M
Human Services M
Library Science M
Mathematics Education M,O
Physical Education M
Reading Education M
Science Education M,O
Secondary Education M,O
Special Education M

MCGILL UNIVERSITY
Accounting M,D,O
Business Administration and Management—General M,D,O
Curriculum and Instruction M,D,O
Education—General M,D,O
Educational Leadership and Administration M,D,O
Educational Psychology M,D,O
Entrepreneurship M,D,O
Finance and Banking M,D,O
Foreign Languages Education M,D,O
Foundations and Philosophy of Education M,D,O
Industrial and Manufacturing Management M,D,O
Information Studies M,D,O
International Business M,D,O
Kinesiology and Movement Studies M,D,O
Law M,D,O
Library Science M,D,O
Management Information Systems M,D,O
Management Strategy and Policy M,D,O
Marketing M,D,O
Music Education M,D
Physical Education M,D,O
Social Work M,D,O
Transportation Management M,D

MCKENDREE UNIVERSITY
Business Administration and Management—General M
Curriculum and Instruction M,D,O
Education—General M,D,O
Educational Leadership and Administration M,D,O
Higher Education M,D,O
Human Resources Management M
International Business M
Music Education M,D,O
Reading Education M,D,O
Special Education M,D,O

MCMASTER UNIVERSITY
Business Administration and Management—General M,D
Human Resources Management M,D
Kinesiology and Movement Studies M,D
Management Information Systems D
Social Work M

MCNEESE STATE UNIVERSITY
Business Administration and Management—General M
Counselor Education M,O
Curriculum and Instruction M
Early Childhood Education M,O
Education—General O
Educational Leadership and Administration M,O
Educational Measurement and Evaluation M,O
Educational Media/Instructional Technology M,O
Elementary Education M,O
Exercise and Sports Science M
Library Science O

Middle School Education O
Music Education O
Reading Education M,O
Science Education M
Secondary Education M,O
Special Education M,O

MCPHERSON COLLEGE
Education—General M

MEDAILLE COLLEGE
Business Administration and Management—General M
Curriculum and Instruction M
Education—General M
Elementary Education M
Organizational Management M
Reading Education M
Secondary Education M
Special Education M

MELBOURNE BUSINESS SCHOOL
Business Administration and Management—General M,D,O
Marketing M,D,O

MEMORIAL UNIVERSITY OF NEWFOUNDLAND
Adult Education M,D,O
Business Administration and Management—General M
Curriculum and Instruction M,D,O
Education—General M,D,O
Educational Leadership and Administration M,D,O
Educational Media/Instructional Technology M,D,O
Educational Psychology M,D,O
Exercise and Sports Science M
Kinesiology and Movement Studies M
Physical Education M
Social Work M,D

MEMPHIS COLLEGE OF ART
Art Education M

MERCER UNIVERSITY
Accounting M
Business Administration and Management—General M
Counselor Education M,D
Curriculum and Instruction M,D,O
Early Childhood Education M,D,O
Education—General M,D,O
Educational Leadership and Administration M,D,O
Entrepreneurship M
Higher Education M,D,O
Human Services M,D
Law D
Management Strategy and Policy M
Middle School Education M,D,O
Organizational Management M
Reading Education M,D,O
Secondary Education M,D,O

MERCY COLLEGE
Accounting M
Business Administration and Management—General M
Counselor Education M,O
Early Childhood Education M
Education—General M,O
Educational Leadership and Administration M,O
Elementary Education M
English as a Second Language M,O
Human Resources Management M
Middle School Education M,O
Organizational Management M
Reading Education M,O
Secondary Education M,O

MERCYHURST UNIVERSITY
Accounting M,O
Educational Leadership and Administration M,O
Entrepreneurship M,O
Higher Education M,O
Human Resources Management M,O
Management Strategy and Policy M,O
Organizational Management M,O
Secondary Education M
Special Education M,O
Sports Management M,O

MEREDITH COLLEGE
Business Administration and Management—General M
Curriculum and Instruction M,O
Education of the Gifted M,O
Education—General M,O
Elementary Education M,O
English as a Second Language M,O
Health Education M,O
Physical Education M,O
Reading Education M,O
Special Education M,O

MERRIMACK COLLEGE
Accounting M
Adult Education M,O
Athletic Training and Sports Medicine M
Business Administration and Management—General M
Curriculum and Instruction M,O
Early Childhood Education M,O
Education—General M,O
Educational Leadership and Administration M,O
Elementary Education M,O
English as a Second Language M,O
Exercise and Sports Science M

Higher Education M,O
Management Strategy and Policy M
Middle School Education M,O
Secondary Education M,O
Special Education M,O
Student Affairs M,O

MESSIAH COLLEGE
Business Administration and Management—General M,O
Counselor Education M,O
Curriculum and Instruction M
English as a Second Language M
Higher Education M
Management Strategy and Policy M,O
Organizational Management M,O
Special Education M,O
Sports Management M
Student Affairs M

METHODIST UNIVERSITY
Business Administration and Management—General M

METROPOLITAN COLLEGE OF NEW YORK
Business Administration and Management—General M
Elementary Education M
Finance and Banking M
Special Education M

METROPOLITAN STATE UNIVERSITY
Business Administration and Management—General M,D,O
Information Studies M,D,O
Management Information Systems M,D,O
Nonprofit Management M,D,O
Project Management M,D,O

METROPOLITAN STATE UNIVERSITY OF DENVER
Accounting M
Education—General M
Elementary Education M
Social Work M
Special Education M
Taxation M

MGH INSTITUTE OF HEALTH PROFESSIONS
Reading Education M,O

MIAMI UNIVERSITY
Accounting M
Art Education M
Business Administration and Management—General M
Education—General M,D,O
Educational Psychology M,O
Exercise and Sports Science M
Mathematics Education M
Music Education M

MICHIGAN SCHOOL OF PROFESSIONAL PSYCHOLOGY
Educational Psychology M,D

MICHIGAN STATE UNIVERSITY
Accounting M,D
Adult Education M,D,O
Advertising and Public Relations M,D
Business Administration and Management—General M,D
Counselor Education M,D,O
Curriculum and Instruction M,D,O
Education—General M,D,O
Educational Leadership and Administration M,D,O
Educational Measurement and Evaluation M,D,O
Educational Media/Instructional Technology M,D,O
Educational Policy D
Educational Psychology M,D,O
English as a Second Language M,D
Finance and Banking M,D
Foreign Languages Education D
Higher Education M,D,O
Hospitality Management M
Human Resources Management M,D
Kinesiology and Movement Studies M,D
Logistics M,D
Management Information Systems M,D
Management Strategy and Policy M,D
Marketing Research M,D
Marketing M,D
Mathematics Education M,D
Music Education M,D
Reading Education M
Recreation and Park Management M,D
Science Education M,D
Social Sciences Education M,D
Social Work M,D
Special Education M,D,O
Supply Chain Management M,D
Taxation M,D

MICHIGAN STATE UNIVERSITY COLLEGE OF LAW
Intellectual Property Law M,D
Law M,D
Legal and Justice Studies M,D

MICHIGAN TECHNOLOGICAL UNIVERSITY
Accounting M
Business Administration and Management—General M
Kinesiology and Movement Studies M
Science Education M,D,O
Sustainability Management M,D,O

MID-AMERICA CHRISTIAN UNIVERSITY
Business Administration and Management—General M
Organizational Management M

MIDAMERICA NAZARENE UNIVERSITY
Business Administration and Management—General M
Education—General M
Educational Media/Instructional Technology M
English as a Second Language M
Reading Education M

MIDDLEBURY INSTITUTE OF INTERNATIONAL STUDIES AT MONTEREY
Business Administration and Management—General M
English as a Second Language M
Foreign Languages Education M
International and Comparative Education M
International Business M
Management Strategy and Policy M

MIDDLE GEORGIA STATE UNIVERSITY
Management Information Systems M

MIDDLE TENNESSEE STATE UNIVERSITY
Accounting M
Actuarial Science M
Archives/Archival Administration M,D,O
Aviation Management M
Business Administration and Management—General M
Business Education M
Counselor Education M
Curriculum and Instruction M,O
Early Childhood Education M,O
Education—General M,D,O
Educational Leadership and Administration M,O
Educational Media/Instructional Technology M,O
Elementary Education M,O
English as a Second Language M,O
Exercise and Sports Science M,D
Foreign Languages Education M
Health Education M
Human Resources Management M
Management Information Systems M
Management Strategy and Policy M
Mathematics Education M,D
Middle School Education M,O
Physical Education M
Reading Education M,D
Recreation and Park Management M
Science Education M,D
Secondary Education M,O
Social Work M
Special Education M
Vocational and Technical Education M

MIDWAY UNIVERSITY
Business Administration and Management—General M
Education—General M
Organizational Management M

MIDWESTERN BAPTIST THEOLOGICAL SEMINARY
Religious Education M,D,O

MIDWESTERN STATE UNIVERSITY
Business Administration and Management—General M
Counselor Education M
Curriculum and Instruction M
Education—General M
Educational Leadership and Administration M
Educational Media/Instructional Technology M
Exercise and Sports Science M
Human Resources Development M
Reading Education M
Special Education M
Sports Management M

MILLENNIA ATLANTIC UNIVERSITY
Accounting M
Business Administration and Management—General M
Human Resources Management M

MILLERSVILLE UNIVERSITY OF PENNSYLVANIA
Art Education M
Distance Education Development M
Early Childhood Education M
Education of the Gifted M,O
Education—General M,D,O
Educational Leadership and Administration M,D
English as a Second Language M
Mathematics Education M
Physical Education M,O
Reading Education M
Science Education M,D
Social Work M,D
Special Education M
Sports Management M,O
Vocational and Technical Education M

MILLIGAN COLLEGE
Business Administration and Management—General M,O
Counselor Education M,O
Early Childhood Education M,D,O
Education—General M,D,O
Educational Leadership and Administration M,D,O

Elementary Education M,D,O
Industrial and Manufacturing Management M,O
Middle School Education M,D,O
Religious Education M,D,O
Secondary Education M,D,O
Special Education M,D,O

MILLIKIN UNIVERSITY
Business Administration and Management—General M

MILLSAPS COLLEGE
Accounting M
Business Administration and Management—General M

MILLS COLLEGE
Business Administration and Management—General M
Early Childhood Education M
Education—General M,D,O
Educational Leadership and Administration

MILWAUKEE SCHOOL OF ENGINEERING
Business Administration and Management—General M
Business Education M
Industrial and Manufacturing Management M
International Business M
Marketing M

MINNESOTA STATE UNIVERSITY MANKATO
Accounting M
Art Education M
Business Administration and Management—General M
Counselor Education M,D
Education—General M,D,O
Educational Leadership and Administration M
English as a Second Language M,O
Foreign Languages Education M
Health Education M,O
Higher Education M
Human Services M
Mathematics Education M
Music Education M
Nonprofit Management M,O
Physical Education M
Science Education M
Social Sciences Education M
Social Work M
Special Education M,O
Student Affairs M,D

MINNESOTA STATE UNIVERSITY MOORHEAD
Accounting M
Business Administration and Management—General M
Counselor Education M,O
Curriculum and Instruction M,O
Education—General M,O
Educational Leadership and Administration M,O
English as a Second Language M
Finance and Banking M
Human Services M,O
Special Education M,O

MINOT STATE UNIVERSITY
Business Administration and Management—General M
Elementary Education M
Management Information Systems M
Mathematics Education M
Middle School Education M
Science Education M
Special Education M

MISERICORDIA UNIVERSITY
Accounting M
Business Administration and Management—General M
Curriculum and Instruction M
Education—General M
Educational Media/Instructional Technology M
Human Resources Management M
Management Information Systems M
Nonprofit Management M
Organizational Management M
Reading Education M
Special Education M
Sports Management M

MISSISSIPPI COLLEGE
Accounting M,O
Advertising and Public Relations M
Art Education M,D,O
Business Administration and Management—General M,O
Business Education M,D,O
Computer Education M,D,O
Counselor Education M,O
Curriculum and Instruction M,D,O
Education—General M,D,O
Educational Leadership and Administration M,D,O
Elementary Education M,D,O
English as a Second Language M
English Education M,D,O
Finance and Banking M,O
Higher Education M,D,O
Kinesiology and Movement Studies M
Law D,O
Legal and Justice Studies M,O
Mathematics Education M,D,O
Music Education M

*M—masters degree; D—doctorate; O—other advanced degree; *—Close-Up and/or Display*

Science Education M,D,O
Secondary Education M,D,O
Social Sciences Education M,D,O
Special Education M,D,O

MISSISSIPPI STATE UNIVERSITY
Accounting M
Agricultural Education M,D
Business Administration and Management—General M,D
Community College Education M,D,O
Counselor Education M,D,O
Curriculum and Instruction M,D,O
Distance Education Development M,D,O
Early Childhood Education M,D,O
Education—General M,D,O
Educational Leadership and Administration M,D,O
Educational Media/Instructional Technology M,D,O
Educational Psychology M,D,O
Elementary Education M,D,O
Exercise and Sports Science M,D
Finance and Banking M,D
Foreign Languages Education M
Human Resources Development M,D,O
Industrial and Manufacturing Management M,D
Kinesiology and Movement Studies M,D
Management Information Systems M,D
Marketing D
Middle School Education M,D,O
Physical Education M,D
Project Management M,D
Reading Education M,D,O
Secondary Education M,D,O
Special Education M,D,O
Sports Management M,D
Student Affairs M,D,O
Taxation M
Vocational and Technical Education M,D,O

MISSISSIPPI UNIVERSITY FOR WOMEN
Curriculum and Instruction M
Education of the Gifted M
Education—General M
Educational Leadership and Administration M
Health Education M
Reading Education M

MISSISSIPPI VALLEY STATE UNIVERSITY
Education—General M

MISSOURI BAPTIST UNIVERSITY
Business Administration and Management—General M,O
Counselor Education M,O
Education—General M,O
Educational Leadership and Administration M,O

MISSOURI SOUTHERN STATE UNIVERSITY
Business Administration and Management—General M
Early Childhood Education M
Education—General M
Educational Media/Instructional Technology M

MISSOURI STATE UNIVERSITY
Accounting M
Athletic Training and Sports Medicine M
Business Administration and Management—General M
Counselor Education M
Early Childhood Education M
Educational Leadership and Administration M,O
Educational Measurement and Evaluation O
Educational Media/Instructional Technology M
Elementary Education M,O
English as a Second Language M,O
English Education M,O
Higher Education M
Kinesiology and Movement Studies M
Management Information Systems M
Mathematics Education M
Physical Education M
Project Management M
Reading Education M
Science Education M
Secondary Education M,O
Social Sciences Education M,O
Social Work M
Special Education M
Sports Management M,O
Student Affairs M

MISSOURI UNIVERSITY OF SCIENCE AND TECHNOLOGY
Business Administration and Management—General M
Mathematics Education M,D

MISSOURI WESTERN STATE UNIVERSITY
Accounting M
Business Administration and Management—General M
Educational Measurement and Evaluation M,O
English as a Second Language M,O
Information Studies M
Special Education M,O
Sports Management M

MITCHELL HAMLINE SCHOOL OF LAW
Law M,D

MOLLOY COLLEGE
Accounting M,O
Business Administration and Management—General M,O
Early Childhood Education M,O
Education—General M,O
Educational Media/Instructional Technology M,O
English as a Second Language M,O
Finance and Banking M,O
Marketing M,O
Multilingual and Multicultural Education M,O
Social Sciences Education M,O
Special Education M,O

MONMOUTH UNIVERSITY
Accounting M,O
Advertising and Public Relations M,O
Business Administration and Management—General M,O*
Early Childhood Education M,D,O
Educational Leadership and Administration M,D,O
Elementary Education M,D,O
English as a Second Language M,D,O
Finance and Banking M,O
Human Resources Management M,O
Marketing M,O
Reading Education M,D,O
Real Estate M,O
Secondary Education M,D,O
Special Education M,D,O
Student Affairs M,D,O

MONROE COLLEGE
Accounting M
Business Administration and Management—General M
Entrepreneurship M
Finance and Banking M
Hospitality Management M
Human Resources Management M
Marketing M

MONTANA STATE UNIVERSITY
Accounting M
Adult Education M,D,O
Agricultural Education M
Curriculum and Instruction M,D,O
Education—General M,D,O
Educational Leadership and Administration M,D,O
Health Education M
Higher Education M,D,O
Home Economics Education M
Mathematics Education M,D
Vocational and Technical Education M,D,O

MONTANA STATE UNIVERSITY BILLINGS
Advertising and Public Relations M
Athletic Training and Sports Medicine M
Counselor Education M
Curriculum and Instruction M
Education—General M,O
Educational Media/Instructional Technology M
Elementary Education M
Reading Education M
Secondary Education M
Special Education M

MONTANA STATE UNIVERSITY–NORTHERN
Counselor Education M
Education—General M

MONTANA TECH OF THE UNIVERSITY OF MONTANA
Project Management M

MONTCLAIR STATE UNIVERSITY
Accounting M,O
Advertising and Public Relations M
Archives/Archival Administration M
Art Education M
Business Administration and Management—General M,O
Counselor Education M,D
Curriculum and Instruction M
Education—General M,D,O
Educational Leadership and Administration M,D
Educational Measurement and Evaluation O
English as a Second Language M,O
English Education M,O
Environmental Education M,O
Environmental Law O
Exercise and Sports Science M,O
Health Education M
Intellectual Property Law M,O
Law M,O
Legal and Justice Studies O
Mathematics Education M,D,O
Music Education M
Physical Education M
Reading Education M
Science Education M
Special Education M
Sports Management M

MOODY THEOLOGICAL SEMINARY–MICHIGAN
Religious Education M,O

MOORE COLLEGE OF ART & DESIGN
Art Education M

MORAVIAN COLLEGE
Accounting M
Athletic Training and Sports Medicine M
Business Administration and Management—General M
Curriculum and Instruction M
Education—General M
Human Resources Development M
Human Resources Management M
Supply Chain Management M

MOREHEAD STATE UNIVERSITY
Adult Education M,O
Art Education M
Business Administration and Management—General M
Business Education M,O
Counselor Education M,O
Curriculum and Instruction M,O
Education of the Gifted M,O
Education—General M,O
Educational Leadership and Administration M,O
Educational Media/Instructional Technology M,O
Elementary Education M,O
English Education M,O
Exercise and Sports Science M
Foreign Languages Education M
Health Education M
Higher Education M,O
International and Comparative Education M,O
Management Information Systems M
Mathematics Education M
Middle School Education M,O
Music Education M
Physical Education M
Reading Education M,O
Science Education M
Secondary Education M,O
Social Sciences Education M,O
Special Education M,O
Sports Management M
Vocational and Technical Education M

MORGAN STATE UNIVERSITY
Business Administration and Management—General D
Community College Education D
Education—General M,D
Educational Leadership and Administration M,D
Elementary Education M
Higher Education M,D
Mathematics Education M,D
Middle School Education M
Science Education M,D
Secondary Education M
Social Work M,D
Transportation Management M
Urban Education D

MORNINGSIDE COLLEGE
Education—General M
Special Education M

MOUNT ALOYSIUS COLLEGE
Accounting M
Business Administration and Management—General M
Nonprofit Management M
Project Management M

MOUNT HOLYOKE COLLEGE
Educational Leadership and Administration M
Mathematics Education M

MOUNT IDA COLLEGE
Business Administration and Management—General M
Human Resources Management M
Sports Management M

MOUNT MARTY COLLEGE
Business Administration and Management—General M

MOUNT MARY UNIVERSITY
Business Administration and Management—General M
Counselor Education M,O
Education—General M

MOUNT MERCY UNIVERSITY
Business Administration and Management—General M
Education—General M
Educational Leadership and Administration M
Human Resources Management M
Management Strategy and Policy M
Quality Management M
Reading Education M
Special Education M

MOUNT ST. JOSEPH UNIVERSITY
Business Administration and Management—General M
Early Childhood Education M,O
Education—General M,O
Middle School Education M,O
Multilingual and Multicultural Education M,O
Organizational Management M
Reading Education M,O
Secondary Education M,O
Special Education M,O

MOUNT SAINT MARY COLLEGE
Business Administration and Management—General M
Education—General M,O
Finance and Banking M
Middle School Education M,O
Reading Education M,O
Special Education M,O

MOUNT SAINT MARY'S UNIVERSITY (CA)
Business Administration and Management—General M,D,O
Education—General M,D,O

MOUNT ST. MARY'S UNIVERSITY (MD)
Business Administration and Management—General M
Education—General M
Sports Management M

MOUNT SAINT VINCENT UNIVERSITY
Adult Education M
Curriculum and Instruction M
Education—General M
Educational Psychology M
Elementary Education M
English as a Second Language M
Foundations and Philosophy of Education M
Middle School Education M
Reading Education M
Special Education M

MOUNT VERNON NAZARENE UNIVERSITY
Business Administration and Management—General M
Education—General M

MULTNOMAH UNIVERSITY
Education—General M
English as a Second Language M

MURRAY STATE UNIVERSITY
Accounting M
Agricultural Education M
Business Administration and Management—General M
Counselor Education M,O
Early Childhood Education M
Education—General M,D,O
Educational Leadership and Administration M,O
Elementary Education M,O
English as a Second Language M
Exercise and Sports Science M
Human Services M
Leisure Studies M
Middle School Education M,O
Music Education M
Physical Education M,O
Reading Education M,O
Secondary Education M,O
Special Education M
Vocational and Technical Education M

MUSKINGUM UNIVERSITY
Education—General M

NAROPA UNIVERSITY
Counselor Education M
Education—General M
Recreation and Park Management M

NATIONAL AMERICAN UNIVERSITY
Business Administration and Management—General M

THE NATIONAL GRADUATE SCHOOL OF QUALITY MANAGEMENT
Quality Management M,D

NATIONAL LOUIS UNIVERSITY
Adult Education M,D,O
Business Administration and Management—General M
Counselor Education M,D,O
Curriculum and Instruction M,D,O
Developmental Education M,D,O
Early Childhood Education M,D,O
Education—General M,D,O
Educational Leadership and Administration M,D,O
Educational Media/Instructional Technology M,D,O
Educational Psychology M,D,O
Elementary Education M,D,O
English Education M,D,O
Human Resources Development M
Human Resources Management M
Human Services M,D,O
Mathematics Education M,D,O
Middle School Education M,D,O
Reading Education M,D,O
Science Education M,D,O
Secondary Education M,D,O
Special Education M,D,O

NATIONAL PARALEGAL COLLEGE
Legal and Justice Studies M
Taxation M

NATIONAL UNIVERSITY
Business Administration and Management—General M,O
Distance Education Development M,O
Education—General M,O
Educational Leadership and Administration M,O
Human Resources Management M,O
Human Services M,D,O
Legal and Justice Studies M

NATIONAL UNIVERSITY COLLEGE
Business Administration and Management—General M
Marketing M
Special Education M

NAVAL POSTGRADUATE SCHOOL
Business Administration and Management—General M
Finance and Banking M
Logistics M
Management Information Systems M,D,O
Supply Chain Management M
Transportation Management M

NAZARETH COLLEGE OF ROCHESTER
Art Education M
Business Administration and Management—General M
Early Childhood Education M

- Education—General M
- Educational Media/Instructional Technology M
- Elementary Education M
- English as a Second Language M
- Human Resources Management M
- Middle School Education M
- Music Education M
- Reading Education M
- Social Work M

NEUMANN UNIVERSITY
- Accounting M
- Business Administration and Management—General M
- Education—General M
- Educational Leadership and Administration M,D
- Elementary Education M
- Information Studies M
- Management Strategy and Policy M
- Organizational Management M
- Secondary Education M
- Special Education M
- Sports Management M

NEW CHARTER UNIVERSITY
- Business Administration and Management—General M
- Finance and Banking M

NEW ENGLAND COLLEGE
- Accounting M
- Business Administration and Management—General M
- Education—General M,D
- Educational Leadership and Administration M,D
- Higher Education M,D
- Human Services M
- Management Strategy and Policy M
- Marketing M
- Nonprofit Management M
- Project Management M
- Recreation and Park Management M
- Special Education M,D
- Sports Management M

NEW ENGLAND COLLEGE OF BUSINESS AND FINANCE
- Finance and Banking M

NEW ENGLAND INSTITUTE OF TECHNOLOGY
- Management Information Systems M

NEW HAMPSHIRE INSTITUTE OF ART
- Art Education M

NEW JERSEY CITY UNIVERSITY
- Accounting M,O
- Art Education M
- Business Administration and Management—General M,O
- Counselor Education M
- Early Childhood Education M
- Education—General M,D
- Educational Leadership and Administration M
- Educational Media/Instructional Technology M,D
- Elementary Education M
- English as a Second Language M
- Finance and Banking M,O
- Health Education M
- Marketing M
- Mathematics Education M
- Multilingual and Multicultural Education M
- Music Education M
- Organizational Management M
- Secondary Education M
- Special Education M
- Urban Education M

NEW JERSEY INSTITUTE OF TECHNOLOGY
- Business Administration and Management—General M,D,O
- International Business M,D,O
- Management Information Systems M,D,O
- Transportation Management M,D

NEWMAN THEOLOGICAL COLLEGE
- Religious Education M,O

NEWMAN UNIVERSITY
- Business Administration and Management—General M
- Curriculum and Instruction M
- Education—General M
- Educational Leadership and Administration M
- English as a Second Language M
- Finance and Banking M
- International Business M
- Management Information Systems M
- Organizational Management M
- Reading Education M
- Social Work M

NEW MEXICO HIGHLANDS UNIVERSITY
- Business Administration and Management—General M
- Counselor Education M
- Curriculum and Instruction M
- Education—General M
- Educational Leadership and Administration M
- Exercise and Sports Science M
- Health Education M
- Human Resources Management M
- International Business M
- Social Work M
- Special Education M
- Sports Management M

NEW MEXICO INSTITUTE OF MINING AND TECHNOLOGY
- Science Education M

NEW MEXICO STATE UNIVERSITY
- Accounting M
- Agricultural Education M
- Business Administration and Management—General M,D
- Counselor Education M,D,O
- Curriculum and Instruction M,D,O
- Distance Education Development O
- Early Childhood Education M,D,O
- Education—General M,D,O
- Educational Leadership and Administration M,D
- Educational Measurement and Evaluation M,D,O
- English as a Second Language M,D,O
- English Education M,D
- Finance and Banking M,O
- Foreign Languages Education M,D,O
- Higher Education M,D
- Kinesiology and Movement Studies D
- Management Information Systems M
- Marketing D
- Multilingual and Multicultural Education M,D,O
- Music Education M
- Reading Education M,D,O
- Social Work M
- Special Education M,D,O
- Travel and Tourism M

NEW ORLEANS BAPTIST THEOLOGICAL SEMINARY
- Religious Education M,D

THE NEW SCHOOL
- English as a Second Language M
- Finance and Banking M,D
- Management Strategy and Policy M,D
- Nonprofit Management M
- Organizational Management M,O
- Sustainability Management M,O

NEW YORK INSTITUTE OF TECHNOLOGY
- Accounting M
- Business Administration and Management—General M
- Counselor Education M,O
- Distance Education Development M,O
- Early Childhood Education M
- Education—General M,O
- Educational Media/Instructional Technology M,O
- Elementary Education M
- Entertainment Management M
- Finance and Banking M,O
- Human Resources Management M,O
- Marketing M
- Mathematics Education M,O
- Middle School Education M
- Science Education M,O
- Secondary Education M
- Supply Chain Management M

NEW YORK LAW SCHOOL
- Law M,D

NEW YORK MEDICAL COLLEGE
- Business Administration and Management—General M,D,O
- Health Education M,D,O

NEW YORK UNIVERSITY
- Accounting M,D
- Advertising and Public Relations M
- Archives/Archival Administration M,D,O
- Art Education M,O
- Business Administration and Management—General M,D,O
- Business Education M,O
- Counselor Education M,D,O
- Early Childhood Education M
- Education—General M,D,O
- Educational Leadership and Administration M,D,O
- Educational Media/Instructional Technology M,D,O
- Educational Policy M,D
- Educational Psychology M,D
- Electronic Commerce M,D,O
- Elementary Education M
- English as a Second Language M,D,O
- English Education M,D,O
- Entrepreneurship M,D,O
- Environmental Education M
- Finance and Banking M,D,O
- Foreign Languages Education M,D,O
- Foundations and Philosophy of Education M,D
- Higher Education M,D
- Hospitality Management M,D,O
- Human Resources Development M,D,O
- Human Resources Management M,D,O
- International and Comparative Education M,D,O
- International Business M,D
- Investment Management M,O
- Kinesiology and Movement Studies M,D,O
- Law M,D,O
- Legal and Justice Studies M,D,O
- Management Information Systems M,D,O
- Management Strategy and Policy M,D,O
- Marketing M,D,O
- Mathematics Education M
- Middle School Education M,D,O
- Multilingual and Multicultural Education M,D,O
- Music Education M,D,O
- Nonprofit Management M,D,O
- Organizational Behavior M,D,O
- Organizational Management M,D,O
- Project Management M,D,O
- Reading Education M
- Real Estate M,O
- Science Education M,D,O
- Secondary Education M,D,O
- Social Sciences Education M,D,O
- Social Work M,D
- Special Education M
- Sports Management M,O
- Student Affairs M,D
- Taxation M,D,O
- Transportation Management M
- Travel and Tourism M,O

NIAGARA UNIVERSITY
- Accounting M
- Business Administration and Management—General M
- Counselor Education M,O
- Early Childhood Education M,O
- Education—General M,O
- Educational Leadership and Administration M,O
- Elementary Education M,O
- English as a Second Language M,O
- Finance and Banking M
- Human Resources Management M
- International Business M
- Management Strategy and Policy M
- Marketing M
- Middle School Education M,O
- Reading Education M
- Secondary Education M,O
- Special Education M,O
- Supply Chain Management M

NICHOLLS STATE UNIVERSITY
- Business Administration and Management—General M
- Counselor Education M,O
- Curriculum and Instruction M
- Education—General M
- Educational Leadership and Administration M
- Elementary Education M
- Health Education M
- Middle School Education M
- Secondary Education M

NICHOLS COLLEGE
- Business Administration and Management—General M
- Organizational Management M

NIPISSING UNIVERSITY
- Education—General M,O

NORFOLK STATE UNIVERSITY
- Early Childhood Education M
- Education of Students with Severe/Multiple Disabilities M
- Education—General M
- Educational Leadership and Administration M
- Music Education M
- Secondary Education M
- Social Work M,D
- Special Education M
- Urban Education M

NORTH AMERICAN UNIVERSITY
- Educational Leadership and Administration M

NORTH CAROLINA AGRICULTURAL AND TECHNICAL STATE UNIVERSITY
- Accounting M
- Adult Education M
- Agricultural Education M
- Business Administration and Management—General M
- Business Education M
- Counselor Education M
- Early Childhood Education M
- Education—General M
- Educational Leadership and Administration M
- Educational Media/Instructional Technology M
- Elementary Education M
- English Education M
- Health Education M
- Human Resources Management M
- Management Information Systems M
- Physical Education M
- Reading Education M
- Science Education M
- Secondary Education M
- Social Work M
- Supply Chain Management M
- Vocational and Technical Education M

NORTH CAROLINA CENTRAL UNIVERSITY
- Business Administration and Management—General M
- Counselor Education M
- Education—General M
- Educational Leadership and Administration M
- Educational Media/Instructional Technology M
- Information Studies M
- Law D
- Library Science M
- Mathematics Education M
- Physical Education M
- Recreation and Park Management M
- Special Education M
- Sports Management M

NORTH CAROLINA STATE UNIVERSITY
- Accounting M
- Adult Education M,D
- Agricultural Education M,O
- Business Administration and Management—General M
- Business Education M
- Community College Education M,D
- Counselor Education M,D
- Curriculum and Instruction M,D
- Developmental Education M,D,O
- Education—General M,D,O
- Educational Leadership and Administration M,D
- Educational Measurement and Evaluation D
- Educational Media/Instructional Technology M,D
- Elementary Education M
- English Education M
- Entrepreneurship M
- Higher Education M,D
- Human Resources Development M
- Mathematics Education M,D
- Middle School Education M
- Nonprofit Management M,D,O
- Recreation and Park Management M,D
- Science Education M,D
- Secondary Education M
- Social Sciences Education M
- Social Work M
- Special Education M
- Sports Management M,D
- Supply Chain Management M
- Travel and Tourism M,D

NORTH CENTRAL COLLEGE
- Business Administration and Management—General M
- Education—General M
- Educational Leadership and Administration M
- Finance and Banking M
- Human Resources Management M
- Management Strategy and Policy M

NORTHCENTRAL UNIVERSITY
- Business Administration and Management—General M,D,O
- Education—General M,D,O

NORTH DAKOTA STATE UNIVERSITY
- Accounting M
- Adult Education M,D,O
- Agricultural Education M
- Athletic Training and Sports Medicine M,D
- Business Administration and Management—General M*
- Counselor Education M,D
- Curriculum and Instruction M
- Education—General M,D,O
- Educational Leadership and Administration M,O
- Exercise and Sports Science M,D
- Higher Education O
- Logistics M,D
- Mathematics Education M,D,O
- Music Education M,D,O
- Science Education M,D,O
- Social Sciences Education M,D,O
- Transportation Management M,D
- Vocational and Technical Education M,D,O

NORTHEASTERN ILLINOIS UNIVERSITY
- Accounting M
- Business Administration and Management—General M
- Counselor Education M
- Early Childhood Education M
- Education of the Gifted M
- Education—General M
- Educational Leadership and Administration M
- Elementary Education M
- English as a Second Language M
- Exercise and Sports Science M
- Finance and Banking M
- Human Resources Development M
- Marketing M
- Mathematics Education M
- Multilingual and Multicultural Education M
- Reading Education M
- Secondary Education M
- Special Education M
- Urban Education M

NORTHEASTERN STATE UNIVERSITY
- Accounting M
- Business Administration and Management—General M
- Counselor Education M
- Early Childhood Education M
- Education—General M
- Educational Leadership and Administration M
- Educational Media/Instructional Technology M
- Finance and Banking M
- Health Education M
- Kinesiology and Movement Studies M
- Mathematics Education M
- Reading Education M
- Science Education M
- Special Education M

NORTHEASTERN UNIVERSITY
- Accounting M

*M—masters degree; D—doctorate; O—other advanced degree; *—Close-Up and/or Display*

- Business Administration and Management—General M,D,O
- Educational Leadership and Administration M
- Elementary Education M
- Entrepreneurship M
- Exercise and Sports Science M,D,O
- Finance and Banking M
- Higher Education M
- Human Services M
- International Business M
- Law M,D
- Legal and Justice Studies M,D
- Management Information Systems M,D,O
- Nonprofit Management M
- Project Management M
- Special Education M
- Sports Management M
- Taxation M

NORTHERN ARIZONA UNIVERSITY
- Business Administration and Management—General M
- Community College Education M,D,O
- Counselor Education M,D,O
- Curriculum and Instruction M,D
- Early Childhood Education M,D
- Education—General M,D,O
- Educational Leadership and Administration M,D,O
- Educational Media/Instructional Technology M,O
- Educational Psychology M,D,O
- Elementary Education M,D
- English as a Second Language M,D,O
- English Education M,D,O
- Foreign Languages Education M
- Foundations and Philosophy of Education M,D,O
- Higher Education M,D,O
- International Business M
- Mathematics Education M,O
- Multilingual and Multicultural Education M,O
- Science Education M,O
- Secondary Education M,D
- Special Education M,O
- Student Affairs M,D,O
- Vocational and Technical Education M,O

NORTHERN ILLINOIS UNIVERSITY
- Accounting M
- Adult Education M,D
- Business Administration and Management—General M
- Counselor Education M,D
- Curriculum and Instruction M,D
- Early Childhood Education M,D
- Education—General M,D,O
- Educational Leadership and Administration M,D,O
- Educational Media/Instructional Technology M,D
- Educational Psychology M,D,O
- Elementary Education M,D
- Foundations and Philosophy of Education M,D,O
- Higher Education M,D
- Industrial and Manufacturing Management M
- Law D
- Management Information Systems M
- Physical Education M
- Reading Education M,D
- Secondary Education M,D
- Special Education M,D
- Taxation M

NORTHERN KENTUCKY UNIVERSITY
- Accounting M,O
- Advertising and Public Relations M,O
- Business Administration and Management—General M,O
- Counselor Education M
- Education—General M,D,O
- Educational Leadership and Administration M,D,O
- Law D
- Nonprofit Management M,O
- Organizational Management M
- Social Work M
- Special Education M,O
- Taxation M,O

NORTHERN MICHIGAN UNIVERSITY
- Business Administration and Management—General M
- Curriculum and Instruction M
- Education—General M
- Educational Leadership and Administration M
- Elementary Education M
- English as a Second Language M,O
- Exercise and Sports Science M
- Higher Education M
- Human Resources Management M
- Reading Education M
- Science Education M
- Secondary Education M
- Special Education M
- Student Affairs M

NORTHERN STATE UNIVERSITY
- Counselor Education M
- Curriculum and Instruction M
- Education—General M
- Educational Leadership and Administration M
- Educational Media/Instructional Technology M
- Finance and Banking M
- Music Education M
- Sports Management M

NORTH GREENVILLE UNIVERSITY
- Education—General M,D
- Finance and Banking M,D
- Human Resources Management M,D

NORTH PARK UNIVERSITY
- Business Administration and Management—General M
- Education—General M
- Nonprofit Management M

NORTHWEST CHRISTIAN UNIVERSITY
- Accounting M
- Business Administration and Management—General M
- Counselor Education M
- Education—General M
- Elementary Education M
- English as a Second Language M
- Secondary Education M

NORTHWESTERN COLLEGE
- Early Childhood Education M,O
- Education—General M,O
- Educational Leadership and Administration M,O

NORTHWESTERN OKLAHOMA STATE UNIVERSITY
- Adult Education M
- Counselor Education M
- Curriculum and Instruction M
- Education—General M
- Educational Leadership and Administration M
- Elementary Education M
- Reading Education M
- Secondary Education M

NORTHWESTERN POLYTECHNIC UNIVERSITY
- Business Administration and Management—General M,D

NORTHWESTERN STATE UNIVERSITY OF LOUISIANA
- Adult Education M
- Counselor Education M,O
- Curriculum and Instruction M
- Early Childhood Education M
- Education—General M,O
- Educational Leadership and Administration M,O
- Educational Media/Instructional Technology M,O
- Elementary Education M,O
- Health Education M
- Middle School Education M
- Reading Education M,O
- Secondary Education M,O
- Special Education M,O
- Student Affairs M

NORTHWESTERN UNIVERSITY
- Accounting M,D
- Business Administration and Management—General M,D
- Education—General M,D*
- Educational Leadership and Administration M
- Educational Media/Instructional Technology M,D
- Electronic Commerce M
- Elementary Education M
- Entrepreneurship M,D
- Finance and Banking M,D
- Human Resources Management M,D
- Industrial and Manufacturing Management M,D
- International Business M,D
- Kinesiology and Movement Studies D
- Law M,D
- Management Information Systems M
- Management Strategy and Policy M,D
- Marketing M,D
- Music Education M,D
- Organizational Behavior M,D
- Organizational Management M,D
- Project Management M
- Quality Management M
- Quantitative Analysis M,D
- Real Estate M,D
- Secondary Education M
- Sports Management M
- Taxation M,D

NORTHWEST MISSOURI STATE UNIVERSITY
- Agricultural Education M
- Business Administration and Management—General M
- Early Childhood Education M,D,O
- Education—General M,D,O
- Educational Leadership and Administration M,D,O
- Educational Media/Instructional Technology M
- Educational Policy M,D,O
- Elementary Education M,D,O
- English as a Second Language M,D,O
- English Education M,O
- Exercise and Sports Science M
- Health Education M
- Higher Education M,D,O
- Human Resources Management M
- Management Information Systems M
- Marketing M
- Mathematics Education M,D,O
- Middle School Education M,D,O
- Physical Education M
- Reading Education M,D,O
- Recreation and Park Management M
- Science Education M,O
- Social Sciences Education M,O
- Special Education M,D,O

NORTHWEST NAZARENE UNIVERSITY
- Business Administration and Management—General M
- Counselor Education M
- Curriculum and Instruction M,D,O
- Education—General M,D,O
- Educational Leadership and Administration M,D,O
- Social Work M
- Special Education M,D,O

NORTHWEST UNIVERSITY
- Business Administration and Management—General M
- Education—General M
- International Business M
- Organizational Management M
- Project Management M

NORTHWOOD UNIVERSITY, MICHIGAN CAMPUS
- Business Administration and Management—General M

NORWICH UNIVERSITY
- Business Administration and Management—General M
- Finance and Banking M
- Human Resources Management M
- International Business M
- Logistics M
- Management Strategy and Policy M
- Nonprofit Management M
- Organizational Management M
- Project Management M
- Supply Chain Management M

NOTRE DAME COLLEGE (OH)
- Reading Education M,O
- Special Education M,O

NOTRE DAME DE NAMUR UNIVERSITY
- Business Administration and Management—General M
- Curriculum and Instruction M,D
- Education—General M,D
- Educational Leadership and Administration M
- Entrepreneurship M
- Finance and Banking M
- Human Resources Management M
- Industrial and Manufacturing Management M
- Marketing M
- Special Education M

NOTRE DAME OF MARYLAND UNIVERSITY
- Business Administration and Management—General M
- Education—General M
- Educational Leadership and Administration M,D
- English as a Second Language M
- Nonprofit Management M

NOVA SOUTHEASTERN UNIVERSITY
- Accounting M
- Business Administration and Management—General M
- Business Education M
- Counselor Education M,D,O
- Distance Education Development M,D,O
- Education—General M,D,O
- Educational Media/Instructional Technology M,D,O
- Entrepreneurship M
- Finance and Banking M
- Health Education M,D,O
- Health Law M,D
- Human Resources Management M
- International Business M
- Law M,D
- Legal and Justice Studies M,D
- Management Information Systems M,D
- Management Strategy and Policy M
- Marketing M
- Student Affairs M,D,O
- Supply Chain Management M
- Taxation M

NYACK COLLEGE
- Business Administration and Management—General M
- Counselor Education M
- Elementary Education M
- English as a Second Language M
- Organizational Management M
- Social Work M
- Special Education M

OAKLAND CITY UNIVERSITY
- Business Administration and Management—General M
- Education—General M,D
- Educational Leadership and Administration M,D

OAKLAND UNIVERSITY
- Accounting M,O
- Business Administration and Management—General M,O
- Early Childhood Education M,D,O
- Education—General M,D,O
- Educational Leadership and Administration M,D,O
- Elementary Education M,O
- English as a Second Language M,O
- Entrepreneurship M,O
- Exercise and Sports Science M,D,O
- Finance and Banking M,O
- Higher Education M,D,O
- Human Resources Management M,O
- Industrial and Manufacturing Management M,O
- International Business M,O
- Management Information Systems M,D,O
- Marketing M,O
- Music Education M,D
- Nonprofit Management M,O
- Organizational Management M,D,O
- Reading Education M,D,O
- Secondary Education M,O
- Special Education M,O

OGLALA LAKOTA COLLEGE
- Business Administration and Management—General M
- Educational Leadership and Administration M

OHIO CHRISTIAN UNIVERSITY
- Accounting M
- Business Administration and Management—General M
- Finance and Banking M
- Human Resources Management M
- Marketing M
- Organizational Management M

OHIO DOMINICAN UNIVERSITY
- Accounting M
- Business Administration and Management—General M
- Curriculum and Instruction M
- Education—General M
- Educational Leadership and Administration M
- English as a Second Language M
- Finance and Banking M
- Management Strategy and Policy M
- Sports Management M

OHIO NORTHERN UNIVERSITY
- Accounting M
- Law M,D

THE OHIO STATE UNIVERSITY
- Accounting M,D
- Actuarial Science M,D
- Agricultural Education M
- Art Education M,D
- Business Administration and Management—General M,D
- Education—General M,D,O
- Educational Leadership and Administration M,D,O
- Educational Policy M,D,O
- Finance and Banking M
- Human Resources Management M,D
- Kinesiology and Movement Studies M,D
- Law M,D
- Logistics M
- Management Information Systems M,D
- Mathematics Education M,D
- Physical Education M,D
- Social Work M,D
- Special Education D

THE OHIO STATE UNIVERSITY AT LIMA
- Social Work M

THE OHIO STATE UNIVERSITY AT MARION
- Education—General M

THE OHIO STATE UNIVERSITY–MANSFIELD CAMPUS
- Education—General M
- Social Work M

THE OHIO STATE UNIVERSITY–NEWARK CAMPUS
- Education—General M
- Social Work M

OHIO UNIVERSITY
- Athletic Training and Sports Medicine M
- Business Administration and Management—General M
- Computer Education M,D
- Counselor Education M,D
- Curriculum and Instruction M,D
- Education—General M,D
- Educational Leadership and Administration M,D
- Educational Measurement and Evaluation M,D
- Educational Media/Instructional Technology M,D
- Exercise and Sports Science M,D
- Finance and Banking M
- Higher Education M,D
- Middle School Education M,D
- Music Education M,O
- Physical Education M
- Reading Education M,D
- Recreation and Park Management M
- Secondary Education M,D
- Social Work M
- Special Education M,D
- Sports Management M
- Student Affairs M,D

OHIO VALLEY UNIVERSITY
- Curriculum and Instruction M
- Education—General M

OKLAHOMA BAPTIST UNIVERSITY
- Business Administration and Management—General M

OKLAHOMA CHRISTIAN UNIVERSITY
- Accounting M
- Business Administration and Management—General M
- Finance and Banking M
- Human Resources Management M
- International Business M
- Marketing M
- Nonprofit Management M
- Organizational Management M
- Project Management M

OKLAHOMA CITY UNIVERSITY
- Business Administration and Management—General M
- Counselor Education M

Early Childhood Education M
Elementary Education M
English as a Second Language M
Law M,D

OKLAHOMA STATE UNIVERSITY
Accounting M,D
Agricultural Education M,D
Business Administration and Management—General M,D
Curriculum and Instruction M,D
Education—General M,D,O
Educational Leadership and Administration M,D
Educational Psychology M,D,O
Entrepreneurship M,D
Finance and Banking M,D
Health Education M,D,O
Higher Education M,D
Hospitality Management M,D
Management Information Systems M,D
Marketing M,D
Mathematics Education M,D
Music Education M
Nonprofit Management M,D,O
Sustainability Management M,D,O

OKLAHOMA WESLEYAN UNIVERSITY
Management Strategy and Policy M

OLD DOMINION UNIVERSITY
Accounting M
Athletic Training and Sports Medicine M
Business Administration and Management—General M,D
Business Education M,D
Community College Education M,D
Counselor Education M,D,O
Curriculum and Instruction M,D
Early Childhood Education M,D
Education—General M,D,O
Educational Leadership and Administration M,D,O
Educational Measurement and Evaluation D
Educational Media/Instructional Technology M,D,O
Educational Psychology D
Elementary Education M,O
English as a Second Language M
Exercise and Sports Science M
Finance and Banking D
Health Education M,D
Higher Education M,D,O
International Business M
Kinesiology and Movement Studies M,D
Library Science M,O
Management Information Systems M,D
Marketing D
Middle School Education M,O
Music Education M
Physical Education M,D
Reading Education M,D
Secondary Education M
Special Education M,D
Sports Management M
Supply Chain Management M
Vocational and Technical Education M,D

OLIVET COLLEGE
Insurance M

OLIVET NAZARENE UNIVERSITY
Business Administration and Management—General M
Curriculum and Instruction M
Education—General M
Educational Leadership and Administration M
Elementary Education M
Library Science M
Organizational Management M
Reading Education M
Secondary Education M

OPEN UNIVERSITY
Business Administration and Management—General M
Education—General M

ORAL ROBERTS UNIVERSITY
Accounting M
Business Administration and Management—General M
Curriculum and Instruction M,D
Education—General M,D
Educational Leadership and Administration M,D
Entrepreneurship M
Finance and Banking M
Higher Education M,D
International Business M
Marketing M
Nonprofit Management M
Religious Education M,D

OREGON STATE UNIVERSITY
Accounting M,D
Actuarial Science M,D
Adult Education M,D
Agricultural Education M,D
Athletic Training and Sports Medicine M
Business Administration and Management—General M,D
Counselor Education M,D
Early Childhood Education M,D
Education—General M,D
Educational Leadership and Administration M,D
Educational Policy M,D
Elementary Education M
English as a Second Language M,D
English Education M
Entrepreneurship M,D
Environmental Education M,D
Finance and Banking M,D
Higher Education M,D
Kinesiology and Movement Studies M,D
Legal and Justice Studies M,D
Management Strategy and Policy M,D
Mathematics Education M,D
Music Education M
Organizational Management M,D
Science Education M,D
Social Sciences Education M,D
Student Affairs M
Supply Chain Management M,D
Sustainability Management M,D

OREGON STATE UNIVERSITY–CASCADES
Education—General M

OTTAWA UNIVERSITY
Business Administration and Management—General M
Counselor Education M
Curriculum and Instruction M
Early Childhood Education M
Education—General M
Educational Leadership and Administration M
Educational Media/Instructional Technology M
Elementary Education M
Finance and Banking M
Human Resources Development M
Human Resources Management M
Marketing M
Special Education M

OTTERBEIN UNIVERSITY
Business Administration and Management—General M
Education—General M

OUR LADY OF THE LAKE UNIVERSITY
Accounting M
Business Administration and Management—General M
Counselor Education M
Curriculum and Instruction M
Education—General M,D
Finance and Banking M
Management Information Systems M
Nonprofit Management M
Organizational Management M,D
Science Education M
Social Work M,D

OXFORD GRADUATE SCHOOL
Organizational Management M,D*

PACE UNIVERSITY
Accounting M,O
Business Administration and Management—General M,D,O
Business Education M,O
Early Childhood Education M,O
Education—General M,O
Educational Media/Instructional Technology M,O
Electronic Commerce O
Elementary Education M,O
Entrepreneurship M
Environmental Law M,D
Finance and Banking M,D,O
Foreign Languages Education M,O
Human Resources Management M,O
International Business M,O
Investment Management M,O
Law M,D
Legal and Justice Studies M,D
Management Information Systems M,D,O
Management Strategy and Policy M
Marketing M,D,O
Nonprofit Management M
Reading Education M,O
Social Sciences Education M,O
Special Education M,O
Taxation M

PACIFIC LUTHERAN UNIVERSITY
Accounting M
Business Administration and Management—General M
Curriculum and Instruction M
Education—General M
Finance and Banking M
Marketing Research M

PACIFIC OAKS COLLEGE
Early Childhood Education M
Education—General M
Special Education M

PACIFIC STATES UNIVERSITY
Accounting M,D
Business Administration and Management—General M,D
Finance and Banking M,D
International Business M,D
Management Information Systems M,D
Real Estate M,D

PACIFIC UNION COLLEGE
Education—General M
Elementary Education M
Secondary Education M

PACIFIC UNIVERSITY
Athletic Training and Sports Medicine M,D
Business Administration and Management—General M
Early Childhood Education M
Education of the Gifted M
Education—General M
Elementary Education M
English as a Second Language M
Finance and Banking M
Middle School Education M
Science Education M
Secondary Education M
Social Work M
Special Education M

PALM BEACH ATLANTIC UNIVERSITY
Business Administration and Management—General M
Counselor Education M
Education—General M
Organizational Management M
Religious Education M

PARK UNIVERSITY
Business Administration and Management—General M,O
Curriculum and Instruction M,O
Education—General M,O
Educational Leadership and Administration M,O
Finance and Banking M,O
International Business M,O
Management Information Systems M,O
Nonprofit Management M,O
Reading Education M,O
Social Work M,O

PEIRCE COLLEGE
Organizational Management M

PENN STATE ERIE, THE BEHREND COLLEGE
Accounting M
Business Administration and Management—General M
Industrial and Manufacturing Management M
Project Management M
Quality Management M

PENN STATE GREAT VALLEY
Business Administration and Management—General M,O
Entrepreneurship M,O
Finance and Banking M,O
Human Resources Development M,O
Human Resources Management M,O
Sustainability Management M,O

PENN STATE HARRISBURG
Accounting M,O
Adult Education M,D,O
Business Administration and Management—General M,O
Curriculum and Instruction M,D,O
Developmental Education M,D,O
Education—General M,D,O
English as a Second Language M,D,O
Finance and Banking M,D,O
Health Education M,D,O
Human Resources Management M,D,O
Management Information Systems M,O
Nonprofit Management M,D,O
Reading Education M,D,O
Supply Chain Management M,O

PENN STATE UNIVERSITY–DICKINSON LAW
Law M,D

PENN STATE UNIVERSITY PARK
Accounting M,D
Adult Education M,D,O
Agricultural Education M,D,O
Art Education M,D,O
Business Administration and Management—General M,D
Counselor Education M,D,O
Curriculum and Instruction M,D,O
Education—General M,D,O
Educational Leadership and Administration M,D,O
Educational Media/Instructional Technology M,D,O
Educational Policy M,D,O
Educational Psychology M,D,O
English as a Second Language M,D
Foundations and Philosophy of Education M,D,O
Higher Education M,D,O
Hospitality Management M,D
Human Resources Development M
Human Resources Management M
Kinesiology and Movement Studies M,D,O
Law M,D
Leisure Studies M,D
Management Information Systems M,D
Music Education M,D,O
Organizational Management M,D
Recreation and Park Management M,D
Special Education M,D,O
Supply Chain Management M,D
Travel and Tourism M,D
Vocational and Technical Education M,D,O

PENN STATE YORK
Curriculum and Instruction M,O
Education—General M,O
English as a Second Language M,O

PENNSYLVANIA COLLEGE OF HEALTH SCIENCES
Health Education M

PENSACOLA CHRISTIAN COLLEGE
Business Administration and Management—General M,D,O
Curriculum and Instruction M,D,O
Educational Leadership and Administration M,D,O

PEPPERDINE UNIVERSITY
Accounting M
Business Administration and Management—General M
Business Education M
Educational Leadership and Administration M,D
Educational Media/Instructional Technology M,D
Finance and Banking M
Human Resources Management M
International Business M
Law D
Organizational Management M,D
Science Education M,D

PERU STATE COLLEGE
Curriculum and Instruction M
Education—General M
Entrepreneurship M
Organizational Management M

PFEIFFER UNIVERSITY
Business Administration and Management—General M
Elementary Education M
Organizational Management M
Religious Education M

PHILADELPHIA UNIVERSITY
Athletic Training and Sports Medicine M
Business Administration and Management—General M
Management Strategy and Policy M
Marketing M
Real Estate M
Taxation M

PHILLIPS GRADUATE UNIVERSITY
Counselor Education M
Organizational Behavior D

PHILLIPS THEOLOGICAL SEMINARY
Business Administration and Management—General M,D
Higher Education M,D
Religious Education M,D
Social Work M,D

PIEDMONT COLLEGE
Art Education M,O
Business Administration and Management—General M
Curriculum and Instruction M,O
Early Childhood Education M,O
Education—General M,O
Educational Media/Instructional Technology M,O
Middle School Education M,O
Music Education M,O
Secondary Education M,O
Special Education M,O

PIEDMONT INTERNATIONAL UNIVERSITY
Curriculum and Instruction M,D
Educational Leadership and Administration M,D

PITTSBURG STATE UNIVERSITY
Accounting M
Business Administration and Management—General M
Counselor Education M
Education—General M,O
Educational Leadership and Administration M,O
Educational Media/Instructional Technology M
Exercise and Sports Science M
Health Education M
Human Resources Development M
International Business M
Music Education M
Physical Education M
Special Education M,O
Sports Management M
Vocational and Technical Education M,O

PLYMOUTH STATE UNIVERSITY
Adult Education D
Art Education M
Athletic Training and Sports Medicine M
Business Administration and Management—General M
Counselor Education M
Curriculum and Instruction M
Education—General O
Educational Leadership and Administration M,O
Educational Media/Instructional Technology M
Elementary Education M
English Education M
Foreign Languages Education M
Health Education M
Higher Education D,O
Mathematics Education M
Music Education M
Physical Education M
Reading Education M
Science Education M
Secondary Education M
Social Sciences Education M
Special Education M

POINT LOMA NAZARENE UNIVERSITY
Business Administration and Management—General M
Counselor Education M

*M—masters degree; D—doctorate; O—other advanced degree; *—Close-Up and/or Display*

Education—General	M
Educational Leadership and Administration	M
Entrepreneurship	M
Exercise and Sports Science	M
Kinesiology and Movement Studies	M
Organizational Management	M
Project Management	M
Special Education	M
Sports Management	M

POINT PARK UNIVERSITY

Business Administration and Management—General	M
Curriculum and Instruction	M
Education—General	M
Educational Leadership and Administration	M,D
Entertainment Management	M
International Business	M
Management Information Systems	M
Organizational Management	M
Special Education	M
Sports Management	M

POLYTECHNIC UNIVERSITY OF PUERTO RICO

Business Administration and Management—General	M
Industrial and Manufacturing Management	M
International Business	M
Management Information Systems	M

POLYTECHNIC UNIVERSITY OF PUERTO RICO, MIAMI CAMPUS

Accounting	M
Business Administration and Management—General	M
Finance and Banking	M
Human Resources Management	M
Industrial and Manufacturing Management	M
International Business	M
Logistics	M
Marketing	M
Project Management	M
Supply Chain Management	M

POLYTECHNIC UNIVERSITY OF PUERTO RICO, ORLANDO CAMPUS

Accounting	M
Business Administration and Management—General	M
Finance and Banking	M
Human Resources Management	M
Industrial and Manufacturing Management	M
International Business	M

PONTIFICAL CATHOLIC UNIVERSITY OF PUERTO RICO

Accounting	M,O
Business Administration and Management—General	M,D,O
Business Education	M,D
Counselor Education	M,D
Curriculum and Instruction	M,D
Education—General	M,D
Educational Leadership and Administration	D
Educational Psychology	M
English as a Second Language	M
Finance and Banking	M
Human Resources Management	M,O
Human Services	M,D
International Business	M
Law	D
Logistics	O
Management Information Systems	M,O
Marketing	M
Religious Education	M
Social Work	M
Transportation Management	O

PONTIFICIA UNIVERSIDAD CATOLICA MADRE Y MAESTRA

Business Administration and Management—General	M
Early Childhood Education	M
Entrepreneurship	M
Finance and Banking	M
Hospitality Management	M
Human Resources Management	M
Insurance	M
International Business	M
Law	M
Logistics	M
Management Strategy and Policy	M
Marketing	M
Real Estate	M
Travel and Tourism	M

PORTLAND STATE UNIVERSITY

Business Administration and Management—General	M,D,O
Education—General	M,D
English as a Second Language	M
Finance and Banking	M
Foreign Languages Education	M
Health Education	M,D,O
Industrial and Manufacturing Management	M,D
International Business	M
Mathematics Education	M,D
Music Education	M
Real Estate	M
Science Education	M,D
Social Sciences Education	M
Social Work	M,D
Supply Chain Management	M

POST UNIVERSITY

Accounting	M
Business Administration and Management—General	M
Distance Education Development	M
Education—General	M
Educational Leadership and Administration	M
Educational Media/Instructional Technology	M
English as a Second Language	M
Entrepreneurship	M
Finance and Banking	M
Human Services	M
Marketing	M
Nonprofit Management	M
Project Management	M

PRAIRIE VIEW A&M UNIVERSITY

Accounting	M
Business Administration and Management—General	M
Counselor Education	M,D
Curriculum and Instruction	M
Education—General	M,D
Educational Leadership and Administration	M,D
Health Education	M
Kinesiology and Movement Studies	M
Legal and Justice Studies	M,D
Management Information Systems	M,D

PRATT INSTITUTE

Art Education	M,O
Facilities Management	M
Information Studies	M,O*
Library Science	M,O
Real Estate	M

PRESCOTT COLLEGE

Counselor Education	M,D
Early Childhood Education	M,D
Education—General	M,D
Educational Leadership and Administration	M,D
Elementary Education	M,D
Environmental Education	M,D
Legal and Justice Studies	M
Leisure Studies	M
Secondary Education	M,D
Special Education	M,D

PRESIDIO GRADUATE SCHOOL (CA)

Business Administration and Management—General	M,O
Sustainability Management	M,O

PRINCETON UNIVERSITY

Finance and Banking	M

PROVIDENCE COLLEGE

Accounting	M
Business Administration and Management—General	M
Counselor Education	M
Educational Leadership and Administration	M
Elementary Education	M
Finance and Banking	M
International Business	M
Marketing	M
Mathematics Education	M
Reading Education	M
Secondary Education	M
Special Education	M
Urban Education	M

PROVIDENCE UNIVERSITY COLLEGE & THEOLOGICAL SEMINARY

English as a Second Language	M,D,O
Religious Education	M,D,O
Student Affairs	M,D,O

PURDUE UNIVERSITY

Agricultural Education	M,D,O
Art Education	M,D,O
Aviation Management	M
Business Administration and Management—General	M,D*
Counselor Education	M,D,O
Curriculum and Instruction	M,D,O
Education of the Gifted	M,D,O
Education—General	M,D,O
Educational Leadership and Administration	M,D,O
Educational Media/Instructional Technology	M,D,O
Educational Psychology	M,D,O
Elementary Education	M,D,O
English Education	M,D,O
Exercise and Sports Science	M,D
Finance and Banking	M
Foreign Languages Education	M,D,O
Foundations and Philosophy of Education	M,D,O
Health Education	M,D
Higher Education	M,D,O
Home Economics Education	M,D,O
Hospitality Management	M,D
Human Resources Management	M,D*
International Business	M
Kinesiology and Movement Studies	M,D
Management Information Systems	M
Mathematics Education	M,D,O
Organizational Behavior	D
Physical Education	M,D
Quantitative Analysis	M,D
Reading Education	M,D,O
Recreation and Park Management	M,D
Science Education	M,D,O
Social Sciences Education	M,D,O
Special Education	M,D,O
Sports Management	M,D
Travel and Tourism	M,D
Vocational and Technical Education	M,D,O

PURDUE UNIVERSITY NORTHWEST

Accounting	M
Business Administration and Management—General	M
Counselor Education	M
Education—General	M
Educational Leadership and Administration	M
Educational Media/Instructional Technology	M
Human Services	M
Mathematics Education	M
Science Education	M
Special Education	M

QUEENS COLLEGE OF THE CITY UNIVERSITY OF NEW YORK

Accounting	M
Art Education	M,O
Counselor Education	M,O
Early Childhood Education	M,O
Education—General	M,O
Educational Leadership and Administration	M,O
Elementary Education	M,O
English as a Second Language	M,O
English Education	M,O
Exercise and Sports Science	M,O
Finance and Banking	M
Foreign Languages Education	M,O
Information Studies	M,O
Library Science	M,O
Mathematics Education	M,O
Middle School Education	M,O
Multilingual and Multicultural Education	M,O
Music Education	M,O
Physical Education	M,O
Reading Education	M,O
Science Education	M,O
Secondary Education	M,O
Social Sciences Education	M,O
Special Education	M,O

QUEEN'S UNIVERSITY AT KINGSTON

Business Administration and Management—General	M
Education—General	M,D
Entrepreneurship	M
Exercise and Sports Science	M,D
Finance and Banking	M
Information Studies	M,D
Law	M,D
Legal and Justice Studies	M,D
Marketing	M
Project Management	M

QUEENS UNIVERSITY OF CHARLOTTE

Business Administration and Management—General	M
Education—General	M
Educational Leadership and Administration	M
Elementary Education	M
Organizational Management	M
Reading Education	M

QUINCY UNIVERSITY

Business Administration and Management—General	M
Counselor Education	M
Curriculum and Instruction	M
Education—General	M
Educational Leadership and Administration	M
English as a Second Language	M
Multilingual and Multicultural Education	M
Reading Education	M
Special Education	M

QUINNIPIAC UNIVERSITY

Advertising and Public Relations	M
Business Administration and Management—General	M
Education—General	M,O
Educational Leadership and Administration	M,O
Educational Media/Instructional Technology	M
Elementary Education	M
English Education	M
Foreign Languages Education	M
Law	M,D
Mathematics Education	M
Middle School Education	M
Organizational Management	M
Science Education	M
Secondary Education	M
Social Sciences Education	M
Social Work	M
Supply Chain Management	M

RADFORD UNIVERSITY

Business Administration and Management—General	M
Counselor Education	M
Early Childhood Education	M
Educational Leadership and Administration	M
Management Information Systems	M
Mathematics Education	M
Reading Education	M
Social Work	M
Special Education	M,O

RAMAPO COLLEGE OF NEW JERSEY

Business Administration and Management—General	M
Educational Leadership and Administration	M
Educational Media/Instructional Technology	M
Social Work	M
Special Education	M

RANDOLPH COLLEGE

Curriculum and Instruction	M
Education—General	M
Special Education	M

REFORMED THEOLOGICAL SEMINARY–JACKSON CAMPUS

Religious Education	M,D,O

REGENT'S UNIVERSITY LONDON

Business Administration and Management—General	M
Finance and Banking	M
Human Resources Management	M
International Business	M
Management Information Systems	M
Marketing	M

REGENT UNIVERSITY

Accounting	M,D,O
Adult Education	M,D,O
Business Administration and Management—General	M,D,O
Counselor Education	M,D,O
Curriculum and Instruction	M,D,O
Distance Education Development	M,D,O
Early Childhood Education	M,D,O
Education of the Gifted	M,D,O
Education—General	M,D,O
Educational Leadership and Administration	M,D,O
Educational Media/Instructional Technology	M,D,O
Educational Psychology	M,D,O
Elementary Education	M,D,O
English as a Second Language	M,D,O
Entrepreneurship	M,D,O
Finance and Banking	M,D,O
Higher Education	M,D,O
Human Resources Development	M,D,O
Human Resources Management	M,D,O
Investment Management	M,D,O
Law	M,D
Legal and Justice Studies	M,D
Management Strategy and Policy	M,D,O
Mathematics Education	M,D,O
Nonprofit Management	M,D,O
Organizational Management	M,D,O
Reading Education	M,D,O
Religious Education	M,D,O
Science Education	M,D,O
Special Education	M,D,O
Student Affairs	M,D,O

REGIS COLLEGE (MA)

Education—General	M,D
Educational Leadership and Administration	M,D
Elementary Education	M,D
Higher Education	M,D
Quality Management	M
Reading Education	M,D
Social Sciences Education	M
Special Education	M,D

REGIS UNIVERSITY

Accounting	M,O
Business Education	M,O
Counselor Education	M,D,O
Curriculum and Instruction	M,O
Education—General	M
Educational Leadership and Administration	M,O
Elementary Education	M,O
Finance and Banking	M,O
Human Resources Management	M,O
Industrial and Manufacturing Management	M,O
Management Information Systems	M,O
Management Strategy and Policy	M,O
Marketing	M,O
Nonprofit Management	M,O
Organizational Management	M,O
Project Management	M,O
Reading Education	M,O
Secondary Education	M,O
Special Education	M,O

REINHARDT UNIVERSITY

Business Administration and Management—General	M
Early Childhood Education	M
Education—General	M

RELAY GRADUATE SCHOOL OF EDUCATION

Education—General	M

RENSSELAER AT HARTFORD

Business Administration and Management—General	M

RENSSELAER POLYTECHNIC INSTITUTE

Business Administration and Management—General	M,D
Entrepreneurship	M
Management Information Systems	M
Supply Chain Management	M

RHODE ISLAND COLLEGE

Accounting	M,O
Art Education	M
Counselor Education	M,O
Early Childhood Education	M
Education—General	D
Educational Leadership and Administration	M,O
Elementary Education	M
English as a Second Language	M
English Education	M
Finance and Banking	M,O
Foreign Languages Education	M
Health Education	M,O
Mathematics Education	M
Music Education	M
Physical Education	M,O
Reading Education	M
Secondary Education	M
Social Sciences Education	M
Social Work	M
Special Education	M,O

RHODE ISLAND SCHOOL OF DESIGN	
Art Education	M

RHODES COLLEGE	
Accounting	M

RICE UNIVERSITY	
Business Administration and Management—General	M
Education—General	M
Science Education	M,D

RICHMONT GRADUATE UNIVERSITY	
Counselor Education	M

RIDER UNIVERSITY	
Accounting	M
Business Administration and Management—General	M
Business Education	O
Counselor Education	M,O
Curriculum and Instruction	M,O
Education—General	M,O
Educational Leadership and Administration	M,O
Elementary Education	O
English as a Second Language	O
English Education	O
Foreign Languages Education	O
Mathematics Education	O
Music Education	M
Organizational Management	M
Reading Education	M,O
Science Education	O
Social Sciences Education	O
Special Education	M,O

RIVIER UNIVERSITY	
Business Administration and Management—General	M
Counselor Education	M,D,O
Curriculum and Instruction	M,D,O
Early Childhood Education	M,D,O
Education—General	M,D,O
Educational Leadership and Administration	M,D,O
Elementary Education	M,D,O
Foreign Languages Education	M
Management Information Systems	M
Reading Education	M,D,O
Social Sciences Education	M
Special Education	M,D,O

ROBERT MORRIS UNIVERSITY	
Business Administration and Management—General	M
Business Education	M,D,O
Education—General	M,D,O
Educational Leadership and Administration	M,D,O
Higher Education	M,D,O
Human Resources Management	M
Management Information Systems	M,D
Organizational Management	M,D
Project Management	M,D
Reading Education	M,D,O
Special Education	M,D,O
Taxation	M

ROBERT MORRIS UNIVERSITY ILLINOIS	
Accounting	M
Business Administration and Management—General	M
Educational Leadership and Administration	M
Educational Media/Instructional Technology	M
Finance and Banking	M
Higher Education	M
Human Resources Management	M
Management Information Systems	M
Management Strategy and Policy	M
Sports Management	M

ROBERTS WESLEYAN COLLEGE	
Business Administration and Management—General	M
Counselor Education	M,D
Early Childhood Education	M
Education—General	M
Human Services	M
Management Strategy and Policy	M
Marketing	M
Middle School Education	M
Reading Education	M
Secondary Education	M
Social Work	M
Special Education	M

ROCHESTER COLLEGE	
Religious Education	M

ROCHESTER INSTITUTE OF TECHNOLOGY	
Accounting	M
Art Education	M
Business Administration and Management—General	M
Entrepreneurship	M
Finance and Banking	M
Hospitality Management	M
Human Resources Development	M
Industrial and Manufacturing Management	M
International Business	M
Management Information Systems	O
Organizational Management	O
Project Management	O
Secondary Education	M
Special Education	M
Sustainability Management	M,D
Travel and Tourism	M

ROCKFORD UNIVERSITY	
Business Administration and Management—General	M
Early Childhood Education	M
Education—General	M
Educational Media/Instructional Technology	M
Elementary Education	M
Reading Education	M
Secondary Education	M
Special Education	M

ROCKHURST UNIVERSITY	
Accounting	M,O
Business Administration and Management—General	M,O
Education—General	M
Entrepreneurship	M,O
Finance and Banking	M,O
Human Resources Development	M,O
International Business	M,O
Management Strategy and Policy	M,O
Nonprofit Management	M,O

ROCKY MOUNTAIN COLLEGE	
Accounting	M
Educational Leadership and Administration	M

ROCKY MOUNTAIN COLLEGE OF ART + DESIGN	
Art Education	M

ROGERS STATE UNIVERSITY	
Business Administration and Management—General	M

ROGER WILLIAMS UNIVERSITY	
Education—General	M
Law	M,D
Reading Education	M

ROLLINS COLLEGE	
Business Administration and Management—General	M,D
Counselor Education	M
Education—General	M
Elementary Education	M
Entrepreneurship	M,D
Finance and Banking	M,D
Human Resources Development	M
Human Resources Management	M
International Business	M,D
Marketing	M,D

ROOSEVELT UNIVERSITY	
Accounting	M
Actuarial Science	M
Business Administration and Management—General	M
Counselor Education	M
Early Childhood Education	M
Education—General	M
Elementary Education	M
Hospitality Management	M
Human Resources Development	M
Human Resources Management	M
Marketing	M
Organizational Management	M
Reading Education	M
Real Estate	M,O
Secondary Education	M
Special Education	M

ROSALIND FRANKLIN UNIVERSITY OF MEDICINE AND SCIENCE	
Health Education	M

ROSE-HULMAN INSTITUTE OF TECHNOLOGY	
Management Information Systems	M

ROSEMAN UNIVERSITY OF HEALTH SCIENCES	
Business Administration and Management—General	M,O

ROSEMONT COLLEGE	
Business Administration and Management—General	M
Counselor Education	M
Education—General	M
Elementary Education	M
Human Services	M

ROWAN UNIVERSITY	
Advertising and Public Relations	M
Business Administration and Management—General	M,O
Counselor Education	M
Education—General	M,D,O
Educational Leadership and Administration	M,D,O
Educational Media/Instructional Technology	M,O
Elementary Education	M
English as a Second Language	O
English Education	O
Exercise and Sports Science	M
Higher Education	M
Library Science	M,D,O
Marketing	O
Mathematics Education	M,O
Middle School Education	O
Multilingual and Multicultural Education	M,O
Reading Education	M,O
Science Education	M
Secondary Education	M
Special Education	M,O

ROYAL MILITARY COLLEGE OF CANADA	
Business Administration and Management—General	M

ROYAL ROADS UNIVERSITY	
Advertising and Public Relations	O
Business Administration and Management—General	M,O
Environmental Education	M,O
Hospitality Management	M,O
Human Resources Management	M,O
Project Management	O
Travel and Tourism	M,O

RUDOLF STEINER COLLEGE	
Early Childhood Education	M
Education—General	M
Elementary Education	M

RUTGERS UNIVERSITY–CAMDEN	
Business Administration and Management—General	M
Educational Leadership and Administration	M
Educational Policy	M
Law	D
Mathematics Education	M

RUTGERS UNIVERSITY–NEWARK	
Accounting	M,D
Business Administration and Management—General	M,D
Finance and Banking	M,D
Health Education	M,D
Human Resources Management	M,D
International Business	D
Law	D
Logistics	M
Management Information Systems	M,D
Marketing	D
Organizational Management	D
Quantitative Analysis	M,O
Real Estate	M
Supply Chain Management	D

RUTGERS UNIVERSITY–NEW BRUNSWICK	
Counselor Education	M
Developmental Education	M
Early Childhood Education	M,D
Education—General	M,D
Educational Leadership and Administration	M,D
Educational Measurement and Evaluation	M
Educational Policy	D
Educational Psychology	M,D
Elementary Education	M,D
English as a Second Language	M,D
English Education	M
Foreign Languages Education	M,D
Foundations and Philosophy of Education	M,D
Health Education	M,D,O
Human Resources Management	M,D
Information Studies	M,D
Legal and Justice Studies	M,D
Library Science	D
Mathematics Education	M,D
Multilingual and Multicultural Education	M,D
Music Education	M,D,O
Quality Management	M,D
Reading Education	M,D
Science Education	M,D
Social Sciences Education	M,D
Social Work	M,D*
Special Education	M,D
Student Affairs	M,D

RYERSON UNIVERSITY	
Business Administration and Management—General	M

SACRED HEART UNIVERSITY	
Accounting	M
Education—General	M,O
Educational Leadership and Administration	O
English as a Second Language	M,O
Exercise and Sports Science	M
Finance and Banking	M,D
Human Resources Management	M
Investment Management	M,D
Marketing	M,O
Reading Education	O
Social Work	M

SAGE GRADUATE SCHOOL	
Business Administration and Management—General	M
Counselor Education	M,O
Education—General	M,D,O
Educational Leadership and Administration	D
Elementary Education	M
Health Education	M
Organizational Management	M
Reading Education	M
Special Education	M

SAGINAW VALLEY STATE UNIVERSITY	
Business Administration and Management—General	M
Distance Education Development	M
Early Childhood Education	M
Education—General	M,O
Educational Leadership and Administration	M,O
Educational Media/Instructional Technology	M
Elementary Education	M
Foreign Languages Education	M
Middle School Education	M
Reading Education	M
Science Education	M
Secondary Education	M
Special Education	M

ST. AMBROSE UNIVERSITY	
Accounting	M
Business Administration and Management—General	M,D
Education—General	M
Educational Leadership and Administration	M
Human Resources Management	M,D
Organizational Management	M
Social Work	M
Special Education	M

ST. AUGUSTINE'S SEMINARY OF TORONTO	
Religious Education	M,O

ST. BONAVENTURE UNIVERSITY	
Accounting	M
Business Administration and Management—General	M
Counselor Education	M,O
Early Childhood Education	M,O
Education of the Gifted	M,O
Education—General	M,O
Educational Leadership and Administration	M,O
Marketing	M
Middle School Education	M
Reading Education	M
Secondary Education	M
Special Education	M,O

ST. CATHERINE UNIVERSITY	
Business Administration and Management—General	M
Curriculum and Instruction	M
Early Childhood Education	M
Education—General	M
Information Studies	M
Library Science	M
Marketing	M
Organizational Management	M
Social Work	M,D

ST. CLOUD STATE UNIVERSITY	
Business Administration and Management—General	M
Counselor Education	M
Curriculum and Instruction	M
Education—General	M,D
Educational Leadership and Administration	M,D
Educational Media/Instructional Technology	M
English as a Second Language	M
Exercise and Sports Science	M
Higher Education	M,D
Music Education	M
Nonprofit Management	M
Social Work	M
Special Education	M
Sports Management	M
Student Affairs	M

ST. EDWARD'S UNIVERSITY	
Accounting	M,O
Business Administration and Management—General	M,O
Counselor Education	M,O
Education—General	M,O
Organizational Management	M
Student Affairs	M

ST. FRANCIS COLLEGE	
Accounting	M

SAINT FRANCIS UNIVERSITY	
Business Administration and Management—General	M
Education—General	M
Educational Leadership and Administration	M
Health Education	M
Human Resources Management	M
Reading Education	M

ST. FRANCIS XAVIER UNIVERSITY	
Adult Education	M
Curriculum and Instruction	M
Education—General	M
Educational Leadership and Administration	M

ST. JOHN FISHER COLLEGE	
Business Administration and Management—General	M
Education—General	M,D,O
Educational Leadership and Administration	M,D
Elementary Education	M,O
English Education	M
Foreign Languages Education	M
Mathematics Education	M
Middle School Education	M
Reading Education	M
Social Sciences Education	M
Special Education	M,O

ST. JOHN'S UNIVERSITY (NY)	
Accounting	M
Actuarial Science	M
Business Administration and Management—General	M
Counselor Education	M,D,O
Early Childhood Education	M
Education of the Gifted	M,D,O
Education—General	M,D,O
Educational Leadership and Administration	M,D,O
Elementary Education	M
English as a Second Language	M,O
Finance and Banking	M
Information Studies	M,O

*M—masters degree; D—doctorate; O—other advanced degree; *—Close-Up and/or Display*

- Insurance M
- International Business M
- Investment Management M
- Law M,D
- Legal and Justice Studies M
- Library Science M,O
- Management Information Systems M
- Management Strategy and Policy M
- Marketing M
- Middle School Education M,O
- Multilingual and Multicultural Education M,O
- Quantitative Analysis M
- Reading Education M,D,O
- Secondary Education M,O
- Special Education M,D,O
- Sports Management M
- Taxation M

ST. JOSEPH'S COLLEGE, LONG ISLAND CAMPUS
- Accounting M
- Business Administration and Management—General M
- Early Childhood Education M
- Educational Leadership and Administration M
- Human Resources Management M
- Human Services M
- Mathematics Education M
- Organizational Management M
- Reading Education M
- Special Education M

ST. JOSEPH'S COLLEGE, NEW YORK
- Accounting M
- Business Administration and Management—General M
- Education—General M
- Educational Leadership and Administration M
- Human Resources Management M
- Human Services M
- Organizational Management M
- Reading Education M
- Special Education M

SAINT JOSEPH'S COLLEGE OF MAINE
- Accounting M
- Adult Education M
- Business Administration and Management—General M
- Education—General M
- Educational Leadership and Administration M
- Health Education M

SAINT JOSEPH'S UNIVERSITY
- Accounting M,O
- Business Administration and Management—General M,O
- Curriculum and Instruction M,D,O
- Early Childhood Education M,D,O
- Education—General M,D,O
- Educational Leadership and Administration M,D,O
- Educational Media/Instructional Technology M,D,O
- Elementary Education M,D,O
- Finance and Banking M,O
- Health Education M
- Human Resources Management M,O
- International Business M,O
- Law M,O
- Management Information Systems M
- Management Strategy and Policy M
- Marketing M,O
- Middle School Education M,D,O
- Reading Education M,D,O
- Secondary Education M,D,O
- Special Education M,D,O

ST. LAWRENCE UNIVERSITY
- Counselor Education M,O
- Education—General M,O
- Educational Leadership and Administration M,O

SAINT LEO UNIVERSITY
- Accounting M,D,O
- Agricultural Education M
- Business Administration and Management—General M,D,O
- Education of the Gifted M,O
- Education—General M,O
- Educational Leadership and Administration M,O
- Educational Media/Instructional Technology M,O
- Human Resources Management M,D,O
- Human Services M
- Legal and Justice Studies M
- Marketing Research M,D,O
- Marketing M,D,O
- Project Management M,D,O
- Reading Education M,O
- Social Work M
- Supply Chain Management M,D,O

SAINT LOUIS UNIVERSITY
- Accounting M
- Athletic Training and Sports Medicine M,D
- Business Administration and Management—General M
- Counselor Education M,D,O
- Curriculum and Instruction M,D
- Education—General M,D
- Educational Leadership and Administration M,D,O
- Finance and Banking M
- Foundations and Philosophy of Education M,D
- Higher Education M,D,O
- International Business M,D
- Law M,D
- Organizational Management M,D,O
- Social Work M
- Special Education M,D
- Student Affairs M,D,O

SAINT MARTIN'S UNIVERSITY
- Business Administration and Management—General M
- Education—General M

SAINT MARY-OF-THE-WOODS COLLEGE
- Management Strategy and Policy M
- Nonprofit Management M
- Organizational Management M

SAINT MARY'S COLLEGE OF CALIFORNIA
- Accounting M
- Business Administration and Management—General M
- Counselor Education M,O
- Early Childhood Education M
- Education—General M,D,O
- Educational Leadership and Administration M,D,O
- Exercise and Sports Science M
- Finance and Banking M
- Investment Management M
- Kinesiology and Movement Studies M
- Organizational Management M
- Special Education M
- Sports Management M

ST. MARY'S COLLEGE OF MARYLAND
- Education—General M

SAINT MARY'S UNIVERSITY (CANADA)
- Business Administration and Management—General M,D

ST. MARY'S UNIVERSITY (UNITED STATES)
- Accounting M
- Business Administration and Management—General M
- Counselor Education D
- Educational Leadership and Administration M
- Law M,D
- Legal and Justice Studies M

SAINT MARY'S UNIVERSITY OF MINNESOTA
- Accounting M
- Business Administration and Management—General M,D
- Education of the Gifted M,O
- Education—General M,O
- Educational Leadership and Administration M,D,O
- Educational Media/Instructional Technology M
- Elementary Education M
- Human Resources Management M
- International Business M
- Multilingual and Multicultural Education M,O
- Organizational Management M
- Project Management M,O
- Reading Education M,O
- Religious Education M
- Secondary Education M
- Special Education M,O

SAINT MICHAEL'S COLLEGE
- Art Education M,O
- Education—General M,O
- Educational Leadership and Administration M,O
- English as a Second Language M,O
- Reading Education M,O
- Special Education M,O

ST. NORBERT COLLEGE
- Business Administration and Management—General M
- Supply Chain Management M

SAINT PETER'S UNIVERSITY
- Accounting M
- Business Administration and Management—General M
- Counselor Education M,O
- Education—General M,D,O
- Educational Leadership and Administration M,D
- Elementary Education M,O
- Finance and Banking M
- Higher Education D
- Human Resources Management M
- International Business M
- Management Information Systems M
- Marketing M
- Mathematics Education M,D,O
- Middle School Education M,O
- Reading Education M,O
- Secondary Education M,O
- Special Education M,O

SAINTS CYRIL AND METHODIUS SEMINARY
- Religious Education M

ST. THOMAS AQUINAS COLLEGE
- Business Administration and Management—General M
- Education—General M,O
- Educational Leadership and Administration M,O
- Elementary Education M,O
- Finance and Banking M
- Marketing M
- Middle School Education M,O
- Reading Education M,O
- Secondary Education M,O
- Special Education M,O

ST. THOMAS UNIVERSITY
- Accounting M,O
- Business Administration and Management—General M,O
- Counselor Education M,O
- Education of the Gifted M,D,O
- Education—General M,D,O
- Educational Leadership and Administration M,D,O
- Educational Media/Instructional Technology M,D,O
- Elementary Education M,D,O
- English as a Second Language M,D,O
- Human Resources Management M,O
- International Business M,O
- Law M,D
- Reading Education M,D,O
- Special Education M,D,O
- Sports Management M,O
- Taxation M,D

SAINT VINCENT COLLEGE
- Business Administration and Management—General M
- Curriculum and Instruction M
- Education—General M
- Educational Leadership and Administration M
- Educational Media/Instructional Technology M
- Special Education M

SAINT XAVIER UNIVERSITY
- Business Administration and Management—General M,O
- Counselor Education M
- Curriculum and Instruction M
- Early Childhood Education M
- Education—General M
- Educational Leadership and Administration M
- Educational Media/Instructional Technology M
- Elementary Education M
- English as a Second Language M
- Finance and Banking M,O
- Foreign Languages Education M
- Marketing M,O
- Music Education M
- Project Management M,O
- Reading Education M
- Science Education M
- Secondary Education M
- Special Education M

SALEM COLLEGE
- Art Education M
- Counselor Education M
- Education—General M
- Elementary Education M
- English as a Second Language M
- Middle School Education M
- Reading Education M
- Secondary Education M
- Special Education M

SALEM INTERNATIONAL UNIVERSITY
- Business Administration and Management—General M
- Curriculum and Instruction M
- Education—General M
- Educational Leadership and Administration M
- International Business M

SALEM STATE UNIVERSITY
- Art Education M
- Business Administration and Management—General M
- Counselor Education M
- Early Childhood Education M
- Educational Leadership and Administration M
- Educational Media/Instructional Technology M
- Elementary Education M
- English as a Second Language M
- Higher Education M
- Mathematics Education M
- Middle School Education M
- Physical Education M
- Reading Education M
- Science Education M
- Secondary Education M
- Social Work M
- Special Education M

SALISBURY UNIVERSITY
- Athletic Training and Sports Medicine M
- Business Administration and Management—General M
- Curriculum and Instruction M
- Educational Leadership and Administration M
- English as a Second Language M
- Mathematics Education M
- Middle School Education M
- Reading Education M,D
- Secondary Education M
- Social Work M

SALUS UNIVERSITY
- Special Education M,O

SALVE REGINA UNIVERSITY
- Business Administration and Management—General M,O
- Entrepreneurship M
- Management Strategy and Policy M,O
- Nonprofit Management M,O

SAMFORD UNIVERSITY
- Accounting M
- Athletic Training and Sports Medicine M,D
- Business Administration and Management—General M
- Early Childhood Education M,D,O
- Education of the Gifted M,D,O
- Education—General M,D,O
- Educational Leadership and Administration M,D,O
- Educational Media/Instructional Technology M,D,O
- Elementary Education M,D,O
- Entrepreneurship M
- Finance and Banking M
- Law M,D
- Marketing M
- Music Education M
- Social Work M
- Special Education M,D,O

SAM HOUSTON STATE UNIVERSITY
- Accounting M
- Business Administration and Management—General M
- Counselor Education M,D
- Curriculum and Instruction M,D
- Developmental Education M,D
- Education—General M,D
- Educational Leadership and Administration M,D
- Finance and Banking M
- Higher Education M,D
- Kinesiology and Movement Studies M
- Library Science M
- Project Management M
- Reading Education M,D
- Special Education M,D
- Sports Management M

SAN DIEGO CHRISTIAN COLLEGE
- Education—General M
- Organizational Management M

SAN DIEGO STATE UNIVERSITY
- Accounting M
- Advertising and Public Relations M
- Business Administration and Management—General M
- Counselor Education M
- Curriculum and Instruction M
- Education—General M,D
- Educational Leadership and Administration M
- Educational Media/Instructional Technology M,D
- Elementary Education M
- English as a Second Language M,O
- Entrepreneurship M
- Exercise and Sports Science M
- Finance and Banking M
- Higher Education M
- Human Resources Management M
- Kinesiology and Movement Studies M
- Management Information Systems M
- Marketing M
- Mathematics Education M,D
- Multilingual and Multicultural Education M,D
- Music Education M
- Reading Education M
- Science Education M,D
- Secondary Education M
- Social Work M
- Special Education M
- Sports Management M

SAN FRANCISCO CONSERVATORY OF MUSIC
- Music Education M,O

SAN FRANCISCO STATE UNIVERSITY
- Accounting M
- Adult Education M
- Business Administration and Management—General M
- Counselor Education M,O
- Early Childhood Education M,D,O
- Education—General M,D,O
- Educational Leadership and Administration M,D,O
- Educational Media/Instructional Technology M
- Elementary Education M
- English as a Second Language M
- English Education M,O
- Entrepreneurship M
- Finance and Banking M
- Health Education M
- Hospitality Management M
- Industrial and Manufacturing Management M
- International Business M
- Kinesiology and Movement Studies M
- Legal and Justice Studies M
- Leisure Studies M
- Management Information Systems M
- Marketing M
- Mathematics Education M,O
- Music Education M
- Nonprofit Management M
- Quantitative Analysis M
- Reading Education M,O
- Recreation and Park Management M
- Secondary Education M,O
- Social Work M
- Special Education M,O
- Sustainability Management M
- Travel and Tourism M

SAN JOAQUIN COLLEGE OF LAW
- Law D

SAN JOSE STATE UNIVERSITY
- Accounting M
- Athletic Training and Sports Medicine M,O
- Counselor Education M,D,O
- Curriculum and Instruction M,D,O

Early Childhood Education M,D,O
Education—General M,D,O
Educational Leadership and Administration M,D,O
Elementary Education M,D,O
English as a Second Language M,O
Exercise and Sports Science M,O
Higher Education M,D,O
Kinesiology and Movement Studies M,O
Legal and Justice Studies M,O
Library Science M,O
Management Strategy and Policy M,O
Mathematics Education M,O
Real Estate M,O
Recreation and Park Management M,O
Science Education M,O
Social Work M,O
Sports Management M,O
Taxation M
Transportation Management M

THE SANTA BARBARA AND VENTURA COLLEGES OF LAW–SANTA BARBARA
Law M,D
Legal and Justice Studies M,D

THE SANTA BARBARA AND VENTURA COLLEGES OF LAW–VENTURA
Law M,D
Legal and Justice Studies M,D

SANTA CLARA UNIVERSITY
Business Administration and Management—General M
Counselor Education M
Education—General M
Educational Leadership and Administration M
Finance and Banking M
Intellectual Property Law M,D
Law M,D
Management Information Systems M
Supply Chain Management M

SARAH LAWRENCE COLLEGE
Education—General M
Kinesiology and Movement Studies M

SAVANNAH COLLEGE OF ART AND DESIGN
Advertising and Public Relations M
Travel and Tourism M

SAVANNAH LAW SCHOOL
Law D

SAVANNAH STATE UNIVERSITY
Business Administration and Management—General M
Human Resources Management M
Social Work M

SAYBROOK UNIVERSITY
Organizational Behavior M,D
Organizational Management M,D

SCHILLER INTERNATIONAL UNIVERSITY (GERMANY)
Business Administration and Management—General M
International Business M
Management Information Systems M

SCHILLER INTERNATIONAL UNIVERSITY
Business Administration and Management—General M
International Business M

SCHILLER INTERNATIONAL UNIVERSITY (SPAIN)
Business Administration and Management—General M
International Business M

SCHILLER INTERNATIONAL UNIVERSITY (UNITED STATES)
Business Administration and Management—General M
Finance and Banking M
Hospitality Management M
International Business M
Management Information Systems M
Travel and Tourism M

SCHOOL OF THE ART INSTITUTE OF CHICAGO
Art Education M

SCHOOL OF VISUAL ARTS (NY)
Art Education M

SCHREINER UNIVERSITY
Business Administration and Management—General M
Education—General M,O
Educational Leadership and Administration M,O

SEATTLE PACIFIC UNIVERSITY
Business Administration and Management—General M
Counselor Education M,D,O
Education—General D
Educational Leadership and Administration M,D,O
Educational Media/Instructional Technology M
English as a Second Language M
Human Resources Management M
Management Information Systems M
Mathematics Education M
Reading Education M
Science Education M
Secondary Education M
Sustainability Management M

SEATTLE UNIVERSITY
Accounting M
Adult Education M,O
Business Administration and Management—General M,O
Counselor Education M,O
Education—General M,D,O
Educational Leadership and Administration M,D,O
English as a Second Language M,O
Finance and Banking M,O
Law D
Organizational Management M,O
Social Work M
Special Education M,O
Sports Management M

SELMA UNIVERSITY
Religious Education M

SETON HALL UNIVERSITY
Accounting M,O
Advertising and Public Relations M
Athletic Training and Sports Medicine M
Business Administration and Management—General M,O
Counselor Education M,D
Education—General M,D,O
Educational Leadership and Administration D,O
Educational Measurement and Evaluation M,D,O
Educational Media/Instructional Technology M
Entrepreneurship M,O
Finance and Banking M,O
Health Law M,D
Higher Education D
International Business M,O
Law M,D
Marketing M,O
Museum Education M
Nonprofit Management M,O
Social Work M
Special Education M
Sports Management M,O
Student Affairs M
Supply Chain Management M,O
Taxation M,O

SETON HILL UNIVERSITY
Accounting M,O
Business Administration and Management—General M,O
Elementary Education M,O
Entrepreneurship M,O
Middle School Education M,O
Special Education M

SHASTA BIBLE COLLEGE
Educational Leadership and Administration M
Religious Education M

SHAWNEE STATE UNIVERSITY
Curriculum and Instruction M
Education—General M

SHAW UNIVERSITY
Curriculum and Instruction M
Early Childhood Education M

SHENANDOAH UNIVERSITY
Athletic Training and Sports Medicine M,D,O
Business Administration and Management—General M,O
Education—General M,D,O
Educational Leadership and Administration M,D,O
Health Education M,D,O
Middle School Education M,D,O
Music Education M,D,O
Physical Education M,D,O
Reading Education M,D,O
Secondary Education M,D,O
Special Education M,D,O

SHEPHERD UNIVERSITY (CA)
Management Information Systems M

SHEPHERD UNIVERSITY (WV)
Curriculum and Instruction M

SHIPPENSBURG UNIVERSITY OF PENNSYLVANIA
Business Administration and Management—General M,O
Counselor Education M,D,O
Curriculum and Instruction M,O
Distance Education Development M,O
Early Childhood Education M,O
Education—General M,D,O
Educational Leadership and Administration M,D
Elementary Education M,O
English as a Second Language M,O
Finance and Banking M,O
Foreign Languages Education M,O
Higher Education M
Logistics M,O
Management Information Systems M,O
Mathematics Education M,O
Middle School Education M,O
Organizational Management M
Reading Education M,O
Science Education M,O
Social Work M
Special Education M,D
Student Affairs M,D,O
Supply Chain Management M,O

SHORTER UNIVERSITY
Accounting M
Business Administration and Management—General M

SIENA COLLEGE
Accounting M
Business Administration and Management—General M

SIENA HEIGHTS UNIVERSITY
Early Childhood Education M,O
Education—General M,O
Educational Leadership and Administration M,O
Elementary Education M,O
Higher Education M,O
Organizational Management M,O
Reading Education M,O
Secondary Education M,O
Special Education M,O

SIERRA NEVADA COLLEGE
Education—General M
Educational Leadership and Administration M
Elementary Education M
Secondary Education M

SILICON VALLEY UNIVERSITY
Business Administration and Management—General M

SILVER LAKE COLLEGE OF THE HOLY FAMILY
Business Administration and Management—General M
Education—General M
Educational Leadership and Administration M

SIMMONS COLLEGE
Business Administration and Management—General M
Education—General M,D,O
Elementary Education M,D,O
Health Education M,D,O
Library Science M,D,O
Nonprofit Management M
Reading Education M,D,O
Social Work M,D,O
Special Education M,D,O

SIMON FRASER UNIVERSITY
Actuarial Science M,D
Art Education M,D
Business Administration and Management—General M,D,O
Counselor Education M
Curriculum and Instruction M,D
Education—General M,D,O
Educational Leadership and Administration M,D
Educational Media/Instructional Technology M,D
Educational Psychology M,D
English as a Second Language M
English Education M,D
Finance and Banking M,D,O
Foundations and Philosophy of Education M,D
Kinesiology and Movement Studies M,D
Legal and Justice Studies M,D
Mathematics Education M,D
Reading Education D

SIMPSON COLLEGE
Education—General M
Secondary Education M

SIMPSON UNIVERSITY
Curriculum and Instruction M
Education—General M
Educational Leadership and Administration M
Organizational Management M

SINTE GLESKA UNIVERSITY
Education—General M
Elementary Education M

SIT GRADUATE INSTITUTE
Business Administration and Management—General M
English as a Second Language M
International and Comparative Education M
International Business M
Organizational Management M

SLIPPERY ROCK UNIVERSITY OF PENNSYLVANIA
Accounting M
Business Administration and Management—General M
Counselor Education M
Education—General M,D
Educational Leadership and Administration M,D
Educational Media/Instructional Technology M,D
Elementary Education M
English as a Second Language M
English Education M
Environmental Education M
Finance and Banking M
Marketing M
Mathematics Education M
Physical Education M
Reading Education M
Recreation and Park Management M
Science Education M
Secondary Education M
Social Sciences Education M
Special Education M,D
Student Affairs M

SMITH COLLEGE
Education—General M
Elementary Education M
English Education M
Exercise and Sports Science M
Foreign Languages Education M
Mathematics Education M
Middle School Education M
Science Education M
Secondary Education M
Social Sciences Education M
Social Work M,D

SOKA UNIVERSITY OF AMERICA
Educational Leadership and Administration M*

SONOMA STATE UNIVERSITY
Business Administration and Management—General M
Curriculum and Instruction M,O
Early Childhood Education M,O
Education—General M,O
Educational Leadership and Administration M,O
Entrepreneurship M
International Business M
Kinesiology and Movement Studies M
Nonprofit Management M,O
Physical Education M
Reading Education M,O
Special Education M,O
Sports Management M

SOUTH CAROLINA STATE UNIVERSITY
Business Administration and Management—General M
Business Education M
Counselor Education M
Early Childhood Education M
Education—General M
Educational Leadership and Administration D,O
Elementary Education M
English Education M
Entrepreneurship M
Home Economics Education M
Human Services M
Mathematics Education M
Science Education M
Secondary Education M
Social Sciences Education M
Special Education M
Vocational and Technical Education M

SOUTH DAKOTA STATE UNIVERSITY
Agricultural Education M
Athletic Training and Sports Medicine M,D
Counselor Education M
Curriculum and Instruction M
Education—General M,D
Educational Leadership and Administration M
Exercise and Sports Science M,D
Human Resources Development M
Recreation and Park Management M,D

SOUTHEASTERN BAPTIST THEOLOGICAL SEMINARY
Religious Education M,D

SOUTHEASTERN LOUISIANA UNIVERSITY
Business Administration and Management—General M
Counselor Education M
Curriculum and Instruction M
Education—General M,D
Educational Leadership and Administration M,D
Elementary Education M
English Education M
Exercise and Sports Science M
Health Education M
Kinesiology and Movement Studies M
Reading Education M
Special Education M

SOUTHEASTERN OKLAHOMA STATE UNIVERSITY
Aviation Management M
Business Administration and Management—General M
Counselor Education M
Education—General M
Educational Leadership and Administration M
Management Information Systems M
Mathematics Education M
Reading Education M

SOUTHEASTERN UNIVERSITY (FL)
Business Administration and Management—General M
Counselor Education M
Curriculum and Instruction M,D
Education of the Gifted M,D
Education—General M,D
Educational Leadership and Administration M,D
Elementary Education M,D
English as a Second Language M,D
Entrepreneurship M
Human Services M
Organizational Management M,D
Reading Education M,D
Social Work M
Sports Management M

*M—masters degree; D—doctorate; O—other advanced degree; *—Close-Up and/or Display*

SOUTHEAST MISSOURI STATE UNIVERSITY
- Accounting M
- Business Administration and Management—General M
- Counselor Education M,O
- Educational Leadership and Administration M,D,O
- Elementary Education M,D,O
- English as a Second Language M
- Entrepreneurship M
- Exercise and Sports Science M
- Finance and Banking M
- Higher Education M,D,O
- Leisure Studies M
- Middle School Education M
- Secondary Education M,D,O
- Special Education M
- Sports Management M

SOUTHERN ADVENTIST UNIVERSITY
- Accounting M
- Business Administration and Management—General M
- Counselor Education M
- Education—General M
- Educational Leadership and Administration M
- Finance and Banking M
- Marketing M
- Nonprofit Management M
- Reading Education M
- Recreation and Park Management M
- Religious Education M
- Social Work M

SOUTHERN ARKANSAS UNIVERSITY–MAGNOLIA
- Adult Education M
- Business Administration and Management—General M
- Counselor Education M
- Curriculum and Instruction M
- Education of the Gifted M
- Education—General M
- Educational Leadership and Administration M
- Higher Education M
- Kinesiology and Movement Studies M
- Library Science M
- Organizational Management M
- Student Affairs M
- Supply Chain Management M

SOUTHERN CONNECTICUT STATE UNIVERSITY
- Art Education M
- Business Administration and Management—General M
- Counselor Education M,O
- Education—General M,D,O
- Educational Leadership and Administration M,D,O
- Educational Measurement and Evaluation M,D,O
- Elementary Education M,O
- English as a Second Language M
- Environmental Education M,O
- Exercise and Sports Science M
- Foreign Languages Education M
- Health Education M
- Information Studies M,O
- Leisure Studies M
- Library Science M,O
- Multilingual and Multicultural Education M
- Physical Education M
- Reading Education M,O
- Recreation and Park Management M
- Science Education M,O
- Social Work M
- Special Education M

SOUTHERN EVANGELICAL SEMINARY
- Religious Education M,D,O

SOUTHERN ILLINOIS UNIVERSITY CARBONDALE
- Accounting M,D
- Business Administration and Management—General M,D
- Curriculum and Instruction M,D
- Education—General M,D
- Educational Leadership and Administration M,D
- Educational Psychology M,D
- English as a Second Language M
- Health Education M,D
- Health Law M
- Higher Education M
- Kinesiology and Movement Studies M
- Law M,D
- Legal and Justice Studies M
- Physical Education M
- Recreation and Park Management M
- Social Work M
- Special Education M,D
- Vocational and Technical Education M,D

SOUTHERN ILLINOIS UNIVERSITY EDWARDSVILLE
- Accounting M
- Advertising and Public Relations M
- Business Administration and Management—General M
- Curriculum and Instruction M
- Education—General M,D,O
- Educational Leadership and Administration M,D,O
- Educational Media/Instructional Technology M,O
- English as a Second Language M,O
- English Education M,O
- Exercise and Sports Science M
- Finance and Banking M
- Foundations and Philosophy of Education M
- Health Education M,D,O
- Higher Education M
- Kinesiology and Movement Studies M
- Management Information Systems M
- Management Strategy and Policy M
- Marketing Research M
- Mathematics Education M
- Music Education M,O
- Physical Education M
- Project Management M
- Reading Education M,O
- Social Work M
- Special Education M,O
- Student Affairs M
- Taxation M

SOUTHERN METHODIST UNIVERSITY
- Accounting M
- Advertising and Public Relations M
- Business Administration and Management—General M
- Counselor Education M
- Education of the Gifted M,D
- Education—General M,D
- Entrepreneurship M
- Finance and Banking M
- Law M,D
- Management Information Systems M
- Management Strategy and Policy M
- Marketing M
- Multilingual and Multicultural Education M,D
- Music Education M
- Reading Education M,D
- Real Estate M
- Special Education M,D
- Sports Management M
- Taxation M,D

SOUTHERN NAZARENE UNIVERSITY
- Business Administration and Management—General M
- Sports Management M

SOUTHERN NEW HAMPSHIRE UNIVERSITY
- Accounting M,O
- Business Administration and Management—General M,O
- Business Education M,D,O
- Curriculum and Instruction M,D,O
- Education—General M,D,O
- Educational Leadership and Administration M,D,O
- Educational Media/Instructional Technology M,D,O
- Elementary Education M,D,O
- English as a Second Language M,D,O
- English Education M,D,O
- Entrepreneurship M,O
- Finance and Banking M,O
- Human Resources Management M,O
- Industrial and Manufacturing Management M,O
- International Business M,O
- Investment Management M,O
- Legal and Justice Studies M,O
- Management Information Systems M,O
- Marketing M,O
- Nonprofit Management M,O
- Organizational Management M,O
- Project Management M,O
- Quality Management M,O
- Reading Education M,D,O
- Secondary Education M,D,O
- Special Education M,D,O
- Sports Management M,O
- Supply Chain Management M,O
- Sustainability Management M,O
- Taxation M,O

SOUTHERN OREGON UNIVERSITY
- Accounting M,O
- Business Administration and Management—General M,O
- Early Childhood Education M
- Education—General M
- Educational Leadership and Administration M
- Elementary Education M
- Environmental Education M
- Foreign Languages Education M
- International Business M,O
- Reading Education M
- Secondary Education M
- Special Education M

SOUTHERN UNIVERSITY AND AGRICULTURAL AND MECHANICAL COLLEGE
- Business Administration and Management—General M
- Counselor Education M
- Education—General M,D
- Educational Leadership and Administration M
- Educational Media/Instructional Technology M
- Elementary Education M
- Law D
- Mathematics Education D
- Recreation and Park Management M
- Science Education D
- Secondary Education M
- Special Education M,D

SOUTHERN UNIVERSITY AT NEW ORLEANS
- Management Information Systems M
- Social Work M

SOUTHERN UTAH UNIVERSITY
- Accounting M
- Business Administration and Management—General M
- Education—General M,O
- Exercise and Sports Science M
- Music Education M

SOUTHERN WESLEYAN UNIVERSITY
- Business Administration and Management—General M
- Education—General M

SOUTH TEXAS COLLEGE OF LAW HOUSTON
- Law D

SOUTH UNIVERSITY (AL)
- Business Administration and Management—General M
- Management Information Systems M

SOUTH UNIVERSITY
- Business Administration and Management—General M
- Management Information Systems M

SOUTH UNIVERSITY
- Business Administration and Management—General M
- Management Information Systems M

SOUTH UNIVERSITY (GA)
- Business Administration and Management—General M
- Entrepreneurship M
- Hospitality Management M
- Organizational Management M
- Sustainability Management M

SOUTH UNIVERSITY (MI)
- Business Administration and Management—General M
- Organizational Management M

SOUTH UNIVERSITY (NC)
- Business Administration and Management—General M

SOUTH UNIVERSITY (OH)
- Business Administration and Management—General M

SOUTH UNIVERSITY (SC)
- Business Administration and Management—General M
- Organizational Management M

SOUTH UNIVERSITY (TX)
- Business Administration and Management—General M
- Management Information Systems M

SOUTH UNIVERSITY
- Business Administration and Management—General M

SOUTH UNIVERSITY
- Business Administration and Management—General M
- Management Information Systems M
- Organizational Management M

SOUTHWEST BAPTIST UNIVERSITY
- Business Administration and Management—General M
- Education—General M,O
- Educational Leadership and Administration M,O

SOUTHWESTERN ADVENTIST UNIVERSITY
- Accounting M
- Business Administration and Management—General M
- Curriculum and Instruction M
- Education—General M
- Educational Leadership and Administration M
- Finance and Banking M
- Reading Education M

SOUTHWESTERN ASSEMBLIES OF GOD UNIVERSITY
- Curriculum and Instruction M
- Education—General M
- Educational Leadership and Administration M
- Religious Education M
- Secondary Education M

SOUTHWESTERN BAPTIST THEOLOGICAL SEMINARY
- Religious Education M,D

SOUTHWESTERN COLLEGE (KS)
- Business Administration and Management—General M
- Curriculum and Instruction M,D
- Early Childhood Education M,D
- Education—General M,D
- Educational Leadership and Administration M,D
- Special Education M,D

SOUTHWESTERN LAW SCHOOL
- Law M,D

SOUTHWESTERN OKLAHOMA STATE UNIVERSITY
- Art Education M
- Business Administration and Management—General M
- Counselor Education M
- Early Childhood Education M
- Education—General M
- Educational Leadership and Administration M
- Educational Measurement and Evaluation M
- Elementary Education M
- English Education M
- Kinesiology and Movement Studies M
- Mathematics Education M
- Music Education M
- Recreation and Park Management M
- Science Education M
- Secondary Education M
- Social Sciences Education M
- Special Education M

SOUTHWEST MINNESOTA STATE UNIVERSITY
- Business Administration and Management—General M
- Early Childhood Education M
- Education—General M
- Educational Leadership and Administration M
- English as a Second Language M
- Marketing M
- Mathematics Education M
- Reading Education M
- Special Education M

SOUTHWEST UNIVERSITY
- Business Administration and Management—General M
- Organizational Management M

SPALDING UNIVERSITY
- Art Education M
- Athletic Training and Sports Medicine M
- Business Education M
- Counselor Education M
- Education—General M,D
- Educational Leadership and Administration M,D
- Elementary Education M
- Foreign Languages Education M
- Middle School Education M
- Secondary Education M
- Social Work M
- Special Education M

SPRING ARBOR UNIVERSITY
- Business Administration and Management—General M
- Education—General M
- Reading Education M
- Special Education M

SPRINGFIELD COLLEGE
- Athletic Training and Sports Medicine M,D
- Business Administration and Management—General M
- Counselor Education M,D,O
- Education—General M
- Exercise and Sports Science M,D
- Human Services M
- Physical Education M,D,O
- Recreation and Park Management M
- Secondary Education M
- Social Work M,O
- Special Education M
- Sports Management M,D,O
- Student Affairs M,D,O

SPRING HILL COLLEGE
- Business Administration and Management—General M
- Early Childhood Education M
- Education—General M
- Elementary Education M
- Foundations and Philosophy of Education M
- Secondary Education M
- Social Sciences Education M,O

STANFORD UNIVERSITY
- Business Administration and Management—General M,D
- Curriculum and Instruction M
- Education—General M,D
- Educational Leadership and Administration M
- Educational Media/Instructional Technology M
- Educational Policy M
- Elementary Education M
- Environmental Law M,D
- International and Comparative Education M,D
- Law M,D
- Legal and Justice Studies M,D
- Secondary Education M

STATE UNIVERSITY OF NEW YORK AT FREDONIA
- Curriculum and Instruction M
- Early Childhood Education M
- Education—General M
- English as a Second Language M
- Middle School Education M
- Music Education M
- Reading Education M
- Secondary Education M

STATE UNIVERSITY OF NEW YORK AT NEW PALTZ
- Accounting M
- Art Education M
- Business Administration and Management—General M
- Counselor Education M,O
- Early Childhood Education M
- Education—General M,O
- Educational Leadership and Administration M,O
- Elementary Education M
- English as a Second Language M,O
- English Education M,O
- Mathematics Education M
- Multilingual and Multicultural Education M,O
- Reading Education M
- Science Education M,O
- Secondary Education M,O

Social Sciences Education M,O
Special Education M

STATE UNIVERSITY OF NEW YORK AT OSWEGO
Agricultural Education M
Art Education M
Business Administration and Management—General M
Business Education M
Curriculum and Instruction M
Early Childhood Education M
Education—General M,O
Educational Leadership and Administration O
Elementary Education M
Middle School Education M
Reading Education M
Secondary Education M
Special Education M
Vocational and Technical Education M

STATE UNIVERSITY OF NEW YORK AT PLATTSBURGH
Counselor Education M,O
Curriculum and Instruction M
Early Childhood Education O
Educational Leadership and Administration O
Elementary Education M,O
English Education M
Foreign Languages Education M
Mathematics Education M
Reading Education M
Science Education M
Secondary Education M
Social Sciences Education M
Special Education M
Student Affairs M,O

STATE UNIVERSITY OF NEW YORK COLLEGE AT CORTLAND
Early Childhood Education M
Education—General M,O
Educational Leadership and Administration O
English as a Second Language M
English Education M
Environmental Education M
Health Education M
Mathematics Education M
Physical Education M
Reading Education M
Recreation and Park Management M
Science Education M
Secondary Education M
Special Education M
Sports Management M

STATE UNIVERSITY OF NEW YORK COLLEGE AT GENESEO
Accounting M
Business Administration and Management—General M
Early Childhood Education M
Education—General M
English Education M
Foreign Languages Education M
Multilingual and Multicultural Education M
Reading Education M
Science Education M
Secondary Education M

STATE UNIVERSITY OF NEW YORK COLLEGE AT OLD WESTBURY
Accounting M
Business Administration and Management—General M
Education—General M
English Education M
Foreign Languages Education M
Mathematics Education M
Science Education M
Social Sciences Education M
Taxation M

STATE UNIVERSITY OF NEW YORK COLLEGE AT ONEONTA
Counselor Education M,O
Education—General M,O
Educational Psychology M,O
Elementary Education M
Reading Education M
Special Education M,O

STATE UNIVERSITY OF NEW YORK COLLEGE AT POTSDAM
Curriculum and Instruction M
Early Childhood Education M
Educational Media/Instructional Technology M
Elementary Education M
English Education M
Mathematics Education M
Middle School Education M
Music Education M
Organizational Management M
Reading Education M
Science Education M
Secondary Education M
Social Sciences Education M
Special Education M

STATE UNIVERSITY OF NEW YORK COLLEGE OF ENVIRONMENTAL SCIENCE AND FORESTRY
Sustainability Management M,D,O

STATE UNIVERSITY OF NEW YORK EMPIRE STATE COLLEGE
Adult Education M
Business Administration and Management—General M
Education—General M
Educational Media/Instructional Technology M
International Business M

STATE UNIVERSITY OF NEW YORK MARITIME COLLEGE
Transportation Management M

STATE UNIVERSITY OF NEW YORK POLYTECHNIC INSTITUTE
Accounting M
Business Administration and Management—General M
Finance and Banking M
Human Resources Management M
Marketing M

STEPHEN F. AUSTIN STATE UNIVERSITY
Accounting M
Agricultural Education M
Athletic Training and Sports Medicine M
Business Administration and Management—General M
Counselor Education M
Early Childhood Education M
Education—General M,D
Educational Leadership and Administration M,D
Elementary Education M
Kinesiology and Movement Studies M
Marketing M
Mathematics Education M
Secondary Education M,D
Social Work M
Special Education M

STEPHENS COLLEGE
Counselor Education M,O

STETSON UNIVERSITY
Accounting M
Business Administration and Management—General M
Counselor Education M
Education—General M
Educational Leadership and Administration M
Law M,D
Legal and Justice Studies M

STEVENS INSTITUTE OF TECHNOLOGY
Business Administration and Management—General M,O
Electronic Commerce M,O
Entrepreneurship M,O
Finance and Banking M,O
Human Resources Management M
Industrial and Manufacturing Management M
International Business M
Logistics O
Management Information Systems M,D,O
Management Strategy and Policy M
Marketing M,O
Project Management M,O
Quality Management M,O

STEVENSON UNIVERSITY
Education—General M
Mathematics Education M
Project Management M
Quality Management M
Science Education M

STOCKTON UNIVERSITY
Business Administration and Management—General M
Education—General M
Educational Media/Instructional Technology M
Organizational Management D
Social Work M

STONY BROOK UNIVERSITY, STATE UNIVERSITY OF NEW YORK
Accounting M,O
Business Administration and Management—General M,O
Computer Education M
Educational Leadership and Administration M,O
Educational Media/Instructional Technology M,O
English as a Second Language M,O
English Education M,D,O
Finance and Banking M,O
Foreign Languages Education M,O
Higher Education M,O
Human Resources Management M,O
Industrial and Manufacturing Management M,O
Management Information Systems M,D,O
Marketing M,O
Mathematics Education M,O
Physical Education M,O
Science Education M,D,O
Social Sciences Education M,O
Social Work M,D

STRATFORD UNIVERSITY (MD)
Hospitality Management M

STRATFORD UNIVERSITY (VA)
Accounting M
Business Administration and Management—General M
Entrepreneurship M
Hospitality Management M
International Business M
Management Information Systems M

STRAYER UNIVERSITY
Accounting M
Business Administration and Management—General M
Education—General M
Educational Media/Instructional Technology M
Finance and Banking M
Hospitality Management M
Human Resources Management M
Management Information Systems M
Marketing M
Supply Chain Management M
Taxation M
Travel and Tourism M

SUFFOLK UNIVERSITY
Accounting M,O
Advertising and Public Relations M
Business Administration and Management—General M
Counselor Education M,D,O
Educational Leadership and Administration M,O
Entrepreneurship M
Finance and Banking M
Health Law M,D
Intellectual Property Law M,D
International Business M
Law M,D
Management Information Systems M
Management Strategy and Policy M
Marketing M
Nonprofit Management M
Organizational Behavior M
Supply Chain Management M
Taxation M,O

SULLIVAN UNIVERSITY
Business Administration and Management—General M,D

SUL ROSS STATE UNIVERSITY
Art Education M
Business Administration and Management—General M
Counselor Education M
Education—General M,O
Educational Leadership and Administration M
Educational Measurement and Evaluation M,O
Elementary Education M
Multilingual and Multicultural Education M
Physical Education M
Reading Education M,O
Secondary Education M

SWEET BRIAR COLLEGE
Education—General M

SYRACUSE UNIVERSITY
Accounting M
Advertising and Public Relations M
Art Education M
Business Administration and Management—General M,D
Counselor Education M,D
Curriculum and Instruction M,D,O
Early Childhood Education M
Education of Students with Severe/Multiple Disabilities M
Education—General M,D,O
Educational Leadership and Administration M,D,O
Educational Measurement and Evaluation M,D,O
Educational Media/Instructional Technology M,O
Educational Policy O
English as a Second Language M,O
English Education M
Entertainment Management M
Entrepreneurship M
Exercise and Sports Science M
Finance and Banking M,D
Foundations and Philosophy of Education M,D,O
Higher Education M,D
Hospitality Management M,O
Information Studies M
Kinesiology and Movement Studies M,D,O
Law M,D
Library Science M*
Management Information Systems M,D,O
Management Strategy and Policy M
Marketing M
Mathematics Education M,D
Music Education M
Organizational Management O
Reading Education M,D
Real Estate M
Science Education M,D
Social Sciences Education M
Social Work M
Special Education M,D
Sports Management M
Student Affairs M
Supply Chain Management M
Sustainability Management O
Travel and Tourism M

TABOR COLLEGE
Accounting M
Business Administration and Management—General M

TAFT UNIVERSITY SYSTEM
Education—General M
Law M,D
Legal and Justice Studies M,D
Taxation M,D

TARLETON STATE UNIVERSITY
Accounting M
Athletic Training and Sports Medicine M
Business Administration and Management—General M
Curriculum and Instruction M
Education—General M,D,O
Educational Leadership and Administration M,D,O
Educational Media/Instructional Technology M
Elementary Education M
Human Resources Management M
Kinesiology and Movement Studies M
Management Information Systems M
Marketing M
Music Education M
Reading Education M
Secondary Education M
Social Work M
Special Education M

TAYLOR COLLEGE AND SEMINARY
English as a Second Language M,O

TAYLOR UNIVERSITY
Business Administration and Management—General M
Higher Education M
International Business M
Management Strategy and Policy M

TEACHERS COLLEGE, COLUMBIA UNIVERSITY
Adult Education M,D
Art Education M,D,O
Computer Education M,D
Curriculum and Instruction M,D
Early Childhood Education M,D
Education of Students with Severe/Multiple Disabilities M,D,O
Education of the Gifted M,D
Education—General M,D
Educational Leadership and Administration M,D
Educational Measurement and Evaluation M,D
Educational Media/Instructional Technology M,D
Educational Policy M,D
Educational Psychology M,D,O
Elementary Education M,D
English as a Second Language M,D,O
English Education M,D,O
Foundations and Philosophy of Education M,D,O
Health Education M,D,O
Higher Education M,D
International and Comparative Education M,D
Kinesiology and Movement Studies M,D
Mathematics Education M,D
Multilingual and Multicultural Education M,D,O
Music Education M,D,O
Physical Education M,D
Reading Education M,D,O
Science Education M,D
Secondary Education M,D
Social Sciences Education M,D,O
Special Education M,D,O
Urban Education M,D

TÉLÉ-UNIVERSITÉ
Distance Education Development M,D
Finance and Banking M,D

TEMPLE UNIVERSITY
Accounting M,D
Actuarial Science M
Art Education M
Athletic Training and Sports Medicine M,D
Business Administration and Management—General M,D
Business Education M
Education—General M,D,O
Educational Psychology M,D,O
English as a Second Language M
English Education M
Entrepreneurship M,D
Finance and Banking M,D
Hospitality Management M,D*
Human Resources Management M
Insurance D
International Business M,D
Kinesiology and Movement Studies M,D
Law M,D
Legal and Justice Studies M,D
Management Information Systems M,D
Management Strategy and Policy D
Marketing M,D
Mathematics Education M
Middle School Education M
Music Education M,D
Physical Education M,D
Recreation and Park Management M,D
Science Education M
Secondary Education M
Social Sciences Education M
Social Work M
Sports Management M,D*
Supply Chain Management M,D
Taxation M,D
Transportation Management M,O
Travel and Tourism M,D
Urban Education M
Vocational and Technical Education M

TENNESSEE STATE UNIVERSITY
Agricultural Education M,D

*M—masters degree; D—doctorate; O—other advanced degree; *—Close-Up and/or Display*

Business Administration and Management—General M
Curriculum and Instruction M,D
Education—General M,D,O
Elementary Education M,D
Exercise and Sports Science M
Human Resources Management M,D
Management Strategy and Policy M,D
Physical Education M
Social Work M,D
Special Education M,D
Sports Management M

TENNESSEE TECHNOLOGICAL UNIVERSITY
Accounting M
Business Administration and Management—General M
Curriculum and Instruction M,O
Early Childhood Education M,O
Education of the Gifted D
Education—General M,D,O
Educational Leadership and Administration M,O
Educational Measurement and Evaluation D
Educational Media/Instructional Technology M,O
Educational Psychology M,O
Elementary Education M,O
Finance and Banking M
Health Education M
Human Resources Management M
International Business M
Kinesiology and Movement Studies M
Library Science M,O
Management Information Systems M
Management Strategy and Policy M
Mathematics Education M,O
Middle School Education M
Music Education M
Physical Education M
Reading Education M,D,O
Science Education M,O
Secondary Education M,O
Special Education M,O
Sports Management M

TENNESSEE WESLEYAN UNIVERSITY
Accounting M
Business Administration and Management—General M

TEXAS A&M INTERNATIONAL UNIVERSITY
Accounting M
Business Administration and Management—General M,D
Counselor Education M
Curriculum and Instruction M
Education—General M
Educational Leadership and Administration M
Finance and Banking M
Foreign Languages Education M,D
International Business M,D
Management Information Systems M,D
Special Education M

TEXAS A&M UNIVERSITY
Accounting M
Agricultural Education M,D
Athletic Training and Sports Medicine M,D
Business Administration and Management—General M
Curriculum and Instruction M,D
Education—General M,D
Educational Leadership and Administration M,D
Educational Media/Instructional Technology M,D
Educational Psychology M,D
Entrepreneurship M
Finance and Banking M
Health Education M,D
Human Resources Development M,D
Human Resources Management M
Kinesiology and Movement Studies M,D
Law M,D
Management Information Systems M
Marketing M
Multilingual and Multicultural Education M,D
Nonprofit Management M,D
Real Estate M
Recreation and Park Management M,D
Special Education M,D
Sports Management M,D
Transportation Management M

TEXAS A&M UNIVERSITY–CENTRAL TEXAS
Accounting M,O
Business Administration and Management—General M,O
Counselor Education M,O
Curriculum and Instruction M,O
Educational Leadership and Administration M,O
Educational Psychology M,O
Human Resources Management M,O
Management Information Systems M,O

TEXAS A&M UNIVERSITY–COMMERCE
Accounting M
Business Administration and Management—General M
Counselor Education M,D,O
Curriculum and Instruction M,D,O
Early Childhood Education M,D,O
Education—General M,D,O
Educational Leadership and Administration M,D,O
Educational Media/Instructional Technology M,D,O
Educational Psychology M,D,O
Elementary Education M,D,O
English as a Second Language M,D,O
Exercise and Sports Science M,D,O
Finance and Banking M
Higher Education M,D,O
Industrial and Manufacturing Management M,D,O
Kinesiology and Movement Studies M,D,O
Library Science M,D,O
Marketing M
Reading Education M,D,O
Secondary Education M,D,O
Social Work M,D,O
Special Education M,D,O

TEXAS A&M UNIVERSITY–CORPUS CHRISTI
Accounting M
Business Administration and Management—General M
Counselor Education M,D
Curriculum and Instruction M,D
Early Childhood Education M,D
Education—General M,D
Educational Leadership and Administration M,D
Educational Media/Instructional Technology M,D
Elementary Education M
Finance and Banking M
International Business M
Kinesiology and Movement Studies M,D
Reading Education M,D
Secondary Education M
Special Education M

TEXAS A&M UNIVERSITY–KINGSVILLE
Adult Education M,D
Business Administration and Management—General M
Counselor Education M,D
Early Childhood Education M
Education—General M,D,O
Educational Leadership and Administration M,D
Educational Media/Instructional Technology M
English as a Second Language M,D
Foreign Languages Education M
Health Education M
Industrial and Manufacturing Management M
Kinesiology and Movement Studies M
Multilingual and Multicultural Education M,D
Music Education M
Reading Education M
Secondary Education M
Special Education M

TEXAS A&M UNIVERSITY–SAN ANTONIO
Accounting M
Business Administration and Management—General M
Counselor Education M
Early Childhood Education M
Educational Leadership and Administration M
Educational Measurement and Evaluation M
Finance and Banking M
Human Resources Management M
International Business M
Kinesiology and Movement Studies M
Management Information Systems M
Multilingual and Multicultural Education M
Project Management M
Reading Education M
Special Education M
Supply Chain Management M

TEXAS A&M UNIVERSITY–TEXARKANA
Accounting M
Adult Education M
Business Administration and Management—General M
Curriculum and Instruction M
Education—General M
Educational Leadership and Administration M
Educational Media/Instructional Technology M
Special Education M

TEXAS CHRISTIAN UNIVERSITY
Accounting M
Business Administration and Management—General M
Counselor Education M,D,O
Curriculum and Instruction M,D,O
Education—General M,D,O
Educational Leadership and Administration M,D,O
Finance and Banking M
Kinesiology and Movement Studies M
Marketing M
Mathematics Education M,O
Music Education M,D
Reading Education M,O
Science Education M,D,O
Social Work M
Special Education M,O
Supply Chain Management M
Taxation M

TEXAS HEALTH AND SCIENCE UNIVERSITY
Business Administration and Management—General M,D

TEXAS LUTHERAN UNIVERSITY
Accounting M

TEXAS SOUTHERN UNIVERSITY
Business Administration and Management—General M
Counselor Education M,D
Curriculum and Instruction M,D
Education—General M,D
Educational Leadership and Administration M,D
Health Education M
Higher Education M,D
Human Services M
Law D
Management Information Systems M
Multilingual and Multicultural Education M,D
Physical Education M
Secondary Education M,D
Transportation Management M

TEXAS STATE UNIVERSITY
Accounting M
Adult Education M,D
Agricultural Education M
Athletic Training and Sports Medicine M
Business Administration and Management—General M
Counselor Education M
Developmental Education M,D
Education—General M,D,O
Educational Leadership and Administration M,D
Educational Media/Instructional Technology M
Elementary Education M
Health Education M
Higher Education M
Human Resources Management M
Legal and Justice Studies M
Leisure Studies M
Management Information Systems M
Mathematics Education M,D
Multilingual and Multicultural Education M
Music Education M
Physical Education M
Reading Education M
Recreation and Park Management M
Secondary Education M
Social Work M
Special Education M
Student Affairs M
Vocational and Technical Education M

TEXAS TECH UNIVERSITY
Accounting M,D
Agricultural Education M,D
Art Education M
Business Administration and Management—General M,D
Counselor Education M,D
Curriculum and Instruction M,D
Distance Education Development M,D
Education—General M,D
Educational Leadership and Administration M,D
Educational Media/Instructional Technology M,D
Educational Psychology M,D
Elementary Education M,D
Exercise and Sports Science M
Finance and Banking M,D
Higher Education M,D
Home Economics Education M,D
Hospitality Management M,D
Kinesiology and Movement Studies M
Law M,D
Legal and Justice Studies M,D
Management Information Systems M,D
Marketing M,D
Multilingual and Multicultural Education M,D
Music Education M,D
Reading Education M,D
Science Education M,D
Secondary Education M,D
Social Work M
Special Education M,D
Sports Management M
Taxation M,D

TEXAS TECH UNIVERSITY HEALTH SCIENCES CENTER
Athletic Training and Sports Medicine M

TEXAS WESLEYAN UNIVERSITY
Business Administration and Management—General M
Counselor Education M,D
Education—General M,D

TEXAS WOMAN'S UNIVERSITY
Accounting M
Business Administration and Management—General M
Counselor Education M,D
Curriculum and Instruction M,D
Early Childhood Education M,D
Education—General M,D
Educational Leadership and Administration M,D
Exercise and Sports Science M,D
Health Education M,D
Kinesiology and Movement Studies M,D
Library Science M,D
Mathematics Education M
Music Education M
Physical Education M,D
Reading Education M,D
Special Education M,D
Sports Management M,D

THEOLOGICAL UNIVERSITY OF THE CARIBBEAN
Early Childhood Education M,D
Middle School Education M,D

THOMAS COLLEGE
Business Administration and Management—General M
Business Education M
Computer Education M
Human Resources Management M

THOMAS EDISON STATE UNIVERSITY
Business Administration and Management—General M
Distance Education Development O
Educational Leadership and Administration M
Educational Media/Instructional Technology O
Human Resources Management M,O
Organizational Management O

THOMAS JEFFERSON SCHOOL OF LAW
Law D

THOMAS JEFFERSON UNIVERSITY
Health Education M,D,O

THOMAS MORE COLLEGE
Business Administration and Management—General M
Education—General M
Educational Leadership and Administration M

THOMAS UNIVERSITY
Business Administration and Management—General M
Education—General M
Human Services M

THOMPSON RIVERS UNIVERSITY
Business Administration and Management—General M
Education—General M
Social Work M

TIFFIN UNIVERSITY
Business Administration and Management—General M
Education—General M
Educational Leadership and Administration M
Educational Media/Instructional Technology M
Finance and Banking M
Higher Education M
Human Resources Management M
International Business M
Marketing M
Nonprofit Management M
Sports Management M

TOURO COLLEGE
Education—General M
Educational Leadership and Administration M
Educational Media/Instructional Technology M
English as a Second Language M
Law M,D
Legal and Justice Studies M,D
Management Information Systems M
Mathematics Education M
Reading Education M
Science Education M
Social Work M
Special Education M

TOURO UNIVERSITY CALIFORNIA
Education—General M,D

TOWSON UNIVERSITY
Accounting M
Art Education M,O
Early Childhood Education M,O
Education—General M
Educational Leadership and Administration M,O
Educational Media/Instructional Technology M,D
Electronic Commerce M,O
Elementary Education M
Human Resources Development M
Management Information Systems M,D,O
Marketing Research M
Mathematics Education M
Music Education M,O
Organizational Behavior O
Reading Education M,O
Religious Education M,O
Secondary Education M
Special Education M,O
Supply Chain Management M,O

TREVECCA NAZARENE UNIVERSITY
Business Administration and Management—General M
Counselor Education M,D
Curriculum and Instruction M,O
Education—General M,O
Educational Leadership and Administration M,D,O
Educational Media/Instructional Technology M
Elementary Education M,O
English as a Second Language M,O
Library Science M,O
Organizational Management M,O
Secondary Education M,O
Special Education M,O

TRIDENT UNIVERSITY INTERNATIONAL
Adult Education M
Business Administration and Management—General M,D
Early Childhood Education M
Education—General M,D
Educational Leadership and Administration M,D

Educational Media/Instructional Technology M,D
Finance and Banking M,D
Health Education M,D,O
Higher Education M,D
Human Resources Management M,D
International Business M,D
Legal and Justice Studies M,D,O
Logistics M,D
Management Information Systems M,D,O
Marketing M,D
Project Management M,D
Quality Management M,D,O
Reading Education M

TRINE UNIVERSITY
Law M

TRINITY BAPTIST COLLEGE
Educational Leadership and Administration M
Special Education M

TRINITY CHRISTIAN COLLEGE
Special Education M

TRINITY INTERNATIONAL UNIVERSITY
Athletic Training and Sports Medicine M
Business Administration and Management—General M,D,O
Education—General M
Human Resources Management M,D
Law M,D
Religious Education M,D,O

TRINITY LUTHERAN SEMINARY
Religious Education M

TRINITY UNIVERSITY
Accounting M
Business Administration and Management—General M
Education—General M
Educational Leadership and Administration M

TRINITY WASHINGTON UNIVERSITY
Business Administration and Management—General M
Counselor Education M
Curriculum and Instruction M
Early Childhood Education M
Education—General M
Educational Leadership and Administration M
Elementary Education M
English Education M
Human Resources Management M
Nonprofit Management M
Organizational Management M
Reading Education M
Secondary Education M
Social Sciences Education M
Special Education M

TRINITY WESTERN UNIVERSITY
Business Administration and Management—General M
Educational Leadership and Administration M,O
English as a Second Language M
International Business M
Nonprofit Management M,O
Organizational Management M,O

TROPICAL AGRICULTURE RESEARCH AND HIGHER EDUCATION CENTER
Travel and Tourism M,D

TROY UNIVERSITY
Accounting M
Adult Education M
Business Administration and Management—General M
Counselor Education M,O
Early Childhood Education M,O
Education—General M,O
Educational Leadership and Administration M,O
Elementary Education M,O
English as a Second Language M
Finance and Banking M
Human Resources Management M
Management Information Systems M
Secondary Education M
Social Work M
Sports Management M
Taxation M,O

TRUMAN STATE UNIVERSITY
Accounting M
Education—General M

TUFTS UNIVERSITY
Art Education M,D,O
Early Childhood Education M,D
Education—General M,D,O
Elementary Education M,D
Entrepreneurship M
International Business M,D
Law M,D
Management Strategy and Policy O
Mathematics Education M,D
Middle School Education M,D
Museum Education M,D
Nonprofit Management O
Science Education M,D
Secondary Education M,D

TULANE UNIVERSITY
Accounting M,D
Business Administration and Management—General M,D
Entrepreneurship M,D
Finance and Banking M,D
International Business M,D
Law M,D
Management Strategy and Policy M,D
Social Work M,D

TUSCULUM COLLEGE
Business Administration and Management—General M
Curriculum and Instruction M
Education—General M
Human Resources Management M
Mathematics Education M
Nonprofit Management M
Special Education M

TUSKEGEE UNIVERSITY
Management Information Systems M

UNIFICATION THEOLOGICAL SEMINARY
Nonprofit Management M,D
Religious Education M,D

UNION COLLEGE (KY)
Education—General M
Educational Leadership and Administration M
Elementary Education M
Health Education M
Middle School Education M
Music Education M
Physical Education M
Reading Education M
Secondary Education M
Special Education M

UNION INSTITUTE & UNIVERSITY
Education—General D
Organizational Management M

UNION PRESBYTERIAN SEMINARY
Religious Education M,D

UNION UNIVERSITY
Accounting M
Business Administration and Management—General M
Education—General M,D,O
Educational Leadership and Administration M,D,O
Higher Education M,D,O
Social Work M

UNITED STATES INTERNATIONAL UNIVERSITY–AFRICA
Business Administration and Management—General M
Entrepreneurship M
Finance and Banking M
Human Resources Management M
International Business M
Management Information Systems M
Management Strategy and Policy M
Marketing M
Organizational Management M

UNITED STATES SPORTS ACADEMY
Athletic Training and Sports Medicine M
Exercise and Sports Science M
Physical Education M
Sports Management M,D

UNIVERSIDAD ADVENTISTA DE LAS ANTILLAS
Curriculum and Instruction M
Educational Leadership and Administration M

UNIVERSIDAD AUTONOMA DE GUADALAJARA
Advertising and Public Relations M,D
Business Administration and Management—General M,D
Education—General M,D
Entertainment Management M,D
International Business M,D
Law M,D
Legal and Justice Studies M,D
Marketing Research M,D
Mathematics Education M,D

UNIVERSIDAD CENTRAL DEL ESTE
Finance and Banking M
Higher Education M
Human Resources Development M
Law D

UNIVERSIDAD DE IBEROAMERICA
Educational Psychology M,D

UNIVERSIDAD DE LAS AMERICAS, A.C.
Business Administration and Management—General M
Education—General M
Finance and Banking M
Marketing Research M
Organizational Behavior M
Quality Management M

UNIVERSIDAD DE LAS AMÉRICAS PUEBLA
Business Administration and Management—General M
Education—General M
Finance and Banking M
Industrial and Manufacturing Management M

UNIVERSIDAD DEL ESTE
Accounting M
Adult Education M
Business Administration and Management—General M
Electronic Commerce M
Elementary Education M
English as a Second Language M
Foreign Languages Education M
Human Resources Management M
Management Information Systems M
Management Strategy and Policy M
Social Work M
Special Education M

UNIVERSIDAD DEL TURABO
Accounting M
Athletic Training and Sports Medicine M
Business Administration and Management—General M,D
Counselor Education M
Curriculum and Instruction M,D
Early Childhood Education M,D
Education—General M,D
Educational Leadership and Administration M,D
English as a Second Language M
Human Resources Management M
Human Services M
Information Studies M
Library Science M
Logistics M
Management Information Systems D
Marketing M
Physical Education M
Project Management M
Quality Management M
Special Education M

UNIVERSIDAD IBEROAMERICANA
Business Administration and Management—General M,D
Educational Leadership and Administration M,D
Human Resources Development M,D
Law M,D
Marketing M,D
Real Estate M,D
Special Education M,D

UNIVERSIDAD METROPOLITANA
Accounting M
Adult Education M
Business Administration and Management—General M
Curriculum and Instruction M
Education—General M
Educational Leadership and Administration M
Elementary Education M
Finance and Banking M
Human Resources Management M
International Business M
Leisure Studies M
Management Information Systems M
Marketing M
Physical Education M
Recreation and Park Management M
Secondary Education M
Special Education M

UNIVERSIDAD NACIONAL PEDRO HENRIQUEZ URENA
Project Management M
Science Education M

UNIVERSITÉ DE MONCTON
Business Administration and Management—General M
Counselor Education M
Education—General M
Educational Leadership and Administration M
Educational Psychology M
Social Work M

UNIVERSITÉ DE MONTRÉAL
Curriculum and Instruction M,D,O
Education—General M,D,O
Educational Leadership and Administration M,D,O
Educational Psychology M,D,O
Electronic Commerce M,D
Human Services D
Information Studies M,D
Kinesiology and Movement Studies M,D,O
Law M,D,O
Library Science M,D
Physical Education M,D,O
Social Work O
Taxation M,D,O

UNIVERSITÉ DE SAINT-BONIFACE
Education—General M

UNIVERSITÉ DE SHERBROOKE
Accounting M
Business Administration and Management—General M,D,O
Education—General M,O
Educational Leadership and Administration M
Electronic Commerce M
Elementary Education M,O
Finance and Banking M
Health Law M,D,O
Higher Education M,O
International Business M
Kinesiology and Movement Studies M,O
Law M,D,O
Management Information Systems M,O
Marketing M
Organizational Behavior M
Physical Education M,O
Social Work M
Special Education M,O
Taxation M,O

UNIVERSITÉ DU QUÉBEC À CHICOUTIMI
Business Administration and Management—General M
Education—General M,D
Project Management M

UNIVERSITÉ DU QUÉBEC À MONTRÉAL
Accounting M,O
Actuarial Science O
Business Administration and Management—General M,D,O
Education—General M,D,O
Environmental Education M,D,O
Finance and Banking O
Kinesiology and Movement Studies M
Law O
Management Information Systems M
Project Management M,O
Social Work M

UNIVERSITÉ DU QUÉBEC À RIMOUSKI
Business Administration and Management—General M,O
Education—General M,D,O
Project Management M,O

UNIVERSITÉ DU QUÉBEC À TROIS-RIVIÈRES
Accounting M
Business Administration and Management—General M,D
Education—General M,D
Educational Leadership and Administration O
Educational Psychology M,D
Finance and Banking O
Leisure Studies M,O
Physical Education M
Travel and Tourism M,O

UNIVERSITÉ DU QUÉBEC, ÉCOLE NATIONALE D'ADMINISTRATION PUBLIQUE
International Business M,O

UNIVERSITÉ DU QUÉBEC EN ABITIBI-TÉMISCAMINGUE
Business Administration and Management—General M
Education—General M,D,O
Project Management M,O
Social Work M

UNIVERSITÉ DU QUÉBEC EN OUTAOUAIS
Accounting M,O
Education—General M,D,O
Educational Psychology M
Finance and Banking M,O
Foreign Languages Education O
Project Management M,O
Social Work M

UNIVERSITÉ LAVAL
Accounting M,O
Advertising and Public Relations O
Business Administration and Management—General M,D,O
Counselor Education M,D
Curriculum and Instruction M,D
Education—General M,D,O
Educational Leadership and Administration M,D,O
Educational Measurement and Evaluation M,D,O
Educational Media/Instructional Technology M,D
Educational Psychology M,D
Electronic Commerce M,O
Entrepreneurship M,O
Facilities Management M,O
Finance and Banking M,O
International Business M,O
Kinesiology and Movement Studies M,D
Law M,D,O
Legal and Justice Studies O
Management Information Systems M,O
Marketing M,O
Music Education M,D
Organizational Management M,O
Social Work M,D

UNIVERSITÉ SAINTE-ANNE
Education—General M

UNIVERSITY AT ALBANY, STATE UNIVERSITY OF NEW YORK
Accounting M
Business Administration and Management—General M
Curriculum and Instruction M,D,O
Education—General M,D,O
Educational Leadership and Administration M,D,O
Educational Measurement and Evaluation M,D,O
Educational Media/Instructional Technology M,D,O
Educational Policy M,D,O
Educational Psychology M,D,O
Entrepreneurship M
Finance and Banking M,D,O
Higher Education M,D,O
Human Resources Management M,D,O
Information Studies M,O
International and Comparative Education M,D,O
Law M
Library Science M,O
Management Information Systems M,D,O
Marketing M
Nonprofit Management M,D,O
Organizational Behavior M,D,O

*M—masters degree; D—doctorate; O—other advanced degree; *—Close-Up and/or Display*

- Reading Education M,D,O
- Social Work M,D
- Special Education M
- Taxation M

UNIVERSITY AT BUFFALO, THE STATE UNIVERSITY OF NEW YORK

- Accounting M,D
- Business Administration and Management—General M,D
- Counselor Education M,D,O
- Curriculum and Instruction M,D,O
- Distance Education Development M,D,O
- Early Childhood Education M,D,O
- Education of the Gifted M,D,O
- Education—General M,D,O
- Educational Leadership and Administration M,D,O
- Educational Media/Instructional Technology M,D,O
- Educational Psychology M,D,O
- Electronic Commerce M,D,O
- Elementary Education M,D,O
- English as a Second Language M,D,O
- English Education M,D,O
- Exercise and Sports Science M,D,O
- Finance and Banking M,D
- Foreign Languages Education M,D,O
- Foundations and Philosophy of Education M,D,O
- Higher Education M,D,O
- Human Resources Management M,D,O
- Information Studies M,O
- International Business M,D
- Law M,D
- Library Science M,O
- Logistics M,O
- Management Information Systems M,D,O
- Management Strategy and Policy M,D
- Marketing M,D
- Mathematics Education M,D,O
- Multilingual and Multicultural Education M,D,O
- Music Education M,D,O
- Quantitative Analysis M,D
- Reading Education M,D,O
- Real Estate M
- Science Education M,D,O
- Social Sciences Education M,D,O
- Social Work M,D
- Special Education M,D,O
- Supply Chain Management M,D

THE UNIVERSITY OF AKRON

- Accounting M
- Art Education M
- Business Administration and Management—General M
- Counselor Education M,D
- Curriculum and Instruction M
- Education—General M
- Educational Leadership and Administration M
- Educational Measurement and Evaluation M,O
- Educational Media/Instructional Technology M
- Elementary Education M
- English Education M
- Exercise and Sports Science M
- Finance and Banking M
- Higher Education M
- International Business M
- Law M,D
- Management Information Systems M
- Marketing M
- Mathematics Education M
- Music Education M
- Physical Education M
- Reading Education M
- Science Education M
- Secondary Education M
- Social Sciences Education M
- Social Work M
- Special Education M
- Supply Chain Management M
- Taxation M

THE UNIVERSITY OF ALABAMA

- Accounting M,D
- Advertising and Public Relations M
- Business Administration and Management—General M,D
- Counselor Education M,D,O
- Education of the Gifted M,D,O
- Educational Leadership and Administration M,D,O
- Elementary Education M,D,O
- English as a Second Language M,D
- Exercise and Sports Science M,D
- Finance and Banking M,D
- Health Education M,D
- Higher Education M,D
- Hospitality Management M
- Industrial and Manufacturing Management M,D
- Information Studies M,D
- Kinesiology and Movement Studies M,D
- Law M,D
- Library Science M,D
- Marketing M,D
- Music Education M,D,O
- Physical Education M,D
- Quality Management M
- Secondary Education M,D,O
- Social Work M,D
- Special Education M,D,O
- Sports Management M
- Taxation M

THE UNIVERSITY OF ALABAMA AT BIRMINGHAM

- Accounting M
- Art Education M
- Business Administration and Management—General M
- Counselor Education M
- Curriculum and Instruction O
- Early Childhood Education M,D
- Education—General M,D,O
- Educational Leadership and Administration M,D,O
- Elementary Education M
- English as a Second Language M,O
- Finance and Banking M
- Health Education D
- Management Information Systems M
- Marketing M
- Quantitative Analysis M,D
- Reading Education M
- Secondary Education M
- Special Education M

THE UNIVERSITY OF ALABAMA IN HUNTSVILLE

- Accounting M,O
- Business Administration and Management—General M,O
- Education—General M,O
- English as a Second Language M,O
- English Education M,O
- Entrepreneurship M,O
- Finance and Banking M,O
- Human Resources Management M,O
- Logistics M,O
- Management Information Systems M,O
- Marketing M,O
- Mathematics Education M,D,O
- Project Management M,O
- Reading Education M,O
- Science Education M,D,O
- Secondary Education M,O
- Social Sciences Education M,O
- Special Education M,O
- Supply Chain Management M,O
- Taxation M

UNIVERSITY OF ALASKA ANCHORAGE

- Business Administration and Management—General M
- Counselor Education M
- Early Childhood Education M,O
- Education—General M,O
- Educational Leadership and Administration M,O
- Logistics M,O
- Project Management M
- Social Work M,O
- Special Education M,O

UNIVERSITY OF ALASKA FAIRBANKS

- Business Administration and Management—General M
- Counselor Education M,O
- Education—General M,O
- Finance and Banking M
- Multilingual and Multicultural Education M
- Special Education M

UNIVERSITY OF ALASKA SOUTHEAST

- Education—General M
- Educational Leadership and Administration M
- Educational Media/Instructional Technology M
- Elementary Education M
- Mathematics Education M
- Reading Education M
- Secondary Education M
- Special Education M

UNIVERSITY OF ALBERTA

- Accounting D
- Adult Education M,D,O
- Business Administration and Management—General M,D
- Counselor Education M,D
- Educational Leadership and Administration M,D,O
- Educational Media/Instructional Technology M,D
- Educational Policy M,D,O
- Educational Psychology M,D
- Elementary Education M,D
- English as a Second Language M,D
- Exercise and Sports Science M,D
- Finance and Banking M,D
- Information Studies M
- International Business M
- Law M,D
- Library Science M
- Marketing D
- Multilingual and Multicultural Education M
- Organizational Management D
- Physical Education M,D
- Recreation and Park Management M,D
- Secondary Education M,D
- Special Education M,D
- Sports Management M

UNIVERSITY OF ANTELOPE VALLEY

- Business Administration and Management—General M

THE UNIVERSITY OF ARIZONA

- Accounting M
- Agricultural Education M,O
- Art Education M,D
- Business Administration and Management—General M,D,O
- Counselor Education M
- Education—General M,D,O
- Educational Leadership and Administration M,D,O
- Educational Psychology M,D,O
- Elementary Education M,D
- English as a Second Language M,D
- English Education M,D
- Finance and Banking M
- Higher Education M,D
- Information Studies M,D
- Law M,D
- Library Science M,D
- Management Information Systems M,O
- Management Strategy and Policy M,D
- Marketing M,D
- Mathematics Education M,D
- Music Education M,D
- Organizational Management M,D
- Reading Education M,D,O
- Secondary Education M,D
- Special Education M,D

UNIVERSITY OF ARKANSAS

- Accounting M
- Adult Education M,D
- Agricultural Education M
- Athletic Training and Sports Medicine M
- Business Administration and Management—General M,D
- Counselor Education M,D,O
- Curriculum and Instruction M,D,O
- Early Childhood Education M
- Education—General M,D,O
- Educational Leadership and Administration M,D,O
- Educational Measurement and Evaluation M,D
- Educational Media/Instructional Technology M
- Educational Policy D
- Health Education M,D
- Higher Education M,D,O
- Human Resources Development M,D,O
- Industrial and Manufacturing Management M
- Kinesiology and Movement Studies M,D
- Law M,D
- Management Information Systems M
- Mathematics Education M
- Middle School Education M,D,O
- Physical Education M
- Recreation and Park Management M,D
- Secondary Education M,O
- Social Work M
- Special Education M
- Sports Management M,D
- Vocational and Technical Education M,D,O

UNIVERSITY OF ARKANSAS AT LITTLE ROCK

- Adult Education M
- Art Education M
- Business Administration and Management—General M,O
- Community College Education M,D
- Counselor Education M
- Curriculum and Instruction M
- Education of the Gifted M,O
- Education—General M,D,O
- Educational Leadership and Administration M,D,O
- Educational Media/Instructional Technology M
- English as a Second Language M
- Entrepreneurship O
- Exercise and Sports Science M
- Foreign Languages Education M
- Health Education M,D
- Higher Education M,D
- Law D
- Management Information Systems M,O
- Middle School Education M
- Nonprofit Management O
- Reading Education M,D,O
- Secondary Education M,O
- Social Work M
- Special Education M,O
- Sports Management M
- Student Affairs M,D

UNIVERSITY OF ARKANSAS AT MONTICELLO

- Education—General M
- Educational Leadership and Administration M

UNIVERSITY OF ARKANSAS AT PINE BLUFF

- Education—General M
- Elementary Education M
- English Education M
- Mathematics Education M
- Science Education M
- Secondary Education M
- Social Sciences Education M

UNIVERSITY OF ARKANSAS FOR MEDICAL SCIENCES

- Health Education M,D,O

UNIVERSITY OF BALTIMORE

- Accounting M,O
- Business Administration and Management—General M,O
- Entrepreneurship M
- Finance and Banking M
- Human Services M
- Intellectual Property Law M,D
- International Business M
- Law M,D
- Legal and Justice Studies M
- Management Information Systems M,O
- Marketing M
- Taxation M,D

UNIVERSITY OF BRIDGEPORT

- Accounting M
- Business Administration and Management—General M
- Computer Education M,D,O
- Early Childhood Education M,D,O
- Education—General M,D,O
- Educational Leadership and Administration M,D,O
- Elementary Education M,D,O
- Entrepreneurship M
- Finance and Banking M
- Human Resources Development M
- Human Resources Management M
- Human Services M
- Industrial and Manufacturing Management M
- International and Comparative Education M,D,O
- International Business M
- Management Information Systems M
- Marketing M
- Middle School Education M,D,O
- Music Education M,D,O
- Reading Education M,D,O
- Secondary Education M,D,O
- Student Affairs M

THE UNIVERSITY OF BRITISH COLUMBIA

- Accounting D
- Adult Education M,D
- Archives/Archival Administration M,D
- Art Education M,D
- Business Administration and Management—General M,D
- Curriculum and Instruction M,D
- Education—General M,D,O
- Educational Leadership and Administration M,D
- Educational Measurement and Evaluation M,D,O
- Educational Policy M,D
- English as a Second Language M,D
- Finance and Banking D
- Foundations and Philosophy of Education M,D
- Higher Education M,D
- Home Economics Education M,D
- Information Studies M,D
- Kinesiology and Movement Studies M,D
- Law M,D
- Library Science M,D
- Management Information Systems D
- Management Strategy and Policy D
- Marketing D
- Mathematics Education M,D
- Music Education M,D
- Organizational Behavior D
- Physical Education M,D
- Quantitative Analysis M,D
- Reading Education M,D
- Science Education M,D
- Social Sciences Education M,D
- Social Work M,D
- Special Education M,D,O
- Sustainability Management M,D
- Taxation M,D
- Transportation Management D
- Vocational and Technical Education M,D

UNIVERSITY OF CALGARY

- Adult Education M,D
- Business Administration and Management—General M,D
- Curriculum and Instruction M,D
- Educational Leadership and Administration M,D
- Educational Measurement and Evaluation M,D
- Environmental Law M,O
- Kinesiology and Movement Studies M,D
- Law M,D,O
- Legal and Justice Studies M,O
- Management Strategy and Policy M,D
- Multilingual and Multicultural Education M,D
- Project Management M,D
- Social Work M,D,O

UNIVERSITY OF CALIFORNIA, BERKELEY

- Accounting D,O
- Business Administration and Management—General M,D,O
- Education—General M,D,O
- Educational Leadership and Administration M,D
- English as a Second Language O
- Facilities Management O
- Finance and Banking D,O
- Human Resources Management O
- Information Studies M,D
- International Business O
- Law M,D
- Legal and Justice Studies D
- Management Information Systems M,D,O
- Marketing D,O
- Mathematics Education M,D
- Organizational Behavior D
- Project Management O
- Real Estate D
- Science Education M,D
- Social Work M,D
- Special Education M,D
- Sustainability Management O

UNIVERSITY OF CALIFORNIA, DAVIS

- Accounting M
- Business Administration and Management—General M
- Curriculum and Instruction M,D
- Education—General M,D
- Educational Psychology M,D
- Exercise and Sports Science M
- Law M,D
- Transportation Management M,D

UNIVERSITY OF CALIFORNIA, HASTINGS COLLEGE OF THE LAW

- Law M,D

UNIVERSITY OF CALIFORNIA, IRVINE
Accounting M
Business Administration and Management—General M,D
Education—General M,D
Educational Leadership and Administration M,D
Educational Media/Instructional Technology M
Elementary Education M,D
Foreign Languages Education M,D
Law D
Secondary Education M,D

UNIVERSITY OF CALIFORNIA, LOS ANGELES
Accounting M,D
Archives/Archival Administration M,D,O
Business Administration and Management—General M,D
Education—General M,D
Educational Leadership and Administration D
English as a Second Language M,D,O
Finance and Banking M,D
Information Studies M,D,O
Law M,D
Library Science M,D,O
Management Strategy and Policy M,D
Marketing M,D
Social Work M,D
Special Education D

UNIVERSITY OF CALIFORNIA, RIVERSIDE
Archives/Archival Administration M,D
Business Administration and Management—General M,D
Education—General M,D,O
Educational Leadership and Administration M,D,O
Educational Psychology M,D,O
English as a Second Language M,D,O
Foundations and Philosophy of Education M,D,O
Higher Education M,D,O
Multilingual and Multicultural Education M,D,O
Reading Education M,D,O
Special Education M,D,O

UNIVERSITY OF CALIFORNIA, SAN DIEGO
Business Administration and Management—General M,D
Curriculum and Instruction M,D
Education—General M,D
Educational Leadership and Administration M,D
Finance and Banking M,D
Health Law M
International Business M
Law M
Legal and Justice Studies M
Management Strategy and Policy M,D
Mathematics Education D
Multilingual and Multicultural Education M,D
Nonprofit Management M
Science Education D

UNIVERSITY OF CALIFORNIA, SAN FRANCISCO
Health Law M

UNIVERSITY OF CALIFORNIA, SANTA BARBARA
Education—General M,D,O
Finance and Banking M,D
Quantitative Analysis M,D
Transportation Management M,D

UNIVERSITY OF CALIFORNIA, SANTA CRUZ
Education—General M,D
Finance and Banking M
Management Information Systems D
Social Sciences Education M

UNIVERSITY OF CENTRAL ARKANSAS
Accounting M
Adult Education M,O
Business Administration and Management—General M
Counselor Education M
Curriculum and Instruction M,O
Education of the Gifted M,O
Education—General M,O
Educational Leadership and Administration M,O
Educational Media/Instructional Technology M
Foreign Languages Education M
Health Education M
Kinesiology and Movement Studies M
Library Science M
Mathematics Education M
Music Education M,O
Organizational Management D
Reading Education M
Special Education M,O
Student Affairs M

UNIVERSITY OF CENTRAL FLORIDA
Accounting M
Art Education M
Business Administration and Management—General M,D,O
Community College Education M,D,O
Counselor Education M,O
Curriculum and Instruction D
Early Childhood Education D
Education—General M,O
Educational Leadership and Administration M,D,O
Educational Media/Instructional Technology M,D,O
Elementary Education M,D
English as a Second Language M,D,O
English Education M
Entrepreneurship M,O
Exercise and Sports Science M,D
Higher Education M,D,O
Hospitality Management M,D,O
Mathematics Education M,D,O
Middle School Education M
Nonprofit Management M,O
Reading Education M,D,O
Science Education M,D,O
Social Sciences Education M,D
Social Work M,O
Special Education M,D,O
Sports Management M
Student Affairs M,D,O
Travel and Tourism M,D,O
Vocational and Technical Education M,D,O

UNIVERSITY OF CENTRAL MISSOURI
Accounting M,D,O
Business Administration and Management—General M,D,O
Counselor Education M,D,O
Early Childhood Education M,D,O
Education—General M,D,O
Educational Leadership and Administration M,D,O
Educational Media/Instructional Technology M,D,O
Elementary Education M,D,O
English as a Second Language M,D,O
Finance and Banking M,D,O
Human Services M,D,O
Industrial and Manufacturing Management M,D,O
Kinesiology and Movement Studies M,D,O
Library Science M,D,O
Management Information Systems M,D,O
Marketing M,D,O
Reading Education M,D,O
Special Education M,D,O
Student Affairs M,D,O
Vocational and Technical Education M,D,O

UNIVERSITY OF CENTRAL OKLAHOMA
Accounting M
Adult Education M
Athletic Training and Sports Medicine M
Counselor Education M
Early Childhood Education M
Education—General M
Educational Leadership and Administration M
Educational Media/Instructional Technology M
Elementary Education M
English as a Second Language M
Exercise and Sports Science M
Higher Education M
Library Science M
Reading Education M
Secondary Education M
Special Education M
Student Affairs M

UNIVERSITY OF CHARLESTON
Accounting M
Business Administration and Management—General M
Legal and Justice Studies M
Management Strategy and Policy M
Organizational Management D

UNIVERSITY OF CHICAGO
Accounting M,O
Business Administration and Management—General M,D,O
Entrepreneurship M,O
Finance and Banking M,O
Industrial and Manufacturing Management M,O
International Business M,O
Law M,D
Management Strategy and Policy M,O
Marketing M,O
Organizational Behavior M,O
Science Education D
Social Work M,D
Urban Education M

UNIVERSITY OF CINCINNATI
Accounting M,D
Adult Education M,D,O
Art Education M
Business Administration and Management—General M,D
Counselor Education M,D,O
Curriculum and Instruction M,D
Early Childhood Education M,D
Education—General M,D,O
Educational Leadership and Administration M,D,O
Elementary Education M
English as a Second Language M,D,O
Finance and Banking M,D
Foundations and Philosophy of Education M,D
Health Education M,D
Industrial and Manufacturing Management D
Law M,D
Management Information Systems M,D
Marketing M,D
Mathematics Education M,D
Music Education M
Organizational Management M
Quantitative Analysis M,D
Reading Education M,D
Science Education M,D,O
Secondary Education M
Social Sciences Education M,D,O
Social Work M
Special Education M,D
Sports Management M
Taxation M

UNIVERSITY OF COLORADO BOULDER
Advertising and Public Relations M,D
Business Administration and Management—General M
Curriculum and Instruction M,D
Education—General M,D
Educational Measurement and Evaluation D
Educational Policy M,D
Educational Psychology M,D
Kinesiology and Movement Studies M,D
Law D
Multilingual and Multicultural Education M,D
Music Education M,D

UNIVERSITY OF COLORADO COLORADO SPRINGS
Business Administration and Management—General M
Counselor Education M,D
Curriculum and Instruction M,D
Education—General M,D
Educational Leadership and Administration M,D
English as a Second Language M,D
Human Services M,D
Special Education M,D

UNIVERSITY OF COLORADO DENVER
Accounting M
Adult Education M
Business Administration and Management—General M
Counselor Education M
Distance Education Development M
Early Childhood Education M,D
Education—General M,D,O
Educational Leadership and Administration M,D,O
Educational Measurement and Evaluation M,D,O
Educational Media/Instructional Technology M
Educational Policy D
Educational Psychology M,D,O
Elementary Education M
English Education M
Entertainment Management M
Entrepreneurship M
Environmental Education M
Environmental Law M,D
Finance and Banking M
Health Education M,D
Human Resources Management M
Insurance M
International Business M
Investment Management M
Management Information Systems M,D
Management Strategy and Policy M
Marketing Research M
Marketing M
Mathematics Education M,D
Multilingual and Multicultural Education M
Nonprofit Management M,D
Quantitative Analysis M
Reading Education M
Science Education M,D
Secondary Education M
Special Education M,D
Sports Management M
Sustainability Management M
Taxation M

UNIVERSITY OF CONNECTICUT
Accounting M
Adult Education M,O
Agricultural Education M,D
Business Administration and Management—General M,D
Counselor Education M,D
Curriculum and Instruction M,D
Education of the Gifted O
Education—General M,D
Educational Leadership and Administration M
Educational Media/Instructional Technology M,D
Educational Psychology M,D,O
Elementary Education M,D
English Education M,D
Exercise and Sports Science M,D
Finance and Banking M,D,O
Foreign Languages Education M,D
Higher Education M
Human Resources Management M
Law D
Marketing M,D
Mathematics Education M,D
Multilingual and Multicultural Education M,D
Music Education M,D
Nonprofit Management M,O
Quantitative Analysis M,O
Reading Education M,D
Science Education M,D
Secondary Education M,D
Social Sciences Education M,D
Sports Management M

UNIVERSITY OF DALLAS
Accounting M,D
Business Administration and Management—General M,D
Entertainment Management M,D
Finance and Banking M,D
Human Resources Management M,D
International Business M,D
Logistics M,D
Management Information Systems M,D
Management Strategy and Policy M,D
Marketing M,D
Organizational Management M,D
Project Management M,D
Sports Management M,D
Supply Chain Management M,D

UNIVERSITY OF DAYTON
Accounting M
Business Administration and Management—General M
Counselor Education M,O
Early Childhood Education M
Educational Leadership and Administration M,D,O
Educational Media/Instructional Technology M
English as a Second Language M
Exercise and Sports Science M
Finance and Banking M
Higher Education D
Law M,D
Marketing M
Mathematics Education M
Middle School Education M
Music Education M
Physical Education M
Reading Education M
Secondary Education M
Student Affairs M,O

UNIVERSITY OF DELAWARE
Accounting M
Agricultural Education M
Business Administration and Management—General M,D
Business Education M,D
Curriculum and Instruction M,D,O
Education—General M,D,O
Educational Leadership and Administration M,D,O
English as a Second Language M,D,O
Entrepreneurship M,D
Finance and Banking M
Foreign Languages Education M
Higher Education M,D,O
Hospitality Management M
Kinesiology and Movement Studies M,D
Management Information Systems M,D
Multilingual and Multicultural Education M,D,O
Music Education M

UNIVERSITY OF DENVER
Accounting M
Art Education M,O
Business Administration and Management—General M
Curriculum and Instruction M,D,O
Early Childhood Education M,D,O
Education—General M,D,O
Educational Leadership and Administration M,D,O
Educational Measurement and Evaluation M,D,O
Educational Policy M,D,O
Finance and Banking M
Higher Education M,D,O
Human Resources Management M,O
Law M,D,O
Legal and Justice Studies M,O
Library Science M,D,O
Management Strategy and Policy M
Marketing M
Music Education M,O
Organizational Management M,O
Project Management M,O
Real Estate M
Social Work M,D,O
Special Education M,D,O
Taxation M

UNIVERSITY OF DETROIT MERCY
Accounting M,O
Business Administration and Management—General M,O
Curriculum and Instruction M,D,O
Educational Leadership and Administration M,D,O
Finance and Banking M,D,O
Law D
Management Information Systems M,D,O
Management Strategy and Policy M,O
Mathematics Education M,D
Religious Education M,D,O
Special Education M,D,O

UNIVERSITY OF DUBUQUE
Business Administration and Management—General M

UNIVERSITY OF EVANSVILLE
Athletic Training and Sports Medicine M

THE UNIVERSITY OF FINDLAY
Accounting M,D
Athletic Training and Sports Medicine M,D
Business Administration and Management—General M,D
Education—General M,D

*M—masters degree; D—doctorate; O—other advanced degree; *—Close-Up and/or Display*

Educational Leadership and Administration M,D
Educational Media/Instructional Technology M,D
English as a Second Language M,D
Hospitality Management M,D
Multilingual and Multicultural Education M,D
Reading Education M,D
Science Education M,D

UNIVERSITY OF FLORIDA

Accounting M,D
Advertising and Public Relations M,D
Agricultural Education M,D
Art Education M,D
Athletic Training and Sports Medicine M,D
Business Administration and Management—General M,D
Counselor Education M,D,O
Curriculum and Instruction M,D,O
Early Childhood Education M,D,O
Education—General M,D,O
Educational Leadership and Administration M,D,O
Educational Measurement and Evaluation M,D,O
Educational Policy M,D,O
Elementary Education M,D,O
English as a Second Language M,D,O
English Education M,D,O
Entrepreneurship M,D,O
Environmental Education M,D,O
Environmental Law M,D
Exercise and Sports Science M,D
Finance and Banking M,D,O
Foreign Languages Education M,D
Health Education M,D,O
Higher Education M,D,O
Human Resources Management M,D
Insurance M,D,O
International Business M,D
Kinesiology and Movement Studies M,D
Law M,D
Management Information Systems M,D,O
Marketing M,D
Mathematics Education M,D,O
Music Education M,D
Nonprofit Management M
Physical Education M,D
Quantitative Analysis M,D,O
Reading Education M,D,O
Real Estate M,D,O
Recreation and Park Management M,D
Science Education M,D,O
Social Sciences Education M,D,O
Special Education M,D,O
Sports Management M,D
Student Affairs M,D,O
Supply Chain Management M,D,O
Taxation M,D
Travel and Tourism M,D

UNIVERSITY OF GEORGIA

Accounting M
Adult Education D,O
Business Administration and Management—General M
Business Education M,D,O
Counselor Education M,D,O
Education—General M,D,O
Educational Leadership and Administration D,O
Educational Media/Instructional Technology M,D,O
Educational Policy D,O
Educational Psychology O
English Education M,D
Health Education M,D
Higher Education M,D
Kinesiology and Movement Studies M,D
Law M,D
Mathematics Education M,D,O
Music Education M,D
Nonprofit Management M,D,O
Physical Education M,D
Reading Education M,D
Science Education M,D,O
Social Work M,D,O
Special Education M,D,O
Student Affairs M,D,O
Vocational and Technical Education M,D,O

UNIVERSITY OF GREAT FALLS

Human Services M

UNIVERSITY OF GUAM

Business Administration and Management—General M
Counselor Education M
Education—General M
Educational Leadership and Administration M
English as a Second Language M
Reading Education M
Secondary Education M
Social Work M
Special Education M

UNIVERSITY OF GUELPH

Business Administration and Management—General M,D
Hospitality Management M
Organizational Management M

UNIVERSITY OF HARTFORD

Accounting M,O
Business Administration and Management—General M
Counselor Education M,O
Early Childhood Education M
Education—General M,D,O
Educational Leadership and Administration D,O
Educational Media/Instructional Technology M
Elementary Education M
Music Education M,D,O
Organizational Behavior M
Taxation M,O

UNIVERSITY OF HAWAII AT HILO

Education—General M
Foreign Languages Education M,D

UNIVERSITY OF HAWAII AT MANOA

Accounting M,D
Business Administration and Management—General M
Curriculum and Instruction M,D
Early Childhood Education M
Education—General M,D,O
Educational Leadership and Administration M,D
Educational Media/Instructional Technology M,D
Educational Policy D
Educational Psychology M,D
English as a Second Language M,D,O
Entrepreneurship M,O
Finance and Banking M,D
Foreign Languages Education M,D,O
Foundations and Philosophy of Education M,D
Human Resources Management M
Information Studies M,O
International Business M,D
Kinesiology and Movement Studies M,D
Law M,D,O
Library Science M,O
Management Information Systems M,D,O
Marketing M,D
Organizational Behavior M
Organizational Management M,D
Real Estate M
Social Work M,D
Special Education M,D
Taxation M
Transportation Management M,D,O
Travel and Tourism M

UNIVERSITY OF HOLY CROSS

Counselor Education M
Curriculum and Instruction M
Education—General M
Educational Leadership and Administration M

UNIVERSITY OF HOUSTON

Accounting M,D
Advertising and Public Relations M
Business Administration and Management—General M,D
Curriculum and Instruction M,D
Education—General M,D
Educational Leadership and Administration M,D
Educational Psychology M,D
Environmental Law M,D
Exercise and Sports Science M,D
Finance and Banking M
Foundations and Philosophy of Education M,D
Health Education M,D
Health Law M,D
Higher Education M,D
Hospitality Management M
Human Resources Development M
Intellectual Property Law M,D
Kinesiology and Movement Studies M,D
Law M,D
Logistics M
Marketing D
Music Education M,D
Physical Education M,D
Project Management M
Social Work M,D
Special Education M,D
Supply Chain Management M
Taxation M,D

UNIVERSITY OF HOUSTON–CLEAR LAKE

Accounting M
Business Administration and Management—General M
Counselor Education M
Curriculum and Instruction M
Early Childhood Education M
Education—General M,D
Educational Leadership and Administration M,D
Educational Media/Instructional Technology M
Exercise and Sports Science M
Finance and Banking M
Foundations and Philosophy of Education M
Human Resources Management M
Library Science M
Management Information Systems M
Multilingual and Multicultural Education M
Reading Education M

UNIVERSITY OF HOUSTON–DOWNTOWN

Business Administration and Management—General M
Curriculum and Instruction M
Finance and Banking M
Human Resources Management M
Investment Management M
Middle School Education M
Nonprofit Management M
Secondary Education M
Social Work M
Supply Chain Management M
Urban Education M

UNIVERSITY OF HOUSTON–VICTORIA

Accounting M
Adult Education M
Business Administration and Management—General M
Counselor Education M
Curriculum and Instruction M
Education—General M
Educational Leadership and Administration M
Educational Media/Instructional Technology M
Entrepreneurship M
Finance and Banking M
Higher Education M
International Business M
Management Information Systems M
Marketing M
Special Education M

UNIVERSITY OF IDAHO

Accounting M
Athletic Training and Sports Medicine M,D
Business Administration and Management—General M,D
Counselor Education M,O
Curriculum and Instruction M,O
Education—General M,D,O
Educational Leadership and Administration M,O
English as a Second Language M
Entrepreneurship D
Environmental Law D
Human Services M,O
Law D
Physical Education M,D
Recreation and Park Management M,D
Special Education M,O
Vocational and Technical Education M,O

UNIVERSITY OF ILLINOIS AT CHICAGO

Accounting M
Business Administration and Management—General M,D
Computer Education D
Curriculum and Instruction M,D
Early Childhood Education M,D
Education—General M,D
Educational Leadership and Administration M,D
Educational Measurement and Evaluation M,D
Educational Policy M,D
Educational Psychology M,D
Elementary Education M,D
English as a Second Language M,D
Finance and Banking M
Foreign Languages Education M,D
Health Education M
Kinesiology and Movement Studies M,D
Management Information Systems M,D
Mathematics Education M,D
Real Estate M
Science Education D
Secondary Education M,D
Social Sciences Education D
Social Work M,D,O
Special Education M,D
Urban Education M,D

UNIVERSITY OF ILLINOIS AT SPRINGFIELD

Accounting M
Business Administration and Management—General M
Distance Education Development M,O
Education—General M,O
Educational Leadership and Administration M,O
Educational Media/Instructional Technology M,O
English as a Second Language M,O
English Education M,O
Health Education M,O
Higher Education M,O
Human Services M,O
Legal and Justice Studies M
Management Information Systems M

UNIVERSITY OF ILLINOIS AT URBANA–CHAMPAIGN

Accounting M,D
Actuarial Science M,D
Advertising and Public Relations M
Agricultural Education M
Art Education M,D
Business Administration and Management—General M,D
Counselor Education M,D,O
Curriculum and Instruction M,D,O
Education of Students with Severe/Multiple Disabilities M,D,O
Education—General M,D,O
Educational Leadership and Administration M,D,O
Educational Policy M,D,O
Educational Psychology M,D,O
English as a Second Language M,D
Finance and Banking M,D
Foreign Languages Education M,D
Human Resources Management M,D,O
Human Services M,D
Information Studies M,D,O
Kinesiology and Movement Studies M,D
Law M,D
Leisure Studies M,D
Library Science M,D,O
Management Information Systems M,D,O
Management Strategy and Policy M,D,O
Mathematics Education M,D
Music Education M,D
Science Education M,D
Social Work M,D
Special Education M,D,O

Taxation M,D

UNIVERSITY OF INDIANAPOLIS

Art Education M
Business Administration and Management—General M,O
Curriculum and Instruction M
Education—General M
Educational Leadership and Administration M
Elementary Education M
English Education M
Foreign Languages Education M
Mathematics Education M
Physical Education M
Science Education M
Secondary Education M
Social Sciences Education M
Sports Management M

THE UNIVERSITY OF IOWA

Accounting M,D
Actuarial Science M,D
Art Education M,D
Athletic Training and Sports Medicine M,D
Business Administration and Management—General M,D
Counselor Education M,D
Developmental Education M,D
Education—General M,D,O
Educational Leadership and Administration M,D,O
Educational Measurement and Evaluation M,D,O
Educational Policy M,D,O
Educational Psychology M,D,O
Elementary Education M,D
English as a Second Language M,D
English Education M,D
Exercise and Sports Science M,D
Finance and Banking D
Foreign Languages Education M,D
Foundations and Philosophy of Education M,D,O
Higher Education M,D
Information Studies M,D
Law M,D
Leisure Studies M,D
Library Science M,D
Marketing D
Mathematics Education M,D
Music Education M,D
Quantitative Analysis M,D,O
Recreation and Park Management M,D
Science Education M,D
Secondary Education M,D
Social Sciences Education M,D
Social Work M,D
Special Education M,D
Sports Management M,D
Student Affairs M,D

UNIVERSITY OF JAMESTOWN

Curriculum and Instruction M
Education—General M

THE UNIVERSITY OF KANSAS

Accounting M,D
Art Education M
Business Administration and Management—General M,D
Curriculum and Instruction M,D
Distance Education Development M,D
Early Childhood Education M,D,O
Education—General M,D,O
Educational Leadership and Administration M,D,O
Educational Measurement and Evaluation M,D
Educational Media/Instructional Technology M,D
Educational Policy M,D
Educational Psychology M,D
Exercise and Sports Science M,D
Finance and Banking M,D
Health Education M,D,O
Higher Education M,D
Human Resources Management M,D
Law D
Logistics M,D
Management Information Systems M
Management Strategy and Policy M,D
Marketing M,D
Music Education M,D
Organizational Behavior M,D
Organizational Management M,D,O
Physical Education M,D
Project Management M
Social Work M,D
Special Education M,D,O
Sports Management M,D
Supply Chain Management M,D

UNIVERSITY OF KENTUCKY

Accounting M
Art Education M
Athletic Training and Sports Medicine M
Business Administration and Management—General M,D
Curriculum and Instruction M,D
Early Childhood Education M,D
Education—General M,D,O
Educational Leadership and Administration M,D,O
Educational Measurement and Evaluation M,D
Educational Media/Instructional Technology M,D
Educational Policy M,D
Educational Psychology M,D,O
Elementary Education M,D
Exercise and Sports Science M,D
Foreign Languages Education M
Higher Education M,D

Hospitality Management M
International Business M
Kinesiology and Movement Studies M,D
Law D
Library Science M
Middle School Education M,D
Music Education M,D
Physical Education M,D
Reading Education M,D
Secondary Education M,D
Social Work M,D
Special Education M,D

UNIVERSITY OF LA VERNE

Accounting M
Business Administration and Management—General M,D,O
Counselor Education M,D,O
Education—General M,O
Educational Leadership and Administration M,D,O
Elementary Education M,D,O
Finance and Banking M
Human Resources Management M,O
International Business M
Law D
Management Information Systems M,O
Marketing M
Nonprofit Management M,O
Organizational Management M,D,O
Reading Education M,O
Secondary Education M,D,O
Special Education M,D,O
Supply Chain Management M

UNIVERSITY OF LETHBRIDGE

Accounting M,D
Business Administration and Management—General M,D
Counselor Education M,D
Education—General M,D
Educational Leadership and Administration M,D
Exercise and Sports Science M,D
Finance and Banking M,D
Human Resources Management M,D
International Business M,D
Kinesiology and Movement Studies M,D
Management Information Systems M,D
Management Strategy and Policy M,D
Marketing M,D

UNIVERSITY OF LOUISIANA AT LAFAYETTE

Business Administration and Management—General M
Counselor Education M
Curriculum and Instruction M
Education of the Gifted M
Education—General M,D
Educational Leadership and Administration M,D
Music Education M

UNIVERSITY OF LOUISIANA AT MONROE

Art Education M,D
Business Administration and Management—General M
Counselor Education M
Curriculum and Instruction M,D
Early Childhood Education M,D
Education of the Gifted M,D
Education—General M,D
Educational Leadership and Administration M,D
Educational Measurement and Evaluation M,D
Elementary Education M,D
English as a Second Language M,D
English Education M,D
Exercise and Sports Science M
Foreign Languages Education M,D
Mathematics Education M,D
Middle School Education M,D
Music Education M,D
Reading Education M,D
Recreation and Park Management M
Science Education M,D
Secondary Education M
Social Sciences Education M,D
Special Education M,D
Sports Management M

UNIVERSITY OF LOUISVILLE

Accounting M
Art Education M,D,O
Business Administration and Management—General M
Counselor Education M,D
Curriculum and Instruction M,D,O
Early Childhood Education M,D,O
Education—General M,D,O
Educational Leadership and Administration M,D,O
Educational Measurement and Evaluation M,D
Educational Psychology M,D
Elementary Education M,D,O
Entrepreneurship M,D
Exercise and Sports Science M,D,O
Health Education M,D,O
Higher Education M,D,O
Human Resources Development M,D,O
Human Resources Management M,D,O
International Business M
Law D
Logistics M,D,O
Middle School Education M,D,O
Music Education M,D,O
Nonprofit Management M,D
Physical Education M,D,O

Secondary Education M,D,O
Social Work M,D,O
Special Education M,D,O
Sports Management M,D,O
Student Affairs M,D
Supply Chain Management M,D,O
Sustainability Management M,D

UNIVERSITY OF MAINE

Business Administration and Management—General M,O
Early Childhood Education M,D,O
Education—General M,D,O
Educational Leadership and Administration M,D,O
Educational Media/Instructional Technology M,D,O
Exercise and Sports Science M,D,O
Finance and Banking M
Foreign Languages Education M
Higher Education M,D,O
Kinesiology and Movement Studies M,D,O
Law D
Physical Education M,D,O
Reading Education M,D,O
Social Sciences Education M,D,O
Social Work M,O
Special Education M,D,O

UNIVERSITY OF MAINE AT FARMINGTON

Early Childhood Education M
Education—General M
Educational Leadership and Administration M
Educational Media/Instructional Technology M

UNIVERSITY OF MANAGEMENT AND TECHNOLOGY

Business Administration and Management—General M,D,O
Management Information Systems M,O
Project Management M,D,O

THE UNIVERSITY OF MANCHESTER

Accounting M
Actuarial Science M,D
Business Administration and Management—General M
Education—General M,D
Educational Psychology M,D
English as a Second Language M,D
Entrepreneurship M
Finance and Banking M
Health Law M,D
Human Resources Management M
Industrial and Manufacturing Management M,D
International Business M
Law M,D
Management Strategy and Policy M
Marketing M
Project Management M
Social Work M,D
Supply Chain Management M

UNIVERSITY OF MANITOBA

Adult Education M
Archives/Archival Administration M,D
Business Administration and Management—General M,D
Counselor Education M
Curriculum and Instruction M
Education—General M,D
Educational Leadership and Administration M
Educational Psychology M
English as a Second Language M
English Education M
Foundations and Philosophy of Education M
Higher Education M
Kinesiology and Movement Studies M
Law M
Physical Education M
Recreation and Park Management M
Social Work M,D
Special Education M

UNIVERSITY OF MARY

Business Administration and Management—General M
Curriculum and Instruction M,D
Education—General M,D
Educational Leadership and Administration M,D
Exercise and Sports Science M
Human Resources Management M
Kinesiology and Movement Studies M
Physical Education M
Project Management M
Reading Education M,D
Special Education M,D
Sports Management M

UNIVERSITY OF MARY HARDIN-BAYLOR

Accounting M
Business Administration and Management—General M
Counselor Education M
Curriculum and Instruction M,D
Education—General M,D
Educational Leadership and Administration M,D
Elementary Education M,D
Exercise and Sports Science M
Higher Education M,D
International Business M
Management Information Systems M
Secondary Education M,D
Sports Management M

UNIVERSITY OF MARYLAND, BALTIMORE

Law M,D
Social Work M,D

UNIVERSITY OF MARYLAND, BALTIMORE COUNTY

Art Education M
Distance Education Development M,O
Early Childhood Education M
Education—General M,O
Educational Media/Instructional Technology M,O
Educational Policy M,D
Elementary Education M
English as a Second Language M,O
English Education M
Foreign Languages Education M
Health Education M,D,O
Human Services M,D
Mathematics Education M
Multilingual and Multicultural Education M,D
Music Education M
Nonprofit Management M,O
Science Education M
Social Sciences Education M

UNIVERSITY OF MARYLAND, COLLEGE PARK

Advertising and Public Relations M,D
Business Administration and Management—General M,D
Counselor Education M,D,O
Curriculum and Instruction M,D,O
Education—General M,D,O
Educational Leadership and Administration M,D,O
Educational Measurement and Evaluation M,D
Educational Media/Instructional Technology M,D,O
English as a Second Language M,D,O
Foreign Languages Education D
Foundations and Philosophy of Education M,D,O
Health Education M,D
Information Studies M,D
Kinesiology and Movement Studies M,D
Law
Library Science
Music Education M,D
Quantitative Analysis M,D
Reading Education M,D,O
Real Estate M
Secondary Education M,D,O
Social Work
Student Affairs M,D,O

UNIVERSITY OF MARYLAND EASTERN SHORE

Counselor Education M
Education—General M
Educational Leadership and Administration D
Organizational Management D
Special Education M
Vocational and Technical Education M

UNIVERSITY OF MARYLAND UNIVERSITY COLLEGE

Accounting M
Business Administration and Management—General M,D,O
Distance Education Development M
Education—General M
Educational Media/Instructional Technology M
Finance and Banking M

UNIVERSITY OF MARY WASHINGTON

Business Administration and Management—General M
Education—General M
Elementary Education M

UNIVERSITY OF MASSACHUSETTS AMHERST

Accounting M,D
Art Education M
Business Administration and Management—General M,D
Counselor Education M,D,O
Early Childhood Education M,D,O
Education—General M,D,O
Educational Leadership and Administration M,D,O
Educational Measurement and Evaluation M,D,O
Educational Media/Instructional Technology M,D,O
Educational Policy M,D,O
Elementary Education M,D,O
English as a Second Language M,D,O
Entertainment Management
Entrepreneurship M,D
Finance and Banking M,D
Foreign Languages Education M
Health Education M,D
Higher Education M,D,O
Hospitality Management M,D
International and Comparative Education M,D,O
Kinesiology and Movement Studies M,D
Management Strategy and Policy M,D
Marketing M,D
Multilingual and Multicultural Education M,D,O
Music Education M,D
Organizational Management M,D
Reading Education M,D,O
Science Education M,D,O

Secondary Education M,D,O
Special Education M,D,O
Sports Management M,D
Travel and Tourism M,D

UNIVERSITY OF MASSACHUSETTS BOSTON

Accounting M
Archives/Archival Administration M
Business Administration and Management—General M
Counselor Education M
Early Childhood Education D
Education—General M,D
Educational Leadership and Administration M,D,O
Educational Media/Instructional Technology M,O
Educational Policy D
Exercise and Sports Science M,D
Finance and Banking M
Higher Education D
Human Services M
International Business M
Management Information Systems M
Quality Management M,O
Special Education M
Urban Education D

UNIVERSITY OF MASSACHUSETTS DARTMOUTH

Accounting M,O
Art Education M
Business Administration and Management—General M,O
Early Childhood Education M,D,O
Education—General M,D,O
Educational Leadership and Administration D
Educational Policy M,D,O
English as a Second Language M,D,O
Finance and Banking M,O
International Business M,O
Law D
Management Information Systems M,O
Management Strategy and Policy M,O
Marketing M,O
Mathematics Education M,D,O
Middle School Education M,D,O
Organizational Management M,O
Science Education M,D,O
Secondary Education M,D,O
Special Education M,O
Supply Chain Management M,O

UNIVERSITY OF MASSACHUSETTS LOWELL

Business Administration and Management—General M,D
Curriculum and Instruction M
Education—General M
Entrepreneurship M,D
Legal and Justice Studies M
Music Education M

UNIVERSITY OF MEMPHIS

Accounting M,D
Adult Education M,D,O
Business Administration and Management—General M,D
Community College Education M,D,O
Counselor Education M,D
Curriculum and Instruction M,D,O
Early Childhood Education M,D,O
Education—General M,D,O
Educational Leadership and Administration M,D,O
Educational Measurement and Evaluation M,D
Educational Media/Instructional Technology M,D,O
Educational Psychology M,D
Elementary Education M,D,O
English as a Second Language M,D,O
Exercise and Sports Science M,O
Finance and Banking M,D
Higher Education M,D,O
Hospitality Management M,O
Human Resources Management M,O
Law D
Management Information Systems M,D,O
Management Strategy and Policy M,O
Marketing M,D
Mathematics Education M,D
Music Education M,D
Nonprofit Management M,O
Physical Education M,O
Reading Education M,D,O
Real Estate M,D
Science Education M,D,O
Secondary Education M,D,O
Social Work M
Special Education M,D,O
Supply Chain Management M,D
Urban Education M,D,O

UNIVERSITY OF MIAMI

Advertising and Public Relations M,D
Athletic Training and Sports Medicine M,D
Business Administration and Management—General M,D
Counselor Education M,O
Early Childhood Education M,O
Education—General M,D,O
Educational Measurement and Evaluation M,D
Exercise and Sports Science M,D
Higher Education M,D,O
Law M,D
Mathematics Education D

*M—masters degree; D—doctorate; O—other advanced degree; *—Close-Up and/or Display*

Multilingual and Multicultural Education D
Music Education M,D,O
Reading Education D
Real Estate M,D
Science Education D
Special Education M,D,O
Sports Management M
Taxation M,D

UNIVERSITY OF MICHIGAN
Accounting M,D
Business Administration and Management—General M,D
Education—General M,D
English Education D
Foreign Languages Education M,D
Health Education M,D
Information Studies M,D
Kinesiology and Movement Studies M,D
Law M,D
Music Education M,D,O
Social Work M,D
Sports Management M,D
Supply Chain Management M,D
Taxation M,D

UNIVERSITY OF MICHIGAN–DEARBORN
Accounting M
Business Administration and Management—General M
Curriculum and Instruction D,O
Early Childhood Education M
Education—General M
Educational Leadership and Administration M,D,O
Educational Measurement and Evaluation M
Educational Media/Instructional Technology M
Finance and Banking M
Management Information Systems M
Management Strategy and Policy M
Project Management M
Science Education M
Special Education M
Supply Chain Management M
Urban Education M,D

UNIVERSITY OF MICHIGAN–FLINT
Accounting M,O
Business Administration and Management—General M,O
Curriculum and Instruction M,D,O
Early Childhood Education M,D,O
Education—General M,D,O
Educational Leadership and Administration M,D,O
Educational Media/Instructional Technology M,D,O
Finance and Banking M,O
Health Education M
Industrial and Manufacturing Management M,O
International Business M,O
Management Information Systems M,O
Marketing M,O
Nonprofit Management M
Organizational Management M,O
Reading Education M,D,O
Secondary Education M,D,O

UNIVERSITY OF MINNESOTA, DULUTH
Business Administration and Management—General M
Education—General M,D
Music Education M
Social Work M

UNIVERSITY OF MINNESOTA ROCHESTER
Business Administration and Management—General M,D

UNIVERSITY OF MINNESOTA, TWIN CITIES CAMPUS
Accounting M,D
Adult Education M,O
Art Education M
Business Administration and Management—General M,D
Counselor Education M
Curriculum and Instruction M,D,O
Early Childhood Education M,D,O
Education of the Gifted M,D,O
Education—General M,D,O
Educational Leadership and Administration M,D
Educational Measurement and Evaluation M,D
Educational Media/Instructional Technology M,D,O
Educational Policy M,D
Educational Psychology M,D,O
Elementary Education M
English as a Second Language M,D,O
English Education M
Entrepreneurship D
Exercise and Sports Science M,D
Finance and Banking M,D
Foreign Languages Education M
Foundations and Philosophy of Education M,D
Higher Education M,D
Human Resources Development M,D,O
Human Resources Management M
Industrial and Manufacturing Management M
International and Comparative Education M,D
Kinesiology and Movement Studies M,D
Law M,D
Management Information Systems M,D
Management Strategy and Policy D
Marketing M,D
Mathematics Education M,D,O

Multilingual and Multicultural Education M,D,O
Quantitative Analysis M,D,O
Reading Education M,D,O
Science Education M
Social Sciences Education M
Social Work M,D
Special Education M,D
Sports Management M,D
Student Affairs M
Supply Chain Management M,D
Taxation M
Travel and Tourism M,D
Vocational and Technical Education M,D,O

UNIVERSITY OF MISSISSIPPI
Accounting M,D
Business Administration and Management—General M,D
Education—General M,D,O
Exercise and Sports Science M,D
Foreign Languages Education M,D
Kinesiology and Movement Studies M,D
Law M,D
Management Information Systems M,D
Recreation and Park Management M,D
Social Work M,D
Taxation M,D

UNIVERSITY OF MISSOURI
Accounting M,D,O
Adult Education M,D,O
Agricultural Education M,D,O
Art Education M,D,O
Business Administration and Management—General M,D
Business Education M,D,O
Curriculum and Instruction M,D,O
Early Childhood Education M,D,O
Education of the Gifted M,D
Education—General M,D,O
Educational Leadership and Administration M,D,O
Educational Media/Instructional Technology M,D,O
Educational Psychology M,D,O
Elementary Education M,D,O
English Education M,D,O
Finance and Banking M,D
Foreign Languages Education M,D,O
Health Education M,D,O
Higher Education M,D,O
Hospitality Management M,D
Information Studies M,D,O
Law M,D
Library Science M,D,O
Marketing M,D
Mathematics Education M,D,O
Music Education M,D,O
Nonprofit Management M,D,O
Organizational Management M,D,O
Reading Education M,D,O
Science Education M,D,O
Social Sciences Education M,D,O
Social Work M,D,O
Special Education M,D
Taxation M,D,O
Vocational and Technical Education M,D,O

UNIVERSITY OF MISSOURI–KANSAS CITY
Accounting M,D
Business Administration and Management—General M,D
Counselor Education M,D,O
Curriculum and Instruction M,D,O
Education—General M,D,O
Educational Leadership and Administration M,D,O
Finance and Banking M,D
Health Education M,D
Higher Education M,D,O
Law M,D
Music Education M,D
Reading Education M,D,O
Social Work M
Special Education M,D,O

UNIVERSITY OF MISSOURI–ST. LOUIS
Accounting M,D,O
Adult Education M,D,O
Business Administration and Management—General M,D,O
Counselor Education M,D
Curriculum and Instruction M
Early Childhood Education M
Education—General M,D,O
Educational Leadership and Administration M,D,O
Educational Measurement and Evaluation M,D,O
Educational Policy M,D,O
Educational Psychology D
Elementary Education M,D
English as a Second Language M
Finance and Banking M,D,O
Higher Education M,D,O
Human Resources Management M,D,O
Industrial and Manufacturing Management M,D,O
International Business M,D,O
Logistics M,D,O
Management Information Systems M,D,O
Management Strategy and Policy M,D,O
Marketing M,D,O
Middle School Education M
Music Education M
Nonprofit Management M,O
Reading Education M
Science Education M,D,O
Secondary Education M,D
Social Work M
Special Education M
Supply Chain Management M,D,O

UNIVERSITY OF MOBILE
Business Administration and Management—General M
Education—General M

UNIVERSITY OF MONTANA
Accounting M
Art Education M
Business Administration and Management—General M
Counselor Education M,D,O
Curriculum and Instruction M,D
Early Childhood Education M,D
Education—General M,D,O
Educational Leadership and Administration M,D,O
English Education M
Exercise and Sports Science M
Health Education M
Law D
Legal and Justice Studies M
Mathematics Education M,D
Physical Education M
Recreation and Park Management M,D
Social Work M

UNIVERSITY OF MONTEVALLO
Business Administration and Management—General M
Counselor Education M
Education—General M,O
Educational Leadership and Administration M,O
Elementary Education M
Secondary Education M

UNIVERSITY OF MOUNT OLIVE
Business Administration and Management—General M

UNIVERSITY OF MOUNT UNION
Educational Leadership and Administration M

UNIVERSITY OF NEBRASKA AT KEARNEY
Accounting M
Art Education M
Business Administration and Management—General M
Counselor Education M,O
Curriculum and Instruction M
Early Childhood Education M
Education of the Gifted M
Education—General M,O
Educational Leadership and Administration M,O
Educational Media/Instructional Technology M
Elementary Education M
English as a Second Language M
Exercise and Sports Science M
Foreign Languages Education M
Human Resources Management M
Human Services M
Leisure Studies M
Library Science M
Management Information Systems M
Marketing M
Mathematics Education M
Music Education M
Physical Education M
Reading Education M
Recreation and Park Management M
Science Education M
Secondary Education M
Special Education M,O
Sports Management M
Student Affairs M,O

UNIVERSITY OF NEBRASKA AT OMAHA
Accounting M
Athletic Training and Sports Medicine M,D
Business Administration and Management—General M,O
Counselor Education M
Education—General M,D,O
Educational Leadership and Administration M,D,O
Elementary Education M
English as a Second Language M,O
Exercise and Sports Science M,D
Foreign Languages Education M
Health Education M,D
Human Resources Development M,D,O
Kinesiology and Movement Studies M,D
Management Information Systems M,D,O
Organizational Management M
Project Management M,D,O
Science Education M,O
Secondary Education M,O
Social Work M
Special Education M
Urban Education M,O

UNIVERSITY OF NEBRASKA–LINCOLN
Accounting M,D
Actuarial Science M
Adult Education M,D,O
Advertising and Public Relations M,D
Agricultural Education M
Business Administration and Management—General M,D
Curriculum and Instruction M,D,O
Early Childhood Education M,D
Educational Leadership and Administration M,D,O
Educational Measurement and Evaluation M,D,O
Educational Psychology M,D,O
Exercise and Sports Science M,D
Finance and Banking M,D
Home Economics Education M,D
Law M,D
Legal and Justice Studies M

Management Information Systems M
Marketing M,D
Music Education M,D
Special Education M,D,O
Vocational and Technical Education M,D,O

UNIVERSITY OF NEVADA, LAS VEGAS
Accounting M,O
Business Administration and Management—General M,O
Counselor Education M,D,O
Curriculum and Instruction M,D,O
Distance Education Development M,D,O
Early Childhood Education M,D,O
Education—General M,D,O
Educational Leadership and Administration M,D,O
Educational Media/Instructional Technology M,D,O
Elementary Education M,D,O
English as a Second Language M,D,O
Exercise and Sports Science M,D
Higher Education M,D,O
Hospitality Management M,D
Kinesiology and Movement Studies M,D
Law M,D
Management Information Systems M,O
Nonprofit Management M,D,O
Secondary Education M,D,O
Social Work M
Special Education M,D,O

UNIVERSITY OF NEVADA, RENO
Accounting M
Business Administration and Management—General M
Counselor Education M,D,O
Curriculum and Instruction D
Education—General M,D,O
Educational Leadership and Administration M,D,O
Educational Psychology M,D,O
Elementary Education M
English as a Second Language M
Finance and Banking M
Foreign Languages Education M
Legal and Justice Studies M,D
Management Information Systems M
Mathematics Education M
Reading Education M,D
Secondary Education M
Social Work M
Special Education M,D

UNIVERSITY OF NEW BRUNSWICK FREDERICTON
Business Administration and Management—General M
Education—General M,D
Entrepreneurship M
Exercise and Sports Science M
Marketing M,D
Physical Education M
Recreation and Park Management M
Sports Management M

UNIVERSITY OF NEW BRUNSWICK SAINT JOHN
Business Administration and Management—General M
Electronic Commerce M
International Business M

UNIVERSITY OF NEW ENGLAND
Curriculum and Instruction M,D,O
Early Childhood Education M,D,O
Education—General M,D,O
Educational Leadership and Administration M,D,O
Reading Education M,D,O
Social Work M,D,O
Vocational and Technical Education M,D,O

UNIVERSITY OF NEW HAMPSHIRE
Accounting M
Business Administration and Management—General M,O
Curriculum and Instruction D,O
Early Childhood Education M,D,O
Education—General M,D,O
Educational Leadership and Administration M,O
Educational Media/Instructional Technology M,O
Elementary Education M,O
Higher Education O
Intellectual Property Law M,D,O
Kinesiology and Movement Studies M,O
Law M,D,O
Legal and Justice Studies M,D,O
Management Information Systems M,O
Mathematics Education M,D,O
Physical Education M,O
Recreation and Park Management M
Science Education M,D
Secondary Education M,O
Social Work M,O
Special Education M
Sustainability Management M,O

UNIVERSITY OF NEW HAVEN
Accounting M,O
Business Administration and Management—General M,O
Facilities Management M,O
Finance and Banking M,O
Human Resources Management M,O
Industrial and Manufacturing Management M,O
International Business M,O
Management Strategy and Policy M,O
Marketing M,O
Organizational Management M,O
Science Education M,O
Sports Management M,O
Taxation M,O

UNIVERSITY OF NEW MEXICO

Accounting	M
Art Education	M
Business Administration and Management—General	M
Counselor Education	M,D
Early Childhood Education	D
Education—General	M,D,O
Educational Leadership and Administration	M,D,O
Educational Media/Instructional Technology	M,D,O
Educational Psychology	M,D
Elementary Education	M
English as a Second Language	M,D
English Education	M,D
Entrepreneurship	M
Exercise and Sports Science	D
Finance and Banking	M
Foundations and Philosophy of Education	M,D
Health Education	M
Higher Education	O
Human Resources Management	M
International Business	M
Law	D
Management Information Systems	M
Management Strategy and Policy	M
Marketing	M
Multilingual and Multicultural Education	M,D
Music Education	M
Organizational Behavior	M
Organizational Management	M
Physical Education	D
Quantitative Analysis	D
Reading Education	M,D
Science Education	O
Secondary Education	M
Special Education	M,D,O
Sports Management	D
Taxation	M

UNIVERSITY OF NEW ORLEANS

Accounting	M
Business Administration and Management—General	M
Counselor Education	M,D
Curriculum and Instruction	M,D
Education—General	M,D
Educational Leadership and Administration	M,D
Finance and Banking	M,D
Hospitality Management	M
Special Education	M,D
Taxation	M
Transportation Management	M
Travel and Tourism	M

UNIVERSITY OF NORTH ALABAMA

Accounting	M
Business Administration and Management—General	M
Counselor Education	M
Education—General	M,O
Educational Leadership and Administration	M
Elementary Education	M,O
Exercise and Sports Science	M
Finance and Banking	M
International Business	M
Kinesiology and Movement Studies	M
Law	M
Management Information Systems	M
Physical Education	M
Project Management	M
Secondary Education	M
Special Education	M

THE UNIVERSITY OF NORTH CAROLINA AT CHAPEL HILL

Accounting	M,D
Athletic Training and Sports Medicine	M
Business Administration and Management—General	M,D
Counselor Education	M,D
Curriculum and Instruction	M,D
Early Childhood Education	M,D
Education—General	M,D
Educational Leadership and Administration	M,D
Educational Measurement and Evaluation	M,D
Educational Psychology	M,D
English as a Second Language	M
English Education	M
Exercise and Sports Science	M
Finance and Banking	D
Foreign Languages Education	M
Information Studies	M,D,O
Kinesiology and Movement Studies	M,D
Law	D
Library Science	M,D,O
Management Information Systems	D
Management Strategy and Policy	D
Marketing	D
Mathematics Education	M
Music Education	M
Organizational Behavior	D
Physical Education	M
Reading Education	M,D
Science Education	M
Secondary Education	M
Social Sciences Education	M
Social Work	M,D
Sports Management	M

THE UNIVERSITY OF NORTH CAROLINA AT CHARLOTTE

Accounting	M
Art Education	M,D,O
Business Administration and Management—General	M,D,O
Business Education	D
Counselor Education	M,D,O
Curriculum and Instruction	M,D,O
Early Childhood Education	M,D,O
Education of the Gifted	M,D,O
Education—General	M,D,O
Educational Leadership and Administration	M,D,O
Educational Media/Instructional Technology	M,D,O
Elementary Education	M,O
English as a Second Language	M,D,O
Facilities Management	M,O
Finance and Banking	M,O
Foreign Languages Education	M,D,O
Industrial and Manufacturing Management	M,D,O
Kinesiology and Movement Studies	M
Logistics	M,O
Management Information Systems	M,D,O
Middle School Education	M,D,O
Nonprofit Management	M,O
Reading Education	M,O
Real Estate	M,O
Secondary Education	M,D,O
Social Work	M
Special Education	M,D,O
Supply Chain Management	M,O

THE UNIVERSITY OF NORTH CAROLINA AT GREENSBORO

Accounting	M,O
Adult Education	M,D,O
Athletic Training and Sports Medicine	M,D
Business Administration and Management—General	M,O
Counselor Education	M,D,O
Curriculum and Instruction	M,D,O
Early Childhood Education	M,D,O
Education—General	M,D,O
Educational Leadership and Administration	M,D,O
Educational Measurement and Evaluation	D
Educational Media/Instructional Technology	M,D,O
Elementary Education	D
English as a Second Language	M,D,O
English Education	M,D
Finance and Banking	M,O
Foreign Languages Education	M,D,O
Higher Education	D
Information Studies	M
Kinesiology and Movement Studies	M,D
Library Science	M
Management Information Systems	M,D,O
Marketing	M,D
Mathematics Education	M,D,O
Middle School Education	M,D,O
Multilingual and Multicultural Education	M,D,O
Music Education	M,D
Nonprofit Management	M,O
Reading Education	M,D,O
Recreation and Park Management	M
Science Education	M,D,O
Social Sciences Education	M,D,O
Social Work	M
Special Education	M,D,O
Supply Chain Management	M,D,O

THE UNIVERSITY OF NORTH CAROLINA AT PEMBROKE

Art Education	M
Business Administration and Management—General	M
Counselor Education	M
Education—General	M
Educational Leadership and Administration	M
Elementary Education	M
English Education	M
Exercise and Sports Science	M
Mathematics Education	M
Physical Education	M
Reading Education	M
Science Education	M
Social Sciences Education	M
Social Work	M

THE UNIVERSITY OF NORTH CAROLINA WILMINGTON

Accounting	M
Business Administration and Management—General	M
Curriculum and Instruction	M,D
Early Childhood Education	M
Education of the Gifted	M
Education—General	M,D
Educational Leadership and Administration	M,D
Educational Media/Instructional Technology	M
Educational Policy	M
Elementary Education	M
English as a Second Language	M
Foreign Languages Education	M
Health Education	M
Higher Education	M,D
International Business	M
Management Information Systems	M
Middle School Education	M
Physical Education	M
Reading Education	M
Secondary Education	M
Social Work	M
Special Education	M

UNIVERSITY OF NORTH DAKOTA

Business Administration and Management—General	M
Early Childhood Education	M
Education—General	M,D,O
Educational Leadership and Administration	M,D,O
Educational Media/Instructional Technology	M
Elementary Education	M
Kinesiology and Movement Studies	M
Music Education	M,D
Reading Education	M
Social Work	M
Special Education	M

UNIVERSITY OF NORTHERN BRITISH COLUMBIA

Education—General	M,D,O
Social Work	M,D,O

UNIVERSITY OF NORTHERN COLORADO

Accounting	M
Art Education	M
Business Administration and Management—General	M
Counselor Education	M
Curriculum and Instruction	M,D
Education of the Gifted	M,D
Education—General	M,D,O
Educational Leadership and Administration	M,D,O
Educational Measurement and Evaluation	M,D
Educational Policy	M,D,O
Educational Psychology	M,D
Elementary Education	M,D
English as a Second Language	M,D
English Education	M,D
Exercise and Sports Science	M,D
Foreign Languages Education	M,D
Health Education	M
Higher Education	M,D
Human Resources Management	M
Mathematics Education	M,D
Multilingual and Multicultural Education	M,D
Music Education	M,D
Physical Education	M,D
Reading Education	M,D
Science Education	M,D
Special Education	M,D
Sports Management	M,D
Student Affairs	M,D

UNIVERSITY OF NORTHERN IOWA

Accounting	M
Art Education	M
Athletic Training and Sports Medicine	M
Business Administration and Management—General	M
Community College Education	M
Counselor Education	M
Curriculum and Instruction	D
Early Childhood Education	M
Education—General	M,D,O
Educational Leadership and Administration	M,D
Educational Measurement and Evaluation	M
Educational Media/Instructional Technology	M
Educational Psychology	M
Elementary Education	M
English as a Second Language	M
English Education	M
Foreign Languages Education	M
Health Education	M
Higher Education	M
Human Services	M
Kinesiology and Movement Studies	M
Mathematics Education	M
Middle School Education	M
Music Education	M
Nonprofit Management	M
Physical Education	M
Reading Education	M
Science Education	M
Secondary Education	M
Social Work	M
Special Education	M
Sports Management	M
Student Affairs	M
Vocational and Technical Education	M,D

UNIVERSITY OF NORTH FLORIDA

Accounting	M
Adult Education	M
Business Administration and Management—General	M
Counselor Education	M,D
Education—General	M,D
Educational Leadership and Administration	M,D
Educational Media/Instructional Technology	M,D
Electronic Commerce	M
Elementary Education	M
English as a Second Language	M
Exercise and Sports Science	M,D
Finance and Banking	M
Human Resources Management	M
International Business	M
Logistics	M
Management Information Systems	M
Nonprofit Management	M,O
Reading Education	M
Secondary Education	M
Special Education	M
Sports Management	M,D

UNIVERSITY OF NORTH GEORGIA

Business Administration and Management—General	M
Early Childhood Education	M,O
Education—General	M,O
Educational Leadership and Administration	M,O
English Education	M,O
Mathematics Education	M,O
Middle School Education	M,O
Physical Education	M,O
Secondary Education	M,O
Social Sciences Education	M,O

UNIVERSITY OF NORTH TEXAS

Accounting	M,D,O
Advertising and Public Relations	M,D,O
Art Education	M,D,O
Business Administration and Management—General	M,D,O
Counselor Education	M,D,O
Curriculum and Instruction	M,D,O
Early Childhood Education	M,D,O
Education of the Gifted	M,D,O
Education—General	M,D,O
Educational Leadership and Administration	M,D,O
Educational Measurement and Evaluation	M,D,O
Educational Psychology	M,D,O
English as a Second Language	M,D,O
Finance and Banking	M,D,O
Higher Education	M,D,O
Hospitality Management	M,D,O
Human Resources Management	M,D,O
Industrial and Manufacturing Management	M,D,O
Kinesiology and Movement Studies	M,D,O
Logistics	M,D,O
Management Information Systems	M,D,O
Management Strategy and Policy	M,D,O
Marketing	M,D,O
Music Education	M,D,O
Nonprofit Management	M,D,O
Quantitative Analysis	M,D,O
Special Education	M,D,O
Supply Chain Management	M,D,O
Travel and Tourism	M,D,O
Vocational and Technical Education	M,D,O

UNIVERSITY OF NORTH TEXAS AT DALLAS

Accounting	M
Business Administration and Management—General	M
Counselor Education	M
Curriculum and Instruction	M
Educational Leadership and Administration	M
Human Resources Management	M
Management Strategy and Policy	M
Organizational Behavior	M

UNIVERSITY OF NORTHWESTERN–ST. PAUL

Business Administration and Management—General	M
Education—General	M
Human Services	M
Organizational Management	M

UNIVERSITY OF NOTRE DAME

Accounting	M
Business Administration and Management—General	M
Education—General	M
Entrepreneurship	M
Finance and Banking	M
Investment Management	M
Law	M,D
Management Strategy and Policy	M
Marketing	M
Nonprofit Management	M
Taxation	M

UNIVERSITY OF OKLAHOMA

Accounting	M,D
Adult Education	M
Business Administration and Management—General	M,D
Curriculum and Instruction	M,D
Early Childhood Education	M,D
Education—General	M,D,O
Educational Leadership and Administration	M,D
Educational Media/Instructional Technology	M,D
Educational Policy	M,D
Educational Psychology	M,D
Elementary Education	M,D
English Education	M,D
Entrepreneurship	M,D
Exercise and Sports Science	M,D
Finance and Banking	M,D
Foreign Languages Education	M,D
Higher Education	M,D,O
Human Resources Management	M,O
Human Services	M,O
Information Studies	M
International Business	M,D
Law	M,D
Library Science	M
Management Information Systems	M,D,O
Marketing	M,D
Mathematics Education	M,D
Music Education	M,D,O
Nonprofit Management	M,O
Organizational Behavior	M,O
Organizational Management	M,O
Project Management	M,O
Reading Education	M,D
Science Education	M,D

*M—masters degree; D—doctorate; O—other advanced degree; *—Close-Up and/or Display*

Social Sciences Education M,D
Social Work M
Special Education M,D
Student Affairs M
Supply Chain Management M,D

UNIVERSITY OF OKLAHOMA HEALTH SCIENCES CENTER
Health Education D
Reading Education M,D,O
Special Education M,D,O

UNIVERSITY OF OREGON
Accounting M,D
Business Administration and Management—General M,D
Education—General M,D
Finance and Banking D
Law M,D
Management Information Systems M
Marketing D
Music Education M,D
Quantitative Analysis M
Sports Management M

UNIVERSITY OF OTTAWA
Business Administration and Management—General M
Education—General M,D,O
Electronic Commerce M,D,O
Finance and Banking D,O
Kinesiology and Movement Studies M
Law M,D
Music Education M,D
Project Management M,O
Social Work M

UNIVERSITY OF PENNSYLVANIA
Accounting M,D
Business Administration and Management—General M,D
Counselor Education M
Education—General M,D,O
Educational Leadership and Administration M,D
Educational Measurement and Evaluation M,D
Educational Media/Instructional Technology M
Educational Policy M,D
Elementary Education M
English as a Second Language M,D
English Education M,D
Entrepreneurship M
Finance and Banking M,D
Foundations and Philosophy of Education M,D
Higher Education M,D
Insurance M,D
International and Comparative Education M
International Business M
Law M,D
Legal and Justice Studies M,D
Management Information Systems M,D
Marketing M,D
Multilingual and Multicultural Education M
Nonprofit Management M,O
Organizational Management M,O
Reading Education M
Real Estate M,D
Science Education M,O
Secondary Education M
Social Work M,D
Urban Education M

UNIVERSITY OF PHOENIX–ATLANTA CAMPUS
Accounting M
Business Administration and Management—General M
Human Resources Management M
International Business M
Management Information Systems M
Marketing M

UNIVERSITY OF PHOENIX–AUGUSTA CAMPUS
Accounting M
Business Administration and Management—General M
Human Resources Management M
International Business M
Management Information Systems M
Marketing M

UNIVERSITY OF PHOENIX–BAY AREA CAMPUS
Accounting M,D
Adult Education M,D,O
Business Administration and Management—General M,D
Early Childhood Education M,D,O
Education—General M,D,O
Educational Leadership and Administration M,D,O
Elementary Education M,D,O
Higher Education M,D,O
Human Resources Management M,D
International Business M,D
Management Information Systems M,D
Marketing M,D
Organizational Management M,D
Project Management M,D
Secondary Education M,D,O
Special Education M,D,O

UNIVERSITY OF PHOENIX–CENTRAL VALLEY CAMPUS
Accounting M
Business Administration and Management—General M
Computer Education M
Curriculum and Instruction M
Education—General M
Elementary Education M
Human Resources Management M
International Business M
Management Information Systems M
Marketing M
Secondary Education M

UNIVERSITY OF PHOENIX–CHARLOTTE CAMPUS
Accounting M
Business Administration and Management—General M
Health Education M
International Business M
Management Information Systems M

UNIVERSITY OF PHOENIX–COLORADO CAMPUS
Accounting M
Business Administration and Management—General M
Curriculum and Instruction M
Education—General M
Educational Leadership and Administration M
Electronic Commerce M
Elementary Education M
Human Resources Management M
International Business M
Management Information Systems M
Marketing M
Secondary Education M

UNIVERSITY OF PHOENIX–COLORADO SPRINGS DOWNTOWN CAMPUS
Accounting M
Business Administration and Management—General M
Curriculum and Instruction M,O
Education—General M,O
Educational Leadership and Administration M,O
Elementary Education M,O
Health Education M
Human Resources Management M
International Business M
Management Information Systems M
Marketing M
Secondary Education M,O

UNIVERSITY OF PHOENIX–COLUMBUS GEORGIA CAMPUS
Accounting M
Business Administration and Management—General M
Electronic Commerce M
Human Resources Management M
International Business M
Management Information Systems M
Marketing M

UNIVERSITY OF PHOENIX–DALLAS CAMPUS
Accounting M
Business Administration and Management—General M
Curriculum and Instruction M
Education—General M
Electronic Commerce M
Human Resources Management M
International Business M
Management Information Systems M
Marketing M

UNIVERSITY OF PHOENIX–HAWAII CAMPUS
Accounting M
Business Administration and Management—General M
Curriculum and Instruction M
Education—General M
Educational Leadership and Administration M
Elementary Education M
Human Resources Management M
International Business M
Management Information Systems M
Marketing M
Secondary Education M
Special Education M

UNIVERSITY OF PHOENIX–HOUSTON CAMPUS
Accounting M
Business Administration and Management—General M
Curriculum and Instruction M
Education—General M
Electronic Commerce M
Human Resources Management M
International Business M
Management Information Systems M
Marketing M

UNIVERSITY OF PHOENIX–JERSEY CITY CAMPUS
Accounting M
Business Administration and Management—General M
Human Resources Management M
International Business M
Management Information Systems M
Marketing M

UNIVERSITY OF PHOENIX–LAS VEGAS CAMPUS
Accounting M
Business Administration and Management—General M
Counselor Education M
Curriculum and Instruction M
Education—General M
Educational Leadership and Administration M
Elementary Education M
Human Resources Management M
International Business M
Management Information Systems M
Marketing M

UNIVERSITY OF PHOENIX–NEW MEXICO CAMPUS
Accounting M
Business Administration and Management—General M
Counselor Education M
Curriculum and Instruction M
Education—General M
Educational Leadership and Administration M
Electronic Commerce M
Elementary Education M
Human Resources Management M
International Business M
Management Information Systems M
Marketing M
Secondary Education M

UNIVERSITY OF PHOENIX–NORTH FLORIDA CAMPUS
Accounting M
Business Administration and Management—General M
Computer Education M
Curriculum and Instruction M
Early Childhood Education M
Education—General M
Educational Leadership and Administration M
Elementary Education M
Human Resources Management M
International Business M
Management Information Systems M
Marketing M
Mathematics Education M
Secondary Education M

UNIVERSITY OF PHOENIX–ONLINE CAMPUS
Accounting M,O
Adult Education M,O
Business Administration and Management—General M,D,O
Computer Education M,O
Curriculum and Instruction M,D,O
Early Childhood Education M,O
Education—General M,O
Educational Leadership and Administration M,D,O
Educational Media/Instructional Technology D,O
Elementary Education M,O
English as a Second Language M,O
English Education M,O
Health Education M,O
Higher Education D,O
Human Resources Management M,O
International Business M,O
Management Information Systems M,O
Marketing M,O
Mathematics Education M,O
Middle School Education M,O
Organizational Management D,O
Project Management M,O
Reading Education M,O
Science Education M,O
Secondary Education M,O
Special Education M,O

UNIVERSITY OF PHOENIX–PHOENIX CAMPUS
Accounting M,O
Adult Education M
Business Administration and Management—General M,O
Counselor Education M
Curriculum and Instruction M
Early Childhood Education M
Education—General M
Educational Leadership and Administration M
Elementary Education M
Human Resources Management M,O
International Business M,O
Marketing M,O
Project Management M,O
Reading Education M
Secondary Education M
Special Education M
Vocational and Technical Education M

UNIVERSITY OF PHOENIX–SACRAMENTO VALLEY CAMPUS
Accounting M
Adult Education M,O
Business Administration and Management—General M
Curriculum and Instruction M,O
Education—General M,O
Elementary Education M,O
Human Resources Management M
International Business M
Management Information Systems M
Marketing M
Secondary Education M,O

UNIVERSITY OF PHOENIX–SAN ANTONIO CAMPUS
Accounting M
Business Administration and Management—General M
Curriculum and Instruction M
Electronic Commerce M
Human Resources Management M
International Business M
Management Information Systems M
Marketing M

UNIVERSITY OF PHOENIX–SAN DIEGO CAMPUS
Accounting M
Business Administration and Management—General M
Computer Education M
Curriculum and Instruction M
Education—General M
Elementary Education M
English as a Second Language M
Human Resources Management M
International Business M
Management Information Systems M
Marketing M
Secondary Education M

UNIVERSITY OF PHOENIX–SOUTHERN ARIZONA CAMPUS
Accounting M
Adult Education M,O
Business Administration and Management—General M
Counselor Education M,O
Curriculum and Instruction M,O
Education—General M,O
Educational Leadership and Administration M,O
Educational Psychology M,O
Elementary Education M,O
Human Resources Management M
International Business M
Management Information Systems M
Marketing M
Secondary Education M,O
Special Education M,O

UNIVERSITY OF PHOENIX–SOUTHERN CALIFORNIA CAMPUS
Accounting M
Adult Education M,O
Business Administration and Management—General M
Counselor Education M
Education—General M,O
Educational Leadership and Administration M,O
Elementary Education M,O
English as a Second Language M,O
Human Resources Management M
International Business M
Marketing M
Project Management M
Secondary Education M,O

UNIVERSITY OF PHOENIX–SOUTH FLORIDA CAMPUS
Accounting M
Business Administration and Management—General M
Computer Education M
Curriculum and Instruction M
Early Childhood Education M
Education—General M
Educational Leadership and Administration M
Elementary Education M
Human Resources Management M
International Business M
Management Information Systems M
Marketing M
Mathematics Education M
Secondary Education M

UNIVERSITY OF PHOENIX–UTAH CAMPUS
Accounting M
Business Administration and Management—General M
Curriculum and Instruction M
Education—General M
Educational Leadership and Administration M
Elementary Education M
Human Resources Management M
International Business M
Management Information Systems M
Marketing M
Secondary Education M
Special Education M

UNIVERSITY OF PHOENIX–WASHINGTON D.C. CAMPUS
Accounting M,D
Adult Education M,D,O
Business Administration and Management—General M,D
Computer Education M,D,O
Curriculum and Instruction M,D,O
Early Childhood Education M,D,O
Education—General M,D,O
Educational Leadership and Administration M,D,O
Educational Media/Instructional Technology M,D,O
Elementary Education M,D,O
English as a Second Language M,D,O
English Education M,D,O
Health Education M,D
Higher Education M,D,O
Human Resources Management M,D
Management Information Systems M,D
Mathematics Education M,D,O
Organizational Management M,D
Secondary Education M,D,O
Special Education M,D,O

UNIVERSITY OF PHOENIX–WESTERN WASHINGTON CAMPUS
Business Administration and Management—General M

UNIVERSITY OF PIKEVILLE
Business Administration and Management—General M
Education—General M
Educational Leadership and Administration M

UNIVERSITY OF PITTSBURGH
Accounting M,D
Athletic Training and Sports Medicine M
Business Administration and Management—General M,D*
Early Childhood Education M
Education—General M,D*
Educational Leadership and Administration M,D
Educational Measurement and Evaluation M,D
Educational Policy D
Elementary Education M
English as a Second Language M,D,O
English Education M,D
Environmental Law M
Exercise and Sports Science M,D
Finance and Banking M,D
Foreign Languages Education M,D
Foundations and Philosophy of Education M,D
Health Education M,D
Health Law M
Higher Education M,D
Human Resources Management M,D
Industrial and Manufacturing Management M
Information Studies M,D
Intellectual Property Law M
International and Comparative Education M,D
International Business O
Law M
Legal and Justice Studies M,D
Library Science M,D
Management Information Systems M,D
Management Strategy and Policy M,D
Marketing M,D
Mathematics Education M,D
Nonprofit Management M
Organizational Behavior M,D
Quantitative Analysis M,D
Reading Education M,D
Science Education M,D
Secondary Education M,D
Social Sciences Education M,D
Social Work M,D,O
Special Education M,D
Supply Chain Management M

UNIVERSITY OF PORTLAND
Business Administration and Management—General M
Education—General M,D
Educational Leadership and Administration M,D
English as a Second Language M,D
Entrepreneurship M
Finance and Banking M
Industrial and Manufacturing Management M
Marketing M
Nonprofit Management M
Organizational Management M,D
Reading Education M,D
Special Education M,D
Sustainability Management M

UNIVERSITY OF PRINCE EDWARD ISLAND
Education—General M
Educational Leadership and Administration M

UNIVERSITY OF PUERTO RICO, MAYAGÜEZ CAMPUS
Agricultural Education M
Business Administration and Management—General M
English Education M
Exercise and Sports Science M
Finance and Banking M
Higher Education M
Human Resources Management M
Industrial and Manufacturing Management M
Kinesiology and Movement Studies M
Mathematics Education M

UNIVERSITY OF PUERTO RICO, MEDICAL SCIENCES CAMPUS
Health Education M
Special Education O

UNIVERSITY OF PUERTO RICO, RÍO PIEDRAS CAMPUS
Accounting M,D
Business Administration and Management—General M,D
Counselor Education M,D
Curriculum and Instruction M,D
Early Childhood Education M
Education—General M,D
Educational Leadership and Administration M,D
Educational Measurement and Evaluation M
English as a Second Language M
Exercise and Sports Science M
Finance and Banking M,D
Foreign Languages Education M,D
Human Resources Management M,D
Industrial and Manufacturing Management M,D
Information Studies M,O
International Business M,D
Law M,D
Library Science M,O
Marketing M,D
Mathematics Education M,D
Quantitative Analysis M,D
Science Education M,D
Social Sciences Education M,D
Social Work M,D
Special Education M

UNIVERSITY OF PUGET SOUND
Counselor Education M
Education—General M
Elementary Education M
Secondary Education M

UNIVERSITY OF REDLANDS
Business Administration and Management—General M
Education—General M,D,O
Management Information Systems M

UNIVERSITY OF REGINA
Adult Education M
Business Administration and Management—General M,O
Curriculum and Instruction M
Education—General M,D,O
Educational Leadership and Administration M
Educational Psychology M
Human Resources Development M
Human Resources Management M,O
International Business M,O
Kinesiology and Movement Studies M,D
Organizational Management M,O
Project Management M,O
Social Work M,D

UNIVERSITY OF RHODE ISLAND
Accounting M,D
Business Administration and Management—General M,D*
Education—General M,D
Entrepreneurship M,D
Exercise and Sports Science M
Finance and Banking M,D
Health Education M
Human Resources Management M,O
Information Studies M
Library Science M
Management Strategy and Policy M,D
Marketing M,D
Music Education M
Physical Education M
Reading Education M,D
Recreation and Park Management M
Special Education M,D
Student Affairs M
Supply Chain Management M,D

UNIVERSITY OF RICHMOND
Business Administration and Management—General M
Law D

UNIVERSITY OF RIO GRANDE
Art Education M
Education—General M
Educational Leadership and Administration M
Physical Education M
Special Education M

UNIVERSITY OF ROCHESTER
Accounting M,D
Archives/Archival Administration M
Business Administration and Management—General M,D
Counselor Education M,D
Curriculum and Instruction M,D
Education—General M,D
Educational Leadership and Administration M,D
Educational Policy M,D
Entrepreneurship M
Finance and Banking M,D
Foundations and Philosophy of Education D
Higher Education M,D
Industrial and Manufacturing Management D
Management Information Systems M,D
Management Strategy and Policy M
Marketing Research M
Marketing M,D
Music Education M,D
Student Affairs M

UNIVERSITY OF ST. AUGUSTINE FOR HEALTH SCIENCES
Athletic Training and Sports Medicine M
Health Education M,D

UNIVERSITY OF ST. FRANCIS (IL)
Accounting M,O
Art Education M,D,O
Business Administration and Management—General M,O
Business Education M,O
Curriculum and Instruction M,D,O
Developmental Education M,O
Education—General M,D,O
Educational Leadership and Administration M,D,O
Educational Media/Instructional Technology M,O
Elementary Education M,D,O
English as a Second Language M,D,O
English Education M,D,O
Finance and Banking M,O
Human Resources Management M,O
Logistics M,O
Management Strategy and Policy M,O
Mathematics Education M,D,O
Reading Education M,D,O
Science Education M,D,O
Secondary Education M,D,O
Social Sciences Education M,D,O
Social Work M,O
Special Education M,D,O

UNIVERSITY OF SAINT FRANCIS (IN)
Business Administration and Management—General M
Counselor Education M,O
Education—General M
Organizational Management M
Secondary Education M
Special Education M
Sustainability Management M

UNIVERSITY OF SAINT JOSEPH
Business Administration and Management—General M
Counselor Education M,O
Curriculum and Instruction M
Education—General M
Educational Media/Instructional Technology M
Reading Education M
Special Education M

UNIVERSITY OF SAINT MARY
Advertising and Public Relations M
Business Administration and Management—General M
Education—General M
Elementary Education M
Finance and Banking M
Human Resources Management M
Marketing M
Special Education M

UNIVERSITY OF ST. MICHAEL'S COLLEGE
Religious Education M,D,O

UNIVERSITY OF ST. THOMAS (MN)
Accounting M
Business Administration and Management—General M
Education—General M,D,O
Educational Leadership and Administration M,D,O
Law M,D
Music Education M,D
Organizational Management M,D
Religious Education M
Social Work M,D
Special Education M,O
Student Affairs M,D,O

UNIVERSITY OF ST. THOMAS (TX)
Accounting M
Business Administration and Management—General M
Counselor Education M,D
Curriculum and Instruction M,D
Education—General M,D
Educational Leadership and Administration M,D
Educational Measurement and Evaluation M,D
Elementary Education M,D
English as a Second Language M,D
Finance and Banking M
International Business M
Multilingual and Multicultural Education M,D
Reading Education M,D
Religious Education M,D
Secondary Education M,D
Special Education M,D

UNIVERSITY OF SAN DIEGO
Accounting M
Business Administration and Management—General M
Counselor Education M
Curriculum and Instruction M
Education—General M,D,O
Educational Leadership and Administration M,D,O
English as a Second Language M
Finance and Banking M
Higher Education M,D,O
International Business M
Law M,D,O
Legal and Justice Studies M,D,O
Nonprofit Management M,D,O
Reading Education M
Real Estate M
Science Education M
Special Education M
Supply Chain Management M,O
Taxation M,D,O

UNIVERSITY OF SAN FRANCISCO
Business Administration and Management—General M
Counselor Education M
Curriculum and Instruction M,D
Education—General M,D
Educational Leadership and Administration M,D
Educational Media/Instructional Technology M,D
Entrepreneurship M
Finance and Banking M
Intellectual Property Law M
International and Comparative Education M,D
International Business M
Law D
Management Information Systems M
Marketing M
Multilingual and Multicultural Education M,D
Nonprofit Management M
Organizational Management M

Reading Education M,D
Religious Education M,D
Special Education M,D
Sports Management M
Urban Education M

UNIVERSITY OF SASKATCHEWAN
Accounting M
Business Administration and Management—General M
Curriculum and Instruction M,D,O
Education—General M,D,O
Educational Leadership and Administration M,D,O
Educational Psychology M,D,O
Finance and Banking M
Foundations and Philosophy of Education M,D,O
International Business M,D
Kinesiology and Movement Studies M,D,O
Law M,D
Marketing M
Special Education M,D,O
Sustainability Management M

THE UNIVERSITY OF SCRANTON
Accounting M
Business Administration and Management—General M
Counselor Education M
Curriculum and Instruction M
Education—General M
Educational Leadership and Administration M
Finance and Banking M
Human Resources Development M
International Business M
Management Information Systems M
Marketing M
Reading Education M
Secondary Education M
Special Education M

UNIVERSITY OF SIOUX FALLS
Business Administration and Management—General M
Education—General M,O
Educational Leadership and Administration M,O
Educational Media/Instructional Technology M,O
Entrepreneurship M
Marketing M
Reading Education M,O

UNIVERSITY OF SOUTH AFRICA
Accounting M,D
Adult Education M,D
Business Administration and Management—General M,D
Counselor Education M,D
Curriculum and Instruction M,D
Education—General M,D
Educational Leadership and Administration M,D
Educational Media/Instructional Technology M,D
Educational Psychology M,D
English as a Second Language M,D
Environmental Education M,D
Foundations and Philosophy of Education M,D
Health Education M,D
Human Resources Development M,D
International and Comparative Education M,D
Law M,D
Logistics M,D
Management Information Systems M
Marketing M,D
Mathematics Education M,D
Quantitative Analysis M,D
Real Estate M,D
Science Education M,D
Social Work M,D
Travel and Tourism M,D
Vocational and Technical Education M,D

UNIVERSITY OF SOUTH ALABAMA
Accounting M
Art Education M,D
Business Administration and Management—General M,D
Counselor Education M,D
Early Childhood Education M,D
Education—General M,D
Educational Leadership and Administration M,D
Educational Media/Instructional Technology M,D
Elementary Education M,D
Exercise and Sports Science M
Health Education M
Kinesiology and Movement Studies M
Management Information Systems M,D
Music Education M
Physical Education M
Reading Education M,D
Science Education M,D
Secondary Education M,D
Special Education M,D
Sports Management M

UNIVERSITY OF SOUTH CAROLINA
Accounting M
Archives/Archival Administration M,O
Art Education M,D
Business Administration and Management—General M,D
Business Education M,D
Counselor Education D,O
Curriculum and Instruction D
Early Childhood Education M,D

*M—masters degree; D—doctorate; O—other advanced degree; *—Close-Up and/or Display*

- Education—General M,D,O
- Educational Leadership and Administration M,D,O
- Educational Measurement and Evaluation M,D
- Educational Media/Instructional Technology M
- Educational Psychology M,D
- Elementary Education M,D
- English as a Second Language M,D,O
- English Education M,D
- Entertainment Management M
- Exercise and Sports Science M,D
- Foreign Languages Education M,D
- Foundations and Philosophy of Education D
- Health Education M,D,O
- Higher Education M
- Hospitality Management M
- Human Resources Management M
- Information Studies M,D,O
- International Business M
- Law D
- Library Science M,D,O
- Mathematics Education M,D
- Music Education M,D,O
- Physical Education M,D
- Reading Education M,D
- Science Education M,D
- Secondary Education M,D
- Social Sciences Education M,D
- Social Work M,D
- Special Education M,D
- Sports Management M
- Student Affairs M
- Travel and Tourism M

UNIVERSITY OF SOUTH CAROLINA AIKEN

- Business Administration and Management—General M
- Educational Media/Instructional Technology M

UNIVERSITY OF SOUTH CAROLINA UPSTATE

- Early Childhood Education M
- Education—General M
- Elementary Education M
- Special Education M

THE UNIVERSITY OF SOUTH DAKOTA

- Accounting M
- Adult Education M,D,O
- Art Education M
- Business Administration and Management—General M
- Counselor Education M,D,O
- Curriculum and Instruction M,D,O
- Early Childhood Education M,D,O
- Education—General M,D,O
- Educational Leadership and Administration M,D,O
- Educational Media/Instructional Technology M
- Educational Psychology M,D,O
- Elementary Education M
- Exercise and Sports Science M
- Higher Education M,D,O
- Human Resources Management M
- Kinesiology and Movement Studies M
- Law D
- Music Education M
- Organizational Management M
- Reading Education M
- Secondary Education M
- Social Work M
- Special Education M,D,O

UNIVERSITY OF SOUTHERN CALIFORNIA

- Accounting M
- Advertising and Public Relations M
- Business Administration and Management—General M,D
- Counselor Education M
- Education—General M,D
- Educational Leadership and Administration D
- Educational Policy D
- Educational Psychology D
- English as a Second Language M
- Entrepreneurship M
- Health Education M
- Higher Education D
- Kinesiology and Movement Studies M,D
- Law M,D
- Multilingual and Multicultural Education D
- Music Education M,D,O
- Nonprofit Management M,O
- Organizational Management M
- Quantitative Analysis M,D
- Real Estate M
- Social Work M,D
- Student Affairs M
- Supply Chain Management M,D,O
- Taxation M
- Urban Education D

UNIVERSITY OF SOUTHERN INDIANA

- Accounting M
- Business Administration and Management—General M
- Education—General M
- Educational Leadership and Administration M
- Elementary Education M
- English as a Second Language M
- Human Resources Management M
- Industrial and Manufacturing Management M
- Mathematics Education M
- Nonprofit Management M
- Organizational Management M,D,O
- Secondary Education M
- Social Work M
- Sports Management M

UNIVERSITY OF SOUTHERN MAINE

- Accounting M
- Adult Education M,O
- Business Administration and Management—General M,O
- Counselor Education M,O
- Education of the Gifted M,O
- Education—General M,D,O
- Educational Leadership and Administration M,O
- Educational Psychology M,O
- English as a Second Language M,O
- Finance and Banking M
- Higher Education M,O
- Music Education M
- Reading Education M,O
- Social Work M
- Special Education M,O
- Sustainability Management M

UNIVERSITY OF SOUTHERN MISSISSIPPI

- Accounting M
- Advertising and Public Relations M,D
- Business Administration and Management—General M
- Curriculum and Instruction M,D
- Education—General M,D,O
- Educational Leadership and Administration M,D,O
- Educational Measurement and Evaluation M,D,O
- Educational Media/Instructional Technology M,D
- Elementary Education M,D
- English Education M,D
- Exercise and Sports Science M,D
- Foreign Languages Education M
- Health Education M
- Higher Education M,D,O
- Library Science M,O
- Logistics M
- Mathematics Education M,D
- Music Education M,D
- Physical Education M,D
- Science Education M,D
- Secondary Education M,D
- Social Work M
- Special Education M,D
- Sports Management M,D
- Student Affairs M,D,O

UNIVERSITY OF SOUTH FLORIDA

- Accounting M,D
- Adult Education M,D,O
- Athletic Training and Sports Medicine M,D
- Business Administration and Management—General M,D
- Community College Education M,D,O
- Counselor Education M,D,O
- Distance Education Development O
- Early Childhood Education M,D,O
- Education—General M,D,O
- Educational Leadership and Administration M,D,O
- Educational Measurement and Evaluation O
- Educational Media/Instructional Technology O
- Educational Psychology M,D,O
- Elementary Education M,D,O
- English as a Second Language M,D,O
- Entrepreneurship M,O
- Finance and Banking M,D
- Foreign Languages Education O
- Health Education M,D
- Higher Education M,D,O
- Human Resources Development O
- Human Resources Management M
- Information Studies M,O
- Legal and Justice Studies O
- Library Science M
- Management Information Systems M,D,O
- Management Strategy and Policy M,D,O
- Marketing M,D
- Music Education M,D
- Nonprofit Management O
- Reading Education M,D,O
- Real Estate M,D
- Secondary Education O
- Social Sciences Education M,D,O
- Social Work M,D,O
- Special Education O
- Student Affairs M,D,O
- Sustainability Management M,O
- Taxation M,D
- Travel and Tourism M,O
- Vocational and Technical Education M,D,O

UNIVERSITY OF SOUTH FLORIDA, ST. PETERSBURG

- Business Administration and Management—General M
- Education—General M
- Educational Leadership and Administration M
- Elementary Education M
- English Education M
- Mathematics Education M
- Middle School Education M
- Reading Education M
- Science Education M

UNIVERSITY OF SOUTH FLORIDA SARASOTA-MANATEE

- Business Administration and Management—General M
- Curriculum and Instruction M
- Educational Leadership and Administration M
- Elementary Education M
- English Education M
- Hospitality Management M
- Social Work M

THE UNIVERSITY OF TAMPA

- Accounting M
- Business Administration and Management—General M
- Curriculum and Instruction M
- Education—General M
- Educational Media/Instructional Technology M
- Entrepreneurship M
- Exercise and Sports Science M
- Finance and Banking M
- International Business M
- Management Information Systems M
- Marketing M
- Nonprofit Management M

THE UNIVERSITY OF TENNESSEE

- Accounting M,D
- Adult Education M,D
- Advertising and Public Relations M,D
- Agricultural Education M
- Art Education M,D,O
- Athletic Training and Sports Medicine M,D
- Business Administration and Management—General M,D
- Counselor Education M,D,O
- Curriculum and Instruction M,D,O
- Early Childhood Education M,D,O
- Education—General M,D,O
- Educational Leadership and Administration M,D,O
- Educational Measurement and Evaluation M,D,O
- Educational Media/Instructional Technology M,D,O
- Educational Psychology M,D,O
- Elementary Education M,D,O
- English as a Second Language M,D,O
- English Education M,D,O
- Exercise and Sports Science M,D,O
- Finance and Banking M,D
- Foreign Languages Education M,D,O
- Foundations and Philosophy of Education M,D,O
- Health Education M
- Hospitality Management M
- Human Resources Development M
- Industrial and Manufacturing Management M,D
- Kinesiology and Movement Studies M,D
- Law D
- Leisure Studies M,D
- Logistics M,D
- Marketing M,D
- Mathematics Education M,D,O
- Multilingual and Multicultural Education M,D,O
- Music Education M
- Reading Education M,D,O
- Recreation and Park Management M,D
- Science Education M,D,O
- Secondary Education M,D,O
- Social Sciences Education M,D,O
- Social Work M,D
- Special Education M,D,O
- Sports Management M,D
- Student Affairs M
- Transportation Management M,D
- Travel and Tourism M

THE UNIVERSITY OF TENNESSEE AT CHATTANOOGA

- Accounting M
- Athletic Training and Sports Medicine M
- Business Administration and Management—General M
- Counselor Education M,D,O
- Education—General M,D,O
- Educational Leadership and Administration M,D,O
- Educational Media/Instructional Technology M,D,O
- Elementary Education M,D,O
- Logistics M,O
- Mathematics Education M,O
- Music Education M,O
- Nonprofit Management M,O
- Physical Education M
- Project Management M,O
- Quality Management M,O
- Secondary Education M,D,O
- Special Education M,D,O
- Supply Chain Management M,O

THE UNIVERSITY OF TENNESSEE AT MARTIN

- Business Administration and Management—General M
- Counselor Education M
- Curriculum and Instruction M
- Education—General M
- Educational Leadership and Administration M
- Elementary Education M
- Finance and Banking M
- Physical Education M
- Secondary Education M
- Special Education M
- Student Affairs M

THE UNIVERSITY OF TEXAS AT ARLINGTON

- Accounting M,D
- Curriculum and Instruction M
- Education—General M,D
- Educational Leadership and Administration M,D
- Educational Policy M,D
- English as a Second Language M
- Finance and Banking M,D
- Higher Education M,D
- Human Resources Management M
- Logistics M
- Management Information Systems M,D
- Marketing Research M
- Marketing M
- Mathematics Education M,D
- Music Education M
- Quantitative Analysis M,D
- Reading Education M
- Real Estate M,D
- Science Education M
- Social Work M,D
- Taxation M,D

THE UNIVERSITY OF TEXAS AT AUSTIN

- Accounting M,D
- Actuarial Science M,D
- Advertising and Public Relations M,D
- Art Education M
- Business Administration and Management—General M,D
- Counselor Education M,D
- Curriculum and Instruction M,D
- Early Childhood Education M,D
- Education—General M,D
- Educational Leadership and Administration M,D
- Educational Media/Instructional Technology M,D
- Educational Psychology M,D
- Entrepreneurship M
- Exercise and Sports Science M,D
- Finance and Banking M,D
- Health Education M,D
- Industrial and Manufacturing Management M,D
- Information Studies M,D
- Kinesiology and Movement Studies M,D
- Law M,D
- Management Information Systems M,D
- Marketing M,D
- Multilingual and Multicultural Education M,D
- Music Education M,D
- Organizational Behavior M
- Physical Education M,D
- Quantitative Analysis M,D
- Reading Education M,D
- Social Work M,D
- Special Education M,D
- Supply Chain Management M,D

THE UNIVERSITY OF TEXAS AT DALLAS

- Accounting M
- Actuarial Science M,D
- Business Administration and Management—General M,D*
- Entrepreneurship M
- Finance and Banking M
- Industrial and Manufacturing Management M,D
- International Business M,D
- Investment Management M
- Law M,D
- Management Information Systems M
- Management Strategy and Policy M
- Marketing M
- Mathematics Education M
- Nonprofit Management M,D
- Project Management M,D
- Real Estate M
- Science Education M
- Supply Chain Management M

THE UNIVERSITY OF TEXAS AT EL PASO

- Accounting M
- Art Education M
- Business Administration and Management—General M,D,O
- Counselor Education M
- Curriculum and Instruction M,D
- Education—General M,D
- Educational Leadership and Administration M,D
- Educational Measurement and Evaluation M
- Educational Psychology M
- English as a Second Language M,O
- English Education M,D,O
- International Business M,D,O
- Kinesiology and Movement Studies M
- Mathematics Education M
- Multilingual and Multicultural Education M,D,O
- Music Education M
- Reading Education M,D
- Science Education M
- Social Work M
- Special Education M

THE UNIVERSITY OF TEXAS AT SAN ANTONIO

- Accounting M,D
- Business Administration and Management—General M,D,O
- Counselor Education M,D
- Curriculum and Instruction M,D
- Early Childhood Education M,D
- Educational Leadership and Administration M,D
- Educational Media/Instructional Technology M,D,O
- English as a Second Language M,D,O
- Finance and Banking M,D
- Health Education M
- Higher Education M,D
- Kinesiology and Movement Studies M
- Marketing M,D
- Mathematics Education M
- Multilingual and Multicultural Education M,D

Organizational Management D
Reading Education M,D
Social Work M
Special Education M,D

THE UNIVERSITY OF TEXAS AT TYLER
Accounting M
Business Administration and Management—General M
Early Childhood Education M
Educational Leadership and Administration M
Health Education M
Human Resources Development M,D
Industrial and Manufacturing Management M
Kinesiology and Movement Studies M
Marketing M
Organizational Management M
Quality Management M
Reading Education M
Special Education M

THE UNIVERSITY OF TEXAS HEALTH SCIENCE CENTER AT HOUSTON
Quantitative Analysis M,D

THE UNIVERSITY OF TEXAS HEALTH SCIENCE CENTER AT SAN ANTONIO
Special Education M,D

THE UNIVERSITY OF TEXAS OF THE PERMIAN BASIN
Accounting M
Business Administration and Management—General M
Counselor Education M
Early Childhood Education M
Education—General M
Educational Leadership and Administration M
English as a Second Language M
Foundations and Philosophy of Education M
Kinesiology and Movement Studies M
Reading Education M
Special Education M

THE UNIVERSITY OF TEXAS RIO GRANDE VALLEY
Accounting M
Advertising and Public Relations M,O
Business Administration and Management—General M,D
Counselor Education M
Curriculum and Instruction M,D
Early Childhood Education M
Education—General M,D
Educational Leadership and Administration M,D
Educational Measurement and Evaluation M
Educational Media/Instructional Technology M,D
Educational Psychology M
Elementary Education M,D
English as a Second Language M
Exercise and Sports Science M
Finance and Banking M,D
Kinesiology and Movement Studies M
Management Information Systems M
Marketing M,D
Multilingual and Multicultural Education M
Music Education M
Reading Education M
Secondary Education M,D
Social Work M
Special Education M

THE UNIVERSITY OF THE ARTS
Art Education M
Museum Education M
Music Education M

UNIVERSITY OF THE CUMBERLANDS
Accounting M
Business Administration and Management—General M
Business Education M,D,O
Counselor Education M,D,O
Education—General M,D,O
Educational Leadership and Administration M,D,O
Elementary Education M,D,O
Marketing M,D,O
Middle School Education M,D,O
Reading Education M,D,O
Secondary Education M,D,O
Special Education M,D,O
Student Affairs M,D,O

UNIVERSITY OF THE DISTRICT OF COLUMBIA
Adult Education O
Business Administration and Management—General M
Early Childhood Education M
Elementary Education M
English Education M
Law M,D
Legal and Justice Studies M,D
Mathematics Education M
Middle School Education M
Secondary Education M
Social Sciences Education M

UNIVERSITY OF THE FRASER VALLEY
Social Work M

UNIVERSITY OF THE INCARNATE WORD
Mathematics Education M

UNIVERSITY OF THE PACIFIC
Business Administration and Management—General M
Curriculum and Instruction M,D
Education—General M,D,O
Educational Leadership and Administration M,D
Educational Psychology M,D,O
Exercise and Sports Science M
Hospitality Management M
Law M,D
Music Education M
Special Education M,D

UNIVERSITY OF THE POTOMAC
Business Administration and Management—General M

UNIVERSITY OF THE SACRED HEART
Accounting M,O
Advertising and Public Relations M
Business Administration and Management—General M,O
Early Childhood Education M,O
Education—General M,O
Educational Media/Instructional Technology M
English Education M,O
Foreign Languages Education M,O
Human Resources Management M
Legal and Justice Studies M
Management Information Systems M
Marketing M
Mathematics Education M,O
Nonprofit Management M
Taxation M

UNIVERSITY OF THE SOUTHWEST
Business Administration and Management—General M
Counselor Education M
Curriculum and Instruction M
Early Childhood Education M
Education—General M
Educational Leadership and Administration M
English as a Second Language M
Multilingual and Multicultural Education M
Special Education M
Sports Management M

UNIVERSITY OF THE VIRGIN ISLANDS
Business Administration and Management—General M
Education—General M,D,O
Educational Leadership and Administration M,D,O
Mathematics Education M
Secondary Education M

UNIVERSITY OF THE WEST
Business Administration and Management—General M
Finance and Banking M
International Business M
Management Information Systems M
Nonprofit Management M

THE UNIVERSITY OF TOLEDO
Accounting M
Art Education M,D,O
Business Administration and Management—General M
Business Education M,D,O
Counselor Education M,D,O
Curriculum and Instruction M,D,O
Early Childhood Education M,D,O
Education of the Gifted M,D,O
Education—General M,D,O
Educational Leadership and Administration M,D,O
Educational Measurement and Evaluation M,D,O
Educational Media/Instructional Technology M,D,O
Educational Psychology M,D,O
Elementary Education M,D,O
English as a Second Language M,D,O
English Education M,D,O
Exercise and Sports Science M,D
Finance and Banking M
Foreign Languages Education M,D,O
Foundations and Philosophy of Education M,D,O
Health Education M,D,O
Higher Education M,D,O
International Business M
Law M,D,O
Leisure Studies M,D
Marketing M
Mathematics Education M,D,O
Middle School Education M,D,O
Music Education M,D,O
Nonprofit Management M,O
Physical Education M,D
Recreation and Park Management M,D
Science Education M,D,O
Secondary Education M,D,O
Social Sciences Education M,D,O
Social Work M,O
Special Education M,D,O
Vocational and Technical Education M,D,O

UNIVERSITY OF TORONTO
Business Administration and Management—General M,D
Education—General M,D
Finance and Banking M
Human Resources Management M,D
Information Studies M,D
Kinesiology and Movement Studies M,D
Law M,D
Music Education M,D
Physical Education M,D
Social Work M,D

THE UNIVERSITY OF TULSA
Accounting M
Business Administration and Management—General M
Education—General M
Elementary Education M
English Education M
Environmental Law M,D,O
Finance and Banking M
Health Law M,D,O
Investment Management M
Kinesiology and Movement Studies M
Law M,D,O
Mathematics Education M
Science Education M
Secondary Education M

UNIVERSITY OF UTAH
Accounting M,D
Art Education M
Athletic Training and Sports Medicine D
Business Administration and Management—General M,D,O
Counselor Education M,D,O
Early Childhood Education M,D,O
Education—General M,D,O
Educational Leadership and Administration M,D
Educational Media/Instructional Technology M,D,O
Educational Psychology M,D,O
Elementary Education M,D,O
Finance and Banking M,D
Foreign Languages Education M,D
Foundations and Philosophy of Education M,D
Health Education M,D
Higher Education M,D
Industrial and Manufacturing Management M,D,O
Kinesiology and Movement Studies M,D
Law M,D
Leisure Studies M,D
Management Information Systems M,D,O
Management Strategy and Policy M,D,O
Marketing M,D
Mathematics Education M,D
Music Education M,D
Organizational Behavior M,D
Reading Education M,D,O
Real Estate M
Recreation and Park Management M,D
Science Education M,D
Secondary Education M,D
Social Work M,D
Special Education M,D
Student Affairs M,D

UNIVERSITY OF VERMONT
Accounting M
Business Administration and Management—General M
Counselor Education M
Curriculum and Instruction M
Education—General M,D
Educational Leadership and Administration M,D
Mathematics Education M
Science Education M,D
Social Work M
Special Education M

UNIVERSITY OF VICTORIA
Art Education M,D
Business Administration and Management—General M
Counselor Education M,D
Curriculum and Instruction M,D
Early Childhood Education M,D
Education—General M,D
Educational Leadership and Administration M,D
Educational Measurement and Evaluation M,D
Educational Psychology M,D
English Education M,D
Environmental Education M,D
Foreign Languages Education M
Foundations and Philosophy of Education M,D
Kinesiology and Movement Studies M
Law M,D
Leisure Studies M
Mathematics Education M,D
Music Education M,D
Physical Education M
Reading Education M,D
Science Education M,D
Social Sciences Education M,D
Social Work M
Special Education M,D
Vocational and Technical Education M,D

UNIVERSITY OF VIRGINIA
Accounting M
Business Administration and Management—General M,D,O
Counselor Education M,D,O
Curriculum and Instruction M,D,O
Early Childhood Education M,D
Education of the Gifted M,D,O
Education—General M,D,O
Educational Leadership and Administration M,D,O
Educational Measurement and Evaluation M,D,O
Educational Media/Instructional Technology M,D,O
Educational Policy D
Educational Psychology M,D,O
Elementary Education M,D,O
English Education M,D,O
Finance and Banking M
Foreign Languages Education M,D,O
Higher Education M,D,O
International Business M,O
Kinesiology and Movement Studies M,D
Law M,O
Management Strategy and Policy M,O
Marketing M
Mathematics Education M,D,O
Physical Education M,D
Reading Education M,D
Science Education M,D,O
Social Sciences Education M,D,O
Special Education M,D,O
Student Affairs M,D,O

UNIVERSITY OF WASHINGTON
Accounting M,D
Business Administration and Management—General M,D
Business Education M,D
Curriculum and Instruction M,D
Education—General M,D
Educational Leadership and Administration M,D
Educational Measurement and Evaluation M,D
Educational Media/Instructional Technology M,D
Educational Policy M,D
Educational Psychology M,D
English as a Second Language M,D
English Education M,D
Entrepreneurship M,D
Foundations and Philosophy of Education M,D
Higher Education M,D
Intellectual Property Law M,D
International Business M,D,O
Law M,D
Legal and Justice Studies M,D
Library Science M,D
Logistics O
Management Information Systems M,D
Mathematics Education M,D
Multilingual and Multicultural Education M,D
Music Education M,D
Physical Education M,D
Reading Education M,D
Science Education M,D
Social Sciences Education M,D
Social Work M,D
Special Education M,D
Supply Chain Management M,D
Taxation M,D
Transportation Management O

UNIVERSITY OF WASHINGTON, BOTHELL
Business Administration and Management—General M
Education—General M
Educational Leadership and Administration M
Middle School Education M
Secondary Education M

UNIVERSITY OF WASHINGTON, TACOMA
Accounting M
Business Administration and Management—General M
Education—General M
Educational Leadership and Administration M
Elementary Education M
Finance and Banking M
Mathematics Education M
Science Education M
Social Work M
Special Education M

UNIVERSITY OF WATERLOO
Accounting M,D
Actuarial Science M,D
Business Administration and Management—General M
Entrepreneurship M
Finance and Banking M,D
Health Education M,D
Kinesiology and Movement Studies M,D
Leisure Studies M,D
Recreation and Park Management M,D
Taxation M,D

THE UNIVERSITY OF WEST ALABAMA
Adult Education M
Business Administration and Management—General M
Counselor Education M,O
Curriculum and Instruction M,O
Early Childhood Education M,O
Education—General M,O
Educational Leadership and Administration M,O
Educational Media/Instructional Technology M,O
Elementary Education M,O
English Education M
Finance and Banking M
Higher Education M
Mathematics Education M
Physical Education M
Science Education M
Secondary Education M

*M—masters degree; D—doctorate; O—other advanced degree; *—Close-Up and/or Display*

Social Sciences Education M
Special Education M,O

THE UNIVERSITY OF WESTERN ONTARIO
Business Administration and Management—General M,D
Curriculum and Instruction M
Education—General M
Educational Policy M
Educational Psychology M
Entrepreneurship M,D
Finance and Banking M,D
Information Studies M,D
International Business M,D
Kinesiology and Movement Studies M,D
Law M,D,O
Library Science M,D
Management Strategy and Policy M,D
Marketing M,D
Special Education M

UNIVERSITY OF WEST FLORIDA
Accounting M
Business Administration and Management—General M
Curriculum and Instruction M,O
Educational Leadership and Administration M,D
Educational Media/Instructional Technology M,D
Elementary Education M
Exercise and Sports Science M
Leisure Studies M
Middle School Education M
Physical Education M,D
Reading Education M
Secondary Education M
Social Work M
Special Education M
Student Affairs M

UNIVERSITY OF WEST GEORGIA
Accounting M
Business Administration and Management—General M
Business Education M,D,O
Counselor Education M,D,O
Early Childhood Education M,D,O
Education—General M,D,O
Educational Leadership and Administration M,D,O
Educational Media/Instructional Technology M,D,O
Music Education M,O
Nonprofit Management M,D,O
Reading Education M,D,O
Secondary Education M,D,O
Special Education M,D,O

UNIVERSITY OF WINDSOR
Business Administration and Management—General M
Education—General M,D
Kinesiology and Movement Studies M
Legal and Justice Studies M
Social Work M

UNIVERSITY OF WISCONSIN–EAU CLAIRE
Business Administration and Management—General M
Education—General M
Library Science M
Reading Education M
Secondary Education M
Special Education M

UNIVERSITY OF WISCONSIN–GREEN BAY
Business Administration and Management—General M
Education—General M
Social Work M
Sustainability Management M

UNIVERSITY OF WISCONSIN–LA CROSSE
Athletic Training and Sports Medicine M
Business Administration and Management—General M
Education—General M,O
English Education M,O
Exercise and Sports Science M
Health Education M
Higher Education M,D
Physical Education M
Reading Education M,O
Recreation and Park Management M
Special Education M,O
Student Affairs M,D

UNIVERSITY OF WISCONSIN–MADISON
Accounting M,D
Art Education M,D
Business Administration and Management—General M
Counselor Education M
Curriculum and Instruction M,D
Education—General M,D,O
Educational Leadership and Administration M,D,O
Educational Policy M,D,O
Educational Psychology M,D
Finance and Banking M,D
Foreign Languages Education M,D
Higher Education M,D,O
Human Resources Management M,D
Information Studies M,D
Insurance M,D
International and Comparative Education M,D,O
Investment Management D
Kinesiology and Movement Studies M,D
Law M,D
Library Science M,D
Management Information Systems D
Management Strategy and Policy M,D
Marketing Research M
Marketing D
Mathematics Education M,D
Music Education M,D
Real Estate M,D
Science Education M,D
Social Work M,D
Special Education M,D
Supply Chain Management M
Taxation M

UNIVERSITY OF WISCONSIN–MILWAUKEE
Actuarial Science M,D
Adult Education M,D,O
Art Education M,D,O
Athletic Training and Sports Medicine M,D
Business Administration and Management—General M,O
Counselor Education M,D,O
Curriculum and Instruction M,D,O
Early Childhood Education M
Education—General M,D,O
Educational Leadership and Administration M,D,O
Educational Measurement and Evaluation M,D,O
Educational Media/Instructional Technology M,O
Educational Policy M,O
Educational Psychology M,D,O
Elementary Education M
English as a Second Language M,D,O
English Education M
Exercise and Sports Science M,D
Foreign Languages Education M,O
Foundations and Philosophy of Education M,D,O
Health Education M,D,O
Higher Education M,O
Human Resources Development M,O
Information Studies M,D,O
International Business M,O
Investment Management M,O
Kinesiology and Movement Studies M,D
Library Science M,D,O
Management Strategy and Policy M,O
Mathematics Education M,D,O
Middle School Education M
Multilingual and Multicultural Education M,D,O
Nonprofit Management M,D,O
Reading Education M
Science Education M
Social Sciences Education M
Social Work M,D,O
Special Education M,D,O
Taxation M,O
Urban Education M,D,O

UNIVERSITY OF WISCONSIN–OSHKOSH
Business Administration and Management—General M
Counselor Education M
Curriculum and Instruction M
Early Childhood Education M
Education—General M
Educational Leadership and Administration M
International Business M
Mathematics Education M
Reading Education M
Social Work M
Special Education M

UNIVERSITY OF WISCONSIN–PARKSIDE
Business Administration and Management—General M

UNIVERSITY OF WISCONSIN–PLATTEVILLE
Adult Education M
Counselor Education M
Education—General M
Human Resources Management M
Organizational Management M
Project Management M
Supply Chain Management M

UNIVERSITY OF WISCONSIN–RIVER FALLS
Agricultural Education M
Business Administration and Management—General M
Counselor Education M,O
Education—General M
Elementary Education M
English as a Second Language M
Mathematics Education M
Reading Education M
Science Education M
Social Sciences Education M

UNIVERSITY OF WISCONSIN–STEVENS POINT
Advertising and Public Relations M
Business Administration and Management—General M
Counselor Education M
Education—General M
Educational Leadership and Administration M
Elementary Education M
Music Education M
Reading Education M
Science Education M
Secondary Education M
Special Education M

UNIVERSITY OF WISCONSIN–STOUT
Education—General M,D,O
Human Resources Development M
Project Management M
Quality Management M
Supply Chain Management M
Sustainability Management M
Vocational and Technical Education M,D,O

UNIVERSITY OF WISCONSIN–SUPERIOR
Art Education M
Counselor Education M
Curriculum and Instruction M
Education—General M
Educational Leadership and Administration M,O
Reading Education M
Special Education M
Sustainability Management M

UNIVERSITY OF WISCONSIN–WHITEWATER
Accounting M
Business Administration and Management—General M
Business Education M
Education—General M,O
Educational Leadership and Administration M
Finance and Banking M
Marketing M
Special Education M,O

UNIVERSITY OF WYOMING
Accounting M
Business Administration and Management—General M
Counselor Education M,D
Curriculum and Instruction M,D
Educational Leadership and Administration M,D,O
Educational Media/Instructional Technology M,D
Exercise and Sports Science M
Finance and Banking M
Health Education M
Kinesiology and Movement Studies M
Law D
Mathematics Education M,D
Music Education M
Physical Education M
Science Education M
Social Work M
Special Education M,D,O
Student Affairs M,D

UPPER IOWA UNIVERSITY
Accounting M
Business Administration and Management—General M
Early Childhood Education M
Education—General M
Educational Leadership and Administration M
English as a Second Language M
Finance and Banking M
Higher Education M
Human Resources Management M
Human Services M
Nonprofit Management M
Organizational Management M
Reading Education M
Sports Management M

URBANA UNIVERSITY
Business Administration and Management—General M
Education—General M

URSULINE COLLEGE
Accounting M
Business Administration and Management—General M
Early Childhood Education M
Educational Leadership and Administration M
Entrepreneurship M
Finance and Banking M
Marketing M
Middle School Education M
Secondary Education M
Special Education M

UTAH STATE UNIVERSITY
Accounting M
Agricultural Education M
Business Administration and Management—General M
Business Education M,D
Counselor Education M,D
Curriculum and Instruction D
Education—General M,D,O
Educational Measurement and Evaluation M,D
Educational Media/Instructional Technology M,D,O
Elementary Education M
Health Education M
Home Economics Education M
Human Resources Management M
Management Information Systems M,D
Multilingual and Multicultural Education M
Physical Education M
Recreation and Park Management M,D
Secondary Education M
Special Education M,D,O
Vocational and Technical Education M

UTAH VALLEY UNIVERSITY
Accounting M
Business Administration and Management—General M
Education—General M
Educational Leadership and Administration M
Educational Media/Instructional Technology M
Elementary Education M
English as a Second Language M
Mathematics Education M
Reading Education M

UTICA COLLEGE
Accounting M
Education—General M,O

VALDOSTA STATE UNIVERSITY
Business Administration and Management—General M
Counselor Education M,O
Early Childhood Education M,O
Educational Leadership and Administration M
English Education M
Information Studies M
Library Science M
Social Work M
Special Education M,O

VALLEY CITY STATE UNIVERSITY
Education—General M
Educational Media/Instructional Technology M
Elementary Education M
English as a Second Language M
English Education M
Library Science M
Vocational and Technical Education M

VALPARAISO UNIVERSITY
Business Administration and Management—General M,O
Education—General M,O
Educational Leadership and Administration M,O
Educational Media/Instructional Technology M,O
English as a Second Language M,O
Entertainment Management M
Entrepreneurship M,O
Finance and Banking M,O
Foreign Languages Education M
Law M,D
Legal and Justice Studies O
Management Information Systems M
Management Strategy and Policy M,O
Marketing M,O
Secondary Education M,O
Sports Management M,O
Sustainability Management M,O

VANCOUVER ISLAND UNIVERSITY
Business Administration and Management—General M
Finance and Banking M
International Business M
Marketing M

VANDERBILT UNIVERSITY
Accounting M
Business Administration and Management—General M
Counselor Education M
Education—General M,D*
Educational Leadership and Administration M,D
Educational Policy M,D
Elementary Education M
English Education M
Finance and Banking M
Foreign Languages Education M,D
Higher Education M,D
International and Comparative Education M,D
Law M,D
Management Strategy and Policy M
Marketing M
Multilingual and Multicultural Education M,D
Organizational Management M,D
Quantitative Analysis M
Reading Education M
Science Education M,D
Secondary Education M
Special Education M,D
Urban Education M

VANDERCOOK COLLEGE OF MUSIC
Music Education M

VANGUARD UNIVERSITY OF SOUTHERN CALIFORNIA
Education—General M

VAUGHN COLLEGE OF AERONAUTICS AND TECHNOLOGY
Aviation Management M

VERMONT COLLEGE OF FINE ARTS
Art Education M

VERMONT LAW SCHOOL
Environmental Law M
Law D
Legal and Justice Studies M

VILLANOVA UNIVERSITY
Accounting M
Business Administration and Management—General M
Counselor Education M
Education—General M
Educational Leadership and Administration M
Finance and Banking M
Human Resources Development M
International Business M
Law D
Management Information Systems M
Management Strategy and Policy M
Marketing M
Nonprofit Management M,O
Real Estate M
Secondary Education M
Taxation M

VIRGINIA COLLEGE IN BIRMINGHAM
- Business Administration and Management—General M

VIRGINIA COMMONWEALTH UNIVERSITY
- Accounting M
- Adult Education M
- Advertising and Public Relations M
- Art Education M,D
- Business Administration and Management—General M,D
- Counselor Education M,D
- Curriculum and Instruction D
- Early Childhood Education M
- Education—General M,D,O
- Educational Leadership and Administration M,D
- Educational Measurement and Evaluation D
- Educational Media/Instructional Technology M
- Educational Psychology D
- Elementary Education M
- Exercise and Sports Science M
- Finance and Banking M
- Human Resources Development M
- Management Information Systems M
- Music Education M
- Nonprofit Management O
- Reading Education M,O
- Real Estate O
- Recreation and Park Management M
- Social Work M,D
- Special Education M,D
- Student Affairs M
- Urban Education D

VIRGINIA INTERNATIONAL UNIVERSITY
- Accounting M,O
- Advertising and Public Relations M,O
- Business Administration and Management—General M,O
- Education—General M,O
- English as a Second Language M
- Entrepreneurship M,O
- Finance and Banking M,O
- Hospitality Management M,O
- Human Resources Management M,O
- International Business M,O
- Logistics M,O
- Management Information Systems M,O
- Marketing M,O
- Project Management M,O

VIRGINIA POLYTECHNIC INSTITUTE AND STATE UNIVERSITY
- Accounting M,D
- Business Administration and Management—General M,D
- Counselor Education M,D,O
- Curriculum and Instruction M,D,O
- Distance Education Development M,O
- Education—General M,O
- Educational Leadership and Administration M,D,O
- Educational Measurement and Evaluation M,D,O
- Educational Media/Instructional Technology M,O
- Educational Policy M,D,O
- Exercise and Sports Science M,D
- Foreign Languages Education M,D,O
- Higher Education M,D,O
- Hospitality Management M,D
- Management Information Systems M,D,O
- Mathematics Education M,O
- Nonprofit Management M,O
- Quantitative Analysis M,O
- Social Sciences Education M,D,O
- Student Affairs M,D,O
- Travel and Tourism M,D
- Vocational and Technical Education M,D,O

VIRGINIA STATE UNIVERSITY
- Counselor Education M
- Education—General M,D
- Educational Leadership and Administration M,D
- Health Education M,D
- Mathematics Education M

VIRGINIA THEOLOGICAL SEMINARY
- Educational Leadership and Administration M,D

VIRGINIA UNION UNIVERSITY
- Curriculum and Instruction M
- Education—General M

VITERBO UNIVERSITY
- Business Administration and Management—General M
- Early Childhood Education M,O
- Education of the Gifted M,O
- Education—General M,O
- Educational Leadership and Administration M,O
- International Business M
- Organizational Management M,O
- Project Management M
- Reading Education M,O
- Special Education M,O

WAGNER COLLEGE
- Accounting M
- Business Administration and Management—General M
- Early Childhood Education M
- Education—General M,O
- Educational Leadership and Administration M,O
- Elementary Education M
- English Education M
- Finance and Banking M
- Foreign Languages Education M
- International Business M
- Marketing M
- Mathematics Education M
- Middle School Education M
- Reading Education M
- Science Education M
- Secondary Education M
- Social Sciences Education M
- Special Education M

WAKE FOREST UNIVERSITY
- Accounting M
- Business Administration and Management—General M
- Counselor Education M
- Education—General M
- Exercise and Sports Science M
- Law M,D
- Secondary Education M
- Taxation M

WALDEN UNIVERSITY
- Accounting M,D,O
- Adult Education M,D,O
- Business Administration and Management—General M,D,O
- Counselor Education M,D
- Curriculum and Instruction M,D,O
- Developmental Education M,D,O
- Distance Education Development M,D,O
- Early Childhood Education M,D,O
- Education—General M,D,O
- Educational Leadership and Administration M,D,O
- Educational Measurement and Evaluation M,D,O
- Educational Media/Instructional Technology M,D,O
- Educational Psychology M,D,O
- Elementary Education M,D,O
- English as a Second Language M,D,O
- Entrepreneurship M,D,O
- Finance and Banking M,D,O
- Health Education M,D,O
- Higher Education M,D,O
- Human Resources Management M,D,O
- Human Services M,D
- International and Comparative Education M,D,O
- International Business M,D,O
- Law M,D,O
- Management Information Systems M,D,O
- Marketing M,D,O
- Mathematics Education M,D,O
- Multilingual and Multicultural Education M,D,O
- Nonprofit Management M,D,O
- Organizational Management M,D,O
- Project Management M,D,O
- Reading Education M,D,O
- Science Education M,D,O
- Social Work M,D
- Special Education M,D,O
- Supply Chain Management M,D,O

WALDORF UNIVERSITY
- Educational Leadership and Administration M
- Human Resources Development M
- Organizational Management M
- Sports Management M

WALLA WALLA UNIVERSITY
- Curriculum and Instruction M
- Education—General M
- Educational Leadership and Administration M
- Reading Education M
- Social Work M
- Special Education M

WALSH COLLEGE OF ACCOUNTANCY AND BUSINESS ADMINISTRATION
- Accounting M
- Business Administration and Management—General M
- Finance and Banking M
- Human Resources Management M
- International Business M
- Management Information Systems M
- Management Strategy and Policy M
- Marketing M
- Taxation M

WALSH UNIVERSITY
- Business Administration and Management—General M
- Counselor Education M
- Education—General M
- Higher Education M
- Marketing M
- Reading Education M
- Religious Education M
- Student Affairs M

WARNER PACIFIC COLLEGE
- Education—General M
- Human Services M
- Nonprofit Management M
- Organizational Management M

WARNER UNIVERSITY
- Accounting M
- Business Administration and Management—General M
- Curriculum and Instruction M
- Education—General M
- Educational Media/Instructional Technology M
- Elementary Education M
- Human Resources Management M
- International Business M
- Science Education M

WASHBURN UNIVERSITY
- Accounting M
- Business Administration and Management—General M
- Curriculum and Instruction M
- Education—General M
- Educational Leadership and Administration M
- Health Education M
- Human Services M
- Law M,D
- Legal and Justice Studies M,D
- Reading Education M
- Social Work M
- Special Education M

WASHINGTON ADVENTIST UNIVERSITY
- Business Administration and Management—General M

WASHINGTON & JEFFERSON COLLEGE
- Accounting M,O

WASHINGTON AND LEE UNIVERSITY
- Law D

WASHINGTON STATE UNIVERSITY
- Accounting M
- Business Administration and Management—General M,D
- Business Education M,D
- Curriculum and Instruction M,D
- Education—General M,D
- Educational Leadership and Administration M,D
- Educational Psychology M,D
- Elementary Education M,D
- English as a Second Language M,D
- Exercise and Sports Science M
- Foreign Languages Education M
- Mathematics Education M,D
- Reading Education M,D
- Secondary Education M,D
- Special Education M,D
- Sports Management M,D
- Vocational and Technical Education M,D

WASHINGTON UNIVERSITY IN ST. LOUIS
- Accounting M
- Business Administration and Management—General M,D
- Education—General M,D
- Educational Measurement and Evaluation D
- Elementary Education M
- Entrepreneurship M
- Finance and Banking M,D
- Kinesiology and Movement Studies D
- Law M,D
- Organizational Management M
- Secondary Education M
- Social Work M,D
- Special Education M,D
- Supply Chain Management M

WAYLAND BAPTIST UNIVERSITY
- Accounting M,D
- Business Administration and Management—General M,D
- Education—General M
- Educational Leadership and Administration M
- Educational Measurement and Evaluation M
- Educational Media/Instructional Technology M
- Elementary Education M
- English as a Second Language M
- English Education M
- Higher Education M
- Human Resources Management M,D
- International Business M,D
- Management Information Systems M,D
- Organizational Management M,D
- Project Management M,D
- Science Education M
- Secondary Education M
- Social Sciences Education M
- Special Education M
- Sports Management M

WAYNESBURG UNIVERSITY
- Business Administration and Management—General M,D
- Counselor Education M,D
- Curriculum and Instruction M,D
- Distance Education Development M,D
- Educational Leadership and Administration M,D
- Educational Media/Instructional Technology M,D
- Finance and Banking M,D
- Human Resources Management M,D
- Organizational Management M,D
- Special Education M,D

WAYNE STATE COLLEGE
- Business Administration and Management—General M
- Business Education M
- Counselor Education M
- Curriculum and Instruction M
- Early Childhood Education M
- Education—General M,O
- Educational Leadership and Administration M,O
- Elementary Education M
- English as a Second Language M
- English Education M
- Exercise and Sports Science M
- Home Economics Education M
- Mathematics Education M
- Music Education M
- Organizational Management M
- Physical Education M
- Science Education M
- Social Sciences Education M
- Special Education M
- Sports Management M
- Vocational and Technical Education M

WAYNE STATE UNIVERSITY
- Accounting M,D,O
- Advertising and Public Relations M,D,O
- Archives/Archival Administration M,O
- Art Education M,D,O
- Business Administration and Management—General M,D,O
- Counselor Education M,D,O
- Curriculum and Instruction M,D,O
- Developmental Education M,D,O
- Distance Education Development M,D,O
- Early Childhood Education M,D,O
- Education—General M,D,O
- Educational Leadership and Administration M,D,O
- Educational Measurement and Evaluation M,D,O
- Educational Media/Instructional Technology M,D,O
- Educational Policy M,D,O
- Educational Psychology M,D,O
- Elementary Education M,D,O
- English as a Second Language M,D,O
- English Education M,D,O
- Entrepreneurship M,D,O
- Exercise and Sports Science M,D
- Finance and Banking M,D,O
- Foreign Languages Education M,D,O
- Foundations and Philosophy of Education M,D,O
- Health Education M,D,O
- Higher Education M,D,O
- Human Resources Management M,D
- Industrial and Manufacturing Management M,D
- Information Studies M,O
- Kinesiology and Movement Studies M,D,O
- Law M,D
- Library Science M,O
- Management Information Systems M,D,O
- Management Strategy and Policy M,D,O
- Mathematics Education M,D,O
- Multilingual and Multicultural Education M,D,O
- Music Education M,D
- Nonprofit Management M,D
- Organizational Behavior M,D
- Organizational Management M,D
- Physical Education M,D
- Reading Education M,D,O
- Science Education M,D,O
- Secondary Education M,D,O
- Social Sciences Education M,D,O
- Social Work M,D,O
- Special Education M,D,O
- Sports Management M,D
- Taxation M,D,O
- Vocational and Technical Education M,D,O

WEBBER INTERNATIONAL UNIVERSITY
- Accounting M
- Business Administration and Management—General M
- International Business M
- Sports Management M

WEBER STATE UNIVERSITY
- Accounting M
- Athletic Training and Sports Medicine M
- Business Administration and Management—General M
- Curriculum and Instruction M
- Education—General M
- Legal and Justice Studies M
- Taxation M

WEBSTER UNIVERSITY
- Accounting M
- Advertising and Public Relations M
- Business Administration and Management—General M,D,O
- Early Childhood Education M,O
- Education—General M,O
- Educational Media/Instructional Technology M,O
- Educational Psychology M,O
- Elementary Education M,O
- English as a Second Language M,O
- Finance and Banking M
- Human Resources Development M,D,O
- Human Resources Management M,D,O
- Human Services M
- International Business M
- Legal and Justice Studies M,O
- Management Information Systems M,D,O
- Marketing M,D,O
- Mathematics Education M,O
- Middle School Education M,O
- Music Education M
- Nonprofit Management M,D,O
- Reading Education M,O
- Secondary Education M,O
- Special Education M,O

WENTWORTH INSTITUTE OF TECHNOLOGY
- Facilities Management M

*M—masters degree; D—doctorate; O—other advanced degree; *—Close-Up and/or Display*

WESLEYAN COLLEGE
Business Administration and Management—General M
Early Childhood Education M
Education—General M

WESLEY BIBLICAL SEMINARY
Religious Education M

WESLEY COLLEGE
Business Administration and Management—General M
Education—General M

WEST CHESTER UNIVERSITY OF PENNSYLVANIA
Athletic Training and Sports Medicine M,O
Business Administration and Management—General M,O
Business Education M,O
Counselor Education M,O
Early Childhood Education M,O
Education—General M,D,O
Educational Leadership and Administration M,D,O
Educational Media/Instructional Technology M,O
Educational Policy D
English as a Second Language M,O
English Education M,O
Entrepreneurship M,O
Exercise and Sports Science M,O
Foreign Languages Education M,O
Health Education M,O
Higher Education M,O
Human Resources Management M,O
Kinesiology and Movement Studies M,O
Management Information Systems M,O
Management Strategy and Policy M,O
Mathematics Education M,O
Music Education M,O
Nonprofit Management M,O
Physical Education M,O
Project Management M,O
Reading Education M,O
Science Education M,O
Secondary Education M,O
Social Work M
Special Education M,O
Sports Management M,O
Student Affairs M,O

WESTERN CAROLINA UNIVERSITY
Accounting M
Business Administration and Management—General M
Education—General M
English as a Second Language M
Entrepreneurship M
Project Management M,O
Social Work M

WESTERN CONNECTICUT STATE UNIVERSITY
Accounting M
Business Administration and Management—General M
Counselor Education M
Curriculum and Instruction M
Education—General M,D
Educational Leadership and Administration D
Educational Media/Instructional Technology M
Music Education M
Reading Education M
Special Education M

WESTERN GOVERNORS UNIVERSITY
Business Administration and Management—General M
Education—General M,O
Educational Leadership and Administration M,O
Educational Measurement and Evaluation M,O
Educational Media/Instructional Technology M,O
Elementary Education M,O
English Education M,O
Higher Education M,O
Management Information Systems M
Management Strategy and Policy M
Mathematics Education M,O
Science Education M,O
Social Sciences Education M,O
Special Education M,O

WESTERN ILLINOIS UNIVERSITY
Accounting M
Business Administration and Management—General M,O
Counselor Education M
Curriculum and Instruction M
Distance Education Development M,O
Education—General M,D,O
Educational Leadership and Administration M,D,O
Educational Media/Instructional Technology M,O
English as a Second Language M,O
Foundations and Philosophy of Education M,O
Health Education M,O
Higher Education M
Kinesiology and Movement Studies M
Reading Education M
Recreation and Park Management M
Special Education M
Sports Management M
Student Affairs M
Supply Chain Management M,O
Travel and Tourism M

WESTERN KENTUCKY UNIVERSITY
Adult Education M,D,O
Art Education M
Business Administration and Management—General M
Counselor Education M
Early Childhood Education M,O
Educational Leadership and Administration M,D,O
Educational Media/Instructional Technology M,O
Elementary Education M,O
English as a Second Language M
English Education M
Foreign Languages Education M
Higher Education M
Middle School Education M,O
Music Education M
Physical Education M
Reading Education M,O
Recreation and Park Management M
Secondary Education M,O
Social Work M
Special Education M,O
Sports Management M
Student Affairs M

WESTERN MICHIGAN UNIVERSITY
Accounting M
Art Education M
Athletic Training and Sports Medicine M
Business Administration and Management—General M
Counselor Education M,D
Education—General M,D,O
Educational Leadership and Administration M,D,O
Educational Measurement and Evaluation M,D,O
Educational Media/Instructional Technology M,D,O
English Education M,D
Exercise and Sports Science M
Health Education D,O
Higher Education M,D
Human Services D,O
Mathematics Education M,D
Music Education M,O
Nonprofit Management M,D,O
Physical Education M
Reading Education M,D
Science Education M,D,O
Social Work M
Special Education M,D
Sports Management M
Vocational and Technical Education M

WESTERN MICHIGAN UNIVERSITY THOMAS M. COOLEY LAW SCHOOL
Environmental Law M,D
Finance and Banking M,D
Insurance M,D
Intellectual Property Law M,D
Law M,D
Legal and Justice Studies M,D
Taxation M,D

WESTERN NEW ENGLAND UNIVERSITY
Accounting M
Advertising and Public Relations M
Business Administration and Management—General M
Curriculum and Instruction M
English Education M
Law M,D
Mathematics Education M
Organizational Management M
Sports Management M

WESTERN NEW MEXICO UNIVERSITY
Business Administration and Management—General M
Education—General M
Educational Leadership and Administration M
Elementary Education M
English as a Second Language M
Multilingual and Multicultural Education M
Reading Education M
Secondary Education M
Social Work M
Special Education M

WESTERN OREGON UNIVERSITY
Early Childhood Education M
Education—General M
Educational Media/Instructional Technology M
Health Education M
Mathematics Education M
Multilingual and Multicultural Education M
Science Education M
Secondary Education M
Social Sciences Education M
Special Education M

WESTERN SEMINARY
Human Resources Development M

WESTERN STATE COLLEGE OF LAW AT ARGOSY UNIVERSITY
Law D

WESTERN STATE COLORADO UNIVERSITY
Education—General M
Educational Leadership and Administration M
Reading Education M

WESTERN UNIVERSITY OF HEALTH SCIENCES
Health Education M

WESTERN WASHINGTON UNIVERSITY
Adult Education M
Business Administration and Management—General M
Counselor Education M
Education of the Gifted M
Education—General M
Educational Leadership and Administration M
Elementary Education M
Environmental Education M
Exercise and Sports Science M
Higher Education M
Physical Education M
Science Education M
Secondary Education M

WESTFIELD STATE UNIVERSITY
Accounting M
Counselor Education M
Early Childhood Education M
Education—General M
Elementary Education M
Mathematics Education M
Nonprofit Management M
Physical Education M
Reading Education M
Science Education M
Secondary Education M
Social Sciences Education M
Social Work M
Special Education M
Vocational and Technical Education M

WEST LIBERTY UNIVERSITY
Education—General M
Organizational Management M

WESTMINSTER COLLEGE (PA)
Counselor Education M,O
Early Childhood Education M,O
Educational Leadership and Administration M,O
Reading Education M,O
Special Education M,O

WESTMINSTER COLLEGE (UT)
Accounting M,O
Business Administration and Management—General M,O
Education—General M

WEST TEXAS A&M UNIVERSITY
Business Administration and Management—General M
Counselor Education M
Curriculum and Instruction M
Education—General M
Educational Leadership and Administration M
Educational Measurement and Evaluation M
Educational Media/Instructional Technology M
Exercise and Sports Science M
Finance and Banking M
Reading Education M
Social Work M
Sports Management M

WEST VIRGINIA UNIVERSITY
Accounting M
Agricultural Education M,D
Art Education M
Athletic Training and Sports Medicine M,D
Business Administration and Management—General M
Counselor Education M
Curriculum and Instruction M,D
Early Childhood Education M,D
Education of Students with Severe/Multiple Disabilities M,D
Education of the Gifted M,D
Education—General M,D
Educational Leadership and Administration M,D
Educational Media/Instructional Technology M,D
Educational Psychology M
Elementary Education M
English as a Second Language M,D
Environmental Education M,D
Exercise and Sports Science M,D
Higher Education M,D
Human Services M,D
Law M,D
Legal and Justice Studies M
Marketing M,O
Mathematics Education M,D
Music Education M,D
Physical Education M,D
Reading Education M
Recreation and Park Management M
Secondary Education M,D
Social Work M
Special Education M,D
Sports Management M,D

WEST VIRGINIA WESLEYAN COLLEGE
Athletic Training and Sports Medicine M
Business Administration and Management—General M
Education—General M

WHEATON COLLEGE
Education—General M
Elementary Education M
English as a Second Language M,O
Religious Education M
Secondary Education M

WHEELING JESUIT UNIVERSITY
Accounting M
Business Administration and Management—General M
Educational Leadership and Administration M
Organizational Management M

WHEELOCK COLLEGE
Early Childhood Education M
Education—General M
Educational Leadership and Administration M
Elementary Education M
Reading Education M
Social Work M
Special Education M

WHITTIER COLLEGE
Education—General M
Educational Leadership and Administration M
Elementary Education M
Secondary Education M

WHITWORTH UNIVERSITY
Business Administration and Management—General M
Counselor Education M
Education of the Gifted M
Education—General M
Educational Leadership and Administration M
Elementary Education M
Secondary Education M
Special Education M

WHU - OTTO BEISHEIM SCHOOL OF MANAGEMENT
Business Administration and Management—General M

WICHITA STATE UNIVERSITY
Accounting M
Business Administration and Management—General M
Counselor Education M,D,O
Curriculum and Instruction M
Early Childhood Education M
Education of the Gifted M
Education—General M,D,O
Educational Leadership and Administration M,D,O
Educational Psychology M,D,O
Entrepreneurship M
Exercise and Sports Science M
Human Services M
Management Information Systems M
Middle School Education M
Music Education M
Secondary Education M
Social Work M
Special Education M
Sports Management M
Taxation M

WIDENER UNIVERSITY
Adult Education M,D
Business Administration and Management—General M
Counselor Education M,D
Early Childhood Education M,D
Education—General M,D
Educational Leadership and Administration M,D
Educational Media/Instructional Technology M,D
Educational Psychology M,D
Elementary Education M,D
English Education M,D
Foundations and Philosophy of Education M,D
Health Education M,D
Health Law M,D
Hospitality Management M,D
Law M,D
Mathematics Education M,D
Middle School Education M,D
Reading Education M,D
Science Education M,D
Social Sciences Education M,D
Social Work M,D
Special Education M,D
Taxation M

WILFRID LAURIER UNIVERSITY
Accounting M,D
Business Administration and Management—General M,D
Finance and Banking M,D
Human Resources Management M,D
Kinesiology and Movement Studies M
Legal and Justice Studies D
Marketing M,D
Organizational Behavior M,D
Organizational Management M,D
Physical Education M
Social Work M,D
Supply Chain Management M,D

WILKES UNIVERSITY
Accounting M
Art Education M,D
Business Administration and Management—General M
Curriculum and Instruction M,D
Distance Education Development M,D
Early Childhood Education M,D
Education—General M,D
Educational Leadership and Administration M,D
Educational Measurement and Evaluation M,D
Educational Media/Instructional Technology M,D
English as a Second Language M,D
Entrepreneurship M
Finance and Banking M
Human Resources Management M
Industrial and Manufacturing Management M
International and Comparative Education M,D

International Business	M
Middle School Education	M,D
Organizational Management	M
Reading Education	M,D
Science Education	M,D
Special Education	M,D

WILLAMETTE UNIVERSITY

Business Administration and Management—General	M
Law	M,D

William Carey University

Art Education	M,O
Business Administration and Management—General	M
Education of the Gifted	M,O
Education—General	M,O
Elementary Education	M,O
English Education	M,O
Secondary Education	M,O
Social Sciences Education	M,O
Special Education	M,O

WILLIAM JAMES COLLEGE

Student Affairs	M,D,O

WILLIAM JESSUP UNIVERSITY

Education—General	M
English Education	M
Mathematics Education	M

WILLIAM JEWELL COLLEGE

Education—General	M

WILLIAM PATERSON UNIVERSITY OF NEW JERSEY

Business Administration and Management—General	M
Counselor Education	M
Education—General	M
Educational Leadership and Administration	M
Elementary Education	M
Exercise and Sports Science	M,D
Foundations and Philosophy of Education	M,D
Reading Education	M
Secondary Education	M
Special Education	M

WILLIAM PENN UNIVERSITY

Organizational Management	M

WILLIAMSON COLLEGE

Organizational Management	M

WILLIAM WOODS UNIVERSITY

Advertising and Public Relations	M,D,O
Business Administration and Management—General	M,D,O
Curriculum and Instruction	M,D,O
Educational Leadership and Administration	M,D,O
Educational Media/Instructional Technology	M,D,O
Human Resources Development	M,D,O
Marketing	M,D,O
Physical Education	M,D,O

WILMINGTON COLLEGE

Education—General	M
Reading Education	M
Special Education	M

WILMINGTON UNIVERSITY

Accounting	M,D
Business Administration and Management—General	M,D
Counselor Education	M,D
Education of the Gifted	M,D
Education—General	M,D
Educational Leadership and Administration	M,D
Educational Media/Instructional Technology	M,D
Elementary Education	M,D
English as a Second Language	M,D
Finance and Banking	M,D
Higher Education	M,D
Human Resources Management	M,D
Human Services	M
Management Information Systems	M,D
Marketing	M,D
Organizational Management	M,D
Reading Education	M,D
Secondary Education	M,D
Special Education	M,D
Vocational and Technical Education	M,D

WILSON COLLEGE

Accounting	M
Business Administration and Management—General	M
Education—General	M
Elementary Education	M
Secondary Education	M

WINGATE UNIVERSITY

Accounting	M
Business Administration and Management—General	M
Community College Education	M,D,O
Education—General	M,D,O
Educational Leadership and Administration	M,D,O
Elementary Education	M,D,O
Entrepreneurship	M
Finance and Banking	M
Marketing	M
Project Management	M
Sports Management	M

WINONA STATE UNIVERSITY

Counselor Education	M
Education—General	M
Educational Leadership and Administration	M,O
Recreation and Park Management	M,O
Special Education	M
Sports Management	M,O

WINSTON-SALEM STATE UNIVERSITY

Business Administration and Management—General	M
Education—General	M
Management Information Systems	M
Middle School Education	M
Special Education	M

WINTHROP UNIVERSITY

Art Education	M
Business Administration and Management—General	M
Counselor Education	M
Education—General	M
Educational Leadership and Administration	M
Music Education	M
Physical Education	M
Secondary Education	M
Social Work	M
Special Education	M

WISCONSIN LUTHERAN COLLEGE

Curriculum and Instruction	M
Educational Leadership and Administration	M
Educational Media/Instructional Technology	M
Science Education	M

WITTENBERG UNIVERSITY

Education—General	M

WOODBURY UNIVERSITY

Business Administration and Management—General	M
Organizational Management	M

WORCESTER POLYTECHNIC INSTITUTE

Business Administration and Management—General	M,D,O
Educational Media/Instructional Technology	M,D
Management Information Systems	M,D,O
Marketing	M,D,O
Organizational Management	M,D,O

WORCESTER STATE UNIVERSITY

Accounting	M
Business Administration and Management—General	M
Early Childhood Education	M
Education—General	M,O
Educational Leadership and Administration	M,O
Elementary Education	M
English as a Second Language	M,O
English Education	M
Foreign Languages Education	M
Health Education	M
Middle School Education	M,O
Nonprofit Management	M
Organizational Management	M
Reading Education	M,O
Secondary Education	M,O
Social Sciences Education	M
Special Education	M,O

WRIGHT STATE UNIVERSITY

Accounting	M
Business Administration and Management—General	M
Counselor Education	M
Curriculum and Instruction	O
Education—General	M,O
Educational Leadership and Administration	O
Elementary Education	M
Health Education	M
Logistics	M
Management Information Systems	M
Mathematics Education	D
Music Education	M
Science Education	M,D
Secondary Education	M
Special Education	M
Supply Chain Management	M

XAVIER UNIVERSITY

Accounting	M
Athletic Training and Sports Medicine	M
Business Administration and Management—General	M
Counselor Education	M
Early Childhood Education	M
Education—General	M,D
Educational Leadership and Administration	M,D
Elementary Education	M
Finance and Banking	M
Human Resources Development	M,D
International Business	M
Management Strategy and Policy	M
Marketing	M
Multilingual and Multicultural Education	M
Reading Education	M
Religious Education	M
Secondary Education	M
Special Education	M
Sports Management	M

XAVIER UNIVERSITY OF LOUISIANA

Counselor Education	M
Curriculum and Instruction	M
Education—General	M
Educational Leadership and Administration	M

YALE UNIVERSITY

Accounting	D
Business Administration and Management—General	M,D
Finance and Banking	D
Law	M,D
Marketing	D
Organizational Management	D

YESHIVA UNIVERSITY

Accounting	M
Business Administration and Management—General	M
Educational Leadership and Administration	M,D,O
Intellectual Property Law	M,D
Law	M,D
Marketing	M
Religious Education	M,D,O
Social Work	M,D

YORK COLLEGE OF PENNSYLVANIA

Business Administration and Management—General	M
Education—General	M
Educational Leadership and Administration	M
Educational Media/Instructional Technology	M
Finance and Banking	M
Marketing	M
Reading Education	M

YORK UNIVERSITY

Accounting	M,D
Business Administration and Management—General	M,D
Education—General	M,D
Finance and Banking	M,D
Human Resources Management	M,D
International Business	M,D
Kinesiology and Movement Studies	M,D
Law	M,D
Social Work	M,D

YOUNGSTOWN STATE UNIVERSITY

Accounting	M
Business Administration and Management—General	M,O
Counselor Education	M
Curriculum and Instruction	M
Early Childhood Education	M
Education of the Gifted	M
Education—General	M,D
Educational Leadership and Administration	M,D
Educational Media/Instructional Technology	M
Finance and Banking	M
Human Services	M
Marketing	M
Mathematics Education	M
Middle School Education	M
Music Education	M
Reading Education	M
Science Education	M
Secondary Education	M
Special Education	M

*M—masters degree; D—doctorate; O—other advanced degree; *—Close-Up and/or Display*

ACADEMIC AND PROFESSIONAL PROGRAMS IN BUSINESS

Section 1
Business Administration and Management

This section contains a directory of institutions offering graduate work in business administration and management, followed by in-depth entries submitted by institutions that chose to prepare detailed program descriptions. Additional information about programs listed in the directory but not augmented by an in-depth entry may be obtained by writing directly to the dean of a graduate school or chair of a department at the address given in the directory.

For programs offering related work, see also in this book Sections 2–18, Education (Business Education), and Sports Management. In the other guides in this series:

Graduate Programs in the Humanities, Arts & Social Sciences

See *Art and Art History (Arts Administration), Economics, Family and Consumer Sciences (Consumer Economics), Political Science and International Affairs, Psychology (Industrial and Organizational Psychology),* and *Public, Regional, and Industrial Affairs (Industrial and Labor Relations)*

Graduate Programs in the Biological/Biomedical Sciences & Health-Related Medical Professions

See *Health Services* and *Nursing (Nursing and Healthcare Administration)*

Graduate Programs in the Physical Sciences, Mathematics, Agricultural Sciences, the Environment & Natural Resources

See *Environmental Sciences and Management (Environmental Management and Policy)* and *Mathematical Sciences*

Graduate Programs in Engineering & Applied Sciences

See *Computer Science and Information Technology, Civil and Environmental Engineering (Construction Engineering and Management), Industrial Engineering,* and *Management of Engineering and Technology*

CONTENTS

Program Directory

Featured Schools: Displays and Close-Ups

See also:

Business Administration and Management—General

Abilene Christian University, Graduate Programs, College of Business Administration, Program in Business Administration, Abilene, TX 79699. Offers MBA. *Program availability:* Part-time, online only, 100% online. *Students:* 45 full-time (19 women), 34 part-time (13 women); includes 28 minority (14 Black or African American, non-Hispanic/Latino; 2 Asian, non-Hispanic/Latino; 11 Hispanic/Latino; 1 Two or more races, non-Hispanic/Latino). 61 applicants, 93% accepted, 52 enrolled. *Entrance requirements:* Additional exam requirements/recommendations for international students: Required—TOEFL (minimum score 80 iBT), IELTS (minimum score 6). *Application deadline:* For fall admission, 8/14 priority date for domestic students; for winter admission, 10/1 priority date for domestic students; for spring admission, 12/15 priority date for domestic students; for summer admission, 4/15 priority date for domestic students. Applications are processed on a rolling basis. Application fee: $50. Electronic applications accepted. *Expenses:* $700 per credit hour. *Financial support:* Application deadline: 4/1; applicants required to submit FAFSA. *Faculty research:* Organizational structure, financial management, cost accounting, unit analysis management. *Unit head:* Jonathan Wilson, Program Director, 214-305-9500, E-mail: jxw15b@acu.edu. *Application contact:* Graduate Admissions, 817-219-7000, E-mail: gradonline@acu.edu.
Website: http://www.acu.edu/online/academics/mba-business-administration.html

Adelphi University, Robert B. Willumstad School of Business, MBA Program, Garden City, NY 11530-0701. Offers accounting (MBA); finance (MBA); health services administration (MBA); human resource management (MBA); management (MBA); management information systems (MBA); marketing (MBA); sport management (MBA). *Accreditation:* AACSB. *Program availability:* Part-time, evening/weekend. *Students:* 172 full-time (74 women), 129 part-time (66 women); includes 30 minority (9 Black or African American, non-Hispanic/Latino; 11 Asian, non-Hispanic/Latino; 9 Hispanic/Latino; 1 Two or more races, non-Hispanic/Latino), 29 international. Average age 32. 4 applicants. In 2016, 130 master's awarded. *Degree requirements:* For master's, capstone course. *Entrance requirements:* For master's, GMAT, 2 letters of recommendation. Additional exam requirements/recommendations for international students: Required—TOEFL (minimum score 550 paper-based; 80 iBT), IELTS (minimum score 6.5). *Application deadline:* For fall admission, 4/1 for international students; for spring admission, 11/1 for international students. Applications are processed on a rolling basis. Application fee: $50. Electronic applications accepted. *Expenses:* Contact institution. *Financial support:* Research assistantships with partial tuition reimbursements, career-related internships or fieldwork, Federal Work-Study, institutionally sponsored loans, scholarships/grants, tuition waivers (partial), and unspecified assistantships available. Financial award application deadline: 3/1; financial award applicants required to submit FAFSA. *Faculty research:* Supply chain management, distribution channels, productivity benchmark analysis, data envelopment analysis, financial portfolio analysis. *Unit head:* Dr. Rakesh Gupta, Associate Dean, 516-877-4629. *Application contact:* Christine Murphy, Director of Admissions, 516-877-3050, Fax: 516-877-3039,
E-mail: graduateadmissions@adelphi.edu.
Website: http://business.adelphi.edu/degree-programs/graduate-degree-programs/m-b-a/

Alabama State University, College of Business Administration, Montgomery, AL 36101-0271. Offers M Acc. *Accreditation:* ACBSP. *Program availability:* Part-time. *Faculty:* 4 full-time (1 woman), 1 part-time/adjunct (0 women). *Students:* 9 full-time (7 women), 2 part-time (both women); includes 6 minority (all Black or African American, non-Hispanic/Latino), 4 international. Average age 29. 24 applicants, 33% accepted, 5 enrolled. In 2016, 10 master's awarded. *Degree requirements:* For master's, comprehensive exam. *Entrance requirements:* For master's, minimum GPA of 2.75 (undergraduate), 3.0 (graduate); bachelor's degree or its equivalent from accredited college or university. Additional exam requirements/recommendations for international students: Required—TOEFL (minimum score 500 paper-based). *Application deadline:* For fall admission, 4/15 for domestic and international students; for spring admission, 11/15 for domestic students, 11/1 for international students; for summer admission, 3/15 for domestic and international students. Application fee: $25. Electronic applications accepted. *Expenses:* Tuition, state resident: full-time $3087; part-time $2744 per credit. Tuition, nonresident: full-time $6174; part-time $5488 per credit. *Required fees:* $2284; $1142 per credit. $571 per semester. Tuition and fees vary according to class time, course level, course load, degree level, program and student level. *Financial support:* Fellowships and unspecified assistantships available. Financial award application deadline: 6/30; financial award applicants required to submit FAFSA. *Unit head:* Dr. Kamal K. Hingorani, Interim Dean, 334-229-4124, E-mail: khingorani@alasu.edu. *Application contact:* Dr. William Person, Dean of Graduate Studies, 334-229-4274, Fax: 334-229-4928, E-mail: wperson@alasu.edu.
Website: http://www.alasu.edu/academics/colleges—departments/college-of-business-administration/index.aspx

Alaska Pacific University, Graduate Programs, Business Administration Department, Program in Business Administration, Anchorage, AK 99508-4672. Offers business administration (MBA); health services administration (MBA). *Program availability:* Part-time, evening/weekend. *Degree requirements:* For master's, capstone course. *Entrance requirements:* For master's, GMAT or GRE General Test, minimum GPA of 3.0.

Albany State University, College of Business, Albany, GA 31705-2717. Offers accounting (MBA); general business administration (MBA); healthcare (MBA); public administration (MBA); supply chain and logistics (MBA). *Accreditation:* ACBSP. *Program availability:* Part-time, evening/weekend. *Degree requirements:* For master's, comprehensive exam, internship, 3 hours of physical education. *Entrance requirements:* For master's, GMAT (minimum score of 450)/GRE (minimum score of 800) for those without earned master's degree or higher, minimum undergraduate GPA of 2.5, 2 letters of reference, official transcript, pre-entrance medical record and certificate of immunization. *Application deadline:* For fall admission, 6/1 for domestic students, 5/1 for international students; for spring admission, 11/1 for domestic students, 10/1 for international students. Applications are processed on a rolling basis. Application fee: $20. Electronic applications accepted. *Financial support:* Application deadline: 4/15; applicants required to submit FAFSA. *Faculty research:* Diversity issues, ancestry, understanding finance through use of technology. *Unit head:* Dr. Alicia Jackson, Dean, 229-430-7009, Fax: 229-430-5119. *Application contact:* Jeffrey Pierce, II, Graduate Counselor, 229-430-4646, Fax: 229-430-4105, E-mail: jeffrey.pierce@asurams.edu.
Website: https://www.asurams.edu/Academics/collegeofbusiness/

Albertus Magnus College, Master of Arts in Leadership Program, New Haven, CT 06511-1189. Offers MA. *Program availability:* Part-time, evening/weekend, blended/hybrid learning. *Faculty:* 2 full-time (0 women), 4 part-time/adjunct (2 women). *Students:* 2 full-time (both women), 10 part-time (7 women); includes 4 minority (3 Black or African American, non-Hispanic/Latino; 1 Hispanic/Latino). Average age 39. In 2016, 8 master's awarded. *Degree requirements:* For master's, thesis optional. *Entrance requirements:* For master's, interview, minimum GPA of 2.7. Additional exam requirements/recommendations for international students: Required—TWE; Recommended—TOEFL (minimum score 550 paper-based; 80 iBT). *Application deadline:* Applications are processed on a rolling basis. Application fee: $50. Electronic applications accepted. *Expenses:* Contact institution. *Financial support:* Federal Work-Study and unspecified assistantships available. Support available to part-time students. Financial award applicants required to submit FAFSA. *Faculty research:* Leadership, quality management, employee motivation. *Unit head:* Dr. Howard Fero, Director, 203-773-4424, E-mail: hfero@albertus.edu. *Application contact:* Anthony Reich, Director of Admission, Division of Professional and Graduate Studies, 203-773-5032, Fax: 203-773-5257, E-mail: leadership@albertus.edu.
Website: http://www.albertus.edu/leadership/ms/

Albertus Magnus College, Master of Business Administration Program, New Haven, CT 06511-1189. Offers MBA. Program also offered in East Hartford, CT. *Program availability:* Part-time, evening/weekend, 100% online, blended/hybrid learning. *Faculty:* 7 full-time (2 women), 24 part-time/adjunct (6 women). *Students:* 82 full-time (53 women), 21 part-time (12 women); includes 61 minority (43 Black or African American, non-Hispanic/Latino; 2 Asian, non-Hispanic/Latino; 13 Hispanic/Latino; 3 Two or more races, non-Hispanic/Latino), 2 international. Average age 34. In 2016, 51 master's awarded. *Degree requirements:* For master's, thesis, capstone project, business plan, minimum cumulative GPA of 3.0, complete all requirements within seven years of matriculation. *Entrance requirements:* For master's, 3 years of management or related experience, minimum GPA of 2.5, 2 letters of recommendation, official transcripts. Additional exam requirements/recommendations for international students: Recommended—TOEFL (minimum score 550 paper-based; 80 iBT). *Application deadline:* Applications are processed on a rolling basis. Application fee: $50. Electronic applications accepted. *Expenses:* Contact institution. *Financial support:* Federal Work-Study and unspecified assistantships available. Support available to part-time students. Financial award applicants required to submit FAFSA. *Faculty research:* Finance, project management, accounting, business administration, generalist. *Unit head:* Dr. Wayne Gineo, Director, MBA Programs, 203-672-6670, E-mail: wgineo@albertus.edu. *Application contact:* Anthony Reich, Director of Admission, Division of Professional and Graduate Studies, 203-773-5302, E-mail: arreich@albertus.edu.
Website: http://www.albertus.edu/business-administration/ms/

Alcorn State University, School of Graduate Studies, School of Business, Lorman, MS 39096-7500. Offers MBA. *Accreditation:* ACBSP.

Alfred University, Graduate School, School of Business, Alfred, NY 14802-1205. Offers accounting (MBA); business administration (MBA). *Accreditation:* AACSB. *Program availability:* Part-time. *Students:* 28 full-time (11 women), 20 part-time (8 women); includes 10 minority (7 Black or African American, non-Hispanic/Latino; 1 Asian, non-Hispanic/Latino; 2 Hispanic/Latino), 1 international. Average age 24. In 2016, 31 master's awarded. *Entrance requirements:* For master's, GMAT. Additional exam requirements/recommendations for international students: Required—TOEFL (minimum score 590 paper-based; 90 iBT), IELTS (minimum score 6.5). *Application deadline:* For fall admission, 8/1 for domestic students, 3/15 for international students; for winter admission, 12/1 for domestic students; for spring admission, 10/1 for international students. Applications are processed on a rolling basis. Application fee: $60. Electronic applications accepted. *Expenses:* *Tuition:* Full-time $38,020; part-time $810 per credit. *Required fees:* $970; $82 per semester. *Financial support:* Research assistantships with partial tuition reimbursements, tuition waivers (partial), and unspecified assistantships available. Financial award applicants required to submit FAFSA. *Unit head:* Dr. Nancy Evangelista, Dean of the College of Professional Studies, 607-871-2124, Fax: 607-871-2114, E-mail: fevangel@alfred.edu. *Application contact:* Sara Love, Coordinator of Graduate Admissions, 607-871-2115, Fax: 607-871-2198, E-mail: gradinquiry@alfred.edu.
Website: http://business.alfred.edu/mba/

Alliant International University–Los Angeles, Marshall Goldsmith School of Management, Business Division, Alhambra, CA 91803. Offers DBA.

Alliant International University–San Diego, Alliant School of Management, Business and Management Division, San Diego, CA 92131. Offers business administration (MBA); MBA/MA; MBA/PhD. *Program availability:* Part-time, evening/weekend. *Entrance requirements:* For master's, GMAT or GRE, minimum GPA of 2.75. Additional exam requirements/recommendations for international students: Required—TOEFL (minimum score 550 paper-based; 80 iBT), TWE (minimum score 5). Electronic applications accepted. *Faculty research:* Financial and commodity markets, market micro-structures, risk measurement, virtual teams, sustainable work environments.

Alvernia University, School of Graduate Studies, Department of Business, Reading, PA 19607-1799. Offers MBA. *Accreditation:* ACBSP. *Program availability:* Part-time, evening/weekend. *Degree requirements:* For master's, thesis optional. *Entrance requirements:* For master's, GMAT, GRE, or MAT. Electronic applications accepted.

Alverno College, School of Business, Milwaukee, WI 53234-3922. Offers MBA. *Program availability:* Evening/weekend. *Faculty:* 4 full-time (3 women), 3 part-time/adjunct (0 women). *Students:* 71 full-time (59 women); includes 28 minority (11 Black or African American, non-Hispanic/Latino; 1 American Indian or Alaska Native, non-Hispanic/Latino; 5 Asian, non-Hispanic/Latino; 8 Hispanic/Latino; 3 Two or more races, non-Hispanic/Latino). Average age 34. 33 applicants, 100% accepted, 29 enrolled. In 2016, 21 master's awarded. *Entrance requirements:* For master's, 3 or more years of relevant work experience. Additional exam requirements/recommendations for international students: Required—TOEFL. *Application deadline:* For fall admission, 7/15 priority date for domestic and international students; for spring admission, 12/15 priority date for domestic and international students. Applications are processed on a rolling basis. Application fee: $0. Electronic applications accepted. *Expenses:* Contact institution. *Financial support:* Federal Work-Study and scholarships/grants available. Support available to part-time students. Financial award applicants required to submit FAFSA. *Unit head:* Eileen Sherman, Dean, School of Business, 414-382-6503, E-mail: eileen.sherman@alverno.edu. *Application contact:* Janet Stikel, Associate Director of Adult and Graduate Admissions, 414-382-6112, Fax: 414-382-6354, E-mail: janet.stikel@alverno.edu.

Amberton University, Graduate School, Department of Business Administration, Garland, TX 75041-5595. Offers general business (MBA); management (MBA); project management (MBA); strategic leadership (MBA). *Program availability:* Part-time, evening/weekend. *Entrance requirements:* For master's, minimum GPA of 3.0.

Amberton University, Graduate School, Program in Managerial Science, Garland, TX 75041-5595. Offers MS.

American Business & Technology University, Programs in Business Administration, Saint Joseph, MO 64506. Offers business administration (MBA); financial management (MBA); global business management (MBA); information systems management (MBA); marketing and social media (MBA); project and operations management (MBA); public accounting (MBA). *Program availability:* Online learning.

The American College of Financial Services, Graduate Programs, Bryn Mawr, PA 19010-2105. Offers financial services (MSFS); leadership (MSM). *Program availability:* Part-time, evening/weekend, online learning. Electronic applications accepted. *Faculty research:* Retirement counseling, social security, aging, family composition, inflation.

American College of Thessaloniki, Department of Business Administration, Pylea, Greece. Offers banking and finance (MBA); entrepreneurship (MBA, Certificate); finance (Certificate); management (MBA, Certificate); marketing (MBA, Certificate). *Program availability:* Part-time, evening/weekend. *Degree requirements:* For master's, thesis. *Entrance requirements:* For master's, bachelor's degree. Additional exam requirements/recommendations for international students: Recommended—TOEFL. Electronic applications accepted.

American Graduate University, Program in Acquisition Management, Covina, CA 91724. Offers MAM, Certificate. *Program availability:* Part-time, online learning. *Degree requirements:* For master's, thesis (for some programs), comprehensive exam or project. *Entrance requirements:* For master's, undergraduate degree from institution accredited by accrediting agency recognized by the U.S. Department of Education. Additional exam requirements/recommendations for international students: Required—TOEFL. *Application deadline:* Applications are processed on a rolling basis. Application fee: $50. Electronic applications accepted. *Unit head:* Paul McDonald, President, 626-966-4576 Ext. 1006, E-mail: paulmcdonald@agu.edu. *Application contact:* Laurie Mejia, Director of Admissions, 626-966-4576 Ext. 1007, Fax: 626-915-1709, E-mail: lauriemejia@agu.edu.
Website: http://www.agu.edu/Acquisition_mgnt/master_aq.html

American Graduate University, Program in Business Administration, Covina, CA 91724. Offers acquisition and contracting (MBA); supply chain management (MBA). *Program availability:* Part-time, online learning. *Degree requirements:* For master's, thesis. *Entrance requirements:* For master's, undergraduate degree from institution accredited by accrediting agency recognized by the U.S. Department of Education. Additional exam requirements/recommendations for international students: Required—TOEFL. *Application deadline:* Applications are processed on a rolling basis. Application fee: $50. Electronic applications accepted. *Unit head:* Paul McDonald, President, 626-966-4576 Ext. 1006, E-mail: paulmcdonald@agu.edu. *Application contact:* Laurie Mejia, Director of Admissions, 626-966-4576 Ext. 1007, Fax: 626-915-1709, E-mail: lauriemejia@agu.edu.

American Graduate University, Program in Contract Management, Covina, CA 91724. Offers MCM, Certificate. *Program availability:* Part-time, online learning. *Degree requirements:* For master's, comprehensive exam (for some programs), thesis (for some programs), comprehensive exam or project. *Entrance requirements:* For master's, undergraduate degree from institution accredited by accrediting agency recognized by the U.S. Department of Education. Additional exam requirements/recommendations for international students: Required—TOEFL. *Application deadline:* Applications are processed on a rolling basis. Application fee: $50. Electronic applications accepted. *Unit head:* Paul McDonald, President, 626-966-4576 Ext. 1006, E-mail: paulmcdonald@agu.edu. *Application contact:* Laurie Mejia, Director of Admissions, 626-966-4576 Ext. 1007, Fax: 626-915-1709, E-mail: lauriemejia@agu.edu.
Website: http://www.agu.edu/Acquisition_mgnt/master_contract.html

American InterContinental University Houston, School of Business, Houston, TX 77042. Offers management (MBA).

American InterContinental University Online, Program in Business Administration, Schaumburg, IL 60173. Offers accounting and finance (MBA); finance (MBA); healthcare management (MBA); human resource management (MBA); international business (MBA); management (MBA); marketing (MBA); operations management (MBA); organizational psychology and development (MBA); project management (MBA). *Accreditation:* ACBSP. *Program availability:* Evening/weekend, online learning. *Entrance requirements:* Additional exam requirements/recommendations for international students: Required—TOEFL (minimum score 550 paper-based). Electronic applications accepted.

American International College, School of Business, Arts and Sciences, Springfield, MA 01109-3189. Offers accounting and taxation (MS); business administration (MBA); clinical psychology (MA); educational psychology (Ed D); forensic psychology (MS); general psychology (MA, CAGS); management (CAGS); resort and casino management (MBA, CAGS). *Program availability:* Part-time, evening/weekend. *Degree requirements:* For master's, comprehensive exam (for some programs), thesis (for some programs), practicum; for doctorate, comprehensive exam (for some programs), thesis/dissertation; for CAGS, comprehensive exam (for some programs), thesis (for some programs). *Entrance requirements:* For master's, BS or BA; for doctorate, interview. Additional exam requirements/recommendations for international students: Required—TOEFL (minimum score 550 paper-based; 80 iBT). *Expenses: Tuition:* Full-time $7902; part-time $750 per semester hour. *Required fees:* $60; $60 per semester hour. $30 per semester. One-time fee: $100. Tuition and fees vary according to course load, degree level, campus/location and program.

American Jewish University, Graduate School of Nonprofit Management, Program in Business Administration, Bel Air, CA 90077-1599. Offers general nonprofit administration (MBA); Jewish nonprofit administration (MBA). *Program availability:* Part-time, evening/weekend. *Degree requirements:* For master's, thesis, internship. *Entrance requirements:* For master's, GMAT or GRE General Test, interview, minimum undergraduate GPA of 3.0. Additional exam requirements/recommendations for international students: Required—TOEFL (minimum score 550 paper-based).

American National University, Program in Business Administration, Salem, VA 24153. Offers MBA.

American Public University System, AMU/APU Graduate Programs, Charles Town, WV 25414. Offers accounting (MBA, MS); applied business analytics (MBA, MS); criminal justice (MA), including business administration, emergency and disaster management, general (MA, MS); educational leadership (M Ed); emergency and disaster management (MA); entrepreneurship (MBA); environmental policy and management (MS), including environmental planning, environmental sustainability, fish and wildlife management, general (MA, MS), global environmental management; finance (MBA); general (MBA); government contracting and acquisition (MBA); health care administration (MBA); health information management (MS); history (MA), including American history, ancient and classical history, European history, global history, public history; homeland security (MA), including business administration, counterterrorism studies, criminal justice, cyber, emergency management and public health, intelligence studies, transportation security; homeland security resource allocation (MBA); humanities (MA); information technology (MS), including digital forensics, enterprise software development, information assurance and security, IT project management; information technology management (MBA); intelligence studies (MA), including criminal intelligence, cyber, general (MA, MS), homeland security, intelligence analysis, intelligence collection, intelligence management, intelligence operations, terrorism studies; international relations and conflict resolution (MA), including comparative and security issues, conflict resolution, international and transnational security issues, peacekeeping; legal studies (MA); management (MA), including strategic consulting; marketing (MBA); military history (MA), including American military history, American Revolution, civil war, war since 1945, World War II; military studies (MA), including joint warfare, strategic leadership; national security studies (MA), including cyber, general (MA, MS), homeland security, regional security studies, security and intelligence analysis, terrorism studies; nonprofit management (MBA); political science (MA), including American politics and government, comparative government and development, general (MA, MS), international relations, public policy; psychology (MA); public administration (MPA), including disaster management, environmental policy, health policy, human resources, national security, organizational management, security management; public health (MPH); reverse logistics management (MA); security management (MA); space studies (MS), including aerospace science, general (MA, MS), planetary science; sports and health sciences (MS); sports management (MBA); teaching (M Ed), including autism spectrum disorder, curriculum and instruction for elementary teachers, elementary reading, English language learners, instructional leadership, online learning, special education, STEAM (STEM plus the arts); transportation and logistics management (MA). *Program availability:* Part-time, evening/weekend, online only, 100% online. *Faculty:* 401 full-time (228 women), 1,678 part-time/adjunct (781 women). *Students:* 378 full-time (184 women), 8,455 part-time (3,484 women); includes 2,972 minority (1,552 Black or African American, non-Hispanic/Latino; 52 American Indian or Alaska Native, non-Hispanic/Latino; 211 Asian, non-Hispanic/Latino; 791 Hispanic/Latino; 70 Native Hawaiian or other Pacific Islander, non-Hispanic/Latino; 296 Two or more races, non-Hispanic/Latino), 109 international. Average age 37. In 2016, 3,185 master's awarded. *Degree requirements:* For master's, comprehensive exam or practicum. *Entrance requirements:* For master's, official transcript showing earned bachelor's degree from institution accredited by recognized accrediting body. Additional exam requirements/recommendations for international students: Required—TOEFL (minimum score 550 paper-based), IELTS (minimum score 6.5). *Application deadline:* Applications are processed on a rolling basis. Application fee: $0. Electronic applications accepted. *Expenses: Tuition:* Part-time $350 per credit hour. *Required fees:* $50 per course. *Financial support:* Scholarships/grants available. Financial award applicants required to submit FAFSA. *Unit head:* Dr. Karan Powell, President, 877-468-6268, Fax: 304-724-3780. *Application contact:* Terry Grant, Vice President of Enrollment Management, 877-468-6268, Fax: 304-724-3780, E-mail: info@apus.edu.
Website: http://www.apus.edu

American Sentinel University, Graduate Programs, Aurora, CO 80014. Offers business administration (MBA); business intelligence (MS); computer science (MSCS); health information management (MS); healthcare (MBA); information systems (MSIS); nursing (MSN). *Program availability:* Part-time, evening/weekend, online learning. *Entrance requirements:* Additional exam requirements/recommendations for international students: Required—TOEFL (minimum score 600 paper-based). Electronic applications accepted.

The American University in Cairo, School of Business, Cairo, Egypt. Offers business administration (MBA); economics (MA); economics in international development (MA, Diploma); finance (MS). *Program availability:* Part-time, evening/weekend. *Faculty:* 24 full-time (4 women), 5 part-time/adjunct (2 women). *Students:* 53 full-time (24 women), 80 part-time (41 women), 1 international. Average age 29. 109 applicants, 45% accepted, 35 enrolled. In 2016, 49 master's awarded. *Degree requirements:* For master's, comprehensive exam (for some programs), thesis (for some programs). *Entrance requirements:* For master's, GMAT, GRE. Additional exam requirements/recommendations for international students: Required—TOEFL (minimum score 450 paper-based; 45 iBT), IELTS (minimum score 5). *Application deadline:* For fall admission, 2/1 priority date for domestic and international students; for spring admission, 10/15 priority date for domestic and international students. Applications are processed on a rolling basis. Application fee: $80. Electronic applications accepted. *Expenses:* Contact institution. *Financial support:* Fellowships with partial tuition reimbursements, scholarships/grants, tuition waivers (partial), and unspecified assistantships available. Financial award application deadline: 3/10. *Faculty research:* Marketing and quality management, banking operations management, economics, finance. *Unit head:* Dr. Nizar Becheikh, Interim Dean, 20-2-2615-2120, E-mail: nbecheikh@aucegypt.edu. *Application contact:* Maha Hegazi, Director of Graduate Admissions, 20-2-2615-1462, E-mail: mahahegazi@aucegypt.edu.
Website: http://www.aucegypt.edu/Business/Pages/default.aspx

The American University in Dubai, Graduate Programs, Dubai, United Arab Emirates. Offers construction management (MS); education (M Ed); finance (MBA); generalist (MBA); marketing (MBA). *Program availability:* Part-time, evening/weekend. *Degree requirements:* For master's, thesis optional. *Entrance requirements:* For master's, GMAT (for MBA); GRE (for M Ed and MS), minimum undergraduate GPA of 3.0, official transcripts, two reference forms, curriculum vitae/resume, statement of career objectives, work experience. Additional exam requirements/recommendations for international students: Required—TOEFL (minimum score 550 paper-based; 79 iBT). Electronic applications accepted.

American University of Armenia, Graduate Programs, Yerevan, Armenia. Offers business administration (MBA); computer and information science (MS), including business management, design and manufacturing, energy (ME, MS), industrial engineering and systems management; economics (MS); industrial engineering and systems management (ME), including business, computer aided design/manufacturing, energy (ME, MS), information technology; law (LL M); political science and international affairs (MPSIA); public health (MPH); teaching English as a foreign language (MA). *Program availability:* Part-time, evening/weekend. *Degree requirements:* For master's, thesis (for some programs), capstone/project. *Entrance requirements:* For master's, GRE, GMAT, or LSAT. Additional exam requirements/recommendations for international students: Recommended—TOEFL (minimum score 79 iBT), IELTS (minimum score 6.5). *Faculty research:* Microfinance, finance (rural/development, international, corporate), firm life cycle theory, TESOL, language proficiency testing, public policy, administrative law, economic development, cryptography, artificial intelligence, energy efficiency/renewable energy, computer-aided design/manufacturing, health financing, tuberculosis control, mother/child health, preventive ophthalmology, post-earthquake psychopathological investigations, tobacco control, environmental health risk assessments.

American University of Beirut, Graduate Programs, Suliman S. Olayan School of Business, Executive MBA Program, 11072020, Lebanon. Offers EMBA. *Faculty:* 6 full-time (0 women), 3 part-time/adjunct (1 woman). *Students:* 13 full-time (2 women).

Average age 36. In 2016, 16 master's awarded. *Expenses:* Contact institution. *Faculty research:* Operations management, corporate governance, corporate finance, strategy, leadership. *Unit head:* Laith Dajani, Executive Director, 961-1350000 Ext. 3707, E-mail: ld28@aub.edu.lb. *Application contact:* Hanaa Mounzer, Administrative Assistant, 961-1350000 Ext. 3797, E-mail: hm89@aub.edu.lb.
Website: http://www.aub.edu.lb/osb/osb_home/program/EMBA/Pages/index.aspx

American University of Beirut, Graduate Programs, Suliman S. Olayan School of Business, MBA Program, 11072020, Lebanon. Offers MBA. *Program availability:* Online learning. *Faculty:* 11 full-time (3 women), 4 part-time/adjunct (1 woman). *Students:* 5 full-time (2 women), 11 part-time (9 women). Average age 26. 42 applicants, 57% accepted, 16 enrolled. In 2016, 20 master's awarded. Terminal master's awarded for partial completion of doctoral program. *Degree requirements:* For master's, thesis. *Entrance requirements:* Additional exam requirements/recommendations for international students: Required—TOEFL (minimum score 583 paper-based; 97 iBT), IELTS (minimum score 7). *Application deadline:* For fall admission, 2/12 for domestic students; for winter admission, 4/1 for domestic students. Application fee: $80. Electronic applications accepted. *Expenses:* Contact institution. *Financial support:* In 2016–17, 4 research assistantships with tuition reimbursements (averaging $1,300 per year) were awarded; scholarships/grants and unspecified assistantships also available. Financial award application deadline: 6/1. *Unit head:* Maya Naim El-Helou, Director of Graduate Programs, 961-1352700 Ext. 3955, Fax: 961-1750214, E-mail: helou@aub.edu.lb. *Application contact:* Maya Naim El-Helou, Director of Graduate Programs, 961-1352700 Ext. 3955, Fax: 961-1750214, E-mail: helou@aub.edu.lb.
Website: http://www.aub.edu.lb/osb/osb_home/program/MBA/Pages/index.aspx

The American University of Paris, Graduate Programs, Paris, France. Offers cross-cultural and sustainable business management (MA); cultural translation (MA); global communications (MA); global communications and civil society (MA); international affairs (MA); international affairs, conflict resolution and civil society development (MA); Middle East and Islamic studies (MA); Middle East and Islamic studies and international affairs (MA); public policy and international affairs (MA); public policy and international law (MA). *Degree requirements:* For master's, thesis (for some programs). *Entrance requirements:* For master's, minimum undergraduate GPA of 3.0. Additional exam requirements/recommendations for international students: Recommended—TOEFL, IELTS. Electronic applications accepted.

American University of Sharjah, Graduate Programs, Sharjah, United Arab Emirates. Offers accounting (MS); biomedical engineering (MSBME); business (MBA); chemical engineering (MS Ch E); civil engineering (MSCE); computer engineering (MS); electrical engineering (MSEE); engineering systems management (MS); mathematics (MS); mechanical engineering (MSME); mechatronics engineering (MS); teaching English to speakers of other languages (MA); translation and interpreting (MA); urban planning (MUP). *Program availability:* Part-time, evening/weekend. *Students:* 123 full-time (53 women), 306 part-time (151 women). Average age 27. 184 applicants, 83% accepted, 92 enrolled. In 2016, 97 master's awarded. *Degree requirements:* For master's, thesis (for some programs). *Entrance requirements:* For master's, GMAT (for MBA). Additional exam requirements/recommendations for international students: Required—TOEFL (minimum score 550 paper-based; 80 iBT), TWE (minimum score 5); Recommended—IELTS (minimum score 6.5). *Application deadline:* For fall admission, 8/28 priority date for domestic students, 8/14 priority date for international students; for spring admission, 1/22 priority date for domestic students, 1/8 for international students; for summer admission, 5/21 for domestic and international students. Applications are processed on a rolling basis. Application fee: $350. Electronic applications accepted. *Expenses: Tuition, area resident:* Part-time 4660 United Arab Emirates dirhams per credit hour. *Financial support:* In 2016–17, 63 students received support, including 28 research assistantships with full and partial tuition reimbursements available, 35 teaching assistantships with full and partial tuition reimbursements available; scholarships/grants also available. *Faculty research:* Water pollution, management and waste water treatment, energy and sustainability, air pollution, Islamic finance, family business and small and medium enterprises. *Unit head:* Ali Shuhaimy, Executive Director of Enrollment Management, 971-6515-1030. *Application contact:* Mona A. Mabrouk, Graduate Admissions/Office of Enrollment Management, 971-65151012, E-mail: graduateadmission@aus.edu.
Website: http://www.aus.edu/programs/graduate/

Anaheim University, Programs in Business Administration, Anaheim, CA 92806-5150. Offers entrepreneurship (ME, DBA); global sustainable management (MBA); international business (MBA, DBA, Certificate, Diploma); management (DBA); sustainable management (DBA, Certificate, Diploma). *Program availability:* Part-time, evening/weekend, online only, 100% online. In 2016, 3 master's, 4 doctorates awarded. *Application deadline:* Applications are processed on a rolling basis. Electronic applications accepted. *Unit head:* Robert Robertson, Dean, Graduate School of Business, 714-772-3330, Fax: 714-772-3331, E-mail: admissions@anaheim.edu.

Anderson University, College of Business, Anderson, SC 29621-4035. Offers business administration (MBA); healthcare leadership (MBA); human resources (MBA); marketing (MBA); supply chain management (MBA). *Accreditation:* ACBSP. *Students:* 7 full-time (0 women), 1 part-time (0 women). *Expenses:* Contact institution. *Financial support:* Tuition waivers available. Financial award application deadline: 3/1; financial award applicants required to submit FAFSA. *Unit head:* Dr. Douglas Goodwin, MBA Director/Associate Dean, 864-MBA-6000. *Application contact:* Mallory Knight, Graduate Admission Counselor, 864-231-2182, Fax: 864-231-2115, E-mail: malloryknight@andersonuniversity.edu.
Website: http://www.andersonuniversity.edu/business

Anderson University, Falls School of Business, Anderson, IN 46012-3495. Offers accountancy (MA); business administration (MBA, DBA). *Accreditation:* ACBSP.

Angelo State University, College of Graduate Studies and Research, College of Business, Department of Management and Marketing, San Angelo, TX 76909. Offers business administration (MBA). *Accreditation:* ACBSP. *Program availability:* Part-time, evening/weekend. *Students:* 33 full-time (20 women), 47 part-time (15 women); includes 20 minority (5 Black or African American, non-Hispanic/Latino; 12 Hispanic/Latino; 3 Two or more races, non-Hispanic/Latino), 4 international. Average age 28. *Entrance requirements:* For master's, GMAT or GRE, essay, resume. Additional exam requirements/recommendations for international students: Required—TOEFL or IELTS. *Application deadline:* For fall admission, 7/15 priority date for domestic students, 6/10 for international students; for spring admission, 12/1 priority date for domestic students, 11/1 for international students. Applications are processed on a rolling basis. Application fee: $40 ($50 for international students). Electronic applications accepted. *Expenses:* Tuition, state resident: full-time $3726; part-time $2484 per year. Tuition, nonresident: full-time $10,746; part-time $7164 per year. *Required fees:* $2538; $1702 per unit. *Financial support:* Career-related internships or fieldwork, Federal Work-Study, and scholarships/grants available. Support available to part-time students. Financial award application deadline: 3/1; financial award applicants required to submit FAFSA. *Unit head:* Dr. Brian W. Kulik, Chair, 325-942-2383, Fax: 325-942-2384, E-mail: brian.kulik@angelo.edu. *Application contact:* Dr. Sharynn Tomlin, MBA Director, 325-486-6635, E-mail: sharynn.tomlin@angelo.edu.
Website: http://www.angelo.edu/dept/management_marketing/

Anna Maria College, Graduate Division, Program in Business Administration, Paxton, MA 01612. Offers MBA, AC. *Program availability:* Part-time, evening/weekend. *Degree requirements:* For master's, capstone project. *Entrance requirements:* For master's, minimum GPA of 2.7. Additional exam requirements/recommendations for international students: Required—TOEFL (minimum score 500 paper-based). Electronic applications accepted. *Faculty research:* Management organization.

Antioch University Los Angeles, Graduate Programs, Program in Organizational Management, Culver City, CA 90230. Offers human resource development (MA); leadership (MA); organizational development (MA). *Program availability:* Part-time, evening/weekend. *Entrance requirements:* For master's, interview. Additional exam requirements/recommendations for international students: Required—TOEFL. *Faculty research:* Systems thinking and chaos theory, technology and organizational structure, nonprofit management, power and empowerment.

Antioch University Midwest, Graduate Programs, Program in Management and Change Leadership, Yellow Springs, OH 45387-1609. Offers MA. *Program availability:* Part-time, evening/weekend, online learning. *Entrance requirements:* For master's, resume, goal statement, interview. *Application deadline:* For fall admission, 9/1 for domestic students; for winter admission, 12/1 for domestic students; for spring admission, 3/10 for domestic students. Applications are processed on a rolling basis. Application fee: $50. Electronic applications accepted. *Expenses:* $799 per credit hour. *Financial support:* Federal Work-Study available. Financial award applicants required to submit FAFSA. *Unit head:* Hays Moulton, Chair, 937-769-1860, Fax: 937-769-1807, E-mail: hmoulton@antioch.edu. *Application contact:* Deena Kent-Hummel, Director of Admissions, 937-769-1816, Fax: 937-769-1804, E-mail: dkent@antioch.edu.
Website: https://www.antioch.edu/midwest/degrees-programs/business-management-leadership/management-and-change-leadership-ma/

Antioch University New England, Graduate School, Department of Management, Program in Sustainability (Green MBA), Keene, NH 03431-3552. Offers MBA. *Program availability:* Part-time. *Entrance requirements:* For master's, GRE, resume, 3 letters of recommendation. Additional exam requirements/recommendations for international students: Required—TOEFL (minimum score 600 paper-based).

Antioch University Santa Barbara, Program in Business Administration, Santa Barbara, CA 93101-1581. Offers non-profit management (MBA); social business (MBA); strategic leadership (MBA).

Appalachian State University, Cratis D. Williams Graduate School, Program in Business Administration, Boone, NC 28608. Offers general management (MBA). *Accreditation:* AACSB. *Program availability:* Part-time, online learning. *Degree requirements:* For master's, comprehensive exam. *Entrance requirements:* For master's, GMAT, 3 letters of recommendation. Additional exam requirements/recommendations for international students: Required—TOEFL (minimum score 550 paper-based; 79 iBT), IELTS (minimum score 6.5). *Application deadline:* For fall admission, 3/1 for domestic students, 2/1 for international students; for spring admission, 7/1 for international students. Applications are processed on a rolling basis. Application fee: $55. Electronic applications accepted. *Expenses:* Tuition, state resident: full-time $4744. Tuition, nonresident: full-time $17,913. Full-time tuition and fees vary according to program. *Financial support:* Fellowships, research assistantships, teaching assistantships, career-related internships or fieldwork, Federal Work-Study, scholarships/grants, and unspecified assistantships available. Financial award application deadline: 4/1; financial award applicants required to submit FAFSA. *Unit head:* Dr. Joseph Cazier, Director/Assistant Dean, College of Business, 828-262-2922, E-mail: cazierja@appstate.edu. *Application contact:* Dr. Sandy Vannoy, Program Director, 828-262-2922, E-mail: vannoysa@appstate.edu.
Website: http://www.mba.appstate.edu

Aquinas College, School of Management, Grand Rapids, MI 49506. Offers marketing management (MM); organizational leadership (MM); sustainable business (MM). *Program availability:* Part-time, evening/weekend. *Entrance requirements:* For master's, GMAT, minimum undergraduate GPA of 2.75, 2 years of work experience. Additional exam requirements/recommendations for international students: Required—TOEFL (minimum score 550 paper-based). *Application deadline:* Applications are processed on a rolling basis. Application fee: $0. *Expenses:* Contact institution. *Financial support:* Scholarships/grants available. Support available to part-time students. Financial award application deadline: 3/15; financial award applicants required to submit FAFSA. *Unit head:* Cynthia G. VanGelderen, Interim Director, 616-632-2922, Fax: 616-732-4489. *Application contact:* Lynn Atkins-Rykert, Program Coordinator, 616-632-2925, Fax: 616-732-4489, E-mail: atkinlyn@aquinas.edu.

Arcadia University, Program in Business Administration, Glenside, PA 19038-3295. Offers MBA. *Accreditation:* ACBSP. *Faculty:* 11 full-time (5 women), 21 part-time/adjunct (8 women). *Students:* 35 part-time (23 women); includes 17 minority (11 Black or African American, non-Hispanic/Latino; 2 Asian, non-Hispanic/Latino; 3 Hispanic/Latino; 1 Two or more races, non-Hispanic/Latino), 2 international. Average age 28. 32 applicants, 69% accepted, 18 enrolled. In 2016, 17 master's awarded. *Entrance requirements:* Additional exam requirements/recommendations for international students: Required—TOEFL. Application fee: $50. *Expenses:* Contact institution. *Unit head:* Dr. Thomas M. Brinker, Executive Director, 215-572-4039. *Application contact:* Office of Enrollment Management, 215-572-2910, Fax: 215-572-4049, E-mail: admiss@arcadia.edu.

Argosy University, Atlanta, College of Business, Atlanta, GA 30328. Offers accounting (DBA); corporate compliance (MBA); customized professional concentration (MBA, DBA); finance (MBA); healthcare administration (MBA); information systems (DBA); information systems management (MBA); international business (MBA, DBA); management (MBA, MSM, DBA); marketing (MBA, DBA). *Accreditation:* ACBSP.

Argosy University, Chicago, College of Business, Chicago, IL 60601. Offers accounting (DBA); customized professional concentration (MBA, DBA); finance (MBA); fraud examination (MBA); global business sustainability (DBA); healthcare administration (MBA); information systems (DBA); information systems management (MBA); international business (MBA, DBA); management (MBA, MSM, DBA); marketing (MBA, DBA); organizational leadership (Ed D); public administration (MBA); sustainable management (MBA). *Accreditation:* ACBSP. *Program availability:* Online learning.

Argosy University, Dallas, College of Business, Farmers Branch, TX 75244. Offers accounting (DBA, AGC); corporate compliance (MBA, Graduate Certificate); customized professional concentration (MBA); finance (MBA, Graduate Certificate); fraud examination (MBA, Graduate Certificate); global business sustainability (DBA, AGC); healthcare administration (Graduate Certificate); healthcare management (MBA); information systems (MBA, DBA, AGC); information systems management (Graduate Certificate); international business (MBA, DBA, AGC, Graduate Certificate); management (MBA, DBA, AGC, Graduate Certificate); marketing (MBA, DBA, AGC, Graduate Certificate); public administration (MBA, Graduate Certificate); sustainable management (MBA, Graduate Certificate). *Accreditation:* ACBSP.

Argosy University, Denver, College of Business, Denver, CO 80231. Offers accounting (DBA); corporate compliance (MBA); customized professional concentration (MBA, DBA); finance (MBA); fraud examination (MBA); global business sustainability (DBA); healthcare administration (MBA); information systems (DBA); information systems management (MBA); international business (MBA, DBA); management (MBA, MSM, DBA); marketing (MBA, DBA); organizational leadership (Ed D); public administration (MBA); sustainable management (MBA). *Accreditation:* ACBSP.

Argosy University, Hawai'i, College of Business, Honolulu, HI 96813. Offers accounting (DBA); corporate compliance (MBA); customized professional concentration (MBA, DBA); finance (MBA, Certificate); fraud examination (MBA); global business sustainability (DBA); healthcare administration (MBA, Certificate); information systems (DBA); information systems management (MBA, Certificate); international business (MBA, DBA, Certificate); management (MBA, MSM, DBA); marketing (MBA, DBA, Certificate); organizational leadership (Ed D); public administration (MBA); sustainable management (MBA).

Argosy University, Inland Empire, College of Business, Ontario, CA 91761. Offers accounting (DBA); corporate compliance (MBA); customized professional concentration (MBA, DBA); finance (MBA); fraud examination (MBA); global business sustainability (DBA); healthcare administration (MBA); information systems (DBA); information systems management (MBA); international business (MBA, DBA); management (MBA, MSM, DBA); marketing (MBA, DBA); organizational leadership (Ed D); public administration (MBA); sustainable management (MBA).

Argosy University, Los Angeles, College of Business, Santa Monica, CA 90045. Offers accounting (DBA); corporate compliance (MBA); customized professional concentration (MBA, DBA); finance (MBA); fraud examination (MBA); global business sustainability (DBA); healthcare administration (MBA); information systems (DBA); information systems management (MBA); international business (MBA, DBA); management (MBA, MSM, DBA); marketing (MBA, DBA); organizational leadership (Ed D); public administration (MBA); sustainable management (MBA).

Argosy University, Nashville, College of Business, Nashville, TN 37214. Offers accounting (DBA); customized professional concentration (MBA, DBA); finance (MBA); healthcare administration (MBA); information systems (MBA, DBA); international business (MBA, DBA); management (MBA, MSM, DBA); marketing (MBA, DBA).

Argosy University, Northern Virginia, College of Business, Arlington, VA 22209. Offers accounting (DBA); customized professional concentration (MBA, DBA); finance (MBA); fraud examination (MBA); global business sustainability (DBA); healthcare administration (MBA); information systems (DBA); information systems management (MBA); international business (MBA, DBA, Certificate); management (MBA, MSM, DBA); marketing (MBA, DBA, Certificate); organizational leadership (Ed D); public administration (MBA); sustainable management (MBA).

Argosy University, Orange County, College of Business, Orange, CA 92868. Offers accounting (DBA, Adv C); corporate compliance (MBA); customized professional concentration (MBA, DBA); finance (MBA, Certificate); fraud examination (MBA); global business sustainability (DBA); healthcare administration (MBA, Certificate); information systems (DBA, Adv C, Certificate); information systems management (MBA); international business (MBA, DBA, Adv C, Certificate); management (MBA, MSM, DBA, Adv C); marketing (MBA, DBA, Adv C, Certificate); organizational leadership (Ed D); public administration (MBA, Certificate); sustainable management (MBA).

Argosy University, Phoenix, College of Business, Phoenix, AZ 85021. Offers accounting (DBA); corporate compliance (MBA); customized professional concentration (MBA, DBA); finance (MBA); fraud examination (MBA); global business sustainability (DBA); healthcare administration (MBA); information systems (DBA); information systems management (MBA); international business (MBA, DBA); management (MBA, DBA); marketing (MBA, DBA); public administration (MBA); sustainable management (MBA).

Argosy University, Salt Lake City, College of Business, Draper, UT 84020. Offers accounting (DBA); corporate compliance (MBA); customized professional concentration (MBA, DBA); finance (MBA); fraud examination (MBA); global business sustainability (DBA); healthcare administration (MBA); information systems (DBA); information systems management (MBA); international business (MBA, DBA); management (MBA, DBA); marketing (MBA, DBA); public administration (MBA); sustainable management (MBA).

Argosy University, San Diego, College of Business, San Diego, CA 92108. Offers accounting (DBA); corporate compliance (MBA); customized professional concentration (MBA, DBA); finance (MBA); fraud examination (MBA); global business sustainability (DBA); information systems (DBA); information systems management (MBA); international business (MBA, DBA); management (MBA, MSM, DBA); marketing (MBA, DBA); organizational leadership (Ed D); public administration (MBA).

Argosy University, San Francisco Bay Area, College of Business, Alameda, CA 94501. Offers accounting (DBA); corporate compliance (MBA); customized professional concentration (MBA, DBA); finance (MBA); fraud examination (MBA); global business sustainability (DBA); healthcare administration (MBA); information systems (DBA); information systems management (MBA); international business (MBA, DBA); management (MBA, MSM, DBA); marketing (MBA, DBA); organizational leadership (Ed D); public administration (MBA); sustainable management (MBA).

Argosy University, Sarasota, College of Business, Sarasota, FL 34235. Offers accounting (DBA, Adv C); corporate compliance (MBA, DBA, Certificate); customized professional concentration (MBA, DBA); finance (MBA, Certificate); fraud examination (MBA, Certificate); global business sustainability (DBA, Adv C); healthcare administration (MBA, Certificate); information systems (DBA, Adv C, Certificate); information systems management (MBA); international business (MBA, DBA, Adv C, Certificate); management (MBA, MSM, DBA, Adv C, Certificate); marketing (MBA, DBA, Adv C, Certificate); organizational leadership (Ed D); public administration (MBA, Certificate); sustainable management (MBA, Certificate).

Argosy University, Schaumburg, Graduate School of Business and Management, Schaumburg, IL 60173-5403. Offers accounting (DBA, Adv C); customized professional concentration (MBA, DBA); finance (MBA, Certificate); fraud examination (MBA); healthcare administration (MBA, Certificate); human resource management (MS); information systems (Adv C, Certificate); information systems management (MBA); international business (MBA, DBA, Adv C, Certificate); management (MBA, MSM, DBA, Adv C, Certificate); marketing (MBA, DBA, Adv C, Certificate); organizational leadership (MS, Ed D); public administration (MBA); sustainable management (MBA).

Argosy University, Seattle, College of Business, Seattle, WA 98121. Offers accounting (DBA); corporate compliance (MBA); customized professional concentration (MBA, DBA); finance (MBA); fraud examination (MBA); global business sustainability (DBA); healthcare administration (MBA); information systems (DBA); information systems management (MBA); international business (MBA, DBA); management (MBA, MSM, DBA); marketing (MBA, DBA); organizational leadership (Ed D); public administration (MBA); sustainable management (MBA).

Argosy University, Tampa, College of Business, Tampa, FL 33607. Offers accounting (DBA); corporate compliance (MBA); customized professional concentration (MBA, DBA); finance (MBA); fraud examination (MBA); global business sustainability (DBA); healthcare administration (MBA); information systems (DBA); information systems management (MBA); international business (MBA, DBA); management (MBA, MSM, DBA); marketing (MBA, DBA); organizational leadership (Ed D); public administration (MBA); sustainable management (MBA).

Argosy University, Twin Cities, College of Business, Eagan, MN 55121. Offers accounting (DBA); customized professional concentration (MBA, DBA); finance (MBA); fraud examination (MBA); global business sustainability (DBA); healthcare administration (MBA); information systems (DBA); information systems management (MBA); international business (MBA, DBA); management (MBA, MSM, DBA); marketing (MBA, DBA); organizational leadership (Ed D); public administration (MBA); sustainable management (MBA).

Arizona State University at the Tempe campus, Thunderbird School of Global Management, Tempe, AZ 85287. Offers global affairs and management (MA); global management (MGM). *Accreditation:* AACSB. *Program availability:* Online learning. *Degree requirements:* For master's, one foreign language. *Entrance requirements:* For master's, GMAT. Additional exam requirements/recommendations for international students: Required—TOEFL.

Arizona State University at the Tempe campus, W. P. Carey School of Business, Program in Business Administration, Tempe, AZ 85287-4906. Offers entrepreneurship (MBA); finance (MBA); health sector management (MBA); international business (MBA); leadership (MBA); marketing (MBA); organizational behavior (PhD); strategic management (PhD); supply chain management (MBA, PhD); JD/MBA; MBA/M Acc; MBA/M Arch. *Accreditation:* AACSB. *Program availability:* Part-time, evening/weekend, online learning. Terminal master's awarded for partial completion of doctoral program. *Degree requirements:* For master's, thesis or alternative, internship, interactive Program of Study (iPOS) submitted before completing 50 percent of required credit hours; for doctorate, comprehensive exam, thesis/dissertation, interactive Program of Study (iPOS) submitted before completing 50 percent of required credit hours. *Entrance requirements:* For master's, GMAT, minimum GPA of 3.0 in last 2 years of work leading to bachelor's degree, 2 letters of recommendation, professional resume, official transcripts, 3 essays; for doctorate, GMAT or GRE, minimum GPA of 3.0 in last 2 years of work leading to bachelor's degree, 3 letters of recommendation, resume, personal statement/essay. Additional exam requirements/recommendations for international students: Required—TOEFL (minimum score 550 paper-based; 80 iBT), IELTS (minimum score 6.5). Electronic applications accepted. *Expenses:* Contact institution.

Arkansas State University, Graduate School, College of Business, Department of Economics and Finance, State University, AR 72467. Offers business administration (MBA). *Accreditation:* AACSB. *Program availability:* Part-time. *Degree requirements:* For master's, comprehensive exam, thesis or alternative. *Entrance requirements:* For master's, GMAT, appropriate bachelor's degree, letters of reference, official transcripts, immunization records. Additional exam requirements/recommendations for international students: Required—TOEFL (minimum score 550 paper-based; 79 iBT), IELTS (minimum score 6), PTE (minimum score 56). Electronic applications accepted. *Expenses:* Contact institution.

Arkansas Tech University, College of Business, Russellville, AR 72801. Offers MSBA. *Accreditation:* AACSB. *Program availability:* Part-time, evening/weekend, online only. *Students:* 4 full-time (all women), 22 part-time (14 women); includes 4 minority (3 Black or African American, non-Hispanic/Latino; 1 Hispanic/Latino), 2 international. Average age 33. In 2016, 10 master's awarded. *Degree requirements:* For master's, completion of all required coursework with minimum cumulative GPA of 3.0 within six years. *Entrance requirements:* For master's, official bachelor's degree transcripts from regionally-accredited university; minimum cumulative undergraduate GPA of 2.5 or 3.0 on last 30 credit hours; business information systems course or equivalent with minimum C grade; business statistics course or its equivalent with minimum C grade. Additional exam requirements/recommendations for international students: Required—TOEFL (minimum score 550 paper-based; 79 iBT), IELTS (minimum score 6). *Application deadline:* For fall admission, 3/1 priority date for domestic students, 5/1 priority date for international students; for spring admission, 10/1 priority date for domestic and international students. Applications are processed on a rolling basis. Application fee: $25 ($75 for international students). Electronic applications accepted. *Expenses:* Tuition, state resident: full-time $4932; part-time $274 per credit hour. Tuition, nonresident: full-time $9864; part-time $548 per credit hour. *Required fees:* $513 per semester. Tuition and fees vary according to course load. *Financial support:* Application deadline: 4/15; applicants required to submit FAFSA. *Unit head:* Dr. Jeff Robertson, Dean, 479-968-0498, E-mail: jrobertson@atu.edu. *Application contact:* Dr. Mary B. Gunter, Dean of Graduate College, 479-968-0398, Fax: 479-964-0542, E-mail: gradcollege@atu.edu.
Website: http://www.atu.edu/business/

Armstrong State University, School of Graduate Studies, Program in Professional Communication and Leadership, Savannah, GA 31419-1997. Offers MA, Certificate. *Program availability:* Part-time, evening/weekend. *Faculty:* 3 full-time (2 women), 1 (woman) part-time/adjunct. *Students:* 26 full-time (17 women), 44 part-time (32 women); includes 43 minority (36 Black or African American, non-Hispanic/Latino; 1 Asian, non-Hispanic/Latino; 3 Hispanic/Latino; 3 Two or more races, non-Hispanic/Latino), 2 international. Average age 25. 50 applicants, 54% accepted, 19 enrolled. In 2016, 27 master's awarded. *Degree requirements:* For master's, comprehensive exam, project. *Entrance requirements:* For master's, minimum GPA of 2.5, letters of recommendation, letter of intent, resume. Additional exam requirements/recommendations for international students: Required—TOEFL (minimum score 523 paper-based; 70 iBT). *Application deadline:* For fall admission, 6/1 priority date for domestic students, 5/1 priority date for international students; for spring admission, 11/15 priority date for domestic students, 9/15 priority date for international students; for summer admission, 4/15 for domestic students, 9/15 priority date for international students. Applications are processed on a rolling basis. Application fee: $30. Electronic applications accepted. *Expenses:* Tuition, state resident: full-time $1781; part-time $161.93 per credit hour. Tuition, nonresident: full-time $6482; part-time $589.27 per credit hour. *Required fees:* $1224 per unit. $612 per semester. Tuition and fees vary according to course load, campus/location and program. *Financial support:* In 2016–17, research assistantships with full tuition reimbursements (averaging $5,000 per year) were awarded; scholarships/grants and unspecified assistantships also available. Financial award application deadline: 3/15; financial award applicants required to submit FAFSA. *Faculty research:* Organizational communication, conflict resolution and mediation, rhetoric and language identity, brand identity and marketing, communication theory. *Unit head:* Dr. Robert Terry, 912-344-3606, E-mail: robert.terry@armstrong.edu. *Application contact:* McKenzie Peterman, Assistant Director of Graduate Admissions, 912-344-2503, Fax: 912-344-3417, E-mail: graduate@armstrong.edu.
Website: http://www.armstrong.edu/Majors/degree/master_professional_communication_leadership

Ashland University, Dauch College of Business and Economics, Ashland, OH 44805-3702. Offers MBA. *Accreditation:* ACBSP. *Program availability:* Part-time, evening/weekend. *Degree requirements:* For master's, thesis optional. *Entrance requirements:* For master's, 2 years of full-time work experience. Additional exam requirements/recommendations for international students: Required—TOEFL. *Application deadline:* For fall admission, 8/1 priority date for domestic students; for spring admission, 12/1 priority date for domestic students. Applications are processed on a rolling basis.

Application fee: $30. Electronic applications accepted. *Expenses:* Contact institution. *Financial support:* Tuition waivers (partial) and unspecified assistantships available. Financial award application deadline: 4/15; financial award applicants required to submit FAFSA. *Faculty research:* Human resource management, statistical analysis, global business issues, organizational development, government and business. *Unit head:* Dr. Raymond Jacobs, Associate Dean, 419-289-5931, E-mail: rjacobs@ashland.edu. *Application contact:* Stephen W. Krispinsky, Executive Director of MBA Program, 419-289-5236, Fax: 419-289-5910, E-mail: skrispin@ashland.edu.
Website: http://www.ashland.edu/mba/

Ashworth College, Graduate Programs, Norcross, GA 30092. Offers business administration (MBA); criminal justice (MS); health care administration (MBA, MS); human resource management (MBA, MS); international business (MBA); management (MS); marketing (MBA, MS).

Aspen University, Program in Business Administration, Denver, CO 80246-1930. Offers business administration (MBA); finance (MBA); information management (MBA); project management (MBA, Certificate). *Program availability:* Part-time, evening/weekend, online learning. *Entrance requirements:* Additional exam requirements/recommendations for international students: Required—TOEFL (minimum score 530 paper-based). Electronic applications accepted.

Assumption College, Business Studies Program, Worcester, MA 01609-1296. Offers accounting (MBA); business studies (CAGS); finance/economics (MBA); human resources (MBA); international business (MBA); management (MBA); marketing (MBA); nonprofit leadership (MBA). *Program availability:* Part-time, evening/weekend. *Faculty:* 4 full-time (1 woman), 19 part-time/adjunct (6 women). *Students:* 44 full-time (16 women), 97 part-time (47 women); includes 20 minority (8 Black or African American, non-Hispanic/Latino; 5 Asian, non-Hispanic/Latino; 6 Hispanic/Latino; 1 Two or more races, non-Hispanic/Latino), 4 international. Average age 29. 34 applicants, 59% accepted, 16 enrolled. In 2016, 97 master's, 1 other advanced degree awarded. *Degree requirements:* For master's, thesis, capstone. *Entrance requirements:* For master's, bachelor's degree, 3 letters of recommendation, official transcripts, personal statement, current resume; for CAGS, MBA or equivalent degree in a closely related field, 3 letters of recommendation, official transcripts, personal statement, current resume. Additional exam requirements/recommendations for international students: Required—TOEFL (minimum score 540 paper-based; 76 iBT), IELTS (minimum score 6). *Application deadline:* For fall admission, 7/1 priority date for domestic and international students; for spring admission, 12/1 priority date for domestic and international students; for summer admission, 4/1 priority date for domestic and international students. Application fee: $30. Electronic applications accepted. *Expenses: Tuition:* Full-time $11,610; part-time $645 per credit. *Required fees:* $70 per term. Tuition and fees vary according to course load and program. *Financial support:* In 2016–17, 19 students received support. Tuition waivers (full and partial), unspecified assistantships, and institutional discounts available. Financial award applicants required to submit FAFSA. *Faculty research:* Workplace diversity, dynamics of team interaction, utilization of leased employees, experiential learning project on due diligence market for prostheses. *Unit head:* Dr. Robin Frkal, Director, 508-767-7622, E-mail: rafrkal@assumption.edu. *Application contact:* Karen Stoyanoff, Director of Recruitment for Graduate Enrollment, 508-767-7442, Fax: 508-799-4412, E-mail: graduate@assumption.edu.
Website: http://graduate.assumption.edu/mba/assumption-mba

Athabasca University, Faculty of Business, Edmonton, AB T5L 4W1, Canada. Offers business administration (MBA); information technology management (MBA), including policing concentration; innovative management (DBA); management (GDM); project management (MBA, GDM). *Program availability:* Part-time, evening/weekend, online learning. *Degree requirements:* For master's, thesis or alternative, applied project. *Entrance requirements:* For master's, 3-8 years of managerial experience, 3 years with undergraduate degree, 5 years' managerial experience with professional designation, 8-10 years' management experience (on exception). Electronic applications accepted. *Expenses:* Contact institution. *Faculty research:* Human resources, project management, operations research, information technology management, corporate stewardship, energy management.

Auburn University, Graduate School, College of Business, Department of Management, Auburn University, AL 36849. Offers management (PhD). *Accreditation:* AACSB. *Program availability:* Part-time. *Faculty:* 42 full-time (8 women), 7 part-time/adjunct (4 women). *Students:* 115 full-time (40 women), 511 part-time (130 women); includes 111 minority (44 Black or African American, non-Hispanic/Latino; 4 American Indian or Alaska Native, non-Hispanic/Latino; 28 Asian, non-Hispanic/Latino; 26 Hispanic/Latino; 9 Two or more races, non-Hispanic/Latino), 46 international. Average age 33. 491 applicants, 63% accepted, 187 enrolled. In 2016, 176 master's, 4 doctorates awarded. *Degree requirements:* For master's, thesis (for some programs); for doctorate, thesis/dissertation. *Entrance requirements:* For master's, GMAT, GRE General Test (for MS); for doctorate, GMAT, GRE General Test. Additional exam requirements/recommendations for international students: Required—TOEFL. *Application deadline:* Applications are processed on a rolling basis. Application fee: $50 ($60 for international students). Electronic applications accepted. *Expenses:* Tuition, state resident: full-time $9072; part-time $504 per credit hour. Tuition, nonresident: full-time $27,216; part-time $1512 per credit hour. *Required fees:* $812 per semester. Tuition and fees vary according to degree level and program. *Financial support:* Teaching assistantships and Federal Work-Study available. Support available to part-time students. Financial award application deadline: 3/15; financial award applicants required to submit FAFSA. *Unit head:* Kevin Mossholder, Department Chair, 334-844-9565. *Application contact:* Dr. George Flowers, Dean of the Graduate School, 334-844-2125.
Website: http://business.auburn.edu/academics/departments/department-of-management/

Auburn University, Graduate School, College of Business, Program in Business Administration, Auburn University, AL 36849. Offers MBA. *Accreditation:* AACSB. *Program availability:* Part-time. *Faculty:* 42 full-time (8 women), 7 part-time/adjunct (4 women). *Students:* 87 full-time (30 women), 462 part-time (120 women); includes 101 minority (38 Black or African American, non-Hispanic/Latino; 4 American Indian or Alaska Native, non-Hispanic/Latino; 26 Asian, non-Hispanic/Latino; 25 Hispanic/Latino; 8 Two or more races, non-Hispanic/Latino), 21 international. Average age 34. 355 applicants, 70% accepted, 169 enrolled. In 2016, 151 master's awarded. *Entrance requirements:* For master's, GMAT. *Application deadline:* Applications are processed on a rolling basis. Application fee: $50 ($60 for international students). Electronic applications accepted. *Expenses:* Tuition, state resident: full-time $9072; part-time $504 per credit hour. Tuition, nonresident: full-time $27,216; part-time $1512 per credit hour. *Required fees:* $812 per semester. Tuition and fees vary according to degree level and program. *Financial support:* Federal Work-Study available. Support available to part-time students. Financial award application deadline: 3/15; financial award applicants required to submit FAFSA. *Unit head:* Dr. Christopher Shook, Head, 334-844-9565. *Application contact:* Dr. George Flowers, Dean of the Graduate School, 334-844-2125.
Website: http://www.auburn.edu/business/mbaprog.html

Auburn University at Montgomery, College of Business, Department of Business Administration, Montgomery, AL 36124-4023. Offers business and management (MBA). *Accreditation:* AACSB. *Faculty:* 9 full-time (1 woman), 1 part-time/adjunct (0 women). *Students:* 34 full-time (18 women), 47 part-time (29 women); includes 19 minority (17 Black or African American, non-Hispanic/Latino; 1 Asian, non-Hispanic/Latino; 1 Hispanic/Latino), 15 international. 72 applicants, 85% accepted, 53 enrolled. In 2016, 56 master's awarded. *Entrance requirements:* For master's, GMAT - College of Business. Additional exam requirements/recommendations for international students: Required—TOEFL (minimum score 500 paper-based; 61 iBT), IELTS (minimum score 5.5), PTE (minimum score 44). *Application deadline:* Applications are processed on a rolling basis. Application fee: $25 ($0 for international students). Electronic applications accepted. *Expenses:* Tuition, state resident: full-time $6462; part-time $359 per credit hour. Tuition, nonresident: full-time $14,526; part-time $807 per credit hour. *Required fees:* $554. *Financial support:* Application deadline: 3/1; applicants required to submit FAFSA. *Unit head:* Ravi Chinta, Head, 334-244-3885, E-mail: rchinta@aum.edu. *Application contact:* Jennifer Taylor, Assistant Director of Graduate Programs, 334-244-3587, Fax: 334-244-3137, E-mail: jtaylor5@aum.edu.
Website: http://business.aum.edu/academic-departments/business-administration

Augsburg College, Program in Business Administration, Minneapolis, MN 55454-1351. Offers MBA. *Program availability:* Evening/weekend. Electronic applications accepted.

Augusta University, Hull College of Business, Augusta, GA 30912. Offers business administration (MBA); information security management (MS). *Accreditation:* AACSB. *Program availability:* Part-time, evening/weekend. *Entrance requirements:* For master's, GMAT. *Application deadline:* For fall admission, 7/2 for domestic and international students; for spring admission, 12/2 priority date for domestic students, 12/2 for international students; for summer admission, 4/2 for domestic and international students. Applications are processed on a rolling basis. Application fee: $20. *Financial support:* Research assistantships with partial tuition reimbursements, Federal Work-Study, and institutionally sponsored loans available. Support available to part-time students. Financial award application deadline: 4/15; financial award applicants required to submit FAFSA. *Unit head:* Dr. Richard Franza, Dean, 706-737-1418, Fax: 706-667-4064, E-mail: rfranza@augusta.edu. *Application contact:* Melissa Furman, Assistant Dean, 706-729-2056, Fax: 706-667-4064, E-mail: mfurman@augusta.edu.
Website: http://www.augusta.edu/hull/

Aurora University, Dunham School of Business and Public Policy, Aurora, IL 60506-4892. Offers accountancy (MS); business (MBA); digital marketing and analytics (MS). *Program availability:* Part-time, evening/weekend, 100% online. *Faculty:* 8 full-time (1 woman), 19 part-time/adjunct (9 women). *Students:* 67 full-time (42 women), 186 part-time (98 women); includes 76 minority (32 Black or African American, non-Hispanic/Latino; 2 Asian, non-Hispanic/Latino; 35 Hispanic/Latino; 7 Two or more races, non-Hispanic/Latino), 5 international. Average age 33. 123 applicants, 99% accepted, 21 enrolled. In 2016, 99 master's awarded. *Entrance requirements:* For master's, minimum GPA of 2.75, 2 years of work experience. Additional exam requirements/recommendations for international students: Required—TOEFL (minimum score 550 paper-based; 79 iBT). *Application deadline:* For fall admission, 6/1 for international students; for spring admission, 10/1 for international students. Applications are processed on a rolling basis. Application fee: $0. Electronic applications accepted. *Expenses:* Contact institution. *Financial support:* In 2016–17, 58 students received support. Federal Work-Study, scholarships/grants, and unspecified assistantships available. Support available to part-time students. Financial award applicants required to submit FAFSA. *Unit head:* Dr. Toby Arquette, Executive Director of School of Business and Policy, 630-844-5614, E-mail: tarquett@aurora.edu. *Application contact:* Ed Miranda, Senior Recruiter for Adult and Graduate Programs, 630-947-8923, E-mail: emiranda@aurora.edu.

Austin Peay State University, College of Graduate Studies, College of Business, Clarksville, TN 37044. Offers management (MS). *Program availability:* Part-time, evening/weekend, online learning. *Faculty:* 6 full-time (3 women). *Students:* 3 full-time (2 women), 68 part-time (35 women); includes 11 minority (3 Black or African American, non-Hispanic/Latino; 2 Asian, non-Hispanic/Latino; 3 Hispanic/Latino; 3 Two or more races, non-Hispanic/Latino). Average age 34. 68 applicants, 49% accepted, 24 enrolled. In 2016, 21 master's awarded. *Degree requirements:* For master's, comprehensive exam. *Entrance requirements:* For master's, GMAT, minimum undergraduate GPA of 2.5. Additional exam requirements/recommendations for international students: Required—TOEFL (minimum score 500 paper-based). *Application deadline:* For fall admission, 8/9 priority date for domestic students. Applications are processed on a rolling basis. Application fee: $45 ($50 for international students). Electronic applications accepted. *Expenses:* Tuition, state resident: full-time $8300; part-time $415 per credit hour. Tuition, nonresident: full-time $22,280; part-time $1114 per credit hour. *Required fees:* $1473; $73.65 per credit hour. *Financial support:* Research assistantships with full tuition reimbursements, career-related internships or fieldwork, Federal Work-Study, institutionally sponsored loans, scholarships/grants, and unspecified assistantships available. Support available to part-time students. Financial award application deadline: 4/1; financial award applicants required to submit FAFSA. *Unit head:* Charles Moses, Interim Dean, 931-221-7674, Fax: 931-221-7355, E-mail: mosesc@apsu.edu. *Application contact:* Brad Averitt, Coordinator of Graduate Admissions, 800-859-4723, Fax: 931-221-7641, E-mail: gradadmissions@apsu.edu.
Website: http://www.apsu.edu/business/

Averett University, Master of Business Administration Program, Danville, VA 24541-3692. Offers business administration (MBA); human resources management (MBA); leadership (MBA); marketing (MBA). *Program availability:* Part-time, evening/weekend, 100% online, blended/hybrid learning. *Faculty:* 6 full-time (0 women), 21 part-time/adjunct (6 women). *Students:* 52 full-time (40 women), 215 part-time (117 women); includes 133 minority (110 Black or African American, non-Hispanic/Latino; 5 American Indian or Alaska Native, non-Hispanic/Latino; 9 Asian, non-Hispanic/Latino; 9 Hispanic/Latino), 6 international. Average age 38. 143 applicants, 78% accepted, 104 enrolled. In 2016, 99 master's awarded. *Degree requirements:* For master's, 41-credit core curriculum, minimum GPA of 3.0 throughout program, no more than 2 grades of C, completion of degree requirements within six years from start of program. *Entrance requirements:* For master's, minimum cumulative GPA of 3.0 over the last 60 semester hours of undergraduate study toward a baccalaureate degree, official transcripts, three years of full-time work experience, three letters of recommendation, current resume. Additional exam requirements/recommendations for international students: Required—TOEFL (minimum score 600 paper-based; 100 iBT). *Application deadline:* Applications are processed on a rolling basis. Electronic applications accepted. *Expenses:* $12,645. *Financial support:* Application deadline: 3/1; applicants required to submit FAFSA. *Unit head:* Dr. Peggy C. Wright, Chair, Business Department, 434-791-7118, E-mail: pwright@averett.edu. *Application contact:* Melissa Anderson, Director of Admissions, Graduate and Professional Studies, 804-729-8285, E-mail: manderson@averett.edu.
Website: http://gps.averett.edu/programs/master-degrees/

Avila University, School of Business, Kansas City, MO 64145-1698. Offers accounting (MBA); finance (MBA); health care administration (MBA); international business (MBA); management (MBA); management information systems (MBA); marketing (MBA). *Program availability:* Part-time, evening/weekend. *Faculty:* 8 full-time (4 women), 4 part-time/adjunct (2 women). *Students:* 58 full-time (22 women), 21 part-time (10 women); includes 20 minority (10 Black or African American, non-Hispanic/Latino; 2 Asian, non-

Hispanic/Latino; 5 Hispanic/Latino; 3 Two or more races, non-Hispanic/Latino), 18 international. Average age 30. 75 applicants, 28% accepted, 14 enrolled. In 2016, 40 master's awarded. *Degree requirements:* For master's, comprehensive exam, capstone course. *Entrance requirements:* For master's, GMAT (minimum score 420), minimum GPA of 3.0, interview. Additional exam requirements/recommendations for international students: Required—TOEFL (minimum score 550 paper-based). *Application deadline:* For fall admission, 7/30 priority date for domestic and international students; for winter admission, 11/30 priority date for domestic and international students; for spring admission, 2/28 priority date for domestic and international students; for summer admission, 6/1 priority date for domestic and international students. Applications are processed on a rolling basis. Application fee: $0. Electronic applications accepted. *Expenses:* $628 per credit hour. *Financial support:* In 2016–17, 11 students received support. Career-related internships or fieldwork and scholarships/grants available. Support available to part-time students. Financial award applicants required to submit FAFSA. *Faculty research:* Leadership characteristics, financial hedging, group dynamics. *Unit head:* Dr. Richard Woodall, Dean, 816-501-3720, Fax: 816-501-2463, E-mail: richard.woodall@avila.edu. *Application contact:* Brandon Black, MBA Admission Advisor, 816-501-3601, Fax: 816-501-2463, E-mail: brandon.black@avila.edu.
Website: https://www.avila.edu/mrk/mba

Avila University, School of Professional Studies, Kansas City, MO 64145-1698. Offers executive leadership development (MS); fundraising (MA); instructional design and technology (MA, MS); leadership coaching (MS); organizational development (MS); project management (MA); strategic human resources (MS). *Program availability:* Part-time-only, evening/weekend, 100% online, blended/hybrid learning. *Faculty:* 15 part-time/adjunct (9 women). *Students:* 90 full-time (59 women), 47 part-time (40 women); includes 50 minority (38 Black or African American, non-Hispanic/Latino; 1 American Indian or Alaska Native, non-Hispanic/Latino; 3 Asian, non-Hispanic/Latino; 7 Hispanic/Latino; 1 Two or more races, non-Hispanic/Latino), 6 international. Average age 38. 95 applicants, 58% accepted, 38 enrolled. In 2016, 37 master's awarded. *Degree requirements:* For master's, thesis optional. *Entrance requirements:* For master's, 2 letters of recommendation, minimum GPA of 3.0 during last 60 hours, resume, statement of intent. Additional exam requirements/recommendations for international students: Required—TOEFL (minimum score 550 paper-based; 79 iBT). *Application deadline:* Applications are processed on a rolling basis. Application fee: $0. Electronic applications accepted. *Expenses:* $545 per credit hour. *Financial support:* In 2016–17, 14 students received support. Unspecified assistantships available. Support available to part-time students. Financial award applicants required to submit FAFSA. *Unit head:* Dr. Steve Iliff, Associate Dean/Director, 816-501-3675, Fax: 816-941-4650, E-mail: advantage@avila.edu. *Application contact:* Jessica Burson, Graduate Admission Advisor, 816-501-2482, Fax: 816-941-4650, E-mail: advantage@avila.edu.
Website: https://www.avila.edu/mrk/advantage-3

Azusa Pacific University, School of Business and Management, Program in Business Administration, Azusa, CA 91702-7000. Offers MBA.

Babson College, F. W. Olin Graduate School of Business, Babson Park, MA 02457-0310. Offers accounting (MSA); advanced management (Certificate); business administration (MBA); global entrepreneurship (MS); technological entrepreneurship (MS). *Accreditation:* AACSB. *Program availability:* Part-time, evening/weekend, online learning. *Entrance requirements:* For master's, GMAT, 2 years of work experience, resume, letters of recommendation. Additional exam requirements/recommendations for international students: Required—TOEFL (minimum score 100 iBT), IELTS (minimum score 6.5). Electronic applications accepted. *Faculty research:* Entrepreneurship, sustainability, global markets, process of innovation, social media and advertising.

Baker College Center for Graduate Studies–Online, Graduate Programs, Flint, MI 48507. Offers accounting (MBA); business administration (DBA); finance (MBA); general business (MBA); health care management (MBA); human resources management (MBA); information management (MBA); leadership studies (MBA); management information systems (MSIS); marketing (MBA). *Program availability:* Part-time, evening/weekend, online learning. *Degree requirements:* For master's, portfolio. *Entrance requirements:* For master's, 3 years of work experience, minimum undergraduate GPA of 2.5, writing sample, 3 letters of recommendation; for doctorate, MBA or acceptable related master's degree from accredited association, 5 years work experience, minimum graduate GPA of 3.25, writing sample, 3 professional references. Additional exam requirements/recommendations for international students: Required—TOEFL (minimum score 550 paper-based). Electronic applications accepted.

Baker University, School of Professional and Graduate Studies, Programs in Business, Baldwin City, KS 66006-0065. Offers MAOL, MBA, MSM, MSSM. Programs also offered in Lee's Summit, MO; Overland Park, KS; Topeka, KS; and Wichita, KS. *Accreditation:* ACBSP. *Program availability:* Part-time, evening/weekend, online learning. *Students:* 116 full-time (63 women), 275 part-time (131 women); includes 86 minority (42 Black or African American, non-Hispanic/Latino; 11 American Indian or Alaska Native, non-Hispanic/Latino; 11 Asian, non-Hispanic/Latino; 18 Hispanic/Latino; 4 Two or more races, non-Hispanic/Latino), 2 international. Average age 34. In 2016, 240 master's awarded. *Entrance requirements:* For master's, 2 years of full-time work experience. Additional exam requirements/recommendations for international students: Required—TOEFL (minimum score 600 paper-based; 100 iBT). *Application deadline:* Applications are processed on a rolling basis. *Financial support:* Applicants required to submit FAFSA. *Unit head:* Dr. Jacob Bucher, Dean of the School of Professional and Graduate Studies, 785-594-8475, E-mail: jacob.bucher@bakeru.edu. *Application contact:* Kelly Belk, Vice President of Enrollment Management, 913-491-4432, E-mail: kelly.belk@learn.bakeru.edu.
Website: https://www.bakeru.edu/spgs/

Bakke Graduate University, Programs in Pastoral Ministry and Business, Dallas, TX 75243-7039. Offers business administration (MBA); church and ministry multiplication (D Min); global urban leadership (MA); leadership (D Min); ministry in complex contexts (D Min); social and civic entrepreneurship (MA); theology of work (D Min); theology reflection (D Min); transformational leadership (DTL); urban youth ministry (D Min). *Program availability:* Part-time, online learning. *Degree requirements:* For master's, thesis; for doctorate, thesis/dissertation. *Entrance requirements:* For master's, 2 years of ministry experience, BA in Biblical studies or theology; for doctorate, 3 years of ministry experience, M Div. Additional exam requirements/recommendations for international students: Required—TOEFL. Electronic applications accepted. *Faculty research:* Theological systems, church management, worship.

Baldwin Wallace University, Graduate Programs, School of Business, Master's in Management Program, Berea, OH 44017-2088. Offers MAM. *Entrance requirements:* Additional exam requirements/recommendations for international students: Required—TOEFL. *Expenses:* Contact institution. *Financial support:* Applicants required to submit FAFSA. *Unit head:* Dale Kramer, MBA Program Director, 440-826-3331, Fax: 440-826-3868, E-mail: dkramer@bw.edu. *Application contact:* Laura Spencer, Graduate Application Specialist, 440-826-2191, Fax: 440-826-3868, E-mail: lspencer@bw.edu.
Website: http://www.bw.edu/academics/master-management/

Baldwin Wallace University, Graduate Programs, School of Business, MBA in Management - Hybrid Program, Berea, OH 44017-2088. Offers MBA. *Program availability:* Part-time, evening/weekend, blended/hybrid learning. *Students:* 35 full-time (15 women); includes 5 minority (3 Black or African American, non-Hispanic/Latino; 1 Asian, non-Hispanic/Latino; 1 Hispanic/Latino). Average age 32. 11 applicants, 73% accepted, 7 enrolled. In 2016, 12 master's awarded. *Entrance requirements:* For master's, GMAT or minimum undergraduate GPA of 3.0, bachelor's degree in any field, work experience. Additional exam requirements/recommendations for international students: Required—TOEFL (minimum score 79 iBT). *Application deadline:* For fall admission, 7/31 for domestic students; for summer admission, 4/15 for domestic students. Applications are processed on a rolling basis. Electronic applications accepted. *Expenses:* $921 per credit hour. *Financial support:* Applicants required to submit FAFSA. *Unit head:* Dale Kramer, Program Director, 440-826-3331, Fax: 440-826-3868, E-mail: dkramer@bw.edu. *Application contact:* Laura Spencer, Graduate Application Specialist, 440-826-2191, Fax: 440-826-3868, E-mail: lspencer@bw.edu.
Website: http://www.bw.edu/graduate/business/mba/

Baldwin Wallace University, Graduate Programs, School of Business, Program in Executive Management, Berea, OH 44017-2088. Offers MBA. *Program availability:* Part-time, evening/weekend. *Students:* 20 full-time (3 women); includes 2 minority (1 Black or African American, non-Hispanic/Latino; 1 Two or more races, non-Hispanic/Latino). Average age 41. 8 applicants, 100% accepted, 6 enrolled. In 2016, 13 master's awarded. *Degree requirements:* For master's, project, minimum overall GPA of 3.0. *Entrance requirements:* For master's, interview, 8 years of work experience, current professional or managerial position, bachelor's degree in any field. Additional exam requirements/recommendations for international students: Required—TOEFL (minimum score 550 paper-based; 79 iBT). *Application deadline:* For fall admission, 7/25 priority date for domestic students, 4/30 priority date for international students; for spring admission, 12/15 priority date for domestic students, 9/30 priority date for international students. Applications are processed on a rolling basis. Application fee: $25. Electronic applications accepted. Application fee is waived when completed online. *Expenses:* $12,480 per semester. *Financial support:* Applicants required to submit FAFSA. *Unit head:* Dale Kramer, MBA/EMBA Director, 440-826-2392, Fax: 440-826-3331, E-mail: dkramer@bw.edu. *Application contact:* Laura Spencer, Graduate Application Specialist, 440-826-2191, Fax: 440-826-3868, E-mail: lspencer@bw.edu.
Website: http://www.bw.edu/graduate/business/executive-mba/

Baldwin Wallace University, Graduate Programs, School of Business, Program in Management, Berea, OH 44017-2088. Offers MBA. *Program availability:* Part-time, evening/weekend. *Students:* 54 full-time (17 women), 39 part-time (16 women); includes 10 minority (4 Black or African American, non-Hispanic/Latino; 3 Asian, non-Hispanic/Latino; 2 Hispanic/Latino; 1 Two or more races, non-Hispanic/Latino), 1 international. Average age 28. 42 applicants, 83% accepted, 31 enrolled. In 2016, 59 master's awarded. *Degree requirements:* For master's, minimum overall GPA of 3.0. *Entrance requirements:* For master's, GMAT or minimum GPA of 3.0, bachelor's degree in any field, work experience. Additional exam requirements/recommendations for international students: Required—TOEFL (minimum score 550 paper-based; 79 iBT). *Application deadline:* For fall admission, 7/25 priority date for domestic students, 4/30 priority date for international students; for spring admission, 12/15 priority date for domestic students, 9/30 priority date for international students; for summer admission, 4/15 priority date for domestic students. Applications are processed on a rolling basis. Application fee: $25. Electronic applications accepted. Application fee is waived when completed online. *Expenses:* $921 per credit hour. *Financial support:* Applicants required to submit FAFSA. *Unit head:* Dale Kramer, MBA/EMBA Director, 440-826-2392, Fax: 440-826-3868, E-mail: dkramer@bw.edu. *Application contact:* Laura Spencer, Graduate Application Specialist, 440-826-2191, Fax: 440-826-3868, E-mail: lspencer@bw.edu.
Website: http://www.bw.edu/graduate/business/mba/

Ball State University, Graduate School, Miller College of Business, Interdepartmental Program in Business Administration, Muncie, IN 47306. Offers business administration (MBA); business essentials (Graduate Certificate); community and economic development (Certificate). *Accreditation:* AACSB. *Program availability:* Part-time, 100% online, blended/hybrid learning. *Entrance requirements:* For master's, GMAT or GRE, minimum baccalaureate GPA of 2.75 or 3.0 in latter half of baccalauareate, resume or curriculum vitae, four professional letters of recommendation. Additional exam requirements/recommendations for international students: Required—TOEFL (minimum score 550 paper-based; 79 iBT), IELTS (minimum score 6.5). Electronic applications accepted. *Expenses:* Contact institution.

Barry University, Andreas School of Business, Graduate Certificate Programs, Miami Shores, FL 33161-6695. Offers finance (Certificate); health services administration (Certificate); international business (Certificate); management (Certificate); management information systems (Certificate); marketing (Certificate).

Barry University, Andreas School of Business, Program in Business Administration, Miami Shores, FL 33161-6695. Offers MBA, DPM/MBA, MBA/MS, MBA/MSN. *Accreditation:* AACSB.

Barry University, School of Adult and Continuing Education, Division of Nursing and Andreas School of Business, Program in Nursing Administration and Business Administration, Miami Shores, FL 33161-6695. Offers MSN/MBA. *Accreditation:* AACN. *Program availability:* Part-time, evening/weekend. Electronic applications accepted. *Faculty research:* Power/empowerment, health delivery systems, managed care, employee health well-being.

Barry University, School of Adult and Continuing Education, Program in Administrative Studies, Miami Shores, FL 33161-6695. Offers MA. *Program availability:* Part-time, evening/weekend. *Entrance requirements:* For master's, GMAT, GRE or MAT, recommendations. Electronic applications accepted.

Barry University, School of Human Performance and Leisure Sciences and Andreas School of Business, Program in Sport Management and Business Administration, Miami Shores, FL 33161-6695. Offers MS/MBA. *Program availability:* Part-time, evening/weekend. Electronic applications accepted. *Faculty research:* Economic impact of professional sports, sport marketing.

Barry University, School of Podiatric Medicine, Podiatric Medicine and Surgery Program and Andreas School of Business, Podiatric Medicine/Business Administration Option, Miami Shores, FL 33161-6695. Offers DPM/MBA.

Baruch College of the City University of New York, Zicklin School of Business, New York, NY 10010-5585. Offers MBA, MS, PhD, Certificate, JD/MBA. JD/MBA offered jointly with Brooklyn Law School and New York Law School. *Accreditation:* AACSB. *Program availability:* Part-time, evening/weekend. *Degree requirements:* For doctorate, comprehensive exam, thesis/dissertation. *Entrance requirements:* For master's, GMAT or GRE, 2 letters of recommendation, resume, 2 years of work experience; for doctorate, GMAT or GRE. Additional exam requirements/recommendations for international students: Required—TOEFL (minimum iBT score of 102) or PTE. Electronic applications accepted.

Baruch College of the City University of New York, Zicklin School of Business, Zicklin Executive Programs, Executive MBA Program, New York, NY 10010-5585. Offers MBA. *Accreditation:* AACSB. *Entrance requirements:* For master's, 5 years of management-level work experience, personal interview. Additional exam requirements/

recommendations for international students: Required—TOEFL. *Expenses:* Contact institution. *Faculty research:* Entrepreneurship, corporate governance, international finance, mergers and acquisitions.

Bayamón Central University, Graduate Programs, Program in Business Administration, Bayamón, PR 00960-1725. Offers accounting (MBA); finance (MBA); general business (MBA); management (MBA); marketing (MBA). *Program availability:* Part-time, evening/weekend. *Degree requirements:* For master's, comprehensive exam (for some programs). *Entrance requirements:* For master's, EXADEP, bachelor's degree in business or related field.

Baylor University, Graduate School, Hankamer School of Business, Program in Business Administration, Waco, TX 76798. Offers MBA, JD/MBA, MBA/MSIS. *Accreditation:* AACSB. *Program availability:* Part-time. *Students:* 180 full-time (63 women), 6 part-time (1 woman); includes 58 minority (20 Black or African American, non-Hispanic/Latino; 12 Asian, non-Hispanic/Latino; 19 Hispanic/Latino; 7 Two or more races, non-Hispanic/Latino), 9 international. 240 applicants, 52% accepted, 83 enrolled. In 2016, 141 master's awarded. *Entrance requirements:* For master's, GMAT, minimum AACSB index of 1050. *Application deadline:* For fall admission, 8/1 for domestic students; for spring admission, 12/1 for domestic students. Applications are processed on a rolling basis. Application fee: $0. *Expenses:* Contact institution. *Financial support:* Research assistantships, teaching assistantships, career-related internships or fieldwork, Federal Work-Study, and institutionally sponsored loans available. *Unit head:* Dr. Gary Carini, Associate Dean, 254-710-3718, Fax: 254-710-1092, E-mail: gary_carini@baylor.edu. *Application contact:* Laurie Wilson, Director, Graduate Business Programs, 254-710-4163, Fax: 254-710-1066, E-mail: laurie_wilson@baylor.edu.

Belhaven University, School of Business, Jackson, MS 39202-1789. Offers business administration (MBA); health administration (MBA, MHA); human resources (MBA, MSL); leadership (MBA); public administration (MPA); sports administration (MBA, MSA). *Program availability:* Part-time, evening/weekend, 100% online. *Faculty:* 16 full-time (3 women), 82 part-time/adjunct (32 women). *Students:* 953 full-time (677 women), 392 part-time (292 women); includes 1,082 minority (1,027 Black or African American, non-Hispanic/Latino; 14 American Indian or Alaska Native, non-Hispanic/Latino; 4 Asian, non-Hispanic/Latino; 20 Hispanic/Latino; 2 Native Hawaiian or other Pacific Islander, non-Hispanic/Latino; 15 Two or more races, non-Hispanic/Latino), 11 international. Average age 35. In 2016, 235 master's awarded. *Degree requirements:* For master's, comprehensive exam (for some programs), thesis (for some programs). *Application deadline:* Applications are processed on a rolling basis. Application fee: $25. Electronic applications accepted. *Expenses:* $535 per credit hour tuition, $75 per course technology fee. *Financial support:* Applicants required to submit FAFSA. *Unit head:* Dr. Ralph Mason, Dean, 601-968-8949, Fax: 601-968-8951, E-mail: cmason@belhaven.edu. *Application contact:* Dr. Audrey Kelleher, Vice President of Adult and Graduate Marketing and Development, 407-804-1424, Fax: 407-620-5210, E-mail: akelleher@belhaven.edu.
Website: http://www.belhaven.edu/campuses/index.htm

Bellarmine University, W. Fielding Rubel School of Business, Louisville, KY 40205. Offers EMBA, MBA, MST. *Accreditation:* AACSB. *Program availability:* Part-time, evening/weekend. *Faculty:* 13 full-time (4 women). *Students:* 54 full-time (21 women), 43 part-time (23 women); includes 14 minority (6 Black or African American, non-Hispanic/Latino; 2 Asian, non-Hispanic/Latino; 4 Hispanic/Latino; 2 Two or more races, non-Hispanic/Latino), 2 international. Average age 29. In 2016, 74 master's awarded. *Degree requirements:* For master's, comprehensive exam. *Entrance requirements:* For master's, GMAT, baccalaureate degree from accredited institution. Additional exam requirements/recommendations for international students: Required—TOEFL (minimum score 550 paper-based; 80 iBT). *Application deadline:* Applications are processed on a rolling basis. Application fee: $40. Electronic applications accepted. *Expenses:* Contact institution. *Financial support:* Career-related internships or fieldwork, scholarships/grants, and unspecified assistantships available. Support available to part-time students. Financial award application deadline: 7/1. *Faculty research:* Marketing, management, small business and entrepreneurship, finance, economics. *Unit head:* Dr. Sharon Kerrick, Dean, 800-272-8249, Fax: 502-272-7443, E-mail: skerrick@bellarmine.edu. *Application contact:* Dr. Sara Pettingill, Dean of Graduate Admission, 800-274-4723 Ext. 8258, Fax: 502-272-8002, E-mail: spettingill@bellarmine.edu.
Website: http://www.bellarmine.edu/business.aspx

Bellevue University, Graduate School, College of Business, Bellevue, NE 68005-3098. Offers acquisition and contract management (MS); business administration (MBA); finance (MS); human capital management (PhD); management (MSM).

Belmont University, Jack C. Massey Graduate School of Business, Nashville, TN 37212. Offers accounting (M Acc); business (AMBA, PMBA); healthcare (MBA). *Accreditation:* AACSB. *Program availability:* Part-time, evening/weekend. *Faculty:* 27 full-time (10 women), 8 part-time/adjunct (3 women). *Students:* 154 full-time (72 women), 49 part-time (25 women); includes 30 minority (12 Black or African American, non-Hispanic/Latino; 11 Asian, non-Hispanic/Latino; 4 Hispanic/Latino; 3 Two or more races, non-Hispanic/Latino), 10 international. Average age 28. 148 applicants, 64% accepted, 77 enrolled. In 2016, 136 master's awarded. *Entrance requirements:* For master's, GMAT, 2 years of work experience (MBA). Additional exam requirements/recommendations for international students: Required—TOEFL (minimum score 550 paper-based). *Application deadline:* For fall admission, 7/1 for domestic and international students; for spring admission, 11/1 for domestic and international students. Applications are processed on a rolling basis. Application fee: $50. Electronic applications accepted. *Expenses:* Contact institution. *Financial support:* Scholarships/grants, tuition waivers (partial), and unspecified assistantships available. Financial award application deadline: 7/1; financial award applicants required to submit FAFSA. *Faculty research:* Music business, strategy, ethics, finance, accounting systems. *Unit head:* Dr. Patrick Raines, Dean, 615-460-6480, Fax: 615-460-6455, E-mail: pat.raines@belmont.edu. *Application contact:* E-mail: masseyadmissions@belmont.edu.
Website: http://www.belmont.edu/business/masseyschool/

Benedictine College, Master of Business Administration Program, Atchison, KS 66002-1499. Offers MBA. *Program availability:* Part-time, evening/weekend. *Faculty:* 6 part-time/adjunct (0 women). *Students:* 36 full-time (12 women), 3 part-time (1 woman); includes 2 minority (1 Black or African American, non-Hispanic/Latino; 1 Hispanic/Latino), 3 international. Average age 27. 34 applicants, 85% accepted, 27 enrolled. In 2016, 12 master's awarded. *Entrance requirements:* For master's, GMAT. Additional exam requirements/recommendations for international students: Recommended—TOEFL, IELTS. *Application deadline:* Applications are processed on a rolling basis. Application fee: $50. Electronic applications accepted. Application fee is waived when completed online. *Expenses:* Contact institution. *Financial support:* In 2016–17, 7 students received support. Unspecified assistantships available. Financial award application deadline: 3/15; financial award applicants required to submit FAFSA. *Faculty research:* Banking, strategic planning, ethics, leadership and entrepreneurship. *Unit head:* Michael King, Chair, School of Business, 913-360-7160, E-mail: mking@benedictine.edu.
Website: http://www.benedictine.edu/mba

Benedictine University, Graduate Programs, Program in Business Administration, Lisle, IL 60532. Offers accounting (MBA); entrepreneurship and managing innovation (MBA); financial management (MBA); health administration (MBA); human resource management (MBA); information systems security (MBA); international business (MBA); management consulting (MBA); management information systems (MBA); marketing management (MBA); operations management and logistics (MBA); organizational leadership (MBA). *Program availability:* Part-time, evening/weekend, online learning. *Faculty:* 4 full-time (2 women), 24 part-time/adjunct (3 women). *Students:* 90 full-time (51 women), 440 part-time (262 women); includes 147 minority (65 Black or African American, non-Hispanic/Latino; 1 American Indian or Alaska Native, non-Hispanic/Latino; 58 Asian, non-Hispanic/Latino; 20 Hispanic/Latino; 3 Native Hawaiian or other Pacific Islander, non-Hispanic/Latino), 2 international. Average age 34. 211 applicants, 89% accepted, 155 enrolled. In 2016, 350 master's awarded. *Entrance requirements:* For master's, GMAT. Additional exam requirements/recommendations for international students: Required—TOEFL (minimum score 550 paper-based). *Application deadline:* For fall admission, 9/1 for domestic students; for winter admission, 12/1 for domestic students; for spring admission, 2/15 for domestic students. Applications are processed on a rolling basis. Application fee: $40. Electronic applications accepted. *Expenses: Tuition:* Full-time $15,600; part-time $650 per hour. *Required fees:* $300. One-time fee: $125 part-time. Tuition and fees vary according to class time, course load, campus/location and program. *Financial support:* Career-related internships or fieldwork and health care benefits available. Support available to part-time students. *Faculty research:* Strategic leadership in professional organizations, sociology of professions, organizational change, social identity theory, applications to change management. *Unit head:* Dr. Sharon Borowicz, Director, 630-829-6219, E-mail: sborowicz@ben.edu. *Application contact:* Kari Gibbons, Director, Admissions, 630-829-6200, Fax: 630-829-6584, E-mail: kgibbons@ben.edu.

Benedictine University, Graduate Programs, Program in Management and Organizational Behavior, Lisle, IL 60532. Offers MS, PhD, MBA/MS, MPH/MS. *Program availability:* Part-time, evening/weekend. *Students:* 38 full-time (21 women), 7 part-time (2 women); includes 6 minority (3 Black or African American, non-Hispanic/Latino; 3 Asian, non-Hispanic/Latino), 3 international. Average age 40. 45 applicants, 96% accepted, 28 enrolled. In 2016, 30 master's, 8 doctorates awarded. *Entrance requirements:* For master's, GMAT. Additional exam requirements/recommendations for international students: Required—TOEFL (minimum score 550 paper-based). *Application deadline:* For fall admission, 9/1 for domestic students; for winter admission, 12/1 for domestic students; for spring admission, 2/15 for domestic students. Applications are processed on a rolling basis. Application fee: $40. Electronic applications accepted. *Expenses: Tuition:* Full-time $15,600; part-time $650 per hour. *Required fees:* $300. One-time fee: $125 part-time. Tuition and fees vary according to class time, course load, campus/location and program. *Financial support:* Career-related internships or fieldwork and health care benefits available. Support available to part-time students. *Faculty research:* Organizational change, transformation, development, learning organizations, career transitions for academics. *Unit head:* Dr. Peter F. Sorensen, Director, 630-829-6220, Fax: 630-960-1126, E-mail: psorensen@ben.edu. *Application contact:* Kari Gibbons, Associate Vice President, Enrollment Center, 630-829-6200, Fax: 630-829-6584, E-mail: kgibbons@ben.edu.

Bentley University, Graduate School of Business, Bentley MBA Program, Waltham, MA 02452-4705. Offers MBA. *Faculty:* 71 full-time (25 women), 33 part-time/adjunct (15 women). *Students:* 29 full-time (20 women); includes 6 minority (4 Black or African American, non-Hispanic/Latino; 2 Hispanic/Latino), 23 international. Average age 33. 88 applicants, 55% accepted, 29 enrolled. In 2016, 25 master's awarded. *Entrance requirements:* For master's, GMAT or GRE General Test, current resume; two letters of recommendation; official copies of all university-level transcripts; in-person interview. Additional exam requirements/recommendations for international students: Required—TOEFL (minimum score 600 paper-based; 100 iBT), IELTS (minimum score 7), or PTE. *Application deadline:* For fall admission, 12/1 for domestic and international students. Applications are processed on a rolling basis. Application fee: $50. Electronic applications accepted. *Expenses: Tuition:* Part-time $1408 per credit. *Required fees:* $160 per credit. *Financial support:* In 2016–17, 29 students received support. Scholarships/grants available. Financial award application deadline: 6/1; financial award applicants required to submit FAFSA. *Faculty research:* Strategy and innovation; personal and group creativity; stakeholder analysis; corporate social responsibility; organizational change and leadership. *Unit head:* Dr. David Schwarzkopf, Director, 781-891-2783, E-mail: dschwarzkopf@bentley.edu. *Application contact:* Sharon Hill, Assistant Dean/Director of Graduate Admissions, 781-891-2108, Fax: 781-891-2464, E-mail: bentleygraduateadmissions@bentley.edu.
Website: http://www.bentley.edu/graduate/mba-programs/bentley-mba

Bentley University, Graduate School of Business, Business PhD Program, Waltham, MA 02452-4705. Offers PhD. *Faculty:* 71 full-time (25 women), 33 part-time/adjunct (15 women). *Students:* 15 full-time (9 women), 2 part-time (1 woman), 13 international. Average age 31. In 2016, 4 doctorates awarded. *Degree requirements:* For doctorate, comprehensive exam, thesis/dissertation. *Entrance requirements:* For doctorate, GMAT or GRE General Test, master's degree; official copies of transcripts; research paper; personal statement; 3 letters of recommendation; curriculum vitae; interview. Additional exam requirements/recommendations for international students: Required—TOEFL (minimum score 600 paper-based; 100 iBT), IELTS (minimum score 7), or PTE. Application fee: $50. Electronic applications accepted. *Expenses: Tuition:* Part-time $1408 per credit. *Required fees:* $160 per credit. *Financial support:* In 2016–17, 18 students received support. Scholarships/grants available. Financial award application deadline: 6/1; financial award applicants required to submit FAFSA. *Faculty research:* Management (including strategy, governance, organization behavior, entrepreneurship, ethics), business analytics, information systems, marketing. *Unit head:* Patricia A. Caffrey, Administrative Director of PhD Programs, 781-891-2541, Fax: 781-891-3121, E-mail: pacaffrey@bentley.edu. *Application contact:* Sharon Hill, Assistant Dean/Director of Graduate Admissions, 781-891-2108, Fax: 781-891-2464, E-mail: bentleygraduateadmissions@bentley.edu.
Website: http://www.bentley.edu/offices/phd/phd-business/

Bentley University, Graduate School of Business, Emerging Leaders MBA Program, Waltham, MA 02452-4705. Offers MBA. *Accreditation:* AACSB. *Faculty:* 71 full-time (25 women), 33 part-time/adjunct (15 women). *Students:* 95 full-time (39 women), 3 part-time (0 women); includes 9 minority (1 Black or African American, non-Hispanic/Latino; 1 American Indian or Alaska Native, non-Hispanic/Latino; 1 Asian, non-Hispanic/Latino; 6 Hispanic/Latino), 56 international. Average age 24. 125 applicants, 77% accepted, 45 enrolled. In 2016, 54 master's awarded. *Entrance requirements:* For master's, GMAT or GRE General Test, interview, current resume, two letters of recommendation, official copies of all university-level transcripts. Additional exam requirements/recommendations for international students: Required—TOEFL (minimum score 600 paper-based; 100 iBT), IELTS (minimum score 7), or PTE. *Application deadline:* Applications are processed on a rolling basis. Application fee: $50. Electronic applications accepted. *Expenses:* $38,965 per year tuition, $480 per year fees. *Financial support:* In 2016–17, 42 students received support. Scholarships/grants, tuition waivers (partial), and unspecified assistantships available. Financial award application deadline: 6/1; financial award applicants required to submit FAFSA. *Faculty research:* Strategy

and innovation, business process management, corporate social responsibility, IT strategy, organizational change and leadership. *Unit head:* Dr. David Schwarzkopf, Associate Professor, 781-891-2783, Fax: 781-891-2464, E-mail: dschwarzkopf@bentley.edu. *Application contact:* Sharon Hill, Assistant Dean/Director of Graduate Admissions, 781-891-2108, Fax: 781-891-2464, E-mail: bentleygraduateadmissions@bentley.edu.
Website: http://www.bentley.edu/graduate/mba-programs/emerging-leaders-mba

Bentley University, Graduate School of Business, Graduate Business Certificate Program, Waltham, MA 02452-4705. Offers accounting (GBC); business analytics (GBC); business ethics (GBC); financial planning (GBC); fraud and forensic accounting (GBC); marketing analytics (GBC); taxation (GBC). *Accreditation:* AACSB. *Program availability:* Part-time, evening/weekend. *Faculty:* 71 full-time (25 women), 33 part-time/adjunct (15 women). *Students:* 10 part-time (5 women); includes 2 minority (1 Black or African American, non-Hispanic/Latino; 1 Asian, non-Hispanic/Latino). Average age 39. 12 applicants, 92% accepted, 6 enrolled. In 2016, 118 GBCs awarded. *Entrance requirements:* For degree, GMAT or GRE General Test, current resume; two letters of recommendation; official copies of all university-level transcripts. Additional exam requirements/recommendations for international students: Required—TOEFL (minimum score 600 paper-based; 100 iBT), IELTS (minimum score 7), or PTE. *Application deadline:* Applications are processed on a rolling basis. Application fee: $50. Electronic applications accepted. *Expenses:* $4,225 per course, $160 fee per year. *Financial support:* Scholarships/grants available. Financial award application deadline: 6/1; financial award applicants required to submit FAFSA. *Unit head:* Dr. Roy A. Wiggins, III, Acting Co-Provost, Dean of Business, 781-891-3166. *Application contact:* Sharon Hill, Senior Assistant Director of Graduate Admissions, 781-891-2108, Fax: 781-891-2464, E-mail: bentleygraduateadmissions@bentley.edu.
Website: http://www.bentley.edu/graduate/special-programs

Bentley University, Graduate School of Business, MS+MBA Program, Waltham, MA 02452-4705. Offers MS/MBA. *Accreditation:* AACSB. *Faculty:* 71 full-time (25 women), 33 part-time/adjunct (15 women). *Students:* 6 full-time (1 woman), 1 part-time (0 women), 5 international. Average age 25. 7 applicants, 71% accepted. *Entrance requirements:* Additional exam requirements/recommendations for international students: Required—TOEFL (minimum score 600 paper-based; 100 iBT), IELTS (minimum score 7), or PTE. *Application deadline:* Applications are processed on a rolling basis. Application fee: $50. Electronic applications accepted. *Expenses:* $38,965 tuition, $480 per year fees. *Financial support:* In 2016–17, 5 students received support. Scholarships/grants and unspecified assistantships available. Financial award application deadline: 6/1; financial award applicants required to submit FAFSA. *Faculty research:* Strategy and innovation, business process management, corporate social responsibility, IT strategy, organizational change and leadership. *Unit head:* Dr. David Schwarzkopf, Associate Professor, 781-891-2783, Fax: 781-891-2464, E-mail: dschwarzkopf@bentley.edu. *Application contact:* Sharon Hill, Associate Dean/Director of Graduate Admissions, 781-891-2108, Fax: 781-891-2464, E-mail: bentleygraduateadmissions@bentley.edu.
Website: http://www.bentley.edu/graduate/mba-programs/elmba/ms-mba

Bentley University, Graduate School of Business, Professional MBA Program, Waltham, MA 02452-4705. Offers MBA. *Accreditation:* AACSB. *Program availability:* Part-time, evening/weekend. *Faculty:* 71 full-time (25 women), 33 part-time/adjunct (15 women). *Students:* 7 full-time (1 woman), 205 part-time (92 women); includes 44 minority (13 Black or African American, non-Hispanic/Latino; 22 Asian, non-Hispanic/Latino; 6 Hispanic/Latino; 3 Two or more races, non-Hispanic/Latino), 5 international. Average age 32. 72 applicants, 88% accepted, 45 enrolled. In 2016, 70 master's awarded. *Entrance requirements:* For master's, GMAT or GRE General Test, current resume; two letters of recommendation; official copies of all university-level transcripts. Additional exam requirements/recommendations for international students: Required—TOEFL (minimum score 600 paper-based; 100 iBT), IELTS (minimum score 7), or PTE. *Application deadline:* Applications are processed on a rolling basis. Application fee: $50. Electronic applications accepted. *Expenses:* $4,225 per course, $160 fee per year. *Financial support:* In 2016–17, 32 students received support. Scholarships/grants available. Financial award application deadline: 6/1; financial award applicants required to submit FAFSA. *Faculty research:* Strategy and innovation, corporate social responsibility, IT strategy, business process management, organizational change and leadership. *Unit head:* Dr. David Schwarzkopf, Associate Professor, 781-891-2783, Fax: 781-891-2464, E-mail: dschwarzkopf@bentley.edu. *Application contact:* Sharon Hill, Associate Dean/Director of Graduate Admissions, 781-891-2108, Fax: 781-891-2464, E-mail: bentleygraduateadmissions@bentley.edu.
Website: http://www.bentley.edu/graduate/mba-programs/professional-mba

Berkeley College–Woodland Park Campus, MBA Program, Woodland Park, NJ 07424. Offers management (MBA).

Berry College, Graduate Programs, Campbell School of Business, Mount Berry, GA 30149-0159. Offers MBA. *Accreditation:* AACSB. *Program availability:* Part-time, evening/weekend. *Faculty:* 6 part-time/adjunct (2 women). *Students:* 2 full-time (1 woman), 21 part-time (7 women); includes 3 minority (2 Black or African American, non-Hispanic/Latino; 1 Hispanic/Latino). Average age 31. In 2016, 11 master's awarded. *Degree requirements:* For master's, thesis. *Entrance requirements:* For master's, GMAT or GRE, minimum GPA of 3.0, essay/goals statement. Additional exam requirements/recommendations for international students: Required—TOEFL (minimum score 550 paper-based). *Application deadline:* For fall admission, 7/21 for domestic students; for spring admission, 12/1 for domestic students. Applications are processed on a rolling basis. Application fee: $25 ($30 for international students). Electronic applications accepted. *Expenses: Tuition:* Full-time $10,890; part-time $605 per credit hour. *Financial support:* In 2016–17, 18 students received support, including 11 research assistantships with full tuition reimbursements available (averaging $6,930 per year); scholarships/grants, tuition waivers (partial), and unspecified assistantships also available. Support available to part-time students. Financial award application deadline: 3/1; financial award applicants required to submit FAFSA. *Faculty research:* Sports economics, human resource management, public choice, applied microeconomics, labor. *Total annual research expenditures:* $6,800. *Unit head:* Dr. Joyce Heames, Dean, 706-236-2233, Fax: 706-802-6728, E-mail: jheames@berry.edu. *Application contact:* Brett Kennedy, Assistant Vice President of Enrollment Management, 706-236-2215, Fax: 706-290-2178, E-mail: admissions@berry.edu.
Website: http://www.berry.edu/mba/

Bethel College, Adult and Graduate Programs, Program in Business Administration, Mishawaka, IN 46545-5591. Offers MBA. *Program availability:* Part-time, evening/weekend, 100% online, blended/hybrid learning. *Faculty:* 9 part-time/adjunct (1 woman). *Students:* 18 full-time (9 women), 63 part-time (33 women); includes 20 minority (15 Black or African American, non-Hispanic/Latino; 5 Hispanic/Latino), 3 international. Average age 37. 44 applicants, 70% accepted, 29 enrolled. In 2016, 24 master's awarded. *Entrance requirements:* For master's, GMAT. Additional exam requirements/recommendations for international students: Required—TOEFL (minimum score 540 paper-based). *Application deadline:* For fall admission, 5/1 for international students; for spring admission, 10/1 for international students. Applications are processed on a rolling basis. Application fee: $0. Electronic applications accepted. *Expenses: Tuition:* Full-time $6750; part-time $3375 per credit hour. *Required fees:* $75 per semester. Tuition and fees vary according to course load and program. *Financial support:* Career-related internships or fieldwork available. Financial award applicants required to submit FAFSA. *Faculty research:* Marketing. *Unit head:* Dale Gadd, Program Director, 574-807-7322, E-mail: dale.gadd@bethelcollege.edu.
Website: http://www.bethelcollege.edu/academics/graduate/mba/

Bethel University, Graduate Programs, McKenzie, TN 38201. Offers administration and supervision (MA Ed); business administration (MBA); conflict resolution (MA); physician assistant studies (MS). *Program availability:* Part-time, evening/weekend. *Degree requirements:* For master's, thesis (for some programs). *Entrance requirements:* For master's, GRE General Test or MAT, minimum undergraduate GPA of 2.5.

Bethel University, Graduate School, St. Paul, MN 55112-6999. Offers business administration (MBA); classroom management (Certificate); counseling (MA); international baccalaureate teaching and learning (Certificate); K-12 education (MA); leadership (Ed D); leadership foundations (Certificate); nurse educator (MS, Certificate); nurse-midwifery (MS); physician assistant (MS); special education (MA); strategic leadership (MA); teaching (MA). *Program availability:* Part-time, evening/weekend, 100% online, blended/hybrid learning. *Faculty:* 19 full-time (15 women), 57 part-time/adjunct (37 women). *Students:* 674 full-time (466 women), 378 part-time (256 women); includes 188 minority (94 Black or African American, non-Hispanic/Latino; 3 American Indian or Alaska Native, non-Hispanic/Latino; 43 Asian, non-Hispanic/Latino; 31 Hispanic/Latino; 1 Native Hawaiian or other Pacific Islander, non-Hispanic/Latino; 16 Two or more races, non-Hispanic/Latino), 33 international. *Degree requirements:* For master's, comprehensive exam (for some programs), thesis (for some programs); for doctorate, comprehensive exam, thesis/dissertation. *Entrance requirements:* Additional exam requirements/recommendations for international students: Required—TOEFL (minimum score 550 paper-based, 80 iBT) or IELTS. *Application deadline:* Applications are processed on a rolling basis. Application fee: $0. Electronic applications accepted. *Expenses:* Contact institution. *Financial support:* Teaching assistantships, career-related internships or fieldwork, and scholarships/grants available. Support available to part-time students. Financial award applicants required to submit FAFSA. *Unit head:* Dick Crombie, Vice-President/Dean, 651-635-8000, Fax: 651-635-8004, E-mail: gs@bethel.edu. *Application contact:* Director of Admissions, 651-635-8000, Fax: 651-635-8004, E-mail: gs@bethel.edu.
Website: https://www.bethel.edu/graduate/

Binghamton University, State University of New York, Graduate School, School of Management, Program in Business Administration, Binghamton, NY 13902-6000. Offers business administration (MBA); corporate executive (MBA); executive business administration (MBA); health care professional executive (MBA); management (PhD); professional business administration (MBA). Executive and Professional MBA programs offered in Manhattan. *Accreditation:* AACSB. *Program availability:* Part-time. *Students:* 126 full-time (43 women), 14 part-time (7 women); includes 24 minority (3 Black or African American, non-Hispanic/Latino; 13 Asian, non-Hispanic/Latino; 8 Hispanic/Latino), 42 international. Average age 25. 288 applicants, 51% accepted, 102 enrolled. In 2016, 92 master's, 4 doctorates awarded. *Degree requirements:* For doctorate, thesis/dissertation. *Entrance requirements:* For master's and doctorate, GMAT. Additional exam requirements/recommendations for international students: Required—TOEFL (minimum score 96 iBT). *Application deadline:* Applications are processed on a rolling basis. Application fee: $75. Electronic applications accepted. *Expenses:* Contact institution. *Financial support:* In 2016–17, 26 students received support, including 10 teaching assistantships with full tuition reimbursements available (averaging $17,000 per year); career-related internships or fieldwork, Federal Work-Study, institutionally sponsored loans, scholarships/grants, health care benefits, tuition waivers (full and partial), and unspecified assistantships also available. Financial award applicants required to submit FAFSA. *Unit head:* Dr. Upinder Dhillon, Dean, 607-777-2314, E-mail: dhillon@binghamton.edu. *Application contact:* Ben Balkaya, Assistant Dean and Director, 607-777-2151, Fax: 607-777-2501, E-mail: balkaya@binghamton.edu.

Biola University, Crowell School of Business, La Mirada, CA 90639-0001. Offers MBA, MP Acc. *Accreditation:* ACBSP. *Program availability:* Part-time, evening/weekend. *Entrance requirements:* For master's, GMAT. Additional exam requirements/recommendations for international students: Required—TOEFL (minimum score 600 paper-based; 100 iBT). Electronic applications accepted. *Faculty research:* Integration of theology with business and accounting principles.

Black Hills State University, Graduate Studies, Program in Business Administration, Spearfish, SD 57799. Offers MBA. *Accreditation:* AACSB. *Program availability:* Evening/weekend. *Entrance requirements:* Additional exam requirements/recommendations for international students: Required—TOEFL (minimum score 500 paper-based; 60 iBT).

Bloomsburg University of Pennsylvania, School of Graduate Studies, Zeigler College of Business, Program in Business Administration, Bloomsburg, PA 17815-1301. Offers business administration (MBA); management (Certificate). *Accreditation:* AACSB. *Program availability:* Part-time, evening/weekend. *Faculty:* 4 full-time (0 women). *Students:* 26 full-time (7 women), 35 part-time (17 women); includes 8 minority (2 Black or African American, non-Hispanic/Latino; 3 Asian, non-Hispanic/Latino; 2 Hispanic/Latino; 1 Native Hawaiian or other Pacific Islander, non-Hispanic/Latino), 1 international. Average age 28. 78 applicants, 64% accepted, 44 enrolled. In 2016, 17 master's awarded. *Degree requirements:* For master's, minimum QPA of 3.0, practicum. *Entrance requirements:* For master's, GMAT, resume, 3 letters of recommendation, personal statement. Additional exam requirements/recommendations for international students: Required—TOEFL (minimum score 550 paper-based; 79 iBT), IELTS (minimum score 7.5). *Application deadline:* Applications are processed on a rolling basis. Application fee: $35 ($60 for international students). Electronic applications accepted. *Expenses:* Tuition, state resident: full-time $9660; part-time $483 per credit. Tuition, nonresident: full-time $14,500; part-time $725 per credit. *Required fees:* $2410; $107 per credit. $75 per term. Tuition and fees vary according to course load, degree level and program. *Financial support:* Federal Work-Study and unspecified assistantships available. *Unit head:* Dr. Darrin Kass, Coordinator, 570-389-4394, Fax: 570-389-3892, E-mail: dkass@bloomu.edu. *Application contact:* Jennifer Kessler, Administrative Assistant, 570-389-4015, Fax: 570-389-3054, E-mail: jkessler@bloomu.edu.
Website: http://www.bloomu.edu/gradschool/mba

Bluffton University, Programs in Business, Bluffton, OH 45817. Offers accounting and financial management (MBA); business administration (MBA); health care management (MBA); leadership (MBA); organizational management (MA); production and operations management (MBA). *Program availability:* Evening/weekend, online learning. *Faculty:* 9 full-time (3 women), 12 part-time/adjunct (4 women). *Students:* 55 full-time (34 women), 2 part-time (1 woman); includes 5 minority (1 Black or African American, non-Hispanic/Latino; 2 Asian, non-Hispanic/Latino; 2 Hispanic/Latino), 2 international. Average age 34. 31 applicants, 77% accepted, 22 enrolled. In 2016, 44 master's awarded. *Entrance requirements:* For master's, current resume, official transcript, two recommendation forms, bachelor's degree, minimum GPA of 3.0, four years of professional experience, interview. Additional exam requirements/recommendations for international students: Recommended—TOEFL. *Application deadline:* For fall admission, 7/31 priority date for domestic and international students. Applications are processed on a rolling basis.

Application fee: $25. Electronic applications accepted. Application fee is waived when completed online. *Expenses:* $550 per credit. *Financial support:* Scholarships/grants and unspecified assistantships available. Financial award application deadline: 5/1. *Unit head:* Dr. Melissa Green, Director of Graduate Programs in Business, 419-358-3447, E-mail: greenm@bluffton.edu. *Application contact:* Carrie Mast, Administrative Assistant, Graduate Programs in Business, 419-358-3065, E-mail: mastc@bluffton.edu.
Website: http://www.bluffton.edu/grad/

Bob Jones University, Graduate Programs, Greenville, SC 29614. Offers accountancy (MS); Bible (MA); Bible translation (MA); Biblical studies (Certificate); broadcast management (MS); business administration (MBA); church history (MA, PhD); church ministries (MA); church music (MM); cinema and video production (MA); counseling (MS); curriculum and instruction (Ed D); divinity (M Div); dramatic production (MA); educational leadership (MS, Ed D, Ed S); elementary education (M Ed, MAT); English (M Ed, MA, MAT); fine arts (MA); graphic design (MA); history (M Ed, MA); illustration (MA); interpretative speech (MA); mathematics (M Ed, MAT); medical missions (Certificate); ministry (MM, D Min); multi-categorical special education (M Ed, MAT); music (M Ed); New Testament interpretation (PhD); Old Testament interpretation (PhD); orchestral instrument performance (MM); organ performance (MM); pastoral studies (MA); personnel services (MS, Ed S); piano pedagogy (MM); piano performance (MM); platform arts (MA); radio and television broadcasting (MS); rhetoric and public address (MA); secondary education (M Ed); studio art (MA); teaching Bible (MA); theology (MA, PhD); voice performance (MM); youth ministries (MA); M Div/MM.

Boise State University, College of Business and Economics, Program in Business Administration, Boise, ID 83725-1600. Offers executive (MBA). *Accreditation:* AACSB. *Program availability:* Part-time, 100% online. *Faculty:* 6. *Students:* 128 full-time (44 women), 159 part-time (46 women); includes 28 minority (3 Black or African American, non-Hispanic/Latino; 1 American Indian or Alaska Native, non-Hispanic/Latino; 6 Asian, non-Hispanic/Latino; 13 Hispanic/Latino; 5 Two or more races, non-Hispanic/Latino), 11 international. Average age 33. 207 applicants, 62% accepted, 104 enrolled. In 2016, 98 master's awarded. *Entrance requirements:* For master's, GMAT, minimum GPA of 3.0. Additional exam requirements/recommendations for international students: Required—TOEFL (minimum score 587 paper-based; 95 iBT), IELTS (minimum score 6.5). *Application deadline:* For fall admission, 4/15 for domestic and international students. Applications are processed on a rolling basis. Application fee: $65 ($95 for international students). Electronic applications accepted. *Expenses:* Tuition, state resident: full-time $6058; part-time $358 per credit hour. Tuition, nonresident: full-time $20,108; part-time $608 per credit hour. *Required fees:* $2108. Tuition and fees vary according to program. *Financial support:* Scholarships/grants and unspecified assistantships available. Financial award application deadline: 2/15; financial award applicants required to submit FAFSA. *Unit head:* Dr. Kirk Smith, Associate Dean, Graduate Studies, 208-426-3180. *Application contact:* Trisha Stevens-Lamb, Director, Career Start MBA, 208-426-1120, E-mail: trishastevenslamb@boisestate.edu.
Website: http://cobe.boisestate.edu/graduate/

Boston College, Carroll School of Management, Business Administration Program, Chestnut Hill, MA 02467-3800. Offers MBA, JD/MBA, MBA/MA, MBA/MS, MBA/MSA, MBA/MSF, MBA/MSW, MBA/PhD. *Accreditation:* AACSB. *Program availability:* Part-time, evening/weekend. *Entrance requirements:* For master's, GMAT, GRE, 2 letters of recommendation, resume, transcript. Additional exam requirements/recommendations for international students: Required—TOEFL (minimum score 600 paper-based, 100 iBT), IELTS (minimum score 7.5), or PTE (minimum score 68). Electronic applications accepted. Tuition and fees vary according to program. *Faculty research:* Investments, corporate finance, management of financial services, strategic management.

Boston University, Metropolitan College, Department of Administrative Sciences, Boston, MA 02215. Offers applied business analytics (MS); economic development and tourism management (MSAS); enterprise risk management (MS); financial management (MS); global marketing management (MS); innovation and technology (MSAS); insurance management (MSM); project management (MS); supply chain management (MS). *Accreditation:* AACSB. *Program availability:* Part-time, evening/weekend, online learning. *Faculty:* 15 full-time (3 women), 22 part-time/adjunct (3 women). *Students:* 301 full-time (146 women), 934 part-time (501 women); includes 237 minority (81 Black or African American, non-Hispanic/Latino; 5 American Indian or Alaska Native, non-Hispanic/Latino; 60 Asian, non-Hispanic/Latino; 76 Hispanic/Latino; 1 Native Hawaiian or other Pacific Islander, non-Hispanic/Latino; 14 Two or more races, non-Hispanic/Latino), 514 international. Average age 31. 593 applicants, 69% accepted, 260 enrolled. In 2016, 263 master's awarded. *Degree requirements:* For master's, thesis optional. *Entrance requirements:* For master's, 1 year of work experience, minimum GPA of 3.0. Additional exam requirements/recommendations for international students: Required—TOEFL (minimum score 84 iBT). *Application deadline:* Applications are processed on a rolling basis. Application fee: $80. Electronic applications accepted. *Expenses:* Contact institution. *Financial support:* In 2016–17, 15 students received support, including 14 research assistantships (averaging $8,400 per year); career-related internships or fieldwork, Federal Work-Study, and unspecified assistantships also available. *Faculty research:* International business, innovative process. *Unit head:* Dr. John Sullivan, Chair, 617-353-3016, E-mail: adminsc@bu.edu. *Application contact:* Fiona Niven, Administrative Sciences Department, 617-353-3016, E-mail: adminsc@bu.edu.
Website: http://www.bu.edu/met/academic-community/departments/administrative-sciences/

Boston University, Questrom School of Business, Boston, MA 02215. Offers business (EMBA, MBA); management (PhD); management studies (MSMS); mathematical finance (MS, PhD); JD/MBA; MBA/MA; MBA/MPH; MBA/MS; MD/MBA; MS/MBA. *Accreditation:* AACSB. *Program availability:* Part-time, evening/weekend. *Faculty:* 77 full-time (21 women), 41 part-time/adjunct (7 women). *Students:* 744 full-time (331 women), 734 part-time (315 women); includes 257 minority (41 Black or African American, non-Hispanic/Latino; 2 American Indian or Alaska Native, non-Hispanic/Latino; 123 Asian, non-Hispanic/Latino; 72 Hispanic/Latino; 1 Native Hawaiian or other Pacific Islander, non-Hispanic/Latino; 18 Two or more races, non-Hispanic/Latino), 441 international. Average age 28. 1,098 applicants, 37% accepted, 159 enrolled. In 2016, 492 master's, 7 doctorates awarded. *Degree requirements:* For doctorate, comprehensive exam, thesis/dissertation. *Entrance requirements:* For master's, GMAT or GRE (for MBA and MS in mathematical finance programs), essay, resume, 2 letters of recommendation, official transcript; for doctorate, GMAT or GRE, personal statement, resume, 3 letters of recommendation, official transcripts. Additional exam requirements/recommendations for international students: Required—TOEFL (minimum score 600 paper-based; 90 iBT). *Application deadline:* For fall admission, 3/19 for domestic and international students; for spring admission, 11/8 for domestic students. Application fee: $125. Electronic applications accepted. *Financial support:* Career-related internships or fieldwork, Federal Work-Study, institutionally sponsored loans, scholarships/grants, and tuition waivers (partial) available. Support available to part-time students. Financial award applicants required to submit FAFSA. *Faculty research:* Entrepreneurship, sustainable energy, corporate social responsibility, risk management, information systems. *Unit head:* Kenneth W. Freeman, Professor/Dean, 617-353-9720, Fax: 617-353-5581, E-mail: kfreeman@bu.edu. *Application contact:* Meredith C. Siegel, Assistant Dean, Graduate Admission, 617-353-2670, Fax: 617-353-7368, E-mail: mba@bu.edu.
Website: http://www.bu.edu/questrom/

Boston University, School of Public Health, Health Law, Policy and Management Department, Boston, MA 02215. Offers health services research (MS). *Accreditation:* CAHME. *Program availability:* Part-time, evening/weekend. *Faculty:* 37 full-time, 31 part-time/adjunct. *Students:* 134 full-time (105 women), 108 part-time (86 women); includes 75 minority (22 Black or African American, non-Hispanic/Latino; 1 American Indian or Alaska Native, non-Hispanic/Latino; 28 Asian, non-Hispanic/Latino; 16 Hispanic/Latino; 8 Two or more races, non-Hispanic/Latino), 23 international. Average age 29. 507 applicants, 44% accepted, 77 enrolled. In 2016, 203 master's, 10 doctorates awarded. *Degree requirements:* For master's, comprehensive exam (for some programs), thesis (for some programs); for doctorate, comprehensive exam, thesis/dissertation. *Entrance requirements:* For master's, GRE, MCAT, GMAT; for doctorate, GRE. Additional exam requirements/recommendations for international students: Required—TOEFL (minimum score 600 paper-based; 100 iBT), IELTS (minimum score 7). *Application deadline:* For fall admission, 12/1 priority date for domestic and international students; for spring admission, 10/15 priority date for domestic students. Applications are processed on a rolling basis. Application fee: $115. Electronic applications accepted. *Financial support:* Career-related internships or fieldwork, Federal Work-Study, institutionally sponsored loans, scholarships/grants, and tuition waivers (partial) available. Support available to part-time students. Financial award application deadline: 3/1; financial award applicants required to submit FAFSA. *Faculty research:* Health policy, health law and ethics, human rights, healthcare management. *Unit head:* Dr. David Rosenbloom, Interim Chair, 617-638-5042. *Application contact:* LePhan Quan, Associate Director of Admissions, 617-638-4640, Fax: 617-638-5299, E-mail: asksph@bu.edu.
Website: http://www.bu.edu/sph/about/departments/health-law-policy-and-management/

Bowie State University, Graduate Programs, Program in Business Administration, Bowie, MD 20715-9465. Offers MBA. *Accreditation:* ACBSP. *Program availability:* Part-time, evening/weekend. *Degree requirements:* For master's, comprehensive exam. *Entrance requirements:* For master's, GMAT, minimum undergraduate GPA of 2.5. Electronic applications accepted.

Bowling Green State University, Graduate College, College of Business, Master of Business Administration Program, Bowling Green, OH 43403. Offers MBA. *Accreditation:* AACSB. *Program availability:* Part-time, evening/weekend. *Degree requirements:* For master's, thesis or alternative, research project. *Entrance requirements:* For master's, GMAT. Additional exam requirements/recommendations for international students: Required—TOEFL. *Application deadline:* For fall admission, 2/15 priority date for domestic students, 1/15 priority date for international students. Application fee: $30. Electronic applications accepted. *Financial support:* Research assistantships with full tuition reimbursements, teaching assistantships with full tuition reimbursements, career-related internships or fieldwork, Federal Work-Study, institutionally sponsored loans, and unspecified assistantships available. Financial award applicants required to submit FAFSA. *Faculty research:* Management of change processes, supply chain management, impacts of money on society, corporate financing strategies, macro-marketing/management of sales staff and services. *Unit head:* Director, E-mail: dchatfi@bgsu.edu. *Application contact:* Dr. Terry L. Lawrence, Assistant Dean for Graduate Admissions and Studies, 419-372-7713, Fax: 419-372-8569, E-mail: tlawren@bgnet.bgsu.edu.
Website: http://www.bgsu.edu/business/students/future-students/graduate-programs/mba.html

Bradley University, The Graduate School, Foster College of Business, Business Administration Program, Peoria, IL 61625-0002. Offers MBA. *Accreditation:* AACSB. *Program availability:* Part-time, evening/weekend. *Degree requirements:* For master's, comprehensive exam. *Entrance requirements:* For master's, GMAT or GRE, minimum undergraduate GPA of 2.75 in major, 2 letters of recommendation. Additional exam requirements/recommendations for international students: Required—TOEFL (minimum score 550 paper-based; 79 iBT), IELTS (minimum score 6.5). *Application deadline:* For fall admission, 5/15 priority date for domestic and international students; for spring admission, 10/15 priority date for domestic and international students. Applications are processed on a rolling basis. Application fee: $40 ($50 for international students). Electronic applications accepted. *Expenses: Tuition:* Full-time $7650; part-time $850 per credit. *Required fees:* $50 per credit. One-time fee: $100 full-time. *Financial support:* Research assistantships with full and partial tuition reimbursements, teaching assistantships with full and partial tuition reimbursements, career-related internships or fieldwork, institutionally sponsored loans, scholarships/grants, tuition waivers (partial), and unspecified assistantships available. Support available to part-time students. Financial award application deadline: 4/1. *Application contact:* Kayla Carroll, Director of International Admission and Student Services, 309-677-2375, E-mail: klcarroll@fsmail.bradley.edu.
Website: http://www.bradley.edu/academic/colleges/fcba/education/grad/mba/

Bradley University, The Graduate School, Foster College of Business, Theresa S. Falcon Executive MBA Program, Peoria, IL 61625-0002. Offers MBA. *Accreditation:* AACSB. *Program availability:* Evening/weekend. *Entrance requirements:* For master's, company sponsorship, 7 years of managerial experience, letters of recommendation. Additional exam requirements/recommendations for international students: Required—TOEFL (minimum score 550 paper-based; 79 iBT), IELTS (minimum score 6.5). *Application deadline:* Applications are processed on a rolling basis. Application fee: $40 ($50 for international students). Electronic applications accepted. *Expenses:* Contact institution. *Unit head:* Rob Johanssen, Director, 309-677-2256, E-mail: rjohannsen@bradley.edu.
Website: http://www.bradley.edu/academic/colleges/fcba/education/grad/emba/

Brandeis University, The Heller School for Social Policy and Management, Program in Nonprofit Management, Waltham, MA 02454-9110. Offers child, youth, and family management (MBA); health care management (MBA); social impact management (MBA); social policy and management (MBA); sustainable development (MBA); MBA/MA; MBA/MD. MBA/MD program offered in conjunction with Tufts University School of Medicine. *Accreditation:* AACSB. *Program availability:* Part-time. *Degree requirements:* For master's, team consulting project. *Entrance requirements:* For master's, GMAT (preferred) or GRE, 2 letters of recommendation, problem statement analysis, 3-5 years of professional experience. Additional exam requirements/recommendations for international students: Required—TOEFL (minimum score 600 paper-based; 100 iBT). Electronic applications accepted. *Expenses:* Contact institution. *Faculty research:* Health care; children and families; elder and disabled services; social impact management; organizations in the non-profit, for-profit, or public sector.

Brandman University, School of Business and Professional Studies, Irvine, CA 92618. Offers accounting (MBA); business administration (MBA); e-business strategic management (MBA); entrepreneurship (MBA); finance (MBA); health administration (MBA); human resources (MBA, MS); international business (MBA); marketing (MBA); organizational leadership (MA, MBA, MPA); public administration (MPA). *Expenses: Tuition:* Full-time $14,880; part-time $620 per credit hour. Tuition and fees vary according to degree level and program. *Unit head:* Dr. Glenn Worthington, Dean, 253-

861-1024, E-mail: gworthin@brandman.edu.
Website: https://www.brandman.edu/business-professional-studies

Brenau University, Sydney O. Smith Graduate School, College of Business and Mass Communication, Gainesville, GA 30501. Offers accounting (MBA); business administration (MBA); healthcare management (MBA); organizational leadership (MS); project management (MBA). *Accreditation:* ACBSP. *Program availability:* Part-time, evening/weekend, online learning. *Degree requirements:* For master's, comprehensive exam (for some programs). *Entrance requirements:* For master's, resume, minimum undergraduate GPA of 2.5. Additional exam requirements/recommendations for international students: Required—TOEFL (minimum score 500 paper-based; 61 iBT); Recommended—IELTS (minimum score 5). Electronic applications accepted. *Expenses:* Contact institution.

Brescia University, Program in Business Administration, Owensboro, KY 42301-3023. Offers MBA. *Program availability:* Part-time, evening/weekend. *Entrance requirements:* For master's, minimum cumulative GPA of 2.5. Additional exam requirements/recommendations for international students: Required—TOEFL (minimum score 100 iBT). Electronic applications accepted. Application fee is waived when completed online.

Brescia University, Program in Management, Owensboro, KY 42301-3023. Offers MSM. *Program availability:* Part-time, evening/weekend. *Entrance requirements:* For master's, minimum GPA of 2.5. Additional exam requirements/recommendations for international students: Required—TOEFL (minimum score 100 iBT).

Bridgewater State University, College of Graduate Studies, Ricciardi College of Business, Department of Management, Bridgewater, MA 02325. Offers MSM. *Entrance requirements:* For master's, GMAT.

Briercrest Seminary, Graduate Programs, Program in Leadership and Management, Caronport, SK S0H 0S0, Canada. Offers organizational leadership (MA). *Program availability:* Part-time. *Degree requirements:* For master's, comprehensive exam, thesis optional. *Entrance requirements:* Additional exam requirements/recommendations for international students: Required—TOEFL (minimum score 550 paper-based).

Brigham Young University, Graduate Studies, Marriott School of Management, Executive Master of Business Administration Program, Provo, UT 84602. Offers MBA. *Accreditation:* AACSB. *Program availability:* Part-time-only, evening/weekend. *Students:* 138 part-time (23 women); includes 9 minority (2 Black or African American, non-Hispanic/Latino; 1 Asian, non-Hispanic/Latino; 3 Hispanic/Latino; 3 Native Hawaiian or other Pacific Islander, non-Hispanic/Latino), 9 international. Average age 40. 141 applicants, 55% accepted, 69 enrolled. In 2016, 54 master's awarded. *Entrance requirements:* For master's, GMAT or GRE, 5 years of management experience, minimum GPA of 3.0 in last 60 undergraduate hours. Additional exam requirements/recommendations for international students: Required—TOEFL (minimum score 590 paper-based; 94 iBT), IELTS (minimum score 7). *Application deadline:* For fall admission, 5/1 for domestic students, 1/15 for international students. Applications are processed on a rolling basis. Application fee: $50. Electronic applications accepted. *Expenses:* Contact institution. *Financial support:* In 2016–17, 1 student received support. Application deadline: 3/1; applicants required to submit FAFSA. *Faculty research:* Finance, marketing, supply chain management, entrepreneurship, strategic human resources. *Unit head:* Dr. Grant McQueen, Director, 801-422-3500, Fax: 801-422-0513, E-mail: emba@byu.edu. *Application contact:* Yvette Anderson, MBA Program Admissions Director, 801-422-3500, Fax: 801-422-0513, E-mail: mba@byu.edu.
Website: http://emba.byu.edu

Brigham Young University, Graduate Studies, Marriott School of Management, Master of Business Administration Program, Provo, UT 84602. Offers entrepreneurship (MBA); finance (MBA); global supply chain management (MBA); marketing (MBA); strategic human resources (MBA); JD/MBA; MBA/MS. *Accreditation:* AACSB. *Students:* 321 full-time (63 women); includes 16 minority (1 Black or African American, non-Hispanic/Latino; 9 Asian, non-Hispanic/Latino; 6 Hispanic/Latino), 69 international. Average age 31. 397 applicants, 49% accepted, 154 enrolled. In 2016, 146 master's awarded. *Entrance requirements:* For master's, GMAT or GRE, minimum GPA of 3.0 in last 60 hours. Additional exam requirements/recommendations for international students: Required—TOEFL (minimum score 590 paper-based; 94 iBT), IELTS (minimum score 7). *Application deadline:* For fall admission, 5/1 for domestic students, 1/15 for international students. Applications are processed on a rolling basis. Application fee: $50. Electronic applications accepted. *Expenses:* Contact institution. *Financial support:* In 2016–17, 247 students received support. Research assistantships, teaching assistantships, career-related internships or fieldwork, institutionally sponsored loans, and scholarships/grants available. Financial award application deadline: 3/1; financial award applicants required to submit FAFSA. *Faculty research:* Finance, marketing, supply chain management, entrepreneurship, strategic human resources. *Unit head:* Dr. Grant McQueen, Director, 801-422-3500, Fax: 801-422-0513, E-mail: mba@byu.edu. *Application contact:* Yvette Anderson, MBA Program Admissions Director, 801-422-3500, Fax: 801-422-0513, E-mail: mba@byu.edu.
Website: http://mba.byu.edu

Bristol University, Program in Business Administration, Anaheim, CA 92806. Offers business administration (MBA); international business (MBA); marketing (MBA); sports management (MBA). *Degree requirements:* For master's, capstone.

Broadview University–West Jordan, Graduate Programs, West Jordan, UT 84088. Offers business administration (MBA); health care management (MSM); information technology (MSM); managerial leadership (MSM).

Brock University, Faculty of Graduate Studies, Faculty of Business, Program in Business Administration, St. Catharines, ON L2S 3A1, Canada. Offers MBA. *Degree requirements:* For master's, thesis or alternative. *Entrance requirements:* For master's, honours degree. Additional exam requirements/recommendations for international students: Required—TOEFL (minimum score 575 paper-based; 89 iBT), IELTS (minimum score 7), TWE (minimum score 4.5). Electronic applications accepted.

Brock University, Faculty of Graduate Studies, Faculty of Business, Program in Management, St. Catharines, ON L2S 3A1, Canada. Offers M Sc. *Program availability:* Part-time. *Degree requirements:* For master's, thesis. *Entrance requirements:* For master's, GMAT, honors degree. Additional exam requirements/recommendations for international students: Required—TOEFL (minimum score 600 paper-based; 100 iBT), IELTS (minimum score 7), TWE (minimum score 4.5). Electronic applications accepted.

Brooklyn College of the City University of New York, School of Business, Brooklyn, NY 11210-2889. Offers accounting (MS); business administration (MS), including economic analysis, general business, global business and finance. *Program availability:* Part-time, evening/weekend. *Degree requirements:* For master's, comprehensive exam, thesis or alternative. *Entrance requirements:* For master's, GMAT, 2 letters of recommendation. Additional exam requirements/recommendations for international students: Required—TOEFL (minimum score 550 paper-based; 79 iBT). Electronic applications accepted. *Faculty research:* Econometrics, environmental economics, microeconomics, macroeconomics, taxation.

Bryan College, MBA Program, Dayton, TN 37321. Offers MBA. *Entrance requirements:* For master's, resume, 2 letters of recommendation. Additional exam requirements/recommendations for international students: Required—TOEFL. Application fee: $50. *Expenses:* $545 per credit hour. *Financial support:* Applicants required to submit FAFSA. *Unit head:* Dr. Adina Scruggs, MBA Director, 423-634-2057, E-mail: adina.scruggs@bryan.edu. *Application contact:* Carla Harle, MBA Coordinator, 423-775-7480, E-mail: carla.harle@bryan.edu.
Website: http://www.bryan.edu/academics/adult-education/graduate/online-mba/

Bryant University, Graduate School of Business, Smithfield, RI 02917. Offers accounting (MPAC); business administration (MBA), including general management, global finance, global supply chain management, international business; business analytics (Graduate Certificate); taxation (MST). *Program availability:* Part-time, evening/weekend. *Faculty:* 16 full-time (3 women), 2 part-time/adjunct (0 women). *Students:* 71 full-time (23 women), 83 part-time (32 women); includes 17 minority (5 Black or African American, non-Hispanic/Latino; 4 Asian, non-Hispanic/Latino; 5 Hispanic/Latino; 3 Two or more races, non-Hispanic/Latino), 17 international. Average age 27. 165 applicants, 57% accepted, 66 enrolled. In 2016, 106 master's, 12 other advanced degrees awarded. *Degree requirements:* For master's, comprehensive exam (for some programs). *Entrance requirements:* For master's, GMAT, resume, recommendation, college transcripts. Additional exam requirements/recommendations for international students: Required—TOEFL (minimum score 580 paper-based; 95 iBT). *Application deadline:* For fall admission, 7/15 for domestic and international students; for spring admission, 11/15 for domestic and international students; for summer admission, 4/15 for domestic and international students. Applications are processed on a rolling basis. Application fee: $80. Electronic applications accepted. *Expenses:* Contact institution. *Financial support:* Research assistantships, scholarships/grants, and unspecified assistantships available. Support available to part-time students. Financial award application deadline: 2/15; financial award applicants required to submit FAFSA. *Faculty research:* International business, public sector auditing, taxation of partnerships, information systems security, financial markets microstructure. *Unit head:* Bjorn Carlsson, Graduate Program Director, 401-232-6707, E-mail: bcarlsson@bryant.edu. *Application contact:* Terri Rogers, Admissions Assistant, 401-232-6230, Fax: 401-232-6494, E-mail: graduateprograms@bryant.edu.
Website: http://gradschool.bryant.edu/business/

Bryan University, Program in Business Administration, Springfield, MO 65804. Offers MBA. *Program availability:* Online learning.

Butler University, Lacy School of Business, Indianapolis, IN 46208-3485. Offers finance (MBA); international business (MBA); leadership (MBA); marketing (MBA); professional accounting (MP Acc). *Accreditation:* AACSB. *Program availability:* Part-time. *Faculty:* 18 full-time (6 women), 14 part-time/adjunct (5 women). *Students:* 31 full-time (11 women), 133 part-time (40 women); includes 10 minority (2 Black or African American, non-Hispanic/Latino; 2 Asian, non-Hispanic/Latino; 6 Hispanic/Latino), 2 international. Average age 31. 122 applicants, 68% accepted, 42 enrolled. In 2016, 89 master's awarded. *Entrance requirements:* For master's, GMAT, minimum AACSB index of 950, personal statement, two letters of recommendation, official transcripts, current resume. Additional exam requirements/recommendations for international students: Required—TOEFL (minimum score 550 paper-based; 79 iBT), IELTS (minimum score 6), Michigan English Language Assessment Battery (minimum score of 80). *Application deadline:* For fall admission, 8/1 for domestic and international students; for spring admission, 12/1 for domestic and international students; for summer admission, 4/1 for domestic and international students. Applications are processed on a rolling basis. Application fee: $0. Electronic applications accepted. *Expenses:* $790 per credit hour. *Financial support:* In 2016–17, 15 students received support. Scholarships/grants, tuition waivers (full and partial), and unspecified assistantships available. Financial award application deadline: 7/15; financial award applicants required to submit FAFSA. *Faculty research:* Higher education and pedagogy; ecotourism; healthcare issues and marketing public policy; domestic public policy, international finance and banking, international and management entrepreneurship, organizational management. *Unit head:* Dr. Stephen Standifird, Dean. *Application contact:* Diane Dubord, Graduate Student Service Specialist, 317-940-8107, Fax: 317-940-8250,
E-mail: ddubord@butler.edu.
Website: https://www.butler.edu/lacyschool

Cairn University, School of Business, Langhorne, PA 19047-2990. Offers accounting (MBA); business administration (MBA); international entrepreneurship (MBA); nonprofit leadership (MBA); organizational leadership (MSOL, Postbaccalaureate Certificate). *Program availability:* Part-time, evening/weekend, 100% online, blended/hybrid learning. *Faculty:* 3 full-time (0 women), 6 part-time/adjunct (1 woman). *Students:* 7 full-time (5 women), 43 part-time (19 women); includes 20 minority (10 Black or African American, non-Hispanic/Latino; 1 American Indian or Alaska Native, non-Hispanic/Latino; 4 Asian, non-Hispanic/Latino; 3 Hispanic/Latino; 2 Two or more races, non-Hispanic/Latino), 4 international. Average age 36. 17 applicants, 100% accepted, 16 enrolled. In 2016, 16 master's awarded. *Entrance requirements:* Additional exam requirements/recommendations for international students: Required—TOEFL (minimum score 550 paper-based). *Application deadline:* Applications are processed on a rolling basis. Application fee: $25. Electronic applications accepted. Application fee is waived when completed online. *Expenses:* $655 per semester credit. *Financial support:* Scholarships/grants available. Support available to part-time students. Financial award applicants required to submit FAFSA. *Unit head:* Yunn Kang, Dean, School of Business, 215-702-4461, Fax: 215-702-4248, E-mail: ykang@cairn.edu. *Application contact:* Gwen Dorsey, Assistant Director, Graduate Admissions, 800-572-2472, Fax: 215-702-4248, E-mail: gdorsey@cairn.edu.
Website: http://cairn.edu/academics/business

Caldwell University, Graduate Studies, Division of Business, Caldwell, NJ 07006-6195. Offers accounting (MS); business administration (MBA). *Accreditation:* ACBSP. *Program availability:* Part-time. *Entrance requirements:* For master's, GMAT, undergraduate accounting, marketing, and finance. Additional exam requirements/recommendations for international students: Required—TOEFL (minimum score 580 paper-based). Electronic applications accepted.

California Baptist University, Program in Business Administration, Riverside, CA 92504-3206. Offers accounting (MBA); construction management (MBA); healthcare management (MBA); management (MBA). *Accreditation:* ACBSP. *Program availability:* Part-time, evening/weekend, 100% online, blended/hybrid learning. *Faculty:* 14 full-time (3 women), 10 part-time/adjunct (1 woman). *Students:* 105 full-time (48 women), 122 part-time (63 women); includes 101 minority (23 Black or African American, non-Hispanic/Latino; 1 American Indian or Alaska Native, non-Hispanic/Latino; 10 Asian, non-Hispanic/Latino; 59 Hispanic/Latino; 2 Native Hawaiian or other Pacific Islander, non-Hispanic/Latino; 6 Two or more races, non-Hispanic/Latino), 54 international. Average age 29. 136 applicants, 65% accepted, 62 enrolled. In 2016, 71 master's awarded. *Degree requirements:* For master's, interdisciplinary capstone project. *Entrance requirements:* For master's, GMAT, minimum GPA of 2.5; two recommendations; comprehensive essay; resume; interview. Additional exam requirements/recommendations for international students: Required—TOEFL (minimum score 80 iBT). *Application deadline:* For fall admission, 8/1 priority date for domestic students, 7/1 for international students; for spring admission, 12/1 priority date for domestic students, 11/1 for international students. Applications are processed on a rolling basis. Application fee: $45. Electronic applications accepted. *Expenses:* Contact

institution. *Financial support:* In 2016–17, 38 students received support. Federal Work-Study and scholarships/grants available. Financial award applicants required to submit CSS PROFILE or FAFSA. *Faculty research:* Behavioral economics, economic indicators, marketing ethics, international business, microfinance. *Unit head:* Dr. Steve Strombeck, Interim Dean, School of Business, 951-343-4701, Fax: 951-343-4361, E-mail: sstrombeck@calbaptist.edu. *Application contact:* Stephanie Fluitt, Graduate Admissions Counselor, 951-343-4696, E-mail: sfluitt@calbaptist.edu.
Website: http://www.calbaptist.edu/mba/about/

California Coast University, School of Administration and Management, Santa Ana, CA 92701. Offers business marketing (MBA); health care management (MBA); human resource management (MBA); management (MBA, MS). *Program availability:* Online learning. Electronic applications accepted.

California Intercontinental University, School of Business, Irvine, CA 92614. Offers banking and finance (MBA); entrepreneurship and business management (DBA); global business leadership (DBA); international management and marketing (MBA); organizational management and human resource management (MBA).

California International Business University, Graduate Programs, San Diego, CA 92101. Offers MBA, MSIM, DBA.

California Lutheran University, Graduate Studies, School of Management, Thousand Oaks, CA 91360-2787. Offers business (IMBA); computer science (MS); econometrics (MBA); economics (MS); entrepreneurship (MBA, Certificate); finance (MBA, Certificate); financial planning (MBA, Certificate); information systems and technology (MS); information technology management (MBA, Certificate); international business (MBA, Certificate); management and organization behavior (MBA); management and organizational behavior (Certificate); marketing (MBA, Certificate); microeconomics (MBA); nonprofit and social enterprise (MBA); public policy and administration (MPPA). *Program availability:* Part-time, evening/weekend, 100% online, blended/hybrid learning. *Faculty:* 25 full-time (10 women), 36 part-time/adjunct (12 women). *Students:* 427 full-time (172 women), 189 part-time (87 women); includes 120 minority (14 Black or African American, non-Hispanic/Latino; 2 American Indian or Alaska Native, non-Hispanic/Latino; 19 Asian, non-Hispanic/Latino; 37 Hispanic/Latino; 48 Two or more races, non-Hispanic/Latino), 338 international. Average age 30. 591 applicants, 64% accepted, 131 enrolled. In 2016, 305 master's awarded. *Entrance requirements:* For master's, GMAT, interview, minimum GPA of 3.0. *Application deadline:* Applications are processed on a rolling basis. Application fee: $50. Electronic applications accepted. *Expenses:* Contact institution. *Unit head:* Dr. Gerhard Apfelthaler, Dean, 805-493-3360. *Application contact:* 805-493-3325, Fax: 805-493-3861, E-mail: clugrad@callutheran.edu.
Website: http://www.callutheran.edu/management/

California Miramar University, Program in Business Administration, San Diego, CA 92108. Offers MBA.

California Polytechnic State University, San Luis Obispo, Orfalea College of Business, Program in Business Administration, San Luis Obispo, CA 93407. Offers MBA. *Students:* 26 full-time (16 women), 16 part-time (7 women); includes 10 minority (3 Asian, non-Hispanic/Latino; 4 Hispanic/Latino; 3 Two or more races, non-Hispanic/Latino), 2 international. Average age 25. In 2016, 24 master's awarded. *Degree requirements:* For master's, comprehensive exam (for some programs), thesis (for some programs). *Entrance requirements:* For master's, GMAT. Additional exam requirements/recommendations for international students: Required—TOEFL (minimum score 80 iBT). *Application deadline:* For fall admission, 4/1 for domestic students, 3/1 for international students. Applications are processed on a rolling basis. Application fee: $55. Electronic applications accepted. *Expenses:* Tuition, state resident: full-time $6738; part-time $3906 per year. Tuition, nonresident: full-time $15,666; part-time $8370 per year. *Required fees:* $3603; $3141 per unit. $1047 per term. *Financial support:* Fellowships, career-related internships or fieldwork, Federal Work-Study, institutionally sponsored loans, scholarships/grants, and unspecified assistantships available. Support available to part-time students. Financial award application deadline: 3/2; financial award applicants required to submit FAFSA. *Faculty research:* Management of high-tech firms, Pacific Rim, capital market structures, economics of environmental policy, marketing of services. *Unit head:* Dr. Scott Dawson, Dean, 805-756-2705, E-mail: scdawson@calpoly.edu. *Application contact:* Dr. Sanjiv Jaggia, Associate Dean, Graduate Programs, 805-756-7519, E-mail: sjaggia@calpoly.edu.
Website: http://www.cob.calpoly.edu/gradbusiness/degree-programs/mba/

California State Polytechnic University, Pomona, Master of Science in Business Administration Program, Pomona, CA 91768-2557. Offers information systems auditing (MS). *Accreditation:* AACSB. *Program availability:* Part-time, evening/weekend. *Students:* 6 part-time (1 woman); includes 4 minority (3 Asian, non-Hispanic/Latino; 1 Hispanic/Latino), 1 international. Average age 34. 2 applicants, 100% accepted, 2 enrolled. In 2016, 4 master's awarded. *Entrance requirements:* Additional exam requirements/recommendations for international students: Required—TOEFL. *Application deadline:* Applications are processed on a rolling basis. Application fee: $55. Electronic applications accepted. *Expenses:* Contact institution. *Financial support:* Application deadline: 3/2; applicants required to submit FAFSA. *Unit head:* Dr. Erik Rolland, Dean, 909-869-2400, Fax: 909-869-6799, E-mail: erolland@cpp.edu. *Application contact:* Andrew M. Wright, Director of Admissions, 909-869-3130, Fax: 909-869-4529, E-mail: awright@cpp.edu.
Website: http://www.cpp.edu/~cba/graduate-business-programs/programs/index.shtml

California State Polytechnic University, Pomona, MBA Program, Pomona, CA 91768-2557. Offers MBA. *Program availability:* Part-time, evening/weekend. *Students:* 7 full-time (3 women), 29 part-time (11 women); includes 18 minority (1 Black or African American, non-Hispanic/Latino; 10 Asian, non-Hispanic/Latino; 7 Hispanic/Latino), 6 international. Average age 29. 20 applicants, 95% accepted, 15 enrolled. In 2016, 29 master's awarded. *Entrance requirements:* Additional exam requirements/recommendations for international students: Required—TOEFL. *Application deadline:* Applications are processed on a rolling basis. Application fee: $55. Electronic applications accepted. *Expenses:* Contact institution. *Financial support:* Application deadline: 3/2; applicants required to submit FAFSA. *Unit head:* Dr. Erik Rolland, Dean, 909-869-2400, E-mail: erolland@cpp.edu. *Application contact:* Andrew M. Wright, Director of Admissions, 909-869-3130, Fax: 909-869-4529, E-mail: awright@cpp.edu.
Website: http://www.cpp.edu/~cba/graduate-business-programs/programs/index.shtml

California State University, Bakersfield, Division of Graduate Studies, Program in Administration, Bakersfield, CA 93311. Offers MSA. *Program availability:* Online learning. *Degree requirements:* For master's, capstone experience. *Entrance requirements:* For master's, official transcripts, three professional references, current resume, statement of purpose. *Application deadline:* For fall admission, 5/5 priority date for domestic students; for spring admission, 10/6 priority date for domestic students; for summer admission, 3/2 priority date for domestic students. Application fee: $75. *Expenses:* $450 per unit. *Financial support:* Application deadline: 3/2; applicants required to submit FAFSA. *Unit head:* Dr. Abbas Grammy, Academic Coordinator, 661-654-2466, E-mail: agrammy@csub.edu. *Application contact:* Debbie Blowers, Assistant Director of Admissions, 661-664-3381, E-mail: dblowers@csub.edu.
Website: http://www.csub.edu/eud/degrees/msa/

California State University, Bakersfield, Division of Graduate Studies, School of Business and Public Administration, Program in Business Administration, Bakersfield, CA 93311. Offers MBA. *Accreditation:* AACSB. *Students:* 28 full-time (13 women), 28 part-time (11 women); includes 21 minority (4 Black or African American, non-Hispanic/Latino; 1 Asian, non-Hispanic/Latino; 15 Hispanic/Latino; 1 Two or more races, non-Hispanic/Latino), 4 international. Average age 32. 72 applicants, 39% accepted, 25 enrolled. In 2016, 50 master's awarded. *Entrance requirements:* For master's, GMAT or GRE, baccalaureate degree, minimum undergraduate GPA of 2.75. *Application deadline:* Applications are processed on a rolling basis. Application fee: $55. *Expenses:* Tuition, state resident: full-time $2246; part-time $1302 per semester. *Financial support:* In 2016–17, fellowships (averaging $1,850 per year) were awarded; Federal Work-Study, scholarships/grants, and tuition waivers (full and partial) also available. Financial award application deadline: 3/2; financial award applicants required to submit FAFSA. *Unit head:* Dr. Michael Way, Director, 661-654-2780. *Application contact:* Kathy Carpenter, Advisor, 661-654-3404, E-mail: mba@csub.edu.
Website: http://www.csub.edu/mba/index.html

California State University Channel Islands, Extended University and International Programs, Master of Business Administration Program, Thousand Oaks, CA 91360. Offers MBA. *Program availability:* Part-time, evening/weekend. *Entrance requirements:* For master's, GMAT, 2 years of work experience. Additional exam requirements/recommendations for international students: Required—TOEFL (minimum score 550 paper-based; 80 iBT), IELTS (minimum score 6). Electronic applications accepted. *Expenses:* Contact institution.

California State University, Chico, Office of Graduate Studies, College of Behavioral and Social Sciences, Political Science and Criminal Justice Department, Program in Public Administration, Chico, CA 95929-0722. Offers health administration (MPA); local government management (MPA). *Accreditation:* NASPAA. *Program availability:* Part-time. *Students:* 24 full-time (15 women), 12 part-time (7 women); includes 14 minority (1 American Indian or Alaska Native, non-Hispanic/Latino; 5 Asian, non-Hispanic/Latino; 5 Hispanic/Latino; 3 Two or more races, non-Hispanic/Latino). 18 applicants, 72% accepted, 9 enrolled. *Degree requirements:* For master's, thesis or culminating practicum. *Entrance requirements:* For master's, 2 letters of recommendation. Additional exam requirements/recommendations for international students: Required—TOEFL (minimum score 550 paper-based; 80 iBT), IELTS (minimum score 6.5), PTE. *Application deadline:* For fall admission, 3/1 priority date for domestic students, 3/1 for international students; for spring admission, 9/15 priority date for domestic students, 9/15 for international students. Applications are processed on a rolling basis. Application fee: $55. Electronic applications accepted. *Financial support:* Fellowships and career-related internships or fieldwork available. Financial award application deadline: 3/1; financial award applicants required to submit FAFSA. *Unit head:* Mahalley Allen, Chair, 530-898-6506, Fax: 530-898-5301, E-mail: mdallen@csuchico.edu. *Application contact:* Judy L. Morris, School of Graduate, International, and Interdisciplinary Studies, 530-898-6880, Fax: 530-898-6889, E-mail: jlmorris@csuchico.edu.
Website: http://catalog.csuchico.edu/viewer/12/POLS/PADMNONEMP.html

California State University, Chico, Office of Graduate Studies, College of Business, Chico, CA 95929-0722. Offers MBA. *Program availability:* Part-time. *Faculty:* 60 full-time (21 women), 54 part-time/adjunct (19 women). *Students:* 33 full-time (15 women), 37 part-time (16 women); includes 29 minority (1 American Indian or Alaska Native, non-Hispanic/Latino; 18 Asian, non-Hispanic/Latino; 8 Hispanic/Latino; 2 Two or more races, non-Hispanic/Latino). 53 applicants, 75% accepted, 24 enrolled. In 2016, 26 master's awarded. *Degree requirements:* For master's, thesis, project, or comprehensive exam. *Entrance requirements:* For master's, GMAT or GRE, two letters of recommendation, statement of purpose, resume. Additional exam requirements/recommendations for international students: Required—TOEFL (minimum score 550 paper-based; 80 iBT), PTE Academic (minimum score 59) or IELTS (6.5). *Application deadline:* For fall admission, 3/1 for domestic and international students; for spring admission, 9/15 for domestic and international students. Application fee: $55. Electronic applications accepted. *Expenses:* Contact institution. *Financial support:* Career-related internships or fieldwork, institutionally sponsored loans, scholarships/grants, traineeships, and unspecified assistantships available. Financial award application deadline: 3/1; financial award applicants required to submit FAFSA. *Unit head:* Dr. Judy Hennessey, Dean, 530-898-6272, Fax: 530-898-4584, E-mail: jehennessey@csuchico.edu. *Application contact:* Dr. Matthew Meuter, MBA Director, 530-898-5880, Fax: 530-898-4584, E-mail: mmeuter@csuchico.edu.
Website: http://www.csuchico.edu/cob/

California State University, Dominguez Hills, College of Business Administration and Public Policy, Program in Business Administration, Carson, CA 90747-0001. Offers MBA. *Program availability:* Part-time, evening/weekend, online learning. *Entrance requirements:* For master's, GMAT, minimum GPA of 2.75. Additional exam requirements/recommendations for international students: Required—TOEFL (minimum score 570 paper-based; 88 iBT). *Faculty research:* Management.

California State University, East Bay, Office of Graduate Studies, College of Business and Economics, MBA Program, Hayward, CA 94542-3000. Offers entrepreneurship (MBA), including small business management; finance (MBA); global innovators (MBA); human resources and organizational behavior (MBA), including human resources/personnel management; information technology management (MBA), including computer information systems; marketing management (MBA), including marketing; operations and supply chain management (MBA); strategy and international business (MBA). *Accreditation:* AACSB. *Program availability:* Part-time, evening/weekend. *Students:* 137 full-time (75 women), 168 part-time (80 women); includes 71 minority (8 Black or African American, non-Hispanic/Latino; 55 Asian, non-Hispanic/Latino; 4 Hispanic/Latino; 2 Native Hawaiian or other Pacific Islander, non-Hispanic/Latino; 2 Two or more races, non-Hispanic/Latino), 70 international. Average age 32. 385 applicants, 48% accepted, 83 enrolled. In 2016, 148 master's awarded. *Degree requirements:* For master's, comprehensive exam or thesis. *Entrance requirements:* For master's, GMAT (minimum 20th percentile verbal and quantitative section), bachelor's degree, minimum GPA of 2.75. Additional exam requirements/recommendations for international students: Required—TOEFL (minimum score 550 paper-based; 79 iBT). *Application deadline:* For fall admission, 6/30 for domestic and international students. Applications are processed on a rolling basis. Application fee: $55. Electronic applications accepted. *Expenses:* Contact institution. *Financial support:* Career-related internships or fieldwork, Federal Work-Study, institutionally sponsored loans, and scholarships/grants available. Support available to part-time students. Financial award application deadline: 3/2; financial award applicants required to submit FAFSA. *Unit head:* Xinjian Lu, Associate Dean, 510-855-3290, E-mail: xinjian.lu@csueastbay.edu. *Application contact:* Dr. Donna Wiley, Interim Associate Vice President for Academic Programs and Graduate Studies, 510-885-3716, Fax: 510-885-4777, E-mail: donna.wiley@csueastbay.edu.
Website: http://www20.csueastbay.edu/ecat/graduate-chapters/g-buad.html#mba

California State University, Fullerton, Graduate Studies, College of Business and Economics, Department of Management, Fullerton, CA 92834-9480. Offers entrepreneurship (MBA); management (MBA). *Accreditation:* AACSB. *Program availability:* Part-time. *Degree requirements:* For master's, project or thesis. *Entrance requirements:* For master's, GMAT, minimum AACSB index of 950. Application fee: $55.

Expenses: Tuition, state resident: full-time $3369; part-time $1953 per unit. Tuition, nonresident: full-time $3915; part-time $2499 per unit. Tuition and fees vary according to course load, degree level and program. *Financial support:* Career-related internships or fieldwork, Federal Work-Study, institutionally sponsored loans, and scholarships/grants available. Support available to part-time students. Financial award application deadline: 3/1; financial award applicants required to submit FAFSA. *Unit head:* Dr. Gus Manoochehri, Chair, 657-278-3071. *Application contact:* Admissions/Applications, 657-278-2371.

California State University, Fullerton, Graduate Studies, College of Business and Economics, Program in Business Administration, Fullerton, CA 92834-9480. Offers business administration (MBA); business analytics (MBA); international business (MBA); organizational leadership (MBA); risk management and insurance (MBA). *Accreditation:* AACSB. *Program availability:* Part-time. *Degree requirements:* For master's, project or thesis. *Entrance requirements:* For master's, GMAT. Application fee: $55. *Expenses:* Tuition, state resident: full-time $3369; part-time $1953 per unit. Tuition, nonresident: full-time $3915; part-time $2499 per unit. Tuition and fees vary according to course load, degree level and program. *Financial support:* Career-related internships or fieldwork, Federal Work-Study, institutionally sponsored loans, and scholarships/grants available. Support available to part-time students. Financial award application deadline: 3/1; financial award applicants required to submit FAFSA. *Unit head:* Shaun Pichler, Director, 657-278-7373, E-mail: spichler@fullerton.edu. *Application contact:* Admissions/Applications, 657-278-2371.

California State University, Long Beach, Graduate Studies, College of Business Administration, Long Beach, CA 90840. Offers MS. *Accreditation:* AACSB. *Program availability:* Part-time, evening/weekend. *Entrance requirements:* For master's, GMAT. *Application deadline:* For fall admission, 3/30 for domestic students. Applications are processed on a rolling basis. Application fee: $55. Electronic applications accepted. *Financial support:* Career-related internships or fieldwork and scholarships/grants available. Financial award application deadline: 3/2; financial award applicants required to submit FAFSA. *Faculty research:* Attitude formation theory, consumer motivation, gift giving, derivative and synthetic securities, financial applications of artificial intelligence. *Unit head:* Dr. Michael E. Solt, Dean, 562-985-5307, E-mail: msolt@csulb.edu. *Application contact:* Dr. H. Michael Chung, Director, Graduate Programs and Executive Education, 562-985-5565, Fax: 562-985-5742, E-mail: hmchung@csulb.edu.
Website: http://www.csulb.edu/mba

California State University, Los Angeles, Graduate Studies, College of Business and Economics, Department of Information Systems, Los Angeles, CA 90032-8530. Offers management (MS). *Program availability:* Part-time, evening/weekend. *Degree requirements:* For master's, comprehensive exam (MBA), thesis (MS). *Entrance requirements:* For master's, GMAT, minimum GPA of 2.5 during previous 2 years of course work. Additional exam requirements/recommendations for international students: Required—TOEFL (minimum score 550 paper-based). Electronic applications accepted.

California State University, Los Angeles, Graduate Studies, College of Business and Economics, Department of Management, Los Angeles, CA 90032-8530. Offers health care management (MS); management (MBA). *Accreditation:* AACSB. *Program availability:* Part-time, evening/weekend. *Entrance requirements:* For master's, GMAT, minimum GPA of 2.5 during previous 2 years of course work. Additional exam requirements/recommendations for international students: Required—TOEFL (minimum score 550 paper-based). Electronic applications accepted.

California State University, Monterey Bay, College of Business, Seaside, CA 93955-8001. Offers MBA. *Program availability:* Part-time, evening/weekend, online learning. *Entrance requirements:* For master's, recommendation, resume, work experience, bachelor's degree from accredited university. Additional exam requirements/recommendations for international students: Recommended—TOEFL (minimum score 550 paper-based; 79 iBT). Electronic applications accepted.

California State University, Northridge, Graduate Studies, College of Business and Economics, Northridge, CA 91330. Offers MBA. *Accreditation:* AACSB. *Program availability:* Part-time. *Students:* 49 full-time (26 women), 94 part-time (50 women); includes 59 minority (6 Black or African American, non-Hispanic/Latino; 29 Asian, non-Hispanic/Latino; 19 Hispanic/Latino; 5 Two or more races, non-Hispanic/Latino), 12 international. Average age 32. 401 applicants, 31% accepted, 59 enrolled. *Degree requirements:* For master's, thesis or alternative. *Entrance requirements:* For master's, GMAT, minimum GPA of 3.0 in last 60 units. Additional exam requirements/recommendations for international students: Required—TOEFL. *Application deadline:* For fall admission, 11/30 for domestic students. Application fee: $55. *Expenses:* Tuition, state resident: full-time $4152. *Financial support:* Teaching assistantships and Federal Work-Study available. Support available to part-time students. Financial award application deadline: 3/1. *Unit head:* Dr. Kenneth Lord, Dean, 818-677-2455. *Application contact:* Dr. Deborah Heisley, Director of Graduate Programs, 818-677-2467, E-mail: deborah.heisley@csun.edu.
Website: http://www.csun.edu/mba

California State University, Northridge, Graduate Studies, The Tseng College of Extended Learning, Program in Public Sector Management and Leadership, Northridge, CA 91330. Offers MPA. *Program availability:* Online learning. *Expenses:* Tuition, state resident: full-time $4152. *Unit head:* Henrik Minassians, Director, 818-677-3332.
Website: http://tsengcollege.csun.edu/programs/MPA/online-PSML

California State University, Sacramento, Office of Graduate Studies, College of Business Administration, Sacramento, CA 95819. Offers accountancy (MS); business administration (IMBA, MBA); human resources (MBA); urban land development (MBA). *Accreditation:* AACSB. *Program availability:* Part-time, evening/weekend. *Students:* 138 full-time (68 women), 129 part-time (63 women); includes 211 minority (12 Black or African American, non-Hispanic/Latino; 132 American Indian or Alaska Native, non-Hispanic/Latino; 63 Asian, non-Hispanic/Latino; 4 Native Hawaiian or other Pacific Islander, non-Hispanic/Latino). Average age 34. 198 applicants, 77% accepted, 85 enrolled. In 2016, 168 master's awarded. *Degree requirements:* For master's, thesis or alternative, writing proficiency exam. *Entrance requirements:* For master's, GMAT. Additional exam requirements/recommendations for international students: Required—TOEFL (minimum score 550 paper-based; 80 iBT). *Application deadline:* For fall admission, 2/1 for domestic students, 3/1 for international students; for spring admission, 9/15 for domestic students, 9/30 for international students. Applications are processed on a rolling basis. Application fee: $55. Electronic applications accepted. *Expenses:* $4,302 full-time tuition and fees per semester, $2,796 part-time. *Financial support:* Research assistantships, teaching assistantships, career-related internships or fieldwork, and Federal Work-Study available. Support available to part-time students. Financial award applicants required to submit FAFSA. *Unit head:* Dr. Pierre A. Balthazard, Dean, 916-278-6578, Fax: 916-278-5793, E-mail: cba@csus.edu. *Application contact:* Jose Martinez, Graduate Admissions Supervisor, 916-278-7871, E-mail: martinj@skymail.csus.edu.
Website: http://www.cba.csus.edu

California State University, San Bernardino, Graduate Studies, College of Business and Public Administration, Program in Business Administration, San Bernardino, CA 92407. Offers accounting (MBA); entrepreneurship (MBA); finance (MBA); global business (MBA); information management (MBA); information security (MBA); management (MBA); supply chain management (MBA). *Accreditation:* AACSB. *Program availability:* Part-time, evening/weekend, online learning. *Faculty:* 7 full-time (4 women), 3 part-time/adjunct (2 women). *Students:* 37 full-time (11 women), 141 part-time (51 women); includes 85 minority (16 Black or African American, non-Hispanic/Latino; 1 American Indian or Alaska Native, non-Hispanic/Latino; 20 Asian, non-Hispanic/Latino; 45 Hispanic/Latino; 3 Two or more races, non-Hispanic/Latino), 46 international. 260 applicants, 37% accepted, 34 enrolled. In 2016, 180 master's awarded. *Degree requirements:* For master's, comprehensive exam, thesis. *Entrance requirements:* Additional exam requirements/recommendations for international students: Required—TOEFL. *Application deadline:* For fall admission, 7/16 for domestic students, 7/20 for international students; for winter admission, 10/23 for domestic students, 10/20 for international students; for spring admission, 1/22 for domestic students, 1/20 for international students. Application fee: $55. *Expenses:* Contact institution. *Financial support:* Application deadline: 3/1. *Unit head:* Dr. Lawrence C. Rose, Dean, 909-537-3703, Fax: 909-537-7026, E-mail: lrose@csusb.edu. *Application contact:* Dr. Vipin Gupta, Associate Dean/MBA Director, 909-537-7380, Fax: 909-537-7026, E-mail: vgupta@csusb.edu.
Website: http://mba.csusb.edu/

California State University, San Marcos, College of Business Administration, San Marcos, CA 92096-0001. Offers MBA. *Program availability:* Evening/weekend. *Degree requirements:* For master's, project. *Entrance requirements:* For master's, GMAT, minimum GPA of 3.0 in last 60 units, 3 years of full-time work experience. Additional exam requirements/recommendations for international students: Required—TOEFL (minimum score 550 paper-based). *Expenses:* Contact institution.

California State University, Stanislaus, College of Business Administration, Program in Business Administration (Executive MBA), Turlock, CA 95382. Offers EMBA. *Accreditation:* AACSB. *Program availability:* Part-time, evening/weekend. *Degree requirements:* For master's, comprehensive exam, thesis or alternative. *Entrance requirements:* For master's, GMAT or GRE, minimum GPA of 2.5, 2 letters of reference, personal statement, interview. Additional exam requirements/recommendations for international students: Required—TOEFL (minimum score 550 paper-based). Electronic applications accepted. *Expenses:* Contact institution.

California State University, Stanislaus, College of Business Administration, Program in Business Administration (MBA), Turlock, CA 95382. Offers MBA. *Accreditation:* AACSB. *Program availability:* Part-time, evening/weekend. *Degree requirements:* For master's, comprehensive exam, thesis or alternative. *Entrance requirements:* For master's, GMAT or GRE, minimum GPA of 2.5, 3 letters of reference, personal statement. Additional exam requirements/recommendations for international students: Required—TOEFL (minimum score 550 paper-based). Electronic applications accepted. *Expenses:* Contact institution. *Faculty research:* Teaching creativity, graduate operations management, curricula data mining, foreign direct investment.

California University of Management and Sciences, Graduate Programs, Anaheim, CA 92801. Offers business administration (MBA, DBA); computer information systems (MS); economics (MS); international business (MS); sports management (MS).

California University of Pennsylvania, School of Graduate Studies and Research, Eberly College of Science and Technology, Program in Business Administration, California, PA 15419-1394. Offers business administration (MBA); business analytics (MBA); entrepreneurship (MBA); nursing administration and leadership (MBA). *Program availability:* Part-time, evening/weekend. *Degree requirements:* For master's, comprehensive exam. *Entrance requirements:* For master's, minimum GPA of 3.0, official transcripts. Additional exam requirements/recommendations for international students: Required—TOEFL (minimum score 550 paper-based). Electronic applications accepted. *Expenses:* Tuition, state resident: full-time $11,592; part-time $483 per credit. Tuition, nonresident: full-time $17,400; part-time $725 per credit. *Required fees:* $3916. Tuition and fees vary according to course load, degree level, campus/location and reciprocity agreements. *Faculty research:* Economics, applied economics, consumer behavior, technology and business, impact of technology.

Cambridge College, School of Management, Cambridge, MA 02138-5304. Offers business negotiation and conflict resolution (M Mgt); general business (M Mgt); health care informatics (M Mgt); health care management (M Mgt); leadership in human and organizational dynamics (M Mgt); non-profit and public organization management (M Mgt); small business development (M Mgt); technology management (M Mgt). *Program availability:* Part-time, evening/weekend. *Degree requirements:* For master's, thesis, seminars. *Entrance requirements:* For master's, resume, 2 professional references. Additional exam requirements/recommendations for international students: Required—TOEFL (minimum score 550 paper-based; 79 iBT), Michigan English Language Assessment Battery (minimum score 85); Recommended—IELTS (minimum score 6). Electronic applications accepted. *Expenses:* Contact institution. *Faculty research:* Negotiation, mediation and conflict resolution; leadership; management of diverse organizations; case studies and simulation methodologies for management education, digital as a second language: social networking for digital immigrants, non-profit and public management.

Cameron University, Office of Graduate Studies, Program in Business Administration, Lawton, OK 73505-6377. Offers MBA. *Accreditation:* ACBSP. *Program availability:* Part-time, evening/weekend, online learning. *Degree requirements:* For master's, comprehensive exam. *Entrance requirements:* Additional exam requirements/recommendations for international students: Required—TOEFL (minimum score 550 paper-based). Electronic applications accepted. *Faculty research:* Financial liberalization, right to work, recession, teaching evaluations, database management.

Campbellsville University, School of Business and Economics, Campbellsville, KY 42718-2799. Offers business administration (MBA). *Program availability:* Part-time, evening/weekend, 100% online, blended/hybrid learning. *Faculty:* 12 full-time (2 women), 11 part-time/adjunct (6 women). *Students:* 35 full-time (17 women), 414 part-time (112 women); includes 35 minority (21 Black or African American, non-Hispanic/Latino; 10 Asian, non-Hispanic/Latino; 4 Hispanic/Latino), 323 international. Average age 28. 351 applicants, 79% accepted, 209 enrolled. In 2016, 47 master's awarded. *Degree requirements:* For master's, comprehensive exam (for some programs), thesis optional. *Entrance requirements:* For master's, GRE or GMAT, letters of recommendation, college transcripts. Additional exam requirements/recommendations for international students: Required—TOEFL (minimum score 550 paper-based; 79 iBT); Recommended—IELTS (minimum score 6). *Application deadline:* Applications are processed on a rolling basis. Application fee: $25. Electronic applications accepted. Application fee is waived when completed online. *Expenses:* $525 per credit hour (for MSITM, PMBA); $499 per credit hour (for MBA, MML). *Financial support:* Application deadline: 6/1; applicants required to submit FAFSA. *Unit head:* Dr. Patricia H. Cowherd, Dean, 270-789-5553, Fax: 270-789-5066, E-mail: phcowherd@campbellsville.edu. *Application contact:* Monica Bamwine, Assistant Director of Graduate Admissions, 270-789-5221, Fax: 270-789-5071, E-mail: mkbamwine@campbellsville.edu.
Website: http://www.campbellsville.edu

Campbell University, Graduate and Professional Programs, Lundy-Fetterman School of Business, Buies Creek, NC 27506. Offers MBA, MTWM. *Accreditation:* ACBSP.

Business Administration and Management—General

Program availability: Part-time, evening/weekend. *Degree requirements:* For master's, comprehensive exam, thesis or alternative. *Entrance requirements:* For master's, GMAT or GRE, minimum GPA of 2.7, 3 letters of reference, resume. Additional exam requirements/recommendations for international students: Required—TOEFL (minimum score 550 paper-based). *Faculty research:* Agricultural economics, investments, leadership, marketing, law and economics.

Canisius College, Graduate Division, Richard J. Wehle School of Business, Department of Management, Buffalo, NY 14208-1098. Offers business administration (MBA); international business (MS). *Accreditation:* AACSB. *Program availability:* Part-time, evening/weekend. *Faculty:* 15 full-time (3 women), 10 part-time/adjunct (2 women). *Students:* 90 full-time (38 women), 123 part-time (43 women); includes 25 minority (12 Black or African American, non-Hispanic/Latino; 1 American Indian or Alaska Native, non-Hispanic/Latino; 6 Asian, non-Hispanic/Latino; 5 Hispanic/Latino; 1 Two or more races, non-Hispanic/Latino), 27 international. Average age 28. 192 applicants, 63% accepted, 91 enrolled. In 2016, 94 master's awarded. *Entrance requirements:* For master's, GMAT, GRE, official transcript from colleges attended, current resume. Additional exam requirements/recommendations for international students: Required—TOEFL (minimum score 550 paper-based, 80 iBT), IELTS (minimum score 6.5), or CAEL (minimum score 70). *Application deadline:* For fall admission, 7/1 priority date for domestic students; for spring admission, 11/1 priority date for domestic students. Applications are processed on a rolling basis. Application fee: $25. Electronic applications accepted. Application fee is waived when completed online. *Expenses: Tuition:* Full-time $14,742. *Required fees:* $724. *Financial support:* Career-related internships or fieldwork, Federal Work-Study, scholarships/grants, tuition waivers (partial), and unspecified assistantships available. Support available to part-time students. Financial award application deadline: 4/30; financial award applicants required to submit FAFSA. *Faculty research:* Global leadership effectiveness, global supply chain management, quality management. *Unit head:* Dr. Gordon W. Meyer, Chair of Management, Entrepreneurship and International Business, 716-888-2634, E-mail: meyerg@canisius.edu. *Application contact:* Kathleen B. Davis, Vice President of Enrollment Management, 716-888-2500, Fax: 716-888-3195, E-mail: daviskb@canisius.edu.
Website: http://www.canisius.edu/graduate/

Cape Breton University, Shannon School of Business, Sydney, NS B1P 6L2, Canada. Offers MBA. *Program availability:* Part-time. *Entrance requirements:* For master's, GMAT. Additional exam requirements/recommendations for international students: Required—TOEFL (minimum score 550 paper-based; 80 iBT), IELTS (minimum score 6.5). Electronic applications accepted.

Capella University, School of Business and Technology, Doctoral Programs in Business, Minneapolis, MN 55402. Offers accounting (DBA, PhD); business intelligence (DBA); finance (DBA, PhD); general business management (PhD); human resource management (DBA, PhD); leadership (DBA, PhD); management education (PhD); marketing (DBA, PhD); project management (DBA, PhD); strategy and innovation (DBA, PhD). *Accreditation:* ACBSP.

Capella University, School of Business and Technology, Master's Programs in Business, Minneapolis, MN 55402. Offers accounting (MBA); business analysis (MS); business intelligence (MBA); entrepreneurship (MBA); finance (MBA); general business administration (MBA); general human resource management (MS); general leadership (MS); health care management (MBA); human resource management (MBA); marketing (MBA); project management (MBA, MS). *Accreditation:* ACBSP.

Capital University, Law School, Program in Business Law and Taxation, Columbus, OH 43209-2394. Offers business (LL M); business and taxation (LL M); taxation (LL M); JD/LL M. *Program availability:* Part-time, evening/weekend. *Degree requirements:* For master's, thesis or alternative. *Entrance requirements:* For master's, previous course work in accounting, business law, and taxation. Additional exam requirements/recommendations for international students: Required—TOEFL (minimum score 600 paper-based). Electronic applications accepted.

Capital University, School of Management, Columbus, OH 43209-2394. Offers leadership (MBA); MBA/JD; MBA/MSN. *Accreditation:* ACBSP. *Program availability:* Part-time, evening/weekend. *Faculty:* 17 full-time (7 women), 23 part-time/adjunct (1 woman). *Students:* 165 (70 women); includes 16 minority (8 Black or African American, non-Hispanic/Latino; 6 Asian, non-Hispanic/Latino; 2 Hispanic/Latino), 6 international. Average age 32. 71 applicants, 56% accepted, 32 enrolled. In 2016, 1 master's awarded. *Entrance requirements:* For master's, 2-3 years of professional work experience. Additional exam requirements/recommendations for international students: Required—TOEFL (minimum score 550 paper-based; 80 iBT); Recommended—IELTS (minimum score 6.5). *Application deadline:* For fall admission, 7/1 priority date for domestic and international students; for winter admission, 11/1 for domestic students; for spring admission, 11/1 priority date for domestic and international students; for summer admission, 4/1 priority date for domestic and international students. Applications are processed on a rolling basis. Electronic applications accepted. Application fee is waived when completed online. *Expenses:* Contact institution. *Financial support:* Unspecified assistantships available. Financial award application deadline: 8/1; financial award applicants required to submit FAFSA. *Faculty research:* Taxation, public policy, health care, management of non-profits. *Unit head:* John Gentner, MBA Director, 614-236-6544, Fax: 614-236-6923, E-mail: jgentner@capital.edu. *Application contact:* Carli Isgrigg, Assistant Director of Adult and Graduate Education Recruitment, 614-236-6546, Fax: 614-236-6923, E-mail: cisgrigg@capital.edu.
Website: http://www.capital.edu/mba/

Capitol Technology University, Graduate Programs, Laurel, MD 20708-9759. Offers business administration (MBA); computer science (MS); electrical engineering (MS); information and telecommunications systems management (MS); information architecture (MS); network security (MS). *Program availability:* Part-time, evening/weekend, online learning. *Entrance requirements:* For master's, minimum GPA of 3.0. Electronic applications accepted.

Cardinal Stritch University, College of Business and Management, Milwaukee, WI 53217-3985. Offers healthcare management (MBA). Programs also offered in Madison, WI. *Accreditation:* ACBSP. *Program availability:* Part-time, evening/weekend, 100% online, blended/hybrid learning. *Students:* 226 full-time (130 women), 84 part-time (47 women); includes 117 minority (78 Black or African American, non-Hispanic/Latino; 1 American Indian or Alaska Native, non-Hispanic/Latino; 20 Asian, non-Hispanic/Latino; 14 Hispanic/Latino; 1 Native Hawaiian or other Pacific Islander, non-Hispanic/Latino; 3 Two or more races, non-Hispanic/Latino), 14 international. Average age 35. 247 applicants, 66% accepted, 120 enrolled. In 2016, 309 master's awarded. *Degree requirements:* For master's, thesis (for some programs), case study, faculty recommendation. *Entrance requirements:* For master's, 3 years of management or related experience, minimum GPA of 2.5. Additional exam requirements/recommendations for international students: Required—TOEFL (minimum score 79 iBT), IELTS (minimum score 6.5). *Application deadline:* Applications are processed on a rolling basis. Application fee: $0. Electronic applications accepted. *Expenses:* Contact institution. *Financial support:* Career-related internships or fieldwork, Federal Work-Study, and scholarships/grants available. Financial award applicants required to submit FAFSA. *Unit head:* Dr. Philip Anderson, Dean, 414-410-4004, E-mail: ptanderson@stritch.edu. *Application contact:* Graduate Admissions, 414-410-4042, E-mail: admissions@stritch.edu.
Website: http://www.stritch.edu/cbm

Carleton University, Faculty of Graduate Studies, Faculty of Business, Sprott School of Business, Ottawa, ON K1S 5B6, Canada. Offers business administration (MBA); management (PhD). *Degree requirements:* For master's, thesis optional; for doctorate, comprehensive exam, thesis/dissertation. *Entrance requirements:* For master's, GMAT, honors degree; for doctorate, GMAT. Additional exam requirements/recommendations for international students: Required—TOEFL. *Faculty research:* Business information systems, finance, international business, marketing, production and operations.

Carlos Albizu University, Miami Campus, Graduate Programs, Miami, FL 33172-2209. Offers clinical psychology (PhD, Psy D); entrepreneurship (MBA); exceptional student education (MS); human services (PhD); industrial/organizational psychology (MS); marriage and family therapy (MS); mental health counseling (MS); nonprofit management (MBA); organizational management (MBA); psychology (MS); school counseling (MS); speech and language pathology (MS); teaching English for speakers of other languages (MS). *Accreditation:* APA. *Program availability:* Part-time, evening/weekend, 100% online. *Faculty:* 28 full-time (22 women), 31 part-time/adjunct (19 women). *Students:* 475 full-time (396 women), 191 part-time (161 women); includes 560 minority (56 Black or African American, non-Hispanic/Latino; 1 American Indian or Alaska Native, non-Hispanic/Latino; 4 Asian, non-Hispanic/Latino; 494 Hispanic/Latino; 5 Two or more races, non-Hispanic/Latino), 15 international. Average age 34. 335 applicants, 46% accepted, 122 enrolled. In 2016, 143 master's, 48 doctorates awarded. Terminal master's awarded for partial completion of doctoral program. *Degree requirements:* For master's, comprehensive exam, integrative project (for MBA); research project (for exceptional student education, teaching English as a second language); for doctorate, comprehensive exam, thesis/dissertation, internship, project. *Entrance requirements:* For master's, 3 letters of recommendation, interview, minimum GPA of 3.0, resume, statement of purpose, official transcripts; for doctorate, 3 letters of recommendation, minimum GPA of 3.0, resume, interview, statement of purpose, official transcripts. Additional exam requirements/recommendations for international students: Required—Michigan Test of English Language Proficiency. *Application deadline:* For fall admission, 4/1 priority date for domestic students, 5/1 priority date for international students; for spring admission, 11/1 priority date for domestic students, 9/1 priority date for international students. Applications are processed on a rolling basis. Application fee: $50. Electronic applications accepted. *Expenses:* Contact institution. *Financial support:* In 2016–17, 131 students received support. Federal Work-Study, scholarships/grants, unspecified assistantships, and tuition discounts available. Financial award application deadline: 6/1; financial award applicants required to submit FAFSA. *Faculty research:* Psychotherapy, forensic psychology, neuropsychology, marketing strategy, entrepreneurship, special education, speech-language pathology. *Unit head:* Dr. Etiony Aldarondo, Provost, 305-593-1223 Ext. 3138, Fax: 305-592-7930, E-mail: ealdarondo@albizu.edu. *Application contact:* Sonia Feliciano, Institutional Director of Student Recruitment, 305-593-1223 Ext. 3108, Fax: 305-477-8983, E-mail: sfeliciano@albizu.edu.

Carlow University, College of Health and Wellness, MSN-MBA Dual Degree Program, Pittsburgh, PA 15213-3165. Offers MSN/MBA. *Program availability:* Part-time, 100% online, blended/hybrid learning. *Students:* 37 full-time (29 women), 4 part-time (all women); includes 2 minority (1 Black or African American, non-Hispanic/Latino; 1 Asian, non-Hispanic/Latino). Average age 35. 12 applicants, 83% accepted, 8 enrolled. *Entrance requirements:* Additional exam requirements/recommendations for international students: Required—TOEFL (minimum score 550 paper-based). *Application deadline:* Applications are processed on a rolling basis. Electronic applications accepted. *Expenses: Tuition:* Full-time $11,855; part-time $801 per credit. *Required fees:* $182; $13 per credit. Tuition and fees vary according to course load, degree level and program. *Financial support:* Application deadline: 4/1; applicants required to submit FAFSA. *Unit head:* Dr. Renee Ingel, Program Director, 412-578-6103, E-mail: rmingel@carlow.edu. *Application contact:* E-mail: gradstudies@carlow.edu.
Website: http://www.carlow.edu/MSN-MBA_Dual_Degree.aspx

Carlow University, College of Leadership and Social Change, MBA Program, Pittsburgh, PA 15213-3165. Offers fraud and forensics (MBA); healthcare management (MBA); human resource management (MBA); leadership and management (MBA); project management (MBA). *Program availability:* Part-time, evening/weekend, 100% online, blended/hybrid learning. *Students:* 87 full-time (65 women), 32 part-time (21 women); includes 31 minority (23 Black or African American, non-Hispanic/Latino; 3 Asian, non-Hispanic/Latino; 2 Hispanic/Latino; 3 Two or more races, non-Hispanic/Latino), 1 international. Average age 33. 54 applicants, 98% accepted, 33 enrolled. In 2016, 29 master's awarded. *Entrance requirements:* For master's, minimum undergraduate GPA of 3.0 (preferred); personal essay; resume; official transcripts; two professional recommendations. Additional exam requirements/recommendations for international students: Required—TOEFL (minimum score 550 paper-based). *Application deadline:* Applications are processed on a rolling basis. Electronic applications accepted. *Expenses: Tuition:* Full-time $11,855; part-time $801 per credit. *Required fees:* $182; $13 per credit. Tuition and fees vary according to course load, degree level and program. *Financial support:* Application deadline: 4/1; applicants required to submit FAFSA. *Unit head:* Dr. Howard Stern, Chair, MBA Program, 412-578-8828, E-mail: hastern@carlow.edu. *Application contact:* 412-578-6059, Fax: 412-578-6321, E-mail: gradstudies@carlow.edu.
Website: http://www.carlow.edu/Business_Administration.aspx

Carnegie Mellon University, Heinz College, School of Public Policy and Management, Master of Entertainment Industry Management Program, Pittsburgh, PA 15213-3891. Offers MEIM. *Accreditation:* AACSB. *Entrance requirements:* For master's, GRE or GMAT, college-level course in advanced algebra/pre-calculus; college-level courses in economics and statistics (recommended). Additional exam requirements/recommendations for international students: Required—TOEFL or IELTS.

Carnegie Mellon University, Heinz College, School of Public Policy and Management, Master of Science Program in Biotechnology and Management, Pittsburgh, PA 15213-3891. Offers MS. *Accreditation:* AACSB. *Entrance requirements:* For master's, GRE or GMAT, college-level course in advanced algebra/pre-calculus; college-level courses in economics and statistics (recommended). Additional exam requirements/recommendations for international students: Required—TOEFL or IELTS.

Carnegie Mellon University, Tepper School of Business, Pittsburgh, PA 15213-3891. Offers accounting (PhD); business management and software engineering (MBMSE); business technologies (PhD); civil engineering and industrial management (MS); computational finance (MSCF); economics (PhD); environmental engineering and management (MEEM); financial economics (PhD); industrial administration (MBA), including administration and public management; marketing (PhD); mathematical finance (PhD); operations management (PhD); operations research (PhD); organizational behavior and theory (PhD); production and operations management (PhD); public policy and management (MS, MSED); software engineering and business management (MS); JD/MS; JD/MSIA; M Div/MS; MOM/MSIA; MSCF/MSIA. JD/MSIA offered jointly with University of Pittsburgh. *Program availability:* Part-time. Terminal master's awarded for partial completion of doctoral program. *Degree requirements:* For doctorate, thesis/dissertation. *Entrance requirements:* For master's, GMAT. Additional exam requirements/recommendations for international students: Required—TOEFL. *Expenses:* Contact institution.

Carroll University, Program in Business Administration, Waukesha, WI 53186-5593. Offers MBA. *Program availability:* Part-time. *Faculty:* 2 full-time (both women). *Students:* 15 part-time (6 women). Average age 28. 54 applicants, 43% accepted. *Entrance requirements:* For master's, GRE or GMAT (waived if GPA is 2.75 or above), resume, transcripts. Additional exam requirements/recommendations for international students: Required—TOEFL. *Application deadline:* Applications are processed on a rolling basis. Electronic applications accepted. *Expenses: Tuition:* Full-time $10,548; part-time $586 per credit. *Required fees:* $520 per semester. Tuition and fees vary according to course load, degree level and program. *Financial support:* Applicants required to submit FAFSA. *Unit head:* Carol Tallarico, Professor and Academic Leader, 262-951-3027, E-mail: ctallari@carrollu.edu. *Application contact:* Kyle Jones, MBA Admission Counselor, 262-524-7225, E-mail: mbainfo@carrollu.edu.
Website: http://www.carrollu.edu/gradprograms/mba/default.asp

Carson-Newman University, Program in Business Administration, Jefferson City, TN 37760. Offers MBA. *Program availability:* Part-time, evening/weekend, 100% online, blended/hybrid learning. *Entrance requirements:* Additional exam requirements/recommendations for international students: Recommended—TOEFL (minimum score 79 iBT), IELTS (minimum score 6.5), TSE (minimum score 53). *Expenses: Tuition:* Full-time $10,142; part-time $461 per credit hour. *Required fees:* $300; $150 per semester. One-time fee: $150.

Case Western Reserve University, Weatherhead School of Management, Executive Doctor of Management Program, Cleveland, OH 44106. Offers management (EDM). *Program availability:* Part-time, evening/weekend. *Degree requirements:* For doctorate, thesis/dissertation. *Entrance requirements:* For doctorate, GMAT. Electronic applications accepted. *Expenses:* Contact institution. *Faculty research:* Information technology and design, emotional intelligence and leadership, entrepreneurship, governing of NP organizations, social ethics.

Case Western Reserve University, Weatherhead School of Management, Executive MBA Program, Cleveland, OH 44106. Offers EMBA. *Accreditation:* AACSB. *Entrance requirements:* For master's, GMAT (if candidate does not have an undergraduate degree from an accredited institution), work experience, interview. Electronic applications accepted. *Expenses:* Contact institution.

Case Western Reserve University, Weatherhead School of Management, Full Time MBA Program, Cleveland, OH 44106. Offers MBA, MBA/JD, MBA/M Acc, MBA/MD, MBA/MIM, MBA/MNO, MBA/MSM, MBA/MSN, MBA/MSSA. *Accreditation:* AACSB. *Entrance requirements:* For master's, GMAT, letters of recommendation, interview, work experience. Additional exam requirements/recommendations for international students: Required—TOEFL (minimum score 600 paper-based). Electronic applications accepted. *Expenses: Tuition:* Full-time $42,576; part-time $1774 per credit hour. *Required fees:* $34. Tuition and fees vary according to course load and program.

Case Western Reserve University, Weatherhead School of Management, Part-time MBA Program, Cleveland, OH 44106. Offers MBA, MBA/M Acc, MBA/MSM, MBA/MSSA. *Accreditation:* AACSB. *Program availability:* Part-time, evening/weekend. *Entrance requirements:* For master's, GMAT, interview, work experience. Additional exam requirements/recommendations for international students: Recommended—TOEFL (minimum score 600 paper-based). Electronic applications accepted. *Expenses: Tuition:* Full-time $42,576; part-time $1774 per credit hour. *Required fees:* $34. Tuition and fees vary according to course load and program.

The Catholic University of America, Busch School of Business and Economics, Washington, DC 20064. Offers accounting (MS); business analysis (MSBA); integral economic development management (MA); integral economic development policy (MA); management (MS), including Federal contract management, human resource management, leadership and management, project management, sales management. *Program availability:* Part-time. *Faculty:* 30 full-time (7 women), 30 part-time/adjunct (5 women). *Students:* 60 full-time (32 women), 26 part-time (14 women); includes 26 minority (11 Black or African American, non-Hispanic/Latino; 8 Asian, non-Hispanic/Latino; 5 Hispanic/Latino; 2 Two or more races, non-Hispanic/Latino), 22 international. Average age 29. 121 applicants, 77% accepted, 64 enrolled. In 2016, 48 master's awarded. *Degree requirements:* For master's, comprehensive exam (for some programs). *Entrance requirements:* For master's, GRE General Test, statement of purpose, official copies of academic transcripts, three letters of recommendation. Additional exam requirements/recommendations for international students: Required—TOEFL (minimum score 550 paper-based; 80 iBT). *Application deadline:* For fall admission, 7/15 priority date for domestic students, 7/1 for international students; for spring admission, 11/15 priority date for domestic students, 11/1 for international students. Applications are processed on a rolling basis. Application fee: $55. Electronic applications accepted. *Expenses:* $42,850 per year; $1,170 per credit; $200 per semester part-time fees. *Financial support:* Fellowships, research assistantships, teaching assistantships, Federal Work-Study, scholarships/grants, tuition waivers (full and partial), and unspecified assistantships available. Financial award application deadline: 2/1; financial award applicants required to submit FAFSA. *Faculty research:* Integrity of the marketing process, economics of energy and the environment, emerging markets, social change, international finance and economic development. *Total annual research expenditures:* $3,698. *Unit head:* Dr. William Bowman, Dean, 202-319-5290, Fax: 202-319-4426, E-mail: otey@cua.edu. *Application contact:* Director of Graduate Admissions, 202-319-5057, Fax: 202-319-6533, E-mail: cua-admissions@cua.edu.
Website: http://business.cua.edu/

The Catholic University of America, Metropolitan School of Professional Studies, Washington, DC 20064. Offers emergency service administration (MS); health administration (MHA); social service administration (MS). *Program availability:* Part-time, evening/weekend, 100% online. *Faculty:* 35 part-time/adjunct (10 women). *Students:* 12 full-time (5 women), 85 part-time (42 women); includes 53 minority (29 Black or African American, non-Hispanic/Latino; 2 Asian, non-Hispanic/Latino; 12 Hispanic/Latino; 10 Two or more races, non-Hispanic/Latino), 2 international. Average age 37. 9 applicants, 89% accepted, 4 enrolled. In 2016, 97 master's awarded. *Degree requirements:* For master's, minimum GPA of 3.0, capstone course. *Entrance requirements:* For master's, statement of purpose, official copies of academic transcripts, three letters of recommendation, resume. Additional exam requirements/recommendations for international students: Required—TOEFL (minimum score 550 paper-based; 80 iBT). *Application deadline:* For fall admission, 7/15 priority date for domestic students, 7/1 for international students; for spring admission, 11/15 priority date for domestic students, 11/1 for international students. Applications are processed on a rolling basis. Application fee: $55. Electronic applications accepted. *Expenses:* $1,035 per credit hour; $905 part-time per credit hour (for online students). *Financial support:* Scholarships/grants available. Financial award application deadline: 3/15; financial award applicants required to submit FAFSA. *Unit head:* Dr. Vince Kiernan, Dean, 202-319-5256, Fax: 202-319-6260, E-mail: kiernan@cua.edu. *Application contact:* Director of Graduate Admissions, 202-319-5057, Fax: 202-319-6533, E-mail: cua-admissions@cua.edu.
Website: http://metro.cua.edu/

Cedar Crest College, Program in Business Administration, Allentown, PA 18104-6196. Offers MBA. *Accreditation:* ACBSP. *Program availability:* Part-time, evening/weekend. *Faculty:* 1 full-time (0 women), 9 part-time/adjunct (5 women). *Students:* 27 full-time (18 women), 18 part-time (13 women); includes 15 minority (8 Black or African American, non-Hispanic/Latino; 7 Hispanic/Latino). Average age 41. *Entrance requirements:* For master's, GRE or GMAT, two letters of recommendation, copy of current resume, official transcripts. *Application deadline:* Applications are processed on a rolling basis. Electronic applications accepted. *Expenses:* $776 per credit. *Unit head:* Ibolya Balog, Chair, 610-437-4471 Ext. 4453, E-mail: ibalog@cedarcrest.edu. *Application contact:* Mary Ellen Hickes, Director of School of Adult and Graduate Education, 610-437-4471, E-mail: sage@cedarcrest.edu.
Website: http://mba.cedarcrest.edu/

Cedarville University, Graduate Programs, Cedarville, OH 45314. Offers business administration (MBA); curriculum (M Ed); educational administration (M Ed); family nurse practitioner (MSN); global health ministries (MSN); instruction (M Ed); ministry (M Min); pharmacy (Pharm D). *Program availability:* Part-time, evening/weekend, online learning. *Degree requirements:* For master's, thesis. *Entrance requirements:* For master's, GRE, 2 professional recommendations; for doctorate, PCAT, professional recommendation from a practicing pharmacist or current employer/supervisor, resume, essay, interview. Additional exam requirements/recommendations for international students: Required—TOEFL (minimum score 550 paper-based; 80 iBT). Electronic applications accepted. *Expenses:* Contact institution.

Centenary College of Louisiana, Graduate Programs, Frost School of Business, Shreveport, LA 71104. Offers MBA. *Program availability:* Part-time, evening/weekend. *Faculty:* 3 full-time, 2 part-time/adjunct (both women). *Students:* 10 part-time (6 women). In 2016, 13 master's awarded. *Degree requirements:* For master's, thesis. *Entrance requirements:* For master's, GMAT, minimum 5 years of professional/managerial experience. *Application deadline:* For fall admission, 8/1 for domestic students; for winter admission, 10/1 for domestic students; for spring admission, 3/1 for domestic students; for summer admission, 5/1 for domestic students. Applications are processed on a rolling basis. Application fee: $20. *Expenses:* $1,425 per course. *Faculty research:* Leadership, organizational change strategy, market behavior, executive compensation. *Unit head:* Dr. Harold Christensen, Dean, 318-869-5141, Fax: 318-869-5139, E-mail: hchriste@centenary.edu. *Application contact:* Patricia F. Gallion, MBA Coordinator, 318-869-5141, Fax: 318-869-5139, E-mail: pgallion@centenary.edu.
Website: http://www.centenary.edu/mba

Centenary University, Program in Business Administration, Hackettstown, NJ 07840-2100. Offers MBA. *Program availability:* Part-time, evening/weekend, online learning. *Entrance requirements:* For master's, GMAT.

Central Connecticut State University, School of Graduate Studies, School of Business, Program in Business Administration, New Britain, CT 06050-4010. Offers MBA. *Program availability:* Part-time, evening/weekend. *Faculty:* 9 full-time (2 women). *Students:* 9 full-time (4 women), 178 part-time (73 women); includes 53 minority (20 Black or African American, non-Hispanic/Latino; 12 Asian, non-Hispanic/Latino; 18 Hispanic/Latino; 3 Two or more races, non-Hispanic/Latino), 1 international. Average age 31. 116 applicants, 69% accepted, 54 enrolled. In 2016, 23 master's awarded. *Degree requirements:* For master's, thesis or alternative. *Entrance requirements:* For master's, GMAT or GRE, minimum undergraduate GPA of 2.7, resume. Additional exam requirements/recommendations for international students: Required—TOEFL (minimum score 550 paper-based; 79 iBT). *Application deadline:* For fall admission, 6/1 for domestic students, 5/1 for international students; for spring admission, 11/1 for domestic and international students. Applications are processed on a rolling basis. Application fee: $50. Electronic applications accepted. *Expenses: Tuition, area resident:* Full-time $6497; part-time $606 per credit. Tuition, state resident: full-time $9748; part-time $622 per credit. Tuition, nonresident: full-time $18,102; part-time $622 per credit. *Required fees:* $4459; $246 per credit. *Financial support:* In 2016–17, 12 students received support. Career-related internships or fieldwork, Federal Work-Study, and scholarships/grants available. Support available to part-time students. Financial award application deadline: 3/1; financial award applicants required to submit FAFSA. *Unit head:* Dr. Jason Snyder, Director, 860-832-3207, E-mail: mba@ccsu.edu. *Application contact:* Patricia Gardner, Associate Director of Graduate Admissions, 860-832-2350, Fax: 860-832-2362.
Website: http://www.ccsu.edu/mba/

Central European University, CEU Business School, Budapest, Hungary. Offers business administration (PhD); business analytics (M Sc); executive business administration (EMBA); finance (M Sc); general management (MBA); information technology management (M Sc); international executive (MBA). *Program availability:* Part-time. *Faculty:* 16 full-time (4 women), 15 part-time/adjunct (5 women). *Students:* 73 full-time (29 women), 108 part-time (28 women). Average age 33. 218 applicants, 57% accepted, 69 enrolled. In 2016, 108 master's awarded. *Degree requirements:* For master's, one foreign language; for doctorate, thesis/dissertation or alternative. *Entrance requirements:* For master's, GMAT. Additional exam requirements/recommendations for international students: Required—TOEFL (minimum score 570 paper-based); Recommended—IELTS (minimum score 6.5). *Application deadline:* For fall admission, 2/4 for domestic and international students. Application fee: $30. Electronic applications accepted. *Expenses:* Contact institution. *Financial support:* Scholarships/grants, health care benefits, and tuition waivers (full and partial) available. *Faculty research:* Social and ethical business, marketing, international business, international trade and investment, management development in Central and East Europe, non-market strategies of emerging-market multinationals, macro and micro analysis of the business environment, international competitive analysis, the transition process from emerging economies to established market economies and its social impact, the regulation of natural monopolies. *Unit head:* Dr. Mel Horwitch, Dean/Managing Director, 36 1 887-5050, E-mail: mhorwitch@ceubusiness.com. *Application contact:* Agnes Schram, Admissions Coordinator, 361-887-5111, E-mail: schrama@business.ceu.edu.
Website: http://business.ceu.hu/

Central Michigan University, Central Michigan University Global Campus, Program in Business Administration, Mount Pleasant, MI 48859. Offers enterprise resource planning (MBA, Certificate); human resource management (MBA); logistics management (MBA, Certificate); marketing (MBA); value-driven organization (MBA). *Program availability:* Part-time, evening/weekend. *Faculty:* 17 full-time (7 women), 3 part-time/adjunct (0 women). *Students:* 189 (82 women); includes 29 minority (17 Black or African American, non-Hispanic/Latino; 2 American Indian or Alaska Native, non-Hispanic/Latino; 3 Asian, non-Hispanic/Latino; 1 Hispanic/Latino; 6 Two or more races, non-Hispanic/Latino). Average age 32. In 2016, 25 master's awarded. *Entrance requirements:* For master's, GMAT. *Financial support:* Scholarships/grants available. Support available to part-time students. *Unit head:* Dr. Debasish Chakraborty, 989-774-3678, E-mail: chakt1d@cmich.edu. *Application contact:* Global Campus Student Services Call Center, 877-268-4636, E-mail: cmuglobal@cmich.edu.

Business Administration and Management—General

Central Michigan University, College of Graduate Studies, College of Business Administration, MBA Program, Mount Pleasant, MI 48859. Offers accounting (MBA); business economics (MBA); consulting (MBA); finance (MBA); general business (MBA); human resource management (MBA); information systems (MBA); international business (MBA); logistics management (MBA); marketing (MBA); value-driven organization (MBA). *Program availability:* Part-time, evening/weekend, online learning. Electronic applications accepted. *Faculty research:* Accounting, consulting, international business, marketing, information systems.

Central Michigan University, College of Graduate Studies, Interdisciplinary Administration Programs, Mount Pleasant, MI 48859. Offers acquisitions administration (MSA, Graduate Certificate); general administration (MSA, Graduate Certificate); health services administration (MSA, Graduate Certificate); human resource administration (Graduate Certificate); human resources administration (MSA); information resource management (MSA, Graduate Certificate); international administration (MSA, Graduate Certificate); leadership (MSA, Graduate Certificate); public administration (MSA, Graduate Certificate); research administration (Graduate Certificate); sport administration (MSA). *Accreditation:* AACSB. *Program availability:* Part-time, evening/weekend, online learning. *Degree requirements:* For master's, thesis or alternative. *Entrance requirements:* For master's, bachelor's degree with minimum GPA of 2.7. Electronic applications accepted. *Faculty research:* Interdisciplinary studies in acquisitions administration, health services administration, sport administration, recreation and park administration, and international administration.

Chadron State College, School of Professional and Graduate Studies, Department of Business and Economics, Chadron, NE 69337. Offers MBA. *Accreditation:* ACBSP. *Program availability:* Part-time, evening/weekend, online learning. *Degree requirements:* For master's, thesis optional. *Entrance requirements:* For master's, GMAT, minimum GPA of 2.75 or 12 graduate hours at CSC with minimum GPA of 3.25. Additional exam requirements/recommendations for international students: Required—TOEFL. Electronic applications accepted.

Chaminade University of Honolulu, Office of Professional and Continuing Education, Program in Business Administration, Honolulu, HI 96816-1578. Offers accounting (MBA); business (MBA); island business (MBA); not-for-profit (MBA). *Program availability:* Part-time, evening/weekend, 100% online, blended/hybrid learning. *Faculty:* 7 full-time (3 women), 7 part-time/adjunct (2 women). *Students:* 71 full-time (47 women), 40 part-time (23 women); includes 78 minority (4 Black or African American, non-Hispanic/Latino; 1 American Indian or Alaska Native, non-Hispanic/Latino; 37 Asian, non-Hispanic/Latino; 5 Hispanic/Latino; 28 Native Hawaiian or other Pacific Islander, non-Hispanic/Latino; 3 Two or more races, non-Hispanic/Latino). Average age 32. 70 applicants, 96% accepted, 45 enrolled. In 2016, 56 master's awarded. *Entrance requirements:* For master's, minimum GPA of 3.0, resume, two years or more of work experience. Additional exam requirements/recommendations for international students: Required—TOEFL (minimum score 550 paper-based; 79 iBT). *Application deadline:* Applications are processed on a rolling basis. Application fee: $40. Electronic applications accepted. *Expenses:* $820 per credit hour with $93 fee per online course. *Financial support:* Applicants required to submit FAFSA. *Unit head:* Dr. Scott J. Schroeder, Dean, 808-739-4612, Fax: 808-735-4734, E-mail: mba@chaminade.edu. *Application contact:* 808-735-4755, E-mail: gradserv@chaminade.edu.
Website: http://www.chaminade.edu/mba

Champlain College, Graduate Studies, Burlington, VT 05402-0670. Offers business (MBA); digital forensic science (MS); early childhood education (M Ed); emergent media (MFA, MS); executive leadership (MS); health care administration (MS); information security operations (MS); law (MS); mediation and applied conflict studies (MS). MS in emergent media program held in Shanghai. *Program availability:* Part-time, online learning. *Degree requirements:* For master's, capstone project. *Entrance requirements:* Additional exam requirements/recommendations for international students: Required—TOEFL (minimum score 550 paper-based; 80 iBT). Electronic applications accepted.

Chapman University, The George L. Argyros School of Business and Economics, Orange, CA 92866. Offers accounting (MS); business administration (Exec MBA, MBA); economic systems design (MS); JD/MBA. *Accreditation:* AACSB. *Program availability:* Part-time, evening/weekend. *Faculty:* 54 full-time (10 women), 35 part-time/adjunct (7 women). *Students:* 179 full-time (83 women), 94 part-time (44 women); includes 77 minority (4 Black or African American, non-Hispanic/Latino; 2 American Indian or Alaska Native, non-Hispanic/Latino; 30 Asian, non-Hispanic/Latino; 30 Hispanic/Latino; 3 Native Hawaiian or other Pacific Islander, non-Hispanic/Latino; 8 Two or more races, non-Hispanic/Latino), 96 international. Average age 28. 250 applicants, 75% accepted, 94 enrolled. In 2016, 114 master's awarded. *Entrance requirements:* Additional exam requirements/recommendations for international students: Required—TOEFL (minimum score 550 paper-based, 80 iBT), IELTS (6.5), PTE Academic (53), or CAE. Application fee: $60. Electronic applications accepted. *Expenses:* Contact institution. *Financial support:* Fellowships, Federal Work-Study, and scholarships/grants available. Financial award applicants required to submit FAFSA. *Unit head:* Reginald Gilyard, Dean, 714-997-6684. *Application contact:* Debra Gonda, Associate Dean, 714-997-6894, E-mail: gonda@chapman.edu.
Website: http://www.chapman.edu/business/

Charleston Southern University, School of Business, Charleston, SC 29423-8087. Offers accounting (MBA); finance (MBA); general management (MBA); human resource management (MS); leadership (MBA); management information systems (MBA); organizational leadership (MA). *Program availability:* Part-time, evening/weekend. *Degree requirements:* For master's, thesis optional. *Entrance requirements:* For master's, GMAT. Additional exam requirements/recommendations for international students: Required—TOEFL (minimum score 550 paper-based; 79 iBT). *Application deadline:* Applications are processed on a rolling basis. Application fee: $40. *Expenses:* *Tuition:* Full-time $6000. Tuition and fees vary according to program. *Financial support:* Research assistantships with full tuition reimbursements available. Financial award application deadline: 4/15; financial award applicants required to submit FAFSA. *Unit head:* Dr. David Palmer, Interim Dean, 843-863-7025, Fax: 843-863-7922, E-mail: dpalmer@csuniv.edu. *Application contact:* Dr. Darin L. Gerdes, Director of the MBA Program, 843-863-7814, Fax: 843-863-7922, E-mail: dgerdes@csuniv.edu.
Website: http://www.csuniv.edu/business/

Chatham University, Program in Business Administration, Pittsburgh, PA 15232-2826. Offers business administration (MBA); healthcare management (MBA); sustainability (MBA); women's leadership (MBA). *Program availability:* Part-time, evening/weekend. *Entrance requirements:* For master's, minimum GPA of 3.0, letters of recommendation. Additional exam requirements/recommendations for international students: Required—TOEFL (minimum score 600 paper-based; 100 iBT), IELTS (minimum score 7), TWE. Electronic applications accepted. Application fee is waived when completed online. *Expenses:* *Tuition:* Full-time $16,254; part-time $903 per credit hour. *Required fees:* $468; $26 per credit hour.

Christian Brothers University, School of Business, Memphis, TN 38104-5581. Offers accountancy (M Acc); business (MBA); international business (MIB); project management (Certificate); MBA/MIB. *Program availability:* Part-time, evening/weekend. *Entrance requirements:* For master's, GMAT, GRE. Additional exam requirements/recommendations for international students: Required—TOEFL.

The Citadel, The Military College of South Carolina, Citadel Graduate College, Tommy and Victoria Baker School of Business, Charleston, SC 29409. Offers MBA. *Accreditation:* AACSB. *Program availability:* Part-time, evening/weekend, 100% online, blended/hybrid learning. *Faculty:* 3 full-time (0 women), 1 part-time/adjunct (0 women). *Students:* 27 full-time (10 women), 137 part-time (51 women); includes 17 minority (7 Black or African American, non-Hispanic/Latino; 1 American Indian or Alaska Native, non-Hispanic/Latino; 2 Asian, non-Hispanic/Latino; 4 Hispanic/Latino; 3 Two or more races, non-Hispanic/Latino), 3 international. 100 applicants, 94% accepted, 56 enrolled. In 2016, 91 master's awarded. *Entrance requirements:* For master's, GMAT or GRE (5 years old or less), 2 letters of recommendation from professor, supervisor, military official, or someone familiar with applicant's academic or professional work; resume detailing professional work experience. Additional exam requirements/recommendations for international students: Required—TOEFL (minimum score 550 paper-based; 79 iBT). *Application deadline:* Applications are processed on a rolling basis. Application fee: $40. Electronic applications accepted. *Expenses:* Tuition, state resident: full-time $5121; part-time $569 per credit hour. Tuition, nonresident: full-time $8613; part-time $957 per credit hour. *Required fees:* $90 per term. *Financial support:* Fellowships and unspecified assistantships available. Support available to part-time students. Financial award application deadline: 7/1; financial award applicants required to submit FAFSA. *Unit head:* Dr. William Sharbrough, MBA Program Director, 843-953-5056, E-mail: sharbroughw@citadel.edu. *Application contact:* Morgan LaForge, MBA Academic Advisor, 843-953-5257, E-mail: mlaforge@citadel.edu. Website: http://www.citadel.edu/root/mba

City College of the City University of New York, Graduate School, Colin Powell School for Civic and Global Leadership, Department of Economics and Business, New York, NY 10031-9198. Offers economics (MA). *Program availability:* Part-time. *Degree requirements:* For master's, comprehensive exam, proficiency in a foreign language or advanced statistics. *Entrance requirements:* Additional exam requirements/recommendations for international students: Required—TOEFL (minimum score 550 paper-based; 79 iBT). Electronic applications accepted. Tuition and fees vary according to course load, degree level and program. *Faculty research:* International economics, health, banking.

City University of Seattle, Graduate Division, School of Management, Seattle, WA 98121. Offers accounting (Certificate); change leadership (MBA, Certificate); computer systems (MS); finance (Certificate); financial management (MBA); general management (MBA); general management-Europe (MBA); global marketing (MBA); human resources management (Certificate); individualized study (MBA); information security (MS); information systems (MBA); leadership (MA); marketing (MBA, Certificate); project management (MBA, MS, Certificate); sustainable business (Certificate); technology management (MBA, Certificate). *Program availability:* Part-time, evening/weekend, online learning. *Degree requirements:* For master's, comprehensive exam (for some programs), thesis (for some programs). *Entrance requirements:* For master's, baccalaureate degree or equivalent from an accredited or otherwise recognized institution. Additional exam requirements/recommendations for international students: Required—TOEFL (minimum score 567 paper-based; 87 iBT); Recommended—IELTS. Electronic applications accepted.

Claflin University, Graduate Programs, Orangeburg, SC 29115. Offers biotechnology (MS); business administration (MBA). *Program availability:* Part-time. *Degree requirements:* For master's, comprehensive exam, thesis. *Entrance requirements:* For master's, GRE, GMAT, baccalaureate degree, 3 letters of recommendation, resume, statement of purpose. Additional exam requirements/recommendations for international students: Recommended—TOEFL (minimum score 550 paper-based).

Claremont Graduate University, Graduate Programs, Peter F. Drucker and Masatoshi Ito Graduate School of Management, Claremont, CA 91711-6160. Offers EMBA, MA, MBA, MS, PhD, Certificate, MBA/MA, MBA/PhD, MS/MBA. *Program availability:* Part-time. *Faculty:* 15 full-time (5 women), 1 part-time/adjunct (0 women). *Students:* 137 full-time (84 women), 73 part-time (34 women); includes 57 minority (10 Black or African American, non-Hispanic/Latino; 22 Asian, non-Hispanic/Latino; 19 Hispanic/Latino; 3 Native Hawaiian or other Pacific Islander, non-Hispanic/Latino; 3 Two or more races, non-Hispanic/Latino), 75 international. Average age 32. In 2016, 102 master's, 2 doctorates, 26 other advanced degrees awarded. *Entrance requirements:* For doctorate, GMAT or GRE General Test. Additional exam requirements/recommendations for international students: Required—TOEFL (minimum score 75 iBT). *Application deadline:* For fall admission, 2/1 priority date for domestic and international students. Applications are processed on a rolling basis. Application fee: $80. Electronic applications accepted. *Expenses:* Contact institution. *Financial support:* Fellowships, research assistantships, teaching assistantships, Federal Work-Study, institutionally sponsored loans, and scholarships/grants available. Support available to part-time students. Financial award application deadline: 2/15; financial award applicants required to submit FAFSA. *Faculty research:* Strategy and leadership, brand management, cost management and control, organizational transformation, general management. *Unit head:* Jenny Darroch, Dean, 909-607-2471, E-mail: jenny.darroch@cgu.edu. *Application contact:* Alice Liu, Assistant Director of Admissions, 909-607-7583, E-mail: alice.liu@cgu.edu.
Website: https://www.cgu.edu/school/drucker-school-of-management/

Claremont Graduate University, Graduate Programs, School of Social Science, Policy and Evaluation, Program in Politics, Economics, and Business, Claremont, CA 91711-6160. Offers MA. *Program availability:* Part-time. *Students:* 2 full-time (1 woman), 1 part-time (0 women); includes 1 minority (Hispanic/Latino). Average age 31. In 2016, 3 master's awarded. *Entrance requirements:* For master's, GRE General Test. Additional exam requirements/recommendations for international students: Required—TOEFL (minimum score 75 iBT). *Application deadline:* For fall admission, 2/1 priority date for domestic and international students. Applications are processed on a rolling basis. Application fee: $80. Electronic applications accepted. *Expenses:* *Tuition:* Full-time $44,328; part-time $1847 per unit. *Required fees:* $600; $300 per semester. Tuition and fees vary according to course load and program. *Financial support:* Federal Work-Study, institutionally sponsored loans, and scholarships/grants available. Support available to part-time students. Financial award application deadline: 2/15; financial award applicants required to submit FAFSA. *Unit head:* Stewart Donaldson, Dean, 909-607-8235, E-mail: stewart.donaldson@cgu.edu. *Application contact:* Paige Piontkowsky, Senior Assistant Director of Admissions, 909-607-3240, E-mail: paige.piontkowsky@cgu.edu.
Website: https://www.cgu.edu/academics/program/politics-economics-and-business/

Clarion University of Pennsylvania, Office of Transfer, Adult and Graduate Admissions, Master of Business Administration Program, Clarion, PA 16214. Offers finance (MBA); health care administration (MBA); innovation and entrepreneurship (MBA). *Accreditation:* AACSB. *Program availability:* Part-time, evening/weekend, 100% online. *Faculty:* 15 full-time (2 women). *Students:* 52 full-time (9 women), 54 part-time (43 women); includes 14 minority (7 Black or African American, non-Hispanic/Latino; 2 Asian, non-Hispanic/Latino; 1 Hispanic/Latino; 4 Two or more races, non-Hispanic/Latino), 4 international. Average age 32. 87 applicants, 86% accepted, 28 enrolled. In 2016, 21 master's awarded. *Degree requirements:* For master's, portfolio. *Entrance*

requirements: For master's, GMAT, minimum QPA of 2.75. Additional exam requirements/recommendations for international students: Required—TOEFL (minimum score 550 paper-based; 80 iBT), IELTS (minimum score 7). *Application deadline:* For fall admission, 8/1 priority date for domestic students, 4/15 priority date for international students; for spring admission, 12/1 priority date for domestic students, 9/15 priority date for international students. Applications are processed on a rolling basis. Application fee: $40. Electronic applications accepted. *Expenses:* $632.55 per credit. *Financial support:* Career-related internships or fieldwork, Federal Work-Study, scholarships/grants, and unspecified assistantships available. Support available to part-time students. Financial award application deadline: 3/1; financial award applicants required to submit FAFSA. *Unit head:* Juanice Vega, Associate Dean of the College of Business Administration and Information Sciences, 814-393-2600, Fax: 814-393-1910, E-mail: mba@clarion.edu. *Application contact:* Dana Bearer, Assistant Director, Graduate Programs, 814-393-2337, Fax: 814-393-2722, E-mail: gradstudies@clarion.edu.
Website: http://www.clarion.edu/admissions/graduate/index.html

Clark Atlanta University, School of Business Administration, Department of Business Administration, Atlanta, GA 30314. Offers MBA. *Accreditation:* AACSB. *Program availability:* Part-time. *Faculty:* 11 full-time (4 women), 2 part-time/adjunct (0 women). *Students:* 44 full-time (25 women), 7 part-time (3 women); includes 34 minority (all Black or African American, non-Hispanic/Latino), 7 international. Average age 26. 63 applicants, 52% accepted, 16 enrolled. In 2016, 26 master's awarded. *Degree requirements:* For master's, thesis (for some programs). *Entrance requirements:* For master's, GMAT. Additional exam requirements/recommendations for international students: Required—TOEFL (minimum score 500 paper-based; 61 iBT). *Application deadline:* For fall admission, 4/1 for domestic and international students; for spring admission, 11/1 for domestic and international students. Applications are processed on a rolling basis. Application fee: $40 ($55 for international students). Electronic applications accepted. *Expenses: Tuition:* Full-time $15,498; part-time $861 per credit hour. *Required fees:* $1326; $1326 per credit hour. Tuition and fees vary according to course load. *Financial support:* Career-related internships or fieldwork, Federal Work-Study, scholarships/grants, and unspecified assistantships available. Support available to part-time students. Financial award application deadline: 4/30; financial award applicants required to submit FAFSA. *Unit head:* Dr. Raphael Boyd, Chairperson, 404-880-6050, E-mail: rboyd@cau.edu. *Application contact:* Graduate Program Admissions, 404-880-8483, E-mail: graduateadmissions@cau.edu.

Clarke University, Graduate Business Programs, Dubuque, IA 52001-3198. Offers MBA, MOL. *Program availability:* Part-time, evening/weekend, blended/hybrid learning. *Faculty:* 6 full-time (3 women). *Students:* 13 full-time (9 women), 26 part-time (16 women); includes 5 minority (2 Black or African American, non-Hispanic/Latino; 1 Asian, non-Hispanic/Latino; 2 Hispanic/Latino), 1 international. Average age 33. 37 applicants, 54% accepted, 12 enrolled. In 2016, 19 master's awarded. *Entrance requirements:* For master's, GMAT if GPA under 3.0, minimum GPA of 2.8, previous undergraduate course work in business, two recommendations, resume, essay, interview. Additional exam requirements/recommendations for international students: Required—TOEFL (minimum score 550 paper-based, 80 iBT) or IELTS (6.5). *Application deadline:* Applications are processed on a rolling basis. Application fee: $35. Electronic applications accepted. *Expenses:* $535 per credit. *Financial support:* Applicants required to submit FAFSA. *Unit head:* B'Ann Dittmar, Director of Graduate Business Studies, 563-588-6419, E-mail: bann.dittmar@clarke.edu. *Application contact:* Kimberly Roush, Director of Admission, Graduate and Adult Programs, 563-588-6539, Fax: 563-552-7994, E-mail: graduate@clarke.edu. Website: https://www.clarke.edu/academics/#graduate

Clarkson University, School of Business, Master's Program in Business Administration, Potsdam, NY 13699. Offers business administration (MBA); business fundamentals (Advanced Certificate); global supply chain management (Advanced Certificate); human resource management (Advanced Certificate); management and leadership (Advanced Certificate). *Accreditation:* AACSB. *Program availability:* Part-time, evening/weekend, 100% online, blended/hybrid learning. *Faculty:* 53 full-time (12 women), 33 part-time/adjunct (6 women). *Students:* 119 full-time (45 women), 51 part-time (19 women); includes 23 minority (5 Black or African American, non-Hispanic/Latino; 1 American Indian or Alaska Native, non-Hispanic/Latino; 10 Asian, non-Hispanic/Latino; 4 Hispanic/Latino; 3 Two or more races, non-Hispanic/Latino), 14 international. 390 applicants, 39% accepted, 101 enrolled. In 2016, 91 master's, 2 other advanced degrees awarded. *Entrance requirements:* For master's, GRE or GMAT. Additional exam requirements/recommendations for international students: Required—TOEFL (minimum score 550 paper-based, 80 iBT) or IELTS (6.5). *Application deadline:* Applications are processed on a rolling basis. Application fee: $50. Electronic applications accepted. *Expenses: Tuition:* Full-time $23,400; part-time $1300 per credit hour. Tuition and fees vary according to campus/location and program. *Financial support:* Scholarships/grants available. *Unit head:* Dr. Alan Bowman, Senior Associate Dean of Graduate Business Programs, 518-631-9887, E-mail: abowman@clarkson.edu. *Application contact:* Erin Wheeler, Graduate Admissions Contact, 518-631-9910, E-mail: ewheeler@clarkson.edu.

Clark University, Graduate School, Graduate School of Management, Business Administration Program, Worcester, MA 01610-1477. Offers accounting (MBA); finance (MBA); information management and business analytics (MBA); management (MBA); marketing (MBA); social change (MBA); sustainability (MBA). *Accreditation:* AACSB. *Program availability:* Part-time, evening/weekend. *Students:* 91 full-time (48 women), 101 part-time (45 women); includes 22 minority (8 Black or African American, non-Hispanic/Latino; 4 Asian, non-Hispanic/Latino; 9 Hispanic/Latino; 1 Native Hawaiian or other Pacific Islander, non-Hispanic/Latino), 45 international. Average age 31. 225 applicants, 58% accepted, 78 enrolled. In 2016, 113 master's awarded. *Degree requirements:* For master's, thesis optional. *Application deadline:* For fall admission, 6/1 priority date for domestic students; for spring admission, 12/1 priority date for domestic students. Applications are processed on a rolling basis. Application fee: $75. Electronic applications accepted. *Expenses: Tuition:* Full-time $44,050. *Required fees:* $80. Tuition and fees vary according to course load and program. *Financial support:* In 2016–17, research assistantships with partial tuition reimbursements (averaging $4,800 per year), teaching assistantships with partial tuition reimbursements (averaging $4,800 per year) were awarded; fellowships, career-related internships or fieldwork, Federal Work-Study, institutionally sponsored loans, and tuition waivers (partial) also available. Support available to part-time students. Financial award application deadline: 5/31. *Faculty research:* Marketing, accounting, human resource management, management information systems, business finance. *Unit head:* Dr. Catherine Usoff, Dean, 508-793-7543, Fax: 508-793-8822. *Application contact:* Ethan Bernstein, Director of Graduate Admissions, 508-793-7543, E-mail: graduateadmissions@clarku.edu.
Website: http://www.clarku.edu/programs/masters-business-administration

Clark University, Graduate School, Graduate School of Management, Program in Management, Worcester, MA 01610-1477. Offers MSM. *Program availability:* Part-time. *Expenses: Tuition:* Full-time $44,050. *Required fees:* $80. Tuition and fees vary according to course load and program. *Unit head:* Dr. Catherine Usoff, Dean, 508-793-8822, Fax: 508-793-8822, E-mail: cusoff@clarku.edu. *Application contact:* Ethan Bernstein, Director of Admissions, 508-793-7543, E-mail: graduateadmissions@clarku.edu.
Website: http://www.clarku.edu/programs/masters-management

Clayton State University, School of Graduate Studies, College of Business, Program in Business Administration, Morrow, GA 30260-0285. Offers accounting (MBA); human resource leadership (MBA); international business (MBA); sports and entertainment management (MBA); supply chain management (MBA). *Accreditation:* AACSB. *Program availability:* Part-time, evening/weekend. *Degree requirements:* For master's, thesis. *Entrance requirements:* For master's, GMAT, 3 letters of recommendation; statement of purpose; 2 official transcripts. Additional exam requirements/recommendations for international students: Required—TOEFL (minimum score 550 paper-based; 80 iBT). Electronic applications accepted. *Expenses:* Contact institution.

Cleary University, Online Program in Business Administration, Howell, MI 48843. Offers analytics, technology, and innovation (MBA, Graduate Certificate); financial planning (Graduate Certificate); global leadership (MBA, Graduate Certificate); health care leadership (MBA, Graduate Certificate). *Program availability:* Part-time, evening/weekend, online learning. *Faculty:* 13 part-time/adjunct (6 women). *Students:* 92 full-time (47 women), 25 part-time (14 women). *Degree requirements:* For master's, thesis. *Entrance requirements:* For master's, bachelor's degree; minimum GPA of 2.5; professional resume indicating minimum of 2 years of management or related experience; undergraduate degree from accredited college or university with at least 18 quarter hours (or 12 semester hours) of accounting study (for MBA in accounting). Additional exam requirements/recommendations for international students: Required—TOEFL (minimum score 550 paper-based; 79 iBT), Michigan English Language Assessment Battery (minimum score 75). *Application deadline:* For fall admission, 8/15 for domestic students, 7/15 for international students; for spring admission, 4/2 for domestic students, 1/2 for international students. Applications are processed on a rolling basis. Application fee: $50. Electronic applications accepted. *Expenses: Tuition:* Full-time $16,560; part-time $920 per credit hour. *Required fees:* $100 per semester. *Financial support:* Fellowships, Federal Work-Study, and scholarships/grants available. Support available to part-time students. Financial award application deadline: 8/15; financial award applicants required to submit FAFSA. *Unit head:* Dr. Lance B. Lewis, Provost and Chief Academic Officer, 800-686-1883, E-mail: llewis@cleary.edu. *Application contact:* Cassandra Tarnowski, Director of Admissions, 800-686-1883, Fax: 517-338-3336, E-mail: ctarnowski@cleary.edu.

Clemson University, Graduate School, College of Business, Department of Management, Clemson, SC 29634. Offers business administration (PhD), including management information systems, supply chain and operations management; management (MS). *Accreditation:* AACSB. *Faculty:* 17 full-time (3 women). *Students:* 17 full-time (5 women), 2 part-time (1 woman), 13 international. Average age 33. 30 applicants, 7% accepted, 2 enrolled. In 2016, 2 master's, 1 doctorate awarded. Terminal master's awarded for partial completion of doctoral program. *Degree requirements:* For master's, comprehensive exam, thesis optional; for doctorate, comprehensive exam, thesis/dissertation. *Entrance requirements:* For master's and doctorate, GMAT or GRE General Test, unofficial transcripts, two letters of reference, curriculum vitae. Additional exam requirements/recommendations for international students: Required—TOEFL (minimum score 94 iBT), IELTS (minimum score 7), PTE (minimum score 64). *Application deadline:* For fall admission, 1/15 priority date for domestic and international students. Application fee: $80 ($90 for international students). Electronic applications accepted. *Expenses:* $5,617 per semester full-time resident, $11,194 per semester full-time non-resident, $697 per credit hour part-time resident, $1,392 per credit hour part-time non-resident. *Financial support:* In 2016–17, 52 students received support, including 11 fellowships with partial tuition reimbursements available (averaging $3,826 per year), 3 research assistantships with partial tuition reimbursements available (averaging $22,667 per year), 32 teaching assistantships with partial tuition reimbursements available (averaging $25,000 per year); unspecified assistantships also available. Financial award application deadline: 1/15. *Faculty research:* Effective use of information technology in business, manufacturing and service operations strategy, lean operations and quality management, healthcare operations, behavioral market design. *Total annual research expenditures:* $89,179. *Unit head:* Dr. V. Sridharan, Department Chair, 864-656-2624, E-mail: suhas@clemson.edu. *Application contact:* Dr. Janis Miller, Graduate Program Coordinator, 864-656-3757, E-mail: janism@clemson.edu.
Website: https://www.clemson.edu/business/departments/management/

Clemson University, Graduate School, College of Business, Master of Business Administration Program, Greenville, SC 29601. Offers business administration (MBA); business analytics (MBA); entrepreneurship and innovation (MBA). *Accreditation:* AACSB. *Program availability:* Part-time, evening/weekend. *Faculty:* 3 full-time (1 woman), 9 part-time/adjunct (1 woman). *Students:* 146 full-time (57 women), 322 part-time (102 women); includes 81 minority (46 Black or African American, non-Hispanic/Latino; 13 Asian, non-Hispanic/Latino; 17 Hispanic/Latino; 1 Native Hawaiian or other Pacific Islander, non-Hispanic/Latino; 4 Two or more races, non-Hispanic/Latino), 35 international. Average age 31. 226 applicants, 63% accepted, 115 enrolled. In 2016, 165 master's awarded. *Entrance requirements:* For master's, GMAT, resume, unofficial transcripts, personal statement, letters of recommendation. Additional exam requirements/recommendations for international students: Required—TOEFL (minimum score 80 iBT), IELTS (minimum score 6.5). *Application deadline:* For fall admission, 7/15 for domestic students, 4/15 for international students; for spring admission, 12/1 for domestic students. Applications are processed on a rolling basis. Application fee: $80 ($90 for international students). Electronic applications accepted. *Expenses:* $9,761 per semester resident, $15,764 per semester non-resident. *Financial support:* In 2016–17, 38 students received support, including 1 research assistantship with partial tuition reimbursement available (averaging $18,000 per year); unspecified assistantships also available. Financial award application deadline: 7/15. *Unit head:* Dr. Gregory Pickett, Senior Associate Dean, 864-656-3975, Fax: 864-370-8061, E-mail: pgregor@clemson.edu. *Application contact:* Kristin Allen, Director of Admissions, 864-656-8173, Fax: 864-370-8061, E-mail: klallen@clemson.edu.
Website: https://www.clemson.edu/business/departments/mba/

Cleveland State University, College of Graduate Studies, Monte Ahuja College of Business, Doctor of Business Administration Program, Cleveland, OH 44115. Offers information systems (DBA); marketing (DBA). *Accreditation:* AACSB. *Program availability:* Part-time, evening/weekend. *Faculty:* 50 full-time (11 women). *Students:* 8 full-time (5 women), 13 part-time (3 women); includes 4 minority (3 Black or African American, non-Hispanic/Latino; 1 Asian, non-Hispanic/Latino), 3 international. Average age 40. In 2016, 2 doctorates awarded. *Degree requirements:* For doctorate, comprehensive exam, thesis/dissertation, oral dissertation defense. *Entrance requirements:* For doctorate, GMAT, MBA or equivalent. Additional exam requirements/recommendations for international students: Required—TOEFL (minimum score 550 paper-based; 78 iBT). *Application deadline:* For fall admission, 2/1 for domestic and international students. Application fee: $40. Electronic applications accepted. *Expenses:* Tuition, state resident: full-time $9565. Tuition, nonresident: full-time $17,980. Tuition and fees vary according to program. *Financial support:* In 2016–17, 5 research assistantships with full tuition reimbursements (averaging $12,700 per year), 4 teaching assistantships with full tuition reimbursements (averaging $12,700 per year) were awarded; tuition waivers (full) and unspecified assistantships also available. *Faculty research:* Supply chain management, international business, strategic management,

risk analysis, consumer behavior. *Unit head:* Dr. Raj Shekhar G. Javalgi, Director, 216-687-3786, Fax: 216-687-9354, E-mail: r.javalgi@csuohio.edu. *Application contact:* Melinda J. Arnold, Administrative Secretary, 216-687-6952, Fax: 216-687-9257, E-mail: m.arnold@csuohio.edu.
Website: http://www.csuohio.edu/business/academics/mbajuris-doctor

Cleveland State University, College of Graduate Studies, Monte Ahuja College of Business, MBA Programs, Cleveland, OH 44115. Offers AMBA, EMBA, MBA, JD/MBA, MSN/MBA. Programs also offered at Progressive Insurance Corporation, The Cleveland Clinic, and Metro Health Medical Center. *Accreditation:* AACSB. *Program availability:* Part-time, evening/weekend, online learning. *Faculty:* 33 full-time (9 women), 16 part-time/adjunct (2 women). *Students:* 195 full-time (101 women), 337 part-time (153 women); includes 96 minority (51 Black or African American, non-Hispanic/Latino; 20 Asian, non-Hispanic/Latino; 16 Hispanic/Latino; 1 Native Hawaiian or other Pacific Islander, non-Hispanic/Latino; 8 Two or more races, non-Hispanic/Latino), 85 international. Average age 30. 674 applicants, 48% accepted, 126 enrolled. In 2016, 272 master's awarded. *Degree requirements:* For master's, variable foreign language requirement, comprehensive exam (for some programs), thesis (for some programs). *Entrance requirements:* For master's, GMAT or GRE, minimum cumulative GPA of 2.75 from bachelor's degree; resume, statement of purpose and two letters of reference (for health care administration MBA). Additional exam requirements/recommendations for international students: Required—TOEFL (minimum score 550 paper-based; 78 iBT). *Application deadline:* For fall admission, 6/1 priority date for domestic students, 6/1 for international students; for spring admission, 11/1 priority date for domestic students, 11/1 for international students. Applications are processed on a rolling basis. Application fee: $40. Electronic applications accepted. *Expenses:* Tuition, state resident: full-time $9565. Tuition, nonresident: full-time $17,980. Tuition and fees vary according to program. *Financial support:* In 2016–17, 594 students received support, including 45 research assistantships with tuition reimbursements available (averaging $6,960 per year), 1 teaching assistantship with tuition reimbursement available (averaging $7,800 per year); tuition waivers (full) and unspecified assistantships also available. Financial award application deadline: 5/15; financial award applicants required to submit FAFSA. *Faculty research:* Accounting and finance, management and organizational behavior, marketing, computer information systems, international business. *Total annual research expenditures:* $70,000. *Unit head:* Ronald John Mickler, Jr., Acting Assistant Director, Graduate Programs, 216-687-3730, Fax: 216-687-5311, E-mail: cbacsu@csuohio.edu. *Application contact:* Kenneth Dippong, Director, Student Services, 216-523-7545, Fax: 216-687-9354, E-mail: k.dippong@csuohio.edu.
Website: http://www.csuohio.edu/cba/

Coastal Carolina University, E. Craig Wall, Sr. College of Business Administration, Conway, SC 29528-6054. Offers accounting (M Acc); business administration (MBA); business foundations (Certificate); fraud examination (Certificate). *Accreditation:* AACSB. *Program availability:* Part-time, evening/weekend. *Faculty:* 14 full-time (7 women), 3 part-time/adjunct (0 women). *Students:* 67 full-time (28 women), 30 part-time (15 women); includes 25 minority (16 Black or African American, non-Hispanic/Latino; 2 Asian, non-Hispanic/Latino; 3 Hispanic/Latino; 1 Native Hawaiian or other Pacific Islander, non-Hispanic/Latino; 3 Two or more races, non-Hispanic/Latino), 11 international. Average age 27. 88 applicants, 78% accepted, 56 enrolled. In 2016, 70 master's, 1 other advanced degree awarded. *Entrance requirements:* For master's, GMAT, official transcripts, 2 letters of recommendation, resume, baccalaureate degree; for Certificate, GMAT, official transcripts; 2 letters of recommendation; baccalaureate degree or evidence of receiving a CPA certificate, law degree, or admittance to an accredited law school. Additional exam requirements/recommendations for international students: Required—TOEFL (minimum score 550 paper-based; 79 iBT), IELTS (minimum score 6.5). *Application deadline:* For fall admission, 6/15 priority date for domestic and international students; for spring admission, 11/15 priority date for domestic and international students; for summer admission, 4/15 priority date for domestic and international students. Applications are processed on a rolling basis. Application fee: $45. Electronic applications accepted. *Expenses:* Tuition, state resident: full-time $9990; part-time $555 per credit hour. Tuition, nonresident: full-time $18,108; part-time $1006 per credit hour. *Required fees:* $90; $5 per credit hour. *Financial support:* Fellowships, research assistantships, and unspecified assistantships available. Support available to part-time students. Financial award application deadline: 3/1; financial award applicants required to submit FAFSA. *Unit head:* Dr. Arlise P. McKinney, Associate Professor/Director of Graduate Programs and Executive Education, 843-349-2390, Fax: 843-349-2455, E-mail: amckinney@coastal.edu. *Application contact:* Dr. James O. Luken, Associate Provost/Interim Vice-Dean of the Coastal Environment, 843-349-2235, Fax: 843-349-6444, E-mail: joluken@coastal.edu.
Website: http://www.coastal.edu/academics/colleges/business/

College of Charleston, Graduate School, School of Business, Program in Business Administration, Charleston, SC 29424-0001. Offers MBA. *Entrance requirements:* For master's, GMAT or GRE, transcripts, recommendations, goal statement, bachelor's degree. Additional exam requirements/recommendations for international students: Required—TOEFL (minimum score 81 iBT), IELTS. *Application deadline:* For fall admission, 6/1 for domestic students. Application fee: $45. Electronic applications accepted. *Financial support:* Federal Work-Study, scholarships/grants, and unspecified assistantships available. Financial award application deadline: 4/1; financial award applicants required to submit FAFSA. *Unit head:* Mark Witte, Director, 843-953-3986, E-mail: wittem@cofc.edu. *Application contact:* Mark Witte, Director, 843-953-3986, E-mail: wittem@cofc.edu.
Website: http://sb.cofc.edu/graduate/MBA/index.php

College of Saint Elizabeth, Department of Business Administration and Management, Morristown, NJ 07960-6989. Offers human resource management (MS); organizational change (MS). *Program availability:* Part-time. *Degree requirements:* For master's, thesis. *Entrance requirements:* For master's, GRE, GMAT, minimum GPA of 3.25; 2 research projects related to the development design of the action research dissertation study and oral dissertation defense. Additional exam requirements/recommendations for international students: Required—TOEFL (minimum score 550 paper-based; 79 iBT), IELTS (minimum score 6.5). Electronic applications accepted. Application fee is waived when completed online. *Expenses:* Contact institution.

College of St. Joseph, Graduate Programs, Division of Business, Program in Business Administration, Rutland, VT 05701-3899. Offers MBA. *Program availability:* Part-time, evening/weekend. *Entrance requirements:* For master's, two letters of reference from academic or professional sources; official transcripts of all graduate and undergraduate study; access to computer; computer literacy. Additional exam requirements/recommendations for international students: Required—TOEFL (minimum score 550 paper-based). *Application deadline:* Applications are processed on a rolling basis. Application fee: $35. Electronic applications accepted. *Expenses:* Contact institution. *Financial support:* Teaching assistantships available. Financial award application deadline: 3/1. *Unit head:* Robert Foley, Chair, 802-773-5900 Ext. 3248, Fax: 802-776-5258, E-mail: rfoley@csj.edu. *Application contact:* Alan Young, Dean of Admissions, 802-773-5900 Ext. 3227, Fax: 802-776-5310, E-mail: alanyoung@csj.edu.

The College of Saint Rose, Graduate Studies, Huether School of Business, Program in Business Administration, Albany, NY 12203-1419. Offers MBA, JD/MBA. JD/MBA offered jointly with Albany Law School. *Accreditation:* ACBSP. *Program availability:* Part-time, evening/weekend. *Students:* 45 full-time (20 women), 55 part-time (24 women); includes 16 minority (11 Black or African American, non-Hispanic/Latino; 1 Asian, non-Hispanic/Latino; 3 Hispanic/Latino; 1 Two or more races, non-Hispanic/Latino), 18 international. Average age 28. 96 applicants, 78% accepted, 25 enrolled. In 2016, 43 master's awarded. *Entrance requirements:* For master's, GMAT, graduate degree, or minimum undergraduate GPA of 3.0. Additional exam requirements/recommendations for international students: Required—TOEFL (minimum score 550 paper-based; 80 iBT), IELTS (minimum score 6), PTE (minimum score 56). *Application deadline:* For fall admission, 4/1 priority date for domestic students, 4/1 for international students; for spring admission, 10/15 priority date for domestic students, 10/15 for international students; for summer admission, 3/15 priority date for domestic and international students. Applications are processed on a rolling basis. Application fee: $40. Electronic applications accepted. *Expenses: Tuition:* Full-time $14,382; part-time $799 per credit. *Required fees:* $814; $32 per credit. $88 per semester. Tuition and fees vary according to course load. *Financial support:* Career-related internships or fieldwork, scholarships/grants, tuition waivers (partial), and unspecified assistantships available. Support available to part-time students. Financial award application deadline: 4/15. *Unit head:* Michael Mathews, Program Coordinator, 518-454-5210, E-mail: mathewsm@strose.edu. *Application contact:* Cris Murray, Assistant Vice President for Graduate Recruitment and Enrollment, 518-485-3390, Fax: 518-458-5479, E-mail: grad@strose.edu.
Website: https://www.strose.edu/mba/

The College of St. Scholastica, Graduate Studies, Department of Management, Duluth, MN 55811-4199. Offers MA, Certificate. *Program availability:* Part-time, evening/weekend, online learning. *Degree requirements:* For master's, thesis. *Entrance requirements:* Additional exam requirements/recommendations for international students: Required—TOEFL (minimum score 550 paper-based; 79 iBT). Electronic applications accepted. *Expenses:* Contact institution. *Faculty research:* Violence in higher education and workplace, screening and selection procedures in law enforcement, Internet use in criminal justice, stress management in law enforcement.

College of Staten Island of the City University of New York, Graduate Programs, School of Business, Program in Business Management, Staten Island, NY 10314-6600. Offers MS. *Program availability:* Part-time, evening/weekend. *Faculty:* 2 full-time, 1 part-time/adjunct. *Students:* 22 part-time. Average age 30. 48 applicants, 29% accepted, 14 enrolled. In 2016, 9 master's awarded. *Degree requirements:* For master's, written paper; 30 credit hours, or ten courses at three credits each. *Entrance requirements:* For master's, GMAT or GRE, baccalaureate degree in business or related field; minimum overall GPA of 3.0; letter of intent; two letters of recommendation; 2 courses each in accounting, economics, and quantitative methods; 1 course each in communications, computer fundamentals, management, and marketing. Additional exam requirements/recommendations for international students: Required—TOEFL (minimum score 600 paper-based; 100 iBT), IELTS (minimum score 7). *Application deadline:* For fall admission, 6/30 priority date for domestic and international students. Applications are processed on a rolling basis. Application fee: $125. Electronic applications accepted. *Expenses:* Tuition, state resident: full-time $10,130; part-time $425 per credit. Tuition, nonresident: full-time $18,720; part-time $780 per credit. *Required fees:* $181.10 per semester. Tuition and fees vary according to program. *Faculty research:* Corporate social responsibility, management innovation, organizational decision-making. *Unit head:* Dr. Deepa Aravind, Graduate Program Coordinator, 718-982-2963, E-mail: deepa.aravind@csi.cuny.edu. *Application contact:* Sasha Spence, Associate Director for Graduate Admissions, 718-982-2019, Fax: 718-982-2500, E-mail: sasha.spence@csi.cuny.edu.
Website: http://www.csi.cuny.edu/schoolofbusiness/programs_graduate.php

The College of William and Mary, Raymond A. Mason School of Business, Williamsburg, VA 23185. Offers EMBA, M Acc, MBA, MS, JD/MBA, MBA/MPP. *Accreditation:* AACSB. *Program availability:* Part-time, evening/weekend, online learning. *Faculty:* 62 full-time (20 women), 10 part-time/adjunct (2 women). *Students:* 279 full-time (88 women), 300 part-time (101 women); includes 131 minority (59 Black or African American, non-Hispanic/Latino; 2 American Indian or Alaska Native, non-Hispanic/Latino; 24 Asian, non-Hispanic/Latino; 33 Hispanic/Latino; 2 Native Hawaiian or other Pacific Islander, non-Hispanic/Latino; 11 Two or more races, non-Hispanic/Latino), 76 international. Average age 33. 791 applicants, 58% accepted, 275 enrolled. In 2016, 193 master's awarded. *Degree requirements:* For master's, three domestic residencies and two international trips (EMBA). *Entrance requirements:* For master's, GMAT or GRE. Additional exam requirements/recommendations for international students: Required—TOEFL (minimum score 600 paper-based; 100 iBT), IELTS (minimum score 6.5), PTE. *Application deadline:* For fall admission, 11/16 for domestic and international students; for winter admission, 1/18 for domestic and international students; for spring admission, 5/16 for domestic and international students; for summer admission, 7/15 for domestic students. Application fee: $100. Electronic applications accepted. *Expenses:* Contact institution. *Financial support:* In 2016–17, 141 students received support. Scholarships/grants and unspecified assistantships available. Financial award applicants required to submit FAFSA. *Faculty research:* Saving and asset allocation decisions in retirement accounts, supply chain management, virtual and networked organizations, healthcare informatics, sustainable business operations. *Total annual research expenditures:* $57,823. *Unit head:* Dr. Lawrence Pulley, Dean, 757-221-2891, Fax: 757-221-2937, E-mail: larry.pulley@mason.wm.edu. *Application contact:* Amanda K. Barth, Director, Full-time MBA Admissions, 757-221-2944, Fax: 757-221-2958, E-mail: amanda.barth@mason.wm.edu.
Website: http://mason.wm.edu/

Colorado Christian University, Program in Business Administration, Lakewood, CO 80226. Offers corporate training (MBA); information security (MA); leadership (MBA); project management (MBA). *Program availability:* Part-time, evening/weekend, online learning. *Degree requirements:* For master's, thesis optional. *Entrance requirements:* For master's, GMAT, 2 letters of recommendation, resume. Additional exam requirements/recommendations for international students: Required—TOEFL. Electronic applications accepted. *Expenses:* Contact institution.

Colorado Mesa University, Department of Business, Grand Junction, CO 81501-3122. Offers MBA. *Program availability:* Part-time, evening/weekend. *Faculty:* 12 full-time (1 woman), 1 part-time/adjunct (0 women). *Students:* 8 full-time (0 women), 18 part-time (11 women); includes 5 minority (4 Hispanic/Latino; 1 Native Hawaiian or other Pacific Islander, non-Hispanic/Latino), 3 international. Average age 27. 30 applicants, 43% accepted, 9 enrolled. In 2016, 10 master's awarded. *Degree requirements:* For master's, thesis or research practicum, written comprehensive exams. *Entrance requirements:* For master's, GMAT, MAT, or GRE, minimum GPA of 3.0 for last 60 undergraduate hours, 2 letters of recommendation. Additional exam requirements/recommendations for international students: Required—TOEFL (minimum score 550 paper-based). *Application deadline:* For fall admission, 4/1 priority date for domestic and international students; for spring admission, 10/1 priority date for domestic and international students. Applications are processed on a rolling basis. Application fee: $50. Electronic applications accepted. *Expenses:* $431.43 per credit hour in-state tuition and fees, $1,160.43 per credit hour out-of-state tuition and fees. *Financial support:* In 2016–17, 4

students received support. Scholarships/grants available. Financial award applicants required to submit FAFSA. *Unit head:* Dr. Steven Norman, Department Head, 970-248-1944, Fax: 970-248-1730, E-mail: snorman@coloradomesa.edu. *Application contact:* Jane Sandoval, MBA Coordinator, 970-248-1778, Fax: 970-248-1730, E-mail: jsandova@coloradomesa.edu.
Website: http://www.coloradomesa.edu/business/degrees/mba/index.html

Colorado State University, College of Business, Early Career MBA Program, Fort Collins, CO 80523. Offers MBA. *Students:* 40 full-time (21 women), 2 part-time (1 woman); includes 1 minority (Hispanic/Latino), 23 international. Average age 25. 64 applicants, 66% accepted, 27 enrolled. In 2016, 19 master's awarded. *Degree requirements:* For master's, practicum or internship. *Entrance requirements:* For master's, GMAT, bachelor's degree from accredited university, minimum GPA of 3.0, transcripts, three letters of recommendation, statement of purpose, resume. Additional exam requirements/recommendations for international students: Required—TOEFL (minimum score 86 iBT); Recommended—IELTS (minimum score 6.5), TSE (minimum score 58). *Application deadline:* For fall admission, 2/1 for domestic students, 6/1 for international students. Applications are processed on a rolling basis. Application fee: $60 ($70 for international students). Electronic applications accepted. *Expenses:* Contact institution. *Financial support:* Scholarships/grants and unspecified assistantships available. Financial award application deadline: 2/15; financial award applicants required to submit FAFSA. *Faculty research:* Organizational communication, digital marketing, career assessment and development, financial markets and investments, managerial accounting. *Unit head:* Dr. Sanjay Ramchander, Associate Dean of Academic Programs, 970-491-5027, E-mail: gradadmissions@business.colostate.edu. *Application contact:* Andrea Fortney, Program Manager, 970-491-5591, E-mail: andrea.fortney@colostate.edu.
Website: https://biz.colostate.edu/Academics/Graduate-Programs/Master-of-Business-Administration/Early-Career-MBA

Colorado State University, College of Business, MBA Program, Fort Collins, CO 80523-1201. Offers MBA, MBA/DVM. *Accreditation:* AACSB. *Program availability:* Part-time, evening/weekend. *Students:* 37 full-time (14 women), 9 part-time (1 woman); includes 12 minority (1 Black or African American, non-Hispanic/Latino; 1 American Indian or Alaska Native, non-Hispanic/Latino; 3 Asian, non-Hispanic/Latino; 4 Hispanic/Latino; 3 Two or more races, non-Hispanic/Latino). Average age 33. 43 applicants, 88% accepted, 30 enrolled. In 2016, 31 master's awarded. *Entrance requirements:* For master's, minimum undergraduate GPA of 3.0, 4 years of professional work experience, official transcripts, three professional recommendations, statement of purpose, resume. Additional exam requirements/recommendations for international students: Required—TOEFL (minimum score 86 iBT); Recommended—IELTS (minimum score 6.5), TSE (minimum score 58). *Application deadline:* For fall admission, 6/1 for domestic and international students. Applications are processed on a rolling basis. Application fee: $60 ($70 for international students). Electronic applications accepted. *Expenses:* Contact institution. *Financial support:* Career-related internships or fieldwork and scholarships/grants available. Support available to part-time students. Financial award application deadline: 2/15; financial award applicants required to submit FAFSA. *Faculty research:* Financial markets and investments; supply chain management; business intelligence; consumer behavior; business economics, financial reporting and analysis. *Unit head:* Dr. Sanjay Ramchander, Associate Dean of Academic Programs, 970-491-5027, E-mail: cobgradinfo@colostate.edu. *Application contact:* Graduate Program Admissions, 970-491-5027, E-mail: gradadmissions@business.colostate.edu.
Website: https://biz.colostate.edu/Academics/Graduate-Programs/Master-of-Business-Administration/Professional-MBA

Colorado State University, College of Business, Online MBA Program, Fort Collins, CO 80523. Offers MBA. *Program availability:* Part-time, 100% online, blended/hybrid learning. *Students:* 718 part-time (231 women); includes 145 minority (21 Black or African American, non-Hispanic/Latino; 4 American Indian or Alaska Native, non-Hispanic/Latino; 46 Asian, non-Hispanic/Latino; 56 Hispanic/Latino; 3 Native Hawaiian or other Pacific Islander, non-Hispanic/Latino; 15 Two or more races, non-Hispanic/Latino), 5 international. Average age 37. 167 applicants, 92% accepted, 113 enrolled. In 2016, 289 master's awarded. *Degree requirements:* For master's, thesis or alternative. *Entrance requirements:* For master's, statement of purpose, resume, 3 professional recommendations, official transcripts, minimum of 4 years' professional work experience. Additional exam requirements/recommendations for international students: Required—TOEFL (minimum score 86 iBT); Recommended—IELTS (minimum score 6.5), TSE (minimum score 58). *Application deadline:* For fall admission, 7/1 priority date for domestic and international students; for winter admission, 12/1 priority date for domestic and international students; for summer admission, 4/1 priority date for domestic and international students. Applications are processed on a rolling basis. Application fee: $60 ($70 for international students). Electronic applications accepted. *Expenses:* $946 per credit hour. *Financial support:* Scholarships/grants, unspecified assistantships, and corporate tuition discounts available. Financial award application deadline: 2/15; financial award applicants required to submit FAFSA. *Faculty research:* Managing human capital; fundamentals of firm valuation; digital marketing and strategic selling; fundamentals of real estate finance; international business. *Unit head:* Dr. Sanjay Ramchander, Associate Dean of Academic Programs, 970-491-5027, E-mail: cobgradinfo@colostate.edu. *Application contact:* Graduate Program Admissions, 970-491-5027, E-mail: gradadmissions@business.colostate.edu.
Website: https://biz.colostate.edu/Academics/Graduate-Programs/Master-of-Business-Administration

Colorado State University–Global Campus, Graduate Programs, Greenwood Village, CO 80111. Offers criminal justice and law enforcement administration (MS); education leadership (MS); finance (MS); healthcare administration and management (MS); human resource management (MHRM); information technology management (MITM); international management (MS); management (MS); organizational leadership (MS); professional accounting (MPA); project management (MS); teaching and learning (MS). *Accreditation:* ACBSP. *Program availability:* Online learning.

Colorado State University–Pueblo, Malik and Seeme Hasan School of Business, Pueblo, CO 81001-4901. Offers MBA. *Accreditation:* AACSB. *Program availability:* Part-time, evening/weekend. *Degree requirements:* For master's, thesis optional. *Entrance requirements:* For master's, GMAT, minimum GPA of 3.0. Additional exam requirements/recommendations for international students: Required—TOEFL (minimum score 550 paper-based). *Faculty research:* Total quality management, leadership, small business studies, case research and writing.

Colorado Technical University Aurora, Programs in Business Administration and Management, Aurora, CO 80014. Offers accounting (MBA); business administration (MBA); business administration and management (EMBA); finance (MBA); human resource management (MBA); marketing (MBA); mediation and dispute resolution (MBA); operations management (MBA); project management (MBA); technology management (MBA). *Program availability:* Part-time, evening/weekend. *Degree requirements:* For master's, thesis or alternative. *Entrance requirements:* For master's, minimum undergraduate GPA of 3.0, resume.

Colorado Technical University Colorado Springs, Graduate Studies, Program in Management, Colorado Springs, CO 80907. Offers accounting (MBA, MSA); business administration (MBA); finance (MBA); human resources management (MBA); logistics/supply chain management (MBA); management (DM); marketing (MBA); mediation and dispute resolution (MBA); operations management (MBA); project management (MBA); technology management (MBA). *Accreditation:* ACBSP. *Program availability:* Part-time, evening/weekend, online learning. *Degree requirements:* For master's, thesis or alternative; for doctorate, thesis/dissertation. *Entrance requirements:* For doctorate, minimum graduate GPA of 3.0, 5 years of related work experience. *Faculty research:* Sexual harassment, performance evaluation, critical thinking.

Columbia College, Master of Business Administration Program, Columbia, MO 65216-0002. Offers accounting (MBA); human resources (MBA). *Program availability:* Part-time, evening/weekend, 100% online, blended/hybrid learning. *Faculty:* 5 full-time (2 women), 39 part-time/adjunct (15 women). *Students:* 76 full-time (51 women), 415 part-time (240 women); includes 109 minority (60 Black or African American, non-Hispanic/Latino; 3 American Indian or Alaska Native, non-Hispanic/Latino; 7 Asian, non-Hispanic/Latino; 25 Hispanic/Latino; 2 Native Hawaiian or other Pacific Islander, non-Hispanic/Latino; 12 Two or more races, non-Hispanic/Latino), 26 international. Average age 36. 121 applicants, 90% accepted, 63 enrolled. In 2016, 194 master's awarded. *Entrance requirements:* For master's, 3 letters of recommendation, minimum cumulative undergraduate GPA of 3.0, resume, goal statement. Additional exam requirements/recommendations for international students: Required—TOEFL (minimum score 550 paper-based; 79 iBT). *Application deadline:* For fall admission, 8/9 priority date for domestic and international students; for spring admission, 12/27 priority date for domestic and international students. Applications are processed on a rolling basis. Application fee: $55. Electronic applications accepted. *Expenses:* Contact institution. *Financial support:* Federal Work-Study and scholarships/grants available. Financial award application deadline: 3/1; financial award applicants required to submit FAFSA. *Unit head:* Dr. Shanda Traiser, Dean, School of Business Administration, 573-875-7561, Fax: 573-876-4493, E-mail: strasier@ccis.edu. *Application contact:* Stephanie Johnson, Director of Admissions, 573-875-7352, Fax: 573-875-7506, E-mail: sjohnson@ccis.edu.
Website: http://www.ccis.edu/graduate/academics/degrees.asp?MBA

Columbia Southern University, DBA Program, Orange Beach, AL 36561. Offers DBA. *Program availability:* Part-time, evening/weekend, online learning. *Entrance requirements:* For doctorate, 2 years professional experience, relevant academic experience. Electronic applications accepted.

Columbia Southern University, MBA Program, Orange Beach, AL 36561. Offers finance (MBA); health care management (MBA); human resource management (MBA); marketing (MBA); project management (MBA); public administration (MBA). *Program availability:* Part-time, evening/weekend, online learning. *Entrance requirements:* For master's, bachelor's degree from accredited/approved institution. Additional exam requirements/recommendations for international students: Required—TOEFL. Electronic applications accepted.

Columbia University, Graduate School of Business, Berkeley-Columbia Executive MBA Program, New York, NY 10027. Offers EMBA. Offered jointly with University of California, Berkeley. *Program availability:* Part-time. *Entrance requirements:* For master's, GMAT, 2 letters of reference, interview, minimum 5 years of work experience, transcripts, resume, employee support, personal essays. Additional exam requirements/recommendations for international students: Required—TOEFL (minimum score 570 paper-based; 68 iBT). Electronic applications accepted. *Expenses:* Contact institution.

Columbia University, Graduate School of Business, Doctoral Program in Business, New York, NY 10027. Offers business (PhD), including accounting, decision, risk, and operations, finance and economics, management, marketing. *Accreditation:* AACSB. *Degree requirements:* For doctorate, comprehensive exam, thesis/dissertation, major field exam, research paper, thesis proposal. *Entrance requirements:* For doctorate, GMAT or GRE (finance), 2 letters of reference, resume. Additional exam requirements/recommendations for international students: Required—TOEFL. Electronic applications accepted. *Expenses:* Contact institution. *Faculty research:* Human decision making and behavioral research; real estate market and mortgage defaults; financial crisis and corporate governance; international business; security analysis and accounting.

Columbia University, Graduate School of Business, Executive MBA Global Program, New York, NY 10027. Offers EMBA. Program offered jointly with London Business School. *Entrance requirements:* For master's, GMAT, 2 letters of reference, interview, minimum 5 years of work experience, curriculum vitae or resume, employer support. Additional exam requirements/recommendations for international students: Recommended—TOEFL, IELTS. Electronic applications accepted. *Expenses:* Contact institution.

Columbia University, Graduate School of Business, Executive MBA Program, New York, NY 10027. Offers EMBA. *Entrance requirements:* For master's, GMAT, minimum 5 years of work experience, 2 letters of reference, interview, company sponsorship. Additional exam requirements/recommendations for international students: Recommended—TOEFL. Electronic applications accepted. *Expenses:* Contact institution. *Faculty research:* Human decision making and behavioral research; real estate market and mortgage defaults; financial crisis and corporate governance; international business; and security analysis and accounting.

Columbia University, Graduate School of Business, MBA Program, New York, NY 10027. Offers accounting (MBA); decision, risk, and operations (MBA); entrepreneurship (MBA); finance and economics (MBA); healthcare and pharmaceutical management (MBA); human resource management (MBA); international business (MBA); leadership and ethics (MBA); management (MBA); marketing (MBA); media (MBA); private equity (MBA); real estate (MBA); social enterprise (MBA); value investing (MBA); DDS/MBA; JD/MBA; MBA/MIA; MBA/MPH; MBA/MS; MD/MBA. *Entrance requirements:* For master's, GMAT, 2 letters of recommendation. Additional exam requirements/recommendations for international students: Required—TOEFL. Electronic applications accepted. *Expenses:* Contact institution. *Faculty research:* Human decision making and behavioral research; real estate market and mortgage defaults; financial crisis and corporate governance; international business; security analysis and accounting.

Columbus State University, Graduate Studies, Turner College of Business, Columbus, GA 31907-5645. Offers applied computer science (MS), including informational assurance, modeling and simulation, software development; business administration (MBA); human resource management (Certificate); information systems security (Certificate); modeling and simulation (Certificate); organizational leadership (MS), including human resource management, leader development, servant leadership; servant leadership (Certificate). *Accreditation:* AACSB. *Program availability:* Part-time, evening/weekend, 100% online, blended/hybrid learning. *Faculty:* 10 full-time (3 women). *Students:* 93 full-time (21 women), 132 part-time (47 women); includes 69 minority (36 Black or African American, non-Hispanic/Latino; 1 American Indian or Alaska Native, non-Hispanic/Latino; 11 Asian, non-Hispanic/Latino; 14 Hispanic/Latino; 7 Two or more races, non-Hispanic/Latino), 35 international. Average age 31. 279 applicants, 44% accepted, 64 enrolled. In 2016, 106 master's awarded. *Entrance requirements:* For master's, GMAT, GRE, minimum undergraduate GPA of 2.75, letters of recommendation. Additional exam requirements/recommendations for international students: Required—TOEFL (minimum score 550 paper-based; 79 iBT). *Application deadline:* For fall admission, 6/30 for domestic students, 5/1 for international students;

for spring admission, 11/1 for domestic and international students; for summer admission, 3/1 for domestic and international students. Applications are processed on a rolling basis. Application fee: $50. Electronic applications accepted. *Expenses:* Contact institution. *Financial support:* In 2016–17, 18 students received support, including 16 research assistantships (averaging $3,000 per year); Federal Work-Study also available. Financial award application deadline: 5/1; financial award applicants required to submit FAFSA. *Unit head:* Dr. Linda U. Hadley, Dean, 706-507-8153, Fax: 706-568-2184, E-mail: hadley_linda@columbusstate.edu. *Application contact:* Kristin Williams, Director of International and Graduate Recruitment, 706-507-8848, Fax: 706-568-5091, E-mail: thornton_katie@colstate.edu.
Website: http://turner.columbusstate.edu/

Concordia University, School of Graduate Studies, John Molson School of Business, Montreal, QC H3H 0A1, Canada. Offers administration (M Sc), including finance, management, marketing; business administration (MBA, PhD, Certificate, Diploma); executive business administration (EMBA); supply chain management (MSCM). PhD program offered jointly with HEC Montreal, McGill University, and Université du Québec à Montréal. *Program availability:* Part-time, evening/weekend. *Degree requirements:* For master's, one foreign language, thesis (for some programs), research project; for doctorate, one foreign language, thesis/dissertation; for other advanced degree, one foreign language. *Entrance requirements:* For master's, GMAT, minimum 2 years of work experience (for MBA); letters of recommendation, bachelor's degree from recognized university with minimum GPA of 3.0, curriculum vitae; for doctorate, GMAT (minimum score of 600), official transcripts, curriculum vitae, 3 letters of reference, statement of purpose; for other advanced degree, minimum GPA of 2.7, 2 letters of reference, statement of purpose, resume. Additional exam requirements/recommendations for international students: Required—TOEFL (minimum score 90 iBT), IELTS (minimum score 7). Electronic applications accepted. *Expenses:* Contact institution. *Faculty research:* General business, capital markets, international business.

Concordia University, School of Management, Portland, OR 97211-6099. Offers MBA. *Accreditation:* ACBSP. *Program availability:* Evening/weekend. *Degree requirements:* For master's, thesis optional. *Entrance requirements:* For master's, GMAT or professional portfolio, minimum GPA of 3.0, 2 letters of recommendation, 5 years of work experience, resume. Additional exam requirements/recommendations for international students: Required—TOEFL (minimum score 525 paper-based). *Faculty research:* Leadership characteristics in internships, marketing of MBA programs, entrepreneurship.

Concordia University Chicago, College of Graduate and Innovative Programs, Program in Business Administration, River Forest, IL 60305-1499. Offers MBA.

Concordia University Irvine, School of Business, Irvine, CA 92612-3299. Offers business administration (MBA). *Program availability:* Part-time, evening/weekend. *Degree requirements:* For master's, capstone project or thesis. *Entrance requirements:* For master's, official college transcript(s), signed statement of intent, resume, two references, interview (MBA); passport photo, photocopies of valid U.S. passport, and college diploma (MAIS). Additional exam requirements/recommendations for international students: Required—TOEFL. Electronic applications accepted. *Expenses:* Contact institution.

Concordia University, St. Paul, College of Business, St. Paul, MN 55104-5494. Offers business administration (MBA), including cyber-security leadership; business and organizational leadership (MBA); health care management (MBA); human resource management (MA); leadership and management (MA); strategic communication management (MA). *Accreditation:* ACBSP. *Program availability:* Part-time, evening/weekend, 100% online, blended/hybrid learning. *Faculty:* 12 full-time (4 women), 36 part-time/adjunct (15 women). *Students:* 462 full-time (288 women), 25 part-time (16 women); includes 123 minority (59 Black or African American, non-Hispanic/Latino; 1 American Indian or Alaska Native, non-Hispanic/Latino; 36 Asian, non-Hispanic/Latino; 10 Hispanic/Latino; 1 Native Hawaiian or other Pacific Islander, non-Hispanic/Latino; 16 Two or more races, non-Hispanic/Latino), 28 international. Average age 34. 269 applicants, 73% accepted, 137 enrolled. In 2016, 192 master's awarded. *Degree requirements:* For master's, thesis (for some programs). *Entrance requirements:* For master's, official transcripts from regionally-accredited institution stating the conferral of a bachelor's degree with minimum cumulative GPA of 3.0; personal statement; professional resume. Additional exam requirements/recommendations for international students: Recommended—TOEFL (minimum score 547 paper-based; 78 iBT), IELTS (minimum score 6). *Application deadline:* For fall admission, 8/1 for domestic and international students; for spring admission, 12/1 for domestic and international students; for summer admission, 5/1 for domestic and international students. Applications are processed on a rolling basis. Application fee: $50. Electronic applications accepted. *Expenses:* Contact institution. *Financial support:* In 2016–17, 259 students received support. Scholarships/grants and unspecified assistantships available. Financial award applicants required to submit FAFSA. *Faculty research:* Alternative dispute resolution, franchising, entrepreneurship, applied business ethics, strategic leadership development. *Unit head:* Dr. Kevin Hall, Dean, 651-603-6165, Fax: 651-641-8807, E-mail: khall@csp.edu. *Application contact:* Kimberly Craig, Associate Vice President, Cohort Enrollment Management, 651-603-6223, Fax: 651-603-6320, E-mail: craig@csp.edu.

Concordia University Wisconsin, Graduate Programs, School of Business Administration, Mequon, WI 53097-2402. Offers MBA, MS. *Unit head:* Dr. Marsha K. Konz, Dean of Graduate Studies, 262-243-4253, Fax: 262-243-4428, E-mail: marsha.konz@cuw.edu. *Application contact:* Mary Eberhardt, Graduate Admissions, 262-243-4551, Fax: 262-243-4428, E-mail: mary.eberhardt@cuw.edu.

Copenhagen Business School, Graduate Programs, Copenhagen, Denmark. Offers business administration (Exec MBA, MBA, PhD); business administration and information systems (M Sc); business, language and culture (M Sc); economics and business administration (M Sc); health management (MHM); international business and politics (M Sc); public administration (MPA); shipping and logistics (Exec MBA); technology, market and organization (MBA).

Corban University, Graduate School, The Corban MBA, Salem, OR 97301-9392. Offers management (MBA); non-profit management (MBA). *Program availability:* Online learning.

Cornell University, Graduate School, Graduate Field of Management, Ithaca, NY 14853. Offers accounting (PhD); finance (PhD); marketing (PhD); organizational behavior (PhD); production and operations management (PhD). *Accreditation:* AACSB. *Degree requirements:* For doctorate, comprehensive exam, thesis/dissertation. *Entrance requirements:* For doctorate, GMAT or GRE General Test. Additional exam requirements/recommendations for international students: Required—TOEFL (minimum score 600 paper-based; 77 iBT). Electronic applications accepted. *Expenses:* Contact institution. *Faculty research:* Operations and manufacturing.

Cornell University, Samuel Curtis Johnson Graduate School of Management, Ithaca, NY 14853. Offers business administration (Exec MBA); management (MBA, PhD); management - accounting (MPS); JD/MBA; M Eng/MBA; MBA/MD; MBA/MHA; MBA/MILR; MBA/MPS. *Accreditation:* AACSB. *Faculty:* 62 full-time (17 women), 65 part-time/adjunct (8 women). *Students:* 580 full-time (174 women); includes 139 minority (18 Black or African American, non-Hispanic/Latino; 2 American Indian or Alaska Native, non-Hispanic/Latino; 77 Asian, non-Hispanic/Latino; 26 Hispanic/Latino; 16 Two or more races, non-Hispanic/Latino), 191 international. Average age 28. 1,960 applicants, 27% accepted, 279 enrolled. *Entrance requirements:* For master's, GMAT or GRE, resume, two essays, two recommendations. Additional exam requirements/recommendations for international students: Required—TOEFL. *Application deadline:* For fall admission, 10/5 for domestic and international students; for winter admission, 11/15 for domestic and international students; for spring admission, 1/10 for domestic and international students; for summer admission, 3/15 for domestic and international students. Application fee: $200. Electronic applications accepted. *Expenses:* $61,584 per year. *Financial support:* Fellowships, research assistantships, career-related internships or fieldwork, Federal Work-Study, institutionally sponsored loans, and tuition waivers (full and partial) available. Financial award applicants required to submit FAFSA. *Unit head:* Dr. Mark Nelson, Dean, 607-255-6418, E-mail: dean@johnson.cornell.edu. *Application contact:* Admissions Office, 800-847-2082, Fax: 607-255-0065, E-mail: mba@johnson.cornell.edu.
Website: http://www.johnson.cornell.edu

Cornerstone University, Graduate Programs, Grand Rapids, MI 49525-5897. Offers business administration (MBA); education (MA Ed); management (MSM); teaching English to speakers of other languages (MA, Graduate Certificate). Programs also offered at Holland, Kalamazoo, and Troy, MI campuses. *Program availability:* Part-time, online learning. *Degree requirements:* For master's, comprehensive exam (for some programs), thesis (for some programs). *Entrance requirements:* For master's, minimum GPA of 2.5, 2 letters of reference. Additional exam requirements/recommendations for international students: Required—TOEFL (minimum score 575 paper-based). Electronic applications accepted.

Creighton University, Graduate School, Heider College of Business, Omaha, NE 68178-0001. Offers accounting (MAC); business administration (MBA); business intelligence and analytics (MS); finance (M Fin); JD/MBA; MBA/MSAPM; MD/MBA; Pharm D/MBA. *Accreditation:* AACSB. *Program availability:* Part-time, evening/weekend, 100% online, blended/hybrid learning. *Faculty:* 33 full-time (10 women), 22 part-time/adjunct (3 women). *Students:* 41 full-time (13 women), 262 part-time (79 women); includes 24 minority (16 Black or African American, non-Hispanic/Latino; 3 Asian, non-Hispanic/Latino; 1 Hispanic/Latino; 2 Native Hawaiian or other Pacific Islander, non-Hispanic/Latino; 2 Two or more races, non-Hispanic/Latino), 21 international. Average age 32. 189 applicants, 73% accepted, 74 enrolled. In 2016, 172 master's awarded. *Degree requirements:* For master's, thesis optional. *Entrance requirements:* For master's, GMAT, resume, 2 letters of recommendation. Additional exam requirements/recommendations for international students: Required—TOEFL (minimum score 90 iBT). *Application deadline:* For fall admission, 7/1 priority date for domestic students, 3/1 for international students; for winter admission, 10/1 priority date for domestic students, 7/1 for international students; for spring admission, 4/1 priority date for domestic students, 10/1 for international students; for summer admission, 5/1 for domestic and international students. Applications are processed on a rolling basis. Application fee: $50. Electronic applications accepted. *Expenses:* Contact institution. *Financial support:* In 2016–17, 10 fellowships with partial tuition reimbursements (averaging $8,448 per year) were awarded; career-related internships or fieldwork, tuition waivers (partial), and unspecified assistantships also available. Financial award application deadline: 3/1. *Faculty research:* Small business issues, economics. *Unit head:* Dr. Deborah Wells, Associate Dean for Graduate Programs, 402-280-2841, E-mail: deborahwells@creighton.edu. *Application contact:* Chris Karasek, Assistant Dean, 402-280-2829, Fax: 402-280-2172, E-mail: chriskarasek@creighton.edu.
Website: http://business.creighton.edu

Culver-Stockton College, MBA Program, Canton, MO 63435-1299. Offers accounting and finance (MBA).

Cumberland University, Program in Business Administration, Lebanon, TN 37087. Offers MBA. *Accreditation:* ACBSP. *Program availability:* Part-time, evening/weekend. *Degree requirements:* For master's, comprehensive exam. *Entrance requirements:* For master's, GMAT or GRE General Test, 3 letters of recommendation. Additional exam requirements/recommendations for international students: Required—TOEFL (minimum score 500 paper-based). *Expenses:* Contact institution.

Curry College, Graduate Studies, Program in Business Administration, Milton, MA 02186-9984. Offers business administration (MBA); finance (Certificate). *Program availability:* Part-time, evening/weekend. *Degree requirements:* For master's, capstone applied project. *Entrance requirements:* For master's, resume, recommendations, interview, written statement. Additional exam requirements/recommendations for international students: Required—TOEFL (minimum score 550 paper-based; 80 iBT). *Expenses:* Contact institution.

Daemen College, Program in Executive Leadership and Change, Amherst, NY 14226-3592. Offers business (MS); health professions (MS); not-for-profit organizations (MS). *Program availability:* Part-time, evening/weekend. *Degree requirements:* For master's, thesis, cohort learning sequence (2 years for weekend cohort; 3 years for weeknight cohort). *Entrance requirements:* For master's, 2 letters of recommendation, interview, goal statement, official transcripts, resume. Additional exam requirements/recommendations for international students: Required—TOEFL (minimum score 500 paper-based; 63 iBT), IELTS (minimum score 5.5). Electronic applications accepted.

Dakota State University, College of Business and Information Systems, Madison, SD 57042-1799. Offers analytics (MSA); applied computer science (MSACS); banking security (Graduate Certificate); business analytics (Graduate Certificate); cyber security (D Sc); ethical hacking (Graduate Certificate); general management (MBA); health informatics (MSHI); information assurance and computer security (MSIA); information systems (MSIS, D Sc IS); information technology (Graduate Certificate). *Accreditation:* ACBSP. *Program availability:* Part-time, evening/weekend, 100% online, blended/hybrid learning. *Degree requirements:* For master's, comprehensive exam, thesis optional, examination, integrative project; for doctorate, comprehensive exam, thesis/dissertation, portfolio. *Entrance requirements:* For master's, GRE General Test, demonstration of information systems skills, minimum GPA of 2.7; for doctorate, GRE General Test, demonstration of information systems skills; for Graduate Certificate, GMAT. Additional exam requirements/recommendations for international students: Required—PTE (minimum score 53), TOEFL (minimum score 550 paper-based, 79 iBT) or IELTS (6.5). *Application deadline:* For fall admission, 6/15 for domestic students, 4/15 for international students; for spring admission, 11/15 for domestic students, 9/15 priority date for international students; for summer admission, 4/15 for domestic and international students. Applications are processed on a rolling basis. Application fee: $35. *Expenses:* Contact institution. *Financial support:* Fellowships with partial tuition reimbursements, research assistantships with partial tuition reimbursements, teaching assistantships with partial tuition reimbursements, career-related internships or fieldwork, Federal Work-Study, scholarships/grants, and unspecified assistantships available. Support available to part-time students. Financial award applicants required to submit FAFSA. *Faculty research:* Data mining and analytics, biometrics and information assurance, decision support systems, health informatics, STEM education for K-12 teachers/students and underrepresented populations. *Unit head:* Mark Hawkes, Dean for Graduate Studies and Research, 605-256-5274, E-mail: mark.hawkes@dsu.edu.

Application contact: Erin Blankespoor, Senior Secretary, Office of Graduate Studies and Research, 605-256-5799, E-mail: erin.blankespoor@dsu.edu.
Website: http://dsu.edu/academics/colleges/college-of-business-and-information-systems

Dalhousie University, Faculty of Management, Centre for Advanced Management Education, Halifax, NS B3H 3J5, Canada. Offers financial services (MBA); information management (MIM); management (MPA); natural resources (MBA). *Program availability:* Part-time, online learning. *Entrance requirements:* For master's, GMAT, minimum GPA of 3.0, resume. Additional exam requirements/recommendations for international students: Required—TOEFL, IELTS, CANTEST, CAEL, or Michigan English Language Assessment Battery. Electronic applications accepted.

Dalhousie University, Faculty of Management, Rowe School of Business, Halifax, NS B3H 3J5, Canada. Offers business administration (MBA); financial services (MBA); LL B/MBA; MBA/MLIS. *Program availability:* Part-time. *Entrance requirements:* For master's, GMAT, letter of non-financial guarantee for non-Canadian students, resume, Corporate Residency Preference Form. Additional exam requirements/recommendations for international students: Required—TOEFL, IELTS, CANTEST, CAEL, or Michigan English Language Assessment Battery. Electronic applications accepted. *Faculty research:* International business, quantitative methods, operations research, MIS, marketing, finance.

Dalhousie University, Faculty of Management, School of Public Administration, Halifax, NS B3H 3J5, Canada. Offers management (MPA); public administration (MPA, GDPA); LL B/MPA; MLIS/MPA. *Program availability:* Part-time. *Entrance requirements:* For master's, GMAT. Additional exam requirements/recommendations for international students: Required—TOEFL, IELTS, CANTEST, CAEL, or Michigan English Language Assessment Battery. Electronic applications accepted. *Expenses:* Contact institution. *Faculty research:* Municipal management, policy and program management, environmental policy, economic and social policy, business and government.

Dallas Baptist University, College of Business, Business Administration Program, Dallas, TX 75211-9299. Offers accounting (MBA); business communication (MBA); conflict resolution management (MBA); entrepreneurship (MBA); finance (MBA); health care management (MBA); international business (MBA); leading the non-profit organization (MBA); management (MBA); management information systems (MBA); marketing (MBA); project management (MBA); technology and engineering management (MBA). *Accreditation:* ACBSP. *Program availability:* Part-time, evening/weekend, 100% online, blended/hybrid learning. *Application deadline:* Applications are processed on a rolling basis. Application fee: $25. Electronic applications accepted. Application fee is waived when completed online. *Expenses: Tuition:* Full-time $15,408; part-time $856 per credit hour. *Required fees:* $400 per semester. Tuition and fees vary according to course load and degree level. *Unit head:* Dr. Sandra Reid, Chair of Graduate Business Programs, 214-333-5280, E-mail: sandra@dbu.edu. *Application contact:* Bobby Soto, Director of Admissions, 214-333-5242, E-mail: graduate@dbu.edu.
Website: http://www3.dbu.edu/graduate/mba.asp

Dallas Baptist University, College of Business, Management Program, Dallas, TX 75211-9299. Offers conflict resolution management (MA); general management (MA, MS); health care management (MA); human resource management (MA); organizational communication (MA); performance management (MA); professional sales and management optimization (MA). *Program availability:* Part-time, evening/weekend, 100% online, blended/hybrid learning. *Application deadline:* Applications are processed on a rolling basis. Application fee: $25. Electronic applications accepted. Application fee is waived when completed online. *Expenses: Tuition:* Full-time $15,408; part-time $856 per credit hour. *Required fees:* $400 per semester. Tuition and fees vary according to course load and degree level. *Unit head:* Richard Nassar, Director, 214-333-5280, E-mail: richardn@dbu.edu. *Application contact:* Bobby Soto, Director of Admissions, 214-333-5242, E-mail: graduate@dbu.edu.
Website: http://www.dbu.edu/gsb/ma-in-management

Dallas Baptist University, Gary Cook School of Leadership, Program in Leadership Studies, Dallas, TX 75211-9299. Offers leadership studies (PhD), including business, general leadership, higher education, ministry. *Program availability:* Part-time. *Degree requirements:* For doctorate, thesis/dissertation. *Application deadline:* Applications are processed on a rolling basis. Application fee: $25. Electronic applications accepted. Application fee is waived when completed online. *Expenses: Tuition:* Full-time $15,408; part-time $856 per credit hour. *Required fees:* $400 per semester. Tuition and fees vary according to course load and degree level. *Unit head:* Dr. Jack Goodyear, Director, 214-333-5595, E-mail: jackg@dbu.edu. *Application contact:* Bobby Soto, Director of Admissions, 214-333-5242, E-mail: graduate@dbu.edu.
Website: http://www3.dbu.edu/leadership/phdLeadership.asp

Dallas Baptist University, Professional Development Program, Dallas, TX 75211-9299. Offers accounting (MA); church leadership (MA); communication (MA); counseling (MA); criminal justice (MA); English as a second language (MA); finance (MA); higher education (MA); leadership studies (MA); management (MA); management information systems (MA); marketing (MA); missions (MA); professional life coaching (MA); training and development (MA). *Program availability:* Part-time, evening/weekend, 100% online, blended/hybrid learning. *Application deadline:* Applications are processed on a rolling basis. Application fee: $25. Electronic applications accepted. Application fee is waived when completed online. *Expenses: Tuition:* Full-time $15,408; part-time $856 per credit hour. *Required fees:* $400 per semester. Tuition and fees vary according to course load and degree level. *Unit head:* Jared Ingram, Director, 214-333-5584, E-mail: jaredi@dbu.edu. *Application contact:* Bobby Soto, Director of Admissions, 214-333-5242, E-mail: graduate@dbu.edu.
Website: http://www3.dbu.edu/graduate/mapd.asp

Dartmouth College, Tuck School of Business at Dartmouth, Hanover, NH 03755-9000. Offers MBA, MBA/MPH, MD/MBA, PhD/MBA. MD/MBA offered with the Geisel School of Medicine; MPH/MBA with The Dartmouth Institute for Health Policy and Clinical Practice. *Accreditation:* AACSB. *Faculty:* 54 full-time (11 women). *Students:* 567 full-time (240 women); includes 111 minority (26 Black or African American, non-Hispanic/Latino; 5 American Indian or Alaska Native, non-Hispanic/Latino; 53 Asian, non-Hispanic/Latino; 22 Hispanic/Latino; 1 Native Hawaiian or other Pacific Islander, non-Hispanic/Latino; 4 Two or more races, non-Hispanic/Latino), 170 international. Average age 28. 2,623 applicants, 22% accepted, 285 enrolled. In 2016, 275 master's awarded. *Entrance requirements:* For master's, GMAT or GRE, 2 letters of recommendation, 2 essays, resume/curriculum vitae. Additional exam requirements/recommendations for international students: Required—TOEFL. *Application deadline:* For fall admission, 10/1 for domestic and international students; for winter admission, 11/1 for domestic and international students; for spring admission, 1/1 for domestic and international students; for summer admission, 4/1 for domestic and international students. Application fee: $250. Electronic applications accepted. *Financial support:* Institutionally sponsored loans and scholarships/grants available. Financial award application deadline: 4/1; financial award applicants required to submit FAFSA. *Faculty research:* Global production sourcing, economic effects of fracking, big data in retailing, cross-border mergers and acquisitions, employment and technological change. *Unit head:* Matthew J. Slaughter, Dean, 603-646-2460, E-mail: tuck.public.relations@tuck.dartmouth.edu. *Application contact:* Amy Mitson, Interim Co-Director, Admissions, 603-646-3162, Fax: 603-646-1441, E-mail: tuck.admissions@tuck.dartmouth.edu.
Website: http://www.tuck.dartmouth.edu

Davenport University, Sneden Graduate School, Grand Rapids, MI 49512. Offers accounting (MBA); business administration (EMBA); finance (MBA); health care management (MBA); human resources (MBA); information assurance (MS); public health (MPH); strategic management (MBA). *Program availability:* Evening/weekend. *Entrance requirements:* For master's, GMAT, minimum undergraduate GPA of 2.75. Additional exam requirements/recommendations for international students: Required—TOEFL. Electronic applications accepted. *Faculty research:* Leadership, management, marketing, organizational culture.

Defiance College, Program in Business Administration, Defiance, OH 43512-1610. Offers leadership (MBA). *Program availability:* Part-time, evening/weekend. *Degree requirements:* For master's, thesis. *Entrance requirements:* For master's, minimum GPA of 2.5. Additional exam requirements/recommendations for international students: Recommended—TOEFL. *Application deadline:* For fall admission, 8/1 for domestic and international students. Applications are processed on a rolling basis. Application fee: $25. Electronic applications accepted. *Expenses: Tuition:* Part-time $524 per credit hour. *Required fees:* $188 per semester. *Unit head:* Dr. Arif Sultan, Assistant Professor, 419-783-2431, Fax: 419-784-0426, E-mail: asultan@defiance.edu.
Website: http://www.defiance.edu/graduate-programs/mba-home.html

Delaware State University, Graduate Programs, College of Business, Program in Business Administration, Dover, DE 19901-2277. Offers MBA. *Accreditation:* AACSB. *Program availability:* Part-time, evening/weekend. *Degree requirements:* For master's, exit exam. *Entrance requirements:* For master's, GMAT (minimum score 400), minimum GPA of 3.0 in major, 2.75 overall. Additional exam requirements/recommendations for international students: Required—TOEFL (minimum score 550 paper-based). Electronic applications accepted. *Faculty research:* Managerial economics, strategic management, qualitative effort, finance.

Delaware Valley University, MBA Program, Doylestown, PA 18901-2697. Offers accounting (MBA); entrepreneurship (MBA); finance (MBA); food and agribusiness (MBA); general business (MBA); global executive leadership (MBA); human resource management (MBA); supply chain management (MBA). *Program availability:* Part-time, evening/weekend, online learning. *Entrance requirements:* For master's, minimum undergraduate GPA of 3.0. Electronic applications accepted. *Expenses:* Contact institution.

Delta State University, Graduate Programs, College of Business, Division of Management, Marketing, and Business Administration, Cleveland, MS 38733-0001. Offers business administration (MBA). *Accreditation:* ACBSP. *Program availability:* Part-time, evening/weekend. *Entrance requirements:* For master's, GMAT.

DePaul University, Kellstadt Graduate School of Business, Chicago, IL 60604. Offers accountancy (M Acc, MS, MSA); applied economics (MBA); banking (MBA); behavioral finance (MBA); brand and product management (MBA); business development (MBA); business information technology (MS); business strategy and decision-making (MBA); computational finance (MS); consumer insights (MBA); corporate finance (MBA); economic policy analysis (MS); entrepreneurship (MBA, MS); finance (MBA, MS); financial analysis (MBA); general business (MBA); health sector management (MBA); hospitality leadership (MBA); hospitality leadership and operational performance (MS); human resource management (MBA); human resources (MS); investment management (MBA); leadership and change management (MBA); management accounting (MBA); marketing (MBA, MS); marketing analysis (MS); marketing strategy and planning (MBA); operations management (MBA); organizational diversity (MBA); real estate (MS); real estate finance and investment (MBA); revenue management (MBA); sports management (MBA); strategic global marketing (MBA); strategy, execution and valuation (MBA); sustainable management (MBA, MS); taxation (MS); wealth management (MS); JD/MBA. *Accreditation:* AACSB. *Program availability:* Part-time, evening/weekend, online learning. *Entrance requirements:* For master's, GMAT, 2 letters of recommendation, resume, essay, official transcripts. Additional exam requirements/recommendations for international students: Required—TOEFL (minimum score 550 paper-based; 80 iBT). Electronic applications accepted. *Expenses:* Contact institution.

DeSales University, Division of Business, Center Valley, PA 18034-9568. Offers accounting (MBA); computer information systems (MBA); finance (MBA); health care systems management (MBA); human resources management (MBA); management (MBA); marketing (MBA); project management (MBA); self-design (MBA); supply chain management (MBA); DNP/MBA; MSN/MBA. *Accreditation:* ACBSP. *Program availability:* Part-time, evening/weekend, 100% online, blended/hybrid learning. *Faculty:* 12 full-time (4 women), 29 part-time/adjunct (5 women). *Students:* 73 full-time (38 women), 323 part-time (163 women); includes 59 minority (16 Black or African American, non-Hispanic/Latino; 23 Asian, non-Hispanic/Latino; 16 Hispanic/Latino; 4 Two or more races, non-Hispanic/Latino). Average age 37. 157 applicants, 87% accepted, 128 enrolled. In 2016, 115 master's awarded. *Entrance requirements:* For master's, GMAT (waived if undergraduate GPA is 3.0 or better), minimum GPA of 3.0 in undergraduate work, literacy in basic software, background or interest in the field of study, personal statement, 2 years of work experience. Additional exam requirements/recommendations for international students: Required—TOEFL. *Application deadline:* Applications are processed on a rolling basis. Application fee: $50. Electronic applications accepted. *Expenses:* Contact institution. *Financial support:* Applicants required to submit FAFSA. *Faculty research:* Quality improvement, executive development, productivity, cross-cultural managerial differences, leadership. *Unit head:* Dr. David M. Gilfoil, Director, MBA Program, 610-282-1100 Ext. 1828, Fax: 610-282-2869, E-mail: david.gilfoil@desales.edu. *Application contact:* Julia Ferraro, Director of Graduate Admissions, 610-282-1100 Ext. 1768, E-mail: gradadmissions@desales.edu.

DeVry College of New York–Midtown Manhattan Campus, Keller Graduate School of Management, New York, NY 10016. Offers M Acc, MAFM, MBA, MHRM, MISM, MNCM, MPA, MPM.

DeVry University, Keller Graduate School of Management, Atlanta, GA 30305-1543. Offers MAFM, MBA, MHRM, MISM, MNCM, MPA, MPM, Graduate Certificate. *Accreditation:* ACBSP.

DeVry University–Alpharetta Campus, Keller Graduate School of Management, Alpharetta, GA 30009. Offers MAFM, MBA, MHRM, MISM, MNCM, MPA, MPM. *Accreditation:* ACBSP.

DeVry University–Arlington Campus, Keller Graduate School of Management, Arlington, VA 22202. Offers M Acc, MAFM, MBA, MHRM, MISM, MPM. *Accreditation:* ACBSP. *Students:* 26 full-time (9 women), 208 part-time (94 women). In 2016, 123 master's awarded. *Application contact:* Student Application Contact, 703-414-4000.
Website: http://www.devry.edu

DeVry University–Charlotte Campus, Keller Graduate School of Management, Charlotte, NC 28273. Offers MAFM, MBA, MHRM, MISM, MNCM, MPA, MPM. *Accreditation:* ACBSP.

Business Administration and Management—General

DeVry University–Chesapeake Campus, Keller Graduate School of Management, Chesapeake, VA 23320. Offers MAFM, MBA, MHRM, MISM, MNCM, MPA, MPM. *Accreditation:* ACBSP.

DeVry University–Chicago Campus, Keller Graduate School of Management, Chicago, IL 60618. Offers M Acc, MAFM, MBA, MHRM, MISM, MPM. *Accreditation:* ACBSP. *Students:* 37 full-time (18 women), 117 part-time (50 women). In 2016, 58 master's awarded. *Application contact:* Student Application Contact, 773-929-8500.
Website: http://www.devry.edu

DeVry University–Chicago Loop Campus, Keller Graduate School of Management, Chicago, IL 60606. Offers MAFM, MBA, MHRM, MISM, MNCM, MPM. *Accreditation:* ACBSP.

DeVry University–Cincinnati Campus, Keller Graduate School of Management, Cincinnati, OH 45249. Offers MAFM, MBA, MHRM, MISM, MNCM, MPA, MPM. *Accreditation:* ACBSP.

DeVry University–Columbus Campus, Keller Graduate School of Management, Columbus, OH 43209. Offers MAFM, MBA, MHRM, MISM, MPM. *Accreditation:* ACBSP. *Students:* 26 full-time (16 women), 153 part-time (81 women). In 2016, 24 master's awarded. *Application contact:* Student Application Contact, 614-253-7291.

DeVry University–Decatur Campus, Keller Graduate School of Management, Decatur, GA 30030. Offers MAFM, MBA, MHRM, MISM, MNCM, MPA, MPM, MSA. *Accreditation:* ACBSP. *Students:* 29 full-time (15 women), 154 part-time (94 women). In 2016, 68 master's awarded. *Application contact:* Student Application Contact, 404-270-2700.

DeVry University–Folsom Campus, Graduate Programs, Folsom, CA 95630. Offers accounting (M Acc); accounting and financial management (MAFM); business administration (MBA); curriculum leadership (M Ed); educational leadership (M Ed); educational technology (M Ed); higher education leadership (M Ed); human resource management (MHRM); information systems management (MISM); network and communications management (MNCM); project management (MPM); public administration (MPA).

DeVry University–Fremont Campus, Keller Graduate School of Management, Fremont, CA 94555. Offers MAFM, MBA, MHRM, MISM, MNCM, MPA, MPM. *Accreditation:* ACBSP.

DeVry University–Ft. Washington Campus, Keller Graduate School of Management, Fort Washington, PA 19034. Offers MAFM, MBA, MHRM, MISM, MNCM, MPA, MPM. *Accreditation:* ACBSP.

DeVry University–Henderson Campus, Keller Graduate School of Management, Henderson, NV 89074. Offers MAFM, MBA, MHRM, MISM, MNCM, MPA, MPM. *Accreditation:* ACBSP.

DeVry University–Irving Campus, Keller Graduate School of Management, Irving, TX 75063. Offers M Acc, MAFM, MBA, MHRM, MISM, MPM. *Accreditation:* ACBSP. *Students:* 29 full-time (14 women), 132 part-time (63 women). In 2016, 102 master's awarded. *Application contact:* Student Application Contact, 972-929-6777.

DeVry University–Jacksonville Campus, Keller Graduate School of Management, Jacksonville, FL 32256. Offers MAFM, MBA, MHRM, MISM, MNCM, MPA, MPM. *Accreditation:* ACBSP.

DeVry University–Long Beach Campus, Keller Graduate School of Management, Long Beach, CA 90806. Offers MAFM, MBA, MHRM, MISM, MNCM, MPA, MPM. *Accreditation:* ACBSP.

DeVry University–Miramar Campus, Keller Graduate School of Management, Miramar, FL 33027. Offers MAFM, MBA, MHRM, MISM, MPM, MSA. *Students:* 42 full-time (19 women), 118 part-time (57 women). In 2016, 76 master's awarded. *Application contact:* Student Application Contact, 954-499-9775.

DeVry University–Morrisville Campus, Keller Graduate School of Management, Morrisville, NC 27560. Offers MBA, MHRM, MISM, MNCM, MPA, MPM. *Accreditation:* ACBSP.

DeVry University–Nashville Campus, Keller Graduate School of Management, Nashville, TN 37211. Offers MAFM, MBA, MHRM, MISM, MNCM, MPA, MPM. *Accreditation:* ACBSP.

DeVry University–North Brunswick Campus, Keller Graduate School of Management, North Brunswick, NJ 08902. Offers MBA. *Accreditation:* ACBSP. *Students:* 22 full-time (8 women), 75 part-time (32 women). In 2016, 48 master's awarded.

DeVry University Online, Keller Graduate School of Management, Addison, IL 60101. Offers M Acc, MAFM, MBA, MHRM, MISM, MNCM, MPA, MPM. *Students:* 451 full-time (271 women), 3,007 part-time (1,854 women). In 2016, 1,519 master's awarded. *Application contact:* Student Application Contact, 877-496-9050.

DeVry University–Orlando Campus, Keller Graduate School of Management, Orlando, FL 32819. Offers MAFM, MBA, MHRM, MISM, MPA, MPM, MSA. *Students:* 42 full-time (19 women), 187 part-time (93 women). In 2016, 123 master's awarded. *Application contact:* Student Application Contact, 407-345-2800.

DeVry University–Phoenix Campus, Keller Graduate School of Management, Phoenix, AZ 85021. Offers MAFM, MBA, MISM, MPM, MSA. *Students:* 14 full-time (3 women), 86 part-time (38 women). In 2016, 31 master's awarded. *Application contact:* Student Application Contact, 602-749-7301.
Website: http://www.devry.edu

DeVry University–Pomona Campus, Keller Graduate School of Management, Pomona, CA 91768. Offers MAFM, MBA, MHRM, MISM, MPM, MSA. *Students:* 37 full-time (14 women), 143 part-time (66 women). In 2016, 96 master's awarded. *Application contact:* Student Application Contact, 909-622-8866.

DeVry University–San Diego Campus, Keller Graduate School of Management, San Diego, CA 92108. Offers MAFM, MBA, MHRM, MISM, MNCM, MPA, MPM, Graduate Certificate. *Accreditation:* ACBSP.

DeVry University–Seven Hills Campus, Keller Graduate School of Management, Seven Hills, OH 44131. Offers MAFM, MBA, MHRM, MISM, MNCM, MPA, MPM, Graduate Certificate. *Accreditation:* ACBSP.

DeVry University–Tinley Park Campus, Keller Graduate School of Management, Tinley Park, IL 60477. Offers MAFM, MBA, MHRM, MISM, MNCM, MPA, MPM. *Accreditation:* ACBSP.

Doane University, Program in Management, Crete, NE 68333-2430. Offers MA. *Program availability:* Part-time, evening/weekend. *Faculty:* 3 full-time (2 women), 21 part-time/adjunct (9 women). *Students:* 109 full-time (64 women), 56 part-time (33 women); includes 27 minority (8 Black or African American, non-Hispanic/Latino; 2 American Indian or Alaska Native, non-Hispanic/Latino; 3 Asian, non-Hispanic/Latino; 13 Hispanic/Latino; 1 Two or more races, non-Hispanic/Latino), 2 international. Average age 36. In 2016, 69 master's awarded. *Degree requirements:* For master's, thesis. *Entrance requirements:* For master's, minimum GPA of 3.0. Additional exam requirements/recommendations for international students: Required—TOEFL. *Application deadline:* Applications are processed on a rolling basis. Application fee: $25. Electronic applications accepted. *Expenses:* Contact institution. *Financial support:* Application deadline: 6/1; applicants required to submit FAFSA. *Unit head:* Larry Hughes, Acting Dean, 880-333-6263, E-mail: larry.hughes@doane.edu. *Application contact:* Kerry Fina, Advisor for Master of Arts in Management, 402-466-4774, Fax: 404-466-4228, E-mail: kerry.fina@doane.edu.

Dominican College, MBA Program, Orangeburg, NY 10962-1210. Offers accounting (MBA); healthcare management (MBA); management (MBA). *Program availability:* Part-time, evening/weekend. *Faculty:* 9 full-time (2 women), 7 part-time/adjunct (1 woman). *Students:* 10 full-time (6 women), 22 part-time (11 women); includes 16 minority (9 Black or African American, non-Hispanic/Latino; 3 Asian, non-Hispanic/Latino; 3 Hispanic/Latino; 1 Two or more races, non-Hispanic/Latino), 1 international. In 2016, 16 master's awarded. *Entrance requirements:* For master's, GMAT, 2 letters of recommendation. Additional exam requirements/recommendations for international students: Required—TOEFL (minimum score 550 paper-based; 90 iBT). *Application deadline:* Applications are processed on a rolling basis. Application fee: $50. Electronic applications accepted. *Expenses:* Contact institution. *Financial support:* Application deadline: 2/1; applicants required to submit FAFSA. *Unit head:* Ken Mias, MBA Director, 845-848-4102, E-mail: ken.mias@dc.edu. *Application contact:* Christina Lifshey, Assistant Director of Graduate Admissions, 845-848-7908, Fax: 845-365-3150, E-mail: admissions@dc.edu.

Dominican University, Brennan School of Business, River Forest, IL 60305-1099. Offers MBA, MSA, JD/MBA, MBA/MLIS, MBA/MSW. JD/MBA offered jointly with John Marshall Law School. *Accreditation:* AACSB. *Program availability:* Part-time, evening/weekend, 100% online, blended/hybrid learning. *Faculty:* 22 full-time (9 women), 13 part-time/adjunct (5 women). *Students:* 91 full-time (71 women), 72 part-time (36 women); includes 25 minority (7 Black or African American, non-Hispanic/Latino; 1 American Indian or Alaska Native, non-Hispanic/Latino; 9 Asian, non-Hispanic/Latino; 7 Hispanic/Latino; 1 Native Hawaiian or other Pacific Islander, non-Hispanic/Latino), 24 international. Average age 29. 84 applicants, 93% accepted, 47 enrolled. In 2016, 85 master's awarded. *Entrance requirements:* For master's, GMAT. Additional exam requirements/recommendations for international students: Required—TOEFL (minimum score 550 paper-based; 79 iBT); Recommended—IELTS (minimum score 6). *Application deadline:* Applications are processed on a rolling basis. Application fee: $25. Electronic applications accepted. *Expenses:* $950 per credit hour. *Financial support:* Research assistantships, career-related internships or fieldwork, scholarships/grants, tuition waivers (partial), and unspecified assistantships available. Financial award application deadline: 3/1; financial award applicants required to submit FAFSA. *Faculty research:* Entrepreneurship, small business finance, business ethics, marketing strategy. *Unit head:* Dr. Roberto Curci, Dean, 708-524-6321, Fax: 708-524-6939, E-mail: rcurci@dom.edu. *Application contact:* Dr. Kathleen Odell, Associate Dean, Brennan School of Business, 708-524-6507, Fax: 708-524-6939, E-mail: mquilty@dom.edu.
Website: http://business.dom.edu/

Dominican University of California, Barowsky School of Business, San Rafael, CA 94901-2298. Offers global business (MBA); strategic leadership (MBA); sustainable enterprise (MBA). *Program availability:* Part-time, evening/weekend. *Degree requirements:* For master's, thesis, capstone (for MBA). *Entrance requirements:* For master's, minimum GPA of 3.0. Additional exam requirements/recommendations for international students: Required—TOEFL (minimum score 550 paper-based; 80 iBT), IELTS (minimum score 6.5). Electronic applications accepted. Application fee is waived when completed online. *Expenses:* Contact institution.

Drake University, College of Business and Public Administration, Des Moines, IA 50311-4516. Offers M Acc, MBA, MFM, MPA, JD/MBA, JD/MPA, Pharm D/MBA, Pharm D/MPA. *Program availability:* Part-time, evening/weekend. *Faculty:* 15 full-time (5 women). *Students:* 29 full-time (15 women), 199 part-time (103 women); includes 20 minority (6 Black or African American, non-Hispanic/Latino; 3 Asian, non-Hispanic/Latino; 8 Hispanic/Latino; 3 Two or more races, non-Hispanic/Latino), 12 international. Average age 32. 131 applicants, 76% accepted, 75 enrolled. In 2016, 166 master's awarded. *Degree requirements:* For master's, comprehensive exam (for some programs), thesis (for some programs), internships. *Entrance requirements:* For master's, GMAT, letters of recommendation, resume. Additional exam requirements/recommendations for international students: Required—TOEFL (minimum score 550 paper-based). *Application deadline:* For fall admission, 8/15 priority date for domestic students; for winter admission, 12/20 priority date for domestic students; for spring admission, 12/1 priority date for domestic students. Applications are processed on a rolling basis. Application fee: $25. Electronic applications accepted. *Expenses:* Contact institution. *Financial support:* Fellowships with tuition reimbursements, teaching assistantships, career-related internships or fieldwork, and institutionally sponsored loans available. Support available to part-time students. Financial award application deadline: 3/1; financial award applicants required to submit FAFSA. *Faculty research:* Venture capital, online commerce, professional ethics, process improvement, project management. *Unit head:* Dr. Terri Vaughan, Dean, 515-271-2871, Fax: 515-271-4518, E-mail: terri.vaughan@drake.edu. *Application contact:* Danette Kenne, Assistant Dean, 515-271-2188, Fax: 515-271-4518, E-mail: cbpa.gradprograms@drake.edu.
Website: http://www.drake.edu/cbpa/

Drexel University, LeBow College of Business, Program in Business Administration, Philadelphia, PA 19104-2875. Offers business administration (MBA, PhD, APC), including accounting (MBA, PhD), decision sciences (PhD), economics (MBA, PhD), finance (MBA, PhD), legal studies (MBA), management (MBA), marketing (MBA, PhD), organizational sciences (PhD), quantitative methods (MBA), strategic management (PhD). *Accreditation:* AACSB. *Program availability:* Part-time, evening/weekend, online learning. *Faculty:* 88 full-time (19 women), 11 part-time/adjunct (2 women). *Students:* 153 full-time (70 women), 388 part-time (168 women); includes 107 minority (31 Black or African American, non-Hispanic/Latino; 1 American Indian or Alaska Native, non-Hispanic/Latino; 48 Asian, non-Hispanic/Latino; 16 Hispanic/Latino; 11 Two or more races, non-Hispanic/Latino), 95 international. Average age 33. In 2016, 174 master's, 8 doctorates, 1 other advanced degree awarded. Terminal master's awarded for partial completion of doctoral program. *Entrance requirements:* For master's, GMAT, minimum GPA of 2.75; for doctorate, GMAT. Additional exam requirements/recommendations for international students: Required—TOEFL. *Application deadline:* For fall admission, 8/21 for domestic students; for spring admission, 3/5 for domestic students. Applications are processed on a rolling basis. Application fee: $50. Electronic applications accepted. *Expenses: Tuition:* Full-time $32,184; part-time $1192 per credit hour. *Required fees:* $280. Tuition and fees vary according to campus/location and program. *Financial support:* Research assistantships, teaching assistantships, career-related internships or fieldwork, and unspecified assistantships available. Financial award application deadline: 2/1. *Faculty research:* Decision support systems, individual and group behavior, operations research, techniques and strategy. *Unit head:* Dr. Thomas Wieckowski, Director of Master's Programs in Business, 215-895-1791, Fax: 215-895-1012. *Application contact:* Director of Graduate Admissions, 215-895-6700, Fax: 215-895-5939, E-mail: enroll@drexel.edu.

Drury University, Master of Business Administration Program, Springfield, MO 65802. Offers MBA. *Accreditation:* AACSB; ACBSP. *Program availability:* Part-time, evening/weekend. *Faculty:* 3 full-time (1 woman), 2 part-time/adjunct (0 women). *Students:* 38 full-time (13 women); includes 17 minority (1 Black or African American, non-Hispanic/Latino; 2 Asian, non-Hispanic/Latino; 7 Hispanic/Latino; 7 Two or more races, non-Hispanic/Latino), 10 international. Average age 25. 38 applicants, 61% accepted, 21 enrolled. In 2016, 26 degrees awarded. *Degree requirements:* For master's, international business trip. *Entrance requirements:* For master's, GMAT, bachelor's degree; minimum GPA of 3.0; prerequisite course requirements: financial accounting, managerial accounting, microeconomics, macroeconomics, marketing, management or organizational behavior, finance, and statistics. Additional exam requirements/recommendations for international students: Recommended—TOEFL (minimum score 80 iBT), IELTS (minimum score 6.5). *Application deadline:* For fall admission, 8/4 priority date for domestic and international students; for spring admission, 1/6 priority date for domestic and international students; for summer admission, 5/26 priority date for domestic and international students. Applications are processed on a rolling basis. Application fee: $25 ($50 for international students). Electronic applications accepted. *Expenses:* $695 tuition per credit hour, includes international travel fee; $27 per credit hour technology/enhancement fee; $100 graduation fee. *Financial support:* In 2016–17, 4 students received support. Career-related internships or fieldwork, scholarships/grants, and unspecified assistantships available. Financial award application deadline: 6/30; financial award applicants required to submit FAFSA. *Faculty research:* Cybersecurity leadership, health care management, cross cultural management, corporate finance, social entrepreneurship. *Unit head:* Angie Adamick, Director, MBA Program, 417-873-7612, E-mail: aadamick@drury.edu.
Website: http://mba.drury.edu/

Duke University, The Fuqua School of Business, The Duke MBA-Cross Continent Program, Durham, NC 27708-0586. Offers business administration (MBA); energy and environment (MBA); entrepreneurship and innovation (MBA); finance (MBA); health sector management (Certificate); marketing (MBA); strategy (MBA). *Faculty:* 88 full-time (19 women), 50 part-time/adjunct (9 women). *Students:* 214 full-time (74 women); includes 58 minority (13 Black or African American, non-Hispanic/Latino; 35 Asian, non-Hispanic/Latino; 10 Hispanic/Latino), 35 international. Average age 30. In 2016, 105 master's awarded. *Entrance requirements:* For master's, GMAT or GRE, transcripts, essays, resume, recommendation letters, letter of company support, interview. *Application deadline:* For fall admission, 10/12 priority date for domestic and international students; for winter admission, 2/7 priority date for domestic and international students; for spring admission, 5/3 priority date for domestic and international students; for summer admission, 5/31 for domestic and international students. Applications are processed on a rolling basis. Application fee: $225. Electronic applications accepted. *Expenses:* Contact institution. *Financial support:* In 2016–17, 49 students received support. Institutionally sponsored loans and scholarships/grants available. Financial award applicants required to submit FAFSA. *Unit head:* Mohan Venkatachalam, Senior Associate Dean, Executive Programs, 919-660-7859, E-mail: mohan.venkatachalam@duke.edu. *Application contact:* Sharon Thompson, Assistant Dean, Office of Admissions, 919-660-7705, Fax: 919-681-8026, E-mail: admissions-info@fuqua.duke.edu.
Website: http://www.fuqua.duke.edu/programs/duke_mba/cross_continent/

Duke University, The Fuqua School of Business, The Duke MBA-Daytime Program, Durham, NC 27708-0586. Offers academic excellence in finance (Certificate); business administration (MBA); decision sciences (MBA); energy and environment (MBA); energy finance (MBA); entrepreneurship and innovation (MBA); finance (MBA); financial analysis (MBA); health sector management (Certificate); leadership and ethics (MBA); management (MBA); marketing (MBA); operations management (MBA); social entrepreneurship (MBA); strategy (MBA). *Faculty:* 88 full-time (19 women), 50 part-time/adjunct (9 women). *Students:* 897 full-time (310 women); includes 174 minority (39 Black or African American, non-Hispanic/Latino; 3 American Indian or Alaska Native, non-Hispanic/Latino; 75 Asian, non-Hispanic/Latino; 51 Hispanic/Latino; 1 Native Hawaiian or other Pacific Islander, non-Hispanic/Latino; 5 Two or more races, non-Hispanic/Latino), 343 international. Average age 28. In 2016, 440 master's awarded. *Entrance requirements:* For master's, GMAT or GRE, transcripts, essays, resume, recommendation letters, interview. *Application deadline:* For fall admission, 9/13 for domestic and international students; for winter admission, 10/13 for domestic and international students; for spring admission, 1/4 for domestic and international students; for summer admission, 3/20 for domestic and international students. Application fee: $225. Electronic applications accepted. *Expenses:* $66,717 (first-year tuition and fees). *Financial support:* In 2016–17, 415 students received support. Institutionally sponsored loans and scholarships/grants available. Financial award applicants required to submit FAFSA. *Unit head:* Russ Morgan, Senior Associate Dean for Full-time Programs, 919-660-2931, Fax: 919-684-8742, E-mail: ruskin.morgan@duke.edu. *Application contact:* Sharon Thompson, Assistant Dean, Office of Admissions, 919-660-7705, Fax: 919-681-8026, E-mail: admissions-info@fuqua.duke.edu.
Website: http://www.fuqua.duke.edu/daytime-mba/

Duke University, The Fuqua School of Business, The Duke MBA-Global Executive Program, Durham, NC 27708-0586. Offers business administration (MBA); energy and environment (MBA); entrepreneurship and innovation (MBA); finance (MBA); health sector management (Certificate); marketing (MBA); strategy (MBA). *Faculty:* 88 full-time (19 women), 50 part-time/adjunct (9 women). *Students:* 48 full-time (14 women); includes 18 minority (3 Black or African American, non-Hispanic/Latino; 11 Asian, non-Hispanic/Latino; 4 Hispanic/Latino), 10 international. Average age 39. In 2016, 27 master's awarded. *Entrance requirements:* For master's, transcripts, essays, resume, recommendation letters, letter of company support, interview. *Application deadline:* For fall admission, 10/12 priority date for domestic and international students; for winter admission, 12/7 priority date for domestic and international students; for spring admission, 3/20 priority date for domestic and international students; for summer admission, 5/31 for domestic and international students. Applications are processed on a rolling basis. Application fee: $225. Electronic applications accepted. *Expenses:* Contact institution. *Financial support:* In 2016–17, 22 students received support. Institutionally sponsored loans and scholarships/grants available. Financial award applicants required to submit FAFSA. *Unit head:* Mohan Venkatachalam, Senior Associate Dean, Executive Programs, 919-660-7859, E-mail: mohan.venkatachalam@duke.edu. *Application contact:* Sharon Thompson, Assistant Dean, Office of Admissions, 919-660-7705, Fax: 919-681-8026, E-mail: admissions-info@fuqua.duke.edu.
Website: http://www.fuqua.duke.edu/programs/duke_mba/global-executive/

Duke University, The Fuqua School of Business, The Duke MBA-Weekend Executive Program, Durham, NC 27708-0586. Offers business administration (MBA); energy and environment (MBA); entrepreneurship and innovation (MBA); finance (MBA); health sector management (Certificate); marketing (MBA); strategy (MBA). *Faculty:* 88 full-time (19 women), 50 part-time/adjunct (9 women). *Students:* 190 full-time (43 women); includes 75 minority (11 Black or African American, non-Hispanic/Latino; 3 American Indian or Alaska Native, non-Hispanic/Latino; 48 Asian, non-Hispanic/Latino; 12 Hispanic/Latino; 1 Two or more races, non-Hispanic/Latino), 26 international. Average age 35. In 2016, 87 master's awarded. *Entrance requirements:* For master's, GMAT or GRE, transcripts, essays, resume, recommendation letters, letter of company support, interview. *Application deadline:* For fall admission, 8/30 priority date for domestic and international students; for winter admission, 10/12 priority date for domestic and international students; for spring admission, 2/7 priority date for domestic and international students; for summer admission, 3/20 for domestic and international students. Applications are processed on a rolling basis. Application fee: $225. Electronic applications accepted. *Expenses:* Contact institution. *Financial support:* In 2016–17, 33 students received support. Institutionally sponsored loans and scholarships/grants available. Financial award applicants required to submit FAFSA. *Unit head:* Mohan Venkatachalam, Senior Associate Dean, Executive Programs, 919-660-7859, E-mail: mohan.venkatachalam@duke.edu. *Application contact:* Sharon Thompson, Assistant Dean, Office of Admissions, 919-660-7705, Fax: 919-681-8026, E-mail: admissions-info@fuqua.duke.edu.
Website: http://www.fuqua.duke.edu/programs/duke_mba/weekend_executive/

Duke University, The Fuqua School of Business, MMS: Foundations of Business Program, Durham, NC 27708-0586. Offers MMS. *Faculty:* 88 full-time (19 women), 50 part-time/adjunct (9 women). *Students:* 116 full-time (52 women); includes 25 minority (2 Black or African American, non-Hispanic/Latino; 20 Asian, non-Hispanic/Latino; 2 Hispanic/Latino; 1 Two or more races, non-Hispanic/Latino), 51 international. Average age 23. In 2016, 130 master's awarded. *Entrance requirements:* For master's, GMAT or GRE, transcripts, essays, resume, recommendation letters, interview. *Application deadline:* For fall admission, 9/13 for domestic and international students; for winter admission, 1/30 for domestic and international students; for spring admission, 3/7 for domestic and international students; for summer admission, 4/4 for domestic and international students. Application fee: $125. Electronic applications accepted. *Expenses:* Contact institution. *Financial support:* In 2016–17, 29 students received support. Institutionally sponsored loans and scholarships/grants available. Financial award applicants required to submit FAFSA. *Unit head:* Jeremy Petranka, Associate Dean for the Master of Management Studies, E-mail: jeremy.petranka@duke.edu. *Application contact:* Sharon Thompson, Assistant Dean, Office of Admissions, 919-660-7705, Fax: 919-681-8026, E-mail: mms-fob-info@fuqua.duke.edu.
Website: http://www.fuqua.duke.edu/mms-foundations-of-business/

Duke University, The Fuqua School of Business, PhD Program, Durham, NC 27708-0586. Offers accounting (PhD); decision sciences (PhD); finance (PhD); management and organizations (PhD); marketing (PhD); operations management (PhD); strategy (PhD). *Faculty:* 100 full-time (19 women). *Students:* 77 full-time (27 women); includes 9 minority (1 Black or African American, non-Hispanic/Latino; 7 Asian, non-Hispanic/Latino; 1 Hispanic/Latino), 46 international. 561 applicants, 7% accepted, 14 enrolled. In 2016, 15 doctorates awarded. *Degree requirements:* For doctorate, thesis/dissertation, major field requirement (exam or major paper, depending upon the area). *Entrance requirements:* For doctorate, GMAT or GRE, transcripts, essays, recommendation letters, statement of purpose. Additional exam requirements/recommendations for international students: Required—TOEFL (minimum score 577 paper-based; 90 iBT), IELTS (minimum score 7). *Application deadline:* For fall admission, 12/31 priority date for domestic and international students. Application fee: $85. Electronic applications accepted. *Expenses:* Contact institution. *Financial support:* In 2016–17, 77 students received support, including 70 fellowships with full tuition reimbursements available (averaging $28,200 per year), 63 research assistantships with full tuition reimbursements available (averaging $7,000 per year); institutionally sponsored loans, scholarships/grants, and tuition waivers (full) also available. Financial award applicants required to submit FAFSA. *Unit head:* William Boulding, Dean, 919-660-7822, Fax: 919-684-8742, E-mail: bb1@duke.edu. *Application contact:* Qi Chen, Director of Graduate Studies, 919-660-7753, Fax: 919-660-7971, E-mail: qc2@duke.edu.

Duke University, Graduate School, Department of Business Administration, Durham, NC 27708. Offers PhD. *Accreditation:* AACSB. *Degree requirements:* For doctorate, thesis/dissertation. *Entrance requirements:* For doctorate, GMAT or GRE General Test. Additional exam requirements/recommendations for international students: Required—TOEFL (minimum score 577 paper-based; 90 iBT) or IELTS (minimum score 7). Electronic applications accepted.

Duquesne University, Palumbo-Donahue School of Business, Pittsburgh, PA 15282-0001. Offers accounting (M Acc); finance (MBA); information systems management (MSISM); management (MBA, MS); marketing (MBA); sports business (MS); sustainability (MBA); JD/MBA; MBA/M Acc; MBA/MA; MBA/MES; MBA/MHMS; MSISM/MBA; Pharm D/MBA. *Accreditation:* AACSB. *Program availability:* Part-time, evening/weekend, 100% online, minimal on-campus study. *Faculty:* 59 full-time (23 women), 25 part-time/adjunct (6 women). *Students:* 92 full-time (43 women), 176 part-time (71 women); includes 20 minority (9 Black or African American, non-Hispanic/Latino; 8 Asian, non-Hispanic/Latino; 2 Hispanic/Latino; 1 Two or more races, non-Hispanic/Latino), 35 international. Average age 28. 272 applicants, 86% accepted, 137 enrolled. In 2016, 137 master's awarded. *Entrance requirements:* For master's, GMAT or GRE, undergraduate transcripts, 2 letters of recommendation, current resume, personal statement. Additional exam requirements/recommendations for international students: Required—TOEFL (minimum score 577 paper-based; 90 iBT), IELTS (minimum score 7). *Application deadline:* For fall admission, 7/1 priority date for domestic and international students; for spring admission, 12/1 for domestic and international students; for summer admission, 4/1 for domestic and international students. Applications are processed on a rolling basis. Application fee: $0. Electronic applications accepted. *Expenses:* Contact institution. *Financial support:* In 2016–17, 211 students received support, including 12 fellowships with partial tuition reimbursements available (averaging $14,200 per year), 20 research assistantships with partial tuition reimbursements available (averaging $22,212 per year); career-related internships or fieldwork, scholarships/grants, and unspecified assistantships also available. Support available to part-time students. Financial award application deadline: 7/1; financial award applicants required to submit FAFSA. *Faculty research:* Investment management, business ethics, technology management, supply chain management, entrepreneurship. *Unit head:* Dr. Karen Donovan, Associate Dean of Graduate Programs and Executive Education, 412-396-6276, Fax: 412-396-1726, E-mail: donovan6@duq.edu. *Application contact:* Jeff Jewett, Director of Admissions and Enrollment Management, 412-396-6244, Fax: 412-396-1726, E-mail: decrostam@duq.edu.
Website: http://www.duq.edu/business/grad

D'Youville College, Department of Business, Buffalo, NY 14201-1084. Offers business administration (MBA); international business (MS). *Program availability:* Part-time, evening/weekend. *Degree requirements:* For master's, one foreign language, project or thesis. *Entrance requirements:* For master's, minimum GPA of 3.0. Additional exam requirements/recommendations for international students: Required—TOEFL (minimum score 500 paper-based). Electronic applications accepted. *Faculty research:* Assessment, accreditation, supply chain, online learning, adult learning.

East Carolina University, Graduate School, College of Business, Greenville, NC 27858-4353. Offers MBA, MSA. *Accreditation:* AACSB. *Program availability:* Part-time, evening/weekend. *Students:* 300 full-time (120 women), 719 part-time (354 women); includes 228 minority (139 Black or African American, non-Hispanic/Latino; 8 American Indian or Alaska Native, non-Hispanic/Latino; 29 Asian, non-Hispanic/Latino; 40 Hispanic/Latino; 12 Two or more races, non-Hispanic/Latino), 17 international. Average age 32. 527 applicants, 88% accepted, 341 enrolled. In 2016, 341 master's awarded.

Business Administration and Management—General

Entrance requirements: For master's, GMAT. Additional exam requirements/ recommendations for international students: Required—TOEFL. *Application deadline:* For fall admission, 6/1 priority date for domestic students. Applications are processed on a rolling basis. Application fee: $75. Electronic applications accepted. *Financial support:* Research assistantships with partial tuition reimbursements, teaching assistantships with partial tuition reimbursements, and Federal Work-Study available. Support available to part-time students. Financial award application deadline: 6/1. *Unit head:* Paul Russell, Interim Director of Graduate Programs, 252-328-6970, E-mail: gradbus@ecu.edu.
Website: http://www.business.ecu.edu

East Carolina University, Graduate School, College of Engineering and Technology, Department of Technology Systems, Greenville, NC 27858-4353. Offers computer network professional (Certificate); information assurance (Certificate); Lean Six Sigma Black Belt (Certificate); network technology (MS), including computer networking management, digital communications technology, information security, Web technologies; occupational safety (MS); technology management (PhD); technology systems (MS), including industrial distribution and logistics, manufacturing systems, performance improvement, quality systems; Website developer (Certificate). *Students:* 23 full-time (1 woman), 199 part-time (55 women); includes 59 minority (39 Black or African American, non-Hispanic/Latino; 3 American Indian or Alaska Native, non-Hispanic/Latino; 4 Asian, non-Hispanic/Latino; 10 Hispanic/Latino; 3 Two or more races, non-Hispanic/Latino), 5 international. Average age 38. 85 applicants, 87% accepted, 61 enrolled. In 2016, 23 master's awarded. *Entrance requirements:* For master's and Certificate, GRE General Test or MAT, minimum GPA of 2.5; for doctorate, GRE General Test, related work experience. *Application deadline:* For fall admission, 6/1 priority date for domestic students. Applications are processed on a rolling basis. Application fee: $50. *Financial support:* Application deadline: 6/1. *Unit head:* Dr. Tijjani Mohammed, Chair, 252-328-9668, E-mail: mohammedt@ecu.edu. *Application contact:* Dean of Graduate School, 252-328-6012, Fax: 252-328-6071, E-mail: gradschool@ecu.edu.

Eastern Illinois University, Graduate School, Lumpkin College of Business and Applied Sciences, Program in Business Administration, Charleston, IL 61920. Offers accountancy (MBA); applied management (MBA); business administration (MBA); research (MBA). *Accreditation:* AACSB. *Program availability:* Part-time, evening/ weekend. *Entrance requirements:* For master's, GMAT or GRE. Additional exam requirements/recommendations for international students: Required—TOEFL (minimum score 500 paper-based; 61 iBT), IELTS (minimum score 6). Electronic applications accepted.

Eastern Kentucky University, The Graduate School, College of Business and Technology, Program in Business Administration, Richmond, KY 40475-3102. Offers MBA. *Accreditation:* AACSB.

Eastern Mennonite University, Program in Business Administration, Harrisonburg, VA 22802-2462. Offers general management (MBA); health services administration (MBA); non-profit leadership (MBA). *Program availability:* Part-time, evening/weekend. *Degree requirements:* For master's, final capstone course. *Entrance requirements:* For master's, GMAT, minimum GPA of 2.5, 2 years of work experience, 2 letters of reference. Additional exam requirements/recommendations for international students: Required—TOEFL (minimum score 500 paper-based). Electronic applications accepted. *Expenses:* Contact institution. *Faculty research:* Information security, Anabaptist/Mennonite experiences and perspectives, limits of multi-cultural education, international development performance criteria.

Eastern Michigan University, Graduate School, College of Business, Department of Management, Ypsilanti, MI 48197. Offers entrepreneurship (Postbaccalaureate Certificate); human resources management and organizational development (MSHROD). *Program availability:* Part-time, evening/weekend, online learning. *Faculty:* 22 full-time (11 women). *Students:* 13 full-time (10 women), 77 part-time (58 women); includes 29 minority (23 Black or African American, non-Hispanic/Latino; 1 Asian, non-Hispanic/Latino; 4 Hispanic/Latino; 1 Two or more races, non-Hispanic/Latino), 8 international. Average age 30. 38 applicants, 74% accepted, 12 enrolled. In 2016, 75 master's awarded. *Degree requirements:* For master's, thesis optional. *Entrance requirements:* For master's, GMAT. Additional exam requirements/recommendations for international students: Required—TOEFL. *Application deadline:* For fall admission, 5/15 priority date for domestic students, 2/15 priority date for international students; for winter admission, 10/15 priority date for domestic students, 9/1 priority date for international students; for summer admission, 3/15 priority date for domestic students, 3/1 priority date for international students. Applications are processed on a rolling basis. Application fee: $45. *Financial support:* Fellowships, research assistantships with full tuition reimbursements, teaching assistantships with full tuition reimbursements, career-related internships or fieldwork, Federal Work-Study, institutionally sponsored loans, scholarships/grants, tuition waivers (partial), and unspecified assistantships available. Support available to part-time students. Financial award applicants required to submit FAFSA. *Unit head:* Dr. Fraya Wagner-Marsh, Department Head, 734-487-3240, Fax: 734-487-4100, E-mail: fraya.wagner@emich.edu.

Eastern Michigan University, Graduate School, College of Business, Programs in Business Administration, Ypsilanti, MI 48197. Offers business administration (MBA, Graduate Certificate); computer information systems (Graduate Certificate); e-business (MBA, Graduate Certificate); enterprise business intelligence (MBA); entrepreneurship (MBA, Graduate Certificate); finance (MBA, Graduate Certificate); human resources (MBA); human resources management (Graduate Certificate); information systems (MBA); internal auditing (MBA); international business (MBA, Graduate Certificate); marketing management (Graduate Certificate); nonprofit management (MBA); organizational development (Graduate Certificate); supply chain management (MBA, Graduate Certificate). *Accreditation:* AACSB. *Program availability:* Part-time, online learning. *Students:* 63 full-time (36 women), 320 part-time (186 women); includes 131 minority (76 Black or African American, non-Hispanic/Latino; 5 American Indian or Alaska Native, non-Hispanic/Latino; 16 Asian, non-Hispanic/Latino; 19 Hispanic/Latino; 15 Two or more races, non-Hispanic/Latino), 23 international. Average age 32. 305 applicants, 70% accepted, 124 enrolled. In 2016, 78 master's, 57 other advanced degrees awarded. *Entrance requirements:* For master's, GMAT (minimum score 450), minimum cumulative undergraduate GPA of 2.75. Additional exam requirements/ recommendations for international students: Required—TOEFL. *Application deadline:* For fall admission, 5/15 priority date for domestic students, 2/15 priority date for international students; for winter admission, 10/15 priority date for domestic students, 9/1 priority date for international students; for summer admission, 3/15 priority date for domestic students, 3/1 priority date for international students. Applications are processed on a rolling basis. Application fee: $45. *Financial support:* Fellowships, research assistantships with full tuition reimbursements, teaching assistantships with full tuition reimbursements, career-related internships or fieldwork, Federal Work-Study, institutionally sponsored loans, scholarships/grants, tuition waivers (partial), and unspecified assistantships available. Support available to part-time students. Financial award applicants required to submit FAFSA. *Unit head:* K. Michelle Henry, Director, Graduate Business Programs, 734-487-4444, Fax: 734-483-1316, E-mail: cob.graduate@emich.edu.
Website: http://www.emich.edu/cob/mba/

Eastern Nazarene College, Adult and Graduate Studies, Program in Management, Quincy, MA 02170. Offers MSM.

Eastern New Mexico University, Graduate School, College of Business, Portales, NM 88130. Offers MBA. *Accreditation:* ACBSP. *Program availability:* Part-time, evening/ weekend, online learning. *Degree requirements:* For master's, comprehensive exam, comprehensive integrative project and presentation. *Entrance requirements:* For master's, GMAT (minimum score 450), minimum undergraduate GPA of 3.0. Additional exam requirements/recommendations for international students: Required—TOEFL (minimum score 550 paper-based; 79 iBT), IELTS (minimum score 6). Electronic applications accepted.

Eastern Oregon University, Program in Business Administration, La Grande, OR 97850-2899. Offers MBA. *Program availability:* Part-time, 100% online. *Faculty:* 10 full-time (1 woman), 2 part-time/adjunct (0 women). *Students:* 34 full-time (16 women), 57 part-time (32 women); includes 17 minority (1 Black or African American, non-Hispanic/ Latino; 3 American Indian or Alaska Native, non-Hispanic/Latino; 3 Asian, non-Hispanic/ Latino; 10 Hispanic/Latino), 1 international. Average age 32. In 2016, 35 master's awarded. *Degree requirements:* For master's, thesis. *Entrance requirements:* For master's, baccalaureate degree in business or related fields (agribusiness, finance, accounting, economics, etc.) from accredited institution with minimum cumulative GPA of 3.0. *Application deadline:* For fall admission, 4/15 priority date for domestic students, 2/1 for international students. Applications are processed on a rolling basis. Application fee: $50. Electronic applications accepted. *Expenses:* Tuition, state resident: full-time $11,808; part-time $328 per credit. Tuition, nonresident: full-time $14,886; part-time $413.50 per credit. *Required fees:* $312 per quarter. One-time fee: $120. Tuition and fees vary according to course load, campus/location and program. *Financial support:* Federal Work-Study, scholarships/grants, and tuition waivers (full and partial) available. Support available to part-time students. Financial award applicants required to submit FAFSA. *Unit head:* Les Mueller, Program Coordinator, 541-962-3225, E-mail: lmueller@eou.edu. *Application contact:* Kristin Johnson, MAT Advisor/Recruiter, 541-962-3529, Fax: 541-962-3701, E-mail: kristin.johnson@eou.edu.

Eastern University, Graduate Programs in Business, St. Davids, PA 19087-3696. Offers health administration (MBA); health services management (MS); management (MBA). *Program availability:* Part-time, evening/weekend, online learning. *Students:* 31 full-time (25 women), 167 part-time (110 women); includes 102 minority (73 Black or African American, non-Hispanic/Latino; 12 Asian, non-Hispanic/Latino; 14 Hispanic/ Latino; 3 Two or more races, non-Hispanic/Latino), 15 international. Average age 33. In 2016, 105 master's awarded. *Entrance requirements:* Additional exam requirements/ recommendations for international students: Required—TOEFL (minimum score 550 paper-based; 79 iBT). *Application deadline:* Applications are processed on a rolling basis. Application fee: $35. Electronic applications accepted. Application fee is waived when completed online. *Expenses:* $743 per credit. *Financial support:* Applicants required to submit FAFSA. *Unit head:* Michael Dziedziak, Executive Director of Enrollment, 800-452-0996, E-mail: gpsadmissions@eastern.edu.
Website: http://www.eastern.edu/academics/programs/graduate-business

Eastern University, Program in Organizational Leadership, St. Davids, PA 19087-3696. Offers organizational leadership (PhD), including business, non-profit. *Students:* 74 full-time (42 women); includes 22 minority (17 Black or African American, non-Hispanic/ Latino; 3 Asian, non-Hispanic/Latino; 1 Hispanic/Latino; 1 Two or more races, non-Hispanic/Latino), 4 international. Average age 46. In 2016, 8 doctorates awarded. *Application deadline:* Applications are processed on a rolling basis. Electronic applications accepted. *Expenses:* $985 per credit. *Unit head:* Michael Dziedziak, Executive Director of Enrollment, 800-452-0996, E-mail: gpsadmissions@eastern.edu.
Website: http://www.eastern.edu/academics/programs/phd-organizational-leadership/ phd-organizational-leadership-0

Eastern University, School of Leadership and Development, St. Davids, PA 19087-3696. Offers economic development (MBA), including international development, urban development (MA, MBA); international development (MA), including global development, urban development (MA, MBA); nonprofit management (MS); organizational leadership (MA); M Div/MBA. *Program availability:* Part-time, evening/ weekend, online learning. *Students:* 59 full-time (32 women), 67 part-time (35 women); includes 40 minority (32 Black or African American, non-Hispanic/Latino; 1 Asian, non-Hispanic/Latino; 5 Hispanic/Latino; 2 Two or more races, non-Hispanic/Latino), 22 international. Average age 33. In 2016, 44 master's awarded. *Entrance requirements:* Additional exam requirements/recommendations for international students: Required—TOEFL (minimum score 550 paper-based; 79 iBT). *Application deadline:* Applications are processed on a rolling basis. Application fee: $35. Electronic applications accepted. Application fee is waived when completed online. *Expenses:* $690 per credit. *Faculty research:* Micro-level economic development, China welfare and economic development, macroethics, micro- and macro-level economic development in transitional economics, organizational effectiveness. *Unit head:* Michael Dziedziak, Executive Director of Enrollment, 800-452-0996, E-mail: gpsadmissions@eastern.edu.
Website: http://www.eastern.edu/academics/programs/graduate-programs-leadership-development

Eastern Washington University, Graduate Studies, College of Business and Public Administration, Business Administration Program, Cheney, WA 99004-2431. Offers MBA, MBA/MPA. *Accreditation:* AACSB. *Faculty:* 17 full-time (6 women). *Students:* 24 full-time (11 women), 30 part-time (18 women); includes 15 minority (7 Black or African American, non-Hispanic/Latino; 1 American Indian or Alaska Native, non-Hispanic/ Latino; 3 Asian, non-Hispanic/Latino; 4 Hispanic/Latino), 3 international. Average age 34. 69 applicants, 43% accepted, 23 enrolled. In 2016, 23 master's awarded. *Degree requirements:* For master's, comprehensive exam, thesis optional. *Entrance requirements:* For master's, GMAT, minimum GPA of 3.0. Additional exam requirements/recommendations for international students: Required—TOEFL (minimum score 580 paper-based; 92 iBT), IELTS (minimum score 7), PTE (minimum score 63). *Application deadline:* For fall admission, 4/1 priority date for domestic students; for spring admission, 1/15 for domestic students. Applications are processed on a rolling basis. Application fee: $75. Electronic applications accepted. *Expenses:* Tuition, state resident: full-time $11,000; part-time $5500 per credit. Tuition, nonresident: full-time $24,000; part-time $12,000 per credit. *Required fees:* $1300. One-time fee: $50 full-time. Part-time tuition and fees vary according to course load, campus/location and program. *Financial support:* In 2016–17, 5 students received support, including 5 teaching assistantships with partial tuition reimbursements available (averaging $10,000 per year); career-related internships or fieldwork, Federal Work-Study, institutionally sponsored loans, scholarships/grants, health care benefits, tuition waivers (partial), and unspecified assistantships also available. Support available to part-time students. Financial award application deadline: 2/1. *Unit head:* Jill Ericson, Director of Graduate Programs, 509-828-1248, E-mail: jericson@ewu.edu. *Application contact:* Lorene Winters, Program Coordinator, Master of Business Administration, 509-828-1232, E-mail: mbaprograms@ewu.edu.
Website: http://www.ewu.edu/cbpa.xml

East Tennessee State University, School of Graduate Studies, College of Business and Technology, Department of Management and Marketing, Johnson City, TN 37614. Offers business administration (MBA, Postbaccalaureate Certificate); digital marketing

(MS); entrepreneurial leadership (Postbaccalaureate Certificate); health care management (Postbaccalaureate Certificate). *Program availability:* Part-time, evening/weekend. *Degree requirements:* For master's, comprehensive exam, capstone. *Entrance requirements:* For master's, GMAT, minimum GPA of 2.5 (for MBA), 3.0 (for MS); for Postbaccalaureate Certificate, minimum GPA of 2.5. Additional exam requirements/recommendations for international students: Required—TOEFL (minimum score 550 paper-based; 79 iBT). Electronic applications accepted. *Faculty research:* Sustainability, healthcare effectiveness, consumer behavior, merchandizing trends, organizational management issues.

East Texas Baptist University, Master of Business Administration Program, Marshall, TX 75670-1498. Offers entrepreneurial leadership (MBA). *Program availability:* Part-time, evening/weekend, 100% online. *Faculty:* 2 full-time (1 woman), 1 part-time/adjunct (0 women). *Students:* 18 full-time (8 women), 16 part-time (7 women); includes 10 minority (7 Black or African American, non-Hispanic/Latino; 2 Hispanic/Latino; 1 Native Hawaiian or other Pacific Islander, non-Hispanic/Latino), 1 international. Average age 27. 19 applicants, 84% accepted, 13 enrolled. In 2016, 8 master's awarded. *Entrance requirements:* Additional exam requirements/recommendations for international students: Recommended—TOEFL (minimum score 550 paper-based; 79 iBT). *Application deadline:* For fall admission, 8/17 for domestic students; for spring admission, 1/10 for domestic students; for summer admission, 5/2 for domestic students. Applications are processed on a rolling basis. Application fee: $50. Electronic applications accepted. *Expenses:* $700 per credit hour tuition; $150 per semester fees (6 or more hours enrolled); $75 per semester fees (1-5 hours enrolled). *Financial support:* In 2016–17, 18 students received support. Federal Work-Study, scholarships/grants, unspecified assistantships, and staff grants available. Financial award applicants required to submit FAFSA. *Unit head:* Den Murley, Director of Graduate Admissions, 903-923-2079, Fax: 903-934-8115, E-mail: dmurley@etbu.edu.
Website: https://www.etbu.edu/business/master-business-administration/

Edgewood College, Program in Business, Madison, WI 53711-1997. Offers accountancy (MS); sustainability leadership (MBA). *Accreditation:* ACBSP. *Program availability:* Part-time, evening/weekend. *Students:* 38 full-time (22 women), 109 part-time (61 women); includes 13 minority (2 Black or African American, non-Hispanic/Latino; 4 Asian, non-Hispanic/Latino; 3 Hispanic/Latino; 1 Native Hawaiian or other Pacific Islander, non-Hispanic/Latino; 3 Two or more races, non-Hispanic/Latino), 13 international. Average age 33. In 2016, 50 master's awarded. *Entrance requirements:* For master's, GMAT (minimum score 430), minimum GPA of 2.75, 2 letters of recommendation. Additional exam requirements/recommendations for international students: Required—TOEFL. *Application deadline:* For fall admission, 8/15 for domestic students, 5/1 for international students; for spring admission, 1/8 for domestic students, 11/1 for international students. Applications are processed on a rolling basis. Application fee: $30. Electronic applications accepted. *Expenses: Tuition:* Part-time $898 per credit. Tuition and fees vary according to course load. *Financial support:* Career-related internships or fieldwork and scholarships/grants available. *Unit head:* Dr. Stevie Watson, Dean, 608-663-2224, Fax: 608-663-3291, E-mail: swatson@edgewood.edu. *Application contact:* Joann Eastman, Admissions Counselor, 608-663-3250, Fax: 608-663-2214, E-mail: gps@edgewood.edu.
Website: https://www.edgewood.edu/academics/schools/school-of-business

Elmhurst College, Graduate Programs, Program in Business Administration, Elmhurst, IL 60126-3296. Offers MBA. *Program availability:* Part-time, evening/weekend, online learning. *Faculty:* 2 full-time (1 woman), 13 part-time/adjunct (2 women). *Students:* 6 full-time (2 women), 103 part-time (41 women); includes 25 minority (6 Black or African American, non-Hispanic/Latino; 8 Asian, non-Hispanic/Latino; 8 Hispanic/Latino; 3 Two or more races, non-Hispanic/Latino). Average age 31. 75 applicants, 84% accepted, 59 enrolled. In 2016, 29 master's awarded. *Entrance requirements:* For master's, 3 recommendations, resume, statement of purpose. Additional exam requirements/recommendations for international students: Required—TOEFL (minimum score 550 paper-based; 79 iBT). *Application deadline:* Applications are processed on a rolling basis. Application fee: $0. Electronic applications accepted. *Expenses:* $845 per semester hour. *Financial support:* In 2016–17, 45 students received support. Scholarships/grants available. Support available to part-time students. Financial award application deadline: 3/1; financial award applicants required to submit FAFSA. *Unit head:* Kelly Cunningham. *Application contact:* Timothy J. Panfil, Director of Enrollment Management, School for Professional Studies, 630-617-3300 Ext. 3256, Fax: 630-617-6471, E-mail: panfilt@elmhurst.edu.
Website: http://www.elmhurst.edu/mba

Elms College, Division of Business, Chicopee, MA 01013-2839. Offers accounting (MBA); financial planning (MBA); healthcare leadership (MBA); management (MBA). *Program availability:* Part-time, evening/weekend. *Faculty:* 4 full-time (all women), 6 part-time/adjunct (3 women). *Students:* 51 part-time (32 women); includes 10 minority (4 Black or African American, non-Hispanic/Latino; 1 Asian, non-Hispanic/Latino; 5 Hispanic/Latino). Average age 34. 26 applicants, 100% accepted, 22 enrolled. In 2016, 24 master's awarded. *Entrance requirements:* For master's, minimum GPA of 3.0. *Application deadline:* Applications are processed on a rolling basis. Application fee: $30. *Expenses: Tuition:* Full-time $13,392. *Required fees:* $200. *Unit head:* Dr. David Kimball, Chair, Division of Business, 413-265-2300, E-mail: kimballd@elms.edu. *Application contact:* Dr. Elizabeth Teahan Hukowicz, Dean, School of Graduate and Professional Studies, 413-265-2360 Ext. 238, Fax: 413-265-2459, E-mail: hukowicze@elms.edu.

Elon University, Program in Business Administration, Elon, NC 27244-2010. Offers MBA, MSM. *Accreditation:* AACSB. *Program availability:* Part-time, evening/weekend. *Faculty:* 39 full-time (22 women), 10 part-time/adjunct (4 women). *Students:* 65 full-time (27 women), 71 part-time (25 women); includes 28 minority (14 Black or African American, non-Hispanic/Latino; 1 American Indian or Alaska Native, non-Hispanic/Latino; 11 Asian, non-Hispanic/Latino; 1 Hispanic/Latino; 1 Two or more races, non-Hispanic/Latino). Average age 33. 128 applicants, 73% accepted, 80 enrolled. In 2016, 49 master's awarded. *Entrance requirements:* For master's, GMAT. Additional exam requirements/recommendations for international students: Required—TOEFL (minimum score 550 paper-based; 79 iBT). *Application deadline:* For fall admission, 8/15 priority date for domestic students; for spring admission, 2/15 priority date for domestic students. Applications are processed on a rolling basis. Application fee: $50. Electronic applications accepted. *Financial support:* Federal Work-Study and scholarships/grants available. Support available to part-time students. Financial award application deadline: 3/15; financial award applicants required to submit FAFSA. *Faculty research:* Business ethics, international business and global economics, sales force management, sustainable business practices, consumer behavior. *Unit head:* Dr. William Burpitt, Director, 336-278-5949, Fax: 336-278-5952, E-mail: wburpitt@elon.edu. *Application contact:* Art Fadde, Director of Graduate Admissions, 800-334-8448 Ext. 3, Fax: 336-278-7699, E-mail: afadde@elon.edu.
Website: http://www.elon.edu/mba/

Embry-Riddle Aeronautical University–Daytona, Department of Management, Marketing and Operations, Daytona Beach, FL 32114-3900. Offers airline management (MBA); airport management (MBA); aviation finance (MSAF); aviation management (MBA-AM); aviation system management (MBA); finance (MBA); supply chain management (MBA). *Accreditation:* ACBSP. *Program availability:* Part-time. *Faculty:* 13 full-time (2 women). *Students:* 93 full-time (37 women), 15 part-time (8 women); includes 12 minority (3 Black or African American, non-Hispanic/Latino; 3 Asian, non-Hispanic/Latino; 1 Hispanic/Latino; 5 Two or more races, non-Hispanic/Latino), 71 international. Average age 26. 130 applicants, 39% accepted, 40 enrolled. In 2016, 44 degrees awarded. *Degree requirements:* For master's, thesis (for some programs). *Entrance requirements:* Additional exam requirements/recommendations for international students: Required—TOEFL (minimum score 550 paper-based, 79 iBT) or IELTS (6). *Application deadline:* For fall admission, 3/1 priority date for domestic students; for spring admission, 11/1 priority date for domestic students; for summer admission, 4/1 priority date for domestic students. Applications are processed on a rolling basis. Application fee: $50. Electronic applications accepted. *Expenses: Tuition:* Full-time $16,296; part-time $1358 per credit hour. *Required fees:* $1294; $647 per semester. One-time fee: $100 full-time. Tuition and fees vary according to course load, degree level and program. *Financial support:* Research assistantships, teaching assistantships, career-related internships or fieldwork, scholarships/grants, unspecified assistantships, and on-campus employment available. Financial award application deadline: 3/15; financial award applicants required to submit FAFSA. *Unit head:* Michael J. Williams, PhD, Dean, College of Business/Professor of Management, 386-226-6293, E-mail: michael.williams@erau.edu. *Application contact:* Graduate Admissions, 386-226-6176, E-mail: graduate.admissions@erau.edu.
Website: https://daytonabeach.erau.edu/college-business/index.html

See Display on page 616 and Close-Up on page 637.

Embry-Riddle Aeronautical University–Worldwide, Department of Business Administration, Daytona Beach, FL 32114-3900. Offers aviation (MBAA). *Program availability:* Part-time, evening/weekend, 100% online, blended/hybrid learning, EagleVision Classroom (between classrooms), EagleVision Home (faculty and students at home), and a blend of Classroom or Home. *Faculty:* 16 full-time (4 women), 64 part-time/adjunct (18 women). *Students:* 368 full-time (81 women), 315 part-time (57 women); includes 173 minority (57 Black or African American, non-Hispanic/Latino; 4 American Indian or Alaska Native, non-Hispanic/Latino; 36 Asian, non-Hispanic/Latino; 35 Hispanic/Latino; 4 Native Hawaiian or other Pacific Islander, non-Hispanic/Latino; 37 Two or more races, non-Hispanic/Latino), 61 international. Average age 35. In 2016, 204 master's awarded. *Degree requirements:* For master's, comprehensive exam. *Entrance requirements:* Additional exam requirements/recommendations for international students: Required—TOEFL (minimum score 550 paper-based, 79 iBT) or IELTS (6). *Application deadline:* Applications are processed on a rolling basis. Application fee: $50. Electronic applications accepted. *Expenses:* $620 per credit (for civilians), $530 per credit (for military). *Financial support:* Career-related internships or fieldwork and scholarships/grants available. Financial award applicants required to submit FAFSA. *Unit head:* Ronald Mau, PhD, Department Chair, E-mail: ronald.mau@erau.edu. *Application contact:* Worldwide Campus, 800-522-6787, E-mail: worldwide@erau.edu.
Website: http://worldwide.erau.edu/degrees-programs/colleges/business/department-of-business-admin/index.html

Embry-Riddle Aeronautical University–Worldwide, Department of Decision Sciences, Daytona Beach, FL 32114-3900. Offers aviation and aerospace (MSPM); aviation/aerospace management (MSEM); financial management (MSEM, MSPM); general management (MSPM); global management (MSPM); human resources management (MSPM); information systems (MSPM); leadership (MSEM, MSPM); logistics and supply chain management (MSEM, MSLSCM, MSPM); management (MSEM, MSPM); project management (MSEM); systems engineering (MSEM, MSPM); technical management (MSPM). *Program availability:* Part-time, evening/weekend, 100% online, blended/hybrid learning, EagleVision is a virtual classroom that combines Web video conferencing and a learning management system. EagleVision Classroom (between classrooms), EagleVision Home (faculty and students at home), and a blend of Classroom or Home. *Degree requirements:* For master's, comprehensive exam (for some programs), thesis (for some programs). *Entrance requirements:* Additional exam requirements/recommendations for international students: Required—TOEFL (minimum score 550 paper-based; 79 iBT), IELTS (minimum score 6), TOEFL or IELTS accepted. Electronic applications accepted. *Expenses:* Contact institution.

Embry-Riddle Aeronautical University–Worldwide, Department of Management, Daytona Beach, FL 32114-3900. Offers global management (MS); human resources management (MS); leadership (MS); operations management (MS); project management (MS). *Program availability:* Part-time, evening/weekend, 100% online, blended/hybrid learning, EagleVision is a virtual classroom that combines Web video conferencing and a learning management system. EagleVision Classroom (between classrooms), EagleVision Home (faculty and students at home), and a blend of Classroom or Home. *Entrance requirements:* Additional exam requirements/recommendations for international students: Required—TOEFL (minimum score 550 paper-based; 79 iBT), IELTS (minimum score 6), TOEFL or IELTS accepted. Electronic applications accepted. *Expenses:* Contact institution.

Emmanuel College, Graduate and Professional Programs, Graduate Programs in Management, Boston, MA 02115. Offers management (MSM); management and leadership (Graduate Certificate); research administration (MSM, Graduate Certificate). *Program availability:* Part-time, evening/weekend, blended/hybrid learning. *Faculty:* 12 part-time/adjunct (1 woman). *Students:* 5 full-time (1 woman), 55 part-time (42 women); includes 19 minority (11 Black or African American, non-Hispanic/Latino; 5 Asian, non-Hispanic/Latino; 3 Hispanic/Latino). Average age 34. 34 applicants, 35% accepted, 7 enrolled. In 2016, 40 master's, 21 other advanced degrees awarded. *Degree requirements:* For master's, 36 credits. *Entrance requirements:* For master's and Graduate Certificate, transcripts from all regionally-accredited institutions attended (showing proof of bachelor's degree completion), 2 letters of recommendation, essay, resume. Additional exam requirements/recommendations for international students: Required—TOEFL. *Application deadline:* Applications are processed on a rolling basis. Electronic applications accepted. *Expenses:* $13,152 (for Graduate Certificate); $24,112 (for MSM). *Financial support:* Application deadline: 2/15; applicants required to submit FAFSA. *Unit head:* Petia Whitmore, Executive Director, Graduate and Professional Programs, 617-732-1740, E-mail: gpp@emmanuel.edu. *Application contact:* Helen Muterperl, Associate Director of Admissions, Graduate and Professional Programs, 617-735-9700, Fax: 617-507-0434, E-mail: gpp@emmanuel.edu.
Website: http://www.emmanuel.edu/graduate-professional-programs/academics/management.html

Emory University, Goizueta Business School, Doctoral Program in Business, Atlanta, GA 30322. Offers accounting (PhD); finance (PhD); information systems and operations management (PhD); marketing (PhD); organization and management (PhD). *Faculty:* 59 full-time (16 women). *Students:* 40 full-time (16 women); includes 6 minority (1 Black or African American, non-Hispanic/Latino; 4 Asian, non-Hispanic/Latino; 1 Hispanic/Latino), 26 international. Average age 28. 145 applicants, 9% accepted, 4 enrolled. In 2016, 5 doctorates awarded. *Degree requirements:* For doctorate, comprehensive exam, thesis/dissertation. *Entrance requirements:* For doctorate, GMAT (strongly preferred) or GRE. Additional exam requirements/recommendations for international students: Required—TOEFL (minimum score 600 paper-based; 100 iBT). *Application* *deadline:* For fall admission, 1/3 priority date for domestic and international students. Application fee: $75. Electronic applications accepted. *Expenses:* $708 fees per year; 100% of tuition covered by scholarship. *Financial support:* In 2016–17, 34 students received support, including 6 fellowships (averaging $3,333 per year); scholarships/grants and health care benefits also available. Financial award application deadline: 1/3. *Faculty research:* Financial and managerial accounting, asset pricing strategy and organizational behavior, information technology marketing analytics and consumer behavior. *Unit head:* Dr. Anand Swaminathan, Associate Dean, Doctoral Program, 404-727-2306, Fax: 404-727-5337, E-mail: anand.swaminathan@emory.edu. *Application contact:* Allison Gilmore, Director of Admissions and Student Services, 404-727-6353, Fax: 404-727-5337, E-mail: allison.gilmore@emory.edu.

Emory University, Goizueta Business School, Evening MBA Program, Atlanta, GA 30322. Offers MBA. *Program availability:* Part-time, evening/weekend. *Faculty:* 61 full-time (10 women), 13 part-time/adjunct (0 women). *Students:* 265 part-time (80 women); includes 77 minority (22 Black or African American, non-Hispanic/Latino; 36 Asian, non-Hispanic/Latino; 17 Hispanic/Latino; 2 Two or more races, non-Hispanic/Latino), 27 international. Average age 29. 200 applicants, 65% accepted, 93 enrolled. In 2016, 85 master's awarded. *Entrance requirements:* For master's, GMAT/GRE, undergraduate degree, interview, essays, recommendation letters. Additional exam requirements/recommendations for international students: Required—TOEFL (minimum score 100 iBT), IELTS (minimum score 7), PTE (minimum score 68). *Application deadline:* For fall admission, 10/28 for domestic students; for winter admission, 3/3 for domestic students; for spring admission, 5/12 for domestic students; for summer admission, 6/30 for domestic students. Application fee: $150. Electronic applications accepted. *Expenses:* Contact institution. *Financial support:* In 2016–17, 85 students received support. Application deadline: 6/6; applicants required to submit FAFSA. *Unit head:* Douglas Bowman, Senior Associate Dean for Working Professionals Program, 404-727-5008, E-mail: doug.bowman@emory.edu. *Application contact:* Julie Barefoot, Associate Dean, 404-727-6311, Fax: 404-727-4612, E-mail: mbaadmissions@emory.edu.
Website: http://www.goizueta.emory.edu/degree/eveningmba/index.html

Emory University, Goizueta Business School, Full Time MBA Program, Atlanta, GA 30322. Offers accounting (MBA); alternative investments (MBA); business process consulting (MBA); business technology management (MBA); capital markets (MBA); corporate finance (MBA); customer relationship management (MBA); decision analytics (MBA); entrepreneurship (MBA); finance (MBA); global management (MBA); investment banking (MBA); management consulting (MBA); marketing (MBA); marketing analytics (MBA); marketing consulting (MBA); operations management (MBA); organization and management (MBA); product and brand management (MBA); real estate (MBA); social enterprise (MBA); strategy consulting (MBA). *Accreditation:* AACSB. *Faculty:* 72 full-time (17 women), 18 part-time/adjunct (5 women). *Students:* 350 full-time (101 women); includes 77 minority (21 Black or African American, non-Hispanic/Latino; 3 American Indian or Alaska Native, non-Hispanic/Latino; 32 Asian, non-Hispanic/Latino; 15 Hispanic/Latino; 2 Native Hawaiian or other Pacific Islander, non-Hispanic/Latino; 4 Two or more races, non-Hispanic/Latino), 117 international. Average age 29. 1,434 applicants, 31% accepted, 181 enrolled. In 2016, 182 master's awarded. *Degree requirements:* For master's, 1 leadership course; 2 mid-semester module programs; 2 global components. *Entrance requirements:* For master's, GMAT/GRE, essays; recommendation letters; undergraduate degree; interview. Additional exam requirements/recommendations for international students: Required—TOEFL (minimum score 100 iBT), IELTS (minimum score 7), PTE (minimum score 68). *Application deadline:* For fall admission, 10/14 priority date for domestic and international students; for winter admission, 11/11 priority date for domestic and international students; for spring admission, 1/4 priority date for domestic students, 1/4 for international students. Application fee: $150. Electronic applications accepted. *Expenses:* $57,580. *Financial support:* In 2016–17, 289 students received support. Career-related internships or fieldwork, institutionally sponsored loans, and scholarships/grants available. Financial award application deadline: 4/1; financial award applicants required to submit FAFSA. *Faculty research:* Social enterprise; micro vs. large business; mobile health data; mutual fund performance; product evaluation. *Unit head:* Brian Mitchell, Associate Dean, 404-727-4824, Fax: 404-712-9648, E-mail: brian.mitchell@emory.edu. *Application contact:* Julie Barefoot, Associate Dean, 404-727-6311, Fax: 404-727-4612, E-mail: mbaadmissions@emory.edu.
Website: http://www.goizueta.emory.edu

Emory University, Goizueta Business School, Modular MBA for Executives Program, Atlanta, GA 30322. Offers MBA. *Faculty:* 64 full-time (8 women), 5 part-time/adjunct (0 women). *Students:* 68 full-time (20 women); includes 26 minority (9 Black or African American, non-Hispanic/Latino; 7 Asian, non-Hispanic/Latino; 10 Hispanic/Latino), 12 international. Average age 38. 66 applicants, 85% accepted, 30 enrolled. In 2016, 25 master's awarded. *Degree requirements:* For master's, completion of lock-step program with minimum of 54 credit hours, one elective course, management practice component, global business practices with 10-day international colloquium. *Entrance requirements:* For master's, GMAT/GRE, interview, essays, letters of recommendation, bachelor's degree. Additional exam requirements/recommendations for international students: Required—TOEFL (minimum score 600 paper-based; 100 iBT), IELTS (minimum score 7), PTE (minimum score 68). *Application deadline:* For fall admission, 12/1 for domestic and international students; for winter admission, 3/1 for domestic and international students; for spring admission, 6/1 for domestic and international students; for summer admission, 8/15 for domestic students, 8/1 for international students. Application fee: $150. Electronic applications accepted. *Expenses:* Contact institution. *Financial support:* In 2016–17, 45 students received support. Scholarships/grants available. Financial award application deadline: 3/1; financial award applicants required to submit FAFSA. *Unit head:* Douglas Bowman, Senior Associate Dean, 404-727-5008, Fax: 404-727-4936, E-mail: doug.bowman@emory.edu. *Application contact:* Julie Barefoot, Associate Dean of Admissions, 404-727-6311, Fax: 404-727-4612, E-mail: mbaadmissions@emory.edu.
Website: http://goizueta.emory.edu/degree/emba/memba/

Emory University, Goizueta Business School, Weekend MBA for Executives Program, Atlanta, GA 30322. Offers MBA. *Program availability:* Evening/weekend. *Faculty:* 64 full-time (8 women), 5 part-time/adjunct (0 women). *Students:* 82 full-time (20 women); includes 35 minority (20 Black or African American, non-Hispanic/Latino; 12 Asian, non-Hispanic/Latino; 2 Hispanic/Latino; 1 Two or more races, non-Hispanic/Latino), 7 international. Average age 37. 100 applicants, 82% accepted, 46 enrolled. In 2016, 39 master's awarded. *Degree requirements:* For master's, minimum of 51 credit hours (30 core; 21 electives). *Entrance requirements:* For master's, GMAT/GRE, interview, essays, letters of recommendation, bachelor's degree, resume. Additional exam requirements/recommendations for international students: Required—TOEFL (minimum score 100 iBT), IELTS (minimum score 7), PTE (minimum score 68). *Application deadline:* For fall admission, 12/1 for domestic and international students; for winter admission, 3/1 for domestic and international students; for spring admission, 5/1 for domestic and international students; for summer admission, 6/1 for domestic and international students. Application fee: $150. Electronic applications accepted. *Expenses:* Contact institution. *Financial support:* In 2016–17, 24 students received support. Institutionally sponsored loans and scholarships/grants available. Financial award application deadline: 3/1; financial award applicants required to submit FAFSA. *Unit head:* Douglas Bowman, Senior Associate Dean, 404-727-5008, E-mail: doug.bowman@emory.edu. *Application contact:* Julie Barefoot, Associate Dean of Admissions, 404-727-6311, Fax: 404-727-4612, E-mail: mbaadmissions@emory.edu.
Website: http://goizueta.emory.edu/degree/emba/wemba/

Emporia State University, Program in Business Administration, Emporia, KS 66801-5415. Offers MBA. *Accreditation:* AACSB. *Program availability:* Part-time, evening/weekend, blended/hybrid learning. *Faculty:* 30 full-time (5 women). *Students:* 51 full-time (19 women), 48 part-time (27 women); includes 6 minority (1 Black or African American, non-Hispanic/Latino; 1 Asian, non-Hispanic/Latino; 2 Hispanic/Latino; 2 Two or more races, non-Hispanic/Latino), 36 international. 64 applicants, 92% accepted, 14 enrolled. In 2016, 30 master's awarded. *Entrance requirements:* For master's, GRE, 15 undergraduate credits in business, minimum undergraduate GPA of 2.7 in last 60 hours. Additional exam requirements/recommendations for international students: Required—TOEFL (minimum score 520 paper-based; 68 iBT). *Application deadline:* For fall admission, 8/15 for domestic students. Applications are processed on a rolling basis. Application fee: $30 ($75 for international students). Electronic applications accepted. *Expenses:* Tuition, state resident: full-time $5922; part-time $246.75 per credit hour. Tuition, nonresident: full-time $18,414; part-time $767.25 per credit hour. *Required fees:* $1884; $78.50 per credit hour. *Financial support:* In 2016–17, 8 research assistantships with full tuition reimbursements (averaging $7,344 per year), 10 teaching assistantships with full tuition reimbursements (averaging $7,344 per year) were awarded; career-related internships or fieldwork, health care benefits, and unspecified assistantships also available. Financial award applicants required to submit FAFSA. *Unit head:* James Willingham, Coordinator, Graduate and Career Services, 620-341-5456, E-mail: jwilling@emporia.edu. *Application contact:* Mary Sewell, Admissions Coordinator, 800-950-GRAD, Fax: 620-341-5909, E-mail: msewell@emporia.edu.
Website: http://www.emporia.edu/business/programs/mba/

Endicott College, Van Loan School of Graduate and Professional Studies, Program in Business Administration, Beverly, MA 01915-2096. Offers MBA. *Program availability:* Part-time, evening/weekend, 100% online, blended/hybrid learning. *Faculty:* 8 full-time (3 women), 34 part-time/adjunct (9 women). *Students:* 149 full-time (69 women), 88 part-time (40 women); includes 36 minority (8 Black or African American, non-Hispanic/Latino; 8 Asian, non-Hispanic/Latino; 16 Hispanic/Latino; 4 Two or more races, non-Hispanic/Latino), 8 international. Average age 29. 116 applicants, 100% accepted, 106 enrolled. In 2016, 140 master's awarded. *Degree requirements:* For master's, thesis, project. *Entrance requirements:* For master's, two recommendations, undergraduate transcript, essay. Additional exam requirements/recommendations for international students: Required—TOEFL. *Application deadline:* Applications are processed on a rolling basis. Application fee: $50. Electronic applications accepted. *Expenses:* Contact institution. *Financial support:* Applicants required to submit FAFSA. *Faculty research:* Adult learning and development, supply chain management, marketing, ethics. *Unit head:* Richard Benedetto, Associate Dean of Graduate School, 978-232-2744, Fax: 978-232-3000, E-mail: rbenedet@endicott.edu. *Application contact:* Ian Menchini, Director, Graduate Enrollment and Advising, 978-232-5292, Fax: 978-232-3000, E-mail: imenchin@endicott.edu.
Website: http://www.endicott.edu/VanLoan/International-Progs/Graduate-Programs/International-Business-Admin.aspx

ESSEC Business School, Graduate Programs, Paris, France. Offers business administration (PhD); executive business administration (MBA); global business administration (MBA); hospitality management (MBA); international luxury brand management (MBA); management (MSM).

Everest University, Department of Business Administration, Tampa, FL 33614. Offers accounting (MBA); human resources (MBA); international business (MBA). *Program availability:* Part-time, evening/weekend. *Degree requirements:* For master's, thesis optional. *Entrance requirements:* For master's, GMAT or GRE General Test, minimum GPA of 3.0.

Everglades University, Graduate Programs, Program in Aviation Science, Boca Raton, FL 33431. Offers aviation operations management (MSA); aviation security (MSA); business administration (MSA). *Program availability:* Part-time, evening/weekend, 100% online. *Entrance requirements:* For master's, GMAT (minimum score of 400) or GRE (minimum score of 290), bachelor's or graduate degree from college accredited by an agency recognized by the U.S. Department of Education; minimum cumulative GPA of 2.0 at the baccalaureate level, 3.0 at the master's level. Additional exam requirements/recommendations for international students: Recommended—TOEFL (minimum score 500 paper-based). Electronic applications accepted. *Expenses:* Contact institution.

Everglades University, Graduate Programs, Program in Business Administration, Boca Raton, FL 33431. Offers accounting for managers (MBA); aviation management (MBA); human resource management (MBA); project management (MBA). *Program availability:* Part-time, evening/weekend, 100% online. *Entrance requirements:* For master's, GMAT (minimum score of 400) or GRE (minimum score of 290), bachelor's or graduate degree from college accredited by an agency recognized by the U.S. Department of Education; minimum cumulative GPA of 2.0 at the baccalaureate level, 3.0 at the master's level. Additional exam requirements/recommendations for international students: Recommended—TOEFL (minimum score 500 paper-based). Electronic applications accepted. *Expenses:* Contact institution.

Excelsior College, School of Business and Technology, Albany, NY 12203-5159. Offers business administration (MBA); cybersecurity management (MBA, Graduate Certificate); general business management (MS); health care management (MBA); human performance technology (MBA); human resource management (MS); human resources management (MBA); leadership (MBA, MS); mediation and arbitration (MBA, MS); social media management (MBA); technology management (MBA). *Program availability:* Part-time, evening/weekend, online learning. *Faculty:* 25 part-time/adjunct (9 women). *Students:* 1,801 part-time (487 women); includes 775 minority (424 Black or African American, non-Hispanic/Latino; 5 American Indian or Alaska Native, non-Hispanic/Latino; 58 Asian, non-Hispanic/Latino; 209 Hispanic/Latino; 15 Native Hawaiian or other Pacific Islander, non-Hispanic/Latino; 64 Two or more races, non-Hispanic/Latino), 11 international. Average age 39. In 2016, 288 master's awarded. *Application deadline:* Applications are processed on a rolling basis. Application fee: $50. Electronic applications accepted. *Expenses: Tuition:* Part-time $645 per credit. *Required fees:* $265 per credit. *Financial support:* Scholarships/grants available. *Unit head:* Dr. Lifang Shih, Dean, 888-647-2388. *Application contact:* Admissions, 888-647-2388 Ext. 133, Fax: 518-464-8777, E-mail: admissions@excelsior.edu.

Fairfield University, Dolan School of Business, Fairfield, CT 06824. Offers accounting (MBA, MS, CAS); business analytics (MS); entrepreneurship (MBA); finance (MBA, MS, CAS); general management (MBA, CAS); global management (MBA); human resource management (MBA, CAS); information systems and business analytics (MBA); marketing (MBA, CAS); taxation (MBA, CAS). *Accreditation:* AACSB. *Program availability:* Part-time, evening/weekend. *Faculty:* 20 full-time (6 women), 4 part-time/adjunct (1 woman). *Students:* 106 full-time (41 women), 57 part-time (26 women); includes 18 minority (4 Black or African American, non-Hispanic/Latino; 1 American Indian or Alaska Native, non-Hispanic/Latino; 4 Asian, non-Hispanic/Latino; 7 Hispanic/Latino; 2 Two or more races, non-Hispanic/Latino), 39 international. Average age 26.

136 applicants, 63% accepted, 35 enrolled. In 2016, 90 master's awarded. *Degree requirements:* For master's, capstone course. *Entrance requirements:* For master's, GMAT (minimum score 500), 2 letters of reference, resume, minimum GPA of 3.0. Additional exam requirements/recommendations for international students: Required—TOEFL (minimum score 550 paper-based; 80 iBT) or IELTS (minimum score 6.5). *Application deadline:* For fall admission, 5/15 for international students; for spring admission, 10/15 for international students. Applications are processed on a rolling basis. Application fee: $60. Electronic applications accepted. *Expenses:* $875 per credit hour. *Financial support:* In 2016–17, 33 students received support. Scholarships/grants and unspecified assistantships available. Financial award applicants required to submit FAFSA. *Faculty research:* International finance, leadership and careers, ethics in accounting, emotions in consumer behavior and organizations, data analytics. *Unit head:* Dr. Donald Gibson, Dean, 203-254-4070, Fax: 203-254-4105, E-mail: dgibson@fairfield.edu. *Application contact:* Marianne Gumpper, Director of Graduate and Continuing Studies Admission, 203-254-4184, Fax: 203-254-4073, E-mail: gradadmis@fairfield.edu.
Website: http://fairfield.edu/mba

Fairleigh Dickinson University, College at Florham, Anthony J. Petrocelli College of Continuing Studies, School of Administrative Science, Program in Administrative Science, Madison, NJ 07940-1099. Offers MAS.

Fairleigh Dickinson University, College at Florham, Silberman College of Business, Madison, NJ 07940-1099. Offers EMBA, MBA, MS, Certificate, MA/MBA, MBA/MA. *Accreditation:* AACSB. *Program availability:* Part-time, evening/weekend.

Fairleigh Dickinson University, College at Florham, Silberman College of Business, Departments of Management, Marketing, and Entrepreneurial Studies, Program in Management, Madison, NJ 07940-1099. Offers evolving technology (Certificate); management (MBA); MBA/MA.

Fairleigh Dickinson University, College at Florham, Silberman College of Business, Executive MBA Programs, Executive MBA Program in Management, Madison, NJ 07940-1099. Offers EMBA.

Fairleigh Dickinson University, Metropolitan Campus, Anthony J. Petrocelli College of Continuing Studies, School of Administrative Science, Program in Administrative Science, Teaneck, NJ 07666-1914. Offers MAS, Certificate.

Fairleigh Dickinson University, Metropolitan Campus, Silberman College of Business, Teaneck, NJ 07666-1914. Offers EMBA, MBA, MS, Certificate, MBA/MA. *Accreditation:* AACSB. *Entrance requirements:* For master's, GMAT.

Fairleigh Dickinson University, Metropolitan Campus, Silberman College of Business, Departments of Management, Marketing, and Entrepreneurial Studies, Program in Management, Teaneck, NJ 07666-1914. Offers management (MBA); management information systems (Certificate). *Accreditation:* AACSB.

Fairmont State University, Program in Business Administration, Fairmont, WV 26554. Offers MBA. *Accreditation:* ACBSP. *Program availability:* Part-time, evening/weekend. *Faculty:* 7 full-time (3 women), 1 part-time/adjunct (0 women). *Students:* 16 full-time (9 women), 17 part-time (10 women); includes 5 minority (1 American Indian or Alaska Native, non-Hispanic/Latino; 2 Asian, non-Hispanic/Latino; 1 Hispanic/Latino; 1 Two or more races, non-Hispanic/Latino). Average age 30. 34 applicants, 79% accepted, 13 enrolled. In 2016, 9 master's awarded. *Entrance requirements:* For master's, GRE, MAT, or GMAT, minimum overall undergraduate GPA of 2.75 or 3.0 on the last 60 hours. Additional exam requirements/recommendations for international students: Required—TOEFL (minimum score 80 iBT), IELTS (minimum score 6.5). *Application deadline:* For fall admission, 5/1 for domestic and international students. Applications are processed on a rolling basis. Application fee: $40. Electronic applications accepted. *Expenses:* Tuition, state resident: full-time $7504; part-time $405 per credit hour. Tuition, nonresident: full-time $16,060; part-time $880 per credit hour. Part-time tuition and fees vary according to course load. *Financial support:* In 2016–17, 11 students received support. Research assistantships, teaching assistantships, scholarships/grants, tuition waivers (full and partial), and unspecified assistantships available. Financial award applicants required to submit FAFSA. *Unit head:* Dr. Sunil Surendran, Director, 304-367-4404, Fax: 304-367-4613, E-mail: sunil.surendran@fairmontstate.edu. *Application contact:* Jack Kirby, Director of Graduate Studies, 304-367-4101, E-mail: jack.kirby@fairmontstate.edu.
Website: http://www.fairmontstate.edu/graduatestudies/MBA_program.asp

Fashion Institute of Technology, School of Graduate Studies, Program in Global Fashion Management, New York, NY 10001-5992. Offers MPS. Offered in collaboration with Hong Kong Polytechnic University and Institute Francais de la Mode. *Students:* 36. 69 applicants, 32% accepted, 20 enrolled. In 2016, 18 master's awarded. *Degree requirements:* For master's, capstone seminar. *Entrance requirements:* Additional exam requirements/recommendations for international students: Required—TOEFL (minimum score 550 paper-based). *Application deadline:* For fall admission, 2/15 priority date for domestic and international students. Applications are processed on a rolling basis. Application fee: $50. Electronic applications accepted. *Expenses:* Tuition, state resident: full-time $10,870; part-time $453 per credit. Tuition, nonresident: full-time $22,210; part-time $925 per credit. *Required fees:* $745. *Unit head:* Pamela Ellsworth, Associate Chairperson, 212-217-4300. *Application contact:* Administrative Secretary, Graduate Admissions, 212-217-4300, Fax: 212-217-5156, E-mail: gradinfo@fitnyc.edu.
Website: http://www.fitnyc.edu/gfm/

See Display below and Close-Up on page 177.

Faulkner University, Harris College of Business and Executive Education, Montgomery, AL 36109-3398. Offers management (MSM).

Fayetteville State University, Graduate School, Program in Business Administration, Fayetteville, NC 28301-4298. Offers MBA. *Accreditation:* AACSB. *Program availability:* Part-time, evening/weekend. *Faculty:* 23 full-time (6 women), 3 part-time/adjunct (1 woman). *Students:* 65 full-time (34 women), 97 part-time (50 women); includes 81 minority (58 Black or African American, non-Hispanic/Latino; 3 American Indian or Alaska Native, non-Hispanic/Latino; 13 Asian, non-Hispanic/Latino; 7 Hispanic/Latino), 4 international. Average age 33. 73 applicants, 100% accepted, 54 enrolled. In 2016, 20 master's awarded. *Entrance requirements:* For master's, GMAT. Additional exam requirements/recommendations for international students: Required—TOEFL. *Application deadline:* For fall admission, 4/15 for domestic students; for spring admission, 10/15 for domestic students. Application fee: $40. *Financial support:* Application deadline: 3/1. *Faculty research:* Business ethics, optimization and business simulation, consumer behavior, e-commerce and supply chain management, financial institutions. *Total annual research expenditures:* $15,000. *Unit head:* Dr. Pamela Jackson, Dean, School of Business and Economics, 910-672-1267, Fax: 910-672-2046, E-mail: pjackson@uncfsu.edu. *Application contact:* Mabel Mayle-Hill, Administrative Support Associate, 910-672-1267, Fax: 910-672-2046, E-mail: mhill@uncfsu.edu.

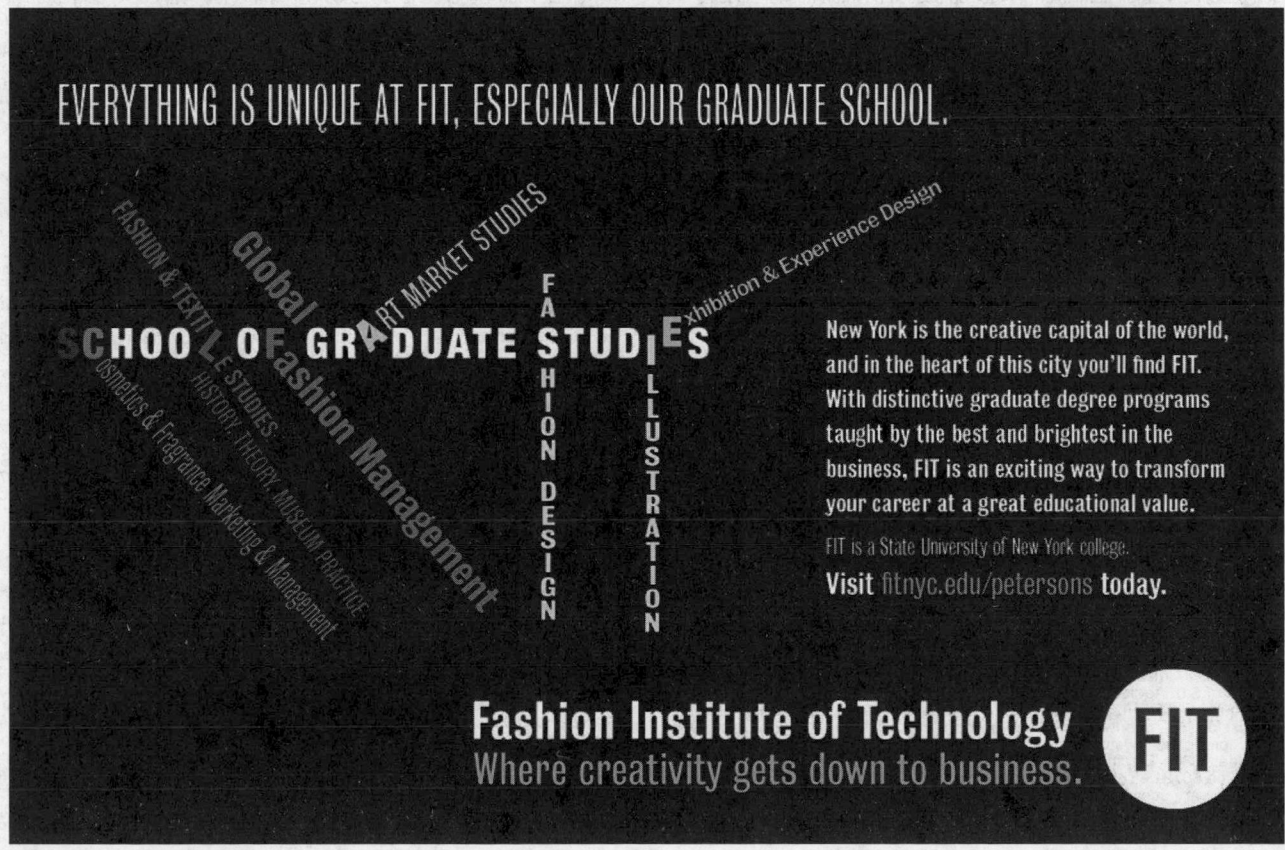

Felician University, Program in Business, Lodi, NJ 07644-2117. Offers business administration (DBA); innovation and entrepreneurship (MBA). *Program availability:* Part-time-only, evening/weekend. *Faculty:* 7 full-time (0 women), 9 part-time/adjunct (2 women). *Students:* 4 full-time (2 women), 85 part-time (46 women); includes 48 minority (24 Black or African American, non-Hispanic/Latino; 10 Asian, non-Hispanic/Latino; 13 Hispanic/Latino; 1 Two or more races, non-Hispanic/Latino), 4 international. Average age 35. 71 applicants, 86% accepted, 40 enrolled. In 2016, 22 master's awarded. Terminal master's awarded for partial completion of doctoral program. *Degree requirements:* For master's, comprehensive exam, thesis, presentation; for doctorate, thesis/dissertation, scholarly project. *Entrance requirements:* For master's and doctorate, GMAT, resume, personal statement, graduation from accredited baccalaureate program. Additional exam requirements/recommendations for international students: Required—TOEFL (minimum score 650 paper-based; 79 iBT), IELTS (minimum score 6.5). *Application deadline:* Applications are processed on a rolling basis. Application fee: $40. Electronic applications accepted. Application fee is waived when completed online. *Expenses:* $1,000 per credit and $55 mandatory fee per term. *Financial support:* Federal Work-Study and scholarships/grants available. Financial award applicants required to submit FAFSA. *Faculty research:* Social media, assessment, small business management, mission integration. *Unit head:* Dr. David M. Turi, Associate Dean/Associate Professor, School of Business, 201-559-3327, E-mail: turid@felician.edu. *Application contact:* Michael Szarek, Assistant Vice-President, Graduate Admissions, 201-559-1450, E-mail: szarekm@felician.edu.

Ferris State University, College of Business, Big Rapids, MI 49307. Offers business intelligence (MBA); design and innovation management (MBA); incident response (MBA); information security and intelligence (MS), including business intelligence, incident response, project management; lean systems and leadership (MBA); performance metrics (MBA); project management (MBA); supply chain management and lean logistics (MBA). *Accreditation:* ACBSP. *Program availability:* Part-time, evening/weekend, 100% online, blended/hybrid learning. *Faculty:* 18 full-time (7 women), 6 part-time/adjunct (3 women). *Students:* 25 full-time (11 women), 113 part-time (47 women); includes 12 minority (2 Black or African American, non-Hispanic/Latino; 1 American Indian or Alaska Native, non-Hispanic/Latino; 3 Asian, non-Hispanic/Latino; 3 Hispanic/Latino; 3 Two or more races, non-Hispanic/Latino), 50 international. Average age 31. 128 applicants, 59% accepted, 39 enrolled. In 2016, 94 master's awarded. *Degree requirements:* For master's, comprehensive exam, thesis. *Entrance requirements:* For master's, GRE or GMAT, minimum GPA of 3.0 in junior-/senior-level classes and overall; statement of purpose; 3 letters of reference; resume; transcripts. Additional exam requirements/recommendations for international students: Required—TOEFL (minimum score 500 paper-based; 70 iBT), IELTS (minimum score 6.5). *Application deadline:* For fall admission, 7/1 priority date for domestic students, 6/15 for international students; for winter admission, 11/1 priority date for domestic students, 10/15 for international students; for spring admission, 3/1 priority date for domestic students, 2/15 for international students. Applications are processed on a rolling basis. Application fee: $0 ($30 for international students). Electronic applications accepted. *Expenses:* Contact institution. *Financial support:* Career-related internships or fieldwork, Federal Work-Study, scholarships/grants, and unspecified assistantships available. Support available to part-time students. Financial award application deadline: 3/15; financial award applicants required to submit FAFSA. *Faculty research:* Lifestyle medicine business models, lean systems value chain pptimization, digital forensics/ incident response, location-based services, passive data capture and analysis. *Unit head:* Dr. David Nicol, College of Business Dean, 231-591-2168, Fax: 231-591-3521, E-mail: davidnicol@ferris.edu. *Application contact:* Dr. Greg Gogolin, Professor, 231-591-3159, Fax: 231-591-3521, E-mail: greggogolin@ferris.edu.
Website: http://cbgp.ferris.edu/

Fisher College, Master of Business Administration Program, Boston, MA 02116-1500. Offers strategic leadership (MBA). *Program availability:* Part-time, evening/weekend, online only, 100% online. *Faculty:* 3 full-time (1 woman), 10 part-time/adjunct (4 women). *Students:* 16 full-time (6 women), 18 part-time (11 women); includes 11 minority (1 Black or African American, non-Hispanic/Latino; 1 American Indian or Alaska Native, non-Hispanic/Latino; 1 Asian, non-Hispanic/Latino; 8 Hispanic/Latino), 5 international. Average age 33. 174 applicants, 17% accepted, 18 enrolled. In 2016, 6 master's awarded. *Degree requirements:* For master's, comprehensive exam. *Entrance requirements:* Additional exam requirements/recommendations for international students: Required—TOEFL (minimum score 80 iBT), IELTS (minimum score 6.5). *Application deadline:* For fall admission, 8/1 for domestic and international students; for winter admission, 11/1 for domestic and international students. Applications are processed on a rolling basis. Electronic applications accepted. *Expenses:* Contact institution. *Financial support:* In 2016–17, 5 students received support. Scholarships/ grants and unspecified assistantships available. Financial award applicants required to submit FAFSA. *Faculty research:* Humanistic management, the role of human resources in employee engagement. *Unit head:* Neil Trotta, Dean, 617-236-8867, Fax: 617-236-5462, E-mail: ntrotta@fisher.edu.
Website: http://www.fisher.edu/mba

Fitchburg State University, Division of Graduate and Continuing Education, Program in Business Administration, Fitchburg, MA 01420-2697. Offers accounting (MBA); human resource management (MBA); management (MBA). *Program availability:* Part-time, evening/weekend, online learning. *Entrance requirements:* Additional exam requirements/recommendations for international students: Required—TOEFL (minimum score 550 paper-based; 79 iBT). Electronic applications accepted. *Expenses:* Tuition, state resident: full-time $2871; part-time $1914 per year. Tuition, nonresident: full-time $2871; part-time $1914 per year. *Required fees:* $3828. Tuition and fees vary according to program.

Florida Agricultural and Mechanical University, Division of Graduate Studies, Research, and Continuing Education, School of Business and Industry, Tallahassee, FL 32307-3200. Offers accounting (MBA); finance (MBA); management information systems (MBA); marketing (MBA). *Accreditation:* ACBSP. *Degree requirements:* For master's, residency. *Entrance requirements:* For master's, GMAT, minimum GPA of 3.0.

Florida Atlantic University, College of Business, Program in Music Business Administration, Boca Raton, FL 33431-0991. Offers MS. *Students:* 3 full-time (all women), 2 part-time (1 woman); includes 1 minority (Hispanic/Latino), 1 international. Average age 46. 1 applicant. *Expenses:* Tuition, state resident: full-time $7392; part-time $369.82 per credit hour. Tuition, nonresident: full-time $19,432; part-time $1024.81 per credit hour. *Unit head:* Dr. Daniel Gropper, Dean, 561-297-3629, Fax: 561-297-3686, E-mail: vhale4@fau.edu. *Application contact:* Dr. Marcy Krugel, Graduate Adviser, 561-297-3940, Fax: 561-297-0801, E-mail: krugel@fau.edu.

Florida Gulf Coast University, Lutgert College of Business, Master of Business Administration Program, Fort Myers, FL 33965-6565. Offers MBA. *Accreditation:* AACSB. *Program availability:* Part-time, evening/weekend. *Faculty:* 58 full-time (23 women), 36 part-time/adjunct (13 women). *Students:* 22 full-time (9 women), 76 part-time (32 women); includes 15 minority (2 Black or African American, non-Hispanic/Latino; 3 Asian, non-Hispanic/Latino; 7 Hispanic/Latino; 3 Two or more races, non-Hispanic/Latino), 4 international. Average age 26. 84 applicants, 48% accepted, 27 enrolled. In 2016, 37 master's awarded. *Entrance requirements:* For master's, GMAT, minimum GPA of 3.0. Additional exam requirements/recommendations for international students: Required—TOEFL (minimum score 550 paper-based). *Application deadline:* For fall admission, 5/1 priority date for domestic students; for spring admission, 9/15 priority date for domestic students. Applications are processed on a rolling basis. Application fee: $30. Electronic applications accepted. *Expenses:* Tuition, state resident: full-time $6721. Tuition, nonresident: full-time $28,170. *Required fees:* $1987. Tuition and fees vary according to course load and degree level. *Financial support:* In 2016–17, 31 students received support. Application deadline: 3/1; applicants required to submit FAFSA. *Faculty research:* Fraud in audits, production planning in cell manufacturing systems, collaborative learning in distance courses, characteristics of minority and women-owned businesses. *Unit head:* Robert Beatty, Dean, 239-590-7300, Fax: 239-590-7330, E-mail: rbeatty@fgcu.edu. *Application contact:* Marisa Ouverson, Director of Enrollment Management, 239-590-7403, Fax: 239-590-7330, E-mail: mouverso@fgcu.edu.

Florida Institute of Technology, Extended Studies Division, Melbourne, FL 32901-6975. Offers acquisition and contract management (MS); aerospace engineering (MS); business administration (MBA, DBA); computer information systems (MS); computer science (MS); electrical engineering (MS); engineering management (MS); human resources management (MS); logistics management (MS), including humanitarian and disaster relief logistics; management (MS), including acquisition and contract management, e-business, human resources management, information systems, logistics management, management, transportation management; material acquisition management (MS); mechanical engineering (MS); operations research (MS); project management (MS), including information systems, operations research; public administration (MPA); quality management (MS); software engineering (MS); space systems (MS); space systems management (MS); supply chain management (MS); systems management (MS), including information systems, operations research; technology management (MS). *Program availability:* Part-time, evening/weekend, online learning. *Faculty:* 10 full-time (3 women), 122 part-time/adjunct (29 women). *Students:* 131 full-time (58 women), 997 part-time (348 women); includes 389 minority (231 Black or African American, non-Hispanic/Latino; 9 American Indian or Alaska Native, non-Hispanic/Latino; 26 Asian, non-Hispanic/Latino; 99 Hispanic/Latino; 3 Native Hawaiian or other Pacific Islander, non-Hispanic/Latino; 21 Two or more races, non-Hispanic/ Latino), 53 international. Average age 36. 962 applicants, 48% accepted, 323 enrolled. In 2016, 403 master's awarded. *Degree requirements:* For master's, comprehensive exam (for some programs). *Entrance requirements:* For master's, GMAT or resume showing 8 years of supervised experience, minimum GPA of 3.0, 2 letters of recommendation, resume. Additional exam requirements/recommendations for international students: Required—TOEFL (minimum score 550 paper-based; 79 iBT). *Application deadline:* For fall admission, 4/1 for international students; for spring admission, 9/30 for international students. Applications are processed on a rolling basis. Electronic applications accepted. *Expenses:* Contact institution. *Financial support:* Application deadline: 3/1; applicants required to submit FAFSA. *Unit head:* Dr. Theodore R. Richardson, III, Dean, 321-674-8123, Fax: 321-674-7597, E-mail: trichardson@fit.edu. *Application contact:* Carolyn Farrior, Director of Graduate Admissions, Online Learning and Off-Campus Programs, 321-674-7118, Fax: 321-674-8216, E-mail: cfarrior@fit.edu.
Website: http://es.fit.edu

Florida Institute of Technology, Nathan M. Bisk College of Business, Melbourne, FL 32901-6975. Offers MBA, MS. *Program availability:* Part-time, online learning. *Faculty:* 7 full-time (1 woman). *Students:* 72 full-time (29 women), 208 part-time (85 women); includes 91 minority (38 Black or African American, non-Hispanic/Latino; 1 American Indian or Alaska Native, non-Hispanic/Latino; 9 Asian, non-Hispanic/Latino; 36 Hispanic/ Latino; 1 Native Hawaiian or other Pacific Islander, non-Hispanic/Latino; 6 Two or more races, non-Hispanic/Latino), 24 international. Average age 33. 206 applicants, 40% accepted, 18 enrolled. In 2016, 192 master's awarded. *Degree requirements:* For master's, comprehensive exam (for some programs), thesis optional, capstone. *Entrance requirements:* For master's, GMAT, GRE or resume showing 8 years of supervised experience, minimum GPA of 3.0 (for MBA), 2 letters of recommendation, resume, statement of objectives. Additional exam requirements/recommendations for international students: Required—TOEFL (minimum score 550 paper-based; 79 iBT). *Application deadline:* For fall admission, 4/1 for international students; for spring admission, 9/30 for international students. Applications are processed on a rolling basis. Electronic applications accepted. *Expenses: Tuition:* Full-time $22,338; part-time $1241 per credit hour. *Required fees:* $250. Tuition and fees vary according to degree level, campus/location and program. *Financial support:* Research assistantships with partial tuition reimbursements, career-related internships or fieldwork, institutionally sponsored loans, and unspecified assistantships available. Support available to part-time students. Financial award application deadline: 3/1; financial award applicants required to submit FAFSA. *Faculty research:* Investment analysis, marketing research, strategy analysis, ethics, small business. *Unit head:* Dr. Theodore R. Richardson, III, Dean, 321-674-8123, Fax: 321-674-7597, E-mail: trichardson@fit.edu. *Application contact:* Cheryl A. Brown, Associate Director of Graduate Admissions, 321-674-7581, Fax: 321-723-9468, E-mail: cbrown@fit.edu.
Website: http://cob.fit.edu

Florida Memorial University, School of Business, Miami-Dade, FL 33054. Offers MBA. *Accreditation:* ACBSP. *Program availability:* Part-time. *Entrance requirements:* For master's, GMAT, 3 letters of recommendation.

Florida National University, Program in Business Administration, Hialeah, FL 33012. Offers finance (MBA); general management (MBA); health services administration (MBA); marketing (MBA); public management and leadership (MBA). *Program availability:* Part-time, blended/hybrid learning. *Degree requirements:* For master's, capstone. *Entrance requirements:* For master's, writing assessment, bachelor's degree from accredited institution; official undergraduate transcripts; minimum undergraduate GPA of 2.5, GMAT (minimum score of 400), or GRE (minimum score of 900); two letters of recommendation. Additional exam requirements/recommendations for international students: Required—TOEFL (minimum score 500 paper-based; 62 iBT), IELTS (minimum score 5.5). *Application deadline:* Applications are processed on a rolling basis. Electronic applications accepted. *Expenses:* Contact institution. *Financial support:* Federal Work-Study, institutionally sponsored loans, scholarships/grants, and tuition waivers available. Financial award applicants required to submit FAFSA. *Unit head:* Dr. Ernesto Gonzalez, Business Department Head, 305-821-3333 Ext. 1070, Fax: 305-362-0595, E-mail: egonzalez@fnu.edu. *Application contact:* Olga Rodriguez, Assistant Campus Dean, 305-821-3333 Ext. 1044, Fax: 305-362-0595, E-mail: orodriguez@fnu.edu.

Florida Southern College, Program in Business Administration, Lakeland, FL 33801-5698. Offers MBA. *Accreditation:* AACSB. *Program availability:* Part-time, evening/ weekend. *Faculty:* 4 full-time (1 woman), 1 part-time/adjunct (0 women). *Students:* 71 full-time (36 women), 6 part-time (4 women); includes 18 minority (4 Black or African American, non-Hispanic/Latino; 3 Asian, non-Hispanic/Latino; 10 Hispanic/Latino; 1 Two or more races, non-Hispanic/Latino), 8 international. Average age 29. 124 applicants, 49% accepted, 52 enrolled. In 2016, 37 master's awarded. *Entrance requirements:* For master's, GMAT or GRE General Test, letter of reference, resume, personal statement. Additional exam requirements/recommendations for international students: Required—TOEFL (minimum score 550 paper-based; 79 iBT), IELTS (minimum score 6.5). *Application deadline:* For fall admission, 6/1 for domestic and international students; for spring admission, 10/1 for domestic and international students. Applications are processed on a rolling basis. Application fee: $30. Electronic applications accepted. *Expenses:* $750 per credit hour tuition, $100 per term fees. *Financial support:* Scholarships/grants and unspecified assistantships available. Support available to part-time students. Financial award application deadline: 3/1; financial award applicants required to submit FAFSA. *Unit head:* Dr. Charles DuVal, Program Coordinator, 863-

680-4280, Fax: 863-680-4355, E-mail: cduval@flsouthern.edu. *Application contact:* Kamalie Morales, Senior Assistant Director of Adult and Graduate Education, 863-680-4205, Fax: 863-680-3872, E-mail: kmorales@flsouthern.edu.
Website: http://www.flsouthern.edu/KCMS/Master-of-Business-Administration.aspx

Florida State University, The Graduate School, College of Business, Tallahassee, FL 32306-1110. Offers accounting (M Acc), including assurance and advisory services, generalist, taxation; business administration (MBA, PhD), including accounting (PhD), finance (PhD), management information systems (PhD), marketing (PhD), organizational behavior and human resources (PhD), risk management and insurance (PhD), strategy (PhD); finance (MS); management information systems (MS); risk management and insurance (MS); JD/MBA; MSW/MBA. *Accreditation:* AACSB. *Program availability:* Part-time, 100% online. *Faculty:* 101 full-time (27 women), 4 part-time/adjunct (2 women). *Students:* 272 full-time (127 women), 351 part-time (133 women); includes 141 minority (45 Black or African American, non-Hispanic/Latino; 2 American Indian or Alaska Native, non-Hispanic/Latino; 20 Asian, non-Hispanic/Latino; 59 Hispanic/Latino; 2 Native Hawaiian or other Pacific Islander, non-Hispanic/Latino; 13 Two or more races, non-Hispanic/Latino), 71 international. Average age 30. 688 applicants, 60% accepted, 273 enrolled. In 2016, 231 master's, 12 doctorates awarded. Terminal master's awarded for partial completion of doctoral program. *Degree requirements:* For doctorate, comprehensive exam, thesis/dissertation. *Entrance requirements:* For master's, GMAT, GRE (for all except MS in finance), work experience (MBA, MS); minimum GPA of 3.0, letters of recommendation; for doctorate, GMAT, GRE (for marketing, organizational behavior, risk management and insurance, management information systems, and human resources only), minimum graduate GPA of 3.5, letters of recommendation. Additional exam requirements/recommendations for international students: Required—TOEFL (minimum score 600 paper-based; 85 iBT); Recommended—IELTS (minimum score 6). *Application deadline:* For fall admission, 6/1 for domestic and international students; for spring admission, 10/1 for domestic and international students; for summer admission, 3/1 for domestic and international students. Applications are processed on a rolling basis. Application fee: $30. Electronic applications accepted. *Expenses:* Contact institution. *Financial support:* In 2016–17, 149 students received support, including 9 fellowships (averaging $1,500 per year), 65 research assistantships with full tuition reimbursements available (averaging $20,000 per year), 75 teaching assistantships with full tuition reimbursements available (averaging $20,000 per year); career-related internships or fieldwork, scholarships/grants, health care benefits, tuition waivers (full and partial), and unspecified assistantships also available. Support available to part-time students. Financial award application deadline: 1/1; financial award applicants required to submit FAFSA. *Faculty research:* Business strategy, marketing, finance, accounting, business analytics. *Total annual research expenditures:* $1.4 million. *Unit head:* Dr. Michael Hartline, Dean, 850-644-4405, Fax: 850-644-0915, E-mail: mhartline@business.fsu.edu. *Application contact:* Jennifer Clark, Director, 850-644-6458, E-mail: gradprograms@business.fsu.edu.
Website: http://business.fsu.edu/

Fontbonne University, Graduate Programs, St. Louis, MO 63105-3098. Offers accounting (MBA, MS); art (MA); art (K-12) (MAT); business (MBA); computer science (MS); deaf education (MA); early intervention in deaf education (MA); education (MA), including autism spectrum disorders, curriculum and instruction, diverse learners, early childhood education, reading, special education; elementary education (MAT); family and consumer sciences (MA), including multidisciplinary health communication studies; fine arts (MFA); instructional design and technology (MS); management and leadership (MM); middle school education (MAT); secondary education (MAT); special education (MAT); speech-language pathology (MS); supply chain management (MS); theatre (MA). *Program availability:* Part-time, evening/weekend, online learning. *Faculty:* 32 full-time (24 women), 43 part-time/adjunct (26 women). *Students:* 456 full-time (313 women), 102 part-time (77 women); includes 138 minority (118 Black or African American, non-Hispanic/Latino; 1 American Indian or Alaska Native, non-Hispanic/Latino; 7 Asian, non-Hispanic/Latino; 9 Hispanic/Latino; 3 Two or more races, non-Hispanic/Latino), 37 international. *Degree requirements:* For master's, comprehensive exam (for some programs), thesis (for some programs). *Entrance requirements:* Additional exam requirements/recommendations for international students: Required—TOEFL (minimum score 500 paper-based; 65 iBT). *Application deadline:* For fall admission, 8/1 for international students; for spring admission, 12/1 for international students. Applications are processed on a rolling basis. Application fee: $25 ($30 for international students). Electronic applications accepted. *Expenses: Tuition:* Full-time $8436; part-time $703 per credit hour. *Required fees:* $18 per credit hour. Tuition and fees vary according to course load. *Financial support:* Teaching assistantships with partial tuition reimbursements and scholarships/grants available. Support available to part-time students. Financial award application deadline: 4/1; financial award applicants required to submit FAFSA. *Unit head:* Dr. Carey Adams, Vice President for Academic Affairs, 314-719-3609, E-mail: cadams@fontbonne.edu. *Application contact:* Lauryn Filip, Coordinator, Graduate Admission and Professional Studies, 314-889-4650, E-mail: admissions@fontbonne.edu.
Website: https://www.fontbonne.edu/academics/graduate-programs/

Fordham University, Gabelli School of Business, New York, NY 10023. Offers accounting (MBA, MS); applied statistics and decision-making (MS); business administration (EMBA); business analytics (MS); communications and media management (MBA); electronic business (MBA); entrepreneurship (MBA); finance (MBA); global finance (MS); global sustainability (MBA); healthcare management (MBA); information systems (MBA, MS); investor relations (MS); management (MBA, MS); marketing (MBA); marketing intelligence (MS); media management (MS); nonprofit leadership (MS); quantitative finance (MS); taxation (MS); JD/MBA; MS/MBA. *Accreditation:* AACSB. *Program availability:* Part-time, evening/weekend. *Faculty:* 132 full-time (44 women), 51 part-time/adjunct (7 women). *Students:* 1,117 full-time (668 women), 553 part-time (282 women); includes 207 minority (44 Black or African American, non-Hispanic/Latino; 92 Asian, non-Hispanic/Latino; 69 Hispanic/Latino; 2 Native Hawaiian or other Pacific Islander, non-Hispanic/Latino), 1,088 international. Average age 27. 4,745 applicants, 46% accepted, 752 enrolled. In 2016, 996 master's awarded. Terminal master's awarded for partial completion of doctoral program. *Degree requirements:* For master's, internships (required for MS in quantitative finance, recommended for MBA). *Entrance requirements:* For master's, GMAT/GRE, 2 letters of recommendation, resume, 2 essays, transcripts. Additional exam requirements/recommendations for international students: Required—TOEFL (minimum score 100 iBT), IELTS (minimum score 7). *Application deadline:* For fall admission, 11/15 priority date for domestic and international students; for winter admission, 1/15 priority date for domestic students, 1/1 priority date for international students; for spring admission, 3/1 for domestic and international students; for summer admission, 6/1 for domestic students. Application fee: $130. Electronic applications accepted. *Expenses:* $1,397 per credit. *Financial support:* In 2016–17, 78 students received support. Career-related internships or fieldwork, institutionally sponsored loans, scholarships/grants, and unspecified assistantships available. Support available to part-time students. Financial award application deadline: 6/30; financial award applicants required to submit FAFSA. *Unit head:* Dr. Donna Rapaccioli, Dean, 212-636-6165, Fax: 212-307-1779, E-mail: rapaccioli@fordham.edu. *Application contact:* Lawrence Murray, Senior Assistant Dean of Graduate Admissions and Advising, 212-636-6200, Fax: 212-636-7076, E-mail: admissionsgb@fordham.edu.
Website: http://www.fordham.edu/gabelli

Fort Hays State University, Graduate School, College of Business and Entrepreneurship, Department of Management, Hays, KS 67601-4099. Offers MBA. *Degree requirements:* For master's, thesis optional. *Entrance requirements:* For master's, GMAT. Additional exam requirements/recommendations for international students: Required—TOEFL (minimum score 550 paper-based). Electronic applications accepted. *Faculty research:* Organizational behavior and performance appraisal, data processing, international marketing.

Framingham State University, Continuing Education, Program in Business Administration, Framingham, MA 01701-9101. Offers MBA. *Program availability:* Part-time, evening/weekend. *Entrance requirements:* For master's, GMAT, GRE, or MAT.

Franciscan University of Steubenville, Graduate Programs, Department of Business, Steubenville, OH 43952-1763. Offers MBA. *Program availability:* Part-time, evening/weekend, 100% online, blended/hybrid learning. *Degree requirements:* For master's, research paper. *Entrance requirements:* For master's, GMAT, minimum undergraduate GPA of 2.5. Additional exam requirements/recommendations for international students: Required—TOEFL (minimum score 550 paper-based; 80 iBT). Electronic applications accepted. Application fee is waived when completed online. *Expenses:* Contact institution.

Francis Marion University, Graduate Programs, School of Business, Florence, SC 29502-0547. Offers business (MBA); health executive management (MBA). *Accreditation:* AACSB. *Program availability:* Part-time, evening/weekend. *Degree requirements:* For master's, comprehensive exam. *Entrance requirements:* For master's, GMAT or GRE, official transcripts, two letters of recommendation. Additional exam requirements/recommendations for international students: Required—TOEFL (minimum score 550 paper-based; 79 iBT). *Expenses:* Tuition, state resident: full-time $10,100; part-time $505 per credit hour. Tuition, nonresident: full-time $20,196; part-time $1009.80 per credit hour. *Required fees:* $14.80 per credit hour. $73 per semester. Tuition and fees vary according to course load and program. *Faculty research:* Ethics, directions of MBA, international business, regional economics, environmental issues.

Franklin Pierce University, Graduate and Professional Studies, Rindge, NH 03461-0060. Offers curriculum and instruction (M Ed); elementary education (MS Ed); emerging network technologies (Graduate Certificate); energy and sustainability studies (MBA, Graduate Certificate); health administration (MBA, Graduate Certificate); human resource management (MBA, Graduate Certificate); information technology (MBA); leadership (MBA); nursing education (MS); nursing leadership (MS); physical therapy (DPT); physician assistant studies (MPAS); special education (M Ed); sports management (MBA). *Accreditation:* APTA. *Program availability:* Part-time, 100% online, blended/hybrid learning. *Faculty:* 47 full-time (36 women), 165 part-time/adjunct (108 women). *Students:* 380 full-time (226 women), 245 part-time (158 women); includes 52 minority (13 Black or African American, non-Hispanic/Latino; 2 American Indian or Alaska Native, non-Hispanic/Latino; 14 Asian, non-Hispanic/Latino; 22 Hispanic/Latino; 1 Native Hawaiian or other Pacific Islander, non-Hispanic/Latino), 13 international. Average age 29. 1,995 applicants, 28% accepted, 267 enrolled. In 2016, 120 master's, 86 doctorates awarded. *Degree requirements:* For master's, concentrated original research projects; student teaching; fieldwork and/or internship; leadership project; PRAXIS I and II (for M Ed); for doctorate, concentrated original research projects, clinical fieldwork and/or internship, leadership project. *Entrance requirements:* For master's, minimum GPA of 2.5, 3 letters of recommendation; competencies in accounting, economics, statistics, and computer skills through life experience or undergraduate coursework (for MBA); certification/e-portfolio, minimum C grade in all education courses (for M Ed); license to practice as RN (for MS); for doctorate, GRE, 80 hours of observation/work in PT settings; completion of anatomy, chemistry, physics, and statistics; minimum GPA of 3.0. Additional exam requirements/recommendations for international students: Required—TOEFL (minimum score 550 paper-based; 61 iBT). *Application deadline:* Applications are processed on a rolling basis. Application fee: $0. Electronic applications accepted. *Expenses: Tuition:* Full-time $15,960; part-time $665 per credit hour. Tuition and fees vary according to program. *Financial support:* Teaching assistantships with tuition reimbursements, career-related internships or fieldwork, and unspecified assistantships available. Support available to part-time students. Financial award applicants required to submit FAFSA. *Faculty research:* Evidence-based practice in sports physical therapy, human resource management in economic crisis, leadership in nursing, innovation in sports facility management, differentiated learning and understanding by design. *Unit head:* Dr. Maria Altobello, Dean, 603-647-3509, Fax: 603-229-4580, E-mail: altobellom@franklinpierce.edu. *Application contact:* Graduate Studies, 800-325-1090, Fax: 603-626-4815, E-mail: cgps@franklinpierce.edu.
Website: http://www.franklinpierce.edu/academics/gradstudies/index.htm

Franklin University, MBA Program, Columbus, OH 43215-5399. Offers MBA. *Program availability:* Part-time, evening/weekend, online learning. *Entrance requirements:* For master's, minimum undergraduate GPA of 2.75. Additional exam requirements/recommendations for international students: Required—TOEFL (minimum score 550 paper-based). Electronic applications accepted.

Freed-Hardeman University, Program in Business Administration, Henderson, TN 38340-2399. Offers accounting (MBA); corporate responsibility (MBA); leadership (MBA). *Accreditation:* ACBSP. *Program availability:* Part-time, evening/weekend, online learning. *Entrance requirements:* For master's, GMAT. Additional exam requirements/recommendations for international students: Required—TOEFL (minimum score 500 paper-based).

Fresno Pacific University, Graduate Programs, MBA Program, Fresno, CA 93702-4709. Offers MBA. *Entrance requirements:* For master's, GMAT, GRE, or MAT, three references; resume; official transcripts verifying BA/BS; minimum GPA of 3.0; prerequisite courses in economics, statistics, and accounting. *Expenses:* Contact institution.

Fresno Pacific University, Graduate Programs, Program in Leadership and Organizational Studies, Fresno, CA 93702-4709. Offers MA. *Program availability:* Part-time, evening/weekend. *Degree requirements:* For master's, thesis. *Entrance requirements:* For master's, MAT, GRE or GMAT, interview, three references. Additional exam requirements/recommendations for international students: Required—TOEFL (minimum score 550 paper-based). Electronic applications accepted. *Expenses:* Contact institution. *Faculty research:* Ethics, servant leadership, communication, creative problem solving.

Frostburg State University, Graduate School, College of Business, Frostburg, MD 21532-1099. Offers MBA. *Accreditation:* AACSB. *Program availability:* Part-time, evening/weekend. *Entrance requirements:* For master's, GMAT. Additional exam requirements/recommendations for international students: Required—TOEFL. Electronic applications accepted. *Faculty research:* Cooperative teaching methods, strategic change processes, political marketing.

Full Sail University, Entertainment Business Master of Science Program - Online, Winter Park, FL 32792-7437. Offers MS. *Program availability:* Online learning. *Entrance* *requirements:* Additional exam requirements/recommendations for international students: Required—TOEFL (minimum score 550 paper-based; 79 iBT).

Gannon University, School of Graduate Studies, College of Engineering and Business, Dahlkemper School of Business, Program in Business Administration, Erie, PA 16541-0001. Offers business administration (MBA); finance (MBA); human resources management (MBA); marketing (MBA). *Accreditation:* ACBSP. *Program availability:* Part-time, evening/weekend, 100% online, blended/hybrid learning. *Students:* 43 full-time (17 women), 67 part-time (34 women); includes 7 minority (4 Black or African American, non-Hispanic/Latino; 2 Asian, non-Hispanic/Latino; 1 Hispanic/Latino), 19 international. Average age 30. 160 applicants, 53% accepted, 28 enrolled. In 2016, 60 master's awarded. *Entrance requirements:* For master's, GMAT, bachelor's degree in any discipline from any accredited college or university, resume, transcripts, 3 letters of recommendation. Additional exam requirements/recommendations for international students: Required—TOEFL (minimum score 79 iBT). *Application deadline:* Applications are processed on a rolling basis. Application fee: $25. Electronic applications accepted. Application fee is waived when completed online. *Expenses: Tuition:* Full-time $17,370. *Required fees:* $550. Tuition and fees vary according to course load and program. *Financial support:* Federal Work-Study and unspecified assistantships available. Financial award application deadline: 7/1; financial award applicants required to submit FAFSA. *Unit head:* Dr. Michael Messina, Director, 814-871-5755, Fax: 814-871-7210, E-mail: messina001@gannon.edu. *Application contact:* Bridget Philip, Director of Graduate Admissions, 814-871-7412, E-mail: graduate@gannon.edu.

Gardner-Webb University, Graduate School of Business, Boiling Springs, NC 28017. Offers IMBA, M Acc, MBA. *Accreditation:* ACBSP. *Program availability:* Part-time, evening/weekend, online learning. *Faculty:* 13 full-time (3 women), 6 part-time/adjunct (2 women). *Students:* 31 full-time (15 women), 250 part-time (134 women); includes 71 minority (54 Black or African American, non-Hispanic/Latino; 4 Asian, non-Hispanic/Latino; 13 Hispanic/Latino). Average age 31. 202 applicants, 65% accepted, 97 enrolled. In 2016, 81 master's awarded. *Entrance requirements:* For master's, GMAT, GRE, 2 semesters of course work each in economics, statistics, and accounting. Additional exam requirements/recommendations for international students: Required—TOEFL (minimum score 500 paper-based; 61 iBT). *Application deadline:* For spring admission, 1/15 for domestic students. Applications are processed on a rolling basis. Electronic applications accepted. *Expenses:* Contact institution. *Financial support:* In 2016–17, 23 students received support. Unspecified assistantships available. Support available to part-time students. Financial award applicants required to submit FAFSA. *Unit head:* Dr. Van Graham, Dean, 704-406-4622, E-mail: vgraham@gardner-webb.edu. *Application contact:* Mischia Taylor, Director of Admissions, 877-498-4723, Fax: 704-406-3895, E-mail: mataylor@gardner-webb.edu.
Website: http://gardner-webb.edu/academic-programs-and-resources/colleges-and-schools/business/index

Geneva College, Program in Business Administration, Beaver Falls, PA 15010-3599. Offers business administration (MBA); finance (MBA); marketing (MBA); operations (MBA). *Accreditation:* ACBSP. *Program availability:* Part-time, evening/weekend. *Students:* 22 full-time (6 women), 29 part-time (10 women); includes 4 minority (1 Black or African American, non-Hispanic/Latino; 1 American Indian or Alaska Native, non-Hispanic/Latino; 2 Asian, non-Hispanic/Latino), 1 international. Average age 35. In 2016, 15 master's awarded. *Degree requirements:* For master's, 36 credit hours of course work (30 of which are required of all students). *Entrance requirements:* For master's, GMAT (if college GPA less than 2.5), undergraduate transcript, 2 letters of recommendation, resume, goals statement. Additional exam requirements/recommendations for international students: Required—TOEFL. *Application deadline:* For fall admission, 3/1 priority date for domestic students; for spring admission, 11/1 priority date for domestic students. Applications are processed on a rolling basis. Electronic applications accepted. *Expenses:* $710 per credit. *Financial support:* In 2016–17, 1 student received support. Scholarships/grants available. Financial award application deadline: 8/1; financial award applicants required to submit FAFSA. *Unit head:* Dr. Gary Vander Plaats, Director of the MBA Program, 724-847-6619, E-mail: gpvander@geneva.edu. *Application contact:* Marina Frazier, Director of Graduate Enrollment, 724-847-6697, E-mail: mba@geneva.edu.
Website: http://www.geneva.edu/page/masters_business

George Fox University, College of Business, Newberg, OR 97132-2697. Offers accounting (DBA); finance (MBA); management (DBA); management and leadership (MBA); marketing (DBA); organizational strategy (MBA); strategic human resource management (MBA). MBA offered in Newberg, OR and in Portland, OR. *Accreditation:* ACBSP. *Program availability:* Part-time, evening/weekend, online learning. *Degree requirements:* For master's, capstone project; for doctorate, credit-applied research project. *Entrance requirements:* For master's, resume (5 years of professional experience); 3 professional references; interview; financial e-learning course; official transcripts; for doctorate, GRE or GMAT, resume; personal mission statement; academic research writing sample; official transcript from each college/university attended; three professional references. Additional exam requirements/recommendations for international students: Required—TOEFL (minimum score 577 paper-based; 90 iBT) or IELTS (minimum score 7). Electronic applications accepted. *Expenses:* Contact institution.

George Mason University, School of Business, Program in Business Administration, Fairfax, VA 22030. Offers MBA. *Accreditation:* AACSB. *Faculty:* 94 full-time (29 women), 58 part-time/adjunct (20 women). *Students:* 201 full-time (83 women), 44 part-time (14 women); includes 83 minority (26 Black or African American, non-Hispanic/Latino; 31 Asian, non-Hispanic/Latino; 24 Hispanic/Latino; 2 Two or more races, non-Hispanic/Latino), 12 international. Average age 32. 251 applicants, 75% accepted, 113 enrolled. In 2016, 87 master's awarded. *Entrance requirements:* For master's, GMAT/GRE, resume; 2 official copies of transcripts; 2 professional letters of recommendation; personal career goals statement; professional essay; interview. Additional exam requirements/recommendations for international students: Required—TOEFL (minimum score 575 paper-based; 88 iBT), IELTS (minimum score 6.5), PTE (minimum score 59). *Application deadline:* For fall admission, 1/15 priority date for domestic students, 3/15 for international students. Application fee: $75 ($80 for international students). Electronic applications accepted. *Expenses:* Contact institution. *Financial support:* In 2016–17, 5 students received support, including 5 teaching assistantships with tuition reimbursements available (averaging $7,226 per year); career-related internships or fieldwork, Federal Work-Study, scholarships/grants, unspecified assistantships, and health care benefits (for full-time research or teaching assistantship recipients) also available. Support available to part-time students. Financial award application deadline: 3/1; financial award applicants required to submit FAFSA. *Faculty research:* Electronic commerce, marketing information systems, group decision-making, corporate governance, risk management. *Unit head:* Victoria Grady, Director, 703-993-8711, Fax: 703-993-1870, E-mail: vgrady3@gmu.edu. *Application contact:* Rebecca Diemer, Director, Graduate Academic Services, 703-993-2216, Fax: 703-993-1778, E-mail: rdiemer@gmu.edu.
Website: http://business.gmu.edu/mba-programs/

Georgetown University, Graduate School of Arts and Sciences, McDonough School of Business, Washington, DC 20057. Offers business administration (EMBA, GEMBA, MBA); finance (MS); leadership (EML). *Accreditation:* AACSB. *Entrance requirements:* For master's, GMAT. Additional exam requirements/recommendations for international students: Required—TOEFL. *Expenses:* Contact institution.

The George Washington University, School of Business, Washington, DC 20052. Offers M Accy, MBA, MS, MSF, MSIST, MTA, PMBA, PhD, Certificate, Professional Certificate, JD/MBA, MBA/MA. PMBA also offered in Alexandria and Ashburn, VA. *Program availability:* Part-time, evening/weekend, online learning. *Faculty:* 121 full-time (38 women). *Students:* 1,022 full-time (540 women), 816 part-time (370 women); includes 522 minority (206 Black or African American, non-Hispanic/Latino; 1 American Indian or Alaska Native, non-Hispanic/Latino; 166 Asian, non-Hispanic/Latino; 103 Hispanic/Latino; 2 Native Hawaiian or other Pacific Islander, non-Hispanic/Latino; 44 Two or more races, non-Hispanic/Latino), 701 international. Average age 32. 3,672 applicants, 47% accepted, 597 enrolled. In 2016, 767 master's, 14 doctorates, 18 other advanced degrees awarded. *Degree requirements:* For doctorate, thesis/dissertation. *Entrance requirements:* For doctorate, GMAT or GRE. Additional exam requirements/recommendations for international students: Required—TOEFL. *Application deadline:* For fall admission, 4/1 priority date for domestic students; for spring admission, 10/1 for domestic students. Applications are processed on a rolling basis. Application fee: $75. Electronic applications accepted. *Financial support:* In 2016–17, 194 students received support. Fellowships with tuition reimbursements available, teaching assistantships with tuition reimbursements available, career-related internships or fieldwork, Federal Work-Study, institutionally sponsored loans, and tuition waivers (partial) available. Financial award application deadline: 4/1. *Unit head:* Dr. Linda Livingstone, Dean. *Application contact:* Christopher Storer, Executive Director, Graduate Admissions, 202-994-1212, E-mail: gwmba@gwu.edu.
Website: http://business.gwu.edu/grad

Georgia Christian University, School of Business, Atlanta, GA 30360. Offers MBA.

Georgia College & State University, Graduate School, The J. Whitney Bunting School of Business, Program in Business Administration, Milledgeville, GA 31061. Offers MBA. *Accreditation:* AACSB. *Program availability:* Part-time, evening/weekend, 100% online, blended/hybrid learning. *Students:* 1 (woman) full-time, 81 part-time (33 women); includes 28 minority (14 Black or African American, non-Hispanic/Latino; 6 Asian, non-Hispanic/Latino; 6 Hispanic/Latino; 2 Two or more races, non-Hispanic/Latino). Average age 34. 50 applicants, 94% accepted, 34 enrolled. In 2016, 64 master's awarded. *Degree requirements:* For master's, minimum GPA of 3.0, complete program within 7 years of start date. *Entrance requirements:* For master's, GRE or GMAT, transcript, certificate of immunization. *Application deadline:* For fall admission, 7/1 priority date for domestic students; for spring admission, 11/1 priority date for domestic students; for summer admission, 4/1 priority date for domestic students. Applications are processed on a rolling basis. Application fee: $40. Electronic applications accepted. *Expenses:* $288 per credit hour in-state, $1,027 per credit hour out-of-state; $733 per credit hour (online); $1,990 per year full-time fees. *Financial support:* In 2016–17, 4 students received support. Unspecified assistantships available. Financial award application deadline: 3/1; financial award applicants required to submit FAFSA. *Unit head:* Dr. Dale Young, Dean, School of Business, 478-445-5497, E-mail: dale.younge@gcsu.edu. *Application contact:* Lynn Hanson, Director of Graduate Programs, 478-445-5115, E-mail: lynn.hanson@gcsu.edu.
Website: http://gcsu.edu/business/gradbusiness/mba

Georgia Institute of Technology, Graduate Studies, Scheller College of Business, Program in Business Administration, Atlanta, GA 30332-0001. Offers business administration (MBA); global business (MBA); management of technology (MBA). *Accreditation:* AACSB. *Program availability:* Part-time, evening/weekend. *Entrance requirements:* For master's, GMAT, two essays, three letters of recommendation, transcript from each college/university attended. Additional exam requirements/recommendations for international students: Required—TOEFL (minimum score 600 paper-based; 100 iBT). Electronic applications accepted. *Expenses:* Contact institution.

Georgia Institute of Technology, Graduate Studies, Scheller College of Business, Program in Management, Atlanta, GA 30332-0001. Offers MS, PhD. *Accreditation:* AACSB. *Program availability:* Part-time. *Degree requirements:* For doctorate, comprehensive exam, thesis/dissertation, oral exams. *Entrance requirements:* For doctorate, GMAT, two essay questions, three letters of recommendation, transcripts from each college/university attended, copy of most recent resume. Additional exam requirements/recommendations for international students: Required—TOEFL (minimum score 600 paper-based; 100 iBT). Electronic applications accepted. *Faculty research:* Management information systems, management of technology, international business, entrepreneurship, operations management.

Georgian Court University, School of Business and Digital Media, Lakewood, NJ 08701-2697. Offers business (MBA); business essentials (Certificate); nonprofit management (Certificate). *Program availability:* Part-time, evening/weekend. *Faculty:* 7 full-time (3 women), 11 part-time/adjunct (4 women). *Students:* 29 full-time (22 women), 40 part-time (26 women); includes 22 minority (7 Black or African American, non-Hispanic/Latino; 2 Asian, non-Hispanic/Latino; 9 Hispanic/Latino; 4 Two or more races, non-Hispanic/Latino). Average age 31. 55 applicants, 49% accepted, 13 enrolled. In 2016, 34 master's, 3 other advanced degrees awarded. *Entrance requirements:* For master's, GMAT or CPA exam, 3 letters of recommendation. Additional exam requirements/recommendations for international students: Required—TOEFL (minimum score 550 paper-based). *Application deadline:* For fall admission, 8/15 priority date for domestic students, 5/1 for international students; for spring admission, 1/15 priority date for domestic students, 10/1 for international students. Applications are processed on a rolling basis. Application fee: $40. Electronic applications accepted. *Expenses: Tuition:* Full-time $15,079; part-time $839 per credit. *Required fees:* $968; $496 per credit. Tuition and fees vary according to campus/location and program. *Financial support:* Scholarships/grants, health care benefits, and unspecified assistantships available. Financial award application deadline: 4/15; financial award applicants required to submit FAFSA. *Unit head:* Dr. Janice Warner, Dean, 732-987-2662, Fax: 732-987-2024, E-mail: jwarner@georgian.edu. *Application contact:* Patrick Givens, Director of Graduate and Professional Studies Admissions, 732-987-2736, Fax: 732-987-2000, E-mail: gps@georgian.edu.
Website: http://georgian.edu/academics/school-of-business/

Georgia Southern University, Jack N. Averitt College of Graduate Studies, College of Business Administration, The Georgia Web MBA, Statesboro, GA 30460. Offers MBA. *Program availability:* Part-time, evening/weekend, blended/hybrid learning. *Students:* 105 part-time (34 women); includes 33 minority (21 Black or African American, non-Hispanic/Latino; 4 Asian, non-Hispanic/Latino; 6 Hispanic/Latino; 2 Two or more races, non-Hispanic/Latino), 5 international. Average age 33. 71 applicants, 92% accepted, 41 enrolled. In 2016, 36 master's awarded. *Entrance requirements:* For master's, GMAT. Additional exam requirements/recommendations for international students: Required—TOEFL (minimum score 550 paper-based; 80 iBT), IELTS (minimum score 6). *Application deadline:* For fall admission, 8/1 for domestic students, 3/1 for international students; for spring admission, 12/1 for domestic students. Applications are processed on a rolling basis. Application fee: $50. Electronic applications accepted. *Expenses:* Contact institution. *Financial support:* In 2016–17, 1 student received support. Unspecified assistantships available. Financial award application deadline: 4/15;

financial award applicants required to submit FAFSA. *Faculty research:* Macroeconomics, international business, leadership, marketing, managerial finance. *Unit head:* Dr. Gordon Smith, Graduate Program Director, 912-478-2357, Fax: 912-478-0292, E-mail: gsmith@georgiasouthern.edu. *Application contact:* Karen Wells, Coordinator for Graduate Student Recruitment, 912-478-5767, Fax: 912-478-0740, E-mail: kwells@georgiasouthern.edu.
Website: http://cogs.georgiasouthern.edu/admission/GraduatePrograms/mbagaweb.php

Georgia Southern University, Jack N. Averitt College of Graduate Studies, College of Business Administration, Program in Business Administration, Statesboro, GA 30458. Offers MBA. *Accreditation:* AACSB. *Program availability:* Part-time, evening/weekend, online learning. *Students:* 59 full-time (29 women), 41 part-time (14 women); includes 20 minority (15 Black or African American, non-Hispanic/Latino; 2 Asian, non-Hispanic/Latino; 2 Hispanic/Latino; 1 Two or more races, non-Hispanic/Latino), 9 international. Average age 30. 71 applicants, 89% accepted, 42 enrolled. In 2016, 60 master's awarded. *Entrance requirements:* For master's, GMAT. Additional exam requirements/recommendations for international students: Required—TOEFL (minimum score 550 paper-based; 80 iBT), IELTS (minimum score 6). *Application deadline:* For fall admission, 3/1 priority date for domestic students, 6/1 for international students; for spring admission, 10/1 priority date for domestic students, 10/1 for international students. Applications are processed on a rolling basis. Application fee: $50. Electronic applications accepted. *Expenses:* Tuition, state resident: full-time $7236; part-time $277 per semester hour. Tuition, nonresident: full-time $27,118; part-time $1105 per semester hour. *Required fees:* $2092. *Financial support:* In 2016–17, 13 students received support, including research assistantships with partial tuition reimbursements available (averaging $7,200 per year), teaching assistantships with partial tuition reimbursements available (averaging $7,200 per year); career-related internships or fieldwork, Federal Work-Study, scholarships/grants, tuition waivers (partial), and unspecified assistantships also available. Support available to part-time students. Financial award application deadline: 4/15; financial award applicants required to submit FAFSA. *Unit head:* Gordon Smith, Graduate Program Director, 912-478-2357, Fax: 912-478-7480, E-mail: gsmith@georgiasouthern.edu. *Application contact:* Karen Wells, Coordinator for Graduate Student Recruitment, 912-478-5767, Fax: 912-478-0740, E-mail: kwells@georgiasouthern.edu.
Website: http://coba.georgiasouthern.edu/mba/

Georgia Southwestern State University, School of Business Administration, Americus, GA 31709-4693. Offers MBA. *Accreditation:* AACSB. *Program availability:* Part-time, online only, 100% online. *Faculty:* 12 full-time (5 women), 2 part-time/adjunct (both women). *Students:* 4 full-time (3 women), 52 part-time (32 women); includes 11 minority (10 Black or African American, non-Hispanic/Latino; 1 Hispanic/Latino). Average age 33. 31 applicants, 71% accepted, 20 enrolled. In 2016, 11 master's awarded. *Degree requirements:* For master's, minimum cumulative GPA of 3.0. *Entrance requirements:* For master's, GMAT or GRE, baccalaureate degree from a regionally-accredited institution; minimum undergraduate overall GPA of 2.7 as reported on official final transcripts; letters of recommendation. *Application deadline:* For fall admission, 6/30 for domestic students; for spring admission, 11/30 for domestic students; for summer admission, 4/30 for domestic students. Applications are processed on a rolling basis. Application fee: $25. Electronic applications accepted. *Expenses:* $215 per credit hour, plus fees, which vary according to number of enrolled credit hours. *Financial support:* Application deadline: 6/1; applicants required to submit FAFSA. *Unit head:* Dr. Liz Wilson, Dean, 229-931-2090. *Application contact:* Whitney Ford, Admissions Specialist, Office of Graduate Admissions, 800-338-0082, Fax: 229-931-2983, E-mail: graduateadmissions@gsw.edu.
Website: https://gsw.edu/academics/schools-and-departments/school-of-business-administration/mba-program

Georgia State University, J. Mack Robinson College of Business, Department of Managerial Sciences, Atlanta, GA 30302-3083. Offers business analysis (MBA, MS); entrepreneurship (MBA); human resources management (MBA, MS); operations management (MBA, MS); organization behavior/human resource management (PhD); organization management (MBA); organizational change (MS); strategic management (PhD). *Accreditation:* AACSB. *Program availability:* Part-time, evening/weekend. *Faculty:* 25 full-time (11 women). *Students:* 30 full-time (20 women), 10 part-time (4 women); includes 14 minority (11 Black or African American, non-Hispanic/Latino; 1 Asian, non-Hispanic/Latino; 1 Hispanic/Latino; 1 Two or more races, non-Hispanic/Latino), 12 international. Average age 31. 79 applicants, 30% accepted, 13 enrolled. In 2016, 23 master's, 2 doctorates awarded. *Degree requirements:* For doctorate, comprehensive exam, thesis/dissertation. *Entrance requirements:* For master's, GRE or GMAT, transcripts from all institutions attended, resume, essays; for doctorate, GMAT, three letters of recommendation, personal statement, transcripts from all institutions attended, resume. Additional exam requirements/recommendations for international students: Required—TOEFL (minimum score 610 paper-based; 101 iBT), IELTS (minimum score 7). *Application deadline:* For fall admission, 5/1 priority date for domestic students, 2/1 priority date for international students; for spring admission, 9/15 priority date for domestic students, 4/1 priority date for international students. Applications are processed on a rolling basis. Application fee: $50. Electronic applications accepted. *Expenses:* Tuition, state resident: full-time $6876; part-time $382 per credit hour. Tuition, nonresident: full-time $22,374; part-time $1243 per credit hour. *Required fees:* $2128; $1064 per term. Part-time tuition and fees vary according to course load and program. *Financial support:* Research assistantships, teaching assistantships, scholarships/grants, tuition waivers, and unspecified assistantships available. Financial award applicants required to submit FAFSA. *Faculty research:* Entrepreneurship and innovation; strategy process; workplace interactions, relationships, and processes; leadership and culture; supply chain management. *Unit head:* Dr. Pamela S. Barr, Interim Chair, 404-413-7525, Fax: 404-413-7571. *Application contact:* Toby McChesney, Assistant Dean for Graduate Recruiting and Student Services, 404-413-7167, Fax: 404-413-7162, E-mail: rcbgradadmissions@gsu.edu.
Website: http://mgmt.robinson.gsu.edu/

Georgia State University, J. Mack Robinson College of Business, Executive Doctorate in Business Program, Atlanta, GA 30302-3083. Offers EDB. *Accreditation:* AACSB. *Program availability:* Part-time, evening/weekend. *Entrance requirements:* Additional exam requirements/recommendations for international students: Required—TOEFL (minimum score 610 paper-based; 101 iBT), IELTS (minimum score 7). *Application deadline:* For fall admission, 5/1 priority date for domestic students, 2/1 priority date for international students. Applications are processed on a rolling basis. Application fee: $100. Electronic applications accepted. *Expenses:* Tuition, state resident: full-time $6876; part-time $382 per credit hour. Tuition, nonresident: full-time $22,374; part-time $1243 per credit hour. *Required fees:* $2128; $1064 per term. Part-time tuition and fees vary according to course load and program. *Financial support:* Scholarships/grants available. *Unit head:* Maury C. Kalnitz, Director of the Executive Doctorate in Business, 404-413-7178. *Application contact:* Heather Jacobs, Assistant Director of the Executive Doctorate in Business, 404-413-7178, E-mail: hjacob3@gsu.edu.
Website: http://robinson.gsu.edu/execdoctorate/index.html

Georgia State University, J. Mack Robinson College of Business, Program in General Business Administration, Atlanta, GA 30302-3083. Offers business administration (MBA); executive business administration (EMBA); global business administration (GMBA); professional business administration (PMBA); PMBA/MHA. *Accreditation:* AACSB. *Program availability:* Part-time, evening/weekend. *Entrance requirements:* For master's, GRE or GMAT, transcripts from all institutions attended, resume, essays. Additional exam requirements/recommendations for international students: Required—TOEFL (minimum score 610 paper-based; 101 iBT), IELTS (minimum score 7). *Application deadline:* For fall admission, 5/1 priority date for domestic students, 2/1 priority date for international students; for spring admission, 9/15 priority date for domestic students, 4/1 priority date for international students. Applications are processed on a rolling basis. Application fee: $50. Electronic applications accepted. *Expenses:* Tuition, state resident: full-time $6876; part-time $382 per credit hour. Tuition, nonresident: full-time $22,374; part-time $1243 per credit hour. *Required fees:* $2128; $1064 per term. Part-time tuition and fees vary according to course load and program. *Financial support:* Research assistantships, scholarships/grants, tuition waivers, and unspecified assistantships available. Financial award application deadline: 5/1. *Unit head:* Dr. Richard D. Phillips, Associate Dean for Academic Initiatives and Innovation, 404-413-7000, Fax: 404-413-7035. *Application contact:* Toby McChesney, Assistant Dean for Graduate Recruiting and Student Services, 404-413-7167, Fax: 404-413-7162, E-mail: rcbgradadmissions@gsu.edu.
Website: http://robinson.gsu.edu/mba/index.html

Goddard College, Graduate Division, Master of Arts in Social Innovation and Sustainability Program, Plainfield, VT 05667-9432. Offers MA. *Program availability:* Part-time, online learning. *Degree requirements:* For master's, thesis. *Entrance requirements:* For master's, 3 letters of recommendation, relevant prior training or experience, interview. Electronic applications accepted.

Golden Gate University, Ageno School of Business, San Francisco, CA 94105-2968. Offers accounting (MBA); business administration (EMBA, MBA, PMBA, DBA); business analytics (MS); finance (MBA, MS, Certificate); financial planning (MS, Certificate); healthcare information systems (Certificate); human resource management (MBA, MS); human resources management (Certificate); information systems (MS); information technology (MBA); information technology management (Certificate); integrated marketing and communications (MS, Certificate); international business (MBA); management (MBA); marketing (MBA, MS, Certificate); operations supply chain management (Certificate); psychology (MA, Certificate); public administration (EMPA); public relations (MS, Certificate); technical market analysis (Certificate); JD/MBA. *Program availability:* Part-time, evening/weekend. *Faculty:* 18 full-time (3 women), 117 part-time/adjunct (44 women). *Students:* 458 full-time (254 women), 664 part-time (331 women); includes 346 minority (75 Black or African American, non-Hispanic/Latino; 2 American Indian or Alaska Native, non-Hispanic/Latino; 132 Asian, non-Hispanic/Latino; 105 Hispanic/Latino; 9 Native Hawaiian or other Pacific Islander, non-Hispanic/Latino; 23 Two or more races, non-Hispanic/Latino), 354 international. Average age 34. 905 applicants, 83% accepted, 165 enrolled. In 2016, 350 master's, 2 doctorates awarded. *Degree requirements:* For doctorate, thesis/dissertation, qualifying examination. *Entrance requirements:* For master's, GMAT (for MBA), minimum GPA of 2.5 (MS). Additional exam requirements/recommendations for international students: Required—TOEFL (minimum score 550 paper-based; 79 iBT). *Application deadline:* For fall admission, 5/15 for domestic and international students; for winter admission, 1/15 for domestic and international students; for spring admission, 9/15 for domestic and international students. Applications are processed on a rolling basis. Application fee: $70 ($110 for international students). Electronic applications accepted. *Expenses:* Contact institution. *Financial support:* In 2016–17, 372 students received support. Career-related internships or fieldwork, Federal Work-Study, institutionally sponsored loans, and scholarships/grants available. Support available to part-time students. Financial award applicants required to submit FAFSA. *Unit head:* Dr. Gordon Swartz, Dean, 415-442-7027, Fax: 415-442-6579, E-mail: gswartz@ggu.edu. *Application contact:* Angela Melero, Enrollment Services, 415-442-7800, Fax: 415-442-7807, E-mail: info@ggu.edu.
Website: http://www.ggu.edu/programs/business-and-management

Goldey-Beacom College, Graduate Program, Wilmington, DE 19808-1999. Offers business administration (MBA); finance (MS); financial management (MBA); health care management (MBA); human resource management (MBA); information technology (MBA); international business management (MBA); major finance (MBA); major taxation (MBA); management (MM); marketing management (MBA); taxation (MBA, MS). *Accreditation:* ACBSP. *Program availability:* Part-time, evening/weekend. *Entrance requirements:* For master's, GMAT, MAT, GRE, minimum GPA of 3.0. Additional exam requirements/recommendations for international students: Required—TOEFL (minimum score 65 iBT); Recommended—IELTS (minimum score 6). Electronic applications accepted.

Gonzaga University, School of Business Administration, Spokane, WA 99258. Offers accountancy (M Acc); American Indian entrepreneurship (MBA); business administration (MBA); taxation (MS); JD/M Acc; JD/MBA. *Accreditation:* AACSB. *Program availability:* Part-time, evening/weekend. *Faculty:* 17 full-time (4 women), 14 part-time/adjunct (2 women). *Students:* 80 full-time (32 women), 135 part-time (60 women); includes 37 minority (2 Black or African American, non-Hispanic/Latino; 10 American Indian or Alaska Native, non-Hispanic/Latino; 5 Asian, non-Hispanic/Latino; 10 Hispanic/Latino; 10 Two or more races, non-Hispanic/Latino), 14 international. Average age 29. 252 applicants, 131 enrolled. In 2016, 113 master's awarded. *Degree requirements:* For master's, capstone course. *Entrance requirements:* For master's, GMAT (minimum score 500), essay, two professional recommendations, resume/curriculum vitae, copy of official transcripts from all colleges attended, minimum GPA of 3.0. Additional exam requirements/recommendations for international students: Required—TOEFL (minimum score 570 paper-based, 89 iBT) or IELTS (minimum score 6.5). *Application deadline:* Applications are processed on a rolling basis. Application fee: $50. Electronic applications accepted. *Expenses:* $975 per credit. *Financial support:* In 2016–17, 134 students received support. Scholarships/grants, tuition waivers, and unspecified assistantships available. Support available to part-time students. Financial award applicants required to submit FAFSA. *Unit head:* Dr. Ken Anderson, Interim Dean, 509-313-5991, E-mail: anderson@gem.gonzaga.edu. *Application contact:* Stacey Chatman, Assistant Director for Admissions, 509-313-4622, E-mail: chatman@gonzaga.edu.
Website: http://www.gonzaga.edu/Academics/Colleges-and-Schools/School-of-Business-Administration

Goucher College, MA and MFA Programs, Baltimore, MD 21204-2794. Offers arts administration (MA); creative nonfiction (MFA); cultural sustainability (MA); digital arts (MA, MFA); environmental studies (MA); historic preservation (MA); management (MA). *Program availability:* Part-time, evening/weekend, blended/hybrid learning. *Faculty:* 6 full-time (4 women), 100 part-time/adjunct (56 women). *Students:* 70 full-time (50 women), 69 part-time (52 women); includes 15 minority (7 Black or African American, non-Hispanic/Latino; 1 American Indian or Alaska Native, non-Hispanic/Latino; 1 Asian, non-Hispanic/Latino; 4 Hispanic/Latino; 2 Two or more races, non-Hispanic/Latino), 2 international. 74 applicants, 88% accepted, 42 enrolled. In 2016, 83 master's awarded.

Business Administration and Management—General

Degree requirements: For master's, thesis, e-portfolio. *Entrance requirements:* For master's, digital portfolio (for MA, MFA in digital arts); writing sample (for MFA in creative nonfiction). Additional exam requirements/recommendations for international students: Required—TOEFL (minimum score 550 paper-based; 80 iBT). *Application deadline:* Applications are processed on a rolling basis. Application fee: $75. Electronic applications accepted. *Expenses:* Contact institution. *Financial support:* Scholarships/ grants and unspecified assistantships available. Financial award application deadline: 4/ 15; financial award applicants required to submit FAFSA. *Unit head:* Leslie Rubinkowski, Assistant Provost, 410-337-6200, E-mail: leslie.rubinkowski@goucher.edu. *Application contact:* Shelby Hillers, Admissions Coordinator, 410-337-6200, Fax: 410-337-6200, E-mail: shelby.hillers@goucher.edu.
Website: http://www.goucher.edu/grad

Governors State University, College of Business, Program in Business Administration, University Park, IL 60484. Offers MBA. *Accreditation:* ACBSP. *Program availability:* Part-time. *Faculty:* 25 full-time (9 women), 30 part-time/adjunct (10 women). *Students:* 26 full-time (11 women), 68 part-time (44 women); includes 63 minority (49 Black or African American, non-Hispanic/Latino; 3 Asian, non-Hispanic/Latino; 6 Hispanic/Latino; 5 Two or more races, non-Hispanic/Latino), 3 international. Average age 36. 157 applicants, 29% accepted, 36 enrolled. In 2016, 37 master's awarded. *Entrance requirements:* Additional exam requirements/recommendations for international students: Required—TOEFL (minimum score 550 paper-based; 80 iBT), IELTS. *Application deadline:* For fall admission, 4/1 for domestic students. Application fee: $50. Electronic applications accepted. *Expenses:* $426 per credit hour; $38 per term or $76 per credit hour fees. *Financial support:* Application deadline: 5/1; applicants required to submit FAFSA. *Unit head:* Olumide Ijose, Interim Chair of Division of Management, Marketing and Entrepreneurship, 708-534-4932, E-mail: oijose@govst.edu. *Application contact:* Yakeea Daniels, Assistant Vice President for Enrollment Services/Director of Admission, 708-534-4510, E-mail: ydaniels@govst.edu.

The Graduate Center, City University of New York, Graduate Studies, Program in Business, New York, NY 10016-4039. Offers accounting (PhD); behavioral science (PhD); finance (PhD); management planning systems (PhD). *Degree requirements:* For doctorate, thesis/dissertation. *Entrance requirements:* For doctorate, GMAT, writing sample (15 pages). Additional exam requirements/recommendations for international students: Required—TOEFL. Electronic applications accepted.

Grand Canyon University, Colangelo College of Business, Phoenix, AZ 85017-1097. Offers accounting (MBA, MS); business analytics (MS); disaster preparedness and executive fire service leadership (MS); finance (MBA); general management (MBA); health systems management (MBA); information technology management (MS); leadership (MBA, MS); marketing (MBA); organizational leadership and entrepreneurship (MS); project management (MBA); sports business (MBA); strategic human resource management (MBA). *Accreditation:* ACBSP. *Program availability:* Part-time, evening/weekend, online learning. *Faculty:* 8 full-time (3 women), 147 part-time/ adjunct (49 women). *Students:* 1 full-time (0 women), 2,121 part-time (1,165 women); includes 341 minority (249 Black or African American, non-Hispanic/Latino; 17 American Indian or Alaska Native, non-Hispanic/Latino; 15 Asian, non-Hispanic/Latino; 29 Hispanic/Latino; 4 Native Hawaiian or other Pacific Islander, non-Hispanic/Latino; 27 Two or more races, non-Hispanic/Latino), 20 international. Average age 38. In 2016, 569 master's awarded. *Entrance requirements:* For master's, equivalent of two years' full-time professional work experience. Additional exam requirements/recommendations for international students: Required—TOEFL (minimum score 575 paper-based; 90 iBT), IELTS (minimum score 7). *Application deadline:* For fall admission, 8/21 for domestic students, 7/2 for international students; for spring admission, 12/24 for domestic students, 11/1 for international students. Applications are processed on a rolling basis. Application fee: $0. Electronic applications accepted. *Financial support:* Federal Work-Study available. Support available to part-time students. Financial award applicants required to submit FAFSA. *Unit head:* Kim Donaldson, Dean, 602-639-6597, E-mail: kdonaldson@gcu.edu. *Application contact:* Matt Tidwell, Enrollment Manager, 602-639-6020, E-mail: mtidwell@gcu.edu.
Website: https://www.gcu.edu/colangelo-college-of-business.php

Grand Canyon University, College of Doctoral Studies, Phoenix, AZ 85017-1097. Offers data analytics (DBA); general psychology (PhD), including cognition and instruction, industrial and organizational psychology, integrating technology, learning, and psychology, performance psychology; management (DBA); marketing (DBA); organizational leadership (Ed D), including behavioral health, Christian ministry, health care administration, organizational development. *Degree requirements:* For doctorate, comprehensive exam, thesis/dissertation. *Entrance requirements:* For doctorate, minimum GPA of 3.4 on earned advanced degree from regionally-accredited institution; transcripts; goals statement. Application fee: $0. *Unit head:* Michael Berger, Dean, 602-639-7255. *Application contact:* Michael Berger, Dean, 602-639-7255.
Website: https://www.gcu.edu/college-of-doctoral-studies.php

Grand Valley State University, Seidman College of Business, Program in Business Administration, Allendale, MI 49401-9403. Offers MBA. *Accreditation:* AACSB. *Program availability:* Part-time, evening/weekend. *Students:* 39 full-time (20 women), 157 part-time (56 women); includes 9 minority (2 Black or African American, non-Hispanic/Latino; 1 Asian, non-Hispanic/Latino; 2 Hispanic/Latino; 4 Two or more races, non-Hispanic/ Latino), 7 international. Average age 33. 68 applicants, 90% accepted, 45 enrolled. In 2016, 97 master's awarded. *Degree requirements:* For master's, capstone course. *Entrance requirements:* For master's, GMAT, personal statement. Additional exam requirements/recommendations for international students: Required—TOEFL. *Application deadline:* For fall admission, 8/1 priority date for domestic students, 5/1 priority date for international students; for winter admission, 12/1 priority date for domestic students, 11/1 priority date for international students; for spring admission, 4/1 priority date for domestic students, 3/1 priority date for international students. Applications are processed on a rolling basis. Application fee: $30. Electronic applications accepted. *Expenses:* $646 per credit hour. *Financial support:* In 2016–17, 52 students received support, including 48 fellowships, 4 research assistantships with full and partial tuition reimbursements available (averaging $4,000 per year); institutionally sponsored loans and unspecified assistantships also available. Support available to part-time students. Financial award application deadline: 2/15. *Faculty research:* E-commerce, continuous improvement, currency futures, manufacturing flexibility. *Unit head:* Dr. Jaideep Motwani, Director, 616-331-7490, Fax: 616-331-7389, E-mail: motwanij@gvsu.edu. *Application contact:* Koleta Moore, Assistant Director, Graduate Business Programs, 616-331-7386, Fax: 616-331-7389, E-mail: moorekol@ gvsu.edu.
Website: http://www.gvsu.edu/business/

Granite State College, MS in Management Program, Concord, NH 03301. Offers MS. *Program availability:* Part-time, 100% online, blended/hybrid learning. *Faculty:* 1 (woman) full-time, 5 part-time/adjunct (1 woman). *Students:* 6 full-time (all women), 16 part-time (10 women); includes 2 minority (both Two or more races, non-Hispanic/ Latino). Average age 35. 8 applicants, 88% accepted, 5 enrolled. In 2016, 4 master's awarded. *Degree requirements:* For master's, capstone. *Entrance requirements:* For master's, bachelor's degree with minimum GPA of 3.0 on last 60 credit hours, 500-1000 word statement of purpose, two letters of professional or academic reference, resume, official transcripts. Additional exam requirements/recommendations for international students: Required—TOEFL (minimum score 80 iBT), IELTS (minimum score 6.5). *Application deadline:* Applications are processed on a rolling basis. Application fee: $0. Electronic applications accepted. *Expenses:* $9,216 full-time in-state, $512 per credit part-time; $9,810 full-time out-of-state, $545 per credit part-time. *Financial support:* Federal Work-Study and National Guard course waivers available. Financial award applicants required to submit FAFSA. *Unit head:* Dr. Johnna Herrick-Phelps, Vice Provost of Academic Affairs, 855-228-3000, E-mail: johnna.herrick-phelps@granite.edu. *Application contact:* Ana Gonzalez, Administrative Assistant, Office of Graduate Studies, 603-822-5433, Fax: 603-513-1387, E-mail: gsc.graduatestudies@granite.edu.
Website: http://www.granite.edu/academics/degrees/masters/management.php

Grantham University, Mark Skousen School of Business, Lenexa, KS 66219. Offers business administration (MBA); business intelligence (MS); human resources management (Certificate); information management (MBA); performance improvement (MS); project management (MBA, Certificate). *Program availability:* Part-time, online only, 100% online. *Faculty:* 1 full-time, 36 part-time/adjunct. *Students:* 73 full-time (37 women), 1,046 part-time (424 women); includes 442 minority (309 Black or African American, non-Hispanic/Latino; 8 American Indian or Alaska Native, non-Hispanic/ Latino; 27 Asian, non-Hispanic/Latino; 63 Hispanic/Latino; 7 Native Hawaiian or other Pacific Islander, non-Hispanic/Latino; 28 Two or more races, non-Hispanic/Latino). Average age 40. 1,324 applicants, 95% accepted, 1123 enrolled. In 2016, 331 master's awarded. *Degree requirements:* For master's, capstone project, PMP Prep Exam; for Certificate, comprehensive exam (for some programs), PMP Prep Exam. *Entrance requirements:* For master's, baccalaureate or master's degree with minimum cumulative GPA of 2.5 from institution accredited by agency recognized by U.S. Department of Education or foreign equivalent. Additional exam requirements/recommendations for international students: Required—PTE (minimum score 50), TOEFL (minimum score 530 paper-based, 71 iBT) or IELTS (minimum score 6.5). *Application deadline:* Applications are processed on a rolling basis. Electronic applications accepted. *Expenses:* $325 per credit hour, $45 per 8-week term technology fee. *Financial support:* Scholarships/grants available. Financial award applicants required to submit FAFSA. *Faculty research:* Organizational structures, e-discovery and project management, decision management, resource-based and ethical perspectives, external finance dependence in corporate investments. *Unit head:* Dr. David Marker, Dean, Mark Skousen School of Business, 800-955-2527, E-mail: dmarker@grantham.edu. *Application contact:* Jared Parlette, Vice President of Student Enrollment, 800-955-2527, E-mail: admissions@grantham.edu.
Website: http://www.grantham.edu/colleges-and-schools/school-of-business/

Green Mountain College, Program in Business Administration, Poultney, VT 05764-1199. Offers MBA. Distance learning only. *Program availability:* Online learning. *Entrance requirements:* For master's, GMAT or Quantitative Skills Assessment, 3 recommendations. Electronic applications accepted. *Faculty research:* Migrant farm workers and world systems theory ecosystem assessments.

Gwynedd Mercy University, School of Graduate and Professional Studies, Gwynedd Valley, PA 19437-0901. Offers health care administration (MBA); management (MSM); strategic management and leadership (MBA). *Program availability:* Part-time, evening/ weekend. *Faculty:* 5 full-time (all women), 22 part-time/adjunct (8 women). *Students:* 73 full-time (48 women); includes 27 minority (20 Black or African American, non-Hispanic/ Latino; 2 Asian, non-Hispanic/Latino; 5 Hispanic/Latino). Average age 39. In 2016, 80 master's awarded. *Degree requirements:* For master's, thesis. *Entrance requirements:* For master's, minimum GPA of 3.0. *Application deadline:* Applications are processed on a rolling basis. *Expenses: Tuition:* Full-time $14,400; part-time $800 per credit hour. One-time fee: $165. Tuition and fees vary according to degree level and program. *Financial support:* Career-related internships or fieldwork, Federal Work-Study, tuition waivers (full and partial), and unspecified assistantships available. Financial award application deadline: 8/31; financial award applicants required to submit FAFSA. *Unit head:* Dr. Mary Sortino, Dean, 215-646-7300, E-mail: sortino.m@gmercyu.edu. *Application contact:* Information Contact, 800-342-5462, Fax: 215-641-5556.

Hallmark University, School of Business, San Antonio, TX 78230. Offers global management (MBA). *Faculty:* 2 full-time (0 women), 3 part-time/adjunct (1 woman). *Students:* 5 full-time (0 women); includes 2 minority (1 Hispanic/Latino; 1 Two or more races, non-Hispanic/Latino). In 2016, 1 master's awarded. *Degree requirements:* For master's, thesis (for some programs). *Entrance requirements:* For master's, bachelor's degree; minimum undergraduate GPA of 2.5; completion of one course each in college-level statistics, quanitative methods, and calculus or pre-calculus; official undergraduate transcripts; professional resume; personal statement; two letters of recommendation; two 200-word typed essays. Additional exam requirements/recommendations for international students: Required—TOEFL (minimum score 450 paper-based; 45 iBT). *Application deadline:* Applications are processed on a rolling basis. Application fee: $60 ($0 for international students). *Expenses:* Contact institution. *Financial support:* Applicants required to submit FAFSA. *Unit head:* Dr. Darla Kenward, Dean of Academics, 210-690-9000 Ext. 242, Fax: 210-697-8225, E-mail: dkenward@ hallmarkuniversity.edu. *Application contact:* Jennifer Sabchez, Director of Admissions, 210-690-9000 Ext. 212, Fax: 210-697-8225, E-mail: jsanchez@hallmarkuniversity.edu.
Website: http://hallmarkuniversity.edu/business/

Hamline University, School of Business, St. Paul, MN 55104-1284. Offers business administration (MBA); nonprofit management (MNM); public administration (MPA, DPA); MBA/MNM; MBA/MPA; MPA/MNM. *Program availability:* Part-time, evening/weekend, blended/hybrid learning. *Faculty:* 21 full-time (7 women), 25 part-time/adjunct (4 women). *Students:* 272 full-time (137 women), 69 part-time (33 women); includes 76 minority (39 Black or African American, non-Hispanic/Latino; 2 American Indian or Alaska Native, non-Hispanic/Latino; 20 Asian, non-Hispanic/Latino; 10 Hispanic/Latino; 5 Two or more races, non-Hispanic/Latino), 19 international. Average age 34. 166 applicants, 64% accepted, 77 enrolled. In 2016, 191 master's, 3 doctorates awarded. *Degree requirements:* For master's, thesis (for some programs); for doctorate, comprehensive exam, thesis/dissertation. *Entrance requirements:* For master's and doctorate, personal statement, official transcripts, resume or curriculum vitae, letters of recommendation, writing sample. Additional exam requirements/recommendations for international students: Required—TOEFL (minimum score 80 iBT). *Application deadline:* For fall admission, 6/1 for domestic and international students; for spring admission, 11/ 1 for domestic students, 10/1 for international students; for summer admission, 3/1 for domestic students, 2/1 for international students. Applications are processed on a rolling basis. Application fee: $0 ($100 for international students). Electronic applications accepted. *Expenses:* Contact institution. *Financial support:* Career-related internships or fieldwork, Federal Work-Study, scholarships/grants, and unspecified assistantships available. Support available to part-time students. Financial award applicants required to submit FAFSA. *Faculty research:* Liberal arts-based business programs, experiential learning, organizational process/politics, gender differences, social equity. *Unit head:* Dr. Anne McCarthy, Dean, 651-523-2284, Fax: 651-523-3098, E-mail: hsb@hamline.edu. *Application contact:* Shawn Skoog, Director of Graduate Recruitment and Admission, 651-523-2900, Fax: 651-523-3058, E-mail: gradprog@hamline.edu.
Website: http://www.hamline.edu/business

Hampton University, Program in Business Administration, Hampton, VA 23668. Offers MBA, PhD. *Program availability:* Part-time, online learning. *Faculty:* 6 full-time (4 women). *Students:* 39 full-time (27 women), 17 part-time (13 women); includes 53 minority (52 Black or African American, non-Hispanic/Latino; 1 Hispanic/Latino), 1 international. Average age 28. 29 applicants, 31% accepted, 9 enrolled. In 2016, 22 master's, 1 doctorate awarded. *Degree requirements:* For master's, comprehensive exam (for some programs), thesis (for some programs); for doctorate, comprehensive exam (for some programs), thesis/dissertation, oral defense, qualifying exam, journal article. *Entrance requirements:* For master's, GMAT. Additional exam requirements/recommendations for international students: Required—TOEFL (minimum score 525 paper-based) or IELTS (6.5). *Application deadline:* For fall admission, 6/1 priority date for domestic students, 4/1 priority date for international students; for spring admission, 11/1 priority date for domestic students, 9/1 priority date for international students; for summer admission, 4/1 priority date for domestic students, 2/1 priority date for international students. Applications are processed on a rolling basis. Application fee: $35. Electronic applications accepted. *Expenses: Tuition:* Full-time $10,776; part-time $548 per credit hour. *Required fees:* $35; $35 per credit hour. Tuition and fees vary according to course load and program. *Financial support:* Teaching assistantships, career-related internships or fieldwork, Federal Work-Study, institutionally sponsored loans, scholarships/grants, unspecified assistantships, and stipends available. Support available to part-time students. Financial award application deadline: 6/30; financial award applicants required to submit FAFSA. *Unit head:* Dr. Sid Credle, Dean, School of Business, 757-727-5361.

Harding University, Paul R. Carter College of Business Administration, Searcy, AR 72149-0001. Offers international business (MBA); leadership and organizational management (MBA). *Accreditation:* ACBSP. *Program availability:* Part-time, evening/weekend, 100% online. *Faculty:* 26 part-time/adjunct (6 women). *Students:* 36 full-time (15 women), 86 part-time (35 women); includes 17 minority (7 Black or African American, non-Hispanic/Latino; 5 Asian, non-Hispanic/Latino; 4 Hispanic/Latino; 1 Two or more races, non-Hispanic/Latino), 12 international. Average age 32. 22 applicants, 100% accepted, 22 enrolled. In 2016, 54 master's awarded. *Degree requirements:* For master's, portfolio. *Entrance requirements:* For master's, GMAT (minimum score of 500) or GRE (minimum score of 300), minimum GPA of 3.0, 2 letters of recommendation, resume, 3 essays, all official transcripts. Additional exam requirements/recommendations for international students: Required—TOEFL (minimum score 550 paper-based; 79 iBT). *Application deadline:* For fall admission, 8/1 priority date for domestic and international students; for spring admission, 12/1 priority date for domestic and international students. Applications are processed on a rolling basis. Application fee: $40. Tuition and fees vary according to degree level and program. *Financial support:* Unspecified assistantships available. Financial award application deadline: 7/30; financial award applicants required to submit FAFSA. *Unit head:* Glen Metheny, Director of Graduate Studies, 501-279-5851, Fax: 501-279-4805, E-mail: gmetheny@harding.edu. *Application contact:* Melanie Kiihnl, Recruiting Manager/Director of Marketing, 501-279-4523, Fax: 501-279-4805, E-mail: mba@harding.edu.
Website: http://www.harding.edu/mba

Hardin-Simmons University, Graduate School, Kelley College of Business, Abilene, TX 79698-0001. Offers business administration (MBA); sports management (MBA). *Accreditation:* ACBSP. *Program availability:* Part-time. *Faculty:* 7 full-time (2 women), 1 part-time/adjunct (0 women). *Students:* 16 full-time (7 women), 11 part-time (3 women); includes 2 minority (1 Hispanic/Latino; 1 Two or more races, non-Hispanic/Latino), 4 international. Average age 23. In 2016, 11 master's awarded. *Degree requirements:* For master's, thesis or alternative. *Entrance requirements:* For master's, GMAT, minimum GPA of 3.0 in upper-level course work, resume, interview. Additional exam requirements/recommendations for international students: Required—TOEFL (minimum score 600 paper-based; 75 iBT). *Application deadline:* For fall admission, 8/15 priority date for domestic students, 4/1 for international students; for spring admission, 1/5 priority date for domestic students, 9/1 for international students. Applications are processed on a rolling basis. Application fee: $50. Electronic applications accepted. *Expenses: Tuition:* Full-time $12,510; part-time $695 per credit hour. *Required fees:* $325; $110 per semester. *Financial support:* In 2016–17, 18 students received support. Fellowships and scholarships/grants available. Support available to part-time students. Financial award application deadline: 6/30; financial award applicants required to submit FAFSA. *Unit head:* Dr. Jennifer Plantier, Program Director, 325-671-2166, Fax: 325-670-1523, E-mail: jplantier@hsutx.edu. *Application contact:* Dr. Nancy Kucinski, Dean of Graduate Studies, 325-670-1298, Fax: 325-670-1564, E-mail: gradoff@hsutx.edu.
Website: http://www.hsutx.edu/academics/kelley/graduate/

Harvard University, Extension School, Cambridge, MA 02138-3722. Offers applied sciences (CAS); biotechnology (ALM); educational technologies (ALM); educational technology (CET); English for graduate and professional studies (DGP); environmental management (ALM, CEM); information technology (ALM); journalism (ALM); liberal arts (ALM); management (ALM, CM); mathematics for teaching (ALM); museum studies (ALM); premedical studies (Diploma); publication and communication (CPC). *Program availability:* Part-time, evening/weekend. *Degree requirements:* For master's, thesis. *Entrance requirements:* For master's, 3 completed graduate courses with grade of B or higher. Additional exam requirements/recommendations for international students: Required—TOEFL (minimum score 600 paper-based), TWE (minimum score 5). *Expenses:* Contact institution.

Harvard University, Harvard Business School, Doctoral Programs in Management, Boston, MA 02163. Offers accounting and management (DBA); business economics (PhD); health policy management (PhD); management (DBA); marketing (DBA); organizational behavior (PhD); science, technology and management (PhD); strategy (DBA); technology and operations management (DBA). *Degree requirements:* For doctorate, comprehensive exam (for some programs), thesis/dissertation. *Entrance requirements:* For doctorate, GRE General Test or GMAT. Additional exam requirements/recommendations for international students: Required—TOEFL.

Harvard University, Harvard Business School, Master's Program in Business Administration, Boston, MA 02163. Offers MBA, JD/MBA. *Entrance requirements:* For master's, GMAT. Additional exam requirements/recommendations for international students: Required—TOEFL.

Hawai`i Pacific University, College of Business, Honolulu, HI 96813. Offers MA, MBA, MSIS. *Program availability:* Part-time, evening/weekend, online learning. *Faculty:* 18 full-time (6 women), 6 part-time/adjunct (0 women). *Students:* 150 full-time (66 women), 72 part-time (29 women); includes 105 minority (10 Black or African American, non-Hispanic/Latino; 1 American Indian or Alaska Native, non-Hispanic/Latino; 32 Asian, non-Hispanic/Latino; 15 Hispanic/Latino; 4 Native Hawaiian or other Pacific Islander, non-Hispanic/Latino; 43 Two or more races, non-Hispanic/Latino), 56 international. Average age 33. 131 applicants, 81% accepted, 70 enrolled. In 2016, 148 master's awarded. *Entrance requirements:* For master's, GMAT or GRE. Additional exam requirements/recommendations for international students: Recommended—TOEFL (minimum score 550 paper-based; 80 iBT), IELTS (minimum score 6), TWE (minimum score 5). *Application deadline:* For fall admission, 2/15 priority date for domestic students; for spring admission, 10/15 priority date for domestic students. Applications are processed on a rolling basis. Application fee: $50. Electronic applications accepted. *Expenses: Tuition:* Full-time $17,190; part-time $955 per credit. *Required fees:* $150; $26 per credit. Tuition and fees vary according to course load and program. *Financial support:* In 2016–17, 30 students received support. Research assistantships, teaching assistantships, career-related internships or fieldwork, Federal Work-Study, scholarships/grants, tuition waivers, and unspecified assistantships available. Financial award application deadline: 3/1; financial award applicants required to submit FAFSA. *Unit head:* Dr. Warren Wee, Associate Dean/Associate Professor of Accounting, 808-544-9325, E-mail: wwee@hpu.edu. *Application contact:* Danny Lam, Assistant Director of Graduate Admissions, 808-544-1135, E-mail: graduate@hpu.edu.
Website: http://www.hpu.edu/CBA/Graduate/index.html

HEC Montreal, School of Business Administration, Doctoral Program in Administration, Montréal, QC H3T 2A7, Canada. Offers PhD. Program offered jointly with Concordia University, McGill University, and Universite du Quebec a Montreal. *Accreditation:* AACSB. *Students:* 122 full-time (49 women). 77 applicants, 42% accepted, 17 enrolled. In 2016, 18 doctorates awarded. *Degree requirements:* For doctorate, one foreign language, thesis/dissertation. *Entrance requirements:* For doctorate, GMAT, GRE, master's degree in administration or related field. *Application deadline:* For fall admission, 1/15 for domestic and international students. Application fee: $86. Electronic applications accepted. *Expenses: Tuition, area resident:* Part-time $77.80 Canadian dollars per credit. Tuition, state resident: full-time $2797 Canadian dollars; part-time $240.92 Canadian dollars per credit. Tuition, nonresident: full-time $8673 Canadian dollars; part-time $531.43 Canadian dollars per credit. *International tuition:* $19,131 Canadian dollars full-time. *Required fees:* $1699 Canadian dollars; $40.58 Canadian dollars per credit. $67.32 Canadian dollars per term. Tuition and fees vary according to degree level and program. *Financial support:* In 2016–17, 814 students received support. Research assistantships, teaching assistantships, and scholarships/grants available. Financial award application deadline: 9/2. *Faculty research:* Art management, business policy, entrepreneurship, new technologies, transportation. *Unit head:* Jacques Robert, Director, 514-340-6853, E-mail: jacques.robert@hec.ca. *Application contact:* Marianne de Moura, Administrative Director, 514-340-7106, Fax: 514-340-6411, E-mail: marianne.de-moura@hec.ca.
Website: http://www.hec.ca/en/programs/phd/index.html

HEC Montreal, School of Business Administration, Graduate Diploma Programs in Administration, Program in Management, Montréal, QC H3T 2A7, Canada. Offers Graduate Diploma. All courses are given in English. *Accreditation:* AACSB. *Students:* 59 full-time (26 women), 265 part-time (161 women). 137 applicants, 69% accepted, 67 enrolled. In 2016, 196 Graduate Diplomas awarded. *Degree requirements:* For Graduate Diploma, one foreign language. *Entrance requirements:* For degree, bachelor's degree (not in administration). *Application deadline:* For fall admission, 4/1 for domestic and international students; for winter admission, 9/15 for domestic and international students. Application fee: $86 Canadian dollars. Electronic applications accepted. *Expenses: Tuition, area resident:* Part-time $77.80 Canadian dollars per credit. Tuition, state resident: full-time $2797 Canadian dollars; part-time $240.92 Canadian dollars per credit. Tuition, nonresident: full-time $8673 Canadian dollars; part-time $531.43 Canadian dollars per credit. *International tuition:* $19,131 Canadian dollars full-time. *Required fees:* $1699 Canadian dollars; $40.58 Canadian dollars per credit. $67.32 Canadian dollars per term. Tuition and fees vary according to degree level and program. *Financial support:* In 2016–17, 814 students received support. Research assistantships, teaching assistantships, and scholarships/grants available. Financial award application deadline: 9/2. *Unit head:* Renaud Lachance, Director, 514-340-7165, E-mail: renaud.lachance@hec.ca. *Application contact:* Anny Caron, Administrative Director, 514-340-3598, Fax: 514-340-6411, E-mail: anny.caron@hec.ca.
Website: http://www.hec.ca/programmes/dess/dess-gestion-management/index.html

HEC Montreal, School of Business Administration, Graduate Diploma Programs in Administration, Program in Management and Sustainable Development, Montréal, QC H3T 2A7, Canada. Offers Graduate Diploma. All courses are given in French. *Students:* 18 full-time (15 women), 39 part-time (24 women). 45 applicants, 69% accepted, 24 enrolled. In 2016, 19 Graduate Diplomas awarded. *Degree requirements:* For Graduate Diploma, one foreign language. *Entrance requirements:* For degree, bachelor's degree (not in administration). *Application deadline:* For fall admission, 4/15 for domestic and international students; for winter admission, 9/15 for domestic and international students. Application fee: $86. Electronic applications accepted. *Expenses: Tuition, area resident:* Part-time $77.80 Canadian dollars per credit. Tuition, state resident: full-time $2797 Canadian dollars; part-time $240.92 Canadian dollars per credit. Tuition, nonresident: full-time $8673 Canadian dollars; part-time $531.43 Canadian dollars per credit. *International tuition:* $19,131 Canadian dollars full-time. *Required fees:* $1699 Canadian dollars; $40.58 Canadian dollars per credit. $67.32 Canadian dollars per term. Tuition and fees vary according to degree level and program. *Financial support:* In 2016–17, 814 students received support. Research assistantships, teaching assistantships, and scholarships/grants available. Financial award application deadline: 9/2. *Unit head:* Renaud Lachance, Director, 514-340-7165, E-mail: renaud.lachance@hec.ca. *Application contact:* Anny Caron, Administrative Director, 514-340-3598, Fax: 514-340-6411, E-mail: anny.caron@hec.ca.
Website: http://www.hec.ca/programmes/dess/dess-gestion-developpement-durable/index.html

HEC Montreal, School of Business Administration, Master of Science Programs in Administration, Montréal, QC H3T 2A7, Canada. Offers applied economics (M Sc); applied financial economics (M Sc); business analytics (M Sc); business intelligence (M Sc); electronic commerce (M Sc); finance (M Sc); financial engineering (M Sc); global supply chain management (M Sc); human resources management (M Sc); information technologies (M Sc); international business (M Sc); international logistics (M Sc); management (M Sc); management and social innovations (M Sc); management control (M Sc); marketing (M Sc); operations management (M Sc); organizational development (M Sc); professional accounting (M Sc); strategy (M Sc). Most courses are given in French. *Accreditation:* AACSB. *Students:* 906 full-time (480 women), 357 part-time (192 women). 794 applicants, 57% accepted, 292 enrolled. In 2016, 441 master's awarded. *Degree requirements:* For master's, one foreign language, thesis. *Entrance requirements:* For master's, bachelor's degree in business administration or equivalent. *Application deadline:* For fall admission, 3/15 for domestic and international students; for winter admission, 9/15 for domestic and international students; for summer admission, 4/15 for domestic and international students. Application fee: $86 Canadian dollars. Electronic applications accepted. *Expenses: Tuition, area resident:* Part-time $77.80 Canadian dollars per credit. Tuition, state resident: full-time $2797 Canadian dollars; part-time $240.92 Canadian dollars per credit. Tuition, nonresident: full-time $8673 Canadian dollars; part-time $531.43 Canadian dollars per credit. *International tuition:* $19,131 Canadian dollars full-time. *Required fees:* $1699 Canadian dollars; $40.58 Canadian dollars per credit. $67.32 Canadian dollars per term. Tuition and fees vary according to degree level and program. *Financial support:* Research assistantships, teaching assistantships, and scholarships/grants available. Financial award application deadline: 9/2. *Unit head:* Dr. Marie-Helene Jobin, Director, 514-340-6283, E-mail: marie-helene.jobin@hec.ca. *Application contact:* Marianne de Moura, Administrative Director, 514-340-7106, Fax: 514-340-6411, E-mail: marianne.de-moura@hec.ca.
Website: http://www.hec.ca/en/programs/masters/index.html

Business Administration and Management—General

HEC Montreal, School of Business Administration, Master's Program in Business Administration and Management, Montréal, QC H3T 2A7, Canada. Offers MBA. *Accreditation:* AACSB. *Students:* 171 full-time (62 women), 139 part-time (49 women). 430 applicants, 56% accepted, 187 enrolled. In 2016, 139 master's awarded. *Degree requirements:* For master's, one foreign language. *Entrance requirements:* For master's, GMAT, 3 years of related work experience. Additional exam requirements/recommendations for international students: Required—TOEFL (minimum iBT score 95 for program in French; 100 for program in English). *Application deadline:* For fall admission, 6/1 for domestic and international students; for summer admission, 1/15 for domestic students, 11/1 for international students. Application fee: $86 Canadian dollars. Electronic applications accepted. *Expenses: Tuition, area resident:* Part-time $77.80 Canadian dollars per credit. Tuition, state resident: full-time $2797 Canadian dollars; part-time $240.92 Canadian dollars per credit. Tuition, nonresident: full-time $8673 Canadian dollars; part-time $531.43 Canadian dollars per credit. *International tuition:* $19,131 Canadian dollars full-time. *Required fees:* $1699 Canadian dollars; $40.58 Canadian dollars per credit. $67.32 Canadian dollars per term. Tuition and fees vary according to degree level and program. *Financial support:* Research assistantships, teaching assistantships, and scholarships/grants available. Financial award application deadline: 9/2. *Unit head:* Louis Hebert, Director, 514-340-6830, E-mail: louis.hebert@hec.ca. *Application contact:* Anik Low, Administrative Director, 514-340-3609, Fax: 514-340-7327, E-mail: anik.low@hec.ca.
Website: http://www.hec.ca/en/programs/mba/index.html

Heidelberg University, Master of Business Administration Program, Tiffin, OH 44883-2462. Offers MBA. *Accreditation:* ACBSP. *Program availability:* Part-time, evening/weekend. *Students:* 5 full-time (1 woman), 28 part-time (13 women). In 2016, 8 master's awarded. *Entrance requirements:* For master's, bachelor's degree, minimum GPA of 2.7. Additional exam requirements/recommendations for international students: Required—TOEFL (minimum score 550 paper-based, 79 iBT) or IELTS (minimum score 6.5). *Application deadline:* Applications are processed on a rolling basis. Electronic applications accepted. *Expenses:* $770 per semester hour. *Financial support:* Scholarships/grants available. Financial award applicants required to submit FAFSA. *Unit head:* Allen Underwood, Director of Graduate Studies in Business, 419-448-2516, E-mail: aunderwo@heidelberg.edu. *Application contact:* Katie Slosser, Graduate Admissions Coordinator, 419-448-2602, Fax: 419-448-2565, E-mail: kslosser@heidelberg.edu.
Website: https://www.heidelberg.edu/academics/programs/master-of-business-administration

Henderson State University, Graduate Studies, School of Business, Arkadelphia, AR 71999-0001. Offers MBA. *Accreditation:* AACSB. *Program availability:* Part-time, 100% online. *Faculty:* 9 full-time (1 woman). *Students:* 15 full-time (7 women), 38 part-time (19 women); includes 16 minority (7 Black or African American, non-Hispanic/Latino; 2 Asian, non-Hispanic/Latino; 5 Hispanic/Latino; 2 Two or more races, non-Hispanic/Latino), 3 international. Average age 29. 26 applicants, 92% accepted, 24 enrolled. In 2016, 27 master's awarded. *Entrance requirements:* For master's, GMAT (minimum score 400), minimum AACSB index of 1000, minimum GPA of 2.7. Additional exam requirements/recommendations for international students: Required—TOEFL (minimum score 600 paper-based); Recommended—IELTS (minimum score 6.5). *Application deadline:* For fall admission, 8/1 priority date for domestic students, 6/30 priority date for international students; for spring admission, 1/1 priority date for domestic students, 11/30 priority date for international students. Applications are processed on a rolling basis. Application fee: $25 ($75 for international students). *Expenses:* Tuition, state resident: full-time $6288; part-time $3144 per credit hour. Tuition, nonresident: full-time $12,888; part-time $6444 per credit hour. *Required fees:* $1429; $1024 per credit hour. Tuition and fees vary according to course load and student level. *Financial support:* In 2016–17, 7 teaching assistantships with partial tuition reimbursements (averaging $4,000 per year) were awarded; scholarships/grants and unspecified assistantships also available. Financial award application deadline: 4/15; financial award applicants required to submit FAFSA. *Unit head:* Dr. Lonnie Jackson, MBA Director, 870-230-5311, Fax: 870-230-5286, E-mail: jacksol@hsu.edu. *Application contact:* Dr. Ken Taylor, Graduate Dean, 870-230-5126, Fax: 870-230-5479, E-mail: taylorke@hsu.edu.
Website: http://www.hsu.edu/Academics/SchoolOfBusiness/MBA/index.html

Herzing University Online, Program in Business Administration, Menomonee Falls, WI 53051. Offers accounting (MBA); business administration (MBA); business management (MBA); healthcare management (MBA); human resources (MBA); marketing (MBA); project management (MBA); technology management (MBA). *Program availability:* Online learning.

High Point University, Norcross Graduate School, High Point, NC 27268. Offers business administration (MBA); educational leadership (M Ed); elementary education (M Ed); history (MA); nonprofit management (MA); secondary math (M Ed); special education (M Ed); strategic communication (MA); teaching elementary education k-6 (MAT); teaching secondary mathematics 9-12 (MAT). *Accreditation:* NCATE. *Program availability:* Part-time, evening/weekend. *Degree requirements:* For master's, comprehensive exam (for some programs), thesis (for some programs). *Entrance requirements:* For master's, GMAT (MBA), GRE, MAT, minimum GPA of 3.0. Additional exam requirements/recommendations for international students: Required—TOEFL (minimum score 550 paper-based). Electronic applications accepted.

Hodges University, Graduate Programs, Naples, FL 34119. Offers accounting (M Acc); business administration (MBA); clinical mental health counseling (MS); health services administration (MS); information systems management (MIS); legal studies (MS); management (MSM). *Program availability:* Part-time, evening/weekend, 100% online, blended/hybrid learning. *Degree requirements:* For master's, comprehensive exam (for some programs), thesis (for some programs). *Entrance requirements:* For master's, essay. Additional exam requirements/recommendations for international students: Recommended—TOEFL. Electronic applications accepted.

Hofstra University, Frank G. Zarb School of Business, Executive Master's Program in Business Administration, Hempstead, NY 11549. Offers EMBA. *Program availability:* Evening/weekend, blended/hybrid learning. *Students:* 21 full-time (8 women); includes 13 minority (5 Black or African American, non-Hispanic/Latino; 6 Asian, non-Hispanic/Latino; 2 Hispanic/Latino). Average age 38. 31 applicants, 58% accepted, 12 enrolled. In 2016, 4 master's awarded. *Entrance requirements:* For master's, 2 letters of recommendation, minimum 7 years of management experience, resume, essay, interview. Additional exam requirements/recommendations for international students: Required—TOEFL (minimum score 550 paper-based; 80 iBT); Recommended—IELTS (minimum score 6). *Application deadline:* Applications are processed on a rolling basis. Application fee: $75. Electronic applications accepted. *Expenses:* Contact institution. *Financial support:* In 2016–17, 11 students received support, including 11 fellowships with full and partial tuition reimbursements available (averaging $6,909 per year); research assistantships with full and partial tuition reimbursements available, career-related internships or fieldwork, Federal Work-Study, institutionally sponsored loans, scholarships/grants, tuition waivers (full and partial), and unspecified assistantships also available. Support available to part-time students. Financial award applicants required to submit FAFSA. *Faculty research:* Marketing strategy; consumer behavior. *Unit head:* Dr. Barry Berman, Director, 516-463-5711, Fax: 516-463-5268, E-mail: barry.berman@hofstra.edu. *Application contact:* Sunil Samuel, Assistant Vice President of Admissions, 516-463-4723, Fax: 516-463-4664, E-mail: graduateadmission@hofstra.edu.
Website: http://www.hofstra.edu/business/

Hofstra University, Frank G. Zarb School of Business, Programs in Accounting and Taxation, Hempstead, NY 11549. Offers accounting (MS, Advanced Certificate); business administration (MBA), including accounting, professional accountancy, taxation; taxation (MS, Advanced Certificate). *Program availability:* Part-time, evening/weekend, blended/hybrid learning. *Students:* 177 full-time (100 women), 36 part-time (17 women); includes 23 minority (4 Black or African American, non-Hispanic/Latino; 1 American Indian or Alaska Native, non-Hispanic/Latino; 6 Asian, non-Hispanic/Latino; 9 Hispanic/Latino; 3 Two or more races, non-Hispanic/Latino), 123 international. Average age 25. 437 applicants, 76% accepted, 104 enrolled. In 2016, 133 master's awarded. *Degree requirements:* For master's, capstone course (for MBA), thesis (for MS), minimum GPA of 3.0. *Entrance requirements:* For master's, GMAT/GRE, 2 letters of recommendation, resume, essay. Additional exam requirements/recommendations for international students: Required—TOEFL (minimum score 550 paper-based; 80 iBT); Recommended—IELTS (minimum score 6). *Application deadline:* Applications are processed on a rolling basis. Application fee: $75. Electronic applications accepted. *Expenses:* $1,170 per credit. *Financial support:* In 2016–17, 64 students received support, including 59 fellowships with full and partial tuition reimbursements available (averaging $4,967 per year), 1 research assistantship with full and partial tuition reimbursement available (averaging $5,800 per year); career-related internships or fieldwork, Federal Work-Study, institutionally sponsored loans, scholarships/grants, tuition waivers (full and partial), and unspecified assistantships also available. Support available to part-time students. Financial award applicants required to submit FAFSA. *Faculty research:* Gender discrimination and professional women; auditor-client interaction in accounting; accounting in prisons; the Fourth Amendment and privacy. *Unit head:* Dr. Martha Weisel, Chairperson, 516-463-5655, E-mail: martha.s.weisel@hofstra.edu. *Application contact:* Sunil Samuel, Assistant Vice President of Admissions, 516-463-4723, Fax: 516-463-4664, E-mail: graduateadmission@hofstra.edu.
Website: http://www.hofstra.edu/business/

Hofstra University, Frank G. Zarb School of Business, Programs in Finance, Hempstead, NY 11549. Offers business administration (MBA), including finance; corporate finance (Advanced Certificate); finance (MS), including financial and risk management, investment analysis; investment management (Advanced Certificate); quantitative finance (MS). *Program availability:* Part-time, evening/weekend, blended/hybrid learning. *Students:* 177 full-time (70 women), 47 part-time (9 women); includes 16 minority (6 Black or African American, non-Hispanic/Latino; 6 Asian, non-Hispanic/Latino; 4 Hispanic/Latino), 167 international. Average age 25. 555 applicants, 72% accepted, 93 enrolled. In 2016, 101 master's awarded. *Degree requirements:* For master's, capstone course (for MBA), thesis (for MS), minimum GPA of 3.0. *Entrance requirements:* For master's, GMAT/GRE, 2 letters of recommendation, resume, essay. Additional exam requirements/recommendations for international students: Required—TOEFL (minimum score 550 paper-based; 80 iBT); Recommended—IELTS (minimum score 6). *Application deadline:* Applications are processed on a rolling basis. Application fee: $75. Electronic applications accepted. *Expenses:* $1,170 per credit. *Financial support:* In 2016–17, 51 students received support, including 43 fellowships with full and partial tuition reimbursements available (averaging $4,829 per year), 1 research assistantship with full and partial tuition reimbursement available (averaging $6,950 per year); career-related internships or fieldwork, Federal Work-Study, institutionally sponsored loans, scholarships/grants, tuition waivers (full and partial), and unspecified assistantships also available. Support available to part-time students. Financial award applicants required to submit FAFSA. *Faculty research:* Individual investors and financial crisis; short-sale constraints and futures trading; social media and sentiment in financial markets; external monitoring of firms; CEO inside debt and insider trading. *Unit head:* Dr. K. G. Viswanathan, Chairperson, 516-463-5699, Fax: 516-463-4834, E-mail: k.g.viswanathan@hofstra.edu. *Application contact:* Sunil Samuel, Assistant Vice President of Admissions, 516-463-4723, Fax: 516-463-4664,
E-mail: graduateadmission@hofstra.edu.
Website: http://www.hofstra.edu/business/

Hofstra University, Frank G. Zarb School of Business, Programs in Management and General Business, Hempstead, NY 11549. Offers business administration (MBA), including health services management, management, sports and entertainment management, strategic business management, strategic healthcare management; general management (Advanced Certificate); human resource management (MS, Advanced Certificate). *Program availability:* Part-time, evening/weekend, blended/hybrid learning. *Students:* 140 full-time (67 women), 159 part-time (70 women); includes 100 minority (24 Black or African American, non-Hispanic/Latino; 41 Asian, non-Hispanic/Latino; 32 Hispanic/Latino; 1 Native Hawaiian or other Pacific Islander, non-Hispanic/Latino; 2 Two or more races, non-Hispanic/Latino), 26 international. Average age 33. 354 applicants, 58% accepted, 94 enrolled. In 2016, 84 master's awarded. *Degree requirements:* For master's, thesis optional, capstone course (for MBA), thesis (for MS), minimum GPA of 3.0. *Entrance requirements:* For master's, GMAT/GRE, 2 letters of recommendation, resume, essay. Additional exam requirements/recommendations for international students: Required—TOEFL (minimum score 550 paper-based; 80 iBT); Recommended—IELTS (minimum score 6). *Application deadline:* Applications are processed on a rolling basis. Application fee: $75. Electronic applications accepted. *Expenses:* $1,170 per credit. *Financial support:* In 2016–17, 65 students received support, including 43 fellowships with full and partial tuition reimbursements available (averaging $4,813 per year); research assistantships with full and partial tuition reimbursements available, career-related internships or fieldwork, Federal Work-Study, institutionally sponsored loans, scholarships/grants, tuition waivers (full and partial), and unspecified assistantships also available. Support available to part-time students. Financial award applicants required to submit FAFSA. *Faculty research:* Organizational change; sustainability; entrepreneurial spawning; family business; global supply chain strategies. *Unit head:* Dr. Kaushik Sengupta, Chairperson, 516-463-7825, Fax: 516-463-4834, E-mail: kaushik.sengupta@hofstra.edu. *Application contact:* Sunil Samuel, Assistant Vice President of Admissions, 516-463-4723, Fax: 516-463-4664, E-mail: graduateadmission@hofstra.edu.
Website: http://www.hofstra.edu/business/

Hofstra University, Frank G. Zarb School of Business, Programs in Marketing and International Business, Hempstead, NY 11549. Offers business administration (MBA), including international business, marketing; international business (Advanced Certificate); marketing (MS, Advanced Certificate); marketing research (MS). *Program availability:* Part-time, evening/weekend, blended/hybrid learning. *Students:* 91 full-time (61 women), 28 part-time (14 women); includes 13 minority (1 Black or African American, non-Hispanic/Latino; 8 Asian, non-Hispanic/Latino; 3 Hispanic/Latino; 1 Two or more races, non-Hispanic/Latino), 84 international. Average age 25. 323 applicants, 67% accepted, 49 enrolled. In 2016, 65 master's awarded. *Degree requirements:* For master's, capstone course (for MBA), thesis (for MS), minimum GPA of 3.0. *Entrance requirements:* For master's, GMAT/GRE, 2 letters of recommendation, resume, essay. Additional exam requirements/recommendations for international students: Required—TOEFL (minimum score 550 paper-based; 80 iBT); Recommended—IELTS (minimum score 6). *Application deadline:* Applications are processed on a rolling basis. Application

fee: $75. Electronic applications accepted. *Expenses:* $1,170 per credit. *Financial support:* In 2016–17, 30 students received support, including 24 fellowships with full and partial tuition reimbursements available (averaging $4,896 per year); research assistantships with full and partial tuition reimbursements available, career-related internships or fieldwork, Federal Work-Study, institutionally sponsored loans, scholarships/grants, tuition waivers (full and partial), and unspecified assistantships also available. Support available to part-time students. Financial award applicants required to submit FAFSA. *Faculty research:* Cross-cultural consumer behavior; social, digital, global, and strategic issues in marketing; consumer health/well-being; ethnocentrism and animosity. *Unit head:* Dr. Anil Mathur, Chairperson, 516-463-5346, Fax: 516-463-4834, E-mail: anil.mathur@hofstra.edu. *Application contact:* Sunil Samuel, Assistant Vice President of Admissions, 516-463-4723, Fax: 516-463-4664, E-mail: graduateadmission@hofstra.edu.
Website: http://www.hofstra.edu/business/

Holy Family University, Graduate and Professional Programs, School of Business Administration, Philadelphia, PA 19114. Offers accountancy (MS); finance (MBA); health care administration (MBA); human resource management (MBA); information systems management (MBA). *Accreditation:* ACBSP. *Program availability:* Part-time, evening/weekend. *Students:* 140 part-time. 58 applicants, 78% accepted, 42 enrolled. In 2016, 44 master's awarded. *Degree requirements:* For master's, comprehensive exam, thesis optional. *Entrance requirements:* For master's, minimum GPA of 3.0, interview, essay/personal statement, current resume, official transcript of all college or university work. Additional exam requirements/recommendations for international students: Required—TOEFL (minimum score 550 paper-based; 79 iBT), IELTS (minimum score 6), PTE (minimum score 54). *Application deadline:* For fall admission, 7/1 priority date for domestic and international students; for winter admission, 1/1 for domestic students; for spring admission, 11/1 priority date for domestic and international students; for summer admission, 4/1 priority date for domestic and international students. Applications are processed on a rolling basis. Application fee: $25. Electronic applications accepted. *Expenses: Tuition:* Part-time $751 per hour. *Required fees:* $140 per semester. One-time fee: $165 part-time. Part-time tuition and fees vary according to degree level and program. *Financial support:* Available to part-time students. Application deadline: 5/1; applicants required to submit FAFSA. *Unit head:* Dr. Barry Dickinson, Dean, 267-341-3440, Fax: 215-637-5937, E-mail: jdickinson@holyfamily.edu. *Application contact:* Gidget Marie Montelibano, Associate Director of Graduate Admissions, 267-341-3558, Fax: 215-637-1478, E-mail: gmontelibano@holyfamily.edu.
Website: http://www.holyfamily.edu/choosing-holy-family-u/academics/schools-of-study/school-of-business-administration

Holy Names University, Graduate Division, Department of Business, Oakland, CA 94619-1699. Offers finance (MBA); management and leadership (MBA); marketing (MBA). *Program availability:* Part-time, evening/weekend. *Students:* 17 full-time (11 women), 15 part-time (10 women); includes 22 minority (9 Black or African American, non-Hispanic/Latino; 2 Asian, non-Hispanic/Latino; 10 Hispanic/Latino; 1 Two or more races, non-Hispanic/Latino), 1 international. Average age 31. 31 applicants, 68% accepted, 15 enrolled. In 2016, 9 master's awarded. *Entrance requirements:* For master's, minimum undergraduate GPA of 2.6 overall, 3.0 in major; two recommendations (letter or form) from previous professors or current or previous work supervisors; 1-3 page personal statement; resume. Additional exam requirements/recommendations for international students: Required—TOEFL (minimum score 550 paper-based; 79 iBT). *Application deadline:* For fall admission, 8/1 priority date for domestic students, 7/15 for international students; for spring admission, 12/1 priority date for domestic students, 12/1 for international students; for summer admission, 5/1 priority date for domestic students, 5/1 for international students. Applications are processed on a rolling basis. Application fee: $65. Electronic applications accepted. Application fee is waived when completed online. *Expenses:* Contact institution. *Financial support:* Career-related internships or fieldwork, Federal Work-Study, scholarships/grants, and unspecified assistantships available. Support available to part-time students. Financial award application deadline: 3/2; financial award applicants required to submit FAFSA. *Faculty research:* Business ethics, sustainable economics, accounting models, cross-cultural management, diversity in organizations. *Unit head:* Russell Jacobus, MBA Program Director, 510-436-1622, E-mail: jacobus@hnu.edu. *Application contact:* 800-430-1321, Fax: 510-436-1325, E-mail: graduateadmissions@hnu.edu.
Website: http://www.hnu.edu

Hood College, Graduate School, Department of Economics and Business Administration, Frederick, MD 21701-8575. Offers accounting (MBA); finance (MBA); human resource management (MBA); information systems (MBA); marketing (MBA); public management (MBA). *Accreditation:* ACBSP. *Program availability:* Part-time, evening/weekend. *Faculty:* 4 full-time, 8 part-time/adjunct. *Students:* 21 full-time (13 women), 106 part-time (60 women); includes 23 minority (12 Black or African American, non-Hispanic/Latino; 4 Asian, non-Hispanic/Latino; 6 Hispanic/Latino; 1 Two or more races, non-Hispanic/Latino), 15 international. Average age 32. 44 applicants, 91% accepted, 25 enrolled. In 2016, 45 master's awarded. *Degree requirements:* For master's, capstone/final research project. *Entrance requirements:* For master's, minimum GPA of 3.0 (or resume and two letters of recommendation), copy of official transcripts, essay. Additional exam requirements/recommendations for international students: Required—TOEFL (minimum score 575 paper-based; 89 iBT), IELTS (minimum score 6.5). *Application deadline:* For fall admission, 8/15 for domestic students, 8/5 for international students; for spring admission, 12/1 for domestic and international students; for summer admission, 5/1 for domestic students, 4/15 for international students. Applications are processed on a rolling basis. Application fee: $35. Electronic applications accepted. *Expenses:* $525 per credit; $110 comprehensive fee per semester. *Financial support:* Tuition waivers (partial) and unspecified assistantships available. Financial award applicants required to submit FAFSA. *Faculty research:* Corporate strategy and sustainable competitive advantages, business ethics, entrepreneurship, investments management, economic development. *Unit head:* April Boulton, Interim Dean of the Graduate School, 301-696-3600, Fax: 301-696-3597, E-mail: gofurther@hood.edu. *Application contact:* Spencer Berk, Assistant Director of Graduate Admissions, 301-696-3604, E-mail: gofurther@hood.edu.

Houston Baptist University, Archie W. Dunham College of Business, Program in Business Administration, Houston, TX 77074-3298. Offers MBA. *Program availability:* Part-time, evening/weekend. *Students:* 49 full-time (24 women), 73 part-time (34 women); includes 65 minority (30 Black or African American, non-Hispanic/Latino; 6 Asian, non-Hispanic/Latino; 25 Hispanic/Latino; 1 Native Hawaiian or other Pacific Islander, non-Hispanic/Latino; 3 Two or more races, non-Hispanic/Latino), 17 international. Average age 31. 322 applicants, 16% accepted, 29 enrolled. In 2016, 53 master's awarded. *Entrance requirements:* For master's, GMAT or GRE, minimum GPA of 2.5, essay/personal statement, resume, bachelor's degree conferred transcript. Additional exam requirements/recommendations for international students: Required—TOEFL (minimum score 80 iBT), IELTS (minimum score 6.5). *Application deadline:* For fall admission, 8/1 for domestic students, 6/1 for international students; for spring admission, 1/1 for domestic students, 11/1 for international students; for summer admission, 5/1 for domestic students, 3/1 for international students. Applications are processed on a rolling basis. Application fee: $0 ($100 for international students). Electronic applications accepted. *Expenses:* $2,850 per 3-hour course; $1,275 annual general fee; $1,060 annual technology fee. *Financial support:* In 2016–17, 8 students received support. Career-related internships or fieldwork, Federal Work-Study, and scholarships/grants available. Support available to part-time students. Financial award application deadline: 4/1; financial award applicants required to submit FAFSA. *Unit head:* Dr. Michael Weeks, Dean, Archie W. Dunham College of Business, 281-649-3014, E-mail: mweeks@hbu.edu. *Application contact:* Laurel Motal, Secretary, 281-649-3306, Fax: 281-649-3436, E-mail: lmotal@hbu.edu.
Website: http://www.hbu.edu/mba

Howard Payne University, Program in Business Administration, Brownwood, TX 76801-2715. Offers MBA. *Program availability:* Part-time, evening/weekend. *Faculty:* 7 full-time (2 women), 2 part-time/adjunct (0 women). *Students:* 12 full-time (4 women), 27 part-time (14 women); includes 16 minority (1 American Indian or Alaska Native, non-Hispanic/Latino; 15 Hispanic/Latino), 1 international. Average age 33. 23 applicants, 78% accepted, 11 enrolled. In 2016, 18 master's awarded. *Degree requirements:* For master's, comprehensive exam, research project. *Entrance requirements:* For master's, minimum undergraduate GPA of 3.0, 3.3 in first 9 hours of coursework; business foundation classes (for those without undergraduate business degree and no business-related coursework). Additional exam requirements/recommendations for international students: Required—TOEFL (minimum score 79 iBT). *Application deadline:* For fall admission, 7/1 for domestic students; for spring admission, 12/1 for domestic students. Applications are processed on a rolling basis. Application fee: $0. Electronic applications accepted. *Financial support:* Application deadline: 3/15; applicants required to submit FAFSA. *Unit head:* Dr. Brad Lemler, Director, 325-649-8149, E-mail: blemler@hputx.edu. *Application contact:* Mary Hill, Administrative Assistant, School of Business, 325-649-8704, E-mail: mhill@hputx.edu.
Website: http://www.hputx.edu/academics/schools/school-of-business/school-of-business-graduate-program/

Howard University, School of Business, Graduate Programs in Business, Washington, DC 20059-0002. Offers accounting (MBA); entrepreneurship (MBA); finance (MBA); general management (MBA); human resources management (MBA); information systems (MBA); international business (MBA); marketing (MBA); supply chain management (MBA); JD/MBA. *Accreditation:* AACSB. *Program availability:* Part-time, evening/weekend, online learning. *Entrance requirements:* For master's, GMAT, minimum 1 year post undergraduate work experience, resume, 3 letters of recommendation, advanced college algebra. Additional exam requirements/recommendations for international students: Required—TOEFL. *Faculty research:* Marketing research in multi-ethnic populations, U.S. trade policies and international relations, risk management (finance).

Hult International Business School, Graduate Programs, Cambridge, MA 02141. Offers business administration (EMBA); business analytics (MBA, MIB); business statistics (MBS); disruptive innovation (MDI); entrepreneurship (MBA, MIB); family business (MBA, MIB); finance (MBA, MF, MIB); international marketing (MIM); marketing (MBA, MIB); project management (MBA, MIB). MDI and MBS offered in San Francisco; MBA also offered in Boston, San Francisco, Dubai, Shanghai, and New York. *Students:* Average age 31. *Entrance requirements:* For master's, GMAT, 3 years of work experience. Additional exam requirements/recommendations for international students: Required—TOEFL. *Application deadline:* For fall admission, 9/1 priority date for domestic and international students; for winter admission, 11/1 priority date for domestic and international students; for spring admission, 12/1 priority date for domestic and international students; for summer admission, 6/1 for domestic and international students. Applications are processed on a rolling basis. Application fee: $150. Electronic applications accepted. *Expenses:* $75,000 (for MBA); $45,000 (for master's); $85,000 (for executive part-time MBA). *Financial support:* Scholarships/grants and tuition waivers (partial) available. Financial award application deadline: 6/1; financial award applicants required to submit FAFSA. *Application contact:* Boston Admissions Office, 617-746-1990, E-mail: postgraduate@hult.edu.
Website: http://www.hult.edu

Humboldt State University, Academic Programs, College of Professional Studies, School of Business, Arcata, CA 95521-8299. Offers MBA. *Program availability:* Part-time, evening/weekend. *Degree requirements:* For master's, thesis or alternative. *Entrance requirements:* For master's, GMAT or GRE, minimum GPA of 2.5. Additional exam requirements/recommendations for international students: Required—TOEFL (minimum score 500 paper-based). *Expenses:* Contact institution. *Faculty research:* International business development, small town entrepreneurship, international trade: Pacific Rim.

Husson University, Master of Business Administration Program, Bangor, ME 04401-2999. Offers athletic administration (MBA); biotechnology and innovation (MBA); general business administration (MBA); healthcare management (MBA); hospitality and tourism management (MBA); organizational management (MBA); risk management (MBA). *Program availability:* Part-time, evening/weekend, 100% online, blended/hybrid learning. *Faculty:* 8 full-time (4 women), 20 part-time/adjunct (5 women). *Students:* 81 full-time (47 women), 249 part-time (142 women); includes 32 minority (9 Black or African American, non-Hispanic/Latino; 2 American Indian or Alaska Native, non-Hispanic/Latino; 17 Asian, non-Hispanic/Latino; 3 Hispanic/Latino; 1 Two or more races, non-Hispanic/Latino), 11 international. Average age 34. 199 applicants, 78% accepted, 119 enrolled. In 2016, 109 master's awarded. *Degree requirements:* For master's, comprehensive exam (for some programs), thesis optional. *Entrance requirements:* For master's, minimum GPA of 3.0, letter of recommendation. Additional exam requirements/recommendations for international students: Required—TOEFL (minimum score 550 paper-based; 80 iBT), IELTS (minimum score 6.5). *Application deadline:* Applications are processed on a rolling basis. Application fee: $50. Electronic applications accepted. *Expenses:* $450 per credit; $450 fees per full-time year or $220 part-time. *Financial support:* Career-related internships or fieldwork, Federal Work-Study, scholarships/grants, and unspecified assistantships available. Financial award application deadline: 4/15; financial award applicants required to submit FAFSA. *Unit head:* Prof. Stephanie Shayne, Director, Graduate and Online Programs, 207-404-5632, Fax: 207-992-4987, E-mail: shaynes@husson.edu. *Application contact:* Kristen Card, Director of Graduate Admissions, 207-404-5660, Fax: 207-941-7935, E-mail: cardk@husson.edu.
Website: http://www.husson.edu/college-of-business/school-of-business-and-management/master-of-business-administration-mba/

Idaho State University, Office of Graduate Studies, College of Business, Pocatello, ID 83209-8020. Offers business administration (MBA, Postbaccalaureate Certificate); computer information systems (MS, Postbaccalaureate Certificate). *Accreditation:* AACSB. *Program availability:* Part-time. *Degree requirements:* For master's, comprehensive exam, thesis (for some programs), oral exam; for Postbaccalaureate Certificate, comprehensive exam, thesis (for some programs), 6 hours of clerkship. *Entrance requirements:* For master's, GMAT, GRE General Test, minimum GPA of 3.0, resume outlining work experience, 2 letters of reference; for Postbaccalaureate Certificate, GMAT, GRE General Test, minimum upper-level GPA of 3.0, resume of work experience. Additional exam requirements/recommendations for international students: Required—TOEFL (minimum score 550 paper-based; 80 iBT). Electronic applications accepted. *Faculty research:* Information assurance, computer information technology, finance management, marketing.

IGlobal University, Graduate Programs, Vienna, VA 22182. Offers accounting (MBA); data management and analytics (MSIT); entrepreneurship (MBA); finance (MBA); global business management (MBA); health care management (MBA); hospitality and tourism management (MBA); human resources management (MBA); information technology (MBA); information technology systems and management (MSIT); leadership and management (MBA); project management (MBA); public service and administration (MBA); software design and management (MSIT).

Illinois Institute of Technology, Stuart School of Business, Program in Business Administration, Chicago, IL 60661. Offers sustainability (MBA); JD/MBA; M Des/MBA; MBA/MS. *Accreditation:* AACSB. *Program availability:* Part-time, evening/weekend. *Entrance requirements:* For master's, GRE (minimum score 298) or GMAT (500). Additional exam requirements/recommendations for international students: Required—TOEFL (minimum score 600 paper-based; 85 iBT); Recommended—IELTS (minimum score 7). Electronic applications accepted. *Expenses:* Contact institution. *Faculty research:* Global management and marketing strategy, technological innovation, management science, financial management, knowledge management.

Illinois Institute of Technology, Stuart School of Business, Program in Management Science, Chicago, IL 60661. Offers PhD. *Accreditation:* AACSB. *Program availability:* Part-time. *Degree requirements:* For doctorate, comprehensive exam, thesis/dissertation. *Entrance requirements:* For doctorate, GRE (minimum score 316) or GMAT (minimum score 650). Additional exam requirements/recommendations for international students: Required—TOEFL (minimum score 600 paper-based; 85 iBT). Electronic applications accepted. *Expenses:* Contact institution. *Faculty research:* Scheduling systems, queuing systems, optimization, quality systems, foreign exchange, enterprise risk management, credit risk modeling.

Illinois State University, Graduate School, College of Business, Program in Business Administration, Normal, IL 61790-2200. Offers MBA. *Accreditation:* AACSB. *Program availability:* Part-time. *Degree requirements:* For master's, thesis optional. *Entrance requirements:* For master's, GMAT, minimum GPA of 2.75 during previous 2 years of course work. Additional exam requirements/recommendations for international students: Required—TOEFL. *Faculty research:* McLean County small business development center.

IMCA–International Management Centres Association, Programs in Business Administration, Buckingham, United Kingdom. Offers M Mgt, M Phil, MBA, MS. *Program availability:* Online learning.

Independence University, Program in Business Administration, Salt Lake City, UT 84107. Offers MBA.

Indiana State University, College of Graduate and Professional Studies, Scott College of Business, Terre Haute, IN 47809. Offers MBA. *Accreditation:* AACSB. *Program availability:* Part-time, evening/weekend. *Degree requirements:* For master's, thesis optional. *Entrance requirements:* For master's, GMAT. Electronic applications accepted. *Faculty research:* Small business and entrepreneurial sciences, production and operations management.

Indiana Tech, Program in Business Administration, Fort Wayne, IN 46803-1297. Offers accounting (MBA); health care management (MBA); human resources (MBA); management (MBA); marketing (MBA). *Program availability:* Part-time, evening/weekend, online learning. *Entrance requirements:* For master's, GMAT, bachelor's degree from regionally-accredited university; minimum undergraduate GPA of 2.5; 2 years of significant work experience; 3 letters of recommendation. Electronic applications accepted.

Indiana Tech, Program in Management, Fort Wayne, IN 46803-1297. Offers MSM. *Program availability:* Part-time, evening/weekend, 100% online. *Entrance requirements:* For master's, bachelor's degree from regionally-accredited university; minimum undergraduate GPA of 2.5; 2 years of significant work experience; 3 letters of recommendation. Electronic applications accepted.

Indiana University Bloomington, Kelley School of Business, Bloomington, IN 47405-7000. Offers MBA, MPA, MS, DBA, PhD, DBA/MIS, JD/MBA, JD/MPA, MBA/MA, PhD/MIS. PhD offered through University Graduate School. *Accreditation:* AACSB. *Faculty:* 167 full-time (32 women). *Students:* 1,488 full-time (417 women), 1,045 part-time (312 women); includes 511 minority (100 Black or African American, non-Hispanic/Latino; 302 Asian, non-Hispanic/Latino; 69 Hispanic/Latino; 2 Native Hawaiian or other Pacific Islander, non-Hispanic/Latino; 38 Two or more races, non-Hispanic/Latino), 493 international. Average age 31. 3,169 applicants, 41% accepted, 744 enrolled. In 2016, 937 master's, 15 doctorates awarded. *Degree requirements:* For doctorate, comprehensive exam, thesis/dissertation. *Entrance requirements:* For master's, GMAT; for doctorate, GMAT, GRE General Test. Additional exam requirements/recommendations for international students: Required—TOEFL (minimum score 100 iBT). *Application deadline:* For fall admission, 12/15 priority date for domestic and international students; for winter admission, 3/1 priority date for domestic students; for spring admission, 4/15 for domestic students, 9/1 for international students. Application fee: $55 ($65 for international students). Electronic applications accepted. *Expenses:* $35,500. *Financial support:* In 2016–17, 41 students received support, including 43 fellowships with full and partial tuition reimbursements available (averaging $5,430 per year), 55 teaching assistantships (averaging $15,003 per year); health care benefits, tuition waivers (full), and fee remissions also available. Financial award application deadline: 12/15; financial award applicants required to submit FAFSA. *Faculty research:* Entrepreneurial ventures, technology-based innovation, on-line price competition, on-line shopping behavior. *Unit head:* Idalene Kesner, Dean, 812-855-8489, E-mail: business@indiana.edu. *Application contact:* Chrystyna Thorbecke, Assistant Director, Doctoral Programs, 812-855-3476, E-mail: chrythor@indiana.edu.
Website: http://kelley.iu.edu/

Indiana University Kokomo, School of Business, Kokomo, IN 46904. Offers accounting (Postbaccalaureate Certificate); business administration (MBA); business fundamentals (Postbaccalaureate Certificate). *Accreditation:* AACSB. *Program availability:* Part-time, evening/weekend. *Faculty:* 14 full-time (6 women). *Students:* 21 full-time (7 women), 34 part-time (14 women); includes 1 minority (Black or African American, non-Hispanic/Latino), 23 international. Average age 31. 33 applicants, 70% accepted, 15 enrolled. In 2016, 36 master's awarded. *Degree requirements:* For master's, thesis optional, research project. *Entrance requirements:* For master's, GMAT. Additional exam requirements/recommendations for international students: Required—TOEFL (minimum score 550 paper-based; 73 iBT). *Application deadline:* For fall admission, 6/15 for domestic students, 6/1 for international students; for spring admission, 11/1 for domestic students, 10/1 for international students; for summer admission, 3/1 for domestic students. Application fee: $40 ($60 for international students). Electronic applications accepted. *Expenses:* $329.79 per credit hour in-state; $739.85 per credit hour out-of-state. *Financial support:* Career-related internships or fieldwork and scholarships/grants available. Financial award application deadline: 3/10; financial award applicants required to submit FAFSA. *Faculty research:* Investments, outsourcing, technology, adoption. *Unit head:* Dr. Alan Krabbenhoff, Dean, 756-455-9275, E-mail: agkrabbe@iuk.edu. *Application contact:* Terri Butler, Administrative Secretary, 765-455-9275, E-mail: tbutler@iuk.edu.
Website: http://www.iuk.edu/business/degrees/masters/business-administration/index.php

Indiana University Northwest, School of Business and Economics, Gary, IN 46408. Offers accounting (Graduate Certificate); management (Certificate); management and administrative studies (MBA). *Accreditation:* AACSB. *Program availability:* Part-time, evening/weekend. *Faculty:* 11 full-time (4 women), 7 part-time/adjunct (1 woman). *Students:* 46 full-time (20 women), 53 part-time (24 women); includes 44 minority (22 Black or African American, non-Hispanic/Latino; 4 Asian, non-Hispanic/Latino; 15 Hispanic/Latino; 3 Two or more races, non-Hispanic/Latino), 2 international. Average age 35. 47 applicants, 94% accepted, 34 enrolled. In 2016, 30 master's, 5 other advanced degrees awarded. *Entrance requirements:* For master's, GMAT (not for Weekend MBA for Professionals), letter of recommendation. *Application deadline:* For fall admission, 7/15 priority date for domestic students; for spring admission, 11/15 for domestic students. Applications are processed on a rolling basis. Application fee: $40 ($60 for international students). Electronic applications accepted. *Expenses:* Contact institution. *Financial support:* Institutionally sponsored loans and unspecified assistantships available. Support available to part-time students. Financial award application deadline: 3/10; financial award applicants required to submit FAFSA. *Faculty research:* International finance, employment law and testing, business ethics, taxation, financial institutions. *Unit head:* Cynthia Roberts, PhD, Dean, 219-980-6552, Fax: 219-980-6916, E-mail: iunbiz@iun.edu.
Website: http://www.iun.edu/business/graduate/index.htm

Indiana University of Pennsylvania, School of Graduate Studies and Research, Eberly College of Business and Information Technology, MBA Executive Track Program, Indiana, PA 15705. Offers MBA. *Program availability:* Part-time, evening/weekend. *Faculty:* 27 full-time (4 women), 1 part-time/adjunct (0 women). *Students:* 2 full-time (both women), 108 part-time (41 women); includes 17 minority (6 Black or African American, non-Hispanic/Latino; 7 Asian, non-Hispanic/Latino; 2 Hispanic/Latino; 2 Two or more races, non-Hispanic/Latino), 40 international. Average age 35. 53 applicants, 72% accepted, 27 enrolled. In 2016, 119 master's awarded. *Entrance requirements:* Additional exam requirements/recommendations for international students: Required—TOEFL (minimum score 540 paper-based). *Application deadline:* Applications are processed on a rolling basis. Application fee: $50. Electronic applications accepted. *Expenses:* Contact institution. *Financial support:* In 2016–17, 1 research assistantship with tuition reimbursement (averaging $1,485 per year) was awarded; fellowships with full tuition reimbursements, career-related internships or fieldwork, Federal Work-Study, scholarships/grants, and unspecified assistantships also available. Financial award application deadline: 4/15; financial award applicants required to submit FAFSA. *Unit head:* Dr. Krish Krishnan, Graduate Coordinator, 724-357-2522, E-mail: krishnan@iup.edu.
Website: http://www.iup.edu/mba/grad/executive-mba/

Indiana University of Pennsylvania, School of Graduate Studies and Research, Eberly College of Business and Information Technology, Program in Business Administration, Indiana, PA 15705. Offers MBA. *Accreditation:* AACSB. *Program availability:* Part-time. *Faculty:* 27 full-time (4 women), 1 part-time/adjunct (0 women). *Students:* 224 full-time (70 women), 17 part-time (5 women); includes 4 minority (2 Black or African American, non-Hispanic/Latino; 2 Asian, non-Hispanic/Latino), 212 international. Average age 23. 213 applicants, 68% accepted, 116 enrolled. In 2016, 109 master's awarded. *Degree requirements:* For master's, thesis optional. *Entrance requirements:* For master's, GMAT, 2 letters of recommendation. Additional exam requirements/recommendations for international students: Required—TOEFL (minimum score 540 paper-based). *Application deadline:* Applications are processed on a rolling basis. Application fee: $50. Electronic applications accepted. *Expenses:* Tuition, state resident: full-time $8694; part-time $483 per credit. Tuition, nonresident: full-time $13,050; part-time $725 per credit. *Required fees:* $157 per credit. $50 per term. Tuition and fees vary according to course load and program. *Financial support:* In 2016–17, 23 research assistantships with tuition reimbursements (averaging $1,577 per year) were awarded; fellowships with full tuition reimbursements, career-related internships or fieldwork, Federal Work-Study, scholarships/grants, and unspecified assistantships also available. Support available to part-time students. Financial award application deadline: 4/15; financial award applicants required to submit FAFSA. *Unit head:* Dr. Krish Krishnan, Graduate Coordinator, 724-357-2522, E-mail: krishnan@iup.edu.
Website: http://www.iup.edu/grad/mba/default.aspx

Indiana University–Purdue University Fort Wayne, Doermer School of Business, Fort Wayne, IN 46805-1499. Offers MBA. *Accreditation:* AACSB. *Program availability:* Part-time. *Entrance requirements:* For master's, GMAT, minimum GPA of 3.0, two letters of recommendation, essay, interview. Additional exam requirements/recommendations for international students: Required—TOEFL (minimum score 600 paper-based; 100 iBT). *Faculty research:* Buddhist ethics education framework, earth orbit pollution, information technology and business school graduates.

Indiana University–Purdue University Indianapolis, Kelley School of Business, Indianapolis, IN 46202-5151. Offers MBA, MSA, MBA/JD, MBA/MD, MBA/MHA, MBA/MS, MBA/MSA, MBA/MSE. *Accreditation:* AACSB. *Unit head:* Philip T. Powell, Associate Dean of Academic Programs, 317-274-2481, E-mail: phpowell@iupui.edu.
Website: http://kelley.iupui.edu

Indiana University South Bend, Judd Leighton School of Business and Economics, South Bend, IN 46634-7111. Offers accounting (MSA); business (Graduate Certificate); business administration (MBA), including finance, human resource management, marketing; MBA/MSA. *Program availability:* Part-time, evening/weekend. *Faculty:* 17 full-time (2 women), 3 part-time/adjunct (1 woman). *Students:* 28 full-time (18 women), 85 part-time (36 women); includes 10 minority (3 Black or African American, non-Hispanic/Latino; 1 Asian, non-Hispanic/Latino; 5 Hispanic/Latino; 1 Two or more races, non-Hispanic/Latino), 22 international. Average age 32. 57 applicants, 68% accepted, 22 enrolled. In 2016, 67 master's, 7 other advanced degrees awarded. *Entrance requirements:* For master's, GMAT. Additional exam requirements/recommendations for international students: Required—TOEFL (minimum score 550 paper-based; 79 iBT). *Application deadline:* For fall admission, 7/15 priority date for domestic and international students; for spring admission, 11/15 priority date for domestic and international students; for summer admission, 4/1 priority date for domestic and international students. Applications are processed on a rolling basis. Application fee: $40 ($60 for international students). Electronic applications accepted. *Expenses:* $329.79 per credit hour in-state; $739.85 per credit hour out-of-state. *Financial support:* Fellowships, Federal Work-Study, and institutionally sponsored loans available. Support available to part-time students. Financial award application deadline: 7/1; financial award applicants required to submit FAFSA. *Faculty research:* Financial accounting, consumer research, capital budgeting research, business strategy research. *Unit head:* Richard Kolbe, Dean, 574-520-4228, Fax: 574-520-4866, E-mail: rkolbe@iusb.edu. *Application contact:* 574-520-4839, Fax: 574-520-4834, E-mail: graduate@iusb.edu.
Website: https://business.iusb.edu/

Indiana University Southeast, School of Business, New Albany, IN 47150-6405. Offers business administration (MBA); strategic finance (MS). *Accreditation:* AACSB.

Program availability: Part-time. *Faculty:* 11 full-time (2 women). *Students:* 14 full-time (2 women), 145 part-time (51 women); includes 19 minority (5 Black or African American, non-Hispanic/Latino; 5 Asian, non-Hispanic/Latino; 4 Hispanic/Latino; 5 Two or more races, non-Hispanic/Latino), 2 international. Average age 32. 52 applicants, 69% accepted, 32 enrolled. In 2016, 50 master's awarded. *Degree requirements:* For master's, community service. *Entrance requirements:* For master's, GMAT, work experience. Additional exam requirements/recommendations for international students: Required—TOEFL. *Application deadline:* For fall admission, 7/20 for domestic and international students; for spring admission, 11/30 for domestic and international students; for summer admission, 4/15 for domestic and international students. Application fee: $40 ($60 for international students). Electronic applications accepted. *Expenses:* $402.33 per credit hour in-state; $828.51 per credit hour out-of-state. *Financial support:* In 2016–17, 2 teaching assistantships (averaging $4,500 per year) were awarded. Financial award applicants required to submit FAFSA. *Unit head:* Sharon Allen, Director of Graduate Business Programs, 812-941-2364, E-mail: allen81@ius.edu. *Application contact:* Admissions Counselor, 812-941-2212, Fax: 812-941-2595, E-mail: admissions@ius.edu.
Website: http://www.ius.edu/business/graduate-programs/index.html

Indiana Wesleyan University, College of Adult and Professional Studies, Graduate Studies in Business, Marion, IN 46953. Offers accounting (MBA, Graduate Certificate); applied management (MBA); business administration (MBA); health care (MBA, Graduate Certificate); human resources (MBA, Graduate Certificate); management (MS); organizational leadership (MA). *Program availability:* Part-time, evening/weekend, online learning. *Degree requirements:* For master's, applied business or management project. *Entrance requirements:* For master's, minimum GPA of 2.5, 2 years of related work experience. Additional exam requirements/recommendations for international students: Required—TOEFL (minimum score 550 paper-based). Electronic applications accepted.

Instituto Centroamericano de Administración de Empresas, Graduate Programs, La Garita, Costa Rica. Offers agribusiness management (MIAM); business administration (EMBA); finance (MBA); real estate management (MGREM); sustainable development (MBA); technology (MBA). *Degree requirements:* For master's, comprehensive exam, essay. *Entrance requirements:* For master's, GMAT or GRE General Test, fluency in Spanish, interview, letters of recommendation, minimum 1 year of work experience. Additional exam requirements/recommendations for international students: Recommended—TOEFL. Electronic applications accepted. *Faculty research:* Competitiveness, production.

Instituto Tecnologico de Santo Domingo, Graduate School, Area of Business, Santo Domingo, Dominican Republic. Offers banking and securities markets (M Mgmt); corporate finance (M Mgmt); human resources management (M Mgmt, Certificate); international trade management (M Mgmt); marketing (M Mgmt); organizational development (M Mgmt); quality and productivity management (Certificate); tax management and planning (M Mgmt); upper management (M Mgmt).

Instituto Tecnológico y de Estudios Superiores de Monterrey, Campus Central de Veracruz, Graduate Programs, Córdoba, Mexico. Offers administration (MA); administration of information technologies (MTI); computer sciences (MCC); education (MEE); educational institution administration (MAD); educational technology (MTE); electronic commerce (MCE); finance (MAF); humanistic studies (MEH); international business for Latin America (MNL); marketing (MMT); science (MCP). *Program availability:* Part-time, evening/weekend, online learning. *Degree requirements:* For master's, thesis (for some programs). *Entrance requirements:* For master's, PAEP College Board. Electronic applications accepted.

Instituto Tecnológico y de Estudios Superiores de Monterrey, Campus Ciudad de México, School of Business Administration, Ciudad de Mexico, Mexico. Offers business administration (EMBA, MBA, PhD); economy (MBA); finance (MBA). EMBA program offered jointly with The University of Texas at Austin. *Program availability:* Part-time, evening/weekend, online learning. *Entrance requirements:* For master's and doctorate, Instituto entrance exam. Additional exam requirements/recommendations for international students: Required—TOEFL.

Instituto Tecnológico y de Estudios Superiores de Monterrey, Campus Ciudad Juárez, Program in Business Administration, Ciudad Juárez, Mexico. Offers MBA. *Program availability:* Part-time, online learning. *Entrance requirements:* Additional exam requirements/recommendations for international students: Required—TOEFL (minimum score 500 paper-based).

Instituto Tecnológico y de Estudios Superiores de Monterrey, Campus Ciudad Obregón, Program in Administration, Ciudad Obregón, Mexico. Offers MA.

Instituto Tecnológico y de Estudios Superiores de Monterrey, Campus Cuernavaca, Programs in Business Administration, Temixco, Mexico. Offers finance (MA); human resources management (MA); international business (MA); marketing (MA).

Instituto Tecnológico y de Estudios Superiores de Monterrey, Campus Estado de México, Professional and Graduate Division, Estado de Mexico, Mexico. Offers administration of information technologies (MITA); architecture (M Arch); business administration (GMBA, MBA); computer sciences (MCS, PhD); education (M Ed); educational institution administration (MAD); educational technology and innovation (PhD); electronic commerce (MEC); environmental systems (MS); finance (MAF); humanistic studies (MHS); information sciences and knowledge management (MISKM); information systems (MS); manufacturing systems (MS); marketing (MEM); quality systems and productivity (MS); science and materials engineering (PhD); telecommunications management (MTM). *Program availability:* Part-time, online learning. *Degree requirements:* For master's, one foreign language, thesis (for some programs); for doctorate, one foreign language, thesis/dissertation. *Entrance requirements:* For master's, E-PAEP 500, interview; for doctorate, E-PAEP 500, research proposal. Additional exam requirements/recommendations for international students: Required—TOEFL (minimum score 550 paper-based). *Faculty research:* Surface treatments by plasmas, mechanical properties, robotics, graphical computing, mechatronics security protocols.

Instituto Tecnológico y de Estudios Superiores de Monterrey, Campus Guadalajara, Program in Business Administration, Zapopan, Mexico. Offers IEMBA, M Ad. *Program availability:* Part-time, evening/weekend, online learning. *Degree requirements:* For master's, one foreign language. *Entrance requirements:* For master's, ITESM admission test. *Faculty research:* Strategic alliances in small business, family business practice in Mexico, competitiveness under NAFTA for Mexican firms.

Instituto Tecnológico y de Estudios Superiores de Monterrey, Campus Irapuato, Graduate Programs, Irapuato, Mexico. Offers administration (MBA); administration of information technology (MAIT); administration of telecommunications (MAT); architecture (M Arch); computer science (MCS); education (M Ed); educational administration (MEA); educational innovation and technology (DEIT); educational technology (MET); electronic commerce (MBA); environmental administration and planning (MEAP); environmental systems (MES); finances (MBA); humanistic studies (MHS); international management for Latin American executives (MIMLAE); library and information science (MLIS); manufacturing quality management (MMQM); marketing research (MBA).

Instituto Tecnológico y de Estudios Superiores de Monterrey, Campus Laguna, Graduate School, Torreón, Mexico. Offers business administration (MBA); industrial engineering (MIE); management information systems (MS). *Program availability:* Part-time. *Entrance requirements:* For master's, GMAT. *Faculty research:* Computer communications from home to the university.

Instituto Tecnológico y de Estudios Superiores de Monterrey, Campus León, Program in Business Administration, León, Mexico. Offers MBA. *Program availability:* Part-time.

Instituto Tecnológico y de Estudios Superiores de Monterrey, Campus Monterrey, Graduate School of Business Administration and Leadership, Program in Business Administration, Monterrey, Mexico. Offers business administration (MA, MBA); finance (M Sc); international business (M Sc); marketing (M Sc). *Program availability:* Part-time. *Degree requirements:* For master's, one foreign language, thesis. *Entrance requirements:* For master's, GMAT. Additional exam requirements/recommendations for international students: Required—TOEFL. *Faculty research:* Technology management, quality management, organizational theory and behavior.

Instituto Tecnológico y de Estudios Superiores de Monterrey, Campus Monterrey, Graduate School of Business Administration and Leadership, Program in Management, Monterrey, Mexico. Offers PhD. *Accreditation:* AACSB. *Program availability:* Part-time. *Degree requirements:* For doctorate, one foreign language, thesis/dissertation. *Entrance requirements:* For doctorate, GMAT. Additional exam requirements/recommendations for international students: Required—TOEFL. *Faculty research:* Quality management, manufacturing and technology management, information systems, managerial economics, business policy.

Instituto Tecnológico y de Estudios Superiores de Monterrey, Campus Querétaro, School of Business, Santiago de Querétaro, Mexico. Offers MBA. *Entrance requirements:* For master's, GRE General Test. *Faculty research:* Organizational analysis, industrial marketing, international trade.

Instituto Tecnológico y de Estudios Superiores de Monterrey, Campus Sonora Norte, Program in Business, Hermosillo, Mexico. Offers MA. *Entrance requirements:* For master's, GMAT.

Instituto Tecnológico y de Estudios Superiores de Monterrey, Campus Toluca, Graduate Programs, Toluca, Mexico. Offers MBA. *Program availability:* Part-time, evening/weekend. *Degree requirements:* For master's, one foreign language. *Faculty research:* Management in the industrial valley of Toluca.

Inter American University of Puerto Rico, Aguadilla Campus, Graduate School, Aguadilla, PR 00605. Offers accounting (MBA); counseling psychology specializing in family (MS); criminal justice (MA); educative management and leadership (MA); elementary education (M Ed); finance (MBA); human resources (MBA); industrial management (MBA); management information systems (MBA); marketing (MBA). *Program availability:* Part-time, evening/weekend. *Degree requirements:* For master's, comprehensive exam. *Entrance requirements:* For master's, EXADEP, 2 letters of recommendation, minimum GPA of 2.5. Electronic applications accepted.

Inter American University of Puerto Rico, Arecibo Campus, Program in Business Administration, Arecibo, PR 00614-4050. Offers accounting (MBA); finance (MBA); human resources (MBA).

Inter American University of Puerto Rico, Barranquitas Campus, Program in Business Administration, Barranquitas, PR 00794. Offers accounting (IMBA); finance (IMBA).

Inter American University of Puerto Rico, Fajardo Campus, Graduate Programs, Fajardo, PR 00738-7003. Offers computer science (MS); educational management and leadership (MA Ed); elementary education (MA Ed); general business (MBA); management information systems (MBA); marketing (MBA); special education (MA Ed).

Inter American University of Puerto Rico, Guayama Campus, Department of Business Administration, Guayama, PR 00785. Offers marketing (MBA).

Inter American University of Puerto Rico, Metropolitan Campus, Graduate Programs, Program in General Business, San Juan, PR 00919-1293. Offers MBA.

Inter American University of Puerto Rico, San Germán Campus, Graduate Studies Center, Program in Business Administration, San Germán, PR 00683-5008. Offers accounting (MBA); finance (MBA); general business administration (MBA); human resources (MBA, PhD); industrial relations (MBA); information systems (MBA); international and interregional business (PhD); management (MBA); marketing (MBA). *Program availability:* Part-time, evening/weekend. *Degree requirements:* For master's, comprehensive exam. *Entrance requirements:* For master's, GRE General Test or EXADEP, minimum GPA of 3.0.

International College of the Cayman Islands, Graduate Program in Management, Newlands, Cayman Islands. Offers business administration (MBA); management (MS), including education, human resources. *Program availability:* Part-time, evening/weekend. *Degree requirements:* For master's, comprehensive exam. *Entrance requirements:* Additional exam requirements/recommendations for international students: Recommended—TOEFL. *Faculty research:* International human resources administration.

International Technological University, Program in Business Administration, San Jose, CA 95134. Offers MBA, DBA. *Program availability:* Part-time, evening/weekend. Terminal master's awarded for partial completion of doctoral program. *Degree requirements:* For master's, thesis or alternative, capstone project; for doctorate, comprehensive exam, thesis/dissertation. *Entrance requirements:* Additional exam requirements/recommendations for international students: Required—TOEFL, IELTS. Electronic applications accepted.

International University in Geneva, Business Programs, Geneva, Switzerland. Offers business administration (MBA, DBA); entrepreneurship (MBA); international business (MIB); international trade (MIT); sales and marketing (MBA). *Accreditation:* ACBSP. *Program availability:* Part-time, evening/weekend. *Degree requirements:* For master's, comprehensive exam. *Entrance requirements:* For master's, GMAT. Additional exam requirements/recommendations for international students: Required—TOEFL. Electronic applications accepted.

The International University of Monaco, Graduate Programs, Monte Carlo, Monaco. Offers entrepreneurship (EMBA, MBA); financial engineering (M Sc); hedge fund and private equity (M Sc); international marketing (EMBA, MBA); international wealth management (M Sc); luxury goods and services (EMBA, M Sc, MBA); wealth and asset management (EMBA, MBA). *Program availability:* Part-time. *Degree requirements:* For master's, comprehensive exam (for some programs), applied research project. *Entrance requirements:* Additional exam requirements/recommendations for international students: Required—TOEFL (minimum score 550 paper-based), IELTS. Electronic applications accepted. *Faculty research:* Gaming, leadership, disintermediation.

Iona College, Hagan School of Business, New Rochelle, NY 10801-1890. Offers MBA, MS, AC, PMC. *Accreditation:* AACSB. *Program availability:* Part-time, evening/weekend,

100% online, blended/hybrid learning. *Faculty:* 35 full-time (8 women), 18 part-time/adjunct (7 women). *Students:* 147 full-time (67 women), 205 part-time (92 women); includes 99 minority (31 Black or African American, non-Hispanic/Latino; 2 American Indian or Alaska Native, non-Hispanic/Latino; 12 Asian, non-Hispanic/Latino; 52 Hispanic/Latino; 1 Native Hawaiian or other Pacific Islander, non-Hispanic/Latino; 1 Two or more races, non-Hispanic/Latino), 68 international. Average age 28. 147 applicants, 99% accepted, 74 enrolled. In 2016, 218 master's, 185 other advanced degrees awarded. *Entrance requirements:* For master's, GMAT, 2 letters of recommendation. Additional exam requirements/recommendations for international students: Required—TOEFL (minimum score 550 paper-based; 80 iBT), IELTS (minimum score 6.5). *Application deadline:* For fall admission, 8/15 priority date for domestic students, 8/1 priority date for international students; for winter admission, 11/15 priority date for domestic students, 11/1 priority date for international students; for spring admission, 2/15 priority date for domestic students, 2/1 priority date for international students; for summer admission, 5/15 priority date for domestic students, 5/1 priority date for international students. Applications are processed on a rolling basis. Application fee: $50. Electronic applications accepted. *Expenses: Tuition:* Full-time $19,692; part-time $1094 per credit. *Required fees:* $245 per term. Tuition and fees vary according to program. *Financial support:* In 2016–17, 151 students received support. Scholarships/grants, tuition waivers (partial), and unspecified assistantships available. Support available to part-time students. Financial award application deadline: 4/15; financial award applicants required to submit FAFSA. *Faculty research:* Artificial intelligence, financial services, value-based management, public policy, business ethics. *Unit head:* Dr. Charles J. Cante, Interim Dean, 914-633-2258, E-mail: ccante@iona.edu. *Application contact:* Katelyn Brunck, Director of MBA Admissions, 914-633-2451, Fax: 914-633-2277, E-mail: kbrunck@iona.edu.
Website: http://www.iona.edu/Academics/Hagan-School-of-Business.aspx

Iowa State University of Science and Technology, Program in Business Administration, Ames, IA 50011. Offers MBA, M Arch/MBA, MBA/MCRP, MBA/MS. *Entrance requirements:* For master's, GMAT, resume. Additional exam requirements/recommendations for international students: Recommended—TOEFL (minimum score 600 paper-based; 100 iBT), IELTS (minimum score 7). *Application deadline:* For fall admission, 7/1 priority date for domestic students, 3/1 priority date for international students; for winter admission, 12/1 for domestic and international students. Application fee: $60 ($90 for international students). Electronic applications accepted. *Application contact:* Debbie Johnson, Application Contact, 515-294-5133, Fax: 515-294-2446, E-mail: busgrad@iastate.edu.

Ithaca College, School of Business, Program in Business Administration, Ithaca, NY 14850. Offers sport management (MBA). *Accreditation:* AACSB. *Faculty:* 15 full-time (6 women), 2 part-time/adjunct (0 women). *Students:* 7 full-time (3 women), 1 part-time (0 women); includes 1 minority (Black or African American, non-Hispanic/Latino), 1 international. Average age 24. 8 applicants, 75% accepted, 4 enrolled. In 2016, 4 master's awarded. *Degree requirements:* For master's, thesis optional. *Entrance requirements:* For master's, GMAT. Additional exam requirements/recommendations for international students: Required—TOEFL (minimum score 550 paper-based; 80 iBT). *Application deadline:* For fall admission, 5/15 for domestic and international students; for spring admission, 11/1 for domestic and international students. Applications are processed on a rolling basis. Application fee: $40. Electronic applications accepted. *Expenses:* Contact institution. *Financial support:* In 2016–17, 6 students received support, including 5 fellowships (averaging $7,700 per year); career-related internships or fieldwork, Federal Work-Study, and scholarships/grants also available. Support available to part-time students. Financial award application deadline: 3/1; financial award applicants required to submit CSS PROFILE or FAFSA. *Unit head:* Rasoul Resvanian, Associate Dean and Director, MBA Programs, 607-274-1762, Fax: 607-274-1263, E-mail: rrezvanian@ithaca.edu. *Application contact:* Nicole Eversley Bradwell, Director, Office of Admission, 607-274-3124, Fax: 607-274-1263, E-mail: admission@ithaca.edu.
Website: http://www.ithaca.edu/business/mba

Jackson State University, Graduate School, College of Business, Department of Economics, Finance and General Business, Jackson, MS 39217. Offers business administration (MBA, PhD). *Accreditation:* AACSB. *Program availability:* Part-time, evening/weekend. *Faculty:* 6 full-time (2 women). *Degree requirements:* For master's, comprehensive exam, thesis. *Entrance requirements:* For master's, GRE General Test, GMAT. Additional exam requirements/recommendations for international students: Required—TOEFL. *Application deadline:* For fall admission, 3/1 priority date for domestic students, 3/1 for international students; for spring admission, 10/1 for domestic and international students. Applications are processed on a rolling basis. Application fee: $25. *Expenses:* Tuition, state resident: full-time $7141. Tuition, nonresident: full-time $17,494. *Required fees:* $1080. Tuition and fees vary according to class time, course level, course load, degree level, campus/location, program and student level. *Financial support:* Federal Work-Study, scholarships/grants, tuition waivers (full and partial), and unspecified assistantships available. Support available to part-time students. Financial award application deadline: 3/1. *Unit head:* Dr. Fidel Ezeala-Harrison, Interim Chair, 601-979-2531. *Application contact:* Dr. Fidel Ezeala-Harrison, Interim Chair, 601-979-2531.
Website: http://www.jsums.edu/economics/

Jacksonville State University, College of Graduate Studies and Continuing Education, College of Commerce and Business Administration, Jacksonville, AL 36265-1602. Offers MBA. *Accreditation:* AACSB. *Program availability:* Part-time, evening/weekend, 100% online, blended/hybrid learning. *Faculty:* 11 full-time (1 woman). *Students:* 23 full-time (15 women), 56 part-time (20 women); includes 8 minority (all Black or African American, non-Hispanic/Latino), 9 international. Average age 32. 102 applicants, 34% accepted, 25 enrolled. In 2016, 17 master's awarded. *Degree requirements:* For master's, comprehensive exam, thesis (for some programs). *Entrance requirements:* For master's, GMAT. Additional exam requirements/recommendations for international students: Required—TOEFL (minimum score 500 paper-based; 61 iBT). *Application deadline:* Applications are processed on a rolling basis. Application fee: $35. Electronic applications accepted. *Financial support:* In 2016–17, 19 students received support. Available to part-time students. Application deadline: 4/1; applicants required to submit FAFSA. *Unit head:* Dr. William Fielding, Dean, 256-782-5508, E-mail: fielding@jsu.edu. *Application contact:* Dr. Jean Pugliese, Associate Dean, 256-782-8278, Fax: 256-782-5321, E-mail: pugliese@jsu.edu.
Website: http://www.jsu.edu/ccba/

Jacksonville University, Davis College of Business, Accelerated Day-time MBA Program, Jacksonville, FL 32211. Offers accounting and finance (MBA); business administration (MBA); consumer goods and services marketing (MBA); management (MBA); management accounting (MBA). *Faculty:* 13 full-time (3 women), 1 part-time/adjunct (0 women). *Students:* 39 full-time (12 women), 8 part-time (4 women); includes 11 minority (5 Black or African American, non-Hispanic/Latino; 4 Hispanic/Latino; 2 Two or more races, non-Hispanic/Latino), 20 international. Average age 25. 80 applicants, 61% accepted, 33 enrolled. In 2016, 44 master's awarded. *Entrance requirements:* For master's, GMAT or GRE (may be waived for 3.3 or higher undergraduate GPA from AACSB-accredited institution), bachelor's degree from regionally-accredited institution, resume, statement of purpose, 2 letters of recommendation. Additional exam requirements/recommendations for international students: Required—TOEFL (minimum score 500 paper-based; 61 iBT), IELTS (minimum score 6). *Application deadline:* For fall admission, 8/1 priority date for domestic students, 7/15 priority date for international students; for spring admission, 12/1 priority date for domestic students, 11/15 priority date for international students. Application fee: $50. Electronic applications accepted. *Expenses:* $740 per credit hour. *Financial support:* In 2016–17, 7 students received support. Scholarships/grants and unspecified assistantships available. Financial award application deadline: 7/1; financial award applicants required to submit FAFSA. *Faculty research:* Behavioral finance, game theory, regional economic integration, information sabotage, public choice and public finance. *Unit head:* Dr. Douglas Johansen, Associate Dean and Graduate Programs Director, 904-256-7763, Fax: 904-256-7168, E-mail: djohans@ju.edu. *Application contact:* AnnaMaria Murphy, Assistant Director of Graduate Admissions, 904-256-7426, Fax: 904-256-7012, E-mail: mba@ju.edu.

See Display on next page and Close-Up on page 179.

Jacksonville University, Davis College of Business, Doctor of Business Administration Program, Jacksonville, FL 32211. Offers DBA. *Program availability:* Evening/weekend. *Faculty:* 12 full-time (1 woman), 2 part-time/adjunct (0 women). *Students:* 40 full-time (19 women), 6 part-time (4 women); includes 17 minority (15 Black or African American, non-Hispanic/Latino; 2 Hispanic/Latino), 3 international. Average age 45. 44 applicants, 61% accepted, 18 enrolled. *Degree requirements:* For doctorate, comprehensive exam, thesis/dissertation. *Entrance requirements:* For doctorate, MBA or master's degree from regionally-accredited institution or comparable foreign institution with minimum GPA of 3.25; curriculum vitae or resume with minimum of 7 years' professional experience in business management or not-for-profit administration; statement of purpose; 3 letters of recommendation. Additional exam requirements/recommendations for international students: Required—TOEFL (minimum score 500 paper-based; 61 iBT), IELTS (minimum score 6). *Application deadline:* For fall admission, 5/1 priority date for domestic students, 4/15 for international students. Application fee: $50. Electronic applications accepted. *Expenses:* Contact institution. *Financial support:* In 2016–17, 7 students received support, including 6 research assistantships with partial tuition reimbursements available (averaging $9,000 per year); scholarships/grants also available. Financial award application deadline: 7/1; financial award applicants required to submit FAFSA. *Unit head:* Dr. Douglas Johansen, Associate Dean and Graduate Programs Director, 904-256-7763, Fax: 904-256-7168, E-mail: djohans@ju.edu. *Application contact:* AnnaMaria Murphy, Assistant Director of Graduate Admissions, 904-256-7426, Fax: 904-256-7012, E-mail: amurphy8@ju.edu.
Website: http://www.ju.edu/dcob/doctorate/

Jacksonville University, Davis College of Business, Executive Master of Business Administration Program, Jacksonville, FL 32211. Offers consumer goods and services marketing (MBA); leadership development (MBA). *Accreditation:* AACSB. *Program availability:* Evening/weekend. *Faculty:* 16 full-time (3 women), 1 part-time/adjunct (0 women). *Students:* 28 full-time (10 women), 8 part-time (4 women); includes 5 minority (4 Black or African American, non-Hispanic/Latino; 1 Asian, non-Hispanic/Latino). Average age 41. 19 applicants, 95% accepted, 16 enrolled. In 2016, 10 master's awarded. *Entrance requirements:* For master's, resume, 5-7 years of professional experience, 3 letters of recommendation, corporate letter of support, statement of purpose, interview. Additional exam requirements/recommendations for international students: Required—TOEFL (minimum score 500 paper-based; 61 iBT), IELTS (minimum score 6). *Application deadline:* For fall admission, 9/1 priority date for domestic students, 8/15 priority date for international students. Application fee: $50. Electronic applications accepted. *Expenses:* Contact institution. *Financial support:* In 2016–17, 4 students received support. Scholarships/grants available. Financial award application deadline: 7/1; financial award applicants required to submit FAFSA. *Faculty research:* Data analytics, emerging markets and economic development, high-performing teams, government deficit, learning from corporate failure. *Unit head:* Dr. Douglas Johansen, Associate Dean and Director of Graduate Studies, 904-256-7763, Fax: 904-256-7168, E-mail: djohans@ju.edu. *Application contact:* AnnaMaria Murphy, Assistant Director of Graduate Admissions, 904-256-7426, Fax: 904-256-7012, E-mail: mba@ju.edu.

See Display on next page and Close-Up on page 179.

Jacksonville University, Davis College of Business, FLEX Master of Business Administration Program, Jacksonville, FL 32211. Offers accounting and finance (MBA); consumer goods and services marketing (MBA); management accounting (MBA); JD/MBA; MBA/MPP; MSN/MBA. JD/MBA offered jointly with Florida School of Law. *Accreditation:* AACSB. *Program availability:* Part-time, evening/weekend, blended/hybrid learning. *Faculty:* 20 full-time (5 women), 1 part-time/adjunct (0 women). *Students:* 32 full-time (13 women), 71 part-time (29 women); includes 29 minority (11 Black or African American, non-Hispanic/Latino; 1 American Indian or Alaska Native, non-Hispanic/Latino; 6 Asian, non-Hispanic/Latino; 10 Hispanic/Latino; 1 Two or more races, non-Hispanic/Latino), 3 international. Average age 32. 32 applicants, 97% accepted, 27 enrolled. In 2016, 57 master's awarded. *Entrance requirements:* For master's, GMAT or GRE (may be waived for 3.3 or higher undergraduate GPA from AACSB-accredited institution), bachelor's degree from regionally-accredited institution, 3 years of full-time work experience (recommended), resume, statement of purpose, 2 letters of recommendation. Additional exam requirements/recommendations for international students: Required—TOEFL (minimum score 500 paper-based; 61 iBT), IELTS (minimum score 6). *Application deadline:* For fall admission, 8/1 priority date for domestic students, 7/15 priority date for international students; for spring admission, 12/1 priority date for domestic students, 11/15 priority date for international students; for summer admission, 4/1 priority date for domestic students, 3/15 priority date for international students. Applications are processed on a rolling basis. Application fee: $50. Electronic applications accepted. *Expenses:* $740 per credit hour. *Financial support:* In 2016–17, 1 student received support. Scholarships/grants available. Financial award application deadline: 7/1; financial award applicants required to submit FAFSA. *Faculty research:* Downsizing with integrity; impact of YouTube videos; game theory; analysis of effective tax rates; creativity innovation and change. *Unit head:* Dr. Douglas Johansen, Associate Dean and Director of Graduate Studies, 904-256-7763, Fax: 904-256-7168, E-mail: djohans@ju.edu. *Application contact:* AnnaMaria Murphy, Assistant Director of Graduate Admissions, 904-256-7426, Fax: 904-256-7012, E-mail: mba@ju.edu.

See Display on next page and Close-Up on page 179.

James Madison University, The Graduate School, College of Business, Program in Business Administration, Harrisonburg, VA 22807. Offers business (MBA), including executive leadership, information security, innovation. *Accreditation:* AACSB. *Program availability:* Part-time, evening/weekend, blended/hybrid learning. *Faculty:* 31 full-time (8 women), 2 part-time/adjunct (1 woman). *Students:* 20 full-time (9 women), 77 part-time (27 women); includes 21 minority (9 Black or African American, non-Hispanic/Latino; 9 Asian, non-Hispanic/Latino; 2 Hispanic/Latino; 1 Two or more races, non-Hispanic/Latino), 1 international. Average age 30. 62 applicants, 82% accepted, 42 enrolled. In 2016, 45 master's awarded. Application fee: $55. Electronic applications accepted. *Financial support:* In 2016–17, 1 student received support. Federal Work-Study and 1

assistantship (averaging $7911) available. Financial award application deadline: 3/1; financial award applicants required to submit FAFSA. *Unit head:* Dr. Matthew A. Rutherford, Department Head, 540-568-8777, E-mail: rutherma@jmu.edu. *Application contact:* Lynette D. Michael, Director of Graduate Admissions, 540-568-6131 Ext. 6395, Fax: 540-568-7860, E-mail: michaeld@jmu.edu.
Website: http://www.jmu.edu/cob/graduate/mba/index.shtml

John Brown University, Soderquist College of Business, Siloam Springs, AR 72761-2121. Offers international business (MBA); leadership and ethics (MBA, MS). *Accreditation:* ACBSP. *Program availability:* Part-time, evening/weekend, online only, 100% online, blended/hybrid learning. *Faculty:* 4 full-time (2 women), 26 part-time/adjunct (7 women). *Students:* 42 full-time (27 women), 246 part-time (129 women); includes 65 minority (25 Black or African American, non-Hispanic/Latino; 7 American Indian or Alaska Native, non-Hispanic/Latino; 6 Asian, non-Hispanic/Latino; 15 Hispanic/Latino; 12 Two or more races, non-Hispanic/Latino), 6 international. Average age 33. 145 applicants, 80% accepted, 88 enrolled. In 2016, 114 master's awarded. *Entrance requirements:* For master's, MAT, GMAT or GRE if undergraduate GPA is less than 3.0, recommendation forms from three people, 200-word essay describing professional plans and reason for seeking acceptance. Additional exam requirements/recommendations for international students: Required—TOEFL (minimum score 550 paper-based; 79 iBT). *Application deadline:* Applications are processed on a rolling basis. Application fee: $35 ($100 for international students). Electronic applications accepted. *Expenses: Tuition:* Full-time $13,000; part-time $6500 per credit hour. Part-time tuition and fees vary according to course load and program. *Financial support:* Fellowships with full tuition reimbursements, scholarships/grants, and unspecified assistantships available. Financial award applicants required to submit FAFSA. *Faculty research:* Ethical leadership. *Unit head:* Kai Togami, Program Director, 479-524-7370, E-mail: ktogami@jbu.edu. *Application contact:* Kent Shaffer, Graduate Business Representative, 479-631-4665, E-mail: kents@jbu.edu.
Website: http://www.jbu.edu/grad/business/

John Carroll University, Graduate Studies, John M. and Mary Jo Boler School of Business, University Heights, OH 44118-4581. Offers accountancy (MS); business (MBA); laboratory administration (MS). *Accreditation:* AACSB. *Program availability:* Part-time, evening/weekend. *Entrance requirements:* For master's, GMAT, minimum GPA of 2.5. Additional exam requirements/recommendations for international students: Required—TOEFL (minimum score 550 paper-based). *Application deadline:* Applications are processed on a rolling basis. Application fee: $25 ($35 for international students). Electronic applications accepted. *Expenses:* Contact institution. *Financial support:* Research assistantships with full tuition reimbursements, scholarships/grants, and unspecified assistantships available. Financial award application deadline: 3/15; financial award applicants required to submit FAFSA. *Faculty research:* Accounting, economics and finance, management, marketing and logistics. *Unit head:* Dr. Alan R. Miciak, Dean, 216-397-4391, Fax: 216-397-1833. *Application contact:* Gayle T. Bruno-Gannon, Assistant to the Dean, 216-397-1970, Fax: 216-397-1728,
E-mail: ggannon@jcu.edu.
Website: http://www.jcu.edu/boler/grads

John F. Kennedy University, School of Management, Program in Business Administration, Pleasant Hill, CA 94523-4817. Offers business administration (MBA); organizational leadership (Certificate). *Program availability:* Part-time, evening/weekend. *Degree requirements:* For master's, thesis or alternative. *Entrance requirements:* For master's, interview. Additional exam requirements/recommendations for international students: Required—TOEFL.

Johns Hopkins University, Carey Business School, Certificate Programs, Baltimore, MD 21218. Offers investments (Certificate). *Program availability:* Part-time, evening/weekend. *Faculty:* 87 full-time (32 women), 51 part-time/adjunct (8 women). *Students:* 37 part-time (17 women); includes 11 minority (4 Black or African American, non-Hispanic/Latino; 5 Asian, non-Hispanic/Latino; 1 Hispanic/Latino; 1 Two or more races, non-Hispanic/Latino), 6 international. Average age 37. 24 applicants, 29% accepted, 6 enrolled. In 2016, 33 Certificates awarded. *Degree requirements:* For Certificate, 16 credits. *Entrance requirements:* Additional exam requirements/recommendations for international students: Required—TOEFL, IELTS. *Application deadline:* Applications are processed on a rolling basis. Application fee: $100. Electronic applications accepted. *Expenses:* $1,290 per credit. *Unit head:* Dr. Kevin Frick, Vice Dean of Education, 410-234-9272, E-mail: kfrick@jhu.edu. *Application contact:* Office of Admissions, 410-234-9220, Fax: 443-529-1554, E-mail: carey.admissions@jhu.edu.
Website: http://carey.jhu.edu/academics/certificate-programs/

Johns Hopkins University, Carey Business School, MBA Full-time Programs, Baltimore, MD 21218. Offers MBA, MBA/MA. MBA/MA offered with Maryland Institute College of Art. *Faculty:* 87 full-time (32 women), 51 part-time/adjunct (8 women). *Students:* 251 full-time (125 women); includes 50 minority (8 Black or African American, non-Hispanic/Latino; 24 Asian, non-Hispanic/Latino; 12 Hispanic/Latino; 6 Two or more races, non-Hispanic/Latino), 113 international. Average age 26. 345 applicants, 64% accepted, 118 enrolled. In 2016, 89 degrees awarded. *Degree requirements:* For master's, 54 credits. *Entrance requirements:* For master's, GMAT or GRE. Additional exam requirements/recommendations for international students: Required—TOEFL, IELTS. *Application deadline:* For fall admission, 5/1 for domestic and international students. Applications are processed on a rolling basis. Application fee: $100. Electronic applications accepted. *Expenses:* $57,000 per year (Global MBA); $97,500 (full program, MBA/MA). *Financial support:* In 2016–17, 82 students received support. Scholarships/grants available. Financial award application deadline: 4/15; financial award applicants required to submit FAFSA. *Unit head:* Dr. Kevin Frick, Vice Dean of Education, 410-234-9272, E-mail: kfrick@jhu.edu. *Application contact:* Office of Admissions, 410-234-9220, Fax: 443-529-1554, E-mail: carey.admissions@jhu.edu.
Website: http://carey.jhu.edu/academics/master-of-business-administration/

Johns Hopkins University, Carey Business School, MBA Part-time Program, Baltimore, MD 21218. Offers MBA, MBA/MA. MBA/MA offered through the Zanvyl Krieger School of Arts and Sciences. *Program availability:* Part-time, evening/weekend, blended/hybrid learning, on-site residency requirement. *Faculty:* 87 full-time (32 women), 51 part-time/adjunct (8 women). *Students:* 663 part-time (272 women); includes 249 minority (72 Black or African American, non-Hispanic/Latino; 1 American Indian or Alaska Native, non-Hispanic/Latino; 119 Asian, non-Hispanic/Latino; 43 Hispanic/Latino; 1 Native Hawaiian or other Pacific Islander, non-Hispanic/Latino; 13 Two or more races, non-Hispanic/Latino), 28 international. Average age 32. 265 applicants, 89% accepted, 143 enrolled. In 2016, 116 master's awarded. *Degree requirements:* For master's, 54 credits. *Entrance requirements:* For master's, GMAT or GRE. Additional exam requirements/recommendations for international students: Required—TOEFL, IELTS. *Application deadline:* For fall admission, 5/1 for domestic and international students. Applications are processed on a rolling basis. Application fee: $100. Electronic applications accepted. *Expenses:* $1,290 per credit. *Financial support:* In 2016–17, 16 students received support. Scholarships/grants available. Support available to part-time students. Financial award application deadline: 4/15; financial award applicants required to submit FAFSA. *Unit head:* Dr. Kevin Frick, Vice Dean of Education, 410-234-9272, E-mail: kfrick@jhu.edu. *Application contact:* Office of Admissions, 410-234-9220, Fax: 443-529-1554, E-mail: carey.admissions@jhu.edu.
Website: http://carey.jhu.edu/academics/master-of-business-administration/flexible-mba

Johnson & Wales University, Graduate Studies, MBA Program, Providence, RI 02903-3703. Offers accounting (MBA); business administration (MBA); finance (MBA); hospitality (MBA); human resource management (MBA); information technology (MBA);

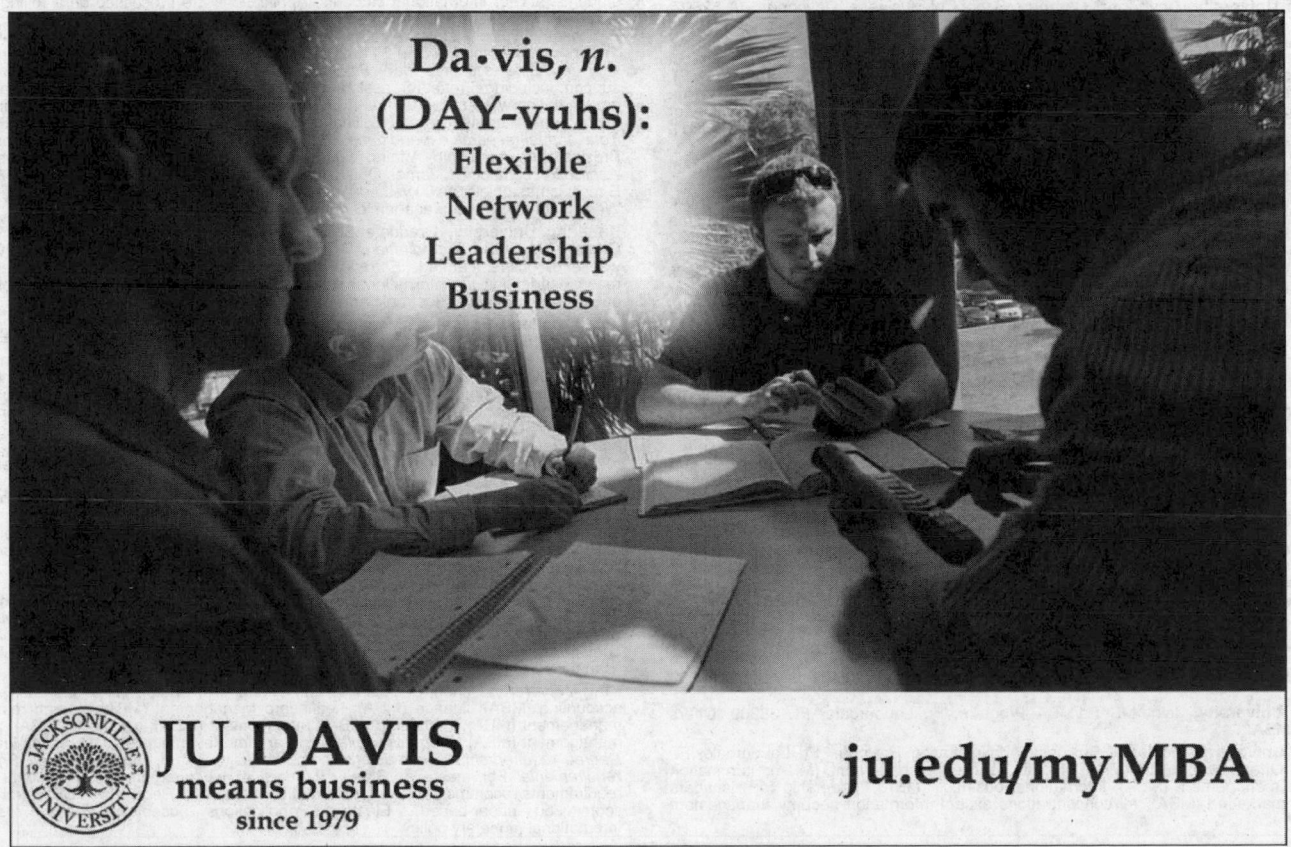

nonprofit management (MBA); operations and supply chain management (MBA). Program also offered on Denver campus. *Program availability:* Part-time, online learning. *Entrance requirements:* For master's, minimum GPA of 2.75. Additional exam requirements/recommendations for international students: Required—TOEFL (minimum score 550 paper-based); Recommended—IELTS, TWE. *Faculty research:* International banking, global economy, international trade, cultural differences.

Judson University, Master of Business Administration Program, Elgin, IL 60123-1498. Offers MBA. *Program availability:* Evening/weekend, 100% online. *Students:* 31 full-time, 22 part-time; includes 20 minority (12 Black or African American, non-Hispanic/Latino; 7 Hispanic/Latino; 1 Two or more races, non-Hispanic/Latino), 2 international. 25 applicants, 80% accepted, 18 enrolled. *Entrance requirements:* For master's, bachelor's degree from college or university; minimum overall undergraduate GPA of 3.0; two years of work experience; two letters of recommendation; professional resume; two letters of reference from pastors and/or other professionals in Christian ministry leadership; personal essay. *Application deadline:* Applications are processed on a rolling basis. Application fee: $35. Electronic applications accepted. *Expenses:* Contact institution. *Financial support:* Applicants required to submit FAFSA. *Faculty research:* Ethics. *Unit head:* Dr. Michelle L. Kilbourne, Chair, 847-268-1515, E-mail: mkilbourne@judsonu.edu. *Application contact:* Maria Aguirre, Student Academic Advisor, 847-628-1160, E-mail: maguirre@judsonu.edu.
Website: http://www.judsonu.edu/Graduate/Master_of_Business_Administration/Overview/

Kansas State University, Graduate School, College of Business, Program in Business Administration, Manhattan, KS 66506. Offers data analytics (MBA); finance (MBA); management (MBA); marketing (MBA); technology entrepreneurship (MBA). *Accreditation:* AACSB. *Program availability:* Part-time, 100% online. *Faculty:* 35 full-time (8 women). *Students:* 50 full-time (19 women), 89 part-time (36 women); includes 25 minority (8 Black or African American, non-Hispanic/Latino; 6 Asian, non-Hispanic/Latino; 4 Hispanic/Latino; 7 Two or more races, non-Hispanic/Latino), 17 international. Average age 32. 78 applicants, 90% accepted, 31 enrolled. In 2016, 26 master's, 3 other advanced degrees awarded. *Entrance requirements:* For master's, GMAT (minimum score of 500), minimum undergraduate GPA of 3.0. Additional exam requirements/recommendations for international students: Required—TOEFL (minimum score 550 paper-based; 79 iBT); Recommended—IELTS (minimum score 7). *Application deadline:* For fall admission, 2/1 priority date for domestic and international students; for spring admission, 10/1 priority date for domestic students, 8/1 priority date for international students. Applications are processed on a rolling basis. Application fee: $70 ($80 for international students). Electronic applications accepted. *Expenses:* Contact institution. *Financial support:* In 2016–17, 6 students received support, including 5 research assistantships (averaging $6,400 per year), 6 teaching assistantships with partial tuition reimbursements available (averaging $6,400 per year); institutionally sponsored loans and scholarships/grants also available. Financial award application deadline: 3/1; financial award applicants required to submit FAFSA. *Faculty research:* Organizational citizenship behavior, service marketing, impression management, human resources management, lean manufacturing and supply chain management, financial market behavior and investment management, data analytics, corporate responsibility, technology entrepreneurship. *Unit head:* Dr. Kevin Gwinner, Dean, 785-532-7227, Fax: 785-532-7216, E-mail: kgwinner@ksu.edu. *Application contact:* Dr. Chwen Sheu, Associate Dean for Academic Programs, 785-532-4363, Fax: 785-532-1339, E-mail: gradbusiness@ksu.edu.
Website: http://www.cba.k-state.edu/

Kansas Wesleyan University, Program in Business Administration, Salina, KS 67401-6196. Offers business administration (MBA); sports management (MBA). *Program availability:* Part-time, evening/weekend. *Entrance requirements:* For master's, GMAT, minimum graduate GPA of 3.0 or undergraduate GPA of 3.25.

Kaplan University, Davenport Campus, School of Business, Davenport, IA 52807. Offers business administration (MBA); change leadership (MS); entrepreneurship (MBA); finance (MBA); health care management (MBA, MS); human resource (MBA); international business (MBA); management (MS); marketing (MBA); project management (MBA, MS); supply chain management and logistics (MBA, MS). *Accreditation:* ACBSP. *Program availability:* Part-time, evening/weekend, online learning. *Entrance requirements:* Additional exam requirements/recommendations for international students: Required—TOEFL (minimum score 550 paper-based; 80 iBT). Electronic applications accepted.

Kean University, Nathan Weiss Graduate College, Program in Educational Administration, Union, NJ 07083. Offers school business administrator (MA); supervisor and principal (MA); supervisors, principals, and school business administrators (MA). *Accreditation:* NCATE. *Program availability:* Part-time, 100% online. *Faculty:* 3 full-time (2 women). *Students:* 12 full-time (8 women), 80 part-time (46 women); includes 32 minority (13 Black or African American, non-Hispanic/Latino; 2 Asian, non-Hispanic/Latino; 17 Hispanic/Latino), 1 international. Average age 33. 184 applicants, 49% accepted, 80 enrolled. In 2016, 31 master's awarded. *Degree requirements:* For master's, comprehensive exam (for some programs), portfolio, field experience, research component, internship, teaching experience. *Entrance requirements:* For master's, GRE General Test or MAT, minimum GPA of 3.0; New Jersey or out-of-state Standard Instructional or Educational Services Certificate; one year of experience under the appropriate certificate; official transcripts from all institutions attended; two letters of recommendation; personal statement; professional resume/curriculum vitae. Additional exam requirements/recommendations for international students: Required—TOEFL (minimum score 550 paper-based; 79 iBT), IELTS (minimum score 6.5). *Application deadline:* For fall admission, 6/1 for domestic and international students; for spring admission, 12/1 for domestic and international students. Applications are processed on a rolling basis. Application fee: $75. Electronic applications accepted. *Expenses:* Tuition, state resident: full-time $13,156; part-time $640 per credit. Tuition, nonresident: full-time $17,831; part-time $785 per credit. *Required fees:* $3316; $151 per credit. Tuition and fees vary according to course level, course load, degree level and program. *Financial support:* Scholarships/grants and unspecified assistantships available. Financial award applicants required to submit FAFSA. *Unit head:* Dr. Steven Locasio, Program Coordinator, 908-737-5977, E-mail: locascst@kean.edu. *Application contact:* Brittany Gerstenhaber, Admissions Counselor, 908-737-7100, E-mail: grad-adm@kean.edu.
Website: http://grad.kean.edu/edleadership/ma-combined

Keiser University, Doctor of Business Administration Program, Ft. Lauderdale, FL 33309. Offers global business (DBA); global organizational leadership (DBA); marketing (DBA).

Keiser University, Joint MS Ed/MBA Program, Ft. Lauderdale, FL 33309. Offers MS Ed/MBA.

Keiser University, Master of Business Administration Program, Ft. Lauderdale, FL 33309. Offers accounting (MBA); health services management (MBA); information security management (MBA); international business (MBA); leadership for managers (MBA); marketing (MBA). All concentrations except information security management also offered in Mandarin; leadership for managers and international business also offered in Spanish. *Program availability:* Part-time, online learning.

Keiser University, MS in Management Program, Ft. Lauderdale, FL 33309. Offers MS. Program also offered in Spanish.

Kennesaw State University, Michael J. Coles College of Business, Doctor of Business Administration Program, Kennesaw, GA 30144. Offers DBA. *Accreditation:* AACSB. *Program availability:* Part-time. *Degree requirements:* For doctorate, thesis/dissertation. *Entrance requirements:* Additional exam requirements/recommendations for international students: Required—TOEFL (minimum score 550 paper-based; 80 iBT), IELTS (minimum score 6.5). Electronic applications accepted. *Expenses:* Contact institution.

Kennesaw State University, Michael J. Coles College of Business, Program in Business Administration, Kennesaw, GA 30144. Offers MBA. *Accreditation:* AACSB. *Program availability:* Part-time, evening/weekend, online learning. *Entrance requirements:* For master's, GMAT (minimum score 530), minimum GPA of 2.8, 1 year of work experience. Additional exam requirements/recommendations for international students: Required—TOEFL (minimum score 550 paper-based; 80 iBT), IELTS (minimum score 6.5). Electronic applications accepted.

Kent State University, College of Business Administration, Master's Program in Business Administration, Kent, OH 44242-0001. Offers MBA. *Accreditation:* AACSB. *Program availability:* Part-time, evening/weekend, 100% online. *Faculty:* 60 full-time (19 women). *Students:* 54 full-time (23 women), 67 part-time (28 women); includes 4 minority (1 Black or African American, non-Hispanic/Latino; 1 Hispanic/Latino; 2 Two or more races, non-Hispanic/Latino), 21 international. Average age 29. 132 applicants, 77% accepted, 38 enrolled. In 2016, 33 master's awarded. *Entrance requirements:* For master's, GMAT or GRE, minimum GPA of 3.0. Additional exam requirements/recommendations for international students: Required—TOEFL (minimum score 550 paper-based; 80 iBT). *Application deadline:* For fall admission, 6/1 for domestic students, 3/15 for international students; for spring admission, 10/15 for domestic students; for summer admission, 5/1 for domestic students. Applications are processed on a rolling basis. Application fee: $45 ($70 for international students). Electronic applications accepted. *Expenses:* Contact institution. *Financial support:* In 2016–17, 12 students received support. Career-related internships or fieldwork, Federal Work-Study, and scholarships/grants available. Financial award application deadline: 3/15; financial award applicants required to submit FAFSA. *Unit head:* Louise M. Ditchey, Administrative Director, 330-672-2282, Fax: 330-672-7303, E-mail: gradbus@kent.edu. *Application contact:* Felecia A. Urbanek, Coordinator, Graduate Programs, 330-672-2282, Fax: 330-672-7303, E-mail: gradbus@kent.edu.
Website: http://www.kent.edu/business/degrees/masters-programs

Kent State University at Stark, Professional MBA Program, Canton, OH 44720-7599. Offers MBA.

Kentucky State University, College of Business and Computer Science, Frankfort, KY 40601. Offers business administration (MBA); computer science technology (MS). *Accreditation:* ACBSP. *Program availability:* Part-time, evening/weekend. *Faculty:* 8 full-time (1 woman), 1 part-time/adjunct (0 women). *Students:* 29 full-time (8 women), 18 part-time (5 women); includes 18 minority (13 Black or African American, non-Hispanic/Latino; 5 Asian, non-Hispanic/Latino), 10 international. Average age 33. 39 applicants, 72% accepted, 20 enrolled. In 2016, 15 master's awarded. *Degree requirements:* For master's, comprehensive exam, thesis optional. *Entrance requirements:* For master's, GMAT, GRE, letters of recommendation, essay, transcript. Additional exam requirements/recommendations for international students: Required—TOEFL (minimum score 525 paper-based). *Application deadline:* For fall admission, 7/1 for domestic students, 4/1 for international students; for spring admission, 11/15 for domestic students, 8/15 for international students; for summer admission, 5/1 for domestic students, 2/1 for international students. Applications are processed on a rolling basis. Application fee: $30 ($100 for international students). Electronic applications accepted. *Expenses:* Tuition, state resident: full-time $7524; part-time $418 per credit hour. Tuition, nonresident: full-time $11,322; part-time $629 per credit hour. Tuition and fees vary according to course load. *Financial support:* In 2016–17, 43 students received support, including 5 research assistantships (averaging $9,200 per year); scholarships/grants, tuition waivers (partial), and unspecified assistantships also available. Financial award application deadline: 4/15; financial award applicants required to submit FAFSA. *Total annual research expenditures:* $303,741. *Unit head:* Dr. Candice L. Jackson, Vice President of Academic Affairs, 502-597-6442, E-mail: candice.jackson@kysu.edu. *Application contact:* Dr. James Obielodan, Director of Graduate Studies, 502-597-4723, E-mail: james.obielodan@kysu.edu.
Website: http://kysu.edu/academics/college-of-business-and-computer-science/

Kettering University, Graduate School, Department of Business, Flint, MI 48504. Offers MBA, MS. *Accreditation:* ACBSP. *Program availability:* Part-time, evening/weekend, online learning. *Entrance requirements:* Additional exam requirements/recommendations for international students: Required—TOEFL (minimum score 550 paper-based; 79 iBT). Electronic applications accepted.

Keuka College, Program in Management, Keuka Park, NY 14478. Offers MS. *Program availability:* Part-time, evening/weekend, 100% online, blended/hybrid learning. *Faculty:* 4 full-time (1 woman), 20 part-time/adjunct (7 women). *Students:* 32 full-time (21 women), 32 part-time (18 women); includes 18 minority (8 Black or African American, non-Hispanic/Latino; 5 Asian, non-Hispanic/Latino; 3 Hispanic/Latino; 2 Two or more races, non-Hispanic/Latino). Average age 35. 56 applicants, 66% accepted, 27 enrolled. In 2016, 53 master's awarded. *Degree requirements:* For master's, thesis, capstone/action research project. *Entrance requirements:* For master's, 2 letters of recommendation, minimum GPA of 3.0. Additional exam requirements/recommendations for international students: Required—TOEFL (minimum score 550 paper-based). *Application deadline:* For fall admission, 8/15 priority date for domestic students; for winter admission, 12/15 priority date for domestic students; for spring admission, 4/15 priority date for domestic students. Applications are processed on a rolling basis. Application fee: $50. *Expenses:* Contact institution. *Financial support:* Scholarships/grants and tuition waivers (full and partial) available. Financial award applicants required to submit FAFSA. *Faculty research:* Inventory control and supply chain management; optimal order policies and supply chain coordination sustainability; using nature as an innovator and designing tool. *Unit head:* Ann Tuttle, Chair, Division of Business and Management, 315-279-5286, E-mail: atuttle@keuka.edu. *Application contact:* Graduate Admissions, 866-255-3852, Fax: 315-279-5386, E-mail: asapadvisor@keuka.edu.

King University, School of Business and Economics, Bristol, TN 37620-2699. Offers accounting (MBA); finance (MBA); healthcare management (MBA); human resources management (MBA); leadership (MBA); management (MBA); marketing (MBA); project management (MBA). *Program availability:* Part-time, evening/weekend, online learning. *Degree requirements:* For master's, comprehensive exam, thesis optional. *Entrance requirements:* For master's, GMAT, 2 years of work experience. Additional exam requirements/recommendations for international students: Required—TOEFL (minimum score 550 paper-based). Electronic applications accepted. *Faculty research:* International monetary policy.

Kutztown University of Pennsylvania, College of Business, Program in Business Administration, Kutztown, PA 19530-0730. Offers MBA. *Accreditation:* AACSB. *Program availability:* Part-time, evening/weekend. *Faculty:* 5 full-time (2 women), 1 part-time/adjunct (0 women). *Students:* 16 full-time (6 women), 18 part-time (7 women); includes 3 minority (2 Black or African American, non-Hispanic/Latino; 1 Asian, non-Hispanic/Latino), 4 international. Average age 30. 31 applicants, 77% accepted, 15 enrolled. In 2016, 16 master's awarded. *Degree requirements:* For master's, comprehensive exam, thesis (for some programs). *Entrance requirements:* For master's, GMAT or GRE, 2 letters of recommendation, resume, goal statement. Additional exam requirements/recommendations for international students: Required—TOEFL (minimum score 550 paper-based, 79 iBT) or IELTS (minimum score 6.5). *Application deadline:* For fall admission, 8/1 priority date for domestic and international students; for spring admission, 12/1 priority date for domestic and international students. Application fee: $35. Electronic applications accepted. *Expenses:* Tuition, state resident: full-time $4347; part-time $483 per credit. Tuition, nonresident: full-time $6525; part-time $725 per credit. *Required fees:* $88 per credit. One-time fee: $50 full-time. *Financial support:* Career-related internships or fieldwork, Federal Work-Study, scholarships/grants, and unspecified assistantships available. Financial award application deadline: 3/1; financial award applicants required to submit FAFSA. *Unit head:* Dr. Ernest Clary, Interim Dean, 610-683-4575, Fax: 610-683-4573, E-mail: clary@kutztown.edu.
Website: http://www.kutztown.edu/MBA

Lake Erie College, School of Business, Painesville, OH 44077-3389. Offers general management (MBA); health care administration (MBA); information technology management (MBA). *Program availability:* Part-time, evening/weekend. *Entrance requirements:* For master's, GMAT or minimum GPA of 3.0, resume, personal statement. Additional exam requirements/recommendations for international students: Required—TOEFL (minimum score 550 paper-based; 79 iBT), IELTS (minimum score 6), STEP Eiken 1st and pre-1st grade level (for Japanese students). Electronic applications accepted. Application fee is waived when completed online. *Expenses:* Contact institution.

Lake Forest Graduate School of Management, The Leadership MBA Program, Lake Forest, IL 60045. Offers finance (MBA); global business (MBA); healthcare management (MBA); management (MBA); marketing (MBA); organizational behavior (MBA). *Program availability:* Part-time, evening/weekend. *Entrance requirements:* For master's, 4 years of work experience in field, interview, 2 letters of recommendation. Electronic applications accepted.

Lakeland University, Graduate Studies Division, Program in Business Administration, Plymouth, WI 53073. Offers accounting (MBA); finance (MBA); healthcare management (MBA); project management (MBA). *Entrance requirements:* For master's, GMAT. *Expenses:* Contact institution.

Lamar University, College of Graduate Studies, College of Business, Beaumont, TX 77710. Offers accounting (MBA); experiential business and entrepreneurship (MBA); healthcare administration (MBA); MSA/MBA. *Accreditation:* AACSB. *Program availability:* Part-time, evening/weekend. *Faculty:* 22 full-time (5 women). *Students:* 23 full-time (12 women), 209 part-time (109 women); includes 96 minority (46 Black or African American, non-Hispanic/Latino; 11 Asian, non-Hispanic/Latino; 32 Hispanic/Latino; 7 Two or more races, non-Hispanic/Latino), 33 international. Average age 33. 151 applicants, 99% accepted, 81 enrolled. In 2016, 104 master's awarded. *Degree requirements:* For master's, comprehensive exam (for some programs), thesis optional. *Entrance requirements:* For master's, GMAT. Additional exam requirements/recommendations for international students: Required—TOEFL (minimum score 550 paper-based; 79 iBT), IELTS (minimum score 6.5). *Application deadline:* For fall admission, 8/10 for domestic students, 7/1 for international students; for spring admission, 1/5 for domestic students, 12/1 for international students. Applications are processed on a rolling basis. Application fee: $25 ($50 for international students). Electronic applications accepted. *Expenses:* $8,134 in-state full-time, $5,574 in-state part-time; $15,604 out-of-state full-time, $10,554 out-of-state part-time per year. *Financial support:* Fellowships with tuition reimbursements, research assistantships with partial tuition reimbursements, career-related internships or fieldwork, Federal Work-Study, institutionally sponsored loans, scholarships/grants, and tuition waivers (partial) available. Support available to part-time students. Financial award application deadline: 4/1; financial award applicants required to submit FAFSA. *Faculty research:* Marketing, finance, quantitative methods, management information systems, legal, environmental. *Unit head:* Dr. Enrique R. Venta, Dean, 409-880-8603, Fax: 409-880-8088, E-mail: henry.venta@lamar.edu. *Application contact:* Deidre Mayer, Interim Director, Admissions and Academic Services, 409-880-8888, Fax: 409-880-7419, E-mail: gradmissions@lamar.edu.
Website: http://business.lamar.edu

La Salle University, School of Business, Master of Business Administration Program, Philadelphia, PA 19141-1199. Offers accounting (MBA, Post-MBA Certificate); business systems and analytics (MBA, Post-MBA Certificate); finance (MBA, Post-MBA Certificate); general business administration (MBA, Post-MBA Certificate); human resource management (MBA, Post-MBA Certificate); management (MBA, Post-MBA Certificate); marketing (Post-MBA Certificate); MBA/MSN. Program also offered in Switzerland. *Accreditation:* AACSB. *Program availability:* Part-time, evening/weekend, online learning. *Faculty:* 19 full-time (6 women), 11 part-time/adjunct (3 women). *Students:* 55 full-time (23 women), 209 part-time (96 women); includes 66 minority (35 Black or African American, non-Hispanic/Latino; 17 Asian, non-Hispanic/Latino; 9 Hispanic/Latino; 5 Two or more races, non-Hispanic/Latino), 17 international. Average age 31. 200 applicants, 59% accepted, 63 enrolled. In 2016, 192 master's, 1 other advanced degree awarded. *Entrance requirements:* For master's, GMAT or GRE, two letters of reference; resume; for Post-MBA Certificate, MBA with minimum GPA of 3.0. Additional exam requirements/recommendations for international students: Required—TOEFL. *Application deadline:* For fall admission, 8/15 priority date for domestic students, 7/15 for international students; for spring admission, 12/15 priority date for domestic students, 11/15 for international students; for summer admission, 4/15 priority date for domestic students, 3/15 for international students. Applications are processed on a rolling basis. Application fee: $35. Electronic applications accepted. Application fee is waived when completed online. *Expenses:* Contact institution. *Financial support:* In 2016–17, 49 students received support. Scholarships/grants available. Support available to part-time students. Financial award application deadline: 8/31; financial award applicants required to submit FAFSA. *Unit head:* Dr. MarySheila McDonald, Interim Dean, 215-951-1040, Fax: 215-951-1886, E-mail: mcdonaldms@lasalle.edu. *Application contact:* Elizabeth Heenan, Director, Graduate and Adult Enrollment, 215-951-1100, Fax: 215-951-1462, E-mail: heenan@lasalle.edu.

Lasell College, Graduate and Professional Studies in Management, Newton, MA 02466-2709. Offers business administration (PMBA); elder care management (MSM, Graduate Certificate); hospitality and event management (MSM, Graduate Certificate); human resources management (MSM, Graduate Certificate); management (MSM, Graduate Certificate); marketing (MSM, Graduate Certificate); non-profit management (MSM, Graduate Certificate); project management (MSM, Graduate Certificate). *Accreditation:* ACBSP. *Program availability:* Part-time, evening/weekend, 100% online, blended/hybrid learning. *Faculty:* 3 full-time (2 women), 16 part-time/adjunct (10 women). *Students:* 47 full-time (34 women), 93 part-time (72 women); includes 28 minority (20 Black or African American, non-Hispanic/Latino; 4 Asian, non-Hispanic/Latino; 3 Hispanic/Latino; 1 Two or more races, non-Hispanic/Latino), 24 international. Average age 31. 121 applicants, 55% accepted, 32 enrolled. In 2016, 61 master's, 3 other advanced degrees awarded. *Degree requirements:* For master's, minimum GPA of 3.0; internship or research paper (for MSM). *Entrance requirements:* For master's, one-page personal statement, 2 letters of recommendation, resume, bachelor's degree transcript; proof of microeconomics and statistics (for PMBA); for Graduate Certificate, bachelor's degree transcript, 2 letters of recommendation, 1-page personal statement, resume. Additional exam requirements/recommendations for international students: Required—TOEFL (minimum score 550 paper-based, 79 iBT) or IELTS (minimum score 6). *Application deadline:* For fall admission, 8/31 priority date for domestic students, 6/30 priority date for international students; for spring admission, 12/31 priority date for domestic students, 10/31 priority date for international students. Applications are processed on a rolling basis. Electronic applications accepted. *Expenses:* $600 per credit. *Financial support:* In 2016–17, 12 students received support. Federal Work-Study, scholarships/grants, and tuition discounts available. Support available to part-time students. Financial award application deadline: 8/31; financial award applicants required to submit FAFSA. *Unit head:* Dr. Joan Dolamore, Dean of Graduate and Professional Studies, 617-243-2485, Fax: 617-243-2450, E-mail: gradinfo@lasell.edu. *Application contact:* Adrienne Franciosi, Director of Graduate Enrollment, 617-243-2214, Fax: 617-243-2450, E-mail: gradinfo@lasell.edu.
Website: http://www.lasell.edu/academics/graduate-and-professional-studies/programs-of-study/master-of-science-in-management.html

La Sierra University, School of Business and Management, Riverside, CA 92515. Offers accounting (MBA); finance (MBA); general management (MBA); human resources management (MBA); leadership, values, and ethics for business and management (Certificate); marketing (MBA). *Degree requirements:* For master's, research project. *Entrance requirements:* For master's, GMAT, minimum GPA of 3.0. Additional exam requirements/recommendations for international students: Required—TOEFL. *Faculty research:* Financial econometrics, institutional assessment and strategic planning, legal issues in management, behavioral finance, content of financial reports.

Laurentian University, School of Graduate Studies and Research, School of Commerce and Administration, Sudbury, ON P3E 2C6, Canada. Offers MBA. *Program availability:* Part-time, evening/weekend. *Entrance requirements:* For master's, GMAT, 2 years of work experience. *Faculty research:* Small business and entrepreneurship development, mutual fund performance, donorship behavior, stress and organizations, quality programs.

Lawrence Technological University, College of Management, Southfield, MI 48075-1058. Offers business administration (MBA), including business analytics (MBA, MS), finance, information technology, marketing, project management (MBA, MS); information technology (MS), including business analytics (MBA, MS), information assurance, project management (MBA, MS); project management (Graduate Certificate). *Accreditation:* ACBSP. *Program availability:* Part-time, evening/weekend, 100% online. *Faculty:* 14 full-time (6 women), 10 part-time/adjunct (2 women). *Students:* 7 full-time (3 women), 323 part-time (120 women); includes 60 minority (29 Black or African American, non-Hispanic/Latino; 2 American Indian or Alaska Native, non-Hispanic/Latino; 17 Asian, non-Hispanic/Latino; 8 Hispanic/Latino; 4 Two or more races, non-Hispanic/Latino), 118 international. Average age 33. 275 applicants, 56% accepted, 72 enrolled. In 2016, 167 master's, 12 other advanced degrees awarded. Terminal master's awarded for partial completion of doctoral program. *Degree requirements:* For master's, thesis (for some programs). *Entrance requirements:* Additional exam requirements/recommendations for international students: Required—TOEFL (minimum score 550 paper-based; 79 iBT), IELTS (minimum score 6.5). *Application deadline:* For fall admission, 5/22 for international students; for spring admission, 10/11 for international students; for summer admission, 2/16 for international students. Applications are processed on a rolling basis. Application fee: $50. Electronic applications accepted. *Expenses: Tuition:* Full-time $14,868; part-time $1062 per credit. *Required fees:* $75 per semester. Tuition and fees vary according to campus/location. *Financial support:* In 2016–17, 35 students received support, including 8 research assistantships with partial tuition reimbursements available (averaging $3,250 per year); career-related internships or fieldwork, unspecified assistantships, and corporate tuition incentives also available. Financial award application deadline: 4/1; financial award applicants required to submit FAFSA. *Faculty research:* Cybersecurity; risk management; IT governance; security controls and countermeasures; threat modeling cyber resilience; autonomous cars; natural language processing; text mining; machine learning; reflective leadership; emerging leadership theories and practice; motivational studies; teaching effectiveness strategies; teamwork; organization development; strategic planning; strengths-based and positive organizational scholarship; global leadership; globalization; corporate governance. *Unit head:* Dr. Bahman Mirshab, Dean, 248-204-3050, E-mail: mgtdean@ltu.edu. *Application contact:* Jane Rohrback, Director of Admissions, 248-204-3160, Fax: 248-204-2228, E-mail: admissions@ltu.edu.
Website: http://www.ltu.edu/management/index.asp

Lebanese American University, School of Business, Beirut, Lebanon. Offers MBA.

Lebanon Valley College, Program in Business Administration, Annville, PA 17003-1400. Offers business administration (MBA); healthcare management (MBA); leadership and ethics (MBA). *Program availability:* Part-time, evening/weekend, 100% online, blended/hybrid learning. *Faculty:* 8 full-time (1 woman), 8 part-time/adjunct (1 woman). *Students:* 17 full-time (12 women), 79 part-time (42 women); includes 14 minority (2 Black or African American, non-Hispanic/Latino; 3 Asian, non-Hispanic/Latino; 8 Hispanic/Latino; 1 Two or more races, non-Hispanic/Latino), 5 international. Average age 34. 23 applicants, 87% accepted, 18 enrolled. In 2016, 49 master's awarded. *Degree requirements:* For master's, capstone course. *Entrance requirements:* For master's, GMAT, 3 years of work experience, resume, professional statement (application form, resume, personal statement, transcripts). Additional exam requirements/recommendations for international students: Required—TOEFL (minimum score 80 iBT), IELTS (minimum score 6.5) or STEP Eiken (grade 1). *Application deadline:* Applications are processed on a rolling basis. Application fee: $0. *Expenses:* $635 per credit hour. *Financial support:* Career-related internships or fieldwork and scholarships/grants available. Financial award application deadline: 3/1; financial award applicants required to submit FAFSA. *Faculty research:* Business intelligence systems, business education as an international aid tool, leadership, business success. *Unit head:* Dr. David Setley, Associate Professor/Chair of Business Administration/Director of the MBA Program, 717-867-6104, Fax: 717-867-6018, E-mail: setley@lvc.edu. *Application contact:* Christine M. Martin, Enrollment and Operations Specialist, 717-867-6486, Fax: 717-867-6013, E-mail: cmartin@lvc.edu.
Website: http://www.lvc.edu/academics/graduate-studies/master-of-buisness-administration/

Lee University, MBA Program, Cleveland, TN 37320-3450. Offers MBA. *Program availability:* Part-time, evening/weekend, 100% online. *Faculty:* 7 full-time (2 women). *Students:* 12 full-time (4 women), 55 part-time (26 women); includes 9 minority (3 Black or African American, non-Hispanic/Latino; 2 American Indian or Alaska Native, non-

Hispanic/Latino; 1 Asian, non-Hispanic/Latino; 3 Hispanic/Latino), 9 international. Average age 30. 41 applicants, 71% accepted, 26 enrolled. In 2016, 26 master's awarded. *Degree requirements:* For master's, variable foreign language requirement, comprehensive exam, thesis optional, practicum. *Entrance requirements:* For master's, GMAT (taken within last 5 years), minimum undergraduate cumulative GPA of 3.0. Additional exam requirements/recommendations for international students: Required—TOEFL (minimum score 61 iBT). *Application deadline:* For fall admission, 4/1 priority date for domestic and international students; for spring admission, 10/1 priority date for domestic and international students. Applications are processed on a rolling basis. Application fee: $25. Electronic applications accepted. *Expenses: Tuition:* Full-time $11,367; part-time $632 per credit hour. *Required fees:* $35 per term. One-time fee: $25. Tuition and fees vary according to program. *Financial support:* In 2016–17, 26 students received support. Scholarships/grants available. Financial award application deadline: 3/1; financial award applicants required to submit FAFSA. *Unit head:* Dr. Shane Griffith, Director, 423-614-8694, E-mail: mba@leeuniversity.edu.
Website: http://www.leeuniversity.edu/academics/graduate/mba/

Lehigh University, College of Business and Economics, Department of Management, Bethlehem, PA 18015. Offers business administration (MBA); project management (MBA); MBA/E; MBA/M Ed. *Accreditation:* AACSB. *Program availability:* Part-time, evening/weekend, 100% online. *Faculty:* 10 full-time (2 women), 1 part-time/adjunct (0 women). *Students:* 40 full-time (25 women), 159 part-time (41 women); includes 31 minority (5 Black or African American, non-Hispanic/Latino; 15 Asian, non-Hispanic/Latino; 9 Hispanic/Latino; 2 Two or more races, non-Hispanic/Latino), 20 international. Average age 32. 188 applicants, 69% accepted, 47 enrolled. In 2016, 47 master's awarded. *Entrance requirements:* For master's, GMAT or GRE. Additional exam requirements/recommendations for international students: Required—TOEFL (minimum score 600 paper-based; 94 iBT). *Application deadline:* For fall admission, 7/15 for domestic students, 5/1 for international students; for spring admission, 12/1 for domestic students. Application fee: $75. Electronic applications accepted. Tuition and fees vary according to program. *Financial support:* In 2016–17, 33 students received support, including 10 fellowships (averaging $5,250 per year), 10 teaching assistantships with tuition reimbursements available (averaging $14,200 per year); scholarships/grants, health care benefits, tuition waivers (full and partial), and unspecified assistantships also available. Support available to part-time students. Financial award application deadline: 1/15. *Faculty research:* Information systems, organizational behavior, supply chain management, strategic management, entrepreneurship. *Total annual research expenditures:* $2,418. *Unit head:* Dr. Yuliang Yao, Department Chair, 610-758-6726, Fax: 610-758-6941, E-mail: yuy3@lehigh.edu. *Application contact:* Michael Tarantino, Director of Recruitment and Admissions, 610-758-3418, Fax: 610-758-5283, E-mail: mgt215@lehigh.edu.
Website: http://www4.lehigh.edu/business/academics/depts/management

Le Moyne College, Madden School of Business, Syracuse, NY 13214. Offers business administration (MBA); information systems (MS). *Accreditation:* AACSB. *Program availability:* Part-time, evening/weekend. *Faculty:* 9 full-time (2 women), 6 part-time/adjunct (2 women). *Students:* 42 full-time (19 women), 58 part-time (23 women); includes 7 minority (3 Black or African American, non-Hispanic/Latino; 1 Asian, non-Hispanic/Latino; 3 Hispanic/Latino), 1 international. Average age 28. 82 applicants, 88% accepted, 67 enrolled. In 2016, 61 master's awarded. *Degree requirements:* For master's, capstone-level course. *Entrance requirements:* For master's, GMAT or GRE General Test, bachelor's degree with minimum GPA of 3.0, resume, 2 letters of recommendation, personal statement, transcripts, interview. Additional exam requirements/recommendations for international students: Required—TOEFL (minimum score 550 paper-based; 79 iBT); Recommended—IELTS (minimum score 6.5). *Application deadline:* For fall admission, 7/1 priority date for domestic and international students; for spring admission, 11/1 priority date for domestic and international students; for summer admission, 4/1 priority date for domestic and international students. Applications are processed on a rolling basis. Application fee: $0. Electronic applications accepted. *Expenses:* $797 per credit hour. *Financial support:* In 2016–17, 27 students received support. Career-related internships or fieldwork, scholarships/grants, health care benefits, and unspecified assistantships available. Support available to part-time students. Financial award applicants required to submit FAFSA. *Faculty research:* Performance evaluation outcomes assessment, technology outsourcing, international business, systems for Web-based information-seeking, non-profit business practices, business sustainability practices, management/leadership development, operations management optimization applications. *Unit head:* James Joseph, Dean of Madden School of Business, 315-445-4280, Fax: 315-445-4787, E-mail: josepjae@lemoyne.edu. *Application contact:* Kristen P. Richards, Senior Director of Enrollment Management, 315-445-5444, Fax: 315-445-6092, E-mail: trapaskp@lemoyne.edu.
Website: http://www.lemoyne.edu/madden

Lenoir-Rhyne University, Graduate Programs, Charles M. Snipes School of Business, Hickory, NC 28601. Offers accounting (MBA); business analytics and information technology (MBA); entrepreneurship (MBA); global business (MBA); healthcare administration (MBA); innovation and change management (MBA); leadership development (MBA). *Accreditation:* ACBSP. *Program availability:* Part-time, evening/weekend, online learning. *Degree requirements:* For master's, capstone course. *Entrance requirements:* For master's, GMAT, GRE, MAT, minimum undergraduate GPA of 2.7, graduate 3.0. Additional exam requirements/recommendations for international students: Required—TOEFL (minimum score 600 paper-based). Electronic applications accepted. *Expenses:* Contact institution.

LeTourneau University, Graduate Programs, Longview, TX 75607-7001. Offers business (MBA); counseling (MA), including licensed professional counselor, marriage and family therapy, school counseling; curriculum and instruction (M Ed); educational administration (M Ed); engineering (ME, MS); engineering management (MEM); health care administration (MS); marriage and family therapy (MA); psychology (MA); strategic leadership (MSL); teacher leadership (M Ed); teaching and learning (M Ed). *Program availability:* Part-time, 100% online, blended/hybrid learning. *Faculty:* 24 full-time (7 women), 40 part-time/adjunct (15 women). *Students:* 82 full-time (48 women), 428 part-time (331 women); includes 234 minority (138 Black or African American, non-Hispanic/Latino; 5 American Indian or Alaska Native, non-Hispanic/Latino; 5 Asian, non-Hispanic/Latino; 50 Hispanic/Latino; 36 Two or more races, non-Hispanic/Latino), 15 international. Average age 37. 257 applicants, 60% accepted, 141 enrolled. In 2016, 136 master's awarded. *Degree requirements:* For master's, thesis (for some programs). *Entrance requirements:* Additional exam requirements/recommendations for international students: Required—TOEFL. *Application deadline:* For fall admission, 8/22 for domestic students, 8/29 for international students; for winter admission, 10/10 for domestic students; for spring admission, 1/2 for domestic students, 1/10 for international students; for summer admission, 5/1 for domestic and international students. Applications are processed on a rolling basis. Electronic applications accepted. *Expenses:* $10,890-$18,450 tuition per year (depending on program). *Financial support:* Research assistantships, institutionally sponsored loans, and unspecified assistantships available. Financial award applicants required to submit FAFSA. *Application contact:* Chris Fontaine, Assistant Vice President for Enrollment Services and Global Admissions, 903-233-4312, E-mail: chrisfontaine@letu.edu.
Website: http://www.letu.edu

Lewis University, College of Business, Graduate School of Management, Romeoville, IL 60446. Offers business administration (MBA), including accounting, custom elective option, e-business, finance, healthcare management, human resources management, international business, management information systems, marketing, project management, technology and operations management; business analytics (MS), including financial analytics, healthcare analytics, marketing analytics, operations analytics; finance (MS); information security (MS); project management (MS). *Accreditation:* ACBSP. *Program availability:* Part-time, evening/weekend, 100% online, blended/hybrid learning. *Students:* 2 part-time (1 woman). Average age 32. *Entrance requirements:* Additional exam requirements/recommendations for international students: Required—TOEFL. *Application deadline:* Applications are processed on a rolling basis. Application fee: $40. Electronic applications accepted. *Expenses: Tuition:* Full-time $13,860; part-time $770 per credit hour. *Required fees:* $75 per semester. Tuition and fees vary according to degree level and program. *Financial support:* Career-related internships or fieldwork, Federal Work-Study, and unspecified assistantships available. Financial award application deadline: 5/1; financial award applicants required to submit FAFSA. *Unit head:* Dr. Rami Khasawneh, Dean, 800-838-0500 Ext. 5360, E-mail: khasawra@lewisu.edu. *Application contact:* Michele Ryan, Director of Admission, 815-836-5384, E-mail: gsm@lewisu.edu.

Lewis University, College of Nursing and Health Professions and College of Business, Program in Nursing/Business, Romeoville, IL 60446. Offers MSN/MBA. *Program availability:* Part-time, evening/weekend. *Entrance requirements:* Additional exam requirements/recommendations for international students: Required—TOEFL (minimum score 550 paper-based; 80 iBT). *Application deadline:* For fall admission, 4/2 priority date for domestic students, 5/1 priority date for international students; for spring admission, 11/15 priority date for international students. Applications are processed on a rolling basis. Electronic applications accepted. *Expenses: Tuition:* Full-time $13,860; part-time $770 per credit hour. *Required fees:* $75 per semester. Tuition and fees vary according to degree level and program. *Financial support:* Scholarships/grants, tuition waivers (full and partial), and unspecified assistantships available. Financial award application deadline: 5/1; financial award applicants required to submit FAFSA. *Faculty research:* Cancer prevention, phenomenological methods, public policy analysis. *Total annual research expenditures:* $1,000. *Unit head:* Dr. Suling Li, Associate Dean and Director, Graduate Studies in Nursing, 815-838-0500 Ext. 5878, E-mail: lisu@lewisu.edu. *Application contact:* Nancy Wiksten, Adult Admission Counselor, 815-838-0500 Ext. 5628, Fax: 815-836-5578, E-mail: wikstena@lewisu.edu.

Liberty University, School of Business, Lynchburg, VA 24515. Offers accounting (MBA, MS); business administration (MBA); criminal justice (MBA); cyber security (MS); executive leadership (MA); information systems (MS), including information assurance, technology management; international business (MBA, DBA); leadership (DBA); marketing (MBA, MS, DBA), including digital marketing and advertising (MS), project management (MS), public relations (MS), sports marketing and media (MS); project management (MBA, DBA); public administration (MBA); public relations (MBA). *Program availability:* Part-time, online learning. *Students:* 1,458 full-time (807 women), 4,188 part-time (2,041 women); includes 1,372 minority (1,060 Black or African American, non-Hispanic/Latino; 19 American Indian or Alaska Native, non-Hispanic/Latino; 85 Asian, non-Hispanic/Latino; 75 Hispanic/Latino; 10 Native Hawaiian or other Pacific Islander, non-Hispanic/Latino; 123 Two or more races, non-Hispanic/Latino), 124 international. Average age 35. 5,424 applicants, 45% accepted, 1242 enrolled. In 2016, 1,859 master's, 87 other advanced degrees awarded. *Entrance requirements:* For master's, minimum undergraduate GPA of 3.0, 15 hours of upper-level business courses. Additional exam requirements/recommendations for international students: Required—TOEFL (minimum score 600 paper-based; 100 iBT). *Application deadline:* Applications are processed on a rolling basis. Application fee: $50. Electronic applications accepted. *Expenses:* Contact institution. *Financial support:* Applicants required to submit FAFSA. *Unit head:* Dr. Scott Hicks, Dean, 434-592-4808, Fax: 434-582-2366, E-mail: smhicks@liberty.edu. *Application contact:* Jay Bridge, Director of Graduate Admissions, 800-424-9595, Fax: 800-628-7977, E-mail: gradadmissions@liberty.edu.
Website: http://www.liberty.edu/academics/business/index.cfm?PID-149

LIM College, MBA Program, New York, NY 10022-5268. Offers entrepreneurship (MBA); fashion management (MBA). *Accreditation:* ACBSP. *Entrance requirements:* For master's, interview. Additional exam requirements/recommendations for international students: Required—TOEFL (minimum score 550 paper-based; 80 iBT), IELTS (minimum score 6.5).

LIM College, MPS Program, New York, NY 10022-5268. Offers fashion marketing (MPS); fashion merchandising and retail management (MPS); visual merchandising (MPS). *Accreditation:* ACBSP.

Limestone College, MBA Program, Gaffney, SC 29340. Offers MBA. *Program availability:* Part-time, evening/weekend, online learning. *Faculty:* 10 full-time (2 women), 1 (woman) part-time/adjunct. *Students:* 41 full-time (28 women), 28 part-time (16 women); includes 30 minority (25 Black or African American, non-Hispanic/Latino; 3 Asian, non-Hispanic/Latino; 2 Two or more races, non-Hispanic/Latino). Average age 40. 74 applicants, 33 enrolled. In 2016, 20 master's awarded. *Degree requirements:* For master's, comprehensive exam, three weekend residency seminars (on campus). *Entrance requirements:* For master's, GMAT/GRE, two letters of recommendation, official transcript(s). Additional exam requirements/recommendations for international students: Required—TOEFL (minimum score 500 paper-based; 90 iBT). *Application deadline:* For fall admission, 8/1 priority date for domestic and international students; for winter admission, 12/12 priority date for domestic and international students; for spring admission, 4/1 priority date for domestic and international students. Applications are processed on a rolling basis. Application fee: $25. Electronic applications accepted. Application fee is waived when completed online. *Expenses:* $1,875 per course. *Financial support:* Scholarships/grants available. Financial award application deadline: 6/15; financial award applicants required to submit FAFSA. *Faculty research:* Management. *Unit head:* Shannon Creighton, Director, MBA Program, 864-488-4371, Fax: 864-487-8706, E-mail: screighton@limestone.edu. *Application contact:* Adair Haynes, Administrative Assistant, MBA Program, 800-795-7151 Ext. 4370, Fax: 864-467-8706, E-mail: ahaynes@limestone.edu.
Website: http://www.limestone.edu/mba-program

Lincoln Memorial University, School of Business, Harrogate, TN 37752-1901. Offers MBA. *Accreditation:* ACBSP. *Program availability:* Part-time, evening/weekend. *Degree requirements:* For master's, comprehensive exam, thesis. *Entrance requirements:* For master's, GMAT, resume, letters of recommendation, interview. Additional exam requirements/recommendations for international students: Required—TOEFL (minimum score 500 paper-based).

Lincoln University, Graduate Studies, Oakland, CA 94612. Offers finance and investments (DBA); finance management (MS); finance management and investments (MBA); general business (MBA); human resource management (MBA, DBA); international business (MBA, MS); management information systems (MBA). *Program availability:* Part-time. *Faculty:* 13 full-time (1 woman), 16 part-time/adjunct (3 women). *Students:* 542 full-time (215 women), 3 part-time (1 woman); includes 10 minority (8 Asian, non-Hispanic/Latino; 1 Hispanic/Latino; 1 Two or more races, non-Hispanic/Latino), 531 international. Average age 26. 800 applicants, 71% accepted, 81 enrolled.

In 2016, 109 master's, 1 doctorate awarded. *Degree requirements:* For master's, research project (thesis), internship report, or comprehensive exam; for doctorate, comprehensive exam, thesis/dissertation. *Entrance requirements:* For master's, minimum GPA of 2.7; for doctorate, GMAT (minimum score: 550), GRE (minimum score: 1000), or equivalent test results (waived for master's degree with minimum cumulative GPA of 3.3). Additional exam requirements/recommendations for international students: Required—TOEFL (minimum score 525 paper-based; 71 iBT) or IELTS (minimum score 5.5) for MBA; TOEFL (minimum score 550 paper-based; 79 iBT) or IELTS (minimum score 6) for DBA; Recommended—TOEFL (minimum score 71 iBT), IELTS (minimum score 6), TSE. *Application deadline:* For fall admission, 8/7 for domestic students, 7/14 for international students; for spring admission, 11/30 for domestic students, 10/31 for international students; for summer admission, 5/29 for domestic students, 5/5 for international students. Applications are processed on a rolling basis. Application fee: $75. Electronic applications accepted. *Expenses: Tuition:* Full-time $7920. *Required fees:* $400. Tuition and fees vary according to course level, course load, degree level and program. *Financial support:* Teaching assistantships, career-related internships or fieldwork, and scholarships/grants available. Financial award applicants required to submit FAFSA. *Unit head:* Dr. Marshall Burak, Director of Graduate Programs, 510-628-8016, Fax: 510-628-8012, E-mail: mburak@lincolnuca.edu. *Application contact:* Reenu Shrestha, Assistant to the President, 510-628-8017, Fax: 510-208-2826, E-mail: sreenu@lincolnuca.edu.
Website: http://www.lincolnuca.edu/

Lincoln University, Graduate Studies, Jefferson City, MO 65101. Offers business administration (MBA), including accounting, management, management information systems, public administration/policy; elementary teaching (M Ed); environmental science (MS); guidance and counseling (M Ed), including community/agency counseling, elementary school, secondary school; higher education (MA); history (MA); integrated agricultural systems (MS); middle school (M Ed); natural sciences (MS); secondary teaching (M Ed); sociology (MA); sociology/criminal justice (MA). *Program availability:* Part-time, evening/weekend, 100% online, blended/hybrid learning. *Students:* 50 full-time (29 women), 68 part-time (39 women); includes 40 minority (37 Black or African American, non-Hispanic/Latino; 1 Asian, non-Hispanic/Latino; 2 Two or more races, non-Hispanic/Latino), 14 international. Average age 33. 75 applicants, 80% accepted, 34 enrolled. In 2016, 51 master's awarded. *Degree requirements:* For master's, comprehensive exam, thesis optional. *Entrance requirements:* For master's, GRE, MAT or GMAT, minimum GPA of 2.75 overall, 3.0 in courses related to specialization; 3 letters of recommendation; minimum C average in English composition; personal statement of purpose. Additional exam requirements/recommendations for international students: Required—TOEFL (minimum score 500 paper-based; 61 iBT), IELTS (minimum score 5.5), Michigan English Language Assessment Battery (minimum score 80). *Application deadline:* For fall admission, 7/1 priority date for domestic students, 5/1 priority date for international students; for spring admission, 11/1 priority date for domestic students, 10/1 priority date for international students; for summer admission, 6/1 priority date for domestic students. Applications are processed on a rolling basis. Application fee: $30. Electronic applications accepted. *Expenses:* Tuition, state resident: full-time $6840; part-time $5130 per year. Tuition, nonresident: full-time $12,720; part-time $9540 per year. *Required fees:* $852; $811 per unit. Tuition and fees vary according to course load. *Financial support:* In 2016–17, 2 fellowships with tuition reimbursements, 8 research assistantships with tuition reimbursements were awarded; Federal Work-Study, scholarships/grants, and unspecified assistantships also available. Support available to part-time students. Financial award application deadline: 3/1; financial award applicants required to submit FAFSA. *Unit head:* Dr. Rolundus R. Rice, Dean, 573-681-5247, Fax: 573-681-5106, E-mail: gradschool@lincolnu.edu. *Application contact:* Irasema Steck, Administrative Assistant, 573-681-5247, Fax: 573-681-5106, E-mail: gradschool@lincolnu.edu.
Website: http://www.lincolnu.edu/web/graduate-studies/graduate-studies

Lindenwood University, Graduate Programs, Plaster School of Business and Entrepreneurship, St. Charles, MO 63301-1695. Offers accountancy (M Acc); accounting (MBA); business administration (MBA); entrepreneurial studies (MBA); finance (MBA, MS); human resource management (MBA); international business (MBA); leadership (MA); management (MBA); marketing (MBA, MS); nonprofit administration (MA); public administration (MBA); sport management (MA); supply chain management (MBA). *Accreditation:* ACBSP. *Program availability:* Part-time, evening/weekend, 100% online. *Faculty:* 15 full-time (6 women), 25 part-time/adjunct (7 women). *Students:* 197 full-time (97 women), 213 part-time (132 women); includes 81 minority (62 Black or African American, non-Hispanic/Latino; 1 American Indian or Alaska Native, non-Hispanic/Latino; 4 Asian, non-Hispanic/Latino; 9 Hispanic/Latino; 5 Two or more races, non-Hispanic/Latino), 83 international. Average age 31. 279 applicants, 54% accepted, 133 enrolled. In 2016, 269 master's awarded. *Degree requirements:* For master's, comprehensive exam (for some programs), thesis (for some programs), minimum GPA of 3.0. *Entrance requirements:* For master's, interview, minimum undergraduate cumulative GPA of 3.0, letter of recommendation. Additional exam requirements/recommendations for international students: Required—TOEFL (minimum score 550 paper-based; 80 iBT); Recommended—IELTS (minimum score 6.5). *Application deadline:* For fall admission, 8/28 priority date for domestic and international students; for winter admission, 1/8 priority date for domestic and international students; for spring admission, 3/5 for domestic students, 3/5 priority date for international students; for summer admission, 6/4 priority date for domestic and international students. Applications are processed on a rolling basis. Application fee: $30 ($100 for international students). Electronic applications accepted. *Expenses:* Contact institution. *Financial support:* In 2016–17, 256 students received support. Career-related internships or fieldwork, Federal Work-Study, institutionally sponsored loans, scholarships/grants, tuition waivers (partial), and unspecified assistantships available. Financial award application deadline: 6/30; financial award applicants required to submit FAFSA. *Unit head:* Roger Ellis, Dean, School of Business and Entrepreneurship, 636-949-4839, E-mail: rellis@lindenwood.edu. *Application contact:* Tyler Kostich, Director, Evening and Graduate Admissions, 636-949-4138, Fax: 636-949-4109, E-mail: adultadmissions@lindenwood.edu.
Website: http://www.lindenwood.edu/academics/academic-schools/robert-w-plaster-school-of-business-entrepreneurship/

Lindenwood University, Graduate Programs, School of Accelerated Degree Programs, St. Charles, MO 63301-1695. Offers administration (MSA), including management, marketing, project management; business administration (MBA); communications (MA), including digital and multimedia, media management, promotions, training and development; criminal justice and administration (MS); healthcare administration (MS); human resource management (MS); information technology (Certificate); managing information security (MS); managing information technology (MS); managing virtualization and cloud computing (MS); writing (MFA). *Program availability:* Part-time, evening/weekend, 100% online. *Faculty:* 16 full-time (7 women), 75 part-time/adjunct (27 women). *Students:* 609 full-time (386 women), 179 part-time (121 women); includes 257 minority (202 Black or African American, non-Hispanic/Latino; 4 American Indian or Alaska Native, non-Hispanic/Latino; 5 Asian, non-Hispanic/Latino; 28 Hispanic/Latino; 1 Native Hawaiian or other Pacific Islander, non-Hispanic/Latino; 17 Two or more races, non-Hispanic/Latino), 28 international. Average age 36. 332 applicants, 70% accepted, 205 enrolled. In 2016, 479 master's awarded. *Degree requirements:* For master's, thesis (for some programs), minimum cumulative GPA of 3.0; for Certificate, minimum cumulative GPA of 3.0. *Entrance requirements:* For master's, resume, personal statement, official undergraduate transcript, minimum undergraduate cumulative GPA of 3.0. Additional exam requirements/recommendations for international students: Required—TOEFL (minimum score 550 paper-based; 80 iBT); Recommended—IELTS (minimum score 6.5). *Application deadline:* For fall admission, 9/26 priority date for domestic and international students; for winter admission, 1/3 priority date for domestic and international students; for spring admission, 3/31 priority date for domestic and international students; for summer admission, 7/3 priority date for domestic and international students. Applications are processed on a rolling basis. Application fee: $30 ($100 for international students). Electronic applications accepted. *Expenses: Tuition:* Full-time $15,672; part-time $453 per credit hour. *Required fees:* $205 per semester. Tuition and fees vary according to course level, course load and degree level. *Financial support:* In 2016–17, 467 students received support. Career-related internships or fieldwork, institutionally sponsored loans, scholarships/grants, tuition waivers (partial), and unspecified assistantships available. Financial award application deadline: 6/30; financial award applicants required to submit FAFSA. *Unit head:* Dr. Gina Ganahl, Dean, Accelerated Degree Programs, 636-949-4501, Fax: 636-949-4505, E-mail: gganahl@lindenwood.edu. *Application contact:* Tyler Kostich, Director, Evening and Graduate Admissions, 636-949-4138, Fax: 636-949-4109, E-mail: adultadmissions@lindenwood.edu.
Website: http://www.lindenwood.edu/academics/academic-schools/school-of-accelerated-degree-programs/

Lindenwood University–Belleville, Graduate Programs, Belleville, IL 62226. Offers business administration (MBA); communications (MA), including digital and multimedia, media management, promotions, training and development; counseling (MA); criminal justice administration (MS); education (MA); healthcare administration (MS); human resource management (MS); school administration (MA); teaching (MAT).

Lipscomb University, College of Business, Nashville, TN 37204-3951. Offers accountancy (M Acc); accounting (MBA); business administration (MM); conflict management (MBA); financial services (MBA); health care informatics (MBA); healthcare management (MBA); information security (MBA); leadership (MBA); nonprofit management (MBA); professional accountancy (Certificate); sports management (MBA); strategic human resources (MBA); sustainability (MBA); MBA/MS; Pharm D/MM. *Accreditation:* ACBSP. *Program availability:* Part-time, evening/weekend. *Faculty:* 22 full-time (4 women), 12 part-time/adjunct (4 women). *Students:* 112 full-time (51 women), 69 part-time (34 women); includes 30 minority (17 Black or African American, non-Hispanic/Latino; 3 Asian, non-Hispanic/Latino; 8 Hispanic/Latino; 2 Two or more races, non-Hispanic/Latino), 5 international. Average age 32. 244 applicants, 55% accepted, 54 enrolled. In 2016, 164 master's awarded. *Entrance requirements:* For master's, GMAT, transcripts, interview, 2 references, resume. Additional exam requirements/recommendations for international students: Required—TOEFL (minimum score 570 paper-based). *Application deadline:* For fall admission, 6/15 for domestic students, 2/1 for international students; for winter admission, 6/1 for international students; for spring admission, 11/15 for domestic students. Applications are processed on a rolling basis. Application fee: $50 ($75 for international students). Electronic applications accepted. *Expenses:* $1,150-$1,290 per hour, depending on program. *Financial support:* Career-related internships or fieldwork, scholarships/grants, tuition waivers (partial), and unspecified assistantships available. Support available to part-time students. Financial award application deadline: 7/1; financial award applicants required to submit FAFSA. *Faculty research:* Impact of spirituality on organization commitment, women in corporate leadership, psychological empowerment, training. *Unit head:* Allison Duke, Associate Dean of Graduate Business Programs, 615-966-5732, Fax: 615-966-1818, E-mail: allison.duke@lipscomb.edu. *Application contact:* Karen Risley, Manager, Graduate Business Recruiting, 615-966-5145, E-mail: karen.risley@lipscomb.edu.
Website: http://www.lipscomb.edu/business/Graduate-Programs

Long Island University–Hudson, Graduate School, Purchase, NY 10577. Offers autism (Advanced Certificate); childhood education (MS Ed); early childhood education (MS Ed); educational leadership (MS Ed); finance (MBA); health administration (MPA); healthcare sector management (MBA); literacy (MS Ed); management (MBA); marriage and family therapy (MS); mental health counseling (MS), including credentialed alcoholism and substance abuse counselor; middle childhood and adolescence education (MS Ed); pharmaceutics (MS), including cosmetic science, industrial pharmacy; public administration (MPA); school counseling (MS Ed, Advanced Certificate); school psychology (MS Ed); special education (MS Ed); TESOL (all grades) (Advanced Certificate); TESOL and bilingual education (MS Ed); the business of pharmaceutics and biotechnology (MBA). *Program availability:* Part-time, evening/weekend, online learning. *Faculty:* 7 full-time (5 women), 42 part-time/adjunct (25 women). *Students:* 55 full-time (41 women), 158 part-time (123 women); includes 40 minority (8 Black or African American, non-Hispanic/Latino; 1 Asian, non-Hispanic/Latino; 31 Hispanic/Latino). Average age 35. *Entrance requirements:* Additional exam requirements/recommendations for international students: Required—TOEFL (minimum score 550 paper-based; 79 iBT). *Application deadline:* Applications are processed on a rolling basis. Application fee: $50. Electronic applications accepted. *Expenses:* Contact institution. *Unit head:* Dr. Sylvia Blake, Dean and Chief Operating Officer, 914-831-2700, E-mail: westchester@liu.edu. *Application contact:* Cindy Pagnotta, Director of Marketing and Enrollment, 914-831-2701, Fax: 914-251-5959, E-mail: cindy.pagnotta@liu.edu.

Long Island University–LIU Brooklyn, School of Business, Public Administration and Information Sciences, Brooklyn, NY 11201-8423. Offers accounting (MBA); accounting (MS); business administration (MBA); computer science (MS); gerontology (Advanced Certificate); health administration (MPA); human resources management (MS); not-for-profit management (Advanced Certificate); public administration (MPA); taxation (MS). *Program availability:* Part-time, evening/weekend, blended/hybrid learning. *Faculty:* 18 full-time (9 women), 32 part-time/adjunct (10 women). *Students:* 275 full-time (150 women), 238 part-time (161 women); includes 281 minority (200 Black or African American, non-Hispanic/Latino; 2 American Indian or Alaska Native, non-Hispanic/Latino; 38 Asian, non-Hispanic/Latino; 36 Hispanic/Latino; 1 Native Hawaiian or other Pacific Islander, non-Hispanic/Latino; 4 Two or more races, non-Hispanic/Latino), 140 international. 796 applicants, 66% accepted, 143 enrolled. In 2016, 185 master's, 17 other advanced degrees awarded. *Entrance requirements:* Additional exam requirements/recommendations for international students: Required—TOEFL (minimum score 527 paper-based; 75 iBT). *Application deadline:* Applications are processed on a rolling basis. Application fee: $50. Electronic applications accepted. *Expenses: Tuition:* Full-time $28,272; part-time $1178 per credit. *Required fees:* $451 per term. Tuition and fees vary according to degree level, program and student level. *Financial support:* In 2016–17, 94 students received support. Career-related internships or fieldwork, Federal Work-Study, institutionally sponsored loans, scholarships/grants, and unspecified assistantships available. Support available to part-time students. Financial award application deadline: 2/15; financial award applicants required to submit FAFSA. *Faculty research:* Corporate social responsibility; executive compensation and corporate governance; combinatorics; secure mobile coding; social equity and justice, particularly among the Latino population; public and healthcare finance. *Unit head:* Dr. Edward Rogoff, Dean, 718-488-1159, E-mail: edward.rogoff@liu.edu. *Application contact:*

Business Administration and Management—General

Gabrielle Gannon, Director of Graduate Admissions, 718-488-1011, Fax: 718-780-6110, E-mail: bkln-admissions@liu.edu.
Website: http://liu.edu/Brooklyn/Academics/School-of-Business-Public-Administration-and-Information-Sciences

Long Island University–LIU Post, College of Management, Brookville, NY 11548-1300. Offers accountancy (MS); finance (MBA); information systems (MS); international business (MBA); management (MBA); management engineering (MS); marketing (MBA); taxation (MS); technical project management (MS); JD/MBA. *Accreditation:* AACSB. *Program availability:* Part-time, 100% online, blended/hybrid learning. *Faculty:* 35 full-time (12 women), 25 part-time/adjunct (6 women). *Students:* 153 full-time (61 women), 68 part-time (22 women); includes 44 minority (8 Black or African American, non-Hispanic/Latino; 24 Asian, non-Hispanic/Latino; 11 Hispanic/Latino; 1 Two or more races, non-Hispanic/Latino), 79 international. 429 applicants, 58% accepted, 74 enrolled. In 2016, 124 master's awarded. *Degree requirements:* For master's, thesis (for some programs). *Entrance requirements:* For master's, GMAT, GRE, or LSAT. Additional exam requirements/recommendations for international students: Required—PTE, TOEFL (minimum score 550 paper-based, 75 iBT) or IELTS. *Application deadline:* Applications are processed on a rolling basis. Application fee: $50. Electronic applications accepted. *Expenses: Tuition:* Full-time $28,272; part-time $1178 per credit. *Required fees:* $451 per term. Tuition and fees vary according to degree level and program. *Financial support:* In 2016–17, 68 students received support. Career-related internships or fieldwork, Federal Work-Study, institutionally sponsored loans, and scholarships/grants available. Support available to part-time students. Financial award application deadline: 2/15; financial award applicants required to submit FAFSA. *Faculty research:* Finance and sustainability, innovation and intellectual property rights, marketing: data analytics and business intelligence, social networking local and international. *Unit head:* Dr. Robert M. Valli, Dean, 516-299-4192, E-mail: rob.valli@liu.edu. *Application contact:* Carol Zerah, Director of Graduate and International Admissions, 516-299-2900, Fax: 516-299-2137, E-mail: post-enroll@liu.edu.
Website: http://liu.edu/CWPost/Academics/Schools/COM

Longwood University, College of Graduate and Professional Studies, College of Business and Economics, Farmville, VA 23909. Offers general business (MBA); real estate (MBA); retail management (MBA). *Accreditation:* AACSB. *Program availability:* Part-time, online only, 100% online. *Degree requirements:* For master's, internship. *Entrance requirements:* For master's, GMAT or GRE, personal essay, 3 recommendations, official transcripts from all colleges and universities attended. Additional exam requirements/recommendations for international students: Required—TOEFL (minimum score 570 paper-based), IELTS (minimum score 6.5). Electronic applications accepted. *Expenses:* Contact institution.

Louisiana State University and Agricultural & Mechanical College, Graduate School, E. J. Ourso College of Business, Department of Finance, Baton Rouge, LA 70803. Offers business administration (PhD), including finance; finance (MS).

Louisiana State University and Agricultural & Mechanical College, Graduate School, E. J. Ourso College of Business, Flores MBA Program, Baton Rouge, LA 70803. Offers EMBA, MBA, PMBA, JD/IMBA. *Accreditation:* AACSB.

Louisiana State University in Shreveport, College of Business, Education, and Human Development, Program in Business Administration, Shreveport, LA 71115-2399. Offers MBA. *Accreditation:* AACSB. *Program availability:* Part-time, evening/weekend. *Students:* 191 full-time (108 women), 984 part-time (465 women); includes 388 minority (248 Black or African American, non-Hispanic/Latino; 7 American Indian or Alaska Native, non-Hispanic/Latino; 39 Asian, non-Hispanic/Latino; 69 Hispanic/Latino; 1 Native Hawaiian or other Pacific Islander, non-Hispanic/Latino; 24 Two or more races, non-Hispanic/Latino). Average age 33. 952 applicants, 90% accepted, 416 enrolled. In 2016, 156 master's awarded. *Degree requirements:* For master's, comprehensive exam. *Entrance requirements:* For master's, minimum undergraduate GPA of 2.5, 2.75 for last 60 credits. Additional exam requirements/recommendations for international students: Required—TOEFL (minimum score 550 paper-based; 61 iBT). *Application deadline:* For fall admission, 6/30 for domestic and international students; for spring admission, 11/30 for domestic and international students; for summer admission, 4/30 for domestic and international students. Applications are processed on a rolling basis. Application fee: $20 ($30 for international students). Electronic applications accepted. *Expenses:* Tuition, state resident: full-time $5163; part-time $350 per credit hour. Tuition, nonresident: full-time $15,578; part-time $1038 per credit hour. *Required fees:* $63 per credit hour. Tuition and fees vary according to course load and program. *Financial support:* In 2016–17, 5 research assistantships (averaging $5,000 per year) were awarded; scholarships/grants also available. *Unit head:* Dr. Tami Knotts, Program Director, 318-797-5268, Fax: 318-797-5176, E-mail: tami.knotts@lsus.edu. *Application contact:* Mary Catherine Harvison, Director, Admissions, 318-797-2400, Fax: 318-797-5286, E-mail: mary.harvison@lsus.edu.

Louisiana Tech University, Graduate School, College of Business, Ruston, LA 71272. Offers MBA, MPA, DBA. *Accreditation:* AACSB. *Program availability:* Part-time. *Degree requirements:* For doctorate, thesis/dissertation. *Entrance requirements:* For master's and doctorate, GMAT. *Application deadline:* For fall admission, 7/29 for domestic students; for spring admission, 2/3 for domestic students. Application fee: $20 ($30 for international students). *Financial support:* Fellowships, research assistantships, and teaching assistantships available. *Unit head:* Dr. Christopher D. Martin, Dean, 318-257-4526, Fax: 318-257-4253. *Application contact:* Marilyn J. Robinson, Assistant to the Dean, 318-257-2924, Fax: 318-257-4487.
Website: http://www.business.latech.edu/

Lourdes University, Graduate School, Sylvania, OH 43560-2898. Offers business (MBA); leadership (M Ed); nurse anesthesia (MSN); nurse educator (MSN); nurse leader (MSN); organizational leadership (MOL); reading (M Ed); teaching and curriculum (M Ed); theology (MA). *Program availability:* Evening/weekend. *Entrance requirements:* Additional exam requirements/recommendations for international students: Required—TOEFL.

Loyola Marymount University, College of Business Administration, Los Angeles, CA 90045-2659. Offers MBA, MS, MBA/JD, MBA/MS. *Accreditation:* AACSB. *Faculty:* 37 full-time (7 women), 12 part-time/adjunct (1 woman). *Expenses:* Contact institution. *Unit head:* Bill Semos, Interim Associate Dean and Director, MBA Program, 310-338-2848, Fax: 310-338-2899, E-mail: william.semos@lmu.edu. *Application contact:* Chake H Kouyoumjian, Associate Dean of Graduate Studies, 310-338-2721, E-mail: ckouyoum@lmu.edu.
Website: http://cba.lmu.edu/

Loyola University Chicago, Quinlan School of Business, Chicago, IL 60611. Offers EMBA, MBA, MSA, MSF, MSHR, MSIMC, MSSCM, Certificate, MBA/MSA, MBA/MSF, MBA/MSHR, MSIMC/MBA. *Accreditation:* AACSB. *Program availability:* Part-time, evening/weekend. *Faculty:* 79 full-time (22 women), 10 part-time/adjunct (4 women). *Students:* 484 full-time (273 women), 106 part-time (52 women); includes 109 minority (33 Black or African American, non-Hispanic/Latino; 36 Asian, non-Hispanic/Latino; 34 Hispanic/Latino; 6 Two or more races, non-Hispanic/Latino), 180 international. Average age 28. 969 applicants, 56% accepted, 218 enrolled. In 2016, 336 master's, 40 other advanced degrees awarded. *Entrance requirements:* For master's, GMAT or GRE, official transcripts, two letters of recommendation, statement of purpose, resume. Additional exam requirements/recommendations for international students: Required—TOEFL (minimum score 90 iBT) or IELTS (minimum score 6.5). *Application deadline:* For fall admission, 7/15 for domestic and international students; for winter admission, 10/1 for domestic and international students; for spring admission, 1/15 for domestic and international students; for summer admission, 4/1 for domestic and international students. Applications are processed on a rolling basis. Application fee: $50. Electronic applications accepted. Application fee is waived when completed online. *Expenses:* Contact institution. *Financial support:* Federal Work-Study, scholarships/grants, health care benefits, and unspecified assistantships available. Support available to part-time students. *Faculty research:* Social enterprise and responsibility, emerging markets, supply chain management, risk management. *Unit head:* Katherine Acles, Assistant Dean for Graduate Programs, 312-915-6124, Fax: 312-915-7207, E-mail: kacles@luc.edu. *Application contact:* Lauren Griffin, Enrollment Advisor, Quinlan School of Business Graduate Programs, 312-915-8908, Fax: 312-915-7207, E-mail: lgriffin3@luc.edu.
Website: http://www.luc.edu/quinlan/mba/index.shtml

Loyola University Maryland, Graduate Programs, Sellinger School of Business, Emerging Leaders MBA Program, Baltimore, MD 21210-2699. Offers MBA. *Program availability:* Part-time. *Faculty:* 26 full-time (8 women), 13 part-time/adjunct (5 women). *Students:* 20 full-time (10 women); includes 9 minority (1 Black or African American, non-Hispanic/Latino; 2 Asian, non-Hispanic/Latino; 5 Hispanic/Latino; 1 Two or more races, non-Hispanic/Latino), 1 international. Average age 24. 42 applicants, 74% accepted, 20 enrolled. In 2016, 20 master's awarded. *Entrance requirements:* For master's, GMAT, essay, 2 letters of recommendation, resume, transcripts. Additional exam requirements/recommendations for international students: Required—TOEFL (minimum score 550 paper-based, 80 iBT) or IELTS (minimum score 7). *Application deadline:* For fall admission, 2/1 priority date for domestic students, 2/1 for international students. Applications are processed on a rolling basis. Application fee: $60. Electronic applications accepted. *Expenses:* Contact institution. *Financial support:* In 2016–17, 11 students received support. Fellowships, scholarships/grants, and traineeships available. Financial award application deadline: 4/15; financial award applicants required to submit FAFSA. *Application contact:* Maureen Faux, 410-617-5067, E-mail: mba@loyola.edu.
Website: http://www.loyola.edu/sellinger/academics/graduate/elmba.aspx

Loyola University Maryland, Graduate Programs, Sellinger School of Business, Professional MBA Program, Baltimore, MD 21210-2699. Offers accounting (MBA); information systems operations management (MBA). *Accreditation:* AACSB. *Program availability:* Part-time, evening/weekend. *Faculty:* 26 full-time (8 women), 13 part-time/adjunct (5 women). *Students:* 59 applicants, 88% accepted, 47 enrolled. In 2016, 125 master's awarded. *Entrance requirements:* For master's, GMAT, resume, essay, official transcripts, professional letter of recommendation. Additional exam requirements/recommendations for international students: Required—TOEFL (minimum score 550 paper-based, 80 iBT) or IELTS (minimum score 7). *Application deadline:* For fall admission, 8/1 for domestic students, 5/1 for international students; for winter admission, 9/1 for international students; for spring admission, 12/1 for domestic students; for summer admission, 5/1 for domestic students. Applications are processed on a rolling basis. Application fee: $60. Electronic applications accepted. *Expenses:* Contact institution. *Financial support:* In 2016–17, 26 students received support. Scholarships/grants available. Financial award application deadline: 4/15; financial award applicants required to submit FAFSA.

Loyola University Maryland, Graduate Programs, Sellinger School of Business, Program in Executive Business Administration, Baltimore, MD 21210-2699. Offers MBA. *Accreditation:* AACSB. *Faculty:* 26 full-time (8 women), 13 part-time/adjunct (5 women). *Students:* 15 full-time (8 women), 312 part-time (120 women); includes 44 minority (14 Black or African American, non-Hispanic/Latino; 13 Asian, non-Hispanic/Latino; 13 Hispanic/Latino; 4 Two or more races, non-Hispanic/Latino), 2 international. Average age 31. 26 applicants, 92% accepted, 20 enrolled. In 2016, 16 master's awarded. *Entrance requirements:* For master's, resume, letter of recommendation, essay. Additional exam requirements/recommendations for international students: Required—TOEFL (minimum score 550 paper-based, 80 iBT) or IELTS (minimum score 7). *Application deadline:* For fall admission, 8/1 priority date for domestic students, 4/1 for international students. Applications are processed on a rolling basis. Application fee: $60. Electronic applications accepted. *Expenses:* Contact institution. *Financial support:* In 2016–17, 26 students received support. Research assistantships and scholarships/grants available. Financial award application deadline: 4/15; financial award applicants required to submit FAFSA. *Unit head:* 410-617-5067, E-mail: emba@loyola.edu.

Loyola University New Orleans, Joseph A. Butt, S.J., College of Business, Program in Business Administration, New Orleans, LA 70118-6195. Offers entrepreneurship and marketing innovation (MBA); organizational performance excellence (MBA); JD/MBA; MBA/MPS. *Accreditation:* AACSB. *Program availability:* Part-time, evening/weekend, online learning. *Faculty:* 8 full-time (4 women), 3 part-time/adjunct (0 women). *Students:* 71 full-time (35 women), 13 part-time (9 women); includes 27 minority (14 Black or African American, non-Hispanic/Latino; 1 American Indian or Alaska Native, non-Hispanic/Latino; 3 Asian, non-Hispanic/Latino; 8 Hispanic/Latino; 1 Two or more races, non-Hispanic/Latino), 3 international. Average age 29. 52 applicants, 96% accepted, 28 enrolled. In 2016, 25 master's awarded. *Degree requirements:* For master's, capstone project. *Entrance requirements:* For master's, GMAT or GRE, minimum GPA of 3.0, transcript, resume, 2 letters of recommendation, work experience in field, personal statement. Additional exam requirements/recommendations for international students: Required—TOEFL (minimum score 580 paper-based; 92 iBT). *Application deadline:* For fall admission, 6/15 priority date for domestic students, 5/15 priority date for international students; for spring admission, 11/15 priority date for domestic students, 10/15 priority date for international students. Applications are processed on a rolling basis. Application fee: $50. Electronic applications accepted. *Financial support:* Research assistantships, scholarships/grants, tuition waivers (partial), and unspecified assistantships available. Financial award application deadline: 5/1; financial award applicants required to submit FAFSA. *Faculty research:* Ethics, international business, entrepreneurship, quality management, risk management. *Unit head:* Dr. William B. Locander, Dean, 504-864-7979, Fax: 504-864-7970, E-mail: mba@loyno.edu. *Application contact:* Ashley Francis, Director of Graduate Programs, 504-864-7979, Fax: 504-864-7970, E-mail: mba@loyno.edu.
Website: http://www.business.loyno.edu/mba/programs

Lynchburg College, Graduate Studies, MBA Program, Lynchburg, VA 24501-3199. Offers MBA. *Accreditation:* ACBSP. *Program availability:* Part-time, evening/weekend. *Students:* 3 full-time (1 woman), 35 part-time (7 women), 1 international. In 2016, 23 master's awarded. *Degree requirements:* For master's, capstone course. *Entrance requirements:* For master's, GMAT (minimum score of 400) or GRE, personal essay, 3 letters of recommendation, official transcripts (bachelor's, others as relevant), career goals statement. Additional exam requirements/recommendations for international students: Required—TOEFL (minimum score 550 paper-based; 79 iBT), IELTS (minimum score 6.5). *Application deadline:* For fall admission, 7/31 for domestic students, 6/1 for international students; for spring admission, 11/30 for domestic students, 10/15 for international students. Applications are processed on a rolling basis.

Application fee: $30. Electronic applications accepted. Application fee is waived when completed online. *Expenses:* Contact institution. *Financial support:* Federal Work-Study, scholarships/grants, health care benefits, and unspecified assistantships available. Support available to part-time students. Financial award application deadline: 7/31; financial award applicants required to submit FAFSA. *Unit head:* Dr. Lee Schimmoeller, Associate Professor/Director of MBA Program, 434-522-8897, E-mail: schimmoeller@lynchburg.edu.
Website: http://www.lynchburg.edu/graduate/master-of-business-administration/

Lynn University, College of Business and Management, Boca Raton, FL 33431-5598. Offers business administration (MBA), including aviation management, financial valuation and investment management, hospitality management, human resource management, international business management, marketing, media management, sports management. *Program availability:* Part-time, evening/weekend, 100% online, blended/hybrid learning. *Faculty:* 24 full-time (9 women), 24 part-time/adjunct (4 women). *Students:* 265 full-time (125 women), 182 part-time (96 women); includes 100 minority (41 Black or African American, non-Hispanic/Latino; 11 Asian, non-Hispanic/Latino; 42 Hispanic/Latino; 6 Two or more races, non-Hispanic/Latino), 119 international. Average age 28. 280 applicants, 94% accepted, 181 enrolled. In 2016, 219 master's awarded. *Degree requirements:* For master's, strategic management seminar, simulation capstone. *Entrance requirements:* For master's, bachelor's degree from accredited institution, resume, letter of recommendation, official transcripts, essay/personal statement. Additional exam requirements/recommendations for international students: Required—TOEFL (minimum score 550 paper-based; 80 iBT), IELTS (minimum score 6.5). *Application deadline:* For fall admission, 8/18 for domestic students, 8/4 for international students; for spring admission, 12/15 for domestic students, 12/1 for international students; for summer admission, 4/17 for domestic students, 4/3 for international students. Applications are processed on a rolling basis. Application fee: $45. Electronic applications accepted. *Expenses:* $725 per credit. *Financial support:* In 2016–17, 115 students received support. Career-related internships or fieldwork, Federal Work-Study, scholarships/grants, tuition waivers (full and partial), and unspecified assistantships available. Support available to part-time students. Financial award application deadline: 3/1; financial award applicants required to submit FAFSA. *Faculty research:* Market volatility investing, biometric research, sports legal history, organizational leadership, urban economic development and productivity. *Unit head:* Dr. RT Good, Dean of the College of Business and Management, 561-237-7458, E-mail: rgood@lynn.edu. *Application contact:* Steven Pruitt, Director of Graduate and Undergraduate Evening Admission, 561-237-7834, Fax: 561-237-7100, E-mail: spruitt@lynn.edu.
Website: http://www.lynn.edu/academics/colleges/business-and-management

Maastricht School of Management, Graduate Programs, Maastricht, Netherlands. Offers business administration (MBA, DBA, PhD); facility management (Exec MBA); management (M Sc); sustainability (Exec MBA).

Madonna University, School of Business, Livonia, MI 48150-1173. Offers business administration (MBA); international business (MSBA); leadership studies (MSBA); leadership studies in criminal justice (MSBA); quality and operations management (MSBA). *Program availability:* Part-time, evening/weekend, online learning. *Degree requirements:* For master's, thesis (for some programs), foreign language proficiency (international business). *Entrance requirements:* For master's, GMAT, GRE General Test, minimum GPA of 3.0. Electronic applications accepted. *Faculty research:* Management, women in management, future studies.

Maharishi University of Management, Graduate Studies, Program in Business Administration, Fairfield, IA 52557. Offers accounting (MBA); management (PhD); sustainability (MBA). *Program availability:* Evening/weekend, online learning. *Degree requirements:* For doctorate, thesis/dissertation. *Entrance requirements:* For master's, GMAT, minimum GPA of 3.0; for doctorate, minimum GPA of 3.0. Additional exam requirements/recommendations for international students: Required—TOEFL. *Faculty research:* Leadership, effects of the group dynamics of consciousness on the economy, innovation, employee development, cooperative strategy.

Malone University, Graduate Program in Business, Canton, OH 44709. Offers MBA. *Accreditation:* ACBSP. *Program availability:* Part-time, evening/weekend, online learning. *Entrance requirements:* For master's, minimum GPA of 3.0. Additional exam requirements/recommendations for international students: Required—TOEFL (minimum score 550 paper-based; 79 iBT). *Expenses:* Contact institution. *Faculty research:* Leadership, business ethics, sustainability, globalization, non-profit financial management.

Manhattan College, Graduate Programs, School of Business, Riverdale, NY 10471. Offers MBA. *Accreditation:* AACSB. *Program availability:* Part-time, 100% online, blended/hybrid learning. *Faculty:* 35 full-time (19 women), 2 part-time/adjunct (1 woman). *Students:* 45 full-time (24 women), 7 part-time (4 women). Average age 24. In 2016, 36 master's awarded. *Entrance requirements:* For master's, GMAT, minimum overall GPA of 3.0, official transcripts, current resume, 2 letters of recommendation. Additional exam requirements/recommendations for international students: Required—TOEFL, IELTS. *Application deadline:* For fall admission, 8/1 for domestic and international students; for spring admission, 1/1 for domestic and international students; for summer admission, 4/1 for domestic and international students. Applications are processed on a rolling basis. Application fee: $75. Electronic applications accepted. *Financial support:* Research assistantships, career-related internships or fieldwork, scholarships/grants, and unspecified assistantships available. *Faculty research:* Supply chain networks, industrial/organizational psychology, emerging economies, financial modeling, business analytics. *Unit head:* Dr. Salwa Ammar, Dean, 718-862-7440, Fax: 718-862-8032, E-mail: salwa.ammar@manhattan.edu. *Application contact:* Dr. Marc Waldman, MBA Program Director, 718-862-3856, E-mail: marc.waldman@manhattan.edu.
Website: https://manhattan.edu/academics/schools-and-departments/school-of-business/index.php

Marconi International University, Graduate Programs, Pembroke Pines, FL 33028. Offers business administration (DBA); education leadership (Ed D); education leadership, management and emerging technologies (M Ed); international business administration (IMBA).

Marian University, School of Business and Public Safety, Fond du Lac, WI 54935-4699. Offers organizational leadership (MS). *Program availability:* Part-time, evening/weekend. *Faculty:* 4 part-time/adjunct (2 women). *Students:* 60 part-time (32 women); includes 9 minority (6 Black or African American, non-Hispanic/Latino; 1 Asian, non-Hispanic/Latino; 2 Hispanic/Latino). Average age 36. In 2016, 26 master's awarded. *Degree requirements:* For master's, comprehensive group project. *Entrance requirements:* For master's, 3 years of managerial experience, minimum GPA of 2.75, letters of professional reference. Additional exam requirements/recommendations for international students: Required—TOEFL (minimum score 525 paper-based; 70 iBT). *Application deadline:* Applications are processed on a rolling basis. Application fee: $25. Electronic applications accepted. *Expenses:* Contact institution. *Financial support:* Application deadline: 3/1; applicants required to submit FAFSA. *Faculty research:* Organizational values, statistical decision-making, learning organization, quality planning, customer research. *Unit head:* Dr. Jeffrey G. Reed, Dean, Marian School of Business, 920-923-8759, Fax: 920-923-7167, E-mail: jreed@marianuniversity.edu.

Marist College, Graduate Programs, School of Management, Business Administration Program, Poughkeepsie, NY 12601-1387. Offers business administration (MBA); executive leadership (Adv C). *Accreditation:* AACSB. *Program availability:* Part-time, evening/weekend. *Entrance requirements:* For master's, GMAT, resume, 2 letters of recommendation. Additional exam requirements/recommendations for international students: Required—TOEFL (minimum score 550 paper-based; 80 iBT); Recommended—IELTS (minimum score 6.5). Electronic applications accepted. *Faculty research:* International trade law, process management, AIDS and the medical provider, mid-Hudson region economics, time quality management and organizational behavior.

Marist College, Graduate Programs, School of Management, Online MBA Program, Poughkeepsie, NY 12601-1387. Offers MBA. *Program availability:* Online learning.

Marlboro College, Graduate and Professional Studies, Program in Business Administration, Brattleboro, VT 05301. Offers collaborative leadership (MBA); conscious business (MBA); mission driven organizations (MBA); project management (MBA); social innovation (MBA); sustainable food systems (MBA). *Program availability:* Part-time, evening/weekend, blended/hybrid learning. *Faculty:* 1 (woman) full-time, 22 part-time/adjunct (13 women). *Students:* 4 full-time (3 women), 13 part-time (11 women); includes 3 minority (1 Hispanic/Latino; 2 Two or more races, non-Hispanic/Latino). Average age 39. 5 applicants, 100% accepted, 3 enrolled. In 2016, 3 master's awarded. *Degree requirements:* For master's, 45 credits including a Master Workshop. *Entrance requirements:* For master's, letter of intent, essay, transcripts, 2 letters of recommendation. *Application deadline:* For fall admission, 7/1 priority date for domestic students; for winter admission, 11/1 priority date for domestic students. Applications are processed on a rolling basis. Application fee: $0. Electronic applications accepted. *Expenses:* $765 per credit. *Financial support:* In 2016–17, 2 students received support. Scholarships/grants available. Financial award applicants required to submit FAFSA. *Unit head:* Tristan Toleno, Degree Chair, 802-258-9200, Fax: 802-258-9201, E-mail: tristant@gradschool.marlboro.edu. *Application contact:* Kelley Barton, Admissions Counselor, 802-258-9209, Fax: 802-258-9201, E-mail: graduateadmissions@marlboro.edu.
Website: https://www.marlboro.edu/academics/graduate/management

Marlboro College, Graduate and Professional Studies, Program in Management, Marlboro, VT 05344. Offers collaborative leadership (MS); conscious business (MS); mission driven organizations (MS); project management (MS); social innovation (MS); sustainable food systems (MS). *Program availability:* Part-time, evening/weekend, blended/hybrid learning. *Faculty:* 1 (woman) full-time, 23 part-time/adjunct (14 women). *Students:* 2 full-time (both women), 12 part-time (9 women). Average age 34. 6 applicants, 33% accepted, 2 enrolled. In 2016, 13 master's awarded. *Degree requirements:* For master's, capstone project. *Entrance requirements:* For master's, statement of intent, 2 letters of recommendation. Additional exam requirements/recommendations for international students: Recommended—TOEFL (minimum score 577 paper-based; 90 iBT), IELTS (minimum score 7). *Application deadline:* For fall admission, 8/5 for domestic students; for winter admission, 12/5 for domestic students; for spring admission, 4/5 for domestic students. Applications are processed on a rolling basis. Application fee: $0. Electronic applications accepted. *Expenses:* $765 per credit. *Financial support:* Scholarships/grants available. Financial award applicants required to submit FAFSA. *Unit head:* Tristan Toleno, Degree Chair, 802-258-9200, Fax: 802-258-9201, E-mail: tristant@gradschool.marlboro.edu. *Application contact:* Kelley Barton, Admissions Counselor, 802-258-9209, Fax: 802-258-9201, E-mail: graduateadmissions@marlboro.edu.
Website: https://www.marlboro.edu/academics/graduate/management

Marquette University, Graduate School of Management, Executive MBA Program, Milwaukee, WI 53201-1881. Offers economics (MBA); finance (MBA); human resources (MBA); international business (MBA); management information systems (MBA); marketing (MBA); operations and supply chain management (MBA); sports business (MBA). *Accreditation:* AACSB. *Students:* 39 full-time (12 women); includes 7 minority (4 Black or African American, non-Hispanic/Latino; 2 Asian, non-Hispanic/Latino; 1 Hispanic/Latino). Average age 38. 25 applicants, 96% accepted, 29 enrolled. In 2016, 14 master's awarded. *Degree requirements:* For master's, international trip. *Entrance requirements:* For master's, GMAT or GRE, two letters of recommendation, official transcripts from current and previous colleges/universities. Additional exam requirements/recommendations for international students: Required—TOEFL (minimum score 550 paper-based; 88 iBT), IELTS (minimum score 6.5), PTE. *Application deadline:* For fall admission, 2/15 for domestic and international students. Application fee: $50. Electronic applications accepted. *Expenses:* Contact institution. *Financial support:* Application deadline: 2/15. *Faculty research:* International trade and finance, customer relationship management, consumer satisfaction, customer service. *Unit head:* Dr. Brian Till, Dean, 414-288-5724. *Application contact:* Dr. Jeanne Simmons, Associate Dean, 414-288-7145.
Website: http://www.busadm.mu.edu/emba/

Marquette University, Graduate School of Management, Program in Business Administration, Milwaukee, WI 53201-1881. Offers business administration (MBA); economics (MBA); entrepreneurship (Certificate); finance (MBA); human resources (MBA); international business (MBA); management information systems (MBA); marketing (MBA); operations and supply chain management (MBA); sports business (MBA); JD/MBA; MBA/MA; MBA/MSN. *Accreditation:* AACSB. *Program availability:* Part-time, evening/weekend. *Students:* 25 full-time (12 women), 202 part-time (57 women); includes 17 minority (5 Black or African American, non-Hispanic/Latino; 6 Asian, non-Hispanic/Latino; 2 Hispanic/Latino; 1 Native Hawaiian or other Pacific Islander, non-Hispanic/Latino; 3 Two or more races, non-Hispanic/Latino), 7 international. Average age 31. 107 applicants, 87% accepted, 113 enrolled. In 2016, 107 master's, 5 other advanced degrees awarded. *Degree requirements:* For Certificate, business plan. *Entrance requirements:* For master's, GMAT or GRE, letters of recommendation. Additional exam requirements/recommendations for international students: Required—TOEFL (minimum score 550 paper-based; 88 iBT), IELTS (minimum score 6.5), PTE. *Application deadline:* For fall admission, 2/15 for domestic and international students. Applications are processed on a rolling basis. Application fee: $50. Electronic applications accepted. *Financial support:* Fellowships, research assistantships, teaching assistantships, Federal Work-Study, institutionally sponsored loans, scholarships/grants, and tuition waivers (full and partial) available. Support available to part-time students. Financial award application deadline: 2/15. *Faculty research:* Ethics in the professions, services marketing, technology impact on decision-making, mentoring. *Unit head:* Dr. Brian Till, Dean, 414-288-5724. *Application contact:* Dr. Jeanne Simmons, Associate Dean, 414-288-7145.
Website: http://business.marquette.edu/academics/mba

Marshall University, Academic Affairs Division, College of Business, Program in Business Administration, Huntington, WV 25755. Offers MBA. *Accreditation:* AACSB. *Program availability:* Part-time, evening/weekend. *Degree requirements:* For master's, comprehensive assessment. *Entrance requirements:* For master's, GMAT.

Business Administration and Management—General

Maryland Institute College of Art, Graduate Studies, Design Leadership MBA/MA Program, Baltimore, MD 21201. Offers MBA/MA. Program offered in collaboration with The Johns Hopkins University. *Students:* 20 full-time (10 women); includes 7 minority (2 Black or African American, non-Hispanic/Latino; 2 Asian, non-Hispanic/Latino; 1 Hispanic/Latino; 2 Two or more races, non-Hispanic/Latino), 3 international. *Entrance requirements:* Additional exam requirements/recommendations for international students: Required—TOEFL (minimum score 100 iBT) or IELTS (minimum score 7). *Application deadline:* For fall admission, 1/15 priority date for domestic and international students; for spring admission, 4/1 for domestic and international students. Applications are processed on a rolling basis. Application fee: $100. Electronic applications accepted. *Expenses:* Contact institution. *Financial support:* Scholarships/grants available. Financial award applicants required to submit FAFSA. *Unit head:* David Gracyalny, Vice Provost for Research/Dean, 410-225-5273, E-mail: dgracyalny@mica.edu. *Application contact:* Chris D. Harring, Director of Graduate Admission, 410-225-2256, Fax: 410-225-5275, E-mail: graduate@mica.edu.
Website: http://www.designleadershipmba.com/

Maryland Institute College of Art, Graduate Studies, MPS Program in Business of Art and Design, Baltimore, MD 21201. Offers MPS. *Program availability:* Part-time. *Faculty:* 15 part-time/adjunct (6 women). *Students:* 20 part-time (10 women); includes 5 minority (2 Black or African American, non-Hispanic/Latino; 1 Asian, non-Hispanic/Latino; 2 Hispanic/Latino). Average age 27. 53 applicants, 47% accepted, 20 enrolled. In 2016, 20 master's awarded. *Degree requirements:* For master's, business plan presentation. *Entrance requirements:* For master's, essay, resume. Additional exam requirements/recommendations for international students: Required—TOEFL (minimum score 550 paper-based; 80 iBT), IELTS (minimum score 6.5). *Application deadline:* For fall admission, 1/15 for domestic and international students; for spring admission, 4/1 for domestic and international students. Application fee: $70. Electronic applications accepted. *Expenses:* Contact institution. *Financial support:* In 2016–17, 20 students received support, including 20 fellowships (averaging $3,400 per year); scholarships/grants also available. Financial award application deadline: 1/15; financial award applicants required to submit FAFSA. *Unit head:* Heather Bradbury, Manager, 410-225-2220, Fax: 410-225-2229, E-mail: hbradbury@mica.edu. *Application contact:* Chris D. Harring, Director of Graduate Admission, 410-225-2256, Fax: 410-225-5275, E-mail: graduate@mica.edu.
Website: http://www.mica.edu/Programs_of_Study/Graduate_Programs/The_Business_of_Art_and_Design_(Online_MPS).html

Marylhurst University, Master of Business Administration Program, Marylhurst, OR 97036-0261. Offers health care management (MBA); real estate (MBA); sustainable business (MBA). *Program availability:* Part-time, evening/weekend, 100% online, blended/hybrid learning. *Students:* 153 (82 women); includes 34 minority (5 Black or African American, non-Hispanic/Latino; 1 American Indian or Alaska Native, non-Hispanic/Latino; 12 Asian, non-Hispanic/Latino; 12 Hispanic/Latino; 4 Two or more races, non-Hispanic/Latino), 1 international. Average age 38. In 2016, 173 master's awarded. *Degree requirements:* For master's, capstone course. *Entrance requirements:* For master's, resume, official transcript from regionally-accredited institution, recommendations, five years of full-time professional experience, statement of intent. Additional exam requirements/recommendations for international students: Required—TOEFL (minimum score 79 iBT), PTE or IELTS (6.5). *Application deadline:* Applications are processed on a rolling basis. Application fee: $0. Electronic applications accepted. *Expenses:* Contact institution. *Financial support:* Career-related internships or fieldwork and scholarships/grants available. Support available to part-time students. Financial award applicants required to submit FAFSA. *Unit head:* Stuart Noble-Goodman, School of Business Director, 503-699-6315, E-mail: snoblegoodman@marylhurst.edu. *Application contact:* Laura Sequeira, Graduate Admissions Counselor, 503-699-6268, E-mail: lsequeira@marylhurst.edu.
Website: http://www.marylhurst.edu/

Marymount California University, Program in Business Administration, Rancho Palos Verdes, CA 90275-6299. Offers MBA. *Degree requirements:* For master's, field project experience.

Marymount University, School of Business Administration, Program in Business Administration, Arlington, VA 22207-4299. Offers MBA, Certificate, MBA/MA, MS/MBA. *Accreditation:* ACBSP. *Program availability:* Part-time, evening/weekend. *Faculty:* 13 full-time (10 women), 2 part-time/adjunct (both women). *Students:* 30 full-time (19 women), 60 part-time (36 women); includes 31 minority (16 Black or African American, non-Hispanic/Latino; 1 American Indian or Alaska Native, non-Hispanic/Latino; 8 Asian, non-Hispanic/Latino; 5 Hispanic/Latino; 1 Two or more races, non-Hispanic/Latino), 12 international. Average age 31. 55 applicants, 96% accepted, 22 enrolled. In 2016, 43 master's awarded. *Degree requirements:* For master's, thesis or alternative. *Entrance requirements:* For master's, GMAT or GRE General Test, resume. Additional exam requirements/recommendations for international students: Required—TOEFL (minimum score 600 paper-based; 96 iBT), IELTS (minimum score 6.5). *Application deadline:* For fall admission, 7/16 priority date for domestic and international students; for spring admission, 11/16 priority date for domestic and international students; for summer admission, 4/16 for domestic and international students. Applications are processed on a rolling basis. Application fee: $40. Electronic applications accepted. *Expenses:* $960 per credit hour. *Financial support:* In 2016–17, 6 students received support, including 3 research assistantships with tuition reimbursements available, 2 teaching assistantships with tuition reimbursements available; career-related internships or fieldwork, Federal Work-Study, scholarships/grants, and unspecified assistantships also available. Support available to part-time students. Financial award applicants required to submit FAFSA. *Unit head:* Dr. Linda Christie, MBA Director, 703-284-5918, E-mail: linda.christie@marymount.edu. *Application contact:* Francesca Reed, Director, Graduate Admissions, 703-284-5901, Fax: 703-527-3815, E-mail: grad.admissions@marymount.edu.
Website: http://www.marymount.edu/Academics/School-of-Business-Administration/Graduate-Programs/Business-Administration

Marymount University, School of Business Administration, Program in Leadership and Management, Arlington, VA 22207-4299. Offers association and nonprofit management (Certificate); leadership and management (MS); management studies (Certificate). *Program availability:* Part-time, evening/weekend. *Faculty:* 1 (woman) full-time. *Students:* 1 (woman) full-time, 13 part-time (8 women); includes 4 minority (2 Black or African American, non-Hispanic/Latino; 1 Asian, non-Hispanic/Latino; 1 Hispanic/Latino). Average age 43. 5 applicants, 100% accepted, 4 enrolled. In 2016, 3 master's, 2 other advanced degrees awarded. *Degree requirements:* For master's, thesis or alternative. *Entrance requirements:* For master's, GMAT or GRE General Test, resume, interview, at least 3 years of managerial experience, essay on a topic provided by School of Business Administration; for Certificate, resume, at least 3 years of managerial experience. Additional exam requirements/recommendations for international students: Required—TOEFL (minimum score 600 paper-based; 96 iBT), IELTS (minimum score 6.5). *Application deadline:* For fall admission, 7/16 priority date for domestic and international students; for spring admission, 11/16 priority date for domestic and international students; for summer admission, 4/16 for domestic and international students. Applications are processed on a rolling basis. Application fee: $40. Electronic applications accepted. *Expenses:* $960 per credit hour. *Financial support:* Research assistantships with tuition reimbursements, career-related internships or fieldwork, Federal Work-Study, scholarships/grants, and unspecified assistantships available. Support available to part-time students. Financial award applicants required to submit FAFSA. *Unit head:* Dr. Lorri Cooper, Chair, Management and Marketing/Director, 703-284-5950, Fax: 703-527-3830, E-mail: lorri.cooper@marymount.edu. *Application contact:* Francesca Reed, Director, Graduate Admissions, 703-284-5901, Fax: 703-527-3815, E-mail: grad.admissions@marymount.edu.
Website: http://www.marymount.edu/Academics/School-of-Business-Administration/Graduate-Programs/Leadership-Management-(M-S-)

Maryville University of Saint Louis, The John E. Simon School of Business, St. Louis, MO 63141-7299. Offers accounting (MBA, Certificate); business studies (Certificate); cyber security (MBA); cybersecurity (Certificate); financial services (MBA, Certificate); healthcare practice management (MBA, Certificate); human resource management (MBA); information technology (MBA, Certificate); management (MBA, Certificate); management and leadership (MA); marketing (MBA, Certificate); project management (MBA); sport business management (MBA); supply chain management/logistics (MBA). *Accreditation:* ACBSP. *Program availability:* Part-time, evening/weekend, 100% online, blended/hybrid learning. *Faculty:* 7 full-time (3 women), 34 part-time/adjunct (9 women). *Students:* 84 full-time (40 women), 223 part-time (118 women); includes 67 minority (40 Black or African American, non-Hispanic/Latino; 2 American Indian or Alaska Native, non-Hispanic/Latino; 8 Asian, non-Hispanic/Latino; 12 Hispanic/Latino; 1 Native Hawaiian or other Pacific Islander, non-Hispanic/Latino; 4 Two or more races, non-Hispanic/Latino), 15 international. Average age 32. In 2016, 67 master's awarded. *Entrance requirements:* Additional exam requirements/recommendations for international students: Required—TOEFL (minimum score 563 paper-based; 85 iBT). *Application deadline:* Applications are processed on a rolling basis. Electronic applications accepted. *Expenses:* $650 per credit hour. *Financial support:* Career-related internships or fieldwork, Federal Work-Study, tuition waivers (partial), and campus employment available. Financial award application deadline: 3/1; financial award applicants required to submit FAFSA. *Faculty research:* Global business, e-marketing, strategic planning, interpersonal management skills, financial analysis. *Unit head:* Pam Horwitz, Interim Dean, 314-529-9680, Fax: 314-529-9975. *Application contact:* Dustin Loeffler, Director for Graduate Studies in Business, 314-529-9571, Fax: 314-529-9975, E-mail: dloeffler@maryville.edu.
Website: http://www.maryville.edu/bu/business-administration-masters/

Marywood University, Academic Affairs, Munley College of Liberal Arts and Sciences, School of Business and Global Innovation, Scranton, PA 18509-1598. Offers finance/investment (MBA); general management (MBA); management information systems (MBA, MS). *Accreditation:* ACBSP. *Program availability:* Part-time, online learning. Electronic applications accepted. *Faculty research:* Problem formulation in ill-structured situations, corporate tax structures.

Massachusetts College of Liberal Arts, Graduate Programs, North Adams, MA 01247-4100. Offers business (MBA); educational administration (M Ed); educational leadership (CAGS); instruction and curriculum (M Ed); instructional technology (M Ed); physical education and health (M Ed); reading (M Ed); special education (M Ed). *Program availability:* Part-time, evening/weekend. *Degree requirements:* For master's, thesis. *Entrance requirements:* For master's, writing sample.

Massachusetts Institute of Technology, MIT Sloan School of Management, Cambridge, MA 02142. Offers M Fin, MBA, MS, SM, PhD. *Accreditation:* AACSB. *Degree requirements:* For master's, thesis (for some programs); for doctorate, thesis/dissertation, exams. Electronic applications accepted. *Expenses:* Contact institution. *Financial support:* Fellowships with tuition reimbursements, research assistantships with tuition reimbursements, teaching assistantships with tuition reimbursements, Federal Work-Study, institutionally sponsored loans, scholarships/grants, health care benefits, and unspecified assistantships available. Support available to part-time students. *Unit head:* David C. Schmittlein, Dean, 617-253-2804, Fax: 617-258-6617, E-mail: dschmitt@mit.edu. *Application contact:* Rod Garcia, Director of Admissions, 617-253-5434, Fax: 617-253-6405, E-mail: mbaadmissions@sloan.mit.edu.
Website: http://mitsloan.mit.edu/

McGill University, Faculty of Graduate and Postdoctoral Studies, Desautels Faculty of Management, Montréal, QC H3A 2T5, Canada. Offers administration (PhD); entrepreneurial studies (MBA); finance (MBA); general management (Post Master's Certificate); information systems (MBA); international business (MBA); international practicing management (MM); management (MBA); management for development (MBA); manufacturing management (MMM); marketing (MBA); operations management (MBA); public accountancy (Diploma); strategic management (MBA); MBA/LL B; MD/MBA. MMM offered jointly with Faculty of Engineering; PhD with Concordia University, HEC Montreal, Université de Montréal, Université du Québec à Montréal.

McKendree University, Graduate Programs, Master of Business Administration Program, Lebanon, IL 62254-1299. Offers business administration (MBA); human resource management (MBA); international business (MBA). *Program availability:* Part-time, evening/weekend, online learning. *Entrance requirements:* For master's, official transcripts from all institutions attended, essay, minimum GPA of 3.0, three references, resume. Additional exam requirements/recommendations for international students: Required—TOEFL. Electronic applications accepted.

McMaster University, School of Graduate Studies, DeGroote School of Business, Hamilton, ON L8S 4M2, Canada. Offers MBA, PhD. *Program availability:* Part-time. *Degree requirements:* For doctorate, comprehensive exam, thesis/dissertation. *Entrance requirements:* For master's, GMAT; for doctorate, GMAT or GRE, master's degree. Additional exam requirements/recommendations for international students: Required—TOEFL (minimum score 580 paper-based). *Faculty research:* Mergers, acquisitions, and restructuring; business investment; capital structure and dividend policy; employee pay/reward systems; pay and employment equity.

McNeese State University, Doré School of Graduate Studies, College of Business, Master of Business Administration Program, Lake Charles, LA 70609. Offers MBA. *Accreditation:* AACSB. *Program availability:* Evening/weekend. *Degree requirements:* For master's, written exam. *Entrance requirements:* For master's, GMAT. *Faculty research:* Management development, integrating technology into the work force, union/management relations, economic development.

Medaille College, Program in Business Administration - Amherst, Amherst, NY 14221. Offers business administration (MBA); organizational leadership (MA). *Program availability:* Evening/weekend. *Degree requirements:* For master's, thesis or alternative. *Entrance requirements:* For master's, GMAT, minimum undergraduate GPA of 2.7, 3 years of work experience. Additional exam requirements/recommendations for international students: Required—TOEFL (minimum score 550 paper-based). Electronic applications accepted. *Expenses:* Contact institution.

Medaille College, Program in Business Administration - Rochester, Rochester, NY 14623. Offers business administration (MBA); organizational leadership (MA). *Program availability:* Evening/weekend. *Degree requirements:* For master's, thesis or alternative. *Entrance requirements:* For master's, GMAT, 3 years of work experience, minimum undergraduate GPA of 2.7. Additional exam requirements/recommendations for international students: Required—TOEFL (minimum score 550 paper-based). *Expenses:* Contact institution.

Melbourne Business School, Graduate Programs, Carlton, Australia. Offers business administration (Exec MBA, MBA); management (PhD); management science (PhD); marketing (PhD); social impact (Graduate Certificate); JD/MBA.

Memorial University of Newfoundland, School of Graduate Studies, Faculty of Business Administration, St. John's, NL A1C 5S7, Canada. Offers MBA. *Program availability:* Part-time. *Degree requirements:* For master's, thesis (for some programs). *Entrance requirements:* For master's, GMAT. Electronic applications accepted. *Faculty research:* International business, marketing, organizational theory and behavior, management science and information systems, small business.

Mercer University, Graduate Studies, Cecil B. Day Campus, Eugene W. Stetson School of Business and Economics (Atlanta), Atlanta, GA 30341. Offers accounting (M Acc); business analytics (MS); innovation (PMBA), including entrepreneurship; international business (MBA); MBA/M Acc; Pharm D/MBA. *Accreditation:* AACSB. *Program availability:* Part-time, evening/weekend, 100% online, blended/hybrid learning. *Faculty:* 19 full-time (7 women), 7 part-time/adjunct (1 woman). *Students:* 183 full-time (91 women), 129 part-time (69 women); includes 136 minority (99 Black or African American, non-Hispanic/Latino; 2 American Indian or Alaska Native, non-Hispanic/Latino; 22 Asian, non-Hispanic/Latino; 10 Hispanic/Latino; 3 Two or more races, non-Hispanic/Latino), 43 international. Average age 32. 207 applicants, 77% accepted, 110 enrolled. In 2016, 176 master's awarded. *Entrance requirements:* For master's, GMAT or GRE. Additional exam requirements/recommendations for international students: Required—TOEFL (minimum score 550 paper-based, 80 iBT) or IELTS. *Application deadline:* For fall admission, 6/15 priority date for domestic and international students; for spring admission, 11/1 priority date for domestic and international students; for summer admission, 3/15 priority date for domestic and international students. Applications are processed on a rolling basis. Application fee: $50 ($100 for international students). Electronic applications accepted. *Expenses:* $795 per credit full-time, $727 per credit part-time. *Financial support:* Federal Work-Study available. Financial award application deadline: 5/1; financial award applicants required to submit FAFSA. *Faculty research:* Entrepreneurship, market studies, international business strategy, financial analysis. *Unit head:* Dr. Susan P. Gilbert, Dean, 678-547-6438, Fax: 678-547-6337, E-mail: gilbert_sp@mercer.edu. *Application contact:* Lael Whiteside, Director of Admissions, 678-547-6300, Fax: 678-547-6160, E-mail: whiteside_l@mercer.edu. Website: http://business.mercer.edu

Mercer University, Graduate Studies, Macon Campus, Eugene W. Stetson School of Business and Economics (Macon), Macon, GA 31207. Offers MBA. *Accreditation:* AACSB. *Program availability:* Part-time, evening/weekend. *Faculty:* 7 full-time (2 women), 3 part-time/adjunct (1 woman). *Students:* 51 full-time (14 women), 31 part-time (18 women); includes 31 minority (21 Black or African American, non-Hispanic/Latino; 1 American Indian or Alaska Native, non-Hispanic/Latino; 5 Asian, non-Hispanic/Latino; 2 Hispanic/Latino; 2 Two or more races, non-Hispanic/Latino), 1 international. Average age 30. In 2016, 56 master's awarded. *Entrance requirements:* For master's, GMAT/GRE. Additional exam requirements/recommendations for international students: Required—TOEFL (minimum score 550 paper-based). *Application deadline:* For fall admission, 8/1 for domestic students; for spring admission, 12/1 for domestic students; for summer admission, 4/1 for domestic students. Applications are processed on a rolling basis. Application fee: $50 ($100 for international students). Electronic applications accepted. Tuition and fees vary according to degree level, campus/location and program. *Faculty research:* Federal reserve system, management of nurses, sales promotion, systems for common stock selection, interest rate premiums. *Unit head:* Dr. Susan P. Gilbert, Dean, 478-301-6438, E-mail: gilbert_sp@mercer.edu. *Application contact:* Dr. James L. Hunt, Professor/Associate Dean, 478-301-2833, Fax: 478-301-2635, E-mail: maconmba@mercer.edu. Website: http://business.mercer.edu/

Mercy College, School of Business, Program in Business Administration, Dobbs Ferry, NY 10522-1189. Offers MBA. *Program availability:* Part-time, evening/weekend, 100% online, blended/hybrid learning. *Students:* 261 full-time (143 women), 72 part-time (44 women); includes 207 minority (88 Black or African American, non-Hispanic/Latino; 2 American Indian or Alaska Native, non-Hispanic/Latino; 23 Asian, non-Hispanic/Latino; 90 Hispanic/Latino; 1 Native Hawaiian or other Pacific Islander, non-Hispanic/Latino; 3 Two or more races, non-Hispanic/Latino), 35 international. Average age 32. 354 applicants, 68% accepted, 134 enrolled. In 2016, 134 master's awarded. *Entrance requirements:* For master's, interview, two letters of recommendation, undergraduate transcripts. Additional exam requirements/recommendations for international students: Required—TOEFL (minimum score 600 paper-based; 100 iBT), IELTS (minimum score 8). *Application deadline:* For fall admission, 8/1 for international students. Applications are processed on a rolling basis. Application fee: $40. Electronic applications accepted. *Expenses:* Contact institution. *Financial support:* Career-related internships or fieldwork, Federal Work-Study, scholarships/grants, and unspecified assistantships available. Support available to part-time students. Financial award applicants required to submit FAFSA. *Unit head:* Ed Weis, Dean, School of Business, 914-674-7490, E-mail: eweis@mercy.edu. *Application contact:* Allison Gurdineer, Senior Director of Admissions, 877-637-2946, Fax: 914-674-7382, E-mail: admissions@mercy.edu. Website: https://www.mercy.edu/degrees-programs/mba-business-administration

Meredith College, School of Business, Raleigh, NC 27607-5298. Offers business administration (MBA). *Accreditation:* AACSB. *Program availability:* Part-time, evening/weekend. *Degree requirements:* For master's, thesis optional. *Entrance requirements:* For master's, GMAT, interview, minimum GPA of 2.5, letters of recommendation. Additional exam requirements/recommendations for international students: Required—TOEFL. Electronic applications accepted. *Expenses:* Contact institution.

Merrimack College, Girard School of Business, North Andover, MA 01845-5800. Offers accounting (MS); business analytics (MS); management (MS). *Program availability:* Part-time, evening/weekend, 100% online. *Faculty:* 7 full-time, 17 part-time/adjunct. *Students:* 101 full-time (45 women), 35 part-time (13 women); includes 6 minority (2 Asian, non-Hispanic/Latino; 3 Hispanic/Latino; 1 Two or more races, non-Hispanic/Latino), 55 international. Average age 27. 116 applicants, 81% accepted, 53 enrolled. In 2016, 57 master's awarded. *Degree requirements:* For master's, comprehensive exam (for some programs), thesis optional, capstone. *Entrance requirements:* For master's, official college transcripts, resume, personal statement, 2 recommendations. Additional exam requirements/recommendations for international students: Required—TOEFL (minimum score 84 iBT), IELTS (minimum score 6.5), PTE (minimum score 56). *Application deadline:* For fall admission, 8/13 for domestic students, 7/15 for international students; for spring admission, 1/10 for domestic and international students; for summer admission, 5/10 for domestic students, 4/10 for international students. Applications are processed on a rolling basis. Application fee: $0. Electronic applications accepted. *Expenses:* Contact institution. *Financial support:* Career-related internships or fieldwork, scholarships/grants, health care benefits, and unspecified assistantships available. Support available to part-time students. Financial award application deadline: 5/1; financial award applicants required to submit FAFSA. *Application contact:* Jennifer Greenwood, Graduate Admission Counselor, 978-837-3563, E-mail: graduate@merrimack.edu. Website: http://www.merrimack.edu/academics/graduate/

Messiah College, Program in Business and Leadership, Mechanicsburg, PA 17055. Offers leadership (MBA, Certificate); management (Certificate); strategic leadership (MA). *Program availability:* Online learning.

Methodist University, School of Graduate Studies, Professional Master of Business Administration Program, Fayetteville, NC 28311. Offers MBA. *Accreditation:* ACBSP. *Program availability:* Part-time, evening/weekend. *Degree requirements:* For master's, thesis. *Entrance requirements:* For master's, GMAT or MAT. Additional exam requirements/recommendations for international students: Required—TOEFL (minimum score 500 paper-based; 60 iBT). Electronic applications accepted. Application fee is waived when completed online. *Faculty research:* Governmental accounting, public economics, systems modeling, organizational culture.

Metropolitan College of New York, Program in Business Administration, New York, NY 10006. Offers financial services (MBA); general management (MBA); health services and risk management (MBA); media management (MBA). *Accreditation:* ACBSP. *Program availability:* Evening/weekend. *Students:* 167 full-time (117 women), 43 part-time (30 women); includes 161 minority (114 Black or African American, non-Hispanic/Latino; 3 American Indian or Alaska Native, non-Hispanic/Latino; 10 Asian, non-Hispanic/Latino; 32 Hispanic/Latino; 2 Two or more races, non-Hispanic/Latino), 26 international. Average age 37. In 2016, 111 master's awarded. *Degree requirements:* For master's, thesis, 10-day study abroad. *Entrance requirements:* For master's, GMAT. Additional exam requirements/recommendations for international students: Required—TOEFL (minimum score 600 paper-based). *Application deadline:* For fall admission, 7/15 priority date for domestic students; for winter admission, 11/15 priority date for domestic students; for spring admission, 3/30 priority date for domestic students. Applications are processed on a rolling basis. Application fee: $45. Electronic applications accepted. *Expenses:* Contact institution. *Financial support:* Scholarships/grants available. Financial award application deadline: 8/15; financial award applicants required to submit FAFSA. *Unit head:* Dr. Tilokie Depoo, Dean and Professor, School for Business, 212-343-1234 Ext. 2204. *Application contact:* Steebo Varghese, Assistant Director of Admissions, 212-343-1234 Ext. 2708, Fax: 212-343-8470.

Metropolitan State University, College of Management, St. Paul, MN 55106-5000. Offers business administration (MBA, DBA); database administration (Graduate Certificate); healthcare information technology management (Graduate Certificate); information assurance security (Graduate Certificate); management information systems (MMIS); MIS generalist (Graduate Certificate); MIS systems analysis and design (Graduate Certificate); project management (Graduate Certificate); public and nonprofit administration (MPNA). *Program availability:* Part-time, evening/weekend. *Degree requirements:* For master's, thesis optional, computer language (MMIS). *Entrance requirements:* For master's, GMAT (for MBA), resume. Additional exam requirements/recommendations for international students: Required—TOEFL (minimum score 550 paper-based). Electronic applications accepted. *Faculty research:* Yugoslav economic system, workers' cooperatives, participative management and job enrichment, global business systems.

Miami University, Farmer School of Business, Oxford, OH 45056. Offers M Acc, MA, MBA. *Accreditation:* AACSB. *Expenses:* Tuition, state resident: full-time $12,890; part-time $564 per credit hour. Tuition, nonresident: full-time $29,604; part-time $1260 per credit hour. *Required fees:* $638. Part-time tuition and fees vary according to course load and program. *Unit head:* Dr. Matthew Myers, Dean/Chair of Business Leadership, 513-529-3631, E-mail: deanofbusiness@miamioh.edu. *Application contact:* Admission Coordinator, 513-529-3734, E-mail: applygrad@miamioh.edu. Website: http://www.fsb.miamioh.edu/

Michigan State University, The Graduate School, Eli Broad College of Business, Department of Management, East Lansing, MI 48224. Offers management (PhD); management, strategy, and leadership (MS). *Program availability:* Part-time, online learning. *Degree requirements:* For doctorate, comprehensive exam, thesis/dissertation. *Entrance requirements:* For master's, full-time managerial experience in a supervisory role; for doctorate, GMAT or GRE, letters of recommendation, experience in teaching and conducting research, work experience in business contexts, personal essay. Additional exam requirements/recommendations for international students: Required—TOEFL (minimum score 600 paper-based). Electronic applications accepted.

Michigan State University, The Graduate School, Eli Broad College of Business, Program in Business Administration, East Lansing, MI 48224. Offers finance (MBA); human resource management (MBA); integrative management (MBA); marketing (MBA); supply chain management (MBA). MBA in integrative management is through Weekend MBA Program; other 4 concentrations are through Full-Time MBA Program. *Program availability:* Evening/weekend. *Degree requirements:* For master's, enrichment experience. *Entrance requirements:* For master's, GMAT or GRE, 4-year bachelor's degree; resume; work experience (minimum of 5 years for Weekend MBA); 2-3 personal essays; 2 letters of recommendation; personal interview. Additional exam requirements/recommendations for international students: Required—PTE (minimum score 70), TOEFL (minimum score 100 iBT) or IELTS (minimum score 7) for full-time MBA applicants. Electronic applications accepted. *Expenses:* Contact institution.

Michigan Technological University, Graduate School, School of Business and Economics, Houghton, MI 49931. Offers accounting (MS); applied natural resource economics (MS); business administration (MBA). *Accreditation:* AACSB. *Program availability:* Part-time, evening/weekend. *Faculty:* 23 full-time (7 women), 1 part-time/adjunct. *Students:* 18 full-time (8 women), 23 part-time (12 women); includes 3 minority (1 Black or African American, non-Hispanic/Latino; 1 Asian, non-Hispanic/Latino; 1 Hispanic/Latino), 10 international. Average age 29. 122 applicants, 30% accepted, 16 enrolled. In 2016, 27 master's awarded. *Degree requirements:* For master's, thesis (for some programs). *Entrance requirements:* For master's, GMAT/GRE (recommended minimum score in the 50th percentile), statement of purpose, personal statement, official transcripts, 2 letters of recommendation, resume/curriculum vitae. Additional exam requirements/recommendations for international students: Required—TOEFL (recommended minimum score 95 iBT) or IELTS (minimum score 7). *Application deadline:* For fall admission, 7/1 for domestic and international students; for spring admission, 12/1 for domestic and international students. Applications are processed on a rolling basis. Electronic applications accepted. *Expenses:* Tuition, state resident: full-time $16,290; part-time $905 per credit. Tuition, nonresident: full-time $16,290; part-time $905 per credit. *Required fees:* $248; $124 per term. Tuition and fees vary according to course load and program. *Financial support:* In 2016–17, 13 students received support. Health care benefits and unspecified assistantships available. Financial award application deadline: 2/1; financial award applicants required to submit FAFSA. *Faculty research:* Natural resource and mineral economics, entrepreneurship, management of technology and innovation, engineering management, management information systems. *Unit head:* Dr. Dean Johnson, Dean, 906-487-2668, Fax: 906-487-1863, E-mail: dean@mtu.edu. *Application contact:* Carol T. Wingerson, Administrative Aide, 906-487-2328, Fax: 906-487-2284, E-mail: gradadms@mtu.edu. Website: http://www.mtu.edu/business/

Business Administration and Management—General

Mid-America Christian University, Program in Business Administration, Oklahoma City, OK 73170-4504. Offers MBA. *Entrance requirements:* For master's, bachelor's degree from regionally-accredited college or university, minimum overall cumulative GPA of 2.75 on undergraduate course work. Additional exam requirements/recommendations for international students: Required—TOEFL (minimum score 550 paper-based).

MidAmerica Nazarene University, School of Business, Olathe, KS 66062-1899. Offers management (MBA, MSM). *Program availability:* Part-time, evening/weekend, 100% online, blended/hybrid learning. *Faculty:* 7 full-time (2 women), 17 part-time/adjunct (5 women). *Students:* 3 full-time (1 woman), 106 part-time (55 women); includes 32 minority (21 Black or African American, non-Hispanic/Latino; 1 Asian, non-Hispanic/Latino; 3 Hispanic/Latino; 7 Two or more races, non-Hispanic/Latino). Average age 30. 54 applicants, 100% accepted, 52 enrolled. In 2016, 50 master's awarded. Terminal master's awarded for partial completion of doctoral program. *Entrance requirements:* For master's, official transcript for bachelor's degree from regionally-accredited college or university; minimum GPA of 3.0 in last 60 hours of undergraduate coursework; completion of college algebra, statistics, or other higher level math with minimum grade of B-. Additional exam requirements/recommendations for international students: Required—TOEFL (minimum score 81 iBT), IELTS (minimum score 6). *Application deadline:* Applications are processed on a rolling basis. Electronic applications accepted. *Expenses:* Contact institution. *Financial support:* Scholarships/grants and unspecified assistantships available. Financial award applicants required to submit FAFSA. *Faculty research:* Project management, global business, entrepreneurship, experience learning. *Unit head:* Dr. Graydon Dawson, Professor and Chair, Graduate Studies in Management, 913-971-3873, Fax: 913-791-3409, E-mail: rgdawson@mnu.edu. *Application contact:* Piper Childs, Director of School of Professional and Graduate Studies Enrollment Services, 913-971-3804, E-mail: pmchilds@mnu.edu.
Website: http://www.mnu.edu/mba/

Middlebury Institute of International Studies at Monterey, Graduate School of International Policy and Management, Fisher MBA in Global Impact Management Program, Monterey, CA 93940-2691. Offers corporate risk management and compliance (MBA). *Accreditation:* AACSB. *Degree requirements:* For master's, one foreign language, thesis. *Entrance requirements:* For master's, GMAT, minimum GPA of 3.0, proficiency in a foreign language. Additional exam requirements/recommendations for international students: Required—TOEFL (minimum score 550 paper-based; 80 iBT). Electronic applications accepted. *Expenses: Tuition:* Full-time $38,250; part-time $1820 per credit. *Required fees:* $78 per semester. *Faculty research:* Cross-cultural consumer behavior, foreign direct investment, marketing and entrepreneurial orientation, political risk analysis and area studies, managing international human resources.

Middle Tennessee State University, College of Graduate Studies, Jennings A. Jones College of Business, Department of Management and Marketing, Murfreesboro, TN 37132. Offers business administration (MBA); management (MS). *Accreditation:* AACSB. *Program availability:* Part-time, evening/weekend, online learning. *Degree requirements:* For master's, comprehensive exam. *Entrance requirements:* For master's, GMAT (minimum score of 400). Additional exam requirements/recommendations for international students: Required—TOEFL (minimum score 525 paper-based; 71 iBT) or IELTS (minimum score 6). Electronic applications accepted.

Midway University, Graduate Programs, Midway, KY 40347-1120. Offers education (MAT); leadership (MBA). *Degree requirements:* For master's, capstone course. *Entrance requirements:* For master's, GMAT (for MBA); GRE or PRAXIS I (for MAT), bachelor's degree; interview; minimum GPA of 3.0 (for MBA), 2.75 (for MAT); 3 years of professional work experience (for MBA). Additional exam requirements/recommendations for international students: Required—TOEFL (minimum score 550 paper-based; 80 iBT).

Midwestern State University, Billie Doris McAda Graduate School, Dillard College of Business Administration, Wichita Falls, TX 76308. Offers MBA. *Accreditation:* AACSB. *Program availability:* Part-time, evening/weekend. *Degree requirements:* For master's, comprehensive exam, thesis optional. *Entrance requirements:* For master's, GMAT. Additional exam requirements/recommendations for international students: Required—TOEFL (minimum score 550 paper-based). Electronic applications accepted. *Faculty research:* Citizenship behavior, software solutions, mediations, sales force training, stock trading volume.

Millennia Atlantic University, Graduate Programs, Doral, FL 33178. Offers accounting (MBA); business administration (MBA); health information management (MS); human resource management (MA). *Program availability:* Online learning.

Milligan College, Area of Business Administration, Milligan College, TN 37682. Offers health sector management (MBA, Graduate Certificate); leadership (MBA, Graduate Certificate); operations management (MBA, Graduate Certificate). *Program availability:* Blended/hybrid learning. *Faculty:* 3 full-time (1 woman), 1 part-time/adjunct (0 women). *Students:* 38 full-time (19 women), 12 part-time (5 women); includes 2 minority (1 Black or African American, non-Hispanic/Latino; 1 Hispanic/Latino). Average age 37. 25 applicants, 100% accepted, 19 enrolled. In 2016, 32 master's awarded. *Degree requirements:* For master's, thesis or alternative. *Entrance requirements:* For master's, GMAT if undergraduate GPA less than 3.0, undergraduate degree and supporting transcripts, relevant full-time work experience, essay/personal statement, professional recommendations. Additional exam requirements/recommendations for international students: Required—TOEFL (minimum score 550 paper-based, 79 iBT) or IELTS (6.5). *Application deadline:* For fall admission, 8/1 for domestic students, 6/1 for international students; for spring admission, 1/15 for domestic students, 12/1 for international students. Applications are processed on a rolling basis. Application fee: $30. Electronic applications accepted. *Expenses:* Contact institution. *Financial support:* Scholarships/grants available. Financial award application deadline: 12/1; financial award applicants required to submit FAFSA. *Faculty research:* International microfinance; economic development in Appalachia; job satisfaction; business ethics; internal migration. *Unit head:* Dr. David Campbell, Area Chair of Business, 423-461-8674, Fax: 423-461-8677, E-mail: dacampbell@milligan.edu. *Application contact:* Rebecca Banton, Graduate Admissions Recruiter, Business Area, 423-461-8662, Fax: 423-461-8789, E-mail: rbbanton@milligan.edu.
Website: http://www.milligan.edu/GPS

Millikin University, Tabor School of Business, Decatur, IL 62522-2084. Offers MBA. *Accreditation:* ACBSP. *Program availability:* Evening/weekend. *Faculty:* 5 full-time (1 woman), 9 part-time/adjunct (3 women). *Students:* 31 full-time (11 women); includes 10 minority (3 Black or African American, non-Hispanic/Latino; 2 Hispanic/Latino; 5 Two or more races, non-Hispanic/Latino). Average age 31. 66 applicants, 55% accepted, 33 enrolled. In 2016, 16 master's awarded. *Entrance requirements:* For master's, GMAT or GRE, resume, 3 reference letters, interview, statement of purpose, transcripts. Additional exam requirements/recommendations for international students: Required—TOEFL (minimum score 650 paper-based; 81 iBT). *Application deadline:* For fall admission, 6/1 priority date for domestic students, 4/1 for international students; for spring admission, 11/1 priority date for domestic students, 8/1 priority date for international students. Applications are processed on a rolling basis. Application fee: $0. Electronic applications accepted. *Expenses:* $750 per credit hour. *Financial support:* In 2016–17, 6 students received support, including 1 research assistantship with partial tuition reimbursement available (averaging $6,000 per year), 1 teaching assistantship with partial tuition reimbursement available (averaging $6,000 per year). Financial award applicants required to submit FAFSA. *Faculty research:* E-commerce, international marketing, pedagogy, total quality management, auditing. *Unit head:* Dr. Anthony Liberatore, MBA Director/Associate Professor, 217-424-6338, E-mail: aliberatore@millikin.edu.
Website: http://www.millikin.edu/mba

Millsaps College, Else School of Management, Jackson, MS 39210-0001. Offers accounting (M Acc); business administration (MBA). *Accreditation:* AACSB. *Program availability:* Part-time. *Entrance requirements:* For master's, GMAT. Additional exam requirements/recommendations for international students: Required—TOEFL. Electronic applications accepted. *Faculty research:* Ethics, audit independence, satisfaction with assurance services, political business cycles, economic development, commercialization of new products.

Mills College, Graduate Studies, Joint MBA/MPP Program, Oakland, CA 94613-1000. Offers MBA/MPP. *Faculty:* 4 full-time (3 women), 14 part-time/adjunct (8 women). *Students:* 12 full-time (10 women), 3 part-time (all women); includes 8 minority (2 Black or African American, non-Hispanic/Latino; 5 Hispanic/Latino; 1 Two or more races, non-Hispanic/Latino). Average age 33. 12 applicants, 83% accepted, 6 enrolled. *Entrance requirements:* Additional exam requirements/recommendations for international students: Required—TOEFL (minimum score 550 paper-based; 80 iBT) or IELTS (minimum score 6). *Application deadline:* For winter admission, 2/1 priority date for domestic students, 12/15 priority date for international students. Application fee: $50. Electronic applications accepted. *Expenses:* Contact institution. *Financial support:* In 2016–17, 17 students received support, including 17 fellowships (averaging $10,220 per year). Financial award application deadline: 2/1; financial award applicants required to submit FAFSA. *Faculty research:* Diversity and inclusion, applied econometrics, non-profit management, business communication and effective public speaking, social media, Internet marketing, organizational and cultural chance, economics of the family, urbanization and land conservation, gender and science, comparative race and ethnic relations. *Unit head:* Lori Bamberger, Professor of Public Policy, 510-430-3375, Fax: 510-430-2159, E-mail: lbamberger@mills.edu. *Application contact:* Robynne Lofton, Director of Admissions, 510-430-3295, Fax: 510-430-2159, E-mail: grad-admission@mills.edu.
Website: http://www.mills.edu/academics/graduate/ppol/program/joint_MPPMBA.php

Mills College, Graduate Studies, Lorry I. Lokey Graduate School of Business, Oakland, CA 94613-1000. Offers applied economics (MA); management (MBA). *Program availability:* Part-time. *Faculty:* 3 full-time (all women), 9 part-time/adjunct (5 women). *Students:* 38 full-time (34 women), 20 part-time (16 women); includes 38 minority (15 Black or African American, non-Hispanic/Latino; 3 Asian, non-Hispanic/Latino; 15 Hispanic/Latino; 5 Two or more races, non-Hispanic/Latino), 3 international. Average age 33. 47 applicants, 81% accepted, 22 enrolled. In 2016, 35 master's awarded. *Entrance requirements:* For master's, GRE, SAT, or ACT, 3 letters of recommendation, 2 transcripts. Additional exam requirements/recommendations for international students: Required—TOEFL (minimum score 550 paper-based; 80 iBT) or IELTS (minimum score 6). *Application deadline:* For fall admission, 2/1 priority date for domestic students, 12/15 for international students; for spring admission, 10/1 for domestic students. Applications are processed on a rolling basis. Application fee: $50. *Expenses:* Contact institution. *Financial support:* In 2016–17, 62 students received support, including 62 fellowships with tuition reimbursements available (averaging $8,048 per year); teaching assistantships with tuition reimbursements available, scholarships/grants, and unspecified assistantships also available. Support available to part-time students. Financial award application deadline: 2/1; financial award applicants required to submit FAFSA. *Faculty research:* Diversity and inclusion, applied econometrics, non-profit management, business communication and effective public speaking, social media and Internet marketing. *Unit head:* Dr. Carolyn Sherwood Call, Department Chair, 510-430-3365, Fax: 510-430-2159, E-mail: csherwoodcall@mills.edu. *Application contact:* Robynne Lofton, Director of Admissions, 510-430-3295, Fax: 510-430-2159, E-mail: grad-admission@mills.edu.
Website: http://www.mills.edu/mba

Milwaukee School of Engineering, Rader School of Business, Program in Business Administration, Milwaukee, WI 53202-3109. Offers MBA. *Program availability:* Part-time, evening/weekend. *Faculty:* 1 full-time (0 women), 4 part-time/adjunct (3 women). *Students:* 14 full-time (8 women), 48 part-time (10 women); includes 9 minority (4 Black or African American, non-Hispanic/Latino; 2 Asian, non-Hispanic/Latino; 3 Hispanic/Latino), 3 international. Average age 25. 28 applicants, 64% accepted, 14 enrolled. In 2016, 12 master's awarded. *Entrance requirements:* For master's, GRE General Test or GMAT if undergraduate GPA less than 2.8, 2 letters of recommendation, BS. Additional exam requirements/recommendations for international students: Required—TOEFL (minimum score 90 iBT), IELTS (minimum score 6.5). *Application deadline:* Applications are processed on a rolling basis. Electronic applications accepted. *Expenses: Tuition:* Full-time $31,440; part-time $655 per credit. *Financial support:* In 2016–17, 30 students received support. Fellowships, career-related internships or fieldwork, scholarships/grants, and tuition waivers (partial) available. Financial award application deadline: 3/15; financial award applicants required to submit FAFSA. *Unit head:* David Schmitz, Program Director, 414-277-2487, Fax: 414-277-7479, E-mail: schmitz@msoe.edu. *Application contact:* Ian Dahlinghaus, Graduate Admissions Counselor, 414-277-7208, E-mail: dahlinghaus@msoe.edu.
Website: http://www.msoe.edu/community/academics/business/page/2328/mba

Minnesota State University Mankato, College of Graduate Studies and Research, College of Business, Mankato, MN 56001. Offers accounting (MSA); business (MBA). *Accreditation:* AACSB. *Students:* 21 full-time (5 women), 73 part-time (31 women). *Entrance requirements:* For master's, GMAT, 2 letters of reference, resume. Additional exam requirements/recommendations for international students: Required—TOEFL. *Application deadline:* For fall admission, 7/1 for domestic students, 5/1 for international students; for spring admission, 11/1 for domestic students, 10/1 for international students. Electronic applications accepted. *Unit head:* Dr. Brenda Flannery, Dean, 507-389-5420, E-mail: brenda.flannery@mnsu.edu.
Website: http://cob.mnsu.edu/

Minnesota State University Moorhead, Graduate Studies, College of Business and Innovation, Moorhead, MN 56563. Offers accounting and finance (MS); business administration (MBA); health care management (MBA). *Accreditation:* AACSB. *Program availability:* Part-time. *Students:* 15 full-time (8 women), 27 part-time (11 women). Average age 32. 20 applicants, 100% accepted. In 2016, 9 master's awarded. *Degree requirements:* For master's, comprehensive exam (for some programs), thesis, final oral exam. *Entrance requirements:* For master's, GMAT, minimum GPA of 3.0. Additional exam requirements/recommendations for international students: Required—TOEFL (minimum score 550 paper-based); Recommended—IELTS (minimum score 6.5). *Application deadline:* For fall admission, 3/15 for domestic students; for spring admission, 10/15 for domestic students. Applications are processed on a rolling basis. Application fee: $20. Electronic applications accepted. *Expenses:* Tuition, state resident: full-time $9000; part-time $4500 per credit. Tuition, nonresident: full-time

$18,000; part-time $9000 per credit. *Required fees:* $942; $39.25 per credit. One-time fee: $90 full-time. Full-time tuition and fees vary according to course load, degree level, program and reciprocity agreements. *Financial support:* Federal Work-Study and unspecified assistantships available. Financial award application deadline: 10/1; financial award applicants required to submit FAFSA. *Faculty research:* Union decertification, small business development, business innovation, pedagogy, curriculum design. *Unit head:* Dr. Marsha Weber, Dean, 218-477-2076, E-mail: marsha.weber@mnstate.edu. *Application contact:* Karla Wenger, Coordinator, 218-477-2344, E-mail: wengerk@mnstate.edu.
Website: http://www.mnstate.edu/cbi/

Minot State University, Graduate School, Program in Management, Minot, ND 58707-0002. Offers MSM. *Program availability:* Part-time. *Degree requirements:* For master's, comprehensive exam (for some programs), thesis optional. *Entrance requirements:* For master's, GRE, minimum GPA of 2.75. Additional exam requirements/recommendations for international students: Required—TOEFL (minimum score 79 iBT), IELTS (minimum score 6).

Misericordia University, College of Business, Master of Business Administration Program, Dallas, PA 18612-1098. Offers accounting (MBA); healthcare management (MBA); human resources (MBA); management (MBA); sport management (MBA). *Program availability:* Part-time, evening/weekend, online learning. *Entrance requirements:* For master's, GMAT, MAT, GRE (50th percentile or higher), or minimum undergraduate GPA of 3.0, interview. Additional exam requirements/recommendations for international students: Required—TOEFL. Electronic applications accepted. Application fee is waived when completed online.

Misericordia University, College of Business, Program in Organizational Management, Dallas, PA 18612-1098. Offers healthcare management (MS); human resource management (MS); information technology management (MS); management (MS); not-for-profit management (MS). *Program availability:* Part-time, evening/weekend, online learning. *Entrance requirements:* For master's, GRE General Test, MAT (35th percentile or higher), or minimum undergraduate GPA of 3.0. Additional exam requirements/recommendations for international students: Required—TOEFL. Electronic applications accepted. Application fee is waived when completed online. *Expenses:* Contact institution.

Mississippi College, Graduate School, School of Business, Clinton, MS 39058. Offers accounting (Certificate); business administration (MBA), including accounting; business education (M Ed); finance (MBA, Certificate); JD/MBA. *Accreditation:* ACBSP. *Program availability:* Part-time, evening/weekend. *Degree requirements:* For master's, comprehensive exam, thesis optional. *Entrance requirements:* For master's, GMAT, minimum GPA of 2.5, 24 hours of undergraduate course work in business. Additional exam requirements/recommendations for international students: Recommended—TOEFL, IELTS. Electronic applications accepted.

Mississippi State University, College of Business, Department of Management and Information Systems, Mississippi State, MS 39762. Offers business administration (MBA); information systems (MSIS, PhD); management (PhD); project management (MBA). *Program availability:* Part-time. *Faculty:* 18 full-time (4 women). *Students:* 66 full-time (15 women), 200 part-time (39 women); includes 25 minority (10 Black or African American, non-Hispanic/Latino; 1 American Indian or Alaska Native, non-Hispanic/Latino; 4 Asian, non-Hispanic/Latino; 6 Hispanic/Latino; 4 Two or more races, non-Hispanic/Latino), 20 international. Average age 31. 186 applicants, 39% accepted, 53 enrolled. In 2016, 84 master's, 2 doctorates awarded. *Degree requirements:* For master's, comprehensive exam; for doctorate, comprehensive exam, thesis/dissertation. *Entrance requirements:* For master's, GMAT, minimum GPA of 3.0 in last 60 hours of undergraduate course work; for doctorate, GMAT (minimum score of 550), minimum GPA of 3.25 on all graduate work; BS with minimum GPA of 3.0 cumulative and last 60 hours. Additional exam requirements/recommendations for international students: Required—TOEFL (minimum score 575 paper-based; 84 iBT); Recommended—IELTS (minimum score 7). *Application deadline:* For fall admission, 7/1 for domestic students, 5/1 for international students; for spring admission, 11/1 for domestic students, 9/1 for international students. Applications are processed on a rolling basis. Application fee: $60. Electronic applications accepted. *Expenses:* Tuition, state resident: full-time $7670; part-time $852.50 per credit hour. Tuition, nonresident: full-time $20,790; part-time $2310.50 per credit hour. Part-time tuition and fees vary according to course load. *Financial support:* Career-related internships or fieldwork, Federal Work-Study, institutionally sponsored loans, scholarships/grants, and unspecified assistantships available. Financial award applicants required to submit FAFSA. *Faculty research:* Electronic commerce, management of information technology. *Total annual research expenditures:* $1.3 million. *Unit head:* Dr. James J. Chrisman, Professor and Head, 662-325-1991, Fax: 662-325-8651, E-mail: jchrisman@business.msstate.edu. *Application contact:* Lakan Drinker, Admissions and Enrollment Assistant, 662-325-8951, E-mail: ldrinker@grad.msstate.edu.
Website: http://www.business.msstate.edu/programs/mis/index.php

Missouri Baptist University, Graduate Programs, St. Louis, MO 63141-8660. Offers business administration (MBA); Christian ministries (MACM); counseling (MAC); education (MSE); education administration (MEA); educational leadership (MSE, Ed S); teaching (MAT).

Missouri Southern State University, Program in Business Administration, Joplin, MO 64801-1595. Offers MBA. Program offered jointly with Northwest Missouri State University. *Program availability:* Online learning. *Degree requirements:* For master's, capstone seminar.

Missouri State University, Graduate College, College of Business Administration, Program in Business Administration, Springfield, MO 65897. Offers MBA. *Accreditation:* AACSB. *Program availability:* Part-time, evening/weekend. *Faculty:* 17 full-time (5 women). *Students:* 314 full-time (150 women), 209 part-time (83 women); includes 40 minority (10 Black or African American, non-Hispanic/Latino; 7 Asian, non-Hispanic/Latino; 13 Hispanic/Latino; 10 Two or more races, non-Hispanic/Latino), 256 international. Average age 28. 391 applicants, 59% accepted, 163 enrolled. In 2016, 316 master's awarded. *Degree requirements:* For master's, thesis optional. *Entrance requirements:* For master's, GMAT or GRE, minimum GPA of 2.75. Additional exam requirements/recommendations for international students: Required—TOEFL (minimum score 550 paper-based; 79 iBT), IELTS (minimum score 6). *Application deadline:* For fall admission, 7/20 priority date for domestic students, 5/1 for international students; for spring admission, 12/20 priority date for domestic students, 9/1 for international students; for summer admission, 5/20 priority date for domestic students. Applications are processed on a rolling basis. Application fee: $35 ($50 for international students). Electronic applications accepted. *Expenses:* Tuition, state resident: full-time $5830. Tuition, nonresident: full-time $10,708. *Required fees:* $1130. Tuition and fees vary according to class time, course level, course load and program. *Financial support:* Federal Work-Study, institutionally sponsored loans, scholarships/grants, and unspecified assistantships available. Support available to part-time students. Financial award application deadline: 3/31; financial award applicants required to submit FAFSA. *Unit head:* Dr. Elizabeth Rozell, MBA Program Director, 417-836-5616, Fax: 417-836-4407, E-mail: mbaprogram@missouristate.edu. *Application contact:* Michael Edwards, Coordinator of Graduate Admissions, 417-836-5330, Fax: 417-836-6200, E-mail: michaeledwards@missouristate.edu.
Website: http://mba.missouristate.edu

Missouri University of Science and Technology, Graduate School, Department of Business and Information Technology, Rolla, MO 65409. Offers business and management systems (MBA); information science and technology (MS). *Degree requirements:* For master's, thesis or alternative. *Entrance requirements:* Additional exam requirements/recommendations for international students: Required—TOEFL (minimum score 600 paper-based); Recommended—IELTS. Electronic applications accepted.

Missouri Western State University, Program in Applied Science, St. Joseph, MO 64507-2294. Offers chemistry (MAS); engineering technology management (MAS); human factors and usability testing (MAS); industrial life science (MAS); sport and fitness management (MAS). *Accreditation:* AACSB. *Program availability:* Part-time. *Students:* 41 full-time (18 women), 27 part-time (11 women); includes 7 minority (6 Black or African American, non-Hispanic/Latino; 1 Two or more races, non-Hispanic/Latino), 15 international. Average age 29. 43 applicants, 88% accepted, 30 enrolled. In 2016, 34 master's awarded. *Entrance requirements:* Additional exam requirements/recommendations for international students: Recommended—TOEFL (minimum score 79 iBT), IELTS (minimum score 6). *Application deadline:* For fall admission, 7/15 for domestic and international students; for spring admission, 10/1 for domestic and international students; for summer admission, 3/15 for domestic students. Applications are processed on a rolling basis. Application fee: $50. Electronic applications accepted. *Expenses:* Tuition, state resident: full-time $6548; part-time $327.39 per credit hour. Tuition, nonresident: full-time $11,848; part-time $592.39 per credit hour. *Required fees:* $542; $99 per credit hour. $176 per semester. One-time fee: $50. Tuition and fees vary according to course load and program. *Financial support:* Scholarships/grants and unspecified assistantships available. Support available to part-time students. *Unit head:* Dr. Benjamin D. Caldwell, Dean of the Graduate School, 816-271-4394, Fax: 816-271-4525, E-mail: graduate@missouriwestern.edu.

Missouri Western State University, Program in Business Administration, St. Joseph, MO 64507-2294. Offers animal and life sciences (MBA); enterprise resource planning (MBA); forensic accounting (MBA); general business (MBA). *Program availability:* Part-time. *Entrance requirements:* Additional exam requirements/recommendations for international students: Recommended—TOEFL (minimum score 79 iBT), IELTS (minimum score 6). *Application deadline:* For fall admission, 7/15 for domestic and international students; for spring admission, 10/1 for domestic and international students; for summer admission, 3/15 for domestic students. Applications are processed on a rolling basis. Application fee: $50. Electronic applications accepted. *Expenses:* Tuition, state resident: full-time $6548; part-time $327.39 per credit hour. Tuition, nonresident: full-time $11,848; part-time $592.39 per credit hour. *Required fees:* $542; $99 per credit hour. $176 per semester. One-time fee: $50. Tuition and fees vary according to course load and program. *Financial support:* Scholarships/grants and unspecified assistantships available. Support available to part-time students. *Unit head:* Dr. Logan Jones, Director, 816-271-4351, E-mail: jjones81@missouriwestern.edu. *Application contact:* Dr. Benjamin D. Caldwell, Dean of the Graduate School, 816-271-4394, Fax: 816-271-4525, E-mail: graduate@missouriwestern.edu.
Website: http://www.missouriwestern.edu/mba/

Molloy College, Graduate Business Program, Rockville Centre, NY 11571-5002. Offers accounting (MBA); finance (MBA, Advanced Certificate); healthcare (MBA, Advanced Certificate); management (MBA); marketing (MBA, Advanced Certificate); personal financial planning (MBA). *Program availability:* Part-time, evening/weekend. *Faculty:* 6 full-time (3 women), 14 part-time/adjunct (5 women). *Students:* 66 full-time (32 women), 178 part-time (92 women); includes 96 minority (38 Black or African American, non-Hispanic/Latino; 24 Asian, non-Hispanic/Latino; 32 Hispanic/Latino; 1 Native Hawaiian or other Pacific Islander, non-Hispanic/Latino; 1 Two or more races, non-Hispanic/Latino), 5 international. Average age 40. 198 applicants, 69% accepted, 108 enrolled. In 2016, 55 master's awarded. *Entrance requirements:* Additional exam requirements/recommendations for international students: Required—TOEFL (minimum score 550 paper-based; 79 iBT). *Application deadline:* Applications are processed on a rolling basis. Application fee: $60. Electronic applications accepted. *Expenses: Tuition:* Full-time $19,170; part-time $1065 per credit. *Required fees:* $950; $790 per credit. Tuition and fees vary according to course load. *Financial support:* Applicants required to submit FAFSA. *Faculty research:* Leadership profiles that provide lessons of strength and purpose applicable to business; pedagogy and student learning outcomes for graduate business education; mobilizing social networks for innovation and qualitative analysis of sociocentric (whole) network measures; the ethical considerations of covenants not to compete in employment contracts and the use of liquidated damages clauses in employment contracts. *Unit head:* Dr. Maureen Mackenzie, Dean, Division of Business/Director of Graduate Programs, 516-323-3080, E-mail: mmackenzie@molloy.edu. *Application contact:* Jaclyn Machowicz, Assistant Director for Admissions, 516-323-4010, E-mail: jmachowicz@molloy.edu.
Website: http://www.molloy.edu/academics/graduate-programs/graduate-business

Monmouth University, Graduate Studies, Leon Hess Business School, West Long Branch, NJ 07764-1898. Offers accounting (MBA, Post-Master's Certificate); business administration (MBA); finance (MBA); management (MBA); marketing (MBA); real estate (MBA). *Accreditation:* AACSB. *Program availability:* Part-time, evening/weekend. *Faculty:* 20 full-time (4 women), 8 part-time/adjunct (0 women). *Students:* 76 full-time (37 women), 94 part-time (43 women); includes 17 minority (2 Black or African American, non-Hispanic/Latino; 6 Asian, non-Hispanic/Latino; 6 Hispanic/Latino; 1 Native Hawaiian or other Pacific Islander, non-Hispanic/Latino; 2 Two or more races, non-Hispanic/Latino), 8 international. Average age 30. 105 applicants, 90% accepted, 67 enrolled. In 2016, 93 master's, 1 other advanced degree awarded. *Degree requirements:* For master's, capstone course. *Entrance requirements:* For master's, GMAT or GRE, current resume; essay (500 words or less). Additional exam requirements/recommendations for international students: Required—TOEFL (minimum score 550 paper-based; 79 iBT), IELTS (minimum score 6), Michigan English Language Assessment Battery (minimum score 77) or Certificate of Advanced English (minimum score B2). *Application deadline:* For fall admission, 7/15 priority date for domestic students, 6/1 for international students; for spring admission, 12/1 priority date for domestic students, 11/1 for international students; for summer admission, 5/1 for domestic students. Applications are processed on a rolling basis. Application fee: $50. Electronic applications accepted. *Expenses: Tuition, area resident:* Full-time $19,764; part-time $1098 per credit hour. *Required fees:* $175 per semester. Tuition and fees vary according to program. *Financial support:* In 2016–17, 191 students received support, including 137 fellowships (averaging $2,643 per year), 20 teaching assistantships with full and partial tuition reimbursements available (averaging $10,034 per year); research assistantships, institutionally sponsored loans, scholarships/grants, and unspecified assistantships also available. Support available to part-time students. Financial award application deadline: 2/1; financial award applicants required to submit FAFSA. *Faculty research:* Information technology and marketing, behavioral research in accounting, human resources, management of technology. *Unit head:* Dr. Susan Gupta, MBA Program Director, 732-571-3639, Fax: 732-263-5517, E-mail: sgupta@

monmouth.edu. *Application contact:* Laurie Kuhn, Associate Director of Graduate Admission, 732-571-3452, Fax: 732-263-5123, E-mail: gradadm@monmouth.edu.
Website: https://www.monmouth.edu/business-school/leon-hess-business-school.aspx
See Display on this page and Close-Up on page 181.

Monroe College, King Graduate School, Bronx, NY 10468. Offers accounting (MS); business administration (MBA), including entrepreneurship, finance, general business administration, healthcare management, human resources, information technology, marketing; computer science (MS); criminal justice (MS); hospitality management (MS); public health (MPH), including biostatistics and epidemiology, community health, health administration and leadership. *Program availability:* Online learning. Application fee: $50.
Website: https://www.monroecollege.edu/Degrees/King-Graduate-School/

Montclair State University, The Graduate School, College of Humanities and Social Sciences, MA Program in Law and Governance, Montclair, NJ 07043-1624. Offers conflict management and peace studies (MA); governance, compliance and regulation (MA); intellectual property (MA); law and governance (MA); legal management (MA). *Program availability:* Part-time, evening/weekend. *Degree requirements:* For master's, thesis or comprehensive exam. *Entrance requirements:* For master's, GRE General Test, minimum cumulative GPA of 2.75 for undergraduate work, 2 letters of recommendation, essay. Additional exam requirements/recommendations for international students: Required—TOEFL (minimum score 83 iBT) or IELTS (minimum score 6.5). Electronic applications accepted. *Expenses:* Tuition, state resident: part-time $553 per credit. Tuition, nonresident: part-time $854 per credit. *Required fees:* $91 per credit. Tuition and fees vary according to program.

Montclair State University, The Graduate School, Feliciano School of Business, General MBA Program, Montclair, NJ 07043-1624. Offers MBA. *Program availability:* Part-time, evening/weekend. *Degree requirements:* For master's, culminating experience. *Entrance requirements:* For master's, GMAT or GRE General Test, 2 letters of recommendation, resume, essay. Additional exam requirements/recommendations for international students: Required—TOEFL (minimum score 83 iBT), IELTS (minimum score 6.5). Electronic applications accepted. *Expenses:* Tuition, state resident: part-time $553 per credit. Tuition, nonresident: part-time $854 per credit. *Required fees:* $91 per credit. Tuition and fees vary according to program. *Faculty research:* Accounting, management, marketing.

Moravian College, Graduate and Continuing Studies, Business and Management Programs, Bethlehem, PA 18018-6650. Offers accounting (MBA); business analytics (MBA); general management (MBA); health administration (MHA); healthcare management (MBA); human resource management (MBA); leadership (MSHRM); learning and performance management (MSHRM); supply chain management (MBA). *Program availability:* Part-time, evening/weekend. *Faculty:* 4 full-time (1 woman), 9 part-time/adjunct (4 women). *Students:* 14 full-time (7 women), 88 part-time (46 women); includes 17 minority (7 Black or African American, non-Hispanic/Latino; 1 American Indian or Alaska Native, non-Hispanic/Latino; 3 Asian, non-Hispanic/Latino; 6 Hispanic/Latino), 1 international. Average age 33. 25 applicants, 92% accepted, 18 enrolled. In 2016, 11 master's awarded. *Entrance requirements:* For master's, current resume, offical transcripts, 2 letters of recommendation. Additional exam requirements/recommendations for international students: Required—TOEFL (minimum score 550 paper-based), IELTS (minimum score 6.5). *Application deadline:* For fall admission, 8/1 priority date for domestic and international students; for spring admission, 1/1 priority date for domestic and international students; for summer admission, 5/1 priority date for domestic and international students. Applications are processed on a rolling basis. Electronic applications accepted. *Expenses: Tuition:* Full-time $2619. Tuition and fees vary according to course load and program. *Financial support:* Applicants required to submit FAFSA. *Faculty research:* Leadership, change management, human resources. *Unit head:* Dr. Liz Kleintop, Associate Chair of Graduate Business, 610-861-1400, Fax: 610-861-1466, E-mail: mba@moravian.edu. *Application contact:* Kristy Sullivan, Director of Student Recruitment Operations, 610-861-1400, Fax: 610-861-1466, E-mail: graduate@moravian.edu.
Website: https://www.moravian.edu/graduate

Morehead State University, Graduate Programs, College of Business and Public Affairs, Morehead, KY 40351. Offers MA, MBA, MPA, MSIS. *Accreditation:* AACSB. *Program availability:* Part-time, evening/weekend, online learning. *Entrance requirements:* For master's, GMAT, GRE General Test, minimum GPA of 2.5 on undergraduate work. Additional exam requirements/recommendations for international students: Required—TOEFL (minimum score 525 paper-based). Electronic applications accepted. *Faculty research:* Regional economic development, accounting systems, banking market structures, macroeconomics, distance learning.

Morgan State University, School of Graduate Studies, Earl G. Graves School of Business and Management, PhD Program in Business Administration, Baltimore, MD 21251. Offers PhD. *Accreditation:* AACSB. *Degree requirements:* For doctorate, thesis/dissertation. *Entrance requirements:* For doctorate, GMAT. Additional exam requirements/recommendations for international students: Required—TOEFL (minimum score 550 paper-based).

Mount Aloysius College, Program in Business Administration, Cresson, PA 16630-1999. Offers accounting (MBA); health and human services administration (MBA); non-profit management (MBA); project management (MBA). *Program availability:* Part-time, evening/weekend. *Entrance requirements:* Additional exam requirements/recommendations for international students: Required—IELTS (minimum score 5.5); Recommended—TOEFL. *Application deadline:* For fall admission, 8/1 for domestic students; for spring admission, 12/1 for domestic students. Applications are processed on a rolling basis. Application fee: $30. Electronic applications accepted. Application fee is waived when completed online. *Expenses: Tuition:* Full-time $6750; part-time $750 per credit. *Required fees:* $285 per semester. *Financial support:* Unspecified assistantships available. Financial award applicants required to submit FAFSA. *Application contact:* Matthew P. Bodenschatz, Director of Graduate and Continuing Education Admissions, 814-886-6556, Fax: 814-886-6441, E-mail: mbodenschatz@mtaloy.edu.
Website: http://www.mtaloy.edu

Mount Ida College, Program in Management, Newton, MA 02459-3310. Offers healthcare management (MSM); human resource management (MSM); interior architecture (MSM); leadership in sport (MSM); management (MSM). *Program availability:* Part-time, evening/weekend, online learning. *Entrance requirements:* For master's, resume, undergraduate transcripts, letters of reference, personal essay. Additional exam requirements/recommendations for international students: Required—TOEFL (minimum score 550 paper-based; 79 iBT); Recommended—IELTS (minimum score 5.5). Electronic applications accepted. *Expenses:* Contact institution.

Mount Marty College, Graduate Studies Division, Yankton, SD 57078-3724. Offers business administration (MBA); nurse anesthesia (MS); nursing (MSN); pastoral ministries (MPM). *Accreditation:* AANA/CANAEP (one or more programs are accredited). *Degree requirements:* For master's, thesis or alternative. *Entrance requirements:* For master's, GRE General Test, minimum GPA of 3.0. Electronic applications accepted. *Faculty research:* Clinical anesthesia, professional characteristics, motivations of applicants.

Mount Mary University, Graduate Programs, Program in Business Administration, Milwaukee, WI 53222-4597. Offers general management (MBA); health systems leadership (MBA). *Program availability:* Part-time, evening/weekend. *Faculty:* 2 full-time (1 woman), 7 part-time/adjunct (1 woman). *Students:* 28 full-time (26 women), 11 part-time (8 women); includes 11 minority (7 Black or African American, non-Hispanic/Latino; 2 Hispanic/Latino; 2 Two or more races, non-Hispanic/Latino). Average age 33. 24 applicants, 33% accepted, 6 enrolled. In 2016, 14 master's awarded. *Degree requirements:* For master's, terminal project. *Entrance requirements:* For master's, minimum GPA of 2.75. Additional exam requirements/recommendations for international students: Required—TOEFL (minimum score 550 paper-based; 80 iBT); Recommended—IELTS (minimum score 6.5). *Application deadline:* For fall admission, 7/15 for domestic and international students; for winter admission, 9/15 for domestic and international students; for spring admission, 12/1 for domestic and international students; for summer admission, 5/1 for domestic and international students. Applications are processed on a rolling basis. Application fee: $45. Electronic applications accepted. *Expenses:* Contact institution. *Financial support:* Career-related internships or fieldwork and Federal Work-Study available. Support available to part-time students. Financial award application deadline: 5/1; financial award applicants required to submit FAFSA. *Faculty research:* Economics, quantitative analysis, accounting, finance. *Unit head:* Dr. Kristen Roche, Director, 414-930-3419, E-mail: rochek@mtmary.edu. *Application contact:* Kirk Heller de Messer, Director, Graduate Admissions, 414-930-3221, E-mail: hellerk@mtmary.edu.
Website: http://www.mtmary.edu/majors-programs/graduate/mba/index.html

Mount Mercy University, Program in Business Administration, Cedar Rapids, IA 52402-4797. Offers human resource (MBA); quality management (MBA). *Program availability:* Evening/weekend. *Entrance requirements:* For master's, minimum cumulative GPA of 3.0, 2 letters of recommendation, resume. Additional exam requirements/recommendations for international students: Required—TOEFL (minimum score 570 paper-based; 88 iBT). Electronic applications accepted.

Mount St. Joseph University, Master of Business Administration Program, Cincinnati, OH 45233-1670. Offers MBA. *Program availability:* Part-time, evening/weekend. *Faculty:* 8 full-time (4 women), 2 part-time/adjunct (0 women). *Students:* 11 full-time (3 women), 41 part-time (23 women); includes 6 minority (4 Black or African American, non-Hispanic/Latino; 1 Asian, non-Hispanic/Latino; 1 Two or more races, non-Hispanic/Latino). Average age 32. In 2016, 28 master's awarded. *Degree requirements:* For master's, 15 hours of foundational course work, 36 hours of MBA coursework, minimum GPA of 3.0, integrative project. *Entrance requirements:* For master's, official undergraduate transcript with minimum cumulative GPA of 3.0; MBA Required Foundational Course form; two references; one-page personal statement; interview with MBA program director or designee. Additional exam requirements/recommendations for international students: Required—TOEFL (minimum score 560 paper-based; 83 iBT). *Application deadline:* Applications are processed on a rolling basis. Application fee: $50. Electronic applications accepted. *Expenses:* Contact institution. *Financial support:* Applicants required to submit FAFSA. *Faculty research:* Gender and cultural effects on management education, group identity formation, leadership skill development, methods for improving instructional effectiveness, technology-based productivity improvement. *Unit head:* Dr. Anna Goldhahn, Interim Dean, 513-244-4924, Fax: 513-244-4270, E-mail: anna.goldhahn@msj.edu. *Application contact:* Amy Wolf, Senior Admissions Counselor for Graduate Studies, 513-244-4204, Fax: 513-745-4629, E-mail: amy.wolf@msj.edu.
Website: http://www.msj.edu/academics/graduate-programs/master-of-business-administration/

Mount Saint Mary College, School of Business, Newburgh, NY 12550-3494. Offers business (MBA); financial planning (MBA); health care management (MBA). *Program availability:* Part-time, evening/weekend. *Faculty:* 6 full-time (2 women), 8 part-time/adjunct (2 women). *Students:* 55 full-time (26 women), 28 part-time (17 women); includes 20 minority (7 Black or African American, non-Hispanic/Latino; 12 Hispanic/Latino; 1 Native Hawaiian or other Pacific Islander, non-Hispanic/Latino), 1 international. Average age 32. 21 applicants, 100% accepted, 15 enrolled. In 2016, 47 master's awarded. *Degree requirements:* For master's, thesis or alternative. *Entrance requirements:* For master's, GMAT or minimum undergraduate GPA of 2.7. Additional exam requirements/recommendations for international students: Required—TOEFL (minimum score 80 iBT). *Application deadline:* Applications are processed on a rolling basis. Application fee: $45. Electronic applications accepted. Application fee is waived when completed online. *Expenses: Tuition:* Full-time $13,914; part-time $773 per credit. *Required fees:* $82 per semester. *Financial support:* In 2016–17, 18 students received support. Unspecified assistantships available. Financial award application deadline: 4/15; financial award applicants required to submit FAFSA. *Faculty research:* Financial reform, entrepreneurship and small business development, global business relations, technology's impact on business decision-making, college-assisted business education. *Unit head:* Dr. Moira Tolan, Graduate Coordinator, 845-569-3121, Fax: 845-562-6762, E-mail: moira.tolan@msmc.edu. *Application contact:* Lisa Gallina, Director of Admissions for Graduate Programs and Adult Degree Completion, 845-569-3166, Fax: 845-569-3450, E-mail: lisa.gallina@msmc.edu.
Website: http://www.msmc.edu/Academics/Graduate_Programs/master_of_business_administration.be

Mount Saint Mary's University, Graduate Division, Los Angeles, CA 90049. Offers business administration (MBA); counseling psychology (MS); creative writing (MFA); education (MS, Certificate); film and television (MFA); health policy and management (MS); humanities (MA); nursing (MSN, Certificate); physical therapy (DPT); religious studies (MA). *Program availability:* Part-time, evening/weekend. *Faculty:* 50 full-time (35 women), 116 part-time/adjunct (81 women). *Students:* 670 full-time (518 women), 147 part-time (116 women); includes 414 minority (73 Black or African American, non-Hispanic/Latino; 4 American Indian or Alaska Native, non-Hispanic/Latino; 60 Asian, non-Hispanic/Latino; 259 Hispanic/Latino; 7 Native Hawaiian or other Pacific Islander, non-Hispanic/Latino; 11 Two or more races, non-Hispanic/Latino), 4 international. Average age 32. 1,398 applicants, 21% accepted, 242 enrolled. In 2016, 170 master's, 28 doctorates, 35 other advanced degrees awarded. *Entrance requirements:* Additional exam requirements/recommendations for international students: Required—TOEFL. *Application deadline:* For fall admission, 6/30 priority date for domestic and international students; for spring admission, 10/30 priority date for domestic and international students; for summer admission, 3/30 priority date for domestic and international students. Applications are processed on a rolling basis. Application fee: $50. Electronic applications accepted. *Expenses: Tuition:* Full-time $9983; part-time $829 per unit. One-time fee: $135. Tuition and fees vary according to degree level and program. *Financial support:* Career-related internships or fieldwork, Federal Work-Study, institutionally sponsored loans, and tuition waivers (full and partial) available. Support available to part-time students. Financial award application deadline: 3/15; financial award applicants required to submit FAFSA. *Unit head:* Albert Ramos, Director of Graduate Admissions, 213-477-2800, E-mail: gradprograms@msmu.edu. *Application contact:* Shawn Peters, Graduate Admission Counselor, 213-477-2676, E-mail: gradprograms@msmu.edu.
Website: http://www.msmu.edu/graduate-programs/

Mount St. Mary's University, Program in Business Administration, Emmitsburg, MD 21727-7799. Offers MBA. *Program availability:* Part-time, evening/weekend. *Faculty:* 11 full-time (4 women), 9 part-time/adjunct (3 women). *Students:* 38 full-time (17 women), 111 part-time (53 women); includes 37 minority (13 Black or African American, non-Hispanic/Latino; 2 American Indian or Alaska Native, non-Hispanic/Latino; 3 Asian, non-Hispanic/Latino; 14 Hispanic/Latino; 2 Native Hawaiian or other Pacific Islander, non-Hispanic/Latino; 3 Two or more races, non-Hispanic/Latino), 6 international. Average age 31. 109 applicants, 89% accepted, 55 enrolled. In 2016, 95 master's awarded. *Degree requirements:* For master's, thesis. *Entrance requirements:* For master's, minimum undergraduate GPA of 2.75, 5 years' relevant professional business experience, or GMAT (minimum score of 500). Additional exam requirements/recommendations for international students: Required—TOEFL (minimum score 550 paper-based; 83 iBT). *Application deadline:* Applications are processed on a rolling basis. Electronic applications accepted. *Expenses:* $610 per credit hour. *Financial support:* Career-related internships or fieldwork and unspecified assistantships available. Financial award applicants required to submit FAFSA. *Unit head:* Carol Rinkoff, Director of Graduate Business Programs, 301-447-5840, E-mail: rinkoff@msmary.edu. *Application contact:* Melissa Flohr, Assistant Director of Graduate Programs, Business, 301-447-5908, E-mail: mflohr@msmary.edu.
Website: http://www.msmary.edu/School_of_business/Graduate_Programs/MBA.html

Mount Vernon Nazarene University, Program in Management, Mount Vernon, OH 43050-9500. Offers MSM. *Accreditation:* ACBSP. *Program availability:* Part-time, evening/weekend.

Murray State University, College of Business and Public Affairs, MBA Program, Murray, KY 42071. Offers MBA. *Accreditation:* AACSB. *Program availability:* Part-time, evening/weekend. *Entrance requirements:* For master's, GMAT. Additional exam requirements/recommendations for international students: Required—TOEFL.

National American University, Graduate Programs, Rapid City, SD 57701. Offers MBA, MM. Programs also offered in Wichita, KS; Albuquerque, NM; Bloomington, MN; Brooklyn Center, MN; Colorado Springs, CO; Denver, CO; Independence, MO; Overland Park, KS; Rio Rancho, NM; Roseville, MN; Zona Rosa, MO. *Program availability:* Part-time, evening/weekend, online learning. *Entrance requirements:* For master's, minimum undergraduate GPA of 2.75. Additional exam requirements/recommendations for international students: Required—TOEFL, TWE. Electronic applications accepted. *Faculty research:* Tourism, finance, marketing.

National Louis University, College of Management and Business, Chicago, IL 60603. Offers business administration (MBA); human resource management and development (MS); management (MS). *Program availability:* Part-time, evening/weekend. *Entrance requirements:* For master's, college-administered critical thinking and writing skills test, minimum GPA of 3.0, resume, 3 references. Additional exam requirements/recommendations for international students: Required—TOEFL (minimum score 550 paper-based; 79 iBT).

National University, Academic Affairs, School of Business and Management, La Jolla, CA 92037-1011. Offers GMBA, M Acc, MA, MBA, MGM, MS, Certificate. *Program availability:* Part-time, evening/weekend, 100% online, blended/hybrid learning. *Faculty:* 34 full-time (10 women), 73 part-time/adjunct (20 women). *Students:* 624 full-time (322 women), 217 part-time (104 women); includes 432 minority (136 Black or African American, non-Hispanic/Latino; 2 American Indian or Alaska Native, non-Hispanic/Latino; 89 Asian, non-Hispanic/Latino; 164 Hispanic/Latino; 15 Native Hawaiian or other Pacific Islander, non-Hispanic/Latino; 26 Two or more races, non-Hispanic/Latino), 110 international. Average age 34. In 2016, 637 master's awarded. *Degree requirements:* For master's, thesis (for some programs). *Entrance requirements:* For master's, interview, minimum GPA of 2.5. Additional exam requirements/recommendations for international students: Required—TOEFL (minimum score 550 paper-based; 79 iBT), IELTS (minimum score 6). *Application deadline:* Applications are processed on a rolling basis. Application fee: $60 ($65 for international students). Electronic applications accepted. *Financial support:* Career-related internships or fieldwork, scholarships/grants, and tuition waivers (partial) available. Support available to part-time students. Financial award application deadline: 6/30; financial award applicants required to submit FAFSA. *Unit head:* School of Business and Management, 800-628-8648, Fax: 858-642-8719, E-mail: sobm@nu.edu. *Application contact:* Brandon Jouganatos, Vice President for Enrollment Services, 800-628-8648, E-mail: advisor@nu.edu.
Website: http://www.nu.edu/OurPrograms/SchoolOfBusinessAndManagement.html

National University College, Graduate Programs, Bayamón, PR 00960. Offers digital marketing (MBA); general business (MBA); special education (M Ed).

Naval Postgraduate School, Departments and Academic Groups, Graduate School of Business and Public Policy, Monterey, CA 93943. Offers acquisition and contract management (MBA); business administration (EMBA, MBA); contract management (MS); defense business management (MBA); defense systems analysis (MS), including management; defense systems management (international) (MBA); financial management (MBA); information management (MBA); manpower systems analysis (MS); material logistics support management (MBA); program management (MS); resource planning and management for international defense (MBA); supply chain management (MBA); systems acquisition management (MBA); transportation management (MBA). Program only open to commissioned officers of the United States and friendly nations and selected United States federal civilian employees. *Accreditation:* AACSB; NASPAA. *Program availability:* Part-time, online learning. *Degree requirements:* For master's, thesis (for some programs), terminal project/capstone (for some programs). *Faculty research:* U.S. and European public procurement policies for small and medium-sized enterprises, examining external validity criticisms in the choice of students as subjects in accounting experiment studies, assurance of learning in contract management education, contracting for cloud computing: opportunities and risks, NPS, Apple App Store as a business model supporting U. S. Navy requirements.

Nazareth College of Rochester, Graduate Studies, Department of Business, Program in Management, Rochester, NY 14618. Offers MS. *Program availability:* Part-time, evening/weekend. *Entrance requirements:* For master's, minimum GPA of 3.0. Additional exam requirements/recommendations for international students: Required—TOEFL (minimum score 550 paper-based, 79 iBT) or IELTS (6.5). *Application deadline:* For fall admission, 8/1 priority date for domestic students; for spring admission, 11/1 priority date for domestic students. Application fee: $40. *Expenses: Tuition:* Part-time $880 per credit hour. Part-time tuition and fees vary according to course load, degree level and program. *Financial support:* Unspecified assistantships available. Financial award application deadline: 3/1; financial award applicants required to submit FAFSA. *Unit head:* Albert Cabral, Program Director, 585-389-2395, E-mail: acabral8@naz.edu. *Application contact:* Judith Baker, Director, Transfer and Graduate Admissions, 585-531-1154, Fax: 585-389-2826, E-mail: gradadmissions@naz.edu.
Website: http://www.naz.edu

Business Administration and Management—General

Neumann University, Graduate Programs in Business and Information Management, Aston, PA 19014-1298. Offers accounting (MS), including forensic and fraud detection; sport business (MS). *Program availability:* Part-time, evening/weekend. *Faculty:* 3 full-time (2 women), 4 part-time/adjunct (1 woman). *Students:* 9 full-time (2 women), 33 part-time (12 women); includes 14 minority (11 Black or African American, non-Hispanic/Latino; 1 Asian, non-Hispanic/Latino; 2 Hispanic/Latino). Average age 31. 58 applicants, 50% accepted, 26 enrolled. In 2016, 16 master's awarded. *Degree requirements:* For master's, thesis (for some programs). *Entrance requirements:* For master's, official transcripts from all institutions attended, resume, letter of intent, 2-3 official letters of recommendation. Additional exam requirements/recommendations for international students: Required—TOEFL (minimum score 70 iBT). *Application deadline:* Applications are processed on a rolling basis. Application fee: $0. Electronic applications accepted. *Expenses:* $600 per credit (for MS in accounting); $495 per credit (MS in sport business). *Financial support:* Scholarships/grants and health care benefits available. Support available to part-time students. Financial award application deadline: 3/15; financial award applicants required to submit FAFSA. *Unit head:* Dr. Eric Wellington, Dean of Business and Information Management, 610-558-5596, Fax: 610-558-5574, E-mail: wellinge@neumann.edu. *Application contact:* Dr. Erika Davis, Director of Adult and Graduate Admissions, 800-9-NEUMANN Ext. 5208, Fax: 610-361-2548, E-mail: GradAdultAdmiss@neumann.edu.

New Charter University, College of Business, Salt Lake City, UT 84101. Offers finance (MBA); health care management (MBA); management (MBA). *Program availability:* Part-time, evening/weekend, online learning. *Entrance requirements:* For master's, course work in calculus, statistics, macroeconomics. Additional exam requirements/recommendations for international students: Required—TOEFL (minimum score 550 paper-based). Electronic applications accepted.

New England College, Program in Management, Henniker, NH 03242-3293. Offers accounting (MSA); healthcare administration (MS); international relations (MA); marketing management (MS); nonprofit leadership (MS); project management (MS); strategic leadership (MS). *Program availability:* Part-time, evening/weekend. *Degree requirements:* For master's, independent research project. Electronic applications accepted.

New Jersey City University, School of Business, Jersey City, NJ 07305-1597. Offers MBA, MS, Graduate Certificate. *Accreditation:* ACBSP. *Program availability:* Part-time, evening/weekend. *Entrance requirements:* Additional exam requirements/recommendations for international students: Required—TOEFL (minimum score 79 iBT).

New Jersey Institute of Technology, Martin Tuchman School of Management, Newark, NJ 07102. Offers business administration (MBA); business data science (PhD); finance for managers (Certificate); international business (MS); management (MS); management essentials (Certificate); management of technology (Certificate). *Accreditation:* AACSB. *Program availability:* Part-time, evening/weekend. *Faculty:* 29 full-time (9 women), 21 part-time/adjunct (3 women). *Students:* 90 full-time (35 women), 147 part-time (53 women); includes 104 minority (30 Black or African American, non-Hispanic/Latino; 30 Asian, non-Hispanic/Latino; 38 Hispanic/Latino; 6 Two or more races, non-Hispanic/Latino), 57 international. Average age 31. 385 applicants, 52% accepted, 80 enrolled. In 2016, 81 master's, 11 other advanced degrees awarded. Terminal master's awarded for partial completion of doctoral program. *Degree requirements:* For master's, thesis optional. *Entrance requirements:* For doctorate, GRE General Test, minimum graduate GPA of 3.5. Additional exam requirements/recommendations for international students: Required—TOEFL (minimum score 550 paper-based; 79 iBT). *Application deadline:* For fall admission, 6/1 priority date for domestic students, 5/1 priority date for international students; for spring admission, 11/15 priority date for domestic and international students. Applications are processed on a rolling basis. Application fee: $75. Electronic applications accepted. *Expenses:* Contact institution. *Financial support:* In 2016–17, 7 students received support, including 3 research assistantships (averaging $9,088 per year), 4 teaching assistantships (averaging $19,250 per year); fellowships, career-related internships or fieldwork, Federal Work-Study, institutionally sponsored loans, and unspecified assistantships also available. Financial award application deadline: 1/15. *Faculty research:* Manufacturing systems analysis, earnings management, knowledge-based view of the firm, data envelopment analysis, human factors in human/machine systems. *Unit head:* Dr. Reggie Caudill, Interim Dean, 973-596-5856, Fax: 973-596-3074, E-mail: reggie.j.caudill@njit.edu. *Application contact:* Stephen Eck, Director of Admissions, 973-596-3300, Fax: 973-596-3461, E-mail: admissions@njit.edu.
Website: http://management.njit.edu

New Jersey Institute of Technology, Ying Wu College of Computing, Newark, NJ 07102. Offers big data management and mining (Certificate); business and information systems (Certificate); computer science (MS, PhD), including bioinformatics (MS), computer science, computing and business (MS), cyber security and privacy (MS), software engineering (MS); data mining (Certificate); information security (Certificate); information systems (MS, PhD), including business and information systems (MS), emergency management and business continuity (MS), information systems; information technology administration and security (MS); IT administration (Certificate); network security and information assurance (Certificate); software engineering analysis/design (Certificate); Web systems development (Certificate). *Program availability:* Part-time, evening/weekend. *Faculty:* 64 full-time (10 women), 38 part-time/adjunct (4 women). *Students:* 818 full-time (241 women), 225 part-time (53 women); includes 162 minority (35 Black or African American, non-Hispanic/Latino; 77 Asian, non-Hispanic/Latino; 41 Hispanic/Latino; 9 Two or more races, non-Hispanic/Latino), 772 international. Average age 27. 2,666 applicants, 51% accepted, 377 enrolled. In 2016, 398 master's, 10 doctorates, 9 other advanced degrees awarded. Terminal master's awarded for partial completion of doctoral program. *Degree requirements:* For master's, thesis optional; for doctorate, thesis/dissertation. *Entrance requirements:* For master's, GRE General Test; for doctorate, GRE General Test, minimum graduate GPA of 3.5. Additional exam requirements/recommendations for international students: Required—TOEFL (minimum score 550 paper-based; 79 iBT). *Application deadline:* For fall admission, 6/1 priority date for domestic students, 5/1 priority date for international students; for spring admission, 11/15 priority date for domestic and international students. Applications are processed on a rolling basis. Application fee: $75. Electronic applications accepted. *Expenses:* Contact institution. *Financial support:* In 2016–17, 57 students received support, including 18 research assistantships (averaging $16,073 per year), 39 teaching assistantships (averaging $20,194 per year); fellowships, career-related internships or fieldwork, Federal Work-Study, institutionally sponsored loans, and unspecified assistantships also available. Financial award application deadline: 1/15. *Faculty research:* Computer systems, communications and networking, artificial intelligence, database engineering, systems analysis, analytics and optimization in crowdsourcing. *Total annual research expenditures:* $3 million. *Unit head:* Dr. Craig Gotsman, Dean, 973-542-5488, Fax: 973-596-5777, E-mail: marek.rusinkiewicz@njit.edu. *Application contact:* Stephen Eck, Director of Admissions, 973-596-3300, Fax: 973-596-3461, E-mail: admissions@njit.edu.
Website: http://computing.njit.edu/

Newman University, MBA Program, Wichita, KS 67213-2097. Offers finance (MBA); international business (MBA); leadership (MBA); management (MBA); management information technology (MBA). *Program availability:* Part-time. *Degree requirements:* For master's, thesis optional. *Entrance requirements:* For master's, minimum GPA of 3.0; 2 letters of recommendation; course work in algebra, statistics, macroeconomics, and financial accounting. Additional exam requirements/recommendations for international students: Required—TOEFL (minimum score 600 paper-based; 100 iBT). Electronic applications accepted. *Expenses:* Contact institution.

New Mexico Highlands University, Graduate Studies, School of Business, Media and Technology, Las Vegas, NM 87701. Offers business administration (MBA), including human resource management, international business, management; media arts and technology (MA), including media arts and computer science. *Accreditation:* ACBSP. *Degree requirements:* For master's, comprehensive exam, thesis or alternative. *Entrance requirements:* For master's, minimum undergraduate GPA of 3.0. Additional exam requirements/recommendations for international students: Required—TOEFL (minimum score 540 paper-based). *Faculty research:* Real estate valuation, studying expert judgments in complex accounting, decision environments, green marketing, environmentalism, marketing research methodology.

New Mexico State University, College of Business, Department of Management, Las Cruces, NM 88003. Offers PhD. *Faculty:* 12 full-time (2 women). *Students:* 16 full-time (8 women); includes 6 minority (1 American Indian or Alaska Native, non-Hispanic/Latino; 2 Asian, non-Hispanic/Latino; 3 Hispanic/Latino), 4 international. Average age 37. 34 applicants, 12% accepted, 4 enrolled. *Degree requirements:* For doctorate, comprehensive exam, thesis/dissertation, qualifying exam at end of first year. *Entrance requirements:* For doctorate, GMAT (preferred) or GRE. Additional exam requirements/recommendations for international students: Required—TOEFL (minimum score 550 paper-based; 79 iBT), IELTS (minimum score 6.5). *Application deadline:* For fall admission, 2/15 for domestic and international students. Application fee: $40 ($50 for international students). Electronic applications accepted. *Expenses:* Tuition, state resident: full-time $4086. Tuition, nonresident: full-time $14,254. *Required fees:* $853. Tuition and fees vary according to course load. *Financial support:* In 2016–17, 11 students received support, including 3 fellowships (averaging $4,088 per year), 10 teaching assistantships (averaging $23,015 per year); career-related internships or fieldwork, Federal Work-Study, scholarships/grants, traineeships, health care benefits, and unspecified assistantships also available. Support available to part-time students. Financial award application deadline: 3/1. *Faculty research:* Supply chain management and integration; enterprise systems; organizational behavior; production/operations; human resource management; entrepreneurship; operations management; electronic commerce; policy and strategy; information systems; governance mechanisms; partnerships and collaborative networks; compensation and staffing; employee safety and attachment; research methodology; critical postmodern studies; storytelling, ethnography, content analysis, deconstruction, and rhetorical analysis. *Unit head:* Dr. Carlo Mora, Interim Department Head, 575-646-1201, Fax: 575-646-1372, E-mail: cmora@nmsu.edu. *Application contact:* Dr. William L. Smith, Director, Management PhD Program, 575-646-1422, Fax: 575-646-1372, E-mail: smith@nmsu.edu.
Website: http://business.nmsu.edu/departments/mgt

New Mexico State University, College of Business, Department of Marketing, Las Cruces, NM 88003. Offers business administration (PhD), including marketing. *Program availability:* Part-time. *Faculty:* 7 full-time (2 women), 1 (woman) part-time/adjunct. *Students:* 10 full-time (6 women), 1 (woman) part-time; includes 3 minority (2 Hispanic/Latino; 1 Two or more races, non-Hispanic/Latino), 4 international. Average age 32. 6 applicants. *Degree requirements:* For doctorate, comprehensive exam, thesis/dissertation. *Entrance requirements:* For doctorate, GMAT or GRE, graduate degree, work experience. Additional exam requirements/recommendations for international students: Required—TOEFL (minimum score 550 paper-based; 79 iBT), IELTS (minimum score 6.5). *Application deadline:* For fall admission, 2/1 for domestic and international students. Application fee: $40 ($50 for international students). Electronic applications accepted. *Expenses:* Tuition, state resident: full-time $4086. Tuition, nonresident: full-time $14,254. *Required fees:* $853. Tuition and fees vary according to course load. *Financial support:* In 2016–17, 10 students received support, including 2 fellowships (averaging $4,088 per year), 10 teaching assistantships (averaging $23,157 per year); career-related internships or fieldwork, Federal Work-Study, scholarships/grants, traineeships, health care benefits, and unspecified assistantships also available. Support available to part-time students. Financial award application deadline: 3/1. *Faculty research:* Consumer behavior, social media marketing, ethics in marketing, advertising, public policy. *Unit head:* Dr. Nancy Orestskin, Department Head, 575-646-3341, Fax: 575-646-1498, E-mail: noretski@nmsu.edu. *Application contact:* Dr. Nancy Oretskin, Coordinator, Marketing PhD Program, 575-646-3341, Fax: 575-646-1498, E-mail: noretski@nmsu.edu.
Website: http://business.nmsu.edu/departments/marketing

New Mexico State University, College of Business, MBA Program, Las Cruces, NM 88003. Offers agribusiness (MBA); finance (MBA); information systems (MBA). *Accreditation:* AACSB. *Program availability:* Part-time-only, evening/weekend, online with required 2-3 day orientation and 2-3 day concluding session in Las Cruces. *Students:* 55 full-time (23 women), 121 part-time (67 women); includes 97 minority (5 Black or African American, non-Hispanic/Latino; 2 American Indian or Alaska Native, non-Hispanic/Latino; 2 Asian, non-Hispanic/Latino; 85 Hispanic/Latino; 3 Two or more races, non-Hispanic/Latino), 10 international. Average age 32. 139 applicants, 62% accepted, 23 enrolled. In 2016, 46 master's awarded. *Degree requirements:* For master's, comprehensive exam, thesis optional. *Entrance requirements:* For master's, GMAT or GRE (depending upon undergraduate or graduate degree institution and GPA), minimum GPA of 3.5 from AACSB international or ACBSP-accredited institution or graduate degree from regionally-accredited U.S. university (without GMAT or GRE). Additional exam requirements/recommendations for international students: Required—TOEFL (minimum score 550 paper-based; 79 iBT), IELTS (minimum score 6.5). *Application deadline:* For fall admission, 7/15 priority date for domestic students, 4/15 priority date for international students; for spring admission, 4/15 priority date for domestic students, 9/15 priority date for international students; for summer admission, 4/15 for domestic students, 1/15 for international students. Applications are processed on a rolling basis. Application fee: $40 ($50 for international students). Electronic applications accepted. *Expenses:* Tuition, state resident: full-time $4086. Tuition, nonresident: full-time $14,254. *Required fees:* $853. Tuition and fees vary according to course load. *Financial support:* In 2016–17, 39 students received support, including 1 fellowship (averaging $4,088 per year); Federal Work-Study, institutionally sponsored loans, scholarships/grants, health care benefits, and unspecified assistantships also available. Financial award application deadline: 3/1. *Unit head:* Dr. Kathleen Brook, Associate Dean, 575-646-5431, Fax: 575-646-6155, E-mail: kbrook@nmsu.edu. *Application contact:* John Shonk, MBA Advisor, 575-646-8003, Fax: 575-646-7977, E-mail: mbaprog@nmsu.edu.
Website: http://business.nmsu.edu/mba

New York Institute of Technology, School of Management, Department of Business Administration, Old Westbury, NY 11568-8000. Offers executive (MBA); management (MBA), including finance, marketing, operations and supply chain management;

professional accounting (MBA). *Accreditation:* AACSB. *Program availability:* Part-time, evening/weekend. *Faculty:* 25 full-time (4 women), 20 part-time/adjunct (6 women). *Students:* 377 full-time (161 women), 149 part-time (88 women); includes 60 minority (17 Black or African American, non-Hispanic/Latino; 1 American Indian or Alaska Native, non-Hispanic/Latino; 28 Asian, non-Hispanic/Latino; 11 Hispanic/Latino; 2 Native Hawaiian or other Pacific Islander, non-Hispanic/Latino; 1 Two or more races, non-Hispanic/Latino), 446 international. Average age 26. 804 applicants, 68% accepted, 215 enrolled. In 2016, 193 master's awarded. *Entrance requirements:* For master's, bachelor's degree; minimum undergraduate GPA of 3.0. Additional exam requirements/recommendations for international students: Required—TOEFL (minimum score 79 iBT), IELTS (minimum score 6). *Application deadline:* Applications are processed on a rolling basis. Application fee: $50. Electronic applications accepted. *Expenses:* $1,215 per credit. *Financial support:* Career-related internships or fieldwork, Federal Work-Study, scholarships/grants, tuition waivers (full and partial), and unspecified assistantships available. Support available to part-time students. Financial award application deadline: 3/1; financial award applicants required to submit FAFSA. *Faculty research:* Accounting, economics, finance, management, marketing. *Unit head:* Dr. Jess Boronico, Dean, 516-686-7838, E-mail: som@nyit.edu. *Application contact:* Alice Dolitsky, Director, Graduate Admissions, 516-686-7520, Fax: 516-686-1116, E-mail: nyitgrad@nyit.edu.
Website: http://www.nyit.edu/degrees/management_mba

New York Medical College, School of Health Sciences and Practice, Valhalla, NY 10595. Offers behavioral sciences and health promotion (MPH); biostatistics (MS); children with special health care (Graduate Certificate); emergency preparedness (Graduate Certificate); environmental health science (MPH); epidemiology (MPH, MS); global health (Graduate Certificate); health education (Graduate Certificate); health policy and management (MPH, Dr PH); industrial hygiene (Graduate Certificate); pediatric dysphagia (Post-Graduate Certificate); physical therapy (DPT); public health (Graduate Certificate); speech-language pathology (MS). *Accreditation:* CEPH. *Program availability:* Part-time, evening/weekend, 100% online, blended/hybrid learning. *Faculty:* 42 full-time (31 women), 236 part-time/adjunct (138 women). *Students:* 235 full-time (165 women), 252 part-time (185 women); includes 188 minority (83 Black or African American, non-Hispanic/Latino; 1 American Indian or Alaska Native, non-Hispanic/Latino; 62 Asian, non-Hispanic/Latino; 36 Hispanic/Latino; 6 Two or more races, non-Hispanic/Latino), 26 international. Average age 27. In 2016, 110 master's, 37 doctorates awarded. *Degree requirements:* For master's, comprehensive exam (for some programs), thesis (for some programs); for doctorate, thesis/dissertation. *Expenses:* $1,070 per credit tuition, $105 fees. *Unit head:* Ben Watson, PhD, Vice Dean, 914-594-4531, E-mail: ben_watson@nymc.edu. *Application contact:* Veronica Jarek-Prinz, Associate Dean for Admissions and Enrollment Management, 914-594-3941, E-mail: veronica_jarekprinz@nymc.edu.
Website: http://www.nymc.edu/school-of-health-sciences-and-practice-shsp/

New York University, Leonard N. Stern School of Business, Department of Marketing, New York, NY 10012-1019. Offers entertainment, media and technology (MBA); general marketing (MBA); marketing (PhD); product management (MBA).

New York University, Polytechnic School of Engineering, Department of Technology Management, New York, NY 10012-1019. Offers construction management (Advanced Certificate); electronic business management (Advanced Certificate); entrepreneurship (Advanced Certificate); human resources management (Advanced Certificate); industrial engineering (MS); information management (Advanced Certificate); management (MS); management of technology (MS); manufacturing engineering (MS); organizational behavior (MS, Advanced Certificate); project management (Advanced Certificate); technology management (MBA, PhD, Advanced Certificate); telecommunications management (Advanced Certificate). *Program availability:* Part-time, evening/weekend. *Degree requirements:* For master's, comprehensive exam (for some programs), thesis (for some programs); for doctorate, comprehensive exam, thesis/dissertation. *Entrance requirements:* For master's, GMAT, minimum B average in undergraduate course work. Additional exam requirements/recommendations for international students: Required—TOEFL (minimum score 550 paper-based; 80 iBT); Recommended—IELTS (minimum score 6.5). Electronic applications accepted. *Faculty research:* Global innovation and research and development strategy, managing emerging technologies, technology and development, service design and innovation, tech entrepreneurship and commercialization, sustainable and clean-tech innovation, impacts of information technology upon individuals, organizations and society.

New York University, School of Law, New York, NY 10012-1019. Offers law (LL M, JD, JSD); law and business (Advanced Certificate); taxation (MSL, Advanced Certificate); JD/JD; JD/LL B; JD/LL M; JD/MA; JD/MBA; JD/MPA; JD/MPP; JD/MSW; JD/MUP; JD/PhD. *Accreditation:* ABA. *Program availability:* Part-time, online learning. *Entrance requirements:* For doctorate, LSAT (for JD). Electronic applications accepted. *Expenses:* Contact institution. *Faculty research:* International law, environmental law, corporate law, globalization of law, philosophy of law.

Niagara University, Graduate Division of Business Administration, Niagara University, NY 14109. Offers accounting (MBA); business administration (MBA); finance (MBA, MS); financial planning (MBA); healthcare administration (MBA, MHA); human resources (MBA); international business (MBA); marketing (MBA); professional accountancy (MBA); strategic management (MBA); supply chain management (MBA). *Accreditation:* AACSB. *Program availability:* Part-time, evening/weekend. *Students:* 172 full-time (69 women), 65 part-time (36 women); includes 25 minority (4 Black or African American, non-Hispanic/Latino; 7 Asian, non-Hispanic/Latino; 7 Hispanic/Latino; 1 Native Hawaiian or other Pacific Islander, non-Hispanic/Latino; 6 Two or more races, non-Hispanic/Latino), 76 international. Average age 27. In 2016, 107 master's awarded. *Entrance requirements:* For master's, GMAT. Additional exam requirements/recommendations for international students: Required—TOEFL (minimum score 550 paper-based; 79 iBT), IELTS (minimum score 6). *Application deadline:* For fall admission, 8/1 for domestic students; for spring admission, 11/1 for domestic students. Applications are processed on a rolling basis. Electronic applications accepted. *Expenses:* $870 per credit hour. *Financial support:* Fellowships, research assistantships, career-related internships or fieldwork, and Federal Work-Study available. Support available to part-time students. Financial award application deadline: 4/15; financial award applicants required to submit FAFSA. *Faculty research:* Capital flows, Federal Reserve policy, human resource management, public policy, issues in marketing, auctions, economics of information, risk and capital markets, management strategy, consumer behavior, Internet and social media marketing. *Unit head:* Dr. Paul Richardson, MBA Director/Chair of the Marketing Department, 716-286-8169, Fax: 716-286-8206, E-mail: psr@niagara.edu. *Application contact:* Evan Pierce, Associate Director for Graduate Recruitment, 716-286-8769, Fax: 716-286-8170, E-mail: epierce@niagara.edu.
Website: http://mba.niagara.edu

Nicholls State University, Graduate Studies, College of Business Administration, Thibodaux, LA 70310. Offers MBA. *Accreditation:* AACSB. *Program availability:* Part-time, evening/weekend. *Degree requirements:* For master's, thesis optional. *Entrance requirements:* For master's, GMAT. Additional exam requirements/recommendations for international students: Required—TOEFL (minimum score 550 paper-based). Electronic applications accepted.

Nichols College, Graduate and Professional Studies, Dudley, MA 01571-5000. Offers business administration (MBA); organizational leadership (MSOL). *Program availability:* Part-time, evening/weekend, online learning. *Degree requirements:* For master's, project (for MOL). *Entrance requirements:* For master's, 2 letters of recommendation, current resume, official transcripts, 800-word personal statement. Additional exam requirements/recommendations for international students: Required—TOEFL (minimum score 500 paper-based). Electronic applications accepted.

North Carolina Agricultural and Technical State University, School of Graduate Studies, School of Business and Economics, Greensboro, NC 27411. Offers accounting (MBA); business education (MAT); human resources management (MBA); supply chain systems (MBA).

North Carolina Central University, School of Business, Durham, NC 27707-3129. Offers MBA. *Accreditation:* AACSB; ACBSP. *Program availability:* Part-time, evening/weekend. *Degree requirements:* For master's, thesis. *Entrance requirements:* For master's, GMAT. Additional exam requirements/recommendations for international students: Required—TOEFL.

North Carolina State University, Graduate School, Poole College of Management, Program in Business Administration, Raleigh, NC 27695. Offers biosciences management (MBA); entrepreneurship and technology commercialization (MBA); financial management (MBA); innovation management (MBA); marketing management (MBA); services management (MBA); supply chain management (MBA). *Accreditation:* AACSB. *Program availability:* Part-time. *Degree requirements:* For master's, thesis optional. *Entrance requirements:* For master's, GMAT, interview, 3 letters of recommendation. Additional exam requirements/recommendations for international students: Required—TOEFL (minimum score 600 paper-based; 100 iBT). Electronic applications accepted. *Faculty research:* Manufacturing strategy, information systems, technology commercialization, managing research and development, historical stock returns.

North Central College, School of Graduate and Professional Studies, Program in Business Administration, Naperville, IL 60566-7063. Offers change management (MBA); finance (MBA); human resource management (MBA); management (MBA). *Program availability:* Part-time, evening/weekend. *Faculty:* 15 full-time (9 women), 13 part-time/adjunct (5 women). *Students:* 30 full-time (14 women), 46 part-time (22 women); includes 11 minority (4 Black or African American, non-Hispanic/Latino; 6 Hispanic/Latino; 1 Two or more races, non-Hispanic/Latino), 6 international. Average age 29. 104 applicants, 50% accepted, 31 enrolled. In 2016, 45 master's awarded. *Degree requirements:* For master's, thesis optional, project. *Entrance requirements:* For master's, interview. Additional exam requirements/recommendations for international students: Required—TOEFL (minimum score 550 paper-based; 80 iBT), IELTS (minimum score 6.5). *Application deadline:* For fall admission, 8/15 for domestic students, 7/15 for international students; for winter admission, 12/1 for domestic students, 11/1 for international students; for spring admission, 2/1 for domestic students, 12/1 for international students. Applications are processed on a rolling basis. Application fee: $25. Electronic applications accepted. Application fee is waived when completed online. *Expenses:* Contact institution. *Financial support:* Scholarships/grants available. Support available to part-time students. Financial award applicants required to submit FAFSA. *Unit head:* Dr. Mary Galvan, Chair of Department of Management and Marketing, 630-637-5473, E-mail: mtgalvan@noctrl.edu. *Application contact:* Wendy Kulpinski, Director of Graduate and Continuing Education Admission, 630-637-5808, Fax: 630-637-5844, E-mail: wekulpinski@noctrl.edu.

North Central College, School of Graduate and Professional Studies, Program in Leadership Studies, Naperville, IL 60566-7063. Offers MLD. *Program availability:* Part-time, evening/weekend. *Faculty:* 8 full-time (5 women), 8 part-time/adjunct (4 women). *Students:* 38 full-time (22 women), 19 part-time (12 women); includes 12 minority (6 Black or African American, non-Hispanic/Latino; 4 Hispanic/Latino; 2 Two or more races, non-Hispanic/Latino), 2 international. Average age 26. 111 applicants, 46% accepted, 25 enrolled. In 2016, 33 master's awarded. *Degree requirements:* For master's, thesis optional, project. *Entrance requirements:* For master's, interview. Additional exam requirements/recommendations for international students: Required—TOEFL (minimum score 550 paper-based; 80 iBT), IELTS (minimum score 6.5). *Application deadline:* For fall admission, 8/15 for domestic students, 7/15 for international students; for winter admission, 12/1 for domestic students, 11/1 for international students; for spring admission, 2/1 for domestic students, 12/1 for international students. Applications are processed on a rolling basis. Application fee: $25. Electronic applications accepted. Application fee is waived when completed online. *Expenses:* Contact institution. *Financial support:* Scholarships/grants available. Support available to part-time students. Financial award applicants required to submit FAFSA. *Unit head:* Dr. Pamela Monaco, Dean of Graduate and Professional Studies, 630-637-5384, E-mail: pjmonaco@noctrl.edu. *Application contact:* Wendy Kulpinski, Director of Graduate and Professional Studies Admission, 630-637-5808, Fax: 630-637-5844, E-mail: wekulpinski@noctrl.edu.

Northcentral University, Graduate Studies, San Diego, CA 92106. Offers business (MBA, DBA, PhD, Postbaccalaureate Certificate); education (M Ed, Ed D, PhD, Ed S, Post-Master's Certificate, Postbaccalaureate Certificate); marriage and family therapy (MA, DMFT, PhD, Post-Master's Certificate, Postbaccalaureate Certificate); psychology (MA, PhD, Post-Master's Certificate, Postbaccalaureate Certificate). *Program availability:* Part-time, evening/weekend, online only, 100% online. *Faculty:* 98 full-time (63 women), 385 part-time/adjunct (203 women). *Students:* 5,036 full-time (3,291 women), 5,747 part-time (3,977 women); includes 3,777 minority (2,550 Black or African American, non-Hispanic/Latino; 76 American Indian or Alaska Native, non-Hispanic/Latino; 192 Asian, non-Hispanic/Latino; 603 Hispanic/Latino; 39 Native Hawaiian or other Pacific Islander, non-Hispanic/Latino; 317 Two or more races, non-Hispanic/Latino). Average age 45. In 2016, 799 master's, 399 doctorates, 230 other advanced degrees awarded. *Degree requirements:* For doctorate, comprehensive exam, thesis/dissertation. *Entrance requirements:* For master's, bachelor's degree from regionally- or nationally-accredited institution, current resume or curriculum vitae, statement of intent, interview, and background check (for marriage and family therapy); for doctorate, post-baccalaureate master's degree and/or doctoral degree from nationally- or regionally-accredited academic institution; for other advanced degree, bachelor's-level or higher degree from accredited institution or university (for Post-Baccalaureate Certificate); master's and/or doctoral degree from regionally- or nationally-accredited academic institution (for Post-Master's Certificate). Additional exam requirements/recommendations for international students: Required—TOEFL (minimum score 550 paper-based; 79 iBT), IELTS (minimum score 6.5), PTE (minimum score 53). *Application deadline:* Applications are processed on a rolling basis. Application fee: $0. Electronic applications accepted. *Expenses: Tuition:* Full-time $16,821; part-time $935 per credit hour. One-time fee: $350. Tuition and fees vary according to degree level and program. *Financial support:* Scholarships/grants available. *Faculty research:* Business management, curriculum and instruction, educational leadership, health psychology, organizational behavior. *Unit head:* Dr. David Harpool, Acting Provost, 888-327-2877

Ext. 8181, E-mail: provost@ncu.edu. *Application contact:* Ken Boutelle, Vice President, Enrollment Services, 888-628-4979, E-mail: enrollmentservices@ncu.edu.

North Dakota State University, College of Graduate and Interdisciplinary Studies, College of Business, Fargo, ND 58102. Offers accountancy (M Acc); business administration (MBA). *Accreditation:* AACSB. *Program availability:* Part-time, evening/weekend. *Entrance requirements:* For master's, GMAT. Additional exam requirements/recommendations for international students: Required—TOEFL (minimum score 550 paper-based; 79 iBT). Electronic applications accepted. *Faculty research:* Labor management, operations, international finance, agency, Internet marketing.

See Display below and Close-Up on page 183.

Northeastern Illinois University, College of Graduate Studies and Research, College of Business and Management, MBA Program, Chicago, IL 60625-4699. Offers MBA.

Northeastern State University, College of Business and Technology, Master of Business Administration Program, Tahlequah, OK 74464-2399. Offers MBA. *Accreditation:* ACBSP. *Program availability:* Part-time, evening/weekend. *Faculty:* 9 full-time (3 women). *Students:* 27 full-time (11 women), 37 part-time (19 women); includes 26 minority (7 Black or African American, non-Hispanic/Latino; 11 American Indian or Alaska Native, non-Hispanic/Latino; 2 Asian, non-Hispanic/Latino; 4 Hispanic/Latino; 2 Two or more races, non-Hispanic/Latino), 9 international. Average age 32. In 2016, 26 master's awarded. *Degree requirements:* For master's, comprehensive exam, thesis, business plan, oral exam. *Entrance requirements:* For master's, GMAT, minimum GPA of 2.5. Additional exam requirements/recommendations for international students: Required—TOEFL. *Application deadline:* For fall admission, 6/1 priority date for domestic students. Applications are processed on a rolling basis. Application fee: $25. Electronic applications accepted. *Expenses:* Tuition, state resident: full-time $2816; part-time $216.60 per credit hour. Tuition, nonresident: full-time $6365; part-time $489.60 per credit hour. *Required fees:* $37.40 per credit hour. *Financial support:* Teaching assistantships and Federal Work-Study available. Financial award application deadline: 3/1. *Unit head:* Dr. Dilene Crockett, Department Chair, 918-444-2940, E-mail: crocketd@nsuok.edu. *Application contact:* Josh McCollum, Graduate Coordinator, 918-444-2093, E-mail: mccolluj@nsuok.edu.
Website: http://academics.nsuok.edu/businesstechnology/Graduate/MBA.aspx

Northeastern State University, College of Business and Technology, Professional Master of Business Administration Program, Tahlequah, OK 74464-2399. Offers PMBA. *Program availability:* Part-time. *Faculty:* 9 full-time (3 women). *Students:* 2 full-time (0 women), 28 part-time (11 women); includes 16 minority (1 Black or African American, non-Hispanic/Latino; 6 American Indian or Alaska Native, non-Hispanic/Latino; 4 Asian, non-Hispanic/Latino; 1 Hispanic/Latino; 4 Two or more races, non-Hispanic/Latino), 1 international. Average age 36. In 2016, 2 master's awarded. *Degree requirements:* For master's, integrative project or research. *Application deadline:* Applications are processed on a rolling basis. Application fee: $25. Electronic applications accepted. *Expenses:* Tuition, state resident: full-time $2816; part-time $216.60 per credit hour. Tuition, nonresident: full-time $6365; part-time $489.60 per credit hour. *Required fees:* $37.40 per credit hour. *Unit head:* Dr. Dilene Crockett, Department Chair, 918-444-2940, E-mail: crocketd@nsuok.edu. *Application contact:* Josh McCollum, Graduate Coordinator, 918-444-2093, E-mail: mccolluj@nsuok.edu.
Website: http://academics.nsuok.edu/businesstechnology/Graduate/PMBA.aspx

Northeastern University, Bouvé College of Health Sciences, Boston, MA 02115-5096. Offers applied behavior analysis (MS); audiology (Au D); counseling psychology (MS, PhD, CAGS); exercise science (MS); nursing (MS, PhD, CAGS), including administration (MS), adult-gerontology acute care nurse practitioner (MS, CAGS), adult-gerontology primary care nurse practitioner (MS, CAGS), anesthesia (MS), family nurse practitioner (MS, CAGS), neonatal nurse practitioner (MS, CAGS), pediatric nurse practitioner (MS, CAGS), psychiatric mental health nurse practitioner (MS, CAGS); nursing practice (DNP); pharmaceutical sciences (MS, PhD), including interdisciplinary concentration, pharmaceutics and drug delivery systems; pharmacology (MS); pharmacy (Pharm D); school psychology (PhD); urban health (MPH); MS/MBA. *Accreditation:* ACPE (one or more programs are accredited). *Program availability:* Part-time, evening/weekend, online learning. *Faculty:* 192 full-time (119 women), 194 part-time/adjunct (156 women). *Students:* 1,371 full-time (1,009 women), 262 part-time (219 women). In 2016, 352 master's, 312 doctorates, 25 other advanced degrees awarded. *Degree requirements:* For doctorate, thesis/dissertation (for some programs); for CAGS, comprehensive exam. Application fee: $75. Electronic applications accepted. *Expenses:* Contact institution. *Financial support:* Fellowships, research assistantships, teaching assistantships, career-related internships or fieldwork, scholarships/grants, health care benefits, tuition waivers, and unspecified assistantships available. Support available to part-time students. Financial award applicants required to submit FAFSA. *Unit head:* Susan L. Parish, Dean, Bouve College of Health Sciences, 617-373-3323, Fax: 617-373-3030. *Application contact:* E-mail: bouvegrad@northeastern.edu.
Website: http://www.northeastern.edu/bouve/

Northeastern University, D'Amore-McKim School of Business, Boston, MA 02115-5096. Offers accounting (MS); business administration (EMBA, MBA); finance (MS); innovation (MS); international business (MS); international management (MS); taxation (MS); technological entrepreneurship (MS); JD/MBA; LL M/MBA; MBA/MSN; MS/MBA. *Accreditation:* AACSB. *Program availability:* Part-time, evening/weekend, online learning. *Faculty:* 185 full-time (66 women), 57 part-time/adjunct (13 women). *Students:* 379 full-time (180 women), 1,182 part-time (514 women). In 2016, 800 master's awarded. *Entrance requirements:* For master's, GMAT or GRE. Application fee: $75. Electronic applications accepted. *Expenses:* Contact institution. *Financial support:* Scholarships/grants available. Financial award applicants required to submit FAFSA. *Unit head:* Dr. Hugh Courtney, Dean, D'Amore-McKim School of Business. *Application contact:* Evelyn Tate, Director, Graduate Recruitment and Admissions, 617-373-3258, Fax: 617-373-8564, E-mail: e.tate@northeastern.edu.
Website: http://damore-mckim.northeastern.edu/

Northern Arizona University, Graduate College, NAU-Yuma, Master of Administration Program, Flagstaff, AZ 86011. Offers M Adm. *Program availability:* Part-time, online learning. *Degree requirements:* For master's, projects. *Entrance requirements:* For master's, five years' related work experience, minimum GPA of 3.0. Additional exam requirements/recommendations for international students: Required—TOEFL (minimum score 550 paper-based; 80 iBT), IELTS (minimum score 7). Electronic applications accepted. *Expenses:* Tuition, state resident: full-time $8971; part-time $444 per credit hour. Tuition, nonresident: full-time $20,958; part-time $1164 per credit hour. *Required fees:* $1018; $644 per credit hour. Tuition and fees vary according to course load, campus/location and program.

Northern Arizona University, Graduate College, The W. A. Franke College of Business, Flagstaff, AZ 86011. Offers MBA. *Accreditation:* AACSB. *Program availability:* Part-time. *Entrance requirements:* For master's, GMAT/GRE. Additional exam requirements/recommendations for international students: Required—TOEFL (minimum score 550 paper-based; 80 iBT), IELTS (minimum score 7). Electronic applications accepted. *Expenses:* Contact institution. *Faculty research:* Data processing applications for business situations and problems, accounting fraud, effects of sales tactics, self-efficacy and performance.

Northern Illinois University, Graduate School, College of Business, MBA Program, De Kalb, IL 60115-2854. Offers MBA. *Accreditation:* AACSB. *Program availability:* Part-time, evening/weekend. *Faculty:* 53 full-time (17 women), 3 part-time/adjunct (0

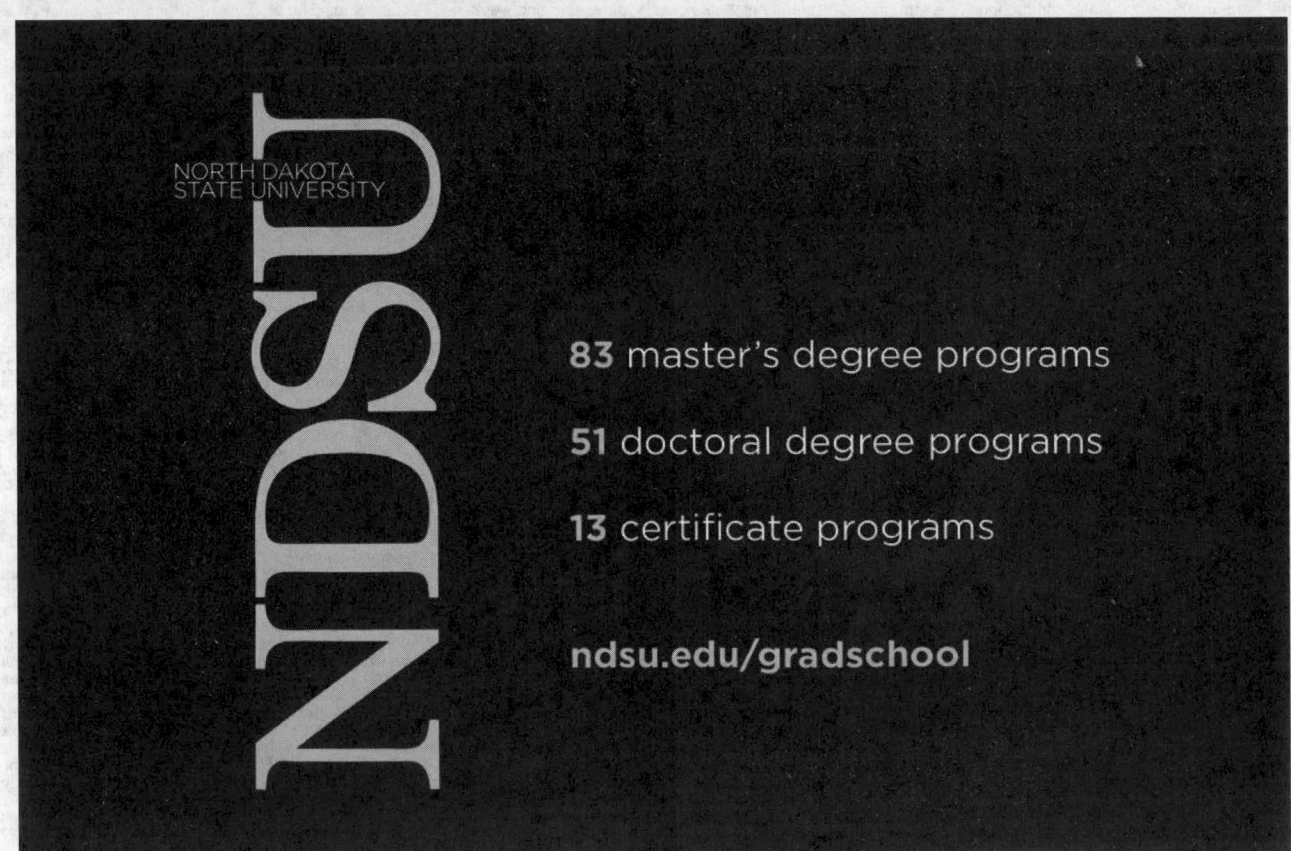

women). *Students:* 146 full-time (53 women), 331 part-time (94 women); includes 148 minority (32 Black or African American, non-Hispanic/Latino; 65 Asian, non-Hispanic/Latino; 33 Hispanic/Latino; 18 Two or more races, non-Hispanic/Latino), 19 international. Average age 34. 175 applicants, 136% accepted, 96 enrolled. In 2016, 307 master's awarded. *Degree requirements:* For master's, thesis optional, seminar. *Entrance requirements:* For master's, GMAT, minimum GPA of 2.75. Additional exam requirements/recommendations for international students: Required—TOEFL (minimum score 550 paper-based). *Application deadline:* For fall admission, 6/1 for domestic students, 5/1 for international students; for spring admission, 11/1 for domestic students, 10/1 for international students. Applications are processed on a rolling basis. Application fee: $40. Electronic applications accepted. *Financial support:* In 2016–17, 9 research assistantships with full tuition reimbursements, 4 teaching assistantships with full tuition reimbursements were awarded; fellowships with full tuition reimbursements, career-related internships or fieldwork, Federal Work-Study, scholarships/grants, tuition waivers (full), and unspecified assistantships also available. Support available to part-time students. Financial award applicants required to submit FAFSA. *Unit head:* Sarah Marsh, Chair, 815-753-1245, E-mail: mba@niu.edu. *Application contact:* Office of Graduate Studies in Business, 815-753-6301.
Website: http://www.cob.niu.edu/mbaprograms/

Northern Kentucky University, Office of Graduate Programs, College of Business, Program in Business Administration, Highland Heights, KY 41099. Offers MBA, Certificate, JD/MBA. *Accreditation:* AACSB. *Program availability:* Part-time, evening/weekend. *Degree requirements:* For master's, thesis optional, capstone course. *Entrance requirements:* For master's, GMAT, 3 years of work experience; undergraduate transcripts; 3 letters of recommendation; resume; essay explaining how MBA will benefit student in life and career. Additional exam requirements/recommendations for international students: Required—TOEFL (minimum score 79 iBT); Recommended—IELTS (minimum score 6.5). Electronic applications accepted. *Expenses:* Contact institution. *Faculty research:* Influence, diversity, organizational culture, ethics, corporate governance, corporate scandals, market research methods, consumer privacy, mergers and acquisitions of financial institutions, sustainability.

Northern Kentucky University, Office of Graduate Programs, College of Business, Program in Executive Leadership and Organizational Change, Highland Heights, KY 41099. Offers MS. *Program availability:* Part-time, evening/weekend. *Entrance requirements:* For master's, resume, current career essay, future career objectives essay, personal statement, 3 letters of recommendation with cover forms, transcripts. Additional exam requirements/recommendations for international students: Required—TOEFL (minimum score 79 iBT); Recommended—IELTS (minimum score 6.5). Electronic applications accepted. *Expenses:* Contact institution. *Faculty research:* Leadership assessment and development, teams and conflict management, organizational strategy development and systems thinking, organizational consultation.

Northern Michigan University, Office of Graduate Education and Research, College of Business, Marquette, MI 49855-5301. Offers MBA. *Accreditation:* AACSB. *Program availability:* Part-time. *Degree requirements:* For master's, strategic analysis research project and report in capstone course. *Entrance requirements:* For master's, GMAT, bachelor's degree; minimum undergraduate GPA of 3.0; statement of purpose; resume. Additional exam requirements/recommendations for international students: Required—TOEFL (minimum score 550 paper-based; 79 iBT), IELTS (minimum score 6.5). Electronic applications accepted.

North Park University, School of Business and Nonprofit Management, Chicago, IL 60625-4895. Offers MBA, MHEA, MHRM, MM, MNA. *Program availability:* Part-time, evening/weekend, online learning. *Entrance requirements:* For master's, GMAT, GRE. Additional exam requirements/recommendations for international students: Required—TOEFL. *Expenses:* Contact institution.

Northwest Christian University, School of Business and Management, Eugene, OR 97401-3745. Offers accounting (MBA); management (MBA). *Program availability:* Part-time, evening/weekend, online only, 100% online. *Faculty:* 4 full-time (1 woman), 5 part-time/adjunct (2 women). *Students:* 22 full-time (11 women), 38 part-time (11 women); includes 18 minority (3 Black or African American, non-Hispanic/Latino; 2 American Indian or Alaska Native, non-Hispanic/Latino; 4 Asian, non-Hispanic/Latino; 6 Hispanic/Latino; 3 Two or more races, non-Hispanic/Latino). Average age 33. In 2016, 32 master's awarded. *Entrance requirements:* For master's, GMAT, GRE, MAT, minimum undergraduate GPA of 3.0, 500-word essay, resume. Additional exam requirements/recommendations for international students: Required—TOEFL (minimum score 550 paper-based; 80 iBT). *Application deadline:* Applications are processed on a rolling basis. Electronic applications accepted. *Expenses:* $625 per credit tuition; $90 per semester technology fee. *Unit head:* Dr. Peter Diffenderfer, Assistant Dean, 541-684-7441, Fax: 541-684-7336, E-mail: pdiffenderfer@nwcu.edu. *Application contact:* Billy Dorsch, Admission Counselor for Graduate Studies, 541-684-7279, Fax: 541-349-5281, E-mail: wdorsch@nwcu.edu.

Northwestern Polytechnic University, School of Business and Information Technology, Fremont, CA 94539-7482. Offers MBA, DBA. *Program availability:* Part-time, evening/weekend. *Degree requirements:* For master's, thesis optional; for doctorate, thesis/dissertation. *Entrance requirements:* For master's, GMAT, minimum GPA of 3.0. Additional exam requirements/recommendations for international students: Required—TOEFL (minimum score 550 paper-based; 79 iBT). *Expenses:* Contact institution. *Faculty research:* Entrepreneurship, accounting, information technology.

Northwestern University, The Graduate School, Kellogg School of Management, Management Programs, Evanston, IL 60208. Offers accounting information and management (MBA, PhD); analytical finance (MBA); business administration (MBA); decision sciences (MBA); entrepreneurship and innovation (MBA); finance (MBA, PhD); health enterprise management (MBA); human resources management (MBA); international business (MBA); management and organizations (MBA, PhD); management and organizations and sociology (PhD); management and strategy (MBA); management studies (MS); managerial analytics (MBA); managerial economics (MBA); managerial economics and strategy (PhD); marketing (MBA, PhD); marketing management (MBA); media management (MBA); operations management (MBA, PhD); real estate (MBA); social enterprise at Kellogg (MBA); JD/MBA. *Program availability:* Part-time, evening/weekend. Terminal master's awarded for partial completion of doctoral program. *Degree requirements:* For doctorate, thesis/dissertation, 2 years of coursework, qualifying (field) exam and candidacy, summer research papers and presentations to faculty, proposal defense, final exam/defense. *Entrance requirements:* For master's, GMAT, GRE, interview, 2 letters of recommendation, college transcripts, resume, essays, Kellogg honor code; for doctorate, GMAT, GRE, statement of purpose, transcripts, 2 letters of recommendation, resume, interview. Additional exam requirements/recommendations for international students: Required—TOEFL, IELTS. Electronic applications accepted. *Expenses:* Contact institution. *Faculty research:* Business cycles and international finance, health policy, networks, non-market strategy, consumer psychology.

Northwestern University, McCormick School of Engineering and Applied Science, MMM Program, Evanston, IL 60208. Offers design innovation (MBA, MS). *Entrance requirements:* For master's, GMAT or GRE, transcripts, two letters of recommendation, resume, evaluative interview report, work experience, two core essays, interest essay, video essay. Additional exam requirements/recommendations for international students: Required—TOEFL, IELTS. *Expenses:* Contact institution.

Northwest Missouri State University, Graduate School, Melvin and Valorie Booth College of Business and Professional Studies, Maryville, MO 64468-6001. Offers agricultural economics (MBA); general management (MBA); human resource management (MBA); marketing (MBA). *Program availability:* Part-time. *Students:* 50 full-time (18 women), 50 part-time (27 women); includes 10 minority (5 Black or African American, non-Hispanic/Latino; 2 Asian, non-Hispanic/Latino; 3 Hispanic/Latino), 16 international. In 2016, 55 master's awarded. *Degree requirements:* For master's, comprehensive exam. *Entrance requirements:* For master's, GMAT, GRE, minimum GPA of 2.5. Additional exam requirements/recommendations for international students: Required—TOEFL (minimum score 550 paper-based). *Application deadline:* For fall admission, 7/1 for domestic and international students; for spring admission, 11/15 for domestic and international students; for summer admission, 4/1 for domestic and international students. Applications are processed on a rolling basis. Application fee: $0 ($50 for international students). Electronic applications accepted. *Expenses:* Tuition, state resident: full-time $3447; part-time $383 per credit hour. Tuition, nonresident: full-time $5724; part-time $636 per credit hour. *Required fees:* $130 per credit hour. *Financial support:* Research assistantships with full tuition reimbursements, teaching assistantships with full tuition reimbursements, career-related internships or fieldwork, and administrative assistantships, tutorial assistantships available. Financial award application deadline: 4/1; financial award applicants required to submit FAFSA. *Unit head:* Dr. Gregory Haddock, Dean of Graduate School, 660-562-1145, Fax: 660-562-1096, E-mail: gradsch@nwmissouri.edu.
Website: http://www.nwmissouri.edu/academics/booth/

Northwest Nazarene University, Program in Business Administration, Nampa, ID 83686-5897. Offers business administration (MBA). *Accreditation:* ACBSP. *Program availability:* Part-time, evening/weekend, 100% online, blended/hybrid learning. *Faculty:* 12 full-time (4 women), 14 part-time/adjunct (2 women). *Students:* 57 full-time (27 women), 30 part-time (10 women); includes 11 minority (1 Black or African American, non-Hispanic/Latino; 2 American Indian or Alaska Native, non-Hispanic/Latino; 2 Asian, non-Hispanic/Latino; 5 Hispanic/Latino; 1 Two or more races, non-Hispanic/Latino), 2 international. Average age 34. 26 applicants, 62% accepted, 11 enrolled. In 2016, 41 master's awarded. *Degree requirements:* For master's, comprehensive exam, thesis or alternative. *Entrance requirements:* For master's, minimum GPA of 3.0. Additional exam requirements/recommendations for international students: Required—TOEFL (minimum score 82 iBT). *Application deadline:* Applications are processed on a rolling basis. Application fee: $50. Electronic applications accepted. *Expenses:* Contact institution. *Faculty research:* Leadership, international business, economic sustainability, teaching pedagogy, teaching abroad. *Unit head:* Dr. Brenda Johnson, Director, 208-467-8415, Fax: 208-467-8440, E-mail: mba@nnu.edu. *Application contact:* Heather Beam, MBA Program Coordinator, 208-467-8100, Fax: 208-467-8440, E-mail: nnu-mba@nnu.edu.
Website: http://nnu.edu/mba

Northwest University, College of Business, Kirkland, WA 98033. Offers business administration (MBA); international business (MBA); project management (MBA); social entrepreneurship (MBA). *Accreditation:* ACBSP. *Program availability:* Part-time, evening/weekend. *Degree requirements:* For master's, formalized research. *Entrance requirements:* For master's, GMAT. Additional exam requirements/recommendations for international students: Required—TOEFL (minimum score 550 paper-based; 75 iBT). Electronic applications accepted. *Expenses:* Contact institution.

Northwood University, Michigan Campus, DeVos Graduate School, Midland, MI 48640-2398. Offers MBA, MSOL. MBA also offered on Florida and Texas campuses; MSOL offered online only. *Program availability:* Part-time, evening/weekend, online learning. *Degree requirements:* For master's, capstone project. *Entrance requirements:* For master's, GMAT, interview, letters of recommendation, resume. Additional exam requirements/recommendations for international students: Required—TOEFL (minimum score 550 paper-based). Electronic applications accepted.

Norwich University, College of Graduate and Continuing Studies, Master of Business Administration Program, Northfield, VT 05663. Offers construction management (MBA); energy management (MBA); finance (MBA); logistics (MBA); organizational leadership (MBA); project management (MBA); supply chain management (MBA). *Accreditation:* ACBSP. *Program availability:* Evening/weekend, online only, mostly all online with a week-long residency requirement. *Faculty:* 24 part-time/adjunct (5 women). *Students:* 228 full-time (54 women); includes 54 minority (23 Black or African American, non-Hispanic/Latino; 1 American Indian or Alaska Native, non-Hispanic/Latino; 6 Asian, non-Hispanic/Latino; 20 Hispanic/Latino; 1 Native Hawaiian or other Pacific Islander, non-Hispanic/Latino; 3 Two or more races, non-Hispanic/Latino), 2 international. Average age 36. 74 applicants, 100% accepted, 57 enrolled. In 2016, 135 master's awarded. *Degree requirements:* For master's, comprehensive exam. *Entrance requirements:* For master's, minimum undergraduate GPA of 2.75. Additional exam requirements/recommendations for international students: Required—TOEFL (minimum score 550 paper-based; 80 iBT), IELTS (minimum score 6.5). *Application deadline:* For fall admission, 8/14 for domestic and international students; for winter admission, 11/13 for domestic and international students; for spring admission, 2/12 for domestic and international students; for summer admission, 6/5 for domestic and international students. Electronic applications accepted. *Expenses:* Contact institution. *Financial support:* In 2016–17, 113 students received support. Scholarships/grants available. Financial award application deadline: 8/4; financial award applicants required to submit FAFSA. *Unit head:* Dr. Jose Cordova, Program Director, 802-485-2567, Fax: 802-485-2533, E-mail: jcordova@norwich.edu. *Application contact:* Admissions Advisor, 800-460-5597 Ext. 3376, Fax: 802-485-2533, E-mail: mba@online.norwich.edu.
Website: https://online.norwich.edu/degree-programs/masters/master-business-administration/overview

Notre Dame de Namur University, Division of Academic Affairs, School of Business and Management, Program in Business Administration, Belmont, CA 94002-1908. Offers business administration (MBA); entrepreneurship (MBA); finance (MBA); human resource management (MBA); marketing (MBA); media and promotion (MBA); technology and operations management (MBA). *Accreditation:* ACBSP. *Program availability:* Part-time, evening/weekend. *Entrance requirements:* For master's, minimum GPA of 2.5. Additional exam requirements/recommendations for international students: Required—TOEFL (minimum score 550 paper-based; 79 iBT). Electronic applications accepted.

Notre Dame de Namur University, Division of Academic Affairs, School of Business and Management, Program in Systems Management, Belmont, CA 94002-1908. Offers MSM. *Program availability:* Part-time, evening/weekend, online learning. *Entrance requirements:* For master's, minimum GPA of 2.5. Additional exam requirements/recommendations for international students: Required—TOEFL (minimum score 550 paper-based; 79 iBT). Electronic applications accepted.

Notre Dame of Maryland University, Graduate Studies, Program in Management, Baltimore, MD 21210-2476. Offers MA. *Program availability:* Part-time, evening/weekend. *Degree requirements:* For master's, thesis optional. *Entrance requirements:*

Business Administration and Management—General

For master's, minimum GPA of 3.0. Additional exam requirements/recommendations for international students: Required—TOEFL (minimum score 500 paper-based; 61 iBT). Electronic applications accepted.

Nova Southeastern University, H. Wayne Huizenga College of Business and Entrepreneurship, Fort Lauderdale, FL 33314-7796. Offers accounting (M Acc); business intelligence/analytics (MBA); entrepreneurship (MBA); finance (MBA); human resource management (MBA); international business (MBA); management (MBA); marketing (MBA); process improvement (MBA); public administration (MPA); real estate development (MS); sport revenue generation (MBA); supply chain management (MBA); taxation (M Tax). *Program availability:* Part-time, evening/weekend, 100% online, blended/hybrid learning. *Faculty:* 65 full-time (26 women), 111 part-time/adjunct (74 women). *Students:* 2,242 full-time (1,400 women), 425 part-time (239 women); includes 1,798 minority (734 Black or African American, non-Hispanic/Latino; 5 American Indian or Alaska Native, non-Hispanic/Latino; 110 Asian, non-Hispanic/Latino; 890 Hispanic/Latino; 2 Native Hawaiian or other Pacific Islander, non-Hispanic/Latino; 57 Two or more races, non-Hispanic/Latino), 255 international. Average age 34. 1,422 applicants, 64% accepted, 672 enrolled. In 2016, 971 master's awarded. *Degree requirements:* For master's, thesis optional. *Entrance requirements:* For master's, GMAT or GRE (depending on undergraduate GPA), official transcripts from all schools attended while in pursuit of bachelor's degree; minimum GPA of 2.5 from regionally-accredited institution. Additional exam requirements/recommendations for international students: Required—TOEFL (minimum score 550 paper-based; 79 iBT), IELTS (minimum score 6), PTE (minimum score 54). *Application deadline:* For fall admission, 8/5 priority date for domestic students, 7/29 priority date for international students; for winter admission, 12/16 priority date for domestic students, 12/9 priority date for international students; for summer admission, 4/21 priority date for domestic and international students. Applications are processed on a rolling basis. Application fee: $50. Electronic applications accepted. *Expenses:* Contact institution. *Financial support:* In 2016–17, 325 students received support. Federal Work-Study and scholarships/grants available. Support available to part-time students. Financial award application deadline: 4/15; financial award applicants required to submit FAFSA. *Faculty research:* Reputation management, call centers, international social capital, corporate earnings guidance, corporate governance. *Unit head:* Dr. J. Preston Jones, Dean, 954-262-5127, E-mail: prestonj@nova.edu. *Application contact:* Zeida Rodriguez, Associate Director of Enrollment Services, 954-262-5163, Fax: 954-262-3822, E-mail: zeida@nova.edu.
Website: http://www.huizenga.nova.edu

Nyack College, School of Business and Leadership, Nyack, NY 10960. Offers business administration (MBA); organizational leadership (MS). *Program availability:* Part-time, evening/weekend, 100% online, blended/hybrid learning. *Students:* 45 full-time (21 women), 20 part-time (15 women); includes 40 minority (26 Black or African American, non-Hispanic/Latino; 1 American Indian or Alaska Native, non-Hispanic/Latino; 4 Asian, non-Hispanic/Latino; 9 Hispanic/Latino), 5 international. Average age 38. In 2016, 40 master's awarded. *Degree requirements:* For master's, thesis (for some programs), capstone project (for MBA). *Entrance requirements:* For master's, GMAT (for MBA only), transcripts, personal goals statement, recommendations, resume, interview. Additional exam requirements/recommendations for international students: Required—TOEFL (minimum score 550 paper-based; 80 iBT), IELTS (minimum score 6.5). *Application deadline:* Applications are processed on a rolling basis. Application fee: $50. Electronic applications accepted. *Expenses:* $700 per credit (for MS); $775 per credit (for MBA). *Financial support:* Scholarships/grants available. Financial award applicants required to submit FAFSA. *Unit head:* Dr. Anita Underwood, Dean, 845-675-4511, Fax: 845-353-5812. *Application contact:* Joseph M. Williams, Graduate Admissions Associate, 800-541-6891, Fax: 845-348-3912, E-mail: admissions.grad@nyack.edu.
Website: http://www.nyack.edu/sbl

Oakland City University, School of Adult and Extended Learning, Oakland City, IN 47660-1099. Offers MBA. *Program availability:* Part-time, evening/weekend. *Degree requirements:* For master's, thesis or alternative. *Entrance requirements:* For master's, GMAT, GRE, or MAT, appropriate bachelor's degree, computer literacy. Additional exam requirements/recommendations for international students: Required—TOEFL. *Faculty research:* Leadership and management styles, international business, new technologies.

Oakland University, Graduate Study and Lifelong Learning, School of Business Administration, Rochester, MI 48309-4401. Offers EMBA, M Acc, MBA, MS, Certificate. *Accreditation:* AACSB. *Program availability:* Part-time, evening/weekend. *Entrance requirements:* For master's, GMAT, minimum GPA of 3.0. Additional exam requirements/recommendations for international students: Required—TOEFL (minimum score 550 paper-based). Electronic applications accepted. *Expenses:* Contact institution.

Oglala Lakota College, Graduate Studies, Program in Lakota Leadership and Management, Kyle, SD 57752-0490. Offers MA. *Program availability:* Part-time, evening/weekend. *Degree requirements:* For master's, thesis. *Entrance requirements:* For master's, minimum GPA of 2.5. *Faculty research:* Curriculum, values, retention of administrators, behavior, graduate follow-up.

Ohio Christian University, Graduate Programs, Circleville, OH 43113-9487. Offers accounting (MBA); business administration (MBA); digital marketing (MBA); finance (MBA); healthcare management (MBA); human resources (MBA); management (MM); organizational leadership (MBA); pastoral care and counseling (MAM); practical theology (MAM).

Ohio Dominican University, Division of Business, Columbus, OH 43219-2099. Offers business administration (MBA), including accounting, data analytics, finance, leadership, risk management, sport management; healthcare administration (MS); sport management (MS). *Accreditation:* ACBSP. *Program availability:* Part-time, evening/weekend, 100% online, blended/hybrid learning. *Faculty:* 11 full-time (5 women), 22 part-time/adjunct (8 women). *Students:* 80 full-time (34 women), 128 part-time (68 women); includes 63 minority (40 Black or African American, non-Hispanic/Latino; 2 American Indian or Alaska Native, non-Hispanic/Latino; 7 Asian, non-Hispanic/Latino; 6 Hispanic/Latino; 2 Native Hawaiian or other Pacific Islander, non-Hispanic/Latino; 6 Two or more races, non-Hispanic/Latino), 9 international. Average age 31. 91 applicants, 53% accepted, 37 enrolled. *Degree requirements:* For master's, thesis or alternative. *Entrance requirements:* Additional exam requirements/recommendations for international students: Required—TOEFL (minimum score 550 paper-based), IELTS (minimum score 6.5). *Application deadline:* For fall admission, 8/15 for domestic students, 6/10 for international students; for spring admission, 1/4 for domestic students, 11/2 for international students; for summer admission, 5/30 for domestic students. Applications are processed on a rolling basis. Application fee: $25. Electronic applications accepted. *Expenses:* Contact institution. *Financial support:* Applicants required to submit FAFSA. *Unit head:* Dr. Kenneth C. Fah, Chair, 614-251-4566, E-mail: fahk@ohiodominican.edu. *Application contact:* John W. Naughton, Director for Graduate Admissions, 614-251-4721, Fax: 614-251-6654, E-mail: grad@ohiodominican.edu.
Website: http://www.ohiodominican.edu/academics/graduate/mba

The Ohio State University, Graduate School, Max M. Fisher College of Business, Program in Business Administration, Columbus, OH 43210. Offers MA, MBA, PhD. *Accreditation:* AACSB. *Students:* 295 full-time (69 women), 297 part-time (89 women); includes 99 minority (23 Black or African American, non-Hispanic/Latino; 56 Asian, non-Hispanic/Latino; 13 Hispanic/Latino; 7 Two or more races, non-Hispanic/Latino), 118 international. Average age 31. In 2016, 256 master's, 6 doctorates awarded. *Degree requirements:* For doctorate, thesis/dissertation. *Entrance requirements:* For master's and doctorate, GMAT. Additional exam requirements/recommendations for international students: Required—TOEFL (minimum score 600 paper-based; 100 iBT), Michigan English Language Assessment Battery (minimum score 86); Recommended—IELTS (minimum score 7). *Application deadline:* For fall admission, 11/15 priority date for domestic and international students. Applications are processed on a rolling basis. Application fee: $60 ($70 for international students). Electronic applications accepted. *Financial support:* Fellowships, research assistantships, teaching assistantships, Federal Work-Study, institutionally sponsored loans, and unspecified assistantships available. Support available to part-time students. *Unit head:* Dr. Walter Zinn, Associate Dean for Students and Programs, 614-292-0797, E-mail: zinn.13@osu.edu. *Application contact:* Graduate and Professional Admissions, 614-292-9444, Fax: 614-292-3895, E-mail: gpadmissions@osu.edu.
Website: http://fisher.osu.edu/

The Ohio State University, Graduate School, Max M. Fisher College of Business, Program in Business Logistics Engineering, Columbus, OH 43210. Offers MBLE. *Students:* 57 full-time (30 women), 56 international. Average age 24. In 2016, 39 master's awarded. *Entrance requirements:* For master's, GRE or GMAT. Additional exam requirements/recommendations for international students: Required—TOEFL (minimum score 550 paper-based; 79 iBT), Michigan English Language Assessment Battery (minimum score 82); Recommended—IELTS (minimum score 7). *Application deadline:* For fall admission, 12/13 priority date for domestic students, 11/30 priority date for international students. Applications are processed on a rolling basis. Application fee: $60 ($70 for international students). Electronic applications accepted. *Financial support:* Scholarships/grants available. *Unit head:* Steve Denunzio, Program Director, 614-769-3155, E-mail: dununzio.4@osu.edu. *Application contact:* Graduate and Professional Admissions, 614-292-9444, Fax: 614-292-3895, E-mail: gpadmissions@osu.edu.
Website: http://fisher.osu.edu/mble

Ohio University, Graduate College, College of Business, Program in Business Administration, Athens, OH 45701-2979. Offers executive management (MBA); MBA/MSA. *Accreditation:* AACSB. *Program availability:* Part-time, evening/weekend, online learning. *Entrance requirements:* For master's, minimum GPA of 3.0. Additional exam requirements/recommendations for international students: Required—TOEFL (minimum score 600 paper-based). *Application deadline:* For fall admission, 7/30 for domestic students, 2/1 for international students; for spring admission, 11/30 for domestic students. Applications are processed on a rolling basis. Application fee: $50 ($55 for international students). Electronic applications accepted. *Expenses:* Contact institution. *Financial support:* Research assistantships with full and partial tuition reimbursements, career-related internships or fieldwork, and institutionally sponsored loans available. Financial award application deadline: 2/1. *Unit head:* Jeffrey Anderson, Director, 740-597-2901, E-mail: andersoj@ohio.edu. *Application contact:* Dr. William Lamb, Associate Dean, 740-593-2068, Fax: 740-593-1388, E-mail: lambw@ohio.edu.
Website: http://aspnet.cob.ohio.edu/isms/cob.aspx

Oklahoma Baptist University, Program in Business Administration, Shawnee, OK 74804. Offers business administration (MBA); energy management (MBA). *Accreditation:* ACBSP. *Program availability:* Online learning.

Oklahoma Christian University, Graduate School of Business, Oklahoma City, OK 73136-1100. Offers accounting (M Acc, MBA); financial services (MBA); general business (MBA); health services management (MBA); human resources (MBA); international business (MBA); leadership and organizational development (MBA); marketing (MBA); nonprofit management (MBA); project management (MBA). *Accreditation:* ACBSP. *Program availability:* Part-time, 100% online. *Faculty:* 10 full-time (2 women), 21 part-time/adjunct (2 women). *Students:* 156 full-time (68 women), 137 part-time (73 women). Average age 30. 374 applicants, 213 enrolled. In 2016, 114 master's awarded. *Entrance requirements:* For master's, bachelor's degree. Additional exam requirements/recommendations for international students: Required—TOEFL (minimum score 550 paper-based). Application fee: $25. Electronic applications accepted. *Expenses:* Contact institution. *Unit head:* Dr. Ken Johnson, Chair, 405-425-5567, Fax: 405-425-5585, E-mail: ken.johnson@oc.edu. *Application contact:* Angie Ricketts, Graduate School Admissions Counselor, 405-425-5587, Fax: 405-425-5585, E-mail: angie.ricketts@oc.edu.
Website: http://www.oc.edu/academics/graduate/business/

Oklahoma City University, Meinders School of Business, Oklahoma City, OK 73106-1402. Offers business (MBA, MSA); computer science (MS); energy legal studies (MS); energy management (MS); JD/MBA. *Program availability:* Part-time, evening/weekend, 100% online. *Faculty:* 17 full-time (3 women), 5 part-time/adjunct (1 woman). *Students:* 170 full-time (68 women), 218 part-time (90 women); includes 82 minority (17 Black or African American, non-Hispanic/Latino; 10 American Indian or Alaska Native, non-Hispanic/Latino; 16 Asian, non-Hispanic/Latino; 24 Hispanic/Latino; 15 Two or more races, non-Hispanic/Latino), 103 international. Average age 30. 592 applicants, 50% accepted, 138 enrolled. In 2016, 171 master's awarded. *Degree requirements:* For master's, practicum/capstone. *Entrance requirements:* For master's, undergraduate degree from accredited institution, minimum GPA of 3.0, essay, letters of recommendation. Additional exam requirements/recommendations for international students: Required—TOEFL (minimum score 550 paper-based; 80 iBT). *Application deadline:* Applications are processed on a rolling basis. Application fee: $50. Electronic applications accepted. *Expenses:* Contact institution. *Financial support:* In 2016–17, 262 students received support. Career-related internships or fieldwork, Federal Work-Study, institutionally sponsored loans, scholarships/grants, and tuition waivers (full and partial) available. Support available to part-time students. Financial award application deadline: 6/1; financial award applicants required to submit FAFSA. *Faculty research:* Group support systems, leadership, decision models in accounting. *Unit head:* Dr. Steve Agee, Dean, 405-208-5275, Fax: 405-208-5008, E-mail: sagee@okcu.edu. *Application contact:* Michael Harrington, Director of Graduate Admission, 800-633-7242, Fax: 405-208-5916, E-mail: gadmissions@okcu.edu.
Website: http://msb.okcu.edu

Oklahoma City University, Petree College of Arts and Sciences, Oklahoma City, OK 73106-1402. Offers applied behavioral studies (M Ed); applied sociology: nonprofit leadership (MA); creative writing (MFA); criminology (MS); early childhood education (M Ed); elementary education (M Ed); general studies (MLA); leadership/management (MLA); moving image arts (MFA); professional counseling (M Ed); teaching (MA); teaching English to speakers of other languages (MA). *Program availability:* Part-time, evening/weekend. *Faculty:* 11 full-time (5 women), 15 part-time/adjunct (6 women). *Students:* 77 full-time (55 women), 46 part-time (30 women); includes 32 minority (13 Black or African American, non-Hispanic/Latino; 1 American Indian or Alaska Native, non-Hispanic/Latino; 2 Asian, non-Hispanic/Latino; 12 Hispanic/Latino; 4 Two or more races, non-Hispanic/Latino), 37 international. Average age 34. 92 applicants, 74% accepted, 46 enrolled. In 2016, 72 master's awarded. *Degree requirements:* For master's, capstone/practicum. *Entrance requirements:* For master's, bachelor's degree

from accredited institution with minimum GPA of 3.0, essay, recommendation letters. Additional exam requirements/recommendations for international students: Required—TOEFL (minimum score 550 paper-based; 80 iBT). *Application deadline:* Applications are processed on a rolling basis. Application fee: $50. Electronic applications accepted. *Expenses:* Contact institution. *Financial support:* In 2016–17, 16 students received support. Federal Work-Study, institutionally sponsored loans, scholarships/grants, and tuition waivers (full and partial) available. Support available to part-time students. Financial award application deadline: 6/1; financial award applicants required to submit FAFSA. *Unit head:* Dr. Amy Cataldi, Dean, 405-208-5446, Fax: 405-208-5447, E-mail: acataldi@okcu.edu. *Application contact:* Michael Harrington, Director of Graduate Admissions, 800-633-7242, Fax: 405-208-5356, E-mail: gadmissions@okcu.edu.
Website: http://www.okcu.edu/petree/

Oklahoma State University, Spears School of Business, Department of Management, Stillwater, OK 74078. Offers MBA, MS, PhD. *Program availability:* Part-time. *Faculty:* 31 full-time (12 women), 3 part-time/adjunct (2 women). *Students:* 4 full-time (3 women), 1 part-time (0 women); includes 1 minority (Black or African American, non-Hispanic/Latino), 2 international. Average age 36. 3 applicants, 100% accepted, 3 enrolled. In 2016, 1 doctorate awarded. *Degree requirements:* For master's, thesis or alternative; for doctorate, comprehensive exam, thesis/dissertation. *Entrance requirements:* For master's and doctorate, GRE or GMAT. Additional exam requirements/recommendations for international students: Required—TOEFL (minimum score 550 paper-based; 79 iBT). *Application deadline:* For fall admission, 3/1 priority date for international students; for spring admission, 8/1 priority date for international students. Applications are processed on a rolling basis. Application fee: $40 ($75 for international students). Electronic applications accepted. *Expenses:* Tuition, state resident: full-time $3775; part-time $209.70 per credit hour. Tuition, nonresident: full-time $14,851; part-time $825.05 per credit hour. *Required fees:* $2027; $112.60 per credit hour. Tuition and fees vary according to campus/location. *Financial support:* In 2016–17, 7 research assistantships (averaging $14,500 per year), 23 teaching assistantships (averaging $6,448 per year) were awarded; career-related internships or fieldwork, Federal Work-Study, scholarships/grants, health care benefits, tuition waivers (partial), and unspecified assistantships also available. Support available to part-time students. Financial award application deadline: 3/1; financial award applicants required to submit FAFSA. *Faculty research:* Telecommunications management, innovative decision support techniques, knowledge networking, organizational research methods, strategic planning. *Unit head:* Dr. James Pappas, Department Head, 405-744-5201, Fax: 405-744-5180, E-mail: james.pappas@okstate.edu. *Application contact:* Dr. Toby Joplin, PhD Coordinator, 405-744-5115, Fax: 405-744-5180, E-mail: toby.joplin@okstate.edu.
Website: http://spears.okstate.edu/management

Old Dominion University, Strome College of Business, Doctoral Program in Business Administration, Norfolk, VA 23529. Offers finance (PhD); information technology (PhD); marketing (PhD); strategic management (PhD). *Accreditation:* AACSB. *Faculty:* 29 full-time (6 women). *Students:* 25 full-time (8 women), 23 part-time (5 women); includes 2 minority (both Asian, non-Hispanic/Latino), 38 international. Average age 34. 71 applicants, 17% accepted, 12 enrolled. In 2016, 15 doctorates awarded. *Degree requirements:* For doctorate, comprehensive exam, thesis/dissertation. *Entrance requirements:* For doctorate, GMAT. Additional exam requirements/recommendations for international students: Required—TOEFL (minimum score 550 paper-based; 79 iBT). *Application deadline:* For fall admission, 1/1 priority date for domestic and international students. Application fee: $50. Electronic applications accepted. *Expenses:* Tuition, state resident: full-time $8604; part-time $478 per credit hour. Tuition, nonresident: full-time $21,510; part-time $1195 per credit hour. *Required fees:* $66 per semester. Tuition and fees vary according to campus/location, program and reciprocity agreements. *Financial support:* In 2016–17, 36 students received support, including 15 research assistantships with full tuition reimbursements available (averaging $7,500 per year), 12 teaching assistantships with full tuition reimbursements available (averaging $7,500 per year); scholarships/grants and unspecified assistantships also available. Financial award application deadline: 3/1; financial award applicants required to submit FAFSA. *Faculty research:* International business, buyer behavior, financial markets, strategy, operations research. *Unit head:* Dr. John B. Ford, Graduate Program Director, 757-683-3587, Fax: 757-683-4076, E-mail: jbford@odu.edu. *Application contact:* Katrina Davenport, Program Coordinator, 757-683-5138, Fax: 757-683-4076,
E-mail: kdavenpo@odu.edu.
Website: http://www.odu.edu/business/academics/graduate/scb-phd

Old Dominion University, Strome College of Business, MBA Program, Norfolk, VA 23529. Offers MBA. *Accreditation:* AACSB. *Program availability:* Part-time, evening/weekend, 100% online, blended/hybrid learning. *Faculty:* 83 full-time (19 women), 1 part-time/adjunct (0 women). *Students:* 18 full-time (9 women), 131 part-time (57 women); includes 29 minority (13 Black or African American, non-Hispanic/Latino; 3 Asian, non-Hispanic/Latino; 6 Hispanic/Latino; 7 Two or more races, non-Hispanic/Latino), 11 international. Average age 32. 90 applicants, 68% accepted, 41 enrolled. In 2016, 56 master's awarded. *Entrance requirements:* For master's, GMAT, GRE, letter of reference, resume, essay, official transcripts from all previously attended institutions. Additional exam requirements/recommendations for international students: Required—TOEFL (minimum score 550 paper-based, 80 iBT) or IELTS. *Application deadline:* For fall admission, 6/1 priority date for domestic students, 4/15 priority date for international students; for spring admission, 11/1 priority date for domestic students, 10/1 priority date for international students; for summer admission, 3/1 priority date for domestic students, 2/1 priority date for international students. Applications are processed on a rolling basis. Application fee: $50. Electronic applications accepted. *Expenses:* $478 per credit hour in-state; $1,195 per credit hour out-of-state. *Financial support:* In 2016–17, 51 students received support, including 48 research assistantships with partial tuition reimbursements available (averaging $8,900 per year); career-related internships or fieldwork, scholarships/grants, and unspecified assistantships also available. Support available to part-time students. Financial award application deadline: 2/15; financial award applicants required to submit FAFSA. *Faculty research:* International business, buyer behavior, financial markets, strategy, operations research, maritime and transportation economics. *Total annual research expenditures:* $302,722. *Unit head:* Dr. David Cook, Assistant Dean for Graduate Studies, 757-683-3585, Fax: 757-683-5750, E-mail: mbainfo@odu.edu. *Application contact:* Sandi Phillips, Assistant MBA Program Manager, 757-683-3585, Fax: 757-683-5750, E-mail: mbainfo@odu.edu.
Website: http://www.odu.edu/mba

Olivet Nazarene University, Graduate School, Department of Business, Bourbonnais, IL 60914. Offers business administration (MBA). *Program availability:* Evening/weekend. *Degree requirements:* For master's, thesis or alternative. *Expenses:* Contact institution.

Open University, Graduate Programs, Milton Keynes, United Kingdom. Offers business (MBA); education (M Ed); engineering (M Eng); history (MA); music (MA); philosophy (MA).

Oral Roberts University, School of Business, Tulsa, OK 74171. Offers accounting (MBA); entrepreneurship (MBA); finance (MBA); international business (MBA); management (MBA); marketing (MBA); non-profit management (MBA); not for profit management (MNM). *Accreditation:* ACBSP. *Program availability:* Part-time, online learning. *Degree requirements:* For master's, thesis optional. *Entrance requirements:* For master's, minimum cumulative GPA of 3.0. Additional exam requirements/recommendations for international students: Required—TOEFL (minimum score 550 paper-based; 79 iBT). Electronic applications accepted. *Faculty research:* Social media, international business and marketing.

Oregon State University, College of Business, Corvallis, OR 97331. Offers MA, MBA, MS, PhD. *Accreditation:* AACSB. *Program availability:* Part-time, blended/hybrid learning. *Faculty:* 53 full-time (19 women), 10 part-time/adjunct (3 women). *Students:* 143 full-time (62 women), 90 part-time (43 women); includes 28 minority (3 Black or African American, non-Hispanic/Latino; 13 Asian, non-Hispanic/Latino; 9 Hispanic/Latino; 1 Native Hawaiian or other Pacific Islander, non-Hispanic/Latino; 2 Two or more races, non-Hispanic/Latino), 100 international. Average age 30. In 2016, 99 master's, 1 doctorate awarded. Application fee: $75 ($85 for international students). *Expenses:* $19,143 resident full-time tuition, $32,616 non-resident (for MBA). *Financial support:* Fellowships, teaching assistantships, career-related internships or fieldwork, Federal Work-Study, and institutionally sponsored loans available. *Faculty research:* Financial and account services, market analysis and planning, innovation, family business, tourism. *Unit head:* Dr. Mitzi Montoya, Dean. *Application contact:* Dr. Jim Coakley, Associate Dean for Academic Programs, 541-737-5510,
E-mail: jim.coakley@bus.oregonstate.edu.
Website: http://business.oregonstate.edu/

Ottawa University, Graduate Studies-Arizona, Programs in Business, Ottawa, KS 66067-3399. Offers business administration (MBA); finance (MBA); human resources (MA, MBA); leadership (MBA); marketing (MBA). Programs offered in Mesa, Phoenix, Tempe and West Valley, AZ. *Program availability:* Part-time, evening/weekend, online learning. *Degree requirements:* For master's, thesis or alternative. *Entrance requirements:* For master's, minimum undergraduate GPA of 3.0. Additional exam requirements/recommendations for international students: Required—TOEFL (minimum score 550 paper-based). Electronic applications accepted.

Ottawa University, Graduate Studies-International, Ottawa, KS 66067-3399. Offers business administration (MBA). *Program availability:* Online learning. *Degree requirements:* For master's, thesis or alternative. *Entrance requirements:* For master's, minimum undergraduate GPA of 3.0. Additional exam requirements/recommendations for international students: Required—TOEFL (minimum score 550 paper-based). Electronic applications accepted. *Expenses:* Contact institution.

Ottawa University, Graduate Studies-Kansas City, Overland Park, KS 66211. Offers business administration (MBA); human resources (MA). *Program availability:* Part-time, evening/weekend, online learning. *Degree requirements:* For master's, thesis or alternative. *Entrance requirements:* For master's, resume, 3 letters of recommendation. Additional exam requirements/recommendations for international students: Required—TOEFL (minimum score 550 paper-based). Electronic applications accepted. *Expenses:* Contact institution.

Ottawa University, Graduate Studies-Wisconsin, Brookfield, WI 53005. Offers business administration (MBA). *Program availability:* Part-time, evening/weekend, online learning. *Degree requirements:* For master's, thesis or alternative. *Entrance requirements:* For master's, resume, 3 letters of recommendation. Additional exam requirements/recommendations for international students: Required—TOEFL (minimum score 550 paper-based). Electronic applications accepted.

Otterbein University, Department of Business, Accounting and Economics, Westerville, OH 43081. Offers MBA. *Program availability:* Part-time, evening/weekend. *Degree requirements:* For master's, consulting project team. *Entrance requirements:* For master's, GMAT, 2 reference forms, resume. Additional exam requirements/recommendations for international students: Required—TOEFL (minimum score 550 paper-based; 79 iBT). *Expenses:* Contact institution. *Faculty research:* Organizational design, dispute resolution international trade, developing economies, marketing consumer goods, human resources development.

Our Lady of the Lake University, School of Business and Leadership, Program in Management, San Antonio, TX 78207-4689. Offers MBA. *Program availability:* Part-time, evening/weekend, 100% online, blended/hybrid learning. *Faculty:* 1 full-time (0 women), 6 part-time/adjunct (1 woman). *Students:* 99 full-time (58 women), 12 part-time (9 women); includes 78 minority (8 Black or African American, non-Hispanic/Latino; 4 Asian, non-Hispanic/Latino; 65 Hispanic/Latino; 1 Native Hawaiian or other Pacific Islander, non-Hispanic/Latino), 1 international. Average age 34. 32 applicants, 91% accepted, 19 enrolled. In 2016, 48 master's awarded. *Entrance requirements:* For master's, official transcripts showing 6 hours of coursework in economics and 3 hours of coursework in each of the following ares: statistics, management, business law, and finance; résumé including detailed work history describing managerial or professional work experience. Additional exam requirements/recommendations for international students: Required—TOEFL. *Application deadline:* For fall admission, 6/15 for domestic and international students; for spring admission, 11/15 for domestic and international students; for summer admission, 4/15 for domestic and international students. Applications are processed on a rolling basis. Application fee: $40 ($50 for international students). Electronic applications accepted. Application fee is waived when completed online. *Expenses: Tuition:* Full-time $14,796. Tuition and fees vary according to course load, degree level, campus/location and program. *Financial support:* In 2016–17, 52 students received support. Federal Work-Study, scholarships/grants, unspecified assistantships, and tuition discounts available. Support available to part-time students. Financial award application deadline: 5/1; financial award applicants required to submit FAFSA. *Application contact:* Office of Graduate Admissions, 210-431-3995, Fax: 210-431-3945, E-mail: gradadm@ollusa.edu.
Website: http://www.ollusa.edu/s/1190/hybrid/default-hybrid-ollu.aspx?sid-1190&gid-1&pgid-7873

Pace University, Lubin School of Business, New York, NY 10038. Offers MBA, MS, DPS, APC. *Accreditation:* AACSB. *Program availability:* Part-time, evening/weekend, blended/hybrid learning. *Students:* 525 full-time (274 women), 409 part-time (216 women); includes 235 minority (59 Black or African American, non-Hispanic/Latino; 2 American Indian or Alaska Native, non-Hispanic/Latino; 109 Asian, non-Hispanic/Latino; 52 Hispanic/Latino; 1 Native Hawaiian or other Pacific Islander, non-Hispanic/Latino; 12 Two or more races, non-Hispanic/Latino), 432 international. Average age 29. 1,148 applicants, 64% accepted, 300 enrolled. In 2016, 409 master's, 4 doctorates awarded. *Degree requirements:* For doctorate, thesis/dissertation, oral and written exam. *Entrance requirements:* For master's, GMAT, GRE, undergraduate degree, transcripts from all accredited colleges/universities attended, two letters of recommendation, resume, personal statement; for doctorate and APC, MBA or similar master's degree, 10 years of experience in business, transcripts from all accredited colleges/universities attended, 4 letters of recommendation, interview. Additional exam requirements/recommendations for international students: Required—TOEFL (minimum score 90 iBT), IELTS (minimum score 7) or PTE (minimum score 61). *Application deadline:* For fall admission, 8/1 priority date for domestic students, 6/1 for international students; for spring admission, 12/1 priority date for domestic students, 10/1 for international students; for summer admission, 5/1 priority date for domestic students, 3/1 for international students. Applications are processed on a rolling basis. Application fee: $70. Electronic applications accepted. *Expenses:* Contact institution. *Financial support:*

Research assistantships, career-related internships or fieldwork, Federal Work-Study, and tuition waivers (full and partial) available. Support available to part-time students. Financial award application deadline: 2/15; financial award applicants required to submit FAFSA. *Faculty research:* Accounting standards and reporting, financial markets and instruments, strategy and entrepreneurship, management learning, marketing and customers. *Total annual research expenditures:* $58,349. *Unit head:* Neil S. Braun, Dean, Lubin School of Business, 212-618-6600, Fax: 212-618-6603, E-mail: nbraun@pace.edu. *Application contact:* Susan Ford-Goldschein, Director of Graduate Admissions, 212-346-1531, Fax: 212-346-1585, E-mail: graduateadmission@pace.edu.
Website: http://www.pace.edu/lubin

Pacific Lutheran University, School of Business, MBA Program, Tacoma, WA 98447. Offers MBA. *Program availability:* Part-time, evening/weekend. *Entrance requirements:* For master's, GMAT or GRE, statement of professional goals, resume, two letters of recommendation. Additional exam requirements/recommendations for international students: Required—TOEFL (minimum score 88 iBT), IELTS (minimum score 6.5). Electronic applications accepted. *Expenses:* Contact institution.

Pacific States University, College of Business, Los Angeles, CA 90010. Offers accounting (MBA); finance (MBA); international business (MBA, DBA); management of information technology (MBA); real estate management (MBA). *Program availability:* Part-time, evening/weekend, online learning. *Degree requirements:* For doctorate, comprehensive exam, thesis/dissertation. *Entrance requirements:* For master's, minimum undergraduate GPA of 2.5 during last 90 hours of course work. Additional exam requirements/recommendations for international students: Required—TOEFL (minimum score 500 paper-based; 61 iBT), IELTS (minimum score 5.5).

Pacific University, College of Business, Forest Grove, OR 97116-1797. Offers business administration (MBA); finance (MSF).

Palm Beach Atlantic University, Rinker School of Business, West Palm Beach, FL 33416-4708. Offers MACC, MBA. *Program availability:* Part-time, evening/weekend. *Faculty:* 1 full-time (0 women), 9 part-time/adjunct (4 women). *Students:* 71 full-time (37 women), 21 part-time (7 women); includes 34 minority (15 Black or African American, non-Hispanic/Latino; 4 Asian, non-Hispanic/Latino; 13 Hispanic/Latino; 1 Native Hawaiian or other Pacific Islander, non-Hispanic/Latino; 1 Two or more races, non-Hispanic/Latino), 22 international. Average age 31. 32 applicants, 97% accepted, 25 enrolled. In 2016, 34 master's awarded. *Entrance requirements:* For master's, minimum GPA of 3.0. Additional exam requirements/recommendations for international students: Required—TOEFL (minimum score 550 paper-based; 79 iBT). *Application deadline:* Applications are processed on a rolling basis. Application fee: $50. Electronic applications accepted. *Expenses: Tuition:* Full-time $6600; part-time $550 per credit hour. Full-time tuition and fees vary according to degree level, campus/location and program. *Financial support:* Scholarships/grants and employee education grants available. Financial award application deadline: 5/1; financial award applicants required to submit FAFSA. *Faculty research:* International business, finance, banking. *Unit head:* Dr. David Smith, MBA Program Director, 561-803-2473, E-mail: david_smith@pba.edu. *Application contact:* Graduate Admissions, 888-468-6722, Fax: 561-803-2115, E-mail: grad@pba.edu.
Website: http://www.pba.edu/bus-mba

Park University, School of Graduate and Professional Studies, Kansas City, MO 54105. Offers adult education (M Ed); business and government leadership (Graduate Certificate); business, government, and global society (MPA); communication and leadership (MA); creative and life writing (Graduate Certificate); disaster and emergency management (MPA, Graduate Certificate); educational leadership (M Ed); finance (MBA, Graduate Certificate); general business (MBA); global business (Graduate Certificate); healthcare administration (MHA); healthcare services management and leadership (Graduate Certificate); international business (MBA); language and literacy (M Ed), including English for speakers of other languages, special reading teacher/literacy coach; leadership of international healthcare organizations (Graduate Certificate); management information systems (MBA, Graduate Certificate); music performance (ADP, Graduate Certificate), including cello (MM, ADP), piano (MM, ADP), viola (MM, ADP), violin (MM, ADP); nonprofit and community services management (MPA); nonprofit leadership (Graduate Certificate); performance (MM), including cello (MM, ADP), piano (MM, ADP), viola (MM, ADP), violin (MM, ADP); public management (MPA); social work (MSW); teacher leadership (M Ed), including curriculum and assessment, instructional leader. *Program availability:* Part-time, evening/weekend, online learning. *Degree requirements:* For master's, comprehensive exam (for some programs), thesis (for some programs), internship (for some programs); exam (for some programs). *Entrance requirements:* For master's, GRE or GMAT (for some programs), teacher certification (for some M Ed programs), letters of recommendation, essay, resume (for some programs). Additional exam requirements/recommendations for international students: Required—TOEFL (minimum score 550 paper-based; 79 iBT), IELTS (minimum score 6). Electronic applications accepted.

Penn State Erie, The Behrend College, Graduate School, Erie, PA 16563. Offers accounting (MPAC); business administration (MBA); project management (MPM); quality and manufacturing management (MMM). *Accreditation:* AACSB. *Program availability:* Part-time. *Students:* 28 full-time (9 women), 118 part-time (31 women); includes 11 minority (5 Black or African American, non-Hispanic/Latino; 2 Asian, non-Hispanic/Latino; 1 Hispanic/Latino; 3 Two or more races, non-Hispanic/Latino), 2 international. Average age 32. 91 applicants, 74% accepted, 55 enrolled. In 2016, 59 master's awarded. *Entrance requirements:* Additional exam requirements/recommendations for international students: Required—TOEFL (minimum score 550 paper-based; 80 iBT), IELTS. *Application deadline:* Applications are processed on a rolling basis. Application fee: $65. Electronic applications accepted. *Financial support:* Federal Work-Study available. Financial award application deadline: 3/1; financial award applicants required to submit FAFSA. *Unit head:* Dr. Ralph M. Ford, Chancellor, 814-898-6160, Fax: 814-898-6461. *Application contact:* Ann M. Burbules, Assistant Director, Graduate Admissions, 866-374-3378, Fax: 814-898-6044, E-mail: behrend.admissions@psu.edu.
Website: http://behrend.psu.edu/

Penn State Great Valley, Graduate Studies, Management Division, Malvern, PA 19355-1488. Offers business administration (MBA); cyber security (Certificate); data analytics (Certificate); distributed energy and grid modernization (Certificate); finance (M Fin, Certificate); health sector management (Certificate); human resource management (Certificate); information science (MSIS); leadership development (MLD); new ventures and entrepreneurship (Certificate); professional studies in data analytics (MPS); sustainable management practices (Certificate). *Accreditation:* AACSB. *Unit head:* Dr. James A. Nemes, Chancellor, 610-648-3202, Fax: 610-725-5296. *Application contact:* JoAnn Kelly, Director of Admissions, 610-648-3315, Fax: 610-725-5296, E-mail: jek2@psu.edu.
Website: http://greatvalley.psu.edu/academics/masters-degrees/engineering-management

Penn State Harrisburg, Graduate School, School of Business Administration, Middletown, PA 17057. Offers accounting (MPAC, Certificate); business administration (MBA); information systems (MS); operations and supply chain management (Certificate). *Program availability:* Part-time, evening/weekend. *Unit head:* Dr. Mukund S. Kulkarni, Chancellor, 717-948-6105, Fax: 717-948-6452. *Application contact:* Robert W. Coffman, Jr., Director of Enrollment Management, Admissions, 717-948-6250, Fax: 717-948-6325, E-mail: hbgadmit@psu.edu.
Website: https://harrisburg.psu.edu/business-administration/

Penn State University Park, Graduate School, Smeal College of Business, University Park, PA 16802. Offers accounting (M Acc); business administration (MBA, MS, PhD); management and organizational leadership (MPS); supply chain management (MPS). *Accreditation:* AACSB. *Students:* 276 full-time (90 women). Average age 30. 1,243 applicants, 26% accepted, 260 enrolled. In 2016, 274 master's, 11 doctorates awarded. *Entrance requirements:* Additional exam requirements/recommendations for international students: Required—TOEFL (minimum score 550 paper-based; 80 iBT), IELTS. *Application deadline:* Applications are processed on a rolling basis. Application fee: $65. Electronic applications accepted. *Financial support:* Fellowships, research assistantships, teaching assistantships, career-related internships or fieldwork, Federal Work-Study, scholarships/grants, traineeships, health care benefits, and unspecified assistantships available. Support available to part-time students. Financial award application deadline: 3/1; financial award applicants required to submit FAFSA. *Unit head:* Dr. Charles H. Whiteman, Dean, 814-863-0448, Fax: 814-865-7064. *Application contact:* Lori Hawn, Director, Graduate Student Services, 814-865-1795, Fax: 814-863-4627, E-mail: l-gswww@lists.psu.edu.
Website: http://smeal.psu.edu/

Pensacola Christian College, Graduate Studies, Pensacola, FL 32503-2267. Offers business administration (MBA); curriculum and instruction (MS, Ed D, Ed S); dramatics (MFA); educational leadership (MS, Ed D, Ed S); graphic design (MA, MFA); music (MA); nursing (MSN); performance studies (MA); studio art (MA, MFA).

Pepperdine University, Graziadio School of Business and Management, Full-Time MBA Programs, Malibu, CA 90263. Offers accounting (MS); applied analytics (MS); applied finance (MS); business administration (MBA); global business (MS); human resources (MS); international business administration (MBA); management and leadership (MS); organization development (MS); real estate investment and finance (MS); JD/MBA; MBA/MPP. *Accreditation:* AACSB. *Students:* 472 full-time (239 women), 3 part-time (2 women); includes 424 minority (111 Black or African American, non-Hispanic/Latino; 7 American Indian or Alaska Native, non-Hispanic/Latino; 216 Asian, non-Hispanic/Latino; 88 Hispanic/Latino; 2 Two or more races, non-Hispanic/Latino), 47 international. Average age 25. 1,991 applicants, 59% accepted, 238 enrolled. In 2016, 419 master's awarded. *Entrance requirements:* For master's, GMAT or GRE, two letters of recommendation. Additional exam requirements/recommendations for international students: Required—TOEFL. *Application deadline:* For fall admission, 5/1 for domestic students, 4/1 for international students. Application fee: $75. Electronic applications accepted. *Financial support:* Applicants required to submit FAFSA. *Unit head:* Dr. Michael L. Williams, Associate Dean, 310-506-4112, Fax: 310-506-4126, E-mail: michael.williams@pepperdine.edu.
Website: http://bschool.pepperdine.edu/masters-degree/

Pepperdine University, Graziadio School of Business and Management, Part-Time MBA Programs, Malibu, CA 90263. Offers MBA. *Students:* 484 full-time (202 women), 844 part-time (420 women); includes 424 minority (111 Black or African American, non-Hispanic/Latino; 7 American Indian or Alaska Native, non-Hispanic/Latino; 216 Asian, non-Hispanic/Latino; 88 Hispanic/Latino; 2 Two or more races, non-Hispanic/Latino), 47 international. Average age 33. 577 applicants, 76% accepted, 285 enrolled. In 2016, 309 master's awarded. *Entrance requirements:* For master's, GMAT or GRE, two letters of recommendation. Additional exam requirements/recommendations for international students: Required—TOEFL. *Application deadline:* For fall admission, 1/10 for domestic students. Application fee: $75. *Financial support:* Scholarships/grants available. Financial award applicants required to submit FAFSA. *Unit head:* Annie Carr, Director of Program Advisement and Student Support, 310-568-5515, E-mail: annie.carr@pepperdine.edu.
Website: http://bschool.pepperdine.edu/masters-degree/

Pepperdine University, Seaver College, Malibu, CA 90263. Offers business (MS), including accounting; communication (MA, MFA), including cinematic media production (MFA), strategic communication (MA); humanities (MA, MFA), including American studies (MA), writing for screen and television (MFA); religion (M Div, MA, MS), including ministry (MS), religion (M Div, MA); JD/M Div. *Program availability:* Part-time, evening/weekend. *Students:* 22 full-time (12 women), 91 part-time (54 women); includes 32 minority (10 Black or African American, non-Hispanic/Latino; 2 American Indian or Alaska Native, non-Hispanic/Latino; 8 Asian, non-Hispanic/Latino; 9 Hispanic/Latino; 1 Native Hawaiian or other Pacific Islander, non-Hispanic/Latino; 2 Two or more races, non-Hispanic/Latino), 10 international. Average age 29. 162 applicants, 51% accepted, 42 enrolled. In 2016, 36 master's awarded. *Entrance requirements:* For master's, GRE General Test. Additional exam requirements/recommendations for international students: Required—TOEFL. *Application deadline:* For fall admission, 2/1 priority date for domestic students. Applications are processed on a rolling basis. Application fee: $55. *Expenses:* $49,770 per academic year; $1,565 per unit. *Financial support:* Fellowships, research assistantships, teaching assistantships, career-related internships or fieldwork, Federal Work-Study, institutionally sponsored loans, scholarships/grants, and tuition waivers (partial) available. Support available to part-time students. Financial award application deadline: 2/15; financial award applicants required to submit FAFSA. *Unit head:* Dr. Dana Dudley, Assistant Dean, Special Academic and Graduate Programs for Seaver College, 310-506-6047, Fax: 310-506-4816, E-mail: dana.dudley@pepperdine.edu. *Application contact:* Joy Brown, Admission Counselor, 310-506-4392, E-mail: joy.brown@pepperdine.edu.
Website: http://seaver.pepperdine.edu/

Pfeiffer University, Program in Business Administration, Misenheimer, NC 28109-0960. Offers MBA, MBA/MHA. *Program availability:* Part-time, evening/weekend, online learning. *Entrance requirements:* For master's, GMAT, minimum GPA of 3.0.

Philadelphia University, School of Business Administration, Program in Business Administration, Philadelphia, PA 19144. Offers general business (MBA); innovation (MBA); management (MBA); marketing (MBA); strategic design (MBA); MBA/MS. *Program availability:* Part-time, evening/weekend, online learning. *Entrance requirements:* For master's, GMAT. Additional exam requirements/recommendations for international students: Required—TOEFL (minimum score 550 paper-based; 79 iBT).

Phillips Theological Seminary, Programs in Theology, Tulsa, OK 74116. Offers administration of church agencies (M Div); campus ministry (M Div); church-related social work (M Div); college and seminary teaching (M Div); global mission work (M Div); institutional chaplaincy (M Div); ministerial vocations in Christian education (M Div); ministry (D Min), including parish ministry, pastoral counseling, practices of ministry; ministry and culture (MAMC), including Christian education, congregational leadership, history and practice of Christian spirituality, theology, ethics, and culture; ministry of music (M Div); pastoral care and counseling (M Div); pastoral ministry (M Div); theological studies (MTS). *Accreditation:* ATS. *Program availability:* Part-time, online learning. *Degree requirements:* For master's, thesis (for some programs); for doctorate, thesis/dissertation. *Entrance requirements:* For master's, minimum GPA of 2.5; for doctorate, M Div, minimum GPA of 3.0. *Faculty research:* Biblical studies, historical studies, theology and culture, practical theology, theology and film.

Piedmont College, School of Business, Demorest, GA 30535. Offers MBA. *Accreditation:* ACBSP. *Program availability:* Part-time, evening/weekend. *Students:* 44 full-time (23 women), 16 part-time (9 women); includes 6 minority (4 Black or African American, non-Hispanic/Latino; 2 Hispanic/Latino). Average age 29. 29 applicants, 62% accepted, 15 enrolled. In 2016, 35 master's awarded. *Degree requirements:* For master's, capstone. *Entrance requirements:* For master's, GMAT, GRE. Additional exam requirements/recommendations for international students: Required—TOEFL (minimum score 550 paper-based). *Application deadline:* For fall admission, 7/15 for domestic students; for spring admission, 12/1 for domestic students. Applications are processed on a rolling basis. Electronic applications accepted. *Expenses: Tuition:* Full-time $8910. *Financial support:* Federal Work-Study and unspecified assistantships available. Financial award applicants required to submit FAFSA. *Unit head:* Dr. Edward Taylor, Dean, 706-778-3000, E-mail: etaylor@piedmont.edu. *Application contact:* Kathleen Carter, Director of Graduate Enrollment Management, 706-778-3000, E-mail: kcarter@piedmont.edu.
Website: http://www.piedmont.edu

Pittsburg State University, Graduate School, Kelce College of Business, Department of Management and Marketing, Pittsburg, KS 66762. Offers general administration (MBA); international business (MBA). *Accreditation:* AACSB. *Program availability:* Part-time. *Students:* 50 (24 women). In 2016, 35 master's awarded. *Degree requirements:* For master's, thesis or alternative. *Entrance requirements:* For master's, GMAT or GRE. Additional exam requirements/recommendations for international students: Required—TOEFL (minimum score 550 paper-based; 79 iBT), IELTS (minimum score 6.5), PTE (minimum score 53). *Application deadline:* For fall admission, 7/15 for domestic students, 6/1 for international students; for spring admission, 12/15 for domestic students, 10/15 for international students; for summer admission, 5/15 for domestic students, 4/1 for international students. Applications are processed on a rolling basis. Application fee: $35 ($60 for international students). Electronic applications accepted. *Expenses:* Contact institution. *Financial support:* In 2016–17, 10 teaching assistantships with full tuition reimbursements (averaging $5,500 per year) were awarded; research assistantships, career-related internships or fieldwork, Federal Work-Study, and unspecified assistantships also available. Financial award application deadline: 2/1; financial award applicants required to submit FAFSA. *Faculty research:* Consumer behavior, productions management, forecasting interest rate swaps, strategy management. *Unit head:* Dr. Bienvenido Cortes, MBA Coordinator, 620-235-4594, E-mail: bcortes@pittstate.edu. *Application contact:* Lisa Allen, Assistant Director of Graduate and Continuing Studies, 620-235-4218, Fax: 620-235-4219, E-mail: lallen@pittstate.edu.
Website: http://www.pittstate.edu/mgmkt/

Plymouth State University, College of Graduate Studies, Graduate Studies in Business, Plymouth, NH 03264-1595. Offers general management (MBA). *Accreditation:* ACBSP. *Program availability:* Part-time, evening/weekend, online learning. *Entrance requirements:* For master's, minimum GPA of 2.5. Additional exam requirements/recommendations for international students: Required—TOEFL (minimum score 550 paper-based). *Expenses:* Contact institution.

Point Loma Nazarene University, Fermanian School of Business, San Diego, CA 92106-2899. Offers general business (MBA); healthcare management (MBA); innovation and entrepreneurship (MBA); organizational leadership (MBA); project management (MBA). *Accreditation:* ACBSP. *Program availability:* Part-time, evening/weekend. *Faculty:* 8 full-time (1 woman), 8 part-time/adjunct (4 women). *Students:* 33 full-time (14 women), 64 part-time (30 women); includes 32 minority (6 Black or African American, non-Hispanic/Latino; 4 Asian, non-Hispanic/Latino; 19 Hispanic/Latino; 3 Two or more races, non-Hispanic/Latino), 7 international. Average age 31. 71 applicants, 79% accepted, 47 enrolled. In 2016, 37 master's awarded. *Entrance requirements:* For master's, GMAT, letters of recommendation, essay, interview. Additional exam requirements/recommendations for international students: Required—TOEFL. *Application deadline:* For fall admission, 7/26 priority date for domestic students; for spring admission, 11/29 priority date for domestic students; for summer admission, 4/2 priority date for domestic students. Applications are processed on a rolling basis. Application fee: $50. Electronic applications accepted. *Expenses:* $825 per credit. *Financial support:* Applicants required to submit FAFSA. *Unit head:* Jamie Ressler, Associate Dean, Graduate Business, 619-849-2721, E-mail: jamieressler@pointloma.edu. *Application contact:* Claire Buckley, Director of Graduate Admission, 866-692-4723, E-mail: gradinfo@pointloma.edu.
Website: http://www.pointloma.edu/discover/graduate-school-san-diego/san-diego-graduate-programs-masters-degree-san-diego/mba

Point Park University, School of Business, Department of Business, Pittsburgh, PA 15222-1984. Offers business analytics (MBA); health systems management (MBA); international business (MBA); management (MBA); management information systems (MBA); sports, arts and entertainment management (MBA). *Program availability:* Evening/weekend, online learning.

Polytechnic University of Puerto Rico, Graduate School, Hato Rey, PR 00918. Offers business administration (MBA), including computer information systems, general management, management of information systems, management of international enterprises; civil engineering (ME, MS); computer engineering (ME, MS); computer science (MCS, MS); electrical engineering (ME, MS); engineering management (MEM); environmental management (MEM); landscape architecture (M Land Arch); manufacturing competitiveness (MMC, MS); manufacturing engineering (ME, MS); mechanical engineering (M Mech E). *Program availability:* Part-time, evening/weekend. *Entrance requirements:* For master's, 3 letters of recommendation.

Polytechnic University of Puerto Rico, Miami Campus, Graduate School, Miami, FL 33166. Offers accounting (MBA); business administration (MBA); construction management (MEM); environmental management (MEM); finance (MBA); human resources management (MBA); logistics and supply chain management (MBA); management of international enterprises (MBA); manufacturing management (MEM); marketing management (MBA); project management (MBA). *Program availability:* Part-time, evening/weekend, online learning. *Entrance requirements:* For master's, minimum GPA of 3.0. Electronic applications accepted.

Polytechnic University of Puerto Rico, Orlando Campus, Graduate School, Orlando, FL 32825. Offers accounting (MBA); business administration (MBA); construction management (MEM); engineering management (MEM); environmental management (MEM); finance (MBA); human resources management (MBA); management of international enterprises (MBA); management of technology (MBA); manufacturing management (MEM). *Program availability:* Part-time, evening/weekend, online learning. *Entrance requirements:* For master's, minimum GPA of 3.0. Additional exam requirements/recommendations for international students: Recommended—TOEFL. Electronic applications accepted.

Pontifical Catholic University of Puerto Rico, College of Business Administration, Ponce, PR 00717-0777. Offers MBA, DBA, PhD, Professional Certificate. *Program availability:* Part-time, evening/weekend. *Degree requirements:* For master's, thesis; for doctorate, comprehensive exam, thesis/dissertation. *Entrance requirements:* For master's, GRE, interview, minimum GPA of 2.75; for doctorate, 2 letters of recommendation, 2 years experience in a related field, interview.

Pontificia Universidad Catolica Madre y Maestra, Graduate School, Faculty of Social and Administrative Sciences, Santiago, Dominican Republic. Offers business administration (MBA), including business development, finance, international business, management skills (M Mgmt, MBA), marketing, operations, strategic cost management, strategy, tourist destination planning and management; law (LL M), including civil law, corporate business law, criminal law, international relations, real estate law; management (M Mgmt), including higher financial management, insurance program administration, management skills (M Mgmt, MBA); psychology (MA), including clinical child and adolescent psychology, forensic psychology; strategic human resources (EMBA).

Portland State University, Graduate Studies, College of Liberal Arts and Sciences, Systems Science Program, Portland, OR 97207-0751. Offers computational intelligence (Certificate); computer modeling and simulation (Certificate); systems science (MS); systems science/anthropology (PhD); systems science/business administration (PhD); systems science/civil engineering (PhD); systems science/economics (PhD); systems science/engineering management (PhD); systems science/general (PhD); systems science/mathematical sciences (PhD); systems science/mechanical engineering (PhD); systems science/psychology (PhD); systems science/sociology (PhD). *Faculty:* 2 full-time (0 women), 3 part-time/adjunct (1 woman). *Students:* 12 full-time (3 women), 21 part-time (5 women); includes 5 minority (1 Black or African American, non-Hispanic/Latino; 2 Hispanic/Latino; 2 Two or more races, non-Hispanic/Latino). Average age 39. 16 applicants, 69% accepted, 9 enrolled. In 2016, 4 master's, 6 doctorates awarded. *Degree requirements:* For master's, comprehensive exam (for some programs), thesis optional; for doctorate, variable foreign language requirement, comprehensive exam (for some programs), thesis/dissertation. *Entrance requirements:* For master's, GRE/GMAT (recommended), minimum GPA of 3.0 undergraduate or graduate work, 2 letters of recommendation, statement of interest; for doctorate, GMAT, GRE General Test, minimum GPA of 3.0 undergraduate, 3.25 graduate; 2 letters of recommendation; statement of interest. Additional exam requirements/recommendations for international students: Required—TOEFL (minimum score 550 paper-based; 80 iBT). *Application deadline:* For fall admission, 1/15 for domestic and international students; for spring admission, 11/1 for domestic students. Application fee: $65. Electronic applications accepted. *Expenses:* Contact institution. *Financial support:* In 2016–17, 2 research assistantships with tuition reimbursements (averaging $7,830 per year) were awarded; teaching assistantships, career-related internships or fieldwork, Federal Work-Study, scholarships/grants, and unspecified assistantships also available. Support available to part-time students. Financial award application deadline: 3/1; financial award applicants required to submit FAFSA. *Faculty research:* Systems theory and methodology, artificial intelligence neural networks, information theory, nonlinear dynamics/chaos, modeling and simulation. *Unit head:* Dr. Wayne Wakeland, Chair, 503-725-4975, E-mail: wakeland@pdx.edu.
Website: http://www.pdx.edu/sysc/

Portland State University, Graduate Studies, School of Business Administration, Program in Business Administration, Portland, OR 97207-0751. Offers MBA. *Accreditation:* AACSB. *Program availability:* Part-time, evening/weekend. *Faculty:* 41 full-time (22 women), 72 part-time/adjunct (18 women). *Students:* 127 full-time (60 women), 58 part-time (24 women); includes 39 minority (5 Black or African American, non-Hispanic/Latino; 1 American Indian or Alaska Native, non-Hispanic/Latino; 17 Asian, non-Hispanic/Latino; 8 Hispanic/Latino; 8 Two or more races, non-Hispanic/Latino), 32 international. Average age 34. 183 applicants, 61% accepted, 80 enrolled. In 2016, 47 master's awarded. *Degree requirements:* For master's, one foreign language, project. *Entrance requirements:* For master's, GMAT or GRE, minimum GPA of 3.0 in upper-division course work, 2 recommendations, resume, interview. Additional exam requirements/recommendations for international students: Required—TOEFL (minimum score 550 paper-based). *Application deadline:* For fall admission, 2/1 priority date for domestic and international students. Applications are processed on a rolling basis. Application fee: $65. Electronic applications accepted. *Expenses:* Contact institution. *Financial support:* In 2016–17, 16 research assistantships with partial tuition reimbursements (averaging $7,987 per year) were awarded; teaching assistantships with partial tuition reimbursements, career-related internships or fieldwork, and Federal Work-Study also available. Support available to part-time students. Financial award application deadline: 3/1; financial award applicants required to submit FAFSA. *Faculty research:* Quality management and organizational excellence, performance measurement, customer satisfaction, values, technology management and technology transfer. *Total annual research expenditures:* $211,260. *Unit head:* Tichelle Sorensen, MBA Academic Director, 503-725-9936, Fax: 503-725-5850, E-mail: sorenset@pdx.edu.
Website: http://www.pdx.edu/sba/master-of-business-administration

Post University, Program in Business Administration, Waterbury, CT 06723-2540. Offers accounting (MSA); business administration (MBA); corporate innovation (MBA); entrepreneurship (MBA); finance (MBA); healthcare (MBA); leadership (MBA); marketing (MBA); project management (MBA). *Accreditation:* ACBSP. *Program availability:* Online learning.

Prairie View A&M University, College of Business, Prairie View, TX 77446. Offers accounting (MS); business administration (MBA). *Accreditation:* AACSB. *Program availability:* Part-time, evening/weekend. *Faculty:* 16 full-time (2 women). *Students:* 81 full-time (49 women), 157 part-time (89 women); includes 205 minority (181 Black or African American, non-Hispanic/Latino; 14 Asian, non-Hispanic/Latino; 10 Hispanic/Latino), 18 international. Average age 32. 172 applicants, 94% accepted, 104 enrolled. In 2016, 87 master's awarded. *Degree requirements:* For master's, comprehensive exam, thesis optional. *Entrance requirements:* For master's, GMAT, GRE, minimum GPA of 2.45, essay. Additional exam requirements/recommendations for international students: Required—TOEFL (minimum score 550 paper-based; 79 iBT). *Application deadline:* For fall admission, 5/1 for domestic students, 5/1 priority date for international students; for spring admission, 10/1 for domestic students, 9/1 priority date for international students; for summer admission, 3/1 for domestic students, 2/1 for international students. Applications are processed on a rolling basis. Application fee: $50. Electronic applications accepted. *Expenses:* Contact institution. *Financial support:* In 2016–17, 5 students received support, including 2 research assistantships (averaging $24,000 per year), 5 teaching assistantships (averaging $60,000 per year); scholarships/grants and unspecified assistantships also available. Financial award application deadline: 4/1; financial award applicants required to submit FAFSA. *Faculty research:* Accounting (energy, oil and gas); finance (international finance, personal finance, real estate markets and institutions); marketing management (supply chain, human resources, entrepreneurship, small business ownership, ethics); management information systems (cyber-security, managing social media during crises). *Unit head:* Dr. Munir Quddus, Dean, 936-261-9200, Fax: 936-261-9241, E-mail: cob@pvamu.edu. *Application contact:* Gabriel Crosby, Director, Graduate Programs in Business, 936-261-9217, Fax: 936-261-9232, E-mail: mba@pvamu.edu.
Website: http://www.pvamu.edu/business/

Business Administration and Management—General

Presidio Graduate School, MBA Programs - Seattle, San Francisco, CA 94129. Offers co-operative management (Certificate); food and agriculture systems (Certificate); sustainable business (MBA); sustainable systems (MBA). *Program availability:* Part-time, evening/weekend, blended/hybrid learning. *Students:* Average age 34. *Entrance requirements:* For master's and Certificate, Quantitative Assessment Summary, GRE, or GMAT, resume, two letters of recommendation, essay, transcripts. Additional exam requirements/recommendations for international students: Required—TOEFL (minimum score 90 iBT), IELTS (minimum score 6.5). *Application deadline:* For fall admission, 6/1 priority date for domestic and international students. Applications are processed on a rolling basis. Application fee: $75. Electronic applications accepted. *Financial support:* Scholarships/grants available. Financial award application deadline: 6/15; financial award applicants required to submit FAFSA. *Unit head:* Steven Crane, Provost, 415-651-6555, E-mail: info@presidio.edu. *Application contact:* Kari Dorth, Director of Admissions, 415-655-8912, E-mail: admissions@presidio.edu.
Website: https://www.presidio.edu/seattle-mbas-overview/

Providence College, School of Business, Providence, RI 02918. Offers accounting (MBA); finance (MBA); international business (MBA); management (MBA); marketing (MBA). *Accreditation:* AACSB. *Program availability:* Part-time, evening/weekend. *Faculty:* 10 full-time (3 women), 5 part-time/adjunct (2 women). *Students:* 84 full-time (39 women), 66 part-time (23 women); includes 15 minority (6 Black or African American, non-Hispanic/Latino; 1 Asian, non-Hispanic/Latino; 8 Hispanic/Latino), 5 international. Average age 26. 116 applicants, 96% accepted, 94 enrolled. In 2016, 80 master's awarded. *Entrance requirements:* For master's, GMAT. Additional exam requirements/recommendations for international students: Required—TOEFL (minimum score 577 paper-based; 90 iBT). *Application deadline:* For fall admission, 5/1 priority date for domestic and international students; for spring admission, 11/1 priority date for domestic and international students; for summer admission, 3/15 priority date for domestic students, 3/15 for international students. Applications are processed on a rolling basis. Application fee: $55. *Expenses:* Contact institution. *Financial support:* Career-related internships or fieldwork, institutionally sponsored loans, and unspecified assistantships available. Support available to part-time students. Financial award application deadline: 8/1; financial award applicants required to submit FAFSA.
Website: http://www.providence.edu/business/Pages/default.aspx

★ **Purdue University,** Graduate School, Krannert School of Management, Doctoral Program in Management, West Lafayette, IN 47907-2056. Offers PhD. *Degree requirements:* For doctorate, comprehensive exam, thesis/dissertation, first-year summer paper, dissertation proposal, dissertation defense. *Entrance requirements:* For doctorate, GMAT or GRE. Additional exam requirements/recommendations for international students: Required—TOEFL (minimum score 575 paper-based); Recommended—TWE. Electronic applications accepted. *Faculty research:* Accounting, finance, marketing, management information systems, operations management, organizational behavior and human resource management, quantitative methods/management science, strategic management.

See Display below and Close-Up on page 187.

★ **Purdue University,** Graduate School, Krannert School of Management, Executive MBA Programs, West Lafayette, IN 47907-2056. Offers EMBA. *Faculty:* 15 full-time (3 women), 6 part-time/adjunct (0 women). *Students:* 52 part-time (10 women); includes 17 minority (3 Black or African American, non-Hispanic/Latino; 1 American Indian or Alaska Native, non-Hispanic/Latino; 10 Asian, non-Hispanic/Latino; 3 Hispanic/Latino). Average age 38. In 2016, 1 master's awarded. *Entrance requirements:* For master's, two professional recommendations; essays; official transcripts and, in some instances, copy of diploma; current professional resume; in-person or virtual interview. *Application deadline:* For fall admission, 7/15 for domestic and international students; for spring admission, 1/31 for domestic and international students. Applications are processed on a rolling basis. Application fee: $60 ($75 for international students). Electronic applications accepted. *Expenses:* Contact institution. *Financial support:* In 2016–17, 40 students received support. Scholarships/grants available. Financial award application deadline: 5/31. *Faculty research:* Trust in organizations, alliances, organizational change, negotiations, risk management. *Unit head:* Dr. Aldas P. Kriauciunas, Executive Director, 765-496-1860, Fax: 765-494-0862, E-mail: akriauci@purdue.edu. *Application contact:* Nancy Smigiel, Associate Director of Admissions, 765-494-4580, Fax: 765-494-0862, E-mail: nks@purdue.edu.
Website: http://www.krannert.purdue.edu/executive/home.php

See Display below and Close-Up on page 187.

★ **Purdue University,** Graduate School, Krannert School of Management, Master of Business Administration Program, West Lafayette, IN 47907. Offers MBA. *Accreditation:* AACSB. *Faculty:* 129 full-time (28 women), 7 part-time/adjunct (1 woman). *Students:* 147 full-time (41 women); includes 23 minority (7 Black or African American, non-Hispanic/Latino; 9 Asian, non-Hispanic/Latino; 1 Hispanic/Latino; 1 Native Hawaiian or other Pacific Islander, non-Hispanic/Latino; 5 Two or more races, non-Hispanic/Latino), 59 international. Average age 27. 453 applicants, 36% accepted, 77 enrolled. In 2016, 81 master's awarded. *Entrance requirements:* For master's, GMAT, four-year baccalaureate degree, minimum GPA of 3.0, essays, recommendation letters, work/internship experience. Additional exam requirements/recommendations for international students: Required—TOEFL (minimum score 600 paper-based; 93 iBT), IELTS (minimum score 7.5), or PTE (minimum score 70). *Application deadline:* For fall admission, 11/15 for domestic and international students; for winter admission, 1/15 for domestic and international students; for spring admission, 3/1 for domestic and international students; for summer admission, 5/1 for domestic students. Applications are processed on a rolling basis. Application fee: $60 ($75 for international students). Electronic applications accepted. *Expenses:* Contact institution. *Financial support:* In 2016–17, 47 students received support. Scholarships/grants and unspecified assistantships available. Financial award applicants required to submit FAFSA. *Faculty research:* Capital market imperfections and the sensitivity of investment to stock prices, identifying beneficial collaboration in decentralized logistics systems, performance periods and the dynamics of the performance-risk relationship, applications of global optimization to process and molecular design. *Unit head:* Dr. David Hummels, Dean/Professor of Economics, 765-494-4366, E-mail: krannertdean@purdue.edu. *Application contact:* Thomas Bates, Associate Director of Admissions, 765-494-0773, Fax: 765-494-9841, E-mail: krannertmasters@purdue.edu.
Website: http://www.krannert.purdue.edu/masters/mba/mba-fulltime/

See Display on next page and Close-Ups on pages 185 and 187.

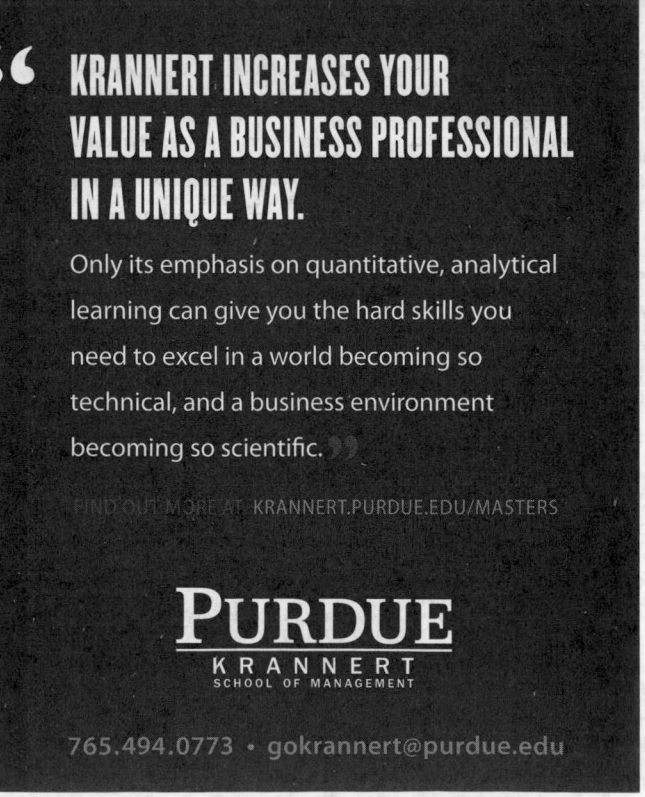

★ **Purdue University,** Graduate School, Krannert School of Management, Weekend Master of Business Administration Program, West Lafayette, IN 47907. Offers MBA. *Program availability:* Part-time-only, evening/weekend. *Faculty:* 12 full-time (3 women), 1 part-time/adjunct (0 women). *Students:* 85 part-time (22 women); includes 15 minority (4 Black or African American, non-Hispanic/Latino; 7 Asian, non-Hispanic/Latino; 1 Hispanic/Latino; 3 Two or more races, non-Hispanic/Latino), 6 international. Average age 34. 77 applicants, 90% accepted, 57 enrolled. In 2016, 30 master's awarded. *Entrance requirements:* For master's, GMAT, minimum GPA of 3.0, four-year baccalaureate degree, essays, letters of recommendation. Additional exam requirements/recommendations for international students: Required—TOEFL (minimum score 600 paper-based; 93 iBT), IELTS (minimum score 7.5), PTE (minimum score 70). *Application deadline:* For fall admission, 11/1 for domestic students, 11/15 for international students; for winter admission, 1/15 for domestic and international students; for spring admission, 3/1 for domestic and

international students; for summer admission, 5/1 for domestic and international students. Applications are processed on a rolling basis. Application fee: $60 ($75 for international students). Electronic applications accepted. *Expenses:* Contact institution. *Financial support:* In 2016–17, 41 students received support. Scholarships/grants available. Financial award applicants required to submit FAFSA. *Unit head:* Dr. David Hummels, Dean/Professor of Economics, 765-494-4366, E-mail: krannertdean@purdue.edu. *Application contact:* Thomas Bates, Associate Director of Admissions, 765-494-0773, Fax: 765-494-9841, E-mail: krannertmasters@purdue.edu.
Website: http://www.krannert.purdue.edu/masters/mba/weekend-mba/

See Display below and Close-Up on page 187.

Purdue University Northwest, Graduate Studies Office, School of Management, Hammond, IN 46323-2094. Offers accountancy (M Acc); business administration (MBA); business administration for executives (EMBA). *Accreditation:* AACSB. *Program availability:* Part-time, evening/weekend. *Entrance requirements:* For master's, GMAT. Additional exam requirements/recommendations for international students: Required—TOEFL. Electronic applications accepted.

Queen's University at Kingston, Queens School of Business, Program in Business Administration, Kingston, ON K7L 3N6, Canada. Offers consulting and project management (MBA); finance (MBA); innovation and entrepreneurship (MBA); marketing (MBA). *Degree requirements:* For master's, thesis optional, research project. *Entrance requirements:* For master's, GMAT, minimum B+ average. Additional exam requirements/recommendations for international students: Required—TOEFL. Electronic applications accepted. *Faculty research:* Management fundamentals, strategic thinking, global business, innovation and change, leadership.

Queens University of Charlotte, McColl School of Business, Charlotte, NC 28274-0002. Offers business administration (EMBA, MBA, PMBA); organization development (MSOD). *Accreditation:* AACSB. *Program availability:* Part-time, evening/weekend, online learning. *Degree requirements:* For master's, capstone course. *Entrance requirements:* For master's, GMAT, minimum GPA of 2.5. Additional exam requirements/recommendations for international students: Required—TOEFL. Electronic applications accepted. *Expenses:* Contact institution.

Quincy University, MBA Program, Quincy, IL 62301-2699. Offers MBA. *Program availability:* Part-time, evening/weekend, online learning. *Entrance requirements:* For master's, GMAT (if GPA less than 3.0), previous course work in accounting, economics, finance, management or marketing, and statistics. Additional exam requirements/recommendations for international students: Required—TOEFL (minimum score 550 paper-based; 79 iBT). Electronic applications accepted. *Expenses:* Contact institution. *Faculty research:* Macroeconomic forecasting.

Quinnipiac University, School of Business and Engineering, Program in Business Administration, Hamden, CT 06518-1940. Offers chartered financial analyst (MBA); health care management (MBA); supply chain management (MBA); JD/MBA. *Accreditation:* AACSB. *Program availability:* Part-time, evening/weekend, 100% online, blended/hybrid learning. *Faculty:* 29 full-time (8 women), 8 part-time/adjunct (2 women). *Students:* 195 full-time (87 women), 257 part-time (123 women); includes 59 minority (9 Black or African American, non-Hispanic/Latino; 19 Asian, non-Hispanic/Latino; 24 Hispanic/Latino; 7 Two or more races, non-Hispanic/Latino), 23 international. 307 applicants, 79% accepted, 223 enrolled. In 2016, 188 master's awarded. *Entrance requirements:* For master's, GMAT or GRE, minimum GPA of 3.0. Additional exam requirements/recommendations for international students: Required—TOEFL (minimum score 575 paper-based; 90 iBT), IELTS (minimum score 6.5). *Application deadline:* For fall admission, 7/30 priority date for domestic students, 4/30 priority date for international students; for spring admission, 12/15 priority date for domestic students, 9/30 priority date for international students. Applications are processed on a rolling basis. Application fee: $45. Electronic applications accepted. *Expenses:* Contact institution. *Financial support:* Career-related internships or fieldwork, Federal Work-Study, scholarships/grants, and unspecified assistantships available. Financial award application deadline: 6/1; financial award applicants required to submit FAFSA. *Faculty research:* Financial markets and investments, international business, supply chain management, health care management, corporate governance. *Unit head:* Lisa Braiewa, Director of the MBA Program, 800-462-1944, Fax: 203-582-3443, E-mail: graduate@qu.edu. *Application contact:* Office of Graduate Admissions, 800-462-1944, Fax: 203-582-3443, E-mail: graduate@qu.edu.
Website: http://www.qu.edu/mba

Radford University, College of Graduate Studies and Research, Program in Business Administration, Radford, VA 24142. Offers MBA. *Accreditation:* AACSB. *Program availability:* Part-time, evening/weekend, online learning. *Faculty:* 7 full-time (4 women). *Students:* 8 full-time (4 women), 29 part-time (10 women); includes 1 minority (Black or African American, non-Hispanic/Latino), 5 international. Average age 32. 37 applicants, 65% accepted, 15 enrolled. In 2016, 21 master's awarded. *Entrance requirements:* For master's, GMAT or GRE (waiver may be submitted based on work experience), minimum GPA of 2.75, 2 letters of reference, letter of intent, resume, official transcripts. Additional exam requirements/recommendations for international students: Required—TOEFL (minimum score 550 paper-based; 79 iBT), IELTS (minimum score 6.5). *Application deadline:* For fall admission, 2/15 priority date for domestic students, 12/1 for international students; for spring admission, 7/1 for international students. Applications are processed on a rolling basis. Application fee: $50. Electronic applications accepted. *Expenses:* Tuition, state resident: full-time $7868; part-time $328 per credit hour. Tuition, nonresident: full-time $16,394; part-time $683 per credit hour. *Required fees:* $3090; $130 per credit hour. Tuition and fees vary according to course load and program. *Financial support:* In 2016–17, 8 students received support, including 3 teaching assistantships (averaging $10,000 per year); scholarships/grants and unspecified assistantships also available. Support available to part-time students. Financial award application deadline: 3/1; financial award applicants required to submit FAFSA. *Unit head:* Dr. Stacey Turmel, Director, MBA Program, 540-831-6905, E-mail: rumba@radford.edu.
Website: http://www.radford.edu/content/cobe/home/programs/mba.html

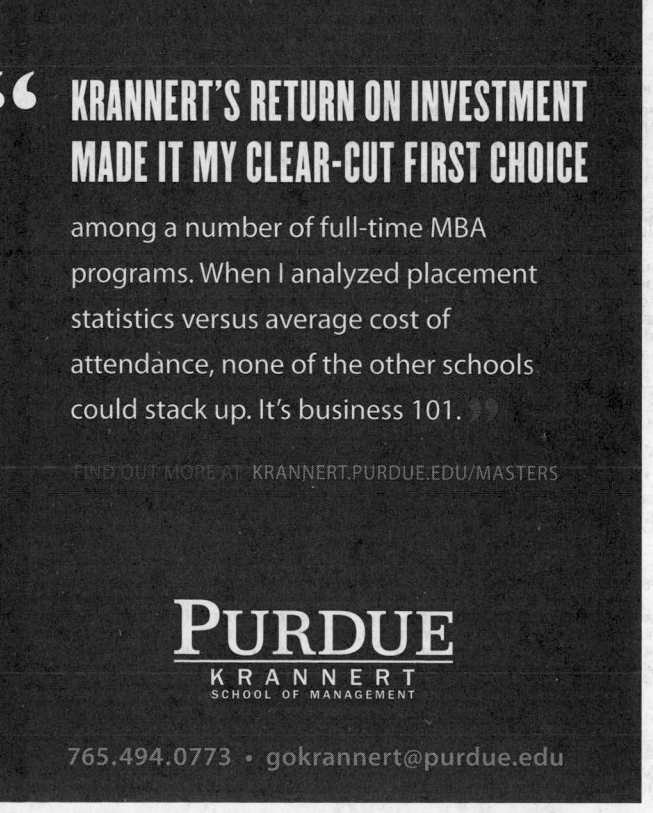

Ramapo College of New Jersey, Master of Business Administration Program, Mahwah, NJ 07430-1680. Offers leadership (MBA). *Accreditation:* AACSB. *Program availability:* Part-time-only, evening/weekend. *Faculty:* 3 full-time (all women). *Students:* 66 part-time (29 women); includes 17 minority (6 Black or African American, non-Hispanic/Latino; 1 American Indian or Alaska Native, non-Hispanic/Latino; 4 Asian, non-Hispanic/Latino; 5 Hispanic/Latino; 1 Two or more races, non-Hispanic/Latino). Average age 32. 115 applicants, 40% accepted, 32 enrolled. In 2016, 28 master's awarded. *Degree requirements:* For master's, capstone course. *Entrance requirements:* For master's, official transcript of baccalaureate degree from accredited institution with minimum recommended GPA of 3.0; personal statement; 2 letters of recommendation; resume. Additional exam requirements/recommendations for international students: Required—TOEFL (minimum score 550 paper-based; 79 iBT); Recommended—IELTS (minimum score 6). *Application deadline:* For fall admission, 5/1 for domestic and international students. Applications are processed on a rolling basis. Application fee: $60. Electronic applications accepted. *Expenses:* $1,098.50 per credit tuition and fees. *Financial support:* Career-related internships or fieldwork and scholarships/grants available. Financial award application deadline: 3/1; financial award applicants required to submit FAFSA. *Faculty research:* Ethical implications of taxation on society, organizational governance, applied labor economics, empirical market microstructure, foreign direct investment. *Unit head:* Dr. Edward Petkus, Dean of the Anisfield School of Business, 201-684-7377, E-mail: epetkus@ramapo.edu. *Application contact:* Timothy

Landers, Assistant Dean/Director of the MBA Program, 201-684-7771, E-mail: tlanders@ramapo.edu.
Website: http://www.ramapo.edu/mba/

Regent's University London, Webster Graduate School, London, United Kingdom. Offers business (MBA); finance (MS); human resources (MA); information technology management (MA); international business (MA); international non-governmental organizations (MA); international relations (MA); management and leadership (MA); marketing (MA). *Program availability:* Part-time.

Regent University, Graduate School, School of Business and Leadership, Virginia Beach, VA 23464-9800. Offers business administration (MBA), including accounting, entrepreneurship, finance and investing, general management, healthcare management (MA, MBA), human resource management, innovation management; leadership (Certificate); organizational leadership (MA, PhD), including ecclesial leadership (PhD), entrepreneurial leadership (PhD), future studies (MA), healthcare management (MA, MBA), human resource development (PhD), interdisciplinary studies (MA), international organizations (MA), leadership coaching and mentoring (MA), not-for-profit management (MA), organizational communication (MA), organizational development consulting (MA); strategic leadership (DSL), including global consulting, leadership coaching, strategic foresight. *Program availability:* Part-time, evening/weekend, 100% online, blended/hybrid learning. *Faculty:* 9 full-time (2 women), 28 part-time/adjunct (10 women). *Students:* 100 full-time (56 women), 1,008 part-time (528 women); includes 562 minority (453 Black or African American, non-Hispanic/Latino; 7 American Indian or Alaska Native, non-Hispanic/Latino; 30 Asian, non-Hispanic/Latino; 51 Hispanic/Latino; 1 Native Hawaiian or other Pacific Islander, non-Hispanic/Latino; 20 Two or more races, non-Hispanic/Latino), 76 international. Average age 40. 1,240 applicants, 45% accepted, 352 enrolled. In 2016, 95 master's, 71 doctorates awarded. *Degree requirements:* For master's, thesis or alternative, 3-credit hour culminating experience; for doctorate, thesis/dissertation. *Entrance requirements:* For master's, college transcripts, resume, essay; for doctorate, college transcripts, resume, essay, writing sample; for Certificate, writing sample, resume, transcripts. Additional exam requirements/recommendations for international students: Required—TOEFL (minimum score 577 paper-based). *Application deadline:* For fall admission, 5/1 priority date for domestic students; for spring admission, 10/1 priority date for domestic students. Applications are processed on a rolling basis. Application fee: $50. Electronic applications accepted. *Expenses:* Contact institution. *Financial support:* In 2016–17, 631 students received support. Career-related internships or fieldwork, scholarships/grants, and unspecified assistantships available. Support available to part-time students. *Faculty research:* Servant leadership, global business, team effectiveness, technology utilization, leadership development. *Unit head:* Dr. Doris Gomez, Dean, 757-352-4686, Fax: 757-352-4634, E-mail: dorigom@regent.edu. *Application contact:* Heidi Cece, Assistant Vice President of Enrollment Management, 800-373-5504, Fax: 757-352-4381, E-mail: admissions@regent.edu.
Website: http://www.regent.edu/sbl/

Reinhardt University, McCamish School of Business, Waleska, GA 30183-2981. Offers MBA. Program offered at the Chattahoochee Technical College campus in downtown Woodstock, GA. *Program availability:* Part-time, evening/weekend. *Degree requirements:* For master's, comprehensive exam. *Entrance requirements:* For master's, GMAT (minimum score 500), bachelor's degree with minimum GPA of 2.75, current resume, interview, 3 professional references. Additional exam requirements/recommendations for international students: Required—TOEFL. *Application deadline:* For fall admission, 5/7 for domestic and international students; for spring admission, 8/9 for domestic and international students. Applications are processed on a rolling basis. Application fee: $25. Electronic applications accepted. *Expenses:* Contact institution. *Financial support:* Application deadline: 5/1; applicants required to submit FAFSA. *Application contact:* Dr. Dana L. Hall, Program Coordinator, 770-720-5756, Fax: 770-720-9236, E-mail: dlh@reinhardt.edu.
Website: http://www.reinhardt.edu/Graduate/MBA/

Rensselaer at Hartford, Lally School of Management and Technology, Hartford, CT 06120-2991. Offers MBA, MS. *Program availability:* Part-time, evening/weekend, online learning. *Degree requirements:* For master's, capstone course. *Entrance requirements:* For master's, GMAT (MBA). Additional exam requirements/recommendations for international students: Required—TOEFL (minimum score 600 paper-based; 100 iBT). Electronic applications accepted.

Rensselaer Polytechnic Institute, Graduate School, Lally School of Management, Troy, NY 12180-3590. Offers MBA, MS, PhD, MS/MBA. *Accreditation:* AACSB. *Program availability:* Part-time, evening/weekend. *Faculty:* 35 full-time (10 women), 7 part-time/adjunct (0 women). *Students:* 172 full-time (84 women). 1,019 applicants, 38% accepted, 104 enrolled. In 2016, 79 master's, 7 doctorates awarded. *Degree requirements:* For doctorate, thesis/dissertation. *Entrance requirements:* For master's and doctorate, GMAT or GRE. Additional exam requirements/recommendations for international students: Required—TOEFL (minimum score 570 paper-based; 88 iBT), IELTS (minimum score 6.5), PTE (minimum score 60). *Application deadline:* For fall admission, 1/1 priority date for domestic and international students; for spring admission, 8/15 priority date for domestic and international students. Applications are processed on a rolling basis. Application fee: $75. Electronic applications accepted. *Expenses:* Contact institution. *Financial support:* In 2016–17, 64 students received support. Scholarships/grants available. Financial award application deadline: 1/1; financial award applicants required to submit FAFSA. *Faculty research:* Business analytics, quantitative finance and risk analytics, management, supply chain management, technology commercialization and entrepreneurship. *Total annual research expenditures:* $639,851. *Unit head:* Dr. Gina O'Connor, Associate Dean, Lally School of Management, 518-276-6842, E-mail: oconng@rpi.edu. *Application contact:* Office of Graduate Admissions, 518-276-6216, E-mail: gradadmissions@rpi.edu.
Website: http://lallyschool.rpi.edu/

Rice University, Graduate Programs, Jesse H. Jones Graduate School of Business, Houston, TX 77251-1892. Offers business administration (EMBA, MBA, PMBA); MBA/M Eng; MD/MBA. *Accreditation:* AACSB. *Program availability:* Evening/weekend. *Faculty:* 64 full-time, 68 part-time/adjunct. *Students:* 110 full-time (27 women), 145 part-time (25 women); includes 66 minority (5 Black or African American, non-Hispanic/Latino; 3 American Indian or Alaska Native, non-Hispanic/Latino; 39 Asian, non-Hispanic/Latino; 19 Hispanic/Latino), 52 international. Average age 28. 840 applicants, 53% accepted, 296 enrolled. In 2016, 217 master's awarded. *Entrance requirements:* For master's, GMAT. Additional exam requirements/recommendations for international students: Required—TOEFL (minimum score 600 paper-based). *Application deadline:* For fall admission, 10/5 priority date for domestic students; for winter admission, 1/9 priority date for domestic students; for spring admission, 4/7 priority date for domestic students. Applications are processed on a rolling basis. Application fee: $200. Electronic applications accepted. *Expenses:* Contact institution. *Financial support:* In 2016–17, 97 students received support. Fellowships, career-related internships or fieldwork, Federal Work-Study, institutionally sponsored loans, scholarships/grants, and tuition waivers (full and partial) available. Financial award applicants required to submit FAFSA. *Faculty research:* Marketing strategy, technology transfer initiatives, management accounting, leadership and change management, financial management. *Unit head:* Dr. Peter Rodriguez, Dean, E-mail: prod@rice.edu. *Application contact:* Sue Oldham, Executive Director of Recruiting and Admissions, 713-348-6153, E-mail: ricemba@rice.edu.
Website: https://business.rice.edu/

Rider University, College of Business Administration, Lawrenceville, NJ 08648-3001. Offers EMBA, M Acc, MBA. *Accreditation:* AACSB. *Program availability:* Part-time, evening/weekend. *Entrance requirements:* For master's, GMAT, minimum AACSB index of 1050, resume. Additional exam requirements/recommendations for international students: Required—TOEFL (minimum score 550 paper-based). Electronic applications accepted. *Expenses:* Contact institution.

Rivier University, School of Graduate Studies, Department of Business Administration, Nashua, NH 03060. Offers MBA. *Program availability:* Part-time, evening/weekend. *Entrance requirements:* Additional exam requirements/recommendations for international students: Recommended—TOEFL.

Robert Morris University, School of Business, Moon Township, PA 15108-1189. Offers business administration (MBA); human resource management (MS); taxation (MS); MBA/MS. *Accreditation:* AACSB. *Program availability:* Part-time-only, evening/weekend, 100% online. *Faculty:* 24 full-time (8 women), 4 part-time/adjunct (3 women). *Students:* 148 part-time (64 women); includes 9 minority (3 Black or African American, non-Hispanic/Latino; 6 Asian, non-Hispanic/Latino), 1 international. Average age 27. 147 applicants, 23% accepted, 32 enrolled. In 2016, 96 master's awarded. *Entrance requirements:* For master's, GMAT, letters of recommendation. Additional exam requirements/recommendations for international students: Required—TOEFL (minimum score 550 paper-based; 79 iBT). *Application deadline:* For fall admission, 7/1 priority date for domestic and international students; for spring admission, 11/1 priority date for domestic and international students. Applications are processed on a rolling basis. Application fee: $35. Electronic applications accepted. Application fee is waived when completed online. *Expenses:* $925 per credit. *Financial support:* Institutionally sponsored loans available. Support available to part-time students. Financial award application deadline: 5/1; financial award applicants required to submit FAFSA. *Unit head:* Dr. Michelle L. Patrick, Dean, 412-397-5445, Fax: 412-397-2585, E-mail: patrick@rmu.edu. *Application contact:* E-mail: graduateadmissions@rmu.edu.
Website: http://sbus.rmu.edu

Robert Morris University Illinois, Morris Graduate School of Management, Chicago, IL 60605. Offers accounting (MBA); accounting/finance (MBA); business analytics (MIS); design and media (MM); design management (MM); educational technology (MM); health care administration (MM); higher education administration (MM); human resource management (MBA); information security (MIS); information systems (MBA, MIS); law enforcement administration (MM); management (MBA); management/finance (MBA); management/human resource management (MBA); mobile computing (MIS); sports administration (MM). *Program availability:* Part-time, evening/weekend. *Faculty:* 4 full-time (1 woman), 25 part-time/adjunct (5 women). *Students:* 196 full-time (98 women), 151 part-time (85 women); includes 200 minority (114 Black or African American, non-Hispanic/Latino; 17 Asian, non-Hispanic/Latino; 67 Hispanic/Latino; 2 Two or more races, non-Hispanic/Latino), 23 international. Average age 33. 174 applicants, 61% accepted, 97 enrolled. In 2016, 190 master's awarded. *Entrance requirements:* For master's, official transcripts and letters of recommendation (for some programs); written personal statement. Additional exam requirements/recommendations for international students: Required—TOEFL (minimum score 550 paper-based). *Application deadline:* Applications are processed on a rolling basis. Application fee: $20 ($100 for international students). Electronic applications accepted. *Expenses: Tuition:* Full-time $16,500; part-time $2750 per course. *Financial support:* In 2016–17, 444 students received support. Federal Work-Study, scholarships/grants, and unspecified assistantships available. Support available to part-time students. Financial award applicants required to submit FAFSA. *Unit head:* Kayed Akkawi, Dean, 312-935-6050, Fax: 312-935-6020, E-mail: kakkawi@robertmorris.edu. *Application contact:* Danielle Naffziger, Vice President of Marketing and Enrollment, 312-935-4812, Fax: 312-935-6020, E-mail: dnaffziger@robertmorris.edu.

Roberts Wesleyan College, Graduate Business Programs, Rochester, NY 14624-1997. Offers strategic leadership (MS); strategic marketing (MS). *Program availability:* Evening/weekend. *Degree requirements:* For master's, thesis or alternative. *Entrance requirements:* For master's, GMAT, minimum GPA of 2.75, verifiable work experience. *Expenses:* Contact institution.

Rochester Institute of Technology, Graduate Enrollment Services, Saunders College of Business, Rochester, NY 14623-5608. Offers Exec MBA, MBA, MS. *Program availability:* Part-time, evening/weekend, 100% online, blended/hybrid learning. *Students:* 251 full-time (112 women), 95 part-time (54 women); includes 21 minority (6 Black or African American, non-Hispanic/Latino; 1 American Indian or Alaska Native, non-Hispanic/Latino; 2 Asian, non-Hispanic/Latino; 10 Hispanic/Latino; 2 Two or more races, non-Hispanic/Latino), 117 international. Average age 27. 687 applicants, 55% accepted, 157 enrolled. In 2016, 109 master's awarded. *Degree requirements:* For master's, comprehensive exam (for some programs), thesis or alternative. *Entrance requirements:* For master's, GMAT or GRE, minimum GPA of 3.0 (recommended). Additional exam requirements/recommendations for international students: Required—PTE (minimum score 58), TOEFL (minimum score 550 paper-based, 79 iBT) or IELTS (minimum score 6.5). *Application deadline:* Applications are processed on a rolling basis. Application fee: $60. Electronic applications accepted. *Expenses:* $1,742 per credit hour. *Financial support:* In 2016–17, 192 students received support. Research assistantships with partial tuition reimbursements available, teaching assistantships with partial tuition reimbursements available, career-related internships or fieldwork, Federal Work-Study, scholarships/grants, and unspecified assistantships available. Support available to part-time students. Financial award applicants required to submit FAFSA. *Faculty research:* Corporate environmental strategy and sustainability, lean manufacturing and environmental performance, entrepreneurship, data analytics, computational finance, technology and information management, marketing and digital marketing. *Unit head:* Dr. Jacqueline Mozrall, Dean, 585-475-6025, E-mail: gradbus@saunders.rit.edu. *Application contact:* Diane Ellison, Associate Vice President, Graduate Enrollment Services, 585-475-2229, Fax: 585-475-7164, E-mail: gradinfo@rit.edu.
Website: http://saunders.rit.edu/

Rochester Institute of Technology, Graduate Enrollment Services, Saunders College of Business, Marketing and Management Department, MBA Program, Rochester, NY 14623. Offers MBA. *Accreditation:* AACSB. *Program availability:* Part-time, evening/weekend. *Students:* 103 full-time (48 women), 35 part-time (15 women); includes 7 minority (2 Asian, non-Hispanic/Latino; 4 Hispanic/Latino; 1 Two or more races, non-Hispanic/Latino), 64 international. Average age 26. 240 applicants, 53% accepted, 55 enrolled. In 2016, 53 master's awarded. *Degree requirements:* For master's, comprehensive exam (for some programs), thesis or alternative. *Entrance requirements:* For master's, GMAT or GRE, minimum GPA of 3.0 (recommended). Additional exam requirements/recommendations for international students: Required—TOEFL (minimum score 580 paper-based; 92 iBT), IELTS (minimum score 7), PTE (minimum score 63). *Application deadline:* Applications are processed on a rolling basis. Application fee: $60. Electronic applications accepted. *Expenses:* $1,742 per credit hour. *Financial support:* In 2016–17, 87 students received support. Research assistantships with partial tuition reimbursements available, teaching assistantships with partial tuition reimbursements

available, career-related internships or fieldwork, scholarships/grants, and unspecified assistantships available. Support available to part-time students. Financial award applicants required to submit FAFSA. *Faculty research:* Health IT adoption; technology management, creativity, and innovation; social media and entrepreneurship; leadership; cybersecurity; and corporate social responsibility and business ethics. *Unit head:* Jenna Lenhardt, Graduate Admissions Advisor, 585-475-6916, E-mail: jlenhardt@saunders.rit.edu. *Application contact:* Diane Ellison, Associate Vice President, Graduate Enrollment Services, 585-475-2229, Fax: 585-475-7164, E-mail: gradinfo@rit.edu.
Website: http://saunders.rit.edu/programs/graduate/mba_main.php

Rochester Institute of Technology, Graduate Enrollment Services, Saunders College of Business, Marketing and Management Department, MBA Program–Executive Option, Rochester, NY 14623. Offers Exec MBA. *Accreditation:* AACSB. *Program availability:* Part-time-only, evening/weekend. *Students:* 39 full-time (18 women), 36 part-time (23 women); includes 3 minority (2 Black or African American, non-Hispanic/Latino; 1 American Indian or Alaska Native, non-Hispanic/Latino), 2 international. Average age 38. 27 applicants, 67% accepted, 13 enrolled. In 2016, 15 master's awarded. *Degree requirements:* For master's, thesis or alternative, capstone. *Entrance requirements:* For master's, minimum of 6 years of work experience, minimum GPA of 3.0 (recommended). Additional exam requirements/recommendations for international students: Required—TOEFL, IELTS, PTE (minimum score 58). *Application deadline:* For fall admission, 6/30 priority date for domestic and international students. Applications are processed on a rolling basis. Application fee: $60. Electronic applications accepted. *Expenses:* $70,000 all-inclusive tuition including iPad, course materials and week of international travel. *Financial support:* In 2016–17, 35 students received support. Scholarships/grants available. Support available to part-time students. Financial award applicants required to submit FAFSA. *Faculty research:* Active learning pedagogy; consumer experience; relationship marketing; virtual ethnography; online learning; globalization of manufacturing R&D and engineering; competitive dynamics and internal vs. external network idea sourcing new products; creativity, cognitive learning style and innovation outcomes; R&D project management in resource-constrained business conditions; crowd sourcing vs. mergers and acquisitions as open innovation strategies; cultural impacts on technology adoption. *Unit head:* Amanda Williams, Admissions Officer, 585-475-2729, E-mail: awilliams@saunders.rit.edu. *Application contact:* Diane Ellison, Associate Vice President, Graduate Enrollment Services, 585-475-2229, Fax: 585-475-7164, E-mail: gradinfo@rit.edu.
Website: https://www.rit.edu/emba/on-campus-emba-program

Rochester Institute of Technology, Graduate Enrollment Services, Saunders College of Business, Marketing and Management Department, MBA Program–Online, Rochester, NY 14623. Offers MBA. *Program availability:* Part-time, evening/weekend, online only, 100% online. *Students:* 23 full-time (11 women), 1 (woman) part-time, 1 international. Average age 38. 27 applicants, 74% accepted, 14 enrolled. In 2016, 17 master's awarded. *Degree requirements:* For master's, thesis or alternative. *Entrance requirements:* For master's, minimum GPA of 3.0 (recommended), five years of work experience. Additional exam requirements/recommendations for international students: Required—PTE (minimum score 58). *Application deadline:* For fall admission, 6/1 priority date for domestic and international students. Applications are processed on a rolling basis. Application fee: $60. Electronic applications accepted. *Expenses:* $70,000 all-inclusive tuition including iPad, course materials and week of international travel. *Financial support:* In 2016–17, 31 students received support. Scholarships/grants available. Support available to part-time students. Financial award applicants required to submit FAFSA. *Faculty research:* Active learning pedagogy; consumer experience; relationship marketing; virtual ethnography; online learning; globalization of manufacturing R&D and engineering; competitive dynamics and internal vs. external network idea sourcing new products; creativity, cognitive learning style and innovation outcomes; R&D project management in resource-constrained business conditions; crowd sourcing vs. mergers and acquisitions as open innovation strategies; cultural impacts on technology adoption. *Unit head:* Amanda Williams, Admissions Officer, 585-475-2729, E-mail: awilliams@saunders.rit.edu. *Application contact:* Diane Ellison, Associate Vice President, Graduate Enrollment Services, 585-475-2229, Fax: 585-475-7164, E-mail: gradinfo@rit.edu.
Website: http://executivembaonline.rit.edu/

Rockford University, Graduate Studies, Program in Business Administration, Rockford, IL 61108-2393. Offers MBA. *Program availability:* Part-time, evening/weekend. *Entrance requirements:* For master's, GMAT, 3 letters of recommendation. Additional exam requirements/recommendations for international students: Required—TOEFL (minimum score 550 paper-based; 79 iBT). *Application deadline:* Applications are processed on a rolling basis. Application fee: $50. Electronic applications accepted. *Expenses:* *Tuition:* Part-time $710 per credit. *Required fees:* $50 per semester. *Financial support:* Scholarships/grants and unspecified assistantships available. Support available to part-time students. Financial award application deadline: 3/1; financial award applicants required to submit FAFSA. *Faculty research:* Entrepreneurship, leadership, international business, services marketing, project management. *Unit head:* Prof. Jeff Fahrenwald, MBA Director, 815-226-4040, E-mail: jfahrenwald@rockford.edu. *Application contact:* Michele Mehren, Assistant Director, Office of Graduate Studies, 815-226-4040, E-mail: mmehren@rockford.edu.
Website: https://www.rockford.edu/admission/graduate/mba/

Rockhurst University, Helzberg School of Management, Kansas City, MO 64110-2561. Offers accounting (MBA); business intelligence (MBA, Certificate); data science (MBA, Certificate); entrepreneurship (MBA); finance (MBA); fundraising leadership (MBA, Certificate); healthcare management (MBA, Certificate); human capital (Certificate); international business (Certificate); management (MBA, Certificate); nonprofit administration (Certificate); organizational development (Certificate); science leadership (Certificate). *Accreditation:* AACSB. *Program availability:* Part-time, evening/weekend. *Entrance requirements:* For master's, GMAT or GRE. Additional exam requirements/recommendations for international students: Required—TOEFL (minimum score 550 paper-based; 79 iBT). Electronic applications accepted. Application fee is waived when completed online. *Faculty research:* Offshoring/outsourcing, systems analysis/synthesis, work teams, multilateral trade, path dependencies/creation.

Rogers State University, Program in Business Administration, Claremore, OK 74017-3252. Offers MBA.

Rollins College, Crummer Graduate School of Business, Winter Park, FL 32789-4499. Offers business administration (EDBA); entrepreneurship (MBA); finance (MBA); international business (MBA); management (MBA); marketing (MBA); operations and technology management (MBA). *Accreditation:* AACSB. *Program availability:* Part-time, evening/weekend, online learning. *Faculty:* 22 full-time (5 women), 4 part-time/adjunct (3 women). *Students:* 254 full-time (105 women), 83 part-time (36 women); includes 63 minority (15 Black or African American, non-Hispanic/Latino; 9 Asian, non-Hispanic/Latino; 35 Hispanic/Latino; 4 Two or more races, non-Hispanic/Latino), 48 international. Average age 31. 360 applicants, 74% accepted, 207 enrolled. In 2016, 159 master's awarded. *Degree requirements:* For master's, minimum GPA of 2.85; for doctorate, thesis/dissertation, minimum GPA of 3.0. *Entrance requirements:* For master's, GMAT or GRE, official transcripts, two letters of recommendation, essay, current resume/curriculum vitae, interview; for doctorate, official transcripts, two letters of recommendation, essays, current resume/curriculum vitae, interview. Additional exam requirements/recommendations for international students: Required—TOEFL (minimum score 100 iBT) or IELTS (minimum score 7). *Application deadline:* Applications are processed on a rolling basis. Application fee: $50. Electronic applications accepted. *Expenses:* Contact institution. *Financial support:* In 2016–17, 125 students received support. Federal Work-Study and scholarships/grants available. Support available to part-time students. Financial award applicants required to submit FAFSA. *Faculty research:* Sustainability, world financial markets, international business, market research, strategic marketing. *Unit head:* Deborah Crown, Dean, 407-646-2249, Fax: 407-646-1550, E-mail: dcrown@rollins.edu. *Application contact:* Maralyn E. Graham, Admissions Coordinator, 407-646-2405, Fax: 407-646-1550,
E-mail: mbaadmissions@rollins.edu.
Website: http://www.rollins.edu/mba/

Roosevelt University, Graduate Division, Walter E. Heller College of Business, Program in Business Administration, Chicago, IL 60605. Offers MBA. *Accreditation:* ACBSP. *Program availability:* Part-time, evening/weekend. *Students:* 89 full-time (46 women), 231 part-time (144 women); includes 163 minority (93 Black or African American, non-Hispanic/Latino; 27 Asian, non-Hispanic/Latino; 35 Hispanic/Latino; 8 Two or more races, non-Hispanic/Latino), 55 international. Average age 31. 172 applicants, 92% accepted, 72 enrolled. In 2016, 140 master's awarded. *Entrance requirements:* For master's, GMAT. *Application deadline:* For fall admission, 6/1 priority date for domestic students. Applications are processed on a rolling basis. Application fee: $40. *Expenses:* *Tuition, area resident:* Full-time $19,566; part-time $880 per credit hour. *Required fees:* $175 per semester. One-time fee: $200. Part-time tuition and fees vary according to course load, degree level and program. *Financial support:* Application deadline: 2/15. *Unit head:* Erica Poremba, Director, 312-281-3326, E-mail: eporemba01@roosevelt.edu. *Application contact:* Angela Ryan, Director of Graduate Enrollment, 877-APPLY RU, Fax: 312-281-3356, E-mail: applyru@roosevelt.edu.
Website: https://www.roosevelt.edu/academics/programs/masters-in-business-administration-mba

Roseman University of Health Sciences, College of Dental Medicine - Henderson Campus, Henderson, NV 89014. Offers business administration (MBA); dental medicine (Post-Doctoral Certificate). *Faculty:* 6 full-time (2 women), 5 part-time/adjunct (0 women). *Students:* 30 full-time (10 women); includes 14 minority (13 Asian, non-Hispanic/Latino; 1 Hispanic/Latino). Average age 30. 132 applicants, 8% accepted, 10 enrolled. In 2016, 12 other advanced degrees awarded. *Degree requirements:* For master's, comprehensive exam, thesis or alternative. *Entrance requirements:* For master's, National Board Dental Examination 1 and 2, graduation from U.S. or Canadian dental school, Nevada dental license. *Application deadline:* For fall admission, 1/31 for domestic and international students. Application fee: $50. *Expenses:* $73,000 per year. *Financial support:* Application deadline: 6/15; applicants required to submit FAFSA. *Faculty research:* Oral cancer; CBCT (Cone Beam Computed Tomography) 3D scan data related projects; in-vitro biomaterial testing such as orthodontic bond strength studies using Instron; nanotechnology and orthodontic practice management research. *Unit head:* Dr. Jaleh Pourhamidi, Dean, 702-968-1652, Fax: 702-968-5277, E-mail: jpourhamidi@roseman.edu. *Application contact:* Rochelle Sharp, Administrative Assistant to the Dean, 702-968-1682, E-mail: rsharp@roseman.edu.
Website: http://www.roseman.edu

Roseman University of Health Sciences, MBA Program, Henderson, NV 89014. Offers MBA. *Program availability:* Part-time, evening/weekend. *Faculty:* 2 full-time (1 woman), 11 part-time/adjunct (5 women). *Students:* 2 full-time (1 woman), 23 part-time (14 women); includes 10 minority (4 Black or African American, non-Hispanic/Latino; 5 Asian, non-Hispanic/Latino; 1 Hispanic/Latino). Average age 37. 10 applicants, 100% accepted, 7 enrolled. In 2016, 68 master's awarded. *Degree requirements:* For master's, comprehensive exam, entrepreneurial project, summative assessment and capstone. *Entrance requirements:* For master's, GMAT or leveling course (for applicants whose overall GPA is below 3.0), bachelor's degree. Additional exam requirements/recommendations for international students: Required—TOEFL (minimum score 550 paper-based; 79 iBT). *Application deadline:* For fall admission, 5/15 for domestic and international students. Application fee: $100. *Expenses:* *Tuition:* Full-time $30,069; part-time $771 per credit. *Required fees:* $469 per credit. Tuition and fees vary according to program. *Financial support:* Application deadline: 5/1; applicants required to submit FAFSA. *Faculty research:* Using a cash flow-based Z-score to access the progressive solvency of the U.S. commercial banking system; identifying the causes and consequences associated with; groups and retirement preparedness; evaluating the performance of individual stocks relative to indexes. *Unit head:* Dr. Okeleke Nzeogwu, Program Director, 702-968-1659, Fax: 702-968-1685,
E-mail: onzeogwu@roseman.edu.
Website: http://www.roseman.edu

Rosemont College, Schools of Graduate and Professional Studies, Business Administration and Leadership Programs, Rosemont, PA 19010-1699. Offers business administration (MBA); leadership (MS); management (MS). *Program availability:* Part-time, evening/weekend, online learning. *Degree requirements:* For master's, thesis (for some programs). *Entrance requirements:* For master's, minimum college GPA of 3.0, 3 letters of recommendation. Application fee is waived when completed online. *Expenses:* Contact institution.

Rowan University, Graduate School, Rohrer College of Business, Department of Business Administration, Glassboro, NJ 08028-1701. Offers MBA. *Accreditation:* AACSB. *Program availability:* Part-time, evening/weekend. *Degree requirements:* For master's, comprehensive exam, thesis. *Entrance requirements:* For master's, GRE General Test. Additional exam requirements/recommendations for international students: Required—TOEFL. Electronic applications accepted.

Rowan University, Graduate School, Rohrer College of Business, Department of Marketing and Business Information Systems, Program in Business, Glassboro, NJ 08028-1701. Offers CGS. *Program availability:* Part-time, evening/weekend. *Entrance requirements:* Additional exam requirements/recommendations for international students: Required—TOEFL. Electronic applications accepted.

Royal Military College of Canada, Division of Graduate Studies and Research, Continuing Studies, Department of Business Administration, Kingston, ON K7K 7B4, Canada. Offers MBA. *Degree requirements:* For master's, thesis. *Entrance requirements:* For master's, GMAT, honours degree with second-class standing. Electronic applications accepted.

Royal Roads University, Graduate Studies, Applied Leadership and Management Program, Victoria, BC V9B 5Y2, Canada. Offers executive coaching (Graduate Certificate); health systems leadership (Graduate Certificate); project management (Graduate Certificate); public relations management (Graduate Certificate); strategic human resources management (Graduate Certificate).

Royal Roads University, Graduate Studies, Faculty of Management, Victoria, BC V9B 5Y2, Canada. Offers digital technologies management (MBA); executive management (MBA), including global aviation management, knowledge management, leadership; human resources management (MBA). *Program availability:* Online learning. *Degree requirements:* For master's, thesis. *Entrance requirements:* For master's, 5-7 years of related work experience. Additional exam requirements/recommendations for international students: Required—TOEFL (paper-based 570) or IELTS (7) recommended. Electronic applications accepted. *Expenses:* Contact institution. *Faculty research:* Global venture analysis standards; computer assisted venture opportunity screening; teaching philosophies, instructions and methods.

Rutgers University–Camden, School of Business, Camden, NJ 08102-1401. Offers MBA, JD/MBA. *Accreditation:* AACSB. *Program availability:* Part-time, evening/weekend. *Entrance requirements:* For master's, GMAT, 2 letters of recommendation. Additional exam requirements/recommendations for international students: Required—TOEFL (minimum score 89 iBT). Electronic applications accepted. *Expenses:* Contact institution. *Faculty research:* Efficiency in utility industry, management information systems development, management/labor relations.

Rutgers University–Newark, Graduate School, Program in Management, Newark, NJ 07102. Offers accounting (PhD); accounting information systems (PhD); computer information systems (PhD); finance (PhD); information technology (PhD); international business (PhD); management science (PhD); marketing (PhD); organization management (PhD). Program offered jointly with New Jersey Institute of Technology. *Accreditation:* AACSB. *Degree requirements:* For doctorate, thesis/dissertation, cumulative exams. *Entrance requirements:* For doctorate, GMAT or GRE General Test, minimum undergraduate B average. Additional exam requirements/recommendations for international students: Required—TOEFL. Electronic applications accepted. *Faculty research:* Technology management, leadership and teams, consumer behavior, financial and markets, logistics.

Rutgers University–Newark, Rutgers Business School–Newark and New Brunswick, Program in Business Administration, Newark, NJ 07102. Offers MBA. *Entrance requirements:* For master's, GMAT. Additional exam requirements/recommendations for international students: Required—TOEFL.

Ryerson University, School of Graduate Studies, Ted Rogers School of Management, Toronto, ON M5B 2K3, Canada. Offers global business administration (MBA); management (MSM); management of technology and innovation (MBA).

Sage Graduate School, School of Management, Program in Business Administration, Troy, NY 12180-4115. Offers MBA. *Program availability:* Part-time, evening/weekend. *Faculty:* 3 full-time (2 women), 13 part-time/adjunct (4 women). *Students:* 41 full-time (27 women), 55 part-time (39 women); includes 24 minority (9 Black or African American, non-Hispanic/Latino; 1 American Indian or Alaska Native, non-Hispanic/Latino; 9 Asian, non-Hispanic/Latino; 4 Hispanic/Latino; 1 Two or more races, non-Hispanic/Latino), 6 international. Average age 31. 73 applicants, 48% accepted, 25 enrolled. In 2016, 21 master's awarded. *Entrance requirements:* For master's, minimum GPA of 2.75, resume, 2 letters of recommendation. Additional exam requirements/recommendations for international students: Required—TOEFL (minimum score 550 paper-based). *Application deadline:* Applications are processed on a rolling basis. Application fee: $40. *Expenses: Tuition:* Full-time $12,240; part-time $680 per credit hour. Tuition and fees vary according to degree level and program. *Financial support:* Fellowships, research assistantships, Federal Work-Study, scholarships/grants, and unspecified assistantships available. Support available to part-time students. Financial award application deadline: 3/1; financial award applicants required to submit FAFSA. *Unit head:* Dr. Kimberly Fredericks, Dean, School of Management, 518-292-1782, Fax: 518-292-1964, E-mail: fredek1@sage.edu. *Application contact:* Wendy D. Diefendorf, Director of Graduate and Adult Admission, 518-244-2443, Fax: 518-244-6880, E-mail: diefew@sage.edu.

Saginaw Valley State University, College of Business and Management, Program in Business Administration, University Center, MI 48710. Offers MBA. *Accreditation:* AACSB. *Program availability:* Part-time, evening/weekend, online only, 100% online, blended/hybrid learning. *Faculty:* 10 full-time (3 women). *Students:* 29 full-time (8 women), 37 part-time (13 women); includes 3 minority (2 Black or African American, non-Hispanic/Latino; 1 Asian, non-Hispanic/Latino), 36 international. Average age 28. 53 applicants, 51% accepted, 12 enrolled. In 2016, 48 master's awarded. *Degree requirements:* For master's, thesis optional. *Entrance requirements:* For master's, GMAT. Additional exam requirements/recommendations for international students: Required—TOEFL (minimum score 550 paper-based; 79 iBT). *Application deadline:* For fall admission, 7/15 for international students; for winter admission, 11/15 for international students; for spring admission, 4/15 for international students. Applications are processed on a rolling basis. Application fee: $30 ($90 for international students). Electronic applications accepted. *Expenses:* Tuition, state resident: full-time $9652; part-time $536 per credit hour. Tuition, nonresident: full-time $12,259; part-time $1022 per credit hour. *Required fees:* $263; $14.60 per credit hour. Tuition and fees vary according to degree level. *Financial support:* Federal Work-Study and scholarships/grants available. Support available to part-time students. Financial award application deadline: 4/15; financial award applicants required to submit FAFSA. *Unit head:* Dr. Mark McCartney, MBA Program Coordinator, 989-964-4064. *Application contact:* Jenna Briggs, Director, Graduate and International Admissions, 989-964-6096, Fax: 989-964-2788, E-mail: gradadm@svsu.edu.
Website: http://www.svsu.edu/mba/

St. Ambrose University, College of Business, Program in Business Administration, Davenport, IA 52803-2898. Offers business administration (DBA); health care (MBA); human resources (MBA). *Accreditation:* ACBSP. *Program availability:* Part-time, evening/weekend. *Degree requirements:* For master's, comprehensive exam (for some programs), thesis or alternative, capstone seminar; for doctorate, comprehensive exam, thesis/dissertation, oral and written exams. *Entrance requirements:* For master's, GMAT; for doctorate, GMAT, master's degree. Additional exam requirements/recommendations for international students: Required—TOEFL. Electronic applications accepted. *Expenses:* Contact institution.

St. Bonaventure University, School of Graduate Studies, School of Business, St. Bonaventure, NY 14778-2284. Offers general business (MBA); professional accountancy (MBA). *Accreditation:* AACSB. *Program availability:* Part-time, evening/weekend, 100% online. *Faculty:* 6 full-time (1 woman), 14 part-time/adjunct (4 women). *Students:* 60 full-time (19 women), 58 part-time (29 women); includes 19 minority (4 Black or African American, non-Hispanic/Latino; 3 American Indian or Alaska Native, non-Hispanic/Latino; 4 Asian, non-Hispanic/Latino; 7 Hispanic/Latino; 1 Two or more races, non-Hispanic/Latino), 3 international. Average age 28. 123 applicants, 84% accepted, 73 enrolled. In 2016, 68 master's awarded. *Entrance requirements:* For master's, GMAT or GRE, undergraduate degree, transcripts, current resume. Additional exam requirements/recommendations for international students: Required—TOEFL (minimum score 550 paper-based; 79 iBT). *Application deadline:* For fall admission, 6/15 priority date for domestic students, 2/1 priority date for international students; for spring admission, 11/1 priority date for domestic students, 7/1 priority date for international students. Applications are processed on a rolling basis. Application fee: $0. Electronic applications accepted. *Expenses:* $733 per credit, $100 graduation fee. *Financial support:* Career-related internships or fieldwork, Federal Work-Study, scholarships/grants, health care benefits, and unspecified assistantships available. Support available to part-time students. Financial award application deadline: 4/15; financial award applicants required to submit FAFSA. *Faculty research:* Impact of Pathways Commission on accounting education, sovereign credit ratings, acculturation, advertising, and cross-cultural research of ethnic consumers. *Unit head:* Dr. Matrecia James, Dean, 716-375-2200, Fax: 716-372-2191, E-mail: mjames@sbu.edu. *Application contact:* Bruce Campbell, Director of Graduate Admissions, 716-375-2429, Fax: 716-375-4015, E-mail: gradsch@sbu.edu.
Website: http://www.sbu.edu/academics/schools/business/graduate-degrees/master-of-business-administration-(mba)

St. Catherine University, Graduate Programs, Program in Business Administration, St. Paul, MN 55105. Offers healthcare (MBA); integrated marketing communications (MBA); management (MBA). *Program availability:* Part-time, evening/weekend. *Entrance requirements:* For master's, GMAT (if undergraduate GPA is less than 3.0), 2+ years' work or volunteer experience in professional setting(s). Additional exam requirements/recommendations for international students: Required—TOEFL. *Expenses:* Contact institution.

St. Cloud State University, School of Graduate Studies, Herberger Business School, Program in Business Administration, St. Cloud, MN 56301-4498. Offers business administration (MBA); information assurance (MS). *Accreditation:* AACSB. *Program availability:* Part-time, evening/weekend. *Degree requirements:* For master's, thesis or alternative. *Entrance requirements:* For master's, GMAT, minimum GPA of 2.75. Additional exam requirements/recommendations for international students: Required—Michigan English Language Assessment Battery; Recommended—TOEFL (minimum score 550 paper-based), IELTS (minimum score 6.5).

St. Edward's University, Bill Munday School of Business, Austin, TX 78704. Offers accounting (M Ac); business (Certificate); business administration (MBA), including accounting, business administration, digital management; leadership and change (MS). *Program availability:* Part-time, evening/weekend. *Students:* 53 full-time (19 women), 183 part-time (103 women); includes 100 minority (19 Black or African American, non-Hispanic/Latino; 11 Asian, non-Hispanic/Latino; 59 Hispanic/Latino; 1 Native Hawaiian or other Pacific Islander, non-Hispanic/Latino; 10 Two or more races, non-Hispanic/Latino), 16 international. Average age 32. 221 applicants, 58% accepted, 80 enrolled. In 2016, 78 master's awarded. *Degree requirements:* For master's, minimum of 24 hours in residence with minimum cumulative GPA of 3.0. *Entrance requirements:* For master's, minimum GPA of 2.75 in last 60 hours of course work. Additional exam requirements/recommendations for international students: Required—TOEFL (minimum score 79 iBT), IELTS (minimum score 6). *Application deadline:* For fall admission, 6/1 priority date for domestic and international students; for spring admission, 10/1 priority date for domestic and international students; for summer admission, 3/1 priority date for domestic and international students. Applications are processed on a rolling basis. Application fee: $50. Electronic applications accepted. *Expenses:* Contact institution. *Unit head:* Dr. Nancy Schreiber, Dean, 512-428-1287, Fax: 512-428-1217, E-mail: nschreib@stedwards.edu. *Application contact:* Mike Leveriza, Graduate Recruiter, 512-448-8745, Fax: 512-464-8877, E-mail: mleveriz@stedwards.edu.
Website: http://www.stedwards.edu

Saint Francis University, School of Business, Loretto, PA 15940-0600. Offers business administration (MBA); human resource management (MHRM). *Program availability:* Part-time, evening/weekend. *Degree requirements:* For master's, comprehensive exam (for some programs), thesis (for some programs). *Entrance requirements:* For master's, GMAT (waived if undergraduate QPA is 3.3 or above), 2 letters of recommendation, minimum GPA of 2.75, two essays. Additional exam requirements/recommendations for international students: Required—TOEFL (minimum score 550 paper-based; 57 iBT). *Expenses:* Contact institution.

St. John Fisher College, School of Business, MBA Program, Rochester, NY 14618-3597. Offers MBA. *Accreditation:* AACSB. *Program availability:* Part-time, evening/weekend. *Faculty:* 13 full-time (3 women), 3 part-time/adjunct (1 woman). *Students:* 47 full-time (19 women), 83 part-time (41 women); includes 13 minority (4 Black or African American, non-Hispanic/Latino; 3 Asian, non-Hispanic/Latino; 5 Hispanic/Latino; 1 Two or more races, non-Hispanic/Latino), 2 international. Average age 28. 78 applicants, 83% accepted, 39 enrolled. In 2016, 73 master's awarded. *Degree requirements:* For master's, capstone project. *Entrance requirements:* For master's, 2 letters of recommendation, personal statement, current resume, interview. Additional exam requirements/recommendations for international students: Required—TOEFL (minimum score 575 paper-based; 80 iBT). *Application deadline:* Applications are processed on a rolling basis. Application fee: $30. Electronic applications accepted. *Expenses:* $1,050 per credit hour. *Financial support:* Scholarships/grants available. Financial award applicants required to submit FAFSA. *Faculty research:* Business strategy, consumer behavior, cross-cultural management practices, international finance, organizational trust. *Unit head:* Dr. David Kunsch, Program Director, 585-385-5245, E-mail: dkunsch@sjfc.edu. *Application contact:* Michelle Gosier, Associate Director of Transfer and Graduate Admissions, 585-385-8064, E-mail: mgosier@sjfc.edu.
Website: https://www.sjfc.edu/graduate-programs/master-of-business-administration-mba/

St. John Fisher College, School of Business, MS in Management Program, Rochester, NY 14618-3597. Offers MS. *Program availability:* Evening/weekend. *Faculty:* 1 full-time (0 women), 2 part-time/adjunct (1 woman). *Students:* 22 full-time (13 women); includes 1 minority (Asian, non-Hispanic/Latino), 1 international. Average age 27. 34 applicants, 88% accepted, 22 enrolled. *Entrance requirements:* For master's, baccalaureate degree, official transcripts, two letters of recommendation, current resume, personal goals statement. Additional exam requirements/recommendations for international students: Required—TOEFL (minimum score 575 paper-based; 80 iBT). *Application deadline:* Applications are processed on a rolling basis. Application fee: $30. Electronic applications accepted. *Expenses:* $885 per credit hour. *Financial support:* Scholarships/grants available. Financial award applicants required to submit FAFSA. *Unit head:* Dr. David Kunsch, Director, 585-385-5245, E-mail: dkunsch@sjfc.edu. *Application contact:* Michelle Gosier, Associate Director of Transfer and Graduate Admissions, 585-385-8064, E-mail: mgosier@sjfc.edu.
Website: https://www.sjfc.edu/graduate-programs/ms-in-management/

St. John's University, The Peter J. Tobin College of Business, Queens, NY 11439. Offers MBA, MS, JD/MBA, MS/JD. *Accreditation:* AACSB. *Program availability:* Part-time, evening/weekend, online learning. *Degree requirements:* For master's, comprehensive exam (for some programs), thesis optional. *Entrance requirements:* For master's, GMAT, 2 letters of recommendation, resume, statement of goals, minimum GPA of 3.0. Additional exam requirements/recommendations for international students: Required—TOEFL (minimum score 600 paper-based; 100 iBT), IELTS (minimum score 7). Electronic applications accepted. *Expenses:* Contact institution.

St. Joseph's College, Long Island Campus, Programs in Business Management and Administration, Field in Business Administration, Patchogue, NY 11772-2399. Offers MBA. *Program availability:* Part-time, evening/weekend. *Faculty:* 1 (woman) full-time, 12 part-time/adjunct (3 women). *Entrance requirements:* Additional exam requirements/recommendations for international students: Recommended—TOEFL (minimum score 550 paper-based). Application fee: $25. *Expenses:* Contact institution. *Unit head:* Eileen White Jahn, Professor and Chair, 631-687-1296, E-mail: ejahn@sjcny.edu. *Application* *contact:* Paige A. Napoli, Coordinator of Graduate Admissions, 631-447-3383, Fax: 631-447-1734, E-mail: pnapoli@sjcny.edu.

St. Joseph's College, Long Island Campus, Programs in Business Management and Administration, Field of Executive Business Administration, Patchogue, NY 11772-2399. Offers EMBA. *Program availability:* Part-time, evening/weekend, 100% online, blended/hybrid learning. *Faculty:* 1 (woman) full-time, 12 part-time/adjunct (3 women). *Students:* 19 full-time (6 women), 81 part-time (50 women); includes 34 minority (13 Black or African American, non-Hispanic/Latino; 7 Asian, non-Hispanic/Latino; 13 Hispanic/Latino; 1 Two or more races, non-Hispanic/Latino). Average age 35. 72 applicants, 75% accepted, 38 enrolled. In 2016, 20 master's awarded. *Entrance requirements:* For master's, official transcripts, minimum undergraduate GPA of 3.0, 2 letters of recommendation, resume, verification of employment, essay. Additional exam requirements/recommendations for international students: Recommended—TOEFL (minimum score 550 paper-based; 79 iBT), IELTS (minimum score 7). *Application deadline:* Applications are processed on a rolling basis. Application fee: $25. Electronic applications accepted. *Expenses:* Contact institution. *Financial support:* In 2016–17, 27 students received support. *Unit head:* Charles Pendola, Director and Assistant Professor, 631-687-1297, E-mail: cpendola@sjcny.edu. *Application contact:* Jodi A. Duffy, Senior Associate Director of Graduate Admissions, 631-687-4501, E-mail: jduffy@sjcny.edu.
Website: http://www.sjcny.edu

St. Joseph's College, Long Island Campus, Programs in Management, Patchogue, NY 11772-2399. Offers health care management (MS); human resources management (MS); human services leadership (MS); organizational management (MS). *Entrance requirements:* For master's, official transcripts, minimum undergraduate GPA of 3.0, 2 letters of recommendation, resume, verification of employment, essay. Additional exam requirements/recommendations for international students: Recommended—TOEFL (minimum score 550 paper-based; 79 iBT), IELTS (minimum score 7). Electronic applications accepted. *Expenses: Tuition:* Full-time $16,182; part-time $899 per credit. *Required fees:* $440.

St. Joseph's College, New York, Programs in Business Management and Administration, Field of Business Administration, Brooklyn, NY 11205-3688. Offers MBA. *Program availability:* Part-time, evening/weekend. *Faculty:* 2 part-time/adjunct (both women). *Students:* 1 (woman) part-time. Average age 51. In 2016, 1 master's awarded. *Entrance requirements:* For master's, official transcripts, resume, two letters of reference, verification of employment. Additional exam requirements/recommendations for international students: Required—TOEFL (minimum score 80 iBT). Application fee: $25. *Expenses:* Contact institution. *Unit head:* John Capela, Associate Chair, 718-940-5843, E-mail: jcapela@sjcny.edu.
Website: https://www.sjcny.edu

Saint Joseph's College of Maine, Master of Business Administration in Leadership Program, Standish, ME 04084. Offers MBA. *Program availability:* Part-time, online learning. *Entrance requirements:* For master's, two years of work experience.

Saint Joseph's University, Erivan K. Haub School of Business, Philadelphia, PA 19131-1395. Offers MBA, MS, Post Master's Certificate, Postbaccalaureate Certificate, DO/MBA. *Accreditation:* AACSB. *Program availability:* Part-time, evening/weekend, 100% online, blended/hybrid learning. *Faculty:* 51 full-time (15 women), 46 part-time/adjunct (11 women). *Students:* 261 full-time (114 women), 761 part-time (330 women); includes 188 minority (96 Black or African American, non-Hispanic/Latino; 52 Asian, non-Hispanic/Latino; 31 Hispanic/Latino; 1 Native Hawaiian or other Pacific Islander, non-Hispanic/Latino; 8 Two or more races, non-Hispanic/Latino), 221 international. Average age 32. 742 applicants, 65% accepted, 236 enrolled. In 2016, 401 master's, 3 other advanced degrees awarded. *Degree requirements:* For master's and other advanced degree, minimum GPA of 3.0. *Entrance requirements:* For master's, GMAT, MAT, GRE, letters of recommendation, resume, personal statement, official undergraduate and graduate transcripts; structured interview (for some programs); for other advanced degree, official master's-level transcripts. Additional exam requirements/recommendations for international students: Required—TOEFL (minimum score 550 paper-based, 80 iBT), IELTS (minimum score 6.5), or PTE (minimum score 60). *Application deadline:* For fall admission, 7/15 priority date for domestic students, 5/15 priority date for international students; for spring admission, 11/15 priority date for domestic students, 10/15 priority date for international students; for summer admission, 4/15 priority date for domestic students, 2/15 priority date for international students. Applications are processed on a rolling basis. Application fee: $35. Electronic applications accepted. Tuition and fees vary according to program. *Financial support:* In 2016–17, 293 students received support, including research assistantships with partial tuition reimbursements available (averaging $2,000 per year); scholarships/grants and unspecified assistantships also available. Support available to part-time students. Financial award application deadline: 5/1; financial award applicants required to submit FAFSA. *Faculty research:* Ethical business practices, sustainability, marketing vitamin D, mushrooms, nutrition marketing for specialty groups, transforming food marketing education and research, business value of information technology and the use of software to manage the business value chain, virtual world-based project. *Total annual research expenditures:* $655,873. *Unit head:* Dr. Joseph A. DiAngelo, Dean, 610-660-1645, Fax: 610-660-1649, E-mail: jodiange@sju.edu. *Application contact:* Dr. Patricia Rafferty, Director, MBA Program, 610-660-1318, Fax: 610-660-1599, E-mail: praffert@sju.edu.
Website: https://www.sju.edu/majors-programs/graduate-business

Saint Leo University, Graduate Business Studies, Saint Leo, FL 33574-6665. Offers accounting (M Acc, MBA, Certificate); cybersecurity (MS); health care management (MBA, Certificate); human resource management (MBA, Certificate); information security management (MBA, Certificate); management (MBA, DBA); marketing (MBA, Certificate); marketing research and social media analytics (MBA, Certificate); project management (MBA, Certificate); sport business (MBA); supply chain global integration management (MBA, Certificate). *Accreditation:* ACBSP. *Program availability:* Part-time, evening/weekend, 100% online, blended/hybrid learning. *Faculty:* 53 full-time (18 women), 53 part-time/adjunct (19 women). *Students:* 8 full-time (4 women), 2,001 part-time (1,160 women); includes 928 minority (650 Black or African American, non-Hispanic/Latino; 5 American Indian or Alaska Native, non-Hispanic/Latino; 43 Asian, non-Hispanic/Latino; 193 Hispanic/Latino; 2 Native Hawaiian or other Pacific Islander, non-Hispanic/Latino; 35 Two or more races, non-Hispanic/Latino), 51 international. Average age 37. 922 applicants, 85% accepted, 517 enrolled. In 2016, 874 master's, 17 other advanced degrees awarded. *Degree requirements:* For doctorate, comprehensive exam, thesis/dissertation. *Entrance requirements:* For master's, GMAT (minimum score 500), official transcripts, current resume, 2 professional recommendations, personal statement, bachelor's degree from regionally-accredited university; undergraduate degree in accounting and minimum undergraduate GPA of 3.0 (for M Acc); minimum undergraduate GPA of 3.0 in final 2 years of undergraduate study and 2 years' work experience (for MBA); for doctorate, GMAT (minimum score of 550) if master's GPA is under 3.25, official transcripts, current resume, 2 professional recommendations, personal statement, master's degree from regionally-accredited university with minimum GPA of 3.25, 3 years' work experience, interview. Additional exam requirements/recommendations for international students: Required—TOEFL (minimum score 550 paper-based; 80 iBT). *Application deadline:* For fall admission, 7/1 priority date for domestic and international students; for spring admission, 11/12 priority date for domestic students, 11/1 for international students. Applications are processed on a rolling basis. Application fee: $80. Electronic applications accepted. *Expenses:* Contact institution. *Financial support:* In 2016–17, 118 students received support. Career-related internships or fieldwork, scholarships/grants, and health care benefits available. Financial award application deadline: 3/1; financial award applicants required to submit FAFSA. *Unit head:* Dr. Lorrie McGovern, Associate Dean, School of Business, 352-588-7869, Fax: 352-588-8912, E-mail: mbaslu@saintleo.edu. *Application contact:* Jennifer Shelley, Senior Associate Director of Graduate Admissions, 800-707-8846, Fax: 352-588-7873, E-mail: grad.admissions@saintleo.edu.
Website: http://www.saintleo.edu/academics/graduate.aspx

Saint Louis University, Graduate Education, John Cook School of Business, Program in Business Administration, St. Louis, MO 63103. Offers MBA. *Accreditation:* AACSB. *Program availability:* Part-time, evening/weekend. *Entrance requirements:* For master's, GMAT, letter of recommendation, resume. Additional exam requirements/recommendations for international students: Required—TOEFL (minimum score 570 paper-based; 88 iBT). Electronic applications accepted. *Expenses:* Contact institution.

Saint Martin's University, Office of Graduate Studies, School of Business, Lacey, WA 98503. Offers MBA. *Accreditation:* ACBSP. *Program availability:* Part-time, evening/weekend. *Faculty:* 6 full-time (4 women), 8 part-time/adjunct (3 women). *Students:* 72 full-time (30 women), 9 part-time (3 women); includes 28 minority (8 Black or African American, non-Hispanic/Latino; 5 Asian, non-Hispanic/Latino; 8 Hispanic/Latino; 1 Native Hawaiian or other Pacific Islander, non-Hispanic/Latino; 6 Two or more races, non-Hispanic/Latino), 21 international. Average age 31. 46 applicants, 74% accepted, 25 enrolled. In 2016, 38 master's awarded. *Entrance requirements:* For master's, personal essay. Additional exam requirements/recommendations for international students: Required—TOEFL (minimum score 550 paper-based; 79 iBT); Recommended—IELTS (minimum score 6.5). *Application deadline:* For fall admission, 7/1 priority date for domestic and international students; for spring admission, 12/1 for domestic students, 12/1 priority date for international students. Applications are processed on a rolling basis. Application fee: $50. Electronic applications accepted. *Expenses: Tuition:* Full-time $13,800; part-time $1150 per credit hour. *Required fees:* $720; $60 per credit hour. Tuition and fees vary according to course level and program. *Financial support:* Career-related internships or fieldwork and scholarships/grants available. Support available to part-time students. Financial award application deadline: 3/1; financial award applicants required to submit FAFSA. *Unit head:* Dr. Donald Conant, Director, MBA Program, 360-556-7359, E-mail: dconant@stmartin.edu. *Application contact:* Casey Caronna, Administrative Assistant, 360-412-6128, E-mail: ccaronna@stmartin.edu.
Website: https://www.stmartin.edu

Saint Mary's College of California, School of Economics and Business Administration, Executive MBA Program, Moraga, CA 94556. Offers MBA. *Accreditation:* AACSB. *Program availability:* Part-time, evening/weekend, blended/hybrid learning. *Entrance requirements:* For master's, 5 years of management experience. Additional exam requirements/recommendations for international students: Required—TOEFL. *Expenses:* Contact institution.

Saint Mary's College of California, School of Economics and Business Administration, MS in Management Program, Moraga, CA 94575. Offers MS.

Saint Mary's College of California, School of Economics and Business Administration, Professional MBA Program, Moraga, CA 94556. Offers MBA. *Accreditation:* AACSB. *Program availability:* Part-time, evening/weekend. *Degree requirements:* For master's, 4 half-day management practica. *Entrance requirements:* For master's, GMAT. Additional exam requirements/recommendations for international students: Required—TOEFL. *Expenses:* Contact institution.

St. Mary's University, Graduate Studies, Greehey School of Business, San Antonio, TX 78228-8507. Offers business administration (MBA), including professional accountancy, values-driven leaders; JD/MBA. *Accreditation:* AACSB. *Program availability:* Part-time, evening/weekend. *Students:* 51 full-time (21 women); includes 23 minority (3 Black or African American, non-Hispanic/Latino; 1 Asian, non-Hispanic/Latino; 19 Hispanic/Latino), 10 international. Average age 27. 133 applicants, 39% accepted, 40 enrolled. In 2016, 22 master's awarded. *Degree requirements:* For master's, comprehensive exam. *Entrance requirements:* For master's, GMAT (minimum score of 525) or GRE (minimum score of 306), undergraduate degree from accredited institution, letters of reference, current resume. Additional exam requirements/recommendations for international students: Required—TOEFL (minimum score 570 paper-based; 87 iBT); Recommended—IELTS (minimum score 6.5), TSE. *Application deadline:* For fall admission, 7/1 for domestic students; for spring admission, 11/15 for domestic students; for summer admission, 4/1 for domestic students. Application fee: $0. Electronic applications accepted. *Expenses: Tuition:* Full-time $15,600; part-time $865 per credit hour. *Required fees:* $148 per semester. *Financial support:* Research assistantships, institutionally sponsored loans, scholarships/grants, and unspecified assistantships available. Financial award application deadline: 3/31; financial award applicants required to submit FAFSA. *Faculty research:* Investment strategies, cross-culture marketing, organizational culture, supply chain management, small-firm internalization. *Application contact:* Jeremy Grace, Director, Master of Business Administration Programs, 210-431-2027, E-mail: jmgrace@stmarytx.edu.

Saint Mary's University, Sobey School of Business, Halifax, NS B3H 3C3, Canada. Offers MBA, MF, PhD. *Program availability:* Part-time, evening/weekend. *Degree requirements:* For master's, research project; for doctorate, thesis/dissertation. *Entrance requirements:* For master's, GMAT, minimum B average; for doctorate, GMAT or GRE, MBA or other master's-level degree, minimum B+ average. *Expenses:* Contact institution.

Saint Mary's University of Minnesota, Schools of Graduate and Professional Programs, Graduate School of Business and Technology, Business Administration Program, Winona, MN 55987-1399. Offers MBA, DBA. Tuition and fees vary according to degree level and program. *Unit head:* Holly Tapper, Director, 612-238-4547, Fax: 612-728-5121, E-mail: htapper@smumn.edu. *Application contact:* James Callinan, Director of Admissions for Graduate and Professional Programs, 612-728-5185, Fax: 612-728-5121, E-mail: jcallina@smumn.edu.
Website: http://www.smumn.edu/graduate-home/areas-of-study/graduate-school-of-business-technology/master-of-business-administration-mba

Saint Mary's University of Minnesota, Schools of Graduate and Professional Programs, Graduate School of Business and Technology, Management Program, Winona, MN 55987-1399. Offers MA. *Degree requirements:* For master's, capstone course. *Entrance requirements:* For master's, undergraduate degree from regionally-accredited institution with minimum overall GPA of 2.75, official transcripts, personal statement, two letters of recommendation, resume. Additional exam requirements/recommendations for international students: Required—TOEFL, IELTS, or Michigan English Language Assessment Battery. Application fee: $25. Electronic applications accepted. Tuition and fees vary according to degree level and program. *Unit head:* Paula Justich, Director, 612-728-5165, E-mail: pjustich@smumn.edu. *Application*

Business Administration and Management—General

contact: James Callinan, Director of Admissions for Graduate and Professional Programs, 612-728-5185, Fax: 612-728-5121, E-mail: jcallina@smumn.edu.
Website: http://www.smumn.edu/graduate-home/areas-of-study/graduate-school-of-business-technology/ma-in-management

St. Norbert College, Master of Business Administration Program, De Pere, WI 54115-2099. Offers business (MBA); health care (MBA); supply chain and manufacturing (MBA). *Program availability:* Part-time. *Faculty:* 9 full-time (3 women), 3 part-time/adjunct (0 women). *Students:* 64 part-time (33 women); includes 6 minority (1 American Indian or Alaska Native, non-Hispanic/Latino; 2 Asian, non-Hispanic/Latino; 2 Hispanic/Latino; 1 Two or more races, non-Hispanic/Latino), 1 international. Average age 33. 17 applicants, 100% accepted, 16 enrolled. *Entrance requirements:* For master's, official transcripts, letters of recommendation, professional resume, essay. *Application deadline:* For fall admission, 8/5 for domestic students; for winter admission, 12/16 for domestic students; for spring admission, 3/3 for domestic students; for summer admission, 4/22 for domestic students. Applications are processed on a rolling basis. Application fee: $50. Electronic applications accepted. *Expenses:* $675 per credit tuition. *Financial support:* Federal Work-Study available. Financial award application deadline: 1/1; financial award applicants required to submit FAFSA. *Unit head:* Lisa Gray, Executive Assistant, 920-403-3449, E-mail: lisa.gray@snc.edu. *Application contact:* Brenda Busch, Associate Director of Graduate Recruitment, 920-403-3942, Fax: 920-403-4072, E-mail: brenda.busch@snc.edu.
Website: http://www.snc.edu/mba/

Saint Peter's University, Graduate Business Programs, MBA Program, Jersey City, NJ 07306-5997. Offers finance (MBA); health care administration (MBA); human resource management (MBA); international business (MBA); management (MBA); management information systems (MBA); marketing (MBA); risk management (MBA); MBA/MS. *Program availability:* Part-time, evening/weekend. *Entrance requirements:* Additional exam requirements/recommendations for international students: Required—TOEFL. Electronic applications accepted. *Faculty research:* Finance, health care management, human resource management, international business, management, management information systems, marketing, risk management.

St. Thomas Aquinas College, Division of Business Administration, Sparkill, NY 10976. Offers business administration (MBA); finance (MBA); management (MBA); marketing (MBA). *Program availability:* Part-time, evening/weekend. *Entrance requirements:* For master's, GMAT. Additional exam requirements/recommendations for international students: Required—TOEFL. Electronic applications accepted.

St. Thomas University, School of Business, Department of Business Administration, Miami Gardens, FL 33054-6459. Offers M Acc, MBA, Certificate. *Program availability:* Part-time, evening/weekend. *Degree requirements:* For master's, comprehensive exam. *Entrance requirements:* Additional exam requirements/recommendations for international students: Required—TOEFL (minimum score 550 paper-based; 79 iBT). Electronic applications accepted.

St. Thomas University, School of Business, Department of Management, Miami Gardens, FL 33054-6459. Offers accounting (MBA); general management (MSM, Certificate); health management (MBA, MSM, Certificate); human resource management (MBA, MSM, Certificate); international business (MBA, MIB, MSM, Certificate); justice administration (MSM, Certificate); management accounting (MSM, Certificate); public management (MSM, Certificate); sports administration (MS). *Program availability:* Part-time, evening/weekend. *Degree requirements:* For master's, comprehensive exam. *Entrance requirements:* For master's, interview, minimum GPA of 3.0 or GMAT. Additional exam requirements/recommendations for international students: Required—TOEFL (minimum score 550 paper-based; 79 iBT). Electronic applications accepted.

St. Thomas University, School of Leadership Studies, Program in Professional Studies, Miami Gardens, FL 33054-6459. Offers executive management (MPS). *Entrance requirements:* Additional exam requirements/recommendations for international students: Required—TOEFL (minimum score 550 paper-based; 79 iBT).

Saint Vincent College, Program in Business, Latrobe, PA 15650-2690. Offers MS. *Entrance requirements:* For master's, bachelor's degree, minimum overall GPA of 3.0, three recommendations, personal statement, curriculum vitae or resume. Additional exam requirements/recommendations for international students: Required—TOEFL (minimum score 91 iBT), IELTS (minimum score 6.5).

Saint Xavier University, Graduate Studies, Graham School of Management, Chicago, IL 60655-3105. Offers employee health benefits (Certificate); finance (MBA); financial fraud examination and management (MBA, Certificate); financial planning (MBA, Certificate); generalist/individualized (MBA); health administration (MBA); managed care (Certificate); management (MBA); marketing (MBA); project management (MBA, Certificate); MBA/MS. *Accreditation:* AACSB; ACBSP. *Program availability:* Part-time, evening/weekend. *Entrance requirements:* For master's, GMAT, minimum GPA of 3.0, 2 years of work experience. Electronic applications accepted. *Expenses:* Contact institution.

Salem International University, School of Business, Salem, WV 26426-0500. Offers information security (MBA); international business (MBA). *Program availability:* Part-time, online learning. *Entrance requirements:* For master's, minimum undergraduate GPA of 2.5, course work in business, resume. Additional exam requirements/recommendations for international students: Recommended—TOEFL (minimum score 550 paper-based), IELTS (minimum score 6.5). Electronic applications accepted. *Expenses:* Contact institution. *Faculty research:* Organizational behavior strategy, marketing services.

Salem State University, School of Graduate Studies, Program in Business Administration, Salem, MA 01970-5353. Offers MBA. *Program availability:* Part-time, evening/weekend. *Entrance requirements:* For master's, GMAT. Additional exam requirements/recommendations for international students: Required—TOEFL (minimum score 550 paper-based; 80 iBT) or IELTS (minimum score 5.5).

Salisbury University, Perdue School of Business, Salisbury, MD 21801-6837. Offers business administration (MBA). *Accreditation:* AACSB. *Program availability:* Part-time, evening/weekend, 100% online, blended/hybrid learning. *Faculty:* 6 full-time (2 women). *Students:* 38 full-time (15 women), 25 part-time (13 women); includes 8 minority (4 Black or African American, non-Hispanic/Latino; 3 Asian, non-Hispanic/Latino; 1 Two or more races, non-Hispanic/Latino), 5 international. Average age 29. 64 applicants, 64% accepted, 36 enrolled. In 2016, 27 master's awarded. *Entrance requirements:* Additional exam requirements/recommendations for international students: Required—TOEFL (minimum score 550 paper-based, 79 iBT) or IELTS (6.5). *Application deadline:* For fall admission, 3/1 priority date for domestic and international students. Applications are processed on a rolling basis. Application fee: $65. Electronic applications accepted. *Expenses:* $381 per credit hour resident, $670 per credit hour non-resident; $84 per credit hour fees; $750 per credit hour (online). *Financial support:* In 2016–17, 2 students received support, including 6 teaching assistantships with full tuition reimbursements available (averaging $8,208 per year); career-related internships or fieldwork and scholarships/grants also available. Support available to part-time students. Financial award application deadline: 3/1; financial award applicants required to submit FAFSA. *Faculty research:* Supply chain management; enterprise resource planning; shared entrepreneurship. *Unit head:* Yvonne Downie Hanley, Graduate Program Director, Business Administration, 410-548-3983, E-mail: yxdownie@salisbury.edu.
Website: http://www.salisbury.edu/gsr/gradstudies/MBApage.html

Salve Regina University, Program in Business Administration, Newport, RI 02840-4192. Offers cybersecurity issues in business (MBA); entrepreneurial enterprise (MBA); health care administration and management (MBA); social ventures (MBA). *Program availability:* Part-time, evening/weekend, online learning. *Entrance requirements:* For master's, GMAT, GRE General Test, or MAT, 6 undergraduate credits each in accounting, economics, quantitative analysis and calculus or statistics. Additional exam requirements/recommendations for international students: Required—TOEFL (minimum score 600 paper-based; 100 iBT) or IELTS. Electronic applications accepted.

Salve Regina University, Program in Management, Newport, RI 02840-4192. Offers innovation and strategic management (MS); nonprofit management (CGS). *Program availability:* Part-time, evening/weekend, online learning. *Entrance requirements:* For master's, GMAT, GRE General Test, or MAT. Additional exam requirements/recommendations for international students: Required—TOEFL (minimum score 600 paper-based; 100 iBT). Electronic applications accepted.

Samford University, Brock School of Business, Birmingham, AL 35229. Offers accounting (M Acc); business administration (MBA); entrepreneurship (MBA); finance (MBA); marketing (MBA); JD/M Acc; JD/MBA; MBA/M Acc; MBA/M Div; MBA/MSEM; MBA/Pharm D. *Accreditation:* AACSB. *Program availability:* Part-time-only, evening/weekend, 100% online, blended/hybrid learning. *Faculty:* 9 full-time (2 women), 3 part-time/adjunct (0 women). *Students:* 87 full-time (33 women), 14 part-time (6 women); includes 10 minority (7 Black or African American, non-Hispanic/Latino; 1 Asian, non-Hispanic/Latino; 1 Hispanic/Latino; 1 Two or more races, non-Hispanic/Latino), 6 international. Average age 28. 148 applicants, 41% accepted, 32 enrolled. In 2016, 63 master's awarded. *Degree requirements:* For master's, capstone course. *Entrance requirements:* For master's, GMAT or GRE. Additional exam requirements/recommendations for international students: Required—TOEFL (minimum score 90 iBT), IELTS (minimum score 6.5). *Application deadline:* For fall admission, 7/1 for domestic and international students; for spring admission, 12/1 for domestic and international students; for summer admission, 4/1 for domestic and international students. Applications are processed on a rolling basis. Application fee: $35. Electronic applications accepted. *Expenses: Tuition:* Full-time $18,530; part-time $789 per credit hour. *Required fees:* $610. Tuition and fees vary according to course load, degree level, program and student level. *Financial support:* In 2016–17, 55 students received support. Career-related internships or fieldwork, institutionally sponsored loans, scholarships/grants, and tuition waivers (partial) available. Support available to part-time students. Financial award application deadline: 3/1; financial award applicants required to submit FAFSA. *Faculty research:* Entrepreneurship, accounting, finance, marketing, economics. *Total annual research expenditures:* $25,000. *Unit head:* Dr. Barbara Cartledge, Assistant Dean, 205-726-2935, Fax: 205-726-2540, E-mail: bhcartle@samford.edu. *Application contact:* Elizabeth Anne Gambrell, Assistant Director of Academic Programs, 205-726-2040, Fax: 205-726-2540, E-mail: eagambre@samford.edu.
Website: http://www.samford.edu/business/

Sam Houston State University, College of Business Administration, Department of General Business and Finance, Huntsville, TX 77341. Offers banking and financial institutions (EMBA); business administration (MBA). *Accreditation:* AACSB. *Program availability:* Part-time, evening/weekend, online learning. *Degree requirements:* For master's, comprehensive exam (for some programs). *Entrance requirements:* For master's, GMAT, interview (for EMBA); resume, transcript(s). Additional exam requirements/recommendations for international students: Required—TOEFL (minimum score 550 paper-based; 79 iBT), IELTS (minimum score 6.5). Electronic applications accepted.

San Diego State University, Graduate and Research Affairs, College of Business Administration, Department of Management, San Diego, CA 92182. Offers entrepreneurship (MS); human resources management (MS); management science (MS). *Program availability:* Part-time, evening/weekend. *Degree requirements:* For master's, thesis or alternative. *Entrance requirements:* For master's, GMAT, resume, letters of reference. Additional exam requirements/recommendations for international students: Required—TOEFL. Electronic applications accepted.

San Diego State University, Graduate and Research Affairs, College of Business Administration, Program in Business Administration, San Diego, CA 92182. Offers MBA. *Accreditation:* AACSB. *Program availability:* Part-time. *Degree requirements:* For master's, thesis or alternative. *Entrance requirements:* For master's, GMAT, resume, letters of reference. Additional exam requirements/recommendations for international students: Required—TOEFL. Electronic applications accepted.

San Francisco State University, Division of Graduate Studies, College of Business, San Francisco, CA 94132-1722. Offers EMBA, MA, MBA, MSA. *Expenses:* Tuition, state resident: full-time $6738. Tuition, nonresident: full-time $15,666. *Required fees:* $1012. Tuition and fees vary according to degree level and program. *Unit head:* Linda Oubre, Dean, 415-338-3650, Fax: 415-338-6237, E-mail: loubre@sfsu.edu. *Application contact:* Dr. Yim-Yu Wong, Associate Dean, 415-338-1276, Fax: 415-338-6237, E-mail: yywong@sfsu.edu.
Website: http://gbp.cob.sfsu.edu/

Santa Clara University, Leavey School of Business, Santa Clara, CA 95053. Offers business administration (MBA); business analytics (MS); finance (MS); information systems (MS); supply chain management and analytics (MS); JD/MBA. *Accreditation:* AACSB. *Program availability:* Part-time, evening/weekend. *Faculty:* 92 full-time (27 women), 44 part-time/adjunct (18 women). *Students:* 330 full-time (192 women), 323 part-time (136 women); includes 190 minority (7 Black or African American, non-Hispanic/Latino; 140 Asian, non-Hispanic/Latino; 28 Hispanic/Latino; 2 Native Hawaiian or other Pacific Islander, non-Hispanic/Latino; 13 Two or more races, non-Hispanic/Latino), 275 international. Average age 30. 388 applicants, 53% accepted, 107 enrolled. In 2016, 339 master's awarded. *Entrance requirements:* For master's, GMAT or GRE, resume, 2 letters of recommendation, 2 transcripts. Additional exam requirements/recommendations for international students: Required—TOEFL (minimum score 100 iBT) or IELTS (7.0). Application fee: $100 ($150 for international students). Electronic applications accepted. *Expenses:* $1,022 per unit tuition (for MBA); $1,124 per unit tuition (for other master's programs). *Financial support:* Fellowships, research assistantships, teaching assistantships, career-related internships or fieldwork, Federal Work-Study, scholarships/grants, traineeships, health care benefits, tuition waivers, and unspecified assistantships available. Support available to part-time students. Financial award applicants required to submit FAFSA. *Faculty research:* Intellectual property, research and development, international trade. *Unit head:* Caryn Beck-Dudley, Dean. *Application contact:* Taryn Upchurch, Director, Graduate Admissions and Recruitment, 408-551-7858, E-mail: upchurch@scu.edu.
Website: http://www.scu.edu/business/

Savannah State University, Master of Business Administration Program, Savannah, GA 31404. Offers MBA. *Accreditation:* AACSB. *Program availability:* Part-time, evening/

weekend. *Entrance requirements:* For master's, GMAT, GRE, or successful completion of pre-MBA program, BA/BS from an accredited institution, official transcripts, essay, 3 letters of recommendation, immunization certificate, current resume. Additional exam requirements/recommendations for international students: Required—TOEFL. Electronic applications accepted. *Expenses:* Contact institution.

Schiller International University, MBA Program, Madrid, Spain, Madrid, Spain. Offers international business (MBA). *Program availability:* Part-time. *Degree requirements:* For master's, comprehensive exam, thesis optional. *Entrance requirements:* Additional exam requirements/recommendations for international students: Required—TOEFL (minimum score 550 paper-based).

Schiller International University, MBA Program Paris, France, Paris, France. Offers international business (MBA). Bilingual French/English MBA available for native French speakers. *Program availability:* Part-time, evening/weekend, online learning. *Degree requirements:* For master's, comprehensive exam, thesis or alternative. *Entrance requirements:* Additional exam requirements/recommendations for international students: Required—TOEFL (minimum score 550 paper-based).

Schiller International University, MBA Programs, Florida, Largo, FL 33771. Offers financial planning (MBA); information technology (MBA); international business (MBA); international hotel and tourism management (MBA). *Program availability:* Part-time, evening/weekend, online learning. *Degree requirements:* For master's, thesis optional. *Entrance requirements:* Additional exam requirements/recommendations for international students: Required—TOEFL (minimum score 550 paper-based).

Schiller International University, MBA Programs, Heidelberg, Germany, Heidelberg, Germany. Offers international business (MBA, MIM); management of information technology (MBA). *Program availability:* Part-time, evening/weekend. *Degree requirements:* For master's, thesis optional. *Entrance requirements:* Additional exam requirements/recommendations for international students: Required—TOEFL (minimum score 550 paper-based). *Faculty research:* Leadership, international economy, foreign direct investment.

Schreiner University, MBA Program, Kerrville, TX 78028-5697. Offers ethical leadership (MBA). *Program availability:* Part-time, online learning. *Entrance requirements:* For master's, 3 recommendations; personal essay; transcripts; resume. Additional exam requirements/recommendations for international students: Required—TOEFL. Electronic applications accepted. *Expenses:* Contact institution.

Seattle Pacific University, Master of Arts in Management Program, Seattle, WA 98119-1997. Offers faith and business (MA); human resources (MA); social and sustainable management (MA). *Entrance requirements:* For master's, GMAT or GRE (waived with cumulative GPA of 3.3 or above), bachelor's degree from accredited college or university, resume, essay, official transcript.

Seattle Pacific University, Master of Business Administration Program, Seattle, WA 98119-1997. Offers business administration (MBA); social and sustainable enterprise (MBA). *Accreditation:* AACSB. *Program availability:* Part-time. *Entrance requirements:* For master's, GMAT (minimum score of 500 preferred; 25 verbal, 30 quantitative, 4.4 analytical writing); GRE (minimum score of 295 preferred; 150 verbal/450 old scoring, 145 quantitative/525 old scoring), BA, resume as evidence of substantive work experience. Additional exam requirements/recommendations for international students: Required—TOEFL. Electronic applications accepted.

Seattle University, Albers School of Business and Economics, Bridge MBA Program, Seattle, WA 98122-1090. Offers MBA. *Faculty:* 27 full-time (9 women), 9 part-time/adjunct (3 women). *Students:* 27 full-time (14 women); includes 9 minority (4 Asian, non-Hispanic/Latino; 3 Hispanic/Latino; 2 Two or more races, non-Hispanic/Latino), 8 international. Average age 23. 56 applicants, 63% accepted, 27 enrolled. In 2016, 25 master's awarded. *Entrance requirements:* For master's, GMAT. Additional exam requirements/recommendations for international students: Required—TOEFL or IELTS. *Application deadline:* For fall admission, 7/1 for domestic students. Applications are processed on a rolling basis. Application fee: $55. Electronic applications accepted. *Expenses:* Contact institution. *Financial support:* In 2016–17, 8 students received support. Scholarships/grants available. Financial award application deadline: 6/1. *Unit head:* John Merle, Director, 206-398-4628, E-mail: merlej@seattleu.edu. *Application contact:* Jeff Millard, Assistant Dean of Graduate Programs, 206-296-5700, E-mail: albersgrad@seattleu.edu.
Website: http://www.seattleu.edu/albers/bridgemba/

Seattle University, Albers School of Business and Economics, Master of Business Administration Program, Seattle, WA 98122-1090. Offers MBA, Certificate, JD/MBA, MBA/MSF, MBA/MSMBA. *Accreditation:* AACSB. *Program availability:* Part-time, evening/weekend. *Faculty:* 31 full-time (11 women), 9 part-time/adjunct (3 women). *Students:* 77 full-time (45 women), 281 part-time (111 women); includes 105 minority (6 Black or African American, non-Hispanic/Latino; 2 American Indian or Alaska Native, non-Hispanic/Latino; 68 Asian, non-Hispanic/Latino; 15 Hispanic/Latino; 2 Native Hawaiian or other Pacific Islander, non-Hispanic/Latino; 12 Two or more races, non-Hispanic/Latino), 49 international. Average age 31. 143 applicants, 64% accepted, 57 enrolled. In 2016, 128 master's, 44 other advanced degrees awarded. *Entrance requirements:* For master's, GMAT, minimum GPA of 3.0, 2 years of related work experience. Additional exam requirements/recommendations for international students: Required—TOEFL (minimum score 580 paper-based; 92 iBT). *Application deadline:* For fall admission, 8/20 priority date for domestic students, 4/1 priority date for international students; for winter admission, 11/20 priority date for domestic students, 9/1 priority date for international students; for spring admission, 2/20 priority date for domestic students, 12/1 priority date for international students. Applications are processed on a rolling basis. Application fee: $55. Electronic applications accepted. *Expenses:* Contact institution. *Financial support:* In 2016–17, 105 students received support. Career-related internships or fieldwork and Federal Work-Study available. Support available to part-time students. Financial award applicants required to submit FAFSA. *Unit head:* Dr. Greg Magnan, Director, 206-296-5700, Fax: 206-296-5795, E-mail: gmagnan@seattleu.edu. *Application contact:* Janet Shandley, Director of Graduate Admissions, 206-296-5900, Fax: 206-298-5656, E-mail: grad_admissions@seattleu.edu.
Website: http://www.seattleu.edu/albers/mba/

Seton Hall University, Stillman School of Business, South Orange, NJ 07079. Offers MBA, MS, Certificate. *Accreditation:* AACSB. *Program availability:* Part-time, evening/weekend. *Degree requirements:* For master's, 20 hours of community service (Social Responsibility Project). *Entrance requirements:* For master's, GMAT or GRE, MS in a business discipline, professional degree or designation (MD, JD, PhD, DVM, DDS, CPA, etc.), minimum undergraduate GPA of 3.0. Additional exam requirements/recommendations for international students: Required—TOEFL (minimum score 607 paper-based; 102 iBT), IELTS (minimum score 6), PTE. Electronic applications accepted. *Expenses:* Contact institution. *Faculty research:* Sport, hedge funds, executive compensation, social media, and legal issues.

Seton Hill University, Program in Business Administration, Greensburg, PA 15601. Offers accounting (MBA); entrepreneurship (MBA, Certificate); management (MBA). *Program availability:* Part-time, evening/weekend. *Entrance requirements:* For master's, resume, 3 letters of recommendation, personal statement, transcripts. Additional exam requirements/recommendations for international students: Required—TOEFL (minimum score 600 paper-based; 100 iBT), IELTS (minimum score 6.5). Electronic applications accepted.

Shenandoah University, Harry F. Byrd, Jr. School of Business, Winchester, VA 22601-5195. Offers business administration (MBA); healthcare management (Certificate). *Accreditation:* AACSB. *Program availability:* Part-time, evening/weekend. *Faculty:* 17 full-time (7 women), 4 part-time/adjunct (1 woman). *Students:* 35 full-time (19 women), 46 part-time (23 women); includes 16 minority (9 Black or African American, non-Hispanic/Latino; 1 American Indian or Alaska Native, non-Hispanic/Latino; 2 Asian, non-Hispanic/Latino; 3 Hispanic/Latino; 1 Native Hawaiian or other Pacific Islander, non-Hispanic/Latino), 18 international. Average age 31. 46 applicants, 63% accepted, 20 enrolled. In 2016, 28 master's awarded. *Entrance requirements:* For master's, transcripts from all institutions of higher learning; minimum GPA of 3.0 in appropriate undergraduate course work; 2 letters of recommendation; resume; interview; brief narrative essay (2-3 pages) of career, professional development and goals, as they relate to the completion of an MBA; for Certificate, 2 letters of recommendation, resume, interview, brief narrative, transcripts from all institutions of higher learning attended. Additional exam requirements/recommendations for international students: Required—TOEFL (minimum score 550 paper-based; 79 iBT), IELTS (minimum score 6.5). *Application deadline:* For fall admission, 5/1 for domestic students, 4/15 for international students; for spring admission, 11/15 for domestic students, 10/15 for international students; for summer admission, 2/15 for domestic students, 3/1 for international students. Application fee: $30. Electronic applications accepted. *Expenses:* Contact institution. *Financial support:* In 2016–17, 21 students received support. Scholarships/grants and unspecified assistantships available. Financial award applicants required to submit FAFSA. *Faculty research:* Sustainability, green initiatives, lean manufacturing, healthcare economics. *Unit head:* Miles K. Davis, PhD, Dean, 540-665-4572, Fax: 540-665-5437, E-mail: mdavi3@su.edu. *Application contact:* Andrew Woodall, Executive Director of Recruitment and Admissions, 540-665-4581, Fax: 540-665-4627, E-mail: admit@su.edu.
Website: http://www.su.edu/business/

Shippensburg University of Pennsylvania, School of Graduate Studies, College of Arts and Sciences, Department of Sociology and Anthropology, Shippensburg, PA 17257-2299. Offers organizational development and leadership (MS), including business, higher education structure and policy, historical administration, leadership in society, management information systems, public organizations. *Program availability:* Part-time, evening/weekend. *Faculty:* 4 full-time (3 women). *Students:* 11 full-time (6 women), 29 part-time (18 women); includes 9 minority (7 Black or African American, non-Hispanic/Latino; 1 Hispanic/Latino; 1 Two or more races, non-Hispanic/Latino). Average age 29. 58 applicants, 67% accepted, 21 enrolled. In 2016, 24 master's awarded. *Degree requirements:* For master's, capstone experience including internship. *Entrance requirements:* For master's, interview (if GPA less than 2.75), current resume, personal goals statement. Additional exam requirements/recommendations for international students: Required—TOEFL (minimum score 550 paper-based, 68 iBT) or IELTS (minimum score 6). *Application deadline:* For fall admission, 4/30 for international students; for spring admission, 9/30 for international students. Applications are processed on a rolling basis. Application fee: $45. Electronic applications accepted. *Expenses:* Tuition, state resident: part-time $483 per credit. Tuition, nonresident: part-time $725 per credit. *Required fees:* $141 per credit. *Financial support:* In 2016–17, 9 students received support. Career-related internships or fieldwork, scholarships/grants, unspecified assistantships, and resident hall director and student payroll positions available. Support available to part-time students. Financial award application deadline: 3/1; financial award applicants required to submit FAFSA. *Unit head:* Dr. Barbara J. Denison, Departmental Chair and Program Coordinator, 717-477-1735, Fax: 717-477-4011, E-mail: bjdeni@ship.edu. *Application contact:* Megan N. Luft, Assistant Dean of Graduate Admissions, 717-477-1231, Fax: 717-477-4016, E-mail: mnluft@ship.edu.
Website: http://www.ship.edu/odl/

Shippensburg University of Pennsylvania, School of Graduate Studies, John L. Grove College of Business, Shippensburg, PA 17257-2299. Offers advanced studies in business (Certificate); advanced supply chain and logistics management (Certificate); business administration (MBA), including business administration, finance, healthcare management, management information systems, supply chain management; finance (Certificate); health care management (Certificate); management information systems (Certificate). *Accreditation:* AACSB. *Program availability:* Part-time, evening/weekend, 100% online, blended/hybrid learning. *Faculty:* 23 full-time (4 women), 4 part-time/adjunct (1 woman). *Students:* 58 full-time (17 women), 195 part-time (59 women); includes 26 minority (12 Black or African American, non-Hispanic/Latino; 8 Asian, non-Hispanic/Latino; 5 Hispanic/Latino; 1 Two or more races, non-Hispanic/Latino), 26 international. Average age 32. 224 applicants, 55% accepted, 70 enrolled. In 2016, 101 master's awarded. *Degree requirements:* For master's, thesis optional, practicum. *Entrance requirements:* For master's, GMAT (minimum score 450 if less than 5 years of mid-level experience, including management experience), current resume; relevant work/classroom experience; 500-word statement of purpose; prerequisites of quantitative analysis, computer usage, and oral and written communications; laptop computer. Additional exam requirements/recommendations for international students: Required—TOEFL (minimum score 550 paper-based, 68 iBT) or IELTS (minimum score 6). *Application deadline:* For fall admission, 4/30 for international students; for spring admission, 9/30 for international students. Applications are processed on a rolling basis. Application fee: $45. Electronic applications accepted. *Expenses:* Tuition, state resident: part-time $483 per credit. Tuition, nonresident: part-time $725 per credit. *Required fees:* $141 per credit. *Financial support:* In 2016–17, 12 students received support. Career-related internships or fieldwork, scholarships/grants, unspecified assistantships, and resident hall director and student payroll positions available. Support available to part-time students. Financial award application deadline: 3/1; financial award applicants required to submit FAFSA. *Unit head:* Dr. John G. Kooti, Dean of the College of Business, 717-477-1435, Fax: 717-477-4003, E-mail: jgkooti@ship.edu. *Application contact:* Megan N. Luft, Associate Dean of Graduate Admissions, 717-477-1231, Fax: 717-477-4016, E-mail: mnluft@ship.edu.
Website: http://www.ship.edu/business

Shorter University, Professional Studies, Rome, GA 30165. Offers accountancy (MAC); business administration (MBA); management (MM). *Program availability:* Evening/weekend. *Degree requirements:* For master's, project. *Entrance requirements:* For master's, minimum undergraduate GPA of 2.75 in last 60 hours, 3 years of work experience. Additional exam requirements/recommendations for international students: Required—TOEFL (minimum score 550 paper-based; 79 iBT). Electronic applications accepted.

Siena College, School of Business, Loudonville, NY 12211-1462. Offers accounting (MS). *Program availability:* Evening/weekend. *Degree requirements:* For master's, internship.

Silicon Valley University, Graduate Programs, San Jose, CA 95131. Offers business administration (MBA); computer engineering (MSCE); computer science (MSCS). *Degree requirements:* For master's, project (MSCS).

Business Administration and Management—General

Silver Lake College of the Holy Family, Graduate School, Graduate Business Program, Manitowoc, WI 54220-9319. Offers leadership and organizational development (MS). *Program availability:* Part-time, evening/weekend. *Faculty:* 1 full-time (0 women), 4 part-time/adjunct (2 women). *Students:* 14 full-time (10 women), 9 part-time (7 women); includes 4 minority (1 Black or African American, non-Hispanic/Latino; 2 American Indian or Alaska Native, non-Hispanic/Latino; 1 Asian, non-Hispanic/Latino). Average age 39. In 2016, 12 master's awarded. *Degree requirements:* For master's, comprehensive exam (for some programs), thesis optional, capstone culminating project, thesis research, comprehensive portfolio, or public presentation of project. *Entrance requirements:* For master's, ACT (preferred) or SAT, minimum undergraduate GPA of 3.0. Additional exam requirements/recommendations for international students: Required—TOEFL (minimum score 550 paper-based; 89 iBT). *Application deadline:* For fall admission, 8/1 for domestic and international students; for spring admission, 12/1 for domestic and international students. Applications are processed on a rolling basis. Application fee: $50. Electronic applications accepted. *Expenses:* $540 per credit; $220 comprehensive fee. *Financial support:* Career-related internships or fieldwork, Federal Work-Study, scholarships/grants, and unspecified assistantships available. Support available to part-time students. Financial award application deadline: 6/1; financial award applicants required to submit FAFSA. *Faculty research:* Leadership development; organizational change; organizational behavior. *Unit head:* Nancy Sim, Director of Graduate Education Programs, 920-686-6117, Fax: 920-684-6322, E-mail: nancy.sim@sl.edu. *Application contact:* Jamie A. Grant, Executive Director of Enrollment Management, 920-686-6175, Fax: 920-686-6322, E-mail: jamie.grant@sl.edu.
Website: http://www.sl.edu/future-students/graduate-programs/degrees-offered/master-of-science-in-leadership-and-organizational-development

Simmons College, School of Management, Boston, MA 02115. Offers business administration (MBA); health care (MBA); management (MS, MSM), including communications management (MS), non-profit management (MS); MBA/MSW; MS/MA. *Accreditation:* AACSB. *Program availability:* Part-time, evening/weekend. *Faculty:* 14 full-time (10 women), 5 part-time/adjunct (3 women). *Students:* 23 full-time (20 women), 141 part-time (126 women); includes 41 minority (20 Black or African American, non-Hispanic/Latino; 7 Asian, non-Hispanic/Latino; 13 Hispanic/Latino; 1 Two or more races, non-Hispanic/Latino), 7 international. Average age 32. 62 applicants, 74% accepted, 32 enrolled. In 2016, 58 master's awarded. *Entrance requirements:* For master's, GMAT or GRE. Additional exam requirements/recommendations for international students: Required—TOEFL. *Application deadline:* For fall admission, 7/18 priority date for domestic students; for summer admission, 4/24 priority date for domestic students. Applications are processed on a rolling basis. Application fee: $75. Electronic applications accepted. *Expenses:* $1,374 per credit, $4,122 per course, $102 activity fee per semester. *Financial support:* Scholarships/grants and unspecified assistantships available. Financial award applicants required to submit FAFSA. *Faculty research:* Gender and organizations, leadership, health care management. *Unit head:* Patricia Deyton, Associate Dean for Graduate Programs, 617-521-3876.
Website: http://www.simmons.edu/som

Simon Fraser University, Office of Graduate Studies and Postdoctoral Fellows, Faculty of Business Administration, Vancouver, BC V6B 5K3, Canada. Offers business administration (EMBA, PhD, Graduate Diploma); finance (M Sc); management of technology (MBA); management of technology/biotechnology (MBA). *Program availability:* Online learning. *Faculty:* 91 full-time (33 women). *Students:* 554 full-time (252 women), 161 part-time (58 women). 928 applicants, 45% accepted, 279 enrolled. In 2016, 178 master's, 3 doctorates, 78 other advanced degrees awarded. *Degree requirements:* For master's, thesis (for some programs); for doctorate, comprehensive exam, thesis/dissertation. *Entrance requirements:* For master's, GMAT, minimum GPA of 3.0 (on scale of 4.33) or 3.33 based on last 60 credits of undergraduate courses; for doctorate, minimum GPA of 3.5 (on scale of 4.33); for Graduate Diploma, minimum GPA of 2.5 (on scale of 4.33) or 2.67 based on last 60 credits of undergraduate courses. Additional exam requirements/recommendations for international students: Recommended—TOEFL (minimum score 580 paper-based; 93 iBT), IELTS (minimum score 7), TWE (minimum score 5). *Application deadline:* For fall admission, 4/2 for domestic students; for winter admission, 10/1 for domestic students; for spring admission, 2/2 for domestic students. Application fee: $90 ($125 for international students). *Expenses:* Contact institution. *Financial support:* In 2016–17, 71 students received support, including 9 fellowships (averaging $6,139 per year), teaching assistantships (averaging $5,608 per year); research assistantships, career-related internships or fieldwork, and scholarships/grants also available. *Faculty research:* Accounting, management and organizational studies, technology and operations management, finance, international business. *Unit head:* Dr. Ian McCarthy, Associate Dean, Graduate Programs, 778-782-9255, Fax: 778-782-4920, E-mail: grad-business@sfu.ca. *Application contact:* Graduate Secretary, 778-782-5013, Fax: 778-782-5122, E-mail: grad-business@sfu.ca.
Website: http://beedie.sfu.ca/graduate/index.php

SIT Graduate Institute, Graduate Programs, Master's Programs in Intercultural Service, Leadership, and Management, Brattleboro, VT 05302-0676. Offers intercultural service, leadership, and management (self-designed) (MA); international education (MA); peacebuilding and conflict transformation (MA); sustainable development (MA). *Program availability:* Online learning. *Degree requirements:* For master's, one foreign language, thesis. *Entrance requirements:* For master's, 3 letters of reference. Additional exam requirements/recommendations for international students: Required—TOEFL, IELTS. *Faculty research:* Intercultural communication, conflict resolution, international education, world issues, international affairs.

Slippery Rock University of Pennsylvania, Graduate Studies (Recruitment), College of Business, School of Business, Slippery Rock, PA 16057-1383. Offers accounting/finance (MBA); general (MBA); marketing/management (MBA). *Program availability:* Part-time, evening/weekend. *Faculty:* 6 full-time (4 women), 1 part-time/adjunct (0 women). *Students:* 16 full-time (9 women), 9 part-time (6 women); includes 1 minority (Black or African American, non-Hispanic/Latino). Average age 29. 109 applicants, 26% accepted, 13 enrolled. In 2016, 26 master's awarded. *Degree requirements:* For master's, comprehensive exam (for some programs), thesis (for some programs). *Entrance requirements:* For master's, minimum cumulative GPA of 3.0, official transcripts, three references. Additional exam requirements/recommendations for international students: Required—TOEFL (minimum score 550 paper-based; 80 iBT). *Application deadline:* For fall admission, 3/1 priority date for domestic students, 5/1 priority date for international students; for spring admission, 10/1 priority date for domestic students, 9/1 priority date for international students. Applications are processed on a rolling basis. Application fee: $25 ($30 for international students). Electronic applications accepted. *Expenses:* $646.50 per credit in-state, $936.80 per credit out-of-state; $581.45 per online credit in-state, $648.65 per online credit out-of-state. *Financial support:* In 2016–17, 5 students received support. Career-related internships or fieldwork, Federal Work-Study, institutionally sponsored loans, scholarships/grants, tuition waivers (partial), and unspecified assistantships available. Support available to part-time students. Financial award application deadline: 5/1; financial award applicants required to submit FAFSA. *Unit head:* Dr. Larry McCarthy, Graduate Coordinator, 724-738-2552, Fax: 724-738-2959, E-mail: larry.mccarthy@sru.edu. *Application contact:* Brandi Weber-Mortimer, Director of Graduate Admissions, 724-738-2051, Fax: 724-738-2146, E-mail: graduate.admissions@sru.edu.
Website: http://www.sru.edu/academics/graduate-programs/mba-master-of-business-administration

Sonoma State University, School of Business and Economics, Rohnert Park, CA 94928-3609. Offers business administration (MBA), including contemporary business issues, global business, leadership and entrepreneurship; executive business administration (MBA); wine business (MBA). *Accreditation:* AACSB. *Program availability:* Part-time, evening/weekend. *Degree requirements:* For master's, thesis or alternative. *Entrance requirements:* For master's, GMAT. Additional exam requirements/recommendations for international students: Required—TOEFL (minimum score 500 paper-based). *Application deadline:* For fall admission, 1/31 priority date for domestic students; for spring admission, 8/31 for domestic students. Applications are processed on a rolling basis. Application fee: $55. *Expenses:* Tuition, state resident: full-time $6738; part-time $3906 per unit. *Required fees:* $1916; $1916 per year. Tuition and fees vary according to course load, degree level and program. *Financial support:* Career-related internships or fieldwork, Federal Work-Study, institutionally sponsored loans, and scholarships/grants available. Support available to part-time students. Financial award application deadline: 3/2; financial award applicants required to submit FAFSA. *Unit head:* Dr. William Silver, Dean, 707-664-2377. *Application contact:* John Stayton, Executive Director, Graduate and Executive Programs, 707-664-3954, E-mail: john.stayton@sonoma.edu.
Website: http://web.sonoma.edu/sbe/

South Carolina State University, College of Graduate and Professional Studies, School of Business, Orangeburg, SC 29117-0001. Offers agribusiness (MBA); entrepreneurship (MBA); general business administration (MBA); healthcare management (MBA). *Program availability:* Part-time, evening/weekend. *Faculty:* 7 full-time (3 women). *Students:* 19 full-time (11 women), 10 part-time (5 women); includes 27 minority (all Black or African American, non-Hispanic/Latino). Average age 27. 17 applicants, 94% accepted, 15 enrolled. In 2016, 6 master's awarded. *Degree requirements:* For master's, comprehensive exam, business plan. *Entrance requirements:* For master's, GMAT, minimum GPA of 2.8. Additional exam requirements/recommendations for international students: Required—TOEFL. *Application deadline:* For fall admission, 6/15 for domestic and international students; for spring admission, 11/1 for domestic and international students. Application fee: $25. Electronic applications accepted. *Expenses:* Tuition, state resident: full-time $8938; part-time $579 per credit hour. Tuition, nonresident: full-time $19,018; part-time $1139 per credit hour. *Required fees:* $1482; $82 per credit hour. *Financial support:* Fellowships, research assistantships, career-related internships or fieldwork, Federal Work-Study, scholarships/grants, and unspecified assistantships available. Financial award application deadline: 6/1. *Unit head:* Dr. Matthew Guah, Chair, 803-516-4834, Fax: 803-536-8078, E-mail: mguah@scsu.edu. *Application contact:* Ellen R. Ricoma, MBA Program Director, 803-533-3777, Fax: 803-516-4651, E-mail: ericoma1@scsu.edu.

Southeastern Louisiana University, College of Business, Hammond, LA 70402. Offers MBA. *Accreditation:* AACSB. *Faculty:* 13 full-time (1 woman). *Students:* 69 full-time (32 women), 10 part-time (4 women); includes 14 minority (3 Black or African American, non-Hispanic/Latino; 8 Hispanic/Latino; 3 Two or more races, non-Hispanic/Latino), 11 international. Average age 25. 81 applicants, 57% accepted, 26 enrolled. In 2016, 31 master's awarded. *Entrance requirements:* Additional exam requirements/recommendations for international students: Required—TOEFL (minimum score 500 paper-based; 61 iBT), IELTS (minimum score 5.5). *Application deadline:* For fall admission, 7/15 priority date for domestic students, 6/1 priority date for international students; for spring admission, 12/1 priority date for domestic students, 10/1 priority date for international students. Applications are processed on a rolling basis. Application fee: $20 ($30 for international students). Electronic applications accepted. *Expenses:* Tuition, state resident: full-time $6540; part-time $465 per credit hour. Tuition, nonresident: full-time $19,017; part-time $1158 per credit hour. *Required fees:* $1829. *Financial support:* In 2016–17, 18 students received support. Research assistantships, career-related internships or fieldwork, Federal Work-Study, institutionally sponsored loans, scholarships/grants, and unspecified assistantships available. Support available to part-time students. Financial award application deadline: 5/1; financial award applicants required to submit FAFSA. *Faculty research:* Ethical decision-making in accounting, entrepreneurship and emerging information, leadership and organizational performance. *Unit head:* Dr. Antoinette Phillips, Interim Dean, 985-549-2258, Fax: 985-549-5038, E-mail: business@southeastern.edu. *Application contact:* Amanda Harper, Graduate Admissions Analyst, 985-549-5620, Fax: 985-549-5882, E-mail: admissions@southeastern.edu.
Website: http://www.selu.edu/acad_research/colleges/bus/index.html

Southeastern Oklahoma State University, John Massey School of Business, Durant, OK 74701-0609. Offers MBA. *Accreditation:* AACSB. *Program availability:* Part-time, evening/weekend. *Degree requirements:* For master's, thesis optional. *Entrance requirements:* For master's, GMAT, minimum GPA of 3.0 in last 60 hours or 2.75 overall. Additional exam requirements/recommendations for international students: Required—TOEFL (minimum score 550 paper-based; 79 iBT). Electronic applications accepted.

Southeastern University, Jannetides College of Business and Entrepreneurial Leadership, Lakeland, FL 33801-6099. Offers executive leadership (MBA); missional leadership (MBA); sport management (MBA). *Accreditation:* ACBSP. *Program availability:* Evening/weekend, online learning. *Entrance requirements:* For master's, GMAT, minimum cumulative GPA of 3.0, writing sample. Electronic applications accepted. *Expenses: Tuition:* Full-time $9450; part-time $6300 per credit. *Required fees:* $500; $250 per semester. One-time fee: $150. Tuition and fees vary according to degree level, campus/location and program. *Unit head:* Lyle L. Bowlin, Dean, 863-667-5118, E-mail: llbowlin@seu.edu.
Website: http://www.seu.edu/business/

Southeast Missouri State University, School of Graduate Studies, Harrison College of Business, Cape Girardeau, MO 63701-4799. Offers accounting (MBA); entrepreneurship (MBA); financial management (MBA); sport management (MBA). *Accreditation:* AACSB. *Program availability:* Part-time, evening/weekend, 100% online. *Faculty:* 27 full-time (7 women), 1 (woman) part-time/adjunct. *Students:* 72 full-time (39 women), 112 part-time (41 women); includes 20 minority (10 Black or African American, non-Hispanic/Latino; 6 Asian, non-Hispanic/Latino; 4 Hispanic/Latino), 64 international. Average age 29. 106 applicants, 70% accepted, 55 enrolled. In 2016, 65 master's awarded. *Degree requirements:* For master's, variable foreign language requirement, comprehensive exam (for some programs), thesis or alternative. *Entrance requirements:* For master's, GMAT or GRE, minimum undergraduate GPA of 2.5, minimum grade of C in prerequisite courses. Additional exam requirements/recommendations for international students: Required—TOEFL (minimum score 550 paper-based; 79 iBT), IELTS (minimum score 6), PTE (minimum score 53). *Application deadline:* For fall admission, 8/1 for domestic students, 6/1 for international students; for spring admission, 11/21 for domestic students, 10/1 for international students; for summer admission, 5/15 for domestic students. Applications are processed on a rolling basis. Application fee: $30 ($40 for international students). Electronic applications accepted.

Expenses: Tuition, state resident: full-time $3130; part-time $260.80 per credit hour. Tuition, nonresident: full-time $5842; part-time $486.80 per credit hour. *Required fees:* $33.70 per credit hour. *Financial support:* In 2016–17, 61 students received support. Career-related internships or fieldwork, Federal Work-Study, scholarships/grants, traineeships, tuition waivers (full), and unspecified assistantships available. Financial award application deadline: 6/30; financial award applicants required to submit FAFSA. *Faculty research:* Organizational justice, ethics, leadership, corporate finance, generational differences. *Unit head:* Dr. James L. Caldwell, Director, Graduate Business Studies, 573-651-2851, Fax: 573-651-5032, E-mail: jcaldwell@semo.edu. *Application contact:* Gail Amick, Admissions Specialist, 573-651-2590, Fax: 573-651-5936, E-mail: gamick@semo.edu.
Website: http://www.semo.edu/mba

Southern Adventist University, School of Business and Management, Collegedale, TN 37315-0370. Offers accounting (MBA); church administration (MSA); church and nonprofit leadership (MBA); financial management (MFM); healthcare administration (MBA); management (MBA); marketing management (MBA); outdoor education (MSA). *Program availability:* Part-time, evening/weekend, online learning. *Entrance requirements:* For master's, GMAT. Additional exam requirements/recommendations for international students: Required—TOEFL (minimum score 600 paper-based; 100 iBT). Electronic applications accepted.

Southern Arkansas University–Magnolia, School of Graduate Studies, Magnolia, AR 71753. Offers agriculture (MS); business administration (MBA), including agri-business, social entrepreneurship, supply chain management; clinical and mental health counseling (MS); computer and information sciences (MS), including cyber security and privacy, data science, information technology; gifted and talented (M Ed), including curriculum and instruction, educational administration and supervision, gifted and talented P-8/7-12, instructional specialist P-4; higher, adult and lifelong education (M Ed); kinesiology (M Ed), including coaching; library media and information specialist (M Ed); public administration (MPA); school counseling K-12 (M Ed); student affairs and college counseling (M Ed); teaching (MAT). *Accreditation:* NCATE. *Program availability:* Part-time, 100% online, blended/hybrid learning. *Faculty:* 36 full-time (19 women), 33 part-time/adjunct (14 women). *Students:* 605 full-time (143 women), 879 part-time (352 women); includes 130 minority (113 Black or African American, non-Hispanic/Latino; 7 American Indian or Alaska Native, non-Hispanic/Latino; 2 Asian, non-Hispanic/Latino; 2 Hispanic/Latino; 6 Two or more races, non-Hispanic/Latino), 1,048 international. Average age 28. 904 applicants, 81% accepted, 262 enrolled. In 2016, 278 master's awarded. *Degree requirements:* For master's, comprehensive exam (for some programs), thesis optional. *Entrance requirements:* For master's, GRE, MAT or GMAT, minimum GPA of 2.5. Additional exam requirements/recommendations for international students: Required—TOEFL (minimum score 550 paper-based), IELTS (minimum score 6). *Application deadline:* For fall admission, 7/20 for domestic students, 7/10 for international students; for spring admission, 12/1 for domestic students, 11/15 for international students; for summer admission, 4/1 for domestic students, 5/1 for international students. Applications are processed on a rolling basis. Application fee: $25 ($50 for international students). Electronic applications accepted. *Expenses:* Tuition, state resident: full-time $2511; part-time $279 per credit hour. Tuition, nonresident: full-time $3726; part-time $414 per credit hour. *Required fees:* $307 per semester. Tuition and fees vary according to course load and program. *Financial support:* Career-related internships or fieldwork, Federal Work-Study, scholarships/grants, tuition waivers (full), and unspecified assistantships available. Financial award applicants required to submit FAFSA. *Faculty research:* Alternative certification for teachers, supervision of instruction, instructional leadership, counseling. *Unit head:* Dr. Kim Bloss, Dean, School of Graduate Studies, 870-235-4150, Fax: 870-235-5227, E-mail: kkbloss@saumag.edu. *Application contact:* Shrijana Malakar, Admissions Specialist, 870-235-4150, Fax: 870-235-5227, E-mail: smalakar@saumag.edu.
Website: http://www.saumag.edu/graduate

Southern Connecticut State University, School of Graduate Studies, School of Business, Program in Business Administration, New Haven, CT 06515-1355. Offers MBA. *Program availability:* Part-time, evening/weekend. *Faculty:* 17 full-time (2 women), 5 part-time/adjunct (1 woman). *Students:* 92 full-time (46 women), 82 part-time (45 women); includes 63 minority (35 Black or African American, non-Hispanic/Latino; 7 Asian, non-Hispanic/Latino; 17 Hispanic/Latino; 4 Two or more races, non-Hispanic/Latino), 8 international. Average age 31. 102 applicants, 66% accepted, 49 enrolled. In 2016, 54 master's awarded. *Entrance requirements:* For master's, GMAT, interview. *Application deadline:* For fall admission, 7/1 priority date for domestic students. Applications are processed on a rolling basis. Application fee: $50. Electronic applications accepted. *Expenses:* Tuition, state resident: full-time $6497; part-time $519 per credit hour. Tuition, nonresident: full-time $18,102; part-time $535 per credit hour. *Required fees:* $4722; $55 per semester. Tuition and fees vary according to program. *Financial support:* Career-related internships or fieldwork, scholarships/grants, and unspecified assistantships available. Financial award application deadline: 4/15; financial award applicants required to submit FAFSA. *Unit head:* Dr. James Thorson, Director, 203-392-5626, Fax: 203-392-5988, E-mail: thorsonj1@southernct.edu. *Application contact:* Lisa Galvin, Director of Graduate Admissions, 203-392-5240, Fax: 203-392-5235, E-mail: galvinl1@southernct.edu.

Southern Illinois University Carbondale, Graduate School, College of Business and Administration, Department of Business Administration, Carbondale, IL 62901-4701. Offers MBA, PhD, JD/MBA, MBA/MA, MBA/MS. *Accreditation:* AACSB. *Degree requirements:* For doctorate, thesis/dissertation. *Entrance requirements:* For master's, GMAT, minimum GPA of 2.7; for doctorate, GMAT, minimum graduate GPA of 3.25. Additional exam requirements/recommendations for international students: Required—TOEFL (minimum score 550 paper-based; 80 iBT). Electronic applications accepted. *Faculty research:* Marketing, corporate finance, organizational behavior, accounting, management information systems, international business.

Southern Illinois University Edwardsville, Graduate School, School of Business, Program in Business Administration, Edwardsville, IL 62026. Offers business analytics (MBA); management information systems (MBA); project management (MBA). *Accreditation:* AACSB. *Program availability:* Part-time, evening/weekend. *Degree requirements:* For master's, comprehensive exam. *Entrance requirements:* For master's, GMAT. Additional exam requirements/recommendations for international students: Required—TOEFL (minimum score 550 paper-based; 79 iBT), IELTS (minimum score 6.5). Electronic applications accepted.

Southern Methodist University, Cox School of Business, Dallas, TX 75275. Offers accounting (MSA); business (Exec MBA); business administration (MBA), including accounting, finance, information technology and operations management, management, marketing, strategy and entrepreneurship; entrepreneurship (MS); finance (MSF); management (MSM); JD/MBA. *Accreditation:* AACSB. *Program availability:* Part-time, evening/weekend. *Entrance requirements:* For master's, GMAT. Additional exam requirements/recommendations for international students: Required—TOEFL, PTE. Electronic applications accepted. *Expenses:* Contact institution. *Faculty research:* Financial markets structure, international finance, accounting disclosure, corporate finance, leadership, change management, organizational behavior, entrepreneurship, strategic marketing, corporate strategy, product innovation, information systems, knowledge management, energy markets, customer relationship management.

Southern Nazarene University, College of Professional and Graduate Studies, School of Business, Bethany, OK 73008. Offers business administration (MBA); health care management (MBA); management (MS Mgt). *Accreditation:* ACBSP. *Program availability:* Part-time, evening/weekend, online learning. *Degree requirements:* For master's, thesis optional. *Entrance requirements:* For master's, resume. Additional exam requirements/recommendations for international students: Required—TOEFL (minimum score 550 paper-based; 80 iBT), IELTS (minimum score 7). Electronic applications accepted.

Southern New Hampshire University, School of Business, Manchester, NH 03106-1045. Offers accounting (MBA, MS, Graduate Certificate); accounting finance (MS); accounting/auditing (MS); accounting/forensic accounting (MS); accounting/taxation (MS); athletic administration (MBA, Graduate Certificate); business administration (IMBA, MBA, Certificate, Graduate Certificate), including accounting (Certificate), business administration (MBA), business information systems (Graduate Certificate), human resource management (Certificate); corporate social responsibility (MBA); entrepreneurship (MBA); finance (MBA, MS, Graduate Certificate); finance/corporate finance (MS); finance/investments and securities (MS); forensic accounting (MBA); healthcare informatics (MBA); healthcare management (MBA); human resource management (Graduate Certificate); information technology (MS, Graduate Certificate); information technology management (MBA); international business (Graduate Certificate); international business and information technology (Graduate Certificate); international finance (Graduate Certificate); international sport management (Graduate Certificate); justice studies (MBA); leadership of nonprofit organizations (Graduate Certificate); management (MS); marketing (MBA, MS, Graduate Certificate); operations and project management (MS); operations and supply chain management (MBA, Graduate Certificate); organizational leadership (MS); project management (MBA, Graduate Certificate); Six Sigma (MBA); Six Sigma quality (Graduate Certificate); social media marketing (MBA); sport management (MBA, MS, Graduate Certificate); sustainability and environmental compliance (MBA); workplace conflict management (MBA); MBA/Certificate. *Accreditation:* ACBSP. *Program availability:* Part-time, evening/weekend, online learning. Terminal master's awarded for partial completion of doctoral program. *Degree requirements:* For master's, one foreign language, comprehensive exam (for some programs), thesis or alternative. *Entrance requirements:* For master's, minimum GPA of 2.5. Additional exam requirements/recommendations for international students: Required—TOEFL (minimum score 500 paper-based). Electronic applications accepted.

Southern Oregon University, Graduate Studies, School of Business, Ashland, OR 97520. Offers accounting (Postbaccalaureate Certificate); business administration (MBA); international management (MIM). *Accreditation:* ACBSP. *Program availability:* Part-time, evening/weekend, online learning. *Faculty:* 18 full-time (6 women), 8 part-time/adjunct (5 women). *Students:* 28 full-time (13 women), 30 part-time (10 women); includes 13 minority (1 Black or African American, non-Hispanic/Latino; 2 Asian, non-Hispanic/Latino; 7 Hispanic/Latino; 3 Two or more races, non-Hispanic/Latino), 19 international. Average age 33. 65 applicants, 49% accepted, 25 enrolled. In 2016, 16 master's awarded. *Degree requirements:* For master's, comprehensive exam. *Entrance requirements:* For master's, GMAT, minimum cumulative GPA of 3.0 in the last 90 quarter credits (60 semester credits) of undergraduate coursework. Additional exam requirements/recommendations for international students: Required—TOEFL (minimum score 540 paper-based; 76 iBT), IELTS (minimum score 6), ELPT (minimum score 964) or ELS (minimum score 112). *Application deadline:* For fall admission, 7/31 priority date for domestic and international students; for winter admission, 11/15 priority date for domestic students, 11/14 priority date for international students; for spring admission, 1/7 priority date for domestic and international students. Applications are processed on a rolling basis. Application fee: $60. Electronic applications accepted. *Expenses:* Tuition, state resident: full-time $10,719; part-time $397 per credit. Tuition, nonresident: full-time $13,419; part-time $497 per credit. *Required fees:* $548. *Financial support:* In 2016–17, 1 student received support, including 1 research assistantship with partial tuition reimbursement available; career-related internships or fieldwork, institutionally sponsored loans, scholarships/grants, and unspecified assistantships also available. *Unit head:* Dr. Mark Siders, Graduate Program Coordinator, 541-552-6709, E-mail: sidersm@sou.edu. *Application contact:* Kelly Moutsatson, Director of Admissions, 541-552-6411, Fax: 541-552-8403, E-mail: admissions@sou.edu.
Website: http://www.sou.edu/business/graduate-programs.html

Southern University and Agricultural and Mechanical College, College of Business, Baton Rouge, LA 70813. Offers MBA. *Accreditation:* AACSB. *Degree requirements:* For master's, comprehensive exam. *Entrance requirements:* For master's, GMAT. Additional exam requirements/recommendations for international students: Required—TOEFL (minimum score 525 paper-based). *Faculty research:* Accounting theory, auditing, governmental and non-profit accounting.

Southern Utah University, Master of Accountancy/MBA Dual Degree Program, Cedar City, UT 84720-2498. Offers MBA/M Acc. *Program availability:* Part-time, 100% online. *Students:* 1 full-time (0 women). Average age 29. 3 applicants, 100% accepted, 1 enrolled. *Entrance requirements:* Additional exam requirements/recommendations for international students: Required—TOEFL (minimum score 550 paper-based, 79 iBT) or IELTS (minimum score 6). *Application deadline:* For fall admission, 3/1 for domestic and international students; for spring admission, 10/1 for domestic and international students; for summer admission, 3/1 for domestic and international students. Applications are processed on a rolling basis. Application fee: $60 ($65 for international students). Electronic applications accepted. *Expenses:* $8,722 per year, in-state or online, full-time; $23,814 per year, out-of-state, full-time. *Financial support:* Unspecified assistantships available. *Application contact:* Patricia Palmer, Academic Advisor and Graduate Program Coordinator, 435-865-8167, Fax: 435-586-5493, E-mail: patriciapalmer@suu.edu.
Website: http://www.suu.edu/business/grad.html

Southern Utah University, Program in Business Administration, Cedar City, UT 84720-2498. Offers MBA. *Accreditation:* AACSB. *Program availability:* Part-time, evening/weekend, 100% online. *Faculty:* 8 full-time (0 women). *Students:* 18 full-time (5 women), 37 part-time (11 women); includes 4 minority (2 Black or African American, non-Hispanic/Latino; 2 Hispanic/Latino). Average age 33. 63 applicants, 40% accepted, 13 enrolled. In 2016, 13 master's awarded. *Entrance requirements:* For master's, GMAT or GRE. Additional exam requirements/recommendations for international students: Required—TOEFL (minimum score 550 paper-based, 79 iBT) or IELTS (minimum score 6). *Application deadline:* For fall admission, 3/1 for domestic and international students; for spring admission, 10/1 for domestic and international students; for summer admission, 3/1 for domestic students, 2/1 for international students. Applications are processed on a rolling basis. Application fee: $60 ($65 for international students). Electronic applications accepted. *Expenses:* $8,722 per year, in-state or online, full-time; $23,814 per year, out-of-state, full-time. *Financial support:* Unspecified assistantships available. *Unit head:* Dr. Kim Craft, Department Chair/MBA Program Director, 435-586-5414, Fax: 435-586-5493, E-mail: craft@suu.edu. *Application contact:* Patricia Palmer, Academic Advisor and Graduate Program Coordinator, 435-865-8167, Fax: 435-586-

5493, E-mail: patriciapalmer@suu.edu.
Website: https://www.suu.edu/business/mgmt/mba.html

Southern Wesleyan University, Program in Business Administration, Central, SC 29630-1020. Offers MBA. *Program availability:* Evening/weekend. *Degree requirements:* For master's, comprehensive exam. *Entrance requirements:* For master's, GMAT, GRE, or MAT, minimum of 3 undergraduate semester credit hours each in accounting, economics, and statistics; minimum of 18 undergraduate semester credit hours in business administration; minimum of 2 years' significant work experience. Additional exam requirements/recommendations for international students: Required—TOEFL (minimum score 500 paper-based).

Southern Wesleyan University, Program in Management, Central, SC 29630-1020. Offers MSM. *Program availability:* Evening/weekend. *Entrance requirements:* For master's, GMAT, GRE, or MAT, minimum of 18 undergraduate semester credit hours in business administration; minimum of 2 years significant work experience. Additional exam requirements/recommendations for international students: Required—TOEFL (minimum score 500 paper-based). *Expenses:* Contact institution.

South University, Graduate Programs, College of Business, Savannah, GA 31406. Offers corrections (MBA); entrepreneurship and small business (MBA); healthcare administration (MBA); hospitality management (MBA); leadership (MS); public administration (MPA); sustainability (MBA).

South University, Program in Business Administration, Royal Palm Beach, FL 33411. Offers business administration (MBA); healthcare administration (MBA).

South University, Program in Business Administration, Montgomery, AL 36116-1120. Offers MBA.

South University, Program in Business Administration, Columbia, SC 29203. Offers MBA.

South University, Program in Business Administration, Glen Allen, VA 23060. Offers MBA.

South University, Program in Business Administration, Virginia Beach, VA 23452. Offers MBA.

South University, Program in Business Administration, Round Rock, TX 78681. Offers MBA.

South University, Program in Business Administration, Novi, MI 48377. Offers MBA.

South University, Program in Business Administration, Tampa, FL 33614. Offers MBA.

South University, Program in Business Administration, High Point, NC 27265. Offers MBA.

South University, Program in Business Administration, Cleveland, OH 44128. Offers MBA.

Southwest Baptist University, Program in Business, Bolivar, MO 65613-2597. Offers business administration (MBA); health administration (MBA). *Accreditation:* ACBSP. *Program availability:* Part-time, online learning. *Degree requirements:* For master's, comprehensive exam. *Entrance requirements:* For master's, interviews, minimum GPA of 2.75. Additional exam requirements/recommendations for international students: Required—TOEFL (minimum score 550 paper-based).

Southwestern Adventist University, Business Administration Department, Keene, TX 76059. Offers accounting (MBA); finance (MBA); management/leadership (MBA). *Program availability:* Part-time, evening/weekend. *Degree requirements:* For master's, capstone course. *Entrance requirements:* For master's, GMAT, GRE General Test.

Southwestern College, Fifth-Year Graduate Programs, Winfield, KS 67156-2499. Offers management (MBA). *Program availability:* Part-time. *Faculty:* 3 full-time (2 women), 1 part-time/adjunct (0 women). *Students:* 22 full-time (7 women), 11 part-time (6 women); includes 10 minority (5 Black or African American, non-Hispanic/Latino; 2 American Indian or Alaska Native, non-Hispanic/Latino; 2 Hispanic/Latino; 1 Two or more races, non-Hispanic/Latino), 12 international. Average age 24. 33 applicants, 100% accepted, 24 enrolled. In 2016, 17 master's awarded. *Entrance requirements:* For master's, baccalaureate degree, minimum GPA of 3.0. Additional exam requirements/recommendations for international students: Required—TOEFL (minimum score 550 paper-based; 80 iBT). *Application deadline:* For fall admission, 8/28 for domestic students; for spring admission, 1/23 for domestic students. Applications are processed on a rolling basis. Application fee: $25. Electronic applications accepted. *Expenses:* $665 per credit hour. *Financial support:* In 2016–17, 14 students received support, including 1 fellowship (averaging $23,940 per year); scholarships/grants and unspecified assistantships also available. Financial award applicants required to submit FAFSA. *Unit head:* Dr. Kurt Keiser, Professor/Division Chair, 620-229-6361, E-mail: kurt.keiser@sckans.edu. *Application contact:* Dean Clark, Executive Vice President, 800-846-1543 Ext. 6364, Fax: 620-229-6344, E-mail: dean.clark@sckans.edu.
Website: http://www.sckans.edu/graduate

Southwestern College, Professional Studies Programs, Wichita, KS 67207. Offers business administration (MBA); leadership (MS); management (MS); security administration (MS); specialized ministries (MA). *Program availability:* Part-time, evening/weekend, online only, 100% online. *Faculty:* 1 full-time (0 women), 12 part-time/adjunct (4 women). *Students:* 81 part-time (26 women); includes 24 minority (10 Black or African American, non-Hispanic/Latino; 4 American Indian or Alaska Native, non-Hispanic/Latino; 1 Asian, non-Hispanic/Latino; 9 Hispanic/Latino). Average age 37. 61 applicants, 75% accepted, 18 enrolled. In 2016, 61 master's awarded. *Degree requirements:* For master's, thesis (for some programs), practicum/capstone project. *Entrance requirements:* For master's, baccalaureate degree; minimum GPA of 3.0. Additional exam requirements/recommendations for international students: Required—TOEFL (minimum score 550 paper-based; 80 iBT). *Application deadline:* Applications are processed on a rolling basis. Application fee: $40. Electronic applications accepted. *Expenses:* Contact institution. *Financial support:* In 2016–17, 9 students received support. Unspecified assistantships and employee tuition benefits available. Financial award applicants required to submit FAFSA. *Unit head:* Dennis Russell, Director of Admissions and Student Services, 888-684-5335 Ext. 3372, Fax: 316-688-5218, E-mail: dennis.russell@sckans.edu.
Website: http://www.southwesterncollege.org

Southwestern Oklahoma State University, College of Professional and Graduate Studies, School of Business and Technology, Weatherford, OK 73096-3098. Offers MBA. MBA distance learning degree program offered to Oklahoma residents only. *Program availability:* Part-time, evening/weekend, online learning. *Degree requirements:* For master's, comprehensive exam. *Entrance requirements:* For master's, GMAT, minimum GPA of 2.5. Additional exam requirements/recommendations for international students: Required—TOEFL.

Southwest Minnesota State University, Department of Business and Public Affairs, Marshall, MN 56258. Offers leadership (MBA); management (MBA); marketing (MBA). *Program availability:* Part-time, evening/weekend, online learning. *Degree requirements:* For master's, thesis. *Entrance requirements:* For master's, GMAT (minimum score: 450). Additional exam requirements/recommendations for international students: Recommended—TOEFL (minimum score 550 paper-based; 79 iBT), IELTS. Electronic applications accepted.

Southwest University, MBA Program, Kenner, LA 70062. Offers business administration (MBA); management (MBA); organizational management (MBA).

Southwest University, Program in Management, Kenner, LA 70062. Offers MA.

Spring Arbor University, Gainey School of Business, Spring Arbor, MI 49283-9799. Offers MBA. *Program availability:* Part-time, evening/weekend, online learning. *Degree requirements:* For master's, thesis. *Entrance requirements:* For master's, minimum overall GPA of 3.0 for all undergraduate coursework, bachelor's degree from regionally-accredited college or university, two recommendation forms from professional/academic individuals. Additional exam requirements/recommendations for international students: Required—TOEFL (minimum score 600 paper-based).

Springfield College, Graduate Programs, Program in Business Administration, Springfield, MA 01109-3797. Offers MBA. *Program availability:* Part-time, evening/weekend. *Expenses: Tuition:* Full-time $29,640; part-time $988 per credit. *Required fees:* $195.

Spring Hill College, Graduate Programs, Program in Business Administration, Mobile, AL 36608-1791. Offers MBA. *Program availability:* Part-time, evening/weekend. *Faculty:* 4 full-time (2 women). *Students:* 7 part-time (2 women); includes 1 minority (Black or African American, non-Hispanic/Latino). Average age 34. In 2016, 4 master's awarded. *Degree requirements:* For master's, comprehensive exam, capstone course, completion of program within 6 calendar years. *Entrance requirements:* For master's, GMAT, bachelor's degree. Additional exam requirements/recommendations for international students: Required—TOEFL (minimum score 550 paper-based; 80 iBT), IELTS (minimum score 6.5), CPE or CAE (minimum score C), Michigan English Language Assessment Battery (minimum score 90). *Application deadline:* For fall admission, 8/1 priority date for domestic and international students; for spring admission, 12/1 priority date for domestic and international students. Applications are processed on a rolling basis. Application fee: $25 ($35 for international students). Electronic applications accepted. *Expenses:* Contact institution. *Financial support:* Applicants required to submit FAFSA. *Unit head:* Dr. Sergio Castello, Director, 251-380-4123, Fax: 251-460-2178, E-mail: scastello@shc.edu. *Application contact:* Robert Stewart, Vice President of Enrollment, 251-380-3030, Fax: 251-460-2186, E-mail: rstewart@shc.edu.
Website: http://ug.shc.edu/graduate-degrees/master-business-administration/

Stanford University, Graduate School of Business, Stanford, CA 94305-2004. Offers MBA, PhD, JD/MBA, MBA/MS. *Accreditation:* AACSB. Terminal master's awarded for partial completion of doctoral program. *Degree requirements:* For doctorate, thesis/dissertation. *Entrance requirements:* For master's, GMAT; for doctorate, GMAT, GRE. Electronic applications accepted. *Expenses:* Contact institution.

State University of New York at New Paltz, Graduate School, School of Business, New Paltz, NY 12561. Offers business administration (MBA); public accountancy (MBA). *Accreditation:* AACSB. *Program availability:* Part-time, evening/weekend. *Students:* 57 full-time (27 women), 23 part-time (13 women); includes 23 minority (3 Black or African American, non-Hispanic/Latino; 7 Asian, non-Hispanic/Latino; 10 Hispanic/Latino; 3 Two or more races, non-Hispanic/Latino), 12 international. 57 applicants, 72% accepted, 27 enrolled. In 2016, 55 master's awarded. *Entrance requirements:* For master's, GMAT or GRE, minimum GPA of 3.0. Additional exam requirements/recommendations for international students: Required—TOEFL (minimum score 550 paper-based; 80 iBT), IELTS (minimum score 6.5). *Application deadline:* Applications are processed on a rolling basis. Application fee: $50. Electronic applications accepted. *Expenses:* Contact institution. *Financial support:* In 2016–17, 6 research assistantships with partial tuition reimbursements (averaging $5,000 per year), 1 teaching assistantship with partial tuition reimbursement (averaging $5,000 per year) were awarded; scholarships/grants, traineeships, and unspecified assistantships also available. Financial award application deadline: 8/1. *Faculty research:* Cognitive styles in management education, supporting SME e-commerce migration through e-learning, earnings management and board activity, trading future spread portfolio, global equity market correlation and volatility. *Unit head:* Dr. Kristin Backhaus, Dean, 845-257-2930, E-mail: mba@newpaltz.edu. *Application contact:* Aaron Hines, Director of MBA Program, 845-257-2968, E-mail: mba@newpaltz.edu.
Website: http://mba.newpaltz.edu

State University of New York at Oswego, Graduate Studies, School of Business, Oswego, NY 13126. Offers MBA. *Program availability:* Part-time, evening/weekend. *Entrance requirements:* For master's, GMAT, minimum GPA of 2.6. Additional exam requirements/recommendations for international students: Required—TOEFL (minimum score 560 paper-based).

State University of New York College at Geneseo, Graduate Studies, School of Business, Geneseo, NY 14454. Offers accounting (MS). *Accreditation:* AACSB. *Faculty:* 5 full-time (2 women). *Students:* 17 full-time (8 women). Average age 22. 29 applicants, 76% accepted, 17 enrolled. In 2016, 15 master's awarded. *Degree requirements:* For master's, thesis. *Entrance requirements:* For master's, GMAT, bachelor's degree in accounting. Additional exam requirements/recommendations for international students: Required—TOEFL, IELTS, PTE. *Application deadline:* For fall admission, 6/1 priority date for domestic students. Applications are processed on a rolling basis. Application fee: $50. Electronic applications accepted. *Expenses:* Tuition, state resident: full-time $10,870; part-time $453 per credit. Tuition, nonresident: full-time $22,210; part-time $925 per credit. *Required fees:* $865; $35.85 per credit hour. *Financial support:* Research assistantships with full tuition reimbursements available. Financial award application deadline: 4/1; financial award applicants required to submit FAFSA. *Unit head:* Dr. Denise Rotondo, Dean of the School of Business, 585-245-5367, Fax: 585-245-5467, E-mail: rotondo@geneseo.edu. *Application contact:* Michael R. George, Graduate Enrollment Coordinator, 585-245-5148, Fax: 585-245-5550, E-mail: georgem@geneseo.edu.
Website: http://www.geneseo.edu/business/accounting_ms

State University of New York College at Old Westbury, School of Business, Old Westbury, NY 11568-0210. Offers accounting (MS); taxation (MS). *Program availability:* Part-time, evening/weekend. *Faculty:* 10 full-time (2 women), 1 part-time/adjunct (0 women). *Students:* 30 full-time (13 women), 47 part-time (15 women); includes 19 minority (3 Black or African American, non-Hispanic/Latino; 11 Asian, non-Hispanic/Latino; 5 Hispanic/Latino). Average age 31. 35 applicants, 91% accepted, 25 enrolled. In 2016, 25 master's awarded. *Entrance requirements:* For master's, GMAT, 2 letters of recommendation. Additional exam requirements/recommendations for international students: Required—TOEFL (minimum score 550 paper-based). *Application deadline:* For fall admission, 6/15 priority date for domestic students; for spring admission, 11/15 priority date for domestic students. Applications are processed on a rolling basis. Application fee: $50. Electronic applications accepted. *Expenses:* Tuition, state resident: full-time $10,870; part-time $453 per credit. Tuition, nonresident: full-time $22,210; part-time $925 per credit. *Required fees:* $24.35 per credit. $76 per semester. Tuition and fees vary according to course load. *Financial support:* Applicants required to submit FAFSA. *Faculty research:* Corporate governance, asset pricing, corporate finance, hedge funds, taxation. *Unit head:* Rita Buttermilch, Director of Graduate Business Programs, 516-876-3900, E-mail: langec@oldwestbury.edu. *Application*

contact: Philip D'Angelo, Graduate Admissions Office, 516-876-3073, E-mail: enroll@oldwestbury.edu.
Website: http://www.oldwestbury.edu/schools/business

State University of New York Empire State College, School for Graduate Studies, Program in Business Administration, Saratoga Springs, NY 12866-4391. Offers global leadership (MBA); management (MBA). *Program availability:* Part-time, online learning. *Degree requirements:* For master's, thesis or alternative. *Entrance requirements:* For master's, previous course work in statistics, macroeconomics, microeconomics, and accounting. Additional exam requirements/recommendations for international students: Required—TOEFL (minimum score 600 paper-based). Electronic applications accepted. *Expenses:* Contact institution. *Faculty research:* Corporate strategy, managerial competencies, decision analysis, economics in transition, organizational communication.

State University of New York Polytechnic Institute, Program in Business Administration in Technology Management, Utica, NY 13502. Offers accounting and finance (MBA); business management (MBA); health services management (MBA); human resource management (MBA); marketing management (MBA). *Program availability:* Part-time, online learning. *Degree requirements:* For master's, capstone course. *Entrance requirements:* For master's, GMAT, resume, one letter of reference. Additional exam requirements/recommendations for international students: Required—TOEFL (minimum score 550 paper-based; 79 iBT), IELTS (minimum score 6.5). Electronic applications accepted. *Faculty research:* Technology management, writing schools, leadership, new products.

Stephen F. Austin State University, Graduate School, College of Business, Program in Business Administration, Nacogdoches, TX 75962. Offers business (MBA); management and marketing (MBA). *Accreditation:* AACSB. *Program availability:* Part-time, evening/weekend. *Degree requirements:* For master's, comprehensive exam. *Entrance requirements:* For master's, GMAT, minimum AACSB index of 1000. Additional exam requirements/recommendations for international students: Required—TOEFL (minimum score 550 paper-based). *Faculty research:* Strategic implications, information search, multinational firms, philosophical guidance.

Stetson University, School of Business Administration, Program in Business Administration, DeLand, FL 32723. Offers EMBA, MBA, JD/MBA, MBA/MS. *Accreditation:* AACSB. *Program availability:* Part-time, evening/weekend, online learning. *Faculty:* 17 full-time (3 women), 5 part-time/adjunct (0 women). *Students:* 72 full-time (32 women), 34 part-time (25 women); includes 20 minority (6 Black or African American, non-Hispanic/Latino; 2 Asian, non-Hispanic/Latino; 11 Hispanic/Latino; 1 Two or more races, non-Hispanic/Latino), 10 international. Average age 32. 86 applicants, 63% accepted, 37 enrolled. In 2016, 65 master's awarded. *Entrance requirements:* For master's, GMAT, GRE, transcripts, resume, two letters of recommendation, personal statement. Additional exam requirements/recommendations for international students: Required—TOEFL (minimum score 90 iBT), IELTS (minimum score 7.5). *Application deadline:* For fall admission, 8/1 for domestic students; for spring admission, 1/1 for domestic students; for summer admission, 5/1 for domestic students. Applications are processed on a rolling basis. Application fee: $50. Electronic applications accepted. *Expenses:* Contact institution. *Financial support:* In 2016–17, 30 students received support. Career-related internships or fieldwork, Federal Work-Study, scholarships/grants, unspecified assistantships, and tuition waivers for staff and dependents available. Support available to part-time students. *Unit head:* Mary Jo Jackson, Executive Director of Graduate and Professional Programs, 386-822-7410, E-mail: mjackson1@stetson.edu. *Application contact:* Jamie Vanderlip, Senior Associate Director of Graduate Admissions, 386-822-7100, Fax: 386-822-7112, E-mail: jlvander@stetson.edu.

Stevens Institute of Technology, Graduate School, School of Business, Program in Business Administration, Hoboken, NJ 07030. Offers business intelligence and analytics (MBA); engineering management (MBA); finance (MBA); information systems (MBA); innovation and entrepreneurship (MBA); marketing (MBA); pharmaceutical management (MBA); project management (MBA, Certificate); technology management (MBA); telecommunications management (MBA). *Accreditation:* AACSB. *Program availability:* Part-time, evening/weekend. *Students:* 35 full-time (15 women), 181 part-time (79 women); includes 53 minority (10 Black or African American, non-Hispanic/Latino; 2 American Indian or Alaska Native, non-Hispanic/Latino; 36 Asian, non-Hispanic/Latino; 5 Hispanic/Latino), 30 international. Average age 32. 215 applicants, 53% accepted, 61 enrolled. In 2016, 61 master's awarded. *Degree requirements:* For master's, thesis optional, minimum B average in major field and overall; for Certificate, minimum B average. *Entrance requirements:* Additional exam requirements/recommendations for international students: Required—TOEFL (minimum score 74 iBT), IELTS (minimum score 6). *Application deadline:* For fall admission, 6/1 for domestic students, 4/15 for international students; for spring admission, 11/30 for domestic students, 11/1 for international students. Applications are processed on a rolling basis. Application fee: $65. Electronic applications accepted. *Expenses:* Contact institution. *Financial support:* Fellowships, research assistantships, teaching assistantships, career-related internships or fieldwork, Federal Work-Study, scholarships/grants, and unspecified assistantships available. Financial award application deadline: 2/15; financial award applicants required to submit FAFSA. *Unit head:* Dr. Gregory Prastacos, Dean, 201-216-8366, E-mail: gprastac@stevens.edu. *Application contact:* Graduate Admissions, 888-783-8367, Fax: 888-511-1306, E-mail: graduate@stevens.edu.
Website: https://www.stevens.edu/school-business/masters-programs/mbaemba

Stevens Institute of Technology, Graduate School, School of Business, Program in Management, Hoboken, NJ 07030. Offers general management (MS); global innovation management (MS); human resource management (MS); information management (MS); project management (MS); technology commercialization (MS); technology management (MS). *Program availability:* Part-time, evening/weekend. *Students:* 83 full-time (28 women), 82 part-time (36 women); includes 30 minority (6 Black or African American, non-Hispanic/Latino; 1 American Indian or Alaska Native, non-Hispanic/Latino; 21 Asian, non-Hispanic/Latino; 2 Hispanic/Latino), 73 international. Average age 29. 381 applicants, 64% accepted, 53 enrolled. In 2016, 66 master's awarded. *Degree requirements:* For master's, thesis optional, minimum B average in major field and overall. *Entrance requirements:* Additional exam requirements/recommendations for international students: Required—TOEFL (minimum score 74 iBT), IELTS (minimum score 6). *Application deadline:* For fall admission, 6/1 for domestic students, 4/15 for international students; for spring admission, 11/30 for domestic students, 11/1 for international students. Applications are processed on a rolling basis. Application fee: $65. Electronic applications accepted. *Expenses:* Contact institution. *Financial support:* Fellowships, research assistantships, teaching assistantships, career-related internships or fieldwork, Federal Work-Study, scholarships/grants, and unspecified assistantships available. Financial award application deadline: 2/15; financial award applicants required to submit FAFSA. *Unit head:* Brian Rothschild, Director, 201-216-3677, E-mail: brian.rothschild@stevens.edu. *Application contact:* Graduate Admissions, 888-783-8367, Fax: 888-511-1306, E-mail: graduate@stevens.edu.
Website: https://www.stevens.edu/school-business/masters-programs/management

Stockton University, Office of Graduate Studies, Program in Business Administration, Galloway, NJ 08205-9441. Offers MBA. *Accreditation:* AACSB. *Program availability:* Part-time, evening/weekend. *Faculty:* 9 full-time (3 women). *Students:* 22 full-time (6 women), 63 part-time (34 women); includes 23 minority (2 Black or African American, non-Hispanic/Latino; 5 Asian, non-Hispanic/Latino; 14 Hispanic/Latino; 2 Two or more races, non-Hispanic/Latino), 2 international. Average age 33. 41 applicants, 71% accepted, 24 enrolled. In 2016, 45 master's awarded. *Degree requirements:* For master's, project. *Entrance requirements:* For master's, GMAT. Additional exam requirements/recommendations for international students: Required—TOEFL (minimum score 550 paper-based; 80 iBT). *Application deadline:* For fall admission, 7/1 for domestic and international students; for spring admission, 12/1 for domestic students, 11/1 for international students. Applications are processed on a rolling basis. Application fee: $50. Electronic applications accepted. *Expenses:* $772 per credit in-state. *Financial support:* Fellowships, research assistantships with partial tuition reimbursements, career-related internships or fieldwork, Federal Work-Study, scholarships/grants, and unspecified assistantships available. Support available to part-time students. Financial award application deadline: 3/1; financial award applicants required to submit FAFSA. *Faculty research:* Business ethics, marketing channels development, event studies, total quality management. *Unit head:* Dr. Diane Holtzman, Graduate Program Director, 609-626-3640, E-mail: mba@stockton.edu. *Application contact:* Tara Williams, Assistant Director of Graduate Enrollment Management, 609-626-3640, Fax: 609-626-6050, E-mail: gradschool@stockton.edu.

Stony Brook University, State University of New York, Graduate School, College of Business, Program in Business Administration, Stony Brook, NY 11794. Offers accounting (MBA); business administration (MBA); finance (MBA, Certificate); health care management (MBA); innovation, human resources, management, or operations management (MBA); marketing (MBA). *Faculty:* 37 full-time (12 women), 12 part-time/adjunct (4 women). *Students:* 199 full-time (109 women), 139 part-time (64 women); includes 81 minority (19 Black or African American, non-Hispanic/Latino; 41 Asian, non-Hispanic/Latino; 17 Hispanic/Latino; 1 Native Hawaiian or other Pacific Islander, non-Hispanic/Latino; 3 Two or more races, non-Hispanic/Latino), 88 international. Average age 29. 246 applicants, 65% accepted, 91 enrolled. In 2016, 116 master's awarded. *Entrance requirements:* For master's, GMAT, 3 letters of recommendation from current or former employers or professors, transcripts, personal statement, resume. Additional exam requirements/recommendations for international students: Required—TOEFL (minimum score 550 paper-based; 90 iBT), IELTS (minimum score 6.5). *Application deadline:* For fall admission, 5/15 for domestic students, 3/15 for international students; for spring admission, 11/15 for domestic students, 10/15 for international students. Application fee: $100. *Expenses:* Contact institution. *Financial support:* Teaching assistantships available. *Total annual research expenditures:* $5,325. *Unit head:* Dr. Manuel London, Dean, 631-632-7159, E-mail: manuel.london@stonybrook.edu. *Application contact:* Dr. Jadranka Skorin-Kapov, Graduate Program Director, 631-632-7171, Fax: 631-632-8181, E-mail: jadranka.skorin-kapov@stonybrook.edu.

Stratford University, School of Graduate Studies, Falls Church, VA 22043. Offers accounting (MS); business administration (IMBA, MBA); cyber security (MS); cyber security leadership and policy (MS); digital forensics (MS); enterprise business management (MS); entrepreneurial management (MS); healthcare administration (MS); information systems (MS); international hospitality management (MS); networking and telecommunications (MS); software engineering (MS). *Program availability:* Part-time, evening/weekend, 100% online, blended/hybrid learning. *Students:* 505 full-time (186 women), 172 part-time (88 women); includes 532 minority (165 Black or African American, non-Hispanic/Latino; 18 American Indian or Alaska Native, non-Hispanic/Latino; 324 Asian, non-Hispanic/Latino; 13 Hispanic/Latino; 10 Native Hawaiian or other Pacific Islander, non-Hispanic/Latino; 2 Two or more races, non-Hispanic/Latino). Average age 27. In 2016, 520 master's awarded. *Degree requirements:* For master's, comprehensive exam, capstone project. *Entrance requirements:* For master's, GRE or GMAT, baccalaureate degree. Additional exam requirements/recommendations for international students: Required—TOEFL (minimum score 79 iBT), IELTS (minimum score 6.5), PTE (minimum score 5). *Application deadline:* Applications are processed on a rolling basis. Application fee: $50. Electronic applications accepted. *Expenses: Tuition:* Full-time $4455; part-time $2227.50 per course. One-time fee: $100. *Financial support:* Federal Work-Study and scholarships/grants available. Financial award applicants required to submit FAFSA. *Unit head:* Dr. Richard R. Shurtz, President, 703-539-6890, Fax: 703-539-6960. *Application contact:* Admissions, 800-444-0804, E-mail: fcadmissions@stratford.edu.

Strayer University, Graduate Studies, Washington, DC 20005-2603. Offers accounting (MS); acquisition (MBA); business administration (MBA); communications technology (MS); educational management (M Ed); finance (MBA); health services administration (MHSA); hospitality and tourism management (MBA); human resource management (MBA); information systems (MS), including computer security management, decision support system management, enterprise resource management, network management, software engineering management, systems development management; management (MBA); management information systems (MS); marketing (MBA); professional accounting (MS), including accounting information systems, controllership, taxation; public administration (MPA); supply chain management (MBA); technology in education (M Ed). Programs also offered at campus locations in Birmingham, AL; Chamblee, GA; Cobb County, GA; Morrow, GA; White Marsh, MD; Charleston, SC; Columbia, SC; Greensboro, NC; Greenville, SC; Lexington, KY; Louisville, KY; Nashville, TN; North Raleigh, NC; Washington, DC. *Accreditation:* ACBSP. *Program availability:* Part-time, evening/weekend, online learning. *Degree requirements:* For master's, thesis. *Entrance requirements:* For master's, GMAT, GRE General Test, bachelor's degree from an accredited college or university, minimum undergraduate GPA of 2.75. Electronic applications accepted.

Suffolk University, Sawyer Business School, Master of Business Administration Program, Boston, MA 02108-2770. Offers accounting (MBA); entrepreneurship (MBA); executive business administration (EMBA); finance (MBA); global business administration (GMBA); health administration (MBA); international business (MBA); marketing (MBA); nonprofit management (MBA); organizational behavior (MBA); strategic management (MBA); supply chain management (MBA); taxation (MBA); JD/MBA; MBA/MHA; MBA/MSA; MBA/MSF; MBA/MST. *Accreditation:* AACSB. *Program availability:* Part-time, evening/weekend, 100% online. *Faculty:* 17 full-time (6 women), 10 part-time/adjunct (1 woman). *Students:* 137 full-time (70 women), 265 part-time (138 women); includes 78 minority (20 Black or African American, non-Hispanic/Latino; 22 Asian, non-Hispanic/Latino; 31 Hispanic/Latino; 5 Two or more races, non-Hispanic/Latino), 46 international. Average age 30. 416 applicants, 70% accepted, 128 enrolled. In 2016, 165 degrees awarded. *Entrance requirements:* For master's, GMAT, minimum undergraduate GPA of 2.75 (MBA), 5 years of managerial experience (EMBA). Additional exam requirements/recommendations for international students: Required—TOEFL (minimum score 550 paper-based; 80 iBT). *Application deadline:* For fall admission, 3/15 priority date for domestic students, 10/15 priority date for international students; for spring admission, 10/15 priority date for domestic and international students. Applications are processed on a rolling basis. Application fee: $50. Electronic applications accepted. *Expenses: Tuition:* Full-time $41,490; part-time $1383 per credit hour. *Required fees:* $52; $52 per credit hour. Part-time tuition and fees vary according to course load and program. *Financial support:* In 2016–17, 209 students received support, including 176 fellowships (averaging $8,581 per year); career-related

internships or fieldwork, Federal Work-Study, institutionally sponsored loans, and scholarships/grants also available. Support available to part-time students. Financial award application deadline: 4/1; financial award applicants required to submit FAFSA. *Faculty research:* Foreign investments; career strategies and boundaryless careers; corporate ethics codes; interest rates, inflation, and growth options; innovation and product development performance. *Unit head:* Jodi Detjen, Director of MBA Programs, 617-573-8306, E-mail: jdetjen@suffolk.edu. *Application contact:* Mara Marzocchi, Associate Director of Graduate Admissions, 617-573-8302, Fax: 617-305-1733, E-mail: grad.admission@suffolk.edu.
Website: http://www.suffolk.edu/mba

Sullivan University, School of Business, Louisville, KY 40205. Offers EMBA, MBA, MPM, MSCM, MSCS, MSHRL, MSM, MSMIT, PhD, Pharm D. *Program availability:* Part-time, online learning. *Degree requirements:* For doctorate, comprehensive exam, thesis/dissertation. *Entrance requirements:* Additional exam requirements/recommendations for international students: Required—TOEFL.

Sul Ross State University, College of Professional Studies, Department of Business Administration, Alpine, TX 79832. Offers EMBA, MBA. Two-year Executive MBA program in cooperation with La Universidad de Chihuahua, Mexico (UACH). *Program availability:* Part-time, evening/weekend. *Degree requirements:* For master's, thesis optional. *Entrance requirements:* For master's, GMAT or GRE General Test, minimum GPA of 2.5 in last 60 hours of undergraduate work. *Faculty research:* Cross-cultural comparisons, U.S.-Mexico management relations.

Sul Ross State University, Rio Grande College of Sul Ross State University, Alpine, TX 79832. Offers business administration (MBA); teacher education (M Ed), including bilingual education, counseling, educational diagnostics, elementary education, general education, reading, school administration, secondary education. *Program availability:* Part-time, evening/weekend, online learning. *Degree requirements:* For master's, comprehensive exam, thesis optional, minimum GPA of 3.0. *Entrance requirements:* For master's, GMAT or GRE General Test, minimum GPA of 2.5 in last 60 hours of undergraduate work. Additional exam requirements/recommendations for international students: Required—TOEFL.

Syracuse University, Martin J. Whitman School of Management, Syracuse, NY 13244. Offers MBA, MS, PhD, JD/MBA. *Accreditation:* AACSB. *Program availability:* Part-time, 100% online. *Faculty:* 73 full-time (24 women), 53 part-time/adjunct (18 women). *Students:* 307 full-time (143 women), 890 part-time (299 women); includes 356 minority (142 Black or African American, non-Hispanic/Latino; 3 American Indian or Alaska Native, non-Hispanic/Latino; 82 Asian, non-Hispanic/Latino; 99 Hispanic/Latino; 3 Native Hawaiian or other Pacific Islander, non-Hispanic/Latino; 27 Two or more races, non-Hispanic/Latino), 209 international. Average age 33. 1,579 applicants, 49% accepted, 308 enrolled. In 2016, 294 master's, 3 doctorates awarded. *Degree requirements:* For master's, comprehensive exam (for MS in business analytics); for doctorate, comprehensive exam, thesis/dissertation, summer research paper. *Entrance requirements:* For master's and doctorate, GMAT or GRE. Additional exam requirements/recommendations for international students: Required—PTE (minimum score 68), TOEFL (minimum iBT score of 100) or IELTS (7); GMAT; GRE. *Application deadline:* For fall admission, 11/30 for domestic and international students; for winter admission, 1/1 for domestic and international students; for spring admission, 2/15 for domestic and international students; for summer admission, 4/19 for domestic students. Application fee: $75. Electronic applications accepted. *Expenses: Tuition:* Full-time $25,974; part-time $1443 per credit hour. *Required fees:* $802; $50 per course. Tuition and fees vary according to course load and program. *Financial support:* In 2016–17, 45 students received support. Fellowships with full tuition reimbursements available, research assistantships with tuition reimbursements available, teaching assistantships with tuition reimbursements available, career-related internships or fieldwork, and scholarships/grants available. Financial award application deadline: 2/15. *Faculty research:* Marketing, supply chain management, management, finance, entrepreneurship. *Unit head:* Don Harter, Associate Dean for Master's Programs, 315-443-3502, Fax: 315-443-9517, E-mail: dharter@syr.edu. *Application contact:* Shri Ramakrishnan, Assistant Director, Graduate Recruitment, 315-443-3497, Fax: 315-443-9517, E-mail: sramak01@syr.edu.
Website: http://whitman.syr.edu

Tabor College, Graduate Program, Hillsboro, KS 67063. Offers accounting (MBA). Program offered at the Wichita campus only.

Tarleton State University, College of Graduate Studies, College of Business Administration, Master of Business Administration Program, Stephenville, TX 76402. Offers MBA. *Program availability:* Part-time, evening/weekend, 100% online, blended/hybrid learning. *Students:* 59 full-time (30 women), 181 part-time (103 women); includes 55 minority (15 Black or African American, non-Hispanic/Latino; 3 Asian, non-Hispanic/Latino; 26 Hispanic/Latino; 11 Two or more races, non-Hispanic/Latino), 3 international. 102 applicants, 85% accepted, 67 enrolled. In 2016, 33 master's awarded. *Entrance requirements:* Additional exam requirements/recommendations for international students: Required—TOEFL (minimum score 550 paper-based; 80 iBT). *Application deadline:* Applications are processed on a rolling basis. Application fee: $45 ($145 for international students). Electronic applications accepted. *Expenses:* $3,672 tuition; $2,437 fees. *Financial support:* Applicants required to submit FAFSA. *Unit head:* Dr. Adolfo Benavides, Dean, 254-968-9496, Fax: 254-968-9496, E-mail: benavides@tarleton.edu. *Application contact:* Information Contact, 254-968-9104, Fax: 254-968-9670, E-mail: gradoffice@tarleton.edu.

Taylor University, Master of Business Administration Program, Upland, IN 46989-1001. Offers emerging business strategies (MBA); global leadership (MBA). *Program availability:* Part-time.

Temple University, Fox School of Business, Doctoral Programs in Business, Philadelphia, PA 19122-6096. Offers accounting (PhD); entrepreneurship (PhD); finance (PhD); international business (PhD); management information systems (PhD); marketing (PhD); risk management and insurance (PhD); statistics (PhD); strategic management (PhD); tourism and sport (PhD). *Accreditation:* AACSB. *Degree requirements:* For doctorate, thesis/dissertation. *Entrance requirements:* For doctorate, GRE General Test, GMAT, minimum GPA of 3.0, master's degree. Additional exam requirements/recommendations for international students: Required—TOEFL (minimum score 600 paper-based; 100 iBT), IELTS (minimum score 7.5). Electronic applications accepted.

Temple University, Fox School of Business, MBA Programs, Philadelphia, PA 19122-6096. Offers accounting (MBA); business management (MBA); financial management (MBA); healthcare and life sciences innovation (MBA); human resource management (MBA); international business (IMBA); IT management (MBA); marketing management (MBA); pharmaceutical management (MBA); strategic management (EMBA, MBA). EMBA offered in Philadelphia, PA and Tokyo, Japan. *Accreditation:* AACSB. *Program availability:* Part-time, evening/weekend, online learning. *Entrance requirements:* For master's, GMAT, minimum undergraduate GPA of 3.0. Additional exam requirements/recommendations for international students: Required—TOEFL (minimum score 600 paper-based; 100 iBT), IELTS (minimum score 7.5).

Temple University, Fox School of Business, Specialized Master's Programs, Philadelphia, PA 19122-6096. Offers accountancy (MS); actuarial science (MS); finance (MS); financial engineering (MS); human resource management (MS); innovation management and entrepreneurship (MS); marketing (MS); statistics (MS). MS in innovation management and entrepreneurship delivered jointly with College of Engineering. *Accreditation:* AACSB. *Program availability:* Part-time. *Entrance requirements:* For master's, GRE General Test or GMAT, minimum undergraduate GPA of 3.0. Additional exam requirements/recommendations for international students: Required—TOEFL (minimum score 600 paper-based; 100 iBT), IELTS (minimum score 7.5).

Tennessee State University, The School of Graduate Studies and Research, College of Business, Nashville, TN 37209-1561. Offers MBA. *Accreditation:* AACSB. *Program availability:* Part-time, evening/weekend, online learning. *Entrance requirements:* For master's, GMAT. Additional exam requirements/recommendations for international students: Required—TOEFL (minimum score 500 paper-based). Electronic applications accepted. *Faculty research:* Supply chain management, health economics, accounting, e-commerce, international business.

Tennessee Technological University, College of Graduate Studies, College of Business, Cookeville, TN 38505. Offers accounting (MBA); finance (MBA); human resource management (MBA); international business (MBA); management information systems (MBA). *Accreditation:* AACSB. *Program availability:* Part-time, evening/weekend, online learning. *Faculty:* 28 full-time (5 women). *Students:* 45 full-time (22 women), 167 part-time (51 women); includes 18 minority (5 Black or African American, non-Hispanic/Latino; 4 Asian, non-Hispanic/Latino; 4 Hispanic/Latino; 5 Two or more races, non-Hispanic/Latino), 14 international. Average age 25. 173 applicants, 54% accepted, 52 enrolled. In 2016, 78 master's awarded. *Entrance requirements:* For master's, GMAT, GRE. Additional exam requirements/recommendations for international students: Required—TOEFL (minimum score 550 paper-based; 79 iBT), IELTS (minimum score 5.5), PTE (minimum score 53), or TOEIC (Test of English as an International Communication). *Application deadline:* For fall admission, 8/1 for domestic students, 5/1 for international students; for spring admission, 12/1 for domestic students, 10/1 for international students; for summer admission, 5/1 for domestic students, 2/1 for international students. Applications are processed on a rolling basis. Application fee: $35 ($40 for international students). Electronic applications accepted. *Expenses:* Tuition, state resident: full-time $9375; part-time $534 per credit hour. Tuition, nonresident: full-time $22,443; part-time $1260 per credit hour. *Financial support:* In 2016–17, 5 fellowships (averaging $10,000 per year), 1 teaching assistantship (averaging $5,200 per year) were awarded; research assistantships also available. Support available to part-time students. Financial award application deadline: 4/1. *Unit head:* Kate Nicewicz, Director, 931-372-3600, Fax: 931-372-6249, E-mail: knicewicz@tntech.edu. *Application contact:* Shelia K. Kendrick, Coordinator of Graduate Studies, 931-372-3808, Fax: 931-372-3497, E-mail: skendrick@tntech.edu.
Website: http://www.tntech.edu/mba

Tennessee Wesleyan University, Graduate Programs, Athens, TN 37303. Offers accounting (MBA); management (MBA). *Program availability:* Evening/weekend. *Faculty:* 8 full-time (4 women), 3 part-time/adjunct (2 women). *Students:* 4 full-time (2 women), 18 part-time (11 women). *Entrance requirements:* For master's, GMAT, official transcripts, three letters of recommendation, current curriculum vitae or resume. *Expenses: Tuition:* Full-time $9000; part-time $500 per hour. *Application contact:* Mark Bucco, Adult and Graduate Admissions Counselor, 423-252-1114, Fax: 423-745-9335, E-mail: mbucco@tnwesleyan.edu.
Website: http://www.tnwesleyan.edu/academics/graduate-programs/

Texas A&M International University, Office of Graduate Studies and Research, A.R. Sanchez, Jr. School of Business, Laredo, TX 78041-1900. Offers MBA, MP Acc, MSIS, PhD. *Accreditation:* AACSB. *Program availability:* Part-time, evening/weekend. *Degree requirements:* For master's, thesis (for some programs). *Entrance requirements:* For master's, GMAT or GRE General Test. Additional exam requirements/recommendations for international students: Required—TOEFL (minimum score 550 paper-based; 79 iBT), IELTS (minimum score 6.5).

Texas A&M University, Mays Business School, Department of Management, College Station, TX 77843. Offers entrepreneurial leadership (MS); human resource management (MS); management (MS). *Faculty:* 30. *Students:* 93 full-time (51 women), 1 part-time (0 women); includes 22 minority (3 Black or African American, non-Hispanic/Latino; 1 American Indian or Alaska Native, non-Hispanic/Latino; 6 Asian, non-Hispanic/Latino; 9 Hispanic/Latino; 3 Two or more races, non-Hispanic/Latino), 5 international. Average age 25. 164 applicants, 29% accepted, 37 enrolled. In 2016, 84 master's awarded. Terminal master's awarded for partial completion of doctoral program. *Degree requirements:* For master's, comprehensive exam. *Entrance requirements:* For master's, GMAT or GRE. Additional exam requirements/recommendations for international students: Required—TOEFL (minimum score 550 paper-based; 80 iBT), IELTS (minimum score 6), PTE (minimum score 53). *Application deadline:* For fall admission, 5/26 for domestic and international students. Applications are processed on a rolling basis. Application fee: $50 ($90 for international students). Electronic applications accepted. *Expenses:* Contact institution. *Financial support:* In 2016–17, 75 students received support, including 2 fellowships with tuition reimbursements available (averaging $6,000 per year), 33 research assistantships with tuition reimbursements available (averaging $3,826 per year), 20 teaching assistantships with tuition reimbursements available (averaging $4,191 per year); career-related internships or fieldwork, institutionally sponsored loans, scholarships/grants, traineeships, health care benefits, tuition waivers (full and partial), and unspecified assistantships also available. Support available to part-time students. Financial award application deadline: 3/15; financial award applicants required to submit FAFSA. *Faculty research:* Strategic and human resource management, business and public policy, organizational behavior, organizational theory. *Unit head:* Dr. Wendy R. Boswell, Head, 979-845-4045, Fax: 979-845-9641, E-mail: wboswell@mays.tamu.edu. *Application contact:* Kristi R. Mora, Senior Academic Advisor II, 979-845-6127, Fax: 979-845-9641, E-mail: kmora@mays.tamu.edu.
Website: http://mays.tamu.edu/mgmt/

Texas A&M University–Central Texas, Graduate Studies and Research, Killeen, TX 76549. Offers accounting (MS); business administration (MBA); clinical mental health counseling (MS); criminal justice (MCJ); curriculum and instruction (M Ed); educational administration (M Ed); educational psychology - experimental psychology (MS); history (MA); human resource management (MS); information systems (MS); liberal studies (MS); management and leadership (MS); marriage and family therapy (MS); mathematics (MS); political science (MA); school counseling (M Ed); school psychology (Ed S).

Texas A&M University–Commerce, College of Business, Commerce, TX 75429-3011. Offers accounting (MSA); business administration (MBA); business analytics (MS); finance (MSF); management (MS); marketing (MS). *Accreditation:* AACSB. *Program availability:* Part-time, evening/weekend, 100% online, blended/hybrid learning. *Faculty:* 48 full-time (17 women), 8 part-time/adjunct (2 women). *Students:* 463 full-time (232 women), 1,109 part-time (539 women); includes 653 minority (280 Black or African American, non-Hispanic/Latino; 7 American Indian or Alaska Native, non-Hispanic/

Latino; 131 Asian, non-Hispanic/Latino; 202 Hispanic/Latino; 1 Native Hawaiian or other Pacific Islander, non-Hispanic/Latino; 32 Two or more races, non-Hispanic/Latino), 211 international. Average age 33. 1,021 applicants, 59% accepted, 424 enrolled. In 2016, 617 master's awarded. *Degree requirements:* For master's, comprehensive exam. *Entrance requirements:* For master's, GRE General Test, GMAT, letter of recommendation. Additional exam requirements/recommendations for international students: Required—TOEFL (minimum score 550 paper-based; 79 iBT), IELTS (minimum score 6). *Application deadline:* For fall admission, 5/15 priority date for international students; for spring admission, 10/1 priority date for international students; for summer admission, 2/1 priority date for international students. Applications are processed on a rolling basis. Application fee: $50 ($75 for international students). Electronic applications accepted. *Expenses:* Contact institution. *Financial support:* In 2016–17, 90 students received support, including 20 research assistantships with partial tuition reimbursements available (averaging $8,000 per year); Federal Work-Study, institutionally sponsored loans, scholarships/grants, health care benefits, and unspecified assistantships also available. Financial award application deadline: 5/1; financial award applicants required to submit FAFSA. *Faculty research:* Applied economics emphasis on industries that are important to the region including health, energy and agriculture; finance research on banking, investments, financial institutions and risk management; marketing and big data decisions of product choice behavior and channel behavior of consumers; strategic management and organizational behavior phenomena; International Accounting in Governmental Sectors. *Total annual research expenditures:* $1,920. *Unit head:* Dr. Shanan G. Gibson, Dean of College of Business, 903-886-5191, Fax: 903-886-5650, E-mail: shanan.gibson@tamuc.edu. *Application contact:* Shanna Hoskison, Director, Graduate Advising, 903-886-5190, E-mail: shanna.hoskison@tamuc.edu.
Website: http://www.tamuc.edu/academics/graduateSchool/programs/businessEntrepreneurship/default.aspx

Texas A&M University–Corpus Christi, College of Graduate Studies, College of Business, Corpus Christi, TX 78412-5503. Offers accounting (M Acc); business (MBA); finance (MBA); health care administration (MBA); international business (MBA). *Accreditation:* AACSB. *Program availability:* Part-time, evening/weekend, 100% online, blended/hybrid learning. *Faculty:* 31 full-time (11 women), 2 part-time/adjunct (0 women). *Students:* 132 full-time (71 women), 495 part-time (232 women); includes 261 minority (49 Black or African American, non-Hispanic/Latino; 44 Asian, non-Hispanic/Latino; 160 Hispanic/Latino; 8 Two or more races, non-Hispanic/Latino), 111 international. Average age 32. 444 applicants, 55% accepted, 192 enrolled. In 2016, 205 master's awarded. *Degree requirements:* For master's, 30 to 42 hours (for MBA; varies by concentration area, delivery format, and necessity for foundational courses for students with nonbusiness degrees). *Entrance requirements:* For master's, GMAT, GRE. Additional exam requirements/recommendations for international students: Required—TOEFL (minimum score 550 paper-based), IELTS (minimum score 6.5). *Application deadline:* For fall admission, 7/15 priority date for domestic students, 5/1 priority date for international students; for spring admission, 11/15 priority date for domestic students, 9/1 priority date for international students; for summer admission, 4/15 priority date for domestic students, 2/1 priority date for international students. Applications are processed on a rolling basis. Application fee: $50 ($70 for international students). Electronic applications accepted. *Financial support:* Research assistantships, teaching assistantships, career-related internships or fieldwork, Federal Work-Study, institutionally sponsored loans, scholarships/grants, health care benefits, and unspecified assistantships available. Support available to part-time students. Financial award application deadline: 3/15; financial award applicants required to submit FAFSA. *Unit head:* Dr. John Gamble, Dean, 361-825-6045, Fax: 361-825-2725, E-mail: john.gamble@tamucc.edu. *Application contact:* Sharon Polansky, Director, Master's Program, 361-825-3448, Fax: 361-825-2755, E-mail: gradweb@tamucc.edu.
Website: http://cob.tamucc.edu

Texas A&M University–Kingsville, College of Graduate Studies, College of Business Administration, Kingsville, TX 78363. Offers MBA. *Program availability:* Online only, 100% online, blended/hybrid learning. *Entrance requirements:* Additional exam requirements/recommendations for international students: Required—TOEFL (minimum score 550 paper-based; 79 iBT); Recommended—IELTS. Electronic applications accepted.

Texas A&M University–San Antonio, School of Business, San Antonio, TX 78224. Offers business administration (MBA); enterprise resource planning systems (MBA); finance (MBA); healthcare management (MBA); human resources management (MBA); information assurance and security (MBA); international business (MBA); professional accounting (MPA); project management (MBA); supply chain management (MBA). *Program availability:* Part-time, evening/weekend. *Entrance requirements:* For master's, GMAT. Additional exam requirements/recommendations for international students: Required—TOEFL (minimum score 550 paper-based; 80 iBT), IELTS (minimum score 6). Electronic applications accepted.

Texas A&M University–Texarkana, Graduate Studies and Research, College of Business, Texarkana, TX 75505-5518. Offers accounting (MSA); business administration (MBA, MS). *Program availability:* Part-time, evening/weekend. *Degree requirements:* For master's, thesis or alternative. *Entrance requirements:* For master's, minimum GPA of 2.5 in last 60 hours of bachelor's degree. Additional exam requirements/recommendations for international students: Required—TOEFL. Electronic applications accepted.

Texas Christian University, Neeley School of Business, Executive MBA Program, Fort Worth, TX 76129-0002. Offers MBA. *Faculty:* 60 full-time (17 women), 17 part-time/adjunct (4 women). *Students:* 61 full-time (15 women); includes 13 minority (5 Black or African American, non-Hispanic/Latino; 8 Hispanic/Latino). Average age 40. *Expenses:* *Tuition:* Full-time $26,640; part-time $1480 per credit hour. *Required fees:* $48. Tuition and fees vary according to program. *Unit head:* Dr. Suzanne M. Carter, EMBA Executive Director/Professor of Strategy Practice, 817-257-7543, E-mail: s.carter@tcu.edu. *Application contact:* Kevin T. Davis, Director, Executive MBA Recruiting and External Relations, 817-257-4681, Fax: 817-257-7719, E-mail: kevin.davis@tcu.edu.

Texas Christian University, Neeley School of Business, Full-time Master's Program in Business Administration and Accelerated MBA, Fort Worth, TX 76129. Offers accounting (MBA); finance (MBA), including corporate finance, investments; marketing (MBA), including marketing management, product and brand management; supply and value chain management (MBA). *Accreditation:* AACSB. *Program availability:* Part-time, evening/weekend. *Faculty:* 60 full-time (17 women), 17 part-time/adjunct (4 women). *Students:* 92 full-time (26 women); includes 14 minority (3 Black or African American, non-Hispanic/Latino; 1 American Indian or Alaska Native, non-Hispanic/Latino; 3 Asian, non-Hispanic/Latino; 7 Hispanic/Latino), 30 international. Average age 28. 205 applicants, 50% accepted, 47 enrolled. In 2016, 43 master's awarded. *Entrance requirements:* For master's, GMAT (preferred); GRE. Additional exam requirements/recommendations for international students: Required—TOEFL (minimum score 100 iBT); Recommended—IELTS (minimum score 7), TSE (minimum score 68). *Application deadline:* For fall admission, 3/1 for domestic and international students; for winter admission, 1/15 for domestic and international students; for spring admission, 11/1 for domestic and international students; for summer admission, 1/15 for domestic and international students. Applications are processed on a rolling basis. Application fee: $100. Electronic applications accepted. Application fee is waived when completed online. *Expenses:* Contact institution. *Financial support:* In 2016–17, 94 students received support. Career-related internships or fieldwork, scholarships/grants, and unspecified assistantships available. Financial award application deadline: 4/1; financial award applicants required to submit FAFSA. *Faculty research:* Emerging financial markets, derivative trading activity, salesforce deployment, examining sales activity, litigation against tax practitioners. *Unit head:* Anne Rooney, Executive Director, Graduate Programs, 817-257-7991, Fax: 817-257-6431, E-mail: mbainfo@tcu.edu. *Application contact:* Peggy Conway, Director, Full-time MBA Admissions, 817-257-7989, Fax: 817-257-6431, E-mail: mbainfo@tcu.edu.
Website: http://www.neeley.tcu.edu/mba

Texas Christian University, Neeley School of Business, Professional MBA Program, Fort Worth, TX 76129. Offers MBA. *Program availability:* Part-time-only, evening/weekend. *Faculty:* 60 full-time (17 women), 17 part-time/adjunct (4 women). *Students:* 128 full-time (29 women), 24 part-time (7 women); includes 23 minority (3 Black or African American, non-Hispanic/Latino; 4 American Indian or Alaska Native, non-Hispanic/Latino; 9 Asian, non-Hispanic/Latino; 7 Hispanic/Latino), 5 international. Average age 30. 107 applicants, 81% accepted, 65 enrolled. In 2016, 80 master's awarded. *Entrance requirements:* For master's, GMAT (preferred) or GRE. *Application deadline:* For fall admission, 11/1 for domestic and international students; for winter admission, 1/15 for domestic and international students; for spring admission, 4/15 for domestic and international students. Applications are processed on a rolling basis. Application fee: $100. Electronic applications accepted. Application fee is waived when completed online. *Expenses:* $1,480 per hour tuition, $1,600 per semester fees. *Financial support:* Application deadline: 5/1. *Unit head:* Kelli Kilpatrick, Director, Evening Graduate Programs, 817-257-5148, E-mail: k.kilpatrick@tcu.edu.
Website: http://www.neeley.tcu.edu/Professional_MBA.aspx

Texas Health and Science University, Graduate Programs, Austin, TX 78704. Offers acupuncture and Oriental medicine (MS, DAOM); business administration (MBA); healthcare management (MBA). *Accreditation:* ACAOM. *Entrance requirements:* For master's, 60 hours applicable to bachelor's degree. Additional exam requirements/recommendations for international students: Required—TOEFL (minimum score 500 paper-based), TWE. Electronic applications accepted.

Texas Southern University, Jesse H. Jones School of Business, Program in Business Administration, Houston, TX 77004-4584. Offers MBA. *Accreditation:* AACSB. *Program availability:* Part-time, evening/weekend. *Degree requirements:* For master's, comprehensive exam. *Entrance requirements:* For master's, GMAT, minimum GPA of 2.5. Electronic applications accepted.

Texas State University, The Graduate College, Emmett and Miriam McCoy College of Business Administration, Program in Business Administration, San Marcos, TX 78666. Offers MBA. *Accreditation:* AACSB. *Program availability:* Part-time. *Faculty:* 28 full-time (9 women), 1 part-time/adjunct (0 women). *Students:* 99 full-time (46 women), 158 part-time (75 women); includes 71 minority (12 Black or African American, non-Hispanic/Latino; 10 Asian, non-Hispanic/Latino; 42 Hispanic/Latino; 7 Two or more races, non-Hispanic/Latino), 15 international. Average age 31. 223 applicants, 46% accepted, 57 enrolled. In 2016, 100 master's awarded. *Degree requirements:* For master's, comprehensive exam, thesis optional. *Entrance requirements:* For master's, GMAT or GRE, baccalaureate degree from regionally-accredited university; two letters or forms of recommendation from persons best able to assess applicant's ability to succeed in graduate school; essay; detailed resume showing work experience, extracurricular and community activities, and honors and achievements. Additional exam requirements/recommendations for international students: Required—TOEFL (minimum score 550 paper-based; 78 iBT), IELTS (minimum score 6.5). *Application deadline:* For fall admission, 2/1 priority date for domestic and international students; for spring admission, 10/1 for domestic and international students. Application fee: $40 ($90 for international students). Electronic applications accepted. *Expenses:* $4,851 per semester. *Financial support:* In 2016–17, 111 students received support, including 1 research assistantship (averaging $14,500 per year), 13 teaching assistantships (averaging $13,807 per year); Federal Work-Study, institutionally sponsored loans, scholarships/grants, health care benefits, and unspecified assistantships also available. Support available to part-time students. Financial award application deadline: 3/1; financial award applicants required to submit FAFSA. *Unit head:* Dr. William Chittenden, Graduate Advisor, 512-245-3591, Fax: 512-245-7973, E-mail: wc10@txstate.edu. *Application contact:* Dr. Andrea Golato, Dean of Graduate School, 512-245-2581, Fax: 512-245-8365, E-mail: gradcollege@txstate.edu.
Website: http://graduate.mccoy.txstate.edu/grad_programs/MBA.html

Texas Tech University, Rawls College of Business Administration, Lubbock, TX 79409-2101. Offers accounting (MSA, PhD), including audit/financial reporting (MSA), taxation (MSA); business statistics (MS, PhD); data science (MS); finance (PhD); general business (MBA); healthcare management (MS); information systems and operations management (PhD); management (PhD); marketing (PhD); STEM (MBA); JD/MBA; JD/MSA; MBA/M Arch; MBA/MD; MBA/MS; MBA/Pharm D. *Accreditation:* AACSB; CAHME (one or more programs are accredited). *Program availability:* Evening/weekend. *Faculty:* 74 full-time (13 women). *Students:* 741 full-time (275 women); includes 198 minority (38 Black or African American, non-Hispanic/Latino; 1 American Indian or Alaska Native, non-Hispanic/Latino; 24 Asian, non-Hispanic/Latino; 116 Hispanic/Latino; 1 Native Hawaiian or other Pacific Islander, non-Hispanic/Latino; 18 Two or more races, non-Hispanic/Latino), 95 international. Average age 28. 905 applicants, 48% accepted, 251 enrolled. In 2016, 545 master's, 13 doctorates awarded. *Degree requirements:* For master's, capstone course; for doctorate, comprehensive exam, thesis/dissertation, qualifying exams. *Entrance requirements:* For master's, GMAT, GRE, MCAT, PCAT, LSAT, or DAT, holistic review of academic credentials, resume, essay, letters of recommendation; for doctorate, GMAT, GRE, holistic review of academic credentials, resume, statement of purpose, letters of recommendation. Additional exam requirements/recommendations for international students: Required—TOEFL (minimum score 95 iBT), IELTS. *Application deadline:* For fall admission, 7/1 priority date for domestic students, 1/15 for international students; for spring admission, 12/1 priority date for domestic students, 6/15 for international students; for summer admission, 5/1 for domestic students. Applications are processed on a rolling basis. Application fee: $60. Electronic applications accepted. *Expenses:* $48,000 (MBA for Working Professionals); $20,000 (STEM MBA). *Financial support:* In 2016–17, 157 students received support, including 25 research assistantships (averaging $22,725 per year), 27 teaching assistantships (averaging $22,725 per year); fellowships, career-related internships or fieldwork, Federal Work-Study, scholarships/grants, health care benefits, and unspecified assistantships also available. Financial award application deadline: 3/1; financial award applicants required to submit FAFSA. *Faculty research:* Governmental and nonprofit accounting, securities and options futures, statistical analysis and design, leadership, consumer behavior. *Unit head:* Dr. Margaret Williams, Dean, 806-742-3188, Fax: 806-742-1092, E-mail: margaret.l.williams@ttu.edu. *Application contact:* Chathry Keaton, Applications Manager, Graduate and Professional Programs, 806-742-3184, Fax: 806-742-3958, E-mail: rawlsgrad@ttu.edu.
Website: http://www.depts.ttu.edu/rawlsbusiness/graduate/

Business Administration and Management—General

Texas Wesleyan University, Graduate Programs, Graduate Business Programs, Fort Worth, TX 76105. Offers MBA. *Accreditation:* AACSB; ACBSP. *Program availability:* Part-time, evening/weekend. *Faculty:* 7 full-time (1 woman), 4 part-time/adjunct (all women). *Students:* 22 full-time (9 women), 9 part-time (5 women); includes 8 minority (3 Black or African American, non-Hispanic/Latino; 1 Asian, non-Hispanic/Latino; 3 Hispanic/Latino; 1 Two or more races, non-Hispanic/Latino), 17 international. Average age 28. 39 applicants, 28% accepted, 9 enrolled. In 2016, 12 master's awarded. *Degree requirements:* For master's, capstone course. *Entrance requirements:* For master's, GMAT or GRE, bachelor's degree, minimum overall undergraduate GPA of 2.6, three letters of recommendation, written essay that shows objectives in pursuing an MBA. Additional exam requirements/recommendations for international students: Required—TOEFL (minimum score 550 paper-based; 79 iBT), IELTS (minimum score 6.5). *Application deadline:* Applications are processed on a rolling basis. Application fee: $64. Electronic applications accepted. *Expenses:* $900 per credit hour. *Financial support:* In 2016–17, 6 students received support. Federal Work-Study and tuition waivers (full and partial) available. Support available to part-time students. Financial award application deadline: 3/15; financial award applicants required to submit FAFSA. *Unit head:* Dr. Hector Quintanilla, Dean, 817-531-4840, Fax: 817-531-6585. *Application contact:* Amy Orcutt, Interim Director of Graduate Admissions, 817-531-4288, E-mail: arorcutt@txwes.edu.
Website: https://txwes.edu/academics/business-administration/

Texas Woman's University, Graduate School, School of Management, Denton, TX 76204-5738. Offers accounting (MBA); business administration (MBA); health systems management (MHSM). *Accreditation:* ACBSP. *Program availability:* Part-time. *Students:* 432 full-time (357 women), 442 part-time (356 women); includes 598 minority (341 Black or African American, non-Hispanic/Latino; 2 American Indian or Alaska Native, non-Hispanic/Latino; 111 Asian, non-Hispanic/Latino; 121 Hispanic/Latino; 3 Native Hawaiian or other Pacific Islander, non-Hispanic/Latino; 20 Two or more races, non-Hispanic/Latino), 46 international. Average age 35. In 2016, 604 master's awarded. *Degree requirements:* For master's, thesis optional. *Entrance requirements:* For master's, 2 letters of reference, resume, 5 years of relevant experience (EMBA only). Additional exam requirements/recommendations for international students: Required—TOEFL (minimum score 550 paper-based; 79 iBT). *Application deadline:* For fall admission, 8/1 priority date for domestic students, 3/1 for international students; for spring admission, 12/1 priority date for domestic students, 7/1 for international students. Applications are processed on a rolling basis. Application fee: $50 ($75 for international students). Electronic applications accepted. *Expenses:* Contact institution. *Financial support:* Research assistantships, career-related internships or fieldwork, Federal Work-Study, institutionally sponsored loans, scholarships/grants, traineeships, health care benefits, and unspecified assistantships available. Support available to part-time students. Financial award application deadline: 3/1; financial award applicants required to submit FAFSA. *Faculty research:* Tax research, privacy issues in Web-based marketing, multitasking, leadership, women in management, global comparative studies, corporate sustainability and responsibility. *Unit head:* Dr. Margaret A. Young, Director, 940-898-2105, Fax: 940-898-2120, E-mail: myoung13@twu.edu. *Application contact:* Dr. Samuel Wheeler, Assistant Director of Admissions, 940-898-3188, Fax: 940-898-3081, E-mail: wheelersr@twu.edu.
Website: http://www.twu.edu/som/

Thomas College, Graduate School, Programs in Business, Waterville, ME 04901-5097. Offers business (MBA); computer technology education (MS); education (MS); human resource management (MBA). *Program availability:* Part-time, evening/weekend. *Entrance requirements:* For master's, GMAT, GRE, MAT or minimum GPA of 3.3 in first 3 graduate-level courses. Additional exam requirements/recommendations for international students: Recommended—TOEFL.

Thomas Edison State University, School of Business and Management, Program in Management, Trenton, NJ 08608. Offers MSM. *Program availability:* Part-time, online learning. *Degree requirements:* For master's, final capstone project. *Entrance requirements:* For master's, bachelor's degree from a regionally-accredited college or university; minimum 2 letters of recommendation; 3-5 years of related working experience; current resume. Additional exam requirements/recommendations for international students: Required—TOEFL (minimum score 550 paper-based; 79 iBT). Electronic applications accepted.

Thomas More College, Program in Business Administration, Crestview Hills, KY 41017-3495. Offers MBA. *Accreditation:* ACBSP. *Program availability:* Evening/weekend, 100% online. *Degree requirements:* For master's, comprehensive exam, final project. *Entrance requirements:* For master's, GMAT, minimum GPA of 2.7. Additional exam requirements/recommendations for international students: Required—TOEFL (minimum score 600 paper-based; 100 iBT). Electronic applications accepted. *Expenses:* Contact institution. *Faculty research:* Leadership, elder abuse and neglect, community health asset mapping, critical thinking in higher education, business communication, corporate social responsibility.

Thomas University, Department of Business Administration, Thomasville, GA 31792-7499. Offers MBA. *Program availability:* Part-time. *Entrance requirements:* For master's, resume, 3 professional or academic references. Additional exam requirements/recommendations for international students: Required—TOEFL (minimum score 600 paper-based). Electronic applications accepted.

Thompson Rivers University, Program in Business Administration, Kamloops, BC V2C 0C8, Canada. Offers MBA. *Program availability:* Part-time. *Entrance requirements:* For master's, GMAT, undergraduate degree with minimum B- average in last 60 credits, personal resume. Additional exam requirements/recommendations for international students: Required—TOEFL (570 paper-based, 88 iBT), IELTS (6.5), or CAEL (70).

Tiffin University, Program in Business Administration, Tiffin, OH 44883-2161. Offers finance (MBA); general management (MBA); healthcare administration (MBA); human resource management (MBA); international business (MBA); leadership (MBA); marketing (MBA); non-profit management (MBA); sports management (MBA). *Accreditation:* ACBSP. *Program availability:* Part-time, evening/weekend, online learning. *Students:* 10 full-time (4 women), 497 part-time (240 women); includes 91 minority (67 Black or African American, non-Hispanic/Latino; 1 American Indian or Alaska Native, non-Hispanic/Latino; 5 Asian, non-Hispanic/Latino; 15 Hispanic/Latino; 3 Two or more races, non-Hispanic/Latino), 102 international. Average age 31. 214 applicants, 86% accepted, 146 enrolled. In 2016, 183 master's awarded. *Entrance requirements:* For master's, minimum undergraduate GPA of 2.5, work experience. Additional exam requirements/recommendations for international students: Required—TOEFL (minimum score 550 paper-based; 79 iBT), IELTS. *Application deadline:* For fall admission, 8/15 for domestic students, 8/1 for international students; for spring admission, 1/9 for domestic students, 12/1 for international students. Applications are processed on a rolling basis. Application fee: $50. Electronic applications accepted. Application fee is waived when completed online. *Expenses: Tuition:* Full-time $21,000; part-time $700 per credit hour. *Required fees:* $150. Tuition and fees vary according to program. *Financial support:* Unspecified assistantships available. Support available to part-time students. Financial award application deadline: 7/31; financial award applicants required to submit FAFSA. *Faculty research:* Small business, executive development operations, research and statistical analysis, market research, management information systems. *Unit head:* Dr. Bonnie Tiell, Dean of Graduate Studies, 419-448-3261, Fax: 419-443-5002, E-mail: btiell@tiffin.edu. *Application contact:* Nikki Hintze, Director of Graduate and Distance Education Academic Advising, 800-968-6446 Ext. 3596, Fax: 419-443-5002, E-mail: hintzenm@tiffin.edu.
Website: http://www.tiffin.edu/graduateprograms/

Trevecca Nazarene University, Graduate Business Programs, Nashville, TN 37210-2877. Offers business administration (MBA); management (MSM). *Program availability:* Evening/weekend, online learning. *Faculty:* 8 full-time (1 woman), 8 part-time/adjunct (3 women). *Students:* 168 full-time (108 women), 24 part-time (13 women); includes 98 minority (81 Black or African American, non-Hispanic/Latino; 6 Asian, non-Hispanic/Latino; 8 Hispanic/Latino; 1 Native Hawaiian or other Pacific Islander, non-Hispanic/Latino; 2 Two or more races, non-Hispanic/Latino), 3 international. Average age 32. In 2016, 44 master's awarded. *Entrance requirements:* For master's, minimum GPA of 2.75, resume, official transcript from regionally accredited institution, minimum math grade of C, minimum English composition grade of C. Additional exam requirements/recommendations for international students: Required—TOEFL (minimum score 550 paper-based; 80 iBT). *Application deadline:* Applications are processed on a rolling basis. Application fee: $0. Electronic applications accepted. *Expenses:* $520 per credit hour. *Financial support:* Applicants required to submit FAFSA. *Unit head:* Dr. Rick Mann, Director of Graduate and Professional Programs for School of Business, 615-248-1529, E-mail: management@trevecca.edu. *Application contact:* 615-248-1529, E-mail: sgcsadmissions@trevecca.edu.
Website: http://www.trevecca.edu/mba

Trident University International, College of Business Administration, Program in Business Administration, Cypress, CA 90630. Offers business administration (PhD); conflict and negotiation management (MBA); criminal justice administration (MBA); entrepreneurship (MBA); finance (MBA); general management (MBA); government accounting (MBA); human resource management (MBA); information security and digital assurance management (MBA); information technology management (MBA); international business (MBA); logistics management (MBA); marketing (MBA); project management (MBA); public management (MBA); quality management (MBA); strategic leadership (MBA). *Program availability:* Part-time, evening/weekend, online learning. *Degree requirements:* For doctorate, comprehensive exam, thesis/dissertation, defense of dissertation. *Entrance requirements:* For master's, minimum GPA of 2.5 (students with GPA 3.0 or greater may transfer up to 30% of graduate level credits); for doctorate, minimum GPA of 3.4, curriculum vitae, course work in research methods or statistics. Additional exam requirements/recommendations for international students: Required—TOEFL. Electronic applications accepted.

Trinity International University, Trinity Evangelical Divinity School, Deerfield, IL 60015-1284. Offers academic ministry (M Div); Biblical and Near Eastern archaeology and languages (MA); chaplaincy and ministry care (MA); Christian studies (Certificate); church and parachurch ministry (M Div); church history (MA, Th M); counseling (Th M); educational ministries (MA); educational ministry (Th M); educational studies (PhD); intercultural studies (MA, PhD); leadership and management (D Min); mental health counseling (MA); military chaplaincy (D Min); ministry (MA); missions (Th M); missions and evangelism (D Min); New Testament (MA, Th M); Old Testament (Th M); Old Testament and Semitic languages (MA); pastoral ministry and care (D Min); pastoral theology (Th M); preaching and teaching (D Min); spiritual formation and education (D Min); systematic theology (MA, Th M); theological studies (MA, PhD); urban ministry (MA). *Program availability:* Part-time, online learning. *Students:* 578 full-time (141 women), 711 part-time (202 women). *Degree requirements:* For master's, comprehensive exam, thesis, fieldwork; for doctorate, comprehensive exam (for some programs), thesis/dissertation; for Certificate, comprehensive exam, integrative papers. *Entrance requirements:* For master's, GRE, MAT, minimum cumulative undergraduate GPA of 3.0; for doctorate, GRE, minimum cumulative graduate GPA of 3.2; for Certificate, GRE, MAT, minimum undergraduate GPA of 2.5. Additional exam requirements/recommendations for international students: Required—TOEFL (minimum score 580 paper-based), TWE (minimum score 4). *Application deadline:* For fall admission, 7/15 priority date for domestic and international students. Applications are processed on a rolling basis. Application fee: $25. Electronic applications accepted. *Expenses: Tuition:* Full-time $19,898. *Required fees:* $200. *Financial support:* Fellowships with partial tuition reimbursements, teaching assistantships with partial tuition reimbursements, career-related internships or fieldwork, Federal Work-Study, scholarships/grants, and tuition waivers (partial) available. Financial award application deadline: 4/1; financial award applicants required to submit FAFSA. *Unit head:* Dr. Tite Tienou, Academic Dean, 847-317-8086, Fax: 847-317-8014, E-mail: ttienou@teds.edu. *Application contact:* Ron Campbell, Director of Admissions, 800-345-8337, Fax: 847-317-8097, E-mail: rcampbel@tiu.edu.
Website: https://divinity.tiu.edu/

Trinity University, School of Business, San Antonio, TX 78212-7200. Offers accounting (MS). *Accreditation:* AACSB. *Entrance requirements:* For master's, GMAT, minimum GPA of 3.0, course work in accounting and business law, letters of recommendation. Electronic applications accepted. *Expenses: Tuition:* Full-time $38,974. *Required fees:* $586.

Trinity Washington University, School of Business and Graduate Studies, Washington, DC 20017-1094. Offers business administration (MBA); communication (MA); international security studies (MA); organizational management (MSA), including federal program management, human resource management, nonprofit management, organizational development, public and community health. *Program availability:* Part-time, evening/weekend. *Degree requirements:* For master's, thesis (for some programs), capstone project (MSA). *Entrance requirements:* For master's, minimum GPA of 2.5. Additional exam requirements/recommendations for international students: Required—TOEFL (minimum score 550 paper-based).

Trinity Western University, School of Graduate Studies, Program in Business Administration, Langley, BC V2Y 1Y1, Canada. Offers international business (MBA); management of the growing enterprise (MBA); non-profit and charitable organization management (MBA). *Program availability:* Part-time, online learning. *Degree requirements:* For master's, thesis or alternative, applied project. *Entrance requirements:* For master's, GMAT (minimum score of 550 recommended). Additional exam requirements/recommendations for international students: Required—TOEFL (minimum score 600 paper-based; 100 iBT), IELTS. Electronic applications accepted.

Troy University, Graduate School, College of Business, Program in Business Administration, Troy, AL 36082. Offers accounting (EMBA, MBA); criminal justice (EMBA); finance (MBA); general management (EMBA, MBA); healthcare management (EMBA); information systems (EMBA, MBA); international economic development (MBA). *Accreditation:* ACBSP. *Program availability:* Part-time, evening/weekend. *Faculty:* 10 full-time (3 women), 2 part-time/adjunct (0 women). *Students:* 44 full-time (23 women), 131 part-time (69 women); includes 58 minority (38 Black or African American, non-Hispanic/Latino; 13 Asian, non-Hispanic/Latino; 4 Hispanic/Latino; 3 Two or more races, non-Hispanic/Latino). Average age 30. 285 applicants, 91% accepted, 22 enrolled. In 2016, 78 master's awarded. *Degree requirements:* For master's, minimum GPA of 3.0, capstone course, research course. *Entrance requirements:* For master's, GMAT (minimum score 500) or GRE (minimum score 900 on old exam or 294 on new exam), bachelor's degree; minimum undergraduate GPA of 2.5 or 3.0 on last 30 semester hours, letter of recommendation. Additional exam requirements/recommendations for international students: Required—TOEFL (minimum score 523 paper-based; 70 iBT), IELTS (minimum score 6). *Application deadline:* Applications are processed on a rolling basis. Application fee: $50. Electronic applications accepted. *Expenses:* Tuition, state resident: full-time $7146; part-time $397 per credit hour. Tuition, nonresident: full-time $14,292; part-time $794 per credit hour. *Required fees:* $802; $50 per semester. Tuition and fees vary according to campus/location and program. *Financial support:* Fellowships, career-related internships or fieldwork, and scholarships/grants available. Support available to part-time students. Financial award applicants required to submit FAFSA. *Unit head:* Dr. Phillip Mixon, MBA Director, 334-670-3140, Fax: 334-670-3708, E-mail: pamixon@troy.edu. *Application contact:* Jessica A. Kimbro, Director of Graduate Admissions, 334-670-3178, E-mail: jacord@troy.edu.

Troy University, Graduate School, College of Business, Program in Management, Troy, AL 36082. Offers MS, MSM. *Accreditation:* ACBSP. *Program availability:* Part-time, evening/weekend. *Faculty:* 14 full-time (6 women). *Students:* 48 full-time (22 women), 215 part-time (102 women); includes 80 minority (63 Black or African American, non-Hispanic/Latino; 1 American Indian or Alaska Native, non-Hispanic/Latino; 1 Asian, non-Hispanic/Latino; 7 Hispanic/Latino; 8 Two or more races, non-Hispanic/Latino). Average age 36. 156 applicants, 99% accepted, 54 enrolled. In 2016, 84 master's awarded. *Degree requirements:* For master's, Graduate Educational Testing Service Major Field Test, capstone exam, minimum GPA of 3.0. *Entrance requirements:* For master's, GRE (minimum score of 900 on old exam or 294 on new exam) or GMAT (minimum score of 500), bachelor's degree; minimum undergraduate GPA of 2.5 or 3.0 on last 30 semester hours, letter of recommendation. Additional exam requirements/recommendations for international students: Required—TOEFL (minimum score 523 paper-based; 70 iBT), IELTS (minimum score 6). *Application deadline:* Applications are processed on a rolling basis. Application fee: $50. Electronic applications accepted. *Expenses:* Contact institution. *Financial support:* Fellowships, career-related internships or fieldwork, and scholarships/grants available. Support available to part-time students. *Unit head:* Dr. Bob Wheatley, Director, Graduate Business Programs, 334-670-3143, Fax: 334-670-3599, E-mail: rwheat@troy.edu. *Application contact:* Jessica A. Kimbro, Director of Graduate Admissions, 334-670-3178, E-mail: kimbro@troy.edu.

Tulane University, A. B. Freeman School of Business, New Orleans, LA 70118-5669. Offers accounting (M Acct); analytics (MBA); banking and financial services (M Fin); energy (M Fin, MBA); entrepreneurship (MBA); finance (MBA, PhD); international business (MBA); international management (MBA); strategic management and leadership (MBA); JD/M Acct; JD/MBA; MBA/M Acc; MBA/MA; MBA/MD; MBA/ME; MBA/MPH. *Accreditation:* AACSB. *Program availability:* Part-time, evening/weekend. *Faculty:* 46 full-time (11 women), 36 part-time/adjunct (3 women). *Students:* 488 full-time (240 women), 414 part-time (198 women); includes 81 minority (31 Black or African American, non-Hispanic/Latino; 1 American Indian or Alaska Native, non-Hispanic/Latino; 17 Asian, non-Hispanic/Latino; 29 Hispanic/Latino; 3 Two or more races, non-Hispanic/Latino), 575 international. Average age 27. 2,038 applicants, 71% accepted, 511 enrolled. In 2016, 694 master's, 9 doctorates awarded. Terminal master's awarded for partial completion of doctoral program. *Degree requirements:* For master's, one foreign language, comprehensive exam (for some programs); for doctorate, one foreign language, comprehensive exam, thesis/dissertation. *Entrance requirements:* For master's and doctorate, GMAT or GRE, interview. Additional exam requirements/recommendations for international students: Required—TOEFL or IELTS. *Application deadline:* For fall admission, 11/1 priority date for domestic and international students; for winter admission, 1/6 for domestic and international students; for spring admission, 3/1 priority date for domestic and international students; for summer admission, 5/5 for domestic students. Applications are processed on a rolling basis. Application fee: $125. Electronic applications accepted. *Expenses:* Contact institution. *Financial support:* In 2016–17, 153 students received support. Fellowships with tuition reimbursements available, research assistantships, teaching assistantships, career-related internships or fieldwork, Federal Work-Study, tuition waivers (full and partial), and unspecified assistantships available. Support available to part-time students. Financial award application deadline: 4/15; financial award applicants required to submit FAFSA. *Faculty research:* Corporate finance, managerial accounting and financial reporting, strategic management and leadership, consumer behavior and decision making, organizational behavior and human resource management. *Unit head:* Ira Solomon, PhD, Dean, 504-865-5407, Fax: 504-865-5491, E-mail: businessdean@tulane.edu. *Application contact:* Melissa Booth, Director of Graduate Admissions and Financial Aid, 800-223-5402, E-mail: freeman.admissions@tulane.edu.
Website: http://www.freeman.tulane.edu

Tusculum College, Graduate and Professional Studies, Program in Business Administration, Greeneville, TN 37743-9997. Offers general management (MBA); healthcare administration (MBA); human resources (MBA); nonprofit management (MBA). *Program availability:* Evening/weekend. *Entrance requirements:* For master's, GMAT, GRE, 3 years of work experience, minimum GPA of 2.75. *Expenses:* Tuition: Full-time $7497; part-time $357 per credit hour. *Unit head:* Dr. Michael Dillon, Dean of the School of Business, 423-636-7300 Ext. 5022, E-mail: mdillon@tusculum.edu. *Application contact:* Lindsey Seal, Director of Enrollment, 423-636-7300 Ext. 5006, E-mail: lseal@tusculum.edu.
Website: http://home.tusculum.edu/gps/graduate-degrees/master-business-administration/

Union University, McAfee School of Business Administration, Jackson, TN 38305-3697. Offers accountancy (M Acc). Program also available at Germantown campus. *Program availability:* Evening/weekend, online learning. *Entrance requirements:* For master's, GMAT, minimum GPA of 2.5. Electronic applications accepted. *Expenses:* Contact institution. *Faculty research:* Personal financial management, strategy, accounting, marketing, economics.

United States International University–Africa, School of Business Administration, Nairobi, Kenya. Offers business administration (GEMBA); entrepreneurship (MBA); finance (MBA); human resource management (MBA); information technology management (MBA); integrated studies (MBA); international business administration (MBA); management and organizational development (MS); marketing (MBA); organizational development (EMS); strategic management (MBA). *Program availability:* Part-time, evening/weekend. *Degree requirements:* For master's, thesis. *Entrance requirements:* For master's, GMAT, 2 letters of reference, resume. Additional exam requirements/recommendations for international students: Required—TOEFL (minimum score 550 paper-based). *Faculty research:* Marketing in small business enterprises, total quality management in Kenya.

Universidad Autonoma de Guadalajara, Graduate Programs, Guadalajara, Mexico. Offers administrative law and justice (LL M); advertising and corporate communications (MA); architecture (M Arch); business (MBA); computational science (MCC); education (Ed M, Ed D); English-Spanish translation (MA); entrepreneurship and management (MBA); integrated management of digital animation (MA); international business (MIB); international corporate law (LL M); internet technologies (MS); manufacturing systems (MMS); occupational health (MS); philosophy (MA, PhD); power electronics (MS); quality systems (MQS); renewable energy (MS); social evaluation of projects (MBA); strategic market research (MBA); tax law (MA); teaching mathematics (MA).

Universidad de las Americas, A.C., Program in Business Administration, Mexico City, Mexico. Offers finance (MBA); marketing research (MBA); production and quality (MBA).

Universidad de las Américas Puebla, Division of Graduate Studies, School of Business and Economics, Puebla, Mexico. Offers business administration (MBA); finance (M Adm). *Program availability:* Part-time, evening/weekend. *Degree requirements:* For master's, one foreign language, thesis. *Entrance requirements:* Additional exam requirements/recommendations for international students: Required—TOEFL. *Faculty research:* System dynamics, information technology, marketing, international business, strategic planning, quality.

Universidad del Este, Graduate School, Carolina, PR 00984. Offers accounting (MBA); adult education (M Ed); agribusiness (MBA); criminal justice and criminology (MA); curriculum and instruction - early education (M Ed); curriculum and instruction - elementary (M Ed); curriculum and instruction - English (M Ed); curriculum and instruction - Spanish (M Ed); human resources (MBA); information security management (MBA); information technology and Web business development (MBA); management (MBA); public policy (MPA); social work (MA), including clinical social work; special education (M Ed); strategic leadership (MBA).

Universidad del Turabo, Graduate Programs, School of Business and Entrepreneurship, Program in Management, Gurabo, PR 00778-3030. Offers MBA, DBA. *Program availability:* Part-time, evening/weekend. *Students:* 27 full-time (15 women), 80 part-time (40 women); all minorities (all Hispanic/Latino). Average age 39. 144 applicants, 34% accepted, 37 enrolled. In 2016, 6 master's, 5 doctorates awarded. *Entrance requirements:* For master's, GRE, EXADEP or GMAT, interview, essay, official transcript, recommendation letters; for doctorate, GRE, EXADEP or GMAT, official transcript, recommendation letters, essay, curriculum vitae, interview. *Application deadline:* For fall admission, 8/5 for domestic students. Application fee: $25. Electronic applications accepted. *Financial support:* Institutionally sponsored loans available. Financial award applicants required to submit FAFSA. *Unit head:* Juan Sosa, Dean, 787-743-7979 Ext. 4118, E-mail: negocios_ut@suagm.edu. *Application contact:* Diriee Rodríguez, Admissions Director, 787-743-7979 Ext. 4453, E-mail: admisiones-ut@suagm.edu.
Website: http://ut.suagm.edu/es/negocios

Universidad Iberoamericana, Graduate School, Santo Domingo D.N., Dominican Republic. Offers business administration (MBA, PMBA); constitutional law (LL M); dentistry (DMD); educational management (MA); integrated marketing communication (MA); psychopedagogical intervention (M Ed); real estate law (LL M); strategic management of human talent (MM).

Universidad Metropolitana, School of Business Administration, San Juan, PR 00928-1150. Offers accounting (MBA); finance (MBA); human resources management (MBA); international business (MBA); management (MBA); management information systems (MBA); marketing (MBA). *Program availability:* Part-time, evening/weekend. *Degree requirements:* For master's, thesis or alternative. Electronic applications accepted. *Faculty research:* Latin American trade, international investments, central city business development, Hispanic consumer research, Caribbean and Asian trade cooperation.

Université de Moncton, Faculty of Administration, Moncton, NB E1A 3E9, Canada. Offers MBA, JD/MBA. *Program availability:* Part-time, evening/weekend, online learning. *Faculty:* 25 full-time (10 women), 16 part-time/adjunct (5 women). *Students:* 38 full-time (15 women), 18 international. Average age 28. 125 applicants, 41% accepted, 17 enrolled. In 2016, 20 master's awarded. *Degree requirements:* For master's, one foreign language, thesis. *Entrance requirements:* For master's, minimum undergraduate GPA of 3.0. *Application deadline:* For fall admission, 6/1 for domestic students, 2/1 for international students; for winter admission, 11/15 for domestic students, 9/1 for international students; for spring admission, 3/31 for domestic students, 1/1 for international students; for summer admission, 3/31 for domestic students, 1/1 for international students. Applications are processed on a rolling basis. Application fee: $60. Electronic applications accepted. *Financial support:* In 2016–17, 7 fellowships (averaging $2,500 per year) were awarded; teaching assistantships and institutionally sponsored loans also available. Support available to part-time students. Financial award application deadline: 5/30. *Faculty research:* Service management, corporate reputation, financial management, accounting, supply chain. *Total annual research expenditures:* $150,000. *Unit head:* Dr. Nha Nguyen, Director, 506-858-4231, Fax: 506-858-4093, E-mail: nha.nguyen@umoncton.ca. *Application contact:* Natalie Allain, Admission Counselor, 506-858-4273, Fax: 506-858-4093, E-mail: natalie.allain@umoncton.ca.
Website: http://www.umoncton.ca/umcm-administration/

Université de Sherbrooke, Faculty of Administration, Doctoral Program in Business Administration, Sherbrooke, QC J1K 2R1, Canada. Offers DBA. *Degree requirements:* For doctorate, one foreign language, comprehensive exam, thesis/dissertation. *Entrance requirements:* For doctorate, 3 years of related work experience, interview, fluency in French, advanced English, good oral and written French comprehension (tested with an interview). Electronic applications accepted. *Faculty research:* Change management, international business and finance, work organization, information technology implementation and impact on organizations, strategic management.

Université de Sherbrooke, Faculty of Administration, Master of Business Administration Program, Sherbrooke, QC J1K 2R1, Canada. Offers executive business administration (EMBA); general management (MBA). *Program availability:* Part-time, evening/weekend. *Entrance requirements:* For master's, bachelor's degree, minimum GPA of 2.7 (on 4.3 scale), minimum of two years of work experience, letters of recommendation. Electronic applications accepted.

Université de Sherbrooke, Faculty of Law, Sherbrooke, QC J1K 2R1, Canada. Offers alternative dispute resolution (LL M, Diploma); business law (Diploma); common law (JD); criminal and penal law (Diploma); health law (LL M, Diploma); international law (LL M); law (LL D); legal management (Diploma); notarial law (Diploma); transnational law (Diploma). *Program availability:* Part-time, evening/weekend. *Degree requirements:* For master's, thesis; for Diploma, one foreign language. *Entrance requirements:* For master's and Diploma, LL B. Electronic applications accepted.

Université du Québec à Chicoutimi, Graduate Programs, Program in Small and Medium-Sized Organization Management, Chicoutimi, QC G7H 2B1, Canada. Offers M Sc. *Program availability:* Part-time. *Degree requirements:* For master's, thesis. *Entrance requirements:* For master's, appropriate bachelor's degree, proficiency in French.

Université du Québec à Montréal, Graduate Programs, PhD Program in Business Administration, Montréal, QC H3C 3P8, Canada. Offers PhD. *Program availability:* Part-time. *Degree requirements:* For doctorate, thesis/dissertation. *Entrance requirements:* For doctorate, appropriate master's degree or equivalent, proficiency in French.

Université du Québec à Montréal, Graduate Programs, Program in Business Administration (Professional), Montréal, QC H3C 3P8, Canada. Offers business administration (MBA); management consultant (Diploma). *Program availability:* Part-time. *Entrance requirements:* For master's and Diploma, appropriate bachelor's degree or equivalent, proficiency in French.

Université du Québec à Montréal, Graduate Programs, Program in Business Administration (Research), Montréal, QC H3C 3P8, Canada. Offers MBA. *Program availability:* Part-time. *Entrance requirements:* For master's, appropriate bachelor's degree or equivalent and proficiency in French.

Université du Québec à Rimouski, Graduate Programs, Program in Business Administration, Rimouski, QC G5L 3A1, Canada. Offers MBA.

Université du Québec à Rimouski, Graduate Programs, Program in Management of People in Working Situation, Rimouski, QC G5L 3A1, Canada. Offers M Sc, Diploma.

Université du Québec à Trois-Rivières, Graduate Programs, Program in Business Administration, Trois-Rivières, QC G9A 5H7, Canada. Offers MBA, DBA. DBA offered jointly with Université de Sherbrooke. *Degree requirements:* For doctorate, thesis/dissertation.

Université du Québec en Abitibi-Témiscamingue, Graduate Programs, Program in Business Administration, Rouyn-Noranda, QC J9X 5E4, Canada. Offers MBA.

Université du Québec en Abitibi-Témiscamingue, Graduate Programs, Program in Organization Management, Rouyn-Noranda, QC J9X 5E4, Canada. Offers M Sc. *Program availability:* Part-time. *Degree requirements:* For master's, thesis. *Entrance requirements:* For master's, appropriate bachelor's degree, proficiency in French.

Université Laval, Faculty of Administrative Sciences, Program in Organizations Management and Development, Québec, QC G1K 7P4, Canada. Offers Diploma. *Program availability:* Part-time. *Entrance requirements:* For degree, knowledge of French. Electronic applications accepted.

Université Laval, Faculty of Administrative Sciences, Programs in Administrative Studies, Québec, QC G1K 7P4, Canada. Offers administrative studies (M Sc, PhD); financial engineering (M Sc). *Accreditation:* AACSB. Terminal master's awarded for partial completion of doctoral program. *Degree requirements:* For master's, thesis (for some programs); for doctorate, comprehensive exam, thesis/dissertation. *Entrance requirements:* For master's and doctorate, knowledge of French and English. Electronic applications accepted.

Université Laval, Faculty of Administrative Sciences, Programs in Business Administration, Québec, QC G1K 7P4, Canada. Offers accounting (MBA); agri-food management (MBA); electronic business (MBA, Diploma); factory management and logistics (MBA); finance (MBA); firm management (MBA); geomatic management (MBA); information technology management (MBA); international management (MBA); management (MBA); management accounting (MBA, Diploma); marketing (MBA); modeling and organizational decision (MBA); occupational health and safety management (MBA); pharmacy management (MBA); social and environmental responsibility (MBA); technological entrepreneurship (Diploma). *Accreditation:* AACSB. *Program availability:* Part-time, evening/weekend, online learning. *Entrance requirements:* For master's and Diploma, knowledge of French and English. Electronic applications accepted.

University at Albany, State University of New York, School of Business, Albany, NY 12222-0001. Offers MBA, MS. *Accreditation:* AACSB. *Program availability:* Part-time, evening/weekend. *Faculty:* 21 full-time (5 women), 20 part-time/adjunct (7 women). *Students:* 270 full-time (116 women), 200 part-time (81 women); includes 100 minority (21 Black or African American, non-Hispanic/Latino; 1 American Indian or Alaska Native, non-Hispanic/Latino; 47 Asian, non-Hispanic/Latino; 22 Hispanic/Latino; 9 Two or more races, non-Hispanic/Latino), 49 international. 489 applicants, 70% accepted, 260 enrolled. In 2016, 225 master's awarded. Terminal master's awarded for partial completion of doctoral program. *Degree requirements:* For master's, project. *Entrance requirements:* For master's, GMAT. Additional exam requirements/recommendations for international students: Required—TOEFL (minimum score 550 paper-based). *Application deadline:* For fall admission, 3/1 for domestic students, 5/1 for international students. Applications are processed on a rolling basis. Application fee: $75. Electronic applications accepted. *Expenses:* $14,410 per year in-state tuition, $24,390 per year out-of-state tuition. *Financial support:* Fellowships, research assistantships, career-related internships or fieldwork, and Federal Work-Study available. *Total annual research expenditures:* $194,980. *Unit head:* Donald S. Siegel, Dean, 518-956-8370, E-mail: dsiegel@albany.edu. *Application contact:* Michael DeRensis, Director, Graduate Admissions, 518-442-3980, Fax: 518-442-3922, E-mail: graduate@albany.edu.
Website: http://www.albany.edu/business

University at Buffalo, the State University of New York, Graduate School, School of Management, Buffalo, NY 14620. Offers accounting (MS); analytics (MBA); business administration (PMBA); consulting (MBA); finance (MBA, MS), including financial risk management (MS), quantitative finance (MS); healthcare (MBA); information assurance (MBA); information systems (MBA); international management (MBA); management (EMBA, PhD); management information systems (MS); marketing (MBA); supply chain and operations (MBA); supply chains and operations management (MS); Au D/MBA; DDS/MBA; JD/MBA; M Arch/MBA; MD/MBA; MPH/MBA; MSW/MBA; Pharm D/MBA. *Accreditation:* AACSB. *Program availability:* Part-time, evening/weekend. *Faculty:* 80 full-time (26 women), 36 part-time/adjunct (6 women). *Students:* 683 full-time (277 women), 196 part-time (63 women); includes 76 minority (23 Black or African American, non-Hispanic/Latino; 1 American Indian or Alaska Native, non-Hispanic/Latino; 48 Asian, non-Hispanic/Latino; 3 Hispanic/Latino; 1 Two or more races, non-Hispanic/Latino), 371 international. Average age 31. 2,451 applicants, 42% accepted, 484 enrolled. In 2016, 515 master's, 10 doctorates awarded. *Degree requirements:* For master's, thesis (for some programs); for doctorate, comprehensive exam, thesis/dissertation. *Entrance requirements:* For master's, GMAT (for MS in accounting, finance); GRE or GMAT (for MBA, PMBA, other MS concentrations), essays, letters of recommendation; for doctorate, GMAT or GRE, essays, writing sample, letters of recommendation. Additional exam requirements/recommendations for international students: Required—TOEFL (minimum score 95 iBT) or IELTS (minimum score 6.5); Recommended—TSE (minimum score 73). *Application deadline:* For fall admission, 10/15 priority date for domestic and international students; for winter admission, 2/1 priority date for domestic and international students; for spring admission, 4/15 for domestic students; for summer admission, 5/15 for domestic students. Application fee: $100. Electronic applications accepted. *Expenses:* Contact institution. *Financial support:* Fellowships with full and partial tuition reimbursements, research assistantships with full and partial tuition reimbursements, teaching assistantships with full and partial tuition reimbursements, career-related internships or fieldwork, Federal Work-Study, institutionally sponsored loans, scholarships/grants, health care benefits, and unspecified assistantships available. Financial award application deadline: 2/15. *Faculty research:* Data analytics, accounting information and corporate finance, consumer behavior, supply chain logistics, leadership and team effectiveness. *Total annual research expenditures:* $1.5 million. *Unit head:* Erin K. O'Brien, Assistant Dean and Director of Graduate Programs, 716-645-3204, Fax: 716-645-2341, E-mail: ekobrien@buffalo.edu. *Application contact:* Meghan Felser, Associate Director of Admissions and Recruiting, 716-645-3204, Fax: 716-645-2341, E-mail: mpwood@buffalo.edu.
Website: http://mgt.buffalo.edu/

The University of Akron, Graduate School, College of Business Administration, Department of Management, Program in Management, Akron, OH 44325. Offers MBA. *Students:* 34 full-time (16 women), 42 part-time (16 women); includes 8 minority (1 Black or African American, non-Hispanic/Latino; 4 Asian, non-Hispanic/Latino; 1 Hispanic/Latino; 2 Two or more races, non-Hispanic/Latino), 21 international. Average age 29. 25 applicants, 92% accepted, 19 enrolled. In 2016, 32 master's awarded. *Entrance requirements:* For master's, GMAT, minimum GPA of 3.0 (preferred), two letters of recommendation, resume, statement of purpose. Additional exam requirements/recommendations for international students: Required—TOEFL (minimum score 550 paper-based; 79 iBT), IELTS (minimum score 6.5). *Application deadline:* For fall admission, 7/15 for domestic and international students; for spring admission, 11/15 for domestic and international students; for summer admission, 4/15 for domestic and international students. Application fee: $45 ($75 for international students). Electronic applications accepted. *Expenses:* Tuition, state resident: full-time $8618; part-time $359 per credit hour. Tuition, nonresident: full-time $17,149; part-time $715 per credit hour. *Required fees:* $1652. *Unit head:* Dr. Steve Ash, Chair, 330-972-6429, E-mail: ash@uakron.edu. *Application contact:* Dr. William Hauser, Director of Graduate Business Programs, 330-972-7043, Fax: 330-972-6588, E-mail: whauser@uakron.edu.
Website: http://www.uakron.edu/cba/graduate/programs/mba/management.dot

The University of Alabama, Graduate School, Manderson Graduate School of Business, Department of Management, Tuscaloosa, AL 35487. Offers MA, MS, PhD. *Accreditation:* AACSB. *Program availability:* Part-time, evening/weekend, online learning. *Faculty:* 25 full-time (7 women). *Students:* 8 full-time (4 women), 52 part-time (17 women); includes 10 minority (8 Black or African American, non-Hispanic/Latino; 1 Hispanic/Latino; 1 Two or more races, non-Hispanic/Latino), 3 international. Average age 33. 57 applicants, 40% accepted, 17 enrolled. In 2016, 21 master's, 3 doctorates awarded. Terminal master's awarded for partial completion of doctoral program. *Degree requirements:* For master's, comprehensive exam (for some programs), thesis (for some programs), formal project paper; for doctorate, comprehensive exam, thesis/dissertation. *Entrance requirements:* For master's and doctorate, GMAT or GRE, minimum GPA of 3.0. Additional exam requirements/recommendations for international students: Required—TOEFL (minimum score 600 paper-based) or IELTS (minimum score 6.5). *Application deadline:* For fall admission, 6/30 priority date for domestic students, 1/31 for international students; for spring admission, 10/30 for domestic students. Applications are processed on a rolling basis. Application fee: $50 ($60 for international students). *Expenses:* Tuition, state resident: full-time $10,470. Tuition, nonresident: full-time $26,950. *Financial support:* In 2016–17, 15 students received support, including 5 fellowships with full tuition reimbursements available (averaging $15,000 per year), 2 research assistantships with full tuition reimbursements available (averaging $18,000 per year), 2 teaching assistantships with tuition reimbursements available (averaging $18,000 per year); scholarships/grants, health care benefits, and unspecified assistantships also available. *Faculty research:* Leadership, entrepreneurship, health care management, organizational behavior, strategy. *Unit head:* Dr. William E. Jackson, III, Department Head, 205-348-6183, Fax: 205-348-6695, E-mail: wjackson@cba.ua.edu. *Application contact:* Courtney Cox, Office Associate II, 205-348-6183, Fax: 205-348-6695, E-mail: crhodes@cba.ua.edu.
Website: http://cba.ua.edu/mgt

The University of Alabama, Graduate School, Manderson Graduate School of Business, Program in General Commerce and Business, Tuscaloosa, AL 35487. Offers EMBA, MBA. *Accreditation:* AACSB. *Students:* 214 full-time (63 women), 1 part-time (0 women); includes 34 minority (21 Black or African American, non-Hispanic/Latino; 4 Asian, non-Hispanic/Latino; 5 Hispanic/Latino; 1 Native Hawaiian or other Pacific Islander, non-Hispanic/Latino; 3 Two or more races, non-Hispanic/Latino), 11 international. Average age 28. 281 applicants, 60% accepted, 66 enrolled. In 2016, 122 master's awarded. *Entrance requirements:* For master's, GMAT or GRE. Additional exam requirements/recommendations for international students: Required—TOEFL (minimum score 550 paper-based). *Application deadline:* For winter admission, 1/5 priority date for domestic and international students; for spring admission, 4/15 for domestic and international students. Applications are processed on a rolling basis. Application fee: $50 ($60 for international students). Electronic applications accepted. *Expenses:* Tuition, state resident: full-time $10,470. Tuition, nonresident: full-time $26,950. *Financial support:* In 2016–17, 26 students received support, including 22 research assistantships with partial tuition reimbursements available (averaging $6,800 per year); teaching assistantships, scholarships/grants, health care benefits, and unspecified assistantships also available. Financial award application deadline: 4/15. *Unit head:* Dr. J. Brian Gray, Associate Dean, Manderson Graduate School of Business, 205-348-8912, Fax: 205-348-4504, E-mail: bgray@cba.ua.edu. *Application contact:* Patricia Wilson, Director of MBA Recruiting and Admissions, 205-348-9122, Fax: 205-348-4504, E-mail: pewilson@cba.ua.edu.

The University of Alabama at Birmingham, Collat School of Business, Birmingham, AL 35294. Offers M Acct, MBA, MS, MD/MBA. MD/MBA program offered in partnership with the School of Medicine. *Accreditation:* AACSB. *Program availability:* Part-time, online learning. *Entrance requirements:* For master's, GMAT. Additional exam requirements/recommendations for international students: Required—TOEFL. Electronic applications accepted. Full-time tuition and fees vary according to course load and program.

The University of Alabama in Huntsville, School of Graduate Studies, College of Business Administration, Programs in Business and Management, Huntsville, AL 35899. Offers business analytics (MSMS); federal contracting and procurement management (Certificate); human resource management (MSM); management (MBA), including acquisition management, entrepreneurship, federal contract accounting, finance, human resource management, logistics and supply chain management, marketing, project management; supply chain management (Certificate); technology and innovation management (Certificate). *Accreditation:* AACSB. *Program availability:* Part-time, evening/weekend. *Degree requirements:* For master's, comprehensive exam, thesis or alternative. *Entrance requirements:* For master's, GMAT (minimum score 500), minimum AACSB index of 1080. Additional exam requirements/recommendations for international students: Required—TOEFL (minimum score 550 paper-based; 80 iBT), IELTS (minimum score 6.5). Electronic applications accepted. *Expenses:* Tuition, state resident: full-time $9834; part-time $600 per credit hour. Tuition, nonresident: full-time $21,830; part-time $1325 per credit hour. *Faculty research:* Supply chain management, management of research and development, international marketing and branding, organizational behavior and human resource management, social networks and computational economics.

University of Alaska Anchorage, College of Business and Public Policy, Program in Business Administration, Anchorage, AK 99508. Offers MBA. *Accreditation:* AACSB. *Program availability:* Part-time. *Degree requirements:* For master's, comprehensive exam, thesis (for some programs), capstone projects. *Entrance requirements:* Additional exam requirements/recommendations for international students: Required—TOEFL (minimum score 550 paper-based). *Faculty research:* Complex global environments.

University of Alaska Fairbanks, School of Management, Department of Business Administration, Fairbanks, AK 99775-6080. Offers capital markets (MBA); general

management (MBA). *Accreditation:* AACSB. *Program availability:* Part-time, online only, 100% online. *Faculty:* 10 full-time (4 women). *Students:* 32 full-time (18 women), 55 part-time (28 women); includes 21 minority (3 Black or African American, non-Hispanic/Latino; 7 American Indian or Alaska Native, non-Hispanic/Latino; 3 Asian, non-Hispanic/Latino; 3 Hispanic/Latino; 1 Native Hawaiian or other Pacific Islander, non-Hispanic/Latino; 4 Two or more races, non-Hispanic/Latino), 7 international. Average age 31. 62 applicants, 66% accepted, 29 enrolled. In 2016, 30 master's awarded. *Degree requirements:* For master's, comprehensive exam, thesis or alternative. *Entrance requirements:* For master's, GRE General Test, GMAT, bachelor's degree from accredited institution with minimum cumulative undergraduate and major GPA of 3.0. Additional exam requirements/recommendations for international students: Required—TOEFL (minimum score 550 paper-based; 79 iBT), IELTS (minimum score 6.5). *Application deadline:* For fall admission, 3/1 priority date for domestic students, 2/1 for international students; for spring admission, 9/1 priority date for domestic students, 9/1 for international students. Applications are processed on a rolling basis. Application fee: $60. Electronic applications accepted. *Expenses:* $533 per credit resident tuition, $673 per semester resident fees; $1,088 per credit non-resident tuition, $835 per semester non-resident fees. *Financial support:* In 2016–17, 5 teaching assistantships with full tuition reimbursements (averaging $9,699 per year) were awarded; fellowships with full tuition reimbursements, research assistantships with full tuition reimbursements, career-related internships or fieldwork, Federal Work-Study, scholarships/grants, health care benefits, and unspecified assistantships also available. Support available to part-time students. Financial award application deadline: 2/15; financial award applicants required to submit FAFSA. *Faculty research:* Consumer behavior, marketing, international finance and business, strategic risk, organization theory. *Unit head:* Dr. Nicole Cundiff, Program Director, 907-474-7461, Fax: 907-474-5219, E-mail: uaf-som@alaska.edu. *Application contact:* Mary Kreta, Director of Admissions, 907-474-7500, Fax: 907-474-7097, E-mail: admissions@uaf.edu.
Website: http://www.uaf.edu/som/degrees/graduate/mba/

University of Alberta, Faculty of Graduate Studies and Research, Doctoral Program in Business, Edmonton, AB T6G 2E1, Canada. Offers accounting (PhD); finance (PhD); human resources/industrial relations (PhD); management science (PhD); marketing (PhD); organizational analysis (PhD); MBA/PhD. *Accreditation:* AACSB. *Program availability:* Part-time. *Degree requirements:* For doctorate, comprehensive exam, thesis/dissertation. *Entrance requirements:* For doctorate, GMAT. Additional exam requirements/recommendations for international students: Required—TOEFL (minimum score 550 paper-based). Electronic applications accepted. *Faculty research:* Accounting, capital markets and corporate finance, organizational change and human resource management, marketing, strategic management.

University of Alberta, Faculty of Graduate Studies and Research, Executive MBA Program, Edmonton, AB T6G 2E1, Canada. Offers Exec MBA. Program offered jointly with University of Calgary. *Accreditation:* AACSB. *Entrance requirements:* For master's, GMAT. Additional exam requirements/recommendations for international students: Required—TOEFL. Electronic applications accepted. *Expenses:* Contact institution.

University of Alberta, Faculty of Graduate Studies and Research, Program in Business Administration, Edmonton, AB T6G 2E1, Canada. Offers international business (MBA); leisure and sport management (MBA); natural resources and energy (MBA); technology commercialization (MBA); MBA/LL B; MBA/M Ag; MBA/M Eng; MBA/MF; MBA/PhD. *Accreditation:* AACSB. *Program availability:* Part-time, evening/weekend. *Degree requirements:* For master's, thesis or alternative. *Entrance requirements:* For master's, GMAT. Additional exam requirements/recommendations for international students: Required—TOEFL (minimum score 600 paper-based). Electronic applications accepted. *Faculty research:* Natural resources and energy/management and policy/family enterprise/international business/healthcare research management.

University of Antelope Valley, Program in Business Management, Lancaster, CA 93534. Offers MS. *Degree requirements:* For master's, capstone. *Entrance requirements:* For master's, official transcripts documenting earned bachelor's degree from nationally- or regionally-accredited institution with minimum cumulative GPA of 2.0.

The University of Arizona, Eller College of Management, Tucson, AZ 85721. Offers M Ac, MA, MBA, MS, PhD, Graduate Certificate, JD/MBA. *Accreditation:* AACSB. *Program availability:* Evening/weekend. *Degree requirements:* For doctorate, thesis/dissertation. *Entrance requirements:* Additional exam requirements/recommendations for international students: Required—TOEFL (minimum score 550 paper-based; 79 iBT). Electronic applications accepted. *Expenses:* Contact institution.

University of Arkansas, Graduate School, Sam M. Walton College of Business Administration, Program in Business Administration, Fayetteville, AR 72701. Offers MBA, PhD. *Accreditation:* AACSB. *Program availability:* Part-time, evening/weekend, online learning. In 2016, 105 master's, 5 doctorates awarded. *Degree requirements:* For doctorate, thesis/dissertation. *Entrance requirements:* For master's and doctorate, GMAT. Application fee: $40 ($50 for international students). *Financial support:* In 2016–17, 23 research assistantships were awarded; fellowships with tuition reimbursements, teaching assistantships, career-related internships or fieldwork, and Federal Work-Study also available. Support available to part-time students. Financial award application deadline: 4/1; financial award applicants required to submit FAFSA. *Unit head:* Dr. Vikas Anand, MBA Director, 479-575-2851, E-mail: vikas@uark.edu. *Application contact:* Marion Dunagan, Assistant Director of Marketing and Recruiting, 479-575-2996, E-mail: gsb@walton.uark.edu.
Website: http://gsb.uark.edu/

University of Arkansas at Little Rock, Graduate School, College of Business, Little Rock, AR 72204-1099. Offers business administration (MBA); business information systems (MS, Graduate Certificate); management (Graduate Certificate). *Accreditation:* AACSB. *Program availability:* Part-time, evening/weekend. *Entrance requirements:* For master's, GMAT, minimum undergraduate GPA of 2.7. Additional exam requirements/recommendations for international students: Required—TOEFL (minimum score 525 paper-based).

University of Baltimore, Graduate School, Merrick School of Business, Baltimore, MD 21201-5779. Offers MBA, MS, Graduate Certificate, JD/MBA, MBA/MSN, MBA/Pharm D. *Accreditation:* AACSB. *Program availability:* Part-time, evening/weekend, online learning. *Entrance requirements:* For master's, GMAT. Additional exam requirements/recommendations for international students: Required—TOEFL (minimum score 550 paper-based). Electronic applications accepted. *Faculty research:* Finance, economics, accounting, health care, management information systems.

University of Baltimore, Joint University of Baltimore/Towson University (UB/Towson) MBA Program, Baltimore, MD 21201-5779. Offers MBA, JD/MBA, MBA/MSN, MBA/Pharm D. MBA/MSN, MBA/Pharm D offered jointly with University of Maryland, Baltimore. *Accreditation:* AACSB. *Program availability:* Part-time, evening/weekend, online learning. *Entrance requirements:* For master's, GMAT. Additional exam requirements/recommendations for international students: Required—TOEFL (minimum score 550 paper-based).

University of Bridgeport, School of Business, Bridgeport, CT 06604. Offers accounting (MBA); finance (MBA); general business (MBA); global financial services (MBA); human resource management (MBA); information systems and knowledge management (MBA); international business (MBA); management (MBA); marketing (MBA); operations management (MBA); small business and entrepreneurship (MBA); specialized business (MBA). *Accreditation:* ACBSP. *Program availability:* Part-time, evening/weekend. *Degree requirements:* For master's, thesis optional. *Entrance requirements:* For master's, GMAT. Additional exam requirements/recommendations for international students: Recommended—TOEFL (minimum score 550 paper-based; 80 iBT), IELTS (minimum score 6.5). Electronic applications accepted. *Expenses:* Contact institution.

The University of British Columbia, Sauder School of Business, Doctoral Program in Business Administration, Vancouver, BC V6T 1Z2, Canada. Offers accounting (PhD); finance (PhD); management information systems (PhD); management science (PhD); marketing (PhD); organizational behavior (PhD); strategy and business economics (PhD); transportation and logistics (PhD); urban land economics (PhD). *Degree requirements:* For doctorate, comprehensive exam, thesis/dissertation. *Entrance requirements:* For doctorate, GMAT or GRE. Additional exam requirements/recommendations for international students: Required—TOEFL (minimum score 600 paper-based; 100 iBT). *Application deadline:* Applications are processed on a rolling basis. Application fee: $102 Canadian dollars ($165 Canadian dollars for international students). Electronic applications accepted. *Expenses:* $4,802 per year tuition and fees, $8,436 per year international. *Financial support:* Fellowships with full tuition reimbursements, research assistantships with full tuition reimbursements, and teaching assistantships with full tuition reimbursements available. *Application contact:* Elaine Cho, Administrator, PhD and M Sc Programs, 604-822-8366, Fax: 604-822-8755, E-mail: phd.program@sauder.ubc.ca.
Website: http://www.sauder.ubc.ca/Programs/PhD_in_Business_Administration

The University of British Columbia, Sauder School of Business, MBA Program, Vancouver, BC V6T 1Z2, Canada. Offers IMBA, MBA. Application fee: $138. *Expenses:* Contact institution. *Unit head:* Robert Helsley, Dean, 604-822-8559, Fax: 604-822-8468.
Website: http://www.sauder.ubc.ca/Programs/MBA

University of Calgary, Faculty of Graduate Studies, Haskayne School of Business, Alberta/Haskayne Executive MBA Program, Calgary, AB T2N 1N4, Canada. Offers EMBA. Program offered with School of Business at University of Alberta. *Accreditation:* AACSB. *Program availability:* Part-time. *Entrance requirements:* For master's, GMAT, minimum GPA of 3.0, minimum 7 years of work experience, 3 letters of reference. Additional exam requirements/recommendations for international students: Required—TOEFL (minimum score 600 paper-based; 100 iBT). *Expenses:* Contact institution. *Faculty research:* Accounting, data analysis and modeling, strategy, entrepreneurship, negotiations.

University of Calgary, Faculty of Graduate Studies, Haskayne School of Business, Program in Business Administration, Calgary, AB T2N 1N4, Canada. Offers MBA, MBA/LL B, MBA/MBT, MBA/MD, MBA/MSW. *Accreditation:* AACSB. *Program availability:* Part-time, evening/weekend. *Degree requirements:* For master's, comprehensive exam, thesis optional. *Entrance requirements:* For master's, GMAT (minimum score 550), minimum GPA of 3.0, resume, 3 years of work experience, 3 letters of reference, 4 year bachelor degree. Additional exam requirements/recommendations for international students: Required—TOEFL (minimum score 600 paper-based). Electronic applications accepted. *Expenses:* Contact institution. *Faculty research:* Entrepreneurship, ethics, strategy, finance energy management and sustainability.

University of Calgary, Faculty of Graduate Studies, Haskayne School of Business, Program in Management, Calgary, AB T2N 1N4, Canada. Offers MBA, PhD. *Accreditation:* AACSB. Terminal master's awarded for partial completion of doctoral program. *Degree requirements:* For master's, one foreign language, comprehensive exam, thesis; for doctorate, one foreign language, comprehensive exam, thesis/dissertation, written and oral exams. *Entrance requirements:* For master's, GMAT, GRE, minimum GPA of 3.3 in last 2 years of course work, 2 letters of reference; for doctorate, GMAT, GRE, minimum GPA of 3.5 in last 2 years of course work, 2 letters of reference. Additional exam requirements/recommendations for international students: Required—TOEFL (minimum score 600 paper-based; 100 iBT), IELTS (minimum score 7). Electronic applications accepted. *Faculty research:* Operations management, international business, management information systems, accounting, finance, sustainable development.

University of California, Berkeley, Graduate Division, Haas School of Business, The Berkeley MBA for Executives Program, Berkeley, CA 94720. Offers EMBA. *Accreditation:* AACSB. *Program availability:* Part-time. *Students:* 139 part-time (45 women); includes 59 minority (4 Black or African American, non-Hispanic/Latino; 44 Asian, non-Hispanic/Latino; 4 Hispanic/Latino; 7 Two or more races, non-Hispanic/Latino). Average age 36. *Entrance requirements:* For master's, GMAT or GRE, BA or BS. Additional exam requirements/recommendations for international students: Required—TOEFL (minimum score 570 paper-based, 90 iBT) or IELTS (minimum score 7). *Application deadline:* For fall admission, 11/15 for domestic students, 11/17 for international students; for winter admission, 1/3 for domestic students, 1/5 for international students; for spring admission, 2/8 for domestic students, 2/10 for international students. Applications are processed on a rolling basis. Application fee: $200. Electronic applications accepted. *Expenses:* Contact institution. *Financial support:* Fellowships with partial tuition reimbursements, teaching assistantships with partial tuition reimbursements, institutionally sponsored loans, scholarships/grants, and tuition waivers available. Support available to part-time students. Financial award application deadline: 4/4. *Unit head:* Jamie Breen, Assistant Dean, Berkeley MBA for Executives, 415-990-9115, E-mail: jamiebreen@berkeley.edu. *Application contact:* E-mail: mbaforexecs@haas.berkeley.edu.
Website: http://mbaforexecs.haas.berkeley.edu/

University of California, Berkeley, Graduate Division, Haas School of Business and School of Law, Concurrent JD/MBA Program, Berkeley, CA 94720-1500. Offers JD/MBA. *Accreditation:* AACSB; ABA. *Students:* 1 full-time (0 women). Average age 29. *Entrance requirements:* Additional exam requirements/recommendations for international students: Required—TOEFL (minimum score 570 paper-based; 90 iBT). *Application deadline:* For fall admission, 10/1 for domestic and international students; for winter admission, 1/7 for domestic and international students; for spring admission, 3/31 for domestic and international students. Application fee: $200. Electronic applications accepted. *Expenses:* Contact institution. *Financial support:* Fellowships, research assistantships with partial tuition reimbursements, teaching assistantships with partial tuition reimbursements, career-related internships or fieldwork, institutionally sponsored loans, scholarships/grants, and non-resident tuition waivers for some students, such as veterans available. Financial award application deadline: 5/18; financial award applicants required to submit FAFSA. *Faculty research:* Accounting, business and public policy, economic analysis and public policy, entrepreneurship, finance, management of organizations, marketing, operations and information technology management, real estate. *Application contact:* Morgan Bernstein, Executive Director, Full-time MBA Admissions, 510-642-1405, Fax: 510-643-6659, E-mail: mbernstein@haas.berkeley.edu.
Website: http://mba.haas.berkeley.edu/academics/concurrentdegrees.html

University of California, Berkeley, Graduate Division, Haas School of Business and School of Public Health, Concurrent MBA/MPH Program, Berkeley, CA 94720-1500.

Business Administration and Management—General

Offers MBA/MPH. *Accreditation:* AACSB; CEPH. *Students:* 37 full-time (20 women); includes 12 minority (1 Black or African American, non-Hispanic/Latino; 11 Asian, non-Hispanic/Latino), 3 international. Average age 28. *Entrance requirements:* Additional exam requirements/recommendations for international students: Required—TOEFL (minimum score 570 paper-based; 90 iBT); Recommended—IELTS (minimum score 7). *Application deadline:* For fall admission, 10/1 for domestic and international students; for winter admission, 1/7 for domestic and international students; for spring admission, 3/31 for domestic students, 3/11 for international students. Application fee: $200. Electronic applications accepted. *Expenses:* Contact institution. *Financial support:* Fellowships, research assistantships with partial tuition reimbursements, teaching assistantships with partial tuition reimbursements, career-related internships or fieldwork, institutionally sponsored loans, scholarships/grants, and non-resident tuition waivers for some students, such as veterans available. Financial award application deadline: 5/18. *Faculty research:* Accounting, business and public policy, economic analysis and public policy, entrepreneurship, finance, management of organizations, marketing, operations and information technology management, real estate. *Unit head:* Prof. Kim MacPherson, Associate Director, Health Services Management Program, 510-642-9175, Fax: 510-643-6659, E-mail: kmacpherson@haas.berkeley.edu. *Application contact:* Morgan Bernstein, Executive Director of Admissions, 510-642-1405, Fax: 510-643-6659, E-mail: mbaadm@haas.berkeley.edu.
Website: http://www.haas.berkeley.edu/

University of California, Berkeley, Graduate Division, Haas School of Business, Evening and Weekend MBA Program, Berkeley, CA 94720-1500. Offers MBA. *Accreditation:* AACSB. *Program availability:* Part-time, evening/weekend. *Students:* 726 part-time (209 women); includes 399 minority (15 Black or African American, non-Hispanic/Latino; 335 Asian, non-Hispanic/Latino; 28 Hispanic/Latino; 21 Two or more races, non-Hispanic/Latino), 1 international. Average age 33. *Degree requirements:* For master's, comprehensive exam, academic retreat, experiential learning course. *Entrance requirements:* For master's, GMAT or GRE, BA or BS. Additional exam requirements/recommendations for international students: Required—TOEFL (minimum score 570 paper-based; 90 iBT); Recommended—IELTS (minimum score 7). *Application deadline:* For fall admission, 11/16 for domestic students, 11/18 for international students; for winter admission, 1/17 for domestic students, 1/19 for international students; for spring admission, 3/8 for domestic students, 3/9 for international students; for summer admission, 4/24 for domestic students, 4/25 for international students. Application fee: $200. Electronic applications accepted. *Expenses:* Contact institution. *Financial support:* Fellowships, research assistantships with partial tuition reimbursements, teaching assistantships with partial tuition reimbursements, career-related internships or fieldwork, institutionally sponsored loans, scholarships/grants, and non-resident tuition waivers for some students, such as veterans available. Support available to part-time students. Financial award application deadline: 6/9; financial award applicants required to submit CSS PROFILE. *Faculty research:* Accounting, business and public policy, economic analysis and public policy, finance, management of organizations, marketing, operations and information technology management, real estate. *Unit head:* Courtney Chandler, Assistant Dean, 510-643-0434, Fax: 510-643-5902, E-mail: ewmbaadm@haas.berkeley.edu. *Application contact:* Marjorie DeGraca, Evening and Weekend MBA Admissions Office, 510-642-0292, Fax: 510-643-5902, E-mail: ewmbaadm@haas.berkeley.edu.
Website: http://ewmba.haas.berkeley.edu/

University of California, Berkeley, Graduate Division, Haas School of Business, Full-Time MBA Program, Berkeley, CA 94720-1902. Offers MBA. *Accreditation:* AACSB. *Students:* 464 full-time (182 women); includes 97 minority (27 Black or African American, non-Hispanic/Latino; 1 American Indian or Alaska Native, non-Hispanic/Latino; 55 Asian, non-Hispanic/Latino; 9 Hispanic/Latino; 5 Two or more races, non-Hispanic/Latino), 179 international. Average age 29. 4,031 applicants, 252 enrolled. In 2016, 235 master's awarded. *Degree requirements:* For master's, 51 units, one experiential learning course. *Entrance requirements:* For master's, GMAT or GRE, four-year degree (BA/BS). Additional exam requirements/recommendations for international students: Required—TOEFL (minimum score 570 paper-based, 90 iBT) or IELTS (minimum score 7). *Application deadline:* For fall admission, 9/21 for domestic and international students; for winter admission, 1/4 for domestic and international students; for spring admission, 4/5 for domestic and international students. Application fee: $200. Electronic applications accepted. *Expenses:* Contact institution. *Financial support:* In 2016–17, 224 fellowships (averaging $24,496 per year) were awarded; research assistantships with partial tuition reimbursements, teaching assistantships, career-related internships or fieldwork, institutionally sponsored loans, scholarships/grants, and non-resident tuition waivers for some students, such as veterans also available. Financial award application deadline: 6/18. *Unit head:* Peter Johnson, Assistant Dean, Full-time MBA Program and Admissions, 510-642-1405, Fax: 510-643-6659, E-mail: pjohnson@haas.berkeley.edu. *Application contact:* Morgan Bernstein, Executive Director, Full-time MBA Admissions, 510-642-1405, Fax: 510-643-6659, E-mail: mbaadm@haas.berkeley.edu.
Website: http://mba.haas.berkeley.edu/

University of California, Berkeley, Graduate Division, Haas School of Business, PhD in Business Administration Program, Berkeley, CA 94720-1500. Offers accounting (PhD); business and public policy (PhD); finance (PhD); management of organizations (PhD); marketing (PhD); real estate (PhD). *Accreditation:* AACSB. *Students:* 78 full-time (28 women); includes 34 minority (29 Asian, non-Hispanic/Latino; 5 Hispanic/Latino). Average age 27. *Degree requirements:* For doctorate, comprehensive exam, thesis/dissertation, written preliminary exams, oral qualifying exam. *Entrance requirements:* For doctorate, GMAT or GRE, minimum GPA of 3.0 in undergraduate and graduate coursework. Additional exam requirements/recommendations for international students: Required—TOEFL (minimum score 570 paper-based; 70 iBT), IELTS (minimum score 7). *Application deadline:* For fall admission, 12/1 for domestic and international students. Application fee: $90 ($110 for international students). Electronic applications accepted. *Expenses:* Contact institution. *Financial support:* Fellowships with tuition reimbursements, research assistantships with tuition reimbursements, teaching assistantships with tuition reimbursements, scholarships/grants, health care benefits, tuition waivers (full), unspecified assistantships, and transit passes, travel grants available. Financial award application deadline: 12/10. *Faculty research:* Accounting, business and public policy, entrepreneurship, finance, management of organizations, marketing, operations and information technology management, real estate. *Unit head:* Dr. Nicolae Garleanu, Director, 510-643-6349, Fax: 510-643-4255. *Application contact:* Melissa Hacker, Director, Student Affairs, 510-642-3944, Fax: 510-643-4255, E-mail: melhacker@haas.berkeley.edu.
Website: http://www.haas.berkeley.edu/Phd/

University of California, Berkeley, UC Berkeley Extension, Certificate Programs in Business, Berkeley, CA 94720-1500. Offers accounting (Certificate); business administration (Certificate); finance (Certificate); human resource management (Certificate); management (Certificate); marketing (Certificate); project management (Certificate). *Accreditation:* AACSB. *Program availability:* Online learning.

University of California, Berkeley, UC Berkeley Extension, International Diploma Programs, Berkeley, CA 94720-1500. Offers business administration (Certificate); finance (Certificate); global business management (Certificate); marketing (Certificate); project management (Certificate). *Accreditation:* AACSB.

University of California, Davis, Graduate School of Management, Full-Time MBA Program, Davis, CA 95616. Offers MBA, DVM/MBA, JD/MBA, M Engr/MBA, MBA/MPH, MBA/MS, MD/MBA, MSN/MBA, PhD/MBA. *Faculty:* 30 full-time (10 women), 43 part-time/adjunct (7 women). *Students:* 99 full-time (30 women); includes 18 minority (14 Asian, non-Hispanic/Latino; 2 Hispanic/Latino; 2 Two or more races, non-Hispanic/Latino), 35 international. Average age 29. 351 applicants, 15% accepted, 47 enrolled. In 2016, 39 master's awarded. *Degree requirements:* For master's, thesis or alternative, integrated management project. *Entrance requirements:* For master's, GMAT or GRE, letters of recommendation, resume, essays, equivalent of a 4-year U.S. undergraduate degree. Additional exam requirements/recommendations for international students: Required—TOEFL (minimum score 600 paper-based; 100 iBT), IELTS (minimum score 7). *Application deadline:* For fall admission, 11/2 priority date for domestic and international students. Application fee: $125. Electronic applications accepted. *Expenses:* Contact institution. *Financial support:* In 2016–17, 80 students received support. Fellowships, teaching assistantships with partial tuition reimbursements available, career-related internships or fieldwork, institutionally sponsored loans, scholarships/grants, health care benefits, tuition waivers (partial), and unspecified assistantships available. Financial award application deadline: 3/2; financial award applicants required to submit FAFSA. *Faculty research:* Finance, marketing, organizational behavior, business analytics, accounting. *Unit head:* James Stevens, Senior Assistant Dean of Student Affairs, 530-752-7658, Fax: 530-754-9355, E-mail: admissions@gsm.ucdavis.edu. *Application contact:* Kathy Gleed, Senior Director of Admission, 530-752-7658, Fax: 530-754-9355, E-mail: admissions@gsm.ucdavis.edu.
Website: http://gsm.ucdavis.edu/daytime-mba-program

University of California, Davis, Graduate School of Management, MBA Programs in Sacramento and San Francisco Bay Area, Davis, CA 95616. Offers MBA. *Program availability:* Part-time, evening/weekend. *Faculty:* 30 full-time (10 women), 43 part-time/adjunct (7 women). *Students:* 352 part-time (138 women); includes 171 minority (6 Black or African American, non-Hispanic/Latino; 103 Asian, non-Hispanic/Latino; 38 Hispanic/Latino; 4 Native Hawaiian or other Pacific Islander, non-Hispanic/Latino; 20 Two or more races, non-Hispanic/Latino), 25 international. Average age 30. 197 applicants, 58% accepted, 111 enrolled. In 2016, 145 master's awarded. *Degree requirements:* For master's, thesis or alternative, integrated management project. *Entrance requirements:* For master's, GMAT or GRE, letters of recommendation, resume, equivalent of a 4-year undergraduate degree. Additional exam requirements/recommendations for international students: Required—TOEFL (minimum score 600 paper-based; 100 iBT), IELTS (minimum score 7). *Application deadline:* For fall admission, 11/2 priority date for domestic and international students. Application fee: $125. Electronic applications accepted. *Expenses:* Contact institution. *Financial support:* In 2016–17, 39 students received support. Fellowships, teaching assistantships, scholarships/grants, and unspecified assistantships available. Support available to part-time students. Financial award application deadline: 3/2; financial award applicants required to submit FAFSA. *Faculty research:* Finance, marketing, organizational behavior, business analytics, accounting. *Unit head:* James Stevens, Senior Assistant Dean of Student Affairs, 530-752-7658, Fax: 530-754-9355, E-mail: admissions@gsm.ucdavis.edu. *Application contact:* Kathy Gleed, Senior Director of Admissions, 530-752-7658, Fax: 530-754-9355, E-mail: admissions@gsm.ucdavis.edu.
Website: http://gsm.ucdavis.edu/mba-programs

University of California, Irvine, The Paul Merage School of Business, Doctoral Program in Management, Irvine, CA 92697. Offers PhD. *Students:* 52 full-time (27 women); includes 7 minority (1 American Indian or Alaska Native, non-Hispanic/Latino; 5 Asian, non-Hispanic/Latino; 1 Native Hawaiian or other Pacific Islander, non-Hispanic/Latino), 35 international. Average age 31. 257 applicants, 4% accepted, 9 enrolled. In 2016, 6 doctorates awarded. Application fee: $105 ($125 for international students). *Unit head:* Dr. Terry Shevlin, Director, 949-824-6149, E-mail: tshevlin@uci.edu. *Application contact:* Noel Negrete, Associate Director, 949-824-8318, Fax: 949-824-1592, E-mail: nnegrete@uci.edu.
Website: http://merage.uci.edu/PhD/Default.aspx

University of California, Irvine, The Paul Merage School of Business, Executive MBA Program, Irvine, CA 92697. Offers EMBA. *Students:* 40 full-time (13 women), 31 part-time (13 women); includes 36 minority (2 Black or African American, non-Hispanic/Latino; 3 American Indian or Alaska Native, non-Hispanic/Latino; 29 Asian, non-Hispanic/Latino; 2 Hispanic/Latino), 15 international. Average age 40. 63 applicants, 83% accepted, 37 enrolled. In 2016, 44 master's awarded. Application fee: $105 ($125 for international students). *Unit head:* Anthony Hansford, Senior Assistant Dean, 949-824-3801, E-mail: hansfora@uci.edu. *Application contact:* Jon Masciana, Senior Director, 949-824-8595, E-mail: jmascian@uci.edu.
Website: http://merage.uci.edu/ExecutiveMBA/

University of California, Irvine, The Paul Merage School of Business, Full-Time MBA Program, Irvine, CA 92697. Offers MBA. *Students:* 164 full-time (49 women), 10 part-time (4 women); includes 48 minority (2 Black or African American, non-Hispanic/Latino; 46 Asian, non-Hispanic/Latino), 98 international. Average age 30. 738 applicants, 27% accepted, 83 enrolled. In 2016, 104 master's awarded. Application fee: $105 ($125 for international students). *Unit head:* Jon Kaplan, Assistant Dean, 949-824-9654, E-mail: jbkaplan@uci.edu. *Application contact:* Courtney Watts, Director of Recruitment and Admissions, 949-824-0462, Fax: 949-824-2235, E-mail: courtney.elmes@uci.edu.
Website: http://merage.uci.edu/FullTimeMBA/default.aspx

University of California, Irvine, The Paul Merage School of Business, Fully Employed MBA Program, Irvine, CA 92697. Offers MBA. *Program availability:* Part-time. *Students:* 139 full-time (47 women), 190 part-time (68 women); includes 159 minority (5 Black or African American, non-Hispanic/Latino; 12 American Indian or Alaska Native, non-Hispanic/Latino; 135 Asian, non-Hispanic/Latino; 7 Hispanic/Latino), 34 international. Average age 30. 203 applicants, 71% accepted, 100 enrolled. In 2016, 130 master's awarded. *Application deadline:* For fall admission, 7/11 for domestic students. Application fee: $105 ($125 for international students). *Unit head:* Anthony Hansford, Senior Assistant Dean, 949-824-3801, Fax: 949-824-2944, E-mail: hansfora@uci.edu. *Application contact:* Melanie Coburn, Senior Associate Director, Admissions, 949-824-7505, E-mail: mcoburn@uci.edu.
Website: http://merage.uci.edu/FullyEmployedMBA/default.aspx

University of California, Los Angeles, Graduate Division, UCLA Anderson School of Management, Los Angeles, CA 90095-1481. Offers accounting (PhD); behavioral decision making (PhD); business administration (EMBA, MBA); decisions, operations, and technology management (PhD); finance (PhD); financial engineering (MFE); global economics and management (PhD); management and organizations (PhD); marketing (PhD); strategy and policy (PhD); DDS/MBA; MBA/JD; MBA/MD; MBA/MLAS; MBA/MLIS; MBA/MN; MBA/MPH; MBA/MPP; MBA/MSCS; MBA/MURP. *Accreditation:* AACSB. *Program availability:* Part-time, evening/weekend. *Faculty:* 90 full-time (20 women), 98 part-time/adjunct (19 women). *Students:* 865 full-time (263 women), 1,201 part-time (337 women); includes 710 minority (48 Black or African American, non-Hispanic/Latino; 1 American Indian or Alaska Native, non-Hispanic/Latino; 505 Asian, non-Hispanic/Latino; 88 Hispanic/Latino; 4 Native Hawaiian or other Pacific Islander,

non-Hispanic/Latino; 64 Two or more races, non-Hispanic/Latino), 451 international. Average age 31. 5,643 applicants, 26% accepted, 881 enrolled. In 2016, 807 master's, 7 doctorates awarded. *Degree requirements:* For master's, comprehensive exam, field consulting project; internship (for MBA); thesis/dissertation (for MFE); for doctorate, comprehensive exam, thesis/dissertation, oral and written qualifying exams. *Entrance requirements:* For master's, GMAT or GRE, 4-year bachelor's degree or equivalent; 2 letters of recommendation; essays (1 for MBA, 2 for FEMBA and MFE); 4-8 years of full-time work experience (for FEMBA); minimum eight years of work experience with at least three years at management level (for EMBA); for doctorate, GMAT or GRE, bachelor's degree from college or university of fully-recognized standing, minimum B average during junior and senior years of undergraduate years, 3 letters of recommendation, statement of purpose. Additional exam requirements/recommendations for international students: Required—TOEFL (minimum score 560 paper-based; 87 iBT), IELTS (minimum score 7). *Application deadline:* For fall admission, 10/6 priority date for domestic and international students; for winter admission, 1/5 for domestic and international students; for spring admission, 4/12 for domestic and international students. Applications are processed on a rolling basis. Application fee: $200. Electronic applications accepted. *Expenses:* Contact institution. *Financial support:* In 2016–17, 633 students received support, including 455 fellowships (averaging $30,253 per year); research assistantships with partial tuition reimbursements available, teaching assistantships with partial tuition reimbursements available, career-related internships or fieldwork, institutionally sponsored loans, and scholarships/grants also available. Support available to part-time students. *Faculty research:* Finance/global economics, entrepreneurship, accounting, human resources/organizational behavior, marketing, behavioral decision making. *Total annual research expenditures:* $1.1 million. *Unit head:* Dr. Judy D. Olian, Dean/Chair in Management, 310-825-7982, Fax: 310-206-2073, E-mail: judy.olian@anderson.ucla.edu. *Application contact:* Alex Lawrence, Assistant Dean and Director of MBA Admissions, 310-825-6944, Fax: 310-825-8582, E-mail: mba.admissions@anderson.ucla.edu.
Website: http://www.anderson.ucla.edu/

University of California, Riverside, Graduate Division, The A. Gary Anderson Graduate School of Management, Riverside, CA 92521-0102. Offers business administration (MBA, PhD). *Accreditation:* AACSB. *Program availability:* Part-time, evening/weekend. Terminal master's awarded for partial completion of doctoral program. *Degree requirements:* For master's, thesis optional; for doctorate, comprehensive exam, thesis/dissertation. *Entrance requirements:* For master's and doctorate, GMAT or GRE. Additional exam requirements/recommendations for international students: Required—TOEFL (minimum score 550 paper-based; 80 iBT), IELTS. Electronic applications accepted. *Expenses:* Contact institution. *Faculty research:* Option pricing, marketing, decision modeling, new technologies in cost accounting, supply chain management, operations, production and inventory systems, entrepreneurial finance, e-commerce.

University of California, San Diego, Graduate Division, Rady School of Management, La Jolla, CA 92093. Offers business administration (MBA); business analytics (MS); finance (MF); management (PhD). *Accreditation:* AACSB. *Program availability:* Part-time, evening/weekend. *Faculty:* 28 full-time (5 women), 5 part-time/adjunct (1 woman). *Students:* 433 full-time (183 women), 89 part-time (35 women). 2,021 applicants, 32% accepted, 313 enrolled. In 2016, 152 master's, 5 doctorates awarded. *Degree requirements:* For master's, capstone project; for doctorate, comprehensive exam, thesis/dissertation. *Entrance requirements:* For master's, GMAT (for MBA); GMAT or GRE General Test (for MF); for doctorate, GMAT or GRE General Test. Additional exam requirements/recommendations for international students: Required—TOEFL (minimum score 550 paper-based; 80 iBT), IELTS (minimum score 7). *Application deadline:* Applications are processed on a rolling basis. Application fee: $200. Electronic applications accepted. *Expenses:* Contact institution. *Financial support:* Fellowships, teaching assistantships, and scholarships/grants available. Financial award applicants required to submit FAFSA. *Faculty research:* Innovation technology, operations management, finance, behavioral economics, organizational strategy, marketing, business analytics. *Unit head:* Robert Sullivan, Dean, 858-822-0830, E-mail: rssullivan@ucsd.edu. *Application contact:* Jay Bryant, Director of Graduate Recruitment and Admissions, 858-534-0864, E-mail: radygradadmissions@ucsd.edu.
Website: http://rady.ucsd.edu/

University of Central Arkansas, Graduate School, College of Business Administration, Program in Business Administration, Conway, AR 72035-0001. Offers MBA. *Accreditation:* AACSB. *Program availability:* Part-time, evening/weekend. *Entrance requirements:* For master's, GMAT or GRE, minimum GPA of 2.7. Additional exam requirements/recommendations for international students: Required—TOEFL (minimum score 550 paper-based).

University of Central Florida, College of Business Administration, Department of Management, Orlando, FL 32816. Offers entrepreneurship (Graduate Certificate); management (MSM); technology ventures (Graduate Certificate). *Accreditation:* AACSB. *Faculty:* 23 full-time (7 women), 3 part-time/adjunct (1 woman). *Students:* 55 part-time (38 women); includes 24 minority (7 Black or African American, non-Hispanic/Latino; 1 American Indian or Alaska Native, non-Hispanic/Latino; 1 Asian, non-Hispanic/Latino; 12 Hispanic/Latino; 3 Two or more races, non-Hispanic/Latino), 1 international. Average age 33. 19 applicants, 84% accepted, 13 enrolled. In 2016, 30 master's, 13 other advanced degrees awarded. *Degree requirements:* For master's, capstone course. *Entrance requirements:* For master's, GMAT, minimum GPA of 3.0 in last 60 hours. Additional exam requirements/recommendations for international students: Required—TOEFL. *Application deadline:* For fall admission, 7/1 for domestic students; for spring admission, 12/1 for domestic students. Application fee: $30. Electronic applications accepted. *Expenses:* Tuition, state resident: part-time $288.16 per credit hour. Tuition, nonresident: part-time $1071.31 per credit hour. *Financial support:* Fellowships available. Financial award application deadline: 3/1; financial award applicants required to submit FAFSA. *Unit head:* Dr. Stephen Goodman, Chair, 407-823-2675, Fax: 407-823-3725, E-mail: sgoodman@bus.ucf.edu. *Application contact:* Assistant Director, Graduate Admissions, 407-823-2776, Fax: 407-823-6224, E-mail: gradadmissions@ucf.edu.
Website: http://business.ucf.edu/departments-schools/management/

University of Central Florida, College of Business Administration, Program in Business Administration, Orlando, FL 32816. Offers MBA, PhD. *Accreditation:* AACSB. *Program availability:* Part-time, evening/weekend. *Students:* 119 full-time (52 women), 452 part-time (196 women); includes 210 minority (45 Black or African American, non-Hispanic/Latino; 1 American Indian or Alaska Native, non-Hispanic/Latino; 38 Asian, non-Hispanic/Latino; 119 Hispanic/Latino; 7 Two or more races, non-Hispanic/Latino), 28 international. Average age 32. 606 applicants, 42% accepted, 204 enrolled. In 2016, 192 master's, 7 doctorates awarded. *Degree requirements:* For master's, exam; for doctorate, thesis/dissertation, departmental candidacy exam. *Entrance requirements:* For master's and doctorate, GMAT, minimum GPA of 3.0 in last 60 hours. Additional exam requirements/recommendations for international students: Required—TOEFL. *Application deadline:* For fall admission, 1/15 priority date for domestic students. Application fee: $30. Electronic applications accepted. *Expenses:* Tuition, state resident: part-time $288.16 per credit hour. Tuition, nonresident: part-time $1071.31 per credit hour. *Financial support:* In 2016–17, 40 students received support, including 14 fellowships with partial tuition reimbursements available (averaging $6,390 per year), 38 teaching assistantships with partial tuition reimbursements available (averaging $15,998 per year); career-related internships or fieldwork, Federal Work-Study, institutionally sponsored loans, tuition waivers (partial), and unspecified assistantships also available. Financial award application deadline: 3/1; financial award applicants required to submit FAFSA. *Unit head:* Dr. Paul Jarley, Dean, 407-823-5133, E-mail: pjarley@bus.ucf.edu. *Application contact:* Assistant Director, Graduate Admissions, 407-823-2776, Fax: 407-823-6442, E-mail: gradadmissions@ucf.edu.
Website: http://www.bus.ucf.edu

University of Central Missouri, The Graduate School, Warrensburg, MO 64093. Offers accountancy (MA); accounting (MBA); applied mathematics (MS); aviation safety (MA); biology (MS); business administration (MBA); career and technical education leadership (MS); college student personnel administration (MS); communication (MA); computer science (MS); counseling (MS); criminal justice (MS); educational leadership (Ed D); educational technology (MS); elementary and early childhood education (MSE); English (MA); environmental studies (MA); finance (MBA); history (MA); human services/educational technology (Ed S); human services/learning resources (Ed S); human services/professional counseling (Ed S); industrial hygiene (MS); industrial management (MS); information systems (MBA); information technology (MS); kinesiology (MS); library science and information services (MS); literacy education (MSE); marketing (MBA); mathematics (MS); music (MA); occupational safety management (MS); psychology (MS); rural family nursing (MS); school administration (MSE); social gerontology (MS); sociology (MA); special education (MSE); speech language pathology (MS); superintendency (Ed S); teaching (MAT); teaching English as a second language (MA); technology (MS); technology management (PhD); theatre (MA). *Program availability:* Part-time, 100% online, blended/hybrid learning. *Degree requirements:* For master's and Ed S, comprehensive exam (for some programs), thesis (for some programs). *Entrance requirements:* Additional exam requirements/recommendations for international students: Required—TOEFL (minimum score 550 paper-based; 79 iBT). Electronic applications accepted.

University of Charleston, Master of Business Administration Program, Charleston, WV 25304-1099. Offers MBA. *Program availability:* Part-time, evening/weekend. *Students:* 51 full-time (20 women); includes 6 minority (5 Black or African American, non-Hispanic/Latino; 1 Two or more races, non-Hispanic/Latino), 5 international. Average age 31. In 2016, 36 master's awarded. *Entrance requirements:* Additional exam requirements/recommendations for international students: Required—TOEFL, IELTS. *Application deadline:* Applications are processed on a rolling basis. Application fee: $50. Electronic applications accepted. *Expenses: Tuition:* Full-time $20,602; part-time $425 per credit. *Required fees:* $200. Tuition and fees vary according to course load, campus/location, program and student level. *Financial support:* Scholarships/grants and unspecified assistantships available. Financial award application deadline: 3/1; financial award applicants required to submit FAFSA. *Unit head:* Rick Ferris, Program Director, 304-720-6680, E-mail: mba@ucwv.edu. *Application contact:* Bobby Redd, Admissions Representative, 304-860-5621, E-mail: bobbyredd@ucwv.edu.
Website: http://www.ucwv.edu/School-of-Business-Leadership/Graduate-Programs/Master-of-Business-Administration-MBA/

University of Chicago, Booth School of Business, Doctoral Program in Business, Chicago, IL 60637-1513. Offers PhD. *Accreditation:* AACSB. *Students:* 115 full-time (29 women). In 2016, 25 doctorates awarded. *Degree requirements:* For doctorate, thesis/dissertation, workshops, curriculum paper. *Entrance requirements:* For doctorate, GMAT or GRE (for most programs), transcripts, resume, letters of reference, essay. Additional exam requirements/recommendations for international students: Required—TOEFL, IELTS. *Application deadline:* For winter admission, 12/1 for domestic and international students. Electronic applications accepted. *Expenses:* Contact institution. *Unit head:* Associate Director, 773-702-0093.
Website: https://www.chicagobooth.edu/programs/phd

University of Chicago, Booth School of Business, Evening MBA Program, Chicago, IL 60611. Offers MBA. *Accreditation:* AACSB. *Program availability:* Part-time, evening/weekend. *Students:* 82 full-time (25 women), 820 part-time (221 women). *Entrance requirements:* For master's, GMAT or GRE, transcripts, resume, 2 letters of recommendation, essay, interview. Additional exam requirements/recommendations for international students: Required—TOEFL (minimum score 600 paper-based; 104 iBT), IELTS (minimum score 7). *Application deadline:* For fall admission, 7/1 for domestic and international students; for winter admission, 10/1 for domestic and international students; for summer admission, 4/1 for domestic and international students. Applications are processed on a rolling basis. Electronic applications accepted. *Expenses:* Contact institution. *Unit head:* Associate Dean for Evening and Weekend MBA Programs, 312-464-8675. *Application contact:* Evening and Weekend MBA Programs Admissions, 312-464-8700, E-mail: eveningweekend-admissions@chicagobooth.edu.
Website: http://www.chicagobooth.edu/programs/evening

University of Chicago, Booth School of Business, Full-Time MBA Program, Chicago, IL 60637. Offers accounting (MBA); analytic finance (MBA); analytic management (MBA); econometrics and statistics (MBA); economics (MBA); entrepreneurship (MBA); finance (MBA); general management (MBA); health administration and policy (Certificate); international business (MBA); managerial and organizational behavior (MBA); marketing analytics (MBA); marketing management (MBA); operations management (MBA); strategic management (MBA); MBA/AM; MBA/JD; MBA/MA; MBA/MD; MBA/MPP. *Accreditation:* AACSB. *Students:* 1,151 full-time (443 women), 17 part-time (9 women). Terminal master's awarded for partial completion of doctoral program. *Entrance requirements:* For master's, GMAT or GRE, transcripts, resume, 2 letters of recommendation, essay, interview. Additional exam requirements/recommendations for international students: Required—TOEFL (minimum score 600 paper-based; 104 iBT), IELTS (minimum score 7), PTE (minimum score 70). *Application deadline:* For spring admission, 4/1 for domestic and international students. Electronic applications accepted. *Expenses:* Contact institution. *Unit head:* Stacey Kole, Deputy Dean, 773-702-7121. *Application contact:* Full-time MBA Program Admissions, 773-702-7369, Fax: 773-702-9085, E-mail: admissions@chicagobooth.edu.
Website: https://www.chicagobooth.edu/programs/full-time

University of Chicago, Booth School of Business, Part-Time Weekend MBA Program, Chicago, IL 60611. Offers MBA. *Accreditation:* AACSB. *Program availability:* Part-time, evening/weekend. *Students:* 48 full-time (9 women), 339 part-time (65 women). *Entrance requirements:* For master's, GMAT or GRE, transcripts, resume, 2 letters of recommendation, essay, interview. Additional exam requirements/recommendations for international students: Required—TOEFL (minimum score 600 paper-based; 104 iBT), IELTS (minimum score 7). *Application deadline:* For fall admission, 5/1 for domestic and international students. Applications are processed on a rolling basis. Electronic applications accepted. *Expenses:* Contact institution. *Unit head:* Glenn Sykes, Associate Dean for Evening and Weekend MBA Programs, 312-464-8675. *Application contact:* Evening and Weekend MBA Programs Admissions, 312-464-8700, E-mail: eveningweekend-admissions@chicagobooth.edu.
Website: https://www.chicagobooth.edu/programs/weekend

Business Administration and Management—General

University of Cincinnati, Graduate School, Carl H. Lindner College of Business, MBA Program, Cincinnati, OH 45221. Offers MBA. *Accreditation:* AACSB. *Program availability:* Part-time, evening/weekend, 100% online, blended/hybrid learning. *Faculty:* 32 full-time (7 women), 12 part-time/adjunct (6 women). *Students:* 91 full-time (33 women), 266 part-time (105 women); includes 63 minority (21 Black or African American, non-Hispanic/Latino; 1 American Indian or Alaska Native, non-Hispanic/Latino; 26 Asian, non-Hispanic/Latino; 9 Hispanic/Latino; 1 Native Hawaiian or other Pacific Islander, non-Hispanic/Latino; 5 Two or more races, non-Hispanic/Latino), 44 international. Average age 31. 351 applicants, 46% accepted, 127 enrolled. In 2016, 184 master's awarded. *Degree requirements:* For master's, capstone project. *Entrance requirements:* For master's, GMAT or GRE, resume, letters of recommendation, essays, official transcripts. Additional exam requirements/recommendations for international students: Required—TOEFL (minimum score 577 paper-based; 90 iBT), IELTS (minimum score 6.5). *Application deadline:* For fall admission, 8/1 priority date for domestic students, 3/15 for international students; for spring admission, 12/15 for domestic students, 9/15 for international students; for summer admission, 4/15 for domestic and international students. Applications are processed on a rolling basis. Application fee: $65 ($70 for international students). Electronic applications accepted. *Expenses:* Contact institution. *Financial support:* In 2016–17, 77 students received support. Scholarships/grants, tuition waivers (full and partial), and unspecified assistantships available. Financial award application deadline: 3/15; financial award applicants required to submit FAFSA. *Unit head:* Dr. David Szymanski, Dean, 513-556-7001, Fax: 513-556-4891, E-mail: david.szymanski@uc.edu. *Application contact:* Dona Clary, Director, Graduate Programs, 513-556-3546, Fax: 513-558-7006, E-mail: dona.clary@uc.edu.
Website: http://www.business.uc.edu/mba

University of Cincinnati, Graduate School, Carl H. Lindner College of Business, PhD Programs, Cincinnati, OH 45211. Offers accounting (PhD); economics (PhD); finance (PhD); information systems (PhD); management (PhD); marketing (PhD); operations and business analytics (PhD). *Faculty:* 72 full-time (18 women). *Students:* 37 full-time (19 women); includes 4 minority (1 Black or African American, non-Hispanic/Latino; 3 Asian, non-Hispanic/Latino), 19 international. Average age 30. 92 applicants, 16% accepted, 7 enrolled. In 2016, 4 doctorates awarded. *Degree requirements:* For doctorate, comprehensive exam, thesis/dissertation. *Entrance requirements:* For doctorate, GMAT, GRE, transcripts, essays, resume, letters of recommendation. Additional exam requirements/recommendations for international students: Required—TOEFL (minimum score 600 paper-based; 100 iBT), IELTS (minimum score 7). *Application deadline:* For fall admission, 1/15 for domestic and international students. Application fee: $65 ($70 for international students). Electronic applications accepted. *Expenses:* Contact institution. *Financial support:* In 2016–17, 38 students received support, including 25 research assistantships with tuition reimbursements available (averaging $23,250 per year); scholarships/grants, tuition waivers (full and partial), and unspecified assistantships also available. Financial award application deadline: 1/15; financial award applicants required to submit FAFSA. *Faculty research:* Bayesian Prediction Theory, organizational fairness, consumer insight and market research, EGARCH idiosyncratic volatility and expected stock returns, consumer insight and market research, density estimation from correlated data. *Unit head:* Dr. Suzanne Masterson, Director, 513-556-7125, Fax: 513-556-5499, E-mail: suzanne.masterson@uc.edu. *Application contact:* Angel Elvin, Assistant Director, 513-556-7190, Fax: 513-558-7006, E-mail: angel.elvin@uc.edu.
Website: http://www.business.uc.edu/phd

University of Colorado Boulder, Leeds School of Business, MBA Programs, Boulder, CO 80309. Offers MBA. *Accreditation:* AACSB. *Students:* 316 full-time (106 women), 2 part-time (0 women); includes 33 minority (2 Black or African American, non-Hispanic/Latino; 11 Asian, non-Hispanic/Latino; 17 Hispanic/Latino; 3 Two or more races, non-Hispanic/Latino), 46 international. Average age 30. 433 applicants, 78% accepted, 107 enrolled. In 2016, 119 master's awarded. *Entrance requirements:* For master's, GMAT, minimum undergraduate GPA of 2.75. *Application deadline:* Applications are processed on a rolling basis. Application fee: $60 ($80 for international students). Electronic applications accepted. Application fee is waived when completed online. *Financial support:* In 2016–17, 272 students received support, including 205 fellowships (averaging $5,962 per year), 1 teaching assistantship with full and partial tuition reimbursement available (averaging $10,173 per year); institutionally sponsored loans, scholarships/grants, health care benefits, and unspecified assistantships also available. Financial award applicants required to submit FAFSA. *Application contact:* E-mail: leedsmba@colorado.edu.
Website: http://www.colorado.edu/leedsmba/

University of Colorado Colorado Springs, College of Business, Colorado Springs, CO 80918. Offers MBA, MSA. *Accreditation:* AACSB. *Program availability:* Part-time, evening/weekend, 100% online, blended/hybrid learning. *Faculty:* 24 full-time (9 women), 14 part-time/adjunct (3 women). *Students:* 67 full-time (27 women), 241 part-time (112 women); includes 59 minority (8 Black or African American, non-Hispanic/Latino; 14 Asian, non-Hispanic/Latino; 20 Hispanic/Latino; 17 Two or more races, non-Hispanic/Latino), 13 international. Average age 34. 107 applicants, 66% accepted, 50 enrolled. In 2016, 98 master's awarded. *Entrance requirements:* Additional exam requirements/recommendations for international students: Recommended—TOEFL (minimum score 500 paper-based; 80 iBT). *Application deadline:* For fall admission, 6/1 for domestic and international students; for spring admission, 11/1 for domestic and international students; for summer admission, 4/1 for domestic and international students. Applications are processed on a rolling basis. Application fee: $60 ($100 for international students). Electronic applications accepted. *Expenses:* Contact institution. *Financial support:* In 2016–17, 37 students received support. Career-related internships or fieldwork, Federal Work-Study, and scholarships/grants available. Support available to part-time students. Financial award application deadline: 3/1; financial award applicants required to submit FAFSA. *Faculty research:* Management information systems, marketing science, organizational behavior and human decision processes, accounting. *Unit head:* Dr. Cathy Claiborne, Interim Dean, 719-255-3113, Fax: 719-255-3100, E-mail: cclaibor@uccs.edu. *Application contact:* Whitney Porter, Assistant Director of Graduate Programs, 719-255-3408, E-mail: cobgrad@uccs.edu.
Website: http://www.uccs.edu/mba

University of Colorado Denver, Business School, Master of Business Administration Program, Denver, CO 80217. Offers bioinnovation and entrepreneurship (MBA); business intelligence (MBA); business strategy (MBA); business to business marketing (MBA); business to consumer marketing (MBA); change management (MBA); corporate financial management (MBA); enterprise technology management (MBA); entrepreneurship (MBA); health administration (MBA), including financial management, health administration, health information technologies, international health management and policy; human resources management (MBA); international business (MBA); investment management (MBA); managing for sustainability (MBA); sports and entertainment management (MBA). *Accreditation:* AACSB. *Program availability:* Part-time, evening/weekend, 100% online, blended/hybrid learning. *Students:* 544 full-time (210 women), 112 part-time (22 women); includes 99 minority (15 Black or African American, non-Hispanic/Latino; 4 American Indian or Alaska Native, non-Hispanic/Latino; 38 Asian, non-Hispanic/Latino; 36 Hispanic/Latino; 6 Two or more races, non-Hispanic/Latino), 22 international. Average age 32. 335 applicants, 73% accepted, 179 enrolled. In 2016, 251 master's awarded. *Degree requirements:* For master's, 48 semester hours, including 30 of core courses, 3 in international business, and 15 in electives from over 50 other business courses. *Entrance requirements:* For master's, GMAT, resume, official transcripts, essay, two letters of recommendation, financial statements (for international applicants). Additional exam requirements/recommendations for international students: Required—TOEFL (minimum score 560 paper-based; 83 iBT); Recommended—IELTS (minimum score 6.5). *Application deadline:* For fall admission, 4/15 priority date for domestic students, 3/15 priority date for international students; for spring admission, 10/15 priority date for domestic students, 9/15 priority date for international students; for summer admission, 2/15 priority date for domestic students, 1/15 priority date for international students. Applications are processed on a rolling basis. Application fee: $50 ($75 for international students). Electronic applications accepted. *Expenses:* Contact institution. *Financial support:* In 2016–17, 171 students received support. Fellowships, research assistantships, teaching assistantships, Federal Work-Study, institutionally sponsored loans, scholarships/grants, traineeships, and unspecified assistantships available. Financial award application deadline: 4/1; financial award applicants required to submit FAFSA. *Faculty research:* Marketing, management, entrepreneurship, finance, health administration. *Unit head:* Woodrow Eckard, MBA Director, 303-315-8470, E-mail: woody.eckard@ucdenver.edu. *Application contact:* Shelly Townley, Admissions Director, Graduate Programs, 303-315-8202, E-mail: shelly.townley@ucdenver.edu.
Website: http://www.ucdenver.edu/academics/colleges/business/degrees/mba/Pages/MBA.aspx

University of Colorado Denver, Business School, Program in Management and Organization, Denver, CO 80217. Offers business strategy (MS); change and innovation (MS); enterprise technology management (MS); entrepreneurship and innovation (MS); global management (MS); leadership (MS); managing for sustainability (MS); managing human resources (MS); sports and entertainment management (MS). *Accreditation:* AACSB. *Program availability:* Part-time, evening/weekend, online learning. *Students:* 20 full-time (13 women), 17 part-time (10 women); includes 6 minority (3 Black or African American, non-Hispanic/Latino; 1 American Indian or Alaska Native, non-Hispanic/Latino; 1 Hispanic/Latino; 1 Two or more races, non-Hispanic/Latino), 6 international. Average age 33. 24 applicants, 58% accepted, 6 enrolled. In 2016, 19 master's awarded. *Degree requirements:* For master's, 30 semester hours (12 of required courses, 12 of management electives, and 6 of free electives). *Entrance requirements:* For master's, GMAT, resume, two letters of recommendation, essay, financial statements (for international applicants). Additional exam requirements/recommendations for international students: Required—TOEFL (minimum score 525 paper-based; 71 iBT); Recommended—IELTS (minimum score 6.5). *Application deadline:* For fall admission, 4/15 priority date for domestic students, 3/15 priority date for international students; for spring admission, 10/15 priority date for domestic students, 9/15 priority date for international students; for summer admission, 2/15 priority date for domestic students, 1/15 priority date for international students. Applications are processed on a rolling basis. Application fee: $50 ($75 for international students). Electronic applications accepted. *Expenses:* Contact institution. *Financial support:* In 2016–17, 7 students received support. Fellowships, research assistantships, teaching assistantships, Federal Work-Study, institutionally sponsored loans, scholarships/grants, and traineeships available. Financial award application deadline: 4/1; financial award applicants required to submit FAFSA. *Faculty research:* Human resource management, management of catastrophe, turnaround strategies. *Unit head:* Dr. Kenneth Bettenhausen, Associate Professor/Director of MS in Management, 303-315-8425, E-mail: kenneth.bettenhausen@ucdenver.edu. *Application contact:* 303-315-8200, E-mail: bschool.admissions@ucdenver.edu.
Website: http://www.ucdenver.edu/academics/colleges/business/degrees/ms/management/Pages/Management.aspx

University of Connecticut, Graduate School, School of Business, Storrs, CT 06269. Offers accounting (MS, PhD); business administration (MBA, PhD); finance (PhD); health care management and insurance studies (MBA); management (PhD); management consulting (MBA); marketing (PhD); marketing intelligence (MBA). *Accreditation:* AACSB. *Degree requirements:* For master's, comprehensive exam; for doctorate, thesis/dissertation. *Entrance requirements:* For master's and doctorate, GMAT. Additional exam requirements/recommendations for international students: Required—TOEFL (minimum score 550 paper-based). Electronic applications accepted.

University of Dallas, Satish and Yasmin Gupta College of Business, Irving, TX 75062-4736. Offers accounting (MBA, MS); business administration (DBA); business analytics (MS); business management (MBA); corporate finance (MBA); cybersecurity (MS); finance (MS); financial services (MBA); global business (MBA, MS); health services management (MBA); human resource management (MBA); information and technology management (MS); information assurance (MBA); information technology (MBA); information technology service management (MBA); marketing management (MBA); organization development (MBA); project management (MBA); sports and entertainment management (MBA); strategic leadership (MBA); supply chain management (MBA). *Accreditation:* AACSB. *Program availability:* Part-time, evening/weekend, online learning. *Entrance requirements:* Additional exam requirements/recommendations for international students: Required—TOEFL. Electronic applications accepted. *Expenses:* Contact institution.

University of Dayton, School of Business Administration, Dayton, OH 45469. Offers accounting (MBA); cyber security (MBA); finance (MBA); marketing (MBA); JD/MBA. *Accreditation:* AACSB. *Program availability:* Part-time, evening/weekend, blended/hybrid learning. *Faculty:* 23 full-time (5 women), 18 part-time/adjunct (9 women). *Students:* 94 full-time (35 women), 85 part-time (38 women); includes 14 minority (5 Black or African American, non-Hispanic/Latino; 4 Asian, non-Hispanic/Latino; 5 Hispanic/Latino), 26 international. Average age 30. 269 applicants, 31% accepted. In 2016, 93 master's awarded. *Entrance requirements:* For master's, GMAT (minimum score of 500 total, 19 verbal); GRE (minimum score of 149 verbal, 146 quantitative), minimum GPA of 3.0, current resume. Additional exam requirements/recommendations for international students: Required—TOEFL (minimum score 550 paper-based; 80 iBT); Recommended—IELTS (minimum score 6.5). *Application deadline:* Applications are processed on a rolling basis. Application fee: $0 ($50 for international students). Electronic applications accepted. *Expenses:* $970 per credit hour, $25 registration fee per term. *Financial support:* In 2016–17, 7 research assistantships with partial tuition reimbursements (averaging $8,535 per year), 2 teaching assistantships with partial tuition reimbursements (averaging $8,535 per year) were awarded; institutionally sponsored loans, health care benefits, and unspecified assistantships also available. Financial award application deadline: 3/1; financial award applicants required to submit FAFSA. *Faculty research:* Asset pricing, applied microeconomics, financial reporting and auditing, entrepreneurship. *Unit head:* Scott MacDonald, Director, MBA Program, 937-229-3733, Fax: 937-229-3882, E-mail: smacdonald1@udayton.edu. *Application contact:* Mandy Bingaman, MBA Program Manager, 937-229-3733, Fax: 937-229-3882, E-mail: mbingaman1@udayton.edu.
Website: https://www.udayton.edu/business/academics/master_of_business_administration/index.php

University of Delaware, Alfred Lerner College of Business and Economics, Program in Business Administration, Newark, DE 19716. Offers MBA, MA/MBA, MBA/MIB, MBA/MS. *Accreditation:* AACSB. *Program availability:* Part-time, evening/weekend. *Entrance requirements:* For master's, GMAT, 2 letters of recommendation, resume. Additional exam requirements/recommendations for international students: Required—TOEFL (minimum score 600 paper-based; 70 iBT). Electronic applications accepted. *Expenses:* Contact institution. *Faculty research:* Finance, corporate governance, information systems, leadership, marketing.

University of Delaware, College of Agriculture and Natural Resources, Department of Entomology and Wildlife Ecology, Newark, DE 19716. Offers entomology and applied ecology (MS, PhD), including avian ecology, evolution and taxonomy, insect biological control, insect ecology and behavior (MS), insect genetics, pest management, plant-insect interactions, wildlife ecology and management. *Program availability:* Part-time. *Degree requirements:* For master's, comprehensive exam, thesis, oral exam, seminar; for doctorate, comprehensive exam, thesis/dissertation, qualifying exam, seminar. *Entrance requirements:* For master's, GRE General Test, minimum GPA of 3.0 in field, 2.8 overall; for doctorate, GRE General Test, GRE Subject Test (biology), minimum GPA of 3.0 in field, 2.8 overall. Additional exam requirements/recommendations for international students: Required—TOEFL. Electronic applications accepted. *Faculty research:* Ecology and evolution of plant-insect interactions, ecology of wildlife conservation management, habitat restoration, biological control, applied ecosystem management.

University of Denver, Daniels College of Business, Denver, CO 80208. Offers M Acc, MBA, MS. *Accreditation:* AACSB. *Program availability:* Part-time, evening/weekend. *Faculty:* 104 full-time (36 women), 48 part-time/adjunct (12 women). *Students:* 417 full-time (176 women), 314 part-time (134 women); includes 127 minority (22 Black or African American, non-Hispanic/Latino; 33 Asian, non-Hispanic/Latino; 53 Hispanic/Latino; 19 Two or more races, non-Hispanic/Latino), 147 international. Average age 30. 1,266 applicants, 60% accepted, 341 enrolled. In 2016, 501 master's awarded. *Entrance requirements:* For master's, GRE General Test or GMAT, bachelor's degree, transcripts, essays, resume, two letters of recommendation, interview. Additional exam requirements/recommendations for international students: Required—TOEFL (minimum score 550 paper-based; 80 iBT). *Application deadline:* For fall admission, 11/15 priority date for domestic and international students; for spring admission, 10/1 priority date for domestic and international students. Applications are processed on a rolling basis. Application fee: $100. Electronic applications accepted. *Expenses:* $43,458 per year full-time. *Financial support:* In 2016–17, 525 students received support, including 34 teaching assistantships with tuition reimbursements available (averaging $1,864 per year); career-related internships or fieldwork, Federal Work-Study, institutionally sponsored loans, scholarships/grants, and unspecified assistantships also available. Support available to part-time students. Financial award application deadline: 2/15; financial award applicants required to submit FAFSA. *Faculty research:* Corporate governance, decision making, emerging economies, ethics, leadership. *Unit head:* Dr. Brent Chrite, Dean, 303-871-4324, Fax: 303-871-2156, E-mail: brent.chrite@du.edu. *Application contact:* Information Contact, 303-871-3416, Fax: 303-871-4466, E-mail: daniels@du.edu.
Website: http://daniels.du.edu/

University of Detroit Mercy, College of Business Administration, Detroit, MI 48221. Offers business administration (MBA); business fundamentals (Certificate); business turnaround management (Certificate); ethical leadership and change management (Certificate); finance (Certificate); forensic accounting (Certificate); JD/MBA; MBA/MHSA. *Program availability:* Part-time, evening/weekend, 100% online, blended/hybrid learning. *Entrance requirements:* For master's, GMAT, resume, letter of recommendation, transcripts; for Certificate, resume, letter of recommendation, transcripts. Electronic applications accepted. Application fee is waived when completed online. *Expenses:* Contact institution. *Faculty research:* Ethics, international finance, trade policy, leadership, information technology.

University of Dubuque, Program in Business Administration, Dubuque, IA 52001-5099. Offers MBA. *Program availability:* Part-time, evening/weekend. *Entrance requirements:* For master's, 2 letters of recommendation. Electronic applications accepted.

The University of Findlay, Office of Graduate Admissions, Findlay, OH 45840-3653. Offers applied security and analytics (MSAS); athletic training (MAT); business (MBA), including certified management accountant, certified public accountant, health care management, hospitality management; education (MA Ed, Ed D), including children's literature (MA Ed), curriculum and teaching (MA Ed), education (MA Ed), educational administration (MA Ed), human resource development (MA Ed), reading (MA Ed), science education (MA Ed), superintendent (Ed D), teaching (Ed D), technology (MA Ed); environmental, safety and health management (MSEM); health informatics (MS); occupational therapy (MOT); pharmacy (Pharm D); physical therapy (DPT); physician assistant (MPA); rhetoric and writing (MA); teaching English to speakers of other languages (TESOL) and bilingual education (MA). *Program availability:* Part-time, evening/weekend, 100% online, blended/hybrid learning. *Faculty:* 114 full-time (63 women), 44 part-time/adjunct (18 women). *Students:* 751 full-time (452 women), 573 part-time (323 women); includes 164 minority (82 Black or African American, non-Hispanic/Latino; 1 American Indian or Alaska Native, non-Hispanic/Latino; 27 Asian, non-Hispanic/Latino; 37 Hispanic/Latino; 17 Two or more races, non-Hispanic/Latino), 280 international. Average age 28. 661 applicants, 52% accepted, 288 enrolled. In 2016, 366 master's, 137 doctorates awarded. *Degree requirements:* For master's, comprehensive exam (for some programs), thesis, cumulative project, capstone project; for doctorate, thesis/dissertation. *Entrance requirements:* For master's, GRE (for some programs), bachelor's degree from accredited institution, minimum undergraduate GPA of 3.0 in last 64 hours of course work; for doctorate, MAT, minimum cumulative GPA of 3.0, master's degree. Additional exam requirements/recommendations for international students: Recommended—TOEFL (minimum score 79 iBT), IELTS (minimum score 7). *Application deadline:* For fall admission, 6/15 for international students; for spring admission, 12/1 for international students; for summer admission, 4/1 for international students. Applications are processed on a rolling basis. Electronic applications accepted. *Expenses:* Contact institution. *Financial support:* In 2016–17, 139 students received support, including 15 research assistantships with partial tuition reimbursements available (averaging $7,200 per year), 25 teaching assistantships with partial tuition reimbursements available (averaging $7,200 per year); Federal Work-Study, institutionally sponsored loans, and unspecified assistantships also available. Financial award application deadline: 4/1; financial award applicants required to submit FAFSA. *Unit head:* Christopher M. Harris, Director of Admissions, 419-434-4347, E-mail: harrisc1@findlay.edu. *Application contact:* Madeline Fauser Brennan, Graduate Admissions Counselor, 419-434-4636, Fax: 419-434-4898, E-mail: fauserbrennan@findlay.edu.
Website: http://www.findlay.edu/admissions/graduate/Pages/default.aspx

University of Florida, Graduate School, Warrington College of Business Administration, Hough Graduate School of Business, Department of Management, Gainesville, FL 32611. Offers health care risk management (MS); international business (MA); management (MS, PhD). *Accreditation:* AACSB. *Program availability:* Online learning. *Degree requirements:* For master's, comprehensive exam, thesis. *Entrance requirements:* For master's, GMAT (minimum score of 465) or GRE General Test, minimum GPA of 3.0. Additional exam requirements/recommendations for international students: Required—TOEFL (minimum score 550 paper-based; 80 iBT), IELTS (minimum score 6). Electronic applications accepted. *Faculty research:* Job attitudes, personality and individual differences, organizational entry and exit, knowledge management, competitive dynamics.

University of Florida, Graduate School, Warrington College of Business Administration, Hough Graduate School of Business, Programs in Business Administration, Gainesville, FL 32611. Offers business administration (MA, MS, PhD); competitive strategy (MBA); finance (MBA); global management (MBA); Graham-Buffett security analysis (MBA); human resource management (MBA); information systems and operations management (MBA); international studies (MBA); management (MBA); real estate (MBA); JD/MBA; MBA/MS; MBA/PhD; MBA/Pharm D; MD/MBA. *Accreditation:* AACSB. *Program availability:* Part-time, evening/weekend, online learning. *Degree requirements:* For master's, capstone course. *Entrance requirements:* For master's and doctorate, GMAT (minimum score 465), minimum GPA of 3.0, interview. Additional exam requirements/recommendations for international students: Required—TOEFL (minimum score 550 paper-based; 80 iBT), IELTS (minimum score 6). Electronic applications accepted. *Faculty research:* Accounting, finance, insurance, management, real estate, urban analysis marketing.

University of Georgia, Terry College of Business, Program in Business Administration, Athens, GA 30602. Offers Exec MBA, MBA. *Accreditation:* AACSB. *Degree requirements:* For master's, thesis (MA). *Entrance requirements:* For master's, GMAT (for MBA), GRE General Test (for MA). *Application deadline:* For fall admission, 7/1 priority date for domestic students; for spring admission, 11/15 for domestic students. Application fee: $50. Electronic applications accepted. *Financial support:* Fellowships, research assistantships, teaching assistantships, and unspecified assistantships available. *Unit head:* Dr. Richard L. Daniels, Director, 404-842-4862, Fax: 706-542-5351, E-mail: rdaniels@terry.uga.edu.
Website: http://mba.terry.uga.edu/

University of Guam, Office of Graduate Studies, School of Business and Public Administration, Business Administration Program, Mangilao, GU 96923. Offers PMBA. *Entrance requirements:* For master's, GMAT. Additional exam requirements/recommendations for international students: Required—TOEFL.

University of Guelph, Graduate Studies, College of Management and Economics, Guelph, ON N1G 2W1, Canada. Offers M Sc, MA, MBA, PhD.

University of Hartford, Barney School of Business, Program in Business Administration, West Hartford, CT 06117-1599. Offers MBA, MBA/M Eng. *Accreditation:* AACSB. *Program availability:* Part-time, evening/weekend. *Entrance requirements:* For master's, GMAT, 2 letters of recommendation, resume. Additional exam requirements/recommendations for international students: Required—TOEFL (minimum score 550 paper-based). Electronic applications accepted.

University of Hartford, College of Education, Nursing, and Health Professions, Program in Nursing, West Hartford, CT 06117-1599. Offers community/public health nursing (MSN); nursing education (MSN); nursing management (MSN). *Accreditation:* AACN. *Program availability:* Part-time, evening/weekend. *Degree requirements:* For master's, research project. *Entrance requirements:* For master's, BSN, Connecticut RN license. Additional exam requirements/recommendations for international students: Required—TOEFL (minimum score 550 paper-based). Electronic applications accepted. *Expenses:* Contact institution. *Faculty research:* Child development, women in doctoral study, applying feminist theory in teaching methods, near death experience, grandmothers as primary care providers.

University of Hawaii at Manoa, Graduate Division, Shidler College of Business, Executive MBA Programs, Honolulu, HI 96822. Offers executive business administration (EMBA); Vietnam focused business administration (EMBA). *Accreditation:* AACSB. *Program availability:* Part-time. *Entrance requirements:* For master's, GMAT, minimum GPA of 3.0.

University of Hawaii at Manoa, Graduate Division, Shidler College of Business, Program in Business Administration, Honolulu, HI 96822. Offers Asian business studies (MBA); Chinese business studies (MBA); decision sciences (MBA); entrepreneurship (MBA); finance (MBA); finance and banking (MBA); human resources management (MBA); information management (MBA); information technology (MBA); international business (MBA); Japanese business studies (MBA); marketing (MBA); organizational behavior (MBA); organizational management (MBA); real estate (MBA); student-designed track (MBA). *Accreditation:* AACSB. *Program availability:* Part-time, evening/weekend. *Degree requirements:* For master's, thesis optional. *Entrance requirements:* For master's, GMAT, minimum GPA of 3.0. Additional exam requirements/recommendations for international students: Required—TOEFL (minimum score 600 paper-based; 100 iBT), IELTS (minimum score 7). *Expenses:* Contact institution.

University of Houston, Bauer College of Business, Houston, TX 77204. Offers MBA, MS, MS Accy, PhD. *Accreditation:* AACSB. *Program availability:* Part-time, evening/weekend. *Degree requirements:* For master's, 30 hours completed in residence, minimum cumulative GPA of 3.0 at UH, no more than 11 semester hours of 'C' grades or below in graduate courses taken at UH; for doctorate, comprehensive exam, thesis/dissertation, minimum GPA of 3.25, continuous full time enrollment, dissertation defense within 6 years of entering the program. *Entrance requirements:* For master's, GMAT or GRE (MBA), official transcripts from all higher education institutions attended, resume, letters of recommendation, self appraisal and goal statement (MBA); for doctorate, GMAT or GRE, letter of financial backing, statement of understanding, reference letters, statement of academic and research interests. Additional exam requirements/recommendations for international students: Required—TOEFL (minimum score 603 paper-based; 100 iBT), IELTS (minimum score 6.5), PTE (minimum score 70). Electronic applications accepted. *Faculty research:* Accountancy and taxation, finance, international business, management.

University of Houston–Clear Lake, School of Business, Program in Business Administration, Houston, TX 77058-1002. Offers MBA. *Accreditation:* AACSB. *Program availability:* Part-time, evening/weekend. *Degree requirements:* For master's, thesis optional. *Entrance requirements:* For master's, GMAT. Additional exam requirements/recommendations for international students: Required—TOEFL (minimum score 550 paper-based). Electronic applications accepted.

University of Houston–Downtown, Davies College of Business, MBA Program, Houston, TX 77002. Offers finance (MBA); human resource management (MBA); investment management (MBA); leadership (MBA); sales management and business development (MBA); supply chain management (MBA). *Accreditation:* AACSB. *Program availability:* Part-time, evening/weekend. *Faculty:* 33 full-time (12 women), 1 part-time/adjunct (0 women). *Students:* 7 full-time (3 women), 1,037 part-time (565 women); includes 773 minority (361 Black or African American, non-Hispanic/Latino; 2 American Indian or Alaska Native, non-Hispanic/Latino; 132 Asian, non-Hispanic/Latino; 278 Hispanic/Latino), 32 international. Average age 33. 583 applicants, 86% accepted, 409 enrolled. In 2016, 181 master's awarded. *Entrance requirements:* For master's, GMAT, two letters of recommendation from professional references, personal statement,

resume. Additional exam requirements/recommendations for international students: Required—TOEFL (minimum score 81 iBT). *Application deadline:* For fall admission, 7/15 for domestic and international students. Application fee: $35 ($60 for international students). Electronic applications accepted. *Expenses:* $428 in-state per credit; $786 non-resident per credit. *Financial support:* Federal Work-Study and scholarships/grants available. Financial award application deadline: 4/1; financial award applicants required to submit FAFSA. *Unit head:* Dr. D. Michael Fields, Dean, Davies College of Business, 713-221-8179, Fax: 713-221-8675, E-mail: fieldsd@uhd.edu. *Application contact:* Ceshia Love, Director of Graduate and International Admissions, 713-221-8093, Fax: 713-223-7408, E-mail: gradadmissions@uhd.edu.
Website: http://mba.uhd.edu/

University of Houston–Victoria, School of Business Administration, Victoria, TX 77901-4450. Offers accounting (MBA); economic development and entrepreneurship (MS); finance (GMBA, MBA); general business (MBA); international business (MBA); management (GMBA, MBA); marketing (MBA). *Accreditation:* AACSB. *Program availability:* Part-time, evening/weekend, online learning. *Entrance requirements:* For master's, GMAT. Additional exam requirements/recommendations for international students: Required—TOEFL (minimum score 550 paper-based). Electronic applications accepted. *Faculty research:* Economic development, marketing, finance.

University of Idaho, College of Graduate Studies, College of Business and Economics, Department of Business and Economics, Moscow, ID 83844. Offers general management (MBA). *Faculty:* 8 full-time. *Students:* 25 full-time (8 women). Average age 41. In 2016, 14 master's awarded. *Entrance requirements:* For master's, minimum GPA of 3.0. Additional exam requirements/recommendations for international students: Required—TOEFL. *Application deadline:* For fall admission, 8/1 for domestic students; for spring admission, 12/15 for domestic students. Applications are processed on a rolling basis. Application fee: $60. Electronic applications accepted. *Expenses:* Tuition, state resident: full-time $6460; part-time $414 per credit hour. Tuition, nonresident: full-time $21,268; part-time $1237 per credit hour. *Required fees:* $2070; $60 per credit hour. Full-time tuition and fees vary according to course load and reciprocity agreements. *Financial support:* Applicants required to submit FAFSA. *Unit head:* Dr. Metlen Scott, Department Head, 208-885-6295, E-mail: canthony@uidaho.edu. *Application contact:* Sean Scoggin, Graduate Recruitment Coordinator, 208-885-4001, Fax: 208-885-4406, E-mail: graduateadmissions@uidaho.edu.
Website: http://www.uidaho.edu/cbe

University of Idaho, College of Law, Moscow, ID 83844-2321. Offers business law and entrepreneurship (JD); law (JD); litigation and alternative dispute resolution (JD); Native American law (JD); natural resources and environmental law (JD). *Accreditation:* ABA. *Faculty:* 32 full-time, 11 part-time/adjunct. *Students:* Average age 28. *Entrance requirements:* For doctorate, LSAT, Law School Admission Council Credential Assembly Service (CAS) Report. Additional exam requirements/recommendations for international students: Required—TOEFL. *Application deadline:* For fall admission, 3/15 priority date for domestic students. Applications are processed on a rolling basis. Application fee: $50 ($60 for international students). Electronic applications accepted. *Expenses:* Contact institution. *Financial support:* Career-related internships or fieldwork, Federal Work-Study, and institutionally sponsored loans available. Financial award applicants required to submit FAFSA. *Faculty research:* Transboundary river governance, tribal protection and stewardship, regional water issues, environmental law. *Unit head:* Mark Adams, Dean, 208-885-4977, E-mail: uilaw@uidaho.edu. *Application contact:* Carole Wells, Director of Admissions, 208-885-2300, Fax: 208-885-2252, E-mail: lawadmit@uidaho.edu.
Website: http://www.uidaho.edu/law/

University of Illinois at Chicago, Liautaud Graduate School of Business, Program in Business Administration, Chicago, IL 60607-7128. Offers MBA, PhD, MBA/MA, MBA/MD, MBA/MPH, MBA/MS. *Accreditation:* AACSB. *Program availability:* Part-time. *Entrance requirements:* For master's, GMAT, minimum GPA of 2.75; for doctorate, GMAT. Additional exam requirements/recommendations for international students: Required—TOEFL. Electronic applications accepted. *Expenses:* Contact institution.

University of Illinois at Springfield, Graduate Programs, College of Business and Management, Program in Business Administration, Springfield, IL 62703-5407. Offers MBA. *Accreditation:* AACSB. *Program availability:* Part-time, evening/weekend. *Faculty:* 8 full-time (1 woman), 3 part-time/adjunct (1 woman). *Students:* 58 full-time (23 women), 44 part-time (22 women); includes 13 minority (4 Black or African American, non-Hispanic/Latino; 6 Asian, non-Hispanic/Latino; 2 Hispanic/Latino; 1 Two or more races, non-Hispanic/Latino), 12 international. Average age 32. 105 applicants, 43% accepted, 29 enrolled. In 2016, 50 master's awarded. *Degree requirements:* For master's, closure course. *Entrance requirements:* For master's, GMAT or substantial supervisory experience and managerial responsibility, minimum cumulative GPA of 2.0 (2.5 preferred); 3 letters of reference; resume; single-spaced essay, no more than two pages, discussing career goals and/or professional aspirations. Additional exam requirements/recommendations for international students: Required—TOEFL (minimum score 550 paper-based; 61 iBT). *Application deadline:* Applications are processed on a rolling basis. Application fee: $60 ($75 for international students). Electronic applications accepted. *Expenses:* $609.00 per hour off-campus in-state; $955.00 per hour off-campus out-of-state. *Financial support:* In 2016–17, fellowships with full tuition reimbursements (averaging $9,900 per year), research assistantships with full tuition reimbursements (averaging $9,991 per year), teaching assistantships with full tuition reimbursements (averaging $10,059 per year) were awarded; career-related internships or fieldwork, Federal Work-Study, scholarships/grants, health care benefits, and unspecified assistantships also available. Support available to part-time students. Financial award application deadline: 11/15; financial award applicants required to submit FAFSA. *Unit head:* Dr. Jorge Villegas, Program Administrator, 217-206-6780, Fax: 217-206-7541, E-mail: jvill2@uis.edu. *Application contact:* Dr. Cecelia Cornell, Associate Vice Chancellor for Graduate Education, 217-206-7230, E-mail: ccorn1@uis.edu.
Website: http://www.uis.edu/mba/

University of Illinois at Urbana–Champaign, Graduate College, College of Business, Department of Business Administration, Champaign, IL 61820. Offers business administration (MS, PhD); technology management (MS). *Accreditation:* AACSB. *Expenses:* Contact institution.

University of Illinois at Urbana–Champaign, Graduate College, College of Business, Program in Business Administration, Champaign, IL 61820. Offers MBA, Ed M/MBA, JD/MBA, M Arch/MBA, MCS/MBA, MHRIR/MBA, MS/MBA. *Accreditation:* AACSB.

University of Indianapolis, Graduate Programs, School of Business, Indianapolis, IN 46227-3697. Offers EMBA, MBA, Graduate Certificate. *Program availability:* Part-time, evening/weekend. *Entrance requirements:* For master's, GMAT, interview, minimum GPA of 2.8, 2 letters of recommendation, resume. Additional exam requirements/recommendations for international students: Required—TOEFL (minimum score 550 paper-based).

The University of Iowa, Henry B. Tippie College of Business, Department of Finance, Iowa City, IA 52242-1316. Offers PhD. *Faculty:* 22 full-time (4 women), 10 part-time/adjunct (1 woman). *Students:* 13 full-time (2 women); includes 1 minority (Asian, non-Hispanic/Latino), 6 international. Average age 31. 73 applicants, 3% accepted, 2 enrolled. In 2016, 1 doctorate awarded. *Degree requirements:* For doctorate, comprehensive exam, thesis/dissertation. *Entrance requirements:* For doctorate, GMAT or GRE. Additional exam requirements/recommendations for international students: Required—TOEFL (minimum score 100 iBT) or IELTS (minimum score 7.0). *Application deadline:* For fall admission, 1/15 priority date for domestic and international students. Application fee: $60 ($100 for international students). Electronic applications accepted. *Financial support:* In 2016–17, 13 students received support, including 13 fellowships (averaging $6,000 per year), 13 teaching assistantships with full tuition reimbursements available (averaging $18,809 per year); health care benefits and unspecified assistantships also available. Financial award application deadline: 1/15. *Faculty research:* International finance, real estate finance, theoretical and empirical corporate finance, theoretical and empirical asset pricing, bond pricing and derivatives. *Unit head:* Prof. Thomas Rietz, Department Executive Officer, 319-335-0929, Fax: 319-335-3690, E-mail: thomas-rietz@uiowa.edu. *Application contact:* Renea L. Jay, Associate Director, Non-MBA Graduate Programs, 319-335-0830, Fax: 319-335-0860, E-mail: renea-jay@uiowa.edu.
Website: https://tippie.uiowa.edu/finance

The University of Iowa, Henry B. Tippie College of Business, Department of Management and Organizations, Iowa City, IA 52242-1316. Offers PhD. *Accreditation:* AACSB. *Faculty:* 33 full-time (11 women), 19 part-time/adjunct (5 women). *Students:* 13 full-time (6 women); includes 1 minority (Asian, non-Hispanic/Latino), 5 international. Average age 30. 45 applicants, 9% accepted, 2 enrolled. In 2016, 6 doctorates awarded. *Degree requirements:* For doctorate, comprehensive exam, thesis/dissertation. *Entrance requirements:* For doctorate, GMAT or GRE. Additional exam requirements/recommendations for international students: Required—TOEFL (minimum score 100 iBT). *Application deadline:* For fall admission, 1/15 priority date for domestic and international students. Application fee: $60 ($100 for international students). Electronic applications accepted. *Financial support:* In 2016–17, 13 students received support, including 13 fellowships (averaging $3,000 per year), 3 research assistantships with full tuition reimbursements available (averaging $18,809 per year), 10 teaching assistantships with full tuition reimbursements available (averaging $18,809 per year); health care benefits and unspecified assistantships also available. Financial award application deadline: 1/15; financial award applicants required to submit FAFSA. *Faculty research:* Decision-making, human resources, personal selection, organizational behavior, training. *Unit head:* Prof. Amy Kristof-Brown, Department Executive Officer, 319-335-0927, Fax: 319-335-1956, E-mail: amy-kristofbrown@uiowa.edu. *Application contact:* Renea L. Jay, Associate Director, Non-MBA Graduate Programs, 319-335-0830, Fax: 319-335-0860, E-mail: renea-jay@uiowa.edu.
Website: https://tippie.uiowa.edu/management-and-organizations

The University of Iowa, Henry B. Tippie College of Business, Department of Management Sciences, Iowa City, IA 52242-1316. Offers PhD. *Accreditation:* AACSB. *Faculty:* 24 full-time (4 women), 4 part-time/adjunct (0 women). *Students:* 11 full-time (3 women), 9 international. Average age 29. 41 applicants, 20% accepted, 2 enrolled. In 2016, 3 doctorates awarded. *Degree requirements:* For doctorate, comprehensive exam, thesis/dissertation. *Entrance requirements:* For doctorate, GRE General Test or GMAT. Additional exam requirements/recommendations for international students: Required—TOEFL (minimum score 100 iBT) or IELTS (minimum score 7.0). *Application deadline:* For fall admission, 1/15 priority date for domestic and international students. Application fee: $60 ($100 for international students). Electronic applications accepted. *Financial support:* In 2016–17, 11 students received support, including 11 fellowships (averaging $3,000 per year), 1 research assistantship with full tuition reimbursement available (averaging $18,809 per year), 10 teaching assistantships with full tuition reimbursements available (averaging $18,809 per year); health care benefits and unspecified assistantships also available. Financial award application deadline: 1/15. *Faculty research:* Optimization, supply chain management, data mining, logistics, database management. *Unit head:* Prof. Nick Street, Department Executive Officer, 319-335-0858, Fax: 319-335-1956, E-mail: nick-street@uiowa.edu. *Application contact:* Renea L. Jay, Associate Director, Non-MBA Graduate Programs, 319-335-0830, Fax: 319-335-0860, E-mail: renea-jay@uiowa.edu.
Website: https://tippie.uiowa.edu/management-sciences

The University of Iowa, Henry B. Tippie College of Business, MBA Program, Iowa City, IA 52242. Offers EMBA, MBA, JD/MBA, MBA/MA, MBA/MD, MBA/MHA, MBA/MSN. *Accreditation:* AACSB. *Program availability:* Part-time, evening/weekend. *Faculty:* 133 full-time (34 women), 70 part-time/adjunct (18 women). *Students:* 118 full-time (31 women), 837 part-time (280 women); includes 109 minority (21 Black or African American, non-Hispanic/Latino; 1 American Indian or Alaska Native, non-Hispanic/Latino; 57 Asian, non-Hispanic/Latino; 19 Hispanic/Latino; 1 Native Hawaiian or other Pacific Islander, non-Hispanic/Latino; 10 Two or more races, non-Hispanic/Latino), 130 international. Average age 27. 656 applicants, 63% accepted, 313 enrolled. In 2016, 382 master's awarded. *Entrance requirements:* For master's, GMAT, GRE (waived for EMBA), quality work experience and leadership as shown through resume, references, and essays. Additional exam requirements/recommendations for international students: Required—TOEFL (minimum score 600 paper-based; 100 iBT). *Application deadline:* For fall admission, 7/30 for domestic students, 3/1 for international students. Applications are processed on a rolling basis. Application fee: $60 ($100 for international students). Electronic applications accepted. *Expenses:* Contact institution. *Financial support:* Fellowships, research assistantships, career-related internships or fieldwork, scholarships/grants, health care benefits, and unspecified assistantships available. Financial award application deadline: 7/15; financial award applicants required to submit FAFSA. *Faculty research:* Capital markets, econometrics, optimization, investments and empirical corporate finance, Iowa electronic markets. *Unit head:* Prof. David W. Frasier, Associate Dean, Tippie MBA Programs, 319-335-1030, Fax: 319-335-3604, E-mail: david-frasier@uiowa.edu. *Application contact:* David Deyak, Assistant Dean, Full-time MBA Program, 319-335-0864, Fax: 319-335-3604, E-mail: david-deyak@uiowa.edu.
Website: https://tippie.uiowa.edu/future-graduate-students/mba-programs

The University of Kansas, Graduate Studies, School of Business, Program in Business, Lawrence, KS 66045. Offers accounting (PhD); business and organizational leadership (MS); decision sciences and supply chain management (PhD); finance (PhD); human resources management (PhD); marketing (PhD); organizational behavior (PhD); strategic management (PhD); supply chain management and logistics (MS). *Accreditation:* AACSB. *Program availability:* Part-time. *Students:* 76 full-time (11 women), 170 part-time (83 women); includes 41 minority (15 Black or African American, non-Hispanic/Latino; 3 American Indian or Alaska Native, non-Hispanic/Latino; 6 Asian, non-Hispanic/Latino; 5 Hispanic/Latino; 12 Two or more races, non-Hispanic/Latino), 25 international. Average age 32. 294 applicants, 69% accepted, 152 enrolled. In 2016, 36 master's, 9 doctorates awarded. *Entrance requirements:* For master's, GMAT, official transcript, three letters of recommendation, resume, statement of purpose; for doctorate, GMAT or GRE, official transcript, three letters of recommendation, resume, statement of purpose. Additional exam requirements/recommendations for international students: Required—TOEFL (minimum score 600 paper-based; 100 iBT). *Application deadline:* For fall admission, 1/10 for domestic and international students. Application fee: $65 ($85 for international students). Electronic applications accepted. *Financial support:* Fellowships, research assistantships, teaching assistantships, scholarships/grants,

health care benefits, tuition waivers (full), and unspecified assistantships available. Financial award application deadline: 1/10. *Faculty research:* Strategic human resource management, business ethics, organizational theory/behavior, corporate strategy, international business, supply chain management, Bayesian networks, game theory, decision analysis and time/series analysis, pricing, consumer effects, advertising and emotion. *Unit head:* Charly Edmonds, Director, 785-864-3841, E-mail: bschoolphd@ku.edu. *Application contact:* Graduate Admission Contact, 785-864-7500, E-mail: bschoolphd@ku.edu.
Website: http://www.business.ku.edu/

The University of Kansas, Graduate Studies, School of Business, Program in Business Administration and Management, Lawrence, KS 66045. Offers finance (MBA); human resources management (MBA); information systems (MBA); international business (MBA); management (MBA); marketing (MBA); strategic management (MBA); JD/MBA; MBA/MA; MBA/MM; MBA/MS; MBA/Pharm D. *Accreditation:* AACSB. *Program availability:* Part-time, online learning. *Students:* 67 full-time (13 women), 213 part-time (70 women); includes 44 minority (8 Black or African American, non-Hispanic/Latino; 4 American Indian or Alaska Native, non-Hispanic/Latino; 7 Asian, non-Hispanic/Latino; 12 Hispanic/Latino; 13 Two or more races, non-Hispanic/Latino), 13 international. Average age 32. 218 applicants, 69% accepted, 123 enrolled. In 2016, 91 degrees awarded. *Entrance requirements:* For master's, GMAT, official transcript; two recommendation forms; current resume; three essays; acknowledge the University Honor Code. Additional exam requirements/recommendations for international students: Required—TOEFL or IELTS. *Application deadline:* For fall admission, 8/4 for domestic students, 5/1 for international students. Application fee: $65 ($85 for international students). Electronic applications accepted. *Financial support:* Research assistantships, career-related internships or fieldwork, Federal Work-Study, institutionally sponsored loans, scholarships/grants, and unspecified assistantships available. Financial award application deadline: 1/15; financial award applicants required to submit FAFSA. *Unit head:* Dr. Duane Myer, Director of MBA Programs, 785-864-4276, E-mail: dmyer@ku.edu. *Application contact:* Marysa Sacerdote, Master's Admissions Coordinator, 785-864-7556, E-mail: marysa@ku.edu.
Website: http://www.business.ku.edu/

University of Kentucky, Graduate School, Gatton College of Business and Economics, Program in Business Administration, Lexington, KY 40506-0032. Offers MBA, PhD. *Accreditation:* AACSB. *Degree requirements:* For master's, comprehensive exam; for doctorate, comprehensive exam, thesis/dissertation. *Entrance requirements:* For master's, GMAT, minimum undergraduate GPA of 2.75; for doctorate, GMAT, minimum undergraduate GPA of 3.0. Additional exam requirements/recommendations for international students: Required—TOEFL (minimum score 550 paper-based). Electronic applications accepted. *Faculty research:* Expert systems in manufacturing, knowledge acquisition and management, financial institutions, market in service organizations, strategic planning.

University of La Verne, College of Business and Public Management, Graduate Programs in Business Administration, La Verne, CA 91750-4443. Offers accounting (MBA, MBA-EP); finance (MBA, MBA-EP); health services management (MBA); information technology (MBA, MBA-EP); international business (MBA, MBA-EP); management and leadership (MBA, MBA-EP); marketing (MBA, MBA-EP); supply chain management (MBA, MBA-EP). *Program availability:* Part-time, evening/weekend. *Students:* 385 full-time (177 women), 89 part-time (46 women); includes 92 minority (4 Black or African American, non-Hispanic/Latino; 1 American Indian or Alaska Native, non-Hispanic/Latino; 14 Asian, non-Hispanic/Latino; 71 Hispanic/Latino; 1 Native Hawaiian or other Pacific Islander, non-Hispanic/Latino; 1 Two or more races, non-Hispanic/Latino), 319 international. Average age 28. *Entrance requirements:* For master's, GMAT, MAT, or GRE, minimum undergraduate GPA of 3.0, 2 letters of recommendation, resume, statement of purpose. Additional exam requirements/recommendations for international students: Required—TOEFL (minimum score 550 paper-based; 85 iBT). *Application deadline:* Applications are processed on a rolling basis. Application fee: $50. *Expenses: Tuition:* Part-time $795 per credit hour. Tuition and fees vary according to campus/location and program. *Financial support:* Institutionally sponsored loans and scholarships/grants available. Financial award application deadline: 3/2; financial award applicants required to submit FAFSA. *Unit head:* Dr. Abe Helou, Chairperson, 909-448-4455, Fax: 909-392-2704, E-mail: ihelou@laverne.edu. *Application contact:* Rina Lazarian-Chehab, Senior Associate Director of Graduate Admissions, 909-448-4317, Fax: 909-971-2295, E-mail: rlazarian@laverne.edu.
Website: https://laverne.edu/business-and-public-administration/mba-2/

University of La Verne, College of Business and Public Management, Program in Health Administration, La Verne, CA 91750-4443. Offers financial management (MHA); management and leadership (MHA); marketing and business development (MHA). *Program availability:* Part-time. *Students:* 45 full-time (33 women), 32 part-time (22 women); includes 31 minority (5 Black or African American, non-Hispanic/Latino; 1 American Indian or Alaska Native, non-Hispanic/Latino; 7 Asian, non-Hispanic/Latino; 18 Hispanic/Latino), 11 international. Average age 32. *Entrance requirements:* For master's, bachelor's degree, experience in health services industry (preferred). Additional exam requirements/recommendations for international students: Required—TOEFL (minimum score 550 paper-based). *Application deadline:* Applications are processed on a rolling basis. Application fee: $50. *Expenses:* Contact institution. *Financial support:* Federal Work-Study, institutionally sponsored loans, and scholarships/grants available. Financial award application deadline: 3/2; financial award applicants required to submit FAFSA. *Unit head:* Dr. Kathy Duncan, Program Chairperson, 909-448-4415, E-mail: kduncan2@laverne.edu. *Application contact:* Barbara Cox, Program and Admissions Specialist, 909-448-4004, Fax: 909-971-2295, E-mail: bcox@laverne.edu.
Website: http://laverne.edu/business-and-public-administration/mha-2/

University of La Verne, College of Business and Public Management, Program in Leadership and Management, La Verne, CA 91750-4443. Offers human resource management (Certificate); leadership and management (MS), including human resource management, nonprofit management, organizational development; nonprofit management (Certificate); organizational leadership (Certificate). *Program availability:* Part-time. *Students:* 47 full-time (32 women), 44 part-time (25 women); includes 42 minority (2 Black or African American, non-Hispanic/Latino; 3 Asian, non-Hispanic/Latino; 37 Hispanic/Latino), 14 international. Average age 32. *Degree requirements:* For master's, thesis or research project. *Entrance requirements:* For master's, bachelor's degree, minimum undergraduate GPA of 2.75, 2 letters of recommendation, interview, resume. Additional exam requirements/recommendations for international students: Required—TOEFL (minimum score 550 paper-based). *Application deadline:* Applications are processed on a rolling basis. Application fee: $50. *Expenses: Tuition:* Part-time $795 per credit hour. Tuition and fees vary according to campus/location and program. *Financial support:* Federal Work-Study, institutionally sponsored loans, and scholarships/grants available. Financial award application deadline: 3/2; financial award applicants required to submit FAFSA. *Unit head:* Dr. Kathy Duncan, Program Director, 909-448-4415, E-mail: kduncan2@laverne.edu. *Application contact:* Barbara Cox, Associate Director of Graduate Admissions, 909-448-4004, E-mail: bcox@laverne.edu.
Website: http://laverne.edu/business-and-public-administration/

University of La Verne, Regional and Online Campuses, Graduate Programs, Central Coast/Vandenberg Air Force Base Campuses, La Verne, CA 91750-4443. Offers business administration for experienced professionals (MBA), including health services management, information technology, education (special emphasis) (M Ed); educational counseling (MS); educational leadership (M Ed); multiple subject (elementary) (Credential); preliminary administrative services (Credential); pupil personnel services (Credential); single subject (secondary) (Credential). *Program availability:* Part-time. *Expenses:* Contact institution.

University of La Verne, Regional and Online Campuses, Graduate Programs, High Desert Campus, Victorville, CA 92392. Offers business administration for experienced professionals (MBA); educational counseling (MS); educational leadership (M Ed); multiple subject (elementary) (Credential); preliminary administrative services (Credential); pupil personnel services (Credential); single subject (secondary) (Credential). *Expenses:* Contact institution.

University of La Verne, Regional and Online Campuses, Graduate Programs, Inland Empire Campus, Ontario, CA 91730. Offers business administration (MBA, MBA-EP), including accounting (MBA), finance (MBA), health services management (MBA-EP), information technology (MBA-EP), international business (MBA), managed care (MBA), management and leadership (MBA-EP), marketing (MBA-EP), supply chain management (MBA); leadership and management (MS), including human resource management, nonprofit management, organizational development. *Program availability:* Part-time, evening/weekend. *Expenses:* Contact institution.

University of La Verne, Regional and Online Campuses, Graduate Programs, Kern County Campus, Bakersfield, CA 93301. Offers business administration for experienced professionals (MBA-EP); education (special emphasis) (M Ed); educational counseling (MS); educational leadership (M Ed); health administration (MHA); leadership and management (MS); mild/moderate education specialist (Credential); multiple subject (elementary) (Credential); organizational leadership (Ed D); preliminary administrative services (Credential); single subject (secondary) (Credential); special education studies (MS). *Program availability:* Part-time, evening/weekend. *Expenses:* Contact institution.

University of La Verne, Regional and Online Campuses, Graduate Programs, Orange County Campus, Irvine, CA 92840. Offers business administration for experienced professionals (MBA); educational counseling (MS); educational leadership (M Ed); health administration (MHA); leadership and management (MS); preliminary administrative services (Credential); pupil personnel services (Credential). *Program availability:* Part-time. *Expenses:* Contact institution.

University of La Verne, Regional and Online Campuses, Graduate Programs, San Fernando Valley Campus, Burbank, CA 91505. Offers business administration for experienced professionals (MBA-EP); educational counseling (MS); educational leadership (M Ed); leadership and management (MS); preliminary administrative services (Credential); pupil personnel services (Credential). *Program availability:* Part-time, evening/weekend. *Expenses:* Contact institution.

University of La Verne, Regional and Online Campuses, Graduate Programs, Ventura County/Point Mugu Naval Air Station Campuses, Oxnard, CA 93036. Offers business administration for experienced professionals (MS); educational counseling (MS); educational leadership (M Ed); leadership and management (MS); multiple subject (elementary) (Credential); pupil personnel services (Credential); single subject (secondary) (Credential). *Program availability:* Part-time, evening/weekend. *Expenses:* Contact institution.

University of La Verne, Regional and Online Campuses, Graduate Program, ULV Online, La Verne, CA 91750-4443. Offers business administration for experienced professionals (MBA). *Program availability:* Part-time, evening/weekend, online learning. *Entrance requirements:* For master's, GMAT, MAT, or GRE, minimum undergraduate GPA of 3.0, 2 letters of recommendation, resume, statement of purpose. *Expenses: Tuition:* Part-time $795 per credit hour. Tuition and fees vary according to campus/location and program.

University of Lethbridge, School of Graduate Studies, Lethbridge, AB T1K 3M4, Canada. Offers addictions counseling (M Sc); agricultural biotechnology (M Sc); agricultural studies (M Sc, MA); anthropology (MA); archaeology (M Sc, MA); art (MA, MFA); biochemistry (M Sc); biological sciences (M Sc); biomolecular science (PhD); biosystems and biodiversity (PhD); Canadian studies (MA); chemistry (M Sc); computer science (M Sc); computer science and geographical information science (M Sc); counseling (MC); counseling psychology (M Ed); dramatic arts (MA); earth, space, and physical science (PhD); economics (MA); education (MA, PhD); educational leadership (M Ed); English (MA); environmental science (M Sc); evolution and behavior (PhD); exercise science (M Sc); French (MA); French/German (MA); French/Spanish (MA); general education (M Ed); geography (M Sc, MA); German (MA); health sciences (M Sc); individualized multidisciplinary (M Sc, MA); kinesiology (M Sc, MA); management (M Sc), including accounting, finance, human resource management and labor relations, information systems, international management, marketing, policy and strategy; mathematics (M Sc); music (M Mus, MA); Native American studies (MA); neuroscience (M Sc, PhD); new media (MA, MFA); nursing (M Sc, MN); philosophy (MA); physics (M Sc); political science (MA); psychology (M Sc, MA); religious studies (MA); sociology (MA); theatre and dramatic arts (MFA); theoretical and computational science (PhD); urban and regional studies (MA); women and gender studies (MA). *Program availability:* Part-time, evening/weekend. *Degree requirements:* For master's, thesis (for some programs); for doctorate, comprehensive exam, thesis/dissertation. *Entrance requirements:* For master's, GMAT (for M Sc in management), bachelor's degree in related field, minimum GPA of 3.0 during previous 20 graded semester courses, 2 years' teaching or related experience (M Ed); for doctorate, master's degree, minimum graduate GPA of 3.5. Additional exam requirements/recommendations for international students: Required—TOEFL (minimum score 580 paper-based; 93 iBT). Electronic applications accepted. *Faculty research:* Movement and brain plasticity, gibberellin physiology, photosynthesis, carbon cycling, molecular properties of main-group ring components.

University of Louisiana at Lafayette, BI Moody III College of Business Administration MBA Program, Lafayette, LA 70504. Offers MBA. *Accreditation:* AACSB. *Program availability:* Part-time, evening/weekend. *Entrance requirements:* For master's, GRE General Test. Additional exam requirements/recommendations for international students: Required—TOEFL (minimum score 550 paper-based).

University of Louisiana at Monroe, Graduate School, College of Business and Social Sciences, MBA Program, Monroe, LA 71209-0001. Offers MBA. Program also offered Shue Yan University in Hong Kong. *Program availability:* Evening/weekend. *Faculty:* 9 full-time (4 women). *Students:* 21 full-time (6 women), 10 part-time (4 women); includes 3 minority (2 Black or African American, non-Hispanic/Latino; 1 Two or more races, non-Hispanic/Latino), 16 international. Average age 27. 214 applicants, 32% accepted, 13 enrolled. In 2016, 22 master's awarded. *Expenses:* Tuition, state resident: full-time $6489. Tuition, nonresident: full-time $18,589. *Required fees:* $8984. Tuition and fees vary according to course level, course load, degree level and program. *Financial*

support: Teaching assistantships and unspecified assistantships available. *Unit head:* Dr. Ronald Berry, Dean, 318-342-1103, E-mail: rberry@ulm.edu.
Website: http://www.ulm.edu/cbss/mba/

University of Louisville, Graduate School, College of Business, MBA Programs, Louisville, KY 40292-0001. Offers entrepreneurship (MBA); global business (MBA); health sector management (MBA). *Accreditation:* AACSB. *Program availability:* Part-time, evening/weekend. *Students:* 251 full-time (83 women), 9 part-time (0 women); includes 35 minority (10 Black or African American, non-Hispanic/Latino; 1 American Indian or Alaska Native, non-Hispanic/Latino; 11 Asian, non-Hispanic/Latino; 8 Hispanic/Latino; 5 Two or more races, non-Hispanic/Latino), 18 international. Average age 31. 304 applicants, 61% accepted, 159 enrolled. In 2016, 52 master's awarded. *Degree requirements:* For master's, international learning experience. *Entrance requirements:* For master's, GMAT, 2 letters of reference, personal interview, resume, personal statement, college transcript(s). Additional exam requirements/recommendations for international students: Required—TOEFL (minimum score 83 iBT). *Application deadline:* For fall admission, 7/1 for domestic students; for spring admission, 12/1 for domestic students. Applications are processed on a rolling basis. Application fee: $60. *Expenses:* Tuition, state resident: full-time $12,246; part-time $681 per credit hour. Tuition, nonresident: full-time $25,486; part-time $1417 per credit hour. *Required fees:* $196. Tuition and fees vary according to program and reciprocity agreements. *Financial support:* Fellowships with full tuition reimbursements, research assistantships with full tuition reimbursements, health care benefits, and unspecified assistantships available. Financial award application deadline: 3/31; financial award applicants required to submit FAFSA. *Faculty research:* Entrepreneurship, venture capital, retailing/franchising, corporate governance and leadership, supply chain management. *Total annual research expenditures:* $859,000. *Unit head:* Dr. Todd Mooradian, Dean, 502-852-6443, Fax: 502-852-7557, E-mail: todd.mooradian@louisville.edu. *Application contact:* Susan E. Hildebrand, Program Director, 502-852-7257, Fax: 502-852-4901, E-mail: s.hildebrand@louisville.edu.
Website: http://business.louisville.edu/mba

University of Maine, Graduate School, The Maine Business School, Orono, ME 04469. Offers MBA, CGS. *Accreditation:* AACSB. *Program availability:* Part-time, evening/weekend, online learning. *Faculty:* 24 full-time (6 women), 1 (woman) part-time/adjunct. *Students:* 42 full-time (15 women), 38 part-time (20 women); includes 8 minority (1 Black or African American, non-Hispanic/Latino; 3 American Indian or Alaska Native, non-Hispanic/Latino; 2 Asian, non-Hispanic/Latino; 2 Two or more races, non-Hispanic/Latino), 6 international. Average age 29. 72 applicants, 90% accepted, 45 enrolled. In 2016, 22 master's, 4 other advanced degrees awarded. *Entrance requirements:* For master's, GMAT. Additional exam requirements/recommendations for international students: Required—TOEFL (minimum score 550 paper-based; 80 iBT), IELTS (minimum score 6.5). *Application deadline:* For fall admission, 2/1 priority date for domestic students, 5/1 priority date for international students; for spring admission, 11/1 priority date for domestic students, 9/1 priority date for international students; for summer admission, 4/1 priority date for domestic students, 2/1 priority date for international students. Applications are processed on a rolling basis. Application fee: $65. Electronic applications accepted. *Expenses:* Contact institution. *Financial support:* In 2016–17, 11 students received support, including 3 teaching assistantships (averaging $14,600 per year); career-related internships or fieldwork, Federal Work-Study, institutionally sponsored loans, scholarships/grants, tuition waivers (full and partial), and unspecified assistantships also available. Financial award application deadline: 3/1. *Faculty research:* Audit quality and its impact on financial markets, socially responsible investing, human capital acquisition, management in multinational corporations, corporate social responsibility. *Unit head:* Richard Borgman, Manager of MBA Programs, Executive Education and Internships, 207-581-1870, Fax: 207-581-1930, E-mail: borgman@maine.edu. *Application contact:* Scott G. Delcourt, Assistant Vice President for Graduate Studies and Senior Associate Dean, 207-581-3291, Fax: 207-581-3232, E-mail: graduate@maine.edu.
Website: http://www.umaine.edu/business/

University of Management and Technology, Program in Business Administration, Arlington, VA 22209-1609. Offers general management (MBA, DBA); project management (MBA). *Program availability:* Part-time, evening/weekend, online learning. *Degree requirements:* For master's, comprehensive exam; for doctorate, thesis/dissertation. *Entrance requirements:* For master's, 3 recommendations, resume. Additional exam requirements/recommendations for international students: Required—TOEFL (minimum score 530 paper-based; 71 iBT). Electronic applications accepted.

University of Management and Technology, Program in Management, Arlington, VA 22209-1609. Offers acquisition management (MS, AC); criminal justice administration (MS); general management (MS); project management (MS, AC). *Program availability:* Part-time, evening/weekend, online learning. *Entrance requirements:* For master's, 3 recommendations, resume. Additional exam requirements/recommendations for international students: Required—TOEFL (minimum score 530 paper-based; 71 iBT). Electronic applications accepted.

The University of Manchester, Alliance Manchester Business School, M15 6PB, United Kingdom. Offers accounting and finance (M Sc); business (M Ent); business analysis and strategic management (M Sc); business analytics: operational research and risk analysis (M Sc); business psychology (M Sc); corporate communications and reputation management (M Sc); finance (M Sc); finance and business economics (M Sc); human resource management and industrial relations (M Sc); innovation management and entrepreneurship (M Sc); international business and management (M Sc); international human resource management and comparative industrial relations (M Sc); management (M Sc); marketing (M Sc); operations, project and supply chain management (M Sc); organizational psychology (M Sc); quantitative finance (M Sc). *Entrance requirements:* For master's, UK 2:1 honours degree or overseas equivalent. Additional exam requirements/recommendations for international students: Required—TOEFL (minimum score 100 iBT), IELTS (minimum score 7), PTE. Electronic applications accepted. *Faculty research:* Accounting and finance, management sciences and marketing, people management and organization, innovation management and policy, decision sciences.

University of Manitoba, Faculty of Graduate Studies, Asper School of Business, Winnipeg, MB R3T 2N2, Canada. Offers M Sc, MBA, PhD. *Accreditation:* AACSB.

University of Mary, Gary Tharaldson School of Business, Bismarck, ND 58504-9652. Offers business administration (MBA); energy management (MBA, MS); executive (MBA, MS); health care (MBA, MS); human resource management (MBA); project management (MBA, MPM); virtuous leadership (MBA, MPM, MS). *Program availability:* Part-time, evening/weekend. *Entrance requirements:* For master's, minimum GPA of 2.5. Additional exam requirements/recommendations for international students: Required—TOEFL (minimum score 550 paper-based; 80 iBT). Electronic applications accepted.

University of Mary Hardin-Baylor, Graduate Studies in Business Administration, Belton, TX 76513. Offers accounting (MBA); information systems management (MBA); international business (MBA); management (MBA). *Program availability:* Part-time, evening/weekend. *Faculty:* 11 full-time (5 women), 6 part-time/adjunct (2 women). *Students:* 21 full-time (12 women), 44 part-time (14 women); includes 23 minority (12 Black or African American, non-Hispanic/Latino; 1 Asian, non-Hispanic/Latino; 10 Hispanic/Latino), 11 international. Average age 29. 96 applicants, 70% accepted, 21 enrolled. In 2016, 22 master's awarded. *Degree requirements:* For master's, comprehensive exam. *Entrance requirements:* For master's, minimum GPA of 3.0, interview. Additional exam requirements/recommendations for international students: Required—TOEFL (minimum score 60 iBT), IELTS (minimum score 4.5). *Application deadline:* For fall admission, 6/1 for domestic students, 4/30 priority date for international students; for spring admission, 11/1 for domestic students, 9/30 priority date for international students. Applications are processed on a rolling basis. Application fee: $35 ($135 for international students). Electronic applications accepted. *Expenses:* *Tuition:* Full-time $14,940; part-time $830 per credit hour. *Required fees:* $1350; $75 per credit hour. $50 per term. Tuition and fees vary according to course load and degree level. *Financial support:* In 2016–17, 33 students received support. Federal Work-Study, unspecified assistantships, and scholarships for some active duty military personnel available. Financial award applicants required to submit FAFSA. *Faculty research:* Experiential learning, case studies in systems analysis and design, forecasting methodologies, short-selling in the stock market, open educational resources. *Total annual research expenditures:* $17,500. *Unit head:* Dr. Kirk Fischer, Assistant Professor/Director, Graduate Programs in McLane College of Business, 254-295-4655, E-mail: kfischer@umhb.edu. *Application contact:* Sharon Aguilera, Assistant Director, Graduate Admissions, 254-295-4835, Fax: 254-295-5038, E-mail: saguilera@umhb.edu.
Website: http://www.graduate.umhb.edu/mba

University of Maryland, College Park, Academic Affairs, Joint Program in Business and Management/Public Policy, College Park, MD 20742. Offers MBA/MPM. *Accreditation:* AACSB. Electronic applications accepted.

University of Maryland, College Park, Academic Affairs, Robert H. Smith School of Business, Combined MSW/MBA Program, College Park, MD 20742. Offers MSW/MBA. *Accreditation:* AACSB. *Entrance requirements:* Additional exam requirements/recommendations for international students: Required—TOEFL.

University of Maryland, College Park, Academic Affairs, Robert H. Smith School of Business, Executive MBA Program, College Park, MD 20742. Offers EMBA. *Accreditation:* AACSB. *Entrance requirements:* For master's, minimum GPA of 3.0, 7-12 years of professional experience. Additional exam requirements/recommendations for international students: Required—TOEFL.

University of Maryland, College Park, Academic Affairs, Robert H. Smith School of Business, Joint Program in Business and Management, College Park, MD 20742. Offers MBA/MS. *Accreditation:* AACSB. *Entrance requirements:* Additional exam requirements/recommendations for international students: Required—TOEFL. Electronic applications accepted.

University of Maryland, College Park, Academic Affairs, Robert H. Smith School of Business, Program in Business Administration, College Park, MD 20742. Offers MBA. *Accreditation:* AACSB. *Program availability:* Part-time, evening/weekend, online learning. *Entrance requirements:* For master's, GMAT, minimum GPA of 3.0, resume, 3 letters of recommendation. Additional exam requirements/recommendations for international students: Required—TOEFL. Electronic applications accepted. *Faculty research:* Accounting, entrepreneurship, finance management and organization, management server and statistical information systems.

University of Maryland, College Park, Academic Affairs, Robert H. Smith School of Business, Program in Business and Management, College Park, MD 20742. Offers MS, PhD. *Accreditation:* AACSB. *Program availability:* Part-time. *Degree requirements:* For master's, thesis optional; for doctorate, comprehensive exam, thesis/dissertation. *Entrance requirements:* For master's, GMAT, minimum GPA of 3.0, resume, 2 letters of recommendation; for doctorate, GMAT or GRE General Test, minimum GPA of 3.0, resume, 2 letters of recommendation. Additional exam requirements/recommendations for international students: Required—TOEFL. Electronic applications accepted.

University of Maryland, College Park, Academic Affairs, Robert H. Smith School of Business, Program in Business Management/Law, College Park, MD 20742. Offers JD/MBA. *Accreditation:* AACSB. *Entrance requirements:* Additional exam requirements/recommendations for international students: Required—TOEFL.

University of Maryland University College, The Graduate School, Doctoral Program in Management, Adelphi, MD 20783. Offers DM. *Accreditation:* AACSB. *Program availability:* Part-time. *Students:* 141 part-time (79 women); includes 66 minority (47 Black or African American, non-Hispanic/Latino; 4 Asian, non-Hispanic/Latino; 7 Hispanic/Latino; 8 Two or more races, non-Hispanic/Latino), 4 international. Average age 43. 62 applicants, 100% accepted, 4 enrolled. In 2016, 49 doctorates awarded. *Degree requirements:* For doctorate, comprehensive exam, thesis/dissertation. *Application deadline:* Applications are processed on a rolling basis. Application fee: $100. Electronic applications accepted. *Expenses:* Tuition, state resident: part-time $458 per credit. Tuition, nonresident: part-time $659 per credit. *Financial support:* Federal Work-Study and scholarships/grants available. Support available to part-time students. Financial award application deadline: 6/1; financial award applicants required to submit FAFSA. *Unit head:* Dr. Leslie Dinauer, Program Chair, 240-684-2400, Fax: 240-684-2401, E-mail: leslie.dinauer@umuc.edu. *Application contact:* Admissions Coordinator, 800-888-8682, Fax: 240-684-2151, E-mail: newgrad@umuc.edu.
Website: http://www.umuc.edu/academic-programs/doctor-of-management.cfm

University of Maryland University College, The Graduate School, Program in Business Administration, Adelphi, MD 20783. Offers MBA. *Accreditation:* AACSB. *Program availability:* Part-time, evening/weekend, online learning. *Students:* 1,569 full-time (890 women), 582 part-time (302 women); includes 1,228 minority (863 Black or African American, non-Hispanic/Latino; 10 American Indian or Alaska Native, non-Hispanic/Latino; 123 Asian, non-Hispanic/Latino; 137 Hispanic/Latino; 7 Native Hawaiian or other Pacific Islander, non-Hispanic/Latino; 88 Two or more races, non-Hispanic/Latino), 29 international. Average age 33. 1,182 applicants, 100% accepted, 564 enrolled. In 2016, 910 master's awarded. *Degree requirements:* For master's, thesis or alternative, capstone course. *Application deadline:* Applications are processed on a rolling basis. Application fee: $50. Electronic applications accepted. *Expenses:* Tuition, state resident: part-time $458 per credit. Tuition, nonresident: part-time $659 per credit. *Financial support:* Federal Work-Study and scholarships/grants available. Support available to part-time students. Financial award application deadline: 6/1; financial award applicants required to submit FAFSA. *Unit head:* Ravi Mittal, Professor, 240-684-2143, Fax: 240-684-2960, E-mail: ravi.mittal@umuc.edu. *Application contact:* Coordinator, Graduate Admissions, 800-888-8682, Fax: 240-684-2151, E-mail: newgrad@umuc.edu.
Website: http://www.umuc.edu/academic-programs/masters-degrees/master-of-business-administration.cfm

University of Maryland University College, The Graduate School, Program in Management, Adelphi, MD 20783. Offers MS, Certificate. *Program availability:* Part-time, online learning. *Students:* 30 full-time (17 women), 3,216 part-time (2,066 women); includes 1,952 minority (1,491 Black or African American, non-Hispanic/Latino; 8 American Indian or Alaska Native, non-Hispanic/Latino; 106 Asian, non-Hispanic/Latino;

242 Hispanic/Latino; 5 Native Hawaiian or other Pacific Islander, non-Hispanic/Latino; 100 Two or more races, non-Hispanic/Latino), 44 international. Average age 33. 856 applicants, 100% accepted, 612 enrolled. In 2016, 837 master's, 222 other advanced degrees awarded. *Degree requirements:* For master's, thesis or alternative. *Application deadline:* Applications are processed on a rolling basis. Application fee: $50. Electronic applications accepted. *Expenses:* Tuition, state resident: part-time $458 per credit. Tuition, nonresident: part-time $659 per credit. *Financial support:* Federal Work-Study and scholarships/grants available. Support available to part-time students. Financial award application deadline: 6/1; financial award applicants required to submit FAFSA. *Unit head:* Harriet Smith, Program Director, 240-684-2423, Fax: 240-684-2401, E-mail: harriet.smith@umuc.edu. *Application contact:* Coordinator, Graduate Admissions, 888-888-8682, Fax: 240-684-2151, E-mail: newgrad@umuc.edu.
Website: http://www.umuc.edu/academic-programs/masters-degrees/management.cfm

University of Mary Washington, College of Business, Fredericksburg, VA 22401-5300. Offers MBA. *Program availability:* Part-time-only, evening/weekend. *Faculty:* 12 full-time (3 women), 1 part-time/adjunct (0 women). *Students:* 112 applicants, 52% accepted, 49 enrolled. *Entrance requirements:* For master's, GMAT or GRE, minimum GPA of 3.0. Additional exam requirements/recommendations for international students: Required—TOEFL (minimum score 570 paper-based; 80 iBT), IELTS (minimum score 6.5). *Application deadline:* For fall admission, 6/1 priority date for domestic students, 6/1 for international students; for spring admission, 10/1 for domestic and international students. Applications are processed on a rolling basis. Application fee: $50. Electronic applications accepted. Application fee is waived when completed online. *Expenses:* $531 per credit hour resident; $1,024 per credit hour non-resident. *Financial support:* In 2016–17, 8 students received support. Available to part-time students. Application deadline: 3/15; applicants required to submit FAFSA. *Faculty research:* Power laws/CEO compensation, sustainable competitive advantage, resistance to security implementation, profiling sustainable curriculums, perceived customer value. *Unit head:* Dr. Lynne D. Richardson, Dean, 540-654-2470, Fax: 540-654-2430, E-mail: lynne.richardson@umw.edu. *Application contact:* Christy Pack, Director of Graduate Admissions, 540-286-8086, Fax: 540-286-8085, E-mail: dpack@umw.edu.
Website: http://business.umw.edu/

University of Massachusetts Amherst, Graduate School, Interdisciplinary Programs, Dual Degree Program in Management and Public Policy and Administration, Amherst, MA 01003. Offers MPPA/MBA. *Accreditation:* AACSB. *Program availability:* Part-time. *Entrance requirements:* Additional exam requirements/recommendations for international students: Required—TOEFL (minimum score 600 paper-based; 100 iBT), IELTS (minimum score 7). Electronic applications accepted.

University of Massachusetts Amherst, Graduate School, Interdisciplinary Programs, Dual Degree Program in Management and Sport Management, Amherst, MA 01003. Offers MBA/MS. *Program availability:* Part-time. *Entrance requirements:* Additional exam requirements/recommendations for international students: Required—TOEFL (minimum score 600 paper-based; 100 iBT), IELTS (minimum score 7). Electronic applications accepted.

University of Massachusetts Amherst, Graduate School, Interdisciplinary Programs, Dual Degree Programs in Management and Engineering, Amherst, MA 01003. Offers MBA/MIE, MBA/MSEWRE, MSCE/MBA, MSME/MBA. *Program availability:* Part-time. *Entrance requirements:* Additional exam requirements/recommendations for international students: Required—TOEFL (minimum score 600 paper-based; 100 iBT), IELTS (minimum score 7). Electronic applications accepted.

University of Massachusetts Amherst, Graduate School, Isenberg School of Management, Program in Management, Amherst, MA 01003. Offers accounting (PhD); business administration (MBA); entrepreneurship (MBA); finance (MBA, PhD); healthcare administration (MBA); hospitality and tourism management (PhD); management science (PhD); marketing (MBA, PhD); organization studies (PhD); sport management (PhD); strategic management (PhD); MBA/MS. *Accreditation:* AACSB. *Program availability:* Part-time, evening/weekend, online learning. Terminal master's awarded for partial completion of doctoral program. *Degree requirements:* For doctorate, comprehensive exam, thesis/dissertation. *Entrance requirements:* For master's and doctorate, GMAT or GRE General Test. Additional exam requirements/recommendations for international students: Required—TOEFL (minimum score 550 paper-based; 80 iBT), IELTS (minimum score 6.5). Electronic applications accepted.

University of Massachusetts Boston, College of Management, Program in Business Administration, Boston, MA 02125-3393. Offers MBA. *Accreditation:* AACSB. *Program availability:* Part-time, evening/weekend. *Students:* 172 full-time (75 women), 164 part-time (76 women); includes 70 minority (16 Black or African American, non-Hispanic/Latino; 26 Asian, non-Hispanic/Latino; 23 Hispanic/Latino; 5 Two or more races, non-Hispanic/Latino), 90 international. Average age 30. 314 applicants, 48% accepted, 106 enrolled. In 2016, 84 master's awarded. *Degree requirements:* For master's, capstone project. *Entrance requirements:* For master's, GMAT, minimum GPA of 3.0. *Application deadline:* For fall admission, 3/1 for domestic students; for spring admission, 11/1 for domestic students. *Expenses:* Tuition, state resident: full-time $16,863. Tuition, nonresident: full-time $32,913. *Required fees:* $177. *Financial support:* Research assistantships with full tuition reimbursements, teaching assistantships with full tuition reimbursements, career-related internships or fieldwork, Federal Work-Study, and unspecified assistantships available. Support available to part-time students. Financial award application deadline: 3/1; financial award applicants required to submit FAFSA. *Faculty research:* International finance, human resource management, management information systems, investment and corporate finance, international marketing. *Application contact:* Peggy Roldan Patel, Graduate Admissions Coordinator, 617-287-6400, Fax: 617-287-6236, E-mail: bos.gadm@dpc.umassp.edu.

University of Massachusetts Dartmouth, Graduate School, Charlton College of Business, North Dartmouth, MA 02747-2300. Offers accounting and finance (MS, Postbaccalaureate Certificate), including accounting, finance (Postbaccalaureate Certificate); business administration (MBA, Graduate Certificate, Postbaccalaureate Certificate), including business administration (MBA), business foundations (Graduate Certificate), international business (Graduate Certificate), management (Postbaccalaureate Certificate), marketing (Postbaccalaureate Certificate), organizational leadership (Graduate Certificate), supply chain management and information systems (Postbaccalaureate Certificate); decision and information sciences (MS), including healthcare management, technology management. *Program availability:* Part-time, 100% online, blended/hybrid learning. *Faculty:* 41 full-time (15 women), 20 part-time/adjunct (9 women). *Students:* 169 full-time (72 women), 215 part-time (125 women); includes 63 minority (13 Black or African American, non-Hispanic/Latino; 1 American Indian or Alaska Native, non-Hispanic/Latino; 24 Asian, non-Hispanic/Latino; 18 Hispanic/Latino; 7 Two or more races, non-Hispanic/Latino), 122 international. Average age 32. 312 applicants, 80% accepted, 171 enrolled. In 2016, 143 master's, 13 other advanced degrees awarded. *Entrance requirements:* For master's, GMAT, statement of purpose (minimum of 300 words), resume, official transcripts, 2 letters of recommendation; for other advanced degree, statement of purpose (minimum of 300 words), resume, official transcripts. Additional exam requirements/recommendations for international students: Required—TOEFL (minimum score 533 paper-based; 72 iBT). Application fee: $60. Electronic applications accepted. *Expenses:* Tuition, state resident: full-time $14,994; part-time $624.75 per credit. Tuition, nonresident: full-time $27,068; part-time $1127.83 per credit. *Required fees:* $405; $25.88 per credit. Tuition and fees vary according to course load and reciprocity agreements. *Financial support:* In 2016–17, 2 research assistantships (averaging $2,667 per year) were awarded; institutionally sponsored loans, scholarships/grants, and unspecified assistantships also available. Support available to part-time students. Financial award application deadline: 3/1; financial award applicants required to submit FAFSA. *Faculty research:* Managing diversity, e-commerce, agile manufacturing, green business, activity-based management, build-to-order supply chain management, process management, corporate governance. *Total annual research expenditures:* $413,000. *Unit head:* Melissa Pacheco, Assistant Dean of Graduate Studies, 508-999-8543, Fax: 508-999-8646, E-mail: mpacheco@umassd.edu. *Application contact:* Steven Briggs, Director of Recruitment and Marketing for Graduate Studies, 508-999-8604, Fax: 508-999-8183, E-mail: graduate@umassd.edu.
Website: http://www.umassd.edu/charlton/programs/graduate

University of Massachusetts Lowell, Manning School of Business, Lowell, MA 01854. Offers business administration (MBA, PhD); healthcare innovation and entrepreneurship (MS). *Accreditation:* AACSB. *Program availability:* Part-time, evening/weekend. *Entrance requirements:* For master's, GMAT.

University of Memphis, Graduate School, Fogelman College of Business and Economics, Program in Business Administration, Memphis, TN 38152. Offers accounting (MBA, PhD); business administration (IMBA); economics (PhD); executive business administration (MBA); finance (PhD); management (PhD); marketing (MS); marketing and supply chain management (PhD); real estate development (MS); JD/MBA. *Accreditation:* AACSB. *Faculty:* 44 full-time (9 women), 5 part-time/adjunct (0 women). *Students:* 167 full-time (64 women), 341 part-time (119 women); includes 154 minority (80 Black or African American, non-Hispanic/Latino; 1 American Indian or Alaska Native, non-Hispanic/Latino; 43 Asian, non-Hispanic/Latino; 12 Hispanic/Latino; 1 Native Hawaiian or other Pacific Islander, non-Hispanic/Latino; 17 Two or more races, non-Hispanic/Latino), 96 international. Average age 33. 306 applicants, 64% accepted, 154 enrolled. In 2016, 273 master's, 7 doctorates awarded. *Degree requirements:* For master's, comprehensive exam; for doctorate, comprehensive exam, thesis/dissertation. *Entrance requirements:* For master's, GMAT, resume; for doctorate, GMAT, interview, minimum GPA of 3.4, resume, letter of recommendation. Additional exam requirements/recommendations for international students: Required—TOEFL (minimum score 550 paper-based). *Application deadline:* For fall admission, 8/1 for domestic students; for spring admission, 12/1 for domestic students. Application fee: $35 ($60 for international students). *Expenses:* Tuition, state resident: full-time $10,463; part-time $9483 per year. Tuition, nonresident: full-time $19,247; part-time $17,291 per year. *Required fees:* $821.50 per semester. Tuition and fees vary according to course load and program. *Financial support:* In 2016–17, 164 students received support. Research assistantships with full tuition reimbursements available, teaching assistantships with full tuition reimbursements available, career-related internships or fieldwork, Federal Work-Study, scholarships/grants, and unspecified assistantships available. Financial award application deadline: 2/15; financial award applicants required to submit FAFSA. *Faculty research:* Competitive business strategy, finance microstructures, supply chain management innovations, health care economics, litigation risks and corporate audits. *Unit head:* Dr. Rajiv Grover, Dean, 901-678-3759, E-mail: rgrover@memphis.edu. *Application contact:* Dr. Carol V. Danehower, Associate Dean, 901-678-5402, Fax: 901-678-3579, E-mail: fcbegp@memphis.edu.
Website: https://web0.memphis.edu/gradcatalog/degreeprog/fcbe/fcbe.php

University of Miami, Graduate School, School of Business Administration, Coral Gables, FL 33124. Offers MA, MBA, MP Acc, MS, MS Tax, MSPM, PhD, JD/MBA, MBA/MSIE. *Accreditation:* AACSB; CAHME (one or more programs are accredited). *Program availability:* Part-time, evening/weekend. *Degree requirements:* For master's, comprehensive exam; for doctorate, comprehensive exam, thesis/dissertation. *Entrance requirements:* For master's, GMAT; for doctorate, GRE General Test. Additional exam requirements/recommendations for international students: Required—TOEFL (minimum score 550 paper-based; 59 iBT). Electronic applications accepted. *Faculty research:* Calculating efficiency of multinational operations, efficiency and effectiveness of retail locations, evolution of contractual intent.

University of Michigan, Ross School of Business, Ann Arbor, MI 48109-1234. Offers accounting (M Acc); business (MBA); business administration (PhD); supply chain management (MSCM); JD/MBA; MBA/M Arch; MBA/M Eng; MBA/MA; MBA/MEM; MBA/MHSA; MBA/MM; MBA/MPP; MBA/MS; MBA/MSE; MBA/MSI; MBA/MSW; MBA/MUP; MD/MBA; MHSA/MBA. *Accreditation:* AACSB. *Program availability:* Part-time, evening/weekend. *Degree requirements:* For doctorate, comprehensive exam, thesis/dissertation, oral defense of dissertation, preliminary exam. *Entrance requirements:* For master's, GMAT or GRE, completion of equivalent of four-year U.S. bachelor's degree, two letters of recommendation, essays, resume; for doctorate, GMAT or GRE. Additional exam requirements/recommendations for international students: Required—TOEFL (minimum score 600 paper-based; 100 iBT). Electronic applications accepted. *Expenses:* Tuition, state resident: full-time $21,466; part-time $1152 per credit hour. Tuition, nonresident: full-time $43,346; part-time $2367 per credit hour. Part-time tuition and fees vary according to course load, degree level and program. *Faculty research:* Finance and accounting, marketing, technology and operations management, corporate strategy, management and organizations.

University of Michigan–Dearborn, College of Business, MBA Program, Dearborn, MI 48126. Offers MBA. *Accreditation:* AACSB. *Program availability:* Part-time, evening/weekend, 100% online. *Faculty:* 33 full-time (14 women), 10 part-time/adjunct (5 women). *Students:* 28 full-time (14 women), 171 part-time (54 women); includes 30 minority (8 Black or African American, non-Hispanic/Latino; 13 Asian, non-Hispanic/Latino; 6 Hispanic/Latino; 3 Two or more races, non-Hispanic/Latino), 14 international. Average age 30. 122 applicants, 43% accepted, 37 enrolled. In 2016, 50 master's awarded. *Entrance requirements:* For master's, GMAT or GRE, equivalent of four-year U.S. bachelor's degree from regionally-accredited institution, undergraduate course in finite math, pre-calculus, or calculus. Additional exam requirements/recommendations for international students: Required—TOEFL (minimum score 560 paper-based; 84 iBT), IELTS (minimum score 6.5). *Application deadline:* For fall admission, 8/1 for domestic students, 5/1 for international students; for winter admission, 12/1 for domestic students, 9/1 for international students; for spring admission, 4/1 for domestic students, 1/1 for international students. Applications are processed on a rolling basis. Application fee: $60. Electronic applications accepted. *Expenses:* Contact institution. *Financial support:* In 2016–17, 29 students received support. Scholarships/grants and non-resident tuition scholarships available. Financial award application deadline: 3/1; financial award applicants required to submit FAFSA. *Faculty research:* Business intelligence, information technology, brand management and new media, management education, operations strategy. *Unit head:* Dr. Michael Kamen, Director, COB Graduate Programs, 313-593-5460, E-mail: mkamen@umich.edu. *Application contact:* Joan Doherty, Academic Advisor/Counselor, 313-593-5460, Fax: 313-271-9838, E-mail: umd-gradbusiness@umich.edu.
Website: http://umdearborn.edu/cob/mba-program/

Business Administration and Management—General

University of Michigan–Flint, School of Management, Flint, MI 48502. Offers accounting (MSA); business (Graduate Certificate); business administration (MBA, Post-Master's Certificate), including accounting, computer information systems (MBA), finance, general business administration (MBA), health care management (MBA), international business, lean manufacturing (MBA), marketing, organizational leadership. *Accreditation:* AACSB. *Program availability:* Part-time, evening/weekend, mixed mode programs. *Faculty:* 33 full-time (9 women), 6 part-time/adjunct (1 woman). *Students:* 29 full-time (13 women), 171 part-time (58 women); includes 45 minority (21 Black or African American, non-Hispanic/Latino; 2 American Indian or Alaska Native, non-Hispanic/Latino; 12 Asian, non-Hispanic/Latino; 6 Hispanic/Latino; 1 Native Hawaiian or other Pacific Islander, non-Hispanic/Latino; 3 Two or more races, non-Hispanic/Latino), 23 international. Average age 33. 198 applicants, 51% accepted, 49 enrolled. In 2016, 86 master's, 3 other advanced degrees awarded. *Degree requirements:* For master's, thesis or alternative. *Entrance requirements:* For master's, GMAT or GRE, bachelor's degree in arts, sciences, engineering, or business administration from regionally-accredited college or university with minimum GPA of 3.0; for other advanced degree, bachelor's degree from regionally-accredited college with minimum GPA of 3.0 and completion of college-level math, statistics, or quantitative course (for Graduate Certificate); MBA or equivalent from accredited college or university (for Post-Master's Certificate). Additional exam requirements/recommendations for international students: Required—TOEFL (minimum score 84 iBT), IELTS (minimum score 6.5). *Application deadline:* For fall admission, 8/1 for domestic students, 5/1 for international students; for winter admission, 11/15 for domestic students, 9/1 for international students; for spring admission, 3/15 for domestic students; for summer admission, 5/15 for domestic students. Applications are processed on a rolling basis. Application fee: $55. Electronic applications accepted. *Expenses:* Contact institution. *Financial support:* Federal Work-Study, scholarships/grants, and unspecified assistantships available. Support available to part-time students. Financial award application deadline: 3/1; financial award applicants required to submit FAFSA. *Unit head:* Dr. Scott Johnson, Dean, School of Management, 810-762-6579, Fax: 810-237-6685, E-mail: scotjohn@umflint.edu. *Application contact:* Bradley T. Maki, Director of Graduate Admissions, 810-762-3171, Fax: 810-766-6789, E-mail: bmaki@umflint.edu.
Website: http://www.umflint.edu/som

University of Minnesota, Duluth, Graduate School, Labovitz School of Business and Economics, Program in Business Administration, Duluth, MN 55812-2496. Offers MBA. *Accreditation:* AACSB. *Program availability:* Part-time, evening/weekend. *Entrance requirements:* For master's, GMAT, minimum GPA of 3.0; course work in accounting, business administration, and economics. Additional exam requirements/recommendations for international students: Required—TOEFL (minimum score 550 paper-based; 79 iBT). *Expenses:* Contact institution. *Faculty research:* Regional economic analysis, marketing, management, human resources, organizational behavior.

University of Minnesota Rochester, Graduate Programs, Rochester, MN 55904. Offers bioinformatics and computational biology (MS, PhD); business administration (MBA); occupational therapy (MOT).

University of Minnesota, Twin Cities Campus, Carlson School of Management, Minneapolis, MN 55455. Offers EMBA, M Acc, MA, MBA, MBT, MS, PhD, JD/MBA, MBA/MPP, MBA/MSBA, MD/MBA, MHA/MBA, Pharm D/MBA. *Accreditation:* AACSB. *Program availability:* Part-time, evening/weekend. *Faculty:* 139 full-time (39 women), 49 part-time/adjunct (10 women). *Students:* 556 full-time (248 women), 1,142 part-time (393 women); includes 175 minority (32 Black or African American, non-Hispanic/Latino; 5 American Indian or Alaska Native, non-Hispanic/Latino; 79 Asian, non-Hispanic/Latino; 32 Hispanic/Latino; 1 Native Hawaiian or other Pacific Islander, non-Hispanic/Latino; 26 Two or more races, non-Hispanic/Latino), 329 international. Average age 27. In 2016, 609 master's, 10 doctorates awarded. Terminal master's awarded for partial completion of doctoral program. *Degree requirements:* For doctorate, comprehensive exam, thesis/dissertation. Electronic applications accepted. *Expenses:* Contact institution. *Financial support:* Fellowships with full and partial tuition reimbursements, research assistantships with full tuition reimbursements, teaching assistantships with full and partial tuition reimbursements, career-related internships or fieldwork, Federal Work-Study, institutionally sponsored loans, scholarships/grants, health care benefits, tuition waivers (full and partial), and unspecified assistantships available. Support available to part-time students. Financial award application deadline: 4/1; financial award applicants required to submit FAFSA. *Faculty research:* Finance and accounting: financial reporting, asset pricing models and corporate finance; information and decision sciences: on-line auctions, information transparency and recommender systems; marketing: psychological influences on consumer behavior, brand equity, pricing and marketing channels; operations: lean manufacturing, quality management and global supply chains; strategic management and organization: global strategy, networks, entrepreneurship and innovation, sustainability. *Unit head:* Prof. Alok Gupta, Associate Dean of Faculty and Research, 612-626-0276, Fax: 612-624-6374, E-mail: gupta037@umn.edu. *Application contact:* Graduate School Admissions, 612-625-3014, Fax: 612-625-6002, E-mail: gsquest@umn.edu.
Website: http://www.carlsonschool.umn.edu

University of Mississippi, Graduate School, School of Business Administration, University, MS 38677. Offers business administration (PhD); systems management (MS); JD/MBA. *Accreditation:* AACSB. *Faculty:* 56 full-time (40 women), 9 part-time/adjunct (4 women). *Students:* 78 full-time (25 women), 111 part-time (20 women); includes 18 minority (3 Black or African American, non-Hispanic/Latino; 5 Asian, non-Hispanic/Latino; 6 Hispanic/Latino; 4 Two or more races, non-Hispanic/Latino), 19 international. Average age 28. In 2016, 83 master's, 6 doctorates awarded. *Degree requirements:* For doctorate, thesis/dissertation. *Entrance requirements:* For master's, GMAT, minimum GPA of 3.0; for doctorate, GMAT. Additional exam requirements/recommendations for international students: Required—TOEFL. *Application deadline:* For fall admission, 2/1 for domestic students; for spring admission, 10/1 for domestic students. Applications are processed on a rolling basis. Application fee: $40. Electronic applications accepted. *Financial support:* Fellowships, career-related internships or fieldwork, scholarships/grants, tuition waivers (full), and unspecified assistantships available. Financial award application deadline: 3/1; financial award applicants required to submit FAFSA. *Unit head:* Dr. Ken Cyree, Dean, 662-915-5820, Fax: 662-915-5821, E-mail: info@bus.olemiss.edu. *Application contact:* Dr. Christy M. Wyandt, Associate Dean, 662-915-7474, Fax: 662-915-7577, E-mail: cwyandt@olemiss.edu.
Website: http://www.olemissbusiness.com/

University of Missouri, Office of Research and Graduate Studies, Robert J. Trulaske, Sr. College of Business, Program in Business Administration, Columbia, MO 65211. Offers business administration (MBA); executive business administration (MBA); finance (PhD); management (PhD); marketing (PhD); MBA/JD; MBA/MHA; MBA/MSIE. *Accreditation:* AACSB. *Degree requirements:* For doctorate, thesis/dissertation. *Entrance requirements:* For master's and doctorate, GMAT, minimum GPA of 3.0. Additional exam requirements/recommendations for international students: Required—TOEFL (minimum score 500 paper-based; 61 iBT). Electronic applications accepted. *Expenses:* Tuition, state resident: full-time $6347; part-time $352.60 per credit hour. Tuition, nonresident: full-time $17,379; part-time $965.50 per credit hour. *Required fees:* $1035. Tuition and fees vary according to course load, campus/location and program.

University of Missouri–Kansas City, Henry W. Bloch School of Management, Kansas City, MO 64110-2499. Offers accounting (MS); finance (MS); public affairs (MPA, PhD); JD/MBA; LL M/MPA. PhD (interdisciplinary) offered through the School of Graduate Studies. *Accreditation:* AACSB; NASPAA. *Program availability:* Part-time, evening/weekend. *Faculty:* 60 full-time (19 women), 40 part-time/adjunct (11 women). *Students:* 204 full-time (97 women), 308 part-time (151 women); includes 70 minority (29 Black or African American, non-Hispanic/Latino; 1 American Indian or Alaska Native, non-Hispanic/Latino; 17 Asian, non-Hispanic/Latino; 18 Hispanic/Latino; 5 Two or more races, non-Hispanic/Latino), 82 international. Average age 30. 389 applicants, 49% accepted, 190 enrolled. In 2016, 248 master's, 2 doctorates awarded. Terminal master's awarded for partial completion of doctoral program. *Entrance requirements:* For master's, GMAT, GRE, 2 essays, 2 references, support of employer; for doctorate, GRE, minimum GPA of 3.0. Additional exam requirements/recommendations for international students: Required—TOEFL (minimum score 550 paper-based; 80 iBT). *Application deadline:* For fall admission, 5/1 priority date for domestic and international students; for spring admission, 10/1 priority date for domestic and international students. Applications are processed on a rolling basis. Application fee: $45 ($50 for international students). Electronic applications accepted. *Financial support:* In 2016–17, 31 research assistantships with partial tuition reimbursements (averaging $10,597 per year), 10 teaching assistantships with partial tuition reimbursements (averaging $14,592 per year) were awarded; career-related internships or fieldwork, Federal Work-Study, institutionally sponsored loans, scholarships/grants, tuition waivers (full and partial), and unspecified assistantships also available. Support available to part-time students. Financial award application deadline: 3/1; financial award applicants required to submit FAFSA. *Faculty research:* Entrepreneurship, finance, non-profit, risk management. *Unit head:* Dr. David Donnelly, Dean, 816-235-1333, Fax: 816-235-2206, E-mail: donnellyd@umkc.edu. *Application contact:* 816-235-1111, E-mail: admit@umkc.edu.
Website: http://www.bloch.umkc.edu

University of Missouri–St. Louis, College of Business Administration, Program in Business Administration, St. Louis, MO 63121. Offers accounting (MBA); business administration (Certificate); business intelligence (Certificate); cybersecurity (Certificate); digital and social media marketing (Certificate); finance (MBA); human resources management (Certificate); information systems (MBA); international business (MBA); logistics and supply chain management (MBA, PhD, Certificate); management (MBA); marketing (MBA); marketing management (Certificate); operations management (MBA). *Accreditation:* AACSB. *Program availability:* Part-time, evening/weekend. *Faculty:* 32 full-time (10 women), 14 part-time/adjunct (3 women). *Students:* 181 full-time (88 women), 357 part-time (154 women); includes 83 minority (30 Black or African American, non-Hispanic/Latino; 36 Asian, non-Hispanic/Latino; 12 Hispanic/Latino; 2 Native Hawaiian or other Pacific Islander, non-Hispanic/Latino; 3 Two or more races, non-Hispanic/Latino), 100 international. Average age 31. 245 applicants, 83% accepted, 139 enrolled. *Degree requirements:* For doctorate, thesis/dissertation. *Entrance requirements:* For master's, GMAT, 2 letters of recommendation. Additional exam requirements/recommendations for international students: Recommended—TOEFL (minimum score 550 paper-based; 79 iBT), IELTS (minimum score 6.5). *Application deadline:* For fall admission, 7/1 for domestic and international students; for spring admission, 12/1 for domestic and international students. Applications are processed on a rolling basis. Application fee: $50 ($40 for international students). Electronic applications accepted. *Financial support:* Research assistantships with tuition reimbursements, teaching assistantships with tuition reimbursements, career-related internships or fieldwork, Federal Work-Study, and institutionally sponsored loans available. Support available to part-time students. Financial award application deadline: 4/1; financial award applicants required to submit FAFSA. *Faculty research:* Human resources, strategic management, marketing strategy, consumer behavior product development, advertising. *Unit head:* Dr. Thomas H. Eyssell, Associate Dean and Director of Graduate Studies, 314-516-5885, Fax: 314-516-6420, E-mail: mba@umsl.edu. *Application contact:* 314-516-5458, Fax: 314-516-6996, E-mail: gradadm@umsl.edu.

University of Missouri–St. Louis, Graduate School, Program in Public Policy Administration, St. Louis, MO 63121. Offers local government management (MPPA, Certificate); nonprofit management and leadership (MPPA, Certificate); policy and program evaluation (MPPA, Certificate). *Accreditation:* NASPAA. *Program availability:* Part-time, evening/weekend. *Faculty:* 2 full-time (both women), 6 part-time/adjunct (2 women). *Students:* 10 full-time (5 women), 43 part-time (26 women); includes 14 minority (12 Black or African American, non-Hispanic/Latino; 2 Asian, non-Hispanic/Latino). Average age 33. 28 applicants, 89% accepted, 17 enrolled. *Degree requirements:* For master's, exit project. *Entrance requirements:* For master's, 3 letters of recommendation, personal statement. Additional exam requirements/recommendations for international students: Recommended—TOEFL (minimum score 550 paper-based), IELTS (minimum score 6.5). *Application deadline:* For fall admission, 7/1 priority date for domestic and international students; for spring admission, 12/1 priority date for domestic and international students. Applications are processed on a rolling basis. Application fee: $50 ($40 for international students). Electronic applications accepted. *Financial support:* Research assistantships with tuition reimbursements and career-related internships or fieldwork available. Financial award application deadline: 4/1; financial award applicants required to submit FAFSA. *Faculty research:* Urban policy, public finance, evaluation. *Unit head:* Dr. Deborah Balser, Director, 314-516-5146, Fax: 314-516-5210, E-mail: balserd@umsl.edu. *Application contact:* 314-516-5458, Fax: 314-516-6996, E-mail: gradadm@umsl.edu.
Website: http://www.umsl.edu/gradschool/ppa/

University of Mobile, Graduate Studies, Program in Business Administration, Mobile, AL 36613. Offers MBA. *Accreditation:* ACBSP. *Program availability:* Part-time, evening/weekend. *Degree requirements:* For master's, comprehensive exam. *Entrance requirements:* For master's, GMAT. Additional exam requirements/recommendations for international students: Required—TOEFL (minimum score 550 paper-based; 80 iBT). Electronic applications accepted. *Faculty research:* Management, personnel management, small business, diversity.

University of Montana, Graduate School, School of Business Administration, MBA Program, Missoula, MT 59812-0002. Offers MBA, JD/MBA, MBA/Pharm D. *Accreditation:* AACSB. *Program availability:* Part-time, evening/weekend, online learning. *Degree requirements:* For master's, thesis optional. *Entrance requirements:* For master's, GMAT. Additional exam requirements/recommendations for international students: Required—TOEFL. *Faculty research:* Information systems, research methods, international business, human resource management, marketing.

University of Montevallo, Stephens College of Business, Montevallo, AL 35115. Offers MBA. *Accreditation:* AACSB. *Program availability:* Part-time, evening/weekend. *Students:* 16 full-time (8 women), 19 part-time (9 women); includes 7 minority (4 Black or African American, non-Hispanic/Latino; 2 Hispanic/Latino; 1 Two or more races, non-Hispanic/Latino), 7 international. In 2016, 12 master's awarded. *Degree requirements:* For master's, comprehensive exam. *Entrance requirements:* Additional exam requirements/recommendations for international students: Required—TOEFL (minimum score 550 paper-based). *Application deadline:* For fall admission, 7/15 for domestic students; for spring admission, 11/15 for domestic students. Application fee: $25.

Expenses: Tuition, state resident: full-time $9936. Tuition, nonresident: full-time $20,592. *Required fees:* $640. *Unit head:* Dr. Stephen H. Craft, Dean, 205-665-6540. *Application contact:* Kevin Thornthwaite, Director, Graduate Admissions and Records, 205-665-6350, E-mail: graduate@montevallo.edu.
Website: http://www.montevallo.edu/business/college-of-business/

University of Mount Olive, Graduate Programs, Mount Olive, NC 28365. Offers business (MBA); education (M Ed); nursing (MSN). *Program availability:* Online learning.

University of Nebraska at Kearney, College of Business and Technology, Department of Business, Kearney, NE 68849-0001. Offers accounting (MBA); generalist (MBA); human resources (MBA); human services (MBA); marketing (MBA). *Accreditation:* AACSB. *Program availability:* Part-time, evening/weekend. *Faculty:* 32 full-time (13 women). *Students:* 11 full-time (5 women), 30 part-time (14 women), 8 international. Average age 39. 13 applicants, 100% accepted, 10 enrolled. In 2016, 6 master's awarded. *Degree requirements:* For master's, thesis optional, capstone course. *Entrance requirements:* For master's, GRE or GMAT (if no significant managerial experience), letters of recommendation, essay, resume. Additional exam requirements/recommendations for international students: Recommended—TOEFL (minimum score 550 paper-based; 79 iBT), IELTS (minimum score 6.5). *Application deadline:* For fall admission, 6/15 for domestic and international students; for spring admission, 10/15 for domestic and international students; for summer admission, 3/15 for domestic and international students. Application fee: $45. Electronic applications accepted. *Expenses:* Tuition, state resident: full-time $4064; part-time $225.75 per credit hour. Tuition, nonresident: full-time $8915; part-time $495.25 per credit hour. *Required fees:* $772; $23 per credit hour. Part-time tuition and fees vary according to course load, campus/location, program and reciprocity agreements. *Financial support:* In 2016–17, 2 research assistantships with full tuition reimbursements (averaging $10,500 per year), 2 teaching assistantships with full tuition reimbursements (averaging $10,500 per year) were awarded; career-related internships or fieldwork, scholarships/grants, health care benefits, and unspecified assistantships also available. Support available to part-time students. Financial award application deadline: 2/28; financial award applicants required to submit FAFSA. *Faculty research:* Small business financial management, employment law, expert systems, international trade and marketing, environmental economics. *Unit head:* Dr. Sri Seshadri, Director, 308-865-8346, Fax: 308-865-8114. *Application contact:* Linda Johnson, Director, Graduate Admissions and Programs, 800-717-7881, Fax: 308-865-8837, E-mail: gradstudies@unk.edu.

University of Nebraska at Omaha, Graduate Studies, College of Business Administration, Program in Business Administration, Omaha, NE 68182. Offers business administration (MBA); business for bioscientists (Certificate); executive business administration (EMBA); human resources and training (Certificate). *Accreditation:* AACSB. *Program availability:* Part-time, evening/weekend. *Faculty:* 9 full-time (3 women). *Students:* 80 full-time (31 women), 207 part-time (78 women); includes 35 minority (6 Black or African American, non-Hispanic/Latino; 1 American Indian or Alaska Native, non-Hispanic/Latino; 11 Asian, non-Hispanic/Latino; 12 Hispanic/Latino; 5 Two or more races, non-Hispanic/Latino), 29 international. Average age 30. 185 applicants, 48% accepted, 78 enrolled. In 2016, 128 master's, 5 other advanced degrees awarded. *Degree requirements:* For master's, thesis (for some programs), capstone course. *Entrance requirements:* For master's, GMAT or GRE, minimum GPA of 3.0, official transcripts, resume; for Certificate, minimum GPA of 3.0, official transcripts, resume, letter of recommendation, statement of purpose. Additional exam requirements/recommendations for international students: Required—TOEFL, IELTS, PTE. *Application deadline:* For fall admission, 7/1 for domestic and international students; for spring admission, 11/1 for domestic and international students; for summer admission, 4/1 for domestic and international students. Applications are processed on a rolling basis. Application fee: $45. Electronic applications accepted. *Financial support:* In 2016–17, 15 students received support, including 9 research assistantships with tuition reimbursements available, 6 teaching assistantships with tuition reimbursements available; Federal Work-Study, institutionally sponsored loans, scholarships/grants, health care benefits, tuition waivers (partial), and unspecified assistantships also available. Support available to part-time students. Financial award application deadline: 3/1; financial award applicants required to submit FAFSA. *Unit head:* Lex Kaczmarek, Graduate Program Chair, 402-554-2341, E-mail: graduate@unomaha.edu.

University of Nebraska–Lincoln, Graduate College, College of Business Administration, Interdepartmental Area of Business, Lincoln, NE 68588. Offers accountancy (PhD); business (MBA); finance (MA, PhD), including business; management (MA, PhD), including business; marketing (MA, PhD), including business; JD/MBA; M Arch/MBA. *Accreditation:* AACSB. *Program availability:* Part-time, online learning. *Degree requirements:* For doctorate, comprehensive exam, thesis/dissertation. *Entrance requirements:* For master's and doctorate, GMAT. Additional exam requirements/recommendations for international students: Required—TOEFL (minimum score 550 paper-based). Electronic applications accepted.

University of Nevada, Las Vegas, Graduate College, Lee Business School, Program in Business Administration, Las Vegas, NV 89154-6031. Offers Exec MBA, MBA, Certificate, DMD/MBA, MBA/JD, MBA/MS. *Accreditation:* AACSB. *Program availability:* Part-time, evening/weekend. *Faculty:* 3 part-time/adjunct (2 women). *Students:* 122 full-time (49 women), 81 part-time (27 women); includes 57 minority (6 Black or African American, non-Hispanic/Latino; 25 Asian, non-Hispanic/Latino; 16 Hispanic/Latino; 1 Native Hawaiian or other Pacific Islander, non-Hispanic/Latino; 9 Two or more races, non-Hispanic/Latino), 21 international. Average age 32. 100 applicants, 55% accepted, 40 enrolled. In 2016, 77 master's awarded. *Degree requirements:* For master's, capstone course. *Entrance requirements:* For master's, GMAT, 2 letters of recommendation; statement of purpose. Additional exam requirements/recommendations for international students: Required—TOEFL (minimum score 550 paper-based; 80 iBT), IELTS (minimum score 7). *Application deadline:* For fall admission, 7/15 for domestic students, 2/15 for international students; for spring admission, 11/15 for domestic students, 10/1 for international students; for summer admission, 4/1 for domestic students. Application fee: $60 ($95 for international students). Electronic applications accepted. *Expenses:* $269.25 per credit, $792 per 3-credit course; $9,634 per year resident; $23,274 per year non-resident; $7,094 fees non-resident (7 credits or more); $1,307 annual health insurance fee. *Financial support:* In 2016–17, 4 research assistantships with partial tuition reimbursements (averaging $10,890 per year), 7 teaching assistantships with partial tuition reimbursements (averaging $10,000 per year) were awarded; institutionally sponsored loans, scholarships/grants, health care benefits, and unspecified assistantships also available. Financial award application deadline: 3/15. *Faculty research:* Economic effects on wages; benefits and economic effects of risk, uncertainty; asymmetric information: adverse selection, moral hazard; business processes. *Unit head:* Dr. Vincent Hsu, Director of Academic Programs/Professor, 702-895-3842, Fax: 702-895-3632, E-mail: vincent.hsu@unlv.edu.
Website: http://business.unlv.edu/mba/

University of Nevada, Reno, Graduate School, College of Business Administration, Department of Business Administration, Reno, NV 89557. Offers MBA. *Accreditation:* AACSB. *Program availability:* Part-time, evening/weekend, online learning. *Entrance requirements:* For master's, GMAT, minimum GPA of 2.75. Additional exam requirements/recommendations for international students: Required—TOEFL (minimum score 500 paper-based; 61 iBT), IELTS (minimum score 6). Electronic applications accepted.

University of New Brunswick Fredericton, School of Graduate Studies, Faculty of Business Administration, Fredericton, NB E3B 5A3, Canada. Offers business administration (MBA); engineering management (MBA); entrepreneurship (MBA); sports and recreation management (MBA); MBA/LL B. *Program availability:* Part-time. *Degree requirements:* For master's, thesis optional. *Entrance requirements:* For master's, GMAT (minimum score 550), minimum GPA of 3.0; 3-5 years of work experience; 3 letters of reference with at least one academic reference. Additional exam requirements/recommendations for international students: Required—TOEFL (minimum score 580 paper-based; 92 iBT) or IELTS (minimum score 7). Electronic applications accepted. *Faculty research:* Entrepreneurship, finance, law, sport and recreation management, engineering management.

University of New Brunswick Saint John, Faculty of Business, Saint John, NB E2L 4L5, Canada. Offers administration (MBA); electronic commerce (MBA); international business (MBA); natural resource management (MBA). *Program availability:* Part-time. *Entrance requirements:* For master's, GMAT (minimum score of 550) or GRE (minimum 54th percentile), minimum GPA of 3.0. Additional exam requirements/recommendations for international students: Required—TOEFL (minimum score 580 paper-based; 93 iBT), TWE (minimum score 4.5). Electronic applications accepted. *Expenses:* Contact institution. *Faculty research:* International business, project management, innovation and technology management; business use of Weblogs and podcasts to communicate; corporate governance; high-involvement work systems; international competitiveness; supply chain management and logistics.

University of New Hampshire, Graduate School Manchester Campus, Manchester, NH 03101. Offers business administration (MBA); educational administration and supervision (Ed S); educational studies (M Ed); elementary teacher education (M Ed); information technology (MS); public administration (MPA); public health (MPH, Certificate); secondary teacher education (M Ed, MAT); social work (MSW); substance use disorders (Certificate). *Program availability:* Part-time, evening/weekend. *Degree requirements:* For master's, thesis or alternative. *Entrance requirements:* Additional exam requirements/recommendations for international students: Required—TOEFL (minimum score 550 paper-based; 80 iBT). Electronic applications accepted.

University of New Haven, Graduate School, College of Business, Executive Program in Business Administration, West Haven, CT 06516. Offers EMBA. *Accreditation:* AACSB. *Program availability:* Part-time, evening/weekend. *Students:* 24 full-time (9 women); includes 3 minority (1 Black or African American, non-Hispanic/Latino; 2 Hispanic/Latino). Average age 43. *Entrance requirements:* Additional exam requirements/recommendations for international students: Required—TOEFL (minimum score 80 iBT), IELTS, PTE. *Application deadline:* Applications are processed on a rolling basis. Application fee: $50. Electronic applications accepted. Application fee is waived when completed online. *Expenses:* Contact institution. *Financial support:* Application deadline: 5/1. *Unit head:* Darell Singleterry, Program Director, 203-932-1085, E-mail: dsingleterry@newhaven.edu. *Application contact:* Michelle Mason, Director of Graduate Enrollment, 203-932-7067, E-mail: mmason@newhaven.edu.
Website: http://www.newhaven.edu/6465/

University of New Haven, Graduate School, College of Business, Program in Business Administration, West Haven, CT 06516. Offers accounting (MBA), including CPA; business administration (MBA); business intelligence (MBA); business management (Graduate Certificate); business policy and strategic leadership (MBA); finance (MBA), including CFA; global marketing (MBA); human resources management (MBA, Graduate Certificate); sport management (MBA). *Accreditation:* AACSB. *Program availability:* Part-time, evening/weekend. *Students:* 123 full-time (56 women), 74 part-time (29 women); includes 46 minority (24 Black or African American, non-Hispanic/Latino; 8 Asian, non-Hispanic/Latino; 10 Hispanic/Latino; 4 Two or more races, non-Hispanic/Latino), 57 international. Average age 27. In 2016, 100 master's awarded. *Entrance requirements:* For master's, GMAT. Additional exam requirements/recommendations for international students: Required—TOEFL (minimum score 80 iBT), IELTS, PTE. *Application deadline:* Applications are processed on a rolling basis. Application fee: $50. Electronic applications accepted. Application fee is waived when completed online. *Expenses: Tuition:* Full-time $15,660; part-time $870 per credit hour. *Required fees:* $200; $85 per term. Tuition and fees vary according to program. *Financial support:* Research assistantships with partial tuition reimbursements, teaching assistantships with partial tuition reimbursements, career-related internships or fieldwork, Federal Work-Study, scholarships/grants, and unspecified assistantships available. Support available to part-time students. Financial award applicants required to submit FAFSA. *Unit head:* Darell Singleterry, Director, 203-932-1085, E-mail: dsingleterry@newhaven.edu. *Application contact:* Michelle Mason, Director of Graduate Enrollment, 203-932-7067, E-mail: mmason@newhaven.edu.
Website: http://www.newhaven.edu/business/programs/EMBA/

University of New Mexico, Anderson School of Management, Albuquerque, NM 87131. Offers EMBA, M Acct, MBA, MS, JD/M Acct, JD/MBA, MBA/MA, MBA/MEME, MBA/Pharm D. *Accreditation:* AACSB. *Program availability:* Part-time, evening/weekend. *Faculty:* 64 full-time (24 women), 23 part-time/adjunct (11 women). *Students:* 277 full-time (118 women), 357 part-time (182 women); includes 284 minority (10 Black or African American, non-Hispanic/Latino; 20 American Indian or Alaska Native, non-Hispanic/Latino; 23 Asian, non-Hispanic/Latino; 206 Hispanic/Latino; 25 Two or more races, non-Hispanic/Latino), 61 international. Average age 31. 338 applicants, 56% accepted, 176 enrolled. In 2016, 246 master's awarded. *Degree requirements:* For master's, minimum of 33 credit hours, capstone course, minimum GPA of 3.0. *Entrance requirements:* For master's, GMAT or GRE (minimum score of 500), minimum GPA of 3.0 on last 60 hours of college coursework including any post baccalaureate work. Additional exam requirements/recommendations for international students: Required—TOEFL (minimum score 550 paper-based; 79 iBT), IELTS (minimum score 6.5). *Application deadline:* For fall admission, 4/1 priority date for domestic and international students; for spring admission, 10/1 priority date for domestic and international students. Applications are processed on a rolling basis. Application fee: $50. Electronic applications accepted. *Expenses:* Contact institution. *Financial support:* In 2016–17, 101 students received support, including 30 fellowships (averaging $13,838 per year), 52 research assistantships with partial tuition reimbursements available (averaging $8,655 per year); career-related internships or fieldwork, Federal Work-Study, scholarships/grants, and unspecified assistantships also available. Support available to part-time students. Financial award application deadline: 6/1; financial award applicants required to submit FAFSA. *Faculty research:* Organizational and social aspects of accounting, international management of technology and entrepreneurship, business ethics and corporate social responsibility, marketing, information assurance and fraud. *Unit head:* Dr. Shawn Berman, Acting Dean, 505-277-1792, E-mail: sberman@unm.edu. *Application contact:* Lisa Beauchene, Student Recruitment Specialist, 505-277-6471, E-mail: andersonadvising@unm.edu.
Website: http://www.mgt.unm.edu

University of New Orleans, Graduate School, College of Business Administration, Program in Business Administration, New Orleans, LA 70148. Offers MBA.

Business Administration and Management—General

Accreditation: AACSB. *Degree requirements:* For master's, thesis optional. *Entrance requirements:* For master's, GMAT. Additional exam requirements/recommendations for international students: Required—TOEFL (minimum score 550 paper-based; 79 iBT). Electronic applications accepted.

University of North Alabama, College of Business, Florence, AL 35632-0001. Offers business administration (MBA), including accounting, enterprise resource planning systems, executive, finance, health care management, information systems, international business, project management. *Accreditation:* AACSB; ACBSP. *Program availability:* Part-time, 100% online, blended/hybrid learning. *Faculty:* 24 full-time (2 women), 6 part-time/adjunct (3 women). *Students:* 180 full-time (77 women), 411 part-time (199 women); includes 208 minority (84 Black or African American, non-Hispanic/Latino; 4 American Indian or Alaska Native, non-Hispanic/Latino; 106 Asian, non-Hispanic/Latino; 6 Hispanic/Latino; 8 Two or more races, non-Hispanic/Latino), 37 international. Average age 34. 263 applicants, 84% accepted, 173 enrolled. In 2016, 156 master's awarded. *Entrance requirements:* For master's, GMAT, GRE, minimum GPA of 2.75 in last 60 hours, 2.5 overall (on a 3.0 scale); 27 hours of course work in business and economics. Additional exam requirements/recommendations for international students: Required—TOEFL (minimum score 79 iBT), IELTS (minimum score 6), PTE (minimum score 54). *Application deadline:* Applications are processed on a rolling basis. Application fee: $50 ($100 for international students). Electronic applications accepted. *Expenses:* Tuition, state resident: full-time $2799; part-time $1866 per semester. Tuition, nonresident: full-time $5598; part-time $3732 per semester. *Required fees:* $915; $642 per semester. Tuition and fees vary according to course load. *Financial support:* In 2016–17, 114 students received support. Scholarships/grants available. Financial award application deadline: 2/1; financial award applicants required to submit FAFSA. *Unit head:* Dr. Gregory A. Carnes, Dean, 256-765-4261, Fax: 256-765-4170, E-mail: gacarnes@una.edu. *Application contact:* Hillary N. Coats, Graduate Admissions Coordinator, 256-765-4447, E-mail: graduate@una.edu.
Website: http://www.una.edu/business/

The University of North Carolina at Chapel Hill, Kenan-Flagler Business School, Doctoral Program in Business Administration, Chapel Hill, NC 27599. Offers accounting (PhD); finance (PhD); marketing (PhD); operations management (PhD); organizational behavior (PhD); strategy (PhD). *Accreditation:* AACSB. *Degree requirements:* For doctorate, thesis/dissertation. *Entrance requirements:* For doctorate, GMAT or GRE General Test. Electronic applications accepted. *Expenses:* Contact institution.

The University of North Carolina at Chapel Hill, Kenan-Flagler Business School, Executive MBA Programs, Chapel Hill, NC 27599. Offers MBA. *Accreditation:* AACSB. *Program availability:* Evening/weekend, online learning. *Degree requirements:* For master's, exams, project. *Entrance requirements:* For master's, GMAT, 5 years of full-time work experience, interview. Electronic applications accepted. *Expenses:* Contact institution.

The University of North Carolina at Chapel Hill, Kenan-Flagler Business School, MBA Program, Chapel Hill, NC 27599. Offers MBA, MBA/JD, MBA/MHA, MBA/MRP, MBA/MSIS. *Accreditation:* AACSB. *Degree requirements:* For master's, exams, practicum. *Entrance requirements:* For master's, GMAT, interview, minimum 2 years of work experience. Additional exam requirements/recommendations for international students: Required—TOEFL. Electronic applications accepted.

The University of North Carolina at Charlotte, Belk College of Business, Department of Management, Charlotte, NC 28223-0001. Offers business administration (MBA, DBA, PhD); business foundations (Graduate Certificate); management (Post-Master's Certificate). *Program availability:* Part-time, evening/weekend. *Faculty:* 13 full-time (4 women). *Students:* 88 full-time (35 women), 266 part-time (74 women); includes 54 minority (15 Black or African American, non-Hispanic/Latino; 15 Asian, non-Hispanic/Latino; 16 Hispanic/Latino; 8 Two or more races, non-Hispanic/Latino), 121 international. Average age 31. 225 applicants, 70% accepted, 98 enrolled. In 2016, 129 master's, 3 doctorates, 1 other advanced degree awarded. Terminal master's awarded for partial completion of doctoral program. *Degree requirements:* For doctorate, comprehensive exam, thesis/dissertation. *Entrance requirements:* For master's, GMAT or GRE, bachelor's degree from regionally-accredited college or university; at least three evaluations from persons familiar with applicant's personal and professional qualifications; essay describing applicant's experience and objectives; resume; for doctorate, GMAT (minimum score of 650) or GRE (minimum 700 on quantitative section, 500 on verbal), baccalaureate or master's degree in business, economics, or related field such as mathematical finance, mathematics, or physics with minimum undergraduate GPA of 3.5 (3.25 graduate); three letters of recommendation; statement of purpose; for other advanced degree, transcripts, minimum undergraduate GPA of 2.75, essay describing experience and objectives. Additional exam requirements/recommendations for international students: Required—TOEFL (minimum score 523 paper-based, 70 iBT) or IELTS (6.5). *Application deadline:* For fall admission, 1/15 for domestic and international students; for spring admission, 10/1 priority date for domestic and international students; for summer admission, 4/1 priority date for domestic and international students. Applications are processed on a rolling basis. Application fee: $75. Electronic applications accepted. *Expenses:* Contact institution. *Financial support:* In 2016–17, 1 student received support, including 1 research assistantship (averaging $17,600 per year); career-related internships or fieldwork, institutionally sponsored loans, scholarships/grants, and unspecified assistantships also available. Support available to part-time students. Financial award application deadline: 3/1; financial award applicants required to submit FAFSA. *Total annual research expenditures:* $139,850. *Unit head:* Dr. David J. Woehr, Department Chair, 704-687-7684, Fax: 704-687-1380, E-mail: dwoehr@uncc.edu. *Application contact:* Kathy B. Giddings, Director of Graduate Admissions, 704-687-5503, Fax: 704-687-1668, E-mail: gradadm@uncc.edu.
Website: https://belkcollege.uncc.edu/departments/management

The University of North Carolina at Greensboro, Graduate School, Bryan School of Business and Economics, Department of Business Administration, Greensboro, NC 27412-5001. Offers MBA, PMC, Postbaccalaureate Certificate, MS/MBA, MSN/MBA. *Accreditation:* AACSB. *Entrance requirements:* For master's, GMAT, GRE General Test, managerial experience. Additional exam requirements/recommendations for international students: Required—TOEFL. Electronic applications accepted.

The University of North Carolina at Pembroke, The Graduate School, School of Business, Pembroke, NC 28372-1510. Offers MBA. *Accreditation:* AACSB. *Program availability:* Part-time, evening/weekend. *Degree requirements:* For master's, thesis optional. *Entrance requirements:* For master's, GMAT, minimum GPA of 3.0 in major or 2.5 overall. Additional exam requirements/recommendations for international students: Required—TOEFL.

The University of North Carolina Wilmington, Cameron School of Business, Business Administration Program, Wilmington, NC 28403-3297. Offers business administration (MBA); international business administration (MBA). *Accreditation:* AACSB. *Program availability:* Part-time-only. *Faculty:* 41 full-time (11 women). *Students:* 87 full-time (43 women), 45 part-time (18 women); includes 19 minority (7 Black or African American, non-Hispanic/Latino; 1 American Indian or Alaska Native, non-Hispanic/Latino; 4 Asian, non-Hispanic/Latino; 4 Hispanic/Latino; 3 Two or more races, non-Hispanic/Latino), 17 international. Average age 31. 115 applicants, 83% accepted, 75 enrolled. In 2016, 30 master's awarded. *Degree requirements:* For master's, written case analysis, oral competency presentation. *Entrance requirements:* For master's, GMAT or GRE, 2 years of appropriate work experience, 3 letters of recommendation. Additional exam requirements/recommendations for international students: Required—TOEFL (minimum score 79 iBT), IELTS (minimum score 6.5). *Application deadline:* For fall admission, 6/1 for domestic students. Applications are processed on a rolling basis. Application fee: $60. Electronic applications accepted. *Expenses:* Contact institution. *Financial support:* Scholarships/grants and unspecified assistantships available. Financial award application deadline: 3/15; financial award applicants required to submit FAFSA. *Unit head:* Dr. Thom Porter, Interim MBA Director, 910-962-7466, E-mail: portert@uncw.edu. *Application contact:* Candace Wilhelm, Graduate Programs Coordinator, 910-962-3903, Fax: 910-962-2184, E-mail: wilhelmc@uncw.edu.
Website: http://www.csb.uncw.edu/mba/

University of North Dakota, Graduate School, College of Business and Public Administration, Business Administration Program, Grand Forks, ND 58202. Offers MBA, MBA/JD. *Accreditation:* AACSB. *Program availability:* Part-time, evening/weekend, online learning. *Degree requirements:* For master's, comprehensive exam, thesis or alternative, project. *Entrance requirements:* For master's, GMAT, minimum GPA of 3.25. Additional exam requirements/recommendations for international students: Required—TOEFL (minimum score 550 paper-based; 79 iBT), IELTS (minimum score 6.5). *Application deadline:* For fall admission, 8/1 priority date for domestic students, 5/1 priority date for international students; for spring admission, 12/1 priority date for domestic students, 9/1 priority date for international students. Applications are processed on a rolling basis. Application fee: $35. Electronic applications accepted. *Financial support:* Fellowships with full and partial tuition reimbursements, research assistantships with full tuition reimbursements, teaching assistantships with full and partial tuition reimbursements, Federal Work-Study, institutionally sponsored loans, scholarships/grants, health care benefits, tuition waivers (full and partial), and unspecified assistantships available. Support available to part-time students. Financial award application deadline: 3/15; financial award applicants required to submit FAFSA. *Unit head:* Dr. Timothy P. O'Keefe, Graduate Director, 701-777-2135, Fax: 701-777-2019, E-mail: mba@mail.business.und.edu. *Application contact:* Matt Anderson, Admissions Specialist, 701-777-2947, Fax: 701-777-3619, E-mail: matthew.anderson@gradschool.und.edu.

University of Northern Colorado, Graduate School, Monfort College of Business, Greeley, CO 80639. Offers accounting (MA); general business management (MBA); healthcare administration (MBA); human resources management (MBA). *Accreditation:* AACSB. *Unit head:* Donald Gudmundson, Dean, 970-351-2411, E-mail: don.gudmundson@unco.edu. *Application contact:* Linda Sisson, Graduate Student Admission Coordinator, 970-351-1807, Fax: 970-351-2371, E-mail: linda.sisson@unco.edu.
Website: http://mcb.unco.edu/

University of Northern Iowa, Graduate College, College of Business Administration, MBA Program, Cedar Falls, IA 50614. Offers MBA. *Accreditation:* AACSB. *Program availability:* Part-time, evening/weekend. *Entrance requirements:* For master's, GMAT (minimum score 500), minimum GPA of 3.0. Additional exam requirements/recommendations for international students: Required—TOEFL (minimum score 500 paper-based; 61 iBT). Electronic applications accepted.

University of North Florida, Coggin College of Business, MBA Program, Jacksonville, FL 32224. Offers accounting (MBA); construction management (MBA); e-commerce (MBA); economics (MBA); finance (MBA); human resource management (MBA); international business (MBA); logistics (MBA); management applications (MBA). *Accreditation:* AACSB. *Program availability:* Part-time, evening/weekend. *Faculty:* 16 full-time (4 women), 1 (woman) part-time/adjunct. *Students:* 105 full-time (50 women), 162 part-time (68 women); includes 57 minority (14 Black or African American, non-Hispanic/Latino; 1 American Indian or Alaska Native, non-Hispanic/Latino; 17 Asian, non-Hispanic/Latino; 18 Hispanic/Latino; 7 Two or more races, non-Hispanic/Latino), 41 international. Average age 28. 231 applicants, 46% accepted, 84 enrolled. In 2016, 114 master's awarded. *Entrance requirements:* For master's, GMAT or GRE, U.S. bachelor's degree from regionally-accredited university or equivalent foreign degree. Additional exam requirements/recommendations for international students: Required—TOEFL (minimum score 550 paper-based; 79 iBT). *Application deadline:* For fall admission, 8/1 priority date for domestic students, 5/1 for international students; for spring admission, 12/1 priority date for domestic students, 10/1 for international students; for summer admission, 4/29 priority date for domestic students, 2/1 for international students. Application fee: $30. Tuition and fees vary according to course load, campus/location and program. *Financial support:* In 2016–17, 22 students received support, including 1 research assistantship (averaging $2,501 per year); teaching assistantships, Federal Work-Study, and tuition waivers (partial) also available. Support available to part-time students. Financial award application deadline: 4/1; financial award applicants required to submit FAFSA. *Faculty research:* Performance measures, costing, and inventory issues in logistics and supply chain management; inter-organizational systems; international management and marketing practices; e-commerce; organizational learning and socialization processes. *Total annual research expenditures:* $17,654. *Unit head:* Dr. Parvez Ahmed, Graduate Program Director, 904-620-1678, E-mail: pahmed@unf.edu. *Application contact:* Amy Bishop, MSM Advisor, 904-620-2575, Fax: 904-620-2832, E-mail: coggin.students@unf.edu.
Website: http://www.unf.edu/graduateschool/academics/programs/MBA.aspx

University of North Georgia, Mike Cottrell College of Business, Dahlonega, GA 30597. Offers MBA. *Accreditation:* AACSB. *Program availability:* Part-time, evening/weekend. *Faculty:* 5 full-time (3 women), 1 part-time/adjunct (0 women). *Students:* 56 part-time (25 women); includes 11 minority (3 Black or African American, non-Hispanic/Latino; 6 Asian, non-Hispanic/Latino; 2 Hispanic/Latino). Average age 35. 69 applicants, 83% accepted, 43 enrolled. In 2016, 11 master's awarded. *Degree requirements:* For master's, capstone leadership experience. *Entrance requirements:* For master's, GRE or GMAT, references, resume. Additional exam requirements/recommendations for international students: Required—TOEFL (minimum score 550 paper-based; 79 iBT), IELTS (minimum score 6.5). *Application deadline:* For fall admission, 4/1 priority date for domestic and international students. Application fee: $40. Electronic applications accepted. *Expenses:* Contact institution. *Financial support:* Unspecified assistantships available. Financial award application deadline: 3/17; financial award applicants required to submit CSS PROFILE or FAFSA. *Unit head:* Dr. Donna Mayo, Dean, 706-864-1620, E-mail: donna.mayo@ung.edu. *Application contact:* Melinda Maxwell, Director of Graduate Admissions, 706-864-1543, E-mail: melinda.maxwell@ung.edu.
Website: http://www.ung.edu/graduate/MBA

University of North Texas, Robert B. Toulouse School of Graduate Studies, Denton, TX 76203-5459. Offers accounting (MS); applied anthropology (MA, MS); applied behavior analysis (Certificate); applied geography (MA); applied technology and performance improvement (M Ed, MS); art education (MA); art history (MA); art museum education (Certificate); arts leadership (Certificate); audiology (Au D); behavior analysis (MS); behavioral science (PhD); biochemistry and molecular biology (MS); biology (MA, MS); biomedical engineering (MS); business analysis (MS); chemistry (MS); clinical health psychology (PhD); communication studies (MA, MS); computer engineering (MS); computer science (MS); counseling (M Ed, MS), including clinical mental health counseling (MS), college and university counseling, elementary school counseling, secondary school counseling; creative writing (MA); criminal justice (MS); curriculum and instruction (M Ed); decision sciences (MBA); design (MA, MFA), including fashion design (MFA), innovation studies, interior design (MFA); early childhood studies (MS); economics (MS); educational leadership (M Ed, Ed D); educational psychology (MS, PhD), including family studies (MS), gifted and talented (MS), human development (MS), learning and cognition (MS), research, measurement and evaluation (MS); electrical engineering (MS); emergency management (MPA); engineering technology (MS); English (MA); English as a second language (MA); environmental science (MS); finance (MBA, MS); financial management (MPA); French (MA); health services management (MBA); higher education (M Ed, Ed D); history (MA, MS); hospitality management (MS); human resources management (MPA); information science (MS); information systems (PhD); information technologies (MBA); interdisciplinary studies (MA, MS); international studies (MA); international sustainable tourism (MS); jazz studies (MM); journalism (MA, MJ, Graduate Certificate), including interactive and virtual digital communication (Graduate Certificate), narrative journalism (Graduate Certificate), public relations (Graduate Certificate); kinesiology (MS); linguistics (MA); local government management (MPA); logistics (PhD); logistics and supply chain management (MBA); long-term care, senior housing, and aging services (MA); management (PhD); marketing (MBA); mathematics (MA, MS); mechanical and energy engineering (MS, PhD); music (MA), including ethnomusicology, music theory, musicology, performance; music composition (PhD); music education (MM Ed, PhD); nonprofit management (MPA); operations and supply chain management (MBA); performance (MM, DMA); philosophy (MA); political science (MA); professional and technical communication (MA); radio, television and film (MA, MFA); rehabilitation counseling (Certificate); sociology (MA); Spanish (MA); special education (M Ed); speech-language pathology (MA); strategic management (MBA); studio art (MFA); teaching (M Ed); MBA/MS. *Program availability:* Part-time, evening/weekend, online learning. Terminal master's awarded for partial completion of doctoral program. *Degree requirements:* For master's, variable foreign language requirement, comprehensive exam (for some programs), thesis (for some programs); for doctorate, variable foreign language requirement, comprehensive exam (for some programs), thesis/dissertation; for other advanced degree, variable foreign language requirement, comprehensive exam (for some programs). *Entrance requirements:* For master's and doctorate, GRE, GMAT. Additional exam requirements/ recommendations for international students: Required—TOEFL (minimum score 550 paper-based; 79 iBT). Electronic applications accepted.

University of North Texas at Dallas, Graduate School, Dallas, TX 75241. Offers accounting (MBA); counseling (M Ed, MS); criminal justice (MS); curriculum and instruction (M Ed); educational administration (M Ed); human resources and organizational behavior (MBA); public leadership (MS); strategic management (MBA).

University of Northwestern–St. Paul, Master of Business Administration Program, St. Paul, MN 55113-1598. Offers MBA. *Program availability:* Part-time, evening/weekend, online learning. *Application deadline:* Applications are processed on a rolling basis. Electronic applications accepted. *Application contact:* College of Adult and Graduate Studies Admissions, 651-631-5200, E-mail: gradstudies@unwsp.edu.
Website: https://www.unwsp.edu/web/graduate-studies/master-of-business-administration

University of Notre Dame, Mendoza College of Business, Executive Master of Business Administration Program, Notre Dame, IN 46556. Offers MBA. Program offered at the Stayer Center for Executive Education in Notre Dame, Indiana and also at Notre Dame Chicago Commons in downtown Chicago, IL. *Accreditation:* AACSB. *Program availability:* Part-time. *Faculty:* 12 full-time (2 women), 6 part-time/adjunct (0 women). *Students:* 164 full-time (32 women); includes 37 minority (14 Black or African American, non-Hispanic/Latino; 1 American Indian or Alaska Native, non-Hispanic/Latino; 7 Asian, non-Hispanic/Latino; 10 Hispanic/Latino; 1 Native Hawaiian or other Pacific Islander, non-Hispanic/Latino; 4 Two or more races, non-Hispanic/Latino), 2 international. Average age 38. In 2016, 113 master's awarded. *Entrance requirements:* For master's, five or more years of significant experience managing people, projects or business units. Additional exam requirements/recommendations for international students: Required—TOEFL. *Application deadline:* For fall admission, 10/15 for domestic students, 6/1 for international students; for winter admission, 11/1 for international students; for summer admission, 6/1 for domestic students. Applications are processed on a rolling basis. Application fee: $100. Electronic applications accepted. *Expenses:* Contact institution. *Financial support:* In 2016–17, 45 fellowships (averaging $9,388 per year) were awarded. Financial award application deadline: 6/1; financial award applicants required to submit FAFSA. *Faculty research:* Economic determinants of multinational firm behavior and foreign direct investment; psychology of ethical decision making - examining why individuals behave unethically; role of corporate governance on voluntary financial statement disclosures; proactive personality and behavior at work; strategy design and implementation. *Unit head:* Paul Slaggert, Director, Executive Education, 574-631-4856, Fax: 574-631-6783, E-mail: slaggert4@nd.edu. *Application contact:* Terron J. Phillips, Admissions Coordinator, 574-631-3188, Fax: 574-631-6783, E-mail: terron.j.phillips.146@nd.edu.
Website: https://mendoza.nd.edu

University of Notre Dame, Mendoza College of Business, Master of Business Administration Program, Notre Dame, IN 46556. Offers business analytics (MBA); business leadership (MBA); consulting (MBA); corporate finance (MBA); innovation and entrepreneurship (MBA); investments (MBA); marketing (MBA). *Accreditation:* AACSB. *Faculty:* 62 full-time (13 women), 26 part-time/adjunct (7 women). *Students:* 304 full-time (78 women); includes 38 minority (10 Black or African American, non-Hispanic/Latino; 7 Asian, non-Hispanic/Latino; 15 Hispanic/Latino; 6 Two or more races, non-Hispanic/ Latino), 80 international. Average age 27. 647 applicants, 41% accepted, 121 enrolled. In 2016, 177 master's awarded. *Entrance requirements:* For master's, GMAT or GRE, work experience, essay, four-slide presentation, two recommendations, transcripts from all colleges and/or universities attended, interview. Additional exam requirements/ recommendations for international students: Required—TOEFL (minimum score 600 paper-based; 100 iBT), IELTS (minimum score 7), PTE (minimum score 68). *Application deadline:* For fall admission, 11/1 for domestic and international students; for winter admission, 1/10 for domestic and international students; for spring admission, 2/21 for domestic and international students; for summer admission, 3/28 for domestic and international students. Application fee: $175. Electronic applications accepted. *Expenses:* Contact institution. *Financial support:* In 2016–17, 251 students received support, including 243 fellowships (averaging $26,417 per year); career-related internships or fieldwork, Federal Work-Study, institutionally sponsored loans, scholarships/grants, and unspecified assistantships also available. Financial award application deadline: 2/28; financial award applicants required to submit FAFSA. *Faculty research:* Market micro-structure; marketing and public policy; corporate finance and accounting; corporate governance and ethical behavior; high performing organizations. *Unit head:* Dr. Katherine Speiss, Associate Dean, Graduate Business Programs, 574-631-3759, E-mail: spiess.1@nd.edu. *Application contact:* Kristin McAndrew, Director of Admissions, Graduate Business Programs, 574-631-8488, E-mail: kmcadre@nd.edu.
Website: http://mendoza.nd.edu/programs/mba-programs/

University of Notre Dame, Mendoza College of Business, Master of Science in Management Program, Notre Dame, IN 46556. Offers MSM. *Faculty:* 12 full-time (3 women), 3 part-time/adjunct (1 woman). *Students:* 48 full-time (21 women); includes 10 minority (2 Black or African American, non-Hispanic/Latino; 1 American Indian or Alaska Native, non-Hispanic/Latino; 2 Asian, non-Hispanic/Latino; 5 Hispanic/Latino), 4 international. Average age 22. 173 applicants, 49% accepted, 48 enrolled. In 2016, 50 master's awarded. *Entrance requirements:* For master's, GMAT or GRE, essay, two recommendations, transcript from all colleges or universities attended, resume, interview. Additional exam requirements/recommendations for international students: Required—TOEFL (minimum score 600 paper-based; 100 iBT), IELTS (minimum score 7). *Application deadline:* For fall admission, 11/1 for domestic and international students; for winter admission, 1/17 for domestic and international students; for spring admission, 3/28 for domestic and international students. Application fee: $50. Electronic applications accepted. *Expenses:* Contact institution. *Financial support:* In 2016–17, 33 students received support, including 32 fellowships (averaging $16,438 per year). Financial award application deadline: 2/28; financial award applicants required to submit FAFSA. *Unit head:* Dr. Katherine Spiess, Associate Dean, Graduate Business Programs, 574-631-3759, E-mail: spiess.1@nd.edu. *Application contact:* Kristin McAndrew, Director of Admissions, Graduate Business Programs, 574-631-8488, E-mail: kmcadre@nd.edu.
Website: http://mendoza.nd.edu/programs/specialized-masters/ms-in-management/

University of Oklahoma, Price College of Business, Program in Business Administration, Norman, OK 73019. Offers accounting (PhD); business administration (MBA, PhD); entrepreneurship and economic development (PhD); finance (PhD); management and international business (PhD); management of information systems (PhD); marketing/supply chain (PhD); JD/MBA; MBA/MS. *Accreditation:* AACSB. *Program availability:* Part-time, evening/weekend. *Students:* 122 full-time (27 women), 146 part-time (30 women); includes 36 minority (5 Black or African American, non-Hispanic/Latino; 6 American Indian or Alaska Native, non-Hispanic/Latino; 8 Asian, non-Hispanic/Latino; 11 Hispanic/Latino; 6 Two or more races, non-Hispanic/Latino), 37 international. Average age 30. 261 applicants, 27% accepted, 59 enrolled. In 2016, 127 master's, 5 doctorates awarded. *Degree requirements:* For doctorate, comprehensive exam, thesis/dissertation. *Entrance requirements:* For master's, GMAT or GRE, resume, statement of goals; for doctorate, GMAT or GRE, resume, statement of goals, 3 letters of recommendation. Additional exam requirements/recommendations for international students: Required—TOEFL (minimum score 100 iBT) or IELTS (minimum score 7). *Application deadline:* For fall admission, 11/15 priority date for domestic and international students; for spring admission, 3/15 priority date for domestic and international students; for summer admission, 5/15 for domestic and international students. Application fee: $50 ($100 for international students). Electronic applications accepted. *Expenses:* Contact institution. *Financial support:* In 2016–17, 107 students received support, including 10 fellowships with partial tuition reimbursements available (averaging $3,295 per year); research assistantships with full and partial tuition reimbursements available, teaching assistantships with full and partial tuition reimbursements available, career-related internships or fieldwork, scholarships/grants, health care benefits, and unspecified assistantships also available. Support available to part-time students. Financial award application deadline: 6/1; financial award applicants required to submit FAFSA. *Faculty research:* Energy finance; international accounting; organizational behavior and entrepreneurship; management information systems; supply chain. *Unit head:* Laku Chidambaram, Associate Dean for Academic Programs and Engagement. *Application contact:* Director of MBA Admissions, 405-325-5623.
Website: http://www.ou.edu/content/price/divisions/graduate.html

University of Oregon, Graduate School, Charles H. Lundquist College of Business, Department of Management, Eugene, OR 97403. Offers PhD. *Accreditation:* AACSB. *Program availability:* Part-time. Terminal master's awarded for partial completion of doctoral program. *Degree requirements:* For doctorate, thesis/dissertation, 2 comprehensive exams. *Entrance requirements:* For doctorate, GMAT. Additional exam requirements/recommendations for international students: Required—TOEFL.

University of Oregon, Graduate School, Charles H. Lundquist College of Business, Department of Management: General Business, Eugene, OR 97403. Offers MBA. *Accreditation:* AACSB. *Entrance requirements:* For master's, GMAT. Additional exam requirements/recommendations for international students: Required—TOEFL.

University of Ottawa, Faculty of Graduate and Postdoctoral Studies, Telfer School of Management, Executive Business Administration Program, Ottawa, ON K1N 6N5, Canada. Offers EMBA. *Accreditation:* AACSB. *Program availability:* Evening/weekend. *Entrance requirements:* For master's, bachelor's degree or equivalent, minimum B average, business experience. Additional exam requirements/recommendations for international students: Recommended—TOEFL. Electronic applications accepted. *Expenses:* Contact institution.

University of Ottawa, Faculty of Graduate and Postdoctoral Studies, Telfer School of Management, MBA Program, Ottawa, ON K1N 6N5, Canada. Offers MBA. *Accreditation:* AACSB. *Program availability:* Part-time, evening/weekend. *Degree requirements:* For master's, thesis optional. *Entrance requirements:* For master's, GMAT, bachelor's degree or equivalent, minimum B average, minimum 2 years of work experience. Additional exam requirements/recommendations for international students: Recommended—TOEFL. Electronic applications accepted.

University of Pennsylvania, Wharton School, Management Department, Philadelphia, PA 19104. Offers MBA, PhD. *Accreditation:* AACSB. *Entrance requirements:* For master's, GMAT; for doctorate, GMAT or GRE. *Expenses: Tuition:* Full-time $31,068; part-time $5762 per course. *Required fees:* $3200; $336 per course. Full-time tuition and fees vary according to degree level, program and student level. Part-time tuition and fees vary according to course load, degree level and program. *Faculty research:* Cross-cultural leadership, international technology transfers, human resource management, financial services.

University of Pennsylvania, Wharton School, Wharton Doctoral Programs, Philadelphia, PA 19104. Offers accounting (PhD); applied economics (PhD); ethics and legal studies (PhD); finance (PhD); health care management and economics (PhD); management (PhD); marketing (PhD); operations and information management (PhD); statistics (PhD). *Accreditation:* AACSB. *Degree requirements:* For doctorate, thesis/ dissertation. *Entrance requirements:* For doctorate, GMAT or GRE, letters of recommendation. Additional exam requirements/recommendations for international students: Required—TOEFL, TWE. Electronic applications accepted. *Expenses: Tuition:* Full-time $31,068; part-time $5762 per course. *Required fees:* $3200; $336 per course. Full-time tuition and fees vary according to degree level, program and student level. Part-time tuition and fees vary according to course load, degree level and program.

University of Pennsylvania, Wharton School, The Wharton MBA Program, Philadelphia, PA 19104. Offers MBA, DMD/MBA, JD/MBA, MBA/MA, MBA/MS, MBA/ MSN, MBA/MSW, MBA/PhD, MD/MBA, VMD/MBA. *Accreditation:* AACSB. *Entrance requirements:* For master's, GMAT, interview, 2 letters of recommendation, resume/ curriculum vitae. Additional exam requirements/recommendations for international students: Required—TOEFL. Electronic applications accepted. *Expenses: Tuition:* Full-time $31,068; part-time $5762 per course. *Required fees:* $3200; $336 per course. Full-time tuition and fees vary according to degree level, program and student level. Part-time tuition and fees vary according to course load, degree level and program. *Faculty research:* Entrepreneurial studies, finance, management of technology.

University of Pennsylvania, Wharton School, The Wharton MBA Program for Executives, Wharton Executive MBA East, Philadelphia, PA 19104. Offers MBA. *Accreditation:* AACSB. *Program availability:* Evening/weekend. *Entrance requirements:* For master's, GMAT. Additional exam requirements/recommendations for international students: Recommended—TOEFL. *Expenses: Tuition:* Full-time $31,068; part-time $5762 per course. *Required fees:* $3200; $336 per course. Full-time tuition and fees vary according to degree level, program and student level. Part-time tuition and fees vary according to course load, degree level and program.

University of Pennsylvania, Wharton School, The Wharton MBA Program for Executives, Wharton Executive MBA West, Philadelphia, PA 19104. Offers MBA. *Accreditation:* AACSB. *Program availability:* Evening/weekend. *Entrance requirements:* For master's, GMAT. Additional exam requirements/recommendations for international students: Recommended—TOEFL. *Expenses: Tuition:* Full-time $31,068; part-time $5762 per course. *Required fees:* $3200; $336 per course. Full-time tuition and fees vary according to degree level, program and student level. Part-time tuition and fees vary according to course load, degree level and program.

University of Phoenix–Atlanta Campus, School of Business, Sandy Springs, GA 30350-4147. Offers accounting (MBA); business administration (MBA); global management (MBA); human resources management (MBA, MM); management (MM); marketing (MBA); public administration (MM). *Accreditation:* ACBSP. *Program availability:* Evening/weekend, online learning. *Degree requirements:* For master's, thesis (for some programs). *Entrance requirements:* For master's, minimum undergraduate GPA of 3.0, 3 years of work experience. Additional exam requirements/recommendations for international students: Required—TOEFL (minimum score 550 paper-based; 79 iBT).

University of Phoenix–Augusta Campus, School of Business, Augusta, GA 30909-4583. Offers accounting (MBA); business administration (MBA); business and management (MBA, MM); global management (MBA); human resources management (MBA, MM); management (MM); marketing (MBA); public administration (MBA, MM). *Accreditation:* ACBSP. *Program availability:* Online learning.

University of Phoenix–Bay Area Campus, School of Business, San Jose, CA 95134-1805. Offers accountancy (MS); accounting (MBA); business administration (MBA, DBA); energy management (MBA); global management (MBA); health care management (MBA); human resource management (MBA); human resources management (MM); management (MM); marketing (MBA); organizational leadership (DM); project management (MBA); public administration (MPA); technology management (MBA). *Accreditation:* ACBSP. *Program availability:* Evening/weekend, online learning. *Degree requirements:* For master's, thesis (for some programs). *Entrance requirements:* For master's, minimum undergraduate GPA of 3.0, 3 years of work experience. Additional exam requirements/recommendations for international students: Required—TOEFL (minimum score 550 paper-based; 79 iBT). Electronic applications accepted.

University of Phoenix–Central Valley Campus, School of Business, Fresno, CA 93720-1552. Offers accounting (MBA); business administration (MBA); global management (MBA); human resources management (MBA, MM); management (MM); marketing (MBA); public administration (MBA, MM). *Accreditation:* ACBSP.

University of Phoenix–Charlotte Campus, School of Business, Charlotte, NC 28273-3409. Offers accounting (MBA); business administration (MBA); global management (MBA). *Accreditation:* ACBSP. *Program availability:* Evening/weekend. *Degree requirements:* For master's, thesis (for some programs). *Entrance requirements:* For master's, minimum undergraduate GPA of 3.0, 3 years work experience. Additional exam requirements/recommendations for international students: Required—TOEFL (minimum score 550 paper-based; 79 iBT). Electronic applications accepted.

University of Phoenix–Colorado Campus, College of Information Systems and Technology, Lone Tree, CO 80124-5453. Offers e-business (MBA); management (MIS); technology management (MBA). *Program availability:* Evening/weekend, online learning. *Degree requirements:* For master's, thesis (for some programs). *Entrance requirements:* For master's, minimum undergraduate GPA of 3.0, 3 years of work experience. Additional exam requirements/recommendations for international students: Required—TOEFL (minimum score 550 paper-based; 79 iBT). Electronic applications accepted.

University of Phoenix–Colorado Campus, School of Business, Lone Tree, CO 80124-5453. Offers accountancy (MSA); accounting (MBA); business administration (MBA); e-business (MBA); global management (MBA); human resources management (MBA, MM); management (MM); marketing (MBA); public administration (MBA, MM). *Accreditation:* ACBSP. *Program availability:* Evening/weekend, online learning. *Degree requirements:* For master's, thesis (for some programs). *Entrance requirements:* For master's, minimum undergraduate GPA of 3.0, 3 years work experience. Additional exam requirements/recommendations for international students: Required—TOEFL (minimum score 550 paper-based; 79 iBT). Electronic applications accepted.

University of Phoenix–Colorado Springs Downtown Campus, School of Business, Colorado Springs, CO 80903. Offers accounting (MBA); business administration (MBA); global management (MBA); human resources management (MBA, MM); management (MM); marketing (MBA); public administration (MM). *Program availability:* Evening/weekend. *Degree requirements:* For master's, thesis (for some programs). *Entrance requirements:* For master's, minimum undergraduate GPA of 3.0, 3 years of work experience. Additional exam requirements/recommendations for international students: Required—TOEFL (minimum score 550 paper-based; 79 iBT). Electronic applications accepted.

University of Phoenix–Columbus Georgia Campus, School of Business, Columbus, GA 31909. Offers accounting (MBA); business administration (MBA); global management (MBA); human resources management (MBA, MM); management (MM); marketing (MBA); public administration (MBA). *Accreditation:* ACBSP. *Program availability:* Evening/weekend. *Degree requirements:* For master's, thesis (for some programs). *Entrance requirements:* For master's, minimum undergraduate GPA of 3.0, 3 years of work experience. Additional exam requirements/recommendations for international students: Required—TOEFL (minimum score 550 paper-based; 79 iBT). Electronic applications accepted.

University of Phoenix–Dallas Campus, School of Business, Dallas, TX 75251. Offers accounting (MBA); business administration (MBA); global management (MBA); human resources management (MBA, MM); management (MM); marketing (MBA); public administration (MBA, MM). *Accreditation:* ACBSP. *Program availability:* Evening/weekend, online learning. *Degree requirements:* For master's, thesis (for some programs). *Entrance requirements:* For master's, 3 years of work experience, minimum undergraduate GPA of 3.0. Additional exam requirements/recommendations for international students: Required—TOEFL (minimum score 550 paper-based; 79 iBT). Electronic applications accepted.

University of Phoenix–Hawaii Campus, School of Business, Honolulu, HI 96813-3800. Offers accounting (MBA); business administration (MBA); global management (MBA); human resources management (MBA, MM); management (MM); marketing (MBA); public administration (MBA, MM). *Accreditation:* ACBSP. *Program availability:* Evening/weekend. *Degree requirements:* For master's, thesis (for some programs). *Entrance requirements:* For master's, minimum undergraduate GPA of 3.0, 3 years of work experience. Additional exam requirements/recommendations for international students: Required—TOEFL (minimum score 550 paper-based; 79 iBT). Electronic applications accepted.

University of Phoenix–Houston Campus, School of Business, Houston, TX 77079-2004. Offers accounting (MBA); business administration (MBA); global management (MBA); human resources management (MBA, MM); management (MM); marketing (MBA); public administration (MBA, MM). *Accreditation:* ACBSP. *Program availability:* Evening/weekend, online learning. *Degree requirements:* For master's, thesis (for some programs). *Entrance requirements:* For master's, 3 years of work experience, minimum undergraduate GPA of 3.0. Additional exam requirements/recommendations for international students: Required—TOEFL (minimum score 550 paper-based; 79 iBT). Electronic applications accepted.

University of Phoenix–Jersey City Campus, School of Business, Jersey City, NJ 07310. Offers accounting (MBA); business administration (MBA); global management (MBA); human resources management (MBA, MM); management (MM); marketing (MBA); public administration (MBA, MM). *Accreditation:* ACBSP.

University of Phoenix–Las Vegas Campus, School of Business, Las Vegas, NV 89135. Offers accounting (MBA); business administration (MBA); global management (MBA); human resources management (MBA, MM); management (MM); marketing (MBA); public administration (MM). *Accreditation:* ACBSP. *Program availability:* Evening/weekend, online learning. *Degree requirements:* For master's, thesis (for some programs). *Entrance requirements:* For master's, minimum undergraduate GPA of 3.0, 3 years of work experience. Additional exam requirements/recommendations for international students: Required—TOEFL (minimum score 550 paper-based; 79 iBT). Electronic applications accepted.

University of Phoenix–New Mexico Campus, School of Business, Albuquerque, NM 87113-1570. Offers accounting (MBA); business administration (MBA); global management (MBA); human resources management (MBA, MM); management (MM); marketing (MBA). *Accreditation:* ACBSP. *Program availability:* Evening/weekend. *Degree requirements:* For master's, thesis (for some programs). *Entrance requirements:* For master's, 3 years of work experience, minimum undergraduate GPA of 3.0. Additional exam requirements/recommendations for international students: Required—TOEFL (minimum score 550 paper-based; 79 iBT). Electronic applications accepted.

University of Phoenix–North Florida Campus, College of Information Systems and Technology, Jacksonville, FL 32216-0959. Offers information systems (MIS); management (MIS). *Program availability:* Evening/weekend. *Degree requirements:* For master's, thesis (for some programs). *Entrance requirements:* For master's, minimum undergraduate GPA of 3.0, 3 years work experience. Additional exam requirements/recommendations for international students: Required—TOEFL (minimum score 550 paper-based; 79 iBT). Electronic applications accepted.

University of Phoenix–North Florida Campus, School of Business, Jacksonville, FL 32216-0959. Offers accounting (MBA); business administration (MBA); global management (MBA); human resources management (MBA, MM); management (MM); marketing (MBA); public administration (MBA, MM). *Accreditation:* ACBSP. *Program availability:* Evening/weekend. *Degree requirements:* For master's, thesis (for some programs). *Entrance requirements:* For master's, minimum undergraduate GPA of 3.0, 3 years work experience. Additional exam requirements/recommendations for international students: Required—TOEFL (minimum score 550 paper-based; 79 iBT). Electronic applications accepted.

University of Phoenix–Online Campus, School of Advanced Studies, Phoenix, AZ 85034-7209. Offers business administration (DBA); education (Ed S); educational leadership (Ed D), including curriculum and instruction, education technology, educational leadership; health administration (DHA); higher education administration (PhD); industrial/organizational psychology (PhD); nursing (PhD); organizational leadership (DM), including information systems and technology, organizational leadership. *Program availability:* Evening/weekend, online learning. *Degree requirements:* For doctorate, thesis/dissertation. *Entrance requirements:* Additional exam requirements/recommendations for international students: Required—TOEFL, TOEIC (Test of English as an International Communication), Berlitz Online English Proficiency Exam, PTE, or IELTS. Electronic applications accepted. *Expenses:* Contact institution.

University of Phoenix–Online Campus, School of Business, Phoenix, AZ 85034-7209. Offers accountancy (MS); accounting (MBA, Certificate); business administration (MBA); energy management (MBA); global management (MBA); health care management (MBA); human resource management (MBA, Certificate); human resources management (MM); management (MM); marketing (MBA, Certificate); project management (MBA, Certificate); public administration (MBA, MM); technology management (MBA). *Program availability:* Evening/weekend, online learning. *Entrance requirements:* Additional exam requirements/recommendations for international students: Required—TOEFL, TOEIC (Test of English as an International Communication), Berlitz Online English Proficiency Exam, PTE, or IELTS. Electronic applications accepted. *Expenses:* Contact institution.

University of Phoenix–Phoenix Campus, School of Business, Tempe, AZ 85282-2371. Offers accounting (MBA, MS, Certificate); business administration (MBA); energy management (MBA); global management (MBA); health care management (MBA); human resource management (MBA, Certificate); management (MM); marketing (MBA); project management (MBA); technology management (MBA). *Program availability:* Evening/weekend, online learning. *Entrance requirements:* Additional exam requirements/recommendations for international students: Required—TOEFL, TOEIC (Test of English as an International Communication), Berlitz Online English Proficiency Exam, PTE, or IELTS. Electronic applications accepted. *Expenses:* Contact institution.

University of Phoenix–Sacramento Valley Campus, College of Information Systems and Technology, Sacramento, CA 95833-4334. Offers management (MIS); technology management (MBA). *Program availability:* Evening/weekend. *Degree requirements:* For master's, thesis (for some programs). *Entrance requirements:* For master's, minimum undergraduate GPA of 3.0, 3 years work experience. Additional exam requirements/recommendations for international students: Required—TOEFL (minimum score 550 paper-based; 79 iBT). Electronic applications accepted.

University of Phoenix–Sacramento Valley Campus, School of Business, Sacramento, CA 95833-4334. Offers accounting (MBA); business administration (MBA); global management (MBA); human resources management (MBA, MM); management (MM); marketing (MBA); public administration (MBA, MM). *Accreditation:* ACBSP. *Program availability:* Evening/weekend. *Degree requirements:* For master's, thesis (for some programs). *Entrance requirements:* For master's, minimum undergraduate GPA of 3.0, 3 years work experience. Additional exam requirements/recommendations for

international students: Required—TOEFL (minimum score 550 paper-based; 79 iBT). Electronic applications accepted.

University of Phoenix–San Antonio Campus, School of Business, San Antonio, TX 78230. Offers accounting (MBA); business administration (MBA); e-business (MBA); global management (MBA); human resources management (MBA, MM); management (MM); marketing (MBA); public administration (MBA, MM). *Accreditation:* ACBSP.

University of Phoenix–San Diego Campus, College of Information Systems and Technology, San Diego, CA 92123. Offers management (MIS); technology management (MBA). *Program availability:* Evening/weekend. *Degree requirements:* For master's, thesis (for some programs). *Entrance requirements:* For master's, minimum undergraduate GPA of 3.0, 3 years work experience. Additional exam requirements/recommendations for international students: Required—TOEFL (minimum score 550 paper-based; 79 iBT). Electronic applications accepted.

University of Phoenix–San Diego Campus, School of Business, San Diego, CA 92123. Offers accounting (MBA); business administration (MBA); global management (MBA); human resources management (MBA, MM); management (MM); marketing (MBA); public administration (MBA). *Accreditation:* ACBSP. *Program availability:* Evening/weekend. *Degree requirements:* For master's, thesis (for some programs). *Entrance requirements:* For master's, 3 years of work experience, minimum undergraduate GPA of 3.0. Additional exam requirements/recommendations for international students: Required—TOEFL (minimum score 550 paper-based; 79 iBT). Electronic applications accepted.

University of Phoenix–Southern Arizona Campus, School of Business, Tucson, AZ 85711. Offers accountancy (MS); accounting (MBA); business administration (MBA); global management (MBA); human resources management (MBA); management (MM); marketing (MBA). *Accreditation:* ACBSP. *Program availability:* Evening/weekend. *Degree requirements:* For master's, thesis (for some programs). *Entrance requirements:* For master's, minimum undergraduate GPA of 3.0, 3 years of work experience. Additional exam requirements/recommendations for international students: Required—TOEFL (minimum score 550 paper-based; 79 iBT). Electronic applications accepted.

University of Phoenix–Southern California Campus, School of Business, Costa Mesa, CA 92626. Offers accounting (MBA); business administration (MBA); energy management (MBA); global management (MBA); health care management (MBA); human resource management (MBA); management (MM); marketing (MBA); project management (MBA); technology management (MBA). *Program availability:* Evening/weekend, online learning. *Entrance requirements:* Additional exam requirements/recommendations for international students: Required—TOEFL, TOEIC (Test of English as an International Communication), Berlitz Online English Proficiency Exam, PTE, or IELTS. Electronic applications accepted. *Expenses:* Contact institution.

University of Phoenix–South Florida Campus, College of Information Systems and Technology, Miramar, FL 33027-4145. Offers management (MIS); technology management (MBA). *Program availability:* Evening/weekend. *Degree requirements:* For master's, thesis (for some programs). *Entrance requirements:* For master's, minimum undergraduate GPA of 3.0, 3 years of work experience. Additional exam requirements/recommendations for international students: Required—TOEFL (minimum score 550 paper-based; 79 iBT). Electronic applications accepted.

University of Phoenix–South Florida Campus, School of Business, Miramar, FL 33027-4145. Offers accounting (MBA); business administration (MBA); global management (MBA); human resource management (MBA); human resources management (MM); management (MM); marketing (MBA); public administration (MBA, MM). *Accreditation:* ACBSP. *Program availability:* Evening/weekend. *Degree requirements:* For master's, thesis (for some programs). *Entrance requirements:* For master's, minimum undergraduate GPA of 3.0, 3 years of work experience. Additional exam requirements/recommendations for international students: Required—TOEFL (minimum score 550 paper-based; 79 iBT). Electronic applications accepted.

University of Phoenix–Utah Campus, School of Business, Salt Lake City, UT 84123-4642. Offers accounting (MBA); business administration (MBA); global management (MBA); human resource management (MBA, MM); management (MM); marketing (MBA); technology management (MBA). *Accreditation:* ACBSP. *Program availability:* Evening/weekend. *Degree requirements:* For master's, thesis (for some programs). *Entrance requirements:* For master's, minimum undergraduate GPA of 3.0, 3 years of work experience. Additional exam requirements/recommendations for international students: Required—TOEFL (minimum score 550 paper-based; 79 iBT). Electronic applications accepted.

University of Phoenix–Washington D.C. Campus, School of Business, Washington, DC 20001. Offers accountancy (MS); business administration (MBA, DBA); human resources management (MM); management (MM); organizational leadership (DM); public administration (MPA). *Accreditation:* ACBSP.

University of Phoenix–Western Washington Campus, School of Business, Tukwila, WA 98188. Offers MBA. *Accreditation:* ACBSP. *Program availability:* Evening/weekend. *Degree requirements:* For master's, thesis (for some programs). *Entrance requirements:* For master's, minimum undergraduate GPA of 3.0, 3 years of work experience. Additional exam requirements/recommendations for international students: Required—TOEFL (minimum score 550 paper-based; 79 iBT). Electronic applications accepted.

University of Pikeville, Coleman College of Business, Pikeville, KY 41501. Offers MBA. *Program availability:* Part-time, evening/weekend. *Faculty:* 4 part-time/adjunct (0 women). *Students:* 44 full-time (23 women), 1 part-time (0 women); includes 4 minority (all Black or African American, non-Hispanic/Latino), 6 international. Average age 28. In 2016, 17 master's awarded. *Degree requirements:* For master's, comprehensive exam (for some programs). *Entrance requirements:* For master's, official transcripts, two professional letters of recommendation, three years of work experience. *Application deadline:* For fall admission, 8/15 for domestic students, 7/1 for international students. Applications are processed on a rolling basis. Application fee: $50. *Expenses:* Contact institution. *Financial support:* Tuition waivers (full) and university employee grants available. Financial award application deadline: 2/15; financial award applicants required to submit FAFSA. *Unit head:* Dr. Howard V. Roberts, Dean, 606-218-5019, Fax: 606-218-5031, E-mail: howardroberts@upike.edu. *Application contact:* Cathy Maynard, Secretary, Business and Economics, 606-218-5020, Fax: 606-218-5031, E-mail: cathymaynard@upike.edu.
Website: http://www.upike.edu/Colleges/CCOB/

★ **University of Pittsburgh,** Katz Graduate School of Business, Doctoral Program in Business Administration, Pittsburgh, PA 15260. Offers accounting (PhD); business analytics and operations (PhD); finance (PhD); information systems and technology management (PhD); marketing (PhD); organizational behavior and human resources (PhD); strategic management (PhD). *Accreditation:* AACSB. *Program availability:* Evening/weekend. *Faculty:* 88 full-time (27 women), 42 part-time/adjunct (15 women). *Students:* 51 full-time (23 women), 1 part-time (0 women); includes 4 minority (1 Black or African American, non-Hispanic/Latino; 2 Asian, non-Hispanic/Latino; 1 Two or more races, non-Hispanic/Latino), 31 international. Average age 31. 344 applicants, 6% accepted, 9 enrolled. In 2016, 5 doctorates awarded. *Degree requirements:* For doctorate, comprehensive exam, thesis/dissertation, student teaching. *Entrance requirements:* For doctorate, GMAT or GRE, 3 recommendations, statement of purpose, transcripts of all previous course work and degrees. Additional exam requirements/recommendations for international students: Required—TOEFL (minimum score 100 iBT) or IELTS (minimum score 7.0). *Application deadline:* For fall admission, 4/1 priority date for domestic students, 2/1 priority date for international students. Applications are processed on a rolling basis. Application fee: $50. Electronic applications accepted. *Expenses:* Contact institution. *Financial support:* In 2016–17, 40 students received support, including 27 research assistantships with full tuition reimbursements available (averaging $26,000 per year), 9 teaching assistantships with full tuition reimbursements available (averaging $26,700 per year); Federal Work-Study, scholarships/grants, health care benefits, and unspecified assistantships also available. Financial award application deadline: 6/1; financial award applicants required to submit FAFSA. *Faculty research:* Accounting systems/financial reporting, corporate finance, shopper marketing/consumer behavior, management information systems, organizational behavior and entrepreneurship. *Total annual research expenditures:* $493,036. *Unit head:* Dr. Arjang A. Assad, Dean, 412-648-1556, Fax: 412-648-1552, E-mail: aassad@katz.pitt.edu. *Application contact:* Dr. Dennis Galletta, Director, 412-648-1699, Fax: 412-648-3633, E-mail: galletta@katz.pitt.edu.
Website: http://www.business.pitt.edu/katz/phd/

See Display on next page and Close-Up on page 189.

★ **University of Pittsburgh,** Katz Graduate School of Business, Executive MBA Program, Pittsburgh, PA 15260. Offers EMBA. *Accreditation:* AACSB. *Faculty:* 88 full-time (27 women), 42 part-time/adjunct (15 women). *Students:* 51 full-time (11 women); includes 8 minority (7 Asian, non-Hispanic/Latino; 1 Hispanic/Latino), 11 international. Average age 39. 56 applicants, 100% accepted, 46 enrolled. In 2016, 59 master's awarded. *Entrance requirements:* For master's, GMAT (for candidates with less than 10 years experience, GPA less than 3.0, or limited quantitative background), minimum 5 years of management experience, resume, 2 letters of recommendation, essay, interview. Additional exam requirements/recommendations for international students: Required—TOEFL (minimum score 100 iBT) or IELTS (minimum score 7.0). *Application deadline:* For winter admission, 12/1 for domestic students, 3/1 for international students; for spring admission, 4/1 for domestic and international students. Applications are processed on a rolling basis. Application fee: $50. Electronic applications accepted. *Expenses:* Contact institution. *Financial support:* Scholarships/grants available. Financial award applicants required to submit FAFSA. *Faculty research:* Accounting systems/financial reporting, corporate finance, shopper marketing/consumer behavior, management information systems, organizational behavior and entrepreneurship. *Total annual research expenditures:* $493,036. *Unit head:* Dr. Arjang A. Assad, Dean, 412-648-1556, Fax: 412-648-1552, E-mail: aassad@katz.pitt.edu. *Application contact:* William T. Valenta, Jr., Assistant Dean, MBA and Executive Programs, 412-648-1610, Fax: 412-648-1787, E-mail: valenta@pitt.edu.
Website: http://www.business.pitt.edu/katz/emba/

See Display on next page and Close-Up on page 189.

★ **University of Pittsburgh,** Katz Graduate School of Business, Master of Business Administration Programs, Pittsburgh, PA 15260. Offers finance (MBA); information systems (MBA); marketing (MBA); operations (MBA); organizational behavior and human resources (MBA); strategy, environment and organizations (MBA); MBA/JD; MBA/MSE. *Accreditation:* AACSB. *Program availability:* Part-time, evening/weekend, blended/hybrid learning. *Faculty:* 88 full-time (27 women), 42 part-time/adjunct (15 women). *Students:* 165 full-time (59 women), 330 part-time (103 women); includes 70 minority (29 Black or African American, non-Hispanic/Latino; 20 Asian, non-Hispanic/Latino; 13 Hispanic/Latino; 8 Two or more races, non-Hispanic/Latino), 73 international. Average age 29. 786 applicants, 41% accepted, 179 enrolled. In 2016, 477 master's awarded. *Degree requirements:* For master's, minimum GPA of 3.0. *Entrance requirements:* For master's, GMAT, GRE. Additional exam requirements/recommendations for international students: Required—TOEFL (minimum score 100 iBT) or IELTS (minimum score 7.0). *Application deadline:* For fall admission, 4/1 priority date for domestic students, 2/1 priority date for international students. Application fee: $50. Electronic applications accepted. *Expenses:* Contact institution. *Financial support:* In 2016–17, 110 students received support. Scholarships/grants available. Financial award application deadline: 6/1; financial award applicants required to submit FAFSA. *Faculty research:* Accounting systems/financial reporting, corporate finance, shopper marketing/consumer behavior, management information systems, organizational behavior and entrepreneurship. *Total annual research expenditures:* $493,036. *Unit head:* Dr. Arjang A. Assad, Dean, 412-648-1556, Fax: 412-648-1552, E-mail: aassad@katz.pitt.edu. *Application contact:* Thomas Keller, Director of MBA Admissions, 412-648-1700, Fax: 412-648-1659, E-mail: mba@katz.pitt.edu.
Website: http://www.business.pitt.edu/katz/mba/

See Display on next page and Close-Up on page 189.

★ **University of Pittsburgh,** Katz Graduate School of Business, MBA/Juris Doctor Program, Pittsburgh, PA 15260. Offers MBA/JD. *Program availability:* Evening/weekend. *Faculty:* 88 full-time (27 women), 42 part-time/adjunct (15 women). *Students:* 8 full-time (2 women); includes 1 minority (Black or African American, non-Hispanic/Latino), 1 international. Average age 28. 5 applicants, 80% accepted, 2 enrolled. *Entrance requirements:* Additional exam requirements/recommendations for international students: Required—TOEFL (minimum score 100 iBT) or IELTS (minimum score 7.0). *Application deadline:* For fall admission, 4/1 priority date for domestic students, 2/1 priority date for international students. Application fee: $50. Electronic applications accepted. *Expenses:* Contact institution. *Financial support:* Scholarships/grants available. Financial award application deadline: 6/1; financial award applicants required to submit FAFSA. *Faculty research:* Accounting systems/financial reporting, corporate finance, shopper marketing/consumer behavior, management information systems, organizational behavior and entrepreneurship. *Total annual research expenditures:* $493,036. *Unit head:* Dr. Arjang A. Assad, Dean, 412-648-1556, Fax: 412-648-1552, E-mail: aassad@katz.pitt.edu. *Application contact:* Thomas Keller, Director of MBA Admissions, 412-648-1700, Fax: 412-648-1659, E-mail: mba@katz.pitt.edu.
Website: http://www.business.pitt.edu/katz/mba/academics/programs/mba-jd.php

See Display on next page and Close-Up on page 189.

★ **University of Pittsburgh,** Katz Graduate School of Business, MBA/Master of International Business Dual Degree Program, Pittsburgh, PA 15260. Offers MBA/MIB. *Program availability:* Part-time, evening/weekend. *Faculty:* 88 full-time (27 women), 42 part-time/adjunct (15 women). *Students:* 1 (woman) full-time, 2 part-time (both women); includes 2 minority (both Black or African American, non-Hispanic/Latino). Average age 31. 13 applicants, 8% accepted. *Entrance requirements:* Additional exam requirements/recommendations for international students: Required—TOEFL (minimum score 100 iBT) or IELTS (minimum score 7.0). *Application deadline:* For fall admission, 4/1 priority date for domestic students, 2/1 priority date for international students. Application fee: $50. Electronic applications

accepted. Tuition and fees vary according to program. *Financial support:* Scholarships/grants available. Financial award application deadline: 6/1; financial award applicants required to submit FAFSA. *Faculty research:* Accounting systems/financial reporting, corporate finance, shopper marketing/consumer behavior, management information systems, organizational behavior and entrepreneurship. *Total annual research expenditures:* $493,036. *Unit head:* Dr. Arjang A. Assad, Dean, 412-648-1556, Fax: 412-648-1552, E-mail: aassad@katz.pitt.edu. *Application contact:* Thomas Keller, Director of MBA Admissions, 412-648-1700, Fax: 412-648-1659, E-mail: mba@katz.pitt.edu.
Website: http://www.business.pitt.edu/katz/mba/academics/programs/mba-mib.php

See Display below and Close-Up on page 189.

University of Pittsburgh, Katz Graduate School of Business, MBA/Master of International Development Joint Degree Program, Pittsburgh, PA 15260. Offers MID/MBA. *Accreditation:* AACSB. *Program availability:* Part-time, evening/weekend. *Faculty:* 88 full-time (27 women), 42 part-time/adjunct (15 women). *Students:* 1 (woman) full-time. Average age 26. 6 applicants, 33% accepted, 1 enrolled. *Entrance requirements:* Additional exam requirements/recommendations for international students: Required—TOEFL (minimum score 100 iBT) or IELTS (minimum score 7.0). *Application deadline:* For fall admission, 4/1 priority date for domestic students, 2/1 priority date for international students. Application fee: $50. Electronic applications accepted. Tuition and fees vary according to program. *Financial support:* Scholarships/grants available. Financial award application deadline: 6/1; financial award applicants required to submit FAFSA. *Faculty research:* Accounting systems/financial reporting, corporate finance, shopper marketing/consumer behavior, management information systems, organizational behavior and entrepreneurship. *Total annual research expenditures:* $493,036. *Unit head:* Dr. Arjang A. Assad, Dean, 412-648-1556, Fax: 412-648-1552, E-mail: aassad@katz.pitt.edu. *Application contact:* Thomas Keller, Director of MBA Admissions, 412-648-1700, Fax: 412-648-1659,
E-mail: mba@katz.pitt.edu.
Website: http://www.business.pitt.edu/katz/mba/academics/programs/mba-mid.php

See Display below and Close-Up on page 189.

University of Pittsburgh, Katz Graduate School of Business, MBA/Master of Public and International Affairs Dual-Degree Program, Pittsburgh, PA 15260. Offers MBA/MPIA. *Accreditation:* AACSB. *Program availability:* Part-time, evening/weekend. *Faculty:* 88 full-time (27 women), 42 part-time/adjunct (15 women). *Students:* 3 applicants, 33% accepted. *Entrance requirements:* Additional exam requirements/recommendations for international students: Required—TOEFL (minimum score 100 iBT) or IELTS (minimum score 7.0). *Application deadline:* For fall admission, 4/1 priority date for domestic students, 2/1 priority date for international students. Application fee: $50. Electronic applications accepted. Tuition and fees vary according to program. *Financial support:* Scholarships/grants available. Financial award application deadline: 6/1; financial award applicants required to submit FAFSA. *Faculty research:* Accounting systems/financial reporting, corporate finance, shopper marketing/consumer behavior, management information systems, organizational behavior and entrepreneurship. *Total annual research expenditures:* $493,036. *Unit head:* Dr. Arjang A. Assad, Dean, 412-648-1556, Fax: 412-648-1552, E-mail: aassad@katz.pitt.edu. *Application contact:* Thomas Keller, Director of MBA Admissions, 412-648-1700,
Fax: 412-648-1659, E-mail: mba@katz.pitt.edu.
Website: http://www.business.pitt.edu/katz/mba/academics/programs/mba-mpia.php

See Display below and Close-Up on page 189.

University of Pittsburgh, Katz Graduate School of Business, MBA/Master of Science in Engineering Joint Degree Program, Pittsburgh, PA 15260. Offers MBA/MSE. *Accreditation:* AACSB. *Program availability:* Part-time, evening/weekend. *Faculty:* 88 full-time (27 women), 42 part-time/adjunct (15 women). *Students:* 17 full-time (4 women), 18 part-time (0 women); includes 5 minority (1 Black or African American, non-Hispanic/Latino; 2 Hispanic/Latino; 2 Two or more races, non-Hispanic/Latino), 4 international. Average age 27. 42 applicants, 71% accepted, 18 enrolled. *Entrance requirements:* Additional exam requirements/recommendations for international students: Required—TOEFL (minimum score 100 iBT) or IELTS (minimum score 7.0). *Application deadline:* For fall admission, 4/1 priority date for domestic students, 2/1 priority date for international students. Application fee: $50. Electronic applications accepted. Tuition and fees vary according to program. *Financial support:* Scholarships/grants available. Financial award application deadline: 6/1; financial award applicants required to submit FAFSA. *Faculty research:* Accounting systems/financial reporting, corporate finance, shopper marketing/consumer behavior, management information systems, organizational behavior and entrepreneurship. *Total annual research expenditures:* $493,036. *Unit head:* Dr. Arjang A. Assad, Dean, 412-648-1556, Fax: 412-648-1552, E-mail: aassad@katz.pitt.edu. *Application contact:* Thomas Keller, Director of MBA Admissions, 412-648-1700, Fax: 412-648-1659,
E-mail: mba@katz.pitt.edu.
Website: http://www.business.pitt.edu/katz/mba/academics/programs/mba-msengineering.php

See Display below and Close-Up on page 189.

University of Portland, Dr. Robert B. Pamplin, Jr. School of Business, Portland, OR 97203-5798. Offers entrepreneurship (MBA); finance (MBA, MS); health care management (MBA); marketing (MBA); nonprofit management (EMBA); operations and technology management (MBA, MS); sustainability (MBA). *Accreditation:* AACSB. *Program availability:* Part-time, evening/weekend. *Entrance requirements:* For master's, GMAT, minimum GPA of 3.0, resume, 2 letters of recommendation. Additional exam requirements/recommendations for international students: Required—TOEFL (minimum score 570 paper-based; 89 iBT), IELTS (minimum score 7). *Expenses:* Contact institution.

University of Puerto Rico, Mayagüez Campus, Graduate Studies, College of Business Administration, Mayagüez, PR 00681-9000. Offers business administration (MBA); finance (MBA); human resources (MBA); industrial management (MBA). *Program availability:* Part-time, evening/weekend. *Faculty:* 24 full-time (10 women). *Students:* 37 full-time (24 women), 27 part-time (18 women); includes 60 minority (all Hispanic/Latino). Average age 25. 22 applicants, 68% accepted, 12 enrolled. In 2016, 6 master's awarded. *Degree requirements:* For master's, one foreign language, comprehensive exam, thesis (for some programs). *Entrance requirements:* For master's, GMAT or EXADEP, bachelor's degree with courses in calculus, microeconomics, accounting and statistics. Additional exam requirements/recommendations for international students: Required—TOEFL (minimum score 500 paper-based; 173 iBT), GMAT or EXADEP. *Application deadline:* For fall admission, 2/15 for domestic and international students; for spring admission, 9/15 for domestic and international students. Applications are processed on a rolling basis. Application fee: $25. Electronic applications accepted. *Expenses: Tuition, area resident:* Full-time $2466. *International tuition:* $7166 full-time. *Required fees:* $210. Tuition and fees vary according to course level, campus/location, program and student level. *Financial support:* In 2016–17, 6 students received support, including 5 research assistantships with full and partial tuition reimbursements available (averaging $4,489 per year), 4 teaching assistantships with full and partial tuition reimbursements available (averaging $4,605 per year); unspecified assistantships also available. *Faculty research:* Organizational studies, management, accounting, entrepreneurship, leadership and motivation. *Unit head:* Roberto L. Seijo, PhD, Department Head, 787-832-4040 Ext. 3887, Fax: 787-832-5320, E-mail: roberto.seijo@upr.edu. *Application contact:* Judith Valentín, Administrative Secretary,

787-265-3887, Fax: 787-832-5320, E-mail: grad.adem@uprm.edu.
Website: http://enterprise.uprm.edu/

University of Puerto Rico, Río Piedras Campus, College of Business Administration, San Juan, PR 00931-3300. Offers accounting (MBA); finance (MBA, PhD); general business (MBA); human resources management (MBA); international trade and business (MBA, PhD); marketing (MBA); operations management (MBA); quantitative methods (MBA). *Accreditation:* AACSB. *Program availability:* Part-time. *Degree requirements:* For master's, comprehensive exam, thesis or alternative, research project. *Entrance requirements:* For master's, GMAT or PAEG, minimum GPA of 3.0, letter of recommendation; for doctorate, GMAT, PAEG, minimum GPA of 3.0, master degree. *Faculty research:* Management.

University of Redlands, School of Business, Redlands, CA 92373-0999. Offers business (MBA); information technology (MS); management (MA). *Program availability:* Evening/weekend. *Entrance requirements:* For master's, minimum GPA of 3.0, 2 letters of recommendation. *Faculty research:* Human resources management, educational leadership, humanities, teacher education.

University of Regina, Faculty of Graduate Studies and Research, Kenneth Levene Graduate School of Business, Regina, SK S4S 0A2, Canada. Offers EMBA, M Admin, MBA, MHRM, Master's Certificate, PGD. *Program availability:* Part-time, evening/weekend. *Faculty:* 43 full-time (15 women), 7 part-time/adjunct (5 women). *Students:* 83 full-time (47 women), 76 part-time (54 women). 175 applicants, 41% accepted. In 2016, 57 master's, 13 other advanced degrees awarded. *Degree requirements:* For master's, project (for some programs). *Entrance requirements:* For master's, two years of relevant work experience (MHRM, M Admin); three years of relevant work experience (MBA); for other advanced degree, two years of relevant work experience (Master's Certificate); three years' relevant work experience (PGD). Additional exam requirements/recommendations for international students: Required—TOEFL (minimum score 580 paper-based; 80 iBT), IELTS (minimum score 6.5), PTE (minimum score 59). *Application deadline:* Applications are processed on a rolling basis. Application fee: $100. Electronic applications accepted. *Expenses:* Contact institution. *Financial support:* In 2016–17, 8 fellowships (averaging $6,000 per year), 7 teaching assistantships (averaging $2,501 per year) were awarded; career-related internships or fieldwork and scholarships/grants also available. Financial award application deadline: 6/15. *Faculty research:* Management of public and private sector organizations. *Unit head:* Dr. Andrew Gaudes, Dean, 306-585-4435, Fax: 306-585-4805, E-mail: andrew.gaudes@uregina.ca. *Application contact:* Dr. Gina Grandy, Associate Dean, Research and Graduate Programs/Director of Kenneth Levene Graduate School, 306-585-5647, Fax: 306-585-5361, E-mail: gina.grandy@uregina.ca.
Website: http://www.uregina.ca/business/levene/

★ **University of Rhode Island,** Graduate School, College of Business Administration, Kingston, RI 02881. Offers accounting (MS); business administration (PhD), including finance and insurance, marketing, supply chain management; finance (MBA, MS); general business (MBA); health care management (MBA); management (MBA); marketing (MBA); oceanography (MBA); strategic innovation (MBA); supply chain management (MBA); Pharm D/MBA. *Accreditation:* AACSB. *Program availability:* Part-time, evening/weekend. *Faculty:* 57 full-time (24 women). *Students:* 94 full-time (45 women), 166 part-time (84 women); includes 37 minority (6 Black or African American, non-Hispanic/Latino; 1 American Indian or Alaska Native, non-Hispanic/Latino; 22 Asian, non-Hispanic/Latino; 3 Hispanic/Latino; 5 Two or more races, non-Hispanic/Latino), 18 international. In 2016, 124 master's, 4 doctorates awarded. *Degree requirements:* For master's, comprehensive exam (for some programs), thesis optional; for doctorate, comprehensive exam, thesis/dissertation. *Entrance requirements:* For master's, GMAT or GRE, 2 letters of recommendation, resume; for doctorate, GMAT or GRE, 3 letters of recommendation, resume. Additional exam requirements/recommendations for international students: Required—TOEFL. *Application deadline:* For fall admission, 2/1 for domestic and international students. Application fee: $65. Electronic applications accepted. *Expenses:* Tuition, state resident: full-time $11,796; part-time $655 per credit. Tuition, nonresident: full-time $24,206; part-time $1345 per credit. *Required fees:* $1546; $44 per credit. One-time fee: $155 full-time; $35 part-time. *Financial support:* In 2016–17, 17 teaching assistantships with tuition reimbursements (averaging $15,347 per year) were awarded; research assistantships also available. Financial award application deadline: 2/1; financial award applicants required to submit FAFSA. *Unit head:* Dr. Maling Ebrahimpour, Dean, 401-874-4348, Fax: 401-874-4312, E-mail: mebrahimpour@uri.edu. *Application contact:* Lisa Lancellotta, Coordinator, MBA Programs, 401-874-4241, Fax: 401-874-4312, E-mail: mba@uri.edu.
Website: http://www.cba.uri.edu/

See Display on this page and Close-Up on page 191.

University of Richmond, Robins School of Business, University of Richmond, VA 23173. Offers MBA, JD/MBA. *Accreditation:* AACSB. *Program availability:* Part-time, evening/weekend. *Degree requirements:* For master's, capstone project. *Entrance requirements:* For master's, GMAT or GRE, minimum of two years' professional work experience. Additional exam requirements/recommendations for international students: Required—TOEFL (minimum score 600 paper-based; 100 iBT). Electronic applications accepted. *Faculty research:* Entrepreneurship, investments, auditing, consumer behavior, strategic management.

University of Rochester, Simon Business School, Doctoral Program in Business Administration, Rochester, NY 14627. Offers accounting (PhD); computer information systems (PhD); finance (PhD); marketing (PhD); operations management (PhD). *Accreditation:* AACSB. *Faculty:* 66 full-time (13 women), 22 part-time/adjunct (2 women). *Students:* 52 full-time (19 women); includes 2 minority (both Asian, non-Hispanic/Latino), 42 international. Average age 29. 210 applicants, 16% accepted, 15 enrolled. In 2016, 6 doctorates awarded. *Degree requirements:* For doctorate, comprehensive exam, thesis/dissertation, qualifying exam. *Entrance requirements:* For doctorate, GMAT or GRE. Additional exam requirements/recommendations for international students: Required—TOEFL. *Application deadline:* For fall admission, 1/5 for domestic and international students. Application fee: $100. Electronic applications accepted. *Expenses:* $1,800 per credit hour. *Financial support:* In 2016–17, 52 students received support. Fellowships, research assistantships, teaching assistantships, and tuition waivers (full) available. Financial award application deadline: 1/5. *Unit head:* Dr. Ron Kaniel, Committee Chair, 585-275-2959. *Application contact:* Sue Harris, PhD Administrator, 585-275-2959, E-mail: phdoffice@simon.rochester.edu.
Website: http://www.simon.rochester.edu/programs/phd/index.aspx

University of Rochester, Simon Business School, Executive MBA Program, Rochester, NY 14627. Offers MBA. *Program availability:* Part-time, evening/weekend. *Faculty:* 66 full-time (13 women), 22 part-time/adjunct (2 women). *Students:* 69 part-time (23 women); includes 13 minority (1 Black or African American, non-Hispanic/Latino; 8 Asian, non-Hispanic/Latino; 3 Hispanic/Latino; 1 Two or more races, non-Hispanic/Latino), 2 international. Average age 37. 38 applicants, 97% accepted, 34 enrolled. In 2016, 32 master's awarded. *Application deadline:* For spring admission, 6/15 for domestic students. Applications are processed on a rolling basis. Electronic applications accepted. *Expenses:* Contact institution. *Financial support:* In 2016–17, 49 students

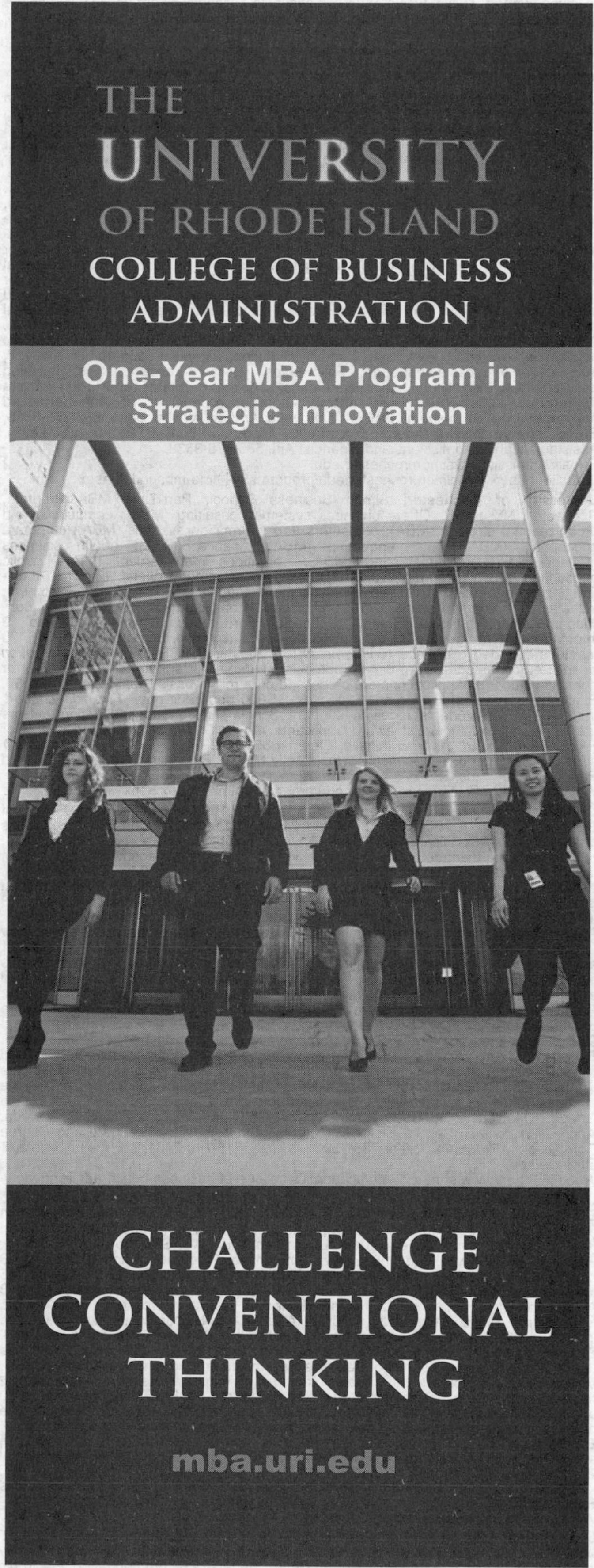

received support. Tuition waivers (partial) available. Financial award applicants required to submit CSS PROFILE or FAFSA. *Unit head:* Andrew Ainslie, Dean, 585-275-3316, E-mail: andrew.ainslie@simon.rochester.edu. *Application contact:* Molly Mesko, Executive Director, EMBA and Part-Time Programs, 585-275-4277, E-mail: molly.mesko@simon.rochester.edu.
Website: http://www.simon.rochester.edu/programs/executive-mba/index.aspx

University of Rochester, Simon Business School, Full-Time Master's Program in Business Administration, Rochester, NY 14627. Offers business systems consulting (MBA); competitive and organizational strategy (MBA); computers and information systems (MBA); corporate accounting (MBA); entrepreneurship (MBA); finance (MBA); health sciences management (MBA); marketing (MBA); operations management (MBA); public accounting (MBA). *Accreditation:* AACSB. *Program availability:* Part-time, evening/weekend. *Faculty:* 66 full-time (13 women), 22 part-time/adjunct (2 women). *Students:* 202 full-time (78 women); includes 50 minority (30 Black or African American, non-Hispanic/Latino; 10 Asian, non-Hispanic/Latino; 9 Hispanic/Latino; 1 Two or more races, non-Hispanic/Latino), 107 international. Average age 27. 915 applicants, 30% accepted, 86 enrolled. In 2016, 110 master's awarded. *Entrance requirements:* For master's, GMAT/GRE. Additional exam requirements/recommendations for international students: Required—TOEFL. *Application deadline:* For fall admission, 10/15 for domestic and international students; for winter admission, 1/5 for domestic and international students; for spring admission, 3/15 for domestic and international students; for summer admission, 5/15 for domestic and international students. Applications are processed on a rolling basis. Application fee: $150. Electronic applications accepted. *Expenses:* Contact institution. *Financial support:* In 2016–17, 190 students received support. Fellowships, research assistantships, teaching assistantships, institutionally sponsored loans, scholarships/grants, and tuition waivers (full and partial) available. Financial award application deadline: 1/5; financial award applicants required to submit FAFSA. *Unit head:* Andrew Ainslie, Dean, 585-275-3316, E-mail: andrew.ainslie@simon.rochester.edu. *Application contact:* Rebekah S. Lewin, Assistant Dean of Admissions and Financial Aid, 585-275-3533,
E-mail: admissions@simon.rochester.edu.
Website: http://www.simon.rochester.edu/programs/full-time-mba/index.aspx

University of Rochester, Simon Business School, Part-Time MBA Program, Rochester, NY 14627. Offers business systems consulting (MBA); competitive and organizational strategy (MBA); computers and information systems (MBA); corporate accounting (MBA); entrepreneurship (MBA); finance (MBA); health sciences management (MBA); marketing (MBA); operations management (MBA); public accounting (MBA). *Program availability:* Part-time, evening/weekend. *Faculty:* 66 full-time (13 women), 22 part-time/adjunct (2 women). *Students:* 185 part-time (65 women); includes 29 minority (6 Black or African American, non-Hispanic/Latino; 13 Asian, non-Hispanic/Latino; 8 Hispanic/Latino; 2 Two or more races, non-Hispanic/Latino), 9 international. Average age 32. 33 applicants, 100% accepted, 31 enrolled. In 2016, 70 master's awarded. *Entrance requirements:* For master's, GRE or GMAT. *Application deadline:* For fall admission, 8/1 for domestic students; for spring admission, 2/15 for domestic students. Applications are processed on a rolling basis. Application fee: $150. Electronic applications accepted. *Expenses:* $1,800 per credit hour. *Financial support:* In 2016–17, 75 students received support. Scholarships/grants and tuition waivers (partial) available. Financial award applicants required to submit CSS PROFILE or FAFSA. *Unit head:* Andrew Ainslie, Dean, 585-275-3316, E-mail: andrew.ainslie@simon.rochester.edu. *Application contact:* Molly Mesko, Executive Director, EMBA and Part-Time Programs, 585-275-4277, E-mail: molly.mesko@simon.rochester.edu.
Website: http://www.simon.rochester.edu/programs/ptmba/index.aspx

University of St. Francis, College of Business and Health Administration, School of Business, Joliet, IL 60435-6169. Offers accounting (MBA, Certificate); business analytics (MBA, Certificate); finance (MBA, Certificate); health administration (MBA); human resource management (MBA); logistics (Certificate); management (MBA, MSM); training and development (MBA); transportation and logistics (MBA). *Accreditation:* ACBSP. *Program availability:* Part-time, evening/weekend, 100% online, blended/hybrid learning. *Faculty:* 6 full-time (3 women), 12 part-time/adjunct (6 women). *Students:* 78 full-time (28 women), 110 part-time (62 women); includes 41 minority (22 Black or African American, non-Hispanic/Latino; 3 Asian, non-Hispanic/Latino; 15 Hispanic/Latino; 1 Two or more races, non-Hispanic/Latino), 8 international. Average age 36. 171 applicants, 44% accepted, 58 enrolled. In 2016, 62 master's, 3 other advanced degrees awarded. *Entrance requirements:* For master's, GMAT or 2 years of managerial experience. Additional exam requirements/recommendations for international students: Required—TOEFL (minimum score 550 paper-based; 79 iBT), IELTS (minimum score 6). *Application deadline:* Applications are processed on a rolling basis. Application fee: $30. Electronic applications accepted. Application fee is waived when completed online. *Expenses:* $798 per credit. *Financial support:* In 2016–17, 51 students received support. Career-related internships or fieldwork, scholarships/grants, tuition waivers (partial), and unspecified assistantships available. Support available to part-time students. Financial award applicants required to submit FAFSA. *Unit head:* Dr. Orlando Griego, Dean, 815-740-3395, Fax: 815-740-3537, E-mail: ogriego@stfrancis.edu. *Application contact:* Sandra Sloka, Director of Admissions for Graduate and Degree Completion Programs, 800-735-7500, Fax: 815-740-3431, E-mail: ssloka@stfrancis.edu.
Website: http://www.stfrancis.edu/academics/college-of-business-health-administration/

University of Saint Francis, Graduate School, Keith Busse School of Business and Entrepreneurial Leadership, Fort Wayne, IN 46808-3994. Offers business administration (MBA), including sustainability; environmental health (MEH); healthcare administration (MHA); organizational leadership (MOL). *Accreditation:* ACBSP. *Program availability:* Part-time, evening/weekend, online only, 100% online. *Faculty:* 6 full-time (3 women), 13 part-time/adjunct (4 women). *Students:* 77 full-time (51 women), 102 part-time (45 women); includes 40 minority (22 Black or African American, non-Hispanic/Latino; 3 Asian, non-Hispanic/Latino; 12 Hispanic/Latino; 1 Native Hawaiian or other Pacific Islander, non-Hispanic/Latino; 2 Two or more races, non-Hispanic/Latino). Average age 33. 71 applicants, 100% accepted, 46 enrolled. In 2016, 107 master's awarded. *Entrance requirements:* For master's, GMAT if cumulative GPA is below 2.75 with less than five years' professional work experience), minimum undergraduate GPA of 2.75; statement of professional goals; resume. Additional exam requirements/recommendations for international students: Required—TOEFL (minimum score 550 paper-based) or IELTS (minimum score 6.5). *Application deadline:* Applications are processed on a rolling basis. Application fee: $0. Electronic applications accepted. *Expenses:* $475 per credit hour. *Financial support:* Application deadline: 3/10; applicants required to submit FAFSA. *Unit head:* Dr. Karen Palumbo, Director of Virtual Campus Business Programs, 260-399-7700 Ext. 8312, Fax: 260-399-8174, E-mail: kpalumbo@sf.edu. *Application contact:* Kyle Richardson, Enrollment Services Specialist, 260-399-7700 Ext. 6310, Fax: 260-399-8152, E-mail: krichardson@sf.edu.
Website: http://business.sf.edu/graduate/

University of Saint Joseph, Department of Business Administration, West Hartford, CT 06117-2700. Offers management (MS). *Program availability:* Part-time, evening/weekend. *Entrance requirements:* For master's, 2 letters of recommendation. Electronic applications accepted. Application fee is waived when completed online. *Expenses: Tuition:* Full-time $14,580; part-time $729 per credit hour. *Required fees:* $920; $46 per credit hour. Tuition and fees vary according to course load, degree level and program.

University of Saint Mary, Graduate Programs, Program in Business Administration, Leavenworth, KS 66048-5082. Offers enterprise risk management (MBA); finance (MBA); general management (MBA); health care management (MBA); human resource management (MBA); marketing and advertising management (MBA). *Program availability:* Part-time, evening/weekend, 100% online, blended/hybrid learning. *Students:* 201 full-time (110 women), 62 part-time (38 women); includes 83 minority (29 Black or African American, non-Hispanic/Latino; 3 American Indian or Alaska Native, non-Hispanic/Latino; 14 Asian, non-Hispanic/Latino; 32 Hispanic/Latino; 1 Native Hawaiian or other Pacific Islander, non-Hispanic/Latino; 4 Two or more races, non-Hispanic/Latino), 7 international. Average age 34. In 2016, 73 master's awarded. *Degree requirements:* For master's, thesis. *Entrance requirements:* For master's, minimum undergraduate GPA of 2.75, official transcripts, two letters of recommendation. *Application deadline:* Applications are processed on a rolling basis. Application fee: $25. Electronic applications accepted. *Expenses:* $595 per hour. *Unit head:* Rick Gunter, Director, 913-319-3007. *Application contact:* Mark Harvey, Program Manager, 913-319-3007, E-mail: mark.harvey@stmary.edu.
Website: http://www.stmary.edu/success/Grad-Program/Master-of-Business-Administration-MBA.aspx

University of St. Thomas, Cameron School of Business, Houston, TX 77006-4696. Offers MBA, MCTM, MIB, MSA, MSF. *Program availability:* Part-time, evening/weekend. *Faculty:* 26 full-time (8 women), 7 part-time/adjunct (2 women). *Students:* 178 full-time (86 women), 222 part-time (127 women); includes 182 minority (38 Black or African American, non-Hispanic/Latino; 36 Asian, non-Hispanic/Latino; 104 Hispanic/Latino; 4 Two or more races, non-Hispanic/Latino), 115 international. Average age 31. 144 applicants, 97% accepted, 72 enrolled. In 2016, 164 master's awarded. *Degree requirements:* For master's, capstone (for some programs), additional course requirements for those sitting for state accountancy exam. *Entrance requirements:* For master's, minimum GPA of 2.5, 3 letters of recommendation. Additional exam requirements/recommendations for international students: Required—TOEFL (minimum score 550 paper-based; 79 iBT), IELTS (minimum score 6.5), PTE (minimum score 53). *Application deadline:* For fall admission, 7/15 for domestic and international students; for winter admission, 7/15 for domestic and international students; for spring admission, 11/15 for domestic students, 10/15 for international students. Applications are processed on a rolling basis. Application fee: $35. Electronic applications accepted. *Expenses: Tuition:* Full-time $20,934; part-time $1163 per credit hour. *Required fees:* $81 per semester. One-time fee: $100. Part-time tuition and fees vary according to course level, course load, campus/location and program. *Financial support:* In 2016–17, 56 students received support, including research assistantships with partial tuition reimbursements available (averaging $3,000 per year); Federal Work-Study, scholarships/grants, unspecified assistantships, and state work-study, institutional employment also available. Support available to part-time students. Financial award application deadline: 4/15; financial award applicants required to submit FAFSA. *Unit head:* Dr. Beena George, Dean, 713-525-2100, Fax: 713-525-2110, E-mail: cameron@stthom.edu. *Application contact:* Fran Wilson Mayes, Academic Coordinator, 713-525-2100, Fax: 713-525-2110, E-mail: cameron@stthom.edu.
Website: http://www.stthom.edu/Academics/Cameron_School_of_Business/Index.aqf

University of St. Thomas, Graduate Studies, Opus College of Business, Executive UST MBA Program, Minneapolis, MN 55403. Offers MBA. *Program availability:* Part-time. *Entrance requirements:* For master's, five years of significant management or leadership experience. *Application deadline:* For fall admission, 7/15 for domestic and international students. Applications are processed on a rolling basis. Application fee: $100. Electronic applications accepted. *Expenses:* Contact institution. *Unit head:* Sandy Bauer, Coordinator, 651-962-8800, Fax: 651-962-4235, E-mail: execmba@stthomas.edu.
Website: http://www.stthomas.edu/execmba

University of St. Thomas, Graduate Studies, Opus College of Business, Full-time UST MBA Program, Minneapolis, MN 55403. Offers MBA. *Entrance requirements:* For master's, GMAT, GRE. Additional exam requirements/recommendations for international students: Required—TOEFL (minimum score 90 iBT), IELTS (minimum score 7), or Michigan English Language Assessment Battery. *Application deadline:* For fall admission, 12/15 priority date for domestic and international students. Applications are processed on a rolling basis. Application fee: $60. Electronic applications accepted. *Expenses: Tuition:* Full-time $19,354; part-time $1320 per credit. One-time fee: $214. Tuition and fees vary according to course load, degree level, program and reciprocity agreements. *Financial support:* Scholarships/grants, tuition waivers (full and partial), and unspecified assistantships available. Financial award application deadline: 4/15. *Unit head:* Sandy Bauer, Coordinator, 651-962-8800. *Application contact:* Tiffany Cork, Director of Recruiting and Admissions, 651-962-8801, Fax: 651-962-4129, E-mail: ustmba@stthomas.edu.
Website: http://www.stthomas.edu/mba

University of St. Thomas, Graduate Studies, Opus College of Business, Part-time UST MBA Program, Minneapolis, MN 55403. Offers MBA. *Program availability:* Part-time, evening/weekend. *Entrance requirements:* For master's, GMAT. Additional exam requirements/recommendations for international students: Required—TOEFL (minimum score 80 iBT), IELTS, or Michigan English Language Assessment Battery. *Application deadline:* For fall admission, 5/1 priority date for domestic students; for spring admission, 11/1 priority date for domestic students; for summer admission, 4/1 priority date for domestic students. Applications are processed on a rolling basis. Application fee: $60. Electronic applications accepted. *Expenses: Tuition:* Full-time $19,354; part-time $1320 per credit. One-time fee: $214. Tuition and fees vary according to course load, degree level, program and reciprocity agreements. *Financial support:* Scholarships/grants available. Financial award application deadline: 6/1. *Unit head:* Corey Eakins, Program Director, 651-962-4228, Fax: 651-962-4129. *Application contact:* Tiffany Cork, Director of Recruiting and Admissions, 651-962-8801, Fax: 651-962-4129.
Website: http://www.stthomas.edu/eveningmba

University of San Diego, School of Business, MBA Program, San Diego, CA 92110-2492. Offers MBA, JD/MBA. *Program availability:* Part-time, evening/weekend. *Students:* 100 full-time (35 women), 63 part-time (27 women); includes 32 minority (3 Black or African American, non-Hispanic/Latino; 11 Asian, non-Hispanic/Latino; 11 Hispanic/Latino; 3 Native Hawaiian or other Pacific Islander, non-Hispanic/Latino; 4 Two or more races, non-Hispanic/Latino), 54 international. Average age 30. In 2016, 92 master's awarded. *Degree requirements:* For master's, community service, capstone project. *Entrance requirements:* For master's, GMAT (minimum score 600 for full-time, 550 for part-time), minimum GPA of 3.0, minimum 2 years of full-time professional experience. Additional exam requirements/recommendations for international students: Required—TOEFL (minimum score 580 paper-based; 92 iBT), TWE. *Application deadline:* For fall admission, 11/1 priority date for domestic students; for spring admission, 10/1 priority date for domestic students. Applications are processed on a rolling basis. Application fee: $80. Electronic applications accepted. *Financial support:* In 2016–17, 122 students received support. Career-related internships or fieldwork,

Federal Work-Study, institutionally sponsored loans, and unspecified assistantships available. Support available to part-time students. Financial award application deadline: 4/1; financial award applicants required to submit FAFSA. *Faculty research:* Exchange rate forecasting, corporate governance, performance of private equity funds, economic geography, food banking. *Unit head:* Dr. Manzur Rahman, Academic Director, MBA Programs, 619-260-2388, E-mail: mba@sandiego.edu. *Application contact:* Monica Mahon, Associate Director of Graduate Admissions, 619-260-4524, Fax: 619-260-4158, E-mail: grads@sandiego.edu.
Website: http://www.sandiego.edu/business/graduate/mba/

University of San Diego, School of Business, Program in Executive Leadership, San Diego, CA 92110-2492. Offers MS. *Program availability:* Evening/weekend. *Students:* 20 full-time (6 women), 19 part-time (10 women); includes 10 minority (3 Black or African American, non-Hispanic/Latino; 1 Asian, non-Hispanic/Latino; 6 Hispanic/Latino). Average age 41. In 2016, 17 master's awarded. *Entrance requirements:* For master's, GMAT (taken within the last 5 years) or professional product that demonstrates ability to analyze complex problems. Additional exam requirements/recommendations for international students: Required—TOEFL (minimum score 580 paper-based; 92 iBT), TWE. *Application deadline:* For fall admission, 5/1 for domestic students. Applications are processed on a rolling basis. Application fee: $80. Electronic applications accepted. *Financial support:* In 2016–17, 8 students received support. Career-related internships or fieldwork and scholarships/grants available. Financial award application deadline: 4/1; financial award applicants required to submit FAFSA. *Unit head:* Director, MS in Executive Leadership, 619-260-4860, E-mail: msel@sandiego.edu. *Application contact:* Monica Mahon, Associate Director of Graduate Admissions, 619-260-4524, Fax: 619-260-4158, E-mail: grads@sandiego.edu.
Website: http://www.sandiego.edu/business/programs/ms-executive-leadership/

University of San Francisco, School of Management, Executive Master of Business Administration Program, San Francisco, CA 94117. Offers MBA. *Accreditation:* AACSB. *Program availability:* Part-time, evening/weekend. *Faculty:* 7 full-time (3 women), 2 part-time/adjunct (1 woman). *Students:* 42 full-time (25 women); includes 18 minority (5 Black or African American, non-Hispanic/Latino; 8 Asian, non-Hispanic/Latino; 5 Hispanic/Latino). Average age 38. 38 applicants, 95% accepted, 24 enrolled. In 2016, 16 master's awarded. *Entrance requirements:* For master's, GMAT (for applicants with less than eight years of post-undergraduate professional experience), resume demonstrating minimum of eight years of professional work experience, transcripts from each college or university attended, two letters of recommendation, essays, interview. Additional exam requirements/recommendations for international students: Required—TOEFL (minimum score 600 paper-based, 100 iBT), IELTS (minimum score 7) or PTE (minimum score 68). *Application deadline:* Applications are processed on a rolling basis. Application fee: $55. Electronic applications accepted. *Expenses:* Contact institution. *Financial support:* In 2016–17, 22 students received support. Scholarships/grants available. Financial award application deadline: 3/2; financial award applicants required to submit FAFSA. *Unit head:* Dr. Richard Stackman, Chair, 415-422-6939, E-mail: emba@usfca.edu. *Application contact:* Office of Graduate Recruiting and Admissions, 415-422-2221, Fax: 415-422-6315, E-mail: management@usfca.edu.
Website: http://www.usfca.edu/emba

University of San Francisco, School of Management, Master of Business Administration Program, San Francisco, CA 94117. Offers entrepreneurship and innovation (MBA); finance (MBA); marketing (MBA); organization development (MBA); DDS/MBA; JD/MBA; MBA/MAPS. *Accreditation:* AACSB. *Program availability:* Part-time, evening/weekend. *Faculty:* 17 full-time (6 women), 5 part-time/adjunct (2 women). *Students:* 146 full-time (70 women), 2 part-time (1 woman); includes 50 minority (5 Black or African American, non-Hispanic/Latino; 27 Asian, non-Hispanic/Latino; 15 Hispanic/Latino; 1 Native Hawaiian or other Pacific Islander, non-Hispanic/Latino; 2 Two or more races, non-Hispanic/Latino), 51 international. Average age 29. 282 applicants, 63% accepted, 70 enrolled. In 2016, 91 master's awarded. *Entrance requirements:* For master's, GMAT or GRE, resume (two years of professional work experience required for part-time students, preferred for full-time), transcripts from each college or university attended, two letters of recommendation, personal statement, interview. Additional exam requirements/recommendations for international students: Required—TOEFL (minimum score 600 paper-based, 100 iBT), IELTS (minimum score 7) or PTE (minimum score 68). *Application deadline:* For fall admission, 6/5 for domestic students, 5/15 for international students; for spring admission, 11/30 for domestic students. Application fee: $55. Electronic applications accepted. *Expenses: Tuition:* Full-time $23,310; part-time $1295 per credit. Tuition and fees vary according to course load, degree level, campus/location and program. *Financial support:* In 2016–17, 60 students received support. Fellowships and scholarships/grants available. Financial award application deadline: 3/2; financial award applicants required to submit FAFSA. *Faculty research:* International financial markets, technology transfer licensing, international marketing, strategic planning. *Total annual research expenditures:* $50,000. *Unit head:* Dr. Frank Fletcher, Director, 415-422-2221, Fax: 415-422-6315, E-mail: management@usfca.edu. *Application contact:* Office of Graduate Recruiting and Admissions, 415-422-2221, Fax: 415-422-6315, E-mail: management@usfca.edu.
Website: http://www.usfca.edu/mba

University of Saskatchewan, College of Graduate Studies and Research, Edwards School of Business, Saskatoon, SK S7N 5A2, Canada. Offers M Sc, MBA, MP Acc. *Program availability:* Part-time. *Degree requirements:* For master's, thesis (for some programs). *Entrance requirements:* For master's, GMAT. Additional exam requirements/recommendations for international students: Required—TOEFL.

The University of Scranton, Kania School of Management, Program in Business Administration, Scranton, PA 18510. Offers accounting (MBA); finance (MBA); general business administration (MBA); health care management (MBA); international business (MBA); management information systems (MBA); marketing (MBA); operations management (MBA). *Accreditation:* AACSB. *Program availability:* Part-time, evening/weekend, 100% online. *Entrance requirements:* For master's, GMAT (for MBA). *Faculty research:* Financial markets, strategic impact of total quality management, internal accounting controls, consumer preference, information systems and the Internet.

University of Sioux Falls, Vucurevich School of Business, Sioux Falls, SD 57105-1699. Offers entrepreneurial leadership (MBA); general management (MBA); health care management (MBA); marketing (MBA). *Program availability:* Part-time, evening/weekend. *Degree requirements:* For master's, project. *Entrance requirements:* For master's, minimum GPA of 3.0. Additional exam requirements/recommendations for international students: Required—TOEFL. *Expenses:* Contact institution.

University of South Africa, College of Economic and Management Sciences, Pretoria, South Africa. Offers accounting (D Admin, D Com); accounting science (DA); auditing (D Admin, D Com); business administration (M Tech); business economics (D Admin); business leadership (DBL); business management (D Admin, D Com); economic management analysis (M Tech); economics (D Admin, D Com, PhD); human resource development (M Tech); industrial psychology (D Admin, D Com, PhD); logistics (D Com); marketing (M Tech); public administration (D Admin, D Com, DPA, PhD); public management (M Tech); quantitative management (D Admin, D Com); real estate (M Tech); statistics (D Admin, PhD); tourism management (D Admin, D Com); transport economics (D Admin, D Com).

University of South Africa, Graduate School of Business Leadership, Pretoria, South Africa. Offers MBA, MBL, DBL.

University of South Alabama, Mitchell College of Business, Program in Business Administration, Mobile, AL 36688. Offers MBA, DBA. *Accreditation:* AACSB. *Program availability:* Part-time, evening/weekend. *Faculty:* 8 full-time (1 woman). *Students:* 67 full-time (24 women), 7 part-time (1 woman); includes 15 minority (8 Black or African American, non-Hispanic/Latino; 1 American Indian or Alaska Native, non-Hispanic/Latino; 3 Asian, non-Hispanic/Latino; 2 Hispanic/Latino; 1 Two or more races, non-Hispanic/Latino), 6 international. Average age 33. 87 applicants, 37% accepted, 24 enrolled. In 2016, 22 master's, 3 doctorates awarded. *Degree requirements:* For master's, comprehensive exam; for doctorate, comprehensive exam, three manuscripts. *Entrance requirements:* For master's, GMAT (minimum score of 450 with minimum score of 3.0 in Analytical Writing section), minimum undergraduate GPA of 3.0; for doctorate, MBA/specialized master's degree, 5 years of professional experience, 3 letters of reference, curriculum vitae, interview. Additional exam requirements/recommendations for international students: Required—TOEFL (minimum score 525 paper-based; 71 iBT). *Application deadline:* For fall admission, 7/15 for domestic students, 6/15 for international students; for summer admission, 1/31 for domestic students. Application fee: $35. Electronic applications accepted. *Expenses:* Contact institution. *Financial support:* Research assistantships and unspecified assistantships available. Support available to part-time students. Financial award application deadline: 5/31; financial award applicants required to submit FAFSA. *Unit head:* Dr. Bob Wood, Dean of Business, 251-460-7167, Fax: 251-460-6529, E-mail: bgwood@southalabama.edu. *Application contact:* Dr. Alex Sharland, Assistant Dean and Director of Graduate Studies, 251-460-6412, Fax: 251-460-6529, E-mail: mcobgraduate@southalabama.edu.

University of South Carolina, The Graduate School, Darla Moore School of Business, Columbia, SC 29208. Offers accountancy (M Acc), including business measurement and assurance; business administration (MBA, PhD), including business administration (PhD), economics (PhD); economics (MA); human resources (MHR); international business administration (IMBA); JD/M Acc; JD/MA; JD/MHR. *Accreditation:* AACSB. *Program availability:* Part-time, evening/weekend, online learning. *Degree requirements:* For doctorate, one foreign language, thesis/dissertation. *Entrance requirements:* For master's, GMAT, GRE, minimum GPA of 3.0; for doctorate, GMAT or GRE. Additional exam requirements/recommendations for international students: Required—TOEFL (minimum score 600 paper-based). Electronic applications accepted. *Expenses:* Contact institution. *Faculty research:* Finance, marketing, strategic management, international management, operations.

University of South Carolina Aiken, Program in Business Administration for STEM and Liberal Arts, Aiken, SC 29801. Offers MBA. *Program availability:* Part-time-only, evening/weekend. *Faculty:* 4 full-time (2 women). *Students:* 1 full-time (0 women), 22 part-time (12 women); includes 1 minority (Black or African American, non-Hispanic/Latino), 1 international. Average age 34. 11 applicants, 82% accepted, 7 enrolled. *Degree requirements:* For master's, capstone course(s). *Entrance requirements:* For master's, GMAT or GRE. Additional exam requirements/recommendations for international students: Required—TOEFL (minimum score 550 paper-based; 80 iBT). *Application deadline:* For fall admission, 8/1 for domestic and international students; for spring admission, 12/3 for domestic and international students. Applications are processed on a rolling basis. Application fee: $45. Electronic applications accepted. *Expenses:* Tuition, state resident: full-time $12,798; part-time $533 per credit hour. Tuition, nonresident: full-time $27,408; part-time $1142 per credit hour. *Required fees:* $11 per credit hour. $25 per semester. Full-time tuition and fees vary according to course load. *Financial support:* In 2016–17, 8 students received support. Scholarships/grants and tuition waivers (partial) available. Support available to part-time students. Financial award application deadline: 3/15; financial award applicants required to submit FAFSA. *Faculty research:* Corporate financial distress; corporate restructuring and control; and valuation. *Unit head:* Dr. Michael J. Fekula, Dean for School of Business Administration, 803-641-3340, E-mail: mickf@usca.edu. *Application contact:* Dan Robb, Associate Vice Chancellor for Enrollment Management, 803-641-3487, Fax: 803-641-3727, E-mail: danr@usca.edu.
Website: http://www.usca.edu/soba/graduate-program/

The University of South Dakota, Graduate School, Beacom School of Business, Department of Business Administration, Vermillion, SD 57069. Offers business administration (MBA); business analytics (MBA); health services administration (MBA); JD/MBA. *Accreditation:* AACSB. *Program availability:* Part-time, evening/weekend, online learning. *Degree requirements:* For master's, thesis or alternative. *Entrance requirements:* For master's, GMAT, minimum GPA of 2.7, resume. Additional exam requirements/recommendations for international students: Required—TOEFL (minimum score 550 paper-based; 79 iBT). Electronic applications accepted. *Expenses:* Contact institution.

The University of South Dakota, Graduate School, College of Arts and Sciences, Program in Administrative Studies, Vermillion, SD 57069. Offers addiction studies (MSA); criminal justice studies (MSA); health services administration (MSA); human resources (MSA); interdisciplinary studies (MSA); long term care administration (MSA); organizational leadership (MSA). *Program availability:* Part-time, evening/weekend, online learning. *Degree requirements:* For master's, thesis or alternative. *Entrance requirements:* For master's, 3 years of work or experience, minimum GPA of 2.7, resume. Additional exam requirements/recommendations for international students: Required—TOEFL (minimum score 550 paper-based; 79 iBT). Electronic applications accepted.

University of Southern California, Graduate School, Marshall School of Business, Los Angeles, CA 90089. Offers M Acc, MBA, MBT, MBV, MMM, MS, PhD, DDS/MBA, JD/MBT, MBA/Ed D, MBA/M Pl, MBA/MD, MBA/MRED, MBA/MS, MBA/MSW, MBA/Pharm D. *Accreditation:* AACSB. *Degree requirements:* For doctorate, thesis/dissertation. *Entrance requirements:* For master's, GMAT and/or CPA Exam; for doctorate, GMAT or GRE. Additional exam requirements/recommendations for international students: Required—TOEFL. Electronic applications accepted.

University of Southern Indiana, Graduate Studies, Romain College of Business, Program in Business Administration, Evansville, IN 47712-3590. Offers accounting (MBA); business administration (MBA); data analytics (MBA); engineering management (MBA); health administration (MBA); human resources (MBA). *Accreditation:* AACSB. *Program availability:* Part-time, evening/weekend, 100% online, blended/hybrid learning. *Faculty:* 22 full-time (4 women), 2 part-time/adjunct (0 women). *Students:* 149 full-time (70 women), 64 part-time (29 women); includes 25 minority (17 Black or African American, non-Hispanic/Latino; 1 Asian, non-Hispanic/Latino; 5 Hispanic/Latino; 2 Two or more races, non-Hispanic/Latino), 5 international. Average age 32. In 2016, 36 master's awarded. *Entrance requirements:* For master's, GMAT or GRE, minimum GPA of 2.5, resume, 3 professional references. Additional exam requirements/recommendations for international students: Required—TOEFL (minimum score 550 paper-based; 79 iBT), IELTS (minimum score 6). *Application deadline:* For fall admission, 8/1 for domestic students, 3/1 priority date for international students. Applications are processed on a rolling basis. Application fee: $40. Electronic applications accepted. *Expenses:* Tuition, state resident: full-time $8497. Tuition,

nonresident: full-time $16,691. *Required fees:* $500. *Financial support:* In 2016–17, 8 students received support. Federal Work-Study, scholarships/grants, tuition waivers (full and partial), and unspecified assistantships available. Financial award application deadline: 3/1; financial award applicants required to submit FAFSA. *Unit head:* Dr. Jack E. Smothers, Program Director, 812-461-5248, E-mail: jesmothers@usi.edu. *Application contact:* Michelle Simmons, MBA Program Assistant, 812-464-1926, Fax: 812-465-1044, E-mail: masimmons3@usi.edu.
Website: http://www.usi.edu/business/mba

University of Southern Maine, College of Management and Human Service, School of Business, Portland, ME 04104-9300. Offers accounting (MBA); business administration (MBA); finance (MBA); health management and policy (MBA); sustainability (MBA); JD/MBA; MBA/MSA; MBA/MSN; MS/MBA. *Accreditation:* AACSB. *Program availability:* Part-time, evening/weekend. *Entrance requirements:* For master's, GMAT or GRE, minimum AACSB index of 1100. Additional exam requirements/recommendations for international students: Required—TOEFL (minimum score 550 paper-based; 79 iBT). Electronic applications accepted. *Faculty research:* Economic development, management information systems, real options, system dynamics, simulation.

University of Southern Maine, Lewiston-Auburn College, Program in Leadership Studies, Portland, ME 04103. Offers creative leadership/global strategies (CGS); leadership studies (MA). *Program availability:* Part-time, online learning.

University of Southern Mississippi, Graduate School, College of Business, Program in Business Administration, Hattiesburg, MS 39406-0001. Offers business administration (MBA); sport security management (MBA). *Accreditation:* AACSB. *Program availability:* Part-time, evening/weekend. *Degree requirements:* For master's, comprehensive exam. *Entrance requirements:* For master's, GMAT, minimum GPA of 2.75 on last 60 hours. Additional exam requirements/recommendations for international students: Required—TOEFL, IELTS. *Application deadline:* For fall admission, 7/15 priority date for domestic students, 7/15 for international students; for spring admission, 11/15 priority date for domestic students, 11/15 for international students. Application fee: $60. Electronic applications accepted. *Expenses:* Tuition, area resident: Full-time $15,708; part-time $437 per credit hour. *Financial support:* Research assistantships with full and partial tuition reimbursements, teaching assistantships with full tuition reimbursements, Federal Work-Study, institutionally sponsored loans, scholarships/grants, health care benefits, and unspecified assistantships available. Support available to part-time students. Financial award application deadline: 3/15; financial award applicants required to submit FAFSA. *Faculty research:* Inflation accounting, self-esteem training, international trade policy, health care marketing, ethics in strategic planning. *Unit head:* Heather Adams Sison, Advisor, 601-266-3496, E-mail: h.l.adams@usm.edu.

University of South Florida, Muma College of Business, Department of Management, Tampa, FL 33620-9951. Offers management (MS), including human resources. *Accreditation:* AACSB. *Program availability:* Part-time, online learning. *Faculty:* 3 full-time (2 women). *Students:* 22 full-time (5 women), 8 part-time (4 women); includes 1 minority (Black or African American, non-Hispanic/Latino), 23 international. Average age 26. 40 applicants, 38% accepted, 13 enrolled. In 2016, 48 master's awarded. Terminal master's awarded for partial completion of doctoral program. *Degree requirements:* For master's, comprehensive exam, thesis (for some programs). *Entrance requirements:* For master's, GMAT, letters of recommendation, resume, statement of purpose, relevant work experience. Additional exam requirements/recommendations for international students: Required—TOEFL (minimum score 550 paper-based; 79 iBT) or IELTS (minimum score 6.5). *Application deadline:* For fall admission, 6/1 for domestic students, 2/1 for international students; for spring admission, 10/15 for domestic students, 7/1 for international students. Application fee: $30. Electronic applications accepted. *Expenses:* Tuition, state resident: full-time $7766; part-time $431.43 per credit hour. Tuition, nonresident: full-time $15,789; part-time $877.17 per credit hour. *Required fees:* $37 per term. *Financial support:* In 2016–17, 1 student received support, including 1 research assistantship with tuition reimbursement available (averaging $9,002 per year), 3 teaching assistantships with tuition reimbursements available (averaging $9,002 per year); tuition waivers also available. Financial award applicants required to submit FAFSA. *Faculty research:* Leadership and employment relations, time management, personal motivation, crew resource management in aviation, psychology of gambling, organizational culture, issues of fairness, employment law, marketing strategy/implementation, organizational diversity, ethics, environmentally-friendly business practices, green business, sustainable business plans, institutional theory, social movement theory, diffusion of innovations, stakeholder human resources management, social responsibility. *Unit head:* Dr. Sally Fuller, Interim Department Chair/Associate Professor, 813-974-1766, Fax: 813-905-9964, E-mail: sfuller@usf.edu. *Application contact:* Carrie Fischer, Office Manager, 813-974-1714, Fax: 813-974-9964, E-mail: cfischer1@usf.edu.
Website: http://www.usf.edu/business/graduate/masters/management/

University of South Florida, Muma College of Business, Lynn Pippenger School of Accountancy, Tampa, FL 33620-9951. Offers accountancy (M Acc), including audit/systems, tax; business administration (PhD), including accounting. *Accreditation:* AACSB. *Program availability:* Part-time, evening/weekend. *Faculty:* 10 full-time (4 women). *Students:* 67 full-time (36 women), 34 part-time (16 women); includes 22 minority (2 Black or African American, non-Hispanic/Latino; 3 Asian, non-Hispanic/Latino; 15 Hispanic/Latino; 2 Two or more races, non-Hispanic/Latino), 9 international. Average age 26. 89 applicants, 56% accepted, 41 enrolled. In 2016, 67 master's, 2 doctorates awarded. Terminal master's awarded for partial completion of doctoral program. *Degree requirements:* For master's, comprehensive exam, thesis or alternative; for doctorate, comprehensive exam, thesis/dissertation. *Entrance requirements:* For master's, GMAT, minimum overall GPA of 3.0 in general upper-level coursework and in upper-level accounting coursework (minimum of 21 hours at a U.S. accredited program within past 5 years); for doctorate, GMAT or GRE, personal statement, recommendations, interview. Additional exam requirements/recommendations for international students: Required—TOEFL (minimum score 550 paper-based; 79 iBT) or IELTS (minimum score 6.5). *Application deadline:* For fall admission, 1/2 for domestic and international students; for spring admission, 10/1 for domestic students, 9/15 for international students; for summer admission, 2/15 for domestic students, 1/15 for international students. Application fee: $30. Electronic applications accepted. *Expenses:* Tuition, state resident: full-time $7766; part-time $431.43 per credit hour. Tuition, nonresident: full-time $15,789; part-time $877.17 per credit hour. *Required fees:* $37 per term. *Financial support:* In 2016–17, 41 students received support, including 18 teaching assistantships with tuition reimbursements available (averaging $12,273 per year); scholarships/grants, health care benefits, and unspecified assistantships also available. Financial award applicants required to submit FAFSA. *Faculty research:* Auditing, auditor independence, audit committee decisions, fraud detection and reporting, disclosure effects, effects of information technology on accounting, governmental accounting/auditing, accounting information systems, data modeling and design methodologies for accounting systems, auditing computer-based systems, expert systems, group support systems in accounting, fair value accounting issues, corporate governance, financial accounting, financial reporting quality. *Unit head:* Dr. Uday Murthy, Interim Director, School of Accountancy, 813-974-6516, Fax: 813-974-6528, E-mail: umurthy@usf.edu. *Application contact:* Christy Ward, Advisor and Graduation Specialist, 813-974-4290, Fax: 813-974-2797, E-mail: cward@usf.edu.
Website: http://business.usf.edu/departments/accountancy/

University of South Florida, St. Petersburg, Kate Tiedemann College of Business, St. Petersburg, FL 33701. Offers MBA. *Accreditation:* AACSB. *Program availability:* Part-time. *Entrance requirements:* For master's, GMAT (minimum score of 500), bachelor's degree with minimum GPA of 3.0 overall or in upper two years from regionally-accredited institution; resume. Additional exam requirements/recommendations for international students: Required—TOEFL (minimum score 550 paper-based; 79 iBT); Recommended—IELTS. Electronic applications accepted.

University of South Florida Sarasota-Manatee, College of Business, Sarasota, FL 34243. Offers MBA. *Accreditation:* AACSB. *Program availability:* Part-time, evening/weekend. *Faculty:* 10 full-time (1 woman). *Students:* 32 full-time (14 women), 56 part-time (26 women); includes 27 minority (6 Black or African American, non-Hispanic/Latino; 1 American Indian or Alaska Native, non-Hispanic/Latino; 10 Asian, non-Hispanic/Latino; 10 Hispanic/Latino). Average age 33. 79 applicants, 47% accepted, 30 enrolled. In 2016, 15 master's awarded. *Degree requirements:* For master's, capstone project. *Entrance requirements:* For master's, GMAT (minimum score 500) or GRE (minimum score 1050 if taken before August 1, 2011 or 300 if taken after August 1, 2011), two years of full-time work experience (preferred); resume; two letters of recommendation; statement of purpose. Additional exam requirements/recommendations for international students: Required—TOEFL (minimum score 550 paper-based; 79 iBT), IELTS (minimum score 6.5). *Application deadline:* For fall admission, 3/1 priority date for domestic students, 3/1 for international students; for spring admission, 10/1 priority date for domestic students, 10/1 for international students. Applications are processed on a rolling basis. Application fee: $30. Electronic applications accepted. *Expenses:* $453.81 per credit hour tuition and fees. *Financial support:* In 2016–17, 6 students received support. Federal Work-Study, scholarships/grants, health care benefits, and unspecified assistantships available. Support available to part-time students. Financial award application deadline: 3/1; financial award applicants required to submit FAFSA. *Faculty research:* Mergers and acquisitions, customer loyalty, employment discrimination, measurement of quality, efficiency of markets. *Unit head:* Dr. James M. Curran, Dean, 941-359-4605, Fax: 941-359-4367, E-mail: jmcurran@sar.usf.edu. *Application contact:* Andy Telatovich, Director, Admissions, 941-359-4330, E-mail: atelatovich@sar.usf.edu.
Website: http://usfsm.edu/college-of-business/

The University of Tampa, Sykes College of Business, Tampa, FL 33606-1490. Offers accounting (MS); entrepreneurship (MBA); finance (MBA, MS); information systems management (MBA); innovation management (MBA); international business (MBA); marketing (MBA, MS); nonprofit management (MBA). *Accreditation:* AACSB. *Program availability:* Part-time, evening/weekend. *Faculty:* 43 full-time (19 women), 9 part-time/adjunct (3 women). *Students:* 438 full-time (176 women), 126 part-time (57 women); includes 37 minority (22 Black or African American, non-Hispanic/Latino; 11 Asian, non-Hispanic/Latino; 4 Two or more races, non-Hispanic/Latino), 203 international. Average age 28. 1,305 applicants, 39% accepted, 192 enrolled. In 2016, 266 master's awarded. *Degree requirements:* For master's, capstone. *Entrance requirements:* For master's, GMAT or GRE, official transcripts from all colleges and/or universities previously attended, resume, personal statement, letters of recommendation. Additional exam requirements/recommendations for international students: Required—TOEFL (minimum score 577 paper-based, 90 iBT) or IELTS (7.5). *Application deadline:* Applications are processed on a rolling basis. Application fee: $40. Electronic applications accepted. *Expenses:* $588 per credit tuition, $40 per term fees. *Financial support:* In 2016–17, 116 students received support. Career-related internships or fieldwork, scholarships/grants, and unspecified assistantships available. Financial award applicants required to submit FAFSA. *Faculty research:* Job market signaling, on-line shopping behaviors and social media, the Tampa Bay economy, digital literacy, entrepreneurship in small businesses. *Unit head:* Dr. Natasha F. Veltri, Associate Dean, 813-253-6289, E-mail: nveltri@ut.edu. *Application contact:* Chanelle Cox, Staff Assistant, Admissions for Graduate and Continuing Studies, 813-253-6249, E-mail: ccox@ut.edu.
Website: http://www.ut.edu/business/

The University of Tennessee, Graduate School, College of Business Administration, Program in Business Administration, Knoxville, TN 37996. Offers accounting (PhD); finance (MBA, PhD); logistics and transportation (MBA, PhD); management (PhD); marketing (MBA, PhD); operations management (MBA); professional business administration (MBA); statistics (PhD); JD/MBA; MS/MBA; Pharm D/MBA. Pharm D/MBA offered jointly with The University of Tennessee Health Science Center. *Accreditation:* AACSB. *Program availability:* Online learning. *Degree requirements:* For master's, thesis or alternative; for doctorate, thesis/dissertation. *Entrance requirements:* For master's and doctorate, GMAT, minimum GPA of 2.7. Additional exam requirements/recommendations for international students: Required—TOEFL. Electronic applications accepted.

The University of Tennessee, Graduate School, College of Business Administration, Program in Management Science, Knoxville, TN 37996. Offers MS, PhD. *Accreditation:* AACSB. *Degree requirements:* For master's, thesis or alternative; for doctorate, thesis/dissertation. *Entrance requirements:* For master's and doctorate, GMAT or GRE General Test, minimum GPA of 2.7. Additional exam requirements/recommendations for international students: Required—TOEFL. Electronic applications accepted.

The University of Tennessee at Chattanooga, Program in Business Administration, Chattanooga, TN 37403. Offers EMBA, MBA, PMBA. *Accreditation:* AACSB. *Program availability:* Part-time, evening/weekend. *Faculty:* 17 full-time (7 women), 1 part-time/adjunct (0 women). *Students:* 49 full-time (22 women), 108 part-time (50 women); includes 22 minority (8 Black or African American, non-Hispanic/Latino; 3 Asian, non-Hispanic/Latino; 3 Hispanic/Latino; 8 Two or more races, non-Hispanic/Latino), 6 international. Average age 29. 151 applicants, 90% accepted, 92 enrolled. In 2016, 102 master's awarded. *Entrance requirements:* For master's, GMAT (minimum score 450) or GRE General Test (minimum score 146 on verbal and 144 on quantitative), minimum overall undergraduate GPA of 2.7 or 3.0 in final two years. Additional exam requirements/recommendations for international students: Required—TOEFL (minimum score 550 paper-based; 79 iBT), IELTS (minimum score 6). *Application deadline:* For fall admission, 6/15 priority date for domestic students, 7/1 for international students; for spring admission, 11/1 priority date for domestic students, 11/1 for international students. Applications are processed on a rolling basis. Application fee: $35 ($40 for international students). Electronic applications accepted. *Expenses:* $9,876 full-time in-state; $25,994 full-time out-of-state; $450 per credit part-time in-state; $1,345 per credit part-time out-of-state. *Financial support:* In 2016–17, 11 research assistantships were awarded; teaching assistantships, career-related internships or fieldwork, scholarships/grants, health care benefits, tuition waivers (partial), and unspecified assistantships also available. Support available to part-time students. Financial award application deadline: 7/1. *Faculty research:* Diversity, operations/production management, entrepreneurial processes, customer satisfaction and retention, branding. *Unit head:* Elizabeth Bell, Director of Graduate Programs, 423-425-2326, Fax: 423-425-5255, E-mail: elizabeth-bell@utc.edu. *Application contact:* Dr. Joanne Romagni, Dean of the Graduate School, 423-425-4478, Fax: 423-425-5223, E-mail: joanne-romagni@utc.edu.

Website: http://www.utc.edu/college-business/academic-programs/graduate-programs/index.php

The University of Tennessee at Martin, Graduate Programs, College of Business and Global Affairs, Program in Business, Martin, TN 38238. Offers agricultural business (MBA); financial services (MBA); general business (MBA). *Accreditation:* AACSB. *Program availability:* Part-time, online only, 100% online, blended/hybrid learning. *Faculty:* 31. *Students:* 15 full-time (6 women), 79 part-time (28 women); includes 13 minority (6 Black or African American, non-Hispanic/Latino; 2 Asian, non-Hispanic/Latino; 4 Hispanic/Latino; 1 Two or more races, non-Hispanic/Latino). Average age 33. 62 applicants, 40% accepted, 20 enrolled. In 2016, 34 master's awarded. *Degree requirements:* For master's, comprehensive exam. *Entrance requirements:* For master's, GMAT, GRE, minimum GPA of 2.5, resume. Additional exam requirements/recommendations for international students: Required—TOEFL (minimum score 525 paper-based; 71 iBT). *Application deadline:* For fall admission, 7/27 priority date for domestic students, 7/27 for international students; for spring admission, 12/17 priority date for domestic students, 12/17 for international students; for summer admission, 5/10 priority date for domestic and international students. Applications are processed on a rolling basis. Application fee: $30 ($130 for international students). Electronic applications accepted. *Expenses:* Tuition, state resident: full-time $8254; part-time $459 per credit hour. Tuition, nonresident: full-time $22,198; part-time $1234 per credit hour. *Required fees:* $79 per credit hour. Part-time tuition and fees vary according to course load and campus/location. *Financial support:* In 2016–17, 10 students received support, including 5 research assistantships with full tuition reimbursements available (averaging $7,540 per year), 5 teaching assistantships with full tuition reimbursements available (averaging $7,560 per year); career-related internships or fieldwork, scholarships/grants, and unspecified assistantships also available. Support available to part-time students. Financial award application deadline: 2/1; financial award applicants required to submit FAFSA. *Unit head:* Dr. Ashley Kilburn, Coordinator, 731-881-7245, Fax: 731-881-7231, E-mail: mba@utm.edu. *Application contact:* Jolene L. Cunningham, Student Services Specialist, 731-881-7012, Fax: 731-881-7499, E-mail: jcunningham@utm.edu.

The University of Texas at Austin, Graduate School, McCombs School of Business, Department of Management, Austin, TX 78712-1111. Offers PhD. *Accreditation:* AACSB. *Degree requirements:* For doctorate, thesis/dissertation. *Entrance requirements:* For doctorate, GMAT or GRE. Electronic applications accepted.

The University of Texas at Austin, Graduate School, McCombs School of Business, Executive MBA Program at Mexico City, Austin, TX 78712-1111. Offers MBA. Program offered jointly with Instituto Tecnológico y de Estudios Superiores de Monterrey, Campus Ciudad de México. *Accreditation:* AACSB. *Entrance requirements:* For master's, GMAT, 5 years of work experience. Additional exam requirements/recommendations for international students: Required—TOEFL.

The University of Texas at Austin, Graduate School, McCombs School of Business, MBA Programs, Austin, TX 78712-1111. Offers MBA, JD/MBA, MBA/MA, MBA/MP Aff, MBA/MSN. *Accreditation:* AACSB. *Program availability:* Part-time. *Entrance requirements:* For master's, GMAT, minimum 2 years of full-time work experience. Additional exam requirements/recommendations for international students: Required—TOEFL. Electronic applications accepted.

The University of Texas at Dallas, Naveen Jindal School of Management, Richardson, TX 75080. Offers EMBA, MBA, MS, PhD, MS/MBA, MSEE/MBA. *Program availability:* Part-time, evening/weekend, online learning. *Faculty:* 105 full-time (19 women), 79 part-time/adjunct (23 women). *Students:* 3,051 full-time (1,320 women), 1,667 part-time (757 women); includes 805 minority (157 Black or African American, non-Hispanic/Latino; 4 American Indian or Alaska Native, non-Hispanic/Latino; 414 Asian, non-Hispanic/Latino; 152 Hispanic/Latino; 1 Native Hawaiian or other Pacific Islander, non-Hispanic/Latino; 77 Two or more races, non-Hispanic/Latino), 2,974 international. Average age 29. 6,998 applicants, 58% accepted, 1816 enrolled. In 2016, 1,920 master's, 13 doctorates awarded. *Degree requirements:* For doctorate, thesis/dissertation. *Entrance requirements:* For master's and doctorate, GMAT. Additional exam requirements/recommendations for international students: Required—TOEFL (minimum score 550 paper-based). *Application deadline:* For fall admission, 7/15 for domestic students, 5/1 priority date for international students; for spring admission, 11/15 for domestic students, 9/1 priority date for international students. Applications are processed on a rolling basis. Application fee: $50 ($100 for international students). Electronic applications accepted. *Expenses:* Tuition, state resident: full-time $12,418; part-time $690 per semester hour. Tuition, nonresident: full-time $24,150; part-time $1342 per semester hour. Tuition and fees vary according to course load. *Financial support:* In 2016–17, 1,138 students received support, including 1 fellowship (averaging $1,000 per year), 26 research assistantships with partial tuition reimbursements available (averaging $23,618 per year), 140 teaching assistantships with partial tuition reimbursements available (averaging $13,437 per year); career-related internships or fieldwork, Federal Work-Study, institutionally sponsored loans, scholarships/grants, and unspecified assistantships also available. Support available to part-time students. Financial award application deadline: 4/30; financial award applicants required to submit FAFSA. *Faculty research:* Finance, marketing and organization, strategy, management education for physicians. *Total annual research expenditures:* $3.3 million. *Unit head:* Dr. Hasan Pirkul, Dean, 972-883-2705, Fax: 972-883-2799, E-mail: hpirkul@utdallas.edu. *Application contact:* 972-883-2750, Fax: 972-883-6425, E-mail: jindal@utdallas.edu. Website: http://jindal.utdallas.edu/

See Display on this page and Close-Up on page 193.

The University of Texas at El Paso, Graduate School, College of Business Administration, Programs in Business Administration, El Paso, TX 79968-0001. Offers business administration (MBA, Certificate); international business (PhD). *Accreditation:* AACSB. *Program availability:* Part-time, evening/weekend, online learning. *Degree requirements:* For master's, comprehensive exam. *Entrance requirements:* For master's and doctorate, GMAT. Additional exam requirements/recommendations for international students: Required—TOEFL. Electronic applications accepted. *Faculty research:* Cross-border modeling, human resources, and outsourcing and manufacturing; global information technology transfer; international investments and risk management.

The University of Texas at San Antonio, College of Business, Department of Information Systems and Cyber Security, San Antonio, TX 78249-0617. Offers cyber security (MSIT); information technology (MS, PhD); management of technology (MBA); technology entrepreneurship and management (Certificate). *Program availability:* Part-time, evening/weekend. *Faculty:* 10 full-time (2 women), 4 part-time/adjunct (0 women). *Students:* 70 full-time (19 women), 73 part-time (21 women); includes 38 minority (6 Black or African American, non-Hispanic/Latino; 6 Asian, non-Hispanic/Latino; 24 Hispanic/Latino; 2 Two or more races, non-Hispanic/Latino), 38 international. Average age 30. 141 applicants, 59% accepted, 55 enrolled. In 2016, 45 master's, 1 doctorate, 6 other advanced degrees awarded. *Degree requirements:* For master's, comprehensive exam (for some programs), thesis optional; for doctorate, comprehensive exam, thesis/dissertation. *Entrance requirements:* For master's and doctorate, GMAT/GRE, official transcripts, statement of purpose, letters of recommendation. Additional exam requirements/recommendations for international students: Required—TOEFL (minimum score 550 paper-based; 79 iBT), IELTS (minimum score 6.5). *Application deadline:* For

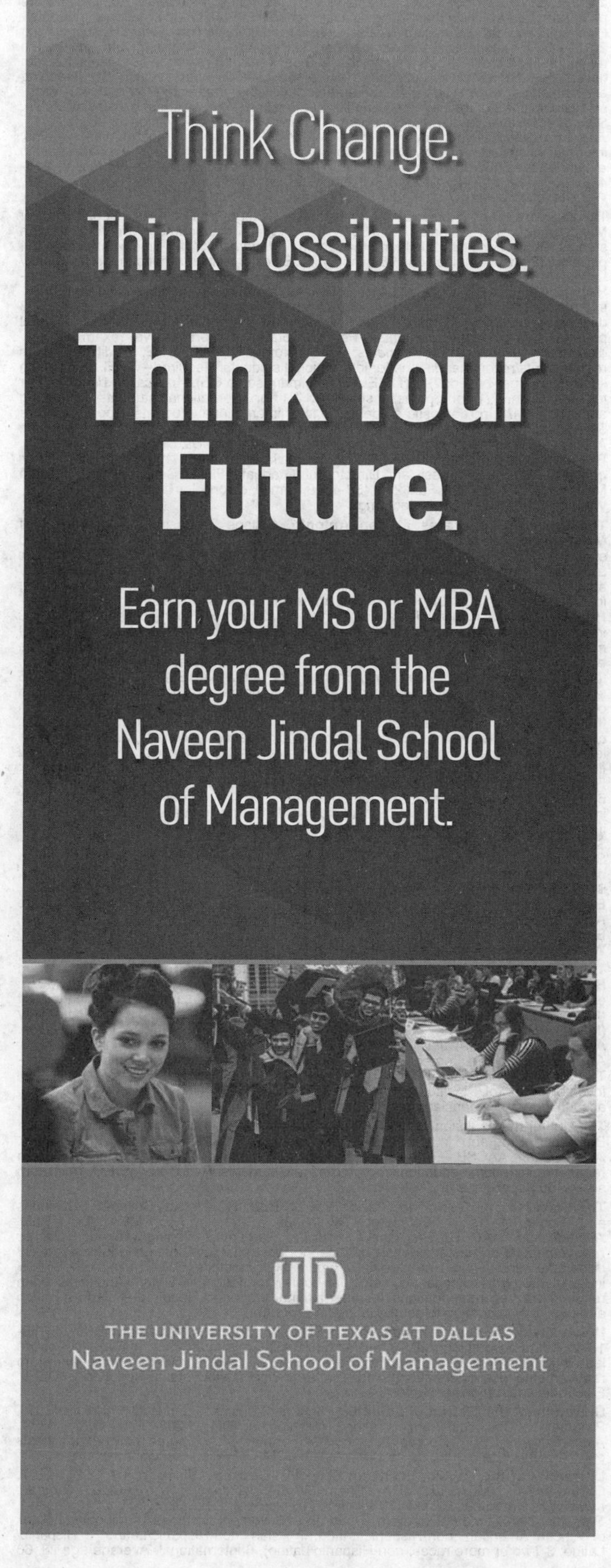

fall admission, 7/1 for domestic students, 4/1 for international students; for spring admission, 11/1 for domestic students, 9/1 for international students. Applications are processed on a rolling basis. Application fee: $45 ($80 for international students). Electronic applications accepted. *Expenses:* Contact institution. *Financial support:* In 2016–17, 15 students received support, including 1 fellowship with full tuition reimbursement available (averaging $25,000 per year), 10 research assistantships with tuition reimbursements available (averaging $9,000 per year), 12 teaching assistantships with tuition reimbursements available (averaging $9,000 per year); scholarships/grants, health care benefits, and unspecified assistantships also available. Support available to part-time students. Financial award application deadline: 2/15. *Faculty research:* Cyber security, digital forensics, economics of information systems, information systems privacy, information technology adoption. *Total annual research expenditures:* $650,902. *Unit head:* Dr. Yoris A. Au, Chair/Associate Professor, 210-458-6300, Fax: 210-458-6305, E-mail: yoris.au@utsa.edu.
Website: http://business.utsa.edu/directory/index.aspx?DepID-16

The University of Texas at San Antonio, College of Business, Department of Management, San Antonio, TX 78249-0617. Offers management and organization studies (PhD). *Faculty:* 12 full-time (5 women). *Students:* 151 full-time (46 women), 64 part-time (20 women); includes 95 minority (12 Black or African American, non-Hispanic/Latino; 1 American Indian or Alaska Native, non-Hispanic/Latino; 13 Asian, non-Hispanic/Latino; 66 Hispanic/Latino; 3 Two or more races, non-Hispanic/Latino), 11 international. Average age 33. 134 applicants, 77% accepted, 77 enrolled. In 2016, 3 doctorates awarded. Terminal master's awarded for partial completion of doctoral program. *Degree requirements:* For doctorate, comprehensive exam, thesis/dissertation. *Entrance requirements:* For doctorate, GMAT, GRE. Additional exam requirements/recommendations for international students: Required—TOEFL (minimum score 550 paper-based; 79 iBT), IELTS (minimum score 6.5). *Application deadline:* For fall admission, 7/1 for domestic students, 4/1 for international students; for spring admission, 11/1 for domestic students, 9/1 for international students. Application fee: $45 ($80 for international students). Electronic applications accepted. *Financial support:* Application deadline: 3/31. *Total annual research expenditures:* $18,948. *Unit head:* Dr. Robert L. Cardy, Chair, 210-458-4310, E-mail: robert.cardy@utsa.edu. *Application contact:* Caron Kiley, Assistant Director of Graduate Fiscal Services/PhD Program Manager, 210-458-7324, Fax: 210-458-4398, E-mail: caron.kiley@utsa.edu.
Website: http://business.utsa.edu/mgt/

The University of Texas at San Antonio, College of Business, Department of Management Science and Statistics, San Antonio, TX 78249-0617. Offers applied statistics (MS, PhD); management science (MBA). *Accreditation:* AACSB. *Program availability:* Part-time, evening/weekend. *Faculty:* 13 full-time (1 woman), 4 part-time/adjunct (1 woman). *Students:* 96 full-time (35 women), 39 part-time (17 women); includes 52 minority (4 Black or African American, non-Hispanic/Latino; 16 Asian, non-Hispanic/Latino; 31 Hispanic/Latino; 1 Two or more races, non-Hispanic/Latino), 23 international. Average age 32. 139 applicants, 77% accepted, 81 enrolled. In 2016, 19 master's, 3 doctorates awarded. *Degree requirements:* For master's, comprehensive exam (for some programs), thesis or alternative; for doctorate, comprehensive exam, thesis/dissertation. *Entrance requirements:* For master's, GMAT, minimum of 36 semester credit hours of coursework beyond any hours acquired in the MBA-leveling courses; statement of purpose; for doctorate, GRE, minimum cumulative GPA of 3.3 in the last 60 hours of coursework; transcripts from all colleges and universities attended; curriculum vitae; statement of academic work experiences, interests, and goals; three letters of recommendation; BA, BS, or MS in mathematics, statistics, or closely-related field. Additional exam requirements/recommendations for international students: Required—TOEFL (minimum score 550 paper-based; 79 iBT), IELTS (minimum score 6.5). *Application deadline:* For fall admission, 7/1 for domestic students, 4/1 for international students; for spring admission, 11/1 for domestic students, 9/1 for international students. Applications are processed on a rolling basis. Application fee: $45 ($80 for international students). Electronic applications accepted. *Faculty research:* Statistical signal processing, reliability and life-testing experiments, modeling decompression sickness using survival analysis. *Total annual research expenditures:* $155,894. *Unit head:* Dr. Raydel Tullous, Chair, 210-458-6345, Fax: 210-458-6350, E-mail: raydel.tullous@utsa.edu. *Application contact:* Katherine Pope, Graduate Assistant of Record, 210-458-7316, Fax: 210-458-4398,
E-mail: katherine.pope@utsa.edu.
Website: http://business.utsa.edu/mss/

The University of Texas at Tyler, College of Business and Technology, Program in Business Administration, Tyler, TX 75799-0001. Offers cyber security (MBA); engineering management (MBA); general management (MBA); healthcare management (MBA); internal assurance and consulting (MBA); marketing (MBA); oil, gas and energy (MBA); organizational development (MBA); quality management (MBA). *Accreditation:* AACSB. *Program availability:* Part-time, online learning. *Entrance requirements:* Additional exam requirements/recommendations for international students: Required—TOEFL (minimum score 550 paper-based). *Faculty research:* General business, inventory control, institutional markets, service marketing, product distribution, accounting fraud, financial reporting and recognition.

The University of Texas of the Permian Basin, Office of Graduate Studies, School of Business, Program in Management, Odessa, TX 79762-0001. Offers MBA. *Accreditation:* AACSB. *Entrance requirements:* For master's, GMAT. Additional exam requirements/recommendations for international students: Required—TOEFL (minimum score 550 paper-based).

The University of Texas Rio Grande Valley, Robert C. Vackar College of Business and Entrepreneurship, Edinburg, TX 78539. Offers M Acc, MBA, MS, PhD. *Accreditation:* AACSB. *Program availability:* Part-time, evening/weekend. *Degree requirements:* For master's, thesis optional; for doctorate, one foreign language, thesis/dissertation, internship. *Entrance requirements:* For master's, GMAT, minimum AACSB index of 1000 (based on last 60 semester hours); for doctorate, GMAT. Additional exam requirements/recommendations for international students: Required—TOEFL. Tuition and fees vary according to course load and program.

University of the Cumberlands, Hutton School of Business, Williamsburg, KY 40769-1372. Offers accounting (MBA); business (MBA). *Program availability:* Part-time, online learning. *Entrance requirements:* For master's, GMAT, GRE. Additional exam requirements/recommendations for international students: Required—TOEFL. Electronic applications accepted.

University of the District of Columbia, School of Business and Public Administration, Program in Business Administration, Washington, DC 20008-1175. Offers MBA. *Accreditation:* ACBSP. *Degree requirements:* For master's, comprehensive exam, thesis optional. *Entrance requirements:* For master's, GMAT, writing proficiency exam.

University of the Pacific, Eberhardt School of Business, Stockton, CA 95211-0197. Offers M Acc, MBA, JD/MBA, Pharm D/MBA. *Accreditation:* AACSB. *Program availability:* Part-time. *Faculty:* 30 full-time (15 women), 2 part-time/adjunct (1 woman). *Students:* 24 full-time (12 women), 7 part-time (3 women); includes 14 minority (1 Black or African American, non-Hispanic/Latino; 7 Asian, non-Hispanic/Latino; 3 Hispanic/Latino; 3 Two or more races, non-Hispanic/Latino), 6 international. Average age 28. 66 applicants, 53% accepted, 10 enrolled. In 2016, 32 master's awarded. *Entrance requirements:* For master's, GMAT. Additional exam requirements/recommendations for international students: Required—TOEFL. *Application deadline:* For fall admission, 7/31 priority date for domestic students; for spring admission, 11/30 for domestic students. Applications are processed on a rolling basis. Application fee: $75. *Financial support:* Fellowships, research assistantships, Federal Work-Study, and institutionally sponsored loans available. Support available to part-time students. Financial award application deadline: 3/1; financial award applicants required to submit FAFSA. *Unit head:* Dr. David Dauwalder, Interim Dean, 209-946-7710, E-mail: ddauwalder@pacific.edu. *Application contact:* 209-946-2239, E-mail: business@pacific.edu.
Website: http://www.pacific.edu/mba/

University of the Potomac, Program in Business Administration, Washington, DC 20005. Offers MBA. Program also offered at Vienna, VA campus. *Program availability:* Online learning.

University of the Sacred Heart, Graduate Programs, Department of Business Administration, San Juan, PR 00914-0383. Offers human resource management (MBA); information systems auditing (MS); information technology (Certificate); international marketing (MBA); management information systems (MBA); production and marketing of special events (Certificate); taxation (MBA). *Program availability:* Part-time, evening/weekend. *Degree requirements:* For master's, thesis. *Entrance requirements:* For master's, EXADEP, minimum undergraduate GPA of 2.75, interview.

University of the Southwest, Graduate Programs, Hobbs, NM 88240-9129. Offers business administration (MBA); curriculum and instruction (MSE); curriculum and instruction: bilingual (MSE); curriculum and instruction: TESOL (MSE); early childhood education (MSE); educational administration (MSE); mental health counseling (MSE); school counseling (MSE); special education (MSE); sports management (MBA). *Program availability:* Part-time, evening/weekend, online learning. *Degree requirements:* For master's, comprehensive exam, thesis (for some programs). *Entrance requirements:* Additional exam requirements/recommendations for international students: Recommended—TOEFL. Electronic applications accepted.

University of the Virgin Islands, School of Business, St. Thomas, VI 00802. Offers EMBA, MBA. *Program availability:* Part-time, evening/weekend. *Faculty:* 8 full-time (0 women). *Students:* 32 full-time (20 women), 15 part-time (11 women); includes 31 minority (30 Black or African American, non-Hispanic/Latino; 1 Asian, non-Hispanic/Latino), 5 international. Average age 31. 39 applicants, 87% accepted, 29 enrolled. In 2016, 3 master's awarded. *Degree requirements:* For master's, comprehensive exam or thesis. *Entrance requirements:* For master's, GMAT, minimum GPA of 2.5. Additional exam requirements/recommendations for international students: Required—TOEFL (minimum score 550 paper-based). *Application deadline:* For fall admission, 4/30 for domestic and international students; for spring admission, 10/30 for domestic and international students. Applications are processed on a rolling basis. Application fee: $30. Electronic applications accepted. *Expenses:* Contact institution. *Financial support:* Application deadline: 4/15; applicants required to submit FAFSA. *Unit head:* Dr. Stephen Reames, Dean, 340-693-1301, Fax: 340-693-1305, E-mail: stephen.reames@uvi.edu. *Application contact:* Xuri M Allen, Director of Admissions, 340-693-1224, Fax: 340-693-1167, E-mail: xallen@uvi.edu.
Website: http://www.uvi.edu/academics/school-business/

University of the West, Department of Business Administration, Rosemead, CA 91770. Offers business administration (EMBA); computer information systems (MBA); finance (MBA); international business (MBA); nonprofit organization management (MBA). *Program availability:* Part-time, evening/weekend. *Faculty:* 3 full-time (1 woman), 6 part-time/adjunct (2 women). *Students:* 54 full-time (31 women), 14 part-time (3 women); includes 8 minority (4 Asian, non-Hispanic/Latino; 4 Hispanic/Latino), 59 international. Average age 29. *Entrance requirements:* Additional exam requirements/recommendations for international students: Required—TOEFL. *Application deadline:* For fall admission, 6/15 for domestic and international students; for winter admission, 4/1 for domestic and international students; for spring admission, 11/15 for domestic and international students. Applications are processed on a rolling basis. Application fee: $50 ($100 for international students). *Expenses: Tuition:* Full-time $9324; part-time $4662 per year. *Required fees:* $900; $640 per unit. $320 per semester. Tuition and fees vary according to program. *Financial support:* Career-related internships or fieldwork, Federal Work-Study, scholarships/grants, and tuition waivers (partial) available. Financial award applicants required to submit FAFSA. *Unit head:* Dr. Bill Y. Chen, Chair, 626-656-2125, Fax: 626-571-1413, E-mail: billchen@uwest.edu. *Application contact:* Rica Toribio, Director of Enrollment Services, 626-571-8811 Ext. 311, Fax: 626-571-1413, E-mail: ricat@uwest.edu.
Website: http://www.uwest.edu/site/
index.php?option=com_content&view=article&id=119&Itemid=162

The University of Toledo, College of Graduate Studies, College of Business and Innovation, Department of Management, Toledo, OH 43606-3390. Offers MBA. *Program availability:* Part-time, evening/weekend. *Entrance requirements:* For master's, GMAT, GRE, or LSAT, minimum GPA of 2.7 for all prior academic work, three letters of recommendation, statement of purpose, transcripts from all prior institutions attended. Additional exam requirements/recommendations for international students: Required—TOEFL (minimum score 550 paper-based; 80 iBT). Electronic applications accepted. *Faculty research:* Stress, deviation, workplace, globalization, recruitment.

University of Toronto, School of Graduate Studies, Rotman School of Management, Toronto, ON M5S 1A1, Canada. Offers MBA, MF, PhD, JD/MBA. *Accreditation:* AACSB. *Program availability:* Part-time, evening/weekend. *Degree requirements:* For doctorate, thesis/dissertation. *Entrance requirements:* For master's, GMAT (MBA), minimum mid-B average in final undergraduate year; minimum 2 years of full-time work experience; 2-3 letters of reference; for doctorate, GMAT or GRE, minimum B+ average, master's degree in business administration, 2-3 letters of reference. *Expenses:* Contact institution. *Faculty research:* Natural resources, organizational behavior, finance, marketing, strategic management.

The University of Tulsa, Graduate School, Collins College of Business, Business Administration/Computer Science Program, Tulsa, OK 74104-3189. Offers MBA/MS. *Program availability:* Part-time. *Entrance requirements:* Additional exam requirements/recommendations for international students: Required—TOEFL (minimum score 577 paper-based; 91 iBT), IELTS (minimum score 6.5). *Application deadline:* Applications are processed on a rolling basis. Application fee: $55. Electronic applications accepted. *Expenses: Tuition:* Full-time $22,230; part-time $1235 per credit hour. *Required fees:* $990 per semester. Tuition and fees vary according to course load. *Financial support:* Fellowships, research assistantships with full tuition reimbursements, teaching assistantships, career-related internships or fieldwork, Federal Work-Study, institutionally sponsored loans, scholarships/grants, health care benefits, tuition waivers (full and partial), and unspecified assistantships available. Support available to part-time students. Financial award application deadline: 2/1; financial award applicants required to submit FAFSA. *Unit head:* Dr. Ralph Jackson, Associate Dean, 918-631-2242, Fax: 918-631-2142, E-mail: ralph-jackson@utulsa.edu. *Application contact:* Information Contact, 918-631-2242, E-mail: graduate-business@utulsa.edu.

The University of Tulsa, Graduate School, Collins College of Business, Master of Business Administration Program, Tulsa, OK 74104-3189. Offers MBA, JD/MBA, MBA/MSCS, MBA/MSF. *Accreditation:* AACSB. *Program availability:* Part-time, evening/weekend. *Faculty:* 32 full-time (6 women). *Students:* 42 full-time (18 women), 50 part-time (18 women); includes 12 minority (1 Black or African American, non-Hispanic/Latino; 2 American Indian or Alaska Native, non-Hispanic/Latino; 4 Asian, non-Hispanic/Latino; 4 Hispanic/Latino; 1 Two or more races, non-Hispanic/Latino), 13 international. Average age 28. 115 applicants, 52% accepted, 34 enrolled. In 2016, 36 master's awarded. *Entrance requirements:* For master's, GMAT. Additional exam requirements/recommendations for international students: Required—TOEFL (minimum score 577 paper-based; 91 iBT), IELTS (minimum score 6.5). *Application deadline:* Applications are processed on a rolling basis. Application fee: $55. Electronic applications accepted. *Expenses: Tuition:* Full-time $22,230; part-time $1235 per credit hour. *Required fees:* $990 per semester. Tuition and fees vary according to course load. *Financial support:* In 2016–17, 23 students received support, including 1 research assistantship with full tuition reimbursement available (averaging $6,759 per year), 29 teaching assistantships with full tuition reimbursements available (averaging $7,238 per year); fellowships, career-related internships or fieldwork, institutionally sponsored loans, scholarships/grants, health care benefits, tuition waivers (full and partial), and unspecified assistantships also available. Support available to part-time students. Financial award application deadline: 2/1; financial award applicants required to submit FAFSA. *Faculty research:* Accounting, energy management, finance, international business, management information systems, taxation. *Unit head:* Dr. Ralph Jackson, Associate Dean of the Collins College of Business, 918-631-2242, Fax: 918-631-2142, E-mail: ralph-jackson@utulsa.edu. *Application contact:* Information Contact, 918-631-2242, E-mail: graduate-business@utulsa.edu.

University of Utah, Graduate School, David Eccles School of Business, Salt Lake City, UT 84112. Offers EMBA, M Acc, MBA, MHA, MRED, MS, MSF, PMBA, PhD, Graduate Certificate, MBA/JD, MBA/MHA, MBA/MS, MHA/MPA, MPH/MHA, MRED/JD, MRED/M Arch, MRED/MCMP, PMBA/MHA. *Accreditation:* AACSB. *Program availability:* Part-time, evening/weekend. *Faculty:* 64 full-time (22 women), 45 part-time/adjunct (10 women). *Students:* 1,018 full-time (296 women), 323 part-time (77 women); includes 157 minority (3 Black or African American, non-Hispanic/Latino; 1 American Indian or Alaska Native, non-Hispanic/Latino; 41 Asian, non-Hispanic/Latino; 84 Hispanic/Latino; 2 Native Hawaiian or other Pacific Islander, non-Hispanic/Latino; 26 Two or more races, non-Hispanic/Latino), 227 international. Average age 30. 1,122 applicants, 74% accepted, 580 enrolled. In 2016, 604 master's, 6 doctorates awarded. *Degree requirements:* For master's, comprehensive exam (for some programs), thesis (for some programs); for doctorate, comprehensive exam (for some programs), thesis/dissertation. *Entrance requirements:* Additional exam requirements/recommendations for international students: Required—TOEFL. Application fee: $55 ($65 for international students). Electronic applications accepted. *Expenses:* Contact institution. *Financial support:* Fellowships with partial tuition reimbursements, research assistantships with partial tuition reimbursements, teaching assistantships with tuition reimbursements, scholarships/grants, tuition waivers (full and partial), and unspecified assistantships available. Financial award applicants required to submit FAFSA. *Faculty research:* Information systems, investment, financial accounting, international strategy. *Total annual research expenditures:* $129,423. *Unit head:* Dr. Taylor Randall, Dean, 801-581-3074, E-mail: dean@business.utah.edu. *Application contact:* Andrea Miller, Director of Graduate Admissions, 801-585-7366, E-mail: andrea.miller@business.utah.edu.
Website: http://www.business.utah.edu/

University of Vermont, Graduate College, School of Business Administration, Burlington, VT 05405. Offers M Acc, MBA. *Accreditation:* AACSB. *Program availability:* Part-time. *Entrance requirements:* For master's, GMAT, resume. Additional exam requirements/recommendations for international students: Required—TOEFL (minimum score 550 paper-based; 80 iBT). Electronic applications accepted. *Expenses:* Tuition, state resident: full-time $5814. Tuition, nonresident: full-time $14,670.

University of Victoria, Faculty of Graduate Studies, Peter B. Gustavson School of Business, Victoria, BC V8W 2Y2, Canada. Offers MBA, MBA/LL B. *Accreditation:* AACSB. *Program availability:* Part-time. *Entrance requirements:* For master's, GMAT, minimum B average. Additional exam requirements/recommendations for international students: Required—TOEFL (minimum score 575 paper-based), IELTS (minimum score 7). Electronic applications accepted. *Expenses:* Contact institution. *Faculty research:* Organizational design and analysis, negotiation and conflict management, human resources management, entrepreneurship, international marketing and tourism.

University of Virginia, Darden School of Business, Charlottesville, VA 22903. Offers MBA, PhD, MBA/JD, MBA/M Ed, MBA/MA, MBA/MD, MBA/ME, MBA/MPP, MBA/MS, MBA/MSN. *Accreditation:* AACSB. *Faculty:* 62 full-time (16 women), 3 part-time/adjunct (1 woman). *Students:* 905 full-time (312 women), 2 part-time (0 women); includes 172 minority (48 Black or African American, non-Hispanic/Latino; 2 American Indian or Alaska Native, non-Hispanic/Latino; 62 Asian, non-Hispanic/Latino; 43 Hispanic/Latino; 1 Native Hawaiian or other Pacific Islander, non-Hispanic/Latino; 16 Two or more races, non-Hispanic/Latino), 228 international. Average age 30. 2,747 applicants, 31% accepted, 467 enrolled. In 2016, 415 master's awarded. *Degree requirements:* For doctorate, thesis/dissertation. *Entrance requirements:* For master's, GMAT, resume; 2 letters of recommendation; interview; for doctorate, GMAT, resume; essay; 2 letters of recommendation; interview. Additional exam requirements/recommendations for international students: Required—TOEFL. *Application deadline:* For fall admission, 3/1 for domestic students, 3/2 for international students. Applications are processed on a rolling basis. Application fee: $200. Electronic applications accepted. *Expenses:* $57,790 tuition, $2,716 fees in-state; $60,108 tuition, $3,392 fees out-of-state. *Financial support:* Career-related internships or fieldwork available. Financial award applicants required to submit FAFSA. *Unit head:* Scott C. Beardsley, Dean, 434-924-7481, E-mail: dean@virginia.edu. *Application contact:* Sara Neher, Assistant Dean of MBA Admissions, 434-924-3900, E-mail: darden@virginia.edu.
Website: http://www.darden.virginia.edu/

University of Virginia, McIntire School of Commerce, Charlottesville, VA 22904. Offers MS, MSC, Certificate, JD/MS. *Accreditation:* AACSB. *Faculty:* 69 full-time (23 women), 1 (woman) part-time/adjunct. *Students:* 230 full-time (103 women); includes 46 minority (11 Black or African American, non-Hispanic/Latino; 20 Asian, non-Hispanic/Latino; 15 Hispanic/Latino), 35 international. Average age 23. 734 applicants, 49% accepted, 245 enrolled. In 2016, 240 master's awarded. *Entrance requirements:* For master's, GMAT, 2 letters of recommendation. Additional exam requirements/recommendations for international students: Required—TOEFL (minimum score 100 iBT) or IELTS (minimum score 7.5). *Application deadline:* Applications are processed on a rolling basis. Application fee: $75. Electronic applications accepted. *Expenses:* Contact institution. *Financial support:* In 2016–17, 65 students received support. Federal Work-Study, scholarships/grants, and unspecified assistantships available. Financial award application deadline: 2/1; financial award applicants required to submit FAFSA. *Unit head:* Carl Zeithaml, Dean, 877-349-2620, Fax: 434-924-7074, E-mail: mcintiregrad@virginia.edu. *Application contact:* Emma Candelier, Director of Graduate Recruiting, 434-243-4992, Fax: 434-924-4511, E-mail: ecandelier@virginia.edu.
Website: http://www.commerce.virginia.edu

University of Washington, Graduate School, Michael G. Foster School of Business, Seattle, WA 98195-3200. Offers auditing and assurance (MP Acc); business administration (MBA, PhD); entrepreneurship (MS); executive business administration (MBA); global executive business administration (MBA); information systems (MSIS); supply chain management (MSSCM); taxation (MP Acc); technology management (MBA); JD/MBA; MBA/MAIS; MBA/MHA. *Accreditation:* AACSB. *Program availability:* Part-time, evening/weekend. Terminal master's awarded for partial completion of doctoral program. *Degree requirements:* For doctorate, comprehensive exam, thesis/dissertation. *Entrance requirements:* For master's and doctorate, GMAT, GRE. Additional exam requirements/recommendations for international students: Required—TOEFL (minimum score 600 paper-based; 100 iBT). Electronic applications accepted. *Expenses:* Contact institution. *Faculty research:* Finance, marketing, organizational behavior, information technology, strategy.

University of Washington, Bothell, School of Business, Bothell, WA 98011. Offers leadership (MBA); technology (MBA). *Accreditation:* AACSB. *Program availability:* Part-time, evening/weekend. *Degree requirements:* For master's, 72 credits, minimum cumulative GPA of 3.0. *Entrance requirements:* For master's, GMAT or GRE General Test. Additional exam requirements/recommendations for international students: Required—TOEFL (minimum score 580 paper-based; 92 iBT), IELTS (minimum score 7). Electronic applications accepted. *Expenses:* Contact institution. *Faculty research:* Leadership, supply chain management, entrepreneurship, game theory, corporate finance, marketing innovation.

University of Washington, Tacoma, Graduate Programs, MBA Programs, Tacoma, WA 98402-3100. Offers accounting (MBA); business administration (MBA); certified financial analyst (MBA). *Accreditation:* AACSB. *Program availability:* Part-time, evening/weekend. *Entrance requirements:* For master's, GMAT, minimum GPA of 3.0 in final graded 90 quarter credits or 60 graded semester credits; at least 2 years of professional/management work experience. Additional exam requirements/recommendations for international students: Required—TOEFL (minimum score 580 paper-based; 92 iBT). Electronic applications accepted. *Expenses:* Contact institution. *Faculty research:* International accounting, marketing, change management, investments, corporate social responsibility.

University of Waterloo, Graduate Studies, Faculty of Engineering, Conrad Business, Entrepreneurship and Technology Center, Waterloo, ON N2L 3G1, Canada. Offers MBET. *Entrance requirements:* For master's, honors degree. Additional exam requirements/recommendations for international students: Required—TOEFL (minimum score 90 iBT), IELTS (minimum score 7), PTE (minimum score 63). Electronic applications accepted.

The University of West Alabama, School of Graduate Studies, College of Business, Livingston, AL 35470. Offers finance (MBA); general business (MBA). *Program availability:* Part-time, evening/weekend, 100% online. *Faculty:* 5 full-time (1 woman), 11 part-time/adjunct (8 women). *Students:* 70 (48 women); includes 39 minority (33 Black or African American, non-Hispanic/Latino; 1 American Indian or Alaska Native, non-Hispanic/Latino; 1 Asian, non-Hispanic/Latino; 3 Hispanic/Latino; 1 Two or more races, non-Hispanic/Latino). Average age 30. 42 applicants, 90% accepted, 31 enrolled. In 2016, 9 master's awarded. *Degree requirements:* For master's, project or six additional hours in emphasis area and comprehensive examination. *Entrance requirements:* For master's, GMAT, bachelor's degree with minimum GPA of 2.75 or master's degree with minimum GPA of 3.0. Additional exam requirements/recommendations for international students: Required—TOEFL (minimum score 500 paper-based; 61 iBT). *Application deadline:* Applications are processed on a rolling basis. Application fee: $40. Electronic applications accepted. *Expenses:* Tuition, state resident: part-time $355 per credit hour. Tuition, nonresident: part-time $710 per credit hour. *Required fees:* $130 per semester. *Financial support:* Federal Work-Study and scholarships/grants available. Support available to part-time students. Financial award application deadline: 3/1; financial award applicants required to submit FAFSA. *Unit head:* Dr. Wayne Bedford, Dean, 205-652-3687, Fax: 205-652-3776, E-mail: dbedford@uwa.edu.
Website: http://www.uwa.edu/cob/

The University of Western Ontario, Richard Ivey School of Business, London, ON N6A 3K7, Canada. Offers business (EMBA, PhD); corporate strategy and leadership elective (MBA); entrepreneurship elective (MBA); finance elective (MBA); health sector stream (MBA); international management elective (MBA); marketing elective (MBA); JD/MBA. *Degree requirements:* For master's, thesis (for some programs); for doctorate, thesis/dissertation. *Entrance requirements:* For master's, GMAT, 2 years of full-time work experience, interview. Additional exam requirements/recommendations for international students: Required—TOEFL (minimum score 100 iBT) or IELTS (minimium score 6). Electronic applications accepted. *Faculty research:* Strategy, organizational behavior, international business, finance, operations management.

University of West Florida, College of Business, Program in Business Administration, Pensacola, FL 32514-5750. Offers MBA. *Accreditation:* AACSB. *Program availability:* Part-time, evening/weekend. *Degree requirements:* For master's, industry portfolio project based on information from five of the core MBA courses. *Entrance requirements:* For master's, GMAT or GRE, official transcripts; minimum undergraduate GPA of 3.0; bachelor's degree; business course academic preparation; graduate-level motivation and writing abilities as noted in essay responses; two letters of recommendation; appropriate employment at increasing levels of responsibility via resume. Additional exam requirements/recommendations for international students: Required—TOEFL (minimum score 550 paper-based). *Application deadline:* For fall admission, 6/30 for domestic students, 6/1 for international students; for spring admission, 10/1 for domestic and international students. Applications are processed on a rolling basis. Application fee: $30. *Expenses:* Tuition, state resident: full-time $5316.12. Tuition, nonresident: full-time $11,308. *Required fees:* $583.92. Tuition and fees vary according to course load and program. *Financial support:* Fellowships, research assistantships with partial tuition reimbursements, and unspecified assistantships available. Financial award application deadline: 4/15; financial award applicants required to submit FAFSA. *Faculty research:* Robotics, corporate behavior, international trade, franchising, counterfeiting. *Unit head:* Melissa Brode, Director, E-mail: mbrode@uwf.edu. *Application contact:* Cheryl Powell, Academic Advisor, 850-474-2348.
Website: http://uwf.edu/mba/gradprograms.cfm

University of West Georgia, Richards College of Business, Carrollton, GA 30118. Offers accounting (MP Acc); business administration (MBA). *Program availability:* Part-time, evening/weekend, 100% online, blended/hybrid learning. *Faculty:* 38 full-time (14 women). *Students:* 56 full-time (24 women), 132 part-time (64 women); includes 61 minority (49 Black or African American, non-Hispanic/Latino; 1 American Indian or Alaska Native, non-Hispanic/Latino; 3 Asian, non-Hispanic/Latino; 7 Hispanic/Latino; 1 Two or more races, non-Hispanic/Latino), 12 international. Average age 29. 121 applicants, 94% accepted, 77 enrolled. In 2016, 123 master's awarded. *Entrance requirements:* Additional exam requirements/recommendations for international students: Required—TOEFL (minimum score 550 paper-based; 79 iBT); Recommended—IELTS (minimum score 6.5). *Application deadline:* For fall admission, 7/15 for domestic students, 6/1 for international students; for spring admission, 11/15 for domestic students, 10/15 for international students; for summer admission, 5/15 for domestic students, 3/30 for international students. Applications are processed on a

rolling basis. Application fee: $40. Electronic applications accepted. *Expenses:* Tuition, state resident: full-time $5316; part-time $222 per semester hour. Tuition, nonresident: full-time $20,658; part-time $861 per semester hour. *Required fees:* $1962. Tuition and fees vary according to course load, degree level and program. *Financial support:* Fellowships, research assistantships, teaching assistantships, career-related internships or fieldwork, Federal Work-Study, institutionally sponsored loans, scholarships/grants, and unspecified assistantships available. Support available to part-time students. Financial award application deadline: 4/1; financial award applicants required to submit FAFSA. *Unit head:* Dr. Faye S. McIntyre, Dean of Richards College of Business, 678-839-6467, Fax: 678-839-5040, E-mail: fmcintyr@westga.edu. *Application contact:* Dr. Toby Ziglar, Assistant Dean of the Graduate School, 678-839-1394, Fax: 678-839-1395, E-mail: graduate@westga.edu.
Website: https://www.westga.edu/business

University of Windsor, Faculty of Graduate Studies, Odette School of Business, Windsor, ON N9B 3P4, Canada. Offers MBA, MM, MBA/LL B. *Program availability:* Evening/weekend. *Degree requirements:* For master's, thesis or alternative. *Entrance requirements:* For master's, GMAT, minimum B average. Additional exam requirements/recommendations for international students: Required—TOEFL (minimum score 600 paper-based). Electronic applications accepted. *Faculty research:* Accounting, administrative studies, finance, marketing, business policy and strategy.

University of Wisconsin–Eau Claire, College of Business, Program in Business Administration, Eau Claire, WI 54702-4004. Offers MBA. *Accreditation:* AACSB. *Program availability:* Part-time, evening/weekend, online learning. Terminal master's awarded for partial completion of doctoral program. *Degree requirements:* For master's, thesis optional, applied field project. *Entrance requirements:* For master's, GMAT or GRE, minimum GPA of 2.75 overall. Additional exam requirements/recommendations for international students: Required—TOEFL (minimum score 79 iBT). *Expenses:* Contact institution.

University of Wisconsin–Green Bay, Graduate Studies, Program in Management, Green Bay, WI 54311-7001. Offers MS. *Program availability:* Part-time, evening/weekend. *Faculty:* 5 full-time (0 women). *Students:* 7 full-time (4 women), 13 part-time (3 women); includes 3 minority (2 Asian, non-Hispanic/Latino; 1 Hispanic/Latino), 4 international. Average age 33. 10 applicants, 100% accepted, 6 enrolled. In 2016, 11 master's awarded. *Degree requirements:* For master's, thesis or alternative. *Entrance requirements:* For master's, GMAT or GRE General Test, minimum GPA of 3.0. *Application deadline:* For fall admission, 8/1 for domestic students; for spring admission, 11/1 for domestic students. Applications are processed on a rolling basis. Application fee: $56. Electronic applications accepted. *Expenses:* Tuition, state resident: full-time $7640; part-time $424 per credit hour. Tuition, nonresident: full-time $16,771; part-time $932 per credit hour. *Required fees:* $1580; $88 per credit hour. Tuition and fees vary according to program and reciprocity agreements. *Financial support:* In 2016–17, 6 students received support. Scholarships/grants and unspecified assistantships available. Financial award application deadline: 7/15; financial award applicants required to submit FAFSA. *Faculty research:* Planning methods, budgeting, decision-making, organizational behavior and theory, management. *Unit head:* Dr. David Radosevich, Chair, 920-465-2051, E-mail: radosevd@uwgb.edu. *Application contact:* Mary Valitchka, Graduate Studies Coordinator, 920-465-2123, Fax: 920-465-2043,
E-mail: valitchm@uwgb.edu.
Website: http://www.uwgb.edu/management/

University of Wisconsin–La Crosse, College of Business Administration, La Crosse, WI 54601-3742. Offers MBA. *Accreditation:* AACSB. *Program availability:* Part-time, evening/weekend. *Faculty:* 10 full-time (3 women). *Students:* 8 full-time (3 women), 19 part-time (7 women); includes 2 minority (1 Black or African American, non-Hispanic/Latino; 1 Asian, non-Hispanic/Latino), 6 international. Average age 30. 29 applicants, 90% accepted, 15 enrolled. In 2016, 16 master's awarded. *Degree requirements:* For master's, thesis optional. *Entrance requirements:* For master's, GMAT. Additional exam requirements/recommendations for international students: Required—TOEFL (minimum score 550 paper-based; 79 iBT). *Application deadline:* For fall admission, 6/15 priority date for domestic and international students; for spring admission, 11/15 priority date for domestic and international students. Applications are processed on a rolling basis. Electronic applications accepted. *Expenses:* Contact institution. *Financial support:* Research assistantships with partial tuition reimbursements, Federal Work-Study, scholarships/grants, health care benefits, and tuition waivers (partial) available. Support available to part-time students. Financial award application deadline: 3/15; financial award applicants required to submit FAFSA. *Faculty research:* Tax regulation, accounting standards, public sector information technology, corporate social responsibility, economics of sports. *Unit head:* Dr. Laura Milner, Dean, 608-785-8090, Fax: 608-785-6700, E-mail: lmilner@uwlax.edu. *Application contact:* Brandon Schaller, Senior Graduate Student Status Examiner, 608-785-8941, Fax: 608-785-6700,
E-mail: bschaller@uwlax.edu.
Website: https://www.uwlax.edu/cba/

University of Wisconsin–Madison, Graduate School, Wisconsin School of Business, Wisconsin Evening MBA Program, Madison, WI 53706. Offers general management (MBA). *Program availability:* Part-time-only, evening/weekend. *Faculty:* 14 full-time (2 women), 8 part-time/adjunct (0 women). *Students:* 168 part-time (54 women); includes 16 minority (3 Black or African American, non-Hispanic/Latino; 11 Asian, non-Hispanic/Latino; 2 Hispanic/Latino), 5 international. Average age 29. 73 applicants, 96% accepted, 54 enrolled. In 2016, 46 master's awarded. *Entrance requirements:* For master's, GMAT, essay, resume, 2 professional recommendations, official college transcripts, two years of professional experience, minimum GPA of 3.0. Additional exam requirements/recommendations for international students: Required—TOEFL (minimum score 600 paper-based; 106 iBT). *Application deadline:* For fall admission, 5/1 priority date for domestic and international students. Applications are processed on a rolling basis. Application fee: $75 ($81 for international students). Electronic applications accepted. *Expenses:* $22,526 per academic year tuition and fees. *Financial support:* In 2016–17, 29 students received support. Scholarships/grants available. Support available to part-time students. Financial award application deadline: 7/1. *Faculty research:* Creativity, leadership, healthcare operations, financial accounting, compensation. *Unit head:* Dr. Don Hausch, Associate Dean, 608-262-2535, Fax: 608-262-3607, E-mail: emba@wsb.wisc.edu. *Application contact:* Jean Sink, Director of Admissions, 608-262-9141, Fax: 608-262-3607, E-mail: emba@wsb.wisc.edu.
Website: https://wsb.wisc.edu/programs-degrees/mba/evening

University of Wisconsin–Madison, Graduate School, Wisconsin School of Business, Wisconsin Executive MBA Program, Madison, WI 53706. Offers general management (MBA). *Program availability:* Part-time-only, evening/weekend. *Faculty:* 13 full-time (1 woman), 6 part-time/adjunct (2 women). *Students:* 79 full-time (21 women); includes 10 minority (1 Black or African American, non-Hispanic/Latino; 5 Asian, non-Hispanic/Latino; 3 Hispanic/Latino; 1 Two or more races, non-Hispanic/Latino), 9 international. Average age 40. 56 applicants, 93% accepted, 41 enrolled. In 2016, 43 master's awarded. *Entrance requirements:* For master's, essay, two professional recommendations, official college transcripts, resume, interview, eight years of professional work experience, five years of leadership experience, minimum GPA of 3.0, employer authorization form. Additional exam requirements/recommendations for international students: Required—TOEFL (minimum score 600 paper-based; 106 iBT). *Application deadline:* For fall admission, 5/1 priority date for domestic and international students. Applications are processed on a rolling basis. Application fee: $75 ($81 for international students). Electronic applications accepted. *Expenses:* $41,899. *Financial support:* In 2016–17, 21 students received support. Scholarships/grants available. Support available to part-time students. Financial award application deadline: 7/1. *Faculty research:* Entrepreneurship, environmental issues in supply chain, leadership, marketing channels. *Unit head:* Dr. Don Hausch, Associate Dean, 608-262-2535, Fax: 608-262-3607, E-mail: emba@wsb.wisc.edu. *Application contact:* Jean Sink, Director of Admissions, 608-262-9141, Fax: 608-262-3607, E-mail: emba@wsb.wisc.edu.
Website: https://wsb.wisc.edu/programs-degrees/mba/executive

University of Wisconsin–Madison, Graduate School, Wisconsin School of Business, Wisconsin Full-Time MBA Program, Madison, WI 53706. Offers applied security analysis (MBA); arts administration (MBA); brand and product management (MBA); corporate finance and investment banking (MBA); marketing research (MBA); operations and technology management (MBA); real estate (MBA); risk management and insurance (MBA); strategic human resource management (MBA); supply chain management (MBA). *Faculty:* 125 full-time (32 women), 48 part-time/adjunct (11 women). *Students:* 197 full-time (73 women); includes 30 minority (11 Black or African American, non-Hispanic/Latino; 9 Asian, non-Hispanic/Latino; 10 Hispanic/Latino), 42 international. Average age 29. 728 applicants, 26% accepted, 99 enrolled. In 2016, 100 master's awarded. *Entrance requirements:* For master's, GMAT or GRE, bachelor's or equivalent degree, 2 years of work experience, essay, letter of recommendation, resume. Additional exam requirements/recommendations for international students: Required—TOEFL (minimum score 100 iBT), IELTS (minimum score 7.5). *Application deadline:* For fall admission, 9/28 for domestic students, 11/1 for international students; for winter admission, 11/2 for domestic students, 12/16 for international students; for spring admission, 1/11 for domestic students, 2/24 for international students; for summer admission, 3/1 for domestic students, 4/14 for international students. Applications are processed on a rolling basis. Application fee: $75 ($81 for international students). Electronic applications accepted. *Expenses:* $7,947 per semester resident tuition, $2,430 fees; $16,082 per semester resident tuition, $2,830 fees. *Financial support:* In 2016–17, 178 students received support, including 8 fellowships with full tuition reimbursements available (averaging $56,413 per year), 23 research assistantships with full tuition reimbursements available (averaging $42,151 per year), 51 teaching assistantships with full tuition reimbursements available (averaging $39,963 per year); scholarships/grants, health care benefits, and unspecified assistantships also available. Financial award application deadline: 4/11. *Faculty research:* Forms of competition and outcomes in dual distribution systems; explaining the accuracy of revised forecasts; supply chain planning for random demand surges; advanced demand information in a multi-product system; the effects of presentation salience and measurement subjectivity on nonprofessional investors' fair value judgments. *Unit head:* Prof. Ella Mae Matsumura, Associate Dean, Full-time MBA Program, 608-262-9731, E-mail: ematsumura@bus.wisc.edu. *Application contact:* Mary Lewitzke, Assistant Director of Admissions and Recruiting, Full-time MBA Program, 608-262-4000,
E-mail: mlewitzke@bus.wisc.edu.
Website: http://www.bus.wisc.edu/mba

University of Wisconsin–Milwaukee, Graduate School, Lubar School of Business, Milwaukee, WI 53201-0742. Offers business administration (MBA); executive business administration (EMBA); management science (MS, Graduate Certificate), including business analytics (Graduate Certificate), enterprise resource planning (Graduate Certificate), information technology management (MS), investment management (Graduate Certificate), nonprofit management (Graduate Certificate), nonprofit management and leadership (MS), state and local taxation (Graduate Certificate). *Accreditation:* AACSB. *Program availability:* Part-time, evening/weekend. *Students:* 304 full-time (120 women), 268 part-time (95 women); includes 107 minority (36 Black or African American, non-Hispanic/Latino; 1 American Indian or Alaska Native, non-Hispanic/Latino; 34 Asian, non-Hispanic/Latino; 10 Hispanic/Latino; 26 Two or more races, non-Hispanic/Latino), 79 international. Average age 32. 461 applicants, 62% accepted, 210 enrolled. In 2016, 300 master's, 32 other advanced degrees awarded. *Degree requirements:* For master's, comprehensive exam (for some programs). *Entrance requirements:* For master's, GMAT or GRE General Test. Additional exam requirements/recommendations for international students: Required—TOEFL (minimum score 550 paper-based; 79 iBT), IELTS (minimum score 6.5). *Application deadline:* For fall admission, 1/1 priority date for domestic students; for spring admission, 9/1 for domestic students. Applications are processed on a rolling basis. Application fee: $56 ($96 for international students). Electronic applications accepted. *Expenses:* Contact institution. *Financial support:* Fellowships with full tuition reimbursements, research assistantships with full tuition reimbursements, teaching assistantships with full tuition reimbursements, career-related internships or fieldwork, Federal Work-Study, health care benefits, unspecified assistantships, and project assistantships available. Support available to part-time students. Financial award application deadline: 4/15; financial award applicants required to submit FAFSA. *Faculty research:* Applied management research in finance, management information systems, marketing, operations research, organizational sciences. *Unit head:* V. Kanti Prasad, Dean, 414-229-6256, E-mail: dean-prasad@uwm.edu. *Application contact:* Business Graduate Student Services, 414-229-5403, E-mail: mba-ms@uwm.edu.
Website: https://uwm.edu/business/

University of Wisconsin–Oshkosh, Graduate Studies, College of Business, Program in Business Administration, Oshkosh, WI 54901. Offers MBA. *Accreditation:* AACSB. *Program availability:* Part-time. *Degree requirements:* For master's, integrative seminar. *Entrance requirements:* For master's, GMAT, GRE, minimum undergraduate GPA of 2.75. Additional exam requirements/recommendations for international students: Required—TOEFL (minimum score 550 paper-based; 79 iBT). Electronic applications accepted.

University of Wisconsin–Parkside, School of Business and Technology, Kenosha, WI 53141-2000. Offers MBA, MSCIS. *Accreditation:* AACSB. *Program availability:* Part-time, evening/weekend. *Entrance requirements:* For master's, GMAT. Additional exam requirements/recommendations for international students: Required—TOEFL (minimum score 550 paper-based; 79 iBT). Electronic applications accepted. *Expenses:* Contact institution. *Faculty research:* Business strategy, ethics in accounting and finance, mutual funds, decision analysis and neural networks, management skills.

University of Wisconsin–River Falls, Outreach and Graduate Studies, College of Business and Economics, River Falls, WI 54022. Offers MBA, MM. *Accreditation:* AACSB. *Degree requirements:* For master's, thesis or alternative. *Entrance requirements:* Additional exam requirements/recommendations for international students: Required—TOEFL (minimum score 550 paper-based; 79 iBT). Electronic applications accepted.

University of Wisconsin–Stevens Point, College of Letters and Science, Division of Business and Economics, Stevens Point, WI 54481-3897. Offers MBA. Program offered jointly with University of Wisconsin–Oshkosh.

University of Wisconsin–Whitewater, School of Graduate Studies, College of Business and Economics, Program in Business Administration, Whitewater, WI 53190-

1790. Offers finance (MBA). *Accreditation:* AACSB. *Program availability:* Part-time, evening/weekend, online learning. *Entrance requirements:* For master's, GMAT or GRE, minimum AACSB index of 1000, minimum GPA of 2.75. Additional exam requirements/recommendations for international students: Required—TOEFL (minimum score 550 paper-based; 80 iBT), IELTS (minimum score 6). Electronic applications accepted. *Faculty research:* Interface between social institutions and individual behavior, technology and innovation management, occupational mental health, workplace deviance and workplace romance.

University of Wyoming, College of Business, Program in Business Administration, Laramie, WY 82071. Offers MBA. *Accreditation:* AACSB. *Program availability:* Part-time, evening/weekend, online learning. *Degree requirements:* For master's, comprehensive exam, thesis or alternative. *Entrance requirements:* For master's, GMAT, GRE General Test, minimum GPA of 3.0. Additional exam requirements/recommendations for international students: Required—TOEFL (minimum score 550 paper-based; 80 iBT). Electronic applications accepted. *Faculty research:* Natural resource marketing and product development, work place violence.

Upper Iowa University, Online Master's Programs, Fayette, IA 52142-1857. Offers accounting (MBA); corporate financial management (MBA); emergency management and homeland security (MPA); general management (MBA); general studies (MPA); government administration (MPA); health and human services (MPA); human resources management (MBA); nonprofit organizational management (MPA); organizational development (MBA); public management (MPA); sport administration (MSA). MBA also available at Madison, WI campus. *Program availability:* Part-time, online learning. *Degree requirements:* For master's, research project. *Entrance requirements:* For master's, GMAT, GRE, or minimum GPA of 2.7 during last 60 hours. Additional exam requirements/recommendations for international students: Required—TOEFL (minimum score 570 paper-based). Electronic applications accepted. *Faculty research:* Total quality management, teams, organization culture and climate, management.

Urbana University, Division of Business Administration, Urbana, OH 43078-2091. Offers MBA. *Program availability:* Part-time, evening/weekend. *Degree requirements:* For master's, comprehensive exam, thesis or alternative. *Entrance requirements:* For master's, GMAT, minimum GPA of 2.7, BS in business, 3 letters of recommendation, work experience. Additional exam requirements/recommendations for international students: Required—TOEFL (minimum score 550 paper-based). *Faculty research:* Organizational behavior, taxation, segmentation, information systems, retail gravitation.

Ursuline College, School of Graduate Studies, Program in Business Administration, Pepper Pike, OH 44124-4398. Offers ethical and entrepreneurial leadership (MBA); financial planning and accounting (MBA); health services management (MBA); management (MBA); management and leadership (MBA); marketing and communications management (MBA). *Program availability:* Part-time. *Faculty:* 2 full-time (both women), 1 (woman) part-time/adjunct. *Students:* 27 full-time (25 women), 9 part-time (all women); includes 15 minority (14 Black or African American, non-Hispanic/Latino; 1 Hispanic/Latino), 2 international. Average age 38. 31 applicants, 71% accepted, 18 enrolled. In 2016, 34 master's awarded. *Degree requirements:* For master's, comprehensive exam (for some programs). *Entrance requirements:* For master's, GRE. Additional exam requirements/recommendations for international students: Required—TOEFL (minimum score 500 paper-based) or GRE. Application fee: $25. Electronic applications accepted. *Expenses:* Contact institution. *Financial support:* In 2016–17, 6 students received support. Scholarships/grants available. Financial award applicants required to submit FAFSA. *Faculty research:* Gift economy; sharing economy; cooperative business models; collaborative leadership; corporate social responsibility and the triple bottom line, defined as the three P's: people, planet and profit. *Unit head:* Dr. Nurete Brenner, Executive Director, 440-684-6038, Fax: 440-684-6088, E-mail: nurete.brenner@ursuline.edu. *Application contact:* Melanie Steele, Director of Graduate Admission, 440-646-8146, Fax: 440-684-6138, E-mail: graduateadmissions@ursuline.edu.

Utah State University, School of Graduate Studies, College of Business, Program in Business Administration, Logan, UT 84322. Offers MBA. *Accreditation:* AACSB. *Program availability:* Part-time, evening/weekend, online learning. *Degree requirements:* For master's, comprehensive exam. *Entrance requirements:* For master's, GMAT or GRE, minimum GPA of 3.0. Additional exam requirements/recommendations for international students: Required—TOEFL. Electronic applications accepted. *Faculty research:* Marketing strategy, technology and innovation, public utility finance, international competitiveness.

Utah Valley University, MBA Program, Orem, UT 84058-5999. Offers accounting (MBA); management (MBA). *Accreditation:* AACSB. *Program availability:* Part-time, evening/weekend. *Entrance requirements:* For master's, GMAT, official transcripts, current resume, three letters of recommendation, essay. Additional exam requirements/recommendations for international students: Required—TOEFL (minimum score 79 iBT). Electronic applications accepted. *Expenses:* Contact institution.

Valdosta State University, Master of Business Administration Program, Valdosta, GA 31698. Offers business administration (MBA); healthcare administration (MBA). Program is a member of the Georgia WebMBA. *Accreditation:* AACSB. *Program availability:* Part-time, evening/weekend, 100% online, blended/hybrid learning. *Degree requirements:* For master's, comprehensive written and/or oral exams. *Entrance requirements:* For master's, GMAT or GRE, minimum GPA of 2.75. Additional exam requirements/recommendations for international students: Required—TOEFL (minimum score 523 paper-based); Recommended—IELTS. Electronic applications accepted. *Expenses:* Contact institution.

Valparaiso University, Graduate School and Continuing Education, College of Business, Valparaiso, IN 46383. Offers business administration (MBA); business intelligence (Certificate); engineering management (Certificate); entrepreneurship (Certificate); finance (Certificate); general business (Certificate); management (Certificate); marketing (Certificate); sustainability (Certificate); JD/MBA; MSN/MBA. *Accreditation:* AACSB. *Program availability:* Part-time, evening/weekend, online learning. *Entrance requirements:* For master's, GMAT, GRE, minimum GPA of 3.0. Additional exam requirements/recommendations for international students: Required—TOEFL (minimum score 550 paper-based; 80 iBT), IELTS (minimum score 6). Electronic applications accepted. *Expenses:* Contact institution.

Vancouver Island University, Master of Business Administration Program, Nanaimo, BC V9R 5S5, Canada. Offers international business (MBA), including finance, marketing. Program offered jointly with University of Hertfordshire. *Accreditation:* ACBSP. *Program availability:* Part-time. *Degree requirements:* For master's, thesis. *Entrance requirements:* Additional exam requirements/recommendations for international students: Required—TOEFL (minimum score 88 iBT), IELTS (minimum score 6.5). Electronic applications accepted. *Expenses:* Contact institution. *Faculty research:* Tourism development, entrepreneurship, organizational development, strategic planning, international business strategy, intercultural team work.

Vanderbilt University, Vanderbilt University Owen Graduate School of Management, Vanderbilt Executive MBA Programs, Nashville, TN 37203. Offers EMBA, MBA. *Accreditation:* AACSB. *Program availability:* Evening/weekend. *Entrance requirements:* For master's, GMAT, minimum of 5 years of professional work experience. Electronic applications accepted. *Expenses:* Contact institution.

Vanderbilt University, Vanderbilt University Owen Graduate School of Management, Vanderbilt MBA Program, Nashville, TN 37203. Offers accounting (MBA); finance (MBA); general management (MBA); health care (MBA); human and organizational performance (MBA); marketing (MBA); operations (MBA); strategy (MBA); MBA/JD; MBA/M Div; MBA/MD; MBA/MSN; MBA/MTS; MBA/PhD. *Accreditation:* AACSB. *Degree requirements:* For master's, 62 credit hours of coursework; completion of ethics course; minimum GPA of 3.0. *Entrance requirements:* For master's, GMAT (preferred) or GRE, 2 years of work experience (recommended). Additional exam requirements/recommendations for international students: Required—TOEFL (minimum score 100 iBT). Electronic applications accepted. *Expenses:* Contact institution. *Faculty research:* Accounting and finance, business strategy and economics, marketing, operations management, organization studies.

Villanova University, Villanova School of Business, Executive MBA Program, Radnor, PA 19087. Offers EMBA. *Accreditation:* AACSB. *Program availability:* Evening/weekend. *Faculty:* 108 full-time (39 women), 32 part-time/adjunct (8 women). *Students:* 52 part-time (17 women); includes 12 minority (6 Black or African American, non-Hispanic/Latino; 1 Asian, non-Hispanic/Latino; 3 Hispanic/Latino; 2 Two or more races, non-Hispanic/Latino), 1 international. Average age 39. In 2016, 28 master's awarded. *Degree requirements:* For master's, minimum cumulative GPA of 3.0. *Entrance requirements:* For master's, 2 letters of recommendation, essay, resume, official transcript, significant managerial or executive work experience, employer approval. Additional exam requirements/recommendations for international students: Required—TOEFL (minimum score 550 paper-based; 100 iBT). *Application deadline:* For fall admission, 6/30 for domestic and international students. Applications are processed on a rolling basis. Application fee: $50. Electronic applications accepted. *Expenses:* Contact institution. *Financial support:* Scholarships/grants available. Financial award application deadline: 6/30; financial award applicants required to submit FAFSA. *Faculty research:* Business analytics; creativity, innovation and entrepreneurship; global leadership; real estate; church management; business ethics. *Unit head:* Michael L. Capella, Associate Dean of Graduate and Executive Programs, 610-523-4336, E-mail: michael.l.capella@villanova.edu. *Application contact:* Jennifer Wiess, Director, Executive Programs, 610-523-1794, E-mail: jennifer.wiess@villanova.edu.
Website: http://www.emba.villanova.edu/

Villanova University, Villanova School of Business, MBA - The Fast Track Program, Villanova, PA 19085. Offers analytics (MBA); cybersecurity (MBA); finance (MBA); healthcare (MBA); international business (MBA); management information systems (MBA); marketing (MBA); real estate (MBA); strategic management (MBA); sustainability (MBA). *Accreditation:* AACSB. *Program availability:* Part-time, evening/weekend. *Faculty:* 108 full-time (39 women), 32 part-time/adjunct (8 women). *Students:* 127 part-time (58 women); includes 18 minority (3 Black or African American, non-Hispanic/Latino; 7 Asian, non-Hispanic/Latino; 6 Hispanic/Latino; 2 Two or more races, non-Hispanic/Latino), 2 international. Average age 30. 88 applicants, 90% accepted, 66 enrolled. In 2016, 75 master's awarded. *Degree requirements:* For master's, minimum GPA of 3.0. *Entrance requirements:* For master's, GMAT or GRE, work experience, 2 letters of recommendation, 2 essays, resume, official transcripts, interview. Additional exam requirements/recommendations for international students: Required—TOEFL (minimum score 550 paper-based; 100 iBT). *Application deadline:* For fall admission, 6/30 for domestic and international students. Application fee: $65. Electronic applications accepted. *Expenses:* Contact institution. *Financial support:* Scholarships/grants available. Financial award application deadline: 6/30; financial award applicants required to submit FAFSA. *Faculty research:* Business analytics; creativity, innovation and entrepreneurship; global leadership; real estate; church management; business ethics; marketing and consumer insights. *Unit head:* Michael L. Capella, Associate Dean of Graduate and Executive Business Programs, 610-519-4336, Fax: 610-519-6273, E-mail: michael.l.capella@villanova.edu. *Application contact:* Kimberly Kane, Manager of Admissions, 610-519-3701, Fax: 610-519-6273, E-mail: kimberly.kane@villanova.edu.
Website: http://www1.villanova.edu/villanova/business/graduate/mba.html

Villanova University, Villanova School of Business, MBA - The Flex Track Program, Villanova, PA 19085. Offers analytics (MBA); finance (MBA); healthcare (MBA); international business (MBA); marketing (MBA); real estate (MBA); strategic management (MBA); JD/MBA. *Accreditation:* AACSB. *Program availability:* Part-time, evening/weekend, online learning. *Faculty:* 108 full-time (39 women), 32 part-time/adjunct (8 women). *Students:* 13 full-time (5 women), 399 part-time (134 women); includes 73 minority (21 Black or African American, non-Hispanic/Latino; 32 Asian, non-Hispanic/Latino; 19 Hispanic/Latino; 1 Two or more races, non-Hispanic/Latino), 11 international. Average age 31. 93 applicants, 94% accepted, 80 enrolled. In 2016, 133 master's awarded. *Degree requirements:* For master's, minimum GPA of 3.0. *Entrance requirements:* For master's, GMAT or GRE, work experience, 2 letters of recommendation, 2 essays, resume, official transcript. Additional exam requirements/recommendations for international students: Required—TOEFL (minimum score 550 paper-based; 100 iBT). *Application deadline:* For fall admission, 6/30 for domestic and international students; for spring admission, 11/15 for domestic and international students; for summer admission, 3/31 for domestic and international students. Applications are processed on a rolling basis. Application fee: $65. Electronic applications accepted. *Expenses:* Contact institution. *Financial support:* In 2016–17, 13 research assistantships with full tuition reimbursements (averaging $13,100 per year) were awarded; scholarships/grants also available. Financial award application deadline: 6/30; financial award applicants required to submit FAFSA. *Faculty research:* Business analytics; creativity, innovation and entrepreneurship; global leadership; real estate; church management; business ethics. *Unit head:* Michael L. Capella, Associate Dean of Graduate and Executive Business Programs, 610-610-4336, Fax: 610-519-6273, E-mail: michael.l.capella@villanova.edu. *Application contact:* Claire Bruno, Director of Recruitment and Enrollment Management, 610-519-4336, Fax: 610-519-6273, E-mail: claire.bruno@villanova.edu.
Website: http://www1.villanova.edu/villanova/business/graduate/mba.html

Villanova University, Villanova School of Business, Online MBA Program, Villanova, PA 19085-1699. Offers MBA. *Program availability:* Part-time-only, evening/weekend, 100% online, blended/hybrid learning. *Faculty:* 108 full-time (39 women), 27 part-time/adjunct (6 women). *Students:* 180 part-time (69 women); includes 29 minority (12 Black or African American, non-Hispanic/Latino; 1 American Indian or Alaska Native, non-Hispanic/Latino; 10 Asian, non-Hispanic/Latino; 4 Hispanic/Latino; 2 Two or more races, non-Hispanic/Latino), 1 international. Average age 33. *Degree requirements:* For master's, minimum cumulative GPA of 3.0. *Entrance requirements:* For master's, GMAT or GRE. Additional exam requirements/recommendations for international students: Required—TOEFL. *Application deadline:* For spring admission, 11/15 for domestic and international students; for summer admission, 3/31 for domestic and international students. Applications are processed on a rolling basis. Application fee: $65. Electronic applications accepted. *Expenses:* Contact institution. *Financial support:* Institutionally sponsored loans and scholarships/grants available. Financial award application deadline: 6/30; financial award applicants required to submit FAFSA. *Faculty research:*

Real estate; business analytics; global leadership; innovation, creativity and entrepreneurship; church management; business ethics; marketing and consumer insights. *Unit head:* Michael L. Capella, Associate Dean of Graduate and Executive Business Programs, 610-519-4336, Fax: 610-519-6273, E-mail: michael.l.capella@villanova.edu. *Application contact:* Claire Bruno, Director of Recruitment and Enrollment Management, 610-519-4336, Fax: 610-519-6273, E-mail: claire.bruno@villanova.edu.

Virginia College in Birmingham, Program in Business Administration, Birmingham, AL 35209. Offers healthcare (MBA); management (MBA). *Program availability:* Part-time, evening/weekend, online learning. *Entrance requirements:* For master's, bachelor's degree in related academic area.

Virginia College in Birmingham, Virginia College Online, Birmingham, AL 35209. Offers business administration (MBA); criminal justice (MCJ); cybersecurity (MC). *Program availability:* Part-time, evening/weekend, online learning.

Virginia Commonwealth University, Graduate School, School of Business, Program in Business Administration, Richmond, VA 23284-9005. Offers MBA, PhD. *Degree requirements:* For doctorate, thesis/dissertation. *Entrance requirements:* For master's and doctorate, GMAT. Additional exam requirements/recommendations for international students: Required—TOEFL (minimum score 600 paper-based; 100 iBT). *Application deadline:* For fall admission, 7/1 for domestic students; for spring admission, 11/1 for domestic students. Applications are processed on a rolling basis. Application fee: $50. Electronic applications accepted. *Financial support:* Fellowships, research assistantships, teaching assistantships, Federal Work-Study, institutionally sponsored loans, and tuition waivers (full and partial) available. Financial award application deadline: 3/15; financial award applicants required to submit FAFSA. *Unit head:* Dr. E. G. Miller, Interim Chair, 804-827-7404, Fax: 804-828-8884, E-mail: egmiller@vcu.edu. *Application contact:* Colleen A. Davis, Graduate Program Director, 804-828-4622, E-mail: androvichcm@vcu.edu.
Website: http://www.business.vcu.edu/graduate.html

Virginia International University, School of Business, Fairfax, VA 22030. Offers accounting (MBA, MS); entrepreneurship (MBA); executive management (Graduate Certificate); global logistics (MBA); health care management (MBA); hospitality and tourism management (MBA); human resources management (MBA); international business management (MBA); international finance (MBA); marketing management (MBA); mass media and public relations (MBA); project management (MBA, MS). *Program availability:* Part-time, online learning. *Entrance requirements:* For master's and Graduate Certificate, bachelor's degree. Additional exam requirements/recommendations for international students: Required—TOEFL (minimum score 550 paper-based; 80 iBT), IELTS (minimum score 6). Electronic applications accepted.

Virginia Polytechnic Institute and State University, Graduate School, Pamplin College of Business, Blacksburg, VA 24061. Offers accounting and information systems (MACIS); business (PhD); business administration (MBA, MS); hospitality and tourism management (MS, PhD). *Faculty:* 126 full-time (38 women), 3 part-time/adjunct (1 woman). *Students:* 255 full-time (101 women), 156 part-time (56 women); includes 95 minority (21 Black or African American, non-Hispanic/Latino; 49 Asian, non-Hispanic/Latino; 13 Hispanic/Latino; 12 Two or more races, non-Hispanic/Latino), 73 international. Average age 33. 310 applicants, 59% accepted, 150 enrolled. In 2016, 167 master's, 8 doctorates awarded. *Degree requirements:* For master's, comprehensive exam (for some programs), thesis (for some programs); for doctorate, comprehensive exam (for some programs), thesis/dissertation (for some programs). *Entrance requirements:* For master's and doctorate, GRE/GMAT. Additional exam requirements/recommendations for international students: Required—TOEFL (minimum score 80 iBT). *Application deadline:* For fall admission, 8/1 for domestic students, 4/1 for international students; for spring admission, 1/1 for domestic students, 9/1 for international students. Applications are processed on a rolling basis. Application fee: $75. Electronic applications accepted. *Expenses:* Tuition, state resident: full-time $12,467; part-time $692.50 per credit hour. Tuition, nonresident: full-time $25,095; part-time $1394.25 per credit hour. *Required fees:* $2669; $491.50 per semester. Tuition and fees vary according to course load, campus/location and program. *Financial support:* In 2016–17, 2 fellowships with full tuition reimbursements (averaging $21,222 per year), 3 research assistantships with full tuition reimbursements (averaging $24,988 per year), 46 teaching assistantships with full tuition reimbursements (averaging $20,054 per year) were awarded. Financial award application deadline: 3/1; financial award applicants required to submit FAFSA. *Total annual research expenditures:* $2.7 million. *Unit head:* Dr. Robert T. Sumichrast, Dean, 540-231-6601, Fax: 540-231-4487, E-mail: busdean@vt.edu. *Application contact:* Kimberly Ridpath, Executive Assistant, 540-231-6601, Fax: 540-231-4487, E-mail: ridpathk@vt.edu.
Website: http://www.pamplin.vt.edu/

Viterbo University, Master of Business Administration Program, La Crosse, WI 54601-4797. Offers general business administration (MBA); health care management (MBA); international business (MBA); leadership (MBA); project management (MBA). *Accreditation:* ACBSP. *Program availability:* Part-time, evening/weekend. *Degree requirements:* For master's, 34 semester credits. *Entrance requirements:* For master's, bachelor's degree, transcripts, minimum undergraduate cumulative GPA of 3.0, 2 letters of reference, 3-5 page essay. Additional exam requirements/recommendations for international students: Recommended—TOEFL (minimum score 550 paper-based). Electronic applications accepted. *Expenses:* Contact institution.

Wagner College, Division of Graduate Studies, Department of Business Administration, Staten Island, NY 10301-4495. Offers accounting (MS); business administration (MBA); finance (MBA); health care administration (MBA); international business (MBA); management (Exec MBA); marketing (MBA). *Accreditation:* ACBSP. *Program availability:* Part-time, evening/weekend. *Faculty:* 8 full-time (3 women), 17 part-time/adjunct (5 women). *Students:* 90 full-time (25 women), 16 part-time (8 women); includes 21 minority (12 Black or African American, non-Hispanic/Latino; 1 American Indian or Alaska Native, non-Hispanic/Latino; 3 Asian, non-Hispanic/Latino; 5 Hispanic/Latino), 5 international. Average age 26. 88 applicants, 85% accepted, 62 enrolled. In 2016, 72 master's awarded. *Degree requirements:* For master's, thesis optional. *Entrance requirements:* For master's, minimum GPA of 2.75, proficiency in computers and math. Additional exam requirements/recommendations for international students: Required—TOEFL (minimum score 550 paper-based; 79 iBT). *Application deadline:* For fall admission, 5/1 priority date for domestic students, 3/1 priority date for international students; for spring admission, 12/1 for domestic students, 11/1 for international students. Applications are processed on a rolling basis. Application fee: $50. Tuition and fees vary according to degree level. *Financial support:* In 2016–17, 93 students received support. Career-related internships or fieldwork, unspecified assistantships, and alumni fellowship grants available. Financial award application deadline: 4/1; financial award applicants required to submit FAFSA. *Unit head:* Dr. Donald Crooks, Director, 718-390-3429, Fax: 718-390-3429, E-mail: dcrooks@wagner.edu. *Application contact:* Patricia Clancy, Assistant Director for Enrollment, 718-420-4464, Fax: 718-390-3105, E-mail: patricia.clancy@wagner.edu.

Wake Forest University, School of Business, Charlotte Evening MBA Program, Charlotte, NC 28211. Offers MBA. *Accreditation:* AACSB. *Program availability:* Part-time-only, evening/weekend. *Faculty:* 19 full-time (3 women). *Students:* 117 full-time (37 women); includes 22 minority (11 Black or African American, non-Hispanic/Latino; 1 American Indian or Alaska Native, non-Hispanic/Latino; 6 Asian, non-Hispanic/Latino; 3 Hispanic/Latino; 1 Two or more races, non-Hispanic/Latino), 1 international. Average age 32. 81 applicants, 93% accepted, 59 enrolled. In 2016, 55 master's awarded. *Degree requirements:* For master's, 54 total credit hours. *Entrance requirements:* For master's, GMAT or GRE, letters of recommendation, official transcripts, current resume or curriculum vitae, three years of work experience. Additional exam requirements/recommendations for international students: Required—TOEFL (minimum score 600 paper-based; 100 iBT). *Application deadline:* For fall admission, 8/1 for domestic and international students. Applications are processed on a rolling basis. Application fee: $100. Electronic applications accepted. *Expenses:* Contact institution. *Financial support:* Scholarships/grants available. Financial award application deadline: 4/15; financial award applicants required to submit FAFSA. *Faculty research:* Influence of personal relationships on business decision-making and management of change; drivers of perceived value and consumer behavior; impact of accounting on auditing, financial, managerial, systems and taxation stakeholders; corporate governance and executive compensation; impact of operations strategies on competitiveness. *Unit head:* Tim Janke, Associate Dean of Working Professional Programs, 704-365-1717, Fax: 704-365-3511, E-mail: cltbusadmissions@wfu.edu. *Application contact:* Judi Affeldt, Administrative Assistant, 704-365-1717, Fax: 704-365-3511,
E-mail: cltbusadmissions@wfu.edu.
Website: http://business.wfu.edu/charlotte-evening-mba/

Wake Forest University, School of Business, Evening MBA Program–Winston-Salem, Winston-Salem, NC 27106. Offers MBA, PhD/MBA. *Accreditation:* AACSB. *Program availability:* Part-time-only, evening/weekend. *Faculty:* 14 full-time (1 woman), 1 part-time/adjunct (0 women). *Students:* 102 full-time (41 women); includes 19 minority (10 Black or African American, non-Hispanic/Latino; 2 Asian, non-Hispanic/Latino; 6 Hispanic/Latino; 1 Two or more races, non-Hispanic/Latino), 2 international. Average age 32. 77 applicants, 74% accepted, 50 enrolled. In 2016, 45 master's awarded. *Degree requirements:* For master's, 54 total credit hours. *Entrance requirements:* For master's, GMAT or GRE, letters of recommendation, official transcripts, current resume or curriculum vitae, three years of work experience. Additional exam requirements/recommendations for international students: Required—TOEFL (minimum score 600 paper-based; 100 iBT). *Application deadline:* For fall admission, 8/1 for domestic and international students. Applications are processed on a rolling basis. Application fee: $100. Electronic applications accepted. *Expenses:* Contact institution. *Financial support:* In 2016–17, 48 students received support. Scholarships/grants available. Financial award application deadline: 4/15; financial award applicants required to submit FAFSA. *Faculty research:* Influence of personal relationships on business decision-making and management of change; drivers of perceived value and consumer behavior; impact of accounting on auditing, financial, managerial, systems and taxation stakeholders; corporate governance and executive compensation; impact of operations strategies on competitiveness. *Unit head:* Tim Jamkme, Associate Dean of Working Professional Programs, 336-758-5422, Fax: 336-758-5830, E-mail: busadmissions@wfu.edu. *Application contact:* Tamara Paquee, Administrative Assistant, 336-758-5422, Fax: 336-758-5830, E-mail: busadmissions@wfu.edu.
Website: http://business.wfu.edu/evening-mba/

Wake Forest University, School of Business, MA in Management Program, Winston-Salem, NC 27106. Offers MA. *Faculty:* 16 full-time (6 women), 7 part-time/adjunct (3 women). *Students:* 151 full-time (88 women); includes 42 minority (31 Black or African American, non-Hispanic/Latino; 3 Asian, non-Hispanic/Latino; 6 Hispanic/Latino; 2 Two or more races, non-Hispanic/Latino), 10 international. Average age 23. 283 applicants, 87% accepted, 151 enrolled. In 2016, 148 master's awarded. *Degree requirements:* For master's, 41.5 credit hours. *Entrance requirements:* For master's, GMAT or GRE, letters of recommendation, official transcripts, current resume or curriculum vitae. Additional exam requirements/recommendations for international students: Required—TOEFL (minimum score 600 paper-based; 100 iBT). *Application deadline:* For fall admission, 6/15 for domestic and international students. Applications are processed on a rolling basis. Application fee: $100. Electronic applications accepted. *Expenses:* Contact institution. *Financial support:* Scholarships/grants available. Financial award application deadline: 4/1; financial award applicants required to submit FAFSA. *Faculty research:* Influence of personal relationships on business decision-making and management of change; drivers of perceived value and consumer behavior; impact of accounting on auditing, financial, managerial, systems and taxation stakeholders; corporate governance and executive compensation; impact of operations strategies on competitiveness. *Unit head:* Scott Shafer, Associate Dean, MA in Management, 336-758-5422, Fax: 336-758-5830, E-mail: busadmissions@wfu.edu. *Application contact:* John Montana, Senior Associate Director, MA Enrollment Management, 336-758-5422, Fax: 336-758-5830, E-mail: busadmissions@wfu.edu.
Website: http://www.business.wfu.edu/ma-management

Wake Forest University, School of Business, Saturday MBA Program–Charlotte, Charlotte, NC 28211. Offers MBA. *Accreditation:* AACSB. *Program availability:* Part-time, evening/weekend. *Faculty:* 19 full-time (3 women), 1 part-time/adjunct (0 women). *Students:* 86 full-time (29 women); includes 27 minority (10 Black or African American, non-Hispanic/Latino; 3 American Indian or Alaska Native, non-Hispanic/Latino; 7 Asian, non-Hispanic/Latino; 5 Hispanic/Latino; 2 Two or more races, non-Hispanic/Latino). Average age 34. 60 applicants, 95% accepted, 45 enrolled. In 2016, 41 master's awarded. *Degree requirements:* For master's, 54 total credit hours. *Entrance requirements:* For master's, GMAT or GRE, letters of recommendation, official transcripts, current resume or curriculum vitae, three years of work experience. Additional exam requirements/recommendations for international students: Required—TOEFL (minimum score 600 paper-based; 100 iBT), PTE. *Application deadline:* For spring admission, 11/1 for domestic and international students. Applications are processed on a rolling basis. Application fee: $100. Electronic applications accepted. *Expenses:* Contact institution. *Financial support:* In 2016–17, 51 students received support. Scholarships/grants available. Financial award application deadline: 9/1; financial award applicants required to submit FAFSA. *Faculty research:* Influence of personal relationships on business decision-making and management of change; drivers of perceived value and consumer behavior; impact of accounting on auditing, financial, managerial, systems and taxation stakeholders; corporate governance and executive compensation; impact of operations strategies on competitiveness. *Unit head:* Tim Janke, Associate Dean of Working Professional Programs, 704-365-1717, Fax: 704-365-3511, E-mail: cltbusadmissions@wfu.edu. *Application contact:* Judi Affeldt, Administrative Assistant, 704-365-1717, Fax: 704-365-3511,
E-mail: cltbusadmissions@wfu.edu.
Website: http://business.wfu.edu/charlotte-saturday-mba/

Walden University, Graduate Programs, School of Management, Minneapolis, MN 55401. Offers accounting (MBA, MS, DBA), including accounting for the professional (MS), accounting with CPA emphasis (MS), self-designed (MS); advanced project management (Graduate Certificate); applied project management (Graduate Certificate); auditing (Graduate Certificate); bridge to business administration (Post-Doctoral Certificate); bridge to management (Post-Doctoral Certificate); business management (Graduate Certificate); communication (MBA); corporate finance (MBA); digital marketing (Graduate Certificate); entrepreneurship (DBA); entrepreneurship and small business (MBA); finance (MS, DBA), including finance for the professional (MS), finance with CFA/investment (MS), finance with CPA emphasis (MS); global supply chain management (DBA); healthcare management (MBA, DBA); human resource management (MBA, MS, Graduate Certificate), including functional human resource management (MS), general program (MS), integrating functional and strategic human resource management (MS), organizational strategy (MS); human resources management (DBA); information systems management (DBA); international business (MBA, DBA); leadership (MBA, MS, DBA, Graduate Certificate), including general program (MS), human resource leadership (MS), leader development (MS), self-designed (MS); management (MS, PhD), including communications (MS), finance (PhD), general program (MS), healthcare management (MS), human resource management (MS), human resources management (PhD), information systems management (PhD), international business (MS), leadership (MS), leadership and organizational change (PhD), marketing (MS), project management (MS), strategy and operations (MS); managerial accounting (Graduate Certificate); marketing (MBA, MS, DBA); project management (MBA, MS, DBA); self-designed (MBA, DBA); social impact management (DBA); technology entrepreneurship (DBA). *Accreditation:* ACBSP. *Program availability:* Part-time, evening/weekend, online only, 100% online. *Degree requirements:* For master's, thesis (for some programs), residency (for EMBA); for doctorate, thesis/dissertation (for some programs), residency. *Entrance requirements:* For master's, bachelor's degree or higher; minimum GPA of 2.5; official transcripts; goal statement (for some programs); access to computer and Internet; for doctorate, master's degree or higher; three years of related professional or academic experience (preferred); minimum GPA of 3.0; goal statement and current resume (for select programs); official transcripts; access to computer and Internet; for other advanced degree, relevant work experience; access to computer and Internet. Additional exam requirements/recommendations for international students: Required—TOEFL (minimum score 550 paper-based, 79 iBT), IELTS (minimum score 6.5), Michigan English Language Assessment Battery (minimum score 82), or PTE (minimum score 53). Electronic applications accepted.

Walden University, Graduate Programs, School of Public Policy and Administration, Minneapolis, MN 55401. Offers criminal justice (MPA, MPP, MS, Graduate Certificate), including emergency management (MS, PhD), general program (MS), global leadership (MS, PhD), homeland security and policy coordination (MS, PhD), law and public policy (MS, PhD), policy analysis (MS, PhD), public management and leadership (MS, PhD), self-designed (MS), terrorism, mediation, and peace (MS, PhD); criminal justice and executive management (MS), including global leadership (MS, PhD); criminal justice leadership and executive management (MS), including emergency management (MS, PhD), general program, homeland security and policy coordination (MS, PhD), law and public policy (MS, PhD), policy analysis (MS, PhD), public management and leadership (MS, PhD), self-designed, terrorism, mediation, and peace (MS, PhD); emergency management (MPA, MPP, MS), including criminal justice (MS, PhD), general program (MS), homeland security (MS), public management and leadership (MS, PhD), terrorism and emergency management (MS); general program (MPA, MPP); global leadership (MPA, MPP); government management (Graduate Certificate); health policy (MPA, MPP); homeland security (Graduate Certificate); homeland security and policy coordination (MPA, MPP); international nongovernmental organizations (MPA, MPP); law and public policy (MPA, MPP); local government management for sustainable communities (MPA, MPP); nonprofit management (Graduate Certificate); nonprofit management and leadership (MPA, MPP, MS), including global leadership (MS, PhD), international nongovernmental organization (MS), local government for sustainable communities (MS), self designed (MS); online teaching in higher education (Post-Master's Certificate); policy analysis (MPA); public management and leadership (MPA, MPP, Graduate Certificate); public policy (Graduate Certificate); public policy and administration (PhD), including criminal justice (MS, PhD), emergency management (MS, PhD), global leadership (MS, PhD), health policy, homeland security and policy coordination (MS, PhD), international nongovernmental organizations, law and public policy (MS, PhD), local government management for sustainable communities, nonprofit management and leadership, policy analysis (MS, PhD), public management and leadership (MS, PhD), terrorism, mediation, and peace (MS, PhD); strategic planning and public policy (Graduate Certificate); terrorism, mediation, and peace (MPA, MPP). *Program availability:* Part-time, evening/weekend, online only, 100% online. *Degree requirements:* For doctorate, thesis/dissertation, residency. *Entrance requirements:* For master's, bachelor's degree or higher; minimum GPA of 2.5; official transcripts; goal statement (for some programs); access to computer and Internet; for doctorate, master's degree or higher; three years of related professional or academic experience (preferred); minimum GPA of 3.0; goal statement and current resume (for select programs); official transcripts; access to computer and Internet; for other advanced degree, relevant work experience; access to computer and Internet. Additional exam requirements/recommendations for international students: Required—TOEFL (minimum score 550 paper-based, 79 iBT), IELTS (minimum score 6.5), Michigan English Language Assessment Battery (minimum score 82), or PTE (minimum score 53). Electronic applications accepted.

Walsh College of Accountancy and Business Administration, Graduate Programs, Program in Business Administration, Troy, MI 48083. Offers MBA, MBA/MSF, MBA/MSITL, MBA/MSM, MBA/MSMKT. *Accreditation:* ACBSP. *Program availability:* Part-time, evening/weekend, 100% online, blended/hybrid learning. *Faculty:* 16 full-time (7 women), 15 part-time/adjunct (6 women). *Students:* 536 (270 women); includes 121 minority (70 Black or African American, non-Hispanic/Latino; 3 American Indian or Alaska Native, non-Hispanic/Latino; 23 Asian, non-Hispanic/Latino; 19 Hispanic/Latino; 6 Two or more races, non-Hispanic/Latino), 23 international. Average age 33. 151 applicants, 89% accepted, 99 enrolled. In 2016, 188 master's awarded. *Entrance requirements:* For master's, minimum overall cumulative GPA of 2.75 from all colleges previously attended. Additional exam requirements/recommendations for international students: Required—TOEFL (minimum score 550 paper-based, 79 iBT), IELTS (6.5), Michigan English Language Assessment Battery, or MTELP. *Application deadline:* Applications are processed on a rolling basis. Application fee: $35. Electronic applications accepted. *Expenses:* $740 per semester credit hour, $125 registration fee per semester. *Financial support:* In 2016–17, 16 students received support. Career-related internships or fieldwork and scholarships/grants available. Financial award application deadline: 6/30; financial award applicants required to submit FAFSA. *Faculty research:* Strategy practice and process, management learning and decision making, consumer behavior, data and decision making. *Unit head:* Dr. Michael Rinkus, Interim Executive Vice President/Chief Academic Officer, 248-823-1269, Fax: 248-689-0920, E-mail: mrinkus@walshcollege.edu. *Application contact:* Heather Rigby, Director, Admissions and Academic Advising, 248-823-1294, Fax: 248-823-1611, E-mail: hrigby@walshcollege.edu.

Walsh College of Accountancy and Business Administration, Graduate Programs, Program in Management, Troy, MI 48083. Offers human resources management (MS); international business (MS); strategic management (MS). *Program availability:* Part-time, evening/weekend. *Faculty:* 12 full-time (6 women), 12 part-time/adjunct (5 women). *Students:* 54 (43 women); includes 20 minority (15 Black or African American, non-Hispanic/Latino; 1 American Indian or Alaska Native, non-Hispanic/Latino; 2 Asian, non-Hispanic/Latino; 1 Hispanic/Latino; 1 Two or more races, non-Hispanic/Latino). Average age 33. 27 applicants, 70% accepted, 13 enrolled. In 2016, 2 master's awarded. *Entrance requirements:* For master's, minimum overall cumulative GPA of 2.75 from all colleges previously attended. Additional exam requirements/recommendations for international students: Required—TOEFL (minimum score 550 paper-based, 79 iBT), IELTS (6.5), Michigan English Language Assessment Battery, or MTELP. *Application deadline:* Applications are processed on a rolling basis. Application fee: $35. Electronic applications accepted. *Expenses:* $740 per credit hour, $125 registration fee per semester. *Financial support:* In 2016–17, 2 students received support. Career-related internships or fieldwork and scholarships/grants available. Financial award application deadline: 6/30; financial award applicants required to submit FAFSA. *Faculty research:* Strategy practice and process, management learning and decision-making, human capital development, global leadership and citizenship, use of systems and complexity theory and management practice. *Unit head:* Dr. Sheila Ronis, Chair, Management, 248-823-1635, Fax: 248-689-0920, E-mail: sronis@walshcollege.edu. *Application contact:* Heather Rigby, Director, Admissions and Academic Advising, 248-823-1610, Fax: 248-689-0938, E-mail: hrigby@walshcollege.edu.

Walsh University, Graduate Programs, MBA Program, North Canton, OH 44720-3396. Offers healthcare management (MBA); management (MBA); marketing (MBA). *Program availability:* Part-time, evening/weekend, online only, 100% online. *Faculty:* 10 full-time (4 women), 22 part-time/adjunct (5 women). *Students:* 37 full-time (14 women), 137 part-time (84 women); includes 21 minority (17 Black or African American, non-Hispanic/Latino; 1 Asian, non-Hispanic/Latino; 2 Hispanic/Latino; 1 Two or more races, non-Hispanic/Latino), 7 international. Average age 35. 66 applicants, 76% accepted, 34 enrolled. In 2016, 66 master's awarded. *Degree requirements:* For master's, capstone course in strategic management. *Entrance requirements:* For master's, GMAT (minimum score of 490), minimum GPA of 3.0. Additional exam requirements/recommendations for international students: Required—TOEFL (minimum score 500 paper-based; 61 iBT). *Application deadline:* For fall admission, 7/15 priority date for domestic students. Applications are processed on a rolling basis. Application fee: $25. Electronic applications accepted. Application fee is waived when completed online. *Expenses:* $665 per credit hour. *Financial support:* In 2016–17, 6 students received support, including 6 research assistantships with partial tuition reimbursements available (averaging $7,395 per year); teaching assistantships and tuition discounts also available. Financial award application deadline: 12/31; financial award applicants required to submit FAFSA. *Faculty research:* Medical tourism, familial influence in financial fitness, pedagogy in finance courses, sociocultural aspects of women entrepreneurs, patient satisfaction. *Unit head:* Dr. Michael Petrochuk, Director of the MBA Program/Associate Professor of Marketing and Healthcare Management, 330-244-4764, Fax: 330-490-7359, E-mail: mpetrochuk@walsh.edu. *Application contact:* Audra Dice, Graduate and Transfer Admissions Counselor, 330-490-7181, Fax: 330-244-4925, E-mail: adice@walsh.edu.
Website: http://www.walsh.edu/mba-program

Warner University, School of Business, Lake Wales, FL 33859. Offers accounting (MBA); business administration (MBA); human resource management (MBA); international business (MBA); management (MSMC). *Program availability:* Part-time, evening/weekend, online learning. *Degree requirements:* For master's, comprehensive exam, thesis. *Entrance requirements:* For master's, minimum GPA of 3.0, letters of recommendation (2). Additional exam requirements/recommendations for international students: Required—TOEFL. *Application deadline:* Applications are processed on a rolling basis. Application fee: $50. Electronic applications accepted. *Financial support:* Scholarships/grants available. Financial award applicants required to submit FAFSA. *Unit head:* Cindy Polston, Program Director, 863-638-7689. *Application contact:* Judianne Steibly, Graduate Academic Advisor, 863-638-3702, Fax: 863-638-4907, E-mail: admissions@warner.edu.

Washburn University, School of Business, Topeka, KS 66621. Offers accountancy (M Acc). *Accreditation:* AACSB. *Program availability:* Part-time, evening/weekend. *Entrance requirements:* For master's, GMAT, minimum GPA of 2.75. Additional exam requirements/recommendations for international students: Required—TOEFL (minimum score 550 paper-based; 80 iBT); Recommended—IELTS (minimum score 6.5). Electronic applications accepted. *Faculty research:* Ethics in information technology, forecasting for shareholder value creation, model for measuring expected losses from litigation contingencies, business vs. family commitment in family businesses, calculated intangible value and brand recognition.

Washington Adventist University, MBA Program, Takoma Park, MD 20912. Offers MBA. *Program availability:* Part-time, evening/weekend, online learning. *Entrance requirements:* For master's, minimum undergraduate GPA of 2.75, curriculum vitae, interview, essay, personal statement. Additional exam requirements/recommendations for international students: Required—TOEFL (minimum score 550 paper-based), IELTS (minimum score 5).

Washington State University, Carson College of Business, Pullman, WA 99164-4750. Offers M Acc, MBA, PhD. Programs also offered at the Tri-Cities, Vancouver, and Global (online) campuses. *Program availability:* Online learning. *Degree requirements:* For master's, comprehensive exam (for some programs), thesis (for some programs); for doctorate, comprehensive exam, thesis/dissertation. *Entrance requirements:* For master's and doctorate, GMAT (minimum score of 600), resume; statement of purpose identifying area of interest, experiences, and intended research focus; minimum GPA of 3.25. Additional exam requirements/recommendations for international students: Required—TOEFL (minimum score 580 paper-based), IELTS.

Washington University in St. Louis, Olin Business School, Executive MBA Program, St. Louis, MO 63130-4899. Offers EMBA. *Program availability:* Evening/weekend. *Faculty:* 97 full-time (22 women), 44 part-time/adjunct (13 women). *Students:* 164 part-time (56 women); includes 24 minority (10 Black or African American, non-Hispanic/Latino; 6 Asian, non-Hispanic/Latino; 1 Hispanic/Latino; 7 Two or more races, non-Hispanic/Latino), 17 international. Average age 40. 111 applicants, 95% accepted, 96 enrolled. In 2016, 87 master's awarded. *Entrance requirements:* For master's, two letters of recommendation, letter of commitment/sponsorship, transcripts. Additional exam requirements/recommendations for international students: Recommended—TOEFL. *Application deadline:* For fall admission, 8/19 for domestic and international students; for spring admission, 3/24 for domestic and international students. Applications are processed on a rolling basis. Application fee: $0. Electronic applications accepted. *Expenses:* Contact institution. *Financial support:* Applicants required to submit FAFSA. *Unit head:* Dr. Stuart Bunderson, Associate Dean/Director of Executive Programs/Professor of Organizational Ethics and Governance, 314-935-9009, Fax: 314-935-7161, E-mail: bunderson@wustl.edu. *Application contact:* Meg Shuff, Assistant Dean of Admissions, Executive MBA Programs, 314-935-9009, Fax: 314-935-7161, E-mail: mshuff@wustl.edu.
Website: http://www.olin.wustl.edu/execed/emba.cfm

Washington University in St. Louis, Olin Business School, Full-time MBA Program, St. Louis, MO 63130-4899. Offers MBA, JD/MBA, M Arch/MBA, M Eng/MBA, MBA/MA, MBA/MPH, MBA/MSW. *Faculty:* 97 full-time (22 women), 44 part-time/adjunct (13 women). *Students:* 269 full-time (86 women); includes 61 minority (15 Black or African American, non-Hispanic/Latino; 2 American Indian or Alaska Native, non-Hispanic/

Latino; 26 Asian, non-Hispanic/Latino; 6 Hispanic/Latino; 12 Two or more races, non-Hispanic/Latino), 98 international. Average age 28. 1,576 applicants, 30% accepted, 128 enrolled. In 2016, 141 master's awarded. *Entrance requirements:* For master's, GMAT or GRE. Additional exam requirements/recommendations for international students: Required—TOEFL. *Application deadline:* For fall admission, 10/1 for domestic and international students; for winter admission, 1/4 for domestic and international students; for spring admission, 4/1 for domestic and international students. Application fee: $0. Electronic applications accepted. *Expenses:* Contact institution. *Financial support:* Application deadline: 4/19; applicants required to submit FAFSA. *Unit head:* Joe Fox, Associate Dean and Director of MBA Programs, 314-935-6322, Fax: 314-935-4464, E-mail: fox@wustl.edu. *Application contact:* Ruthie Pyles, Assistant Dean and Director of Graduate Admissions, 314-935-7301, Fax: 314-935-4464, E-mail: ruthie.pyles@wustl.edu.
Website: http://www.olin.wustl.edu/mba/

Washington University in St. Louis, Olin Business School, IIT Bombay-Washington University Executive MBA Program, St. Louis, MO 63130-4899. Offers EMBA. Program offered in partnership with Shailesh J. Mehta School of Management at the Indian Institute of Technology in Bombay. *Faculty:* 97 full-time (22 women), 44 part-time/adjunct (13 women). *Students:* 49 full-time (9 women), all international. Average age 41. 29 applicants, 100% accepted, 22 enrolled. In 2016, 27 master's awarded. *Application deadline:* Applications are processed on a rolling basis. Application fee: $0. Electronic applications accepted. *Expenses:* Contact institution. *Unit head:* Dr. Mark Taylor, Dean, 314-935-6344. *Application contact:* Kiran Shesh, Academy Chief Executive Officer, 314-935-3383, E-mail: kiran.shesh@wustl.edu.

Washington University in St. Louis, Olin Business School, PhD Program in Business Administration, St. Louis, MO 63130-4899. Offers PhD. *Faculty:* 97 full-time (22 women), 44 part-time/adjunct (13 women). *Students:* 60 full-time (17 women); includes 7 minority (6 Asian, non-Hispanic/Latino; 1 Two or more races, non-Hispanic/Latino), 39 international. Average age 26. 390 applicants, 8% accepted, 12 enrolled. In 2016, 9 doctorates awarded. *Degree requirements:* For doctorate, comprehensive exam, thesis/dissertation. *Entrance requirements:* For doctorate, GMAT or GRE. Additional exam requirements/recommendations for international students: Required—TOEFL or IELTS. *Application deadline:* For fall admission, 1/15 for domestic and international students. Application fee: $100. Electronic applications accepted. *Expenses:* Contact institution. *Financial support:* In 2016–17, fellowships with full tuition reimbursements (averaging $25,000 per year) were awarded; health care benefits and travel support for conferences also available. *Unit head:* Prof. Anjan Thakor, Professor/Director, 314-935-7197, Fax: 314-935-6359, E-mail: thakor@wust.edu. *Application contact:* Erin Murdock, Associate Director of Doctoral Admissions, 314-935-6340, Fax: 314-935-9484, E-mail: murdockel@wustl.edu.
Website: http://www.olin.wustl.edu/prospective/phd.cfm

Washington University in St. Louis, Olin Business School, Professional MBA Program, St. Louis, MO 63130-4899. Offers MBA. *Program availability:* Part-time, evening/weekend. *Faculty:* 97 full-time (22 women), 44 part-time/adjunct (13 women). *Students:* 295 part-time (93 women); includes 61 minority (13 Black or African American, non-Hispanic/Latino; 34 Asian, non-Hispanic/Latino; 7 Hispanic/Latino; 7 Two or more races, non-Hispanic/Latino), 15 international. Average age 29. 162 applicants, 83% accepted, 108 enrolled. In 2016, 110 master's awarded. Terminal master's awarded for partial completion of doctoral program. *Degree requirements:* For master's, 54 credits. *Entrance requirements:* For master's, GMAT or GRE. Additional exam requirements/recommendations for international students: Required—TOEFL. *Application deadline:* Applications are processed on a rolling basis. Application fee: $0. Electronic applications accepted. *Expenses:* $1,620 per credit hour. *Financial support:* Applicants required to submit FAFSA. *Unit head:* Joe Fox, Associate Dean and Director of MBA Programs, 314-935-6322, Fax: 314-935-4464, E-mail: fox@wustl.edu. *Application contact:* Ruthie Pyles, Assistant Dean and Director of Graduate Admissions, 314-935-7301, Fax: 314-935-4464, E-mail: ruthie.pyles@wustl.edu.
Website: http://www.olin.wustl.edu/prospective/pmba.cfm

Washington University in St. Louis, Olin Business School, Washington University-Fudan University Executive MBA Program, Shanghai, MO 63130-4899, China. Offers EMBA. *Program availability:* Part-time. *Faculty:* 97 full-time (22 women), 44 part-time/adjunct (13 women). *Students:* 67 part-time (27 women); includes 55 minority (54 Asian, non-Hispanic/Latino; 1 Hispanic/Latino). Average age 39. 255 applicants, 22% accepted, 53 enrolled. In 2016, 32 master's awarded. *Degree requirements:* For master's, thesis optional. *Application deadline:* For spring admission, 4/30 for domestic and international students. Applications are processed on a rolling basis. Application fee: 1,200 Chinese yuans. Electronic applications accepted. *Expenses:* Contact institution. *Unit head:* Dr. Stuart Bunderson, Associate Dean, 314-935-3622, E-mail: bunderson@wustl.edu. *Application contact:* Chen Zhang, Recruiting Director, 314-935-3622, E-mail: czhang30@wustl.edu.
Website: http://www.olin.wustl.edu/EN-US/executive-programs/executive-mba-shanghai/Pages/default.aspx

Wayland Baptist University, Graduate Programs, Programs in Business Administration/Management, Plainview, TX 79072-6998. Offers accounting (MBA); general business (MBA); health care administration (MAM, MBA); human resource management (MAM, MBA); international management (MBA); management (MBA, D Mgt); management information systems (MBA); organization management (MAM); project management (MBA). *Program availability:* Part-time, evening/weekend, online learning. *Degree requirements:* For master's, capstone course. *Entrance requirements:* For master's, GMAT, GRE or MAT. Additional exam requirements/recommendations for international students: Required—TOEFL (minimum score 500 paper-based; 61 iBT). Electronic applications accepted.

Waynesburg University, Graduate and Professional Studies, Canonsburg, PA 15370. Offers business (MBA), including energy management, finance, health systems, human resources, leadership, market development; counseling (MA), including addictions counseling, clinical mental health; counselor education and supervision (PhD); criminal investigation (MA); education (M Ed), including autism, curriculum and instruction, educational leadership, online teaching; nursing (MSN), including administration, education, informatics; nursing practice (DNP); special education (M Ed); technology (M Ed); MSN/MBA. *Accreditation:* AACN. *Program availability:* Part-time, evening/weekend. *Degree requirements:* For doctorate, thesis/dissertation. *Entrance requirements:* Additional exam requirements/recommendations for international students: Required—TOEFL. Electronic applications accepted.

Wayne State College, School of Business and Technology, Wayne, NE 68787. Offers MBA. *Program availability:* Part-time, evening/weekend, online learning. *Entrance requirements:* For master's, GMAT, minimum overall GPA of 3.0. Additional exam requirements/recommendations for international students: Required—TOEFL (minimum score 550 paper-based).

Wayne State University, Mike Ilitch School of Business, Detroit, MI 48202. Offers accounting (MS, Postbaccalaureate Certificate); business (Graduate Certificate); business administration (MBA, PhD); data science (MS), including business analytics; entrepreneurship and innovation (Postbaccalaureate Certificate); finance (MS); information systems management (Postbaccalaureate Certificate); taxation (MST); JD/MBA. Application deadline for PhD is February 15. *Accreditation:* AACSB. *Program availability:* Part-time, evening/weekend. *Faculty:* 32. *Students:* 219 full-time (105 women), 941 part-time (406 women); includes 314 minority (186 Black or African American, non-Hispanic/Latino; 3 American Indian or Alaska Native, non-Hispanic/Latino; 68 Asian, non-Hispanic/Latino; 33 Hispanic/Latino; 24 Two or more races, non-Hispanic/Latino), 88 international. Average age 30. 1,119 applicants, 49% accepted, 329 enrolled. In 2016, 203 master's, 1 doctorate, 3 other advanced degrees awarded. *Degree requirements:* For doctorate, thesis/dissertation. *Entrance requirements:* For master's, GMAT, GRE, LSAT, MCAT, at least three years of relevant work experience that shows increased responsibility, or minimum GPA of 3.0 from AACSB-accredited program or 3.2 from regionally-accredited program, undergraduate degree from accredited institution; undergraduate degree in accounting, business administration, or area of business administration (for MS and MST); for doctorate, GMAT (minimum score of 600), minimum undergraduate GPA of 3.0, 3.5 upper-division or graduate; three letters of recommendation; brief essay; undergraduate degree from accredited institution; personal statement; for other advanced degree, bachelor's degree from accredited institution. Additional exam requirements/recommendations for international students: Required—TOEFL (minimum score 550 paper-based; 79 iBT), Michigan English Language Assessment Battery (minimum score 85); Recommended—IELTS (minimum score 6.5), TWE (minimum score 5.5). *Application deadline:* For fall admission, 7/1 for domestic students, 5/1 priority date for international students; for winter admission, 11/1 for domestic students, 9/1 priority date for international students; for spring admission, 3/1 for domestic students, 1/1 priority date for international students. Applications are processed on a rolling basis. Application fee: $50. Electronic applications accepted. *Expenses:* $18,871 per year resident tuition and fees, $36,065 per year non-resident tuition and fees. *Financial support:* In 2016–17, 174 students received support, including 1 fellowship with tuition reimbursement available (averaging $18,000 per year), 2 research assistantships with tuition reimbursements available (averaging $18,000 per year), 5 teaching assistantships with tuition reimbursements available (averaging $18,000 per year); scholarships/grants, health care benefits, and unspecified assistantships also available. Support available to part-time students. Financial award applicants required to submit FAFSA. *Faculty research:* Executive compensation and stock performance, consumer reactions to pricing strategies, communication across the automotive supply chain, performance of firms in sub-Saharan Africa, implementation issues with ERP software. *Unit head:* Dr. Robert Forsythe, Dean, School of Business Administration, 313-577-4501, E-mail: robert.forsythe@wayne.edu. *Application contact:* Kiantee N. Rupert-Jones, Director, 313-577-4511, Fax: 313-577-9442, E-mail: gradbusiness@wayne.edu.
Website: http://ilitchbusiness.wayne.edu/

Webber International University, Graduate School of Business, Babson Park, FL 33827-0096. Offers accounting (MBA); business (MBA); criminal justice management (MBA); international business (MBA); sport business management (MBA). *Program availability:* Part-time, evening/weekend, 100% online. *Faculty:* 11 full-time (3 women), 1 part-time/adjunct (0 women). *Students:* 44 full-time (21 women), 6 part-time (2 women); includes 11 minority (5 Black or African American, non-Hispanic/Latino; 5 Hispanic/Latino; 1 Two or more races, non-Hispanic/Latino), 11 international. Average age 27. 32 applicants, 69% accepted, 18 enrolled. In 2016, 16 master's awarded. *Degree requirements:* For master's, class trip (for international business); practicum (for criminal justice management). *Entrance requirements:* For master's, three recommendation letters, résumé, essay, official transcripts from all colleges and universities attended. Additional exam requirements/recommendations for international students: Recommended—TOEFL (minimum score 500 paper-based; 61 iBT), IELTS (minimum score 6). *Application deadline:* For fall admission, 7/1 for international students. Applications are processed on a rolling basis. Application fee: $50 ($75 for international students). Electronic applications accepted. *Expenses:* $2,013 tuition per course; $207 technology fee per course (for online courses only). *Financial support:* In 2016–17, 11 students received support. Scholarships/grants and unspecified assistantships available. Financial award application deadline: 8/16; financial award applicants required to submit FAFSA. *Unit head:* Dr. Nikos Orphanoudakis, Dean, 863-638-2910, Fax: 863-638-1591, E-mail: orphanoudakisn@webber.edu. *Application contact:* Lacy Edwards, Admissions Counselor and MBA Coordinator, 863-638-2910, Fax: 863-638-1591, E-mail: admissions@webber.edu.

Weber State University, John B. Goddard School of Business and Economics, Program in Business Administration, Ogden, UT 84408-1001. Offers MBA. *Accreditation:* AACSB. *Program availability:* Part-time, evening/weekend. *Faculty:* 13 full-time (3 women), 2 part-time/adjunct (0 women). *Students:* 72 full-time (15 women), 111 part-time (28 women); includes 6 minority (1 Black or African American, non-Hispanic/Latino; 1 American Indian or Alaska Native, non-Hispanic/Latino; 1 Asian, non-Hispanic/Latino; 2 Hispanic/Latino; 1 Two or more races, non-Hispanic/Latino), 5 international. Average age 35. In 2016, 66 master's awarded. *Entrance requirements:* For master's, GMAT or GRE, resume, letters of recommendation. Additional exam requirements/recommendations for international students: Required—TOEFL (minimum score 550 paper-based). *Application deadline:* For fall admission, 5/1 for domestic and international students; for spring admission, 11/1 for domestic and international students. Application fee: $60 ($90 for international students). Electronic applications accepted. *Expenses:* Contact institution. *Financial support:* In 2016–17, 13 students received support. Scholarships/grants available. Financial award application deadline: 4/1; financial award applicants required to submit FAFSA. *Unit head:* Dr. Matt Mouritsen, MBA Program Director/Associate Professor of Accounting, 801-626-8151, Fax: 801-626-7423, E-mail: mmouritsen@weber.edu. *Application contact:* Dr. Mark A. Stevenson, MBA Enrollment Director, 801-395-3528, Fax: 801-395-3525, E-mail: mba@weber.edu.
Website: http://www.weber.edu/mba/

Webster University, George Herbert Walker School of Business and Technology, Department of Business, St. Louis, MO 63119-3194. Offers business and organizational security management (MBA); decision support systems (MBA); environmental management (MBA); finance (MBA, MS); forensic accounting (MS); gerontology (MBA); human resources development (MBA); human resources management (MBA); information technology management (MBA); international business (MA, MBA); international relations (MBA); management and leadership (MBA); marketing (MBA); media communications (MBA); procurement and acquisitions management (MBA); Web services (MBA). *Accreditation:* ACBSP. *Program availability:* Part-time, evening/weekend, online learning. *Degree requirements:* For master's, comprehensive exam (for some programs), thesis (for some programs). *Entrance requirements:* Additional exam requirements/recommendations for international students: Required—TOEFL. *Application deadline:* Applications are processed on a rolling basis. Application fee: $35 ($50 for international students). *Expenses: Tuition:* Full-time $21,900; part-time $730 per credit hour. Tuition and fees vary according to campus/location and program. *Financial support:* Federal Work-Study available. Support available to part-time students. Financial award application deadline: 4/1; financial award applicants required to submit FAFSA. *Unit head:* David Porras, Chair, 314-246-8621, E-mail: porrasd@webster.edu. *Application contact:* Sarah Nandor, Director, Graduate and Transfer Admissions, 314-968-7109, E-mail: gadmit@webster.edu.

Webster University, George Herbert Walker School of Business and Technology, Department of Management, St. Louis, MO 63119-3194. Offers business and organizational security management (MA); digital marketing management (Graduate Certificate); government contracting (Graduate Certificate); health administration (MHA); health care management (MA); health services management (MA); human resources development (MA); human resources management (MA); information technology management (MA, MS); management (D Mgt); management and leadership (MA); marketing (MA); nonprofit leadership (MA); nonprofit revenue development (Graduate Certificate); organizational development (Graduate Certificate); procurement and acquisitions management (MA); public administration (MPA); space systems operations management (MS). *Program availability:* Part-time, evening/weekend, online learning. *Degree requirements:* For master's, thesis (for some programs); for doctorate, thesis/dissertation, written exam. *Entrance requirements:* For doctorate, GMAT, 3 years of work experience, MBA. Additional exam requirements/recommendations for international students: Required—TOEFL. *Application deadline:* Applications are processed on a rolling basis. Application fee: $25 ($50 for international students). *Expenses: Tuition:* Full-time $21,900; part-time $730 per credit hour. Tuition and fees vary according to campus/location and program. *Financial support:* Federal Work-Study available. Support available to part-time students. Financial award application deadline: 4/1; financial award applicants required to submit FAFSA. *Unit head:* Barrett Baebler, Chair, 314-246-7940, E-mail: baeblerb@webster.edu. *Application contact:* Sarah Nandor, Director, Graduate and Transfer Admissions, 314-968-7109, E-mail: gadmit@webster.edu.

Wesleyan College, Department of Business and Economics, EMBA Program, Macon, GA 31210-4462. Offers EMBA. *Program availability:* Evening/weekend. *Entrance requirements:* For master's, GMAT, LSAT, GRE or MAT, 5 years of work experience, 5 years of management experience. Additional exam requirements/recommendations for international students: Required—TOEFL (minimum score 550 paper-based). Electronic applications accepted.

Wesley College, Business Program, Dover, DE 19901-3875. Offers environmental management (MBA); executive leadership (MBA); management (MBA). Executive leadership concentration also offered at New Castle, DE location. *Program availability:* Part-time, evening/weekend. *Entrance requirements:* For master's, GMAT or GRE, minimum undergraduate GPA of 2.75.

West Chester University of Pennsylvania, College of Business and Public Management, School of Business, West Chester, PA 19383. Offers business analytics (Certificate); business education (MBA); entrepreneurship (Certificate); project management (Certificate). *Accreditation:* AACSB. *Program availability:* Part-time, evening/weekend, 100% online. *Faculty:* 13 full-time (6 women), 2 part-time/adjunct (1 woman). *Students:* 44 full-time (23 women), 213 part-time (82 women); includes 37 minority (16 Black or African American, non-Hispanic/Latino; 11 Asian, non-Hispanic/Latino; 9 Hispanic/Latino; 1 Two or more races, non-Hispanic/Latino). Average age 32. 202 applicants, 83% accepted, 126 enrolled. In 2016, 41 master's, 16 other advanced degrees awarded. *Degree requirements:* For master's, minimum GPA of 3.0. *Entrance requirements:* For master's, GMAT or GRE, statement of professional goals, resume, two letters of recommendation, transcripts. Additional exam requirements/recommendations for international students: Required—TOEFL or IELTS. *Application deadline:* For fall admission, 5/15 for international students; for spring admission, 10/15 for international students. Applications are processed on a rolling basis. Application fee: $50. Electronic applications accepted. *Expenses:* Tuition, state resident: full-time $8694; part-time $483 per credit. Tuition, nonresident: full-time $13,050; part-time $725 per credit. *Required fees:* $2399; $119.05 per credit. Tuition and fees vary according to campus/location and program. *Financial support:* Scholarships/grants and unspecified assistantships available. Financial award application deadline: 2/15; financial award applicants required to submit FAFSA. *Unit head:* Dr. Brian Halsey, MBA Director/Graduate Coordinator, 610-425-5000 Ext. 4444, E-mail: mba@wcupa.edu. *Application contact:* Office of Graduate Studies and Extended Education, 610-436-2943, Fax: 610-436-2763, E-mail: gradstudy@wcupa.edu.
Website: http://www.wcupa.edu/mba

Western Carolina University, Graduate School, College of Business, Program in Business Administration, Cullowhee, NC 28723. Offers MBA. *Accreditation:* AACSB. *Program availability:* Part-time, evening/weekend. *Entrance requirements:* For master's, GMAT, appropriate undergraduate degree, 3 letters of recommendation. Additional exam requirements/recommendations for international students: Required—TOEFL (minimum score 550 paper-based; 79 iBT). *Expenses:* Tuition, state resident: full-time $2174. Tuition, nonresident: full-time $7377. *Required fees:* $1442. Part-time tuition and fees vary according to course load. *Faculty research:* Marketing strategy, biotechnology, executive education, business statistics, supply chain management, innovation.

Western Connecticut State University, Division of Graduate Studies, Ancell School of Business, Program in Business Administration, Danbury, CT 06810-6885. Offers accounting (MBA); business administration (MBA). *Program availability:* Part-time. *Degree requirements:* For master's, comprehensive exam, completion of program within 8 years. *Entrance requirements:* For master's, GMAT. Additional exam requirements/recommendations for international students: Recommended—TOEFL (minimum score 550 paper-based; 79 iBT), IELTS (minimum score 6). *Faculty research:* Global strategic marketing planning, project management and team coordination; email, discussion boards that act as blogs and videoconferencing.

Western Governors University, College of Business, Salt Lake City, UT 84107. Offers information technology management (MBA); integrated healthcare management (MS); management and strategy (MBA); strategic leadership (MBA). *Program availability:* Evening/weekend. *Degree requirements:* For master's, capstone project. *Entrance requirements:* For master's, Readiness Assessment, transcripts. Additional exam requirements/recommendations for international students: Required—TOEFL (minimum score 450 paper-based; 80 iBT). Electronic applications accepted.

Western Illinois University, School of Graduate Studies, College of Business and Technology, Program in Business Administration, Macomb, IL 61455-1390. Offers business administration (MBA, Certificate); supply chain management (Certificate). *Accreditation:* AACSB. *Program availability:* Part-time. *Students:* 37 full-time (17 women), 40 part-time (14 women); includes 6 minority (2 Black or African American, non-Hispanic/Latino; 1 Asian, non-Hispanic/Latino; 3 Hispanic/Latino), 9 international. Average age 31. 63 applicants, 79% accepted, 27 enrolled. In 2016, 42 master's, 6 other advanced degrees awarded. *Degree requirements:* For master's, thesis or alternative. *Entrance requirements:* For master's, GMAT. Additional exam requirements/recommendations for international students: Required—TOEFL (minimum score 550 paper-based; 80 iBT). *Application deadline:* Applications are processed on a rolling basis. Application fee: $30. Electronic applications accepted. *Financial support:* In 2016–17, 13 students received support, including 1 research assistantship with full tuition reimbursement available; unspecified assistantships also available. Financial award applicants required to submit FAFSA. *Unit head:* Dr. Bill Polley, Associate Dean, 309-298-2442. *Application contact:* Dr. Nancy Parsons, Associate Provost and Director of Graduate Studies, 309-298-1806, Fax: 309-298-2345, E-mail: grad-office@wiu.edu.
Website: http://wiu.edu/cbt

Western Kentucky University, Graduate Studies, Gordon Ford College of Business, MBA Program, Bowling Green, KY 42101. Offers MBA. *Accreditation:* AACSB. *Program availability:* Part-time, evening/weekend. *Degree requirements:* For master's, comprehensive exam, thesis optional. *Entrance requirements:* For master's, GMAT, minimum GPA of 2.5. Additional exam requirements/recommendations for international students: Required—TOEFL (minimum score 555 paper-based; 70 iBT). *Faculty research:* Business and international education, web page development, management training, international studies, globalization.

Western Michigan University, Graduate College, Haworth College of Business, Department of Interdisciplinary Business, Kalamazoo, MI 49008. Offers business administration (MBA). *Accreditation:* AACSB.

Western New England University, College of Business, Program in Business Administration, Springfield, MA 01119. Offers general business (MBA); sport management (MBA); JD/MBA; Pharm D/MBA. *Accreditation:* AACSB. *Program availability:* Part-time, evening/weekend, online learning. *Faculty:* 7 full-time (5 women). *Students:* 85 part-time (35 women); includes 11 minority (6 Black or African American, non-Hispanic/Latino; 3 Asian, non-Hispanic/Latino; 2 Hispanic/Latino), 4 international. Average age 31. 73 applicants, 27% accepted, 18 enrolled. In 2016, 66 master's awarded. *Entrance requirements:* For master's, GMAT or GRE, official transcript, two letters of recommendation, essay, resume. Additional exam requirements/recommendations for international students: Required—TOEFL (minimum score 79 iBT). *Application deadline:* Applications are processed on a rolling basis. Application fee: $30. Electronic applications accepted. *Expenses:* Contact institution. *Financial support:* Application deadline: 4/15; applicants required to submit FAFSA. *Unit head:* Dr. Rob Kleine, Dean, 413-782-1395, E-mail: rob.kleine@wne.edu. *Application contact:* Matthew Fox, Director of Admissions for Graduate Students and Adult Learners, 413-782-1410, Fax: 413-782-1777, E-mail: study@wne.edu.
Website: http://www1.wne.edu/academics/graduate/mba.cfm

Western New Mexico University, Graduate Division, School of Business, Silver City, NM 88062-0680. Offers business administration (MBA). *Accreditation:* ACBSP. *Program availability:* Part-time, online learning. *Entrance requirements:* For master's, GMAT. Additional exam requirements/recommendations for international students: Required—TOEFL (minimum score 550 paper-based). Electronic applications accepted. *Faculty research:* Migration: an analysis of Puerto Rican interest to migrate to the united states using Internet search trends, entrepreneurship management in rural U.S. areas, exports and maritime ports: Puerto Rico and the port of Las Americas, female labor force participation in the border states.

Western Washington University, Graduate School, College of Business and Economics, Bellingham, WA 98225-5996. Offers MBA, MP Acc. *Accreditation:* AACSB. *Program availability:* Part-time, evening/weekend. *Degree requirements:* For master's, comprehensive exam. *Entrance requirements:* For master's, GMAT, minimum GPA of 3.0 in last 60 semester hours or last 90 quarter hours. Additional exam requirements/recommendations for international students: Required—TOEFL (minimum score 567 paper-based). Electronic applications accepted. *Faculty research:* Enterprise strategy/corporate social performance, sustainability/environmental management/nonprofit marketing, managerial/environmental accounting, organizational applications of collaborative technology, environmental and resource economics.

Westminster College, The Bill and Vieve Gore School of Business, Salt Lake City, UT 84105. Offers accountancy (M Acc); business administration (MBA, Certificate); technology commercialization (MBA). *Program availability:* Part-time, evening/weekend, 100% online. *Faculty:* 19 full-time (5 women), 20 part-time/adjunct (7 women). *Students:* 120 full-time (43 women), 124 part-time (45 women); includes 47 minority (8 Black or African American, non-Hispanic/Latino; 1 American Indian or Alaska Native, non-Hispanic/Latino; 15 Asian, non-Hispanic/Latino; 18 Hispanic/Latino; 5 Two or more races, non-Hispanic/Latino), 12 international. Average age 34. 97 applicants, 79% accepted, 56 enrolled. In 2016, 119 master's, 10 other advanced degrees awarded. *Entrance requirements:* For master's, GMAT, 2 professional recommendations, employer letter of support, personal resume, essay, official transcripts. Additional exam requirements/recommendations for international students: Required—TOEFL (minimum score 600 paper-based; 84 iBT), IELTS (minimum score 7.5). *Application deadline:* For fall admission, 5/20 priority date for domestic and international students; for spring admission, 10/7 priority date for domestic and international students; for summer admission, 2/5 priority date for domestic and international students. Applications are processed on a rolling basis. Application fee: $50. Electronic applications accepted. *Expenses:* Contact institution. *Financial support:* In 2016–17, 87 students received support. Career-related internships or fieldwork, scholarships/grants, unspecified assistantships, and tuition reimbursements, tuition remission available. Financial award applicants required to submit FAFSA. *Faculty research:* Innovation and entrepreneurship, business strategy and change, financial analysis and capital budgeting, leadership development, knowledge management. *Unit head:* Melissa Koerner, Interim Dean, Bill and Vieve Gore School of Business, 801-832-2600, Fax: 801-832-3106, E-mail: mkoerner@westminstercollege.edu. *Application contact:* Ashley Williams, Director of Graduate Admissions, 801-832-2213, Fax: 801-832-3101, E-mail: awilliams@westminstercollege.edu.
Website: http://www.westminstercollege.edu/mba/

West Texas A&M University, College of Business, Department of Management, Marketing and General Business, Canyon, TX 79016-0001. Offers business administration (MBA). *Accreditation:* AACSB. *Program availability:* Part-time, evening/weekend, 100% online. *Entrance requirements:* For master's, GMAT. Additional exam requirements/recommendations for international students: Required—TOEFL (minimum score 550 paper-based). *Application deadline:* For fall admission, 8/1 for domestic students, 5/1 for international students; for spring admission, 12/1 for domestic students, 10/30 for international students; for summer admission, 5/1 for domestic students. Applications are processed on a rolling basis. Application fee: $40 ($75 for international students). Electronic applications accepted. *Financial support:* Research assistantships, teaching assistantships with partial tuition reimbursements, career-related internships or fieldwork, Federal Work-Study, institutionally sponsored loans, and tuition waivers (partial) available. Support available to part-time students. Financial award applicants required to submit CSS PROFILE or FAFSA. *Faculty research:* Human resources, international business, southern Asian markets, global strategies, international trade composition. *Unit head:* Dr. LaVelle Mills, Associate Dean, 806-651-3866, E-mail: lmills@wtamu.edu. *Application contact:* Dr. Jonathan Shaffer, Associate Professor, 806-651-2489, E-mail: jshaffer@wtamu.edu.
Website: http://www.wtamu.edu/academics/management-marketing-general-business.aspx

West Virginia University, College of Business and Economics, Program in Business Administration, Morgantown, WV 26506. Offers MBA, JD/MBA. *Accreditation:* AACSB. *Program availability:* Part-time, evening/weekend. *Entrance requirements:* For master's, GMAT. Additional exam requirements/recommendations for international students: Required—TOEFL. Electronic applications accepted. *Faculty research:* Financial management, managerial accounting, marketing, planning, corporate finance.

Business Administration and Management—General

West Virginia Wesleyan College, MBA Program, Buckhannon, WV 26201. Offers MBA. *Program availability:* Part-time, evening/weekend. *Degree requirements:* For master's, exit evaluation. *Entrance requirements:* For master's, GMAT. Additional exam requirements/recommendations for international students: Required—TOEFL.

Wheeling Jesuit University, Department of Business, Wheeling, WV 26003-6295. Offers accounting (MSA); business administration (MBA). *Accreditation:* ACBSP. *Program availability:* Part-time, evening/weekend. *Entrance requirements:* For master's, minimum undergraduate GPA of 2.8. Additional exam requirements/recommendations for international students: Required—TOEFL (minimum score 600 paper-based; 100 iBT). Electronic applications accepted. *Faculty research:* Forensic economics, consumer behavior, economic development, capitalism, leadership.

Whitworth University, School of Business, Spokane, WA 99251-0001. Offers MBA. *Program availability:* Part-time, evening/weekend. *Degree requirements:* For master's, variable foreign language requirement. *Entrance requirements:* For master's, GMAT or GRE, minimum undergraduate GPA of 3.25, or alternate exam, two letters of recommendation; resume; completion of prerequisite courses in micro-economics, macro-economics, financial accounting, finance, and marketing; interview with director. Additional exam requirements/recommendations for international students: Required—TOEFL (minimum score 88 iBT), TWE. Electronic applications accepted. *Faculty research:* International business (European, Central America and Asian topics), entrepreneurship and business plan development.

WHU - Otto Beisheim School of Management, Graduate Programs, Vallendar, Germany. Offers EMBA, MBA, MS. EMBA offered jointly with Kellogg School of Management.

Wichita State University, Graduate School, W. Frank Barton School of Business, Department of Business, Wichita, KS 67260. Offers EMBA, MBA. *Accreditation:* AACSB. *Program availability:* Part-time, evening/weekend. *Unit head:* Liz McLain, Director, 316-978-3230, E-mail: liz.mclain@wichita.edu. *Application contact:* Jordan Oleson, Admissions Coordinator, 316-978-3095, Fax: 316-978-3253,
E-mail: jordan.oleson@wichita.edu.
Website: http://www.wichita.edu/mba

Widener University, School of Business Administration, Chester, PA 19013-5792. Offers MBA, MHA, MS, JD/MBA, MD/MBA, MD/MHA, ME/MBA, Psy D/MBA, Psy D/MHA. *Accreditation:* AACSB. *Program availability:* Part-time, evening/weekend, 100% online, blended/hybrid learning. *Faculty:* 14 full-time (6 women), 6 part-time/adjunct (2 women). *Students:* 50 full-time (26 women), 129 part-time (53 women); includes 48 minority (35 Black or African American, non-Hispanic/Latino; 6 Asian, non-Hispanic/Latino; 5 Hispanic/Latino; 1 Native Hawaiian or other Pacific Islander, non-Hispanic/Latino; 1 Two or more races, non-Hispanic/Latino), 27 international. Average age 34. 154 applicants, 49% accepted, 43 enrolled. In 2016, 45 master's awarded. *Entrance requirements:* For master's, minimum GPA of 2.5. *Application deadline:* For fall admission, 8/1 priority date for domestic students; for spring admission, 12/1 for domestic students. Applications are processed on a rolling basis. Application fee: $25 ($300 for international students). Electronic applications accepted. *Expenses:* Contact institution. *Financial support:* In 2016–17, 11 research assistantships with full tuition reimbursements were awarded; career-related internships or fieldwork, Federal Work-Study, and traineeships also available. Support available to part-time students. Financial award application deadline: 5/1. *Faculty research:* Cost containment in health care, human resource management, productivity, globalization. *Unit head:* Dr. Catherine Morgan, Interim Dean, 610-499-4300, Fax: 610-499-4615. *Application contact:* Ann Seltzer, Graduate Enrollment Administrator, 610-499-4305, E-mail: apseltzer@widener.edu.
Website: http://www.widener.edu

Wilfrid Laurier University, Faculty of Graduate and Postdoctoral Studies, School of Business and Economics, Business Administration Program, Waterloo, ON N2L 3C5, Canada. Offers co-op (MBA); full-time (MBA); part-time (MBA). *Accreditation:* AACSB. *Program availability:* Part-time, evening/weekend. *Degree requirements:* For master's, thesis. *Entrance requirements:* For master's, GMAT, minimum 2 years of business experience (for 12-month or part-time MBA formats), minimum B average in 4-year BA program. Additional exam requirements/recommendations for international students: Required—TOEFL (minimum score 89 iBT). Electronic applications accepted.

Wilfrid Laurier University, Faculty of Graduate and Postdoctoral Studies, School of Business and Economics, Department of Business, Waterloo, ON N2L 3C5, Canada. Offers accounting (PhD); finance (M Fin); financial economics (PhD); marketing (PhD); operations and supply chain management (PhD); organizational behavior and human resource management (M Sc); organizational behaviour and human resource management (PhD); supply chain management (M Sc); technology management (EMTM). *Accreditation:* AACSB. *Program availability:* Part-time, evening/weekend. *Degree requirements:* For master's, thesis optional; for doctorate, comprehensive exam, thesis/dissertation. *Entrance requirements:* For master's, GMAT, 4-year honors degree with minimum B+ average; for doctorate, GMAT, master's degree, minimum B+ average. Additional exam requirements/recommendations for international students: Required—TOEFL (minimum score 89 iBT). Electronic applications accepted. *Faculty research:* Financial economics, management and organizational behavior, operations and supply chain management.

Wilkes University, College of Graduate and Professional Studies, Jay S. Sidhu School of Business and Leadership, Wilkes-Barre, PA 18766-0002. Offers accounting (MBA); entrepreneurship (MBA); finance (MBA); health care administration (MBA); human resource management (MBA); international business (MBA); operations management (MBA); organizational leadership and development (MBA). *Accreditation:* ACBSP. *Program availability:* Part-time, evening/weekend. *Students:* 35 full-time (17 women), 112 part-time (55 women); includes 17 minority (6 Black or African American, non-Hispanic/Latino; 4 Asian, non-Hispanic/Latino; 5 Hispanic/Latino; 2 Two or more races, non-Hispanic/Latino), 16 international. Average age 31. In 2016, 59 master's awarded. *Entrance requirements:* For master's, GMAT. Additional exam requirements/recommendations for international students: Required—TOEFL (minimum score 550 paper-based; 79 iBT). *Application deadline:* Applications are processed on a rolling basis. Application fee: $45 ($65 for international students). Electronic applications accepted. *Expenses:* Contact institution. *Financial support:* Unspecified assistantships available. Financial award application deadline: 3/1; financial award applicants required to submit FAFSA. *Unit head:* Dr. Abel Adekola, Dean, 570-408-4701, Fax: 570-408-7846, E-mail: abel.adekola@wilkes.edu. *Application contact:* Director of Graduate Enrollment, 570-408-4234, Fax: 570-408-7846.
Website: http://www.wilkes.edu/academics/colleges/sidhu-school-of-business-leadership/index.aspx

Willamette University, Atkinson Graduate School of Management, Salem, OR 97301-3931. Offers MBA, JD/MBA. JD/MBA offered jointly with College of Law. *Accreditation:* AACSB; NASPAA. *Program availability:* Part-time, evening/weekend. *Faculty:* 17 full-time (3 women), 18 part-time/adjunct (7 women). *Students:* 155 full-time (69 women), 120 part-time (67 women); includes 39 minority (6 Black or African American, non-Hispanic/Latino; 2 American Indian or Alaska Native, non-Hispanic/Latino; 18 Asian, non-Hispanic/Latino; 8 Hispanic/Latino; 3 Native Hawaiian or other Pacific Islander, non-Hispanic/Latino; 2 Two or more races, non-Hispanic/Latino), 66 international. Average age 29. 208 applicants, 96% accepted, 104 enrolled. In 2016, 138 master's awarded. *Degree requirements:* For master's, minimum cumulative GPA of 3.0. *Entrance requirements:* For master's, GMAT or GRE, essays, transcripts, references, resume, interview. Additional exam requirements/recommendations for international students: Required—TOEFL (minimum score 570 paper-based, 88 iBT) or IELTS (minimum score 6.5). *Application deadline:* 5/1 priority date for domestic and international students. Applications are processed on a rolling basis. Application fee: $100. Electronic applications accepted. Application fee is waived when completed online. *Expenses:* $39,280 full-time; $34,600 part-time. *Financial support:* In 2016–17, 220 students received support. Federal Work-Study, scholarships/grants, and unspecified assistantships available. Financial award application deadline: 5/1; financial award applicants required to submit FAFSA. *Faculty research:* Entrepreneurship and angel investing, corporate finance and investment, political economy and public management, organizational behavior, sustainability and corporate responsibility, marketing, operations. *Unit head:* Dr. Debra J. Ringold, Dean and Professor of Free Enterprise, 503-370-6790, Fax: 503-370-3011, E-mail: dringold@willamette.edu. *Application contact:* Aimee Akimoff, Director of Recruitment, 503-370-6167, Fax: 503-370-3011, E-mail: aakimoff@willamette.edu.
Website: http://www.willamette.edu/mba/

William Carey University, School of Business, Hattiesburg, MS 39401-5499. Offers MBA. *Program availability:* Part-time. *Entrance requirements:* For master's, GMAT. Additional exam requirements/recommendations for international students: Required—TOEFL (minimum score 500 paper-based).

William Paterson University of New Jersey, Cotsakos College of Business, Wayne, NJ 07470-8420. Offers business administration (MBA). *Accreditation:* AACSB. *Program availability:* Part-time, evening/weekend. *Faculty:* 19 full-time (5 women), 1 (woman) part-time/adjunct. *Students:* 74 full-time (37 women), 161 part-time (77 women); includes 86 minority (25 Black or African American, non-Hispanic/Latino; 13 Asian, non-Hispanic/Latino; 39 Hispanic/Latino; 9 Two or more races, non-Hispanic/Latino), 30 international. Average age 31. 176 applicants, 69% accepted, 89 enrolled. In 2016, 41 master's awarded. *Entrance requirements:* For master's, GMAT (minimum score 500) or GRE (minimum 152 Verbal, 152 Quantitative), minimum GPA of 3.0, professional resume. Additional exam requirements/recommendations for international students: Required—TOEFL (minimum score 550 paper-based; 79 iBT), IELTS (minimum score 6). *Application deadline:* For fall admission, 8/1 for domestic students, 4/1 for international students; for spring admission, 12/1 for domestic students, 11/1 for international students; for summer admission, 5/1 for domestic students, 2/1 for international students. Applications are processed on a rolling basis. Application fee: $50. Electronic applications accepted. *Expenses:* Tuition, state resident: full-time $12,480; part-time $611 per credit. Tuition, nonresident: full-time $20,263; part-time $992 per credit. *Required fees:* $1573; $77 per credit. Tuition and fees vary according to course load, degree level and program. *Financial support:* Career-related internships or fieldwork, Federal Work-Study, scholarships/grants, and unspecified assistantships available. Support available to part-time students. Financial award applicants required to submit FAFSA. *Faculty research:* Social media communities, impact of public health campaigns, racioethnicity and gender in sales recruiting, non-profit organization investment strategies, life expectancy in china. *Unit head:* Dr. Siamack Shojai, Dean, 973-720-2964, Fax: 973-720-2809, E-mail: shojais@wpunj.edu. *Application contact:* Tinu Adeniran, Assistant Director, Graduate Admissions, 973-720-2764, Fax: 973-720-2035, E-mail: adenirant@wpunj.edu.
Website: http://www.wpunj.edu/ccob

William Woods University, Graduate and Adult Studies, Fulton, MO 65251-1098. Offers administration (M Ed, Ed S); athletic/activities administration (M Ed); curriculum and instruction (M Ed, Ed S); educational leadership (Ed D); equestrian education (M Ed); health management (MBA); human resources (MBA); leadership (MBA); marketing, advertising, and public relations (MBA); teaching and technology (M Ed). *Program availability:* Part-time, evening/weekend. *Degree requirements:* For master's, capstone course (MBA), action research (M Ed); for Ed S, field experience. *Entrance requirements:* Additional exam requirements/recommendations for international students: Required—TOEFL (minimum score 550 paper-based). Electronic applications accepted. *Expenses:* Contact institution.

Wilmington University, College of Business, New Castle, DE 19720-6491. Offers accounting (MBA, MS); business administration (MBA, DBA); environmental stewardship (MBA); finance (MBA); health care administration (MBA, MSM); homeland security (MBA, MSM); human resource management (MSM); management information systems (MBA, MSN); marketing (MSM); marketing management (MBA); military leadership (MSM); organizational leadership (MBA, MSM); public administration (MSM). *Program availability:* Part-time, evening/weekend. *Faculty:* 17 full-time (7 women), 106 part-time/adjunct (46 women). *Students:* 436 full-time (237 women), 1,202 part-time (739 women); includes 594 minority (474 Black or African American, non-Hispanic/Latino; 19 American Indian or Alaska Native, non-Hispanic/Latino; 64 Asian, non-Hispanic/Latino; 30 Hispanic/Latino; 3 Native Hawaiian or other Pacific Islander, non-Hispanic/Latino; 4 Two or more races, non-Hispanic/Latino), 153 international. Average age 35. 814 applicants, 98% accepted, 426 enrolled. In 2016, 594 master's, 23 doctorates awarded. *Entrance requirements:* Additional exam requirements/recommendations for international students: Required—TOEFL (minimum score 500 paper-based). *Application deadline:* Applications are processed on a rolling basis. Application fee: $35. Electronic applications accepted. *Expenses: Tuition:* Full-time $8388; part-time $466 per credit. *Required fees:* $25 per semester. Tuition and fees vary according to degree level. *Financial support:* Applicants required to submit FAFSA. *Unit head:* Dr. Robert W. Rescigno, Dean. *Application contact:* Laura Morris, Director of Admissions, 877-967-5456, E-mail: infocenter@wilmu.edu.
Website: http://www.wilmu.edu/business/

Wilson College, Graduate Programs, Chambersburg, PA 17201-1285. Offers accounting (M Acc); choreography and visual art (MFA); education (M Ed); healthcare management for sustainability (MHM); humanities (MA), including art and culture, critical/cultural theory, English language and literature, women's studies; management (MSM); nursing (MSN), including nursing education, nursing leadership and management. *Program availability:* Evening/weekend. *Degree requirements:* For master's, project. *Entrance requirements:* For master's, PRAXIS, minimum undergraduate cumulative GPA of 3.0, 2 letters of recommendation, current certification for eligibility to teach in grades K-12, resume, personal interview. Electronic applications accepted.

Wingate University, Porter B. Byrum School of Business, Wingate, NC 28174. Offers accounting (MAC); corporate innovation (MBA); finance (MBA); general management (MBA); healthcare management (MBA); marketing (MBA); project management (MBA). *Accreditation:* ACBSP. *Program availability:* Part-time, evening/weekend. *Entrance requirements:* For master's, GMAT, work experience, 2 letters of recommendation. *Application deadline:* For fall admission, 8/15 priority date for domestic students; for spring admission, 12/15 priority date for domestic students. Applications are processed on a rolling basis. Application fee: $50. Electronic applications accepted. *Expenses:* Contact institution. *Financial support:* Federal Work-Study and scholarships/grants

available. Support available to part-time students. Financial award application deadline: 8/1; financial award applicants required to submit FAFSA. *Faculty research:* Stochastic processes, business ethics, regional economic development, municipal finance, consumer behavior. *Unit head:* Dr. Peter Frank, Dean, 704-233-8148, Fax: 704-233-8146, E-mail: pfrank@wingate.edu. *Application contact:* Mary Maye, Administrative Assistant to the Dean, 704-233-8148, Fax: 704-233-8146.
Website: http://www.wingate.edu/academics/school-of-business

Winston-Salem State University, Program in Business Administration, Winston-Salem, NC 27110-0003. Offers MBA. *Accreditation:* AACSB. *Program availability:* Part-time, evening/weekend, online learning. *Entrance requirements:* For master's, GMAT, resume, 3 letters of recommendation. Electronic applications accepted. *Faculty research:* Innovative entrepreneurship and customer service, econometrics and operations research.

Winthrop University, College of Business Administration, Program in Business Administration, Rock Hill, SC 29733. Offers MBA. *Accreditation:* AACSB. *Program availability:* Part-time. *Entrance requirements:* For master's, GMAT. Additional exam requirements/recommendations for international students: Required—TOEFL (minimum score 550 paper-based; 79 iBT), IELTS (minimum score 6). *Expenses:* Tuition, state resident: full-time $14,312; part-time $599 per credit hour. Tuition, nonresident: full-time $27,570; part-time $1153 per credit hour.

Woodbury University, School of Business, Burbank, CA 91504-1099. Offers business administration (MBA); organizational leadership (MA). *Accreditation:* AACSB; ACBSP. *Program availability:* Part-time, evening/weekend. *Entrance requirements:* For master's, GMAT, transcripts, resume. Additional exam requirements/recommendations for international students: Required—TOEFL (minimum score 550 paper-based; 83 iBT), IELTS (minimum score 6.5). *Faculty research:* Total quality management, leadership.

Worcester Polytechnic Institute, Graduate Studies and Research, Foisie Business School, Worcester, MA 01609-2280. Offers information technology (MS), including information security management; management (Graduate Certificate); marketing and technological innovation (MS); operations design and leadership (MS); technology (MBA, MS). *Accreditation:* AACSB. *Program availability:* Part-time, evening/weekend, 100% online, blended/hybrid learning. *Faculty:* 20 full-time (12 women), 16 part-time/adjunct (1 woman). *Students:* 237 full-time (139 women), 186 part-time (67 women); includes 35 minority (4 Black or African American, non-Hispanic/Latino; 17 Asian, non-Hispanic/Latino; 12 Hispanic/Latino; 2 Two or more races, non-Hispanic/Latino), 221 international. 645 applicants, 62% accepted, 144 enrolled. In 2016, 150 master's awarded. *Degree requirements:* For master's, thesis optional. *Entrance requirements:* For master's, GMAT (MBA); GMAT or GRE General Test (MS), statement of purpose, 3 letters of recommendation, resume; for Graduate Certificate, GMAT or GRE General Test, statement of purpose, 3 letters of recommendation. Additional exam requirements/recommendations for international students: Required—TOEFL (minimum score 563 paper-based; 84 iBT), IELTS (minimum score 7). *Application deadline:* For fall admission, 6/1 priority date for domestic and international students; for spring admission, 11/1 priority date for domestic students, 10/1 priority date for international students. Applications are processed on a rolling basis. Application fee: $70. Electronic applications accepted. *Financial support:* Career-related internships or fieldwork, institutionally sponsored loans, scholarships/grants, and unspecified assistantships available. Financial award application deadline: 6/1; financial award applicants required to submit FAFSA. *Unit head:* Melissa Terrio, Executive Director, 508-831-4665, Fax: 508-831-4665, E-mail: biz@wpi.edu. *Application contact:* Eileen Dagostino, Recruiting Operations Coordinator, 508-831-4665, Fax: 508-831-5720, E-mail: edag@wpi.edu.
Website: https://www.wpi.edu/academics/business

Worcester State University, Graduate Studies, Program in Management, Worcester, MA 01602-2597. Offers accounting (MS); managerial leadership (MS). *Program availability:* Part-time, evening/weekend. *Faculty:* 7 full-time (3 women). *Students:* 9 full-time (5 women), 36 part-time (22 women); includes 11 minority (5 Black or African American, non-Hispanic/Latino; 2 Asian, non-Hispanic/Latino; 3 Hispanic/Latino; 1 Two or more races, non-Hispanic/Latino), 3 international. Average age 32. 44 applicants, 70% accepted, 15 enrolled. In 2016, 10 master's awarded. *Degree requirements:* For master's, comprehensive exam (for some programs), thesis optional. *Entrance requirements:* For master's, GMAT, 3 letters of recommendation from professors and/or supervisors. Additional exam requirements/recommendations for international students: Required—TOEFL (minimum score 550 paper-based; 79 iBT). *Application deadline:* For fall admission, 6/15 for domestic and international students; for spring admission, 11/1 for domestic and international students; for summer admission, 4/1 for domestic and international students. Applications are processed on a rolling basis. Application fee: $50. Electronic applications accepted. *Expenses:* Tuition, state resident: part-time $150 per credit. Tuition, nonresident: part-time $150 per credit. *Financial support:* Career-related internships or fieldwork, scholarships/grants, and unspecified assistantships available. Financial award application deadline: 3/1; financial award applicants required to submit FAFSA. *Unit head:* Dr. Elizabeth Wark, Program Coordinator, 508-929-8743, E-mail: ewark@worcester.edu. *Application contact:* Sara Grady, Associate Dean, Graduate Studies and Professional Development, 508-929-8787, Fax: 508-929-8100, E-mail: sara.grady@worcester.edu.

Wright State University, Graduate School, Raj Soin College of Business, Program in Business Administration, Dayton, OH 45435. Offers MBA. *Expenses:* Tuition, state resident: full-time $9952; part-time $622 per credit hour. Tuition, nonresident: full-time $16,960; part-time $1060 per credit hour. *Unit head:* Michael Evans, Director of MBA Programs, 937-775-2437, Fax: 937-775-3545, E-mail: michael.evans@wright.edu. *Application contact:* Michael Evans, Director of MBA Programs, 937-775-2437, Fax: 937-775-3545, E-mail: michael.evans@wright.edu.

Xavier University, Williams College of Business, Master of Business Administration Program, Cincinnati, OH 45207. Offers business administration (Exec MBA, MBA); business intelligence (MBA); finance (MBA); health industry (MBA); international business (MBA); marketing (MBA); values-based leadership (MBA); MBA/MHSA; MSN/MBA. *Accreditation:* AACSB. *Program availability:* Part-time, evening/weekend. *Degree requirements:* For master's, capstone course. *Entrance requirements:* For master's, GMAT or GRE, official transcript; resume. Additional exam requirements/recommendations for international students: Required—TOEFL (minimum score 550 paper-based; 79 iBT). Electronic applications accepted. Application fee is waived when completed online. *Expenses:* Contact institution.

Yale University, Yale School of Management and Graduate School of Arts and Sciences, Doctoral Program in Management, New Haven, CT 06520. Offers accounting (PhD); financial economics (PhD); marketing (PhD); organizations and management (PhD). *Accreditation:* AACSB. *Degree requirements:* For doctorate, comprehensive exam, thesis/dissertation. *Entrance requirements:* For doctorate, GMAT or GRE General Test. Additional exam requirements/recommendations for international students: Required—TOEFL or IELTS. Electronic applications accepted. *Expenses:* Contact institution. *Faculty research:* Pricing of options and futures, term structure of interest rates, use of accounting numbers in debt contracts, product differentiation, e-commerce and marketing, behavioral finance.

Yale University, Yale School of Management, Program in Business Administration, New Haven, CT 06520. Offers MBA, MBA/JD, MBA/M Arch, MBA/M Div, MBA/MA, MBA/MEM, MBA/MF, MBA/MFA, MBA/MPH, MBA/PhD, MD/MBA. *Accreditation:* AACSB. Terminal master's awarded for partial completion of doctoral program. *Degree requirements:* For master's, international experience. *Entrance requirements:* For master's, GMAT or GRE. Additional exam requirements/recommendations for international students: Required—TOEFL, PTE, or IELTS. Electronic applications accepted. *Expenses:* Contact institution. *Faculty research:* Finance, strategy, marketing, leadership, operations.

Yeshiva University, Sy Syms School of Business, New York, NY 10016. Offers accounting (MS); business (EMBA); marketing (MS). *Program availability:* Part-time. *Entrance requirements:* For master's, minimum GPA of 3.5 or GMAT.

York College of Pennsylvania, Graham School of Business, York, PA 17403-3651. Offers continuous improvement (MBA); financial management (MBA); health care management (MBA); management (MBA); marketing (MBA); self-designed (MBA). *Accreditation:* ACBSP. *Program availability:* Part-time, evening/weekend. *Faculty:* 11 full-time (3 women), 4 part-time/adjunct (1 woman). *Students:* 2 full-time (1 woman), 68 part-time (31 women); includes 7 minority (2 Black or African American, non-Hispanic/Latino; 1 Asian, non-Hispanic/Latino; 1 Hispanic/Latino; 3 Two or more races, non-Hispanic/Latino). Average age 32. 39 applicants, 79% accepted, 20 enrolled. In 2016, 22 master's awarded. *Degree requirements:* For master's, directed study. *Entrance requirements:* For master's, GMAT. Additional exam requirements/recommendations for international students: Required—TOEFL (minimum score 530 paper-based; 72 iBT), IELTS (minimum score 6). *Application deadline:* For fall admission, 7/15 priority date for domestic students, 5/1 for international students; for spring admission, 11/15 priority date for domestic students, 9/1 for international students; for summer admission, 4/15 priority date for domestic students. Applications are processed on a rolling basis. Application fee: $0. Electronic applications accepted. *Expenses:* $795 per credit. *Financial support:* In 2016–17, 3 students received support. Scholarships/grants available. Financial award applicants required to submit FAFSA. *Unit head:* Nicole Cornell Sadowski, MBA Director, 717-815-1491, Fax: 717-600-3999, E-mail: ncornell@ycp.edu. *Application contact:* MBA Office, 717-815-1491, Fax: 717-600-3999, E-mail: mba@ycp.edu.
Website: http://www.ycp.edu/mba

York University, Faculty of Graduate Studies, Schulich School of Business, Toronto, ON M3J 1P3, Canada. Offers accounting (M Acc); administration (PhD); business (MBA); business analytics (MBA); finance (MF); international business (IMBA); MBA/JD; MBA/MA; MBA/MFA. *Program availability:* Part-time, evening/weekend. *Degree requirements:* For master's, advanced proficiency in a second language, work term (IMBA); for doctorate, comprehensive exam, thesis/dissertation. *Entrance requirements:* For master's, GMAT or GRE, minimum GPA of 3.0 (3.3 for MF, MBA in business analytics, and IMBA); for doctorate, GMAT or GRE, minimum GPA of 3.3. Additional exam requirements/recommendations for international students: Required—TOEFL (minimum score 600 paper-based; 100 iBT), IELTS (minimum score 7), York English Language Test (minimum score 1); PearsonVUE (minimum score 64). Electronic applications accepted. *Faculty research:* Accounting, finance, marketing, operations management and information systems, organizational studies, strategic management.

Youngstown State University, Graduate School, Williamson College of Business Administration, Youngstown, OH 44555-0001. Offers MBA, Certificate. *Accreditation:* AACSB. *Program availability:* Part-time, evening/weekend. *Degree requirements:* For master's, thesis optional. *Entrance requirements:* For master's, GMAT, minimum GPA of 2.7. Additional exam requirements/recommendations for international students: Required—TOEFL. *Faculty research:* Taxation and compliance, business ethics, operations management, organizational behavior, gender issues.

FASHION INSTITUTE OF TECHNOLOGY

State University of New York

M.P.S. in Global Fashion Management

 For more information, visit http://petersons.to/fitglobalfashion

Programs of Study

The Fashion Institute of Technology (FIT), a State University of New York (SUNY) college of art and design, business, and technology, is home to a mix of innovative achievers, creative thinkers, and industry pioneers. FIT fosters interdisciplinary initiatives, advances research, and provides access to an international network of professionals. With a reputation for excellence, FIT offers its diverse student body access to world-class faculty, dynamic and relevant curricula, and a superior education at an affordable cost. It offers seven programs of graduate study. The programs in Art Market Studies; Exhibition and Experience Design; and Fashion and Textile Studies: History, Theory, Museum Practice lead to the Master of Arts (M.A.) degree. The Illustration and Fashion Design programs lead to the Master of Fine Arts (M.F.A.) degree. The Master of Professional Studies (M.P.S.) degree programs are Cosmetics and Fragrance Marketing and Management, and Global Fashion Management.

Global Fashion Management is a 36-credit, full-time Master of Professional Studies program offered in collaboration with Hong Kong Polytechnic University in Hong Kong and the Institut Français de la Mode in Paris. The program is designed to prepare current apparel industry managers for senior- and executive-level positions. The course of study is completed in three semesters and brings students from all three institutions together for intensive seminars held at each of the three participating institutions, thus providing a unique international experience for those involved. The curriculum includes courses in production and supply chain management, global marketing and fashion brand management, international retail management, business policy, international culture and business, finance, politics, and world trade. Students devote a year to research in preparation for delivering a capstone project that is judged by industry executives.

Research Facilities

The School of Graduate Studies is primarily located in the campus's Shirley Goodman Resource Center, which also houses the Gladys Marcus Library and The Museum at FIT. School of Graduate Studies facilities include conference rooms; a fully equipped conservation laboratory; a multipurpose laboratory for conservation projects and the dressing of mannequins; storage facilities for costume and textile materials; a graduate student lounge with computer and printer access; a graduate student library reading room with computers, reference materials, and copies of past classes' qualifying and thesis papers; specialized wireless classrooms; traditional and digital illustration studios; and classrooms equipped with model stands, easels, and drafting tables.

The Gladys Marcus Library houses more than 300,000 volumes of print, nonprint, and digital resources. Specialized holdings include industry reference materials, manufacturers' catalogs, original fashion sketches and scrapbooks, photographs, portfolios of plates, and sample books. The FIT Digital Library provides access to over 90 searchable online databases.

The Museum at FIT houses one of the world's most important collections of clothing and textiles and is the only museum in New York City dedicated to the art of fashion. The permanent collection encompasses more than 50,000 garments and accessories dating from the eighteenth century to the present, with particular strength in twentieth-century fashion, as well as 30,000 textiles and 100,000 textile swatches. Each year, nearly 100,000 visitors are drawn to the museum's award-winning exhibitions and public programs.

Financial Aid

FIT directly administers its institutional grants, scholarships, and loans. Federal funding administered by the college may include Federal Perkins Loans, federally subsidized and unsubsidized Direct Loans for students, Grad PLUS loans, and the Federal Work-Study Program. Priority for institutionally administered funds is given to students enrolled and designated as full-time.

Cost of Study

Tuition for New York State residents is $5,603 per semester, or $467 per credit. Out-of-state residents' tuition is $11,449 per semester, or $954 per credit. Tuition and fees are subject to change at the discretion of FIT's Board of Trustees. Additional expenses—for class materials, textbooks, and travel—may apply and vary per program.

Living and Housing Costs

On-campus housing is available to graduate students. Traditional residence hall accommodations (including meal plan) cost from $5,887 to $7,074 per semester. Apartment-style housing options (not including meal plan) cost from $6,299 to $10,495 per semester.

Student Group

Enrollment in the School of Graduate Studies is approximately 200 students per academic year, allowing considerable individualized advisement. Students come to FIT from throughout the country and around the world.

Student Outcomes

Students in the Global Fashion Management program maintain full-time employment in the industry while working toward their degree, which provides the basis for advancement to positions of upper-level managerial responsibility.

Location

FIT is located in Manhattan's Chelsea neighborhood, at the heart of the advertising, visual arts, marketing, fashion, business, design, and communications industries. Students are connected to New York City and gain unparalleled exposure to their field through guest lectures, field trips, internships, and sponsored competitions. The location provides access to major museums, galleries, and auction houses as well as dining, entertainment, and shopping options. The campus is near subway, bus, and commuter rail lines.

Applying

Applicants to all School of Graduate Studies programs must hold a baccalaureate degree in an appropriate major from a college or university, with a cumulative GPA of 3.0 or higher. International students from non-English-speaking countries are required to submit minimum TOEFL scores of 550 on the written test, 213 on the computer test, or 80 on the Internet test. Students applying to the Global Fashion Management program must submit GRE scores. Each major has additional, specialized prerequisites for admission; for detailed information, students should visit the School of Graduate Studies on FIT's website.

Domestic and international students use the same application when seeking admission. The deadline for completed applications with transcripts and supplemental materials is February 15 for the Global Fashion Management program. After the deadline date, applicants are considered on a rolling admissions basis. Candidates may apply online at fitnyc.edu/gradstudies.

Correspondence and Information

School of Graduate Studies
Shirley Goodman Resource Center, Room E315
Fashion Institute of Technology
227 West 27 Street
New York, New York 10001-5992
Phone: 212-217-4300
Fax: 212-217-4301
E-mail: gradinfo@fitnyc.edu
Website: fitnyc.edu/gradstudies
fitnyc.edu/GFM

THE FACULTY

The faculty members listed below constitute a partial listing. Guest lecturers are not included.

Pamela Ellsworth, Chairperson; M.P.S., Fashion Institute of Technology.
Raja Akram, M.A., Texas A&M.
Jim Biolos, M.B.A., International University of Japan, Niigata.
Praveen Chaudhry, Ph.D., Pennsylvania.
James Gutman, Ed.M., Harvard.
Meg Joseph, M.B.A., Columbia.
Christine Russo, B.S., Cornell.

JACKSONVILLE UNIVERSITY

Davis College of Business

 For more information, visit http://petersons.to/jacksonvilleubusiness

Programs of Study

Jacksonville University's (JU) Davis College of Business offers flexible and accelerated Master of Business Administration (M.B.A.) programs designed for all types of working professionals, both those seeking career changes and those who want to move up within their current fields. Graduates earn promotions into senior managerial roles in their professions by incorporating their accumulated theory and practice into their respective roles as managers and leaders. Management training serves as a foundation for both the Flex M.B.A. and Accelerated M.B.A. programs.

The M.B.A. Program: It combines accounting, decision sciences, economics, finance, information technology, international business, management, and marketing—all included so that students are well-equipped for management and decision-making roles in both small companies and large corporations. Students can choose to follow a general M.B.A. path (36 credits) or concentrate in one of four concentration areas (39 credits): Accounting and Finance, Management, Management Accounting, or Consumer Goods and Services Marketing. More than half of the students choose to pursue one of the four concentration areas.

The Flex program is highly adaptable to the student's career goals: students choose the pace of coursework based on how quickly they want to complete their program. Most students are able to complete the program in two years as part-time students. The Accelerated M.B.A. program is a full-time, structured cohort, enabling students to complete the program in just twelve months regardless of their undergraduate degree.

Executive M.B.A. Program: With concentrations in Leadership Development (LD) and Consumer Goods and Services Marketing (CGSM), the JU Davis Executive Masters of Business Administration (E.M.B.A.) is an intensive 19-month (LD) or 29-month (CGSM) program designed to develop a leader's strategic mindset, business expertise, and creative instincts. Grounded in a compelling holistic management framework, the program recognizes that sustainable high-performance in the business world today requires attention to mind, body, and spirit. The E.M.B.A. is designed for rising and midcareer executives, both in context and convenience. The curriculum is taught in a team-oriented environment where courses are integrated to emphasize broader strategic management and leadership skills.

Master of Science in Organizational Leadership: The Master of Science in Organizational Leadership (M.S.O.L.) degree program is a 30-credit program designed for experienced professionals who want the practical knowledge and skills to lead people engaged in innovation, change, and transformation initiatives. It is particularly appropriate for human resource, technical, or functional specialists who are preparing for greater leadership roles. It is tailored for nonbusiness undergraduate majors who seek to earn graduate degrees that focus more on management and leadership rather than the quantitative focus of the M.B.A. degree.

Doctor of Business Administration: The 63-credit doctoral program for executives takes business intelligence and the art of informed intuition to a new level. The D.B.A. curriculum builds on the skills students have mastered professionally, while heightening their ability to be agile and fluid as managers. The JU D.B.A. program is based on the three pillars of leadership, globalization, and business analytics. The three-year, 63-credit D.B.A. program prepares candidates to explore the best paths for data discovery, innovation, quantitative analysis, and global challenges.

Joint Program Graduate Business Degrees: There are three joint M.B.A. programs at Jacksonville University: the Master of Science in Nursing (M.S.N.)/M.B.A. degree program; the Master of Public Policy (M.P.P.)/M.B.A. degree program; and the Juris Doctor (J.D.)/M.B.A. degree program. The first two programs are offered entirely at JU, while the J.D./M.B.A. is conducted in conjunction with the Florida Coastal School of Law.

Four+1 Bachelor's/M.B.A.: Jacksonville University offers a unique 4-year+1 bachelor's/M.B.A. program that is designed for highly motivated high school students with interests in any major. If qualified, students are conditionally admitted to the Accelerated (full-time day) M.B.A. program when they apply to JU as high school seniors. Students who maintain at least 3.3 cumulative GPAs in their undergraduate studies are automatically accepted into the Accelerated M.B.A. program upon graduation from JU.

Accreditation

Jacksonville University is regionally accredited by the Southern Association of Colleges and Schools (SACS). In addition, the Davis College of Business has been accredited by the Association to Advance Collegiate Schools of Business (AACSB) since 2010. Only 5 percent of all the business schools in the world are accredited by AACSB, making it the most challenging, prestigious accreditation for a school to earn. Very strict standards apply in every area—faculty quality, teaching resources and technology, facilities, connections with the business community, and services for students.

Financial Aid

Most graduate students at Jacksonville University receive some type of financial aid through scholarships, loans, or assistantships. Many working students receive partial financial support for their education from their employers. JU is a voluntary participant in the Yellow Ribbon Program for Post-9/11 G.I. Bill recipients.

Cost of Study

The graduate programs at Jacksonville University are competitively priced. Costs shown are for the 2017–18 academic year and may vary depending on foundation needs, concentration(s) pursued, and the amount of time each student needs to complete the program.

The Flex and Accelerated M.B.A. programs cost $770 per credit hour, with a total program cost of $27,720 for a general M.B.A. with no foundation courses.

The Executive M.B.A.–Leadership Development program cost is $11,800 per semester for a total cost of $59,000 (five semesters).

The Executive M.B.A.–Consumer Goods and Services Markıng program cost is $7,375 per semester for a total cost of $59,000 (eight semesters).

The Master of Science in Organizational Leadership program costs $770 per credit hour and has a total cost of $23,000.

The Doctor of Business Administration program costs $30,000 per year, for a total cost of $90,000.

Student Group

More than 200 graduate students attend classes at the Davis College of Business (DCOB) and the majority of students enroll part-time.

Student Outcomes

The JU Career Resource Center supports all Jacksonville University students and alumni, including graduate students. Staff members provide a variety of services to help students and alumni succeed in graduate and professional school and in the world of work. These include individual career consulting and counseling, career assessments, career workshops, an annual career and internship expo, information sessions, special speakers and events, on-campus recruiting, job and internship postings, mock interviewing, resume/cover letter preparation and revision, and much more.

Location

Jacksonville is a rapidly growing metropolitan city, the largest in Florida, with approximately 850,000 residents. Miles of beaches and waterways, a major symphony orchestra, NFL football, a myriad of restaurants, and annual special events enhance the quality of life. Jacksonville is also a leading international business hub, with world-renowned port and air cargo facilities and rail and trucking routes. According to Forbes magazine, Jacksonville's growing population, strong economy, diverse cultural and recreational opportunities, abundant natural resources, and growing financial and tech environment make Jacksonville one of the nation's top-rated job markets.

The University and the Business School

Jacksonville University (JU) is located in a beautiful riverfront setting in suburban Jacksonville, across the St. Johns River from downtown and just minutes from the Atlantic Ocean. The 190-acre campus includes a riverfront, oak-lined paths, and a state-of-the-art business building. JU offers seven bachelor's degree programs and more than 70 majors, programs, and concentrations. There are graduate programs in nursing, business, education, marine science, fine arts, math, applied health sciences, and public policy. Doctoral programs include the Doctor of Nursing Practice (D.N.P.) program, a Doctor of Business Administration (D.B.A.) program, and a nationally known postgraduate certification in orthodontics.

The Davis College of Business (DCOB) offers both undergraduate and graduate business degrees. The college is the only private business college in North Florida that is accredited by the Association to Advance Collegiate Schools of Business (AACSB) International. The college has been recognized by *CEO Magazine* for having one of the Top 100 M.B.A. programs in North America.

The Faculty

Graduate students benefit from in-depth business instruction. Classes are taught by both Ph.D.-credentialed faculty members from the world's best universities and experienced professionals who have earned excellent records of accomplishment in the industry. The flexible graduate programs are tailored to each student's particular needs and goals.

Applying

Prospective students can apply to Jacksonville University's graduate business programs online at www.ju.edu/apply.

Correspondence and Information

For more information, students should contact:

Davis College of Business
Jacksonville University
2800 University Boulevard North
Jacksonville, Florida 32211
United States
Phone: 904-256-7426
E-mail: amurphy8@ju.edu
Website: www.ju.edu/dcob

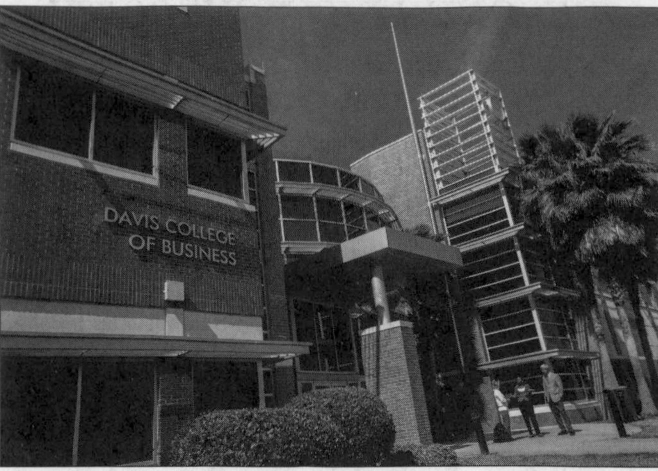

This Jacksonville University state-of-the-art campus building features executive training rooms, conference rooms, computer labs, media conference room, and study rooms.

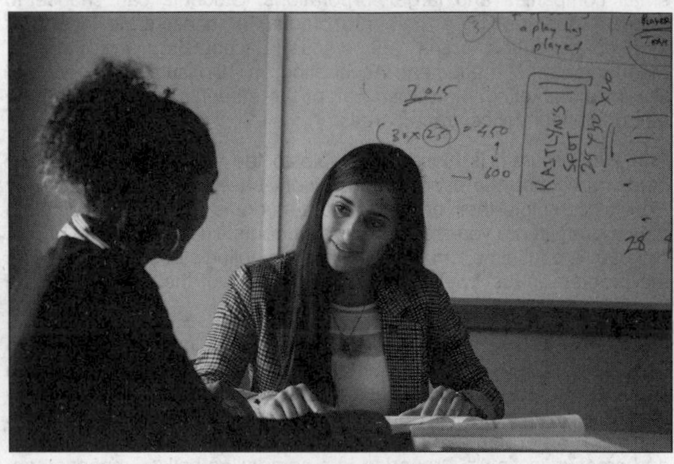

Jacksonville University's more than 25,000 alumni come from all 50 states and 92 countries.

MONMOUTH UNIVERSITY

Leon Hess Business School

Programs of Study

Monmouth University is a leading private institution that helps students of all ages to increase their professional skills and enhance their intellectual development. Graduate programs are offered within six academic schools: the Leon Hess Business School (M.B.A.), the Wayne D. McMurray School of Humanities and Social Sciences (M.A., M.S.), the Marjorie K. Unterberg School of Nursing and Health Studies (M.S.N., M.S., D.N.P.), the School of Education (M.A.T., M.S.Ed., M.Ed., Ed.D.), the School of Science (M.S.), and the School of Social Work (M.S.W.).

Monmouth provides high-quality graduate and certificate programs in areas that are in demand in the work-place. The University also offers a Doctor of Nursing Practice (D.N.P.) and Doctor of Education in Educational Leadership program. M.B.A. students can customize their program by pursuing a concentration in accounting, finance, management, marketing, or real estate. Monmouth's programs offer hands-on, personalized attention to improve students' leadership qualities and prepare them for career advancement, career changes, or further study. Graduate students also have opportunities to engage in scholarly research with the University's innovative faculty. To view all of Monmouth's graduate studies offerings, visit www.monmouth.edu/graduate.

Many of Monmouth's graduate students work or intern on a full-time basis and attend classes in the evening. To provide flexibility, some programs offer courses in hybrid format, consisting of face-to-face classes interspersed with online sessions on alternate weeks. The online component is asynchronous, allowing students to participate when it is most convenient for them. The University encourages students to accelerate their program by taking summer course work.

Research Facilities

The Monmouth University Library holds approximately 360,000 print and electronic monographs, 68,000 print and electronic periodicals, 157 databases, and 1,100 media assets (CDs and DVDs). All academic programs are amply supported by state-of-the-art computer hardware and software and classroom/laboratory facilities. The major components supporting Monmouth's academic programs include Windows, Mac OS, and Unix systems connected via an expansive wired and wireless network, which spans twenty-three buildings and encompasses more than 2,400 workstations in general and specialty labs and classrooms.

Financial Aid

To help students realize their goals, graduate scholarships are available to eligible matriculated students in most master's degree and doctoral programs and are renewable each semester. Qualified students may also be eligible for graduate assistantships in which on-campus work is performed in exchange for tuition. These positions include graduate teaching and research assistantship opportunities, and there is a competitive application process.

To obtain federal loans, applicants must file the FAFSA form at www.fafsa.ed.gov. Monmouth University participates in the Federal Direct Student Loan Program, which makes loans available to all students who file the FAFSA. Alternative loan funding sources are available to those students who might not otherwise qualify for federal funding or need additional funding above and beyond the amount that has already been provided.

Cost of Study

Tuition for study in 2017–18 is $1,142 per credit. A University fee is assessed each semester.

Living and Housing Costs

Due to Monmouth's proximity to the beach, there are ample off-campus housing opportunities that are conveniently located near the University. A rental listing website is maintained by the Office of Off-Campus and Commuter Services and can be found at http://www.monmouth.edu/commuter. Graduate students may also apply for University housing; these apartment-style accommodations are located in University-owned or -sponsored housing.

Student Group

Monmouth University enrolls approximately 6,400 students, roughly 1,700 of whom are enrolled in Graduate Studies. The diverse student body includes international students representing thirty-four different countries.

Location

Monmouth University is located less than a mile from the Atlantic Ocean on a 159-acre campus in the safe, suburban town of West Long Branch, New Jersey. The campus is approximately an hour from New York City and Philadelphia. The University's proximity to high-technology firms, financial institutions, and a thriving business-industrial sector provides Monmouth students and graduates with a wide variety of employment possibilities. The surrounding area also has numerous activities, theaters, restaurants, and cultural events.

The University

Monmouth University provides a learning environment that enables students to pursue their educational goals and realize their full potential as leaders. Small classes allow for individual attention and student-faculty dialogue, and the Center for Student Success offers a hub of academic and career counseling services.

At Monmouth, students enjoy one of the most beautiful campuses in New Jersey. The centerpiece of campus is Woodrow Wilson Hall, a National Historic Landmark, which was used as Daddy Warbucks' mansion in the film *Annie*. Other unique buildings include the Jules L. Plangere Jr. Center for Communication, which provides state-of-the-art studios and editing facilities, and Bey Hall, which houses the financial markets lab.

Throughout the year, students and employees cheer on Monmouth's Division I athletic teams. The school fields 23 teams for men and women. The University's basketball and track and field teams compete in the 153,200-square-foot OceanFirst Bank Center, which features a 4,100-seat arena with premium suites, as well as a fitness center and a 200-meter, six-lane indoor track.

Applying

An application for graduate admission includes a completed application form with fee, official transcripts of the undergraduate record, score reports from the appropriate entrance examination, and transcripts of any graduate work done elsewhere. Students should contact the Office of Graduate Admission for details, or visit http://www.monmouth.edu/gradbook. International students must also provide evidence of English proficiency.

The application deadlines are July 15 for the fall term, December 1 for the spring term, and May 1 for the summer sessions. (Please note that some programs have different application deadlines and only accept students once per year.) An initial review of the complete application for admission is conducted by the Office of Graduate Admission; the file is then forwarded to the faculty program director for an admission decision. All correspondence should be directed to the Office of Graduate Admission.

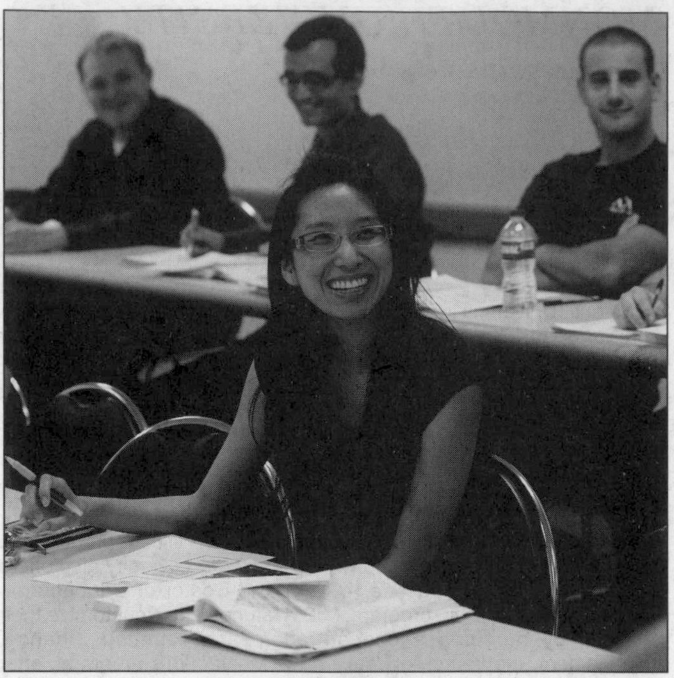

Correspondence and Information

Office of Graduate Admission
Monmouth University
400 Cedar Avenue
West Long Branch, New Jersey 07764-1898
United States
Phone: 732-571-3452
Fax: 732-263-5123
E-mail: gradadm@monmouth.edu
Website: http://www.monmouth.edu/gradbook

THE FACULTY AND THEIR RESEARCH AREAS

Faculty members at Monmouth University are committed teachers with extensive academic and professional experience who have established themselves as important scholars in their respective fields. Their work has been published in a variety of major journals, the proceedings of national and international conferences, books, and other outlets.

Students at Monmouth learn in small classes that promote close interaction with this knowledgeable faculty. Each faculty member strives to provide students with the foundation to succeed. Teaching and learning are not just confined to the classroom; professors and students often continue their discussions in the hallways, faculty offices, and dining facilities on campus.

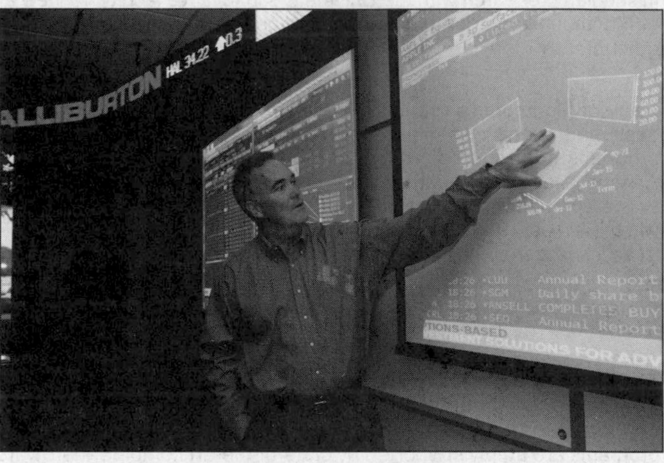

NORTH DAKOTA STATE UNIVERSITY

College of Business

NDSU GRADUATE SCHOOL

 For more information, visit http://petersons.to/ndstatebusiness

Programs of Study

The College of Business at North Dakota State University offers two graduate programs: the Master of Business Administration (MBA) and the Master of Accountancy (M.Acc.).

These programs integrate case study and applied learning to prepare students for career advancement. Accreditation from AACSB International, which accredits less than five percent of the business schools worldwide, ensures that these programs meet the highest academic standards.

In addition to providing high-quality programs, the college offers a collaborative learning environment. Students learn from fellow students' experiences and network with leaders from top businesses.

Master of Business Administration program: The MBA program provides analytical skills, an expansive view of how organizations operate, and in-depth understanding of business functional areas. Its curriculum consists of 24 credits of core courses in finance, information resources, management, marketing, and organizational behavior. The curriculum also includes six credits of elective courses in accounting, finance, management, and information systems. In addition, concentrations are offered in health care industry and in supply chain/ logistics.

Required courses are generally offered during the evening to accommodate working professionals, while elective courses are offered during the day and in the evening, as well as in the summer. The program is also available to distance students via teleconferencing technology.

Master of Accountancy program: The 30-credit M.Acc. program is ideal for students who want to advance their careers in corporate accounting, government accounting, or public accounting. The program's curriculum consists of four required courses, five additional accounting courses, and one management course. It emphasizes the analytical, decision-making, and research skills involved with identifying and solving accounting problems. It also prepares students for the Certified Public Accounting (CPA) exam.

Research

Faculty members in the College of Business conduct innovative research to advance business education, theory, and practice. They investigate an extensive range of topics, including the following:

- auditing
- entrepreneurship/small business strategy
- financial accounting
- fraud in nonprofits
- intellectual capital
- international accounting
- managerial accounting
- market structure and performance
- personal selling
- public-private partnerships
- sales management
- services marketing
- strategic leadership
- strategic management in nonprofit organizations
- transport economics

Students assist faculty members with their research and conduct their own research through course work. For example, the Marketing Research course emphasizes research design, data collection, and data analysis. The Applied Professional Research course focuses on the research methods used to address complex accounting issues.

Financial Aid

Graduate students in the College of Business may qualify for graduate assistantships and scholarships. Assistantships provide stipends and tuition waivers.

Students may also qualify for loans through federal programs or private lenders and receive tuition reimbursement from their employers.

Cost of Study

The most current information on tuition and fees can be found online at https://www.ndsu.edu/onestop/accounts/.

Living and Housing Costs

Information about on-campus housing for graduate students can be found at www.ndsu.edu/reslife/general_apartment_information/. While there is no specific residence hall for graduate students, they are able to live in the University apartments. There are also numerous housing options in the Fargo community.

Faculty

Graduate faculty members in the College of Business have considerable academic expertise and practical experience working at Fortune 500 companies.

For example, Professor of Accounting Peggy Andersen has more than 30 years of academic experience. A prolific researcher, she has investigated issues concerning corporate responsibility, business ethics, target costing, new product costing, real estate, and mutual funds. Her work has been published in numerous scholarly journals, and she has received several grants and awards for her research.

Associate Professor of Management Derek Lehmberg holds graduate degrees from schools in Asia, Europe, and North America. His research primarily examines issues relating to strategic management in the context of Japanese business. He has authored numerous academic journal articles and also written several widely used teaching case studies. Prior to entering academia, Lehmberg was a management consultant in areas of operations and strategic management, serving clients in the Consumer and Industrial Products industry based in Japan, the U.S., and Germany.

Student Life

The College of Business provides a supportive environment where students with diverse academic, cultural, and professional backgrounds thrive. Students build productive relationships with each other, faculty members, and business leaders. They have access to co-curricular activities that enhance academic and professional achievement, including student organizations, events, speakers, and study abroad opportunities.

Support services like the Career Center, Counseling Center, Disability Services, Military and Veterans Services, Office of Multicultural Programs, and Wallman Wellness Center also enhance students' academic, professional, and personal growth.

Students take classes in Richard H. Barry Hall in downtown Fargo. This 135,000-square-foot facility includes a state-of-the-art trading room, 250-seat auditorium, and a Business Learning Center, as well as wireless Internet. Its three-story atrium also has a coffee bar and study lounges.

Location

North Dakota State University is located on the eastern edge of North Dakota in Fargo, the state's largest community. With its sister city, Moorhead, Minnesota, directly across the Red River, Fargo is one of the largest metropolitan centers between Minneapolis and Seattle and offers a family-friendly environment with excellent schools, safe neighborhoods, and a low crime rate; an active arts and cultural scene, including a symphony, civic opera company, art museums, and community theater; and many places to shop and eat, including numerous restaurants, coffee shops, and a newly refurbished downtown district.

The University

North Dakota State University, a student-focused, land-grant, research institution provides student-centered education for more than 14,400 students (and nearly 2,100 graduate students) who represent forty-eight states and sixty-nine countries. Its rigorous academic programs integrate theory and practice to create a comprehensive learning experience. The National Science Foundation ranked several of its programs among the top 100 in the country. Challenging academic programs coupled with outstanding co-curricular activities allow students to achieve academic excellence and contribute to the world.

Applying

North The North Dakota State University graduate school application procedure places responsibility on the applicant to gather all supporting credentials and verifying that the application file is complete. The deadline for submission is dependent upon the program. If no deadline is listed on the program's bulletin page, all application materials are due at least one month prior the start of the semester.

Prospective students must file their application online. There is a $35 nonrefundable application fee. A statement of purpose—covering reasons for pursing graduate study, special interests within the chosen discipline, and preparation, skills, and experience in the proposed field of study—is required for admission consideration and must be uploaded with the online application. Other requirements include three letters of recommendation; official transcripts from each college or university attended; and official GRE or GMAT scores if required. Some programs may have additional requirements, as stated on the individual program pages.

The online application and additional details regarding the application process are available at https://www.ndsu.edu/gradschool/prospective_students.

Correspondence and Information

College of Business
Graduate School
Department 2820, P.O. Box 6050
North Dakota State University
Fargo, North Dakota 58108-6050
Phone: 701-231-7033
800-608-6378 (toll-free)
E-mail: ndsu.grad.school@ndsu.edu
Website: www.ndsu.edu/gradschool
facebook.com/ndsugradschool (Facebook)
@NDSUGradSchool (Twitter)

MBA and M.Acc. students work with top NDSU graduate faculty members with extensive expertise from prominent research institutions and work experience—including management of billion-dollar portfolios and applied engineering management at Fortune 500 firms. NDSU's approach to learning combines case study and applied learning in a collaborative environment at an institution that has earned accreditation by AACSB International.

PURDUE UNIVERSITY

Krannert School of Management

PURDUE
KRANNERT
SCHOOL OF MANAGEMENT

 For more information, visit http://petersons.to/purduekrannert

Programs of Study

Purdue University's Krannert School of Management emphasizes quantitative analysis alongside the qualitative, establishing a strong foundation of business knowledge. Krannert's cohort-based approach and emphasis on the team dynamic simulates a true corporate working environment. Case studies help to develop critical thinking and problem-solving skills that translate to the business world. Specialization areas add depth to the broad base of management knowledge covered in the core curriculum and enhance skills in a specific business function. For these reasons and many others, the Krannert MBA has been ranked the #7 MBA at a U.S. public institution (*Financial Times*).

The Krannert School of Management offers two unique MBA programs, a Full-Time MBA as well as a hybrid Weekend MBA. The school also offers a full suite of Master of Science programs in accounting, business analytics and information management, economics, finance, global supply chain management, human resource management, and marketing.

Research and Extension Centers

Students in the Krannert School of Management go beyond theory and actually get down to business. In addition to classrooms, Krannert offers numerous real-world, practical R&D, and business-startup 'ecosystems' to offer an unparalleled learning experience. On campus, this higher-education/private-enterprise merger is where investors, manufacturing partners, entrepreneurs, researchers, professors, alumni, and students work together. By association, Krannert students have access to needs-based opportunities where they receive hands-on experience commercializing, and optimizing in real operational settings, taking the very latest technologies to market.

Human networking and the priceless utility of professional social-skill development are value-add hallmarks of the Krannert School of Management. Students are able to leverage an array of career resources and opportunities that range from leadership coursework and one-on-one coaching, to an alumni network and a full slate of career fairs.

The Krannert School of Management connects to campus and community through its extension centers.

The Business Information and Analytics Center (BIAC) merges two highly regarded areas in the Krannert School—Management Information Systems and Quantitative Methods—to leverage the breadth and depth of its research and corporate collaborations. The Dr. Cornell A. Bell Business Opportunity Program (BOP) was the first program to increase diversity and give all students access to a world-class management education at a major business school. Purdue's Jane Brock-Wilson Women in Management Center supports the leadership development of women from pre-college throughout their careers, while influencing thought and behavior in global business settings. The Purdue University Research Center in Economics (PURCE) conducts research into the effects of government policies in areas such as health care, crime, antitrust, international trade and taxation, to name a few.

For almost three decades, the Dauch Center for the Management of Manufacturing Enterprises (DCMME) and the Global Supply Chain Management Initiative (GSCMI) have been the focal point within Purdue University's Krannert School of Management for promoting education, research and industrial engagement with those interested in operations management, manufacturing management and supply chain management.

Financial Aid

Purdue offers top applicants assistantship opportunities and scholarships, such as the Purdue University MBA Alumnus Scholarship, to help reduce the cost of attending the Krannert School of Management. These merit-based awards do not require any additional application as all applicants are considered.

Graduate Assistantships involve approximately 10 hours of work per week and provide a monthly stipend and significant remission of tuition and fees. (Please note: Graduate Assistantships are only available for MBA and MSHRM applicants)

Many Purdue master's students serve as resident assistants within the Purdue Residence Halls system. All students (first-year, international, and continuing students) are eligible to apply for these positions, which include room and board, a small stipend, partial remission of tuition and fees.

Several forms of need-based financial aid are available, such as Federal Direct Stafford Loans, Federal Graduate Plus Loans, private alternative loans, and additional sources of funding.

Students may also secure graduate assistantships outside of the Krannert School of Management, based upon their special skills and expertise. There are also opportunities for students to find employment outside of the master's programs, working for the University or in the Lafayette/West Lafayette area, although these do not include any type of tuition remission.

Cost of Study

For the 2016–17 academic year, the MBA program fee each semester was $11,290 for Indiana residents and $21,092 for nonresidents. All fees are subject to increase based on approval by the Purdue University Board of Trustees. For the Weekend MBA program, the fee per semester was $49,740 for Indiana residents and $57,750 for nonresidents.

A complete breakdown of tuition and fees for all Krannert School of Management is available at http://www.purdue.edu/bursar/tuition/feerates/2016-2017/graduate/management.html#WL_ManagementGrad.

Living and Housing Costs

West Lafayette, Indiana is an inviting community for students and families alike. In 2016, The American Institute for Economic Research ranked West Lafayette/Lafayette, Indiana the tenth-best college town in America. In 2015, *Forbes* ranked West Lafayette/Lafayette second in its rankings of Best Small Cities for Business and Careers. The community is an affordable place to live compared to other university communities across the United States. Purdue offers an off-campus housing resource for students looking to live within the community.

Student Opportunities

Students have access to a full suite of career assistance services provided by the Krannert Professional Development Center (KPDC). Students also have the opportunity to work with entrepreneurs and technology specialists at Purdue's Discovery Park or Burton D. Morgan Center for Entrepreneurship. Purdue is ranked eighth as a producer of start-up talent among U.S. public universities (Tech.Co) and has the sixth most startups based on university IP among U.S. universities (AUTM U.S. Licensing Survey).

West Lafayette is annually rated among the top college towns in the U.S. (#12 by Business Insider). Purdue's campus is located between Indianapolis and Chicago and offers access to big-city life at a modest cost of living. When combined with tuition rates that have remained static for six straight years, Purdue offers exceptional return on investment for its students. Krannert's Full-Time MBA program has been ranked third by *Bloomberg Businessweek* for highest return on investment (2014).

Purdue University

Purdue has the second-largest international student enrollment among U.S. public institutions and that diversity translates to the Krannert classroom. In its small classroom atmosphere, Krannert students encounter a true cross-continental immersion with classmates from across the globe. In addition, Krannert offers a number of study-abroad opportunities.

Location

West Lafayette/Lafayette is a warm, welcoming community ideally situated between Chicago, Illinois and Indianapolis, Indiana. Home to Purdue University and just over 174,000 residents, the city is known for its diverse community and great quality of life. West Lafayette offers good schools, safe neighborhoods, and excellent public facilities and amenities, including over 40 parks and extensive trail systems. There is a wide spectrum of businesses, including many nationally and internationally known high-tech corporations and institutions.

Other amenities include beautiful turn-of-the-century architecture; a lively downtown with local shopping and restaurants; a sophisticated art scene with galleries and public art; and a full slate of annual festivals throughout the year.

The School and the University

Purdue University's Krannert School of Management provides a vibrant ecosystem for mastering the analytical problem-solving and tech-commercialization skills that move industry forward and change the world.

Krannert is uniquely positioned alongside a globally renowned STEM school, inside a dynamic corporate-partnership R&D community. Operating against that strong science and technology backdrop, Krannert approaches business learning from a research-based, quantitative angle that develops students' analytical skills. Tomorrow's business leaders will be those who speak the language of innovation—who know how to analyze data, develop and statistically justify creative business solutions, and even take new technologies to market.

Krannert School of Management is located on Purdue University's oldest and largest campus with approximately 39,000 students, in West Lafayette, Indiana.

Faculty and Alumni

While part of a Big Ten university, Krannert is proportionately smaller in scale—maintaining a student-professed family feel, a more mutually encouraging atmosphere of competition, and a highly collaborative classroom model that is reflective of the way today's successful business enterprises operate and solve problems.

Krannert students have access to a global and highly engaged alumni network that dramatically enhances learning and career opportunities. The distinguished faculty and alumni serve as student professional mentors. They foster and facilitate career goals, providing students with highly personalized guidance to steer their future careers. Pedagogically, Krannert empowers graduates—emphasizing leadership, professional development, and collaboration to accelerate careers.

Two Krannert faculty members were named to Poets and Quants 2017 Best 40 Under 40 Professors. A complete listing of faculty and their specialties is available at http://www.krannert.purdue.edu/faculty.

Applying

Applications for the Krannert School of Management must be completed using Purdue's Graduate School online application. International applicants must follow a slightly altered application process.

Applications will not be considered until all required materials have been received. This includes submission of a nonrefundable application fee of $60 (U.S. dollars) for domestic applicants and $75 (U.S. dollars) for international applicants, payable online by credit card. Non-degree applicants will not be charged an application fee.

Application deadlines vary by program; specific details can be found online at http://www.krannert.purdue.edu/masters/admissions/application-deadlines/home.php.

Correspondence and Information

Krannert School of Management
Purdue University MBA and M.S. Programs Office
100 South Grant Street
Rawls Hall, Suite 2020
West Lafayette, Indiana 47907-2056
Phone: 765-494-0773
877-MBA-KRAN (toll-free)
Fax: 765-494-9841
E-mail: gokrannert@purdue.edu
Website: www.krannert.purdue.edu

The director of the Purdue Foundry discusses a business venture with three aspiring entrepreneurs.

Welcome to Purdue University, home of the Krannert School of Management.

PURDUE UNIVERSITY

Krannert School of Management

PURDUE
KRANNERT
SCHOOL OF MANAGEMENT

For more information, visit http://petersons.to/purduemba

Program of Study

Purdue University's Krannert School of Management offers a Full-Time MBA program that combines a dynamic classroom experience with hands-on experiential learning, providing students abundant opportunities to fortify their talents outside the classroom. The program immerses students in learning through dynamic course work, leadership portfolio development, consulting projects, and study-abroad opportunities.

The Full-Time MBA is a two-year program (21 months) that begins in August. It spans four semesters (eight modules) and 60 credit hours. Krannert's cohort-based approach and emphasis on the team dynamic simulates a true corporate working environment. Case studies also develop critical thinking and problem-solving skills that translate to the business world. Specialization areas add depth to the broad base of management knowledge covered in the core curriculum and enhance skills in a specific business function. For these reasons and many others, the Krannert MBA has been ranked the #7 MBA at a U.S. public institution (*Financial Times*).

The Full-Time MBA program offers 14 specialization options for students to specialize in, including: accounting, business analytics, finance, global supply chain management, human resource management, international management, management consulting, management information systems, manufacturing/technology management, marketing, operations, organizational behavior, strategic management, and technology innovation and entrepreneurship.

Research and Extension Centers

Students in the Krannert School of Management go beyond theory and actually get down to business. In addition to classrooms, Krannert offers numerous real-world, practical R&D, and business-startup 'ecosystems' to offer an unparalleled learning experience. On campus, this higher-education/private-enterprise merger is where investors, manufacturing partners, entrepreneurs, researchers, professors, alumni, and students work together. By association, Krannert students have access to needs-based opportunities where they receive hands-on experience commercializing, and optimizing in real operational settings, taking the very latest technologies to market.

Human networking and the priceless utility of professional social-skill development are value-add hallmarks of the Krannert School of Management. Students are able to leverage an array of career resources and opportunities that range from leadership coursework and one-on-one coaching, to an alumni network and a full slate of career fairs.

The Krannert School of Management connects to campus and community through its extension centers.

The Business Information and Analytics Center (BIAC) merges two highly regarded areas in the Krannert School—Management Information Systems and Quantitative Methods—to leverage the breadth and depth of its research and corporate collaborations. The Dr. Cornell A. Bell Business Opportunity Program (BOP) was the first program to increase diversity and give all students access to a world-class management education at a major business school. Purdue's Jane Brock-Wilson Women in Management Center supports the leadership development of women from pre-college throughout their careers, while influencing thought and behavior in global business settings. The Purdue University Research Center in Economics (PURCE) conducts research into the effects of government policies in areas such as health care, crime, antitrust, international trade and taxation, to name a few.

For almost three decades, the Dauch Center for the Management of Manufacturing Enterprises (DCMME) and the Global Supply Chain Management Initiative (GSCMI) have been the focal point within Purdue University's Krannert School of Management for promoting education, research and industrial engagement with those interested in operations management, manufacturing management and supply chain management.

Financial Aid

Purdue offers top applicants assistantship opportunities and scholarships, such as the Purdue University MBA Alumnus Scholarship, to help reduce the cost of attending the Krannert School of Management. These merit-based awards do not require any additional application as all applicants are considered.

Graduate Assistantships involve approximately 10 hours of work per week and provide a monthly stipend and significant remission of tuition and fees. (Please note: Graduate Assistantships are only available for MBA and MSHRM applicants)

Many Purdue master's students serve as resident assistants within the Purdue Residence Halls system. All students (first-year, international, and continuing students) are eligible to apply for these positions, which include room and board, a small stipend, partial remission of tuition and fees.

Several forms of need-based financial aid are available, such as Federal Direct Stafford Loans, Federal Graduate Plus Loans, private alternative loans, and additional sources of funding.

Students may also secure graduate assistantships outside of the Krannert School of Management, based upon their special skills and expertise. There are also opportunities for students to find employment outside of the master's programs, working for the University or in the Lafayette/West Lafayette area, although these do not include any type of tuition remission.

Cost of Study

For the 2016–17 academic year, the MBA program fee each semester was $11,209 for Indiana residents and $21,092 for nonresidents. All fees are subject to increase based on approval by the Purdue University Board of Trustees.

A complete breakdown of tuition and fees for all Krannert School of Management is available at http://www.purdue.edu/bursar/tuition/feerates/2016-2017/graduate/management.html#WL_ManagementGrad.

Living and Housing Costs

West Lafayette, Indiana is an inviting community for students and families alike. In 2016, The American Institute for Economic Research ranked West Lafayette/Lafayette, Indiana the tenth-best college town in America. In 2015, *Forbes* ranked West Lafayette/Lafayette second in its rankings of Best Small Cities for Business and Careers. The community is an affordable place to live compared to other university communities across the United States. Purdue offers an off-campus housing resource for students looking to live within the community.

Student Opportunities

Engaging programs such as Launching Global Leaders, provide inclusive professional development opportunities designed to strengthen interpersonal skills.

Students have access to a full suite of career assistance services provided by the Krannert Professional Development Center (KPDC). Students also have the opportunity to work with entrepreneurs and technology specialists at Purdue's Discovery Park or Burton D. Morgan Center for Entrepreneurship. Purdue is ranked eighth as a producer of start-up talent among U.S. public universities (Tech.Co) and has the sixth most startups based on university IP among U.S. universities (AUTM U.S. Licensing Survey).

West Lafayette is annually rated among the top college towns in the U.S. (#12 by Business Insider). Purdue's campus is located between Indianapolis and Chicago and offers access to big-city life at a modest cost of living. When combined with tuition rates that have remained static for six straight years, Purdue offers exceptional return on investment for its students. Krannert's Full-Time MBA program has been ranked third by *Bloomberg Businessweek* for highest return on investment (2014).

Purdue has the second-largest international student enrollment among U.S. public institutions and that diversity translates to the Krannert classroom. In its small classroom atmosphere, Krannert students encounter a true cross-continental immersion with classmates from across the globe. In addition, Krannert offers a number of study-abroad opportunities.

Location

West Lafayette/Lafayette is a warm, welcoming community ideally situated between Chicago, Illinois and Indianapolis, Indiana. Home to Purdue University and just over 174,000 residents, the city is known for its diverse community and great quality of life. West Lafayette offers good schools, safe neighborhoods, and excellent public facilities and amenities, including over 40 parks and extensive trail systems. There is a wide spectrum of businesses, including many nationally and internationally known high-tech corporations and institutions.

Other amenities include beautiful turn-of-the-century architecture; a lively downtown with local shopping and restaurants; a sophisticated art scene with galleries and public art; and a full slate of annual festivals throughout the year.

The School and the University

Purdue University's Krannert School of Management provides a vibrant ecosystem for mastering the analytical problem-solving and tech-commercialization skills that move industry forward and change the world.

Krannert is uniquely positioned alongside a globally renowned STEM school, inside a dynamic corporate-partnership R&D community. Operating against that strong science and technology backdrop, Krannert approaches business learning from a research-based, quantitative angle that develops students' analytical skills. Tomorrow's business leaders will be those who speak the language of innovation—who know how to analyze data, develop and statistically justify creative business solutions, and even take new technologies to market.

Krannert School of Management is located on Purdue University's oldest and largest campus with approximately 39,000 students, in West Lafayette, Indiana.

Faculty

Krannert students have access to a global and highly engaged alumni network that dramatically enhances learning and career opportunities. The distinguished faculty and alumni serve as student professional mentors. They foster and facilitate career goals, providing students with highly personalized guidance to steer their future careers. Pedagogically, Krannert empowers graduates—emphasizing leadership, professional development, and collaboration to accelerate careers. Two Krannert faculty members were named to Poets and Quants 2017 Best 40 Under 40 Professors.

While part of a Big Ten university, Krannert is proportionately smaller in scale—maintaining a student-professed family feel, a more mutually encouraging atmosphere of competition, and a highly collaborative classroom model that is reflective of the way today's successful business enterprises operate and solve problems. A complete listing of faculty and their specialties is available at http://www.krannert.purdue.edu/faculty.

Applying

Applications for the Krannert School of Management must be completed using Purdue's Graduate School online application. International applicants must follow a slightly altered application process. Qualified domestic applicants for the Full-Time MBA program may receive an application fee waiver.

Applications will not be considered until all required materials have been received. This includes submission of a nonrefundable application fee of $60 (U.S. dollars) for domestic applicants and $75 (U.S. dollars) for international applicants, payable online by credit card. Non-degree applicants will not be charged an application fee.

Application deadlines vary by program; specific details can be found online at http://www.krannert.purdue.edu/masters/admissions/application-deadlines/home.php.

Correspondence and Information

Krannert School of Management
Purdue University MBA and M.S. Programs Office
100 South Grant Street
Rawls Hall, Suite 2020
West Lafayette, Indiana 47907-2056
Phone: 765-494-0773
877-MBA-KRAN (toll-free)
Fax: 765-494-9841
E-mail: gokrannert@purdue.edu
Website: www.krannert.purdue.edu

The director of the Purdue Foundry discusses a business venture with three aspiring entrepreneurs.

Welcome to Purdue University, home of the Krannert School of Management.

UNIVERSITY OF PITTSBURGH

Graduate Programs in Education

KATZ UNIVERSITY OF PITTSBURGH JOSEPH M.KATZ GRADUATE SCHOOL OF BUSINESS

 For more information, visit http://petersons.to//upittkatz

Programs of Study

The University of Pittsburgh's Joseph M. Katz Graduate School of Business believes two things to be universally true: business never stops reinventing itself, and neither should businesspersons. As a global, AACSB-accredited institution, Katz offers MBA, Executive MBA, Ph.D., and specialized master's programs in accounting, finance, marketing, management information systems (MIS), and supply chain management that are continually ranked among the world's best by independent publications.

The **One-Year MBA** is a full-time, 51-credit program, with classes in person on campus. The program is designed to be completed in 12 months, beginning in May.

The **Two-Year MBA** is a full-time, 57-credit program, with classes in person on campus. The program requires 21 months of study and begins in August.

The **Professional MBA** is a part-time, 51-credit program, with classes in a blended online format. The program can be completed in 12 to 24 months, with sessions beginning in August and January.

The **Specialized Master's** programs are full-time, 30-credit programs with classes on campus. The programs can be completed in 9 months and begin in August. Programs are available in accounting, finance, marketing, MIS, and supply chain management.

Research Facilities

Led by a world-renowned faculty, the curriculum incorporates groundbreaking research, the entrepreneurial spirit, and an emphasis on experience-based learning. As part of the University of Pittsburgh, Katz students and faculty enjoy an abundance of opportunities for cross-disciplinary collaboration.

Students have opportunities in several Katz research centers, including the Center for Branding, David Berg Center for Ethics and Leadership, Center for Executive Education, Center for Healthcare Management, International Business Center, and Center for Supply Chain Management.

Financial Aid

Tuition scholarships provide the primary source of financial assistance for incoming full-time Katz students. These merit-based scholarships are awarded in various dollar amounts and are directly applied to tuition charges.

Cost of Study

For full-time students who are Pennsylvania residents in the 2017–18 academic year, the One-Year MBA tuition is $44,454 and fees bring the total to $50,229; the Two-Year MBA tuition is $44,452 and fees bring the total to $52,152; and the Specialized Master's programs have tuition costs of $28,540 and fees bring the total to $31,090. Part-time Pennsylvania students in the Professional MBA program pay $65,127 in tuition and fees bring the total to $68,487; those in the Specialized Master's programs pay $32,490 in tuition and fees bring the total to $34,970.

For full-time students who are nonresidents in the 2017–18 academic year, the One-Year MBA tuition is $61,017 and fees bring the total to $66,792; the Two-Year MBA tuition is $61,016 and fees bring the total to $68,716; and the Specialized Master's programs have tuition costs of $38,664 and fees bring the total to $41,214. Part-time nonresident students in the Professional MBA program pay $98,583 in tuition and fees bring the total to $101,943; those in the Specialized Master's programs pay $46,290 in tuition and fees bring the total to $48,770.

Living and Housing Costs

The University of Pittsburgh does not provide graduate student housing; however, there are numerous housing options available in the nearby area.

Living expenses are estimated at $15,740 for the One-Year MBA program, $27,545 for the Two-Year MBA, and $11,805 for the specialized master's programs. Health insurance costs are estimated at an additional $1,697 to $3,960 per program. Students should add $4,160 per year for each dependent family member.

Student Group

Katz students are part of a nurturing community of business professionals who use small class sizes, a collaborative environment, and student-led organizations to form friendships that last a lifetime.

For the Full-Time MBA programs, the most recent entering class had 82 students, with an average work experience of 54 months, average GMAT of 613, and average undergraduate GPA of 3.28. International students made up 46 percent of the group and 34 percent of the students were female.

For the Professional MBA program, the most recent entering class had 100 students, with an average work experience of 47 months, average GMAT of 545, and average undergraduate GPA of 3.24. International students made up 3 percent of the group and 35 percent of the students were female.

For the specialized master's programs, the most recent entering class had 120 students, with an average work experience of 7 months, average GMAT of 660, and average undergraduate GPA of 3.44. International students made up 65 percent of the group and 65 percent of the students were female.

Student Outcomes

The Katz leadership network spans the globe: over 30,000 Pitt Business alumni live in more than 90 countries. Through its Career Management Center, Katz builds partnerships with leading companies and assists students in realizing their full career potential.

Students who have completed the various graduate-level programs in the Katz School of Business went on to further their careers in finance (investment management, banking and financial institutions, corporate finance, financial consulting, etc.), information systems and technology management (IS management, business analysis, IT consulting, product development management, etc.), marketing (brand and product management, marketing research and consumer insights, social media and digital marketing, business development and sales management, etc.), operations (supply chain/logistics management, project management, operations management), organizational behavior and HR management (human resources management, human resources consulting, etc.), and strategy (management consulting, business development analysis, entrepreneurship, etc.).

Firms that have hired Katz graduates include: Accenture, Alcoa, Amazon, American Eagle Outfitters, Anheuser-Busch, Aon, AT Kearney, Bank of America, Bank of New York Mellon, Barclays, Bayer, Booz Allen Hamilton, Bosch,Capgemini, Capital One, Citibank, Cognizant, Colgate Palmolive, Corning, Crane, Deloitte, Dick's Sporting Goods, Direct Energy, Eaton, eBay, EQT, Ericcson, Ernst & Young, FDIC, FedEx, Ford, General Electric, General Mills, Georgia Pacific, GNC, Goodyear, Highmark, Honeywell, HSBC, IBM, Key Bank, KPMG, Kraft Heinz, McKinsey, Merck, Microsoft, Nationwide Insurance, Nielson, Olympus, Oracle, Philips, PNC, PPG, PricewaterhouseCoopers, Samsung, Starkist, Sungard, Target, Texas

Instruments, Hershey, The Vanguard Group, Thermo Fisher Scientific, TriState Capital Bank, United Technologies, UPMC, Volkswagon, Westinghouse Electric Company, Wipro Technologies, and others.

Location

Pittsburgh's unique and eclectic heritage, energy, and diversity are a source of inspiration and opportunity for Katz students. Nationally renowned for livability and natural beauty, Pittsburgh has a vibrant business community anchored by Fortune 500 companies in banking, manufacturing, consumer goods, and retail, and bolstered by new tech arrivals like Apple, Google, and Uber. University of Pittsburgh students can take advantage of all the amenities the city has to offer. Some students choose to stay in Pittsburgh after they graduate, while others pursue their careers in cities all over the world. Either way, Pittsburgh is a launch pad.

The University's urban campus is home to the Cathedral of Learning and the beautiful 300-acre Schenley Park. Students can also cheer on their Pitt Panthers as they compete for championships and renew rivalries in the Atlantic Coast Conference (ACC).

The University and the School

The University of Pittsburgh is a state-related research university, founded as the Pittsburgh Academy in 1787. Pitt is a member of the Association of American Universities (AAU), which comprises 62 preeminent doctorate-granting research institutions in North America.

The Katz School of Business was established in 1960, but has history dating to 1907, Katz is the first school to offer a one-year MBA and was among the first to offer an Executive MBA. Katz believe that success favors the agile, which is why students are immersed in real-world experiences so they graduate ready to build, lead, and contribute immediately.

Faculty

Katz faculty members anchor a strong research culture and collaborative atmosphere. Their teaching approach ties the latest in business theory to experience-based learning to prepare students to be catalysts for change. They pursue a wide variety of cutting-edge research streams and ask the bold questions needed to unearth and expand globally relevant insights for today's business leaders. Not only do faculty members frequently publish in top academic journals, many serve as journal editors and command leadership roles in academic organizations.

The University's urban location in Pittsburgh gives faculty members opportunities to collaborate with business leaders, which they leverage into opportunities for consulting-based projects, case studies, and guest speakers. Students find that faculty members genuinely care about their education and are committed to help them in their careers.

Applying

Prospective students are required to submit the following: application and fee (waived if entering FT18PE11 in the Fee Waiver Code field of the application), two letters of recommendation, an essay, resume, transcripts from all post-secondary schools attended, GMAT or GRE scores, and TOEFL or ITLTS scores (international applicants).

Application deadlines for the Full-Time MBA and M.S. in Accounting programs are: Round 1, October 1; Round 2, December 1; Round 3, February 1 (also deadline for scholarship consideration); and Round 4, April 1.

Application deadlines for the M.S. in Customer Insights, Finance, MIS, and Supply Chain Management programs are: Round 1, November 1; Round 2, January 1; Round 3, March 1 (also deadline for scholarship consideration); and Round 4, May 1.

Application deadlines for the part-time programs are: spring semester, November 1; summer semester, March 1; and fall semester, July 1.

Correspondence and Information

Admissions Office
Katz Graduate School of Business
University of Pittsburgh
301 Mervis Hall
3950 Roberto Clemente Drive
Pittsburgh, Pennsylvania 15260
Phone: 412-648-1700
E-mail: admissions@katz.pitt.edu
Website: business.pitt.edu

THE UNIVERSITY OF TEXAS AT DALLAS

Naveen Jindal School of Management

 For more information, visit http://petersons.to/texasdallasmanagement

Programs of Study

The University of Texas at Dallas (UT Dallas) Naveen Jindal School of Management's 13 dynamic M.S. programs address the challenges facing today's business leaders. The curriculum for each degree is built around a strong core of classes, then detailed study tackles specific industry issues. The Jindal School offers master's degrees in accounting, business analytics, energy management, financial engineering and risk management, finance, healthcare management, information technology and management, innovation and entrepreneurship, international management studies, management science, marketing, supply chain management, and systems engineering and management. Many of these degrees may be completed fully online—including accounting, information technology and management, and supply chain management. Many degrees also prepare students to take national certification exams, including CPA, CFA, CFP, Certified Internal Auditor, and others. Master's degrees require 36 credit hours for completion. More information is available at jindal.utdallas.edu/masters.

The Jindal School also offers five MBA program formats (Full-Time, Professional Flex, Professional Cohort, Professional Online, and Executive) with more than 200 electives. Employers seek the strong analytical skills Jindal School students develop during their MBA studies, and students may focus their course work to match their individual career goals. Additional details are at jindal.utdallas.edu/mba.

Those seeking a greater breadth of study may enroll in a dual M.S./MBA degree program at the Jindal School. While earning the two degrees would typically require 89 credit hours, with careful planning, both degrees can be earned with a total of 63 credit hours.

Research Facilities

The Jindal School faculty has been recognized globally for its research productivity. The faculty ranks No. 5 in North America and No. 5 globally based on research contributions to major journals, according to *The UTD Top 100 Business School Research Rankings,* and ranks fifteenth worldwide according to *Financial Times.* Research by the information systems faculty is ranked No. 1 based on publications in three prestigious journals and operations management faculty ranks No. 2 nationally based on publications in three prestigious journals, according to the *UTD Top 100* rankings. The Jindal School also houses several Centers of Excellence which cover topics ranging from healthcare to audit. In these centers, faculty and students take on issues faced by local businesses. Students participate in meetings and lectures sponsored by the centers for industry professionals.

Financial Aid

The Jindal School Scholarship Committee makes awards based on merit. The Jindal School's annual Scholarship Breakfast generates scholarships for all students. Students may also apply for the Dean's Excellence Scholarships, several of which are awarded each year. Full-time MBA students with strong academic potential are eligible for significant scholarship and grant assistance. The University participates in most federal and state aid programs. Short-term loans are available. Prospective students should visit the Jindal School's website at jindal.utdallas.edu/scholarships for information.

Cost of Study

Tuition for in-state full-time graduate students (9 hours) for fall 2017 is $6,209. For part-time graduate students, tuition is $2,760 for 3 hours and $4,408 for 6 hours. These prices exclude fees and other charges. More information is available at utdallas.edu/bursar.

Living and Housing Costs

On-campus apartments, University Village, offer a variety of floorplans, are competitively priced, and fill quickly. Interested students should visit utdallas.edu/housing for on-campus housing information.

The surrounding metropolitan area offers off-campus housing options in a wide range of prices and amenities. An array of shopping and dining establishments, representing everything from large chains to small, single proprietor–run shops, are within bicycling distance of campus.

Students

With more than 9,000 students, the Jindal School is the largest of UT Dallas' eight schools. About 4,800 Jindal School students are in graduate studies. Most graduate students have at least five years of work experience. Women make up about 40 percent of master's students. About 35 percent of Jindal School students are international.

Location

The UT Dallas campus is in Richardson, Texas, a close suburb to the vibrant city of Dallas. Dallas and Fort Worth both have an array of cultural activities, from world-class museums and opera to internationally recognized symphony performances and concert appearances from the best in pop, folk, and country music. Many professional sports teams call the Dallas-Fort Worth area home including the Dallas Cowboys, Texas Rangers, and Dallas Stars.

The University and the School

UT Dallas was established in 1969 by the Texas Legislature in response to the developing high-tech industry in North Texas. A little more than four decades later, the University has almost 27,000 students in undergraduate, graduate, and doctoral programs. The University of Texas at Dallas is ranked No. 1 in the United States among universities founded less than 50 years ago, according to the 2017 Young University Rankings report from Times Higher Education.

The Jindal School was established in 1975 and is fully accredited by AACSB International (The Association to Advance Collegiate Schools of Business).

Applying

Prerequisites for all Jindal School graduate admissions include a bachelor's degree from an accredited institution. Many programs also require calculus and spreadsheet proficiency. Undergraduate work in business-related courses is not required. Additional requirements include GMAT or GRE scores, a complete application, an essay of educational intent, and three recent letters of reference. A TOEFL score is required from those for whom English is not the native language. Application requirements and deadlines are available on the school's website at jindal.utdallas.edu.

Applicants to programs which require calculus but do not meet the calculus requirement may be admitted but must make up the deficiency in the first semester at UT Dallas.

The University of Texas at Dallas

Most programs enroll students in the next semester after acceptance. Certain programs, including the Full-Time MBA, Executive MBA, and Global Leadership Executive MBA, admit students only once each year.

Correspondence and Information

Joanna Fowler, Director, Admissions and Operations
Naveen Jindal School of Management, SM21
The University of Texas at Dallas
800 West Campbell Road
Richardson, Texas 75080
Phone: 972-883-6282
Fax: 972-883-6823
E-mail: joanna.fowler@utdallas.edu
Website: jindal.utdallas.edu

THE FACULTY AND THEIR RESEARCH

Faculty research at the Naveen Jindal School of Management covers a range of topics, from findings of corruption in Asia to developing models for predicting the timing and frequency of future patient re-admissions related to congestive heart failure. Jindal School faculty members are globally ranked for their research productivity. They are well-represented in professional associations and publications and speak at events worldwide. A complete list of faculty members and their research publications is available at jindal.utdallas.edu/faculty.

Faculty research highlights include:

Healthcare Quality v. Costs
Indranil Bardhan, Professor, Information Systems.

Negotiation, Reputation Building, Bargaining
Gary Bolton, O.P. Jindal Distinguished Chair and Professor, Managerial Economics.

Inventory Management
Metin Cakanyildirim, Professor, Operations Management.

Product Diffusion
Jianqing Chen, Associate Professor, Information Systems.

Financial Misconduct in Firms
Rebecca Files, Assistant Professor, Accounting.

Breach of Contract
Berhard Ganglmair, Assistant Professor, Finance and Managerial Economics.

Trade and Investment
Umit Gurun, Professor, Accounting.

Performance of Financial Institutions
Vikram Nanda, Professor, O.P. Jindal Distinguished Chair in Finance.

Management and Decisions of Global Businesses
Özalp Özer, Ashbel Smith Professor, Management Science.

Outsourcing Decisions
Srinivasan Raghunathan, Professor, Information Systems.

Digital Advertising
Ram Rao, Founders Professor, Marketing.

Flexible Manufacturing Systems
Kathryn E. Stecke, Ashbel Smith Professor, Operations Management.

Chinese Agricultural Futures Markets
Feng Zhao, Associate Professor, Finance and Managerial Economics.

The strong North Texas economy provides many job opportunities in fields such as accounting, healthcare, information technology, and marketing for graduates of the Naveen Jindal School of Management.

UNIVERSITY OF RHODE ISLAND

College of Business Administration

THE UNIVERSITY OF RHODE ISLAND

 For more information, visit http://petersons.to/uri-business

Programs of Study

The University of Rhode Island's (URI) College of Business Administration, the first accredited business school in Rhode Island, is recognized for its leadership in business education, research, and outreach.

URI offers a variety of AACSB-accredited M.B.A. programs to a meet the needs of students with different goals and schedules. The University recognizes that students' time is valuable, so it has created programs to allow them to finish their degrees in a rapid timeframe and quickly move to the next phase of their careers. URI keeps its classes small, helping students feel more comfortable networking in a smaller environment and encouraging interaction and intellectual debate in a community atmosphere.

The URI M.B.A. programs offer personalized academic advising, faculty members with a broad range of experience and research, value, and technologically enhanced facilities.

One-Year Program in Strategic Innovation: To meet the needs of a global business environment that requires a workforce capable of critical and innovative thinking, URI redesigned its one-year M.B.A. that challenged the traditional look and feel of a full-time M.B.A. program. The program offers a unique, hands-on approach to learning that breaks down the functional barriers of business education, by offering cross-disciplined courses that directly map onto solving real business problems in a strategically innovative way. Students will meet Monday through Friday from 9 a.m. to 4 p.m. at the Providence campus during the fall and spring semesters, followed by a summer internship, electives, or research projects.

The URI One-Year M.B.A. program walks students through the strategic process of defining how to define their change goals, measure them, analyze the results, make improvements, and control that process to ensure that the goals have been met. This is accomplished by using a small dedicated group of faculty members that will work with the students for the entire year, combining forces within the classroom to integrate different disciplines; a live case study with a local global company; hands-on consulting projects with such companies as Fidelity Investments, CVS Health, Hasbro, IGT, and Ocean State Job Lot; either a Business Innovation or Product Innovation project; and team and individual papers, homework, and exams. To complete the program, students will participate in a summer internship, electives, or research project.

Part-Time Evening M.B.A.: The URI evening M.B.A. program is aimed at individuals who want to pursue a degree while maintaining their professional commitments and who value flexibility, convenience, diversity, and a return on investment. The program is designed to emphasize conceptual, analytical, technical, and interpersonal skills. Material for this non-thesis program is presented through lectures, discussions, case studies, and both individual and group projects. Students learn from both the instructor and the network of fellow students who work in a broad range of industries. A goal of the program is to take the new ideas discussed and learned in class that evening straight to the workplace the next day.

This program requires the completion of 45 credits, or 15 courses. Classes (with a maximum of 30 students) meet one night a week during the fall, spring, and summer sessions in Providence or Kingston. Students are allowed to enroll in as many classes as they wish per semester. Concentrations include finance, healthcare management, general management, marketing, and supply chain management. Web-based and Saturday courses are also available to enable students to finish in their desired timeframes. The M.B.A. program does not require previous instruction in business administration.

Blue M.B.A.—Dual Degree M.B.A. and Master of Oceanography: Climate change represents both a major challenge and opportunity to a broad range of businesses and the global economy. In turn, there is a growing demand for leaders with skills in both business and science, particularly climate-related sciences. To address this need, URI created a unique dual-degree program that merges the M.B.A. with a Master of Oceanography (M.B.A./M.O.) dubbed the Blue M.B.A.

The Blue M.B.A. program requires students to take both M.B.A. and M.O. classes at the Providence and Narragansett Bay campuses, choosing one of three schedule options. The program provides students with the knowledge and skills needed to develop business models to ensure an environmentally sustainable world for future generations. It allows for a summer internship anywhere in the world. At the end of the program, students graduate with two degrees: the M.B.A. and the M.O.

This program is designed for students with pure science, environmental science, or engineering undergraduate degrees who want to develop their management skills and broaden their marketability. Students are expected to be successful in both GSO science courses and M.B.A. courses. The program will be particularly beneficial to those seeking management careers in industries such as energy, ocean technology and engineering, hazard risk management, water resources, fisheries, marine navigation, and tourism, as well as ocean and human health.

Accreditation

The College of Business Administration has been accredited since 1972 by AACSB—The Association to Advance Collegiate Schools of Business. AACSB accreditation is highly sought-after by universities; its high level of academic merit and accreditation has been achieved by less than 15 percent of the institutions teaching management education.

Research

Research is central to the University of Rhode Island. Faculty research within the College of Business Administration covers a broad range of interests and specializations, and students have a variety of opportunities to benefit from it.

PACAP Research Center: The Sandra Ann Morsilli Pacific-Basin Capital Markets Research Center was established in 1989 at the University of Rhode Island to meet the growing demand for information on the capital markets in the Pacific-Basin region. The PACAP Research Center, which serves the securities industry, financial service industry, government, multilateral development institutions, and academia, has become recognized internationally as the leading research institute on Asian capital markets.

For current information on faculty research, prospective students should visit http://web.uri.edu/business/research/.

Financial Aid

Financial support is available in the form of assistantships, scholarships and fellowships.

Recommendations for the appointment of teaching, research, and administrative assistants are usually made by individual departments or programs. Assistantships are awarded with the expectation that service will be provided by the recipient.

Scholarships are available from a variety of professional societies and organizations, and often the best sources of advice for these awards will be the major professor, Graduate Director or Department Chair. The Graduate School provides a limited number of scholarships that are awarded on a competitive basis.

Fellowships are available from a number of organizations and agencies. Information on grants and loans is available from Enrollment Services/ Financial Aid (www.uri.edu/es/menus/finaid.html).

Costs

Tuition and fees for full-time graduate students (9–15 credits) in the 2017–18 academic year are estimated at $19,669 for in-state students and $37,780 for out-of-state students. Part-time M.B.A. students are charged per credit: $706/credit for in-state students, $1,059/credit for regional students, and $1,401 for out-of-state students.

Student Outcomes

More than 220 students are currently enrolled in URI's M.B.A. programs. Alumni of these programs are given exit surveys and here are just some of their comments about their experiences at URI:

"As I progressed through the program, I realized that I was not only getting a wonderful business education, but I was also getting a fantastic real-world education."

"The professors taught with passion and were always there for the students. It was evident that the professors wanted the students to excel."

"With a great emphasis on team projects, I believe I grew not only academically, but also professionally as the program was very similar to a real-world business atmosphere."

By combining learning modules and self-directed projects, the program prepared me for the difficult decisions I now make as a manager."

"The education I received at URI's Providence campus provided some of the momentum I needed to launch my businesses. In fact, I visualized my marketing company during an entrepreneurship class project, and it is a dream that the business is now growing so fast. There's no doubt that I have URI to thank for laying a solid groundwork for the success I've achieved as a business owner."

"Having an engineering degree with no business background except on the job, the program was very effective at providing me with a broad yet in-depth knowledge that will be very useful in the future."

"Excellent exposure to public speaking and business interaction such as debating issues and negotiating. I have found this is the area where any person interacting with others in today's business world must excel at and feel comfortable with in order to succeed."

Location

The ocean is a big part of the University of Rhode Island's history, culture, and everyday life and contributes to its ranking of #3 in Best Value College's list of the 30 Most Beautiful Coastal College Campuses. But there's more than just the Kingston campus; URI maintains 315 buildings on four campuses.

The University and the College

The University of Rhode Island is the State's public learner-centered research university. The University is committed to enriching the lives of its students through its land, sea, and urban grant traditions. URI is the only public institution in Rhode Island offering undergraduate, graduate, and professional students the distinctive educational opportunities of a major research university. Students, faculty, staff, and alumni are united in one common purpose: to learn and lead together.

The College of Business Administration strives to be one of the leading business programs in New England, and highly responsive to the needs of the Rhode Island and regional business community. The College offers multi-disciplinary business programs that align with the financial, health, environmental, science, and technological sectors of the economy.

Applying

Applicants with a bachelor's degree in any major, from any accredited college or university may apply for admission to the Master of Business Administration Program. The application includes submission of the following: brief statement of purpose; a $65 non-refundable application fee; two letters of recommendation; current resume; official college transcript(s) from a baccalaureate degree at an accredited institution in the U.S. or the equivalent of a four-year degree at an international institution; official score report for the Graduate Management Admission Test (GMAT) or GRE taken within the last five years (waived for students who meet specific criteria); Residency Application or Certificate of Residency for in-state or qualified regional students; and TOEFL or IELTS scores (taken within the last two years) for all international students who completed their bachelor's degree from a non-English speaking foreign University. Most of this material can be submitted online.

More specific information regarding the M.B.A. admission process is available at http://web.uri.edu/business/mba-admission/.

Correspondence and Information

Ms. Lisa Lancellotta, Coordinator
M.B.A. Programs
College of Business Administration
University of Rhode Island
Kingston, Rhode Island 02881
United States
Phone: 401-874-4241
Fax: 401-874-4312
E-mail: mba@uri.edu
Website: http://web.uri.edu/business/mba/

Section 2
Accounting and Finance

This section contains a directory of institutions offering graduate work in accounting and finance. Additional information about programs listed in the directory but not augmented by an in-depth entry may be obtained by writing directly to the dean of a graduate school or chair of a department at the address given in the directory.

For programs offering related work, see also in this book *Business Administration and Management, International Business,* and *Nonprofit Management.* In the other guides in this series:

Graduate Programs in the Humanities, Arts & Social Sciences
See *Economics* and *Family and Consumer Sciences (Consumer Economics)*

Graduate Programs in the Physical Sciences, Mathematics, Agricultural Sciences, the Environment & Natural Resources
See *Mathematical Sciences*

Graduate Programs in Engineering & Applied Sciences
See *Computer Science and Information Technology*

CONTENTS

Program Directories

Featured Schools: Displays and Close-Ups

See:

Accounting

Abilene Christian University, Graduate Programs, College of Business Administration, Program in Accountancy, Abilene, TX 79699. Offers M Acc. *Program availability:* Part-time. *Faculty:* 7 part-time/adjunct (0 women). *Students:* 13 full-time (4 women), 1 (woman) part-time; includes 1 minority (Hispanic/Latino), 2 international. 45 applicants, 40% accepted, 10 enrolled. In 2016, 28 master's awarded. *Entrance requirements:* For master's, GMAT. Additional exam requirements/recommendations for international students: Required—TOEFL (minimum score 80 iBT), IELTS (minimum score 6). *Application deadline:* For fall admission, 8/11 for domestic students; for spring admission, 11/1 for domestic students. Applications are processed on a rolling basis. Application fee: $50. Electronic applications accepted. *Expenses: Tuition:* Full-time $19,890; part-time $1105 per credit hour. Tuition and fees vary according to course load and program. *Financial support:* In 2016–17, 11 students received support. Federal Work-Study and scholarships/grants available. Support available to part-time students. Financial award application deadline: 4/1; financial award applicants required to submit FAFSA. *Unit head:* John Neill, Chair, 325-674-2053, Fax: 325-674-2564, E-mail: john.neill@acu.edu. *Application contact:* Corey Patterson, Director of Graduate Admissions and Recruiting, 325-674-6566, Fax: 325-674-6717, E-mail: gradinfo@acu.edu. Website: http://www.acu.edu/graduate/academics/accounting.html

Adelphi University, Robert B. Willumstad School of Business, MBA Program, Garden City, NY 11530-0701. Offers accounting (MBA); finance (MBA); health services administration (MBA); human resource management (MBA); management (MBA); management information systems (MBA); marketing (MBA); sport management (MBA). *Accreditation:* AACSB. *Program availability:* Part-time, evening/weekend. *Students:* 172 full-time (74 women), 129 part-time (66 women); includes 30 minority (9 Black or African American, non-Hispanic/Latino; 11 Asian, non-Hispanic/Latino; 9 Hispanic/Latino; 1 Two or more races, non-Hispanic/Latino), 29 international. Average age 32. 4 applicants. In 2016, 130 master's awarded. *Degree requirements:* For master's, capstone course. *Entrance requirements:* For master's, GMAT, 2 letters of recommendation. Additional exam requirements/recommendations for international students: Required—TOEFL (minimum score 550 paper-based; 80 iBT), IELTS (minimum score 6.5). *Application deadline:* For fall admission, 4/1 for international students; for spring admission, 11/1 for international students. Applications are processed on a rolling basis. Application fee: $50. Electronic applications accepted. *Expenses:* Contact institution. *Financial support:* Research assistantships with partial tuition reimbursements, career-related internships or fieldwork, Federal Work-Study, institutionally sponsored loans, scholarships/grants, tuition waivers (partial), and unspecified assistantships available. Financial award application deadline: 3/1; financial award applicants required to submit FAFSA. *Faculty research:* Supply chain management, distribution channels, productivity benchmark analysis, data envelopment analysis, financial portfolio analysis. *Unit head:* Dr. Rakesh Gupta, Associate Dean, 516-877-4629. *Application contact:* Christine Murphy, Director of Admissions, 516-877-3050, Fax: 516-877-3039, E-mail: graduateadmissions@adelphi.edu.
Website: http://business.adelphi.edu/degree-programs/graduate-degree-programs/m-b-a/

Adrian College, Graduate Programs, Adrian, MI 49221-2575. Offers accounting (MS); athletic training (MS); criminal justice (MA). *Degree requirements:* For master's, comprehensive exam (for some programs), thesis (for some programs), thesis, internship or practicum with corresponding in-depth paper and/or presentation. *Entrance requirements:* For master's, appropriate undergraduate degree, minimum cumulative and major GPA of 3.0, personal statement.

Alabama State University, College of Business Administration, Department of Accounting and Finance, Montgomery, AL 36101-0271. Offers accountancy (M Acc). *Faculty:* 4 full-time (1 woman), 1 part-time/adjunct (0 women). *Students:* 9 full-time (7 women), 2 part-time (both women); includes 6 minority (all Black or African American, non-Hispanic/Latino), 4 international. Average age 29. 31 applicants, 42% accepted, 8 enrolled. In 2016, 10 master's awarded. *Degree requirements:* For master's, comprehensive exam. *Entrance requirements:* For master's, minimum GPA of 2.75 (undergraduate), 3.0 (graduate). Additional exam requirements/recommendations for international students: Required—TOEFL (minimum score 500 paper-based). *Application deadline:* For fall admission, 4/15 for domestic and international students; for spring admission, 11/15 for domestic and international students; for summer admission, 3/15 for domestic and international students. Applications are processed on a rolling basis. Application fee: $25. Electronic applications accepted. *Expenses:* Tuition, state resident: full-time $3087; part-time $2744 per credit. Tuition, nonresident: full-time $6174; part-time $5488 per credit. *Required fees:* $2284; $1142 per credit. $571 per semester. Tuition and fees vary according to class time, course level, course load, degree level, program and student level. *Financial support:* In 2016–17, 11 students received support. Fellowships and unspecified assistantships available. Financial award applicants required to submit FAFSA. *Unit head:* Dr. Dave Thompson, Chair, 334-229-4134, Fax: 334-229-4870, E-mail: dthompson@asunet.alasu.edu. *Application contact:* Dr. William Person, Dean of Graduate Studies, 334-229-4274, Fax: 334-229-4928, E-mail: wperson@alasu.edu.
Website: http://www.alasu.edu/academics/colleges—departments/college-of-business-administration/college-of-business-academics/accounting—finance/index.aspx

Albany State University, College of Business, Albany, GA 31705-2717. Offers accounting (MBA); general business administration (MBA); healthcare (MBA); public administration (MBA); supply chain and logistics (MBA). *Accreditation:* ACBSP. *Program availability:* Part-time, evening/weekend. *Degree requirements:* For master's, comprehensive exam, internship, 3 hours of physical education. *Entrance requirements:* For master's, GMAT (minimum score of 450)/GRE (minimum score of 800) for those without earned master's degree or higher, minimum undergraduate GPA of 2.5, 2 letters of reference, official transcript, pre-entrance medical record and certificate of immunization. *Application deadline:* For fall admission, 6/1 for domestic students, 5/1 for international students; for spring admission, 11/1 for domestic students, 10/1 for international students. Applications are processed on a rolling basis. Application fee: $20. Electronic applications accepted. *Financial support:* Application deadline: 4/15; applicants required to submit FAFSA. *Faculty research:* Diversity issues, ancestry, understanding finance through use of technology. *Unit head:* Dr. Alicia Jackson, Dean, 229-430-7009, Fax: 229-430-5119. *Application contact:* Jeffrey Pierce, II, Graduate Counselor, 229-430-4646, Fax: 229-430-4105, E-mail: jeffrey.pierce@asurams.edu.
Website: https://www.asurams.edu/Academics/collegeofbusiness/

Albertus Magnus College, Master of Science in Accounting Program, New Haven, CT 06511-1189. Offers MSA. *Program availability:* Part-time, evening/weekend, 100% online, blended/hybrid learning. *Faculty:* 7 full-time (2 women), 24 part-time/adjunct (6 women). *Students:* 14 full-time (8 women), 8 part-time (5 women); includes 7 minority (3 Black or African American, non-Hispanic/Latino; 3 Hispanic/Latino; 1 Two or more races, non-Hispanic/Latino). Average age 36. In 2016, 9 master's awarded. *Degree requirements:* For master's, project. *Entrance requirements:* For master's, bachelor's degree; minimum cumulative GPA of 3.0; 24 undergraduate credits in accounting, 22 in business (separate from accounting); 2 letters of recommendation; essay. Additional exam requirements/recommendations for international students: Recommended—TOEFL (minimum score 550 paper-based; 80 iBT). *Application deadline:* Applications are processed on a rolling basis. Application fee: $50. Electronic applications accepted. *Expenses:* Contact institution. *Financial support:* Federal Work-Study and unspecified assistantships available. Support available to part-time students. Financial award applicants required to submit FAFSA. *Unit head:* Dr. Nancy Fallon, Director of the Business Programs, 203-773-8567, E-mail: nfallon@albertus.edu. *Application contact:* Dr. Sean O'Connell, Vice President for Academic Affairs, 203-777-8539, Fax: 203-777-3701, E-mail: soconnell@albertus.edu.
Website: http://www.albertus.edu/graduate-degrees/graduate-degree-programs/accounting/

Alfred University, Graduate School, School of Business, Alfred, NY 14802-1205. Offers accounting (MBA); business administration (MBA). *Accreditation:* AACSB. *Program availability:* Part-time. *Students:* 28 full-time (11 women), 20 part-time (8 women); includes 10 minority (7 Black or African American, non-Hispanic/Latino; 1 Asian, non-Hispanic/Latino; 2 Hispanic/Latino), 1 international. Average age 24. In 2016, 31 master's awarded. *Entrance requirements:* For master's, GMAT. Additional exam requirements/recommendations for international students: Required—TOEFL (minimum score 590 paper-based; 90 iBT), IELTS (minimum score 6.5). *Application deadline:* For fall admission, 8/1 for domestic students, 3/15 for international students; for winter admission, 12/1 for domestic students; for spring admission, 10/1 for international students. Applications are processed on a rolling basis. Application fee: $60. Electronic applications accepted. *Expenses: Tuition:* Full-time $38,020; part-time $810 per credit. *Required fees:* $970; $82 per semester. *Financial support:* Research assistantships with partial tuition reimbursements, tuition waivers (partial), and unspecified assistantships available. Financial award applicants required to submit FAFSA. *Unit head:* Dr. Nancy Evangelista, Dean of the College of Professional Studies, 607-871-2124, Fax: 607-871-2114, E-mail: fevangel@alfred.edu. *Application contact:* Sara Love, Coordinator of Graduate Admissions, 607-871-2115, Fax: 607-871-2198, E-mail: gradinquiry@alfred.edu.
Website: http://business.alfred.edu/mba/

American Business & Technology University, Programs in Business Administration, Saint Joseph, MO 64506. Offers business administration (MBA); financial management (MBA); global business management (MBA); information systems management (MBA); marketing and social media (MBA); project and operations management (MBA); public accounting (MBA). *Program availability:* Online learning.

American InterContinental University Online, Program in Business Administration, Schaumburg, IL 60173. Offers accounting and finance (MBA); finance (MBA); healthcare management (MBA); human resource management (MBA); international business (MBA); management (MBA); marketing (MBA); operations management (MBA); organizational psychology and development (MBA); project management (MBA). *Accreditation:* ACBSP. *Program availability:* Evening/weekend, online learning. *Entrance requirements:* Additional exam requirements/recommendations for international students: Required—TOEFL (minimum score 550 paper-based). Electronic applications accepted.

American International College, School of Business, Arts and Sciences, Springfield, MA 01109-3189. Offers accounting and taxation (MS); business administration (MBA); clinical psychology (MA); educational psychology (Ed D); forensic psychology (MS); general psychology (MA, CAGS); management (CAGS); resort and casino management (MBA, CAGS). *Program availability:* Part-time, evening/weekend. *Degree requirements:* For master's, comprehensive exam (for some programs), thesis (for some programs), practicum; for doctorate, comprehensive exam (for some programs), thesis/dissertation; for CAGS, comprehensive exam (for some programs), thesis (for some programs). *Entrance requirements:* For master's, BS or BA; for doctorate, interview. Additional exam requirements/recommendations for international students: Required—TOEFL (minimum score 550 paper-based; 80 iBT). *Expenses: Tuition:* Full-time $7902; part-time $750 per semester hour. *Required fees:* $60; $60 per semester hour. $30 per semester. One-time fee: $100. Tuition and fees vary according to course load, degree level, campus/location and program.

American Public University System, AMU/APU Graduate Programs, Charles Town, WV 25414. Offers accounting (MBA, MS); applied business analytics (MBA, MS); criminal justice (MA), including business administration, emergency and disaster management, general (MA, MS); educational leadership (M Ed); emergency and disaster management (MA); entrepreneurship (MBA); environmental policy and management (MS), including environmental planning, environmental sustainability, fish and wildlife management, general (MA, MS), global environmental management; finance (MBA); general (MBA); government contracting and acquisition (MBA); health care administration (MBA); health information management (MS); history (MA), including American history, ancient and classical history, European history, global history, public history; homeland security (MA), including business administration, counterterrorism studies, criminal justice, cyber, emergency management and public health, intelligence studies, transportation security; homeland security resource allocation (MBA); humanities (MA); information technology (MS), including digital forensics, enterprise software development, information assurance and security, IT project management; information technology management (MBA); intelligence studies (MA), including criminal intelligence, cyber, general (MA, MS), homeland security, intelligence analysis, intelligence collection, intelligence management, intelligence operations, terrorism studies; international relations and conflict resolution (MA), including comparative and security issues, conflict resolution, international and transnational security issues, peacekeeping; legal studies (MA); management (MA), including strategic consulting; marketing (MBA); military history (MA), including American military history, American Revolution, civil war, war since 1945, World War II; military studies (MA), including joint warfare, strategic leadership; national security studies (MA), including cyber, general (MA, MS), homeland security, regional security studies, security and intelligence analysis, terrorism studies; nonprofit management (MBA); political science (MA), including American politics and government, comparative government and development, general (MA, MS), international relations, public policy; psychology (MA); public administration (MPA), including disaster management, environmental policy, health policy, human resources, national security, organizational management, security management; public health (MPH); reverse logistics management (MA); security management (MA); space studies (MS), including aerospace science, general (MA, MS), planetary science; sports and health sciences (MS); sports management (MBA); teaching (M Ed), including autism spectrum disorder, curriculum and instruction for elementary teachers, elementary reading, English language learners, instructional leadership, online learning, special education, STEAM (STEM plus the arts); transportation and logistics management (MA). *Program availability:* Part-time, evening/weekend, online only, 100% online. *Faculty:* 401 full-time (228 women), 1,678 part-time/adjunct (781 women). *Students:* 378 full-time (184 women), 8,455 part-time (3,484 women); includes 2,972 minority (1,552 Black or African American, non-Hispanic/Latino; 52 American Indian or Alaska Native, non-Hispanic/Latino; 211 Asian, non-Hispanic/Latino; 791 Hispanic/Latino; 70 Native Hawaiian or other Pacific Islander, non-Hispanic/Latino; 296 Two or more races, non-Hispanic/Latino), 109 international. Average age 37. In 2016, 3,185 master's awarded. *Degree requirements:* For master's, comprehensive exam or practicum. *Entrance requirements:* For master's, official transcript showing earned bachelor's degree from institution accredited by recognized accrediting body. Additional exam requirements/recommendations for international students: Required—TOEFL (minimum score 550 paper-based), IELTS (minimum score 6.5). *Application deadline:* Applications are processed on a rolling basis. Application fee: $0. Electronic applications accepted. *Expenses: Tuition:* Part-time $350 per credit hour. *Required fees:* $50 per course. *Financial support:* Scholarships/grants available. Financial award applicants required to submit FAFSA. *Unit head:* Dr. Karan Powell, President, 877-468-6268, Fax: 304-724-3780. *Application contact:* Terry Grant, Vice President of Enrollment Management, 877-468-6268, Fax: 304-724-3780, E-mail: info@apus.edu. Website: http://www.apus.edu

American University, Kogod School of Business, Department of Accounting, Program in Accounting, Washington, DC 20016-8044. Offers accounting (MS); forensic accounting (Certificate). *Accreditation:* AACSB. *Program availability:* Part-time, evening/weekend. *Students:* 34 full-time (21 women), 35 part-time (21 women); includes 23 minority (12 Black or African American, non-Hispanic/Latino; 3 Asian, non-Hispanic/Latino; 8 Hispanic/Latino), 17 international. Average age 28. 120 applicants, 58% accepted, 31 enrolled. In 2016, 48 master's, 20 other advanced degrees awarded. *Entrance requirements:* For master's, GMAT/GRE, resume, personal statement, interview, two letters of recommendation, transcripts. Additional exam requirements/recommendations for international students: Required—TOEFL, IELTS, PTE. *Application deadline:* For fall admission, 2/20 priority date for domestic students, 2/20 for international students; for spring admission, 12/10 priority date for domestic students, 11/15 for international students. Applications are processed on a rolling basis. Application fee: $100. *Expenses:* $1,579 per credit tuition; $690 mandatory fees. *Financial support:* Institutionally sponsored loans and unspecified assistantships available. Financial award application deadline: 2/1; financial award applicants required to submit FAFSA. *Unit head:* Dr. Donald T. Williamson, Chair, Department of Accounting, 202-885-1942, Fax: 202-885-1992, E-mail: dwillia@american.edu. *Application contact:* Jason Kennedy, Associate Director of Graduate Admissions, 202-885-1968, E-mail: jkennedy@american.edu. Website: http://www.american.edu/kogod/

American University of Sharjah, Graduate Programs, Sharjah, United Arab Emirates. Offers accounting (MS); biomedical engineering (MSBME); business (MBA); chemical engineering (MS Ch E); civil engineering (MSCE); computer engineering (MS); electrical engineering (MSEE); engineering systems management (MS); mathematics (MS); mechanical engineering (MSME); mechatronics engineering (MS); teaching English to speakers of other languages (MA); translation and interpreting (MA); urban planning (MUP). *Program availability:* Part-time, evening/weekend. *Students:* 123 full-time (53 women), 306 part-time (151 women). Average age 27. 184 applicants, 83% accepted, 92 enrolled. In 2016, 97 master's awarded. *Degree requirements:* For master's, thesis (for some programs). *Entrance requirements:* For master's, GMAT (for MBA). Additional exam requirements/recommendations for international students: Required—TOEFL (minimum score 550 paper-based; 80 iBT), TWE (minimum score 5); Recommended—IELTS (minimum score 6.5). *Application deadline:* For fall admission, 8/28 priority date for domestic students, 8/14 priority date for international students; for spring admission, 1/22 priority date for domestic students, 1/8 for international students; for summer admission, 5/21 for domestic and international students. Applications are processed on a rolling basis. Application fee: $350. Electronic applications accepted. *Expenses: Tuition, area resident:* Part-time 4660 United Arab Emirates dirhams per credit hour. *Financial support:* In 2016–17, 63 students received support, including 28 research assistantships with full and partial tuition reimbursements available, 35 teaching assistantships with full and partial tuition reimbursements available; scholarships/grants also available. *Faculty research:* Water pollution, management and waste water treatment, energy and sustainability, air pollution, Islamic finance, family business and small and medium enterprises. *Unit head:* Ali Shuhaimy, Executive Director of Enrollment Management, 971-6515-1030. *Application contact:* Mona A. Mabrouk, Graduate Admissions/Office of Enrollment Management, 971-65151012, E-mail: graduateadmission@aus.edu. Website: http://www.aus.edu/programs/graduate/

Anderson University, Falls School of Business, Anderson, IN 46012-3495. Offers accountancy (MA); business administration (MBA, DBA). *Accreditation:* ACBSP.

Andrews University, School of Graduate Studies, School of Business, Graduate Programs in Business, Berrien Springs, MI 49104. Offers MBA, MSA. *Faculty:* 8 full-time (3 women). *Students:* 16 full-time (7 women), 29 part-time (15 women); includes 19 minority (6 Black or African American, non-Hispanic/Latino; 3 Asian, non-Hispanic/Latino; 8 Hispanic/Latino; 2 Two or more races, non-Hispanic/Latino), 12 international. Average age 32. In 2016, 29 master's awarded. *Entrance requirements:* For master's, GMAT. Additional exam requirements/recommendations for international students: Required—TOEFL (minimum score 550 paper-based). Application fee: $40. *Unit head:* Dr. Leonard K. Gashugi, Chair, 769-471-3429, E-mail: gashugi@andrews.edu. *Application contact:* Justina Clayburn, Supervisor of Graduate Admission, 800-253-2874, Fax: 269-471-6321, E-mail: graduate@andrews.edu.

Angelo State University, College of Graduate Studies and Research, College of Business, Department of Accounting, Economics and Finance, San Angelo, TX 76909. Offers professional accountancy (MPAC). *Program availability:* Part-time, evening/weekend. *Students:* 11 full-time (5 women), 3 part-time (2 women); includes 4 minority (1 American Indian or Alaska Native, non-Hispanic/Latino; 3 Hispanic/Latino), 2 international. Average age 26. *Degree requirements:* For master's, comprehensive exam. *Entrance requirements:* For master's, GMAT, essay. Additional exam requirements/recommendations for international students: Required—TOEFL or IELTS. *Application deadline:* For fall admission, 7/15 priority date for domestic students, 6/10 for international students; for spring admission, 12/1 priority date for domestic students, 11/1 for international students. Applications are processed on a rolling basis. Application fee: $40 ($50 for international students). Electronic applications accepted. *Expenses:* Tuition, state resident: full-time $3726; part-time $2484 per year. Tuition, nonresident: full-time $10,746; part-time $7164 per year. *Required fees:* $2538; $1702 per unit. *Financial support:* Career-related internships or fieldwork, Federal Work-Study, and scholarships/grants available. Support available to part-time students. Financial award application deadline: 3/1; financial award applicants required to submit FAFSA. *Unit head:* Dr. Charles Aaron Pier, Chair, 325-486-6479, Fax: 325-942-2285, E-mail: chuck.pier@angelo.edu. *Application contact:* Dr. Norman A. Sunderman, Graduate Advisor, 325-942-2046 Ext. 245, E-mail: norman.sunderman@angelo.edu. Website: http://www.angelo.edu/dept/aef/

Appalachian State University, Cratis D. Williams Graduate School, Department of Accounting, Boone, NC 28608. Offers taxation (MS). *Program availability:* Part-time. *Degree requirements:* For master's, comprehensive exam, thesis optional. *Entrance requirements:* For master's, GMAT, 3 letters of recommendation. Additional exam requirements/recommendations for international students: Required—TOEFL (minimum score 550 paper-based; 79 iBT), IELTS (minimum score 6.5). *Application deadline:* For fall admission, 3/15 priority date for domestic students, 2/1 for international students; for spring admission, 11/1 for domestic students, 7/1 for international students. Applications are processed on a rolling basis. Application fee: $55. Electronic applications accepted. *Expenses:* Tuition, state resident: full-time $4744. Tuition, nonresident: full-time $17,913. Full-time tuition and fees vary according to program. *Financial support:* Fellowships, research assistantships, teaching assistantships, Federal Work-Study, scholarships/grants, and unspecified assistantships available. Financial award application deadline: 4/1; financial award applicants required to submit FAFSA. *Faculty research:* Audit assurance risk, state taxation, financial accounting inconsistencies, management information systems, charitable contribution taxation. *Unit head:* Dr. Timothy Forsyth, Chairman, 828-262-2036, Fax: 828-262-6640. *Application contact:* Dr. William Pollard, Director, 828-262-6206, Fax: 828-262-6640, E-mail: pollardwb@appstate.edu. Website: http://www.acc.appstate.edu

Argosy University, Atlanta, College of Business, Atlanta, GA 30328. Offers accounting (DBA); corporate compliance (MBA); customized professional concentration (MBA, DBA); finance (MBA); healthcare administration (MBA); information systems (DBA); information systems management (MBA); international business (MBA, DBA); management (MBA, MSM, DBA); marketing (MBA, DBA). *Accreditation:* ACBSP.

Argosy University, Chicago, College of Business, Chicago, IL 60601. Offers accounting (DBA); customized professional concentration (MBA, DBA); finance (MBA); fraud examination (MBA); global business sustainability (DBA); healthcare administration (MBA); information systems (DBA); information systems management (MBA); international business (MBA, DBA); management (MBA, MSM, DBA); marketing (MBA, DBA); organizational leadership (Ed D); public administration (MBA); sustainable management (MBA). *Accreditation:* ACBSP. *Program availability:* Online learning.

Argosy University, Dallas, College of Business, Farmers Branch, TX 75244. Offers accounting (DBA, AGC); corporate compliance (MBA, Graduate Certificate); customized professional concentration (MBA); finance (MBA, Graduate Certificate); fraud examination (MBA, Graduate Certificate); global business sustainability (DBA, AGC); healthcare administration (Graduate Certificate); healthcare management (MBA); information systems (MBA, DBA, AGC); information systems management (Graduate Certificate); international business (MBA, DBA, AGC, Graduate Certificate); management (MBA, DBA, AGC, Graduate Certificate); marketing (MBA, DBA, AGC, Graduate Certificate); public administration (MBA, Graduate Certificate); sustainable management (MBA, Graduate Certificate). *Accreditation:* ACBSP.

Argosy University, Denver, College of Business, Denver, CO 80231. Offers accounting (DBA); corporate compliance (MBA); customized professional concentration (MBA, DBA); finance (MBA); fraud examination (MBA); global business sustainability (DBA); healthcare administration (MBA); information systems (DBA); information systems management (MBA); international business (MBA, DBA); management (MBA, MSM, DBA); marketing (MBA, DBA); organizational leadership (Ed D); public administration (MBA); sustainable management (MBA). *Accreditation:* ACBSP.

Argosy University, Hawai`i, College of Business, Honolulu, HI 96813. Offers accounting (DBA); corporate compliance (MBA); customized professional concentration (MBA, DBA); finance (MBA, Certificate); fraud examination (MBA); global business sustainability (DBA); healthcare administration (MBA, Certificate); information systems (DBA); information systems management (MBA, Certificate); international business (MBA, DBA, Certificate); management (MBA, MSM, DBA); marketing (MBA, DBA, Certificate); organizational leadership (Ed D); public administration (MBA); sustainable management (MBA).

Argosy University, Inland Empire, College of Business, Ontario, CA 91761. Offers accounting (DBA); corporate compliance (MBA); customized professional concentration (MBA, DBA); finance (MBA); fraud examination (MBA); global business sustainability (DBA); healthcare administration (MBA); information systems (DBA); information systems management (MBA); international business (MBA, DBA); management (MBA, MSM, DBA); marketing (MBA, DBA); organizational leadership (Ed D); public administration (MBA); sustainable management (MBA).

Argosy University, Los Angeles, College of Business, Santa Monica, CA 90045. Offers accounting (DBA); corporate compliance (MBA); customized professional concentration (MBA, DBA); finance (MBA); fraud examination (MBA); global business sustainability (DBA); healthcare administration (MBA); information systems (DBA); information systems management (MBA); international business (MBA, DBA); management (MBA, MSM, DBA); marketing (MBA, DBA); organizational leadership (Ed D); public administration (MBA); sustainable management (MBA).

Argosy University, Nashville, College of Business, Nashville, TN 37214. Offers accounting (DBA); customized professional concentration (MBA, DBA); finance (MBA); healthcare administration (MBA); information systems (MBA, DBA); international business (MBA, DBA); management (MBA, MSM, DBA); marketing (MBA, DBA).

Argosy University, Northern Virginia, College of Business, Arlington, VA 22209. Offers accounting (DBA); customized professional concentration (MBA, DBA); finance (MBA); fraud examination (MBA); global business sustainability (DBA); healthcare administration (MBA); information systems (DBA); information systems management (MBA); international business (MBA, DBA, Certificate); management (MBA, MSM, DBA); marketing (MBA, DBA, Certificate); organizational leadership (Ed D); public administration (MBA); sustainable management (MBA).

Argosy University, Orange County, College of Business, Orange, CA 92868. Offers accounting (DBA, Adv C); corporate compliance (MBA); customized professional concentration (MBA, DBA); finance (MBA, Certificate); fraud examination (MBA); global business sustainability (DBA); healthcare administration (MBA, Certificate); information systems (DBA, Adv C, Certificate); information systems management (MBA); international business (MBA, DBA, Adv C, Certificate); management (MBA, MSM, DBA, Adv C); marketing (MBA, DBA, Adv C, Certificate); organizational leadership (Ed D); public administration (MBA, Certificate); sustainable management (MBA).

Argosy University, Phoenix, College of Business, Phoenix, AZ 85021. Offers accounting (DBA); corporate compliance (MBA); customized professional concentration (MBA, DBA); finance (MBA); fraud examination (MBA); global business sustainability (DBA); healthcare administration (MBA); information systems (DBA); information systems management (MBA); international business (MBA, DBA); management (MBA, DBA); marketing (MBA, DBA); public administration (MBA); sustainable management (MBA).

Argosy University, Salt Lake City, College of Business, Draper, UT 84020. Offers accounting (DBA); corporate compliance (MBA); customized professional concentration (MBA, DBA); finance (MBA); fraud examination (MBA); global business sustainability (DBA); healthcare administration (MBA); information systems (DBA); information systems management (MBA); international business (MBA, DBA); management (MBA, DBA); marketing (MBA, DBA); public administration (MBA); sustainable management (MBA).

Accounting

Argosy University, San Diego, College of Business, San Diego, CA 92108. Offers accounting (DBA); corporate compliance (MBA); customized professional concentration (MBA, DBA); finance (MBA); fraud examination (MBA); global business sustainability (DBA); information systems (DBA); information systems management (MBA); international business (MBA, DBA); management (MBA, MSM, DBA); marketing (MBA, DBA); organizational leadership (Ed D); public administration (MBA).

Argosy University, San Francisco Bay Area, College of Business, Alameda, CA 94501. Offers accounting (DBA); corporate compliance (MBA); customized professional concentration (MBA, DBA); finance (MBA); fraud examination (MBA); global business sustainability (DBA); healthcare administration (MBA); information systems (DBA); information systems management (MBA); international business (MBA, DBA); management (MBA, MSM, DBA); marketing (MBA, DBA); organizational leadership (Ed D); public administration (MBA); sustainable management (MBA).

Argosy University, Sarasota, College of Business, Sarasota, FL 34235. Offers accounting (DBA, Adv C); corporate compliance (MBA, DBA, Certificate); customized professional concentration (MBA, DBA); finance (MBA, Certificate); fraud examination (MBA, Certificate); global business sustainability (DBA, Adv C); healthcare administration (MBA, Certificate); information systems (DBA, Adv C, Certificate); information systems management (MBA); international business (MBA, DBA, Adv C, Certificate); management (MBA, MSM, DBA, Adv C, Certificate); marketing (MBA, DBA, Adv C, Certificate); organizational leadership (Ed D); public administration (MBA, Certificate); sustainable management (MBA, Certificate).

Argosy University, Schaumburg, Graduate School of Business and Management, Schaumburg, IL 60173-5403. Offers accounting (DBA, Adv C); customized professional concentration (MBA, DBA); finance (MBA, Certificate); fraud examination (MBA); healthcare administration (MBA, Certificate); human resource management (MS); information systems (Adv C, Certificate); information systems management (MBA); international business (MBA, DBA, Adv C, Certificate); management (MBA, MSM, DBA, Adv C, Certificate); marketing (MBA, DBA, Adv C, Certificate); organizational leadership (MS, Ed D); public administration (MBA); sustainable management (MBA).

Argosy University, Seattle, College of Business, Seattle, WA 98121. Offers accounting (DBA); corporate compliance (MBA); customized professional concentration (MBA, DBA); finance (MBA); fraud examination (MBA); global business sustainability (DBA); healthcare administration (MBA); information systems (DBA); information systems management (MBA); international business (MBA, DBA); management (MBA, MSM, DBA); marketing (MBA, DBA); organizational leadership (Ed D); public administration (MBA); sustainable management (MBA).

Argosy University, Tampa, College of Business, Tampa, FL 33607. Offers accounting (DBA); corporate compliance (MBA); customized professional concentration (MBA, DBA); finance (MBA); fraud examination (MBA); global business sustainability (DBA); healthcare administration (MBA); information systems (DBA); information systems management (MBA); international business (MBA, DBA); management (MBA, MSM, DBA); marketing (MBA, DBA); organizational leadership (Ed D); public administration (MBA); sustainable management (MBA).

Argosy University, Twin Cities, College of Business, Eagan, MN 55121. Offers accounting (DBA); customized professional concentration (MBA, DBA); finance (MBA); fraud examination (MBA); global business sustainability (DBA); healthcare administration (MBA); information systems (DBA); information systems management (MBA); international business (MBA, DBA); management (MBA, MSM, DBA); marketing (MBA, DBA); organizational leadership (Ed D); public administration (MBA); sustainable management (MBA).

Arizona State University at the Tempe campus, W. P. Carey School of Business, School of Accountancy, Tempe, AZ 85287-3606. Offers accountancy (M Acc, M Tax); business administration (PhD), including accountancy. *Accreditation:* AACSB. *Program availability:* Part-time, evening/weekend. *Degree requirements:* For master's, thesis optional, interactive Program of Study (iPOS) submitted before completing 50 percent of required credit hours. *Entrance requirements:* For master's, GMAT (waivers may apply for ASU accountancy undergraduates), minimum GPA of 3.0 in last 2 years of work leading to bachelor's degree, 2 letters of recommendation, professional resume, official transcripts, responses to 3 essay questions. Additional exam requirements/recommendations for international students: Required—TOEFL (minimum score 550 paper-based; 80 iBT), IELTS (minimum score 6.5). Electronic applications accepted. *Expenses:* Contact institution.

Arkansas State University, Graduate School, College of Business, Department of Accounting, State University, AR 72467. Offers accountancy (M Acc). *Program availability:* Part-time. *Degree requirements:* For master's, comprehensive exam, thesis or alternative. *Entrance requirements:* For master's, GMAT, appropriate bachelor's degree, letters of reference, official transcript, immunization records. Additional exam requirements/recommendations for international students: Required—TOEFL (minimum score 550 paper-based; 79 iBT), IELTS (minimum score 6), PTE (minimum score 56). Electronic applications accepted. *Expenses:* Contact institution.

Assumption College, Business Studies Program, Worcester, MA 01609-1296. Offers accounting (MBA); business studies (CAGS); finance/economics (MBA); human resources (MBA); international business (MBA); management (MBA); marketing (MBA); nonprofit leadership (MBA). *Program availability:* Part-time, evening/weekend. *Faculty:* 4 full-time (1 woman), 19 part-time/adjunct (6 women). *Students:* 44 full-time (16 women), 97 part-time (47 women); includes 20 minority (8 Black or African American, non-Hispanic/Latino; 5 Asian, non-Hispanic/Latino; 6 Hispanic/Latino; 1 Two or more races, non-Hispanic/Latino), 4 international. Average age 29. 34 applicants, 59% accepted, 16 enrolled. In 2016, 97 master's, 1 other advanced degree awarded. *Degree requirements:* For master's, thesis, capstone. *Entrance requirements:* For master's, bachelor's degree, 3 letters of recommendation, official transcripts, personal statement, current resume; for CAGS, MBA or equivalent degree in a closely related field, 3 letters of recommendation, official transcripts, personal statement, current resume. Additional exam requirements/recommendations for international students: Required—TOEFL (minimum score 540 paper-based; 76 iBT), IELTS (minimum score 6). *Application deadline:* For fall admission, 7/1 priority date for domestic and international students; for spring admission, 12/1 priority date for domestic and international students; for summer admission, 4/1 priority date for domestic and international students. Application fee: $30. Electronic applications accepted. *Expenses: Tuition:* Full-time $11,610; part-time $645 per credit. *Required fees:* $70 per term. Tuition and fees vary according to course load and program. *Financial support:* In 2016–17, 19 students received support. Tuition waivers (full and partial), unspecified assistantships, and institutional discounts available. Financial award applicants required to submit FAFSA. *Faculty research:* Workplace diversity, dynamics of team interaction, utilization of leased employees, experiential learning project on due diligence market for prostheses. *Unit head:* Dr. Robin Frkal, Director, 508-767-7622, E-mail: rafrkal@assumption.edu. *Application contact:* Karen Stoyanoff, Director of Recruitment for Graduate Enrollment, 508-767-7442, Fax: 508-799-4412, E-mail: graduate@assumption.edu.
Website: http://graduate.assumption.edu/mba/assumption-mba

Auburn University, Graduate School, College of Business, School of Accountancy, Auburn University, AL 36849. Offers M Acc. *Accreditation:* AACSB. *Program availability:* Part-time. *Faculty:* 16 full-time (8 women). *Students:* 63 full-time (39 women), 65 part-time (30 women); includes 11 minority (2 Black or African American, non-Hispanic/Latino; 1 American Indian or Alaska Native, non-Hispanic/Latino; 2 Asian, non-Hispanic/Latino; 4 Hispanic/Latino; 2 Two or more races, non-Hispanic/Latino). Average age 29. 168 applicants, 59% accepted, 75 enrolled. In 2016, 86 master's awarded. *Entrance requirements:* For master's, GMAT, GRE General Test. Additional exam requirements/recommendations for international students: Required—TOEFL. *Application deadline:* Applications are processed on a rolling basis. Application fee: $50 ($60 for international students). Electronic applications accepted. *Expenses:* Tuition, state resident: full-time $9072; part-time $504 per credit hour. Tuition, nonresident: full-time $27,216; part-time $1512 per credit hour. *Required fees:* $812 per semester. Tuition and fees vary according to degree level and program. *Financial support:* Teaching assistantships and Federal Work-Study available. Support available to part-time students. Financial award application deadline: 3/15; financial award applicants required to submit FAFSA. *Unit head:* Jennifer Mueller-Phillips, Director, 334-844-5827. *Application contact:* Dr. George Flowers, Dean of the Graduate School, 334-844-2125.
Website: http://business.auburn.edu/academics/departments/school-of-accountancy

Auburn University at Montgomery, College of Business, School of Accountancy, Montgomery, AL 36124-4023. Offers M Acc. *Program availability:* Part-time. *Faculty:* 5 full-time (3 women). *Students:* 5 full-time (2 women), 26 part-time (19 women); includes 6 minority (5 Black or African American, non-Hispanic/Latino; 1 Two or more races, non-Hispanic/Latino), 4 international. 28 applicants, 93% accepted, 20 enrolled. *Entrance requirements:* For master's, GMAT, official transcripts. Additional exam requirements/recommendations for international students: Required—TOEFL (minimum score 500 paper-based; 61 iBT), IELTS (minimum score 5.5), PTE (minimum score 44). *Application deadline:* Applications are processed on a rolling basis. Application fee: $25 ($0 for international students). Electronic applications accepted. *Expenses:* Tuition, state resident: full-time $6462; part-time $359 per credit hour. Tuition, nonresident: full-time $14,526; part-time $807 per credit hour. *Required fees:* $554. *Financial support:* Scholarships/grants available. *Application contact:* Rhonda Seay, Graduate Advisor, 334-244-3115, E-mail: rseay@aum.edu.
Website: http://business.aum.edu/academic-departments/accounting

Aurora University, Dunham School of Business and Public Policy, Aurora, IL 60506-4892. Offers accountancy (MS); business (MBA); digital marketing and analytics (MS). *Program availability:* Part-time, evening/weekend, 100% online. *Faculty:* 8 full-time (1 woman), 19 part-time/adjunct (9 women). *Students:* 67 full-time (42 women), 186 part-time (98 women); includes 76 minority (32 Black or African American, non-Hispanic/Latino; 2 Asian, non-Hispanic/Latino; 35 Hispanic/Latino; 7 Two or more races, non-Hispanic/Latino), 5 international. Average age 33. 123 applicants, 99% accepted, 21 enrolled. In 2016, 99 master's awarded. *Entrance requirements:* For master's, minimum GPA of 2.75, 2 years of work experience. Additional exam requirements/recommendations for international students: Required—TOEFL (minimum score 550 paper-based; 79 iBT). *Application deadline:* For fall admission, 6/1 for international students; for spring admission, 10/1 for international students. Applications are processed on a rolling basis. Application fee: $0. Electronic applications accepted. *Expenses:* Contact institution. *Financial support:* In 2016–17, 58 students received support. Federal Work-Study, scholarships/grants, and unspecified assistantships available. Support available to part-time students. Financial award applicants required to submit FAFSA. *Unit head:* Dr. Toby Arquette, Executive Director of School of Business and Policy, 630-844-5614, E-mail: tarquett@aurora.edu. *Application contact:* Ed Miranda, Senior Recruiter for Adult and Graduate Programs, 630-947-8923, E-mail: emiranda@aurora.edu.

Averett University, Master of Accountancy Program, Danville, VA 24541-3692. Offers M Acc. *Program availability:* Part-time, online only, 100% online. *Faculty:* 2 full-time (1 woman). *Students:* 1 full-time (0 women), 5 part-time (3 women); includes 1 minority (Black or African American, non-Hispanic/Latino). Average age 29. 6 applicants, 100% accepted, 6 enrolled. In 2016, 1 master's awarded. *Degree requirements:* For master's, 30 credit hours, minimum GPA of 3.0 throughout program, completion of degree requirements within six years from start of program. *Entrance requirements:* For master's, GMAT, minimum cumulative GPA of 3.0, undergraduate degree in accounting, work experience. Additional exam requirements/recommendations for international students: Required—TOEFL. *Application deadline:* Applications are processed on a rolling basis. Electronic applications accepted. *Expenses:* $9,630. *Financial support:* In 2016–17, 1 student received support. Application deadline: 3/1; applicants required to submit FAFSA. *Unit head:* Dr. Peggy C. Wright, Director of the Master in Accountancy Program, 434-791-7118, E-mail: pwright@averett.edu. *Application contact:* Melissa Anderson, Director of Admissions, Graduate and Professional Studies, 804-729-8285, E-mail: manderson@averett.edu.

Avila University, School of Business, Kansas City, MO 64145-1698. Offers accounting (MBA); finance (MBA); health care administration (MBA); international business (MBA); management (MBA); management information systems (MBA); marketing (MBA). *Program availability:* Part-time, evening/weekend. *Faculty:* 8 full-time (4 women), 4 part-time/adjunct (2 women). *Students:* 58 full-time (22 women), 21 part-time (10 women); includes 20 minority (10 Black or African American, non-Hispanic/Latino; 2 Asian, non-Hispanic/Latino; 5 Hispanic/Latino; 3 Two or more races, non-Hispanic/Latino), 18 international. Average age 30. 75 applicants, 28% accepted, 14 enrolled. In 2016, 40 master's awarded. *Degree requirements:* For master's, comprehensive exam, capstone course. *Entrance requirements:* For master's, GMAT (minimum score 420), minimum GPA of 3.0, interview. Additional exam requirements/recommendations for international students: Required—TOEFL (minimum score 550 paper-based). *Application deadline:* For fall admission, 7/30 priority date for domestic and international students; for winter admission, 11/30 priority date for domestic and international students; for spring admission, 2/28 priority date for domestic and international students; for summer admission, 6/1 priority date for domestic and international students. Applications are processed on a rolling basis. Application fee: $0. Electronic applications accepted. *Expenses:* $628 per credit hour. *Financial support:* In 2016–17, 11 students received support. Career-related internships or fieldwork and scholarships/grants available. Support available to part-time students. Financial award applicants required to submit FAFSA. *Faculty research:* Leadership characteristics, financial hedging, group dynamics. *Unit head:* Dr. Richard Woodall, Dean, 816-501-3720, Fax: 816-501-2463, E-mail: richard.woodall@avila.edu. *Application contact:* Brandon Black, MBA Admission Advisor, 816-501-3601, Fax: 816-501-2463, E-mail: brandon.black@avila.edu.
Website: https://www.avila.edu/mrk/mba

Babson College, F. W. Olin Graduate School of Business, Babson Park, MA 02457-0310. Offers accounting (MSA); advanced management (Certificate); business administration (MBA); global entrepreneurship (MS); technological entrepreneurship (MS). *Accreditation:* AACSB. *Program availability:* Part-time, evening/weekend, online learning. *Entrance requirements:* For master's, GMAT, 2 years of work experience, resume, letters of recommendation. Additional exam requirements/recommendations for international students: Required—TOEFL (minimum score 100 iBT), IELTS (minimum score 6.5). Electronic applications accepted. *Faculty research:* Entrepreneurship, sustainability, global markets, process of innovation, social media and advertising.

Baker College Center for Graduate Studies–Online, Graduate Programs, Flint, MI 48507. Offers accounting (MBA); business administration (DBA); finance (MBA); general business (MBA); health care management (MBA); human resources management (MBA); information management (MBA); leadership studies (MBA); management information systems (MSIS); marketing (MBA). *Program availability:* Part-time, evening/weekend, online learning. *Degree requirements:* For master's, portfolio. *Entrance requirements:* For master's, 3 years of work experience, minimum undergraduate GPA of 2.5, writing sample, 3 letters of recommendation; for doctorate, MBA or acceptable related master's degree from accredited association, 5 years work experience, minimum graduate GPA of 3.25, writing sample, 3 professional references. Additional exam requirements/recommendations for international students: Required—TOEFL (minimum score 550 paper-based). Electronic applications accepted.

Baldwin Wallace University, Graduate Programs, School of Business, Program in Accounting, Berea, OH 44017-2088. Offers MBA. *Program availability:* Part-time, evening/weekend. *Students:* 10 full-time (4 women), 9 part-time (4 women); includes 1 minority (Black or African American, non-Hispanic/Latino). Average age 34. 12 applicants, 25% accepted, 2 enrolled. In 2016, 37 master's awarded. *Degree requirements:* For master's, minimum overall GPA of 3.0. *Entrance requirements:* For master's, GMAT or minimum undergraduate GPA of 3.0, minimum GPA of 3.0, work experience, bachelor's degree in any field, undergraduate accounting coursework. Additional exam requirements/recommendations for international students: Required—TOEFL (minimum score 550 paper-based; 79 iBT). *Application deadline:* For fall admission, 7/25 priority date for domestic students, 4/30 priority date for international students; for spring admission, 12/15 priority date for domestic students, 9/30 priority date for international students. Applications are processed on a rolling basis. Application fee: $25. Electronic applications accepted. Application fee is waived when completed online. *Expenses:* $921 per credit hour. *Financial support:* Applicants required to submit FAFSA. *Unit head:* Dale Kramer, Director, 440-826-3331, Fax: 440-826-3868, E-mail: dkramer@bw.edu. *Application contact:* Laura Spencer, Graduate Application Specialist, 440-826-2191, Fax: 440-826-3868, E-mail: lspencer@bw.edu.
Website: http://www.bw.edu/graduate/business/mba-accounting/

Ball State University, Graduate School, Miller College of Business, Department of Accounting, Muncie, IN 47306. Offers MS. *Accreditation:* AACSB. *Program availability:* Part-time. *Entrance requirements:* For master's, GMAT, minimum baccalaureate GPA of 2.75 or 3.0 in latter half of baccalauareate. Additional exam requirements/recommendations for international students: Required—TOEFL (minimum score 550 paper-based; 79 iBT), IELTS (minimum score 6.5). Electronic applications accepted. *Expenses:* Contact institution.

Barry University, Andreas School of Business, Program in Accounting, Miami Shores, FL 33161-6695. Offers MSA.

Baruch College of the City University of New York, Zicklin School of Business, Department of Accounting, Program in Accounting, New York, NY 10010-5585. Offers MBA, MS, PhD. PhD offered jointly with Graduate School and University Center of the City University of New York. *Accreditation:* AACSB. *Program availability:* Part-time, evening/weekend. *Degree requirements:* For doctorate, comprehensive exam, thesis/dissertation. *Entrance requirements:* For master's, GMAT, 2 letters of recommendation, resume, 2 years of work experience; for doctorate, GMAT. Additional exam requirements/recommendations for international students: Required—TOEFL (minimum score 590 paper-based), TWE (minimum score 5).

Bayamón Central University, Graduate Programs, Program in Business Administration, Bayamón, PR 00960-1725. Offers accounting (MBA); finance (MBA); general business (MBA); management (MBA); marketing (MBA). *Program availability:* Part-time, evening/weekend. *Degree requirements:* For master's, comprehensive exam (for some programs). *Entrance requirements:* For master's, EXADEP, bachelor's degree in business or related field.

Baylor University, Graduate School, Hankamer School of Business, Department of Accounting and Business Law, Waco, TX 76798. Offers M Acc, MT, JD/MT. *Accreditation:* AACSB. *Program availability:* Part-time. *Faculty:* 8 full-time (5 women). *Students:* 66 full-time (39 women), 22 part-time (10 women); includes 14 minority (1 Black or African American, non-Hispanic/Latino; 1 Asian, non-Hispanic/Latino; 10 Hispanic/Latino; 2 Two or more races, non-Hispanic/Latino), 6 international. In 2016, 86 master's awarded. *Entrance requirements:* For master's, GMAT. Additional exam requirements/recommendations for international students: Required—TOEFL (minimum score 100 iBT). *Application deadline:* For fall admission, 2/15 priority date for domestic and international students; for spring admission, 8/15 priority date for domestic and international students; for summer admission, 2/15 priority date for domestic and international students. Application fee: $50. Electronic applications accepted. *Expenses: Tuition:* Full-time $28,494; part-time $1583 per credit hour. *Required fees:* $167 per credit hour. Tuition and fees vary according to course load and program. *Financial support:* Research assistantships, career-related internships or fieldwork, Federal Work-Study, and institutionally sponsored loans available. *Faculty research:* Financial reporting, auditing, professional skepticism, tax policy, international financial reporting. *Unit head:* Dr. Gia Chevis, Adviser, 254-710-1328, Fax: 254-710-1067, E-mail: gia_chevis@baylor.edu. *Application contact:* Drew Snyder, Assistant Director of Admissions, 254-710-6281, E-mail: drew_snyder@baylor.edu.

Bay Path University, Program in Accounting, Longmeadow, MA 01106-2292. Offers forensic accounting (MS); private accounting (MS); public accounting (tax and audit) (MS). *Program availability:* Part-time, online only, 100% online. *Students:* 1 (woman) full-time, 27 part-time (25 women); includes 12 minority (5 Black or African American, non-Hispanic/Latino; 2 Asian, non-Hispanic/Latino; 4 Hispanic/Latino; 1 Two or more races, non-Hispanic/Latino). Average age 34. 18 applicants, 83% accepted, 11 enrolled. In 2016, 3 master's awarded. *Entrance requirements:* For master's, minimum GPA of 3.0; completion of accounting principles I and II, intermediate accounting, cost accounting, accounting information systems, auditing, federal taxation, business law, and managerial finance. *Application deadline:* Applications are processed on a rolling basis. Application fee: $45. Electronic applications accepted. Application fee is waived when completed online. *Expenses:* $14,310; $795 per credit. *Financial support:* In 2016–17, 2 students received support. Scholarships/grants and unspecified assistantships available. Financial award applicants required to submit FAFSA. *Unit head:* Kara Stevens, Director, 413-565-1344, E-mail: kastevens@baypath.edu. *Application contact:* Diane Ranaldi, Dean of Graduate Admissions, 413-565-1332, Fax: 413-565-1250, E-mail: dranaldi@baypath.edu.
Website: http://graduate.baypath.edu/graduate-programs/programs-online/ms-programs/accounting

Belmont University, Jack C. Massey Graduate School of Business, Nashville, TN 37212. Offers accounting (M Acc); business (AMBA, PMBA); healthcare (MBA). *Accreditation:* AACSB. *Program availability:* Part-time, evening/weekend. *Faculty:* 27 full-time (10 women), 8 part-time/adjunct (3 women). *Students:* 154 full-time (72 women), 49 part-time (25 women); includes 30 minority (12 Black or African American, non-Hispanic/Latino; 11 Asian, non-Hispanic/Latino; 4 Hispanic/Latino; 3 Two or more races, non-Hispanic/Latino), 10 international. Average age 28. 148 applicants, 64% accepted, 77 enrolled. In 2016, 136 master's awarded. *Entrance requirements:* For master's, GMAT, 2 years of work experience (MBA). Additional exam requirements/recommendations for international students: Required—TOEFL (minimum score 550 paper-based). *Application deadline:* For fall admission, 7/1 for domestic and international students; for spring admission, 11/1 for domestic and international students. Applications are processed on a rolling basis. Application fee: $50. Electronic applications accepted. *Expenses:* Contact institution. *Financial support:* Scholarships/grants, tuition waivers (partial), and unspecified assistantships available. Financial award application deadline: 7/1; financial award applicants required to submit FAFSA. *Faculty research:* Music business, strategy, ethics, finance, accounting systems. *Unit head:* Dr. Patrick Raines, Dean, 615-460-6480, Fax: 615-460-6455, E-mail: pat.raines@belmont.edu. *Application contact:* E-mail: masseyadmissions@belmont.edu.
Website: http://www.belmont.edu/business/masseyschool/

Benedictine University, Graduate Programs, Program in Accountancy, Lisle, IL 60532. Offers MS. *Program availability:* Evening/weekend. *Students:* 4 full-time (all women), 34 part-time (17 women); includes 16 minority (3 Black or African American, non-Hispanic/Latino; 8 Asian, non-Hispanic/Latino; 5 Hispanic/Latino), 3 international. 19 applicants, 68% accepted, 6 enrolled. In 2016, 22 master's awarded. *Entrance requirements:* For master's, official transcripts, 2 letters of reference, resume. Additional exam requirements/recommendations for international students: Required—TOEFL. *Application deadline:* Applications are processed on a rolling basis. Electronic applications accepted. *Expenses: Tuition:* Full-time $15,600; part-time $650 per hour. *Required fees:* $300. One-time fee: $125 part-time. Tuition and fees vary according to class time, course load, campus/location and program. *Unit head:* Dr. Sharon Borowicz, Director, 630-829-6219, E-mail: sborowicz@ben.edu. *Application contact:* Kari Gibbons, Associate Vice President, Enrollment Center, 630-829-6200, Fax: 630-829-6584, E-mail: kgibbons@ben.edu.

Benedictine University, Graduate Programs, Program in Business Administration, Lisle, IL 60532. Offers accounting (MBA); entrepreneurship and managing innovation (MBA); financial management (MBA); health administration (MBA); human resource management (MBA); information systems security (MBA); international business (MBA); management consulting (MBA); management information systems (MBA); marketing management (MBA); operations management and logistics (MBA); organizational leadership (MBA). *Program availability:* Part-time, evening/weekend, online learning. *Faculty:* 4 full-time (2 women), 24 part-time/adjunct (3 women). *Students:* 90 full-time (51 women), 440 part-time (262 women); includes 147 minority (65 Black or African American, non-Hispanic/Latino; 1 American Indian or Alaska Native, non-Hispanic/Latino; 58 Asian, non-Hispanic/Latino; 20 Hispanic/Latino; 3 Native Hawaiian or other Pacific Islander, non-Hispanic/Latino), 2 international. Average age 34. 211 applicants, 89% accepted, 155 enrolled. In 2016, 350 master's awarded. *Entrance requirements:* For master's, GMAT. Additional exam requirements/recommendations for international students: Required—TOEFL (minimum score 550 paper-based). *Application deadline:* For fall admission, 9/1 for domestic students; for winter admission, 12/1 for domestic students; for spring admission, 2/15 for domestic students. Applications are processed on a rolling basis. Application fee: $40. Electronic applications accepted. *Expenses: Tuition:* Full-time $15,600; part-time $650 per hour. *Required fees:* $300. One-time fee: $125 part-time. Tuition and fees vary according to class time, course load, campus/location and program. *Financial support:* Career-related internships or fieldwork and health care benefits available. Support available to part-time students. *Faculty research:* Strategic leadership in professional organizations, sociology of professions, organizational change, social identity theory, applications to change management. *Unit head:* Dr. Sharon Borowicz, Director, 630-829-6219, E-mail: sborowicz@ben.edu. *Application contact:* Kari Gibbons, Director, Admissions, 630-829-6200, Fax: 630-829-6584, E-mail: kgibbons@ben.edu.

Bentley University, Graduate School of Business, Accountancy PhD Program, Waltham, MA 02452-4705. Offers PhD. *Faculty:* 71 full-time (25 women), 33 part-time/adjunct (15 women). *Students:* 7 full-time (6 women). Average age 30. In 2016, 2 doctorates awarded. *Degree requirements:* For doctorate, comprehensive exam, thesis/dissertation. *Entrance requirements:* For doctorate, GMAT or GRE General Test, master's degree; official copies of transcripts; research paper; personal statement; 3 letters of recommendation; curriculum vitae; interview. Additional exam requirements/recommendations for international students: Required—TOEFL (minimum score 600 paper-based; 100 iBT), IELTS (minimum score 7), or PTE. *Application deadline:* For fall admission, 1/15 for domestic and international students. Application fee: $50. Electronic applications accepted. *Expenses: Tuition:* Part-time $1408 per credit. *Required fees:* $160 per credit. *Financial support:* In 2016–17, 7 students received support. Scholarships/grants available. Financial award application deadline: 6/1; financial award applicants required to submit FAFSA. *Faculty research:* Auditing; accounting information systems; capitol markets; governance and control; judgment and decision-making. *Unit head:* Patricia A. Caffrey, Administrative Director of PhD Programs, 781-891-2541, E-mail: pacaffrey@bentley.edu. *Application contact:* Sharon Hill, Assistant Dean/Director of Graduate Admissions, 781-891-2108, Fax: 781-891-2464, E-mail: bentleygraduateadmissions@bentley.edu.
Website: http://www.bentley.edu/offices/phd/phd-accountancy

Bentley University, Graduate School of Business, Master's Program in Accounting, Waltham, MA 02452-4705. Offers MSA. *Accreditation:* AACSB. *Program availability:* Part-time, evening/weekend. *Faculty:* 71 full-time (25 women), 33 part-time/adjunct (15 women). *Students:* 249 full-time (191 women), 54 part-time (34 women); includes 25 minority (1 Black or African American, non-Hispanic/Latino; 1 American Indian or Alaska Native, non-Hispanic/Latino; 19 Asian, non-Hispanic/Latino; 4 Hispanic/Latino), 192 international. Average age 25. 470 applicants, 74% accepted, 163 enrolled. In 2016, 154 master's awarded. *Entrance requirements:* For master's, GMAT or GRE General Test, current resume; two letters of recommendation; official copies of all university-level transcripts. Additional exam requirements/recommendations for international students: Required—TOEFL (minimum score 600 paper-based; 100 iBT), IELTS (minimum score 7), or PTE. *Application deadline:* Applications are processed on a rolling basis. Application fee: $50. Electronic applications accepted. *Expenses:* $4,225 per course, $480 fee per year. *Financial support:* In 2016–17, 57 students received support. Scholarships/grants and unspecified assistantships available. Financial award application deadline: 6/1; financial award applicants required to submit FAFSA. *Faculty research:* Audit risk assessment; ethics in accounting; corporate governance; accounting information systems and management control; tax policy, forensic accounting. *Unit head:* Dr. Donna McConville, Senior Lecturer, 781-891-2433, E-mail: dmcconville@bentley.edu. *Application contact:* Sharon Hill, Assistant Dean/Director of Graduate Admissions, 781-891-2108, Fax: 781-891-2464, E-mail: bentleygraduateadmissions@bentley.edu.
Website: http://www.bentley.edu/graduate/ms-programs/masters-in-accountancy

Binghamton University, State University of New York, Graduate School, School of Management, Program in Accounting, Binghamton, NY 13902-6000. Offers MS. *Program availability:* Part-time, evening/weekend. *Students:* 225 full-time (124 women), 50 part-time (38 women); includes 53 minority (44 Asian, non-Hispanic/Latino; 8 Hispanic/Latino; 1 Two or more races, non-Hispanic/Latino), 140 international. Average age 24. 555 applicants, 58% accepted, 167 enrolled. In 2016, 170 master's awarded. *Entrance requirements:* For master's, GMAT. Additional exam requirements/

recommendations for international students: Required—TOEFL (minimum score 90 iBT). *Application deadline:* For fall admission, 3/1 priority date for domestic and international students. Application fee: $75. Electronic applications accepted. *Financial support:* In 2016–17, 15 students received support, including 6 teaching assistantships (averaging $10,000 per year); career-related internships or fieldwork, Federal Work-Study, institutionally sponsored loans, scholarships/grants, health care benefits, and unspecified assistantships also available. Financial award applicants required to submit FAFSA. *Unit head:* Dr. Upinder Dhillon, Dean of School of Management, 607-777-2314, E-mail: dhillon@binghamton.edu. *Application contact:* Ben Balkaya, Assistant Dean and Director, 607-777-2151, Fax: 607-777-2501, E-mail: balkaya@binghamton.edu.

Bloomfield College, Program in Accounting, Bloomfield, NJ 07003-9981. Offers MS.

Bloomsburg University of Pennsylvania, School of Graduate Studies, Zeigler College of Business, Program in Accounting, Bloomsburg, PA 17815-1301. Offers M Acc. *Program availability:* Part-time, evening/weekend. *Faculty:* 3 full-time (1 woman). *Students:* 10 full-time (5 women), 2 part-time (0 women); includes 2 minority (1 Black or African American, non-Hispanic/Latino; 1 Two or more races, non-Hispanic/Latino), 1 international. Average age 23. 24 applicants, 46% accepted, 9 enrolled. In 2016, 17 master's awarded. *Degree requirements:* For master's, minimum QPA of 3.0. *Entrance requirements:* For master's, GRE, GMAT, 2 letters of recommendation, resume. Additional exam requirements/recommendations for international students: Required—TOEFL, IELTS. *Application deadline:* Applications are processed on a rolling basis. Application fee: $35 ($60 for international students). Electronic applications accepted. *Expenses:* Tuition, state resident: full-time $9660; part-time $483 per credit. Tuition, nonresident: full-time $14,500; part-time $725 per credit. *Required fees:* $2410; $107 per credit. $75 per term. Tuition and fees vary according to course load, degree level and program. *Financial support:* Federal Work-Study, scholarships/grants, and unspecified assistantships available. *Unit head:* Dr. Gary Robson, Chair, 570-389-4519, Fax: 570-389-3892, E-mail: grobson@bloomu.edu. *Application contact:* Jennifer Kessler, Administrative Assistant, 570-389-4015, Fax: 570-389-3054, E-mail: jkessler@bloomu.edu. Website: http://www.bloomu.edu/gradschool/accounting

Bluffton University, Programs in Business, Bluffton, OH 45817. Offers accounting and financial management (MBA); business administration (MBA); health care management (MBA); leadership (MBA); organizational management (MA); production and operations management (MBA). *Program availability:* Evening/weekend, online learning. *Faculty:* 9 full-time (3 women), 12 part-time/adjunct (4 women). *Students:* 55 full-time (34 women), 2 part-time (1 woman); includes 5 minority (1 Black or African American, non-Hispanic/Latino; 2 Asian, non-Hispanic/Latino; 2 Hispanic/Latino), 2 international. Average age 34. 31 applicants, 77% accepted, 22 enrolled. In 2016, 44 master's awarded. *Entrance requirements:* For master's, current resume, official transcript, two recommendation forms, bachelor's degree, minimum GPA of 3.0, four years of professional experience, interview. Additional exam requirements/recommendations for international students: Recommended—TOEFL. *Application deadline:* For fall admission, 7/31 priority date for domestic and international students. Applications are processed on a rolling basis. Application fee: $25. Electronic applications accepted. Application fee is waived when completed online. *Expenses:* $550 per credit. *Financial support:* Scholarships/grants and unspecified assistantships available. Financial award application deadline: 5/1. *Unit head:* Dr. Melissa Green, Director of Graduate Programs in Business, 419-358-3447, E-mail: greenm@bluffton.edu. *Application contact:* Carrie Mast, Administrative Assistant, Graduate Programs in Business, 419-358-3065, E-mail: mastc@bluffton.edu. Website: http://www.bluffton.edu/grad/

Bob Jones University, Graduate Programs, Greenville, SC 29614. Offers accountancy (MS); Bible (MA); Bible translation (MA); Biblical studies (Certificate); broadcast management (MS); business administration (MBA); church history (MA, PhD); church ministries (MA); church music (MM); cinema and video production (MA); counseling (MS); curriculum and instruction (Ed D); divinity (M Div); dramatic production (MA); educational leadership (MS, Ed D, Ed S); elementary education (M Ed, MAT); English (M Ed, MA, MAT); fine arts (MA); graphic design (MA); history (M Ed, MA); illustration (MA); interpretative speech (MA); mathematics (M Ed, MAT); medical missions (Certificate); ministry (MM, D Min); multi-categorical special education (M Ed, MAT); music (M Ed); New Testament interpretation (PhD); Old Testament interpretation (PhD); orchestral instrument performance (MM); organ performance (MM); pastoral studies (MA); personnel services (MS, Ed S); piano pedagogy (MM); piano performance (MM); platform arts (MA); radio and television broadcasting (MS); rhetoric and public address (MA); secondary education (M Ed); studio art (MA); teaching Bible (MA); theology (MA, PhD); voice performance (MM); youth ministries (MA); M Div/MM.

Boise State University, College of Business and Economics, Department of Accountancy, Boise, ID 83725-1600. Offers accountancy (MSA); accountancy taxation (MSAT). *Accreditation:* AACSB. *Program availability:* Part-time. *Faculty:* 7. *Students:* 18 full-time (8 women), 28 part-time (13 women); includes 5 minority (2 Asian, non-Hispanic/Latino; 3 Hispanic/Latino), 1 international. Average age 32. 27 applicants, 74% accepted, 12 enrolled. In 2016, 27 master's awarded. *Entrance requirements:* For master's, GMAT, minimum GPA of 3.0. Additional exam requirements/recommendations for international students: Required—TOEFL (minimum score 587 paper-based; 95 iBT), IELTS (minimum score 6.5). *Application deadline:* For fall admission, 6/1 for domestic and international students; for spring admission, 10/1 for domestic and international students; for summer admission, 3/1 for domestic and international students. Application fee: $65 ($95 for international students). Electronic applications accepted. *Expenses:* Tuition, state resident: full-time $6058; part-time $358 per credit hour. Tuition, nonresident: full-time $20,108; part-time $608 per credit hour. *Required fees:* $2108. Tuition and fees vary according to program. *Financial support:* In 2016–17, 12 students received support. Scholarships/grants and unspecified assistantships available. Financial award application deadline: 2/15; financial award applicants required to submit FAFSA. *Unit head:* Dr. Troy Hyatt, Director, 208-426-3412, E-mail: troyhyatt@boisestate.edu. *Application contact:* Trisha Stevens Lamb, Program Director, 208-426-1120, E-mail: trishastevenslamb@boisestate.edu.
Website: http://cobe.boisestate.edu/graduate/

Boston College, Carroll School of Management, Programs in Accounting, Chestnut Hill, MA 02467-3800. Offers MSA. *Entrance requirements:* For master's, GMAT, GRE, recommendations, resume, transcript. Additional exam requirements/recommendations for international students: Required—TOEFL (minimum score 600 paper-based, 100 iBT), IELTS (minimum score 7.5), or PTE (minimum score 68). Electronic applications accepted. Tuition and fees vary according to program. *Faculty research:* Financial reporting, auditing, tax planning, financial statement analysis.

Bowling Green State University, Graduate College, College of Business, Program in Accountancy, Bowling Green, OH 43403. Offers M Acc. *Accreditation:* AACSB. *Program availability:* Part-time. *Degree requirements:* For master's, thesis or alternative. *Entrance requirements:* For master's, GMAT. Additional exam requirements/recommendations for international students: Required—TOEFL. *Application deadline:* For fall admission, 2/15 priority date for domestic students. Application fee: $30. Electronic applications accepted. *Financial support:* Research assistantships with full tuition reimbursements, teaching assistantships with full tuition reimbursements, Federal Work-Study, and unspecified assistantships available. Financial award applicants required to submit FAFSA. *Faculty research:* Financial reporting and auditing, accounting information systems, taxation. *Unit head:* Earl McKinney, Interim Chair, E-mail: emckinn@bgsu.edu. *Application contact:* Alan Lord, Director, 419-372-8045.

Bradley University, The Graduate School, Foster College of Business, Program in Accounting, Peoria, IL 61625-0002. Offers MSA. *Accreditation:* AACSB. *Program availability:* Part-time, evening/weekend. *Degree requirements:* For master's, comprehensive exam. *Entrance requirements:* For master's, GMAT, 2 letters of recommendation. Additional exam requirements/recommendations for international students: Required—TOEFL (minimum score 550 paper-based; 79 iBT), IELTS (minimum score 6.5). *Application deadline:* For fall admission, 5/15 priority date for domestic and international students; for spring admission, 10/15 priority date for domestic and international students. Applications are processed on a rolling basis. Application fee: $40 ($50 for international students). Electronic applications accepted. *Expenses:* *Tuition:* Full-time $7650; part-time $850 per credit. *Required fees:* $50 per credit. One-time fee: $100 full-time. *Financial support:* Research assistantships with full and partial tuition reimbursements, career-related internships or fieldwork, institutionally sponsored loans, scholarships/grants, tuition waivers (partial), and unspecified assistantships available. Support available to part-time students. Financial award application deadline: 4/1. *Unit head:* Stephen Kerr, Chairperson, 309-677-2283, E-mail: skerr@bradley.edu. *Application contact:* Kayla Carroll, Director of International Admissions and Student Services, 309-677-2375, E-mail: klcarroll@fsmail.bradley.edu. Website: http://www.bradley.edu/academic/colleges/fcba/education/grad/msa/

Brandman University, School of Business and Professional Studies, Irvine, CA 92618. Offers accounting (MBA); business administration (MBA); e-business strategic management (MBA); entrepreneurship (MBA); finance (MBA); health administration (MBA); human resources (MBA, MS); international business (MBA); marketing (MBA); organizational leadership (MA, MBA, MPA); public administration (MPA). *Expenses:* *Tuition:* Full-time $14,880; part-time $620 per credit hour. Tuition and fees vary according to degree level and program. *Unit head:* Dr. Glenn Worthington, Dean, 253-861-1024, E-mail: gworthin@brandman.edu.
Website: https://www.brandman.edu/business-professional-studies

Brenau University, Sydney O. Smith Graduate School, College of Business and Mass Communication, Gainesville, GA 30501. Offers accounting (MBA); business administration (MBA); healthcare management (MBA); organizational leadership (MS); project management (MBA). *Accreditation:* ACBSP. *Program availability:* Part-time, evening/weekend, online learning. *Degree requirements:* For master's, comprehensive exam (for some programs). *Entrance requirements:* For master's, resume, minimum undergraduate GPA of 2.5. Additional exam requirements/recommendations for international students: Required—TOEFL (minimum score 500 paper-based; 61 iBT); Recommended—IELTS (minimum score 5). Electronic applications accepted. *Expenses:* Contact institution.

Bridgewater State University, College of Graduate Studies, Ricciardi College of Business, Department of Accounting and Finance, Bridgewater, MA 02325. Offers MSM. *Program availability:* Part-time, evening/weekend. *Entrance requirements:* For master's, GMAT.

Brock University, Faculty of Graduate Studies, Faculty of Business, Program in Accountancy, St. Catharines, ON L2S 3A1, Canada. Offers M Acc. *Degree requirements:* For master's, thesis or alternative. *Entrance requirements:* For master's, honours degree. Additional exam requirements/recommendations for international students: Required—TOEFL (minimum score 550 paper-based; 80 iBT), IELTS (minimum score 6.5), TWE (minimum score 4.5). Electronic applications accepted.

Brooklyn College of the City University of New York, School of Business, Brooklyn, NY 11210-2889. Offers accounting (MS); business administration (MS), including economic analysis, general business, global business and finance. *Program availability:* Part-time, evening/weekend. *Degree requirements:* For master's, comprehensive exam, thesis or alternative. *Entrance requirements:* For master's, GMAT, 2 letters of recommendation. Additional exam requirements/recommendations for international students: Required—TOEFL (minimum score 550 paper-based; 79 iBT). Electronic applications accepted. *Faculty research:* Econometrics, environmental economics, microeconomics, macroeconomics, taxation.

Bryant University, Graduate School of Business, Smithfield, RI 02917. Offers accounting (MPAC); business administration (MBA), including general management, global finance, global supply chain management, international business; business analytics (Graduate Certificate); taxation (MST). *Program availability:* Part-time, evening/weekend. *Faculty:* 16 full-time (3 women), 2 part-time/adjunct (0 women). *Students:* 71 full-time (23 women), 83 part-time (32 women); includes 17 minority (5 Black or African American, non-Hispanic/Latino; 4 Asian, non-Hispanic/Latino; 5 Hispanic/Latino; 3 Two or more races, non-Hispanic/Latino), 17 international. Average age 27. 165 applicants, 57% accepted, 66 enrolled. In 2016, 106 master's, 12 other advanced degrees awarded. *Degree requirements:* For master's, comprehensive exam (for some programs). *Entrance requirements:* For master's, GMAT, resume, recommendation, college transcripts. Additional exam requirements/recommendations for international students: Required—TOEFL (minimum score 580 paper-based; 95 iBT). *Application deadline:* For fall admission, 7/15 for domestic and international students; for spring admission, 11/15 for domestic and international students; for summer admission, 4/15 for domestic and international students. Applications are processed on a rolling basis. Application fee: $80. Electronic applications accepted. *Expenses:* Contact institution. *Financial support:* Research assistantships, scholarships/grants, and unspecified assistantships available. Support available to part-time students. Financial award application deadline: 2/15; financial award applicants required to submit FAFSA. *Faculty research:* International business, public sector auditing, taxation of partnerships, information systems security, financial markets microstructure. *Unit head:* Bjorn Carlsson, Graduate Program Director, 401-232-6707, E-mail: bcarlsson@bryant.edu. *Application contact:* Terri Rogers, Admissions Assistant, 401-232-6230, Fax: 401-232-6494, E-mail: graduateprograms@bryant.edu.
Website: http://gradschool.bryant.edu/business/

Butler University, Lacy School of Business, Indianapolis, IN 46208-3485. Offers finance (MBA); international business (MBA); leadership (MBA); marketing (MBA); professional accounting (MP Acc). *Accreditation:* AACSB. *Program availability:* Part-time. *Faculty:* 18 full-time (6 women), 14 part-time/adjunct (5 women). *Students:* 31 full-time (11 women), 133 part-time (40 women); includes 10 minority (2 Black or African American, non-Hispanic/Latino; 2 Asian, non-Hispanic/Latino; 6 Hispanic/Latino), 2 international. Average age 31. 122 applicants, 68% accepted, 42 enrolled. In 2016, 89 master's awarded. *Entrance requirements:* For master's, GMAT, minimum AACSB index of 950, personal statement, two letters of recommendation, official transcripts, current resume. Additional exam requirements/recommendations for international students: Required—TOEFL (minimum score 550 paper-based; 79 iBT), IELTS (minimum score 6), Michigan English Language Assessment Battery (minimum score of 80). *Application deadline:* For fall admission, 8/1 for domestic and international students; for spring admission, 12/1 for domestic and international students; for summer admission, 4/1 for domestic and international students. Applications are processed on a rolling basis. Application fee: $0. Electronic applications accepted. *Expenses:* $790 per credit hour. *Financial support:* In 2016–17, 15 students received support. Scholarships/grants,

tuition waivers (full and partial), and unspecified assistantships available. Financial award application deadline: 7/15; financial award applicants required to submit FAFSA. *Faculty research:* Higher education and pedagogy; ecotourism; healthcare issues and marketing public policy; domestic public policy, international finance and banking, international and management entrepreneurship, organizational management. *Unit head:* Dr. Stephen Standifird, Dean. *Application contact:* Diane Dubord, Graduate Student Service Specialist, 317-940-8107, Fax: 317-940-8250, E-mail: ddubord@butler.edu.
Website: https://www.butler.edu/lacyschool

Cabrini University, Graduate Studies, Radnor, PA 19087. Offers accounting (M Acc); education (M Ed); leadership (MS). *Program availability:* Part-time, evening/weekend. *Degree requirements:* For master's, thesis optional. *Entrance requirements:* For master's, GRE and/or MAT (in some cases), bachelor's degree with minimum GPA of 3.0, one-page personal essay/statement, professional letter of recommendation. Additional exam requirements/recommendations for international students: Required—TOEFL. Electronic applications accepted.

Cairn University, School of Business, Langhorne, PA 19047-2990. Offers accounting (MBA); business administration (MBA); international entrepreneurship (MBA); nonprofit leadership (MBA); organizational leadership (MSOL, Postbaccalaureate Certificate). *Program availability:* Part-time, evening/weekend, 100% online, blended/hybrid learning. *Faculty:* 3 full-time (0 women), 6 part-time/adjunct (1 woman). *Students:* 7 full-time (5 women), 43 part-time (19 women); includes 20 minority (10 Black or African American, non-Hispanic/Latino; 1 American Indian or Alaska Native, non-Hispanic/Latino; 4 Asian, non-Hispanic/Latino; 3 Hispanic/Latino; 2 Two or more races, non-Hispanic/Latino), 4 international. Average age 36. 17 applicants, 100% accepted, 16 enrolled. In 2016, 16 master's awarded. *Entrance requirements:* Additional exam requirements/recommendations for international students: Required—TOEFL (minimum score 550 paper-based). *Application deadline:* Applications are processed on a rolling basis. Application fee: $25. Electronic applications accepted. Application fee is waived when completed online. *Expenses:* $655 per semester credit. *Financial support:* Scholarships/grants available. Support available to part-time students. Financial award applicants required to submit FAFSA. *Unit head:* Yunn Kang, Dean, School of Business, 215-702-4461, Fax: 215-702-4248, E-mail: ykang@cairn.edu. *Application contact:* Gwen Dorsey, Assistant Director, Graduate Admissions, 800-572-2472, Fax: 215-702-4248, E-mail: gdorsey@cairn.edu.
Website: http://cairn.edu/academics/business

Caldwell University, Graduate Studies, Division of Business, Caldwell, NJ 07006-6195. Offers accounting (MS); business administration (MBA). *Accreditation:* ACBSP. *Program availability:* Part-time. *Entrance requirements:* For master's, GMAT, undergraduate accounting, marketing, and finance. Additional exam requirements/recommendations for international students: Required—TOEFL (minimum score 580 paper-based). Electronic applications accepted.

California Baptist University, Program in Accounting, Riverside, CA 92504-3206. Offers MS. *Program availability:* Part-time, evening/weekend, online only, 100% online. *Faculty:* 8 full-time (2 women). *Students:* 13 full-time (9 women), 12 part-time (7 women); includes 15 minority (5 Black or African American, non-Hispanic/Latino; 1 Asian, non-Hispanic/Latino; 6 Hispanic/Latino; 1 Native Hawaiian or other Pacific Islander, non-Hispanic/Latino; 2 Two or more races, non-Hispanic/Latino). Average age 33. 13 applicants, 62% accepted, 4 enrolled. In 2016, 2 master's awarded. *Degree requirements:* For master's, interdisciplinary capstone project. *Entrance requirements:* For master's, minimum cumulative GPA of 2.5, prerequisite courses completed with minimum C grade, two letters of recommendation, 500-word essay, current resume. Additional exam requirements/recommendations for international students: Required—TOEFL (minimum score 80 iBT). *Application deadline:* For fall admission, 8/1 priority date for domestic students, 7/1 priority date for international students; for spring admission, 12/1 priority date for domestic students, 11/1 priority date for international students. Applications are processed on a rolling basis. Application fee: $45. Electronic applications accepted. Application fee is waived when completed online. *Expenses:* Contact institution. *Financial support:* In 2016–17, 5 students received support. Federal Work-Study and scholarships/grants available. Financial award applicants required to submit CSS PROFILE or FAFSA. *Faculty research:* Financial stability, social entrepreneurship, cross-sector collaboration, business and government relations. *Unit head:* Dr. David Poole, Vice President, Online and Professional Studies, 951-343-3902, E-mail: dpoole@calbaptist.edu. *Application contact:* Karin Nelson, Program Director, Accounting, 951-552-8777, E-mail: knelson@calbaptist.edu.
Website: http://www.cbuonline.edu/programs/program/master-of-science-in-accounting

California Baptist University, Program in Business Administration, Riverside, CA 92504-3206. Offers accounting (MBA); construction management (MBA); healthcare management (MBA); management (MBA). *Accreditation:* ACBSP. *Program availability:* Part-time, evening/weekend, 100% online, blended/hybrid learning. *Faculty:* 14 full-time (3 women), 10 part-time/adjunct (1 woman). *Students:* 105 full-time (48 women), 122 part-time (63 women); includes 101 minority (23 Black or African American, non-Hispanic/Latino; 1 American Indian or Alaska Native, non-Hispanic/Latino; 10 Asian, non-Hispanic/Latino; 59 Hispanic/Latino; 2 Native Hawaiian or other Pacific Islander, non-Hispanic/Latino; 6 Two or more races, non-Hispanic/Latino), 54 international. Average age 29. 136 applicants, 65% accepted, 62 enrolled. In 2016, 71 master's awarded. *Degree requirements:* For master's, interdisciplinary capstone project. *Entrance requirements:* For master's, GMAT, minimum GPA of 2.5; two recommendations; comprehensive essay; resume; interview. Additional exam requirements/recommendations for international students: Required—TOEFL (minimum score 80 iBT). *Application deadline:* For fall admission, 8/1 priority date for domestic students, 7/1 for international students; for spring admission, 12/1 priority date for domestic students, 11/1 for international students. Applications are processed on a rolling basis. Application fee: $45. Electronic applications accepted. *Expenses:* Contact institution. *Financial support:* In 2016–17, 38 students received support. Federal Work-Study and scholarships/grants available. Financial award applicants required to submit CSS PROFILE or FAFSA. *Faculty research:* Behavioral economics, economic indicators, marketing ethics, international business, microfinance. *Unit head:* Dr. Steve Strombeck, Interim Dean, School of Business, 951-343-4701, Fax: 951-343-4361, E-mail: sstrombeck@calbaptist.edu. *Application contact:* Stephanie Fluitt, Graduate Admissions Counselor, 951-343-4696, E-mail: sfluitt@calbaptist.edu.
Website: http://www.calbaptist.edu/mba/about/

California Polytechnic State University, San Luis Obispo, Orfalea College of Business, Program in Accounting, San Luis Obispo, CA 93407. Offers MS. *Students:* 49 full-time (24 women); includes 15 minority (10 Asian, non-Hispanic/Latino; 4 Hispanic/Latino; 1 Two or more races, non-Hispanic/Latino). Average age 22. In 2016, 47 master's awarded. *Degree requirements:* For master's, comprehensive exam (for some programs), thesis (for some programs). *Entrance requirements:* For master's, GMAT. Additional exam requirements/recommendations for international students: Required—TOEFL (minimum score 80 iBT). *Application deadline:* For fall admission, 4/1 for domestic students, 3/1 for international students. Applications are processed on a rolling basis. Application fee: $55. Electronic applications accepted. *Expenses:* Tuition, state resident: full-time $6738; part-time $3906 per year. Tuition, nonresident: full-time $15,666; part-time $8370 per year. *Required fees:* $3603; $3141 per unit. $1047 per term. *Financial support:* Fellowships, career-related internships or fieldwork, Federal Work-Study, institutionally sponsored loans, scholarships/grants, and unspecified assistantships available. Support available to part-time students. Financial award application deadline: 3/2; financial award applicants required to submit FAFSA. *Faculty research:* Management of high-tech firms, Pacific Rim, capital market structures, economics of environmental policy, marketing of services. *Unit head:* Dr. Scott Dawson, Dean, 805-756-2705, E-mail: scdawson@calpoly.edu. *Application contact:* Dr. Sanjiv Jaggia, Associate Dean, Graduate Programs, 805-756-7519, E-mail: sjaggia@calpoly.edu.
Website: http://www.cob.calpoly.edu/gradbusiness/degree-programs/ms-accounting/

California State Polytechnic University, Pomona, Master of Science in Business Administration Program, Pomona, CA 91768-2557. Offers information systems auditing (MS). *Accreditation:* AACSB. *Program availability:* Part-time, evening/weekend. *Students:* 6 part-time (1 woman); includes 4 minority (3 Asian, non-Hispanic/Latino; 1 Hispanic/Latino), 1 international. Average age 34. 2 applicants, 100% accepted, 2 enrolled. In 2016, 4 master's awarded. *Entrance requirements:* Additional exam requirements/recommendations for international students: Required—TOEFL. *Application deadline:* Applications are processed on a rolling basis. Application fee: $55. Electronic applications accepted. *Expenses:* Contact institution. *Financial support:* Application deadline: 3/2; applicants required to submit FAFSA. *Unit head:* Dr. Erik Rolland, Dean, 909-869-2400, Fax: 909-869-6799, E-mail: erolland@cpp.edu. *Application contact:* Andrew M. Wright, Director of Admissions, 909-869-3130, Fax: 909-869-4529, E-mail: awright@cpp.edu.
Website: http://www.cpp.edu/~cba/graduate-business-programs/programs/index.shtml

California State Polytechnic University, Pomona, Program in Accountancy, Pomona, CA 91768-2557. Offers MS. *Program availability:* Part-time, evening/weekend. *Students:* 12 full-time (6 women), 10 part-time (7 women); includes 10 minority (7 Asian, non-Hispanic/Latino; 2 Hispanic/Latino; 1 Two or more races, non-Hispanic/Latino), 7 international. Average age 29. 30 applicants, 100% accepted, 19 enrolled. In 2016, 8 master's awarded. *Entrance requirements:* Additional exam requirements/recommendations for international students: Required—TOEFL. *Application deadline:* Applications are processed on a rolling basis. Application fee: $55. Electronic applications accepted. *Expenses:* Contact institution. *Financial support:* Application deadline: 3/2; applicants required to submit FAFSA. *Unit head:* Dr. Meihua Koo, Program Coordinator, 909-869-4531, Fax: 909-869-4511, E-mail: mkoo@cpp.edu. *Application contact:* Andrew M. Wright, Director of Admissions, 909-869-3130, Fax: 909-869-4529, E-mail: awright@cpp.edu.
Website: http://www.cpp.edu/~cba/graduate-business-programs/programs/index.shtml

California State University, East Bay, Office of Graduate Studies, College of Business and Economics, Department of Accounting and Finance, Hayward, CA 94542-3000. Offers accountancy (MS). *Program availability:* Part-time, evening/weekend. *Degree requirements:* For master's, comprehensive exam or thesis. *Entrance requirements:* For master's, GMAT, minimum GPA of 2.75. Additional exam requirements/recommendations for international students: Required—TOEFL (minimum score 550 paper-based). Electronic applications accepted.

California State University, Fullerton, Graduate Studies, College of Business and Economics, Department of Accounting, Fullerton, CA 92834-9480. Offers accounting (MBA, MS). *Accreditation:* AACSB. *Program availability:* Part-time. *Degree requirements:* For master's, thesis or alternative, project. *Entrance requirements:* For master's, GMAT, minimum AACSB index of 950. *Application deadline:* Applications are processed on a rolling basis. Application fee: $55. Electronic applications accepted. *Expenses:* Tuition, state resident: full-time $3369; part-time $1953 per unit. Tuition, nonresident: full-time $3915; part-time $2499 per unit. Tuition and fees vary according to course load, degree level and program. *Financial support:* Career-related internships or fieldwork, Federal Work-Study, institutionally sponsored loans, and scholarships/grants available. Support available to part-time students. Financial award application deadline: 3/1; financial award applicants required to submit FAFSA. *Unit head:* Dr. Betty Chavis, Chair, 657-278-2225. *Application contact:* Admissions/Applications, 657-278-2371.

California State University, Los Angeles, Graduate Studies, College of Business and Economics, Department of Accounting, Los Angeles, CA 90032-8530. Offers MBA. *Program availability:* Part-time, evening/weekend. *Degree requirements:* For master's, comprehensive exam (MBA), thesis (MS). *Entrance requirements:* For master's, GMAT, minimum GPA of 2.5 during previous 2 years of course work. Additional exam requirements/recommendations for international students: Required—TOEFL (minimum score 550 paper-based). Electronic applications accepted.

California State University, Sacramento, Office of Graduate Studies, College of Business Administration, Sacramento, CA 95819. Offers accountancy (MS); business administration (IMBA, MBA); human resources (MBA); urban land development (MBA). *Accreditation:* AACSB. *Program availability:* Part-time, evening/weekend. *Students:* 138 full-time (68 women), 129 part-time (63 women); includes 211 minority (12 Black or African American, non-Hispanic/Latino; 132 American Indian or Alaska Native, non-Hispanic/Latino; 63 Asian, non-Hispanic/Latino; 4 Native Hawaiian or other Pacific Islander, non-Hispanic/Latino). Average age 34. 198 applicants, 77% accepted, 85 enrolled. In 2016, 168 master's awarded. *Degree requirements:* For master's, thesis or alternative, writing proficiency exam. *Entrance requirements:* For master's, GMAT. Additional exam requirements/recommendations for international students: Required—TOEFL (minimum score 550 paper-based; 80 iBT). *Application deadline:* For fall admission, 2/1 for domestic students, 3/1 for international students; for spring admission, 9/15 for domestic students, 9/30 for international students. Applications are processed on a rolling basis. Application fee: $55. Electronic applications accepted. *Expenses:* $4,302 full-time tuition and fees per semester, $2,796 part-time. *Financial support:* Research assistantships, teaching assistantships, career-related internships or fieldwork, and Federal Work-Study available. Support available to part-time students. Financial award applicants required to submit FAFSA. *Unit head:* Dr. Pierre A. Balthazard, Dean, 916-278-6578, Fax: 916-278-5793, E-mail: cba@csus.edu. *Application contact:* Jose Martinez, Graduate Admissions Supervisor, 916-278-7871, E-mail: martinj@skymail.csus.edu.
Website: http://www.cba.csus.edu

California State University, San Bernardino, Graduate Studies, College of Business and Public Administration, Program in Accountancy, San Bernardino, CA 92407. Offers MSA. *Faculty:* 8 full-time (0 women). *Students:* 34 full-time (18 women), 30 part-time (13 women); includes 30 minority (1 Black or African American, non-Hispanic/Latino; 1 American Indian or Alaska Native, non-Hispanic/Latino; 8 Asian, non-Hispanic/Latino; 18 Hispanic/Latino; 2 Two or more races, non-Hispanic/Latino), 21 international. 69 applicants, 57% accepted, 29 enrolled. In 2016, 40 master's awarded. *Application deadline:* For fall admission, 7/16 for domestic students. Application fee: $55. *Expenses:* Tuition, state resident: full-time $7843; part-time $5011.20 per year. Tuition and fees vary according to course load, degree level, program and reciprocity agreements. *Unit head:* Dr. Lawrence C. Rose, Dean, 909-537-3703, E-mail: lrose@csusb.edu. *Application contact:* Dr. Francisca Beer, Dean of Graduate Studies, 909-537-5058, Fax: 909-537-5078, E-mail: fbeer@csusb.edu.

Accounting

California State University, San Bernardino, Graduate Studies, College of Business and Public Administration, Program in Business Administration, San Bernardino, CA 92407. Offers accounting (MBA); entrepreneurship (MBA); finance (MBA); global business (MBA); information management (MBA); information security (MBA); management (MBA); supply chain management (MBA). *Accreditation:* AACSB. *Program availability:* Part-time, evening/weekend, online learning. *Faculty:* 7 full-time (4 women), 3 part-time/adjunct (2 women). *Students:* 37 full-time (11 women), 141 part-time (51 women); includes 85 minority (16 Black or African American, non-Hispanic/Latino; 1 American Indian or Alaska Native, non-Hispanic/Latino; 20 Asian, non-Hispanic/Latino; 45 Hispanic/Latino; 3 Two or more races, non-Hispanic/Latino), 46 international. 260 applicants, 37% accepted, 34 enrolled. In 2016, 180 master's awarded. *Degree requirements:* For master's, comprehensive exam, thesis. *Entrance requirements:* Additional exam requirements/recommendations for international students: Required—TOEFL. *Application deadline:* For fall admission, 7/16 for domestic students, 7/20 for international students; for winter admission, 10/23 for domestic students, 10/20 for international students; for spring admission, 1/22 for domestic students, 1/20 for international students. Application fee: $55. *Expenses:* Contact institution. *Financial support:* Application deadline: 3/1. *Unit head:* Dr. Lawrence C. Rose, Dean, 909-537-3703, Fax: 909-537-7026, E-mail: lrose@csusb.edu. *Application contact:* Dr. Vipin Gupta, Associate Dean/MBA Director, 909-537-7380, Fax: 909-537-7026, E-mail: vgupta@csusb.edu. Website: http://mba.csusb.edu/

California Western School of Law, Graduate and Professional Programs, San Diego, CA 92101-3090. Offers law (JD); Spanish language in trial advocacy (LL M); JD/MBA; JD/MSW; MCL/LL M. JD/MSW and JD/MBA offered jointly with San Diego State University. *Accreditation:* ABA. *Program availability:* Part-time. *Faculty:* 43 full-time (18 women), 48 part-time/adjunct (20 women). *Students:* 568 full-time (339 women), 189 part-time (84 women); includes 267 minority (41 Black or African American, non-Hispanic/Latino; 9 American Indian or Alaska Native, non-Hispanic/Latino; 42 Asian, non-Hispanic/Latino; 123 Hispanic/Latino; 9 Native Hawaiian or other Pacific Islander, non-Hispanic/Latino; 43 Two or more races, non-Hispanic/Latino), 12 international. Average age 27. 1,408 applicants, 70% accepted, 230 enrolled. *Entrance requirements:* For doctorate, LSAT. Additional exam requirements/recommendations for international students: Required—TOEFL. *Application deadline:* For fall admission, 4/1 for domestic students; for spring admission, 11/1 for domestic students. Applications are processed on a rolling basis. Electronic applications accepted. *Expenses: Tuition:* Full-time $48,800; part-time $34,200 per year. *Required fees:* $100; $100 per unit. Tuition and fees vary according to degree level. *Financial support:* Career-related internships or fieldwork, Federal Work-Study, institutionally sponsored loans, and scholarships/grants available. Support available to part-time students. Financial award applicants required to submit FAFSA. *Faculty research:* Biotechnology, health law, international law, labor and employment law, business law. *Unit head:* Niels B. Schaumann, Dean, 619-239-0391, Fax: 619-685-2916. *Application contact:* Traci D. Howard, Assistant Dean for Admissions, 619-525-1404, Fax: 619-615-1404, E-mail: admissions@cwsl.edu.
Website: http://www.californiawestern.edu/

Canisius College, Graduate Division, Richard J. Wehle School of Business, Department of Accounting, Buffalo, NY 14208-1098. Offers accounting (MBA); forensic accounting (MS); professional accounting (MBA). *Program availability:* Part-time, evening/weekend. *Faculty:* 8 full-time (1 woman), 4 part-time/adjunct (1 woman). *Students:* 61 full-time (27 women), 25 part-time (7 women); includes 11 minority (4 Black or African American, non-Hispanic/Latino; 4 Asian, non-Hispanic/Latino; 3 Hispanic/Latino), 3 international. Average age 27. 82 applicants, 73% accepted, 19 enrolled. In 2016, 56 master's awarded. *Entrance requirements:* For master's, GMAT, GRE, official transcript from colleges attended, current resume. Additional exam requirements/recommendations for international students: Required—TOEFL (minimum score 550 paper-based, 80 iBT), IELTS (minimum score 6.5), or CAEL (minimum score 70). *Application deadline:* For fall admission, 7/1 priority date for domestic students; for spring admission, 11/1 priority date for domestic students. Applications are processed on a rolling basis. Application fee: $25. Electronic applications accepted. Application fee is waived when completed online. *Expenses: Tuition:* Full-time $14,742. *Required fees:* $724. *Financial support:* Career-related internships or fieldwork, Federal Work-Study, scholarships/grants, and unspecified assistantships available. Financial award application deadline: 4/30; financial award applicants required to submit FAFSA. *Faculty research:* Auditing (process and operational factors), fraud from a global perspective, managing risk in software development, valuation of intellectual property. *Unit head:* Dr. Joseph B. O'Donnell, Chair/Professor, 716-888-2868, E-mail: odonnelj@canisius.edu. *Application contact:* Kathleen B. Davis, Vice President of Enrollment Management, 716-888-2500, Fax: 716-888-3195, E-mail: daviskb@canisius.edu.
Website: http://www.canisius.edu/graduate/

Capella University, School of Business and Technology, Doctoral Programs in Business, Minneapolis, MN 55402. Offers accounting (DBA, PhD); business intelligence (DBA); finance (DBA, PhD); general business management (PhD); human resource management (DBA, PhD); leadership (DBA, PhD); management education (PhD); marketing (DBA, PhD); project management (DBA, PhD); strategy and innovation (DBA, PhD). *Accreditation:* ACBSP.

Capella University, School of Business and Technology, Master's Programs in Business, Minneapolis, MN 55402. Offers accounting (MBA); business analysis (MS); business intelligence (MBA); entrepreneurship (MBA); finance (MBA); general business administration (MBA); general human resource management (MS); general leadership (MS); health care management (MBA); human resource management (MBA); marketing (MBA); project management (MBA, MS). *Accreditation:* ACBSP.

Carnegie Mellon University, Tepper School of Business, Program in Accounting, Pittsburgh, PA 15213-3891. Offers PhD. *Accreditation:* AACSB. *Degree requirements:* For doctorate, thesis/dissertation. *Entrance requirements:* For doctorate, GRE.

Case Western Reserve University, Weatherhead School of Management, Department of Accountancy, Cleveland, OH 44106. Offers M Acc, PhD, MBA/M Acc. *Accreditation:* AACSB. *Program availability:* Evening/weekend. *Degree requirements:* For doctorate, thesis/dissertation. *Entrance requirements:* For master's and doctorate, GMAT. *Expenses: Tuition:* Full-time $42,576; part-time $1774 per credit hour. *Required fees:* $34. Tuition and fees vary according to course load and program. *Faculty research:* Auditing, regulation, financial reporting, public interest, efficient markets.

The Catholic University of America, Busch School of Business and Economics, Washington, DC 20064. Offers accounting (MS); business analysis (MSBA); integral economic development management (MA); integral economic development policy (MA); management (MS), including Federal contract management, human resource management, leadership and management, project management, sales management. *Program availability:* Part-time. *Faculty:* 30 full-time (7 women), 30 part-time/adjunct (5 women). *Students:* 60 full-time (32 women), 26 part-time (14 women); includes 26 minority (11 Black or African American, non-Hispanic/Latino; 8 Asian, non-Hispanic/Latino; 5 Hispanic/Latino; 2 Two or more races, non-Hispanic/Latino), 22 international. Average age 29. 121 applicants, 77% accepted, 64 enrolled. In 2016, 48 master's awarded. *Degree requirements:* For master's, comprehensive exam (for some programs). *Entrance requirements:* For master's, GRE General Test, statement of purpose, official copies of academic transcripts, three letters of recommendation. Additional exam requirements/recommendations for international students: Required—TOEFL (minimum score 550 paper-based; 80 iBT). *Application deadline:* For fall admission, 7/15 priority date for domestic students, 7/1 for international students; for spring admission, 11/15 priority date for domestic students, 11/1 for international students. Applications are processed on a rolling basis. Application fee: $55. Electronic applications accepted. *Expenses:* $42,850 per year; $1,170 per credit; $200 per semester part-time fees. *Financial support:* Fellowships, research assistantships, teaching assistantships, Federal Work-Study, scholarships/grants, tuition waivers (full and partial), and unspecified assistantships available. Financial award application deadline: 2/1; financial award applicants required to submit FAFSA. *Faculty research:* Integrity of the marketing process, economics of energy and the environment, emerging markets, social change, international finance and economic development. *Total annual research expenditures:* $3,698. *Unit head:* Dr. William Bowman, Dean, 202-319-5290, Fax: 202-319-4426, E-mail: otey@cua.edu. *Application contact:* Director of Graduate Admissions, 202-319-5057, Fax: 202-319-6533, E-mail: cua-admissions@cua.edu.
Website: http://business.cua.edu/

Centenary University, Program in Professional Accounting, Hackettstown, NJ 07840-2100. Offers MS. *Program availability:* Part-time, evening/weekend, online learning.

Central Connecticut State University, School of Graduate Studies, School of Business, Department of Accounting, New Britain, CT 06050-4010. Offers MSA. *Program availability:* Part-time, evening/weekend. *Faculty:* 7 full-time (2 women), 1 part-time/adjunct (0 women). *Students:* 12 full-time (8 women), 16 part-time (10 women); includes 12 minority (5 Black or African American, non-Hispanic/Latino; 5 Asian, non-Hispanic/Latino; 1 Hispanic/Latino; 1 Two or more races, non-Hispanic/Latino). Average age 29. 42 applicants, 81% accepted, 22 enrolled. *Degree requirements:* For master's, thesis or alternative. *Entrance requirements:* For master's, GMAT or GRE, minimum undergraduate GPA of 2.7, resume. Additional exam requirements/recommendations for international students: Required—TOEFL (minimum score 550 paper-based; 79 iBT). *Application deadline:* For fall admission, 6/1 for domestic students, 5/1 for international students; for spring admission, 11/1 for domestic and international students. Applications are processed on a rolling basis. Application fee: $50. Electronic applications accepted. *Expenses: Tuition, area resident:* Full-time $6497; part-time $606 per credit. Tuition, state resident: full-time $9748; part-time $622 per credit. Tuition, nonresident: full-time $18,102; part-time $622 per credit. *Required fees:* $4459; $246 per credit. *Financial support:* In 2016–17, 2 students received support. Career-related internships or fieldwork, Federal Work-Study, scholarships/grants, and unspecified assistantships available. Support available to part-time students. Financial award application deadline: 3/1; financial award applicants required to submit FAFSA. *Unit head:* Lawrence Grasso, Chair, 860-832-3226, E-mail: grassola@ccsu.edu. *Application contact:* Patricia Gardner, Associate Director of Graduate Admissions, 860-832-2350, Fax: 860-832-2362.
Website: http://www.ccsu.edu/accounting/

Central Michigan University, College of Graduate Studies, College of Business Administration, Department of Business Information Systems, Mount Pleasant, MI 48859. Offers business computing (Graduate Certificate); information systems (MS), including accounting information systems, business informatics, enterprise systems using SAP software, information systems. *Program availability:* Part-time, evening/weekend. *Degree requirements:* For master's, thesis or alternative. Electronic applications accepted. *Faculty research:* Enterprise software, electronic commerce, decision support systems, ethical issues in information systems, information technology management and teaching issues.

Central Michigan University, College of Graduate Studies, College of Business Administration, MBA Program, Mount Pleasant, MI 48859. Offers accounting (MBA); business economics (MBA); consulting (MBA); finance (MBA); general business (MBA); human resource management (MBA); information systems (MBA); international business (MBA); logistics management (MBA); marketing (MBA); value-driven organization (MBA). *Program availability:* Part-time, evening/weekend, online learning. Electronic applications accepted. *Faculty research:* Accounting, consulting, international business, marketing, information systems.

Central Washington University, Graduate Studies and Research, College of Business, Department of Accounting, Ellensburg, WA 98926. Offers MPA. *Accreditation:* AACSB. *Program availability:* Part-time. *Degree requirements:* For master's, comprehensive exam. *Entrance requirements:* For master's, GMAT, minimum GPA of 3.0. Additional exam requirements/recommendations for international students: Required—TOEFL (minimum score 550 paper-based; 79 iBT), IELTS (minimum score 6.5). Electronic applications accepted.

Chaminade University of Honolulu, Office of Professional and Continuing Education, Program in Business Administration, Honolulu, HI 96816-1578. Offers accounting (MBA); business (MBA); island business (MBA); not-for-profit (MBA). *Program availability:* Part-time, evening/weekend, 100% online, blended/hybrid learning. *Faculty:* 7 full-time (3 women), 7 part-time/adjunct (2 women). *Students:* 71 full-time (47 women), 40 part-time (23 women); includes 78 minority (4 Black or African American, non-Hispanic/Latino; 1 American Indian or Alaska Native, non-Hispanic/Latino; 37 Asian, non-Hispanic/Latino; 5 Hispanic/Latino; 28 Native Hawaiian or other Pacific Islander, non-Hispanic/Latino; 3 Two or more races, non-Hispanic/Latino). Average age 32. 70 applicants, 96% accepted, 45 enrolled. In 2016, 56 master's awarded. *Entrance requirements:* For master's, minimum GPA of 3.0, resume, two years or more of work experience. Additional exam requirements/recommendations for international students: Required—TOEFL (minimum score 550 paper-based; 79 iBT). *Application deadline:* Applications are processed on a rolling basis. Application fee: $40. Electronic applications accepted. *Expenses:* $820 per credit hour with $93 fee per online course. *Financial support:* Applicants required to submit FAFSA. *Unit head:* Dr. Scott J. Schroeder, Dean, 808-739-4612, Fax: 808-735-4734, E-mail: mba@chaminade.edu. *Application contact:* 808-735-4755, E-mail: gradserv@chaminade.edu.
Website: http://www.chaminade.edu/mba

Chapman University, The George L. Argyros School of Business and Economics, Orange, CA 92866. Offers accounting (MS); business administration (Exec MBA, MBA); economic systems design (MS); JD/MBA. *Accreditation:* AACSB. *Program availability:* Part-time, evening/weekend. *Faculty:* 54 full-time (10 women), 35 part-time/adjunct (7 women). *Students:* 179 full-time (83 women), 94 part-time (44 women); includes 77 minority (4 Black or African American, non-Hispanic/Latino; 2 American Indian or Alaska Native, non-Hispanic/Latino; 30 Asian, non-Hispanic/Latino; 30 Hispanic/Latino; 3 Native Hawaiian or other Pacific Islander, non-Hispanic/Latino; 8 Two or more races, non-Hispanic/Latino), 96 international. Average age 28. 250 applicants, 75% accepted, 94 enrolled. In 2016, 114 master's awarded. *Entrance requirements:* Additional exam requirements/recommendations for international students: Required—TOEFL (minimum score 550 paper-based, 80 iBT), IELTS (6.5), PTE Academic (53), or CAE. Application fee: $60. Electronic applications accepted. *Expenses:* Contact institution. *Financial support:* Fellowships, Federal Work-Study, and scholarships/grants available. Financial award applicants required to submit FAFSA. *Unit head:* Reginald Gilyard, Dean, 714-997-6684. *Application contact:* Debra Gonda, Associate Dean, 714-997-6894, E-mail: gonda@chapman.edu.
Website: http://www.chapman.edu/business/

Charleston Southern University, School of Business, Charleston, SC 29423-8087. Offers accounting (MBA); finance (MBA); general management (MBA); human resource management (MS); leadership (MBA); management information systems (MBA); organizational leadership (MA). *Program availability:* Part-time, evening/weekend. *Degree requirements:* For master's, thesis optional. *Entrance requirements:* For master's, GMAT. Additional exam requirements/recommendations for international students: Required—TOEFL (minimum score 550 paper-based; 79 iBT). *Application deadline:* Applications are processed on a rolling basis. Application fee: $40. *Expenses: Tuition:* Full-time $6000. Tuition and fees vary according to program. *Financial support:* Research assistantships with full tuition reimbursements available. Financial award application deadline: 4/15; financial award applicants required to submit FAFSA. *Unit head:* Dr. David Palmer, Interim Dean, 843-863-7025, Fax: 843-863-7922, E-mail: dpalmer@csuniv.edu. *Application contact:* Dr. Darin L. Gerdes, Director of the MBA Program, 843-863-7814, Fax: 843-863-7922, E-mail: dgerdes@cusniv.edu.
Website: http://www.csuniv.edu/business/

Chatham University, Program in Accounting, Pittsburgh, PA 15232-2826. Offers M Acc, MAC. *Program availability:* Part-time, evening/weekend. *Entrance requirements:* Additional exam requirements/recommendations for international students: Required—TOEFL (minimum score 600 paper-based; 100 iBT), IELTS (minimum score 7), TWE. Electronic applications accepted. Application fee is waived when completed online. *Expenses: Tuition:* Full-time $16,254; part-time $903 per credit hour. *Required fees:* $468; $26 per credit hour.

Christian Brothers University, School of Business, Memphis, TN 38104-5581. Offers accountancy (M Acc); business (MBA); international business (MIB); project management (Certificate); MBA/MIB. *Program availability:* Part-time, evening/weekend. *Entrance requirements:* For master's, GMAT, GRE. Additional exam requirements/recommendations for international students: Required—TOEFL.

City University of Seattle, Graduate Division, School of Management, Seattle, WA 98121. Offers accounting (Certificate); change leadership (MBA, Certificate); computer systems (MS); finance (Certificate); financial management (MBA); general management (MBA); general management-Europe (MBA); global marketing (MBA); human resources management (Certificate); individualized study (MBA); information security (MS); information systems (MBA); leadership (MA); marketing (MBA, Certificate); project management (MBA, MS, Certificate); sustainable business (Certificate); technology management (MBA, Certificate). *Program availability:* Part-time, evening/weekend, online learning. *Degree requirements:* For master's, comprehensive exam (for some programs), thesis (for some programs). *Entrance requirements:* For master's, baccalaureate degree or equivalent from an accredited or otherwise recognized institution. Additional exam requirements/recommendations for international students: Required—TOEFL (minimum score 567 paper-based; 87 iBT); Recommended—IELTS. Electronic applications accepted.

Clarion University of Pennsylvania, Office of Transfer, Adult and Graduate Admissions, Online Master of Science Programs, Clarion, PA 16214. Offers accounting (MS); applied data analytics (MS); clinical mental health counseling (MS); library science (MSLS); mass media arts and journalism (MS). *Program availability:* Part-time, 100% online. *Faculty:* 15 full-time (7 women), 3 part-time/adjunct (2 women). *Students:* 84 full-time (69 women), 304 part-time (246 women); includes 36 minority (19 Black or African American, non-Hispanic/Latino; 3 Asian, non-Hispanic/Latino; 10 Hispanic/Latino; 4 Two or more races, non-Hispanic/Latino), 1 international. Average age 34. 179 applicants, 93% accepted, 131 enrolled. In 2016, 146 master's awarded. *Degree requirements:* For master's, comprehensive exam, thesis or alternative. *Entrance requirements:* For master's, minimum QPA of 3.0. Additional exam requirements/recommendations for international students: Required—TOEFL (minimum score 600 paper-based; 100 iBT), IELTS (minimum score 7.5). *Application deadline:* For fall admission, 8/1 priority date for domestic students, 4/15 priority date for international students; for spring admission, 12/1 priority date for domestic students, 9/15 priority date for international students. Applications are processed on a rolling basis. Application fee: $40. Electronic applications accepted. *Expenses:* $632.35 per credit. *Financial support:* Career-related internships or fieldwork, Federal Work-Study, scholarships/grants, and unspecified assistantships available. Support available to part-time students. Financial award application deadline: 3/1. *Application contact:* Dana Bearer, Associate Director, Transfer, Adult, and Graduate Programs, 814-393-2337, Fax: 814-393-2772, E-mail: gradstudies@clarion.edu.
Website: http://www.clarion.edu/admissions/graduate/index.html

Clark Atlanta University, School of Business Administration, Department of Accounting, Atlanta, GA 30314. Offers MA. *Program availability:* Part-time. *Faculty:* 3 full-time (2 women), 1 (woman) part-time/adjunct. *Students:* 16 full-time (14 women), 2 part-time (both women); includes 10 minority (all Black or African American, non-Hispanic/Latino), 6 international. Average age 26. 20 applicants, 80% accepted, 10 enrolled. In 2016, 6 master's awarded. *Entrance requirements:* For master's, GMAT, minimum undergraduate GPA of 2.5. Additional exam requirements/recommendations for international students: Required—TOEFL (minimum score 500 paper-based; 61 iBT). *Application deadline:* For fall admission, 4/1 for domestic and international students; for spring admission, 11/1 for domestic and international students. Applications are processed on a rolling basis. Application fee: $40 ($55 for international students). Electronic applications accepted. *Expenses: Tuition:* Full-time $15,498; part-time $861 per credit hour. *Required fees:* $1326; $1326 per credit hour. Tuition and fees vary according to course load. *Financial support:* Career-related internships or fieldwork, Federal Work-Study, scholarships/grants, and unspecified assistantships available. Support available to part-time students. Financial award application deadline: 4/30; financial award applicants required to submit FAFSA. *Unit head:* Dr. Kasim Alli, Chairperson, 404-880-8740, E-mail: kalli@cau.edu. *Application contact:* Graduate Program Admissions, 404-880-8483, E-mail: graduateadmissions@cau.edu.

Clark University, Graduate School, Graduate School of Management, Business Administration Program, Worcester, MA 01610-1477. Offers accounting (MBA); finance (MBA); information management and business analytics (MBA); management (MBA); marketing (MBA); social change (MBA); sustainability (MBA). *Accreditation:* AACSB. *Program availability:* Part-time, evening/weekend. *Students:* 91 full-time (48 women), 101 part-time (45 women); includes 22 minority (8 Black or African American, non-Hispanic/Latino; 4 Asian, non-Hispanic/Latino; 9 Hispanic/Latino; 1 Native Hawaiian or other Pacific Islander, non-Hispanic/Latino), 45 international. Average age 31. 225 applicants, 58% accepted, 78 enrolled. In 2016, 113 master's awarded. *Degree requirements:* For master's, thesis optional. *Application deadline:* For fall admission, 6/1 priority date for domestic students; for spring admission, 12/1 priority date for domestic students. Applications are processed on a rolling basis. Application fee: $75. Electronic applications accepted. *Expenses: Tuition:* Full-time $44,050. *Required fees:* $80. Tuition and fees vary according to course load and program. *Financial support:* In 2016–17, research assistantships with partial tuition reimbursements (averaging $4,800 per year), teaching assistantships with partial tuition reimbursements (averaging $4,800 per year) were awarded; fellowships, career-related internships or fieldwork, Federal Work-Study, institutionally sponsored loans, and tuition waivers (partial) also available. Support available to part-time students. Financial award application deadline: 5/31. *Faculty research:* Marketing, accounting, human resource management, management information systems, business finance. *Unit head:* Dr. Catherine Usoff, Dean, 508-793-7543, Fax: 508-793-8822. *Application contact:* Ethan Bernstein, Director of Graduate Admissions, 508-793-7543, E-mail: graduateadmissions@clarku.edu.
Website: http://www.clarku.edu/programs/masters-business-administration

Clark University, Graduate School, Graduate School of Management, Program in Accounting, Worcester, MA 01610-1477. Offers MSA. *Program availability:* Part-time. *Students:* 52 full-time (41 women), 18 part-time (13 women); includes 2 minority (1 Black or African American, non-Hispanic/Latino; 1 Asian, non-Hispanic/Latino), 54 international. Average age 27. 259 applicants, 80% accepted, 31 enrolled. In 2016, 10 master's awarded. *Entrance requirements:* For master's, GMAT or GRE, statement of purpose, resume, two letters of recommendation. Additional exam requirements/recommendations for international students: Required—TOEFL (minimum score 577 paper-based; 90 iBT) or IELTS (minimum score 6.5). *Application deadline:* For fall admission, 6/1 for domestic students. Application fee: $75. Electronic applications accepted. *Expenses: Tuition:* Full-time $44,050. *Required fees:* $80. Tuition and fees vary according to course load and program. *Financial support:* Research assistantships and teaching assistantships available. *Unit head:* Dr. Catherine Usoff, Dean, 508-793-7543, Fax: 508-793-8822. *Application contact:* Patrick Oroszko, Enrollment and Marketing Director, 508-793-7543, Fax: 508-793-8822, E-mail: poroszko@clarku.edu.
Website: http://www.clarku.edu/programs/masters-accounting

Clayton State University, School of Graduate Studies, College of Business, Program in Business Administration, Morrow, GA 30260-0285. Offers accounting (MBA); human resource leadership (MBA); international business (MBA); sports and entertainment management (MBA); supply chain management (MBA). *Accreditation:* AACSB. *Program availability:* Part-time, evening/weekend. *Degree requirements:* For master's, thesis. *Entrance requirements:* For master's, GMAT, 3 letters of recommendation; statement of purpose; 2 official transcripts. Additional exam requirements/recommendations for international students: Required—TOEFL (minimum score 550 paper-based; 80 iBT). Electronic applications accepted. *Expenses:* Contact institution.

Clemson University, Graduate School, College of Business, School of Accountancy, Clemson, SC 29634. Offers accounting (MP Acc). *Accreditation:* AACSB. *Program availability:* Part-time. *Faculty:* 5 full-time (1 woman), 5 part-time/adjunct (0 women). *Students:* 94 full-time (41 women), 8 part-time (4 women); includes 14 minority (6 Black or African American, non-Hispanic/Latino; 3 Asian, non-Hispanic/Latino; 2 Hispanic/Latino; 3 Two or more races, non-Hispanic/Latino), 5 international. Average age 23. 161 applicants, 65% accepted, 82 enrolled. In 2016, 85 master's awarded. *Entrance requirements:* For master's, GMAT, unofficial transcripts, letters of recommendation. Additional exam requirements/recommendations for international students: Required—TOEFL (minimum score 80 iBT), IELTS (minimum score 6.5). *Application deadline:* For fall admission, 6/1 priority date for domestic students, 4/15 priority date for international students; for spring admission, 11/1 priority date for domestic students, 9/30 priority date for international students. Applications are processed on a rolling basis. Application fee: $80 ($90 for international students). Electronic applications accepted. *Expenses:* $4,841 per semester full-time resident, $9,640 per semester full-time non-resident, $612 per credit hour part-time resident, $1,223 per credit hour part-time non-resident. *Financial support:* In 2016–17, 18 students received support, including 4 fellowships with partial tuition reimbursements available (averaging $1,500 per year); career-related internships or fieldwork and unspecified assistantships also available. Financial award application deadline: 12/31. *Faculty research:* Financial accounting, auditing, managerial accounting. *Unit head:* Dr. Jeffrey McMillan, Interim Director, 864-656-4880, E-mail: mjeffre@clemson.edu. *Application contact:* Dr. Carl Hollingsworth, Program Coordinator, 864-656-4883, E-mail: chollin@clemson.edu.
Website: https://www.clemson.edu/business/departments/accountancy/index.html

Cleveland State University, College of Graduate Studies, Monte Ahuja College of Business, Department of Accounting, Cleveland, OH 44115. Offers financial accounting/audit (M Acc). *Accreditation:* AACSB. *Program availability:* Part-time, evening/weekend. *Faculty:* 13 full-time (3 women), 11 part-time/adjunct (3 women). *Students:* 54 full-time (27 women), 81 part-time (44 women); includes 32 minority (12 Black or African American, non-Hispanic/Latino; 1 American Indian or Alaska Native, non-Hispanic/Latino; 13 Asian, non-Hispanic/Latino; 4 Hispanic/Latino; 2 Two or more races, non-Hispanic/Latino), 20 international. Average age 31. 89 applicants, 85% accepted, 36 enrolled. In 2016, 85 master's awarded. *Entrance requirements:* For master's, GMAT, minimum GPA of 2.75. Additional exam requirements/recommendations for international students: Required—TOEFL (minimum score 550 paper-based; 78 iBT). *Application deadline:* For fall admission, 7/1 priority date for domestic students, 5/15 for international students; for spring admission, 11/15 priority date for domestic students, 11/1 for international students; for summer admission, 4/1 for domestic students, 3/15 for international students. Applications are processed on a rolling basis. Application fee: $40. Electronic applications accepted. *Expenses:* Tuition, state resident: full-time $9565. Tuition, nonresident: full-time $17,980. Tuition and fees vary according to program. *Financial support:* In 2016–17, 3 research assistantships with tuition reimbursements (averaging $6,960 per year) were awarded; career-related internships or fieldwork, Federal Work-Study, scholarships/grants, and unspecified assistantships also available. Financial award applicants required to submit FAFSA. *Faculty research:* Internal auditing, computer auditing, accounting education, managerial accounting. *Unit head:* Bruce W. McClain, Chair, 216-687-3652, Fax: 216-687-9212, E-mail: b.mcclain@csuohio.edu. *Application contact:* Bruce Gottschalk, MBA Programs Administrator, 216-687-3730, Fax: 216-687-5311, E-mail: cbacsu@csuohio.edu.
Website: http://www.csuohio.edu/business/academics/master-accountancy

Coastal Carolina University, E. Craig Wall, Sr. College of Business Administration, Conway, SC 29528-6054. Offers accounting (M Acc); business administration (MBA); business foundations (Certificate); fraud examination (Certificate). *Accreditation:* AACSB. *Program availability:* Part-time, evening/weekend. *Faculty:* 14 full-time (7 women), 3 part-time/adjunct (0 women). *Students:* 67 full-time (28 women), 30 part-time (15 women); includes 25 minority (16 Black or African American, non-Hispanic/Latino; 2 Asian, non-Hispanic/Latino; 3 Hispanic/Latino; 1 Native Hawaiian or other Pacific Islander, non-Hispanic/Latino; 3 Two or more races, non-Hispanic/Latino), 11 international. Average age 27. 88 applicants, 78% accepted, 56 enrolled. In 2016, 70 master's, 1 other advanced degree awarded. *Entrance requirements:* For master's, GMAT, official transcripts, 2 letters of recommendation, resume, baccalaureate degree; for Certificate, GMAT, official transcripts; 2 letters of recommendation; baccalaureate degree or evidence of receiving a CPA certificate, law degree, or admittance to an accredited law school. Additional exam requirements/recommendations for international students: Required—TOEFL (minimum score 550 paper-based; 79 iBT), IELTS (minimum score 6.5). *Application deadline:* For fall admission, 6/15 priority date for domestic and international students; for spring admission, 11/15 priority date for domestic and international students; for summer admission, 4/15 priority date for domestic and international students. Applications are processed on a rolling basis. Application fee: $45. Electronic applications accepted. *Expenses:* Tuition, state resident: full-time $9990; part-time $555 per credit hour. Tuition, nonresident: full-time $18,108; part-time $1006 per credit hour. *Required fees:* $90; $5 per credit hour. *Financial support:* Fellowships, research assistantships, and unspecified assistantships available. Support available to part-time students. Financial award application deadline:

3/1; financial award applicants required to submit FAFSA. *Unit head:* Dr. Arlise P. McKinney, Associate Professor/Director of Graduate Programs and Executive Education, 843-349-2390, Fax: 843-349-2455, E-mail: amckinney@coastal.edu. *Application contact:* Dr. James O. Luken, Associate Provost/Interim Vice-Dean of the Coastal Environment, 843-349-2235, Fax: 843-349-6444, E-mail: joluken@coastal.edu. Website: http://www.coastal.edu/academics/colleges/business/

The College at Brockport, State University of New York, School of Business and Management, Brockport, NY 14420-2997. Offers forensic accounting (MS); public administration (MPA, AGC), including arts administration (AGC), nonprofit management (AGC), public administration (MPA). *Program availability:* Part-time. *Faculty:* 5 full-time (1 woman), 1 part-time/adjunct (0 women). *Students:* 13 full-time (5 women), 8 part-time (5 women); includes 4 minority (3 Black or African American, non-Hispanic/Latino; 1 Asian, non-Hispanic/Latino). 29 applicants, 79% accepted, 19 enrolled. In 2016, 17 master's awarded. *Entrance requirements:* For master's, GMAT or GRE General Test. Additional exam requirements/recommendations for international students: Required—TOEFL (minimum score 550 paper-based; 79 iBT), IELTS (minimum score 6.5). *Application deadline:* For fall admission, 7/1 priority date for domestic and international students; for spring admission, 12/1 priority date for domestic and international students. Application fee: $50. Electronic applications accepted. *Expenses:* Contact institution. *Financial support:* Career-related internships or fieldwork, Federal Work-Study, scholarships/grants, and unspecified assistantships available. Financial award application deadline: 3/15; financial award applicants required to submit FAFSA. *Unit head:* Dr. James Cordeiro, Department Chair, 585-395-5793, Fax: 585-395-2542. *Application contact:* Dr. Donald A. Kent, Graduate Director, 585-395-5521, Fax: 585-395-2515, E-mail: dkent@brockport.edu.
Website: http://www.brockport.edu/academics/school_business_management/

College of Charleston, Graduate School, School of Business, Program in Accountancy, Charleston, SC 29424-0001. Offers MS. *Accreditation:* AACSB. *Program availability:* Evening/weekend. *Entrance requirements:* For master's, GMAT, minimum GPA of 3.0 in last 60 hours of undergraduate course work, 24 hours of course work in accounting, 2 letters of reference. Additional exam requirements/recommendations for international students: Required—TOEFL (minimum score 81 iBT). *Application deadline:* For fall admission, 7/1 for domestic students. Applications are processed on a rolling basis. Application fee: $45. Electronic applications accepted. *Financial support:* Research assistantships, Federal Work-Study, institutionally sponsored loans, scholarships/grants, and unspecified assistantships available. Support available to part-time students. Financial award application deadline: 3/1; financial award applicants required to submit FAFSA. *Unit head:* Dr. Roger B. Daniels, Director, 843-953-8041, E-mail: danielsr@cofc.edu. *Application contact:* Susan Hallatt, Director of Graduate Admissions, 843-953-5614, Fax: 843-953-1434, E-mail: hallatts@cofc.edu.
Website: http://sb.cofc.edu/graduate/accountancy/index.php

The College of Saint Rose, Graduate Studies, Huether School of Business, Program in Accounting, Albany, NY 12203-1419. Offers MS. *Program availability:* Part-time, evening/weekend. *Students:* 25 full-time (17 women), 10 part-time (5 women); includes 9 minority (6 Black or African American, non-Hispanic/Latino; 2 Hispanic/Latino; 1 Two or more races, non-Hispanic/Latino), 2 international. Average age 28. 16 applicants, 69% accepted, 7 enrolled. In 2016, 24 master's awarded. *Entrance requirements:* For master's, GMAT, graduate degree, or minimum undergraduate GPA of 3.0. Additional exam requirements/recommendations for international students: Required—TOEFL (minimum score 550 paper-based; 80 iBT), IELTS (minimum score 6), PTE (minimum score 56). *Application deadline:* For fall admission, 4/1 priority date for domestic and international students; for spring admission, 10/15 priority date for domestic and international students; for summer admission, 3/15 priority date for domestic and international students. Applications are processed on a rolling basis. Application fee: $40. Electronic applications accepted. *Expenses: Tuition:* Full-time $14,382; part-time $799 per credit. *Required fees:* $814; $32 per credit. $88 per semester. Tuition and fees vary according to course load. *Financial support:* Career-related internships or fieldwork, scholarships/grants, tuition waivers (partial), and unspecified assistantships available. Support available to part-time students. Financial award application deadline: 4/15; financial award applicants required to submit FAFSA. *Unit head:* Gretchen Guenther-Collins, Program Coordinator, 518-458-5304, Fax: 518-458-5449, E-mail: guentheg@strose.edu. *Application contact:* Cris Murray, Assistant Vice President for Graduate Recruitment and Enrollment, 518-485-3390, Fax: 518-458-5479, E-mail: grad@strose.edu. Website: https://www.strose.edu/accounting-ms/

College of Staten Island of the City University of New York, Graduate Programs, School of Business, Program in Accounting, Staten Island, NY 10314-6600. Offers MS. *Program availability:* Part-time, evening/weekend. *Faculty:* 5 full-time, 1 part-time/adjunct. *Students:* 5 full-time, 31 part-time. Average age 31. 29 applicants, 55% accepted, 12 enrolled. In 2016, 13 master's awarded. *Degree requirements:* For master's, 30 credits or 10 courses worth 3 credits each; capstone course. *Entrance requirements:* For master's, GMAT or College of Staten Island degree with minimum GPA of 3.2 in accounting or business pre-major and major. TOEFL or IETLS is a requirement of students whom English is a second language, baccalaureate degree in accounting or related field; letter of intent; minimum GPA of 3.0; two letters of recommendation from instructors or employers; proficiency in business fundamentals and in-depth knowledge of accounting through undergraduate coursework. Additional exam requirements/recommendations for international students: Required—TOEFL (minimum score 600 paper-based; 100 iBT), IELTS (minimum score 7). *Application deadline:* For fall admission, 6/30 priority date for domestic and international students; for spring admission, 11/25 priority date for domestic and international students. Applications are processed on a rolling basis. Application fee: $125. Electronic applications accepted. *Expenses:* Tuition, state resident: full-time $10,130; part-time $425 per credit. Tuition, nonresident: full-time $18,720; part-time $780 per credit. *Required fees:* $181.10 per semester. Tuition and fees vary according to program. *Faculty research:* Fair value reporting, forensic accounting, pension asset allocation, archival empirical analysis. *Unit head:* Prof. John Sandler, Graduate Program Coordinator, 718-982-2963, E-mail: john.sandler@csi.cuny.edu. *Application contact:* Sasha Spence, Associate Director for Graduate Admissions, 718-982-2019, Fax: 718-982-2500, E-mail: sasha.spence@csi.cuny.edu.
Website: http://www.csi.cuny.edu/schoolofbusiness/programs_graduate.php

The College of William and Mary, Raymond A. Mason School of Business, Master of Accounting Program, Williamsburg, VA 23185. Offers M Acc. *Accreditation:* AACSB. *Faculty:* 10 full-time (3 women), 7 part-time/adjunct (0 women). *Students:* 116 full-time (55 women); includes 19 minority (8 Black or African American, non-Hispanic/Latino; 5 Asian, non-Hispanic/Latino; 3 Hispanic/Latino; 3 Two or more races, non-Hispanic/Latino), 22 international. Average age 23. 452 applicants, 38% accepted, 107 enrolled. In 2016, 112 master's awarded. *Degree requirements:* For master's, 30 credit hours. *Entrance requirements:* For master's, GMAT, 2 written recommendations, interview, transcripts. Additional exam requirements/recommendations for international students: Required—TOEFL (minimum score 620 paper-based; 102 IBT) or IELTS (minimum score 7). *Application deadline:* Applications are processed on a rolling basis. Application fee: $80. Electronic applications accepted. *Expenses:* Contact institution. *Financial support:* In 2016–17, 70 students received support, including 12 research assistantships (averaging $4,000 per year); fellowships, scholarships/grants, and unspecified assistantships also available. Financial award application deadline: 3/15; financial award applicants required to submit FAFSA. *Faculty research:* Valuation, voluntary disclosure, auditing, taxation, executive compensation. *Unit head:* Phil Shane, Accounting Department Chair, 757-221-1504, Fax: 757-221-7862, E-mail: phil.shane@mason.wm.edu. *Application contact:* Beth McGraw, Associate Director, 757-221-2879, Fax: 757-221-7862, E-mail: beth.mcgraw@mason.wm.edu.
Website: http://mason.wm.edu/programs/macc/index.php

Colorado State University, College of Business, Department of Accounting, Fort Collins, CO 80523-1271. Offers accounting (M Acc); taxation (M Acc). *Faculty:* 5 full-time (3 women), 5 part-time/adjunct (1 woman). *Students:* 27 full-time (12 women), 14 part-time (8 women); includes 8 minority (5 Hispanic/Latino; 3 Two or more races, non-Hispanic/Latino), 6 international. Average age 30. 55 applicants, 73% accepted, 27 enrolled. In 2016, 37 master's awarded. *Degree requirements:* For master's, thesis or alternative. *Entrance requirements:* For master's, GMAT (minimum score of 600) or GRE (minimum score of 315), minimum GPA of 3.25, BA/BS, 3 letters of reference, official transcripts, statement of purpose, resume. Additional exam requirements/recommendations for international students: Required—TOEFL (minimum score 95 iBT); Recommended—IELTS (minimum score 7), TSE (minimum score 70). *Application deadline:* For fall admission, 5/1 for domestic and international students. Applications are processed on a rolling basis. Application fee: $60 ($70 for international students). Electronic applications accepted. *Expenses:* Contact institution. *Financial support:* Scholarships/grants and unspecified assistantships available. Financial award application deadline: 2/1; financial award applicants required to submit FAFSA. *Faculty research:* Financial analysis, auditing and reporting; taxation; data analytics and systems; managerial accounting; corporate social responsibility. *Total annual research expenditures:* $5,000. *Unit head:* Dr. Audrey A. Gramling, Department Chair, 970-491-6268, E-mail: audrey.gramling@colostate.edu. *Application contact:* Jennifer Ivan, Program Manager, 970-491-1184, E-mail: jennifer.ivan@colostate.edu.
Website: https://biz.colostate.edu/About/Departments/Department-of-Accounting

Colorado State University–Global Campus, Graduate Programs, Greenwood Village, CO 80111. Offers criminal justice and law enforcement administration (MS); education leadership (MS); finance (MS); healthcare administration and management (MS); human resource management (MHRM); information technology management (MITM); international management (MS); management (MS); organizational leadership (MS); professional accounting (MPA); project management (MS); teaching and learning (MS). *Accreditation:* ACBSP. *Program availability:* Online learning.

Colorado Technical University Aurora, Programs in Business Administration and Management, Aurora, CO 80014. Offers accounting (MBA); business administration (MBA); business administration and management (EMBA); finance (MBA); human resource management (MBA); marketing (MBA); mediation and dispute resolution (MBA); operations management (MBA); project management (MBA); technology management (MBA). *Program availability:* Part-time, evening/weekend. *Degree requirements:* For master's, thesis or alternative. *Entrance requirements:* For master's, minimum undergraduate GPA of 3.0, resume.

Colorado Technical University Colorado Springs, Graduate Studies, Program in Management, Colorado Springs, CO 80907. Offers accounting (MBA, MSA); business administration (MBA); finance (MBA); human resources management (MBA); logistics/supply chain management (MBA); management (DM); marketing (MBA); mediation and dispute resolution (MBA); operations management (MBA); project management (MBA); technology management (MBA). *Accreditation:* ACBSP. *Program availability:* Part-time, evening/weekend, online learning. *Degree requirements:* For master's, thesis or alternative; for doctorate, thesis/dissertation. *Entrance requirements:* For doctorate, minimum graduate GPA of 3.0, 5 years of related work experience. *Faculty research:* Sexual harassment, performance evaluation, critical thinking.

Columbia College, Master of Business Administration Program, Columbia, MO 65216-0002. Offers accounting (MBA); human resources (MBA). *Program availability:* Part-time, evening/weekend, 100% online, blended/hybrid learning. *Faculty:* 5 full-time (2 women), 39 part-time/adjunct (15 women). *Students:* 76 full-time (51 women), 415 part-time (240 women); includes 109 minority (60 Black or African American, non-Hispanic/Latino; 3 American Indian or Alaska Native, non-Hispanic/Latino; 7 Asian, non-Hispanic/Latino; 25 Hispanic/Latino; 2 Native Hawaiian or other Pacific Islander, non-Hispanic/Latino; 12 Two or more races, non-Hispanic/Latino), 26 international. Average age 36. 121 applicants, 90% accepted, 63 enrolled. In 2016, 194 master's awarded. *Entrance requirements:* For master's, 3 letters of recommendation, minimum cumulative undergraduate GPA of 3.0, resume, goal statement. Additional exam requirements/recommendations for international students: Required—TOEFL (minimum score 550 paper-based; 79 iBT). *Application deadline:* For fall admission, 8/9 priority date for domestic and international students; for spring admission, 12/27 priority date for domestic and international students. Applications are processed on a rolling basis. Application fee: $55. Electronic applications accepted. *Expenses:* Contact institution. *Financial support:* Federal Work-Study and scholarships/grants available. Financial award application deadline: 3/1; financial award applicants required to submit FAFSA. *Unit head:* Dr. Shanda Traiser, Dean, School of Business Administration, 573-875-7561, Fax: 573-876-4493, E-mail: strasier@ccis.edu. *Application contact:* Stephanie Johnson, Director of Admissions, 573-875-7352, Fax: 573-875-7506, E-mail: sjohnson@ccis.edu.
Website: http://www.ccis.edu/graduate/academics/degrees.asp?MBA

Columbia University, Graduate School of Business, Doctoral Program in Business, New York, NY 10027. Offers business (PhD), including accounting, decision, risk, and operations, finance and economics, management, marketing. *Accreditation:* AACSB. *Degree requirements:* For doctorate, comprehensive exam, thesis/dissertation, major field exam, research paper, thesis proposal. *Entrance requirements:* For doctorate, GMAT or GRE (finance), 2 letters of reference, resume. Additional exam requirements/recommendations for international students: Required—TOEFL. Electronic applications accepted. *Expenses:* Contact institution. *Faculty research:* Human decision making and behavioral research; real estate market and mortgage defaults; financial crisis and corporate governance; international business; security analysis and accounting.

Columbia University, Graduate School of Business, MBA Program, New York, NY 10027. Offers accounting (MBA); decision, risk, and operations (MBA); entrepreneurship (MBA); finance and economics (MBA); healthcare and pharmaceutical management (MBA); human resource management (MBA); international business (MBA); leadership and ethics (MBA); management (MBA); marketing (MBA); media (MBA); private equity (MBA); real estate (MBA); social enterprise (MBA); value investing (MBA); DDS/MBA; JD/MBA; MBA/MIA; MBA/MPH; MBA/MS; MD/MBA. *Entrance requirements:* For master's, GMAT, 2 letters of recommendation. Additional exam requirements/recommendations for international students: Required—TOEFL. Electronic applications accepted. *Expenses:* Contact institution. *Faculty research:* Human decision making and behavioral research; real estate market and mortgage defaults; financial crisis and corporate governance; international business; security analysis and accounting.

Cornell University, Graduate School, Graduate Field of Management, Ithaca, NY 14853. Offers accounting (PhD); finance (PhD); marketing (PhD); organizational behavior (PhD); production and operations management (PhD). *Accreditation:* AACSB.

Degree requirements: For doctorate, comprehensive exam, thesis/dissertation. *Entrance requirements:* For doctorate, GMAT or GRE General Test. Additional exam requirements/recommendations for international students: Required—TOEFL (minimum score 600 paper-based; 77 iBT). Electronic applications accepted. *Expenses:* Contact institution. *Faculty research:* Operations and manufacturing.

Cornell University, Samuel Curtis Johnson Graduate School of Management, Ithaca, NY 14853. Offers business administration (Exec MBA); management (MBA, PhD); management - accounting (MPS); JD/MBA; M Eng/MBA; MBA/MD; MBA/MHA; MBA/MILR; MBA/MPS. *Accreditation:* AACSB. *Faculty:* 62 full-time (17 women), 65 part-time/adjunct (8 women). *Students:* 580 full-time (174 women); includes 139 minority (18 Black or African American, non-Hispanic/Latino; 2 American Indian or Alaska Native, non-Hispanic/Latino; 77 Asian, non-Hispanic/Latino; 26 Hispanic/Latino; 16 Two or more races, non-Hispanic/Latino), 191 international. Average age 28. 1,960 applicants, 27% accepted, 279 enrolled. *Entrance requirements:* For master's, GMAT or GRE, resume, two essays, two recommendations. Additional exam requirements/recommendations for international students: Required—TOEFL. *Application deadline:* For fall admission, 10/5 for domestic and international students; for winter admission, 11/15 for domestic and international students; for spring admission, 1/10 for domestic and international students; for summer admission, 3/15 for domestic and international students. Application fee: $200. Electronic applications accepted. *Expenses:* $61,584 per year. *Financial support:* Fellowships, research assistantships, career-related internships or fieldwork, Federal Work-Study, institutionally sponsored loans, and tuition waivers (full and partial) available. Financial award applicants required to submit FAFSA. *Unit head:* Dr. Mark Nelson, Dean, 607-255-6418, E-mail: dean@johnson.cornell.edu. *Application contact:* Admissions Office, 800-847-2082, Fax: 607-255-0065, E-mail: mba@johnson.cornell.edu.
Website: http://www.johnson.cornell.edu

Creighton University, Graduate School, Heider College of Business, Omaha, NE 68178-0001. Offers accounting (MAC); business administration (MBA); business intelligence and analytics (MS); finance (M Fin); JD/MBA; MBA/MSAPM; MD/MBA; Pharm D/MBA. *Accreditation:* AACSB. *Program availability:* Part-time, evening/weekend, 100% online, blended/hybrid learning. *Faculty:* 33 full-time (10 women), 22 part-time/adjunct (3 women). *Students:* 41 full-time (13 women), 262 part-time (79 women); includes 24 minority (16 Black or African American, non-Hispanic/Latino; 3 Asian, non-Hispanic/Latino; 1 Hispanic/Latino; 2 Native Hawaiian or other Pacific Islander, non-Hispanic/Latino; 2 Two or more races, non-Hispanic/Latino), 21 international. Average age 32. 189 applicants, 73% accepted, 74 enrolled. In 2016, 172 master's awarded. *Degree requirements:* For master's, thesis optional. *Entrance requirements:* For master's, GMAT, resume, 2 letters of recommendation. Additional exam requirements/recommendations for international students: Required—TOEFL (minimum score 90 iBT). *Application deadline:* For fall admission, 7/1 priority date for domestic students, 3/1 for international students; for winter admission, 10/1 priority date for domestic students, 7/1 for international students; for spring admission, 4/1 priority date for domestic students, 10/1 for international students; for summer admission, 5/1 for domestic and international students. Applications are processed on a rolling basis. Application fee: $50. Electronic applications accepted. *Expenses:* Contact institution. *Financial support:* In 2016–17, 10 fellowships with partial tuition reimbursements (averaging $8,448 per year) were awarded; career-related internships or fieldwork, tuition waivers (partial), and unspecified assistantships also available. Financial award application deadline: 3/1. *Faculty research:* Small business issues, economics. *Unit head:* Dr. Deborah Wells, Associate Dean for Graduate Programs, 402-280-2841, E-mail: deborahwells@creighton.edu. *Application contact:* Chris Karasek, Assistant Dean, 402-280-2829, Fax: 402-280-2172, E-mail: chriskarasek@creighton.edu.
Website: http://business.creighton.edu

Culver-Stockton College, MBA Program, Canton, MO 63435-1299. Offers accounting and finance (MBA).

Daemen College, Department of Accounting/Information Systems, Amherst, NY 14226-3592. Offers global business (MS), including accounting, global business, management information systems, marketing. *Program availability:* Part-time, evening/weekend. *Degree requirements:* For master's, minimum GPA of 3.0. *Entrance requirements:* For master's, GMAT if undergraduate GPA is less than 3.0, 2 letters of recommendation; goal statement; transcripts; demonstration of satisfactory oral and written English. Additional exam requirements/recommendations for international students: Required—TOEFL (minimum score 500 paper-based; 63 iBT), IELTS (minimum score 5.5). Electronic applications accepted. *Faculty research:* Internationalization of small business, cultural influences on business practices, international human resource practices.

Dallas Baptist University, College of Business, Business Administration Program, Dallas, TX 75211-9299. Offers accounting (MBA); business communication (MBA); conflict resolution management (MBA); entrepreneurship (MBA); finance (MBA); health care management (MBA); international business (MBA); leading the non-profit organization (MBA); management (MBA); management information systems (MBA); marketing (MBA); project management (MBA); technology and engineering management (MBA). *Accreditation:* ACBSP. *Program availability:* Part-time, evening/weekend, 100% online, blended/hybrid learning. *Application deadline:* Applications are processed on a rolling basis. Application fee: $25. Electronic applications accepted. Application fee is waived when completed online. *Expenses: Tuition:* Full-time $15,408; part-time $856 per credit hour. *Required fees:* $400 per semester. Tuition and fees vary according to course load and degree level. *Unit head:* Dr. Sandra Reid, Chair of Graduate Business Programs, 214-333-5280, E-mail: sandra@dbu.edu. *Application contact:* Bobby Soto, Director of Admissions, 214-333-5242, E-mail: graduate@dbu.edu.
Website: http://www3.dbu.edu/graduate/mba.asp

Dallas Baptist University, Professional Development Program, Dallas, TX 75211-9299. Offers accounting (MA); church leadership (MA); communication (MA); counseling (MA); criminal justice (MA); English as a second language (MA); finance (MA); higher education (MA); leadership studies (MA); management (MA); management information systems (MA); marketing (MA); missions (MA); professional life coaching (MA); training and development (MA). *Program availability:* Part-time, evening/weekend, 100% online, blended/hybrid learning. *Application deadline:* Applications are processed on a rolling basis. Application fee: $25. Electronic applications accepted. Application fee is waived when completed online. *Expenses: Tuition:* Full-time $15,408; part-time $856 per credit hour. *Required fees:* $400 per semester. Tuition and fees vary according to course load and degree level. *Unit head:* Jared Ingram, Director, 214-333-5584, E-mail: jaredi@dbu.edu. *Application contact:* Bobby Soto, Director of Admissions, 214-333-5242, E-mail: graduate@dbu.edu.
Website: http://www3.dbu.edu/graduate/mapd.asp

Davenport University, Sneden Graduate School, Grand Rapids, MI 49512. Offers accounting (MBA); business administration (EMBA); finance (MBA); health care management (MBA); human resources (MBA); information assurance (MS); public health (MPH); strategic management (MBA). *Program availability:* Evening/weekend. *Entrance requirements:* For master's, GMAT, minimum undergraduate GPA of 2.75. Additional exam requirements/recommendations for international students: Required—TOEFL. Electronic applications accepted. *Faculty research:* Leadership, management, marketing, organizational culture.

Delaware Valley University, MBA Program, Doylestown, PA 18901-2697. Offers accounting (MBA); entrepreneurship (MBA); finance (MBA); food and agribusiness (MBA); general business (MBA); global executive leadership (MBA); human resource management (MBA); supply chain management (MBA). *Program availability:* Part-time, evening/weekend, online learning. *Entrance requirements:* For master's, minimum undergraduate GPA of 3.0. Electronic applications accepted. *Expenses:* Contact institution.

Delta State University, Graduate Programs, College of Business, Division of Accounting, Computer Information Systems, and Finance, Cleveland, MS 38733-0001. Offers accountancy (MPA).

DePaul University, Kellstadt Graduate School of Business, Chicago, IL 60604. Offers accountancy (M Acc, MS, MSA); applied economics (MBA); banking (MBA); behavioral finance (MBA); brand and product management (MBA); business development (MBA); business information technology (MS); business strategy and decision-making (MBA); computational finance (MS); consumer insights (MBA); corporate finance (MBA); economic policy analysis (MS); entrepreneurship (MBA, MS); finance (MBA, MS); financial analysis (MBA); general business (MBA); health sector management (MBA); hospitality leadership (MBA); hospitality leadership and operational performance (MS); human resource management (MBA); human resources (MS); investment management (MBA); leadership and change management (MBA); management accounting (MBA); marketing (MBA, MS); marketing analysis (MS); marketing strategy and planning (MBA); operations management (MBA); organizational diversity (MBA); real estate (MS); real estate finance and investment (MBA); revenue management (MBA); sports management (MBA); strategic global marketing (MBA); strategy, execution and valuation (MBA); sustainable management (MBA, MS); taxation (MS); wealth management (MS); JD/MBA. *Accreditation:* AACSB. *Program availability:* Part-time, evening/weekend, online learning. *Entrance requirements:* For master's, GMAT, 2 letters of recommendation, resume, essay, official transcripts. Additional exam requirements/recommendations for international students: Required—TOEFL (minimum score 550 paper-based; 80 iBT). Electronic applications accepted. *Expenses:* Contact institution.

DeSales University, Division of Business, Center Valley, PA 18034-9568. Offers accounting (MBA); computer information systems (MBA); finance (MBA); health care systems management (MBA); human resources management (MBA); management (MBA); marketing (MBA); project management (MBA); self-design (MBA); supply chain management (MBA); DNP/MBA; MSN/MBA. *Accreditation:* ACBSP. *Program availability:* Part-time, evening/weekend, 100% online, blended/hybrid learning. *Faculty:* 12 full-time (4 women), 29 part-time/adjunct (5 women). *Students:* 73 full-time (38 women), 323 part-time (163 women); includes 59 minority (16 Black or African American, non-Hispanic/Latino; 23 Asian, non-Hispanic/Latino; 16 Hispanic/Latino; 4 Two or more races, non-Hispanic/Latino). Average age 37. 157 applicants, 87% accepted, 128 enrolled. In 2016, 115 master's awarded. *Entrance requirements:* For master's, GMAT (waived if undergraduate GPA is 3.0 or better), minimum GPA of 3.0 in undergraduate work, literacy in basic software, background or interest in the field of study, personal statement, 2 years of work experience. Additional exam requirements/recommendations for international students: Required—TOEFL. *Application deadline:* Applications are processed on a rolling basis. Application fee: $50. Electronic applications accepted. *Expenses:* Contact institution. *Financial support:* Applicants required to submit FAFSA. *Faculty research:* Quality improvement, executive development, productivity, cross-cultural managerial differences, leadership. *Unit head:* Dr. David M. Gilfoil, Director, MBA Program, 610-282-1100 Ext. 1828, Fax: 610-282-2869, E-mail: david.gilfoil@desales.edu. *Application contact:* Julia Ferraro, Director of Graduate Admissions, 610-282-1100 Ext. 1768, E-mail: gradadmissions@desales.edu.

DeVry University–Folsom Campus, Graduate Programs, Folsom, CA 95630. Offers accounting (M Acc); accounting and financial management (MAFM); business administration (MBA); curriculum leadership (M Ed); educational leadership (M Ed); educational technology (M Ed); higher education leadership (M Ed); human resource management (MHRM); information systems management (MISM); network and communications management (MNCM); project management (MPM); public administration (MPA).

Dominican College, MBA Program, Orangeburg, NY 10962-1210. Offers accounting (MBA); healthcare management (MBA); management (MBA). *Program availability:* Part-time, evening/weekend. *Faculty:* 9 full-time (2 women), 7 part-time/adjunct (1 woman). *Students:* 10 full-time (6 women), 22 part-time (11 women); includes 16 minority (9 Black or African American, non-Hispanic/Latino; 3 Asian, non-Hispanic/Latino; 3 Hispanic/Latino; 1 Two or more races, non-Hispanic/Latino), 1 international. In 2016, 16 master's awarded. *Entrance requirements:* For master's, GMAT, 2 letters of recommendation. Additional exam requirements/recommendations for international students: Required—TOEFL (minimum score 550 paper-based; 90 iBT). *Application deadline:* Applications are processed on a rolling basis. Application fee: $50. Electronic applications accepted. *Expenses:* Contact institution. *Financial support:* Application deadline: 2/1; applicants required to submit FAFSA. *Unit head:* Ken Mias, MBA Director, 845-848-4102, E-mail: ken.mias@dc.edu. *Application contact:* Christina Lifshey, Assistant Director of Graduate Admissions, 845-848-7908, Fax: 845-365-3150, E-mail: admissions@dc.edu.

Dominican University, Brennan School of Business, River Forest, IL 60305-1099. Offers MBA, MSA, JD/MBA, MBA/MLIS, MBA/MSW. JD/MBA offered jointly with John Marshall Law School. *Accreditation:* AACSB. *Program availability:* Part-time, evening/weekend, 100% online, blended/hybrid learning. *Faculty:* 22 full-time (9 women), 13 part-time/adjunct (5 women). *Students:* 91 full-time (71 women), 72 part-time (36 women); includes 25 minority (7 Black or African American, non-Hispanic/Latino; 1 American Indian or Alaska Native, non-Hispanic/Latino; 9 Asian, non-Hispanic/Latino; 7 Hispanic/Latino; 1 Native Hawaiian or other Pacific Islander, non-Hispanic/Latino), 24 international. Average age 29. 84 applicants, 93% accepted, 47 enrolled. In 2016, 85 master's awarded. *Entrance requirements:* For master's, GMAT. Additional exam requirements/recommendations for international students: Required—TOEFL (minimum score 550 paper-based; 79 iBT); Recommended—IELTS (minimum score 6). *Application deadline:* Applications are processed on a rolling basis. Application fee: $25. Electronic applications accepted. *Expenses:* $950 per credit hour. *Financial support:* Research assistantships, career-related internships or fieldwork, scholarships/grants, tuition waivers (partial), and unspecified assistantships available. Financial award application deadline: 3/1; financial award applicants required to submit FAFSA. *Faculty research:* Entrepreneurship, small business finance, business ethics, marketing strategy. *Unit head:* Dr. Roberto Curci, Dean, 708-524-6321, Fax: 708-524-6939, E-mail: rcurci@dom.edu. *Application contact:* Dr. Kathleen Odell, Associate Dean, Brennan School of Business, 708-524-6507, Fax: 708-524-6939, E-mail: mquilty@dom.edu.
Website: http://business.dom.edu/

Drexel University, LeBow College of Business, Department of Accounting, Program in Accounting, Philadelphia, PA 19104-2875. Offers MS. *Faculty:* 17 full-time (8 women), 4 part-time/adjunct (1 woman). *Students:* 70 full-time (49 women), 8 part-time (5 women);

includes 2 minority (both Hispanic/Latino), 66 international. Average age 24. In 2016, 56 master's awarded. *Entrance requirements:* For master's, GMAT, minimum GPA of 2.75. Additional exam requirements/recommendations for international students: Required—TOEFL. *Application deadline:* For fall admission, 8/21 for domestic students. Applications are processed on a rolling basis. Application fee: $50. Electronic applications accepted. *Expenses: Tuition:* Full-time $32,184; part-time $1192 per credit hour. *Required fees:* $280. Tuition and fees vary according to campus/location and program. *Financial support:* Teaching assistantships available. Financial award application deadline: 2/1. *Total annual research expenditures:* $23,152. *Unit head:* Dr. Michael J. Gombola, Interim Head, 215-895-2116. *Application contact:* Director of Graduate Admissions, 215-895-6700, Fax: 215-895-5939, E-mail: enroll@drexel.edu.

Drexel University, LeBow College of Business, Program in Business Administration, Philadelphia, PA 19104-2875. Offers business administration (MBA, PhD, APC), including accounting (MBA, PhD), decision sciences (PhD), economics (MBA, PhD), finance (MBA, PhD), legal studies (MBA), management (MBA), marketing (MBA, PhD), organizational sciences (PhD), quantitative methods (MBA), strategic management (PhD). *Accreditation:* AACSB. *Program availability:* Part-time, evening/weekend, online learning. *Faculty:* 88 full-time (19 women), 11 part-time/adjunct (2 women). *Students:* 153 full-time (70 women), 388 part-time (168 women); includes 107 minority (31 Black or African American, non-Hispanic/Latino; 1 American Indian or Alaska Native, non-Hispanic/Latino; 48 Asian, non-Hispanic/Latino; 16 Hispanic/Latino; 11 Two or more races, non-Hispanic/Latino), 95 international. Average age 33. In 2016, 174 master's, 8 doctorates, 1 other advanced degree awarded. Terminal master's awarded for partial completion of doctoral program. *Entrance requirements:* For master's, GMAT, minimum GPA of 2.75; for doctorate, GMAT. Additional exam requirements/recommendations for international students: Required—TOEFL. *Application deadline:* For fall admission, 8/21 for domestic students; for spring admission, 3/5 for domestic students. Applications are processed on a rolling basis. Application fee: $50. Electronic applications accepted. *Expenses: Tuition:* Full-time $32,184; part-time $1192 per credit hour. *Required fees:* $280. Tuition and fees vary according to campus/location and program. *Financial support:* Research assistantships, teaching assistantships, career-related internships or fieldwork, and unspecified assistantships available. Financial award application deadline: 2/1. *Faculty research:* Decision support systems, individual and group behavior, operations research, techniques and strategy. *Unit head:* Dr. Thomas Wieckowski, Director of Master's Programs in Business, 215-895-1791, Fax: 215-895-1012. *Application contact:* Director of Graduate Admissions, 215-895-6700, Fax: 215-895-5939, E-mail: enroll@drexel.edu.

Duke University, The Fuqua School of Business, PhD Program, Durham, NC 27708-0586. Offers accounting (PhD); decision sciences (PhD); finance (PhD); management and organizations (PhD); marketing (PhD); operations management (PhD); strategy (PhD). *Faculty:* 100 full-time (19 women). *Students:* 77 full-time (27 women); includes 9 minority (1 Black or African American, non-Hispanic/Latino; 7 Asian, non-Hispanic/Latino; 1 Hispanic/Latino), 46 international. 561 applicants, 7% accepted, 14 enrolled. In 2016, 15 doctorates awarded. *Degree requirements:* For doctorate, thesis/dissertation, major field requirement (exam or major paper, depending upon the area). *Entrance requirements:* For doctorate, GMAT or GRE, transcripts, essays, recommendation letters, statement of purpose. Additional exam requirements/recommendations for international students: Required—TOEFL (minimum score 577 paper-based; 90 iBT), IELTS (minimum score 7). *Application deadline:* For fall admission, 12/31 priority date for domestic and international students. Application fee: $85. Electronic applications accepted. *Expenses:* Contact institution. *Financial support:* In 2016–17, 77 students received support, including 70 fellowships with full tuition reimbursements available (averaging $28,200 per year), 63 research assistantships with full tuition reimbursements available (averaging $7,000 per year); institutionally sponsored loans, scholarships/grants, and tuition waivers (full) also available. Financial award applicants required to submit FAFSA. *Unit head:* William Boulding, Dean, 919-660-7822, Fax: 919-684-8742, E-mail: bb1@duke.edu. *Application contact:* Qi Chen, Director of Graduate Studies, 919-660-7753, Fax: 919-660-7971, E-mail: qc2@duke.edu.

Duquesne University, Palumbo-Donahue School of Business, Pittsburgh, PA 15282-0001. Offers accounting (M Acc); finance (MBA); information systems management (MSISM); management (MBA, MS); marketing (MBA); sports business (MS); sustainability (MBA); JD/MBA; MBA/M Acc; MBA/MA; MBA/MES; MBA/MHMS; MSISM/MBA; Pharm D/MBA. *Accreditation:* AACSB. *Program availability:* Part-time, evening/weekend, 100% online, minimal on-campus study. *Faculty:* 59 full-time (23 women), 25 part-time/adjunct (6 women). *Students:* 92 full-time (43 women), 176 part-time (71 women); includes 20 minority (9 Black or African American, non-Hispanic/Latino; 8 Asian, non-Hispanic/Latino; 2 Hispanic/Latino; 1 Two or more races, non-Hispanic/Latino), 35 international. Average age 28. 272 applicants, 86% accepted, 137 enrolled. In 2016, 137 master's awarded. *Entrance requirements:* For master's, GMAT or GRE, undergraduate transcripts, 2 letters of recommendation, current resume, personal statement. Additional exam requirements/recommendations for international students: Required—TOEFL (minimum score 577 paper-based; 90 iBT), IELTS (minimum score 7). *Application deadline:* For fall admission, 7/1 priority date for domestic and international students; for spring admission, 12/1 for domestic and international students; for summer admission, 4/1 for domestic and international students. Applications are processed on a rolling basis. Application fee: $0. Electronic applications accepted. *Expenses:* Contact institution. *Financial support:* In 2016–17, 211 students received support, including 12 fellowships with partial tuition reimbursements available (averaging $14,200 per year), 20 research assistantships with partial tuition reimbursements available (averaging $22,212 per year); career-related internships or fieldwork, scholarships/grants, and unspecified assistantships also available. Support available to part-time students. Financial award application deadline: 7/1; financial award applicants required to submit FAFSA. *Faculty research:* Investment management, business ethics, technology management, supply chain management, entrepreneurship. *Unit head:* Dr. Karen Donovan, Associate Dean of Graduate Programs and Executive Education, 412-396-6276, Fax: 412-396-1726, E-mail: donovan6@duq.edu. *Application contact:* Jeff Jewett, Director of Admissions and Enrollment Management, 412-396-6244, Fax: 412-396-1726, E-mail: decrostam@duq.edu.
Website: http://www.duq.edu/business/grad

East Carolina University, Graduate School, College of Business, Department of Accounting, Greenville, NC 27858-4353. Offers MSA. *Students:* 76 full-time (29 women), 10 part-time (6 women); includes 15 minority (7 Black or African American, non-Hispanic/Latino; 2 American Indian or Alaska Native, non-Hispanic/Latino; 1 Asian, non-Hispanic/Latino; 3 Hispanic/Latino; 2 Two or more races, non-Hispanic/Latino), 3 international. Average age 26. 82 applicants, 80% accepted, 42 enrolled. In 2016, 33 master's awarded. *Unit head:* Dr. Dan L. Schisler, Chair, 252-328-6055, E-mail: gradbus@ecu.edu.
Website: http://www.ecu.edu/cs-bus/acct/index.cfm

Eastern Connecticut State University, School of Education and Professional Studies/Graduate Division, Program in Accounting, Willimantic, CT 06226-2295. Offers MS. *Accreditation:* NCATE. *Program availability:* Part-time, evening/weekend. *Faculty:* 5 full-time (3 women), 3 part-time/adjunct (0 women). *Students:* 10 full-time (7 women), 8 part-time (4 women); includes 8 minority (2 Black or African American, non-Hispanic/Latino; 6 Asian, non-Hispanic/Latino). Average age 31. 14 applicants, 50% accepted, 7 enrolled. In 2016, 3 master's awarded. *Entrance requirements:* For master's, minimum GPA of 2.7, bachelor's degree from accredited institution. Additional exam requirements/recommendations for international students: Required—TOEFL (minimum score 550 paper-based; 79 iBT); Recommended—IELTS (minimum score 6). *Application deadline:* For fall admission, 7/6 priority date for domestic and international students; for spring admission, 11/3 priority date for domestic and international students. Applications are processed on a rolling basis. Application fee: $50. Electronic applications accepted. *Expenses: Tuition, area resident:* Full-time $11,781; part-time $560 per credit. Tuition, state resident: full-time $15,031; part-time $568 per credit. Tuition, nonresident: full-time $24,581; part-time $568 per credit. *Required fees:* $40 per semester. Full-time tuition and fees vary according to course level, course load and reciprocity agreements. *Financial support:* Research assistantships, career-related internships or fieldwork, institutionally sponsored loans, scholarships/grants, and unspecified assistantships available. Financial award application deadline: 3/1; financial award applicants required to submit FAFSA. *Unit head:* Dr. Moh'd RuJoub, Advisor, 860-465-5284, Fax: 860-465-5099, E-mail: rujoubm@easternct.edu. *Application contact:* Paula Goyette, Graduate Division, School of Education and Professional Studies, 860-465-5292, Fax: 860-465-4538, E-mail: graduateadmissions@easternct.edu.

Eastern Illinois University, Graduate School, Lumpkin College of Business and Applied Sciences, Program in Business Administration, Charleston, IL 61920. Offers accountancy (MBA); applied management (MBA); business administration (MBA); research (MBA). *Accreditation:* AACSB. *Program availability:* Part-time, evening/weekend. *Entrance requirements:* For master's, GMAT or GRE. Additional exam requirements/recommendations for international students: Required—TOEFL (minimum score 500 paper-based; 61 iBT), IELTS (minimum score 6). Electronic applications accepted.

Eastern Michigan University, Graduate School, College of Business, Department of Accounting and Finance, Ypsilanti, MI 48197. Offers accounting (MS); accounting information systems (MS). *Program availability:* Part-time, evening/weekend, online learning. *Faculty:* 25 full-time (10 women). *Students:* 51 full-time (22 women), 47 part-time (26 women); includes 17 minority (4 Black or African American, non-Hispanic/Latino; 1 American Indian or Alaska Native, non-Hispanic/Latino; 6 Asian, non-Hispanic/Latino; 5 Hispanic/Latino; 1 Two or more races, non-Hispanic/Latino), 13 international. Average age 28. 73 applicants, 63% accepted, 30 enrolled. In 2016, 45 master's awarded. *Entrance requirements:* For master's, GMAT. Additional exam requirements/recommendations for international students: Required—TOEFL. *Application deadline:* Applications are processed on a rolling basis. Application fee: $45. *Financial support:* Fellowships, research assistantships with full tuition reimbursements, teaching assistantships with full tuition reimbursements, career-related internships or fieldwork, Federal Work-Study, institutionally sponsored loans, scholarships/grants, tuition waivers (partial), and unspecified assistantships available. Support available to part-time students. Financial award applicants required to submit FAFSA. *Unit head:* Dr. Zafar Khan, Department Head, 734-487-3320, Fax: 734-487-0806, E-mail: zafar.khan@emich.edu. *Application contact:* Dr. Phil Lewis, Director, 734-487-3320, Fax: 734-482-0806, E-mail: cob.graduate@emich.edu.
Website: http://www.accfin.emich.edu

East Tennessee State University, School of Graduate Studies, College of Business and Technology, Department of Accountancy, Johnson City, TN 37614. Offers M Acc. *Accreditation:* AACSB. *Program availability:* Part-time, evening/weekend. *Degree requirements:* For master's, comprehensive exam, capstone, professional accounting experience. *Entrance requirements:* For master's, GMAT, minimum GPA of 2.5. Additional exam requirements/recommendations for international students: Required—TOEFL (minimum score 550 paper-based; 79 iBT). Electronic applications accepted. *Faculty research:* Smaller firm practice management, personal financial planning, accounting education, taxation issues.

Edgewood College, Program in Business, Madison, WI 53711-1997. Offers accountancy (MS); sustainability leadership (MBA). *Accreditation:* ACBSP. *Program availability:* Part-time, evening/weekend. *Students:* 38 full-time (22 women), 109 part-time (61 women); includes 13 minority (2 Black or African American, non-Hispanic/Latino; 4 Asian, non-Hispanic/Latino; 3 Hispanic/Latino; 1 Native Hawaiian or other Pacific Islander, non-Hispanic/Latino; 3 Two or more races, non-Hispanic/Latino), 13 international. Average age 33. In 2016, 50 master's awarded. *Entrance requirements:* For master's, GMAT (minimum score 430), minimum GPA of 2.75, 2 letters of recommendation. Additional exam requirements/recommendations for international students: Required—TOEFL. *Application deadline:* For fall admission, 8/15 for domestic students, 5/1 for international students; for spring admission, 1/8 for domestic students, 11/1 for international students. Applications are processed on a rolling basis. Application fee: $30. Electronic applications accepted. *Expenses: Tuition:* Part-time $898 per credit. Tuition and fees vary according to course load. *Financial support:* Career-related internships or fieldwork and scholarships/grants available. *Unit head:* Dr. Stevie Watson, Dean, 608-663-2224, Fax: 608-663-3291, E-mail: swatson@edgewood.edu. *Application contact:* Joann Eastman, Admissions Counselor, 608-663-3250, Fax: 608-663-2214, E-mail: gps@edgewood.edu.
Website: https://www.edgewood.edu/academics/schools/school-of-business

Elms College, Division of Business, Chicopee, MA 01013-2839. Offers accounting (MBA); financial planning (MBA); healthcare leadership (MBA); management (MBA). *Program availability:* Part-time, evening/weekend. *Faculty:* 4 full-time (all women), 6 part-time/adjunct (3 women). *Students:* 51 part-time (32 women); includes 10 minority (4 Black or African American, non-Hispanic/Latino; 1 Asian, non-Hispanic/Latino; 5 Hispanic/Latino). Average age 34. 26 applicants, 100% accepted, 22 enrolled. In 2016, 24 master's awarded. *Entrance requirements:* For master's, minimum GPA of 3.0. *Application deadline:* Applications are processed on a rolling basis. Application fee: $30. *Expenses: Tuition:* Full-time $13,392. *Required fees:* $200. *Unit head:* Dr. David Kimball, Chair, Division of Business, 413-265-2300, E-mail: kimballd@elms.edu. *Application contact:* Dr. Elizabeth Teahan Hukowicz, Dean, School of Graduate and Professional Studies, 413-265-2360 Ext. 238, Fax: 413-265-2459, E-mail: hukowiczе@elms.edu.

Emory University, Goizueta Business School, Doctoral Program in Business, Atlanta, GA 30322. Offers accounting (PhD); finance (PhD); information systems and operations management (PhD); marketing (PhD); organization and management (PhD). *Faculty:* 59 full-time (16 women). *Students:* 40 full-time (16 women); includes 6 minority (1 Black or African American, non-Hispanic/Latino; 4 Asian, non-Hispanic/Latino; 1 Hispanic/Latino), 26 international. Average age 28. 145 applicants, 9% accepted, 4 enrolled. In 2016, 5 doctorates awarded. *Degree requirements:* For doctorate, comprehensive exam, thesis/dissertation. *Entrance requirements:* For doctorate, GMAT (strongly preferred) or GRE. Additional exam requirements/recommendations for international students: Required—TOEFL (minimum score 600 paper-based; 100 iBT). *Application deadline:* For fall admission, 1/3 priority date for domestic and international students. Application fee: $75. Electronic applications accepted. *Expenses:* $708 fees per year; 100% of tuition covered by scholarship. *Financial support:* In 2016–17, 34 students received support, including 6 fellowships (averaging $3,333 per year); scholarships/

grants and health care benefits also available. Financial award application deadline: 1/3. *Faculty research:* Financial and managerial accounting, asset pricing strategy and organizational behavior, information technology marketing analytics and consumer behavior. *Unit head:* Dr. Anand Swaminathan, Associate Dean, Doctoral Program, 404-727-2306, Fax: 404-727-5337, E-mail: anand.swaminathan@emory.edu. *Application contact:* Allison Gilmore, Director of Admissions and Student Services, 404-727-6353, Fax: 404-727-5337, E-mail: allison.gilmore@emory.edu.

Emory University, Goizueta Business School, Full Time MBA Program, Atlanta, GA 30322. Offers accounting (MBA); alternative investments (MBA); business process consulting (MBA); business technology management (MBA); capital markets (MBA); corporate finance (MBA); customer relationship management (MBA); decision analytics (MBA); entrepreneurship (MBA); finance (MBA); global management (MBA); investment banking (MBA); management consulting (MBA); marketing (MBA); marketing analytics (MBA); marketing consulting (MBA); operations management (MBA); organization and management (MBA); product and brand management (MBA); real estate (MBA); social enterprise (MBA); strategy consulting (MBA). *Accreditation:* AACSB. *Faculty:* 72 full-time (17 women), 18 part-time/adjunct (5 women). *Students:* 350 full-time (101 women); includes 77 minority (21 Black or African American, non-Hispanic/Latino; 3 American Indian or Alaska Native, non-Hispanic/Latino; 32 Asian, non-Hispanic/Latino; 15 Hispanic/Latino; 2 Native Hawaiian or other Pacific Islander, non-Hispanic/Latino; 4 Two or more races, non-Hispanic/Latino), 117 international. Average age 29. 1,434 applicants, 31% accepted, 181 enrolled. In 2016, 182 master's awarded. *Degree requirements:* For master's, 1 leadership course; 2 mid-semester module programs; 2 global components. *Entrance requirements:* For master's, GMAT/GRE, essays; recommendation letters; undergraduate degree; interview. Additional exam requirements/recommendations for international students: Required—TOEFL (minimum score 100 iBT), IELTS (minimum score 7), PTE (minimum score 68). *Application deadline:* For fall admission, 10/14 priority date for domestic and international students; for winter admission, 11/11 priority date for domestic and international students; for spring admission, 1/4 priority date for domestic students, 1/4 for international students. Application fee: $150. Electronic applications accepted. *Expenses:* $57,580. *Financial support:* In 2016–17, 289 students received support. Career-related internships or fieldwork, institutionally sponsored loans, and scholarships/grants available. Financial award application deadline: 4/1; financial award applicants required to submit FAFSA. *Faculty research:* Social enterprise; micro vs. large business; mobile health data; mutual fund performance; product evaluation. *Unit head:* Brian Mitchell, Associate Dean, 404-727-4824, Fax: 404-712-9648, E-mail: brian.mitchell@emory.edu. *Application contact:* Julie Barefoot, Associate Dean, 404-727-6311, Fax: 404-727-4612, E-mail: mbaadmissions@emory.edu. Website: http://www.goizueta.emory.edu

Emporia State University, Program in Accountancy, Emporia, KS 66801-5415. Offers M Acc. *Program availability:* Part-time, 100% online, blended/hybrid learning. *Faculty:* 30 full-time (5 women). *Students:* 17 full-time (12 women), 22 part-time (13 women); includes 3 minority (1 American Indian or Alaska Native, non-Hispanic/Latino; 2 Hispanic/Latino), 11 international. 20 applicants, 95% accepted, 6 enrolled. In 2016, 11 master's awarded. *Entrance requirements:* For master's, bachelor's degree in accounting. Additional exam requirements/recommendations for international students: Required—TOEFL (minimum score 550 paper-based). *Application deadline:* Applications are processed on a rolling basis. Application fee: $40. Electronic applications accepted. *Expenses:* Tuition, state resident: full-time $5922; part-time $246.75 per credit hour. Tuition, nonresident: full-time $18,414; part-time $767.25 per credit hour. *Required fees:* $1884; $78.50 per credit hour. *Financial support:* In 2016–17, 3 research assistantships with full tuition reimbursements (averaging $7,353 per year), 3 teaching assistantships with full tuition reimbursements (averaging $7,335 per year) were awarded; unspecified assistantships also available. Financial award applicants required to submit FAFSA. *Unit head:* Dr. Shawn Keough, Chair of the Faculty, 620-341-5408, E-mail: skeough@emporia.edu. *Application contact:* April Huddleston, Recruitment and Development Specialist, 800-950-GRAD, Fax: 620-341-5909, E-mail: ahuddles@emporia.edu.

Everest University, Department of Business Administration, Tampa, FL 33614. Offers accounting (MBA); human resources (MBA); international business (MBA). *Program availability:* Part-time, evening/weekend. *Degree requirements:* For master's, thesis optional. *Entrance requirements:* For master's, GMAT or GRE General Test, minimum GPA of 3.0.

Everglades University, Graduate Programs, Program in Business Administration, Boca Raton, FL 33431. Offers accounting for managers (MBA); aviation management (MBA); human resource management (MBA); project management (MBA). *Program availability:* Part-time, evening/weekend, 100% online. *Entrance requirements:* For master's, GMAT (minimum score of 400) or GRE (minimum score of 290), bachelor's or graduate degree from college accredited by an agency recognized by the U.S. Department of Education; minimum cumulative GPA of 2.0 at the baccalaureate level, 3.0 at the master's level. Additional exam requirements/recommendations for international students: Recommended—TOEFL (minimum score 500 paper-based). Electronic applications accepted. *Expenses:* Contact institution.

Fairfield University, Dolan School of Business, Fairfield, CT 06824. Offers accounting (MBA, MS, CAS); business analytics (MS); entrepreneurship (MBA); finance (MBA, MS, CAS); general management (MBA, CAS); global management (MBA); human resource management (MBA, CAS); information systems and business analytics (MBA); marketing (MBA, CAS); taxation (MBA, CAS). *Accreditation:* AACSB. *Program availability:* Part-time, evening/weekend. *Faculty:* 20 full-time (6 women), 4 part-time/adjunct (1 woman). *Students:* 106 full-time (41 women), 57 part-time (26 women); includes 18 minority (4 Black or African American, non-Hispanic/Latino; 1 American Indian or Alaska Native, non-Hispanic/Latino; 4 Asian, non-Hispanic/Latino; 7 Hispanic/Latino; 2 Two or more races, non-Hispanic/Latino), 39 international. Average age 26. 136 applicants, 63% accepted, 35 enrolled. In 2016, 90 master's awarded. *Degree requirements:* For master's, capstone course. *Entrance requirements:* For master's, GMAT (minimum score 500), 2 letters of reference, resume, minimum GPA of 3.0. Additional exam requirements/recommendations for international students: Required—TOEFL (minimum score 550 paper-based; 80 iBT) or IELTS (minimum score 6.5). *Application deadline:* For fall admission, 5/15 for international students; for spring admission, 10/15 for international students. Applications are processed on a rolling basis. Application fee: $60. Electronic applications accepted. *Expenses:* $875 per credit hour. *Financial support:* In 2016–17, 33 students received support. Scholarships/grants and unspecified assistantships available. Financial award applicants required to submit FAFSA. *Faculty research:* International finance, leadership and careers, ethics in accounting, emotions in consumer behavior and organizations, data analytics. *Unit head:* Dr. Donald Gibson, Dean, 203-254-4070, Fax: 203-254-4105, E-mail: dgibson@fairfield.edu. *Application contact:* Marianne Gumpper, Director of Graduate and Continuing Studies Admission, 203-254-4184, Fax: 203-254-4073, E-mail: gradadmis@fairfield.edu.
Website: http://fairfield.edu/mba

Fairleigh Dickinson University, College at Florham, Silberman College of Business, Department of Accounting, Law, and Tax, Program in Accounting, Madison, NJ 07940-1099. Offers MS. *Entrance requirements:* For master's, GMAT.

Fairleigh Dickinson University, Metropolitan Campus, Silberman College of Business, Department of Accounting, Law, and Tax, Program in Accounting, Teaneck, NJ 07666-1914. Offers MBA, MS, Certificate. *Faculty research:* Corporate accounting, legal issues.

Fitchburg State University, Division of Graduate and Continuing Education, Program in Business Administration, Fitchburg, MA 01420-2697. Offers accounting (MBA); human resource management (MBA); management (MBA). *Program availability:* Part-time, evening/weekend, online learning. *Entrance requirements:* Additional exam requirements/recommendations for international students: Required—TOEFL (minimum score 550 paper-based; 79 iBT). Electronic applications accepted. *Expenses:* Tuition, state resident: full-time $2871; part-time $1914 per year. Tuition, nonresident: full-time $2871; part-time $1914 per year. *Required fees:* $3828. Tuition and fees vary according to program.

Florida Agricultural and Mechanical University, Division of Graduate Studies, Research, and Continuing Education, School of Business and Industry, Tallahassee, FL 32307-3200. Offers accounting (MBA); finance (MBA); management information systems (MBA); marketing (MBA). *Accreditation:* ACBSP. *Degree requirements:* For master's, residency. *Entrance requirements:* For master's, GMAT, minimum GPA of 3.0.

Florida Atlantic University, College of Business, School of Accounting, Boca Raton, FL 33431-0991. Offers MAC. *Accreditation:* AACSB. *Program availability:* Part-time, evening/weekend, online learning. *Faculty:* 17 full-time (7 women), 4 part-time/adjunct (2 women). *Students:* 142 full-time (54 women), 457 part-time (264 women); includes 287 minority (79 Black or African American, non-Hispanic/Latino; 32 Asian, non-Hispanic/Latino; 150 Hispanic/Latino; 2 Native Hawaiian or other Pacific Islander, non-Hispanic/Latino; 24 Two or more races, non-Hispanic/Latino), 21 international. Average age 32. 500 applicants, 61% accepted, 238 enrolled. In 2016, 158 master's awarded. *Degree requirements:* For master's, comprehensive exam, thesis optional. *Entrance requirements:* For master's, GMAT with minimum score 500 (preferred) or GRE (minimum score 1000 old test, 153 Verbal, 144 Quantitative, 4 Writing) taken within last 5 years, BS in accounting or equivalent, minimum GPA of 3.0 in last 60 hours of undergraduate study. Additional exam requirements/recommendations for international students: Required—TOEFL (minimum score 600 paper-based; 61 iBT), IELTS (minimum score 6). *Application deadline:* For fall admission, 7/1 priority date for domestic students, 2/15 priority date for international students; for spring admission, 11/1 priority date for domestic students, 7/15 priority date for international students. Applications are processed on a rolling basis. Application fee: $30. *Expenses:* Tuition, state resident: full-time $7392; part-time $369.82 per credit hour. Tuition, nonresident: full-time $19,432; part-time $1024.81 per credit hour. *Financial support:* Fellowships, research assistantships with partial tuition reimbursements, teaching assistantships, career-related internships or fieldwork, Federal Work-Study, institutionally sponsored loans, scholarships/grants, and tuition waivers (partial) available. Support available to part-time students. Financial award application deadline: 3/1. *Faculty research:* Systems and computer applications, accounting theory, information systems. *Unit head:* 561-297-3636, E-mail: soa@fau.edu.
Website: http://business.fau.edu/departments/accounting/index.aspx

Florida Gulf Coast University, Lutgert College of Business, Program in Accounting and Taxation, Fort Myers, FL 33965-6565. Offers MS. *Program availability:* Part-time, evening/weekend. *Faculty:* 58 full-time (23 women), 36 part-time/adjunct (13 women). *Students:* 13 full-time (6 women), 22 part-time (12 women); includes 10 minority (2 Black or African American, non-Hispanic/Latino; 7 Hispanic/Latino; 1 Two or more races, non-Hispanic/Latino). Average age 26. 31 applicants, 71% accepted, 18 enrolled. In 2016, 19 master's awarded. *Degree requirements:* For master's, thesis or alternative. *Entrance requirements:* For master's, GMAT, minimum GPA of 3.0. Additional exam requirements/recommendations for international students: Required—TOEFL (minimum score 550 paper-based). *Application deadline:* For fall admission, 5/1 priority date for domestic students; for spring admission, 9/15 for domestic students. Applications are processed on a rolling basis. Application fee: $30. Electronic applications accepted. *Expenses:* Tuition, state resident: full-time $6721. Tuition, nonresident: full-time $28,170. *Required fees:* $1987. Tuition and fees vary according to course load and degree level. *Financial support:* In 2016–17, 13 students received support. Application deadline: 3/1; applicants required to submit FAFSA. *Faculty research:* Stock petitions, mergers and acquisitions, deferred taxes, fraud and accounting regulations, graphical reporting practices. *Unit head:* Dr. Tanya Benford, Chair, 239-590-7342, Fax: 239-590-7330, E-mail: tbenford@fgcu.edu. *Application contact:* Marisa Ouverson, Director of Enrollment Management, 239-590-7403, Fax: 239-590-7330, E-mail: mouverso@fgcu.edu.

Florida International University, Chapman Graduate School of Business, School of Accounting, Miami, FL 33199. Offers M Acc. *Program availability:* Part-time, evening/weekend. *Faculty:* 26 full-time (9 women), 10 part-time/adjunct (1 woman). *Students:* 98 full-time (53 women), 19 part-time (7 women); includes 105 minority (4 Black or African American, non-Hispanic/Latino; 9 Asian, non-Hispanic/Latino; 88 Hispanic/Latino; 1 Native Hawaiian or other Pacific Islander, non-Hispanic/Latino; 3 Two or more races, non-Hispanic/Latino), 2 international. Average age 27. 242 applicants, 50% accepted, 90 enrolled. In 2016, 153 master's awarded. *Entrance requirements:* For master's, GMAT or GRE, minimum GPA of 3.0 in upper-level coursework. Additional exam requirements/recommendations for international students: Required—TOEFL (minimum score 550 paper-based; 80 iBT) or IELTS (minimum score 6.5). *Application deadline:* For fall admission, 6/1 for domestic students, 4/1 for international students; for spring admission, 10/1 for domestic students, 9/1 for international students. Applications are processed on a rolling basis. Application fee: $30. Electronic applications accepted. *Expenses:* Contact institution. *Financial support:* Institutionally sponsored loans and scholarships/grants available. Financial award application deadline: 3/1; financial award applicants required to submit FAFSA. *Faculty research:* Financial and managerial accounting. *Unit head:* Ruth Ann McEwen, Director, 305-348-2581, E-mail: rmcewen@fiu.edu. *Application contact:* Cynthia Teljeiro, Program Manager, 305-348-7564, E-mail: cteijeir@fiu.edu.

Florida Southern College, Program in Accounting, Lakeland, FL 33801-5698. Offers M Acc. *Program availability:* Part-time, evening/weekend, blended/hybrid learning. *Faculty:* 4 full-time (2 women). *Students:* 27 full-time (15 women), 2 part-time (0 women); includes 7 minority (2 Black or African American, non-Hispanic/Latino; 5 Hispanic/Latino), 2 international. Average age 28. 27 applicants, 70% accepted, 17 enrolled. In 2016, 8 master's awarded. *Entrance requirements:* For master's, GMAT or GRE General Test, letter of reference, resume, personal statement. Additional exam requirements/recommendations for international students: Required—TOEFL (minimum score 550 paper-based, 79 iBT) or IELTS (6.5). *Application deadline:* For fall admission, 6/1 for domestic and international students; for spring admission, 10/1 for domestic and international students. Applications are processed on a rolling basis. Application fee: $30. Electronic applications accepted. *Expenses:* $750 per credit hour tuition, $100 per term fees. *Financial support:* Federal Work-Study and unspecified assistantships available. Financial award applicants required to submit FAFSA. *Unit head:* Dr. Lynn Clements, Director, 863-680-5022, E-mail: lclements@flsouthern.edu. *Application contact:* Jared Welling, Director, Office of Adult and Graduate Education, 863-680-4914, Fax: 863-680-3872, E-mail: jwelling@flsouthern.edu.

Accounting

Florida State University, The Graduate School, College of Business, Tallahassee, FL 32306-1110. Offers accounting (M Acc), including assurance and advisory services, generalist, taxation; business administration (MBA, PhD), including accounting (PhD), finance (PhD), management information systems (PhD), marketing (PhD), organizational behavior and human resources (PhD), risk management and insurance (PhD), strategy (PhD); finance (MS); management information systems (MS); risk management and insurance (MS); JD/MBA; MSW/MBA. *Accreditation:* AACSB. *Program availability:* Part-time, 100% online. *Faculty:* 101 full-time (27 women), 4 part-time/adjunct (2 women). *Students:* 272 full-time (127 women), 351 part-time (133 women); includes 141 minority (45 Black or African American, non-Hispanic/Latino; 2 American Indian or Alaska Native, non-Hispanic/Latino; 20 Asian, non-Hispanic/Latino; 59 Hispanic/Latino; 2 Native Hawaiian or other Pacific Islander, non-Hispanic/Latino; 13 Two or more races, non-Hispanic/Latino), 71 international. Average age 30. 688 applicants, 60% accepted, 273 enrolled. In 2016, 231 master's, 12 doctorates awarded. Terminal master's awarded for partial completion of doctoral program. *Degree requirements:* For doctorate, comprehensive exam, thesis/dissertation. *Entrance requirements:* For master's, GMAT, GRE (for all except MS in finance), work experience (MBA, MS); minimum GPA of 3.0, letters of recommendation; for doctorate, GMAT, GRE (for marketing, organizational behavior, risk management and insurance, management information systems, and human resources only), minimum graduate GPA of 3.5, letters of recommendation. Additional exam requirements/recommendations for international students: Required—TOEFL (minimum score 600 paper-based; 85 iBT); Recommended—IELTS (minimum score 6). *Application deadline:* For fall admission, 6/1 for domestic and international students; for spring admission, 10/1 for domestic and international students; for summer admission, 3/1 for domestic and international students. Applications are processed on a rolling basis. Application fee: $30. Electronic applications accepted. *Expenses:* Contact institution. *Financial support:* In 2016–17, 149 students received support, including 9 fellowships (averaging $1,500 per year), 65 research assistantships with full tuition reimbursements available (averaging $20,000 per year), 75 teaching assistantships with full tuition reimbursements available (averaging $20,000 per year); career-related internships or fieldwork, scholarships/grants, health care benefits, tuition waivers (full and partial), and unspecified assistantships also available. Support available to part-time students. Financial award application deadline: 1/1; financial award applicants required to submit FAFSA. *Faculty research:* Business strategy, marketing, finance, accounting, business analytics. *Total annual research expenditures:* $1.4 million. *Unit head:* Dr. Michael Hartline, Dean, 850-644-4405, Fax: 850-644-0915, E-mail: mhartline@business.fsu.edu. *Application contact:* Jennifer Clark, Director, 850-644-6458, E-mail: gradprograms@business.fsu.edu.
Website: http://business.fsu.edu/

Fontbonne University, Graduate Programs, St. Louis, MO 63105-3098. Offers accounting (MBA, MS); art (MA); art (K-12) (MAT); business (MBA); computer science (MS); deaf education (MA); early intervention in deaf education (MA); education (MA), including autism spectrum disorders, curriculum and instruction, diverse learners, early childhood education, reading, special education; elementary education (MAT); family and consumer sciences (MA), including multidisciplinary health communication studies; fine arts (MFA); instructional design and technology (MS); management and leadership (MM); middle school education (MAT); secondary education (MAT); special education (MAT); speech-language pathology (MS); supply chain management (MS); theatre (MA). *Program availability:* Part-time, evening/weekend, online learning. *Faculty:* 32 full-time (24 women), 43 part-time/adjunct (26 women). *Students:* 456 full-time (313 women), 102 part-time (77 women); includes 138 minority (118 Black or African American, non-Hispanic/Latino; 1 American Indian or Alaska Native, non-Hispanic/Latino; 7 Asian, non-Hispanic/Latino; 9 Hispanic/Latino; 3 Two or more races, non-Hispanic/Latino), 37 international. *Degree requirements:* For master's, comprehensive exam (for some programs), thesis (for some programs). *Entrance requirements:* Additional exam requirements/recommendations for international students: Required—TOEFL (minimum score 500 paper-based; 65 iBT). *Application deadline:* For fall admission, 8/1 for international students; for spring admission, 12/1 for international students. Applications are processed on a rolling basis. Application fee: $25 ($30 for international students). Electronic applications accepted. *Expenses: Tuition:* Full-time $8436; part-time $703 per credit hour. *Required fees:* $18 per credit hour. Tuition and fees vary according to course load. *Financial support:* Teaching assistantships with partial tuition reimbursements and scholarships/grants available. Support available to part-time students. Financial award application deadline: 4/1; financial award applicants required to submit FAFSA. *Unit head:* Dr. Carey Adams, Vice President for Academic Affairs, 314-719-3609, E-mail: cadams@fontbonne.edu. *Application contact:* Lauryn Filip, Coordinator, Graduate Admission and Professional Studies, 314-889-4650, E-mail: admissions@fontbonne.edu.
Website: https://www.fontbonne.edu/academics/graduate-programs/

Fordham University, Gabelli School of Business, New York, NY 10023. Offers accounting (MBA, MS); applied statistics and decision-making (MS); business administration (EMBA); business analytics (MS); communications and media management (MBA); electronic business (MBA); entrepreneurship (MBA); finance (MBA); global finance (MS); global sustainability (MBA); healthcare management (MBA); information systems (MBA, MS); investor relations (MS); management (MBA, MS); marketing (MBA); marketing intelligence (MS); media management (MS); nonprofit leadership (MS); quantitative finance (MS); taxation (MS); JD/MBA; MS/MBA. *Accreditation:* AACSB. *Program availability:* Part-time, evening/weekend. *Faculty:* 132 full-time (44 women), 51 part-time/adjunct (7 women). *Students:* 1,117 full-time (668 women), 553 part-time (282 women); includes 207 minority (44 Black or African American, non-Hispanic/Latino; 92 Asian, non-Hispanic/Latino; 69 Hispanic/Latino; 2 Native Hawaiian or other Pacific Islander, non-Hispanic/Latino), 1,088 international. Average age 27. 4,745 applicants, 46% accepted, 752 enrolled. In 2016, 996 master's awarded. Terminal master's awarded for partial completion of doctoral program. *Degree requirements:* For master's, internships (required for MS in quantitative finance, recommended for MBA). *Entrance requirements:* For master's, GMAT/GRE, 2 letters of recommendation, resume, 2 essays, transcripts. Additional exam requirements/recommendations for international students: Required—TOEFL (minimum score 100 iBT), IELTS (minimum score 7). *Application deadline:* For fall admission, 11/15 priority date for domestic and international students; for winter admission, 1/15 priority date for domestic students, 1/1 priority date for international students; for spring admission, 3/1 for domestic and international students; for summer admission, 6/1 for domestic students. Application fee: $130. Electronic applications accepted. *Expenses:* $1,397 per credit. *Financial support:* In 2016–17, 78 students received support. Career-related internships or fieldwork, institutionally sponsored loans, scholarships/grants, and unspecified assistantships available. Support available to part-time students. Financial award application deadline: 6/30; financial award applicants required to submit FAFSA. *Unit head:* Dr. Donna Rapaccioli, Dean, 212-636-6165, Fax: 212-307-1779, E-mail: rapaccioli@fordham.edu. *Application contact:* Lawrence Murray, Senior Assistant Dean of Graduate Admissions and Advising, 212-636-6200, Fax: 212-636-7076, E-mail: admissionsgb@fordham.edu.
Website: http://www.fordham.edu/gabelli

Franklin University, Accounting Program, Columbus, OH 43215-5399. Offers MSA. *Program availability:* Online learning.

Freed-Hardeman University, Program in Business Administration, Henderson, TN 38340-2399. Offers accounting (MBA); corporate responsibility (MBA); leadership (MBA). *Accreditation:* ACBSP. *Program availability:* Part-time, evening/weekend, online learning. *Entrance requirements:* For master's, GMAT. Additional exam requirements/recommendations for international students: Required—TOEFL (minimum score 500 paper-based).

Friends University, Graduate School, Wichita, KS 67213. Offers family therapy (MSFT); global business administration (MBA), including accounting, business law, change management, health care leadership, management information systems, supply chain management and logistics; health care leadership (MHCL); management information systems (MMIS); professional business administration (MBA), including accounting, business law, change management, health care leadership, management information systems, supply chain management and logistics. *Program availability:* Part-time, evening/weekend, online learning. *Degree requirements:* For master's, research project. *Entrance requirements:* For master's, bachelor's degree from accredited institution, official transcripts, interview with program director, letter(s) of recommendation. Additional exam requirements/recommendations for international students: Required—TOEFL (minimum score 560 paper-based). Electronic applications accepted.

George Fox University, College of Business, Newberg, OR 97132-2697. Offers accounting (DBA); finance (MBA); management (DBA); management and leadership (MBA); marketing (DBA); organizational strategy (MBA); strategic human resource management (MBA). MBA offered in Newberg, OR and in Portland, OR. *Accreditation:* ACBSP. *Program availability:* Part-time, evening/weekend, online learning. *Degree requirements:* For master's, capstone project; for doctorate, credit-applied research project. *Entrance requirements:* For master's, resume (5 years of professional experience); 3 professional references; interview; financial e-learning course; official transcripts; for doctorate, GRE or GMAT, resume; personal mission statement; academic research writing sample; official transcript from each college/university attended; three professional references. Additional exam requirements/recommendations for international students: Required—TOEFL (minimum score 577 paper-based; 90 iBT) or IELTS (minimum score 7). Electronic applications accepted. *Expenses:* Contact institution.

George Mason University, School of Business, Program in Accounting, Fairfax, VA 22030. Offers MS, Certificate. *Accreditation:* AACSB. *Faculty:* 20 full-time (7 women), 18 part-time/adjunct (7 women). *Students:* 68 full-time (48 women), 29 part-time (19 women); includes 40 minority (12 Black or African American, non-Hispanic/Latino; 22 Asian, non-Hispanic/Latino; 5 Hispanic/Latino; 1 Two or more races, non-Hispanic/Latino), 17 international. Average age 29. 119 applicants, 79% accepted, 62 enrolled. In 2016, 35 master's awarded. *Entrance requirements:* For master's, GMAT/GRE, resume; official transcripts; 2 letters of recommendation; personal statement; professional essay; interview. Additional exam requirements/recommendations for international students: Required—TOEFL (minimum score 575 paper-based; 88 iBT), IELTS (minimum score 6.5), PTE (minimum score 59). *Application deadline:* For fall admission, 1/15 priority date for domestic students, 3/15 for international students. Application fee: $75 ($80 for international students). Electronic applications accepted. *Expenses:* Contact institution. *Financial support:* In 2016–17, 11 students received support, including 5 research assistantships with tuition reimbursements available (averaging $7,584 per year), 6 teaching assistantships with tuition reimbursements available (averaging $8,553 per year); career-related internships or fieldwork, Federal Work-Study, scholarships/grants, unspecified assistantships, and health care benefits (for full-time research or teaching assistantship recipients) also available. Support available to part-time students. Financial award application deadline: 3/1; financial award applicants required to submit FAFSA. *Faculty research:* Current leading global business issues, including offshore outsourcing, international financial risk, and comparative systems of innovation; business management/practices; emerging technology and generating new business. *Unit head:* JK Aier, Chair, 703-993-4546, Fax: 703-993-1809, E-mail: jaier@gmu.edu. *Application contact:* Mary Hayes Colllins, Program Manager, 703-993-9093, E-mail: mhayesco@gmu.edu.
Website: http://business.gmu.edu/masters-in-accounting/

The George Washington University, School of Business, Department of Accountancy, Washington, DC 20052. Offers M Accy. *Accreditation:* AACSB. *Program availability:* Part-time, evening/weekend. *Faculty:* 18 full-time (7 women). *Students:* 184 full-time (142 women), 45 part-time (25 women); includes 30 minority (10 Black or African American, non-Hispanic/Latino; 9 Asian, non-Hispanic/Latino; 7 Hispanic/Latino; 1 Native Hawaiian or other Pacific Islander, non-Hispanic/Latino; 3 Two or more races, non-Hispanic/Latino), 163 international. Average age 25. 658 applicants, 41% accepted, 108 enrolled. In 2016, 113 master's awarded. *Entrance requirements:* For master's, GMAT. Additional exam requirements/recommendations for international students: Required—TOEFL. *Application deadline:* For fall admission, 4/1 priority date for domestic students; for spring admission, 10/1 for domestic students. Applications are processed on a rolling basis. Application fee: $75. *Financial support:* In 2016–17, 50 students received support. Fellowships, teaching assistantships, career-related internships or fieldwork, Federal Work-Study, and institutionally sponsored loans available. Financial award application deadline: 4/1. *Faculty research:* Management accounting and capital markets, financial accounting and the analytic hierarchy process, ethics and accounting, accounting information systems. *Unit head:* Dr. Angela Gore, Chair, 202-994-6195, E-mail: agore@gwu.edu. *Application contact:* Tatyana I. Kuzina, Administrative Manager, 202-994-4181, Fax: 202-994-5164, E-mail: tkuzina@gwu.edu.
Website: http://business.gwu.edu/about-us/departments/department-of-accountancy/

Georgia College & State University, Graduate School, The J. Whitney Bunting School of Business, Program in Accounting, Milledgeville, GA 31061. Offers M Acc. *Program availability:* Part-time, evening/weekend. *Students:* 17 full-time (7 women), 3 part-time (1 woman); includes 4 minority (3 Black or African American, non-Hispanic/Latino; 1 Hispanic/Latino), 1 international. Average age 26. 15 applicants, 80% accepted, 5 enrolled. In 2016, 36 master's awarded. *Degree requirements:* For master's, minimum GPA of 3.0, complete program within 7 years of start date. *Entrance requirements:* For master's, GRE or GMAT (not required if graduated from AASCB-accredited business school with accounting degree, overall GPA of 3.25, and major GPA of 3.0), transcript, certification of immunization. *Application deadline:* For fall admission, 7/1 priority date for domestic students; for spring admission, 11/1 priority date for domestic students; for summer admission, 4/1 priority date for domestic students. Applications are processed on a rolling basis. Application fee: $40. Electronic applications accepted. *Expenses:* $288 per credit hour in-state, $1,027 out-of-state; $1,990 full-time annual fees. *Financial support:* In 2016–17, 10 students received support. Unspecified assistantships available. Financial award application deadline: 3/1; financial award applicants required to submit FAFSA. *Unit head:* Dr. Dale Young, Dean, School of Business, 478-445-5497, E-mail: dale.younge@gcsu.edu. *Application contact:* Lynn Hanson, Director of Graduate Programs, 478-445-5115, E-mail: lynn.hanson@gcsu.edu.
Website: http://gcsu.edu/business/gradbusiness/macc

Georgia Southern University, Jack N. Averitt College of Graduate Studies, College of Business Administration, Program in Accounting, Statesboro, GA 30460. Offers forensic accounting (M Acc); taxation (M Acc). *Accreditation:* AACSB. *Program availability:* Part-time, evening/weekend. *Students:* 46 full-time (25 women), 58 part-time (38 women); includes 29 minority (22 Black or African American, non-Hispanic/Latino; 1 Asian, non-Hispanic/Latino; 5 Hispanic/Latino; 1 Two or more races, non-Hispanic/Latino), 6 international. Average age 27. 60 applicants, 78% accepted, 39 enrolled. In 2016, 32 master's awarded. *Entrance requirements:* For master's, GMAT. Additional exam requirements/recommendations for international students: Required—TOEFL (minimum score 550 paper-based; 80 iBT), IELTS (minimum score 6). *Application deadline:* For fall admission, 3/1 priority date for domestic and international students; for spring admission, 10/1 priority date for domestic students, 10/1 for international students. Applications are processed on a rolling basis. Application fee: $50. Electronic applications accepted. *Expenses:* Contact institution. *Financial support:* In 2016–17, 21 students received support, including 1 research assistantship with full tuition reimbursement available (averaging $7,750 per year), 1 teaching assistantship with full tuition reimbursement available (averaging $7,750 per year); career-related internships or fieldwork, Federal Work-Study, scholarships/grants, tuition waivers (full), and unspecified assistantships also available. Support available to part-time students. Financial award application deadline: 4/15; financial award applicants required to submit FAFSA. *Faculty research:* Consolidation of fraud in the financial statement, reasons why firms switch auditions for the financial audit, internalization of accounting standards, pedagogy issues in accounting and law courses. *Unit head:* Dr. Timothy Pearson, Graduate Program Director, 912-478-0103, Fax: 912-478-0292, E-mail: tpearson@georgiasouthern.edu. *Application contact:* Jordan Wilburn, Coordinator for Graduate Student Recruitment, 912-478-5767, Fax: 912-478-0740, E-mail: macccoordinator@georgiasouthern.edu.
Website: http://coba.georgiasouthern.edu/soa/graduate/

Georgia State University, J. Mack Robinson College of Business, School of Accountancy, Program in Professional Accountancy, Atlanta, GA 30303. Offers MPA. *Accreditation:* AACSB. *Program availability:* Part-time, evening/weekend. *Entrance requirements:* For master's, GRE or GMAT, transcripts from all institutions attended, resume, essays. Additional exam requirements/recommendations for international students: Required—TOEFL (minimum score 610 paper-based; 101 iBT), IELTS (minimum score 7). *Application deadline:* For fall admission, 5/1 priority date for domestic students, 2/1 priority date for international students; for spring admission, 9/15 priority date for domestic students, 4/1 priority date for international students. Applications are processed on a rolling basis. Application fee: $50. Electronic applications accepted. *Expenses:* Tuition, state resident: full-time $6876; part-time $382 per credit hour. Tuition, nonresident: full-time $22,374; part-time $1243 per credit hour. *Required fees:* $2128; $1064 per term. Part-time tuition and fees vary according to course load and program. *Financial support:* Research assistantships, scholarships/grants, tuition waivers, and unspecified assistantships available. *Unit head:* Dr. Galen R. Sevcik, Director of the School of Accountancy, 404-413-7200, Fax: 404-413-7203. *Application contact:* Toby McChesney, Assistant Dean for Graduate Recruiting and Student Services, 404-413-7167, Fax: 404-413-7162, E-mail: rcbgradadmissions@gsu.edu.
Website: http://robinson.gsu.edu/accountancy/mpa.html

Golden Gate University, Ageno School of Business, San Francisco, CA 94105-2968. Offers accounting (MBA); business administration (EMBA, MBA, PMBA, DBA); business analytics (MS); finance (MBA, MS, Certificate); financial planning (MS, Certificate); healthcare information systems (Certificate); human resource management (MBA, MS); human resources management (Certificate); information systems (MS); information technology (MBA); information technology management (Certificate); integrated marketing and communications (MS, Certificate); international business (MBA); management (MBA); marketing (MBA, MS, Certificate); operations supply chain management (Certificate); psychology (MA, Certificate); public administration (EMPA); public relations (MS, Certificate); technical market analysis (Certificate); JD/MBA. *Program availability:* Part-time, evening/weekend. *Faculty:* 18 full-time (3 women), 117 part-time/adjunct (44 women). *Students:* 458 full-time (254 women), 664 part-time (331 women); includes 346 minority (75 Black or African American, non-Hispanic/Latino; 2 American Indian or Alaska Native, non-Hispanic/Latino; 132 Asian, non-Hispanic/Latino; 105 Hispanic/Latino; 9 Native Hawaiian or other Pacific Islander, non-Hispanic/Latino; 23 Two or more races, non-Hispanic/Latino), 354 international. Average age 34. 905 applicants, 83% accepted, 165 enrolled. In 2016, 350 master's, 2 doctorates awarded. *Degree requirements:* For doctorate, thesis/dissertation, qualifying examination. *Entrance requirements:* For master's, GMAT (for MBA), minimum GPA of 2.5 (MS). Additional exam requirements/recommendations for international students: Required—TOEFL (minimum score 550 paper-based; 79 iBT). *Application deadline:* For fall admission, 5/15 for domestic and international students; for winter admission, 1/15 for domestic and international students; for spring admission, 9/15 for domestic and international students. Applications are processed on a rolling basis. Application fee: $70 ($110 for international students). Electronic applications accepted. *Expenses:* Contact institution. *Financial support:* In 2016–17, 372 students received support. Career-related internships or fieldwork, Federal Work-Study, institutionally sponsored loans, and scholarships/grants available. Support available to part-time students. Financial award applicants required to submit FAFSA. *Unit head:* Dr. Gordon Swartz, Dean, 415-442-7027, Fax: 415-442-6579, E-mail: gswartz@ggu.edu. *Application contact:* Angela Melero, Enrollment Services, 415-442-7800, Fax: 415-442-7807, E-mail: info@ggu.edu.
Website: http://www.ggu.edu/programs/business-and-management

Golden Gate University, School of Accounting, San Francisco, CA 94105-2968. Offers accounting (M Ac, MSA, Graduate Certificate); forensic accounting (M Ac, MSA, Graduate Certificate); taxation (M Ac). *Program availability:* Part-time, evening/weekend. *Faculty:* 4 full-time (1 woman), 46 part-time/adjunct (14 women). *Students:* 121 full-time (88 women), 135 part-time (77 women); includes 68 minority (5 Black or African American, non-Hispanic/Latino; 1 American Indian or Alaska Native, non-Hispanic/Latino; 40 Asian, non-Hispanic/Latino; 20 Hispanic/Latino; 1 Native Hawaiian or other Pacific Islander, non-Hispanic/Latino; 1 Two or more races, non-Hispanic/Latino), 107 international. Average age 32. 128 applicants, 71% accepted, 48 enrolled. In 2016, 80 master's awarded. *Entrance requirements:* For master's, minimum GPA of 3.0. Additional exam requirements/recommendations for international students: Required—TOEFL (minimum score 550 paper-based), IELTS (minimum score 6.5). *Application deadline:* For fall admission, 5/15 for international students; for winter admission, 1/15 for international students; for spring admission, 9/15 for international students. Applications are processed on a rolling basis. Application fee: $70 ($100 for international students). Electronic applications accepted. *Expenses:* Contact institution. *Financial support:* In 2016–17, 38 students received support. Career-related internships or fieldwork, Federal Work-Study, institutionally sponsored loans, and scholarships/grants available. Support available to part-time students. Financial award applicants required to submit FAFSA. *Faculty research:* Forensic accounting, audit, tax, CPA exam. *Unit head:* Fred Sroka, Dean, 415-369-5285, Fax: 415-543-2607. *Application contact:* Angela Melero, Enrollment Services, 415-442-7800, Fax: 415-442-7807, E-mail: info@ggu.edu.

Gonzaga University, School of Business Administration, Spokane, WA 99258. Offers accountancy (M Acc); American Indian entrepreneurship (MBA); business administration (MBA); taxation (MS); JD/M Acc; JD/MBA. *Accreditation:* AACSB. *Program availability:* Part-time, evening/weekend. *Faculty:* 17 full-time (4 women), 14 part-time/adjunct (2 women). *Students:* 80 full-time (32 women), 135 part-time (60 women); includes 37 minority (2 Black or African American, non-Hispanic/Latino; 10 American Indian or Alaska Native, non-Hispanic/Latino; 5 Asian, non-Hispanic/Latino; 10 Hispanic/Latino; 10 Two or more races, non-Hispanic/Latino), 14 international. Average age 29. 252 applicants, 131 enrolled. In 2016, 113 master's awarded. *Degree requirements:* For master's, capstone course. *Entrance requirements:* For master's, GMAT (minimum score 500), essay, two professional recommendations, resume/curriculum vitae, copy of official transcripts from all colleges attended, minimum GPA of 3.0. Additional exam requirements/recommendations for international students: Required—TOEFL (minimum score 570 paper-based, 89 iBT) or IELTS (minimum score 6.5). *Application deadline:* Applications are processed on a rolling basis. Application fee: $50. Electronic applications accepted. *Expenses:* $975 per credit. *Financial support:* In 2016–17, 134 students received support. Scholarships/grants, tuition waivers, and unspecified assistantships available. Support available to part-time students. Financial award applicants required to submit FAFSA. *Unit head:* Dr. Ken Anderson, Interim Dean, 509-313-5991, E-mail: anderson@gem.gonzaga.edu. *Application contact:* Stacey Chatman, Assistant Director for Admissions, 509-313-4622, E-mail: chatman@gonzaga.edu.
Website: http://www.gonzaga.edu/Academics/Colleges-and-Schools/School-of-Business-Administration

Governors State University, College of Business, Program in Accounting, University Park, IL 60484. Offers MS. *Program availability:* Part-time. *Faculty:* 25 full-time (9 women), 30 part-time/adjunct (10 women). *Students:* 17 full-time (9 women), 31 part-time (12 women); includes 22 minority (19 Black or African American, non-Hispanic/Latino; 1 Asian, non-Hispanic/Latino; 2 Hispanic/Latino), 1 international. Average age 39. 59 applicants, 59% accepted, 28 enrolled. In 2016, 15 master's awarded. *Entrance requirements:* Additional exam requirements/recommendations for international students: Required—TOEFL (minimum score 550 paper-based; 80 iBT), IELTS. *Application deadline:* For fall admission, 4/1 for domestic students. Application fee: $50. Electronic applications accepted. *Expenses:* $307 per credit hour; $38 per term or $76 per credit hour fees. *Financial support:* Application deadline: 5/1; applicants required to submit FAFSA. *Unit head:* David Green, Chair of Division of Accounting, Finance, Management and Economics, 708-534-4967, E-mail: dgreen@govst.edu. *Application contact:* Yakeea Daniels, Assistant Vice President for Enrollment Services/Director of Admission, 708-534-4510, E-mail: ydaniels@govst.edu.

The Graduate Center, City University of New York, Graduate Studies, Program in Business, New York, NY 10016-4039. Offers accounting (PhD); behavioral science (PhD); finance (PhD); management planning systems (PhD). *Degree requirements:* For doctorate, thesis/dissertation. *Entrance requirements:* For doctorate, GMAT, writing sample (15 pages). Additional exam requirements/recommendations for international students: Required—TOEFL. Electronic applications accepted.

Grand Canyon University, Colangelo College of Business, Phoenix, AZ 85017-1097. Offers accounting (MBA, MS); business analytics (MS); disaster preparedness and executive fire service leadership (MS); finance (MBA); general management (MBA); health systems management (MBA); information technology management (MS); leadership (MBA, MS); marketing (MBA); organizational leadership and entrepreneurship (MS); project management (MBA); sports business (MBA); strategic human resource management (MBA). *Accreditation:* ACBSP. *Program availability:* Part-time, evening/weekend, online learning. *Faculty:* 8 full-time (3 women), 147 part-time/adjunct (49 women). *Students:* 1 full-time (0 women), 2,121 part-time (1,165 women); includes 341 minority (249 Black or African American, non-Hispanic/Latino; 17 American Indian or Alaska Native, non-Hispanic/Latino; 15 Asian, non-Hispanic/Latino; 29 Hispanic/Latino; 4 Native Hawaiian or other Pacific Islander, non-Hispanic/Latino; 27 Two or more races, non-Hispanic/Latino), 20 international. Average age 38. In 2016, 569 master's awarded. *Entrance requirements:* For master's, equivalent of two years' full-time professional work experience. Additional exam requirements/recommendations for international students: Required—TOEFL (minimum score 575 paper-based; 90 iBT), IELTS (minimum score 7). *Application deadline:* For fall admission, 8/21 for domestic students, 7/2 for international students; for spring admission, 12/24 for domestic students, 11/1 for international students. Applications are processed on a rolling basis. Application fee: $0. Electronic applications accepted. *Financial support:* Federal Work-Study available. Support available to part-time students. Financial award applicants required to submit FAFSA. *Unit head:* Kim Donaldson, Dean, 602-639-6597, E-mail: kdonaldson@gcu.edu. *Application contact:* Matt Tidwell, Enrollment Manager, 602-639-6020, E-mail: mtidwell@gcu.edu.
Website: https://www.gcu.edu/colangelo-college-of-business.php

Grand Valley State University, Seidman College of Business, Program in Accounting, Allendale, MI 49401-9403. Offers MSA. *Accreditation:* AACSB. *Program availability:* Part-time, evening/weekend. *Faculty:* 9 full-time (3 women), 5 part-time/adjunct (1 woman). *Students:* 65 full-time (21 women), 27 part-time (9 women); includes 7 minority (1 Black or African American, non-Hispanic/Latino; 4 Asian, non-Hispanic/Latino; 1 Hispanic/Latino; 1 Two or more races, non-Hispanic/Latino), 5 international. Average age 25. 45 applicants, 82% accepted, 31 enrolled. In 2016, 41 master's awarded. *Degree requirements:* For master's, comprehensive exam. *Entrance requirements:* For master's, GMAT, personal statement. Additional exam requirements/recommendations for international students: Required—TOEFL. *Application deadline:* For fall admission, 8/1 priority date for domestic students, 5/1 priority date for international students; for winter admission, 11/1 priority date for domestic and international students; for spring admission, 4/1 priority date for domestic students, 3/1 priority date for international students. Applications are processed on a rolling basis. Application fee: $30. *Expenses:* $646 per credit hour. *Financial support:* In 2016–17, 25 students received support, including 10 fellowships, 18 research assistantships with full and partial tuition reimbursements available (averaging $4,000 per year); Federal Work-Study, scholarships/grants, and unspecified assistantships also available. Support available to part-time students. Financial award application deadline: 2/15; financial award applicants required to submit FAFSA. *Faculty research:* Public trust, capacity measurement, theoretical capacity, economic order quantity. *Unit head:* Dr. Steve Goldberg, Director, 616-331-7410, Fax: 616-331-7412, E-mail: goldbers@gvsu.edu. *Application contact:* Koleta Moore, Assistant Director, Graduate Business Programs, 616-331-7386, Fax: 616-331-7389, E-mail: moorekol@gvsu.edu.
Website: http://www.gvsu.edu/business/

Harvard University, Harvard Business School, Doctoral Programs in Management, Boston, MA 02163. Offers accounting and management (DBA); business economics (PhD); health policy management (PhD); management (DBA); marketing (DBA); organizational behavior (PhD); science, technology and management (PhD); strategy (DBA); technology and operations management (DBA). *Degree requirements:* For doctorate, comprehensive exam (for some programs), thesis/dissertation. *Entrance requirements:* For doctorate, GRE General Test or GMAT. Additional exam requirements/recommendations for international students: Required—TOEFL.

Accounting

Hawai`i Pacific University, College of Business, Program in Business Administration, Honolulu, HI 96813. Offers accounting (MBA); economics (MBA); finance (MBA); hospitality and tourism management (MBA); human resource management (MBA); information systems (MBA); international business (MBA); management (MBA); marketing (MBA); organizational change and development (MBA). *Program availability:* Part-time, evening/weekend, online learning. *Faculty:* 13 full-time (4 women), 1 part-time/adjunct (0 women). *Students:* 106 full-time (47 women), 33 part-time (13 women); includes 66 minority (5 Black or African American, non-Hispanic/Latino; 1 American Indian or Alaska Native, non-Hispanic/Latino; 23 Asian, non-Hispanic/Latino; 11 Hispanic/Latino; 1 Native Hawaiian or other Pacific Islander, non-Hispanic/Latino; 25 Two or more races, non-Hispanic/Latino), 36 international. Average age 33. 77 applicants, 84% accepted, 44 enrolled. In 2016, 78 master's awarded. *Entrance requirements:* For master's, GMAT or GRE. Additional exam requirements/recommendations for international students: Recommended—TOEFL (minimum score 550 paper-based; 80 iBT), IELTS (minimum score 6), TWE (minimum score 5). *Application deadline:* For fall admission, 2/15 priority date for domestic students; for spring admission, 10/15 priority date for domestic students. Applications are processed on a rolling basis. Application fee: $50. Electronic applications accepted. *Expenses: Tuition:* Full-time $17,190; part-time $955 per credit. *Required fees:* $150; $26 per credit. Tuition and fees vary according to course load and program. *Financial support:* In 2016–17, 27 students received support. Research assistantships, career-related internships or fieldwork, Federal Work-Study, scholarships/grants, tuition waivers, and unspecified assistantships available. Financial award application deadline: 3/1; financial award applicants required to submit FAFSA. *Unit head:* Dr. Warren Wee, Associate Dean/Associate Professor of Accounting, 808-544-9325, E-mail: wwee@hpu.edu. *Application contact:* Danny Lam, Assistant Director of Graduate Admissions, 808-544-1135, E-mail: graduate@hpu.edu.
Website: http://www.hpu.edu/CBA/Graduate/MBA/index.html

HEC Montreal, School of Business Administration, Graduate Diploma Programs in Administration, Program in Professional Accounting, Montréal, QC H3T 2A7, Canada. Offers Graduate Diploma. All courses are given in French. *Students:* 193 full-time (105 women), 63 part-time (27 women). 326 applicants, 72% accepted, 220 enrolled. In 2016, 173 Graduate Diplomas awarded. *Degree requirements:* For Graduate Diploma, one foreign language. *Entrance requirements:* For degree, bachelor's degree in accounting. *Application deadline:* For winter admission, 9/15 for domestic and international students; for spring admission, 2/15 for domestic and international students. Application fee: $86 Canadian dollars. Electronic applications accepted. *Expenses: Tuition, area resident:* Part-time $77.80 Canadian dollars per credit. Tuition, state resident: full-time $2797 Canadian dollars; part-time $240.92 Canadian dollars per credit. Tuition, nonresident: full-time $8673 Canadian dollars; part-time $531.43 Canadian dollars per credit. *International tuition:* $19,131 Canadian dollars full-time. *Required fees:* $1699 Canadian dollars; $40.58 Canadian dollars per credit. $67.32 Canadian dollars per term. Tuition and fees vary according to degree level and program. *Financial support:* In 2016–17, 814 students received support. Research assistantships, teaching assistantships, and scholarships/grants available. Financial award application deadline: 9/2. *Unit head:* Renaud Lachance, Director, 514-340-7165, E-mail: renaud.lachance@hec.ca. *Application contact:* Anny Caron, Administrative Director, 514-340-3598, Fax: 514-340-6411, E-mail: anny.caron@hec.ca.
Website: http://www.hec.ca/programmes/dess/dess-comptabilite-professionnelle-cpa/index.html

HEC Montreal, School of Business Administration, Master of Science Programs in Administration, Program in Management Control, Montréal, QC H3T 2A7, Canada. Offers M Sc. All courses are given in French. *Students:* 7 full-time (4 women), 7 part-time (5 women). 8 applicants. In 2016, 7 master's awarded. *Degree requirements:* For master's, one foreign language, thesis. *Entrance requirements:* For master's, Test de francais international (TFI) with minimum score of 850 (for those who have never studied in French), BBA, undergraduate degree in another field, degree deemed equivalent by program director and minimum GPA of 3.0 on 4.3 scale. *Application deadline:* For fall admission, 3/15 for domestic and international students; for winter admission, 9/15 for domestic and international students. Application fee: $86 Canadian dollars. Electronic applications accepted. *Expenses: Tuition, area resident:* Part-time $77.80 Canadian dollars per credit. Tuition, state resident: full-time $2797 Canadian dollars; part-time $240.92 Canadian dollars per credit. Tuition, nonresident: full-time $8673 Canadian dollars; part-time $531.43 Canadian dollars per credit. *International tuition:* $19,131 Canadian dollars full-time. *Required fees:* $1699 Canadian dollars; $40.58 Canadian dollars per credit. $67.32 Canadian dollars per term. Tuition and fees vary according to degree level and program. *Financial support:* Research assistantships, teaching assistantships, and scholarships/grants available. Financial award application deadline: 9/2. *Unit head:* Dr. Marie-Helene Jobin, Director, 514-340-6283, E-mail: marie-helene.jobin@hec.ca. *Application contact:* Marianne de Moura, Administrative Director, 514-340-7106, Fax: 514-340-6411, E-mail: marianne.de-moura@hec.ca.
Website: http://www.hec.ca/programmes/maitrises/maitrise-controle-de-gestion/index.html

HEC Montreal, School of Business Administration, Master of Science Programs in Administration, Program in Professional Accounting, Montréal, QC H3T 2A7, Canada. Offers M Sc. All courses are given in English. *Students:* 10 full-time (7 women), 6 part-time (3 women). 3 applicants, 100% accepted, 3 enrolled. In 2016, 6 master's awarded. *Degree requirements:* For master's, one foreign language, thesis. *Entrance requirements:* For master's, short graduate program in public accounting from HEC Montreal, minimum GPA of 3.0 on 4.3 scale. *Application deadline:* For fall admission, 3/15 for domestic and international students; for winter admission, 9/15 for domestic and international students. Application fee: $86. Electronic applications accepted. *Expenses: Tuition, area resident:* Part-time $77.80 Canadian dollars per credit. Tuition, state resident: full-time $2797 Canadian dollars; part-time $240.92 Canadian dollars per credit. Tuition, nonresident: full-time $8673 Canadian dollars; part-time $531.43 Canadian dollars per credit. *International tuition:* $19,131 Canadian dollars full-time. *Required fees:* $1699 Canadian dollars; $40.58 Canadian dollars per credit. $67.32 Canadian dollars per term. Tuition and fees vary according to degree level and program. *Financial support:* Research assistantships, teaching assistantships, and scholarships/grants available. Financial award application deadline: 9/2. *Unit head:* Dr. Marie-Helene Jobin, Director, 514-340-6283, E-mail: marie-helene.jobin@hec.ca. *Application contact:* Marianne de Moura, Administrative Director, 514-340-7106, Fax: 514-340-6411, E-mail: marianne.de-moura@hec.ca.
Website: http://www.hec.ca/programmes/maitrises/maitrise-comptabilite-professionnelle/index.html

Hendrix College, Program in Accounting, Conway, AR 72032-3080. Offers MA. *Program availability:* Part-time. *Entrance requirements:* For master's, GMAT. Additional exam requirements/recommendations for international students: Required—TOEFL. *Faculty research:* Meta-analysis, utility regulatory entities.

Herzing University Online, Program in Business Administration, Menomonee Falls, WI 53051. Offers accounting (MBA); business administration (MBA); business management (MBA); healthcare management (MBA); human resources (MBA); marketing (MBA); project management (MBA); technology management (MBA). *Program availability:* Online learning.

Hodges University, Graduate Programs, Naples, FL 34119. Offers accounting (M Acc); business administration (MBA); clinical mental health counseling (MS); health services administration (MS); information systems management (MIS); legal studies (MS); management (MSM). *Program availability:* Part-time, evening/weekend, 100% online, blended/hybrid learning. *Degree requirements:* For master's, comprehensive exam (for some programs), thesis (for some programs). *Entrance requirements:* For master's, essay. Additional exam requirements/recommendations for international students: Recommended—TOEFL. Electronic applications accepted.

Hofstra University, Frank G. Zarb School of Business, Programs in Accounting and Taxation, Hempstead, NY 11549. Offers accounting (MS, Advanced Certificate); business administration (MBA), including accounting, professional accountancy, taxation; taxation (MS, Advanced Certificate). *Program availability:* Part-time, evening/weekend, blended/hybrid learning. *Students:* 177 full-time (100 women), 36 part-time (17 women); includes 23 minority (4 Black or African American, non-Hispanic/Latino; 1 American Indian or Alaska Native, non-Hispanic/Latino; 6 Asian, non-Hispanic/Latino; 9 Hispanic/Latino; 3 Two or more races, non-Hispanic/Latino), 123 international. Average age 25. 437 applicants, 76% accepted, 104 enrolled. In 2016, 133 master's awarded. *Degree requirements:* For master's, capstone course (for MBA), thesis (for MS), minimum GPA of 3.0. *Entrance requirements:* For master's, GMAT/GRE, 2 letters of recommendation, resume, essay. Additional exam requirements/recommendations for international students: Required—TOEFL (minimum score 550 paper-based; 80 iBT); Recommended—IELTS (minimum score 6). *Application deadline:* Applications are processed on a rolling basis. Application fee: $75. Electronic applications accepted. *Expenses:* $1,170 per credit. *Financial support:* In 2016–17, 64 students received support, including 59 fellowships with full and partial tuition reimbursements available (averaging $4,967 per year), 1 research assistantship with full and partial tuition reimbursement available (averaging $5,800 per year); career-related internships or fieldwork, Federal Work-Study, institutionally sponsored loans, scholarships/grants, tuition waivers (full and partial), and unspecified assistantships also available. Support available to part-time students. Financial award applicants required to submit FAFSA. *Faculty research:* Gender discrimination and professional women; auditor-client interaction in accounting; accounting in prisons; the Fourth Amendment and privacy. *Unit head:* Dr. Martha Weisel, Chairperson, 516-463-5655, E-mail: martha.s.weisel@hofstra.edu. *Application contact:* Sunil Samuel, Assistant Vice President of Admissions, 516-463-4723, Fax: 516-463-4664, E-mail: graduateadmission@hofstra.edu.
Website: http://www.hofstra.edu/business/

Holy Family University, Division of Academic Affairs, Philadelphia, PA 19114. Offers accountancy (MS); business administration (MBA); counseling psychology (MS); criminal justice (MA); education (M Ed); educational leadership (Ed D); nursing (MS). *Accreditation:* ACBSP. *Program availability:* Part-time, evening/weekend. *Faculty:* 28 full-time (19 women), 66 part-time/adjunct (36 women). *Students:* 329 full-time (281 women), 458 part-time (327 women); includes 153 minority (83 Black or African American, non-Hispanic/Latino; 1 American Indian or Alaska Native, non-Hispanic/Latino; 27 Asian, non-Hispanic/Latino; 41 Hispanic/Latino; 1 Native Hawaiian or other Pacific Islander, non-Hispanic/Latino), 4 international. Average age 34. 467 applicants, 69% accepted, 262 enrolled. In 2016, 6 master's, 2 doctorates awarded. *Degree requirements:* For master's, comprehensive exam, thesis or alternative; for doctorate, comprehensive exam, thesis/dissertation. *Entrance requirements:* For master's, minimum GPA of 3.0, interview, essay/professional statement, 2 recommendations, current resume, official transcripts of college or university work. Additional exam requirements/recommendations for international students: Required—TOEFL (minimum score 550 paper-based; 79 iBT), IELTS (minimum score 6). *Application deadline:* For fall admission, 7/1 priority date for domestic and international students; for spring admission, 11/1 priority date for domestic and international students; for summer admission, 4/1 priority date for domestic and international students. Applications are processed on a rolling basis. Application fee: $25. Electronic applications accepted. *Expenses:* $9,292 per year. *Financial support:* Available to part-time students. Applicants required to submit FAFSA. *Unit head:* Dr. Michael Markowitz, Vice President of Academic Affairs, 267-341-3286, E-mail: mmarkowitz@holyfamily.edu. *Application contact:* Don Reinmold, Director of Graduate Admissions, 267-341-5001 Ext. 3230, Fax: 215-633-0558, E-mail: dreinmold@holyfamily.edu.

Holy Family University, Graduate and Professional Programs, School of Business Administration, Philadelphia, PA 19114. Offers accountancy (MS); finance (MBA); health care administration (MBA); human resource management (MBA); information systems management (MBA). *Accreditation:* ACBSP. *Program availability:* Part-time, evening/weekend. *Students:* 140 part-time. 58 applicants, 78% accepted, 42 enrolled. In 2016, 44 master's awarded. *Degree requirements:* For master's, comprehensive exam, thesis optional. *Entrance requirements:* For master's, minimum GPA of 3.0, interview, essay/personal statement, current resume, official transcript of all college or university work. Additional exam requirements/recommendations for international students: Required—TOEFL (minimum score 550 paper-based; 79 iBT), IELTS (minimum score 6), PTE (minimum score 54). *Application deadline:* For fall admission, 7/1 priority date for domestic and international students; for winter admission, 1/1 for domestic students; for spring admission, 11/1 priority date for domestic and international students; for summer admission, 4/1 priority date for domestic and international students. Applications are processed on a rolling basis. Application fee: $25. Electronic applications accepted. *Expenses: Tuition:* Part-time $751 per hour. *Required fees:* $140 per semester. One-time fee: $165 part-time. Part-time tuition and fees vary according to degree level and program. *Financial support:* Available to part-time students. Application deadline: 5/1; applicants required to submit FAFSA. *Unit head:* Dr. Barry Dickinson, Dean, 267-341-3440, Fax: 215-637-5937, E-mail: jdickinson@holyfamily.edu. *Application contact:* Gidget Marie Montelibano, Associate Director of Graduate Admissions, 267-341-3558, Fax: 215-637-1478, E-mail: gmontelibano@holyfamily.edu.
Website: http://www.holyfamily.edu/choosing-holy-family-u/academics/schools-of-study/school-of-business-administration

Hood College, Graduate School, Department of Economics and Business Administration, Frederick, MD 21701-8575. Offers accounting (MBA); finance (MBA); human resource management (MBA); information systems (MBA); marketing (MBA); public management (MBA). *Accreditation:* ACBSP. *Program availability:* Part-time, evening/weekend. *Faculty:* 4 full-time, 8 part-time/adjunct. *Students:* 21 full-time (13 women), 106 part-time (60 women); includes 23 minority (12 Black or African American, non-Hispanic/Latino; 4 Asian, non-Hispanic/Latino; 6 Hispanic/Latino; 1 Two or more races, non-Hispanic/Latino), 15 international. Average age 32. 44 applicants, 91% accepted, 25 enrolled. In 2016, 45 master's awarded. *Degree requirements:* For master's, capstone/final research project. *Entrance requirements:* For master's, minimum GPA of 3.0 (or resume and two letters of recommendation), copy of official transcripts, essay. Additional exam requirements/recommendations for international students: Required—TOEFL (minimum score 575 paper-based; 89 iBT), IELTS (minimum score 6.5). *Application deadline:* For fall admission, 8/15 for domestic students, 8/5 for international students; for spring admission, 12/1 for domestic and international students; for summer admission, 5/1 for domestic students, 4/15 for international students. Applications are processed on a rolling basis. Application fee: $35. Electronic applications accepted. *Expenses:* $525 per credit; $110 comprehensive fee per semester. *Financial support:* Tuition waivers (partial) and unspecified assistantships available. Financial award applicants required to submit FAFSA. *Faculty research:* Corporate strategy and sustainable competitive advantages, business ethics, entrepreneurship, investments management, economic development. *Unit head:* April Boulton, Interim Dean of the Graduate School, 301-696-3600, Fax: 301-696-3597, E-mail: gofurther@hood.edu. *Application contact:* Spencer Berk, Assistant Director of Graduate Admissions, 301-696-3604, E-mail: gofurther@hood.edu.

Howard University, School of Business, Graduate Programs in Business, Washington, DC 20059-0002. Offers accounting (MBA); entrepreneurship (MBA); finance (MBA); general management (MBA); human resources management (MBA); information systems (MBA); international business (MBA); marketing (MBA); supply chain management (MBA); JD/MBA. *Accreditation:* AACSB. *Program availability:* Part-time, evening/weekend, online learning. *Entrance requirements:* For master's, GMAT, minimum 1 year post undergraduate work experience, resume, 3 letters of recommendation, advanced college algebra. Additional exam requirements/recommendations for international students: Required—TOEFL. *Faculty research:* Marketing research in multi-ethnic populations, U.S. trade policies and international relations, risk management (finance).

Hunter College of the City University of New York, Graduate School, School of Arts and Sciences, Department of Economics, Program in Accounting, New York, NY 10065-5085. Offers MS. *Students:* 13 full-time (12 women), 19 part-time (8 women); includes 14 minority (3 Black or African American, non-Hispanic/Latino; 9 Asian, non-Hispanic/Latino; 2 Hispanic/Latino), 5 international. Average age 28. 45 applicants, 69% accepted, 19 enrolled. In 2016, 20 master's awarded. *Entrance requirements:* For master's, GMAT, statement of purpose, bachelor's degree, official transcripts, two letters of recommendation. Additional exam requirements/recommendations for international students: Required—TOEFL (minimum score 550 paper-based; 60 iBT). *Application deadline:* For fall admission, 4/1 for domestic students, 2/1 for international students; for spring admission, 11/1 for domestic students, 9/1 for international students. Electronic applications accepted. *Unit head:* Dr. Toshi Mitsudome, Director, 212-772-5430, E-mail: toshiaki.mitsudome@hunter.cuny.edu. *Application contact:* Milena Solo, Graduate Admissions Director, 212-772-4480, E-mail: admissions@hunter.cuny.edu.
Website: http://econ.hunter.cuny.edu/accounting-program/m-s-in-accounting/

IGlobal University, Graduate Programs, Vienna, VA 22182. Offers accounting (MBA); data management and analytics (MSIT); entrepreneurship (MBA); finance (MBA); global business management (MBA); health care management (MBA); hospitality and tourism management (MBA); human resources management (MBA); information technology (MBA); information technology systems and management (MSIT); leadership and management (MBA); project management (MBA); public service and administration (MBA); software design and management (MSIT).

Illinois State University, Graduate School, College of Business, Department of Accounting, Normal, IL 61790-2200. Offers MPA, MS. *Accreditation:* AACSB. *Degree requirements:* For master's, comprehensive exam. *Entrance requirements:* For master's, GMAT, minimum GPA of 2.75 in last 60 hours of course work. Additional exam requirements/recommendations for international students: Required—TOEFL.

Indiana Tech, Program in Business Administration, Fort Wayne, IN 46803-1297. Offers accounting (MBA); health care management (MBA); human resources (MBA); management (MBA); marketing (MBA). *Program availability:* Part-time, evening/weekend, online learning. *Entrance requirements:* For master's, GMAT, bachelor's degree from regionally-accredited university; minimum undergraduate GPA of 2.5; 2 years of significant work experience; 3 letters of recommendation. Electronic applications accepted.

Indiana University Kokomo, School of Business, Kokomo, IN 46904. Offers accounting (Postbaccalaureate Certificate); business administration (MBA); business fundamentals (Postbaccalaureate Certificate). *Accreditation:* AACSB. *Program availability:* Part-time, evening/weekend. *Faculty:* 14 full-time (6 women). *Students:* 21 full-time (7 women), 34 part-time (14 women); includes 1 minority (Black or African American, non-Hispanic/Latino), 23 international. Average age 31. 33 applicants, 70% accepted, 15 enrolled. In 2016, 36 master's awarded. *Degree requirements:* For master's, thesis optional, research project. *Entrance requirements:* For master's, GMAT. Additional exam requirements/recommendations for international students: Required—TOEFL (minimum score 550 paper-based; 73 iBT). *Application deadline:* For fall admission, 6/15 for domestic students, 6/1 for international students; for spring admission, 11/1 for domestic students, 10/1 for international students; for summer admission, 3/1 for domestic students. Application fee: $40 ($60 for international students). Electronic applications accepted. *Expenses:* $329.79 per credit hour in-state; $739.85 per credit hour out-of-state. *Financial support:* Career-related internships or fieldwork and scholarships/grants available. Financial award application deadline: 3/10; financial award applicants required to submit FAFSA. *Faculty research:* Investments, outsourcing, technology, adoption. *Unit head:* Dr. Alan Krabbenhoff, Dean, 756-455-9275, E-mail: agkrabbe@iuk.edu. *Application contact:* Terri Butler, Administrative Secretary, 765-455-9275, E-mail: tbutler@iuk.edu.
Website: http://www.iuk.edu/business/degrees/masters/business-administration/index.php

Indiana University Northwest, School of Business and Economics, Gary, IN 46408. Offers accounting (Graduate Certificate); management (Certificate); management and administrative studies (MBA). *Accreditation:* AACSB. *Program availability:* Part-time, evening/weekend. *Faculty:* 11 full-time (4 women), 7 part-time/adjunct (1 woman). *Students:* 46 full-time (20 women), 53 part-time (24 women); includes 44 minority (22 Black or African American, non-Hispanic/Latino; 4 Asian, non-Hispanic/Latino; 15 Hispanic/Latino; 3 Two or more races, non-Hispanic/Latino), 2 international. Average age 35. 47 applicants, 94% accepted, 34 enrolled. In 2016, 30 master's, 5 other advanced degrees awarded. *Entrance requirements:* For master's, GMAT (not for Weekend MBA for Professionals), letter of recommendation. *Application deadline:* For fall admission, 7/15 priority date for domestic students; for spring admission, 11/15 for domestic students. Applications are processed on a rolling basis. Application fee: $40 ($60 for international students). Electronic applications accepted. *Expenses:* Contact institution. *Financial support:* Institutionally sponsored loans and unspecified assistantships available. Support available to part-time students. Financial award application deadline: 3/10; financial award applicants required to submit FAFSA. *Faculty research:* International finance, employment law and testing, business ethics, taxation, financial institutions. *Unit head:* Cynthia Roberts, PhD, Dean, 219-980-6552, Fax: 219-980 6916, E-mail: iunbiz@iun.edu.
Website: http://www.iun.edu/business/graduate/index.htm

Indiana University–Purdue University Indianapolis, Kelley School of Business, Evening MBA Program, Indianapolis, IN 46202-5151. Offers accounting (MBA); entrepreneurship (MBA); finance (MBA); general administration (MBA); marketing (MBA); supply chain management (MBA); MBA/JD; MBA/MD; MBA/MHA; MBA/MS; MBA/MSA; MBA/MSE. *Program availability:* Part-time-only, evening/weekend, online learning. *Faculty:* 30 full-time (7 women), 4 part-time/adjunct (0 women). *Students:* 294 part-time (46 women); includes 41 minority (11 Black or African American, non-Hispanic/Latino; 22 Asian, non-Hispanic/Latino; 8 Hispanic/Latino), 106 international. Average age 31. 129 applicants, 53% accepted, 61 enrolled. In 2016, 103 degrees awarded. *Entrance requirements:* For master's, GMAT or GRE, 2 years of professional work experience. Additional exam requirements/recommendations for international students: Required—TOEFL or IELTS. *Application deadline:* For fall admission, 6/1 for domestic and international students; for spring admission, 11/1 for domestic and international students. Applications are processed on a rolling basis. Application fee: $60 ($65 for international students). Electronic applications accepted. *Expenses:* $772.34 per credit hour in-state tuition, $1,456.56 per credit hour out-of-state tuition. *Financial support:* Scholarships/grants available. Financial award application deadline: 6/1. *Faculty research:* Entrepreneurship; corporate finance; international business; consumer behavior; supply chain; business law. *Unit head:* Mary Johnson, Associate Director, Evening MBA Program, 317-274-4895, E-mail: mbaindy@iupui.edu. *Application contact:* Kristen Peters, Program Assistant, 317-274-4895, E-mail: mbaindy@iupui.edu.
Website: http://kelley.iupui.edu/evemba

Indiana University–Purdue University Indianapolis, Kelley School of Business, Graduate Accounting Program, Indianapolis, IN 46202-5151. Offers MBA, MSA. *Faculty:* 10 full-time (3 women), 8 part-time/adjunct (0 women). *Students:* 54 full-time (27 women), 72 part-time (33 women); includes 55 minority (13 Black or African American, non-Hispanic/Latino; 40 Asian, non-Hispanic/Latino; 2 Hispanic/Latino), 37 international. Average age 29. 73 applicants, 97% accepted, 59 enrolled. In 2016, 74 degrees awarded. *Entrance requirements:* For master's, GMAT, previous coursework in accounting and statistics. *Application deadline:* For fall admission, 8/1 for domestic students, 6/1 for international students; for spring admission, 12/1 for domestic students, 10/15 for international students. Application fee: $60 ($65 for international students). *Financial support:* Application deadline: 3/1. *Faculty research:* Auditing analytics; international accounting; taxation; financial accounting; corporate finance. *Unit head:* Susan E. Cauble, Director, 317-274-3451, E-mail: ksbigap@iupui.edu.
Website: http://kelley.iupui.edu/programs/graduate-accounting/

Indiana University South Bend, Judd Leighton School of Business and Economics, South Bend, IN 46634-7111. Offers accounting (MSA); business (Graduate Certificate); business administration (MBA), including finance, human resource management, marketing; MBA/MSA. *Program availability:* Part-time, evening/weekend. *Faculty:* 17 full-time (2 women), 3 part-time/adjunct (1 woman). *Students:* 28 full-time (18 women), 85 part-time (36 women); includes 10 minority (3 Black or African American, non-Hispanic/Latino; 1 Asian, non-Hispanic/Latino; 5 Hispanic/Latino; 1 Two or more races, non-Hispanic/Latino), 22 international. Average age 32. 57 applicants, 68% accepted, 22 enrolled. In 2016, 67 master's, 7 other advanced degrees awarded. *Entrance requirements:* For master's, GMAT. Additional exam requirements/recommendations for international students: Required—TOEFL (minimum score 550 paper-based; 79 iBT). *Application deadline:* For fall admission, 7/15 priority date for domestic and international students; for spring admission, 11/15 priority date for domestic and international students; for summer admission, 4/1 priority date for domestic and international students. Applications are processed on a rolling basis. Application fee: $40 ($60 for international students). Electronic applications accepted. *Expenses:* $329.79 per credit hour in-state; $739.85 per credit hour out-of-state. *Financial support:* Fellowships, Federal Work-Study, and institutionally sponsored loans available. Support available to part-time students. Financial award application deadline: 7/1; financial award applicants required to submit FAFSA. *Faculty research:* Financial accounting, consumer research, capital budgeting research, business strategy research. *Unit head:* Richard Kolbe, Dean, 574-520-4228, Fax: 574-520-4866, E-mail: rkolbe@iusb.edu. *Application contact:* 574-520-4839, Fax: 574-520-4834, E-mail: graduate@iusb.edu.
Website: https://business.iusb.edu/

Indiana Wesleyan University, College of Adult and Professional Studies, Graduate Studies in Business, Marion, IN 46953. Offers accounting (MBA, Graduate Certificate); applied management (MBA); business administration (MBA); health care (MBA, Graduate Certificate); human resources (MBA, Graduate Certificate); management (MS); organizational leadership (MA). *Program availability:* Part-time, evening/weekend, online learning. *Degree requirements:* For master's, applied business or management project. *Entrance requirements:* For master's, minimum GPA of 2.5, 2 years of related work experience. Additional exam requirements/recommendations for international students: Required—TOEFL (minimum score 550 paper-based). Electronic applications accepted.

Instituto Tecnologico de Santo Domingo, Graduate School, Area of Humanities and Social Sciences, Santo Domingo, Dominican Republic. Offers accounting (Certificate); adult education (Certificate); applied linguistics (MA); economics (MA); education (M Ed); educational psychology (MA, Certificate); gender and development (MA, Certificate); humanistic studies (MA); international marketing management (Certificate); international relations in the Caribbean basin (Certificate); intervention systems in family therapy (MA); linguistic and literary communication (Certificate); pedagogical support (MA); social science education (M Ed); sustainable human development (MA); terminal illness and death psychology (Certificate); youth and adult education (M Ed).

Inter American University of Puerto Rico, Aguadilla Campus, Graduate School, Aguadilla, PR 00605. Offers accounting (MBA); counseling psychology specializing in family (MS); criminal justice (MA); educative management and leadership (MA); elementary education (M Ed); finance (MBA); human resources (MBA); industrial management (MBA); management information systems (MBA); marketing (MBA). *Program availability:* Part-time, evening/weekend. *Degree requirements:* For master's, comprehensive exam. *Entrance requirements:* For master's, EXADEP, 2 letters of recommendation, minimum GPA of 2.5. Electronic applications accepted.

Inter American University of Puerto Rico, Arecibo Campus, Program in Business Administration, Arecibo, PR 00614-4050. Offers accounting (MBA); finance (MBA); human resources (MBA).

Inter American University of Puerto Rico, Barranquitas Campus, Program in Business Administration, Barranquitas, PR 00794. Offers accounting (IMBA); finance (IMBA).

Inter American University of Puerto Rico, Metropolitan Campus, Graduate Programs, Program in Accounting, San Juan, PR 00919-1293. Offers MBA. *Degree requirements:* For master's, comprehensive exam. *Entrance requirements:* For master's, GRE or EXADEP, interview. Electronic applications accepted.

Inter American University of Puerto Rico, Ponce Campus, Graduate School, Mercedita, PR 00715-1602. Offers accounting (MBA); biology (M Ed); chemistry (M Ed); criminal justice (MA); elementary education (M Ed); English as a Second Language (M Ed); finance (MBA); history (M Ed); human resources (MBA); marketing (MBA); mathematics (M Ed); Spanish (M Ed). *Entrance requirements:* For master's, minimum GPA of 2.5.

Inter American University of Puerto Rico, San Germán Campus, Graduate Studies Center, Program in Business Administration, San Germán, PR 00683-5008. Offers accounting (MBA); finance (MBA); general business administration (MBA); human resources (MBA, PhD); industrial relations (MBA); information systems (MBA); international and interregional business (PhD); management (MBA); marketing (MBA).

Program availability: Part-time, evening/weekend. *Degree requirements:* For master's, comprehensive exam. *Entrance requirements:* For master's, GRE General Test or EXADEP, minimum GPA of 3.0.

Iona College, Hagan School of Business, Department of Accounting, New Rochelle, NY 10801-1890. Offers general accounting (MBA, AC); public accounting (MBA, MS, AC). *Program availability:* Part-time, evening/weekend. *Faculty:* 6 full-time (1 woman). *Students:* 42 full-time (22 women), 41 part-time (17 women); includes 23 minority (6 Black or African American, non-Hispanic/Latino; 3 Asian, non-Hispanic/Latino; 14 Hispanic/Latino), 11 international. Average age 28. 31 applicants, 100% accepted, 20 enrolled. In 2016, 39 master's, 14 other advanced degrees awarded. *Entrance requirements:* For master's, GMAT, two letters of recommendation, minimum GPA of 3.0; for AC, GMAT, minimum GPA of 3.0. Additional exam requirements/ recommendations for international students: Required—TOEFL (minimum score 550 paper-based; 80 iBT), IELTS (minimum score 6.5). *Application deadline:* For fall admission, 8/15 priority date for domestic students, 8/1 priority date for international students; for winter admission, 11/15 priority date for domestic students, 11/1 priority date for international students; for spring admission, 2/15 priority date for domestic students, 2/1 priority date for international students; for summer admission, 5/15 priority date for domestic students, 5/1 priority date for international students. Applications are processed on a rolling basis. Application fee: $50. Electronic applications accepted. *Expenses: Tuition:* Full-time $19,692; part-time $1094 per credit. *Required fees:* $245 per term. Tuition and fees vary according to program. *Financial support:* In 2016–17, 41 students received support. Scholarships/grants, tuition waivers (partial), and unspecified assistantships available. Support available to part-time students. Financial award application deadline: 4/15; financial award applicants required to submit FAFSA. *Faculty research:* Tax policy, investment returns, international accounting standards. *Unit head:* Dr. Jeffrey Haber, Chair, 914-633-2244, E-mail: jhaber@iona.edu. *Application contact:* Katelyn Brunck, Director of MBA Admissions, 914-633-2451, Fax: 914-633-2277, E-mail: kbrunck@iona.edu.
Website: http://www.iona.edu/Academics/Hagan-School-of-Business/Departments/Accounting/Graduate-Programs.aspx

Iona College, Hagan School of Business, Department of Information Systems, New Rochelle, NY 10801-1890. Offers accounting and information systems (MS); business continuity and risk management (AC); information systems (MBA, MS, PMC); project management (MS). *Program availability:* Part-time, evening/weekend. *Faculty:* 6 full-time (1 woman), 1 part-time/adjunct (0 women). *Students:* 6 full-time (4 women), 14 part-time (5 women); includes 4 minority (1 Black or African American, non-Hispanic/Latino; 1 American Indian or Alaska Native, non-Hispanic/Latino; 2 Hispanic/Latino), 6 international. Average age 30. 14 applicants, 100% accepted, 6 enrolled. In 2016, 12 master's awarded. *Entrance requirements:* For master's, GMAT, 2 letters of recommendation, minimum GPA of 3.0; for other advanced degree, GMAT, minimum GPA of 3.0. Additional exam requirements/recommendations for international students: Required—TOEFL (minimum score 550 paper-based; 80 iBT), IELTS (minimum score 6.5). *Application deadline:* For fall admission, 8/15 priority date for domestic students, 8/1 priority date for international students; for winter admission, 11/15 priority date for domestic students, 11/1 priority date for international students; for spring admission, 2/15 priority date for domestic students, 2/1 priority date for international students; for summer admission, 5/15 priority date for domestic students, 5/1 priority date for international students. Applications are processed on a rolling basis. Application fee: $50. Electronic applications accepted. *Expenses:* Contact institution. *Financial support:* In 2016–17, 9 students received support. Scholarships/grants, tuition waivers (partial), and unspecified assistantships available. Support available to part-time students. Financial award application deadline: 4/15; financial award applicants required to submit FAFSA. *Faculty research:* Fuzzy sets, risk management, computer security, competence set analysis, investment strategies. *Unit head:* Dr. Shoshana Altschuller, Department Chair, 914-637-7726, E-mail: saltschuller@iona.edu. *Application contact:* Katelyn Brunck, Director of MBA Admissions, 914-633-2451, Fax: 914-633-2277, E-mail: kbrunck@iona.edu.
Website: http://www.iona.edu/Academics/Hagan-School-of-Business/Departments/Information-Systems/Graduate-Programs.aspx

Iowa State University of Science and Technology, Department of Accounting, Ames, IA 50011. Offers M Acc. *Accreditation:* AACSB. *Degree requirements:* For master's, thesis or alternative. *Entrance requirements:* For master's, GMAT, resume. Additional exam requirements/recommendations for international students: Recommended—TOEFL (minimum score 600 paper-based; 100 iBT), IELTS (minimum score 7). *Application deadline:* For fall admission, 7/1 priority date for domestic students, 6/1 priority date for international students; for spring admission, 11/1 priority date for domestic students, 10/1 priority date for international students. Application fee: $60 ($90 for international students). Electronic applications accepted. *Unit head:* 515-294-8118, Fax: 515-294-2446, E-mail: busgrad@iastate.edu. *Application contact:* Meleah Cue, Application Contact, 515-294-8118, Fax: 515-294-2446, E-mail: busgrad@iastate.edu.
Website: http://www.business.iastate.edu/masters/macc

Ithaca College, School of Business, Program in Accounting, Ithaca, NY 14850. Offers MS. *Program availability:* Part-time. *Faculty:* 6 full-time (2 women), 1 (woman) part-time/adjunct. *Students:* 8 full-time (3 women); includes 2 minority (both Black or African American, non-Hispanic/Latino). Average age 22. *Degree requirements:* For master's, thesis optional. *Entrance requirements:* For master's, GMAT. Additional exam requirements/recommendations for international students: Required—TOEFL (minimum score 550 paper-based; 80 iBT). *Application deadline:* For fall admission, 5/15 for domestic and international students; for spring admission, 11/1 for domestic and international students. Applications are processed on a rolling basis. Application fee: $40. Electronic applications accepted. *Expenses:* Contact institution. *Financial support:* In 2016–17, 8 students received support, including 8 fellowships (averaging $13,750 per year); career-related internships or fieldwork, Federal Work-Study, and scholarships/grants also available. Support available to part-time students. Financial award application deadline: 3/1; financial award applicants required to submit CSS PROFILE or FAFSA. *Unit head:* Rasoul Rezvanian, Associate Dean and Director, MBA Programs, 607-274-1762, Fax: 607-274-1263, E-mail: rrezvanian@ithaca.edu. *Application contact:* Nicole Eversley Bradwell, Director, Office of Admission, 607-274-3124, Fax: 607-274-1263, E-mail: admission@ithaca.edu.
Website: https://www.ithaca.edu/gps/gradprograms/programsites/mba/msaccounting/

Jackson State University, Graduate School, College of Business, Department of Accounting, Jackson, MS 39217. Offers MPA. *Accreditation:* AACSB. *Program availability:* Part-time, evening/weekend. *Degree requirements:* For master's, comprehensive exam. *Entrance requirements:* For master's, GRE General Test, GMAT. Additional exam requirements/recommendations for international students: Required—TOEFL (minimum score 520 paper-based; 67 iBT). *Application deadline:* For fall admission, 3/1 priority date for domestic students, 3/1 for international students; for spring admission, 10/1 for domestic and international students. Applications are processed on a rolling basis. Application fee: $25. *Expenses:* Tuition, state resident: full-time $7141. Tuition, nonresident: full-time $17,494. *Required fees:* $1080. Tuition and fees vary according to class time, course level, course load, degree level, campus/location, program and student level. *Financial support:* Career-related internships or fieldwork, Federal Work-Study, and tuition waivers (full and partial) available. Support available to part-time students. Financial award application deadline: 3/1. *Unit head:* Dr. Quinton Booker, Chair, 601-979-2414. *Application contact:* Fatoumatta Sisay, Manager of Graduate Admissions, 601-979-0342, Fax: 601-979-4325, E-mail: fatoumatta.sisay@jsums.edu.
Website: http://www.jsums.edu/accounting/

Jacksonville University, Davis College of Business, Accelerated Day-time MBA Program, Jacksonville, FL 32211. Offers accounting and finance (MBA); business administration (MBA); consumer goods and services marketing (MBA); management (MBA); management accounting (MBA). *Faculty:* 13 full-time (3 women), 1 part-time/adjunct (0 women). *Students:* 39 full-time (12 women), 8 part-time (4 women); includes 11 minority (5 Black or African American, non-Hispanic/Latino; 4 Hispanic/Latino; 2 Two or more races, non-Hispanic/Latino), 20 international. Average age 25. 80 applicants, 61% accepted, 33 enrolled. In 2016, 44 master's awarded. *Entrance requirements:* For master's, GMAT or GRE (may be waived for 3.3 or higher undergraduate GPA from AACSB-accredited institution), bachelor's degree from regionally-accredited institution, resume, statement of purpose, 2 letters of recommendation. Additional exam requirements/recommendations for international students: Required—TOEFL (minimum score 500 paper-based; 61 iBT), IELTS (minimum score 6). *Application deadline:* For fall admission, 8/1 priority date for domestic students, 7/15 priority date for international students; for spring admission, 12/1 priority date for domestic students, 11/15 priority date for international students. Application fee: $50. Electronic applications accepted. *Expenses:* $740 per credit hour. *Financial support:* In 2016–17, 7 students received support. Scholarships/grants and unspecified assistantships available. Financial award application deadline: 7/1; financial award applicants required to submit FAFSA. *Faculty research:* Behavioral finance, game theory, regional economic integration, information sabotage, public choice and public finance. *Unit head:* Dr. Douglas Johansen, Associate Dean and Graduate Programs Director, 904-256-7763, Fax: 904-256-7168, E-mail: djohans@ju.edu. *Application contact:* AnnaMaria Murphy, Assistant Director of Graduate Admissions, 904-256-7426, Fax: 904-256-7012, E-mail: mba@ju.edu.

See Display on page 107 and Close-Up on page 179.

Jacksonville University, Davis College of Business, FLEX Master of Business Administration Program, Jacksonville, FL 32211. Offers accounting and finance (MBA); consumer goods and services marketing (MBA); management accounting (MBA); JD/MBA; MBA/MPP; MSN/MBA. JD/MBA offered jointly with Florida School of Law. *Accreditation:* AACSB. *Program availability:* Part-time, evening/weekend, blended/hybrid learning. *Faculty:* 20 full-time (5 women), 1 part-time/adjunct (0 women). *Students:* 32 full-time (13 women), 71 part-time (29 women); includes 29 minority (11 Black or African American, non-Hispanic/Latino; 1 American Indian or Alaska Native, non-Hispanic/Latino; 6 Asian, non-Hispanic/Latino; 10 Hispanic/Latino; 1 Two or more races, non-Hispanic/Latino), 3 international. Average age 32. 32 applicants, 97% accepted, 27 enrolled. In 2016, 57 master's awarded. *Entrance requirements:* For master's, GMAT or GRE (may be waived for 3.3 or higher undergraduate GPA from AACSB-accredited institution), bachelor's degree from regionally-accredited institution, 3 years of full-time work experience (recommended), resume, statement of purpose, 2 letters of recommendation. Additional exam requirements/recommendations for international students: Required—TOEFL (minimum score 500 paper-based; 61 iBT), IELTS (minimum score 6). *Application deadline:* For fall admission, 8/1 priority date for domestic students, 7/15 priority date for international students; for spring admission, 12/1 priority date for domestic students, 11/15 priority date for international students; for summer admission, 4/1 priority date for domestic students, 3/15 priority date for international students. Applications are processed on a rolling basis. Application fee: $50. Electronic applications accepted. *Expenses:* $740 per credit hour. *Financial support:* In 2016–17, 1 student received support. Scholarships/grants available. Financial award application deadline: 7/1; financial award applicants required to submit FAFSA. *Faculty research:* Downsizing with integrity; impact of YouTube videos; game theory; analysis of effective tax rates; creativity innovation and change. *Unit head:* Dr. Douglas Johansen, Associate Dean and Director of Graduate Studies, 904-256-7763, Fax: 904-256-7168, E-mail: djohans@ju.edu. *Application contact:* AnnaMaria Murphy, Assistant Director of Graduate Admissions, 904-256-7426, Fax: 904-256-7012, E-mail: mba@ju.edu.

See Display on page 107 and Close-Up on page 179.

James Madison University, The Graduate School, College of Business, Program in Accounting, Harrisonburg, VA 22807. Offers accounting information systems (MS); taxation (MS). *Accreditation:* AACSB. *Program availability:* Part-time, evening/weekend. *Students:* 67 full-time (27 women); includes 5 minority (1 Black or African American, non-Hispanic/Latino; 1 Asian, non-Hispanic/Latino; 1 Hispanic/Latino; 2 Two or more races, non-Hispanic/Latino), 1 international. Average age 30. 91 applicants, 80% accepted, 60 enrolled. In 2016, 72 master's awarded. Application fee: $55. Electronic applications accepted. *Financial support:* In 2016–17, 23 students received support. Federal Work-Study and 23 assistantships (averaging $6911) available. Financial award application deadline: 3/1; financial award applicants required to submit FAFSA. *Unit head:* Dr. Tim J. Louwers, Director of the School of Accounting, 540-568-3027, E-mail: louwertj@jmu.edu. *Application contact:* Lynette D. Michael, Director of Graduate Admissions, 540-568-6131 Ext. 6395, Fax: 540-568-7860, E-mail: michaeld@jmu.edu.
Website: https://www.jmu.edu/cob/accounting/masters/index.shtml

John Carroll University, Graduate Studies, John M. and Mary Jo Boler School of Business, University Heights, OH 44118-4581. Offers accountancy (MS); business (MBA); laboratory administration (MS). *Accreditation:* AACSB. *Program availability:* Part-time, evening/weekend. *Entrance requirements:* For master's, GMAT, minimum GPA of 2.5. Additional exam requirements/recommendations for international students: Required—TOEFL (minimum score 550 paper-based). *Application deadline:* Applications are processed on a rolling basis. Application fee: $25 ($35 for international students). Electronic applications accepted. *Expenses:* Contact institution. *Financial support:* Research assistantships with full tuition reimbursements, scholarships/grants, and unspecified assistantships available. Financial award application deadline: 3/15; financial award applicants required to submit FAFSA. *Faculty research:* Accounting, economics and finance, management, marketing and logistics. *Unit head:* Dr. Alan R. Miciak, Dean, 216-397-4391, Fax: 216-397-1833. *Application contact:* Gayle T. Bruno-Gannon, Assistant to the Dean, 216-397-1970, Fax: 216-397-1728, E-mail: ggannon@jcu.edu.
Website: http://www.jcu.edu/boler/grads

Johnson & Wales University, Graduate Studies, MBA Program, Providence, RI 02903-3703. Offers accounting (MBA); business administration (MBA); finance (MBA); hospitality (MBA); human resource management (MBA); information technology (MBA); nonprofit management (MBA); operations and supply chain management (MBA). Program also offered on Denver campus. *Program availability:* Part-time, online learning. *Entrance requirements:* For master's, minimum GPA of 2.75. Additional exam requirements/recommendations for international students: Required—TOEFL (minimum score 550 paper-based); Recommended—IELTS, TWE. *Faculty research:* International banking, global economy, international trade, cultural differences.

Juniata College, Department of Accounting, Business, and Economics, Huntingdon, PA 16652-2119. Offers accounting (M Acc). *Students:* 3 full-time (1 woman); includes 1 minority (Black or African American, non-Hispanic/Latino). Average age 22. In 2016, 8 master's awarded. *Entrance requirements:* For master's, GMAT. *Expenses: Tuition:* Full-time $24,800; part-time $775 per credit. *Required fees:* $560. *Unit head:* Dr. Dominick Peruso, Chair, 814-641-3661, E-mail: peruso@juniata.edu.
Website: http://www.juniata.edu/departments/accounting-business-economics/

Kansas State University, Graduate School, College of Business, Department of Accounting, Manhattan, KS 66506. Offers M Acc. *Accreditation:* AACSB. *Program availability:* Part-time. *Faculty:* 11 full-time (4 women). *Students:* 58 full-time (36 women), 3 part-time (2 women); includes 4 minority (1 Black or African American, non-Hispanic/Latino; 1 Asian, non-Hispanic/Latino; 1 Hispanic/Latino; 1 Two or more races, non-Hispanic/Latino), 5 international. Average age 23. 58 applicants, 93% accepted, 34 enrolled. In 2016, 27 master's awarded. *Entrance requirements:* For master's, GMAT (minimum score of 500), minimum undergraduate GPA of 3.0. Additional exam requirements/recommendations for international students: Required—TOEFL (minimum score 550 paper-based; 79 iBT); Recommended—IELTS (minimum score 7). *Application deadline:* For fall admission, 2/1 priority date for domestic and international students; for spring admission, 10/1 priority date for domestic students, 8/1 priority date for international students. Applications are processed on a rolling basis. Application fee: $70 ($80 for international students). Electronic applications accepted. *Expenses:* Tuition, state resident: full-time $9670. Tuition, nonresident: full-time $21,828. *Required fees:* $862. *Financial support:* In 2016–17, 3 research assistantships (averaging $5,760 per year), 6 teaching assistantships with full tuition reimbursements (averaging $7,840 per year) were awarded; institutionally sponsored loans and scholarships/grants also available. Financial award application deadline: 3/1; financial award applicants required to submit FAFSA. *Faculty research:* Accounting education, accounting ethics, capital markets (empirical/archival), research in tax and financial reporting, behavioral research in accounting. *Unit head:* Dr. Brett Wilkinson, Head, 785-532-6184, Fax: 785-532-5959, E-mail: bwilkinson@ksu.edu. *Application contact:* Lynn Waugh, Graduate Program Coordinator, 785-532-7190, Fax: 785-532-7809, E-mail: lwaugh@ksu.edu.
Website: http://cba.k-state.edu/about/departments-initiatives/accounting/index.html

Kean University, College of Business and Public Management, Program in Accounting, Union, NJ 07083. Offers MS. *Program availability:* Part-time, evening/weekend. *Faculty:* 12 full-time (3 women). *Students:* 23 full-time (14 women), 28 part-time (14 women); includes 27 minority (10 Black or African American, non-Hispanic/Latino; 7 Asian, non-Hispanic/Latino; 9 Hispanic/Latino; 1 Two or more races, non-Hispanic/Latino), 7 international. Average age 31. 42 applicants, 60% accepted, 23 enrolled. In 2016, 19 master's awarded. *Entrance requirements:* For master's, GMAT/GRE, two letters of recommendation; professional resume/curriculum vitae; personal statement; minimum cumulative GPA of 3.0; official transcripts from all institutions attended. Additional exam requirements/recommendations for international students: Required—TOEFL (minimum score 550 paper-based; 79 iBT), IELTS (minimum score 6.5). *Application deadline:* For fall admission, 6/1 for domestic and international students; for spring admission, 12/1 for domestic and international students. Applications are processed on a rolling basis. Application fee: $75. Electronic applications accepted. *Expenses:* Tuition, state resident: full-time $13,156; part-time $640 per credit. Tuition, nonresident: full-time $17,831; part-time $785 per credit. *Required fees:* $3316; $151 per credit. Tuition and fees vary according to course level, course load, degree level and program. *Financial support:* Scholarships/grants and unspecified assistantships available. Financial award applicants required to submit FAFSA. *Unit head:* Dr. Veysel Yucetepe, Program Coordinator, 908-737-4762, E-mail: vyucetep@kean.edu. *Application contact:* Pedro Lopes, Office of Graduate Admissions, 908-737-7100, E-mail: grad-adm@kean.edu.
Website: http://grad.kean.edu/masters-programs/accounting

Keiser University, Master of Accountancy Program, Ft. Lauderdale, FL 33309. Offers forensic accounting (M Acc); general accounting (M Acc). *Entrance requirements:* For master's, baccalaureate degree from accredited institution in accounting, business or a related discipline.

Keiser University, Master of Business Administration Program, Ft. Lauderdale, FL 33309. Offers accounting (MBA); health services management (MBA); information security management (MBA); international business (MBA); leadership for managers (MBA); marketing (MBA). All concentrations except information security management also offered in Mandarin; leadership for managers and international business also offered in Spanish. *Program availability:* Part-time, online learning.

Kennesaw State University, Michael J. Coles College of Business, Program in Accounting, Kennesaw, GA 30144. Offers M Acc. *Accreditation:* AACSB. *Program availability:* Part-time, evening/weekend. *Entrance requirements:* For master's, GMAT, minimum GPA of 2.8. Additional exam requirements/recommendations for international students: Required—TOEFL (minimum score 550 paper-based; 80 iBT), IELTS (minimum score 6.5). Electronic applications accepted.

Kent State University, College of Business Administration, Doctoral Program in Accounting, Kent, OH 44242. Offers PhD. *Faculty:* 9 full-time (4 women). *Students:* 12 full-time (5 women); includes 1 minority (Asian, non-Hispanic/Latino), 8 international. Average age 33. 16 applicants, 19% accepted, 2 enrolled. *Degree requirements:* For doctorate, comprehensive exam, thesis/dissertation, oral defense. *Entrance requirements:* For doctorate, GMAT. Additional exam requirements/recommendations for international students: Required—TOEFL (minimum score 600 paper-based; 100 iBT). *Application deadline:* For fall admission, 12/15 for domestic and international students. Application fee: $45 ($70 for international students). Electronic applications accepted. *Expenses:* Tuition, state resident: full-time $10,864; part-time $495 per credit hour. Tuition, nonresident: full-time $18,380; part-time $837 per credit hour. *Financial support:* In 2016–17, 11 students received support, including 11 teaching assistantships with full tuition reimbursements available (averaging $23,000 per year); fellowships and Federal Work-Study also available. Financial award application deadline: 12/15; financial award applicants required to submit FAFSA. *Faculty research:* Information economics, capital management, use of accounting information, curriculum design. *Unit head:* Dr. Linda Zucca, Chair and Associate Professor, 330-672-2545, Fax: 330-672-2548, E-mail: lzucca@kent.edu. *Application contact:* Felecia A. Urbanek, Coordinator, Graduate Programs, 330-672-2282, Fax: 330-672-7303, E-mail: gradbus@kent.edu.
Website: http://www.kent.edu/business/phd

Kent State University, College of Business Administration, Master of Science Program in Accounting, Kent, OH 44242. Offers MS. *Program availability:* Part-time, evening/weekend. *Faculty:* 9 full-time (3 women). *Students:* 29 full-time (17 women), 7 part-time (3 women); includes 1 minority (Black or African American, non-Hispanic/Latino), 16 international. Average age 26. 33 applicants, 91% accepted, 10 enrolled. In 2016, 25 master's awarded. *Degree requirements:* For master's, internship. *Entrance requirements:* For master's, GMAT, minimum GPA of 3.0. Additional exam requirements/recommendations for international students: Required—TOEFL (minimum score 550 paper-based; 80 iBT). *Application deadline:* For fall admission, 3/15 priority date for domestic students, 3/15 for international students; for spring admission, 10/15 for domestic and international students; for summer admission, 5/1 for domestic and international students. Applications are processed on a rolling basis. Application fee: $45 ($70 for international students). Electronic applications accepted. *Expenses:* Tuition, state resident: full-time $10,864; part-time $495 per credit hour. Tuition, nonresident: full-time $18,380; part-time $837 per credit hour. *Financial support:* In 2016–17, 7 students received support, including 7 research assistantships with full tuition reimbursements available (averaging $4,000 per year); Federal Work-Study also available. Financial award application deadline: 3/15; financial award applicants required to submit FAFSA. *Faculty research:* Financial accounting, managerial accounting, auditing, accounting systems. *Unit head:* Dr. Linda Zucca, Chair and Associate Professor, 330-672-2545, Fax: 330-672-2548, E-mail: lzucca@kent.edu. *Application contact:* Louise M. Ditchey, Administrative Director, 330-672-2282, Fax: 330-672-7303, E-mail: gradbus@kent.edu.
Website: http://www.kent.edu/business/ms-accounting

Keystone College, Program in Accountancy, La Plume, PA 18440. Offers M Acc. *Program availability:* Part-time, online only, 100% online. *Faculty:* 2 full-time (1 woman), 3 part-time/adjunct (1 woman). *Students:* 2 applicants, 50% accepted. *Degree requirements:* For master's, thesis. *Entrance requirements:* For master's, GMAT, college transcripts, resume or curriculum vitae. Additional exam requirements/recommendations for international students: Required—TOEFL (minimum score 80 iBT) or IELTS (minimum score 6.5). *Application deadline:* For fall admission, 8/1 for domestic students; for spring admission, 12/1 for domestic students; for summer admission, 5/1 for domestic students. Applications are processed on a rolling basis. Application fee: $50. Electronic applications accepted. *Expenses:* Contact institution. *Financial support:* Unspecified assistantships available. Financial award application deadline: 5/1; financial award applicants required to submit FAFSA. *Unit head:* Patricia Davis, PhD, Professor, 570-945-8424, E-mail: patricia.davis@keystone.edu. *Application contact:* Jennifer Sekol, Director of Admissions, 570-945-8117, Fax: 570-945-7916, E-mail: jennifer.sekol@keystone.edu.

King University, School of Business and Economics, Bristol, TN 37620-2699. Offers accounting (MBA); finance (MBA); healthcare management (MBA); human resources management (MBA); leadership (MBA); management (MBA); marketing (MBA); project management (MBA). *Program availability:* Part-time, evening/weekend, online learning. *Degree requirements:* For master's, comprehensive exam, thesis optional. *Entrance requirements:* For master's, GMAT, 2 years of work experience. Additional exam requirements/recommendations for international students: Required—TOEFL (minimum score 550 paper-based). Electronic applications accepted. *Faculty research:* International monetary policy.

Lakeland University, Graduate Studies Division, Program in Business Administration, Plymouth, WI 53073. Offers accounting (MBA); finance (MBA); healthcare management (MBA); project management (MBA). *Entrance requirements:* For master's, GMAT. *Expenses:* Contact institution.

Lamar University, College of Graduate Studies, College of Business, Beaumont, TX 77710. Offers accounting (MBA); experiential business and entrepreneurship (MBA); healthcare administration (MBA); MSA/MBA. *Accreditation:* AACSB. *Program availability:* Part-time, evening/weekend. *Faculty:* 22 full-time (5 women). *Students:* 23 full-time (12 women), 209 part-time (109 women); includes 96 minority (46 Black or African American, non-Hispanic/Latino; 11 Asian, non-Hispanic/Latino; 32 Hispanic/Latino; 7 Two or more races, non-Hispanic/Latino), 33 international. Average age 33. 151 applicants, 99% accepted, 81 enrolled. In 2016, 104 master's awarded. *Degree requirements:* For master's, comprehensive exam (for some programs), thesis optional. *Entrance requirements:* For master's, GMAT. Additional exam requirements/recommendations for international students: Required—TOEFL (minimum score 550 paper-based; 79 iBT), IELTS (minimum score 6.5). *Application deadline:* For fall admission, 8/10 for domestic students, 7/1 for international students; for spring admission, 1/5 for domestic students, 12/1 for international students. Applications are processed on a rolling basis. Application fee: $25 ($50 for international students). Electronic applications accepted. *Expenses:* $8,134 in-state full-time, $5,574 in-state part-time; $15,604 out-of-state full-time, $10,554 out-of-state part-time per year. *Financial support:* Fellowships with tuition reimbursements, research assistantships with partial tuition reimbursements, career-related internships or fieldwork, Federal Work-Study, institutionally sponsored loans, scholarships/grants, and tuition waivers (partial) available. Support available to part-time students. Financial award application deadline: 4/1; financial award applicants required to submit FAFSA. *Faculty research:* Marketing, finance, quantitative methods, management information systems, legal, environmental. *Unit head:* Dr. Enrique R. Venta, Dean, 409-880-8603, Fax: 409-880-8088, E-mail: henry.venta@lamar.edu. *Application contact:* Deidre Mayer, Interim Director, Admissions and Academic Services, 409-880-8888, Fax: 409-880-7419, E-mail: gradmissions@lamar.edu.
Website: http://business.lamar.edu

La Roche College, School of Graduate Studies and Adult Education, Program in Accounting, Pittsburgh, PA 15237-5898. Offers MS. *Accreditation:* ACBSP. *Program availability:* Part-time, evening/weekend. *Faculty:* 2 full-time (1 woman), 3 part-time/adjunct (0 women). *Students:* 7 full-time (4 women), 7 part-time (4 women), 3 international. Average age 27. 10 applicants, 80% accepted, 8 enrolled. In 2016, 13 master's awarded. *Entrance requirements:* For master's, baccalaureate degree in business, accounting or finance from accredited college or university; two letters of recommendation; resume; personal essay. *Application deadline:* For fall admission, 8/15 for domestic and international students; for spring admission, 12/15 for domestic and international students. Applications are processed on a rolling basis. Application fee: $50. Electronic applications accepted. *Expenses: Tuition:* Full-time $12,600; part-time $700 per credit. *Required fees:* $25 per semester. *Unit head:* Mark Dawson, Professor/Department Chair of Accounting and Finance, 412-536-1190, Fax: 412-536-1179, E-mail: mark.dawson@laroche.edu. *Application contact:* Hope Schiffgens, Director of Graduate Studies and Adult Education, 412-536-1266, Fax: 412-536-1283, E-mail: schombh1@laroche.edu.

La Salle University, School of Business, Master of Business Administration Program, Philadelphia, PA 19141-1199. Offers accounting (MBA, Post-MBA Certificate); business systems and analytics (MBA, Post-MBA Certificate); finance (MBA, Post-MBA Certificate); general business administration (MBA, Post-MBA Certificate); human resource management (MBA, Post-MBA Certificate); management (MBA, Post-MBA Certificate); marketing (Post-MBA Certificate); MBA/MSN. Program also offered in Switzerland. *Accreditation:* AACSB. *Program availability:* Part-time, evening/weekend, online learning. *Faculty:* 19 full-time (6 women), 11 part-time/adjunct (3 women). *Students:* 55 full-time (23 women), 209 part-time (96 women); includes 66 minority (35 Black or African American, non-Hispanic/Latino; 17 Asian, non-Hispanic/Latino; 9 Hispanic/Latino; 5 Two or more races, non-Hispanic/Latino), 17 international. Average age 31. 200 applicants, 59% accepted, 63 enrolled. In 2016, 192 master's, 1 other advanced degree awarded. *Entrance requirements:* For master's, GMAT or GRE, two letters of reference; resume; for Post-MBA Certificate, MBA with minimum GPA of 3.0. Additional exam requirements/recommendations for international students: Required—TOEFL. *Application deadline:* For fall admission, 8/15 priority date for domestic students, 7/15 for international students; for spring admission, 12/15 priority date for domestic students, 11/15 for international students; for summer admission, 4/15 priority date for domestic students, 3/15 for international students. Applications are processed on a rolling basis. Application fee: $35. Electronic applications accepted. Application fee is waived when completed online. *Expenses:* Contact institution. *Financial support:* In 2016–17, 49 students received support. Scholarships/grants available. Support available to part-time students. Financial award application deadline: 8/31; financial award applicants required to submit FAFSA. *Unit head:* Dr. MarySheila McDonald, Interim Dean, 215-951-1040, Fax: 215-951-1886, E-mail: mcdonaldms@lasalle.edu. *Application contact:* Elizabeth Heenan, Director, Graduate and Adult Enrollment, 215-951-1100, Fax: 215-951-1462, E-mail: heenan@lasalle.edu.

La Sierra University, School of Business and Management, Riverside, CA 92515. Offers accounting (MBA); finance (MBA); general management (MBA); human resources management (MBA); leadership, values, and ethics for business and management (Certificate); marketing (MBA). *Degree requirements:* For master's, research project. *Entrance requirements:* For master's, GMAT, minimum GPA of 3.0. Additional exam requirements/recommendations for international students: Required—TOEFL. *Faculty research:* Financial econometrics, institutional assessment and strategic planning, legal issues in management, behavioral finance, content of financial reports.

Lehigh University, College of Business and Economics, Department of Accounting, Bethlehem, PA 18015. Offers accounting and information analysis (MS). *Accreditation:* AACSB. *Faculty:* 6 full-time (0 women), 1 part-time/adjunct (0 women). *Students:* 31 full-time (16 women), 3 part-time (2 women); includes 4 minority (1 Black or African American, non-Hispanic/Latino; 1 Asian, non-Hispanic/Latino; 2 Hispanic/Latino), 20 international. Average age 23. 118 applicants, 42% accepted, 10 enrolled. In 2016, 76 master's awarded. *Entrance requirements:* For master's, GMAT. Additional exam requirements/recommendations for international students: Required—TOEFL (minimum score 105 iBT). *Application deadline:* For fall admission, 2/28 for domestic and international students. Applications are processed on a rolling basis. Application fee: $75. Electronic applications accepted. *Expenses:* $1,200 per credit hour. *Financial support:* In 2016–17, 19 students received support. Research assistantships, scholarships/grants, tuition waivers, and unspecified assistantships available. Financial award application deadline: 1/15. *Faculty research:* Behavioral accounting, internal control, information systems, supply chain management, financial accounting. *Unit head:* Dr. C. Bryan Cloyd, Chairman, 610-758-2816, Fax: 610-758-6429, E-mail: cbc215@lehigh.edu. *Application contact:* Michael Tarantino, Director of Recruitment and Admissions, 610-758-3418, Fax: 610-758-5283, E-mail: mgt215@lehigh.edu.
Website: http://www4.lehigh.edu/business/academics/depts/accounting

Lehman College of the City University of New York, School of Natural and Social Sciences, Department of Economics and Accounting, Bronx, NY 10468-1589. Offers accounting (MS). *Entrance requirements:* For master's, GMAT.

Lenoir-Rhyne University, Graduate Programs, Charles M. Snipes School of Business, Hickory, NC 28601. Offers accounting (MBA); business analytics and information technology (MBA); entrepreneurship (MBA); global business (MBA); healthcare administration (MBA); innovation and change management (MBA); leadership development (MBA). *Accreditation:* ACBSP. *Program availability:* Part-time, evening/weekend, online learning. *Degree requirements:* For master's, capstone course. *Entrance requirements:* For master's, GMAT, GRE, MAT, minimum undergraduate GPA of 2.7, graduate 3.0. Additional exam requirements/recommendations for international students: Required—TOEFL (minimum score 600 paper-based). Electronic applications accepted. *Expenses:* Contact institution.

Lewis University, College of Business, Graduate School of Management, Program in Business Administration, Romeoville, IL 60446. Offers accounting (MBA); custom elective option (MBA); e-business (MBA); finance (MBA); healthcare management (MBA); human resources management (MBA); international business (MBA); management information systems (MBA); marketing (MBA); project management (MBA); technology and operations management (MBA). *Program availability:* Part-time, evening/weekend. *Students:* 145 full-time (72 women), 213 part-time (123 women); includes 101 minority (46 Black or African American, non-Hispanic/Latino; 2 American Indian or Alaska Native, non-Hispanic/Latino; 7 Asian, non-Hispanic/Latino; 41 Hispanic/Latino; 1 Native Hawaiian or other Pacific Islander, non-Hispanic/Latino; 4 Two or more races, non-Hispanic/Latino), 47 international. Average age 31. In 2016, 99 master's awarded. *Degree requirements:* For master's, comprehensive exam. *Entrance requirements:* For master's, interview, bachelor's degree, resume, 2 recommendations. Additional exam requirements/recommendations for international students: Required—TOEFL (minimum score 550 paper-based). *Application deadline:* For fall admission, 8/15 priority date for domestic students, 5/1 priority date for international students; for spring admission, 11/15 priority date for international students. Applications are processed on a rolling basis. Application fee: $40. Electronic applications accepted. *Expenses: Tuition:* Full-time $13,860; part-time $770 per credit hour. *Required fees:* $75 per semester. Tuition and fees vary according to degree level and program. *Financial support:* Career-related internships or fieldwork, Federal Work-Study, scholarships/grants, and unspecified assistantships available. Financial award application deadline: 5/1; financial award applicants required to submit FAFSA. *Unit head:* Dr. Maureen Culleeney, Academic Program Director, 815-838-0500 Ext. 5631, E-mail: culleema@lewisu.edu. *Application contact:* Michele Ryan, Director of Admission, 815-838-0500 Ext. 5384, E-mail: gsm@lewisu.edu.

Liberty University, School of Business, Lynchburg, VA 24515. Offers accounting (MBA, MS); business administration (MBA); criminal justice (MBA); cyber security (MS); executive leadership (MA); information systems (MS), including information assurance, technology management; international business (MBA, DBA); leadership (DBA); marketing (MBA, MS, DBA), including digital marketing and advertising (MS), project management (MS), public relations (MS), sports marketing and media (MS); project management (MBA, DBA); public administration (MBA); public relations (MBA). *Program availability:* Part-time, online learning. *Students:* 1,458 full-time (807 women), 4,188 part-time (2,041 women); includes 1,372 minority (1,060 Black or African American, non-Hispanic/Latino; 19 American Indian or Alaska Native, non-Hispanic/Latino; 85 Asian, non-Hispanic/Latino; 75 Hispanic/Latino; 10 Native Hawaiian or other Pacific Islander, non-Hispanic/Latino; 123 Two or more races, non-Hispanic/Latino), 124 international. Average age 35. 5,424 applicants, 45% accepted, 1242 enrolled. In 2016, 1,859 master's, 87 other advanced degrees awarded. *Entrance requirements:* For master's, minimum undergraduate GPA of 3.0, 15 hours of upper-level business courses. Additional exam requirements/recommendations for international students: Required—TOEFL (minimum score 600 paper-based; 100 iBT). *Application deadline:* Applications are processed on a rolling basis. Application fee: $50. Electronic applications accepted. *Expenses:* Contact institution. *Financial support:* Applicants required to submit FAFSA. *Unit head:* Dr. Scott Hicks, Dean, 434-592-4808, Fax: 434-582-2366, E-mail: smhicks@liberty.edu. *Application contact:* Jay Bridge, Director of Graduate Admissions, 800-424-9595, Fax: 800-628-7977, E-mail: gradadmissions@liberty.edu.
Website: http://www.liberty.edu/academics/business/index.cfm?PID-149

Lincoln University, Graduate Studies, Jefferson City, MO 65101. Offers business administration (MBA), including accounting, management, management information systems, public administration/policy; elementary teaching (M Ed); environmental science (MS); guidance and counseling (M Ed), including community/agency counseling, elementary school, secondary school; higher education (MA); history (MA); integrated agricultural systems (MS); middle school (M Ed); natural sciences (MS); secondary teaching (M Ed); sociology (MA); sociology/criminal justice (MA). *Program availability:* Part-time, evening/weekend, 100% online, blended/hybrid learning. *Students:* 50 full-time (29 women), 68 part-time (39 women); includes 40 minority (37 Black or African American, non-Hispanic/Latino; 1 Asian, non-Hispanic/Latino; 2 Two or more races, non-Hispanic/Latino), 14 international. Average age 33. 75 applicants, 80% accepted, 34 enrolled. In 2016, 51 master's awarded. *Degree requirements:* For master's, comprehensive exam, thesis optional. *Entrance requirements:* For master's, GRE, MAT or GMAT, minimum GPA of 2.75 overall, 3.0 in courses related to specialization; 3 letters of recommendation; minimum C average in English composition; personal statement of purpose. Additional exam requirements/recommendations for international students: Required—TOEFL (minimum score 500 paper-based; 61 iBT), IELTS (minimum score 5.5), Michigan English Language Assessment Battery (minimum score 80). *Application deadline:* For fall admission, 7/1 priority date for domestic students, 5/1 priority date for international students; for spring admission, 11/1 priority date for domestic students, 10/1 priority date for international students; for summer admission, 6/1 priority date for domestic students. Applications are processed on a rolling basis. Application fee: $30. Electronic applications accepted. *Expenses:* Tuition, state resident: full-time $6840; part-time $5130 per year. Tuition, nonresident: full-time $12,720; part-time $9540 per year. *Required fees:* $852; $811 per unit. Tuition and fees vary according to course load. *Financial support:* In 2016–17, 2 fellowships with tuition reimbursements, 8 research assistantships with tuition reimbursements were awarded; Federal Work-Study, scholarships/grants, and unspecified assistantships also available. Support available to part-time students. Financial award application deadline: 3/1; financial award applicants required to submit FAFSA. *Unit head:* Dr. Rolundus R. Rice, Dean, 573-681-5247, Fax: 573-681-5106, E-mail: gradschool@lincolnu.edu. *Application contact:* Irasema Steck, Administrative Assistant, 573-681-5247, Fax: 573-681-5106, E-mail: gradschool@lincolnu.edu.
Website: http://www.lincolnu.edu/web/graduate-studies/graduate-studies

Lindenwood University, Graduate Programs, Plaster School of Business and Entrepreneurship, St. Charles, MO 63301-1695. Offers accountancy (M Acc); accounting (MBA); business administration (MBA); entrepreneurial studies (MBA); finance (MBA, MS); human resource management (MBA); international business (MBA); leadership (MA); management (MBA); marketing (MBA, MS); nonprofit administration (MA); public administration (MBA); sport management (MA); supply chain management (MBA). *Accreditation:* ACBSP. *Program availability:* Part-time, evening/weekend, 100% online. *Faculty:* 15 full-time (6 women), 25 part-time/adjunct (7 women). *Students:* 197 full-time (97 women), 213 part-time (132 women); includes 81 minority (62 Black or African American, non-Hispanic/Latino; 1 American Indian or Alaska Native, non-Hispanic/Latino; 4 Asian, non-Hispanic/Latino; 9 Hispanic/Latino; 5 Two or more races, non-Hispanic/Latino), 83 international. Average age 31. 279 applicants, 54% accepted, 133 enrolled. In 2016, 269 master's awarded. *Degree requirements:* For master's, comprehensive exam (for some programs), thesis (for some programs), minimum GPA of 3.0. *Entrance requirements:* For master's, interview, minimum undergraduate cumulative GPA of 3.0, letter of recommendation. Additional exam requirements/recommendations for international students: Required—TOEFL (minimum score 550 paper-based; 80 iBT); Recommended—IELTS (minimum score 6.5). *Application deadline:* For fall admission, 8/28 priority date for domestic and international students; for winter admission, 1/8 priority date for domestic and international students; for spring admission, 3/5 for domestic students, 3/5 priority date for international students; for summer admission, 6/4 priority date for domestic and international students. Applications are processed on a rolling basis. Application fee: $30 ($100 for international students). Electronic applications accepted. *Expenses:* Contact institution. *Financial support:* In 2016–17, 256 students received support. Career-related internships or fieldwork, Federal Work-Study, institutionally sponsored loans, scholarships/grants, tuition waivers (partial), and unspecified assistantships available. Financial award application deadline: 6/30; financial award applicants required to submit FAFSA. *Unit head:* Roger Ellis, Dean, School of Business and Entrepreneurship, 636-949-4839, E-mail: rellis@lindenwood.edu. *Application contact:* Tyler Kostich, Director, Evening and Graduate Admissions, 636-949-4138, Fax: 636-949-4109, E-mail: adultadmissions@lindenwood.edu.
Website: http://www.lindenwood.edu/academics/academic-schools/robert-w-plaster-school-of-business-entrepreneurship/

Lipscomb University, College of Business, Nashville, TN 37204-3951. Offers accountancy (M Acc); accounting (MBA); business administration (MM); conflict management (MBA); financial services (MBA); health care informatics (MBA); healthcare management (MBA); information security (MBA); leadership (MBA); nonprofit management (MBA); professional accountancy (Certificate); sports management (MBA); strategic human resources (MBA); sustainability (MBA); MBA/MS; Pharm D/MM. *Accreditation:* ACBSP. *Program availability:* Part-time, evening/weekend. *Faculty:* 22 full-time (4 women), 12 part-time/adjunct (4 women). *Students:* 112 full-time (51 women), 69 part-time (34 women); includes 30 minority (17 Black or African American, non-Hispanic/Latino; 3 Asian, non-Hispanic/Latino; 8 Hispanic/Latino; 2 Two or more races, non-Hispanic/Latino), 5 international. Average age 32. 244 applicants, 55% accepted, 54 enrolled. In 2016, 164 master's awarded. *Entrance requirements:* For master's, GMAT, transcripts, interview, 2 references, resume. Additional exam requirements/recommendations for international students: Required—TOEFL (minimum score 570 paper-based). *Application deadline:* For fall admission, 6/15 for domestic students, 2/1 for international students; for winter admission, 6/1 for international students; for spring admission, 11/15 for domestic students. Applications are processed on a rolling basis. Application fee: $50 ($75 for international students). Electronic applications accepted. *Expenses:* $1,150-$1,290 per hour, depending on program. *Financial support:* Career-related internships or fieldwork, scholarships/grants, tuition waivers (partial), and unspecified assistantships available. Support available to part-time students. Financial award application deadline: 7/1; financial award applicants required to submit FAFSA. *Faculty research:* Impact of spirituality on organization commitment, women in corporate leadership, psychological empowerment, training. *Unit head:* Allison Duke, Associate Dean of Graduate Business Programs, 615-966-5732, Fax: 615-966-1818, E-mail: allison.duke@lipscomb.edu. *Application contact:* Karen Risley, Manager, Graduate Business Recruiting, 615-966-5145, E-mail: karen.risley@lipscomb.edu.
Website: http://www.lipscomb.edu/business/Graduate-Programs

Long Island University–LIU Brooklyn, School of Business, Public Administration and Information Sciences, Brooklyn, NY 11201-8423. Offers accounting (MBA); accounting (MS); business administration (MBA); computer science (MS); gerontology (Advanced Certificate); health administration (MPA); human resources management (MS); not-for-profit management (Advanced Certificate); public administration (MPA); taxation (MS). *Program availability:* Part-time, evening/weekend, blended/hybrid learning. *Faculty:* 18 full-time (9 women), 32 part-time/adjunct (10 women). *Students:* 275 full-time (150 women), 238 part-time (161 women); includes 281 minority (200 Black or African American, non-Hispanic/Latino; 2 American Indian or Alaska Native, non-Hispanic/Latino; 38 Asian, non-Hispanic/Latino; 36 Hispanic/Latino; 1 Native Hawaiian or other Pacific Islander, non-Hispanic/Latino; 4 Two or more races, non-Hispanic/Latino), 140 international. 796 applicants, 66% accepted, 143 enrolled. In 2016, 185 master's, 17 other advanced degrees awarded. *Entrance requirements:* Additional exam requirements/recommendations for international students: Required—TOEFL (minimum

score 527 paper-based; 75 iBT). *Application deadline:* Applications are processed on a rolling basis. Application fee: $50. Electronic applications accepted. *Expenses: Tuition:* Full-time $28,272; part-time $1178 per credit. *Required fees:* $451 per term. Tuition and fees vary according to degree level, program and student level. *Financial support:* In 2016–17, 94 students received support. Career-related internships or fieldwork, Federal Work-Study, institutionally sponsored loans, scholarships/grants, and unspecified assistantships available. Support available to part-time students. Financial award application deadline: 2/15; financial award applicants required to submit FAFSA. *Faculty research:* Corporate social responsibility; executive compensation and corporate governance; combinatorics; secure mobile coding; social equity and justice, particularly among the Latino population; public and healthcare finance. *Unit head:* Dr. Edward Rogoff, Dean, 718-488-1159, E-mail: edward.rogoff@liu.edu. *Application contact:* Gabrielle Gannon, Director of Graduate Admissions, 718-488-1011, Fax: 718-780-6110, E-mail: bkln-admissions@liu.edu.
Website: http://liu.edu/Brooklyn/Academics/School-of-Business-Public-Administration-and-Information-Sciences

Long Island University–LIU Post, College of Management, Brookville, NY 11548-1300. Offers accountancy (MS); finance (MBA); information systems (MS); international business (MBA); management (MBA); management engineering (MS); marketing (MBA); taxation (MS); technical project management (MS); JD/MBA. *Accreditation:* AACSB. *Program availability:* Part-time, 100% online, blended/hybrid learning. *Faculty:* 35 full-time (12 women), 25 part-time/adjunct (6 women). *Students:* 153 full-time (61 women), 68 part-time (22 women); includes 44 minority (8 Black or African American, non-Hispanic/Latino; 24 Asian, non-Hispanic/Latino; 11 Hispanic/Latino; 1 Two or more races, non-Hispanic/Latino), 79 international. 429 applicants, 58% accepted, 74 enrolled. In 2016, 124 master's awarded. *Degree requirements:* For master's, thesis (for some programs). *Entrance requirements:* For master's, GMAT, GRE, or LSAT. Additional exam requirements/recommendations for international students: Required—PTE, TOEFL (minimum score 550 paper-based, 75 iBT) or IELTS. *Application deadline:* Applications are processed on a rolling basis. Application fee: $50. Electronic applications accepted. *Expenses: Tuition:* Full-time $28,272; part-time $1178 per credit. *Required fees:* $451 per term. Tuition and fees vary according to degree level and program. *Financial support:* In 2016–17, 68 students received support. Career-related internships or fieldwork, Federal Work-Study, institutionally sponsored loans, and scholarships/grants available. Support available to part-time students. Financial award application deadline: 2/15; financial award applicants required to submit FAFSA. *Faculty research:* Finance and sustainability, innovation and intellectual property rights, marketing: data analytics and business intelligence, social networking local and international. *Unit head:* Dr. Robert M. Valli, Dean, 516-299-4192, E-mail: rob.valli@liu.edu. *Application contact:* Carol Zerah, Director of Graduate and International Admissions, 516-299-2900, Fax: 516-299-2137, E-mail: post-enroll@liu.edu.
Website: http://liu.edu/CWPost/Academics/Schools/COM

Louisiana State University and Agricultural & Mechanical College, Graduate School, E. J. Ourso College of Business, Department of Accounting, Baton Rouge, LA 70803. Offers MS, PhD.

Louisiana Tech University, Graduate School, College of Business, School of Accountancy, Ruston, LA 71272. Offers accounting (MPA, DBA). *Accreditation:* AACSB. *Program availability:* Part-time. *Degree requirements:* For doctorate, thesis/dissertation. *Entrance requirements:* For master's and doctorate, GMAT. *Application deadline:* For fall admission, 7/29 for domestic students; for spring admission, 2/3 for domestic students. Application fee: $20 ($30 for international students). *Financial support:* Fellowships, research assistantships, and teaching assistantships available. Financial award application deadline: 2/1. *Unit head:* Dr. Andrea Drake, Director, 318-257-2822, Fax: 318-257-4253, E-mail: adrake@latech.edu. *Application contact:* Marilyn J. Robinson, Assistant to the Dean, 318-257-2924, Fax: 318-257-4487.
Website: http://www.business.latech.edu/accounting/

Loyola Marymount University, College of Business Administration, Master of Science in Accounting Program, Los Angeles, CA 90045-2659. Offers MS. *Program availability:* Part-time. *Students:* 12 full-time (7 women), 2 part-time (both women); includes 4 minority (2 Asian, non-Hispanic/Latino; 1 Hispanic/Latino; 1 Two or more races, non-Hispanic/Latino), 8 international. Average age 26. 24 applicants, 54% accepted, 7 enrolled. In 2016, 8 master's awarded. *Entrance requirements:* For master's, GMAT/GRE. Additional exam requirements/recommendations for international students: Required—TOEFL (minimum score 600 paper-based; 100 iBT). *Application deadline:* Applications are processed on a rolling basis. Application fee: $50. Electronic applications accepted. *Financial support:* In 2016–17, 8 students received support, including 4 research assistantships. Financial award application deadline: 6/30; financial award applicants required to submit FAFSA. *Unit head:* Dr. Michael Moore, Director, Master of Science in Accounting Program, 310-568-6266. *Application contact:* Chake H Kouyoumjian, Associate Dean of Graduate Studies, 310-338-2721, E-mail: ckouyoum@lmu.edu.
Website: http://cba.lmu.edu/academics/msinaccounting/

Loyola University Chicago, Quinlan School of Business, Master of Science in Accountancy Program, Chicago, IL 60611. Offers MSA, MBA/MSA. *Accreditation:* AACSB. *Program availability:* Part-time, evening/weekend. *Faculty:* 11 full-time (3 women), 9 part-time/adjunct (3 women). *Students:* 84 full-time (59 women), 10 part-time (8 women); includes 7 minority (2 Black or African American, non-Hispanic/Latino; 2 Asian, non-Hispanic/Latino; 3 Hispanic/Latino), 74 international. Average age 24. 217 applicants, 66% accepted, 49 enrolled. In 2016, 48 master's awarded. *Entrance requirements:* For master's, GMAT or GRE, official transcripts, two letters of recommendation, statement of purpose, resume. Additional exam requirements/recommendations for international students: Required—TOEFL (minimum score 90 iBT) or IELTS (minimum score 6.5). *Application deadline:* For fall admission, 7/15 for domestic and international students; for winter admission, 10/1 for domestic and international students; for spring admission, 1/15 for domestic and international students; for summer admission, 4/1 for domestic and international students. Applications are processed on a rolling basis. Application fee: $50. Electronic applications accepted. Application fee is waived when completed online. *Expenses:* $4,488 per course. *Financial support:* In 2016–17, 37 students received support. Federal Work-Study, scholarships/grants, health care benefits, and unspecified assistantships available. Support available to part-time students. *Faculty research:* Investigate taxonomy of financial ratios across industries and financial reporting standards, federal transfer taxation, federal fiduciary taxation, estate planning, fraud in local governments, multi-disciplinary instructional cases for class use, impact of changes in accounting standards and business practices on the use of financial ratios, employment attributes for college graduates, credit relevance of litigation materiality disclosures. *Unit head:* Dr. Brian Stanko, Chair, 312-915-7100, Fax: 312-915-7224, E-mail: bstanko@luc.edu. *Application contact:* Lauren Griffin, Enrollment Advisor, Quinlan School of Business Graduate Programs, 312-915-8908, Fax: 312-915-7207, E-mail: lgriffin3@luc.edu.
Website: http://www.luc.edu/quinlan/mba/masters-in-accounting/

Loyola University Chicago, Quinlan School of Business, MBA Programs, Chicago, IL 60611. Offers accounting (MBA); business administration (EMBA); business ethics (MBA); economics (MBA); entrepreneurship (MBA); finance (MBA); healthcare management (MBA); human resources management (MBA); international business (MBA); management (MBA); marketing (MBA); operation management (MBA); risk management (MBA); supply chain management (MBA). *Program availability:* Part-time, evening/weekend. *Faculty:* 79 full-time (22 women), 10 part-time/adjunct (6 women). *Students:* 309 full-time (151 women), 65 part-time (31 women); includes 82 minority (25 Black or African American, non-Hispanic/Latino; 27 Asian, non-Hispanic/Latino; 27 Hispanic/Latino; 3 Two or more races, non-Hispanic/Latino), 49 international. Average age 30. 371 applicants, 53% accepted, 114 enrolled. In 2016, 216 master's awarded. *Entrance requirements:* For master's, GMAT or GRE, official transcripts, two letters of recommendation, statement of purpose, resume. Additional exam requirements/recommendations for international students: Required—TOEFL (minimum score 90 iBT) or IELTS (minimum score 6.5). *Application deadline:* For fall admission, 7/15 for domestic and international students; for winter admission, 10/1 for domestic and international students; for spring admission, 1/15 for domestic and international students; for summer admission, 4/1 for domestic and international students. Applications are processed on a rolling basis. Application fee: $50. Electronic applications accepted. Application fee is waived when completed online. *Expenses:* $4,488 per course. *Financial support:* In 2016–17, 83 students received support. Federal Work-Study, scholarships/grants, health care benefits, and unspecified assistantships available. Support available to part-time students. *Faculty research:* Social enterprise and responsibility, emerging markets, supply chain management, risk management. *Unit head:* Katherine Acles, Assistant Dean for Graduate Programs, 312-915-6124, Fax: 312-915-7207, E-mail: kacles@luc.edu. *Application contact:* Lauren Griffin, Enrollment Advisor, Quinlan School of Business Graduate Programs, 312-915-6124, Fax: 312-915-7207, E-mail: lgriffin3@luc.edu.

Loyola University Maryland, Graduate Programs, Sellinger School of Business, Professional MBA Program, Baltimore, MD 21210-2699. Offers accounting (MBA); information systems operations management (MBA). *Accreditation:* AACSB. *Program availability:* Part-time, evening/weekend. *Faculty:* 26 full-time (8 women), 13 part-time/adjunct (5 women). *Students:* 59 applicants, 88% accepted, 47 enrolled. In 2016, 125 master's awarded. *Entrance requirements:* For master's, GMAT, resume, essay, official transcripts, professional letter of recommendation. Additional exam requirements/recommendations for international students: Required—TOEFL (minimum score 550 paper-based, 80 iBT) or IELTS (minimum score 7). *Application deadline:* For fall admission, 8/1 for domestic students, 5/1 for international students; for winter admission, 9/1 for international students; for spring admission, 12/1 for domestic students; for summer admission, 5/1 for domestic students. Applications are processed on a rolling basis. Application fee: $60. Electronic applications accepted. *Expenses:* Contact institution. *Financial support:* In 2016–17, 26 students received support. Scholarships/grants available. Financial award application deadline: 4/15; financial award applicants required to submit FAFSA.

Maharishi University of Management, Graduate Studies, Program in Business Administration, Fairfield, IA 52557. Offers accounting (MBA); management (PhD); sustainability (MBA). *Program availability:* Evening/weekend, online learning. *Degree requirements:* For doctorate, thesis/dissertation. *Entrance requirements:* For master's, GMAT, minimum GPA of 3.0; for doctorate, minimum GPA of 3.0. Additional exam requirements/recommendations for international students: Required—TOEFL. *Faculty research:* Leadership, effects of the group dynamics of consciousness on the economy, innovation, employee development, cooperative strategy.

Manhattanville College, School of Business, Master of Science in Finance Program, Purchase, NY 10577-2132. Offers accounting (MS); corporate finance (MS); investment management (MS). *Program availability:* Part-time, evening/weekend. *Students:* 30 (14 women); includes 13 minority (7 Black or African American, non-Hispanic/Latino; 3 Asian, non-Hispanic/Latino; 1 Hispanic/Latino; 2 Two or more races, non-Hispanic/Latino). Average age 28. 23 applicants, 30% accepted, 7 enrolled. In 2016, 9 master's awarded. *Degree requirements:* For master's, thesis (for some programs), final project. *Entrance requirements:* For master's, transcripts, 2 letters of recommendation, resume. Additional exam requirements/recommendations for international students: Required—TOEFL (minimum score 563 paper-based; 85 iBT). *Application deadline:* Applications are processed on a rolling basis. Application fee: $75. Electronic applications accepted. *Expenses: Tuition:* Full-time $16,470; part-time $915 per credit. *Required fees:* $60 per semester. Part-time tuition and fees vary according to course load and program. *Financial support:* Federal Work-Study, institutionally sponsored loans, scholarships/grants, and unspecified assistantships available. Financial award applicants required to submit FAFSA. *Faculty research:* Life transitions: theory, strategies and practice. *Unit head:* Laura Persky, Graduate Program Director, 914-323-5188, E-mail: laura.persky@mville.edu. *Application contact:* Monika Pottgen, Assistant Director, Recruitment and Admissions, 914-323-5150, E-mail: business@mville.edu.
Website: https://www.mville.edu/programs/ms-finance

Marquette University, Graduate School of Management, Program in Accounting, Milwaukee, WI 53201-1881. Offers MSA. *Accreditation:* AACSB. *Program availability:* Part-time, evening/weekend. *Faculty:* 11 full-time (5 women), 3 part-time/adjunct (1 woman). *Students:* 52 full-time (35 women), 4 part-time (3 women), 42 international. Average age 23. 149 applicants, 80% accepted, 28 enrolled. In 2016, 49 master's awarded. *Entrance requirements:* For master's, GMAT or GRE, letters of recommendation (if applying for financial aid). Additional exam requirements/recommendations for international students: Required—TOEFL (minimum score 550 paper-based; 88 iBT), IELTS (minimum score 6.5), PTE. *Application deadline:* For fall admission, 2/15 for domestic and international students. Applications are processed on a rolling basis. Application fee: $50. Electronic applications accepted. *Financial support:* Fellowships, research assistantships, and teaching assistantships available. Financial award application deadline: 2/15. *Faculty research:* Financial (accounting) literacy, international perception of corruption, effect of carbon credits on accounting and tax transactions, targeted tax breaks. *Total annual research expenditures:* $8,250. *Unit head:* Dr. Brian Till, Dean, 414-288-5724. *Application contact:* Dr. Jeanne Simmons, Associate Dean, 414-288-7145.
Website: http://www.busadm.mu.edu/graduate/

Marshall University, Academic Affairs Division, College of Business, Program in Accountancy, Huntington, WV 25755. Offers MS. *Entrance requirements:* For master's, undergraduate degree in accounting with minimum GPA of 3.0 or GMAT.

Maryville University of Saint Louis, The John E. Simon School of Business, St. Louis, MO 63141-7299. Offers accounting (MBA, Certificate); business studies (Certificate); cyber security (MBA); cybersecurity (Certificate); financial services (MBA, Certificate); healthcare practice management (MBA, Certificate); human resource management (MBA); information technology (MBA, Certificate); management (MBA, Certificate); management and leadership (MA); marketing (MBA, Certificate); project management (MBA); sport business management (MBA); supply chain management/logistics (MBA). *Accreditation:* ACBSP. *Program availability:* Part-time, evening/weekend, 100% online, blended/hybrid learning. *Faculty:* 7 full-time (3 women), 34 part-time/adjunct (9 women). *Students:* 84 full-time (40 women), 223 part-time (118 women); includes 67 minority (40 Black or African American, non-Hispanic/Latino; 2 American Indian or Alaska Native, non-Hispanic/Latino; 8 Asian, non-Hispanic/Latino; 12 Hispanic/Latino; 1 Native

Hawaiian or other Pacific Islander, non-Hispanic/Latino; 4 Two or more races, non-Hispanic/Latino), 15 international. Average age 32. In 2016, 67 master's awarded. *Entrance requirements:* Additional exam requirements/recommendations for international students: Required—TOEFL (minimum score 563 paper-based; 85 iBT). *Application deadline:* Applications are processed on a rolling basis. Electronic applications accepted. *Expenses:* $650 per credit hour. *Financial support:* Career-related internships or fieldwork, Federal Work-Study, tuition waivers (partial), and campus employment available. Financial award application deadline: 3/1; financial award applicants required to submit FAFSA. *Faculty research:* Global business, e-marketing, strategic planning, interpersonal management skills, financial analysis. *Unit head:* Pam Horwitz, Interim Dean, 314-529-9680, Fax: 314-529-9975. *Application contact:* Dustin Loeffler, Director for Graduate Studies in Business, 314-529-9571, Fax: 314-529-9975, E-mail: dloeffler@maryville.edu.
Website: http://www.maryville.edu/bu/business-administration-masters/

McGill University, Faculty of Graduate and Postdoctoral Studies, Desautels Faculty of Management, Montréal, QC H3A 2T5, Canada. Offers administration (PhD); entrepreneurial studies (MBA); finance (MBA); general management (Post Master's Certificate); information systems (MBA); international business (MBA); international practicing management (MM); management (MBA); management for development (MBA); manufacturing management (MMM); marketing (MBA); operations management (MBA); public accountancy (Diploma); strategic management (MBA); MBA/LL B; MD/MBA. MMM offered jointly with Faculty of Engineering; PhD with Concordia University, HEC Montreal, Université de Montréal, Université du Québec à Montréal.

Mercer University, Graduate Studies, Cecil B. Day Campus, Eugene W. Stetson School of Business and Economics (Atlanta), Atlanta, GA 30341. Offers accounting (M Acc); business analytics (MS); innovation (PMBA), including entrepreneurship; international business (MBA); MBA/M Acc; Pharm D/MBA. *Accreditation:* AACSB. *Program availability:* Part-time, evening/weekend, 100% online, blended/hybrid learning. *Faculty:* 19 full-time (7 women), 7 part-time/adjunct (1 woman). *Students:* 183 full-time (91 women), 129 part-time (69 women); includes 136 minority (99 Black or African American, non-Hispanic/Latino; 2 American Indian or Alaska Native, non-Hispanic/Latino; 22 Asian, non-Hispanic/Latino; 10 Hispanic/Latino; 3 Two or more races, non-Hispanic/Latino), 43 international. Average age 32. 207 applicants, 77% accepted, 110 enrolled. In 2016, 176 master's awarded. *Entrance requirements:* For master's, GMAT or GRE. Additional exam requirements/recommendations for international students: Required—TOEFL (minimum score 550 paper-based, 80 iBT) or IELTS. *Application deadline:* For fall admission, 6/15 priority date for domestic and international students; for spring admission, 11/1 priority date for domestic and international students; for summer admission, 3/15 priority date for domestic and international students. Applications are processed on a rolling basis. Application fee: $50 ($100 for international students). Electronic applications accepted. *Expenses:* $795 per credit full-time, $727 per credit part-time. *Financial support:* Federal Work-Study available. Financial award application deadline: 5/1; financial award applicants required to submit FAFSA. *Faculty research:* Entrepreneurship, market studies, international business strategy, financial analysis. *Unit head:* Dr. Susan P. Gilbert, Dean, 678-547-6438, Fax: 678-547-6337, E-mail: gilbert_sp@mercer.edu. *Application contact:* Lael Whiteside, Director of Admissions, 678-547-6300, Fax: 678-547-6160, E-mail: whiteside_l@mercer.edu.
Website: http://business.mercer.edu

Mercy College, School of Business, Program in Public Accounting, Dobbs Ferry, NY 10522-1189. Offers accounting (MS). *Program availability:* Part-time, evening/weekend. *Students:* 33 full-time (19 women), 2 part-time (1 woman); includes 24 minority (5 Black or African American, non-Hispanic/Latino; 1 Asian, non-Hispanic/Latino; 17 Hispanic/Latino; 1 Two or more races, non-Hispanic/Latino). Average age 32. 29 applicants, 31% accepted, 8 enrolled. In 2016, 14 master's awarded. *Entrance requirements:* For master's, interview, essay, two letters of reference, undergraduate transcripts. Additional exam requirements/recommendations for international students: Required—TOEFL (minimum score 600 paper-based; 100 iBT), IELTS (minimum score 8). *Application deadline:* For fall admission, 8/1 for international students. Applications are processed on a rolling basis. Application fee: $40. Electronic applications accepted. *Expenses:* Contact institution. *Financial support:* Career-related internships or fieldwork, Federal Work-Study, scholarships/grants, and unspecified assistantships available. Support available to part-time students. Financial award applicants required to submit FAFSA. *Unit head:* Ed Weis, Dean, School of Business, 914-674-7490, E-mail: eweis@mercy.edu. *Application contact:* Allison Gurdineer, Senior Director of Admissions, 877-637-2946, Fax: 914-674-7382, E-mail: admissions@mercy.edu.
Website: https://www.mercy.edu/degrees-programs/ms-public-accounting

Mercyhurst University, Graduate Studies, Program in Organizational Leadership, Erie, PA 16546. Offers accounting (MS); higher education administration (MS); human resources (MS); organizational leadership (MS, Certificate); sports leadership (MS); strategy and innovation (MS). *Program availability:* Part-time, evening/weekend. *Degree requirements:* For master's, thesis. *Entrance requirements:* For master's, GRE General Test or MAT, interview, resume, essay, three professional references, transcripts. Additional exam requirements/recommendations for international students: Required—TOEFL (minimum score 80 iBT), IELTS (minimum score 6.5). Electronic applications accepted. *Faculty research:* Leadership training, organizational communication, leadership pedagogy.

Merrimack College, Girard School of Business, North Andover, MA 01845-5800. Offers accounting (MS); business analytics (MS); management (MS). *Program availability:* Part-time, evening/weekend, 100% online. *Faculty:* 7 full-time, 17 part-time/adjunct. *Students:* 101 full-time (45 women), 35 part-time (13 women); includes 6 minority (2 Asian, non-Hispanic/Latino; 3 Hispanic/Latino; 1 Two or more races, non-Hispanic/Latino), 55 international. Average age 27. 116 applicants, 81% accepted, 53 enrolled. In 2016, 57 master's awarded. *Degree requirements:* For master's, comprehensive exam (for some programs), thesis optional, capstone. *Entrance requirements:* For master's, official college transcripts, resume, personal statement, 2 recommendations. Additional exam requirements/recommendations for international students: Required—TOEFL (minimum score 84 iBT), IELTS (minimum score 6.5), PTE (minimum score 56). *Application deadline:* For fall admission, 8/13 for domestic students, 7/15 for international students; for spring admission, 1/10 for domestic and international students; for summer admission, 5/10 for domestic students, 4/10 for international students. Applications are processed on a rolling basis. Application fee: $0. Electronic applications accepted. *Expenses:* Contact institution. *Financial support:* Career-related internships or fieldwork, scholarships/grants, health care benefits, and unspecified assistantships available. Support available to part-time students. Financial award application deadline: 5/1; financial award applicants required to submit FAFSA. *Application contact:* Jennifer Greenwood, Graduate Admission Counselor, 978-837-3563, E-mail: graduate@merrimack.edu.
Website: http://www.merrimack.edu/academics/graduate/

Metropolitan State University of Denver, School of Business, Denver, CO 80204. Offers accounting (MP Acc); fraud exam and forensic auditing (MP Acc); internal audit (MP Acc); public accounting (MP Acc); taxation (MP Acc). *Accreditation:* AACSB. *Faculty:* 11 full-time (2 women), 1 (woman) part-time/adjunct. *Students:* 76 full-time (41 women), 36 part-time (16 women); includes 22 minority (4 Black or African American, non-Hispanic/Latino; 1 American Indian or Alaska Native, non-Hispanic/Latino; 11 Asian, non-Hispanic/Latino; 6 Hispanic/Latino). Average age 34. In 2016, 38 master's awarded. *Entrance requirements:* For master's, GMAT. *Application deadline:* For fall admission, 6/5 for domestic and international students; for spring admission, 10/2 for domestic and international students. Application fee: $50. *Expenses:* $8,220.60 full-time residents, $997.40 per credit hour part-time residents, $17,953.20 full-time non-residents. *Unit head:* Ann Murphy, Dean, 303-556-4695, E-mail: murphann@msudenver.edu. *Application contact:* Kim Bernie, Graduate Student Outreach, CBUS Graduate Programs, 303-556-5161, E-mail: kbernie1@msudenver.edu.
Website: http://www.msudenver.edu/business/

Miami University, Farmer School of Business, Department of Accountancy, Oxford, OH 45056. Offers M Acc. *Accreditation:* AACSB. *Students:* 18 full-time (8 women); includes 2 minority (1 Asian, non-Hispanic/Latino; 1 Hispanic/Latino), 3 international. Average age 22. In 2016, 33 master's awarded. *Expenses:* Tuition, state resident: full-time $12,890; part-time $564 per credit hour. Tuition, nonresident: full-time $29,604; part-time $1260 per credit hour. *Required fees:* $638. Part-time tuition and fees vary according to course load and program. *Unit head:* Marc Rubin, Chair, 513-529-3381, E-mail: rubinma@miamioh.edu. *Application contact:* Amanda Pyzoha, Academic Program Coordinator, 513-529-3372, E-mail: shickar@miamioh.edu.
Website: http://www.MiamiOH.edu/accountancy

Michigan State University, The Graduate School, Eli Broad College of Business, Department of Accounting and Information Systems, East Lansing, MI 48224. Offers accounting (MS, PhD), including information systems (MS), public and corporate accounting (MS), taxation (MS); business information systems (PhD). *Accreditation:* AACSB. *Degree requirements:* For doctorate, comprehensive exam, thesis/dissertation. *Entrance requirements:* For master's, GMAT (minimum score 550), bachelor's degree in accounting; minimum cumulative GPA of 3.0 at any institution attended and in any junior-/senior-level accounting courses taken; 3 letters of recommendation (at least 1 from faculty); working knowledge of computers including word processing, spreadsheets, networking, and database management system; for doctorate, GMAT (minimum score 600), bachelor's degree; transcripts; 3 letters of recommendation; statement of purpose; resume; on-campus interview; personal qualifications of sound character, perseverance, intellectual curiosity, and interest in scholarly research. Additional exam requirements/recommendations for international students: Required—TOEFL (minimum score 600 paper-based; 100 iBT), IELTS (minimum score 7) accepted for MS only. Electronic applications accepted.

Michigan Technological University, Graduate School, School of Business and Economics, Houghton, MI 49931. Offers accounting (MS); applied natural resource economics (MS); business administration (MBA). *Accreditation:* AACSB. *Program availability:* Part-time, evening/weekend. *Faculty:* 23 full-time (7 women), 1 part-time/adjunct. *Students:* 18 full-time (8 women), 23 part-time (12 women); includes 3 minority (1 Black or African American, non-Hispanic/Latino; 1 Asian, non-Hispanic/Latino; 1 Hispanic/Latino), 10 international. Average age 29. 122 applicants, 30% accepted, 16 enrolled. In 2016, 27 master's awarded. *Degree requirements:* For master's, thesis (for some programs). *Entrance requirements:* For master's, GMAT/GRE (recommended minimum score in the 50th percentile), statement of purpose, personal statement, official transcripts, 2 letters of recommendation, resume/curriculum vitae. Additional exam requirements/recommendations for international students: Required—TOEFL (recommended minimum score 95 iBT) or IELTS (minimum score 7). *Application deadline:* For fall admission, 7/1 for domestic and international students; for spring admission, 12/1 for domestic and international students. Applications are processed on a rolling basis. Electronic applications accepted. *Expenses:* Tuition, state resident: full-time $16,290; part-time $905 per credit. Tuition, nonresident: full-time $16,290; part-time $905 per credit. *Required fees:* $248; $124 per term. Tuition and fees vary according to course load and program. *Financial support:* In 2016–17, 13 students received support. Health care benefits and unspecified assistantships available. Financial award application deadline: 2/1; financial award applicants required to submit FAFSA. *Faculty research:* Natural resource and mineral economics, entrepreneurship, management of technology and innovation, engineering management, management information systems. *Unit head:* Dr. Dean Johnson, Dean, 906-487-2668, Fax: 906-487-1863, E-mail: dean@mtu.edu. *Application contact:* Carol T. Wingerson, Administrative Aide, 906-487-2328, Fax: 906-487-2284, E-mail: gradadms@mtu.edu.
Website: http://www.mtu.edu/business/

Middle Tennessee State University, College of Graduate Studies, Jennings A. Jones College of Business, Department of Accounting, Murfreesboro, TN 37132. Offers M Acc. *Accreditation:* AACSB. *Program availability:* Part-time, evening/weekend, online learning. *Entrance requirements:* For master's, GMAT (minimum score of 400). Additional exam requirements/recommendations for international students: Required—TOEFL (minimum score 525 paper-based; 71 iBT) or IELTS (minimum score 6). Electronic applications accepted.

Millennia Atlantic University, Graduate Programs, Doral, FL 33178. Offers accounting (MBA); business administration (MBA); health information management (MS); human resource management (MA). *Program availability:* Online learning.

Millsaps College, Else School of Management, Jackson, MS 39210-0001. Offers accounting (M Acc); business administration (MBA). *Accreditation:* AACSB. *Program availability:* Part-time. *Entrance requirements:* For master's, GMAT. Additional exam requirements/recommendations for international students: Required—TOEFL. Electronic applications accepted. *Faculty research:* Ethics, audit independence, satisfaction with assurance services, political business cycles, economic development, commercialization of new products.

Minnesota State University Mankato, College of Graduate Studies and Research, College of Business, Mankato, MN 56001. Offers accounting (MSA); business (MBA). *Accreditation:* AACSB. *Students:* 21 full-time (5 women), 73 part-time (31 women). *Entrance requirements:* For master's, GMAT, 2 letters of reference, resume. Additional exam requirements/recommendations for international students: Required—TOEFL. *Application deadline:* For fall admission, 7/1 for domestic students, 5/1 for international students; for spring admission, 11/1 for domestic students, 10/1 for international students. Electronic applications accepted. *Unit head:* Dr. Brenda Flannery, Dean, 507-389-5420, E-mail: brenda.flannery@mnsu.edu.
Website: http://cob.mnsu.edu/

Minnesota State University Moorhead, Graduate Studies, College of Business and Innovation, Moorhead, MN 56563. Offers accounting and finance (MS); business administration (MBA); health care management (MBA). *Accreditation:* AACSB. *Program availability:* Part-time. *Students:* 15 full-time (8 women), 27 part-time (11 women). Average age 32. 20 applicants, 100% accepted. In 2016, 9 master's awarded. *Degree requirements:* For master's, comprehensive exam (for some programs), thesis, final oral exam. *Entrance requirements:* For master's, GMAT, minimum GPA of 3.0. Additional exam requirements/recommendations for international students: Required—TOEFL (minimum score 550 paper-based); Recommended—IELTS (minimum score 6.5). *Application deadline:* For fall admission, 3/15 for domestic students; for spring admission, 10/15 for domestic students. Applications are processed on a rolling basis. Application fee: $20. Electronic applications accepted. *Expenses:* Tuition, state

resident: full-time $9000; part-time $4500 per credit. Tuition, nonresident: full-time $18,000; part-time $9000 per credit. *Required fees:* $942; $39.25 per credit. One-time fee: $90 full-time. Full-time tuition and fees vary according to course load, degree level, program and reciprocity agreements. *Financial support:* Federal Work-Study and unspecified assistantships available. Financial award application deadline: 10/1; financial award applicants required to submit FAFSA. *Faculty research:* Union decertification, small business development, business innovation, pedagogy, curriculum design. *Unit head:* Dr. Marsha Weber, Dean, 218-477-2076, E-mail: marsha.weber@mnstate.edu. *Application contact:* Karla Wenger, Coordinator, 218-477-2344, E-mail: wengerk@mnstate.edu.
Website: http://www.mnstate.edu/cbi/

Misericordia University, College of Business, Master of Business Administration Program, Dallas, PA 18612-1098. Offers accounting (MBA); healthcare management (MBA); human resources (MBA); management (MBA); sport management (MBA). *Program availability:* Part-time, evening/weekend, online learning. *Entrance requirements:* For master's, GMAT, MAT, GRE (50th percentile or higher), or minimum undergraduate GPA of 3.0, interview. Additional exam requirements/recommendations for international students: Required—TOEFL. Electronic applications accepted. Application fee is waived when completed online.

Mississippi College, Graduate School, School of Business, Clinton, MS 39058. Offers accounting (Certificate); business administration (MBA), including accounting; business education (M Ed); finance (MBA, Certificate); JD/MBA. *Accreditation:* ACBSP. *Program availability:* Part-time, evening/weekend. *Degree requirements:* For master's, comprehensive exam, thesis optional. *Entrance requirements:* For master's, GMAT, minimum GPA of 2.5, 24 hours of undergraduate course work in business. Additional exam requirements/recommendations for international students: Recommended—TOEFL, IELTS. Electronic applications accepted.

Mississippi State University, College of Business, Adkerson School of Accountancy, Mississippi State, MS 39762. Offers accountancy (MPA, MTX); systems (MPA). *Accreditation:* AACSB. *Faculty:* 10 full-time (2 women). *Students:* 49 full-time (23 women), 1 (woman) part-time; includes 1 minority (Asian, non-Hispanic/Latino), 3 international. Average age 23. 37 applicants, 54% accepted, 18 enrolled. In 2016, 39 master's awarded. *Degree requirements:* For master's, comprehensive exam. *Entrance requirements:* For master's, GMAT (minimum score of 510), minimum GPA of 3.0 over last 60 hours of undergraduate course work. Additional exam requirements/recommendations for international students: Required—TOEFL (minimum score 575 paper-based; 84 iBT); Recommended—IELTS (minimum score 7). *Application deadline:* For fall admission, 7/1 for domestic students, 5/1 for international students; for spring admission, 11/1 for domestic students, 9/1 for international students. Applications are processed on a rolling basis. Application fee: $60. Electronic applications accepted. *Expenses:* Tuition, state resident: full-time $7670; part-time $852.50 per credit hour. Tuition, nonresident: full-time $20,790; part-time $2310.50 per credit hour. Part-time tuition and fees vary according to course load. *Financial support:* Career-related internships or fieldwork, Federal Work-Study, institutionally sponsored loans, scholarships/grants, and unspecified assistantships available. Support available to part-time students. Financial award application deadline: 4/1; financial award applicants required to submit FAFSA. *Faculty research:* Income tax, financial accounting system, managerial accounting, auditing. *Unit head:* Dr. Shawn Mauldin, Director and Professor, 662-325-3710, Fax: 662-325-1646, E-mail: smauldin@business.msstate.edu. *Application contact:* Lakan Drinker, Admissions and Enrollment Assistant, 662-325-8951, E-mail: ldrinker@grad.msstate.edu.
Website: http://www.business.msstate.edu/programs/adkerson

Missouri State University, Graduate College, College of Business Administration, School of Accountancy, Springfield, MO 65897. Offers M Acc. *Accreditation:* AACSB. *Program availability:* Part-time, evening/weekend. *Faculty:* 13 full-time (3 women). *Students:* 32 full-time (21 women), 17 part-time (11 women); includes 5 minority (3 Asian, non-Hispanic/Latino; 2 Hispanic/Latino), 12 international. Average age 28. 50 applicants, 28% accepted, 5 enrolled. In 2016, 40 master's awarded. *Entrance requirements:* For master's, GMAT (minimum composite score of 500), minimum GPA of 3.2 in last 60 hours of coursework. Additional exam requirements/recommendations for international students: Required—TOEFL (minimum score 90 iBT). *Application deadline:* For fall admission, 7/20 priority date for domestic students, 5/1 for international students; for spring admission, 12/20 priority date for domestic students, 9/1 for international students; for summer admission, 5/20 priority date for domestic students. Applications are processed on a rolling basis. Application fee: $35 ($50 for international students). Electronic applications accepted. *Expenses:* Tuition, state resident: full-time $5830. Tuition, nonresident: full-time $10,708. *Required fees:* $1130. Tuition and fees vary according to class time, course level, course load and program. *Financial support:* Career-related internships or fieldwork, Federal Work-Study, institutionally sponsored loans, scholarships/grants, tuition waivers (partial), and unspecified assistantships available. Support available to part-time students. Financial award application deadline: 3/31; financial award applicants required to submit FAFSA. *Faculty research:* Forensic accounting, accounting information systems, accounting education, tax compliance. *Unit head:* Dr. John R. Williams, Director, 417-836-5414, Fax: 417-836-6337, E-mail: accountancy@missouristate.edu. *Application contact:* Michael Edwards, Coordinator for Graduate Admissions, 417-836-5330, Fax: 417-836-6200, E-mail: michaeledwards@missouristate.edu.
Website: http://www.missouristate.edu/soa/

Missouri Western State University, Program in Business Administration, St. Joseph, MO 64507-2294. Offers animal and life sciences (MBA); enterprise resource planning (MBA); forensic accounting (MBA); general business (MBA). *Program availability:* Part-time. *Entrance requirements:* Additional exam requirements/recommendations for international students: Recommended—TOEFL (minimum score 79 iBT), IELTS (minimum score 6). *Application deadline:* For fall admission, 7/15 for domestic and international students; for spring admission, 10/1 for domestic and international students; for summer admission, 3/15 for domestic students. Applications are processed on a rolling basis. Application fee: $50. Electronic applications accepted. *Expenses:* Tuition, state resident: full-time $6548; part-time $327.39 per credit hour. Tuition, nonresident: full-time $11,848; part-time $592.39 per credit hour. *Required fees:* $542; $99 per credit hour. $176 per semester. One-time fee: $50. Tuition and fees vary according to course load and program. *Financial support:* Scholarships/grants and unspecified assistantships available. Support available to part-time students. *Unit head:* Dr. Logan Jones, Director, 816-271-4351, E-mail: jjones81@missouriwestern.edu. *Application contact:* Dr. Benjamin D. Caldwell, Dean of the Graduate School, 816-271-4394, Fax: 816-271-4525, E-mail: graduate@missouriwestern.edu.
Website: http://www.missouriwestern.edu/mba/

Molloy College, Graduate Business Program, Rockville Centre, NY 11571-5002. Offers accounting (MBA); finance (MBA, Advanced Certificate); healthcare (MBA, Advanced Certificate); management (MBA); marketing (MBA, Advanced Certificate); personal financial planning (MBA). *Program availability:* Part-time, evening/weekend. *Faculty:* 6 full-time (3 women), 14 part-time/adjunct (5 women). *Students:* 66 full-time (32 women), 178 part-time (92 women); includes 96 minority (38 Black or African American, non-Hispanic/Latino; 24 Asian, non-Hispanic/Latino; 32 Hispanic/Latino; 1 Native Hawaiian or other Pacific Islander, non-Hispanic/Latino; 1 Two or more races, non-Hispanic/Latino), 5 international. Average age 40. 198 applicants, 69% accepted, 108 enrolled. In 2016, 55 master's awarded. *Entrance requirements:* Additional exam requirements/recommendations for international students: Required—TOEFL (minimum score 550 paper-based; 79 iBT). *Application deadline:* Applications are processed on a rolling basis. Application fee: $60. Electronic applications accepted. *Expenses: Tuition:* Full-time $19,170; part-time $1065 per credit. *Required fees:* $950; $790 per credit. Tuition and fees vary according to course load. *Financial support:* Applicants required to submit FAFSA. *Faculty research:* Leadership profiles that provide lessons of strength and purpose applicable to business; pedagogy and student learning outcomes for graduate business education; mobilizing social networks for innovation and qualitative analysis of sociocentric (whole) network measures; the ethical considerations of covenants not to compete in employment contracts and the use of liquidated damages clauses in employment contracts. *Unit head:* Dr. Maureen Mackenzie, Dean, Division of Business/Director of Graduate Programs, 516-323-3080, E-mail: mmackenzie@molloy.edu. *Application contact:* Jaclyn Machowicz, Assistant Director for Admissions, 516-323-4010, E-mail: jmachowicz@molloy.edu.
Website: http://www.molloy.edu/academics/graduate-programs/graduate-business

Monmouth University, Graduate Studies, Leon Hess Business School, West Long Branch, NJ 07764-1898. Offers accounting (MBA, Post-Master's Certificate); business administration (MBA); finance (MBA); management (MBA); marketing (MBA); real estate (MBA). *Accreditation:* AACSB. *Program availability:* Part-time, evening/weekend. *Faculty:* 20 full-time (4 women), 8 part-time/adjunct (0 women). *Students:* 76 full-time (37 women), 94 part-time (43 women); includes 17 minority (2 Black or African American, non-Hispanic/Latino; 6 Asian, non-Hispanic/Latino; 6 Hispanic/Latino; 1 Native Hawaiian or other Pacific Islander, non-Hispanic/Latino; 2 Two or more races, non-Hispanic/Latino), 8 international. Average age 30. 105 applicants, 90% accepted, 67 enrolled. In 2016, 93 master's, 1 other advanced degree awarded. *Degree requirements:* For master's, capstone course. *Entrance requirements:* For master's, GMAT or GRE, current resume; essay (500 words or less). Additional exam requirements/recommendations for international students: Required—TOEFL (minimum score 550 paper-based; 79 iBT), IELTS (minimum score 6), Michigan English Language Assessment Battery (minimum score 77) or Certificate of Advanced English (minimum score B2). *Application deadline:* For fall admission, 7/15 priority date for domestic students, 6/1 for international students; for spring admission, 12/1 priority date for domestic students, 11/1 for international students; for summer admission, 5/1 for domestic students. Applications are processed on a rolling basis. Application fee: $50. Electronic applications accepted. *Expenses: Tuition, area resident:* Full-time $19,764; part-time $1098 per credit hour. *Required fees:* $175 per semester. Tuition and fees vary according to program. *Financial support:* In 2016–17, 191 students received support, including 137 fellowships (averaging $2,643 per year), 20 teaching assistantships with full and partial tuition reimbursements available (averaging $10,034 per year); research assistantships, institutionally sponsored loans, scholarships/grants, and unspecified assistantships also available. Support available to part-time students. Financial award application deadline: 2/1; financial award applicants required to submit FAFSA. *Faculty research:* Information technology and marketing, behavioral research in accounting, human resources, management of technology. *Unit head:* Dr. Susan Gupta, MBA Program Director, 732-571-3639, Fax: 732-263-5517, E-mail: sgupta@monmouth.edu. *Application contact:* Laurie Kuhn, Associate Director of Graduate Admission, 732-571-3452, Fax: 732-263-5123, E-mail: gradadm@monmouth.edu.
Website: https://www.monmouth.edu/business-school/leon-hess-business-school.aspx

See Display on page 118 and Close-Up on page 181.

Monroe College, King Graduate School, Bronx, NY 10468. Offers accounting (MS); business administration (MBA), including entrepreneurship, finance, general business administration, healthcare management, human resources, information technology, marketing; computer science (MS); criminal justice (MS); hospitality management (MS); public health (MPH), including biostatistics and epidemiology, community health, health administration and leadership. *Program availability:* Online learning. Application fee: $50.
Website: https://www.monroecollege.edu/Degrees/King-Graduate-School/

Montana State University, The Graduate School, College of Business, Bozeman, MT 59717. Offers professional accountancy (MP Ac). *Accreditation:* AACSB. *Program availability:* Part-time. *Degree requirements:* For master's, comprehensive exam. *Entrance requirements:* For master's, GRE General Test, GMAT, minimum undergraduate GPA of 3.1 (preferred). Additional exam requirements/recommendations for international students: Required—TOEFL (minimum score 550 paper-based). Electronic applications accepted. *Faculty research:* Tax research, accounting education, fraud issues, CPA exams.

Montclair State University, The Graduate School, Feliciano School of Business, Post Master's Certificate Program in Accounting, Montclair, NJ 07043-1624. Offers Post Master's Certificate. *Program availability:* Part-time, evening/weekend. *Entrance requirements:* For degree, 2 letters of recommendation, essay. Additional exam requirements/recommendations for international students: Required—TOEFL (minimum score 83 iBT), IELTS (minimum score 6.5). Electronic applications accepted. *Expenses:* Tuition, state resident: part-time $553 per credit. Tuition, nonresident: part-time $854 per credit. *Required fees:* $91 per credit. Tuition and fees vary according to program. *Faculty research:* Economic costs and benefits of tax incentive programs, sustainability and financial accounting, auditors' expanded role post-Great Recession; revising rules for restructuring charges, aggressive accounting and ethical behavior.

Montclair State University, The Graduate School, Feliciano School of Business, Program in Accounting, Montclair, NJ 07043-1624. Offers MS. *Program availability:* Part-time, evening/weekend. *Degree requirements:* For master's, culminating experience. *Entrance requirements:* For master's, GMAT, 2 letters of recommendation, resume, essay. Additional exam requirements/recommendations for international students: Required—TOEFL (minimum score 83 iBT), IELTS (minimum score 6.5). Electronic applications accepted. *Expenses:* Tuition, state resident: part-time $553 per credit. Tuition, nonresident: part-time $854 per credit. *Required fees:* $91 per credit. Tuition and fees vary according to program. *Faculty research:* Economic costs and benefits of tax incentive programs, sustainability and financial accounting, auditors' expanded role post-Great Recession, revising rules for restructuring charges, aggressive accounting and ethical behavior.

Montclair State University, The Graduate School, Feliciano School of Business, Program in Forensic Accounting, Montclair, NJ 07043-1624. Offers Graduate Certificate. *Expenses:* Tuition, state resident: part-time $553 per credit. Tuition, nonresident: part-time $854 per credit. *Required fees:* $91 per credit. Tuition and fees vary according to program.

Moravian College, Graduate and Continuing Studies, Business and Management Programs, Bethlehem, PA 18018-6650. Offers accounting (MBA); business analytics (MBA); general management (MBA); health administration (MHA); healthcare management (MBA); human resource management (MBA); leadership (MSHRM); learning and performance management (MSHRM); supply chain management (MBA). *Program availability:* Part-time, evening/weekend. *Faculty:* 4 full-time (1 woman), 9 part-

time/adjunct (4 women). *Students:* 14 full-time (7 women), 88 part-time (46 women); includes 17 minority (7 Black or African American, non-Hispanic/Latino; 1 American Indian or Alaska Native, non-Hispanic/Latino; 3 Asian, non-Hispanic/Latino; 6 Hispanic/Latino), 1 international. Average age 33. 25 applicants, 92% accepted, 18 enrolled. In 2016, 11 master's awarded. *Entrance requirements:* For master's, current resume, offical transcripts, 2 letters of recommendation. Additional exam requirements/recommendations for international students: Required—TOEFL (minimum score 550 paper-based), IELTS (minimum score 6.5). *Application deadline:* For fall admission, 8/1 priority date for domestic and international students; for spring admission, 1/1 priority date for domestic and international students; for summer admission, 5/1 priority date for domestic and international students. Applications are processed on a rolling basis. Electronic applications accepted. *Expenses: Tuition:* Full-time $2619. Tuition and fees vary according to course load and program. *Financial support:* Applicants required to submit FAFSA. *Faculty research:* Leadership, change management, human resources. *Unit head:* Dr. Liz Kleintop, Associate Chair of Graduate Business, 610-861-1400, Fax: 610-861-1466, E-mail: mba@moravian.edu. *Application contact:* Kristy Sullivan, Director of Student Recruitment Operations, 610-861-1400, Fax: 610-861-1466, E-mail: graduate@moravian.edu.
Website: https://www.moravian.edu/graduate

Mount Aloysius College, Program in Business Administration, Cresson, PA 16630-1999. Offers accounting (MBA); health and human services administration (MBA); non-profit management (MBA); project management (MBA). *Program availability:* Part-time, evening/weekend. *Entrance requirements:* Additional exam requirements/recommendations for international students: Required—IELTS (minimum score 5.5); Recommended—TOEFL. *Application deadline:* For fall admission, 8/1 for domestic students; for spring admission, 12/1 for domestic students. Applications are processed on a rolling basis. Application fee: $30. Electronic applications accepted. Application fee is waived when completed online. *Expenses: Tuition:* Full-time $6750; part-time $750 per credit. *Required fees:* $285 per semester. *Financial support:* Unspecified assistantships available. Financial award applicants required to submit FAFSA. *Application contact:* Matthew P. Bodenschatz, Director of Graduate and Continuing Education Admissions, 814-886-6556, Fax: 814-886-6441, E-mail: mbodenschatz@mtaloy.edu.
Website: http://www.mtaloy.edu

Murray State University, College of Business and Public Affairs, Master of Professional Accountancy (MPAC) Program, Murray, KY 42071. Offers MPAC. *Program availability:* Part-time. *Degree requirements:* For master's, thesis. *Entrance requirements:* For master's, GMAT or GRE. Additional exam requirements/recommendations for international students: Required—TOEFL (minimum score 525 paper-based). *Faculty research:* Corporate governance, information systems innovations, public finances, accounting education.

Neumann University, Graduate Programs in Business and Information Management, Aston, PA 19014-1298. Offers accounting (MS), including forensic and fraud detection; sport business (MS). *Program availability:* Part-time, evening/weekend. *Faculty:* 3 full-time (2 women), 4 part-time/adjunct (1 woman). *Students:* 9 full-time (2 women), 33 part-time (12 women); includes 14 minority (11 Black or African American, non-Hispanic/Latino; 1 Asian, non-Hispanic/Latino; 2 Hispanic/Latino). Average age 31. 58 applicants, 50% accepted, 26 enrolled. In 2016, 16 master's awarded. *Degree requirements:* For master's, thesis (for some programs). *Entrance requirements:* For master's, official transcripts from all institutions attended, resume, letter of intent, 2-3 official letters of recommendation. Additional exam requirements/recommendations for international students: Required—TOEFL (minimum score 70 iBT). *Application deadline:* Applications are processed on a rolling basis. Application fee: $0. Electronic applications accepted. *Expenses:* $600 per credit (for MS in accounting); $495 per credit (MS in sport business). *Financial support:* Scholarships/grants and health care benefits available. Support available to part-time students. Financial award application deadline: 3/15; financial award applicants required to submit FAFSA. *Unit head:* Dr. Eric Wellington, Dean of Business and Information Management, 610-558-5596, Fax: 610-558-5574, E-mail: wellinge@neumann.edu. *Application contact:* Dr. Erika Davis, Director of Adult and Graduate Admissions, 800-9-NEUMANN Ext. 5208, Fax: 610-361-2548, E-mail: GradAdultAdmiss@neumann.edu.

New England College, Program in Management, Henniker, NH 03242-3293. Offers accounting (MSA); healthcare administration (MS); international relations (MA); marketing management (MS); nonprofit leadership (MS); project management (MS); strategic leadership (MS). *Program availability:* Part-time, evening/weekend. *Degree requirements:* For master's, independent research project. Electronic applications accepted.

New Jersey City University, School of Business, Program in Accounting, Jersey City, NJ 07305-1597. Offers MS, Graduate Certificate. *Program availability:* Part-time, evening/weekend. *Entrance requirements:* Additional exam requirements/recommendations for international students: Required—TOEFL (minimum score 79 iBT).

New Mexico State University, College of Business, Department of Accounting and Information Systems, Las Cruces, NM 88003. Offers accountancy (MACCT). *Accreditation:* AACSB. *Program availability:* Part-time. *Faculty:* 13 full-time (5 women). *Students:* 31 full-time (20 women), 11 part-time (4 women); includes 22 minority (3 American Indian or Alaska Native, non-Hispanic/Latino; 1 Asian, non-Hispanic/Latino; 16 Hispanic/Latino; 2 Two or more races, non-Hispanic/Latino), 3 international. Average age 28. 29 applicants, 69% accepted, 14 enrolled. In 2016, 20 master's awarded. *Degree requirements:* For master's, comprehensive exam, thesis optional. *Entrance requirements:* For master's, GMAT, minimum undergraduate accounting GPA of 3.0 (upper-division). Additional exam requirements/recommendations for international students: Required—TOEFL (minimum score 550 paper-based; 79 iBT), IELTS (minimum score 6.5). *Application deadline:* For fall admission, 7/1 priority date for domestic students, 3/1 priority date for international students; for spring admission, 11/1 priority date for domestic students. Applications are processed on a rolling basis. Application fee: $40 ($50 for international students). Electronic applications accepted. *Expenses:* Tuition, state resident: full-time $4086. Tuition, nonresident: full-time $14,254. *Required fees:* $853. Tuition and fees vary according to course load. *Financial support:* In 2016–17, 28 students received support, including 16 teaching assistantships (averaging $9,012 per year); career-related internships or fieldwork, Federal Work-Study, scholarships/grants, traineeships, health care benefits, and unspecified assistantships also available. Support available to part-time students. Financial award application deadline: 3/1. *Faculty research:* Taxation, financial accounting, managerial accounting, accounting systems, accounting education. *Total annual research expenditures:* $361. *Unit head:* Dr. Larry Tunnell, Department Head, 575-646-4901, Fax: 575-646-1552, E-mail: ltunnell@nmsu.edu. *Application contact:* Dr. Cindy L. Tunnell, Director, Master of Accountancy Program, 575-646-5206, Fax: 575-646-1552, E-mail: cseipel@nmsu.edu.
Website: http://business.nmsu.edu/departments/accounting

New York Institute of Technology, School of Management, Department of Business Administration, Old Westbury, NY 11568-8000. Offers executive (MBA); management (MBA), including finance, marketing, operations and supply chain management; professional accounting (MBA). *Accreditation:* AACSB. *Program availability:* Part-time, evening/weekend. *Faculty:* 25 full-time (4 women), 20 part-time/adjunct (6 women). *Students:* 377 full-time (161 women), 149 part-time (88 women); includes 60 minority (17 Black or African American, non-Hispanic/Latino; 1 American Indian or Alaska Native, non-Hispanic/Latino; 28 Asian, non-Hispanic/Latino; 11 Hispanic/Latino; 2 Native Hawaiian or other Pacific Islander, non-Hispanic/Latino; 1 Two or more races, non-Hispanic/Latino), 446 international. Average age 26. 804 applicants, 68% accepted, 215 enrolled. In 2016, 193 master's awarded. *Entrance requirements:* For master's, bachelor's degree; minimum undergraduate GPA of 3.0. Additional exam requirements/recommendations for international students: Required—TOEFL (minimum score 79 iBT), IELTS (minimum score 6). *Application deadline:* Applications are processed on a rolling basis. Application fee: $50. Electronic applications accepted. *Expenses:* $1,215 per credit. *Financial support:* Career-related internships or fieldwork, Federal Work-Study, scholarships/grants, tuition waivers (full and partial), and unspecified assistantships available. Support available to part-time students. Financial award application deadline: 3/1; financial award applicants required to submit FAFSA. *Faculty research:* Accounting, economics, finance, management, marketing. *Unit head:* Dr. Jess Boronico, Dean, 516-686-7838, E-mail: som@nyit.edu. *Application contact:* Alice Dolitsky, Director, Graduate Admissions, 516-686-7520, Fax: 516-686-1116, E-mail: nyitgrad@nyit.edu.
Website: http://www.nyit.edu/degrees/management_mba

New York University, Leonard N. Stern School of Business, Department of Accounting, New York, NY 10012-1019. Offers MBA, PhD. *Accreditation:* AACSB. *Faculty research:* Earnings management and financial analysis effectiveness and accounting policy, value-relevance of financial reporting, intangibles-related reporting and analysis, equity.

Niagara University, Graduate Division of Business Administration, Niagara University, NY 14109. Offers accounting (MBA); business administration (MBA); finance (MBA, MS); financial planning (MBA); healthcare administration (MBA, MHA); human resources (MBA); international business (MBA); marketing (MBA); professional accountancy (MBA); strategic management (MBA); supply chain management (MBA). *Accreditation:* AACSB. *Program availability:* Part-time, evening/weekend. *Students:* 172 full-time (69 women), 65 part-time (36 women); includes 25 minority (4 Black or African American, non-Hispanic/Latino; 7 Asian, non-Hispanic/Latino; 7 Hispanic/Latino; 1 Native Hawaiian or other Pacific Islander, non-Hispanic/Latino; 6 Two or more races, non-Hispanic/Latino), 76 international. Average age 27. In 2016, 107 master's awarded. *Entrance requirements:* For master's, GMAT. Additional exam requirements/recommendations for international students: Required—TOEFL (minimum score 550 paper-based; 79 iBT), IELTS (minimum score 6). *Application deadline:* For fall admission, 8/1 for domestic students; for spring admission, 11/1 for domestic students. Applications are processed on a rolling basis. Electronic applications accepted. *Expenses:* $870 per credit hour. *Financial support:* Fellowships, research assistantships, career-related internships or fieldwork, and Federal Work-Study available. Support available to part-time students. Financial award application deadline: 4/15; financial award applicants required to submit FAFSA. *Faculty research:* Capital flows, Federal Reserve policy, human resource management, public policy, issues in marketing, auctions, economics of information, risk and capital markets, management strategy, consumer behavior, Internet and social media marketing. *Unit head:* Dr. Paul Richardson, MBA Director/Chair of the Marketing Department, 716-286-8169, Fax: 716-286-8206, E-mail: psr@niagara.edu. *Application contact:* Evan Pierce, Associate Director for Graduate Recruitment, 716-286-8769, Fax: 716-286-8170, E-mail: epierce@niagara.edu.
Website: http://mba.niagara.edu

North Carolina Agricultural and Technical State University, School of Graduate Studies, School of Business and Economics, Greensboro, NC 27411. Offers accounting (MBA); business education (MAT); human resources management (MBA); supply chain systems (MBA).

North Carolina State University, Graduate School, Poole College of Management, Program in Accounting, Raleigh, NC 27695. Offers MAC. *Program availability:* Part-time. *Degree requirements:* For master's, thesis optional. *Entrance requirements:* For master's, GMAT, interview. Additional exam requirements/recommendations for international students: Required—TOEFL. Electronic applications accepted. *Faculty research:* Financial reporting issues using positive economic models and empirical studies of human behavior related to accounting decisions.

North Dakota State University, College of Graduate and Interdisciplinary Studies, College of Business, Fargo, ND 58102. Offers accountancy (M Acc); business administration (MBA). *Accreditation:* AACSB. *Program availability:* Part-time, evening/weekend. *Entrance requirements:* For master's, GMAT. Additional exam requirements/recommendations for international students: Required—TOEFL (minimum score 550 paper-based; 79 iBT). Electronic applications accepted. *Faculty research:* Labor management, operations, international finance, agency, Internet marketing.

See Display on page 122 and Close-Up on page 183.

Northeastern Illinois University, College of Graduate Studies and Research, College of Business and Management, Master of Science in Accounting Program, Chicago, IL 60625-4699. Offers MSA.

Northeastern State University, College of Business and Technology, Program in Accounting and Financial Analysis, Tahlequah, OK 74464-2399. Offers MS. *Program availability:* Part-time, evening/weekend. *Faculty:* 6 full-time (1 woman). *Students:* 6 full-time (1 woman), 59 part-time (31 women); includes 21 minority (2 Black or African American, non-Hispanic/Latino; 9 American Indian or Alaska Native, non-Hispanic/Latino; 5 Hispanic/Latino; 5 Two or more races, non-Hispanic/Latino), 2 international. Average age 33. In 2016, 21 master's awarded. *Entrance requirements:* For master's, GMAT. Additional exam requirements/recommendations for international students: Required—TOEFL. *Application deadline:* For fall admission, 6/1 priority date for domestic students. Applications are processed on a rolling basis. Application fee: $25. Electronic applications accepted. *Expenses:* Tuition, state resident: full-time $2816; part-time $216.60 per credit hour. Tuition, nonresident: full-time $6365; part-time $489.60 per credit hour. *Required fees:* $37.40 per credit hour. *Faculty research:* Information systems and organizational performance, capital markets, sustainability. *Unit head:* Dr. Justin Halpern, Department Chair, 918-449-6525, E-mail: halpernj@nsuok.edu. *Application contact:* Josh McCollum, Graduate Coordinator, 918-444-2093, E-mail: mccolluj@nsuok.edu.
Website: http://academics.nsuok.edu/businesstechnology/Graduate/MAFA.aspx

Northeastern University, D'Amore-McKim School of Business, Boston, MA 02115-5096. Offers accounting (MS); business administration (EMBA, MBA); finance (MS); innovation (MS); international business (MS); international management (MS); taxation (MS); technological entrepreneurship (MS); JD/MBA; LL M/MBA; MBA/MSN; MS/MBA. *Accreditation:* AACSB. *Program availability:* Part-time, evening/weekend, online learning. *Faculty:* 185 full-time (66 women), 57 part-time/adjunct (13 women). *Students:* 379 full-time (180 women), 1,182 part-time (514 women). In 2016, 800 master's awarded. *Entrance requirements:* For master's, GMAT or GRE. Application fee: $75. Electronic applications accepted. *Expenses:* Contact institution. *Financial support:* Scholarships/grants available. Financial award applicants required to submit FAFSA.

Unit head: Dr. Hugh Courtney, Dean, D'Amore-McKim School of Business. *Application contact:* Evelyn Tate, Director, Graduate Recruitment and Admissions, 617-373-3258, Fax: 617-373-8564, E-mail: e.tate@northeastern.edu.
Website: http://damore-mckim.northeastern.edu/

Northern Illinois University, Graduate School, College of Business, Department of Accountancy, De Kalb, IL 60115-2854. Offers MAS, MST. *Accreditation:* AACSB. *Program availability:* Part-time, evening/weekend. *Faculty:* 14 full-time (4 women). *Students:* 130 full-time (58 women), 80 part-time (42 women); includes 56 minority (10 Black or African American, non-Hispanic/Latino; 25 Asian, non-Hispanic/Latino; 19 Hispanic/Latino; 2 Two or more races, non-Hispanic/Latino), 31 international. Average age 29. 141 applicants, 72% accepted, 63 enrolled. In 2016, 121 master's awarded. *Degree requirements:* For master's, thesis optional. *Entrance requirements:* For master's, GMAT, minimum GPA of 2.75. Additional exam requirements/recommendations for international students: Required—TOEFL (minimum score 550 paper-based). *Application deadline:* For fall admission, 4/1 priority date for domestic students, 5/1 for international students; for spring admission, 9/15 priority date for domestic students, 10/1 for international students. Applications are processed on a rolling basis. Application fee: $40. Electronic applications accepted. *Financial support:* In 2016–17, 31 research assistantships with full tuition reimbursements, 9 teaching assistantships with full tuition reimbursements were awarded; fellowships with full tuition reimbursements, career-related internships or fieldwork, Federal Work-Study, scholarships/grants, tuition waivers (full), and unspecified assistantships also available. Support available to part-time students. Financial award applicants required to submit FAFSA. *Faculty research:* Accounting fraud, governmental accounting, corporate income tax planning, auditing, ethics. *Unit head:* Rebecca Shortridge, Chair, 815-753-1250, Fax: 815-753-8515. *Application contact:* Graduate Advising, 815-753-1325, E-mail: cobadvising@niu.edu.
Website: http://www.cob.niu.edu/accy/

Northern Kentucky University, Office of Graduate Programs, College of Business, Program in Accountancy, Highland Heights, KY 41099. Offers accountancy (M Acc); advanced taxation (Certificate). *Program availability:* Part-time, evening/weekend. *Degree requirements:* For master's, capstone course. *Entrance requirements:* For master's, GMAT, master's degree, MD, or PhD, official transcripts, current resume, 3 years of work experience (strongly suggested), statement of purpose. Additional exam requirements/recommendations for international students: Required—TOEFL (minimum score 79 iBT); Recommended—IELTS (minimum score 6.5). Electronic applications accepted. *Faculty research:* Ethics, accounting history, financial reporting.

Northwest Christian University, School of Business and Management, Eugene, OR 97401-3745. Offers accounting (MBA); management (MBA). *Program availability:* Part-time, evening/weekend, online only, 100% online. *Faculty:* 4 full-time (1 woman), 5 part-time/adjunct (2 women). *Students:* 22 full-time (11 women), 38 part-time (11 women); includes 18 minority (3 Black or African American, non-Hispanic/Latino; 2 American Indian or Alaska Native, non-Hispanic/Latino; 4 Asian, non-Hispanic/Latino; 6 Hispanic/Latino; 3 Two or more races, non-Hispanic/Latino). Average age 33. In 2016, 32 master's awarded. *Entrance requirements:* For master's, GMAT, GRE, MAT, minimum undergraduate GPA of 3.0, 500-word essay, resume. Additional exam requirements/recommendations for international students: Required—TOEFL (minimum score 550 paper-based; 80 iBT). *Application deadline:* Applications are processed on a rolling basis. Electronic applications accepted. *Expenses:* $625 per credit tuition; $90 per semester technology fee. *Unit head:* Dr. Peter Diffenderfer, Assistant Dean, 541-684-7441, Fax: 541-684-7336, E-mail: pdiffenderfer@nwcu.edu. *Application contact:* Billy Dorsch, Admission Counselor for Graduate Studies, 541-684-7279, Fax: 541-349-5281, E-mail: wdorsch@nwcu.edu.

Northwestern University, The Graduate School, Kellogg School of Management, Department of Accounting Information and Management, Evanston, IL 60208. Offers PhD. Admissions and degree offered through The Graduate School. *Accreditation:* AACSB. *Degree requirements:* For doctorate, comprehensive exam, thesis/dissertation. *Entrance requirements:* For doctorate, GMAT or GRE General Test. Additional exam requirements/recommendations for international students: Required—TOEFL. Electronic applications accepted. *Faculty research:* Managerial and financial accounting theory, financial accounting/theory, managerial accounting and performance measurement, international accounting, joint cost allocation.

Northwestern University, The Graduate School, Kellogg School of Management, Management Programs, Evanston, IL 60208. Offers accounting information and management (MBA, PhD); analytical finance (MBA); business administration (MBA); decision sciences (MBA); entrepreneurship and innovation (MBA); finance (MBA, PhD); health enterprise management (MBA); human resources management (MBA); international business (MBA); management and organizations (MBA, PhD); management and organizations and sociology (PhD); management and strategy (MBA); management studies (MS); managerial analytics (MBA); managerial economics (MBA); managerial economics and strategy (PhD); marketing (MBA, PhD); marketing management (MBA); media management (MBA); operations management (MBA, PhD); real estate (MBA); social enterprise at Kellogg (MBA); JD/MBA. *Program availability:* Part-time, evening/weekend. Terminal master's awarded for partial completion of doctoral program. *Degree requirements:* For doctorate, thesis/dissertation, 2 years of coursework, qualifying (field) exam and candidacy, summer research papers and presentations to faculty, proposal defense, final exam/defense. *Entrance requirements:* For master's, GMAT, GRE, interview, 2 letters of recommendation, college transcripts, resume, essays, Kellogg honor code; for doctorate, GMAT, GRE, statement of purpose, transcripts, 2 letters of recommendation, resume, interview. Additional exam requirements/recommendations for international students: Required—TOEFL, IELTS. Electronic applications accepted. *Expenses:* Contact institution. *Faculty research:* Business cycles and international finance, health policy, networks, non-market strategy, consumer psychology.

Nova Southeastern University, H. Wayne Huizenga College of Business and Entrepreneurship, Fort Lauderdale, FL 33314-7796. Offers accounting (M Acc); business intelligence/analytics (MBA); entrepreneurship (MBA); finance (MBA); human resource management (MBA); international business (MBA); management (MBA); marketing (MBA); process improvement (MBA); public administration (MPA); real estate development (MS); sport revenue generation (MBA); supply chain management (MBA); taxation (M Tax). *Program availability:* Part-time, evening/weekend, 100% online, blended/hybrid learning. *Faculty:* 65 full-time (26 women), 111 part-time/adjunct (74 women). *Students:* 2,242 full-time (1,400 women), 425 part-time (239 women); includes 1,798 minority (734 Black or African American, non-Hispanic/Latino; 5 American Indian or Alaska Native, non-Hispanic/Latino; 110 Asian, non-Hispanic/Latino; 890 Hispanic/Latino; 2 Native Hawaiian or other Pacific Islander, non-Hispanic/Latino; 57 Two or more races, non-Hispanic/Latino), 255 international. Average age 34. 1,422 applicants, 64% accepted, 672 enrolled. In 2016, 971 master's awarded. *Degree requirements:* For master's, thesis optional. *Entrance requirements:* For master's, GMAT or GRE (depending on undergraduate GPA), official transcripts from all schools attended while in pursuit of bachelor's degree; minimum GPA of 2.5 from regionally-accredited institution. Additional exam requirements/recommendations for international students: Required—TOEFL (minimum score 550 paper-based; 79 iBT), IELTS (minimum score 6), PTE (minimum score 54). *Application deadline:* For fall admission, 8/5 priority date for domestic students, 7/29 priority date for international students; for winter admission, 12/16 priority date for domestic students, 12/9 priority date for international students; for summer admission, 4/21 priority date for domestic and international students. Applications are processed on a rolling basis. Application fee: $50. Electronic applications accepted. *Expenses:* Contact institution. *Financial support:* In 2016–17, 325 students received support. Federal Work-Study and scholarships/grants available. Support available to part-time students. Financial award application deadline: 4/15; financial award applicants required to submit FAFSA. *Faculty research:* Reputation management, call centers, international social capital, corporate earnings guidance, corporate governance. *Unit head:* Dr. J. Preston Jones, Dean, 954-262-5127, E-mail: prestonj@nova.edu. *Application contact:* Zeida Rodriguez, Associate Director of Enrollment Services, 954-262-5163, Fax: 954-262-3822, E-mail: zeida@nova.edu.
Website: http://www.huizenga.nova.edu

Oakland University, Graduate Study and Lifelong Learning, School of Business Administration, Department of Accounting and Finance, Rochester, MI 48309-4401. Offers accounting (M Acc, Certificate); finance (Certificate).

Ohio Christian University, Graduate Programs, Circleville, OH 43113-9487. Offers accounting (MBA); business administration (MBA); digital marketing (MBA); finance (MBA); healthcare management (MBA); human resources (MBA); management (MM); organizational leadership (MBA); pastoral care and counseling (MAM); practical theology (MAM).

Ohio Dominican University, Division of Business, Program in Business Administration, Columbus, OH 43219-2099. Offers accounting (MBA); data analytics (MBA); finance (MBA); leadership (MBA); risk management (MBA); sport management (MBA). *Program availability:* Part-time, evening/weekend, 100% online, blended/hybrid learning. *Faculty:* 8 full-time (4 women), 17 part-time/adjunct (3 women). *Students:* 63 full-time (26 women), 112 part-time (59 women); includes 50 minority (29 Black or African American, non-Hispanic/Latino; 2 American Indian or Alaska Native, non-Hispanic/Latino; 6 Asian, non-Hispanic/Latino; 6 Hispanic/Latino; 1 Native Hawaiian or other Pacific Islander, non-Hispanic/Latino; 6 Two or more races, non-Hispanic/Latino), 7 international. Average age 31. 65 applicants, 51% accepted, 26 enrolled. In 2016, 120 master's awarded. *Entrance requirements:* For master's, minimum overall GPA of 3.0 in undergraduate degree from regionally-accredited institution or 2.75 in last 60 semester hours of bachelor's degree. Additional exam requirements/recommendations for international students: Required—TOEFL (minimum score 550 paper-based), IELTS (minimum score 6.5). *Application deadline:* For fall admission, 8/15 for domestic students, 6/10 for international students; for spring admission, 1/4 for domestic students, 11/2 for international students; for summer admission, 5/30 for domestic students. Applications are processed on a rolling basis. Application fee: $25. Electronic applications accepted. *Expenses:* $590 per credit hour; $225 fees per semester. *Financial support:* Applicants required to submit FAFSA. *Unit head:* Dr. Steve Vickner, Director of Master of Business Administration Program, 614-251-4569, E-mail: vickners@ohiodominican.edu. *Application contact:* John W. Naughton, Director for Graduate Admissions, 614-251-4721, Fax: 614-251-6654, E-mail: grad@ohiodominican.edu.
Website: http://www.ohiodominican.edu/academics/graduate/mba

Ohio Northern University, College of Business, Ada, OH 45810-1599. Offers MSA.

The Ohio State University, Graduate School, Max M. Fisher College of Business, Department of Accounting and Management Information Systems, Columbus, OH 43210. Offers M Acc, PhD. *Accreditation:* AACSB. *Faculty:* 21. *Students:* 88 full-time (61 women); includes 6 minority (all Two or more races, non-Hispanic/Latino), 43 international. Average age 23. In 2016, 78 master's, 1 doctorate awarded. Terminal master's awarded for partial completion of doctoral program. *Degree requirements:* For doctorate, thesis/dissertation. *Entrance requirements:* For master's, GMAT (minimum score of 550 recommended, 600 preferred) or GRE; for doctorate, GMAT. Additional exam requirements/recommendations for international students: Required—TOEFL (minimum score 600 paper-based; 100 iBT), Michigan English Language Assessment Battery (minimum score 86); Recommended—IELTS (minimum score 7). *Application deadline:* For fall admission, 11/15 priority date for domestic and international students. Applications are processed on a rolling basis. Application fee: $60 ($70 for international students). Electronic applications accepted. *Financial support:* Fellowships with tuition reimbursements, research assistantships with tuition reimbursements, teaching assistantships with tuition reimbursements, career-related internships or fieldwork, Federal Work-Study, and institutionally sponsored loans available. Support available to part-time students. *Faculty research:* Artificial intelligence, protocol analysis, database design in decision-supporting systems. *Unit head:* Dr. Brian Mittendorf, Chair and Professor, 614-292-1720, E-mail: mittendorf.3@osu.edu. *Application contact:* Graduate and Professional Admissions, 614-292-6031, Fax: 614-292-3656, E-mail: gpadmissions@osu.edu.
Website: http://fisher.osu.edu/departments/accounting-and-mis/

The Ohio State University, Graduate School, Max M. Fisher College of Business, Program in Accounting, Columbus, OH 43210. Offers M Acc. *Faculty:* 21. *Students:* 79 full-time (56 women); includes 5 minority (all Two or more races, non-Hispanic/Latino), 40 international. Average age 22. In 2016, 78 master's awarded. *Entrance requirements:* For master's, GMAT. Additional exam requirements/recommendations for international students: Required—TOEFL (minimum score 600 paper-based; 100 iBT), Michigan English Language Assessment Battery (minimum score 86); Recommended—IELTS (minimum score 7). *Application deadline:* For fall admission, 11/18 priority date for domestic and international students. Applications are processed on a rolling basis. Application fee: $60 ($70 for international students). Electronic applications accepted. *Financial support:* Fellowships with tuition reimbursements available. *Unit head:* Dr. Brian Mittendorf, Professor and Chair, 614-292-1720, E-mail: mittendorf.3@osu.edu. *Application contact:* 614-292-8511, Fax: 614-292-9006, E-mail: fisher_macc@fisher.osu.edu.
Website: http://fisher.osu.edu/macc

Oklahoma Christian University, Graduate School of Business, Oklahoma City, OK 73136-1100. Offers accounting (M Acc, MBA); financial services (MBA); general business (MBA); health services management (MBA); human resources (MBA); international business (MBA); leadership and organizational development (MBA); marketing (MBA); nonprofit management (MBA); project management (MBA). *Accreditation:* ACBSP. *Program availability:* Part-time, 100% online. *Faculty:* 10 full-time (2 women), 21 part-time/adjunct (2 women). *Students:* 156 full-time (68 women), 137 part-time (73 women). Average age 30. 374 applicants, 213 enrolled. In 2016, 114 master's awarded. *Entrance requirements:* For master's, bachelor's degree. Additional exam requirements/recommendations for international students: Required—TOEFL (minimum score 550 paper-based). Application fee: $25. Electronic applications accepted. *Expenses:* Contact institution. *Unit head:* Dr. Ken Johnson, Chair, 405-425-5567, Fax: 405-425-5585, E-mail: ken.johnson@oc.edu. *Application contact:* Angie Ricketts, Graduate School Admissions Counselor, 405-425-5587, Fax: 405-425-5585, E-mail: angie.ricketts@oc.edu.
Website: http://www.oc.edu/academics/graduate/business/

Accounting

Oklahoma State University, Spears School of Business, School of Accounting, Stillwater, OK 74078. Offers MS, PhD. *Accreditation:* AACSB. *Program availability:* Part-time. *Faculty:* 17 full-time (8 women), 5 part-time/adjunct (4 women). *Students:* 39 full-time (15 women), 11 part-time (5 women); includes 10 minority (1 Black or African American, non-Hispanic/Latino; 2 American Indian or Alaska Native, non-Hispanic/Latino; 1 Asian, non-Hispanic/Latino; 1 Hispanic/Latino; 5 Two or more races, non-Hispanic/Latino), 3 international. Average age 23. 33 applicants, 21% accepted, 7 enrolled. In 2016, 42 master's, 4 doctorates awarded. *Degree requirements:* For master's, thesis or alternative; for doctorate, comprehensive exam, thesis/dissertation. *Entrance requirements:* For master's and doctorate, GRE or GMAT. Additional exam requirements/recommendations for international students: Required—TOEFL (minimum score 550 paper-based; 79 iBT). *Application deadline:* For fall admission, 3/1 priority date for international students; for spring admission, 8/1 priority date for international students. Applications are processed on a rolling basis. Application fee: $40 ($75 for international students). Electronic applications accepted. *Expenses:* Tuition, state resident: full-time $3775; part-time $209.70 per credit hour. Tuition, nonresident: full-time $14,851; part-time $825.05 per credit hour. *Required fees:* $2027; $112.60 per credit hour. Tuition and fees vary according to campus/location. *Financial support:* In 2016–17, 6 research assistantships (averaging $15,818 per year), 23 teaching assistantships (averaging $5,404 per year) were awarded; career-related internships or fieldwork, Federal Work-Study, scholarships/grants, health care benefits, tuition waivers (partial), and unspecified assistantships also available. Support available to part-time students. Financial award application deadline: 3/1; financial award applicants required to submit FAFSA. *Faculty research:* International accounting, accounting education, cost-management, taxation, oil and gas. *Unit head:* Dr. Rick Wilson, Department Head, 405-744-3551, Fax: 405-744-1680, E-mail: rick.wilson@okstate.edu. *Application contact:* Dr. Alyssa Vowell, Graduate Coordinator, 405-744-6635, Fax: 405-744-1680, E-mail: alyssa.vowell@okstate.edu.
Website: http://spears.okstate.edu/accounting

Old Dominion University, Strome College of Business, Program in Accounting, Norfolk, VA 23529. Offers MS. *Accreditation:* AACSB. *Program availability:* Part-time, evening/weekend. *Faculty:* 7 full-time (3 women), 4 part-time/adjunct (2 women). *Students:* 22 full-time (14 women), 29 part-time (13 women); includes 21 minority (9 Black or African American, non-Hispanic/Latino; 7 Asian, non-Hispanic/Latino; 1 Hispanic/Latino; 4 Two or more races, non-Hispanic/Latino), 9 international. Average age 32. 25 applicants, 88% accepted, 18 enrolled. In 2016, 11 master's awarded. *Degree requirements:* For master's, comprehensive exam. *Entrance requirements:* For master's, GMAT, minimum GPA of 3.0. Additional exam requirements/recommendations for international students: Required—TOEFL (minimum score 550 paper-based). *Application deadline:* For fall admission, 7/1 priority date for domestic students, 4/15 priority date for international students; for spring admission, 11/1 priority date for domestic students, 10/1 priority date for international students. Applications are processed on a rolling basis. Application fee: $50. *Expenses:* Contact institution. *Financial support:* In 2016–17, 4 students received support, including 8 research assistantships with partial tuition reimbursements available (averaging $6,400 per year); career-related internships or fieldwork and unspecified assistantships also available. Financial award application deadline: 2/15; financial award applicants required to submit FAFSA. *Faculty research:* Assurance services, auditing, managerial accounting, financial accounting, accounting history. *Unit head:* Dr. Yin Xu, Graduate Program Director, 757-683-3554, Fax: 757-683-5639, E-mail: yxu@odu.edu.
Website: http://www.odu.edu/business/departments/accounting

Oral Roberts University, School of Business, Tulsa, OK 74171. Offers accounting (MBA); entrepreneurship (MBA); finance (MBA); international business (MBA); management (MBA); marketing (MBA); non-profit management (MBA); not for profit management (MNM). *Accreditation:* ACBSP. *Program availability:* Part-time, online learning. *Degree requirements:* For master's, thesis optional. *Entrance requirements:* For master's, minimum cumulative GPA of 3.0. Additional exam requirements/recommendations for international students: Required—TOEFL (minimum score 550 paper-based; 79 iBT). Electronic applications accepted. *Faculty research:* Social media, international business and marketing.

Oregon State University, College of Business, Program in Accounting, Corvallis, OR 97331. Offers MBA. *Program availability:* Part-time, online learning. *Faculty:* 47 full-time (13 women), 10 part-time/adjunct (3 women). *Students:* 7 full-time (2 women), 3 part-time (all women); includes 1 minority (Asian, non-Hispanic/Latino), 6 international. Average age 32. 5 applicants, 100% accepted, 3 enrolled. In 2016, 16 master's awarded. *Entrance requirements:* For master's, GMAT. Additional exam requirements/recommendations for international students: Required—TOEFL (minimum score 91 iBT), IELTS (minimum score 7). Application fee: $75 ($85 for international students). *Expenses:* $19,143 resident full-time tuition, $32,616 non-resident (for MBA). *Unit head:* Dr. David Baldridge, Director for Business Master's Programs, 541-737-6062, E-mail: osumba@bus.oregonstate.edu.

Oregon State University, College of Business, Program in Business Administration, Corvallis, OR 97331. Offers business administration (PhD), including accounting, innovation/commercialization; business analytics (MBA); corporate finance (MBA); innovation management (MBA); organizational leadership (MBA); research thesis (MBA); supply chain and logistics management (MBA). *Program availability:* Part-time, blended/hybrid learning. *Faculty:* 47 full-time (13 women), 10 part-time/adjunct (3 women). *Students:* 132 full-time (58 women), 83 part-time (36 women); includes 24 minority (3 Black or African American, non-Hispanic/Latino; 11 Asian, non-Hispanic/Latino; 8 Hispanic/Latino; 1 Native Hawaiian or other Pacific Islander, non-Hispanic/Latino; 1 Two or more races, non-Hispanic/Latino), 91 international. Average age 30. 203 applicants, 38% accepted, 67 enrolled. In 2016, 81 master's awarded. *Entrance requirements:* For master's, GMAT. Additional exam requirements/recommendations for international students: Required—TOEFL (minimum score 91 iBT), IELTS (minimum score 7). *Application deadline:* For fall admission, 2/1 priority date for domestic and international students; for winter admission, 9/15 priority date for domestic and international students; for spring admission, 1/1 priority date for domestic and international students. Applications are processed on a rolling basis. Application fee: $75 ($85 for international students). *Expenses:* $19,143 resident full-time tuition, $32,616 non-resident (for MBA). *Financial support:* Application deadline: 1/15. *Unit head:* Dr. David Baldridge, Director for Business Master's Program, 541-737-6062, E-mail: david.baldridge@bus.oregonstate.edu. *Application contact:* E-mail: osumba@bus.oregonstate.edu.
Website: http://business.oregonstate.edu/graduate-programs

Our Lady of the Lake University, School of Business and Leadership, Program in Accounting, San Antonio, TX 78207-4689. Offers MS. *Program availability:* Part-time, evening/weekend. *Faculty:* 4 full-time (2 women), 4 part-time/adjunct (0 women). *Students:* 11 full-time (7 women), 8 part-time (6 women); includes 16 minority (2 Black or African American, non-Hispanic/Latino; 1 Asian, non-Hispanic/Latino; 13 Hispanic/Latino). Average age 31. 8 applicants, 63% accepted, 4 enrolled. In 2016, 8 master's awarded. *Entrance requirements:* For master's, GMAT, GRE General Test, or MAT, official transcripts showing undergraduate degree in accounting or 30 hours of accounting courses previously taken with minimum cumulative GPA of 2.5; 2 letters of recommendation; resume highlighting managerial or professional work experience. Additional exam requirements/recommendations for international students: Required—TOEFL. *Application deadline:* For fall admission, 6/15 for domestic and international students; for spring admission, 11/15 for domestic and international students; for summer admission, 4/15 for domestic and international students. Applications are processed on a rolling basis. Application fee: $40 ($50 for international students). Electronic applications accepted. Application fee is waived when completed online. *Expenses: Tuition:* Full-time $14,796. Tuition and fees vary according to course load, degree level, campus/location and program. *Financial support:* In 2016–17, 8 students received support. Federal Work-Study, scholarships/grants, unspecified assistantships, and tuition discounts available. Support available to part-time students. Financial award application deadline: 5/1; financial award applicants required to submit FAFSA. *Unit head:* Kathryn Winney, Associate Dean, 210-434-6711 Ext. 2297, E-mail: kmwinney@ollusa.edu. *Application contact:* Graduate Admission, 210-431-3995, Fax: 210-431-3945, E-mail: gradadm@ollusa.edu.
Website: http://www.ollusa.edu/s/1190/hybrid/default-hybrid-ollu.aspx?sid-1190&gid-1&pgid-7870

Pace University, Lubin School of Business, Accounting Program, New York, NY 10038. Offers public accounting (MBA, MS). *Accreditation:* AACSB. *Program availability:* Evening/weekend. *Students:* 201 full-time (117 women), 89 part-time (56 women); includes 70 minority (9 Black or African American, non-Hispanic/Latino; 1 American Indian or Alaska Native, non-Hispanic/Latino; 43 Asian, non-Hispanic/Latino; 15 Hispanic/Latino; 2 Two or more races, non-Hispanic/Latino), 153 international. Average age 26. 293 applicants, 69% accepted, 93 enrolled. In 2016, 162 master's awarded. *Entrance requirements:* For master's, GMAT, GRE, undergraduate degree, transcripts from all accredited colleges/universities attended, two letters of recommendation, resume, personal statement. Additional exam requirements/recommendations for international students: Required—TOEFL (minimum score 90 iBT), IELTS (minimum score 7) or PTE (minimum score 61). *Application deadline:* For fall admission, 8/1 priority date for domestic students, 6/1 for international students; for spring admission, 12/1 priority date for domestic students, 10/1 for international students. Applications are processed on a rolling basis. Application fee: $70. Electronic applications accepted. *Expenses: Tuition:* Part-time $1195 per credit. *Required fees:* $260 per semester. Tuition and fees vary according to degree level, campus/location and program. *Financial support:* Research assistantships, career-related internships or fieldwork, and Federal Work-Study available. Support available to part-time students. Financial award application deadline: 2/15; financial award applicants required to submit FAFSA. *Unit head:* Dr. Rudolph Jacob, Chairperson, 212-618-6425, E-mail: rjacob@pace.edu. *Application contact:* Susan Ford-Goldschein, Director of Graduate Admissions, 212-346-1531, Fax: 212-346-1585, E-mail: graduateadmission@pace.edu.
Website: http://www.pace.edu/lubin/departments-and-research-centers/accounting-department/graduate-accounting-programs

Pace University, Lubin School of Business, Advanced Professional Certificate Program, New York, NY 10038. Offers business economics (APC); e-business (APC); financial management (APC); international business (APC); international economics (APC); investment management (APC); marketing (APC); public accounting (APC). *Program availability:* Evening/weekend. *Students:* 1 applicant, 100% accepted, 1 enrolled. *Entrance requirements:* For degree, MBA or MS in business discipline, relevant professional experience. Additional exam requirements/recommendations for international students: Required—TOEFL (minimum score 90 iBT), IELTS (minimum score 7) or PTE (minimum score 61). *Application deadline:* For fall admission, 8/1 priority date for domestic students, 6/1 for international students; for spring admission, 12/1 for domestic students, 10/1 for international students. Applications are processed on a rolling basis. Application fee: $70. Electronic applications accepted. *Expenses: Tuition:* Part-time $1195 per credit. *Required fees:* $260 per semester. Tuition and fees vary according to degree level, campus/location and program. *Unit head:* Dr. Jack Yurkiewicz, Director, 212-618-6567, E-mail: jyurkiewicz@pace.edu. *Application contact:* Susan Ford-Goldschein, Director of Graduate Admissions, 212-346-1531, Fax: 212-346-1585, E-mail: graduateadmission@pace.edu.
Website: http://www.pace.edu/lubin/agc

Pacific Lutheran University, School of Business, Master of Science in Accounting Program, Tacoma, WA 98447. Offers MSA. *Program availability:* Part-time. *Entrance requirements:* For master's, GMAT or GRE. Additional exam requirements/recommendations for international students: Required—TOEFL (minimum score 550 paper-based; 88 iBT). *Expenses:* Contact institution.

Pacific States University, College of Business, Los Angeles, CA 90010. Offers accounting (MBA); finance (MBA); international business (MBA, DBA); management of information technology (MBA); real estate management (MBA). *Program availability:* Part-time, evening/weekend, online learning. *Degree requirements:* For doctorate, comprehensive exam, thesis/dissertation. *Entrance requirements:* For master's, minimum undergraduate GPA of 2.5 during last 90 hours of course work. Additional exam requirements/recommendations for international students: Required—TOEFL (minimum score 500 paper-based; 61 iBT), IELTS (minimum score 5.5).

Penn State Erie, The Behrend College, Graduate School, Erie, PA 16563. Offers accounting (MPAC); business administration (MBA); project management (MPM); quality and manufacturing management (MMM). *Accreditation:* AACSB. *Program availability:* Part-time. *Students:* 28 full-time (9 women), 118 part-time (31 women); includes 11 minority (5 Black or African American, non-Hispanic/Latino; 2 Asian, non-Hispanic/Latino; 1 Hispanic/Latino; 3 Two or more races, non-Hispanic/Latino), 2 international. Average age 32. 91 applicants, 74% accepted, 55 enrolled. In 2016, 59 master's awarded. *Entrance requirements:* Additional exam requirements/recommendations for international students: Required—TOEFL (minimum score 550 paper-based; 80 iBT), IELTS. *Application deadline:* Applications are processed on a rolling basis. Application fee: $65. Electronic applications accepted. *Financial support:* Federal Work-Study available. Financial award application deadline: 3/1; financial award applicants required to submit FAFSA. *Unit head:* Dr. Ralph M. Ford, Chancellor, 814-898-6160, Fax: 814-898-6461. *Application contact:* Ann M. Burbules, Assistant Director, Graduate Admissions, 866-374-3378, Fax: 814-898-6044, E-mail: behrend.admissions@psu.edu.
Website: http://behrend.psu.edu/

Penn State Harrisburg, Graduate School, School of Business Administration, Middletown, PA 17057. Offers accounting (MPAC, Certificate); business administration (MBA); information systems (MS); operations and supply chain management (Certificate). *Program availability:* Part-time, evening/weekend. *Unit head:* Dr. Mukund S. Kulkarni, Chancellor, 717-948-6105, Fax: 717-948-6452. *Application contact:* Robert W. Coffman, Jr., Director of Enrollment Management, Admissions, 717-948-6250, Fax: 717-948-6325, E-mail: hbgadmit@psu.edu.
Website: https://harrisburg.psu.edu/business-administration/

Penn State University Park, Graduate School, Smeal College of Business, University Park, PA 16802. Offers accounting (M Acc); business administration (MBA, MS, PhD); management and organizational leadership (MPS); supply chain management (MPS). *Accreditation:* AACSB. *Students:* 276 full-time (90 women). Average age 30. 1,243 applicants, 26% accepted, 260 enrolled. In 2016, 274 master's, 11 doctorates awarded.

Entrance requirements: Additional exam requirements/recommendations for international students: Required—TOEFL (minimum score 550 paper-based; 80 iBT), IELTS. *Application deadline:* Applications are processed on a rolling basis. Application fee: $65. Electronic applications accepted. *Financial support:* Fellowships, research assistantships, teaching assistantships, career-related internships or fieldwork, Federal Work-Study, scholarships/grants, traineeships, health care benefits, and unspecified assistantships available. Support available to part-time students. Financial award application deadline: 3/1; financial award applicants required to submit FAFSA. *Unit head:* Dr. Charles H. Whiteman, Dean, 814-863-0448, Fax: 814-865-7064. *Application contact:* Lori Hawn, Director, Graduate Student Services, 814-865-1795, Fax: 814-863-4627, E-mail: l-gswww@lists.psu.edu. Website: http://smeal.psu.edu/

Pepperdine University, Graziadio School of Business and Management, Full-Time MBA Programs, Malibu, CA 90263. Offers accounting (MS); applied analytics (MS); applied finance (MS); business administration (MBA); global business (MS); human resources (MS); international business administration (MBA); management and leadership (MS); organization development (MS); real estate investment and finance (MS); JD/MBA; MBA/MPP. *Accreditation:* AACSB. *Students:* 472 full-time (239 women), 3 part-time (2 women); includes 424 minority (111 Black or African American, non-Hispanic/Latino; 7 American Indian or Alaska Native, non-Hispanic/Latino; 216 Asian, non-Hispanic/Latino; 88 Hispanic/Latino; 2 Two or more races, non-Hispanic/Latino), 47 international. Average age 25. 1,991 applicants, 59% accepted, 238 enrolled. In 2016, 419 master's awarded. *Entrance requirements:* For master's, GMAT or GRE, two letters of recommendation. Additional exam requirements/recommendations for international students: Required—TOEFL. *Application deadline:* For fall admission, 5/1 for domestic students, 4/1 for international students. Application fee: $75. Electronic applications accepted. *Financial support:* Applicants required to submit FAFSA. *Unit head:* Dr. Michael L. Williams, Associate Dean, 310-506-4112, Fax: 310-506-4126, E-mail: michael.williams@pepperdine.edu.
Website: http://bschool.pepperdine.edu/masters-degree/

Pepperdine University, Seaver College, Division of Business, Malibu, CA 90263. Offers accounting (MS). *Students:* 1 full-time (0 women), 1 (woman) part-time, 1 international. Average age 22. In 2016, 2 master's awarded. *Entrance requirements:* For master's, GRE General Test, statement of purpose and intent for writing as a vocation, script writing sample, letters of recommendation. Additional exam requirements/recommendations for international students: Required—TOEFL. *Application deadline:* For fall admission, 2/1 priority date for domestic students. Application fee: $55. Electronic applications accepted. *Unit head:* Dr. Dean Baim, Divisional Dean/Professor of Economics and Finance, 310-506-4237, E-mail: dean.baim@pepperdine.edu. *Application contact:* Hayley Wolf, Director of Admission, 310-506-4392, E-mail: hayley.wolf@pepperdine.edu.
Website: http://seaver.pepperdine.edu/humanities/graduate/screenwriting/

Pittsburg State University, Graduate School, Kelce College of Business, Department of Accounting, Pittsburg, KS 66762. Offers MBA. *Program availability:* Part-time. *Students:* 12. In 2016, 20 master's awarded. *Degree requirements:* For master's, thesis or alternative. *Entrance requirements:* For master's, GMAT or GRE. Additional exam requirements/recommendations for international students: Required—TOEFL (minimum score 550 paper-based; 79 iBT), IELTS (minimum score 6.5), PTE (minimum score 53). *Application deadline:* For fall admission, 7/15 for domestic students, 7/1 for international students; for spring admission, 12/15 for domestic students, 10/15 for international students; for summer admission, 5/15 for domestic students, 4/1 for international students. Applications are processed on a rolling basis. Application fee: $35 ($60 for international students). Electronic applications accepted. *Expenses:* Contact institution. *Financial support:* In 2016–17, 5 teaching assistantships with full tuition reimbursements (averaging $5,500 per year) were awarded; research assistantships, career-related internships or fieldwork, Federal Work-Study, and unspecified assistantships also available. Financial award application deadline: 2/1; financial award applicants required to submit FAFSA. *Faculty research:* Accountant's legal liability, computer audit. *Unit head:* Dr. Bienvenido Cortes, MBA Coordinator, 620-235-4594, E-mail: bcortes@pittstate.edu. *Application contact:* Lisa Allen, Assistant Director of Graduate and Continuing Studies, 620-235-4218, Fax: 620-235-4219, E-mail: lallen@pittstate.edu.

Polytechnic University of Puerto Rico, Miami Campus, Graduate School, Miami, FL 33166. Offers accounting (MBA); business administration (MBA); construction management (MEM); environmental management (MEM); finance (MBA); human resources management (MBA); logistics and supply chain management (MBA); management of international enterprises (MBA); manufacturing management (MEM); marketing management (MBA); project management (MBA). *Program availability:* Part-time, evening/weekend, online learning. *Entrance requirements:* For master's, minimum GPA of 3.0. Electronic applications accepted.

Polytechnic University of Puerto Rico, Orlando Campus, Graduate School, Orlando, FL 32825. Offers accounting (MBA); business administration (MBA); construction management (MEM); engineering management (MEM); environmental management (MEM); finance (MBA); human resources management (MBA); management of international enterprises (MBA); management of technology (MBA); manufacturing management (MEM). *Program availability:* Part-time, evening/weekend, online learning. *Entrance requirements:* For master's, minimum GPA of 3.0. Additional exam requirements/recommendations for international students: Recommended—TOEFL. Electronic applications accepted.

Pontifical Catholic University of Puerto Rico, College of Business Administration, Program in Accounting, Ponce, PR 00717-0777. Offers MBA. *Program availability:* Part-time, evening/weekend. *Degree requirements:* For master's, thesis. *Entrance requirements:* For master's, GRE, interview, minimum GPA of 2.75.

Pontifical Catholic University of Puerto Rico, College of Business Administration, Program in Management and Accounting, Ponce, PR 00717-0777. Offers Professional Certificate.

Post University, Program in Business Administration, Waterbury, CT 06723-2540. Offers accounting (MSA); business administration (MBA); corporate innovation (MBA); entrepreneurship (MBA); finance (MBA); healthcare (MBA); leadership (MBA); marketing (MBA); project management (MBA). *Accreditation:* ACBSP. *Program availability:* Online learning.

Prairie View A&M University, College of Business, Prairie View, TX 77446. Offers accounting (MS); business administration (MBA). *Accreditation:* AACSB. *Program availability:* Part-time, evening/weekend. *Faculty:* 16 full-time (2 women). *Students:* 81 full-time (49 women), 157 part-time (89 women); includes 205 minority (101 Black or African American, non-Hispanic/Latino; 14 Asian, non-Hispanic/Latino; 10 Hispanic/Latino), 18 international. Average age 32. 172 applicants, 94% accepted, 104 enrolled. In 2016, 87 master's awarded. *Degree requirements:* For master's, comprehensive exam, thesis optional. *Entrance requirements:* For master's, GMAT, GRE, minimum GPA of 2.45, essay. Additional exam requirements/recommendations for international students: Required—TOEFL (minimum score 550 paper-based; 79 iBT). *Application deadline:* For fall admission, 5/1 for domestic students, 5/1 priority date for international students; for spring admission, 10/1 for domestic students, 9/1 priority date for international students; for summer admission, 3/1 for domestic students, 2/1 for international students. Applications are processed on a rolling basis. Application fee: $50. Electronic applications accepted. *Expenses:* Contact institution. *Financial support:* In 2016–17, 5 students received support, including 2 research assistantships (averaging $24,000 per year), 5 teaching assistantships (averaging $60,000 per year); scholarships/grants and unspecified assistantships also available. Financial award application deadline: 4/1; financial award applicants required to submit FAFSA. *Faculty research:* Accounting (energy, oil and gas); finance (international finance, personal finance, real estate markets and institutions); marketing management (supply chain, human resources, entrepreneurship, small business ownership, ethics); management information systems (cyber-security, managing social media during crises). *Unit head:* Dr. Munir Quddus, Dean, 936-261-9200, Fax: 936-261-9241, E-mail: cob@pvamu.edu. *Application contact:* Gabriel Crosby, Director, Graduate Programs in Business, 936-261-9217, Fax: 936-261-9232, E-mail: mba@pvamu.edu.
Website: http://www.pvamu.edu/business/

Providence College, School of Business, Providence, RI 02918. Offers accounting (MBA); finance (MBA); international business (MBA); management (MBA); marketing (MBA). *Accreditation:* AACSB. *Program availability:* Part-time, evening/weekend. *Faculty:* 10 full-time (3 women), 5 part-time/adjunct (2 women). *Students:* 84 full-time (39 women), 66 part-time (23 women); includes 15 minority (6 Black or African American, non-Hispanic/Latino; 1 Asian, non-Hispanic/Latino; 8 Hispanic/Latino), 5 international. Average age 26. 116 applicants, 96% accepted, 94 enrolled. In 2016, 80 master's awarded. *Entrance requirements:* For master's, GMAT. Additional exam requirements/recommendations for international students: Required—TOEFL (minimum score 577 paper-based; 90 iBT). *Application deadline:* For fall admission, 5/1 priority date for domestic and international students; for spring admission, 11/1 priority date for domestic and international students; for summer admission, 3/15 priority date for domestic students, 3/15 for international students. Applications are processed on a rolling basis. Application fee: $55. *Expenses:* Contact institution. *Financial support:* Career-related internships or fieldwork, institutionally sponsored loans, and unspecified assistantships available. Support available to part-time students. Financial award application deadline: 8/1; financial award applicants required to submit FAFSA.
Website: http://www.providence.edu/business/Pages/default.aspx

Purdue University Northwest, Graduate Studies Office, School of Management, Hammond, IN 46323-2094. Offers accountancy (M Acc); business administration (MBA); business administration for executives (EMBA). *Accreditation:* AACSB. *Program availability:* Part-time, evening/weekend. *Entrance requirements:* For master's, GMAT. Additional exam requirements/recommendations for international students: Required—TOEFL. Electronic applications accepted.

Queens College of the City University of New York, Division of Social Sciences, Department of Accounting, Queens, NY 11367-1597. Offers MS. *Program availability:* Part-time. *Faculty:* 22 full-time (4 women), 38 part-time/adjunct (9 women). *Students:* 25 full-time (13 women), 138 part-time (73 women); includes 117 minority (13 Black or African American, non-Hispanic/Latino; 66 Asian, non-Hispanic/Latino; 36 Hispanic/Latino; 2 Two or more races, non-Hispanic/Latino), 9 international. Average age 30. 142 applicants, 79% accepted, 54 enrolled. In 2016, 110 master's awarded. *Degree requirements:* For master's, comprehensive exam. *Entrance requirements:* For master's, minimum GPA of 3.0. Additional exam requirements/recommendations for international students: Required—TOEFL (minimum score 100 iBT), IELTS (minimum score 7). *Application deadline:* For fall admission, 4/1 for domestic students; for spring admission, 11/1 for domestic students. Application fee: $125. Electronic applications accepted. *Expenses:* Tuition, state resident: full-time $5065; part-time $425 per credit. Tuition, nonresident: part-time $780 per credit. *Required fees:* $522; $397 per credit. Part-time tuition and fees vary according to course load and program. *Financial support:* Career-related internships or fieldwork and unspecified assistantships available. *Unit head:* Dr. Israel Blumenfrucht, Chairperson, 718-997-5070, E-mail: israel.blumenfrucht@qc.cuny.edu.

Queens College of the City University of New York, Division of Social Sciences, Department of Economics, Queens, NY 11367-1597. Offers risk management-accounting (MS); risk management-dynamic finance analysis (MS); risk management-finance (MS). *Degree requirements:* For master's, thesis. *Entrance requirements:* For master's, minimum GPA of 3.0. Additional exam requirements/recommendations for international students: Required—TOEFL (minimum score 100 iBT), IELTS (minimum score 7). *Expenses:* Tuition, state resident: full-time $5065; part-time $425 per credit. Tuition, nonresident: part-time $780 per credit. *Required fees:* $522; $397 per credit. Part-time tuition and fees vary according to course load and program. *Faculty research:* Business economics, urban economic problems, international economics, economics of nonprofit sector.

Regent University, Graduate School, School of Business and Leadership, Virginia Beach, VA 23464-9800. Offers business administration (MBA), including accounting, entrepreneurship, finance and investing, general management, healthcare management (MA, MBA), human resource management, innovation management; leadership (Certificate); organizational leadership (MA, PhD), including ecclesial leadership (PhD), entrepreneurial leadership (PhD), future studies (MA), healthcare management (MA, MBA), human resource development (PhD), interdisciplinary studies (MA), international organizations (MA), leadership coaching and mentoring (MA), not-for-profit management (MA), organizational communication (MA), organizational development consulting (MA); strategic leadership (DSL), including global consulting, leadership coaching, strategic foresight. *Program availability:* Part-time, evening/weekend, 100% online, blended/hybrid learning. *Faculty:* 9 full-time (2 women), 28 part-time/adjunct (10 women). *Students:* 100 full-time (56 women), 1,008 part-time (528 women); includes 562 minority (453 Black or African American, non-Hispanic/Latino; 7 American Indian or Alaska Native, non-Hispanic/Latino; 30 Asian, non-Hispanic/Latino; 51 Hispanic/Latino; 1 Native Hawaiian or other Pacific Islander, non-Hispanic/Latino; 20 Two or more races, non-Hispanic/Latino), 76 international. Average age 40. 1,240 applicants, 45% accepted, 352 enrolled. In 2016, 95 master's, 71 doctorates awarded. *Degree requirements:* For master's, thesis or alternative, 3-credit hour culminating experience; for doctorate, thesis/dissertation. *Entrance requirements:* For master's, college transcripts, resume, essay; for doctorate, college transcripts, resume, essay, writing sample; for Certificate, writing sample, resume, transcripts. Additional exam requirements/recommendations for international students: Required—TOEFL (minimum score 577 paper-based). *Application deadline:* For fall admission, 5/1 priority date for domestic students; for spring admission, 10/1 priority date for domestic students. Applications are processed on a rolling basis. Application fee: $50. Electronic applications accepted. *Expenses:* Contact institution. *Financial support:* In 2016–17, 631 students received support. Career-related internships or fieldwork, scholarships/grants, and unspecified assistantships available. Support available to part-time students. *Faculty research:* Servant leadership, global business, team effectiveness, technology utilization, leadership development. *Unit head:* Dr. Doris Gomez, Dean, 757-352-4686, Fax: 757-352-4634, E-mail: dorigom@regent.edu. *Application contact:* Heidi Cece, Assistant Vice President of Enrollment Management, 800-373-5504, Fax: 757-352-4381, E-mail: admissions@regent.edu.
Website: http://www.regent.edu/sbl/

Accounting

Regis University, College of Business and Economics, Denver, CO 80221-1099. Offers accounting (MS); executive leadership (Certificate); finance (MS); finance and accounting (MBA); health industry leadership (MBA); human resource management and leadership (MSOL); management (MBA); marketing (MBA); nonprofit leadership (Post-Graduate Certificate); nonprofit management (MNM); nonprofit organizational capacity building (Certificate); operations management (MBA); organizational leadership and management (MSOL); project leadership and management (MS, MSOL); strategic business management (Certificate); strategic human resource integration (Certificate); strategic management (MBA). Programs offered at Colorado Springs Campus, Northwest Denver Campus, Southeast Denver Campus, Fort Collins Campus, Broomfield Campus, Henderson (Nevada) Campus, and Summerlin (Nevada) Campus. *Program availability:* Part-time, evening/weekend, 100% online, blended/hybrid learning. *Faculty:* 15 full-time (5 women), 43 part-time/adjunct (16 women). *Students:* 622 full-time (350 women), 460 part-time (170 women); includes 317 minority (88 Black or African American, non-Hispanic/Latino; 7 American Indian or Alaska Native, non-Hispanic/Latino; 44 Asian, non-Hispanic/Latino; 151 Hispanic/Latino; 1 Native Hawaiian or other Pacific Islander, non-Hispanic/Latino; 26 Two or more races, non-Hispanic/Latino), 44 international. Average age 36. 307 applicants, 73% accepted, 134 enrolled. In 2016, 394 master's awarded. *Degree requirements:* For master's, thesis (for some programs), capstone or final research project. *Entrance requirements:* For master's, official transcript reflecting baccalaureate degree awarded from regionally-accredited college or university, interview, 2 years of full-time related work experience, resume, letters of recommendation. Additional exam requirements/recommendations for international students: Required—TOEFL (minimum score 550 paper-based; 82 iBT). *Application deadline:* For fall admission, 8/15 priority date for domestic students, 8/13 for international students; for winter admission, 10/10 priority date for domestic students, 9/8 for international students; for spring admission, 1/10 priority date for domestic students, 11/17 for international students; for summer admission, 5/1 priority date for domestic students. Applications are processed on a rolling basis. Application fee: $75. Electronic applications accepted. *Expenses:* $780 per credit hour. *Financial support:* Scholarships/grants available. Financial award application deadline: 4/15; financial award applicants required to submit FAFSA. *Faculty research:* Impact of information technology on small business regulation of accounting, international project financing, mineral development, delivery of healthcare to rural indigenous communities. *Unit head:* Dr. Timothy Keane, Academic Dean. *Application contact:* Cate Clark, Director of Admissions, 303-458-4900, Fax: 303-964-5534, E-mail: ruadmissions@regis.edu.
Website: http://www.regis.edu/CBE.aspx

Rhode Island College, School of Graduate Studies, School of Management, Department of Accounting and Computer Information Systems, Providence, RI 02908-1991. Offers accounting (MP Ac); financial planning (CGS). *Program availability:* Part-time, evening/weekend. *Faculty:* 1 (woman) full-time, 2 part-time/adjunct (1 woman). *Students:* 6 full-time (2 women), 17 part-time (10 women); includes 3 minority (1 Black or African American, non-Hispanic/Latino; 2 Asian, non-Hispanic/Latino). Average age 31. In 2016, 10 master's awarded. *Entrance requirements:* For master's, GMAT (unless applicant is a CPA or has passed a state bar exam); for CGS, GMAT, bachelor's degree from an accredited college or university, official transcripts of all undergraduate and graduate records. Additional exam requirements/recommendations for international students: Recommended—TOEFL (minimum score 550 paper-based; 79 iBT). *Application deadline:* For fall admission, 3/1 for domestic students. Applications are processed on a rolling basis. Application fee: $50. Electronic applications accepted. *Expenses:* Tuition, state resident: full-time $8928; part-time $372 per credit. Tuition, nonresident: full-time $17,376; part-time $724 per credit. *Required fees:* $604; $22 per credit. One-time fee: $74. *Financial support:* In 2016–17, 1 teaching assistantship with full tuition reimbursement (averaging $1,500 per year) was awarded; Federal Work-Study, scholarships/grants, and health care benefits also available. Support available to part-time students. Financial award application deadline: 5/15; financial award applicants required to submit FAFSA. *Unit head:* Prof. Jane Przybyla, Chair, 401-456-8036. *Application contact:* Graduate Studies, 401-456-8700.
Website: http://www.ric.edu/accountingComputerInformationSystems/

Rhodes College, Department of Commerce and Business, Memphis, TN 38112-1690. Offers accounting (MS). *Program availability:* Part-time. *Entrance requirements:* For master's, GMAT. Additional exam requirements/recommendations for international students: Required—TOEFL (minimum score 550 paper-based).

Rider University, College of Business Administration, Program in Accountancy, Lawrenceville, NJ 08648-3001. Offers M Acc. *Accreditation:* AACSB. *Entrance requirements:* For master's, GMAT, resume. Additional exam requirements/recommendations for international students: Required—TOEFL (minimum score 550 paper-based). Electronic applications accepted. *Faculty research:* Financial reporting, corporate governance, information technology, ethics, pedagogy.

Robert Morris University Illinois, Morris Graduate School of Management, Chicago, IL 60605. Offers accounting (MBA); accounting/finance (MBA); business analytics (MIS); design and media (MM); design management (MM); educational technology (MM); health care administration (MM); higher education administration (MM); human resource management (MBA); information security (MIS); information systems (MBA, MIS); law enforcement administration (MM); management (MBA); management/finance (MBA); management/human resource management (MBA); mobile computing (MIS); sports administration (MM). *Program availability:* Part-time, evening/weekend. *Faculty:* 4 full-time (1 woman), 25 part-time/adjunct (5 women). *Students:* 196 full-time (98 women), 151 part-time (85 women); includes 200 minority (114 Black or African American, non-Hispanic/Latino; 17 Asian, non-Hispanic/Latino; 67 Hispanic/Latino; 2 Two or more races, non-Hispanic/Latino), 23 international. Average age 33. 174 applicants, 61% accepted, 97 enrolled. In 2016, 190 master's awarded. *Entrance requirements:* For master's, official transcripts and letters of recommendation (for some programs); written personal statement. Additional exam requirements/recommendations for international students: Required—TOEFL (minimum score 550 paper-based). *Application deadline:* Applications are processed on a rolling basis. Application fee: $20 ($100 for international students). Electronic applications accepted. *Expenses: Tuition:* Full-time $16,500; part-time $2750 per course. *Financial support:* In 2016–17, 444 students received support. Federal Work-Study, scholarships/grants, and unspecified assistantships available. Support available to part-time students. Financial award applicants required to submit FAFSA. *Unit head:* Kayed Akkawi, Dean, 312-935-6050, Fax: 312-935-6020, E-mail: kakkawi@robertmorris.edu. *Application contact:* Danielle Naffziger, Vice President of Marketing and Enrollment, 312-935-4812, Fax: 312-935-6020, E-mail: dnaffziger@robertmorris.edu.

Rochester Institute of Technology, Graduate Enrollment Services, Saunders College of Business, Accounting and Finance Department, MBA Program in Accounting, Rochester, NY 14623-5603. Offers MBA. *Program availability:* Part-time, evening/weekend. *Students:* 16 full-time (5 women), 5 part-time (2 women); includes 2 minority (1 Black or African American, non-Hispanic/Latino; 1 Two or more races, non-Hispanic/Latino), 2 international. Average age 25. 33 applicants, 52% accepted, 9 enrolled. In 2016, 8 master's awarded. *Degree requirements:* For master's, comprehensive exam. *Entrance requirements:* For master's, GRE or GMAT, minimum GPA of 3.0 (recommended). Additional exam requirements/recommendations for international students: Required—TOEFL (minimum score 580 paper-based; 92 iBT), IELTS (minimum score 7), PTE (minimum score 63). *Application deadline:* Applications are processed on a rolling basis. Application fee: $60. Electronic applications accepted. *Expenses:* $1,742 per credit hour. *Financial support:* In 2016–17, 11 students received support. Research assistantships with partial tuition reimbursements available, teaching assistantships with partial tuition reimbursements available, career-related internships or fieldwork, scholarships/grants, and unspecified assistantships available. Support available to part-time students. Financial award applicants required to submit FAFSA. *Faculty research:* Corporate financial reporting disclosure and quality, fraud and litigation risk, audit quality, opinion, and pricing decision, financial regulations, information technology performance. *Unit head:* Jenna Lenhardt, Graduate Admissions Advisor, 585-475-6916, E-mail: gradbus@saunders.rit.edu. *Application contact:* Diane Ellison, Associate Vice President, 585-475-2229, Fax: 585-475-7164, E-mail: gradinfo@rit.edu.
Website: http://saunders.rit.edu/programs/graduate/mba_accounting.php

Rochester Institute of Technology, Graduate Enrollment Services, Saunders College of Business, Accounting and Finance Department, MS Program in Accounting, Rochester, NY 14623. Offers MS. *Program availability:* Part-time, evening/weekend. *Students:* 4 full-time (2 women). 29 applicants, 34% accepted, 3 enrolled. In 2016, 5 master's awarded. *Degree requirements:* For master's, thesis or alternative. *Entrance requirements:* For master's, GMAT or GRE, minimum GPA of 3.0 (recommended). Additional exam requirements/recommendations for international students: Required—TOEFL (minimum score 92 iBT), IELTS (minimum score 7), PTE (minimum score 63). *Application deadline:* Applications are processed on a rolling basis. Application fee: $60. Electronic applications accepted. *Expenses:* $1,742 per credit hour. *Financial support:* In 2016–17, 4 students received support. Research assistantships with partial tuition reimbursements available, teaching assistantships with partial tuition reimbursements available, career-related internships or fieldwork, and unspecified assistantships available. Support available to part-time students. Financial award applicants required to submit FAFSA. *Faculty research:* Corporate financial reporting disclosure and quality, fraud and litigation risk, audit quality, opinion, and pricing decision, financial regulations, information technology performance. *Unit head:* Jenna Lenhardt, Graduate Program Advisor, 585-475-6916, E-mail: jlenhardt@saunders.rit.edu. *Application contact:* Diane Ellison, Associate Vice President, Graduate Enrollment Services, 585-475-2229, Fax: 585-475-7164, E-mail: gradinfo@rit.edu.
Website: http://saunders.rit.edu/programs/graduate/ms_accounting.php

Rockhurst University, Helzberg School of Management, Kansas City, MO 64110-2561. Offers accounting (MBA); business intelligence (MBA, Certificate); data science (MBA, Certificate); entrepreneurship (MBA); finance (MBA); fundraising leadership (MBA, Certificate); healthcare management (MBA, Certificate); human capital (Certificate); international business (Certificate); management (MBA, Certificate); nonprofit administration (Certificate); organizational development (Certificate); science leadership (Certificate). *Accreditation:* AACSB. *Program availability:* Part-time, evening/weekend. *Entrance requirements:* For master's, GMAT or GRE. Additional exam requirements/recommendations for international students: Required—TOEFL (minimum score 550 paper-based; 79 iBT). Electronic applications accepted. Application fee is waived when completed online. *Faculty research:* Offshoring/outsourcing, systems analysis/synthesis, work teams, multilateral trade, path dependencies/creation.

Rocky Mountain College, Program in Accountancy, Billings, MT 59102-1796. Offers M Acc. *Program availability:* Part-time-only. *Faculty:* 2 full-time (0 women). *Students:* 1 (woman) part-time. Average age 27. In 2016, 3 master's awarded. *Entrance requirements:* For master's, GMAT. Additional exam requirements/recommendations for international students: Required—TOEFL (minimum score 570 paper-based; 88 iBT), IELTS (minimum score 6.5). *Application deadline:* Applications are processed on a rolling basis. Application fee: $35 ($40 for international students). Electronic applications accepted. Application fee is waived when completed online. *Expenses:* Contact institution. *Financial support:* Applicants required to submit FAFSA. *Unit head:* Anthony Piltz, Professor of Business Administration and Economics, 406-657-1069, E-mail: piltza@rocky.edu. *Application contact:* Austin Mapston, Dean of Enrollment Services, 406-657-1026, Fax: 406-657-1189, E-mail: admissions@rocky.edu.
Website: http://www.rocky.edu/academics/academic-programs/undergraduate-majors/accountancy/index.php

Roosevelt University, Graduate Division, Walter E. Heller College of Business, Program in Accounting, Chicago, IL 60605. Offers MSA. *Program availability:* Part-time, evening/weekend. *Students:* 30 full-time (19 women), 67 part-time (38 women); includes 47 minority (22 Black or African American, non-Hispanic/Latino; 10 Asian, non-Hispanic/Latino; 12 Hispanic/Latino; 1 Native Hawaiian or other Pacific Islander, non-Hispanic/Latino; 2 Two or more races, non-Hispanic/Latino), 19 international. Average age 31. 58 applicants, 93% accepted, 30 enrolled. In 2016, 53 master's awarded. *Entrance requirements:* For master's, GMAT. *Application deadline:* For fall admission, 6/1 priority date for domestic students. Applications are processed on a rolling basis. Application fee: $40. *Expenses: Tuition, area resident:* Full-time $19,566; part-time $880 per credit hour. *Required fees:* $175 per semester. One-time fee: $200. Part-time tuition and fees vary according to course load, degree level and program. *Financial support:* Application deadline: 2/15. *Unit head:* Deborah Pavelka, Director, 312-281-3328, E-mail: dpavelka@roosevelt.edu. *Application contact:* Angela Ryan, Director of Graduate Enrollment, 877-APPLY RU, Fax: 312-281-3356, E-mail: applyru@roosevelt.edu.
Website: https://www.roosevelt.edu/academics/programs/masters-of-accounting-msa

Rutgers University–Newark, Graduate School, Program in Management, Newark, NJ 07102. Offers accounting (PhD); accounting information systems (PhD); computer information systems (PhD); finance (PhD); information technology (PhD); international business (PhD); management science (PhD); marketing (PhD); organization management (PhD). Program offered jointly with New Jersey Institute of Technology. *Accreditation:* AACSB. *Degree requirements:* For doctorate, thesis/dissertation, cumulative exams. *Entrance requirements:* For doctorate, GMAT or GRE General Test, minimum undergraduate B average. Additional exam requirements/recommendations for international students: Required—TOEFL. Electronic applications accepted. *Faculty research:* Technology management, leadership and teams, consumer behavior, financial and markets, logistics.

Rutgers University–Newark, Rutgers Business School–Newark and New Brunswick, Doctoral Programs in Management, Newark, NJ 07102. Offers accounting (PhD); accounting information systems (PhD); economics (PhD); finance (PhD); individualized study (PhD); information technology (PhD); international business (PhD); management science (PhD); marketing science (PhD); organizational management (PhD); science, technology and management (PhD); supply chain management (PhD). *Degree requirements:* For doctorate, comprehensive exam, thesis/dissertation. *Entrance requirements:* For doctorate, GRE or GMAT. Additional exam requirements/recommendations for international students: Required—TOEFL (minimum score 550 paper-based; 79 iBT). Electronic applications accepted.

Rutgers University–Newark, Rutgers Business School–Newark and New Brunswick, Program in Accountancy, Newark, NJ 07102. Offers M Accy. *Accreditation:* AACSB. *Program availability:* Online learning.

Rutgers University–Newark, Rutgers Business School–Newark and New Brunswick, Program in Professional Accounting, Newark, NJ 07102. Offers MBA. *Accreditation:* AACSB. *Entrance requirements:* For master's, GMAT. Additional exam requirements/recommendations for international students: Required—TOEFL. Electronic applications accepted.

Sacred Heart University, Graduate Programs, Jack Welch College of Business, Department of Accounting, Fairfield, CT 06825. Offers MS. *Program availability:* Part-time, evening/weekend. *Faculty:* 5 full-time (2 women), 2 part-time/adjunct (0 women). *Students:* 32 full-time (17 women), 1 part-time (0 women); includes 9 minority (2 Black or African American, non-Hispanic/Latino; 1 Asian, non-Hispanic/Latino; 6 Hispanic/Latino). Average age 25. 40 applicants, 98% accepted, 33 enrolled. In 2016, 25 master's awarded. *Entrance requirements:* For master's, bachelor's degree with minimum GPA of 3.0. Additional exam requirements/recommendations for international students: Required—TOEFL (minimum score 570 paper-based, 80 iBT), TWE, or IELTS (6.5); Recommended—TSE. *Application deadline:* Applications are processed on a rolling basis. Application fee: $75. Electronic applications accepted. *Expenses:* $875 per credit. *Financial support:* Unspecified assistantships available. Financial award applicants required to submit FAFSA. *Unit head:* Barbara Tarasovich, Director of MS in Accounting Program, 203-416-3513, E-mail: tarasovichb@sacredheart.edu. *Application contact:* William Sweeney, Director of Graduate Admissions Operations, 203-365-4827, Fax: 203-365-4732, E-mail: graduatestudies@sacredheart.edu.
Website: http://www.sacredheart.edu/academics/johnfwelchcollegeofbusiness/graduateprogramscertificates/msinaccounting/

St. Ambrose University, College of Business, Program in Accounting, Davenport, IA 52803-2898. Offers MAC. *Program availability:* Part-time, evening/weekend. *Degree requirements:* For master's, comprehensive exam (for some programs), thesis or alternative, capstone seminar. *Entrance requirements:* For master's, GMAT. Electronic applications accepted.

St. Bonaventure University, School of Graduate Studies, School of Business, St. Bonaventure, NY 14778-2284. Offers general business (MBA); professional accountancy (MBA). *Accreditation:* AACSB. *Program availability:* Part-time, evening/weekend, 100% online. *Faculty:* 6 full-time (1 woman), 14 part-time/adjunct (4 women). *Students:* 60 full-time (19 women), 58 part-time (29 women); includes 19 minority (4 Black or African American, non-Hispanic/Latino; 3 American Indian or Alaska Native, non-Hispanic/Latino; 4 Asian, non-Hispanic/Latino; 7 Hispanic/Latino; 1 Two or more races, non-Hispanic/Latino), 3 international. Average age 28. 123 applicants, 84% accepted, 73 enrolled. In 2016, 68 master's awarded. *Entrance requirements:* For master's, GMAT or GRE, undergraduate degree, transcripts, current resume. Additional exam requirements/recommendations for international students: Required—TOEFL (minimum score 550 paper-based; 79 iBT). *Application deadline:* For fall admission, 6/15 priority date for domestic students, 2/1 priority date for international students; for spring admission, 11/1 priority date for domestic students, 7/1 priority date for international students. Applications are processed on a rolling basis. Application fee: $0. Electronic applications accepted. *Expenses:* $733 per credit, $100 graduation fee. *Financial support:* Career-related internships or fieldwork, Federal Work-Study, scholarships/grants, health care benefits, and unspecified assistantships available. Support available to part-time students. Financial award application deadline: 4/15; financial award applicants required to submit FAFSA. *Faculty research:* Impact of Pathways Commission on accounting education, sovereign credit ratings, acculturation, advertising, and cross-cultural research of ethnic consumers. *Unit head:* Dr. Matrecia James, Dean, 716-375-2200, Fax: 716-372-2191, E-mail: mjames@sbu.edu. *Application contact:* Bruce Campbell, Director of Graduate Admissions, 716-375-2429, Fax: 716-375-4015, E-mail: gradsch@sbu.edu.
Website: http://www.sbu.edu/academics/schools/business/graduate-degrees/master-of-business-administration-(mba)

St. Edward's University, Bill Munday School of Business, Area of Business Administration, Austin, TX 78704. Offers accounting (MBA); business administration (MBA). *Program availability:* Part-time, evening/weekend. *Students:* 38 full-time (9 women), 117 part-time (61 women); includes 60 minority (9 Black or African American, non-Hispanic/Latino; 8 Asian, non-Hispanic/Latino; 36 Hispanic/Latino; 1 Native Hawaiian or other Pacific Islander, non-Hispanic/Latino; 6 Two or more races, non-Hispanic/Latino), 12 international. Average age 32. 141 applicants, 54% accepted, 47 enrolled. In 2016, 68 master's awarded. *Degree requirements:* For master's, completion of at least 24 semester hours of the 36 semester hours at St. Edward's University with minimum cumulative GPA of 3.0. *Entrance requirements:* For master's, minimum GPA of 2.75 in final 60 undergraduate semester credit hours of study. Additional exam requirements/recommendations for international students: Required—TOEFL (minimum score 79 iBT), IELTS (minimum score 6). *Application deadline:* For fall admission, 6/1 priority date for domestic and international students; for spring admission, 10/1 priority date for domestic and international students; for summer admission, 3/1 priority date for domestic and international students. Applications are processed on a rolling basis. Application fee: $50. Electronic applications accepted. *Expenses: Tuition:* Full-time $25,092; part-time $1394 per credit hour. *Required fees:* $75 per trimester. Full-time tuition and fees vary according to course load and program. *Unit head:* Dr. Ali Dadpay, Associate Dean of Academic Programs/Professor of Economics, 512-485-4616, Fax: 512-428-1217, E-mail: adadpay@stedwards.edu. *Application contact:* Mike Leveriza, Graduate Recruiter, 512-448-8745, Fax: 512-464-8877, E-mail: mleveriz@stedwards.edu.

St. Edward's University, Bill Munday School of Business, Program in Accounting, Austin, TX 78704. Offers M Ac. *Program availability:* Part-time, evening/weekend. *Students:* 9 full-time (6 women), 20 part-time (12 women); includes 9 minority (1 Black or African American, non-Hispanic/Latino; 1 Asian, non-Hispanic/Latino; 7 Hispanic/Latino), 3 international. Average age 30. 39 applicants, 59% accepted, 13 enrolled. In 2016, 10 master's awarded. *Degree requirements:* For master's, completion of at least 21 semester hours of the 30 semester hours at St. Edward's University with minimum cumulative GPA of 3.0. *Entrance requirements:* For master's, minimum GPA of 2.75 in final 60 undergraduate semester credit hours of study and in all accounting coursework. Additional exam requirements/recommendations for international students: Required—TOEFL (minimum score 79 iBT), IELTS (minimum score 6). *Application deadline:* For fall admission, 6/1 priority date for domestic and international students; for spring admission, 10/1 priority date for domestic and international students; for summer admission, 3/1 priority date for domestic and international students. Applications are processed on a rolling basis. Application fee: $50. Electronic applications accepted. *Expenses: Tuition:* Full-time $25,092; part-time $1394 per credit hour. *Required fees:* $75 per trimester. Full-time tuition and fees vary according to course load and program. *Unit head:* Dr. Louise Single, Program Director/Professor of Accounting, 512 402-3114, Fax: 512-428-1217, E-mail: louises@stedwards.edu. *Application contact:* Mike Leveriza, Graduate Recruiter, 512-448-8745, Fax: 512-464-8877, E-mail: mleveriz@stedwards.edu.
Website: http://www.stedwards.edu

St. Francis College, Program in Professional Accountancy, Brooklyn Heights, NY 11201-4398. Offers MS.

St. John's University, The Peter J. Tobin College of Business, Department of Accounting and Taxation, Program in Accounting, Queens, NY 11439. Offers accounting (MBA, MS); controllership (MBA). *Accreditation:* AACSB. *Program availability:* Part-time, evening/weekend, online learning. *Degree requirements:* For master's, comprehensive exam (for some programs), thesis optional. *Entrance requirements:* For master's, GMAT, 2 letters of recommendation, resume, transcripts, statement of goals, bachelor's degree in business. Additional exam requirements/recommendations for international students: Required—TOEFL (minimum score 600 paper-based; 100 iBT), IELTS (minimum score 7). Electronic applications accepted. *Expenses:* Contact institution.

St. Joseph's College, Long Island Campus, Programs in Business Management and Administration, Program in Accounting, Patchogue, NY 11772-2399. Offers MBA. *Program availability:* Part-time, evening/weekend. *Faculty:* 1 (woman) full-time, 12 part-time/adjunct (3 women). *Students:* 40 full-time (21 women), 57 part-time (22 women); includes 15 minority (1 Black or African American, non-Hispanic/Latino; 6 Asian, non-Hispanic/Latino; 7 Hispanic/Latino; 1 Native Hawaiian or other Pacific Islander, non-Hispanic/Latino). Average age 29. 64 applicants, 83% accepted, 37 enrolled. In 2016, 22 master's awarded. *Entrance requirements:* For master's, official transcripts, minimum undergraduate GPA of 3.0, 2 letters of recommendation, resume, verification of employment, essay. Additional exam requirements/recommendations for international students: Recommended—TOEFL (minimum score 550 paper-based; 79 iBT), IELTS (minimum score 7). *Application deadline:* Applications are processed on a rolling basis. Application fee: $25. Electronic applications accepted. *Expenses:* Contact institution. *Financial support:* In 2016–17, 23 students received support. *Unit head:* Mary Chance, Assistant Professor and Chair, 631-687-1288, E-mail: mchance@sjcny.edu. *Application contact:* Jodi A. Duffy, Senior Associate Director of Graduate Admissions, 631-687-4525, E-mail: jduffy@sjcny.edu.
Website: http://www.sjcny.edu

St. Joseph's College, New York, Programs in Business Management and Administration, Program in Accounting, Brooklyn, NY 11205-3688. Offers MBA. *Program availability:* Part-time, evening/weekend. *Faculty:* 2 full-time (both women), 6 part-time/adjunct (3 women). *Students:* 1 (woman) full-time, 5 part-time (2 women); includes 3 minority (2 Black or African American, non-Hispanic/Latino; 1 Hispanic/Latino). Average age 27. 12 applicants, 50% accepted, 2 enrolled. In 2016, 1 master's awarded. *Entrance requirements:* For master's, official transcripts, resume, two letters of reference, verification of employment. Additional exam requirements/recommendations for international students: Required—TOEFL (minimum score 80 iBT). *Application deadline:* Applications are processed on a rolling basis. Application fee: $25. Electronic applications accepted. *Expenses:* Contact institution. *Financial support:* In 2016–17, 2 students received support. *Unit head:* Christopher Smith, Assistant Professor/Associate Chair, 718-940-5786, E-mail: csmith2@sjcny.edu.
Website: http://www.sjcny.edu

Saint Joseph's College of Maine, Master of Accountancy Program, Standish, ME 04084. Offers M Acc. *Program availability:* Part-time, online learning. *Entrance requirements:* For master's, baccalaureate degree with minimum cumulative GPA of 2.5; successful completion of each of the following prior to program enrollment: financial accounting, managerial accounting, introduction of finance/business finance and macroeconomics. Electronic applications accepted.

Saint Joseph's University, Erivan K. Haub School of Business, MBA Program, Philadelphia, PA 19131-1395. Offers accounting (MBA, Postbaccalaureate Certificate); business intelligence (MBA); finance (MBA); general business (MBA); health and medical services administration (MBA); international business (MBA); international marketing (MBA); managing human capital (MBA); marketing (MBA); DO/MBA. DO/MBA offered jointly with Philadelphia College of Osteopathic Medicine. *Program availability:* Part-time, evening/weekend, 100% online, blended/hybrid learning. *Faculty:* 31 full-time (10 women), 28 part-time/adjunct (7 women). *Students:* 95 full-time (40 women), 348 part-time (137 women); includes 64 minority (29 Black or African American, non-Hispanic/Latino; 17 Asian, non-Hispanic/Latino; 14 Hispanic/Latino; 1 Native Hawaiian or other Pacific Islander, non-Hispanic/Latino; 3 Two or more races, non-Hispanic/Latino), 47 international. Average age 30. 237 applicants, 60% accepted, 76 enrolled. In 2016, 144 master's awarded. *Degree requirements:* For master's and Postbaccalaureate Certificate, minimum GPA of 3.0. *Entrance requirements:* For master's, GMAT or GRE, 2 letters of recommendation, resume, personal statement, official undergraduate and graduate transcripts; for Postbaccalaureate Certificate, official master's-level transcripts. Additional exam requirements/recommendations for international students: Required—TOEFL (minimum score 550 paper-based, 80 iBT), IELTS (minimum score 6.5), or PTE (minimum score 60). *Application deadline:* For fall admission, 7/15 priority date for domestic students, 5/15 priority date for international students; for spring admission, 11/15 priority date for domestic students, 10/15 priority date for international students; for summer admission, 4/15 priority date for domestic students, 2/15 priority date for international students. Applications are processed on a rolling basis. Application fee: $35. Electronic applications accepted. *Expenses:* $1,003 per credit. *Financial support:* In 2016–17, 105 students received support, including 2 research assistantships with partial tuition reimbursements available (averaging $4,000 per year); scholarships/grants and unspecified assistantships also available. Support available to part-time students. Financial award application deadline: 5/1; financial award applicants required to submit FAFSA. *Unit head:* Dr. Patricia Rafferty, Director, 610-660-1318, E-mail: praffert@sju.edu. *Application contact:* Kate Sonstein, Program Manager/Recruiter, 610-660-1693, E-mail: kate.sonstein@sju.edu.
Website: http://www.sju.edu/haubmba

Saint Leo University, Graduate Business Studies, Saint Leo, FL 33574-6665. Offers accounting (M Acc, MBA, Certificate); cybersecurity (MS); health care management (MBA, Certificate); human resource management (MBA, Certificate); information security management (MBA, Certificate); management (MBA, DBA); marketing (MBA, Certificate); marketing research and social media analytics (MBA, Certificate); project management (MBA, Certificate); sport business (MBA); supply chain global integration management (MBA, Certificate). *Accreditation:* ACBSP. *Program availability:* Part-time, evening/weekend, 100% online, blended/hybrid learning. *Faculty:* 53 full-time (18 women), 53 part-time/adjunct (19 women). *Students:* 8 full-time (4 women), 2,001 part-time (1,160 women); includes 928 minority (650 Black or African American, non-Hispanic/Latino; 5 American Indian or Alaska Native, non-Hispanic/Latino; 43 Asian, non-Hispanic/Latino; 193 Hispanic/Latino; 2 Native Hawaiian or other Pacific Islander, non-Hispanic/Latino; 35 Two or more races, non-Hispanic/Latino), 51 international. Average age 37. 922 applicants, 85% accepted, 517 enrolled. In 2016, 874 master's, 17 other advanced degrees awarded. *Degree requirements:* For doctorate, comprehensive exam, thesis/dissertation. *Entrance requirements:* For master's, GMAT (minimum score 500), official transcripts, current resume, 2 professional recommendations, personal statement, bachelor's degree from regionally-accredited university; undergraduate degree in accounting and minimum undergraduate GPA of 3.0 (for M Acc); minimum undergraduate GPA of 3.0 in final 2 years of undergraduate study and 2 years' work experience (for MBA); for doctorate, GMAT (minimum score of 550) if master's GPA is under 3.25, official transcripts, current resume, 2 professional recommendations, personal statement, master's degree from regionally-accredited university with minimum

GPA of 3.25, 3 years' work experience, interview. Additional exam requirements/recommendations for international students: Required—TOEFL (minimum score 550 paper-based; 80 iBT). *Application deadline:* For fall admission, 7/1 priority date for domestic and international students; for spring admission, 11/12 priority date for domestic students, 11/1 for international students. Applications are processed on a rolling basis. Application fee: $80. Electronic applications accepted. *Expenses:* Contact institution. *Financial support:* In 2016–17, 118 students received support. Career-related internships or fieldwork, scholarships/grants, and health care benefits available. Financial award application deadline: 3/1; financial award applicants required to submit FAFSA. *Unit head:* Dr. Lorrie McGovern, Associate Dean, School of Business, 352-588-7869, Fax: 352-588-8912, E-mail: mbaslu@saintleo.edu. *Application contact:* Jennifer Shelley, Senior Associate Director of Graduate Admissions, 800-707-8846, Fax: 352-588-7873, E-mail: grad.admissions@saintleo.edu.
Website: http://www.saintleo.edu/academics/graduate.aspx

Saint Louis University, Graduate Education, John Cook School of Business, Department of Accounting, St. Louis, MO 63103. Offers M Acct, MBA. *Program availability:* Part-time, evening/weekend. *Entrance requirements:* For master's, GMAT. Additional exam requirements/recommendations for international students: Required—TOEFL (minimum score 570 paper-based; 88 iBT). Electronic applications accepted. *Expenses:* Contact institution. *Faculty research:* Tax policy, market valuation/corporate governance, foreign currency translation, accounting for income taxes, earnings quality.

Saint Mary's College of California, School of Economics and Business Administration, MS in Accounting Program, Moraga, CA 94575. Offers MS.

St. Mary's University, Graduate Studies, Greehey School of Business, San Antonio, TX 78228-8507. Offers business administration (MBA), including professional accountancy, values-driven leaders; JD/MBA. *Accreditation:* AACSB. *Program availability:* Part-time, evening/weekend. *Students:* 51 full-time (21 women); includes 23 minority (3 Black or African American, non-Hispanic/Latino; 1 Asian, non-Hispanic/Latino; 19 Hispanic/Latino), 10 international. Average age 27. 133 applicants, 39% accepted, 40 enrolled. In 2016, 22 master's awarded. *Degree requirements:* For master's, comprehensive exam. *Entrance requirements:* For master's, GMAT (minimum score of 525) or GRE (minimum score of 306), undergraduate degree from accredited institution, letters of reference, current resume. Additional exam requirements/recommendations for international students: Required—TOEFL (minimum score 570 paper-based; 87 iBT); Recommended—IELTS (minimum score 6.5), TSE. *Application deadline:* For fall admission, 7/1 for domestic students; for spring admission, 11/15 for domestic students; for summer admission, 4/1 for domestic students. Application fee: $0. Electronic applications accepted. *Expenses: Tuition:* Full-time $15,600; part-time $865 per credit hour. *Required fees:* $148 per semester. *Financial support:* Research assistantships, institutionally sponsored loans, scholarships/grants, and unspecified assistantships available. Financial award application deadline: 3/31; financial award applicants required to submit FAFSA. *Faculty research:* Investment strategies, cross-culture marketing, organizational culture, supply chain management, small-firm internalization. *Application contact:* Jeremy Grace, Director, Master of Business Administration Programs, 210-431-2027, E-mail: jmgrace@stmarytx.edu.

Saint Mary's University of Minnesota, Schools of Graduate and Professional Programs, Graduate School of Business and Technology, Accountancy Program, Winona, MN 55987-1399. Offers MS. *Program availability:* Online learning. Tuition and fees vary according to degree level and program. *Unit head:* Melanie Torborg, Program Director, 612-238-4525, E-mail: mtorborg@smumn.edu. *Application contact:* James Callinan, Director of Admissions for Graduate and Professional Programs, 612-728-5185, Fax: 612-728-5121, E-mail: jcallina@smumn.edu.
Website: http://www.smumn.edu/graduate-home/areas-of-study/graduate-school-of-business-technology/ms-in-accountancy

Saint Peter's University, Graduate Business Programs, Program in Accountancy, Jersey City, NJ 07306-5997. Offers MS, MBA/MS. *Program availability:* Part-time, evening/weekend. *Entrance requirements:* Additional exam requirements/recommendations for international students: Required—TOEFL. Electronic applications accepted.

St. Thomas University, School of Business, Department of Management, Miami Gardens, FL 33054-6459. Offers accounting (MBA); general management (MSM, Certificate); health management (MBA, MSM, Certificate); human resource management (MBA, MSM, Certificate); international business (MBA, MIB, MSM, Certificate); justice administration (MSM, Certificate); management accounting (MSM, Certificate); public management (MSM, Certificate); sports administration (MS). *Program availability:* Part-time, evening/weekend. *Degree requirements:* For master's, comprehensive exam. *Entrance requirements:* For master's, interview, minimum GPA of 3.0 or GMAT. Additional exam requirements/recommendations for international students: Required—TOEFL (minimum score 550 paper-based; 79 iBT). Electronic applications accepted.

Samford University, Brock School of Business, Birmingham, AL 35229. Offers accounting (M Acc); business administration (MBA); entrepreneurship (MBA); finance (MBA); marketing (MBA); JD/M Acc; JD/MBA; MBA/M Acc; MBA/M Div; MBA/MSEM; MBA/Pharm D. *Accreditation:* AACSB. *Program availability:* Part-time-only, evening/weekend, 100% online, blended/hybrid learning. *Faculty:* 9 full-time (2 women), 3 part-time/adjunct (0 women). *Students:* 87 full-time (33 women), 14 part-time (6 women); includes 10 minority (7 Black or African American, non-Hispanic/Latino; 1 Asian, non-Hispanic/Latino; 1 Hispanic/Latino; 1 Two or more races, non-Hispanic/Latino), 6 international. Average age 28. 148 applicants, 41% accepted, 32 enrolled. In 2016, 63 master's awarded. *Degree requirements:* For master's, capstone course. *Entrance requirements:* For master's, GMAT or GRE. Additional exam requirements/recommendations for international students: Required—TOEFL (minimum score 90 iBT), IELTS (minimum score 6.5). *Application deadline:* For fall admission, 7/1 for domestic and international students; for spring admission, 12/1 for domestic and international students; for summer admission, 4/1 for domestic and international students. Applications are processed on a rolling basis. Application fee: $35. Electronic applications accepted. *Expenses: Tuition:* Full-time $18,530; part-time $789 per credit hour. *Required fees:* $610. Tuition and fees vary according to course load, degree level, program and student level. *Financial support:* In 2016–17, 55 students received support. Career-related internships or fieldwork, institutionally sponsored loans, scholarships/grants, and tuition waivers (partial) available. Support available to part-time students. Financial award application deadline: 3/1; financial award applicants required to submit FAFSA. *Faculty research:* Entrepreneurship, accounting, finance, marketing, economics. *Total annual research expenditures:* $25,000. *Unit head:* Dr. Barbara Cartledge, Assistant Dean, 205-726-2935, Fax: 205-726-2540, E-mail: bhcartle@samford.edu. *Application contact:* Elizabeth Anne Gambrell, Assistant Director of Academic Programs, 205-726-2040, Fax: 205-726-2540, E-mail: eagambre@samford.edu.
Website: http://www.samford.edu/business/

Sam Houston State University, College of Business Administration, Department of Accounting, Huntsville, TX 77341. Offers MS. *Program availability:* Part-time. *Degree requirements:* For master's, comprehensive exam. *Entrance requirements:* For master's, GMAT. Additional exam requirements/recommendations for international students: Required—TOEFL (minimum score 550 paper-based; 79 iBT), IELTS (minimum score 6.5). Electronic applications accepted.

San Diego State University, Graduate and Research Affairs, College of Business Administration, Charles W. Lamden School of Accountancy, San Diego, CA 92182. Offers MS. *Accreditation:* AACSB. *Degree requirements:* For master's, thesis or alternative. *Entrance requirements:* For master's, GMAT, resume, letters of reference. Additional exam requirements/recommendations for international students: Required—TOEFL. Electronic applications accepted.

San Francisco State University, Division of Graduate Studies, College of Business, Department of Accounting, San Francisco, CA 94132-1722. Offers MSA. *Program availability:* Part-time. *Entrance requirements:* For master's, GMAT, copy of transcripts, written statement of purpose, resume, two letters of reference. Additional exam requirements/recommendations for international students: Required—TOEFL or IELTS. Electronic applications accepted. *Expenses:* Tuition, state resident: full-time $6738. Tuition, nonresident: full-time $15,666. *Required fees:* $1012. Tuition and fees vary according to degree level and program. *Unit head:* Dr. Jiunn C. Huang, Chair, 415-338-1910, Fax: 415-338-0596, E-mail: jchuang@sfsu.edu. *Application contact:* Dr. Theresa Hammond, Graduate Coordinator, 415-338-6283, Fax: 415-338-0596, E-mail: thammond@sfsu.edu.
Website: http://cob.sfsu.edu/accounting

San Jose State University, Graduate Studies and Research, Lucas Graduate School of Business, San Jose, CA 95192-0001. Offers accountancy (MS); business administration (MBA); taxation (MS); transportation management (MS). *Program availability:* Part-time, evening/weekend, online learning. *Degree requirements:* For master's, comprehensive exam, thesis or alternative. *Entrance requirements:* For master's, GMAT, minimum GPA of 3.0. Electronic applications accepted.

Seattle University, Albers School of Business and Economics, Master of Professional Accounting Program, Seattle, WA 98122-1090. Offers MPAC, JD/MPAC, MBA/MPAC, MPAC/MSF. *Program availability:* Part-time, evening/weekend. *Faculty:* 9 full-time (3 women), 1 (woman) part-time/adjunct. *Students:* 77 full-time (52 women), 38 part-time (24 women); includes 27 minority (3 Black or African American, non-Hispanic/Latino; 1 American Indian or Alaska Native, non-Hispanic/Latino; 18 Asian, non-Hispanic/Latino; 4 Hispanic/Latino; 1 Two or more races, non-Hispanic/Latino), 72 international. Average age 26. 104 applicants, 55% accepted, 24 enrolled. In 2016, 57 master's awarded. *Entrance requirements:* For master's, GMAT, minimum GPA of 3.0. Additional exam requirements/recommendations for international students: Required—TOEFL (minimum score 580 paper-based; 92 iBT). *Application deadline:* For fall admission, 5/1 priority date for domestic students, 4/1 priority date for international students; for winter admission, 11/20 priority date for domestic students, 9/1 priority date for international students; for spring admission, 2/20 priority date for domestic students, 12/1 priority date for international students. Applications are processed on a rolling basis. Application fee: $55. Electronic applications accepted. *Expenses:* Contact institution. *Financial support:* In 2016–17, 34 students received support. Career-related internships or fieldwork and Federal Work-Study available. Support available to part-time students. Financial award applicants required to submit FAFSA. *Unit head:* Dr. Bruce Koch, Program Director, 206-296-5700, Fax: 206-296-5795, E-mail: kochb@seattleu.edu. *Application contact:* Janet Shandley, Director of Graduate Admissions, 206-296-5900, Fax: 206-298-5656, E-mail: grad_admissions@seattleu.edu.
Website: http://www.seattleu.edu/albers/mpac/

Seton Hall University, Stillman School of Business, Department of Accounting, South Orange, NJ 07079-2697. Offers accounting (MS, Certificate); CPA (Certificate); professional accounting (MS); taxation (Certificate). *Program availability:* Part-time, evening/weekend. *Entrance requirements:* For master's, GMAT or GRE (waived based on work experience), MS in a business discipline, professional degree (MD, JD, PhD, DVM, DDS, CPA, etc.), minimum undergraduate GPA of 3.0. Additional exam requirements/recommendations for international students: Required—TOEFL (minimum score 607 paper-based; 102 iBT), IELTS (minimum score 6), PTE. Electronic applications accepted. *Expenses:* Contact institution. *Faculty research:* Nonfinancial metrics, pension accounting, integrated reporting, multinational enterprises.

Seton Hall University, Stillman School of Business, Programs in Business Administration, South Orange, NJ 07079-2697. Offers accounting (MBA); entrepreneurship (Certificate); finance (MBA, Certificate); information technology management (MBA); international business (MBA); management (MBA); marketing (MBA); sport management (MBA); supply chain management (MBA, Certificate). *Program availability:* Part-time, evening/weekend. *Degree requirements:* For master's, 20 hours of community service (Social Responsibility Project). *Entrance requirements:* For master's, GMAT or CPA, GRE (waived based on work experience or advanced degree from AACSB institution), MS in business discipline, professional degree (MD, JD, PhD, DVM, DDS, CPA, etc.), minimum undergraduate GPA of 3.0. Additional exam requirements/recommendations for international students: Required—TOEFL (minimum score 607 paper-based; 102 iBT), IELTS (minimum score 6), PTE. Electronic applications accepted. *Expenses:* Contact institution. *Faculty research:* Sport, hedge funds, executive compensation, social media, legal studies.

Seton Hill University, Program in Business Administration, Greensburg, PA 15601. Offers accounting (MBA); entrepreneurship (MBA, Certificate); management (MBA). *Program availability:* Part-time, evening/weekend. *Entrance requirements:* For master's, resume, 3 letters of recommendation, personal statement, transcripts. Additional exam requirements/recommendations for international students: Required—TOEFL (minimum score 600 paper-based; 100 iBT), IELTS (minimum score 6.5). Electronic applications accepted.

Shorter University, Professional Studies, Rome, GA 30165. Offers accountancy (MAC); business administration (MBA); management (MM). *Program availability:* Evening/weekend. *Degree requirements:* For master's, project. *Entrance requirements:* For master's, minimum undergraduate GPA of 2.75 in last 60 hours, 3 years of work experience. Additional exam requirements/recommendations for international students: Required—TOEFL (minimum score 550 paper-based; 79 iBT). Electronic applications accepted.

Siena College, School of Business, Loudonville, NY 12211-1462. Offers accounting (MS). *Program availability:* Evening/weekend. *Degree requirements:* For master's, internship.

Slippery Rock University of Pennsylvania, Graduate Studies (Recruitment), College of Business, School of Business, Slippery Rock, PA 16057-1383. Offers accounting/finance (MBA); general (MBA); marketing/management (MBA). *Program availability:* Part-time, evening/weekend. *Faculty:* 6 full-time (4 women), 1 part-time/adjunct (0 women). *Students:* 16 full-time (9 women), 9 part-time (6 women); includes 1 minority (Black or African American, non-Hispanic/Latino). Average age 29. 109 applicants, 26% accepted, 13 enrolled. In 2016, 26 master's awarded. *Degree requirements:* For master's, comprehensive exam (for some programs), thesis (for some programs). *Entrance requirements:* For master's, minimum cumulative GPA of 3.0, official transcripts, three references. Additional exam requirements/recommendations for international students: Required—TOEFL (minimum score 550 paper-based; 80 iBT).

Application deadline: For fall admission, 3/1 priority date for domestic students, 5/1 priority date for international students; for spring admission, 10/1 priority date for domestic students, 9/1 priority date for international students. Applications are processed on a rolling basis. Application fee: $25 ($30 for international students). Electronic applications accepted. *Expenses:* $646.50 per credit in-state, $936.80 per credit out-of-state; $581.45 per online credit in-state, $648.65 per online credit out-of-state. *Financial support:* In 2016–17, 5 students received support. Career-related internships or fieldwork, Federal Work-Study, institutionally sponsored loans, scholarships/grants, tuition waivers (partial), and unspecified assistantships available. Support available to part-time students. Financial award application deadline: 5/1; financial award applicants required to submit FAFSA. *Unit head:* Dr. Larry McCarthy, Graduate Coordinator, 724-738-2552, Fax: 724-738-2959, E-mail: larry.mccarthy@sru.edu. *Application contact:* Brandi Weber-Mortimer, Director of Graduate Admissions, 724-738-2051, Fax: 724-738-2146, E-mail: graduate.admissions@sru.edu.
Website: http://www.sru.edu/academics/graduate-programs/mba-master-of-business-administration

Southeast Missouri State University, School of Graduate Studies, Harrison College of Business, Cape Girardeau, MO 63701-4799. Offers accounting (MBA); entrepreneurship (MBA); financial management (MBA); sport management (MBA). *Accreditation:* AACSB. *Program availability:* Part-time, evening/weekend, 100% online. *Faculty:* 27 full-time (7 women), 1 (woman) part-time/adjunct. *Students:* 72 full-time (39 women), 112 part-time (41 women); includes 20 minority (10 Black or African American, non-Hispanic/Latino; 6 Asian, non-Hispanic/Latino; 4 Hispanic/Latino), 64 international. Average age 29. 106 applicants, 70% accepted, 55 enrolled. In 2016, 65 master's awarded. *Degree requirements:* For master's, variable foreign language requirement, comprehensive exam (for some programs), thesis or alternative. *Entrance requirements:* For master's, GMAT or GRE, minimum undergraduate GPA of 2.5, minimum grade of C in prerequisite courses. Additional exam requirements/recommendations for international students: Required—TOEFL (minimum score 550 paper-based; 79 iBT), IELTS (minimum score 6), PTE (minimum score 53). *Application deadline:* For fall admission, 8/1 for domestic students, 6/1 for international students; for spring admission, 11/21 for domestic students, 10/1 for international students; for summer admission, 5/15 for domestic students. Applications are processed on a rolling basis. Application fee: $30 ($40 for international students). Electronic applications accepted. *Expenses:* Tuition, state resident: full-time $3130; part-time $260.80 per credit hour. Tuition, nonresident: full-time $5842; part-time $486.80 per credit hour. *Required fees:* $33.70 per credit hour. *Financial support:* In 2016–17, 61 students received support. Career-related internships or fieldwork, Federal Work-Study, scholarships/grants, traineeships, tuition waivers (full), and unspecified assistantships available. Financial award application deadline: 6/30; financial award applicants required to submit FAFSA. *Faculty research:* Organizational justice, ethics, leadership, corporate finance, generational differences. *Unit head:* Dr. James L. Caldwell, Director, Graduate Business Studies, 573-651-2851, Fax: 573-651-5032, E-mail: jcaldwell@semo.edu. *Application contact:* Gail Amick, Admissions Specialist, 573-651-2590, Fax: 573-651-5936, E-mail: gamick@semo.edu.
Website: http://www.semo.edu/mba

Southern Adventist University, School of Business and Management, Collegedale, TN 37315-0370. Offers accounting (MBA); church administration (MSA); church and nonprofit leadership (MBA); financial management (MFM); healthcare administration (MBA); management (MBA); marketing management (MBA); outdoor education (MSA). *Program availability:* Part-time, evening/weekend, online learning. *Entrance requirements:* For master's, GMAT. Additional exam requirements/recommendations for international students: Required—TOEFL (minimum score 600 paper-based; 100 iBT). Electronic applications accepted.

Southern Illinois University Carbondale, Graduate School, College of Business and Administration, School of Accountancy, Carbondale, IL 62901-4701. Offers M Acc, PhD, JD/M Acc. *Accreditation:* AACSB. *Program availability:* Part-time. *Degree requirements:* For doctorate, thesis/dissertation. *Entrance requirements:* For master's, GMAT, minimum GPA of 2.7; for doctorate, GMAT, minimum graduate GPA of 3.25. Additional exam requirements/recommendations for international students: Required—TOEFL (minimum score 550 paper-based; 80 iBT). Electronic applications accepted. *Faculty research:* Not-for-profit accounting, SEC regulations, computers and accounting education, taxation.

Southern Illinois University Edwardsville, Graduate School, School of Business, Department of Accounting, Edwardsville, IL 62026. Offers accountancy (MSA); taxation (MSA). *Accreditation:* AACSB. *Program availability:* Part-time, evening/weekend. *Degree requirements:* For master's, thesis or alternative, final exam. *Entrance requirements:* For master's, GMAT. Additional exam requirements/recommendations for international students: Required—TOEFL (minimum score 550 paper-based; 79 iBT), IELTS (minimum score 6.5). Electronic applications accepted.

Southern Methodist University, Cox School of Business, MBA Program, Dallas, TX 75275. Offers accounting (MBA, PMBA); business administration (EMBA); finance (MBA); financial statement analysis (PMBA); general business (MBA); information technology and operations management (MBA); management (MBA); marketing (MBA); real estate (MBA); strategy (MBA); strategy and entrepreneurship (MBA); JD/MBA; MA/MBA. *Program availability:* Part-time, evening/weekend. *Entrance requirements:* For master's, GMAT. Additional exam requirements/recommendations for international students: Required—TOEFL. Electronic applications accepted. *Expenses:* Contact institution. *Faculty research:* Corporate finance, financial reporting, modeling consumer decision-making, competition between national brands and store brands, institutional determinants of firms' strategy.

Southern Methodist University, Cox School of Business, Program in Accounting, Dallas, TX 75275. Offers MSA. *Program availability:* Part-time, evening/weekend. *Entrance requirements:* For master's, GMAT. Additional exam requirements/recommendations for international students: Required—TOEFL. *Expenses:* Contact institution. *Faculty research:* Capital markets, taxation, business combinations, intangibles accounting, accounting history.

Southern New Hampshire University, School of Business, Manchester, NH 03106-1045. Offers accounting (MBA, MS, Graduate Certificate); accounting finance (MS); accounting/auditing (MS); accounting/forensic accounting (MS); accounting/taxation (MS); athletic administration (MBA, Graduate Certificate); business administration (IMBA, MBA, Certificate, Graduate Certificate), including accounting (Certificate), business administration (MBA), business information systems (Graduate Certificate), human resource management (Certificate); corporate social responsibility (MBA); entrepreneurship (MBA); finance (MBA, MS, Graduate Certificate); finance/corporate finance (MS); finance/investments and securities (MS); forensic accounting (MBA); healthcare informatics (MBA); healthcare management (MBA); human resource management (Graduate Certificate); information technology (MS, Graduate Certificate); information technology management (MBA); international business (Graduate Certificate); international business and information technology (Graduate Certificate); international finance (Graduate Certificate); international sport management (Graduate Certificate); justice studies (MBA); leadership of nonprofit organizations (Graduate Certificate); management (MS); marketing (MBA, MS, Graduate Certificate); operations and project management (MS); operations and supply chain management (MBA, Graduate Certificate); organizational leadership (MS); project management (MBA, Graduate Certificate); Six Sigma (MBA); Six Sigma quality (Graduate Certificate); social media marketing (MBA); sport management (MBA, MS, Graduate Certificate); sustainability and environmental compliance (MBA); workplace conflict management (MBA); MBA/Certificate. *Accreditation:* ACBSP. *Program availability:* Part-time, evening/weekend, online learning. Terminal master's awarded for partial completion of doctoral program. *Degree requirements:* For master's, one foreign language, comprehensive exam (for some programs), thesis or alternative. *Entrance requirements:* For master's, minimum GPA of 2.5. Additional exam requirements/recommendations for international students: Required—TOEFL (minimum score 500 paper-based). Electronic applications accepted.

Southern Oregon University, Graduate Studies, School of Business, Ashland, OR 97520. Offers accounting (Postbaccalaureate Certificate); business administration (MBA); international management (MIM). *Accreditation:* ACBSP. *Program availability:* Part-time, evening/weekend, online learning. *Faculty:* 18 full-time (6 women), 8 part-time/adjunct (5 women). *Students:* 28 full-time (13 women), 30 part-time (10 women); includes 13 minority (1 Black or African American, non-Hispanic/Latino; 2 Asian, non-Hispanic/Latino; 7 Hispanic/Latino; 3 Two or more races, non-Hispanic/Latino), 19 international. Average age 33. 65 applicants, 49% accepted, 25 enrolled. In 2016, 16 master's awarded. *Degree requirements:* For master's, comprehensive exam. *Entrance requirements:* For master's, GMAT, minimum cumulative GPA of 3.0 in the last 90 quarter credits (60 semester credits) of undergraduate coursework. Additional exam requirements/recommendations for international students: Required—TOEFL (minimum score 540 paper-based; 76 iBT), IELTS (minimum score 6), ELPT (minimum score 964) or ELS (minimum score 112). *Application deadline:* For fall admission, 7/31 priority date for domestic and international students; for winter admission, 11/15 priority date for domestic students, 11/14 priority date for international students; for spring admission, 1/7 priority date for domestic and international students. Applications are processed on a rolling basis. Application fee: $60. Electronic applications accepted. *Expenses:* Tuition, state resident: full-time $10,719; part-time $397 per credit. Tuition, nonresident: full-time $13,419; part-time $497 per credit. *Required fees:* $548. *Financial support:* In 2016–17, 1 student received support, including 1 research assistantship with partial tuition reimbursement available; career-related internships or fieldwork, institutionally sponsored loans, scholarships/grants, and unspecified assistantships also available. *Unit head:* Dr. Mark Siders, Graduate Program Coordinator, 541-552-6709, E-mail: sidersm@sou.edu. *Application contact:* Kelly Moutsatson, Director of Admissions, 541-552-6411, Fax: 541-552-8403, E-mail: admissions@sou.edu.
Website: http://www.sou.edu/business/graduate-programs.html

Southern Utah University, Master of Accountancy/MBA Dual Degree Program, Cedar City, UT 84720-2498. Offers MBA/M Acc. *Program availability:* Part-time, 100% online. *Students:* 1 full-time (0 women). Average age 29. 3 applicants, 100% accepted, 1 enrolled. *Entrance requirements:* Additional exam requirements/recommendations for international students: Required—TOEFL (minimum score 550 paper-based, 79 iBT) or IELTS (minimum score 6). *Application deadline:* For fall admission, 3/1 for domestic and international students; for spring admission, 10/1 for domestic and international students; for summer admission, 3/1 for domestic and international students. Applications are processed on a rolling basis. Application fee: $60 ($65 for international students). Electronic applications accepted. *Expenses:* $8,722 per year, in-state or online, full-time; $23,814 per year, out-of-state, full-time. *Financial support:* Unspecified assistantships available. *Application contact:* Patricia Palmer, Academic Advisor and Graduate Program Coordinator, 435-865-8167, Fax: 435-586-5493, E-mail: patriciapalmer@suu.edu. Website: http://www.suu.edu/business/grad.html

Southern Utah University, Program in Accounting, Cedar City, UT 84720-2498. Offers M Acc. *Program availability:* Part-time, online learning. *Faculty:* 5 full-time (0 women). *Students:* 46 full-time (15 women), 36 part-time (13 women); includes 4 minority (1 Black or African American, non-Hispanic/Latino; 1 Asian, non-Hispanic/Latino; 1 Hispanic/Latino; 1 Two or more races, non-Hispanic/Latino). Average age 27. 46 applicants, 74% accepted, 28 enrolled. In 2016, 61 master's awarded. *Entrance requirements:* For master's, GMAT or GRE, official transcripts of all academic work prior to admission with transcripts verifying minimum GPA of 3.0 for all work completed; three letters of recommendation from former/current college professors, assigned mentors, supervisors or associates (for non-SUU business majors). Additional exam requirements/recommendations for international students: Required—TOEFL (minimum scores: 550 paper-based, 79 iBT) or IELTS (minimum score 6). *Application deadline:* For fall admission, 3/1 for domestic and international students; for spring admission, 10/1 for domestic and international students; for summer admission, 3/1 for domestic and international students. Applications are processed on a rolling basis. Application fee: $60 ($65 for international students). Electronic applications accepted. *Expenses:* $8,722 per year, in-state or online, full-time; $23,814 per year, out-of-state, full-time. *Financial support:* Unspecified assistantships available. *Faculty research:* Cost accounting, intermediate accounting text, GAAP policy, Statements on Standards for Accounting and Review Services (SSARS). *Unit head:* Dr. Robin Boneck, Chair, Accounting Department, 435-586-7773, Fax: 435-586-5493, E-mail: boneck@suu.edu. *Application contact:* Patricia Palmer, Academic Advisor and Graduate Program Coordinator, 435-865-8167, Fax: 435-586-5493, E-mail: patriciapalmer@suu.edu.
Website: https://www.suu.edu/business/acct/macc.html

Southwestern Adventist University, Business Administration Department, Keene, TX 76059. Offers accounting (MBA); finance (MBA); management/leadership (MBA). *Program availability:* Part-time, evening/weekend. *Degree requirements:* For master's, capstone course. *Entrance requirements:* For master's, GMAT, GRE General Test.

State University of New York at New Paltz, Graduate School, School of Business, New Paltz, NY 12561. Offers business administration (MBA); public accountancy (MBA). *Accreditation:* AACSB. *Program availability:* Part-time, evening/weekend. *Students:* 57 full-time (27 women), 23 part-time (13 women); includes 23 minority (3 Black or African American, non-Hispanic/Latino; 7 Asian, non-Hispanic/Latino; 10 Hispanic/Latino; 3 Two or more races, non-Hispanic/Latino), 12 international. 57 applicants, 72% accepted, 27 enrolled. In 2016, 55 master's awarded. *Entrance requirements:* For master's, GMAT or GRE, minimum GPA of 3.0. Additional exam requirements/recommendations for international students: Required—TOEFL (minimum score 550 paper-based; 80 iBT), IELTS (minimum score 6.5). *Application deadline:* Applications are processed on a rolling basis. Application fee: $50. Electronic applications accepted. *Expenses:* Contact institution. *Financial support:* In 2016–17, 6 research assistantships with partial tuition reimbursements (averaging $5,000 per year), 1 teaching assistantship with partial tuition reimbursement (averaging $5,000 per year) were awarded; scholarships/grants, traineeships, and unspecified assistantships also available. Financial award application deadline: 8/1. *Faculty research:* Cognitive styles in management education, supporting SME e-commerce migration through e-learning, earnings management and board activity, trading future spread portfolio, global equity market correlation and volatility. *Unit head:* Dr. Kristin Backhaus, Dean, 845-257-2930, E-mail: mba@newpaltz.edu. *Application contact:* Aaron Hines, Director of MBA Program, 845-257-2968, E-mail: mba@newpaltz.edu.
Website: http://mba.newpaltz.edu

Accounting

State University of New York College at Geneseo, Graduate Studies, School of Business, Geneseo, NY 14454. Offers accounting (MS). *Accreditation:* AACSB. *Faculty:* 5 full-time (2 women). *Students:* 17 full-time (8 women). Average age 22. 29 applicants, 76% accepted, 17 enrolled. In 2016, 15 master's awarded. *Degree requirements:* For master's, thesis. *Entrance requirements:* For master's, GMAT, bachelor's degree in accounting. Additional exam requirements/recommendations for international students: Required—TOEFL, IELTS, PTE. *Application deadline:* For fall admission, 6/1 priority date for domestic students. Applications are processed on a rolling basis. Application fee: $50. Electronic applications accepted. *Expenses:* Tuition, state resident: full-time $10,870; part-time $453 per credit. Tuition, nonresident: full-time $22,210; part-time $925 per credit. *Required fees:* $865; $35.85 per credit hour. *Financial support:* Research assistantships with full tuition reimbursements available. Financial award application deadline: 4/1; financial award applicants required to submit FAFSA. *Unit head:* Dr. Denise Rotondo, Dean of the School of Business, 585-245-5367, Fax: 585-245-5467, E-mail: rotondo@geneseo.edu. *Application contact:* Michael R. George, Graduate Enrollment Coordinator, 585-245-5148, Fax: 585-245-5550, E-mail: georgem@geneseo.edu.
Website: http://www.geneseo.edu/business/accounting_ms

State University of New York College at Old Westbury, School of Business, Old Westbury, NY 11568-0210. Offers accounting (MS); taxation (MS). *Program availability:* Part-time, evening/weekend. *Faculty:* 10 full-time (2 women), 1 part-time/adjunct (0 women). *Students:* 30 full-time (13 women), 47 part-time (15 women); includes 19 minority (3 Black or African American, non-Hispanic/Latino; 11 Asian, non-Hispanic/Latino; 5 Hispanic/Latino). Average age 31. 35 applicants, 91% accepted, 25 enrolled. In 2016, 25 master's awarded. *Entrance requirements:* For master's, GMAT, 2 letters of recommendation. Additional exam requirements/recommendations for international students: Required—TOEFL (minimum score 550 paper-based). *Application deadline:* For fall admission, 6/15 priority date for domestic students; for spring admission, 11/15 priority date for domestic students. Applications are processed on a rolling basis. Application fee: $50. Electronic applications accepted. *Expenses:* Tuition, state resident: full-time $10,870; part-time $453 per credit. Tuition, nonresident: full-time $22,210; part-time $925 per credit. *Required fees:* $24.35 per credit. $76 per semester. Tuition and fees vary according to course load. *Financial support:* Applicants required to submit FAFSA. *Faculty research:* Corporate governance, asset pricing, corporate finance, hedge funds, taxation. *Unit head:* Rita Buttermilch, Director of Graduate Business Programs, 516-876-3900, E-mail: langec@oldwestbury.edu. *Application contact:* Philip D'Angelo, Graduate Admissions Office, 516-876-3073, E-mail: enroll@oldwestbury.edu.
Website: http://www.oldwestbury.edu/schools/business

State University of New York Polytechnic Institute, Program in Accountancy, Utica, NY 13502. Offers MS. *Accreditation:* AACSB. *Program availability:* Part-time, online learning. *Degree requirements:* For master's, capstone courses. *Entrance requirements:* For master's, GMAT, one letter of reference, resume. Additional exam requirements/recommendations for international students: Required—TOEFL (minimum score 550 paper-based; 79 iBT), IELTS (minimum score 6.5). Electronic applications accepted. *Faculty research:* Cash flows, accounting earnings, stock price analysis.

State University of New York Polytechnic Institute, Program in Business Administration in Technology Management, Utica, NY 13502. Offers accounting and finance (MBA); business management (MBA); health services management (MBA); human resource management (MBA); marketing management (MBA). *Program availability:* Part-time, online learning. *Degree requirements:* For master's, capstone course. *Entrance requirements:* For master's, GMAT, resume, one letter of reference. Additional exam requirements/recommendations for international students: Required—TOEFL (minimum score 550 paper-based; 79 iBT), IELTS (minimum score 6.5). Electronic applications accepted. *Faculty research:* Technology management, writing schools, leadership, new products.

Stephen F. Austin State University, Graduate School, College of Business, Program in Professional Accountancy, Nacogdoches, TX 75962. Offers MPAC. Students admitted at the undergraduate level. *Degree requirements:* For master's, comprehensive exam. *Entrance requirements:* For master's, GMAT. Additional exam requirements/recommendations for international students: Required—TOEFL.

Stetson University, School of Business Administration, Program in Accounting, DeLand, FL 32723. Offers M Acc. *Accreditation:* AACSB. *Program availability:* Part-time, online learning. *Faculty:* 17 full-time (3 women), 5 part-time/adjunct (0 women). *Students:* 27 full-time (16 women), 1 (woman) part-time; includes 9 minority (2 Black or African American, non-Hispanic/Latino; 1 Asian, non-Hispanic/Latino; 3 Hispanic/Latino; 3 Two or more races, non-Hispanic/Latino), 2 international. Average age 30. 40 applicants, 68% accepted, 19 enrolled. In 2016, 28 master's awarded. *Entrance requirements:* For master's, GMAT, GRE, transcripts, resume, two letters of recommendation, personal statement. Additional exam requirements/recommendations for international students: Required—TOEFL (minimum score 90 iBT), IELTS (minimum score 7.5). *Application deadline:* For fall admission, 8/1 for domestic students; for spring admission, 1/1 for domestic students; for summer admission, 5/1 for domestic students. Applications are processed on a rolling basis. Application fee: $50. Electronic applications accepted. *Expenses:* $981 per credit hour; $784 per credit hour (online). *Financial support:* In 2016–17, 10 students received support. Career-related internships or fieldwork, Federal Work-Study, institutionally sponsored loans, unspecified assistantships, and tuition waivers for staff and dependents available. Support available to part-time students. Financial award application deadline: 3/15. *Faculty research:* Oil and gas reserve accounting, the impact of dependent tuition policies on behavior, tax scams and frauds, auditor conservatism in going concern decisions, tax implications of NCAA travel benefits. *Unit head:* Dr. Michael E. Bitter, Director, 386-822-7410. *Application contact:* Jamie Vanderlip, Senior Associate Director of Graduate Admissions, 386-822-7100, Fax: 386-822-7112, E-mail: jlvander@stetson.edu.

Stony Brook University, State University of New York, Graduate School, College of Business, Program in Accounting, Stony Brook, NY 11794. Offers MS. *Program availability:* Part-time. *Students:* 56 applicants, 39% accepted, 12 enrolled. *Degree requirements:* For master's, capstone. *Entrance requirements:* For master's, GMAT or GRE. Additional exam requirements/recommendations for international students: Required—TOEFL (minimum score 85 iBT). *Application deadline:* For fall admission, 5/15 for domestic students, 3/15 for international students; for spring admission, 11/15 for domestic students, 10/15 for international students. *Expenses:* Contact institution. *Unit head:* Dr. Manuel London, Dean, 631-632-7159, E-mail: manuel.london@stonybrook.edu. *Application contact:* Erica Robey, Graduate Coordinator, 631-632-7171, Fax: 631-632-8181, E-mail: oss@stonybrook.edu.
Website: http://www.stonybrook.edu/commcms/business/academics/graduate-program/ms-accounting.html

Stony Brook University, State University of New York, Graduate School, College of Business, Program in Business Administration, Stony Brook, NY 11794. Offers accounting (MBA); business administration (MBA); finance (MBA, Certificate); health care management (MBA); innovation, human resources, management, or operations management (MBA); marketing (MBA). *Faculty:* 37 full-time (12 women), 12 part-time/adjunct (4 women). *Students:* 199 full-time (109 women), 139 part-time (64 women); includes 81 minority (19 Black or African American, non-Hispanic/Latino; 41 Asian, non-Hispanic/Latino; 17 Hispanic/Latino; 1 Native Hawaiian or other Pacific Islander, non-Hispanic/Latino; 3 Two or more races, non-Hispanic/Latino), 88 international. Average age 29. 246 applicants, 65% accepted, 91 enrolled. In 2016, 116 master's awarded. *Entrance requirements:* For master's, GMAT, 3 letters of recommendation from current or former employers or professors, transcripts, personal statement, resume. Additional exam requirements/recommendations for international students: Required—TOEFL (minimum score 550 paper-based; 90 iBT), IELTS (minimum score 6.5). *Application deadline:* For fall admission, 5/15 for domestic students, 3/15 for international students; for spring admission, 11/15 for domestic students, 10/15 for international students. Application fee: $100. *Expenses:* Contact institution. *Financial support:* Teaching assistantships available. *Total annual research expenditures:* $5,325. *Unit head:* Dr. Manuel London, Dean, 631-632-7159, E-mail: manuel.london@stonybrook.edu. *Application contact:* Dr. Jadranka Skorin-Kapov, Graduate Program Director, 631-632-7171, Fax: 631-632-8181, E-mail: jadranka.skorin-kapov@stonybrook.edu.

Stratford University, School of Graduate Studies, Falls Church, VA 22043. Offers accounting (MS); business administration (IMBA, MBA); cyber security (MS); cyber security leadership and policy (MS); digital forensics (MS); enterprise business management (MS); entrepreneurial management (MS); healthcare administration (MS); information systems (MS); international hospitality management (MS); networking and telecommunications (MS); software engineering (MS). *Program availability:* Part-time, evening/weekend, 100% online, blended/hybrid learning. *Students:* 505 full-time (186 women), 172 part-time (88 women); includes 532 minority (165 Black or African American, non-Hispanic/Latino; 18 American Indian or Alaska Native, non-Hispanic/Latino; 324 Asian, non-Hispanic/Latino; 13 Hispanic/Latino; 10 Native Hawaiian or other Pacific Islander, non-Hispanic/Latino; 2 Two or more races, non-Hispanic/Latino). Average age 27. In 2016, 520 master's awarded. *Degree requirements:* For master's, comprehensive exam, capstone project. *Entrance requirements:* For master's, GRE or GMAT, baccalaureate degree. Additional exam requirements/recommendations for international students: Required—TOEFL (minimum score 79 iBT), IELTS (minimum score 6.5), PTE (minimum score 5). *Application deadline:* Applications are processed on a rolling basis. Application fee: $50. Electronic applications accepted. *Expenses: Tuition:* Full-time $4455; part-time $2227.50 per course. One-time fee: $100. *Financial support:* Federal Work-Study and scholarships/grants available. Financial award applicants required to submit FAFSA. *Unit head:* Dr. Richard R. Shurtz, President, 703-539-6890, Fax: 703-539-6960. *Application contact:* Admissions, 800-444-0804, E-mail: fcadmissions@stratford.edu.

Strayer University, Graduate Studies, Washington, DC 20005-2603. Offers accounting (MS); acquisition (MBA); business administration (MBA); communications technology (MS); educational management (M Ed); finance (MBA); health services administration (MHSA); hospitality and tourism management (MBA); human resource management (MBA); information systems (MS), including computer security management, decision support system management, enterprise resource management, network management, software engineering management, systems development management; management (MBA); management information systems (MS); marketing (MBA); professional accounting (MS), including accounting information systems, controllership, taxation; public administration (MPA); supply chain management (MBA); technology in education (M Ed). Programs also offered at campus locations in Birmingham, AL; Chamblee, GA; Cobb County, GA; Morrow, GA; White Marsh, MD; Charleston, SC; Columbia, SC; Greensboro, NC; Greenville, SC; Lexington, KY; Louisville, KY; Nashville, TN; North Raleigh, NC; Washington, DC. *Accreditation:* ACBSP. *Program availability:* Part-time, evening/weekend, online learning. *Degree requirements:* For master's, thesis. *Entrance requirements:* For master's, GMAT, GRE General Test, bachelor's degree from an accredited college or university, minimum undergraduate GPA of 2.75. Electronic applications accepted.

Suffolk University, Sawyer Business School, Department of Accounting, Boston, MA 02108-2770. Offers accounting (MSA, Graduate Certificate); taxation (MST); MBA/MSA; MBA/MST. *Accreditation:* AACSB. *Program availability:* Part-time, evening/weekend, 100% online. *Faculty:* 13 full-time (6 women), 5 part-time/adjunct (1 woman). *Students:* 82 full-time (55 women), 115 part-time (73 women); includes 48 minority (16 Black or African American, non-Hispanic/Latino; 21 Asian, non-Hispanic/Latino; 11 Hispanic/Latino), 55 international. Average age 29. 217 applicants, 85% accepted, 91 enrolled. In 2016, 95 master's, 2 other advanced degrees awarded. *Entrance requirements:* For master's, GMAT. Additional exam requirements/recommendations for international students: Required—TOEFL (minimum score 550 paper-based; 80 iBT). *Application deadline:* For fall admission, 3/15 priority date for domestic and international students; for spring admission, 10/15 priority date for domestic and international students. Applications are processed on a rolling basis. Application fee: $50. Electronic applications accepted. *Expenses: Tuition:* Full-time $41,490; part-time $1383 per credit hour. *Required fees:* $52; $52 per credit hour. Part-time tuition and fees vary according to course load and program. *Financial support:* In 2016–17, 116 students received support, including 111 fellowships (averaging $11,442 per year); career-related internships or fieldwork, Federal Work-Study, institutionally sponsored loans, and scholarships/grants also available. Support available to part-time students. Financial award application deadline: 4/1; financial award applicants required to submit FAFSA. *Faculty research:* Tax policy, tax research, decision-making in accounting, accounting information systems, capital markets and strategic planning. *Unit head:* Tracy Riley, Chair, 617-994-4276, E-mail: triley@suffolk.edu. *Application contact:* Mara Marzocchi, Associate Director of Graduate Admissions, 617-573-8302, Fax: 617-305-1733, E-mail: grad.admission@suffolk.edu.
Website: http://www.suffolk.edu/msa

Suffolk University, Sawyer Business School, Master of Business Administration Program, Boston, MA 02108-2770. Offers accounting (MBA); entrepreneurship (MBA); executive business administration (EMBA); finance (MBA); global business administration (GMBA); health administration (MBA); international business (MBA); marketing (MBA); nonprofit management (MBA); organizational behavior (MBA); strategic management (MBA); supply chain management (MBA); taxation (MBA); JD/MBA; MBA/MHA; MBA/MSA; MBA/MSF; MBA/MST. *Accreditation:* AACSB. *Program availability:* Part-time, evening/weekend, 100% online. *Faculty:* 17 full-time (6 women), 10 part-time/adjunct (1 woman). *Students:* 137 full-time (70 women), 265 part-time (138 women); includes 78 minority (20 Black or African American, non-Hispanic/Latino; 22 Asian, non-Hispanic/Latino; 31 Hispanic/Latino; 5 Two or more races, non-Hispanic/Latino), 46 international. Average age 30. 416 applicants, 70% accepted, 128 enrolled. In 2016, 165 degrees awarded. *Entrance requirements:* For master's, GMAT, minimum undergraduate GPA of 2.75 (MBA), 5 years of managerial experience (EMBA). Additional exam requirements/recommendations for international students: Required—TOEFL (minimum score 550 paper-based; 80 iBT). *Application deadline:* For fall admission, 3/15 priority date for domestic students, 10/15 priority date for international students; for spring admission, 10/15 priority date for domestic and international students. Applications are processed on a rolling basis. Application fee: $50. Electronic applications accepted. *Expenses: Tuition:* Full-time $41,490; part-time $1383 per credit hour. *Required fees:* $52; $52 per credit hour. Part-time tuition and fees vary according to course load and program. *Financial support:* In 2016–17, 209 students received support, including 176 fellowships (averaging $8,581 per year); career-related

internships or fieldwork, Federal Work-Study, institutionally sponsored loans, and scholarships/grants also available. Support available to part-time students. Financial award application deadline: 4/1; financial award applicants required to submit FAFSA. *Faculty research:* Foreign investments; career strategies and boundaryless careers; corporate ethics codes; interest rates, inflation, and growth options; innovation and product development performance. *Unit head:* Jodi Detjen, Director of MBA Programs, 617-573-8306, E-mail: jdetjen@suffolk.edu. *Application contact:* Mara Marzocchi, Associate Director of Graduate Admissions, 617-573-8302, Fax: 617-305-1733, E-mail: grad.admission@suffolk.edu.
Website: http://www.suffolk.edu/mba

Syracuse University, Martin J. Whitman School of Management, Master of Business Administration Program, Syracuse, NY 13244. Offers accounting (MBA); business analytics (MBA); entrepreneurship (MBA); marketing management (MBA); real estate (MBA); supply chain management (MBA); JD/MBA. *Program availability:* Part-time, 100% online. *Students:* 22 full-time (9 women), 495 part-time (147 women); includes 182 minority (81 Black or African American, non-Hispanic/Latino; 3 American Indian or Alaska Native, non-Hispanic/Latino; 42 Asian, non-Hispanic/Latino; 52 Hispanic/Latino; 4 Native Hawaiian or other Pacific Islander, non-Hispanic/Latino), 22 international. Average age 32. 1,086 applicants, 73% accepted, 518 enrolled. In 2016, 84 master's awarded. *Entrance requirements:* For master's, GMAT or GRE, resume, essay, 5-minute video interview, two letters of recommendation, transcripts (unofficial). Additional exam requirements/recommendations for international students: Required—TOEFL (minimum score 100 iBT), IELTS (minimum score 7), PTE (minimum score 68). *Application deadline:* For fall admission, 11/30 for domestic students, 11/30 priority date for international students; for winter admission, 1/1 for domestic students, 1/1 priority date for international students; for spring admission, 2/15 for domestic and international students; for summer admission, 4/19 for domestic students. Application fee: $75. Electronic applications accepted. *Expenses:* Contact institution. *Financial support:* In 2016–17, 22 students received support. Merit scholarships available. Financial award application deadline: 2/15. *Faculty research:* Data analysis, economics of international business, financial markets and institutions, operations management, supply chain management. *Unit head:* Don Harter, Associate Dean, Graduate Programs, 315-443-3502, E-mail: dharter@syr.edu. *Application contact:* Shri Ramakrishnan, Assistant Director, Graduate Recruitment, 315-443-3497, Fax: 315-443-9517, E-mail: busgrad@syr.edu.
Website: http://whitman.syr.edu/ftmba/

Syracuse University, Martin J. Whitman School of Management, MS Program in Professional Accounting, Syracuse, NY 13244. Offers MS. *Program availability:* Part-time, evening/weekend, 100% online. *Students:* 43 full-time (27 women), 60 part-time (33 women); includes 33 minority (12 Black or African American, non-Hispanic/Latino; 1 American Indian or Alaska Native, non-Hispanic/Latino; 13 Asian, non-Hispanic/Latino; 7 Hispanic/Latino), 24 international. Average age 23. 429 applicants, 55% accepted, 103 enrolled. In 2016, 76 master's awarded. *Entrance requirements:* For master's, GMAT or GRE, resume, essay, 5-minute video interview, two letters of recommendation, transcripts (unofficial). Additional exam requirements/recommendations for international students: Required—TOEFL (minimum score 100 iBT), IELTS (minimum score 7), PTE (minimum score 68). *Application deadline:* For fall admission, 11/30 for domestic students, 11/30 priority date for international students; for winter admission, 1/1 for domestic students, 1/1 priority date for international students; for spring admission, 2/15 for domestic and international students; for summer admission, 4/19 for domestic students. Application fee: $75. Electronic applications accepted. *Expenses:* Contact institution. *Financial support:* In 2016–17, 41 students received support. Merit-based scholarships available. Financial award application deadline: 2/15. *Faculty research:* Financial statement analysis, international reporting and analysis, advanced auditing, taxes and business strategy, principles of fraud examination. *Unit head:* Dr. Joseph Comprix, Chair/Associate Professor, 315-443-3674, E-mail: jjcompri@syr.edu. *Application contact:* Shri Ramakrishnan, Assistant Director, Graduate Recruitment, 315-443-3497, Fax: 315-443-9517, E-mail: busgrad@syr.edu.
Website: http://whitman.syr.edu/msacc/

Tabor College, Graduate Program, Hillsboro, KS 67063. Offers accounting (MBA). Program offered at the Wichita campus only.

Tarleton State University, College of Graduate Studies, College of Business Administration, Department of Accounting, Finance and Economics, Stephenville, TX 76402. Offers accounting (M Acc). *Program availability:* Part-time, evening/weekend. *Faculty:* 11 full-time (2 women), 3 part-time/adjunct (0 women). *Students:* 9 full-time (6 women), 11 part-time (5 women); includes 5 minority (2 Black or African American, non-Hispanic/Latino; 3 Hispanic/Latino), 1 international. 20 applicants, 85% accepted, 11 enrolled. In 2016, 9 master's awarded. *Degree requirements:* For master's, comprehensive exam. *Entrance requirements:* For master's, GRE or GMAT, minimum GPA of 3.0. Additional exam requirements/recommendations for international students: Required—TOEFL (minimum score 550 paper-based; 80 iBT). *Application deadline:* For fall admission, 8/5 priority date for domestic students; for spring admission, 12/1 for domestic students. Applications are processed on a rolling basis. Application fee: $45 ($145 for international students). Electronic applications accepted. *Expenses:* $3,672 tuition; $2,437 fees. *Financial support:* Research assistantships and teaching assistantships available. Financial award application deadline: 5/1; financial award applicants required to submit FAFSA. *Unit head:* Dr. Keldon Bauer, Department Head, 254-968-9909, Fax: 254-968-9665, E-mail: kbauer@tarleton.edu. *Application contact:* Information Contact, 254-968-9104, Fax: 254-968-9670, E-mail: gradoffice@tarleton.edu.
Website: http://www.tarleton.edu/afe/

Temple University, Fox School of Business, Doctoral Programs in Business, Philadelphia, PA 19122-6096. Offers accounting (PhD); entrepreneurship (PhD); finance (PhD); international business (PhD); management information systems (PhD); marketing (PhD); risk management and insurance (PhD); statistics (PhD); strategic management (PhD); tourism and sport (PhD). *Accreditation:* AACSB. *Degree requirements:* For doctorate, thesis/dissertation. *Entrance requirements:* For doctorate, GRE General Test, GMAT, minimum GPA of 3.0, master's degree. Additional exam requirements/recommendations for international students: Required—TOEFL (minimum score 600 paper-based; 100 iBT), IELTS (minimum score 7.5). Electronic applications accepted.

Temple University, Fox School of Business, MBA Programs, Philadelphia, PA 19122-6096. Offers accounting (MBA); business management (MBA); financial management (MBA); healthcare and life sciences innovation (MBA); human resource management (MBA); international business (IMBA); IT management (MBA); marketing management (MBA); pharmaceutical management (MBA); strategic management (EMBA, MBA). EMBA offered in Philadelphia, PA and Tokyo, Japan. *Accreditation:* AACSB. *Program availability:* Part-time, evening/weekend, online learning. *Entrance requirements:* For master's, GMAT, minimum undergraduate GPA of 3.0. Additional exam requirements/recommendations for international students: Required—TOEFL (minimum score 600 paper-based; 100 iBT), IELTS (minimum score 7.5).

Temple University, Fox School of Business, Specialized Master's Programs, Philadelphia, PA 19122-6096. Offers accountancy (MS); actuarial science (MS); finance (MS); financial engineering (MS); human resource management (MS); innovation management and entrepreneurship (MS); marketing (MS); statistics (MS). MS in innovation management and entrepreneurship delivered jointly with College of Engineering. *Accreditation:* AACSB. *Program availability:* Part-time. *Entrance requirements:* For master's, GRE General Test or GMAT, minimum undergraduate GPA of 3.0. Additional exam requirements/recommendations for international students: Required—TOEFL (minimum score 600 paper-based; 100 iBT), IELTS (minimum score 7.5).

Tennessee Technological University, College of Graduate Studies, College of Business, Cookeville, TN 38505. Offers accounting (MBA); finance (MBA); human resource management (MBA); international business (MBA); management information systems (MBA). *Accreditation:* AACSB. *Program availability:* Part-time, evening/weekend, online learning. *Faculty:* 28 full-time (5 women). *Students:* 45 full-time (22 women), 167 part-time (51 women); includes 18 minority (5 Black or African American, non-Hispanic/Latino; 4 Asian, non-Hispanic/Latino; 4 Hispanic/Latino; 5 Two or more races, non-Hispanic/Latino), 14 international. Average age 25. 173 applicants, 54% accepted, 52 enrolled. In 2016, 78 master's awarded. *Entrance requirements:* For master's, GMAT, GRE. Additional exam requirements/recommendations for international students: Required—TOEFL (minimum score 550 paper-based; 79 iBT), IELTS (minimum score 5.5), PTE (minimum score 53), or TOEIC (Test of English as an International Communication). *Application deadline:* For fall admission, 8/1 for domestic students, 5/1 for international students; for spring admission, 12/1 for domestic students, 10/1 for international students; for summer admission, 5/1 for domestic students, 2/1 for international students. Applications are processed on a rolling basis. Application fee: $35 ($40 for international students). Electronic applications accepted. *Expenses:* Tuition, state resident: full-time $9375; part-time $534 per credit hour. Tuition, nonresident: full-time $22,443; part-time $1260 per credit hour. *Financial support:* In 2016–17, 5 fellowships (averaging $10,000 per year), 1 teaching assistantship (averaging $5,200 per year) were awarded; research assistantships also available. Support available to part-time students. Financial award application deadline: 4/1. *Unit head:* Kate Nicewicz, Director, 931-372-3600, Fax: 931-372-6249, E-mail: knicewicz@tntech.edu. *Application contact:* Shelia K. Kendrick, Coordinator of Graduate Studies, 931-372-3808, Fax: 931-372-3497, E-mail: skendrick@tntech.edu.
Website: http://www.tntech.edu/mba

Tennessee Wesleyan University, Graduate Programs, Athens, TN 37303. Offers accounting (MBA); management (MBA). *Program availability:* Evening/weekend. *Faculty:* 8 full-time (4 women), 3 part-time/adjunct (2 women). *Students:* 4 full-time (2 women), 18 part-time (11 women). *Entrance requirements:* For master's, GMAT, official transcripts, three letters of recommendation, current curriculum vitae or resume. *Expenses: Tuition:* Full-time $9000; part-time $500 per hour. *Application contact:* Mark Bucco, Adult and Graduate Admissions Counselor, 423-252-1114, Fax: 423-745-9335, E-mail: mbucco@tnwesleyan.edu.
Website: http://www.tnwesleyan.edu/academics/graduate-programs/

Texas A&M International University, Office of Graduate Studies and Research, A.R. Sanchez, Jr. School of Business, Division of International Banking and Finance Studies, Laredo, TX 78041-1900. Offers accounting (MP Acc); international banking and finance (MBA). *Entrance requirements:* For master's, GMAT or GRE General Test. Additional exam requirements/recommendations for international students: Required—TOEFL (minimum score 550 paper-based; 79 iBT).

Texas A&M University, Mays Business School, Department of Accounting, College Station, TX 77843. Offers MS. *Accreditation:* AACSB. *Faculty:* 27. *Students:* 167 full-time (98 women), 6 part-time (4 women); includes 34 minority (1 Black or African American, non-Hispanic/Latino; 10 Asian, non-Hispanic/Latino; 21 Hispanic/Latino; 2 Two or more races, non-Hispanic/Latino), 7 international. Average age 24. 220 applicants, 14% accepted, 23 enrolled. In 2016, 138 master's awarded. Terminal master's awarded for partial completion of doctoral program. *Degree requirements:* For master's, comprehensive exam. *Entrance requirements:* For master's, GMAT or GRE. Additional exam requirements/recommendations for international students: Required—TOEFL (minimum score 550 paper-based; 80 iBT), IELTS (minimum score 6), PTE (minimum score 53). *Application deadline:* For fall admission, 3/15 for domestic students, 2/15 for international students; for spring admission, 10/15 for domestic and international students. Applications are processed on a rolling basis. Application fee: $50 ($90 for international students). *Expenses:* Contact institution. *Financial support:* In 2016–17, 80 students received support, including 8 fellowships with tuition reimbursements available (averaging $9,738 per year), 15 research assistantships with tuition reimbursements available (averaging $7,799 per year), 1 teaching assistantship with tuition reimbursement available (averaging $1,631 per year); career-related internships or fieldwork, institutionally sponsored loans, scholarships/grants, traineeships, health care benefits, tuition waivers (full and partial), and unspecified assistantships also available. Support available to part-time students. Financial award application deadline: 3/15; financial award applicants required to submit FAFSA. *Faculty research:* Financial reporting, taxation management, decision-making, accounting information systems, government accounting. *Unit head:* Dr. James J. Benjamin, Head, 979-845-0356, Fax: 979-845-0028, E-mail: jbenjamin@mays.tamu.edu. *Application contact:* Dr. Bala Shetty, Interim Associate Dean for Graduate Programs, 979-845-7024, Fax: 979-845-0028, E-mail: bshetty@mays.tamu.edu.
Website: http://mays.tamu.edu/acct/

Texas A&M University–Central Texas, Graduate Studies and Research, Killeen, TX 76549. Offers accounting (MS); business administration (MBA); clinical mental health counseling (MS); criminal justice (MCJ); curriculum and instruction (M Ed); educational administration (M Ed); educational psychology - experimental psychology (MS); history (MA); human resource management (MS); information systems (MS); liberal studies (MS); management and leadership (MS); marriage and family therapy (MS); mathematics (MS); political science (MA); school counseling (M Ed); school psychology (Ed S).

Texas A&M University–Commerce, College of Business, Commerce, TX 75429-3011. Offers accounting (MSA); business administration (MBA); business analytics (MS); finance (MSF); management (MS); marketing (MS). *Accreditation:* AACSB. *Program availability:* Part-time, evening/weekend, 100% online, blended/hybrid learning. *Faculty:* 48 full-time (17 women), 8 part-time/adjunct (2 women). *Students:* 463 full-time (232 women), 1,109 part-time (539 women); includes 653 minority (280 Black or African American, non-Hispanic/Latino; 7 American Indian or Alaska Native, non-Hispanic/Latino; 131 Asian, non-Hispanic/Latino; 202 Hispanic/Latino; 1 Native Hawaiian or other Pacific Islander, non-Hispanic/Latino; 32 Two or more races, non-Hispanic/Latino), 211 international. Average age 33. 1,021 applicants, 59% accepted, 424 enrolled. In 2016, 617 master's awarded. *Degree requirements:* For master's, comprehensive exam. *Entrance requirements:* For master's, GRE General Test, GMAT, letter of recommendation. Additional exam requirements/recommendations for international students: Required—TOEFL (minimum score 550 paper-based; 79 iBT), IELTS (minimum score 6). *Application deadline:* For fall admission, 5/15 priority date for international students; for spring admission, 10/1 priority date for international students; for summer admission, 2/1 priority date for international students. Applications are processed on a rolling basis. Application fee: $50 ($75 for international students).

Electronic applications accepted. *Expenses:* Contact institution. *Financial support:* In 2016–17, 90 students received support, including 20 research assistantships with partial tuition reimbursements available (averaging $8,000 per year); Federal Work-Study, institutionally sponsored loans, scholarships/grants, health care benefits, and unspecified assistantships also available. Financial award application deadline: 5/1; financial award applicants required to submit FAFSA. *Faculty research:* Applied economics emphasis on industries that are important to the region including health, energy and agriculture; finance research on banking, investments, financial institutions and risk management; marketing and big data decisions of product choice behavior and channel behavior of consumers; strategic management and organizational behavior phenomena; International Accounting in Governmental Sectors. *Total annual research expenditures:* $1,920. *Unit head:* Dr. Shanan G. Gibson, Dean of College of Business, 903-886-5191, Fax: 903-886-5650, E-mail: shanan.gibson@tamuc.edu. *Application contact:* Shanna Hoskison, Director, Graduate Advising, 903-886-5190, E-mail: shanna.hoskison@tamuc.edu.
Website: http://www.tamuc.edu/academics/graduateSchool/programs/businessEntrepreneurship/default.aspx

Texas A&M University–Corpus Christi, College of Graduate Studies, College of Business, Corpus Christi, TX 78412-5503. Offers accounting (M Acc); business (MBA); finance (MBA); health care administration (MBA); international business (MBA). *Accreditation:* AACSB. *Program availability:* Part-time, evening/weekend, 100% online, blended/hybrid learning. *Faculty:* 31 full-time (11 women), 2 part-time/adjunct (0 women). *Students:* 132 full-time (71 women), 495 part-time (232 women); includes 261 minority (49 Black or African American, non-Hispanic/Latino; 44 Asian, non-Hispanic/Latino; 160 Hispanic/Latino; 8 Two or more races, non-Hispanic/Latino), 111 international. Average age 32. 444 applicants, 55% accepted, 192 enrolled. In 2016, 205 master's awarded. *Degree requirements:* For master's, 30 to 42 hours (for MBA; varies by concentration area, delivery format, and necessity for foundational courses for students with nonbusiness degrees). *Entrance requirements:* For master's, GMAT, GRE. Additional exam requirements/recommendations for international students: Required—TOEFL (minimum score 550 paper-based), IELTS (minimum score 6.5). *Application deadline:* For fall admission, 7/15 priority date for domestic students, 5/1 priority date for international students; for spring admission, 11/15 priority date for domestic students, 9/1 priority date for international students; for summer admission, 4/15 priority date for domestic students, 2/1 priority date for international students. Applications are processed on a rolling basis. Application fee: $50 ($70 for international students). Electronic applications accepted. *Financial support:* Research assistantships, teaching assistantships, career-related internships or fieldwork, Federal Work-Study, institutionally sponsored loans, scholarships/grants, health care benefits, and unspecified assistantships available. Support available to part-time students. Financial award application deadline: 3/15; financial award applicants required to submit FAFSA. *Unit head:* Dr. John Gamble, Dean, 361-825-6045, Fax: 361-825-2725, E-mail: john.gamble@tamucc.edu. *Application contact:* Sharon Polansky, Director, Master's Program, 361-825-3448, Fax: 361-825-2755, E-mail: gradweb@tamucc.edu.
Website: http://cob.tamucc.edu

Texas A&M University–San Antonio, School of Business, San Antonio, TX 78224. Offers business administration (MBA); enterprise resource planning systems (MBA); finance (MBA); healthcare management (MBA); human resources management (MBA); information assurance and security (MBA); international business (MBA); professional accounting (MPA); project management (MBA); supply chain management (MBA). *Program availability:* Part-time, evening/weekend. *Entrance requirements:* For master's, GMAT. Additional exam requirements/recommendations for international students: Required—TOEFL (minimum score 550 paper-based; 80 iBT), IELTS (minimum score 6). Electronic applications accepted.

Texas A&M University–Texarkana, Graduate Studies and Research, College of Business, Texarkana, TX 75505-5518. Offers accounting (MSA); business administration (MBA, MS). *Program availability:* Part-time, evening/weekend. *Degree requirements:* For master's, thesis or alternative. *Entrance requirements:* For master's, minimum GPA of 2.5 in last 60 hours of bachelor's degree. Additional exam requirements/recommendations for international students: Required—TOEFL. Electronic applications accepted.

Texas Christian University, Neeley School of Business, Full-time Master's Program in Business Administration and Accelerated MBA, Fort Worth, TX 76129. Offers accounting (MBA); finance (MBA), including corporate finance, investments; marketing (MBA), including marketing management, product and brand management; supply and value chain management (MBA). *Accreditation:* AACSB. *Program availability:* Part-time, evening/weekend. *Faculty:* 60 full-time (17 women), 17 part-time/adjunct (4 women). *Students:* 92 full-time (26 women); includes 14 minority (3 Black or African American, non-Hispanic/Latino; 1 American Indian or Alaska Native, non-Hispanic/Latino; 3 Asian, non-Hispanic/Latino; 7 Hispanic/Latino), 30 international. Average age 28. 205 applicants, 50% accepted, 47 enrolled. In 2016, 43 master's awarded. *Entrance requirements:* For master's, GMAT (preferred); GRE. Additional exam requirements/recommendations for international students: Required—TOEFL (minimum score 100 iBT); Recommended—IELTS (minimum score 7), TSE (minimum score 68). *Application deadline:* For fall admission, 3/1 for domestic and international students; for winter admission, 1/15 for domestic and international students; for spring admission, 11/1 for domestic and international students; for summer admission, 1/15 for domestic and international students. Applications are processed on a rolling basis. Application fee: $100. Electronic applications accepted. Application fee is waived when completed online. *Expenses:* Contact institution. *Financial support:* In 2016–17, 94 students received support. Career-related internships or fieldwork, scholarships/grants, and unspecified assistantships available. Financial award application deadline: 4/1; financial award applicants required to submit FAFSA. *Faculty research:* Emerging financial markets, derivative trading activity, salesforce deployment, examining sales activity, litigation against tax practitioners. *Unit head:* Anne Rooney, Executive Director, Graduate Programs, 817-257-7991, Fax: 817-257-6431, E-mail: mbainfo@tcu.edu. *Application contact:* Peggy Conway, Director, Full-time MBA Admissions, 817-257-7989, Fax: 817-257-6431, E-mail: mbainfo@tcu.edu.
Website: http://www.neeley.tcu.edu/mba

Texas Christian University, Neeley School of Business, Master of Accounting Program, Fort Worth, TX 76129. Offers audit (M Ac); taxation (M Ac); valuation and reporting (M Ac). *Accreditation:* AACSB. *Faculty:* 12 full-time (6 women), 1 part-time/adjunct (0 women). *Students:* 63 full-time (27 women); includes 4 minority (all Hispanic/Latino), 2 international. Average age 22. 71 applicants, 97% accepted, 61 enrolled. In 2016, 69 master's awarded. *Entrance requirements:* Additional exam requirements/recommendations for international students: Recommended—TOEFL. *Application deadline:* For fall admission, 2/15 for domestic and international students; for spring admission, 9/15 for domestic and international students. Application fee: $0. Electronic applications accepted. *Expenses:* $1,480 per semester hour tuition, $1,450 per semester fees. *Financial support:* In 2016–17, 33 students received support. Unspecified assistantships available. Financial award application deadline: 1/31. *Faculty research:* Financial accounting, market valuation of accounting information, corporate governance, managerial compensation and incentives, taxation. *Unit head:* Dr. Mary A. Stanford, Department Chair, 817-257-7483, Fax: 817-257-7227, E-mail: m.stanford@tcu.edu. *Application contact:* Emily Davis, Director, 817-257-5112, Fax: 817-257-7227, E-mail: e.k.davis@tcu.edu.
Website: http://www.neeley.tcu.edu/Academics/Master_of_Accounting/MAc.aspx

Texas Lutheran University, Program in Accounting, Seguin, TX 78155-5999. Offers M Acy.

Texas State University, The Graduate College, Emmett and Miriam McCoy College of Business Administration, Program in Accounting, San Marcos, TX 78666. Offers M Acy. *Program availability:* Part-time. *Faculty:* 13 full-time (6 women), 3 part-time/adjunct (0 women). *Students:* 75 full-time (36 women), 29 part-time (15 women); includes 36 minority (9 Black or African American, non-Hispanic/Latino; 1 American Indian or Alaska Native, non-Hispanic/Latino; 4 Asian, non-Hispanic/Latino; 19 Hispanic/Latino; 3 Two or more races, non-Hispanic/Latino), 6 international. Average age 27. 87 applicants, 53% accepted, 31 enrolled. In 2016, 67 master's awarded. *Degree requirements:* For master's, comprehensive exam. *Entrance requirements:* For master's, GMAT or GRE, baccalaureate degree from regionally-accredited university; two forms of recommendation from persons best able to assess the applicant's ability to succeed in graduate school; essays; resume showing work experience, extracurricular and community activities, and honors and achievements. Additional exam requirements/recommendations for international students: Required—TOEFL (minimum score 550 paper-based; 78 iBT); Recommended—IELTS (minimum score 6.5). *Application deadline:* For fall admission, 2/1 priority date for domestic and international students; for spring admission, 10/1 for domestic and international students. Application fee: $40 ($90 for international students). Electronic applications accepted. *Expenses:* $4,851 per semester. *Financial support:* In 2016–17, 67 students received support, including 1 research assistantship (averaging $13,502 per year), 7 teaching assistantships (averaging $13,612 per year); Federal Work-Study, institutionally sponsored loans, scholarships/grants, health care benefits, and unspecified assistantships also available. Support available to part-time students. Financial award application deadline: 3/1; financial award applicants required to submit FAFSA. *Unit head:* Dr. William Chittenden, Graduate Advisor, 512-245-3591, Fax: 512-245-8365, E-mail: wc10@txstate.edu. *Application contact:* Dr. Andrea Golato, Dean of Graduate School, 512-245-2581, Fax: 512-245-8365, E-mail: gradcollege@txstate.edu.
Website: http://accounting.mccoy.txstate.edu/degress-programs/macy.html

Texas State University, The Graduate College, Emmett and Miriam McCoy College of Business Administration, Program in Accounting and Information Technology, San Marcos, TX 78666. Offers MS. *Program availability:* Part-time. *Faculty:* 4 full-time (1 woman). *Students:* 11 full-time (5 women), 7 part-time (2 women); includes 5 minority (2 Asian, non-Hispanic/Latino; 3 Hispanic/Latino), 6 international. Average age 35. 16 applicants, 63% accepted, 6 enrolled. In 2016, 5 master's awarded. *Degree requirements:* For master's, comprehensive exam. *Entrance requirements:* For master's, GMAT or GRE, baccalaureate degree from regionally-accredited university; two letters or forms of recommendation from persons best able to assess applicant's ability to succeed in graduate school; essay; resume showing work experience, extracurricular and community activities, and honors and achievements. Additional exam requirements/recommendations for international students: Required—TOEFL (minimum score 550 paper-based; 78 iBT), IELTS (minimum score 6.5). *Application deadline:* For fall admission, 2/1 priority date for domestic and international students; for spring admission, 10/1 for domestic and international students. Application fee: $40 ($90 for international students). Electronic applications accepted. *Expenses:* $4,851 per semester. *Financial support:* In 2016–17, 9 students received support, including 5 teaching assistantships (averaging $13,641 per year); research assistantships, Federal Work-Study, institutionally sponsored loans, scholarships/grants, health care benefits, and unspecified assistantships also available. Support available to part-time students. Financial award application deadline: 3/1; financial award applicants required to submit FAFSA. *Faculty research:* Aerospace MIS evaluation; learning the science of climate change with commuting. *Total annual research expenditures:* $15,531. *Unit head:* Dr. William Chittenden, Graduate Advisor, 512-245-3591, Fax: 512-245-8365, E-mail: wc10@txstate.edu. *Application contact:* Dr. Andrea Golato, Dean of Graduate School, 512-245-2581, Fax: 512-245-8365, E-mail: gradcollege@txstate.edu.
Website: http://mycatalog.txstate.edu/graduate/mccoy-business-administration/accounting/information-technology-ms/

Texas Tech University, Rawls College of Business Administration, Lubbock, TX 79409-2101. Offers accounting (MSA, PhD), including audit/financial reporting (MSA), taxation (MSA); business statistics (MS, PhD); data science (MS); finance (PhD); general business (MBA); healthcare management (MS); information systems and operations management (PhD); management (PhD); marketing (PhD); STEM (MBA); JD/MBA; JD/MSA; MBA/M Arch; MBA/MD; MBA/MS; MBA/Pharm D. *Accreditation:* AACSB; CAHME (one or more programs are accredited). *Program availability:* Evening/weekend. *Faculty:* 74 full-time (13 women). *Students:* 741 full-time (275 women); includes 198 minority (38 Black or African American, non-Hispanic/Latino; 1 American Indian or Alaska Native, non-Hispanic/Latino; 24 Asian, non-Hispanic/Latino; 116 Hispanic/Latino; 1 Native Hawaiian or other Pacific Islander, non-Hispanic/Latino; 18 Two or more races, non-Hispanic/Latino), 95 international. Average age 28. 905 applicants, 48% accepted, 251 enrolled. In 2016, 545 master's, 13 doctorates awarded. *Degree requirements:* For master's, capstone course; for doctorate, comprehensive exam, thesis/dissertation, qualifying exams. *Entrance requirements:* For master's, GMAT, GRE, MCAT, PCAT, LSAT, or DAT, holistic review of academic credentials, resume, essay, letters of recommendation; for doctorate, GMAT, GRE, holistic review of academic credentials, resume, statement of purpose, letters of recommendation. Additional exam requirements/recommendations for international students: Required—TOEFL (minimum score 95 iBT), IELTS. *Application deadline:* For fall admission, 7/1 priority date for domestic students, 1/15 for international students; for spring admission, 12/1 priority date for domestic students, 6/15 for international students; for summer admission, 5/1 for domestic students. Applications are processed on a rolling basis. Application fee: $60. Electronic applications accepted. *Expenses:* $48,000 (MBA for Working Professionals); $20,000 (STEM MBA). *Financial support:* In 2016–17, 157 students received support, including 25 research assistantships (averaging $22,725 per year), 27 teaching assistantships (averaging $22,725 per year); fellowships, career-related internships or fieldwork, Federal Work-Study, scholarships/grants, health care benefits, and unspecified assistantships also available. Financial award application deadline: 3/1; financial award applicants required to submit FAFSA. *Faculty research:* Governmental and nonprofit accounting, securities and options futures, statistical analysis and design, leadership, consumer behavior. *Unit head:* Dr. Margaret Williams, Dean, 806-742-3188, Fax: 806-742-1092, E-mail: margaret.l.williams@ttu.edu. *Application contact:* Chathry Keaton, Applications Manager, Graduate and Professional Programs, 806-742-3184, Fax: 806-742-3958, E-mail: rawlsgrad@ttu.edu.
Website: http://www.depts.ttu.edu/rawlsbusiness/graduate/

Texas Woman's University, Graduate School, School of Management, Denton, TX 76204-5738. Offers accounting (MBA); business administration (MBA); health systems management (MHSM). *Accreditation:* ACBSP. *Program availability:* Part-time. *Students:* 432 full-time (357 women), 442 part-time (356 women); includes 598 minority (341 Black or African American, non-Hispanic/Latino; 2 American Indian or Alaska Native, non-

Hispanic/Latino; 111 Asian, non-Hispanic/Latino; 121 Hispanic/Latino; 3 Native Hawaiian or other Pacific Islander, non-Hispanic/Latino; 20 Two or more races, non-Hispanic/Latino), 46 international. Average age 35. In 2016, 604 master's awarded. *Degree requirements:* For master's, thesis optional. *Entrance requirements:* For master's, 2 letters of reference, resume, 5 years of relevant experience (EMBA only). Additional exam requirements/recommendations for international students: Required—TOEFL (minimum score 550 paper-based; 79 iBT). *Application deadline:* For fall admission, 8/1 priority date for domestic students, 3/1 for international students; for spring admission, 12/1 priority date for domestic students, 7/1 for international students. Applications are processed on a rolling basis. Application fee: $50 ($75 for international students). Electronic applications accepted. *Expenses:* Contact institution. *Financial support:* Research assistantships, career-related internships or fieldwork, Federal Work-Study, institutionally sponsored loans, scholarships/grants, traineeships, health care benefits, and unspecified assistantships available. Support available to part-time students. Financial award application deadline: 3/1; financial award applicants required to submit FAFSA. *Faculty research:* Tax research, privacy issues in Web-based marketing, multitasking, leadership, women in management, global comparative studies, corporate sustainability and responsibility. *Unit head:* Dr. Margaret A. Young, Director, 940-898-2105, Fax: 940-898-2120, E-mail: myoung13@twu.edu. *Application contact:* Dr. Samuel Wheeler, Assistant Director of Admissions, 940-898-3188, Fax: 940-898-3081, E-mail: wheelersr@twu.edu.
Website: http://www.twu.edu/som/

Towson University, Program in Accounting and Business Advisory Services, Towson, MD 21252-0001. Offers MS. Program offered jointly with University of Baltimore. *Accreditation:* AACSB. *Program availability:* Part-time, evening/weekend. *Students:* 27 full-time (12 women), 14 part-time (6 women); includes 12 minority (4 Black or African American, non-Hispanic/Latino; 8 Asian, non-Hispanic/Latino), 10 international. *Entrance requirements:* For master's, GMAT, GRE General Test, minimum GPA of 3.0; prerequisite courses in accounting, economics, communications, math, marketing, finance, business law, and business ethics. *Application deadline:* Applications are processed on a rolling basis. Application fee: $45. Electronic applications accepted. *Expenses:* Tuition, state resident: full-time $7580; part-time $379 per unit. Tuition, nonresident: full-time $15,700; part-time $785 per unit. *Required fees:* $2480. *Unit head:* Dr. Martin Freedman, Graduate Program Director, 410-704-4143, E-mail: mfreedman@towson.edu. *Application contact:* University Admissions, 410-704-2113, Fax: 410-704-3030, E-mail: grads@towson.edu.
Website: https://www.towson.edu/cbe/departments/accounting/gradaccounting/

Trinity University, School of Business, San Antonio, TX 78212-7200. Offers accounting (MS). *Accreditation:* AACSB. *Entrance requirements:* For master's, GMAT, minimum GPA of 3.0, course work in accounting and business law, letters of recommendation. Electronic applications accepted. *Expenses: Tuition:* Full-time $38,974. *Required fees:* $586.

Troy University, Graduate School, College of Business, Program in Accountancy, Troy, AL 36082. Offers M Acc. *Program availability:* Part-time, evening/weekend. *Faculty:* 3 full-time (1 woman). *Students:* 26 full-time (16 women), 11 part-time (2 women); includes 7 minority (1 Black or African American, non-Hispanic/Latino; 1 American Indian or Alaska Native, non-Hispanic/Latino; 3 Asian, non-Hispanic/Latino; 1 Hispanic/Latino; 1 Two or more races, non-Hispanic/Latino). Average age 25. 33 applicants, 88% accepted. In 2016, 17 master's awarded. *Degree requirements:* For master's, minimum GPA of 3.0, research course. *Entrance requirements:* For master's, GMAT (minimum score of 500), bachelor's degree; minimum undergraduate GPA of 2.5 or 3.0 on last 30 semester hours, letter of recommendation. Additional exam requirements/recommendations for international students: Required—TOEFL (minimum score 523 paper-based; 70 iBT), IELTS (minimum score 6). *Application deadline:* Applications are processed on a rolling basis. Application fee: $50. Electronic applications accepted. *Expenses:* Tuition, state resident: full-time $7146; part-time $397 per credit hour. Tuition, nonresident: full-time $14,292; part-time $794 per credit hour. *Required fees:* $802; $50 per semester. Tuition and fees vary according to campus/location and program. *Financial support:* Fellowships, career-related internships or fieldwork, and scholarships/grants available. Support available to part-time students. Financial award applicants required to submit FAFSA. *Unit head:* Dr. Steve Grice, Chairman, Master of Accountancy, 334-670-3154, Fax: 334-670-3592, E-mail: sgrice@troy.edu. *Application contact:* Jessica A. Kimbro, Director of Graduate Admissions, 334-670-3178, E-mail: jacord@troy.edu.

Troy University, Graduate School, College of Business, Program in Business Administration, Troy, AL 36082. Offers accounting (EMBA, MBA); criminal justice (EMBA); finance (MBA); general management (EMBA, MBA); healthcare management (EMBA); information systems (EMBA, MBA); international economic development (MBA). *Accreditation:* ACBSP. *Program availability:* Part-time, evening/weekend. *Faculty:* 10 full-time (3 women), 2 part-time/adjunct (0 women). *Students:* 44 full-time (23 women), 131 part-time (69 women); includes 58 minority (38 Black or African American, non-Hispanic/Latino; 13 Asian, non-Hispanic/Latino; 4 Hispanic/Latino; 3 Two or more races, non-Hispanic/Latino). Average age 30. 285 applicants, 91% accepted, 22 enrolled. In 2016, 78 master's awarded. *Degree requirements:* For master's, minimum GPA of 3.0, capstone course, research course. *Entrance requirements:* For master's, GMAT (minimum score 500) or GRE (minimum score 900 on old exam or 294 on new exam), bachelor's degree; minimum undergraduate GPA of 2.5 or 3.0 on last 30 semester hours, letter of recommendation. Additional exam requirements/recommendations for international students: Required—TOEFL (minimum score 523 paper-based; 70 iBT), IELTS (minimum score 6). *Application deadline:* Applications are processed on a rolling basis. Application fee: $50. Electronic applications accepted. *Expenses:* Tuition, state resident: full-time $7146; part-time $397 per credit hour. Tuition, nonresident: full time $14,292; part-time $794 per credit hour. *Required fees:* $802; $50 per semester. Tuition and fees vary according to campus/location and program. *Financial support:* Fellowships, career-related internships or fieldwork, and scholarships/grants available. Support available to part-time students. Financial award applicants required to submit FAFSA. *Unit head:* Dr. Phillip Mixon, MBA Director, 334-670-3140, Fax: 334-670-3708, E-mail: pamixon@troy.edu. *Application contact:* Jessica A. Kimbro, Director of Graduate Admissions, 334-670-3178, E-mail: jacord@troy.edu.

Truman State University, Graduate School, School of Business, Program in Accounting, Kirksville, MO 63501-4221. Offers M Ac. *Accreditation:* AACSB. *Students:* 30 full-time (16 women), 2 part-time (1 woman); includes 7 minority (1 Black or African American, non-Hispanic/Latino; 6 Asian, non-Hispanic/Latino). Average age 23. In 2016, 34 master's awarded. *Degree requirements:* For master's, comprehensive exam. *Entrance requirements:* For master's, GMAT, minimum GPA of 3.0. Additional exam requirements/recommendations for international students: Required—TOEFL (minimum score 550 paper-based). *Application deadline:* For fall admission, 6/1 for domestic and international students; for spring admission, 11/1 for domestic and international students; for summer admission, 4/1 for domestic and international students. Applications are processed on a rolling basis. Application fee: $40. Electronic applications accepted. *Expenses:* Tuition, state resident: full-time $6300; part-time $350 per credit hour. Tuition, nonresident: full-time $10,818; part-time $601 per credit hour. Tuition and fees vary according to course load and program. *Financial support:* In 2016–17, 12 research assistantships with full and partial tuition reimbursements (averaging $2,500 per year) were awarded; teaching assistantships also available. Financial award application deadline: 5/1; financial award applicants required to submit FAFSA. *Unit head:* Dr. Alan Davis, Director, 660-785-5550, Fax: 660-785-7471, E-mail: abdavis@truman.edu. *Application contact:* Stephanie Rudolph, Graduate Office Secretary, 660-785-4109, Fax: 660-785-7460, E-mail: gradinfo@truman.edu.

Tulane University, A. B. Freeman School of Business, New Orleans, LA 70118-5669. Offers accounting (M Acct); analytics (MBA); banking and financial services (M Fin); energy (M Fin, MBA); entrepreneurship (MBA); finance (MBA, PhD); international business (MBA); international management (MBA); strategic management and leadership (MBA); JD/M Acct; JD/MBA; MBA/M Acc; MBA/MA; MBA/MD; MBA/ME; MBA/MPH. *Accreditation:* AACSB. *Program availability:* Part-time, evening/weekend. *Faculty:* 46 full-time (11 women), 36 part-time/adjunct (3 women). *Students:* 488 full-time (240 women), 414 part-time (198 women); includes 81 minority (31 Black or African American, non-Hispanic/Latino; 1 American Indian or Alaska Native, non-Hispanic/Latino; 17 Asian, non-Hispanic/Latino; 29 Hispanic/Latino; 3 Two or more races, non-Hispanic/Latino), 575 international. Average age 27. 2,038 applicants, 71% accepted, 511 enrolled. In 2016, 694 master's, 9 doctorates awarded. Terminal master's awarded for partial completion of doctoral program. *Degree requirements:* For master's, one foreign language, comprehensive exam (for some programs); for doctorate, one foreign language, comprehensive exam, thesis/dissertation. *Entrance requirements:* For master's and doctorate, GMAT or GRE, interview. Additional exam requirements/recommendations for international students: Required—TOEFL or IELTS. *Application deadline:* For fall admission, 11/1 priority date for domestic and international students; for winter admission, 1/6 for domestic and international students; for spring admission, 3/1 priority date for domestic and international students; for summer admission, 5/5 for domestic students. Applications are processed on a rolling basis. Application fee: $125. Electronic applications accepted. *Expenses:* Contact institution. *Financial support:* In 2016–17, 153 students received support. Fellowships with tuition reimbursements available, research assistantships, teaching assistantships, career-related internships or fieldwork, Federal Work-Study, tuition waivers (full and partial), and unspecified assistantships available. Support available to part-time students. Financial award application deadline: 4/15; financial award applicants required to submit FAFSA. *Faculty research:* Corporate finance, managerial accounting and financial reporting, strategic management and leadership, consumer behavior and decision making, organizational behavior and human resource management. *Unit head:* Ira Solomon, PhD, Dean, 504-865-5407, Fax: 504-865-5491, E-mail: businessdean@tulane.edu. *Application contact:* Melissa Booth, Director of Graduate Admissions and Financial Aid, 800-223-5402, E-mail: freeman.admissions@tulane.edu.
Website: http://www.freeman.tulane.edu

Union University, McAfee School of Business Administration, Jackson, TN 38305-3697. Offers accountancy (M Acc). Program also available at Germantown campus. *Program availability:* Evening/weekend, online learning. *Entrance requirements:* For master's, GMAT, minimum GPA of 2.5. Electronic applications accepted. *Expenses:* Contact institution. *Faculty research:* Personal financial management, strategy, accounting, marketing, economics.

Universidad del Este, Graduate School, Carolina, PR 00984. Offers accounting (MBA); adult education (M Ed); agribusiness (MBA); criminal justice and criminology (MA); curriculum and instruction - early education (M Ed); curriculum and instruction - elementary (M Ed); curriculum and instruction - English (M Ed); curriculum and instruction - Spanish (M Ed); human resources (MBA); information security management (MBA); information technology and Web business development (MBA); management (MBA); public policy (MPA); social work (MA), including clinical social work; special education (M Ed); strategic leadership (MBA).

Universidad del Turabo, Graduate Programs, School of Business and Entrepreneurship, Program in Accounting, Gurabo, PR 00778-3030. Offers MBA. *Program availability:* Part-time, evening/weekend. *Students:* 8 full-time (7 women), 17 part-time (9 women); all minorities (all Hispanic/Latino). Average age 33. 16 applicants, 56% accepted, 9 enrolled. In 2016, 5 master's awarded. *Entrance requirements:* For master's, GRE, EXADEP, GMAT, interview, essay, official transcript, recommendation letters. *Application deadline:* For fall admission, 8/5 for domestic students. Applications are processed on a rolling basis. Application fee: $25. Electronic applications accepted. *Financial support:* Institutionally sponsored loans available. Financial award applicants required to submit FAFSA. *Unit head:* Juan Sosa, Dean, 787-743-7979 Ext. 4118, E-mail: negocios_ut@suagm.edu. *Application contact:* Diriee Rodríguez, Admissions Director, 787-743-7979 Ext. 4453, E-mail: admisiones-ut@suagm.edu.
Website: http://ut.suagm.edu/es/negocios

Universidad Metropolitana, School of Business Administration, Program in Accounting, San Juan, PR 00928-1150. Offers MBA. *Program availability:* Part-time. *Degree requirements:* For master's, thesis or alternative. *Entrance requirements:* For master's, GMAT, PAEG, interview. Electronic applications accepted.

Université de Sherbrooke, Faculty of Administration, Program in Accounting, Sherbrooke, QC J1K 2R1, Canada. Offers M Sc. *Degree requirements:* For master's, one foreign language, thesis. *Entrance requirements:* For master's, bachelor's degree in related field, minimum GPA of 3.0 (on 4.3 scale). Electronic applications accepted. *Faculty research:* Financial analysis, management accounting, certification, system and control.

Université du Québec à Montréal, Graduate Programs, Program in Accounting, Montréal, QC H3C 3P8, Canada. Offers M Sc, MPA, Diploma. *Program availability:* Part-time. *Degree requirements:* For master's, thesis (for some programs). *Entrance requirements:* For master's, appropriate bachelor's degree or equivalent and proficiency in French.

Université du Québec à Trois-Rivières, Graduate Programs, Program in Accounting Science, Trois-Rivières, QC G9A 5H7, Canada. Offers MBA.

Université du Québec en Outaouais, Graduate Programs, Program in Accounting, Gatineau, QC J8X 3X7, Canada. Offers MA, DESS, Diploma. *Program availability:* Part-time, evening/weekend.

Université du Québec en Outaouais, Graduate Programs, Program in Executive Certified Management Accounting, Gatineau, QC J8X 3X7, Canada. Offers MA, MBA, DESS. *Program availability:* Part-time, evening/weekend. *Degree requirements:* For master's, thesis (for some programs).

Université Laval, Faculty of Administrative Sciences, Programs in Business Administration, Québec, QC G1K 7P4, Canada. Offers accounting (MBA); agri-food management (MBA); electronic business (MBA, Diploma); factory management and logistics (MBA); finance (MBA); firm management (MBA); geomatic management (MBA); information technology management (MBA); international management (MBA); management (MBA); management accounting (MBA, Diploma); marketing (MBA); modeling and organizational decision (MBA); occupational health and safety management (MBA); pharmacy management (MBA); social and environmental responsibility (MBA); technological entrepreneurship (Diploma). *Accreditation:* AACSB. *Program availability:* Part-time, evening/weekend, online learning. *Entrance*

Accounting

requirements: For master's and Diploma, knowledge of French and English. Electronic applications accepted.

Université Laval, Faculty of Administrative Sciences, Programs in Public Accountancy, Québec, QC G1K 7P4, Canada. Offers MBA, Diploma. *Program availability:* Part-time. *Entrance requirements:* For master's and Diploma, knowledge of French and English. Electronic applications accepted.

University at Albany, State University of New York, School of Business, Department of Accounting and Law, Albany, NY 12222-0001. Offers accounting (MS); forensic accounting (MS); professional accounting (MS); tax practice (MS); taxation (MS). *Accreditation:* AACSB. *Faculty:* 9 full-time (2 women), 8 part-time/adjunct (3 women). *Students:* 137 full-time (62 women), 9 part-time (4 women); includes 31 minority (7 Black or African American, non-Hispanic/Latino; 11 Asian, non-Hispanic/Latino; 9 Hispanic/Latino; 4 Two or more races, non-Hispanic/Latino), 22 international. 257 applicants, 67% accepted, 117 enrolled. In 2016, 110 master's awarded. *Degree requirements:* For master's, research project. *Entrance requirements:* For master's, GMAT. Additional exam requirements/recommendations for international students: Required—TOEFL (minimum score 550 paper-based). *Application deadline:* For fall admission, 3/1 priority date for domestic students, 4/1 for international students. Applications are processed on a rolling basis. Application fee: $75. Electronic applications accepted. *Expenses:* Tuition, state resident: full-time $10,870; part-time $453 per credit hour. Tuition, nonresident: full-time $22,210; part-time $925 per credit hour. *International tuition:* $21,550 full-time. *Required fees:* $1864; $96 per credit hour. *Financial support:* Application deadline: 4/1. *Faculty research:* Professional ethics, statistical analysis, cost management systems, accounting theory. *Unit head:* Ingrid Fisher, Chair, 518-956-8365, E-mail: ifisher@albany.edu. *Application contact:* Michael DeRensis, Director, Graduate Admissions, 518-442-3980, Fax: 518-442-3922, E-mail: graduate@albany.edu.
Website: http://www.albany.edu/business/accounting_index.shtml

University at Buffalo, the State University of New York, Graduate School, School of Management, Buffalo, NY 14620. Offers accounting (MS); analytics (MBA); business administration (PMBA); consulting (MBA); finance (MBA, MS), including financial risk management (MS), quantitative finance (MS); healthcare (MBA); information assurance (MBA); information systems (MBA); international management (MBA); management (EMBA, PhD); management information systems (MS); marketing (MBA); supply chain and operations (MBA); supply chains and operations management (MS); Au D/MBA; DDS/MBA; JD/MBA; M Arch/MBA; MD/MBA; MPH/MBA; MSW/MBA; Pharm D/MBA. *Accreditation:* AACSB. *Program availability:* Part-time, evening/weekend. *Faculty:* 80 full-time (26 women), 36 part-time/adjunct (6 women). *Students:* 683 full-time (277 women), 196 part-time (63 women); includes 76 minority (23 Black or African American, non-Hispanic/Latino; 1 American Indian or Alaska Native, non-Hispanic/Latino; 48 Asian, non-Hispanic/Latino; 3 Hispanic/Latino; 1 Two or more races, non-Hispanic/Latino), 371 international. Average age 31. 2,451 applicants, 42% accepted, 484 enrolled. In 2016, 515 master's, 10 doctorates awarded. *Degree requirements:* For master's, thesis (for some programs); for doctorate, comprehensive exam, thesis/dissertation. *Entrance requirements:* For master's, GMAT (for MS in accounting, finance); GRE or GMAT (for MBA, PMBA, other MS concentrations), essays, letters of recommendation; for doctorate, GMAT or GRE, essays, writing sample, letters of recommendation. Additional exam requirements/recommendations for international students: Required—TOEFL (minimum score 95 iBT) or IELTS (minimum score 6.5); Recommended—TSE (minimum score 73). *Application deadline:* For fall admission, 10/15 priority date for domestic and international students; for winter admission, 2/1 priority date for domestic and international students; for spring admission, 4/15 for domestic students; for summer admission, 5/15 for domestic students. Application fee: $100. Electronic applications accepted. *Expenses:* Contact institution. *Financial support:* Fellowships with full and partial tuition reimbursements, research assistantships with full and partial tuition reimbursements, teaching assistantships with full and partial tuition reimbursements, career-related internships or fieldwork, Federal Work-Study, institutionally sponsored loans, scholarships/grants, health care benefits, and unspecified assistantships available. Financial award application deadline: 2/15. *Faculty research:* Data analytics, accounting information and corporate finance, consumer behavior, supply chain logistics, leadership and team effectiveness. *Total annual research expenditures:* $1.5 million. *Unit head:* Erin K. O'Brien, Assistant Dean and Director of Graduate Programs, 716-645-3204, Fax: 716-645-2341, E-mail: ekobrien@buffalo.edu. *Application contact:* Meghan Felser, Associate Director of Admissions and Recruiting, 716-645-3204, Fax: 716-645-2341, E-mail: mpwood@buffalo.edu.
Website: http://mgt.buffalo.edu/

The University of Akron, Graduate School, College of Business Administration, The George W. Daverio School of Accountancy, Program in Accounting, Akron, OH 44325. Offers MSA. *Expenses:* Tuition, state resident: full-time $8618; part-time $359 per credit hour. Tuition, nonresident: full-time $17,149; part-time $715 per credit hour. *Required fees:* $1652. *Unit head:* Dr. Thomas Calderon, Chair, 330-972-6099, E-mail: tcalderon@uakron.edu. *Application contact:* Dr. William Hauser, Director of Graduate Business Programs, 330-972-7043, Fax: 330-972-6588, E-mail: whauser@uakron.edu.

The University of Alabama, Graduate School, Manderson Graduate School of Business, Culverhouse School of Accountancy, Tuscaloosa, AL 35487. Offers accounting (M Acc, PhD); tax accounting (MTA). *Accreditation:* AACSB. *Faculty:* 19 full-time (4 women). *Students:* 115 full-time (47 women), 3 part-time (all women); includes 14 minority (6 Black or African American, non-Hispanic/Latino; 1 American Indian or Alaska Native, non-Hispanic/Latino; 4 Asian, non-Hispanic/Latino; 1 Hispanic/Latino; 2 Two or more races, non-Hispanic/Latino), 4 international. Average age 24. 221 applicants, 58% accepted, 100 enrolled. In 2016, 102 master's, 4 doctorates awarded. *Degree requirements:* For doctorate, thesis/dissertation. *Entrance requirements:* For master's, GMAT, minimum GPA of 3.0 overall or on last 60 hours; for doctorate, GMAT, minimum GPA of 3.0. Additional exam requirements/recommendations for international students: Required—TOEFL. *Application deadline:* For fall admission, 7/1 priority date for domestic students, 6/1 priority date for international students; for spring admission, 11/1 priority date for domestic students, 9/1 priority date for international students. Applications are processed on a rolling basis. Application fee: $50 ($60 for international students). Electronic applications accepted. *Expenses:* Tuition, state resident: full-time $10,470. Tuition, nonresident: full-time $26,950. *Financial support:* In 2016–17, 79 students received support, including 4 fellowships with full tuition reimbursements available (averaging $15,000 per year), 23 research assistantships with tuition reimbursements available (averaging $9,765 per year), 19 teaching assistantships with tuition reimbursements available (averaging $13,352 per year); career-related internships or fieldwork, Federal Work-Study, institutionally sponsored loans, scholarships/grants, health care benefits, and unspecified assistantships also available. Financial award application deadline: 3/31. *Faculty research:* Corporate governance, audit decision-making, earning management, valuation, executive compensation. *Total annual research expenditures:* $44,946. *Unit head:* Dr. Richard Houston, Director, 205-348-8392, E-mail: rhouston@culverhouse.ua.edu. *Application contact:* Sandy D. Davidson, Advisor, 205-348-6131, Fax: 205-348-8453, E-mail: sdavidso@cba.ua.edu.
Website: http://www.cba.ua.edu/accounting/

The University of Alabama at Birmingham, Collat School of Business, Program in Accounting, Birmingham, AL 35294. Offers accounting (M Acct), including internal auditing. *Accreditation:* AACSB. *Program availability:* Part-time, evening/weekend, online learning. *Entrance requirements:* For master's, GMAT (minimum score of 500). Additional exam requirements/recommendations for international students: Required—TOEFL (minimum score 80 iBT). Electronic applications accepted. Full-time tuition and fees vary according to course load and program.

The University of Alabama in Huntsville, School of Graduate Studies, College of Business Administration, Program in Accounting, Huntsville, AL 35899. Offers accounting (M Acc), including CPA preparatory with an emphasis in taxation, CPA preparatory with emphasis in assurance and financial reporting, general accounting, information systems audit and control (ISAC). *Accreditation:* AACSB. *Program availability:* Part-time, evening/weekend. *Degree requirements:* For master's, comprehensive exam, thesis or alternative. *Entrance requirements:* For master's, GMAT (minimum score 500), minimum AACSB index of 1080. Additional exam requirements/recommendations for international students: Required—TOEFL (minimum score 550 paper-based; 80 iBT), IELTS (minimum score 6.5). Electronic applications accepted. *Expenses:* Tuition, state resident: full-time $9834; part-time $600 per credit hour. Tuition, nonresident: full-time $21,830; part-time $1325 per credit hour. *Faculty research:* Accounting information systems, managerial accounting, behavioral accounting, state and local taxation, financial accounting.

The University of Alabama in Huntsville, School of Graduate Studies, College of Business Administration, Programs in Business and Management, Huntsville, AL 35899. Offers business analytics (MSMS); federal contracting and procurement management (Certificate); human resource management (MSM); management (MBA), including acquisition management, entrepreneurship, federal contract accounting, finance, human resource management, logistics and supply chain management, marketing, project management; supply chain management (Certificate); technology and innovation management (Certificate). *Accreditation:* AACSB. *Program availability:* Part-time, evening/weekend. *Degree requirements:* For master's, comprehensive exam, thesis or alternative. *Entrance requirements:* For master's, GMAT (minimum score 500), minimum AACSB index of 1080. Additional exam requirements/recommendations for international students: Required—TOEFL (minimum score 550 paper-based; 80 iBT), IELTS (minimum score 6.5). Electronic applications accepted. *Expenses:* Tuition, state resident: full-time $9834; part-time $600 per credit hour. Tuition, nonresident: full-time $21,830; part-time $1325 per credit hour. *Faculty research:* Supply chain management, management of research and development, international marketing and branding, organizational behavior and human resource management, social networks and computational economics.

University of Alberta, Faculty of Graduate Studies and Research, Doctoral Program in Business, Edmonton, AB T6G 2E1, Canada. Offers accounting (PhD); finance (PhD); human resources/industrial relations (PhD); management science (PhD); marketing (PhD); organizational analysis (PhD); MBA/PhD. *Accreditation:* AACSB. *Program availability:* Part-time. *Degree requirements:* For doctorate, comprehensive exam, thesis/dissertation. *Entrance requirements:* For doctorate, GMAT. Additional exam requirements/recommendations for international students: Required—TOEFL (minimum score 550 paper-based). Electronic applications accepted. *Faculty research:* Accounting, capital markets and corporate finance, organizational change and human resource management, marketing, strategic management.

The University of Arizona, Eller College of Management, Department of Accounting, Tucson, AZ 85721. Offers M Ac, MS. *Accreditation:* AACSB. *Program availability:* Part-time. *Degree requirements:* For master's, comprehensive exam, 1-year residency. *Entrance requirements:* For master's, GMAT (minimum score 550), 2 letters of recommendation, 3 writing samples, resume. Additional exam requirements/recommendations for international students: Required—TOEFL (minimum score 600 paper-based; 100 iBT). Electronic applications accepted. *Expenses:* Contact institution. *Faculty research:* Auditing, financial reporting and financial markets, taxation policy and markets, behavioral research in accounting.

University of Arkansas, Graduate School, Sam M. Walton College of Business Administration, Department of Accounting, Fayetteville, AR 72701. Offers M Acc. *Accreditation:* AACSB. In 2016, 51 master's awarded. *Entrance requirements:* For master's, GMAT. Application fee: $40 ($50 for international students). *Financial support:* In 2016–17, 18 research assistantships, 2 teaching assistantships were awarded; fellowships with tuition reimbursements, career-related internships or fieldwork, and Federal Work-Study also available. Support available to part-time students. Financial award application deadline: 4/1; financial award applicants required to submit FAFSA. *Unit head:* Dr. Gary Peters, Chair, 479-575-4051, Fax: 479-575-2863, E-mail: peters@walton.uark.edu.
Website: http://gsb.uark.edu/

University of Baltimore, Graduate School, Merrick School of Business, Department of Accounting, Baltimore, MD 21201-5779. Offers accounting and business advisory services (MS); accounting fundamentals (Graduate Certificate); forensic accounting (Graduate Certificate); taxation (MS). *Program availability:* Part-time, evening/weekend. *Entrance requirements:* For master's, GMAT. Additional exam requirements/recommendations for international students: Required—TOEFL (minimum score 550 paper-based). Electronic applications accepted. *Faculty research:* Health care, accounting and administration, managerial accounting, financial accounting theory, accounting information.

University of Baltimore, Graduate School, Merrick School of Business, Department of Information Systems and Decision Science, Baltimore, MD 21201-5779. Offers accounting and business advisory services (MS).

University of Bridgeport, School of Business, Bridgeport, CT 06604. Offers accounting (MBA); finance (MBA); general business (MBA); global financial services (MBA); human resource management (MBA); information systems and knowledge management (MBA); international business (MBA); management (MBA); marketing (MBA); operations management (MBA); small business and entrepreneurship (MBA); specialized business (MBA). *Accreditation:* ACBSP. *Program availability:* Part-time, evening/weekend. *Degree requirements:* For master's, thesis optional. *Entrance requirements:* For master's, GMAT. Additional exam requirements/recommendations for international students: Recommended—TOEFL (minimum score 550 paper-based; 80 iBT), IELTS (minimum score 6.5). Electronic applications accepted. *Expenses:* Contact institution.

The University of British Columbia, Sauder School of Business, Doctoral Program in Business Administration, Vancouver, BC V6T 1Z2, Canada. Offers accounting (PhD); finance (PhD); management information systems (PhD); management science (PhD); marketing (PhD); organizational behavior (PhD); strategy and business economics (PhD); transportation and logistics (PhD); urban land economics (PhD). *Degree requirements:* For doctorate, comprehensive exam, thesis/dissertation. *Entrance requirements:* For doctorate, GMAT or GRE. Additional exam requirements/recommendations for international students: Required—TOEFL (minimum score 600 paper-based; 100 iBT). *Application deadline:* Applications are processed on a rolling basis. Application fee: $102 Canadian dollars ($165 Canadian dollars for international students). Electronic applications accepted. *Expenses:* $4,802 per year tuition and fees,

$8,436 per year international. *Financial support:* Fellowships with full tuition reimbursements, research assistantships with full tuition reimbursements, and teaching assistantships with full tuition reimbursements available. *Application contact:* Elaine Cho, Administrator, PhD and M Sc Programs, 604-822-8366, Fax: 604-822-8755, E-mail: phd.program@sauder.ubc.ca.
Website: http://www.sauder.ubc.ca/Programs/PhD_in_Business_Administration

University of California, Berkeley, Graduate Division, Haas School of Business, PhD in Business Administration Program, Berkeley, CA 94720-1500. Offers accounting (PhD); business and public policy (PhD); finance (PhD); management of organizations (PhD); marketing (PhD); real estate (PhD). *Accreditation:* AACSB. *Students:* 78 full-time (28 women); includes 34 minority (29 Asian, non-Hispanic/Latino; 5 Hispanic/Latino). Average age 27. *Degree requirements:* For doctorate, comprehensive exam, thesis/dissertation, written preliminary exams, oral qualifying exam. *Entrance requirements:* For doctorate, GMAT or GRE, minimum GPA of 3.0 in undergraduate and graduate coursework. Additional exam requirements/recommendations for international students: Required—TOEFL (minimum score 570 paper-based; 70 iBT), IELTS (minimum score 7). *Application deadline:* For fall admission, 12/1 for domestic and international students. Application fee: $90 ($110 for international students). Electronic applications accepted. *Expenses:* Contact institution. *Financial support:* Fellowships with tuition reimbursements, research assistantships with tuition reimbursements, teaching assistantships with tuition reimbursements, scholarships/grants, health care benefits, tuition waivers (full), unspecified assistantships, and transit passes, travel grants available. Financial award application deadline: 12/10. *Faculty research:* Accounting, business and public policy, entrepreneurship, finance, management of organizations, marketing, operations and information technology management, real estate. *Unit head:* Dr. Nicolae Garleanu, Director, 510-643-6349, Fax: 510-643-4255. *Application contact:* Melissa Hacker, Director, Student Affairs, 510-642-3944, Fax: 510-643-4255, E-mail: melhacker@haas.berkeley.edu.
Website: http://www.haas.berkeley.edu/Phd/

University of California, Berkeley, UC Berkeley Extension, Certificate Programs in Business, Berkeley, CA 94720-1500. Offers accounting (Certificate); business administration (Certificate); finance (Certificate); human resource management (Certificate); management (Certificate); marketing (Certificate); project management (Certificate). *Accreditation:* AACSB. *Program availability:* Online learning.

University of California, Davis, Graduate School of Management, Master of Professional Accountancy Program, Davis, CA 95616. Offers MP Ac. *Faculty:* 4 full-time (3 women), 3 part-time/adjunct (1 woman). *Students:* 56 full-time (35 women); includes 8 minority (1 Black or African American, non-Hispanic/Latino; 3 Asian, non-Hispanic/Latino; 2 Hispanic/Latino; 2 Two or more races, non-Hispanic/Latino), 19 international. Average age 25. 512 applicants, 17% accepted, 56 enrolled. In 2016, 46 master's awarded. *Degree requirements:* For master's, comprehensive exam. *Entrance requirements:* For master's, GMAT or GRE, letters of recommendation, resume, essays, equivalent of a 4-year U.S. undergraduate degree. Additional exam requirements/recommendations for international students: Required—TOEFL (minimum score 600 paper-based; 100 iBT), IELTS (minimum score 7). *Application deadline:* For fall admission, 11/2 priority date for domestic and international students. Applications are processed on a rolling basis. Application fee: $125. Electronic applications accepted. *Expenses:* Contact institution. *Financial support:* In 2016–17, 28 students received support. Fellowships, teaching assistantships, scholarships/grants, and health care benefits available. Financial award application deadline: 3/2; financial award applicants required to submit FAFSA. *Faculty research:* Accounting, finance, organizational behavior, business ethics, taxation. *Unit head:* James Stevens, Senior Assistant Dean of Student Affairs, 530-752-7658, Fax: 530-754-9355, E-mail: admissions@gsm.ucdavis.edu. *Application contact:* Kathy Gleed, Senior Director of Admission, 530-752-7658, Fax: 530-754-9355, E-mail: admissions@gsm.ucdavis.edu.
Website: http://gsm.ucdavis.edu/master-professional-accountancy

University of California, Irvine, The Paul Merage School of Business, Program in Professional Accountancy, Irvine, CA 92697. Offers MPA. *Students:* 108 full-time (80 women), 1 (woman) part-time; includes 11 minority (1 Black or African American, non-Hispanic/Latino; 9 Asian, non-Hispanic/Latino; 1 Native Hawaiian or other Pacific Islander, non-Hispanic/Latino), 69 international. Average age 25. 674 applicants, 29% accepted, 108 enrolled. In 2016, 94 master's awarded. Application fee: $105 ($125 for international students). *Unit head:* Morton Pincus, Director, 949-824-4062, E-mail: mpincus@uci.edu. *Application contact:* Burt Slusher, Senior Associate Director, Recruitment and Admissions, 949-824-1609, E-mail: bslusher@uci.edu.
Website: http://merage.uci.edu/MPAc/

University of California, Los Angeles, Graduate Division, UCLA Anderson School of Management, Los Angeles, CA 90095-1481. Offers accounting (PhD); behavioral decision making (PhD); business administration (EMBA, MBA); decisions, operations, and technology management (PhD); finance (PhD); financial engineering (MFE); global economics and management (PhD); management and organizations (PhD); marketing (PhD); strategy and policy (PhD); DDS/MBA; MBA/JD; MBA/MD; MBA/MLAS; MBA/MLIS; MBA/MN; MBA/MPH; MBA/MPP; MBA/MSCS; MBA/MURP. *Accreditation:* AACSB. *Program availability:* Part-time, evening/weekend. *Faculty:* 90 full-time (20 women), 98 part-time/adjunct (19 women). *Students:* 865 full-time (263 women), 1,201 part-time (337 women); includes 710 minority (48 Black or African American, non-Hispanic/Latino; 1 American Indian or Alaska Native, non-Hispanic/Latino; 505 Asian, non-Hispanic/Latino; 88 Hispanic/Latino; 4 Native Hawaiian or other Pacific Islander, non-Hispanic/Latino; 64 Two or more races, non-Hispanic/Latino), 451 international. Average age 31. 5,643 applicants, 26% accepted, 881 enrolled. In 2016, 807 master's, 7 doctorates awarded. *Degree requirements:* For master's, comprehensive exam, field consulting project; internship (for MBA); thesis/dissertation (for MFE); for doctorate, comprehensive exam, thesis/dissertation, oral and written qualifying exams. *Entrance requirements:* For master's, GMAT or GRE, 4-year bachelor's degree or equivalent; 2 letters of recommendation; essays (1 for MBA, 2 for FEMBA and MFE); 4-8 years of full-time work experience (for FEMBA); minimum eight years of work experience with at least three years at management level (for EMBA); for doctorate, GMAT or GRE, bachelor's degree from college or university of fully-recognized standing, minimum B average during junior and senior years of undergraduate years, 3 letters of recommendation, statement of purpose. Additional exam requirements/recommendations for international students: Required—TOEFL (minimum score 560 paper-based; 87 iBT), IELTS (minimum score 7). *Application deadline:* For fall admission, 10/6 priority date for domestic and international students; for winter admission, 1/5 for domestic and international students; for spring admission, 4/12 for domestic and international students. Applications are processed on a rolling basis. Application fee: $200. Electronic applications accepted. *Expenses:* Contact institution. *Financial support:* In 2016–17, 633 students received support, including 455 fellowships (averaging $30,253 per year); research assistantships with partial tuition reimbursements available, teaching assistantships with partial tuition reimbursements available, career-related internships or fieldwork, institutionally sponsored loans, and scholarships/grants also available. Support available to part-time students. *Faculty research:* Finance/global economics, entrepreneurship, accounting, human resources/organizational behavior, marketing, behavioral decision making. *Total annual research expenditures:* $1.1 million. *Unit head:* Dr. Judy D. Olian, Dean/Chair in Management, 310-825-7982, Fax: 310-206-2073, E-mail: judy.olian@anderson.ucla.edu. *Application contact:* Alex Lawrence, Assistant Dean and Director of MBA Admissions, 310-825-6944, Fax: 310-825-8582, E-mail: mba.admissions@anderson.ucla.edu.
Website: http://www.anderson.ucla.edu/

University of Central Arkansas, Graduate School, College of Business Administration, Program in Accounting, Conway, AR 72035-0001. Offers M Acc. *Program availability:* Part-time. *Degree requirements:* For master's, capstone course. *Entrance requirements:* For master's, GMAT or GRE, minimum GPA of 2.7. Additional exam requirements/recommendations for international students: Required—TOEFL (minimum score 550 paper-based; 80 iBT).

University of Central Florida, College of Business Administration, Kenneth G. Dixon School of Accounting, Orlando, FL 32816. Offers MSA. *Accreditation:* AACSB. *Program availability:* Part-time, evening/weekend. *Faculty:* 24 full-time (11 women), 3 part-time/adjunct (2 women). *Students:* 79 full-time (34 women), 83 part-time (42 women); includes 44 minority (17 Asian, non-Hispanic/Latino; 20 Hispanic/Latino; 7 Two or more races, non-Hispanic/Latino), 5 international. Average age 27. 109 applicants, 55% accepted, 47 enrolled. In 2016, 68 master's awarded. *Degree requirements:* For master's, comprehensive exam. *Entrance requirements:* For master's, GMAT, minimum GPA of 3.0 in last 60 hours. Additional exam requirements/recommendations for international students: Required—TOEFL. *Application deadline:* For fall admission, 7/15 for domestic students; for spring admission, 12/1 for domestic students. Application fee: $30. Electronic applications accepted. *Expenses:* Tuition, state resident: part-time $288.16 per credit hour. Tuition, nonresident: part-time $1071.31 per credit hour. *Financial support:* In 2016–17, 23 students received support, including 1 research assistantship with partial tuition reimbursement available (averaging $9,416 per year), 22 teaching assistantships with partial tuition reimbursements available (averaging $9,542 per year); fellowships, career-related internships or fieldwork, Federal Work-Study, institutionally sponsored loans, tuition waivers (partial), and unspecified assistantships also available. Financial award application deadline: 3/1; financial award applicants required to submit FAFSA. *Unit head:* Dr. Sean Robb, Director, 407-823-2876, Fax: 407-823-3881, E-mail: srobb@ucf.edu. *Application contact:* Assistant Director, Graduate Admissions, 407-823-2776, Fax: 407-823-6442, E-mail: gradadmissions@ucf.edu.
Website: https://business.ucf.edu/departments-schools/kenneth-g-dixon-school-of-accounting/

University of Central Missouri, The Graduate School, Warrensburg, MO 64093. Offers accountancy (MA); accounting (MBA); applied mathematics (MS); aviation safety (MA); biology (MS); business administration (MBA); career and technical education leadership (MS); college student personnel administration (MS); communication (MA); computer science (MS); counseling (MS); criminal justice (MS); educational leadership (Ed D); educational technology (MS); elementary and early childhood education (MSE); English (MA); environmental studies (MA); finance (MBA); history (MA); human services/educational technology (Ed S); human services/learning resources (Ed S); human services/professional counseling (Ed S); industrial hygiene (MS); industrial management (MS); information systems (MBA); information technology (MS); kinesiology (MS); library science and information services (MS); literacy education (MSE); marketing (MBA); mathematics (MS); music (MA); occupational safety management (MS); psychology (MS); rural family nursing (MS); school administration (MSE); social gerontology (MS); sociology (MA); special education (MSE); speech language pathology (MS); superintendency (Ed S); teaching (MAT); teaching English as a second language (MA); technology (MS); technology management (PhD); theatre (MA). *Program availability:* Part-time, 100% online, blended/hybrid learning. *Degree requirements:* For master's and Ed S, comprehensive exam (for some programs), thesis (for some programs). *Entrance requirements:* Additional exam requirements/recommendations for international students: Required—TOEFL (minimum score 550 paper-based; 79 iBT). Electronic applications accepted.

University of Central Oklahoma, The Jackson College of Graduate Studies, College of Business, Edmond, OK 73034-5209. Offers accounting (MBA); management (MBA). *Program availability:* Part-time. *Degree requirements:* For master's, comprehensive exam (for some programs), thesis optional. *Entrance requirements:* For master's, GMAT, GRE. Additional exam requirements/recommendations for international students: Required—TOEFL (minimum score 550 paper-based; 79 iBT), IELTS (minimum score 6.5). Electronic applications accepted. *Expenses:* Contact institution.

University of Charleston, Master of Forensic Accounting Program, Charleston, WV 25304-1099. Offers EMFA. *Program availability:* Part-time, blended/hybrid learning. *Students:* 23 full-time (16 women); includes 4 minority (2 Black or African American, non-Hispanic/Latino; 1 Hispanic/Latino; 1 Native Hawaiian or other Pacific Islander, non-Hispanic/Latino), 1 international. Average age 36. *Entrance requirements:* Additional exam requirements/recommendations for international students: Required—TOEFL. *Application deadline:* Applications are processed on a rolling basis. Application fee: $50. Electronic applications accepted. *Expenses: Tuition:* Full-time $20,602; part-time $425 per credit. *Required fees:* $200. Tuition and fees vary according to course load, campus/location, program and student level. *Financial support:* Applicants required to submit FAFSA. *Unit head:* Christina Chard, Program Director, 304-352-0033, E-mail: christinachard@ucwv.edu. *Application contact:* Bobby Redd, Admissions Representative, 304-860-5621, E-mail: bobbyredd@ucwv.edu.
Website: http://www.ucwv.edu/Forensic-Accounting/

University of Chicago, Booth School of Business, Full-Time MBA Program, Chicago, IL 60637. Offers accounting (MBA); analytic finance (MBA); analytic management (MBA); econometrics and statistics (MBA); economics (MBA); entrepreneurship (MBA); finance (MBA); general management (MBA); health administration and policy (Certificate); international business (MBA); managerial and organizational behavior (MBA); marketing analytics (MBA); marketing management (MBA); operations management (MBA); strategic management (MBA); MBA/AM; MBA/JD; MBA/MA; MBA/MD; MBA/MPP. *Accreditation:* AACSB. *Students:* 1,151 full-time (443 women), 17 part-time (9 women). Terminal master's awarded for partial completion of doctoral program. *Entrance requirements:* For master's, GMAT or GRE, transcripts, resume, 2 letters of recommendation, essay, interview. Additional exam requirements/recommendations for international students: Required—TOEFL (minimum score 600 paper-based; 104 iBT), IELTS (minimum score 7), PTE (minimum score 70). *Application deadline:* For spring admission, 4/1 for domestic and international students. Electronic applications accepted. *Expenses:* Contact institution. *Unit head:* Stacey Kole, Deputy Dean, 773-702-7121. *Application contact:* Full-time MBA Program Admissions, 773-702-7369, Fax: 773-702-9085, E-mail: admissions@chicagobooth.edu.
Website: https://www.chicagobooth.edu/programs/full-time

University of Cincinnati, Graduate School, Carl H. Lindner College of Business, MS Program, Cincinnati, OH 45221. Offers accounting (MS); business analytics (MS); finance (MS); information systems (MS); marketing (MS); taxation (MS). *Program availability:* Part-time, evening/weekend. *Faculty:* 74 full-time (17 women), 33 part-time/adjunct (8 women). *Students:* 307 full-time (128 women), 246 part-time (106 women); includes 60 minority (22 Black or African American, non-Hispanic/Latino; 20 Asian, non-Hispanic/Latino; 9 Hispanic/Latino; 1 Native Hawaiian or other Pacific Islander, non-

Hispanic/Latino; 8 Two or more races, non-Hispanic/Latino), 321 international. Average age 28. 1,756 applicants, 24% accepted, 351 enrolled. In 2016, 334 master's awarded. *Degree requirements:* For master's, thesis (for some programs). *Entrance requirements:* For master's, GMAT, GRE, resume, transcripts, essays, letters of recommendation. Additional exam requirements/recommendations for international students: Required—TOEFL (minimum score 577 paper-based; 90 iBT), IELTS (minimum score 6.5). *Application deadline:* For fall admission, 8/1 priority date for domestic students, 3/15 for international students; for spring admission, 12/15 for domestic students, 9/15 for international students; for summer admission, 4/15 for domestic and international students. Applications are processed on a rolling basis. Application fee: $65 ($70 for international students). Electronic applications accepted. *Expenses:* Contact institution. *Financial support:* In 2016–17, 251 students received support, including 12 teaching assistantships with tuition reimbursements available (averaging $3,500 per year); scholarships/grants, tuition waivers (full and partial), and unspecified assistantships also available. Financial award application deadline: 2/1; financial award applicants required to submit FAFSA. *Faculty research:* Real estate, empirical pricing, organization information pricing, strategic management, portfolio choice in institutional investment. *Unit head:* Dr. David Szymanski, Dean, 513-556-7001, Fax: 513-556-4891, E-mail: david.szymanski@uc.edu. *Application contact:* Dona Clary, Director, Graduate Programs, 513-556-3546, Fax: 513-558-7006, E-mail: dona.clary@uc.edu.

University of Cincinnati, Graduate School, Carl H. Lindner College of Business, PhD Programs, Cincinnati, OH 45211. Offers accounting (PhD); economics (PhD); finance (PhD); information systems (PhD); management (PhD); marketing (PhD); operations and business analytics (PhD). *Faculty:* 72 full-time (18 women). *Students:* 37 full-time (19 women); includes 4 minority (1 Black or African American, non-Hispanic/Latino; 3 Asian, non-Hispanic/Latino), 19 international. Average age 30. 92 applicants, 16% accepted, 7 enrolled. In 2016, 4 doctorates awarded. *Degree requirements:* For doctorate, comprehensive exam, thesis/dissertation. *Entrance requirements:* For doctorate, GMAT, GRE, transcripts, essays, resume, letters of recommendation. Additional exam requirements/recommendations for international students: Required—TOEFL (minimum score 600 paper-based; 100 iBT), IELTS (minimum score 7). *Application deadline:* For fall admission, 1/15 for domestic and international students. Application fee: $65 ($70 for international students). Electronic applications accepted. *Expenses:* Contact institution. *Financial support:* In 2016–17, 38 students received support, including 25 research assistantships with tuition reimbursements available (averaging $23,250 per year); scholarships/grants, tuition waivers (full and partial), and unspecified assistantships also available. Financial award application deadline: 1/15; financial award applicants required to submit FAFSA. *Faculty research:* Bayesian Prediction Theory, organizational fairness, consumer insight and market research, EGARCH idiosyncratic volatility and expected stock returns, consumer insight and market research, density estimation from correlated data. *Unit head:* Dr. Suzanne Masterson, Director, 513-556-7125, Fax: 513-556-5499, E-mail: suzanne.masterson@uc.edu. *Application contact:* Angel Elvin, Assistant Director, 513-556-7190, Fax: 513-558-7006, E-mail: angel.elvin@uc.edu.
Website: http://www.business.uc.edu/phd

University of Colorado Denver, Business School, Program in Accounting, Denver, CO 80217. Offers accounting and information systems audit control (MS); auditing and forensic accounting (MS); controllership and financial leadership (MS). *Accreditation:* AACSB. *Program availability:* Part-time, evening/weekend. *Students:* 90 full-time (42 women), 54 part-time (32 women); includes 36 minority (1 American Indian or Alaska Native, non-Hispanic/Latino; 21 Asian, non-Hispanic/Latino; 11 Hispanic/Latino; 3 Two or more races, non-Hispanic/Latino), 23 international. Average age 30. 93 applicants, 66% accepted, 38 enrolled. In 2016, 69 master's awarded. *Degree requirements:* For master's, 30 semester hours. *Entrance requirements:* For master's, GMAT (waived for students who already hold a graduate degree, or an undergraduate degree from CU Denver), essay, resume, two letters of recommendation; financial statements (for international students). Additional exam requirements/recommendations for international students: Required—TOEFL (minimum score 537 paper-based; 75 iBT); Recommended—IELTS (minimum score 6.5). *Application deadline:* For fall admission, 4/15 priority date for domestic students, 3/15 priority date for international students; for spring admission, 10/15 priority date for domestic students, 9/15 priority date for international students; for summer admission, 2/15 priority date for domestic students, 1/15 priority date for international students. Applications are processed on a rolling basis. Application fee: $50 ($75 for international students). Electronic applications accepted. *Expenses:* Contact institution. *Financial support:* In 2016–17, 28 students received support. Fellowships, research assistantships, teaching assistantships, Federal Work-Study, institutionally sponsored loans, scholarships/grants, and traineeships available. Financial award application deadline: 4/1; financial award applicants required to submit FAFSA. *Faculty research:* Transportation, energy, communications, healthcare, nano-science and engineering, unmanned aircraft systems, biomedical applications, aerosol mechanics, interface mechanics during rapid evaporation, low SWAP-C inertial navigation systems. *Unit head:* Clifford Young, Associate Dean, 303-315-8000, E-mail: clifford.young@ucdenver.edu. *Application contact:* Admissions Director, Graduate Programs, 303-315-8200, E-mail: bschool.admissions@ucdenver.edu.
Website: http://www.ucdenver.edu/academics/colleges/business/degrees/ms/accounting/Pages/Accounting.aspx

University of Colorado Denver, Business School, Program in Information Systems, Denver, CO 80217. Offers accounting and information systems audit and control (MS); business intelligence systems (MS); digital health entrepreneurship (MS); enterprise risk management (MS); enterprise technology management (MS); geographic information systems (MS); health information technology (MS); technology innovation and entrepreneurship (MS); Web and mobile computing (MS). *Program availability:* Part-time, evening/weekend, online learning. *Students:* 110 full-time (44 women), 33 part-time (11 women); includes 19 minority (1 Black or African American, non-Hispanic/Latino; 8 Asian, non-Hispanic/Latino; 6 Hispanic/Latino; 4 Two or more races, non-Hispanic/Latino), 79 international. Average age 29. 140 applicants, 71% accepted, 38 enrolled. In 2016, 50 master's awarded. *Degree requirements:* For master's, 30 credit hours. *Entrance requirements:* For master's, GMAT, resume, essay, two letters of recommendation, financial statements (for international applicants). Additional exam requirements/recommendations for international students: Required—TOEFL (minimum score 525 paper-based; 71 iBT); Recommended—IELTS (minimum score 6.5). *Application deadline:* For fall admission, 4/15 priority date for domestic students, 3/15 priority date for international students; for spring admission, 10/15 priority date for domestic students, 9/15 priority date for international students; for summer admission, 2/15 priority date for domestic students, 1/15 priority date for international students. Applications are processed on a rolling basis. Application fee: $50 ($75 for international students). Electronic applications accepted. *Expenses:* Contact institution. *Financial support:* In 2016–17, 24 students received support. Fellowships, research assistantships, teaching assistantships, Federal Work-Study, institutionally sponsored loans, scholarships/grants, and traineeships available. Financial award application deadline: 4/1; financial award applicants required to submit FAFSA. *Faculty research:* Human-computer interaction, expert systems, database management, electronic commerce, object-oriented software development. *Unit head:* Dr. Jahangir Karimi, Director of Information Systems Programs, 303-315-8430, E-mail: jahangir.karimi@ucdenver.edu. *Application contact:* 303-315-8200, E-mail: bschool.admissions@ucdenver.edu.
Website: http://www.ucdenver.edu/academics/colleges/business/degrees/ms/IS/Pages/Information-Systems.aspx

University of Connecticut, Graduate School, School of Business, Field of Accounting, Storrs, CT 06269. Offers MS. *Accreditation:* AACSB. *Entrance requirements:* Additional exam requirements/recommendations for international students: Required—TOEFL (minimum score 550 paper-based). Electronic applications accepted.

University of Dallas, Satish and Yasmin Gupta College of Business, Irving, TX 75062-4736. Offers accounting (MBA, MS); business administration (DBA); business analytics (MS); business management (MBA); corporate finance (MBA); cybersecurity (MS); finance (MS); financial services (MBA); global business (MBA, MS); health services management (MBA); human resource management (MBA); information and technology management (MS); information assurance (MBA); information technology (MBA); information technology service management (MBA); marketing management (MBA); organization development (MBA); project management (MBA); sports and entertainment management (MBA); strategic leadership (MBA); supply chain management (MBA). *Accreditation:* AACSB. *Program availability:* Part-time, evening/weekend, online learning. *Entrance requirements:* Additional exam requirements/recommendations for international students: Required—TOEFL. Electronic applications accepted. *Expenses:* Contact institution.

University of Dayton, School of Business Administration, Dayton, OH 45469. Offers accounting (MBA); cyber security (MBA); finance (MBA); marketing (MBA); JD/MBA. *Accreditation:* AACSB. *Program availability:* Part-time, evening/weekend, blended/hybrid learning. *Faculty:* 23 full-time (5 women), 18 part-time/adjunct (9 women). *Students:* 94 full-time (35 women), 85 part-time (38 women); includes 14 minority (5 Black or African American, non-Hispanic/Latino; 4 Asian, non-Hispanic/Latino; 5 Hispanic/Latino), 26 international. Average age 30. 269 applicants, 31% accepted. In 2016, 93 master's awarded. *Entrance requirements:* For master's, GMAT (minimum score of 500 total, 19 verbal); GRE (minimum score of 149 verbal, 146 quantitative), minimum GPA of 3.0, current resume. Additional exam requirements/recommendations for international students: Required—TOEFL (minimum score 550 paper-based; 80 iBT); Recommended—IELTS (minimum score 6.5). *Application deadline:* Applications are processed on a rolling basis. Application fee: $0 ($50 for international students). Electronic applications accepted. *Expenses:* $970 per credit hour, $25 registration fee per term. *Financial support:* In 2016–17, 7 research assistantships with partial tuition reimbursements (averaging $8,535 per year), 2 teaching assistantships with partial tuition reimbursements (averaging $8,535 per year) were awarded; institutionally sponsored loans, health care benefits, and unspecified assistantships also available. Financial award application deadline: 3/1; financial award applicants required to submit FAFSA. *Faculty research:* Asset pricing, applied microeconomics, financial reporting and auditing, entrepreneurship. *Unit head:* Scott MacDonald, Director, MBA Program, 937-229-3733, Fax: 937-229-3882, E-mail: smacdonald1@udayton.edu. *Application contact:* Mandy Bingaman, MBA Program Manager, 937-229-3733, Fax: 937-229-3882, E-mail: mbingaman1@udayton.edu.
Website: https://www.udayton.edu/business/academics/master_of_business_administration/index.php

University of Delaware, Alfred Lerner College of Business and Economics, Department of Accounting and Management Information Systems, Newark, DE 19716. Offers accounting (MS); information systems and technology management (MS). *Accreditation:* AACSB. *Program availability:* Part-time, evening/weekend. *Degree requirements:* For master's, thesis optional. *Entrance requirements:* For master's, GMAT. Additional exam requirements/recommendations for international students: Required—TOEFL (minimum score 550 paper-based). Electronic applications accepted. *Faculty research:* External reporting, managerial accounting, auditing information systems, taxation.

University of Denver, Daniels College of Business, School of Accountancy, Denver, CO 80208. Offers accounting (M Acc, MBA). *Accreditation:* AACSB. *Program availability:* Part-time, evening/weekend. *Faculty:* 19 full-time (8 women), 7 part-time/adjunct (1 woman). *Students:* 34 full-time (18 women), 49 part-time (31 women); includes 13 minority (5 Asian, non-Hispanic/Latino; 8 Hispanic/Latino), 41 international. Average age 26. 258 applicants, 61% accepted, 44 enrolled. In 2016, 123 master's awarded. *Entrance requirements:* For master's, GRE General Test or GMAT, bachelor's degree, transcripts, resume, two letters of recommendation, essays, interview. Additional exam requirements/recommendations for international students: Required—TOEFL (minimum score 570 paper-based; 88 iBT). *Application deadline:* For fall admission, 11/15 priority date for domestic and international students; for spring admission, 10/1 priority date for domestic and international students. Applications are processed on a rolling basis. Application fee: $100. Electronic applications accepted. *Expenses:* $43,458 per year full-time. *Financial support:* In 2016–17, 70 students received support, including 3 teaching assistantships with tuition reimbursements available (averaging $1,242 per year); career-related internships or fieldwork, Federal Work-Study, institutionally sponsored loans, scholarships/grants, and unspecified assistantships also available. Support available to part-time students. Financial award application deadline: 2/15; financial award applicants required to submit FAFSA. *Faculty research:* Financial accounting and reporting, financial analysis, corporate governance and responsibility, public policy, repatriation of foreign earning by mining companies. *Unit head:* Dr. Sharon Lassar, Professor/Director, School of Accountancy, 303-871-2032, Fax: 303-871-2016, E-mail: slassar@du.edu.
Website: https://daniels.du.edu/accountancy

University of Detroit Mercy, College of Business Administration, Detroit, MI 48221. Offers business administration (MBA); business fundamentals (Certificate); business turnaround management (Certificate); ethical leadership and change management (Certificate); finance (Certificate); forensic accounting (Certificate); JD/MBA; MBA/MHSA. *Program availability:* Part-time, evening/weekend, 100% online, blended/hybrid learning. *Entrance requirements:* For master's, GMAT, resume, letter of recommendation, transcripts; for Certificate, resume, letter of recommendation, transcripts. Electronic applications accepted. Application fee is waived when completed online. *Expenses:* Contact institution. *Faculty research:* Ethics, international finance, trade policy, leadership, information technology.

The University of Findlay, Office of Graduate Admissions, Findlay, OH 45840-3653. Offers applied security and analytics (MSAS); athletic training (MAT); business (MBA), including certified management accountant, certified public accountant, health care management, hospitality management; education (MA Ed, Ed D), including children's literature (MA Ed), curriculum and teaching (MA Ed), education (MA Ed), educational administration (MA Ed), human resource development (MA Ed), reading (MA Ed), science education (MA Ed), superintendent (Ed D), teaching (Ed D), technology (MA Ed); environmental, safety and health management (MSEM); health informatics (MS); occupational therapy (MOT); pharmacy (Pharm D); physical therapy (DPT); physician assistant (MPA); rhetoric and writing (MA); teaching English to speakers of other languages (TESOL) and bilingual education (MA). *Program availability:* Part-time, evening/weekend, 100% online, blended/hybrid learning. *Faculty:* 114 full-time (63 women), 44 part-time/adjunct (18 women). *Students:* 751 full-time (452 women), 573 part-time (323 women); includes 164 minority (82 Black or African American, non-

Hispanic/Latino; 1 American Indian or Alaska Native, non-Hispanic/Latino; 27 Asian, non-Hispanic/Latino; 37 Hispanic/Latino; 17 Two or more races, non-Hispanic/Latino), 280 international. Average age 28. 661 applicants, 52% accepted, 288 enrolled. In 2016, 366 master's, 137 doctorates awarded. *Degree requirements:* For master's, comprehensive exam (for some programs), thesis, cumulative project, capstone project; for doctorate, thesis/dissertation. *Entrance requirements:* For master's, GRE (for some programs), bachelor's degree from accredited institution, minimum undergraduate GPA of 3.0 in last 64 hours of course work; for doctorate, MAT, minimum cumulative GPA of 3.0, master's degree. Additional exam requirements/recommendations for international students: Recommended—TOEFL (minimum score 79 iBT), IELTS (minimum score 7). *Application deadline:* For fall admission, 6/15 for international students; for spring admission, 12/1 for international students; for summer admission, 4/1 for international students. Applications are processed on a rolling basis. Electronic applications accepted. *Expenses:* Contact institution. *Financial support:* In 2016–17, 139 students received support, including 15 research assistantships with partial tuition reimbursements available (averaging $7,200 per year), 25 teaching assistantships with partial tuition reimbursements available (averaging $7,200 per year); Federal Work-Study, institutionally sponsored loans, and unspecified assistantships also available. Financial award application deadline: 4/1; financial award applicants required to submit FAFSA. *Unit head:* Christopher M. Harris, Director of Admissions, 419-434-4347, E-mail: harrisc1@findlay.edu. *Application contact:* Madeline Fauser Brennan, Graduate Admissions Counselor, 419-434-4636, Fax: 419-434-4898, E-mail: fauserbrennan@findlay.edu.
Website: http://www.findlay.edu/admissions/graduate/Pages/default.aspx

University of Florida, Graduate School, Warrington College of Business Administration, Fisher School of Accounting, Gainesville, FL 32611. Offers M Acc, PhD, JD/M Acc. *Accreditation:* AACSB. *Program availability:* Part-time. *Degree requirements:* For master's, comprehensive exam, thesis optional; for doctorate, comprehensive exam, thesis/dissertation. *Entrance requirements:* For master's, GMAT (minimum score of 465) or GRE General Test, minimum GPA of 3.0. Additional exam requirements/recommendations for international students: Required—TOEFL (minimum score 550 paper-based; 80 iBT), IELTS (minimum score 6). Electronic applications accepted. *Faculty research:* Financial reporting, managerial accounting, auditing, taxation.

University of Georgia, Terry College of Business, J.M. Tull School of Accounting, Athens, GA 30602. Offers M Acc. *Accreditation:* AACSB. *Entrance requirements:* For master's, GMAT. *Application deadline:* For fall admission, 7/1 priority date for domestic students; for spring admission, 11/15 for domestic students. Application fee: $50. Electronic applications accepted. *Financial support:* Fellowships, research assistantships, teaching assistantships, and unspecified assistantships available. *Application contact:* Jennifer Chapman, Graduate Coordinator, 706-542-3601, E-mail: jennchap@uga.edu.
Website: http://www.terry.uga.edu/accounting/

University of Hartford, Barney School of Business, Department of Accounting and Taxation, West Hartford, CT 06117-1599. Offers professional accounting (Certificate); taxation (MSAT). *Program availability:* Part-time, evening/weekend. *Entrance requirements:* For master's, GMAT, 2 letters of recommendation, resume. Additional exam requirements/recommendations for international students: Required—TOEFL (minimum score 550 paper-based). Electronic applications accepted.

University of Hawaii at Manoa, Graduate Division, Shidler College of Business, Program in Accounting, Honolulu, HI 96822. Offers accounting (M Acc); accounting law (M Acc); information systems (M Acc); taxation (M Acc). *Program availability:* Part-time. *Entrance requirements:* For master's, GMAT, bachelor's degree in accounting, minimum GPA of 3.0. Additional exam requirements/recommendations for international students: Required—TOEFL (minimum score 550 paper-based; 79 iBT), IELTS (minimum score 5). *Faculty research:* International accounting, current tax topics, insurance industry financial reporting, behavioral accounting, auditing.

University of Hawaii at Manoa, Graduate Division, Shidler College of Business, Program in International Management, Honolulu, HI 96822. Offers Asian finance (PhD); global information technology management (PhD); international accounting (PhD); international marketing (PhD); international organization and strategy (PhD). *Program availability:* Part-time. *Degree requirements:* For doctorate, comprehensive exam, thesis/dissertation. *Entrance requirements:* For doctorate, GMAT or GRE General Test, minimum GPA of 3.0. Additional exam requirements/recommendations for international students: Required—TOEFL (minimum score 600 paper-based; 100 iBT), IELTS (minimum score 7). *Expenses:* Contact institution.

University of Houston, Bauer College of Business, Accountancy and Taxation Program, Houston, TX 77204. Offers accountancy (MS Accy); accountancy and taxation (PhD). *Accreditation:* AACSB. *Program availability:* Part-time, evening/weekend. *Degree requirements:* For master's, 30 hours completed in residence, minimum cumulative GPA of 3.0 at UH, no more than 11 semester hours of 'C' grades or below in graduate courses taken at UH; for doctorate, continuous full time enrollment, dissertation defense within 6 years of entering the program. *Entrance requirements:* For master's, GMAT, official transcripts from all higher education institutions attended, letters of recommendation, resume, goals statement; for doctorate, GMAT or GRE, letter of financial backing, statement of understanding, reference letters, statement of academic and research interests. Additional exam requirements/recommendations for international students: Required—TOEFL (minimum score 550 paper-based; 79 iBT), IELTS (minimum score 6.5), PTE (minimum score 70). Electronic applications accepted. *Faculty research:* Accountancy and taxation, finance, international business, management.

University of Houston–Clear Lake, School of Business, Program in Accounting, Houston, TX 77058-1002. Offers accounting (MS); professional accounting (MS). *Accreditation:* AACSB. *Program availability:* Part-time, evening/weekend. *Degree requirements:* For master's, thesis optional. *Entrance requirements:* For master's, GMAT. Additional exam requirements/recommendations for international students: Required—TOEFL (minimum score 550 paper-based). Electronic applications accepted.

University of Houston–Victoria, School of Business Administration, Victoria, TX 77901-4450. Offers accounting (MBA); economic development and entrepreneurship (MS); finance (GMBA, MBA); general business (MBA); international business (MBA); management (GMBA, MBA); marketing (MBA). *Accreditation:* AACSB. *Program availability:* Part-time, evening/weekend, online learning. *Entrance requirements:* For master's, GMAT. Additional exam requirements/recommendations for international students: Required—TOEFL (minimum score 550 paper-based). Electronic applications accepted. *Faculty research:* Economic development, marketing, finance.

University of Idaho, College of Graduate Studies, College of Business and Economics, Department of Accounting, Moscow, ID 83844. Offers accountancy (M Acct). *Accreditation:* AACSB. *Faculty:* 5 full-time, 1 part-time/adjunct. *Students:* 24 full-time (13 women), 5 part-time (all women). Average age 29. In 2016, 25 master's awarded. *Entrance requirements:* For master's, GMAT (minimum score 450), minimum GPA of 3.0. *Application deadline:* For fall admission, 8/1 for domestic students; for spring admission, 12/15 for domestic students. Applications are processed on a rolling basis. Application fee: $60. Electronic applications accepted. *Expenses:* Tuition, state resident: full-time $6460; part-time $414 per credit hour. Tuition, nonresident: full-time $21,268; part-time $1237 per credit hour. *Required fees:* $2070; $60 per credit hour. Full-time tuition and fees vary according to course load and reciprocity agreements. *Financial support:* Research assistantships and teaching assistantships available. Financial award applicants required to submit FAFSA. *Unit head:* Dr. Marla Kraut, Head, 208-885-6453, Fax: 208-885-6296, E-mail: amberg@uidaho.edu. *Application contact:* Sean Scoggin, Graduate Recruitment Coordinator, 208-885-4001, Fax: 208-885-4406, E-mail: graduateadmissions@uidaho.edu.
Website: http://www.uidaho.edu/cbe

University of Illinois at Chicago, Liautaud Graduate School of Business, Department of Accounting, Chicago, IL 60607-7128. Offers MS, MBA/MS. *Accreditation:* AACSB. *Program availability:* Part-time. *Entrance requirements:* For master's, GMAT, minimum GPA of 2.75. Additional exam requirements/recommendations for international students: Required—TOEFL. Electronic applications accepted. *Expenses:* Contact institution. *Faculty research:* Governmental accounting, managerial accounting, auditing.

University of Illinois at Springfield, Graduate Programs, College of Business and Management, Program in Accountancy, Springfield, IL 62703-5407. Offers MA. *Program availability:* Part-time, evening/weekend. *Faculty:* 6 full-time (1 woman), 1 part-time/adjunct (0 women). *Students:* 53 full-time (34 women), 42 part-time (26 women); includes 10 minority (8 Black or African American, non-Hispanic/Latino; 2 Asian, non-Hispanic/Latino), 33 international. Average age 27. 57 applicants, 58% accepted, 19 enrolled. In 2016, 30 master's awarded. *Degree requirements:* For master's, closure exercise including capstone courses, theses or projects. *Entrance requirements:* For master's, minimum undergraduate GPA of 2.7 in prerequisite coursework; introductory course in financial and managerial accounting, college math through business calculus, principles of economics (micro and macro), and statistics. Additional exam requirements/recommendations for international students: Required—TOEFL (minimum score 550 paper-based). *Application deadline:* Applications are processed on a rolling basis. Application fee: $60 ($75 for international students). Electronic applications accepted. *Expenses:* Tuition, state resident: part-time $329 per credit hour. Tuition, nonresident: part-time $675 per credit hour. *Financial support:* In 2016–17, fellowships with full tuition reimbursements (averaging $9,900 per year), research assistantships with full tuition reimbursements (averaging $9,991 per year), teaching assistantships with full tuition reimbursements (averaging $10,059 per year) were awarded; career-related internships or fieldwork, Federal Work-Study, scholarships/grants, health care benefits, and unspecified assistantships also available. Support available to part-time students. Financial award application deadline: 11/15; financial award applicants required to submit FAFSA. *Unit head:* Dr. Leonard Branson, Program Administrator, 217-206-6299, Fax: 217-206-7541, E-mail: lbran1@uis.edu. *Application contact:* Dr. Cecelia Cornell, Associate Vice Chancellor for Graduate Education, 217-206-7230, E-mail: ccorn1@uis.edu.
Website: http://www.uis.edu/accountancy

University of Illinois at Urbana–Champaign, Graduate College, College of Business, Department of Accountancy, Champaign, IL 61820. Offers accountancy (MAS, MS, PhD); taxation (MS). *Accreditation:* AACSB.

The University of Iowa, Henry B. Tippie College of Business, M Ac Program in Accounting, Iowa City, IA 52242-1316. Offers M Ac, PhD, JD/M Ac. *Faculty:* 18 full-time (5 women), 7 part-time/adjunct (1 woman). *Students:* 39 full-time (21 women). Average age 25. 121 applicants, 20% accepted, 17 enrolled. In 2016, 27 master's, 1 doctorate awarded. *Degree requirements:* For doctorate, comprehensive exam, thesis/dissertation. *Entrance requirements:* Additional exam requirements/recommendations for international students: Required—TOEFL (minimum score 100 iBT). *Application deadline:* For fall admission, 7/15 for domestic students, 4/15 priority date for international students; for spring admission, 12/1 for domestic students, 10/1 priority date for international students; for summer admission, 4/1 for domestic students, 3/1 priority date for international students. Application fee: $60 ($100 for international students). Electronic applications accepted. *Expenses:* Contact institution. *Financial support:* In 2016–17, 39 students received support, including 25 fellowships (averaging $4,400 per year), 14 teaching assistantships with partial tuition reimbursements available (averaging $18,809 per year); scholarships/grants and health care benefits also available. Financial award application deadline: 3/1; financial award applicants required to submit FAFSA. *Unit head:* Prof. Daniel W. Collins, Dean, 319-335-0910, Fax: 319-335-1956, E-mail: daniel-collins@uiowa.edu. *Application contact:* Renea L. Jay, Associate Director, Non-MBA Graduate Programs, 319-335-0930, Fax: 319-335-0860, E-mail: renea-jay@uiowa.edu.
Website: https://tippie.uiowa.edu/accounting

The University of Iowa, Henry B. Tippie College of Business, PhD Program in Accounting, Iowa City, IA 52242-1316. Offers PhD. *Accreditation:* AACSB. *Faculty:* 18 full-time (5 women), 7 part-time/adjunct (1 woman). *Students:* 12 full-time (5 women); includes 3 minority (2 Asian, non-Hispanic/Latino; 1 Hispanic/Latino), 6 international. Average age 32. 47 applicants, 11% accepted, 3 enrolled. In 2016, 3 doctorates awarded. *Degree requirements:* For doctorate, comprehensive exam, thesis/dissertation. *Entrance requirements:* For doctorate, GMAT. Additional exam requirements/recommendations for international students: Required—TOEFL (minimum score 100 iBT). *Application deadline:* For fall admission, 1/15 priority date for domestic students, 1/15 for international students. Application fee: $60 ($100 for international students). Electronic applications accepted. *Financial support:* In 2016–17, 12 students received support, including 12 fellowships with full tuition reimbursements available (averaging $11,200 per year), 12 teaching assistantships with full tuition reimbursements available (averaging $18,809 per year); scholarships/grants, health care benefits, and unspecified assistantships also available. Financial award application deadline: 1/15. *Faculty research:* Corporate financial reporting issues; financial statement information and capital markets; cost structure: analysis, estimation, and management; experimental and prediction economics; income taxes and interaction of financial and tax reporting systems. *Unit head:* Prof. Daniel W. Collins, Department Executive Officer, 319-335-0910, Fax: 319-335-1956, E-mail: daniel-collins@uiowa.edu. *Application contact:* Renea L. Jay, Associate Director, Non-MBA Graduate Programs, 319-335-0830, Fax: 319-335-0860, E-mail: renea-jay@uiowa.edu.
Website: https://tippie.uiowa.edu/accounting/

The University of Kansas, Graduate Studies, School of Business, Master of Accounting Program, Lawrence, KS 66045. Offers M Acc. *Accreditation:* AACSB. *Program availability:* Part-time. *Students:* 144 full-time (65 women), 38 part-time (22 women); includes 23 minority (1 Black or African American, non-Hispanic/Latino; 1 American Indian or Alaska Native, non-Hispanic/Latino; 8 Asian, non-Hispanic/Latino; 11 Hispanic/Latino; 2 Two or more races, non-Hispanic/Latino), 18 international. Average age 26. 132 applicants, 76% accepted, 86 enrolled. In 2016, 129 master's awarded. *Entrance requirements:* For master's, GMAT, official transcript, two letters of recommendation, pledge to support Honor System of School of Business, current resume, three essays. Additional exam requirements/recommendations for international students: Required—TOEFL or IELTS. *Application deadline:* For fall admission, 9/15 for domestic students, 12/15 for international students; for spring admission, 8/1 for domestic and international students; for summer admission, 12/15 for domestic and international students. Application fee: $65 ($85 for international students). Electronic

applications accepted. *Financial support:* Fellowships, research assistantships, teaching assistantships, career-related internships or fieldwork, Federal Work-Study, institutionally sponsored loans, and scholarships/grants available. Financial award application deadline: 2/15; financial award applicants required to submit FAFSA. *Faculty research:* Earnings quality, financial reporting conservatism, internal control systems, auditing and corporate governance, financial reporting restatements. *Unit head:* Dr. John T. Sweeney, Director, 785-864-7507, E-mail: jtsweeney@ku.edu. *Application contact:* Karen Heintzen, Assistant Director, M Acc Program, 785-864-7558, E-mail: heintzen@ku.edu.
Website: https://business.ku.edu/degrees/accounting/macc/

The University of Kansas, Graduate Studies, School of Business, Program in Business, Lawrence, KS 66045. Offers accounting (PhD); business and organizational leadership (MS); decision sciences and supply chain management (PhD); finance (PhD); human resources management (PhD); marketing (PhD); organizational behavior (PhD); strategic management (PhD); supply chain management and logistics (MS). *Accreditation:* AACSB. *Program availability:* Part-time. *Students:* 76 full-time (11 women), 170 part-time (83 women); includes 41 minority (15 Black or African American, non-Hispanic/Latino; 3 American Indian or Alaska Native, non-Hispanic/Latino; 6 Asian, non-Hispanic/Latino; 5 Hispanic/Latino; 12 Two or more races, non-Hispanic/Latino), 25 international. Average age 32. 294 applicants, 69% accepted, 152 enrolled. In 2016, 36 master's, 9 doctorates awarded. *Entrance requirements:* For master's, GMAT, official transcript, three letters of recommendation, resume, statement of purpose; for doctorate, GMAT or GRE, official transcript, three letters of recommendation, resume, statement of purpose. Additional exam requirements/recommendations for international students: Required—TOEFL (minimum score 600 paper-based; 100 iBT). *Application deadline:* For fall admission, 1/10 for domestic and international students. Application fee: $65 ($85 for international students). Electronic applications accepted. *Financial support:* Fellowships, research assistantships, teaching assistantships, scholarships/grants, health care benefits, tuition waivers (full), and unspecified assistantships available. Financial award application deadline: 1/10. *Faculty research:* Strategic human resource management, business ethics, organizational theory/behavior, corporate strategy, international business, supply chain management, Bayesian networks, game theory, decision analysis and time/series analysis, pricing, consumer effects, advertising and emotion. *Unit head:* Charly Edmonds, Director, 785-864-3841, E-mail: bschoolphd@ku.edu. *Application contact:* Graduate Admission Contact, 785-864-7500, E-mail: bschoolphd@ku.edu. Website: http://www.business.ku.edu/

University of Kentucky, Graduate School, Gatton College of Business and Economics, Program in Accounting, Lexington, KY 40506-0032. Offers MSACC. *Accreditation:* AACSB. *Degree requirements:* For master's, comprehensive exam. *Entrance requirements:* For master's, GRE General Test, minimum undergraduate GPA of 2.75. Additional exam requirements/recommendations for international students: Required—TOEFL (minimum score 550 paper-based). Electronic applications accepted. *Faculty research:* Taxation, financial accounting and auditing, managerial accounting, not-for-profit accounting.

University of La Verne, College of Business and Public Management, Graduate Programs in Business Administration, La Verne, CA 91750-4443. Offers accounting (MBA, MBA-EP); finance (MBA, MBA-EP); health services management (MBA); information technology (MBA, MBA-EP); international business (MBA, MBA-EP); management and leadership (MBA, MBA-EP); marketing (MBA, MBA-EP); supply chain management (MBA, MBA-EP). *Program availability:* Part-time, evening/weekend. *Students:* 385 full-time (177 women), 89 part-time (46 women); includes 92 minority (4 Black or African American, non-Hispanic/Latino; 1 American Indian or Alaska Native, non-Hispanic/Latino; 14 Asian, non-Hispanic/Latino; 71 Hispanic/Latino; 1 Native Hawaiian or other Pacific Islander, non-Hispanic/Latino; 1 Two or more races, non-Hispanic/Latino), 319 international. Average age 28. *Entrance requirements:* For master's, GMAT, MAT, or GRE, minimum undergraduate GPA of 3.0, 2 letters of recommendation, resume, statement of purpose. Additional exam requirements/recommendations for international students: Required—TOEFL (minimum score 550 paper-based; 85 iBT). *Application deadline:* Applications are processed on a rolling basis. Application fee: $50. *Expenses: Tuition:* Part-time $795 per credit hour. Tuition and fees vary according to campus/location and program. *Financial support:* Institutionally sponsored loans and scholarships/grants available. Financial award application deadline: 3/2; financial award applicants required to submit FAFSA. *Unit head:* Dr. Abe Helou, Chairperson, 909-448-4455, Fax: 909-392-2704, E-mail: ihelou@laverne.edu. *Application contact:* Rina Lazarian-Chehab, Senior Associate Director of Graduate Admissions, 909-448-4317, Fax: 909-971-2295, E-mail: rlazarian@laverne.edu.
Website: https://laverne.edu/business-and-public-administration/mba-2/

University of La Verne, College of Business and Public Management, Program in Accounting, La Verne, CA 91750-4443. Offers MS. *Program availability:* Part-time. *Students:* 85 full-time (59 women), 6 part-time (3 women); includes 9 minority (3 Asian, non-Hispanic/Latino; 6 Hispanic/Latino), 76 international. Average age 27. *Entrance requirements:* For master's, GMAT, MAT, or GRE, minimum undergraduate GPA of 3.0, 2 letters of recommendation, resume, statement of purpose. Additional exam requirements/recommendations for international students: Required—TOEFL (minimum score 550 paper-based; 85 iBT). *Application deadline:* Applications are processed on a rolling basis. Application fee: $50. *Expenses:* Contact institution. *Financial support:* Institutionally sponsored loans and scholarships/grants available. Financial award application deadline: 3/2; financial award applicants required to submit FAFSA. *Unit head:* Renee Miller, Program Chair, 909-448-4766, E-mail: rmiller@laverne.edu. *Application contact:* Rina Lazarian-Chehab, Senior Associate Director of Graduate Admissions, 909-448-4317, Fax: 909-971-2295, E-mail: rlazarian@laverne.edu.
Website: https://laverne.edu/business-and-public-administration/master-of-science-in-accounting/

University of La Verne, Regional and Online Campuses, Graduate Programs, Inland Empire Campus, Ontario, CA 91730. Offers business administration (MBA, MBA-EP), including accounting (MBA), finance (MBA), health services management (MBA-EP), information technology (MBA-EP), international business (MBA), managed care (MBA), management and leadership (MBA-EP), marketing (MBA-EP), supply chain management (MBA); leadership and management (MS), including human resource management, nonprofit management, organizational development. *Program availability:* Part-time, evening/weekend. *Expenses:* Contact institution.

University of Lethbridge, School of Graduate Studies, Lethbridge, AB T1K 3M4, Canada. Offers addictions counseling (M Sc); agricultural biotechnology (M Sc); agricultural studies (M Sc, MA); anthropology (MA); archaeology (M Sc, MA); art (MA, MFA); biochemistry (M Sc); biological sciences (M Sc); biomolecular science (PhD); biosystems and biodiversity (PhD); Canadian studies (MA); chemistry (M Sc); computer science (M Sc); computer science and geographical information science (M Sc); counseling (MC); counseling psychology (M Ed); dramatic arts (MA); earth, space, and physical science (PhD); economics (MA); education (MA, PhD); educational leadership (M Ed); English (MA); environmental science (M Sc); evolution and behavior (PhD); exercise science (M Sc); French (MA); French/German (MA); French/Spanish (MA); general education (M Ed); geography (M Sc, MA); German (MA); health sciences (M Sc); individualized multidisciplinary (M Sc, MA); kinesiology (M Sc, MA); management (M Sc), including accounting, finance, human resource management and labor relations, information systems, international management, marketing, policy and strategy; mathematics (M Sc); music (M Mus, MA); Native American studies (MA); neuroscience (M Sc, PhD); new media (MA, MFA); nursing (M Sc, MN); philosophy (MA); physics (M Sc); political science (MA); psychology (M Sc, MA); religious studies (MA); sociology (MA); theatre and dramatic arts (MFA); theoretical and computational science (PhD); urban and regional studies (MA); women and gender studies (MA). *Program availability:* Part-time, evening/weekend. *Degree requirements:* For master's, thesis (for some programs); for doctorate, comprehensive exam, thesis/dissertation. *Entrance requirements:* For master's, GMAT (for M Sc in management), bachelor's degree in related field, minimum GPA of 3.0 during previous 20 graded semester courses, 2 years' teaching or related experience (M Ed); for doctorate, master's degree, minimum graduate GPA of 3.5. Additional exam requirements/recommendations for international students: Required—TOEFL (minimum score 580 paper-based; 93 iBT). Electronic applications accepted. *Faculty research:* Movement and brain plasticity, gibberellin physiology, photosynthesis, carbon cycling, molecular properties of main-group ring components.

University of Louisville, Graduate School, College of Business, School of Accountancy, Louisville, KY 40292-0001. Offers MAC, MBA/MAC. *Accreditation:* AACSB. *Program availability:* Part-time, evening/weekend. *Faculty:* 14 full-time (8 women), 2 part-time/adjunct (1 woman). *Students:* 20 full-time (14 women), 26 part-time (13 women); includes 9 minority (5 Black or African American, non-Hispanic/Latino; 2 Asian, non-Hispanic/Latino; 2 Hispanic/Latino), 4 international. Average age 31. 33 applicants, 73% accepted, 18 enrolled. *Entrance requirements:* For master's, GMAT, 2 letters of reference, resume, personal statement, personal interview, transcript. Additional exam requirements/recommendations for international students: Required—TOEFL (minimum score 83 iBT). *Application deadline:* For fall admission, 5/15 priority date for domestic students. Applications are processed on a rolling basis. Application fee: $60. *Expenses:* Tuition, state resident: full-time $12,246; part-time $681 per credit hour. Tuition, nonresident: full-time $25,486; part-time $1417 per credit hour. *Required fees:* $196. Tuition and fees vary according to program and reciprocity agreements. *Financial support:* In 2016–17, research assistantships with full tuition reimbursements (averaging $1,200 per year) were awarded; health care benefits and unspecified assistantships also available. Financial award application deadline: 3/15; financial award applicants required to submit FAFSA. *Faculty research:* Audit judgment and decision-making, information systems, taxation, cost and managerial accounting. *Total annual research expenditures:* $19,347. *Unit head:* Dr. Todd Mooradian, Dean, 502-852-6443, Fax: 502-852-7557, E-mail: todd.mooradian@louisville.edu. *Application contact:* Susan E. Hildebrand, Director of IT and Master's Programs Admissions/Recruiting Manager, 502-852-7257, Fax: 502-852-4901, E-mail: s.hildebrand@louisville.edu.
Website: http://business.louisville.edu/graduate-programs/

The University of Manchester, Alliance Manchester Business School, M15 6PB, United Kingdom. Offers accounting and finance (M Sc); business (M Ent); business analysis and strategic management (M Sc); business analytics: operational research and risk analysis (M Sc); business psychology (M Sc); corporate communications and reputation management (M Sc); finance (M Sc); finance and business economics (M Sc); human resource management and industrial relations (M Sc); innovation management and entrepreneurship (M Sc); international business and management (M Sc); international human resource management and comparative industrial relations (M Sc); management (M Sc); marketing (M Sc); operations, project and supply chain management (M Sc); organizational psychology (M Sc); quantitative finance (M Sc). *Entrance requirements:* For master's, UK 2:1 honours degree or overseas equivalent. Additional exam requirements/recommendations for international students: Required—TOEFL (minimum score 100 iBT), IELTS (minimum score 7), PTE. Electronic applications accepted. *Faculty research:* Accounting and finance, management sciences and marketing, people management and organization, innovation management and policy, decision sciences.

University of Mary Hardin-Baylor, Graduate Studies in Business Administration, Belton, TX 76513. Offers accounting (MBA); information systems management (MBA); international business (MBA); management (MBA). *Program availability:* Part-time, evening/weekend. *Faculty:* 11 full-time (5 women), 6 part-time/adjunct (2 women). *Students:* 21 full-time (12 women), 44 part-time (14 women); includes 23 minority (12 Black or African American, non-Hispanic/Latino; 1 Asian, non-Hispanic/Latino; 10 Hispanic/Latino), 11 international. Average age 29. 96 applicants, 70% accepted, 21 enrolled. In 2016, 22 master's awarded. *Degree requirements:* For master's, comprehensive exam. *Entrance requirements:* For master's, minimum GPA of 3.0, interview. Additional exam requirements/recommendations for international students: Required—TOEFL (minimum score 60 iBT), IELTS (minimum score 4.5). *Application deadline:* For fall admission, 6/1 for domestic students, 4/30 priority date for international students; for spring admission, 11/1 for domestic students, 9/30 priority date for international students. Applications are processed on a rolling basis. Application fee: $35 ($135 for international students). Electronic applications accepted. *Expenses: Tuition:* Full-time $14,940; part-time $830 per credit hour. *Required fees:* $1350; $75 per credit hour. $50 per term. Tuition and fees vary according to course load and degree level. *Financial support:* In 2016–17, 33 students received support. Federal Work-Study, unspecified assistantships, and scholarships for some active duty military personnel available. Financial award applicants required to submit FAFSA. *Faculty research:* Experiential learning, case studies in systems analysis and design, forecasting methodologies, short-selling in the stock market, open educational resources. *Total annual research expenditures:* $17,500. *Unit head:* Dr. Kirk Fischer, Assistant Professor/Director, Graduate Programs in McLane College of Business, 254-295-4655, E-mail: kfischer@umhb.edu. *Application contact:* Sharon Aguilera, Assistant Director, Graduate Admissions, 254-295-4835, Fax: 254-295-5038, E-mail: saguilera@umhb.edu.
Website: http://www.graduate.umhb.edu/mba

University of Maryland University College, The Graduate School, Program in Accounting and Financial Management, Adelphi, MD 20783. Offers MS. *Accreditation:* AACSB. *Program availability:* Part-time, evening/weekend, online learning. *Students:* 11 full-time (8 women), 399 part-time (260 women); includes 248 minority (166 Black or African American, non-Hispanic/Latino; 3 American Indian or Alaska Native, non-Hispanic/Latino; 39 Asian, non-Hispanic/Latino; 29 Hispanic/Latino; 2 Native Hawaiian or other Pacific Islander, non-Hispanic/Latino; 9 Two or more races, non-Hispanic/Latino), 17 international. Average age 33. 139 applicants, 100% accepted, 110 enrolled. In 2016, 100 master's awarded. *Degree requirements:* For master's, thesis or alternative, capstone course. *Application deadline:* Applications are processed on a rolling basis. Application fee: $50. Electronic applications accepted. *Expenses:* Tuition, state resident: part-time $458 per credit. Tuition, nonresident: part-time $659 per credit. *Financial support:* Federal Work-Study and scholarships/grants available. Support available to part-time students. Financial award application deadline: 6/1; financial award applicants required to submit FAFSA. *Application contact:* Coordinator, Graduate Admissions, 800-888-8682, Fax: 240-684-2151, E-mail: newgrad@umuc.edu.
Website: http://www.umuc.edu/academic-programs/masters-degrees/accounting-and-financial-management.cfm

University of Massachusetts Amherst, Graduate School, Isenberg School of Management, Department of Accounting, Amherst, MA 01003. Offers MSA. *Accreditation:* AACSB. *Program availability:* Part-time. *Entrance requirements:* For master's, GMAT. Additional exam requirements/recommendations for international students: Required—TOEFL (minimum score 550 paper-based; 80 iBT), IELTS (minimum score 6.5). Electronic applications accepted.

University of Massachusetts Amherst, Graduate School, Isenberg School of Management, Program in Management, Amherst, MA 01003. Offers accounting (PhD); business administration (MBA); entrepreneurship (MBA); finance (MBA, PhD); healthcare administration (MBA); hospitality and tourism management (PhD); management science (PhD); marketing (MBA, PhD); organization studies (PhD); sport management (PhD); strategic management (PhD); MBA/MS. *Accreditation:* AACSB. *Program availability:* Part-time, evening/weekend, online learning. Terminal master's awarded for partial completion of doctoral program. *Degree requirements:* For doctorate, comprehensive exam, thesis/dissertation. *Entrance requirements:* For master's and doctorate, GMAT or GRE General Test. Additional exam requirements/ recommendations for international students: Required—TOEFL (minimum score 550 paper-based; 80 iBT), IELTS (minimum score 6.5). Electronic applications accepted.

University of Massachusetts Boston, College of Management, Program in Accounting, Boston, MA 02125-3393. Offers MS. *Faculty:* 27 full-time (8 women), 11 part-time/adjunct (0 women). *Students:* 44 full-time (28 women), 54 part-time (20 women); includes 31 minority (5 Black or African American, non-Hispanic/Latino; 18 Asian, non-Hispanic/Latino; 6 Hispanic/Latino; 2 Two or more races, non-Hispanic/ Latino), 28 international. Average age 30. 54 applicants, 54% accepted, 17 enrolled. In 2016, 38 master's awarded. *Expenses:* Tuition, state resident: full-time $16,863. Tuition, nonresident: full-time $32,913. *Required fees:* $177. *Application contact:* Peggy Roldan Patel, Graduate Admissions Coordinator, 617-287-6400, Fax: 617-287-6236, E-mail: bos.gadm@dpc.umassp.edu.

University of Massachusetts Dartmouth, Graduate School, Charlton College of Business, Department of Accounting and Finance, North Dartmouth, MA 02747-2300. Offers accounting (MS, Postbaccalaureate Certificate); finance (Postbaccalaureate Certificate). *Program availability:* Part-time. *Faculty:* 13 full-time (3 women), 6 part-time/ adjunct (5 women). *Students:* 26 full-time (14 women), 15 part-time (10 women); includes 10 minority (2 Black or African American, non-Hispanic/Latino; 4 Asian, non-Hispanic/Latino; 3 Hispanic/Latino; 1 Two or more races, non-Hispanic/Latino), 7 international. Average age 29. 38 applicants, 87% accepted, 20 enrolled. In 2016, 1 master's awarded. *Entrance requirements:* For master's, GMAT, statement of purpose (minimum 300 words), resume, official transcript, 2 letters of recommendation; for Postbaccalaureate Certificate, statement of purpose (minimum 300 words), resume, official transcript. Additional exam requirements/recommendations for international students: Required—TOEFL (minimum score 533 paper-based; 72 iBT). *Application deadline:* For fall admission, 7/1 priority date for domestic students, 6/1 priority date for international students; for spring admission, 11/15 priority date for domestic students, 10/15 priority date for international students. Application fee: $60. Electronic applications accepted. *Expenses:* Tuition, state resident: full-time $14,994; part-time $624.75 per credit. Tuition, nonresident: full-time $27,068; part-time $1127.83 per credit. *Required fees:* $405; $25.88 per credit. Tuition and fees vary according to course load and reciprocity agreements. *Financial support:* Institutionally sponsored loans and scholarships/grants available. Support available to part-time students. Financial award application deadline: 3/1; financial award applicants required to submit FAFSA. *Faculty research:* Accounting information systems, analytical controls in continuous auditing, accounting education, managerial accounting, e-commerce, corporate governance, executive compensation, financial statement analysis, efficiency of emerging capital markets. *Unit head:* Dr. Jia Wu, Program Coordinator, Accounting, 508-999-8428, E-mail: jwu@umassd.edu. *Application contact:* Steven Briggs, Director of Marketing and Recruitment for Graduate Studies, 508-999-8604, Fax: 508-999-8183, E-mail: graduate@umassd.edu.
Website: http://www.umassd.edu/charlton/programs/graduate/msaccounting/

University of Memphis, Graduate School, Fogelman College of Business and Economics, Program in Business Administration, Memphis, TN 38152. Offers accounting (MBA, PhD); business administration (IMBA); economics (PhD); executive business administration (MBA); finance (PhD); management (PhD); marketing (MS); marketing and supply chain management (PhD); real estate development (MS); JD/ MBA. *Accreditation:* AACSB. *Faculty:* 44 full-time (9 women), 5 part-time/adjunct (0 women). *Students:* 167 full-time (64 women), 341 part-time (119 women); includes 154 minority (80 Black or African American, non-Hispanic/Latino; 1 American Indian or Alaska Native, non-Hispanic/Latino; 43 Asian, non-Hispanic/Latino; 12 Hispanic/Latino; 1 Native Hawaiian or other Pacific Islander, non-Hispanic/Latino; 17 Two or more races, non-Hispanic/Latino), 96 international. Average age 33. 306 applicants, 64% accepted, 154 enrolled. In 2016, 273 master's, 7 doctorates awarded. *Degree requirements:* For master's, comprehensive exam; for doctorate, comprehensive exam, thesis/dissertation. *Entrance requirements:* For master's, GMAT, resume; for doctorate, GMAT, interview, minimum GPA of 3.4, resume, letter of recommendation. Additional exam requirements/ recommendations for international students: Required—TOEFL (minimum score 550 paper-based). *Application deadline:* For fall admission, 8/1 for domestic students; for spring admission, 12/1 for domestic students. Application fee: $35 ($60 for international students). *Expenses:* Tuition, state resident: full-time $10,463; part-time $9483 per year. Tuition, nonresident: full-time $19,247; part-time $17,291 per year. *Required fees:* $821.50 per semester. Tuition and fees vary according to course load and program. *Financial support:* In 2016–17, 164 students received support. Research assistantships with full tuition reimbursements available, teaching assistantships with full tuition reimbursements available, career-related internships or fieldwork, Federal Work-Study, scholarships/grants, and unspecified assistantships available. Financial award application deadline: 2/15; financial award applicants required to submit FAFSA. *Faculty research:* Competitive business strategy, finance microstructures, supply chain management innovations, health care economics, litigation risks and corporate audits. *Unit head:* Dr. Rajiv Grover, Dean, 901-678-3759, E-mail: rgrover@memphis.edu. *Application contact:* Dr. Carol V. Danehower, Associate Dean, 901-678-5402, Fax: 901-678-3579, E-mail: fcbegp@memphis.edu.
Website: https://web0.memphis.edu/gradcatalog/degreeprog/fcbe/fcbe.php

University of Memphis, Graduate School, Fogelman College of Business and Economics, School of Accountancy, Memphis, TN 38152. Offers accounting (MS). *Accreditation:* AACSB. *Faculty:* 9 full-time (1 woman), 1 part-time/adjunct (0 women). *Students:* 35 full-time (21 women), 21 part-time (6 women); includes 19 minority (8 Black or African American, non-Hispanic/Latino; 6 Asian, non-Hispanic/Latino; 4 Hispanic/ Latino; 1 Two or more races, non-Hispanic/Latino), 6 international. Average age 28. 52 applicants, 83% accepted, 26 enrolled. In 2016, 57 master's awarded. *Degree requirements:* For master's, comprehensive exam. *Entrance requirements:* For master's, GMAT. Additional exam requirements/recommendations for international students: Required—TOEFL (minimum score 550 paper-based; 79 iBT). *Application deadline:* For fall admission, 8/1 for domestic students; for spring admission, 12/1 for domestic students. Application fee: $35 ($60 for international students). Electronic applications accepted. *Expenses:* $5,231.50 per semester full-time in-state, $9,623.50 full-time out-of-state. *Financial support:* In 2016–17, 32 students received support, including 9 research assistantships with full tuition reimbursements available (averaging $12,000 per year); teaching assistantships with full tuition reimbursements available, Federal Work-Study, scholarships/grants, and unspecified assistantships also available. Financial award application deadline: 2/1; financial award applicants required to submit FAFSA. *Faculty research:* Financial accounting, corporate governance, EDP auditing, evolution of system analysis, investor behavior and investment decisions. *Unit head:* Dr. Kenton Walker, Director, 901-678-4569, E-mail: kbwalker@memphis.edu. *Application contact:* Dr. Zabihollah Rezaee, PhD Program Coordinator, 901-678-4652, E-mail: zrezaee@memphis.edu.
Website: http://www.memphis.edu/accountancy/

University of Michigan, Ross School of Business, Ann Arbor, MI 48109-1234. Offers accounting (M Acc); business (MBA); business administration (PhD); supply chain management (MSCM); JD/MBA; MBA/M Arch; MBA/M Eng; MBA/MA; MBA/MEM; MBA/ MHSA; MBA/MM; MBA/MPP; MBA/MS; MBA/MSE; MBA/MSI; MBA/MSW; MBA/MUP; MD/MBA; MHSA/MBA. *Accreditation:* AACSB. *Program availability:* Part-time, evening/ weekend. *Degree requirements:* For doctorate, comprehensive exam, thesis/ dissertation, oral defense of dissertation, preliminary exam. *Entrance requirements:* For master's, GMAT or GRE, completion of equivalent of four-year U.S. bachelor's degree, two letters of recommendation, essays, resume; for doctorate, GMAT or GRE. Additional exam requirements/recommendations for international students: Required—TOEFL (minimum score 600 paper-based; 100 iBT). Electronic applications accepted. *Expenses:* Tuition, state resident: full-time $21,466; part-time $1152 per credit hour. Tuition, nonresident: full-time $43,346; part-time $2367 per credit hour. Part-time tuition and fees vary according to course load, degree level and program. *Faculty research:* Finance and accounting, marketing, technology and operations management, corporate strategy, management and organizations.

University of Michigan–Dearborn, College of Business, MS Program in Accounting, Dearborn, MI 48126. Offers MS. *Program availability:* Part-time, evening/weekend. *Faculty:* 33 full-time (14 women), 10 part-time/adjunct (5 women). *Students:* 9 full-time (7 women), 13 part-time (4 women); includes 5 minority (1 Black or African American, non-Hispanic/Latino; 3 Asian, non-Hispanic/Latino; 1 Two or more races, non-Hispanic/ Latino), 6 international. Average age 30. 46 applicants, 76% accepted, 16 enrolled. In 2016, 20 master's awarded. *Entrance requirements:* For master's, GMAT or GRE, equivalent of four-year U.S. bachelor's degree from regionally-accredited institution, undergraduate course in finite math, pre-calculus, or calculus. Additional exam requirements/recommendations for international students: Required—TOEFL (minimum score 560 paper-based; 84 iBT), IELTS (minimum score 6.5). *Application deadline:* For fall admission, 8/1 for domestic students, 5/1 for international students; for winter admission, 12/1 for domestic students, 9/1 for international students; for spring admission, 4/1 for domestic students, 1/1 for international students. Applications are processed on a rolling basis. Application fee: $60. Electronic applications accepted. *Expenses:* Contact institution. *Financial support:* In 2016–17, 12 students received support. Scholarships/grants and non-resident tuition scholarships available. Financial award application deadline: 3/1; financial award applicants required to submit FAFSA. *Faculty research:* Business intelligence, information technology, brand management and new media, management education, operations strategy. *Unit head:* Dr. Michael Kamen, Director, COB Graduate Programs, 313-593-5460, E-mail: mkamen@ umich.edu. *Application contact:* Joan Doherty, Academic Advisor/Counselor, 313-593-5460, Fax: 313-271-9838, E-mail: umd-gradbusiness@umich.edu.
Website: http://umdearborn.edu/cob/ms-accounting/

University of Michigan–Flint, School of Management, Program in Accounting, Flint, MI 48502. Offers MSA. *Program availability:* Part-time, evening/weekend, mixed mode program. *Faculty:* 33 full-time (9 women), 6 part-time/adjunct (1 woman). *Students:* 3 full-time (1 woman), 23 part-time (9 women); includes 8 minority (4 Black or African American, non-Hispanic/Latino; 2 Asian, non-Hispanic/Latino; 2 Hispanic/Latino), 4 international. Average age 31. 31 applicants, 68% accepted, 9 enrolled. In 2016, 13 master's awarded. *Entrance requirements:* For master's, GMAT or GRE, bachelor's degree in arts, sciences, engineering, or business administration from regionally-accredited college or university with minimum GPA of 3.0. Additional exam requirements/recommendations for international students: Required—TOEFL (minimum score 84 iBT), IELTS (minimum score 3.5). *Application deadline:* For fall admission, 8/1 for domestic students, 5/1 for international students; for winter admission, 11/15 for domestic students, 9/1 for international students; for spring admission, 2/15 for domestic students; for summer admission, 5/15 for domestic students. Applications are processed on a rolling basis. Application fee: $55. Electronic applications accepted. *Financial support:* Federal Work-Study, scholarships/grants, and unspecified assistantships available. Support available to part-time students. Financial award application deadline: 3/1; financial award applicants required to submit FAFSA. *Unit head:* Dr. Scott Johnson, Dean, School of Management, 810-762-3164, Fax: 810-237-6685, E-mail: scotjohn@ umflint.edu. *Application contact:* Bradley T. Maki, Director of Graduate Admissions, 810-762-3171, Fax: 810-766-6789, E-mail: bmaki@umflint.edu.
Website: http://www.umflint.edu/graduateprograms/accounting-msa

University of Michigan–Flint, School of Management, Program in Business Administration, Flint, MI 48502. Offers accounting (MBA, Post-Master's Certificate); computer information systems (MBA); finance (MBA, Post-Master's Certificate); general business (Graduate Certificate); general business administration (MBA); health care management (MBA); international business (MBA, Post-Master's Certificate); lean manufacturing (MBA); marketing (MBA, Post-Master's Certificate); organizational leadership (MBA, Post-Master's Certificate). *Program availability:* Part-time, evening/ weekend, mixed mode programs. *Faculty:* 33 full-time (9 women), 6 part-time/adjunct (1 woman). *Students:* 24 full-time (12 women), 146 part-time (49 women); includes 37 minority (17 Black or African American, non-Hispanic/Latino; 2 American Indian or Alaska Native, non-Hispanic/Latino; 10 Asian, non-Hispanic/Latino; 4 Hispanic/Latino; 1 Native Hawaiian or other Pacific Islander, non-Hispanic/Latino; 3 Two or more races, non-Hispanic/Latino), 17 international. Average age 33. 167 applicants, 47% accepted, 40 enrolled. In 2016, 73 master's, 3 other advanced degrees awarded. *Entrance requirements:* For master's, GMAT or GRE, bachelor's degree in arts, sciences, engineering, or business administration from regionally-accredited college or university with minimum GPA of 3.0; for other advanced degree, bachelor's degree in arts, sciences, engineering, or business administration from regionally-accredited college or university with minimum GPA of 3.0, college-level math, statistics, or quantitative course (for Graduate Certificate); MBA or equivalent degree from regionally-accredited college or university (for Post Master's Certificate). Additional exam requirements/ recommendations for international students: Required—TOEFL (minimum score 84 iBT), IELTS (minimum score 6.5). *Application deadline:* For fall admission, 8/1 for domestic students, 5/1 for international students; for winter admission, 11/15 for domestic students, 9/1 for international students; for spring admission, 3/15 for domestic students, 1/1 for international students; for summer admission, 5/15 for domestic students. Applications are processed on a rolling basis. Application fee: $55. Electronic applications accepted. *Financial support:* Federal Work-Study, scholarships/grants, and unspecified assistantships available. Support available to part-time students. Financial award application deadline: 3/1; financial award applicants required to submit FAFSA. *Unit head:* Dr. Scott Johnson, Dean, School of Management, 810-762-3164, Fax: 810-

237-6685, E-mail: scotjohn@umflint.edu. *Application contact:* Bradley T. Maki, Director of Graduate Admissions, 810-762-3171, E-mail: bmaki@umflint.edu.
Website: http://www.umflint.edu/graduateprograms/business-administration-mba

University of Minnesota, Twin Cities Campus, Carlson School of Management, Doctoral Program in Business Administration, Minneapolis, MN 55455. Offers accounting (PhD); finance (PhD); information and decision sciences (PhD); marketing (PhD); strategic management and entrepreneurship (PhD); supply chain and operations (PhD); work and organizations (PhD). *Faculty:* 101 full-time (32 women). *Students:* 90 full-time (29 women); includes 7 minority (2 Black or African American, non-Hispanic/Latino; 3 Asian, non-Hispanic/Latino; 2 Hispanic/Latino), 64 international. Average age 30. 352 applicants, 7% accepted, 15 enrolled. In 2016, 20 doctorates awarded. *Degree requirements:* For doctorate, comprehensive exam, thesis/dissertation, written and oral preliminary exams, proposal defense, final defense. *Entrance requirements:* For doctorate, GMAT, GRE General Test, minimum undergraduate GPA of 3.0, graduate 3.5 (recommended). Additional exam requirements/recommendations for international students: Required—TOEFL (minimum score 600 paper-based, 100 iBT) or IELTS (minimum score 7.0). *Application deadline:* For fall admission, 12/15 for domestic students, 12/15 priority date for international students. Applications are processed on a rolling basis. Application fee: $75 ($95 for international students). Electronic applications accepted. *Expenses:* Contact institution. *Financial support:* In 2016–17, 80 students received support, including 80 fellowships with full tuition reimbursements available (averaging $13,500 per year), 72 research assistantships with full tuition reimbursements available (averaging $7,371 per year), 72 teaching assistantships with full tuition reimbursements available (averaging $7,371 per year); institutionally sponsored loans, scholarships/grants, health care benefits, unspecified assistantships, and full student service fee waivers also available. Financial award application deadline: 12/15. *Faculty research:* Finance, strategy and entrepreneurship, marketing, information and decision science, operations, accounting, supply chain, human resources and industrial relations, organizational behavior. *Unit head:* Dr. Shawn P. Curley, Director, 612-624-6546, Fax: 612-624-8221, E-mail: curley@umn.edu. *Application contact:* Sandy Herzan, Associate Director, 612-624-0875, Fax: 612-624-8221, E-mail: herza002@umn.edu.
Website: http://carlsonschool.umn.edu/degrees/phd

University of Minnesota, Twin Cities Campus, Carlson School of Management, Master's Program in Accountancy, Minneapolis, MN 55455-0213. Offers M Acc. *Accreditation:* AACSB. *Program availability:* Part-time, evening/weekend. *Faculty:* 23 full-time (5 women), 1 part-time/adjunct (0 women). *Students:* 56 full-time (31 women), 7 part-time (2 women); includes 5 minority (1 American Indian or Alaska Native, non-Hispanic/Latino; 3 Asian, non-Hispanic/Latino; 1 Hispanic/Latino), 30 international. Average age 23. 188 applicants, 36% accepted, 47 enrolled. In 2016, 43 master's awarded. *Entrance requirements:* For master's, GMAT, letters of recommendation. Additional exam requirements/recommendations for international students: Required—TOEFL (minimum score 550 paper-based; 79 iBT), IELTS (minimum score 6.5). *Application deadline:* For fall admission, 2/1 priority date for domestic and international students; for spring admission, 10/1 priority date for domestic and international students. Applications are processed on a rolling basis. Application fee: $75 ($95 for international students). Electronic applications accepted. *Expenses:* $22,155 resident, $35,065 non-resident tuition and fees to complete the degree in two semesters. *Financial support:* In 2016–17, 42 students received support, including 11 fellowships (averaging $2,750 per year), 6 teaching assistantships with partial tuition reimbursements available (averaging $9,000 per year); institutionally sponsored loans and scholarships/grants also available. Financial award application deadline: 7/15. *Faculty research:* Capital market-based accounting, cognitive skill acquisition in auditing, incentives and control in organizations, economic consequences of securities regulation, earnings management. *Unit head:* Larry Kallio, Director of Graduate Studies, 612-624-9818, Fax: 612-626-7795, E-mail: kalli008@umn.edu. *Application contact:* Information Contact, 612-624-7511, Fax: 612-626-7795, E-mail: macct@umn.edu.
Website: http://carlsonschool.umn.edu/degrees/master-accountancy

University of Mississippi, Graduate School, School of Accountancy, University, MS 38677. Offers accountancy (M Acc, PhD); taxation accounting (M Tax). *Accreditation:* AACSB. *Faculty:* 17 full-time (12 women), 4 part-time/adjunct (3 women). *Students:* 143 full-time (64 women), 7 part-time (4 women); includes 12 minority (7 Black or African American, non-Hispanic/Latino; 1 American Indian or Alaska Native, non-Hispanic/Latino; 1 Asian, non-Hispanic/Latino; 1 Hispanic/Latino; 2 Two or more races, non-Hispanic/Latino), 6 international. Average age 22. *Degree requirements:* For doctorate, thesis/dissertation. *Entrance requirements:* For master's, GMAT, minimum GPA of 3.0; for doctorate, GMAT. Additional exam requirements/recommendations for international students: Required—TOEFL. *Application deadline:* For fall admission, 4/1 for domestic students; for spring admission, 10/1 for domestic students. Applications are processed on a rolling basis. Application fee: $40. *Financial support:* Scholarships/grants available. Financial award application deadline: 3/1; financial award applicants required to submit FAFSA. *Unit head:* Dr. W. Mark Wilder, Dean, School of Accountancy, 662-915-7468, Fax: 662-915-7483, E-mail: umaccy@olemiss.edu. *Application contact:* Dr. Christy M. Wyandt, Associate Dean, 662-915-7474, Fax: 662-915-7577, E-mail: cwyandt@olemiss.edu.
Website: https://www.olemiss.edu

University of Missouri, Office of Research and Graduate Studies, Robert J. Trulaske, Sr. College of Business, School of Accountancy, Columbia, MO 65211. Offers accountancy (M Acc, PhD); taxation (Certificate). *Accreditation:* AACSB. *Program availability:* Part-time. *Degree requirements:* For master's, thesis or alternative; for doctorate, thesis/dissertation. *Entrance requirements:* For master's and doctorate, GMAT, minimum GPA of 3.0. Additional exam requirements/recommendations for international students: Required—TOEFL (minimum score 600 paper-based; 100 iBT). Electronic applications accepted. *Expenses:* Tuition, state resident: full-time $6347; part-time $352.60 per credit hour. Tuition, nonresident: full-time $17,379; part-time $965.50 per credit hour. *Required fees:* $1035. Tuition and fees vary according to course load, campus/location and program.

University of Missouri–Kansas City, Henry W. Bloch School of Management, Kansas City, MO 64110-2499. Offers accounting (MS); finance (MS); public affairs (MPA, PhD); JD/MBA; LL M/MPA. PhD (interdisciplinary) offered through the School of Graduate Studies. *Accreditation:* AACSB; NASPAA. *Program availability:* Part-time, evening/weekend. *Faculty:* 60 full-time (19 women), 40 part-time/adjunct (11 women). *Students:* 204 full-time (97 women), 308 part-time (151 women); includes 70 minority (29 Black or African American, non-Hispanic/Latino; 1 American Indian or Alaska Native, non-Hispanic/Latino; 17 Asian, non-Hispanic/Latino; 18 Hispanic/Latino; 5 Two or more races, non-Hispanic/Latino), 82 international. Average age 30. 389 applicants, 49% accepted, 190 enrolled. In 2016, 248 master's, 2 doctorates awarded. Terminal master's awarded for partial completion of doctoral program. *Entrance requirements:* For master's, GMAT, GRE, 2 essays, 2 references, support of employer; for doctorate, GRE, minimum GPA of 3.0. Additional exam requirements/recommendations for international students: Required—TOEFL (minimum score 550 paper-based; 80 iBT). *Application deadline:* For fall admission, 5/1 priority date for domestic and international students; for spring admission, 10/1 priority date for domestic and international students. Applications are processed on a rolling basis. Application fee: $45 ($50 for international students). Electronic applications accepted. *Financial support:* In 2016–17, 31 research assistantships with partial tuition reimbursements (averaging $10,597 per year), 10 teaching assistantships with partial tuition reimbursements (averaging $14,592 per year) were awarded; career-related internships or fieldwork, Federal Work-Study, institutionally sponsored loans, scholarships/grants, tuition waivers (full and partial), and unspecified assistantships also available. Support available to part-time students. Financial award application deadline: 3/1; financial award applicants required to submit FAFSA. *Faculty research:* Entrepreneurship, finance, non-profit, risk management. *Unit head:* Dr. David Donnelly, Dean, 816-235-1333, Fax: 816-235-2206, E-mail: donnellyd@umkc.edu. *Application contact:* 816-235-1111, E-mail: admit@umkc.edu.
Website: http://www.bloch.umkc.edu

University of Missouri–St. Louis, College of Business Administration, Program in Accounting, St. Louis, MO 63121. Offers M Acc. *Accreditation:* AACSB. *Program availability:* Part-time, evening/weekend. *Faculty:* 10 full-time (7 women), 5 part-time/adjunct (3 women). *Entrance requirements:* For master's, GMAT, 2 letters of recommendation. Additional exam requirements/recommendations for international students: Recommended—TOEFL (minimum score 550 paper-based; 79 iBT), IELTS (minimum score 6.5). *Application deadline:* For fall admission, 3/15 for domestic and international students; for spring admission, 10/15 for domestic and international students. Application fee: $50 ($40 for international students). Electronic applications accepted. *Financial support:* Research assistantships with tuition reimbursements, career-related internships or fieldwork, Federal Work-Study, and institutionally sponsored loans available. Support available to part-time students. Financial award application deadline: 4/1; financial award applicants required to submit FAFSA. *Faculty research:* Accounting information in contracts, financial reporting issues, empirical valuation issues. *Unit head:* Dr. Stephen Moehrle, Chair, 314-516-6142, Fax: 314-516-6420, E-mail: moehrle@umsl.edu. *Application contact:* 314-516-5458, Fax: 314-516-6996, E-mail: gradadm@umsl.edu.
Website: http://www.umsl.edu/divisions/business/accounting/

University of Missouri–St. Louis, College of Business Administration, Program in Business Administration, St. Louis, MO 63121. Offers accounting (MBA); business administration (Certificate); business intelligence (Certificate); cybersecurity (Certificate); digital and social media marketing (Certificate); finance (MBA); human resources management (Certificate); information systems (MBA); international business (MBA); logistics and supply chain management (MBA, PhD, Certificate); management (MBA); marketing (MBA); marketing management (Certificate); operations management (MBA). *Accreditation:* AACSB. *Program availability:* Part-time, evening/weekend. *Faculty:* 32 full-time (10 women), 14 part-time/adjunct (3 women). *Students:* 181 full-time (88 women), 357 part-time (154 women); includes 83 minority (30 Black or African American, non-Hispanic/Latino; 36 Asian, non-Hispanic/Latino; 12 Hispanic/Latino; 2 Native Hawaiian or other Pacific Islander, non-Hispanic/Latino; 3 Two or more races, non-Hispanic/Latino), 100 international. Average age 31. 245 applicants, 83% accepted, 139 enrolled. *Degree requirements:* For doctorate, thesis/dissertation. *Entrance requirements:* For master's, GMAT, 2 letters of recommendation. Additional exam requirements/recommendations for international students: Recommended—TOEFL (minimum score 550 paper-based; 79 iBT), IELTS (minimum score 6.5). *Application deadline:* For fall admission, 7/1 for domestic and international students; for spring admission, 12/1 for domestic and international students. Applications are processed on a rolling basis. Application fee: $50 ($40 for international students). Electronic applications accepted. *Financial support:* Research assistantships with tuition reimbursements, teaching assistantships with tuition reimbursements, career-related internships or fieldwork, Federal Work-Study, and institutionally sponsored loans available. Support available to part-time students. Financial award application deadline: 4/1; financial award applicants required to submit FAFSA. *Faculty research:* Human resources, strategic management, marketing strategy, consumer behavior product development, advertising. *Unit head:* Dr. Thomas H. Eyssell, Associate Dean and Director of Graduate Studies, 314-516-5885, Fax: 314-516-6420, E-mail: mba@umsl.edu. *Application contact:* 314-516-5458, Fax: 314-516-6996, E-mail: gradadm@umsl.edu.

University of Montana, Graduate School, School of Business Administration, Department of Accounting and Finance, Missoula, MT 59812-0002. Offers accounting (M Acct). *Accreditation:* AACSB. *Degree requirements:* For master's, thesis optional. *Entrance requirements:* For master's, GMAT. Additional exam requirements/recommendations for international students: Required—TOEFL (minimum score 580 paper-based). *Faculty research:* Income tax, financial markets, nonprofit accounting, accounting information systems, auditing.

University of Nebraska at Kearney, College of Business and Technology, Department of Business, Kearney, NE 68849-0001. Offers accounting (MBA); generalist (MBA); human resources (MBA); human services (MBA); marketing (MBA). *Accreditation:* AACSB. *Program availability:* Part-time, evening/weekend. *Faculty:* 32 full-time (13 women). *Students:* 11 full-time (5 women), 30 part-time (14 women), 8 international. Average age 39. 13 applicants, 100% accepted, 10 enrolled. In 2016, 6 master's awarded. *Degree requirements:* For master's, thesis optional, capstone course. *Entrance requirements:* For master's, GRE or GMAT (if no significant managerial experience), letters of recommendation, essay, resume. Additional exam requirements/recommendations for international students: Recommended—TOEFL (minimum score 550 paper-based; 79 iBT), IELTS (minimum score 6.5). *Application deadline:* For fall admission, 6/15 for domestic and international students; for spring admission, 10/15 for domestic and international students; for summer admission, 3/15 for domestic and international students. Application fee: $45. Electronic applications accepted. *Expenses:* Tuition, state resident: full-time $4064; part-time $225.75 per credit hour. Tuition, nonresident: full-time $8915; part-time $495.25 per credit hour. *Required fees:* $772; $23 per credit hour. Part-time tuition and fees vary according to course load, campus/location, program and reciprocity agreements. *Financial support:* In 2016–17, 2 research assistantships with full tuition reimbursements (averaging $10,500 per year), 2 teaching assistantships with full tuition reimbursements (averaging $10,500 per year) were awarded; career-related internships or fieldwork, scholarships/grants, health care benefits, and unspecified assistantships also available. Support available to part-time students. Financial award application deadline: 2/28; financial award applicants required to submit FAFSA. *Faculty research:* Small business financial management, employment law, expert systems, international trade and marketing, environmental economics. *Unit head:* Dr. Sri Seshadri, Director, 308-865-8346, Fax: 308-865-8114. *Application contact:* Linda Johnson, Director, Graduate Admissions and Programs, 800-717-7881, Fax: 308-865-8837, E-mail: gradstudies@unk.edu.

University of Nebraska at Omaha, Graduate Studies, College of Business Administration, Department of Accounting, Omaha, NE 68182. Offers M Acc. *Program availability:* Part-time, evening/weekend. *Faculty:* 5 full-time (4 women). *Students:* 15 full-time (5 women), 24 part-time (12 women); includes 7 minority (3 Asian, non-Hispanic/Latino; 1 Hispanic/Latino; 3 Two or more races, non-Hispanic/Latino), 4 international. Average age 29. 22 applicants, 50% accepted, 7 enrolled. In 2016, 13 master's awarded. *Degree requirements:* For master's, comprehensive exam (for some programs), thesis (for some programs). *Entrance requirements:* For master's, GMAT, minimum GPA of 3.0 in undergraduate courses related to accounting, official transcript. Additional exam requirements/recommendations for international students: Required—TOEFL, IELTS, PTE. *Application deadline:* Applications are processed on a rolling basis. Application fee: $45. Electronic applications accepted. *Financial support:* In 2016–17, 2 students received support, including 2 research assistantships with tuition reimbursements available; Federal Work-Study, institutionally sponsored loans, scholarships/grants, health care benefits, tuition waivers (partial), and unspecified assistantships also available. Support available to part-time students. Financial award application deadline: 3/1; financial award applicants required to submit FAFSA. *Unit head:* Dr. Susan Eldridge, Chairperson, 402-554-2341, E-mail: graduate@unomaha.edu. *Application contact:* Dr. Jennifer Riley, Graduate Program Chair, 402-554-2341, E-mail: graduate@unomaha.edu.

University of Nebraska–Lincoln, Graduate College, College of Business Administration, Interdepartmental Area of Business, Lincoln, NE 68588. Offers accountancy (PhD); business (MBA); finance (MA, PhD), including business; management (MA, PhD), including business; marketing (MA, PhD), including business; JD/MBA; M Arch/MBA. *Accreditation:* AACSB. *Program availability:* Part-time, online learning. *Degree requirements:* For doctorate, comprehensive exam, thesis/dissertation. *Entrance requirements:* For master's and doctorate, GMAT. Additional exam requirements/recommendations for international students: Required—TOEFL (minimum score 550 paper-based). Electronic applications accepted.

University of Nebraska–Lincoln, Graduate College, College of Business Administration, School of Accountancy, Lincoln, NE 68588. Offers MPA, PhD, JD/MPA. *Accreditation:* AACSB. *Entrance requirements:* For master's, GMAT. Additional exam requirements/recommendations for international students: Required—TOEFL (minimum score 550 paper-based). Electronic applications accepted. *Faculty research:* Auditing, financial accounting, managerial accounting, capital markets, tax accounting.

University of Nevada, Las Vegas, Graduate College, Lee Business School, Department of Accounting, Las Vegas, NV 89154-6003. Offers MS, Advanced Certificate, Certificate. *Accreditation:* AACSB. *Program availability:* Part-time. *Faculty:* 7 full-time (2 women), 6 part-time/adjunct (2 women). *Students:* 61 full-time (32 women), 36 part-time (22 women); includes 46 minority (1 Black or African American, non-Hispanic/Latino; 17 Asian, non-Hispanic/Latino; 16 Hispanic/Latino; 2 Native Hawaiian or other Pacific Islander, non-Hispanic/Latino; 10 Two or more races, non-Hispanic/Latino), 11 international. Average age 30. 34 applicants, 79% accepted, 21 enrolled. In 2016, 73 master's awarded. *Entrance requirements:* For master's, GMAT, bachelor's degree with minimum GPA 3.0. Additional exam requirements/recommendations for international students: Required—TOEFL (minimum score 550 paper-based; 80 iBT), IELTS (minimum score 7). *Application deadline:* For fall admission, 8/1 for domestic students, 5/1 for international students; for spring admission, 12/1 for domestic students, 10/1 for international students; for summer admission, 5/15 for domestic students, 4/15 for international students. Application fee: $60 ($95 for international students). Electronic applications accepted. *Expenses:* $269.25 per credit, $792 per 3-credit course; $9,634 per year resident; $23,274 per year non-resident; $7,094 fees non-resident (7 credits or more); $1,307 annual health insurance fee. *Financial support:* In 2016–17, 13 research assistantships with partial tuition reimbursements (averaging $10,131 per year), 2 teaching assistantships with partial tuition reimbursements (averaging $10,000 per year) were awarded; institutionally sponsored loans, scholarships/grants, health care benefits, and unspecified assistantships also available. Financial award application deadline: 3/15. *Faculty research:* Audit judgments and decision-making, fraud, corporate governance, information systems technology and decision-making, internal audit. *Total annual research expenditures:* $9,740. *Unit head:* Dr. Kimberly Charron, Chair/Associate Professor, 702-895-4323, Fax: 702-895-4306, E-mail: kim.charron@unlv.edu. *Application contact:* Dr. Tammy Perri, Graduate Coordinator, 702-895-3768, Fax: 702-895-4306, E-mail: tammy.perri@unlv.edu.
Website: http://business.unlv.edu/accounting/

University of Nevada, Reno, Graduate School, College of Business Administration, Department of Accounting and Information Systems, Reno, NV 89557. Offers M Acc. *Accreditation:* AACSB. *Entrance requirements:* For master's, GMAT or GRE (if undergraduate degree is not from an AACSB-accredited business school with minimum GPA of 3.5), minimum GPA of 2.75. Additional exam requirements/recommendations for international students: Required—TOEFL (minimum score 500 paper-based; 61 iBT), IELTS (minimum score 6). Electronic applications accepted. *Faculty research:* Financial reporting/auditing, taxation.

University of New Hampshire, Graduate School, Peter T. Paul College of Business and Economics, Department of Accounting and Finance, Durham, NH 03824. Offers accounting (MS). *Program availability:* Part-time. *Entrance requirements:* For master's, GMAT. Additional exam requirements/recommendations for international students: Required—TOEFL (minimum score 550 paper-based; 80 iBT). *Application deadline:* For fall admission, 5/1 priority date for domestic students, 4/1 for international students; for spring admission, 12/1 for domestic students. Applications are processed on a rolling basis. Application fee: $65. Electronic applications accepted. *Financial support:* Fellowships, research assistantships, and teaching assistantships available. Financial award application deadline: 2/15. *Unit head:* Stephen Ciccone, Chair, 603-862-3343, E-mail: stephen.ciccone@unh.edu. *Application contact:* Sinthy Kounlasa, Administrative Assistant III, 603-862-3380, E-mail: sinthy.kounlasa@unh.edu.
Website: http://paulcollege.unh.edu/academics/graduate-programs/ms-accounting

University of New Haven, Graduate School, College of Business, Program in Accounting, West Haven, CT 06516. Offers Graduate Certificate. *Accreditation:* AACSB. *Students:* 7 full-time (3 women), 19 part-time (8 women); includes 8 minority (4 Black or African American, non-Hispanic/Latino; 3 Asian, non-Hispanic/Latino; 1 Two or more races, non-Hispanic/Latino). Average age 32. 11 applicants, 100% accepted, 8 enrolled. In 2016, 1 Graduate Certificate awarded. *Application deadline:* Applications are processed on a rolling basis. Application fee: $50. *Expenses: Tuition:* Full-time $15,660; part-time $870 per credit hour. *Required fees:* $200; $85 per term. Tuition and fees vary according to program. *Financial support:* Research assistantships with partial tuition reimbursements, teaching assistantships with partial tuition reimbursements, and Federal Work-Study available. Support available to part-time students. Financial award application deadline: 5/1; financial award applicants required to submit FAFSA. *Unit head:* Michael Rolleri, Chair of Accounting, E-mail: mrolleri@newhaven.edu. *Application contact:* Michelle Mason, Director of Graduate Enrollment, 203-932-7067, E-mail: mmason@newhaven.edu.

University of New Haven, Graduate School, College of Business, Program in Business Administration, West Haven, CT 06516. Offers accounting (MBA), including CPA; business administration (MBA); business intelligence (MBA); business management (Graduate Certificate); business policy and strategic leadership (MBA); finance (MBA), including CFA; global marketing (MBA); human resources management (MBA, Graduate Certificate); sport management (MBA). *Accreditation:* AACSB. *Program availability:* Part-time, evening/weekend. *Students:* 123 full-time (56 women), 74 part-time (29 women); includes 46 minority (24 Black or African American, non-Hispanic/Latino; 8 Asian, non-Hispanic/Latino; 10 Hispanic/Latino; 4 Two or more races, non-Hispanic/Latino), 57 international. Average age 27. In 2016, 100 master's awarded. *Entrance requirements:* For master's, GMAT. Additional exam requirements/recommendations for international students: Required—TOEFL (minimum score 80 iBT), IELTS, PTE. *Application deadline:* Applications are processed on a rolling basis. Application fee: $50. Electronic applications accepted. Application fee is waived when completed online. *Expenses: Tuition:* Full-time $15,660; part-time $870 per credit hour. *Required fees:* $200; $85 per term. Tuition and fees vary according to program. *Financial support:* Research assistantships with partial tuition reimbursements, teaching assistantships with partial tuition reimbursements, career-related internships or fieldwork, Federal Work-Study, scholarships/grants, and unspecified assistantships available. Support available to part-time students. Financial award applicants required to submit FAFSA. *Unit head:* Darell Singleterry, Director, 203-932-1085, E-mail: dsingleterry@newhaven.edu. *Application contact:* Michelle Mason, Director of Graduate Enrollment, 203-932-7067, E-mail: mmason@newhaven.edu.
Website: http://www.newhaven.edu/business/programs/EMBA/

University of New Mexico, Anderson School of Management, Department of Accounting, Albuquerque, NM 87131. Offers accounting (MBA); advanced accounting (M Acct); information assurance (M Acct); professional accounting (M Acct); tax accounting (M Acct); JD/M Acct. *Accreditation:* AACSB. *Program availability:* Part-time, evening/weekend. *Faculty:* 15 full-time (7 women), 3 part-time/adjunct (all women). *Students:* 81 applicants, 70% accepted, 51 enrolled. In 2016, 39 master's awarded. *Entrance requirements:* For master's, GMAT/GRE (minimum score of 500), minimum GPA of 3.25, 3.0 on last 60 hours of coursework (for M Acct in professional accounting). Additional exam requirements/recommendations for international students: Required—TOEFL (minimum score 550 paper-based; 79 iBT), IELTS (minimum score 6.5). *Application deadline:* For fall admission, 4/1 priority date for domestic and international students; for spring admission, 10/1 priority date for domestic and international students. Applications are processed on a rolling basis. Application fee: $50. Electronic applications accepted. *Expenses:* Contact institution. *Financial support:* In 2016–17, 2 fellowships (averaging $20,800 per year), 12 research assistantships with partial tuition reimbursements (averaging $15,488 per year) were awarded; career-related internships or fieldwork, Federal Work-Study, scholarships/grants, and unspecified assistantships also available. Support available to part-time students. Financial award application deadline: 6/1; financial award applicants required to submit FAFSA. *Faculty research:* Critical accounting, accounting pedagogy, theory, taxation, information fraud. *Unit head:* Dr. Leslie Oakes, Chair, 505-277-6471, E-mail: loakes@unm.edu. *Application contact:* Dr. Rich Brody, Professor, 505-277-6471, E-mail: tmarmijo@unm.edu.
Website: https://www.mgt.unm.edu/acct/default.asp?mm=faculty

University of New Orleans, Graduate School, College of Business Administration, Department of Accounting, Program in Accounting, New Orleans, LA 70148. Offers MS. *Accreditation:* AACSB. *Program availability:* Part-time, evening/weekend. *Degree requirements:* For master's, thesis optional. *Entrance requirements:* For master's, GMAT. Additional exam requirements/recommendations for international students: Required—TOEFL (minimum score 550 paper-based; 79 iBT). Electronic applications accepted.

University of North Alabama, College of Business, Florence, AL 35632-0001. Offers business administration (MBA), including accounting, enterprise resource planning systems, executive, finance, health care management, information systems, international business, project management. *Accreditation:* AACSB; ACBSP. *Program availability:* Part-time, 100% online, blended/hybrid learning. *Faculty:* 24 full-time (2 women), 6 part-time/adjunct (3 women). *Students:* 180 full-time (77 women), 411 part-time (199 women); includes 208 minority (84 Black or African American, non-Hispanic/Latino; 4 American Indian or Alaska Native, non-Hispanic/Latino; 106 Asian, non-Hispanic/Latino; 6 Hispanic/Latino; 8 Two or more races, non-Hispanic/Latino), 37 international. Average age 34. 263 applicants, 84% accepted, 173 enrolled. In 2016, 156 master's awarded. *Entrance requirements:* For master's, GMAT, GRE, minimum GPA of 2.75 in last 60 hours, 2.5 overall (on a 3.0 scale); 27 hours of course work in business and economics. Additional exam requirements/recommendations for international students: Required—TOEFL (minimum score 79 iBT), IELTS (minimum score 6), PTE (minimum score 54). *Application deadline:* Applications are processed on a rolling basis. Application fee: $50 ($100 for international students). Electronic applications accepted. *Expenses:* Tuition, state resident: full-time $2799; part-time $1866 per semester. Tuition, nonresident: full-time $5598; part-time $3732 per semester. *Required fees:* $915; $642 per semester. Tuition and fees vary according to course load. *Financial support:* In 2016–17, 114 students received support. Scholarships/grants available. Financial award application deadline: 2/1; financial award applicants required to submit FAFSA. *Unit head:* Dr. Gregory A. Carnes, Dean, 256-765-4261, Fax: 256-765-4170, E-mail: gacarnes@una.edu. *Application contact:* Hillary N. Coats, Graduate Admissions Coordinator, 256-765-4447, E-mail: graduate@una.edu.
Website: http://www.una.edu/business/

The University of North Carolina at Chapel Hill, Kenan-Flagler Business School, Accounting Program, Chapel Hill, NC 27599. Offers MAC. *Entrance requirements:* For master's, GMAT. Additional exam requirements/recommendations for international students: Required—TOEFL. *Expenses:* Contact institution. *Faculty research:* Corporate taxation, international taxation, financial accounting, corporate governance, strategy.

The University of North Carolina at Chapel Hill, Kenan-Flagler Business School, Doctoral Program in Business Administration, Chapel Hill, NC 27599. Offers accounting (PhD); finance (PhD); marketing (PhD); operations management (PhD); organizational behavior (PhD); strategy (PhD). *Accreditation:* AACSB. *Degree requirements:* For doctorate, thesis/dissertation. *Entrance requirements:* For doctorate, GMAT or GRE General Test. Electronic applications accepted. *Expenses:* Contact institution.

The University of North Carolina at Charlotte, Belk College of Business, Turner School of Accountancy, Charlotte, NC 28223-0001. Offers M Acct. *Accreditation:* AACSB. *Program availability:* Part-time, evening/weekend. *Faculty:* 10 full-time (4 women), 1 part-time/adjunct (0 women). *Students:* 68 full-time (40 women), 38 part-time (19 women); includes 14 minority (4 Black or African American, non-Hispanic/Latino; 4 Asian, non-Hispanic/Latino; 3 Hispanic/Latino; 3 Two or more races, non-Hispanic/Latino), 10 international. Average age 27. 138 applicants, 79% accepted, 76 enrolled. In 2016, 73 master's awarded. *Degree requirements:* For master's, thesis or alternative. *Entrance requirements:* For master's, GMAT or GRE, bachelor's degree from accredited college or university; official transcript of all previous academic work; minimum overall GPA of 3.0 on previous work beyond high school; completion of a principles of financial accounting course with minimum B grade; at least three evaluations; essay. Additional exam requirements/recommendations for international students: Required—TOEFL (minimum score 523 paper-based, 70 iBT) or IELTS (6.5). *Application deadline:* For fall admission, 3/1 priority date for domestic and international students; for spring admission, 10/1 priority date for domestic and international students; for summer admission, 4/1 priority date for domestic and international students. Applications are processed on a rolling basis. Application fee: $75. Electronic applications accepted. *Expenses:* Contact institution. *Financial support:* Career-related internships or fieldwork, institutionally sponsored loans, scholarships/grants, and unspecified assistantships available. Support available to part-time students. Financial award application deadline: 3/1; financial award applicants required to submit FAFSA. *Faculty research:* Corporate financial reporting trends, use of latest software for accounting and business applications, latest developments in federal and international taxation. *Unit*

head: Dr. Hughlene Burton, Chair, 704-687-7701, Fax: 704-687-1382, E-mail: haburton@uncc.edu. *Application contact:* Kathy B. Giddings, Director of Graduate Admissions, 704-687-5503, Fax: 704-687-1668, E-mail: gradadm@uncc.edu.
Website: http://belkcollege.uncc.edu/departments/accounting

The University of North Carolina at Greensboro, Graduate School, Bryan School of Business and Economics, Department of Accounting and Finance, Greensboro, NC 27412-5001. Offers accounting (MS); financial analysis (PMC). *Accreditation:* AACSB. *Entrance requirements:* For master's, GMAT, GRE General Test, previous course work in accounting and business. Additional exam requirements/recommendations for international students: Required—TOEFL. Electronic applications accepted.

The University of North Carolina Wilmington, Cameron School of Business, Accountancy Program, Wilmington, NC 28403-3297. Offers MSA. *Faculty:* 14 full-time (7 women). *Students:* 44 full-time (19 women); includes 6 minority (2 Black or African American, non-Hispanic/Latino; 1 Asian, non-Hispanic/Latino; 2 Hispanic/Latino; 1 Two or more races, non-Hispanic/Latino). Average age 25. 67 applicants, 73% accepted, 39 enrolled. In 2016, 66 master's awarded. *Degree requirements:* For master's, written and oral project (for systems advisory), written research paper (for tax services). *Entrance requirements:* For master's, GMAT, 3 letters of recommendation, resume. Additional exam requirements/recommendations for international students: Required—TOEFL (minimum score 79 iBT), IELTS (minimum score 6.5). *Application deadline:* For fall admission, 4/1 for domestic students; for summer admission, 4/1 for domestic students. Applications are processed on a rolling basis. Application fee: $60. Electronic applications accepted. *Expenses:* Contact institution. *Financial support:* Teaching assistantships, scholarships/grants, and unspecified assistantships available. Financial award application deadline: 3/15; financial award applicants required to submit FAFSA. *Unit head:* Dr. David Mautz, Department Chair, 910-962-2280, Fax: 910-962-3663, E-mail: mautzr@uncw.edu. *Application contact:* Dr. William Kerler, Program Director, 910-962-7632, Fax: 910-962-3663, E-mail: kerlerw@uncw.edu.
Website: http://www.csb.uncw.edu/msa/index.html

University of Northern Colorado, Graduate School, Monfort College of Business, Greeley, CO 80639. Offers accounting (MA); general business management (MBA); healthcare administration (MBA); human resources management (MBA). *Accreditation:* AACSB. *Unit head:* Donald Gudmundson, Dean, 970-351-2411, E-mail: don.gudmundson@unco.edu. *Application contact:* Linda Sisson, Graduate Student Admission Coordinator, 970-351-1807, Fax: 970-351-2371, E-mail: linda.sisson@unco.edu.
Website: http://mcb.unco.edu/

University of Northern Iowa, Graduate College, College of Business Administration, M Acc Program in Accounting, Cedar Falls, IA 50614. Offers M Acc. *Degree requirements:* For master's, thesis or alternative. *Entrance requirements:* For master's, GMAT. Additional exam requirements/recommendations for international students: Required—TOEFL (minimum score 575 paper-based; 89 iBT).

University of North Florida, Coggin College of Business, M Acc Program, Jacksonville, FL 32224. Offers M Acc. *Accreditation:* AACSB. *Program availability:* Part-time, evening/weekend. *Faculty:* 14 full-time (2 women), 1 part-time/adjunct (0 women). *Students:* 20 full-time (11 women), 34 part-time (16 women); includes 11 minority (3 Black or African American, non-Hispanic/Latino; 3 Asian, non-Hispanic/Latino; 3 Hispanic/Latino; 2 Two or more races, non-Hispanic/Latino), 1 international. Average age 29. 51 applicants, 51% accepted, 16 enrolled. In 2016, 21 master's awarded. *Entrance requirements:* For master's, GMAT or GRE, U.S. bachelor's degree from regionally-accredited university or equivalent foreign degree. Additional exam requirements/recommendations for international students: Required—TOEFL (minimum score 550 paper-based; 79 iBT). *Application deadline:* For fall admission, 8/1 priority date for domestic students, 5/1 for international students; for spring admission, 12/1 priority date for domestic students, 10/1 for international students; for summer admission, 3/15 priority date for domestic students, 2/1 for international students. Application fee: $30. Electronic applications accepted. Tuition and fees vary according to course load, campus/location and program. *Financial support:* In 2016–17, 9 students received support. Career-related internships or fieldwork, Federal Work-Study, and tuition waivers (partial) available. Financial award application deadline: 4/1; financial award applicants required to submit FAFSA. *Faculty research:* Enterprise-wide risk management, accounting input in the strategic planning process, accounting information systems, taxation issues in lawsuits and damage awards, database design. *Total annual research expenditures:* $1,206. *Unit head:* Dr. David Jaeger, Chair, 904-620-2630, E-mail: djaeger@unf.edu. *Application contact:* Dr. Amanda Pascale, Director, The Graduate School, 904-620-1360, Fax: 904-620-1362, E-mail: graduateschool@unf.edu.
Website: http://www.unf.edu/coggin/academics/graduate/macc.aspx

University of North Florida, Coggin College of Business, MBA Program, Jacksonville, FL 32224. Offers accounting (MBA); construction management (MBA); e-commerce (MBA); economics (MBA); finance (MBA); human resource management (MBA); international business (MBA); logistics (MBA); management applications (MBA). *Accreditation:* AACSB. *Program availability:* Part-time, evening/weekend. *Faculty:* 16 full-time (4 women), 1 (woman) part-time/adjunct. *Students:* 105 full-time (50 women), 162 part-time (68 women); includes 57 minority (14 Black or African American, non-Hispanic/Latino; 1 American Indian or Alaska Native, non-Hispanic/Latino; 17 Asian, non-Hispanic/Latino; 18 Hispanic/Latino; 7 Two or more races, non-Hispanic/Latino), 41 international. Average age 28. 231 applicants, 46% accepted, 84 enrolled. In 2016, 114 master's awarded. *Entrance requirements:* For master's, GMAT or GRE, U.S. bachelor's degree from regionally-accredited university or equivalent foreign degree. Additional exam requirements/recommendations for international students: Required—TOEFL (minimum score 550 paper-based; 79 iBT). *Application deadline:* For fall admission, 8/1 priority date for domestic students, 5/1 for international students; for spring admission, 12/1 priority date for domestic students, 10/1 for international students; for summer admission, 4/29 priority date for domestic students, 2/1 for international students. Application fee: $30. Tuition and fees vary according to course load, campus/location and program. *Financial support:* In 2016–17, 22 students received support, including 1 research assistantship (averaging $2,501 per year); teaching assistantships, Federal Work-Study, and tuition waivers (partial) also available. Support available to part-time students. Financial award application deadline: 4/1; financial award applicants required to submit FAFSA. *Faculty research:* Performance measures, costing, and inventory issues in logistics and supply chain management; inter-organizational systems; international management and marketing practices; e-commerce; organizational learning and socialization processes. *Total annual research expenditures:* $17,654. *Unit head:* Dr. Parvez Ahmed, Graduate Program Director, 904-620-1678, E-mail: pahmed@unf.edu. *Application contact:* Amy Bishop, MSM Advisor, 904-620-2575, Fax: 904-620-2832, E-mail: coggin.students@unf.edu.
Website: http://www.unf.edu/graduateschool/academics/programs/MBA.aspx

University of North Texas, Robert B. Toulouse School of Graduate Studies, Denton, TX 76203-5459. Offers accounting (MS); applied anthropology (MA, MS); applied behavior analysis (Certificate); applied geography (MA); applied technology and performance improvement (M Ed, MS); art education (MA); art history (MA); art museum education (Certificate); arts leadership (Certificate); audiology (Au D); behavior analysis (MS); behavioral science (PhD); biochemistry and molecular biology (MS); biology (MA, MS); biomedical engineering (MS); business analysis (MS); chemistry (MS); clinical health psychology (PhD); communication studies (MA, MS); computer engineering (MS); computer science (MS); counseling (M Ed, MS), including clinical mental health counseling (MS), college and university counseling, elementary school counseling, secondary school counseling; creative writing (MA); criminal justice (MS); curriculum and instruction (M Ed); decision sciences (MBA); design (MA, MFA), including fashion design (MFA), innovation studies, interior design (MFA); early childhood studies (MS); economics (MS); educational leadership (M Ed, Ed D); educational psychology (MS, PhD), including family studies (MS), gifted and talented (MS), human development (MS), learning and cognition (MS), research, measurement and evaluation (MS); electrical engineering (MS); emergency management (MPA); engineering technology (MS); English (MA); English as a second language (MA); environmental science (MS); finance (MBA, MS); financial management (MPA); French (MA); health services management (MBA); higher education (M Ed, Ed D); history (MA, MS); hospitality management (MS); human resources management (MPA); information science (MS); information systems (PhD); information technologies (MBA); interdisciplinary studies (MA, MS); international studies (MA); international sustainable tourism (MS); jazz studies (MM); journalism (MA, MJ, Graduate Certificate), including interactive and virtual digital communication (Graduate Certificate), narrative journalism (Graduate Certificate), public relations (Graduate Certificate); kinesiology (MS); linguistics (MA); local government management (MPA); logistics (PhD); logistics and supply chain management (MBA); long-term care, senior housing, and aging services (MA); management (PhD); marketing (MBA); mathematics (MA, MS); mechanical and energy engineering (MS, PhD); music (MA), including ethnomusicology, music theory, musicology, performance; music composition (PhD); music education (MM Ed, PhD); nonprofit management (MPA); operations and supply chain management (MBA); performance (MM, DMA); philosophy (MA); political science (MA); professional and technical communication (MA); radio, television and film (MA, MFA); rehabilitation counseling (Certificate); sociology (MA); Spanish (MA); special education (M Ed); speech-language pathology (MA); strategic management (MBA); studio art (MFA); teaching (M Ed); MBA/MS. *Program availability:* Part-time, evening/weekend, online learning. Terminal master's awarded for partial completion of doctoral program. *Degree requirements:* For master's, variable foreign language requirement, comprehensive exam (for some programs), thesis (for some programs); for doctorate, variable foreign language requirement, comprehensive exam (for some programs), thesis/dissertation; for other advanced degree, variable foreign language requirement, comprehensive exam (for some programs). *Entrance requirements:* For master's and doctorate, GRE, GMAT. Additional exam requirements/recommendations for international students: Required—TOEFL (minimum score 550 paper-based; 79 iBT). Electronic applications accepted.

University of North Texas at Dallas, Graduate School, Dallas, TX 75241. Offers accounting (MBA); counseling (M Ed, MS); criminal justice (MS); curriculum and instruction (M Ed); educational administration (M Ed); human resources and organizational behavior (MBA); public leadership (MS); strategic management (MBA).

University of Notre Dame, Mendoza College of Business, Master of Science in Accountancy Program, Notre Dame, IN 46556. Offers assurance and advisory services (MSA); tax services (MSA). *Accreditation:* AACSB. *Faculty:* 38 full-time (8 women), 15 part-time/adjunct (3 women). *Students:* 95 full-time (39 women); includes 16 minority (1 Black or African American, non-Hispanic/Latino; 1 American Indian or Alaska Native, non-Hispanic/Latino; 1 Asian, non-Hispanic/Latino; 13 Hispanic/Latino), 20 international. Average age 22. 391 applicants, 31% accepted, 95 enrolled. In 2016, 93 master's awarded. *Entrance requirements:* For master's, GMAT, essay, two recommendations, transcripts from all colleges or universities attended, resume. Additional exam requirements/recommendations for international students: Required—TOEFL (minimum score 630 paper-based; 109 iBT), IELTS (minimum score 7.5). *Application deadline:* For fall admission, 10/1 for domestic and international students; for spring admission, 5/1 for domestic and international students. Applications are processed on a rolling basis. Application fee: $50 ($100 for international students). Electronic applications accepted. *Expenses:* Contact institution. *Financial support:* In 2016–17, 88 students received support, including 88 fellowships (averaging $15,748 per year); scholarships/grants and unspecified assistantships also available. Financial award application deadline: 2/28; financial award applicants required to submit FAFSA. *Faculty research:* Stock valuation, accounting information in decision-making, choice of accounting method, taxes cost on capital. *Unit head:* Dr. Katherine Spiess, Associate Dean, Graduate Business Programs, 574-631-3759, E-mail: spiess.1@nd.edu. *Application contact:* Kristin McAndrew, Director of Admissions, Graduate Business Programs, 574-631-8488, E-mail: kmcadre@nd.edu.
Website: http://mendoza.nd.edu/programs/specialized-masters/ms-in-accountancy/

University of Oklahoma, Price College of Business, John T. Steed School of Accounting, Norman, OK 73019. Offers M Acc. *Accreditation:* AACSB. *Program availability:* Part-time, 100% online. *Faculty:* 12 full-time (4 women). *Students:* 25 full-time (11 women), 3 part-time (2 women); includes 7 minority (1 Black or African American, non-Hispanic/Latino; 1 American Indian or Alaska Native, non-Hispanic/Latino; 3 Asian, non-Hispanic/Latino; 2 Two or more races, non-Hispanic/Latino), 6 international. Average age 27. 27 applicants, 41% accepted, 11 enrolled. In 2016, 11 master's awarded. *Entrance requirements:* For master's, GMAT or GRE, resume, statement of goals, 3 letters of recommendation. Additional exam requirements/recommendations for international students: Required—TOEFL (minimum score 100 iBT) or IELTS (minimum score 7). *Application deadline:* For fall admission, 6/15 for domestic students, 3/1 for international students; for spring admission, 11/15 for domestic students, 8/1 for international students; for summer admission, 3/15 for domestic students, 1/1 for international students. Applications are processed on a rolling basis. Application fee: $50 ($100 for international students). Electronic applications accepted. *Expenses:* Tuition, state resident: full-time $4886; part-time $203.60 per credit hour. Tuition, nonresident: full-time $18,989; part-time $791.20 per credit hour. *Required fees:* $3283; $126.25 per credit hour. $126.50 per semester. *Financial support:* In 2016–17, 12 students received support, including 4 research assistantships with partial tuition reimbursements available (averaging $16,364 per year), 10 teaching assistantships with partial tuition reimbursements available (averaging $11,896 per year); career-related internships or fieldwork, scholarships/grants, and unspecified assistantships also available. Support available to part-time students. Financial award application deadline: 6/1; financial award applicants required to submit FAFSA. *Faculty research:* Tax professional judgment and taxpayer compliance; financial disclosure and reporting decisions; regulation and auditing profession; behavioral issues of auditor-client dyad; market based accounting research. *Unit head:* Ervin Black, Director/Chair, 405-325-2401, Fax: 405-325-7348, E-mail: ervblack@ou.edu. *Application contact:* Jennifer Aragon, Academic Advisor, 405-325-2074, Fax: 405-325-7118, E-mail: jhardman@ou.edu.
Website: http://www.ou.edu/content/price/accounting.html

University of Oklahoma, Price College of Business, Program in Business Administration, Norman, OK 73019. Offers accounting (PhD); business administration (MBA, PhD); entrepreneurship and economic development (PhD); finance (PhD); management and international business (PhD); management of information systems (PhD); marketing/supply chain (PhD); JD/MBA; MBA/MS. *Accreditation:* AACSB. *Program availability:* Part-time, evening/weekend. *Students:* 122 full-time (27 women),

146 part-time (30 women); includes 36 minority (5 Black or African American, non-Hispanic/Latino; 6 American Indian or Alaska Native, non-Hispanic/Latino; 8 Asian, non-Hispanic/Latino; 11 Hispanic/Latino; 6 Two or more races, non-Hispanic/Latino), 37 international. Average age 30. 261 applicants, 27% accepted, 59 enrolled. In 2016, 127 master's, 5 doctorates awarded. *Degree requirements:* For doctorate, comprehensive exam, thesis/dissertation. *Entrance requirements:* For master's, GMAT or GRE, resume, statement of goals; for doctorate, GMAT or GRE, resume, statement of goals, 3 letters of recommendation. Additional exam requirements/recommendations for international students: Required—TOEFL (minimum score 100 iBT) or IELTS (minimum score 7). *Application deadline:* For fall admission, 11/15 priority date for domestic and international students; for spring admission, 3/15 priority date for domestic and international students; for summer admission, 5/15 for domestic and international students. Application fee: $50 ($100 for international students). Electronic applications accepted. *Expenses:* Contact institution. *Financial support:* In 2016–17, 107 students received support, including 10 fellowships with partial tuition reimbursements available (averaging $3,295 per year); research assistantships with full and partial tuition reimbursements available, teaching assistantships with full and partial tuition reimbursements available, career-related internships or fieldwork, scholarships/grants, health care benefits, and unspecified assistantships also available. Support available to part-time students. Financial award application deadline: 6/1; financial award applicants required to submit FAFSA. *Faculty research:* Energy finance; international accounting; organizational behavior and entrepreneurship; management information systems; supply chain. *Unit head:* Laku Chidambaram, Associate Dean for Academic Programs and Engagement. *Application contact:* Director of MBA Admissions, 405-325-5623. Website: http://www.ou.edu/content/price/divisions/graduate.html

University of Oregon, Graduate School, Charles H. Lundquist College of Business, Department of Accounting, Eugene, OR 97403. Offers M Actg, PhD. *Accreditation:* AACSB. *Program availability:* Part-time. *Degree requirements:* For doctorate, thesis/dissertation, 2 comprehensive exams. *Entrance requirements:* For master's, GMAT, minimum GPA of 3.0, bachelor's degree in accounting or equivalent; for doctorate, GMAT. Additional exam requirements/recommendations for international students: Required—TOEFL. *Faculty research:* Empirical financial accounting, effects of regulation on accounting standards, use of protocol analysis as a research methodology in accounting.

University of Pennsylvania, Wharton School, Accounting Department, Philadelphia, PA 19104. Offers MBA, PhD. *Accreditation:* AACSB. Terminal master's awarded for partial completion of doctoral program. *Degree requirements:* For doctorate, thesis/dissertation. *Entrance requirements:* For master's, GMAT; for doctorate, GMAT or GRE. *Expenses: Tuition:* Full-time $31,068; part-time $5762 per course. *Required fees:* $3200; $336 per course. Full-time tuition and fees vary according to degree level, program and student level. Part-time tuition and fees vary according to course load, degree level and program. *Faculty research:* Financial reporting, information disclosure, performance measurement, executive compensation, corporate governance.

University of Phoenix–Atlanta Campus, School of Business, Sandy Springs, GA 30350-4147. Offers accounting (MBA); business administration (MBA); global management (MBA); human resources management (MBA, MM); management (MM); marketing (MBA); public administration (MM). *Accreditation:* ACBSP. *Program availability:* Evening/weekend, online learning. *Degree requirements:* For master's, thesis (for some programs). *Entrance requirements:* For master's, minimum undergraduate GPA of 3.0, 3 years of work experience. Additional exam requirements/recommendations for international students: Required—TOEFL (minimum score 550 paper-based; 79 iBT).

University of Phoenix–Augusta Campus, School of Business, Augusta, GA 30909-4583. Offers accounting (MBA); business administration (MBA); business and management (MBA, MM); global management (MBA); human resources management (MBA, MM); management (MM); marketing (MBA); public administration (MBA, MM). *Accreditation:* ACBSP. *Program availability:* Online learning.

University of Phoenix–Bay Area Campus, School of Business, San Jose, CA 95134-1805. Offers accountancy (MS); accounting (MBA); business administration (MBA, DBA); energy management (MBA); global management (MBA); health care management (MBA); human resource management (MBA); human resources management (MM); management (MM); marketing (MBA); organizational leadership (DM); project management (MBA); public administration (MPA); technology management (MBA). *Accreditation:* ACBSP. *Program availability:* Evening/weekend, online learning. *Degree requirements:* For master's, thesis (for some programs). *Entrance requirements:* For master's, minimum undergraduate GPA of 3.0, 3 years of work experience. Additional exam requirements/recommendations for international students: Required—TOEFL (minimum score 550 paper-based; 79 iBT). Electronic applications accepted.

University of Phoenix–Central Valley Campus, School of Business, Fresno, CA 93720-1552. Offers accounting (MBA); business administration (MBA); global management (MBA); human resources management (MBA, MM); management (MM); marketing (MBA); public administration (MBA, MM). *Accreditation:* ACBSP.

University of Phoenix–Charlotte Campus, School of Business, Charlotte, NC 28273-3409. Offers accounting (MBA); business administration (MBA); global management (MBA). *Accreditation:* ACBSP. *Program availability:* Evening/weekend. *Degree requirements:* For master's, thesis (for some programs). *Entrance requirements:* For master's, minimum undergraduate GPA of 3.0, 3 years work experience. Additional exam requirements/recommendations for international students: Required—TOEFL (minimum score 550 paper-based; 79 iBT). Electronic applications accepted.

University of Phoenix–Colorado Campus, School of Business, Lone Tree, CO 80124-5453. Offers accountancy (MSA); accounting (MBA); business administration (MBA); e-business (MBA); global management (MBA); human resources management (MBA, MM); management (MM); marketing (MBA); public administration (MBA, MM). *Accreditation:* ACBSP. *Program availability:* Evening/weekend, online learning. *Degree requirements:* For master's, thesis (for some programs). *Entrance requirements:* For master's, minimum undergraduate GPA of 3.0, 3 years work experience. Additional exam requirements/recommendations for international students: Required—TOEFL (minimum score 550 paper-based; 79 iBT). Electronic applications accepted.

University of Phoenix–Colorado Springs Downtown Campus, School of Business, Colorado Springs, CO 80903. Offers accounting (MBA); business administration (MBA); global management (MBA); human resources management (MBA, MM); management (MM); marketing (MBA); public administration (MM). *Program availability:* Evening/weekend. *Degree requirements:* For master's, thesis (for some programs). *Entrance requirements:* For master's, minimum undergraduate GPA of 3.0, 3 years of work experience. Additional exam requirements/recommendations for international students: Required—TOEFL (minimum score 550 paper-based; 79 iBT). Electronic applications accepted.

University of Phoenix–Columbus Georgia Campus, School of Business, Columbus, GA 31909. Offers accounting (MBA); business administration (MBA); global management (MBA); human resources management (MBA, MM); management (MM); marketing (MBA); public administration (MBA). *Accreditation:* ACBSP. *Program availability:* Evening/weekend. *Degree requirements:* For master's, thesis (for some programs). *Entrance requirements:* For master's, minimum undergraduate GPA of 3.0, 3 years of work experience. Additional exam requirements/recommendations for international students: Required—TOEFL (minimum score 550 paper-based; 79 iBT). Electronic applications accepted.

University of Phoenix–Dallas Campus, School of Business, Dallas, TX 75251. Offers accounting (MBA); business administration (MBA); global management (MBA); human resources management (MBA, MM); management (MM); marketing (MBA); public administration (MBA, MM). *Accreditation:* ACBSP. *Program availability:* Evening/weekend, online learning. *Degree requirements:* For master's, thesis (for some programs). *Entrance requirements:* For master's, 3 years of work experience, minimum undergraduate GPA of 3.0. Additional exam requirements/recommendations for international students: Required—TOEFL (minimum score 550 paper-based; 79 iBT). Electronic applications accepted.

University of Phoenix–Hawaii Campus, School of Business, Honolulu, HI 96813-3800. Offers accounting (MBA); business administration (MBA); global management (MBA); human resources management (MBA, MM); management (MM); marketing (MBA); public administration (MBA, MM). *Accreditation:* ACBSP. *Program availability:* Evening/weekend. *Degree requirements:* For master's, thesis (for some programs). *Entrance requirements:* For master's, minimum undergraduate GPA of 3.0, 3 years of work experience. Additional exam requirements/recommendations for international students: Required—TOEFL (minimum score 550 paper-based; 79 iBT). Electronic applications accepted.

University of Phoenix–Houston Campus, School of Business, Houston, TX 77079-2004. Offers accounting (MBA); business administration (MBA); global management (MBA); human resources management (MBA, MM); management (MM); marketing (MBA); public administration (MBA, MM). *Accreditation:* ACBSP. *Program availability:* Evening/weekend, online learning. *Degree requirements:* For master's, thesis (for some programs). *Entrance requirements:* For master's, 3 years of work experience, minimum undergraduate GPA of 3.0. Additional exam requirements/recommendations for international students: Required—TOEFL (minimum score 550 paper-based; 79 iBT). Electronic applications accepted.

University of Phoenix–Jersey City Campus, School of Business, Jersey City, NJ 07310. Offers accounting (MBA); business administration (MBA); global management (MBA); human resources management (MBA, MM); management (MM); marketing (MBA); public administration (MBA, MM). *Accreditation:* ACBSP.

University of Phoenix–Las Vegas Campus, School of Business, Las Vegas, NV 89135. Offers accounting (MBA); business administration (MBA); global management (MBA); human resources management (MBA, MM); management (MM); marketing (MBA); public administration (MM). *Accreditation:* ACBSP. *Program availability:* Evening/weekend, online learning. *Degree requirements:* For master's, thesis (for some programs). *Entrance requirements:* For master's, minimum undergraduate GPA of 3.0, 3 years of work experience. Additional exam requirements/recommendations for international students: Required—TOEFL (minimum score 550 paper-based; 79 iBT). Electronic applications accepted.

University of Phoenix–New Mexico Campus, School of Business, Albuquerque, NM 87113-1570. Offers accounting (MBA); business administration (MBA); global management (MBA); human resources management (MBA, MM); management (MM); marketing (MBA). *Accreditation:* ACBSP. *Program availability:* Evening/weekend. *Degree requirements:* For master's, thesis (for some programs). *Entrance requirements:* For master's, 3 years of work experience, minimum undergraduate GPA of 3.0. Additional exam requirements/recommendations for international students: Required—TOEFL (minimum score 550 paper-based; 79 iBT). Electronic applications accepted.

University of Phoenix–North Florida Campus, School of Business, Jacksonville, FL 32216-0959. Offers accounting (MBA); business administration (MBA); global management (MBA); human resources management (MBA, MM); management (MM); marketing (MBA); public administration (MBA, MM). *Accreditation:* ACBSP. *Program availability:* Evening/weekend. *Degree requirements:* For master's, thesis (for some programs). *Entrance requirements:* For master's, minimum undergraduate GPA of 3.0, 3 years work experience. Additional exam requirements/recommendations for international students: Required—TOEFL (minimum score 550 paper-based; 79 iBT). Electronic applications accepted.

University of Phoenix–Online Campus, School of Business, Phoenix, AZ 85034-7209. Offers accountancy (MS); accounting (MBA, Certificate); business administration (MBA); energy management (MBA); global management (MBA); health care management (MBA); human resource management (MBA, Certificate); human resources management (MM); management (MM); marketing (MBA, Certificate); project management (MBA, Certificate); public administration (MBA, MM); technology management (MBA). *Program availability:* Evening/weekend, online learning. *Entrance requirements:* Additional exam requirements/recommendations for international students: Required—TOEFL, TOEIC (Test of English as an International Communication), Berlitz Online English Proficiency Exam, PTE, or IELTS. Electronic applications accepted. *Expenses:* Contact institution.

University of Phoenix–Phoenix Campus, School of Business, Tempe, AZ 85282-2371. Offers accounting (MBA, MS, Certificate); business administration (MBA); energy management (MBA); global management (MBA); health care management (MBA); human resource management (MBA, Certificate); management (MM); marketing (MBA); project management (MBA); technology management (MBA). *Program availability:* Evening/weekend, online learning. *Entrance requirements:* Additional exam requirements/recommendations for international students: Required—TOEFL, TOEIC (Test of English as an International Communication), Berlitz Online English Proficiency Exam, PTE, or IELTS. Electronic applications accepted. *Expenses:* Contact institution.

University of Phoenix–Sacramento Valley Campus, School of Business, Sacramento, CA 95833-4334. Offers accounting (MBA); business administration (MBA); global management (MBA); human resources management (MBA, MM); management (MM); marketing (MBA); public administration (MBA, MM). *Accreditation:* ACBSP. *Program availability:* Evening/weekend. *Degree requirements:* For master's, thesis (for some programs). *Entrance requirements:* For master's, minimum undergraduate GPA of 3.0, 3 years work experience. Additional exam requirements/recommendations for international students: Required—TOEFL (minimum score 550 paper-based; 79 iBT). Electronic applications accepted.

University of Phoenix–San Antonio Campus, School of Business, San Antonio, TX 78230. Offers accounting (MBA); business administration (MBA); e-business (MBA); global management (MBA); human resources management (MBA, MM); management (MM); marketing (MBA); public administration (MBA, MM). *Accreditation:* ACBSP.

University of Phoenix–San Diego Campus, School of Business, San Diego, CA 92123. Offers accounting (MBA); business administration (MBA); global management (MBA); human resources management (MBA, MM); management (MM); marketing (MBA); public administration (MBA). *Accreditation:* ACBSP. *Program availability:* Evening/weekend. *Degree requirements:* For master's, thesis (for some programs). *Entrance requirements:* For master's, 3 years of work experience, minimum undergraduate GPA of 3.0. Additional exam requirements/recommendations for international students: Required—TOEFL (minimum score 550 paper-based; 79 iBT). Electronic applications accepted.

University of Phoenix–Southern Arizona Campus, School of Business, Tucson, AZ 85711. Offers accountancy (MS); accounting (MBA); business administration (MBA); global management (MBA); human resources management (MBA); management (MM); marketing (MBA). *Accreditation:* ACBSP. *Program availability:* Evening/weekend. *Degree requirements:* For master's, thesis (for some programs). *Entrance requirements:* For master's, minimum undergraduate GPA of 3.0, 3 years of work experience. Additional exam requirements/recommendations for international students: Required—TOEFL (minimum score 550 paper-based; 79 iBT). Electronic applications accepted.

University of Phoenix–Southern California Campus, School of Business, Costa Mesa, CA 92626. Offers accounting (MBA); business administration (MBA); energy management (MBA); global management (MBA); health care management (MBA); human resource management (MBA); management (MM); marketing (MBA); project management (MBA); technology management (MBA). *Program availability:* Evening/weekend, online learning. *Entrance requirements:* Additional exam requirements/recommendations for international students: Required—TOEFL, TOEIC (Test of English as an International Communication), Berlitz Online English Proficiency Exam, PTE, or IELTS. Electronic applications accepted. *Expenses:* Contact institution.

University of Phoenix–South Florida Campus, School of Business, Miramar, FL 33027-4145. Offers accounting (MBA); business administration (MBA); global management (MBA); human resource management (MBA); human resources management (MM); management (MM); marketing (MBA); public administration (MBA, MM). *Accreditation:* ACBSP. *Program availability:* Evening/weekend. *Degree requirements:* For master's, thesis (for some programs). *Entrance requirements:* For master's, minimum undergraduate GPA of 3.0, 3 years work experience. Additional exam requirements/recommendations for international students: Required—TOEFL (minimum score 550 paper-based; 79 iBT). Electronic applications accepted.

University of Phoenix–Utah Campus, School of Business, Salt Lake City, UT 84123-4642. Offers accounting (MBA); business administration (MBA); global management (MBA); human resource management (MBA, MM); management (MM); marketing (MBA); technology management (MBA). *Accreditation:* ACBSP. *Program availability:* Evening/weekend. *Degree requirements:* For master's, thesis (for some programs). *Entrance requirements:* For master's, minimum undergraduate GPA of 3.0, 3 years of work experience. Additional exam requirements/recommendations for international students: Required—TOEFL (minimum score 550 paper-based; 79 iBT). Electronic applications accepted.

University of Phoenix–Washington D.C. Campus, School of Business, Washington, DC 20001. Offers accountancy (MS); business administration (MBA, DBA); human resources management (MM); management (MM); organizational leadership (DM); public administration (MPA). *Accreditation:* ACBSP.

University of Pittsburgh, Katz Graduate School of Business, Doctoral Program in Business Administration, Pittsburgh, PA 15260. Offers accounting (PhD); business analytics and operations (PhD); finance (PhD); information systems and technology management (PhD); marketing (PhD); organizational behavior and human resources (PhD); strategic management (PhD). *Accreditation:* AACSB. *Program availability:* Evening/weekend. *Faculty:* 88 full-time (27 women), 42 part-time/adjunct (15 women). *Students:* 51 full-time (23 women), 1 part-time (0 women); includes 4 minority (1 Black or African American, non-Hispanic/Latino; 2 Asian, non-Hispanic/Latino; 1 Two or more races, non-Hispanic/Latino), 31 international. Average age 31. 344 applicants, 6% accepted, 9 enrolled. In 2016, 5 doctorates awarded. *Degree requirements:* For doctorate, comprehensive exam, thesis/dissertation, student teaching. *Entrance requirements:* For doctorate, GMAT or GRE, 3 recommendations, statement of purpose, transcripts of all previous course work and degrees. Additional exam requirements/recommendations for international students: Required—TOEFL (minimum score 100 iBT) or IELTS (minimum score 7.0). *Application deadline:* For fall admission, 4/1 priority date for domestic students, 2/1 priority date for international students. Applications are processed on a rolling basis. Application fee: $50. Electronic applications accepted. *Expenses:* Contact institution. *Financial support:* In 2016–17, 40 students received support, including 27 research assistantships with full tuition reimbursements available (averaging $26,000 per year), 9 teaching assistantships with full tuition reimbursements available (averaging $26,700 per year); Federal Work-Study, scholarships/grants, health care benefits, and unspecified assistantships also available. Financial award application deadline: 6/1; financial award applicants required to submit FAFSA. *Faculty research:* Accounting systems/financial reporting, corporate finance, shopper marketing/consumer behavior, management information systems, organizational behavior and entrepreneurship. *Total annual research expenditures:* $493,036. *Unit head:* Dr. Arjang A. Assad, Dean, 412-648-1556, Fax: 412-648-1552, E-mail: aassad@katz.pitt.edu. *Application contact:* Dr. Dennis Galletta, Director, 412-648-1699, Fax: 412-648-3633, E-mail: galletta@katz.pitt.edu.
Website: http://www.business.pitt.edu/katz/phd/

See Display on page 160 and Close-Up on page 189.

University of Pittsburgh, Katz Graduate School of Business, Master of Science in Accounting Program, Pittsburgh, PA 15260. Offers MS. *Program availability:* Part-time, blended/hybrid learning. *Faculty:* 88 full-time (27 women), 42 part-time/adjunct (15 women). *Students:* 117 full-time (84 women), 10 part-time (6 women); includes 5 minority (3 Asian, non-Hispanic/Latino; 1 Hispanic/Latino; 1 Two or more races, non-Hispanic/Latino), 86 international. Average age 25. 363 applicants, 44% accepted, 66 enrolled. In 2016, 84 master's awarded. *Degree requirements:* For master's, 30 credits; minimum cumulative GPA of 3.0. *Entrance requirements:* For master's, GMAT, GRE. Additional exam requirements/recommendations for international students: Required—TOEFL (minimum score 100 iBT) or IELTS (minimum score 7.0). *Application deadline:* For fall admission, 4/1 priority date for domestic students, 2/1 priority date for international students. Application fee: $50. Electronic applications accepted. Tuition and fees vary according to program. *Financial support:* Scholarships/grants available. Financial award application deadline: 6/1; financial award applicants required to submit FAFSA. *Faculty research:* Accounting systems/financial reporting, corporate finance, shopper marketing/consumer behavior, management information systems, organizational behavior and entrepreneurship. *Total annual research expenditures:* $493,036. *Unit head:* Sandra Douglas, Director, 412-648-1556, Fax: 412-624-5198, E-mail: srdouglas@katz.pitt.edu. *Application contact:* Jessica Quarterman, Assistant Director, 412-624-0147, E-mail: macc@katz.pitt.edu.
Website: http://www.business.pitt.edu/katz/macc/

University of Puerto Rico, Río Piedras Campus, College of Business Administration, San Juan, PR 00931-3300. Offers accounting (MBA); finance (MBA, PhD); general business (MBA); human resources management (MBA); international trade and business (MBA, PhD); marketing (MBA); operations management (MBA); quantitative methods (MBA). *Accreditation:* AACSB. *Program availability:* Part-time. *Degree requirements:* For master's, comprehensive exam, thesis or alternative, research project. *Entrance requirements:* For master's, GMAT or PAEG, minimum GPA of 3.0, letter of recommendation; for doctorate, GMAT, PAEG, minimum GPA of 3.0, master degree. *Faculty research:* Management.

University of Rhode Island, Graduate School, College of Business Administration, Kingston, RI 02881. Offers accounting (MS); business administration (PhD), including finance and insurance, marketing, supply chain management; finance (MBA, MS); general business (MBA); health care management (MBA); management (MBA); marketing (MBA); oceanography (MBA); strategic innovation (MBA); supply chain management (MBA); Pharm D/MBA. *Accreditation:* AACSB. *Program availability:* Part-time, evening/weekend. *Faculty:* 57 full-time (24 women). *Students:* 94 full-time (45 women), 166 part-time (84 women); includes 37 minority (6 Black or African American, non-Hispanic/Latino; 1 American Indian or Alaska Native, non-Hispanic/Latino; 22 Asian, non-Hispanic/Latino; 3 Hispanic/Latino; 5 Two or more races, non-Hispanic/Latino), 18 international. In 2016, 124 master's, 4 doctorates awarded. *Degree requirements:* For master's, comprehensive exam (for some programs), thesis optional; for doctorate, comprehensive exam, thesis/dissertation. *Entrance requirements:* For master's, GMAT or GRE, 2 letters of recommendation, resume; for doctorate, GMAT or GRE, 3 letters of recommendation, resume. Additional exam requirements/recommendations for international students: Required—TOEFL. *Application deadline:* For fall admission, 2/1 for domestic and international students. Application fee: $65. Electronic applications accepted. *Expenses:* Tuition, state resident: full-time $11,796; part-time $655 per credit. Tuition, nonresident: full-time $24,206; part-time $1345 per credit. *Required fees:* $1546; $44 per credit. One-time fee: $155 full-time; $35 part-time. *Financial support:* In 2016–17, 17 teaching assistantships with tuition reimbursements (averaging $15,347 per year) were awarded; research assistantships also available. Financial award application deadline: 2/1; financial award applicants required to submit FAFSA. *Unit head:* Dr. Maling Ebrahimpour, Dean, 401-874-4348, Fax: 401-874-4312, E-mail: mebrahimpour@uri.edu. *Application contact:* Lisa Lancellotta, Coordinator, MBA Programs, 401-874-4241, Fax: 401-874-4312, E-mail: mba@uri.edu.
Website: http://www.cba.uri.edu/

See Display on page 161 and Close-Up on page 191.

University of Rochester, Simon Business School, Doctoral Program in Business Administration, Rochester, NY 14627. Offers accounting (PhD); computer information systems (PhD); finance (PhD); marketing (PhD); operations management (PhD). *Accreditation:* AACSB. *Faculty:* 66 full-time (13 women), 22 part-time/adjunct (2 women). *Students:* 52 full-time (19 women); includes 2 minority (both Asian, non-Hispanic/Latino), 42 international. Average age 29. 210 applicants, 16% accepted, 15 enrolled. In 2016, 6 doctorates awarded. *Degree requirements:* For doctorate, comprehensive exam, thesis/dissertation, qualifying exam. *Entrance requirements:* For doctorate, GMAT or GRE. Additional exam requirements/recommendations for international students: Required—TOEFL. *Application deadline:* For fall admission, 1/5 for domestic and international students. Application fee: $100. Electronic applications accepted. *Expenses:* $1,800 per credit hour. *Financial support:* In 2016–17, 52 students received support. Fellowships, research assistantships, teaching assistantships, and tuition waivers (full) available. Financial award application deadline: 1/5. *Unit head:* Dr. Ron Kaniel, Committee Chair, 585-275-2959. *Application contact:* Sue Harris, PhD Administrator, 585-275-2959, E-mail: phdoffice@simon.rochester.edu.
Website: http://www.simon.rochester.edu/programs/phd/index.aspx

University of Rochester, Simon Business School, Full-Time Master's Program in Business Administration, Rochester, NY 14627. Offers business systems consulting (MBA); competitive and organizational strategy (MBA); computers and information systems (MBA); corporate accounting (MBA); entrepreneurship (MBA); finance (MBA); health sciences management (MBA); marketing (MBA); operations management (MBA); public accounting (MBA). *Accreditation:* AACSB. *Program availability:* Part-time, evening/weekend. *Faculty:* 66 full-time (13 women), 22 part-time/adjunct (2 women). *Students:* 202 full-time (78 women); includes 50 minority (30 Black or African American, non-Hispanic/Latino; 10 Asian, non-Hispanic/Latino; 9 Hispanic/Latino; 1 Two or more races, non-Hispanic/Latino), 107 international. Average age 27. 915 applicants, 30% accepted, 86 enrolled. In 2016, 110 master's awarded. *Entrance requirements:* For master's, GMAT/GRE. Additional exam requirements/recommendations for international students: Required—TOEFL. *Application deadline:* For fall admission, 10/15 for domestic and international students; for winter admission, 1/5 for domestic and international students; for spring admission, 3/15 for domestic and international students; for summer admission, 5/15 for domestic and international students. Applications are processed on a rolling basis. Application fee: $150. Electronic applications accepted. *Expenses:* Contact institution. *Financial support:* In 2016–17, 190 students received support. Fellowships, research assistantships, teaching assistantships, institutionally sponsored loans, scholarships/grants, and tuition waivers (full and partial) available. Financial award application deadline: 1/5; financial award applicants required to submit FAFSA. *Unit head:* Andrew Ainslie, Dean, 585-275-3316, E-mail: andrew.ainslie@simon.rochester.edu. *Application contact:* Rebekah S. Lewin, Assistant Dean of Admissions and Financial Aid, 585-275-3533, E-mail: admissions@simon.rochester.edu.
Website: http://www.simon.rochester.edu/programs/full-time-mba/index.aspx

University of Rochester, Simon Business School, Master of Science Program in Accountancy, Rochester, NY 14627. Offers MS. *Faculty:* 66 full-time (13 women), 22 part-time/adjunct (2 women). *Students:* 62 full-time (48 women); includes 4 minority (1 Black or African American, non-Hispanic/Latino; 1 Asian, non-Hispanic/Latino; 1 Hispanic/Latino; 1 Two or more races, non-Hispanic/Latino), 55 international. Average age 22. 592 applicants, 30% accepted, 62 enrolled. In 2016, 60 master's awarded. *Entrance requirements:* For master's, GMAT/GRE. Additional exam requirements/recommendations for international students: Required—TOEFL. *Application deadline:* For fall admission, 10/15 for domestic and international students; for winter admission, 1/5 for domestic and international students; for spring admission, 3/15 for domestic and international students; for summer admission, 5/15 for domestic and international students. Applications are processed on a rolling basis. Application fee: $150. Electronic applications accepted. *Expenses:* Contact institution. *Financial support:* In 2016–17, 42 students received support. Institutionally sponsored loans, scholarships/grants, and tuition waivers (partial) available. Financial award application deadline: 1/5; financial award applicants required to submit FAFSA. *Unit head:* Andrew Ainslie, Dean, 585-275-3316, E-mail: andrew.ainslie@simon.rochester.edu. *Application contact:* Rebekah S. Lewin, Assistant Dean of Admissions and Financial Aid, 585-275-3533, E-mail: admissions@simon.rochester.edu.
Website: http://www.simon.rochester.edu/programs/full-time-ms-in-accountancy/index.aspx

University of Rochester, Simon Business School, Part-Time MBA Program, Rochester, NY 14627. Offers business systems consulting (MBA); competitive and organizational strategy (MBA); computers and information systems (MBA); corporate accounting (MBA); entrepreneurship (MBA); finance (MBA); health sciences management (MBA); marketing (MBA); operations management (MBA); public accounting (MBA). *Program availability:* Part-time, evening/weekend. *Faculty:* 66 full-time (13 women), 22 part-time/adjunct (2 women). *Students:* 185 part-time (65 women); includes 29 minority (6 Black or African American, non-Hispanic/Latino; 13 Asian, non-Hispanic/Latino; 8 Hispanic/Latino; 2 Two or more races, non-Hispanic/Latino), 9

international. Average age 32. 33 applicants, 100% accepted, 31 enrolled. In 2016, 70 master's awarded. *Entrance requirements:* For master's, GRE or GMAT. *Application deadline:* For fall admission, 8/1 for domestic students; for spring admission, 2/15 for domestic students. Applications are processed on a rolling basis. Application fee: $150. Electronic applications accepted. *Expenses:* $1,800 per credit hour. *Financial support:* In 2016–17, 75 students received support. Scholarships/grants and tuition waivers (partial) available. Financial award applicants required to submit CSS PROFILE or FAFSA. *Unit head:* Andrew Ainslie, Dean, 585-275-3316, E-mail: andrew.ainslie@simon.rochester.edu. *Application contact:* Molly Mesko, Executive Director, EMBA and Part-Time Programs, 585-275-4277, E-mail: molly.mesko@simon.rochester.edu.
Website: http://www.simon.rochester.edu/programs/ptmba/index.aspx

University of St. Francis, College of Business and Health Administration, School of Business, Joliet, IL 60435-6169. Offers accounting (MBA, Certificate); business analytics (MBA, Certificate); finance (MBA, Certificate); health administration (MBA); human resource management (MBA); logistics (Certificate); management (MBA, MSM); training and development (MBA); transportation and logistics (MBA). *Accreditation:* ACBSP. *Program availability:* Part-time, evening/weekend, 100% online, blended/hybrid learning. *Faculty:* 6 full-time (3 women), 12 part-time/adjunct (6 women). *Students:* 78 full-time (28 women), 110 part-time (62 women); includes 41 minority (22 Black or African American, non-Hispanic/Latino; 3 Asian, non-Hispanic/Latino; 15 Hispanic/Latino; 1 Two or more races, non-Hispanic/Latino), 8 international. Average age 36. 171 applicants, 44% accepted, 58 enrolled. In 2016, 62 master's, 3 other advanced degrees awarded. *Entrance requirements:* For master's, GMAT or 2 years of managerial experience. Additional exam requirements/recommendations for international students: Required—TOEFL (minimum score 550 paper-based; 79 iBT), IELTS (minimum score 6). *Application deadline:* Applications are processed on a rolling basis. Application fee: $30. Electronic applications accepted. Application fee is waived when completed online. *Expenses:* $798 per credit. *Financial support:* In 2016–17, 51 students received support. Career-related internships or fieldwork, scholarships/grants, tuition waivers (partial), and unspecified assistantships available. Support available to part-time students. Financial award applicants required to submit FAFSA. *Unit head:* Dr. Orlando Griego, Dean, 815-740-3395, Fax: 815-740-3537, E-mail: ogriego@stfrancis.edu. *Application contact:* Sandra Sloka, Director of Admissions for Graduate and Degree Completion Programs, 800-735-7500, Fax: 815-740-3431, E-mail: ssloka@stfrancis.edu.
Website: http://www.stfrancis.edu/academics/college-of-business-health-administration/

University of St. Thomas, Cameron School of Business, Houston, TX 77006-4696. Offers MBA, MCTM, MIB, MSA, MSF. *Program availability:* Part-time, evening/weekend. *Faculty:* 26 full-time (8 women), 7 part-time/adjunct (2 women). *Students:* 178 full-time (86 women), 222 part-time (127 women); includes 182 minority (38 Black or African American, non-Hispanic/Latino; 36 Asian, non-Hispanic/Latino; 104 Hispanic/Latino; 4 Two or more races, non-Hispanic/Latino), 115 international. Average age 31. 144 applicants, 97% accepted, 72 enrolled. In 2016, 164 master's awarded. *Degree requirements:* For master's, capstone (for some programs), additional course requirements for those sitting for state accountancy exam. *Entrance requirements:* For master's, minimum GPA of 2.5, 3 letters of recommendation. Additional exam requirements/recommendations for international students: Required—TOEFL (minimum score 550 paper-based; 79 iBT), IELTS (minimum score 6.5), PTE (minimum score 53). *Application deadline:* For fall admission, 7/15 for domestic and international students; for winter admission, 7/15 for domestic and international students; for spring admission, 11/15 for domestic students, 10/15 for international students. Applications are processed on a rolling basis. Application fee: $35. Electronic applications accepted. *Expenses: Tuition:* Full-time $20,934; part-time $1163 per credit hour. *Required fees:* $81 per semester. One-time fee: $100. Part-time tuition and fees vary according to course level, course load, campus/location and program. *Financial support:* In 2016–17, 56 students received support, including research assistantships with partial tuition reimbursements available (averaging $3,000 per year); Federal Work-Study, scholarships/grants, unspecified assistantships, and state work-study, institutional employment also available. Support available to part-time students. Financial award application deadline: 4/15; financial award applicants required to submit FAFSA. *Unit head:* Dr. Beena George, Dean, 713-525-2100, Fax: 713-525-2110, E-mail: cameron@stthom.edu. *Application contact:* Fran Wilson Mayes, Academic Coordinator, 713-525-2100, Fax: 713-525-2110, E-mail: cameron@stthom.edu.
Website: http://www.stthom.edu/Academics/Cameron_School_of_Business/Index.aqf

University of St. Thomas, Graduate Studies, Opus College of Business, Master of Science in Accountancy Program, Minneapolis, MN 55403. Offers MS. *Entrance requirements:* For master's, GMAT. Additional exam requirements/recommendations for international students: Required—TOEFL (minimum score 94 iBT), IELTS (minimum score 7). *Application deadline:* For spring admission, 5/4 for domestic students, 1/13 for international students. Applications are processed on a rolling basis. Application fee: $60. Electronic applications accepted. *Expenses: Tuition:* Full-time $19,354; part-time $1320 per credit. One-time fee: $214. Tuition and fees vary according to course load, degree level, program and reciprocity agreements. *Financial support:* Career-related internships or fieldwork and scholarships/grants available. *Unit head:* Kristine Sharockman DeVinck, Director, 651-962-4124, Fax: 651-962-4141, E-mail: msacct@stthomas.edu. *Application contact:* Cathy Davis, Program Manager, 651-962-4110, Fax: 651-962-4141, E-mail: msacct@stthomas.edu.
Website: http://www.stthomas.edu/accountancy

University of San Diego, School of Business, Programs in Accountancy and Taxation, San Diego, CA 92110-2492. Offers accountancy (MS); taxation (MS). *Program availability:* Part-time, evening/weekend. *Students:* 21 full-time (15 women), 4 part-time (1 woman); includes 4 minority (1 Asian, non-Hispanic/Latino; 2 Hispanic/Latino; 1 Two or more races, non-Hispanic/Latino), 17 international. Average age 25. In 2016, 35 master's awarded. *Entrance requirements:* For master's, GMAT (minimum score of 550), minimum GPA of 3.0. Additional exam requirements/recommendations for international students: Required—TOEFL (minimum score 580 paper-based; 92 iBT), TWE. *Application deadline:* For fall admission, 4/1 for domestic students, 6/1 for international students; for spring admission, 10/1 for domestic students, 12/1 for international students. Application fee: $80. *Financial support:* In 2016–17, 9 students received support. Career-related internships or fieldwork, Federal Work-Study, institutionally sponsored loans, scholarships/grants, and unspecified assistantships available. Support available to part-time students. Financial award application deadline: 4/1; financial award applicants required to submit FAFSA. *Faculty research:* Accounting, financial report, taxation, Sarbanes-Oxley. *Unit head:* Dr. Diane Pattison, Academic Director, Accountancy Programs, 619-260-4850, E-mail: pattison@sandiego.edu. *Application contact:* Monica Mahon, Associate Director of Graduate Admissions, 619-260-4524, Fax: 619-260-4158, E-mail: grads@sandiego.edu.
Website: http://www.sandiego.edu/business/programs/accounting-tax/

University of Saskatchewan, College of Graduate Studies and Research, Edwards School of Business, Department of Accounting, Saskatoon, SK S7N 5A2, Canada. Offers M Sc, MP Acc. *Program availability:* Part-time. *Degree requirements:* For master's, thesis (for some programs). *Entrance requirements:* For master's, GMAT. Additional exam requirements/recommendations for international students: Required—TOEFL.

The University of Scranton, Kania School of Management, Program in Accountancy, Scranton, PA 18510. Offers M Acc.

The University of Scranton, Kania School of Management, Program in Business Administration, Scranton, PA 18510. Offers accounting (MBA); finance (MBA); general business administration (MBA); health care management (MBA); international business (MBA); management information systems (MBA); marketing (MBA); operations management (MBA). *Accreditation:* AACSB. *Program availability:* Part-time, evening/weekend, 100% online. *Entrance requirements:* For master's, GMAT (for MBA). *Faculty research:* Financial markets, strategic impact of total quality management, internal accounting controls, consumer preference, information systems and the Internet.

University of South Africa, College of Economic and Management Sciences, Pretoria, South Africa. Offers accounting (D Admin, D Com); accounting science (DA); auditing (D Admin, D Com); business administration (M Tech); business economics (D Admin); business leadership (DBL); business management (D Admin, D Com); economic management analysis (M Tech); economics (D Admin, D Com, PhD); human resource development (M Tech); industrial psychology (D Admin, D Com, PhD); logistics (D Com); marketing (M Tech); public administration (D Admin, D Com, DPA, PhD); public management (M Tech); quantitative management (D Admin, D Com); real estate (M Tech); statistics (D Admin, PhD); tourism management (D Admin, D Com); transport economics (D Admin, D Com).

University of South Alabama, Mitchell College of Business, Department of Accounting, Mobile, AL 36688. Offers M Acc. *Program availability:* Part-time, evening/weekend. *Faculty:* 3 full-time (0 women). *Students:* 10 full-time (4 women), 2 part-time (0 women); includes 1 minority (Black or African American, non-Hispanic/Latino), 1 international. Average age 24. 21 applicants, 62% accepted, 8 enrolled. In 2016, 9 master's awarded. *Degree requirements:* For master's, comprehensive exam. *Entrance requirements:* For master's, GMAT (minimum score of 450 with minimum score of 3.0 in Analytical Writing section), minimum undergraduate GPA of 3.0. Additional exam requirements/recommendations for international students: Required—TOEFL (minimum score 525 paper-based; 71 iBT), IELTS (minimum score 6). *Application deadline:* For fall admission, 7/15 for domestic students, 6/15 for international students; for spring admission, 12/1 for domestic students, 11/1 for international students. Application fee: $35. Electronic applications accepted. *Expenses:* Contact institution. *Financial support:* Fellowships, research assistantships, teaching assistantships, career-related internships or fieldwork, Federal Work-Study, institutionally sponsored loans, scholarships/grants, and unspecified assistantships available. Support available to part-time students. Financial award application deadline: 5/31; financial award applicants required to submit FAFSA. *Unit head:* Dr. Russell Hardin, Chair, 251-460-7140, E-mail: rhardin@southalabama.edu. *Application contact:* Dr. Alex Sharland, Assistant Dean and Director of Graduate Studies, 251-460-6412, Fax: 251-460-6529, E-mail: mcobgraduate@southalabama.edu.
Website: http://www.southalabama.edu/colleges/mcob/macc/index.html

University of South Carolina, The Graduate School, Darla Moore School of Business, Master of Accountancy Program, Columbia, SC 29208. Offers business measurement and assurance (M Acc); JD/M Acc. *Accreditation:* AACSB. *Program availability:* Part-time. *Degree requirements:* For master's, comprehensive exam. *Entrance requirements:* For master's, GMAT. Additional exam requirements/recommendations for international students: Required—TOEFL (minimum score 100 iBT); Recommended—IELTS. Electronic applications accepted. *Faculty research:* Judgment modeling, international accounting, accounting information systems, behavioral accounting, cost/management accounting.

The University of South Dakota, Graduate School, Beacom School of Business, Department of Accounting, Vermillion, SD 57069. Offers professional accountancy (MP Acc); JD/MP Acc. *Program availability:* Part-time, online learning. *Degree requirements:* For master's, comprehensive exam. *Entrance requirements:* For master's, GMAT, minimum GPA of 2.7, resume. Additional exam requirements/recommendations for international students: Required—TOEFL (minimum score 550 paper-based; 79 iBT). Electronic applications accepted.

University of Southern California, Graduate School, Marshall School of Business, Leventhal School of Accounting, Los Angeles, CA 90089. Offers accounting (M Acc); business taxation (MBT); JD/MBT. *Program availability:* Part-time. *Degree requirements:* For master's, 30-48 units of study. *Entrance requirements:* For master's, GMAT, undergraduate degree, communication skills. Additional exam requirements/recommendations for international students: Required—TOEFL. Electronic applications accepted. *Faculty research:* State and local taxation, Securities and Exchange Commission, governance, auditing fees, financial accounting, enterprise zones, women in business.

University of Southern Indiana, Graduate Studies, Romain College of Business, Program in Business Administration, Evansville, IN 47712-3590. Offers accounting (MBA); business administration (MBA); data analytics (MBA); engineering management (MBA); health administration (MBA); human resources (MBA). *Accreditation:* AACSB. *Program availability:* Part-time, evening/weekend, 100% online, blended/hybrid learning. *Faculty:* 22 full-time (4 women), 2 part-time/adjunct (0 women). *Students:* 149 full-time (70 women), 64 part-time (29 women); includes 25 minority (17 Black or African American, non-Hispanic/Latino; 1 Asian, non-Hispanic/Latino; 5 Hispanic/Latino; 2 Two or more races, non-Hispanic/Latino), 5 international. Average age 32. In 2016, 36 master's awarded. *Entrance requirements:* For master's, GMAT or GRE, minimum GPA of 2.5, resume, 3 professional references. Additional exam requirements/recommendations for international students: Required—TOEFL (minimum score 550 paper-based; 79 iBT), IELTS (minimum score 6). *Application deadline:* For fall admission, 8/1 for domestic students, 3/1 priority date for international students. Applications are processed on a rolling basis. Application fee: $40. Electronic applications accepted. *Expenses:* Tuition, state resident: full-time $8497. Tuition, nonresident: full-time $16,691. *Required fees:* $500. *Financial support:* In 2016–17, 8 students received support. Federal Work-Study, scholarships/grants, tuition waivers (full and partial), and unspecified assistantships available. Financial award application deadline: 3/1; financial award applicants required to submit FAFSA. *Unit head:* Dr. Jack E. Smothers, Program Director, 812-461-5248, E-mail: jesmothers@usi.edu. *Application contact:* Michelle Simmons, MBA Program Assistant, 812-464-1926, Fax: 812-465-1044, E-mail: masimmons3@usi.edu.
Website: http://www.usi.edu/business/mba

University of Southern Maine, College of Management and Human Service, School of Business, Portland, ME 04104-9300. Offers accounting (MBA); business administration (MBA); finance (MBA); health management and policy (MBA); sustainability (MBA); JD/MBA; MBA/MSA; MBA/MSN; MS/MBA. *Accreditation:* AACSB. *Program availability:* Part-time, evening/weekend. *Entrance requirements:* For master's, GMAT or GRE, minimum AACSB index of 1100. Additional exam requirements/recommendations for international students: Required—TOEFL (minimum score 550 paper-based; 79 iBT). Electronic applications accepted. *Faculty research:* Economic development, management information systems, real options, system dynamics, simulation.

Accounting

University of Southern Mississippi, Graduate School, College of Business, School of Accountancy, Hattiesburg, MS 39406. Offers accountancy (MPA). *Accreditation:* AACSB. *Program availability:* Part-time, evening/weekend. *Degree requirements:* For master's, comprehensive exam. *Entrance requirements:* For master's, GMAT, minimum GPA of 2.75 on last 60 hours. Additional exam requirements/recommendations for international students: Required—TOEFL, IELTS. *Application deadline:* For fall admission, 7/15 priority date for domestic students, 7/15 for international students; for spring admission, 11/15 priority date for domestic students, 11/15 for international students. Applications are processed on a rolling basis. Application fee: $60. Electronic applications accepted. *Expenses: Tuition, area resident:* Full-time $15,708; part-time $437 per credit hour. *Financial support:* Research assistantships with full tuition reimbursements, Federal Work-Study, institutionally sponsored loans, scholarships/grants, health care benefits, and unspecified assistantships available. Support available to part-time students. Financial award application deadline: 3/15; financial award applicants required to submit FAFSA. *Faculty research:* Bank liquidity, subchapter S corporations, internal auditing, governmental accounting, inflation accounting. *Unit head:* Gwen Pate, Director, 601-266-4641, Fax: 601-266-4642.
Website: https://www.usm.edu/business/accounting

University of South Florida, Muma College of Business, Lynn Pippenger School of Accountancy, Tampa, FL 33620-9951. Offers accountancy (M Acc), including audit/systems, tax; business administration (PhD), including accounting. *Accreditation:* AACSB. *Program availability:* Part-time, evening/weekend. *Faculty:* 10 full-time (4 women). *Students:* 67 full-time (36 women), 34 part-time (16 women); includes 22 minority (2 Black or African American, non-Hispanic/Latino; 3 Asian, non-Hispanic/Latino; 15 Hispanic/Latino; 2 Two or more races, non-Hispanic/Latino), 9 international. Average age 26. 89 applicants, 56% accepted, 41 enrolled. In 2016, 67 master's, 2 doctorates awarded. Terminal master's awarded for partial completion of doctoral program. *Degree requirements:* For master's, comprehensive exam, thesis or alternative; for doctorate, comprehensive exam, thesis/dissertation. *Entrance requirements:* For master's, GMAT, minimum overall GPA of 3.0 in general upper-level coursework and in upper-level accounting coursework (minimum of 21 hours at a U.S. accredited program within past 5 years); for doctorate, GMAT or GRE, personal statement, recommendations, interview. Additional exam requirements/recommendations for international students: Required—TOEFL (minimum score 550 paper-based; 79 iBT) or IELTS (minimum score 6.5). *Application deadline:* For fall admission, 1/2 for domestic and international students; for spring admission, 10/1 for domestic students, 9/15 for international students; for summer admission, 2/15 for domestic students, 1/15 for international students. Application fee: $30. Electronic applications accepted. *Expenses:* Tuition, state resident: full-time $7766; part-time $431.43 per credit hour. Tuition, nonresident: full-time $15,789; part-time $877.17 per credit hour. *Required fees:* $37 per term. *Financial support:* In 2016–17, 41 students received support, including 18 teaching assistantships with tuition reimbursements available (averaging $12,273 per year); scholarships/grants, health care benefits, and unspecified assistantships also available. Financial award applicants required to submit FAFSA. *Faculty research:* Auditing, auditor independence, audit committee decisions, fraud detection and reporting, disclosure effects, effects of information technology on accounting, governmental accounting/auditing, accounting information systems, data modeling and design methodologies for accounting systems, auditing computer-based systems, expert systems, group support systems in accounting, fair value accounting issues, corporate governance, financial accounting, financial reporting quality. *Unit head:* Dr. Uday Murthy, Interim Director, School of Accountancy, 813-974-6516, Fax: 813-974-6528, E-mail: umurthy@usf.edu. *Application contact:* Christy Ward, Advisor and Graduation Specialist, 813-974-4290, Fax: 813-974-2797, E-mail: cward@usf.edu.
Website: http://business.usf.edu/departments/accountancy/

The University of Tampa, Sykes College of Business, Tampa, FL 33606-1490. Offers accounting (MS); entrepreneurship (MBA); finance (MBA, MS); information systems management (MBA); innovation management (MBA); international business (MBA); marketing (MBA, MS); nonprofit management (MBA). *Accreditation:* AACSB. *Program availability:* Part-time, evening/weekend. *Faculty:* 43 full-time (19 women), 9 part-time/adjunct (3 women). *Students:* 438 full-time (176 women), 126 part-time (57 women); includes 37 minority (22 Black or African American, non-Hispanic/Latino; 11 Asian, non-Hispanic/Latino; 4 Two or more races, non-Hispanic/Latino), 203 international. Average age 28. 1,305 applicants, 39% accepted, 192 enrolled. In 2016, 266 master's awarded. *Degree requirements:* For master's, capstone. *Entrance requirements:* For master's, GMAT or GRE, official transcripts from all colleges and/or universities previously attended, resume, personal statement, letters of recommendation. Additional exam requirements/recommendations for international students: Required—TOEFL (minimum score 577 paper-based, 90 iBT) or IELTS (7.5). *Application deadline:* Applications are processed on a rolling basis. Application fee: $40. Electronic applications accepted. *Expenses:* $588 per credit tuition, $40 per term fees. *Financial support:* In 2016–17, 116 students received support. Career-related internships or fieldwork, scholarships/grants, and unspecified assistantships available. Financial award applicants required to submit FAFSA. *Faculty research:* Job market signaling, on-line shopping behaviors and social media, the Tampa Bay economy, digital literacy, entrepreneurship in small businesses. *Unit head:* Dr. Natasha F. Veltri, Associate Dean, 813-253-6289, E-mail: nveltri@ut.edu. *Application contact:* Chanelle Cox, Staff Assistant, Admissions for Graduate and Continuing Studies, 813-253-6249, E-mail: ccox@ut.edu.
Website: http://www.ut.edu/business/

The University of Tennessee, Graduate School, College of Business Administration, Department of Accounting, Knoxville, TN 37996. Offers accounting (M Acc), including assurance; systems (M Acc); taxation (M Acc). *Accreditation:* AACSB. *Degree requirements:* For master's, thesis or alternative. *Entrance requirements:* For master's, GMAT, minimum GPA of 2.7. Additional exam requirements/recommendations for international students: Required—TOEFL. Electronic applications accepted.

The University of Tennessee, Graduate School, College of Business Administration, Program in Business Administration, Knoxville, TN 37996. Offers accounting (PhD); finance (MBA, PhD); logistics and transportation (MBA, PhD); management (PhD); marketing (MBA, PhD); operations management (MBA); professional business administration (MBA); statistics (PhD); JD/MBA; MS/MBA; Pharm D/MBA. Pharm D/MBA offered jointly with The University of Tennessee Health Science Center. *Accreditation:* AACSB. *Program availability:* Online learning. *Degree requirements:* For master's, thesis or alternative; for doctorate, thesis/dissertation. *Entrance requirements:* For master's and doctorate, GMAT, minimum GPA of 2.7. Additional exam requirements/recommendations for international students: Required—TOEFL. Electronic applications accepted.

The University of Tennessee at Chattanooga, Program in Accountancy, Chattanooga, TN 37403. Offers M Acc. *Accreditation:* AACSB. *Program availability:* Part-time, evening/weekend. *Faculty:* 4 full-time (2 women). *Students:* 12 full-time (7 women), 14 part-time (6 women); includes 7 minority (1 Black or African American, non-Hispanic/Latino; 2 Asian, non-Hispanic/Latino; 1 Hispanic/Latino; 3 Two or more races, non-Hispanic/Latino). Average age 26. 24 applicants, 67% accepted, 13 enrolled. In 2016, 13 master's awarded. *Entrance requirements:* For master's, GMAT (minimum score 450). Additional exam requirements/recommendations for international students: Required—TOEFL (minimum score 550 paper-based; 79 iBT), IELTS (minimum score 6). *Application deadline:* For fall admission, 6/15 priority date for domestic students, 7/1 for international students; for spring admission, 11/1 priority date for domestic students, 11/1 for international students. Applications are processed on a rolling basis. Application fee: $35 ($40 for international students). Electronic applications accepted. *Expenses:* $9,876 full-time in-state; $25,994 full-time out-of-state; $450 per credit part-time in-state; $1,345 per credit part-time out-of-state. *Financial support:* In 2016–17, 2 research assistantships were awarded; teaching assistantships, career-related internships or fieldwork, scholarships/grants, and unspecified assistantships also available. Support available to part-time students. Financial award application deadline: 7/1; financial award applicants required to submit FAFSA. *Faculty research:* Performance measurement, auditing, income taxation, corporate efficiency, portfolio management and performance. *Unit head:* Dr. Dan Hollingsworth, Department Head, 423-425-4664, Fax: 423-425-5255, E-mail: dan-hollingsworth@utc.edu. *Application contact:* Dr. Joanne Romagni, Dean of the Graduate School, 413-425-4478, Fax: 423-425-5223, E-mail: randy-walker@utc.edu.
Website: http://www.utc.edu/college-business/academic-programs/graduate-programs/macc/index.php

The University of Texas at Arlington, Graduate School, College of Business, Accounting Department, Arlington, TX 76019. Offers accounting (MP Acc, MS, PhD); taxation (MS). *Accreditation:* AACSB. *Program availability:* Part-time, evening/weekend. *Degree requirements:* For master's, thesis optional; for doctorate, comprehensive exam, thesis/dissertation. *Entrance requirements:* For master's and doctorate, GMAT. Additional exam requirements/recommendations for international students: Required—TOEFL (minimum score 550 paper-based; 79 iBT). *Application deadline:* For fall admission, 6/1 for domestic students, 4/1 for international students; for spring admission, 10/15 for domestic students, 9/15 for international students. Applications are processed on a rolling basis. Application fee: $40 ($70 for international students). *Financial support:* Fellowships, research assistantships, teaching assistantships, career-related internships or fieldwork, scholarships/grants, and unspecified assistantships available. Financial award application deadline: 6/1; financial award applicants required to submit FAFSA. *Unit head:* Dr. Chandra Subramaniam, Chair, 817-272-7029, Fax: 817-282-5793, E-mail: subramaniam@uta.edu. *Application contact:* Carly S. Andrews, Graduate Advisor, 817-272-3047, Fax: 817-272-5793, E-mail: graduate.accounting.advisor@uta.edu.
Website: http://www2.uta.edu/accounting/

The University of Texas at Austin, Graduate School, McCombs School of Business, Department of Accounting, Austin, TX 78712-1111. Offers MPA, PhD. *Accreditation:* AACSB. *Degree requirements:* For doctorate, comprehensive exam, thesis/dissertation. *Entrance requirements:* For master's and doctorate, GMAT. Additional exam requirements/recommendations for international students: Required—TOEFL. Electronic applications accepted.

The University of Texas at Dallas, Naveen Jindal School of Management, Program in Accounting, Richardson, TX 75080. Offers MS. *Accreditation:* AACSB. *Faculty:* 22 full-time (7 women), 20 part-time/adjunct (8 women). *Students:* 536 full-time (356 women), 261 part-time (153 women); includes 158 minority (17 Black or African American, non-Hispanic/Latino; 1 American Indian or Alaska Native, non-Hispanic/Latino; 94 Asian, non-Hispanic/Latino; 34 Hispanic/Latino; 1 Native Hawaiian or other Pacific Islander, non-Hispanic/Latino; 11 Two or more races, non-Hispanic/Latino), 482 international. Average age 28. 785 applicants, 68% accepted, 243 enrolled. In 2016, 321 master's awarded. *Entrance requirements:* For master's, GMAT, minimum GPA of 3.0 in upper-level course work in field. Additional exam requirements/recommendations for international students: Required—TOEFL (minimum score 550 paper-based). *Application deadline:* For fall admission, 7/15 for domestic students, 5/1 priority date for international students; for spring admission, 11/15 for domestic students, 9/1 priority date for international students. Applications are processed on a rolling basis. Application fee: $50 ($100 for international students). Electronic applications accepted. *Expenses:* Tuition, state resident: full-time $12,418; part-time $690 per semester hour. Tuition, nonresident: full-time $24,150; part-time $1342 per semester hour. Tuition and fees vary according to course load. *Financial support:* In 2016–17, 188 students received support, including 13 teaching assistantships with partial tuition reimbursements available (averaging $10,050 per year); research assistantships with partial tuition reimbursements available, career-related internships or fieldwork, Federal Work-Study, institutionally sponsored loans, scholarships/grants, and unspecified assistantships also available. Support available to part-time students. Financial award application deadline: 4/30; financial award applicants required to submit FAFSA. *Faculty research:* Privatization and accounting/auditing, corporate performance and executive compensation, risk management, information technology in accounting. *Unit head:* Dr. William Cready, Area Coordinator, 972-883-4185, Fax: 972-883-6823, E-mail: cready@utdallas.edu. *Application contact:* Van Dam, Senior Academic Support Coordinator, 972-883-2703, Fax: 972-883-6823, E-mail: vanchi@utdallas.edu.
Website: http://jindal.utdallas.edu/accounting

The University of Texas at El Paso, Graduate School, College of Business Administration, Department of Accounting, El Paso, TX 79968-0001. Offers M Acc. *Accreditation:* AACSB. *Program availability:* Part-time, evening/weekend. *Entrance requirements:* For master's, GMAT, minimum GPA of 3.0. Additional exam requirements/recommendations for international students: Required—TOEFL; Recommended—IELTS. Electronic applications accepted. *Faculty research:* Financial and managerial accounting, auditing and accounting information systems.

The University of Texas at San Antonio, College of Business, Department of Accounting, San Antonio, TX 78249-0617. Offers M Acy, PhD. *Accreditation:* AACSB. *Program availability:* Part-time, evening/weekend. *Faculty:* 8 full-time (2 women), 4 part-time/adjunct (2 women). *Students:* 73 full-time (39 women), 51 part-time (18 women); includes 52 minority (5 Black or African American, non-Hispanic/Latino; 6 Asian, non-Hispanic/Latino; 38 Hispanic/Latino; 3 Two or more races, non-Hispanic/Latino), 13 international. Average age 33. 102 applicants, 71% accepted, 26 enrolled. In 2016, 47 master's awarded. *Degree requirements:* For master's, thesis or alternative. *Entrance requirements:* For master's, GMAT, bachelor's degree, transcripts, statement of purpose. Additional exam requirements/recommendations for international students: Required—TOEFL (minimum score 550 paper-based; 79 iBT), IELTS (minimum score 6.5). *Application deadline:* For fall admission, 7/1 for domestic students, 4/1 for international students; for spring admission, 11/1 for domestic students, 9/1 for international students. Application fee: $45 ($80 for international students). Electronic applications accepted. *Expenses:* Contact institution. *Financial support:* Teaching assistantships, Federal Work-Study, and scholarships/grants available. *Faculty research:* Capital markets, corporate governance, auditing, health care accounting, fraud. *Total annual research expenditures:* $29,872. *Unit head:* Dr. Sharad Asthana, Chair, 210-458-4320, E-mail: sharad.asthana@utsa.edu. *Application contact:* Dr. Jeff Boone, Advisor of Record for Accounting Doctoral Programs, 210-458-7091, E-mail: jeff.boone@utsa.edu.
Website: http://business.utsa.edu/accounting/

The University of Texas at Tyler, College of Business and Technology, Program in Accountancy, Tyler, TX 75799-0001. Offers M Acc. *Entrance requirements:* For master's, GMAT, official transcripts, current resume.

The University of Texas of the Permian Basin, Office of Graduate Studies, School of Business, Program in Accountancy, Odessa, TX 79762-0001. Offers MPA. *Entrance requirements:* For master's, GMAT. Additional exam requirements/recommendations for international students: Required—TOEFL (minimum score 550 paper-based).

The University of Texas Rio Grande Valley, Robert C. Vackar College of Business and Entrepreneurship, Program in Accounting, Edinburg, TX 78539. Offers M Acc, MS. *Program availability:* Part-time, evening/weekend. *Entrance requirements:* For master's, GMAT. Additional exam requirements/recommendations for international students: Required—TOEFL (minimum score 500 paper-based). Electronic applications accepted. Tuition and fees vary according to course load and program. *Faculty research:* Financial and managerial accounting, international accounting, taxation, ethics.

University of the Cumberlands, Hutton School of Business, Williamsburg, KY 40769-1372. Offers accounting (MBA); business (MBA). *Program availability:* Part-time, online learning. *Entrance requirements:* For master's, GMAT, GRE. Additional exam requirements/recommendations for international students: Required—TOEFL. Electronic applications accepted.

University of the Sacred Heart, Graduate Programs, Department of Business Administration, San Juan, PR 00914-0383. Offers human resource management (MBA); information systems auditing (MS); information technology (Certificate); international marketing (MBA); management information systems (MBA); production and marketing of special events (Certificate); taxation (MBA). *Program availability:* Part-time, evening/weekend. *Degree requirements:* For master's, thesis. *Entrance requirements:* For master's, EXADEP, minimum undergraduate GPA of 2.75, interview.

The University of Toledo, College of Graduate Studies, College of Business and Innovation, Department of Accounting, Toledo, OH 43606-3390. Offers MBA, MSA. *Accreditation:* AACSB. *Program availability:* Part-time, evening/weekend. *Entrance requirements:* For master's, GMAT, GRE, or LSAT, minimum GPA of 2.7 for all prior academic work, three letters of recommendation, statement of purpose, transcripts from all prior institutions attended. Additional exam requirements/recommendations for international students: Required—TOEFL (minimum score 550 paper-based; 80 iBT). Electronic applications accepted. *Faculty research:* Estate gift tax, audit and legal liability, corporate tax, accounting information systems.

The University of Tulsa, Graduate School, Collins College of Business, Program in Accounting, Tulsa, OK 74104-3189. Offers M Acc. *Program availability:* Part-time. *Faculty:* 10 full-time (4 women). *Students:* 14 full-time (6 women), 10 part-time (3 women); includes 3 minority (1 Black or African American, non-Hispanic/Latino; 1 American Indian or Alaska Native, non-Hispanic/Latino; 1 Asian, non-Hispanic/Latino), 7 international. Average age 25. 42 applicants, 31% accepted, 7 enrolled. In 2016, 27 master's awarded. *Entrance requirements:* For master's, GMAT. Additional exam requirements/recommendations for international students: Required—TOEFL (minimum score 577 paper-based; 91 iBT). *Application deadline:* Applications are processed on a rolling basis. Application fee: $55. Electronic applications accepted. *Expenses: Tuition:* Full-time $22,230; part-time $1235 per credit hour. *Required fees:* $990 per semester. Tuition and fees vary according to course load. *Financial support:* In 2016–17, 10 students received support, including 10 teaching assistantships with full tuition reimbursements available (averaging $9,558 per year); fellowships, research assistantships, career-related internships or fieldwork, Federal Work-Study, scholarships/grants, health care benefits, tuition waivers (full and partial), and unspecified assistantships also available. Support available to part-time students. Financial award application deadline: 2/1; financial award applicants required to submit FAFSA. *Faculty research:* Capital markets, financial reporting, innovation in accounting. *Unit head:* Dr. Ralph Jackson, Associate Dean, 918-631-2242, Fax: 918-631-2142, E-mail: ralph-jackson@utulsa.edu. *Application contact:* Information Contact, 918-631-2242, E-mail: graduate-business@utulsa.edu.

University of Utah, Graduate School, David Eccles School of Business, Business Administration Program, Salt Lake City, UT 84112. Offers accounting (PhD); business administration (EMBA, MBA, PMBA); finance (PhD); information systems (PhD); marketing (PhD); operations management (PhD); organizational behavior (PhD); strategic management (PhD); MBA/JD; MBA/MHA; MBA/MS. *Program availability:* Part-time, evening/weekend, online learning. *Faculty:* 58 full-time (21 women), 37 part-time/adjunct (7 women). *Students:* 578 full-time (149 women), 89 part-time (28 women); includes 71 minority (1 American Indian or Alaska Native, non-Hispanic/Latino; 17 Asian, non-Hispanic/Latino; 45 Hispanic/Latino; 8 Two or more races, non-Hispanic/Latino), 50 international. Average age 32. 442 applicants, 70% accepted, 226 enrolled. In 2016, 246 master's, 6 doctorates awarded. *Degree requirements:* For doctorate, comprehensive exam, thesis/dissertation. *Entrance requirements:* For master's, GMAT or GRE; for doctorate, GMAT. Additional exam requirements/recommendations for international students: Required—TOEFL (minimum score 600 paper-based; 100 iBT), IELTS (minimum score 7). *Application deadline:* For fall admission, 11/1 priority date for domestic students, 3/1 priority date for international students; for spring admission, 11/1 for domestic and international students. Applications are processed on a rolling basis. Application fee: $55 ($65 for international students). Electronic applications accepted. *Expenses:* Contact institution. *Financial support:* In 2016–17, 53 students received support, including 53 fellowships with partial tuition reimbursements available (averaging $8,600 per year); scholarships/grants and unspecified assistantships also available. Financial award application deadline: 2/1; financial award applicants required to submit FAFSA. *Faculty research:* Corporate finance, strategy services, consumer behavior, financial disclosures, operations. *Unit head:* Kristina Diekmann, Department Chair, 801-581-8524, Fax: 801-581-3380, E-mail: mastersinfo@business.utah.edu. *Application contact:* Christine Harris, Coordinator, 801-581-7785, Fax: 801-585-3962, E-mail: execch@business.utah.edu.
Website: http://www.business.utah.edu/

University of Utah, Graduate School, David Eccles School of Business, School of Accounting, Salt Lake City, UT 84112. Offers accounting (PhD); accounting information systems (M Acc); financial/audit (M Acc); tax (M Acc). *Accreditation:* AACSB. *Program availability:* Part-time, evening/weekend. *Faculty:* 15 full-time (6 women), 8 part-time/adjunct (3 women). *Students:* 168 full-time (61 women), 33 part-time (13 women); includes 33 minority (1 Black or African American, non-Hispanic/Latino; 12 Asian, non-Hispanic/Latino; 13 Hispanic/Latino; 1 Native Hawaiian or other Pacific Islander, non-Hispanic/Latino; 6 Two or more races, non-Hispanic/Latino), 22 international. Average age 27. 138 applicants, 83% accepted, 110 enrolled. In 2016, 154 master's awarded. *Degree requirements:* For doctorate, comprehensive exam, thesis/dissertation, oral qualifying exams, written qualifying exams. *Entrance requirements:* For master's, GMAT, minimum undergraduate GPA of 3.0; for doctorate, GMAT. Additional exam requirements/recommendations for international students: Required—TOEFL (minimum score 600 paper-based; 100 iBT), IELTS (minimum score 7). *Application deadline:* For fall admission, 3/1 priority date for domestic and international students; for spring admission, 10/15 priority date for domestic students, 8/1 priority date for international students. Applications are processed on a rolling basis. Application fee: $55 ($65 for international students). Electronic applications accepted. *Expenses:* $27,700 full-time resident; $51,500 full-time non-resident; $29,400 part-time resident; $52,600 part-time non-resident. *Financial support:* In 2016–17, 32 students received support. Scholarships/grants and tuition waivers (partial) available. Financial award application deadline: 3/1; financial award applicants required to submit FAFSA. *Faculty research:* Auditing, taxation, information systems, financial accounting, accounting theory, international accounting. *Total annual research expenditures:* $86,000. *Unit head:* Dr. Martha Eining, Chair, 801-581-7673, Fax: 801-581-3581, E-mail: martha.eining@utah.edu. *Application contact:* Olivia Hansen, M Acc Admissions Coordinator, 801-587-3282, Fax: 801-581-3581, E-mail: olivia.hansen@business.utah.edu.
Website: http://www.business.utah.edu/accounting/

University of Vermont, Graduate College, School of Business Administration, Program in Accounting, Burlington, VT 05405. Offers M Acc. *Entrance requirements:* For master's, GMAT, GRE, resume. Additional exam requirements/recommendations for international students: Required—TOEFL (minimum score 550 paper-based; 80 iBT). Electronic applications accepted. *Expenses:* Tuition, state resident: full-time $5814. Tuition, nonresident: full-time $14,670.

University of Virginia, McIntire School of Commerce, Program in Accounting, Charlottesville, VA 22903. Offers MS, JD/MS. *Accreditation:* AACSB. *Entrance requirements:* For master's, GMAT, 2 letters of recommendation, 12 hours of accounting courses. Additional exam requirements/recommendations for international students: Required—TOEFL (minimum score 600 paper-based; 100 iBT), IELTS (minimum score 7). Electronic applications accepted. *Expenses:* Contact institution.

University of Washington, Graduate School, Michael G. Foster School of Business, Seattle, WA 98195-3200. Offers auditing and assurance (MP Acc); business administration (MBA, PhD); entrepreneurship (MS); executive business administration (MBA); global executive business administration (MBA); information systems (MSIS); supply chain management (MSSCM); taxation (MP Acc); technology management (MBA); JD/MBA; MBA/MAIS; MBA/MHA. *Accreditation:* AACSB. *Program availability:* Part-time, evening/weekend. Terminal master's awarded for partial completion of doctoral program. *Degree requirements:* For doctorate, comprehensive exam, thesis/dissertation. *Entrance requirements:* For master's and doctorate, GMAT, GRE. Additional exam requirements/recommendations for international students: Required—TOEFL (minimum score 600 paper-based; 100 iBT). Electronic applications accepted. *Expenses:* Contact institution. *Faculty research:* Finance, marketing, organizational behavior, information technology, strategy.

University of Washington, Tacoma, Graduate Programs, MBA Programs, Tacoma, WA 98402-3100. Offers accounting (MBA); business administration (MBA); certified financial analyst (MBA). *Accreditation:* AACSB. *Program availability:* Part-time, evening/weekend. *Entrance requirements:* For master's, GMAT, minimum GPA of 3.0 in final graded 90 quarter credits or 60 graded semester credits; at least 2 years of professional/management work experience. Additional exam requirements/recommendations for international students: Required—TOEFL (minimum score 580 paper-based; 92 iBT). Electronic applications accepted. *Expenses:* Contact institution. *Faculty research:* International accounting, marketing, change management, investments, corporate social responsibility.

University of Waterloo, Graduate Studies, Faculty of Arts, School of Accounting and Finance, Waterloo, ON N2L 3G1, Canada. Offers accounting (M Acc, PhD); finance (M Acc); taxation (M Tax). *Degree requirements:* For master's, thesis or alternative; for doctorate, thesis/dissertation. *Entrance requirements:* For master's, honors degree, minimum B average, resume; for doctorate, GMAT, master's degree, minimum A- average, resume. Additional exam requirements/recommendations for international students: Required—TOEFL, IELTS, PTE. Electronic applications accepted. *Expenses:* Contact institution. *Faculty research:* Auditing, management accounting.

University of West Florida, College of Business, Program in Accounting, Pensacola, FL 32514-5750. Offers M Acc. *Program availability:* Part-time, evening/weekend. *Entrance requirements:* For master's, GMAT (minimum score 450) or equivalent GRE score, official transcripts; bachelor's degree; two letters of recommendation; letter of intent. Additional exam requirements/recommendations for international students: Required—TOEFL (minimum score 550 paper-based). *Application deadline:* For fall admission, 6/30 priority date for domestic students, 6/1 for international students; for spring admission, 10/1 for domestic and international students. Application fee: $30. *Expenses:* Tuition, state resident: full-time $5316.12. Tuition, nonresident: full-time $11,308. *Required fees:* $583.92. Tuition and fees vary according to course load and program. *Financial support:* Fellowships, research assistantships with partial tuition reimbursements, and unspecified assistantships available. Financial award application deadline: 4/15; financial award applicants required to submit FAFSA. *Faculty research:* Audit risk, tax legislation, product costing, bank core deposit intangibles, financial reporting. *Unit head:* Dr. Doug Waggle, Director, 850-474-2719, E-mail: dwaggle@uwf.edu. *Application contact:* Terry McCray, Assistant Director of Graduate Admissions, 850-473-7718, Fax: 850-473-7714, E-mail: gradadmissions@uwf.edu.
Website: http://uwf.edu/account/gradprograms.cfm

University of West Georgia, Richards College of Business, Carrollton, GA 30118. Offers accounting (MP Acc); business administration (MBA). *Program availability:* Part-time, evening/weekend, 100% online, blended/hybrid learning. *Faculty:* 38 full-time (14 women). *Students:* 56 full-time (24 women), 132 part-time (64 women); includes 61 minority (49 Black or African American, non-Hispanic/Latino; 1 American Indian or Alaska Native, non-Hispanic/Latino; 3 Asian, non-Hispanic/Latino; 7 Hispanic/Latino; 1 Two or more races, non-Hispanic/Latino), 12 international. Average age 29. 121 applicants, 94% accepted, 77 enrolled. In 2016, 123 master's awarded. *Entrance requirements:* Additional exam requirements/recommendations for international students: Required—TOEFL (minimum score 550 paper-based; 79 iBT); Recommended—IELTS (minimum score 6.5). *Application deadline:* For fall admission, 7/15 for domestic students, 6/1 for international students; for spring admission, 11/15 for domestic students, 10/15 for international students; for summer admission, 5/15 for domestic students, 3/30 for international students. Applications are processed on a rolling basis. Application fee: $40. Electronic applications accepted. *Expenses:* Tuition, state resident: full-time $5316; part-time $222 per semester hour. Tuition, nonresident: full-time $20,658; part-time $861 per semester hour. *Required fees:* $1962. Tuition and fees vary according to course load, degree level and program. *Financial support:* Fellowships, research assistantships, teaching assistantships, career-related internships or fieldwork, Federal Work-Study, institutionally sponsored loans, scholarships/grants, and unspecified assistantships available. Support available to part-time students. Financial award application deadline: 4/1; financial award applicants required to submit FAFSA. *Unit head:* Dr. Faye S. McIntyre, Dean of Richards College of Business, 678-839-6467, Fax: 678-839-5040, E-mail: fmcintyr@westga.edu. *Application contact:* Dr. Toby Ziglar, Assistant Dean of the Graduate School, 678-839-1394, Fax: 678-839-1395, E-mail: graduate@westga.edu.
Website: https://www.westga.edu/business

University of Wisconsin–Madison, Graduate School, Wisconsin School of Business, Doctoral Program in Accounting and Information Systems, Madison, WI 53706-1380. Offers PhD. *Accreditation:* AACSB. *Degree requirements:* For doctorate, comprehensive exam, thesis/dissertation. *Entrance requirements:* For doctorate, GMAT or GRE. Additional exam requirements/recommendations for international students: Recommended—TOEFL (minimum score 623 paper-based; 106 iBT), IELTS (minimum score 7.5). Electronic applications accepted. *Expenses:* Contact institution. *Faculty research:* Auditing, financial reporting, economic theory, strategy, computer models, Internal audit and fraud, health care fiscal management, tax reporting, incentives used in nonprofit hospitals, CFO compensation, state and local taxation, audit quality, FASB pronouncements, financial statement analysis.

University of Wisconsin–Madison, Graduate School, Wisconsin School of Business, Master of Accountancy Program, Madison, WI 53706-1380. Offers accountancy (M Acc); taxation (M Acc). *Degree requirements:* For master's, minimum GPA of 3.0. *Entrance requirements:* For master's, GMAT, essays. Additional exam requirements/recommendations for international students: Required—TOEFL (minimum score 104 iBT), IELTS (minimum score 8), GMAT. Electronic applications accepted. *Faculty research:* Tax reserves, audit committee incentives, internal audit, accounting report's impact on management decisions.

University of Wisconsin–Whitewater, School of Graduate Studies, College of Business and Economics, Department of Accounting, Whitewater, WI 53190-1790. Offers MPA. *Program availability:* Part-time, evening/weekend, online learning. *Degree requirements:* For master's, thesis or alternative. *Entrance requirements:* For master's, GMAT or GRE, minimum AACSB index of 1000, minimum GPA of 2.75. Additional exam requirements/recommendations for international students: Required—TOEFL (minimum score 550 paper-based; 80 iBT), IELTS (minimum score 6). Electronic applications accepted. *Faculty research:* Laws/economy/quality of life; tax, accounting and public policy.

University of Wyoming, College of Business, Program in Accounting, Laramie, WY 82071. Offers MS. *Degree requirements:* For master's, thesis optional. *Entrance requirements:* For master's, GMAT or GRE, minimum GPA of 3.0. Additional exam requirements/recommendations for international students: Required—TOEFL (minimum score 540 paper-based; 76 iBT). Electronic applications accepted. *Faculty research:* Taxation, accounting education, assessment, not-for-profit accounting, fraud examination, ethics, management accounting.

Upper Iowa University, Online Master's Programs, Fayette, IA 52142-1857. Offers accounting (MBA); corporate financial management (MBA); emergency management and homeland security (MPA); general management (MBA); general studies (MPA); government administration (MPA); health and human services (MPA); human resources management (MBA); nonprofit organizational management (MPA); organizational development (MBA); public management (MPA); sport administration (MSA). MBA also available at Madison, WI campus. *Program availability:* Part-time, online learning. *Degree requirements:* For master's, research project. *Entrance requirements:* For master's, GMAT, GRE, or minimum GPA of 2.7 during last 60 hours. Additional exam requirements/recommendations for international students: Required—TOEFL (minimum score 570 paper-based). Electronic applications accepted. *Faculty research:* Total quality management, teams, organization culture and climate, management.

Ursuline College, School of Graduate Studies, Program in Business Administration, Pepper Pike, OH 44124-4398. Offers ethical and entrepreneurial leadership (MBA); financial planning and accounting (MBA); health services management (MBA); management (MBA); management and leadership (MBA); marketing and communications management (MBA). *Program availability:* Part-time. *Faculty:* 2 full-time (both women), 1 (woman) part-time/adjunct. *Students:* 27 full-time (25 women), 9 part-time (all women); includes 15 minority (14 Black or African American, non-Hispanic/Latino; 1 Hispanic/Latino), 2 international. Average age 38. 31 applicants, 71% accepted, 18 enrolled. In 2016, 34 master's awarded. *Degree requirements:* For master's, comprehensive exam (for some programs). *Entrance requirements:* For master's, GRE. Additional exam requirements/recommendations for international students: Required—TOEFL (minimum score 500 paper-based) or GRE. Application fee: $25. Electronic applications accepted. *Expenses:* Contact institution. *Financial support:* In 2016–17, 6 students received support. Scholarships/grants available. Financial award applicants required to submit FAFSA. *Faculty research:* Gift economy; sharing economy; cooperative business models; collaborative leadership; corporate social responsibility and the triple bottom line, defined as the three P's: people, planet and profit. *Unit head:* Dr. Nurete Brenner, Executive Director, 440-684-6038, Fax: 440-684-6088, E-mail: nurete.brenner@ursuline.edu. *Application contact:* Melanie Steele, Director of Graduate Admission, 440-646-8146, Fax: 440-684-6138, E-mail: graduateadmissions@ursuline.edu.

Utah State University, School of Graduate Studies, College of Business, School of Accountancy, Logan, UT 84322. Offers M Acc. *Accreditation:* AACSB. *Program availability:* Part-time. *Entrance requirements:* For master's, GMAT, minimum GPA of 3.0, 3 recommendation letters. Additional exam requirements/recommendations for international students: Required—TOEFL. *Faculty research:* Relationship theory, enterprise systems, just in time/loan, reported earnings measures, accounting education.

Utah Valley University, MBA Program, Orem, UT 84058-5999. Offers accounting (MBA); management (MBA). *Accreditation:* AACSB. *Program availability:* Part-time, evening/weekend. *Entrance requirements:* For master's, GMAT, official transcripts, current resume, three letters of recommendation, essay. Additional exam requirements/recommendations for international students: Required—TOEFL (minimum score 79 iBT). Electronic applications accepted. *Expenses:* Contact institution.

Utica College, Program in Accountancy, Utica, NY 13502-4892. Offers MBA. *Program availability:* Part-time, evening/weekend. *Faculty:* 3 full-time (1 woman). *Students:* 9 full-time (6 women), 13 part-time (9 women); includes 2 minority (both Hispanic/Latino). Average age 31. 16 applicants, 88% accepted, 11 enrolled. *Entrance requirements:* For master's, BS, minimum GPA of 3.0. Additional exam requirements/recommendations for international students: Required—TOEFL (minimum score 525 paper-based). *Application deadline:* Applications are processed on a rolling basis. Application fee: $50. Electronic applications accepted. *Expenses:* Contact institution. *Financial support:* Career-related internships or fieldwork, scholarships/grants, tuition waivers (partial), and unspecified assistantships available. Support available to part-time students. Financial award application deadline: 3/15; financial award applicants required to submit FAFSA. *Unit head:* Dr. Zhaodan Huang, MBA Director, 315-792-3247, E-mail: zhuang@utica.edu. *Application contact:* John D. Rowe, Director of Graduate Admissions, 315-792-3824, Fax: 315-792-3003, E-mail: jrowe@utica.edu.
Website: http://www.utica.edu/academic/ssm/accounting/mba/

Vanderbilt University, Vanderbilt University Owen Graduate School of Management, Master of Accountancy in Valuation Program, Nashville, TN 37203. Offers M Acc. *Entrance requirements:* For master's, GMAT or GRE. Additional exam requirements/recommendations for international students: Required—TOEFL, IELTS. Electronic applications accepted. *Expenses: Tuition:* Part-time $1854 per credit hour.

Vanderbilt University, Vanderbilt University Owen Graduate School of Management, Master of Accountancy Program, Nashville, TN 37240-1001. Offers M Acc. *Accreditation:* AACSB. *Entrance requirements:* For master's, GMAT or GRE. Additional exam requirements/recommendations for international students: Required—TOEFL, IELTS. Electronic applications accepted. *Expenses:* Contact institution.

Vanderbilt University, Vanderbilt University Owen Graduate School of Management, Vanderbilt MBA Program, Nashville, TN 37203. Offers accounting (MBA); finance (MBA); general management (MBA); health care (MBA); human and organizational performance (MBA); marketing (MBA); operations (MBA); strategy (MBA); MBA/JD; MBA/M Div; MBA/MD; MBA/MSN; MBA/MTS; MBA/PhD. *Accreditation:* AACSB. *Degree requirements:* For master's, 62 credit hours of coursework; completion of ethics course; minimum GPA of 3.0. *Entrance requirements:* For master's, GMAT (preferred) or GRE, 2 years of work experience (recommended). Additional exam requirements/recommendations for international students: Required—TOEFL (minimum score 100 iBT). Electronic applications accepted. *Expenses:* Contact institution. *Faculty research:* Accounting and finance, business strategy and economics, marketing, operations management, organization studies.

Villanova University, Villanova School of Business, Master of Accountancy Program, Villanova, PA 19085. Offers MAC. *Accreditation:* AACSB. *Faculty:* 108 full-time (39 women), 32 part-time/adjunct (8 women). *Students:* 31 part-time (14 women); includes 7 minority (2 Black or African American, non-Hispanic/Latino; 2 Asian, non-Hispanic/Latino; 3 Hispanic/Latino), 1 international. Average age 23. 56 applicants, 66% accepted, 28 enrolled. In 2016, 35 master's awarded. *Degree requirements:* For master's, minimum cumulative GPA of 3.0. *Entrance requirements:* For master's, undergraduate accounting major or the following prerequisite courses: intermediate accounting I and II, federal income tax and auditing; 2 letters of recommendation; 2 essays; resume; official transcripts. Additional exam requirements/recommendations for international students: Required—TOEFL (minimum score 550 paper-based; 100 iBT). *Application deadline:* For fall admission, 6/30 for domestic and international students; for spring admission, 11/15 for domestic and international students; for summer admission, 3/31 for domestic and international students. Applications are processed on a rolling basis. Application fee: $65. Electronic applications accepted. *Expenses:* Contact institution. *Financial support:* Scholarships/grants available. Financial award application deadline: 6/30; financial award applicants required to submit FAFSA. *Faculty research:* Business analytics; creativity, innovation and entrepreneurship; global leadership; real estate; church management; business ethics; marketing and consumer insights. *Unit head:* Michael L. Capella, Associate Dean of Graduate and Executive Business Programs, 610-519-4336, Fax: 610-519-6273, E-mail: michael.l.capella@villanova.edu. *Application contact:* Claire Bruno, Manager of Recruiting, 610-519-4336, Fax: 610-519-6273, E-mail: claire.bruno@villanova.edu.
Website: http://www1.villanova.edu/villanova/business/graduate/specializedprograms/mac.html

Virginia Commonwealth University, Graduate School, School of Business, Program in Accounting, Richmond, VA 23284-9005. Offers M Acc. *Accreditation:* AACSB. *Entrance requirements:* For master's, GMAT. Additional exam requirements/recommendations for international students: Required—TOEFL (minimum score 600 paper-based; 100 iBT). *Application deadline:* For fall admission, 7/1 for domestic students; for spring admission, 11/1 for domestic students. Applications are processed on a rolling basis. Application fee: $50. Electronic applications accepted. *Financial support:* Fellowships, research assistantships, teaching assistantships, Federal Work-Study, institutionally sponsored loans, and tuition waivers (full and partial) available. Financial award application deadline: 3/15; financial award applicants required to submit FAFSA. *Unit head:* Dr. Carolyn S. Norman, Professor/Interim Chair, 804-828-3160, E-mail: castrand@vcu.edu. *Application contact:* Colleen A. Davis, Graduate Program Director, 804-828-4622, E-mail: androvichcm@vcu.edu.

Virginia International University, School of Business, Fairfax, VA 22030. Offers accounting (MBA, MS); entrepreneurship (MBA); executive management (Graduate Certificate); global logistics (MBA); health care management (MBA); hospitality and tourism management (MBA); human resources management (MBA); international business management (MBA); international finance (MBA); marketing management (MBA); mass media and public relations (MBA); project management (MBA, MS). *Program availability:* Part-time, online learning. *Entrance requirements:* For master's and Graduate Certificate, bachelor's degree. Additional exam requirements/recommendations for international students: Required—TOEFL (minimum score 550 paper-based; 80 iBT), IELTS (minimum score 6). Electronic applications accepted.

Virginia Polytechnic Institute and State University, Graduate School, Pamplin College of Business, Blacksburg, VA 24061. Offers accounting and information systems (MACIS); business (PhD); business administration (MBA, MS); hospitality and tourism management (MS, PhD). *Faculty:* 126 full-time (38 women), 3 part-time/adjunct (1 woman). *Students:* 255 full-time (101 women), 156 part-time (56 women); includes 95 minority (21 Black or African American, non-Hispanic/Latino; 49 Asian, non-Hispanic/Latino; 13 Hispanic/Latino; 12 Two or more races, non-Hispanic/Latino), 73 international. Average age 33. 310 applicants, 59% accepted, 150 enrolled. In 2016, 167 master's, 8 doctorates awarded. *Degree requirements:* For master's, comprehensive exam (for some programs), thesis (for some programs); for doctorate, comprehensive exam (for some programs), thesis/dissertation (for some programs). *Entrance requirements:* For master's and doctorate, GRE/GMAT. Additional exam requirements/recommendations for international students: Required—TOEFL (minimum score 80 iBT). *Application deadline:* For fall admission, 8/1 for domestic students, 4/1 for international students; for spring admission, 1/1 for domestic students, 9/1 for international students. Applications are processed on a rolling basis. Application fee: $75. Electronic applications accepted. *Expenses:* Tuition, state resident: full-time $12,467; part-time $692.50 per credit hour. Tuition, nonresident: full-time $25,095; part-time $1394.25 per credit hour. *Required fees:* $2669; $491.50 per semester. Tuition and fees vary according to course load, campus/location and program. *Financial support:* In 2016–17, 2 fellowships with full tuition reimbursements (averaging $21,222 per year), 3 research assistantships with full tuition reimbursements (averaging $24,988 per year), 46 teaching assistantships with full tuition reimbursements (averaging $20,054 per year) were awarded. Financial award application deadline: 3/1; financial award applicants required to submit FAFSA. *Total annual research expenditures:* $2.7 million. *Unit head:* Dr. Robert T. Sumichrast, Dean, 540-231-6601, Fax: 540-231-4487, E-mail: busdean@vt.edu. *Application contact:* Kimberly Ridpath, Executive Assistant, 540-231-6601, Fax: 540-231-4487, E-mail: ridpathk@vt.edu.
Website: http://www.pamplin.vt.edu/

Wagner College, Division of Graduate Studies, Department of Business Administration, Staten Island, NY 10301-4495. Offers accounting (MS); business administration (MBA); finance (MBA); health care administration (MBA); international business (MBA); management (Exec MBA); marketing (MBA). *Accreditation:* ACBSP. *Program availability:* Part-time, evening/weekend. *Faculty:* 8 full-time (3 women), 17 part-time/adjunct (5 women). *Students:* 90 full-time (25 women), 16 part-time (8 women); includes 21 minority (12 Black or African American, non-Hispanic/Latino; 1 American Indian or Alaska Native, non-Hispanic/Latino; 3 Asian, non-Hispanic/Latino; 5 Hispanic/Latino), 5 international. Average age 26. 88 applicants, 85% accepted, 62 enrolled. In 2016, 72 master's awarded. *Degree requirements:* For master's, thesis optional. *Entrance requirements:* For master's, minimum GPA of 2.75, proficiency in computers and math. Additional exam requirements/recommendations for international students: Required—

TOEFL (minimum score 550 paper-based; 79 iBT). *Application deadline:* For fall admission, 5/1 priority date for domestic students, 3/1 priority date for international students; for spring admission, 12/1 for domestic students, 11/1 for international students. Applications are processed on a rolling basis. Application fee: $50. Tuition and fees vary according to degree level. *Financial support:* In 2016–17, 93 students received support. Career-related internships or fieldwork, unspecified assistantships, and alumni fellowship grants available. Financial award application deadline: 4/1; financial award applicants required to submit FAFSA. *Unit head:* Dr. Donald Crooks, Director, 718-390-3429, Fax: 718-390-3429, E-mail: dcrooks@wagner.edu. *Application contact:* Patricia Clancy, Assistant Director for Enrollment, 718-420-4464, Fax: 718-390-3105, E-mail: patricia.clancy@wagner.edu.

Wake Forest University, Graduate School of Arts and Sciences, Department of Accountancy, Winston-Salem, NC 27106. Offers MSA. *Accreditation:* AACSB. *Entrance requirements:* For master's, GMAT. Additional exam requirements/recommendations for international students: Required—TOEFL. Electronic applications accepted.

Wake Forest University, School of Business, MS in Accountancy Program, Winston-Salem, NC 27106. Offers assurance services (MSA); tax consulting (MSA); transaction services (MSA). *Faculty:* 19 full-time (3 women), 2 part-time/adjunct (0 women). *Students:* 206 full-time (101 women); includes 30 minority (15 Black or African American, non-Hispanic/Latino; 5 Asian, non-Hispanic/Latino; 6 Hispanic/Latino; 4 Two or more races, non-Hispanic/Latino), 38 international. Average age 23. 549 applicants, 46% accepted, 142 enrolled. In 2016, 157 master's awarded. *Degree requirements:* For master's, 30 credit hours. *Entrance requirements:* For master's, GMAT/GRE, letters of recommendation, official transcripts, current resume or curriculum vitae. Additional exam requirements/recommendations for international students: Required—TOEFL (minimum score 600 paper-based; 100 iBT). *Application deadline:* For fall admission, 6/1 for domestic students, 1/1 for international students. Applications are processed on a rolling basis. Application fee: $100. Electronic applications accepted. *Expenses:* Contact institution. *Financial support:* Career-related internships or fieldwork and scholarships/grants available. Financial award application deadline: 4/15; financial award applicants required to submit FAFSA. *Faculty research:* Influence of personal relationships on business decision-making and management of change; drivers of perceived value and consumer behavior; impact of accounting on auditing, financial, managerial, systems and taxation stakeholders; corporate governance and executive compensation; impact of operations strategies on competitiveness. *Unit head:* James Willis, Associate Dean for Accountancy, 336-758-5422, Fax: 336-758-5830, E-mail: busadmissions@wfu.edu. *Application contact:* Tamara Paquee, Administrative Assistant, 336-758-5422, Fax: 336-758-5830, E-mail: busadmissions@wfu.edu.
Website: http://business.wfu.edu/ms-accountancy

Walden University, Graduate Programs, School of Management, Minneapolis, MN 55401. Offers accounting (MBA, MS, DBA), including accounting for the professional (MS), accounting with CPA emphasis (MS), self-designed (MS); advanced project management (Graduate Certificate); applied project management (Graduate Certificate); auditing (Graduate Certificate); bridge to business administration (Post-Doctoral Certificate); bridge to management (Post-Doctoral Certificate); business management (Graduate Certificate); communication (MBA); corporate finance (MBA); digital marketing (Graduate Certificate); entrepreneurship (DBA); entrepreneurship and small business (MBA); finance (MS, DBA), including finance for the professional (MS), finance with CFA/investment (MS), finance with CPA emphasis (MS); global supply chain management (DBA); healthcare management (MBA, DBA); human resource management (MBA, MS, Graduate Certificate), including functional human resource management (MS), general program (MS), integrating functional and strategic human resource management (MS), organizational strategy (MS); human resources management (DBA); information systems management (DBA); international business (MBA, DBA); leadership (MBA, MS, DBA, Graduate Certificate), including general program (MS), human resource leadership (MS), leader development (MS), self-designed (MS); management (MS, PhD), including communications (MS), finance (PhD), general program (MS), healthcare management (MS), human resource management (MS), human resources management (PhD), information systems management (PhD), international business (MS), leadership (MS), leadership and organizational change (PhD), marketing (MS), project management (MS), strategy and operations (MS); managerial accounting (Graduate Certificate); marketing (MBA, MS, DBA); project management (MBA, MS, DBA); self-designed (MBA, DBA); social impact management (DBA); technology entrepreneurship (DBA). *Accreditation:* ACBSP. *Program availability:* Part-time, evening/weekend, online only, 100% online. *Degree requirements:* For master's, thesis (for some programs), residency (for EMBA); for doctorate, thesis/dissertation (for some programs), residency. *Entrance requirements:* For master's, bachelor's degree or higher; minimum GPA of 2.5; official transcripts; goal statement (for some programs); access to computer and Internet; for doctorate, master's degree or higher; three years of related professional or academic experience (preferred); minimum GPA of 3.0; goal statement and current resume (for select programs); official transcripts; access to computer and Internet; for other advanced degree, relevant work experience; access to computer and Internet. Additional exam requirements/recommendations for international students: Required—TOEFL (minimum score 550 paper-based, 79 iBT), IELTS (minimum score 6.5), Michigan English Language Assessment Battery (minimum score 82), or PTE (minimum score 53). Electronic applications accepted.

Walsh College of Accountancy and Business Administration, Graduate Programs, Program in Accountancy, Troy, MI 48083. Offers finance (MAC); taxation (MAC). *Program availability:* Part-time, evening/weekend. *Faculty:* 8 full-time (4 women), 24 part-time/adjunct (6 women). *Students:* 278 (159 women); includes 55 minority (23 Black or African American, non-Hispanic/Latino; 1 American Indian or Alaska Native, non-Hispanic/Latino; 21 Asian, non-Hispanic/Latino; 7 Hispanic/Latino; 3 Two or more races, non-Hispanic/Latino), 24 international. Average age 32. 94 applicants, 76% accepted, 71 enrolled. In 2016, 93 master's awarded. *Degree requirements:* For master's, thesis optional. *Entrance requirements:* For master's, minimum overall cumulative GPA of 2.75 from all colleges previously attended. Additional exam requirements/recommendations for international students: Required—TOEFL (minimum score 550 paper-based, 79 iBT), IELTS (6.5), Michigan English Language Assessment Battery, or MTELP. *Application deadline:* Applications are processed on a rolling basis. Application fee: $35. Electronic applications accepted. *Expenses:* $740 per semester credit hour, $125 registration fee per semester. *Financial support:* In 2016–17, 19 students received support. Career-related internships or fieldwork and scholarships/grants available. Financial award application deadline: 6/30; financial award applicants required to submit FAFSA. *Unit head:* John Black, Chair, Accounting, Tax and Business Law, 248-823-1635, Fax: 248-689-0920, E-mail: jblack@walshcollege.edu. *Application contact:* Heather Rigby, Director, Admissions and Academic Advising, 248-823-1294, Fax: 248-823-1611, E-mail: hrigby@walshcollege.edu.

Warner University, School of Business, Lake Wales, FL 33859. Offers accounting (MBA); business administration (MBA); human resource management (MBA); international business (MBA); management (MSMC). *Program availability:* Part-time, evening/weekend, online learning. *Degree requirements:* For master's, comprehensive exam, thesis. *Entrance requirements:* For master's, minimum GPA of 3.0, letters of recommendation (2). Additional exam requirements/recommendations for international students: Required—TOEFL. *Application deadline:* Applications are processed on a rolling basis. Application fee: $50. Electronic applications accepted. *Financial support:* Scholarships/grants available. Financial award applicants required to submit FAFSA. *Unit head:* Cindy Polston, Program Director, 863-638-7689. *Application contact:* Judianne Steibly, Graduate Academic Advisor, 863-638-3702, Fax: 863-638-4907, E-mail: admissions@warner.edu.

Washburn University, School of Business, Topeka, KS 66621. Offers accountancy (M Acc). *Accreditation:* AACSB. *Program availability:* Part-time, evening/weekend. *Entrance requirements:* For master's, GMAT, minimum GPA of 2.75. Additional exam requirements/recommendations for international students: Required—TOEFL (minimum score 550 paper-based; 80 iBT); Recommended—IELTS (minimum score 6.5). Electronic applications accepted. *Faculty research:* Ethics in information technology, forecasting for shareholder value creation, model for measuring expected losses from litigation contingencies, business vs. family commitment in family businesses, calculated intangible value and brand recognition.

Washington & Jefferson College, Graduate and Continuing Studies, Washington, PA 15301. Offers applied health care economics and outcomes management (MS); professional accounting (MAC); professional writing (Graduate Certificate); thanatology (Graduate Certificate).

Washington State University, Carson College of Business, Department of Accounting, Pullman, WA 99164-4729. Offers M Acc. Program also offered at the Vancouver campus. *Accreditation:* AACSB. *Program availability:* Part-time. *Degree requirements:* For master's, comprehensive exam, thesis or alternative. *Entrance requirements:* For master's, GMAT (minimum score of 500), minimum GPA of 3.0, statement of purpose. Additional exam requirements/recommendations for international students: Required—TOEFL (minimum score 580 paper-based; 93 iBT), IELTS (minimum score 7.5). Electronic applications accepted. *Faculty research:* Ethics, taxation, auditing, finance.

Washington University in St. Louis, Olin Business School, Program in Accounting, St. Louis, MO 63130-4899. Offers MS. *Program availability:* Part-time. *Faculty:* 97 full-time (22 women), 44 part-time/adjunct (13 women). *Students:* 84 full-time (54 women), 1 part-time (0 women); includes 7 minority (1 Black or African American, non-Hispanic/Latino; 5 Asian, non-Hispanic/Latino; 1 Two or more races, non-Hispanic/Latino), 65 international. Average age 24. 479 applicants, 23% accepted, 54 enrolled. In 2016, 63 master's awarded. *Entrance requirements:* For master's, GMAT or GRE. Additional exam requirements/recommendations for international students: Required—TOEFL, IELTS. *Application deadline:* For fall admission, 10/3 for domestic students, 2/1 priority date for international students; for winter admission, 12/1 for domestic students; for spring admission, 4/3 for domestic students. Applications are processed on a rolling basis. Application fee: $100. Electronic applications accepted. *Financial support:* Institutionally sponsored loans and scholarships/grants available. Financial award applicants required to submit FAFSA. *Unit head:* Joe Fox, Associate Dean/Director of Specialized Master's Programs, 314-935-6322, Fax: 314-935-4464, E-mail: fox@wustl.edu. *Application contact:* 314-935-7301, E-mail: olingradadmissions@wustl.edu.

Wayland Baptist University, Graduate Programs, Programs in Business Administration/Management, Plainview, TX 79072-6998. Offers accounting (MBA); general business (MBA); health care administration (MAM, MBA); human resource management (MAM, MBA); international management (MBA); management (MBA, D Mgt); management information systems (MBA); organization management (MAM); project management (MBA). *Program availability:* Part-time, evening/weekend, online learning. *Degree requirements:* For master's, capstone course. *Entrance requirements:* For master's, GMAT, GRE or MAT. Additional exam requirements/recommendations for international students: Required—TOEFL (minimum score 500 paper-based; 61 iBT). Electronic applications accepted.

Wayne State University, Mike Ilitch School of Business, Detroit, MI 48202. Offers accounting (MS, Postbaccalaureate Certificate); business (Graduate Certificate); business administration (MBA, PhD); data science (MS), including business analytics; entrepreneurship and innovation (Postbaccalaureate Certificate); finance (MS); information systems management (Postbaccalaureate Certificate); taxation (MST); JD/MBA. Application deadline for PhD is February 15. *Accreditation:* AACSB. *Program availability:* Part-time, evening/weekend. *Faculty:* 32. *Students:* 219 full-time (105 women), 941 part-time (406 women); includes 314 minority (186 Black or African American, non-Hispanic/Latino; 3 American Indian or Alaska Native, non-Hispanic/Latino; 68 Asian, non-Hispanic/Latino; 33 Hispanic/Latino; 24 Two or more races, non-Hispanic/Latino), 88 international. Average age 30. 1,119 applicants, 49% accepted, 329 enrolled. In 2016, 203 master's, 1 doctorate, 3 other advanced degrees awarded. *Degree requirements:* For doctorate, thesis/dissertation. *Entrance requirements:* For master's, GMAT, GRE, LSAT, MCAT, at least three years of relevant work experience that shows increased responsibility, or minimum GPA of 3.0 from AACSB-accredited program or 3.2 from regionally-accredited program, undergraduate degree from accredited institution; undergraduate degree in accounting, business administration, or area of business administration (for MS and MST); for doctorate, GMAT (minimum score of 600), minimum undergraduate GPA of 3.0, 3.5 upper-division or graduate; three letters of recommendation; brief essay; undergraduate degree from accredited institution; personal statement; for other advanced degree, bachelor's degree from accredited institution. Additional exam requirements/recommendations for international students: Required—TOEFL (minimum score 550 paper-based; 79 iBT), Michigan English Language Assessment Battery (minimum score 85); Recommended—IELTS (minimum score 6.5), TWE (minimum score 5.5). *Application deadline:* For fall admission, 7/1 for domestic students, 5/1 priority date for international students; for winter admission, 11/1 for domestic students, 9/1 priority date for international students; for spring admission, 3/1 for domestic students, 1/1 priority date for international students. Applications are processed on a rolling basis. Application fee: $50. Electronic applications accepted. *Expenses:* $18,871 per year resident tuition and fees, $36,065 per year non-resident tuition and fees. *Financial support:* In 2016–17, 174 students received support, including 1 fellowship with tuition reimbursement available (averaging $18,000 per year), 2 research assistantships with tuition reimbursements available (averaging $18,000 per year), 5 teaching assistantships with tuition reimbursements available (averaging $18,000 per year); scholarships/grants, health care benefits, and unspecified assistantships also available. Support available to part-time students. Financial award applicants required to submit FAFSA. *Faculty research:* Executive compensation and stock performance, consumer reactions to pricing strategies, communication across the automotive supply chain, performance of firms in sub-Saharan Africa, implementation issues with ERP software. *Unit head:* Dr. Robert Forsythe, Dean, School of Business Administration, 313-577-4501, E-mail: robert.forsythe@wayne.edu. *Application contact:* Kiantee N. Rupert-Jones, Director, 313-577-4511, Fax: 313-577-9442, E-mail: gradbusiness@wayne.edu.
Website: http://ilitchbusiness.wayne.edu/

Webber International University, Graduate School of Business, Babson Park, FL 33827-0096. Offers accounting (MBA); business (MBA); criminal justice management (MBA); international business (MBA); sport business management (MBA). *Program availability:* Part-time, evening/weekend, 100% online. *Faculty:* 11 full-time (3 women), 1 part-time/adjunct (0 women). *Students:* 44 full-time (21 women), 6 part-time (2 women);

includes 11 minority (5 Black or African American, non-Hispanic/Latino; 5 Hispanic/Latino; 1 Two or more races, non-Hispanic/Latino), 11 international. Average age 27. 32 applicants, 69% accepted, 18 enrolled. In 2016, 16 master's awarded. *Degree requirements:* For master's, class trip (for international business); practicum (for criminal justice management). *Entrance requirements:* For master's, three recommendation letters, résumé, essay, official transcripts from all colleges and universities attended. Additional exam requirements/recommendations for international students: Recommended—TOEFL (minimum score 500 paper-based; 61 iBT), IELTS (minimum score 6). *Application deadline:* For fall admission, 7/1 for international students. Applications are processed on a rolling basis. Application fee: $50 ($75 for international students). Electronic applications accepted. *Expenses:* $2,013 tuition per course; $207 technology fee per course (for online courses only). *Financial support:* In 2016–17, 11 students received support. Scholarships/grants and unspecified assistantships available. Financial award application deadline: 8/16; financial award applicants required to submit FAFSA. *Unit head:* Dr. Nikos Orphanoudakis, Dean, 863-638-2910, Fax: 863-638-1591, E-mail: orphanoudakisn@webber.edu. *Application contact:* Lacy Edwards, Admissions Counselor and MBA Coordinator, 863-638-2910, Fax: 863-638-1591, E-mail: admissions@webber.edu.

Weber State University, John B. Goddard School of Business and Economics, School of Accounting and Taxation, Ogden, UT 84408-1001. Offers accounting (M Acc); taxation (M Tax). *Accreditation:* AACSB. *Program availability:* Part-time, evening/weekend. *Faculty:* 7 full-time (2 women). *Students:* 25 full-time (12 women), 12 part-time (4 women); includes 3 minority (1 Asian, non-Hispanic/Latino; 2 Hispanic/Latino), 6 international. Average age 30. In 2016, 42 master's awarded. *Entrance requirements:* For master's, GMAT. Additional exam requirements/recommendations for international students: Required—TOEFL (minimum score 80 iBT). *Application deadline:* For fall admission, 8/1 for domestic students; for spring admission, 12/1 for domestic students; for summer admission, 4/1 for domestic students. Application fee: $60 ($90 for international students). Electronic applications accepted. *Expenses:* Contact institution. *Financial support:* In 2016–17, 19 students received support. Scholarships/grants available. Financial award application deadline: 4/1; financial award applicants required to submit FAFSA. *Unit head:* Dr. Ryan Pace, Program Director, 801-626-7562, Fax: 801-626-7423, E-mail: rpace@weber.edu. *Application contact:* Dr. Larry A. Deppe, Graduate Coordinator, 801-626-7838, Fax: 801-626-7423, E-mail: ldeppe1@weber.edu.
Website: http://www.weber.edu/goddard/accounting-taxation.html

Webster University, George Herbert Walker School of Business and Technology, Department of Business, St. Louis, MO 63119-3194. Offers business and organizational security management (MBA); decision support systems (MBA); environmental management (MBA); finance (MBA, MS); forensic accounting (MS); gerontology (MBA); human resources development (MBA); human resources management (MBA); information technology management (MBA); international business (MA, MBA); international relations (MBA); management and leadership (MBA); marketing (MBA); media communications (MBA); procurement and acquisitions management (MBA); Web services (MBA). *Accreditation:* ACBSP. *Program availability:* Part-time, evening/weekend, online learning. *Degree requirements:* For master's, comprehensive exam (for some programs), thesis (for some programs). *Entrance requirements:* Additional exam requirements/recommendations for international students: Required—TOEFL. *Application deadline:* Applications are processed on a rolling basis. Application fee: $35 ($50 for international students). *Expenses: Tuition:* Full-time $21,900; part-time $730 per credit hour. Tuition and fees vary according to campus/location and program. *Financial support:* Federal Work-Study available. Support available to part-time students. Financial award application deadline: 4/1; financial award applicants required to submit FAFSA. *Unit head:* David Porras, Chair, 314-246-8621, E-mail: porrasd@webster.edu. *Application contact:* Sarah Nandor, Director, Graduate and Transfer Admissions, 314-968-7109, E-mail: gadmit@webster.edu.

Western Carolina University, Graduate School, College of Business, Program in Accountancy, Cullowhee, NC 28723. Offers M Ac. *Program availability:* Part-time, evening/weekend. *Entrance requirements:* For master's, GMAT, appropriate undergraduate degree, 3 letters of recommendation. Additional exam requirements/recommendations for international students: Required—TOEFL (minimum score 550 paper-based; 79 iBT). *Expenses:* Tuition, state resident: full-time $2174. Tuition, nonresident: full-time $7377. *Required fees:* $1442. Part-time tuition and fees vary according to course load.

Western Connecticut State University, Division of Graduate Studies, Ancell School of Business, Program in Business Administration, Danbury, CT 06810-6885. Offers accounting (MBA); business administration (MBA). *Program availability:* Part-time. *Degree requirements:* For master's, comprehensive exam, completion of program within 8 years. *Entrance requirements:* For master's, GMAT. Additional exam requirements/recommendations for international students: Recommended—TOEFL (minimum score 550 paper-based; 79 iBT), IELTS (minimum score 6). *Faculty research:* Global strategic marketing planning, project management and team coordination; email, discussion boards that act as blogs and videoconferencing.

Western Illinois University, School of Graduate Studies, College of Business and Technology, Department of Accountancy, Macomb, IL 61455-1390. Offers M Acct. *Accreditation:* AACSB. *Program availability:* Part-time. *Students:* 16 full-time (13 women), 6 part-time (5 women); includes 2 minority (1 Black or African American, non-Hispanic/Latino; 1 Asian, non-Hispanic/Latino), 2 international. Average age 30. 12 applicants, 42% accepted, 2 enrolled. In 2016, 12 master's awarded. *Degree requirements:* For master's, thesis or alternative. *Entrance requirements:* For master's, GMAT. Additional exam requirements/recommendations for international students: Required—TOEFL (minimum score 550 paper-based; 80 iBT). *Application deadline:* Applications are processed on a rolling basis. Application fee: $30. Electronic applications accepted. *Financial support:* In 2016–17, 12 students received support. Unspecified assistantships available. Financial award applicants required to submit FAFSA. *Unit head:* Dr. Gregg Woodruff, Chairperson, 309-298-1152. *Application contact:* Dr. Nancy Parsons, Assistant Director of Graduate Studies, 309-298-1806, Fax: 309-298-2345, E-mail: grad-office@wiu.edu. Website: http://wiu.edu/accountancy

Western Michigan University, Graduate College, Haworth College of Business, Department of Accountancy, Kalamazoo, MI 49008. Offers MSA. *Accreditation:* AACSB.

Western New England University, College of Business, Program in Accounting, Springfield, MA 01119. Offers MSA, JD/MSA. *Program availability:* Part-time, evening/weekend. *Faculty:* 11 full-time (3 women). *Students:* 33 part-time (15 women); includes 2 minority (1 Asian, non-Hispanic/Latino; 1 Hispanic/Latino). Average age 26. 22 applicants, 55% accepted, 11 enrolled. In 2016, 26 master's awarded. *Entrance requirements:* For master's, GMAT, official transcript, two letters of recommendation, essay, resume. Additional exam requirements/recommendations for international students: Required—TOEFL (minimum score 79 iBT). *Application deadline:* Applications are processed on a rolling basis. Application fee: $30. Electronic applications accepted. *Expenses:* Contact institution. *Financial support:* Application deadline: 4/15; applicants required to submit FAFSA. *Unit head:* Dr. John Coulter, Chair, Accounting and Finance, 413-782-1720, E-mail: jcoulter@wne.edu. *Application contact:* Matthew Fox, Director of Admissions for Graduate Students and Adult Learners, 413-782-1410, Fax: 413-782-1779, E-mail: study@wne.edu.
Website: http://www1.wne.edu/academics/graduate/msa.cfm

Westfield State University, College of Graduate and Continuing Education, Department of Economics and Business Management, Westfield, MA 01086. Offers accounting (MS). *Program availability:* Part-time, evening/weekend. *Faculty:* 3 full-time (2 women), 4 part-time/adjunct (1 woman). *Students:* 7 full-time (3 women), 14 part-time (8 women); includes 3 minority (1 Black or African American, non-Hispanic/Latino; 1 American Indian or Alaska Native, non-Hispanic/Latino; 1 Hispanic/Latino), 1 international. Average age 27. 13 applicants, 92% accepted, 7 enrolled. In 2016, 5 master's awarded. *Degree requirements:* For master's, comprehensive exam, thesis (for some programs). *Entrance requirements:* For master's, GRE General Test or MAT, minimum undergraduate GPA of 2.8. Additional exam requirements/recommendations for international students: Recommended—TOEFL (minimum score 550 paper-based; 79 iBT). *Application deadline:* For fall admission, 6/30 for domestic students; for spring admission, 10/31 for domestic students; for summer admission, 3/31 for domestic students. Application fee: $50. *Expenses:* Tuition, state resident: part-time $318 per semester hour. Tuition, nonresident: part-time $318 per semester hour. *Required fees:* $75 per semester. Tuition and fees vary according to course load and program. *Financial support:* Unspecified assistantships available. Financial award application deadline: 3/1; financial award applicants required to submit FAFSA. *Unit head:* Dr. Michelle Maggio, Acting Chair, 413-572-5591, Fax: 413-572-8787, E-mail: mmaggio@westfield.ma.edu. *Application contact:* Shelly Henrichon, Admissions Coordinator, 413-572-8022, Fax: 413-572-5227, E-mail: mhenrichon@westfield.ma.edu.

Westminster College, The Bill and Vieve Gore School of Business, Salt Lake City, UT 84105. Offers accountancy (M Acc); business administration (MBA, Certificate); technology commercialization (MBA). *Program availability:* Part-time, evening/weekend, 100% online. *Faculty:* 19 full-time (5 women), 20 part-time/adjunct (7 women). *Students:* 120 full-time (43 women), 124 part-time (45 women); includes 47 minority (8 Black or African American, non-Hispanic/Latino; 1 American Indian or Alaska Native, non-Hispanic/Latino; 15 Asian, non-Hispanic/Latino; 18 Hispanic/Latino; 5 Two or more races, non-Hispanic/Latino), 12 international. Average age 34. 97 applicants, 79% accepted, 56 enrolled. In 2016, 119 master's, 10 other advanced degrees awarded. *Entrance requirements:* For master's, GMAT, 2 professional recommendations, employer letter of support, personal resume, essay, official transcripts. Additional exam requirements/recommendations for international students: Required—TOEFL (minimum score 600 paper-based; 84 iBT), IELTS (minimum score 7.5). *Application deadline:* For fall admission, 5/20 priority date for domestic and international students; for spring admission, 10/7 priority date for domestic and international students; for summer admission, 2/5 priority date for domestic and international students. Applications are processed on a rolling basis. Application fee: $50. Electronic applications accepted. *Expenses:* Contact institution. *Financial support:* In 2016–17, 87 students received support. Career-related internships or fieldwork, scholarships/grants, unspecified assistantships, and tuition reimbursements, tuition remission available. Financial award applicants required to submit FAFSA. *Faculty research:* Innovation and entrepreneurship, business strategy and change, financial analysis and capital budgeting, leadership development, knowledge management. *Unit head:* Melissa Koerner, Interim Dean, Bill and Vieve Gore School of Business, 801-832-2600, Fax: 801-832-3106, E-mail: mkoerner@westminstercollege.edu. *Application contact:* Ashley Williams, Director of Graduate Admissions, 801-832-2213, Fax: 801-832-3101, E-mail: awilliams@westminstercollege.edu.
Website: http://www.westminstercollege.edu/mba/

West Virginia University, College of Business and Economics, Division of Accounting, Morgantown, WV 26506. Offers MPA. *Accreditation:* AACSB. *Program availability:* Part-time, evening/weekend. *Entrance requirements:* For master's, GMAT (minimum 50th percentile), BS in accounting or equivalent, minimum GPA of 3.0. Additional exam requirements/recommendations for international students: Required—TOEFL. Electronic applications accepted. *Faculty research:* Financial reporting, government/not-for-profit accounting, information systems/technology, forensic accounting, internal control.

Wheeling Jesuit University, Department of Business, Wheeling, WV 26003-6295. Offers accounting (MSA); business administration (MBA). *Accreditation:* ACBSP. *Program availability:* Part-time, evening/weekend. *Entrance requirements:* For master's, minimum undergraduate GPA of 2.8. Additional exam requirements/recommendations for international students: Required—TOEFL (minimum score 600 paper-based; 100 iBT). Electronic applications accepted. *Faculty research:* Forensic economics, consumer behavior, economic development, capitalism, leadership.

Wichita State University, Graduate School, W. Frank Barton School of Business, School of Accountancy, Wichita, KS 67260. Offers accounting information systems (M Acc); taxation (M Acc). *Accreditation:* AACSB. *Program availability:* Part-time, evening/weekend. *Unit head:* Dr. Paul D. Harrison, Director, 316-978-3215, Fax: 316-978-3660, E-mail: paul.harrison@wichita.edu. *Application contact:* Jordan Oleson, Admissions Coordinator, 316-978-3095, Fax: 316-978-3253, E-mail: jordan.oleson@wichita.edu.
Website: http://www.wichita.edu/acct

Wilfrid Laurier University, Faculty of Graduate and Postdoctoral Studies, School of Business and Economics, Department of Business, Waterloo, ON N2L 3C5, Canada. Offers accounting (PhD); finance (M Fin); financial economics (PhD); marketing (PhD); operations and supply chain management (PhD); organizational behavior and human resource management (M Sc); organizational behaviour and human resource management (PhD); supply chain management (M Sc); technology management (EMTM). *Accreditation:* AACSB. *Program availability:* Part-time, evening/weekend. *Degree requirements:* For master's, thesis optional; for doctorate, comprehensive exam, thesis/dissertation. *Entrance requirements:* For master's, GMAT, 4-year honors degree with minimum B+ average; for doctorate, GMAT, master's degree, minimum B+ average. Additional exam requirements/recommendations for international students: Required—TOEFL (minimum score 89 iBT). Electronic applications accepted. *Faculty research:* Financial economics, management and organizational behavior, operations and supply chain management.

Wilkes University, College of Graduate and Professional Studies, Jay S. Sidhu School of Business and Leadership, Wilkes-Barre, PA 18766-0002. Offers accounting (MBA); entrepreneurship (MBA); finance (MBA); health care administration (MBA); human resource management (MBA); international business (MBA); operations management (MBA); organizational leadership and development (MBA). *Accreditation:* ACBSP. *Program availability:* Part-time, evening/weekend. *Students:* 35 full-time (17 women), 112 part-time (55 women); includes 17 minority (6 Black or African American, non-Hispanic/Latino; 4 Asian, non-Hispanic/Latino; 5 Hispanic/Latino; 2 Two or more races, non-Hispanic/Latino), 16 international. Average age 31. In 2016, 59 master's awarded. *Entrance requirements:* For master's, GMAT. Additional exam requirements/recommendations for international students: Required—TOEFL (minimum score 550 paper-based; 79 iBT). *Application deadline:* Applications are processed on a rolling basis. Application fee: $45 ($65 for international students). Electronic applications accepted. *Expenses:* Contact institution. *Financial support:* Unspecified assistantships

available. Financial award application deadline: 3/1; financial award applicants required to submit FAFSA. *Unit head:* Dr. Abel Adekola, Dean, 570-408-4701, Fax: 570-408-7846, E-mail: abel.adekola@wilkes.edu. *Application contact:* Director of Graduate Enrollment, 570-408-4234, Fax: 570-408-7846.
Website: http://www.wilkes.edu/academics/colleges/sidhu-school-of-business-leadership/index.aspx

Wilmington University, College of Business, New Castle, DE 19720-6491. Offers accounting (MBA, MS); business administration (MBA, DBA); environmental stewardship (MBA); finance (MBA); health care administration (MBA, MSM); homeland security (MBA, MSM); human resource management (MSM); management information systems (MBA, MSN); marketing (MSM); marketing management (MBA); military leadership (MSM); organizational leadership (MBA, MSM); public administration (MSM). *Program availability:* Part-time, evening/weekend. *Faculty:* 17 full-time (7 women), 106 part-time/adjunct (46 women). *Students:* 436 full-time (237 women), 1,202 part-time (739 women); includes 594 minority (474 Black or African American, non-Hispanic/Latino; 19 American Indian or Alaska Native, non-Hispanic/Latino; 64 Asian, non-Hispanic/Latino; 30 Hispanic/Latino; 3 Native Hawaiian or other Pacific Islander, non-Hispanic/Latino; 4 Two or more races, non-Hispanic/Latino), 153 international. Average age 35. 814 applicants, 98% accepted, 426 enrolled. In 2016, 594 master's, 23 doctorates awarded. *Entrance requirements:* Additional exam requirements/recommendations for international students: Required—TOEFL (minimum score 500 paper-based). *Application deadline:* Applications are processed on a rolling basis. Application fee: $35. Electronic applications accepted. *Expenses: Tuition:* Full-time $8388; part-time $466 per credit. *Required fees:* $25 per semester. Tuition and fees vary according to degree level. *Financial support:* Applicants required to submit FAFSA. *Unit head:* Dr. Robert W. Rescigno, Dean. *Application contact:* Laura Morris, Director of Admissions, 877-967-5456, E-mail: infocenter@wilmu.edu.
Website: http://www.wilmu.edu/business/

Wilson College, Graduate Programs, Chambersburg, PA 17201-1285. Offers accounting (M Acc); choreography and visual art (MFA); education (M Ed); healthcare management for sustainability (MHM); humanities (MA), including art and culture, critical/cultural theory, English language and literature, women's studies; management (MSM); nursing (MSN), including nursing education, nursing leadership and management. *Program availability:* Evening/weekend. *Degree requirements:* For master's, project. *Entrance requirements:* For master's, PRAXIS, minimum undergraduate cumulative GPA of 3.0, 2 letters of recommendation, current certification for eligibility to teach in grades K-12, resume, personal interview. Electronic applications accepted.

Wingate University, Porter B. Byrum School of Business, Wingate, NC 28174. Offers accounting (MAC); corporate innovation (MBA); finance (MBA); general management (MBA); healthcare management (MBA); marketing (MBA); project management (MBA). *Accreditation:* ACBSP. *Program availability:* Part-time, evening/weekend. *Entrance requirements:* For master's, GMAT, work experience, 2 letters of recommendation. *Application deadline:* For fall admission, 8/15 priority date for domestic students; for spring admission, 12/15 priority date for domestic students. Applications are processed on a rolling basis. Application fee: $50. Electronic applications accepted. *Expenses:* Contact institution. *Financial support:* Federal Work-Study and scholarships/grants available. Support available to part-time students. Financial award application deadline: 8/1; financial award applicants required to submit FAFSA. *Faculty research:* Stochastic processes, business ethics, regional economic development, municipal finance, consumer behavior. *Unit head:* Dr. Peter Frank, Dean, 704-233-8148, Fax: 704-233-8146, E-mail: pfrank@wingate.edu. *Application contact:* Mary Maye, Administrative Assistant to the Dean, 704-233-8148, Fax: 704-233-8146.
Website: http://www.wingate.edu/academics/school-of-business

Worcester State University, Graduate Studies, Program in Management, Worcester, MA 01602-2597. Offers accounting (MS); managerial leadership (MS). *Program availability:* Part-time, evening/weekend. *Faculty:* 7 full-time (3 women). *Students:* 9 full-time (5 women), 36 part-time (22 women); includes 11 minority (5 Black or African American, non-Hispanic/Latino; 2 Asian, non-Hispanic/Latino; 3 Hispanic/Latino; 1 Two or more races, non-Hispanic/Latino), 3 international. Average age 32. 44 applicants, 70% accepted, 15 enrolled. In 2016, 10 master's awarded. *Degree requirements:* For master's, comprehensive exam (for some programs), thesis optional. *Entrance requirements:* For master's, GMAT, 3 letters of recommendation from professors and/or supervisors. Additional exam requirements/recommendations for international students: Required—TOEFL (minimum score 550 paper-based; 79 iBT). *Application deadline:* For fall admission, 6/15 for domestic and international students; for spring admission, 11/1 for domestic and international students; for summer admission, 4/1 for domestic and international students. Applications are processed on a rolling basis. Application fee: $50. Electronic applications accepted. *Expenses:* Tuition, state resident: part-time $150 per credit. Tuition, nonresident: part-time $150 per credit. *Financial support:* Career-related internships or fieldwork, scholarships/grants, and unspecified assistantships available. Financial award application deadline: 3/1; financial award applicants required to submit FAFSA. *Unit head:* Dr. Elizabeth Wark, Program Coordinator, 508-929-8743, E-mail: ewark@worcester.edu. *Application contact:* Sara Grady, Associate Dean, Graduate Studies and Professional Development, 508-929-8787, Fax: 508-929-8100, E-mail: sara.grady@worcester.edu.

Wright State University, Graduate School, Raj Soin College of Business, Department of Accountancy, Accountancy Program, Dayton, OH 45435. Offers M Acc. *Expenses:* Tuition, state resident: full-time $9952; part-time $622 per credit hour. Tuition, nonresident: full-time $16,960; part-time $1060 per credit hour. *Unit head:* Dr. Susan S. Lightle, Director, 937-775-4169, Fax: 937-775-2310, E-mail: susan.lightle@wright.edu. *Application contact:* Dr. Susan S. Lightle, Director, 937-775-4169, Fax: 937-775-2310, E-mail: susan.lightle@wright.edu.

Xavier University, Williams College of Business, Master of Science in Accountancy Program, Cincinnati, OH 45207. Offers MS. *Entrance requirements:* For master's, GMAT, official transcript; resume; 3 letters of recommendation. Additional exam requirements/recommendations for international students: Required—TOEFL (minimum score 550 paper-based; 70 iBT) or IELTS. Electronic applications accepted. Application fee is waived when completed online. *Expenses:* Contact institution.

Yale University, Yale School of Management and Graduate School of Arts and Sciences, Doctoral Program in Management, New Haven, CT 06520. Offers accounting (PhD); financial economics (PhD); marketing (PhD); organizations and management (PhD). *Accreditation:* AACSB. *Degree requirements:* For doctorate, comprehensive exam, thesis/dissertation. *Entrance requirements:* For doctorate, GMAT or GRE General Test. Additional exam requirements/recommendations for international students: Required—TOEFL or IELTS. Electronic applications accepted. *Expenses:* Contact institution. *Faculty research:* Pricing of options and futures, term structure of interest rates, use of accounting numbers in debt contracts, product differentiation, e-commerce and marketing, behavioral finance.

Yeshiva University, Sy Syms School of Business, New York, NY 10016. Offers accounting (MS); business (EMBA); marketing (MS). *Program availability:* Part-time. *Entrance requirements:* For master's, minimum GPA of 3.5 or GMAT.

York University, Faculty of Graduate Studies, Schulich School of Business, Toronto, ON M3J 1P3, Canada. Offers accounting (M Acc); administration (PhD); business (MBA); business analytics (MBA); finance (MF); international business (IMBA); MBA/JD; MBA/MA; MBA/MFA. *Program availability:* Part-time, evening/weekend. *Degree requirements:* For master's, advanced proficiency in a second language, work term (IMBA); for doctorate, comprehensive exam, thesis/dissertation. *Entrance requirements:* For master's, GMAT or GRE, minimum GPA of 3.0 (3.3 for MF, MBA in business analytics, and IMBA); for doctorate, GMAT or GRE, minimum GPA of 3.3. Additional exam requirements/recommendations for international students: Required—TOEFL (minimum score 600 paper-based; 100 iBT), IELTS (minimum score 7), York English Language Test (minimum score 1); PearsonVUE (minimum score 64). Electronic applications accepted. *Faculty research:* Accounting, finance, marketing, operations management and information systems, organizational studies, strategic management.

Youngstown State University, Graduate School, Williamson College of Business Administration, Department of Accounting and Finance, Youngstown, OH 44555-0001. Offers accounting (MBA). *Accreditation:* AACSB. *Program availability:* Part-time, evening/weekend. *Degree requirements:* For master's, thesis optional. *Entrance requirements:* For master's, GMAT, minimum GPA of 2.7. Additional exam requirements/recommendations for international students: Required—TOEFL. *Faculty research:* Taxation and compliance, capital markets, accounting information systems, accounting theory, tax and government accounting.

Finance and Banking

Adelphi University, Robert B. Willumstad School of Business, MBA Program, Garden City, NY 11530-0701. Offers accounting (MBA); finance (MBA); health services administration (MBA); human resource management (MBA); management (MBA); management information systems (MBA); marketing (MBA); sport management (MBA). *Accreditation:* AACSB. *Program availability:* Part-time, evening/weekend. *Students:* 172 full-time (74 women), 129 part-time (66 women); includes 30 minority (9 Black or African American, non-Hispanic/Latino; 11 Asian, non-Hispanic/Latino; 9 Hispanic/Latino; 1 Two or more races, non-Hispanic/Latino), 29 international. Average age 32. 4 applicants. In 2016, 130 master's awarded. *Degree requirements:* For master's, capstone course. *Entrance requirements:* For master's, GMAT, 2 letters of recommendation. Additional exam requirements/recommendations for international students: Required—TOEFL (minimum score 550 paper-based; 80 iBT), IELTS (minimum score 6.5). *Application deadline:* For fall admission, 4/1 for international students; for spring admission, 11/1 for international students. Applications are processed on a rolling basis. Application fee: $50. Electronic applications accepted. *Expenses:* Contact institution. *Financial support:* Research assistantships with partial tuition reimbursements, career-related internships or fieldwork, Federal Work-Study, institutionally sponsored loans, scholarships/grants, tuition waivers (partial), and unspecified assistantships available. Financial award application deadline: 3/1; financial award applicants required to submit FAFSA. *Faculty research:* Supply chain management, distribution channels, productivity benchmark analysis, data envelopment analysis, financial portfolio analysis. *Unit head:* Dr. Rakesh Gupta, Associate Dean, 516-877-4629. *Application contact:* Christine Murphy, Director of Admissions, 516-877-3050, Fax: 516-877-3039, E-mail: graduateadmissions@adelphi.edu.
Website: http://business.adelphi.edu/degree-programs/graduate-degree-programs/m-b-a/

American Business & Technology University, Programs in Business Administration, Saint Joseph, MO 64506. Offers business administration (MBA); financial management (MBA); global business management (MBA); information systems management (MBA); marketing and social media (MBA); project and operations management (MBA); public accounting (MBA). *Program availability:* Online learning.

The American College of Financial Services, Graduate Programs, Bryn Mawr, PA 19010-2105. Offers financial services (MSFS); leadership (MSM). *Program availability:* Part-time, evening/weekend, online learning. Electronic applications accepted. *Faculty research:* Retirement counseling, social security, aging, family composition, inflation.

American College of Thessaloniki, Department of Business Administration, Pylea, Greece. Offers banking and finance (MBA); entrepreneurship (MBA, Certificate); finance (Certificate); management (MBA, Certificate); marketing (MBA, Certificate). *Program availability:* Part-time, evening/weekend. *Degree requirements:* For master's, thesis. *Entrance requirements:* For master's, bachelor's degree. Additional exam requirements/recommendations for international students: Recommended—TOEFL. Electronic applications accepted.

American InterContinental University Online, Program in Business Administration, Schaumburg, IL 60173. Offers accounting and finance (MBA); finance (MBA); healthcare management (MBA); human resource management (MBA); international business (MBA); management (MBA); marketing (MBA); operations management (MBA); organizational psychology and development (MBA); project management (MBA). *Accreditation:* ACBSP. *Program availability:* Evening/weekend, online learning. *Entrance requirements:* Additional exam requirements/recommendations for international students: Required—TOEFL (minimum score 550 paper-based). Electronic applications accepted.

American Public University System, AMU/APU Graduate Programs, Charles Town, WV 25414. Offers accounting (MBA, MS); applied business analytics (MBA, MS); criminal justice (MA), including business administration, emergency and disaster management, general (MA, MS); educational leadership (M Ed); emergency and disaster management (MA); entrepreneurship (MBA); environmental policy and management (MS), including environmental planning, environmental sustainability, fish and wildlife management, general (MA, MS), global environmental management; finance (MBA); general (MBA); government contracting and acquisition (MBA); health care administration (MBA); health information management (MS); history (MA), including American history, ancient and classical history, European history, global history, public

history; homeland security (MA), including business administration, counterterrorism studies, criminal justice, cyber, emergency management and public health, intelligence studies, transportation security; homeland security resource allocation (MBA); humanities (MA); information technology (MS), including digital forensics, enterprise software development, information assurance and security, IT project management; information technology management (MBA); intelligence studies (MA), including criminal intelligence, cyber, general (MA, MS), homeland security, intelligence analysis, intelligence collection, intelligence management, intelligence operations, terrorism studies; international relations and conflict resolution (MA), including comparative and security issues, conflict resolution, international and transnational security issues, peacekeeping; legal studies (MA); management (MA), including strategic consulting; marketing (MBA); military history (MA), including American military history, American Revolution, civil war, war since 1945, World War II; military studies (MA), including joint warfare, strategic leadership; national security studies (MA), including cyber, general (MA, MS), homeland security, regional security studies, security and intelligence analysis, terrorism studies; nonprofit management (MBA); political science (MA), including American politics and government, comparative government and development, general (MA, MS), international relations, public policy; psychology (MA); public administration (MPA), including disaster management, environmental policy, health policy, human resources, national security, organizational management, security management; public health (MPH); reverse logistics management (MA); security management (MA); space studies (MS), including aerospace science, general (MA, MS), planetary science; sports and health sciences (MS); sports management (MBA); teaching (M Ed), including autism spectrum disorder, curriculum and instruction for elementary teachers, elementary reading, English language learners, instructional leadership, online learning, special education, STEAM (STEM plus the arts); transportation and logistics management (MA). *Program availability:* Part-time, evening/weekend, online only, 100% online. *Faculty:* 401 full-time (228 women), 1,678 part-time/adjunct (781 women). *Students:* 378 full-time (184 women), 8,455 part-time (3,484 women); includes 2,972 minority (1,552 Black or African American, non-Hispanic/Latino; 52 American Indian or Alaska Native, non-Hispanic/Latino; 211 Asian, non-Hispanic/Latino; 791 Hispanic/Latino; 70 Native Hawaiian or other Pacific Islander, non-Hispanic/Latino; 296 Two or more races, non-Hispanic/Latino), 109 international. Average age 37. In 2016, 3,185 master's awarded. *Degree requirements:* For master's, comprehensive exam or practicum. *Entrance requirements:* For master's, official transcript showing earned bachelor's degree from institution accredited by recognized accrediting body. Additional exam requirements/recommendations for international students: Required—TOEFL (minimum score 550 paper-based), IELTS (minimum score 6.5). *Application deadline:* Applications are processed on a rolling basis. Application fee: $0. Electronic applications accepted. *Expenses: Tuition:* Part-time $350 per credit hour. *Required fees:* $50 per course. *Financial support:* Scholarships/grants available. Financial award applicants required to submit FAFSA. *Unit head:* Dr. Karan Powell, President, 877-468-6268, Fax: 304-724-3780. *Application contact:* Terry Grant, Vice President of Enrollment Management, 877-468-6268, Fax: 304-724-3780, E-mail: info@apus.edu.
Website: http://www.apus.edu

American University, Kogod School of Business, Department of Finance, Program in Finance, Washington, DC 20016-8044. Offers MS. *Program availability:* Part-time, evening/weekend. *Students:* 40 full-time (12 women), 17 part-time (7 women); includes 9 minority (6 Black or African American, non-Hispanic/Latino; 1 Asian, non-Hispanic/Latino; 2 Hispanic/Latino), 34 international. Average age 27. 174 applicants, 46% accepted, 22 enrolled. In 2016, 21 master's awarded. *Entrance requirements:* For master's, GMAT/GRE, resume, personal statement, interview, two letters of recommendation, transcript. Additional exam requirements/recommendations for international students: Required—TOEFL, IELTS, PTE. *Application deadline:* For fall admission, 2/20 priority date for domestic students, 2/20 for international students; for spring admission, 12/10 priority date for domestic students, 11/15 for international students. Applications are processed on a rolling basis. Application fee: $100. *Expenses:* $1,579 per credit tuition; $690 mandatory fees. *Financial support:* In 2016–17, 15 students received support. Institutionally sponsored loans and unspecified assistantships available. Financial award application deadline: 2/1; financial award applicants required to submit FAFSA. *Faculty research:* Development finance, market microstructure, international investment, real estate finance, quantitative modeling. *Unit head:* Dr. Jeffery Harris, Department Chair, Finance and Real Estate, 202-885-6669, Fax: 202-885-1946, E-mail: jharris@american.edu. *Application contact:* Jason Kennedy, Associate Director of Graduate Admissions, 202-885-1968, E-mail: jkennedy@american.edu.
Website: http://www.american.edu/kogod/

The American University in Cairo, School of Business, Cairo, Egypt. Offers business administration (MBA); economics (MA); economics in international development (MA, Diploma); finance (MS). *Program availability:* Part-time, evening/weekend. *Faculty:* 24 full-time (4 women), 5 part-time/adjunct (2 women). *Students:* 53 full-time (24 women), 80 part-time (41 women), 1 international. Average age 29. 109 applicants, 45% accepted, 35 enrolled. In 2016, 49 master's awarded. *Degree requirements:* For master's, comprehensive exam (for some programs), thesis (for some programs). *Entrance requirements:* For master's, GMAT, GRE. Additional exam requirements/recommendations for international students: Required—TOEFL (minimum score 450 paper-based; 45 iBT), IELTS (minimum score 5). *Application deadline:* For fall admission, 2/1 priority date for domestic and international students; for spring admission, 10/15 priority date for domestic and international students. Applications are processed on a rolling basis. Application fee: $80. Electronic applications accepted. *Expenses:* Contact institution. *Financial support:* Fellowships with partial tuition reimbursements, scholarships/grants, tuition waivers (partial), and unspecified assistantships available. Financial award application deadline: 3/10. *Faculty research:* Marketing and quality management, banking operations management, economics, finance. *Unit head:* Dr. Nizar Becheikh, Interim Dean, 20-2-2615-2120, E-mail: nbecheikh@aucegypt.edu. *Application contact:* Maha Hegazi, Director of Graduate Admissions, 20-2-2615-1462, E-mail: mahahegazi@aucegypt.edu.
Website: http://www.aucegypt.edu/Business/Pages/default.aspx

The American University in Dubai, Graduate Programs, Dubai, United Arab Emirates. Offers construction management (MS); education (M Ed); finance (MBA); generalist (MBA); marketing (MBA). *Program availability:* Part-time, evening/weekend. *Degree requirements:* For master's, thesis optional. *Entrance requirements:* For master's, GMAT (for MBA); GRE (for M Ed and MS), minimum undergraduate GPA of 3.0, official transcripts, two reference forms, curriculum vitae/resume, statement of career objectives, work experience. Additional exam requirements/recommendations for international students: Required—TOEFL (minimum score 550 paper-based; 79 iBT). Electronic applications accepted.

American University of Beirut, Graduate Programs, Faculty of Arts and Sciences, Beirut, Lebanon. Offers anthropology (MA); Arab and Middle Eastern history (PhD); Arabic language and literature (MA, PhD); archaeology (MA); art history and curating (MA); biology (MS); cell and molecular biology (PhD); chemistry (MS); clinical psychology (MA); computational sciences (MS); computer science (MS); economics (MA); education (MA); English language (MA); English literature (MA); environmental policy planning (MS); financial economics (MAFE); geology (MS); history (MA); Islamic studies (MA); mathematics (MS); media studies (MA); Middle Eastern studies (MA); physics (MS); political studies (MA); psychology (MA); public administration (MA); public policy and international affairs (MA); sociology (MA); statistics (MA, MS); theoretical physics (PhD); transnational American studies (MA). *Program availability:* Part-time. *Faculty:* 133 full-time (42 women), 6 part-time/adjunct (2 women). *Students:* 240 full-time (172 women), 227 part-time (166 women). Average age 27. 286 applicants, 67% accepted, 108 enrolled. In 2016, 60 master's, 3 doctorates awarded. Terminal master's awarded for partial completion of doctoral program. *Degree requirements:* For master's, one foreign language, comprehensive exam, thesis (for some programs); for doctorate, one foreign language, comprehensive exam, thesis/dissertation. *Entrance requirements:* For master's, GRE (for some MA, MS programs), letters of recommendation; for doctorate, GRE, letters of recommendation. Additional exam requirements/recommendations for international students: Required—TOEFL (minimum score 600 paper-based; 97 iBT), IELTS (minimum score 7). *Application deadline:* For fall admission, 4/3 for domestic students; for winter admission, 11/3 for domestic students. Application fee: $50. Electronic applications accepted. *Expenses:* Contact institution. *Financial support:* In 2016–17, 4 fellowships (averaging $11,200 per year), 18 research assistantships (averaging $5,400 per year) were awarded; teaching assistantships, career-related internships or fieldwork, Federal Work-Study, institutionally sponsored loans, scholarships/grants, traineeships, health care benefits, tuition waivers (full), and unspecified assistantships also available. Support available to part-time students. *Faculty research:* Development economics, spatial econometrics, health economics, labor economics, energy economics, hydrogeology, geophysics, petrophysics, structural geology, mineralogy, petrology, geochemistry, multilingualism, comparative/world literature, translation studies, book histories/ cultures, biocatalysis, molecular recognition, photocatalysis, photophysical and biophysical chemistry, probe chemistry, machine learning, data science. *Unit head:* Dr. Nadia Maria El Cheikh, Dean, Faculty of Arts and Sciences, 961-1374374 Ext. 3800, Fax: 961-1744461, E-mail: nmcheikh@aub.edu.lb. *Application contact:* Dr. Salim Kanaan, Director, Admissions Office, 961-1350000 Ext. 2590, Fax: 961-1750775, E-mail: sk00@aub.edu.lb.
Website: http://www.aub.edu.lb/fas/

American University of Beirut, Graduate Programs, Suliman S. Olayan School of Business, Master's in Finance Program, 11072020, Lebanon. Offers M Fin. *Program availability:* Evening/weekend, online learning. *Faculty:* 8 full-time (0 women), 3 part-time/adjunct (0 women). *Students:* 30 full-time (21 women), 11 part-time (3 women). Average age 23. 98 applicants, 73% accepted, 41 enrolled. In 2016, 41 master's awarded. *Entrance requirements:* Additional exam requirements/recommendations for international students: Required—TOEFL (minimum score 583 paper-based; 97 iBT), IELTS (minimum score 7). *Application deadline:* For fall admission, 2/12 for domestic students; for winter admission, 4/1 for domestic students. Application fee: $80. Electronic applications accepted. *Expenses:* Contact institution. *Financial support:* In 2016–17, 20 research assistantships with tuition reimbursements (averaging $1,300 per year) were awarded; scholarships/grants and unspecified assistantships also available. Financial award application deadline: 6/1. *Unit head:* Maya Naim El-Helou, Director of Graduate Programs, 961-1352700 Ext. 3955, Fax: 961-1750214, E-mail: helou@aub.edu.lb. *Application contact:* Maya Naim El-Helou, Director of Graduate Programs, 961-1352700 Ext. 3955, Fax: 961-1750214, E-mail: helou@aub.edu.lb.
Website: https://www.aub.edu.lb/osb/osb_home/program/MFIN/Pages/programOverview.aspx

Andrews University, School of Graduate Studies, School of Business, Graduate Programs in Business, Berrien Springs, MI 49104. Offers MBA, MSA. *Faculty:* 8 full-time (3 women). *Students:* 16 full-time (7 women), 29 part-time (15 women); includes 19 minority (6 Black or African American, non-Hispanic/Latino; 3 Asian, non-Hispanic/Latino; 8 Hispanic/Latino; 2 Two or more races, non-Hispanic/Latino), 12 international. Average age 32. In 2016, 29 master's awarded. *Entrance requirements:* For master's, GMAT. Additional exam requirements/recommendations for international students: Required—TOEFL (minimum score 550 paper-based). Application fee: $40. *Unit head:* Dr. Leonard K. Gashugi, Chair, 769-471-3429, E-mail: gashugi@andrews.edu. *Application contact:* Justina Clayburn, Supervisor of Graduate Admission, 800-253-2874, Fax: 269-471-6321, E-mail: graduate@andrews.edu.

Argosy University, Atlanta, College of Business, Atlanta, GA 30328. Offers accounting (DBA); corporate compliance (MBA); customized professional concentration (MBA, DBA); finance (MBA); healthcare administration (MBA); information systems (DBA); information systems management (MBA); international business (MBA, DBA); management (MBA, MSM, DBA); marketing (MBA, DBA). *Accreditation:* ACBSP.

Argosy University, Chicago, College of Business, Chicago, IL 60601. Offers accounting (DBA); customized professional concentration (MBA, DBA); finance (MBA); fraud examination (MBA); global business sustainability (DBA); healthcare administration (MBA); information systems (DBA); information systems management (MBA); international business (MBA, DBA); management (MBA, MSM, DBA); marketing (MBA, DBA); organizational leadership (Ed D); public administration (MBA); sustainable management (MBA). *Accreditation:* ACBSP. *Program availability:* Online learning.

Argosy University, Dallas, College of Business, Farmers Branch, TX 75244. Offers accounting (DBA, AGC); corporate compliance (MBA, Graduate Certificate); customized professional concentration (MBA); finance (MBA, Graduate Certificate); fraud examination (MBA, Graduate Certificate); global business sustainability (DBA, AGC); healthcare administration (Graduate Certificate); healthcare management (MBA); information systems (MBA, DBA, AGC); information systems management (Graduate Certificate); international business (MBA, DBA, AGC, Graduate Certificate); management (MBA, DBA, AGC, Graduate Certificate); marketing (MBA, DBA, AGC, Graduate Certificate); public administration (MBA, Graduate Certificate); sustainable management (MBA, Graduate Certificate). *Accreditation:* ACBSP.

Argosy University, Denver, College of Business, Denver, CO 80231. Offers accounting (DBA); corporate compliance (MBA); customized professional concentration (MBA, DBA); finance (MBA); fraud examination (MBA); global business sustainability (DBA); healthcare administration (MBA); information systems (DBA); information systems management (MBA); international business (MBA, DBA); management (MBA, MSM, DBA); marketing (MBA, DBA); organizational leadership (Ed D); public administration (MBA); sustainable management (MBA). *Accreditation:* ACBSP.

Argosy University, Hawai`i, College of Business, Honolulu, HI 96813. Offers accounting (DBA); corporate compliance (MBA); customized professional concentration (MBA, DBA); finance (MBA, Certificate); fraud examination (MBA); global business sustainability (DBA); healthcare administration (MBA, Certificate); information systems (DBA); information systems management (MBA, Certificate); international business (MBA, DBA, Certificate); management (MBA, MSM, DBA); marketing (MBA, DBA, Certificate); organizational leadership (Ed D); public administration (MBA); sustainable management (MBA).

Argosy University, Inland Empire, College of Business, Ontario, CA 91761. Offers accounting (DBA); corporate compliance (MBA); customized professional concentration (MBA, DBA); finance (MBA); fraud examination (MBA); global business sustainability (DBA); healthcare administration (MBA); information systems (DBA); information systems management (MBA); international business (MBA, DBA); management (MBA,

MSM, DBA); marketing (MBA, DBA); organizational leadership (Ed D); public administration (MBA); sustainable management (MBA).

Argosy University, Los Angeles, College of Business, Santa Monica, CA 90045. Offers accounting (DBA); corporate compliance (MBA); customized professional concentration (MBA, DBA); finance (MBA); fraud examination (MBA); global business sustainability (DBA); healthcare administration (MBA); information systems (DBA); information systems management (MBA); international business (MBA, DBA); management (MBA, MSM, DBA); marketing (MBA, DBA); organizational leadership (Ed D); public administration (MBA); sustainable management (MBA).

Argosy University, Nashville, College of Business, Nashville, TN 37214. Offers accounting (DBA); customized professional concentration (MBA, DBA); finance (MBA); healthcare administration (MBA); information systems (MBA, DBA); international business (MBA, DBA); management (MBA, MSM, DBA); marketing (MBA, DBA).

Argosy University, Northern Virginia, College of Business, Arlington, VA 22209. Offers accounting (DBA); customized professional concentration (MBA, DBA); finance (MBA); fraud examination (MBA); global business sustainability (DBA); healthcare administration (MBA); information systems (DBA); information systems management (MBA); international business (MBA, DBA, Certificate); management (MBA, MSM, DBA); marketing (MBA, DBA, Certificate); organizational leadership (Ed D); public administration (MBA); sustainable management (MBA).

Argosy University, Orange County, College of Business, Orange, CA 92868. Offers accounting (DBA, Adv C); corporate compliance (MBA); customized professional concentration (MBA, DBA); finance (MBA, Certificate); fraud examination (MBA); global business sustainability (DBA); healthcare administration (MBA, Certificate); information systems (DBA, Adv C, Certificate); information systems management (MBA); international business (MBA, DBA, Adv C, Certificate); management (MBA, MSM, DBA, Adv C); marketing (MBA, DBA, Adv C, Certificate); organizational leadership (Ed D); public administration (MBA, Certificate); sustainable management (MBA).

Argosy University, Phoenix, College of Business, Phoenix, AZ 85021. Offers accounting (DBA); corporate compliance (MBA); customized professional concentration (MBA, DBA); finance (MBA); fraud examination (MBA); global business sustainability (DBA); healthcare administration (MBA); information systems (DBA); information systems management (MBA); international business (MBA, DBA); management (MBA, DBA); marketing (MBA, DBA); public administration (MBA); sustainable management (MBA).

Argosy University, Salt Lake City, College of Business, Draper, UT 84020. Offers accounting (DBA); corporate compliance (MBA); customized professional concentration (MBA, DBA); finance (MBA); fraud examination (MBA); global business sustainability (DBA); healthcare administration (MBA); information systems (DBA); information systems management (MBA); international business (MBA, DBA); management (MBA, DBA); marketing (MBA, DBA); public administration (MBA); sustainable management (MBA).

Argosy University, San Diego, College of Business, San Diego, CA 92108. Offers accounting (DBA); corporate compliance (MBA); customized professional concentration (MBA, DBA); finance (MBA); fraud examination (MBA); global business sustainability (DBA); information systems (DBA); information systems management (MBA); international business (MBA, DBA); management (MBA, MSM, DBA); marketing (MBA, DBA); organizational leadership (Ed D); public administration (MBA).

Argosy University, San Francisco Bay Area, College of Business, Alameda, CA 94501. Offers accounting (DBA); corporate compliance (MBA); customized professional concentration (MBA, DBA); finance (MBA); fraud examination (MBA); global business sustainability (DBA); healthcare administration (MBA); information systems (DBA); information systems management (MBA); international business (MBA, DBA); management (MBA, MSM, DBA); marketing (MBA, DBA); organizational leadership (Ed D); public administration (MBA); sustainable management (MBA).

Argosy University, Sarasota, College of Business, Sarasota, FL 34235. Offers accounting (DBA, Adv C); corporate compliance (MBA, DBA, Certificate); customized professional concentration (MBA, DBA); finance (MBA, Certificate); fraud examination (MBA, Certificate); global business sustainability (DBA, Adv C); healthcare administration (MBA, Certificate); information systems (DBA, Adv C, Certificate); information systems management (MBA); international business (MBA, DBA, Adv C, Certificate); management (MBA, MSM, DBA, Adv C, Certificate); marketing (MBA, DBA, Adv C, Certificate); organizational leadership (Ed D); public administration (MBA, Certificate); sustainable management (MBA, Certificate).

Argosy University, Schaumburg, Graduate School of Business and Management, Schaumburg, IL 60173-5403. Offers accounting (DBA, Adv C); customized professional concentration (MBA, DBA); finance (MBA, Certificate); fraud examination (MBA); healthcare administration (MBA, Certificate); human resource management (MS); information systems (Adv C, Certificate); information systems management (MBA); international business (MBA, DBA, Adv C, Certificate); management (MBA, MSM, DBA, Adv C, Certificate); marketing (MBA, DBA, Adv C, Certificate); organizational leadership (MS, Ed D); public administration (MBA); sustainable management (MBA).

Argosy University, Seattle, College of Business, Seattle, WA 98121. Offers accounting (DBA); corporate compliance (MBA); customized professional concentration (MBA, DBA); finance (MBA); fraud examination (MBA); global business sustainability (DBA); healthcare administration (MBA); information systems (DBA); information systems management (MBA); international business (MBA, DBA); management (MBA, MSM, DBA); marketing (MBA, DBA); organizational leadership (Ed D); public administration (MBA); sustainable management (MBA).

Argosy University, Tampa, College of Business, Tampa, FL 33607. Offers accounting (DBA); corporate compliance (MBA); customized professional concentration (MBA, DBA); finance (MBA); fraud examination (MBA); global business sustainability (DBA); healthcare administration (MBA); information systems (DBA); information systems management (MBA); international business (MBA, DBA); management (MBA, MSM, DBA); marketing (MBA, DBA); organizational leadership (Ed D); public administration (MBA); sustainable management (MBA).

Argosy University, Twin Cities, College of Business, Eagan, MN 55121. Offers accounting (DBA); customized professional concentration (MBA, DBA); finance (MBA); fraud examination (MBA); global business sustainability (DBA); healthcare administration (MBA); information systems (DBA); information systems management (MBA); international business (MBA, DBA); management (MBA, MSM, DBA); marketing (MBA, DBA); organizational leadership (Ed D); public administration (MBA); sustainable management (MBA).

Arizona State University at the Tempe campus, W. P. Carey School of Business, Program in Business Administration, Tempe, AZ 85287-4906. Offers entrepreneurship (MBA); finance (MBA); health sector management (MBA); international business (MBA); leadership (MBA); marketing (MBA); organizational behavior (PhD); strategic management (PhD); supply chain management (MBA, PhD); JD/MBA; MBA/M Acc; MBA/M Arch. *Accreditation:* AACSB. *Program availability:* Part-time, evening/weekend, online learning. Terminal master's awarded for partial completion of doctoral program. *Degree requirements:* For master's, thesis or alternative, internship, interactive Program of Study (iPOS) submitted before completing 50 percent of required credit hours; for doctorate, comprehensive exam, thesis/dissertation, interactive Program of Study (iPOS) submitted before completing 50 percent of required credit hours. *Entrance requirements:* For master's, GMAT, minimum GPA of 3.0 in last 2 years of work leading to bachelor's degree, 2 letters of recommendation, professional resume, official transcripts, 3 essays; for doctorate, GMAT or GRE, minimum GPA of 3.0 in last 2 years of work leading to bachelor's degree, 3 letters of recommendation, resume, personal statement/essay. Additional exam requirements/recommendations for international students: Required—TOEFL (minimum score 550 paper-based; 80 iBT), IELTS (minimum score 6.5). Electronic applications accepted. *Expenses:* Contact institution.

Aspen University, Program in Business Administration, Denver, CO 80246-1930. Offers business administration (MBA); finance (MBA); information management (MBA); project management (MBA, Certificate). *Program availability:* Part-time, evening/weekend, online learning. *Entrance requirements:* Additional exam requirements/recommendations for international students: Required—TOEFL (minimum score 530 paper-based). Electronic applications accepted.

Assumption College, Business Studies Program, Worcester, MA 01609-1296. Offers accounting (MBA); business studies (CAGS); finance/economics (MBA); human resources (MBA); international business (MBA); management (MBA); marketing (MBA); nonprofit leadership (MBA). *Program availability:* Part-time, evening/weekend. *Faculty:* 4 full-time (1 woman), 19 part-time/adjunct (6 women). *Students:* 44 full-time (16 women), 97 part-time (47 women); includes 20 minority (8 Black or African American, non-Hispanic/Latino; 5 Asian, non-Hispanic/Latino; 6 Hispanic/Latino; 1 Two or more races, non-Hispanic/Latino), 4 international. Average age 29. 34 applicants, 59% accepted, 16 enrolled. In 2016, 97 master's, 1 other advanced degree awarded. *Degree requirements:* For master's, thesis, capstone. *Entrance requirements:* For master's, bachelor's degree, 3 letters of recommendation, official transcripts, personal statement, current resume; for CAGS, MBA or equivalent degree in a closely related field, 3 letters of recommendation, official transcripts, personal statement, current resume. Additional exam requirements/recommendations for international students: Required—TOEFL (minimum score 540 paper-based; 76 iBT), IELTS (minimum score 6). *Application deadline:* For fall admission, 7/1 priority date for domestic and international students; for spring admission, 12/1 priority date for domestic and international students; for summer admission, 4/1 priority date for domestic and international students. Application fee: $30. Electronic applications accepted. *Expenses: Tuition:* Full-time $11,610; part-time $645 per credit. *Required fees:* $70 per term. Tuition and fees vary according to course load and program. *Financial support:* In 2016–17, 19 students received support. Tuition waivers (full and partial), unspecified assistantships, and institutional discounts available. Financial award applicants required to submit FAFSA. *Faculty research:* Workplace diversity, dynamics of team interaction, utilization of leased employees, experiential learning project on due diligence market for prostheses. *Unit head:* Dr. Robin Frkal, Director, 508-767-7622, E-mail: rafrkal@assumption.edu. *Application contact:* Karen Stoyanoff, Director of Recruitment for Graduate Enrollment, 508-767-7442, Fax: 508-799-4412, E-mail: graduate@assumption.edu.
Website: http://graduate.assumption.edu/mba/assumption-mba

Auburn University, Graduate School, College of Business, Department of Finance, Auburn University, AL 36849. Offers MS. *Faculty:* 15 full-time (3 women), 2 part-time/adjunct (1 woman). *Students:* 19 full-time (6 women), 14 part-time (4 women); includes 2 minority (1 Hispanic/Latino; 1 Two or more races, non-Hispanic/Latino), 12 international. Average age 30. 133 applicants, 30% accepted, 11 enrolled. In 2016, 14 master's awarded. Application fee: $50 ($60 for international students). *Expenses:* Tuition, state resident: full-time $9072; part-time $504 per credit hour. Tuition, nonresident: full-time $27,216; part-time $1512 per credit hour. *Required fees:* $812 per semester. Tuition and fees vary according to degree level and program. *Financial support:* Applicants required to submit FAFSA. *Unit head:* Dr. Larry L. Colquitt, Jr., Chair, 334-844-3000. *Application contact:* Dr. George Flowers, Dean of the Graduate School, 334-844-2125.

Avila University, School of Business, Kansas City, MO 64145-1698. Offers accounting (MBA); finance (MBA); health care administration (MBA); international business (MBA); management (MBA); management information systems (MBA); marketing (MBA). *Program availability:* Part-time, evening/weekend. *Faculty:* 8 full-time (4 women), 4 part-time/adjunct (2 women). *Students:* 58 full-time (22 women), 21 part-time (10 women); includes 20 minority (10 Black or African American, non-Hispanic/Latino; 2 Asian, non-Hispanic/Latino; 5 Hispanic/Latino; 3 Two or more races, non-Hispanic/Latino), 18 international. Average age 30. 75 applicants, 28% accepted, 14 enrolled. In 2016, 40 master's awarded. *Degree requirements:* For master's, comprehensive exam, capstone course. *Entrance requirements:* For master's, GMAT (minimum score 420), minimum GPA of 3.0, interview. Additional exam requirements/recommendations for international students: Required—TOEFL (minimum score 550 paper-based). *Application deadline:* For fall admission, 7/30 priority date for domestic and international students; for winter admission, 11/30 priority date for domestic and international students; for spring admission, 2/28 priority date for domestic and international students; for summer admission, 6/1 priority date for domestic and international students. Applications are processed on a rolling basis. Application fee: $0. Electronic applications accepted. *Expenses:* $628 per credit hour. *Financial support:* In 2016–17, 11 students received support. Career-related internships or fieldwork and scholarships/grants available. Support available to part-time students. Financial award applicants required to submit FAFSA. *Faculty research:* Leadership characteristics, financial hedging, group dynamics. *Unit head:* Dr. Richard Woodall, Dean, 816-501-3720, Fax: 816-501-2463, E-mail: richard.woodall@avila.edu. *Application contact:* Brandon Black, MBA Admission Advisor, 816-501-3601, Fax: 816-501-2463, E-mail: brandon.black@avila.edu.
Website: https://www.avila.edu/mrk/mba

Azusa Pacific University, School of Business and Management, Azusa, CA 91702-7000. Offers business administration (MBA); diversity for strategic advantage (MA); entrepreneurship (MBA); finance (MBA); human and organizational development (MA); human resources and organizational development (MBA); human resources management (MA); international business (MBA); marketing (MBA); non-profit management (MA); organizational development and change (MA); performance improvement (MA); public administration (MA); strategic management (MBA). *Program availability:* Part-time, evening/weekend. *Degree requirements:* For master's, thesis (for some programs), final project. *Entrance requirements:* For master's, GMAT, minimum GPA of 3.0. Additional exam requirements/recommendations for international students: Required—TOEFL (minimum score 600 paper-based). *Expenses:* Contact institution. *Faculty research:* Gender issues, financial risk, leadership and ethics, marketing strategy.

Baker College Center for Graduate Studies–Online, Graduate Programs, Flint, MI 48507. Offers accounting (MBA); business administration (DBA); finance (MBA); general business (MBA); health care management (MBA); human resources management (MBA); information management (MBA); leadership studies (MBA); management information systems (MSIS); marketing (MBA). *Program availability:* Part-time, evening/weekend, online learning. *Degree requirements:* For master's, portfolio. *Entrance requirements:* For master's, 3 years of work experience, minimum undergraduate GPA of 2.5, writing sample, 3 letters of recommendation; for doctorate, MBA or acceptable related master's degree from accredited association, 5 years work experience, minimum graduate GPA of 3.25, writing sample, 3 professional references. Additional exam requirements/recommendations for international students: Required—TOEFL (minimum score 550 paper-based). Electronic applications accepted.

Barry University, Andreas School of Business, Graduate Certificate Programs, Miami Shores, FL 33161-6695. Offers finance (Certificate); health services administration (Certificate); international business (Certificate); management (Certificate); management information systems (Certificate); marketing (Certificate).

Baruch College of the City University of New York, Zicklin School of Business, Department of Economics and Finance, Program in Finance, New York, NY 10010-5585. Offers MBA, MS, PhD. PhD offered jointly with Graduate School and University Center of the City University of New York. *Program availability:* Part-time, evening/weekend. *Degree requirements:* For doctorate, comprehensive exam, thesis/dissertation. *Entrance requirements:* For master's, GMAT, 2 letters of recommendation, resume, 2 years of work experience; for doctorate, GMAT. Additional exam requirements/recommendations for international students: Required—TOEFL (minimum score 590 paper-based), TWE (minimum score 5).

Baruch College of the City University of New York, Zicklin School of Business, Zicklin Executive Programs, Executive Program in Finance, New York, NY 10010-5585. Offers MS. *Program availability:* Evening/weekend. *Entrance requirements:* For master's, personal interview, work experience. *Expenses:* Contact institution. *Faculty research:* Corporate finance, investments, options, securities, system risk.

Bayamón Central University, Graduate Programs, Program in Business Administration, Bayamón, PR 00960-1725. Offers accounting (MBA); finance (MBA); general business (MBA); management (MBA); marketing (MBA). *Program availability:* Part-time, evening/weekend. *Degree requirements:* For master's, comprehensive exam (for some programs). *Entrance requirements:* For master's, EXADEP, bachelor's degree in business or related field.

Bellevue University, Graduate School, College of Business, Bellevue, NE 68005-3098. Offers acquisition and contract management (MS); business administration (MBA); finance (MS); human capital management (PhD); management (MSM).

Benedictine University, Graduate Programs, Program in Business Administration, Lisle, IL 60532. Offers accounting (MBA); entrepreneurship and managing innovation (MBA); financial management (MBA); health administration (MBA); human resource management (MBA); information systems security (MBA); international business (MBA); management consulting (MBA); management information systems (MBA); marketing management (MBA); operations management and logistics (MBA); organizational leadership (MBA). *Program availability:* Part-time, evening/weekend, online learning. *Faculty:* 4 full-time (2 women), 24 part-time/adjunct (3 women). *Students:* 90 full-time (51 women), 440 part-time (262 women); includes 147 minority (65 Black or African American, non-Hispanic/Latino; 1 American Indian or Alaska Native, non-Hispanic/Latino; 58 Asian, non-Hispanic/Latino; 20 Hispanic/Latino; 3 Native Hawaiian or other Pacific Islander, non-Hispanic/Latino), 2 international. Average age 34. 211 applicants, 89% accepted, 155 enrolled. In 2016, 350 master's awarded. *Entrance requirements:* For master's, GMAT. Additional exam requirements/recommendations for international students: Required—TOEFL (minimum score 550 paper-based). *Application deadline:* For fall admission, 9/1 for domestic students; for winter admission, 12/1 for domestic students; for spring admission, 2/15 for domestic students. Applications are processed on a rolling basis. Application fee: $40. Electronic applications accepted. *Expenses: Tuition:* Full-time $15,600; part-time $650 per hour. *Required fees:* $300. One-time fee: $125 part-time. Tuition and fees vary according to class time, course load, campus/location and program. *Financial support:* Career-related internships or fieldwork and health care benefits available. Support available to part-time students. *Faculty research:* Strategic leadership in professional organizations, sociology of professions, organizational change, social identity theory, applications to change management. *Unit head:* Dr. Sharon Borowicz, Director, 630-829-6219, E-mail: sborowicz@ben.edu. *Application contact:* Kari Gibbons, Director, Admissions, 630-829-6200, Fax: 630-829-6584, E-mail: kgibbons@ben.edu.

Bentley University, Graduate School of Business, Master's Program in Financial Planning, Waltham, MA 02452-4705. Offers MSFP. *Program availability:* Part-time, evening/weekend, 100% online, blended/hybrid learning. *Faculty:* 71 full-time (25 women), 33 part-time/adjunct (15 women). *Students:* 6 full-time (2 women), 20 part-time (8 women); includes 2 minority (1 Black or African American, non-Hispanic/Latino; 1 Asian, non-Hispanic/Latino), 3 international. Average age 33. 18 applicants, 83% accepted, 7 enrolled. In 2016, 14 master's awarded. *Entrance requirements:* For master's, GMAT or GRE General Test, current resume; two letters of recommendation; official copies of all university-level transcripts. Additional exam requirements/recommendations for international students: Required—TOEFL (minimum score 600 paper-based; 100 iBT), IELTS (minimum score 7), or PTE. *Application deadline:* Applications are processed on a rolling basis. Application fee: $50. Electronic applications accepted. *Expenses:* $4,225 per course, $480 fee per year. *Financial support:* In 2016–17, 1 student received support. Scholarships/grants available. Financial award application deadline: 6/1; financial award applicants required to submit FAFSA. *Faculty research:* International financial planning, compensation and benefits, retirement planning. *Unit head:* John Lynch, Jr., Senior Lecturer, 781-891-2624, E-mail: jlynch@bentley.edu. *Application contact:* Sharon Hill, Assistant Dean/Director of Graduate Admission, 781-891-2108, Fax: 781-891-2464, E-mail: bentleygraduateadmissions@bentley.edu.
Website: http://www.bentley.edu/graduate/ms-programs/masters-in-financial-planning

Bentley University, Graduate School of Business, Program in Finance, Waltham, MA 02452-4705. Offers MSF. *Program availability:* Part-time, evening/weekend. *Faculty:* 71 full-time (25 women), 33 part-time/adjunct (15 women). *Students:* 85 full-time (36 women), 16 part-time (4 women); includes 11 minority (2 Black or African American, non-Hispanic/Latino; 5 Asian, non-Hispanic/Latino; 2 Hispanic/Latino; 2 Two or more races, non-Hispanic/Latino), 68 international. Average age 24. 240 applicants, 65% accepted, 47 enrolled. In 2016, 41 master's awarded. *Entrance requirements:* For master's, GMAT or GRE General Test, current resume; two letters of recommendation; official copies of all university-level transcripts. Additional exam requirements/recommendations for international students: Required—TOEFL (minimum score 600 paper-based; 100 iBT), IELTS (minimum score 7), or PTE. *Application deadline:* Applications are processed on a rolling basis. Application fee: $50. Electronic applications accepted. *Expenses:* $4,225 per course, $480 fee per year. *Financial support:* In 2016–17, 13 students received support. Scholarships/grants and unspecified assistantships available. Financial award application deadline: 6/1; financial award applicants required to submit FAFSA. *Faculty research:* Management of financial institutions; corporate governance and executive compensation; asset valuation; international mergers and acquisitions; hedging, risk management and derivatives. *Unit head:* Claude Cicchetti, Lecturer, 781-891-2511, E-mail: ccicchetti@bentley.edu. *Application contact:* Sharon Hill, Assistant Dean/Director of Graduate Admissions, 781-891-2108, Fax: 781-891-2464, E-mail: bentleygraduateadmissions@bentley.edu.
Website: http://www.bentley.edu/graduate/ms-programs/masters-in-finance

Bluffton University, Programs in Business, Bluffton, OH 45817. Offers accounting and financial management (MBA); business administration (MBA); health care management (MBA); leadership (MBA); organizational management (MA); production and operations management (MBA). *Program availability:* Evening/weekend, online learning. *Faculty:* 9 full-time (3 women), 12 part-time/adjunct (4 women). *Students:* 55 full-time (34 women), 2 part-time (1 woman); includes 5 minority (1 Black or African American, non-Hispanic/Latino; 2 Asian, non-Hispanic/Latino; 2 Hispanic/Latino), 2 international. Average age 34. 31 applicants, 77% accepted, 22 enrolled. In 2016, 44 master's awarded. *Entrance requirements:* For master's, current resume, official transcript, two recommendation forms, bachelor's degree, minimum GPA of 3.0, four years of professional experience, interview. Additional exam requirements/recommendations for international students: Recommended—TOEFL. *Application deadline:* For fall admission, 7/31 priority date for domestic and international students. Applications are processed on a rolling basis. Application fee: $25. Electronic applications accepted. Application fee is waived when completed online. *Expenses:* $550 per credit. *Financial support:* Scholarships/grants and unspecified assistantships available. Financial award application deadline: 5/1. *Unit head:* Dr. Melissa Green, Director of Graduate Programs in Business, 419-358-3447, E-mail: greenm@bluffton.edu. *Application contact:* Carrie Mast, Administrative Assistant, Graduate Programs in Business, 419-358-3065, E-mail: mastc@bluffton.edu.
Website: http://www.bluffton.edu/grad/

Boston College, Carroll School of Management, Graduate Finance Programs, Chestnut Hill, MA 02467-3800. Offers MSF, PhD, MBA/MSF. *Program availability:* Part-time. *Degree requirements:* For doctorate, thesis/dissertation. *Entrance requirements:* For master's, GMAT or GRE, resume, recommendations; for doctorate, GMAT or GRE, curriculum vitae, recommendations. Additional exam requirements/recommendations for international students: Required—TOEFL (minimum score 600 paper-based, 100 iBT), IELTS (minimum score 7.5), or PTE (minimum score 68). Electronic applications accepted. Tuition and fees vary according to program. *Faculty research:* Security and derivative markets, financial institutions, corporate finance and capital markets, market macrostructure, investments, portfolio analysis.

Boston University, Metropolitan College, Department of Administrative Sciences, Boston, MA 02215. Offers applied business analytics (MS); economic development and tourism management (MSAS); enterprise risk management (MS); financial management (MS); global marketing management (MS); innovation and technology (MSAS); insurance management (MSM); project management (MS); supply chain management (MS). *Accreditation:* AACSB. *Program availability:* Part-time, evening/weekend, online learning. *Faculty:* 15 full-time (3 women), 22 part-time/adjunct (3 women). *Students:* 301 full-time (146 women), 934 part-time (501 women); includes 237 minority (81 Black or African American, non-Hispanic/Latino; 5 American Indian or Alaska Native, non-Hispanic/Latino; 60 Asian, non-Hispanic/Latino; 76 Hispanic/Latino; 1 Native Hawaiian or other Pacific Islander, non-Hispanic/Latino; 14 Two or more races, non-Hispanic/Latino), 514 international. Average age 31. 593 applicants, 69% accepted, 260 enrolled. In 2016, 263 master's awarded. *Degree requirements:* For master's, thesis optional. *Entrance requirements:* For master's, 1 year of work experience, minimum GPA of 3.0. Additional exam requirements/recommendations for international students: Required—TOEFL (minimum score 84 iBT). *Application deadline:* Applications are processed on a rolling basis. Application fee: $80. Electronic applications accepted. *Expenses:* Contact institution. *Financial support:* In 2016–17, 15 students received support, including 14 research assistantships (averaging $8,400 per year); career-related internships or fieldwork, Federal Work-Study, and unspecified assistantships also available. *Faculty research:* International business, innovative process. *Unit head:* Dr. John Sullivan, Chair, 617-353-3016, E-mail: adminsc@bu.edu. *Application contact:* Fiona Niven, Administrative Sciences Department, 617-353-3016, E-mail: adminsc@bu.edu.
Website: http://www.bu.edu/met/academic-community/departments/administrative-sciences/

Brandeis University, International Business School (IBS), Master of Arts in International Economics and Finance Program, Waltham, MA 02454-9110. Offers business economics (MA). *Faculty:* 29 full-time (10 women), 27 part-time/adjunct (3 women). *Students:* 150 full-time (77 women). Average age 23. 741 applicants, 28% accepted, 68 enrolled. In 2016, 79 master's awarded. *Entrance requirements:* For master's, GMAT or GRE. Additional exam requirements/recommendations for international students: Required—TOEFL (minimum score 600 paper-based; 100 iBT), IELTS (minimum score 7), PTE (minimum score 68). *Application deadline:* For fall admission, 11/1 priority date for domestic and international students; for winter admission, 1/15 priority date for domestic and international students; for spring admission, 3/15 priority date for domestic and international students; for summer admission, 5/15 for domestic and international students. Application fee: $55. Electronic applications accepted. *Expenses:* Contact institution. *Financial support:* In 2016–17, 112 students received support. Institutionally sponsored loans and scholarships/grants available. Financial award application deadline: 3/15; financial award applicants required to submit FAFSA. *Faculty research:* International economic policy analysis, macroeconomics, econometrics, business economics, economic development. *Unit head:* Peter Petri, Dean, 781-736-2256. *Application contact:* Kelly Sugrue, Director of Admissions, 781-736-2252, Fax: 781-736-2263, E-mail: admission@lemberg.brandeis.edu.
Website: http://www.brandeis.edu/global/ma

Brandeis University, International Business School (IBS), Master of Science in Finance Program, Waltham, MA 02454-9110. Offers asset management (MSF); corporate finance (MSF); risk management (MSF); transfer pricing and valuation (MSF). *Faculty:* 29 full-time (10 women), 27 part-time/adjunct (3 women). *Students:* 74 full-time (40 women); includes 55 minority (2 Black or African American, non-Hispanic/Latino; 49 Asian, non-Hispanic/Latino; 4 Hispanic/Latino). Average age 22. 663 applicants, 29% accepted, 74 enrolled. In 2016, 50 master's awarded. *Entrance requirements:* For master's, GMAT or GRE. Additional exam requirements/recommendations for international students: Required—TOEFL (minimum score 600 paper-based; 100 iBT), IELTS (minimum score 7), PTE (minimum score 68). *Application deadline:* For fall admission, 11/1 priority date for domestic and international students; for winter admission, 1/15 priority date for domestic and international students; for spring admission, 3/15 priority date for domestic and international students; for summer admission, 5/15 for domestic and international students. Application fee: $55. *Expenses:* Contact institution. *Financial support:* Institutionally sponsored loans and scholarships/grants available. Support available to part-time students. Financial award application deadline: 3/15; financial award applicants required to submit FAFSA. *Faculty research:* Asset management, municipal finance, corporate finance, venture capital, international trade. *Unit head:* Peter Petri, Interim Dean, 781-736-2256. *Application contact:* Kelly Sugrue, Director of Admissions, 781-736-2252, Fax: 781-736-2263, E-mail: admission@lemberg.brandeis.edu.
Website: https://www.brandeis.edu/global/msf

Brandeis University, International Business School (IBS), PhD in International Economics and Finance Program, Waltham, MA 02454-9110. Offers global trade (PhD); macroeconomics (PhD). *Faculty:* 11 full-time (5 women). *Students:* 7 full-time (3 women). Average age 32. 107 applicants, 19% accepted, 7 enrolled. In 2016, 3 doctorates awarded. *Degree requirements:* For doctorate, thesis/dissertation. *Entrance*

requirements: Additional exam requirements/recommendations for international students: Required—TOEFL (minimum score 600 paper-based; 100 iBT), IELTS (minimum score 7), PTE (minimum score 68). *Application deadline:* For winter admission, 1/15 priority date for domestic and international students. Application fee: $55. *Expenses:* Contact institution. *Financial support:* In 2016–17, 16 students received support, including 11 fellowships (averaging $9,545 per year), research assistantships (averaging $6,000 per year), teaching assistantships (averaging $6,000 per year); institutionally sponsored loans, scholarships/grants, health care benefits, and tuition waivers (full and partial) also available. Financial award application deadline: 1/15; financial award applicants required to submit FAFSA. *Faculty research:* Global business, global trade, global finance, macroeconomics, development and institutions. *Unit head:* Peter Petri, Interim Dean, 781-736-2256. *Application contact:* Kelly Sugrue, Director of Admissions, 781-736-2252, Fax: 781-736-2263, E-mail: admission@lemberg.brandeis.edu.
Website: https://www.brandeis.edu/global/academics/phd/

Brandman University, School of Business and Professional Studies, Irvine, CA 92618. Offers accounting (MBA); business administration (MBA); e-business strategic management (MBA); entrepreneurship (MBA); finance (MBA); health administration (MBA); human resources (MBA, MS); international business (MBA); marketing (MBA); organizational leadership (MA, MBA, MPA); public administration (MPA). *Expenses: Tuition:* Full-time $14,880; part-time $620 per credit hour. Tuition and fees vary according to degree level and program. *Unit head:* Dr. Glenn Worthington, Dean, 253-861-1024, E-mail: gworthin@brandman.edu.
Website: https://www.brandman.edu/business-professional-studies

Bridgewater State University, College of Graduate Studies, Ricciardi College of Business, Department of Accounting and Finance, Bridgewater, MA 02325. Offers MSM. *Program availability:* Part-time, evening/weekend. *Entrance requirements:* For master's, GMAT.

Brigham Young University, Graduate Studies, Marriott School of Management, Master of Business Administration Program, Provo, UT 84602. Offers entrepreneurship (MBA); finance (MBA); global supply chain management (MBA); marketing (MBA); strategic human resources (MBA); JD/MBA; MBA/MS. *Accreditation:* AACSB. *Students:* 321 full-time (63 women); includes 16 minority (1 Black or African American, non-Hispanic/Latino; 9 Asian, non-Hispanic/Latino; 6 Hispanic/Latino), 69 international. Average age 31. 397 applicants, 49% accepted, 154 enrolled. In 2016, 146 master's awarded. *Entrance requirements:* For master's, GMAT or GRE, minimum GPA of 3.0 in last 60 hours. Additional exam requirements/recommendations for international students: Required—TOEFL (minimum score 590 paper-based; 94 iBT), IELTS (minimum score 7). *Application deadline:* For fall admission, 5/1 for domestic students, 1/15 for international students. Applications are processed on a rolling basis. Application fee: $50. Electronic applications accepted. *Expenses:* Contact institution. *Financial support:* In 2016–17, 247 students received support. Research assistantships, teaching assistantships, career-related internships or fieldwork, institutionally sponsored loans, and scholarships/grants available. Financial award application deadline: 3/1; financial award applicants required to submit FAFSA. *Faculty research:* Finance, marketing, supply chain management, entrepreneurship, strategic human resources. *Unit head:* Dr. Grant McQueen, Director, 801-422-3500, Fax: 801-422-0513, E-mail: mba@byu.edu. *Application contact:* Yvette Anderson, MBA Program Admissions Director, 801-422-3500, Fax: 801-422-0513, E-mail: mba@byu.edu.
Website: http://mba.byu.edu

Brooklyn College of the City University of New York, School of Business, Brooklyn, NY 11210-2889. Offers accounting (MS); business administration (MS), including economic analysis, general business, global business and finance. *Program availability:* Part-time, evening/weekend. *Degree requirements:* For master's, comprehensive exam, thesis or alternative. *Entrance requirements:* For master's, GMAT, 2 letters of recommendation. Additional exam requirements/recommendations for international students: Required—TOEFL (minimum score 550 paper-based; 79 iBT). Electronic applications accepted. *Faculty research:* Econometrics, environmental economics, microeconomics, macroeconomics, taxation.

Bryant University, Graduate School of Business, Smithfield, RI 02917. Offers accounting (MPAC); business administration (MBA), including general management, global finance, global supply chain management, international business; business analytics (Graduate Certificate); taxation (MST). *Program availability:* Part-time, evening/weekend. *Faculty:* 16 full-time (3 women), 2 part-time/adjunct (0 women). *Students:* 71 full-time (23 women), 83 part-time (32 women); includes 17 minority (5 Black or African American, non-Hispanic/Latino; 4 Asian, non-Hispanic/Latino; 5 Hispanic/Latino; 3 Two or more races, non-Hispanic/Latino), 17 international. Average age 27. 165 applicants, 57% accepted, 66 enrolled. In 2016, 106 master's, 12 other advanced degrees awarded. *Degree requirements:* For master's, comprehensive exam (for some programs). *Entrance requirements:* For master's, GMAT, resume, recommendation, college transcripts. Additional exam requirements/recommendations for international students: Required—TOEFL (minimum score 580 paper-based; 95 iBT). *Application deadline:* For fall admission, 7/15 for domestic and international students; for spring admission, 11/15 for domestic and international students; for summer admission, 4/15 for domestic and international students. Applications are processed on a rolling basis. Application fee: $80. Electronic applications accepted. *Expenses:* Contact institution. *Financial support:* Research assistantships, scholarships/grants, and unspecified assistantships available. Support available to part-time students. Financial award application deadline: 2/15; financial award applicants required to submit FAFSA. *Faculty research:* International business, public sector auditing, taxation of partnerships, information systems security, financial markets microstructure. *Unit head:* Bjorn Carlsson, Graduate Program Director, 401-232-6707, E-mail: bcarlsson@bryant.edu. *Application contact:* Terri Rogers, Admissions Assistant, 401-232-6230, Fax: 401-232-6494, E-mail: graduateprograms@bryant.edu.
Website: http://gradschool.bryant.edu/business/

Butler University, Lacy School of Business, Indianapolis, IN 46208-3485. Offers finance (MBA); international business (MBA); leadership (MBA); marketing (MBA); professional accounting (MP Acc). *Accreditation:* AACSB. *Program availability:* Part-time. *Faculty:* 18 full-time (6 women), 14 part-time/adjunct (5 women). *Students:* 31 full-time (11 women), 133 part-time (40 women); includes 10 minority (2 Black or African American, non-Hispanic/Latino; 2 Asian, non-Hispanic/Latino; 6 Hispanic/Latino), 2 international. Average age 31. 122 applicants, 68% accepted, 42 enrolled. In 2016, 89 master's awarded. *Entrance requirements:* For master's, GMAT, minimum AACSB index of 950, personal statement, two letters of recommendation, official transcripts, current resume. Additional exam requirements/recommendations for international students: Required—TOEFL (minimum score 550 paper-based; 79 iBT), IELTS (minimum score 6), Michigan English Language Assessment Battery (minimum score of 80). *Application deadline:* For fall admission, 8/1 for domestic and international students; for spring admission, 12/1 for domestic and international students; for summer admission, 4/1 for domestic and international students. Applications are processed on a rolling basis. Application fee: $0. Electronic applications accepted. *Expenses:* $790 per credit hour. *Financial support:* In 2016–17, 15 students received support. Scholarships/grants, tuition waivers (full and partial), and unspecified assistantships available. Financial award application deadline: 7/15; financial award applicants required to submit FAFSA. *Faculty research:* Higher education and pedagogy; ecotourism; healthcare issues and marketing public policy; domestic public policy, international finance and banking, international and management entrepreneurship, organizational management. *Unit head:* Dr. Stephen Standifird, Dean. *Application contact:* Diane Dubord, Graduate Student Service Specialist, 317-940-8107, Fax: 317-940-8250, E-mail: ddubord@butler.edu.
Website: https://www.butler.edu/lacyschool

California College of the Arts, Graduate Programs, MBA in Design Strategy Program, San Francisco, CA 94107. Offers MBA. *Accreditation:* NASAD. *Faculty:* 2 full-time (1 woman), 14 part-time/adjunct (3 women). *Students:* 86 full-time (57 women); includes 23 minority (4 Black or African American, non-Hispanic/Latino; 11 Asian, non-Hispanic/Latino; 7 Hispanic/Latino; 1 Native Hawaiian or other Pacific Islander, non-Hispanic/Latino), 35 international. Average age 30. 141 applicants, 94% accepted, 39 enrolled. In 2016, 54 master's awarded. *Degree requirements:* For master's, thesis. *Entrance requirements:* Additional exam requirements/recommendations for international students: Required—TOEFL, IELTS, or PTE. *Application deadline:* For fall admission, 1/10 for domestic and international students. Applications are processed on a rolling basis. Application fee: $70. Electronic applications accepted. *Expenses:* $1,641 per unit, $49,230 per year tuition; $490 fees. *Financial support:* Federal Work-Study and scholarships/grants available. Financial award application deadline: 7/31; financial award applicants required to submit FAFSA. *Unit head:* Nathan Shedroff, Program Chair, 800-447-1ART, E-mail: nshedroff@cca.edu. *Application contact:* Wes Fanelli, Assistant Director of Graduate Admissions, 415-703-9533, Fax: 415-703-9539, E-mail: wfanelli@cca.edu.

California Intercontinental University, School of Business, Irvine, CA 92614. Offers banking and finance (MBA); entrepreneurship and business management (DBA); global business leadership (DBA); international management and marketing (MBA); organizational management and human resource management (MBA).

California Lutheran University, Graduate Studies, School of Management, Thousand Oaks, CA 91360-2787. Offers business (IMBA); computer science (MS); econometrics (MBA); economics (MS); entrepreneurship (MBA, Certificate); finance (MBA, Certificate); financial planning (MBA, Certificate); information systems and technology (MS); information technology management (MBA, Certificate); international business (MBA, Certificate); management and organization behavior (MBA); management and organizational behavior (Certificate); marketing (MBA, Certificate); microeconomics (MBA); nonprofit and social enterprise (MBA); public policy and administration (MPPA). *Program availability:* Part-time, evening/weekend, 100% online, blended/hybrid learning. *Faculty:* 25 full-time (10 women), 36 part-time/adjunct (12 women). *Students:* 427 full-time (172 women), 189 part-time (87 women); includes 120 minority (14 Black or African American, non-Hispanic/Latino; 2 American Indian or Alaska Native, non-Hispanic/Latino; 19 Asian, non-Hispanic/Latino; 37 Hispanic/Latino; 48 Two or more races, non-Hispanic/Latino), 338 international. Average age 30. 591 applicants, 64% accepted, 131 enrolled. In 2016, 305 master's awarded. *Entrance requirements:* For master's, GMAT, interview, minimum GPA of 3.0. *Application deadline:* Applications are processed on a rolling basis. Application fee: $50. Electronic applications accepted. *Expenses:* Contact institution. *Unit head:* Dr. Gerhard Apfelthaler, Dean, 805-493-3360. *Application contact:* 805-493-3325, Fax: 805-493-3861, E-mail: clugrad@callutheran.edu.
Website: http://www.callutheran.edu/management/

California State University, East Bay, Office of Graduate Studies, College of Business and Economics, MBA Program, Option in Finance, Hayward, CA 94542-3000. Offers MBA. *Students:* 29 full-time (12 women), 38 part-time (14 women); includes 32 minority (7 Black or African American, non-Hispanic/Latino; 19 Asian, non-Hispanic/Latino; 4 Hispanic/Latino; 2 Native Hawaiian or other Pacific Islander, non-Hispanic/Latino), 22 international. Average age 33. 41 applicants, 34% accepted, 12 enrolled. In 2016, 26 master's awarded. *Degree requirements:* For master's, comprehensive exam or thesis. *Entrance requirements:* For master's, GMAT, minimum GPA of 2.75. Additional exam requirements/recommendations for international students: Required—TOEFL (minimum score 550 paper-based). *Application deadline:* For fall admission, 6/30 for domestic and international students. Applications are processed on a rolling basis. Application fee: $55. Electronic applications accepted. *Financial support:* Career-related internships or fieldwork, Federal Work-Study, and institutionally sponsored loans available. Support available to part-time students. Financial award application deadline: 3/1; financial award applicants required to submit FAFSA. *Application contact:* Dr. Donna Wiley, Interim Associate Vice President for Academic Programs and Graduate Studies, 510-885-3716, Fax: 510-885-4777, E-mail: donna.wiley@csueastbay.edu.

California State University, Fullerton, Graduate Studies, College of Business and Economics, Department of Finance, Fullerton, CA 92834-9480. Offers MBA. *Program availability:* Part-time. *Degree requirements:* For master's, project or thesis. *Entrance requirements:* For master's, GMAT, minimum AACSB index of 950. Application fee: $55. *Expenses:* Tuition, state resident: full-time $3369; part-time $1953 per unit. Tuition, nonresident: full-time $3915; part-time $2499 per unit. Tuition and fees vary according to course load, degree level and program. *Financial support:* Career-related internships or fieldwork, Federal Work-Study, institutionally sponsored loans, and scholarships/grants available. Support available to part-time students. Financial award application deadline: 3/1; financial award applicants required to submit FAFSA. *Unit head:* Mark Hoven Stohs, Chair, 657-278-2217. *Application contact:* Admissions/Applications, 657-278-2371.

California State University, Los Angeles, Graduate Studies, College of Business and Economics, Department of Finance and Law, Los Angeles, CA 90032-8530. Offers finance and banking (MBA, MS). *Program availability:* Part-time, evening/weekend. *Degree requirements:* For master's, comprehensive exam (MBA), thesis (MS). *Entrance requirements:* For master's, GMAT, minimum GPA of 2.5 during previous 2 years of course work. Additional exam requirements/recommendations for international students: Required—TOEFL (minimum score 550 paper-based). Electronic applications accepted.

California State University, San Bernardino, Graduate Studies, College of Business and Public Administration, Program in Business Administration, San Bernardino, CA 92407. Offers accounting (MBA); entrepreneurship (MBA); finance (MBA); global business (MBA); information management (MBA); information security (MBA); management (MBA); supply chain management (MBA). *Accreditation:* AACSB. *Program availability:* Part-time, evening/weekend, online learning. *Faculty:* 7 full-time (4 women), 3 part-time/adjunct (2 women). *Students:* 37 full-time (11 women), 141 part-time (51 women); includes 85 minority (16 Black or African American, non-Hispanic/Latino; 1 American Indian or Alaska Native, non-Hispanic/Latino; 20 Asian, non-Hispanic/Latino; 45 Hispanic/Latino; 3 Two or more races, non-Hispanic/Latino), 46 international. 260 applicants, 37% accepted, 34 enrolled. In 2016, 180 master's awarded. *Degree requirements:* For master's, comprehensive exam, thesis. *Entrance requirements:* Additional exam requirements/recommendations for international students: Required—TOEFL. *Application deadline:* For fall admission, 7/16 for domestic students, 7/20 for international students; for winter admission, 10/23 for domestic students, 10/20 for international students; for spring admission, 1/22 for domestic students, 1/20 for international students. Application fee: $55. *Expenses:* Contact institution. *Financial support:* Application deadline: 3/1. *Unit head:* Dr. Lawrence C. Rose, Dean, 909-537-3703, Fax: 909-537-7026, E-mail: lrose@csusb.edu. *Application contact:* Dr. Vipin

Gupta, Associate Dean/MBA Director, 909-537-7380, Fax: 909-537-7026, E-mail: vgupta@csusb.edu.
Website: http://mba.csusb.edu/

Capella University, School of Business and Technology, Doctoral Programs in Business, Minneapolis, MN 55402. Offers accounting (DBA, PhD); business intelligence (DBA); finance (DBA, PhD); general business management (PhD); human resource management (DBA, PhD); leadership (DBA, PhD); management education (PhD); marketing (DBA, PhD); project management (DBA, PhD); strategy and innovation (DBA, PhD). *Accreditation:* ACBSP.

Capella University, School of Business and Technology, Master's Programs in Business, Minneapolis, MN 55402. Offers accounting (MBA); business analysis (MS); business intelligence (MBA); entrepreneurship (MBA); finance (MBA); general business administration (MBA); general human resource management (MS); general leadership (MS); health care management (MBA); human resource management (MBA); marketing (MBA); project management (MBA, MS). *Accreditation:* ACBSP.

Carnegie Mellon University, Tepper School of Business, Program in Financial Economics, Pittsburgh, PA 15213-3891. Offers PhD. *Degree requirements:* For doctorate, thesis/dissertation. *Entrance requirements:* For doctorate, GRE General Test.

Case Western Reserve University, Weatherhead School of Management, Department of Banking and Finance, Cleveland, OH 44106. Offers finance (MSM). *Entrance requirements:* For master's, GMAT. *Expenses: Tuition:* Full-time $42,576; part-time $1774 per credit hour. *Required fees:* $34. Tuition and fees vary according to course load and program. *Faculty research:* Monetary and fiscal policy, corporate finance, future markets, derivative pricing, capital market efficiency.

Central European University, CEU Business School, Budapest, Hungary. Offers business administration (PhD); business analytics (M Sc); executive business administration (EMBA); finance (M Sc); general management (MBA); information technology management (M Sc); international executive (MBA). *Program availability:* Part-time. *Faculty:* 16 full-time (4 women), 15 part-time/adjunct (5 women). *Students:* 73 full-time (29 women), 108 part-time (28 women). Average age 33. 218 applicants, 57% accepted, 69 enrolled. In 2016, 108 master's awarded. *Degree requirements:* For master's, one foreign language; for doctorate, thesis/dissertation or alternative. *Entrance requirements:* For master's, GMAT. Additional exam requirements/recommendations for international students: Required—TOEFL (minimum score 570 paper-based); Recommended—IELTS (minimum score 6.5). *Application deadline:* For fall admission, 2/4 for domestic and international students. Application fee: $30. Electronic applications accepted. *Expenses:* Contact institution. *Financial support:* Scholarships/grants, health care benefits, and tuition waivers (full and partial) available. *Faculty research:* Social and ethical business, marketing, international business, international trade and investment, management development in Central and East Europe, non-market strategies of emerging-market multinationals, macro and micro analysis of the business environment, international competitive analysis, the transition process from emerging economies to established market economies and its social impact, the regulation of natural monopolies. *Unit head:* Dr. Mel Horwitch, Dean/Managing Director, 36 1 887-5050, E-mail: mhorwitch@ceubusiness.com. *Application contact:* Agnes Schram, Admissions Coordinator, 361-887-5111, E-mail: schrama@business.ceu.edu.
Website: http://business.ceu.hu/

Central Michigan University, College of Graduate Studies, College of Business Administration, MBA Program, Mount Pleasant, MI 48859. Offers accounting (MBA); business economics (MBA); consulting (MBA); finance (MBA); general business (MBA); human resource management (MBA); information systems (MBA); international business (MBA); logistics management (MBA); marketing (MBA); value-driven organization (MBA). *Program availability:* Part-time, evening/weekend, online learning. Electronic applications accepted. *Faculty research:* Accounting, consulting, international business, marketing, information systems.

Charleston Southern University, School of Business, Charleston, SC 29423-8087. Offers accounting (MBA); finance (MBA); general management (MBA); human resource management (MS); leadership (MBA); management information systems (MBA); organizational leadership (MA). *Program availability:* Part-time, evening/weekend. *Degree requirements:* For master's, thesis optional. *Entrance requirements:* For master's, GMAT. Additional exam requirements/recommendations for international students: Required—TOEFL (minimum score 550 paper-based; 79 iBT). *Application deadline:* Applications are processed on a rolling basis. Application fee: $40. *Expenses: Tuition:* Full-time $6000. Tuition and fees vary according to program. *Financial support:* Research assistantships with full tuition reimbursements available. Financial award application deadline: 4/15; financial award applicants required to submit FAFSA. *Unit head:* Dr. David Palmer, Interim Dean, 843-863-7025, Fax: 843-863-7922, E-mail: dpalmer@csuniv.edu. *Application contact:* Dr. Darin L. Gerdes, Director of the MBA Program, 843-863-7814, Fax: 843-863-7922, E-mail: dgerdes@csuniv.edu.
Website: http://www.csuniv.edu/business/

City University of Seattle, Graduate Division, School of Management, Seattle, WA 98121. Offers accounting (Certificate); change leadership (MBA, Certificate); computer systems (MS); finance (Certificate); financial management (MBA); general management (MBA); general management-Europe (MBA); global marketing (MBA); human resources management (Certificate); individualized study (MBA); information security (MS); information systems (MBA); leadership (MA); marketing (MBA, Certificate); project management (MBA, MS, Certificate); sustainable business (Certificate); technology management (MBA, Certificate). *Program availability:* Part-time, evening/weekend, online learning. *Degree requirements:* For master's, comprehensive exam (for some programs), thesis (for some programs). *Entrance requirements:* For master's, baccalaureate degree or equivalent from an accredited or otherwise recognized institution. Additional exam requirements/recommendations for international students: Required—TOEFL (minimum score 567 paper-based; 87 iBT); Recommended—IELTS. Electronic applications accepted.

Claremont McKenna College, Robert Day School of Economics and Finance, Claremont, CA 91711. Offers finance (MA). *Entrance requirements:* For master's, GMAT or GRE, 2 letters of recommendation, resume, interview. Additional exam requirements/recommendations for international students: Required—TOEFL. Electronic applications accepted.

Clarion University of Pennsylvania, Office of Transfer, Adult and Graduate Admissions, Master of Business Administration Program, Clarion, PA 16214. Offers finance (MBA); health care administration (MBA); innovation and entrepreneurship (MBA). *Accreditation:* AACSB. *Program availability:* Part-time, evening/weekend, 100% online. *Faculty:* 15 full-time (2 women). *Students:* 52 full-time (9 women), 54 part-time (43 women); includes 14 minority (7 Black or African American, non-Hispanic/Latino; 2 Asian, non-Hispanic/Latino; 1 Hispanic/Latino; 4 Two or more races, non-Hispanic/Latino), 4 international. Average age 32. 87 applicants, 86% accepted, 28 enrolled. In 2016, 21 master's awarded. *Degree requirements:* For master's, portfolio. *Entrance requirements:* For master's, GMAT, minimum QPA of 2.75. Additional exam requirements/recommendations for international students: Required—TOEFL (minimum score 550 paper-based; 80 iBT), IELTS (minimum score 7). *Application deadline:* For fall admission, 8/1 priority date for domestic students, 4/15 priority date for international students; for spring admission, 12/1 priority date for domestic students, 9/15 priority date for international students. Applications are processed on a rolling basis. Application fee: $40. Electronic applications accepted. *Expenses:* $632.55 per credit. *Financial support:* Career-related internships or fieldwork, Federal Work-Study, scholarships/grants, and unspecified assistantships available. Support available to part-time students. Financial award application deadline: 3/1; financial award applicants required to submit FAFSA. *Unit head:* Juanice Vega, Associate Dean of the College of Business Administration and Information Sciences, 814-393-2600, Fax: 814-393-1910, E-mail: mba@clarion.edu. *Application contact:* Dana Bearer, Assistant Director, Graduate Programs, 814-393-2337, Fax: 814-393-2722, E-mail: gradstudies@clarion.edu.
Website: http://www.clarion.edu/admissions/graduate/index.html

Clark University, Graduate School, Graduate School of Management, Business Administration Program, Worcester, MA 01610-1477. Offers accounting (MBA); finance (MBA); information management and business analytics (MBA); management (MBA); marketing (MBA); social change (MBA); sustainability (MBA). *Accreditation:* AACSB. *Program availability:* Part-time, evening/weekend. *Students:* 91 full-time (48 women), 101 part-time (45 women); includes 22 minority (8 Black or African American, non-Hispanic/Latino; 4 Asian, non-Hispanic/Latino; 9 Hispanic/Latino; 1 Native Hawaiian or other Pacific Islander, non-Hispanic/Latino), 45 international. Average age 31. 225 applicants, 58% accepted, 78 enrolled. In 2016, 113 master's awarded. *Degree requirements:* For master's, thesis optional. *Application deadline:* For fall admission, 6/1 priority date for domestic students; for spring admission, 12/1 priority date for domestic students. Applications are processed on a rolling basis. Application fee: $75. Electronic applications accepted. *Expenses: Tuition:* Full-time $44,050. *Required fees:* $80. Tuition and fees vary according to course load and program. *Financial support:* In 2016–17, research assistantships with partial tuition reimbursements (averaging $4,800 per year), teaching assistantships with partial tuition reimbursements (averaging $4,800 per year) were awarded; fellowships, career-related internships or fieldwork, Federal Work-Study, institutionally sponsored loans, and tuition waivers (partial) also available. Support available to part-time students. Financial award application deadline: 5/31. *Faculty research:* Marketing, accounting, human resource management, management information systems, business finance. *Unit head:* Dr. Catherine Usoff, Dean, 508-793-7543, Fax: 508-793-8822. *Application contact:* Ethan Bernstein, Director of Graduate Admissions, 508-793-7543, E-mail: graduateadmissions@clarku.edu.
Website: http://www.clarku.edu/programs/masters-business-administration

Clark University, Graduate School, Graduate School of Management, Program in Finance, Worcester, MA 01610-1477. Offers MSF. *Students:* 164 full-time (80 women), 1 part-time (0 women); includes 3 minority (2 Asian, non-Hispanic/Latino; 1 Hispanic/Latino), 160 international. Average age 24. 699 applicants, 85% accepted, 74 enrolled. In 2016, 91 master's awarded. *Degree requirements:* For master's, thesis optional. *Application deadline:* For fall admission, 6/1 priority date for domestic students; for spring admission, 12/1 priority date for domestic students. Applications are processed on a rolling basis. Application fee: $75. Electronic applications accepted. *Expenses: Tuition:* Full-time $44,050. *Required fees:* $80. Tuition and fees vary according to course load and program. *Financial support:* Fellowships, research assistantships with partial tuition reimbursements, teaching assistantships with partial tuition reimbursements, and tuition waivers (partial) available. Financial award application deadline: 5/31. *Faculty research:* Marketing, accounting, human resource management, management information systems, business finance. *Unit head:* Dr. Catherine Usoff, Dean, 508-793-8822, Fax: 508-793-8822, E-mail: clarkmba@clarku.edu. *Application contact:* Patrick Oroszko, Enrollment and Marketing Director, 508-793-8822, Fax: 508-793-8822, E-mail: clarkmsfambassasor@clarku.edu.
Website: http://www.clarku.edu/programs/masters-finance

Cleary University, Online Program in Business Administration, Howell, MI 48843. Offers analytics, technology, and innovation (MBA, Graduate Certificate); financial planning (Graduate Certificate); global leadership (MBA, Graduate Certificate); health care leadership (MBA, Graduate Certificate). *Program availability:* Part-time, evening/weekend, online learning. *Faculty:* 13 part-time/adjunct (6 women). *Students:* 92 full-time (47 women), 25 part-time (14 women). *Degree requirements:* For master's, thesis. *Entrance requirements:* For master's, bachelor's degree; minimum GPA of 2.5; professional resume indicating minimum of 2 years of management or related experience; undergraduate degree from accredited college or university with at least 18 quarter hours (or 12 semester hours) of accounting study (for MBA in accounting). Additional exam requirements/recommendations for international students: Required—TOEFL (minimum score 550 paper-based; 79 iBT), Michigan English Language Assessment Battery (minimum score 75). *Application deadline:* For fall admission, 8/15 for domestic students, 7/15 for international students; for spring admission, 4/2 for domestic students, 1/2 for international students. Applications are processed on a rolling basis. Application fee: $50. Electronic applications accepted. *Expenses: Tuition:* Full-time $16,560; part-time $920 per credit hour. *Required fees:* $100 per semester. *Financial support:* Fellowships, Federal Work-Study, and scholarships/grants available. Support available to part-time students. Financial award application deadline: 8/15; financial award applicants required to submit FAFSA. *Unit head:* Dr. Lance B. Lewis, Provost and Chief Academic Officer, 800-686-1883, E-mail: llewis@cleary.edu. *Application contact:* Cassandra Tarnowski, Director of Admissions, 800-686-1883, Fax: 517-338-3336, E-mail: ctarnowski@cleary.edu.

College for Financial Planning, Graduate Programs, Centennial, CO 80112. Offers finance (MSF); personal financial planning (MS). *Program availability:* Part-time, evening/weekend, online only, 100% online. *Faculty:* 9 full-time (2 women), 32 part-time/adjunct (6 women). *Students:* 4,318 full-time. *Degree requirements:* For master's, capstone course or thesis. *Entrance requirements:* Additional exam requirements/recommendations for international students: Required—TOEFL (minimum score 550 paper-based). *Application deadline:* Applications are processed on a rolling basis. Electronic applications accepted. *Expenses: Tuition:* Full-time $6750; part-time $450 per credit hour. *Unit head:* John Sears, President, 303-220-4918, E-mail: john.sears@cffp.edu. *Application contact:* Alicia Christensen, Director of Enrollment, 303-220-4835, Fax: 303-220-1810, E-mail: alicia.mead@cffp.edu.
Website: http://www.cffpinfo.com/graduate.html

The College of Saint Rose, Graduate Studies, Huether School of Business, Program in Financial Planning, Albany, NY 12203-1419. Offers Advanced Certificate. *Program availability:* Part-time, evening/weekend. *Students:* 2 part-time (0 women). Average age 49. 2 applicants, 100% accepted, 1 enrolled. In 2016, 4 Advanced Certificates awarded. *Degree requirements:* For Advanced Certificate, comprehensive exam. *Entrance requirements:* Additional exam requirements/recommendations for international students: Required—TOEFL (minimum score 550 paper-based; 80 iBT), IELTS (minimum score 6), PTE (minimum score 56). *Application deadline:* For fall admission, 4/1 priority date for domestic and international students; for spring admission, 10/15 priority date for domestic students, 10/15 for international students; for summer admission, 3/15 priority date for domestic and international students. Applications are processed on a rolling basis. Application fee: $40. Electronic applications accepted. *Expenses: Tuition:* Full-time $14,382; part-time $799 per credit. *Required fees:* $814; $32 per credit. $88 per semester. Tuition and fees vary according to course load. *Financial support:* Career-related internships or fieldwork and scholarships/grants

available. Support available to part-time students. Financial award application deadline: 4/15. *Unit head:* Gretchen Guenther-Collins, Program Coordinator, 518-458-5304, E-mail: guentheg@strose.edu. *Application contact:* Cris Murray, Assistant Vice President for Graduate Recruitment and Enrollment, 518-485-3390, Fax: 518-458-5479, E-mail: grad@strose.edu.
Website: https://www.strose.edu/academics/graduate-programs/graduate-studies/financial-planning/

Colorado State University, College of Business, Program in Finance, Fort Collins, CO 80523. Offers M Fin. *Program availability:* Part-time. *Faculty:* 12 full-time (3 women). *Students:* 22 full-time (10 women), 4 part-time (1 woman); includes 1 minority (Asian, non-Hispanic/Latino), 21 international. Average age 27. 80 applicants, 80% accepted, 58 enrolled. In 2016, 31 master's awarded. *Degree requirements:* For master's, thesis or alternative, scholarly paper. *Entrance requirements:* For master's, GMAT or GRE, undergraduate degree with minimum GPA of 3.0; coursework in business finance, probability and statistics, and calculus; academic experience with computer programming; current resume; 3 letters of recommendation; official transcripts; statement of purpose. Additional exam requirements/recommendations for international students: Required—TOEFL (minimum score 86 iBT); Recommended—IELTS (minimum score 6.5), TSE (minimum score 58). *Application deadline:* For fall admission, 6/1 for domestic students, 5/1 for international students. Applications are processed on a rolling basis. Application fee: $60 ($70 for international students). Electronic applications accepted. *Expenses:* Contact institution. *Financial support:* Scholarships/grants and unspecified assistantships available. Financial award application deadline: 2/15; financial award applicants required to submit FAFSA. *Faculty research:* Enterprise valuation; financial modeling and investments; financial engineering; international finance; debt securities analysis. *Total annual research expenditures:* $166,486. *Unit head:* Dr. Sanjay Ramchander, Department Chair, 970-491-5027, E-mail: gradadmissions@business.colostate.edu. *Application contact:* Jennifer Ivan, Program Manager, 970-491-1184, E-mail: jennifer.ivan@colostate.edu.
Website: https://biz.colostate.edu/Academics/Graduate-Programs/Master-of-Finance#Overview

Colorado State University–Global Campus, Graduate Programs, Greenwood Village, CO 80111. Offers criminal justice and law enforcement administration (MS); education leadership (MS); finance (MS); healthcare administration and management (MS); human resource management (MHRM); information technology management (MITM); international management (MS); management (MS); organizational leadership (MS); professional accounting (MPA); project management (MS); teaching and learning (MS). *Accreditation:* ACBSP. *Program availability:* Online learning.

Colorado Technical University Aurora, Programs in Business Administration and Management, Aurora, CO 80014. Offers accounting (MBA); business administration (MBA); business administration and management (EMBA); finance (MBA); human resource management (MBA); marketing (MBA); mediation and dispute resolution (MBA); operations management (MBA); project management (MBA); technology management (MBA). *Program availability:* Part-time, evening/weekend. *Degree requirements:* For master's, thesis or alternative. *Entrance requirements:* For master's, minimum undergraduate GPA of 3.0, resume.

Colorado Technical University Colorado Springs, Graduate Studies, Program in Management, Colorado Springs, CO 80907. Offers accounting (MBA, MSA); business administration (MBA); finance (MBA); human resources management (MBA); logistics/supply chain management (MBA); management (DM); marketing (MBA); mediation and dispute resolution (MBA); operations management (MBA); project management (MBA); technology management (MBA). *Accreditation:* ACBSP. *Program availability:* Part-time, evening/weekend, online learning. *Degree requirements:* For master's, thesis or alternative; for doctorate, thesis/dissertation. *Entrance requirements:* For doctorate, minimum graduate GPA of 3.0, 5 years of related work experience. *Faculty research:* Sexual harassment, performance evaluation, critical thinking.

Columbia Southern University, MBA Program, Orange Beach, AL 36561. Offers finance (MBA); health care management (MBA); human resource management (MBA); marketing (MBA); project management (MBA); public administration (MBA). *Program availability:* Part-time, evening/weekend, online learning. *Entrance requirements:* For master's, bachelor's degree from accredited/approved institution. Additional exam requirements/recommendations for international students: Required—TOEFL. Electronic applications accepted.

Columbia University, Graduate School of Arts and Sciences, New York, NY 10027. Offers African-American studies (MA); American studies (MA); anthropology (MA, PhD); art history and archaeology (MA, PhD); astronomy (PhD); biological sciences (PhD); biotechnology (MA); chemical physics (PhD); chemistry (PhD); classical studies (MA, PhD); classics (MA, PhD); climate and society (MA); conservation biology (MA); earth and environmental sciences (PhD); East Asia: regional studies (MA); East Asian languages and cultures (MA, PhD); ecology, evolution and environmental biology (MA), including conservation biology; ecology, evolution, and environmental biology (PhD), including ecology and evolutionary biology, evolutionary primatology; economics (MA, PhD); English and comparative literature (MA, PhD); French and Romance philology (MA, PhD); Germanic languages (MA, PhD); global French studies (MA); global thought (MA); Hispanic cultural studies (MA); history (PhD); history and literature (MA); human rights studies (MA); Islamic studies (MA); Italian (MA, PhD); Japanese pedagogy (MA); Jewish studies (MA); Latin America and the Caribbean: regional studies (MA); Latin American and Iberian cultures (PhD); mathematics (MA, PhD), including finance (MA); medieval and Renaissance studies (MA); Middle Eastern, South Asian, and African studies (MA, PhD); modern art: critical and curatorial studies (MA); modern European studies (MA); museum anthropology (MA); music (DMA, PhD); oral history (MA); philosophical foundations of physics (MA); philosophy (MA, PhD); physics (PhD); political science (MA, PhD); psychology (PhD); quantitative methods in the social sciences (MA); religion (MA, PhD); Russia, Eurasia and East Europe: regional studies (MA); Russian translation (MA); Slavic cultures (MA); Slavic languages (MA, PhD); sociology (MA, PhD); South Asian studies (MA); statistics (MA, PhD); theatre (PhD). Dual-degree programs require admission to both Graduate School of Arts and Sciences and another Columbia school. *Program availability:* Part-time. Terminal master's awarded for partial completion of doctoral program. *Degree requirements:* For master's, variable foreign language requirement, comprehensive exam (for some programs), thesis (for some programs); for doctorate, variable foreign language requirement, comprehensive exam (for some programs), thesis/dissertation. *Entrance requirements:* For master's and doctorate, GRE General Test, GRE Subject Test (for some programs). Additional exam requirements/recommendations for international students: Required—TOEFL, IELTS. Electronic applications accepted.

Columbia University, Graduate School of Business, Doctoral Program in Business, New York, NY 10027. Offers business (PhD), including accounting, decision, risk, and operations, finance and economics, management, marketing. *Accreditation:* AACSB. *Degree requirements:* For doctorate, comprehensive exam, thesis/dissertation, major field exam, research paper, thesis proposal. *Entrance requirements:* For doctorate, GMAT or GRE (finance), 2 letters of reference, resume. Additional exam requirements/recommendations for international students: Required—TOEFL. Electronic applications accepted. *Expenses:* Contact institution. *Faculty research:* Human decision making and behavioral research; real estate market and mortgage defaults; financial crisis and corporate governance; international business; security analysis and accounting.

Columbia University, Graduate School of Business, MBA Program, New York, NY 10027. Offers accounting (MBA); decision, risk, and operations (MBA); entrepreneurship (MBA); finance and economics (MBA); healthcare and pharmaceutical management (MBA); human resource management (MBA); international business (MBA); leadership and ethics (MBA); management (MBA); marketing (MBA); media (MBA); private equity (MBA); real estate (MBA); social enterprise (MBA); value investing (MBA); DDS/MBA; JD/MBA; MBA/MIA; MBA/MPH; MBA/MS; MD/MBA. *Entrance requirements:* For master's, GMAT, 2 letters of recommendation. Additional exam requirements/recommendations for international students: Required—TOEFL. Electronic applications accepted. *Expenses:* Contact institution. *Faculty research:* Human decision making and behavioral research; real estate market and mortgage defaults; financial crisis and corporate governance; international business; security analysis and accounting.

Concordia University, School of Graduate Studies, John Molson School of Business, Montreal, QC H3H 0A1, Canada. Offers administration (M Sc), including finance, management, marketing; business administration (MBA, PhD, Certificate, Diploma); executive business administration (EMBA); supply chain management (MSCM). PhD program offered jointly with HEC Montreal, McGill University, and Université du Québec à Montréal. *Program availability:* Part-time, evening/weekend. *Degree requirements:* For master's, one foreign language, thesis (for some programs), research project; for doctorate, one foreign language, thesis/dissertation; for other advanced degree, one foreign language. *Entrance requirements:* For master's, GMAT, minimum 2 years of work experience (for MBA); letters of recommendation, bachelor's degree from recognized university with minimum GPA of 3.0, curriculum vitae; for doctorate, GMAT (minimum score of 600), official transcripts, curriculum vitae, 3 letters of reference, statement of purpose; for other advanced degree, minimum GPA of 2.7, 2 letters of reference, statement of purpose, resume. Additional exam requirements/recommendations for international students: Required—TOEFL (minimum score 90 iBT), IELTS (minimum score 7). Electronic applications accepted. *Expenses:* Contact institution. *Faculty research:* General business, capital markets, international business.

Concordia University Wisconsin, Graduate Programs, School of Business Administration, MBA Program, Mequon, WI 53097-2402. Offers finance (MBA); health care administration (MBA); human resource management (MBA); international business (MBA); international business-bilingual English/Chinese (MBA); management (MBA); management information systems (MBA); managerial communications (MBA); marketing (MBA); public administration (MBA); risk management (MBA). *Program availability:* Online learning. *Degree requirements:* For master's, comprehensive exam, thesis or alternative. *Entrance requirements:* Additional exam requirements/recommendations for international students: Required—TOEFL. *Application deadline:* For fall admission, 8/1 priority date for domestic students; for spring admission, 1/15 for domestic students. Applications are processed on a rolling basis. Application fee: $50. *Expenses:* Contact institution. *Financial support:* Application deadline: 8/1. *Unit head:* Dr. David Borst, Director, 262-243-4298, Fax: 262-243-4428, E-mail: david.borst@cuw.edu. *Application contact:* Mary Eberhardt, Graduate Admissions, 262-243-4551, Fax: 262-243-4428, E-mail: mary.eberhardt@cuw.edu.

Cornell University, Graduate School, Graduate Field of Management, Ithaca, NY 14853. Offers accounting (PhD); finance (PhD); marketing (PhD); organizational behavior (PhD); production and operations management (PhD). *Accreditation:* AACSB. *Degree requirements:* For doctorate, comprehensive exam, thesis/dissertation. *Entrance requirements:* For doctorate, GMAT or GRE General Test. Additional exam requirements/recommendations for international students: Required—TOEFL (minimum score 600 paper-based; 77 iBT). Electronic applications accepted. *Expenses:* Contact institution. *Faculty research:* Operations and manufacturing.

Cornell University, Graduate School, Graduate Fields of Arts and Sciences, Field of Economics, Ithaca, NY 14853. Offers applied economics (PhD); basic analytical economics (PhD); econometrics and economic statistics (PhD); economic development and planning (PhD); economic theory (PhD); industrial organization and control (PhD); international economics (PhD); labor economics (PhD); monetary and macro economics (PhD); public finance (PhD). *Degree requirements:* For doctorate, comprehensive exam, thesis/dissertation. *Entrance requirements:* For doctorate, GRE General Test, 3 letters of recommendation. Additional exam requirements/recommendations for international students: Required—TOEFL (minimum score 550 paper-based; 77 iBT). Electronic applications accepted. *Faculty research:* Learning and games, economics of education, political economy, transfer payments, time series and nonparametrics.

Creighton University, Graduate School, Heider College of Business, Omaha, NE 68178-0001. Offers accounting (MAC); business administration (MBA); business intelligence and analytics (MS); finance (M Fin); JD/MBA; MBA/MSAPM; MD/MBA; Pharm D/MBA. *Accreditation:* AACSB. *Program availability:* Part-time, evening/weekend, 100% online, blended/hybrid learning. *Faculty:* 33 full-time (10 women), 22 part-time/adjunct (3 women). *Students:* 41 full-time (13 women), 262 part-time (79 women); includes 24 minority (16 Black or African American, non-Hispanic/Latino; 3 Asian, non-Hispanic/Latino; 1 Hispanic/Latino; 2 Native Hawaiian or other Pacific Islander, non-Hispanic/Latino; 2 Two or more races, non-Hispanic/Latino), 21 international. Average age 32. 189 applicants, 73% accepted, 74 enrolled. In 2016, 172 master's awarded. *Degree requirements:* For master's, thesis optional. *Entrance requirements:* For master's, GMAT, resume, 2 letters of recommendation. Additional exam requirements/recommendations for international students: Required—TOEFL (minimum score 90 iBT). *Application deadline:* For fall admission, 7/1 priority date for domestic students, 3/1 for international students; for winter admission, 10/1 priority date for domestic students, 7/1 for international students; for spring admission, 4/1 priority date for domestic students, 10/1 for international students; for summer admission, 5/1 for domestic and international students. Applications are processed on a rolling basis. Application fee: $50. Electronic applications accepted. *Expenses:* Contact institution. *Financial support:* In 2016–17, 10 fellowships with partial tuition reimbursements (averaging $8,448 per year) were awarded; career-related internships or fieldwork, tuition waivers (partial), and unspecified assistantships also available. Financial award application deadline: 3/1. *Faculty research:* Small business issues, economics. *Unit head:* Dr. Deborah Wells, Associate Dean for Graduate Programs, 402-280-2841, E-mail: deborahwells@creighton.edu. *Application contact:* Chris Karasek, Assistant Dean, 402-280-2829, Fax: 402-280-2172, E-mail: chriskarasek@creighton.edu.
Website: http://business.creighton.edu

Culver-Stockton College, MBA Program, Canton, MO 63435-1299. Offers accounting and finance (MBA).

Curry College, Graduate Studies, Program in Business Administration, Milton, MA 02186-9984. Offers business administration (MBA); finance (Certificate). *Program availability:* Part-time, evening/weekend. *Degree requirements:* For master's, capstone applied project. *Entrance requirements:* For master's, resume, recommendations, interview, written statement. Additional exam requirements/recommendations for international students: Required—TOEFL (minimum score 550 paper-based; 80 iBT). *Expenses:* Contact institution.

Finance and Banking

Dalhousie University, Faculty of Management, Centre for Advanced Management Education, Halifax, NS B3H 3J5, Canada. Offers financial services (MBA); information management (MIM); management (MPA); natural resources (MBA). *Program availability:* Part-time, online learning. *Entrance requirements:* For master's, GMAT, minimum GPA of 3.0, resume. Additional exam requirements/recommendations for international students: Required—TOEFL, IELTS, CANTEST, CAEL, or Michigan English Language Assessment Battery. Electronic applications accepted.

Dalhousie University, Faculty of Management, Rowe School of Business, Halifax, NS B3H 3J5, Canada. Offers business administration (MBA); financial services (MBA); LL B/MBA; MBA/MLIS. *Program availability:* Part-time. *Entrance requirements:* For master's, GMAT, letter of non-financial guarantee for non-Canadian students, resume, Corporate Residency Preference Form. Additional exam requirements/recommendations for international students: Required—TOEFL, IELTS, CANTEST, CAEL, or Michigan English Language Assessment Battery. Electronic applications accepted. *Faculty research:* International business, quantitative methods, operations research, MIS, marketing, finance.

Dallas Baptist University, College of Business, Business Administration Program, Dallas, TX 75211-9299. Offers accounting (MBA); business communication (MBA); conflict resolution management (MBA); entrepreneurship (MBA); finance (MBA); health care management (MBA); international business (MBA); leading the non-profit organization (MBA); management (MBA); management information systems (MBA); marketing (MBA); project management (MBA); technology and engineering management (MBA). *Accreditation:* ACBSP. *Program availability:* Part-time, evening/weekend, 100% online, blended/hybrid learning. *Application deadline:* Applications are processed on a rolling basis. Application fee: $25. Electronic applications accepted. Application fee is waived when completed online. *Expenses: Tuition:* Full-time $15,408; part-time $856 per credit hour. *Required fees:* $400 per semester. Tuition and fees vary according to course load and degree level. *Unit head:* Dr. Sandra Reid, Chair of Graduate Business Programs, 214-333-5280, E-mail: sandra@dbu.edu. *Application contact:* Bobby Soto, Director of Admissions, 214-333-5242, E-mail: graduate@dbu.edu.
Website: http://www3.dbu.edu/graduate/mba.asp

Dallas Baptist University, Professional Development Program, Dallas, TX 75211-9299. Offers accounting (MA); church leadership (MA); communication (MA); counseling (MA); criminal justice (MA); English as a second language (MA); finance (MA); higher education (MA); leadership studies (MA); management (MA); management information systems (MA); marketing (MA); missions (MA); professional life coaching (MA); training and development (MA). *Program availability:* Part-time, evening/weekend, 100% online, blended/hybrid learning. *Application deadline:* Applications are processed on a rolling basis. Application fee: $25. Electronic applications accepted. Application fee is waived when completed online. *Expenses: Tuition:* Full-time $15,408; part-time $856 per credit hour. *Required fees:* $400 per semester. Tuition and fees vary according to course load and degree level. *Unit head:* Jared Ingram, Director, 214-333-5584, E-mail: jaredi@dbu.edu. *Application contact:* Bobby Soto, Director of Admissions, 214-333-5242, E-mail: graduate@dbu.edu.
Website: http://www3.dbu.edu/graduate/mapd.asp

Davenport University, Sneden Graduate School, Grand Rapids, MI 49512. Offers accounting (MBA); business administration (EMBA); finance (MBA); health care management (MBA); human resources (MBA); information assurance (MS); public health (MPH); strategic management (MBA). *Program availability:* Evening/weekend. *Entrance requirements:* For master's, GMAT, minimum undergraduate GPA of 2.75. Additional exam requirements/recommendations for international students: Required—TOEFL. Electronic applications accepted. *Faculty research:* Leadership, management, marketing, organizational culture.

Delaware Valley University, MBA Program, Doylestown, PA 18901-2697. Offers accounting (MBA); entrepreneurship (MBA); finance (MBA); food and agribusiness (MBA); general business (MBA); global executive leadership (MBA); human resource management (MBA); supply chain management (MBA). *Program availability:* Part-time, evening/weekend, online learning. *Entrance requirements:* For master's, minimum undergraduate GPA of 3.0. Electronic applications accepted. *Expenses:* Contact institution.

DePaul University, Kellstadt Graduate School of Business, Chicago, IL 60604. Offers accountancy (M Acc, MS, MSA); applied economics (MBA); banking (MBA); behavioral finance (MBA); brand and product management (MBA); business development (MBA); business information technology (MS); business strategy and decision-making (MBA); computational finance (MS); consumer insights (MBA); corporate finance (MBA); economic policy analysis (MS); entrepreneurship (MBA, MS); finance (MBA, MS); financial analysis (MBA); general business (MBA); health sector management (MBA); hospitality leadership (MBA); hospitality leadership and operational performance (MS); human resource management (MBA); human resources (MS); investment management (MBA); leadership and change management (MBA); management accounting (MBA); marketing (MBA, MS); marketing analysis (MS); marketing strategy and planning (MBA); operations management (MBA); organizational diversity (MBA); real estate (MS); real estate finance and investment (MBA); revenue management (MBA); sports management (MBA); strategic global marketing (MBA); strategy, execution and valuation (MBA); sustainable management (MBA, MS); taxation (MS); wealth management (MS); JD/MBA. *Accreditation:* AACSB. *Program availability:* Part-time, evening/weekend, online learning. *Entrance requirements:* For master's, GMAT, 2 letters of recommendation, resume, essay, official transcripts. Additional exam requirements/recommendations for international students: Required—TOEFL (minimum score 550 paper-based; 80 iBT). Electronic applications accepted. *Expenses:* Contact institution.

DeSales University, Division of Business, Center Valley, PA 18034-9568. Offers accounting (MBA); computer information systems (MBA); finance (MBA); health care systems management (MBA); human resources management (MBA); management (MBA); marketing (MBA); project management (MBA); self-design (MBA); supply chain management (MBA); DNP/MBA; MSN/MBA. *Accreditation:* ACBSP. *Program availability:* Part-time, evening/weekend, 100% online, blended/hybrid learning. *Faculty:* 12 full-time (4 women), 29 part-time/adjunct (5 women). *Students:* 73 full-time (38 women), 323 part-time (163 women); includes 59 minority (16 Black or African American, non-Hispanic/Latino; 23 Asian, non-Hispanic/Latino; 16 Hispanic/Latino; 4 Two or more races, non-Hispanic/Latino). Average age 37. 157 applicants, 87% accepted, 128 enrolled. In 2016, 115 master's awarded. *Entrance requirements:* For master's, GMAT (waived if undergraduate GPA is 3.0 or better), minimum GPA of 3.0 in undergraduate work, literacy in basic software, background or interest in the field of study, personal statement, 2 years of work experience. Additional exam requirements/recommendations for international students: Required—TOEFL. *Application deadline:* Applications are processed on a rolling basis. Application fee: $50. Electronic applications accepted. *Expenses:* Contact institution. *Financial support:* Applicants required to submit FAFSA. *Faculty research:* Quality improvement, executive development, productivity, cross-cultural managerial differences, leadership. *Unit head:* Dr. David M. Gilfoil, Director, MBA Program, 610-282-1100 Ext. 1828, Fax: 610-282-2869, E-mail: david.gilfoil@desales.edu. *Application contact:* Julia Ferraro, Director of Graduate Admissions, 610-282-1100 Ext. 1768, E-mail: gradadmissions@desales.edu.

DeVry University–Folsom Campus, Graduate Programs, Folsom, CA 95630. Offers accounting (M Acc); accounting and financial management (MAFM); business administration (MBA); curriculum leadership (M Ed); educational leadership (M Ed); educational technology (M Ed); higher education leadership (M Ed); human resource management (MHRM); information systems management (MISM); network and communications management (MNCM); project management (MPM); public administration (MPA).

Drexel University, LeBow College of Business, Department of Finance, Philadelphia, PA 19104-2875. Offers MS. *Faculty:* 18 full-time (4 women), 2 part-time/adjunct (0 women). *Students:* 88 full-time (42 women), 2 part-time (both women); includes 3 minority (1 Black or African American, non-Hispanic/Latino; 1 Asian, non-Hispanic/Latino; 1 Hispanic/Latino), 85 international. Average age 24. In 2016, 21 master's awarded. *Degree requirements:* For master's, seminar paper. *Entrance requirements:* For master's, GMAT, minimum GPA of 2.75. Additional exam requirements/recommendations for international students: Required—TOEFL. *Application deadline:* For fall admission, 8/21 for domestic students. Applications are processed on a rolling basis. Application fee: $50. Electronic applications accepted. *Expenses: Tuition:* Full-time $32,184; part-time $1192 per credit hour. *Required fees:* $280. Tuition and fees vary according to campus/location and program. *Financial support:* Research assistantships, teaching assistantships, career-related internships or fieldwork, and unspecified assistantships available. Financial award application deadline: 2/1. *Faculty research:* Investment analysis, portfolio mix, capital budgeting, banking and financial institutions, international finance. *Unit head:* Dr. Michael J. Gombola, Head, 215-895-1741. *Application contact:* Director of Graduate Admissions, 215-895-6700, Fax: 215-895-5939, E-mail: enroll@drexel.edu.

Drexel University, LeBow College of Business, Program in Business Administration, Philadelphia, PA 19104-2875. Offers business administration (MBA, PhD, APC), including accounting (MBA, PhD), decision sciences (PhD), economics (MBA, PhD), finance (MBA, PhD), legal studies (MBA), management (MBA), marketing (MBA, PhD), organizational sciences (PhD), quantitative methods (MBA), strategic management (PhD). *Accreditation:* AACSB. *Program availability:* Part-time, evening/weekend, online learning. *Faculty:* 88 full-time (19 women), 11 part-time/adjunct (2 women). *Students:* 153 full-time (70 women), 388 part-time (168 women); includes 107 minority (31 Black or African American, non-Hispanic/Latino; 1 American Indian or Alaska Native, non-Hispanic/Latino; 48 Asian, non-Hispanic/Latino; 16 Hispanic/Latino; 11 Two or more races, non-Hispanic/Latino), 95 international. Average age 33. In 2016, 174 master's, 8 doctorates, 1 other advanced degree awarded. Terminal master's awarded for partial completion of doctoral program. *Entrance requirements:* For master's, GMAT, minimum GPA of 2.75; for doctorate, GMAT. Additional exam requirements/recommendations for international students: Required—TOEFL. *Application deadline:* For fall admission, 8/21 for domestic students; for spring admission, 3/5 for domestic students. Applications are processed on a rolling basis. Application fee: $50. Electronic applications accepted. *Expenses: Tuition:* Full-time $32,184; part-time $1192 per credit hour. *Required fees:* $280. Tuition and fees vary according to campus/location and program. *Financial support:* Research assistantships, teaching assistantships, career-related internships or fieldwork, and unspecified assistantships available. Financial award application deadline: 2/1. *Faculty research:* Decision support systems, individual and group behavior, operations research, techniques and strategy. *Unit head:* Dr. Thomas Wieckowski, Director of Master's Programs in Business, 215-895-1791, Fax: 215-895-1012. *Application contact:* Director of Graduate Admissions, 215-895-6700, Fax: 215-895-5939, E-mail: enroll@drexel.edu.

Duke University, The Fuqua School of Business, The Duke MBA-Cross Continent Program, Durham, NC 27708-0586. Offers business administration (MBA); energy and environment (MBA); entrepreneurship and innovation (MBA); finance (MBA); health sector management (Certificate); marketing (MBA); strategy (MBA). *Faculty:* 88 full-time (19 women), 50 part-time/adjunct (9 women). *Students:* 214 full-time (74 women); includes 58 minority (13 Black or African American, non-Hispanic/Latino; 35 Asian, non-Hispanic/Latino; 10 Hispanic/Latino), 35 international. Average age 30. In 2016, 105 master's awarded. *Entrance requirements:* For master's, GMAT or GRE, transcripts, essays, resume, recommendation letters, letter of company support, interview. *Application deadline:* For fall admission, 10/12 priority date for domestic and international students; for winter admission, 2/7 priority date for domestic and international students; for spring admission, 5/3 priority date for domestic and international students; for summer admission, 5/31 for domestic and international students. Applications are processed on a rolling basis. Application fee: $225. Electronic applications accepted. *Expenses:* Contact institution. *Financial support:* In 2016–17, 49 students received support. Institutionally sponsored loans and scholarships/grants available. Financial award applicants required to submit FAFSA. *Unit head:* Mohan Venkatachalam, Senior Associate Dean, Executive Programs, 919-660-7859, E-mail: mohan.venkatachalam@duke.edu. *Application contact:* Sharon Thompson, Assistant Dean, Office of Admissions, 919-660-7705, Fax: 919-681-8026, E-mail: admissions-info@fuqua.duke.edu.
Website: http://www.fuqua.duke.edu/programs/duke_mba/cross_continent/

Duke University, The Fuqua School of Business, The Duke MBA-Daytime Program, Durham, NC 27708-0586. Offers academic excellence in finance (Certificate); business administration (MBA); decision sciences (MBA); energy and environment (MBA); energy finance (MBA); entrepreneurship and innovation (MBA); finance (MBA); financial analysis (MBA); health sector management (Certificate); leadership and ethics (MBA); management (MBA); marketing (MBA); operations management (MBA); social entrepreneurship (MBA); strategy (MBA). *Faculty:* 88 full-time (19 women), 50 part-time/adjunct (9 women). *Students:* 897 full-time (310 women); includes 174 minority (39 Black or African American, non-Hispanic/Latino; 3 American Indian or Alaska Native, non-Hispanic/Latino; 75 Asian, non-Hispanic/Latino; 51 Hispanic/Latino; 1 Native Hawaiian or other Pacific Islander, non-Hispanic/Latino; 5 Two or more races, non-Hispanic/Latino), 343 international. Average age 28. In 2016, 440 master's awarded. *Entrance requirements:* For master's, GMAT or GRE, transcripts, essays, resume, recommendation letters, interview. *Application deadline:* For fall admission, 9/13 for domestic and international students; for winter admission, 10/13 for domestic and international students; for spring admission, 1/4 for domestic and international students; for summer admission, 3/20 for domestic and international students. Application fee: $225. Electronic applications accepted. *Expenses:* $66,717 (first-year tuition and fees). *Financial support:* In 2016–17, 415 students received support. Institutionally sponsored loans and scholarships/grants available. Financial award applicants required to submit FAFSA. *Unit head:* Russ Morgan, Senior Associate Dean for Full-time Programs, 919-660-2931, Fax: 919-684-8742, E-mail: ruskin.morgan@duke.edu. *Application contact:* Sharon Thompson, Assistant Dean, Office of Admissions, 919-660-7705, Fax: 919-681-8026, E-mail: admissions-info@fuqua.duke.edu.
Website: http://www.fuqua.duke.edu/daytime-mba/

Duke University, The Fuqua School of Business, The Duke MBA-Global Executive Program, Durham, NC 27708-0586. Offers business administration (MBA); energy and environment (MBA); entrepreneurship and innovation (MBA); finance (MBA); health

sector management (Certificate); marketing (MBA); strategy (MBA). *Faculty:* 88 full-time (19 women), 50 part-time/adjunct (9 women). *Students:* 48 full-time (14 women); includes 18 minority (3 Black or African American, non-Hispanic/Latino; 11 Asian, non-Hispanic/Latino; 4 Hispanic/Latino), 10 international. Average age 39. In 2016, 27 master's awarded. *Entrance requirements:* For master's, transcripts, essays, resume, recommendation letters, letter of company support, interview. *Application deadline:* For fall admission, 10/12 priority date for domestic and international students; for winter admission, 12/7 priority date for domestic and international students; for spring admission, 3/20 priority date for domestic and international students; for summer admission, 5/31 for domestic and international students. Applications are processed on a rolling basis. Application fee: $225. Electronic applications accepted. *Expenses:* Contact institution. *Financial support:* In 2016–17, 22 students received support. Institutionally sponsored loans and scholarships/grants available. Financial award applicants required to submit FAFSA. *Unit head:* Mohan Venkatachalam, Senior Associate Dean, Executive Programs, 919-660-7859, E-mail: mohan.venkatachalam@duke.edu. *Application contact:* Sharon Thompson, Assistant Dean, Office of Admissions, 919-660-7705, Fax: 919-681-8026, E-mail: admissions-info@fuqua.duke.edu.
Website: http://www.fuqua.duke.edu/programs/duke_mba/global-executive/

Duke University, The Fuqua School of Business, The Duke MBA-Weekend Executive Program, Durham, NC 27708-0586. Offers business administration (MBA); energy and environment (MBA); entrepreneurship and innovation (MBA); finance (MBA); health sector management (Certificate); marketing (MBA); strategy (MBA). *Faculty:* 88 full-time (19 women), 50 part-time/adjunct (9 women). *Students:* 190 full-time (43 women); includes 75 minority (11 Black or African American, non-Hispanic/Latino; 3 American Indian or Alaska Native, non-Hispanic/Latino; 48 Asian, non-Hispanic/Latino; 12 Hispanic/Latino; 1 Two or more races, non-Hispanic/Latino), 26 international. Average age 35. In 2016, 87 master's awarded. *Entrance requirements:* For master's, GMAT or GRE, transcripts, essays, resume, recommendation letters, letter of company support, interview. *Application deadline:* For fall admission, 8/30 priority date for domestic and international students; for winter admission, 10/12 priority date for domestic and international students; for spring admission, 2/7 priority date for domestic and international students; for summer admission, 3/20 for domestic and international students. Applications are processed on a rolling basis. Application fee: $225. Electronic applications accepted. *Expenses:* Contact institution. *Financial support:* In 2016–17, 33 students received support. Institutionally sponsored loans and scholarships/grants available. Financial award applicants required to submit FAFSA. *Unit head:* Mohan Venkatachalam, Senior Associate Dean, Executive Programs, 919-660-7859, E-mail: mohan.venkatachalam@duke.edu. *Application contact:* Sharon Thompson, Assistant Dean, Office of Admissions, 919-660-7705, Fax: 919-681-8026, E-mail: admissions-info@fuqua.duke.edu.
Website: http://www.fuqua.duke.edu/programs/duke_mba/weekend_executive/

Duke University, The Fuqua School of Business, Master of Quantitative Management Program, Durham, NC 27708-0586. Offers finance (MQM); forensics (MQM); marketing (MQM); strategy (MQM). *Entrance requirements:* For master's, GMAT/GRE, transcripts, essays, resume, recommendation letters. *Application deadline:* For fall admission, 9/21 for domestic and international students; for winter admission, 11/20 for domestic and international students; for spring admission, 2/16 for domestic and international students; for summer admission, 4/4 for domestic and international students. Application fee: $125. Electronic applications accepted. *Unit head:* Jeremy Petranka, Associate Dean, E-mail: jeremy.petranka@duke.edu. *Application contact:* Sharon Thompson, Assistant Dean, Office of Admissions, 919-660-7705, Fax: 919-681-8026, E-mail: admissions-info@fuqua.duke.edu.
Website: http://www.fuqua.duke.edu/master-quantitative-management/

Duke University, The Fuqua School of Business, PhD Program, Durham, NC 27708-0586. Offers accounting (PhD); decision sciences (PhD); finance (PhD); management and organizations (PhD); marketing (PhD); operations management (PhD); strategy (PhD). *Faculty:* 100 full-time (19 women). *Students:* 77 full-time (27 women); includes 9 minority (1 Black or African American, non-Hispanic/Latino; 7 Asian, non-Hispanic/Latino; 1 Hispanic/Latino), 46 international. 561 applicants, 7% accepted, 14 enrolled. In 2016, 15 doctorates awarded. *Degree requirements:* For doctorate, thesis/dissertation, major field requirement (exam or major paper, depending upon the area). *Entrance requirements:* For doctorate, GMAT or GRE, transcripts, essays, recommendation letters, statement of purpose. Additional exam requirements/recommendations for international students: Required—TOEFL (minimum score 577 paper-based; 90 iBT), IELTS (minimum score 7). *Application deadline:* For fall admission, 12/31 priority date for domestic and international students. Application fee: $85. Electronic applications accepted. *Expenses:* Contact institution. *Financial support:* In 2016–17, 77 students received support, including 70 fellowships with full tuition reimbursements available (averaging $28,200 per year), 63 research assistantships with full tuition reimbursements available (averaging $7,000 per year); institutionally sponsored loans, scholarships/grants, and tuition waivers (full) also available. Financial award applicants required to submit FAFSA. *Unit head:* William Boulding, Dean, 919-660-7822, Fax: 919-684-8742, E-mail: bb1@duke.edu. *Application contact:* Qi Chen, Director of Graduate Studies, 919-660-7753, Fax: 919-660-7971, E-mail: qc2@duke.edu.

Duquesne University, Palumbo-Donahue School of Business, Pittsburgh, PA 15282-0001. Offers accounting (M Acc); finance (MBA); information systems management (MSISM); management (MBA, MS); marketing (MBA); sports business (MS); sustainability (MBA); JD/MBA; MBA/M Acc; MBA/MA; MBA/MES; MBA/MHMS; MSISM/MBA; Pharm D/MBA. *Accreditation:* AACSB. *Program availability:* Part-time, evening/weekend, 100% online, minimal on-campus study. *Faculty:* 59 full-time (23 women), 25 part-time/adjunct (6 women). *Students:* 92 full-time (43 women), 176 part-time (71 women); includes 20 minority (9 Black or African American, non-Hispanic/Latino; 8 Asian, non-Hispanic/Latino; 2 Hispanic/Latino; 1 Two or more races, non-Hispanic/Latino), 35 international. Average age 28. 272 applicants, 86% accepted, 137 enrolled. In 2016, 137 master's awarded. *Entrance requirements:* For master's, GMAT or GRE, undergraduate transcripts, 2 letters of recommendation, current resume, personal statement. Additional exam requirements/recommendations for international students: Required—TOEFL (minimum score 577 paper-based; 90 iBT), IELTS (minimum score 7). *Application deadline:* For fall admission, 7/1 priority date for domestic and international students; for spring admission, 12/1 for domestic and international students; for summer admission, 4/1 for domestic and international students. Applications are processed on a rolling basis. Application fee: $0. Electronic applications accepted. *Expenses:* Contact institution. *Financial support:* In 2016–17, 211 students received support, including 12 fellowships with partial tuition reimbursements available (averaging $14,200 per year), 20 research assistantships with partial tuition reimbursements available (averaging $22,212 per year); career-related internships or fieldwork, scholarships/grants, and unspecified assistantships also available. Support available to part-time students. Financial award application deadline: 7/1; financial award applicants required to submit FAFSA. *Faculty research:* Investment management, business ethics, technology management, supply chain management, entrepreneurship. *Unit head:* Dr. Karen Donovan, Associate Dean of Graduate Programs and Executive Education, 412-396-6276, Fax: 412-396-1726, E-mail: donovan6@duq.edu. *Application contact:* Jeff Jewett, Director of Admissions and Enrollment Management, 412-396-6244, Fax: 412-396-1726, E-mail: decrostam@duq.edu.
Website: http://www.duq.edu/business/grad

Eastern Michigan University, Graduate School, College of Business, Programs in Business Administration, Ypsilanti, MI 48197. Offers business administration (MBA, Graduate Certificate); computer information systems (Graduate Certificate); e-business (MBA, Graduate Certificate); enterprise business intelligence (MBA); entrepreneurship (MBA, Graduate Certificate); finance (MBA, Graduate Certificate); human resources (MBA); human resources management (Graduate Certificate); information systems (MBA); internal auditing (MBA); international business (MBA, Graduate Certificate); marketing management (Graduate Certificate); nonprofit management (MBA); organizational development (Graduate Certificate); supply chain management (MBA, Graduate Certificate). *Accreditation:* AACSB. *Program availability:* Part-time, online learning. *Students:* 63 full-time (36 women), 320 part-time (186 women); includes 131 minority (76 Black or African American, non-Hispanic/Latino; 5 American Indian or Alaska Native, non-Hispanic/Latino; 16 Asian, non-Hispanic/Latino; 19 Hispanic/Latino; 15 Two or more races, non-Hispanic/Latino), 23 international. Average age 32. 305 applicants, 70% accepted, 124 enrolled. In 2016, 78 master's, 57 other advanced degrees awarded. *Entrance requirements:* For master's, GMAT (minimum score 450), minimum cumulative undergraduate GPA of 2.75. Additional exam requirements/recommendations for international students: Required—TOEFL. *Application deadline:* For fall admission, 5/15 priority date for domestic students, 2/15 priority date for international students; for winter admission, 10/15 priority date for domestic students, 9/1 priority date for international students; for summer admission, 3/15 priority date for domestic students, 3/1 priority date for international students. Applications are processed on a rolling basis. Application fee: $45. *Financial support:* Fellowships, research assistantships with full tuition reimbursements, teaching assistantships with full tuition reimbursements, career-related internships or fieldwork, Federal Work-Study, institutionally sponsored loans, scholarships/grants, tuition waivers (partial), and unspecified assistantships available. Support available to part-time students. Financial award applicants required to submit FAFSA. *Unit head:* K. Michelle Henry, Director, Graduate Business Programs, 734-487-4444, Fax: 734-483-1316, E-mail: cob.graduate@emich.edu.
Website: http://www.emich.edu/cob/mba/

East Tennessee State University, School of Graduate Studies, College of Arts and Sciences, Department of Political Science, International Affairs and Public Administration, Johnson City, TN 37614. Offers economic development (Postbaccalaureate Certificate); not-for-profit administration (MPA); planning and development (MPA); public financial management (MPA); urban planning (Postbaccalaureate Certificate). *Program availability:* Part-time. *Degree requirements:* For master's, internship. *Entrance requirements:* For master's, GRE General Test, three letters of recommendation; for Postbaccalaureate Certificate, GRE General Test. Additional exam requirements/recommendations for international students: Required—TOEFL (minimum score 550 paper-based; 79 iBT). Electronic applications accepted. *Faculty research:* Labor issues, presidency, public law in American politics, East Asian politics, European politics, Middle Eastern politics, development in comparative politics, international political economy, international relations, world politics in international affairs.

Elms College, Division of Business, Chicopee, MA 01013-2839. Offers accounting (MBA); financial planning (MBA); healthcare leadership (MBA); management (MBA). *Program availability:* Part-time, evening/weekend. *Faculty:* 4 full-time (all women), 6 part-time/adjunct (3 women). *Students:* 51 part-time (32 women); includes 10 minority (4 Black or African American, non-Hispanic/Latino; 1 Asian, non-Hispanic/Latino; 5 Hispanic/Latino). Average age 34. 26 applicants, 100% accepted, 22 enrolled. In 2016, 24 master's awarded. *Entrance requirements:* For master's, minimum GPA of 3.0. *Application deadline:* Applications are processed on a rolling basis. Application fee: $30. *Expenses: Tuition:* Full-time $13,392. *Required fees:* $200. *Unit head:* Dr. David Kimball, Chair, Division of Business, 413-265-2300, E-mail: kimballd@elms.edu. *Application contact:* Dr. Elizabeth Teahan Hukowicz, Dean, School of Graduate and Professional Studies, 413-265-2360 Ext. 238, Fax: 413-265-2459, E-mail: hukowicze@elms.edu.

Embry-Riddle Aeronautical University–Daytona, Department of Management, Marketing and Operations, Daytona Beach, FL 32114-3900. Offers airline management (MBA); airport management (MBA); aviation finance (MSAF); aviation management (MBA-AM); aviation system management (MBA); finance (MBA); supply chain management (MBA). *Accreditation:* ACBSP. *Program availability:* Part-time. *Faculty:* 13 full-time (2 women). *Students:* 93 full-time (37 women), 15 part-time (8 women); includes 12 minority (3 Black or African American, non-Hispanic/Latino; 3 Asian, non-Hispanic/Latino; 1 Hispanic/Latino; 5 Two or more races, non-Hispanic/Latino), 71 international. Average age 26. 130 applicants, 39% accepted, 40 enrolled. In 2016, 44 degrees awarded. *Degree requirements:* For master's, thesis (for some programs). *Entrance requirements:* Additional exam requirements/recommendations for international students: Required—TOEFL (minimum score 550 paper-based, 79 iBT) or IELTS (6). *Application deadline:* For fall admission, 3/1 priority date for domestic students; for spring admission, 11/1 priority date for domestic students; for summer admission, 4/1 priority date for domestic students. Applications are processed on a rolling basis. Application fee: $50. Electronic applications accepted. *Expenses: Tuition:* Full-time $16,296; part-time $1358 per credit hour. *Required fees:* $1294; $647 per semester. One-time fee: $100 full-time. Tuition and fees vary according to course load, degree level and program. *Financial support:* Research assistantships, teaching assistantships, career-related internships or fieldwork, scholarships/grants, unspecified assistantships, and on-campus employment available. Financial award application deadline: 3/15; financial award applicants required to submit FAFSA. *Unit head:* Michael J. Williams, PhD, Dean, College of Business/Professor of Management, 386-226-6293, E-mail: michael.williams@erau.edu. *Application contact:* Graduate Admissions, 386-226-6176, E-mail: graduate.admissions@erau.edu.
Website: https://daytonabeach.erau.edu/college-business/index.html

See Display on page 616 and Close-Up on page 637.

Embry-Riddle Aeronautical University–Worldwide, Department of Decision Sciences, Daytona Beach, FL 32114-3900. Offers aviation and aerospace (MSPM); aviation/aerospace management (MSEM); financial management (MSEM, MSPM); general management (MSPM); global management (MSPM); human resources management (MSPM); information systems (MSPM); leadership (MSEM, MSPM); logistics and supply chain management (MSEM, MSLSCM, MSPM); management (MSEM, MSPM); project management (MSEM); systems engineering (MSEM, MSPM); technical management (MSPM). *Program availability:* Part-time, evening/weekend, 100% online, blended/hybrid learning, EagleVision is a virtual classroom that combines Web video conferencing and a learning management system. EagleVision Classroom (between classrooms), EagleVision Home (faculty and students at home), and a blend of Classroom or Home. *Degree requirements:* For master's, comprehensive exam (for some programs), thesis (for some programs). *Entrance requirements:* Additional exam requirements/recommendations for international students: Required—TOEFL (minimum score 550 paper-based; 79 iBT), IELTS (minimum score 6), TOEFL or IELTS accepted. Electronic applications accepted. *Expenses:* Contact institution.

Finance and Banking

Emory University, Goizueta Business School, Doctoral Program in Business, Atlanta, GA 30322. Offers accounting (PhD); finance (PhD); information systems and operations management (PhD); marketing (PhD); organization and management (PhD). *Faculty:* 59 full-time (16 women). *Students:* 40 full-time (16 women); includes 6 minority (1 Black or African American, non-Hispanic/Latino; 4 Asian, non-Hispanic/Latino; 1 Hispanic/Latino), 26 international. Average age 28. 145 applicants, 9% accepted, 4 enrolled. In 2016, 5 doctorates awarded. *Degree requirements:* For doctorate, comprehensive exam, thesis/dissertation. *Entrance requirements:* For doctorate, GMAT (strongly preferred) or GRE. Additional exam requirements/recommendations for international students: Required—TOEFL (minimum score 600 paper-based; 100 iBT). *Application deadline:* For fall admission, 1/3 priority date for domestic and international students. Application fee: $75. Electronic applications accepted. *Expenses:* $708 fees per year; 100% of tuition covered by scholarship. *Financial support:* In 2016–17, 34 students received support, including 6 fellowships (averaging $3,333 per year); scholarships/grants and health care benefits also available. Financial award application deadline: 1/3. *Faculty research:* Financial and managerial accounting, asset pricing strategy and organizational behavior, information technology marketing analytics and consumer behavior. *Unit head:* Dr. Anand Swaminathan, Associate Dean, Doctoral Program, 404-727-2306, Fax: 404-727-5337, E-mail: anand.swaminathan@emory.edu. *Application contact:* Allison Gilmore, Director of Admissions and Student Services, 404-727-6353, Fax: 404-727-5337, E-mail: allison.gilmore@emory.edu.

Emory University, Goizueta Business School, Full Time MBA Program, Atlanta, GA 30322. Offers accounting (MBA); alternative investments (MBA); business process consulting (MBA); business technology management (MBA); capital markets (MBA); corporate finance (MBA); customer relationship management (MBA); decision analytics (MBA); entrepreneurship (MBA); finance (MBA); global management (MBA); investment banking (MBA); management consulting (MBA); marketing (MBA); marketing analytics (MBA); marketing consulting (MBA); operations management (MBA); organization and management (MBA); product and brand management (MBA); real estate (MBA); social enterprise (MBA); strategy consulting (MBA). *Accreditation:* AACSB. *Faculty:* 72 full-time (17 women), 18 part-time/adjunct (5 women). *Students:* 350 full-time (101 women); includes 77 minority (21 Black or African American, non-Hispanic/Latino; 3 American Indian or Alaska Native, non-Hispanic/Latino; 32 Asian, non-Hispanic/Latino; 15 Hispanic/Latino; 2 Native Hawaiian or other Pacific Islander, non-Hispanic/Latino; 4 Two or more races, non-Hispanic/Latino), 117 international. Average age 29. 1,434 applicants, 31% accepted, 181 enrolled. In 2016, 182 master's awarded. *Degree requirements:* For master's, 1 leadership course; 2 mid-semester module programs; 2 global components. *Entrance requirements:* For master's, GMAT/GRE, essays; recommendation letters; undergraduate degree; interview. Additional exam requirements/recommendations for international students: Required—TOEFL (minimum score 100 iBT), IELTS (minimum score 7), PTE (minimum score 68). *Application deadline:* For fall admission, 10/14 priority date for domestic and international students; for winter admission, 11/11 priority date for domestic and international students; for spring admission, 1/4 priority date for domestic students, 1/4 for international students. Application fee: $150. Electronic applications accepted. *Expenses:* $57,580. *Financial support:* In 2016–17, 289 students received support. Career-related internships or fieldwork, institutionally sponsored loans, and scholarships/grants available. Financial award application deadline: 4/1; financial award applicants required to submit FAFSA. *Faculty research:* Social enterprise; micro vs. large business; mobile health data; mutual fund performance; product evaluation. *Unit head:* Brian Mitchell, Associate Dean, 404-727-4824, Fax: 404-712-9648, E-mail: brian.mitchell@emory.edu. *Application contact:* Julie Barefoot, Associate Dean, 404-727-6311, Fax: 404-727-4612, E-mail: mbaadmissions@emory.edu.
Website: http://www.goizueta.emory.edu

Fairfield University, Dolan School of Business, Fairfield, CT 06824. Offers accounting (MBA, MS, CAS); business analytics (MS); entrepreneurship (MBA); finance (MBA, MS, CAS); general management (MBA, CAS); global management (MBA); human resource management (MBA, CAS); information systems and business analytics (MBA); marketing (MBA, CAS); taxation (MBA, CAS). *Accreditation:* AACSB. *Program availability:* Part-time, evening/weekend. *Faculty:* 20 full-time (6 women), 4 part-time/adjunct (1 woman). *Students:* 106 full-time (41 women), 57 part-time (26 women); includes 18 minority (4 Black or African American, non-Hispanic/Latino; 1 American Indian or Alaska Native, non-Hispanic/Latino; 4 Asian, non-Hispanic/Latino; 7 Hispanic/Latino; 2 Two or more races, non-Hispanic/Latino), 39 international. Average age 26. 136 applicants, 63% accepted, 35 enrolled. In 2016, 90 master's awarded. *Degree requirements:* For master's, capstone course. *Entrance requirements:* For master's, GMAT (minimum score 500), 2 letters of reference, resume, minimum GPA of 3.0. Additional exam requirements/recommendations for international students: Required—TOEFL (minimum score 550 paper-based; 80 iBT) or IELTS (minimum score 6.5). *Application deadline:* For fall admission, 5/15 for international students; for spring admission, 10/15 for international students. Applications are processed on a rolling basis. Application fee: $60. Electronic applications accepted. *Expenses:* $875 per credit hour. *Financial support:* In 2016–17, 33 students received support. Scholarships/grants and unspecified assistantships available. Financial award applicants required to submit FAFSA. *Faculty research:* International finance, leadership and careers, ethics in accounting, emotions in consumer behavior and organizations, data analytics. *Unit head:* Dr. Donald Gibson, Dean, 203-254-4070, Fax: 203-254-4105, E-mail: dgibson@fairfield.edu. *Application contact:* Marianne Gumpper, Director of Graduate and Continuing Studies Admission, 203-254-4184, Fax: 203-254-4073, E-mail: gradadmis@fairfield.edu.
Website: http://fairfield.edu/mba

Fairleigh Dickinson University, College at Florham, Silberman College of Business, Department of Economics, Finance, and International Business, Program in Finance, Madison, NJ 07940-1099. Offers MBA, Certificate.

Fairleigh Dickinson University, Metropolitan Campus, Silberman College of Business, Department of Economics, Finance and International Business, Program in Finance, Teaneck, NJ 07666-1914. Offers MBA, Certificate.

Florida Agricultural and Mechanical University, Division of Graduate Studies, Research, and Continuing Education, School of Business and Industry, Tallahassee, FL 32307-3200. Offers accounting (MBA); finance (MBA); management information systems (MBA); marketing (MBA). *Accreditation:* ACBSP. *Degree requirements:* For master's, residency. *Entrance requirements:* For master's, GMAT, minimum GPA of 3.0.

Florida Atlantic University, College of Business, Department of Finance, Boca Raton, FL 33431-0991. Offers MS. *Faculty:* 14 full-time (3 women). *Students:* 41 full-time (8 women), 4 part-time (2 women); includes 22 minority (5 Black or African American, non-Hispanic/Latino; 1 Asian, non-Hispanic/Latino; 11 Hispanic/Latino; 5 Two or more races, non-Hispanic/Latino), 8 international. Average age 30. 38 applicants, 74% accepted, 20 enrolled. *Expenses:* Tuition, state resident: full-time $7392; part-time $369.82 per credit hour. Tuition, nonresident: full-time $19,432; part-time $1024.81 per credit hour. *Unit head:* Megan Hall, 561-297-6000, E-mail: msfinance@fau.edu.

Florida International University, Chapman Graduate School of Business, Department of Finance, Miami, FL 33199. Offers MSF. *Program availability:* Part-time, evening/weekend. *Faculty:* 25 full-time (5 women), 10 part-time/adjunct (0 women). *Students:* 97 full-time (37 women), 7 part-time (4 women); includes 66 minority (10 Black or African American, non-Hispanic/Latino; 4 Asian, non-Hispanic/Latino; 51 Hispanic/Latino; 1 Two or more races, non-Hispanic/Latino), 24 international. Average age 29. 212 applicants, 47% accepted, 68 enrolled. In 2016, 109 master's awarded. *Entrance requirements:* For master's, GMAT or GRE, minimum GPA of 3.0 in upper-level coursework; letter of intent; resume. Additional exam requirements/recommendations for international students: Required—TOEFL (minimum score 550 paper-based; 80 iBT) or IELTS (minimum score 6.5). *Application deadline:* For fall admission, 6/1 for domestic students, 4/1 for international students; for spring admission, 10/1 for domestic students, 9/1 for international students. Applications are processed on a rolling basis. Application fee: $30. Electronic applications accepted. *Expenses:* Contact institution. *Financial support:* Institutionally sponsored loans and scholarships/grants available. Financial award application deadline: 3/1; financial award applicants required to submit FAFSA. *Faculty research:* Investment, corporate and international finance. *Unit head:* Shahid Hamid, Chair, 305-348-2681, E-mail: hamids@fiu.edu. *Application contact:* Paula Alger, Program Manager, 305-348-7466, E-mail: palger@fiu.edu.

Florida National University, Program in Business Administration, Hialeah, FL 33012. Offers finance (MBA); general management (MBA); health services administration (MBA); marketing (MBA); public management and leadership (MBA). *Program availability:* Part-time, blended/hybrid learning. *Degree requirements:* For master's, capstone. *Entrance requirements:* For master's, writing assessment, bachelor's degree from accredited institution; official undergraduate transcripts; minimum undergraduate GPA of 2.5, GMAT (minimum score of 400), or GRE (minimum score of 900); two letters of recommendation. Additional exam requirements/recommendations for international students: Required—TOEFL (minimum score 500 paper-based; 62 iBT), IELTS (minimum score 5.5). *Application deadline:* Applications are processed on a rolling basis. Electronic applications accepted. *Expenses:* Contact institution. *Financial support:* Federal Work-Study, institutionally sponsored loans, scholarships/grants, and tuition waivers available. Financial award applicants required to submit FAFSA. *Unit head:* Dr. Ernesto Gonzalez, Business Department Head, 305-821-3333 Ext. 1070, Fax: 305-362-0595, E-mail: egonzalez@fnu.edu. *Application contact:* Olga Rodriguez, Assistant Campus Dean, 305-821-3333 Ext. 1044, Fax: 305-362-0595, E-mail: orodriguez@fnu.edu.

Florida State University, The Graduate School, College of Business, Tallahassee, FL 32306-1110. Offers accounting (M Acc), including assurance and advisory services, generalist, taxation; business administration (MBA, PhD), including accounting (PhD), finance (PhD), management information systems (PhD), marketing (PhD), organizational behavior and human resources (PhD), risk management and insurance (PhD), strategy (PhD); finance (MS); management information systems (MS); risk management and insurance (MS); JD/MBA; MSW/MBA. *Accreditation:* AACSB. *Program availability:* Part-time, 100% online. *Faculty:* 101 full-time (27 women), 4 part-time/adjunct (2 women). *Students:* 272 full-time (127 women), 351 part-time (133 women); includes 141 minority (45 Black or African American, non-Hispanic/Latino; 2 American Indian or Alaska Native, non-Hispanic/Latino; 20 Asian, non-Hispanic/Latino; 59 Hispanic/Latino; 2 Native Hawaiian or other Pacific Islander, non-Hispanic/Latino; 13 Two or more races, non-Hispanic/Latino), 71 international. Average age 30. 688 applicants, 60% accepted, 273 enrolled. In 2016, 231 master's, 12 doctorates awarded. Terminal master's awarded for partial completion of doctoral program. *Degree requirements:* For doctorate, comprehensive exam, thesis/dissertation. *Entrance requirements:* For master's, GMAT, GRE (for all except MS in finance), work experience (MBA, MS); minimum GPA of 3.0, letters of recommendation; for doctorate, GMAT, GRE (for marketing, organizational behavior, risk management and insurance, management information systems, and human resources only), minimum graduate GPA of 3.5, letters of recommendation. Additional exam requirements/recommendations for international students: Required—TOEFL (minimum score 600 paper-based; 85 iBT); Recommended—IELTS (minimum score 6). *Application deadline:* For fall admission, 6/1 for domestic and international students; for spring admission, 10/1 for domestic and international students; for summer admission, 3/1 for domestic and international students. Applications are processed on a rolling basis. Application fee: $30. Electronic applications accepted. *Expenses:* Contact institution. *Financial support:* In 2016–17, 149 students received support, including 9 fellowships (averaging $1,500 per year), 65 research assistantships with full tuition reimbursements available (averaging $20,000 per year), 75 teaching assistantships with full tuition reimbursements available (averaging $20,000 per year); career-related internships or fieldwork, scholarships/grants, health care benefits, tuition waivers (full and partial), and unspecified assistantships also available. Support available to part-time students. Financial award application deadline: 1/1; financial award applicants required to submit FAFSA. *Faculty research:* Business strategy, marketing, finance, accounting, business analytics. *Total annual research expenditures:* $1.4 million. *Unit head:* Dr. Michael Hartline, Dean, 850-644-4405, Fax: 850-644-0915, E-mail: mhartline@business.fsu.edu. *Application contact:* Jennifer Clark, Director, 850-644-6458, E-mail: gradprograms@business.fsu.edu.
Website: http://business.fsu.edu/

Fordham University, Gabelli School of Business, New York, NY 10023. Offers accounting (MBA, MS); applied statistics and decision-making (MS); business administration (EMBA); business analytics (MS); communications and media management (MBA); electronic business (MBA); entrepreneurship (MBA); finance (MBA); global finance (MS); global sustainability (MBA); healthcare management (MBA); information systems (MBA, MS); investor relations (MS); management (MBA, MS); marketing (MBA); marketing intelligence (MS); media management (MS); nonprofit leadership (MS); quantitative finance (MS); taxation (MS); JD/MBA; MS/MBA. *Accreditation:* AACSB. *Program availability:* Part-time, evening/weekend. *Faculty:* 132 full-time (44 women), 51 part-time/adjunct (7 women). *Students:* 1,117 full-time (668 women), 553 part-time (282 women); includes 207 minority (44 Black or African American, non-Hispanic/Latino; 92 Asian, non-Hispanic/Latino; 69 Hispanic/Latino; 2 Native Hawaiian or other Pacific Islander, non-Hispanic/Latino), 1,088 international. Average age 27. 4,745 applicants, 46% accepted, 752 enrolled. In 2016, 996 master's awarded. Terminal master's awarded for partial completion of doctoral program. *Degree requirements:* For master's, internships (required for MS in quantitative finance, recommended for MBA). *Entrance requirements:* For master's, GMAT/GRE, 2 letters of recommendation, resume, 2 essays, transcripts. Additional exam requirements/recommendations for international students: Required—TOEFL (minimum score 100 iBT), IELTS (minimum score 7). *Application deadline:* For fall admission, 11/15 priority date for domestic and international students; for winter admission, 1/15 priority date for domestic students, 1/1 priority date for international students; for spring admission, 3/1 for domestic and international students; for summer admission, 6/1 for domestic students. Application fee: $130. Electronic applications accepted. *Expenses:* $1,397 per credit. *Financial support:* In 2016–17, 78 students received support. Career-related internships or fieldwork, institutionally sponsored loans, scholarships/grants, and unspecified assistantships available. Support available to part-time students. Financial award application deadline: 6/30; financial award applicants required to submit FAFSA. *Unit head:* Dr. Donna Rapaccioli, Dean, 212-636-6165, Fax: 212-307-1779, E-mail: rapaccioli@fordham.edu. *Application contact:* Lawrence Murray, Senior Assistant Dean of Graduate Admissions and Advising, 212-636-6200, Fax: 212-636-7076, E-mail:

admissionsgb@fordham.edu.
Website: http://www.fordham.edu/gabelli

Gannon University, School of Graduate Studies, College of Engineering and Business, Dahlkemper School of Business, Program in Business Administration, Erie, PA 16541-0001. Offers business administration (MBA); finance (MBA); human resources management (MBA); marketing (MBA). *Accreditation:* ACBSP. *Program availability:* Part-time, evening/weekend, 100% online, blended/hybrid learning. *Students:* 43 full-time (17 women), 67 part-time (34 women); includes 7 minority (4 Black or African American, non-Hispanic/Latino; 2 Asian, non-Hispanic/Latino; 1 Hispanic/Latino), 19 international. Average age 30. 160 applicants, 53% accepted, 28 enrolled. In 2016, 60 master's awarded. *Entrance requirements:* For master's, GMAT, bachelor's degree in any discipline from any accredited college or university, resume, transcripts, 3 letters of recommendation. Additional exam requirements/recommendations for international students: Required—TOEFL (minimum score 79 iBT). *Application deadline:* Applications are processed on a rolling basis. Application fee: $25. Electronic applications accepted. Application fee is waived when completed online. *Expenses: Tuition:* Full-time $17,370. *Required fees:* $550. Tuition and fees vary according to course load and program. *Financial support:* Federal Work-Study and unspecified assistantships available. Financial award application deadline: 7/1; financial award applicants required to submit FAFSA. *Unit head:* Dr. Michael Messina, Director, 814-871-5755, Fax: 814-871-7210, E-mail: messina001@gannon.edu. *Application contact:* Bridget Philip, Director of Graduate Admissions, 814-871-7412, E-mail: graduate@gannon.edu.

Geneva College, Program in Business Administration, Beaver Falls, PA 15010-3599. Offers business administration (MBA); finance (MBA); marketing (MBA); operations (MBA). *Accreditation:* ACBSP. *Program availability:* Part-time, evening/weekend. *Students:* 22 full-time (6 women), 29 part-time (10 women); includes 4 minority (1 Black or African American, non-Hispanic/Latino; 1 American Indian or Alaska Native, non-Hispanic/Latino; 2 Asian, non-Hispanic/Latino), 1 international. Average age 35. In 2016, 15 master's awarded. *Degree requirements:* For master's, 36 credit hours of course work (30 of which are required of all students). *Entrance requirements:* For master's, GMAT (if college GPA less than 2.5), undergraduate transcript, 2 letters of recommendation, resume, goals statement. Additional exam requirements/recommendations for international students: Required—TOEFL. *Application deadline:* For fall admission, 3/1 priority date for domestic students; for spring admission, 11/1 priority date for domestic students. Applications are processed on a rolling basis. Electronic applications accepted. *Expenses:* $710 per credit. *Financial support:* In 2016–17, 1 student received support. Scholarships/grants available. Financial award application deadline: 8/1; financial award applicants required to submit FAFSA. *Unit head:* Dr. Gary Vander Plaats, Director of the MBA Program, 724-847-6619, E-mail: gpvander@geneva.edu. *Application contact:* Marina Frazier, Director of Graduate Enrollment, 724-847-6697, E-mail: mba@geneva.edu.
Website: http://www.geneva.edu/page/masters_business

George Fox University, College of Business, Newberg, OR 97132-2697. Offers accounting (DBA); finance (MBA); management (DBA); management and leadership (MBA); marketing (DBA); organizational strategy (MBA); strategic human resource management (MBA). MBA offered in Newberg, OR and in Portland, OR. *Accreditation:* ACBSP. *Program availability:* Part-time, evening/weekend, online learning. *Degree requirements:* For master's, capstone project; for doctorate, credit-applied research project. *Entrance requirements:* For master's, resume (5 years of professional experience); 3 professional references; interview; financial e-learning course; official transcripts; for doctorate, GRE or GMAT, resume; personal mission statement; academic research writing sample; official transcript from each college/university attended; three professional references. Additional exam requirements/recommendations for international students: Required—TOEFL (minimum score 577 paper-based; 90 iBT) or IELTS (minimum score 7). Electronic applications accepted. *Expenses:* Contact institution.

Georgetown University, Graduate School of Arts and Sciences, Department of Economics, Washington, DC 20057. Offers econometrics (PhD); economic development (PhD); economic theory (PhD); industrial organization (PhD); international macro and finance (PhD); international trade (PhD); labor economics (PhD); macroeconomics (PhD); public economics and political economy (PhD); MA/PhD; MS/MA. *Degree requirements:* For doctorate, comprehensive exam, thesis/dissertation. *Entrance requirements:* For doctorate, GRE General Test. Additional exam requirements/recommendations for international students: Required—TOEFL. *Faculty research:* International economics, economic development.

Georgetown University, Graduate School of Arts and Sciences, McDonough School of Business, Washington, DC 20057. Offers business administration (EMBA, GEMBA, MBA); finance (MS); leadership (EML). *Accreditation:* AACSB. *Entrance requirements:* For master's, GMAT. Additional exam requirements/recommendations for international students: Required—TOEFL. *Expenses:* Contact institution.

The George Washington University, School of Business, Department of Finance, Washington, DC 20052. Offers finance (MSF, PhD); finance and investments (MBA). *Program availability:* Part-time, evening/weekend. *Faculty:* 18 full-time (5 women). *Students:* 176 full-time (86 women), 19 part-time (4 women); includes 13 minority (6 Black or African American, non-Hispanic/Latino; 6 Asian, non-Hispanic/Latino; 1 Hispanic/Latino), 173 international. Average age 26. 881 applicants, 28% accepted, 2 enrolled. In 2016, 125 master's awarded. *Degree requirements:* For doctorate, thesis/dissertation. *Entrance requirements:* For master's, GMAT; for doctorate, GMAT or GRE. Additional exam requirements/recommendations for international students: Required—TOEFL. *Application deadline:* For fall admission, 4/1 priority date for domestic students; for spring admission, 10/1 for domestic students. Applications are processed on a rolling basis. Application fee: $75. *Financial support:* In 2016–17, 38 students received support. Fellowships, teaching assistantships, career-related internships or fieldwork, Federal Work-Study, and institutionally sponsored loans available. Financial award application deadline: 4/1. *Unit head:* Robert Van Order, Chair, 202-994-3427, E-mail: rvo@gwu.edu. *Application contact:* Christopher Storer, Executive Director, Graduate Admissions, 202-994-1212, E-mail: gwmba@gwu.edu.

The George Washington University, School of Business, Program in Government Contracts, Washington, DC 20052. Offers MS. *Program availability:* Part-time, evening/weekend. *Students:* 12 full-time (5 women), 51 part-time (24 women); includes 30 minority (21 Black or African American, non-Hispanic/Latino; 1 Asian, non-Hispanic/Latino; 7 Hispanic/Latino; 1 Two or more races, non-Hispanic/Latino), 3 international. Average age 40. 34 applicants, 82% accepted, 16 enrolled. In 2016, 9 master's awarded. *Entrance requirements:* For master's, GMAT/GRE or seven years of full-time, relevant professional work experience. *Application deadline:* For fall admission, 7/31 for domestic students. *Unit head:* Dr. George Jabbour, Associate Dean, 202-994-3879, E-mail: wemba@gwu.edu. *Application contact:* Neal Couture, Director, 202-994-2693, E-mail: ncouture@gwu.edu.
Website: http://gwsbwebsite.com/programs/specialized-masters/m-s-in-government-contracts/

Georgia State University, Andrew Young School of Policy Studies, Department of Economics, Atlanta, GA 30302. Offers economics (MA); environmental economics (PhD); experimental economics (PhD); labor economics (PhD); policy (MA); public finance (PhD); urban and regional economics (PhD). MA offered through the College of Arts and Sciences. *Program availability:* Part-time. *Faculty:* 26 full-time (4 women). *Students:* 112 full-time (37 women), 10 part-time (3 women); includes 17 minority (8 Black or African American, non-Hispanic/Latino; 3 Asian, non-Hispanic/Latino; 4 Hispanic/Latino; 2 Two or more races, non-Hispanic/Latino), 62 international. Average age 28. 168 applicants, 45% accepted, 31 enrolled. In 2016, 26 master's, 9 doctorates awarded. Terminal master's awarded for partial completion of doctoral program. *Degree requirements:* For master's, thesis optional; for doctorate, comprehensive exam, thesis/dissertation. *Entrance requirements:* For master's and doctorate, GRE. Additional exam requirements/recommendations for international students: Required—TOEFL (minimum score 603 paper-based; 100 iBT) or IELTS (minimum score 7). *Application deadline:* For fall admission, 1/15 for domestic and international students. Application fee: $50. Electronic applications accepted. *Expenses:* Tuition, state resident: full-time $6876; part-time $382 per credit hour. Tuition, nonresident: full-time $22,374; part-time $1243 per credit hour. *Required fees:* $2128; $1064 per term. Part-time tuition and fees vary according to course load and program. *Financial support:* In 2016–17, fellowships with full tuition reimbursements (averaging $11,333 per year), research assistantships with full tuition reimbursements (averaging $9,788 per year), teaching assistantships with full tuition reimbursements (averaging $3,000 per year) were awarded; career-related internships or fieldwork also available. Financial award application deadline: 2/15; financial award applicants required to submit FAFSA. *Faculty research:* Public, experimental, urban/environmental, labor, and health economics. *Unit head:* Dr. Rusty Tchernis, Director of the Doctoral Program, 404-413-0154, Fax: 404-413-0145, E-mail: rtchernis@gsu.edu.
Website: http://economics.gsu.edu/

Georgia State University, Andrew Young School of Policy Studies, Department of Public Management and Policy, Atlanta, GA 30303. Offers criminal justice (MPA); disaster management (Certificate); disaster policy (MPA); environmental policy (PhD); health policy (PhD); management and finance (MPA); nonprofit management (MPA, Certificate); nonprofit policy (MPA); planning and economic development (MPP, Certificate); policy analysis and evaluation (MPA), including planning and economic development; public and nonprofit management (PhD); public finance and budgeting (PhD), including science and technology policy, urban and regional economic development; public finance policy (MPA), including social policy; public health (MPA). *Accreditation:* NASPAA (one or more programs are accredited). *Program availability:* Part-time. *Faculty:* 17 full-time (9 women). *Students:* 123 full-time (77 women), 79 part-time (49 women); includes 84 minority (59 Black or African American, non-Hispanic/Latino; 5 Asian, non-Hispanic/Latino; 14 Hispanic/Latino; 6 Two or more races, non-Hispanic/Latino), 34 international. Average age 30. 237 applicants, 60% accepted, 65 enrolled. In 2016, 59 master's, 4 doctorates, 8 other advanced degrees awarded. Terminal master's awarded for partial completion of doctoral program. *Degree requirements:* For master's, thesis optional; for doctorate, comprehensive exam, thesis/dissertation. *Entrance requirements:* For master's and doctorate, GRE. Additional exam requirements/recommendations for international students: Required—TOEFL (minimum score 603 paper-based; 100 iBT) or IELTS (minimum score 7). *Application deadline:* For fall admission, 1/15 for domestic and international students. Application fee: $50. Electronic applications accepted. *Expenses:* Tuition, state resident: full-time $6876; part-time $382 per credit hour. Tuition, nonresident: full-time $22,374; part-time $1243 per credit hour. *Required fees:* $2128; $1064 per term. Part-time tuition and fees vary according to course load and program. *Financial support:* In 2016–17, fellowships (averaging $8,194 per year), research assistantships (averaging $8,068 per year), teaching assistantships (averaging $3,600 per year) were awarded; institutionally sponsored loans, scholarships/grants, health care benefits, and unspecified assistantships also available. Financial award application deadline: 2/1. *Faculty research:* Public budgeting and finance, public management, nonprofit management, performance measurement and management, urban development. *Unit head:* Dr. Carolyn Bourdeaux, Chair and Professor, 404-413-0013, Fax: 404-413-0104, E-mail: cbourdeaux@gsu.edu.
Website: http://aysps.gsu.edu/pmap/

Georgia State University, J. Mack Robinson College of Business, Department of Finance, Atlanta, GA 30302-3083. Offers MBA, MS, PhD. *Program availability:* Part-time, evening/weekend. *Faculty:* 20 full-time (4 women). *Students:* 59 full-time (22 women), 2 part-time (0 women); includes 15 minority (10 Black or African American, non-Hispanic/Latino; 3 Asian, non-Hispanic/Latino; 2 Two or more races, non-Hispanic/Latino), 37 international. Average age 28. 160 applicants, 39% accepted, 33 enrolled. In 2016, 30 master's, 3 doctorates awarded. *Degree requirements:* For doctorate, comprehensive exam, thesis/dissertation. *Entrance requirements:* For master's, GRE or GMAT, transcripts from all institutions attended, resume, essays; for doctorate, GRE or GMAT, three letters of recommendation, personal statement, transcripts from all institutions attended, resume. Additional exam requirements/recommendations for international students: Required—TOEFL (minimum score 610 paper-based; 101 iBT), IELTS (minimum score 7). *Application deadline:* For fall admission, 5/1 priority date for domestic students, 2/1 priority date for international students; for spring admission, 9/15 priority date for domestic students, 4/1 priority date for international students. Applications are processed on a rolling basis. Application fee: $50. Electronic applications accepted. *Expenses:* Tuition, state resident: full-time $6876; part-time $382 per credit hour. Tuition, nonresident: full-time $22,374; part-time $1243 per credit hour. *Required fees:* $2128; $1064 per term. Part-time tuition and fees vary according to course load and program. *Financial support:* Research assistantships, teaching assistantships, scholarships/grants, tuition waivers, and unspecified assistantships available. *Faculty research:* Mergers and acquisitions, asset pricing, mutual and hedge funds, derivatives, corporate governance. *Unit head:* Dr. Gerald D. Gay, Professor/Chair, 404-413-7310, Fax: 404-413-7312. *Application contact:* Toby McChesney, Assistant Dean for Graduate Recruiting and Student Services, 404-413-7167, Fax: 404-413-7162, E-mail: rcbgradadmissions@gsu.edu.
Website: http://www.robinson.gsu.edu/finance/

Georgia State University, J. Mack Robinson College of Business, Department of Risk Management and Insurance, Program in Risk Management and Insurance, Atlanta, GA 30302-3083. Offers enterprise risk management (MBA, Certificate); financial risk management (MBA); mathematical risk management (MS); risk and insurance (MS); risk management and insurance (MBA, PhD); MAS/MRM. *Program availability:* Part-time, evening/weekend. *Degree requirements:* For doctorate, comprehensive exam, thesis/dissertation. *Entrance requirements:* For master's, GRE or GMAT, transcripts from all institutions attended, resume, essays. Additional exam requirements/recommendations for international students: Required—TOEFL (minimum score 610 paper-based; 101 iBT), IELTS (minimum score 7). *Application deadline:* For fall admission, 5/1 priority date for domestic students, 2/1 priority date for international students; for spring admission, 9/15 priority date for domestic students, 4/1 priority date for international students. Applications are processed on a rolling basis. Application fee: $50. Electronic applications accepted. *Expenses:* Tuition, state resident: full-time $6876; part-time $382 per credit hour. Tuition, nonresident: full-time $22,374; part-time $1243 per credit hour. *Required fees:* $2128; $1064 per term. Part-time tuition and fees vary according to course load and program. *Financial support:* Research assistantships, scholarships/

grants, tuition waivers, and unspecified assistantships available. *Faculty research:* Insurance economics, structure and performance of insurance markets, regulation and policy in insurance markets, asset pricing theory, financial econometrics. *Unit head:* Dr. Martin Grace, Professor of Risk Management and Legal Studies/Chair of the Department of Risk Management and Insurance, 404-413-7500, Fax: 404-413-7499. *Application contact:* Toby McChesney, Graduate Recruiting Contact, 404-413-7167, Fax: 404-413-7162, E-mail: rcbgradadmissions@gsu.edu.
Website: http://rmi.robinson.gsu.edu/academic-programs/ms-rmi/

Golden Gate University, Ageno School of Business, San Francisco, CA 94105-2968. Offers accounting (MBA); business administration (EMBA, MBA, PMBA, DBA); business analytics (MS); finance (MBA, MS, Certificate); financial planning (MS, Certificate); healthcare information systems (Certificate); human resource management (MBA, MS); human resources management (Certificate); information systems (MS); information technology (MBA); information technology management (Certificate); integrated marketing and communications (MS, Certificate); international business (MBA); management (MBA); marketing (MBA, MS, Certificate); operations supply chain management (Certificate); psychology (MA, Certificate); public administration (EMPA); public relations (MS, Certificate); technical market analysis (Certificate); JD/MBA. *Program availability:* Part-time, evening/weekend. *Faculty:* 18 full-time (3 women), 117 part-time/adjunct (44 women). *Students:* 458 full-time (254 women), 664 part-time (331 women); includes 346 minority (75 Black or African American, non-Hispanic/Latino; 2 American Indian or Alaska Native, non-Hispanic/Latino; 132 Asian, non-Hispanic/Latino; 105 Hispanic/Latino; 9 Native Hawaiian or other Pacific Islander, non-Hispanic/Latino; 23 Two or more races, non-Hispanic/Latino), 354 international. Average age 34. 905 applicants, 83% accepted, 165 enrolled. In 2016, 350 master's, 2 doctorates awarded. *Degree requirements:* For doctorate, thesis/dissertation, qualifying examination. *Entrance requirements:* For master's, GMAT (for MBA), minimum GPA of 2.5 (MS). Additional exam requirements/recommendations for international students: Required—TOEFL (minimum score 550 paper-based; 79 iBT). *Application deadline:* For fall admission, 5/15 for domestic and international students; for winter admission, 1/15 for domestic and international students; for spring admission, 9/15 for domestic and international students. Applications are processed on a rolling basis. Application fee: $70 ($110 for international students). Electronic applications accepted. *Expenses:* Contact institution. *Financial support:* In 2016–17, 372 students received support. Career-related internships or fieldwork, Federal Work-Study, institutionally sponsored loans, and scholarships/grants available. Support available to part-time students. Financial award applicants required to submit FAFSA. *Unit head:* Dr. Gordon Swartz, Dean, 415-442-7027, Fax: 415-442-6579, E-mail: gswartz@ggu.edu. *Application contact:* Angela Melero, Enrollment Services, 415-442-7800, Fax: 415-442-7807, E-mail: info@ggu.edu.
Website: http://www.ggu.edu/programs/business-and-management

Golden Gate University, School of Taxation, San Francisco, CA 94105-2968. Offers advanced studies in taxation (Certificate); estate planning (Certificate); financial planning and taxation (MS); international tax (Certificate); state and local taxation (Certificate); tax (Certificate); taxation (MS). *Program availability:* Part-time, evening/weekend. *Faculty:* 7 full-time (1 woman), 65 part-time/adjunct (19 women). *Students:* 72 full-time (44 women), 539 part-time (281 women); includes 156 minority (17 Black or African American, non-Hispanic/Latino; 3 American Indian or Alaska Native, non-Hispanic/Latino; 100 Asian, non-Hispanic/Latino; 23 Hispanic/Latino; 7 Native Hawaiian or other Pacific Islander, non-Hispanic/Latino; 6 Two or more races, non-Hispanic/Latino), 82 international. Average age 36. 252 applicants, 84% accepted, 105 enrolled. In 2016, 193 master's awarded. *Entrance requirements:* For master's, minimum GPA of 3.0. Additional exam requirements/recommendations for international students: Required—TOEFL (minimum score 550 paper-based), IELTS (minimum score 6.5). *Application deadline:* For fall admission, 5/15 for international students; for winter admission, 1/15 for international students; for spring admission, 9/15 for international students. Applications are processed on a rolling basis. Application fee: $70 ($100 for international students). Electronic applications accepted. *Expenses:* Contact institution. *Financial support:* In 2016–17, 66 students received support. Career-related internships or fieldwork, Federal Work-Study, institutionally sponsored loans, and scholarships/grants available. Support available to part-time students. Financial award applicants required to submit FAFSA. *Unit head:* Fred Sroka, Dean, 415-369-5285, Fax: 415-442-7807. *Application contact:* Angela Melero, Enrollment Services, 415-442-7800, Fax: 415-442-7807, E-mail: info@ggu.edu.
Website: http://www.ggu.edu/programs/taxation/master-of-science-in-taxation

Goldey-Beacom College, Graduate Program, Wilmington, DE 19808-1999. Offers business administration (MBA); finance (MS); financial management (MBA); health care management (MBA); human resource management (MBA); information technology (MBA); international business management (MBA); major finance (MBA); major taxation (MBA); management (MM); marketing management (MBA); taxation (MBA, MS). *Accreditation:* ACBSP. *Program availability:* Part-time, evening/weekend. *Entrance requirements:* For master's, GMAT, MAT, GRE, minimum GPA of 3.0. Additional exam requirements/recommendations for international students: Required—TOEFL (minimum score 65 iBT); Recommended—IELTS (minimum score 6). Electronic applications accepted.

The Graduate Center, City University of New York, Graduate Studies, Program in Business, New York, NY 10016-4039. Offers accounting (PhD); behavioral science (PhD); finance (PhD); management planning systems (PhD). *Degree requirements:* For doctorate, thesis/dissertation. *Entrance requirements:* For doctorate, GMAT, writing sample (15 pages). Additional exam requirements/recommendations for international students: Required—TOEFL. Electronic applications accepted.

Grand Canyon University, Colangelo College of Business, Phoenix, AZ 85017-1097. Offers accounting (MBA, MS); business analytics (MS); disaster preparedness and executive fire service leadership (MS); finance (MBA); general management (MBA); health systems management (MBA); information technology management (MS); leadership (MBA, MS); marketing (MBA); organizational leadership and entrepreneurship (MS); project management (MBA); sports business (MBA); strategic human resource management (MBA). *Accreditation:* ACBSP. *Program availability:* Part-time, evening/weekend, online learning. *Faculty:* 8 full-time (3 women), 147 part-time/adjunct (49 women). *Students:* 1 full-time (0 women), 2,121 part-time (1,165 women); includes 341 minority (249 Black or African American, non-Hispanic/Latino; 17 American Indian or Alaska Native, non-Hispanic/Latino; 15 Asian, non-Hispanic/Latino; 29 Hispanic/Latino; 4 Native Hawaiian or other Pacific Islander, non-Hispanic/Latino; 27 Two or more races, non-Hispanic/Latino), 20 international. Average age 38. In 2016, 569 master's awarded. *Entrance requirements:* For master's, equivalent of two years' full-time professional work experience. Additional exam requirements/recommendations for international students: Required—TOEFL (minimum score 575 paper-based; 90 iBT), IELTS (minimum score 7). *Application deadline:* For fall admission, 8/21 for domestic students, 7/2 for international students; for spring admission, 12/24 for domestic students, 11/1 for international students. Applications are processed on a rolling basis. Application fee: $0. Electronic applications accepted. *Financial support:* Federal Work-Study available. Support available to part-time students. Financial award applicants required to submit FAFSA. *Unit head:* Kim Donaldson, Dean, 602-639-6597, E-mail: kdonaldson@gcu.edu. *Application contact:* Matt Tidwell, Enrollment Manager, 602-639-6020, E-mail: mtidwell@gcu.edu.
Website: https://www.gcu.edu/colangelo-college-of-business.php

Hawai`i Pacific University, College of Business, Program in Business Administration, Honolulu, HI 96813. Offers accounting (MBA); economics (MBA); finance (MBA); hospitality and tourism management (MBA); human resource management (MBA); information systems (MBA); international business (MBA); management (MBA); marketing (MBA); organizational change and development (MBA). *Program availability:* Part-time, evening/weekend, online learning. *Faculty:* 13 full-time (4 women), 1 part-time/adjunct (0 women). *Students:* 106 full-time (47 women), 33 part-time (13 women); includes 66 minority (5 Black or African American, non-Hispanic/Latino; 1 American Indian or Alaska Native, non-Hispanic/Latino; 23 Asian, non-Hispanic/Latino; 11 Hispanic/Latino; 1 Native Hawaiian or other Pacific Islander, non-Hispanic/Latino; 25 Two or more races, non-Hispanic/Latino), 36 international. Average age 33. 77 applicants, 84% accepted, 44 enrolled. In 2016, 78 master's awarded. *Entrance requirements:* For master's, GMAT or GRE. Additional exam requirements/recommendations for international students: Recommended—TOEFL (minimum score 550 paper-based; 80 iBT), IELTS (minimum score 6), TWE (minimum score 5). *Application deadline:* For fall admission, 2/15 priority date for domestic students; for spring admission, 10/15 priority date for domestic students. Applications are processed on a rolling basis. Application fee: $50. Electronic applications accepted. *Expenses: Tuition:* Full-time $17,190; part-time $955 per credit. *Required fees:* $150; $26 per credit. Tuition and fees vary according to course load and program. *Financial support:* In 2016–17, 27 students received support. Research assistantships, career-related internships or fieldwork, Federal Work-Study, scholarships/grants, tuition waivers, and unspecified assistantships available. Financial award application deadline: 3/1; financial award applicants required to submit FAFSA. *Unit head:* Dr. Warren Wee, Associate Dean/Associate Professor of Accounting, 808-544-9325, E-mail: wwee@hpu.edu. *Application contact:* Danny Lam, Assistant Director of Graduate Admissions, 808-544-1135, E-mail: graduate@hpu.edu.
Website: http://www.hpu.edu/CBA/Graduate/MBA/index.html

HEC Montreal, School of Business Administration, Graduate Diploma Programs in Administration, Program in Financial Professions, Montréal, QC H3T 2A7, Canada. Offers Graduate Diploma. All courses are given in English. *Students:* 20 full-time (8 women), 1 part-time (0 women). 81 applicants, 51% accepted, 20 enrolled. In 2016, 19 Graduate Diplomas awarded. *Entrance requirements:* For degree, bachelor's degree in administration (for finance option). *Application deadline:* For fall admission, 4/15 for domestic and international students. Application fee: $86. Electronic applications accepted. *Expenses: Tuition, area resident:* Part-time $77.80 Canadian dollars per credit. Tuition, state resident: full-time $2797 Canadian dollars; part-time $240.92 Canadian dollars per credit. Tuition, nonresident: full-time $8673 Canadian dollars; part-time $531.43 Canadian dollars per credit. *International tuition:* $19,131 Canadian dollars full-time. *Required fees:* $1699 Canadian dollars; $40.58 Canadian dollars per credit. $67.32 Canadian dollars per term. Tuition and fees vary according to degree level and program. *Financial support:* In 2016–17, 814 students received support. Research assistantships, teaching assistantships, and scholarships/grants available. Financial award application deadline: 9/2. *Unit head:* Renaud Lachance, Academic Supervisor, 514-340-7165, E-mail: renaud.lachance@hec.ca. *Application contact:* Anny Caron, Administrative Director, 514-340-3598, Fax: 514-340-6411, E-mail: anny.caron@hec.ca.
Website: http://www.hec.ca/programmes/dess/dess-professions-financieres/index.html

HEC Montreal, School of Business Administration, Master of Science Programs in Administration, Program in Applied Financial Economics, Montréal, QC H3T 2A7, Canada. Offers M Sc. All courses are given in French. *Students:* 19 full-time (6 women), 10 part-time (0 women). 25 applicants, 68% accepted, 10 enrolled. In 2016, 11 master's awarded. *Degree requirements:* For master's, one foreign language, thesis. *Entrance requirements:* For master's, Test de francais international (TFI) with minimum score of 850 (for those who have never studied in French), BBA, undergraduate degree in another field, degree deemed equivalent by program director and minimum GPA of 3.0 on 4.3 scale. *Application deadline:* For fall admission, 3/15 for domestic and international students; for winter admission, 9/15 for domestic and international students. Application fee: $86 Canadian dollars. Electronic applications accepted. *Expenses: Tuition, area resident:* Part-time $77.80 Canadian dollars per credit. Tuition, state resident: full-time $2797 Canadian dollars; part-time $240.92 Canadian dollars per credit. Tuition, nonresident: full-time $8673 Canadian dollars; part-time $531.43 Canadian dollars per credit. *International tuition:* $19,131 Canadian dollars full-time. *Required fees:* $1699 Canadian dollars; $40.58 Canadian dollars per credit. $67.32 Canadian dollars per term. Tuition and fees vary according to degree level and program. *Financial support:* Research assistantships, teaching assistantships, and scholarships/grants available. Financial award application deadline: 9/2. *Unit head:* Dr. Marie-Helene Jobin, Director, 514-340-6283, E-mail: marie-helene.jobin@hec.ca. *Application contact:* Marianne de Moura, Administrative Director, 514-340-7106, Fax: 514-340-6411, E-mail: marianne.de-moura@hec.ca.
Website: http://www.hec.ca/programmes/maitrises/maitrise-economie-financiere-appliquee/index.html

HEC Montreal, School of Business Administration, Master of Science Programs in Administration, Program in Finance, Montréal, QC H3T 2A7, Canada. Offers M Sc. All courses are given in French. *Students:* 75 full-time (24 women), 29 part-time (6 women). 100 applicants, 46% accepted, 32 enrolled. In 2016, 24 master's awarded. *Degree requirements:* For master's, one foreign language. *Entrance requirements:* For master's, Test de francais international (TFI) with minimum score of 850 (for those who have never studied in French), BBA, undergraduate degree in another field, degree deemed equivalent by program director and minimum GPA of 3.0 on 4.3 scale. *Application deadline:* For fall admission, 3/15 for domestic and international students; for winter admission, 9/15 for domestic and international students. Application fee: $86 Canadian dollars. Electronic applications accepted. *Expenses: Tuition, area resident:* Part-time $77.80 Canadian dollars per credit. Tuition, state resident: full-time $2797 Canadian dollars; part-time $240.92 Canadian dollars per credit. Tuition, nonresident: full-time $8673 Canadian dollars; part-time $531.43 Canadian dollars per credit. *International tuition:* $19,131 Canadian dollars full-time. *Required fees:* $1699 Canadian dollars; $40.58 Canadian dollars per credit. $67.32 Canadian dollars per term. Tuition and fees vary according to degree level and program. *Financial support:* Research assistantships, teaching assistantships, and scholarships/grants available. Financial award application deadline: 9/2. *Unit head:* Dr. Marie-Helene Jobin, Director, 514-340-6283, E-mail: marie-helene.jobin@hec.ca. *Application contact:* Marianne de Moura, Administrative Director, 514-340-7106, Fax: 514-340-6411, E-mail: marianne.de-moura@hec.ca.
Website: http://www.hec.ca/programmes/maitrises/maitrise-finance/index.html

Hofstra University, Frank G. Zarb School of Business, Programs in Finance, Hempstead, NY 11549. Offers business administration (MBA), including finance; corporate finance (Advanced Certificate); finance (MS), including financial and risk management, investment analysis; investment management (Advanced Certificate); quantitative finance (MS). *Program availability:* Part-time, evening/weekend, blended/hybrid learning. *Students:* 177 full-time (70 women), 47 part-time (9 women); includes 16

minority (6 Black or African American, non-Hispanic/Latino; 6 Asian, non-Hispanic/Latino; 4 Hispanic/Latino), 167 international. Average age 25. 555 applicants, 72% accepted, 93 enrolled. In 2016, 101 master's awarded. *Degree requirements:* For master's, capstone course (for MBA), thesis (for MS), minimum GPA of 3.0. *Entrance requirements:* For master's, GMAT/GRE, 2 letters of recommendation, resume, essay. Additional exam requirements/recommendations for international students: Required—TOEFL (minimum score 550 paper-based; 80 iBT); Recommended—IELTS (minimum score 6). *Application deadline:* Applications are processed on a rolling basis. Application fee: $75. Electronic applications accepted. *Expenses:* $1,170 per credit. *Financial support:* In 2016–17, 51 students received support, including 43 fellowships with full and partial tuition reimbursements available (averaging $4,829 per year), 1 research assistantship with full and partial tuition reimbursement available (averaging $6,950 per year); career-related internships or fieldwork, Federal Work-Study, institutionally sponsored loans, scholarships/grants, tuition waivers (full and partial), and unspecified assistantships also available. Support available to part-time students. Financial award applicants required to submit FAFSA. *Faculty research:* Individual investors and financial crisis; short-sale constraints and futures trading; social media and sentiment in financial markets; external monitoring of firms; CEO inside debt and insider trading. *Unit head:* Dr. K. G. Viswanathan, Chairperson, 516-463-5699, Fax: 516-463-4834, E-mail: k.g.viswanathan@hofstra.edu. *Application contact:* Sunil Samuel, Assistant Vice President of Admissions, 516-463-4723, Fax: 516-463-4664, E-mail: graduateadmission@hofstra.edu.
Website: http://www.hofstra.edu/business/

Holy Family University, Graduate and Professional Programs, School of Business Administration, Philadelphia, PA 19114. Offers accountancy (MS); finance (MBA); health care administration (MBA); human resource management (MBA); information systems management (MBA). *Accreditation:* ACBSP. *Program availability:* Part-time, evening/weekend. *Students:* 140 part-time. 58 applicants, 78% accepted, 42 enrolled. In 2016, 44 master's awarded. *Degree requirements:* For master's, comprehensive exam, thesis optional. *Entrance requirements:* For master's, minimum GPA of 3.0, interview, essay/personal statement, current resume, official transcript of all college or university work. Additional exam requirements/recommendations for international students: Required—TOEFL (minimum score 550 paper-based; 79 iBT), IELTS (minimum score 6), PTE (minimum score 54). *Application deadline:* For fall admission, 7/1 priority date for domestic and international students; for winter admission, 1/1 for domestic students; for spring admission, 11/1 priority date for domestic and international students; for summer admission, 4/1 priority date for domestic and international students. Applications are processed on a rolling basis. Application fee: $25. Electronic applications accepted. *Expenses: Tuition:* Part-time $751 per hour. *Required fees:* $140 per semester. One-time fee: $165 part-time. Part-time tuition and fees vary according to degree level and program. *Financial support:* Available to part-time students. Application deadline: 5/1; applicants required to submit FAFSA. *Unit head:* Dr. Barry Dickinson, Dean, 267-341-3440, Fax: 215-637-5937, E-mail: jdickinson@holyfamily.edu. *Application contact:* Gidget Marie Montelibano, Associate Director of Graduate Admissions, 267-341-3558, Fax: 215-637-1478, E-mail: gmontelibano@holyfamily.edu.
Website: http://www.holyfamily.edu/choosing-holy-family-u/academics/schools-of-study/school-of-business-administration

Holy Names University, Graduate Division, Department of Business, Oakland, CA 94619-1699. Offers finance (MBA); management and leadership (MBA); marketing (MBA). *Program availability:* Part-time, evening/weekend. *Students:* 17 full-time (11 women), 15 part-time (10 women); includes 22 minority (9 Black or African American, non-Hispanic/Latino; 2 Asian, non-Hispanic/Latino; 10 Hispanic/Latino; 1 Two or more races, non-Hispanic/Latino), 1 international. Average age 31. 31 applicants, 68% accepted, 15 enrolled. In 2016, 9 master's awarded. *Entrance requirements:* For master's, minimum undergraduate GPA of 2.6 overall, 3.0 in major; two recommendations (letter or form) from previous professors or current or previous work supervisors; 1-3 page personal statement; resume. Additional exam requirements/recommendations for international students: Required—TOEFL (minimum score 550 paper-based; 79 iBT). *Application deadline:* For fall admission, 8/1 priority date for domestic students, 7/15 for international students; for spring admission, 12/1 priority date for domestic students, 12/1 for international students; for summer admission, 5/1 priority date for domestic students, 5/1 for international students. Applications are processed on a rolling basis. Application fee: $65. Electronic applications accepted. Application fee is waived when completed online. *Expenses:* Contact institution. *Financial support:* Career-related internships or fieldwork, Federal Work-Study, scholarships/grants, and unspecified assistantships available. Support available to part-time students. Financial award application deadline: 3/2; financial award applicants required to submit FAFSA. *Faculty research:* Business ethics, sustainable economics, accounting models, cross-cultural management, diversity in organizations. *Unit head:* Russell Jacobus, MBA Program Director, 510-436-1622, E-mail: jacobus@hnu.edu. *Application contact:* 800-430-1321, Fax: 510-436-1325, E-mail: graduateadmissions@hnu.edu.
Website: http://www.hnu.edu

Hood College, Graduate School, Department of Economics and Business Administration, Frederick, MD 21701-8575. Offers accounting (MBA); finance (MBA); human resource management (MBA); information systems (MBA); marketing (MBA); public management (MBA). *Accreditation:* ACBSP. *Program availability:* Part-time, evening/weekend. *Faculty:* 4 full-time, 8 part-time/adjunct. *Students:* 21 full-time (13 women), 106 part-time (60 women); includes 23 minority (12 Black or African American, non-Hispanic/Latino; 4 Asian, non-Hispanic/Latino; 6 Hispanic/Latino; 1 Two or more races, non-Hispanic/Latino), 15 international. Average age 32. 44 applicants, 91% accepted, 25 enrolled. In 2016, 45 master's awarded. *Degree requirements:* For master's, capstone/final research project. *Entrance requirements:* For master's, minimum GPA of 3.0 (or resume and two letters of recommendation), copy of official transcripts, essay. Additional exam requirements/recommendations for international students: Required—TOEFL (minimum score 575 paper-based; 89 iBT), IELTS (minimum score 6.5). *Application deadline:* For fall admission, 8/15 for domestic students, 8/5 for international students; for spring admission, 12/1 for domestic and international students; for summer admission, 5/1 for domestic students, 4/15 for international students. Applications are processed on a rolling basis. Application fee: $35. Electronic applications accepted. *Expenses:* $525 per credit; $110 comprehensive fee per semester. *Financial support:* Tuition waivers (partial) and unspecified assistantships available. Financial award applicants required to submit FAFSA. *Faculty research:* Corporate strategy and sustainable competitive advantages, business ethics, entrepreneurship, investments management, economic development. *Unit head:* April Boulton, Interim Dean of the Graduate School, 301-696-3600, Fax: 301-696-3597, E-mail: gofurther@hood.edu. *Application contact:* Spencer Berk, Assistant Director of Graduate Admissions, 301-696-3604, E-mail: gofurther@hood.edu.

Howard University, School of Business, Graduate Programs in Business, Washington, DC 20059-0002. Offers accounting (MBA); entrepreneurship (MBA); finance (MBA); general management (MBA); human resources management (MBA); information systems (MBA); international business (MBA); marketing (MBA); supply chain management (MBA); JD/MBA. *Accreditation:* AACSB. *Program availability:* Part-time, evening/weekend, online learning. *Entrance requirements:* For master's, GMAT, minimum 1 year post undergraduate work experience, resume, 3 letters of recommendation, advanced college algebra. Additional exam requirements/recommendations for international students: Required—TOEFL. *Faculty research:* Marketing research in multi-ethnic populations, U.S. trade policies and international relations, risk management (finance).

Hult International Business School, Graduate Programs, Cambridge, MA 02141. Offers business administration (EMBA); business analytics (MBA, MIB); business statistics (MBS); disruptive innovation (MDI); entrepreneurship (MBA, MIB); family business (MBA, MIB); finance (MBA, MF, MIB); international marketing (MIM); marketing (MBA, MIB); project management (MBA, MIB). MDI and MBS offered in San Francisco; MBA also offered in Boston, San Francisco, Dubai, Shanghai, and New York. *Students:* Average age 31. *Entrance requirements:* For master's, GMAT, 3 years of work experience. Additional exam requirements/recommendations for international students: Required—TOEFL. *Application deadline:* For fall admission, 9/1 priority date for domestic and international students; for winter admission, 11/1 priority date for domestic and international students; for spring admission, 12/1 priority date for domestic and international students; for summer admission, 6/1 for domestic and international students. Applications are processed on a rolling basis. Application fee: $150. Electronic applications accepted. *Expenses:* $75,000 (for MBA); $45,000 (for master's); $85,000 (for executive part-time MBA). *Financial support:* Scholarships/grants and tuition waivers (partial) available. Financial award application deadline: 6/1; financial award applicants required to submit FAFSA. *Application contact:* Boston Admissions Office, 617-746-1990, E-mail: postgraduate@hult.edu.
Website: http://www.hult.edu

IGlobal University, Graduate Programs, Vienna, VA 22182. Offers accounting (MBA); data management and analytics (MSIT); entrepreneurship (MBA); finance (MBA); global business management (MBA); health care management (MBA); hospitality and tourism management (MBA); human resources management (MBA); information technology (MBA); information technology systems and management (MSIT); leadership and management (MBA); project management (MBA); public service and administration (MBA); software design and management (MSIT).

Illinois Institute of Technology, Chicago-Kent College of Law, Chicago, IL 60661-3691. Offers family law (LL M); financial services law (LL M); international intellectual property law (LL M); law (JD); legal studies (JSD); taxation (LL M); U.S., international, and transnational law (LL M); JD/LL M; JD/MBA; JD/MPA; JD/MPH; JD/MS. *Accreditation:* ABA. *Program availability:* Part-time, evening/weekend. Terminal master's awarded for partial completion of doctoral program. *Entrance requirements:* For master's, 1st degree in law or certified license to practice law; for doctorate, LSAT. Additional exam requirements/recommendations for international students: Required—TOEFL (minimum score 600 paper-based; 100 iBT); Recommended—IELTS (minimum score 7). Electronic applications accepted. *Expenses:* Contact institution. *Faculty research:* Constitutional law, bioethics, environmental law, intellectual property.

Illinois Institute of Technology, Graduate College, College of Science, Department of Computer Science, Chicago, IL 60616. Offers business (MCS); computational intelligence (MCS); computer science (MCS, MS, PhD); cyber-physical systems (MCS); data analytics (MCS); data science (MAS); database systems (MCS); distributed and cloud computing (MCS); education (MCS); finance (MCS); information security and assurance (MCS); networking and communications (MCS); software engineering (MCS); telecommunications and software engineering (MAS); MS/MAS. *Program availability:* Part-time, evening/weekend, online learning. Terminal master's awarded for partial completion of doctoral program. *Degree requirements:* For master's, thesis optional; for doctorate, comprehensive exam, thesis/dissertation. *Entrance requirements:* For master's, GRE General Test with minimum scores of 298 Quantitative and Verbal, 3.0 Analytical Writing (for MS); GRE General Test with minimum scores of 292 Quantitative and Verbal, 2.5 Analytical Writing (for MAS), minimum undergraduate GPA of 3.0; for doctorate, GRE General Test (minimum scores: 304 Quantitative and Verbal, 3.5 Analytical Writing), minimum undergraduate GPA of 3.0. Additional exam requirements/recommendations for international students: Required—TOEFL (minimum score 523 paper-based; 70 iBT). Electronic applications accepted. *Faculty research:* Parallel and distributed processing, high-performance computing, computational linguistics, information retrieval, data mining, grid computing.

Illinois Institute of Technology, Stuart School of Business, Program in Finance, Chicago, IL 60661. Offers MS, JD/MS, MBA/MS. *Program availability:* Part-time, evening/weekend. *Entrance requirements:* For master's, GRE (minimum score 1200) or GMAT (600). Additional exam requirements/recommendations for international students: Required—TOEFL (minimum score 600 paper-based; 85 iBT); Recommended—IELTS (minimum score 7). Electronic applications accepted. *Expenses:* Contact institution. *Faculty research:* Factor models for investment management, credit rating and credit risk management, hedge fund performance analysis, option trading and risk management, global asset allocation strategies.

Indiana University Bloomington, School of Public and Environmental Affairs, Public Affairs Programs, Bloomington, IN 47405. Offers economic development (MPA); energy (MPA); environmental policy (PhD); environmental policy and natural resource management (MPA); information systems (MPA); international development (MPA); local government management (MPA); nonprofit management (MPA, Certificate); policy analysis (MPA); public budgeting and financial management (Certificate); public finance (PhD); public financial administration (MPA); public management (MPA, PhD, Certificate); public policy analysis (PhD); social entrepreneurship (Certificate); specialized public affairs (MPA); sustainability and sustainable development (MPA); JD/MPA; MPA/MA; MPA/MIS; MPA/MLS; MSES/MPA. *Accreditation:* NASPAA (one or more programs are accredited). *Program availability:* Part-time. *Degree requirements:* For master's, capstone, internship; for doctorate, comprehensive exam, thesis/dissertation. *Entrance requirements:* For master's, GRE General Test or GMAT, official transcripts, 3 letters of recommendation, resume, personal statement; for doctorate, GRE General Test, official transcripts, 3 letters of recommendation, statement of purpose. Additional exam requirements/recommendations for international students: Required—TOEFL (minimum score 600 paper-based; 96 iBT); Recommended—IELTS (minimum score 7). Electronic applications accepted. *Faculty research:* International development, environmental policy and resource management, policy analysis, public finance, public management, urban management, nonprofit management, energy policy, social policy, public finance.

Indiana University–Purdue University Indianapolis, Kelley School of Business, Evening MBA Program, Indianapolis, IN 46202-5151. Offers accounting (MBA); entrepreneurship (MBA); finance (MBA); general administration (MBA); marketing (MBA); supply chain management (MBA); MBA/JD; MBA/MD; MBA/MHA; MBA/MS; MBA/MSA; MBA/MSE. *Program availability:* Part-time-only, evening/weekend, online learning. *Faculty:* 30 full-time (7 women), 4 part-time/adjunct (0 women). *Students:* 294 part-time (46 women); includes 41 minority (11 Black or African American, non-Hispanic/Latino; 22 Asian, non-Hispanic/Latino; 8 Hispanic/Latino), 106 international. Average age 31. 129 applicants, 53% accepted, 61 enrolled. In 2016, 103 degrees awarded. *Entrance requirements:* For master's, GMAT or GRE, 2 years of professional work experience. Additional exam requirements/recommendations for international students: Required—TOEFL or IELTS. *Application deadline:* For fall admission, 6/1 for domestic

and international students; for spring admission, 11/1 for domestic and international students. Applications are processed on a rolling basis. Application fee: $60 ($65 for international students). Electronic applications accepted. *Expenses:* $772.34 per credit hour in-state tuition, $1,456.56 per credit hour out-of-state tuition. *Financial support:* Scholarships/grants available. Financial award application deadline: 6/1. *Faculty research:* Entrepreneurship; corporate finance; international business; consumer behavior; supply chain; business law. *Unit head:* Mary Johnson, Associate Director, Evening MBA Program, 317-274-4895, E-mail: mbaindy@iupui.edu. *Application contact:* Kristen Peters, Program Assistant, 317-274-4895, E-mail: mbaindy@iupui.edu.
Website: http://kelley.iupui.edu/evemba

Indiana University South Bend, Judd Leighton School of Business and Economics, South Bend, IN 46634-7111. Offers accounting (MSA); business (Graduate Certificate); business administration (MBA), including finance, human resource management, marketing; MBA/MSA. *Program availability:* Part-time, evening/weekend. *Faculty:* 17 full-time (2 women), 3 part-time/adjunct (1 woman). *Students:* 28 full-time (18 women), 85 part-time (36 women); includes 10 minority (3 Black or African American, non-Hispanic/Latino; 1 Asian, non-Hispanic/Latino; 5 Hispanic/Latino; 1 Two or more races, non-Hispanic/Latino), 22 international. Average age 32. 57 applicants, 68% accepted, 22 enrolled. In 2016, 67 master's, 7 other advanced degrees awarded. *Entrance requirements:* For master's, GMAT. Additional exam requirements/recommendations for international students: Required—TOEFL (minimum score 550 paper-based; 79 iBT). *Application deadline:* For fall admission, 7/15 priority date for domestic and international students; for spring admission, 11/15 priority date for domestic and international students; for summer admission, 4/1 priority date for domestic and international students. Applications are processed on a rolling basis. Application fee: $40 ($60 for international students). Electronic applications accepted. *Expenses:* $329.79 per credit hour in-state; $739.85 per credit hour out-of-state. *Financial support:* Fellowships, Federal Work-Study, and institutionally sponsored loans available. Support available to part-time students. Financial award application deadline: 7/1; financial award applicants required to submit FAFSA. *Faculty research:* Financial accounting, consumer research, capital budgeting research, business strategy research. *Unit head:* Richard Kolbe, Dean, 574-520-4228, Fax: 574-520-4866, E-mail: rkolbe@iusb.edu. *Application contact:* 574-520-4839, Fax: 574-520-4834, E-mail: graduate@iusb.edu.
Website: https://business.iusb.edu/

Indiana University Southeast, School of Business, New Albany, IN 47150-6405. Offers business administration (MBA); strategic finance (MS). *Accreditation:* AACSB. *Program availability:* Part-time. *Faculty:* 11 full-time (2 women). *Students:* 14 full-time (2 women), 145 part-time (51 women); includes 19 minority (5 Black or African American, non-Hispanic/Latino; 5 Asian, non-Hispanic/Latino; 4 Hispanic/Latino; 5 Two or more races, non-Hispanic/Latino), 2 international. Average age 32. 52 applicants, 69% accepted, 32 enrolled. In 2016, 50 master's awarded. *Degree requirements:* For master's, community service. *Entrance requirements:* For master's, GMAT, work experience. Additional exam requirements/recommendations for international students: Required—TOEFL. *Application deadline:* For fall admission, 7/20 for domestic and international students; for spring admission, 11/30 for domestic and international students; for summer admission, 4/15 for domestic and international students. Application fee: $40 ($60 for international students). Electronic applications accepted. *Expenses:* $402.33 per credit hour in-state; $828.51 per credit hour out-of-state. *Financial support:* In 2016–17, 2 teaching assistantships (averaging $4,500 per year) were awarded. Financial award applicants required to submit FAFSA. *Unit head:* Sharon Allen, Director of Graduate Business Programs, 812-941-2364, E-mail: allen81@ius.edu. *Application contact:* Admissions Counselor, 812-941-2212, Fax: 812-941-2595, E-mail: admissions@ius.edu.
Website: http://www.ius.edu/business/graduate-programs/index.html

Instituto Centroamericano de Administración de Empresas, Graduate Programs, La Garita, Costa Rica. Offers agribusiness management (MIAM); business administration (EMBA); finance (MBA); real estate management (MGREM); sustainable development (MBA); technology (MBA). *Degree requirements:* For master's, comprehensive exam, essay. *Entrance requirements:* For master's, GMAT or GRE General Test, fluency in Spanish, interview, letters of recommendation, minimum 1 year of work experience. Additional exam requirements/recommendations for international students: Recommended—TOEFL. Electronic applications accepted. *Faculty research:* Competitiveness, production.

Instituto Tecnologico de Santo Domingo, Graduate School, Area of Business, Santo Domingo, Dominican Republic. Offers banking and securities markets (M Mgmt); corporate finance (M Mgmt); human resources management (M Mgmt, Certificate); international trade management (M Mgmt); marketing (M Mgmt); organizational development (M Mgmt); quality and productivity management (Certificate); tax management and planning (M Mgmt); upper management (M Mgmt).

Instituto Tecnológico y de Estudios Superiores de Monterrey, Campus Central de Veracruz, Graduate Programs, Córdoba, Mexico. Offers administration (MA); administration of information technologies (MTI); computer sciences (MCC); education (MEE); educational institution administration (MAD); educational technology (MTE); electronic commerce (MCE); finance (MAF); humanistic studies (MEH); international business for Latin America (MNL); marketing (MMT); science (MCP). *Program availability:* Part-time, evening/weekend, online learning. *Degree requirements:* For master's, thesis (for some programs). *Entrance requirements:* For master's, PAEP College Board. Electronic applications accepted.

Instituto Tecnológico y de Estudios Superiores de Monterrey, Campus Ciudad de México, School of Business Administration, Ciudad de Mexico, Mexico. Offers business administration (EMBA, MBA, PhD); economy (MBA); finance (MBA). EMBA program offered jointly with The University of Texas at Austin. *Program availability:* Part-time, evening/weekend, online learning. *Entrance requirements:* For master's and doctorate, Instituto entrance exam. Additional exam requirements/recommendations for international students: Required—TOEFL.

Instituto Tecnológico y de Estudios Superiores de Monterrey, Campus Ciudad Obregón, Program in Finance, Ciudad Obregón, Mexico. Offers MF.

Instituto Tecnológico y de Estudios Superiores de Monterrey, Campus Cuernavaca, Programs in Business Administration, Temixco, Mexico. Offers finance (MA); human resources management (MA); international business (MA); marketing (MA).

Instituto Tecnológico y de Estudios Superiores de Monterrey, Campus Estado de México, Professional and Graduate Division, Estado de Mexico, Mexico. Offers administration of information technologies (MITA); architecture (M Arch); business administration (GMBA, MBA); computer sciences (MCS, PhD); education (M Ed); educational institution administration (MAD); educational technology and innovation (PhD); electronic commerce (MEC); environmental systems (MS); finance (MAF); humanistic studies (MHS); information sciences and knowledge management (MISKM); information systems (MS); manufacturing systems (MS); marketing (MEM); quality systems and productivity (MS); science and materials engineering (PhD); telecommunications management (MTM). *Program availability:* Part-time, online learning. *Degree requirements:* For master's, one foreign language, thesis (for some programs); for doctorate, one foreign language, thesis/dissertation. *Entrance requirements:* For master's, E-PAEP 500, interview; for doctorate, E-PAEP 500, research proposal. Additional exam requirements/recommendations for international students: Required—TOEFL (minimum score 550 paper-based). *Faculty research:* Surface treatments by plasmas, mechanical properties, robotics, graphical computing, mechatronics security protocols.

Instituto Tecnológico y de Estudios Superiores de Monterrey, Campus Guadalajara, Program in Finance, Zapopan, Mexico. Offers MF. *Degree requirements:* For master's, one foreign language, thesis. *Entrance requirements:* For master's, ITESM admission test.

Instituto Tecnológico y de Estudios Superiores de Monterrey, Campus Irapuato, Graduate Programs, Irapuato, Mexico. Offers administration (MBA); administration of information technology (MAIT); administration of telecommunications (MAT); architecture (M Arch); computer science (MCS); education (M Ed); educational administration (MEA); educational innovation and technology (DEIT); educational technology (MET); electronic commerce (MBA); environmental administration and planning (MEAP); environmental systems (MES); finances (MBA); humanistic studies (MHS); international management for Latin American executives (MIMLAE); library and information science (MLIS); manufacturing quality management (MMQM); marketing research (MBA).

Instituto Tecnológico y de Estudios Superiores de Monterrey, Campus Monterrey, Graduate School of Business Administration and Leadership, Program in Business Administration, Monterrey, Mexico. Offers business administration (MA, MBA); finance (M Sc); international business (M Sc); marketing (M Sc). *Program availability:* Part-time. *Degree requirements:* For master's, one foreign language, thesis. *Entrance requirements:* For master's, GMAT. Additional exam requirements/recommendations for international students: Required—TOEFL. *Faculty research:* Technology management, quality management, organizational theory and behavior.

Inter American University of Puerto Rico, Aguadilla Campus, Graduate School, Aguadilla, PR 00605. Offers accounting (MBA); counseling psychology specializing in family (MS); criminal justice (MA); educative management and leadership (MA); elementary education (M Ed); finance (MBA); human resources (MBA); industrial management (MBA); management information systems (MBA); marketing (MBA). *Program availability:* Part-time, evening/weekend. *Degree requirements:* For master's, comprehensive exam. *Entrance requirements:* For master's, EXADEP, 2 letters of recommendation, minimum GPA of 2.5. Electronic applications accepted.

Inter American University of Puerto Rico, Arecibo Campus, Program in Business Administration, Arecibo, PR 00614-4050. Offers accounting (MBA); finance (MBA); human resources (MBA).

Inter American University of Puerto Rico, Barranquitas Campus, Program in Business Administration, Barranquitas, PR 00794. Offers accounting (IMBA); finance (IMBA).

Inter American University of Puerto Rico, Metropolitan Campus, Graduate Programs, Program in Finance, San Juan, PR 00919-1293. Offers MBA. *Degree requirements:* For master's, comprehensive exam. *Entrance requirements:* For master's, GRE or EXADEP, interview. Electronic applications accepted.

Inter American University of Puerto Rico, Ponce Campus, Graduate School, Mercedita, PR 00715-1602. Offers accounting (MBA); biology (M Ed); chemistry (M Ed); criminal justice (MA); elementary education (M Ed); English as a Second Language (M Ed); finance (MBA); history (M Ed); human resources (MBA); marketing (MBA); mathematics (M Ed); Spanish (M Ed). *Entrance requirements:* For master's, minimum GPA of 2.5.

Inter American University of Puerto Rico, San Germán Campus, Graduate Studies Center, Program in Business Administration, San Germán, PR 00683-5008. Offers accounting (MBA); finance (MBA); general business administration (MBA); human resources (MBA, PhD); industrial relations (MBA); information systems (MBA); international and interregional business (PhD); management (MBA); marketing (MBA). *Program availability:* Part-time, evening/weekend. *Degree requirements:* For master's, comprehensive exam. *Entrance requirements:* For master's, GRE General Test or EXADEP, minimum GPA of 3.0.

The International University of Monaco, Graduate Programs, Monte Carlo, Monaco. Offers entrepreneurship (EMBA, MBA); financial engineering (M Sc); hedge fund and private equity (M Sc); international marketing (EMBA, MBA); international wealth management (M Sc); luxury goods and services (EMBA, M Sc, MBA); wealth and asset management (EMBA, MBA). *Program availability:* Part-time. *Degree requirements:* For master's, comprehensive exam (for some programs), applied research project. *Entrance requirements:* Additional exam requirements/recommendations for international students: Required—TOEFL (minimum score 550 paper-based), IELTS. Electronic applications accepted. *Faculty research:* Gaming, leadership, disintermediation.

Iona College, Hagan School of Business, Department of Finance, Business Economics and Legal Studies, New Rochelle, NY 10801-1890. Offers finance (MS); financial management (MBA, PMC); financial services (MS); international finance (MS). *Program availability:* Part-time, evening/weekend. *Faculty:* 10 full-time (4 women), 4 part-time/adjunct (1 woman). *Students:* 37 full-time (14 women), 57 part-time (19 women); includes 24 minority (6 Black or African American, non-Hispanic/Latino; 1 American Indian or Alaska Native, non-Hispanic/Latino; 2 Asian, non-Hispanic/Latino; 14 Hispanic/Latino; 1 Native Hawaiian or other Pacific Islander, non-Hispanic/Latino), 23 international. Average age 28. 38 applicants, 100% accepted, 17 enrolled. In 2016, 72 master's awarded. *Entrance requirements:* For master's, GMAT, 2 letters of recommendation, minimum GPA of 3.0; for PMC, minimum GPA of 3.0. Additional exam requirements/recommendations for international students: Required—TOEFL (minimum score 550 paper-based; 80 iBT), IELTS (minimum score 6.5). *Application deadline:* For fall admission, 8/15 priority date for domestic students, 8/1 priority date for international students; for winter admission, 11/15 priority date for domestic students, 11/1 priority date for international students; for spring admission, 2/15 priority date for domestic students, 2/1 priority date for international students; for summer admission, 5/15 priority date for domestic students, 5/1 priority date for international students. Applications are processed on a rolling basis. Application fee: $50. Electronic applications accepted. *Expenses:* Contact institution. *Financial support:* In 2016–17, 40 students received support. Scholarships/grants, tuition waivers (partial), and unspecified assistantships available. Support available to part-time students. Financial award application deadline: 4/15; financial award applicants required to submit FAFSA. *Faculty research:* Options, insurance financing, asset depreciation ranges, international finance, emerging markets. *Unit head:* Dr. John F. Manley, Department Chair, 914-633-2284, E-mail: jmanley@iona.edu. *Application contact:* Katelyn Brunck, Director of MBA Admissions, 914-633-2451, Fax: 914-633-2277, E-mail: kbrunck@iona.edu.
Website: http://www.iona.edu/Academics/Hagan-School-of-Business/Departments/Finance-Business-Economics-Legal-Studies/Graduate-Programs.aspx

Iowa State University of Science and Technology, Program in Finance, Ames, IA 50011. Offers M Fin. *Entrance requirements:* For master's, GMAT, GRE Writing Test, minimum undergraduate GPA of 3.25, resume, three letters of recommendation,

personal essay. Additional exam requirements/recommendations for international students: Required—TOEFL (minimum score 600 paper-based; 100 iBT), IELTS (minimum score 7). *Application deadline:* For fall admission, 7/1 for domestic students; for spring admission, 11/1 for domestic students. *Application contact:* Meleah Cue, Application Contact, 515-294-8118, Fax: 515-294-2592, E-mail: busgrad@iastate.edu.
Website: http://www.business.iastate.edu/masters/mfin/

Jacksonville University, Davis College of Business, Accelerated Day-time MBA Program, Jacksonville, FL 32211. Offers accounting and finance (MBA); business administration (MBA); consumer goods and services marketing (MBA); management (MBA); management accounting (MBA). *Faculty:* 13 full-time (3 women), 1 part-time/adjunct (0 women). *Students:* 39 full-time (12 women), 8 part-time (4 women); includes 11 minority (5 Black or African American, non-Hispanic/Latino; 4 Hispanic/Latino; 2 Two or more races, non-Hispanic/Latino), 20 international. Average age 25. 80 applicants, 61% accepted, 33 enrolled. In 2016, 44 master's awarded. *Entrance requirements:* For master's, GMAT or GRE (may be waived for 3.3 or higher undergraduate GPA from AACSB-accredited institution), bachelor's degree from regionally-accredited institution, resume, statement of purpose, 2 letters of recommendation. Additional exam requirements/recommendations for international students: Required—TOEFL (minimum score 500 paper-based; 61 iBT), IELTS (minimum score 6). *Application deadline:* For fall admission, 8/1 priority date for domestic students, 7/15 priority date for international students; for spring admission, 12/1 priority date for domestic students, 11/15 priority date for international students. Application fee: $50. Electronic applications accepted. *Expenses:* $740 per credit hour. *Financial support:* In 2016–17, 7 students received support. Scholarships/grants and unspecified assistantships available. Financial award application deadline: 7/1; financial award applicants required to submit FAFSA. *Faculty research:* Behavioral finance, game theory, regional economic integration, information sabotage, public choice and public finance. *Unit head:* Dr. Douglas Johansen, Associate Dean and Graduate Programs Director, 904-256-7763, Fax: 904-256-7168, E-mail: djohans@ju.edu. *Application contact:* AnnaMaria Murphy, Assistant Director of Graduate Admissions, 904-256-7426, Fax: 904-256-7012, E-mail: mba@ju.edu.

See Display on page 107 and Close-Up on page 179.

Jacksonville University, Davis College of Business, FLEX Master of Business Administration Program, Jacksonville, FL 32211. Offers accounting and finance (MBA); consumer goods and services marketing (MBA); management accounting (MBA); JD/MBA; MBA/MPP; MSN/MBA. JD/MBA offered jointly with Florida School of Law. *Accreditation:* AACSB. *Program availability:* Part-time, evening/weekend, blended/hybrid learning. *Faculty:* 20 full-time (5 women), 1 part-time/adjunct (0 women). *Students:* 32 full-time (13 women), 71 part-time (29 women); includes 29 minority (11 Black or African American, non-Hispanic/Latino; 1 American Indian or Alaska Native, non-Hispanic/Latino; 6 Asian, non-Hispanic/Latino; 10 Hispanic/Latino; 1 Two or more races, non-Hispanic/Latino), 3 international. Average age 32. 32 applicants, 97% accepted, 27 enrolled. In 2016, 57 master's awarded. *Entrance requirements:* For master's, GMAT or GRE (may be waived for 3.3 or higher undergraduate GPA from AACSB-accredited institution), bachelor's degree from regionally-accredited institution, 3 years of full-time work experience (recommended), resume, statement of purpose, 2 letters of recommendation. Additional exam requirements/recommendations for international students: Required—TOEFL (minimum score 500 paper-based; 61 iBT), IELTS (minimum score 6). *Application deadline:* For fall admission, 8/1 priority date for domestic students, 7/15 priority date for international students; for spring admission, 12/1 priority date for domestic students, 11/15 priority date for international students; for summer admission, 4/1 priority date for domestic students, 3/15 priority date for international students. Applications are processed on a rolling basis. Application fee: $50. Electronic applications accepted. *Expenses:* $740 per credit hour. *Financial support:* In 2016–17, 1 student received support. Scholarships/grants available. Financial award application deadline: 7/1; financial award applicants required to submit FAFSA. *Faculty research:* Downsizing with integrity; impact of YouTube videos; game theory; analysis of effective tax rates; creativity innovation and change. *Unit head:* Dr. Douglas Johansen, Associate Dean and Director of Graduate Studies, 904-256-7763, Fax: 904-256-7168, E-mail: djohans@ju.edu. *Application contact:* AnnaMaria Murphy, Assistant Director of Graduate Admissions, 904-256-7426, Fax: 904-256-7012, E-mail: mba@ju.edu.

See Display on page 107 and Close-Up on page 179.

Johns Hopkins University, Carey Business School, MS in Finance Programs, Baltimore, MD 21218. Offers finance (MS). *Program availability:* Part-time, evening/weekend, blended/hybrid learning, on-site residency requirement. *Faculty:* 87 full-time (32 women), 51 part-time/adjunct (8 women). *Students:* 503 full-time (285 women), 73 part-time (19 women); includes 35 minority (7 Black or African American, non-Hispanic/Latino; 21 Asian, non-Hispanic/Latino; 4 Hispanic/Latino; 3 Two or more races, non-Hispanic/Latino), 488 international. Average age 23. 2,609 applicants, 60% accepted, 535 enrolled. In 2016, 337 master's awarded. *Degree requirements:* For master's, 36 credits. *Entrance requirements:* For master's, GMAT or GRE. Additional exam requirements/recommendations for international students: Required—TOEFL, IELTS. *Application deadline:* For fall admission, 4/3 for domestic and international students. Applications are processed on a rolling basis. Application fee: $100. Electronic applications accepted. *Expenses:* $64,000 (full-time); $1,290 per credit (part-time). *Financial support:* In 2016–17, 26 students received support. Scholarships/grants available. Support available to part-time students. Financial award application deadline: 4/15; financial award applicants required to submit FAFSA. *Faculty research:* Derivatives, financial institutions, fixed income securities, international finance, investments. *Unit head:* Dr. Kevin Frick, Vice Dean of Education, 410-234-9272, E-mail: kfrick@jhu.edu. *Application contact:* Office of Admissions, 410-234-9220, Fax: 443-529-1554, E-mail: carey.admissions@jhu.edu.
Website: http://carey.jhu.edu/academics/master-of-science/ms-in-finance

Johns Hopkins University, School of Advanced International Studies, Washington, DC 20036. Offers global risk (MA); international development (MA, Certificate), including international economics (MA); international economics and finance (MA); international public policy (MIPP); international relations (PhD); international studies (Certificate); Japan studies (MA), including international economics; Korea studies (MA), including international economics; South Asia studies (MA), including international economics; Southeast Asia studies (MA), including international economics; JD/MA; MBA/MA; MHS/MA. Terminal master's awarded for partial completion of doctoral program. *Degree requirements:* For master's, 4-6 international economics courses, 5-6 functional or regional concentration courses, 2 core examinations, proficiency in language other than native language, capstone project; for doctorate, 2 foreign languages, thesis/dissertation, 3 comprehensive exams, economics, quantitative and qualitative course, dissertation prospectus and defense. *Entrance requirements:* For master's, GMAT or GRE General Test, previous course work in economics, foreign language, undergraduate degree; for doctorate, GRE General Test, master's degree. Additional exam requirements/recommendations for international students: Required—TOEFL (minimum score 600 paper-based; 100 iBT) or IELTS (minimum score 7). Electronic applications accepted. *Expenses:* Contact institution. *Faculty research:* Regional studies, international relations, international economics, energy and environment, international development.

Johnson & Wales University, Graduate Studies, MBA Program, Providence, RI 02903-3703. Offers accounting (MBA); business administration (MBA); finance (MBA); hospitality (MBA); human resource management (MBA); information technology (MBA); nonprofit management (MBA); operations and supply chain management (MBA). Program also offered on Denver campus. *Program availability:* Part-time, online learning. *Entrance requirements:* For master's, minimum GPA of 2.75. Additional exam requirements/recommendations for international students: Required—TOEFL (minimum score 550 paper-based); Recommended—IELTS, TWE. *Faculty research:* International banking, global economy, international trade, cultural differences.

Johnson & Wales University, Graduate Studies, MS Program in Finance, Providence, RI 02903-3703. Offers MS. *Program availability:* Online learning.

Kansas State University, Graduate School, College of Business, Program in Business Administration, Manhattan, KS 66506. Offers data analytics (MBA); finance (MBA); management (MBA); marketing (MBA); technology entrepreneurship (MBA). *Accreditation:* AACSB. *Program availability:* Part-time, 100% online. *Faculty:* 35 full-time (8 women). *Students:* 50 full-time (19 women), 89 part-time (36 women); includes 25 minority (8 Black or African American, non-Hispanic/Latino; 6 Asian, non-Hispanic/Latino; 4 Hispanic/Latino; 7 Two or more races, non-Hispanic/Latino), 17 international. Average age 32. 78 applicants, 90% accepted, 31 enrolled. In 2016, 26 master's, 3 other advanced degrees awarded. *Entrance requirements:* For master's, GMAT (minimum score of 500), minimum undergraduate GPA of 3.0. Additional exam requirements/recommendations for international students: Required—TOEFL (minimum score 550 paper-based; 79 iBT); Recommended—IELTS (minimum score 7). *Application deadline:* For fall admission, 2/1 priority date for domestic and international students; for spring admission, 10/1 priority date for domestic students, 8/1 priority date for international students. Applications are processed on a rolling basis. Application fee: $70 ($80 for international students). Electronic applications accepted. *Expenses:* Contact institution. *Financial support:* In 2016–17, 6 students received support, including 5 research assistantships (averaging $6,400 per year), 6 teaching assistantships with partial tuition reimbursements available (averaging $6,400 per year); institutionally sponsored loans and scholarships/grants also available. Financial award application deadline: 3/1; financial award applicants required to submit FAFSA. *Faculty research:* Organizational citizenship behavior, service marketing, impression management, human resources management, lean manufacturing and supply chain management, financial market behavior and investment management, data analytics, corporate responsibility, technology entrepreneurship. *Unit head:* Dr. Kevin Gwinner, Dean, 785-532-7227, Fax: 785-532-7216, E-mail: kgwinner@ksu.edu. *Application contact:* Dr. Chwen Sheu, Associate Dean for Academic Programs, 785-532-4363, Fax: 785-532-1339, E-mail: gradbusiness@ksu.edu.
Website: http://www.cba.k-state.edu/

Kansas State University, Graduate School, College of Human Ecology, School of Family Studies and Human Services, Manhattan, KS 66506-1403. Offers applied family sciences (MS); communication sciences and disorders (MS); conflict resolution (Graduate Certificate); couple and family therapy (MS); early childhood education (MS); family and community service (MS); life-span human development (MS); personal financial planning (MS, PhD, Graduate Certificate); youth development (MS, Graduate Certificate). *Accreditation:* AAMFT/COAMFTE; ASHA. *Program availability:* Part-time, online learning. *Faculty:* 43 full-time (30 women), 4 part-time/adjunct (3 women). *Students:* 55 full-time (45 women), 87 part-time (73 women); includes 30 minority (9 Black or African American, non-Hispanic/Latino; 1 American Indian or Alaska Native, non-Hispanic/Latino; 1 Asian, non-Hispanic/Latino; 14 Hispanic/Latino; 1 Native Hawaiian or other Pacific Islander, non-Hispanic/Latino; 4 Two or more races, non-Hispanic/Latino), 6 international. Average age 29. 182 applicants, 29% accepted, 38 enrolled. In 2016, 39 master's, 17 other advanced degrees awarded. *Degree requirements:* For master's, comprehensive exam (for some programs), thesis optional. *Entrance requirements:* For master's, GRE, minimum GPA of 3.0 in last 2 years (60 semester hours) of undergraduate study; for doctorate, GRE. Additional exam requirements/recommendations for international students: Required—TOEFL (minimum score 600 paper-based). *Application deadline:* For fall admission, 2/1 priority date for domestic students, 1/1 priority date for international students; for spring admission, 10/1 priority date for domestic students, 8/1 priority date for international students; for summer admission, 2/1 priority date for domestic students, 12/1 priority date for international students. Applications are processed on a rolling basis. Application fee: $50 ($75 for international students). Electronic applications accepted. *Expenses:* Tuition, state resident: full-time $9670. Tuition, nonresident: full-time $21,828. *Required fees:* $862. *Financial support:* In 2016–17, 35 students received support, including 25 research assistantships (averaging $10,000 per year), 9 teaching assistantships with full tuition reimbursements available (averaging $10,000 per year); unspecified assistantships also available. Financial award application deadline: 3/1. *Faculty research:* Health and security of military families, training in and evaluation of professional human services (marriage and couple therapy, family life education, treatment of speech and swallowing disorders, financial therapy), disorders of communication and swallowing, family and relationship development and health, financial decision-making. *Total annual research expenditures:* $8.4 million. *Unit head:* Dr. Dottie Durband, Director, 785-532-5510, Fax: 785-532-5505, E-mail: dottie@ksu.edu. *Application contact:* Kristi Hageman, Administrative Specialist, 785-532-5510, Fax: 785-532-5505, E-mail: klsmith@ksu.edu.
Website: http://www.he.k-state.edu/fshs/

Kaplan University, Davenport Campus, School of Business, Davenport, IA 52807. Offers business administration (MBA); change leadership (MS); entrepreneurship (MBA); finance (MBA); health care management (MBA, MS); human resource (MBA); international business (MBA); management (MS); marketing (MBA); project management (MBA, MS); supply chain management and logistics (MBA, MS). *Accreditation:* ACBSP. *Program availability:* Part-time, evening/weekend, online learning. *Entrance requirements:* Additional exam requirements/recommendations for international students: Required—TOEFL (minimum score 550 paper-based; 80 iBT). Electronic applications accepted.

Kent State University, College of Business Administration, Doctoral Program in Finance, Kent, OH 44242-0001. Offers PhD. *Faculty:* 9 full-time (3 women). *Students:* 13 full-time (5 women), 11 international. Average age 33. 23 applicants, 17% accepted, 1 enrolled. In 2016, 1 doctorate awarded. *Degree requirements:* For doctorate, comprehensive exam, thesis/dissertation, oral defense. *Entrance requirements:* For doctorate, GMAT or GRE. Additional exam requirements/recommendations for international students: Required—TOEFL (minimum score 600 paper-based; 100 iBT). *Application deadline:* For fall admission, 12/15 for domestic and international students. Application fee: $45 ($70 for international students). Electronic applications accepted. *Expenses:* Tuition, state resident: full-time $10,864; part-time $495 per credit hour. Tuition, nonresident: full-time $18,380; part-time $837 per credit hour. *Financial support:* In 2016–17, 12 students received support, including 12 teaching assistantships with full tuition reimbursements available (averaging $23,000 per year); Federal Work-Study also available. Financial award application deadline: 12/15; financial award applicants

required to submit FAFSA. *Faculty research:* Corporate finance, investments, international finance, futures and options, risk and insurance. *Unit head:* Dr. Steven Dennis, Chair and Associate Professor, 330-672-2426, Fax: 330-672-9806, E-mail: sdenni14@kent.edu. *Application contact:* Felecia A. Urbanek, Coordinator, Graduate Programs, 330-672-2282, Fax: 330-672-7303, E-mail: gradbus@kent.edu.
Website: http://www.kent.edu/business/phd

King University, School of Business and Economics, Bristol, TN 37620-2699. Offers accounting (MBA); finance (MBA); healthcare management (MBA); human resources management (MBA); leadership (MBA); management (MBA); marketing (MBA); project management (MBA). *Program availability:* Part-time, evening/weekend, online learning. *Degree requirements:* For master's, comprehensive exam, thesis optional. *Entrance requirements:* For master's, GMAT, 2 years of work experience. Additional exam requirements/recommendations for international students: Required—TOEFL (minimum score 550 paper-based). Electronic applications accepted. *Faculty research:* International monetary policy.

Lake Forest Graduate School of Management, The Leadership MBA Program, Lake Forest, IL 60045. Offers finance (MBA); global business (MBA); healthcare management (MBA); management (MBA); marketing (MBA); organizational behavior (MBA). *Program availability:* Part-time, evening/weekend. *Entrance requirements:* For master's, 4 years of work experience in field, interview, 2 letters of recommendation. Electronic applications accepted.

Lakeland University, Graduate Studies Division, Program in Business Administration, Plymouth, WI 53073. Offers accounting (MBA); finance (MBA); healthcare management (MBA); project management (MBA). *Entrance requirements:* For master's, GMAT. *Expenses:* Contact institution.

La Salle University, School of Business, Master of Business Administration Program, Philadelphia, PA 19141-1199. Offers accounting (MBA, Post-MBA Certificate); business systems and analytics (MBA, Post-MBA Certificate); finance (MBA, Post-MBA Certificate); general business administration (MBA, Post-MBA Certificate); human resource management (MBA, Post-MBA Certificate); management (MBA, Post-MBA Certificate); marketing (Post-MBA Certificate); MBA/MSN. Program also offered in Switzerland. *Accreditation:* AACSB. *Program availability:* Part-time, evening/weekend, online learning. *Faculty:* 19 full-time (6 women), 11 part-time/adjunct (3 women). *Students:* 55 full-time (23 women), 209 part-time (96 women); includes 66 minority (35 Black or African American, non-Hispanic/Latino; 17 Asian, non-Hispanic/Latino; 9 Hispanic/Latino; 5 Two or more races, non-Hispanic/Latino), 17 international. Average age 31. 200 applicants, 59% accepted, 63 enrolled. In 2016, 192 master's, 1 other advanced degree awarded. *Entrance requirements:* For master's, GMAT or GRE, two letters of reference; resume; for Post-MBA Certificate, MBA with minimum GPA of 3.0. Additional exam requirements/recommendations for international students: Required—TOEFL. *Application deadline:* For fall admission, 8/15 priority date for domestic students, 7/15 for international students; for spring admission, 12/15 priority date for domestic students, 11/15 for international students; for summer admission, 4/15 priority date for domestic students, 3/15 for international students. Applications are processed on a rolling basis. Application fee: $35. Electronic applications accepted. Application fee is waived when completed online. *Expenses:* Contact institution. *Financial support:* In 2016–17, 49 students received support. Scholarships/grants available. Support available to part-time students. Financial award application deadline: 8/31; financial award applicants required to submit FAFSA. *Unit head:* Dr. MarySheila McDonald, Interim Dean, 215-951-1040, Fax: 215-951-1886, E-mail: mcdonaldms@lasalle.edu. *Application contact:* Elizabeth Heenan, Director, Graduate and Adult Enrollment, 215-951-1100, Fax: 215-951-1462, E-mail: heenan@lasalle.edu.

La Sierra University, School of Business and Management, Riverside, CA 92515. Offers accounting (MBA); finance (MBA); general management (MBA); human resources management (MBA); leadership, values, and ethics for business and management (Certificate); marketing (MBA). *Degree requirements:* For master's, research project. *Entrance requirements:* For master's, GMAT, minimum GPA of 3.0. Additional exam requirements/recommendations for international students: Required—TOEFL. *Faculty research:* Financial econometrics, institutional assessment and strategic planning, legal issues in management, behavioral finance, content of financial reports.

Lawrence Technological University, College of Management, Southfield, MI 48075-1058. Offers business administration (MBA), including business analytics (MBA, MS), finance, information technology, marketing, project management (MBA, MS); information technology (MS), including business analytics (MBA, MS), information assurance, project management (MBA, MS); project management (Graduate Certificate). *Accreditation:* ACBSP. *Program availability:* Part-time, evening/weekend, 100% online. *Faculty:* 14 full-time (6 women), 10 part-time/adjunct (2 women). *Students:* 7 full-time (3 women), 323 part-time (120 women); includes 60 minority (29 Black or African American, non-Hispanic/Latino; 2 American Indian or Alaska Native, non-Hispanic/Latino; 17 Asian, non-Hispanic/Latino; 8 Hispanic/Latino; 4 Two or more races, non-Hispanic/Latino), 118 international. Average age 33. 275 applicants, 56% accepted, 72 enrolled. In 2016, 167 master's, 12 other advanced degrees awarded. Terminal master's awarded for partial completion of doctoral program. *Degree requirements:* For master's, thesis (for some programs). *Entrance requirements:* Additional exam requirements/recommendations for international students: Required—TOEFL (minimum score 550 paper-based; 79 iBT), IELTS (minimum score 6.5). *Application deadline:* For fall admission, 5/22 for international students; for spring admission, 10/11 for international students; for summer admission, 2/16 for international students. Applications are processed on a rolling basis. Application fee: $50. Electronic applications accepted. *Expenses: Tuition:* Full-time $14,868; part-time $1062 per credit. *Required fees:* $75 per semester. Tuition and fees vary according to campus/location. *Financial support:* In 2016–17, 35 students received support, including 8 research assistantships with partial tuition reimbursements available (averaging $3,250 per year); career-related internships or fieldwork, unspecified assistantships, and corporate tuition incentives also available. Financial award application deadline: 4/1; financial award applicants required to submit FAFSA. *Faculty research:* Cybersecurity; risk management; IT governance; security controls and countermeasures; threat modeling cyber resilience; autonomous cars; natural language processing; text mining; machine learning; reflective leadership; emerging leadership theories and practice; motivational studies; teaching effectiveness strategies; teamwork; organization development; strategic planning; strengths-based and positive organizational scholarship; global leadership; globalization; corporate governance. *Unit head:* Dr. Bahman Mirshab, Dean, 248-204-3050, E-mail: mgtdean@ltu.edu. *Application contact:* Jane Rohrback, Director of Admissions, 248-204-3160, Fax: 248-204-2228, E-mail: admissions@ltu.edu.
Website: http://www.ltu.edu/management/index.asp

Lehigh University, College of Business and Economics, Department of Finance, Bethlehem, PA 18015. Offers analytical finance (MS). *Faculty:* 4 full-time (0 women). *Students:* 79 full-time (46 women), 1 part-time (0 women); includes 1 minority (Asian, non-Hispanic/Latino), 77 international. Average age 23. 309 applicants, 41% accepted, 40 enrolled. In 2016, 40 master's awarded. *Degree requirements:* For master's, capstone project. *Entrance requirements:* For master's, GMAT or GRE, bachelor's degree from a mathematically rigorous program, minimum GPA of 3.0. Additional exam requirements/recommendations for international students: Required—TOEFL (minimum score 600 paper-based; 94 iBT), IELTS (minimum score 7). *Application deadline:* For fall admission, 7/15 for domestic students, 2/15 for international students. Application fee: $75. Electronic applications accepted. Tuition and fees vary according to program. *Financial support:* Fellowships, research assistantships, teaching assistantships, and health care benefits available. Financial award application deadline: 1/15. *Total annual research expenditures:* $51,538. *Unit head:* Nandu Nayar, Department Chair, 610-758-4161, E-mail: nan2@lehigh.edu. *Application contact:* Michael Tarantino, Director of Recruitment and Admissions, 610-758-3418, Fax: 610-758-5283, E-mail: mgt215@lehigh.edu.
Website: http://www4.lehigh.edu/business/academics/depts/finance

Lewis University, College of Business, Graduate School of Management, Program in Business Administration, Romeoville, IL 60446. Offers accounting (MBA); custom elective option (MBA); e-business (MBA); finance (MBA); healthcare management (MBA); human resources management (MBA); international business (MBA); management information systems (MBA); marketing (MBA); project management (MBA); technology and operations management (MBA). *Program availability:* Part-time, evening/weekend. *Students:* 145 full-time (72 women), 213 part-time (123 women); includes 101 minority (46 Black or African American, non-Hispanic/Latino; 2 American Indian or Alaska Native, non-Hispanic/Latino; 7 Asian, non-Hispanic/Latino; 41 Hispanic/Latino; 1 Native Hawaiian or other Pacific Islander, non-Hispanic/Latino; 4 Two or more races, non-Hispanic/Latino), 47 international. Average age 31. In 2016, 99 master's awarded. *Degree requirements:* For master's, comprehensive exam. *Entrance requirements:* For master's, interview, bachelor's degree, resume, 2 recommendations. Additional exam requirements/recommendations for international students: Required—TOEFL (minimum score 550 paper-based). *Application deadline:* For fall admission, 8/15 priority date for domestic students, 5/1 priority date for international students; for spring admission, 11/15 priority date for international students. Applications are processed on a rolling basis. Application fee: $40. Electronic applications accepted. *Expenses: Tuition:* Full-time $13,860; part-time $770 per credit hour. *Required fees:* $75 per semester. Tuition and fees vary according to degree level and program. *Financial support:* Career-related internships or fieldwork, Federal Work-Study, scholarships/grants, and unspecified assistantships available. Financial award application deadline: 5/1; financial award applicants required to submit FAFSA. *Unit head:* Dr. Maureen Culleeney, Academic Program Director, 815-838-0500 Ext. 5631, E-mail: culleema@lewisu.edu. *Application contact:* Michele Ryan, Director of Admission, 815-838-0500 Ext. 5384, E-mail: gsm@lewisu.edu.

Lewis University, College of Business, Graduate School of Management, Program in Finance, Romeoville, IL 60446. Offers MS. *Program availability:* Part-time, evening/weekend. *Students:* 6 full-time (2 women), 13 part-time (4 women); includes 5 minority (4 Black or African American, non-Hispanic/Latino; 1 Hispanic/Latino), 4 international. Average age 31. *Entrance requirements:* For master's, bachelor's degree, interview, resume, 2 recommendations, minimum GPA of 2.75. Additional exam requirements/recommendations for international students: Required—TOEFL (minimum score 550 paper-based; 80 iBT). *Application deadline:* For fall admission, 5/1 priority date for international students; for spring admission, 11/15 priority date for international students. Applications are processed on a rolling basis. Application fee: $40. Electronic applications accepted. *Expenses: Tuition:* Full-time $13,860; part-time $770 per credit hour. *Required fees:* $75 per semester. Tuition and fees vary according to degree level and program. *Financial support:* Career-related internships or fieldwork, Federal Work-Study, scholarships/grants, and unspecified assistantships available. Support available to part-time students. Financial award application deadline: 5/1; financial award applicants required to submit FAFSA. *Unit head:* Dr. Robert Atra, Academic Program Director, 815-838-0500 Ext. 5804, E-mail: atraro@lewisu.edu. *Application contact:* Michele Ryan, Director of Admission, 815-838-0500 Ext. 5384, E-mail: gsm@lewisu.edu.

Lincoln University, Graduate Programs, Philadelphia, PA 19104. Offers counseling (MSC); early childhood education (M Ed), including PreK-4; early childhood education and special education (M Ed); educational leadership (M Ed), including principal certification; finance (MSB); human resources management (MSB); human services (MAHS). *Program availability:* Part-time, evening/weekend. *Faculty:* 11 full-time (5 women), 45 part-time/adjunct (24 women). *Students:* 191 full-time (131 women), 77 part-time (60 women); includes 245 minority (236 Black or African American, non-Hispanic/Latino; 1 American Indian or Alaska Native, non-Hispanic/Latino; 7 Hispanic/Latino; 1 Two or more races, non-Hispanic/Latino), 4 international. Average age 34. 221 applicants, 58% accepted, 55 enrolled. In 2016, 97 master's awarded. *Degree requirements:* For master's, thesis or alternative. *Entrance requirements:* For master's, official academic transcript from accredited institution presenting conferred bachelor's degree. *Application deadline:* For fall admission, 6/1 priority date for domestic and international students. Applications are processed on a rolling basis. Application fee: $50. Electronic applications accepted. *Expenses:* Tuition, state resident: full-time $12,264; part-time $511 per credit hour. Tuition, nonresident: full-time $21,264; part-time $886 per credit hour. *Required fees:* $1344; $56 per credit hour. Tuition and fees vary according to course load. *Financial support:* In 2016–17, 9 students received support. Scholarships/grants available. Financial award application deadline: 8/1; financial award applicants required to submit FAFSA. *Unit head:* Dr. Patricia Joseph, Dean, College of Professional, Graduate and Extended Studies, 484-365-7659, E-mail: joseph@lincoln.edu. *Application contact:* Jernice Lea, Director of Graduate Admissions, 215-590-8231, Fax: 215-387-3859, E-mail: jlea@lincoln.edu.
Website: http://www.lincoln.edu/academics/graduate-programs

Lincoln University, Graduate Studies, Oakland, CA 94612. Offers finance and investments (DBA); finance management (MS); finance management and investments (MBA); general business (MBA); human resource management (MBA, DBA); international business (MBA, MS); management information systems (MBA). *Program availability:* Part-time. *Faculty:* 13 full-time (1 woman), 16 part-time/adjunct (3 women). *Students:* 542 full-time (215 women), 3 part-time (1 woman); includes 10 minority (8 Asian, non-Hispanic/Latino; 1 Hispanic/Latino; 1 Two or more races, non-Hispanic/Latino), 531 international. Average age 26. 800 applicants, 71% accepted, 81 enrolled. In 2016, 109 master's, 1 doctorate awarded. *Degree requirements:* For master's, research project (thesis), internship report, or comprehensive exam; for doctorate, comprehensive exam, thesis/dissertation. *Entrance requirements:* For master's, minimum GPA of 2.7; for doctorate, GMAT (minimum score: 550), GRE (minimum score: 1000), or equivalent test results (waived for master's degree with minimum cumulative GPA of 3.3). Additional exam requirements/recommendations for international students: Required—TOEFL (minimum score 525 paper-based; 71 iBT) or IELTS (minimum score 5.5) for MBA; TOEFL (minimum score 550 paper-based; 79 iBT) or IELTS (minimum score 6) for DBA; Recommended—TOEFL (minimum score 71 iBT), IELTS (minimum score 6), TSE. *Application deadline:* For fall admission, 8/7 for domestic students, 7/14 for international students; for spring admission, 11/30 for domestic students, 10/31 for international students; for summer admission, 5/29 for domestic students, 5/5 for international students. Applications are processed on a rolling basis. Application fee: $75. Electronic applications accepted. *Expenses: Tuition:* Full-time $7920. *Required fees:* $400. Tuition and fees vary according to course level, course load, degree level and program. *Financial support:* Teaching assistantships,

career-related internships or fieldwork, and scholarships/grants available. Financial award applicants required to submit FAFSA. *Unit head:* Dr. Marshall Burak, Director of Graduate Programs, 510-628-8016, Fax: 510-628-8012, E-mail: mburak@lincolnuca.edu. *Application contact:* Reenu Shrestha, Assistant to the President, 510-628-8017, Fax: 510-208-2826, E-mail: sreenu@lincolnuca.edu.
Website: http://www.lincolnuca.edu/

Lindenwood University, Graduate Programs, Plaster School of Business and Entrepreneurship, St. Charles, MO 63301-1695. Offers accountancy (M Acc); accounting (MBA); business administration (MBA); entrepreneurial studies (MBA); finance (MBA, MS); human resource management (MBA); international business (MBA); leadership (MA); management (MBA); marketing (MBA, MS); nonprofit administration (MA); public administration (MBA); sport management (MA); supply chain management (MBA). *Accreditation:* ACBSP. *Program availability:* Part-time, evening/weekend, 100% online. *Faculty:* 15 full-time (6 women), 25 part-time/adjunct (7 women). *Students:* 197 full-time (97 women), 213 part-time (132 women); includes 81 minority (62 Black or African American, non-Hispanic/Latino; 1 American Indian or Alaska Native, non-Hispanic/Latino; 4 Asian, non-Hispanic/Latino; 9 Hispanic/Latino; 5 Two or more races, non-Hispanic/Latino), 83 international. Average age 31. 279 applicants, 54% accepted, 133 enrolled. In 2016, 269 master's awarded. *Degree requirements:* For master's, comprehensive exam (for some programs), thesis (for some programs), minimum GPA of 3.0. *Entrance requirements:* For master's, interview, minimum undergraduate cumulative GPA of 3.0, letter of recommendation. Additional exam requirements/recommendations for international students: Required—TOEFL (minimum score 550 paper-based; 80 iBT); Recommended—IELTS (minimum score 6.5). *Application deadline:* For fall admission, 8/28 priority date for domestic and international students; for winter admission, 1/8 priority date for domestic and international students; for spring admission, 3/5 for domestic students, 3/5 priority date for international students; for summer admission, 6/4 priority date for domestic and international students. Applications are processed on a rolling basis. Application fee: $30 ($100 for international students). Electronic applications accepted. *Expenses:* Contact institution. *Financial support:* In 2016–17, 256 students received support. Career-related internships or fieldwork, Federal Work-Study, institutionally sponsored loans, scholarships/grants, tuition waivers (partial), and unspecified assistantships available. Financial award application deadline: 6/30; financial award applicants required to submit FAFSA. *Unit head:* Roger Ellis, Dean, School of Business and Entrepreneurship, 636-949-4839, E-mail: rellis@lindenwood.edu. *Application contact:* Tyler Kostich, Director, Evening and Graduate Admissions, 636-949-4138, Fax: 636-949-4109, E-mail: adultadmissions@lindenwood.edu.
Website: http://www.lindenwood.edu/academics/academic-schools/robert-w-plaster-school-of-business-entrepreneurship/

Lipscomb University, College of Business, Nashville, TN 37204-3951. Offers accountancy (M Acc); accounting (MBA); business administration (MM); conflict management (MBA); financial services (MBA); health care informatics (MBA); healthcare management (MBA); information security (MBA); leadership (MBA); nonprofit management (MBA); professional accountancy (Certificate); sports management (MBA); strategic human resources (MBA); sustainability (MBA); MBA/MS; Pharm D/MM. *Accreditation:* ACBSP. *Program availability:* Part-time, evening/weekend. *Faculty:* 22 full-time (4 women), 12 part-time/adjunct (4 women). *Students:* 112 full-time (51 women), 69 part-time (34 women); includes 30 minority (17 Black or African American, non-Hispanic/Latino; 3 Asian, non-Hispanic/Latino; 8 Hispanic/Latino; 2 Two or more races, non-Hispanic/Latino), 5 international. Average age 32. 244 applicants, 55% accepted, 54 enrolled. In 2016, 164 master's awarded. *Entrance requirements:* For master's, GMAT, transcripts, interview, 2 references, resume. Additional exam requirements/recommendations for international students: Required—TOEFL (minimum score 570 paper-based). *Application deadline:* For fall admission, 6/15 for domestic students, 2/1 for international students; for winter admission, 6/1 for international students; for spring admission, 11/15 for domestic students. Applications are processed on a rolling basis. Application fee: $50 ($75 for international students). Electronic applications accepted. *Expenses:* $1,150-$1,290 per hour, depending on program. *Financial support:* Career-related internships or fieldwork, scholarships/grants, tuition waivers (partial), and unspecified assistantships available. Support available to part-time students. Financial award application deadline: 7/1; financial award applicants required to submit FAFSA. *Faculty research:* Impact of spirituality on organization commitment, women in corporate leadership, psychological empowerment, training. *Unit head:* Allison Duke, Associate Dean of Graduate Business Programs, 615-966-5732, Fax: 615-966-1818, E-mail: allison.duke@lipscomb.edu. *Application contact:* Karen Risley, Manager, Graduate Business Recruiting, 615-966-5145, E-mail: karen.risley@lipscomb.edu.
Website: http://www.lipscomb.edu/business/Graduate-Programs

Long Island University–Hudson, Graduate School, Purchase, NY 10577. Offers autism (Advanced Certificate); childhood education (MS Ed); early childhood education (MS Ed); educational leadership (MS Ed); finance (MBA); health administration (MPA); healthcare sector management (MBA); literacy (MS Ed); management (MBA); marriage and family therapy (MS); mental health counseling (MS), including credentialed alcoholism and substance abuse counselor; middle childhood and adolescence education (MS Ed); pharmaceutics (MS), including cosmetic science, industrial pharmacy; public administration (MPA); school counseling (MS Ed, Advanced Certificate); school psychology (MS Ed); special education (MS Ed); TESOL (all grades) (Advanced Certificate); TESOL and bilingual education (MS Ed); the business of pharmaceutics and biotechnology (MBA). *Program availability:* Part-time, evening/weekend, online learning. *Faculty:* 7 full-time (5 women), 42 part-time/adjunct (25 women). *Students:* 55 full-time (41 women), 158 part-time (123 women); includes 40 minority (8 Black or African American, non-Hispanic/Latino; 1 Asian, non-Hispanic/Latino; 31 Hispanic/Latino). Average age 35. *Entrance requirements:* Additional exam requirements/recommendations for international students: Required—TOEFL (minimum score 550 paper-based; 79 iBT). *Application deadline:* Applications are processed on a rolling basis. Application fee: $50. Electronic applications accepted. *Expenses:* Contact institution. *Unit head:* Dr. Sylvia Blake, Dean and Chief Operating Officer, 914-831-2700, E-mail: westchester@liu.edu. *Application contact:* Cindy Pagnotta, Director of Marketing and Enrollment, 914-831-2701, Fax: 914-251-5959, E-mail: cindy.pagnotta@liu.edu.

Long Island University–LIU Post, College of Management, Brookville, NY 11548-1300. Offers accountancy (MS); finance (MBA); information systems (MS); international business (MBA); management (MBA); management engineering (MS); marketing (MBA); taxation (MS); technical project management (MS); JD/MBA. *Accreditation:* AACSB. *Program availability:* Part-time, 100% online, blended/hybrid learning. *Faculty:* 35 full-time (12 women), 25 part-time/adjunct (6 women). *Students:* 153 full-time (61 women), 68 part-time (22 women); includes 44 minority (8 Black or African American, non-Hispanic/Latino; 24 Asian, non-Hispanic/Latino; 11 Hispanic/Latino; 1 Two or more races, non-Hispanic/Latino), 79 international. 429 applicants, 58% accepted, 74 enrolled. In 2016, 124 master's awarded. *Degree requirements:* For master's, thesis (for some programs). *Entrance requirements:* For master's, GMAT, GRE, or LSAT. Additional exam requirements/recommendations for international students: Required—PTE, TOEFL (minimum score 550 paper-based, 75 iBT) or IELTS. *Application deadline:* Applications are processed on a rolling basis. Application fee: $50. Electronic applications accepted. *Expenses: Tuition:* Full-time $28,272; part-time $1178 per credit. *Required fees:* $451 per term. Tuition and fees vary according to degree level and program. *Financial support:* In 2016–17, 68 students received support. Career-related internships or fieldwork, Federal Work-Study, institutionally sponsored loans, and scholarships/grants available. Support available to part-time students. Financial award application deadline: 2/15; financial award applicants required to submit FAFSA. *Faculty research:* Finance and sustainability, innovation and intellectual property rights, marketing: data analytics and business intelligence, social networking local and international. *Unit head:* Dr. Robert M. Valli, Dean, 516-299-4192, E-mail: rob.valli@liu.edu. *Application contact:* Carol Zerah, Director of Graduate and International Admissions, 516-299-2900, Fax: 516-299-2137, E-mail: post-enroll@liu.edu.
Website: http://liu.edu/CWPost/Academics/Schools/COM

Louisiana State University and Agricultural & Mechanical College, Graduate School, E. J. Ourso College of Business, Department of Finance, Baton Rouge, LA 70803. Offers business administration (PhD), including finance; finance (MS).

Louisiana Tech University, Graduate School, College of Business, Department of Economics and Finance, Ruston, LA 71272. Offers finance (MBA, DBA); finance and economics (DBA). *Program availability:* Part-time. *Degree requirements:* For doctorate, thesis/dissertation. *Entrance requirements:* For master's and doctorate, GMAT. *Application deadline:* For fall admission, 7/29 for domestic students; for spring admission, 2/3 for domestic students. Application fee: $20 ($30 for international students). *Financial support:* Fellowships, research assistantships, and teaching assistantships available. Financial award application deadline: 2/1. *Unit head:* Dr. Otis Gilley, Director, 318-257-4140, Fax: 318-257-4253, E-mail: gilley@latech.edu. *Application contact:* Marilyn J. Robinson, Assistant to the Dean, 318-257-2924, Fax: 318-257-4487.
Website: http://www.business.latech.edu/econ_fin/

Loyola University Chicago, Quinlan School of Business, Master of Science in Finance Program, Chicago, IL 60611. Offers asset management (MSF); corporate finance (MSF); risk management (MSF); MBA/MSF. *Program availability:* Part-time, evening/weekend. *Faculty:* 11 full-time (3 women), 5 part-time/adjunct (1 woman). *Students:* 29 full-time (15 women), 4 part-time (1 woman); includes 4 minority (3 Asian, non-Hispanic/Latino; 1 Two or more races, non-Hispanic/Latino), 21 international. Average age 24. 152 applicants, 53% accepted, 19 enrolled. In 2016, 22 master's awarded. *Entrance requirements:* For master's, GMAT or GRE, official transcripts, letters of recommendation, statement of purpose, resume. Additional exam requirements/recommendations for international students: Required—TOEFL (minimum score 90 iBT) or IELTS (minimum score 6.5). *Application deadline:* For fall admission, 7/15 for domestic and international students; for winter admission, 10/1 for domestic and international students; for spring admission, 1/15 for domestic and international students; for summer admission, 4/1 for domestic and international students. Applications are processed on a rolling basis. Application fee: $50. Electronic applications accepted. Application fee is waived when completed online. *Expenses:* Contact institution. *Financial support:* In 2016–17, 14 students received support. Federal Work-Study, scholarships/grants, health care benefits, and unspecified assistantships available. Support available to part-time students. *Faculty research:* Corporate finance, banking, risk management and derivatives, investment, theoretical finance. *Unit head:* Dr. Abol Jalilvand, Chair, Department of Finance, 312-915-7101, Fax: 312-915-8508, E-mail: ajalilv@luc.edu. *Application contact:* Lauren Griffin, Enrollment Advisor, Quinlan School of Business Graduate Programs, 312-915-8908, Fax: 312-915-7207, E-mail: lgriffin3@luc.edu.
Website: http://www.luc.edu/quinlan/mba/masters/masters-in-finance/

Loyola University Chicago, Quinlan School of Business, MBA Programs, Chicago, IL 60611. Offers accounting (MBA); business administration (EMBA); business ethics (MBA); economics (MBA); entrepreneurship (MBA); finance (MBA); healthcare management (MBA); human resources management (MBA); international business (MBA); management (MBA); marketing (MBA); operation management (MBA); risk management (MBA); supply chain management (MBA). *Program availability:* Part-time, evening/weekend. *Faculty:* 79 full-time (22 women), 10 part-time/adjunct (6 women). *Students:* 309 full-time (151 women), 65 part-time (31 women); includes 82 minority (25 Black or African American, non-Hispanic/Latino; 27 Asian, non-Hispanic/Latino; 27 Hispanic/Latino; 3 Two or more races, non-Hispanic/Latino), 49 international. Average age 30. 371 applicants, 53% accepted, 114 enrolled. In 2016, 216 master's awarded. *Entrance requirements:* For master's, GMAT or GRE, official transcripts, two letters of recommendation, statement of purpose, resume. Additional exam requirements/recommendations for international students: Required—TOEFL (minimum score 90 iBT) or IELTS (minimum score 6.5). *Application deadline:* For fall admission, 7/15 for domestic and international students; for winter admission, 10/1 for domestic and international students; for spring admission, 1/15 for domestic and international students; for summer admission, 4/1 for domestic and international students. Applications are processed on a rolling basis. Application fee: $50. Electronic applications accepted. Application fee is waived when completed online. *Expenses:* $1,488 per course. *Financial support:* In 2016–17, 83 students received support. Federal Work-Study, scholarships/grants, health care benefits, and unspecified assistantships available. Support available to part-time students. *Faculty research:* Social enterprise and responsibility, emerging markets, supply chain management, risk management. *Unit head:* Katherine Acles, Assistant Dean for Graduate Programs, 312-915-6124, Fax: 312-915-7207, E-mail: kacles@luc.edu. *Application contact:* Lauren Griffin, Enrollment Advisor, Quinlan School of Business Graduate Programs, 312-915-6124, Fax: 312-915-7207, E-mail: lgriffin3@luc.edu.

Loyola University Maryland, Graduate Programs, Sellinger School of Business, Master of Science in Finance Program, Baltimore, MD 21210-2699. Offers MSF. *Program availability:* Part-time. *Faculty:* 26 full-time (8 women), 13 part-time/adjunct (5 women). *Students:* 8 part-time. 8 applicants, 100% accepted, 7 enrolled. In 2016, 7 master's awarded. *Entrance requirements:* For master's, GMAT, resume, essay, official transcripts, professional letter of recommendation. Additional exam requirements/recommendations for international students: Required—TOEFL (minimum score 550 paper-based, 80 iBT) or IELTS (minimum score 7). *Application deadline:* For fall admission, 8/1 priority date for domestic students; for spring admission, 12/1 priority date for domestic students; for summer admission, 5/1 priority date for domestic students. Applications are processed on a rolling basis. Application fee: $60. Electronic applications accepted. *Expenses:* Contact institution. *Financial support:* In 2016–17, 6 students received support. Scholarships/grants available. Financial award application deadline: 4/15; financial award applicants required to submit FAFSA. *Application contact:* Maureen Faux, Executive Director, Graduate Admissions, 410-617-5020, Fax: 410-617-2002, E-mail: graduate@loyola.edu.

Manhattanville College, School of Business, Master of Science in Finance Program, Purchase, NY 10577-2132. Offers accounting (MS); corporate finance (MS), investment management (MS). *Program availability:* Part-time, evening/weekend. *Students:* 30 (14 women); includes 13 minority (7 Black or African American, non-Hispanic/Latino; 3 Asian, non-Hispanic/Latino; 1 Hispanic/Latino; 2 Two or more races, non-Hispanic/Latino). Average age 28. 23 applicants, 30% accepted, 7 enrolled. In 2016, 9 master's awarded. *Degree requirements:* For master's, thesis (for some programs), final project. *Entrance requirements:* For master's, transcripts, 2 letters of recommendation, resume.

Finance and Banking

Additional exam requirements/recommendations for international students: Required—TOEFL (minimum score 563 paper-based; 85 iBT). *Application deadline:* Applications are processed on a rolling basis. Application fee: $75. Electronic applications accepted. *Expenses: Tuition:* Full-time $16,470; part-time $915 per credit. *Required fees:* $60 per semester. Part-time tuition and fees vary according to course load and program. *Financial support:* Federal Work-Study, institutionally sponsored loans, scholarships/grants, and unspecified assistantships available. Financial award applicants required to submit FAFSA. *Faculty research:* Life transitions: theory, strategies and practice. *Unit head:* Laura Persky, Graduate Program Director, 914-323-5188, E-mail: laura.persky@mville.edu. *Application contact:* Monika Pottgen, Assistant Director, Recruitment and Admissions, 914-323-5150, E-mail: business@mville.edu.
Website: https://www.mville.edu/programs/ms-finance

Manhattanville College, School of Business, Master of Science in International Management Program, Purchase, NY 10577-2132. Offers business leadership (MS); finance (MS); human resource management (MS); marketing communication management (MS). *Program availability:* Part-time, evening/weekend. *Students:* 10 (9 women); includes 6 minority (2 Black or African American, non-Hispanic/Latino; 3 Hispanic/Latino; 1 Two or more races, non-Hispanic/Latino). Average age 30. 17 applicants, 35% accepted, 3 enrolled. In 2016, 1 master's awarded. *Degree requirements:* For master's, thesis (for some programs), final project. *Entrance requirements:* For master's, transcripts, 2 letters of recommendation, resume. Additional exam requirements/recommendations for international students: Required—TOEFL (minimum score 563 paper-based; 85 iBT). *Application deadline:* Applications are processed on a rolling basis. Application fee: $75. Electronic applications accepted. *Expenses: Tuition:* Full-time $16,470; part-time $915 per credit. *Required fees:* $60 per semester. Part-time tuition and fees vary according to course load and program. *Financial support:* Federal Work-Study, institutionally sponsored loans, scholarships/grants, and unspecified assistantships available. Financial award applicants required to submit FAFSA. *Faculty research:* Market entry in Cuba, linking strategy and customer satisfaction. *Unit head:* Laura Persky, Graduate Program Director, 914-323-5188, E-mail: laura.persky@mville.edu. *Application contact:* Monika Pottgen, Assistant Director, Recruitment and Admissions, 914-323-5150, E-mail: business@mville.edu.
Website: https://www.mville.edu/programs/ms-international-management

Marquette University, Graduate School of Management, Executive MBA Program, Milwaukee, WI 53201-1881. Offers economics (MBA); finance (MBA); human resources (MBA); international business (MBA); management information systems (MBA); marketing (MBA); operations and supply chain management (MBA); sports business (MBA). *Accreditation:* AACSB. *Students:* 39 full-time (12 women); includes 7 minority (4 Black or African American, non-Hispanic/Latino; 2 Asian, non-Hispanic/Latino; 1 Hispanic/Latino). Average age 38. 25 applicants, 96% accepted, 29 enrolled. In 2016, 14 master's awarded. *Degree requirements:* For master's, international trip. *Entrance requirements:* For master's, GMAT or GRE, two letters of recommendation, official transcripts from current and previous colleges/universities. Additional exam requirements/recommendations for international students: Required—TOEFL (minimum score 550 paper-based; 88 iBT), IELTS (minimum score 6.5), PTE. *Application deadline:* For fall admission, 2/15 for domestic and international students. Application fee: $50. Electronic applications accepted. *Expenses:* Contact institution. *Financial support:* Application deadline: 2/15. *Faculty research:* International trade and finance, customer relationship management, consumer satisfaction, customer service. *Unit head:* Dr. Brian Till, Dean, 414-288-5724. *Application contact:* Dr. Jeanne Simmons, Associate Dean, 414-288-7145.
Website: http://www.busadm.mu.edu/emba/

Marquette University, Graduate School of Management, Program in Business Administration, Milwaukee, WI 53201-1881. Offers business administration (MBA); economics (MBA); entrepreneurship (Certificate); finance (MBA); human resources (MBA); international business (MBA); management information systems (MBA); marketing (MBA); operations and supply chain management (MBA); sports business (MBA); JD/MBA; MBA/MA; MBA/MSN. *Accreditation:* AACSB. *Program availability:* Part-time, evening/weekend. *Students:* 25 full-time (12 women), 202 part-time (57 women); includes 17 minority (5 Black or African American, non-Hispanic/Latino; 6 Asian, non-Hispanic/Latino; 2 Hispanic/Latino; 1 Native Hawaiian or other Pacific Islander, non-Hispanic/Latino; 3 Two or more races, non-Hispanic/Latino), 7 international. Average age 31. 107 applicants, 87% accepted, 113 enrolled. In 2016, 107 master's, 5 other advanced degrees awarded. *Degree requirements:* For Certificate, business plan. *Entrance requirements:* For master's, GMAT or GRE, letters of recommendation. Additional exam requirements/recommendations for international students: Required—TOEFL (minimum score 550 paper-based; 88 iBT), IELTS (minimum score 6.5), PTE. *Application deadline:* For fall admission, 2/15 for domestic and international students. Applications are processed on a rolling basis. Application fee: $50. Electronic applications accepted. *Financial support:* Fellowships, research assistantships, teaching assistantships, Federal Work-Study, institutionally sponsored loans, scholarships/grants, and tuition waivers (full and partial) available. Support available to part-time students. Financial award application deadline: 2/15. *Faculty research:* Ethics in the professions, services marketing, technology impact on decision-making, mentoring. *Unit head:* Dr. Brian Till, Dean, 414-288-5724. *Application contact:* Dr. Jeanne Simmons, Associate Dean, 414-288-7145.
Website: http://business.marquette.edu/academics/mba

Maryville University of Saint Louis, The John E. Simon School of Business, St. Louis, MO 63141-7299. Offers accounting (MBA, Certificate); business studies (Certificate); cyber security (MBA); cybersecurity (Certificate); financial services (MBA, Certificate); healthcare practice management (MBA, Certificate); human resource management (MBA); information technology (MBA, Certificate); management (MBA, Certificate); management and leadership (MA); marketing (MBA, Certificate); project management (MBA); sport business management (MBA); supply chain management/logistics (MBA). *Accreditation:* ACBSP. *Program availability:* Part-time, evening/weekend, 100% online, blended/hybrid learning. *Faculty:* 7 full-time (3 women), 34 part-time/adjunct (9 women). *Students:* 84 full-time (40 women), 223 part-time (118 women); includes 67 minority (40 Black or African American, non-Hispanic/Latino; 2 American Indian or Alaska Native, non-Hispanic/Latino; 8 Asian, non-Hispanic/Latino; 12 Hispanic/Latino; 1 Native Hawaiian or other Pacific Islander, non-Hispanic/Latino; 4 Two or more races, non-Hispanic/Latino), 15 international. Average age 32. In 2016, 67 master's awarded. *Entrance requirements:* Additional exam requirements/recommendations for international students: Required—TOEFL (minimum score 563 paper-based; 85 iBT). *Application deadline:* Applications are processed on a rolling basis. Electronic applications accepted. *Expenses:* $650 per credit hour. *Financial support:* Career-related internships or fieldwork, Federal Work-Study, tuition waivers (partial), and campus employment available. Financial award application deadline: 3/1; financial award applicants required to submit FAFSA. *Faculty research:* Global business, e-marketing, strategic planning, interpersonal management skills, financial analysis. *Unit head:* Pam Horwitz, Interim Dean, 314-529-9680, Fax: 314-529-9975. *Application contact:* Dustin Loeffler, Director for Graduate Studies in Business, 314-529-9571, Fax: 314-529-9975, E-mail: dloeffler@maryville.edu.
Website: http://www.maryville.edu/bu/business-administration-masters/

Marywood University, Academic Affairs, Munley College of Liberal Arts and Sciences, School of Business and Global Innovation, Emphasis in Finance/Investment, Scranton, PA 18509-1598. Offers MBA. *Entrance requirements:* For master's, GMAT. Electronic applications accepted.

McGill University, Faculty of Graduate and Postdoctoral Studies, Desautels Faculty of Management, Montréal, QC H3A 2T5, Canada. Offers administration (PhD); entrepreneurial studies (MBA); finance (MBA); general management (Post Master's Certificate); information systems (MBA); international business (MBA); international practicing management (MM); management (MBA); management for development (MBA); manufacturing management (MMM); marketing (MBA); operations management (MBA); public accountancy (Diploma); strategic management (MBA); MBA/LL B; MD/MBA. MMM offered jointly with Faculty of Engineering; PhD with Concordia University, HEC Montreal, Université de Montréal, Université du Québec à Montréal.

Metropolitan College of New York, Program in Business Administration, New York, NY 10006. Offers financial services (MBA); general management (MBA); health services and risk management (MBA); media management (MBA). *Accreditation:* ACBSP. *Program availability:* Evening/weekend. *Students:* 167 full-time (117 women), 43 part-time (30 women); includes 161 minority (114 Black or African American, non-Hispanic/Latino; 3 American Indian or Alaska Native, non-Hispanic/Latino; 10 Asian, non-Hispanic/Latino; 32 Hispanic/Latino; 2 Two or more races, non-Hispanic/Latino), 26 international. Average age 37. In 2016, 111 master's awarded. *Degree requirements:* For master's, thesis, 10-day study abroad. *Entrance requirements:* For master's, GMAT. Additional exam requirements/recommendations for international students: Required—TOEFL (minimum score 600 paper-based). *Application deadline:* For fall admission, 7/15 priority date for domestic students; for winter admission, 11/15 priority date for domestic students; for spring admission, 3/30 priority date for domestic students. Applications are processed on a rolling basis. Application fee: $45. Electronic applications accepted. *Expenses:* Contact institution. *Financial support:* Scholarships/grants available. Financial award application deadline: 8/15; financial award applicants required to submit FAFSA. *Unit head:* Dr. Tilokie Depoo, Dean and Professor, School for Business, 212-343-1234 Ext. 2204. *Application contact:* Steebo Varghese, Assistant Director of Admissions, 212-343-1234 Ext. 2708, Fax: 212-343-8470.

Michigan State University, The Graduate School, Eli Broad College of Business, Department of Finance, East Lansing, MI 48224. Offers MS, PhD. PhD program admits students only in odd-numbered years. *Degree requirements:* For doctorate, comprehensive exam, thesis/dissertation. *Entrance requirements:* For master's, GMAT (minimum score 550) or GRE (minimum score 1050 verbal and quantitative taken within 5 years), 4-year bachelor's degree or equivalent with minimum cumulative GPA of 3.0, transcripts, at least 2 years' work experience, 2 letters of recommendation, working knowledge of computers, laptop computer; for doctorate, GMAT or GRE, transcripts from all colleges/universities attended, 3 letters of recommendation, statement of purpose. Additional exam requirements/recommendations for international students: Required—TOEFL (minimum score 600 paper-based; 100 iBT), IELTS (minimum score 7) accepted for MS only. Electronic applications accepted.

Michigan State University, The Graduate School, Eli Broad College of Business, Program in Business Administration, East Lansing, MI 48224. Offers finance (MBA); human resource management (MBA); integrative management (MBA); marketing (MBA); supply chain management (MBA). MBA in integrative management is through Weekend MBA Program; other 4 concentrations are through Full-Time MBA Program. *Program availability:* Evening/weekend. *Degree requirements:* For master's, enrichment experience. *Entrance requirements:* For master's, GMAT or GRE, 4-year bachelor's degree; resume; work experience (minimum of 5 years for Weekend MBA); 2-3 personal essays; 2 letters of recommendation; personal interview. Additional exam requirements/recommendations for international students: Required—PTE (minimum score 70), TOEFL (minimum score 100 iBT) or IELTS (minimum score 7) for full-time MBA applicants. Electronic applications accepted. *Expenses:* Contact institution.

Minnesota State University Moorhead, Graduate Studies, College of Business and Innovation, Moorhead, MN 56563. Offers accounting and finance (MS); business administration (MBA); health care management (MBA). *Accreditation:* AACSB. *Program availability:* Part-time. *Students:* 15 full-time (8 women), 27 part-time (11 women). Average age 32. 20 applicants, 100% accepted. In 2016, 9 master's awarded. *Degree requirements:* For master's, comprehensive exam (for some programs), thesis, final oral exam. *Entrance requirements:* For master's, GMAT, minimum GPA of 3.0. Additional exam requirements/recommendations for international students: Required—TOEFL (minimum score 550 paper-based); Recommended—IELTS (minimum score 6.5). *Application deadline:* For fall admission, 3/15 for domestic students; for spring admission, 10/15 for domestic students. Applications are processed on a rolling basis. Application fee: $20. Electronic applications accepted. *Expenses:* Tuition, state resident: full-time $9000; part-time $4500 per credit. Tuition, nonresident: full-time $18,000; part-time $9000 per credit. *Required fees:* $942; $39.25 per credit. One-time fee: $90 full-time. Full-time tuition and fees vary according to course load, degree level, program and reciprocity agreements. *Financial support:* Federal Work-Study and unspecified assistantships available. Financial award application deadline: 10/1; financial award applicants required to submit FAFSA. *Faculty research:* Union decertification, small business development, business innovation, pedagogy, curriculum design. *Unit head:* Dr. Marsha Weber, Dean, 218-477-2076, E-mail: marsha.weber@mnstate.edu. *Application contact:* Karla Wenger, Coordinator, 218-477-2344, E-mail: wengerk@mnstate.edu.
Website: http://www.mnstate.edu/cbi/

Mississippi College, Graduate School, School of Business, Clinton, MS 39058. Offers accounting (Certificate); business administration (MBA), including accounting; business education (M Ed); finance (MBA, Certificate); JD/MBA. *Accreditation:* ACBSP. *Program availability:* Part-time, evening/weekend. *Degree requirements:* For master's, comprehensive exam, thesis optional. *Entrance requirements:* For master's, GMAT, minimum GPA of 2.5, 24 hours of undergraduate course work in business. Additional exam requirements/recommendations for international students: Recommended—TOEFL, IELTS. Electronic applications accepted.

Mississippi State University, College of Business, Department of Finance and Economics, Mississippi State, MS 39762. Offers MA, PhD. PhD in applied economics offered jointly with Department of Agricultural Economics. *Program availability:* Part-time. *Faculty:* 18 full-time (6 women), 1 part-time/adjunct (0 women). *Students:* 6 full-time (3 women), 1 part-time (0 women), 5 international. Average age 29. Terminal master's awarded for partial completion of doctoral program. *Degree requirements:* For master's, comprehensive exam, thesis optional; for doctorate, comprehensive exam, thesis/dissertation, written and oral exams. *Entrance requirements:* For master's, GRE, previously-completed intermediate microeconomics and macroeconomics; for doctorate, GRE, BS with minimum GPA of 3.0 cumulative and over last 60 hours of undergraduate work, 3.25 on all graduate work. Additional exam requirements/recommendations for international students: Required—TOEFL (minimum score 575 paper-based; 84 iBT); Recommended—IELTS (minimum score 6.5). *Application deadline:* For fall admission, 7/1 for domestic students, 5/1 for international students; for spring admission, 11/1 for domestic students, 10/1 for international students. Applications are processed on a rolling basis. Application fee: $60. Electronic applications accepted. *Expenses:* Tuition,

state resident: full-time $7670; part-time $852.50 per credit hour. Tuition, nonresident: full-time $20,790; part-time $2310.50 per credit hour. Part-time tuition and fees vary according to course load. *Financial support:* Federal Work-Study, scholarships/grants, health care benefits, and unspecified assistantships available. Financial award application deadline: 4/1; financial award applicants required to submit FAFSA. *Faculty research:* Economics development, mergers, event studies, economic education, bank performance. *Total annual research expenditures:* $979,000. *Unit head:* Dr. Mike Highfield, Department Head, 662-325-3928, Fax: 662-325-1977, E-mail: mhighfield@msstate.edu. *Application contact:* Lakan Drinker, Admissions and Enrollment Assistant, 662-325-8951, E-mail: ldrinker@grad.msstate.edu.
Website: http://www.business.msstate.edu/programs/fe/index.php

Molloy College, Graduate Business Program, Rockville Centre, NY 11571-5002. Offers accounting (MBA); finance (MBA, Advanced Certificate); healthcare (MBA, Advanced Certificate); management (MBA); marketing (MBA, Advanced Certificate); personal financial planning (MBA). *Program availability:* Part-time, evening/weekend. *Faculty:* 6 full-time (3 women), 14 part-time/adjunct (5 women). *Students:* 66 full-time (32 women), 178 part-time (92 women); includes 96 minority (38 Black or African American, non-Hispanic/Latino; 24 Asian, non-Hispanic/Latino; 32 Hispanic/Latino; 1 Native Hawaiian or other Pacific Islander, non-Hispanic/Latino; 1 Two or more races, non-Hispanic/Latino), 5 international. Average age 40. 198 applicants, 69% accepted, 108 enrolled. In 2016, 55 master's awarded. *Entrance requirements:* Additional exam requirements/recommendations for international students: Required—TOEFL (minimum score 550 paper-based; 79 iBT). *Application deadline:* Applications are processed on a rolling basis. Application fee: $60. Electronic applications accepted. *Expenses: Tuition:* Full-time $19,170; part-time $1065 per credit. *Required fees:* $950; $790 per credit. Tuition and fees vary according to course load. *Financial support:* Applicants required to submit FAFSA. *Faculty research:* Leadership profiles that provide lessons of strength and purpose applicable to business; pedagogy and student learning outcomes for graduate business education; mobilizing social networks for innovation and qualitative analysis of sociocentric (whole) network measures; the ethical considerations of covenants not to compete in employment contracts and the use of liquidated damages clauses in employment contracts. *Unit head:* Dr. Maureen Mackenzie, Dean, Division of Business/Director of Graduate Programs, 516-323-3080, E-mail: mmackenzie@molloy.edu. *Application contact:* Jaclyn Machowicz, Assistant Director for Admissions, 516-323-4010, E-mail: jmachowicz@molloy.edu.
Website: http://www.molloy.edu/academics/graduate-programs/graduate-business

Monmouth University, Graduate Studies, Leon Hess Business School, West Long Branch, NJ 07764-1898. Offers accounting (MBA, Post-Master's Certificate); business administration (MBA); finance (MBA); management (MBA); marketing (MBA); real estate (MBA). *Accreditation:* AACSB. *Program availability:* Part-time, evening/weekend. *Faculty:* 20 full-time (4 women), 8 part-time/adjunct (0 women). *Students:* 76 full-time (37 women), 94 part-time (43 women); includes 17 minority (2 Black or African American, non-Hispanic/Latino; 6 Asian, non-Hispanic/Latino; 6 Hispanic/Latino; 1 Native Hawaiian or other Pacific Islander, non-Hispanic/Latino; 2 Two or more races, non-Hispanic/Latino), 8 international. Average age 30. 105 applicants, 90% accepted, 67 enrolled. In 2016, 93 master's, 1 other advanced degree awarded. *Degree requirements:* For master's, capstone course. *Entrance requirements:* For master's, GMAT or GRE, current resume; essay (500 words or less). Additional exam requirements/recommendations for international students: Required—TOEFL (minimum score 550 paper-based; 79 iBT), IELTS (minimum score 6), Michigan English Language Assessment Battery (minimum score 77) or Certificate of Advanced English (minimum score B2). *Application deadline:* For fall admission, 7/15 priority date for domestic students, 6/1 for international students; for spring admission, 12/1 priority date for domestic students, 11/1 for international students; for summer admission, 5/1 for domestic students. Applications are processed on a rolling basis. Application fee: $50. Electronic applications accepted. *Expenses: Tuition, area resident:* Full-time $19,764; part-time $1098 per credit hour. *Required fees:* $175 per semester. Tuition and fees vary according to program. *Financial support:* In 2016–17, 191 students received support, including 137 fellowships (averaging $2,643 per year), 20 teaching assistantships with full and partial tuition reimbursements available (averaging $10,034 per year); research assistantships, institutionally sponsored loans, scholarships/grants, and unspecified assistantships also available. Support available to part-time students. Financial award application deadline: 2/1; financial award applicants required to submit FAFSA. *Faculty research:* Information technology and marketing, behavioral research in accounting, human resources, management of technology. *Unit head:* Dr. Susan Gupta, MBA Program Director, 732-571-3639, Fax: 732-263-5517, E-mail: sgupta@monmouth.edu. *Application contact:* Laurie Kuhn, Associate Director of Graduate Admission, 732-571-3452, Fax: 732-263-5123, E-mail: gradadm@monmouth.edu.
Website: https://www.monmouth.edu/business-school/leon-hess-business-school.aspx

See Display on page 118 and Close-Up on page 181.

Monroe College, King Graduate School, Bronx, NY 10468. Offers accounting (MS); business administration (MBA), including entrepreneurship, finance, general business administration, healthcare management, human resources, information technology, marketing; computer science (MS); criminal justice (MS); hospitality management (MS); public health (MPH), including biostatistics and epidemiology, community health, health administration and leadership. *Program availability:* Online learning. Application fee: $50.
Website: https://www.monroecollege.edu/Degrees/King-Graduate-School/

Mount Saint Mary College, School of Business, Newburgh, NY 12550-3494. Offers business (MBA); financial planning (MBA); health care management (MBA). *Program availability:* Part-time, evening/weekend. *Faculty:* 6 full-time (2 women), 8 part-time/adjunct (2 women). *Students:* 55 full-time (26 women), 28 part-time (17 women); includes 20 minority (7 Black or African American, non-Hispanic/Latino; 12 Hispanic/Latino; 1 Native Hawaiian or other Pacific Islander, non-Hispanic/Latino), 1 international. Average age 32. 21 applicants, 100% accepted, 15 enrolled. In 2016, 47 master's awarded. *Degree requirements:* For master's, thesis or alternative. *Entrance requirements:* For master's, GMAT or minimum undergraduate GPA of 2.7. Additional exam requirements/recommendations for international students: Required—TOEFL (minimum score 80 iBT). *Application deadline:* Applications are processed on a rolling basis. Application fee: $45. Electronic applications accepted. Application fee is waived when completed online. *Expenses: Tuition:* Full-time $13,914; part-time $773 per credit. *Required fees:* $82 per semester. *Financial support:* In 2016–17, 18 students received support. Unspecified assistantships available. Financial award application deadline: 4/15; financial award applicants required to submit FAFSA. *Faculty research:* Financial reform, entrepreneurship and small business development, global business relations, technology's impact on business decision-making, college-assisted business education. *Unit head:* Dr. Moira Tolan, Graduate Coordinator, 845-569-3121, Fax: 845-562-6762, E-mail: moira.tolan@msmc.edu. *Application contact:* Lisa Gallina, Director of Admissions for Graduate Programs and Adult Degree Completion, 845-569-3166, Fax: 845-569-3450, E-mail: lisa.gallina@msmc.edu.
Website: http://www.msmc.edu/Academics/Graduate_Programs/master_of_business_administration.be

Naval Postgraduate School, Departments and Academic Groups, Department of Defense Analysis, Monterey, CA 93943. Offers command and control (MS); communications (MS); defense analysis (MS), including astronautics; financial management (MS); information operations (MS); irregular warfare (MS); national security affairs (MS); operations analysis (MS); special operations (MA, MS), including command and control (MS), communications (MS), financial management (MS), information operations (MS), irregular warfare (MS), national security affairs, operations analysis (MS), tactile missiles (MS), terrorist operations and financing (MS); tactile missiles (MS); terrorist operations and financing (MS). Program only open to commissioned officers of the United States and friendly nations and selected United States federal civilian employees. *Program availability:* Part-time. *Degree requirements:* For master's, thesis. *Faculty research:* CTF Global Ecco Project, Afghanistan endgames, core lab Philippines project, Defense Manpower Data Center (DMDC) data vulnerability.

Naval Postgraduate School, Departments and Academic Groups, Graduate School of Business and Public Policy, Monterey, CA 93943. Offers acquisition and contract management (MBA); business administration (EMBA, MBA); contract management (MS); defense business management (MBA); defense systems analysis (MS), including management; defense systems management (international) (MBA); financial management (MBA); information management (MBA); manpower systems analysis (MS); material logistics support management (MBA); program management (MS); resource planning and management for international defense (MBA); supply chain management (MBA); systems acquisition management (MBA); transportation management (MBA). Program only open to commissioned officers of the United States and friendly nations and selected United States federal civilian employees. *Accreditation:* AACSB; NASPAA. *Program availability:* Part-time, online learning. *Degree requirements:* For master's, thesis (for some programs), terminal project/capstone (for some programs). *Faculty research:* U.S. and European public procurement policies for small and medium-sized enterprises, examining external validity criticisms in the choice of students as subjects in accounting experiment studies, assurance of learning in contract management education, contracting for cloud computing: opportunities and risks, NPS, Apple App Store as a business model supporting U. S. Navy requirements.

New Charter University, College of Business, Salt Lake City, UT 84101. Offers finance (MBA); health care management (MBA); management (MBA). *Program availability:* Part-time, evening/weekend, online learning. *Entrance requirements:* For master's, course work in calculus, statistics, macroeconomics. Additional exam requirements/recommendations for international students: Required—TOEFL (minimum score 550 paper-based). Electronic applications accepted.

New England College of Business and Finance, Program in Finance, Boston, MA 02111-2645. Offers MSF. *Program availability:* Online learning.

New Jersey City University, School of Business, Program in Finance, Jersey City, NJ 07305-1597. Offers MBA, MS, Graduate Certificate. *Program availability:* Part-time, evening/weekend. *Degree requirements:* For master's, thesis. *Entrance requirements:* Additional exam requirements/recommendations for international students: Required—TOEFL (minimum score 79 iBT).

Newman University, MBA Program, Wichita, KS 67213-2097. Offers finance (MBA); international business (MBA); leadership (MBA); management (MBA); management information technology (MBA). *Program availability:* Part-time. *Degree requirements:* For master's, thesis optional. *Entrance requirements:* For master's, minimum GPA of 3.0; 2 letters of recommendation; course work in algebra, statistics, macroeconomics, and financial accounting. Additional exam requirements/recommendations for international students: Required—TOEFL (minimum score 600 paper-based; 100 iBT). Electronic applications accepted. *Expenses:* Contact institution.

New Mexico State University, College of Business, Department of Finance, Las Cruces, NM 88003. Offers finance (MBA, Graduate Certificate). *Program availability:* Part-time. *Faculty:* 9 full-time (2 women). *Students:* 2 applicants. *Entrance requirements:* Additional exam requirements/recommendations for international students: Required—TOEFL (minimum score 550 paper-based; 79 iBT), IELTS (minimum score 6.5). *Application deadline:* Applications are processed on a rolling basis. Application fee: $40 ($50 for international students). Electronic applications accepted. *Expenses:* Tuition, state resident: full-time $4086. Tuition, nonresident: full-time $14,254. *Required fees:* $853. Tuition and fees vary according to course load. *Financial support:* Career-related internships or fieldwork, Federal Work-Study, scholarships/grants, traineeships, health care benefits, and unspecified assistantships available. Support available to part-time students. Financial award application deadline: 3/1. *Faculty research:* Tribal finance, international business finance and trade, market microstructure issues, business law, executive compensation. *Unit head:* Dr. Harikumar Sankaran, Department Head, 575-646-4901, Fax: 575-646-2820, E-mail: sankaran@nmsu.edu. *Application contact:* 575-646-3201, Fax: 575-646-2820.
Website: http://business.nmsu.edu/departments/finance/

New Mexico State University, College of Business, MBA Program, Las Cruces, NM 88003. Offers agribusiness (MBA); finance (MBA); information systems (MBA). *Accreditation:* AACSB. *Program availability:* Part-time-only, evening/weekend, online with required 2-3 day orientation and 2-3 day concluding session in Las Cruces. *Students:* 55 full-time (23 women), 121 part-time (67 women); includes 97 minority (5 Black or African American, non-Hispanic/Latino; 2 American Indian or Alaska Native, non-Hispanic/Latino; 2 Asian, non-Hispanic/Latino; 85 Hispanic/Latino; 3 Two or more races, non-Hispanic/Latino), 10 international. Average age 32. 139 applicants, 62% accepted, 23 enrolled. In 2016, 46 master's awarded. *Degree requirements:* For master's, comprehensive exam, thesis optional. *Entrance requirements:* For master's, GMAT or GRE (depending upon undergraduate or graduate degree institution and GPA), minimum GPA of 3.5 from AACSB international or ACBSP-accredited institution or graduate degree from regionally-accredited U.S. university (without GMAT or GRE). Additional exam requirements/recommendations for international students: Required—TOEFL (minimum score 550 paper-based; 79 iBT), IELTS (minimum score 6.5). *Application deadline:* For fall admission, 7/15 priority date for domestic students, 4/15 priority date for international students; for spring admission, 4/15 priority date for domestic students, 9/15 priority date for international students; for summer admission, 4/15 for domestic students, 1/15 for international students. Applications are processed on a rolling basis. Application fee: $40 ($50 for international students). Electronic applications accepted. *Expenses:* Tuition, state resident: full-time $4086. Tuition, nonresident: full-time $14,254. *Required fees:* $853. Tuition and fees vary according to course load. *Financial support:* In 2016–17, 39 students received support, including 1 fellowship (averaging $4,088 per year); Federal Work-Study, institutionally sponsored loans, scholarships/grants, health care benefits, and unspecified assistantships also available. Financial award application deadline: 3/1. *Unit head:* Dr. Kathleen Brook, Associate Dean, 575-646-5431, Fax: 575-646-6155, E-mail: kbrook@nmsu.edu. *Application contact:* John Shonk, MBA Advisor, 575-646-8003, Fax: 575-646-7977, E-mail: mbaprog@nmsu.edu.
Website: http://business.nmsu.edu/mba

The New School, The New School for Social Research, Department of Economics, New York, NY 10003. Offers economics (M Phil, MA, MS, PhD); global political economy and finance (MA). *Program availability:* Part-time. *Faculty:* 5 full-time (1 woman), 12 part-time/adjunct (4 women). *Students:* 82 full-time (26 women), 21 part-time (6 women); includes 15 minority (5 Black or African American, non-Hispanic/Latino; 4 Asian, non-Hispanic/Latino; 6 Hispanic/Latino), 53 international. Average age 31. 143 applicants, 69% accepted, 18 enrolled. In 2016, 21 master's, 11 doctorates awarded. Terminal master's awarded for partial completion of doctoral program. *Degree requirements:* For master's, mentored research/internship, exam; for doctorate, one foreign language, comprehensive exam, thesis/dissertation. *Entrance requirements:* For master's, GRE, letters of recommendation, writing sample, essays, unofficial transcript; for doctorate, letters of recommendation, writing sample, essays, unofficial transcript. Additional exam requirements/recommendations for international students: Required—TOEFL (minimum score 100 iBT), IELTS (minimum score 7), PTE (minimum score 68). *Application deadline:* For fall admission, 5/5 priority date for domestic and international students; for spring admission, 10/15 priority date for domestic and international students. Applications are processed on a rolling basis. Application fee: $50. Electronic applications accepted. *Expenses:* Contact institution. *Financial support:* Fellowships, research assistantships, teaching assistantships, career-related internships or fieldwork, Federal Work-Study, scholarships/grants, and tuition waivers (full and partial) available. Support available to part-time students. Financial award application deadline: 2/1; financial award applicants required to submit FAFSA. *Faculty research:* Keynesian and post-Keynesian economics; classical political economy of Smith, Ricardo, and Marx; structuralist and institutionalist approaches to economics, and neoclassical economics;. *Unit head:* Dr. William Milberg, Dean, The New School for Social Research, 212-229-5777, E-mail: milbergw@newschool.edu. *Application contact:* Dana Messinger, Director of Graduate Admission, 212-229-5150 Ext. 2300, E-mail: socialresearchadmit@newschool.edu.
Website: http://www.newschool.edu/

New York Institute of Technology, School of Management, Department of Business Administration, Old Westbury, NY 11568-8000. Offers executive (MBA); management (MBA), including finance, marketing, operations and supply chain management; professional accounting (MBA). *Accreditation:* AACSB. *Program availability:* Part-time, evening/weekend. *Faculty:* 25 full-time (4 women), 20 part-time/adjunct (6 women). *Students:* 377 full-time (161 women), 149 part-time (88 women); includes 60 minority (17 Black or African American, non-Hispanic/Latino; 1 American Indian or Alaska Native, non-Hispanic/Latino; 28 Asian, non-Hispanic/Latino; 11 Hispanic/Latino; 2 Native Hawaiian or other Pacific Islander, non-Hispanic/Latino; 1 Two or more races, non-Hispanic/Latino), 446 international. Average age 26. 804 applicants, 68% accepted, 215 enrolled. In 2016, 193 master's awarded. *Entrance requirements:* For master's, bachelor's degree; minimum undergraduate GPA of 3.0. Additional exam requirements/recommendations for international students: Required—TOEFL (minimum score 79 iBT), IELTS (minimum score 6). *Application deadline:* Applications are processed on a rolling basis. Application fee: $50. Electronic applications accepted. *Expenses:* $1,215 per credit. *Financial support:* Career-related internships or fieldwork, Federal Work-Study, scholarships/grants, tuition waivers (full and partial), and unspecified assistantships available. Support available to part-time students. Financial award application deadline: 3/1; financial award applicants required to submit FAFSA. *Faculty research:* Accounting, economics, finance, management, marketing. *Unit head:* Dr. Jess Boronico, Dean, 516-686-7838, E-mail: som@nyit.edu. *Application contact:* Alice Dolitsky, Director, Graduate Admissions, 516-686-7520, Fax: 516-686-1116, E-mail: nyitgrad@nyit.edu.
Website: http://www.nyit.edu/degrees/management_mba

New York University, Leonard N. Stern School of Business, Department of Finance, New York, NY 10012-1019. Offers MBA, PhD. *Faculty research:* Derivative securities, pricing of assets, credit risk, portfolio management, international finance.

New York University, Polytechnic School of Engineering, Department of Finance and Risk Engineering, New York, NY 10012-1019. Offers financial engineering (MS, Advanced Certificate), including capital markets (MS), computational finance (MS), financial technology (MS); financial technology management (Advanced Certificate); organizational behavior (Advanced Certificate); risk management (Advanced Certificate); technology management (Advanced Certificate). MS program also offered in Manhattan. *Program availability:* Part-time, evening/weekend. *Degree requirements:* For master's, comprehensive exam (for some programs), thesis (for some programs). *Entrance requirements:* For master's, GMAT, minimum B average in undergraduate course work. Additional exam requirements/recommendations for international students: Required—TOEFL (minimum score 550 paper-based; 80 iBT); Recommended—IELTS (minimum score 6.5). Electronic applications accepted. *Faculty research:* Optimal control theory, general modeling and analysis, risk parity optimality, a new algorithmic approach to entangled political economy.

New York University, School of Continuing and Professional Studies, Schack Institute of Real Estate, Program in Real Estate, New York, NY 10012-1019. Offers finance and investment (MS); real estate (Advanced Certificate); real estate management (MS). *Program availability:* Part-time, evening/weekend. *Degree requirements:* For master's, thesis, capstone. *Entrance requirements:* For master's, GRE or GMAT (only upon request), bachelor's degree, resume with relevant professional work, internship or volunteer experience, two letters of recommendation, statement of purpose. Additional exam requirements/recommendations for international students: Required—TOEFL (minimum score 600 paper-based; 100 iBT), IELTS (minimum score 7). Electronic applications accepted. *Faculty research:* Economics and market cycles, international property rights, comparative metropolitan economies, current market trends.

New York University, School of Continuing and Professional Studies, Tisch Center for Hospitality and Tourism, Program in Hospitality Industry Studies, New York, NY 10012-1019. Offers brand strategy (MS); hospitality industry studies (Advanced Certificate); hotel finance (MS); lodging operations (MS); revenue management (MS). *Program availability:* Part-time, evening/weekend. *Degree requirements:* For master's, thesis. *Entrance requirements:* For master's, GRE or GMAT (only upon request), bachelor's degree, resume with relevant professional work, internship or volunteer experience, two letters of recommendation, statement of purpose. Additional exam requirements/recommendations for international students: Required—TOEFL (minimum score 600 paper-based; 100 iBT), IELTS (minimum score 7). Electronic applications accepted.

Niagara University, Graduate Division of Business Administration, Niagara University, NY 14109. Offers accounting (MBA); business administration (MBA); finance (MBA, MS); financial planning (MBA); healthcare administration (MBA, MHA); human resources (MBA); international business (MBA); marketing (MBA); professional accountancy (MBA); strategic management (MBA); supply chain management (MBA). *Accreditation:* AACSB. *Program availability:* Part-time, evening/weekend. *Students:* 172 full-time (69 women), 65 part-time (36 women); includes 25 minority (4 Black or African American, non-Hispanic/Latino; 7 Asian, non-Hispanic/Latino; 7 Hispanic/Latino; 1 Native Hawaiian or other Pacific Islander, non-Hispanic/Latino; 6 Two or more races, non-Hispanic/Latino), 76 international. Average age 27. In 2016, 107 master's awarded. *Entrance requirements:* For master's, GMAT. Additional exam requirements/recommendations for international students: Required—TOEFL (minimum score 550 paper-based; 79 iBT), IELTS (minimum score 6). *Application deadline:* For fall admission, 8/1 for domestic students; for spring admission, 11/1 for domestic students. Applications are processed on a rolling basis. Electronic applications accepted. *Expenses:* $870 per credit hour. *Financial support:* Fellowships, research assistantships, career-related internships or fieldwork, and Federal Work-Study available. Support available to part-time students. Financial award application deadline: 4/15; financial award applicants required to submit FAFSA. *Faculty research:* Capital flows, Federal Reserve policy, human resource management, public policy, issues in marketing, auctions, economics of information, risk and capital markets, management strategy, consumer behavior, Internet and social media marketing. *Unit head:* Dr. Paul Richardson, MBA Director/Chair of the Marketing Department, 716-286-8169, Fax: 716-286-8206, E-mail: psr@niagara.edu. *Application contact:* Evan Pierce, Associate Director for Graduate Recruitment, 716-286-8769, Fax: 716-286-8170, E-mail: epierce@niagara.edu.
Website: http://mba.niagara.edu

North Central College, School of Graduate and Professional Studies, Program in Business Administration, Naperville, IL 60566-7063. Offers change management (MBA); finance (MBA); human resource management (MBA); management (MBA). *Program availability:* Part-time, evening/weekend. *Faculty:* 15 full-time (9 women), 13 part-time/adjunct (5 women). *Students:* 30 full-time (14 women), 46 part-time (22 women); includes 11 minority (4 Black or African American, non-Hispanic/Latino; 6 Hispanic/Latino; 1 Two or more races, non-Hispanic/Latino), 6 international. Average age 29. 104 applicants, 50% accepted, 31 enrolled. In 2016, 45 master's awarded. *Degree requirements:* For master's, thesis optional, project. *Entrance requirements:* For master's, interview. Additional exam requirements/recommendations for international students: Required—TOEFL (minimum score 550 paper-based; 80 iBT), IELTS (minimum score 6.5). *Application deadline:* For fall admission, 8/15 for domestic students, 7/15 for international students; for winter admission, 12/1 for domestic students, 11/1 for international students; for spring admission, 2/1 for domestic students, 12/1 for international students. Applications are processed on a rolling basis. Application fee: $25. Electronic applications accepted. Application fee is waived when completed online. *Expenses:* Contact institution. *Financial support:* Scholarships/grants available. Support available to part-time students. Financial award applicants required to submit FAFSA. *Unit head:* Dr. Mary Galvan, Chair of Department of Management and Marketing, 630-637-5473, E-mail: mtgalvan@noctrl.edu. *Application contact:* Wendy Kulpinski, Director of Graduate and Continuing Education Admission, 630-637-5808, Fax: 630-637-5844, E-mail: wekulpinski@noctrl.edu.

Northeastern Illinois University, College of Graduate Studies and Research, College of Business and Management, Chicago, IL 60625-4699. Offers accounting (MSA); business administration (MBA); finance (MBA); management (MBA); marketing (MBA). *Program availability:* Part-time, evening/weekend. *Degree requirements:* For master's, thesis optional. *Entrance requirements:* For master's, GMAT, minimum GPA of 2.75. Additional exam requirements/recommendations for international students: Required—TOEFL (minimum score 550 paper-based; 79 iBT). Electronic applications accepted. *Faculty research:* Perception of accountants and non-accountants toward the future of the accounting industry, asynchronous learning outcomes, cost and efficiency of financial markets, impact of deregulation on airline industry, analysis of derivational instruments.

Northeastern State University, College of Business and Technology, Program in Accounting and Financial Analysis, Tahlequah, OK 74464-2399. Offers MS. *Program availability:* Part-time, evening/weekend. *Faculty:* 6 full-time (1 woman). *Students:* 6 full-time (1 woman), 59 part-time (31 women); includes 21 minority (2 Black or African American, non-Hispanic/Latino; 9 American Indian or Alaska Native, non-Hispanic/Latino; 5 Hispanic/Latino; 5 Two or more races, non-Hispanic/Latino), 2 international. Average age 33. In 2016, 21 master's awarded. *Entrance requirements:* For master's, GMAT. Additional exam requirements/recommendations for international students: Required—TOEFL. *Application deadline:* For fall admission, 6/1 priority date for domestic students. Applications are processed on a rolling basis. Application fee: $25. Electronic applications accepted. *Expenses:* Tuition, state resident: full-time $2816; part-time $216.60 per credit hour. Tuition, nonresident: full-time $6365; part-time $489.60 per credit hour. *Required fees:* $37.40 per credit hour. *Faculty research:* Information systems and organizational performance, capital markets, sustainability. *Unit head:* Dr. Justin Halpern, Department Chair, 918-449-6525, E-mail: halpernj@nsuok.edu. *Application contact:* Josh McCollum, Graduate Coordinator, 918-444-2093, E-mail: mccolluj@nsuok.edu.
Website: http://academics.nsuok.edu/businesstechnology/Graduate/MAFA.aspx

Northeastern University, D'Amore-McKim School of Business, Boston, MA 02115-5096. Offers accounting (MS); business administration (EMBA, MBA); finance (MS); innovation (MS); international business (MS); international management (MS); taxation (MS); technological entrepreneurship (MS); JD/MBA; LL M/MBA; MBA/MSN; MS/MBA. *Accreditation:* AACSB. *Program availability:* Part-time, evening/weekend, online learning. *Faculty:* 185 full-time (66 women), 57 part-time/adjunct (13 women). *Students:* 379 full-time (180 women), 1,182 part-time (514 women). In 2016, 800 master's awarded. *Entrance requirements:* For master's, GMAT or GRE. Application fee: $75. Electronic applications accepted. *Expenses:* Contact institution. *Financial support:* Scholarships/grants available. Financial award applicants required to submit FAFSA. *Unit head:* Dr. Hugh Courtney, Dean, D'Amore-McKim School of Business. *Application contact:* Evelyn Tate, Director, Graduate Recruitment and Admissions, 617-373-3258, Fax: 617-373-8564, E-mail: e.tate@northeastern.edu.
Website: http://damore-mckim.northeastern.edu/

Northern State University, MS Program in Banking and Financial Services, Aberdeen, SD 57401-7198. Offers MS. *Program availability:* Part-time, online learning. *Degree requirements:* For master's, capstone course. *Entrance requirements:* For master's, GMAT or GRE, minimum GPA of 2.75. Additional exam requirements/recommendations for international students: Required—TOEFL (minimum score 550 paper-based; 78 iBT), IELTS (minimum score 6). Electronic applications accepted.

North Greenville University, T. Walter Brashier Graduate School, Greer, SC 29651. Offers Christian ministry (MCM, D Min); education (M Ed, MAT); financial planning (MBA); human resources (MBA). *Program availability:* Part-time, evening/weekend, online learning. *Degree requirements:* For master's, comprehensive exam (for some programs), thesis or alternative, capstone course. *Entrance requirements:* For master's, minimum GPA of 2.25 overall, 2.5 in major; for doctorate, MAT. Additional exam requirements/recommendations for international students: Required—TOEFL (minimum score 550 paper-based). Electronic applications accepted. *Faculty research:* Organizational behavior, church growth, homiletics, human resources, business strategy.

Northwestern University, The Graduate School, Kellogg School of Management, Department of Finance, Evanston, IL 60208. Offers PhD. Admissions and degree offered through The Graduate School. *Degree requirements:* For doctorate, comprehensive exam, thesis/dissertation. *Entrance requirements:* For doctorate, GMAT or GRE General Test, 2 years of undergraduate course work in mathematics. Additional exam requirements/recommendations for international students: Required—TOEFL.

Electronic applications accepted. *Faculty research:* Corporate finance, asset pricing, international finance, micro-structure, empirical finance.

Northwestern University, The Graduate School, Kellogg School of Management, Management Programs, Evanston, IL 60208. Offers accounting information and management (MBA, PhD); analytical finance (MBA); business administration (MBA); decision sciences (MBA); entrepreneurship and innovation (MBA); finance (MBA, PhD); health enterprise management (MBA); human resources management (MBA); international business (MBA); management and organizations (MBA, PhD); management and organizations and sociology (PhD); management and strategy (MBA); management studies (MS); managerial analytics (MBA); managerial economics (MBA); managerial economics and strategy (PhD); marketing (MBA, PhD); marketing management (MBA); media management (MBA); operations management (MBA, PhD); real estate (MBA); social enterprise at Kellogg (MBA); JD/MBA. *Program availability:* Part-time, evening/weekend. Terminal master's awarded for partial completion of doctoral program. *Degree requirements:* For doctorate, thesis/dissertation, 2 years of coursework, qualifying (field) exam and candidacy, summer research papers and presentations to faculty, proposal defense, final exam/defense. *Entrance requirements:* For master's, GMAT, GRE, interview, 2 letters of recommendation, college transcripts, resume, essays, Kellogg honor code; for doctorate, GMAT, GRE, statement of purpose, transcripts, 2 letters of recommendation, resume, interview. Additional exam requirements/recommendations for international students: Required—TOEFL, IELTS. Electronic applications accepted. *Expenses:* Contact institution. *Faculty research:* Business cycles and international finance, health policy, networks, non-market strategy, consumer psychology.

Norwich University, College of Graduate and Continuing Studies, Master of Business Administration Program, Northfield, VT 05663. Offers construction management (MBA); energy management (MBA); finance (MBA); logistics (MBA); organizational leadership (MBA); project management (MBA); supply chain management (MBA). *Accreditation:* ACBSP. *Program availability:* Evening/weekend, online only, mostly all online with a week-long residency requirement. *Faculty:* 24 part-time/adjunct (5 women). *Students:* 228 full-time (54 women); includes 54 minority (23 Black or African American, non-Hispanic/Latino; 1 American Indian or Alaska Native, non-Hispanic/Latino; 6 Asian, non-Hispanic/Latino; 20 Hispanic/Latino; 1 Native Hawaiian or other Pacific Islander, non-Hispanic/Latino; 3 Two or more races, non-Hispanic/Latino), 2 international. Average age 36. 74 applicants, 100% accepted, 57 enrolled. In 2016, 135 master's awarded. *Degree requirements:* For master's, comprehensive exam. *Entrance requirements:* For master's, minimum undergraduate GPA of 2.75. Additional exam requirements/recommendations for international students: Required—TOEFL (minimum score 550 paper-based; 80 iBT), IELTS (minimum score 6.5). *Application deadline:* For fall admission, 8/14 for domestic and international students; for winter admission, 11/13 for domestic and international students; for spring admission, 2/12 for domestic and international students; for summer admission, 6/5 for domestic and international students. Electronic applications accepted. *Expenses:* Contact institution. *Financial support:* In 2016–17, 113 students received support. Scholarships/grants available. Financial award application deadline: 8/4; financial award applicants required to submit FAFSA. *Unit head:* Dr. Jose Cordova, Program Director, 802-485-2567, Fax: 802-485-2533, E-mail: jcordova@norwich.edu. *Application contact:* Admissions Advisor, 800-460-5597 Ext. 3376, Fax: 802-485-2533, E-mail: mba@online.norwich.edu.
Website: https://online.norwich.edu/degree-programs/masters/master-business-administration/overview

Notre Dame de Namur University, Division of Academic Affairs, School of Business and Management, Program in Business Administration, Belmont, CA 94002-1908. Offers business administration (MBA); entrepreneurship (MBA); finance (MBA); human resource management (MBA); marketing (MBA); media and promotion (MBA); technology and operations management (MBA). *Accreditation:* ACBSP. *Program availability:* Part-time, evening/weekend. *Entrance requirements:* For master's, minimum GPA of 2.5. Additional exam requirements/recommendations for international students: Required—TOEFL (minimum score 550 paper-based; 79 iBT). Electronic applications accepted.

Nova Southeastern University, H. Wayne Huizenga College of Business and Entrepreneurship, Fort Lauderdale, FL 33314-7796. Offers accounting (M Acc); business intelligence/analytics (MBA); entrepreneurship (MBA); finance (MBA); human resource management (MBA); international business (MBA); management (MBA); marketing (MBA); process improvement (MBA); public administration (MPA); real estate development (MS); sport revenue generation (MBA); supply chain management (MBA); taxation (M Tax). *Program availability:* Part-time, evening/weekend, 100% online, blended/hybrid learning. *Faculty:* 65 full-time (26 women), 111 part-time/adjunct (74 women). *Students:* 2,242 full-time (1,400 women), 425 part-time (239 women); includes 1,798 minority (734 Black or African American, non-Hispanic/Latino; 5 American Indian or Alaska Native, non-Hispanic/Latino; 110 Asian, non-Hispanic/Latino; 890 Hispanic/Latino; 2 Native Hawaiian or other Pacific Islander, non-Hispanic/Latino; 57 Two or more races, non-Hispanic/Latino), 255 international. Average age 34. 1,422 applicants, 64% accepted, 672 enrolled. In 2016, 971 master's awarded. *Degree requirements:* For master's, thesis optional. *Entrance requirements:* For master's, GMAT or GRE (depending on undergraduate GPA), official transcripts from all schools attended while in pursuit of bachelor's degree; minimum GPA of 2.5 from regionally-accredited institution. Additional exam requirements/recommendations for international students: Required—TOEFL (minimum score 550 paper-based; 79 iBT), IELTS (minimum score 6), PTE (minimum score 54). *Application deadline:* For fall admission, 8/5 priority date for domestic students, 7/29 priority date for international students; for winter admission, 12/16 priority date for domestic students, 12/9 priority date for international students; for summer admission, 4/21 priority date for domestic and international students. Applications are processed on a rolling basis. Application fee: $50. Electronic applications accepted. *Expenses:* Contact institution. *Financial support:* In 2016–17, 325 students received support. Federal Work-Study and scholarships/grants available. Support available to part-time students. Financial award application deadline: 4/15; financial award applicants required to submit FAFSA. *Faculty research:* Reputation management, call centers, international social capital, corporate earnings guidance, corporate governance. *Unit head:* Dr. J. Preston Jones, Dean, 954-262-5127, E-mail: prestonj@nova.edu. *Application contact:* Zeida Rodriguez, Associate Director of Enrollment Services, 954-262-5163, Fax: 954-262-3822, E-mail: zeida@nova.edu.
Website: http://www.huizenga.nova.edu

Oakland University, Graduate Study and Lifelong Learning, School of Business Administration, Department of Accounting and Finance, Rochester, MI 48309-4401. Offers accounting (M Acc, Certificate); finance (Certificate).

Ohio Christian University, Graduate Programs, Circleville, OH 43113-9487. Offers accounting (MBA); business administration (MBA); digital marketing (MBA); finance (MBA); healthcare management (MBA); human resources (MBA); management (MM); organizational leadership (MBA); pastoral care and counseling (MAM); practical theology (MAM).

Ohio Dominican University, Division of Business, Program in Business Administration, Columbus, OH 43219-2099. Offers accounting (MBA); data analytics (MBA); finance (MBA); leadership (MBA); risk management (MBA); sport management (MBA). *Program availability:* Part-time, evening/weekend, 100% online, blended/hybrid learning. *Faculty:* 8 full-time (4 women), 17 part-time/adjunct (3 women). *Students:* 63 full-time (26 women), 112 part-time (59 women); includes 50 minority (29 Black or African American, non-Hispanic/Latino; 2 American Indian or Alaska Native, non-Hispanic/Latino; 6 Asian, non-Hispanic/Latino; 6 Hispanic/Latino; 1 Native Hawaiian or other Pacific Islander, non-Hispanic/Latino; 6 Two or more races, non-Hispanic/Latino), 7 international. Average age 31. 65 applicants, 51% accepted, 26 enrolled. In 2016, 120 master's awarded. *Entrance requirements:* For master's, minimum overall GPA of 3.0 in undergraduate degree from regionally-accredited institution or 2.75 in last 60 semester hours of bachelor's degree. Additional exam requirements/recommendations for international students: Required—TOEFL (minimum score 550 paper-based), IELTS (minimum score 6.5). *Application deadline:* For fall admission, 8/15 for domestic students, 6/10 for international students; for spring admission, 1/4 for domestic students, 11/2 for international students; for summer admission, 5/30 for domestic students. Applications are processed on a rolling basis. Application fee: $25. Electronic applications accepted. *Expenses:* $590 per credit hour; $225 fees per semester. *Financial support:* Applicants required to submit FAFSA. *Unit head:* Dr. Steve Vickner, Director of Master of Business Administration Program, 614-251-4569, E-mail: vickners@ohiodominican.edu. *Application contact:* John W. Naughton, Director for Graduate Admissions, 614-251-4721, Fax: 614-251-6654, E-mail: grad@ohiodominican.edu.
Website: http://www.ohiodominican.edu/academics/graduate/mba

The Ohio State University, Graduate School, Max M. Fisher College of Business, Program in Finance, Columbus, OH 43210. Offers MF. *Students:* 45 full-time (24 women), 33 international. Average age 24. In 2016, 50 master's awarded. *Entrance requirements:* For master's, GMAT (preferred with minimum score of 550 recommended, 600 preferred) or GRE. Additional exam requirements/recommendations for international students: Required—TOEFL (minimum score 600 paper-based; 100 iBT). *Application deadline:* For fall admission, 11/15 priority date for domestic and international students; for spring admission, 10/1 for domestic students. Applications are processed on a rolling basis. Application fee: $60 ($70 for international students). Electronic applications accepted. *Financial support:* Fellowships with tuition reimbursements available. *Unit head:* George Pinteris, Graduate Studies Chair, 614-292-4334, E-mail: pinteris.1@osu.edu. *Application contact:* Graduate and Professional Admissions, 614-292-9444, Fax: 614-292-3895, E-mail: gpadmissions@osu.edu.
Website: http://fisher.osu.edu/smf

Ohio University, Graduate College, College of Arts and Sciences, Department of Economics, Athens, OH 45701-2979. Offers applied economics (MA); financial economics (MFE). *Program availability:* Part-time, evening/weekend. *Degree requirements:* For master's, thesis or alternative. *Entrance requirements:* For master's, GRE or GMAT (recommended), minimum GPA of 3.0. Additional exam requirements/recommendations for international students: Required—TOEFL (minimum score 550 paper-based; 80 iBT) or IELTS (minimum score 6.5). *Application deadline:* For fall admission, 2/15 priority date for domestic and international students; for winter admission, 12/1 for domestic students, 10/1 priority date for international students. Application fee: $50 ($55 for international students). Electronic applications accepted. *Financial support:* Research assistantships with full and partial tuition reimbursements, Federal Work-Study, tuition waivers (partial), and unspecified assistantships available. Financial award application deadline: 2/15. *Faculty research:* Macroeconomics, public finance, international economics and finance, monetary theory, healthcare economics. *Unit head:* Dr. Rosmary Rossiter, Chair, 740-593-2040, E-mail: rossiter@ohio.edu. *Application contact:* Dr. K. Doroodian, Graduate Chair, 740-593-2046, E-mail: doroodia@ohio.edu.
Website: http://www.ohiou.edu/economics/

Oklahoma Christian University, Graduate School of Business, Oklahoma City, OK 73136-1100. Offers accounting (M Acc, MBA); financial services (MBA); general business (MBA); health services management (MBA); human resources (MBA); international business (MBA); leadership and organizational development (MBA); marketing (MBA); nonprofit management (MBA); project management (MBA). *Accreditation:* ACBSP. *Program availability:* Part-time, 100% online. *Faculty:* 10 full-time (2 women), 21 part-time/adjunct (2 women). *Students:* 156 full-time (68 women), 137 part-time (73 women). Average age 30. 374 applicants, 213 enrolled. In 2016, 114 master's awarded. *Entrance requirements:* For master's, bachelor's degree. Additional exam requirements/recommendations for international students: Required—TOEFL (minimum score 550 paper-based). Application fee: $25. Electronic applications accepted. *Expenses:* Contact institution. *Unit head:* Dr. Ken Johnson, Chair, 405-425-5567, Fax: 405-425-5585, E-mail: ken.johnson@oc.edu. *Application contact:* Angie Ricketts, Graduate School Admissions Counselor, 405-425-5587, Fax: 405-425-5585, E-mail: angie.ricketts@oc.edu.
Website: http://www.oc.edu/academics/graduate/business/

Oklahoma State University, Spears School of Business, Department of Finance, Stillwater, OK 74078. Offers MS, PhD. *Program availability:* Part-time. *Faculty:* 14 full-time (2 women), 3 part-time/adjunct (0 women). *Students:* 19 full-time (6 women), 3 part-time (0 women); includes 1 minority (Two or more races, non-Hispanic/Latino), 15 international. Average age 26. 24 applicants, 54% accepted, 9 enrolled. In 2016, 5 master's, 3 doctorates awarded. *Degree requirements:* For master's, thesis or alternative; for doctorate, comprehensive exam, thesis/dissertation. *Entrance requirements:* For master's and doctorate, GRE or GMAT. Additional exam requirements/recommendations for international students: Required—TOEFL (minimum score 550 paper-based; 79 iBT). *Application deadline:* For fall admission, 3/1 priority date for international students; for spring admission, 8/1 priority date for international students. Applications are processed on a rolling basis. Application fee: $40 ($75 for international students). Electronic applications accepted. *Expenses:* Tuition, state resident: full-time $3775; part-time $209.70 per credit hour. Tuition, nonresident: full-time $14,851; part-time $825.05 per credit hour. *Required fees:* $2027; $112.60 per credit hour. Tuition and fees vary according to campus/location. *Financial support:* In 2016–17, 19 research assistantships (averaging $11,556 per year), 4 teaching assistantships (averaging $10,928 per year) were awarded; career-related internships or fieldwork, Federal Work-Study, scholarships/grants, health care benefits, tuition waivers (partial), and unspecified assistantships also available. Support available to part-time students. Financial award application deadline: 3/1; financial award applicants required to submit FAFSA. *Faculty research:* Corporate risk management, derivatives banking, investments and securities issuance, corporate governance, banking. *Unit head:* Dr. Betty Simkins, Interim Department Head, 405-744-8625, Fax: 405-744-5180, E-mail: betty.simkins@okstate.edu.
Website: http://spears.okstate.edu/finance/

Old Dominion University, Strome College of Business, Doctoral Program in Business Administration, Norfolk, VA 23529. Offers finance (PhD); information technology (PhD); marketing (PhD); strategic management (PhD). *Accreditation:* AACSB. *Faculty:* 29 full-time (6 women). *Students:* 25 full-time (8 women), 23 part-time (5 women); includes 2 minority (both Asian, non-Hispanic/Latino), 38 international. Average age 34. 71 applicants, 17% accepted, 12 enrolled. In 2016, 15 doctorates awarded. *Degree requirements:* For doctorate, comprehensive exam, thesis/dissertation. *Entrance requirements:* For doctorate, GMAT. Additional exam requirements/recommendations

for international students: Required—TOEFL (minimum score 550 paper-based; 79 iBT). *Application deadline:* For fall admission, 1/1 priority date for domestic and international students. Application fee: $50. Electronic applications accepted. *Expenses:* Tuition, state resident: full-time $8604; part-time $478 per credit hour. Tuition, nonresident: full-time $21,510; part-time $1195 per credit hour. *Required fees:* $66 per semester. Tuition and fees vary according to campus/location, program and reciprocity agreements. *Financial support:* In 2016–17, 36 students received support, including 15 research assistantships with full tuition reimbursements available (averaging $7,500 per year), 12 teaching assistantships with full tuition reimbursements available (averaging $7,500 per year); scholarships/grants and unspecified assistantships also available. Financial award application deadline: 3/1; financial award applicants required to submit FAFSA. *Faculty research:* International business, buyer behavior, financial markets, strategy, operations research. *Unit head:* Dr. John B. Ford, Graduate Program Director, 757-683-3587, Fax: 757-683-4076, E-mail: jbford@odu.edu. *Application contact:* Katrina Davenport, Program Coordinator, 757-683-5138, Fax: 757-683-4076, E-mail: kdavenpo@odu.edu.
Website: http://www.odu.edu/business/academics/graduate/scb-phd

Oral Roberts University, School of Business, Tulsa, OK 74171. Offers accounting (MBA); entrepreneurship (MBA); finance (MBA); international business (MBA); management (MBA); marketing (MBA); non-profit management (MBA); not for profit management (MNM). *Accreditation:* ACBSP. *Program availability:* Part-time, online learning. *Degree requirements:* For master's, thesis optional. *Entrance requirements:* For master's, minimum cumulative GPA of 3.0. Additional exam requirements/recommendations for international students: Required—TOEFL (minimum score 550 paper-based; 79 iBT). Electronic applications accepted. *Faculty research:* Social media, international business and marketing.

Oregon State University, College of Business, Program in Business Administration, Corvallis, OR 97331. Offers business administration (PhD), including accounting, innovation/commercialization; business analytics (MBA); corporate finance (MBA); innovation management (MBA); organizational leadership (MBA); research thesis (MBA); supply chain and logistics management (MBA). *Program availability:* Part-time, blended/hybrid learning. *Faculty:* 47 full-time (13 women), 10 part-time/adjunct (3 women). *Students:* 132 full-time (58 women), 83 part-time (36 women); includes 24 minority (3 Black or African American, non-Hispanic/Latino; 11 Asian, non-Hispanic/Latino; 8 Hispanic/Latino; 1 Native Hawaiian or other Pacific Islander, non-Hispanic/Latino; 1 Two or more races, non-Hispanic/Latino), 91 international. Average age 30. 203 applicants, 38% accepted, 67 enrolled. In 2016, 81 master's awarded. *Entrance requirements:* For master's, GMAT. Additional exam requirements/recommendations for international students: Required—TOEFL (minimum score 91 iBT), IELTS (minimum score 7). *Application deadline:* For fall admission, 2/1 priority date for domestic and international students; for winter admission, 9/15 priority date for domestic and international students; for spring admission, 1/1 priority date for domestic and international students. Applications are processed on a rolling basis. Application fee: $75 ($85 for international students). *Expenses:* $19,143 resident full-time tuition, $32,616 non-resident (for MBA). *Financial support:* Application deadline: 1/15. *Unit head:* Dr. David Baldridge, Director for Business Master's Program, 541-737-6062, E-mail: david.baldridge@bus.oregonstate.edu. *Application contact:* E-mail: osumba@bus.oregonstate.edu.
Website: http://business.oregonstate.edu/graduate-programs

Ottawa University, Graduate Studies-Arizona, Programs in Business, Ottawa, KS 66067-3399. Offers business administration (MBA); finance (MBA); human resources (MA, MBA); leadership (MBA); marketing (MBA). Programs offered in Mesa, Phoenix, Tempe and West Valley, AZ. *Program availability:* Part-time, evening/weekend, online learning. *Degree requirements:* For master's, thesis or alternative. *Entrance requirements:* For master's, minimum undergraduate GPA of 3.0. Additional exam requirements/recommendations for international students: Required—TOEFL (minimum score 550 paper-based). Electronic applications accepted.

Our Lady of the Lake University, School of Business and Leadership, Program in Finance, San Antonio, TX 78207-4689. Offers MBA. *Program availability:* Part-time, evening/weekend. *Faculty:* 2 full-time (both women), 1 part-time/adjunct (0 women). *Students:* 10 full-time (6 women), 2 part-time (1 woman); includes 7 minority (all Hispanic/Latino), 1 international. Average age 35. 3 applicants, 100% accepted, 3 enrolled. In 2016, 8 master's awarded. *Entrance requirements:* For master's, official transcripts showing 6 hours of coursework in economics and 3 hours of coursework in each of the following ares: statistics, management, business law, and finance; résumé including detailed work history describing managerial or professional work experience. Additional exam requirements/recommendations for international students: Required—TOEFL. *Application deadline:* For fall admission, 6/15 for domestic students, 7/15 for international students; for spring admission, 11/15 for domestic and international students; for summer admission, 4/15 for domestic and international students. Applications are processed on a rolling basis. Application fee: $40 ($50 for international students). Electronic applications accepted. Application fee is waived when completed online. *Expenses: Tuition:* Full-time $14,796. Tuition and fees vary according to course load, degree level, campus/location and program. *Financial support:* In 2016–17, 3 students received support. Federal Work-Study, unspecified assistantships, and tuition discounts available. Support available to part-time students. Financial award application deadline: 5/1; financial award applicants required to submit FAFSA. *Application contact:* Office of Graduate Admissions, 210-431-3995, Fax: 210-431-3945, E-mail: gradadm@ollusa.edu.

Pace University, Lubin School of Business, Advanced Professional Certificate Program, New York, NY 10038. Offers business economics (APC); e-business (APC); financial management (APC); international business (APC); international economics (APC); investment management (APC); marketing (APC); public accounting (APC). *Program availability:* Evening/weekend. *Students:* 1 applicant, 100% accepted, 1 enrolled. *Entrance requirements:* For degree, MBA or MS in business discipline, relevant professional experience. Additional exam requirements/recommendations for international students: Required—TOEFL (minimum score 90 iBT), IELTS (minimum score 7) or PTE (minimum score 61). *Application deadline:* For fall admission, 8/1 priority date for domestic students, 6/1 for international students; for spring admission, 12/1 for domestic students, 10/1 for international students. Applications are processed on a rolling basis. Application fee: $70. Electronic applications accepted. *Expenses: Tuition:* Part-time $1195 per credit. *Required fees:* $260 per semester. Tuition and fees vary according to degree level, campus/location and program. *Unit head:* Dr. Jack Yurkiewicz, Director, 212-618-6567, E-mail: jyurkiewicz@pace.edu. *Application contact:* Susan Ford-Goldschein, Director of Graduate Admissions, 212-346-1531, Fax: 212-346-1585, E-mail: graduateadmission@pace.edu.
Website: http://www.pace.edu/lubin/agc

Pace University, Lubin School of Business, Doctor of Professional Studies Program, New York, NY 10038. Offers finance (DPS); management (DPS); marketing (DPS). *Program availability:* Part-time. *Students:* 6 full-time (1 woman), 78 part-time (33 women); includes 26 minority (15 Black or African American, non-Hispanic/Latino; 5 Asian, non-Hispanic/Latino; 5 Hispanic/Latino; 1 Two or more races, non-Hispanic/Latino), 3 international. Average age 49. 32 applicants, 75% accepted, 14 enrolled. In 2016, 4 doctorates awarded. *Degree requirements:* For doctorate, thesis/dissertation, oral and written exam. *Entrance requirements:* For doctorate, MBA or similar master's degree, 10 years of experience in business, transcripts from all accredited colleges/universities attended, 4 letters of recommendation, interview. Additional exam requirements/recommendations for international students: Required—TOEFL (minimum score 90 iBT), IELTS (minimum score 7) or PTE (minimum score 61). *Application deadline:* For fall admission, 6/1 priority date for domestic students, 6/1 for international students. Applications are processed on a rolling basis. Application fee: $70. Electronic applications accepted. *Expenses: Tuition:* Part-time $1195 per credit. *Required fees:* $260 per semester. Tuition and fees vary according to degree level, campus/location and program. *Unit head:* Dr. John P. Dory, Director, Doctoral Program in Business, 212-618-6660, E-mail: jdory@pace.edu. *Application contact:* Margaret Hanson, Program Coordinator for Doctoral Programs, 212-618-6660, E-mail: dps.bus@pace.edu.
Website: http://www.pace.edu/lubin/dps/

Pace University, Lubin School of Business, Financial Management Program, New York, NY 10038. Offers financial management (MBA, MS); financial risk management (MS); international finance (MBA); investment management (MBA, MS). *Program availability:* Evening/weekend. *Students:* 130 full-time (49 women), 62 part-time (34 women); includes 33 minority (4 Black or African American, non-Hispanic/Latino; 20 Asian, non-Hispanic/Latino; 6 Hispanic/Latino; 1 Native Hawaiian or other Pacific Islander, non-Hispanic/Latino; 2 Two or more races, non-Hispanic/Latino), 124 international. Average age 26. 397 applicants, 65% accepted, 84 enrolled. In 2016, 166 master's awarded. *Entrance requirements:* For master's, GMAT, GRE (GMAT not required for MS with passing of Level 1 of Chartered Financial Analyst exam or Level 1 of Financial Risk Manager Exam), undergraduate degree, transcripts from all accredited colleges/universities attended, two letters of recommendation, resume, personal statement. Additional exam requirements/recommendations for international students: Required—TOEFL (minimum score 90 iBT), IELTS (minimum score 7) or PTE (minimum score 61). *Application deadline:* For fall admission, 8/1 priority date for domestic students, 6/1 for international students; for spring admission, 12/1 for domestic students, 10/1 for international students. Applications are processed on a rolling basis. Application fee: $70. Electronic applications accepted. *Expenses: Tuition:* Part-time $1195 per credit. *Required fees:* $260 per semester. Tuition and fees vary according to degree level, campus/location and program. *Financial support:* Research assistantships, career-related internships or fieldwork, Federal Work-Study, and tuition waivers (full and partial) available. Support available to part-time students. Financial award application deadline: 2/15; financial award applicants required to submit FAFSA. *Unit head:* Dr. P. V. Viswanath, Chairperson, 212-618-6518, E-mail: pviswanath@pace.edu. *Application contact:* Susan Ford-Goldschein, Director of Graduate Admissions, 212-346-1531, Fax: 212-346-1585, E-mail: graduateadmissions@pace.edu.
Website: http://www.pace.edu/lubin/financial-management-mba

Pacific Lutheran University, School of Business, Master of Science in Finance Program, Tacoma, WA 98447. Offers MSF. *Entrance requirements:* For master's, GRE or GMAT. Additional exam requirements/recommendations for international students: Required—TOEFL (minimum score 550 paper-based; 88 iBT). Electronic applications accepted. *Expenses:* Contact institution.

Pacific States University, College of Business, Los Angeles, CA 90010. Offers accounting (MBA); finance (MBA); international business (MBA, DBA); management of information technology (MBA); real estate management (MBA). *Program availability:* Part-time, evening/weekend, online learning. *Degree requirements:* For doctorate, comprehensive exam, thesis/dissertation. *Entrance requirements:* For master's, minimum undergraduate GPA of 2.5 during last 90 hours of course work. Additional exam requirements/recommendations for international students: Required—TOEFL (minimum score 500 paper-based; 61 iBT), IELTS (minimum score 5.5).

Pacific University, College of Business, Forest Grove, OR 97116-1797. Offers business administration (MBA); finance (MSF).

Park University, School of Graduate and Professional Studies, Kansas City, MO 54105. Offers adult education (M Ed); business and government leadership (Graduate Certificate); business, government, and global society (MPA); communication and leadership (MA); creative and life writing (Graduate Certificate); disaster and emergency management (MPA, Graduate Certificate); educational leadership (M Ed); finance (MBA, Graduate Certificate); general business (MBA); global business (Graduate Certificate); healthcare administration (MHA); healthcare services management and leadership (Graduate Certificate); international business (MBA); language and literacy (M Ed), including English for speakers of other languages, special reading teacher/literacy coach; leadership of international healthcare organizations (Graduate Certificate); management information systems (MBA, Graduate Certificate); music performance (ADP, Graduate Certificate), including cello (MM, ADP), piano (MM, ADP), viola (MM, ADP), violin (MM, ADP); nonprofit and community services management (MPA); nonprofit leadership (Graduate Certificate); performance (MM), including cello (MM, ADP), piano (MM, ADP), viola (MM, ADP), violin (MM, ADP); public management (MPA); social work (MSW); teacher leadership (M Ed), including curriculum and assessment, instructional leader. *Program availability:* Part-time, evening/weekend, online learning. *Degree requirements:* For master's, comprehensive exam (for some programs), thesis (for some programs), internship (for some programs); exam (for some programs). *Entrance requirements:* For master's, GRE or GMAT (for some programs), teacher certification (for some M Ed programs), letters of recommendation, essay, resume (for some programs). Additional exam requirements/recommendations for international students: Required—TOEFL (minimum score 550 paper-based; 79 iBT), IELTS (minimum score 6). Electronic applications accepted.

Penn State Great Valley, Graduate Studies, Management Division, Malvern, PA 19355-1488. Offers business administration (MBA); cyber security (Certificate); data analytics (Certificate); distributed energy and grid modernization (Certificate); finance (M Fin, Certificate); health sector management (Certificate); human resource management (Certificate); information science (MSIS); leadership development (MLD); new ventures and entrepreneurship (Certificate); professional studies in data analytics (MPS); sustainable management practices (Certificate). *Accreditation:* AACSB. *Unit head:* Dr. James A. Nemes, Chancellor, 610-648-3202, Fax: 610-725-5296. *Application contact:* JoAnn Kelly, Director of Admissions, 610-648-3315, Fax: 610-725-5296, E-mail: jek2@psu.edu.
Website: http://greatvalley.psu.edu/academics/masters-degrees/engineering-management

Penn State Harrisburg, Graduate School, School of Public Affairs, Middletown, PA 17057. Offers criminal justice (MA); health administration (MHA); health administration: long term care (Certificate); homeland security (Certificate); public administration (MPA, PhD); public administration: non-profit administration (Certificate); public budgeting and financial management (Certificate); public sector human resource management (Certificate). *Accreditation:* NASPAA. *Unit head:* Dr. Mukund S. Kulkarni, Chancellor, 717-948-6105, Fax: 717-948-6452. *Application contact:* Robert W. Coffman, Jr., Director of Enrollment Management, Admissions, 717-948-6250, Fax: 717-948-6325, E-mail: hbgadmit@psu.edu.
Website: https://harrisburg.psu.edu/public-affairs

Pepperdine University, Graziadio School of Business and Management, Full-Time MBA Programs, Malibu, CA 90263. Offers accounting (MS); applied analytics (MS); applied finance (MS); business administration (MBA); global business (MS); human resources (MS); international business administration (MBA); management and leadership (MS); organization development (MS); real estate investment and finance (MS); JD/MBA; MBA/MPP. *Accreditation:* AACSB. *Students:* 472 full-time (239 women), 3 part-time (2 women); includes 424 minority (111 Black or African American, non-Hispanic/Latino; 7 American Indian or Alaska Native, non-Hispanic/Latino; 216 Asian, non-Hispanic/Latino; 88 Hispanic/Latino; 2 Two or more races, non-Hispanic/Latino), 47 international. Average age 25. 1,991 applicants, 59% accepted, 238 enrolled. In 2016, 419 master's awarded. *Entrance requirements:* For master's, GMAT or GRE, two letters of recommendation. Additional exam requirements/recommendations for international students: Required—TOEFL. *Application deadline:* For fall admission, 5/1 for domestic students, 4/1 for international students. Application fee: $75. Electronic applications accepted. *Financial support:* Applicants required to submit FAFSA. *Unit head:* Dr. Michael L. Williams, Associate Dean, 310-506-4112, Fax: 310-506-4126, E-mail: michael.williams@pepperdine.edu.
Website: http://bschool.pepperdine.edu/masters-degree/

Polytechnic University of Puerto Rico, Miami Campus, Graduate School, Miami, FL 33166. Offers accounting (MBA); business administration (MBA); construction management (MEM); environmental management (MEM); finance (MBA); human resources management (MBA); logistics and supply chain management (MBA); management of international enterprises (MBA); manufacturing management (MEM); marketing management (MBA); project management (MBA). *Program availability:* Part-time, evening/weekend, online learning. *Entrance requirements:* For master's, minimum GPA of 3.0. Electronic applications accepted.

Polytechnic University of Puerto Rico, Orlando Campus, Graduate School, Orlando, FL 32825. Offers accounting (MBA); business administration (MBA); construction management (MEM); engineering management (MEM); environmental management (MEM); finance (MBA); human resources management (MBA); management of international enterprises (MBA); management of technology (MBA); manufacturing management (MEM). *Program availability:* Part-time, evening/weekend, online learning. *Entrance requirements:* For master's, minimum GPA of 3.0. Additional exam requirements/recommendations for international students: Recommended—TOEFL. Electronic applications accepted.

Pontifical Catholic University of Puerto Rico, College of Business Administration, Program in Finance, Ponce, PR 00717-0777. Offers MBA. *Program availability:* Part-time, evening/weekend. *Degree requirements:* For master's, thesis. *Entrance requirements:* For master's, GRE, interview, minimum GPA of 2.75.

Pontificia Universidad Catolica Madre y Maestra, Graduate School, Faculty of Social and Administrative Sciences, Santiago, Dominican Republic. Offers business administration (MBA), including business development, finance, international business, management skills (M Mgmt, MBA), marketing, operations, strategic cost management, strategy, tourist destination planning and management; law (LL M), including civil law, corporate business law, criminal law, international relations, real estate law; management (M Mgmt), including higher financial management, insurance program administration, management skills (M Mgmt, MBA); psychology (MA), including clinical child and adolescent psychology, forensic psychology; strategic human resources (EMBA).

Portland State University, Graduate Studies, School of Business Administration, Master of Science in Financial Analysis Program, Portland, OR 97207-0751. Offers MSFA. *Program availability:* Part-time, evening/weekend. *Students:* 34 full-time (19 women), 31 part-time (15 women); includes 12 minority (3 Black or African American, non-Hispanic/Latino; 1 American Indian or Alaska Native, non-Hispanic/Latino; 6 Asian, non-Hispanic/Latino; 2 Hispanic/Latino), 24 international. Average age 31. 100 applicants, 50% accepted, 37 enrolled. In 2016, 52 master's awarded. *Entrance requirements:* For master's, GMAT or GRE, minimum GPA of 2.75, 2 recommendations, resume, interview. Additional exam requirements/recommendations for international students: Required—TOEFL (minimum score 550 paper-based; 80 iBT). *Application deadline:* For fall admission, 2/1 priority date for domestic and international students. Applications are processed on a rolling basis. Application fee: $65. Electronic applications accepted. *Expenses:* Contact institution. *Financial support:* Research assistantships with partial tuition reimbursements, career-related internships or fieldwork, Federal Work-Study, and scholarships/grants available. Financial award application deadline: 3/1; financial award applicants required to submit FAFSA. *Unit head:* David Nickel, Academic Director, 503-725-5931, Fax: 503-725-5850, E-mail: nickel@pdx.edu. *Application contact:* Pamela Dusschee, Director, Graduate Business Programs, 503-725-3714, E-mail: pamela.dusschee@pdx.edu.
Website: https://www.pdx.edu/sba/master-of-science-in-finance

Post University, Program in Business Administration, Waterbury, CT 06723-2540. Offers accounting (MSA); business administration (MBA); corporate innovation (MBA); entrepreneurship (MBA); finance (MBA); healthcare (MBA); leadership (MBA); marketing (MBA); project management (MBA). *Accreditation:* ACBSP. *Program availability:* Online learning.

Princeton University, Graduate School, Bendheim Center for Finance, Princeton, NJ 08544-1019. Offers M Fin. *Entrance requirements:* For master's, GRE General Test. Additional exam requirements/recommendations for international students: Required—TOEFL (minimum score 600 paper-based). Electronic applications accepted.

Providence College, School of Business, Providence, RI 02918. Offers accounting (MBA); finance (MBA); international business (MBA); management (MBA); marketing (MBA). *Accreditation:* AACSB. *Program availability:* Part-time, evening/weekend. *Faculty:* 10 full-time (3 women), 5 part-time/adjunct (2 women). *Students:* 84 full-time (39 women), 66 part-time (23 women); includes 15 minority (6 Black or African American, non-Hispanic/Latino; 1 Asian, non-Hispanic/Latino; 8 Hispanic/Latino), 5 international. Average age 26. 116 applicants, 96% accepted, 94 enrolled. In 2016, 80 master's awarded. *Entrance requirements:* For master's, GMAT. Additional exam requirements/recommendations for international students: Required—TOEFL (minimum score 577 paper-based; 90 iBT). *Application deadline:* For fall admission, 5/1 priority date for domestic and international students; for spring admission, 11/1 priority date for domestic and international students; for summer admission, 3/15 priority date for domestic students, 3/15 for international students. Applications are processed on a rolling basis. Application fee: $55. *Expenses:* Contact institution. *Financial support:* Career-related internships or fieldwork, institutionally sponsored loans, and unspecified assistantships available. Support available to part-time students. Financial award application deadline: 8/1; financial award applicants required to submit FAFSA.
Website: http://www.providence.edu/business/Pages/default.aspx

Purdue University, Graduate School, Krannert School of Management, Master of Science in Finance Program, West Lafayette, IN 47907. Offers MSF. *Faculty:* 129 full-time (28 women), 7 part-time/adjunct (1 woman). *Students:* 51 full-time (22 women); includes 1 minority (Asian, non-Hispanic/Latino), 48 international. Average age 24. 241 applicants, 59% accepted, 51 enrolled. In 2016, 24 master's awarded. *Entrance requirements:* For master's, GMAT or GRE, minimum GPA of 3.0, four-year baccalaureate degree, essays, letters of recommendation. Additional exam requirements/recommendations for international students: Required—TOEFL (minimum score 600 paper-based; 93 iBT), IELTS (minimum score 7.5), PTE (minimum score 70). *Application deadline:* For fall admission, 11/15 priority date for domestic students, 11/15 for international students; for winter admission, 1/15 for domestic students, 1/1 for international students; for spring admission, 3/1 for domestic and international students. Applications are processed on a rolling basis. Application fee: $60 ($75 for international students). Electronic applications accepted. *Expenses:* Contact institution. *Financial support:* In 2016–17, 21 students received support. Scholarships/grants available. Financial award application deadline: 3/1; financial award applicants required to submit FAFSA. *Faculty research:* Capital market imperfections and sensitivity of investment to stock prices, identifying beneficial collaboration in decentralized logistics systems, performance periods and the dynamics of the performance-risk relationship, applications of global optimization to process and molecular design. *Unit head:* Dr. David Hummels, Dean/Professor of Economics, 765-494-4366, E-mail: krannertdean@purdue.edu. *Application contact:* Thomas Bates, Associate Director of Admissions, 765-494-0773, Fax: 765-494-9841, E-mail: krannertmasters@purdue.edu.
Website: http://www.krannert.purdue.edu/masters/programs/ms-f/

Queens College of the City University of New York, Division of Social Sciences, Department of Economics, Queens, NY 11367-1597. Offers risk management-accounting (MS); risk management-dynamic finance analysis (MS); risk management-finance (MS). *Degree requirements:* For master's, thesis. *Entrance requirements:* For master's, minimum GPA of 3.0. Additional exam requirements/recommendations for international students: Required—TOEFL (minimum score 100 iBT), IELTS (minimum score 7). *Expenses:* Tuition, state resident: full-time $5065; part-time $425 per credit. Tuition, nonresident: part-time $780 per credit. *Required fees:* $522; $397 per credit. Part-time tuition and fees vary according to course load and program. *Faculty research:* Business economics, urban economic problems, international economics, economics of nonprofit sector.

Queen's University at Kingston, Queens School of Business, Program in Business Administration, Kingston, ON K7L 3N6, Canada. Offers consulting and project management (MBA); finance (MBA); innovation and entrepreneurship (MBA); marketing (MBA). *Degree requirements:* For master's, thesis optional, research project. *Entrance requirements:* For master's, GMAT, minimum B+ average. Additional exam requirements/recommendations for international students: Required—TOEFL. Electronic applications accepted. *Faculty research:* Management fundamentals, strategic thinking, global business, innovation and change, leadership.

Regent's University London, Webster Graduate School, London, United Kingdom. Offers business (MBA); finance (MS); human resources (MA); information technology management (MA); international business (MA); international non-governmental organizations (MA); international relations (MA); management and leadership (MA); marketing (MA). *Program availability:* Part-time.

Regent University, Graduate School, School of Business and Leadership, Virginia Beach, VA 23464-9800. Offers business administration (MBA), including accounting, entrepreneurship, finance and investing, general management, healthcare management (MA, MBA), human resource management, innovation management; leadership (Certificate); organizational leadership (MA, PhD), including ecclesial leadership (PhD), entrepreneurial leadership (PhD), future studies (MA), healthcare management (MA, MBA), human resource development (PhD), interdisciplinary studies (MA), international organizations (MA), leadership coaching and mentoring (MA), not-for-profit management (MA), organizational communication (MA), organizational development consulting (MA); strategic leadership (DSL), including global consulting, leadership coaching, strategic foresight. *Program availability:* Part-time, evening/weekend, 100% online, blended/hybrid learning. *Faculty:* 9 full-time (2 women), 28 part-time/adjunct (10 women). *Students:* 100 full-time (56 women), 1,008 part-time (528 women); includes 562 minority (453 Black or African American, non-Hispanic/Latino; 7 American Indian or Alaska Native, non-Hispanic/Latino; 30 Asian, non-Hispanic/Latino; 51 Hispanic/Latino; 1 Native Hawaiian or other Pacific Islander, non-Hispanic/Latino; 20 Two or more races, non-Hispanic/Latino), 76 international. Average age 40. 1,240 applicants, 45% accepted, 352 enrolled. In 2016, 95 master's, 71 doctorates awarded. *Degree requirements:* For master's, thesis or alternative, 3-credit hour culminating experience; for doctorate, thesis/dissertation. *Entrance requirements:* For master's, college transcripts, resume, essay; for doctorate, college transcripts, resume, essay, writing sample; for Certificate, writing sample, resume, transcripts. Additional exam requirements/recommendations for international students: Required—TOEFL (minimum score 577 paper-based). *Application deadline:* For fall admission, 5/1 priority date for domestic students; for spring admission, 10/1 priority date for domestic students. Applications are processed on a rolling basis. Application fee: $50. Electronic applications accepted. *Expenses:* Contact institution. *Financial support:* In 2016–17, 631 students received support. Career-related internships or fieldwork, scholarships/grants, and unspecified assistantships available. Support available to part-time students. *Faculty research:* Servant leadership, global business, team effectiveness, technology utilization, leadership development. *Unit head:* Dr. Doris Gomez, Dean, 757-352-4686, Fax: 757-352-4634, E-mail: dorigom@regent.edu. *Application contact:* Heidi Cece, Assistant Vice President of Enrollment Management, 800-373-5504, Fax: 757-352-4381, E-mail: admissions@regent.edu.
Website: http://www.regent.edu/sbl/

Regis University, College of Business and Economics, Denver, CO 80221-1099. Offers accounting (MS); executive leadership (Certificate); finance (MS); finance and accounting (MBA); health industry leadership (MBA); human resource management and leadership (MSOL); management (MBA); marketing (MBA); nonprofit leadership (Post-Graduate Certificate); nonprofit management (MNM); nonprofit organizational capacity building (Certificate); operations management (MBA); organizational leadership and management (MSOL); project leadership and management (MS, MSOL); strategic business management (Certificate); strategic human resource integration (Certificate); strategic management (MBA). Programs offered at Colorado Springs Campus, Northwest Denver Campus, Southeast Denver Campus, Fort Collins Campus, Broomfield Campus, Henderson (Nevada) Campus, and Summerlin (Nevada) Campus. *Program availability:* Part-time, evening/weekend, 100% online, blended/hybrid learning. *Faculty:* 15 full-time (5 women), 43 part-time/adjunct (16 women). *Students:* 622 full-time (350 women), 460 part-time (170 women); includes 317 minority (88 Black or African American, non-Hispanic/Latino; 7 American Indian or Alaska Native, non-Hispanic/Latino; 44 Asian, non-Hispanic/Latino; 151 Hispanic/Latino; 1 Native Hawaiian or other Pacific Islander, non-Hispanic/Latino; 26 Two or more races, non-Hispanic/Latino), 44 international. Average age 36. 307 applicants, 73% accepted, 134 enrolled. In 2016, 394 master's awarded. *Degree requirements:* For master's, thesis (for some programs), capstone or final research project. *Entrance requirements:* For master's, official transcript reflecting baccalaureate degree awarded from regionally-accredited college or university, interview, 2 years of full-time related work experience, resume, letters of recommendation. Additional exam requirements/recommendations for international students: Required—TOEFL (minimum score 550 paper-based; 82 iBT). *Application deadline:* For fall admission, 8/15 priority date for domestic students, 8/13 for international students; for winter admission, 10/10 priority date for domestic students, 9/

8 for international students; for spring admission, 1/10 priority date for domestic students, 11/17 for international students; for summer admission, 5/1 priority date for domestic students. Applications are processed on a rolling basis. Application fee: $75. Electronic applications accepted. *Expenses:* $780 per credit hour. *Financial support:* Scholarships/grants available. Financial award application deadline: 4/15; financial award applicants required to submit FAFSA. *Faculty research:* Impact of information technology on small business regulation of accounting, international project financing, mineral development, delivery of healthcare to rural indigenous communities. *Unit head:* Dr. Timothy Keane, Academic Dean. *Application contact:* Cate Clark, Director of Admissions, 303-458-4900, Fax: 303-964-5534, E-mail: ruadmissions@regis.edu.
Website: http://www.regis.edu/CBE.aspx

Rhode Island College, School of Graduate Studies, School of Management, Department of Accounting and Computer Information Systems, Providence, RI 02908-1991. Offers accounting (MP Ac); financial planning (CGS). *Program availability:* Part-time, evening/weekend. *Faculty:* 1 (woman) full-time, 2 part-time/adjunct (1 woman). *Students:* 6 full-time (2 women), 17 part-time (10 women); includes 3 minority (1 Black or African American, non-Hispanic/Latino; 2 Asian, non-Hispanic/Latino). Average age 31. In 2016, 10 master's awarded. *Entrance requirements:* For master's, GMAT (unless applicant is a CPA or has passed a state bar exam); for CGS, GMAT, bachelor's degree from an accredited college or university, official transcripts of all undergraduate and graduate records. Additional exam requirements/recommendations for international students: Recommended—TOEFL (minimum score 550 paper-based; 79 iBT). *Application deadline:* For fall admission, 3/1 for domestic students. Applications are processed on a rolling basis. Application fee: $50. Electronic applications accepted. *Expenses:* Tuition, state resident: full-time $8928; part-time $372 per credit. Tuition, nonresident: full-time $17,376; part-time $724 per credit. *Required fees:* $604; $22 per credit. One-time fee: $74. *Financial support:* In 2016–17, 1 teaching assistantship with full tuition reimbursement (averaging $1,500 per year) was awarded; Federal Work-Study, scholarships/grants, and health care benefits also available. Support available to part-time students. Financial award application deadline: 5/15; financial award applicants required to submit FAFSA. *Unit head:* Prof. Jane Przybyla, Chair, 401-456-8036. *Application contact:* Graduate Studies, 401-456-8700.
Website: http://www.ric.edu/accountingComputerInformationSystems/

Robert Morris University Illinois, Morris Graduate School of Management, Chicago, IL 60605. Offers accounting (MBA); accounting/finance (MBA); business analytics (MIS); design and media (MM); design management (MM); educational technology (MM); health care administration (MM); higher education administration (MM); human resource management (MBA); information security (MIS); information systems (MBA, MIS); law enforcement administration (MM); management (MBA); management/finance (MBA); management/human resource management (MBA); mobile computing (MIS); sports administration (MM). *Program availability:* Part-time, evening/weekend. *Faculty:* 4 full-time (1 woman), 25 part-time/adjunct (5 women). *Students:* 196 full-time (98 women), 151 part-time (85 women); includes 200 minority (114 Black or African American, non-Hispanic/Latino; 17 Asian, non-Hispanic/Latino; 67 Hispanic/Latino; 2 Two or more races, non-Hispanic/Latino), 23 international. Average age 33. 174 applicants, 61% accepted, 97 enrolled. In 2016, 190 master's awarded. *Entrance requirements:* For master's, official transcripts and letters of recommendation (for some programs); written personal statement. Additional exam requirements/recommendations for international students: Required—TOEFL (minimum score 550 paper-based). *Application deadline:* Applications are processed on a rolling basis. Application fee: $20 ($100 for international students). Electronic applications accepted. *Expenses: Tuition:* Full-time $16,500; part-time $2750 per course. *Financial support:* In 2016–17, 444 students received support. Federal Work-Study, scholarships/grants, and unspecified assistantships available. Support available to part-time students. Financial award applicants required to submit FAFSA. *Unit head:* Kayed Akkawi, Dean, 312-935-6050, Fax: 312-935-6020, E-mail: kakkawi@robertmorris.edu. *Application contact:* Danielle Naffziger, Vice President of Marketing and Enrollment, 312-935-4812, Fax: 312-935-6020, E-mail: dnaffziger@robertmorris.edu.

Rochester Institute of Technology, Graduate Enrollment Services, Saunders College of Business, Accounting and Finance Department, MS Program in Finance, Rochester, NY 14623. Offers MS. *Program availability:* Part-time, evening/weekend. *Students:* 21 full-time (9 women), 5 part-time (3 women); includes 1 minority (Hispanic/Latino), 22 international. Average age 26. 117 applicants, 56% accepted, 20 enrolled. In 2016, 10 master's awarded. *Degree requirements:* For master's, comprehensive exam. *Entrance requirements:* For master's, GMAT or GRE, minimum GPA of 3.0 (recommended). Additional exam requirements/recommendations for international students: Required—TOEFL (minimum score 580 paper-based; 92 iBT), IELTS (minimum score 7), PTE (minimum score 63). *Application deadline:* Applications are processed on a rolling basis. Application fee: $60. Electronic applications accepted. *Expenses:* $1,742 per credit hour. *Financial support:* In 2016–17, 3 students received support. Research assistantships with partial tuition reimbursements available, teaching assistantships with partial tuition reimbursements available, career-related internships or fieldwork, scholarships/grants, and unspecified assistantships available. Support available to part-time students. Financial award applicants required to submit FAFSA. *Faculty research:* Trading algorithms, short selling effects, corporate governance effects, optimal incentive compensation contracts, debt contract parameters, tax policy. *Unit head:* Jenna Lenhardt, Graduate Program Director, 585-475-6916, E-mail: jlenhardt@saunders.rit.edu. *Application contact:* Diane Ellison, Associate Vice President, Graduate Enrollment Services, 585-475-2229, Fax: 585-475-7164, E-mail: gradinfo@rit.edu.
Website: http://saunders.rit.edu/programs/graduate/ms_finance.php

Rockhurst University, Helzberg School of Management, Kansas City, MO 64110-2561. Offers accounting (MBA); business intelligence (MBA, Certificate); data science (MBA, Certificate); entrepreneurship (MBA); finance (MBA); fundraising leadership (MBA, Certificate); healthcare management (MBA, Certificate); human capital (Certificate); international business (Certificate); management (MBA, Certificate); nonprofit administration (Certificate); organizational development (Certificate); science leadership (Certificate). *Accreditation:* AACSB. *Program availability:* Part-time, evening/weekend. *Entrance requirements:* For master's, GMAT or GRE. Additional exam requirements/recommendations for international students: Required—TOEFL (minimum score 550 paper-based; 79 iBT). Electronic applications accepted. Application fee is waived when completed online. *Faculty research:* Offshoring/outsourcing, systems analysis/synthesis, work teams, multilateral trade, path dependencies/creation.

Rollins College, Crummer Graduate School of Business, Winter Park, FL 32789-4499. Offers business administration (EDBA); entrepreneurship (MBA); finance (MBA); international business (MBA); management (MBA); marketing (MBA); operations and technology management (MBA). *Accreditation:* AACSB. *Program availability:* Part-time, evening/weekend, online learning. *Faculty:* 22 full-time (5 women), 4 part-time/adjunct (3 women). *Students:* 254 full-time (105 women), 83 part-time (36 women); includes 63 minority (15 Black or African American, non-Hispanic/Latino; 9 Asian, non-Hispanic/Latino; 35 Hispanic/Latino; 4 Two or more races, non-Hispanic/Latino), 48 international. Average age 31. 360 applicants, 74% accepted, 207 enrolled. In 2016, 159 master's awarded. *Degree requirements:* For master's, minimum GPA of 2.85; for doctorate, thesis/dissertation, minimum GPA of 3.0. *Entrance requirements:* For master's, GMAT or GRE, official transcripts, two letters of recommendation, essay, current resume/curriculum vitae, interview; for doctorate, official transcripts, two letters of recommendation, essays, current resume/curriculum vitae, interview. Additional exam requirements/recommendations for international students: Required—TOEFL (minimum score 100 iBT) or IELTS (minimum score 7). *Application deadline:* Applications are processed on a rolling basis. Application fee: $50. Electronic applications accepted. *Expenses:* Contact institution. *Financial support:* In 2016–17, 125 students received support. Federal Work-Study and scholarships/grants available. Support available to part-time students. Financial award applicants required to submit FAFSA. *Faculty research:* Sustainability, world financial markets, international business, market research, strategic marketing. *Unit head:* Deborah Crown, Dean, 407-646-2249, Fax: 407-646-1550, E-mail: dcrown@rollins.edu. *Application contact:* Maralyn E. Graham, Admissions Coordinator, 407-646-2405, Fax: 407-646-1550, E-mail: mbaadmissions@rollins.edu.
Website: http://www.rollins.edu/mba/

Rutgers University–Newark, Graduate School, Program in Management, Newark, NJ 07102. Offers accounting (PhD); accounting information systems (PhD); computer information systems (PhD); finance (PhD); information technology (PhD); international business (PhD); management science (PhD); marketing (PhD); organization management (PhD). Program offered jointly with New Jersey Institute of Technology. *Accreditation:* AACSB. *Degree requirements:* For doctorate, thesis/dissertation, cumulative exams. *Entrance requirements:* For doctorate, GMAT or GRE General Test, minimum undergraduate B average. Additional exam requirements/recommendations for international students: Required—TOEFL. Electronic applications accepted. *Faculty research:* Technology management, leadership and teams, consumer behavior, financial and markets, logistics.

Rutgers University–Newark, Rutgers Business School–Newark and New Brunswick, Doctoral Programs in Management, Newark, NJ 07102. Offers accounting (PhD); accounting information systems (PhD); economics (PhD); finance (PhD); individualized study (PhD); information technology (PhD); international business (PhD); management science (PhD); marketing science (PhD); organizational management (PhD); science, technology and management (PhD); supply chain management (PhD). *Degree requirements:* For doctorate, comprehensive exam, thesis/dissertation. *Entrance requirements:* For doctorate, GRE or GMAT. Additional exam requirements/recommendations for international students: Required—TOEFL (minimum score 550 paper-based; 79 iBT). Electronic applications accepted.

Rutgers University–Newark, Rutgers Business School–Newark and New Brunswick, Program in Financial Analysis, Newark, NJ 07102. Offers MFA. *Entrance requirements:* For master's, GMAT. Additional exam requirements/recommendations for international students: Required—TOEFL.

Rutgers University–Newark, Rutgers Business School–Newark and New Brunswick, Program in Quantitative Finance, Newark, NJ 07102. Offers MQF. *Entrance requirements:* For master's, GMAT (MBA), GRE General Test (MQF). Additional exam requirements/recommendations for international students: Required—TOEFL.

Sacred Heart University, Graduate Programs, Jack Welch College of Business, Department of Finance, Fairfield, CT 06825. Offers administration (DBA); finance and investment management (MS). *Program availability:* Part-time, evening/weekend. *Faculty:* 8 full-time (3 women), 4 part-time/adjunct (2 women). *Students:* 30 full-time (8 women), 41 part-time (15 women); includes 13 minority (8 Black or African American, non-Hispanic/Latino; 2 Asian, non-Hispanic/Latino; 2 Hispanic/Latino; 1 Two or more races, non-Hispanic/Latino), 28 international. Average age 35. 84 applicants, 82% accepted, 40 enrolled. *Degree requirements:* For doctorate, comprehensive exam. *Entrance requirements:* For master's, GMAT or GRE, official transcripts from all institutions attended; for doctorate, GMAT or GRE with master's degree and 5 years' experience. Additional exam requirements/recommendations for international students: Required—TOEFL (minimum score 570 paper-based, 80 iBT), TWE, or IELTS (6.5); Recommended—TSE. *Application deadline:* Applications are processed on a rolling basis. Application fee: $75. Electronic applications accepted. *Expenses:* $10,674 per trimester full-time. *Financial support:* Unspecified assistantships available. Financial award applicants required to submit FAFSA. *Unit head:* Dr. Kwamie Dunbar, Assistant Professor of Finance/Director of MS in Finance and Investment Management, 203-396-8068, E-mail: dunbark@sacredheart.edu. *Application contact:* William Sweeney, Director of Graduate Admissions Operations, 203-365-4827, E-mail: sweeneyw@sacredheart.edu.
Website: http://www.sacredheart.edu/academics/johnfwelchcollegeofbusiness/aboutthecollege/

St. John's University, The Peter J. Tobin College of Business, Department of Economics and Finance, Program in Finance, Queens, NY 11439. Offers finance (MBA); investment management (MS). *Program availability:* Part-time, evening/weekend. *Degree requirements:* For master's, comprehensive exam (for some programs), thesis optional. *Entrance requirements:* For master's, GMAT, 2 letters of recommendation, resume, transcripts, essay. Additional exam requirements/recommendations for international students: Required—TOEFL (minimum score 600 paper-based; 100 iBT), IELTS (minimum score 7). Electronic applications accepted. *Expenses:* Contact institution.

Saint Joseph's University, Erivan K. Haub School of Business, MBA Program, Philadelphia, PA 19131-1395. Offers accounting (MBA, Postbaccalaureate Certificate); business intelligence (MBA); finance (MBA); general business (MBA); health and medical services administration (MBA); international business (MBA); international marketing (MBA); managing human capital (MBA); marketing (MBA); DO/MBA. DO/MBA offered jointly with Philadelphia College of Osteopathic Medicine. *Program availability:* Part-time, evening/weekend, 100% online, blended/hybrid learning. *Faculty:* 31 full-time (10 women), 28 part-time/adjunct (7 women). *Students:* 95 full-time (40 women), 348 part-time (137 women); includes 64 minority (29 Black or African American, non-Hispanic/Latino; 17 Asian, non-Hispanic/Latino; 14 Hispanic/Latino; 1 Native Hawaiian or other Pacific Islander, non-Hispanic/Latino; 3 Two or more races, non-Hispanic/Latino), 47 international. Average age 30. 237 applicants, 60% accepted, 76 enrolled. In 2016, 144 master's awarded. *Degree requirements:* For master's and Postbaccalaureate Certificate, minimum GPA of 3.0. *Entrance requirements:* For master's, GMAT or GRE, 2 letters of recommendation, resume, personal statement, official undergraduate and graduate transcripts; for Postbaccalaureate Certificate, official master's-level transcripts. Additional exam requirements/recommendations for international students: Required—TOEFL (minimum score 550 paper-based, 80 iBT), IELTS (minimum score 6.5), or PTE (minimum score 60). *Application deadline:* For fall admission, 7/15 priority date for domestic students, 5/15 priority date for international students; for spring admission, 11/15 priority date for domestic students, 10/15 priority date for international students; for summer admission, 4/15 priority date for domestic students, 2/15 priority date for international students. Applications are processed on a rolling basis. Application fee: $35. Electronic applications accepted. *Expenses:* $1,003 per credit. *Financial support:* In 2016–17, 105 students received support, including 2 research assistantships with partial tuition reimbursements available (averaging $4,000 per year); scholarships/grants and unspecified assistantships also available. Support available to part-time students. Financial award application deadline: 5/1; financial

award applicants required to submit FAFSA. *Unit head:* Dr. Patricia Rafferty, Director, 610-660-1318, E-mail: praffert@sju.edu. *Application contact:* Kate Sonstein, Program Manager/Recruiter, 610-660-1693, E-mail: kate.sonstein@sju.edu.
Website: http://www.sju.edu/haubmba

Saint Joseph's University, Erivan K. Haub School of Business, MS in Financial Services Program, Philadelphia, PA 19131-1395. Offers MS. *Program availability:* Part-time, evening/weekend. *Faculty:* 16 full-time (4 women), 13 part-time/adjunct (2 women). *Students:* 34 full-time (11 women), 33 part-time (6 women); includes 5 minority (3 Black or African American, non-Hispanic/Latino; 1 Asian, non-Hispanic/Latino; 1 Hispanic/Latino), 38 international. Average age 29. 85 applicants, 58% accepted, 21 enrolled. In 2016, 34 master's awarded. *Degree requirements:* For master's, minimum GPA of 3.0. *Entrance requirements:* For master's, GMAT or GRE, 2 letters of recommendation, resume, personal statement, official undergraduate and graduate transcripts. Additional exam requirements/recommendations for international students: Required—TOEFL (minimum score 550 paper-based, 80 iBT), IELTS (minimum score 6.5), or PTE (minimum score 60). *Application deadline:* For fall admission, 7/15 priority date for domestic students, 5/15 priority date for international students; for spring admission, 11/15 priority date for domestic students, 10/15 priority date for international students; for summer admission, 4/15 priority date for domestic students. Applications are processed on a rolling basis. Application fee: $35. Electronic applications accepted. *Expenses:* $1,003 per credit. *Financial support:* In 2016–17, 38 students received support. Scholarships/grants available. Support available to part-time students. Financial award application deadline: 5/1; financial award applicants required to submit FAFSA. *Unit head:* Jeannine Lajeunesse, Director, 610-660-1626, Fax: 610-660-1599, E-mail: jlajeune@sju.edu. *Application contact:* Kate Sonstein, Program Manager/ Recruiter, 610-660-1693, Fax: 610-660-1599, E-mail: kate.sonstein@sju.edu.
Website: http://www.sju.edu/msfs

Saint Louis University, Graduate Education, John Cook School of Business, Department of Finance, St. Louis, MO 63103. Offers MBA, MSF. *Program availability:* Part-time, evening/weekend. *Degree requirements:* For master's, thesis. *Entrance requirements:* For master's, GMAT or GRE General Test, letters of recommendation, resume. Additional exam requirements/recommendations for international students: Required—TOEFL (minimum score 570 paper-based; 88 iBT). Electronic applications accepted. *Expenses:* Contact institution. *Faculty research:* Market microstructure, corporate governance, banking, portfolio performance and asset allocation.

Saint Mary's College of California, School of Economics and Business Administration, MS in Financial Analysis and Investment Management Program, Moraga, CA 94556. Offers MS. *Expenses:* Contact institution.

Saint Peter's University, Graduate Business Programs, MBA Program, Jersey City, NJ 07306-5997. Offers finance (MBA); health care administration (MBA); human resource management (MBA); international business (MBA); management (MBA); management information systems (MBA); marketing (MBA); risk management (MBA); MBA/MS. *Program availability:* Part-time, evening/weekend. *Entrance requirements:* Additional exam requirements/recommendations for international students: Required—TOEFL. Electronic applications accepted. *Faculty research:* Finance, health care management, human resource management, international business, management, management information systems, marketing, risk management.

St. Thomas Aquinas College, Division of Business Administration, Sparkill, NY 10976. Offers business administration (MBA); finance (MBA); management (MBA); marketing (MBA). *Program availability:* Part-time, evening/weekend. *Entrance requirements:* For master's, GMAT. Additional exam requirements/recommendations for international students: Required—TOEFL. Electronic applications accepted.

Saint Xavier University, Graduate Studies, Graham School of Management, Chicago, IL 60655-3105. Offers employee health benefits (Certificate); finance (MBA); financial fraud examination and management (MBA, Certificate); financial planning (MBA, Certificate); generalist/individualized (MBA); health administration (MBA); managed care (Certificate); management (MBA); marketing (MBA); project management (MBA, Certificate); MBA/MS. *Accreditation:* AACSB; ACBSP. *Program availability:* Part-time, evening/weekend. *Entrance requirements:* For master's, GMAT, minimum GPA of 3.0, 2 years of work experience. Electronic applications accepted. *Expenses:* Contact institution.

Samford University, Brock School of Business, Birmingham, AL 35229. Offers accounting (M Acc); business administration (MBA); entrepreneurship (MBA); finance (MBA); marketing (MBA); JD/M Acc; JD/MBA; MBA/M Acc; MBA/M Div; MBA/MSEM; MBA/Pharm D. *Accreditation:* AACSB. *Program availability:* Part-time-only, evening/ weekend, 100% online, blended/hybrid learning. *Faculty:* 9 full-time (2 women), 3 part-time/adjunct (0 women). *Students:* 87 full-time (33 women), 14 part-time (6 women); includes 10 minority (7 Black or African American, non-Hispanic/Latino; 1 Asian, non-Hispanic/Latino; 1 Hispanic/Latino; 1 Two or more races, non-Hispanic/Latino), 6 international. Average age 28. 148 applicants, 41% accepted, 32 enrolled. In 2016, 63 master's awarded. *Degree requirements:* For master's, capstone course. *Entrance requirements:* For master's, GMAT or GRE. Additional exam requirements/ recommendations for international students: Required—TOEFL (minimum score 90 iBT), IELTS (minimum score 6.5). *Application deadline:* For fall admission, 7/1 for domestic and international students; for spring admission, 12/1 for domestic and international students; for summer admission, 4/1 for domestic and international students. Applications are processed on a rolling basis. Application fee: $35. Electronic applications accepted. *Expenses: Tuition:* Full-time $18,530; part-time $789 per credit hour. *Required fees:* $610. Tuition and fees vary according to course load, degree level, program and student level. *Financial support:* In 2016–17, 55 students received support. Career-related internships or fieldwork, institutionally sponsored loans, scholarships/grants, and tuition waivers (partial) available. Support available to part-time students. Financial award application deadline: 3/1; financial award applicants required to submit FAFSA. *Faculty research:* Entrepreneurship, accounting, finance, marketing, economics. *Total annual research expenditures:* $25,000. *Unit head:* Dr. Barbara Cartledge, Assistant Dean, 205-726-2935, Fax: 205-726-2540, E-mail: bhcartle@ samford.edu. *Application contact:* Elizabeth Anne Gambrell, Assistant Director of Academic Programs, 205-726-2040, Fax: 205-726-2540, E-mail: eagambre@ samford.edu.
Website: http://www.samford.edu/business/

Sam Houston State University, College of Business Administration, Department of General Business and Finance, Huntsville, TX 77341. Offers banking and financial institutions (EMBA); business administration (MBA). *Accreditation:* AACSB. *Program availability:* Part-time, evening/weekend, online learning. *Degree requirements:* For master's, comprehensive exam (for some programs). *Entrance requirements:* For master's, GMAT, interview (for EMBA); resume, transcript(s). Additional exam requirements/recommendations for international students: Required—TOEFL (minimum score 550 paper-based; 79 iBT), IELTS (minimum score 6.5). Electronic applications accepted.

San Diego State University, Graduate and Research Affairs, College of Business Administration, Department of Finance, San Diego, CA 92182. Offers MS. *Program availability:* Part-time, evening/weekend. *Degree requirements:* For master's, thesis or alternative. *Entrance requirements:* For master's, GMAT, resume, letters of reference. Additional exam requirements/recommendations for international students: Required—TOEFL. Electronic applications accepted.

San Francisco State University, Division of Graduate Studies, College of Business, Program in Business Administration, San Francisco, CA 94132-1722. Offers decision sciences/operations research (MBA); ethics and compliance (MBA); finance (MBA); global business and innovation (MBA); healthcare administration (MBA); hospitality and tourism management (MBA); information systems (MBA); leadership (MBA); marketing (MBA); nonprofit and social enterprise leadership (MBA); sustainable business (MBA). *Accreditation:* AACSB. *Program availability:* Part-time, evening/weekend. *Degree requirements:* For master's, thesis, essay test. *Entrance requirements:* For master's, GMAT, minimum GPA of 2.7 in last 60 units. Additional exam requirements/ recommendations for international students: Required—TOEFL (minimum score 550 paper-based). *Application deadline:* For fall admission, 5/1 priority date for domestic students, 4/1 for international students; for spring admission, 11/1 for domestic students, 10/15 for international students. Applications are processed on a rolling basis. Application fee: $55. *Expenses:* Tuition, state resident: full-time $6738. Tuition, nonresident: full-time $15,666. *Required fees:* $1012. Tuition and fees vary according to degree level and program. *Financial support:* Application deadline: 3/1. *Unit head:* Dr. Sanjit Sengupta, Faculty Director, 415-817-4366, Fax: 415-817-4340, E-mail: sengupta@sfsu.edu. *Application contact:* Zandra Tan, EMBA Program Coordinator, 415-817-4360, Fax: 415-817-4340, E-mail: zandra13@sfsu.edu.
Website: http://cob.sfsu.edu/graduate-programs/mba

Santa Clara University, Leavey School of Business, Santa Clara, CA 95053. Offers business administration (MBA); business analytics (MS); finance (MS); information systems (MS); supply chain management and analytics (MS); JD/MBA. *Accreditation:* AACSB. *Program availability:* Part-time, evening/weekend. *Faculty:* 92 full-time (27 women), 44 part-time/adjunct (18 women). *Students:* 330 full-time (192 women), 323 part-time (136 women); includes 190 minority (7 Black or African American, non-Hispanic/Latino; 140 Asian, non-Hispanic/Latino; 28 Hispanic/Latino; 2 Native Hawaiian or other Pacific Islander, non-Hispanic/Latino; 13 Two or more races, non-Hispanic/ Latino), 275 international. Average age 30. 388 applicants, 53% accepted, 107 enrolled. In 2016, 339 master's awarded. *Entrance requirements:* For master's, GMAT or GRE, resume, 2 letters of recommendation, 2 transcripts. Additional exam requirements/ recommendations for international students: Required—TOEFL (minimum score 100 iBT) or IELTS (7.0). Application fee: $100 ($150 for international students). Electronic applications accepted. *Expenses:* $1,022 per unit tuition (for MBA); $1,124 per unit tuition (for other master's programs). *Financial support:* Fellowships, research assistantships, teaching assistantships, career-related internships or fieldwork, Federal Work-Study, scholarships/grants, traineeships, health care benefits, tuition waivers, and unspecified assistantships available. Support available to part-time students. Financial award applicants required to submit FAFSA. *Faculty research:* Intellectual property, research and development, international trade. *Unit head:* Caryn Beck-Dudley, Dean. *Application contact:* Taryn Upchurch, Director, Graduate Admissions and Recruitment, 408-551-7858, E-mail: upchurch@scu.edu.
Website: http://www.scu.edu/business/

Schiller International University, MBA Programs, Florida, Largo, FL 33771. Offers financial planning (MBA); information technology (MBA); international business (MBA); international hotel and tourism management (MBA). *Program availability:* Part-time, evening/weekend, online learning. *Degree requirements:* For master's, thesis optional. *Entrance requirements:* Additional exam requirements/recommendations for international students: Required—TOEFL (minimum score 550 paper-based).

Seattle University, Albers School of Business and Economics, Master of Science in Finance Program, Seattle, WA 98122-1090. Offers MSF, Certificate, JD/MSF, MPAC/ MSF, MSF/MSBA. *Program availability:* Part-time, evening/weekend. *Faculty:* 13 full-time (3 women), 2 part-time/adjunct (1 woman). *Students:* 35 full-time (15 women), 34 part-time (15 women); includes 15 minority (1 Black or African American, non-Hispanic/ Latino; 12 Asian, non-Hispanic/Latino; 1 Hispanic/Latino; 1 Two or more races, non-Hispanic/Latino), 33 international. Average age 27. 67 applicants, 43% accepted, 17 enrolled. In 2016, 21 master's, 13 Certificates awarded. *Entrance requirements:* For master's, GMAT, minimum GPA of 3.0, 2 years of related work experience. Additional exam requirements/recommendations for international students: Required—TOEFL (minimum score 580 paper-based; 92 iBT). *Application deadline:* For fall admission, 8/20 priority date for domestic students, 4/1 priority date for international students; for winter admission, 11/20 priority date for domestic students, 9/1 priority date for international students; for spring admission, 2/20 priority date for domestic students, 12/1 priority date for international students. Applications are processed on a rolling basis. Application fee: $55. Electronic applications accepted. *Expenses:* Contact institution. *Financial support:* In 2016–17, 21 students received support. Career-related internships or fieldwork and Federal Work-Study available. Support available to part-time students. Financial award applicants required to submit FAFSA. *Unit head:* Dr. Fiona Robertson, Chair, 206-296-5791, Fax: 206-296-5795, E-mail: robertsf@seattleu.edu. *Application contact:* Janet Shandley, Director of Graduate Admissions, 206-296-5900, Fax: 206-298-5656, E-mail: grad_admissions@seattleu.edu.
Website: http://www.seattleu.edu/albers/msf/

Seton Hall University, Stillman School of Business, Programs in Business Administration, South Orange, NJ 07079-2697. Offers accounting (MBA); entrepreneurship (Certificate); finance (MBA, Certificate); information technology management (MBA); international business (MBA); management (MBA); marketing (MBA); sport management (MBA); supply chain management (MBA, Certificate). *Program availability:* Part-time, evening/weekend. *Degree requirements:* For master's, 20 hours of community service (Social Responsibility Project). *Entrance requirements:* For master's, GMAT or CPA, GRE (waived based on work experience or advanced degree from AACSB institution), MS in business discipline, professional degree (MD, JD, PhD, DVM, DDS, CPA, etc.), minimum undergraduate GPA of 3.0. Additional exam requirements/recommendations for international students: Required—TOEFL (minimum score 607 paper-based; 102 iBT), IELTS (minimum score 6), PTE. Electronic applications accepted. *Expenses:* Contact institution. *Faculty research:* Sport, hedge funds, executive compensation, social media, legal studies.

Shippensburg University of Pennsylvania, School of Graduate Studies, John L. Grove College of Business, Shippensburg, PA 17257-2299. Offers advanced studies in business (Certificate); advanced supply chain and logistics management (Certificate); business administration (MBA), including business administration, finance, healthcare management, management information systems, supply chain management; finance (Certificate); health care management (Certificate); management information systems (Certificate). *Accreditation:* AACSB. *Program availability:* Part-time, evening/weekend, 100% online, blended/hybrid learning. *Faculty:* 23 full-time (4 women), 4 part-time/ adjunct (1 woman). *Students:* 58 full-time (17 women), 195 part-time (59 women); includes 26 minority (12 Black or African American, non-Hispanic/Latino; 8 Asian, non-Hispanic/Latino; 5 Hispanic/Latino; 1 Two or more races, non-Hispanic/Latino), 26 international. Average age 32. 224 applicants, 55% accepted, 70 enrolled. In 2016, 101 master's awarded. *Degree requirements:* For master's, thesis optional, practicum. *Entrance requirements:* For master's, GMAT (minimum score 450 if less than 5 years of

mid-level experience, including management experience), current resume; relevant work/classroom experience; 500-word statement of purpose; prerequisites of quantitative analysis, computer usage, and oral and written communications; laptop computer. Additional exam requirements/recommendations for international students: Required—TOEFL (minimum score 550 paper-based, 68 iBT) or IELTS (minimum score 6). *Application deadline:* For fall admission, 4/30 for international students; for spring admission, 9/30 for international students. Applications are processed on a rolling basis. Application fee: $45. Electronic applications accepted. *Expenses:* Tuition, state resident: part-time $483 per credit. Tuition, nonresident: part-time $725 per credit. *Required fees:* $141 per credit. *Financial support:* In 2016–17, 12 students received support. Career-related internships or fieldwork, scholarships/grants, unspecified assistantships, and resident hall director and student payroll positions available. Support available to part-time students. Financial award application deadline: 3/1; financial award applicants required to submit FAFSA. *Unit head:* Dr. John G. Kooti, Dean of the College of Business, 717-477-1435, Fax: 717-477-4003, E-mail: jgkooti@ship.edu. *Application contact:* Megan N. Luft, Associate Dean of Graduate Admissions, 717-477-1231, Fax: 717-477-4016, E-mail: mnluft@ship.edu.
Website: http://www.ship.edu/business

Simon Fraser University, Office of Graduate Studies and Postdoctoral Fellows, Faculty of Business Administration, Vancouver, BC V6B 5K3, Canada. Offers business administration (EMBA, PhD, Graduate Diploma); finance (M Sc); management of technology (MBA); management of technology/biotechnology (MBA). *Program availability:* Online learning. *Faculty:* 91 full-time (33 women). *Students:* 554 full-time (252 women), 161 part-time (58 women). 928 applicants, 45% accepted, 279 enrolled. In 2016, 178 master's, 3 doctorates, 78 other advanced degrees awarded. *Degree requirements:* For master's, thesis (for some programs); for doctorate, comprehensive exam, thesis/dissertation. *Entrance requirements:* For master's, GMAT, minimum GPA of 3.0 (on scale of 4.33) or 3.33 based on last 60 credits of undergraduate courses; for doctorate, minimum GPA of 3.5 (on scale of 4.33); for Graduate Diploma, minimum GPA of 2.5 (on scale of 4.33) or 2.67 based on last 60 credits of undergraduate courses. Additional exam requirements/recommendations for international students: Recommended—TOEFL (minimum score 580 paper-based; 93 iBT), IELTS (minimum score 7), TWE (minimum score 5). *Application deadline:* For fall admission, 4/2 for domestic students; for winter admission, 10/1 for domestic students; for spring admission, 2/2 for domestic students. Application fee: $90 ($125 for international students). *Expenses:* Contact institution. *Financial support:* In 2016–17, 71 students received support, including 9 fellowships (averaging $6,139 per year), teaching assistantships (averaging $5,608 per year); research assistantships, career-related internships or fieldwork, and scholarships/grants also available. *Faculty research:* Accounting, management and organizational studies, technology and operations management, finance, international business. *Unit head:* Dr. Ian McCarthy, Associate Dean, Graduate Programs, 778-782-9255, Fax: 778-782-4920, E-mail: grad-business@sfu.ca. *Application contact:* Graduate Secretary, 778-782-5013, Fax: 778-782-5122, E-mail: grad-business@sfu.ca.
Website: http://beedie.sfu.ca/graduate/index.php

Slippery Rock University of Pennsylvania, Graduate Studies (Recruitment), College of Business, School of Business, Slippery Rock, PA 16057-1383. Offers accounting/finance (MBA); general (MBA); marketing/management (MBA). *Program availability:* Part-time, evening/weekend. *Faculty:* 6 full-time (4 women), 1 part-time/adjunct (0 women). *Students:* 16 full-time (9 women), 9 part-time (6 women); includes 1 minority (Black or African American, non-Hispanic/Latino). Average age 29. 109 applicants, 26% accepted, 13 enrolled. In 2016, 26 master's awarded. *Degree requirements:* For master's, comprehensive exam (for some programs), thesis (for some programs). *Entrance requirements:* For master's, minimum cumulative GPA of 3.0, official transcripts, three references. Additional exam requirements/recommendations for international students: Required—TOEFL (minimum score 550 paper-based; 80 iBT). *Application deadline:* For fall admission, 3/1 priority date for domestic students, 5/1 priority date for international students; for spring admission, 10/1 priority date for domestic students, 9/1 priority date for international students. Applications are processed on a rolling basis. Application fee: $25 ($30 for international students). Electronic applications accepted. *Expenses:* $646.50 per credit in-state, $936.80 per credit out-of-state; $581.45 per online credit in-state, $648.65 per online credit out-of-state. *Financial support:* In 2016–17, 5 students received support. Career-related internships or fieldwork, Federal Work-Study, institutionally sponsored loans, scholarships/grants, tuition waivers (partial), and unspecified assistantships available. Support available to part-time students. Financial award application deadline: 5/1; financial award applicants required to submit FAFSA. *Unit head:* Dr. Larry McCarthy, Graduate Coordinator, 724-738-2552, Fax: 724-738-2959, E-mail: larry.mccarthy@sru.edu. *Application contact:* Brandi Weber-Mortimer, Director of Graduate Admissions, 724-738-2051, Fax: 724-738-2146, E-mail: graduate.admissions@sru.edu.
Website: http://www.sru.edu/academics/graduate-programs/mba-master-of-business-administration

Southeast Missouri State University, School of Graduate Studies, Harrison College of Business, Cape Girardeau, MO 63701-4799. Offers accounting (MBA); entrepreneurship (MBA); financial management (MBA); sport management (MBA). *Accreditation:* AACSB. *Program availability:* Part-time, evening/weekend, 100% online. *Faculty:* 27 full-time (7 women), 1 (woman) part-time/adjunct. *Students:* 72 full-time (39 women), 112 part-time (41 women); includes 20 minority (10 Black or African American, non-Hispanic/Latino; 6 Asian, non-Hispanic/Latino; 4 Hispanic/Latino), 64 international. Average age 29. 106 applicants, 70% accepted, 55 enrolled. In 2016, 65 master's awarded. *Degree requirements:* For master's, variable foreign language requirement, comprehensive exam (for some programs), thesis or alternative. *Entrance requirements:* For master's, GMAT or GRE, minimum undergraduate GPA of 2.5, minimum grade of C in prerequisite courses. Additional exam requirements/recommendations for international students: Required—TOEFL (minimum score 550 paper-based; 79 iBT), IELTS (minimum score 6), PTE (minimum score 53). *Application deadline:* For fall admission, 8/1 for domestic students, 6/1 for international students; for spring admission, 11/21 for domestic students, 10/1 for international students; for summer admission, 5/15 for domestic students. Applications are processed on a rolling basis. Application fee: $30 ($40 for international students). Electronic applications accepted. *Expenses:* Tuition, state resident: full-time $3130; part-time $260.80 per credit hour. Tuition, nonresident: full-time $5842; part-time $486.80 per credit hour. *Required fees:* $33.70 per credit hour. *Financial support:* In 2016–17, 61 students received support. Career-related internships or fieldwork, Federal Work-Study, scholarships/grants, traineeships, tuition waivers (full), and unspecified assistantships available. Financial award application deadline: 6/30; financial award applicants required to submit FAFSA. *Faculty research:* Organizational justice, ethics, leadership, corporate finance, generational differences. *Unit head:* Dr. James L. Caldwell, Director, Graduate Business Studies, 573-651-2851, Fax: 573-651-5032, E-mail: jcaldwell@semo.edu. *Application contact:* Gail Amick, Admissions Specialist, 573-651-2590, Fax: 573-651-5936, E-mail: gamick@semo.edu.
Website: http://www.semo.edu/mba

Southern Adventist University, School of Business and Management, Collegedale, TN 37315-0370. Offers accounting (MBA); church administration (MSA); church and nonprofit leadership (MBA); financial management (MFM); healthcare administration (MBA); management (MBA); marketing management (MBA); outdoor education (MSA). *Program availability:* Part-time, evening/weekend, online learning. *Entrance requirements:* For master's, GMAT. Additional exam requirements/recommendations for international students: Required—TOEFL (minimum score 600 paper-based; 100 iBT). Electronic applications accepted.

Southern Illinois University Edwardsville, Graduate School, School of Business, Department of Economics and Finance, Edwardsville, IL 62026. Offers MA, MS. *Program availability:* Part-time, evening/weekend. *Degree requirements:* For master's, thesis or alternative, final exam, portfolio. *Entrance requirements:* For master's, GMAT or GRE. Additional exam requirements/recommendations for international students: Required—TOEFL (minimum score 550 paper-based; 79 iBT), IELTS (minimum score 6.5). Electronic applications accepted.

Southern Methodist University, Cox School of Business, MBA Program, Dallas, TX 75275. Offers accounting (MBA, PMBA); business administration (EMBA); finance (MBA); financial statement analysis (PMBA); general business (MBA); information technology and operations management (MBA); management (MBA); marketing (MBA); real estate (MBA); strategy (MBA); strategy and entrepreneurship (MBA); JD/MBA; MA/MBA. *Program availability:* Part-time, evening/weekend. *Entrance requirements:* For master's, GMAT. Additional exam requirements/recommendations for international students: Required—TOEFL. Electronic applications accepted. *Expenses:* Contact institution. *Faculty research:* Corporate finance, financial reporting, modeling consumer decision-making, competition between national brands and store brands, institutional determinants of firms' strategy.

Southern New Hampshire University, School of Business, Manchester, NH 03106-1045. Offers accounting (MBA, MS, Graduate Certificate); accounting finance (MS); accounting/auditing (MS); accounting/forensic accounting (MS); accounting/taxation (MS); athletic administration (MBA, Graduate Certificate); business administration (IMBA, MBA, Certificate, Graduate Certificate), including accounting (Certificate), business administration (MBA), business information systems (Graduate Certificate), human resource management (Certificate); corporate social responsibility (MBA); entrepreneurship (MBA); finance (MBA, MS, Graduate Certificate); finance/corporate finance (MS); finance/investments and securities (MS); forensic accounting (MBA); healthcare informatics (MBA); healthcare management (MBA); human resource management (Graduate Certificate); information technology (MS, Graduate Certificate); information technology management (MBA); international business (Graduate Certificate); international business and information technology (Graduate Certificate); international finance (Graduate Certificate); international sport management (Graduate Certificate); justice studies (MBA); leadership of nonprofit organizations (Graduate Certificate); management (MS); marketing (MBA, MS, Graduate Certificate); operations and project management (MS); operations and supply chain management (MBA, Graduate Certificate); organizational leadership (MS); project management (MBA, Graduate Certificate); Six Sigma (MBA); Six Sigma quality (Graduate Certificate); social media marketing (MBA); sport management (MBA, MS, Graduate Certificate); sustainability and environmental compliance (MBA); workplace conflict management (MBA); MBA/Certificate. *Accreditation:* ACBSP. *Program availability:* Part-time, evening/weekend, online learning. Terminal master's awarded for partial completion of doctoral program. *Degree requirements:* For master's, one foreign language, comprehensive exam (for some programs), thesis or alternative. *Entrance requirements:* For master's, minimum GPA of 2.5. Additional exam requirements/recommendations for international students: Required—TOEFL (minimum score 500 paper-based). Electronic applications accepted.

Southwestern Adventist University, Business Administration Department, Keene, TX 76059. Offers accounting (MBA); finance (MBA); management/leadership (MBA). *Program availability:* Part-time, evening/weekend. *Degree requirements:* For master's, capstone course. *Entrance requirements:* For master's, GMAT, GRE General Test.

State University of New York Polytechnic Institute, Program in Business Administration in Technology Management, Utica, NY 13502. Offers accounting and finance (MBA); business management (MBA); health services management (MBA); human resource management (MBA); marketing management (MBA). *Program availability:* Part-time, online learning. *Degree requirements:* For master's, capstone course. *Entrance requirements:* For master's, GMAT, resume, one letter of reference. Additional exam requirements/recommendations for international students: Required—TOEFL (minimum score 550 paper-based; 79 iBT), IELTS (minimum score 6.5). Electronic applications accepted. *Faculty research:* Technology management, writing schools, leadership, new products.

Stevens Institute of Technology, Graduate School, School of Business, Program in Business Administration, Hoboken, NJ 07030. Offers business intelligence and analytics (MBA); engineering management (MBA); finance (MBA); information systems (MBA); innovation and entrepreneurship (MBA); marketing (MBA); pharmaceutical management (MBA); project management (MBA, Certificate); technology management (MBA); telecommunications management (MBA). *Accreditation:* AACSB. *Program availability:* Part-time, evening/weekend. *Students:* 35 full-time (15 women), 181 part-time (79 women); includes 53 minority (10 Black or African American, non-Hispanic/Latino; 2 American Indian or Alaska Native, non-Hispanic/Latino; 36 Asian, non-Hispanic/Latino; 5 Hispanic/Latino), 30 international. Average age 32. 215 applicants, 53% accepted, 61 enrolled. In 2016, 61 master's awarded. *Degree requirements:* For master's, thesis optional, minimum B average in major field and overall; for Certificate, minimum B average. *Entrance requirements:* Additional exam requirements/recommendations for international students: Required—TOEFL (minimum score 74 iBT), IELTS (minimum score 6). *Application deadline:* For fall admission, 6/1 for domestic students, 4/15 for international students; for spring admission, 11/30 for domestic students, 11/1 for international students. Applications are processed on a rolling basis. Application fee: $65. Electronic applications accepted. *Expenses:* Contact institution. *Financial support:* Fellowships, research assistantships, teaching assistantships, career-related internships or fieldwork, Federal Work-Study, scholarships/grants, and unspecified assistantships available. Financial award application deadline: 2/15; financial award applicants required to submit FAFSA. *Unit head:* Dr. Gregory Prastacos, Dean, 201-216-8366, E-mail: gprastac@stevens.edu. *Application contact:* Graduate Admissions, 888-783-8367, Fax: 888-511-1306, E-mail: graduate@stevens.edu.
Website: https://www.stevens.edu/school-business/masters-programs/mbaemba

Stevens Institute of Technology, Graduate School, School of Business, Program in Finance, Hoboken, NJ 07030. Offers MS. *Program availability:* Part-time, evening/weekend. *Students:* 40 full-time (17 women), 1 part-time (0 women), 38 international. Average age 24. 264 applicants, 53% accepted, 26 enrolled. In 2016, 3 master's awarded. *Degree requirements:* For master's, thesis optional, minimum B average in major field and overall. *Entrance requirements:* Additional exam requirements/recommendations for international students: Required—TOEFL (minimum score 74 iBT), IELTS (minimum score 6). *Application deadline:* For fall admission, 6/1 for domestic students, 4/15 for international students; for spring admission, 9/30 for domestic students, 9/1 for international students. Application fee: $65. *Expenses:* Contact institution. *Financial support:* Fellowships, research assistantships, teaching assistantships, career-related internships or fieldwork, Federal Work-Study,

scholarships/grants, and unspecified assistantships available. Financial award application deadline: 2/15; financial award applicants required to submit FAFSA. *Unit head:* Dr. Michael Muehlen, Dean, 201-216-8293, E-mail: michael.zurmuehlen@stevens.edu. *Application contact:* Graduate Admissions, 888-793-8367, Fax: 888-511-1306, E-mail: graduate@stevens.edu.
Website: http://www.stevens.edu/school-business/masters-programs/finance

Stony Brook University, State University of New York, Graduate School, College of Business, Program in Business Administration, Stony Brook, NY 11794. Offers accounting (MBA); business administration (MBA); finance (MBA, Certificate); health care management (MBA); innovation, human resources, management, or operations management (MBA); marketing (MBA). *Faculty:* 37 full-time (12 women), 12 part-time/adjunct (4 women). *Students:* 199 full-time (109 women), 139 part-time (64 women); includes 81 minority (19 Black or African American, non-Hispanic/Latino; 41 Asian, non-Hispanic/Latino; 17 Hispanic/Latino; 1 Native Hawaiian or other Pacific Islander, non-Hispanic/Latino; 3 Two or more races, non-Hispanic/Latino), 88 international. Average age 29. 246 applicants, 65% accepted, 91 enrolled. In 2016, 116 master's awarded. *Entrance requirements:* For master's, GMAT, 3 letters of recommendation from current or former employers or professors, transcripts, personal statement, resume. Additional exam requirements/recommendations for international students: Required—TOEFL (minimum score 550 paper-based; 90 iBT), IELTS (minimum score 6.5). *Application deadline:* For fall admission, 5/15 for domestic students, 3/15 for international students; for spring admission, 11/15 for domestic students, 10/15 for international students. Application fee: $100. *Expenses:* Contact institution. *Financial support:* Teaching assistantships available. *Total annual research expenditures:* $5,325. *Unit head:* Dr. Manuel London, Dean, 631-632-7159, E-mail: manuel.london@stonybrook.edu. *Application contact:* Dr. Jadranka Skorin-Kapov, Graduate Program Director, 631-632-7171, Fax: 631-632-8181, E-mail: jadranka.skorin-kapov@stonybrook.edu.

Stony Brook University, State University of New York, Graduate School, College of Business, Program in Finance, Stony Brook, NY 11794. Offers MS, AGC. *Program availability:* Part-time. *Students:* 8 full-time (2 women), 2 part-time (0 women); includes 3 minority (all Asian, non-Hispanic/Latino), 5 international. 81 applicants, 46% accepted, 6 enrolled. *Degree requirements:* For master's, capstone course. *Entrance requirements:* For master's, GMAT or GRE, letters of recommendation, minimum GPA of 3.0 in prior academic work. Additional exam requirements/recommendations for international students: Required—TOEFL (minimum score 85 iBT). *Application deadline:* For fall admission, 5/15 for domestic students, 3/15 for international students; for spring admission, 11/15 for domestic students, 10/15 for international students; for summer admission, 3/15 for domestic students. *Expenses:* Contact institution. *Unit head:* Dr. Manuel London, Dean, 631-632-7159, E-mail: manuel.london@stonybrook.edu. *Application contact:* Erica Robey, Graduate Coordinator, 631-632-7171, Fax: 631-632-8181, E-mail: oss@stonybrook.edu.
Website: http://www.stonybrook.edu/commcms/business/academics/graduate-program/ms-finance.html

Strayer University, Graduate Studies, Washington, DC 20005-2603. Offers accounting (MS); acquisition (MBA); business administration (MBA); communications technology (MS); educational management (M Ed); finance (MBA); health services administration (MHSA); hospitality and tourism management (MBA); human resource management (MBA); information systems (MS), including computer security management, decision support system management, enterprise resource management, network management, software engineering management, systems development management; management (MBA); management information systems (MS); marketing (MBA); professional accounting (MS), including accounting information systems, controllership, taxation; public administration (MPA); supply chain management (MBA); technology in education (M Ed). Programs also offered at campus locations in Birmingham, AL; Chamblee, GA; Cobb County, GA; Morrow, GA; White Marsh, MD; Charleston, SC; Columbia, SC; Greensboro, NC; Greenville, SC; Lexington, KY; Louisville, KY; Nashville, TN; North Raleigh, NC; Washington, DC. *Accreditation:* ACBSP. *Program availability:* Part-time, evening/weekend, online learning. *Degree requirements:* For master's, thesis. *Entrance requirements:* For master's, GMAT, GRE General Test, bachelor's degree from an accredited college or university, minimum undergraduate GPA of 2.75. Electronic applications accepted.

Suffolk University, Sawyer Business School, Master of Business Administration Program, Boston, MA 02108-2770. Offers accounting (MBA); entrepreneurship (MBA); executive business administration (EMBA); finance (MBA); global business administration (GMBA); health administration (MBA); international business (MBA); marketing (MBA); nonprofit management (MBA); organizational behavior (MBA); strategic management (MBA); supply chain management (MBA); taxation (MBA); JD/MBA; MBA/MHA; MBA/MSA; MBA/MSF; MBA/MST. *Accreditation:* AACSB. *Program availability:* Part-time, evening/weekend, 100% online. *Faculty:* 17 full-time (6 women), 10 part-time/adjunct (1 woman). *Students:* 137 full-time (70 women), 265 part-time (138 women); includes 78 minority (20 Black or African American, non-Hispanic/Latino; 22 Asian, non-Hispanic/Latino; 31 Hispanic/Latino; 5 Two or more races, non-Hispanic/Latino), 46 international. Average age 30. 416 applicants, 70% accepted, 128 enrolled. In 2016, 165 degrees awarded. *Entrance requirements:* For master's, GMAT, minimum undergraduate GPA of 2.75 (MBA), 5 years of managerial experience (EMBA). Additional exam requirements/recommendations for international students: Required—TOEFL (minimum score 550 paper-based; 80 iBT). *Application deadline:* For fall admission, 3/15 priority date for domestic students, 10/15 priority date for international students; for spring admission, 10/15 priority date for domestic and international students. Applications are processed on a rolling basis. Application fee: $50. Electronic applications accepted. *Expenses: Tuition:* Full-time $41,490; part-time $1383 per credit hour. *Required fees:* $52; $52 per credit hour. Part-time tuition and fees vary according to course load and program. *Financial support:* In 2016–17, 209 students received support, including 176 fellowships (averaging $8,581 per year); career-related internships or fieldwork, Federal Work-Study, institutionally sponsored loans, and scholarships/grants also available. Support available to part-time students. Financial award application deadline: 4/1; financial award applicants required to submit FAFSA. *Faculty research:* Foreign investments; career strategies and boundaryless careers; corporate ethics codes; interest rates, inflation, and growth options; innovation and product development performance. *Unit head:* Jodi Detjen, Director of MBA Programs, 617-573-8306, E-mail: jdetjen@suffolk.edu. *Application contact:* Mara Marzocchi, Associate Director of Graduate Admissions, 617-573-8302, Fax: 617-305-1733, E-mail: grad.admission@suffolk.edu.
Website: http://www.suffolk.edu/mba

Suffolk University, Sawyer Business School, Programs in Finance, Boston, MA 02108-2770. Offers MSF, MSFSB, JD/MSF. *Accreditation:* AACSB. *Program availability:* Part-time, evening/weekend. *Faculty:* 7 full-time (4 women), 2 part-time/adjunct (0 women). *Students:* 38 full-time (10 women), 26 part-time (8 women); includes 10 minority (5 Black or African American, non-Hispanic/Latino; 3 Asian, non-Hispanic/Latino; 2 Hispanic/Latino), 30 international. Average age 29. 103 applicants, 65% accepted, 26 enrolled. In 2016, 46 master's awarded. *Entrance requirements:* For master's, GMAT, interview. Additional exam requirements/recommendations for international students: Required—TOEFL (minimum score 550 paper-based; 80 iBT). *Application deadline:* For fall admission, 3/15 priority date for domestic and international students; for spring admission, 10/15 priority date for domestic and international students. Applications are processed on a rolling basis. Application fee: $50. Electronic applications accepted. *Expenses:* $41,490 per year full-time tuition, $1,383 per credit hour part-time tuition, $52 per year student activity fee. *Financial support:* In 2016–17, 33 students received support, including 29 fellowships (averaging $12,212 per year); career-related internships or fieldwork, Federal Work-Study, institutionally sponsored loans, scholarships/grants, and health care benefits also available. Support available to part-time students. Financial award application deadline: 4/1; financial award applicants required to submit FAFSA. *Faculty research:* Financial institutions, corporate finance, ownership structure, dividend policy, corporate restructuring. *Unit head:* Dr. Shahriar Khaksari, Chairperson/Professor of Finance, 617-573-8366, E-mail: skhaksari@suffolk.edu. *Application contact:* Mara Marzocchi, Associate Director of Graduate Admissions, 617-573-8302, Fax: 617-305-1733, E-mail: grad.admission@suffolk.edu.
Website: http://www.suffolk.edu/msf

Syracuse University, Martin J. Whitman School of Management, MS in Finance Program, Syracuse, NY 13244. Offers MS. *Students:* 26 full-time (13 women), all international. Average age 23. 454 applicants, 42% accepted, 26 enrolled. In 2016, 43 master's awarded. *Entrance requirements:* For master's, GMAT or GRE, resume, essay, 5-minute video interview, two letters of recommendation, transcripts (unofficial). Additional exam requirements/recommendations for international students: Required—TOEFL (minimum score 100 iBT), IELTS (minimum score 7), PTE (minimum score 68). *Application deadline:* For fall admission, 11/30 for domestic students, 11/30 priority date for international students; for winter admission, 1/1 for domestic students, 1/1 priority date for international students; for spring admission, 2/15 for domestic and international students; for summer admission, 4/19 for domestic students. Application fee: $75. Electronic applications accepted. *Expenses:* Contact institution. *Financial support:* Merit scholarships available. Financial award application deadline: 2/15. *Faculty research:* Financial accounting, investment analysis, corporate financial policy and strategy, data analysis/business statistics, managerial finance. *Unit head:* Tom Barkley, Director, MS in Finance Program/Professor of Finance Practice, 315-443-8107, E-mail: tbarkley@syr.edu. *Application contact:* Shri Ramakrishnan, Assistant Director, Graduate Recruitment, 315-443-3497, Fax: 315-443-9517, E-mail: sramak01@syr.edu.
Website: http://whitman.syr.edu/msfin/

Syracuse University, Martin J. Whitman School of Management, PhD Programs, Syracuse, NY 13244. Offers finance (PhD); management information systems (PhD). In 2016, 2 doctorates awarded. *Degree requirements:* For doctorate, comprehensive exam, thesis/dissertation, summer research paper. *Entrance requirements:* For doctorate, GMAT (preferred) or GRE, master's degree (preferred), transcripts, three recommendation letters, personal statement. Additional exam requirements/recommendations for international students: Required—TOEFL (minimum score 600 paper-based; 100 iBT). *Application deadline:* For fall admission, 1/15 for domestic and international students. Application fee: $75. Electronic applications accepted. *Expenses: Tuition:* Full-time $25,974; part-time $1443 per credit hour. *Required fees:* $802; $50 per course. Tuition and fees vary according to course load and program. *Financial support:* Fellowships with full tuition reimbursements, research assistantships with full tuition reimbursements, teaching assistantships with full tuition reimbursements, and scholarships/grants available. *Faculty research:* Marketing models, market microstructure, supply chain, auditing, corporate governance. *Unit head:* Dr. Michel Benaroch, Associate Dean for Research and PhD Programs, 315-443-3492, E-mail: mbenaroc@syr.edu. *Application contact:* Lisa Svegl, Executive Assistant for Development and PhD Programs, 315-443-9141, E-mail: lmsvegl@syr.edu.

Télé-université, Graduate Programs, Québec, QC G1K 9H5, Canada. Offers computer science (PhD); corporate finance (MS); distance learning (MS). *Program availability:* Part-time.

Temple University, Fox School of Business, Doctoral Programs in Business, Philadelphia, PA 19122-6096. Offers accounting (PhD); entrepreneurship (PhD); finance (PhD); international business (PhD); management information systems (PhD); marketing (PhD); risk management and insurance (PhD); statistics (PhD); strategic management (PhD); tourism and sport (PhD). *Accreditation:* AACSB. *Degree requirements:* For doctorate, thesis/dissertation. *Entrance requirements:* For doctorate, GRE General Test, GMAT, minimum GPA of 3.0, master's degree. Additional exam requirements/recommendations for international students: Required—TOEFL (minimum score 600 paper-based; 100 iBT), IELTS (minimum score 7.5). Electronic applications accepted.

Temple University, Fox School of Business, Specialized Master's Programs, Philadelphia, PA 19122-6096. Offers accountancy (MS); actuarial science (MS); finance (MS); financial engineering (MS); human resource management (MS); innovation management and entrepreneurship (MS); marketing (MS); statistics (MS). MS in innovation management and entrepreneurship delivered jointly with College of Engineering. *Accreditation:* AACSB. *Program availability:* Part-time. *Entrance requirements:* For master's, GRE General Test or GMAT, minimum undergraduate GPA of 3.0. Additional exam requirements/recommendations for international students: Required—TOEFL (minimum score 600 paper-based; 100 iBT), IELTS (minimum score 7.5).

Tennessee Technological University, College of Graduate Studies, College of Business, Cookeville, TN 38505. Offers accounting (MBA); finance (MBA); human resource management (MBA); international business (MBA); management information systems (MBA). *Accreditation:* AACSB. *Program availability:* Part-time, evening/weekend, online learning. *Faculty:* 28 full-time (5 women). *Students:* 45 full-time (22 women), 167 part-time (51 women); includes 18 minority (5 Black or African American, non-Hispanic/Latino; 4 Asian, non-Hispanic/Latino; 4 Hispanic/Latino; 5 Two or more races, non-Hispanic/Latino), 14 international. Average age 25. 173 applicants, 54% accepted, 52 enrolled. In 2016, 78 master's awarded. *Entrance requirements:* For master's, GMAT, GRE. Additional exam requirements/recommendations for international students: Required—TOEFL (minimum score 550 paper-based; 79 iBT), IELTS (minimum score 5.5), PTE (minimum score 53), or TOEIC (Test of English as an International Communication). *Application deadline:* For fall admission, 8/1 for domestic students, 5/1 for international students; for spring admission, 12/1 for domestic students, 10/1 for international students; for summer admission, 5/1 for domestic students, 2/1 for international students. Applications are processed on a rolling basis. Application fee: $35 ($40 for international students). Electronic applications accepted. *Expenses:* Tuition, state resident: full-time $9375; part-time $534 per credit hour. Tuition, nonresident: full-time $22,443; part-time $1260 per credit hour. *Financial support:* In 2016–17, 5 fellowships (averaging $10,000 per year), 1 teaching assistantship (averaging $5,200 per year) were awarded; research assistantships also available. Support available to part-time students. Financial award application deadline: 4/1. *Unit head:* Kate Nicewicz, Director, 931-372-3600, Fax: 931-372-6249, E-mail: knicewicz@tntech.edu. *Application contact:* Shelia K. Kendrick, Coordinator of Graduate Studies, 931-372-3808, Fax: 931-372-3497, E-mail: skendrick@tntech.edu.
Website: http://www.tntech.edu/mba

Texas A&M International University, Office of Graduate Studies and Research, A.R. Sanchez, Jr. School of Business, Division of International Banking and Finance Studies,

Finance and Banking

Laredo, TX 78041-1900. Offers accounting (MP Acc); international banking and finance (MBA). *Entrance requirements:* For master's, GMAT or GRE General Test. Additional exam requirements/recommendations for international students: Required—TOEFL (minimum score 550 paper-based; 79 iBT).

Texas A&M University, Mays Business School, Department of Finance, College Station, TX 77843. Offers finance (MS); financial management (MFM); land economics and real estate (MRE). *Faculty:* 20. *Students:* 197 full-time (68 women), 21 part-time (3 women); includes 22 minority (8 Asian, non-Hispanic/Latino; 10 Hispanic/Latino; 4 Two or more races, non-Hispanic/Latino), 24 international. Average age 24. 293 applicants, 35% accepted, 76 enrolled. In 2016, 138 master's awarded. Terminal master's awarded for partial completion of doctoral program. *Degree requirements:* For master's, comprehensive exam. *Entrance requirements:* For master's, GMAT or GRE. Additional exam requirements/recommendations for international students: Required—TOEFL (minimum score 550 paper-based; 80 iBT), IELTS (minimum score 6), PTE (minimum score 53). *Application deadline:* For fall admission, 4/7 for domestic students. Applications are processed on a rolling basis. Application fee: $50 ($90 for international students). Electronic applications accepted. *Expenses:* Contact institution. *Financial support:* In 2016–17, 157 students received support, including 9 fellowships with tuition reimbursements available (averaging $3,944 per year), 18 research assistantships with tuition reimbursements available (averaging $5,933 per year), 16 teaching assistantships with tuition reimbursements available (averaging $4,326 per year); career-related internships or fieldwork, institutionally sponsored loans, scholarships/grants, traineeships, health care benefits, tuition waivers (full and partial), and unspecified assistantships also available. Support available to part-time students. Financial award application deadline: 3/15; financial award applicants required to submit FAFSA. *Unit head:* Dr. Sorin Sorescu, Head, 979-458-0380, Fax: 979-845-3884, E-mail: smsorescu@mays.tamu.edu. *Application contact:* Angela G. Degelman, Program Coordinator/Graduate Academic Advisor, 979-845-4858, Fax: 979-845-3884, E-mail: adegelman@mays.tamu.edu.
Website: http://mays.tamu.edu/finc/

Texas A&M University–Commerce, College of Business, Commerce, TX 75429-3011. Offers accounting (MSA); business administration (MBA); business analytics (MS); finance (MSF); management (MS); marketing (MS). *Accreditation:* AACSB. *Program availability:* Part-time, evening/weekend, 100% online, blended/hybrid learning. *Faculty:* 48 full-time (17 women), 8 part-time/adjunct (2 women). *Students:* 463 full-time (232 women), 1,109 part-time (539 women); includes 653 minority (280 Black or African American, non-Hispanic/Latino; 7 American Indian or Alaska Native, non-Hispanic/Latino; 131 Asian, non-Hispanic/Latino; 202 Hispanic/Latino; 1 Native Hawaiian or other Pacific Islander, non-Hispanic/Latino; 32 Two or more races, non-Hispanic/Latino), 211 international. Average age 33. 1,021 applicants, 59% accepted, 424 enrolled. In 2016, 617 master's awarded. *Degree requirements:* For master's, comprehensive exam. *Entrance requirements:* For master's, GRE General Test, GMAT, letter of recommendation. Additional exam requirements/recommendations for international students: Required—TOEFL (minimum score 550 paper-based; 79 iBT), IELTS (minimum score 6). *Application deadline:* For fall admission, 5/15 priority date for international students; for spring admission, 10/1 priority date for international students; for summer admission, 2/1 priority date for international students. Applications are processed on a rolling basis. Application fee: $50 ($75 for international students). Electronic applications accepted. *Expenses:* Contact institution. *Financial support:* In 2016–17, 90 students received support, including 20 research assistantships with partial tuition reimbursements available (averaging $8,000 per year); Federal Work-Study, institutionally sponsored loans, scholarships/grants, health care benefits, and unspecified assistantships also available. Financial award application deadline: 5/1; financial award applicants required to submit FAFSA. *Faculty research:* Applied economics emphasis on industries that are important to the region including health, energy and agriculture; finance research on banking, investments, financial institutions and risk management; marketing and big data decisions of product choice behavior and channel behavior of consumers; strategic management and organizational behavior phenomena; International Accounting in Governmental Sectors. *Total annual research expenditures:* $1,920. *Unit head:* Dr. Shanan G. Gibson, Dean of College of Business, 903-886-5191, Fax: 903-886-5650, E-mail: shanan.gibson@tamuc.edu. *Application contact:* Shanna Hoskison, Director, Graduate Advising, 903-886-5190, E-mail: shanna.hoskison@tamuc.edu.
Website: http://www.tamuc.edu/academics/graduateSchool/programs/businessEntrepreneurship/default.aspx

Texas A&M University–Corpus Christi, College of Graduate Studies, College of Business, Corpus Christi, TX 78412-5503. Offers accounting (M Acc); business (MBA); finance (MBA); health care administration (MBA); international business (MBA). *Accreditation:* AACSB. *Program availability:* Part-time, evening/weekend, 100% online, blended/hybrid learning. *Faculty:* 31 full-time (11 women), 2 part-time/adjunct (0 women). *Students:* 132 full-time (71 women), 495 part-time (232 women); includes 261 minority (49 Black or African American, non-Hispanic/Latino; 44 Asian, non-Hispanic/Latino; 160 Hispanic/Latino; 8 Two or more races, non-Hispanic/Latino), 111 international. Average age 32. 444 applicants, 55% accepted, 192 enrolled. In 2016, 205 master's awarded. *Degree requirements:* For master's, 30 to 42 hours (for MBA; varies by concentration area, delivery format, and necessity for foundational courses for students with nonbusiness degrees). *Entrance requirements:* For master's, GMAT, GRE. Additional exam requirements/recommendations for international students: Required—TOEFL (minimum score 550 paper-based), IELTS (minimum score 6.5). *Application deadline:* For fall admission, 7/15 priority date for domestic students, 5/1 priority date for international students; for spring admission, 11/15 priority date for domestic students, 9/1 priority date for international students; for summer admission, 4/15 priority date for domestic students, 2/1 priority date for international students. Applications are processed on a rolling basis. Application fee: $50 ($70 for international students). Electronic applications accepted. *Financial support:* Research assistantships, teaching assistantships, career-related internships or fieldwork, Federal Work-Study, institutionally sponsored loans, scholarships/grants, health care benefits, and unspecified assistantships available. Support available to part-time students. Financial award application deadline: 3/15; financial award applicants required to submit FAFSA. *Unit head:* Dr. John Gamble, Dean, 361-825-6045, Fax: 361-825-2725, E-mail: john.gamble@tamucc.edu. *Application contact:* Sharon Polansky, Director, Master's Program, 361-825-3448, Fax: 361-825-2755, E-mail: gradweb@tamucc.edu.
Website: http://cob.tamucc.edu

Texas A&M University–San Antonio, School of Business, San Antonio, TX 78224. Offers business administration (MBA); enterprise resource planning systems (MBA); finance (MBA); healthcare management (MBA); human resources management (MBA); information assurance and security (MBA); international business (MBA); professional accounting (MPA); project management (MBA); supply chain management (MBA). *Program availability:* Part-time, evening/weekend. *Entrance requirements:* For master's, GMAT. Additional exam requirements/recommendations for international students: Required—TOEFL (minimum score 550 paper-based; 80 iBT), IELTS (minimum score 6). Electronic applications accepted.

Texas Christian University, Neeley School of Business, Full-time Master's Program in Business Administration and Accelerated MBA, Fort Worth, TX 76129. Offers accounting (MBA); finance (MBA), including corporate finance, investments; marketing (MBA), including marketing management, product and brand management; supply and value chain management (MBA). *Accreditation:* AACSB. *Program availability:* Part-time, evening/weekend. *Faculty:* 60 full-time (17 women), 17 part-time/adjunct (4 women). *Students:* 92 full-time (26 women); includes 14 minority (3 Black or African American, non-Hispanic/Latino; 1 American Indian or Alaska Native, non-Hispanic/Latino; 3 Asian, non-Hispanic/Latino; 7 Hispanic/Latino), 30 international. Average age 28. 205 applicants, 50% accepted, 47 enrolled. In 2016, 43 master's awarded. *Entrance requirements:* For master's, GMAT (preferred); GRE. Additional exam requirements/recommendations for international students: Required—TOEFL (minimum score 100 iBT); Recommended—IELTS (minimum score 7), TSE (minimum score 68). *Application deadline:* For fall admission, 3/1 for domestic and international students; for winter admission, 1/15 for domestic and international students; for spring admission, 11/1 for domestic and international students; for summer admission, 1/15 for domestic and international students. Applications are processed on a rolling basis. Application fee: $100. Electronic applications accepted. Application fee is waived when completed online. *Expenses:* Contact institution. *Financial support:* In 2016–17, 94 students received support. Career-related internships or fieldwork, scholarships/grants, and unspecified assistantships available. Financial award application deadline: 4/1; financial award applicants required to submit FAFSA. *Faculty research:* Emerging financial markets, derivative trading activity, salesforce deployment, examining sales activity, litigation against tax practitioners. *Unit head:* Anne Rooney, Executive Director, Graduate Programs, 817-257-7991, Fax: 817-257-6431, E-mail: mbainfo@tcu.edu. *Application contact:* Peggy Conway, Director, Full-time MBA Admissions, 817-257-7989, Fax: 817-257-6431, E-mail: mbainfo@tcu.edu.
Website: http://www.neeley.tcu.edu/mba

Texas Tech University, Rawls College of Business Administration, Lubbock, TX 79409-2101. Offers accounting (MSA, PhD), including audit/financial reporting (MSA), taxation (MSA); business statistics (MS, PhD); data science (MS); finance (PhD); general business (MBA); healthcare management (MS); information systems and operations management (PhD); management (PhD); marketing (PhD); STEM (MBA); JD/MBA; JD/MSA; MBA/M Arch; MBA/MD; MBA/MS; MBA/Pharm D. *Accreditation:* AACSB; CAHME (one or more programs are accredited). *Program availability:* Evening/weekend. *Faculty:* 74 full-time (13 women). *Students:* 741 full-time (275 women); includes 198 minority (38 Black or African American, non-Hispanic/Latino; 1 American Indian or Alaska Native, non-Hispanic/Latino; 24 Asian, non-Hispanic/Latino; 116 Hispanic/Latino; 1 Native Hawaiian or other Pacific Islander, non-Hispanic/Latino; 18 Two or more races, non-Hispanic/Latino), 95 international. Average age 28. 905 applicants, 48% accepted, 251 enrolled. In 2016, 545 master's, 13 doctorates awarded. *Degree requirements:* For master's, capstone course; for doctorate, comprehensive exam, thesis/dissertation, qualifying exams. *Entrance requirements:* For master's, GMAT, GRE, MCAT, PCAT, LSAT, or DAT, holistic review of academic credentials, resume, essay, letters of recommendation; for doctorate, GMAT, GRE, holistic review of academic credentials, resume, statement of purpose, letters of recommendation. Additional exam requirements/recommendations for international students: Required—TOEFL (minimum score 95 iBT), IELTS. *Application deadline:* For fall admission, 7/1 priority date for domestic students, 1/15 for international students; for spring admission, 12/1 priority date for domestic students, 6/15 for international students; for summer admission, 5/1 for domestic students. Applications are processed on a rolling basis. Application fee: $60. Electronic applications accepted. *Expenses:* $48,000 (MBA for Working Professionals); $20,000 (STEM MBA). *Financial support:* In 2016–17, 157 students received support, including 25 research assistantships (averaging $22,725 per year), 27 teaching assistantships (averaging $22,725 per year); fellowships, career-related internships or fieldwork, Federal Work-Study, scholarships/grants, health care benefits, and unspecified assistantships also available. Financial award application deadline: 3/1; financial award applicants required to submit FAFSA. *Faculty research:* Governmental and nonprofit accounting, securities and options futures, statistical analysis and design, leadership, consumer behavior. *Unit head:* Dr. Margaret Williams, Dean, 806-742-3188, Fax: 806-742-1092, E-mail: margaret.l.williams@ttu.edu. *Application contact:* Chathry Keaton, Applications Manager, Graduate and Professional Programs, 806-742-3184, Fax: 806-742-3958, E-mail: rawlsgrad@ttu.edu.
Website: http://www.depts.ttu.edu/rawlsbusiness/graduate/

Tiffin University, Program in Business Administration, Tiffin, OH 44883-2161. Offers finance (MBA); general management (MBA); healthcare administration (MBA); human resource management (MBA); international business (MBA); leadership (MBA); marketing (MBA); non-profit management (MBA); sports management (MBA). *Accreditation:* ACBSP. *Program availability:* Part-time, evening/weekend, online learning. *Students:* 10 full-time (4 women), 497 part-time (240 women); includes 91 minority (67 Black or African American, non-Hispanic/Latino; 1 American Indian or Alaska Native, non-Hispanic/Latino; 5 Asian, non-Hispanic/Latino; 15 Hispanic/Latino; 3 Two or more races, non-Hispanic/Latino), 102 international. Average age 31. 214 applicants, 86% accepted, 146 enrolled. In 2016, 183 master's awarded. *Entrance requirements:* For master's, minimum undergraduate GPA of 2.5, work experience. Additional exam requirements/recommendations for international students: Required—TOEFL (minimum score 550 paper-based; 79 iBT), IELTS. *Application deadline:* For fall admission, 8/15 for domestic students, 8/1 for international students; for spring admission, 1/9 for domestic students, 12/1 for international students. Applications are processed on a rolling basis. Application fee: $50. Electronic applications accepted. Application fee is waived when completed online. *Expenses: Tuition:* Full-time $21,000; part-time $700 per credit hour. *Required fees:* $150. Tuition and fees vary according to program. *Financial support:* Unspecified assistantships available. Support available to part-time students. Financial award application deadline: 7/31; financial award applicants required to submit FAFSA. *Faculty research:* Small business, executive development operations, research and statistical analysis, market research, management information systems. *Unit head:* Dr. Bonnie Tiell, Dean of Graduate Studies, 419-448-3261, Fax: 419-443-5002, E-mail: btiell@tiffin.edu. *Application contact:* Nikki Hintze, Director of Graduate and Distance Education Academic Advising, 800-968-6446 Ext. 3596, Fax: 419-443-5002, E-mail: hintzenm@tiffin.edu.
Website: http://www.tiffin.edu/graduateprograms/

Trident University International, College of Business Administration, Program in Business Administration, Cypress, CA 90630. Offers business administration (PhD); conflict and negotiation management (MBA); criminal justice administration (MBA); entrepreneurship (MBA); finance (MBA); general management (MBA); government accounting (MBA); human resource management (MBA); information security and digital assurance management (MBA); information technology management (MBA); international business (MBA); logistics management (MBA); marketing (MBA); project management (MBA); public management (MBA); quality management (MBA); strategic leadership (MBA). *Program availability:* Part-time, evening/weekend, online learning. *Degree requirements:* For doctorate, comprehensive exam, thesis/dissertation, defense of dissertation. *Entrance requirements:* For master's, minimum GPA of 2.5 (students with GPA 3.0 or greater may transfer up to 30% of graduate level credits); for doctorate, minimum GPA of 3.4, curriculum vitae, course work in research methods or statistics.

Additional exam requirements/recommendations for international students: Required—TOEFL. Electronic applications accepted.

Troy University, Graduate School, College of Business, Program in Business Administration, Troy, AL 36082. Offers accounting (EMBA, MBA); criminal justice (EMBA); finance (MBA); general management (EMBA, MBA); healthcare management (EMBA); information systems (EMBA, MBA); international economic development (MBA). *Accreditation:* ACBSP. *Program availability:* Part-time, evening/weekend. *Faculty:* 10 full-time (3 women), 2 part-time/adjunct (0 women). *Students:* 44 full-time (23 women), 131 part-time (69 women); includes 58 minority (38 Black or African American, non-Hispanic/Latino; 13 Asian, non-Hispanic/Latino; 4 Hispanic/Latino; 3 Two or more races, non-Hispanic/Latino). Average age 30. 285 applicants, 91% accepted, 22 enrolled. In 2016, 78 master's awarded. *Degree requirements:* For master's, minimum GPA of 3.0, capstone course, research course. *Entrance requirements:* For master's, GMAT (minimum score 500) or GRE (minimum score 900 on old exam or 294 on new exam), bachelor's degree; minimum undergraduate GPA of 2.5 or 3.0 on last 30 semester hours, letter of recommendation. Additional exam requirements/recommendations for international students: Required—TOEFL (minimum score 523 paper-based; 70 iBT), IELTS (minimum score 6). *Application deadline:* Applications are processed on a rolling basis. Application fee: $50. Electronic applications accepted. *Expenses:* Tuition, state resident: full-time $7146; part-time $397 per credit hour. Tuition, nonresident: full-time $14,292; part-time $794 per credit hour. *Required fees:* $802; $50 per semester. Tuition and fees vary according to campus/location and program. *Financial support:* Fellowships, career-related internships or fieldwork, and scholarships/grants available. Support available to part-time students. Financial award applicants required to submit FAFSA. *Unit head:* Dr. Phillip Mixon, MBA Director, 334-670-3140, Fax: 334-670-3708, E-mail: pamixon@troy.edu. *Application contact:* Jessica A. Kimbro, Director of Graduate Admissions, 334-670-3178, E-mail: jacord@troy.edu.

Tulane University, A. B. Freeman School of Business, New Orleans, LA 70118-5669. Offers accounting (M Acct); analytics (MBA); banking and financial services (M Fin); energy (M Fin, MBA); entrepreneurship (MBA); finance (MBA, PhD); international business (MBA); international management (MBA); strategic management and leadership (MBA); JD/M Acct; JD/MBA; MBA/M Acc; MBA/MA; MBA/MD; MBA/ME; MBA/MPH. *Accreditation:* AACSB. *Program availability:* Part-time, evening/weekend. *Faculty:* 46 full-time (11 women), 36 part-time/adjunct (3 women). *Students:* 488 full-time (240 women), 414 part-time (198 women); includes 81 minority (31 Black or African American, non-Hispanic/Latino; 1 American Indian or Alaska Native, non-Hispanic/Latino; 17 Asian, non-Hispanic/Latino; 29 Hispanic/Latino; 3 Two or more races, non-Hispanic/Latino), 575 international. Average age 27. 2,038 applicants, 71% accepted, 511 enrolled. In 2016, 694 master's, 9 doctorates awarded. Terminal master's awarded for partial completion of doctoral program. *Degree requirements:* For master's, one foreign language, comprehensive exam (for some programs); for doctorate, one foreign language, comprehensive exam, thesis/dissertation. *Entrance requirements:* For master's and doctorate, GMAT or GRE, interview. Additional exam requirements/recommendations for international students: Required—TOEFL or IELTS. *Application deadline:* For fall admission, 11/1 priority date for domestic and international students; for winter admission, 1/6 for domestic and international students; for spring admission, 3/1 priority date for domestic and international students; for summer admission, 5/5 for domestic students. Applications are processed on a rolling basis. Application fee: $125. Electronic applications accepted. *Expenses:* Contact institution. *Financial support:* In 2016–17, 153 students received support. Fellowships with tuition reimbursements available, research assistantships, teaching assistantships, career-related internships or fieldwork, Federal Work-Study, tuition waivers (full and partial), and unspecified assistantships available. Support available to part-time students. Financial award application deadline: 4/15; financial award applicants required to submit FAFSA. *Faculty research:* Corporate finance, managerial accounting and financial reporting, strategic management and leadership, consumer behavior and decision making, organizational behavior and human resource management. *Unit head:* Ira Solomon, PhD, Dean, 504-865-5407, Fax: 504-865-5491, E-mail: businessdean@tulane.edu. *Application contact:* Melissa Booth, Director of Graduate Admissions and Financial Aid, 800-223-5402, E-mail: freeman.admissions@tulane.edu.
Website: http://www.freeman.tulane.edu

United States International University–Africa, School of Business Administration, Nairobi, Kenya. Offers business administration (GEMBA); entrepreneurship (MBA); finance (MBA); human resource management (MBA); information technology management (MBA); integrated studies (MBA); international business administration (MBA); management and organizational development (MS); marketing (MBA); organizational development (EMS); strategic management (MBA). *Program availability:* Part-time, evening/weekend. *Degree requirements:* For master's, thesis. *Entrance requirements:* For master's, GMAT, 2 letters of reference, resume. Additional exam requirements/recommendations for international students: Required—TOEFL (minimum score 550 paper-based). *Faculty research:* Marketing in small business enterprises, total quality management in Kenya.

Universidad Central del Este, Graduate School, San Pedro de Macoris, Dominican Republic. Offers environmental engineering (ME); financial management (M Ad); higher education (M Ed), including higher education management, higher education pedagogy; human resources (M Ad). *Entrance requirements:* For master's, letters of recommendation.

Universidad de las Americas, A.C., Program in Business Administration, Mexico City, Mexico. Offers finance (MBA); marketing research (MBA); production and quality (MBA).

Universidad de las Américas Puebla, Division of Graduate Studies, School of Business and Economics, Puebla, Mexico. Offers business administration (MBA); finance (M Adm). *Program availability:* Part-time, evening/weekend. *Degree requirements:* For master's, one foreign language, thesis. *Entrance requirements:* Additional exam requirements/recommendations for international students: Required—TOEFL. *Faculty research:* System dynamics, information technology, marketing, international business, strategic planning, quality.

Universidad de las Américas Puebla, Division of Graduate Studies, School of Social Sciences, Program in Economics, Puebla, Mexico. Offers economics (MA); finance (M Adm). *Program availability:* Part-time, evening/weekend. *Degree requirements:* For master's, one foreign language, thesis. *Faculty research:* Economic models (mathematics), industrial organization, assets and values market.

Universidad Metropolitana, School of Business Administration, Program in Finance, San Juan, PR 00928-1150. Offers MBA.

Université de Sherbrooke, Faculty of Administration, Program in Finance, Sherbrooke, QC J1K 2R1, Canada. Offers M Sc. *Degree requirements:* For master's, one foreign language, thesis. *Entrance requirements:* For master's, bachelor's degree in related field, minimum GPA of 3.0 (on 4.3 scale). Electronic applications accepted. *Faculty research:* Public projects analysis, financial econometrics, risk management, portfolio management.

Université du Québec à Montréal, Graduate Programs, Program in Finance, Montréal, QC H3C 3P8, Canada. Offers Diploma. *Program availability:* Part-time. *Entrance requirements:* For degree, appropriate bachelor's degree or equivalent, proficiency in French.

Université du Québec à Trois-Rivières, Graduate Programs, Program in Finance, Trois-Rivières, QC G9A 5H7, Canada. Offers DESS.

Université du Québec en Outaouais, Graduate Programs, Program in Financial Services, Gatineau, QC J8X 3X7, Canada. Offers MBA, DESS, Diploma. *Program availability:* Part-time, evening/weekend. *Degree requirements:* For master's, thesis (for some programs).

Université Laval, Faculty of Administrative Sciences, Programs in Business Administration, Québec, QC G1K 7P4, Canada. Offers accounting (MBA); agri-food management (MBA); electronic business (MBA, Diploma); factory management and logistics (MBA); finance (MBA); firm management (MBA); geomatic management (MBA); information technology management (MBA); international management (MBA); management (MBA); management accounting (MBA, Diploma); marketing (MBA); modeling and organizational decision (MBA); occupational health and safety management (MBA); pharmacy management (MBA); social and environmental responsibility (MBA); technological entrepreneurship (Diploma). *Accreditation:* AACSB. *Program availability:* Part-time, evening/weekend, online learning. *Entrance requirements:* For master's and Diploma, knowledge of French and English. Electronic applications accepted.

University at Albany, State University of New York, Nelson A. Rockefeller College of Public Affairs and Policy, Department of Public Administration and Policy, Albany, NY 12222-0001. Offers financial management and public economics (MPA); financial market regulation (MPA); health policy (MPA); healthcare management (MPA); homeland security (MPA); human resources management (MPA); information strategy and management (MPA); local government management (MPA); nonprofit management (MPA); nonprofit management and leadership (Certificate); organizational behavior and theory (MPA, PhD); planning and policy analysis (CAS); policy analysis (MPA); politics and administration (PhD); public finance (PhD); public management (PhD); public policy (PhD); public sector management (Certificate); women and public policy (Certificate); JD/MPA. JD/MPA offered jointly with Albany Law School. *Accreditation:* NASPAA (one or more programs are accredited). *Faculty:* 23 full-time (8 women), 14 part-time/adjunct (7 women). *Students:* 117 full-time (65 women), 95 part-time (46 women); includes 41 minority (12 Black or African American, non-Hispanic/Latino; 8 Asian, non-Hispanic/Latino; 19 Hispanic/Latino; 2 Two or more races, non-Hispanic/Latino), 38 international. 223 applicants, 70% accepted, 81 enrolled. In 2016, 52 master's, 10 doctorates, 16 other advanced degrees awarded. *Degree requirements:* For doctorate, one foreign language, thesis/dissertation. *Entrance requirements:* For doctorate, GRE General Test. Additional exam requirements/recommendations for international students: Required—TOEFL (minimum score 550 paper-based). *Application deadline:* For fall admission, 2/1 priority date for domestic students, 5/1 for international students; for spring admission, 12/1 for domestic students. Applications are processed on a rolling basis. Application fee: $75. Electronic applications accepted. *Expenses:* Tuition, state resident: full-time $10,870; part-time $453 per credit hour. Tuition, nonresident: full-time $22,210; part-time $925 per credit hour. *International tuition:* $21,550 full-time. *Required fees:* $1864; $96 per credit hour. *Financial support:* Application deadline: 2/1. *Total annual research expenditures:* $847,949. *Unit head:* Victor Asal, Chair, 518-591-8729, E-mail: vasal@albany.edu.
Website: http://www.albany.edu/rockefeller/pad.shtml

University at Albany, State University of New York, School of Business, MBA Programs, Albany, NY 12222. Offers business administration (MBA); cyber security (MBA); entrepreneurship (MBA); finance (MBA); human resource information systems (MBA); information technology management (MBA); marketing (MBA); JD/MBA. JD/MBA offered with Albany Law School. *Program availability:* Part-time, evening/weekend. *Faculty:* 25 full-time (8 women), 4 part-time/adjunct (1 woman). *Students:* 92 full-time (39 women), 192 part-time (77 women); includes 63 minority (12 Black or African American, non-Hispanic/Latino; 1 American Indian or Alaska Native, non-Hispanic/Latino; 32 Asian, non-Hispanic/Latino; 13 Hispanic/Latino; 5 Two or more races, non-Hispanic/Latino), 27 international. Average age 25. 217 applicants, 73% accepted, 119 enrolled. In 2016, 122 master's awarded. *Degree requirements:* For master's, thesis (for some programs), field or research project. *Entrance requirements:* For master's, GMAT, minimum undergraduate GPA of 3.0; 3 letters of recommendation; resume; statement of goals. Additional exam requirements/recommendations for international students: Required—TOEFL (minimum score 100 iBT); Recommended—IELTS (minimum score 7). *Application deadline:* For fall admission, 4/1 priority date for domestic students, 3/1 for international students; for spring admission, 12/1 for domestic students; for summer admission, 5/1 for domestic students. Applications are processed on a rolling basis. Application fee: $75. Electronic applications accepted. *Expenses:* $16,274 Full-Time MBA per year; $696 Part-Time MBA per credit hour. *Financial support:* In 2016–17, 20 students received support, including 20 fellowships with partial tuition reimbursements available (averaging $6,500 per year); research assistantships, teaching assistantships, and unspecified assistantships also available. Financial award application deadline: 4/1; financial award applicants required to submit FAFSA. *Faculty research:* Cyber security, entrepreneurship, human resource information systems, information technology management, finance, marketing. *Total annual research expenditures:* $136,000. *Unit head:* Dr. Hany A. Shawky, Interim Dean, 518-956-8337, E-mail: hshawky@albany.edu. *Application contact:* Zina Mega Lawrence, Assistant Dean of Graduate Student Services, 518-956-8320, Fax: 518-442-4042, E-mail: zlawrence@albany.edu.
Website: http://graduatebusiness.albany.edu/

University at Buffalo, the State University of New York, Graduate School, School of Management, Buffalo, NY 14620. Offers accounting (MS); analytics (MBA); business administration (PMBA); consulting (MBA); finance (MBA, MS), including financial risk management (MS), quantitative finance (MS); healthcare (MBA); information assurance (MBA); information systems (MBA); international management (MBA); management (EMBA, PhD); management information systems (MS); marketing (MBA); supply chain and operations (MBA); supply chains and operations management (MS); Au D/MBA; DDS/MBA; JD/MBA; M Arch/MBA; MD/MBA; MPH/MBA; MSW/MBA; Pharm D/MBA. *Accreditation:* AACSB. *Program availability:* Part-time, evening/weekend. *Faculty:* 80 full-time (26 women), 36 part-time/adjunct (6 women). *Students:* 683 full-time (277 women), 196 part-time (63 women); includes 76 minority (23 Black or African American, non-Hispanic/Latino; 1 American Indian or Alaska Native, non-Hispanic/Latino; 48 Asian, non-Hispanic/Latino; 3 Hispanic/Latino; 1 Two or more races, non-Hispanic/Latino), 371 international. Average age 31. 2,451 applicants, 42% accepted, 484 enrolled. In 2016, 515 master's, 10 doctorates awarded. *Degree requirements:* For master's, thesis (for some programs); for doctorate, comprehensive exam, thesis/dissertation. *Entrance requirements:* For master's, GMAT (for MS in accounting, finance); GRE or GMAT (for MBA, PMBA, other MS concentrations), essays, letters of recommendation; for doctorate, GMAT or GRE, essays, writing sample, letters of recommendation. Additional exam requirements/recommendations for international students: Required—TOEFL (minimum score 95 iBT) or IELTS (minimum score 6.5); Recommended—TSE (minimum score 73). *Application deadline:* For fall admission, 10/15 priority date for domestic and international students; for winter admission, 2/1 priority date for domestic and international students; for spring admission, 4/15 for domestic

students; for summer admission, 5/15 for domestic students. Application fee: $100. Electronic applications accepted. *Expenses:* Contact institution. *Financial support:* Fellowships with full and partial tuition reimbursements, research assistantships with full and partial tuition reimbursements, teaching assistantships with full and partial tuition reimbursements, career-related internships or fieldwork, Federal Work-Study, institutionally sponsored loans, scholarships/grants, health care benefits, and unspecified assistantships available. Financial award application deadline: 2/15. *Faculty research:* Data analytics, accounting information and corporate finance, consumer behavior, supply chain logistics, leadership and team effectiveness. *Total annual research expenditures:* $1.5 million. *Unit head:* Erin K. O'Brien, Assistant Dean and Director of Graduate Programs, 716-645-3204, Fax: 716-645-2341, E-mail: ekobrien@buffalo.edu. *Application contact:* Meghan Felser, Associate Director of Admissions and Recruiting, 716-645-3204, Fax: 716-645-2341, E-mail: mpwood@buffalo.edu.
Website: http://mgt.buffalo.edu/

The University of Akron, Graduate School, College of Business Administration, Department of Finance, Akron, OH 44325. Offers MBA. *Program availability:* Part-time, evening/weekend. *Faculty:* 11 full-time (3 women), 5 part-time/adjunct (0 women). *Students:* 8 full-time (2 women), 18 part-time (4 women); includes 2 minority (1 Black or African American, non-Hispanic/Latino; 1 Asian, non-Hispanic/Latino), 5 international. Average age 28. 10 applicants, 90% accepted, 3 enrolled. In 2016, 18 master's awarded. *Entrance requirements:* For master's, GMAT, minimum GPA of 3.0 (preferred), two letters of recommendation, statement of purpose, resume. Additional exam requirements/recommendations for international students: Required—TOEFL (minimum score 550 paper-based; 79 iBT), IELTS (minimum score 6.5). *Application deadline:* For fall admission, 7/15 for domestic and international students; for spring admission, 11/15 for domestic and international students; for summer admission, 4/15 for domestic and international students. Application fee: $45 ($75 for international students). Electronic applications accepted. *Expenses:* Tuition, state resident: full-time $8618; part-time $359 per credit hour. Tuition, nonresident: full-time $17,149; part-time $715 per credit hour. *Required fees:* $1652. *Financial support:* Unspecified assistantships and instructional support assistantships available. *Faculty research:* Corporate finance, financial markets and institutions, investment and equity market analysis, personal financial planning, real estate. *Total annual research expenditures:* $15,809. *Unit head:* Dr. James Thomson, Chair, 330-972-6329, E-mail: thomson1@uakron.edu. *Application contact:* Dr. William Hauser, Director of Graduate Business Programs, 330-972-7043, Fax: 330-972-6588, E-mail: whauser@uakron.edu.
Website: http://www.uakron.edu/cba/departments/finance/

The University of Alabama, Graduate School, Manderson Graduate School of Business, Economics, Finance and Legal Studies Department, Tuscaloosa, AL 35487. Offers economics (MA, PhD); finance (MS, PhD). *Faculty:* 25 full-time (3 women). *Students:* 47 full-time (15 women), 7 part-time (1 woman); includes 2 minority (1 Asian, non-Hispanic/Latino; 1 Two or more races, non-Hispanic/Latino), 32 international. Average age 28. 178 applicants, 29% accepted, 13 enrolled. In 2016, 36 master's, 6 doctorates awarded. Terminal master's awarded for partial completion of doctoral program. *Degree requirements:* For master's, comprehensive exam (MA), thesis (MS); for doctorate, comprehensive exam, thesis/dissertation. *Entrance requirements:* For master's, GMAT, GRE; for doctorate, GRE or GMAT. Additional exam requirements/recommendations for international students: Required—TOEFL (minimum score 550 paper-based; 79 iBT). *Application deadline:* For fall admission, 7/1 priority date for domestic students, 1/15 for international students; for spring admission, 11/1 priority date for domestic students, 6/1 for international students. Applications are processed on a rolling basis. Application fee: $50 ($60 for international students). Electronic applications accepted. *Expenses:* Tuition, state resident: full-time $10,470. Tuition, nonresident: full-time $26,950. *Financial support:* In 2016–17, 43 students received support, including 24 research assistantships with tuition reimbursements available (averaging $15,000 per year), 19 teaching assistantships with tuition reimbursements available (averaging $15,000 per year); fellowships, Federal Work-Study, institutionally sponsored loans, and unspecified assistantships also available. Financial award application deadline: 1/15. *Faculty research:* Taxation, futures market, monetary theory and policy, income distribution. *Unit head:* Dr. Laura Razzolini, Department Head, 205-348-6683, E-mail: kcwise@cba.ua.edu. *Application contact:* Debra F. Wheatley, Graduate Programs Secretary, 205-348-6683, Fax: 205-348-0590, E-mail: dwheatle@cba.ua.edu.
Website: http://www.cba.ua.edu/

The University of Alabama at Birmingham, Collat School of Business, Program in Business Administration, Birmingham, AL 35294. Offers business administration (MBA), including finance, health care management, information technology management, marketing. *Program availability:* Part-time, evening/weekend. *Entrance requirements:* For master's, GMAT. Additional exam requirements/recommendations for international students: Required—TOEFL. Full-time tuition and fees vary according to course load and program.

The University of Alabama in Huntsville, School of Graduate Studies, College of Business Administration, Program in Accounting, Huntsville, AL 35899. Offers accounting (M Acc), including CPA preparatory with an emphasis in taxation, CPA preparatory with emphasis in assurance and financial reporting, general accounting, information systems audit and control (ISAC). *Accreditation:* AACSB. *Program availability:* Part-time, evening/weekend. *Degree requirements:* For master's, comprehensive exam, thesis or alternative. *Entrance requirements:* For master's, GMAT (minimum score 500), minimum AACSB index of 1080. Additional exam requirements/recommendations for international students: Required—TOEFL (minimum score 550 paper-based; 80 iBT), IELTS (minimum score 6.5). Electronic applications accepted. *Expenses:* Tuition, state resident: full-time $9834; part-time $600 per credit hour. Tuition, nonresident: full-time $21,830; part-time $1325 per credit hour. *Faculty research:* Accounting information systems, managerial accounting, behavioral accounting, state and local taxation, financial accounting.

The University of Alabama in Huntsville, School of Graduate Studies, College of Business Administration, Programs in Business and Management, Huntsville, AL 35899. Offers business analytics (MSMS); federal contracting and procurement management (Certificate); human resource management (MSM); management (MBA), including acquisition management, entrepreneurship, federal contract accounting, finance, human resource management, logistics and supply chain management, marketing, project management; supply chain management (Certificate); technology and innovation management (Certificate). *Accreditation:* AACSB. *Program availability:* Part-time, evening/weekend. *Degree requirements:* For master's, comprehensive exam, thesis or alternative. *Entrance requirements:* For master's, GMAT (minimum score 500), minimum AACSB index of 1080. Additional exam requirements/recommendations for international students: Required—TOEFL (minimum score 550 paper-based; 80 iBT), IELTS (minimum score 6.5). Electronic applications accepted. *Expenses:* Tuition, state resident: full-time $9834; part-time $600 per credit hour. Tuition, nonresident: full-time $21,830; part-time $1325 per credit hour. *Faculty research:* Supply chain management, management of research and development, international marketing and branding, organizational behavior and human resource management, social networks and computational economics.

University of Alaska Fairbanks, School of Management, Department of Business Administration, Fairbanks, AK 99775-6080. Offers capital markets (MBA); general management (MBA). *Accreditation:* AACSB. *Program availability:* Part-time, online only, 100% online. *Faculty:* 10 full-time (4 women). *Students:* 32 full-time (18 women), 55 part-time (28 women); includes 21 minority (3 Black or African American, non-Hispanic/Latino; 7 American Indian or Alaska Native, non-Hispanic/Latino; 3 Asian, non-Hispanic/Latino; 3 Hispanic/Latino; 1 Native Hawaiian or other Pacific Islander, non-Hispanic/Latino; 4 Two or more races, non-Hispanic/Latino), 7 international. Average age 31. 62 applicants, 66% accepted, 29 enrolled. In 2016, 30 master's awarded. *Degree requirements:* For master's, comprehensive exam, thesis or alternative. *Entrance requirements:* For master's, GRE General Test, GMAT, bachelor's degree from accredited institution with minimum cumulative undergraduate and major GPA of 3.0. Additional exam requirements/recommendations for international students: Required—TOEFL (minimum score 550 paper-based; 79 iBT), IELTS (minimum score 6.5). *Application deadline:* For fall admission, 3/1 priority date for domestic students, 2/1 for international students; for spring admission, 9/1 priority date for domestic students, 9/1 for international students. Applications are processed on a rolling basis. Application fee: $60. Electronic applications accepted. *Expenses:* $533 per credit resident tuition, $673 per semester resident fees; $1,088 per credit non-resident tuition, $835 per semester non-resident fees. *Financial support:* In 2016–17, 5 teaching assistantships with full tuition reimbursements (averaging $9,699 per year) were awarded; fellowships with full tuition reimbursements, research assistantships with full tuition reimbursements, career-related internships or fieldwork, Federal Work-Study, scholarships/grants, health care benefits, and unspecified assistantships also available. Support available to part-time students. Financial award application deadline: 2/15; financial award applicants required to submit FAFSA. *Faculty research:* Consumer behavior, marketing, international finance and business, strategic risk, organization theory. *Unit head:* Dr. Nicole Cundiff, Program Director, 907-474-7461, Fax: 907-474-5219, E-mail: uaf-som@alaska.edu. *Application contact:* Mary Kreta, Director of Admissions, 907-474-7500, Fax: 907-474-7097, E-mail: admissions@uaf.edu.
Website: http://www.uaf.edu/som/degrees/graduate/mba/

University of Alberta, Faculty of Graduate Studies and Research, Department of Economics, Edmonton, AB T6G 2E1, Canada. Offers economics (MA, PhD); economics and finance (MA); environmental and natural resource economics (PhD). *Program availability:* Part-time. *Degree requirements:* For doctorate, thesis/dissertation. *Entrance requirements:* For master's and doctorate, GRE. Additional exam requirements/recommendations for international students: Required—TOEFL. *Faculty research:* Public finance, international trade, industrial organization, Pacific Rim economics, monetary economics.

University of Alberta, Faculty of Graduate Studies and Research, Doctoral Program in Business, Edmonton, AB T6G 2E1, Canada. Offers accounting (PhD); finance (PhD); human resources/industrial relations (PhD); management science (PhD); marketing (PhD); organizational analysis (PhD); MBA/PhD. *Accreditation:* AACSB. *Program availability:* Part-time. *Degree requirements:* For doctorate, comprehensive exam, thesis/dissertation. *Entrance requirements:* For doctorate, GMAT. Additional exam requirements/recommendations for international students: Required—TOEFL (minimum score 550 paper-based). Electronic applications accepted. *Faculty research:* Accounting, capital markets and corporate finance, organizational change and human resource management, marketing, strategic management.

The University of Arizona, Eller College of Management, Department of Finance, Tucson, AZ 85721. Offers MS. *Program availability:* Part-time. Terminal master's awarded for partial completion of doctoral program. *Degree requirements:* For master's, project. *Entrance requirements:* Additional exam requirements/recommendations for international students: Required—TOEFL (minimum score 550 paper-based; 79 iBT). Electronic applications accepted. *Expenses:* Contact institution. *Faculty research:* Corporate finance, banking, investments, stock market.

University of Baltimore, Graduate School, Merrick School of Business, Department of Finance and Economics, Baltimore, MD 21201-5779. Offers business/finance (MS). *Program availability:* Part-time, evening/weekend. *Entrance requirements:* For master's, GMAT. Additional exam requirements/recommendations for international students: Required—TOEFL (minimum score 550 paper-based). Electronic applications accepted. *Faculty research:* International finance, corporate finance, health care, regional economics, small business.

University of Bridgeport, School of Business, Bridgeport, CT 06604. Offers accounting (MBA); finance (MBA); general business (MBA); global financial services (MBA); human resource management (MBA); information systems and knowledge management (MBA); international business (MBA); management (MBA); marketing (MBA); operations management (MBA); small business and entrepreneurship (MBA); specialized business (MBA). *Accreditation:* ACBSP. *Program availability:* Part-time, evening/weekend. *Degree requirements:* For master's, thesis optional. *Entrance requirements:* For master's, GMAT. Additional exam requirements/recommendations for international students: Recommended—TOEFL (minimum score 550 paper-based; 80 iBT), IELTS (minimum score 6.5). Electronic applications accepted. *Expenses:* Contact institution.

The University of British Columbia, Sauder School of Business, Doctoral Program in Business Administration, Vancouver, BC V6T 1Z2, Canada. Offers accounting (PhD); finance (PhD); management information systems (PhD); management science (PhD); marketing (PhD); organizational behavior (PhD); strategy and business economics (PhD); transportation and logistics (PhD); urban land economics (PhD). *Degree requirements:* For doctorate, comprehensive exam, thesis/dissertation. *Entrance requirements:* For doctorate, GMAT or GRE. Additional exam requirements/recommendations for international students: Required—TOEFL (minimum score 600 paper-based; 100 iBT). *Application deadline:* Applications are processed on a rolling basis. Application fee: $102 Canadian dollars ($165 Canadian dollars for international students). Electronic applications accepted. *Expenses:* $4,802 per year tuition and fees, $8,436 per year international. *Financial support:* Fellowships with full tuition reimbursements, research assistantships with full tuition reimbursements, and teaching assistantships with full tuition reimbursements available. *Application contact:* Elaine Cho, Administrator, PhD and M Sc Programs, 604-822-8366, Fax: 604-822-8755, E-mail: phd.program@sauder.ubc.ca.
Website: http://www.sauder.ubc.ca/Programs/PhD_in_Business_Administration

University of California, Berkeley, Graduate Division, Haas School of Business, PhD in Business Administration Program, Berkeley, CA 94720-1500. Offers accounting (PhD); business and public policy (PhD); finance (PhD); management of organizations (PhD); marketing (PhD); real estate (PhD). *Accreditation:* AACSB. *Students:* 78 full-time (28 women); includes 34 minority (29 Asian, non-Hispanic/Latino; 5 Hispanic/Latino). Average age 27. *Degree requirements:* For doctorate, comprehensive exam, thesis/dissertation, written preliminary exams, oral qualifying exam. *Entrance requirements:* For doctorate, GMAT or GRE, minimum GPA of 3.0 in undergraduate and graduate coursework. Additional exam requirements/recommendations for international students: Required—TOEFL (minimum score 570 paper-based; 70 iBT), IELTS (minimum score 7). *Application deadline:* For fall admission, 12/1 for domestic and international students. Application fee: $90 ($110 for international students). Electronic applications accepted. *Expenses:* Contact institution. *Financial support:* Fellowships with tuition

reimbursements, research assistantships with tuition reimbursements, teaching assistantships with tuition reimbursements, scholarships/grants, health care benefits, tuition waivers (full), unspecified assistantships, and transit passes, travel grants available. Financial award application deadline: 12/10. *Faculty research:* Accounting, business and public policy, entrepreneurship, finance, management of organizations, marketing, operations and information technology management, real estate. *Unit head:* Dr. Nicolae Garleanu, Director, 510-643-6349, Fax: 510-643-4255. *Application contact:* Melissa Hacker, Director, Student Affairs, 510-642-3944, Fax: 510-643-4255, E-mail: melhacker@haas.berkeley.edu.
Website: http://www.haas.berkeley.edu/Phd/

University of California, Berkeley, UC Berkeley Extension, Certificate Programs in Business, Berkeley, CA 94720-1500. Offers accounting (Certificate); business administration (Certificate); finance (Certificate); human resource management (Certificate); management (Certificate); marketing (Certificate); project management (Certificate). *Accreditation:* AACSB. *Program availability:* Online learning.

University of California, Berkeley, UC Berkeley Extension, International Diploma Programs, Berkeley, CA 94720-1500. Offers business administration (Certificate); finance (Certificate); global business management (Certificate); marketing (Certificate); project management (Certificate). *Accreditation:* AACSB.

University of California, Los Angeles, Graduate Division, UCLA Anderson School of Management, Los Angeles, CA 90095-1481. Offers accounting (PhD); behavioral decision making (PhD); business administration (EMBA, MBA); decisions, operations, and technology management (PhD); finance (PhD); financial engineering (MFE); global economics and management (PhD); management and organizations (PhD); marketing (PhD); strategy and policy (PhD); DDS/MBA; MBA/JD; MBA/MD; MBA/MLAS; MBA/MLIS; MBA/MN; MBA/MPH; MBA/MPP; MBA/MSCS; MBA/MURP. *Accreditation:* AACSB. *Program availability:* Part-time, evening/weekend. *Faculty:* 90 full-time (20 women), 98 part-time/adjunct (19 women). *Students:* 865 full-time (263 women), 1,201 part-time (337 women); includes 710 minority (48 Black or African American, non-Hispanic/Latino; 1 American Indian or Alaska Native, non-Hispanic/Latino; 505 Asian, non-Hispanic/Latino; 88 Hispanic/Latino; 4 Native Hawaiian or other Pacific Islander, non-Hispanic/Latino; 64 Two or more races, non-Hispanic/Latino), 451 international. Average age 31. 5,643 applicants, 26% accepted, 881 enrolled. In 2016, 807 master's, 7 doctorates awarded. *Degree requirements:* For master's, comprehensive exam, field consulting project; internship (for MBA); thesis/dissertation (for MFE); for doctorate, comprehensive exam, thesis/dissertation, oral and written qualifying exams. *Entrance requirements:* For master's, GMAT or GRE, 4-year bachelor's degree or equivalent; 2 letters of recommendation; essays (1 for MBA, 2 for FEMBA and MFE); 4-8 years of full-time work experience (for FEMBA); minimum eight years of work experience with at least three years at management level (for EMBA); for doctorate, GMAT or GRE, bachelor's degree from college or university of fully-recognized standing, minimum B average during junior and senior years of undergraduate years, 3 letters of recommendation, statement of purpose. Additional exam requirements/recommendations for international students: Required—TOEFL (minimum score 560 paper-based; 87 iBT), IELTS (minimum score 7). *Application deadline:* For fall admission, 10/6 priority date for domestic and international students; for winter admission, 1/5 for domestic and international students; for spring admission, 4/12 for domestic and international students. Applications are processed on a rolling basis. Application fee: $200. Electronic applications accepted. *Expenses:* Contact institution. *Financial support:* In 2016–17, 633 students received support, including 455 fellowships (averaging $30,253 per year); research assistantships with partial tuition reimbursements available, teaching assistantships with partial tuition reimbursements available, career-related internships or fieldwork, institutionally sponsored loans, and scholarships/grants also available. Support available to part-time students. *Faculty research:* Finance/global economics, entrepreneurship, accounting, human resources/organizational behavior, marketing, behavioral decision making. *Total annual research expenditures:* $1.1 million. *Unit head:* Dr. Judy D. Olian, Dean/Chair in Management, 310-825-7982, Fax: 310-206-2073, E-mail: judy.olian@anderson.ucla.edu. *Application contact:* Alex Lawrence, Assistant Dean and Director of MBA Admissions, 310-825-6944, Fax: 310-825-8582, E-mail: mba.admissions@anderson.ucla.edu.
Website: http://www.anderson.ucla.edu/

University of California, San Diego, Graduate Division, Rady School of Management, La Jolla, CA 92093. Offers business administration (MBA); business analytics (MS); finance (MF); management (PhD). *Accreditation:* AACSB. *Program availability:* Part-time, evening/weekend. *Faculty:* 28 full-time (5 women), 5 part-time/adjunct (1 woman). *Students:* 433 full-time (183 women), 89 part-time (35 women). 2,021 applicants, 32% accepted, 313 enrolled. In 2016, 152 master's, 5 doctorates awarded. *Degree requirements:* For master's, capstone project; for doctorate, comprehensive exam, thesis/dissertation. *Entrance requirements:* For master's, GMAT (for MBA); GMAT or GRE General Test (for MF); for doctorate, GMAT or GRE General Test. Additional exam requirements/recommendations for international students: Required—TOEFL (minimum score 550 paper-based; 80 IBT), IELTS (minimum score 7). *Application deadline:* Applications are processed on a rolling basis. Application fee: $200. Electronic applications accepted. *Expenses:* Contact institution. *Financial support:* Fellowships, teaching assistantships, and scholarships/grants available. Financial award applicants required to submit FAFSA. *Faculty research:* Innovation technology, operations management, finance, behavioral economics, organizational strategy, marketing, business analytics. *Unit head:* Robert Sullivan, Dean, 858-822-0830, E-mail: rssullivan@ucsd.edu. *Application contact:* Jay Bryant, Director of Graduate Recruitment and Admissions, 858-534-0864, E-mail: radygradadmissions@ucsd.edu.
Website: http://rady.ucsd.edu/

University of California, Santa Barbara, Graduate Division, College of Letters and Sciences, Division of Social Sciences, Department of Economics, Santa Barbara, CA 93106-9210. Offers economics (MA); mathematical economics (PhD); public finance (PhD); MA/PhD. Terminal master's awarded for partial completion of doctoral program. *Degree requirements:* For master's, comprehensive exam; for doctorate, comprehensive exam, thesis/dissertation. *Entrance requirements:* For master's and doctorate, GRE General Test, 3 letters of recommendation, statement of purpose, personal achievements/contributions statement, resume/curriculum vitae, transcripts for post-secondary institutions attended. Additional exam requirements/recommendations for international students: Required—TOEFL (minimum score 550 paper-based; 80 iBT), IELTS (minimum score 7), TOEFL (minimum score 600 paper-based or 100 iBT) for PhD. Electronic applications accepted. *Faculty research:* Labor economics, econometrics, macroeconomic theory and policy, environmental and natural resources economics, experimental and behavioral economics.

University of California, Santa Cruz, Division of Graduate Studies, Division of Social Sciences, Program in Applied Economics and Finance, Santa Cruz, CA 95064. Offers MS. *Degree requirements:* For master's, thesis or alternative, project. *Entrance requirements:* For master's, GRE General Test, GRE Subject Test. Additional exam requirements/recommendations for international students: Required—TOEFL (minimum score 550 paper-based; 83 iBT); Recommended—IELTS (minimum score 8). Electronic applications accepted. *Faculty research:* Economic decision-making skills for the design and operation of complex institutional systems.

University of Central Missouri, The Graduate School, Warrensburg, MO 64093. Offers accountancy (MA); accounting (MBA); applied mathematics (MS); aviation safety (MA); biology (MS); business administration (MBA); career and technical education leadership (MS); college student personnel administration (MS); communication (MA); computer science (MS); counseling (MS); criminal justice (MS); educational leadership (Ed D); educational technology (MS); elementary and early childhood education (MSE); English (MA); environmental studies (MA); finance (MBA); history (MA); human services/educational technology (Ed S); human services/learning resources (Ed S); human services/professional counseling (Ed S); industrial hygiene (MS); industrial management (MS); information systems (MBA); information technology (MS); kinesiology (MS); library science and information services (MS); literacy education (MSE); marketing (MBA); mathematics (MS); music (MA); occupational safety management (MS); psychology (MS); rural family nursing (MS); school administration (MSE); social gerontology (MS); sociology (MA); special education (MSE); speech language pathology (MS); superintendency (Ed S); teaching (MAT); teaching English as a second language (MA); technology (MS); technology management (PhD); theatre (MA). *Program availability:* Part-time, 100% online, blended/hybrid learning. *Degree requirements:* For master's and Ed S, comprehensive exam (for some programs), thesis (for some programs). *Entrance requirements:* Additional exam requirements/recommendations for international students: Required—TOEFL (minimum score 550 paper-based; 79 iBT). Electronic applications accepted.

University of Chicago, Booth School of Business, Full-Time MBA Program, Chicago, IL 60637. Offers accounting (MBA); analytic finance (MBA); analytic management (MBA); econometrics and statistics (MBA); economics (MBA); entrepreneurship (MBA); finance (MBA); general management (MBA); health administration and policy (Certificate); international business (MBA); managerial and organizational behavior (MBA); marketing analytics (MBA); marketing management (MBA); operations management (MBA); strategic management (MBA); MBA/AM; MBA/JD; MBA/MA; MBA/MD; MBA/MPP. *Accreditation:* AACSB. *Students:* 1,151 full-time (443 women), 17 part-time (9 women). Terminal master's awarded for partial completion of doctoral program. *Entrance requirements:* For master's, GMAT or GRE, transcripts, resume, 2 letters of recommendation, essay, interview. Additional exam requirements/recommendations for international students: Required—TOEFL (minimum score 600 paper-based; 104 iBT), IELTS (minimum score 7), PTE (minimum score 70). *Application deadline:* For spring admission, 4/1 for domestic and international students. Electronic applications accepted. *Expenses:* Contact institution. *Unit head:* Stacey Kole, Deputy Dean, 773-702-7121. *Application contact:* Full-time MBA Program Admissions, 773-702-7369, Fax: 773-702-9085, E-mail: admissions@chicagobooth.edu.
Website: https://www.chicagobooth.edu/programs/full-time

University of Cincinnati, Graduate School, Carl H. Lindner College of Business, MS Program, Cincinnati, OH 45221. Offers accounting (MS); business analytics (MS); finance (MS); information systems (MS); marketing (MS); taxation (MS). *Program availability:* Part-time, evening/weekend. *Faculty:* 74 full-time (17 women), 33 part-time/adjunct (8 women). *Students:* 307 full-time (128 women), 246 part-time (106 women); includes 60 minority (22 Black or African American, non-Hispanic/Latino; 20 Asian, non-Hispanic/Latino; 9 Hispanic/Latino; 1 Native Hawaiian or other Pacific Islander, non-Hispanic/Latino; 8 Two or more races, non-Hispanic/Latino), 321 international. Average age 28. 1,756 applicants, 24% accepted, 351 enrolled. In 2016, 334 master's awarded. *Degree requirements:* For master's, thesis (for some programs). *Entrance requirements:* For master's, GMAT, GRE, resume, transcripts, essays, letters of recommendation. Additional exam requirements/recommendations for international students: Required—TOEFL (minimum score 577 paper-based; 90 iBT), IELTS (minimum score 6.5). *Application deadline:* For fall admission, 8/1 priority date for domestic students, 3/15 for international students; for spring admission, 12/15 for domestic students, 9/15 for international students; for summer admission, 4/15 for domestic and international students. Applications are processed on a rolling basis. Application fee: $65 ($70 for international students). Electronic applications accepted. *Expenses:* Contact institution. *Financial support:* In 2016–17, 251 students received support, including 12 teaching assistantships with tuition reimbursements available (averaging $3,500 per year); scholarships/grants, tuition waivers (full and partial), and unspecified assistantships also available. Financial award application deadline: 2/1; financial award applicants required to submit FAFSA. *Faculty research:* Real estate, empirical pricing, organization information pricing, strategic management, portfolio choice in institutional investment. *Unit head:* Dr. David Szymanski, Dean, 513-556-7001, Fax: 513-556-4891, E-mail: david.szymanski@uc.edu. *Application contact:* Dona Clary, Director, Graduate Programs, 513-556-3546, Fax: 513-558-7006, E-mail: dona.clary@uc.edu.

University of Cincinnati, Graduate School, Carl H. Lindner College of Business, PhD Programs, Cincinnati, OH 45211. Offers accounting (PhD); economics (PhD); finance (PhD); information systems (PhD); management (PhD); marketing (PhD); operations and business analytics (PhD). *Faculty:* 72 full-time (18 women). *Students:* 37 full-time (19 women); includes 4 minority (1 Black or African American, non-Hispanic/Latino; 3 Asian, non-Hispanic/Latino), 19 international. Average age 30. 92 applicants, 16% accepted, 7 enrolled. In 2016, 4 doctorates awarded. *Degree requirements:* For doctorate, comprehensive exam, thesis/dissertation. *Entrance requirements:* For doctorate, GMAT, GRE, transcripts, essays, resume, letters of recommendation. Additional exam requirements/recommendations for international students: Required—TOEFL (minimum score 600 paper-based; 100 iBT), IELTS (minimum score 7). *Application deadline:* For fall admission, 1/15 for domestic and international students. Application fee: $65 ($70 for international students). Electronic applications accepted. *Expenses:* Contact institution. *Financial support:* In 2016–17, 38 students received support, including 25 research assistantships with tuition reimbursements available (averaging $23,250 per year); scholarships/grants, tuition waivers (full and partial), and unspecified assistantships also available. Financial award application deadline: 1/15; financial award applicants required to submit FAFSA. *Faculty research:* Bayesian Prediction Theory, organizational fairness, consumer insight and market research, EGARCH idiosyncratic volatility and expected stock returns, consumer insight and market research, density estimation from correlated data. *Unit head:* Dr. Suzanne Masterson, Director, 513-556-7125, Fax: 513-556-5499, E-mail: suzanne.masterson@uc.edu. *Application contact:* Angel Elvin, Assistant Director, 513-556-7190, Fax: 513-558-7006, E-mail: angel.elvin@uc.edu.
Website: http://www.business.uc.edu/phd

University of Colorado Denver, Business School, Master of Business Administration Program, Denver, CO 80217. Offers bioinnovation and entrepreneurship (MBA); business intelligence (MBA); business strategy (MBA); business to business marketing (MBA); business to consumer marketing (MBA); change management (MBA); corporate financial management (MBA); enterprise technology management (MBA); entrepreneurship (MBA), health administration (MBA), including financial management, health administration, health information technologies, international health management and policy; human resources management (MBA); international business (MBA); investment management (MBA); managing for sustainability (MBA); sports and entertainment management (MBA). *Accreditation:* AACSB. *Program availability:* Part-time, evening/weekend, 100% online, blended/hybrid learning. *Students:* 544 full-time (210 women), 112 part-time (22 women); includes 99 minority (15 Black or African American, non-Hispanic/Latino; 4 American Indian or Alaska Native, non-Hispanic/

Latino; 38 Asian, non-Hispanic/Latino; 36 Hispanic/Latino; 6 Two or more races, non-Hispanic/Latino), 22 international. Average age 32. 335 applicants, 73% accepted, 179 enrolled. In 2016, 251 master's awarded. *Degree requirements:* For master's, 48 semester hours, including 30 of core courses, 3 in international business, and 15 in electives from over 50 other business courses. *Entrance requirements:* For master's, GMAT, resume, official transcripts, essay, two letters of recommendation, financial statements (for international applicants). Additional exam requirements/recommendations for international students: Required—TOEFL (minimum score 560 paper-based; 83 iBT); Recommended—IELTS (minimum score 6.5). *Application deadline:* For fall admission, 4/15 priority date for domestic students, 3/15 priority date for international students; for spring admission, 10/15 priority date for domestic students, 9/15 priority date for international students; for summer admission, 2/15 priority date for domestic students, 1/15 priority date for international students. Applications are processed on a rolling basis. Application fee: $50 ($75 for international students). Electronic applications accepted. *Expenses:* Contact institution. *Financial support:* In 2016–17, 171 students received support. Fellowships, research assistantships, teaching assistantships, Federal Work-Study, institutionally sponsored loans, scholarships/grants, traineeships, and unspecified assistantships available. Financial award application deadline: 4/1; financial award applicants required to submit FAFSA. *Faculty research:* Marketing, management, entrepreneurship, finance, health administration. *Unit head:* Woodrow Eckard, MBA Director, 303-315-8470, E-mail: woody.eckard@ucdenver.edu. *Application contact:* Shelly Townley, Admissions Director, Graduate Programs, 303-315-8202, E-mail: shelly.townley@ucdenver.edu.
Website: http://www.ucdenver.edu/academics/colleges/business/degrees/mba/Pages/MBA.aspx

University of Colorado Denver, Business School, Program in Finance, Denver, CO 80217. Offers economics (MS); finance (MS); financial analysis and management (MS); financial and commodities risk management (MS); risk management and insurance (MS); MS/MA; MS/MBA. *Program availability:* Part-time, evening/weekend. *Students:* 59 full-time (19 women), 25 part-time (4 women); includes 11 minority (1 Black or African American, non-Hispanic/Latino; 4 Asian, non-Hispanic/Latino; 5 Hispanic/Latino; 1 Two or more races, non-Hispanic/Latino), 12 international. Average age 31. 85 applicants, 35% accepted, 12 enrolled. In 2016, 45 master's awarded. *Degree requirements:* For master's, 30 semester hours (18 of required core courses, 9 of finance electives, and 3 of free elective). *Entrance requirements:* For master's, GMAT, essay, resume, two letters of recommendation; financial statements (for international students). Additional exam requirements/recommendations for international students: Required—TOEFL (minimum score 537 paper-based; 75 iBT); Recommended—IELTS (minimum score 6.5). *Application deadline:* For fall admission, 4/15 priority date for domestic students, 3/15 priority date for international students; for spring admission, 10/15 priority date for domestic students, 9/15 priority date for international students; for summer admission, 2/15 priority date for domestic students, 1/15 priority date for international students. Applications are processed on a rolling basis. Application fee: $50 ($75 for international students). Electronic applications accepted. *Expenses:* Contact institution. *Financial support:* In 2016–17, 27 students received support. Teaching assistantships, Federal Work-Study, institutionally sponsored loans, scholarships/grants, and traineeships available. Financial award application deadline: 4/1; financial award applicants required to submit FAFSA. *Faculty research:* Corporate governance, debt maturity policies, regulation and financial markets, option management strategies. *Unit head:* Jian Yang, Director of the Finance Program, 303-315-8423, E-mail: jian.yang@ucdenver.edu. *Application contact:* 303-315-8200, E-mail: bschool.admissions@ucdenver.edu.
Website: http://www.ucdenver.edu/academics/colleges/business/degrees/ms/finance/Pages/Finance.aspx

University of Connecticut, Graduate School, College of Liberal Arts and Sciences, Department of Public Policy, Storrs, CT 06269. Offers public administration (MPA, Graduate Certificate), including nonprofit management (Graduate Certificate), public financial management (Graduate Certificate); survey research (MA, Graduate Certificate), including quantitative research methods (Graduate Certificate), survey research (MA); JD/MPA; MPA/MSW. *Degree requirements:* For master's, comprehensive exam. *Entrance requirements:* For master's, GRE General Test. Additional exam requirements/recommendations for international students: Required—TOEFL (minimum score 550 paper-based). Electronic applications accepted.

University of Connecticut, Graduate School, School of Business, Storrs, CT 06269. Offers accounting (MS, PhD); business administration (MBA, PhD); finance (PhD); health care management and insurance studies (MBA); management (PhD); management consulting (MBA); marketing (PhD); marketing intelligence (MBA). *Accreditation:* AACSB. *Degree requirements:* For master's, comprehensive exam; for doctorate, thesis/dissertation. *Entrance requirements:* For master's and doctorate, GMAT. Additional exam requirements/recommendations for international students: Required—TOEFL (minimum score 550 paper-based). Electronic applications accepted.

University of Dallas, Satish and Yasmin Gupta College of Business, Irving, TX 75062-4736. Offers accounting (MBA, MS); business administration (DBA); business analytics (MS); business management (MBA); corporate finance (MBA); cybersecurity (MS); finance (MS); financial services (MBA); global business (MBA, MS); health services management (MBA); human resource management (MBA); information and technology management (MS); information assurance (MBA); information technology (MBA); information technology service management (MBA); marketing management (MBA); organization development (MBA); project management (MBA); sports and entertainment management (MBA); strategic leadership (MBA); supply chain management (MBA). *Accreditation:* AACSB. *Program availability:* Part-time, evening/weekend, online learning. *Entrance requirements:* Additional exam requirements/recommendations for international students: Required—TOEFL. Electronic applications accepted. *Expenses:* Contact institution.

University of Dayton, School of Business Administration, Dayton, OH 45469. Offers accounting (MBA); cyber security (MBA); finance (MBA); marketing (MBA); JD/MBA. *Accreditation:* AACSB. *Program availability:* Part-time, evening/weekend, blended/hybrid learning. *Faculty:* 23 full-time (5 women), 18 part-time/adjunct (9 women). *Students:* 94 full-time (35 women), 85 part-time (38 women); includes 14 minority (5 Black or African American, non-Hispanic/Latino; 4 Asian, non-Hispanic/Latino; 5 Hispanic/Latino), 26 international. Average age 30. 269 applicants, 31% accepted. In 2016, 93 master's awarded. *Entrance requirements:* For master's, GMAT (minimum score of 500 total, 19 verbal); GRE (minimum score of 149 verbal, 146 quantitative), minimum GPA of 3.0, current resume. Additional exam requirements/recommendations for international students: Required—TOEFL (minimum score 550 paper-based; 80 iBT); Recommended—IELTS (minimum score 6.5). *Application deadline:* Applications are processed on a rolling basis. Application fee: $0 ($50 for international students). Electronic applications accepted. *Expenses:* $970 per credit hour, $25 registration fee per term. *Financial support:* In 2016–17, 7 research assistantships with partial tuition reimbursements (averaging $8,535 per year), 2 teaching assistantships with partial tuition reimbursements (averaging $8,535 per year) were awarded; institutionally sponsored loans, health care benefits, and unspecified assistantships also available. Financial award application deadline: 3/1; financial award applicants required to submit FAFSA. *Faculty research:* Asset pricing, applied microeconomics, financial reporting and auditing, entrepreneurship. *Unit head:* Scott MacDonald, Director, MBA Program, 937-229-3733, Fax: 937-229-3882, E-mail: smacdonald1@udayton.edu. *Application contact:* Mandy Bingaman, MBA Program Manager, 937-229-3733, Fax: 937-229-3882, E-mail: mbingaman1@udayton.edu.
Website: https://www.udayton.edu/business/academics/master_of_business_administration/index.php

University of Delaware, Alfred Lerner College of Business and Economics, Department of Finance, Newark, DE 19716. Offers MS.

University of Denver, Daniels College of Business, Reiman School of Finance, Denver, CO 80208. Offers applied quantitative finance (MS); finance (MBA). *Program availability:* Part-time, evening/weekend. *Faculty:* 18 full-time (4 women), 3 part-time/adjunct (0 women). *Students:* 45 full-time (19 women), 28 part-time (6 women); includes 7 minority (1 Black or African American, non-Hispanic/Latino; 1 Asian, non-Hispanic/Latino; 4 Hispanic/Latino; 1 Two or more races, non-Hispanic/Latino), 38 international. Average age 25. 324 applicants, 48% accepted, 31 enrolled. In 2016, 51 master's awarded. *Entrance requirements:* For master's, GRE General Test or GMAT, bachelor's degree, transcripts, resume, two letters of recommendation, essays, interview. Additional exam requirements/recommendations for international students: Required—TOEFL (minimum score 570 paper-based; 88 iBT). *Application deadline:* For fall admission, 11/15 priority date for domestic and international students; for spring admission, 10/1 priority date for domestic and international students. Applications are processed on a rolling basis. Application fee: $100. Electronic applications accepted. *Expenses:* $43,458 per year full-time. *Financial support:* In 2016–17, 58 students received support, including 3 teaching assistantships with tuition reimbursements available (averaging $2,236 per year); career-related internships or fieldwork, Federal Work-Study, institutionally sponsored loans, scholarships/grants, tuition waivers, and unspecified assistantships also available. Support available to part-time students. Financial award application deadline: 2/15; financial award applicants required to submit FAFSA. *Faculty research:* Sector forecasting, analysts estimates and guidance, derivatives, SEC comment letters, corporate governance. *Unit head:* Dr. Mac Clouse, Interim Director, 303-871-3322, E-mail: mclouse@du.edu.
Website: https://daniels.du.edu/finance

University of Detroit Mercy, College of Business Administration, Detroit, MI 48221. Offers business administration (MBA); business fundamentals (Certificate); business turnaround management (Certificate); ethical leadership and change management (Certificate); finance (Certificate); forensic accounting (Certificate); JD/MBA; MBA/MHSA. *Program availability:* Part-time, evening/weekend, 100% online, blended/hybrid learning. *Entrance requirements:* For master's, GMAT, resume, letter of recommendation, transcripts; for Certificate, resume, letter of recommendation, transcripts. Electronic applications accepted. Application fee is waived when completed online. *Expenses:* Contact institution. *Faculty research:* Ethics, international finance, trade policy, leadership, information technology.

University of Detroit Mercy, College of Liberal Arts and Education, Detroit, MI 48221. Offers addiction counseling (MA); addiction studies (Certificate); clinical mental health counseling (MA); clinical psychology (MA, PhD); computer and information systems (MS); criminal justice (MA); curriculum and instruction (MA); economics (MA); educational administration (MA); financial economics (MA); industrial/organizational psychology (MA); information assurance (MS); intelligence analysis (MA); liberal studies (MALS); religious studies (MA); school counseling (MA, Certificate); school psychology (Spec); security administration (MS); special education: emotionally impaired/behaviorally disordered (MA); special education: learning disabilities (MA). *Program availability:* Part-time, evening/weekend. *Degree requirements:* For doctorate, departmental qualifying exam. *Faculty research:* Psychology of aging, history of technology, Renaissance humanism, U.S. and Japanese economic relations.

University of Florida, Graduate School, Warrington College of Business Administration, Hough Graduate School of Business, Department of Finance, Insurance and Real Estate, Gainesville, FL 32611. Offers entrepreneurship (MS); finance (MS, PhD); financial services (Certificate); insurance (PhD); quantitative finance (PhD); real estate (MS); real estate and urban analysis (PhD); JD/MBA; JD/MS. Terminal master's awarded for partial completion of doctoral program. *Degree requirements:* For master's, comprehensive exam, thesis; for doctorate, comprehensive exam, thesis/dissertation. *Entrance requirements:* For master's, GMAT (minimum score of 465) or GRE General Test, minimum GPA of 3.0 for last 60 hours of undergraduate degree, work experience (preferred); for doctorate, GMAT (minimum score of 465) or GRE General Test, minimum GPA of 3.0. Additional exam requirements/recommendations for international students: Required—TOEFL (minimum score 550 paper-based; 80 iBT), IELTS (minimum score 6). Electronic applications accepted. *Faculty research:* Banking, empirical corporate finance, hedge funds.

University of Florida, Graduate School, Warrington College of Business Administration, Hough Graduate School of Business, Programs in Business Administration, Gainesville, FL 32611. Offers business administration (MA, MS, PhD); competitive strategy (MBA); finance (MBA); global management (MBA); Graham-Buffett security analysis (MBA); human resource management (MBA); information systems and operations management (MBA); international studies (MBA); management (MBA); real estate (MBA); JD/MBA; MBA/MS; MBA/PhD; MBA/Pharm D; MD/MBA. *Accreditation:* AACSB. *Program availability:* Part-time, evening/weekend, online learning. *Degree requirements:* For master's, capstone course. *Entrance requirements:* For master's and doctorate, GMAT (minimum score 465), minimum GPA of 3.0, interview. Additional exam requirements/recommendations for international students: Required—TOEFL (minimum score 550 paper-based; 80 iBT), IELTS (minimum score 6). Electronic applications accepted. *Faculty research:* Accounting, finance, insurance, management, real estate, urban analysis marketing.

University of Hawaii at Manoa, Graduate Division, Shidler College of Business, Program in Business Administration, Honolulu, HI 96822. Offers Asian business studies (MBA); Chinese business studies (MBA); decision sciences (MBA); entrepreneurship (MBA); finance (MBA); finance and banking (MBA); human resources management (MBA); information management (MBA); information technology (MBA); international business (MBA); Japanese business studies (MBA); marketing (MBA); organizational behavior (MBA); organizational management (MBA); real estate (MBA); student-designed track (MBA). *Accreditation:* AACSB. *Program availability:* Part-time, evening/weekend. *Degree requirements:* For master's, thesis optional. *Entrance requirements:* For master's, GMAT, minimum GPA of 3.0. Additional exam requirements/recommendations for international students: Required—TOEFL (minimum score 600 paper-based; 100 iBT), IELTS (minimum score 7). *Expenses:* Contact institution.

University of Hawaii at Manoa, Graduate Division, Shidler College of Business, Program in International Management, Honolulu, HI 96822. Offers Asian finance (PhD); global information technology management (PhD); international accounting (PhD); international marketing (PhD); international organization and strategy (PhD). *Program availability:* Part-time. *Degree requirements:* For doctorate, comprehensive exam, thesis/dissertation. *Entrance requirements:* For doctorate, GMAT or GRE General Test, minimum GPA of 3.0. Additional exam requirements/recommendations for international students: Required—TOEFL (minimum score 600 paper-based; 100 iBT), IELTS (minimum score 7). *Expenses:* Contact institution.

University of Houston, Bauer College of Business, Finance Program, Houston, TX 77204. Offers MS. *Program availability:* Part-time, evening/weekend. *Degree requirements:* For master's, 30 hours completed in residence, minimum cumulative GPA of 3.0 at UH, no more than 11 semester hours of 'C' grades or below in graduate courses taken at UH. *Entrance requirements:* For master's, GMAT or GRE, official transcripts from all higher education institutions attended, resume, goal statement, letters of recommendation. Additional exam requirements/recommendations for international students: Required—TOEFL (minimum score 620 paper-based; 105 iBT), IELTS (minimum score 7.5). Electronic applications accepted. *Faculty research:* Accountancy and taxation, finance, international business, management.

University of Houston–Clear Lake, School of Business, Program in Finance, Houston, TX 77058-1002. Offers MS. *Program availability:* Part-time, evening/weekend. *Degree requirements:* For master's, thesis optional. *Entrance requirements:* For master's, GMAT. Additional exam requirements/recommendations for international students: Required—TOEFL (minimum score 550 paper-based). Electronic applications accepted.

University of Houston–Downtown, Davies College of Business, MBA Program, Houston, TX 77002. Offers finance (MBA); human resource management (MBA); investment management (MBA); leadership (MBA); sales management and business development (MBA); supply chain management (MBA). *Accreditation:* AACSB. *Program availability:* Part-time, evening/weekend. *Faculty:* 33 full-time (12 women), 1 part-time/adjunct (0 women). *Students:* 7 full-time (3 women), 1,037 part-time (565 women); includes 773 minority (361 Black or African American, non-Hispanic/Latino; 2 American Indian or Alaska Native, non-Hispanic/Latino; 132 Asian, non-Hispanic/Latino; 278 Hispanic/Latino), 32 international. Average age 33. 583 applicants, 86% accepted, 409 enrolled. In 2016, 181 master's awarded. *Entrance requirements:* For master's, GMAT, two letters of recommendation from professional references, personal statement, resume. Additional exam requirements/recommendations for international students: Required—TOEFL (minimum score 81 iBT). *Application deadline:* For fall admission, 7/15 for domestic and international students. Application fee: $35 ($60 for international students). Electronic applications accepted. *Expenses:* $428 in-state per credit; $786 non-resident per credit. *Financial support:* Federal Work-Study and scholarships/grants available. Financial award application deadline: 4/1; financial award applicants required to submit FAFSA. *Unit head:* Dr. D. Michael Fields, Dean, Davies College of Business, 713-221-8179, Fax: 713-221-8675, E-mail: fieldsd@uhd.edu. *Application contact:* Ceshia Love, Director of Graduate and International Admissions, 713-221-8093, Fax: 713-223-7408, E-mail: gradadmissions@uhd.edu.
Website: http://mba.uhd.edu/

University of Houston–Victoria, School of Business Administration, Victoria, TX 77901-4450. Offers accounting (MBA); economic development and entrepreneurship (MS); finance (GMBA, MBA); general business (MBA); international business (MBA); management (GMBA, MBA); marketing (MBA). *Accreditation:* AACSB. *Program availability:* Part-time, evening/weekend, online learning. *Entrance requirements:* For master's, GMAT. Additional exam requirements/recommendations for international students: Required—TOEFL (minimum score 550 paper-based). Electronic applications accepted. *Faculty research:* Economic development, marketing, finance.

University of Illinois at Chicago, Liautaud Graduate School of Business, Department of Finance, Chicago, IL 60607-7128. Offers MS. *Entrance requirements:* Additional exam requirements/recommendations for international students: Required—TOEFL. Electronic applications accepted. *Expenses:* Contact institution. *Faculty research:* Global financial markets.

University of Illinois at Urbana–Champaign, Graduate College, College of Business, Department of Finance, Champaign, IL 61820. Offers MS, PhD.

The University of Iowa, Henry B. Tippie College of Business, Department of Finance, Iowa City, IA 52242-1316. Offers PhD. *Faculty:* 22 full-time (4 women), 10 part-time/adjunct (1 woman). *Students:* 13 full-time (2 women); includes 1 minority (Asian, non-Hispanic/Latino), 6 international. Average age 31. 73 applicants, 3% accepted, 2 enrolled. In 2016, 1 doctorate awarded. *Degree requirements:* For doctorate, comprehensive exam, thesis/dissertation. *Entrance requirements:* For doctorate, GMAT or GRE. Additional exam requirements/recommendations for international students: Required—TOEFL (minimum score 100 iBT) or IELTS (minimum score 7.0). *Application deadline:* For fall admission, 1/15 priority date for domestic and international students. Application fee: $60 ($100 for international students). Electronic applications accepted. *Financial support:* In 2016–17, 13 students received support, including 13 fellowships (averaging $6,000 per year), 13 teaching assistantships with full tuition reimbursements available (averaging $18,809 per year); health care benefits and unspecified assistantships also available. Financial award application deadline: 1/15. *Faculty research:* International finance, real estate finance, theoretical and empirical corporate finance, theoretical and empirical asset pricing, bond pricing and derivatives. *Unit head:* Prof. Thomas Rietz, Department Executive Officer, 319-335-0929, Fax: 319-335-3690, E-mail: thomas-rietz@uiowa.edu. *Application contact:* Renea L. Jay, Associate Director, Non-MBA Graduate Programs, 319-335-0830, Fax: 319-335-0860, E-mail: renea-jay@uiowa.edu.
Website: https://tippie.uiowa.edu/finance

The University of Kansas, Graduate Studies, School of Business, Program in Business, Lawrence, KS 66045. Offers accounting (PhD); business and organizational leadership (MS); decision sciences and supply chain management (PhD); finance (PhD); human resources management (PhD); marketing (PhD); organizational behavior (PhD); strategic management (PhD); supply chain management and logistics (MS). *Accreditation:* AACSB. *Program availability:* Part-time. *Students:* 76 full-time (11 women), 170 part-time (83 women); includes 41 minority (15 Black or African American, non-Hispanic/Latino; 3 American Indian or Alaska Native, non-Hispanic/Latino; 6 Asian, non-Hispanic/Latino; 5 Hispanic/Latino; 12 Two or more races, non-Hispanic/Latino), 25 international. Average age 32. 294 applicants, 69% accepted, 152 enrolled. In 2016, 36 master's, 9 doctorates awarded. *Entrance requirements:* For master's, GMAT, official transcript, three letters of recommendation, resume, statement of purpose; for doctorate, GMAT or GRE, official transcript, three letters of recommendation, resume, statement of purpose. Additional exam requirements/recommendations for international students: Required—TOEFL (minimum score 600 paper-based; 100 iBT). *Application deadline:* For fall admission, 1/10 for domestic and international students. Application fee: $65 ($85 for international students). Electronic applications accepted. *Financial support:* Fellowships, research assistantships, teaching assistantships, scholarships/grants, health care benefits, tuition waivers (full), and unspecified assistantships available. Financial award application deadline: 1/10. *Faculty research:* Strategic human resource management, business ethics, organizational theory/behavior, corporate strategy, international business, supply chain management, Bayesian networks, game theory, decision analysis and time/series analysis, pricing, consumer effects, advertising and emotion. *Unit head:* Charly Edmonds, Director, 785-864-3841, E-mail: bschoolphd@ku.edu. *Application contact:* Graduate Admission Contact, 785-864-7500, E-mail: bschoolphd@ku.edu.
Website: http://www.business.ku.edu/

University of La Verne, College of Business and Public Management, Graduate Programs in Business Administration, La Verne, CA 91750-4443. Offers accounting (MBA, MBA-EP); finance (MBA, MBA-EP); health services management (MBA); information technology (MBA, MBA-EP); international business (MBA, MBA-EP); management and leadership (MBA, MBA-EP); marketing (MBA, MBA-EP); supply chain management (MBA, MBA-EP). *Program availability:* Part-time, evening/weekend. *Students:* 385 full-time (177 women), 89 part-time (46 women); includes 92 minority (4 Black or African American, non-Hispanic/Latino; 1 American Indian or Alaska Native, non-Hispanic/Latino; 14 Asian, non-Hispanic/Latino; 71 Hispanic/Latino; 1 Native Hawaiian or other Pacific Islander, non-Hispanic/Latino; 1 Two or more races, non-Hispanic/Latino), 319 international. Average age 28. *Entrance requirements:* For master's, GMAT, MAT, or GRE, minimum undergraduate GPA of 3.0, 2 letters of recommendation, resume, statement of purpose. Additional exam requirements/recommendations for international students: Required—TOEFL (minimum score 550 paper-based; 85 iBT). *Application deadline:* Applications are processed on a rolling basis. Application fee: $50. *Expenses: Tuition:* Part-time $795 per credit hour. Tuition and fees vary according to campus/location and program. *Financial support:* Institutionally sponsored loans and scholarships/grants available. Financial award application deadline: 3/2; financial award applicants required to submit FAFSA. *Unit head:* Dr. Abe Helou, Chairperson, 909-448-4455, Fax: 909-392-2704, E-mail: ihelou@laverne.edu. *Application contact:* Rina Lazarian-Chehab, Senior Associate Director of Graduate Admissions, 909-448-4317, Fax: 909-971-2295, E-mail: rlazarian@laverne.edu.
Website: https://laverne.edu/business-and-public-administration/mba-2/

University of La Verne, College of Business and Public Management, Program in Finance, La Verne, CA 91750-4443. Offers MS. *Program availability:* Part-time. *Students:* 40 full-time (16 women), 2 part-time (both women); includes 6 minority (2 Black or African American, non-Hispanic/Latino; 2 Asian, non-Hispanic/Latino; 2 Hispanic/Latino), 35 international. Average age 26. *Entrance requirements:* For master's, bachelor's degree, minimum preferred GPA of 3.0, 2 recommendations, resume, personal statement. Additional exam requirements/recommendations for international students: Required—TOEFL (minimum score 550 paper-based; 79 iBT). *Application deadline:* Applications are processed on a rolling basis. Application fee: $50. *Expenses:* Contact institution. *Financial support:* Federal Work-Study, institutionally sponsored loans, and scholarships/grants available. *Unit head:* Paul Abbondante, Director, 909-448-4452, E-mail: pabbondante@laverne.edu. *Application contact:* Rina Lazarian-Chehab, Senior Associate Director of Graduate Admissions, 909-448-4317, Fax: 909-971-2295, E-mail: rlazarian@laverne.edu.
Website: https://laverne.edu/business-and-public-administration/master-of-science-in-finance/

University of La Verne, Regional and Online Campuses, Graduate Programs, Inland Empire Campus, Ontario, CA 91730. Offers business administration (MBA, MBA-EP), including accounting (MBA), finance (MBA), health services management (MBA-EP), information technology (MBA-EP), international business (MBA), managed care (MBA), management and leadership (MBA-EP), marketing (MBA-EP), supply chain management (MBA); leadership and management (MS), including human resource management, nonprofit management, organizational development. *Program availability:* Part-time, evening/weekend. *Expenses:* Contact institution.

University of Lethbridge, School of Graduate Studies, Lethbridge, AB T1K 3M4, Canada. Offers addictions counseling (M Sc); agricultural biotechnology (M Sc); agricultural studies (M Sc, MA); anthropology (MA); archaeology (M Sc, MA); art (MA, MFA); biochemistry (M Sc); biological sciences (M Sc); biomolecular science (PhD); biosystems and biodiversity (PhD); Canadian studies (MA); chemistry (M Sc); computer science (M Sc); computer science and geographical information science (M Sc); counseling (MC); counseling psychology (M Ed); dramatic arts (MA); earth, space, and physical science (PhD); economics (MA); education (MA, PhD); educational leadership (M Ed); English (MA); environmental science (M Sc); evolution and behavior (PhD); exercise science (M Sc); French (MA); French/German (MA); French/Spanish (MA); general education (M Ed); geography (M Sc, MA); German (MA); health sciences (M Sc); individualized multidisciplinary (M Sc, MA); kinesiology (M Sc, MA); management (M Sc), including accounting, finance, human resource management and labor relations, information systems, international management, marketing, policy and strategy; mathematics (M Sc); music (M Mus, MA); Native American studies (MA); neuroscience (M Sc, PhD); new media (MA, MFA); nursing (M Sc, MN); philosophy (MA); physics (M Sc); political science (MA); psychology (M Sc, MA); religious studies (MA); sociology (MA); theatre and dramatic arts (MFA); theoretical and computational science (PhD); urban and regional studies (MA); women and gender studies (MA). *Program availability:* Part-time, evening/weekend. *Degree requirements:* For master's, thesis (for some programs); for doctorate, comprehensive exam, thesis/dissertation. *Entrance requirements:* For master's, GMAT (for M Sc in management), bachelor's degree in related field, minimum GPA of 3.0 during previous 20 graded semester courses, 2 years' teaching or related experience (M Ed); for doctorate, master's degree, minimum graduate GPA of 3.5. Additional exam requirements/recommendations for international students: Required—TOEFL (minimum score 580 paper-based; 93 iBT). Electronic applications accepted. *Faculty research:* Movement and brain plasticity, gibberellin physiology, photosynthesis, carbon cycling, molecular properties of main-group ring components.

University of Maine, Graduate School, College of Natural Sciences, Forestry, and Agriculture, School of Economics, Orono, ME 04469. Offers economics (MA); financial economics (MA); resource economics and policy (MS). *Program availability:* Part-time. *Faculty:* 12 full-time (3 women). *Students:* 21 full-time (6 women), 1 part-time (0 women); includes 1 minority (Two or more races, non-Hispanic/Latino), 8 international. Average age 24. 30 applicants, 90% accepted, 9 enrolled. In 2016, 11 master's awarded. *Degree requirements:* For master's, thesis (for some programs). *Entrance requirements:* For master's, GRE General Test. Additional exam requirements/recommendations for international students: Required—TOEFL (minimum score 580 paper-based; 92 iBT), IELTS (minimum score 8.9). *Application deadline:* For fall admission, 2/15 for domestic students, 2/1 for international students; for spring admission, 9/15 for domestic students, 8/15 for international students. Applications are processed on a rolling basis. Application fee: $65. Electronic applications accepted. *Expenses:* Tuition, state resident: full-time $7524; part-time $2508 per credit. Tuition, nonresident: full-time $24,498; part-time $8166 per credit. *Required fees:* $1148; $571 per credit. *Financial support:* In 2016–17, 21 students received support, including 15 research assistantships (averaging $14,600 per year), 6 teaching assistantships with full tuition reimbursements available (averaging $14,600 per year); career-related internships or fieldwork, Federal Work-Study, institutionally sponsored loans, scholarships/grants, and tuition waivers (full and partial) also available. Support available to part-time students. Financial award application deadline: 3/1. *Faculty research:* Food systems, renewable energy; transportation; water quality; economic development. *Total annual research expenditures:* $881,321. *Unit head:* Dr. Mario Teisl, Director, 207-581-3151, Fax: 207-581-4278. *Application contact:* Scott G. Delcourt, Assistant Vice President for Graduate Studies and Senior Associate Dean, 207-581-3291, Fax: 207-581-3232, E-mail: graduate@maine.edu.
Website: http://umaine.edu/soe/

Finance and Banking

The University of Manchester, Alliance Manchester Business School, M15 6PB, United Kingdom. Offers accounting and finance (M Sc); business (M Ent); business analysis and strategic management (M Sc); business analytics: operational research and risk analysis (M Sc); business psychology (M Sc); corporate communications and reputation management (M Sc); finance (M Sc); finance and business economics (M Sc); human resource management and industrial relations (M Sc); innovation management and entrepreneurship (M Sc); international business and management (M Sc); international human resource management and comparative industrial relations (M Sc); management (M Sc); marketing (M Sc); operations, project and supply chain management (M Sc); organizational psychology (M Sc); quantitative finance (M Sc). *Entrance requirements:* For master's, UK 2:1 honours degree or overseas equivalent. Additional exam requirements/recommendations for international students: Required—TOEFL (minimum score 100 iBT), IELTS (minimum score 7), PTE. Electronic applications accepted. *Faculty research:* Accounting and finance, management sciences and marketing, people management and organization, innovation management and policy, decision sciences.

University of Maryland University College, The Graduate School, Program in Accounting and Financial Management, Adelphi, MD 20783. Offers MS. *Accreditation:* AACSB. *Program availability:* Part-time, evening/weekend, online learning. *Students:* 11 full-time (8 women), 399 part-time (260 women); includes 248 minority (166 Black or African American, non-Hispanic/Latino; 3 American Indian or Alaska Native, non-Hispanic/Latino; 39 Asian, non-Hispanic/Latino; 29 Hispanic/Latino; 2 Native Hawaiian or other Pacific Islander, non-Hispanic/Latino; 9 Two or more races, non-Hispanic/Latino), 17 international. Average age 33. 139 applicants, 100% accepted, 110 enrolled. In 2016, 100 master's awarded. *Degree requirements:* For master's, thesis or alternative, capstone course. *Application deadline:* Applications are processed on a rolling basis. Application fee: $50. Electronic applications accepted. *Expenses:* Tuition, state resident: part-time $458 per credit. Tuition, nonresident: part-time $659 per credit. *Financial support:* Federal Work-Study and scholarships/grants available. Support available to part-time students. Financial award application deadline: 6/1; financial award applicants required to submit FAFSA. *Application contact:* Coordinator, Graduate Admissions, 800-888-8682, Fax: 240-684-2151, E-mail: newgrad@umuc.edu.
Website: http://www.umuc.edu/academic-programs/masters-degrees/accounting-and-financial-management.cfm

University of Massachusetts Amherst, Graduate School, Isenberg School of Management, Program in Management, Amherst, MA 01003. Offers accounting (PhD); business administration (MBA); entrepreneurship (MBA); finance (MBA, PhD); healthcare administration (MBA); hospitality and tourism management (PhD); management science (PhD); marketing (MBA, PhD); organization studies (PhD); sport management (PhD); strategic management (PhD); MBA/MS. *Accreditation:* AACSB. *Program availability:* Part-time, evening/weekend, online learning. Terminal master's awarded for partial completion of doctoral program. *Degree requirements:* For doctorate, comprehensive exam, thesis/dissertation. *Entrance requirements:* For master's and doctorate, GMAT or GRE General Test. Additional exam requirements/recommendations for international students: Required—TOEFL (minimum score 550 paper-based; 80 iBT), IELTS (minimum score 6.5). Electronic applications accepted.

University of Massachusetts Boston, College of Management, Program in Finance, Boston, MA 02125-3393. Offers MS. *Faculty:* 27 full-time (9 women), 13 part-time/adjunct (1 woman). *Students:* 38 full-time (17 women), 17 part-time (7 women); includes 3 minority (2 Asian, non-Hispanic/Latino; 1 Hispanic/Latino), 37 international. Average age 28. 87 applicants, 55% accepted, 21 enrolled. In 2016, 20 master's awarded. *Expenses:* Tuition, state resident: full-time $16,863. Tuition, nonresident: full-time $32,913. *Required fees:* $177. *Application contact:* Peggy Roldan Patel, Graduate Admissions Coordinator, 617-287-6400, Fax: 617-287-6236, E-mail: bos.gadm@dpc.umassp.edu.

University of Massachusetts Dartmouth, Graduate School, Charlton College of Business, Department of Accounting and Finance, North Dartmouth, MA 02747-2300. Offers accounting (MS, Postbaccalaureate Certificate); finance (Postbaccalaureate Certificate). *Program availability:* Part-time. *Faculty:* 13 full-time (3 women), 6 part-time/adjunct (5 women). *Students:* 26 full-time (14 women), 15 part-time (10 women); includes 10 minority (2 Black or African American, non-Hispanic/Latino; 4 Asian, non-Hispanic/Latino; 3 Hispanic/Latino; 1 Two or more races, non-Hispanic/Latino), 7 international. Average age 29. 38 applicants, 87% accepted, 20 enrolled. In 2016, 1 master's awarded. *Entrance requirements:* For master's, GMAT, statement of purpose (minimum 300 words), resume, official transcript, 2 letters of recommendation; for Postbaccalaureate Certificate, statement of purpose (minimum 300 words), resume, official transcript. Additional exam requirements/recommendations for international students: Required—TOEFL (minimum score 533 paper-based; 72 iBT). *Application deadline:* For fall admission, 7/1 priority date for domestic students, 6/1 priority date for international students; for spring admission, 11/15 priority date for domestic students, 10/15 priority date for international students. Application fee: $60. Electronic applications accepted. *Expenses:* Tuition, state resident: full-time $14,994; part-time $624.75 per credit. Tuition, nonresident: full-time $27,068; part-time $1127.83 per credit. *Required fees:* $405; $25.88 per credit. Tuition and fees vary according to course load and reciprocity agreements. *Financial support:* Institutionally sponsored loans and scholarships/grants available. Support available to part-time students. Financial award application deadline: 3/1; financial award applicants required to submit FAFSA. *Faculty research:* Accounting information systems, analytical controls in continuous auditing, accounting education, managerial accounting, e-commerce, corporate governance, executive compensation, financial statement analysis, efficiency of emerging capital markets. *Unit head:* Dr. Jia Wu, Program Coordinator, Accounting, 508-999-8428, E-mail: jwu@umassd.edu. *Application contact:* Steven Briggs, Director of Marketing and Recruitment for Graduate Studies, 508-999-8604, Fax: 508-999-8183, E-mail: graduate@umassd.edu.
Website: http://www.umassd.edu/charlton/programs/graduate/msaccounting/

University of Memphis, Graduate School, Fogelman College of Business and Economics, Program in Business Administration, Memphis, TN 38152. Offers accounting (MBA, PhD); business administration (IMBA); economics (PhD); executive business administration (MBA); finance (PhD); management (PhD); marketing (MS); marketing and supply chain management (PhD); real estate development (MS); JD/MBA. *Accreditation:* AACSB. *Faculty:* 44 full-time (9 women), 5 part-time/adjunct (0 women). *Students:* 167 full-time (64 women), 341 part-time (119 women); includes 154 minority (80 Black or African American, non-Hispanic/Latino; 1 American Indian or Alaska Native, non-Hispanic/Latino; 43 Asian, non-Hispanic/Latino; 12 Hispanic/Latino; 1 Native Hawaiian or other Pacific Islander, non-Hispanic/Latino; 17 Two or more races, non-Hispanic/Latino), 96 international. Average age 33. 306 applicants, 64% accepted, 154 enrolled. In 2016, 273 master's, 7 doctorates awarded. *Degree requirements:* For master's, comprehensive exam; for doctorate, comprehensive exam, thesis/dissertation. *Entrance requirements:* For master's, GMAT, resume; for doctorate, GMAT, interview, minimum GPA of 3.4, resume, letter of recommendation. Additional exam requirements/recommendations for international students: Required—TOEFL (minimum score 550 paper-based). *Application deadline:* For fall admission, 8/1 for domestic students; for spring admission, 12/1 for domestic students. Application fee: $35 ($60 for international students). *Expenses:* Tuition, state resident: full-time $10,463; part-time $9483 per year. Tuition, nonresident: full-time $19,247; part-time $17,291 per year. *Required fees:* $821.50 per semester. Tuition and fees vary according to course load and program. *Financial support:* In 2016–17, 164 students received support. Research assistantships with full tuition reimbursements available, teaching assistantships with full tuition reimbursements available, career-related internships or fieldwork, Federal Work-Study, scholarships/grants, and unspecified assistantships available. Financial award application deadline: 2/15; financial award applicants required to submit FAFSA. *Faculty research:* Competitive business strategy, finance microstructures, supply chain management innovations, health care economics, litigation risks and corporate audits. *Unit head:* Dr. Rajiv Grover, Dean, 901-678-3759, E-mail: rgrover@memphis.edu. *Application contact:* Dr. Carol V. Danehower, Associate Dean, 901-678-5402, Fax: 901-678-3579, E-mail: fcbegp@memphis.edu.
Website: https://web0.memphis.edu/gradcatalog/degreeprog/fcbe/fcbe.php

University of Michigan–Dearborn, College of Business, MS Program in Finance, Dearborn, MI 48126. Offers MS. *Program availability:* Part-time, evening/weekend, 100% online. *Faculty:* 33 full-time (14 women), 10 part-time/adjunct (5 women). *Students:* 10 full-time (3 women), 32 part-time (9 women); includes 11 minority (4 Black or African American, non-Hispanic/Latino; 4 Asian, non-Hispanic/Latino; 2 Hispanic/Latino; 1 Two or more races, non-Hispanic/Latino), 7 international. Average age 30. 54 applicants, 50% accepted, 11 enrolled. In 2016, 21 master's awarded. *Entrance requirements:* For master's, GRE or GMAT, equivalent of four-year U.S. bachelor's degree from regionally-accredited institution, undergraduate course in finite math, pre-calculus, or calculus. Additional exam requirements/recommendations for international students: Required—TOEFL (minimum score 560 paper-based; 84 iBT), IELTS (minimum score 6.5). *Application deadline:* For fall admission, 8/1 for domestic students, 5/1 for international students; for winter admission, 12/1 for domestic students, 9/1 for international students; for spring admission, 4/1 for domestic students, 1/1 for international students. Applications are processed on a rolling basis. Application fee: $60. Electronic applications accepted. *Expenses:* Contact institution. *Financial support:* In 2016–17, 7 students received support. Scholarships/grants and non-resident tuition scholarships available. Financial award application deadline: 3/1; financial award applicants required to submit FAFSA. *Faculty research:* Business intelligence, information technology, brand management and new media, management education, operations strategy. *Unit head:* Dr. Michael Kamen, Director, Graduate Programs, 313-593-5460, E-mail: mkamen@umich.edu. *Application contact:* Joan Doherty, Academic Advisor/Counselor, 313-593-5460, Fax: 313-271-9838, E-mail: umd-gradbusiness@umich.edu. Website: http://umdearborn.edu/cob/ms-finance/

University of Michigan–Flint, School of Management, Program in Business Administration, Flint, MI 48502. Offers accounting (MBA, Post-Master's Certificate); computer information systems (MBA); finance (MBA, Post-Master's Certificate); general business (Graduate Certificate); general business administration (MBA); health care management (MBA); international business (MBA, Post-Master's Certificate); lean manufacturing (MBA); marketing (MBA, Post-Master's Certificate); organizational leadership (MBA, Post-Master's Certificate). *Program availability:* Part-time, evening/weekend, mixed mode programs. *Faculty:* 33 full-time (9 women), 6 part-time/adjunct (1 woman). *Students:* 24 full-time (12 women), 146 part-time (49 women); includes 37 minority (17 Black or African American, non-Hispanic/Latino; 2 American Indian or Alaska Native, non-Hispanic/Latino; 10 Asian, non-Hispanic/Latino; 4 Hispanic/Latino; 1 Native Hawaiian or other Pacific Islander, non-Hispanic/Latino; 3 Two or more races, non-Hispanic/Latino), 17 international. Average age 33. 167 applicants, 47% accepted, 40 enrolled. In 2016, 73 master's, 3 other advanced degrees awarded. *Entrance requirements:* For master's, GMAT or GRE, bachelor's degree in arts, sciences, engineering, or business administration from regionally-accredited college or university with minimum GPA of 3.0; for other advanced degree, bachelor's degree in arts, sciences, engineering, or business administration from regionally-accredited college or university with minimum GPA of 3.0, college-level math, statistics, or quantitative course (for Graduate Certificate); MBA or equivalent degree from regionally-accredited college or university (for Post Master's Certificate). Additional exam requirements/recommendations for international students: Required—TOEFL (minimum score 84 iBT), IELTS (minimum score 6.5). *Application deadline:* For fall admission, 8/1 for domestic students, 5/1 for international students; for winter admission, 11/15 for domestic students, 9/1 for international students; for spring admission, 3/15 for domestic students, 1/1 for international students; for summer admission, 5/15 for domestic students. Applications are processed on a rolling basis. Application fee: $55. Electronic applications accepted. *Financial support:* Federal Work-Study, scholarships/grants, and unspecified assistantships available. Support available to part-time students. Financial award application deadline: 3/1; financial award applicants required to submit FAFSA. *Unit head:* Dr. Scott Johnson, Dean, School of Management, 810-762-3164, Fax: 810-237-6685, E-mail: scotjohn@umflint.edu. *Application contact:* Bradley T. Maki, Director of Graduate Admissions, 810-762-3171, E-mail: bmaki@umflint.edu.
Website: http://www.umflint.edu/graduateprograms/business-administration-mba

University of Minnesota, Twin Cities Campus, Carlson School of Management, Carlson Full-Time MBA Program, Minneapolis, MN 55455. Offers finance (MBA); human resources and industrial relations (MA); information technology (MBA); management (MBA); marketing (MBA); medical industry orientation (MBA); supply chain and operations (MBA); JD/MBA; MBA/MPP; MBA/MSBA; MD/MBA; MHA/MBA; Pharm D/MBA. *Accreditation:* AACSB. *Faculty:* 143 full-time (42 women), 24 part-time/adjunct (6 women). *Students:* 193 full-time (59 women); includes 23 minority (2 Black or African American, non-Hispanic/Latino; 1 American Indian or Alaska Native, non-Hispanic/Latino; 9 Asian, non-Hispanic/Latino; 5 Hispanic/Latino; 1 Native Hawaiian or other Pacific Islander, non-Hispanic/Latino; 5 Two or more races, non-Hispanic/Latino), 31 international. Average age 28. 606 applicants, 45% accepted, 104 enrolled. In 2016, 102 master's awarded. *Entrance requirements:* For master's, GMAT or GRE. Additional exam requirements/recommendations for international students: Required—TOEFL (minimum score 580 paper-based; 84 iBT), IELTS (minimum score 7), PTE. *Application deadline:* For fall admission, 4/1 for domestic students, 2/1 for international students. Application fee: $75. Electronic applications accepted. *Expenses:* $39,378 per year resident tuition and fees; $49,766 per year non-resident tuition and fees; $50,084 per year international tuition and fees. *Financial support:* In 2016–17, 148 students received support, including 148 fellowships with tuition reimbursements available (averaging $21,070 per year); research assistantships with partial tuition reimbursements available, teaching assistantships with partial tuition reimbursements available, career-related internships or fieldwork, Federal Work-Study, institutionally sponsored loans, scholarships/grants, health care benefits, and unspecified assistantships also available. Financial award application deadline: 4/1; financial award applicants required to submit FAFSA. *Faculty research:* Market regulation and asset pricing, social networks and data analytics, consumer behavior, innovation and entrepreneurship, workplace wellbeing and labor relationships. *Total annual research expenditures:* $577,440. *Unit head:* Philip J. Miller, Assistant Dean, MBA Programs and Graduate Business Career Center, 612-625-5555, Fax: 612-625-1012, E-mail: mba@umn.edu. *Application contact:* Linh Gilles, Director of Admissions and Recruiting, 612-625-5555, Fax: 612-625-1012, E-mail: ftmba@umn.edu.
Website: http://www.csom.umn.edu/MBA/full-time/

University of Minnesota, Twin Cities Campus, Carlson School of Management, Carlson Part-Time MBA Program, Minneapolis, MN 55455. Offers finance (MBA); information technology (MBA); management (MBA); marketing (MBA); medical industry orientation (MBA); supply chain and operations (MBA). *Program availability:* Part-time-only, evening/weekend, 100% online, blended/hybrid learning. *Faculty:* 143 full-time (42 women), 26 part-time/adjunct (6 women). *Students:* 1,005 part-time (317 women); includes 110 minority (17 Black or African American, non-Hispanic/Latino; 2 American Indian or Alaska Native, non-Hispanic/Latino; 51 Asian, non-Hispanic/Latino; 19 Hispanic/Latino; 21 Two or more races, non-Hispanic/Latino), 58 international. Average age 28. 251 applicants, 86% accepted, 185 enrolled. In 2016, 336 master's awarded. *Entrance requirements:* For master's, GMAT or GRE. Additional exam requirements/recommendations for international students: Required—TOEFL (minimum score 580 paper-based; 84 iBT), IELTS (minimum score 7), PTE. *Application deadline:* For fall admission, 5/15 priority date for domestic and international students; for spring admission, 10/15 priority date for domestic and international students. Applications are processed on a rolling basis. Application fee: $75. Electronic applications accepted. *Expenses:* $1,335 per credit. *Financial support:* Applicants required to submit FAFSA. *Faculty research:* Market regulation and asset pricing, social networks and data analytics, consumer behavior, innovation and entrepreneurship, workplace wellbeing and labor relationships. *Total annual research expenditures:* $577,440. *Unit head:* Philip J. Miller, Assistant Dean, MBA Programs and Graduate Business Career Center, 612-624-2039, Fax: 612-625-1012, E-mail: mba@umn.edu. *Application contact:* Linh Gilles, Director of Admissions and Recruiting, 612-625-5555, Fax: 612-625-1012, E-mail: ptmba@umn.edu.
Website: http://www.carlsonschool.umn.edu/ptmba

University of Minnesota, Twin Cities Campus, Carlson School of Management, Doctoral Program in Business Administration, Minneapolis, MN 55455. Offers accounting (PhD); finance (PhD); information and decision sciences (PhD); marketing (PhD); strategic management and entrepreneurship (PhD); supply chain and operations (PhD); work and organizations (PhD). *Faculty:* 101 full-time (32 women). *Students:* 90 full-time (29 women); includes 7 minority (2 Black or African American, non-Hispanic/Latino; 3 Asian, non-Hispanic/Latino; 2 Hispanic/Latino), 64 international. Average age 30. 352 applicants, 7% accepted, 15 enrolled. In 2016, 20 doctorates awarded. *Degree requirements:* For doctorate, comprehensive exam, thesis/dissertation, written and oral preliminary exams, proposal defense, final defense. *Entrance requirements:* For doctorate, GMAT, GRE General Test, minimum undergraduate GPA of 3.0, graduate 3.5 (recommended). Additional exam requirements/recommendations for international students: Required—TOEFL (minimum score 600 paper-based, 100 iBT) or IELTS (minimum score 7.0). *Application deadline:* For fall admission, 12/15 for domestic students, 12/15 priority date for international students. Applications are processed on a rolling basis. Application fee: $75 ($95 for international students). Electronic applications accepted. *Expenses:* Contact institution. *Financial support:* In 2016–17, 80 students received support, including 80 fellowships with full tuition reimbursements available (averaging $13,500 per year), 72 research assistantships with full tuition reimbursements available (averaging $7,371 per year), 72 teaching assistantships with full tuition reimbursements available (averaging $7,371 per year); institutionally sponsored loans, scholarships/grants, health care benefits, unspecified assistantships, and full student service fee waivers also available. Financial award application deadline: 12/15. *Faculty research:* Finance, strategy and entrepreneurship, marketing, information and decision science, operations, accounting, supply chain, human resources and industrial relations, organizational behavior. *Unit head:* Dr. Shawn P. Curley, Director, 612-624-6546, Fax: 612-624-8221, E-mail: curley@umn.edu. *Application contact:* Sandy Herzan, Associate Director, 612-624-0875, Fax: 612-624-8221, E-mail: herza002@umn.edu.
Website: http://carlsonschool.umn.edu/degrees/phd

University of Missouri, Office of Research and Graduate Studies, Robert J. Trulaske, Sr. College of Business, Program in Business Administration, Columbia, MO 65211. Offers business administration (MBA); executive business administration (MBA); finance (PhD); management (PhD); marketing (PhD); MBA/JD; MBA/MHA; MBA/MSIE. *Accreditation:* AACSB. *Degree requirements:* For doctorate, thesis/dissertation. *Entrance requirements:* For master's and doctorate, GMAT, minimum GPA of 3.0. Additional exam requirements/recommendations for international students: Required—TOEFL (minimum score 500 paper-based; 61 iBT). Electronic applications accepted. *Expenses:* Tuition, state resident: full-time $6347; part-time $352.60 per credit hour. Tuition, nonresident: full-time $17,379; part-time $965.50 per credit hour. *Required fees:* $1035. Tuition and fees vary according to course load, campus/location and program.

University of Missouri–Kansas City, Henry W. Bloch School of Management, Kansas City, MO 64110-2499. Offers accounting (MS); finance (MS); public affairs (MPA, PhD); JD/MBA; LL M/MPA. PhD (interdisciplinary) offered through the School of Graduate Studies. *Accreditation:* AACSB; NASPAA. *Program availability:* Part-time, evening/weekend. *Faculty:* 60 full-time (19 women), 40 part-time/adjunct (11 women). *Students:* 204 full-time (97 women), 308 part-time (151 women); includes 70 minority (29 Black or African American, non-Hispanic/Latino; 1 American Indian or Alaska Native, non-Hispanic/Latino; 17 Asian, non-Hispanic/Latino; 18 Hispanic/Latino; 5 Two or more races, non-Hispanic/Latino), 82 international. Average age 30. 389 applicants, 49% accepted, 190 enrolled. In 2016, 248 master's, 2 doctorates awarded. Terminal master's awarded for partial completion of doctoral program. *Entrance requirements:* For master's, GMAT, GRE, 2 essays, 2 references, support of employer; for doctorate, GRE, minimum GPA of 3.0. Additional exam requirements/recommendations for international students: Required—TOEFL (minimum score 550 paper-based; 80 iBT). *Application deadline:* For fall admission, 5/1 priority date for domestic and international students; for spring admission, 10/1 priority date for domestic and international students. Applications are processed on a rolling basis. Application fee: $45 ($50 for international students). Electronic applications accepted. *Financial support:* In 2016–17, 31 research assistantships with partial tuition reimbursements (averaging $10,597 per year), 10 teaching assistantships with partial tuition reimbursements (averaging $14,592 per year) were awarded; career-related internships or fieldwork, Federal Work-Study, institutionally sponsored loans, scholarships/grants, tuition waivers (full and partial), and unspecified assistantships also available. Support available to part-time students. Financial award application deadline: 3/1; financial award applicants required to submit FAFSA. *Faculty research:* Entrepreneurship, finance, non-profit, risk management. *Unit head:* Dr. David Donnelly, Dean, 816-235-1333, Fax: 816-235-2206, E-mail: donnellyd@umkc.edu. *Application contact:* 816-235-1111, E-mail: admit@umkc.edu.
Website: http://www.bloch.umkc.edu

University of Missouri–St. Louis, College of Business Administration, Program in Business Administration, St. Louis, MO 63121. Offers accounting (MBA); business administration (Certificate); business intelligence (Certificate); cybersecurity (Certificate); digital and social media marketing (Certificate); finance (MBA); human resources management (Certificate); information systems (MBA); international business (MBA); logistics and supply chain management (MBA, PhD, Certificate); management (MBA); marketing (MBA); marketing management (Certificate); operations management (MBA). *Accreditation:* AACSB. *Program availability:* Part-time, evening/weekend. *Faculty:* 32 full-time (10 women), 14 part-time/adjunct (3 women). *Students:* 181 full-time (88 women), 357 part-time (154 women); includes 83 minority (30 Black or African American, non-Hispanic/Latino; 36 Asian, non-Hispanic/Latino; 12 Hispanic/Latino; 2 Native Hawaiian or other Pacific Islander, non-Hispanic/Latino; 3 Two or more races, non-Hispanic/Latino), 100 international. Average age 31. 245 applicants, 83% accepted, 139 enrolled. *Degree requirements:* For doctorate, thesis/dissertation. *Entrance requirements:* For master's, GMAT, 2 letters of recommendation. Additional exam requirements/recommendations for international students: Recommended—TOEFL (minimum score 550 paper-based; 79 iBT), IELTS (minimum score 6.5). *Application deadline:* For fall admission, 7/1 for domestic and international students; for spring admission, 12/1 for domestic and international students. Applications are processed on a rolling basis. Application fee: $50 ($40 for international students). Electronic applications accepted. *Financial support:* Research assistantships with tuition reimbursements, teaching assistantships with tuition reimbursements, career-related internships or fieldwork, Federal Work-Study, and institutionally sponsored loans available. Support available to part-time students. Financial award application deadline: 4/1; financial award applicants required to submit FAFSA. *Faculty research:* Human resources, strategic management, marketing strategy, consumer behavior product development, advertising. *Unit head:* Dr. Thomas H. Eyssell, Associate Dean and Director of Graduate Studies, 314-516-5885, Fax: 314-516-6420, E-mail: mba@umsl.edu. *Application contact:* 314-516-5458, Fax: 314-516-6996, E-mail: gradadm@umsl.edu.

University of Nebraska–Lincoln, Graduate College, College of Business Administration, Interdepartmental Area of Business, Department of Finance, Lincoln, NE 68588. Offers business (MA, PhD). *Degree requirements:* For doctorate, comprehensive exam, thesis/dissertation. *Entrance requirements:* For master's and doctorate, GMAT. Additional exam requirements/recommendations for international students: Required—TOEFL (minimum score 100 iBT). Electronic applications accepted. *Faculty research:* Banking, investments, international finance, insurance, corporate finance.

University of Nevada, Reno, Graduate School, College of Business Administration, Department of Finance, Reno, NV 89557. Offers MS. *Program availability:* Part-time. *Degree requirements:* For master's, thesis optional. *Entrance requirements:* For master's, GMAT or GRE, minimum GPA of 2.75. Additional exam requirements/recommendations for international students: Required—TOEFL (minimum score 500 paper-based; 61 iBT), IELTS (minimum score 6). Electronic applications accepted. *Faculty research:* Financial business problems, economic theory, financial concepts theory.

University of New Haven, Graduate School, College of Business, Program in Business Administration, West Haven, CT 06516. Offers accounting (MBA), including CPA; business administration (MBA); business intelligence (MBA); business management (Graduate Certificate); business policy and strategic leadership (MBA); finance (MBA), including CFA; global marketing (MBA); human resources management (MBA, Graduate Certificate); sport management (MBA). *Accreditation:* AACSB. *Program availability:* Part-time, evening/weekend. *Students:* 123 full-time (56 women), 74 part-time (29 women); includes 46 minority (24 Black or African American, non-Hispanic/Latino; 8 Asian, non-Hispanic/Latino; 10 Hispanic/Latino; 4 Two or more races, non-Hispanic/Latino), 57 international. Average age 27. In 2016, 100 master's awarded. *Entrance requirements:* For master's, GMAT. Additional exam requirements/recommendations for international students: Required—TOEFL (minimum score 80 iBT), IELTS, PTE. *Application deadline:* Applications are processed on a rolling basis. Application fee: $50. Electronic applications accepted. Application fee is waived when completed online. *Expenses: Tuition:* Full-time $15,660; part-time $870 per credit hour. *Required fees:* $200; $85 per term. Tuition and fees vary according to program. *Financial support:* Research assistantships with partial tuition reimbursements, teaching assistantships with partial tuition reimbursements, career-related internships or fieldwork, Federal Work-Study, scholarships/grants, and unspecified assistantships available. Support available to part-time students. Financial award applicants required to submit FAFSA. *Unit head:* Darell Singleterry, Director, 203-932-1085, E-mail: dsingleterry@newhaven.edu. *Application contact:* Michelle Mason, Director of Graduate Enrollment, 203-932-7067, E-mail: mmason@newhaven.edu.
Website: http://www.newhaven.edu/business/programs/EMBA/

University of New Haven, Graduate School, College of Business, Program in Finance, West Haven, CT 06516. Offers Graduate Certificate. *Students:* 5 full-time (2 women), 3 part-time (2 women); includes 1 minority (Asian, non-Hispanic/Latino), 6 international. Average age 28. 21 applicants, 76% accepted, 5 enrolled. In 2016, 1 Graduate Certificate awarded. *Application deadline:* Applications are processed on a rolling basis. Application fee: $50. *Expenses: Tuition:* Full-time $15,660; part-time $870 per credit hour. *Required fees:* $200; $85 per term. Tuition and fees vary according to program. *Financial support:* Research assistantships with partial tuition reimbursements, teaching assistantships with partial tuition reimbursements, career-related internships or fieldwork, and Federal Work-Study available. Financial award application deadline: 5/1; financial award applicants required to submit FAFSA. *Unit head:* Dr. Charlie Boynton, Chair, 203-932-7356, E-mail: cboynton@newhaven.edu. *Application contact:* Michelle Mason, Director of Graduate Enrollment, 203-932-7067, E-mail: mmason@newhaven.edu.
Website: http://www.newhaven.edu/business/programs/graduate/finance/

University of New Mexico, Anderson School of Management, Department of Finance, International, Technology and Entrepreneurship, Albuquerque, NM 87131. Offers entrepreneurship (MBA); finance (MBA); international management (MBA); international management in Latin America (MBA); management of technology (MBA). *Program availability:* Part-time, evening/weekend. *Faculty:* 15 full-time (2 women), 5 part-time/adjunct (0 women). In 2016, 41 master's awarded. *Entrance requirements:* For master's, GMAT or GRE, minimum GPA of 3.0 on last 60 hours of coursework; bachelor's degree from regionally-accredited college or university in U.S. or its equivalent in another country. Additional exam requirements/recommendations for international students: Required—TOEFL (minimum score 550 paper-based; 79 iBT), IELTS (minimum score 6.5). *Application deadline:* For fall admission, 4/1 priority date for domestic and international students; for spring admission, 10/1 priority date for domestic and international students. Applications are processed on a rolling basis. Application fee: $50. Electronic applications accepted. *Expenses:* Contact institution. *Financial support:* In 2016–17, 12 fellowships (averaging $15,441 per year), 12 research assistantships with partial tuition reimbursements (averaging $16,707 per year) were awarded; career-related internships or fieldwork, Federal Work-Study, scholarships/grants, and unspecified assistantships also available. Support available to part-time students. Financial award application deadline: 6/1; financial award applicants required to submit FAFSA. *Faculty research:* Corporate finance, investments, management in Latin America, management of technology, entrepreneurship. *Unit head:* Dr. Sul Kassicieh, Chair, 505-277-6471, E-mail: sul@unm.edu. *Application contact:* Lisa Beauchene, Student Recruitment Specialist, 505-277-6471, E-mail: andersonadvising@unm.edu.
Website: https://www.mgt.unm.edu/fite/default.asp?mm=faculty

University of New Orleans, Graduate School, College of Business Administration, Department of Economics and Finance, New Orleans, LA 70148. Offers economics and finance (MS); financial economics (PhD). *Accreditation:* AACSB. Terminal master's awarded for partial completion of doctoral program. *Degree requirements:* For master's, thesis optional; for doctorate, one foreign language, comprehensive exam, thesis/

dissertation, general exams. *Entrance requirements:* For doctorate, GRE General Test, minimum GPA of 3.0. Additional exam requirements/recommendations for international students: Required—TOEFL (minimum score 550 paper-based; 79 iBT). *Faculty research:* Monetary economics, international economics, urban economics, real estate.

University of North Alabama, College of Business, Florence, AL 35632-0001. Offers business administration (MBA), including accounting, enterprise resource planning systems, executive, finance, health care management, information systems, international business, project management. *Accreditation:* AACSB; ACBSP. *Program availability:* Part-time, 100% online, blended/hybrid learning. *Faculty:* 24 full-time (2 women), 6 part-time/adjunct (3 women). *Students:* 180 full-time (77 women), 411 part-time (199 women); includes 208 minority (84 Black or African American, non-Hispanic/Latino; 4 American Indian or Alaska Native, non-Hispanic/Latino; 106 Asian, non-Hispanic/Latino; 6 Hispanic/Latino; 8 Two or more races, non-Hispanic/Latino), 37 international. Average age 34. 263 applicants, 84% accepted, 173 enrolled. In 2016, 156 master's awarded. *Entrance requirements:* For master's, GMAT, GRE, minimum GPA of 2.75 in last 60 hours, 2.5 overall (on a 3.0 scale); 27 hours of course work in business and economics. Additional exam requirements/recommendations for international students: Required—TOEFL (minimum score 79 iBT), IELTS (minimum score 6), PTE (minimum score 54). *Application deadline:* Applications are processed on a rolling basis. Application fee: $50 ($100 for international students). Electronic applications accepted. *Expenses:* Tuition, state resident: full-time $2799; part-time $1866 per semester. Tuition, nonresident: full-time $5598; part-time $3732 per semester. *Required fees:* $915; $642 per semester. Tuition and fees vary according to course load. *Financial support:* In 2016–17, 114 students received support. Scholarships/grants available. Financial award application deadline: 2/1; financial award applicants required to submit FAFSA. *Unit head:* Dr. Gregory A. Carnes, Dean, 256-765-4261, Fax: 256-765-4170, E-mail: gacarnes@una.edu. *Application contact:* Hillary N. Coats, Graduate Admissions Coordinator, 256-765-4447, E-mail: graduate@una.edu.
Website: http://www.una.edu/business/

The University of North Carolina at Chapel Hill, Kenan-Flagler Business School, Doctoral Program in Business Administration, Chapel Hill, NC 27599. Offers accounting (PhD); finance (PhD); marketing (PhD); operations management (PhD); organizational behavior (PhD); strategy (PhD). *Accreditation:* AACSB. *Degree requirements:* For doctorate, thesis/dissertation. *Entrance requirements:* For doctorate, GMAT or GRE General Test. Electronic applications accepted. *Expenses:* Contact institution.

The University of North Carolina at Charlotte, College of Liberal Arts and Sciences, Department of Political Science and Public Administration, Charlotte, NC 28223-0001. Offers emergency management (Graduate Certificate); non-profit management (Graduate Certificate); public administration (MPA), including arts administration, emergency management, non-profit management, public budgeting and finance, urban management and policy; public budgeting and finance (Graduate Certificate); urban management and policy (Graduate Certificate). *Accreditation:* NASPAA. *Program availability:* Part-time, evening/weekend. *Faculty:* 19 full-time (10 women), 3 part-time/adjunct (0 women). *Students:* 25 full-time (17 women), 57 part-time (39 women); includes 23 minority (14 Black or African American, non-Hispanic/Latino; 1 American Indian or Alaska Native, non-Hispanic/Latino; 2 Asian, non-Hispanic/Latino; 4 Hispanic/Latino; 2 Two or more races, non-Hispanic/Latino). Average age 30. 55 applicants, 73% accepted, 30 enrolled. In 2016, 31 master's, 12 other advanced degrees awarded. *Degree requirements:* For master's, research project or thesis. *Entrance requirements:* For master's, GRE General Test, bachelor's degree, or its equivalent, from accredited college or university; minimum undergraduate GPA of 3.0; 3 letters of recommendation; statement of purpose; for Graduate Certificate, statement of purpose (1-2 pages in length) explaining applicant's career goals, how the Certificate fits into achieving those goals, and any relevant work experience; official transcripts; letters of recommendation. Additional exam requirements/recommendations for international students: Required—TOEFL (minimum score 523 paper-based, 70 iBT) or IELTS (6.5). *Application deadline:* For fall admission, 8/1 for domestic and international students; for spring admission, 12/1 for domestic and international students. Applications are processed on a rolling basis. Application fee: $75. Electronic applications accepted. *Expenses:* Tuition, state resident: full-time $4252. Tuition, nonresident: full-time $17,423. *Required fees:* $3026. Tuition and fees vary according to course load and program. *Financial support:* In 2016–17, 9 students received support, including 9 research assistantships (averaging $7,117 per year); career-related internships or fieldwork, Federal Work-Study, institutionally sponsored loans, scholarships/grants, and unspecified assistantships also available. Support available to part-time students. Financial award application deadline: 3/1; financial award applicants required to submit FAFSA. *Total annual research expenditures:* $477,651. *Unit head:* Dr. Greg Weeks, Chair, 704-687-7574, E-mail: gbweeks@uncc.edu. *Application contact:* Kathy B. Giddings, Director of Graduate Admissions, 704-687-5503, Fax: 704-687-1668, E-mail: gradadm@uncc.edu.
Website: http://politicalscience.uncc.edu/

The University of North Carolina at Greensboro, Graduate School, Bryan School of Business and Economics, Department of Accounting and Finance, Greensboro, NC 27412-5001. Offers accounting (MS); financial analysis (PMC). *Accreditation:* AACSB. *Entrance requirements:* For master's, GMAT, GRE General Test, previous course work in accounting and business. Additional exam requirements/recommendations for international students: Required—TOEFL. Electronic applications accepted.

University of North Florida, Coggin College of Business, MBA Program, Jacksonville, FL 32224. Offers accounting (MBA); construction management (MBA); e-commerce (MBA); economics (MBA); finance (MBA); human resource management (MBA); international business (MBA); logistics (MBA); management applications (MBA). *Accreditation:* AACSB. *Program availability:* Part-time, evening/weekend. *Faculty:* 16 full-time (4 women), 1 (woman) part-time/adjunct. *Students:* 105 full-time (50 women), 162 part-time (68 women); includes 57 minority (14 Black or African American, non-Hispanic/Latino; 1 American Indian or Alaska Native, non-Hispanic/Latino; 17 Asian, non-Hispanic/Latino; 18 Hispanic/Latino; 7 Two or more races, non-Hispanic/Latino), 41 international. Average age 28. 231 applicants, 46% accepted, 84 enrolled. In 2016, 114 master's awarded. *Entrance requirements:* For master's, GMAT or GRE, U.S. bachelor's degree from regionally-accredited university or equivalent foreign degree. Additional exam requirements/recommendations for international students: Required—TOEFL (minimum score 550 paper-based; 79 iBT). *Application deadline:* For fall admission, 8/1 priority date for domestic students, 5/1 for international students; for spring admission, 12/1 priority date for domestic students, 10/1 for international students; for summer admission, 4/29 priority date for domestic students, 2/1 for international students. Application fee: $30. Tuition and fees vary according to course load, campus/location and program. *Financial support:* In 2016–17, 22 students received support, including 1 research assistantship (averaging $2,501 per year); teaching assistantships, Federal Work-Study, and tuition waivers (partial) also available. Support available to part-time students. Financial award application deadline: 4/1; financial award applicants required to submit FAFSA. *Faculty research:* Performance measures, costing, and inventory issues in logistics and supply chain management; inter-organizational systems; international management and marketing practices; e-commerce; organizational learning and socialization processes. *Total annual research expenditures:* $17,654. *Unit head:* Dr. Parvez Ahmed, Graduate Program Director, 904-620-1678, E-mail: pahmed@unf.edu. *Application contact:* Amy Bishop, MSM Advisor, 904-620-2575, Fax: 904-620-2832, E-mail: coggin.students@unf.edu.
Website: http://www.unf.edu/graduateschool/academics/programs/MBA.aspx

University of North Texas, Robert B. Toulouse School of Graduate Studies, Denton, TX 76203-5459. Offers accounting (MS); applied anthropology (MA, MS); applied behavior analysis (Certificate); applied geography (MA); applied technology and performance improvement (M Ed, MS); art education (MA); art history (MA); art museum education (Certificate); arts leadership (Certificate); audiology (Au D); behavior analysis (MS); behavioral science (PhD); biochemistry and molecular biology (MS); biology (MA, MS); biomedical engineering (MS); business analysis (MS); chemistry (MS); clinical health psychology (PhD); communication studies (MA, MS); computer engineering (MS); computer science (MS); counseling (M Ed, MS), including clinical mental health counseling (MS), college and university counseling, elementary school counseling, secondary school counseling; creative writing (MA); criminal justice (MS); curriculum and instruction (M Ed); decision sciences (MBA); design (MA, MFA), including fashion design (MFA), innovation studies, interior design (MFA); early childhood studies (MS); economics (MS); educational leadership (M Ed, Ed D); educational psychology (MS, PhD), including family studies (MS), gifted and talented (MS), human development (MS), learning and cognition (MS), research, measurement and evaluation (MS); electrical engineering (MS); emergency management (MPA); engineering technology (MS); English (MA); English as a second language (MA); environmental science (MS); finance (MBA, MS); financial management (MPA); French (MA); health services management (MBA); higher education (M Ed, Ed D); history (MA, MS); hospitality management (MS); human resources management (MPA); information science (MS); information systems (PhD); information technologies (MBA); interdisciplinary studies (MA, MS); international studies (MA); international sustainable tourism (MS); jazz studies (MM); journalism (MA, MJ, Graduate Certificate), including interactive and virtual digital communication (Graduate Certificate), narrative journalism (Graduate Certificate), public relations (Graduate Certificate); kinesiology (MS); linguistics (MA); local government management (MPA); logistics (PhD); logistics and supply chain management (MBA); long-term care, senior housing, and aging services (MA); management (PhD); marketing (MBA); mathematics (MA, MS); mechanical and energy engineering (MS, PhD); music (MA), including ethnomusicology, music theory, musicology, performance; music composition (PhD); music education (MM Ed, PhD); nonprofit management (MPA); operations and supply chain management (MBA); performance (MM, DMA); philosophy (MA); political science (MA); professional and technical communication (MA); radio, television and film (MA, MFA); rehabilitation counseling (Certificate); sociology (MA); Spanish (MA); special education (M Ed); speech-language pathology (MA); strategic management (MBA); studio art (MFA); teaching (M Ed); MBA/MS. *Program availability:* Part-time, evening/weekend, online learning. Terminal master's awarded for partial completion of doctoral program. *Degree requirements:* For master's, variable foreign language requirement, comprehensive exam (for some programs), thesis (for some programs); for doctorate, variable foreign language requirement, comprehensive exam (for some programs), thesis/dissertation; for other advanced degree, variable foreign language requirement, comprehensive exam (for some programs). *Entrance requirements:* For master's and doctorate, GRE, GMAT. Additional exam requirements/recommendations for international students: Required—TOEFL (minimum score 550 paper-based; 79 iBT). Electronic applications accepted.

University of Notre Dame, Mendoza College of Business, Master of Business Administration Program, Notre Dame, IN 46556. Offers business analytics (MBA); business leadership (MBA); consulting (MBA); corporate finance (MBA); innovation and entrepreneurship (MBA); investments (MBA); marketing (MBA). *Accreditation:* AACSB. *Faculty:* 62 full-time (13 women), 26 part-time/adjunct (7 women). *Students:* 304 full-time (78 women); includes 38 minority (10 Black or African American, non-Hispanic/Latino; 7 Asian, non-Hispanic/Latino; 15 Hispanic/Latino; 6 Two or more races, non-Hispanic/Latino), 80 international. Average age 27. 647 applicants, 41% accepted, 121 enrolled. In 2016, 177 master's awarded. *Entrance requirements:* For master's, GMAT or GRE, work experience, essay, four-slide presentation, two recommendations, transcripts from all colleges and/or universities attended, interview. Additional exam requirements/recommendations for international students: Required—TOEFL (minimum score 600 paper-based; 100 iBT), IELTS (minimum score 7), PTE (minimum score 68). *Application deadline:* For fall admission, 11/1 for domestic and international students; for winter admission, 1/10 for domestic and international students; for spring admission, 2/21 for domestic and international students; for summer admission, 3/28 for domestic and international students. Application fee: $175. Electronic applications accepted. *Expenses:* Contact institution. *Financial support:* In 2016–17, 251 students received support, including 243 fellowships (averaging $26,417 per year); career-related internships or fieldwork, Federal Work-Study, institutionally sponsored loans, scholarships/grants, and unspecified assistantships also available. Financial award application deadline: 2/28; financial award applicants required to submit FAFSA. *Faculty research:* Market micro-structure; marketing and public policy; corporate finance and accounting; corporate governance and ethical behavior; high performing organizations. *Unit head:* Dr. Katherine Speiss, Associate Dean, Graduate Business Programs, 574-631-3759, E-mail: spiess.1@nd.edu. *Application contact:* Kristin McAndrew, Director of Admissions, Graduate Business Programs, 574-631-8488, E-mail: kmcadre@nd.edu.
Website: http://mendoza.nd.edu/programs/mba-programs/

University of Notre Dame, Mendoza College of Business, Master of Science in Finance Program, Notre Dame, IN 46556. Offers MSF. *Program availability:* Part-time-only. *Faculty:* 5 full-time (2 women), 1 part-time/adjunct (0 women). *Students:* 41 part-time (4 women); includes 9 minority (2 Black or African American, non-Hispanic/Latino; 1 Asian, non-Hispanic/Latino; 6 Hispanic/Latino), 2 international. Average age 32. In 2016, 40 master's awarded. *Degree requirements:* For master's, capstone course. *Entrance requirements:* For master's, minimum of two years' work experience and active employment. *Application deadline:* For fall admission, 9/15 for domestic students; for summer admission, 7/15 for domestic students. Applications are processed on a rolling basis. Application fee: $50. Electronic applications accepted. *Expenses:* Contact institution. *Unit head:* Gianna Bern, Academic Director, Master of Science in Finance, 574-631-0434, E-mail: gbern@nd.edu. *Application contact:* Stacey Dickson, Admissions Coordinator, 574-631-1593, Fax: 574-631-6783, E-mail: sdickso1@nd.edu.
Website: http://mendoza.nd.edu/programs/specialized-masters/ms-in-finance/

University of Oklahoma, Price College of Business, Program in Business Administration, Norman, OK 73019. Offers accounting (PhD); business administration (MBA, PhD); entrepreneurship and economic development (PhD); finance (PhD); management and international business (PhD); management of information systems (PhD); marketing/supply chain (PhD); JD/MBA; MBA/MS. *Accreditation:* AACSB. *Program availability:* Part-time, evening/weekend. *Students:* 122 full-time (27 women), 146 part-time (30 women); includes 36 minority (5 Black or African American, non-Hispanic/Latino; 6 American Indian or Alaska Native, non-Hispanic/Latino; 8 Asian, non-Hispanic/Latino; 11 Hispanic/Latino; 6 Two or more races, non-Hispanic/Latino), 37 international. Average age 30. 261 applicants, 27% accepted, 59 enrolled. In 2016, 127 master's, 5 doctorates awarded. *Degree requirements:* For doctorate, comprehensive exam, thesis/dissertation. *Entrance requirements:* For master's, GMAT or GRE, resume, statement of goals; for doctorate, GMAT or GRE, resume, statement of goals, 3 letters of recommendation. Additional exam requirements/recommendations for international students: Required—TOEFL (minimum score 100 iBT) or IELTS (minimum score 7). *Application deadline:* For fall admission, 11/15 priority date for domestic and international students; for spring admission, 3/15 priority date for domestic and international students; for summer admission, 5/15 for domestic and international students. Application fee: $50 ($100 for international students). Electronic applications accepted. *Expenses:* Contact institution. *Financial support:* In 2016–17, 107 students received support, including 10 fellowships with partial tuition reimbursements available (averaging $3,295 per year); research assistantships with full and partial tuition reimbursements available, teaching assistantships with full and partial tuition reimbursements available, career-related internships or fieldwork, scholarships/grants, health care benefits, and unspecified assistantships also available. Support available to part-time students. Financial award application deadline: 6/1; financial award applicants required to submit FAFSA. *Faculty research:* Energy finance; international accounting; organizational behavior and entrepreneurship; management information systems; supply chain. *Unit head:* Laku Chidambaram, Associate Dean for Academic Programs and Engagement. *Application contact:* Director of MBA Admissions, 405-325-5623. Website: http://www.ou.edu/content/price/divisions/graduate.html

University of Oregon, Graduate School, Charles H. Lundquist College of Business, Department of Finance, Eugene, OR 97403. Offers PhD. *Program availability:* Part-time. Terminal master's awarded for partial completion of doctoral program. *Degree requirements:* For doctorate, thesis/dissertation, 2 comprehensive exams. *Entrance requirements:* For doctorate, GMAT. Additional exam requirements/recommendations for international students: Required—TOEFL. *Faculty research:* Changes in firm value in response to corporate takeovers and defenses, capital structure, regulatory changes, financial intermediaries.

University of Ottawa, Faculty of Graduate and Postdoctoral Studies, Interdisciplinary Programs, Ottawa, ON K1N 6N5, Canada. Offers e-business (Certificate); e-commerce (Certificate); finance (Certificate); health services and policies research (Diploma); population health (PhD); population health risk assessment and management (Certificate); public management and governance (Certificate); systems science (Certificate).

University of Pennsylvania, Wharton School, Finance Department, Philadelphia, PA 19104. Offers MBA, PhD. *Degree requirements:* For doctorate, thesis/dissertation. *Entrance requirements:* For doctorate, GMAT or GRE. *Expenses: Tuition:* Full-time $31,068; part-time $5762 per course. *Required fees:* $3200; $336 per course. Full-time tuition and fees vary according to degree level, program and student level. Part-time tuition and fees vary according to course load, degree level and program. *Faculty research:* Corporate finance, investments, macroeconomics, international finance.

University of Pittsburgh, Katz Graduate School of Business, Doctoral Program in Business Administration, Pittsburgh, PA 15260. Offers accounting (PhD); business analytics and operations (PhD); finance (PhD); information systems and technology management (PhD); marketing (PhD); organizational behavior and human resources (PhD); strategic management (PhD). *Accreditation:* AACSB. *Program availability:* Evening/weekend. *Faculty:* 88 full-time (27 women), 42 part-time/adjunct (15 women). *Students:* 51 full-time (23 women), 1 part-time (0 women); includes 4 minority (1 Black or African American, non-Hispanic/Latino; 2 Asian, non-Hispanic/Latino; 1 Two or more races, non-Hispanic/Latino), 31 international. Average age 31. 344 applicants, 6% accepted, 9 enrolled. In 2016, 5 doctorates awarded. *Degree requirements:* For doctorate, comprehensive exam, thesis/dissertation, student teaching. *Entrance requirements:* For doctorate, GMAT or GRE, 3 recommendations, statement of purpose, transcripts of all previous course work and degrees. Additional exam requirements/recommendations for international students: Required—TOEFL (minimum score 100 iBT) or IELTS (minimum score 7.0). *Application deadline:* For fall admission, 4/1 priority date for domestic students, 2/1 priority date for international students. Applications are processed on a rolling basis. Application fee: $50. Electronic applications accepted. *Expenses:* Contact institution. *Financial support:* In 2016–17, 40 students received support, including 27 research assistantships with full tuition reimbursements available (averaging $26,000 per year), 9 teaching assistantships with full tuition reimbursements available (averaging $26,700 per year); Federal Work-Study, scholarships/grants, health care benefits, and unspecified assistantships also available. Financial award application deadline: 6/1; financial award applicants required to submit FAFSA. *Faculty research:* Accounting systems/financial reporting, corporate finance, shopper marketing/consumer behavior, management information systems, organizational behavior and entrepreneurship. *Total annual research expenditures:* $493,036. *Unit head:* Dr. Arjang A. Assad, Dean, 412-648-1556, Fax: 412-648-1552, E-mail: aassad@katz.pitt.edu. *Application contact:* Dr. Dennis Galletta, Director, 412-648-1699, Fax: 412-648-3633, E-mail: galletta@katz.pitt.edu.
Website: http://www.business.pitt.edu/katz/phd/

See Display on page 160 and Close-Up on page 189.

University of Pittsburgh, Katz Graduate School of Business, Master of Business Administration Programs, Pittsburgh, PA 15260. Offers finance (MBA); information systems (MBA); marketing (MBA); operations (MBA); organizational behavior and human resources (MBA); strategy, environment and organizations (MBA); MBA/JD; MBA/MSE. *Accreditation:* AACSB. *Program availability:* Part-time, evening/weekend, blended/hybrid learning. *Faculty:* 88 full-time (27 women), 42 part-time/adjunct (15 women). *Students:* 165 full-time (59 women), 330 part-time (103 women); includes 70 minority (29 Black or African American, non-Hispanic/Latino; 20 Asian, non-Hispanic/Latino; 13 Hispanic/Latino; 8 Two or more races, non-Hispanic/Latino), 73 international. Average age 29. 786 applicants, 41% accepted, 179 enrolled. In 2016, 477 master's awarded. *Degree requirements:* For master's, minimum GPA of 3.0. *Entrance requirements:* For master's, GMAT, GRE. Additional exam requirements/recommendations for international students: Required—TOEFL (minimum score 100 iBT) or IELTS (minimum score 7.0). *Application deadline:* For fall admission, 4/1 priority date for domestic students, 2/1 priority date for international students. Application fee: $50. Electronic applications accepted. *Expenses:* Contact institution. *Financial support:* In 2016–17, 110 students received support. Scholarships/grants available. Financial award application deadline: 6/1; financial award applicants required to submit FAFSA. *Faculty research:* Accounting systems/financial reporting, corporate finance, shopper marketing/consumer behavior, management information systems, organizational behavior and entrepreneurship. *Total annual research expenditures:* $493,036. *Unit head:* Dr. Arjang A. Assad, Dean, 412-648-1556, Fax: 412-648-1552, E-mail: aassad@katz.pitt.edu. *Application contact:* Thomas Keller, Director of MBA Admissions, 412-648-1700, Fax: 412-648-1659, E-mail: mba@katz.pitt.edu.
Website: http://www.business.pitt.edu/katz/mba/

See Display on page 160 and Close-Up on page 189.

University of Pittsburgh, Katz Graduate School of Business, Master of Science in Finance Program, Pittsburgh, PA 15260. Offers MS. *Faculty:* 88 full-time (27 women), 42 part-time/adjunct (15 women). *Students:* 23 full-time (10 women); includes 2 minority (1 Black or African American, non-Hispanic/Latino; 1 Asian, non-Hispanic/Latino), 18 international. Average age 25. 270 applicants, 37% accepted, 23 enrolled. In 2016, 2 master's awarded. *Degree requirements:* For master's, minimum GPA of 3.0. *Entrance requirements:* For master's, GMAT, GRE. Additional exam requirements/recommendations for international students: Required—TOEFL (minimum score 100 iBT), IELTS (minimum score 7). *Application deadline:* For fall admission, 7/1 priority date for domestic students, 5/1 priority date for international students. Applications are processed on a rolling basis. Application fee: $50. Electronic applications accepted. *Expenses:* Contact institution. *Financial support:* Scholarships/grants available. Financial award application deadline: 6/1; financial award applicants required to submit FAFSA. *Faculty research:* Accounting systems/financial reporting, corporate finance, shopper marketing/consumer behavior, management information systems, organizational behavior and entrepreneurship. *Total annual research expenditures:* $493,036. *Unit head:* Dr. Arjang A. Assad, Dean, 412-648-1556, Fax: 412-648-1552, E-mail: aassad@katz.pitt.edu. *Application contact:* Thomas Keller, Director of MBA Admissions, 412-648-1700, Fax: 412-648-1659, E-mail: mba@katz.pitt.edu.
Website: http://www.business.pitt.edu/katz/ms-programs/finance

University of Portland, Dr. Robert B. Pamplin, Jr. School of Business, Portland, OR 97203-5798. Offers entrepreneurship (MBA); finance (MBA, MS); health care management (MBA); marketing (MBA); nonprofit management (EMBA); operations and technology management (MBA, MS); sustainability (MBA). *Accreditation:* AACSB. *Program availability:* Part-time, evening/weekend. *Entrance requirements:* For master's, GMAT, minimum GPA of 3.0, resume, 2 letters of recommendation. Additional exam requirements/recommendations for international students: Required—TOEFL (minimum score 570 paper-based; 89 iBT), IELTS (minimum score 7). *Expenses:* Contact institution.

University of Puerto Rico, Mayagüez Campus, Graduate Studies, College of Business Administration, Mayagüez, PR 00681-9000. Offers business administration (MBA); finance (MBA); human resources (MBA); industrial management (MBA). *Program availability:* Part-time, evening/weekend. *Faculty:* 24 full-time (10 women). *Students:* 37 full-time (24 women), 27 part-time (18 women); includes 60 minority (all Hispanic/Latino). Average age 25. 22 applicants, 68% accepted, 12 enrolled. In 2016, 6 master's awarded. *Degree requirements:* For master's, one foreign language, comprehensive exam, thesis (for some programs). *Entrance requirements:* For master's, GMAT or EXADEP, bachelor's degree with courses in calculus, microeconomics, accounting and statistics. Additional exam requirements/recommendations for international students: Required—TOEFL (minimum score 500 paper-based; 173 iBT), GMAT or EXADEP. *Application deadline:* For fall admission, 2/15 for domestic and international students; for spring admission, 9/15 for domestic and international students. Applications are processed on a rolling basis. Application fee: $25. Electronic applications accepted. *Expenses: Tuition, area resident:* Full-time $2466. *International tuition:* $7166 full-time. *Required fees:* $210. Tuition and fees vary according to course level, campus/location, program and student level. *Financial support:* In 2016–17, 6 students received support, including 5 research assistantships with full and partial tuition reimbursements available (averaging $4,489 per year), 4 teaching assistantships with full and partial tuition reimbursements available (averaging $4,605 per year); unspecified assistantships also available. *Faculty research:* Organizational studies, management, accounting, entrepreneurship, leadership and motivation. *Unit head:* Roberto L. Seijo, PhD, Department Head, 787-832-4040 Ext. 3887, Fax: 787-832-5320, E-mail: roberto.seijo@upr.edu. *Application contact:* Judith Valentín, Administrative Secretary, 787-265-3887, Fax: 787-832-5320, E-mail: grad.adem@uprm.edu.
Website: http://enterprise.uprm.edu/

University of Puerto Rico, Río Piedras Campus, College of Business Administration, San Juan, PR 00931-3300. Offers accounting (MBA); finance (MBA, PhD); general business (MBA); human resources management (MBA); international trade and business (MBA, PhD); marketing (MBA); operations management (MBA); quantitative methods (MBA). *Accreditation:* AACSB. *Program availability:* Part-time. *Degree requirements:* For master's, comprehensive exam, thesis or alternative, research project. *Entrance requirements:* For master's, GMAT or PAEG, minimum GPA of 3.0, letter of recommendation; for doctorate, GMAT, PAEG, minimum GPA of 3.0, master degree. *Faculty research:* Management.

University of Rhode Island, Graduate School, College of Business Administration, Kingston, RI 02881. Offers accounting (MS); business administration (PhD), including finance and insurance, marketing, supply chain management; finance (MBA, MS); general business (MBA); health care management (MBA); management (MBA); marketing (MBA); oceanography (MBA); strategic innovation (MBA); supply chain management (MBA); Pharm D/MBA. *Accreditation:* AACSB. *Program availability:* Part-time, evening/weekend. *Faculty:* 57 full-time (24 women). *Students:* 94 full-time (45 women), 166 part-time (84 women); includes 37 minority (6 Black or African American, non-Hispanic/Latino; 1 American Indian or Alaska Native, non-Hispanic/Latino; 22 Asian, non-Hispanic/Latino; 3 Hispanic/Latino; 5 Two or more races, non-Hispanic/Latino), 18 international. In 2016, 124 master's, 4 doctorates awarded. *Degree requirements:* For master's, comprehensive exam (for some programs), thesis optional; for doctorate, comprehensive exam, thesis/dissertation. *Entrance requirements:* For master's, GMAT or GRE, 2 letters of recommendation, resume; for doctorate, GMAT or GRE, 3 letters of recommendation, resume. Additional exam requirements/recommendations for international students: Required—TOEFL. *Application deadline:* For fall admission, 2/1 for domestic and international students. Application fee: $65. Electronic applications accepted. *Expenses:* Tuition, state resident: full-time $11,796; part-time $655 per credit. Tuition, nonresident: full-time $24,206; part-time $1345 per credit. *Required fees:* $1546; $44 per credit. One-time fee: $155 full-time; $35 part-time. *Financial support:* In 2016–17, 17 teaching assistantships with tuition reimbursements (averaging $15,347 per year) were awarded; research assistantships also available. Financial award application deadline: 2/1; financial award applicants required to submit FAFSA. *Unit head:* Dr. Maling Ebrahimpour, Dean, 401-874-4348, Fax: 401-874-4312, E-mail: mebrahimpour@uri.edu. *Application contact:* Lisa Lancellotta, Coordinator, MBA Programs, 401-874-4241, Fax: 401-874-4312, E-mail: mba@uri.edu.
Website: http://www.cba.uri.edu/

See Display on page 161 and Close-Up on page 191.

University of Rochester, Simon Business School, Doctoral Program in Business Administration, Rochester, NY 14627. Offers accounting (PhD); computer information systems (PhD); finance (PhD); marketing (PhD); operations management (PhD). *Accreditation:* AACSB. *Faculty:* 66 full-time (13 women), 22 part-time/adjunct (2 women). *Students:* 52 full-time (19 women); includes 2 minority (both Asian, non-Hispanic/Latino), 42 international. Average age 29. 210 applicants, 16% accepted, 15 enrolled. In 2016, 6 doctorates awarded. *Degree requirements:* For doctorate, comprehensive exam, thesis/dissertation, qualifying exam. *Entrance requirements:* For doctorate, GMAT or GRE. Additional exam requirements/recommendations for international students: Required—TOEFL. *Application deadline:* For fall admission, 1/5 for domestic and international students. Application fee: $100. Electronic applications accepted. *Expenses:* $1,800 per credit hour. *Financial support:* In 2016–17, 52 students received support. Fellowships, research assistantships, teaching assistantships, and tuition waivers (full) available. Financial award application deadline: 1/5. *Unit head:* Dr. Ron Kaniel, Committee Chair, 585-275-2959. *Application contact:* Sue Harris, PhD Administrator, 585-275-2959, E-mail: phdoffice@simon.rochester.edu.
Website: http://www.simon.rochester.edu/programs/phd/index.aspx

Finance and Banking

University of Rochester, Simon Business School, Full-Time Master's Program in Business Administration, Rochester, NY 14627. Offers business systems consulting (MBA); competitive and organizational strategy (MBA); computers and information systems (MBA); corporate accounting (MBA); entrepreneurship (MBA); finance (MBA); health sciences management (MBA); marketing (MBA); operations management (MBA); public accounting (MBA). *Accreditation:* AACSB. *Program availability:* Part-time, evening/weekend. *Faculty:* 66 full-time (13 women), 22 part-time/adjunct (2 women). *Students:* 202 full-time (78 women); includes 50 minority (30 Black or African American, non-Hispanic/Latino; 10 Asian, non-Hispanic/Latino; 9 Hispanic/Latino; 1 Two or more races, non-Hispanic/Latino), 107 international. Average age 27. 915 applicants, 30% accepted, 86 enrolled. In 2016, 110 master's awarded. *Entrance requirements:* For master's, GMAT/GRE. Additional exam requirements/recommendations for international students: Required—TOEFL. *Application deadline:* For fall admission, 10/15 for domestic and international students; for winter admission, 1/5 for domestic and international students; for spring admission, 3/15 for domestic and international students; for summer admission, 5/15 for domestic and international students. Applications are processed on a rolling basis. Application fee: $150. Electronic applications accepted. *Expenses:* Contact institution. *Financial support:* In 2016–17, 190 students received support. Fellowships, research assistantships, teaching assistantships, institutionally sponsored loans, scholarships/grants, and tuition waivers (full and partial) available. Financial award application deadline: 1/5; financial award applicants required to submit FAFSA. *Unit head:* Andrew Ainslie, Dean, 585-275-3316, E-mail: andrew.ainslie@simon.rochester.edu. *Application contact:* Rebekah S. Lewin, Assistant Dean of Admissions and Financial Aid, 585-275-3533, E-mail: admissions@simon.rochester.edu.
Website: http://www.simon.rochester.edu/programs/full-time-mba/index.aspx

University of Rochester, Simon Business School, Master of Science Program in Finance, Rochester, NY 14627. Offers MS. *Faculty:* 66 full-time (13 women), 22 part-time/adjunct (2 women). *Students:* 183 full-time (90 women); includes 6 minority (3 Asian, non-Hispanic/Latino; 2 Hispanic/Latino; 1 Two or more races, non-Hispanic/Latino), 164 international. Average age 23. 2,230 applicants, 22% accepted, 183 enrolled. In 2016, 141 master's awarded. *Entrance requirements:* For master's, GRE/GMAT. Additional exam requirements/recommendations for international students: Required—TOEFL. *Application deadline:* For fall admission, 10/15 for domestic and international students; for winter admission, 1/5 for domestic and international students; for spring admission, 3/15 for domestic and international students; for summer admission, 5/15 for domestic and international students. Applications are processed on a rolling basis. Application fee: $150. Electronic applications accepted. *Expenses:* Contact institution. *Financial support:* In 2016–17, 102 students received support. Institutionally sponsored loans, scholarships/grants, and tuition waivers (partial) available. Support available to part-time students. Financial award application deadline: 1/5; financial award applicants required to submit FAFSA. *Unit head:* Andrew Ainslie, Dean, 585-275-3316, E-mail: andrew.ainslie@simon.rochester.edu. *Application contact:* Rebekah S. Lewin, Assistant Dean of Admissions and Financial Aid, 585-275-3533, E-mail: admissions@simon.rochester.edu.
Website: http://www.simon.rochester.edu/programs/full-time-ms-in-finance/index.aspx

University of Rochester, Simon Business School, Part-Time MBA Program, Rochester, NY 14627. Offers business systems consulting (MBA); competitive and organizational strategy (MBA); computers and information systems (MBA); corporate accounting (MBA); entrepreneurship (MBA); finance (MBA); health sciences management (MBA); marketing (MBA); operations management (MBA); public accounting (MBA). *Program availability:* Part-time, evening/weekend. *Faculty:* 66 full-time (13 women), 22 part-time/adjunct (2 women). *Students:* 185 part-time (65 women); includes 29 minority (6 Black or African American, non-Hispanic/Latino; 13 Asian, non-Hispanic/Latino; 8 Hispanic/Latino; 2 Two or more races, non-Hispanic/Latino), 9 international. Average age 32. 33 applicants, 100% accepted, 31 enrolled. In 2016, 70 master's awarded. *Entrance requirements:* For master's, GRE or GMAT. *Application deadline:* For fall admission, 8/1 for domestic students; for spring admission, 2/15 for domestic students. Applications are processed on a rolling basis. Application fee: $150. Electronic applications accepted. *Expenses:* $1,800 per credit hour. *Financial support:* In 2016–17, 75 students received support. Scholarships/grants and tuition waivers (partial) available. Financial award applicants required to submit CSS PROFILE or FAFSA. *Unit head:* Andrew Ainslie, Dean, 585-275-3316, E-mail: andrew.ainslie@simon.rochester.edu. *Application contact:* Molly Mesko, Executive Director, EMBA and Part-Time Programs, 585-275-4277, E-mail: molly.mesko@simon.rochester.edu.
Website: http://www.simon.rochester.edu/programs/ptmba/index.aspx

University of St. Francis, College of Business and Health Administration, School of Business, Joliet, IL 60435-6169. Offers accounting (MBA, Certificate); business analytics (MBA, Certificate); finance (MBA, Certificate); health administration (MBA); human resource management (MBA); logistics (Certificate); management (MBA, MSM); training and development (MBA); transportation and logistics (MBA). *Accreditation:* ACBSP. *Program availability:* Part-time, evening/weekend, 100% online, blended/hybrid learning. *Faculty:* 6 full-time (3 women), 12 part-time/adjunct (6 women). *Students:* 78 full-time (28 women), 110 part-time (62 women); includes 41 minority (22 Black or African American, non-Hispanic/Latino; 3 Asian, non-Hispanic/Latino; 15 Hispanic/Latino; 1 Two or more races, non-Hispanic/Latino), 8 international. Average age 36. 171 applicants, 44% accepted, 58 enrolled. In 2016, 62 master's, 3 other advanced degrees awarded. *Entrance requirements:* For master's, GMAT or 2 years of managerial experience. Additional exam requirements/recommendations for international students: Required—TOEFL (minimum score 550 paper-based; 79 iBT), IELTS (minimum score 6). *Application deadline:* Applications are processed on a rolling basis. Application fee: $30. Electronic applications accepted. Application fee is waived when completed online. *Expenses:* $798 per credit. *Financial support:* In 2016–17, 51 students received support. Career-related internships or fieldwork, scholarships/grants, tuition waivers (partial), and unspecified assistantships available. Support available to part-time students. Financial award applicants required to submit FAFSA. *Unit head:* Dr. Orlando Griego, Dean, 815-740-3395, Fax: 815-740-3537, E-mail: ogriego@stfrancis.edu. *Application contact:* Sandra Sloka, Director of Admissions for Graduate and Degree Completion Programs, 800-735-7500, Fax: 815-740-3431, E-mail: ssloka@stfrancis.edu.
Website: http://www.stfrancis.edu/academics/college-of-business-health-administration/

University of Saint Mary, Graduate Programs, Program in Business Administration, Leavenworth, KS 66048-5082. Offers enterprise risk management (MBA); finance (MBA); general management (MBA); health care management (MBA); human resource management (MBA); marketing and advertising management (MBA). *Program availability:* Part-time, evening/weekend, 100% online, blended/hybrid learning. *Students:* 201 full-time (110 women), 62 part-time (38 women); includes 83 minority (29 Black or African American, non-Hispanic/Latino; 3 American Indian or Alaska Native, non-Hispanic/Latino; 14 Asian, non-Hispanic/Latino; 32 Hispanic/Latino; 1 Native Hawaiian or other Pacific Islander, non-Hispanic/Latino; 4 Two or more races, non-Hispanic/Latino), 7 international. Average age 34. In 2016, 73 master's awarded. *Degree requirements:* For master's, thesis. *Entrance requirements:* For master's, minimum undergraduate GPA of 2.75, official transcripts, two letters of recommendation. *Application deadline:* Applications are processed on a rolling basis. Application fee: $25. Electronic applications accepted. *Expenses:* $595 per hour. *Unit head:* Rick Gunter, Director, 913-319-3007. *Application contact:* Mark Harvey, Program Manager, 913-319-3007, E-mail: mark.harvey@stmary.edu.
Website: http://www.stmary.edu/success/Grad-Program/Master-of-Business-Administration-MBA.aspx

University of St. Thomas, Cameron School of Business, Houston, TX 77006-4696. Offers MBA, MCTM, MIB, MSA, MSF. *Program availability:* Part-time, evening/weekend. *Faculty:* 26 full-time (8 women), 7 part-time/adjunct (2 women). *Students:* 178 full-time (86 women), 222 part-time (127 women); includes 182 minority (38 Black or African American, non-Hispanic/Latino; 36 Asian, non-Hispanic/Latino; 104 Hispanic/Latino; 4 Two or more races, non-Hispanic/Latino), 115 international. Average age 31. 144 applicants, 97% accepted, 72 enrolled. In 2016, 164 master's awarded. *Degree requirements:* For master's, capstone (for some programs), additional course requirements for those sitting for state accountancy exam. *Entrance requirements:* For master's, minimum GPA of 2.5, 3 letters of recommendation. Additional exam requirements/recommendations for international students: Required—TOEFL (minimum score 550 paper-based; 79 iBT), IELTS (minimum score 6.5), PTE (minimum score 53). *Application deadline:* For fall admission, 7/15 for domestic and international students; for winter admission, 7/15 for domestic and international students; for spring admission, 11/15 for domestic students, 10/15 for international students. Applications are processed on a rolling basis. Application fee: $35. Electronic applications accepted. *Expenses: Tuition:* Full-time $20,934; part-time $1163 per credit hour. *Required fees:* $81 per semester. One-time fee: $100. Part-time tuition and fees vary according to course level, course load, campus/location and program. *Financial support:* In 2016–17, 56 students received support, including research assistantships with partial tuition reimbursements available (averaging $3,000 per year); Federal Work-Study, scholarships/grants, unspecified assistantships, and state work-study, institutional employment also available. Support available to part-time students. Financial award application deadline: 4/15; financial award applicants required to submit FAFSA. *Unit head:* Dr. Beena George, Dean, 713-525-2100, Fax: 713-525-2110, E-mail: cameron@stthom.edu. *Application contact:* Fran Wilson Mayes, Academic Coordinator, 713-525-2100, Fax: 713-525-2110, E-mail: cameron@stthom.edu.
Website: http://www.stthom.edu/Academics/Cameron_School_of_Business/Index.aqf

University of San Diego, School of Business, Program in Finance, San Diego, CA 92110-2492. Offers MSF. *Program availability:* Part-time, evening/weekend. *Students:* 30 full-time (12 women); includes 5 minority (1 Black or African American, non-Hispanic/Latino; 4 Hispanic/Latino), 19 international. Average age 25. In 2016, 11 master's awarded. *Entrance requirements:* For master's, GMAT (minimum score of 560), minimum GPA of 3.0. Additional exam requirements/recommendations for international students: Required—TOEFL. *Application deadline:* For fall admission, 5/1 for domestic students. Applications are processed on a rolling basis. Application fee: $80. Electronic applications accepted. *Financial support:* In 2016–17, 11 students received support. Career-related internships or fieldwork, Federal Work-Study, institutionally sponsored loans, scholarships/grants, and unspecified assistantships available. Support available to part-time students. Financial award application deadline: 4/1; financial award applicants required to submit FAFSA. *Unit head:* Dr. Marko Svetina, Academic Director, Finance Program, 619-260-7586, E-mail: msf@sandiego.edu. *Application contact:* Monica Mahon, Associate Director of Graduate Admissions, 619-260-4524, Fax: 619-260-4158, E-mail: grads@sandiego.edu.
Website: http://www.sandiego.edu/business/graduate/ms-finance/

University of San Francisco, School of Management, Master of Business Administration Program, San Francisco, CA 94117. Offers entrepreneurship and innovation (MBA); finance (MBA); marketing (MBA); organization development (MBA); DDS/MBA; JD/MBA; MBA/MAPS. *Accreditation:* AACSB. *Program availability:* Part-time, evening/weekend. *Faculty:* 17 full-time (6 women), 5 part-time/adjunct (2 women). *Students:* 146 full-time (70 women), 2 part-time (1 woman); includes 50 minority (5 Black or African American, non-Hispanic/Latino; 27 Asian, non-Hispanic/Latino; 15 Hispanic/Latino; 1 Native Hawaiian or other Pacific Islander, non-Hispanic/Latino; 2 Two or more races, non-Hispanic/Latino), 51 international. Average age 29. 282 applicants, 63% accepted, 70 enrolled. In 2016, 91 master's awarded. *Entrance requirements:* For master's, GMAT or GRE, resume (two years of professional work experience required for part-time students, preferred for full-time), transcripts from each college or university attended, two letters of recommendation, personal statement, interview. Additional exam requirements/recommendations for international students: Required—TOEFL (minimum score 600 paper-based, 100 iBT), IELTS (minimum score 7) or PTE (minimum score 68). *Application deadline:* For fall admission, 6/5 for domestic students, 5/15 for international students; for spring admission, 11/30 for domestic students. Application fee: $55. Electronic applications accepted. *Expenses: Tuition:* Full-time $23,310; part-time $1295 per credit. Tuition and fees vary according to course load, degree level, campus/location and program. *Financial support:* In 2016–17, 60 students received support. Fellowships and scholarships/grants available. Financial award application deadline: 3/2; financial award applicants required to submit FAFSA. *Faculty research:* International financial markets, technology transfer licensing, international marketing, strategic planning. *Total annual research expenditures:* $50,000. *Unit head:* Dr. Frank Fletcher, Director, 415-422-2221, Fax: 415-422-6315, E-mail: management@usfca.edu. *Application contact:* Office of Graduate Recruiting and Admissions, 415-422-2221, Fax: 415-422-6315, E-mail: management@usfca.edu.
Website: http://www.usfca.edu/mba

University of San Francisco, School of Management, Master of Science in Financial Analysis Program, San Francisco, CA 94117. Offers MSFA, MS/MBA. *Program availability:* Part-time, evening/weekend. *Faculty:* 4 full-time (0 women), 3 part-time/adjunct (0 women). *Students:* 148 full-time (63 women), 2 part-time (0 women); includes 21 minority (3 Black or African American, non-Hispanic/Latino; 15 Asian, non-Hispanic/Latino; 3 Hispanic/Latino), 107 international. Average age 26. 291 applicants, 70% accepted, 79 enrolled. In 2016, 88 master's awarded. *Entrance requirements:* For master's, GMAT or GRE, resume (minimum of two years of professional work experience for working professionals format), transcripts from each college or university attended showing completion of required foundation courses, two letters of recommendation, personal statement. Additional exam requirements/recommendations for international students: Required—TOEFL (minimum score 600 paper-based, 100 iBT), IELTS (minimum score 7) or PTE (minimum score 68). *Application deadline:* For fall admission, 6/15 for domestic students, 5/15 for international students; for spring admission, 11/15 for domestic students, 10/15 for international students. Application fee: $55. Electronic applications accepted. *Expenses: Tuition:* Full-time $23,310; part-time $1295 per credit. Tuition and fees vary according to course load, degree level, campus/location and program. *Financial support:* In 2016–17, 56 students received support. Scholarships/grants available. Financial award applicants required to submit FAFSA. *Unit head:* Dr. John Veitch, Director, 415-422-2221, E-mail: management@usfca.edu. *Application contact:* Office of Graduate Recruiting and Admission, 415-422-2221, Fax: 415-422-6315, E-mail: management@usfca.edu.
Website: http://www.usfca.edu/msfa

University of Saskatchewan, College of Graduate Studies and Research, Edwards School of Business, Department of Finance and Management Science, Saskatoon, SK

S7N 5A2, Canada. Offers finance (M Sc). *Program availability:* Part-time. *Degree requirements:* For master's, thesis. *Entrance requirements:* For master's, GMAT. Additional exam requirements/recommendations for international students: Required—TOEFL.

The University of Scranton, Kania School of Management, Program in Business Administration, Scranton, PA 18510. Offers accounting (MBA); finance (MBA); general business administration (MBA); health care management (MBA); international business (MBA); management information systems (MBA); marketing (MBA); operations management (MBA). *Accreditation:* AACSB. *Program availability:* Part-time, evening/weekend, 100% online. *Entrance requirements:* For master's, GMAT (for MBA). *Faculty research:* Financial markets, strategic impact of total quality management, internal accounting controls, consumer preference, information systems and the Internet.

University of Southern Maine, College of Management and Human Service, School of Business, Portland, ME 04104-9300. Offers accounting (MBA); business administration (MBA); finance (MBA); health management and policy (MBA); sustainability (MBA); JD/MBA; MBA/MSA; MBA/MSN; MS/MBA. *Accreditation:* AACSB. *Program availability:* Part-time, evening/weekend. *Entrance requirements:* For master's, GMAT or GRE, minimum AACSB index of 1100. Additional exam requirements/recommendations for international students: Required—TOEFL (minimum score 550 paper-based; 79 iBT). Electronic applications accepted. *Faculty research:* Economic development, management information systems, real options, system dynamics, simulation.

University of South Florida, Muma College of Business, Department of Finance, Tampa, FL 33620-9951. Offers business administration (PhD), including finance; finance (MS); real estate (MSRE). *Program availability:* Part-time, evening/weekend. *Faculty:* 14 full-time (3 women). *Students:* 80 full-time (32 women), 22 part-time (12 women); includes 5 minority (3 Asian, non-Hispanic/Latino; 2 Hispanic/Latino), 75 international. Average age 26. 117 applicants, 63% accepted, 48 enrolled. In 2016, 43 master's, 2 doctorates awarded. Terminal master's awarded for partial completion of doctoral program. *Degree requirements:* For master's, comprehensive exam, thesis or alternative; for doctorate, comprehensive exam, thesis/dissertation. *Entrance requirements:* For master's, GMAT, minimum undergraduate GPA of 3.0 in upper-division coursework; for doctorate, GMAT or GRE, minimum undergraduate GPA of 3.0 in upper-division coursework, personal statement, recommendations, interview. Additional exam requirements/recommendations for international students: Required—TOEFL (minimum score 550 paper-based; 79 iBT) or IELTS (minimum score 6.5). *Application deadline:* For fall admission, 1/2 for domestic and international students; for spring admission, 10/15 for domestic students, 7/1 for international students; for summer admission, 2/15 for domestic students, 1/1 for international students. Application fee: $30. Electronic applications accepted. *Expenses:* Tuition, state resident: full-time $7766; part-time $431.43 per credit hour. Tuition, nonresident: full-time $15,789; part-time $877.17 per credit hour. *Required fees:* $37 per term. *Financial support:* In 2016–17, 9 students received support, including 8 research assistantships (averaging $14,357 per year), 9 teaching assistantships with tuition reimbursements available (averaging $11,972 per year); scholarships/grants, health care benefits, and unspecified assistantships also available. Financial award application deadline: 6/30. *Faculty research:* International corporate finance, corporate finance, market efficiency, mergers and acquisitions, agency theory, corporate governance, investments, mutual fund industry, mergers and acquisitions, corporate creditworthiness, credit risk issues, empirical asset pricing, financial intermediation, corporate finance theory, public offerings, business strategy. *Unit head:* Dr. Scott Besley, Chairperson and Associate Professor, 813-974-6341, Fax: 813-974-3084, E-mail: sbesley@usf.edu. *Application contact:* Amy Dunkel, Office Manager, Finance Department, 813-974-6294, Fax: 813-974-3084, E-mail: adunkel@usf.edu.
Website: http://business.usf.edu/departments/finance/

The University of Tampa, Sykes College of Business, Tampa, FL 33606-1490. Offers accounting (MS); entrepreneurship (MBA); finance (MBA, MS); information systems management (MBA); innovation management (MBA); international business (MBA); marketing (MBA, MS); nonprofit management (MBA). *Accreditation:* AACSB. *Program availability:* Part-time, evening/weekend. *Faculty:* 43 full-time (19 women), 9 part-time/adjunct (3 women). *Students:* 438 full-time (176 women), 126 part-time (57 women); includes 37 minority (22 Black or African American, non-Hispanic/Latino; 11 Asian, non-Hispanic/Latino; 4 Two or more races, non-Hispanic/Latino), 203 international. Average age 28. 1,305 applicants, 39% accepted, 192 enrolled. In 2016, 266 master's awarded. *Degree requirements:* For master's, capstone. *Entrance requirements:* For master's, GMAT or GRE, official transcripts from all colleges and/or universities previously attended, resume, personal statement, letters of recommendation. Additional exam requirements/recommendations for international students: Required—TOEFL (minimum score 577 paper-based, 90 iBT) or IELTS (7.5). *Application deadline:* Applications are processed on a rolling basis. Application fee: $40. Electronic applications accepted. *Expenses:* $588 per credit tuition, $40 per term fees. *Financial support:* In 2016–17, 116 students received support. Career-related internships or fieldwork, scholarships/grants, and unspecified assistantships available. Financial award applicants required to submit FAFSA. *Faculty research:* Job market signaling, on-line shopping behaviors and social media, the Tampa Bay economy, digital literacy, entrepreneurship in small businesses. *Unit head:* Dr. Natasha F. Veltri, Associate Dean, 813-253-6289, E-mail: nveltri@ut.edu. *Application contact:* Chanelle Cox, Staff Assistant, Admissions for Graduate and Continuing Studies, 813-253-6249, E-mail: ccox@ut.edu.
Website: http://www.ut.edu/business/

The University of Tennessee, Graduate School, College of Business Administration, Program in Business Administration, Knoxville, TN 37996. Offers accounting (PhD); finance (MBA, PhD); logistics and transportation (MBA, PhD); management (PhD); marketing (MBA, PhD); operations management (MBA); professional business administration (MBA); statistics (PhD); JD/MBA; MS/MBA; Pharm D/MBA. Pharm D/MBA offered jointly with The University of Tennessee Health Science Center. *Accreditation:* AACSB. *Program availability:* Online learning. *Degree requirements:* For master's, thesis or alternative; for doctorate, thesis/dissertation. *Entrance requirements:* For master's and doctorate, GMAT, minimum GPA of 2.7. Additional exam requirements/recommendations for international students: Required—TOEFL. Electronic applications accepted.

The University of Tennessee at Martin, Graduate Programs, College of Business and Global Affairs, Program in Business, Martin, TN 38238. Offers agricultural business (MBA); financial services (MBA); general business (MBA). *Accreditation:* AACSB. *Program availability:* Part-time, online only, 100% online, blended/hybrid learning. *Faculty:* 31. *Students:* 15 full-time (6 women), 79 part-time (28 women); includes 13 minority (6 Black or African American, non-Hispanic/Latino; 2 Asian, non-Hispanic/Latino; 4 Hispanic/Latino; 1 Two or more races, non-Hispanic/Latino). Average age 33. 62 applicants, 40% accepted, 20 enrolled. In 2016, 34 master's awarded. *Degree requirements:* For master's, comprehensive exam. *Entrance requirements:* For master's, GMAT, GRE, minimum GPA of 2.5, resume. Additional exam requirements/recommendations for international students: Required—TOEFL (minimum score 525 paper-based; 71 iBT). *Application deadline:* For fall admission, 7/27 priority date for domestic students, 7/27 for international students; for spring admission, 12/17 priority date for domestic students, 12/17 for international students; for summer admission, 5/10 priority date for domestic and international students. Applications are processed on a rolling basis. Application fee: $30 ($130 for international students). Electronic applications accepted. *Expenses:* Tuition, state resident: full-time $8254; part-time $459 per credit hour. Tuition, nonresident: full-time $22,198; part-time $1234 per credit hour. *Required fees:* $79 per credit hour. Part-time tuition and fees vary according to course load and campus/location. *Financial support:* In 2016–17, 10 students received support, including 5 research assistantships with full tuition reimbursements available (averaging $7,540 per year), 5 teaching assistantships with full tuition reimbursements available (averaging $7,560 per year); career-related internships or fieldwork, scholarships/grants, and unspecified assistantships also available. Support available to part-time students. Financial award application deadline: 2/1; financial award applicants required to submit FAFSA. *Unit head:* Dr. Ashley Kilburn, Coordinator, 731-881-7245, Fax: 731-881-7231, E-mail: mba@utm.edu. *Application contact:* Jolene L. Cunningham, Student Services Specialist, 731-881-7012, Fax: 731-881-7499, E-mail: jcunningham@utm.edu.

The University of Texas at Arlington, Graduate School, College of Business, Department of Finance and Real Estate, Arlington, TX 76019. Offers finance (PhD); quantitative finance (MS); real estate (MS). *Program availability:* Part-time, evening/weekend. *Degree requirements:* For master's, thesis optional; for doctorate, comprehensive exam, thesis/dissertation. *Entrance requirements:* For master's, GMAT/GRE, minimum GPA of 3.0; for doctorate, GMAT/GRE. Additional exam requirements/recommendations for international students: Required—TOEFL (minimum score 550 paper-based; 79 iBT). *Application deadline:* For fall admission, 6/1 priority date for domestic students, 4/1 for international students; for spring admission, 10/15 for domestic students, 9/15 for international students. Applications are processed on a rolling basis. Application fee: $40 ($70 for international students). *Financial support:* Teaching assistantships, career-related internships or fieldwork, Federal Work-Study, institutionally sponsored loans, and unspecified assistantships available. Financial award application deadline: 6/1; financial award applicants required to submit FAFSA. *Unit head:* Dr. David Diltz, Chair, 817-272-3705, Fax: 817-272-2252, E-mail: diltz@uta.edu. *Application contact:* Dr. Fred Forgey, Graduate Advisor, 817-272-0359, Fax: 817-272-2252, E-mail: realestate@uta.edu.
Website: http://wweb.uta.edu/finance/

The University of Texas at Austin, Graduate School, McCombs School of Business, Department of Finance, Austin, TX 78712-1111. Offers MSF, PhD. *Entrance requirements:* For doctorate, GMAT or GRE. Electronic applications accepted.

The University of Texas at Dallas, Naveen Jindal School of Management, Program in Finance and Managerial Economics, Richardson, TX 75080. Offers finance (MS), including corporate finance/investment banking, energy risk management, enterprise risk management, financial analysis, financial risk management, real estate. *Program availability:* Part-time, evening/weekend. *Faculty:* 24 full-time (2 women), 12 part-time/adjunct (5 women). *Students:* 295 full-time (124 women), 56 part-time (37 women); includes 34 minority (3 Black or African American, non-Hispanic/Latino; 21 Asian, non-Hispanic/Latino; 7 Hispanic/Latino; 3 Two or more races, non-Hispanic/Latino), 279 international. Average age 26. 793 applicants, 66% accepted, 157 enrolled. In 2016, 215 master's awarded. *Entrance requirements:* For master's, GMAT or GRE. Additional exam requirements/recommendations for international students: Required—TOEFL (minimum score 550 paper-based). *Application deadline:* For fall admission, 7/15 for domestic students, 5/1 priority date for international students; for spring admission, 11/15 for domestic students, 9/1 priority date for international students. Applications are processed on a rolling basis. Application fee: $50 ($100 for international students). Electronic applications accepted. *Expenses:* Tuition, state resident: full-time $12,418; part-time $690 per semester hour. Tuition, nonresident: full-time $24,150; part-time $1342 per semester hour. Tuition and fees vary according to course load. *Financial support:* In 2016–17, 55 students received support, including 9 teaching assistantships with partial tuition reimbursements available (averaging $10,050 per year); research assistantships with partial tuition reimbursements available, career-related internships or fieldwork, Federal Work-Study, institutionally sponsored loans, scholarships/grants, and unspecified assistantships also available. Support available to part-time students. Financial award application deadline: 4/30; financial award applicants required to submit FAFSA. *Faculty research:* Econometrics, industrial organization, auction theory, file-sharing copyrights and bundling, international financial management, entrepreneurial finance. *Unit head:* Dr. Harold Zhang, Area Coordinator, 972-883-4777, E-mail: harold.zhang@utdallas.edu. *Application contact:* Kristin Spain, Academic Support Coordinator, 972-883-2373, E-mail: kes160430@utdallas.edu.
Website: http://jindal.utdallas.edu/finance

The University of Texas at San Antonio, College of Business, Department of Finance, San Antonio, TX 78249-0617. Offers MBA, MS, PhD. *Program availability:* Part-time, evening/weekend. *Faculty:* 9 full-time (0 women), 1 part-time/adjunct (0 women). *Students:* 37 full-time (19 women), 54 part-time (8 women); includes 33 minority (5 Asian, non-Hispanic/Latino; 26 Hispanic/Latino; 2 Two or more races, non-Hispanic/Latino), 15 international. Average age 29. 38 applicants, 76% accepted, 19 enrolled. In 2016, 31 master's awarded. *Degree requirements:* For master's, comprehensive exam, thesis or alternative, 33 semester credit hours to be taken from a specified list of courses; for doctorate, comprehensive exam, thesis/dissertation. *Entrance requirements:* For master's and doctorate, GMAT or GRE, statement of purpose; 3 letters of recommendation. Additional exam requirements/recommendations for international students: Required—TOEFL (minimum score 500 paper-based; 61 iBT), IELTS (minimum score 5). *Application deadline:* For fall admission, 7/1 for domestic students, 4/1 for international students; for spring admission, 11/1 for domestic students, 9/1 for international students. Applications are processed on a rolling basis. Application fee: $45 ($80 for international students). Electronic applications accepted. *Financial support:* In 2016–17, 12 students received support, including 1 research assistantship (averaging $10,000 per year), 10 teaching assistantships (averaging $10,000 per year). *Faculty research:* Corporate finance, international finance, options and futures, market microstructure, financial institutions. *Total annual research expenditures:* $240,105. *Unit head:* Dr. Karan Bhanot, Chair, 210-458-6513, E-mail: karan.bhanot@utsa.edu. *Application contact:* Monica Rodriguez, Director of Graduate Admissions, 210-458-4723, Fax: 210-458-4332, E-mail: monica.rodriguez@utsa.edu.

The University of Texas Rio Grande Valley, Robert C. Vackar College of Business and Entrepreneurship, Program in Business Administration, Edinburg, TX 78539. Offers business administration (MBA); finance (PhD); management (PhD); marketing (PhD). *Program availability:* Part-time, evening/weekend, online learning. *Degree requirements:* For master's, thesis optional. *Entrance requirements:* For master's, GMAT, minimum GPA of 3.0. Additional exam requirements/recommendations for international students: Required—TOEFL (minimum score 500 paper-based). Electronic applications accepted. Tuition and fees vary according to course load and program. *Faculty research:* Human resources, border region, entrepreneurship, marketing.

University of the West, Department of Business Administration, Rosemead, CA 91770. Offers business administration (EMBA); computer information systems (MBA); finance (MBA); international business (MBA); nonprofit organization management (MBA). *Program availability:* Part-time, evening/weekend. *Faculty:* 3 full-time (1 woman), 6 part-time/adjunct (2 women). *Students:* 54 full-time (31 women), 14 part-time (3 women); includes 8 minority (4 Asian, non-Hispanic/Latino; 4 Hispanic/Latino), 59 international.

Average age 29. *Entrance requirements:* Additional exam requirements/ recommendations for international students: Required—TOEFL. *Application deadline:* For fall admission, 6/15 for domestic and international students; for winter admission, 4/ 1 for domestic and international students; for spring admission, 11/15 for domestic and international students. Applications are processed on a rolling basis. Application fee: $50 ($100 for international students). *Expenses: Tuition:* Full-time $9324; part-time $4662 per year. *Required fees:* $900; $640 per unit. $320 per semester. Tuition and fees vary according to program. *Financial support:* Career-related internships or fieldwork, Federal Work-Study, scholarships/grants, and tuition waivers (partial) available. Financial award applicants required to submit FAFSA. *Unit head:* Dr. Bill Y. Chen, Chair, 626-656-2125, Fax: 626-571-1413, E-mail: billchen@uwest.edu. *Application contact:* Rica Toribio, Director of Enrollment Services, 626-571-8811 Ext. 311, Fax: 626-571-1413, E-mail: ricat@uwest.edu.
Website: http://www.uwest.edu/site/index.php?option=com_content&view=article&id=119&Itemid=162

The University of Toledo, College of Graduate Studies, College of Business and Innovation, Department of Finance, Toledo, OH 43606-3390. Offers MBA. *Program availability:* Part-time, evening/weekend. *Entrance requirements:* For master's, GMAT, GRE, or LSAT, minimum GPA of 2.7 for all prior academic work, three letters of recommendation, statement of purpose, transcripts from all prior institutions attended. Additional exam requirements/recommendations for international students: Required—TOEFL (minimum score 550 paper-based; 80 iBT). Electronic applications accepted. *Faculty research:* Financial management, banking, international finance, investments.

University of Toronto, School of Graduate Studies, Faculty of Arts and Science, Department of Economics, Program in Financial Economics, Toronto, ON M5S 1A1, Canada. Offers MFE. *Entrance requirements:* Additional exam requirements/ recommendations for international students: Required—TOEFL (minimum score 102 iBT), TWE. Electronic applications accepted.

The University of Tulsa, Graduate School, Collins College of Business, Finance/ Applied Mathematics Program, Tulsa, OK 74104-3189. Offers MS/MS. *Program availability:* Part-time. *Students:* 1 full-time (0 women); minority (Asian, non-Hispanic/ Latino). Average age 28. 5 applicants, 40% accepted. *Entrance requirements:* Additional exam requirements/recommendations for international students: Required—TOEFL (minimum score 577 paper-based; 91 iBT), IELTS (minimum score 6.5). *Application deadline:* Applications are processed on a rolling basis. Application fee: $55. Electronic applications accepted. *Expenses: Tuition:* Full-time $22,230; part-time $1235 per credit hour. *Required fees:* $990 per semester. Tuition and fees vary according to course load. *Financial support:* In 2016–17, 1 student received support, including 1 teaching assistantship with full tuition reimbursement available (averaging $6,705 per year); fellowships, career-related internships or fieldwork, Federal Work-Study, institutionally sponsored loans, scholarships/grants, health care benefits, tuition waivers (full and partial), and unspecified assistantships also available. Support available to part-time students. Financial award application deadline: 2/1; financial award applicants required to submit FAFSA. *Unit head:* Dr. Ralph Jackson, Associate Dean, 918-631-2242, Fax: 918-631-2142, E-mail: ralph-jackson@utulsa.edu. *Application contact:* Information Contact, 918-631-2242, E-mail: graduate-business@utulsa.edu.

The University of Tulsa, Graduate School, Collins College of Business, MBA/MS Program in Finance, Tulsa, OK 74104-3189. Offers MBA/MS. *Program availability:* Part-time, evening/weekend. *Students:* 3 full-time (2 women); includes 1 minority (Two or more races, non-Hispanic/Latino), 2 international. 13 applicants. *Entrance requirements:* Additional exam requirements/recommendations for international students: Required—TOEFL (minimum score 577 paper-based; 91 iBT), IELTS (minimum score 6.5). *Application deadline:* Applications are processed on a rolling basis. Application fee: $55. Electronic applications accepted. *Expenses: Tuition:* Full-time $22,230; part-time $1235 per credit hour. *Required fees:* $990 per semester. Tuition and fees vary according to course load. *Financial support:* In 2016–17, 3 students received support, including 3 teaching assistantships with full tuition reimbursements available (averaging $13,410 per year); fellowships, career-related internships or fieldwork, Federal Work-Study, institutionally sponsored loans, scholarships/grants, health care benefits, tuition waivers (full and partial), and unspecified assistantships also available. Support available to part-time students. Financial award application deadline: 2/1. *Unit head:* Dr. Ralph Jackson, Associate Dean, 918-631-2242, Fax: 918-631-2142, E-mail: ralph-jackson@utulsa.edu. *Application contact:* Information Contact, 918-631-2242, E-mail: graduate-business@utulsa.edu.
Website: http://business.utulsa.edu/academics/graduate-business/

The University of Tulsa, Graduate School, Collins College of Business, Program in Finance, Tulsa, OK 74104-3189. Offers corporate finance (MS); investments and portfolio management (MS); risk management (MS); JD/MSF; MBA/MSF; MSF/MSAM. *Program availability:* Part-time, evening/weekend. *Faculty:* 9 full-time (1 woman). *Students:* 7 full-time (2 women), 4 part-time (0 women); includes 2 minority (both Hispanic/Latino), 3 international. Average age 26. 72 applicants, 39% accepted, 3 enrolled. In 2016, 5 master's awarded. *Degree requirements:* For master's, thesis optional. *Entrance requirements:* For master's, GMAT. Additional exam requirements/ recommendations for international students: Required—TOEFL (minimum score 577 paper-based; 91 iBT), IELTS (minimum score 6.5). *Application deadline:* Applications are processed on a rolling basis. Application fee: $55. Electronic applications accepted. *Expenses: Tuition:* Full-time $22,230; part-time $1235 per credit hour. *Required fees:* $990 per semester. Tuition and fees vary according to course load. *Financial support:* In 2016–17, 3 students received support, including 1 fellowship with full tuition reimbursement available (averaging $10,500 per year), 3 teaching assistantships with full tuition reimbursements available (averaging $10,347 per year); research assistantships with tuition reimbursements available, career-related internships or fieldwork, Federal Work-Study, institutionally sponsored loans, scholarships/grants, health care benefits, tuition waivers (full and partial), and unspecified assistantships also available. Support available to part-time students. Financial award application deadline: 2/1; financial award applicants required to submit FAFSA. *Unit head:* Dr. Ralph Jackson, Associate Dean, 918-631-2242, Fax: 918-631-2142, E-mail: ralph-jackson@utulsa.edu. *Application contact:* Information Contact, 918-631-2242, E-mail: graduate-business@utulsa.edu.

University of Utah, Graduate School, David Eccles School of Business, Business Administration Program, Salt Lake City, UT 84112. Offers accounting (PhD); business administration (EMBA, MBA, PMBA); finance (PhD); information systems (PhD); marketing (PhD); operations management (PhD); organizational behavior (PhD); strategic management (PhD); MBA/JD; MBA/MHA; MBA/MS. *Program availability:* Part-time, evening/weekend, online learning. *Faculty:* 58 full-time (21 women), 37 part-time/ adjunct (7 women). *Students:* 578 full-time (149 women), 89 part-time (28 women); includes 71 minority (1 American Indian or Alaska Native, non-Hispanic/Latino; 17 Asian, non-Hispanic/Latino; 45 Hispanic/Latino; 8 Two or more races, non-Hispanic/ Latino), 50 international. Average age 32. 442 applicants, 70% accepted, 226 enrolled. In 2016, 246 master's, 6 doctorates awarded. *Degree requirements:* For doctorate, comprehensive exam, thesis/dissertation. *Entrance requirements:* For master's, GMAT or GRE; for doctorate, GMAT. Additional exam requirements/recommendations for international students: Required—TOEFL (minimum score 600 paper-based; 100 iBT), IELTS (minimum score 7). *Application deadline:* For fall admission, 11/1 priority date for domestic students, 3/1 priority date for international students; for spring admission, 11/1 for domestic and international students. Applications are processed on a rolling basis. Application fee: $55 ($65 for international students). Electronic applications accepted. *Expenses:* Contact institution. *Financial support:* In 2016–17, 53 students received support, including 53 fellowships with partial tuition reimbursements available (averaging $8,600 per year); scholarships/grants and unspecified assistantships also available. Financial award application deadline: 2/1; financial award applicants required to submit FAFSA. *Faculty research:* Corporate finance, strategy services, consumer behavior, financial disclosures, operations. *Unit head:* Kristina Diekmann, Department Chair, 801-581-8524, Fax: 801-581-3380, E-mail: mastersinfo@business.utah.edu. *Application contact:* Christine Harris, Coordinator, 801-581-7785, Fax: 801-585-3962, E-mail: execch@business.utah.edu.
Website: http://www.business.utah.edu/

University of Utah, Graduate School, David Eccles School of Business, Master of Science in Finance Program, Salt Lake City, UT 84112. Offers MSF. *Program availability:* Part-time. *Faculty:* 16 full-time (3 women), 9 part-time/adjunct (2 women). *Students:* 97 full-time (31 women), 66 part-time (13 women); includes 27 minority (1 Black or African American, non-Hispanic/Latino; 1 American Indian or Alaska Native, non-Hispanic/Latino; 20 Asian, non-Hispanic/Latino; 2 Hispanic/Latino; 1 Native Hawaiian or other Pacific Islander, non-Hispanic/Latino; 2 Two or more races, non-Hispanic/Latino), 43 international. Average age 27. 126 applicants, 93% accepted, 82 enrolled. In 2016, 64 master's awarded. *Degree requirements:* For master's, comprehensive exam. *Entrance requirements:* For master's, GMAT or GRE, minimum undergraduate GPA of 3.0. Additional exam requirements/recommendations for international students: Required—TOEFL (minimum score 90 iBT), IELTS (minimum score 6.5). *Application deadline:* For fall admission, 7/28 for domestic students, 3/1 for international students; for winter admission, 12/7 for domestic students, 9/17 for international students. Applications are processed on a rolling basis. Application fee: $55 ($65 for international students). Electronic applications accepted. *Expenses:* Contact institution. *Financial support:* In 2016–17, 35 students received support, including 35 fellowships with partial tuition reimbursements available (averaging $15,257 per year); tuition waivers (full and partial) and unspecified assistantships also available. Financial award application deadline: 2/1; financial award applicants required to submit FAFSA. *Faculty research:* Investment, corporate finance, risk management, financial analysis, venture capital. *Total annual research expenditures:* $43,423. *Unit head:* Danny Wall, Director, 801-581-8903, E-mail: danny.wall@Eccles.utah.edu. *Application contact:* Regina Mavis, Admissions Coordinator, 801-585-0005, E-mail: regina.mavis@eccles.utah.edu.
Website: http://msf.eccles.utah.edu/

University of Virginia, McIntire School of Commerce, Master's Program in Commerce, Charlottesville, VA 22903. Offers business analytics (MSC); finance (MSC); marketing and management (MSC). *Entrance requirements:* For master's, GMAT, 2 letters of recommendation; prerequisite course work in financial accounting, microeconomics, and introduction to statistics. Additional exam requirements/recommendations for international students: Required—TOEFL (minimum score 600 paper-based; 100 iBT), IELTS (minimum score 7.5). Electronic applications accepted. *Expenses:* Contact institution.

University of Washington, Tacoma, Graduate Programs, MBA Programs, Tacoma, WA 98402-3100. Offers accounting (MBA); business administration (MBA); certified financial analyst (MBA). *Accreditation:* AACSB. *Program availability:* Part-time, evening/ weekend. *Entrance requirements:* For master's, GMAT, minimum GPA of 3.0 in final graded 90 quarter credits or 60 graded semester credits; at least 2 years of professional/ management work experience. Additional exam requirements/recommendations for international students: Required—TOEFL (minimum score 580 paper-based; 92 iBT). Electronic applications accepted. *Expenses:* Contact institution. *Faculty research:* International accounting, marketing, change management, investments, corporate social responsibility.

University of Waterloo, Graduate Studies, Faculty of Arts, School of Accounting and Finance, Waterloo, ON N2L 3G1, Canada. Offers accounting (M Acc, PhD); finance (M Acc); taxation (M Tax). *Degree requirements:* For master's, thesis or alternative; for doctorate, thesis/dissertation. *Entrance requirements:* For master's, honors degree, minimum B average, resume; for doctorate, GMAT, master's degree, minimum A-average, resume. Additional exam requirements/recommendations for international students: Required—TOEFL, IELTS, PTE. Electronic applications accepted. *Expenses:* Contact institution. *Faculty research:* Auditing, management accounting.

The University of West Alabama, School of Graduate Studies, College of Business, Livingston, AL 35470. Offers finance (MBA); general business (MBA). *Program availability:* Part-time, evening/weekend, 100% online. *Faculty:* 5 full-time (1 woman), 11 part-time/adjunct (8 women). *Students:* 70 (48 women); includes 39 minority (33 Black or African American, non-Hispanic/Latino; 1 American Indian or Alaska Native, non-Hispanic/Latino; 1 Asian, non-Hispanic/Latino; 3 Hispanic/Latino; 1 Two or more races, non-Hispanic/Latino). Average age 30. 42 applicants, 90% accepted, 31 enrolled. In 2016, 9 master's awarded. *Degree requirements:* For master's, project or six additional hours in emphasis area and comprehensive examination. *Entrance requirements:* For master's, GMAT, bachelor's degree with minimum GPA of 2.75 or master's degree with minimum GPA of 3.0. Additional exam requirements/recommendations for international students: Required—TOEFL (minimum score 500 paper-based; 61 iBT). *Application deadline:* Applications are processed on a rolling basis. Application fee: $40. Electronic applications accepted. *Expenses:* Tuition, state resident: part-time $355 per credit hour. Tuition, nonresident: part-time $710 per credit hour. *Required fees:* $130 per semester. *Financial support:* Federal Work-Study and scholarships/grants available. Support available to part-time students. Financial award application deadline: 3/1; financial award applicants required to submit FAFSA. *Unit head:* Dr. Wayne Bedford, Dean, 205-652-3687, Fax: 205-652-3776, E-mail: dbedford@uwa.edu.
Website: http://www.uwa.edu/cob/

The University of Western Ontario, Richard Ivey School of Business, London, ON N6A 3K7, Canada. Offers business (EMBA, PhD); corporate strategy and leadership elective (MBA); entrepreneurship elective (MBA); finance elective (MBA); health sector stream (MBA); international management elective (MBA); marketing elective (MBA); JD/ MBA. *Degree requirements:* For master's, thesis (for some programs); for doctorate, thesis/dissertation. *Entrance requirements:* For master's, GMAT, 2 years of full-time work experience, interview. Additional exam requirements/recommendations for international students: Required—TOEFL (minimum score 100 iBT) or IELTS (minimium score 6). Electronic applications accepted. *Faculty research:* Strategy, organizational behavior, international business, finance, operations management.

University of Wisconsin–Madison, Graduate School, Wisconsin School of Business, Doctoral Program in Finance, Investment and Banking, Madison, WI 53706-1380. Offers PhD. *Degree requirements:* For doctorate, comprehensive exam, thesis/dissertation. *Entrance requirements:* For doctorate, GMAT or GRE. Additional exam requirements/ recommendations for international students: Recommended—TOEFL (minimum score 623 paper-based; 106 iBT), IELTS (minimum score 7.5), TSE (minimum score 73). Electronic applications accepted. *Expenses:* Contact institution. *Faculty research:*

Banking and financial institutions, business cycles, investments, derivatives, corporate finance, economics, bankruptcy, foreclosures, mergers and acquisitions, portfolio theory.

University of Wisconsin–Madison, Graduate School, Wisconsin School of Business, Wisconsin Full-Time MBA Program, Madison, WI 53706. Offers applied security analysis (MBA); arts administration (MBA); brand and product management (MBA); corporate finance and investment banking (MBA); marketing research (MBA); operations and technology management (MBA); real estate (MBA); risk management and insurance (MBA); strategic human resource management (MBA); supply chain management (MBA). *Faculty:* 125 full-time (32 women), 48 part-time/adjunct (11 women). *Students:* 197 full-time (73 women); includes 30 minority (11 Black or African American, non-Hispanic/Latino; 9 Asian, non-Hispanic/Latino; 10 Hispanic/Latino), 42 international. Average age 29. 728 applicants, 26% accepted, 99 enrolled. In 2016, 100 master's awarded. *Entrance requirements:* For master's, GMAT or GRE, bachelor's or equivalent degree, 2 years of work experience, essay, letter of recommendation, resume. Additional exam requirements/recommendations for international students: Required—TOEFL (minimum score 100 iBT), IELTS (minimum score 7.5). *Application deadline:* For fall admission, 9/28 for domestic students, 11/1 for international students; for winter admission, 11/2 for domestic students, 12/16 for international students; for spring admission, 1/11 for domestic students, 2/24 for international students; for summer admission, 3/1 for domestic students, 4/14 for international students. Applications are processed on a rolling basis. Application fee: $75 ($81 for international students). Electronic applications accepted. *Expenses:* $7,947 per semester resident tuition, $2,430 fees; $16,082 per semester resident tuition, $2,830 fees. *Financial support:* In 2016–17, 178 students received support, including 8 fellowships with full tuition reimbursements available (averaging $56,413 per year), 23 research assistantships with full tuition reimbursements available (averaging $42,151 per year), 51 teaching assistantships with full tuition reimbursements available (averaging $39,963 per year); scholarships/grants, health care benefits, and unspecified assistantships also available. Financial award application deadline: 4/11. *Faculty research:* Forms of competition and outcomes in dual distribution systems; explaining the accuracy of revised forecasts; supply chain planning for random demand surges; advanced demand information in a multi-product system; the effects of presentation salience and measurement subjectivity on nonprofessional investors' fair value judgments. *Unit head:* Prof. Ella Mae Matsumura, Associate Dean, Full-time MBA Program, 608-262-9731, E-mail: ematsumura@bus.wisc.edu. *Application contact:* Mary Lewitzke, Assistant Director of Admissions and Recruiting, Full-time MBA Program, 608-262-4000, E-mail: mlewitzke@bus.wisc.edu.
Website: http://www.bus.wisc.edu/mba

University of Wisconsin–Whitewater, School of Graduate Studies, College of Business and Economics, Program in Business Administration, Whitewater, WI 53190-1790. Offers finance (MBA). *Accreditation:* AACSB. *Program availability:* Part-time, evening/weekend, online learning. *Entrance requirements:* For master's, GMAT or GRE, minimum AACSB index of 1000, minimum GPA of 2.75. Additional exam requirements/recommendations for international students: Required—TOEFL (minimum score 550 paper-based; 80 iBT), IELTS (minimum score 6). Electronic applications accepted. *Faculty research:* Interface between social institutions and individual behavior, technology and innovation management, occupational mental health, workplace deviance and workplace romance.

University of Wyoming, College of Business, Department of Economics and Finance, Program in Economics and Finance, Laramie, WY 82071. Offers MS. *Degree requirements:* For master's, thesis. *Entrance requirements:* For master's, GRE, minimum GPA of 3.0. Additional exam requirements/recommendations for international students: Required—TOEFL (minimum score 540 paper-based; 76 iBT). *Faculty research:* Financial economics.

University of Wyoming, College of Business, Department of Economics and Finance, Program in Finance, Laramie, WY 82071. Offers MS. *Program availability:* Part-time. *Degree requirements:* For master's, thesis. *Entrance requirements:* For master's, GMAT, GRE, minimum GPA of 3.0. Additional exam requirements/recommendations for international students: Required—TOEFL (minimum score 540 paper-based; 76 iBT). *Faculty research:* Banking.

Upper Iowa University, Online Master's Programs, Fayette, IA 52142-1857. Offers accounting (MBA); corporate financial management (MBA); emergency management and homeland security (MPA); general management (MBA); general studies (MPA); government administration (MPA); health and human services (MPA); human resources management (MBA); nonprofit organizational management (MPA); organizational development (MBA); public management (MPA); sport administration (MSA). MBA also available at Madison, WI campus. *Program availability:* Part-time, online learning. *Degree requirements:* For master's, research project. *Entrance requirements:* For master's, GMAT, GRE, or minimum GPA of 2.7 during last 60 hours. Additional exam requirements/recommendations for international students: Required—TOEFL (minimum score 570 paper-based). Electronic applications accepted. *Faculty research:* Total quality management, teams, organization culture and climate, management.

Ursuline College, School of Graduate Studies, Program in Business Administration, Pepper Pike, OH 44124-4398. Offers ethical and entrepreneurial leadership (MBA); financial planning and accounting (MBA); health services management (MBA); management (MBA); management and leadership (MBA); marketing and communications management (MBA). *Program availability:* Part-time. *Faculty:* 2 full-time (both women), 1 (woman) part-time/adjunct. *Students:* 27 full-time (25 women), 9 part-time (all women); includes 15 minority (14 Black or African American, non-Hispanic/Latino; 1 Hispanic/Latino), 2 international. Average age 38. 31 applicants, 71% accepted, 18 enrolled. In 2016, 34 master's awarded. *Degree requirements:* For master's, comprehensive exam (for some programs). *Entrance requirements:* For master's, GRE. Additional exam requirements/recommendations for international students: Required—TOEFL (minimum score 500 paper-based) or GRE. Application fee: $25. Electronic applications accepted. *Expenses:* Contact institution. *Financial support:* In 2016–17, 6 students received support. Scholarships/grants available. Financial award applicants required to submit FAFSA. *Faculty research:* Gift economy; sharing economy; cooperative business models; collaborative leadership; corporate social responsibility and the triple bottom line, defined as the three P's: people, planet and profit. *Unit head:* Dr. Nurete Brenner, Executive Director, 440-684-6038, Fax: 440-684-6088, E-mail: nurete.brenner@ursuline.edu. *Application contact:* Melanie Steele, Director of Graduate Admission, 440-646-8146, Fax: 440-684-6138, E-mail: graduateadmissions@ursuline.edu.

Valparaiso University, Graduate School and Continuing Education, College of Business, Valparaiso, IN 46383. Offers business administration (MBA); business intelligence (Certificate); engineering management (Certificate); entrepreneurship (Certificate); finance (Certificate); general business (Certificate); management (Certificate); marketing (Certificate); sustainability (Certificate); JD/MBA; MSN/MBA. *Accreditation:* AACSB. *Program availability:* Part-time, evening/weekend, online learning. *Entrance requirements:* For master's, GMAT, GRE, minimum GPA of 3.0. Additional exam requirements/recommendations for international students: Required—TOEFL (minimum score 550 paper-based; 80 iBT), IELTS (minimum score 6). Electronic applications accepted. *Expenses:* Contact institution.

Valparaiso University, Graduate School and Continuing Education, Program in International Economics and Finance, Valparaiso, IN 46383. Offers MS. *Program availability:* Part-time, evening/weekend. *Entrance requirements:* For master's, 1 semester of college-level calculus; 1 statistics or quantitative methods class; 2 semesters of introductory economics (course content in introductory economics must include both introductory microeconomics and macroeconomics); 1 introductory accounting course; minimum undergraduate GPA of 3.0; 2 letters of recommendation. Additional exam requirements/recommendations for international students: Required—TOEFL (minimum score 550 paper-based; 80 iBT), IELTS (minimum score 6). *Expenses: Tuition:* Full-time $11,070; part-time $615 per credit hour. *Required fees:* $116 per semester. Tuition and fees vary according to course load, degree level and program.

Vancouver Island University, Master of Business Administration Program, Nanaimo, BC V9R 5S5, Canada. Offers international business (MBA), including finance, marketing. Program offered jointly with University of Hertfordshire. *Accreditation:* ACBSP. *Program availability:* Part-time. *Degree requirements:* For master's, thesis. *Entrance requirements:* Additional exam requirements/recommendations for international students: Required—TOEFL (minimum score 88 iBT), IELTS (minimum score 6.5). Electronic applications accepted. *Expenses:* Contact institution. *Faculty research:* Tourism development, entrepreneurship, organizational development, strategic planning, international business strategy, intercultural team work.

Vanderbilt University, Vanderbilt University Owen Graduate School of Management, MS in Finance Program, Nashville, TN 37203. Offers MS. *Entrance requirements:* For master's, GMAT and/or GRE. Additional exam requirements/recommendations for international students: Required—TOEFL (minimum score 105 iBT). Electronic applications accepted. *Expenses:* Contact institution.

Vanderbilt University, Vanderbilt University Owen Graduate School of Management, Vanderbilt MBA Program, Nashville, TN 37203. Offers accounting (MBA); finance (MBA); general management (MBA); health care (MBA); human and organizational performance (MBA); marketing (MBA); operations (MBA); strategy (MBA); MBA/JD; MBA/M Div; MBA/MD; MBA/MSN; MBA/MTS; MBA/PhD. *Accreditation:* AACSB. *Degree requirements:* For master's, 62 credit hours of coursework; completion of ethics course; minimum GPA of 3.0. *Entrance requirements:* For master's, GMAT (preferred) or GRE, 2 years of work experience (recommended). Additional exam requirements/recommendations for international students: Required—TOEFL (minimum score 100 iBT). Electronic applications accepted. *Expenses:* Contact institution. *Faculty research:* Accounting and finance, business strategy and economics, marketing, operations management, organization studies.

Villanova University, Villanova School of Business, Master of Science in Finance Program, Villanova, PA 19085. Offers MSF. *Faculty:* 108 full-time (37 women), 32 part-time/adjunct (8 women). *Students:* 23 full-time (5 women); includes 11 minority (10 Asian, non-Hispanic/Latino; 1 Hispanic/Latino), 7 international. Average age 23. 103 applicants, 57% accepted, 25 enrolled. In 2016, 17 master's awarded. *Degree requirements:* For master's, minimum cumulative GPA of 3.0. *Entrance requirements:* For master's, GMAT, prerequisite course in principles of finance, 2 letters of recommendation, 2 essays, resume, official transcripts, interview. Additional exam requirements/recommendations for international students: Required—TOEFL (minimum score 550 paper-based; 100 iBT). *Application deadline:* For spring admission, 3/15 for domestic and international students. Applications are processed on a rolling basis. Application fee: $65. Electronic applications accepted. *Expenses:* Contact institution. *Financial support:* In 2016–17, 4 research assistantships (averaging $6,550 per year) were awarded; scholarships/grants also available. Financial award applicants required to submit FAFSA. *Faculty research:* Business analytics; creativity, innovation and entrepreneurship; global leadership; real estate; church management; business ethics; marketing and consumer insights. *Unit head:* Michael L. Capella, Associate Dean of Graduate and Executive Business Programs, 610-519-4336, Fax: 610-519-6273, E-mail: michael.l.capella@villanova.edu. *Application contact:* Claire Bruno, Director of Recruitment and Enrollment Management, 610-519-4336, Fax: 610-519-6273, E-mail: claire.bruno@villanova.edu.
Website: http://www1.villanova.edu/villanova/business/graduate/specializedprograms/msf.html

Villanova University, Villanova School of Business, MBA - The Fast Track Program, Villanova, PA 19085. Offers analytics (MBA); cybersecurity (MBA); finance (MBA); healthcare (MBA); international business (MBA); management information systems (MBA); marketing (MBA); real estate (MBA); strategic management (MBA); sustainability (MBA). *Accreditation:* AACSB. *Program availability:* Part-time, evening/weekend. *Faculty:* 108 full-time (39 women), 32 part-time/adjunct (8 women). *Students:* 127 part-time (58 women); includes 18 minority (3 Black or African American, non-Hispanic/Latino; 7 Asian, non-Hispanic/Latino; 6 Hispanic/Latino; 2 Two or more races, non-Hispanic/Latino), 2 international. Average age 30. 88 applicants, 90% accepted, 66 enrolled. In 2016, 75 master's awarded. *Degree requirements:* For master's, minimum GPA of 3.0. *Entrance requirements:* For master's, GMAT or GRE, work experience, 2 letters of recommendation, 2 essays, resume, official transcripts, interview. Additional exam requirements/recommendations for international students: Required—TOEFL (minimum score 550 paper-based; 100 iBT). *Application deadline:* For fall admission, 6/30 for domestic and international students. Application fee: $65. Electronic applications accepted. *Expenses:* Contact institution. *Financial support:* Scholarships/grants available. Financial award application deadline: 6/30; financial award applicants required to submit FAFSA. *Faculty research:* Business analytics; creativity, innovation and entrepreneurship; global leadership; real estate; church management; business ethics; marketing and consumer insights. *Unit head:* Michael L. Capella, Associate Dean of Graduate and Executive Business Programs, 610-519-4336, Fax: 610-519-6273, E-mail: michael.l.capella@villanova.edu. *Application contact:* Kimberly Kane, Manager of Admissions, 610-519-3701, Fax: 610-519-6273, E-mail: kimberly.kane@villanova.edu.
Website: http://www1.villanova.edu/villanova/business/graduate/mba.html

Villanova University, Villanova School of Business, MBA - The Flex Track Program, Villanova, PA 19085. Offers analytics (MBA); finance (MBA); healthcare (MBA); international business (MBA); marketing (MBA); real estate (MBA); strategic management (MBA); JD/MBA. *Accreditation:* AACSB. *Program availability:* Part-time, evening/weekend, online learning. *Faculty:* 108 full-time (39 women), 32 part-time/adjunct (8 women). *Students:* 13 full-time (5 women), 399 part-time (134 women); includes 73 minority (21 Black or African American, non-Hispanic/Latino; 32 Asian, non-Hispanic/Latino; 19 Hispanic/Latino; 1 Two or more races, non-Hispanic/Latino), 11 international. Average age 31. 93 applicants, 94% accepted, 80 enrolled. In 2016, 133 master's awarded. *Degree requirements:* For master's, minimum GPA of 3.0. *Entrance requirements:* For master's, GMAT or GRE, work experience, 2 letters of recommendation, 2 essays, resume, official transcript. Additional exam requirements/recommendations for international students: Required—TOEFL (minimum score 550 paper-based; 100 iBT). *Application deadline:* For fall admission, 6/30 for domestic and international students; for spring admission, 11/15 for domestic and international

students; for summer admission, 3/31 for domestic and international students. Applications are processed on a rolling basis. Application fee: $65. Electronic applications accepted. *Expenses:* Contact institution. *Financial support:* In 2016–17, 13 research assistantships with full tuition reimbursements (averaging $13,100 per year) were awarded; scholarships/grants also available. Financial award application deadline: 6/30; financial award applicants required to submit FAFSA. *Faculty research:* Business analytics; creativity, innovation and entrepreneurship; global leadership; real estate; church management; business ethics. *Unit head:* Michael L. Capella, Associate Dean of Graduate and Executive Business Programs, 610-610-4336, Fax: 610-519-6273, E-mail: michael.l.capella@villanova.edu. *Application contact:* Claire Bruno, Director of Recruitment and Enrollment Management, 610-519-4336, Fax: 610-519-6273, E-mail: claire.bruno@villanova.edu.
Website: http://www1.villanova.edu/villanova/business/graduate/mba.html

Virginia Commonwealth University, Graduate School, College of Humanities and Sciences, L. Douglas Wilder School of Government and Public Affairs, Department of Political Science and Public Administration, Richmond, VA 23284-9005. Offers financial management (MPA). *Accreditation:* NASPAA. *Program availability:* Part-time. *Entrance requirements:* For master's, GRE, GMAT or LSAT. Additional exam requirements/recommendations for international students: Required—TOEFL (minimum score 600 paper-based; 100 iBT); Recommended—IELTS (minimum score 6.5). *Application deadline:* For fall admission, 4/1 for domestic students; for spring admission, 10/1 for domestic students. Applications are processed on a rolling basis. Application fee: $50. Electronic applications accepted. *Financial support:* Fellowships, career-related internships or fieldwork, Federal Work-Study, institutionally sponsored loans, and tuition waivers (full and partial) available. Support available to part-time students. Financial award application deadline: 3/1. *Faculty research:* Environmental policy, executive leadership, human resource management, local government management, nonprofit management, public financial management, public policy analysis and evaluation. *Unit head:* Dr. Niraj Verma, Director, L. Douglas Wilder School of Government and Public Affairs, 804-828-2292. *Application contact:* Dr. Richard R. Huff, Graduate Program Director, 804-827-9813, E-mail: rrhuff@vcu.edu.
Website: http://www.wilder.vcu.edu/academic/pubadmin.html

Virginia International University, School of Business, Fairfax, VA 22030. Offers accounting (MBA, MS); entrepreneurship (MBA); executive management (Graduate Certificate); global logistics (MBA); health care management (MBA); hospitality and tourism management (MBA); human resources management (MBA); international business management (MBA); international finance (MBA); marketing management (MBA); mass media and public relations (MBA); project management (MBA, MS). *Program availability:* Part-time, online learning. *Entrance requirements:* For master's and Graduate Certificate, bachelor's degree. Additional exam requirements/recommendations for international students: Required—TOEFL (minimum score 550 paper-based; 80 iBT), IELTS (minimum score 6). Electronic applications accepted.

Wagner College, Division of Graduate Studies, Department of Business Administration, Staten Island, NY 10301-4495. Offers accounting (MS); business administration (MBA); finance (MBA); health care administration (MBA); international business (MBA); management (Exec MBA); marketing (MBA). *Accreditation:* ACBSP. *Program availability:* Part-time, evening/weekend. *Faculty:* 8 full-time (3 women), 17 part-time/adjunct (5 women). *Students:* 90 full-time (25 women), 16 part-time (8 women); includes 21 minority (12 Black or African American, non-Hispanic/Latino; 1 American Indian or Alaska Native, non-Hispanic/Latino; 3 Asian, non-Hispanic/Latino; 5 Hispanic/Latino), 5 international. Average age 26. 88 applicants, 85% accepted, 62 enrolled. In 2016, 72 master's awarded. *Degree requirements:* For master's, thesis optional. *Entrance requirements:* For master's, minimum GPA of 2.75, proficiency in computers and math. Additional exam requirements/recommendations for international students: Required—TOEFL (minimum score 550 paper-based; 79 iBT). *Application deadline:* For fall admission, 5/1 priority date for domestic students, 3/1 priority date for international students; for spring admission, 12/1 for domestic students, 11/1 for international students. Applications are processed on a rolling basis. Application fee: $50. Tuition and fees vary according to degree level. *Financial support:* In 2016–17, 93 students received support. Career-related internships or fieldwork, unspecified assistantships, and alumni fellowship grants available. Financial award application deadline: 4/1; financial award applicants required to submit FAFSA. *Unit head:* Dr. Donald Crooks, Director, 718-390-3429, Fax: 718-390-3429, E-mail: dcrooks@wagner.edu. *Application contact:* Patricia Clancy, Assistant Director for Enrollment, 718-420-4464, Fax: 718-390-3105, E-mail: patricia.clancy@wagner.edu.

Walden University, Graduate Programs, School of Management, Minneapolis, MN 55401. Offers accounting (MBA, MS, DBA), including accounting for the professional (MS), accounting with CPA emphasis (MS), self-designed (MS); advanced project management (Graduate Certificate); applied project management (Graduate Certificate); auditing (Graduate Certificate); bridge to business administration (Post-Doctoral Certificate); bridge to management (Post-Doctoral Certificate); business management (Graduate Certificate); communication (MBA); corporate finance (MBA); digital marketing (Graduate Certificate); entrepreneurship (DBA); entrepreneurship and small business (MBA); finance (MS, DBA), including finance for the professional (MS), finance with CFA/investment (MS), finance with CPA emphasis (MS); global supply chain management (DBA); healthcare management (MBA, DBA); human resource management (MBA, MS, Graduate Certificate), including functional human resource management (MS), general program (MS), integrating functional and strategic human resource management (MS), organizational strategy (MS); human resources management (DBA); information systems management (DBA); international business (MBA, DBA); leadership (MBA, MS, DBA, Graduate Certificate), including general program (MS), human resource leadership (MS), leader development (MS), self-designed (MS); management (MS, PhD), including communications (MS), finance (PhD), general program (MS), healthcare management (MS), human resource management (MS), human resources management (PhD), information systems management (PhD), international business (MS), leadership (MS), leadership and organizational change (PhD), marketing (MS), project management (MS), strategy and operations (MS); managerial accounting (Graduate Certificate); marketing (MBA, MS, DBA); project management (MBA, MS, DBA); self-designed (MBA, DBA); social impact management (DBA); technology entrepreneurship (DBA). *Accreditation:* ACBSP. *Program availability:* Part-time, evening/weekend, online only, 100% online. *Degree requirements:* For master's, thesis (for some programs), residency (for EMBA); for doctorate, thesis/dissertation (for some programs), residency. *Entrance requirements:* For master's, bachelor's degree or higher; minimum GPA of 2.5; official transcripts; goal statement (for some programs); access to computer and Internet; for doctorate, master's degree or higher; three years of related professional or academic experience (preferred); minimum GPA of 3.0; goal statement and current resume (for select programs); official transcripts; access to computer and Internet; for other advanced degree, relevant work experience; access to computer and Internet. Additional exam requirements/recommendations for international students: Required—TOEFL (minimum score 550 paper-based, 79 iBT), IELTS (minimum score 6.5), Michigan English Language Assessment Battery (minimum score 82), or PTE (minimum score 53). Electronic applications accepted.

Walsh College of Accountancy and Business Administration, Graduate Programs, Program in Accountancy, Troy, MI 48083. Offers finance (MAC); taxation (MAC). *Program availability:* Part-time, evening/weekend. *Faculty:* 8 full-time (4 women), 24 part-time/adjunct (6 women). *Students:* 278 (159 women); includes 55 minority (23 Black or African American, non-Hispanic/Latino; 1 American Indian or Alaska Native, non-Hispanic/Latino; 21 Asian, non-Hispanic/Latino; 7 Hispanic/Latino; 3 Two or more races, non-Hispanic/Latino), 24 international. Average age 32. 94 applicants, 76% accepted, 71 enrolled. In 2016, 93 master's awarded. *Degree requirements:* For master's, thesis optional. *Entrance requirements:* For master's, minimum overall cumulative GPA of 2.75 from all colleges previously attended. Additional exam requirements/recommendations for international students: Required—TOEFL (minimum score 550 paper-based, 79 iBT), IELTS (6.5), Michigan English Language Assessment Battery, or MTELP. *Application deadline:* Applications are processed on a rolling basis. Application fee: $35. Electronic applications accepted. *Expenses:* $740 per semester credit hour, $125 registration fee per semester. *Financial support:* In 2016–17, 19 students received support. Career-related internships or fieldwork and scholarships/grants available. Financial award application deadline: 6/30; financial award applicants required to submit FAFSA. *Unit head:* John Black, Chair, Accounting, Tax and Business Law, 248-823-1635, Fax: 248-689-0920, E-mail: jblack@walshcollege.edu. *Application contact:* Heather Rigby, Director, Admissions and Academic Advising, 248-823-1294, Fax: 248-823-1611, E-mail: hrigby@walshcollege.edu.

Walsh College of Accountancy and Business Administration, Graduate Programs, Program in Finance, Troy, MI 48083. Offers financial management (MSF); financial services (MSF). *Program availability:* Part-time, evening/weekend. *Faculty:* 10 full-time (4 women), 12 part-time/adjunct (3 women). *Students:* 93 (43 women); includes 16 minority (7 Black or African American, non-Hispanic/Latino; 6 Asian, non-Hispanic/Latino; 1 Hispanic/Latino; 2 Two or more races, non-Hispanic/Latino), 9 international. Average age 34. 37 applicants, 84% accepted, 21 enrolled. In 2016, 41 master's awarded. *Entrance requirements:* For master's, minimum overall cumulative GPA of 2.75 from all colleges previously attended. Additional exam requirements/recommendations for international students: Required—TOEFL (minimum score 550 paper-based, 79 iBT), IELTS (6.5), Michigan English Language Assessment Battery, or MTELP. *Application deadline:* Applications are processed on a rolling basis. Application fee: $35. Electronic applications accepted. *Expenses:* $740 per credit hour, $125 registration fee per semester. *Financial support:* In 2016–17, 3 students received support. Career-related internships or fieldwork and scholarships/grants available. Financial award application deadline: 6/30; financial award applicants required to submit FAFSA. *Unit head:* Gregory Todd, Chair, Finance and Economics, 248-823-1635, Fax: 248-689-0920, E-mail: gtodd@walshcollehe.edu. *Application contact:* Heather Rigby, Director, Admissions and Academic Advising, 248-823-1610, Fax: 248-689-0938, E-mail: hrigby@walshcollege.edu.

Washington University in St. Louis, Olin Business School, DBA Program in Finance, St. Louis, MO 63130-4899. Offers DBA. *Program availability:* Part-time, evening/weekend. *Faculty:* 93 full-time (22 women), 46 part-time/adjunct (10 women). *Students:* 9 full-time (2 women), 5 part-time (1 woman); includes 4 minority (1 Black or African American, non-Hispanic/Latino; 2 Asian, non-Hispanic/Latino; 1 Hispanic/Latino), 8 international. Average age 34. 22 applicants, 41% accepted, 4 enrolled. In 2016, 1 doctorate awarded. *Degree requirements:* For doctorate, comprehensive exam, thesis/dissertation. *Entrance requirements:* For doctorate, GRE, GMAT. Additional exam requirements/recommendations for international students: Required—TOEFL or IELTS. *Application deadline:* For fall admission, 6/1 for domestic and international students. Applications are processed on a rolling basis. Application fee: $99. Electronic applications accepted. *Unit head:* Prof. Anjan Thakor, Director, 314-935-7197, E-mail: thakor@wustl.edu. *Application contact:* Erin Murdock, Associate Director of Doctoral Admissions and Student Affairs, 314-935-6340, Fax: 314-935-9484, E-mail: murdockel@wustl.edu.
Website: http://www.olin.wustl.edu/EN-US/academic-programs/dba-in-finance/

Washington University in St. Louis, Olin Business School, Program in Finance, St. Louis, MO 63130-4899. Offers corporate finance and investments (MS); quantitative finance (MS). *Program availability:* Part-time. *Faculty:* 97 full-time (22 women), 44 part-time/adjunct (13 women). *Students:* 100 full-time (42 women), 3 part-time (0 women); includes 16 minority (14 Asian, non-Hispanic/Latino; 2 Hispanic/Latino), 66 international. Average age 25. 1,511 applicants, 9% accepted, 71 enrolled. In 2016, 78 master's awarded. *Entrance requirements:* For master's, GMAT or GRE. Additional exam requirements/recommendations for international students: Required—TOEFL, IELTS. *Application deadline:* For fall admission, 10/3 for domestic students, 2/1 priority date for international students; for winter admission, 12/1 for domestic students; for spring admission, 4/3 for domestic students. Applications are processed on a rolling basis. Application fee: $100. Electronic applications accepted. *Expenses:* Contact institution. *Financial support:* Institutionally sponsored loans and scholarships/grants available. Financial award applicants required to submit FAFSA. *Unit head:* Joe Fox, Associate Dean/Director of Specialized Master's Programs, 314-935-6322, Fax: 314-935-4464, E-mail: fox@wustl.edu. *Application contact:* 314-935-7301, Fax: 314-935-4464, E-mail: olingradadmissions@wustl.edu.
Website: http://www.olin.wustl.edu/prospective/

Waynesburg University, Graduate and Professional Studies, Canonsburg, PA 15370. Offers business (MBA), including energy management, finance, health systems, human resources, leadership, market development; counseling (MA), including addictions counseling, clinical mental health; counselor education and supervision (PhD); criminal investigation (MA); education (M Ed), including autism, curriculum and instruction, educational leadership, online teaching; nursing (MSN), including administration, education, informatics; nursing practice (DNP); special education (M Ed); technology (M Ed); MSN/MBA. *Accreditation:* AACN. *Program availability:* Part-time, evening/weekend. *Degree requirements:* For doctorate, thesis/dissertation. *Entrance requirements:* Additional exam requirements/recommendations for international students: Required—TOEFL. Electronic applications accepted.

Wayne State University, Law School, Detroit, MI 48202. Offers corporate and finance law (LL M); labor and employment law (LL M); law (JD); taxation (LL M); United States law (LL M); JD/MA; JD/MADR; JD/MBA; JD/MS. *Accreditation:* ABA. *Faculty:* 40 full-time (15 women), 27 part-time/adjunct (12 women). *Students:* 379 full-time (162 women), 58 part-time (26 women); includes 63 minority (35 Black or African American, non-Hispanic/Latino; 1 American Indian or Alaska Native, non-Hispanic/Latino; 9 Asian, non-Hispanic/Latino; 3 Hispanic/Latino; 15 Two or more races, non-Hispanic/Latino), 13 international. Average age 27. 684 applicants, 53% accepted, 138 enrolled. In 2016, 16 master's, 133 doctorates awarded. *Degree requirements:* For master's, thesis (for some programs). *Entrance requirements:* For master's, JD from ABA-accredited institution and member institution of the AALS; for doctorate, LSAT, LDAS report, bachelor's degree from accredited institution, personal statement, transcripts from all U.S. undergraduate schools attended and an analysis and summary of the transcripts; letter of recommendation (up to two are accepted). Additional exam requirements/recommendations for international students: Required—TOEFL (minimum score 600 paper-based; 100 iBT), Michigan English Language Assessment Battery (minimum score 85); Recommended—IELTS (minimum score 7). *Application deadline:* For fall

admission, 7/1 for domestic students, 5/1 priority date for international students. Applications are processed on a rolling basis. Application fee: $0. Electronic applications accepted. *Expenses:* Contact institution. *Financial support:* In 2016–17, 353 students received support. Fellowships, Federal Work-Study, and scholarships/grants available. Support available to part-time students. Financial award application deadline: 6/30; financial award applicants required to submit FAFSA. *Faculty research:* Public interest law, tax law, international law, environmental law, health law. *Unit head:* Lance Gable, Interim Dean, 313-577-3933, E-mail: jbenson@wayne.edu. *Application contact:* Kathy Fox, Assistant Dean of Admissions, 313-577-3937, Fax: 313-993-8129, E-mail: lawinquire@wayne.edu.
Website: http://law.wayne.edu/

Wayne State University, Mike Ilitch School of Business, Detroit, MI 48202. Offers accounting (MS, Postbaccalaureate Certificate); business (Graduate Certificate); business administration (MBA, PhD); data science (MS), including business analytics; entrepreneurship and innovation (Postbaccalaureate Certificate); finance (MS); information systems management (Postbaccalaureate Certificate); taxation (MST); JD/MBA. Application deadline for PhD is February 15. *Accreditation:* AACSB. *Program availability:* Part-time, evening/weekend. *Faculty:* 32. *Students:* 219 full-time (105 women), 941 part-time (406 women); includes 314 minority (186 Black or African American, non-Hispanic/Latino; 3 American Indian or Alaska Native, non-Hispanic/Latino; 68 Asian, non-Hispanic/Latino; 33 Hispanic/Latino; 24 Two or more races, non-Hispanic/Latino), 88 international. Average age 30. 1,119 applicants, 49% accepted, 329 enrolled. In 2016, 203 master's, 1 doctorate, 3 other advanced degrees awarded. *Degree requirements:* For doctorate, thesis/dissertation. *Entrance requirements:* For master's, GMAT, GRE, LSAT, MCAT, at least three years of relevant work experience that shows increased responsibility, or minimum GPA of 3.0 from AACSB-accredited program or 3.2 from regionally-accredited program, undergraduate degree from accredited institution; undergraduate degree in accounting, business administration, or area of business administration (for MS and MST); for doctorate, GMAT (minimum score of 600), minimum undergraduate GPA of 3.0, 3.5 upper-division or graduate; three letters of recommendation; brief essay; undergraduate degree from accredited institution; personal statement; for other advanced degree, bachelor's degree from accredited institution. Additional exam requirements/recommendations for international students: Required—TOEFL (minimum score 550 paper-based; 79 iBT), Michigan English Language Assessment Battery (minimum score 85); Recommended—IELTS (minimum score 6.5), TWE (minimum score 5.5). *Application deadline:* For fall admission, 7/1 for domestic students, 5/1 priority date for international students; for winter admission, 11/1 for domestic students, 9/1 priority date for international students; for spring admission, 3/1 for domestic students, 1/1 priority date for international students. Applications are processed on a rolling basis. Application fee: $50. Electronic applications accepted. *Expenses:* $18,871 per year resident tuition and fees, $36,065 per year non-resident tuition and fees. *Financial support:* In 2016–17, 174 students received support, including 1 fellowship with tuition reimbursement available (averaging $18,000 per year), 2 research assistantships with tuition reimbursements available (averaging $18,000 per year), 5 teaching assistantships with tuition reimbursements available (averaging $18,000 per year); scholarships/grants, health care benefits, and unspecified assistantships also available. Support available to part-time students. Financial award applicants required to submit FAFSA. *Faculty research:* Executive compensation and stock performance, consumer reactions to pricing strategies, communication across the automotive supply chain, performance of firms in sub-Saharan Africa, implementation issues with ERP software. *Unit head:* Dr. Robert Forsythe, Dean, School of Business Administration, 313-577-4501, E-mail: robert.forsythe@wayne.edu. *Application contact:* Kiantee N. Rupert-Jones, Director, 313-577-4511, Fax: 313-577-9442, E-mail: gradbusiness@wayne.edu.
Website: http://ilitchbusiness.wayne.edu/

Webster University, George Herbert Walker School of Business and Technology, Department of Business, St. Louis, MO 63119-3194. Offers business and organizational security management (MBA); decision support systems (MBA); environmental management (MBA); finance (MBA, MS); forensic accounting (MS); gerontology (MBA); human resources development (MBA); human resources management (MBA); information technology management (MBA); international business (MA, MBA); international relations (MBA); management and leadership (MBA); marketing (MBA); media communications (MBA); procurement and acquisitions management (MBA); Web services (MBA). *Accreditation:* ACBSP. *Program availability:* Part-time, evening/weekend, online learning. *Degree requirements:* For master's, comprehensive exam (for some programs), thesis (for some programs). *Entrance requirements:* Additional exam requirements/recommendations for international students: Required—TOEFL. *Application deadline:* Applications are processed on a rolling basis. Application fee: $35 ($50 for international students). *Expenses: Tuition:* Full-time $21,900; part-time $730 per credit hour. Tuition and fees vary according to campus/location and program. *Financial support:* Federal Work-Study available. Support available to part-time students. Financial award application deadline: 4/1; financial award applicants required to submit FAFSA. *Unit head:* David Porras, Chair, 314-246-8621, E-mail: porrasd@webster.edu. *Application contact:* Sarah Nandor, Director, Graduate and Transfer Admissions, 314-968-7109, E-mail: gadmit@webster.edu.

Western Michigan University Thomas M. Cooley Law School, Graduate Programs, Lansing, MI 48901-3038. Offers administrative law (public law) (JD); business transactions (JD); Canadian law practice (JD); constitutional law/civil rights (public law) (JD); corporate law and finance (LL M); environmental law (public law) (JD); general practice (JD), including solo and small firm; homeland and national security law (LL M); insurance law (LL M); intellectual property (JD); intellectual property law (LL M); international law (JD); litigation (JD); self-directed (LL M, JD); tax law (LL M); taxation (JD); U.S. legal studies for foreign attorneys (LL M); JD/LL M; JD/MBA; JD/MPA; JD/MSW. *Program availability:* Part-time, evening/weekend, 100% online, blended/hybrid learning. *Degree requirements:* For master's, thesis optional; for doctorate, minimum of 3 credits of clinical experience. *Entrance requirements:* For master's, JD or LL B; for doctorate, LSAT. Additional exam requirements/recommendations for international students: Required—TOEFL (for U.S. legal studies for foreign attorneys LL M program); Recommended—TOEFL. Electronic applications accepted. *Faculty research:* Wrongful convictions, civil rights, environmental law, litigation techniques, data mining, intellectual property, practical and skills-based legal education.

West Texas A&M University, College of Business, Department of Accounting, Economics and Finance, Program in Finance and Economics, Canyon, TX 79016-0001. Offers MS. *Program availability:* Part-time, evening/weekend, 100% online, blended/hybrid learning. *Degree requirements:* For master's, comprehensive exam, thesis optional. *Entrance requirements:* For master's, GMAT. Additional exam requirements/recommendations for international students: Required—TOEFL (minimum score 550 paper-based). *Application deadline:* For fall admission, 8/1 for domestic students, 5/1 for international students; for spring admission, 12/1 for domestic students, 10/30 for international students; for summer admission, 5/1 for domestic students. Applications are processed on a rolling basis. Application fee: $40 ($75 for international students). Electronic applications accepted. *Financial support:* Research assistantships, teaching assistantships with partial tuition reimbursements, Federal Work-Study, institutionally sponsored loans, and tuition waivers (partial) available. Support available to part-time students. Financial award applicants required to submit CSS PROFILE or FAFSA. *Faculty research:* International trade composition, cycle of poverty, trade effects in Asian countries, structural problems in Japanese economy, reform and the U.S. sugar program-Nebraska. *Unit head:* Dr. LaVelle Mills, Associate Dean, 806-651-3866, E-mail: lmills@wtamu.edu. *Application contact:* Dr. Jonathan Shaffer, Associate Professor, 806-651-2489, E-mail: jshaffer@wtamu.edu.
Website: http://www.wtamu.edu/academics/finance-economics-graduate-program.aspx

Wilfrid Laurier University, Faculty of Graduate and Postdoctoral Studies, School of Business and Economics, Department of Business, Waterloo, ON N2L 3C5, Canada. Offers accounting (PhD); finance (M Fin); financial economics (PhD); marketing (PhD); operations and supply chain management (PhD); organizational behavior and human resource management (M Sc); organizational behaviour and human resource management (PhD); supply chain management (M Sc); technology management (EMTM). *Accreditation:* AACSB. *Program availability:* Part-time, evening/weekend. *Degree requirements:* For master's, thesis optional; for doctorate, comprehensive exam, thesis/dissertation. *Entrance requirements:* For master's, GMAT, 4-year honors degree with minimum B+ average; for doctorate, GMAT, master's degree, minimum B+ average. Additional exam requirements/recommendations for international students: Required—TOEFL (minimum score 89 iBT). Electronic applications accepted. *Faculty research:* Financial economics, management and organizational behavior, operations and supply chain management.

Wilkes University, College of Graduate and Professional Studies, Jay S. Sidhu School of Business and Leadership, Wilkes-Barre, PA 18766-0002. Offers accounting (MBA); entrepreneurship (MBA); finance (MBA); health care administration (MBA); human resource management (MBA); international business (MBA); operations management (MBA); organizational leadership and development (MBA). *Accreditation:* ACBSP. *Program availability:* Part-time, evening/weekend. *Students:* 35 full-time (17 women), 112 part-time (55 women); includes 17 minority (6 Black or African American, non-Hispanic/Latino; 4 Asian, non-Hispanic/Latino; 5 Hispanic/Latino; 2 Two or more races, non-Hispanic/Latino), 16 international. Average age 31. In 2016, 59 master's awarded. *Entrance requirements:* For master's, GMAT. Additional exam requirements/recommendations for international students: Required—TOEFL (minimum score 550 paper-based; 79 iBT). *Application deadline:* Applications are processed on a rolling basis. Application fee: $45 ($65 for international students). Electronic applications accepted. *Expenses:* Contact institution. *Financial support:* Unspecified assistantships available. Financial award application deadline: 3/1; financial award applicants required to submit FAFSA. *Unit head:* Dr. Abel Adekola, Dean, 570-408-4701, Fax: 570-408-7846, E-mail: abel.adekola@wilkes.edu. *Application contact:* Director of Graduate Enrollment, 570-408-4234, Fax: 570-408-7846.
Website: http://www.wilkes.edu/academics/colleges/sidhu-school-of-business-leadership/index.aspx

Wilmington University, College of Business, New Castle, DE 19720-6491. Offers accounting (MBA, MS); business administration (MBA, DBA); environmental stewardship (MBA); finance (MBA); health care administration (MBA, MSM); homeland security (MBA, MSM); human resource management (MSM); management information systems (MBA, MSN); marketing (MSM); marketing management (MBA); military leadership (MSM); organizational leadership (MBA, MSM); public administration (MSM). *Program availability:* Part-time, evening/weekend. *Faculty:* 17 full-time (7 women), 106 part-time/adjunct (46 women). *Students:* 436 full-time (237 women), 1,202 part-time (739 women); includes 594 minority (474 Black or African American, non-Hispanic/Latino; 19 American Indian or Alaska Native, non-Hispanic/Latino; 64 Asian, non-Hispanic/Latino; 30 Hispanic/Latino; 3 Native Hawaiian or other Pacific Islander, non-Hispanic/Latino; 4 Two or more races, non-Hispanic/Latino), 153 international. Average age 35. 814 applicants, 98% accepted, 426 enrolled. In 2016, 594 master's, 23 doctorates awarded. *Entrance requirements:* Additional exam requirements/recommendations for international students: Required—TOEFL (minimum score 500 paper-based). *Application deadline:* Applications are processed on a rolling basis. Application fee: $35. Electronic applications accepted. *Expenses: Tuition:* Full-time $8388; part-time $466 per credit. *Required fees:* $25 per semester. Tuition and fees vary according to degree level. *Financial support:* Applicants required to submit FAFSA. *Unit head:* Dr. Robert W. Rescigno, Dean. *Application contact:* Laura Morris, Director of Admissions, 877-967-5456, E-mail: infocenter@wilmu.edu.
Website: http://www.wilmu.edu/business/

Wingate University, Porter B. Byrum School of Business, Wingate, NC 28174. Offers accounting (MAC); corporate innovation (MBA); finance (MBA); general management (MBA); healthcare management (MBA); marketing (MBA); project management (MBA). *Accreditation:* ACBSP. *Program availability:* Part-time, evening/weekend. *Entrance requirements:* For master's, GMAT, work experience, 2 letters of recommendation. *Application deadline:* For fall admission, 8/15 priority date for domestic students; for spring admission, 12/15 priority date for domestic students. Applications are processed on a rolling basis. Application fee: $50. Electronic applications accepted. *Expenses:* Contact institution. *Financial support:* Federal Work-Study and scholarships/grants available. Support available to part-time students. Financial award application deadline: 8/1; financial award applicants required to submit FAFSA. *Faculty research:* Stochastic processes, business ethics, regional economic development, municipal finance, consumer behavior. *Unit head:* Dr. Peter Frank, Dean, 704-233-8148, Fax: 704-233-8146, E-mail: pfrank@wingate.edu. *Application contact:* Mary Maye, Administrative Assistant to the Dean, 704-233-8148, Fax: 704-233-8146.
Website: http://www.wingate.edu/academics/school-of-business

Xavier University, Williams College of Business, Master of Business Administration Program, Cincinnati, OH 45207. Offers business administration (Exec MBA, MBA); business intelligence (MBA); finance (MBA); health industry (MBA); international business (MBA); marketing (MBA); values-based leadership (MBA); MBA/MHSA; MSN/MBA. *Accreditation:* AACSB. *Program availability:* Part-time, evening/weekend. *Degree requirements:* For master's, capstone course. *Entrance requirements:* For master's, GMAT or GRE, official transcript; resume. Additional exam requirements/recommendations for international students: Required—TOEFL (minimum score 550 paper-based; 79 iBT). Electronic applications accepted. Application fee is waived when completed online. *Expenses:* Contact institution.

Yale University, Yale School of Management and Graduate School of Arts and Sciences, Doctoral Program in Management, New Haven, CT 06520. Offers accounting (PhD); financial economics (PhD); marketing (PhD); organizations and management (PhD). *Accreditation:* AACSB. *Degree requirements:* For doctorate, comprehensive exam, thesis/dissertation. *Entrance requirements:* For doctorate, GMAT or GRE General Test. Additional exam requirements/recommendations for international students: Required—TOEFL or IELTS. Electronic applications accepted. *Expenses:* Contact institution. *Faculty research:* Pricing of options and futures, term structure of interest rates, use of accounting numbers in debt contracts, product differentiation, e-commerce and marketing, behavioral finance.

York College of Pennsylvania, Graham School of Business, York, PA 17403-3651. Offers continuous improvement (MBA); financial management (MBA); health care management (MBA); management (MBA); marketing (MBA); self-designed (MBA). *Accreditation:* ACBSP. *Program availability:* Part-time, evening/weekend. *Faculty:* 11

full-time (3 women), 4 part-time/adjunct (1 woman). *Students:* 2 full-time (1 woman), 68 part-time (31 women); includes 7 minority (2 Black or African American, non-Hispanic/Latino; 1 Asian, non-Hispanic/Latino; 1 Hispanic/Latino; 3 Two or more races, non-Hispanic/Latino). Average age 32. 39 applicants, 79% accepted, 20 enrolled. In 2016, 22 master's awarded. *Degree requirements:* For master's, directed study. *Entrance requirements:* For master's, GMAT. Additional exam requirements/recommendations for international students: Required—TOEFL (minimum score 530 paper-based; 72 iBT), IELTS (minimum score 6). *Application deadline:* For fall admission, 7/15 priority date for domestic students, 5/1 for international students; for spring admission, 11/15 priority date for domestic students, 9/1 for international students; for summer admission, 4/15 priority date for domestic students. Applications are processed on a rolling basis. Application fee: $0. Electronic applications accepted. *Expenses:* $795 per credit. *Financial support:* In 2016–17, 3 students received support. Scholarships/grants available. Financial award applicants required to submit FAFSA. *Unit head:* Nicole Cornell Sadowski, MBA Director, 717-815-1491, Fax: 717-600-3999, E-mail: ncornell@ycp.edu. *Application contact:* MBA Office, 717-815-1491, Fax: 717-600-3999, E-mail: mba@ycp.edu.
Website: http://www.ycp.edu/mba

York University, Faculty of Graduate Studies, Schulich School of Business, Toronto, ON M3J 1P3, Canada. Offers accounting (M Acc); administration (PhD); business (MBA); business analytics (MBA); finance (MF); international business (IMBA); MBA/JD; MBA/MA; MBA/MFA. *Program availability:* Part-time, evening/weekend. *Degree requirements:* For master's, advanced proficiency in a second language, work term (IMBA); for doctorate, comprehensive exam, thesis/dissertation. *Entrance requirements:* For master's, GMAT or GRE, minimum GPA of 3.0 (3.3 for MF, MBA in business analytics, and IMBA); for doctorate, GMAT or GRE, minimum GPA of 3.3. Additional exam requirements/recommendations for international students: Required—TOEFL (minimum score 600 paper-based; 100 iBT), IELTS (minimum score 7), York English Language Test (minimum score 1); PearsonVUE (minimum score 64). Electronic applications accepted. *Faculty research:* Accounting, finance, marketing, operations management and information systems, organizational studies, strategic management.

Youngstown State University, Graduate School, College of Liberal Arts and Social Sciences, Department of Economics, Youngstown, OH 44555-0001. Offers economics (MA); financial economics (MA). *Program availability:* Part-time. *Degree requirements:* For master's, comprehensive exam, thesis optional. *Entrance requirements:* For master's, minimum GPA of 2.7, 21 hours in economics. Additional exam requirements/recommendations for international students: Required—TOEFL. *Faculty research:* Forecasting, applied econometrics, labor economics, applied macroeconomics, industrial organization.

Youngstown State University, Graduate School, Williamson College of Business Administration, Department of Accounting and Finance, Youngstown, OH 44555-0001. Offers accounting (MBA). *Accreditation:* AACSB. *Program availability:* Part-time, evening/weekend. *Degree requirements:* For master's, thesis optional. *Entrance requirements:* For master's, GMAT, minimum GPA of 2.7. Additional exam requirements/recommendations for international students: Required—TOEFL. *Faculty research:* Taxation and compliance, capital markets, accounting information systems, accounting theory, tax and government accounting.

Investment Management

Alaska Pacific University, Graduate Programs, Business Administration Department, Anchorage, AK 99508-4672. Offers business administration (MBA), including business administration, health services administration; information and communication technology (MBAICT); investment (CGS). *Program availability:* Part-time, evening/weekend. *Degree requirements:* For master's, capstone course. *Entrance requirements:* For master's, GMAT or GRE General Test, minimum GPA of 3.0. Additional exam requirements/recommendations for international students: Required—TOEFL (minimum score 550 paper-based).

DePaul University, Kellstadt Graduate School of Business, Chicago, IL 60604. Offers accountancy (M Acc, MS, MSA); applied economics (MBA); banking (MBA); behavioral finance (MBA); brand and product management (MBA); business development (MBA); business information technology (MS); business strategy and decision-making (MBA); computational finance (MS); consumer insights (MBA); corporate finance (MBA); economic policy analysis (MS); entrepreneurship (MBA, MS); finance (MBA, MS); financial analysis (MBA); general business (MBA); health sector management (MBA); hospitality leadership (MBA); hospitality leadership and operational performance (MS); human resource management (MBA); human resources (MS); investment management (MBA); leadership and change management (MBA); management accounting (MBA); marketing (MBA, MS); marketing analysis (MS); marketing strategy and planning (MBA); operations management (MBA); organizational diversity (MBA); real estate (MS); real estate finance and investment (MBA); revenue management (MBA); sports management (MBA); strategic global marketing (MBA); strategy, execution and valuation (MBA); sustainable management (MBA, MS); taxation (MS); wealth management (MS); JD/MBA. *Accreditation:* AACSB. *Program availability:* Part-time, evening/weekend, online learning. *Entrance requirements:* For master's, GMAT, 2 letters of recommendation, resume, essay, official transcripts. Additional exam requirements/recommendations for international students: Required—TOEFL (minimum score 550 paper-based; 80 iBT). Electronic applications accepted. *Expenses:* Contact institution.

Fordham University, Gabelli School of Business, New York, NY 10023. Offers accounting (MBA, MS); applied statistics and decision-making (MS); business administration (EMBA); business analytics (MS); communications and media management (MBA); electronic business (MBA); entrepreneurship (MBA); finance (MBA); global finance (MS); global sustainability (MBA); healthcare management (MBA); information systems (MBA, MS); investor relations (MS); management (MBA, MS); marketing (MBA); marketing intelligence (MS); media management (MS); nonprofit leadership (MS); quantitative finance (MS); taxation (MS); JD/MBA; MS/MBA. *Accreditation:* AACSB. *Program availability:* Part-time, evening/weekend. *Faculty:* 132 full-time (44 women), 51 part-time/adjunct (7 women). *Students:* 1,117 full-time (668 women), 553 part-time (282 women); includes 207 minority (44 Black or African American, non-Hispanic/Latino; 92 Asian, non-Hispanic/Latino; 69 Hispanic/Latino; 2 Native Hawaiian or other Pacific Islander, non-Hispanic/Latino), 1,088 international. Average age 27. 4,745 applicants, 46% accepted, 752 enrolled. In 2016, 996 master's awarded. Terminal master's awarded for partial completion of doctoral program. *Degree requirements:* For master's, internships (required for MS in quantitative finance, recommended for MBA). *Entrance requirements:* For master's, GMAT/GRE, 2 letters of recommendation, resume, 2 essays, transcripts. Additional exam requirements/recommendations for international students: Required—TOEFL (minimum score 100 iBT), IELTS (minimum score 7). *Application deadline:* For fall admission, 11/15 priority date for domestic and international students; for winter admission, 1/15 priority date for domestic students, 1/1 priority date for international students; for spring admission, 3/1 for domestic and international students; for summer admission, 6/1 for domestic students. Application fee: $130. Electronic applications accepted. *Expenses:* $1,397 per credit. *Financial support:* In 2016–17, 78 students received support. Career-related internships or fieldwork, institutionally sponsored loans, scholarships/grants, and unspecified assistantships available. Support available to part-time students. Financial award application deadline: 6/30; financial award applicants required to submit FAFSA. *Unit head:* Dr. Donna Rapaccioli, Dean, 212-636-6165, Fax: 212-307-1779, E-mail: rapaccioli@fordham.edu. *Application contact:* Lawrence Murray, Senior Assistant Dean of Graduate Admissions and Advising, 212-636-6200, Fax: 212-636-7076, E-mail: admissionsgb@fordham.edu.
Website: http://www.fordham.edu/gabelli

The George Washington University, School of Business, Department of Finance, Washington, DC 20052. Offers finance (MSF, PhD); finance and investments (MBA). *Program availability:* Part-time, evening/weekend. *Faculty:* 18 full-time (5 women). *Students:* 176 full-time (86 women), 19 part-time (4 women); includes 13 minority (6 Black or African American, non-Hispanic/Latino; 6 Asian, non-Hispanic/Latino; 1 Hispanic/Latino), 173 international. Average age 26. 881 applicants, 28% accepted, 2 enrolled. In 2016, 125 master's awarded. *Degree requirements:* For doctorate, thesis/dissertation. *Entrance requirements:* For master's, GMAT; for doctorate, GMAT or GRE. Additional exam requirements/recommendations for international students: Required—TOEFL. *Application deadline:* For fall admission, 4/1 priority date for domestic students; for spring admission, 10/1 for domestic students. Applications are processed on a rolling basis. Application fee: $75. *Financial support:* In 2016–17, 38 students received support. Fellowships, teaching assistantships, career-related internships or fieldwork, Federal Work-Study, and institutionally sponsored loans available. Financial award application deadline: 4/1. *Unit head:* Robert Van Order, Chair, 202-994-3427, E-mail: rvo@gwu.edu. *Application contact:* Christopher Storer, Executive Director, Graduate Admissions, 202-994-1212, E-mail: gwmba@gwu.edu.

Hofstra University, Frank G. Zarb School of Business, Programs in Finance, Hempstead, NY 11549. Offers business administration (MBA), including finance; corporate finance (Advanced Certificate); finance (MS), including financial and risk management, investment analysis; investment management (Advanced Certificate); quantitative finance (MS). *Program availability:* Part-time, evening/weekend, blended/hybrid learning. *Students:* 177 full-time (70 women), 47 part-time (9 women); includes 16 minority (6 Black or African American, non-Hispanic/Latino; 6 Asian, non-Hispanic/Latino; 4 Hispanic/Latino), 167 international. Average age 25. 555 applicants, 72% accepted, 93 enrolled. In 2016, 101 master's awarded. *Degree requirements:* For master's, capstone course (for MBA), thesis (for MS), minimum GPA of 3.0. *Entrance requirements:* For master's, GMAT/GRE, 2 letters of recommendation, resume, essay. Additional exam requirements/recommendations for international students: Required—TOEFL (minimum score 550 paper-based; 80 iBT); Recommended—IELTS (minimum score 6). *Application deadline:* Applications are processed on a rolling basis. Application fee: $75. Electronic applications accepted. *Expenses:* $1,170 per credit. *Financial support:* In 2016–17, 51 students received support, including 43 fellowships with full and partial tuition reimbursements available (averaging $4,829 per year), 1 research assistantship with full and partial tuition reimbursement available (averaging $6,950 per year); career-related internships or fieldwork, Federal Work-Study, institutionally sponsored loans, scholarships/grants, tuition waivers (full and partial), and unspecified assistantships also available. Support available to part-time students. Financial award applicants required to submit FAFSA. *Faculty research:* Individual investors and financial crisis; short-sale constraints and futures trading; social media and sentiment in financial markets; external monitoring of firms; CEO inside debt and insider trading. *Unit head:* Dr. K. G. Viswanathan, Chairperson, 516-463-5699, Fax: 516-463-4834, E-mail: k.g.viswanathan@hofstra.edu. *Application contact:* Sunil Samuel, Assistant Vice President of Admissions, 516-463-4723, Fax: 516-463-4664, E-mail: graduateadmission@hofstra.edu.
Website: http://www.hofstra.edu/business/

Johns Hopkins University, Carey Business School, Certificate Programs, Baltimore, MD 21218. Offers investments (Certificate). *Program availability:* Part-time, evening/weekend. *Faculty:* 87 full-time (32 women), 51 part-time/adjunct (8 women). *Students:* 37 part-time (17 women); includes 11 minority (4 Black or African American, non-Hispanic/Latino; 5 Asian, non-Hispanic/Latino; 1 Hispanic/Latino; 1 Two or more races, non-Hispanic/Latino), 6 international. Average age 37. 24 applicants, 29% accepted, 6 enrolled. In 2016, 33 Certificates awarded. *Degree requirements:* For Certificate, 16 credits. *Entrance requirements:* Additional exam requirements/recommendations for international students: Required—TOEFL, IELTS. *Application deadline:* Applications are processed on a rolling basis. Application fee: $100. Electronic applications accepted. *Expenses:* $1,290 per credit. *Unit head:* Dr. Kevin Frick, Vice Dean of Education, 410-234-9272, E-mail: kfrick@jhu.edu. *Application contact:* Office of Admissions, 410-234-9220, Fax: 443-529-1554, E-mail: carey.admissions@jhu.edu.
Website: http://carey.jhu.edu/academics/certificate-programs/

Johns Hopkins University, Carey Business School, MS in Enterprise Risk Management Program, Baltimore, MD 21218. Offers MS. *Program availability:* Part-time, evening/weekend. *Faculty:* 87 full-time (32 women), 51 part-time/adjunct (8 women). *Students:* 39 full-time (24 women), 12 part-time (4 women); includes 9 minority (7 Black or African American, non-Hispanic/Latino; 2 Asian, non-Hispanic/Latino), 38 international. Average age 23. 140 applicants, 66% accepted, 43 enrolled. In 2016, 14 master's awarded. *Degree requirements:* For master's, 36 credits. *Entrance requirements:* For master's, GMAT or GRE. Additional exam requirements/recommendations for international students: Required—TOEFL, IELTS. *Application deadline:* For fall admission, 5/1 for domestic and international students. Applications are processed on a rolling basis. Application fee: $100. Electronic applications accepted. *Expenses:* $64,000 (full-time); $1,290 per credit (part-time). *Financial support:* In 2016–17, 7 students received support. Scholarships/grants available. Support available to part-time students. Financial award application deadline: 4/15; financial award applicants required to submit FAFSA. *Faculty research:* Emerging issues in risk management, health care/medical services, strategic options and simulation. *Unit head:*

Dr. Kevin Frick, Vice Dean of Education, 410-234-9272, E-mail: kfrick@jhu.edu. *Application contact:* Office of Admissions, 410-234-9220, Fax: 443-529-1554, E-mail: carey.admissions@jhu.edu.
Website: http://carey.jhu.edu/academics/master-of-science/ms-in-enterprise-risk-management

Lincoln University, Graduate Studies, Oakland, CA 94612. Offers finance and investments (DBA); finance management (MS); finance management and investments (MBA); general business (MBA); human resource management (MBA, DBA); international business (MBA, MS); management information systems (MBA). *Program availability:* Part-time. *Faculty:* 13 full-time (1 woman), 16 part-time/adjunct (3 women). *Students:* 542 full-time (215 women), 3 part-time (1 woman); includes 10 minority (8 Asian, non-Hispanic/Latino; 1 Hispanic/Latino; 1 Two or more races, non-Hispanic/Latino), 531 international. Average age 26. 800 applicants, 71% accepted, 81 enrolled. In 2016, 109 master's, 1 doctorate awarded. *Degree requirements:* For master's, research project (thesis), internship report, or comprehensive exam; for doctorate, comprehensive exam, thesis/dissertation. *Entrance requirements:* For master's, minimum GPA of 2.7; for doctorate, GMAT (minimum score: 550), GRE (minimum score: 1000), or equivalent test results (waived for master's degree with minimum cumulative GPA of 3.3). Additional exam requirements/recommendations for international students: Required—TOEFL (minimum score 525 paper-based; 71 iBT) or IELTS (minimum score 5.5) for MBA; TOEFL (minimum score 550 paper-based; 79 iBT) or IELTS (minimum score 6) for DBA; Recommended—TOEFL (minimum score 71 iBT), IELTS (minimum score 6), TSE. *Application deadline:* For fall admission, 8/7 for domestic students, 7/14 for international students; for spring admission, 11/30 for domestic students, 10/31 for international students; for summer admission, 5/29 for domestic students, 5/5 for international students. Applications are processed on a rolling basis. Application fee: $75. Electronic applications accepted. *Expenses: Tuition:* Full-time $7920. *Required fees:* $400. Tuition and fees vary according to course level, course load, degree level and program. *Financial support:* Teaching assistantships, career-related internships or fieldwork, and scholarships/grants available. Financial award applicants required to submit FAFSA. *Unit head:* Dr. Marshall Burak, Director of Graduate Programs, 510-628-8016, Fax: 510-628-8012, E-mail: mburak@lincolnuca.edu. *Application contact:* Reenu Shrestha, Assistant to the President, 510-628-8017, Fax: 510-208-2826, E-mail: sreenu@lincolnuca.edu.
Website: http://www.lincolnuca.edu/

Lynn University, College of Business and Management, Boca Raton, FL 33431-5598. Offers business administration (MBA), including aviation management, financial valuation and investment management, hospitality management, human resource management, international business management, marketing, media management, sports management. *Program availability:* Part-time, evening/weekend, 100% online, blended/hybrid learning. *Faculty:* 24 full-time (9 women), 24 part-time/adjunct (4 women). *Students:* 265 full-time (125 women), 182 part-time (96 women); includes 100 minority (41 Black or African American, non-Hispanic/Latino; 11 Asian, non-Hispanic/Latino; 42 Hispanic/Latino; 6 Two or more races, non-Hispanic/Latino), 119 international. Average age 28. 280 applicants, 94% accepted, 181 enrolled. In 2016, 219 master's awarded. *Degree requirements:* For master's, strategic management seminar, simulation capstone. *Entrance requirements:* For master's, bachelor's degree from accredited institution, resume, letter of recommendation, official transcripts, essay/personal statement. Additional exam requirements/recommendations for international students: Required—TOEFL (minimum score 550 paper-based; 80 iBT), IELTS (minimum score 6.5). *Application deadline:* For fall admission, 8/18 for domestic students, 8/4 for international students; for spring admission, 12/15 for domestic students, 12/1 for international students; for summer admission, 4/17 for domestic students, 4/3 for international students. Applications are processed on a rolling basis. Application fee: $45. Electronic applications accepted. *Expenses:* $725 per credit. *Financial support:* In 2016–17, 115 students received support. Career-related internships or fieldwork, Federal Work-Study, scholarships/grants, tuition waivers (full and partial), and unspecified assistantships available. Support available to part-time students. Financial award application deadline: 3/1; financial award applicants required to submit FAFSA. *Faculty research:* Market volatility investing, biometric research, sports legal history, organizational leadership, urban economic development and productivity. *Unit head:* Dr. RT Good, Dean of the College of Business and Management, 561-237-7458, E-mail: rgood@lynn.edu. *Application contact:* Steven Pruitt, Director of Graduate and Undergraduate Evening Admission, 561-237-7834, Fax: 561-237-7100, E-mail: spruitt@lynn.edu.
Website: http://www.lynn.edu/academics/colleges/business-and-management

Manhattanville College, School of Business, Master of Science in Finance Program, Purchase, NY 10577-2132. Offers accounting (MS); corporate finance (MS); investment management (MS). *Program availability:* Part-time, evening/weekend. *Students:* 30 (14 women); includes 13 minority (7 Black or African American, non-Hispanic/Latino; 3 Asian, non-Hispanic/Latino; 1 Hispanic/Latino; 2 Two or more races, non-Hispanic/Latino). Average age 28. 23 applicants, 30% accepted, 7 enrolled. In 2016, 9 master's awarded. *Degree requirements:* For master's, thesis (for some programs), final project. *Entrance requirements:* For master's, transcripts, 2 letters of recommendation, resume. Additional exam requirements/recommendations for international students: Required—TOEFL (minimum score 563 paper-based; 85 iBT). *Application deadline:* Applications are processed on a rolling basis. Application fee: $75. Electronic applications accepted. *Expenses: Tuition:* Full-time $16,470; part-time $915 per credit. *Required fees:* $60 per semester. Part-time tuition and fees vary according to course load and program. *Financial support:* Federal Work-Study, institutionally sponsored loans, scholarships/grants, and unspecified assistantships available. Financial award applicants required to submit FAFSA. *Faculty research:* Life transitions: theory, strategies and practice. *Unit head:* Laura Persky, Graduate Program Director, 914-323-5188, E-mail: laura.persky@mville.edu. *Application contact:* Monika Pottgen, Assistant Director, Recruitment and Admissions, 914-323-5150, E-mail: business@mville.edu.
Website: https://www.mville.edu/programs/ms-finance

Marywood University, Academic Affairs, Munley College of Liberal Arts and Sciences, School of Business and Global Innovation, Emphasis in Finance/Investment, Scranton, PA 18509-1598. Offers MBA. *Entrance requirements:* For master's, GMAT. Electronic applications accepted.

New York University, School of Continuing and Professional Studies, Schack Institute of Real Estate, Program in Real Estate, New York, NY 10012-1019. Offers finance and investment (MS); real estate (Advanced Certificate); real estate management (MS). *Program availability:* Part-time, evening/weekend. *Degree requirements:* For master's, thesis, capstone. *Entrance requirements:* For master's, GRE or GMAT (only upon request), bachelor's degree, resume with relevant professional work, internship or volunteer experience, two letters of recommendation, statement of purpose. Additional exam requirements/recommendations for international students: Required—TOEFL (minimum score 600 paper-based; 100 iBT), IELTS (minimum score 7). Electronic applications accepted. *Faculty research:* Economics and market cycles, international property rights, comparative metropolitan economies, current market trends.

Pace University, Lubin School of Business, Advanced Professional Certificate Program, New York, NY 10038. Offers business economics (APC); e-business (APC); financial management (APC); international business (APC); international economics (APC); investment management (APC); marketing (APC); public accounting (APC). *Program availability:* Evening/weekend. *Students:* 1 applicant, 100% accepted, 1 enrolled. *Entrance requirements:* For degree, MBA or MS in business discipline, relevant professional experience. Additional exam requirements/recommendations for international students: Required—TOEFL (minimum score 90 iBT), IELTS (minimum score 7) or PTE (minimum score 61). *Application deadline:* For fall admission, 8/1 priority date for domestic students, 6/1 for international students; for spring admission, 12/1 for domestic students, 10/1 for international students. Applications are processed on a rolling basis. Application fee: $70. Electronic applications accepted. *Expenses: Tuition:* Part-time $1195 per credit. *Required fees:* $260 per semester. Tuition and fees vary according to degree level, campus/location and program. *Unit head:* Dr. Jack Yurkiewicz, Director, 212-618-6567, E-mail: jyurkiewicz@pace.edu. *Application contact:* Susan Ford-Goldschein, Director of Graduate Admissions, 212-346-1531, Fax: 212-346-1585, E-mail: graduateadmission@pace.edu.
Website: http://www.pace.edu/lubin/agc

Pace University, Lubin School of Business, Financial Management Program, New York, NY 10038. Offers financial management (MBA, MS); financial risk management (MS); international finance (MBA); investment management (MBA, MS). *Program availability:* Evening/weekend. *Students:* 130 full-time (49 women), 62 part-time (34 women); includes 33 minority (4 Black or African American, non-Hispanic/Latino; 20 Asian, non-Hispanic/Latino; 6 Hispanic/Latino; 1 Native Hawaiian or other Pacific Islander, non-Hispanic/Latino; 2 Two or more races, non-Hispanic/Latino), 124 international. Average age 26. 397 applicants, 65% accepted, 84 enrolled. In 2016, 166 master's awarded. *Entrance requirements:* For master's, GMAT, GRE (GMAT not required for MS with passing of Level 1 of Chartered Financial Analyst exam or Level 1 of Financial Risk Manager Exam), undergraduate degree, transcripts from all accredited colleges/universities attended, two letters of recommendation, resume, personal statement. Additional exam requirements/recommendations for international students: Required—TOEFL (minimum score 90 iBT), IELTS (minimum score 7) or PTE (minimum score 61). *Application deadline:* For fall admission, 8/1 priority date for domestic students, 6/1 for international students; for spring admission, 12/1 for domestic students, 10/1 for international students. Applications are processed on a rolling basis. Application fee: $70. Electronic applications accepted. *Expenses: Tuition:* Part-time $1195 per credit. *Required fees:* $260 per semester. Tuition and fees vary according to degree level, campus/location and program. *Financial support:* Research assistantships, career-related internships or fieldwork, Federal Work-Study, and tuition waivers (full and partial) available. Support available to part-time students. Financial award application deadline: 2/15; financial award applicants required to submit FAFSA. *Unit head:* Dr. P. V. Viswanath, Chairperson, 212-618-6518, E-mail: pviswanath@pace.edu. *Application contact:* Susan Ford-Goldschein, Director of Graduate Admissions, 212-346-1531, Fax: 212-346-1585, E-mail: graduateadmissions@pace.edu.
Website: http://www.pace.edu/lubin/financial-management-mba

Regent University, Graduate School, School of Business and Leadership, Virginia Beach, VA 23464-9800. Offers business administration (MBA), including accounting, entrepreneurship, finance and investing, general management, healthcare management (MA, MBA), human resource management, innovation management; leadership (Certificate); organizational leadership (MA, PhD), including ecclesial leadership (PhD), entrepreneurial leadership (PhD), future studies (MA), healthcare management (MA, MBA), human resource development (PhD), interdisciplinary studies (MA), international organizations (MA), leadership coaching and mentoring (MA), not-for-profit management (MA), organizational communication (MA), organizational development consulting (MA); strategic leadership (DSL), including global consulting, leadership coaching, strategic foresight. *Program availability:* Part-time, evening/weekend, 100% online, blended/hybrid learning. *Faculty:* 9 full-time (2 women), 28 part-time/adjunct (10 women). *Students:* 100 full-time (56 women), 1,008 part-time (528 women); includes 562 minority (453 Black or African American, non-Hispanic/Latino; 7 American Indian or Alaska Native, non-Hispanic/Latino; 30 Asian, non-Hispanic/Latino; 51 Hispanic/Latino; 1 Native Hawaiian or other Pacific Islander, non-Hispanic/Latino; 20 Two or more races, non-Hispanic/Latino), 76 international. Average age 40. 1,240 applicants, 45% accepted, 352 enrolled. In 2016, 95 master's, 71 doctorates awarded. *Degree requirements:* For master's, thesis or alternative, 3-credit hour culminating experience; for doctorate, thesis/dissertation. *Entrance requirements:* For master's, college transcripts, resume, essay; for doctorate, college transcripts, resume, essay, writing sample; for Certificate, writing sample, resume, transcripts. Additional exam requirements/recommendations for international students: Required—TOEFL (minimum score 577 paper-based). *Application deadline:* For fall admission, 5/1 priority date for domestic students; for spring admission, 10/1 priority date for domestic students. Applications are processed on a rolling basis. Application fee: $50. Electronic applications accepted. *Expenses:* Contact institution. *Financial support:* In 2016–17, 631 students received support. Career-related internships or fieldwork, scholarships/grants, and unspecified assistantships available. Support available to part-time students. *Faculty research:* Servant leadership, global business, team effectiveness, technology utilization, leadership development. *Unit head:* Dr. Doris Gomez, Dean, 757-352-4686, Fax: 757-352-4634, E-mail: dorigom@regent.edu. *Application contact:* Heidi Cece, Assistant Vice President of Enrollment Management, 800-373-5504, Fax: 757-352-4381, E-mail: admissions@regent.edu.
Website: http://www.regent.edu/sbl/

Sacred Heart University, Graduate Programs, Jack Welch College of Business, Department of Finance, Fairfield, CT 06825. Offers administration (DBA); finance and investment management (MS). *Program availability:* Part-time, evening/weekend. *Faculty:* 8 full-time (3 women), 4 part-time/adjunct (2 women). *Students:* 30 full-time (8 women), 41 part-time (15 women); includes 13 minority (8 Black or African American, non-Hispanic/Latino; 2 Asian, non-Hispanic/Latino; 2 Hispanic/Latino; 1 Two or more races, non-Hispanic/Latino), 28 international. Average age 35. 84 applicants, 82% accepted, 40 enrolled. *Degree requirements:* For doctorate, comprehensive exam. *Entrance requirements:* For master's, GMAT or GRE, official transcripts from all institutions attended; for doctorate, GMAT or GRE with master's degree and 5 years' experience. Additional exam requirements/recommendations for international students: Required—TOEFL (minimum score 570 paper-based, 80 iBT), TWE, or IELTS (6.5); Recommended—TSE. *Application deadline:* Applications are processed on a rolling basis. Application fee: $75. Electronic applications accepted. *Expenses:* $10,674 per trimester full-time. *Financial support:* Unspecified assistantships available. Financial award applicants required to submit FAFSA. *Unit head:* Dr. Kwamie Dunbar, Assistant Professor of Finance/Director of MS in Finance and Investment Management, 203-396-8068, E-mail: dunbark@sacredheart.edu. *Application contact:* William Sweeney, Director of Graduate Admissions Operations, 203-365-4827, E-mail: sweeneyw@sacredheart.edu.
Website: http://www.sacredheart.edu/academics/johnfwelchcollegeofbusiness/aboutthecollege/

St. John's University, The Peter J. Tobin College of Business, Department of Economics and Finance, Program in Finance, Queens, NY 11439. Offers finance (MBA); investment management (MS). *Program availability:* Part-time, evening/weekend. *Degree requirements:* For master's, comprehensive exam (for some programs), thesis optional. *Entrance requirements:* For master's, GMAT, 2 letters of recommendation, resume, transcripts, essay. Additional exam requirements/ recommendations for international students: Required—TOEFL (minimum score 600 paper-based; 100 iBT), IELTS (minimum score 7). Electronic applications accepted. *Expenses:* Contact institution.

Saint Mary's College of California, School of Economics and Business Administration, MS in Financial Analysis and Investment Management Program, Moraga, CA 94556. Offers MS. *Expenses:* Contact institution.

Southern New Hampshire University, School of Business, Manchester, NH 03106-1045. Offers accounting (MBA, MS, Graduate Certificate); accounting finance (MS); accounting/auditing (MS); accounting/forensic accounting (MS); accounting/taxation (MS); athletic administration (MBA, Graduate Certificate); business administration (IMBA, MBA, Certificate, Graduate Certificate), including accounting (Certificate), business administration (MBA), business information systems (Graduate Certificate), human resource management (Certificate); corporate social responsibility (MBA); entrepreneurship (MBA); finance (MBA, MS, Graduate Certificate); finance/corporate finance (MS); finance/investments and securities (MS); forensic accounting (MBA); healthcare informatics (MBA); healthcare management (MBA); human resource management (Graduate Certificate); information technology (MS, Graduate Certificate); information technology management (MBA); international business (Graduate Certificate); international business and information technology (Graduate Certificate); international finance (Graduate Certificate); international sport management (Graduate Certificate); justice studies (MBA); leadership of nonprofit organizations (Graduate Certificate); management (MS); marketing (MBA, MS, Graduate Certificate); operations and project management (MS); operations and supply chain management (MBA, Graduate Certificate); organizational leadership (MS); project management (MBA, Graduate Certificate); Six Sigma (MBA); Six Sigma quality (Graduate Certificate); social media marketing (MBA); sport management (MBA, MS, Graduate Certificate); sustainability and environmental compliance (MBA); workplace conflict management (MBA); MBA/Certificate. *Accreditation:* ACBSP. *Program availability:* Part-time, evening/ weekend, online learning. Terminal master's awarded for partial completion of doctoral program. *Degree requirements:* For master's, one foreign language, comprehensive exam (for some programs), thesis or alternative. *Entrance requirements:* For master's, minimum GPA of 2.5. Additional exam requirements/recommendations for international students: Required—TOEFL (minimum score 500 paper-based). Electronic applications accepted.

University of Colorado Denver, Business School, Master of Business Administration Program, Denver, CO 80217. Offers bioinnovation and entrepreneurship (MBA); business intelligence (MBA); business strategy (MBA); business to business marketing (MBA); business to consumer marketing (MBA); change management (MBA); corporate financial management (MBA); enterprise technology management (MBA); entrepreneurship (MBA); health administration (MBA), including financial management, health administration, health information technologies, international health management and policy; human resources management (MBA); international business (MBA); investment management (MBA); managing for sustainability (MBA); sports and entertainment management (MBA). *Accreditation:* AACSB. *Program availability:* Part-time, evening/weekend, 100% online, blended/hybrid learning. *Students:* 544 full-time (210 women), 112 part-time (22 women); includes 99 minority (15 Black or African American, non-Hispanic/Latino; 4 American Indian or Alaska Native, non-Hispanic/ Latino; 38 Asian, non-Hispanic/Latino; 36 Hispanic/Latino; 6 Two or more races, non-Hispanic/Latino), 22 international. Average age 32. 335 applicants, 73% accepted, 179 enrolled. In 2016, 251 master's awarded. *Degree requirements:* For master's, 48 semester hours, including 30 of core courses, 3 in international business, and 15 in electives from over 50 other business courses. *Entrance requirements:* For master's, GMAT, resume, official transcripts, essay, two letters of recommendation, financial statements (for international applicants). Additional exam requirements/ recommendations for international students: Required—TOEFL (minimum score 560 paper-based; 83 iBT); Recommended—IELTS (minimum score 6.5). *Application deadline:* For fall admission, 4/15 priority date for domestic students, 3/15 priority date for international students; for spring admission, 10/15 priority date for domestic students, 9/15 priority date for international students; for summer admission, 2/15 priority date for domestic students, 1/15 priority date for international students. Applications are processed on a rolling basis. Application fee: $50 ($75 for international students). Electronic applications accepted. *Expenses:* Contact institution. *Financial support:* In 2016–17, 171 students received support. Fellowships, research assistantships, teaching assistantships, Federal Work-Study, institutionally sponsored loans, scholarships/ grants, traineeships, and unspecified assistantships available. Financial award application deadline: 4/1; financial award applicants required to submit FAFSA. *Faculty research:* Marketing, management, entrepreneurship, finance, health administration. *Unit head:* Woodrow Eckard, MBA Director, 303-315-8470, E-mail: woody.eckard@ ucdenver.edu. *Application contact:* Shelly Townley, Admissions Director, Graduate Programs, 303-315-8202, E-mail: shelly.townley@ucdenver.edu.
Website: http://www.ucdenver.edu/academics/colleges/business/degrees/mba/Pages/ MBA.aspx

University of Houston–Downtown, Davies College of Business, MBA Program, Houston, TX 77002. Offers finance (MBA); human resource management (MBA); investment management (MBA); leadership (MBA); sales management and business development (MBA); supply chain management (MBA). *Accreditation:* AACSB. *Program availability:* Part-time, evening/weekend. *Faculty:* 33 full-time (12 women), 1 part-time/ adjunct (0 women). *Students:* 7 full-time (3 women), 1,037 part-time (565 women); includes 773 minority (361 Black or African American, non-Hispanic/Latino; 2 American Indian or Alaska Native, non-Hispanic/Latino; 132 Asian, non-Hispanic/Latino; 278 Hispanic/Latino), 32 international. Average age 33. 583 applicants, 86% accepted, 409 enrolled. In 2016, 181 master's awarded. *Entrance requirements:* For master's, GMAT, two letters of recommendation from professional references, personal statement, resume. Additional exam requirements/recommendations for international students: Required—TOEFL (minimum score 81 iBT). *Application deadline:* For fall admission, 7/ 15 for domestic and international students. Application fee: $35 ($60 for international students). Electronic applications accepted. *Expenses:* $428 in-state per credit; $786 non-resident per credit. *Financial support:* Federal Work-Study and scholarships/grants available. Financial award application deadline: 4/1; financial award applicants required to submit FAFSA. *Unit head:* Dr. D. Michael Fields, Dean, Davies College of Business, 713-221-8179, Fax: 713-221-8675, E-mail: fieldsd@uhd.edu. *Application contact:* Ceshia Love, Director of Graduate and International Admissions, 713-221-8093, Fax: 713-223-7408, E-mail: gradadmissions@uhd.edu.
Website: http://mba.uhd.edu/

University of Notre Dame, Mendoza College of Business, Master of Business Administration Program, Notre Dame, IN 46556. Offers business analytics (MBA); business leadership (MBA); consulting (MBA); corporate finance (MBA); innovation and entrepreneurship (MBA); investments (MBA); marketing (MBA). *Accreditation:* AACSB. *Faculty:* 62 full-time (13 women), 26 part-time/adjunct (7 women). *Students:* 304 full-time (78 women); includes 38 minority (10 Black or African American, non-Hispanic/Latino; 7 Asian, non-Hispanic/Latino; 15 Hispanic/Latino; 6 Two or more races, non-Hispanic/ Latino), 80 international. Average age 27. 647 applicants, 41% accepted, 121 enrolled. In 2016, 177 master's awarded. *Entrance requirements:* For master's, GMAT or GRE, work experience, essay, four-slide presentation, two recommendations, transcripts from all colleges and/or universities attended, interview. Additional exam requirements/ recommendations for international students: Required—TOEFL (minimum score 600 paper-based; 100 iBT), IELTS (minimum score 7), PTE (minimum score 68). *Application deadline:* For fall admission, 11/1 for domestic and international students; for winter admission, 1/10 for domestic and international students; for spring admission, 2/21 for domestic and international students; for summer admission, 3/28 for domestic and international students. Application fee: $175. Electronic applications accepted. *Expenses:* Contact institution. *Financial support:* In 2016–17, 251 students received support, including 243 fellowships (averaging $26,417 per year); career-related internships or fieldwork, Federal Work-Study, institutionally sponsored loans, scholarships/grants, and unspecified assistantships also available. Financial award application deadline: 2/28; financial award applicants required to submit FAFSA. *Faculty research:* Market micro-structure; marketing and public policy; corporate finance and accounting; corporate governance and ethical behavior; high performing organizations. *Unit head:* Dr. Katherine Speiss, Associate Dean, Graduate Business Programs, 574-631-3759, E-mail: spiess.1@nd.edu. *Application contact:* Kristin McAndrew, Director of Admissions, Graduate Business Programs, 574-631-8488, E-mail: kmcadre@nd.edu.
Website: http://mendoza.nd.edu/programs/mba-programs/

The University of Texas at Dallas, Naveen Jindal School of Management, Program in Finance and Managerial Economics, Richardson, TX 75080. Offers finance (MS), including corporate finance/investment banking, energy risk management, enterprise risk management, financial analysis, financial risk management, real estate. *Program availability:* Part-time, evening/weekend. *Faculty:* 24 full-time (2 women), 12 part-time/ adjunct (5 women). *Students:* 295 full-time (124 women), 56 part-time (37 women); includes 34 minority (3 Black or African American, non-Hispanic/Latino; 21 Asian, non-Hispanic/Latino; 7 Hispanic/Latino; 3 Two or more races, non-Hispanic/Latino), 279 international. Average age 26. 793 applicants, 66% accepted, 157 enrolled. In 2016, 215 master's awarded. *Entrance requirements:* For master's, GMAT or GRE. Additional exam requirements/recommendations for international students: Required—TOEFL (minimum score 550 paper-based). *Application deadline:* For fall admission, 7/15 for domestic students, 5/1 priority date for international students; for spring admission, 11/ 15 for domestic students, 9/1 priority date for international students. Applications are processed on a rolling basis. Application fee: $50 ($100 for international students). Electronic applications accepted. *Expenses:* Tuition, state resident: full-time $12,418; part-time $690 per semester hour. Tuition, nonresident: full-time $24,150; part-time $1342 per semester hour. Tuition and fees vary according to course load. *Financial support:* In 2016–17, 55 students received support, including 9 teaching assistantships with partial tuition reimbursements available (averaging $10,050 per year); research assistantships with partial tuition reimbursements available, career-related internships or fieldwork, Federal Work-Study, institutionally sponsored loans, scholarships/grants, and unspecified assistantships also available. Support available to part-time students. Financial award application deadline: 4/30; financial award applicants required to submit FAFSA. *Faculty research:* Econometrics, industrial organization, auction theory, file-sharing copyrights and bundling, international financial management, entrepreneurial finance. *Unit head:* Dr. Harold Zhang, Area Coordinator, 972-883-4777, E-mail: harold.zhang@utdallas.edu. *Application contact:* Kristin Spain, Academic Support Coordinator, 972-883-2373, E-mail: kes160430@utdallas.edu.
Website: http://jindal.utdallas.edu/finance

The University of Tulsa, Graduate School, Collins College of Business, Program in Finance, Tulsa, OK 74104-3189. Offers corporate finance (MS); investments and portfolio management (MS); risk management (MS); JD/MSF; MBA/MSF; MSF/MSAM. *Program availability:* Part-time, evening/weekend. *Faculty:* 9 full-time (1 woman). *Students:* 7 full-time (2 women), 4 part-time (0 women); includes 2 minority (both Hispanic/Latino), 3 international. Average age 26. 72 applicants, 39% accepted, 3 enrolled. In 2016, 5 master's awarded. *Degree requirements:* For master's, thesis optional. *Entrance requirements:* For master's, GMAT. Additional exam requirements/ recommendations for international students: Required—TOEFL (minimum score 577 paper-based; 91 iBT), IELTS (minimum score 6.5). *Application deadline:* Applications are processed on a rolling basis. Application fee: $55. Electronic applications accepted. *Expenses: Tuition:* Full-time $22,230; part-time $1235 per credit hour. *Required fees:* $990 per semester. Tuition and fees vary according to course load. *Financial support:* In 2016–17, 3 students received support, including 1 fellowship with full tuition reimbursement available (averaging $10,500 per year), 3 teaching assistantships with full tuition reimbursements available (averaging $10,347 per year); research assistantships with tuition reimbursements available, career-related internships or fieldwork, Federal Work-Study, institutionally sponsored loans, scholarships/grants, health care benefits, tuition waivers (full and partial), and unspecified assistantships also available. Support available to part-time students. Financial award application deadline: 2/1; financial award applicants required to submit FAFSA. *Unit head:* Dr. Ralph Jackson, Associate Dean, 918-631-2242, Fax: 918-631-2142, E-mail: ralph-jackson@utulsa.edu. *Application contact:* Information Contact, 918-631-2242, E-mail: graduate-business@ utulsa.edu.

University of Wisconsin–Madison, Graduate School, Wisconsin School of Business, Doctoral Program in Finance, Investment and Banking, Madison, WI 53706-1380. Offers PhD. *Degree requirements:* For doctorate, comprehensive exam, thesis/dissertation. *Entrance requirements:* For doctorate, GMAT or GRE. Additional exam requirements/ recommendations for international students: Recommended—TOEFL (minimum score 623 paper-based; 106 iBT), IELTS (minimum score 7.5), TSE (minimum score 73). Electronic applications accepted. *Expenses:* Contact institution. *Faculty research:* Banking and financial institutions, business cycles, investments, derivatives, corporate finance, economics, bankruptcy, foreclosures, mergers and acquisitions, portfolio theory.

University of Wisconsin–Milwaukee, Graduate School, Lubar School of Business, MS and Certificate Business Programs, Milwaukee, WI 53201-0413. Offers business analytics (Graduate Certificate); enterprise resource planning (Graduate Certificate); information technology management (MS); investment management (Graduate Certificate); nonprofit management (Graduate Certificate); nonprofit management and leadership (MS); state and local taxation (Graduate Certificate). *Students:* 174 full-time (83 women), 157 part-time (64 women); includes 69 minority (23 Black or African American, non-Hispanic/Latino; 27 Asian, non-Hispanic/Latino; 6 Hispanic/Latino; 13 Two or more races, non-Hispanic/Latino), 65 international. Average age 32. 281 applicants, 56% accepted, 116 enrolled. In 2016, 171 master's, 34 other advanced degrees awarded. *Entrance requirements:* Additional exam requirements/ recommendations for international students: Required—TOEFL (minimum score 550 paper-based; 79 iBT), IELTS (minimum score 6.5). *Application deadline:* Applications are processed on a rolling basis. Application fee: $56 ($96 for international students). Electronic applications accepted. *Financial support:* In 2016–17, 12 teaching assistantships were awarded; fellowships, research assistantships, health care benefits, unspecified assistantships, and project assistantships also available. Financial award applicants required to submit FAFSA. *Application contact:* General Information Contact, 414-229-4982, Fax: 414-229-6967, E-mail: gradschool@uwm.edu.

Taxation

American International College, School of Business, Arts and Sciences, Springfield, MA 01109-3189. Offers accounting and taxation (MS); business administration (MBA); clinical psychology (MA); educational psychology (Ed D); forensic psychology (MS); general psychology (MA, CAGS); management (CAGS); resort and casino management (MBA, CAGS). *Program availability:* Part-time, evening/weekend. *Degree requirements:* For master's, comprehensive exam (for some programs), thesis (for some programs), practicum; for doctorate, comprehensive exam (for some programs), thesis/dissertation; for CAGS, comprehensive exam (for some programs), thesis (for some programs). *Entrance requirements:* For master's, BS or BA; for doctorate, interview. Additional exam requirements/recommendations for international students: Required—TOEFL (minimum score 550 paper-based; 80 iBT). *Expenses: Tuition:* Full-time $7902; part-time $750 per semester hour. *Required fees:* $60; $60 per semester hour. $30 per semester. One-time fee: $100. Tuition and fees vary according to course load, degree level, campus/location and program.

American University, Kogod School of Business, Department of Accounting, Program in Taxation, Washington, DC 20016-8044. Offers MS, Certificate. *Program availability:* Part-time, evening/weekend. *Students:* 12 full-time (5 women), 26 part-time (10 women); includes 15 minority (5 Black or African American, non-Hispanic/Latino; 5 Asian, non-Hispanic/Latino; 5 Hispanic/Latino), 5 international. Average age 31. 23 applicants, 78% accepted, 9 enrolled. In 2016, 32 master's, 4 other advanced degrees awarded. *Entrance requirements:* For master's, GMAT/GRE, resume, personal statement, interview, two letters of recommendation, transcripts; for Certificate, bachelor's degree. Additional exam requirements/recommendations for international students: Required—TOEFL, IELTS, PTE. *Application deadline:* For fall admission, 2/20 priority date for domestic students, 2/20 for international students; for spring admission, 12/10 priority date for domestic students, 11/15 for international students. Applications are processed on a rolling basis. Application fee: $100. *Expenses:* $1,579 per credit tuition; $690 mandatory fees. *Financial support:* Application deadline: 2/1; applicants required to submit FAFSA. *Faculty research:* International transactions, corporate partnership, taxation, real estate, estate gift planning. *Unit head:* Dr. Donald T. Williamson, Chair, Department of Accounting, 202-885-1942, Fax: 202-885-1992, E-mail: dwillia@american.edu. *Application contact:* Jason Kennedy, Associate Director of Graduate Admissions, 202-885-1968, E-mail: jkennedy@american.edu.
Website: http://www.american.edu/kogod/

Appalachian State University, Cratis D. Williams Graduate School, Department of Accounting, Boone, NC 28608. Offers taxation (MS). *Program availability:* Part-time. *Degree requirements:* For master's, comprehensive exam, thesis optional. *Entrance requirements:* For master's, GMAT, 3 letters of recommendation. Additional exam requirements/recommendations for international students: Required—TOEFL (minimum score 550 paper-based; 79 iBT), IELTS (minimum score 6.5). *Application deadline:* For fall admission, 3/15 priority date for domestic students, 2/1 for international students; for spring admission, 11/1 for domestic students, 7/1 for international students. Applications are processed on a rolling basis. Application fee: $55. Electronic applications accepted. *Expenses:* Tuition, state resident: full-time $4744. Tuition, nonresident: full-time $17,913. Full-time tuition and fees vary according to program. *Financial support:* Fellowships, research assistantships, teaching assistantships, Federal Work-Study, scholarships/grants, and unspecified assistantships available. Financial award application deadline: 4/1; financial award applicants required to submit FAFSA. *Faculty research:* Audit assurance risk, state taxation, financial accounting inconsistencies, management information systems, charitable contribution taxation. *Unit head:* Dr. Timothy Forsyth, Chairman, 828-262-2036, Fax: 828-262-6640. *Application contact:* Dr. William Pollard, Director, 828-262-6206, Fax: 828-262-6640, E-mail: pollardwb@appstate.edu.
Website: http://www.acc.appstate.edu

Baruch College of the City University of New York, Zicklin School of Business, Department of Accounting, Program in Taxation, New York, NY 10010-5585. Offers MBA, MS. *Program availability:* Part-time, evening/weekend. *Entrance requirements:* For master's, GMAT, 2 letters of recommendation, resume, 2 years of work experience. Additional exam requirements/recommendations for international students: Required—TOEFL (minimum score 590 paper-based), TWE.

Bentley University, Graduate School of Business, Master's Program in Taxation, Waltham, MA 02452-4705. Offers MST. *Program availability:* Part-time, evening/weekend, 100% online, blended/hybrid learning. *Faculty:* 71 full-time (25 women), 33 part-time/adjunct (15 women). *Students:* 37 full-time (22 women), 77 part-time (32 women); includes 13 minority (3 Black or African American, non-Hispanic/Latino; 1 American Indian or Alaska Native, non-Hispanic/Latino; 6 Asian, non-Hispanic/Latino; 3 Two or more races, non-Hispanic/Latino), 26 international. Average age 31. 62 applicants, 89% accepted, 36 enrolled. In 2016, 75 master's awarded. *Entrance requirements:* For master's, GMAT or GRE General Test, current resume, two letters of recommendation, official copies of all university-level transcripts. Additional exam requirements/recommendations for international students: Required—TOEFL (minimum score 600 paper-based; 100 iBT), IELTS (minimum score 7), or PTE. *Application deadline:* Applications are processed on a rolling basis. Application fee: $50. Electronic applications accepted. *Expenses:* $4,225 per course, $480 fee per year. *Financial support:* In 2016–17, 17 students received support. Scholarships/grants and unspecified assistantships available. Financial award application deadline: 6/1; financial award applicants required to submit FAFSA. *Faculty research:* Taxation of intellectual property, tax dispute resolution, corporate tax planning and advocacy, estate and financial planning. *Unit head:* John Lynch, Jr., Senior Lecturer, 781-891-2624, E-mail: jlynch@bentley.edu. *Application contact:* Sharon Hill, Assistant Dean/Director of Graduate Admissions, 781-891-2108, Fax: 781-891-2464, E-mail: bentleygraduateadmissions@bentley.edu.
Website: http://www.bentley.edu/graduate/ms-programs/masters-in-taxation

Boise State University, College of Business and Economics, Department of Accountancy, Boise, ID 83725-1600. Offers accountancy (MSA); accountancy taxation (MSAT). *Accreditation:* AACSB. *Program availability:* Part-time. *Faculty:* 7. *Students:* 18 full-time (8 women), 28 part-time (13 women); includes 5 minority (2 Asian, non-Hispanic/Latino; 3 Hispanic/Latino), 1 international. Average age 32. 27 applicants, 74% accepted, 12 enrolled. In 2016, 27 master's awarded. *Entrance requirements:* For master's, GMAT, minimum GPA of 3.0. Additional exam requirements/recommendations for international students: Required—TOEFL (minimum score 587 paper-based; 95 iBT), IELTS (minimum score 6.5). *Application deadline:* For fall admission, 6/1 for domestic and international students; for spring admission, 10/1 for domestic and international students; for summer admission, 3/1 for domestic and international students. Application fee: $65 ($95 for international students). Electronic applications accepted. *Expenses:* Tuition, state resident: full-time $6058; part-time $358 per credit hour. Tuition, nonresident: full-time $20,108; part-time $608 per credit hour. *Required fees:* $2108. Tuition and fees vary according to program. *Financial support:* In 2016–17, 12 students received support. Scholarships/grants and unspecified assistantships available. Financial award application deadline: 2/15; financial award applicants required to submit FAFSA. *Unit head:* Dr. Troy Hyatt, Director, 208-426-3412, E-mail: troyhyatt@boisestate.edu. *Application contact:* Trisha Stevens Lamb, Program Director, 208-426-1120, E-mail: trishastevenslamb@boisestate.edu.
Website: http://cobe.boisestate.edu/graduate/

Bryant University, Graduate School of Business, Smithfield, RI 02917. Offers accounting (MPAC); business administration (MBA), including general management, global finance, global supply chain management, international business; business analytics (Graduate Certificate); taxation (MST). *Program availability:* Part-time, evening/weekend. *Faculty:* 16 full-time (3 women), 2 part-time/adjunct (0 women). *Students:* 71 full-time (23 women), 83 part-time (32 women); includes 17 minority (5 Black or African American, non-Hispanic/Latino; 4 Asian, non-Hispanic/Latino; 5 Hispanic/Latino; 3 Two or more races, non-Hispanic/Latino), 17 international. Average age 27. 165 applicants, 57% accepted, 66 enrolled. In 2016, 106 master's, 12 other advanced degrees awarded. *Degree requirements:* For master's, comprehensive exam (for some programs). *Entrance requirements:* For master's, GMAT, resume, recommendation, college transcripts. Additional exam requirements/recommendations for international students: Required—TOEFL (minimum score 580 paper-based; 95 iBT). *Application deadline:* For fall admission, 7/15 for domestic and international students; for spring admission, 11/15 for domestic and international students; for summer admission, 4/15 for domestic and international students. Applications are processed on a rolling basis. Application fee: $80. Electronic applications accepted. *Expenses:* Contact institution. *Financial support:* Research assistantships, scholarships/grants, and unspecified assistantships available. Support available to part-time students. Financial award application deadline: 2/15; financial award applicants required to submit FAFSA. *Faculty research:* International business, public sector auditing, taxation of partnerships, information systems security, financial markets microstructure. *Unit head:* Bjorn Carlsson, Graduate Program Director, 401-232-6707, E-mail: bcarlsson@bryant.edu. *Application contact:* Terri Rogers, Admissions Assistant, 401-232-6230, Fax: 401-232-6494, E-mail: graduateprograms@bryant.edu.
Website: http://gradschool.bryant.edu/business/

California Miramar University, Program in Taxation and Trade for Executives, San Diego, CA 92108. Offers MT.

California Polytechnic State University, San Luis Obispo, Orfalea College of Business, Program in Taxation, San Luis Obispo, CA 93407. Offers MS. *Degree requirements:* For master's, comprehensive exam (for some programs), thesis (for some programs). *Entrance requirements:* For master's, GMAT. Additional exam requirements/recommendations for international students: Required—TOEFL. *Application deadline:* For fall admission, 4/1 for domestic students, 3/1 for international students. Applications are processed on a rolling basis. Application fee: $55. Electronic applications accepted. *Expenses:* Tuition, state resident: full-time $6738; part-time $3906 per year. Tuition, nonresident: full-time $15,666; part-time $8370 per year. *Required fees:* $3603; $3141 per unit. $1047 per term. *Financial support:* Fellowships, career-related internships or fieldwork, Federal Work-Study, institutionally sponsored loans, scholarships/grants, and unspecified assistantships available. Support available to part-time students. Financial award application deadline: 3/2; financial award applicants required to submit FAFSA. *Unit head:* Dr. Scott Dawson, Dean, 805-756-2705, E-mail: scdawson@calpoly.edu. *Application contact:* Dr. Sanjiv Jaggia, Associate Dean, Graduate Programs, 805-756-7519, E-mail: sjaggia@calpoly.edu.
Website: http://www.cob.calpoly.edu/gradbusiness/degree-programs/ms-tax/

California State University, Fullerton, Graduate Studies, College of Business and Economics, Department of Accounting, Fullerton, CA 92834-9480. Offers accounting (MBA, MS). *Accreditation:* AACSB. *Program availability:* Part-time. *Degree requirements:* For master's, thesis or alternative, project. *Entrance requirements:* For master's, GMAT, minimum AACSB index of 950. *Application deadline:* Applications are processed on a rolling basis. Application fee: $55. Electronic applications accepted. *Expenses:* Tuition, state resident: full-time $3369; part-time $1953 per unit. Tuition, nonresident: full-time $3915; part-time $2499 per unit. Tuition and fees vary according to course load, degree level and program. *Financial support:* Career-related internships or fieldwork, Federal Work-Study, institutionally sponsored loans, and scholarships/grants available. Support available to part-time students. Financial award application deadline: 3/1; financial award applicants required to submit FAFSA. *Unit head:* Dr. Betty Chavis, Chair, 657-278-2225. *Application contact:* Admissions/Applications, 657-278-2371.

California State University, Northridge, Graduate Studies, The Tseng College of Extended Learning, Northridge, CA 91330. Offers business administration (Graduate Certificate); health administration (MPA); health education (MPH); knowledge management (MKM); music industry administration (MA); nonprofit-sector management (Graduate Certificate); public administration (MPA); public sector management and leadership (MPA); social work (MSW); taxation (MS); tourism, hospitality and recreation management (MS). *Faculty:* 55 part-time/adjunct (28 women). *Students:* 1 (woman) full-time, 1 (woman) part-time. Average age 40. *Entrance requirements:* For master's, GRE (if cumulative undergraduate GPA less than 3.0). *Expenses:* Tuition, state resident: full-time $4152. *Unit head:* Joyce Feucht-Haviar, Dean, 866-873-6439.

See Display on page 1665 and Close-Up on page 1665.

Capital University, Law School, Program in Business Law and Taxation, Columbus, OH 43209-2394. Offers business (LL M); business and taxation (LL M); taxation (LL M); JD/LL M. *Program availability:* Part-time, evening/weekend. *Degree requirements:* For master's, thesis or alternative. *Entrance requirements:* For master's, previous course work in accounting, business law, and taxation. Additional exam requirements/recommendations for international students: Required—TOEFL (minimum score 600 paper-based). Electronic applications accepted.

Capital University, Law School, Program in Taxation, Columbus, OH 43209-2394. Offers taxation (MT). *Program availability:* Part-time, evening/weekend. *Degree requirements:* For master's, thesis or alternative. *Entrance requirements:* For master's, previous course work in accounting, business law, and taxation. Additional exam requirements/recommendations for international students: Required—TOEFL (minimum score 600 paper-based). Electronic applications accepted. *Expenses:* Contact institution.

Chapman University, Fowler School of Law, Orange, CA 92866. Offers advocacy and dispute resolution (JD); business law (LL M, JD); criminal law (JD); entertainment and media law (LL M); entertainment law (JD); environmental, land use, and real estate law (JD); international and comparative law (LL M); international law (JD); law (JD); prosecutorial science (LL M); tax law (JD); taxation (LL M); trial advocacy (LL M); JD/

Taxation

MBA; JD/MFA. *Accreditation:* ABA. *Program availability:* Part-time. *Faculty:* 44 full-time (18 women), 22 part-time/adjunct (6 women). *Students:* 471 full-time (252 women), 38 part-time (19 women); includes 208 minority (8 Black or African American, non-Hispanic/Latino; 3 American Indian or Alaska Native, non-Hispanic/Latino; 76 Asian, non-Hispanic/Latino; 92 Hispanic/Latino; 29 Two or more races, non-Hispanic/Latino), 13 international. Average age 26. 1,499 applicants, 50% accepted, 190 enrolled. In 2016, 21 master's, 159 doctorates awarded. *Entrance requirements:* For doctorate, LSAT. Additional exam requirements/recommendations for international students: Required—TOEFL (minimum score 600 paper-based; 100 iBT). *Application deadline:* For fall admission, 4/15 priority date for domestic students. Applications are processed on a rolling basis. Electronic applications accepted. *Expenses:* Contact institution. *Financial support:* Fellowships, Federal Work-Study, and scholarships/grants available. Financial award applicants required to submit FAFSA. *Unit head:* Matthew J. Parlow, Dean, 714-628-2678, E-mail: parlow@chapman.edu. *Application contact:* Grace Alcantara, Assistant Dean of Admissions and Diversity Initiatives, 714-628-2500, E-mail: lawadmission@chapman.edu.
Website: http://www.chapman.edu/law/

Colorado State University, College of Business, Department of Accounting, Fort Collins, CO 80523-1271. Offers accounting (M Acc); taxation (M Acc). *Faculty:* 5 full-time (3 women), 5 part-time/adjunct (1 woman). *Students:* 27 full-time (12 women), 14 part-time (8 women); includes 8 minority (5 Hispanic/Latino; 3 Two or more races, non-Hispanic/Latino), 6 international. Average age 30. 55 applicants, 73% accepted, 27 enrolled. In 2016, 37 master's awarded. *Degree requirements:* For master's, thesis or alternative. *Entrance requirements:* For master's, GMAT (minimum score of 600) or GRE (minimum score of 315), minimum GPA of 3.25, BA/BS, 3 letters of reference, official transcripts, statement of purpose, resume. Additional exam requirements/recommendations for international students: Required—TOEFL (minimum score 95 iBT); Recommended—IELTS (minimum score 7), TSE (minimum score 70). *Application deadline:* For fall admission, 5/1 for domestic and international students. Applications are processed on a rolling basis. Application fee: $60 ($70 for international students). Electronic applications accepted. *Expenses:* Contact institution. *Financial support:* Scholarships/grants and unspecified assistantships available. Financial award application deadline: 2/1; financial award applicants required to submit FAFSA. *Faculty research:* Financial analysis, auditing and reporting; taxation; data analytics and systems; managerial accounting; corporate social responsibility. *Total annual research expenditures:* $5,000. *Unit head:* Dr. Audrey A. Gramling, Department Chair, 970-491-6268, E-mail: audrey.gramling@colostate.edu. *Application contact:* Jennifer Ivan, Program Manager, 970-491-1184, E-mail: jennifer.ivan@colostate.edu.
Website: https://biz.colostate.edu/About/Departments/Department-of-Accounting

DePaul University, College of Law, Chicago, IL 60604-2287. Offers health law (LL M); intellectual property law (LL M); international law (LL M); law (JD); taxation (LL M); JD/MA; JD/MBA; JD/MPS; JD/MS. *Accreditation:* ABA. *Program availability:* Part-time, evening/weekend. *Entrance requirements:* For doctorate, LSAT, LSAC applicant evaluation/letter of recommendation, personal statement, resume. Additional exam requirements/recommendations for international students: Required—TOEFL (minimum score 577 paper-based; 90 iBT), IELTS (minimum score 6.5). Electronic applications accepted. *Expenses:* Contact institution.

DePaul University, Kellstadt Graduate School of Business, Chicago, IL 60604. Offers accountancy (M Acc, MS, MSA); applied economics (MBA); banking (MBA); behavioral finance (MBA); brand and product management (MBA); business development (MBA); business information technology (MS); business strategy and decision-making (MBA); computational finance (MS); consumer insights (MBA); corporate finance (MBA); economic policy analysis (MS); entrepreneurship (MBA, MS); finance (MBA, MS); financial analysis (MBA); general business (MBA); health sector management (MBA); hospitality leadership (MBA); hospitality leadership and operational performance (MS); human resource management (MBA); human resources (MS); investment management (MBA); leadership and change management (MBA); management accounting (MBA); marketing (MBA, MS); marketing analysis (MS); marketing strategy and planning (MBA); operations management (MBA); organizational diversity (MBA); real estate (MS); real estate finance and investment (MBA); revenue management (MBA); sports management (MBA); strategic global marketing (MBA); strategy, execution and valuation (MBA); sustainable management (MBA, MS); taxation (MS); wealth management (MS); JD/MBA. *Accreditation:* AACSB. *Program availability:* Part-time, evening/weekend, online learning. *Entrance requirements:* For master's, GMAT, 2 letters of recommendation, resume, essay, official transcripts. Additional exam requirements/recommendations for international students: Required—TOEFL (minimum score 550 paper-based; 80 iBT). Electronic applications accepted. *Expenses:* Contact institution.

Fairfield University, Dolan School of Business, Fairfield, CT 06824. Offers accounting (MBA, MS, CAS); business analytics (MS); entrepreneurship (MBA); finance (MBA, MS, CAS); general management (MBA, CAS); global management (MBA); human resource management (MBA, CAS); information systems and business analytics (MBA); marketing (MBA, CAS); taxation (MBA, CAS). *Accreditation:* AACSB. *Program availability:* Part-time, evening/weekend. *Faculty:* 20 full-time (6 women), 4 part-time/adjunct (1 woman). *Students:* 106 full-time (41 women), 57 part-time (26 women); includes 18 minority (4 Black or African American, non-Hispanic/Latino; 1 American Indian or Alaska Native, non-Hispanic/Latino; 4 Asian, non-Hispanic/Latino; 7 Hispanic/Latino; 2 Two or more races, non-Hispanic/Latino), 39 international. Average age 26. 136 applicants, 63% accepted, 35 enrolled. In 2016, 90 master's awarded. *Degree requirements:* For master's, capstone course. *Entrance requirements:* For master's, GMAT (minimum score 500), 2 letters of reference, resume, minimum GPA of 3.0. Additional exam requirements/recommendations for international students: Required—TOEFL (minimum score 550 paper-based; 80 iBT) or IELTS (minimum score 6.5). *Application deadline:* For fall admission, 5/15 for international students; for spring admission, 10/15 for international students. Applications are processed on a rolling basis. Application fee: $60. Electronic applications accepted. *Expenses:* $875 per credit hour. *Financial support:* In 2016–17, 33 students received support. Scholarships/grants and unspecified assistantships available. Financial award applicants required to submit FAFSA. *Faculty research:* International finance, leadership and careers, ethics in accounting, emotions in consumer behavior and organizations, data analytics. *Unit head:* Dr. Donald Gibson, Dean, 203-254-4070, Fax: 203-254-4105, E-mail: dgibson@fairfield.edu. *Application contact:* Marianne Gumpper, Director of Graduate and Continuing Studies Admission, 203-254-4184, Fax: 203-254-4073, E-mail: gradadmis@fairfield.edu.
Website: http://fairfield.edu/mba

Fairleigh Dickinson University, College at Florham, Silberman College of Business, Department of Accounting, Law, and Tax, Program in Taxation, Madison, NJ 07940-1099. Offers MS, Certificate.

Fairleigh Dickinson University, Metropolitan Campus, Silberman College of Business, Department of Accounting, Law, and Tax, Program in Taxation, Teaneck, NJ 07666-1914. Offers MS.

Florida Gulf Coast University, Lutgert College of Business, Program in Accounting and Taxation, Fort Myers, FL 33965-6565. Offers MS. *Program availability:* Part-time, evening/weekend. *Faculty:* 58 full-time (23 women), 36 part-time/adjunct (13 women). *Students:* 13 full-time (6 women), 22 part-time (12 women); includes 10 minority (2 Black or African American, non-Hispanic/Latino; 7 Hispanic/Latino; 1 Two or more races, non-Hispanic/Latino). Average age 26. 31 applicants, 71% accepted, 18 enrolled. In 2016, 19 master's awarded. *Degree requirements:* For master's, thesis or alternative. *Entrance requirements:* For master's, GMAT, minimum GPA of 3.0. Additional exam requirements/recommendations for international students: Required—TOEFL (minimum score 550 paper-based). *Application deadline:* For fall admission, 5/1 priority date for domestic students; for spring admission, 9/15 for domestic students. Applications are processed on a rolling basis. Application fee: $30. Electronic applications accepted. *Expenses:* Tuition, state resident: full-time $6721. Tuition, nonresident: full-time $28,170. *Required fees:* $1987. Tuition and fees vary according to course load and degree level. *Financial support:* In 2016–17, 13 students received support. Application deadline: 3/1; applicants required to submit FAFSA. *Faculty research:* Stock petitions, mergers and acquisitions, deferred taxes, fraud and accounting regulations, graphical reporting practices. *Unit head:* Dr. Tanya Benford, Chair, 239-590-7342, Fax: 239-590-7330, E-mail: tbenford@fgcu.edu. *Application contact:* Marisa Ouverson, Director of Enrollment Management, 239-590-7403, Fax: 239-590-7330, E-mail: mouverso@fgcu.edu.

Florida State University, The Graduate School, College of Business, Tallahassee, FL 32306-1110. Offers accounting (M Acc), including assurance and advisory services, generalist, taxation; business administration (MBA, PhD), including accounting (PhD), finance (PhD), management information systems (PhD), marketing (PhD), organizational behavior and human resources (PhD), risk management and insurance (PhD), strategy (PhD); finance (MS); management information systems (MS); risk management and insurance (MS); JD/MBA; MSW/MBA. *Accreditation:* AACSB. *Program availability:* Part-time, 100% online. *Faculty:* 101 full-time (27 women), 4 part-time/adjunct (2 women). *Students:* 272 full-time (127 women), 351 part-time (133 women); includes 141 minority (45 Black or African American, non-Hispanic/Latino; 2 American Indian or Alaska Native, non-Hispanic/Latino; 20 Asian, non-Hispanic/Latino; 59 Hispanic/Latino; 2 Native Hawaiian or other Pacific Islander, non-Hispanic/Latino; 13 Two or more races, non-Hispanic/Latino), 71 international. Average age 30. 688 applicants, 60% accepted, 273 enrolled. In 2016, 231 master's, 12 doctorates awarded. Terminal master's awarded for partial completion of doctoral program. *Degree requirements:* For doctorate, comprehensive exam, thesis/dissertation. *Entrance requirements:* For master's, GMAT, GRE (for all except MS in finance), work experience (MBA, MS); minimum GPA of 3.0, letters of recommendation; for doctorate, GMAT, GRE (for marketing, organizational behavior, risk management and insurance, management information systems, and human resources only), minimum graduate GPA of 3.5, letters of recommendation. Additional exam requirements/recommendations for international students: Required—TOEFL (minimum score 600 paper-based; 85 iBT); Recommended—IELTS (minimum score 6). *Application deadline:* For fall admission, 6/1 for domestic and international students; for spring admission, 10/1 for domestic and international students; for summer admission, 3/1 for domestic and international students. Applications are processed on a rolling basis. Application fee: $30. Electronic applications accepted. *Expenses:* Contact institution. *Financial support:* In 2016–17, 149 students received support, including 9 fellowships (averaging $1,500 per year), 65 research assistantships with full tuition reimbursements available (averaging $20,000 per year), 75 teaching assistantships with full tuition reimbursements available (averaging $20,000 per year); career-related internships or fieldwork, scholarships/grants, health care benefits, tuition waivers (full and partial), and unspecified assistantships also available. Support available to part-time students. Financial award application deadline: 1/1; financial award applicants required to submit FAFSA. *Faculty research:* Business strategy, marketing, finance, accounting, business analytics. *Total annual research expenditures:* $1.4 million. *Unit head:* Dr. Michael Hartline, Dean, 850-644-4405, Fax: 850-644-0915, E-mail: mhartline@business.fsu.edu. *Application contact:* Jennifer Clark, Director, 850-644-6458, E-mail: gradprograms@business.fsu.edu.
Website: http://business.fsu.edu/

Fordham University, Gabelli School of Business, New York, NY 10023. Offers accounting (MBA, MS); applied statistics and decision-making (MS); business administration (EMBA); business analytics (MS); communications and media management (MBA); electronic business (MBA); entrepreneurship (MBA); finance (MBA); global finance (MS); global sustainability (MBA); healthcare management (MBA); information systems (MBA, MS); investor relations (MS); management (MBA, MS); marketing (MBA); marketing intelligence (MS); media management (MS); nonprofit leadership (MS); quantitative finance (MS); taxation (MS); JD/MBA; MS/MBA. *Accreditation:* AACSB. *Program availability:* Part-time, evening/weekend. *Faculty:* 132 full-time (44 women), 51 part-time/adjunct (7 women). *Students:* 1,117 full-time (668 women), 553 part-time (282 women); includes 207 minority (44 Black or African American, non-Hispanic/Latino; 92 Asian, non-Hispanic/Latino; 69 Hispanic/Latino; 2 Native Hawaiian or other Pacific Islander, non-Hispanic/Latino), 1,088 international. Average age 27. 4,745 applicants, 46% accepted, 752 enrolled. In 2016, 996 master's awarded. Terminal master's awarded for partial completion of doctoral program. *Degree requirements:* For master's, internships (required for MS in quantitative finance, recommended for MBA). *Entrance requirements:* For master's, GMAT/GRE, 2 letters of recommendation, resume, 2 essays, transcripts. Additional exam requirements/recommendations for international students: Required—TOEFL (minimum score 100 iBT), IELTS (minimum score 7). *Application deadline:* For fall admission, 11/15 priority date for domestic and international students; for winter admission, 1/15 priority date for domestic students, 1/1 priority date for international students; for spring admission, 3/1 for domestic and international students; for summer admission, 6/1 for domestic students. Application fee: $130. Electronic applications accepted. *Expenses:* $1,397 per credit. *Financial support:* In 2016–17, 78 students received support. Career-related internships or fieldwork, institutionally sponsored loans, scholarships/grants, and unspecified assistantships available. Support available to part-time students. Financial award application deadline: 6/30; financial award applicants required to submit FAFSA. *Unit head:* Dr. Donna Rapaccioli, Dean, 212-636-6165, Fax: 212-307-1779, E-mail: rapaccioli@fordham.edu. *Application contact:* Lawrence Murray, Senior Assistant Dean of Graduate Admissions and Advising, 212-636-6200, Fax: 212-636-7076, E-mail: admissionsgb@fordham.edu.
Website: http://www.fordham.edu/gabelli

Georgetown University, Law Center, Washington, DC 20001. Offers environmental law (LL M); global health law (LL M); global health law and international institutions (LL M); individualized study (LL M); international business and economic law (LL M); law (JD, SJD); national security law (LL M); securities and financial regulation (LL M); taxation (LL M); JD/LL M; JD/MA; JD/MBA; JD/MPH; JD/PhD. *Accreditation:* ABA. *Program availability:* Part-time, evening/weekend. *Degree requirements:* For master's, thesis; for doctorate, thesis/dissertation (for some programs). *Entrance requirements:* For master's, JD, LL B, or first law degree earned in country of origin; for doctorate, LSAT (for JD). Additional exam requirements/recommendations for international students: Required—TOEFL. *Expenses:* Contact institution. *Faculty research:* Constitutional law, legal history, jurisprudence.

Georgia Southern University, Jack N. Averitt College of Graduate Studies, College of Business Administration, Program in Accounting, Statesboro, GA 30460. Offers forensic accounting (M Acc); taxation (M Acc). *Accreditation:* AACSB. *Program availability:* Part-time, evening/weekend. *Students:* 46 full-time (25 women), 58 part-time (38 women); includes 29 minority (22 Black or African American, non-Hispanic/Latino; 1 Asian, non-Hispanic/Latino; 5 Hispanic/Latino; 1 Two or more races, non-Hispanic/Latino), 6 international. Average age 27. 60 applicants, 78% accepted, 39 enrolled. In 2016, 32 master's awarded. *Entrance requirements:* For master's, GMAT. Additional exam requirements/recommendations for international students: Required—TOEFL (minimum score 550 paper-based; 80 iBT), IELTS (minimum score 6). *Application deadline:* For fall admission, 3/1 priority date for domestic and international students; for spring admission, 10/1 priority date for domestic students, 10/1 for international students. Applications are processed on a rolling basis. Application fee: $50. Electronic applications accepted. *Expenses:* Contact institution. *Financial support:* In 2016–17, 21 students received support, including 1 research assistantship with full tuition reimbursement available (averaging $7,750 per year), 1 teaching assistantship with full tuition reimbursement available (averaging $7,750 per year); career-related internships or fieldwork, Federal Work-Study, scholarships/grants, tuition waivers (full), and unspecified assistantships also available. Support available to part-time students. Financial award application deadline: 4/15; financial award applicants required to submit FAFSA. *Faculty research:* Consolidation of fraud in the financial statement, reasons why firms switch auditions for the financial audit, internalization of accounting standards, pedagogy issues in accounting and law courses. *Unit head:* Dr. Timothy Pearson, Graduate Program Director, 912-478-0103, Fax: 912-478-0292, E-mail: tpearson@georgiasouthern.edu. *Application contact:* Jordan Wilburn, Coordinator for Graduate Student Recruitment, 912-478-5767, Fax: 912-478-0740, E-mail: macccoordinator@georgiasouthern.edu.
Website: http://coba.georgiasouthern.edu/soa/graduate/

Georgia State University, J. Mack Robinson College of Business, School of Accountancy, Program in Taxation, Atlanta, GA 30303. Offers M Tax, JD/M Tax. *Program availability:* Part-time, evening/weekend. *Entrance requirements:* For master's, GRE or GMAT, transcripts from all institutions attended, resume, essays. Additional exam requirements/recommendations for international students: Required—TOEFL (minimum score 610 paper-based; 101 iBT), IELTS (minimum score 7). *Application deadline:* For fall admission, 5/1 priority date for domestic students, 2/1 priority date for international students; for spring admission, 9/1 priority date for domestic students, 4/1 priority date for international students. Applications are processed on a rolling basis. Application fee: $50. Electronic applications accepted. *Expenses:* Tuition, state resident: full-time $6876; part-time $382 per credit hour. Tuition, nonresident: full-time $22,374; part-time $1243 per credit hour. *Required fees:* $2128; $1064 per term. Part-time tuition and fees vary according to course load and program. *Financial support:* Research assistantships, career-related internships or fieldwork, scholarships/grants, tuition waivers, and unspecified assistantships available. Financial award application deadline: 5/1. *Unit head:* Dr. Tad Ransopher, Director, 404-413-7229, Fax: 404-651-1033. *Application contact:* Toby McChesney, Assistant Dean for Graduate Recruiting and Student Services, 404-413-7167, Fax: 404-413-7162, E-mail: rcbgradadmissions@gsu.edu.
Website: http://robinson.gsu.edu/accountancy/mtx.html

Golden Gate University, School of Accounting, San Francisco, CA 94105-2968. Offers accounting (M Ac, MSA, Graduate Certificate); forensic accounting (M Ac, MSA, Graduate Certificate); taxation (M Ac). *Program availability:* Part-time, evening/weekend. *Faculty:* 4 full-time (1 woman), 46 part-time/adjunct (14 women). *Students:* 121 full-time (88 women), 135 part-time (77 women); includes 68 minority (5 Black or African American, non-Hispanic/Latino; 1 American Indian or Alaska Native, non-Hispanic/Latino; 40 Asian, non-Hispanic/Latino; 20 Hispanic/Latino; 1 Native Hawaiian or other Pacific Islander, non-Hispanic/Latino; 1 Two or more races, non-Hispanic/Latino), 107 international. Average age 32. 128 applicants, 71% accepted, 48 enrolled. In 2016, 80 master's awarded. *Entrance requirements:* For master's, minimum GPA of 3.0. Additional exam requirements/recommendations for international students: Required—TOEFL (minimum score 550 paper-based), IELTS (minimum score 6.5). *Application deadline:* For fall admission, 5/15 for international students; for winter admission, 1/15 for international students; for spring admission, 9/15 for international students. Applications are processed on a rolling basis. Application fee: $70 ($100 for international students). Electronic applications accepted. *Expenses:* Contact institution. *Financial support:* In 2016–17, 38 students received support. Career-related internships or fieldwork, Federal Work-Study, institutionally sponsored loans, and scholarships/grants available. Support available to part-time students. Financial award applicants required to submit FAFSA. *Faculty research:* Forensic accounting, audit, tax, CPA exam. *Unit head:* Fred Sroka, Dean, 415-369-5285, Fax: 415-543-2607. *Application contact:* Angela Melero, Enrollment Services, 415-442-7800, Fax: 415-442-7807, E-mail: info@ggu.edu.

Golden Gate University, School of Law, San Francisco, CA 94105-2968. Offers environmental law (LL M); estate planning (LL M); intellectual property law (LL M); international legal studies (LL M, SJD); law (JD); taxation (LL M); U.S. legal studies (LL M); JD/MBA; JD/PhD. *Accreditation:* ABA. *Program availability:* Part-time, evening/weekend. *Faculty:* 41 full-time (19 women), 67 part-time/adjunct (27 women). *Students:* 246 full-time (142 women), 228 part-time (133 women); includes 213 minority (28 Black or African American, non-Hispanic/Latino; 2 American Indian or Alaska Native, non-Hispanic/Latino; 68 Asian, non-Hispanic/Latino; 84 Hispanic/Latino; 7 Native Hawaiian or other Pacific Islander, non-Hispanic/Latino; 24 Two or more races, non-Hispanic/Latino), 58 international. Average age 31. 1,473 applicants, 65% accepted, 189 enrolled. In 2016, 54 master's, 117 doctorates awarded. *Degree requirements:* For doctorate, thesis/dissertation (for some programs). *Entrance requirements:* For doctorate, LSAT (for JD). Additional exam requirements/recommendations for international students: Required—TOEFL (minimum score 600 paper-based). *Application deadline:* For fall admission, 8/18 for domestic students, 4/1 for international students; for spring admission, 1/12 for domestic students; for summer admission, 6/4 for domestic students. Applications are processed on a rolling basis. Electronic applications accepted. *Expenses:* Contact institution. *Financial support:* In 2016–17, 315 students received support. Fellowships, research assistantships, teaching assistantships, career-related internships or fieldwork, Federal Work-Study, institutionally sponsored loans, scholarships/grants, tuition waivers (full and partial), and unspecified assistantships available. Support available to part-time students. Financial award applicants required to submit FAFSA. *Faculty research:* International law, intellectual property law, environmental law, real estate, civil rights. *Unit head:* Rachel Van Cleave, Dean, 415-442-6601, Fax: 415-442-6609. *Application contact:* Greg Egertson, Associate Dean and Director of Admissions, 415-442-6636, Fax: 415-442-6609, E-mail: lawadmit@ggu.edu.
Website: http://www.ggu.edu/law/

Golden Gate University, School of Taxation, San Francisco, CA 94105-2968. Offers advanced studies in taxation (Certificate); estate planning (Certificate); financial planning and taxation (MS); international tax (Certificate); state and local taxation (Certificate); tax (Certificate); taxation (MS). *Program availability:* Part-time, evening/weekend. *Faculty:* 7 full-time (1 woman), 65 part-time/adjunct (19 women). *Students:* 72 full-time (44 women), 539 part-time (281 women); includes 156 minority (17 Black or African American, non-Hispanic/Latino; 3 American Indian or Alaska Native, non-Hispanic/Latino; 100 Asian, non-Hispanic/Latino; 23 Hispanic/Latino; 7 Native Hawaiian or other Pacific Islander, non-Hispanic/Latino; 6 Two or more races, non-Hispanic/Latino), 82 international. Average age 36. 252 applicants, 84% accepted, 105 enrolled. In 2016, 193 master's awarded. *Entrance requirements:* For master's, minimum GPA of 3.0. Additional exam requirements/recommendations for international students: Required—TOEFL (minimum score 550 paper-based), IELTS (minimum score 6.5). *Application deadline:* For fall admission, 5/15 for international students; for winter admission, 1/15 for international students; for spring admission, 9/15 for international students. Applications are processed on a rolling basis. Application fee: $70 ($100 for international students). Electronic applications accepted. *Expenses:* Contact institution. *Financial support:* In 2016–17, 66 students received support. Career-related internships or fieldwork, Federal Work-Study, institutionally sponsored loans, and scholarships/grants available. Support available to part-time students. Financial award applicants required to submit FAFSA. *Unit head:* Fred Sroka, Dean, 415-369-5285, Fax: 415-442-7807. *Application contact:* Angela Melero, Enrollment Services, 415-442-7800, Fax: 415-442-7807, E-mail: info@ggu.edu.
Website: http://www.ggu.edu/programs/taxation/master-of-science-in-taxation

Goldey-Beacom College, Graduate Program, Wilmington, DE 19808-1999. Offers business administration (MBA); finance (MS); financial management (MBA); health care management (MBA); human resource management (MBA); information technology (MBA); international business management (MBA); major finance (MBA); major taxation (MBA); management (MM); marketing management (MBA); taxation (MBA, MS). *Accreditation:* ACBSP. *Program availability:* Part-time, evening/weekend. *Entrance requirements:* For master's, GMAT, MAT, GRE, minimum GPA of 3.0. Additional exam requirements/recommendations for international students: Required—TOEFL (minimum score 65 iBT); Recommended—IELTS (minimum score 6). Electronic applications accepted.

Gonzaga University, School of Business Administration, Spokane, WA 99258. Offers accountancy (M Acc); American Indian entrepreneurship (MBA); business administration (MBA); taxation (MS); JD/M Acc; JD/MBA. *Accreditation:* AACSB. *Program availability:* Part-time, evening/weekend. *Faculty:* 17 full-time (4 women), 14 part-time/adjunct (2 women). *Students:* 80 full-time (32 women), 135 part-time (60 women); includes 37 minority (2 Black or African American, non-Hispanic/Latino; 10 American Indian or Alaska Native, non-Hispanic/Latino; 5 Asian, non-Hispanic/Latino; 10 Hispanic/Latino; 10 Two or more races, non-Hispanic/Latino), 14 international. Average age 29. 252 applicants, 131 enrolled. In 2016, 113 master's awarded. *Degree requirements:* For master's, capstone course. *Entrance requirements:* For master's, GMAT (minimum score 500), essay, two professional recommendations, resume/curriculum vitae, copy of official transcripts from all colleges attended, minimum GPA of 3.0. Additional exam requirements/recommendations for international students: Required—TOEFL (minimum score 570 paper-based, 89 iBT) or IELTS (minimum score 6.5). *Application deadline:* Applications are processed on a rolling basis. Application fee: $50. Electronic applications accepted. *Expenses:* $975 per credit. *Financial support:* In 2016–17, 134 students received support. Scholarships/grants, tuition waivers, and unspecified assistantships available. Support available to part-time students. Financial award applicants required to submit FAFSA. *Unit head:* Dr. Ken Anderson, Interim Dean, 509-313-5991, E-mail: anderson@gem.gonzaga.edu. *Application contact:* Stacey Chatman, Assistant Director for Admissions, 509-313-4622, E-mail: chatman@gonzaga.edu.
Website: http://www.gonzaga.edu/Academics/Colleges-and-Schools/School-of-Business-Administration

Grand Valley State University, Seidman College of Business, Program in Taxation, Allendale, MI 49401-9403. Offers MST. *Program availability:* Part-time, evening/weekend. *Students:* 2 full-time (1 woman), 19 part-time (10 women); includes 1 minority (Black or African American, non-Hispanic/Latino), 1 international. Average age 29. 6 applicants, 100% accepted, 5 enrolled. In 2016, 9 master's awarded. *Degree requirements:* For master's, capstone course. *Entrance requirements:* For master's, GMAT, personal statement. Additional exam requirements/recommendations for international students: Required—TOEFL. *Application deadline:* For fall admission, 8/1 priority date for domestic students, 5/1 priority date for international students; for winter admission, 12/1 priority date for domestic students, 11/1 priority date for international students; for spring admission, 4/1 priority date for domestic students, 3/1 priority date for international students. Applications are processed on a rolling basis. Application fee: $30. Electronic applications accepted. *Expenses:* $646 per credit hour. *Financial support:* In 2016–17, 1 student received support, including 1 fellowship; Federal Work-Study, institutionally sponsored loans, and unspecified assistantships also available. Financial award application deadline: 2/15. *Faculty research:* Individual income taxation, state taxation, pass-through entities, estate and gift taxation, sale-leasebacks. *Unit head:* Dr. Steve` Goldberg, Director, 616-331-7410, Fax: 616-331-7412, E-mail: goldbers@gvsu.edu. *Application contact:* Koleta Moore, Assistant Director, Graduate Business Programs, 616-331-7386, Fax: 616-331-7389, E-mail: moorekol@gvsu.edu.
Website: http://www.gvsu.edu/business/

HEC Montreal, School of Business Administration, Graduate Diploma Programs in Administration, Program in Taxation, Montréal, QC H3T 2A7, Canada. Offers Graduate Diploma. All courses are given in French. *Students:* 40 full-time (15 women), 67 part-time (35 women). 66 applicants, 55% accepted, 28 enrolled. In 2016, 42 Graduate Diplomas awarded. *Degree requirements:* For Graduate Diploma, one foreign language. *Entrance requirements:* For degree, bachelor's diploma in law, accounting, or economics. *Application deadline:* For fall admission, 3/15 for domestic and international students; for winter admission, 9/15 for domestic and international students. Application fee: $86 Canadian dollars. Electronic applications accepted. *Expenses: Tuition, area resident:* Part-time $77.80 Canadian dollars per credit. Tuition, state resident: full-time $2797 Canadian dollars; part-time $240.92 Canadian dollars per credit. Tuition, nonresident: full-time $8673 Canadian dollars; part-time $531.43 Canadian dollars per credit. *International tuition:* $19,131 Canadian dollars full-time. *Required fees:* $1699 Canadian dollars; $40.58 Canadian dollars per credit. $67.32 Canadian dollars per term. Tuition and fees vary according to degree level and program. *Financial support:* In 2016–17, 814 students received support. Research assistantships, teaching assistantships, and scholarships/grants available. Financial award application deadline: 9/2. *Unit head:* Renaud Lachance, Director, 514-340-7165, E-mail: renaud.lachance@hec.ca. *Application contact:* Anny Caron, Administrative Director, 514-340-3598, Fax: 514-340-6411, E-mail: anny.caron@hec.ca.
Website: http://www.hec.ca/programmes/dess/dess-fiscalite/index.html

HEC Montreal, School of Business Administration, Master of Laws in Taxation Program, Montréal, QC H3T 2A7, Canada. Offers LL M. All courses are given in English. *Students:* 11 full-time (5 women), 23 part-time (10 women). In 2016, 27 master's awarded. *Degree requirements:* For master's, one foreign language. *Entrance requirements:* For master's, bachelor's degree in taxation. Application fee: $86. Electronic applications accepted. *Expenses: Tuition, area resident:* Part-time $77.80 Canadian dollars per credit. Tuition, state resident: full-time $2797 Canadian dollars; part-time $240.92 Canadian dollars per credit. Tuition, nonresident: full-time $8673 Canadian dollars; part-time $531.43 Canadian dollars per credit. *International tuition:*

$19,131 Canadian dollars full-time. *Required fees:* $1699 Canadian dollars; $40.58 Canadian dollars per credit. $67.32 Canadian dollars per term. Tuition and fees vary according to degree level and program. *Financial support:* Research assistantships, teaching assistantships, and scholarships/grants available. Financial award application deadline: 9/2. *Unit head:* Dr. Marie-Helene Jobin, Director, 514-340-6283, E-mail: marie-helene.jobin@hec.ca. *Application contact:* Anny Caron, Administrative Director, 514-340-3598, Fax: 514-340-6411, E-mail: anny.caron@hec.ca.
Website: http://www.hec.ca/programmes/maitrises/maitrise-droit-llm-fiscalite/index.html

Hofstra University, Frank G. Zarb School of Business, Programs in Accounting and Taxation, Hempstead, NY 11549. Offers accounting (MS, Advanced Certificate); business administration (MBA), including accounting, professional accountancy, taxation; taxation (MS, Advanced Certificate). *Program availability:* Part-time, evening/weekend, blended/hybrid learning. *Students:* 177 full-time (100 women), 36 part-time (17 women); includes 23 minority (4 Black or African American, non-Hispanic/Latino; 1 American Indian or Alaska Native, non-Hispanic/Latino; 6 Asian, non-Hispanic/Latino; 9 Hispanic/Latino; 3 Two or more races, non-Hispanic/Latino), 123 international. Average age 25. 437 applicants, 76% accepted, 104 enrolled. In 2016, 133 master's awarded. *Degree requirements:* For master's, capstone course (for MBA), thesis (for MS), minimum GPA of 3.0. *Entrance requirements:* For master's, GMAT/GRE, 2 letters of recommendation, resume, essay. Additional exam requirements/recommendations for international students: Required—TOEFL (minimum score 550 paper-based; 80 iBT); Recommended—IELTS (minimum score 6). *Application deadline:* Applications are processed on a rolling basis. Application fee: $75. Electronic applications accepted. *Expenses:* $1,170 per credit. *Financial support:* In 2016–17, 64 students received support, including 59 fellowships with full and partial tuition reimbursements available (averaging $4,967 per year), 1 research assistantship with full and partial tuition reimbursement available (averaging $5,800 per year); career-related internships or fieldwork, Federal Work-Study, institutionally sponsored loans, scholarships/grants, tuition waivers (full and partial), and unspecified assistantships also available. Support available to part-time students. Financial award applicants required to submit FAFSA. *Faculty research:* Gender discrimination and professional women; auditor-client interaction in accounting; accounting in prisons; the Fourth Amendment and privacy. *Unit head:* Dr. Martha Weisel, Chairperson, 516-463-5655, E-mail: martha.s.weisel@hofstra.edu. *Application contact:* Sunil Samuel, Assistant Vice President of Admissions, 516-463-4723, Fax: 516-463-4664, E-mail: graduateadmission@hofstra.edu.
Website: http://www.hofstra.edu/business/

Illinois Institute of Technology, Chicago-Kent College of Law, Chicago, IL 60661-3691. Offers family law (LL M); financial services law (LL M); international intellectual property law (LL M); law (JD); legal studies (JSD); taxation (LL M); U.S., international, and transnational law (LL M); JD/LL M; JD/MBA; JD/MPA; JD/MPH; JD/MS. *Accreditation:* ABA. *Program availability:* Part-time, evening/weekend. Terminal master's awarded for partial completion of doctoral program. *Entrance requirements:* For master's, 1st degree in law or certified license to practice law; for doctorate, LSAT. Additional exam requirements/recommendations for international students: Required—TOEFL (minimum score 600 paper-based; 100 iBT); Recommended—IELTS (minimum score 7). Electronic applications accepted. *Expenses:* Contact institution. *Faculty research:* Constitutional law, bioethics, environmental law, intellectual property.

Instituto Tecnologico de Santo Domingo, Graduate School, Area of Business, Santo Domingo, Dominican Republic. Offers banking and securities markets (M Mgmt); corporate finance (M Mgmt); human resources management (M Mgmt, Certificate); international trade management (M Mgmt); marketing (M Mgmt); organizational development (M Mgmt); quality and productivity management (Certificate); tax management and planning (M Mgmt); upper management (M Mgmt).

James Madison University, The Graduate School, College of Business, Program in Accounting, Harrisonburg, VA 22807. Offers accounting information systems (MS); taxation (MS). *Accreditation:* AACSB. *Program availability:* Part-time, evening/weekend. *Students:* 67 full-time (27 women); includes 5 minority (1 Black or African American, non-Hispanic/Latino; 1 Asian, non-Hispanic/Latino; 1 Hispanic/Latino; 2 Two or more races, non-Hispanic/Latino), 1 international. Average age 30. 91 applicants, 80% accepted, 60 enrolled. In 2016, 72 master's awarded. Application fee: $55. Electronic applications accepted. *Financial support:* In 2016–17, 23 students received support. Federal Work-Study and 23 assistantships (averaging $6911) available. Financial award application deadline: 3/1; financial award applicants required to submit FAFSA. *Unit head:* Dr. Tim J. Louwers, Director of the School of Accounting, 540-568-3027, E-mail: louwertj@jmu.edu. *Application contact:* Lynette D. Michael, Director of Graduate Admissions, 540-568-6131 Ext. 6395, Fax: 540-568-7860, E-mail: michaeld@jmu.edu.
Website: https://www.jmu.edu/cob/accounting/masters/index.shtml

Long Island University–LIU Brooklyn, School of Business, Public Administration and Information Sciences, Brooklyn, NY 11201-8423. Offers accounting (MBA); accounting (MS); business administration (MBA); computer science (MS); gerontology (Advanced Certificate); health administration (MPA); human resources management (MS); not-for-profit management (Advanced Certificate); public administration (MPA); taxation (MS). *Program availability:* Part-time, evening/weekend, blended/hybrid learning. *Faculty:* 18 full-time (9 women), 32 part-time/adjunct (10 women). *Students:* 275 full-time (150 women), 238 part-time (161 women); includes 281 minority (200 Black or African American, non-Hispanic/Latino; 2 American Indian or Alaska Native, non-Hispanic/Latino; 38 Asian, non-Hispanic/Latino; 36 Hispanic/Latino; 1 Native Hawaiian or other Pacific Islander, non-Hispanic/Latino; 4 Two or more races, non-Hispanic/Latino), 140 international. 796 applicants, 66% accepted, 143 enrolled. In 2016, 185 master's, 17 other advanced degrees awarded. *Entrance requirements:* Additional exam requirements/recommendations for international students: Required—TOEFL (minimum score 527 paper-based; 75 iBT). *Application deadline:* Applications are processed on a rolling basis. Application fee: $50. Electronic applications accepted. *Expenses: Tuition:* Full-time $28,272; part-time $1178 per credit. *Required fees:* $451 per term. Tuition and fees vary according to degree level, program and student level. *Financial support:* In 2016–17, 94 students received support. Career-related internships or fieldwork, Federal Work-Study, institutionally sponsored loans, scholarships/grants, and unspecified assistantships available. Support available to part-time students. Financial award application deadline: 2/15; financial award applicants required to submit FAFSA. *Faculty research:* Corporate social responsibility; executive compensation and corporate governance; combinatorics; secure mobile coding; social equity and justice, particularly among the Latino population; public and healthcare finance. *Unit head:* Dr. Edward Rogoff, Dean, 718-488-1159, E-mail: edward.rogoff@liu.edu. *Application contact:* Gabrielle Gannon, Director of Graduate Admissions, 718-488-1011, Fax: 718-780-6110, E-mail: bkln-admissions@liu.edu.
Website: http://liu.edu/Brooklyn/Academics/School-of-Business-Public-Administration-and-Information-Sciences

Long Island University–LIU Post, College of Management, Brookville, NY 11548-1300. Offers accountancy (MS); finance (MBA); information systems (MS); international business (MBA); management (MBA); management engineering (MS); marketing (MBA); taxation (MS); technical project management (MS); JD/MBA. *Accreditation:* AACSB. *Program availability:* Part-time, 100% online, blended/hybrid learning. *Faculty:* 35 full-time (12 women), 25 part-time/adjunct (6 women). *Students:* 153 full-time (61 women), 68 part-time (22 women); includes 44 minority (8 Black or African American, non-Hispanic/Latino; 24 Asian, non-Hispanic/Latino; 11 Hispanic/Latino; 1 Two or more races, non-Hispanic/Latino), 79 international. 429 applicants, 58% accepted, 74 enrolled. In 2016, 124 master's awarded. *Degree requirements:* For master's, thesis (for some programs). *Entrance requirements:* For master's, GMAT, GRE, or LSAT. Additional exam requirements/recommendations for international students: Required—PTE, TOEFL (minimum score 550 paper-based, 75 iBT) or IELTS. *Application deadline:* Applications are processed on a rolling basis. Application fee: $50. Electronic applications accepted. *Expenses: Tuition:* Full-time $28,272; part-time $1178 per credit. *Required fees:* $451 per term. Tuition and fees vary according to degree level and program. *Financial support:* In 2016–17, 68 students received support. Career-related internships or fieldwork, Federal Work-Study, institutionally sponsored loans, and scholarships/grants available. Support available to part-time students. Financial award application deadline: 2/15; financial award applicants required to submit FAFSA. *Faculty research:* Finance and sustainability, innovation and intellectual property rights, marketing: data analytics and business intelligence, social networking local and international. *Unit head:* Dr. Robert M. Valli, Dean, 516-299-4192, E-mail: rob.valli@liu.edu. *Application contact:* Carol Zerah, Director of Graduate and International Admissions, 516-299-2900, Fax: 516-299-2137, E-mail: post-enroll@liu.edu.
Website: http://liu.edu/CWPost/Academics/Schools/COM

Metropolitan State University of Denver, School of Business, Denver, CO 80204. Offers accounting (MP Acc); fraud exam and forensic auditing (MP Acc); internal audit (MP Acc); public accounting (MP Acc); taxation (MP Acc). *Accreditation:* AACSB. *Faculty:* 11 full-time (2 women), 1 (woman) part-time/adjunct. *Students:* 76 full-time (41 women), 36 part-time (16 women); includes 22 minority (4 Black or African American, non-Hispanic/Latino; 1 American Indian or Alaska Native, non-Hispanic/Latino; 11 Asian, non-Hispanic/Latino; 6 Hispanic/Latino). Average age 34. In 2016, 38 master's awarded. *Entrance requirements:* For master's, GMAT. *Application deadline:* For fall admission, 6/5 for domestic and international students; for spring admission, 10/2 for domestic and international students. Application fee: $50. *Expenses:* $8,220.60 full-time residents, $997.40 per credit hour part-time residents, $17,953.20 full-time non-residents. *Unit head:* Ann Murphy, Dean, 303-556-4695, E-mail: murphann@msudenver.edu. *Application contact:* Kim Bernie, Graduate Student Outreach, CBUS Graduate Programs, 303-556-5161, E-mail: kbernie1@msudenver.edu.
Website: http://www.msudenver.edu/business/

Michigan State University, The Graduate School, Eli Broad College of Business, Department of Accounting and Information Systems, East Lansing, MI 48224. Offers accounting (MS, PhD), including information systems (MS), public and corporate accounting (MS), taxation (MS); business information systems (PhD). *Accreditation:* AACSB. *Degree requirements:* For doctorate, comprehensive exam, thesis/dissertation. *Entrance requirements:* For master's, GMAT (minimum score 550), bachelor's degree in accounting; minimum cumulative GPA of 3.0 at any institution attended and in any junior-/senior-level accounting courses taken; 3 letters of recommendation (at least 1 from faculty); working knowledge of computers including word processing, spreadsheets, networking, and database management system; for doctorate, GMAT (minimum score 600), bachelor's degree; transcripts; 3 letters of recommendation; statement of purpose; resume; on-campus interview; personal qualifications of sound character, perseverance, intellectual curiosity, and interest in scholarly research. Additional exam requirements/recommendations for international students: Required—TOEFL (minimum score 600 paper-based; 100 iBT), IELTS (minimum score 7) accepted for MS only. Electronic applications accepted.

Mississippi State University, College of Business, Adkerson School of Accountancy, Mississippi State, MS 39762. Offers accountancy (MPA, MTX); systems (MPA). *Accreditation:* AACSB. *Faculty:* 10 full-time (2 women). *Students:* 49 full-time (23 women), 1 (woman) part-time; includes 1 minority (Asian, non-Hispanic/Latino), 3 international. Average age 23. 37 applicants, 54% accepted, 18 enrolled. In 2016, 39 master's awarded. *Degree requirements:* For master's, comprehensive exam. *Entrance requirements:* For master's, GMAT (minimum score of 510), minimum GPA of 3.0 over last 60 hours of undergraduate course work. Additional exam requirements/recommendations for international students: Required—TOEFL (minimum score 575 paper-based; 84 iBT); Recommended—IELTS (minimum score 7). *Application deadline:* For fall admission, 7/1 for domestic students, 5/1 for international students; for spring admission, 11/1 for domestic students, 9/1 for international students. Applications are processed on a rolling basis. Application fee: $60. Electronic applications accepted. *Expenses:* Tuition, state resident: full-time $7670; part-time $852.50 per credit hour. Tuition, nonresident: full-time $20,790; part-time $2310.50 per credit hour. Part-time tuition and fees vary according to course load. *Financial support:* Career-related internships or fieldwork, Federal Work-Study, institutionally sponsored loans, scholarships/grants, and unspecified assistantships available. Support available to part-time students. Financial award application deadline: 4/1; financial award applicants required to submit FAFSA. *Faculty research:* Income tax, financial accounting system, managerial accounting, auditing. *Unit head:* Dr. Shawn Mauldin, Director and Professor, 662-325-3710, Fax: 662-325-1646, E-mail: smauldin@business.msstate.edu. *Application contact:* Lakan Drinker, Admissions and Enrollment Assistant, 662-325-8951, E-mail: ldrinker@grad.msstate.edu.
Website: http://www.business.msstate.edu/programs/adkerson

National Paralegal College, Graduate Programs, Phoenix, AZ 85014. Offers compliance law (MS); legal studies (MS); taxation (MS). *Program availability:* Part-time. Electronic applications accepted.

New York University, School of Law, New York, NY 10012-1019. Offers law (LL M, JD, JSD); law and business (Advanced Certificate); taxation (MSL, Advanced Certificate); JD/JD; JD/LL B; JD/LL M; JD/MA; JD/MBA; JD/MPA; JD/MPP; JD/MSW; JD/MUP; JD/PhD. *Accreditation:* ABA. *Program availability:* Part-time, online learning. *Entrance requirements:* For doctorate, LSAT (for JD). Electronic applications accepted. *Expenses:* Contact institution. *Faculty research:* International law, environmental law, corporate law, globalization of law, philosophy of law.

Northeastern University, D'Amore-McKim School of Business, Boston, MA 02115-5096. Offers accounting (MS); business administration (EMBA, MBA); finance (MS); innovation (MS); international business (MS); international management (MS); taxation (MS); technological entrepreneurship (MS); JD/MBA; LL M/MBA; MBA/MSN; MS/MBA. *Accreditation:* AACSB. *Program availability:* Part-time, evening/weekend, online learning. *Faculty:* 185 full-time (66 women), 57 part-time/adjunct (13 women). *Students:* 379 full-time (180 women), 1,182 part-time (514 women). In 2016, 800 master's awarded. *Entrance requirements:* For master's, GMAT or GRE. Application fee: $75. Electronic applications accepted. *Expenses:* Contact institution. *Financial support:* Scholarships/grants available. Financial award applicants required to submit FAFSA. *Unit head:* Dr. Hugh Courtney, Dean, D'Amore-McKim School of Business. *Application contact:* Evelyn Tate, Director, Graduate Recruitment and Admissions, 617-373-3258, Fax: 617-373-8564, E-mail: e.tate@northeastern.edu.
Website: http://damore-mckim.northeastern.edu/

Northern Illinois University, Graduate School, College of Business, Department of Accountancy, De Kalb, IL 60115-2854. Offers MAS, MST. *Accreditation:* AACSB. *Program availability:* Part-time, evening/weekend. *Faculty:* 14 full-time (4 women).

Students: 130 full-time (58 women), 80 part-time (42 women); includes 56 minority (10 Black or African American, non-Hispanic/Latino; 25 Asian, non-Hispanic/Latino; 19 Hispanic/Latino; 2 Two or more races, non-Hispanic/Latino), 31 international. Average age 29. 141 applicants, 72% accepted, 63 enrolled. In 2016, 121 master's awarded. *Degree requirements:* For master's, thesis optional. *Entrance requirements:* For master's, GMAT, minimum GPA of 2.75. Additional exam requirements/recommendations for international students: Required—TOEFL (minimum score 550 paper-based). *Application deadline:* For fall admission, 4/1 priority date for domestic students, 5/1 for international students; for spring admission, 9/15 priority date for domestic students, 10/1 for international students. Applications are processed on a rolling basis. Application fee: $40. Electronic applications accepted. *Financial support:* In 2016–17, 31 research assistantships with full tuition reimbursements, 9 teaching assistantships with full tuition reimbursements were awarded; fellowships with full tuition reimbursements, career-related internships or fieldwork, Federal Work-Study, scholarships/grants, tuition waivers (full), and unspecified assistantships also available. Support available to part-time students. Financial award applicants required to submit FAFSA. *Faculty research:* Accounting fraud, governmental accounting, corporate income tax planning, auditing, ethics. *Unit head:* Rebecca Shortridge, Chair, 815-753-1250, Fax: 815-753-8515. *Application contact:* Graduate Advising, 815-753-1325, E-mail: cobadvising@niu.edu.
Website: http://www.cob.niu.edu/accy/

Northern Kentucky University, Office of Graduate Programs, College of Business, Program in Accountancy, Highland Heights, KY 41099. Offers accountancy (M Acc); advanced taxation (Certificate). *Program availability:* Part-time, evening/weekend. *Degree requirements:* For master's, capstone course. *Entrance requirements:* For master's, GMAT, master's degree, MD, or PhD, official transcripts, current resume, 3 years of work experience (strongly suggested), statement of purpose. Additional exam requirements/recommendations for international students: Required—TOEFL (minimum score 79 iBT); Recommended—IELTS (minimum score 6.5). Electronic applications accepted. *Faculty research:* Ethics, accounting history, financial reporting.

Northwestern University, Pritzker School of Law, Chicago, IL 60611-3069. Offers international human rights (LL M); law (JD); law and business (LL M); science law (MSL); tax (LL M in Tax); JD/LL M; JD/MBA; JD/PhD; LL M/Certificate. Executive LL M programs offered in Madrid (Spain), Seoul (South Korea), and Tel Aviv (Israel). *Accreditation:* ABA. *Entrance requirements:* For master's, law degree or equivalent, letter of recommendation, resume; for doctorate, LSAT, 1 letter of recommendation, resume. Additional exam requirements/recommendations for international students: Required—TOEFL. Electronic applications accepted. *Expenses:* Contact institution. *Faculty research:* Constitutional law, corporate law, international law, law and social policy, ethical studies.

Nova Southeastern University, H. Wayne Huizenga College of Business and Entrepreneurship, Fort Lauderdale, FL 33314-7796. Offers accounting (M Acc); business intelligence/analytics (MBA); entrepreneurship (MBA); finance (MBA); human resource management (MBA); international business (MBA); management (MBA); marketing (MBA); process improvement (MBA); public administration (MPA); real estate development (MS); sport revenue generation (MBA); supply chain management (MBA); taxation (M Tax). *Program availability:* Part-time, evening/weekend, 100% online, blended/hybrid learning. *Faculty:* 65 full-time (26 women), 111 part-time/adjunct (74 women). *Students:* 2,242 full-time (1,400 women), 425 part-time (239 women); includes 1,798 minority (734 Black or African American, non-Hispanic/Latino; 5 American Indian or Alaska Native, non-Hispanic/Latino; 110 Asian, non-Hispanic/Latino; 890 Hispanic/Latino; 2 Native Hawaiian or other Pacific Islander, non-Hispanic/Latino; 57 Two or more races, non-Hispanic/Latino), 255 international. Average age 34. 1,422 applicants, 64% accepted, 672 enrolled. In 2016, 971 master's awarded. *Degree requirements:* For master's, thesis optional. *Entrance requirements:* For master's, GMAT or GRE (depending on undergraduate GPA), official transcripts from all schools attended while in pursuit of bachelor's degree; minimum GPA of 2.5 from regionally-accredited institution. Additional exam requirements/recommendations for international students: Required—TOEFL (minimum score 550 paper-based; 79 iBT), IELTS (minimum score 6), PTE (minimum score 54). *Application deadline:* For fall admission, 8/5 priority date for domestic students, 7/29 priority date for international students; for winter admission, 12/16 priority date for domestic students, 12/9 priority date for international students; for summer admission, 4/21 priority date for domestic and international students. Applications are processed on a rolling basis. Application fee: $50. Electronic applications accepted. *Expenses:* Contact institution. *Financial support:* In 2016–17, 325 students received support. Federal Work-Study and scholarships/grants available. Support available to part-time students. Financial award application deadline: 4/15; financial award applicants required to submit FAFSA. *Faculty research:* Reputation management, call centers, international social capital, corporate earnings guidance, corporate governance. *Unit head:* Dr. J. Preston Jones, Dean, 954-262-5127, E-mail: prestonj@nova.edu. *Application contact:* Zeida Rodriguez, Associate Director of Enrollment Services, 954-262-5163, Fax: 954-262-3822, E-mail: zeida@nova.edu.
Website: http://www.huizenga.nova.edu

Pace University, Lubin School of Business, Taxation Program, New York, NY 10038. Offers taxation (MBA, MS). *Program availability:* Part-time, evening/weekend. *Students:* 31 full-time (20 women), 30 part-time (13 women); includes 43 minority (3 Black or African American, non-Hispanic/Latino; 11 American Indian or Alaska Native, non-Hispanic/Latino; 19 Asian, non-Hispanic/Latino; 7 Hispanic/Latino; 3 Two or more races, non-Hispanic/Latino), 10 international. 30 applicants, 93% accepted, 14 enrolled. In 2016, 27 master's awarded. *Entrance requirements:* For master's, GMAT or GRE (waived for anyone who has passed the CPA), undergraduate degree, transcripts from all accredited colleges/universities attended, two letters of recommendation, resume, personal statement. Additional exam requirements/recommendations for international students: Required—TOEFL (minimum score 90 iBT), IELTS (minimum score 7) or PTE (minimum score 61). *Application deadline:* For fall admission, 8/1 priority date for domestic students, 6/1 for international students; for spring admission, 12/1 for domestic students, 10/1 for international students. Applications are processed on a rolling basis. Application fee: $70. Electronic applications accepted. *Expenses: Tuition:* Part-time $1195 per credit. *Required fees:* $260 per semester. Tuition and fees vary according to degree level, campus/location and program. *Financial support:* Research assistantships, career-related internships or fieldwork, and Federal Work-Study available. Support available to part-time students. Financial award application deadline: 2/15; financial award applicants required to submit FAFSA. *Unit head:* Dr. Walter G. Antognini, Chairperson, Legal Studies and Taxation Department, 212-618-6480, E-mail: wantognini@pace.edu. *Application contact:* Susan Ford-Goldschein, Director of Graduate Admissions, 212-346-1531, Fax: 212-346-1585, E-mail: graduateadmission@pace.edu.
Website: http://www.pace.edu/lubin/lubin-academic-programs/graduate-programs

Philadelphia University, School of Business Administration, Program in Taxation, Philadelphia, PA 19144. Offers MS. *Program availability:* Part-time, evening/weekend. *Entrance requirements:* For master's, GMAT. Additional exam requirements/recommendations for international students: Required—TOEFL (minimum score 550 paper-based; 79 iBT). Electronic applications accepted.

Robert Morris University, School of Business, Moon Township, PA 15108-1189. Offers business administration (MBA); human resource management (MS); taxation (MS); MBA/MS. *Accreditation:* AACSB. *Program availability:* Part-time-only, evening/weekend, 100% online. *Faculty:* 24 full-time (8 women), 4 part-time/adjunct (3 women). *Students:* 148 part-time (64 women); includes 9 minority (3 Black or African American, non-Hispanic/Latino; 6 Asian, non-Hispanic/Latino), 1 international. Average age 27. 147 applicants, 23% accepted, 32 enrolled. In 2016, 96 master's awarded. *Entrance requirements:* For master's, GMAT, letters of recommendation. Additional exam requirements/recommendations for international students: Required—TOEFL (minimum score 550 paper-based; 79 iBT). *Application deadline:* For fall admission, 7/1 priority date for domestic and international students; for spring admission, 11/1 priority date for domestic and international students. Applications are processed on a rolling basis. Application fee: $35. Electronic applications accepted. Application fee is waived when completed online. *Expenses:* $925 per credit. *Financial support:* Institutionally sponsored loans available. Support available to part-time students. Financial award application deadline: 5/1; financial award applicants required to submit FAFSA. *Unit head:* Dr. Michelle L. Patrick, Dean, 412-397-5445, Fax: 412-397-2585, E-mail: patrick@rmu.edu. *Application contact:* E-mail: graduateadmissions@rmu.edu.
Website: http://sbus.rmu.edu

St. John's University, The Peter J. Tobin College of Business, Department of Accounting and Taxation, Program in Taxation, Queens, NY 11439. Offers MBA, MS. *Program availability:* Part-time, evening/weekend, online learning. *Degree requirements:* For master's, comprehensive exam (for some programs), thesis optional. *Entrance requirements:* For master's, GMAT (waived for MS applicants who have successfully completed the CPA exam), 2 letters of recommendation, resume, transcripts, statement of goals, bachelor's degree in accounting. Additional exam requirements/recommendations for international students: Required—TOEFL (minimum score 600 paper-based; 100 iBT), IELTS (minimum score 7). Electronic applications accepted. *Expenses:* Contact institution.

St. Thomas University, School of Law, Miami Gardens, FL 33054-6459. Offers international human rights (LL M); international taxation (LL M); law (JD); JD/MBA; JD/MS. *Accreditation:* ABA. *Program availability:* Online learning. *Degree requirements:* For master's, thesis (international taxation). *Entrance requirements:* For doctorate, LSAT. Electronic applications accepted. *Expenses:* Contact institution.

San Jose State University, Graduate Studies and Research, Lucas Graduate School of Business, San Jose, CA 95192-0001. Offers accountancy (MS); business administration (MBA); taxation (MS); transportation management (MS). *Program availability:* Part-time, evening/weekend, online learning. *Degree requirements:* For master's, comprehensive exam, thesis or alternative. *Entrance requirements:* For master's, GMAT, minimum GPA of 3.0. Electronic applications accepted.

Seton Hall University, Stillman School of Business, Department of Accounting, South Orange, NJ 07079-2697. Offers accounting (MS, Certificate); CPA (Certificate); professional accounting (MS); taxation (Certificate). *Program availability:* Part-time, evening/weekend. *Entrance requirements:* For master's, GMAT or GRE (waived based on work experience), MS in a business discipline, professional degree (MD, JD, PhD, DVM, DDS, CPA, etc.), minimum undergraduate GPA of 3.0. Additional exam requirements/recommendations for international students: Required—TOEFL (minimum score 607 paper-based; 102 iBT), IELTS (minimum score 6), PTE. Electronic applications accepted. *Expenses:* Contact institution. *Faculty research:* Nonfinancial metrics, pension accounting, integrated reporting, multinational enterprises.

Seton Hall University, Stillman School of Business, Department of Taxation, South Orange, NJ 07079-2697. Offers Certificate. *Program availability:* Part-time, evening/weekend, blended/hybrid learning. *Entrance requirements:* For degree, GMAT or GRE (waived based on work experience or advanced degree from AACSB institution), MS in a business discipline, professional degree (MD, JD, PhD, DVM, DDS, CPA, etc.), minimum undergraduate GPA of 3.0. Additional exam requirements/recommendations for international students: Required—TOEFL (minimum score 607 paper-based; 102 iBT), IELTS (minimum score 6), PTE. Electronic applications accepted. *Expenses:* Contact institution. *Faculty research:* Third-party settled trusts, family partnership, estate valuation discounts, remainder purchase, marital trusts, offshore asset protection trusts.

Southern Illinois University Edwardsville, Graduate School, School of Business, Department of Accounting, Edwardsville, IL 62026. Offers accountancy (MSA); taxation (MSA). *Accreditation:* AACSB. *Program availability:* Part-time, evening/weekend. *Degree requirements:* For master's, thesis or alternative, final exam. *Entrance requirements:* For master's, GMAT. Additional exam requirements/recommendations for international students: Required—TOEFL (minimum score 550 paper-based; 79 iBT), IELTS (minimum score 6.5). Electronic applications accepted.

Southern Methodist University, Dedman School of Law, Dallas, TX 75275-0110. Offers law (JD, SJD); law (for foreign law school graduates) (LL M); law (general) (LL M); taxation (LL M); JD/MA; JD/MBA. *Accreditation:* ABA. *Program availability:* Part-time, evening/weekend. *Degree requirements:* For master's, thesis optional; for doctorate, thesis/dissertation (for some programs), 30 hours of public service (for JD). *Entrance requirements:* For master's, JD; for doctorate, LSAT (for JD). Additional exam requirements/recommendations for international students: Required—TOEFL (minimum score 575 paper-based; 91 iBT). Electronic applications accepted. *Expenses:* Contact institution. *Faculty research:* Corporate law, intellectual property, international law, commercial law, dispute resolution.

Southern New Hampshire University, School of Business, Manchester, NH 03106-1045. Offers accounting (MBA, MS, Graduate Certificate); accounting finance (MS); accounting/auditing (MS); accounting/forensic accounting (MS); accounting/taxation (MS); athletic administration (MBA, Graduate Certificate); business administration (IMBA, MBA, Certificate, Graduate Certificate), including accounting (Certificate), business administration (MBA), business information systems (Graduate Certificate), human resource management (Certificate); corporate social responsibility (MBA); entrepreneurship (MBA); finance (MBA, MS, Graduate Certificate); finance/corporate finance (MS); finance/investments and securities (MS); forensic accounting (MBA); healthcare informatics (MBA); healthcare management (MBA); human resource management (Graduate Certificate); information technology (MS, Graduate Certificate); information technology management (MBA); international business (Graduate Certificate); international business and information technology (Graduate Certificate); international finance (Graduate Certificate); international sport management (Graduate Certificate); justice studies (MBA); leadership of nonprofit organizations (Graduate Certificate); management (MS); marketing (MBA, MS, Graduate Certificate); operations and project management (MS); operations and supply chain management (MBA, Graduate Certificate); organizational leadership (MS); project management (MBA, Graduate Certificate); Six Sigma (MBA); Six Sigma quality (Graduate Certificate); social media marketing (MBA); sport management (MBA, MS, Graduate Certificate); sustainability and environmental compliance (MBA); workplace conflict management (MBA); MBA/Certificate. *Accreditation:* ACBSP. *Program availability:* Part-time, evening/weekend, online learning. Terminal master's awarded for partial completion of doctoral program. *Degree requirements:* For master's, one foreign language, comprehensive exam (for some programs), thesis or alternative. *Entrance requirements:* For master's, minimum

GPA of 2.5. Additional exam requirements/recommendations for international students: Required—TOEFL (minimum score 500 paper-based). Electronic applications accepted.

State University of New York College at Old Westbury, School of Business, Old Westbury, NY 11568-0210. Offers accounting (MS); taxation (MS). *Program availability:* Part-time, evening/weekend. *Faculty:* 10 full-time (2 women), 1 part-time/adjunct (0 women). *Students:* 30 full-time (13 women), 47 part-time (15 women); includes 19 minority (3 Black or African American, non-Hispanic/Latino; 11 Asian, non-Hispanic/Latino; 5 Hispanic/Latino). Average age 31. 35 applicants, 91% accepted, 25 enrolled. In 2016, 25 master's awarded. *Entrance requirements:* For master's, GMAT, 2 letters of recommendation. Additional exam requirements/recommendations for international students: Required—TOEFL (minimum score 550 paper-based). *Application deadline:* For fall admission, 6/15 priority date for domestic students; for spring admission, 11/15 priority date for domestic students. Applications are processed on a rolling basis. Application fee: $50. Electronic applications accepted. *Expenses:* Tuition, state resident: full-time $10,870; part-time $453 per credit. Tuition, nonresident: full-time $22,210; part-time $925 per credit. *Required fees:* $24.35 per credit. $76 per semester. Tuition and fees vary according to course load. *Financial support:* Applicants required to submit FAFSA. *Faculty research:* Corporate governance, asset pricing, corporate finance, hedge funds, taxation. *Unit head:* Rita Buttermilch, Director of Graduate Business Programs, 516-876-3900, E-mail: langec@oldwestbury.edu. *Application contact:* Philip D'Angelo, Graduate Admissions Office, 516-876-3073, E-mail: enroll@oldwestbury.edu. Website: http://www.oldwestbury.edu/schools/business

Strayer University, Graduate Studies, Washington, DC 20005-2603. Offers accounting (MS); acquisition (MBA); business administration (MBA); communications technology (MS); educational management (M Ed); finance (MBA); health services administration (MHSA); hospitality and tourism management (MBA); human resource management (MBA); information systems (MS), including computer security management, decision support system management, enterprise resource management, network management, software engineering management, systems development management; management (MBA); management information systems (MS); marketing (MBA); professional accounting (MS), including accounting information systems, controllership, taxation; public administration (MPA); supply chain management (MBA); technology in education (M Ed). Programs also offered at campus locations in Birmingham, AL; Chamblee, GA; Cobb County, GA; Morrow, GA; White Marsh, MD; Charleston, SC; Columbia, SC; Greensboro, NC; Greenville, SC; Lexington, KY; Louisville, KY; Nashville, TN; North Raleigh, NC; Washington, DC. *Accreditation:* ACBSP. *Program availability:* Part-time, evening/weekend, online learning. *Degree requirements:* For master's, thesis. *Entrance requirements:* For master's, GMAT, GRE General Test, bachelor's degree from an accredited college or university, minimum undergraduate GPA of 2.75. Electronic applications accepted.

Suffolk University, Sawyer Business School, Department of Accounting, Boston, MA 02108-2770. Offers accounting (MSA, Graduate Certificate); taxation (MST); MBA/MSA; MBA/MST. *Accreditation:* AACSB. *Program availability:* Part-time, evening/weekend, 100% online. *Faculty:* 13 full-time (6 women), 5 part-time/adjunct (1 woman). *Students:* 82 full-time (55 women), 115 part-time (73 women); includes 48 minority (16 Black or African American, non-Hispanic/Latino; 21 Asian, non-Hispanic/Latino; 11 Hispanic/Latino), 55 international. Average age 29. 217 applicants, 85% accepted, 91 enrolled. In 2016, 95 master's, 2 other advanced degrees awarded. *Entrance requirements:* For master's, GMAT. Additional exam requirements/recommendations for international students: Required—TOEFL (minimum score 550 paper-based; 80 iBT). *Application deadline:* For fall admission, 3/15 priority date for domestic and international students; for spring admission, 10/15 priority date for domestic and international students. Applications are processed on a rolling basis. Application fee: $50. Electronic applications accepted. *Expenses: Tuition:* Full-time $41,490; part-time $1383 per credit hour. *Required fees:* $52; $52 per credit hour. Part-time tuition and fees vary according to course load and program. *Financial support:* In 2016–17, 116 students received support, including 111 fellowships (averaging $11,442 per year); career-related internships or fieldwork, Federal Work-Study, institutionally sponsored loans, and scholarships/grants also available. Support available to part-time students. Financial award application deadline: 4/1; financial award applicants required to submit FAFSA. *Faculty research:* Tax policy, tax research, decision-making in accounting, accounting information systems, capital markets and strategic planning. *Unit head:* Tracy Riley, Chair, 617-994-4276, E-mail: triley@suffolk.edu. *Application contact:* Mara Marzocchi, Associate Director of Graduate Admissions, 617-573-8302, Fax: 617-305-1733, E-mail: grad.admission@suffolk.edu. Website: http://www.suffolk.edu/msa

Suffolk University, Sawyer Business School, Master of Business Administration Program, Boston, MA 02108-2770. Offers accounting (MBA); entrepreneurship (MBA); executive business administration (EMBA); finance (MBA); global business administration (GMBA); health administration (MBA); international business (MBA); marketing (MBA); nonprofit management (MBA); organizational behavior (MBA); strategic management (MBA); supply chain management (MBA); taxation (MBA); JD/MBA; MBA/MHA; MBA/MSA; MBA/MSF; MBA/MST. *Accreditation:* AACSB. *Program availability:* Part-time, evening/weekend, 100% online. *Faculty:* 17 full-time (6 women), 10 part-time/adjunct (1 woman). *Students:* 137 full-time (70 women), 265 part-time (138 women); includes 78 minority (20 Black or African American, non-Hispanic/Latino; 22 Asian, non-Hispanic/Latino; 31 Hispanic/Latino; 5 Two or more races, non-Hispanic/Latino), 46 international. Average age 30. 416 applicants, 70% accepted, 128 enrolled. In 2016, 165 degrees awarded. *Entrance requirements:* For master's, GMAT, minimum undergraduate GPA of 2.75 (MBA), 5 years of managerial experience (EMBA). Additional exam requirements/recommendations for international students: Required—TOEFL (minimum score 550 paper-based; 80 iBT). *Application deadline:* For fall admission, 3/15 priority date for domestic students, 10/15 priority date for international students; for spring admission, 10/15 priority date for domestic and international students. Applications are processed on a rolling basis. Application fee: $50. Electronic applications accepted. *Expenses: Tuition:* Full-time $41,490; part-time $1383 per credit hour. *Required fees:* $52; $52 per credit hour. Part-time tuition and fees vary according to course load and program. *Financial support:* In 2016–17, 209 students received support, including 176 fellowships (averaging $8,581 per year); career-related internships or fieldwork, Federal Work-Study, institutionally sponsored loans, and scholarships/grants also available. Support available to part-time students. Financial award application deadline: 4/1; financial award applicants required to submit FAFSA. *Faculty research:* Foreign investments; career strategies and boundaryless careers; corporate ethics codes; interest rates, inflation, and growth options; innovation and product development performance. *Unit head:* Jodi Detjen, Director of MBA Programs, 617-573-8306, E-mail: jdetjen@suffolk.edu. *Application contact:* Mara Marzocchi, Associate Director of Graduate Admissions, 617-573-8302, Fax: 617-305-1733, E-mail: grad.admission@suffolk.edu. Website: http://www.suffolk.edu/mba

Taft University System, Taft Law School, Denver, CO 80246. Offers American jurisprudence (LL M); law (JD); taxation (LL M).

Taft University System, W. Edwards Deming School of Business, Denver, CO 80246. Offers taxation (MS).

Temple University, Beasley School of Law, Philadelphia, PA 19122. Offers law (JD); legal education (SJD); taxation (LL M); transnational law (LL M); trial advocacy (LL M); JD/LL M; JD/MBA; JD/MPH. *Accreditation:* ABA. *Program availability:* Part-time, evening/weekend. *Faculty:* 64 full-time (30 women), 102 part-time/adjunct (37 women). *Students:* 534 full-time (282 women), 153 part-time (66 women); includes 191 minority (59 Black or African American, non-Hispanic/Latino; 2 American Indian or Alaska Native, non-Hispanic/Latino; 60 Asian, non-Hispanic/Latino; 62 Hispanic/Latino; 8 Two or more races, non-Hispanic/Latino), 9 international. Average age 26. 2,046 applicants, 42% accepted, 218 enrolled. In 2016, 202 doctorates awarded. *Entrance requirements:* For doctorate, LSAT (for JD). Additional exam requirements/recommendations for international students: Recommended—TOEFL. *Application deadline:* For fall admission, 3/1 for domestic and international students. Applications are processed on a rolling basis. Application fee: $60. Electronic applications accepted. *Expenses:* $24,786 per year full-time resident tuition; $37,500 per year full-time non-resident tuition; $20,018 per year part-time resident tuition; $30,196 per year part-time non-resident tuition. *Financial support:* In 2016–17, 469 students received support, including research assistantships (averaging $5,500 per year), teaching assistantships (averaging $5,500 per year); fellowships, Federal Work-Study, scholarships/grants, tuition waivers (full and partial), and unspecified assistantships also available. Support available to part-time students. Financial award application deadline: 3/1; financial award applicants required to submit FAFSA. *Faculty research:* Cybersecurity, gender issues, health care law, immigration law, intellectual property law. *Unit head:* Gregory N. Mandel, Dean, 215-204-7863, Fax: 215-204-1185, E-mail: law@temple.edu. *Application contact:* Johanne L. Johnston, Assistant Dean for Admissions and Financial Aid, 800-560-1428, Fax: 215-204-9319, E-mail: lawadmis@temple.edu. Website: http://www.law.temple.edu

Texas Christian University, Neeley School of Business, Master of Accounting Program, Fort Worth, TX 76129. Offers audit (M Ac); taxation (M Ac); valuation and reporting (M Ac). *Accreditation:* AACSB. *Faculty:* 12 full-time (6 women), 1 part-time/adjunct (0 women). *Students:* 63 full-time (27 women); includes 4 minority (all Hispanic/Latino), 2 international. Average age 22. 71 applicants, 97% accepted, 61 enrolled. In 2016, 69 master's awarded. *Entrance requirements:* Additional exam requirements/recommendations for international students: Recommended—TOEFL. *Application deadline:* For fall admission, 2/15 for domestic and international students; for spring admission, 9/15 for domestic and international students. Application fee: $0. Electronic applications accepted. *Expenses:* $1,480 per semester hour tuition, $1,450 per semester fees. *Financial support:* In 2016–17, 33 students received support. Unspecified assistantships available. Financial award application deadline: 1/31. *Faculty research:* Financial accounting, market valuation of accounting information, corporate governance, managerial compensation and incentives, taxation. *Unit head:* Dr. Mary A. Stanford, Department Chair, 817-257-7483, Fax: 817-257-7227, E-mail: m.stanford@tcu.edu. *Application contact:* Emily Davis, Director, 817-257-5112, Fax: 817-257-7227, E-mail: e.k.davis@tcu.edu.
Website: http://www.neeley.tcu.edu/Academics/Master_of_Accounting/MAc.aspx

Texas Tech University, Rawls College of Business Administration, Lubbock, TX 79409-2101. Offers accounting (MSA, PhD), including audit/financial reporting (MSA), taxation (MSA); business statistics (MS, PhD); data science (MS); finance (PhD); general business (MBA); healthcare management (MS); information systems and operations management (PhD); management (PhD); marketing (PhD); STEM (MBA); JD/MBA; JD/MSA; MBA/M Arch; MBA/MD; MBA/MS; MBA/Pharm D. *Accreditation:* AACSB; CAHME (one or more programs are accredited). *Program availability:* Evening/weekend. *Faculty:* 74 full-time (13 women). *Students:* 741 full-time (275 women); includes 198 minority (38 Black or African American, non-Hispanic/Latino; 1 American Indian or Alaska Native, non-Hispanic/Latino; 24 Asian, non-Hispanic/Latino; 116 Hispanic/Latino; 1 Native Hawaiian or other Pacific Islander, non-Hispanic/Latino; 18 Two or more races, non-Hispanic/Latino), 95 international. Average age 28. 905 applicants, 48% accepted, 251 enrolled. In 2016, 545 master's, 13 doctorates awarded. *Degree requirements:* For master's, capstone course; for doctorate, comprehensive exam, thesis/dissertation, qualifying exams. *Entrance requirements:* For master's, GMAT, GRE, MCAT, PCAT, LSAT, or DAT, holistic review of academic credentials, resume, essay, letters of recommendation; for doctorate, GMAT, GRE, holistic review of academic credentials, resume, statement of purpose, letters of recommendation. Additional exam requirements/recommendations for international students: Required—TOEFL (minimum score 95 iBT), IELTS. *Application deadline:* For fall admission, 7/1 priority date for domestic students, 1/15 for international students; for spring admission, 12/1 priority date for domestic students, 6/15 for international students; for summer admission, 5/1 for domestic students. Applications are processed on a rolling basis. Application fee: $60. Electronic applications accepted. *Expenses:* $48,000 (MBA for Working Professionals); $20,000 (STEM MBA). *Financial support:* In 2016–17, 157 students received support, including 25 research assistantships (averaging $22,725 per year), 27 teaching assistantships (averaging $22,725 per year); fellowships, career-related internships or fieldwork, Federal Work-Study, scholarships/grants, health care benefits, and unspecified assistantships also available. Financial award application deadline: 3/1; financial award applicants required to submit FAFSA. *Faculty research:* Governmental and nonprofit accounting, securities and options futures, statistical analysis and design, leadership, consumer behavior. *Unit head:* Dr. Margaret Williams, Dean, 806-742-3188, Fax: 806-742-1092, E-mail: margaret.l.williams@ttu.edu. *Application contact:* Chathry Keaton, Applications Manager, Graduate and Professional Programs, 806-742-3184, Fax: 806-742-3958, E-mail: rawlsgrad@ttu.edu.
Website: http://www.depts.ttu.edu/rawlsbusiness/graduate/

Troy University, Graduate School, College of Business, Program in Taxation, Troy, AL 36082. Offers MTX, Certificate. *Program availability:* Part-time, evening/weekend. *Faculty:* 2 full-time (1 woman). In 2016, 6 master's awarded. *Degree requirements:* For master's, minimum GPA of 3.0, research paper, capstone course. *Entrance requirements:* For master's, GMAT (minimum score of 500), bachelor's degree; minimum undergraduate GPA of 2.5 or 3.0 on last 30 semester hours, letter of recommendation. Additional exam requirements/recommendations for international students: Required—TOEFL (minimum score 523 paper-based; 70 iBT), IELTS (minimum score 6). *Application deadline:* Applications are processed on a rolling basis. Application fee: $50. Electronic applications accepted. *Expenses:* Tuition, state resident: full-time $7146; part-time $397 per credit hour. Tuition, nonresident: full-time $14,292; part-time $794 per credit hour. *Required fees:* $802; $50 per semester. Tuition and fees vary according to campus/location and program. *Financial support:* Fellowships, career-related internships or fieldwork, and scholarships/grants available. Support available to part-time students. *Unit head:* Dr. Kay Sheridan, Director, 334-670-3154, Fax: 334-670-3599, E-mail: ksheridan@troy.edu. *Application contact:* Jessica A. Kimbro, Director of Graduate Admissions, 334-670-3178, Fax: 334-670-3733, E-mail: jacord@troy.edu.

Université de Montréal, Faculty of Law, Montréal, QC H3C 3J7, Canada. Offers business law (DESS); common law (North America) (JD); international law (DESS); law (LL M, LL D, DDN, DESS, LL B); tax law (LL M). *Program availability:* Part-time. *Degree requirements:* For master's, thesis; for doctorate, thesis/dissertation, project; for other advanced degree, thesis (for some programs). Electronic applications accepted. *Faculty research:* Legal theory; constitutional, private, and public law.

Université de Sherbrooke, Faculty of Administration, Program in Taxation, Sherbrooke, QC J1K 2R1, Canada. Offers M Tax, Diploma. *Program availability:* Part-time, evening/weekend. *Degree requirements:* For master's, one foreign language, thesis. *Entrance requirements:* For master's, bachelor's degree in business, law or economics; basic knowledge of Canadian taxation (2 courses). Electronic applications accepted. *Faculty research:* Taxation research, public finances.

University at Albany, State University of New York, School of Business, Department of Accounting and Law, Albany, NY 12222-0001. Offers accounting (MS); forensic accounting (MS); professional accounting (MS); tax practice (MS); taxation (MS). *Accreditation:* AACSB. *Faculty:* 9 full-time (2 women), 8 part-time/adjunct (3 women). *Students:* 137 full-time (62 women), 9 part-time (4 women); includes 31 minority (7 Black or African American, non-Hispanic/Latino; 11 Asian, non-Hispanic/Latino; 9 Hispanic/Latino; 4 Two or more races, non-Hispanic/Latino), 22 international. 257 applicants, 67% accepted, 117 enrolled. In 2016, 110 master's awarded. *Degree requirements:* For master's, research project. *Entrance requirements:* For master's, GMAT. Additional exam requirements/recommendations for international students: Required—TOEFL (minimum score 550 paper-based). *Application deadline:* For fall admission, 3/1 priority date for domestic students, 4/1 for international students. Applications are processed on a rolling basis. Application fee: $75. Electronic applications accepted. *Expenses:* Tuition, state resident: full-time $10,870; part-time $453 per credit hour. Tuition, nonresident: full-time $22,210; part-time $925 per credit hour. *International tuition:* $21,550 full-time. *Required fees:* $1864; $96 per credit hour. *Financial support:* Application deadline: 4/1. *Faculty research:* Professional ethics, statistical analysis, cost management systems, accounting theory. *Unit head:* Ingrid Fisher, Chair, 518-956-8365, E-mail: ifisher@albany.edu. *Application contact:* Michael DeRensis, Director, Graduate Admissions, 518-442-3980, Fax: 518-442-3922, E-mail: graduate@albany.edu.
Website: http://www.albany.edu/business/accounting_index.shtml

The University of Akron, Graduate School, College of Business Administration, The George W. Daverio School of Accountancy, Program in Taxation, Akron, OH 44325. Offers MT, JD/MT. *Students:* 21 full-time (11 women), 23 part-time (10 women); includes 4 minority (1 Black or African American, non-Hispanic/Latino; 1 Asian, non-Hispanic/Latino; 1 Hispanic/Latino; 1 Two or more races, non-Hispanic/Latino), 5 international. Average age 29. 23 applicants, 91% accepted, 21 enrolled. In 2016, 26 master's awarded. *Entrance requirements:* For master's, GMAT, minimum GPA of 3.0 (preferred), two letters of recommendation, resume, statement of purpose. Additional exam requirements/recommendations for international students: Required—TOEFL (minimum score 550 paper-based; 79 iBT), IELTS (minimum score 6.5). *Application deadline:* For fall admission, 8/3 for domestic and international students; for spring admission, 11/15 for domestic and international students; for summer admission, 4/15 for domestic and international students. Application fee: $45 ($75 for international students). Electronic applications accepted. *Expenses:* Tuition, state resident: full-time $8618; part-time $359 per credit hour. Tuition, nonresident: full-time $17,149; part-time $715 per credit hour. *Required fees:* $1652. *Unit head:* Dr. Thomas Calderon, Department Chair, 330-972-6228, E-mail: tcalderon@uakron.edu. *Application contact:* Dr. William Hauser, Director of Graduate Business Programs, 330-972-7043, Fax: 330-972-6588, E-mail: whauser@uakron.edu.
Website: http://www.uakron.edu/cba/graduate/programs/mtax/index.dot

The University of Alabama, Graduate School, Manderson Graduate School of Business, Culverhouse School of Accountancy, Tuscaloosa, AL 35487. Offers accounting (M Acc, PhD); tax accounting (MTA). *Accreditation:* AACSB. *Faculty:* 19 full-time (4 women). *Students:* 115 full-time (47 women), 3 part-time (all women); includes 14 minority (6 Black or African American, non-Hispanic/Latino; 1 American Indian or Alaska Native, non-Hispanic/Latino; 4 Asian, non-Hispanic/Latino; 1 Hispanic/Latino; 2 Two or more races, non-Hispanic/Latino), 4 international. Average age 24. 221 applicants, 58% accepted, 100 enrolled. In 2016, 102 master's, 4 doctorates awarded. *Degree requirements:* For doctorate, thesis/dissertation. *Entrance requirements:* For master's, GMAT, minimum GPA of 3.0 overall or on last 60 hours; for doctorate, GMAT, minimum GPA of 3.0. Additional exam requirements/recommendations for international students: Required—TOEFL. *Application deadline:* For fall admission, 7/1 priority date for domestic students, 6/1 priority date for international students; for spring admission, 11/1 priority date for domestic students, 9/1 priority date for international students. Applications are processed on a rolling basis. Application fee: $50 ($60 for international students). Electronic applications accepted. *Expenses:* Tuition, state resident: full-time $10,470. Tuition, nonresident: full-time $26,950. *Financial support:* In 2016–17, 79 students received support, including 4 fellowships with full tuition reimbursements available (averaging $15,000 per year), 23 research assistantships with tuition reimbursements available (averaging $9,765 per year), 19 teaching assistantships with tuition reimbursements available (averaging $13,352 per year); career-related internships or fieldwork, Federal Work-Study, institutionally sponsored loans, scholarships/grants, health care benefits, and unspecified assistantships also available. Financial award application deadline: 3/31. *Faculty research:* Corporate governance, audit decision-making, earning management, valuation, executive compensation. *Total annual research expenditures:* $44,946. *Unit head:* Dr. Richard Houston, Director, 205-348-8392, E-mail: rhouston@culverhouse.ua.edu. *Application contact:* Sandy D. Davidson, Advisor, 205-348-6131, Fax: 205-348-8453, E-mail: sdavidso@cba.ua.edu.
Website: http://www.cba.ua.edu/accounting/

The University of Alabama, School of Law, Tuscaloosa, AL 35487. Offers business transactions (LL M); comparative law (LL M, JSD); law (JD, JSD); taxation (LL M); JD/MBA. *Accreditation:* ABA. *Faculty:* 40 full-time (16 women), 38 part-time/adjunct (10 women). *Students:* 417 full-time (185 women), 74 part-time (27 women); includes 98 minority (51 Black or African American, non-Hispanic/Latino; 5 American Indian or Alaska Native, non-Hispanic/Latino; 14 Asian, non-Hispanic/Latino; 20 Hispanic/Latino; 8 Two or more races, non-Hispanic/Latino), 7 international. Average age 27. 1,634 applicants, 21% accepted, 172 enrolled. In 2016, 60 master's, 144 doctorates awarded. *Degree requirements:* For master's, 24 hours, exams; for doctorate, 90 hours, including 6 hours of experiential learning, 1 seminar, and 34 required hours. *Entrance requirements:* For master's, LSAT, JD (for business transactions and taxation); undergraduate degree in law, letters of recommendation, personal statement, resume, and official transcripts (for comparative law); for doctorate, LSAT (for JD), undergraduate degree, letter of recommendation, resume, personal statement, and CAS report (for JD). Additional exam requirements/recommendations for international students: Required—TOEFL, IELTS. *Application deadline:* Applications are processed on a rolling basis. Application fee: $40. Electronic applications accepted. *Expenses:* Contact institution. *Financial support:* Applicants required to submit FAFSA. *Faculty research:* Public interest law, Constitutional law, civil rights, international law, tax law. *Total annual research expenditures:* $90,932. *Unit head:* Claude R. Arrington, Associate Dean for Admissions, 205-348-6557, Fax: 205-348-3077, E-mail: carrington@law.ua.edu. *Application contact:* Martha Griffith, Assistant Director for Admissions, 205-348-7945, Fax: 205-348-3917, E-mail: mgriffith@law.ua.edu.
Website: http://www.law.ua.edu/

The University of Alabama in Huntsville, School of Graduate Studies, College of Business Administration, Program in Accounting, Huntsville, AL 35899. Offers accounting (M Acc), including CPA preparatory with an emphasis in taxation, CPA preparatory with emphasis in assurance and financial reporting, general accounting, information systems audit and control (ISAC). *Accreditation:* AACSB. *Program availability:* Part-time, evening/weekend. *Degree requirements:* For master's, comprehensive exam, thesis or alternative. *Entrance requirements:* For master's, GMAT (minimum score 500), minimum AACSB index of 1080. Additional exam requirements/recommendations for international students: Required—TOEFL (minimum score 550 paper-based; 80 iBT), IELTS (minimum score 6.5). Electronic applications accepted. *Expenses:* Tuition, state resident: full-time $9834; part-time $600 per credit hour. Tuition, nonresident: full-time $21,830; part-time $1325 per credit hour. *Faculty research:* Accounting information systems, managerial accounting, behavioral accounting, state and local taxation, financial accounting.

University of Baltimore, Graduate School, Merrick School of Business, Department of Accounting, Program in Taxation, Baltimore, MD 21201-5779. Offers MS. *Program availability:* Part-time, evening/weekend. *Entrance requirements:* For master's, GMAT, minimum GPA of 3.0. Additional exam requirements/recommendations for international students: Required—TOEFL (minimum score 550 paper-based). *Expenses:* Contact institution. *Faculty research:* Taxation of not-for-profit entities.

University of Baltimore, School of Law, Baltimore, MD 21201. Offers business law (JD); criminal practice (JD); estate planning (JD); family law (JD); intellectual property (JD); international law (JD); law (JD, LL M); law of the United States (LL M); litigation and advocacy (JD); public service (JD); real estate practice (JD); taxation (LL M); JD/LL M; JD/MBA; JD/MPA; JD/MS; JD/PhD. JD/MS offered jointly with Division of Criminology, Criminal Justice, and Social Policy; JD/PhD with University of Maryland, Baltimore. *Accreditation:* ABA. *Program availability:* Part-time, evening/weekend. *Faculty:* 53 full-time (25 women), 61 part-time/adjunct (18 women). *Students:* 464 full-time (233 women), 297 part-time (140 women); includes 243 minority (142 Black or African American, non-Hispanic/Latino; 35 Asian, non-Hispanic/Latino; 38 Hispanic/Latino; 28 Two or more races, non-Hispanic/Latino), 20 international. Average age 27. 1,090 applicants, 58% accepted, 208 enrolled. In 2016, 279 doctorates awarded. *Entrance requirements:* For doctorate, LSAT. Additional exam requirements/recommendations for international students: Required—TOEFL (for LL M in law of the United States). *Application deadline:* For fall admission, 7/30 for domestic students, 4/1 priority date for international students. Applications are processed on a rolling basis. Application fee: $60. Electronic applications accepted. *Expenses:* $30,144 per year full-time in-state; $43,972 per year full-time out-of-state. *Financial support:* In 2016–17, 344 students received support. Research assistantships, teaching assistantships, career-related internships or fieldwork, Federal Work-Study, and scholarships/grants available. Support available to part-time students. Financial award application deadline: 4/1; financial award applicants required to submit FAFSA. *Faculty research:* Plain view doctrine, statute of limitations, bankruptcy, family law, international and comparative law, Constitutional law. *Unit head:* Ronald Weich, Dean, 410-837-4458. *Application contact:* Jeffrey L. Zavrotny, Assistant Dean for Admissions, 410-837-5809, Fax: 410-837-4188, E-mail: jzavrotny@ubalt.edu. Website: http://law.ubalt.edu/

The University of British Columbia, Peter A. Allard School of Law, Vancouver, BC V6T 1Z1, Canada. Offers common law (LL M CL); law (LL M, PhD); taxation (LL M). *Program availability:* Part-time. *Degree requirements:* For master's, variable foreign language requirement, thesis, seminar; for doctorate, variable foreign language requirement, comprehensive exam, thesis/dissertation, seminar. *Entrance requirements:* For master's, LL B or JD, thesis proposal, 3 letters of reference; for doctorate, LL B or JD, LL M, thesis proposal, 3 letters of reference. Additional exam requirements/recommendations for international students: Required—TOEFL, IELTS. *Application deadline:* Applications are processed on a rolling basis. Application fee: $100 ($162 for international students). Electronic applications accepted. *Expenses:* Contact institution. *Financial support:* Fellowships, research assistantships, teaching assistantships, Federal Work-Study, scholarships/grants, and unspecified assistantships available. Financial award application deadline: 9/1. *Faculty research:* Aboriginal rights/native law, Asian legal studies, criminal law, environmental law, international law, corporate, human rights, intellectual property, dispute resolution, entertainment. *Application contact:* Joanne Chung, Graduate Administrator, 604-822-6449, Fax: 604-822-4781, E-mail: graduates@law.ubc.ca.
Website: http://www.allard.ubc.ca/

University of Cincinnati, Graduate School, Carl H. Lindner College of Business, MS Program, Cincinnati, OH 45221. Offers accounting (MS); business analytics (MS); finance (MS); information systems (MS); marketing (MS); taxation (MS). *Program availability:* Part-time, evening/weekend. *Faculty:* 74 full-time (17 women), 33 part-time/adjunct (8 women). *Students:* 307 full-time (128 women), 246 part-time (106 women); includes 60 minority (22 Black or African American, non-Hispanic/Latino; 20 Asian, non-Hispanic/Latino; 9 Hispanic/Latino; 1 Native Hawaiian or other Pacific Islander, non-Hispanic/Latino; 8 Two or more races, non-Hispanic/Latino), 321 international. Average age 28. 1,756 applicants, 24% accepted, 351 enrolled. In 2016, 334 master's awarded. *Degree requirements:* For master's, thesis (for some programs). *Entrance requirements:* For master's, GMAT, GRE, resume, transcripts, essays, letters of recommendation. Additional exam requirements/recommendations for international students: Required—TOEFL (minimum score 577 paper-based; 90 iBT), IELTS (minimum score 6.5). *Application deadline:* For fall admission, 8/1 priority date for domestic students, 3/15 for international students; for spring admission, 12/15 for domestic students, 9/15 for international students; for summer admission, 4/15 for domestic and international students. Applications are processed on a rolling basis. Application fee: $65 ($70 for international students). Electronic applications accepted. *Expenses:* Contact institution. *Financial support:* In 2016–17, 251 students received support, including 12 teaching assistantships with tuition reimbursements available (averaging $3,500 per year); scholarships/grants, tuition waivers (full and partial), and unspecified assistantships also available. Financial award application deadline: 2/1; financial award applicants required to submit FAFSA. *Faculty research:* Real estate, empirical pricing, organization information pricing, strategic management, portfolio choice in institutional investment. *Unit head:* Dr. David Szymanski, Dean, 513-556-7001, Fax: 513-556-4891, E-mail: david.szymanski@uc.edu. *Application contact:* Dona Clary, Director, Graduate Programs, 513-556-3546, Fax: 513-558-7006, E-mail: dona.clary@uc.edu.

University of Colorado Denver, Business School, Program in Taxation, Denver, CO 80217. Offers MS. *Students:* 12 full-time (5 women), 5 part-time (2 women); includes 3 minority (1 Asian, non-Hispanic/Latino; 1 Hispanic/Latino; 1 Two or more races, non-Hispanic/Latino). Average age 33. 10 applicants, 70% accepted, 4 enrolled. In 2016, 2 master's awarded. *Degree requirements:* For master's, 30 semester hours of course work. *Entrance requirements:* For master's, GMAT, resume, essay, transcripts from all universities or colleges attended, letters of recommendation (strongly encouraged). Additional exam requirements/recommendations for international students: Required—TOEFL (minimum score 525 paper-based; 71 iBT); Recommended—IELTS (minimum score 6.5). *Application deadline:* For fall admission, 4/15 priority date for domestic students, 3/15 priority date for international students; for spring admission, 10/15 priority date for domestic students, 9/15 priority date for international students; for summer admission, 2/15 priority date for domestic students, 1/15 priority date for international students. Applications are processed on a rolling basis. Application fee: $50 ($75 for international students). Electronic applications accepted. *Expenses:* Tuition, state resident: full-time $11,006; part-time $474 per credit. Tuition, nonresident: full-time $28,212; part-time $1264 per credit hour. *Required fees:* $256 per semester. One-time fee: $94.32. Tuition and fees vary according to campus/location and program. *Financial*

support: In 2016–17, 2 students received support. Federal Work-Study, institutionally sponsored loans, scholarships/grants, and traineeships available. Financial award application deadline: 4/1; financial award applicants required to submit FAFSA. *Unit head:* Eric Zinn, Director of the Taxation Program, E-mail: eric.zinn@ucdenver.edu. *Application contact:* 303-315-8200, E-mail: bschool.admissions@ucdenver.edu.
Website: http://www.ucdenver.edu/academics/colleges/business/degrees/ms/taxation/Pages/default.aspx

University of Denver, Sturm College of Law, Graduate Tax Program, Denver, CO 80208. Offers LL M, MT. *Program availability:* Part-time, evening/weekend. *Faculty:* 4 full-time (2 women), 4 part-time/adjunct (0 women). *Students:* 39 full-time (13 women), 72 part-time (39 women); includes 17 minority (6 Black or African American, non-Hispanic/Latino; 5 Asian, non-Hispanic/Latino; 5 Hispanic/Latino; 1 Two or more races, non-Hispanic/Latino), 22 international. Average age 34. 138 applicants, 92% accepted, 64 enrolled. In 2016, 70 master's awarded. *Entrance requirements:* For master's, LSAT (for LL M), GMAT (for MT), transcripts; JD from ABA-approved institution (for LL M). Additional exam requirements/recommendations for international students: Required—TOEFL (minimum score 550 paper-based; 80 iBT). *Application deadline:* Applications are processed on a rolling basis. Application fee: $65. Electronic applications accepted. *Expenses:* $36,018 per year full-time. *Financial support:* In 2016–17, 83 students received support. Federal Work-Study, institutionally sponsored loans, and scholarships/grants available. Support available to part-time students. Financial award application deadline: 6/30; financial award applicants required to submit FAFSA. *Faculty research:* Individual, estate and gift, and state and local tax; qualified plans; partnerships; c corporations and s corporations; procedural and ethical aspects of the practice of tax. *Unit head:* John Wilson, Professor of the Practice of Taxation/Director, 303-871-6000, E-mail: john.r.wilson@du.edu. *Application contact:* Information Contact, 303-871-6239, Fax: 303-871-6358, E-mail: gtp@du.edu. Website: http://www.du.edu/tax

University of Florida, Levin College of Law, Gainesville, FL 32611. Offers comparative law (LL M), including tropical conservation and development; environmental and land use law (LL M); international taxation (LL M); law (JD); taxation (LL M, SJD). *Accreditation:* ABA. *Entrance requirements:* For doctorate, LSAT (for JD). Electronic applications accepted. *Faculty research:* Environmental and land use law, taxation, dispute resolution, family law, Constitutional law.

University of Hartford, Barney School of Business, Department of Accounting and Taxation, West Hartford, CT 06117-1599. Offers professional accounting (Certificate); taxation (MSAT). *Program availability:* Part-time, evening/weekend. *Entrance requirements:* For master's, GMAT, 2 letters of recommendation, resume. Additional exam requirements/recommendations for international students: Required—TOEFL (minimum score 550 paper-based). Electronic applications accepted.

University of Hawaii at Manoa, Graduate Division, Shidler College of Business, Program in Accounting, Honolulu, HI 96822. Offers accounting (M Acc); accounting law (M Acc); information systems (M Acc); taxation (M Acc). *Program availability:* Part-time. *Entrance requirements:* For master's, GMAT, bachelor's degree in accounting, minimum GPA of 3.0. Additional exam requirements/recommendations for international students: Required—TOEFL (minimum score 550 paper-based; 79 iBT), IELTS (minimum score 5). *Faculty research:* International accounting, current tax topics, insurance industry financial reporting, behavioral accounting, auditing.

University of Houston, Law Center, Houston, TX 77204-6060. Offers energy, environment, and natural resources (LL M); health law (LL M); intellectual property and information law (LL M); international law (LL M); law (LL M, JD); tax law (LL M). *Accreditation:* ABA. *Program availability:* Part-time, evening/weekend. *Entrance requirements:* For doctorate, LSAT. Additional exam requirements/recommendations for international students: Required—TOEFL (minimum score 600 paper-based; 100 iBT). Electronic applications accepted. *Expenses:* Contact institution. *Faculty research:* Health law, international, tax, environmental/energy, information law/intellectual property.

University of Illinois at Urbana–Champaign, Graduate College, College of Business, Department of Accountancy, Champaign, IL 61820. Offers accountancy (MAS, MS, PhD); taxation (MS). *Accreditation:* AACSB.

University of Miami, Graduate School, University of Miami School of Law, Coral Gables, FL 33124-8087. Offers entertainment, arts, and sports law (LL M); estate planning (LL M); international arbitration (LL M); international law (LL M), including general international law, inter-American law, U.S. and transnational law for foreign lawyers; law (JD); maritime law (LL M); real estate/property development (LL M); taxation (LL M); taxation of cross-border investment (LL M); JD/LL M; JD/MA; JD/MBA; JD/MBA/LL M; JD/MD; JD/MM; JD/MPA; JD/MPH; JD/MPS; JD/MS Ed; JD/PhD. *Accreditation:* ABA. *Program availability:* Part-time. *Faculty:* 78 full-time (35 women), 98 part-time/adjunct (22 women). *Students:* 995 full-time (464 women), 74 part-time (33 women); includes 457 minority (69 Black or African American, non-Hispanic/Latino; 3 American Indian or Alaska Native, non-Hispanic/Latino; 31 Asian, non-Hispanic/Latino; 323 Hispanic/Latino; 1 Native Hawaiian or other Pacific Islander, non-Hispanic/Latino; 30 Two or more races, non-Hispanic/Latino), 82 international. 2,443 applicants, 55% accepted, 300 enrolled. *Entrance requirements:* For doctorate, LSAT, 2 letters of recommendation. Additional exam requirements/recommendations for international students: Required—TOEFL (minimum score 580 paper-based; 92 iBT), IELTS (minimum score 7). *Application deadline:* For fall admission, 7/31 for domestic and international students. Applications are processed on a rolling basis. Application fee: $60. Electronic applications accepted. *Expenses:* Contact institution. *Financial support:* Fellowships, research assistantships, career-related internships or fieldwork, Federal Work-Study, institutionally sponsored loans, scholarships/grants, and unspecified assistantships available. Financial award application deadline: 3/1; financial award applicants required to submit FAFSA. *Faculty research:* Energy/climate change, international finance, Internet law/law of electronic commerce, race/social justice, art law/cultural heritage law. *Unit head:* Michael Goodnight, Associate Dean of Admissions and Enrollment Management, 305-284-2527, Fax: 305-284-3084, E-mail: mgoodnig@law.miami.edu. *Application contact:* Therese Lambert, Director of Student Recruitment, 305-284-6746, Fax: 305-284-3084, E-mail: tlambert@law.miami.edu.
Website: http://www.law.miami.edu/

University of Michigan, Law School, Ann Arbor, MI 48109-1215. Offers comparative law (MCL); international tax (LL M); law (LL M, JD, SJD); JD/MA; JD/MBA; JD/MHSA; JD/MPH; JD/MPP; JD/MS; JD/MSI; JD/MSW; JD/MUP; JD/PhD. *Accreditation:* ABA. *Faculty:* 107 full-time (36 women), 36 part-time/adjunct (8 women). *Students:* 933 full-time (438 women); includes 205 minority (35 Black or African American, non-Hispanic/Latino; 8 American Indian or Alaska Native, non-Hispanic/Latino; 78 Asian, non-Hispanic/Latino; 42 Hispanic/Latino; 42 Two or more races, non-Hispanic/Latino), 59 international. 5,076 applicants, 24% accepted, 305 enrolled. In 2016, 36 master's, 328 doctorates awarded. *Entrance requirements:* For doctorate, LSAT. *Application deadline:* For fall admission, 2/15 for domestic students. Applications are processed on a rolling basis. Application fee: $75. Electronic applications accepted. *Expenses:* Contact institution. *Financial support:* In 2016–17, 779 students received support. Career-related internships or fieldwork, Federal Work-Study, institutionally sponsored loans, and scholarships/grants available. Financial award applicants required to submit FAFSA. *Unit head:* Mark D. West, Dean, 734-764-1358. *Application contact:* Sarah C. Zearfoss, Assistant Dean and Director of Admissions, 734-764-0537, Fax: 734-647-3218, E-mail: law.jd.admissions@umich.edu. Website: http://www.law.umich.edu/

University of Minnesota, Twin Cities Campus, Carlson School of Management, Master of Business Taxation Program, Minneapolis, MN 55455-0213. Offers MBT. *Program availability:* Part-time, evening/weekend. *Faculty:* 3 full-time (1 woman), 17 part-time/adjunct (4 women). *Students:* 19 full-time (10 women), 73 part-time (33 women); includes 7 minority (2 Black or African American, non-Hispanic/Latino; 5 Asian, non-Hispanic/Latino), 17 international. Average age 30. 46 applicants, 83% accepted, 31 enrolled. In 2016, 34 master's awarded. *Entrance requirements:* For master's, GMAT or LSAT. Additional exam requirements/recommendations for international students: Required—TOEFL (minimum score 550 paper-based; 79 iBT), IELTS (minimum score 6.5). *Application deadline:* For fall admission, 6/15 priority date for domestic and international students; for spring admission, 10/15 priority date for domestic and international students; for summer admission, 3/15 priority date for domestic and international students. Applications are processed on a rolling basis. Application fee: $75 ($95 for international students). Electronic applications accepted. *Expenses:* $1,295 per credit; Carlson School fee: $290 (for 1-8 credits), $580 (for 9 credits or more); $24 transportation fee; additional fees for international students and health insurance. *Financial support:* In 2016–17, 17 students received support, including 15 fellowships (averaging $2,560 per year), 2 teaching assistantships with partial tuition reimbursements available (averaging $7,500 per year); career-related internships or fieldwork and institutionally sponsored loans also available. Financial award application deadline: 8/1. *Unit head:* Paul Gutterman, Director of Graduate Studies, 612-624-8515, Fax: 612-626-7795, E-mail: pgutterm@umn.edu. *Application contact:* Information Contact, 612-625-6516, E-mail: mbt@umn.edu.
Website: http://carlsonschool.umn.edu/degrees/master-business-taxation

University of Mississippi, Graduate School, School of Accountancy, University, MS 38677. Offers accountancy (M Acc, PhD); taxation accounting (M Tax). *Accreditation:* AACSB. *Faculty:* 17 full-time (12 women), 4 part-time/adjunct (3 women). *Students:* 143 full-time (64 women), 7 part-time (4 women); includes 12 minority (7 Black or African American, non-Hispanic/Latino; 1 American Indian or Alaska Native, non-Hispanic/Latino; 1 Asian, non-Hispanic/Latino; 1 Hispanic/Latino; 2 Two or more races, non-Hispanic/Latino), 6 international. Average age 22. *Degree requirements:* For doctorate, thesis/dissertation. *Entrance requirements:* For master's, GMAT, minimum GPA of 3.0; for doctorate, GMAT. Additional exam requirements/recommendations for international students: Required—TOEFL. *Application deadline:* For fall admission, 4/1 for domestic students; for spring admission, 10/1 for domestic students. Applications are processed on a rolling basis. Application fee: $40. *Financial support:* Scholarships/grants available. Financial award application deadline: 3/1; financial award applicants required to submit FAFSA. *Unit head:* Dr. W. Mark Wilder, Dean, School of Accountancy, 662-915-7468, Fax: 662-915-7483, E-mail: umaccy@olemiss.edu. *Application contact:* Dr. Christy M. Wyandt, Associate Dean, 662-915-7474, Fax: 662-915-7577,
E-mail: cwyandt@olemiss.edu. Website: https://www.olemiss.edu

University of Missouri, Office of Research and Graduate Studies, Robert J. Trulaske, Sr. College of Business, School of Accountancy, Columbia, MO 65211. Offers accountancy (M Acc, PhD); taxation (Certificate). *Accreditation:* AACSB. *Program availability:* Part-time. *Degree requirements:* For master's, thesis or alternative; for doctorate, thesis/dissertation. *Entrance requirements:* For master's and doctorate, GMAT, minimum GPA of 3.0. Additional exam requirements/recommendations for international students: Required—TOEFL (minimum score 600 paper-based; 100 iBT). Electronic applications accepted. *Expenses:* Tuition, state resident: full-time $6347; part-time $352.60 per credit hour. Tuition, nonresident: full-time $17,379; part-time $965.50 per credit hour. *Required fees:* $1035. Tuition and fees vary according to course load, campus/location and program.

University of New Haven, Graduate School, College of Business, Program in Taxation, West Haven, CT 06516. Offers MS, Graduate Certificate. *Program availability:* Part-time, evening/weekend. *Students:* 7 full-time (3 women), 19 part-time (8 women); includes 8 minority (4 Black or African American, non-Hispanic/Latino; 3 Asian, non-Hispanic/Latino; 1 Two or more races, non-Hispanic/Latino). Average age 32. 11 applicants, 100% accepted, 8 enrolled. In 2016, 11 master's, 1 other advanced degree awarded. *Degree requirements:* For master's, thesis or alternative. *Entrance requirements:* For master's, GMAT. Additional exam requirements/recommendations for international students: Required—TOEFL (minimum score 80 iBT), IELTS, PTE. *Application deadline:* Applications are processed on a rolling basis. Application fee: $50. Electronic applications accepted. Application fee is waived when completed online. *Expenses:* Contact institution. *Financial support:* Research assistantships with partial tuition reimbursements, teaching assistantships with partial tuition reimbursements, career-related internships or fieldwork, Federal Work-Study, scholarships/grants, and unspecified assistantships available. Support available to part-time students. Financial award application deadline: 5/1; financial award applicants required to submit FAFSA. *Unit head:* Robert E. Wnek, Chair, 203-932-7111, E-mail: rwnek@newhaven.edu. *Application contact:* Michelle Mason, Director of Graduate Enrollment, 203-932-7067, E-mail: mmason@newhaven.edu. Website: http://www.newhaven.edu/6856/

University of New Mexico, Anderson School of Management, Department of Accounting, Albuquerque, NM 87131. Offers accounting (MBA); advanced accounting (M Acct); information assurance (M Acct); professional accounting (M Acct); tax accounting (M Acct); JD/M Acct. *Accreditation:* AACSB. *Program availability:* Part-time, evening/weekend. *Faculty:* 15 full-time (7 women), 3 part-time/adjunct (all women). *Students:* 81 applicants, 70% accepted, 51 enrolled. In 2016, 39 master's awarded. *Entrance requirements:* For master's, GMAT/GRE (minimum score of 500), minimum GPA of 3.25, 3.0 on last 60 hours of coursework (for M Acct in professional accounting). Additional exam requirements/recommendations for international students: Required—TOEFL (minimum score 550 paper-based; 79 iBT), IELTS (minimum score 6.5). *Application deadline:* For fall admission, 4/1 priority date for domestic and international students; for spring admission, 10/1 priority date for domestic and international students. Applications are processed on a rolling basis. Application fee: $50. Electronic applications accepted. *Expenses:* Contact institution. *Financial support:* In 2016–17, 2 fellowships (averaging $20,800 per year), 12 research assistantships with partial tuition reimbursements (averaging $15,488 per year) were awarded; career-related internships or fieldwork, Federal Work-Study, scholarships/grants, and unspecified assistantships also available. Support available to part-time students. Financial award application deadline: 6/1; financial award applicants required to submit FAFSA. *Faculty research:* Critical accounting, accounting pedagogy, theory, taxation, information fraud. *Unit head:* Dr. Leslie Oakes, Chair, 505-277-6471, E-mail: loakes@unm.edu. *Application contact:* Dr. Rich Brody, Professor, 505-277-6471, E-mail: tmarmijo@unm.edu.
Website: https://www.mgt.unm.edu/acct/default.asp?mm=faculty

University of New Orleans, Graduate School, College of Business Administration, Department of Accounting, Program in Taxation, New Orleans, LA 70148. Offers MS. *Program availability:* Part-time, evening/weekend. *Degree requirements:* For master's, thesis optional. *Entrance requirements:* For master's, GMAT. Additional exam requirements/recommendations for international students: Required—TOEFL (minimum score 550 paper-based; 79 iBT). Electronic applications accepted.

University of Notre Dame, Mendoza College of Business, Master of Science in Accountancy Program, Notre Dame, IN 46556. Offers assurance and advisory services (MSA); tax services (MSA). *Accreditation:* AACSB. *Faculty:* 38 full-time (8 women), 15 part-time/adjunct (3 women). *Students:* 95 full-time (39 women); includes 16 minority (1 Black or African American, non-Hispanic/Latino; 1 American Indian or Alaska Native, non-Hispanic/Latino; 1 Asian, non-Hispanic/Latino; 13 Hispanic/Latino), 20 international. Average age 22. 391 applicants, 31% accepted, 95 enrolled. In 2016, 93 master's awarded. *Entrance requirements:* For master's, GMAT, essay, two recommendations, transcripts from all colleges or universities attended, resume. Additional exam requirements/recommendations for international students: Required—TOEFL (minimum score 630 paper-based; 109 iBT), IELTS (minimum score 7.5). *Application deadline:* For fall admission, 10/1 for domestic and international students; for spring admission, 5/1 for domestic and international students. Applications are processed on a rolling basis. Application fee: $50 ($100 for international students). Electronic applications accepted. *Expenses:* Contact institution. *Financial support:* In 2016–17, 88 students received support, including 88 fellowships (averaging $15,748 per year); scholarships/grants and unspecified assistantships also available. Financial award application deadline: 2/28; financial award applicants required to submit FAFSA. *Faculty research:* Stock valuation, accounting information in decision-making, choice of accounting method, taxes cost on capital. *Unit head:* Dr. Katherine Spiess, Associate Dean, Graduate Business Programs, 574-631-3759, E-mail: spiess.1@nd.edu. *Application contact:* Kristin McAndrew, Director of Admissions, Graduate Business Programs, 574-631-8488,
E-mail: kmcadre@nd.edu.
Website: http://mendoza.nd.edu/programs/specialized-masters/ms-in-accountancy/

University of San Diego, School of Business, Programs in Accountancy and Taxation, San Diego, CA 92110-2492. Offers accountancy (MS); taxation (MS). *Program availability:* Part-time, evening/weekend. *Students:* 21 full-time (15 women), 4 part-time (1 woman); includes 4 minority (1 Asian, non-Hispanic/Latino; 2 Hispanic/Latino; 1 Two or more races, non-Hispanic/Latino), 17 international. Average age 25. In 2016, 35 master's awarded. *Entrance requirements:* For master's, GMAT (minimum score of 550), minimum GPA of 3.0. Additional exam requirements/recommendations for international students: Required—TOEFL (minimum score 580 paper-based; 92 iBT), TWE. *Application deadline:* For fall admission, 4/1 for domestic students, 6/1 for international students; for spring admission, 10/1 for domestic students, 12/1 for international students. Application fee: $80. *Financial support:* In 2016–17, 9 students received support. Career-related internships or fieldwork, Federal Work-Study, institutionally sponsored loans, scholarships/grants, and unspecified assistantships available. Support available to part-time students. Financial award application deadline: 4/1; financial award applicants required to submit FAFSA. *Faculty research:* Accounting, financial report, taxation, Sarbanes-Oxley. *Unit head:* Dr. Diane Pattison, Academic Director, Accountancy Programs, 619-260-4850, E-mail: pattison@sandiego.edu. *Application contact:* Monica Mahon, Associate Director of Graduate Admissions, 619-260-4524, Fax: 619-260-4158, E-mail: grads@sandiego.edu.
Website: http://www.sandiego.edu/business/programs/accounting-tax/

University of San Diego, School of Law, San Diego, CA 92110-2492. Offers business and corporate law (LL M); comparative law (LL M); general studies (LL M); international law (LL M); law (JD); taxation (LL M, Diploma); JD/IMBA; JD/MA; JD/MBA. *Accreditation:* ABA. *Program availability:* Part-time, evening/weekend. *Faculty:* 46 full-time (14 women), 71 part-time/adjunct (21 women). *Students:* 644 full-time (320 women), 118 part-time (46 women); includes 250 minority (24 Black or African American, non-Hispanic/Latino; 11 American Indian or Alaska Native, non-Hispanic/Latino; 96 Asian, non-Hispanic/Latino; 106 Hispanic/Latino; 3 Native Hawaiian or other Pacific Islander, non-Hispanic/Latino; 10 Two or more races, non-Hispanic/Latino), 26 international. Average age 27. 3,106 applicants, 192 enrolled. In 2016, 65 master's, 216 doctorates awarded. *Entrance requirements:* For master's, JD, LL B or equivalent from an ABA-accredited law school; for doctorate, LSAT (less than 5 years old), bachelor's degree, registration with the Credential Assemble Service (CAS). Additional exam requirements/recommendations for international students: Required—TOEFL (minimum score 600 paper-based; 100 iBT). *Application deadline:* For fall admission, 2/1 priority date for domestic students. Applications are processed on a rolling basis. Electronic applications accepted. *Expenses:* Contact institution. *Financial support:* In 2016–17, 567 students received support. Career-related internships or fieldwork, Federal Work-Study, institutionally sponsored loans, and scholarships/grants available. Support available to part-time students. Financial award application deadline: 3/1; financial award applicants required to submit FAFSA. *Faculty research:* Corporate law, children's advocacy, Constitutional and criminal law, international and comparative law, public interest law, intellectual property and tax law. *Unit head:* Dr. Stephen C. Ferruolo, Dean, 619-260-4527, E-mail: lawdean@sandiego.edu. *Application contact:* Jorge Garcia, Assistant Dean, JD Admissions, 619-260-4528, Fax: 619-260-2218,
E-mail: jdinfo@sandiego.edu. Website: http://www.sandiego.edu/law/

University of Southern California, Graduate School, Marshall School of Business, Leventhal School of Accounting, Los Angeles, CA 90089. Offers accounting (M Acc); business taxation (MBT); JD/MBT. *Program availability:* Part-time. *Degree requirements:* For master's, 30-48 units of study. *Entrance requirements:* For master's, GMAT, undergraduate degree, communication skills. Additional exam requirements/recommendations for international students: Required—TOEFL. Electronic applications accepted. *Faculty research:* State and local taxation, Securities and Exchange Commission, governance, auditing fees, financial accounting, enterprise zones, women in business.

University of South Florida, Muma College of Business, Lynn Pippenger School of Accountancy, Tampa, FL 33620-9951. Offers accountancy (M Acc), including audit/systems, tax; business administration (PhD), including accounting. *Accreditation:* AACSB. *Program availability:* Part-time, evening/weekend. *Faculty:* 10 full-time (4 women). *Students:* 67 full-time (36 women), 34 part-time (16 women); includes 22 minority (2 Black or African American, non-Hispanic/Latino; 3 Asian, non-Hispanic/Latino; 15 Hispanic/Latino; 2 Two or more races, non-Hispanic/Latino), 9 international. Average age 26. 89 applicants, 56% accepted, 41 enrolled. In 2016, 67 master's, 2 doctorates awarded. Terminal master's awarded for partial completion of doctoral program. *Degree requirements:* For master's, comprehensive exam, thesis or alternative; for doctorate, comprehensive exam, thesis/dissertation. *Entrance requirements:* For master's, GMAT, minimum overall GPA of 3.0 in general upper-level coursework and in upper-level accounting coursework (minimum of 21 hours at a U.S. accredited program within past 5 years); for doctorate, GMAT or GRE, personal statement, recommendations, interview. Additional exam requirements/recommendations for international students: Required—TOEFL (minimum score 550 paper-based; 79 iBT) or IELTS (minimum score 6.5). *Application deadline:* For fall admission, 1/2 for domestic and international students; for spring admission, 10/1 for domestic students, 9/15 for international students; for summer admission, 2/15 for domestic students, 1/15 for international students. Application fee: $30. Electronic applications accepted. *Expenses:* Tuition, state resident: full-time $7766; part-time $431.43 per credit hour. Tuition, nonresident: full-time $15,789; part-time $877.17 per credit hour. *Required fees:* $37 per term. *Financial support:* In 2016–17, 41 students received support, including 18 teaching assistantships with tuition reimbursements available (averaging $12,273 per year); scholarships/grants, health care benefits, and unspecified assistantships also available. Financial award applicants required to submit FAFSA. *Faculty research:* Auditing, auditor independence, audit committee decisions, fraud detection and reporting, disclosure effects, effects of information technology on accounting, governmental accounting/auditing, accounting information systems, data modeling and design methodologies for accounting systems, auditing computer-based systems, expert systems, group support systems in accounting, fair value accounting issues, corporate governance, financial accounting, financial reporting quality. *Unit head:* Dr. Uday Murthy, Interim Director, School of Accountancy, 813-974-6516, Fax: 813-974-6528, E-mail: umurthy@usf.edu. *Application contact:* Christy Ward, Advisor and Graduation Specialist, 813-974-4290, Fax: 813-974-2797, E-mail: cward@usf.edu.
Website: http://business.usf.edu/departments/accountancy/

The University of Texas at Arlington, Graduate School, College of Business, Accounting Department, Arlington, TX 76019. Offers accounting (MP Acc, MS, PhD); taxation (MS). *Accreditation:* AACSB. *Program availability:* Part-time, evening/weekend. *Degree requirements:* For master's, thesis optional; for doctorate, comprehensive exam, thesis/dissertation. *Entrance requirements:* For master's and doctorate, GMAT. Additional exam requirements/recommendations for international students: Required—TOEFL (minimum score 550 paper-based; 79 iBT). *Application deadline:* For fall admission, 6/1 for domestic students, 4/1 for international students; for spring admission, 10/15 for domestic students, 9/15 for international students. Applications are processed on a rolling basis. Application fee: $40 ($70 for international students). *Financial support:* Fellowships, research assistantships, teaching assistantships, career-related internships or fieldwork, scholarships/grants, and unspecified assistantships available. Financial award application deadline: 6/1; financial award applicants required to submit FAFSA. *Unit head:* Dr. Chandra Subramaniam, Chair, 817-272-7029, Fax: 817-282-5793, E-mail: subramaniam@uta.edu. *Application contact:* Carly S. Andrews, Graduate Advisor, 817-272-3047, Fax: 817-272-5793,
E-mail: graduate.accounting.advisor@uta.edu.
Website: http://www2.uta.edu/accounting/

University of the Sacred Heart, Graduate Programs, Department of Business Administration, Program in Taxation, San Juan, PR 00914-0383. Offers MBA. *Program availability:* Part-time, evening/weekend. *Degree requirements:* For master's, thesis. *Entrance requirements:* For master's, EXADEP, minimum undergraduate GPA of 2.75, interview.

University of Washington, Graduate School, Michael G. Foster School of Business, Seattle, WA 98195-3200. Offers auditing and assurance (MP Acc); business administration (MBA, PhD); entrepreneurship (MS); executive business administration (MBA); global executive business administration (MBA); information systems (MSIS); supply chain management (MSSCM); taxation (MP Acc); technology management (MBA); JD/MBA; MBA/MAIS; MBA/MHA. *Accreditation:* AACSB. *Program availability:* Part-time, evening/weekend. Terminal master's awarded for partial completion of doctoral program. *Degree requirements:* For doctorate, comprehensive exam, thesis/dissertation. *Entrance requirements:* For master's and doctorate, GMAT, GRE. Additional exam requirements/recommendations for international students: Required—TOEFL (minimum score 600 paper-based; 100 iBT). Electronic applications accepted. *Expenses:* Contact institution. *Faculty research:* Finance, marketing, organizational behavior, information technology, strategy.

University of Washington, Graduate School, School of Law, Seattle, WA 98195-3020. Offers Asian law (LL M, PhD); intellectual property law and policy (LL M); law (JD); law of sustainable international development (LL M); taxation (LL M); JD/LL M; JD/MA; JD/MAIS; JD/MBA; JD/MPA; JD/MS; JD/PhD. *Accreditation:* ABA. *Degree requirements:* For master's, thesis; for doctorate, thesis/dissertation (for some programs). *Entrance requirements:* For master's, language proficiency (LL M in Asian law); for doctorate, LSAT (for JD). Additional exam requirements/recommendations for international students: Required—TOEFL. *Expenses:* Contact institution. *Faculty research:* Asian, international and comparative law, intellectual property law, health law, environmental law, taxation.

University of Waterloo, Graduate Studies, Faculty of Arts, School of Accounting and Finance, Waterloo, ON N2L 3G1, Canada. Offers accounting (M Acc, PhD); finance (M Acc); taxation (M Tax). *Degree requirements:* For master's, thesis or alternative; for doctorate, thesis/dissertation. *Entrance requirements:* For master's, honors degree, minimum B average, resume; for doctorate, GMAT, master's degree, minimum A-average, resume. Additional exam requirements/recommendations for international students: Required—TOEFL, IELTS, PTE. Electronic applications accepted. *Expenses:* Contact institution. *Faculty research:* Auditing, management accounting.

University of Wisconsin–Madison, Graduate School, Wisconsin School of Business, Master of Accountancy Program, Madison, WI 53706-1380. Offers accountancy (M Acc); taxation (M Acc). *Degree requirements:* For master's, minimum GPA of 3.0. *Entrance requirements:* For master's, GMAT, essays. Additional exam requirements/recommendations for international students: Required—TOEFL (minimum score 104 iBT), IELTS (minimum score 8), GMAT. Electronic applications accepted. *Faculty research:* Tax reserves, audit committee incentives, internal audit, accounting report's impact on management decisions.

University of Wisconsin–Milwaukee, Graduate School, Lubar School of Business, MS and Certificate Business Programs, Milwaukee, WI 53201-0413. Offers business analytics (Graduate Certificate); enterprise resource planning (Graduate Certificate); information technology management (MS); investment management (Graduate Certificate); nonprofit management (Graduate Certificate); nonprofit management and leadership (MS); state and local taxation (Graduate Certificate). *Students:* 174 full-time (83 women), 157 part-time (64 women); includes 69 minority (23 Black or African American, non-Hispanic/Latino; 27 Asian, non-Hispanic/Latino; 6 Hispanic/Latino; 13 Two or more races, non-Hispanic/Latino), 65 international. Average age 32. 281 applicants, 56% accepted, 116 enrolled. In 2016, 171 master's, 34 other advanced degrees awarded. *Entrance requirements:* Additional exam requirements/recommendations for international students: Required—TOEFL (minimum score 550 paper-based; 79 iBT), IELTS (minimum score 6.5). *Application deadline:* Applications are processed on a rolling basis. Application fee: $56 ($96 for international students). Electronic applications accepted. *Financial support:* In 2016–17, 12 teaching assistantships were awarded; fellowships, research assistantships, health care benefits, unspecified assistantships, and project assistantships also available. Financial award applicants required to submit FAFSA. *Application contact:* General Information Contact, 414-229-4982, Fax: 414-229-6967, E-mail: gradschool@uwm.edu.

Villanova University, School of Law and Villanova School of Business, Tax Program, Villanova, PA 19085-1699. Offers LL M, JD/LL M. *Program availability:* Part-time, evening/weekend. *Entrance requirements:* For master's, LSAT, JD (for LL M). Additional exam requirements/recommendations for international students: Required—TOEFL (minimum score 600 paper-based). Electronic applications accepted. *Expenses:* Contact institution. *Faculty research:* Taxation and estate planning, corporate tax planning, international taxation, state taxation.

Wake Forest University, School of Business, MS in Accountancy Program, Winston-Salem, NC 27106. Offers assurance services (MSA); tax consulting (MSA); transaction services (MSA). *Faculty:* 19 full-time (3 women), 2 part-time/adjunct (0 women). *Students:* 206 full-time (101 women); includes 30 minority (15 Black or African

American, non-Hispanic/Latino; 5 Asian, non-Hispanic/Latino; 6 Hispanic/Latino; 4 Two or more races, non-Hispanic/Latino), 38 international. Average age 23. 549 applicants, 46% accepted, 142 enrolled. In 2016, 157 master's awarded. *Degree requirements:* For master's, 30 credit hours. *Entrance requirements:* For master's, GMAT/GRE, letters of recommendation, official transcripts, current resume or curriculum vitae. Additional exam requirements/recommendations for international students: Required—TOEFL (minimum score 600 paper-based; 100 iBT). *Application deadline:* For fall admission, 6/1 for domestic students, 1/1 for international students. Applications are processed on a rolling basis. Application fee: $100. Electronic applications accepted. *Expenses:* Contact institution. *Financial support:* Career-related internships or fieldwork and scholarships/grants available. Financial award application deadline: 4/15; financial award applicants required to submit FAFSA. *Faculty research:* Influence of personal relationships on business decision-making and management of change; drivers of perceived value and consumer behavior; impact of accounting on auditing, financial, managerial, systems and taxation stakeholders; corporate governance and executive compensation; impact of operations strategies on competitiveness. *Unit head:* James Willis, Associate Dean for Accountancy, 336-758-5422, Fax: 336-758-5830, E-mail: busadmissions@wfu.edu. *Application contact:* Tamara Paquee, Administrative Assistant, 336-758-5422, Fax: 336-758-5830, E-mail: busadmissions@wfu.edu.
Website: http://business.wfu.edu/ms-accountancy

Walsh College of Accountancy and Business Administration, Graduate Programs, Program in Accountancy, Troy, MI 48083. Offers finance (MAC); taxation (MAC). *Program availability:* Part-time, evening/weekend. *Faculty:* 8 full-time (4 women), 24 part-time/adjunct (6 women). *Students:* 278 (159 women); includes 55 minority (23 Black or African American, non-Hispanic/Latino; 1 American Indian or Alaska Native, non-Hispanic/Latino; 21 Asian, non-Hispanic/Latino; 7 Hispanic/Latino; 3 Two or more races, non-Hispanic/Latino), 24 international. Average age 32. 94 applicants, 76% accepted, 71 enrolled. In 2016, 93 master's awarded. *Degree requirements:* For master's, thesis optional. *Entrance requirements:* For master's, minimum overall cumulative GPA of 2.75 from all colleges previously attended. Additional exam requirements/recommendations for international students: Required—TOEFL (minimum score 550 paper-based, 79 iBT), IELTS (6.5), Michigan English Language Assessment Battery, or MTELP. *Application deadline:* Applications are processed on a rolling basis. Application fee: $35. Electronic applications accepted. *Expenses:* $740 per semester credit hour, $125 registration fee per semester. *Financial support:* In 2016–17, 19 students received support. Career-related internships or fieldwork and scholarships/grants available. Financial award application deadline: 6/30; financial award applicants required to submit FAFSA. *Unit head:* John Black, Chair, Accounting, Tax and Business Law, 248-823-1635, Fax: 248-689-0920, E-mail: jblack@walshcollege.edu. *Application contact:* Heather Rigby, Director, Admissions and Academic Advising, 248-823-1294, Fax: 248-823-1611, E-mail: hrigby@walshcollege.edu.

Walsh College of Accountancy and Business Administration, Graduate Programs, Program in Taxation, Troy, MI 48083. Offers MST. *Program availability:* Part-time, evening/weekend. *Faculty:* 2 full-time (1 woman), 4 part-time/adjunct (0 women). *Students:* 63 (24 women); includes 15 minority (9 Black or African American, non-Hispanic/Latino; 3 Asian, non-Hispanic/Latino; 3 Hispanic/Latino), 4 international. Average age 35. 17 applicants, 88% accepted, 11 enrolled. In 2016, 19 master's awarded. *Entrance requirements:* For master's, minimum overall cumulative GPA of 2.75 from all colleges previously attended. Additional exam requirements/recommendations for international students: Required—TOEFL (minimum score 550 paper-based, 79 iBT), IELTS (6.5), Michigan English Language Assessment Battery, or MTELP. *Application deadline:* Applications are processed on a rolling basis. Application fee: $35. Electronic applications accepted. *Expenses:* $740 per credit hour, $125 registration fee per semester. *Financial support:* In 2016–17, 5 students received support. Career-related internships or fieldwork and scholarships/grants available. Financial award application deadline: 6/30; financial award applicants required to submit FAFSA. *Unit head:* Rick Davidson, Vice Chair, Taxation and Business Law, 248-823-1635, Fax: 248-689-0920, E-mail: rdavidson@walshcollege.edu. *Application contact:* Heather Rigby, Director, Admissions and Academic Advising, 248-823-1610, Fax: 248-689-0938, E-mail: hrigby@walshcollege.edu.

Wayne State University, Law School, Detroit, MI 48202. Offers corporate and finance law (LL M); labor and employment law (LL M); law (JD); taxation (LL M); United States law (LL M); JD/MA; JD/MADR; JD/MBA; JD/MS. *Accreditation:* ABA. *Faculty:* 40 full-time (15 women), 27 part-time/adjunct (12 women). *Students:* 379 full-time (162 women), 58 part-time (26 women); includes 63 minority (35 Black or African American, non-Hispanic/Latino; 1 American Indian or Alaska Native, non-Hispanic/Latino; 9 Asian, non-Hispanic/Latino; 3 Hispanic/Latino; 15 Two or more races, non-Hispanic/Latino), 13 international. Average age 27. 684 applicants, 53% accepted, 138 enrolled. In 2016, 16 master's, 133 doctorates awarded. *Degree requirements:* For master's, thesis (for some programs). *Entrance requirements:* For master's, JD from ABA-accredited institution and member institution of the AALS; for doctorate, LSAT, LDAS report, bachelor's degree from accredited institution, personal statement, transcripts from all U.S. undergraduate schools attended and an analysis and summary of the transcripts; letter of recommendation (up to two are accepted). Additional exam requirements/recommendations for international students: Required—TOEFL (minimum score 600 paper-based; 100 iBT), Michigan English Language Assessment Battery (minimum score 85); Recommended—IELTS (minimum score 7). *Application deadline:* For fall admission, 7/1 for domestic students, 5/1 priority date for international students. Applications are processed on a rolling basis. Application fee: $0. Electronic applications accepted. *Expenses:* Contact institution. *Financial support:* In 2016–17, 353 students received support. Fellowships, Federal Work-Study, and scholarships/grants available. Support available to part-time students. Financial award application deadline: 6/30; financial award applicants required to submit FAFSA. *Faculty research:* Public interest law, tax law, international law, environmental law, health law. *Unit head:* Lance Gable, Interim Dean, 313-577-3933, E-mail: jbenson@wayne.edu. *Application contact:* Kathy Fox, Assistant Dean of Admissions, 313-577-3937, Fax: 313-993-8129, E-mail: lawinquire@wayne.edu. Website: http://law.wayne.edu/

Wayne State University, Mike Ilitch School of Business, Detroit, MI 48202. Offers accounting (MS, Postbaccalaureate Certificate); business (Graduate Certificate); business administration (MBA, PhD); data science (MS), including business analytics; entrepreneurship and innovation (Postbaccalaureate Certificate); finance (MS); information systems management (Postbaccalaureate Certificate); taxation (MST); JD/MBA. Application deadline for PhD is February 15. *Accreditation:* AACSB. *Program availability:* Part-time, evening/weekend. *Faculty:* 32. *Students:* 219 full-time (105 women), 941 part-time (406 women); includes 314 minority (186 Black or African American, non-Hispanic/Latino; 3 American Indian or Alaska Native, non-Hispanic/Latino; 68 Asian, non-Hispanic/Latino; 33 Hispanic/Latino; 24 Two or more races, non-Hispanic/Latino), 88 international. Average age 30. 1,119 applicants, 49% accepted, 329 enrolled. In 2016, 203 master's, 1 doctorate, 3 other advanced degrees awarded. *Degree requirements:* For doctorate, thesis/dissertation. *Entrance requirements:* For master's, GMAT, GRE, LSAT, MCAT, at least three years of relevant work experience that shows increased responsibility, or minimum GPA of 3.0 from AACSB-accredited program or 3.2 from regionally-accredited program, undergraduate degree from accredited institution; undergraduate degree in accounting, business administration, or area of business administration (for MS and MST); for doctorate, GMAT (minimum score of 600), minimum undergraduate GPA of 3.0, 3.5 upper-division or graduate; three letters of recommendation; brief essay; undergraduate degree from accredited institution; personal statement; for other advanced degree, bachelor's degree from accredited institution. Additional exam requirements/recommendations for international students: Required—TOEFL (minimum score 550 paper-based; 79 iBT), Michigan English Language Assessment Battery (minimum score 85); Recommended—IELTS (minimum score 6.5), TWE (minimum score 5.5). *Application deadline:* For fall admission, 7/1 for domestic students, 5/1 priority date for international students; for winter admission, 11/1 for domestic students, 9/1 priority date for international students; for spring admission, 3/1 for domestic students, 1/1 priority date for international students. Applications are processed on a rolling basis. Application fee: $50. Electronic applications accepted. *Expenses:* $18,871 per year resident tuition and fees, $36,065 per year non-resident tuition and fees. *Financial support:* In 2016–17, 174 students received support, including 1 fellowship with tuition reimbursement available (averaging $18,000 per year), 2 research assistantships with tuition reimbursements available (averaging $18,000 per year), 5 teaching assistantships with tuition reimbursements available (averaging $18,000 per year); scholarships/grants, health care benefits, and unspecified assistantships also available. Support available to part-time students. Financial award applicants required to submit FAFSA. *Faculty research:* Executive compensation and stock performance, consumer reactions to pricing strategies, communication across the automotive supply chain, performance of firms in sub-Saharan Africa, implementation issues with ERP software. *Unit head:* Dr. Robert Forsythe, Dean, School of Business Administration, 313-577-4501, E-mail: robert.forsythe@wayne.edu. *Application contact:* Kiantee N. Rupert-Jones, Director, 313-577-4511, Fax: 313-577-9442, E-mail: gradbusiness@wayne.edu.
Website: http://ilitchbusiness.wayne.edu/

Weber State University, John B. Goddard School of Business and Economics, School of Accounting and Taxation, Ogden, UT 84408-1001. Offers accounting (M Acc); taxation (M Tax). *Accreditation:* AACSB. *Program availability:* Part-time, evening/weekend. *Faculty:* 7 full-time (2 women). *Students:* 25 full-time (12 women), 12 part-time (4 women); includes 3 minority (1 Asian, non-Hispanic/Latino; 2 Hispanic/Latino), 6 international. Average age 30. In 2016, 42 master's awarded. *Entrance requirements:* For master's, GMAT. Additional exam requirements/recommendations for international students: Required—TOEFL (minimum score 80 iBT). *Application deadline:* For fall admission, 8/1 for domestic students; for spring admission, 12/1 for domestic students; for summer admission, 4/1 for domestic students. Application fee: $60 ($90 for international students). Electronic applications accepted. *Expenses:* Contact institution. *Financial support:* In 2016–17, 19 students received support. Scholarships/grants available. Financial award application deadline: 4/1; financial award applicants required to submit FAFSA. *Unit head:* Dr. Ryan Pace, Program Director, 801-626-7562, Fax: 801-626-7423, E-mail: rpace@weber.edu. *Application contact:* Dr. Larry A. Deppe, Graduate Coordinator, 801-626-7838, Fax: 801-626-7423, E-mail: ldeppe1@weber.edu.
Website: http://www.weber.edu/goddard/accounting-taxation.html

Western Michigan University Thomas M. Cooley Law School, Graduate Programs, Lansing, MI 48901-3038. Offers administrative law (public law) (JD); business transactions (JD); Canadian law practice (JD); constitutional law/civil rights (public law) (JD); corporate law and finance (LL M); environmental law (public law) (JD); general practice (JD), including solo and small firm; homeland and national security law (LL M); insurance law (LL M); intellectual property (JD); intellectual property law (LL M); international law (JD); litigation (JD); self-directed (LL M, JD); tax law (LL M); taxation (JD); U.S. legal studies for foreign attorneys (LL M); JD/LL M; JD/MBA; JD/MPA; JD/MSW. *Program availability:* Part-time, evening/weekend, 100% online, blended/hybrid learning. *Degree requirements:* For master's, thesis optional; for doctorate, minimum of 3 credits of clinical experience. *Entrance requirements:* For master's, JD or LL B; for doctorate, LSAT. Additional exam requirements/recommendations for international students: Required—TOEFL (for U.S. legal studies for foreign attorneys LL M program); Recommended—TOEFL. Electronic applications accepted. *Faculty research:* Wrongful convictions, civil rights, environmental law, litigation techniques, data mining, intellectual property, practical and skills-based legal education.

Wichita State University, Graduate School, W. Frank Barton School of Business, School of Accountancy, Wichita, KS 67260. Offers accounting information systems (M Acc); taxation (M Acc). *Accreditation:* AACSB. *Program availability:* Part-time, evening/weekend. *Unit head:* Dr. Paul D. Harrison, Director, 316-978-3215, Fax: 316-978-3660, E-mail: paul.harrison@wichita.edu. *Application contact:* Jordan Oleson, Admissions Coordinator, 316-978-3095, Fax: 316-978-3253,
E-mail: jordan.oleson@wichita.edu. Website: http://www.wichita.edu/acct

Widener University, School of Business Administration, Program in Taxation, Chester, PA 19013-5792. Offers MS. *Program availability:* Part-time, evening/weekend. *Faculty:* 2 full-time (1 woman), 2 part-time/adjunct (1 woman). *Students:* 7 full-time (5 women), 23 part-time (7 women); includes 7 minority (all Black or African American, non-Hispanic/Latino), 3 international. Average age 35. 10 applicants, 60% accepted, 4 enrolled. In 2016, 11 master's awarded. *Entrance requirements:* For master's, Certified Public Accountant Exam or GMAT. *Application deadline:* For fall admission, 8/1 priority date for domestic students; for spring admission, 12/1 for domestic students. Applications are processed on a rolling basis. Application fee: $25 ($300 for international students). Electronic applications accepted. Tuition and fees vary according to degree level and program. *Financial support:* Available to part-time students. Application deadline: 5/1. *Faculty research:* Financial planning, taxation fraud. *Unit head:* Frank C. Lordi, Head, 610-499-4308, E-mail: frank.c.lordi@widener.edu. *Application contact:* Ann Seltzer, Graduate Enrollment Administrator, 610-499-4305, E-mail: apseltzer@widener.edu.

Section 3
Advertising and Public Relations

This section contains a directory of institutions offering graduate work in electronic commerce. Additional information about programs listed in the directory but not augmented by an in-depth entry may be obtained by writing directly to the dean of a graduate school or chair of a department at the address given in the directory.

For programs offering related work, see also in this book *Business Administration* and *Management and Marketing.* In another guide in this series:

Graduate Programs in the Humanities, Arts & Social Sciences
See *Communication and Media*

CONTENTS

Advertising and Public Relations

Academy of Art University, Graduate Programs, School of Advertising, San Francisco, CA 94105-3410. Offers advertising (MFA); advertising and branded media technology (MA). *Program availability:* Part-time, 100% online. *Faculty:* 6 full-time (2 women), 20 part-time/adjunct (6 women). *Students:* 85 full-time (56 women), 24 part-time (16 women); includes 16 minority (2 Black or African American, non-Hispanic/Latino; 1 American Indian or Alaska Native, non-Hispanic/Latino; 7 Asian, non-Hispanic/Latino; 6 Hispanic/Latino), 72 international. Average age 28. 32 applicants, 100% accepted, 16 enrolled. In 2016, 47 master's awarded. *Degree requirements:* For master's, final review. *Entrance requirements:* For master's, statement of intent; resume; portfolio/reel; official college transcripts. *Application deadline:* Applications are processed on a rolling basis. Application fee: $50. Electronic applications accepted. *Expenses: Tuition:* Part-time $982 per unit. *Financial support:* Career-related internships or fieldwork, Federal Work-Study, and scholarships/grants available. Financial award application deadline: 8/10; financial award applicants required to submit FAFSA. *Unit head:* 800-544-ARTS, E-mail: info@academyart.edu. *Application contact:* 800-544-ARTS, E-mail: info@academyart.edu.
Website: http://www.academyart.edu/advertising-school/index.html

Arcadia University, College of Arts and Sciences, Program in International Public Relations, Glenside, PA 19038-3295. Offers MA. *Students:* 4 full-time (2 women), 5 part-time (3 women); includes 2 minority (1 Black or African American, non-Hispanic/Latino; 1 Asian, non-Hispanic/Latino), 5 international. Average age 29. In 2016, 5 master's awarded. *Degree requirements:* For master's, thesis, internship. *Expenses:* Contact institution. *Application contact:* Office of Enrollment Management, 215-572-2910, Fax: 215-572-4049, E-mail: admiss@arcadia.edu.

Ball State University, Graduate School, College of Communication, Information, and Media, Department of Journalism, Program in Public Relations, Muncie, IN 47306. Offers MA. *Program availability:* Part-time, 100% online, blended/hybrid learning. *Entrance requirements:* For master's, GRE General Test (minimum score 150 verbal), minimum baccalaureate GPA of 2.75 or 3.0 in latter half of baccalauareate, transcripts of all prior course work, current resume or curriculum vitae, statement of purpose, writing sample. Additional exam requirements/recommendations for international students: Required—TOEFL (minimum score 550 paper-based; 79 iBT), IELTS (minimum score 6.5). Electronic applications accepted.

Boston University, College of Communication, Department of Mass Communication, Advertising, and Public Relations, Boston, MA 02215. Offers advertising (MS); JD/MS. *Program availability:* Part-time. *Faculty:* 26 full-time, 33 part-time/adjunct. *Students:* 269 full-time (214 women), 11 part-time (10 women); includes 37 minority (6 Black or African American, non-Hispanic/Latino; 7 Asian, non-Hispanic/Latino; 19 Hispanic/Latino; 5 Two or more races, non-Hispanic/Latino), 173 international. Average age 24. 429 applicants, 48% accepted, 81 enrolled. In 2016, 51 master's awarded. *Degree requirements:* For master's, comprehensive exam (for some programs), thesis (for some programs). *Entrance requirements:* For master's, GRE General Test, resume, letters of recommendation. Additional exam requirements/recommendations for international students: Required—TOEFL (minimum score 600 paper-based; 100 iBT), IELTS. *Application deadline:* For fall admission, 5/1 for domestic and international students. Applications are processed on a rolling basis. Application fee: $80. Electronic applications accepted. *Financial support:* Research assistantships, teaching assistantships with partial tuition reimbursements, career-related internships or fieldwork, Federal Work-Study, institutionally sponsored loans, scholarships/grants, and unspecified assistantships available. Support available to part-time students. Financial award application deadline: 5/1; financial award applicants required to submit FAFSA. *Unit head:* Tobe Berkovitz, Interim Chairman, 617-353-3482, E-mail: tobetv@bu.edu. *Application contact:* Haley Nielsen, Administrator of Admission and Financial Aid, 617-353-3481, E-mail: comgrad@bu.edu.
Website: http://www.bu.edu/com/academics/masscomm-ad-pr/

Boston University, Metropolitan College, Program in Advertising, Boston, MA 02215. Offers MS. *Program availability:* Part-time, evening/weekend. *Faculty:* 1 full-time (0 women), 15 part-time/adjunct (6 women). *Students:* 31 part-time (24 women); includes 2 minority (1 Black or African American, non-Hispanic/Latino; 1 Two or more races, non-Hispanic/Latino). Average age 29. 13 applicants, 69% accepted, 9 enrolled. In 2016, 25 master's awarded. *Entrance requirements:* For master's, undergraduate degree in appropriate field of study. *Application deadline:* Applications are processed on a rolling basis. Application fee: $85. Electronic applications accepted. *Expenses:* Contact institution. *Financial support:* Unspecified assistantships available. Support available to part-time students. Financial award applicants required to submit FAFSA. *Faculty research:* Communication and advertising. *Unit head:* Dr. Christopher Cakebread, Associate Professor, 617-353-3476, E-mail: ccakebr@bu.edu.
Website: http://www.bu.edu/met/advertising

California Baptist University, Program in Public Relations, Riverside, CA 92503. Offers MA. *Program availability:* Part-time, evening/weekend, online learning. *Faculty:* 3 full-time (2 women), 1 (woman) part-time/adjunct. *Students:* 8 full-time (5 women), 8 part-time (6 women); includes 11 minority (6 Black or African American, non-Hispanic/Latino; 3 Hispanic/Latino; 2 Two or more races, non-Hispanic/Latino). Average age 32. 10 applicants, 60% accepted, 5 enrolled. In 2016, 11 master's awarded. *Degree requirements:* For master's, comprehensive capstone. *Entrance requirements:* For master's, minimum undergraduate GPA of 2.5, 2 recommendations, current resume, 500-word essay. Additional exam requirements/recommendations for international students: Required—TOEFL (minimum score 80 iBT). *Application deadline:* For fall admission, 8/1 priority date for domestic students, 7/1 for international students; for spring admission, 12/1 priority date for domestic students, 11/1 priority date for international students. Applications are processed on a rolling basis. Application fee: $45. Electronic applications accepted. *Expenses:* Contact institution. *Financial support:* Applicants required to submit CSS PROFILE or FAFSA. *Faculty research:* New media technologies, media relations, journalism, media effects. *Unit head:* Dr. David Poole, Vice President of Online and Professional Studies, 951-343-3902, E-mail: dpoole@calbaptist.edu. *Application contact:* Dr. MaryAnn Pearson, Program Director, MA in Public Relations, 951-343-3967, E-mail: mpearson@calbaptist.edu.
Website: http://www.cbuonline.edu/programs/program/master-of-arts-in-public-relations

Clarion University of Pennsylvania, Office of Transfer, Adult and Graduate Admissions, Online Certificate Programs, Clarion, PA 16214. Offers family nurse practitioner (Post-Master's Certificate); library science (CAS); nurse educator (Post-Master's Certificate); public relations (Certificate). *Accreditation:* ALA (one or more programs are accredited at the [master's] level). *Program availability:* Part-time, 100% online. *Faculty:* 19 full-time (15 women), 5 part-time/adjunct (all women). *Students:* 6 part-time (5 women); includes 3 minority (1 Black or African American, non-Hispanic/Latino; 1 Asian, non-Hispanic/Latino; 1 Two or more races, non-Hispanic/Latino). Average age 43. 7 applicants, 100% accepted, 1 enrolled. In 2016, 12 CASs awarded. *Entrance requirements:* Additional exam requirements/recommendations for international students: Required—TOEFL (minimum score 550 paper-based; 80 iBT), IELTS (minimum score 7). *Application deadline:* For fall admission, 8/1 priority date for domestic students, 4/15 priority date for international students; for spring admission, 12/1 priority date for domestic students, 9/15 priority date for international students. Applications are processed on a rolling basis. Application fee: $40. Electronic applications accepted. *Expenses:* $687.55 per credit. *Financial support:* Career-related internships or fieldwork, Federal Work-Study, scholarships/grants, and unspecified assistantships available. Support available to part-time students. Financial award application deadline: 3/1. *Unit head:* E-mail: gradstudies@clarion.edu. *Application contact:* Dana Bearer, Associate Director, Transfer, Adult, and Graduate Programs, 814-393-2337, Fax: 814-393-2722, E-mail: gradstudies@clarion.edu.
Website: http://www.clarion.edu/admissions/graduate/index.html

Colorado State University, College of Liberal Arts, Department of Journalism and Media Communication, Fort Collins, CO 80523-1785. Offers communications and media management (MCMM); public communication and technology (MS, PhD). *Program availability:* Part-time. *Faculty:* 13 full-time (6 women). *Students:* 26 full-time (18 women), 40 part-time (29 women); includes 11 minority (1 Black or African American, non-Hispanic/Latino; 2 American Indian or Alaska Native, non-Hispanic/Latino; 4 Hispanic/Latino; 4 Two or more races, non-Hispanic/Latino), 9 international. Average age 32. 28 applicants, 71% accepted, 14 enrolled. In 2016, 9 master's, 4 doctorates awarded. Terminal master's awarded for partial completion of doctoral program. *Degree requirements:* For master's, thesis (for some programs), research project; for doctorate, comprehensive exam, thesis/dissertation. *Entrance requirements:* For master's and doctorate, GRE General Test, minimum GPA of 3.0. Additional exam requirements/recommendations for international students: Required—TOEFL (minimum score 550 paper-based; 80 iBT); Recommended—IELTS (minimum score 6.5). Application fee: $60 ($70 for international students). Electronic applications accepted. *Expenses:* Tuition, state resident: full-time $9628. Tuition, nonresident: full-time $23,603. *Required fees:* $2253; $528.14 per credit hour. $264.07 per semester. Tuition and fees vary according to course load and program. *Financial support:* In 2016–17, 20 students received support, including 1 research assistantship with full and partial tuition reimbursement available (averaging $18,663 per year), 32 teaching assistantships with full and partial tuition reimbursements available (averaging $14,987 per year); fellowships with full and partial tuition reimbursements available, scholarships/grants, and health care benefits also available. Financial award application deadline: 1/15; financial award applicants required to submit FAFSA. *Faculty research:* Media and human behavior; strategic communication; risk, science and health communication; media ethics and policy; news and information. *Total annual research expenditures:* $558,539. *Unit head:* Greg Luft, Professor and Department Chair, 970-491-1979, Fax: 970-491-2908, E-mail: greg.luft@colostate.edu. *Application contact:* Linda Kidder, Graduate Program Administrator, 970-491-5132, Fax: 970-491-2908, E-mail: linda.kidder@colostate.edu.
Website: http://journalism.colostate.edu/

DePaul University, College of Communication, Chicago, IL 60614. Offers digital communication and media arts (MA); health communication (MA); journalism (MA); media and cinema studies (MA); organizational and multicultural communication (MA); public relations and advertising (MA); relational communication (MA). *Program availability:* Part-time, evening/weekend. *Entrance requirements:* Additional exam requirements/recommendations for international students: Required—TOEFL (minimum score 590 paper-based; 96 iBT), IELTS (minimum score 7.5) or PTE. Electronic applications accepted.

Emerson College, Graduate Studies, School of Communication, Department of Marketing Communication, Boston, MA 02116-4624. Offers global marketing communication and advertising (MA); integrated marketing communication (MA). *Faculty:* 16 full-time (6 women), 5 part-time/adjunct (1 woman). *Students:* 106 full-time (87 women), 9 part-time (all women); includes 12 minority (4 Black or African American, non-Hispanic/Latino; 1 Asian, non-Hispanic/Latino; 4 Hispanic/Latino; 3 Two or more races, non-Hispanic/Latino), 70 international. Average age 26. 207 applicants, 86% accepted, 63 enrolled. In 2016, 92 master's awarded. *Entrance requirements:* For master's, GMAT or GRE General Test. Additional exam requirements/recommendations for international students: Required—TOEFL (minimum score 550 paper-based; 80 iBT), IELTS (minimum score 6.5). *Application deadline:* For fall admission, 3/1 priority date for domestic and international students; for spring admission, 11/1 for domestic and international students. Applications are processed on a rolling basis. Application fee: $60 ($75 for international students). Electronic applications accepted. *Financial support:* In 2016–17, 50 students received support, including 57 fellowships with partial tuition reimbursements available (averaging $6,137 per year); research assistantships with partial tuition reimbursements available, Federal Work-Study, scholarships/grants, and unspecified assistantships also available. Financial award application deadline: 3/1; financial award applicants required to submit FAFSA. *Application contact:* Leanda Ferland, Director of Graduate Admission, 617-824-8610, Fax: 617-824-8614.
Website: http://www.emerson.edu/graduate_admission

Georgetown University, Graduate School of Arts and Sciences, School of Continuing Studies, Program in Public Relations and Corporate Communications, Washington, DC 20057. Offers MPS. *Degree requirements:* For master's, capstone course.

Golden Gate University, Ageno School of Business, San Francisco, CA 94105-2968. Offers accounting (MBA); business administration (EMBA, MBA, PMBA, DBA); business analytics (MS); finance (MBA, MS, Certificate); financial planning (MS, Certificate); healthcare information systems (Certificate); human resource management (MBA, MS); human resources management (Certificate); information systems (MS); information technology (MBA); information technology management (Certificate); integrated marketing and communications (MS, Certificate); international business (MBA); management (MBA); marketing (MBA, MS, Certificate); operations supply chain management (Certificate); psychology (MA, Certificate); public administration (EMPA); public relations (MS, Certificate); technical market analysis (Certificate); JD/MBA. *Program availability:* Part-time, evening/weekend. *Faculty:* 18 full-time (3 women), 117 part-time/adjunct (44 women). *Students:* 458 full-time (254 women), 664 part-time (331 women); includes 346 minority (75 Black or African American, non-Hispanic/Latino; 2 American Indian or Alaska Native, non-Hispanic/Latino; 132 Asian, non-Hispanic/Latino; 105 Hispanic/Latino; 9 Native Hawaiian or other Pacific Islander, non-Hispanic/Latino; 23 Two or more races, non-Hispanic/Latino), 354 international. Average age 34. 905 applicants, 83% accepted, 165 enrolled. In 2016, 350 master's, 2 doctorates awarded. *Degree requirements:* For doctorate, thesis/dissertation, qualifying examination. *Entrance requirements:* For master's, GMAT (for MBA), minimum GPA of 2.5 (MS). Additional exam requirements/recommendations for international students: Required—

TOEFL (minimum score 550 paper-based; 79 iBT). *Application deadline:* For fall admission, 5/15 for domestic and international students; for winter admission, 1/15 for domestic and international students; for spring admission, 9/15 for domestic and international students. Applications are processed on a rolling basis. Application fee: $70 ($110 for international students). Electronic applications accepted. *Expenses:* Contact institution. *Financial support:* In 2016–17, 372 students received support. Career-related internships or fieldwork, Federal Work-Study, institutionally sponsored loans, and scholarships/grants available. Support available to part-time students. Financial award applicants required to submit FAFSA. *Unit head:* Dr. Gordon Swartz, Dean, 415-442-7027, Fax: 415-442-6579, E-mail: gswartz@ggu.edu. *Application contact:* Angela Melero, Enrollment Services, 415-442-7800, Fax: 415-442-7807, E-mail: info@ggu.edu.
Website: http://www.ggu.edu/programs/business-and-management

Hofstra University, Lawrence Herbert School of Communication, Programs in Journalism and Public Relations, Hempstead, NY 11549. Offers journalism (MA); public relations (MA). *Program availability:* Part-time, evening/weekend. *Students:* 58 full-time (43 women), 22 part-time (16 women); includes 38 minority (19 Black or African American, non-Hispanic/Latino; 3 Asian, non-Hispanic/Latino; 13 Hispanic/Latino; 3 Two or more races, non-Hispanic/Latino), 8 international. Average age 25. 89 applicants, 73% accepted, 33 enrolled. In 2016, 30 master's awarded. *Degree requirements:* For master's, thesis. *Entrance requirements:* For master's, minimum GPA of 2.75; bachelor's degree. Additional exam requirements/recommendations for international students: Required—TOEFL (minimum score 550 paper-based; 95 iBT). *Application deadline:* Applications are processed on a rolling basis. Application fee: $75. Electronic applications accepted. *Expenses: Tuition:* Full-time $1240. *Required fees:* $970. Tuition and fees vary according to program. *Financial support:* In 2016–17, 43 students received support, including 10 fellowships with full and partial tuition reimbursements available (averaging $3,045 per year), 3 research assistantships with full and partial tuition reimbursements available (averaging $7,125 per year); career-related internships or fieldwork, Federal Work-Study, institutionally sponsored loans, scholarships/grants, tuition waivers (full and partial), and unspecified assistantships also available. Support available to part-time students. Financial award applicants required to submit FAFSA. *Faculty research:* Hybrid media theory, particularly as it relates to journalism and politics; political communication, public relations and international communication; impact of convergence and interactive-based technologies and the impact of immigration and globalization on health information campaigns; mediated message design, rational and emotional appeals in strategic messaging, crisis communications, public relations, persuasion; the crossroads of popular culture, politics, new media, and civic engagement. *Unit head:* Dr. Gregory S. Smith, Chairperson, 516-463-4270, Fax: 516-463-4866, E-mail: gregory.s.smith@hofstra.edu. *Application contact:* Sunil Samuel, Assistant Vice President of Admissions, 516-463-4723, Fax: 516-463-4664, E-mail: graduateadmission@hofstra.edu.
Website: http://www.hofstra.edu/academics/colleges/soc/

Iona College, School of Arts and Science, Department of Mass Communication, New Rochelle, NY 10801-1890. Offers non-profit public relations (Certificate); public relations (MA); sports communication and media (MA). *Accreditation:* ACEJMC (one or more programs are accredited). *Program availability:* Part-time, evening/weekend. *Faculty:* 3 full-time (1 woman), 8 part-time/adjunct (4 women). *Students:* 10 full-time (4 women), 28 part-time (22 women); includes 17 minority (10 Black or African American, non-Hispanic/Latino; 7 Hispanic/Latino), 3 international. Average age 27. 19 applicants, 95% accepted, 11 enrolled. In 2016, 19 master's, 6 other advanced degrees awarded. *Degree requirements:* For master's, comprehensive exam (for some programs), thesis or alternative. *Entrance requirements:* For master's, GRE General Test if undergraduate GPA is below 3.0. Additional exam requirements/recommendations for international students: Required—TOEFL (minimum score 550 paper-based; 80 iBT), IELTS (minimum score 6). *Application deadline:* For fall admission, 8/1 for domestic students, 5/1 for international students; for spring admission, 1/1 for domestic students, 9/1 for international students. Applications are processed on a rolling basis. Application fee: $50. Electronic applications accepted. *Expenses:* Contact institution. *Financial support:* In 2016–17, 15 students received support. Scholarships/grants, tuition waivers (partial), and unspecified assistantships available. Support available to part-time students. Financial award application deadline: 4/15; financial award applicants required to submit FAFSA. *Faculty research:* Media ecology, new media, corporate communication, media images, organizational learning in public relations, media law, medicine ethics. *Unit head:* Anthony Kelso, PhD, Chair, 914-633-7795, E-mail: akelso@iona.edu. *Application contact:* Katelyn Brunck, Assistant Director of Graduate Admissions, 914-633-2492, Fax: 914-633-2277, E-mail: kbrunck@iona.edu.
Website: http://www.iona.edu/Academics/School-of-Arts-Science/Departments/Mass-Communication/Graduate-Programs.aspx

Kansas State University, Graduate School, College of Arts and Sciences, A.Q. Miller School of Journalism and Mass Communications, Manhattan, KS 66506. Offers advertising (MS); community journalism (MS); global communication (MS); health communication (MS); media management (MS); public relations (MS). *Program availability:* Part-time, evening/weekend. *Faculty:* 13 full-time (6 women), 1 (woman) part-time/adjunct. *Students:* 13 full-time (10 women), 6 part-time (4 women); includes 1 minority (Hispanic/Latino), 8 international. Average age 29. 7 applicants, 71% accepted, 3 enrolled. In 2016, 7 master's awarded. *Degree requirements:* For master's, comprehensive exam, thesis. *Entrance requirements:* For master's, GRE General Test, minimum GPA of 3.0. Additional exam requirements/recommendations for international students: Required—TOEFL (minimum score 79 iBT). *Application deadline:* For fall admission, 2/1 priority date for domestic and international students; for spring admission, 8/1 priority date for domestic and international students. Applications are processed on a rolling basis. Application fee: $50 ($75 for international students). Electronic applications accepted. *Expenses:* Tuition, state resident: full-time $9670. Tuition, nonresident: full-time $21,828. *Required fees:* $862. *Financial support:* In 2016–17, 2 research assistantships with full tuition reimbursements (averaging $11,180 per year), 7 teaching assistantships with full tuition reimbursements (averaging $7,729 per year) were awarded; scholarships/grants, health care benefits, and unspecified assistantships also available. Financial award application deadline: 2/1; financial award applicants required to submit FAFSA. *Faculty research:* Health communication, risk communication, strategic communications, community journalism, global communication. *Total annual research expenditures:* $219,641. *Unit head:* Dr. Jean Folkerts, Director, 785-532-6890, Fax: 785-532-5484, E-mail: jeanfolk@ksu.edu. *Application contact:* Dr. Barbara DeSanto, Associate Director of Graduate Studies, 785-532-3890, Fax: 785-532-5484, E-mail: desantoi@ksu.edu.
Website: http://jmc.ksu.edu/

Kent State University, College of Communication and Information, School of Journalism and Mass Communication, Kent, OH 44242-0001. Offers journalism and mass communication (MA), including media management, public relations, reporting and editing-broadcast, reporting and editing-convergence, reporting and editing-journalism educators, reporting and editing-magazine, reporting and editing-newspaper. *Program availability:* Part-time, online learning. *Faculty:* 25 full-time (13 women). *Students:* 12 full-time (7 women), 102 part-time (68 women); includes 19 minority (14 Black or African American, non-Hispanic/Latino; 3 Hispanic/Latino; 2 Two or more races, non-Hispanic/Latino), 5 international. Average age 30. 46 applicants, 67% accepted, 20 enrolled. In 2016, 79 master's awarded. *Degree requirements:* For master's, thesis or project. *Entrance requirements:* For master's, GRE, minimum GPA of 3.0, statement of purpose, 3 online recommendations, resume. Additional exam requirements/recommendations for international students: Required—TOEFL (minimum score of 600 paper-based, 100 iBT), IELTS (minimum score of 7.0), Michigan English Language Assessment Battery (minimum score of 85), or PTE (minimum score of 68). *Application deadline:* For fall admission, 7/1 for domestic and international students. Applications are processed on a rolling basis. Application fee: $45 ($70 for international students). Electronic applications accepted. *Expenses:* Tuition, state resident: full-time $10,864; part-time $495 per credit hour. Tuition, nonresident: full-time $18,380; part-time $837 per credit hour. *Financial support:* Research assistantships with full tuition reimbursements, teaching assistantships with full tuition reimbursements, scholarships/grants, and unspecified assistantships available. Financial award application deadline: 3/1. *Unit head:* Thor Wasbotten, Director and Professor, 330-672-4066, E-mail: thor@kent.edu. *Application contact:* Mark Goodman, Graduate Coordinator/Professor, 330-672-6239, E-mail: mgoodm10@kent.edu.
Website: http://www.kent.edu/jmc

La Salle University, School of Arts and Sciences, Program in Strategic Communication, Philadelphia, PA 19141-1199. Offers communication consulting and development (MA); communication management (MA); general professional communication (MA); professional and business communication (Certificate); public relations (MA); social and new media (Certificate). *Program availability:* Part-time, evening/weekend, online learning. *Faculty:* 4 full-time (all women), 1 (woman) part-time/adjunct. *Students:* 11 full-time (7 women), 39 part-time (29 women); includes 18 minority (15 Black or African American, non-Hispanic/Latino; 2 Hispanic/Latino; 1 Two or more races, non-Hispanic/Latino), 2 international. Average age 27. 13 applicants, 92% accepted, 6 enrolled. In 2016, 41 master's, 4 other advanced degrees awarded. *Degree requirements:* For master's, practicum. *Entrance requirements:* For master's, writing assessment, professional resume; minimum overall B average; two letters of recommendation (if GPA below 3.25); brief personal statement (about 500 words); interview; for Certificate, writing assessment, minimum GPA of 2.75 in undergraduate studies; brief personal statement (about 500 words); interview. Additional exam requirements/recommendations for international students: Required—TOEFL. *Application deadline:* For fall admission, 8/15 priority date for domestic students, 7/15 for international students; for spring admission, 12/15 priority date for domestic students, 11/15 for international students; for summer admission, 4/15 priority date for domestic students, 3/15 for international students. Applications are processed on a rolling basis. Application fee: $35. Electronic applications accepted. Application fee is waived when completed online. *Expenses:* Contact institution. *Financial support:* In 2016–17, 7 students received support. Scholarships/grants available. Support available to part-time students. Financial award application deadline: 8/31; financial award applicants required to submit FAFSA. *Unit head:* Dr. Pamela Lannutti, Director, 215-951-1935, Fax: 215-951-5043, E-mail: annutti95@lasalle.edu. *Application contact:* Elizabeth Heenan, Director, Graduate and Adult Enrollment, 215-951-1100, Fax: 214-951-1462, E-mail: heenan@lasalle.edu.
Website: http://www.lasalle.edu/strategic-communication/

Lasell College, Graduate and Professional Studies in Communication, Newton, MA 02466. Offers health communication (MSC, Graduate Certificate); integrated marketing communication (MSC, Graduate Certificate); public relations (MSC, Graduate Certificate). *Program availability:* Part-time, evening/weekend, 100% online, blended/hybrid learning. *Faculty:* 4 full-time (2 women), 5 part-time/adjunct (2 women). *Students:* 12 full-time (9 women), 38 part-time (28 women); includes 11 minority (8 Black or African American, non-Hispanic/Latino; 1 Asian, non-Hispanic/Latino; 2 Hispanic/Latino), 8 international. Average age 31. 60 applicants, 43% accepted, 13 enrolled. In 2016, 71 master's, 3 other advanced degrees awarded. *Degree requirements:* For master's, comprehensive exam, thesis or alternative, minimum GPA of 3.0; special project or internship. *Entrance requirements:* For master's, one-page personal statement, 2 letters of recommendation, resume, bachelor's degree transcript; for Graduate Certificate, bachelor's degree transcript, 2 letters of recommendation, 1-page personal statement, resume. Additional exam requirements/recommendations for international students: Required—TOEFL (minimum score 550 paper-based, 79 iBT) or IELTS (minimum score 6). *Application deadline:* For fall admission, 8/31 priority date for domestic students, 6/30 priority date for international students; for spring admission, 12/31 priority date for domestic students, 10/31 priority date for international students. Applications are processed on a rolling basis. Electronic applications accepted. *Expenses:* $600 per credit. *Financial support:* In 2016–17, 6 students received support. Federal Work-Study, scholarships/grants, and tuition discounts available. Support available to part-time students. Financial award application deadline: 8/31; financial award applicants required to submit FAFSA. *Faculty research:* Terrorists' use of the internet; refugees' use of cell phones as means of communication in Jordan and Germany; political communication, analysis of the media coverage of the conflict and peace process in northern Ireland; interpersonal communication, strategies to address bullying in online communities, in schools and in the workplace. *Unit head:* Dr. Joan Dolamore, Dean of Graduate and Professional Studies, 617-243-2485, Fax: 617-243-2450, E-mail: gradinfo@lasell.edu. *Application contact:* Adrienne Franciosi, Director of Graduate Enrollment, 617-243-2214, Fax: 617-243-2450, E-mail: gradinfo@lasell.edu.
Website: http://www.lasell.edu/academics/graduate-and-professional-studies/programs-of-study/master-of-science-in-communication.html

La Sierra University, College of Arts and Sciences, Department of English and Communication, Riverside, CA 92515. Offers communication (MA), including public relations/advertising, theory emphasis; English (MA), including literary emphasis, writing emphasis. *Program availability:* Part-time. *Degree requirements:* For master's, one foreign language. *Entrance requirements:* For master's, GRE General Test.

Liberty University, School of Business, Lynchburg, VA 24515. Offers accounting (MBA, MS); business administration (MBA); criminal justice (MBA); cyber security (MS); executive leadership (MA); information systems (MS), including information assurance, technology management; international business (MBA, DBA); leadership (DBA); marketing (MBA, MS, DBA), including digital marketing and advertising (MS), project management (MS), public relations (MS), sports marketing and media (MS); project management (MBA, DBA); public administration (MBA); public relations (MBA). *Program availability:* Part-time, online learning. *Students:* 1,458 full-time (807 women), 4,188 part-time (2,041 women); includes 1,372 minority (1,060 Black or African American, non-Hispanic/Latino; 19 American Indian or Alaska Native, non-Hispanic/Latino; 85 Asian, non-Hispanic/Latino; 75 Hispanic/Latino; 10 Native Hawaiian or other Pacific Islander, non-Hispanic/Latino; 123 Two or more races, non-Hispanic/Latino), 124 international. Average age 35. 5,424 applicants, 45% accepted, 1242 enrolled. In 2016, 1,859 master's, 87 other advanced degrees awarded. *Entrance requirements:* For master's, minimum undergraduate GPA of 3.0, 15 hours of upper-level business courses. Additional exam requirements/recommendations for international students: Required—TOEFL (minimum score 600 paper-based; 100 iBT). *Application deadline:* Applications are processed on a rolling basis. Application fee: $50. Electronic applications accepted. *Expenses:* Contact institution. *Financial support:* Applicants required to submit FAFSA. *Unit head:* Dr. Scott Hicks, Dean, 434-592-4808, Fax: 434-582-2366, E-mail: smhicks@

liberty.edu. *Application contact:* Jay Bridge, Director of Graduate Admissions, 800-424-9595, Fax: 800-628-7977, E-mail: gradadmissions@liberty.edu.
Website: http://www.liberty.edu/academics/business/index.cfm?PID-149

Marquette University, Graduate School, College of Communication, Milwaukee, WI 53201-1881. Offers advertising and public relations (MA); communication studies (MA); digital storytelling (Certificate); journalism (MA); mass communication (MA); science, health and environmental communication (MA). *Accreditation:* ACEJMC (one or more programs are accredited). *Program availability:* Part-time, evening/weekend. *Faculty:* 36 full-time (18 women), 45 part-time/adjunct (20 women). *Students:* 25 full-time (22 women), 23 part-time (16 women); includes 9 minority (3 Black or African American, non-Hispanic/Latino; 1 American Indian or Alaska Native, non-Hispanic/Latino; 4 Hispanic/Latino; 1 Two or more races, non-Hispanic/Latino), 4 international. Average age 28. 55 applicants, 62% accepted, 21 enrolled. In 2016, 10 master's, 1 other advanced degree awarded. *Degree requirements:* For master's, comprehensive exam, thesis or alternative. *Entrance requirements:* For master's, GRE, official transcripts from all current and previous colleges/universities except Marquette, three letters of recommendation, statement of academic and professional goals. Additional exam requirements/recommendations for international students: Required—TOEFL (minimum score 530 paper-based). *Application deadline:* Applications are processed on a rolling basis. Electronic applications accepted. *Financial support:* Fellowships, research assistantships, teaching assistantships, career-related internships or fieldwork, scholarships/grants, health care benefits, tuition waivers (full and partial), and unspecified assistantships available. Support available to part-time students. Financial award application deadline: 2/15. *Faculty research:* Urban journalism, gender and communication, intercultural communication, religious communication. *Total annual research expenditures:* $7,941. *Unit head:* Dr. Sarah Feldner, Associate Dean. *Application contact:* Dr. Sarah Bonewits Feldner.
Website: http://diederich.marquette.edu/

Marshall University, Academic Affairs Division, College of Arts and Media, Program in Journalism, Huntington, WV 25755. Offers journalism (MAJ), including health care public relations. *Degree requirements:* For master's, thesis optional. *Entrance requirements:* For master's, GRE General Test.

Michigan State University, The Graduate School, College of Communication Arts and Sciences, Department of Advertising, Public Relations and Retailing, East Lansing, MI 48824. Offers advertising (MA); public relations (MA); retailing (MS, PhD). *Entrance requirements:* Additional exam requirements/recommendations for international students: Required—TOEFL. Electronic applications accepted.

Mississippi College, Graduate School, College of Arts and Sciences, School of Christian Studies and the Arts, Department of Communication, Clinton, MS 39058. Offers applied communication (MSC); public relations and corporate communication (MSC). *Program availability:* Part-time. *Degree requirements:* For master's, comprehensive exam, thesis optional. *Entrance requirements:* For master's, GRE or NTE, minimum GPA of 2.5. Additional exam requirements/recommendations for international students: Recommended—TOEFL, IELTS. Electronic applications accepted.

Monmouth University, Graduate Studies, Department of Communication, West Long Branch, NJ 07764-1898. Offers corporate and public communication (MA); human resources management and communication (Certificate); public service communication specialist (Certificate); strategic public relations and new media (Certificate). *Program availability:* Part-time, evening/weekend, online learning. *Faculty:* 4 full-time (3 women), 2 part-time/adjunct (both women). *Students:* 11 full-time (9 women), 23 part-time (15 women); includes 8 minority (4 Black or African American, non-Hispanic/Latino; 2 Asian, non-Hispanic/Latino; 2 Hispanic/Latino), 1 international. Average age 27. 27 applicants, 7% accepted, 16 enrolled. In 2016, 8 master's, 2 other advanced degrees awarded. Terminal master's awarded for partial completion of doctoral program. *Degree requirements:* For master's, comprehensive exam (for some programs), thesis (for some programs), project. *Entrance requirements:* For master's, GRE, baccalaureate degree with minimum GPA of 3.0 in major, 2.75 overall; two letters of recommendation; personal essay (750 words or less describing preparation for study and personal objectives); digital or hard copy portfolio of select samples of work including a writing sample; resume. Additional exam requirements/recommendations for international students: Required—TOEFL (minimum score 550 paper-based; 79 iBT), IELTS (minimum score 6), Michigan English Language Assessment Battery (minimum score 77). *Application deadline:* For fall admission, 7/15 priority date for domestic students, 6/1 for international students; for spring admission, 12/1 priority date for domestic students, 11/1 for international students; for summer admission, 5/1 for domestic students. Applications are processed on a rolling basis. Application fee: $50. Electronic applications accepted. *Expenses: Tuition, area resident:* Full-time $19,764; part-time $1098 per credit hour. *Required fees:* $175 per semester. Tuition and fees vary according to program. *Financial support:* In 2016–17, 41 students received support, including 23 fellowships (averaging $2,061 per year), 13 teaching assistantships with full and partial tuition reimbursements available (averaging $5,746 per year); research assistantships, institutionally sponsored loans, scholarships/grants, and unspecified assistantships also available. Support available to part-time students. Financial award application deadline: 2/1; financial award applicants required to submit FAFSA. *Faculty research:* Service-learning, history of television, feminism and the media, executive communication, public relations pedagogy. *Unit head:* Dr. Deanna Shoemaker, Program Director, 732-263-5194, Fax: 732-571-3609, E-mail: dshoemak@monmouth.edu. *Application contact:* Andrea Thompson, Graduate Admission Counselor, 732-571-3452, Fax: 732-263-5123, E-mail: gradadm@monmouth.edu.
Website: http://www.monmouth.edu/cpc

Montana State University Billings, College of Arts and Sciences, Department of Communication and Theater, Billings, MT 59101. Offers public relations (MS). *Program availability:* Part-time, 100% online, blended/hybrid learning. *Faculty:* 4 full-time (1 woman). *Students:* 11. *Degree requirements:* For master's, comprehensive exam, thesis optional. *Entrance requirements:* For master's, GRE General Test, minimum undergraduate GPA of 3.0, letters of recommendation, letter of intent, resume. Additional exam requirements/recommendations for international students: Required—TOEFL (minimum score 79 iBT), IELTS (minimum score 6.5). *Application deadline:* For fall admission, 3/15 for domestic students, 7/15 for international students; for spring admission, 10/15 for domestic students, 12/1 for international students. Applications are processed on a rolling basis. Application fee: $40. Electronic applications accepted. *Expenses:* Tuition, state resident: full-time $5265; part-time $3436 per year. Tuition, nonresident: full-time $14,030; part-time $9280 per year. *International tuition:* $19,295 full-time. Tuition and fees vary according to degree level, campus/location and program. *Financial support:* Research assistantships with partial tuition reimbursements, teaching assistantships with partial tuition reimbursements, career-related internships or fieldwork, Federal Work-Study, institutionally sponsored loans, scholarships/grants, and unspecified assistantships available. Support available to part-time students. Financial award application deadline: 5/1; financial award applicants required to submit FAFSA. *Unit head:* Dr. Sarah Keller, Chair, 406-896-5824, E-mail: skeller@msubillings.edu. *Application contact:* David M. Sullivan, Graduate Studies Counselor, 406-657-2053, Fax: 406-657-2299, E-mail: dsullivan@msubillings.edu.

Montclair State University, The Graduate School, College of the Arts, MA Program in Public and Organizational Relations, Montclair, NJ 07043-1624. Offers MA. *Program availability:* Part-time, evening/weekend. *Degree requirements:* For master's, comprehensive exam. *Entrance requirements:* For master's, GRE General Test, 2 letters of recommendation. Additional exam requirements/recommendations for international students: Required—TOEFL (minimum score 83 iBT) or IELTS (minimum score 6.5). Electronic applications accepted. *Expenses:* Tuition, state resident: part-time $553 per credit. Tuition, nonresident: part-time $854 per credit. *Required fees:* $91 per credit. Tuition and fees vary according to program. *Faculty research:* Organizational problem solving and innovation, social media, health communication, globalization, organizational change management.

New York University, School of Continuing and Professional Studies, Division of Programs in Business, Programs in Marketing and Public Relations, New York, NY 10012-1019. Offers corporate and organizational communication (MS); public relations management (MS). *Program availability:* Part-time, evening/weekend. *Degree requirements:* For master's, thesis. *Entrance requirements:* For master's, GRE or GMAT (only upon request), bachelor's degree, resume with relevant professional work, internship or volunteer experience, two letters of recommendation, statement of purpose. Additional exam requirements/recommendations for international students: Required—TOEFL (minimum score 600 paper-based; 100 iBT), IELTS (minimum score 7). Electronic applications accepted.

Northern Kentucky University, Office of Graduate Programs, College of Informatics, Program in Communication, Highland Heights, KY 41099. Offers communication (MA); communication teaching (Certificate); documentary studies (Certificate); public relations (Certificate); relationships (Certificate). *Program availability:* Part-time, evening/weekend. Terminal master's awarded for partial completion of doctoral program. *Degree requirements:* For master's, comprehensive exams, thesis or applied capstone project. *Entrance requirements:* For master's, GRE, minimum GPA of 3.0, 3 letters of recommendation, letter of intent. Additional exam requirements/recommendations for international students: Required—TOEFL (minimum score 79 iBT); Recommended—IELTS (minimum score 6.5). Electronic applications accepted. *Faculty research:* Mediating effect of health communication, organizational communication, quantitative and qualitative research methods, family and interpersonal communication.

Quinnipiac University, School of Communications, Program in Public Relations, Hamden, CT 06518-1940. Offers public relations (MS), including social media. *Program availability:* Part-time, evening/weekend. *Faculty:* 5 full-time (4 women), 2 part-time/adjunct (1 woman). *Students:* 7 full-time (4 women), 9 part-time (5 women); includes 3 minority (2 Black or African American, non-Hispanic/Latino; 1 Two or more races, non-Hispanic/Latino). 22 applicants, 86% accepted, 9 enrolled. In 2016, 8 master's awarded. *Entrance requirements:* Additional exam requirements/recommendations for international students: Required—TOEFL (minimum score 575 paper-based; 90 iBT), IELTS (minimum score 6.5). *Application deadline:* For fall admission, 7/31 priority date for domestic students, 4/30 for international students. Applications are processed on a rolling basis. Application fee: $45. Electronic applications accepted. *Expenses: Tuition:* Part-time $985 per credit. *Required fees:* $40 per credit. $150 per semester. Tuition and fees vary according to program. *Financial support:* Federal Work-Study, scholarships/grants, and unspecified assistantships available. Financial award application deadline: 6/1; financial award applicants required to submit FAFSA. *Faculty research:* Social media, corporate social responsibility, ethics, international communications and international public relations, public diplomacy, non-profit management, crisis management, investor relations. *Unit head:* Phillip Simon, Program Director, 203-582-8672, E-mail: graduate@qu.edu. *Application contact:* Office of Graduate Admissions, 203-582-8672, Fax: 203-582-3443, E-mail: graduate@qu.edu.
Website: http://www.qu.edu/gradpr

Rowan University, Graduate School, College of Communication and Creative Arts, Program in Public Relations/Advertising, Glassboro, NJ 08028-1701. Offers MA. *Program availability:* Part-time, evening/weekend. *Degree requirements:* For master's, thesis. *Entrance requirements:* For master's, GRE General Test. Additional exam requirements/recommendations for international students: Required—TOEFL. Electronic applications accepted.

Royal Roads University, Graduate Studies, Applied Leadership and Management Program, Victoria, BC V9B 5Y2, Canada. Offers executive coaching (Graduate Certificate); health systems leadership (Graduate Certificate); project management (Graduate Certificate); public relations management (Graduate Certificate); strategic human resources management (Graduate Certificate).

San Diego State University, Graduate and Research Affairs, College of Professional Studies and Fine Arts, School of Communication, San Diego, CA 92182. Offers advertising and public relations (MA); critical-cultural studies (MA); interaction studies (MA); intercultural and international studies (MA); new media studies (MA); news and information studies (MA); telecommunications and media management (MA). *Degree requirements:* For master's, thesis. *Entrance requirements:* For master's, GRE General Test, 3 letters of recommendation. Additional exam requirements/recommendations for international students: Required—TOEFL. Electronic applications accepted.

Savannah College of Art and Design, Graduate School, Program in Advertising, Savannah, GA 31402-3146. Offers MA, MFA. *Program availability:* Part-time. *Faculty:* 9 full-time (3 women), 6 part-time/adjunct (2 women). *Students:* 33 full-time (21 women), 8 part-time (4 women); includes 19 minority (13 Black or African American, non-Hispanic/Latino; 1 American Indian or Alaska Native, non-Hispanic/Latino; 2 Asian, non-Hispanic/Latino; 3 Hispanic/Latino), 12 international. Average age 27. 53 applicants, 26% accepted, 6 enrolled. In 2016, 18 master's awarded. *Degree requirements:* For master's, final project (for MA); thesis (for MFA). *Entrance requirements:* For master's, GRE (recommended), portfolio (submitted in digital format), audition or writing submission, resume, statement of purpose, two letters of recommendation. Additional exam requirements/recommendations for international students: Required—TOEFL (minimum score 550 paper-based, 85 iBT), IELTS (minimum score 6.5), or ACTFL. *Application deadline:* For fall admission, 4/1 for domestic and international students. Applications are processed on a rolling basis. Application fee: $40. Electronic applications accepted. *Expenses: Tuition:* Full-time $36,045. Tuition and fees vary according to course load. *Financial support:* Fellowships, career-related internships or fieldwork, Federal Work-Study, and scholarships/grants available. Financial award application deadline: 4/1; financial award applicants required to submit FAFSA. *Unit head:* Emily Sander, Chair of Advertising Design. *Application contact:* Jenny Jaquillard, Executive Director of Admissions, Recruitment and Events, 912-525-5100, Fax: 912-525-5985, E-mail: admission@scad.edu.
Website: http://www.scad.edu/academics/programs/advertising

Seton Hall University, College of Communication and the Arts, South Orange, NJ 07079-2697. Offers museum professions (MA), including exhibition development, museum education, museum management, museum registration; public relations (MA); strategic communication (MA). *Program availability:* Part-time, evening/weekend, online learning. *Degree requirements:* For master's, thesis. *Entrance requirements:* Additional exam requirements/recommendations for international students: Required—TOEFL.

Electronic applications accepted. *Faculty research:* Managerial communication, communication consulting, communication and development.

Southern Illinois University Edwardsville, Graduate School, College of Arts and Sciences, Department of Applied Communication Studies, Program in Public Relations, Edwardsville, IL 62026. Offers MA. *Program availability:* Part-time, evening/weekend. *Degree requirements:* For master's, comprehensive exam (for some programs), thesis (for some programs). *Entrance requirements:* Additional exam requirements/recommendations for international students: Required—TOEFL (minimum score 550 paper-based, 79 iBT), IELTS (minimum score 6.5), Michigan Test of English Language Proficiency or PTE. Electronic applications accepted.

Southern Methodist University, Meadows School of the Arts, Temerlin Advertising Institute, Dallas, TX 75275. Offers MA. *Entrance requirements:* For master's, GRE, GMAT. Additional exam requirements/recommendations for international students: Required—TOEFL (minimum score 550 paper-based; 80 iBT). Electronic applications accepted.

Suffolk University, College of Arts and Sciences, Advertising and Public Relations Department, Boston, MA 02108-2770. Offers communication studies (MAC); integrated marketing communication (MAC); public relations and advertising (MAC). *Program availability:* Part-time, evening/weekend. *Faculty:* 5 full-time (3 women). *Students:* 14 full-time (9 women), 17 part-time (14 women); includes 5 minority (2 Black or African American, non-Hispanic/Latino; 3 Hispanic/Latino), 12 international. Average age 27. 64 applicants, 66% accepted, 15 enrolled. In 2016, 18 master's awarded. *Degree requirements:* For master's, thesis optional. *Entrance requirements:* For master's, GRE General Test, MAT, or GMAT, 2 letters of recommendation, resume. Additional exam requirements/recommendations for international students: Required—TOEFL (minimum score 550 paper-based; 80 iBT). *Application deadline:* For fall admission, 3/15 priority date for domestic and international students; for spring admission, 10/15 priority date for domestic and international students. Applications are processed on a rolling basis. Application fee: $50. Electronic applications accepted. *Expenses:* $27,456 per year full-time tuition, $1,144 per credit hour part-time tuition, $52 per year student activity fee. *Financial support:* In 2016–17, 22 students received support, including 18 fellowships (averaging $9,186 per year); career-related internships or fieldwork, Federal Work-Study, institutionally sponsored loans, and scholarships/grants also available. Support available to part-time students. Financial award application deadline: 4/1; financial award applicants required to submit FAFSA. *Faculty research:* Branding law and management, health care communication, gender roles and violence in video games, new media, political communication. *Unit head:* Robert Rosenthal, Chair, 617-573-8502, E-mail: rrosenthal@suffolk.edu. *Application contact:* Mara Marzocchi, Associate Director of Graduate Admissions, 617-573-8302, Fax: 617-305-1733, E-mail: grad.admission@suffolk.edu.
Website: http://www.suffolk.edu/college/graduate/69298.php

Syracuse University, S. I. Newhouse School of Public Communications, MA Program in Advertising, Syracuse, NY 13244. Offers MA. *Students:* Average age 24. *Degree requirements:* For master's, capstone course. *Entrance requirements:* For master's, GRE General Test, resume, official transcripts, personal statement, three letters of recommendation. Additional exam requirements/recommendations for international students: Required—TOEFL (minimum score 600 paper-based; 100 iBT). *Application deadline:* For summer admission, 1/15 for domestic and international students. Application fee: $45. Electronic applications accepted. *Expenses: Tuition:* Full-time $25,974; part-time $1443 per credit hour. *Required fees:* $802; $50 per course. Tuition and fees vary according to course load and program. *Financial support:* Fellowships with full tuition reimbursements, research assistantships with partial tuition reimbursements, and teaching assistantships with full tuition reimbursements available. Financial award application deadline: 1/1. *Faculty research:* Advertising management, digital advertising and branding, marketing communication, strategic media planning, advertising campaigns. *Unit head:* Prof. James Tsao, Chair, 315-443-7362, E-mail: jctsao@syr.edu. *Application contact:* Martha Coria, Graduate Records Office, 315-443-4039, Fax: 315-443-1834, E-mail: pcgrad@syr.edu.
Website: http://newhouse.syr.edu/

Syracuse University, S. I. Newhouse School of Public Communications, MS in Public Relations Program, Syracuse, NY 13244. Offers MS. *Students:* Average age 24. *Degree requirements:* For master's, thesis (for some programs). *Entrance requirements:* For master's, GRE General Test, resume, official transcripts, personal statement, three letters of recommendation. Additional exam requirements/recommendations for international students: Required—TOEFL (minimum score 600 paper-based; 100 iBT). *Application deadline:* For summer admission, 1/15 priority date for domestic and international students. Application fee: $45. Electronic applications accepted. *Expenses: Tuition:* Full-time $25,974; part-time $1443 per credit hour. *Required fees:* $802; $50 per course. Tuition and fees vary according to course load and program. *Financial support:* Fellowships with full tuition reimbursements, research assistantships with partial tuition reimbursements, and teaching assistantships with partial tuition reimbursements available. Financial award application deadline: 2/1. *Faculty research:* Media law, visual communication, public relations, financial markets and institutions. *Unit head:* Prof. Rochelle Ford, Chair, 315-443-9347, E-mail: pcgrad@syr.edu. *Application contact:* Martha Coria, Graduate Records Office, 315-443-4039, Fax: 315-443-1834, E-mail: pcgrad@syr.edu.
Website: http://newhouse.syr.edu/

Universidad Autonoma de Guadalajara, Graduate Programs, Guadalajara, Mexico. Offers administrative law and justice (LL M); advertising and corporate communications (MA); architecture (M Arch); business (MBA); computational science (MCC); education (Ed M, Ed D); English-Spanish translation (MA); entrepreneurship and management (MBA); integrated management of digital animation (MA); international business (MIB); international corporate law (LL M); internet technologies (MS); manufacturing systems (MMS); occupational health (MS); philosophy (MA, PhD); power electronics (MS); quality systems (MQS); renewable energy (MS); social evaluation of projects (MBA); strategic market research (MBA); tax law (MA); teaching mathematics (MA).

Université Laval, Faculty of Letters, Program in Public Relations, Québec, QC G1K 7P4, Canada. Offers Diploma. *Program availability:* Part-time, evening/weekend. *Entrance requirements:* For degree, knowledge of French, comprehension of written English. Electronic applications accepted.

The University of Alabama, Graduate School, College of Communication and Information Sciences, Department of Advertising and Public Relations, Tuscaloosa, AL 35487-0172. Offers MA. *Program availability:* Part-time. *Faculty:* 13 full-time (5 women). *Students:* 12 full-time (9 women), 4 part-time (3 women); includes 5 minority (3 Black or African American, non-Hispanic/Latino; 1 Hispanic/Latino; 1 Two or more races, non-Hispanic/Latino), 1 international. Average age 23. 54 applicants, 41% accepted, 9 enrolled. In 2016, 13 master's awarded. *Degree requirements:* For master's, comprehensive exam, thesis or alternative. *Entrance requirements:* For master's, GRE (minimum score: 300 verbal plus quantitative; 4.0 in writing), minimum undergraduate GPA of 3.0 for last 60 hours. Additional exam requirements/recommendations for international students: Required—TOEFL (minimum score 600 paper-based; 100 iBT); Recommended—IELTS (minimum score 7). *Application deadline:* For fall admission, 3/1 priority date for domestic and international students. Applications are processed on a rolling basis. Application fee: $50 ($60 for international students). Electronic applications accepted. *Expenses:* Tuition, state resident: full-time $10,470. Tuition, nonresident: full-time $26,950. *Financial support:* In 2016–17, 2 fellowships, 4 research assistantships with partial tuition reimbursements, 4 teaching assistantships with full tuition reimbursements were awarded; career-related internships or fieldwork, health care benefits, and unspecified assistantships also available. Financial award application deadline: 3/1. *Faculty research:* Advertising and public relations management, leadership, ethics, public opinion, political communication, advertising media, social and digital media, international communication, creativity, consumer privacy, crisis communication, disaster communication, sports communication, advertising and public relations history. *Total annual research expenditures:* $7,500. *Unit head:* Dr. Joseph Edward Phelps, Professor and Chairman, 205-348-8646, E-mail: phelps@apr.ua.edu. *Application contact:* Dr. Kenon Brown, Assistant Professor, 205-348-5326, E-mail: brown@apr.ua.edu.
Website: http://www.apr.ua.edu

University of Colorado Boulder, Graduate School, College of Media, Communication and Information, Department of Advertising, Public Relations and Media Design, Boulder, CO 80309. Offers media research and practice (PhD); strategic communication design (MA). *Faculty:* 8 full-time (4 women). *Students:* 16 full-time (7 women); includes 4 minority (2 Asian, non-Hispanic/Latino; 2 Hispanic/Latino). Average age 29. 23 applicants, 78% accepted, 16 enrolled. Application fee: $60 ($80 for international students). Electronic applications accepted. *Financial support:* In 2016–17, 23 students received support, including 18 fellowships (averaging $7,782 per year), 1 research assistantship with full and partial tuition reimbursement available (averaging $25,432 per year), 2 teaching assistantships with full and partial tuition reimbursements available (averaging $26,510 per year); institutionally sponsored loans, scholarships/grants, health care benefits, and unspecified assistantships also available. Financial award application deadline: 2/1; financial award applicants required to submit FAFSA. *Faculty research:* Advertising; mass communication/media; electronic media; health communication; marketing. *Application contact:* E-mail: gharsha@colorado.edu.
Website: http://www.colorado.edu/cmci/academics/advertising-pr-and-media-design

University of Florida, Graduate School, College of Journalism and Communications, Program in Advertising, Gainesville, FL 32611. Offers M Adv. *Degree requirements:* For master's, thesis or terminal project. *Entrance requirements:* For master's, GRE General Test, minimum GPA of 3.0. Additional exam requirements/recommendations for international students: Required—TOEFL (minimum score 550 paper-based; 80 iBT), IELTS (minimum score 6). Electronic applications accepted. *Faculty research:* Branding, information flow between clients and suppliers, message and media strategies, emotional response.

University of Florida, Graduate School, College of Journalism and Communications, Program in Mass Communication, Gainesville, FL 32611. Offers international/intercultural communication (MAMC); journalism (MAMC); mass communication (MAMC, PhD), including clinical translational science (MAMC); public relations (MAMC); science/health communication (MAMC); telecommunication (MAMC). *Accreditation:* ACEJMC. *Entrance requirements:* For master's and doctorate, GRE General Test, minimum GPA of 3.0.

University of Houston, College of Liberal Arts and Social Sciences, Jack J. Valenti School of Communication, Houston, TX 77204. Offers health communication (MA); mass communication studies (MA); public relations studies (MA); speech communication (MA). *Program availability:* Part-time. *Degree requirements:* For master's, comprehensive exam (for some programs), thesis (for some programs), 30-33 hours. *Entrance requirements:* For master's, GRE. Additional exam requirements/recommendations for international students: Required—TOEFL. Electronic applications accepted.

University of Illinois at Urbana–Champaign, Graduate College, College of Media, Department of Advertising, Champaign, IL 61820. Offers MS.

University of Maryland, College Park, Academic Affairs, College of Arts and Humanities, Department of Communication, College Park, MD 20742. Offers MA, PhD. *Degree requirements:* For master's, thesis optional; for doctorate, comprehensive exam, thesis/dissertation. *Entrance requirements:* For master's, GRE General Test, minimum GPA of 3.0, sample of scholarly writing, 3 letters of recommendation, statement of goals and experiences; for doctorate, GRE General Test. Additional exam requirements/recommendations for international students: Required—TOEFL. Electronic applications accepted. *Faculty research:* Health communication, interpersonal communication, persuasion, intercultural communication, contemporary rhetoric theory.

University of Miami, Graduate School, School of Communication, Coral Gables, FL 33124. Offers communication (PhD); communication studies (MA); film studies (MA, PhD); motion pictures (MFA), including production, producing, and screenwriting; print journalism (MA); public relations (MA); Spanish language journalism (MA); television broadcast journalism (MA). *Program availability:* Part-time. *Degree requirements:* For master's, comprehensive exam (for some programs), thesis (for some programs); for doctorate, comprehensive exam, thesis/dissertation. *Entrance requirements:* For master's, GRE General Test; for doctorate, GRE General Test, master's thesis or scholarly research. Additional exam requirements/recommendations for international students: Required—TOEFL (minimum score 600 paper-based; 100 iBT). Electronic applications accepted. *Faculty research:* Communication studies, mass communication, international/interpersonal communication, film studies, journalism.

University of Nebraska–Lincoln, Graduate College, College of Arts and Sciences, Department of Communication Studies, Lincoln, NE 68588. Offers instructional communication (MA, PhD); interpersonal communication (MA, PhD); marketing, communication studies, and advertising (MA, PhD); organizational communication (MA, PhD); rhetoric and culture (MA, PhD). *Degree requirements:* For master's, thesis optional; for doctorate, comprehensive exam, thesis/dissertation. *Entrance requirements:* For master's and doctorate, GRE General Test, writing sample. Additional exam requirements/recommendations for international students: Required—TOEFL (minimum score 600 paper-based). Electronic applications accepted. *Faculty research:* Message strategies, gender communication, political communication, organizational communication, instructional communication.

University of Nebraska–Lincoln, Graduate College, College of Journalism and Mass Communications, Lincoln, NE 68588. Offers marketing, communication and advertising (MA); professional journalism (MA). *Program availability:* Online learning. *Degree requirements:* For master's, thesis. *Entrance requirements:* For master's, samples of work. Additional exam requirements/recommendations for international students: Required—TOEFL (minimum score 600 paper-based). Electronic applications accepted. *Faculty research:* Interactive media and the Internet, community newspapers, children's radio, advertising involvement, telecommunications policy.

University of North Texas, Robert B. Toulouse School of Graduate Studies, Denton, TX 76203-5459. Offers accounting (MS); applied anthropology (MA, MS); applied behavior analysis (Certificate); applied geography (MA); applied technology and performance improvement (M Ed, MS); art education (MA); art history (MA); art museum education (Certificate); arts leadership (Certificate); audiology (Au D); behavior analysis

(MS); behavioral science (PhD); biochemistry and molecular biology (MS); biology (MA, MS); biomedical engineering (MS); business analysis (MS); chemistry (MS); clinical health psychology (PhD); communication studies (MA, MS); computer engineering (MS); computer science (MS); counseling (M Ed, MS), including clinical mental health counseling (MS), college and university counseling, elementary school counseling, secondary school counseling; creative writing (MA); criminal justice (MS); curriculum and instruction (M Ed); decision sciences (MBA); design (MA, MFA), including fashion design (MFA), innovation studies, interior design (MFA); early childhood studies (MS); economics (MS); educational leadership (M Ed, Ed D); educational psychology (MS, PhD), including family studies (MS), gifted and talented (MS), human development (MS), learning and cognition (MS), research, measurement and evaluation (MS); electrical engineering (MS); emergency management (MPA); engineering technology (MS); English (MA); English as a second language (MA); environmental science (MS); finance (MBA, MS); financial management (MPA); French (MA); health services management (MBA); higher education (M Ed, Ed D); history (MA, MS); hospitality management (MS); human resources management (MPA); information science (MS); information systems (PhD); information technologies (MBA); interdisciplinary studies (MA, MS); international studies (MA); international sustainable tourism (MS); jazz studies (MM); journalism (MA, MJ, Graduate Certificate), including interactive and virtual digital communication (Graduate Certificate), narrative journalism (Graduate Certificate), public relations (Graduate Certificate); kinesiology (MS); linguistics (MA); local government management (MPA); logistics (PhD); logistics and supply chain management (MBA); long-term care, senior housing, and aging services (MA); management (PhD); marketing (MBA); mathematics (MA, MS); mechanical and energy engineering (MS, PhD); music (MA), including ethnomusicology, music theory, musicology, performance; music composition (PhD); music education (MM Ed, PhD); nonprofit management (MPA); operations and supply chain management (MBA); performance (MM, DMA); philosophy (MA); political science (MA); professional and technical communication (MA); radio, television and film (MA, MFA); rehabilitation counseling (Certificate); sociology (MA); Spanish (MA); special education (M Ed); speech-language pathology (MA); strategic management (MBA); studio art (MFA); teaching (M Ed); MBA/MS. *Program availability:* Part-time, evening/weekend, online learning. Terminal master's awarded for partial completion of doctoral program. *Degree requirements:* For master's, variable foreign language requirement, comprehensive exam (for some programs), thesis (for some programs); for doctorate, variable foreign language requirement, comprehensive exam (for some programs), thesis/dissertation; for other advanced degree, variable foreign language requirement, comprehensive exam (for some programs). *Entrance requirements:* For master's and doctorate, GRE, GMAT. Additional exam requirements/recommendations for international students: Required—TOEFL (minimum score 550 paper-based; 79 iBT). Electronic applications accepted.

University of Saint Mary, Graduate Programs, Program in Business Administration, Leavenworth, KS 66048-5082. Offers enterprise risk management (MBA); finance (MBA); general management (MBA); health care management (MBA); human resource management (MBA); marketing and advertising management (MBA). *Program availability:* Part-time, evening/weekend, 100% online, blended/hybrid learning. *Students:* 201 full-time (110 women), 62 part-time (38 women); includes 83 minority (29 Black or African American, non-Hispanic/Latino; 3 American Indian or Alaska Native, non-Hispanic/Latino; 14 Asian, non-Hispanic/Latino; 32 Hispanic/Latino; 1 Native Hawaiian or other Pacific Islander, non-Hispanic/Latino; 4 Two or more races, non-Hispanic/Latino), 7 international. Average age 34. In 2016, 73 master's awarded. *Degree requirements:* For master's, thesis. *Entrance requirements:* For master's, minimum undergraduate GPA of 2.75, official transcripts, two letters of recommendation. *Application deadline:* Applications are processed on a rolling basis. Application fee: $25. Electronic applications accepted. *Expenses:* $595 per hour. *Unit head:* Rick Gunter, Director, 913-319-3007. *Application contact:* Mark Harvey, Program Manager, 913-319-3007, E-mail: mark.harvey@stmary.edu.
Website: http://www.stmary.edu/success/Grad-Program/Master-of-Business-Administration-MBA.aspx

University of Southern California, Graduate School, Annenberg School for Communication and Journalism, School of Journalism, Program in Strategic Public Relations, Los Angeles, CA 90089. Offers MA. *Program availability:* Part-time, evening/weekend. *Students:* 75 full-time (66 women), 5 part-time; includes 36 minority (11 Black or African American, non-Hispanic/Latino; 7 Asian, non-Hispanic/Latino; 16 Hispanic/Latino; 2 Two or more races, non-Hispanic/Latino), 20 international. Average age 24. 153 applicants, 49% accepted, 46 enrolled. In 2016, 41 master's awarded. *Degree requirements:* For master's, comprehensive exam (for some programs), thesis optional. *Entrance requirements:* For master's, GRE General Test, resume, writing samples, letters of recommendation, statement of purpose. Additional exam requirements/recommendations for international students: Required—TOEFL (minimum score 114 iBT), IELTS (minimum score 8). *Application deadline:* For fall admission, 1/1 priority date for domestic students. Application fee: $90. Electronic applications accepted. *Financial support:* In 2016–17, 4 fellowships with full and partial tuition reimbursements (averaging $22,000 per year), 2 teaching assistantships with full and partial tuition reimbursements (averaging $22,000 per year) were awarded; career-related internships or fieldwork, Federal Work-Study, scholarships/grants, and health care benefits also available. Support available to part-time students. Financial award application deadline: 1/1; financial award applicants required to submit FAFSA. *Unit head:* Willow Bay, Director of Journalism School, 213-740-3914, E-mail: jourbks@usc.edu. *Application contact:* Allyson Hill, Associate Dean for Admissions, 213-821-0770, Fax: 213-740-1933, E-mail: ascadm@usc.edu.
Website: http://www.annenberg.usc.edu/

University of Southern Mississippi, Graduate School, College of Arts and Letters, School of Mass Communication and Journalism, Hattiesburg, MS 39406. Offers mass communication (MA, MS, PhD); public relations (MA, MS). *Program availability:* Part-time. *Degree requirements:* For master's, comprehensive exam, thesis optional; for doctorate, comprehensive exam, thesis/dissertation. *Entrance requirements:* For master's, GRE General Test, minimum GPA of 3.0 in field of study, 2.75 in last 2 years; for doctorate, GRE General Test, minimum GPA of 3.5. Additional exam requirements/recommendations for international students: Required—TOEFL, IELTS. *Application deadline:* For fall admission, 3/1 priority date for domestic students, 3/1 for international students; for spring admission, 1/10 priority date for domestic and international students. Applications are processed on a rolling basis. Application fee: $60. *Expenses: Tuition, area resident:* Full-time $15,708; part-time $437 per credit hour. *Financial support:* Fellowships with full tuition reimbursements, research assistantships with full tuition reimbursements, teaching assistantships with full tuition reimbursements, career-related internships or fieldwork, Federal Work-Study, institutionally sponsored loans, scholarships/grants, health care benefits, and unspecified assistantships available. Financial award application deadline: 3/15; financial award applicants required to submit FAFSA. *Unit head:* Dr. David R. Davies, Director, 601-266-4258, Fax: 601-266-4263, E-mail: dave.davies@usm.edu. *Application contact:* Dr. Cheryl Jenkins, Graduate Coordinator, 601-266-6241, Fax: 601-266-6473, E-mail: cheryl.jenkins@usm.edu.
Website: https://www.usm.edu/school-of-journalism-and-media-studies

The University of Tennessee, Graduate School, College of Communication and Information, Knoxville, TN 37996. Offers advertising (MS, PhD); broadcasting (MS, PhD); communications (MS, PhD); information sciences (MS, PhD); journalism (MS, PhD); public relations (MS, PhD); speech communication (MS, PhD). *Program availability:* Part-time, evening/weekend, online learning. *Degree requirements:* For master's, thesis or alternative; for doctorate, thesis/dissertation. *Entrance requirements:* For master's and doctorate, GRE General Test, minimum GPA of 2.7. Additional exam requirements/recommendations for international students: Required—TOEFL. Electronic applications accepted.

The University of Texas at Austin, Graduate School, College of Communication, Department of Advertising, Austin, TX 78712-1111. Offers MA, PhD. *Entrance requirements:* For master's and doctorate, GRE General Test. Electronic applications accepted. *Faculty research:* Interactive advertising, advertising laws and ethics, advertising creativity, media planning and modeling, international advertising.

The University of Texas Rio Grande Valley, College of Liberal Arts, Department of Communication, Edinburg, TX 78539. Offers communication (MA); communication training and consulting (Graduate Certificate); strategic communication and media relations (Graduate Certificate); theatre (MA). *Accreditation:* NAST. *Program availability:* Part-time, evening/weekend. *Degree requirements:* For master's, comprehensive exam, thesis or alternative. *Entrance requirements:* For master's, minimum GPA of 3.0. Additional exam requirements/recommendations for international students: Required—TOEFL. Tuition and fees vary according to course load and program. *Faculty research:* Rhetorical theory, intercultural and mass communication, American theatre, multicultural theatre and drama, television and film.

University of the Sacred Heart, Graduate Programs, Department of Communication, Program in Public Relations, San Juan, PR 00914-0383. Offers MA. *Program availability:* Part-time, evening/weekend. *Degree requirements:* For master's, thesis. *Entrance requirements:* For master's, EXADEP, minimum undergraduate GPA of 2.75, interview.

University of Wisconsin–Stevens Point, College of Fine Arts and Communication, Division of Communication, Stevens Point, WI 54481-3897. Offers interpersonal communication (MA); media studies (MA); organizational communication (MA); public relations (MA). *Program availability:* Part-time. *Degree requirements:* For master's, thesis or alternative. *Entrance requirements:* For master's, GRE. Additional exam requirements/recommendations for international students: Required—TOEFL (minimum score 575 paper-based). *Faculty research:* Communication theory and research, film history.

Virginia Commonwealth University, Graduate School, College of Humanities and Sciences, School of Mass Communications, Program in Mass Communications, Richmond, VA 23284-9005. Offers multimedia journalism (MS); strategic public relations (MS). *Degree requirements:* For master's, comprehensive exam, thesis optional. *Entrance requirements:* For master's, GRE General Test. Additional exam requirements/recommendations for international students: Required—TOEFL (minimum score 600 paper-based; 100 iBT); Recommended—IELTS (minimum score 6.5). *Application deadline:* For fall admission, 3/15 for domestic students. Applications are processed on a rolling basis. Application fee: $50. Electronic applications accepted. *Financial support:* Teaching assistantships, career-related internships or fieldwork, Federal Work-Study, institutionally sponsored loans, and tuition waivers (full and partial) available. Support available to part-time students. Financial award applicants required to submit FAFSA. *Faculty research:* Multimedia journalism, strategic public relations. *Unit head:* Dr. Terry Oggel, Interim Director, School of Mass Communications, 804-828-2660, Fax: 804-828-9175, E-mail: masscomm@vcu.edu. *Application contact:* June O. Nicholson, Director of Graduate Studies, 804-827-0251, Fax: 804-828-9175, E-mail: jonichol@vcu.edu.
Website: http://www.has.vcu.edu/mac/

Virginia International University, School of Business, Fairfax, VA 22030. Offers accounting (MBA, MS); entrepreneurship (MBA); executive management (Graduate Certificate); global logistics (MBA); health care management (MBA); hospitality and tourism management (MBA); human resources management (MBA); international business management (MBA); international finance (MBA); marketing management (MBA); mass media and public relations (MBA); project management (MBA, MS). *Program availability:* Part-time, online learning. *Entrance requirements:* For master's and Graduate Certificate, bachelor's degree. Additional exam requirements/recommendations for international students: Required—TOEFL (minimum score 550 paper-based; 80 iBT), IELTS (minimum score 6). Electronic applications accepted.

Wayne State University, College of Fine, Performing and Communication Arts, Department of Communication, Detroit, MI 48202. Offers communication (PhD), including democratic participation and culture, identity and representation, media, society and culture, risk, crisis and conflict, wellness, work life and relationships; communication and new media (Graduate Certificate); communication studies (MA); dispute resolution (MADR, Graduate Certificate); health communication (Graduate Certificate); journalism (MA); media arts (MA); media studies (MA); public relations and organizational communication (MA); JD/MADR. Doctoral program admits for fall only. *Faculty:* 20. *Students:* 59 full-time (32 women), 113 part-time (75 women); includes 69 minority (54 Black or African American, non-Hispanic/Latino; 2 Asian, non-Hispanic/Latino; 7 Hispanic/Latino; 6 Two or more races, non-Hispanic/Latino), 12 international. Average age 34. 154 applicants, 39% accepted, 41 enrolled. In 2016, 31 master's, 10 doctorates, 4 other advanced degrees awarded. *Degree requirements:* For master's, thesis (for some programs), thesis or essay; for doctorate, thesis/dissertation. *Entrance requirements:* For master's, GRE (if undergraduate GPA less than 3.2), personal statement; BA or BS in communication or related field with minimum upper-division GPA of 3.2 and minimum upper-division undergraduate GPA of 3.0, personal statement, and sample of academic writing (for MA); 3 letters of recommendation (for MADR); for doctorate, GRE, MA in communication or related field with minimum GPA of 3.5; three letters of recommendation; personal statement; sample of written scholarship. Additional exam requirements/recommendations for international students: Required—TOEFL (minimum score 600 paper-based; 100 iBT), IELTS, TWE. Application fee: $50. Electronic applications accepted. *Expenses:* $17,240 per year resident tuition and fees, $34,434 per year non-resident tuition and fees. *Financial support:* In 2016–17, 61 students received support, including 4 fellowships with tuition reimbursements available (averaging $16,000 per year), 2 research assistantships with tuition reimbursements available (averaging $19,570 per year), 21 teaching assistantships with tuition reimbursements available (averaging $17,994 per year); scholarships/grants and unspecified assistantships also available. Financial award applicants required to submit FAFSA. *Faculty research:* Rhetorical theory and criticism; mass media theory and research; argumentation; organizational communication; risk and crisis communication; interpersonal, family, and health communication. *Unit head:* Dr. Lillian Black, Professor and Chair, 313-577-2943, E-mail: eh8899@wayne.edu. *Application contact:* E-mail: communication@wayne.edu.
Website: http://comm.wayne.edu/

Webster University, School of Communications, Program in Advertising and Marketing Communications, St. Louis, MO 63119-3194. Offers MA. *Program availability:* Online learning. *Expenses: Tuition:* Full-time $21,900; part-time $730 per credit hour. Tuition and fees vary according to campus/location and program. *Unit head:* Kristen DiFate, Program Coordinator, 314-246-8238, E-mail: kristendifate41@webster.edu. *Application* *contact:* Sarah Nandor, Director, Graduate and Transfer Admissions, 314-968-7109, E-mail: gadmit@webster.edu.

Webster University, School of Communications, Program in Public Relations, St. Louis, MO 63119-3194. Offers MA. *Expenses: Tuition:* Full-time $21,900; part-time $730 per credit hour. Tuition and fees vary according to campus/location and program. *Unit head:* Gary Ford, Program Facilitator, 314-246-8632, E-mail: fordg@webster.edu. *Application contact:* Sarah Nandor, Director, Graduate and Transfer Admissions, 314-968-7109, E-mail: gadmit@webster.edu.

Western New England University, College of Arts and Sciences, Program in Communication, Springfield, MA 01119. Offers public relations (MA). *Program availability:* Part-time, evening/weekend. *Faculty:* 6 full-time (5 women). *Students:* 17 part-time (11 women); includes 4 minority (2 Black or African American, non-Hispanic/Latino; 1 Asian, non-Hispanic/Latino; 1 Hispanic/Latino). Average age 32. 8 applicants, 88% accepted, 5 enrolled. In 2016, 8 master's awarded. *Degree requirements:* For master's, independent study or thesis. *Entrance requirements:* For master's, official transcript, personal statement, resume, three letters of recommendation. Additional exam requirements/recommendations for international students: Required—TOEFL (minimum score 79 iBT). *Application deadline:* Applications are processed on a rolling basis. Application fee: $30. Electronic applications accepted. *Expenses:* Contact institution. *Financial support:* Application deadline: 4/15; applicants required to submit FAFSA. *Unit head:* Dr. Saeed Ghahramani, Dean, 413-782-1218, Fax: 413-796-2118, E-mail: sghahram@wne.edu. *Application contact:* Matthew Fox, Director of Graduate Admissions, Enrollment Management Group, 413-782-1410, Fax: 413-782-1777, E-mail: study@wne.edu.
Website: http://www1.wne.edu/academics/graduate/ma-communication.cfm

William Woods University, Graduate and Adult Studies, Fulton, MO 65251-1098. Offers administration (M Ed, Ed S); athletic/activities administration (M Ed); curriculum and instruction (M Ed, Ed S); educational leadership (Ed D); equestrian education (M Ed); health management (MBA); human resources (MBA); leadership (MBA); marketing, advertising, and public relations (MBA); teaching and technology (M Ed). *Program availability:* Part-time, evening/weekend. *Degree requirements:* For master's, capstone course (MBA), action research (M Ed); for Ed S, field experience. *Entrance requirements:* Additional exam requirements/recommendations for international students: Required—TOEFL (minimum score 550 paper-based). Electronic applications accepted. *Expenses:* Contact institution.

Section 4
Electronic Commerce

This section contains a directory of institutions offering graduate work in electronic commerce. Additional information about programs listed in the directory but not augmented by an in-depth entry may be obtained by writing directly to the dean of a graduate school or chair of a department at the address given in the directory.

CONTENTS

Program Directory

Electronic Commerce

California State University, Fullerton, Graduate Studies, College of Business and Economics, Department of Information Systems and Decision Sciences, Fullerton, CA 92834-9480. Offers decision science (MBA); information systems (MBA, MS); information systems and decision sciences (MS); information systems and e-commerce (MS); information technology (MS). *Program availability:* Part-time. *Degree requirements:* For master's, project or thesis. *Entrance requirements:* For master's, GMAT, minimum AACSB index of 950. Application fee: $55. *Expenses:* Tuition, state resident: full-time $3369; part-time $1953 per unit. Tuition, nonresident: full-time $3915; part-time $2499 per unit. Tuition and fees vary according to course load, degree level and program. *Financial support:* Career-related internships or fieldwork, Federal Work-Study, institutionally sponsored loans, and scholarships/grants available. Support available to part-time students. Financial award application deadline: 3/1; financial award applicants required to submit FAFSA. *Unit head:* Dr. Bhushan Kapoor, Chair, 657-278-2221. *Application contact:* Admissions/Applications, 657-278-2371.
Website: http://business.fullerton.edu/isds/

Claremont Graduate University, Graduate Programs, Center for Information Systems and Technology, Claremont, CA 91711-6160. Offers cybersecurity and networking (MS); data science and analytics (MS); electronic commerce (PhD); geographic information systems (MS); health informatics (MS); information systems (Certificate); IT strategy and innovation (MS); knowledge management (PhD); systems development (PhD); telecommunications and networking (PhD); MBA/MS. *Program availability:* Part-time. *Faculty:* 8 full-time (1 woman), 1 part-time/adjunct (0 women). *Students:* 60 full-time (18 women), 81 part-time (27 women); includes 34 minority (7 Black or African American, non-Hispanic/Latino; 18 Asian, non-Hispanic/Latino; 7 Hispanic/Latino; 1 Native Hawaiian or other Pacific Islander, non-Hispanic/Latino; 1 Two or more races, non-Hispanic/Latino), 80 international. Average age 35. In 2016, 21 master's, 10 doctorates awarded. *Degree requirements:* For doctorate, comprehensive exam, thesis/dissertation, portfolio. *Entrance requirements:* For master's and doctorate, GMAT, GRE General Test. Additional exam requirements/recommendations for international students: Required—TOEFL (minimum score 75 iBT). *Application deadline:* For fall admission, 2/1 priority date for domestic and international students. Applications are processed on a rolling basis. Application fee: $80. Electronic applications accepted. *Expenses: Tuition:* Full-time $44,328; part-time $1847 per unit. *Required fees:* $600; $300 per semester. Tuition and fees vary according to course load and program. *Financial support:* Fellowships, research assistantships, teaching assistantships, Federal Work-Study, institutionally sponsored loans, and scholarships/grants available. Support available to part-time students. Financial award application deadline: 2/15; financial award applicants required to submit FAFSA. *Faculty research:* Man-machine interaction, organizational aspects of computing, implementation of information systems, information systems practice. *Unit head:* Lorne Olfman, Acting Director, 909-607-3035, E-mail: lorne.olfman@cgu.edu. *Application contact:* Jake Campbell, Senior Assistant Director of Admissions, 909-607-3024, E-mail: jake.campbell@cgu.edu.
Website: https://www.cgu.edu/school/center-for-information-systems-and-technology/

Dalhousie University, Faculty of Computer Science, Halifax, NS B3H 1W5, Canada. Offers computational biology and bioinformatics (M Sc); computer science (MA Sc, MC Sc, PhD); electronic commerce (MEC); health informatics (MHI). *Degree requirements:* For master's, thesis (for some programs); for doctorate, thesis/dissertation. *Entrance requirements:* Additional exam requirements/recommendations for international students: Required—1 of 5 approved tests: TOEFL, IELTS, CANTEST, CAEL, Michigan English Language Assessment Battery. Electronic applications accepted.

DePaul University, College of Computing and Digital Media, Chicago, IL 60604. Offers animation (MA, MFA); business information technology (MS); cinema (MFA); cinema production (MS); computational finance (MS); computer and information sciences (PhD); computer game development (MS); computer information and network security (MS); computer science (MS); e-commerce technology (MS); health informatics (MS); human-computer interaction (MS); information systems (MS); information technology project management (MS); network engineering and management (MS); predictive analytics (MS); screenwriting (MFA); software engineering (MS); JD/MS. *Program availability:* Part-time, evening/weekend, online learning. *Degree requirements:* For master's, thesis (for some programs); for doctorate, comprehensive exam, thesis/dissertation. *Entrance requirements:* For master's, GRE or GMAT (for MS in computational finance only), bachelor's degree, resume (MS in predictive analytics only), IT experience (MS in information technology project management only), portfolio review (all MFA programs and MA in animation); for doctorate, GRE, master's degree in computer science. Additional exam requirements/recommendations for international students: Required—TOEFL (minimum score 590 paper-based; 80 iBT), IELTS (minimum score 6.5), PTE (minimum score 53). Electronic applications accepted. *Expenses:* Contact institution. *Faculty research:* Data mining, computer science, human-computer interaction, security, animation and film.

Eastern Michigan University, Graduate School, College of Business, Department of Marketing, Ypsilanti, MI 48197. Offers e-business (MBA); integrated marketing communications (MS, Postbaccalaureate Certificate); international business (MBA); marketing management (MBA); supply chain management (MBA). *Program availability:* Part-time, evening/weekend, online learning. *Faculty:* 23 full-time (9 women). *Students:* 15 full-time (11 women), 40 part-time (33 women); includes 14 minority (10 Black or African American, non-Hispanic/Latino; 4 Two or more races, non-Hispanic/Latino). Average age 32. 29 applicants, 72% accepted, 15 enrolled. In 2016, 23 master's, 1 other advanced degree awarded. *Entrance requirements:* For master's, GMAT. Additional exam requirements/recommendations for international students: Required—TOEFL. *Application deadline:* For fall admission, 5/15 priority date for domestic students, 2/15 priority date for international students; for winter admission, 10/15 priority date for domestic students, 9/1 priority date for international students; for summer admission, 3/15 priority date for domestic students, 3/1 priority date for international students. Applications are processed on a rolling basis. Application fee: $45. *Financial support:* Fellowships, research assistantships with full tuition reimbursements, teaching assistantships with full tuition reimbursements, career-related internships or fieldwork, Federal Work-Study, institutionally sponsored loans, scholarships/grants, tuition waivers (partial), and unspecified assistantships available. Support available to part-time students. Financial award applicants required to submit FAFSA. *Unit head:* Dr. Lewis Hershey, Department Head, 734-487-3323, Fax: 734-487-7099, E-mail: lhershe1@emich.edu. *Application contact:* K. Michelle Henry, Director, Graduate Business Programs, 734-487-4444, Fax: 734-483-1316, E-mail: cob.graduate@emich.edu.
Website: http://www.mkt.emich.edu/index.html

Eastern Michigan University, Graduate School, College of Business, Programs in Business Administration, Ypsilanti, MI 48197. Offers business administration (MBA, Graduate Certificate); computer information systems (Graduate Certificate); e-business (MBA, Graduate Certificate); enterprise business intelligence (MBA); entrepreneurship (MBA, Graduate Certificate); finance (MBA, Graduate Certificate); human resources (MBA); human resources management (Graduate Certificate); information systems (MBA); internal auditing (MBA); international business (MBA, Graduate Certificate); marketing management (Graduate Certificate); nonprofit management (MBA); organizational development (Graduate Certificate); supply chain management (MBA, Graduate Certificate). *Accreditation:* AACSB. *Program availability:* Part-time, online learning. *Students:* 63 full-time (36 women), 320 part-time (186 women); includes 131 minority (76 Black or African American, non-Hispanic/Latino; 5 American Indian or Alaska Native, non-Hispanic/Latino; 16 Asian, non-Hispanic/Latino; 19 Hispanic/Latino; 15 Two or more races, non-Hispanic/Latino), 23 international. Average age 32. 305 applicants, 70% accepted, 124 enrolled. In 2016, 78 master's, 57 other advanced degrees awarded. *Entrance requirements:* For master's, GMAT (minimum score 450), minimum cumulative undergraduate GPA of 2.75. Additional exam requirements/recommendations for international students: Required—TOEFL. *Application deadline:* For fall admission, 5/15 priority date for domestic students, 2/15 priority date for international students; for winter admission, 10/15 priority date for domestic students, 9/1 priority date for international students; for summer admission, 3/15 priority date for domestic students, 3/1 priority date for international students. Applications are processed on a rolling basis. Application fee: $45. *Financial support:* Fellowships, research assistantships with full tuition reimbursements, teaching assistantships with full tuition reimbursements, career-related internships or fieldwork, Federal Work-Study, institutionally sponsored loans, scholarships/grants, tuition waivers (partial), and unspecified assistantships available. Support available to part-time students. Financial award applicants required to submit FAFSA. *Unit head:* K. Michelle Henry, Director, Graduate Business Programs, 734-487-4444, Fax: 734-483-1316, E-mail: cob.graduate@emich.edu.
Website: http://www.emich.edu/cob/mba/

Fairleigh Dickinson University, Metropolitan Campus, University College: Arts, Sciences, and Professional Studies, School of Computer Sciences and Engineering, Program in E-Commerce, Teaneck, NJ 07666-1914. Offers MS.

Florida Institute of Technology, Extended Studies Division, Melbourne, FL 32901-6975. Offers acquisition and contract management (MS); aerospace engineering (MS); business administration (MBA, DBA); computer information systems (MS); computer science (MS); electrical engineering (MS); engineering management (MS); human resources management (MS); logistics management (MS), including humanitarian and disaster relief logistics; management (MS), including acquisition and contract management, e-business, human resources management, information systems, logistics management, management, transportation management; material acquisition management (MS); mechanical engineering (MS); operations research (MS); project management (MS), including information systems, operations research; public administration (MPA); quality management (MS); software engineering (MS); space systems (MS); space systems management (MS); supply chain management (MS); systems management (MS), including information systems, operations research; technology management (MS). *Program availability:* Part-time, evening/weekend, online learning. *Faculty:* 10 full-time (3 women), 122 part-time/adjunct (29 women). *Students:* 131 full-time (58 women), 997 part-time (348 women); includes 389 minority (231 Black or African American, non-Hispanic/Latino; 9 American Indian or Alaska Native, non-Hispanic/Latino; 26 Asian, non-Hispanic/Latino; 99 Hispanic/Latino; 3 Native Hawaiian or other Pacific Islander, non-Hispanic/Latino; 21 Two or more races, non-Hispanic/Latino), 53 international. Average age 36. 962 applicants, 48% accepted, 323 enrolled. In 2016, 403 master's awarded. *Degree requirements:* For master's, comprehensive exam (for some programs). *Entrance requirements:* For master's, GMAT or resume showing 8 years of supervised experience, minimum GPA of 3.0, 2 letters of recommendation, resume. Additional exam requirements/recommendations for international students: Required—TOEFL (minimum score 550 paper-based; 79 iBT). *Application deadline:* For fall admission, 4/1 for international students; for spring admission, 9/30 for international students. Applications are processed on a rolling basis. Electronic applications accepted. *Expenses:* Contact institution. *Financial support:* Application deadline: 3/1; applicants required to submit FAFSA. *Unit head:* Dr. Theodore R. Richardson, III, Dean, 321-674-8123, Fax: 321-674-7597, E-mail: trichardson@fit.edu. *Application contact:* Carolyn Farrior, Director of Graduate Admissions, Online Learning and Off-Campus Programs, 321-674-7118, Fax: 321-674-8216, E-mail: cfarrior@fit.edu.
Website: http://es.fit.edu

Fordham University, Gabelli School of Business, New York, NY 10023. Offers accounting (MBA, MS); applied statistics and decision-making (MS); business administration (EMBA); business analytics (MS); communications and media management (MBA); electronic business (MBA); entrepreneurship (MBA); finance (MBA); global finance (MS); global sustainability (MBA); healthcare management (MBA); information systems (MBA, MS); investor relations (MS); management (MBA, MS); marketing (MBA); marketing intelligence (MS); media management (MS); nonprofit leadership (MS); quantitative finance (MS); taxation (MS); JD/MBA; MS/MBA. *Accreditation:* AACSB. *Program availability:* Part-time, evening/weekend. *Faculty:* 132 full-time (44 women), 51 part-time/adjunct (7 women). *Students:* 1,117 full-time (668 women), 553 part-time (282 women); includes 207 minority (44 Black or African American, non-Hispanic/Latino; 92 Asian, non-Hispanic/Latino; 69 Hispanic/Latino; 2 Native Hawaiian or other Pacific Islander, non-Hispanic/Latino), 1,088 international. Average age 27. 4,745 applicants, 46% accepted, 752 enrolled. In 2016, 996 master's awarded. Terminal master's awarded for partial completion of doctoral program. *Degree requirements:* For master's, internships (required for MS in quantitative finance, recommended for MBA). *Entrance requirements:* For master's, GMAT/GRE, 2 letters of recommendation, resume, 2 essays, transcripts. Additional exam requirements/recommendations for international students: Required—TOEFL (minimum score 100 iBT), IELTS (minimum score 7). *Application deadline:* For fall admission, 11/15 priority date for domestic and international students; for winter admission, 1/15 priority date for domestic students, 1/1 priority date for international students; for spring admission, 3/1 for domestic and international students; for summer admission, 6/1 for domestic students. Application fee: $130. Electronic applications accepted. *Expenses:* $1,397 per credit. *Financial support:* In 2016–17, 78 students received support. Career-related internships or fieldwork, institutionally sponsored loans, scholarships/grants, and unspecified assistantships available. Support available to part-time students. Financial award application deadline: 6/30; financial award applicants required to submit FAFSA. *Unit head:* Dr. Donna Rapaccioli, Dean, 212-636-6165, Fax: 212-307-1779, E-mail: rapaccioli@fordham.edu. *Application contact:* Lawrence Murray, Senior Assistant Dean of Graduate Admissions and Advising, 212-636-6200, Fax: 212-636-7076, E-mail:

admissionsgb@fordham.edu.
Website: http://www.fordham.edu/gabelli

HEC Montreal, School of Business Administration, Graduate Diploma Programs in Administration, Program in E-Business, Montréal, QC H3T 2A7, Canada. Offers Graduate Diploma. All courses are given in French. *Students:* 9 full-time (4 women), 38 part-time (23 women). 45 applicants, 60% accepted, 21 enrolled. In 2016, 1 Graduate Diploma awarded. *Degree requirements:* For Graduate Diploma, one foreign language. *Entrance requirements:* For degree, bachelor's degree in administration or equivalent. *Application deadline:* For fall admission, 4/15 for domestic and international students; for winter admission, 9/15 for domestic and international students. Application fee: $86 Canadian dollars. Electronic applications accepted. *Expenses: Tuition, area resident:* Part-time $77.80 Canadian dollars per credit. Tuition, state resident: full-time $2797 Canadian dollars; part-time $240.92 Canadian dollars per credit. Tuition, nonresident: full-time $8673 Canadian dollars; part-time $531.43 Canadian dollars per credit. *International tuition:* $19,131 Canadian dollars full-time. *Required fees:* $1699 Canadian dollars; $40.58 Canadian dollars per credit. $67.32 Canadian dollars per term. Tuition and fees vary according to degree level and program. *Financial support:* In 2016–17, 814 students received support. Research assistantships, teaching assistantships, and scholarships/grants available. Financial award application deadline: 9/2. *Unit head:* Renaud Lachance, Director, 514-340-7165, E-mail: renaud.lachance@hec.ca. *Application contact:* Anny Caron, Administrative Director, 514-340-3598, Fax: 514-340-6411, E-mail: anny.caron@hec.ca.
Website: http://www.hec.ca/programmes/dess/dess-gestion-commerce-electronique/index.html

HEC Montreal, School of Business Administration, Master of Science Programs in Administration, Program in Electronic Commerce, Montréal, QC H3T 2A7, Canada. Offers M Sc. Program offered jointly with University of Montreal. *Students:* 29 full-time (16 women), 42 part-time (22 women). 45 applicants, 73% accepted, 21 enrolled. In 2016, 43 master's awarded. *Degree requirements:* For master's, one foreign language. *Entrance requirements:* For master's, bachelor's degree in law, management, information systems or related field. *Application deadline:* For fall admission, 4/1 for domestic and international students. Application fee: $86 Canadian dollars. Electronic applications accepted. *Expenses: Tuition, area resident:* Part-time $77.80 Canadian dollars per credit. Tuition, state resident: full-time $2797 Canadian dollars; part-time $240.92 Canadian dollars per credit. Tuition, nonresident: full-time $8673 Canadian dollars; part-time $531.43 Canadian dollars per credit. *International tuition:* $19,131 Canadian dollars full-time. *Required fees:* $1699 Canadian dollars; $40.58 Canadian dollars per credit. $67.32 Canadian dollars per term. Tuition and fees vary according to degree level and program. *Financial support:* Research assistantships, teaching assistantships, and scholarships/grants available. Financial award application deadline: 9/2. *Unit head:* Renaud Lachance, Director, 514-340-7165, E-mail: renaud.lachance@hec.ca. *Application contact:* Anny Caron, Administrative Director, 514-340-3598, Fax: 514-340-6411, E-mail: anny.caron@hec.ca.
Website: http://www.hec.ca/programmes/maitrises/maitrise-commerce-electronique/index.html

Instituto Tecnológico y de Estudios Superiores de Monterrey, Campus Central de Veracruz, Graduate Programs, Córdoba, Mexico. Offers administration (MA); administration of information technologies (MTI); computer sciences (MCC); education (MEE); educational institution administration (MAD); educational technology (MTE); electronic commerce (MCE); finance (MAF); humanistic studies (MEH); international business for Latin America (MNL); marketing (MMT); science (MCP). *Program availability:* Part-time, evening/weekend, online learning. *Degree requirements:* For master's, thesis (for some programs). *Entrance requirements:* For master's, PAEP College Board. Electronic applications accepted.

Instituto Tecnológico y de Estudios Superiores de Monterrey, Campus Ciudad Juárez, Program in Electronic Commerce, Ciudad Juárez, Mexico. Offers MEC.

Instituto Tecnológico y de Estudios Superiores de Monterrey, Campus Estado de México, Professional and Graduate Division, Estado de Mexico, Mexico. Offers administration of information technologies (MITA); architecture (M Arch); business administration (GMBA, MBA); computer sciences (MCS, PhD); education (M Ed); educational institution administration (MAD); educational technology and innovation (PhD); electronic commerce (MEC); environmental systems (MS); finance (MAF); humanistic studies (MHS); information sciences and knowledge management (MISKM); information systems (MS); manufacturing systems (MS); marketing (MEM); quality systems and productivity (MS); science and materials engineering (PhD); telecommunications management (MTM). *Program availability:* Part-time, online learning. *Degree requirements:* For master's, one foreign language, thesis (for some programs); for doctorate, one foreign language, thesis/dissertation. *Entrance requirements:* For master's, E-PAEP 500, interview; for doctorate, E-PAEP 500, research proposal. Additional exam requirements/recommendations for international students: Required—TOEFL (minimum score 550 paper-based). *Faculty research:* Surface treatments by plasmas, mechanical properties, robotics, graphical computing, mechatronics security protocols.

Instituto Tecnológico y de Estudios Superiores de Monterrey, Campus Irapuato, Graduate Programs, Irapuato, Mexico. Offers administration (MBA); administration of information technology (MAIT); administration of telecommunications (MAT); architecture (M Arch); computer science (MCS); education (M Ed); educational administration (MEA); educational innovation and technology (DEIT); educational technology (MET); electronic commerce (MBA); environmental administration and planning (MEAP); environmental systems (MES); finances (MBA); humanistic studies (MHS); international management for Latin American executives (MIMLAE); library and information science (MLIS); manufacturing quality management (MMQM); marketing research (MBA).

Lewis University, College of Business, Graduate School of Management, Program in Business Administration, Romeoville, IL 60446. Offers accounting (MBA); custom elective option (MBA); e-business (MBA); finance (MBA); healthcare management (MBA); human resources management (MBA); international business (MBA); management information systems (MBA); marketing (MBA); project management (MBA); technology and operations management (MBA). *Program availability:* Part-time, evening/weekend. *Students:* 145 full-time (72 women), 213 part-time (123 women); includes 101 minority (46 Black or African American, non-Hispanic/Latino; 2 American Indian or Alaska Native, non-Hispanic/Latino; 7 Asian, non-Hispanic/Latino; 41 Hispanic/Latino; 1 Native Hawaiian or other Pacific Islander, non-Hispanic/Latino; 4 Two or more races, non-Hispanic/Latino), 47 international. Average age 31. In 2016, 99 master's awarded. *Degree requirements:* For master's, comprehensive exam. *Entrance requirements:* For master's, interview, bachelor's degree, resume, 2 recommendations. Additional exam requirements/recommendations for international students: Required—TOEFL (minimum score 550 paper-based). *Application deadline:* For fall admission, 8/15 priority date for domestic students, 5/1 priority date for international students; for spring admission, 11/15 priority date for international students. Applications are processed on a rolling basis. Application fee: $40. Electronic applications accepted. *Expenses: Tuition:* Full-time $13,860; part-time $770 per credit hour. *Required fees:* $75 per semester. Tuition and fees vary according to degree level and program. *Financial support:* Career-related internships or fieldwork, Federal Work-Study, scholarships/grants, and unspecified assistantships available. Financial award application deadline: 5/1; financial award applicants required to submit FAFSA. *Unit head:* Dr. Maureen Culleeney, Academic Program Director, 815-838-0500 Ext. 5631, E-mail: culleema@lewisu.edu. *Application contact:* Michele Ryan, Director of Admission, 815-838-0500 Ext. 5384, E-mail: gsm@lewisu.edu.

New York University, Polytechnic School of Engineering, Department of Technology Management, New York, NY 10012-1019. Offers construction management (Advanced Certificate); electronic business management (Advanced Certificate); entrepreneurship (Advanced Certificate); human resources management (Advanced Certificate); industrial engineering (MS); information management (Advanced Certificate); management (MS); management of technology (MS); manufacturing engineering (MS); organizational behavior (MS, Advanced Certificate); project management (Advanced Certificate); technology management (MBA, PhD, Advanced Certificate); telecommunications management (Advanced Certificate). *Program availability:* Part-time, evening/weekend. *Degree requirements:* For master's, comprehensive exam (for some programs), thesis (for some programs); for doctorate, comprehensive exam, thesis/dissertation. *Entrance requirements:* For master's, GMAT, minimum B average in undergraduate course work. Additional exam requirements/recommendations for international students: Required—TOEFL (minimum score 550 paper-based; 80 iBT); Recommended—IELTS (minimum score 6.5). Electronic applications accepted. *Faculty research:* Global innovation and research and development strategy, managing emerging technologies, technology and development, service design and innovation, tech entrepreneurship and commercialization, sustainable and clean-tech innovation, impacts of information technology upon individuals, organizations and society.

Northwestern University, Medill School of Journalism, Media, and Integrated Marketing Communications, Integrated Marketing Communications Program, Evanston, IL 60208. Offers brand strategy (MSIMC); content marketing (MSIMC); direct and interactive marketing (MSIMC); marketing analytics (MSIMC); strategic communications (MSIMC). *Program availability:* Part-time. *Entrance requirements:* For master's, GRE General Test or GMAT, full-time work experience (preferred). Additional exam requirements/recommendations for international students: Required—TOEFL. Electronic applications accepted. *Faculty research:* Data mining, business to business marketing, values in advertising, political advertising.

Northwestern University, School of Professional Studies, Program in Predictive Analytics, Evanston, IL 60208. Offers computer-based data mining (MS); marketing analytics (MS); predictive modeling (MS); risk analytics (MS); Web analytics (MS). *Program availability:* Online learning. *Entrance requirements:* For master's, official transcripts, two letters of recommendation, statement of purpose, current resume or curriculum vitae. Additional exam requirements/recommendations for international students: Required—TOEFL (minimum score 600 paper-based; 100 iBT) or IELTS (minimum score 7).

Pace University, Lubin School of Business, Advanced Professional Certificate Program, New York, NY 10038. Offers business economics (APC); e-business (APC); financial management (APC); international business (APC); international economics (APC); investment management (APC); marketing (APC); public accounting (APC). *Program availability:* Evening/weekend. *Students:* 1 applicant, 100% accepted, 1 enrolled. *Entrance requirements:* For degree, MBA or MS in business discipline, relevant professional experience. Additional exam requirements/recommendations for international students: Required—TOEFL (minimum score 90 iBT), IELTS (minimum score 7) or PTE (minimum score 61). *Application deadline:* For fall admission, 8/1 priority date for domestic students, 6/1 for international students; for spring admission, 12/1 for domestic students, 10/1 for international students. Applications are processed on a rolling basis. Application fee: $70. Electronic applications accepted. *Expenses: Tuition:* Part-time $1195 per credit. *Required fees:* $260 per semester. Tuition and fees vary according to degree level, campus/location and program. *Unit head:* Dr. Jack Yurkiewicz, Director, 212-618-6567, E-mail: jyurkiewicz@pace.edu. *Application contact:* Susan Ford-Goldschein, Director of Graduate Admissions, 212-346-1531, Fax: 212-346-1585, E-mail: graduateadmission@pace.edu.
Website: http://www.pace.edu/lubin/agc

Stevens Institute of Technology, Graduate School, School of Business, Program in Information Systems, Hoboken, NJ 07030. Offers computer science (MS); e-commerce (MS); enterprise systems (MS); entrepreneurial information technology (MS); information architecture (MS); information management (MS, Certificate); information security (MS); information technology in financial services industry (MS); information technology in the pharmaceutical industry (MS); information technology outsourcing management (MS); project management (MS, Certificate); software engineering (MS); telecommunications (MS). *Program availability:* Part-time, evening/weekend. *Students:* 280 full-time (100 women), 84 part-time (21 women); includes 23 minority (9 Black or African American, non-Hispanic/Latino; 13 Asian, non-Hispanic/Latino; 1 Hispanic/Latino), 283 international. Average age 26. 925 applicants, 62% accepted, 114 enrolled. In 2016, 212 master's, 32 other advanced degrees awarded. *Degree requirements:* For master's, thesis optional, minimum B average in major field and overall; for Certificate, minimum B average. *Entrance requirements:* Additional exam requirements/recommendations for international students: Required—TOEFL (minimum score 74 iBT), IELTS (minimum score 6). *Application deadline:* For fall admission, 6/1 for domestic students, 4/15 for international students; for spring admission, 11/30 for domestic students, 11/1 for international students. Applications are processed on a rolling basis. Application fee: $65. Electronic applications accepted. *Expenses:* Contact institution. *Financial support:* Fellowships, research assistantships, teaching assistantships, career-related internships or fieldwork, Federal Work-Study, scholarships/grants, and unspecified assistantships available. Financial award application deadline: 2/15; financial award applicants required to submit FAFSA. *Unit head:* Dr. Gregory Prastacos, Dean, 201-216-8366, E-mail: gprastac@stevens.edu. *Application contact:* Graduate Admissions, 888-783-8367, Fax: 888-511-1306, E-mail: graduate@stevens.edu.
Website: https://www.stevens.edu/school-business/masters-programs/information-systems

Towson University, Program in e-Business and Technology Management, Towson, MD 21252-0001. Offers project, program and portfolio management (Postbaccalaureate Certificate); supply chain management (MS, Postbaccalaureate Certificate). *Students:* 2 full-time (1 woman), 22 part-time (8 women); includes 7 minority (3 Black or African American, non-Hispanic/Latino; 1 Asian, non-Hispanic/Latino; 3 Two or more races, non-Hispanic/Latino), 2 international. *Entrance requirements:* For master's and Postbaccalaureate Certificate, GRE or GMAT, bachelor's degree in relevant field and/or three years of post-bachelor's experience working in supply chain related areas; minimum cumulative GPA of 3.0; resume; 2 reference letters. Additional exam requirements/recommendations for international students: Required—TOEFL (minimum score 550 paper-based). *Application deadline:* Applications are processed on a rolling basis. Application fee: $45. Electronic applications accepted. *Expenses:* Tuition, state resident: full-time $7580; part-time $379 per unit. Tuition, nonresident: full-time $15,700; part-time $785 per unit. *Required fees:* $2480. *Unit head:* Dr. Tobin Porterfield, Director, 410-704-3265, E-mail: tporterfield@towson.edu. *Application contact:* Coverley

Electronic Commerce

Beidleman, Assistant Director of Graduate Admissions, 410-704-2113, Fax: 410-704-3030, E-mail: grads@towson.edu.
Website: http://www.towson.edu/cbe/departments/ebusiness/grad/

Universidad del Este, Graduate School, Carolina, PR 00984. Offers accounting (MBA); adult education (M Ed); agribusiness (MBA); criminal justice and criminology (MA); curriculum and instruction - early education (M Ed); curriculum and instruction - elementary (M Ed); curriculum and instruction - English (M Ed); curriculum and instruction - Spanish (M Ed); human resources (MBA); information security management (MBA); information technology and Web business development (MBA); management (MBA); public policy (MPA); social work (MA), including clinical social work; special education (M Ed); strategic leadership (MBA).

Université de Montréal, Faculty of Arts and Sciences, Department of Computer Science and Operational Research, Montréal, QC H3C 3J7, Canada. Offers computer systems (M Sc, PhD); electronic commerce (M Sc). *Program availability:* Part-time. Terminal master's awarded for partial completion of doctoral program. *Degree requirements:* For master's, one foreign language, thesis; for doctorate, one foreign language, thesis/dissertation, general exam. *Entrance requirements:* For master's, B Sc in related field; for doctorate, MA or M Sc in related field. Electronic applications accepted. *Faculty research:* Optimization statistics, programming languages, telecommunications, theoretical computer science, artificial intelligence.

Université de Sherbrooke, Faculty of Administration, Program in E-Commerce, Sherbrooke, QC J1K 2R1, Canada. Offers M Sc. *Degree requirements:* For master's, one foreign language, thesis. *Entrance requirements:* For master's, bachelor's degree in related field, minimum GPA of 3.0 (on 4.3 scale), letters of reference, fluency in French. Electronic applications accepted. *Faculty research:* Radio frequency identification (RFID), Web value concept.

Université Laval, Faculty of Administrative Sciences, Programs in Business Administration, Québec, QC G1K 7P4, Canada. Offers accounting (MBA); agri-food management (MBA); electronic business (MBA, Diploma); factory management and logistics (MBA); finance (MBA); firm management (MBA); geomatic management (MBA); information technology management (MBA); international management (MBA); management (MBA); management accounting (MBA, Diploma); marketing (MBA); modeling and organizational decision (MBA); occupational health and safety management (MBA); pharmacy management (MBA); social and environmental responsibility (MBA); technological entrepreneurship (Diploma). *Accreditation:* AACSB. *Program availability:* Part-time, evening/weekend, online learning. *Entrance requirements:* For master's and Diploma, knowledge of French and English. Electronic applications accepted.

University at Buffalo, the State University of New York, Graduate School, College of Arts and Sciences, Department of Economics, Buffalo, NY 14260. Offers economics (MA, MS, PhD); financial economics (Certificate); health services (Certificate); information and Internet economics (Certificate); international economics (Certificate); law and regulation (Certificate); urban and regional economics (Certificate). *Program availability:* Part-time. Terminal master's awarded for partial completion of doctoral program. *Degree requirements:* For master's, comprehensive exam; for doctorate, comprehensive exam, thesis/dissertation, field and theory exams. *Entrance requirements:* For master's, GRE General Test or GMAT; for doctorate, GRE General Test. Additional exam requirements/recommendations for international students: Required—TOEFL (minimum score 550 paper-based; 79 iBT), TWE. Electronic applications accepted. *Faculty research:* Human capital, international economics, econometrics, applied economics, urban economics, economic growth and development.

University of New Brunswick Saint John, Faculty of Business, Saint John, NB E2L 4L5, Canada. Offers administration (MBA); electronic commerce (MBA); international business (MBA); natural resource management (MBA). *Program availability:* Part-time. *Entrance requirements:* For master's, GMAT (minimum score of 550) or GRE (minimum 54th percentile), minimum GPA of 3.0. Additional exam requirements/recommendations for international students: Required—TOEFL (minimum score 580 paper-based; 93 iBT), TWE (minimum score 4.5). Electronic applications accepted. *Expenses:* Contact institution. *Faculty research:* International business, project management, innovation and technology management; business use of Weblogs and podcasts to communicate; corporate governance; high-involvement work systems; international competitiveness; supply chain management and logistics.

University of North Florida, Coggin College of Business, MBA Program, Jacksonville, FL 32224. Offers accounting (MBA); construction management (MBA); e-commerce (MBA); economics (MBA); finance (MBA); human resource management (MBA); international business (MBA); logistics (MBA); management applications (MBA). *Accreditation:* AACSB. *Program availability:* Part-time, evening/weekend. *Faculty:* 16 full-time (4 women), 1 (woman) part-time/adjunct. *Students:* 105 full-time (50 women), 162 part-time (68 women); includes 57 minority (14 Black or African American, non-Hispanic/Latino; 1 American Indian or Alaska Native, non-Hispanic/Latino; 17 Asian, non-Hispanic/Latino; 18 Hispanic/Latino; 7 Two or more races, non-Hispanic/Latino), 41 international. Average age 28. 231 applicants, 46% accepted, 84 enrolled. In 2016, 114 master's awarded. *Entrance requirements:* For master's, GMAT or GRE, U.S. bachelor's degree from regionally-accredited university or equivalent foreign degree. Additional exam requirements/recommendations for international students: Required—TOEFL (minimum score 550 paper-based; 79 iBT). *Application deadline:* For fall admission, 8/1 priority date for domestic students, 5/1 for international students; for spring admission, 12/1 priority date for domestic students, 10/1 for international students; for summer admission, 4/29 priority date for domestic students, 2/1 for international students. Application fee: $30. Tuition and fees vary according to course load, campus/location and program. *Financial support:* In 2016–17, 22 students received support, including 1 research assistantship (averaging $2,501 per year); teaching assistantships, Federal Work-Study, and tuition waivers (partial) also available. Support available to part-time students. Financial award application deadline: 4/1; financial award applicants required to submit FAFSA. *Faculty research:* Performance measures, costing, and inventory issues in logistics and supply chain management; inter-organizational systems; international management and marketing practices; e-commerce; organizational learning and socialization processes. *Total annual research expenditures:* $17,654. *Unit head:* Dr. Parvez Ahmed, Graduate Program Director, 904-620-1678, E-mail: pahmed@unf.edu. *Application contact:* Amy Bishop, MSM Advisor, 904-620-2575, Fax: 904-620-2832, E-mail: coggin.students@unf.edu.
Website: http://www.unf.edu/graduateschool/academics/programs/MBA.aspx

University of Ottawa, Faculty of Graduate and Postdoctoral Studies, Interdisciplinary Programs, Ottawa, ON K1N 6N5, Canada. Offers e-business (Certificate); e-commerce (Certificate); finance (Certificate); health services and policies research (Diploma); population health (PhD); population health risk assessment and management (Certificate); public management and governance (Certificate); systems science (Certificate).

University of Ottawa, Faculty of Graduate and Postdoctoral Studies, Program in E-Business Technologies, Ottawa, ON K1N 6N5, Canada. Offers M Sc, MEBT. *Degree requirements:* For master's, thesis or alternative, project. *Entrance requirements:* For master's, honours degree or equivalent, minimum B average.

University of Phoenix–Colorado Campus, College of Information Systems and Technology, Lone Tree, CO 80124-5453. Offers e-business (MBA); management (MIS); technology management (MBA). *Program availability:* Evening/weekend, online learning. *Degree requirements:* For master's, thesis (for some programs). *Entrance requirements:* For master's, minimum undergraduate GPA of 3.0, 3 years of work experience. Additional exam requirements/recommendations for international students: Required—TOEFL (minimum score 550 paper-based; 79 iBT). Electronic applications accepted.

University of Phoenix–Colorado Campus, School of Business, Lone Tree, CO 80124-5453. Offers accountancy (MSA); accounting (MBA); business administration (MBA); e-business (MBA); global management (MBA); human resources management (MBA, MM); management (MM); marketing (MBA); public administration (MBA, MM). *Accreditation:* ACBSP. *Program availability:* Evening/weekend, online learning. *Degree requirements:* For master's, thesis (for some programs). *Entrance requirements:* For master's, minimum undergraduate GPA of 3.0, 3 years work experience. Additional exam requirements/recommendations for international students: Required—TOEFL (minimum score 550 paper-based; 79 iBT). Electronic applications accepted.

University of Phoenix–Columbus Georgia Campus, College of Information Systems and Technology, Columbus, GA 31909. Offers e-business (MBA); information systems (MIS); technology management (MBA). *Program availability:* Evening/weekend, online learning. *Degree requirements:* For master's, thesis (for some programs). *Entrance requirements:* For master's, minimum undergraduate GPA of 3.0, 3 years of work experience. Additional exam requirements/recommendations for international students: Required—TOEFL (minimum score 550 paper-based; 79 iBT). Electronic applications accepted.

University of Phoenix–Dallas Campus, College of Information Systems and Technology, Dallas, TX 75251. Offers e-business (MBA); information systems (MIS); technology management (MBA). *Program availability:* Evening/weekend. *Degree requirements:* For master's, thesis (for some programs). *Entrance requirements:* For master's, minimum undergraduate GPA of 3.0, 3 years of work experience. Additional exam requirements/recommendations for international students: Required—TOEFL (minimum score 550 paper-based; 79 iBT). Electronic applications accepted.

University of Phoenix–Houston Campus, College of Information Systems and Technology, Houston, TX 77079-2004. Offers e-business (MBA); information systems (MIS); technology management (MBA). *Program availability:* Evening/weekend, online learning. *Degree requirements:* For master's, comprehensive exam (for some programs), thesis. *Entrance requirements:* For master's, minimum undergraduate GPA of 3.0, 3 years of work experience. Additional exam requirements/recommendations for international students: Required—TOEFL (minimum score 550 paper-based; 79 iBT). Electronic applications accepted.

University of Phoenix–New Mexico Campus, College of Information Systems and Technology, Albuquerque, NM 87113-1570. Offers e-business (MBA); information systems (MS); technology management (MBA). *Program availability:* Evening/weekend. *Degree requirements:* For master's, thesis (for some programs). *Entrance requirements:* For master's, minimum undergraduate GPA of 3.0, 3 years of work experience. Additional exam requirements/recommendations for international students: Required—TOEFL (minimum score 550 paper-based; 79 iBT). Electronic applications accepted.

University of Phoenix–San Antonio Campus, School of Business, San Antonio, TX 78230. Offers accounting (MBA); business administration (MBA); e-business (MBA); global management (MBA); human resources management (MBA, MM); management (MM); marketing (MBA); public administration (MBA, MM). *Accreditation:* ACBSP.

Section 5
Entrepreneurship

This section contains a directory of institutions offering graduate work in entrepreneurship. Additional information about programs listed in the directory but not augmented by an in-depth entry may be obtained by writing directly to the dean of a graduate school or chair of a department at the address given in the directory.

For programs offering related work, see also in this book *Business Administration and Management, International Business,* and *Education (Business Education)*

CONTENTS

Program Directory

Featured School: Display and Close-Up

See:

Entrepreneurship

American College of Thessaloniki, Department of Business Administration, Pylea, Greece. Offers banking and finance (MBA); entrepreneurship (MBA, Certificate); finance (Certificate); management (MBA, Certificate); marketing (MBA, Certificate). *Program availability:* Part-time, evening/weekend. *Degree requirements:* For master's, thesis. *Entrance requirements:* For master's, bachelor's degree. Additional exam requirements/recommendations for international students: Recommended—TOEFL. Electronic applications accepted.

American Public University System, AMU/APU Graduate Programs, Charles Town, WV 25414. Offers accounting (MBA, MS); applied business analytics (MBA, MS); criminal justice (MA), including business administration, emergency and disaster management, general (MA, MS); educational leadership (M Ed); emergency and disaster management (MA); entrepreneurship (MBA); environmental policy and management (MS), including environmental planning, environmental sustainability, fish and wildlife management, general (MA, MS), global environmental management; finance (MBA); general (MBA); government contracting and acquisition (MBA); health care administration (MBA); health information management (MS); history (MA), including American history, ancient and classical history, European history, global history, public history; homeland security (MA), including business administration, counterterrorism studies, criminal justice, cyber, emergency management and public health, intelligence studies, transportation security; homeland security resource allocation (MBA); humanities (MA); information technology (MS), including digital forensics, enterprise software development, information assurance and security, IT project management; information technology management (MBA); intelligence studies (MA), including criminal intelligence, cyber, general (MA, MS), homeland security, intelligence analysis, intelligence collection, intelligence management, intelligence operations, terrorism studies; international relations and conflict resolution (MA), including comparative and security issues, conflict resolution, international and transnational security issues, peacekeeping; legal studies (MA); management (MA), including strategic consulting; marketing (MBA); military history (MA), including American military history, American Revolution, civil war, war since 1945, World War II; military studies (MA), including joint warfare, strategic leadership; national security studies (MA), including cyber, general (MA, MS), homeland security, regional security studies, security and intelligence analysis, terrorism studies; nonprofit management (MBA); political science (MA), including American politics and government, comparative government and development, general (MA, MS), international relations, public policy; psychology (MA); public administration (MPA), including disaster management, environmental policy, health policy, human resources, national security, organizational management, security management; public health (MPH); reverse logistics management (MA); security management (MA); space studies (MS), including aerospace science, general (MA, MS), planetary science; sports and health sciences (MS); sports management (MBA); teaching (M Ed), including autism spectrum disorder, curriculum and instruction for elementary teachers, elementary reading, English language learners, instructional leadership, online learning, special education, STEAM (STEM plus the arts); transportation and logistics management (MA). *Program availability:* Part-time, evening/weekend, online only, 100% online. *Faculty:* 401 full-time (228 women), 1,678 part-time/adjunct (781 women). *Students:* 378 full-time (184 women), 8,455 part-time (3,484 women); includes 2,972 minority (1,552 Black or African American, non-Hispanic/Latino; 52 American Indian or Alaska Native, non-Hispanic/Latino; 211 Asian, non-Hispanic/Latino; 791 Hispanic/Latino; 70 Native Hawaiian or other Pacific Islander, non-Hispanic/Latino; 296 Two or more races, non-Hispanic/Latino), 109 international. Average age 37. In 2016, 3,185 master's awarded. *Degree requirements:* For master's, comprehensive exam or practicum. *Entrance requirements:* For master's, official transcript showing earned bachelor's degree from institution accredited by recognized accrediting body. Additional exam requirements/recommendations for international students: Required—TOEFL (minimum score 550 paper-based), IELTS (minimum score 6.5). *Application deadline:* Applications are processed on a rolling basis. Application fee: $0. Electronic applications accepted. *Expenses: Tuition:* Part-time $350 per credit hour. *Required fees:* $50 per course. *Financial support:* Scholarships/grants available. Financial award applicants required to submit FAFSA. *Unit head:* Dr. Karan Powell, President, 877-468-6268, Fax: 304-724-3780. *Application contact:* Terry Grant, Vice President of Enrollment Management, 877-468-6268, Fax: 304-724-3780, E-mail: info@apus.edu.
Website: http://www.apus.edu

American University, School of International Service, Washington, DC 20016-8071. Offers comparative and regional studies (Certificate); cross-cultural communication (Certificate); development management (MS); ethics, peace, and global affairs (MA); European studies (Certificate); global environmental policy (MA, Certificate); global information technology (Certificate); international affairs (MA), including comparative and international disability policy, comparative and regional studies, international economic relations, international politics, natural resources and sustainable development, U.S. foreign policy; international arts management (Certificate); international communication (MA, Certificate); international development (MA); international economic policy (Certificate); international economic relations (Certificate); international economics (MA); international media (MA); international peace and conflict resolution (MA, Certificate); international politics (Certificate); international relations (MA, PhD); international service (MIS); peacebuilding (Certificate); social enterprise (MA); the Americas (Certificate); United States foreign policy (Certificate); JD/MA. *Program availability:* Part-time, evening/weekend, 100% online. *Faculty:* 116 full-time (53 women), 57 part-time/adjunct (19 women). *Students:* 575 full-time (360 women), 491 part-time (277 women); includes 287 minority (100 Black or African American, non-Hispanic/Latino; 6 American Indian or Alaska Native, non-Hispanic/Latino; 58 Asian, non-Hispanic/Latino; 92 Hispanic/Latino; 1 Native Hawaiian or other Pacific Islander, non-Hispanic/Latino; 30 Two or more races, non-Hispanic/Latino), 151 international. Average age 29. 1,504 applicants, 84% accepted, 403 enrolled. In 2016, 374 master's, 3 doctorates, 1 other advanced degree awarded. Terminal master's awarded for partial completion of doctoral program. *Degree requirements:* For master's, one foreign language, comprehensive exam, thesis or alternative; for doctorate, one foreign language, comprehensive exam, thesis/dissertation. *Entrance requirements:* For master's, GRE; GMAT or GRE (for MA in social enterprise), transcripts, resume, 2 letters of recommendation, statement of purpose; for doctorate, GRE, transcripts, resume, 3 letters of recommendation, statement of purpose. Additional exam requirements/recommendations for international students: Required—TOEFL (minimum score 600 paper-based, 100 iBT), IELTS (minimum score 7), or PTE (minimum score of 68). Application fee: $55. Electronic applications accepted. *Expenses:* $1,579 per credit tuition; $1,930 mandatory fees. *Financial support:* Research assistantships, teaching assistantships, institutionally sponsored loans, scholarships/grants, and unspecified assistantships available. Financial award application deadline: 1/15; financial award applicants required to submit FAFSA. *Unit head:* Dr. James Goldgeier, Dean, 202-885-1603, Fax: 202-885-2494, E-mail: goldgeier@american.edu. *Application contact:* Jia Jiang, Associate Director, Graduate Education Enrollment, 202-885-1689, Fax: 202-885-1109, E-mail: jiang@american.edu. Website: http://www.american.edu/sis/

Anaheim University, Programs in Business Administration, Anaheim, CA 92806-5150. Offers entrepreneurship (ME, DBA); global sustainable management (MBA); international business (MBA, DBA, Certificate, Diploma); management (DBA); sustainable management (DBA, Certificate, Diploma). *Program availability:* Part-time, evening/weekend, online only, 100% online. In 2016, 3 master's, 4 doctorates awarded. *Application deadline:* Applications are processed on a rolling basis. Electronic applications accepted. *Unit head:* Robert Robertson, Dean, Graduate School of Business, 714-772-3330, Fax: 714-772-3331, E-mail: admissions@anaheim.edu.

Arizona State University at the Tempe campus, W. P. Carey School of Business, Program in Business Administration, Tempe, AZ 85287-4906. Offers entrepreneurship (MBA); finance (MBA); health sector management (MBA); international business (MBA); leadership (MBA); marketing (MBA); organizational behavior (PhD); strategic management (PhD); supply chain management (MBA, PhD); JD/MBA; MBA/M Acc; MBA/M Arch. *Accreditation:* AACSB. *Program availability:* Part-time, evening/weekend, online learning. Terminal master's awarded for partial completion of doctoral program. *Degree requirements:* For master's, thesis or alternative, internship, interactive Program of Study (iPOS) submitted before completing 50 percent of required credit hours; for doctorate, comprehensive exam, thesis/dissertation, interactive Program of Study (iPOS) submitted before completing 50 percent of required credit hours. *Entrance requirements:* For master's, GMAT, minimum GPA of 3.0 in last 2 years of work leading to bachelor's degree, 2 letters of recommendation, professional resume, official transcripts, 3 essays; for doctorate, GMAT or GRE, minimum GPA of 3.0 in last 2 years of work leading to bachelor's degree, 3 letters of recommendation, resume, personal statement/essay. Additional exam requirements/recommendations for international students: Required—TOEFL (minimum score 550 paper-based; 80 iBT), IELTS (minimum score 6.5). Electronic applications accepted. *Expenses:* Contact institution.

Azusa Pacific University, School of Business and Management, Azusa, CA 91702-7000. Offers business administration (MBA); diversity for strategic advantage (MA); entrepreneurship (MBA); finance (MBA); human and organizational development (MA); human resources and organizational development (MBA); human resources management (MA); international business (MBA); marketing (MBA); non-profit management (MA); organizational development and change (MA); performance improvement (MA); public administration (MA); strategic management (MBA). *Program availability:* Part-time, evening/weekend. *Degree requirements:* For master's, thesis (for some programs), final project. *Entrance requirements:* For master's, GMAT, minimum GPA of 3.0. Additional exam requirements/recommendations for international students: Required—TOEFL (minimum score 600 paper-based). *Expenses:* Contact institution. *Faculty research:* Gender issues, financial risk, leadership and ethics, marketing strategy.

Babson College, F. W. Olin Graduate School of Business, Babson Park, MA 02457-0310. Offers accounting (MSA); advanced management (Certificate); business administration (MBA); global entrepreneurship (MS); technological entrepreneurship (MS). *Accreditation:* AACSB. *Program availability:* Part-time, evening/weekend, online learning. *Entrance requirements:* For master's, GMAT, 2 years of work experience, resume, letters of recommendation. Additional exam requirements/recommendations for international students: Required—TOEFL (minimum score 100 iBT), IELTS (minimum score 6.5). Electronic applications accepted. *Faculty research:* Entrepreneurship, sustainability, global markets, process of innovation, social media and advertising.

Bakke Graduate University, Programs in Pastoral Ministry and Business, Dallas, TX 75243-7039. Offers business administration (MBA); church and ministry multiplication (D Min); global urban leadership (MA); leadership (D Min); ministry in complex contexts (D Min); social and civic entrepreneurship (MA); theology of work (D Min); theology reflection (D Min); transformational leadership (DTL); urban youth ministry (D Min). *Program availability:* Part-time, online learning. *Degree requirements:* For master's, thesis; for doctorate, thesis/dissertation. *Entrance requirements:* For master's, 2 years of ministry experience, BA in Biblical studies or theology; for doctorate, 3 years of ministry experience, M Div. Additional exam requirements/recommendations for international students: Required—TOEFL. Electronic applications accepted. *Faculty research:* Theological systems, church management, worship.

Baldwin Wallace University, Graduate Programs, School of Business, Program in Entrepreneurship, Berea, OH 44017-2088. Offers MBA. *Program availability:* Part-time, evening/weekend. *Students:* 6 full-time (4 women), 9 part-time (2 women); includes 2 minority (both Asian, non-Hispanic/Latino). Average age 35. 7 applicants, 86% accepted, 6 enrolled. In 2016, 6 master's awarded. *Degree requirements:* For master's, minimum overall GPA of 3.0. *Entrance requirements:* For master's, GMAT or minimum GPA of 3.0, bachelor's degree in any field, work experience. Additional exam requirements/recommendations for international students: Required—TOEFL (minimum score 550 paper-based; 79 iBT). *Application deadline:* For fall admission, 7/25 priority date for domestic students, 4/30 priority date for international students; for spring admission, 12/15 priority date for domestic students, 9/30 priority date for international students; for summer admission, 4/15 priority date for domestic students. Applications are processed on a rolling basis. Application fee: $25. Electronic applications accepted. Application fee is waived when completed online. *Expenses:* $921 per credit hour. *Financial support:* Applicants required to submit FAFSA. *Unit head:* Ven Ochaya, Director, 440-826-2391, Fax: 440-826-3868, E-mail: vochaya@bw.edu. *Application contact:* Laura Spencer, Graduate Application Specialist, 440-826-2191, Fax: 440-826-3868, E-mail: lspencer@bw.edu.
Website: http://www.bw.edu/graduate/business/mba/

Baruch College of the City University of New York, Zicklin School of Business, Department of Management, New York, NY 10010-5585. Offers entrepreneurship (MBA); management (PhD); operations management (MBA); organizational behavior/human resources management (MBA); sustainable business (MBA). PhD offered jointly with Graduate School and University Center of the City University of New York. *Program availability:* Part-time, evening/weekend. *Degree requirements:* For doctorate, comprehensive exam, thesis/dissertation. *Entrance requirements:* For master's, GMAT, 2 letters of recommendation, resume, 2 years of work experience; for doctorate, GMAT. Additional exam requirements/recommendations for international students: Required—TOEFL (minimum score 590 paper-based), TWE.

Baruch College of the City University of New York, Zicklin School of Business, International Executive MS Programs, New York, NY 10010-5585. Offers entrepreneurship (MS). *Program availability:* Part-time, evening/weekend. *Entrance requirements:* For master's, GMAT, 2 letters of recommendation, resume, 2 years of work experience. Additional exam requirements/recommendations for international students: Required—TOEFL (minimum score 590 paper-based), TWE (minimum score 5).

Baylor University, Graduate School, Hankamer School of Business, Department of Entrepreneurship, Waco, TX 76798. Offers PhD. *Entrance requirements:* For doctorate, GMAT or GRE. *Expenses: Tuition:* Full-time $28,494; part-time $1583 per credit hour. *Required fees:* $167 per credit hour. Tuition and fees vary according to course load and program. *Unit head:* Kendall Artz, Chairman, E-mail: kendall_artz@baylor.edu. *Application contact:* Laurie Wilson, Director, Graduate Business Programs, 254-710-4163, Fax: 254-710-1066, E-mail: laurie_wilson@baylor.edu.
Website: http://www.baylor.edu/business/entrepreneurship/

Bay Path University, Program in Entrepreneurial Thinking and Innovative Practices, Longmeadow, MA 01106-2292. Offers MBA. *Program availability:* Part-time, 100% online. *Students:* 21 full-time (19 women), 60 part-time (53 women); includes 17 minority (8 Black or African American, non-Hispanic/Latino; 8 Hispanic/Latino; 1 Two or more races, non-Hispanic/Latino), 2 international. Average age 33. 48 applicants, 92% accepted, 37 enrolled. In 2016, 34 master's awarded. *Degree requirements:* For master's, 12 courses - eight core courses and four electives (each course is eight weeks long). *Application deadline:* Applications are processed on a rolling basis. Application fee: $45. Electronic applications accepted. Application fee is waived when completed online. *Expenses:* $21,465. *Financial support:* Unspecified assistantships available. Financial award applicants required to submit FAFSA. *Unit head:* Mo Sattar, Program Director, 413-565-1228, E-mail: msattar@baypath.edu. *Application contact:* Diane Ranaldi, Dean of Graduate Admissions, 413-565-1332, Fax: 413-565-1250, E-mail: dranaldi@baypath.edu.
Website: http://graduate.baypath.edu/Graduate-Programs/Programs-On-Campus/MBA-Program/Entrepreneurial-Thinking-and-Innovative-Practices

Benedictine University, Graduate Programs, Program in Business Administration, Lisle, IL 60532. Offers accounting (MBA); entrepreneurship and managing innovation (MBA); financial management (MBA); health administration (MBA); human resource management (MBA); information systems security (MBA); international business (MBA); management consulting (MBA); management information systems (MBA); marketing management (MBA); operations management and logistics (MBA); organizational leadership (MBA). *Program availability:* Part-time, evening/weekend, online learning. *Faculty:* 4 full-time (2 women), 24 part-time/adjunct (3 women). *Students:* 90 full-time (51 women), 440 part-time (262 women); includes 147 minority (65 Black or African American, non-Hispanic/Latino; 1 American Indian or Alaska Native, non-Hispanic/Latino; 58 Asian, non-Hispanic/Latino; 20 Hispanic/Latino; 3 Native Hawaiian or other Pacific Islander, non-Hispanic/Latino), 2 international. Average age 34. 211 applicants, 89% accepted, 155 enrolled. In 2016, 350 master's awarded. *Entrance requirements:* For master's, GMAT. Additional exam requirements/recommendations for international students: Required—TOEFL (minimum score 550 paper-based). *Application deadline:* For fall admission, 9/1 for domestic students; for winter admission, 12/1 for domestic students; for spring admission, 2/15 for domestic students. Applications are processed on a rolling basis. Application fee: $40. Electronic applications accepted. *Expenses: Tuition:* Full-time $15,600; part-time $650 per hour. *Required fees:* $300. One-time fee: $125 part-time. Tuition and fees vary according to class time, course load, campus/location and program. *Financial support:* Career-related internships or fieldwork and health care benefits available. Support available to part-time students. *Faculty research:* Strategic leadership in professional organizations, sociology of professions, organizational change, social identity theory, applications to change management. *Unit head:* Dr. Sharon Borowicz, Director, 630-829-6219, E-mail: sborowicz@ben.edu. *Application contact:* Kari Gibbons, Director, Admissions, 630-829-6200, Fax: 630-829-6584, E-mail: kgibbons@ben.edu.

Brandeis University, Rabb School of Continuing Studies, Division of Graduate Professional Studies, Master of Science in Digital Innovation for Finance Technology, Waltham, MA 02454-9110. Offers MS. *Program availability:* Part-time-only. *Faculty:* 45 part-time/adjunct (16 women). *Students:* 2 part-time; both minorities (1 American Indian or Alaska Native, non-Hispanic/Latino; 1 Hispanic/Latino). Average age 37. 2 applicants, 50% accepted, 1 enrolled. *Entrance requirements:* For master's, undergraduate coursework in general finance or economics and at least some basic experience with a programming language; four-year bachelor's degree from regionally-accredited U.S. institution or equivalent; official transcript(s) from every college or university attended; resume or curriculum vitae; statement of goals; letter of recommendation. Additional exam requirements/recommendations for international students: Required—TWE (minimum score 4.5), TOEFL (minimum scores: 600 paper-based, 100 iBT), IELTS (7), or PTE (68). *Application deadline:* For fall admission, 6/21 priority date for domestic and international students; for winter admission, 9/13 priority date for domestic and international students; for spring admission, 12/20 priority date for domestic and international students; for summer admission, 3/14 priority date for domestic and international students. Applications are processed on a rolling basis. Application fee: $50. Electronic applications accepted. *Expenses:* $3,400 per course, $100 graduation fee. *Financial support:* Applicants required to submit FAFSA. *Unit head:* Ashley Nagle Eknaian, Chair, E-mail: aeknaian@brandeis.edu. *Application contact:* Frances Stearns, Director of Admissions and Recruitment, 781-736-8785, E-mail: fstearns@brandeis.edu.
Website: http://www.brandeis.edu/gps/future-students/learn-about-our-programs/fintech-digital-innovation.html

Brandman University, School of Business and Professional Studies, Irvine, CA 92618. Offers accounting (MBA); business administration (MBA); e-business strategic management (MBA); entrepreneurship (MBA); finance (MBA); health administration (MBA); human resources (MBA, MS); international business (MBA); marketing (MBA); organizational leadership (MA, MBA, MPA); public administration (MPA). *Expenses: Tuition:* Full-time $14,880; part-time $620 per credit hour. Tuition and fees vary according to degree level and program. *Unit head:* Dr. Glenn Worthington, Dean, 253-861-1024, E-mail: gworthin@brandman.edu.
Website: https://www.brandman.edu/business-professional-studies

Brigham Young University, Graduate Studies, Marriott School of Management, Master of Business Administration Program, Provo, UT 84602. Offers entrepreneurship (MBA); finance (MBA); global supply chain management (MBA); marketing (MBA); strategic human resources (MBA); JD/MBA; MBA/MS. *Accreditation:* AACSB. *Students:* 321 full-time (63 women); includes 16 minority (1 Black or African American, non-Hispanic/Latino; 9 Asian, non-Hispanic/Latino; 6 Hispanic/Latino), 69 international. Average age 31. 397 applicants, 49% accepted, 154 enrolled. In 2016, 146 master's awarded. *Entrance requirements:* For master's, GMAT or GRE, minimum GPA of 3.0 in last 60 hours. Additional exam requirements/recommendations for international students: Required—TOEFL (minimum score 590 paper-based; 94 iBT), IELTS (minimum score 7). *Application deadline:* For fall admission, 5/1 for domestic students, 1/15 for international students. Applications are processed on a rolling basis. Application fee: $50. Electronic applications accepted. *Expenses:* Contact institution. *Financial support:* In 2016–17, 247 students received support. Research assistantships, teaching assistantships, career-related internships or fieldwork, institutionally sponsored loans, and scholarships/grants available. Financial award application deadline: 3/1; financial award applicants required to submit FAFSA. *Faculty research:* Finance, marketing, supply chain management, entrepreneurship, strategic human resources. *Unit head:* Dr. Grant McQueen, Director, 801-422-3500, Fax: 801-422-0513, E-mail: mba@byu.edu. *Application contact:* Yvette Anderson, MBA Program Admissions Director, 801-422-3500, Fax: 801-422-0513, E-mail: mba@byu.edu.
Website: http://mba.byu.edu

Cairn University, School of Business, Langhorne, PA 19047-2990. Offers accounting (MBA); business administration (MBA); international entrepreneurship (MBA); nonprofit leadership (MBA); organizational leadership (MSOL, Postbaccalaureate Certificate). *Program availability:* Part-time, evening/weekend, 100% online, blended/hybrid learning. *Faculty:* 3 full-time (0 women), 6 part-time/adjunct (1 woman). *Students:* 7 full-time (5 women), 43 part-time (19 women); includes 20 minority (10 Black or African American, non-Hispanic/Latino; 1 American Indian or Alaska Native, non-Hispanic/Latino; 4 Asian, non-Hispanic/Latino; 3 Hispanic/Latino; 2 Two or more races, non-Hispanic/Latino), 4 international. Average age 36. 17 applicants, 100% accepted, 16 enrolled. In 2016, 16 master's awarded. *Entrance requirements:* Additional exam requirements/recommendations for international students: Required—TOEFL (minimum score 550 paper-based). *Application deadline:* Applications are processed on a rolling basis. Application fee: $25. Electronic applications accepted. Application fee is waived when completed online. *Expenses:* $655 per semester credit. *Financial support:* Scholarships/grants available. Support available to part-time students. Financial award applicants required to submit FAFSA. *Unit head:* Yunn Kang, Dean, School of Business, 215-702-4461, Fax: 215-702-4248, E-mail: ykang@cairn.edu. *Application contact:* Gwen Dorsey, Assistant Director, Graduate Admissions, 800-572-2472, Fax: 215-702-4248, E-mail: gdorsey@cairn.edu. Website: http://cairn.edu/academics/business

California Baptist University, Program in Public Administration, Riverside, CA 92504-3206. Offers public administration (MPA); strategic innovation (MPA). *Program availability:* Part-time, evening/weekend, 100% online, blended/hybrid learning. *Faculty:* 5 full-time (3 women), 3 part-time/adjunct (2 women). *Students:* 47 full-time (30 women), 26 part-time (13 women); includes 44 minority (7 Black or African American, non-Hispanic/Latino; 1 American Indian or Alaska Native, non-Hispanic/Latino; 1 Asian, non-Hispanic/Latino; 31 Hispanic/Latino; 4 Two or more races, non-Hispanic/Latino). Average age 34. 59 applicants, 56% accepted, 26 enrolled. In 2016, 47 master's awarded. *Degree requirements:* For master's, comprehensive exam or thesis. *Entrance requirements:* For master's, minimum GPA of 2.75; bachelor's degree in applicable field or any field with five years of managerial experience; three recommendations; resume; 500-word essay. Additional exam requirements/recommendations for international students: Required—TOEFL (minimum score 80 iBT). *Application deadline:* For fall admission, 8/1 priority date for domestic students, 7/1 for international students; for spring admission, 12/1 priority date for domestic students, 11/1 for international students. Applications are processed on a rolling basis. Application fee: $45. Electronic applications accepted. *Expenses:* Contact institution. *Financial support:* In 2016–17, 37 students received support. Federal Work-Study and scholarships/grants available. Financial award applicants required to submit CSS PROFILE or FAFSA. *Faculty research:* Policy networks, water policy, democratic theory, international relations, political theory and philosophy. *Unit head:* Dr. David Poole, Vice President, Online and Professional Studies, 951-343-3902, E-mail: dpoole@calbaptist.edu. *Application contact:* Dr. Elaine Ahumada, Director, MPA Program, 951-343-3929, Fax: 951-343-4661, E-mail: eahumada@calbaptist.edu.
Website: http://www.cbuonline.edu/programs/program/master-of-public-administration

California Intercontinental University, School of Business, Irvine, CA 92614. Offers banking and finance (MBA); entrepreneurship and business management (DBA); global business leadership (DBA); international management and marketing (MBA); organizational management and human resource management (MBA).

California Lutheran University, Graduate Studies, School of Management, Thousand Oaks, CA 91360-2787. Offers business (IMBA); computer science (MS); econometrics (MBA); economics (MS); entrepreneurship (MBA, Certificate); finance (MBA, Certificate); financial planning (MBA, Certificate); information systems and technology (MS); information technology management (MBA, Certificate); international business (MBA, Certificate); management and organization behavior (MBA); management and organizational behavior (Certificate); marketing (MBA, Certificate); microeconomics (MBA); nonprofit and social enterprise (MBA); public policy and administration (MPPA). *Program availability:* Part-time, evening/weekend, 100% online, blended/hybrid learning. *Faculty:* 25 full-time (10 women), 36 part-time/adjunct (12 women). *Students:* 427 full-time (172 women), 189 part-time (87 women); includes 120 minority (14 Black or African American, non-Hispanic/Latino; 2 American Indian or Alaska Native, non-Hispanic/Latino; 19 Asian, non-Hispanic/Latino; 37 Hispanic/Latino; 48 Two or more races, non-Hispanic/Latino), 338 international. Average age 30. 591 applicants, 64% accepted, 131 enrolled. In 2016, 305 master's awarded. *Entrance requirements:* For master's, GMAT, interview, minimum GPA of 3.0. *Application deadline:* Applications are processed on a rolling basis. Application fee: $50. Electronic applications accepted. *Expenses:* Contact institution. *Unit head:* Dr. Gerhard Apfelthaler, Dean, 805-493-3360. *Application contact:* 805-493-3325, Fax: 805-493-3861, E-mail: clugrad@callutheran.edu.
Website: http://www.callutheran.edu/management/

California State University, East Bay, Office of Graduate Studies, College of Business and Economics, MBA Program, Option in Entrepreneurship, Hayward, CA 94542-3000. Offers small business management (MBA). *Students:* 7 full-time (1 woman), 9 part-time (5 women); includes 6 minority (2 Black or African American, non-Hispanic/Latino; 4 Hispanic/Latino), 5 international. Average age 32. 18 applicants, 39% accepted, 5 enrolled. In 2016, 1 master's awarded. *Entrance requirements:* Additional exam requirements/recommendations for international students: Required—TOEFL (minimum score 550 paper-based). *Application deadline:* For fall admission, 6/30 for domestic and international students. *Financial support:* Career-related internships or fieldwork, Federal Work-Study, institutionally sponsored loans, and scholarships/grants available. Support available to part-time students. Financial award applicants required to submit FAFSA. *Unit head:* Dr. Joanna Lee, Program Advisor, 510-885-3290, E-mail: joanna.lee@csueastbay.edu. *Application contact:* Dr. Donna Wiley, Interim Associate Vice President for Academic Programs and Graduate Studies, 510-885-3716, Fax: 510-885-4777, E-mail: donna.wiley@csueastbay.edu.
Website: http://www20.csueastbay.edu/cbe/mba-options/Entrepreneurship-Option.html

California State University, Fullerton, Graduate Studies, College of Business and Economics, Department of Management, Fullerton, CA 92834-9480. Offers entrepreneurship (MBA); management (MBA). *Accreditation:* AACSB. *Program availability:* Part-time. *Degree requirements:* For master's, project or thesis. *Entrance requirements:* For master's, GMAT, minimum AACSB index of 950. Application fee: $55. *Expenses:* Tuition, state resident: full-time $3369; part-time $1953 per unit. Tuition, nonresident: full-time $3915; part-time $2499 per unit. Tuition and fees vary according to course load, degree level and program. *Financial support:* Career-related internships or fieldwork, Federal Work-Study, institutionally sponsored loans, and scholarships/grants available. Support available to part-time students. Financial award application deadline: 3/1; financial award applicants required to submit FAFSA. *Unit head:* Dr. Gus Manoochehri, Chair, 657-278-3071. *Application contact:* Admissions/Applications, 657-278-2371.

California State University, San Bernardino, Graduate Studies, College of Business and Public Administration, Program in Business Administration, San Bernardino, CA 92407. Offers accounting (MBA); entrepreneurship (MBA); finance (MBA); global business (MBA); information management (MBA); information security (MBA);

management (MBA); supply chain management (MBA). *Accreditation:* AACSB. *Program availability:* Part-time, evening/weekend, online learning. *Faculty:* 7 full-time (4 women), 3 part-time/adjunct (2 women). *Students:* 37 full-time (11 women), 141 part-time (51 women); includes 85 minority (16 Black or African American, non-Hispanic/Latino; 1 American Indian or Alaska Native, non-Hispanic/Latino; 20 Asian, non-Hispanic/Latino; 45 Hispanic/Latino; 3 Two or more races, non-Hispanic/Latino), 46 international. 260 applicants, 37% accepted, 34 enrolled. In 2016, 180 master's awarded. *Degree requirements:* For master's, comprehensive exam, thesis. *Entrance requirements:* Additional exam requirements/recommendations for international students: Required—TOEFL. *Application deadline:* For fall admission, 7/16 for domestic students, 7/20 for international students; for winter admission, 10/23 for domestic students, 10/20 for international students; for spring admission, 1/22 for domestic students, 1/20 for international students. Application fee: $55. *Expenses:* Contact institution. *Financial support:* Application deadline: 3/1. *Unit head:* Dr. Lawrence C. Rose, Dean, 909-537-3703, Fax: 909-537-7026, E-mail: lrose@csusb.edu. *Application contact:* Dr. Vipin Gupta, Associate Dean/MBA Director, 909-537-7380, Fax: 909-537-7026, E-mail: vgupta@csusb.edu.
Website: http://mba.csusb.edu/

California University of Pennsylvania, School of Graduate Studies and Research, Eberly College of Science and Technology, Program in Business Administration, California, PA 15419-1394. Offers business administration (MBA); business analytics (MBA); entrepreneurship (MBA); nursing administration and leadership (MBA). *Program availability:* Part-time, evening/weekend. *Degree requirements:* For master's, comprehensive exam. *Entrance requirements:* For master's, minimum GPA of 3.0, official transcripts. Additional exam requirements/recommendations for international students: Required—TOEFL (minimum score 550 paper-based). Electronic applications accepted. *Expenses:* Tuition, state resident: full-time $11,592; part-time $483 per credit. Tuition, nonresident: full-time $17,400; part-time $725 per credit. *Required fees:* $3916. Tuition and fees vary according to course load, degree level, campus/location and reciprocity agreements. *Faculty research:* Economics, applied economics, consumer behavior, technology and business, impact of technology.

Cambridge College, School of Management, Cambridge, MA 02138-5304. Offers business negotiation and conflict resolution (M Mgt); general business (M Mgt); health care informatics (M Mgt); health care management (M Mgt); leadership in human and organizational dynamics (M Mgt); non-profit and public organization management (M Mgt); small business development (M Mgt); technology management (M Mgt). *Program availability:* Part-time, evening/weekend. *Degree requirements:* For master's, thesis, seminars. *Entrance requirements:* For master's, resume, 2 professional references. Additional exam requirements/recommendations for international students: Required—TOEFL (minimum score 550 paper-based; 79 iBT), Michigan English Language Assessment Battery (minimum score 85); Recommended—IELTS (minimum score 6). Electronic applications accepted. *Expenses:* Contact institution. *Faculty research:* Negotiation, mediation and conflict resolution; leadership; management of diverse organizations; case studies and simulation methodologies for management education, digital as a second language: social networking for digital immigrants, non-profit and public management.

Cameron University, Office of Graduate Studies, Program in Entrepreneurial Studies, Lawton, OK 73505-6377. Offers MS. *Program availability:* Part-time, evening/weekend, online learning. *Degree requirements:* For master's, comprehensive exam. *Entrance requirements:* Additional exam requirements/recommendations for international students: Required—TOEFL (minimum score 550 paper-based). Electronic applications accepted. *Faculty research:* Entrepreneurial competition, new venture creation, legal issues, electronic commerce.

Capella University, School of Business and Technology, Doctoral Programs in Business, Minneapolis, MN 55402. Offers accounting (DBA, PhD); business intelligence (DBA); finance (DBA, PhD); general business management (PhD); human resource management (DBA, PhD); leadership (DBA, PhD); management education (PhD); marketing (DBA, PhD); project management (DBA, PhD); strategy and innovation (DBA, PhD). *Accreditation:* ACBSP.

Capella University, School of Business and Technology, Master's Programs in Business, Minneapolis, MN 55402. Offers accounting (MBA); business analysis (MS); business intelligence (MBA); entrepreneurship (MBA); finance (MBA); general business administration (MBA); general human resource management (MS); general leadership (MS); health care management (MBA); human resource management (MBA); marketing (MBA); project management (MBA, MS). *Accreditation:* ACBSP.

Carlos Albizu University, Miami Campus, Graduate Programs, Miami, FL 33172-2209. Offers clinical psychology (PhD, Psy D); entrepreneurship (MBA); exceptional student education (MS); human services (PhD); industrial/organizational psychology (MS); marriage and family therapy (MS); mental health counseling (MS); nonprofit management (MBA); organizational management (MBA); psychology (MS); school counseling (MS); speech and language pathology (MS); teaching English for speakers of other languages (MS). *Accreditation:* APA. *Program availability:* Part-time, evening/weekend, 100% online. *Faculty:* 28 full-time (22 women), 31 part-time/adjunct (19 women). *Students:* 475 full-time (396 women), 191 part-time (161 women); includes 560 minority (56 Black or African American, non-Hispanic/Latino; 1 American Indian or Alaska Native, non-Hispanic/Latino; 4 Asian, non-Hispanic/Latino; 494 Hispanic/Latino; 5 Two or more races, non-Hispanic/Latino), 15 international. Average age 34. 335 applicants, 46% accepted, 122 enrolled. In 2016, 143 master's, 48 doctorates awarded. Terminal master's awarded for partial completion of doctoral program. *Degree requirements:* For master's, comprehensive exam, integrative project (for MBA); research project (for exceptional student education, teaching English as a second language); for doctorate, comprehensive exam, thesis/dissertation, internship, project. *Entrance requirements:* For master's, 3 letters of recommendation, interview, minimum GPA of 3.0, resume, statement of purpose, official transcripts; for doctorate, 3 letters of recommendation, minimum GPA of 3.0, resume, interview, statement of purpose, official transcripts. Additional exam requirements/recommendations for international students: Required—Michigan Test of English Language Proficiency. *Application deadline:* For fall admission, 4/1 priority date for domestic students, 5/1 priority date for international students; for spring admission, 11/1 priority date for domestic students, 9/1 priority date for international students. Applications are processed on a rolling basis. Application fee: $50. Electronic applications accepted. *Expenses:* Contact institution. *Financial support:* In 2016–17, 131 students received support. Federal Work-Study, scholarships/grants, unspecified assistantships, and tuition discounts available. Financial award application deadline: 6/1; financial award applicants required to submit FAFSA. *Faculty research:* Psychotherapy, forensic psychology, neuropsychology, marketing strategy, entrepreneurship, special education, speech-language pathology. *Unit head:* Dr. Etiony Aldarondo, Provost, 305-593-1223 Ext. 3138, Fax: 305-592-7930, E-mail: ealdarondo@albizu.edu. *Application contact:* Sonia Feliciano, Institutional Director of Student Recruitment, 305-593-1223 Ext. 3108, Fax: 305-477-8983, E-mail: sfeliciano@albizu.edu.

Carnegie Mellon University, Dietrich College of Humanities and Social Sciences, Department of Social and Decision Sciences, Pittsburgh, PA 15213-3891. Offers behavioral decision research (PhD); social and decision science (PhD); strategy, entrepreneurship, and technological change (PhD). Terminal master's awarded for partial completion of doctoral program. *Degree requirements:* For doctorate, comprehensive exam, thesis/dissertation, research paper. *Entrance requirements:* For doctorate, GRE General Test. Additional exam requirements/recommendations for international students: Required—TOEFL. Electronic applications accepted. *Faculty research:* Organization theory, political science, sociology, technology studies.

City Vision University, Program in Technology and Ministry, Kansas City, MO 64109-1845. Offers MS. *Program availability:* Online learning. *Degree requirements:* For master's, capstone project.

Clarion University of Pennsylvania, Office of Transfer, Adult and Graduate Admissions, Master of Business Administration Program, Clarion, PA 16214. Offers finance (MBA); health care administration (MBA); innovation and entrepreneurship (MBA). *Accreditation:* AACSB. *Program availability:* Part-time, evening/weekend, 100% online. *Faculty:* 15 full-time (2 women). *Students:* 52 full-time (9 women), 54 part-time (43 women); includes 14 minority (7 Black or African American, non-Hispanic/Latino; 2 Asian, non-Hispanic/Latino; 1 Hispanic/Latino; 4 Two or more races, non-Hispanic/Latino), 4 international. Average age 32. 87 applicants, 86% accepted, 28 enrolled. In 2016, 21 master's awarded. *Degree requirements:* For master's, portfolio. *Entrance requirements:* For master's, GMAT, minimum QPA of 2.75. Additional exam requirements/recommendations for international students: Required—TOEFL (minimum score 550 paper-based; 80 iBT), IELTS (minimum score 7). *Application deadline:* For fall admission, 8/1 priority date for domestic students, 4/15 priority date for international students; for spring admission, 12/1 priority date for domestic students, 9/15 priority date for international students. Applications are processed on a rolling basis. Application fee: $40. Electronic applications accepted. *Expenses:* $632.55 per credit. *Financial support:* Career-related internships or fieldwork, Federal Work-Study, scholarships/grants, and unspecified assistantships available. Support available to part-time students. Financial award application deadline: 3/1; financial award applicants required to submit FAFSA. *Unit head:* Juanice Vega, Associate Dean of the College of Business Administration and Information Sciences, 814-393-2600, Fax: 814-393-1910, E-mail: mba@clarion.edu. *Application contact:* Dana Bearer, Assistant Director, Graduate Programs, 814-393-2337, Fax: 814-393-2722, E-mail: gradstudies@clarion.edu.
Website: http://www.clarion.edu/admissions/graduate/index.html

Clemson University, Graduate School, College of Business, Master of Business Administration Program, Greenville, SC 29601. Offers business administration (MBA); business analytics (MBA); entrepreneurship and innovation (MBA). *Accreditation:* AACSB. *Program availability:* Part-time, evening/weekend. *Faculty:* 3 full-time (1 woman), 9 part-time/adjunct (1 woman). *Students:* 146 full-time (57 women), 322 part-time (102 women); includes 81 minority (46 Black or African American, non-Hispanic/Latino; 13 Asian, non-Hispanic/Latino; 17 Hispanic/Latino; 1 Native Hawaiian or other Pacific Islander, non-Hispanic/Latino; 4 Two or more races, non-Hispanic/Latino), 35 international. Average age 31. 226 applicants, 63% accepted, 115 enrolled. In 2016, 165 master's awarded. *Entrance requirements:* For master's, GMAT, resume, unofficial transcripts, personal statement, letters of recommendation. Additional exam requirements/recommendations for international students: Required—TOEFL (minimum score 80 iBT), IELTS (minimum score 6.5). *Application deadline:* For fall admission, 7/15 for domestic students, 4/15 for international students; for spring admission, 12/1 for domestic students. Applications are processed on a rolling basis. Application fee: $80 ($90 for international students). Electronic applications accepted. *Expenses:* $9,761 per semester resident, $15,764 per semester non-resident. *Financial support:* In 2016–17, 38 students received support, including 1 research assistantship with partial tuition reimbursement available (averaging $18,000 per year); unspecified assistantships also available. Financial award application deadline: 7/15. *Unit head:* Dr. Gregory Pickett, Senior Associate Dean, 864-656-3975, Fax: 864-370-8061, E-mail: pgregor@clemson.edu. *Application contact:* Kristin Allen, Director of Admissions, 864-656-8173, Fax: 864-370-8061, E-mail: klallen@clemson.edu.
Website: https://www.clemson.edu/business/departments/mba/

Cogswell Polytechnical College, Program in Entrepreneurship and Innovation, San Jose, CA 95134. Offers MA.

Columbia University, Graduate School of Business, MBA Program, New York, NY 10027. Offers accounting (MBA); decision, risk, and operations (MBA); entrepreneurship (MBA); finance and economics (MBA); healthcare and pharmaceutical management (MBA); human resource management (MBA); international business (MBA); leadership and ethics (MBA); management (MBA); marketing (MBA); media (MBA); private equity (MBA); real estate (MBA); social enterprise (MBA); value investing (MBA); DDS/MBA; JD/MBA; MBA/MIA; MBA/MPH; MBA/MS; MD/MBA. *Entrance requirements:* For master's, GMAT, 2 letters of recommendation. Additional exam requirements/recommendations for international students: Required—TOEFL. Electronic applications accepted. *Expenses:* Contact institution. *Faculty research:* Human decision making and behavioral research; real estate market and mortgage defaults; financial crisis and corporate governance; international business; security analysis and accounting.

Dallas Baptist University, College of Business, Business Administration Program, Dallas, TX 75211-9299. Offers accounting (MBA); business communication (MBA); conflict resolution management (MBA); entrepreneurship (MBA); finance (MBA); health care management (MBA); international business (MBA); leading the non-profit organization (MBA); management (MBA); management information systems (MBA); marketing (MBA); project management (MBA); technology and engineering management (MBA). *Accreditation:* ACBSP. *Program availability:* Part-time, evening/weekend, 100% online, blended/hybrid learning. *Application deadline:* Applications are processed on a rolling basis. Application fee: $25. Electronic applications accepted. Application fee is waived when completed online. *Expenses: Tuition:* Full-time $15,408; part-time $856 per credit hour. *Required fees:* $400 per semester. Tuition and fees vary according to course load and degree level. *Unit head:* Dr. Sandra Reid, Chair of Graduate Business Programs, 214-333-5280, E-mail: sandra@dbu.edu. *Application contact:* Bobby Soto, Director of Admissions, 214-333-5242, E-mail: graduate@dbu.edu.
Website: http://www3.dbu.edu/graduate/mba.asp

Dallas Baptist University, College of Business, Management Program, Dallas, TX 75211-9299. Offers conflict resolution management (MA); general management (MA, MS); health care management (MA); human resource management (MA); organizational communication (MA); performance management (MA); professional sales and management optimization (MA). *Program availability:* Part-time, evening/weekend, 100% online, blended/hybrid learning. *Application deadline:* Applications are processed on a rolling basis. Application fee: $25. Electronic applications accepted. Application fee is waived when completed online. *Expenses: Tuition:* Full-time $15,408; part-time $856 per credit hour. *Required fees:* $400 per semester. Tuition and fees vary according to course load and degree level. *Unit head:* Richard Nassar, Director, 214-333-5280, E-mail: richardn@dbu.edu. *Application contact:* Bobby Soto, Director of Admissions, 214-333-5242, E-mail: graduate@dbu.edu.
Website: http://www.dbu.edu/gsb/ma-in-management

Dartmouth College, Thayer School of Engineering, PhD in Innovation Program, Hanover, NH 03755. Offers PhD. *Degree requirements:* For doctorate, internship.

Entrance requirements: For doctorate, curriculum vitae. *Application deadline:* For fall admission, 1/1 for domestic students. *Financial support:* Fellowships and research assistantships available. *Unit head:* Prof. Eric Fossum, Director, 603-646-2238, Fax: 603-646-2580, E-mail: eric.r.fossum@dartmouth.edu. *Application contact:* Candace S. Potter, Graduate Admissions and Financial Aid Administrator, 603-646-3844, Fax: 603-646-1620, E-mail: candace.s.potter@dartmouth.edu.
Website: http://engineering.dartmouth.edu/academics/graduate/innovation

Delaware Valley University, MBA Program, Doylestown, PA 18901-2697. Offers accounting (MBA); entrepreneurship (MBA); finance (MBA); food and agribusiness (MBA); general business (MBA); global executive leadership (MBA); human resource management (MBA); supply chain management (MBA). *Program availability:* Part-time, evening/weekend, online learning. *Entrance requirements:* For master's, minimum undergraduate GPA of 3.0. Electronic applications accepted. *Expenses:* Contact institution.

DePaul University, Kellstadt Graduate School of Business, Chicago, IL 60604. Offers accountancy (M Acc, MS, MSA); applied economics (MBA); banking (MBA); behavioral finance (MBA); brand and product management (MBA); business development (MBA); business information technology (MS); business strategy and decision-making (MBA); computational finance (MS); consumer insights (MBA); corporate finance (MBA); economic policy analysis (MS); entrepreneurship (MBA, MS); finance (MBA, MS); financial analysis (MBA); general business (MBA); health sector management (MBA); hospitality leadership (MBA); hospitality leadership and operational performance (MS); human resource management (MBA); human resources (MS); investment management (MBA); leadership and change management (MBA); management accounting (MBA); marketing (MBA, MS); marketing analysis (MS); marketing strategy and planning (MBA); operations management (MBA); organizational diversity (MBA); real estate (MS); real estate finance and investment (MBA); revenue management (MBA); sports management (MBA); strategic global marketing (MBA); strategy, execution and valuation (MBA); sustainable management (MBA, MS); taxation (MS); wealth management (MS); JD/MBA. *Accreditation:* AACSB. *Program availability:* Part-time, evening/weekend, online learning. *Entrance requirements:* For master's, GMAT, 2 letters of recommendation, resume, essay, official transcripts. Additional exam requirements/recommendations for international students: Required—TOEFL (minimum score 550 paper-based; 80 iBT). Electronic applications accepted. *Expenses:* Contact institution.

Drexel University, Goodwin College of Professional Studies, School of Technology and Professional Studies, Philadelphia, PA 19104-2875. Offers construction management (MS); creativity and innovation (MS); engineering technology (MS); food science (MS); hospitality management (MS); professional studies: creativity studies (MS); professional studies: e-learning leadership (MS); professional studies: homeland security management (MS); project management (MS); property management (MS); sport management (MS). *Program availability:* Part-time, evening/weekend. *Faculty:* 37 full-time (14 women). *Students:* 13 full-time, 462 part-time; includes 133 minority (86 Black or African American, non-Hispanic/Latino; 24 Asian, non-Hispanic/Latino; 23 Hispanic/Latino). In 2016, 88 master's awarded. *Entrance requirements:* Additional exam requirements/recommendations for international students: Required—TOEFL, IELTS. *Application deadline:* For fall admission, 9/1 for domestic students; for winter admission, 12/1 for domestic students; for spring admission, 3/1 for domestic students. Applications are processed on a rolling basis. Application fee: $75. Electronic applications accepted. Application fee is waived when completed online. *Expenses: Tuition:* Full-time $32,184; part-time $1192 per credit hour. *Required fees:* $280. Tuition and fees vary according to campus/location and program. *Financial support:* Applicants required to submit FAFSA. *Unit head:* Dr. William F. Lynch, Dean, 215-895-2159, E-mail: goodwin@drexel.edu. *Application contact:* Matthew Gray, Manager, Recruitment and Enrollment, 215-895-6255, Fax: 215-895-2153, E-mail: mdg67@drexel.edu.
Website: http://drexel.edu/grad/programs/goodwin/

Duke University, The Fuqua School of Business, The Duke MBA-Cross Continent Program, Durham, NC 27708-0586. Offers business administration (MBA); energy and environment (MBA); entrepreneurship and innovation (MBA); finance (MBA); health sector management (Certificate); marketing (MBA); strategy (MBA). *Faculty:* 88 full-time (19 women), 50 part-time/adjunct (9 women). *Students:* 214 full-time (74 women); includes 58 minority (13 Black or African American, non-Hispanic/Latino; 35 Asian, non-Hispanic/Latino; 10 Hispanic/Latino), 35 international. Average age 30. In 2016, 105 master's awarded. *Entrance requirements:* For master's, GMAT or GRE, transcripts, essays, resume, recommendation letters, letter of company support, interview. *Application deadline:* For fall admission, 10/12 priority date for domestic and international students; for winter admission, 2/7 priority date for domestic and international students; for spring admission, 5/3 priority date for domestic and international students; for summer admission, 5/31 for domestic and international students. Applications are processed on a rolling basis. Application fee: $225. Electronic applications accepted. *Expenses:* Contact institution. *Financial support:* In 2016–17, 49 students received support. Institutionally sponsored loans and scholarships/grants available. Financial award applicants required to submit FAFSA. *Unit head:* Mohan Venkatachalam, Senior Associate Dean, Executive Programs, 919-660-7859, E-mail: mohan.venkatachalam@duke.edu. *Application contact:* Sharon Thompson, Assistant Dean, Office of Admissions, 919-660-7705, Fax: 919-681-8026, E-mail: admissions-info@fuqua.duke.edu.
Website: http://www.fuqua.duke.edu/programs/duke_mba/cross_continent/

Duke University, The Fuqua School of Business, The Duke MBA-Daytime Program, Durham, NC 27708-0586. Offers academic excellence in finance (Certificate); business administration (MBA); decision sciences (MBA); energy and environment (MBA); energy finance (MBA); entrepreneurship and innovation (MBA); finance (MBA); financial analysis (MBA); health sector management (Certificate); leadership and ethics (MBA); management (MBA); marketing (MBA); operations management (MBA); social entrepreneurship (MBA); strategy (MBA). *Faculty:* 88 full-time (19 women), 50 part-time/adjunct (9 women). *Students:* 897 full-time (310 women); includes 174 minority (39 Black or African American, non-Hispanic/Latino; 3 American Indian or Alaska Native, non-Hispanic/Latino; 75 Asian, non-Hispanic/Latino; 51 Hispanic/Latino; 1 Native Hawaiian or other Pacific Islander, non-Hispanic/Latino; 5 Two or more races, non-Hispanic/Latino), 343 international. Average age 28. In 2016, 440 master's awarded. *Entrance requirements:* For master's, GMAT or GRE, transcripts, essays, resume, recommendation letters, interview. *Application deadline:* For fall admission, 9/13 for domestic and international students; for winter admission, 10/13 for domestic and international students; for spring admission, 1/4 for domestic and international students; for summer admission, 3/20 for domestic and international students. Application fee: $225. Electronic applications accepted. *Expenses:* $66,717 (first-year tuition and fees). *Financial support:* In 2016–17, 415 students received support. Institutionally sponsored loans and scholarships/grants available. Financial award applicants required to submit FAFSA. *Unit head:* Russ Morgan, Senior Associate Dean for Full-time Programs, 919-660-2931, Fax: 919-684-8742, E-mail: ruskin.morgan@duke.edu. *Application contact:* Sharon Thompson, Assistant Dean, Office of Admissions, 919-660-7705, Fax: 919-681-8026, E-mail: admissions-info@fuqua.duke.edu.
Website: http://www.fuqua.duke.edu/daytime-mba/

Duke University, The Fuqua School of Business, The Duke MBA-Global Executive Program, Durham, NC 27708-0586. Offers business administration (MBA); energy and environment (MBA); entrepreneurship and innovation (MBA); finance (MBA); health sector management (Certificate); marketing (MBA); strategy (MBA). *Faculty:* 88 full-time (19 women), 50 part-time/adjunct (9 women). *Students:* 48 full-time (14 women); includes 18 minority (3 Black or African American, non-Hispanic/Latino; 11 Asian, non-Hispanic/Latino; 4 Hispanic/Latino), 10 international. Average age 39. In 2016, 27 master's awarded. *Entrance requirements:* For master's, transcripts, essays, resume, recommendation letters, letter of company support, interview. *Application deadline:* For fall admission, 10/12 priority date for domestic and international students; for winter admission, 12/7 priority date for domestic and international students; for spring admission, 3/20 priority date for domestic and international students; for summer admission, 5/31 for domestic and international students. Applications are processed on a rolling basis. Application fee: $225. Electronic applications accepted. *Expenses:* Contact institution. *Financial support:* In 2016–17, 22 students received support. Institutionally sponsored loans and scholarships/grants available. Financial award applicants required to submit FAFSA. *Unit head:* Mohan Venkatachalam, Senior Associate Dean, Executive Programs, 919-660-7859, E-mail: mohan.venkatachalam@duke.edu. *Application contact:* Sharon Thompson, Assistant Dean, Office of Admissions, 919-660-7705, Fax: 919-681-8026, E-mail: admissions-info@fuqua.duke.edu.
Website: http://www.fuqua.duke.edu/programs/duke_mba/global-executive/

Duke University, The Fuqua School of Business, The Duke MBA-Weekend Executive Program, Durham, NC 27708-0586. Offers business administration (MBA); energy and environment (MBA); entrepreneurship and innovation (MBA); finance (MBA); health sector management (Certificate); marketing (MBA); strategy (MBA). *Faculty:* 88 full-time (19 women), 50 part-time/adjunct (9 women). *Students:* 190 full-time (43 women); includes 75 minority (11 Black or African American, non-Hispanic/Latino; 3 American Indian or Alaska Native, non-Hispanic/Latino; 48 Asian, non-Hispanic/Latino; 12 Hispanic/Latino; 1 Two or more races, non-Hispanic/Latino), 26 international. Average age 35. In 2016, 87 master's awarded. *Entrance requirements:* For master's, GMAT or GRE, transcripts, essays, resume, recommendation letters, letter of company support, interview. *Application deadline:* For fall admission, 8/30 priority date for domestic and international students; for winter admission, 10/12 priority date for domestic and international students; for spring admission, 2/7 priority date for domestic and international students; for summer admission, 3/20 for domestic and international students. Applications are processed on a rolling basis. Application fee: $225. Electronic applications accepted. *Expenses:* Contact institution. *Financial support:* In 2016–17, 33 students received support. Institutionally sponsored loans and scholarships/grants available. Financial award applicants required to submit FAFSA. *Unit head:* Mohan Venkatachalam, Senior Associate Dean, Executive Programs, 919-660-7859, E-mail: mohan.venkatachalam@duke.edu. *Application contact:* Sharon Thompson, Assistant Dean, Office of Admissions, 919-660-7705, Fax: 919-681-8026, E-mail: admissions-info@fuqua.duke.edu.
Website: http://www.fuqua.duke.edu/programs/duke_mba/weekend_executive/

Eastern Michigan University, Graduate School, College of Business, Department of Management, Ypsilanti, MI 48197. Offers entrepreneurship (Postbaccalaureate Certificate); human resources management and organizational development (MSHROD). *Program availability:* Part-time, evening/weekend, online learning. *Faculty:* 22 full-time (11 women). *Students:* 13 full-time (10 women), 77 part-time (58 women); includes 29 minority (23 Black or African American, non-Hispanic/Latino; 1 Asian, non-Hispanic/Latino; 4 Hispanic/Latino; 1 Two or more races, non-Hispanic/Latino), 8 international. Average age 30. 38 applicants, 74% accepted, 12 enrolled. In 2016, 75 master's awarded. *Degree requirements:* For master's, thesis optional. *Entrance requirements:* For master's, GMAT. Additional exam requirements/recommendations for international students: Required—TOEFL. *Application deadline:* For fall admission, 5/15 priority date for domestic students, 2/15 priority date for international students; for winter admission, 10/15 priority date for domestic students, 9/1 priority date for international students; for summer admission, 3/15 priority date for domestic students, 3/1 priority date for international students. Applications are processed on a rolling basis. Application fee: $45. *Financial support:* Fellowships, research assistantships with full tuition reimbursements, teaching assistantships with full tuition reimbursements, career-related internships or fieldwork, Federal Work-Study, institutionally sponsored loans, scholarships/grants, tuition waivers (partial), and unspecified assistantships available. Support available to part-time students. Financial award applicants required to submit FAFSA. *Unit head:* Dr. Fraya Wagner-Marsh, Department Head, 734-487-3240, Fax: 734-487-4100, E-mail: fraya.wagner@emich.edu.

Eastern Michigan University, Graduate School, College of Business, Programs in Business Administration, Ypsilanti, MI 48197. Offers business administration (MBA, Graduate Certificate); computer information systems (Graduate Certificate); e-business (MBA, Graduate Certificate); enterprise business intelligence (MBA); entrepreneurship (MBA, Graduate Certificate); finance (MBA, Graduate Certificate); human resources (MBA); human resources management (Graduate Certificate); information systems (MBA); internal auditing (MBA); international business (MBA, Graduate Certificate); marketing management (Graduate Certificate); nonprofit management (MBA); organizational development (Graduate Certificate); supply chain management (MBA, Graduate Certificate). *Accreditation:* AACSB. *Program availability:* Part-time, online learning. *Students:* 63 full-time (36 women), 320 part-time (186 women); includes 131 minority (76 Black or African American, non-Hispanic/Latino; 5 American Indian or Alaska Native, non-Hispanic/Latino; 16 Asian, non-Hispanic/Latino; 19 Hispanic/Latino; 15 Two or more races, non-Hispanic/Latino), 23 international. Average age 32. 305 applicants, 70% accepted, 124 enrolled. In 2016, 78 master's, 57 other advanced degrees awarded. *Entrance requirements:* For master's, GMAT (minimum score 450), minimum cumulative undergraduate GPA of 2.75. Additional exam requirements/recommendations for international students: Required—TOEFL. *Application deadline:* For fall admission, 5/15 priority date for domestic students, 2/15 priority date for international students; for winter admission, 10/15 priority date for domestic students, 9/1 priority date for international students; for summer admission, 3/15 priority date for domestic students, 3/1 priority date for international students. Applications are processed on a rolling basis. Application fee: $45. *Financial support:* Fellowships, research assistantships with full tuition reimbursements, teaching assistantships with full tuition reimbursements, career-related internships or fieldwork, Federal Work-Study, institutionally sponsored loans, scholarships/grants, tuition waivers (partial), and unspecified assistantships available. Support available to part-time students. Financial award applicants required to submit FAFSA. *Unit head:* K. Michelle Henry, Director, Graduate Business Programs, 734-487-4444, Fax: 734-483-1316,
E-mail: cob.graduate@emich.edu. Website: http://www.emich.edu/cob/mba/

East Tennessee State University, School of Graduate Studies, College of Business and Technology, Department of Management and Marketing, Johnson City, TN 37614. Offers business administration (MBA, Postbaccalaureate Certificate); digital marketing (MS); entrepreneurial leadership (Postbaccalaureate Certificate); health care management (Postbaccalaureate Certificate). *Program availability:* Part-time, evening/weekend. *Degree requirements:* For master's, comprehensive exam, capstone. *Entrance requirements:* For master's, GMAT, minimum GPA of 2.5 (for MBA), 3.0 (for MS); for Postbaccalaureate Certificate, minimum GPA of 2.5. Additional exam requirements/recommendations for international students: Required—TOEFL (minimum score 550 paper-based; 79 iBT). Electronic applications accepted. *Faculty research:* Sustainability, healthcare effectiveness, consumer behavior, merchandizing trends, organizational management issues.

East Texas Baptist University, Master of Business Administration Program, Marshall, TX 75670-1498. Offers entrepreneurial leadership (MBA). *Program availability:* Part-time, evening/weekend, 100% online. *Faculty:* 2 full-time (1 woman), 1 part-time/adjunct (0 women). *Students:* 18 full-time (8 women), 16 part-time (7 women); includes 10 minority (7 Black or African American, non-Hispanic/Latino; 2 Hispanic/Latino; 1 Native Hawaiian or other Pacific Islander, non-Hispanic/Latino), 1 international. Average age 27. 19 applicants, 84% accepted, 13 enrolled. In 2016, 8 master's awarded. *Entrance requirements:* Additional exam requirements/recommendations for international students: Recommended—TOEFL (minimum score 550 paper-based; 79 iBT). *Application deadline:* For fall admission, 8/17 for domestic students; for spring admission, 1/10 for domestic students; for summer admission, 5/2 for domestic students. Applications are processed on a rolling basis. Application fee: $50. Electronic applications accepted. *Expenses:* $700 per credit hour tuition; $150 per semester fees (6 or more hours enrolled); $75 per semester fees (1-5 hours enrolled). *Financial support:* In 2016–17, 18 students received support. Federal Work-Study, scholarships/grants, unspecified assistantships, and staff grants available. Financial award applicants required to submit FAFSA. *Unit head:* Den Murley, Director of Graduate Admissions, 903-923-2079, Fax: 903-934-8115, E-mail: dmurley@etbu.edu.
Website: https://www.etbu.edu/business/master-business-administration/

Emory University, Goizueta Business School, Full Time MBA Program, Atlanta, GA 30322. Offers accounting (MBA); alternative investments (MBA); business process consulting (MBA); business technology management (MBA); capital markets (MBA); corporate finance (MBA); customer relationship management (MBA); decision analytics (MBA); entrepreneurship (MBA); finance (MBA); global management (MBA); investment banking (MBA); management consulting (MBA); marketing (MBA); marketing analytics (MBA); marketing consulting (MBA); operations management (MBA); organization and management (MBA); product and brand management (MBA); real estate (MBA); social enterprise (MBA); strategy consulting (MBA). *Accreditation:* AACSB. *Faculty:* 72 full-time (17 women), 18 part-time/adjunct (5 women). *Students:* 350 full-time (101 women); includes 77 minority (21 Black or African American, non-Hispanic/Latino; 3 American Indian or Alaska Native, non-Hispanic/Latino; 32 Asian, non-Hispanic/Latino; 15 Hispanic/Latino; 2 Native Hawaiian or other Pacific Islander, non-Hispanic/Latino; 4 Two or more races, non-Hispanic/Latino), 117 international. Average age 29. 1,434 applicants, 31% accepted, 181 enrolled. In 2016, 182 master's awarded. *Degree requirements:* For master's, 1 leadership course; 2 mid-semester module programs; 2 global components. *Entrance requirements:* For master's, GMAT/GRE, essays; recommendation letters; undergraduate degree; interview. Additional exam requirements/recommendations for international students: Required—TOEFL (minimum score 100 iBT), IELTS (minimum score 7), PTE (minimum score 68). *Application deadline:* For fall admission, 10/14 priority date for domestic and international students; for winter admission, 11/11 priority date for domestic and international students; for spring admission, 1/4 priority date for domestic students, 1/4 for international students. Application fee: $150. Electronic applications accepted. *Expenses:* $57,580. *Financial support:* In 2016–17, 289 students received support. Career-related internships or fieldwork, institutionally sponsored loans, and scholarships/grants available. Financial award application deadline: 4/1; financial award applicants required to submit FAFSA. *Faculty research:* Social enterprise; micro vs. large business; mobile health data; mutual fund performance; product evaluation. *Unit head:* Brian Mitchell, Associate Dean, 404-727-4824, Fax: 404-712-9648, E-mail: brian.mitchell@emory.edu. *Application contact:* Julie Barefoot, Associate Dean, 404-727-6311, Fax: 404-727-4612, E-mail: mbaadmissions@emory.edu. Website: http://www.goizueta.emory.edu

Everglades University, Graduate Programs, Program in Entrepreneurship, Boca Raton, FL 33431. Offers MS. *Program availability:* Part-time, evening/weekend, 100% online. *Degree requirements:* For master's, capstone course. *Entrance requirements:* For master's, GMAT (minimum score of 400) or GRE (minimum score of 290), bachelor's or graduate degree from college accredited by an agency recognized by the U.S. Department of Education; minimum cumulative GPA of 2.0 at the baccalaureate level, 3.0 at the master's level. Additional exam requirements/recommendations for international students: Recommended—TOEFL (minimum score 500 paper-based). Electronic applications accepted. *Expenses:* Contact institution.

Fairfield University, Dolan School of Business, Fairfield, CT 06824. Offers accounting (MBA, MS, CAS); business analytics (MS); entrepreneurship (MBA); finance (MBA, MS, CAS); general management (MBA, CAS); global management (MBA); human resource management (MBA, CAS); information systems and business analytics (MBA); marketing (MBA, CAS); taxation (MBA, CAS). *Accreditation:* AACSB. *Program availability:* Part-time, evening/weekend. *Faculty:* 20 full-time (6 women), 4 part-time/adjunct (1 woman). *Students:* 106 full-time (41 women), 57 part-time (26 women); includes 18 minority (4 Black or African American, non-Hispanic/Latino; 1 American Indian or Alaska Native, non-Hispanic/Latino; 4 Asian, non-Hispanic/Latino; 7 Hispanic/Latino; 2 Two or more races, non-Hispanic/Latino), 39 international. Average age 26. 136 applicants, 63% accepted, 35 enrolled. In 2016, 90 master's awarded. *Degree requirements:* For master's, capstone course. *Entrance requirements:* For master's, GMAT (minimum score 500), 2 letters of reference, resume, minimum GPA of 3.0. Additional exam requirements/recommendations for international students: Required—TOEFL (minimum score 550 paper-based; 80 iBT) or IELTS (minimum score 6.5). *Application deadline:* For fall admission, 5/15 for international students; for spring admission, 10/15 for international students. Applications are processed on a rolling basis. Application fee: $60. Electronic applications accepted. *Expenses:* $875 per credit hour. *Financial support:* In 2016–17, 33 students received support. Scholarships/grants and unspecified assistantships available. Financial award applicants required to submit FAFSA. *Faculty research:* International finance, leadership and careers, ethics in accounting, emotions in consumer behavior and organizations, data analytics. *Unit head:* Dr. Donald Gibson, Dean, 203-254-4070, Fax: 203-254-4105, E-mail: dgibson@fairfield.edu. *Application contact:* Marianne Gumpper, Director of Graduate and Continuing Studies Admission, 203-254-4184, Fax: 203-254-4073,
E-mail: gradadmis@fairfield.edu. Website: http://fairfield.edu/mba

Fairleigh Dickinson University, College at Florham, Silberman College of Business, Departments of Management, Marketing, and Entrepreneurial Studies, Program in Entrepreneurial Studies, Madison, NJ 07940-1099. Offers MBA, Certificate.

Fairleigh Dickinson University, Metropolitan Campus, Silberman College of Business, Departments of Management, Marketing, and Entrepreneurial Studies, Program in Entrepreneurial Studies, Teaneck, NJ 07666-1914. Offers MBA, Certificate.

Felician University, Program in Business, Lodi, NJ 07644-2117. Offers business administration (DBA); innovation and entrepreneurship (MBA). *Program availability:* Part-time-only, evening/weekend. *Faculty:* 7 full-time (0 women), 9 part-time/adjunct (2 women). *Students:* 4 full-time (2 women), 85 part-time (46 women); includes 48 minority (24 Black or African American, non-Hispanic/Latino; 10 Asian, non-Hispanic/Latino; 13 Hispanic/Latino; 1 Two or more races, non-Hispanic/Latino), 4 international. Average age 35. 71 applicants, 86% accepted, 40 enrolled. In 2016, 22 master's awarded. Terminal master's awarded for partial completion of doctoral program. *Degree requirements:* For master's, comprehensive exam, thesis, presentation; for doctorate, thesis/dissertation, scholarly project. *Entrance requirements:* For master's and doctorate, GMAT, resume, personal statement, graduation from accredited baccalaureate program. Additional exam requirements/recommendations for international students: Required—TOEFL (minimum score 650 paper-based; 79 iBT), IELTS (minimum score 6.5). *Application deadline:* Applications are processed on a rolling basis. Application fee: $40. Electronic applications accepted. Application fee is waived when completed online. *Expenses:* $1,000 per credit and $55 mandatory fee per term. *Financial support:* Federal Work-Study and scholarships/grants available. Financial award applicants required to submit FAFSA. *Faculty research:* Social media, assessment, small business management, mission integration. *Unit head:* Dr. David M. Turi, Associate Dean/Associate Professor, School of Business, 201-559-3327, E-mail: turid@felician.edu. *Application contact:* Michael Szarek, Assistant Vice-President, Graduate Admissions, 201-559-1450, E-mail: szarekm@felician.edu.

Florida Institute of Technology, Nathan M. Bisk College of Business, Program in Innovation and Entrepreneurship, Melbourne, FL 32901-6975. Offers MS. *Program availability:* Part-time, evening/weekend. *Students:* 18 applicants, 11% accepted, 1 enrolled. In 2016, 5 master's awarded. *Degree requirements:* For master's, comprehensive exam (for some programs), thesis optional, 30 credit hours. *Entrance requirements:* For master's, GMAT (minimum score of 500), GRE, or equivalent, bachelor's degree from regionally-accredited institution with minimum GPA of 3.0, 2 letters of recommendation, statement of objectives. Additional exam requirements/recommendations for international students: Required—TOEFL (minimum score 550 paper-based; 79 iBT). *Application deadline:* For fall admission, 4/1 for international students; for spring admission, 9/1 for international students. *Expenses: Tuition:* Full-time $22,338; part-time $1241 per credit hour. *Required fees:* $250. Tuition and fees vary according to degree level, campus/location and program. *Financial support:* Application deadline: 3/1. *Unit head:* Dr. Abram Walton, Associate Professor, 321-674-7327, Fax: 321-674-7494, E-mail: awalton@fit.edu. *Application contact:* Cheryl A. Brown, Associate Director of Graduate Admissions, 321-674-7581, Fax: 321-723-9468, E-mail: cbrown@fit.edu.
Website: http://www.fit.edu/programs/grad/ms_innovation_entrepreneurship

Fordham University, Gabelli School of Business, New York, NY 10023. Offers accounting (MBA, MS); applied statistics and decision-making (MS); business administration (EMBA); business analytics (MS); communications and media management (MBA); electronic business (MBA); entrepreneurship (MBA); finance (MBA); global finance (MS); global sustainability (MBA); healthcare management (MBA); information systems (MBA, MS); investor relations (MS); management (MBA, MS); marketing (MBA); marketing intelligence (MS); media management (MS); nonprofit leadership (MS); quantitative finance (MS); taxation (MS); JD/MBA; MS/MBA. *Accreditation:* AACSB. *Program availability:* Part-time, evening/weekend. *Faculty:* 132 full-time (44 women), 51 part-time/adjunct (7 women). *Students:* 1,117 full-time (668 women), 553 part-time (282 women); includes 207 minority (44 Black or African American, non-Hispanic/Latino; 92 Asian, non-Hispanic/Latino; 69 Hispanic/Latino; 2 Native Hawaiian or other Pacific Islander, non-Hispanic/Latino), 1,088 international. Average age 27. 4,745 applicants, 46% accepted, 752 enrolled. In 2016, 996 master's awarded. Terminal master's awarded for partial completion of doctoral program. *Degree requirements:* For master's, internships (required for MS in quantitative finance, recommended for MBA). *Entrance requirements:* For master's, GMAT/GRE, 2 letters of recommendation, resume, 2 essays, transcripts. Additional exam requirements/recommendations for international students: Required—TOEFL (minimum score 100 iBT), IELTS (minimum score 7). *Application deadline:* For fall admission, 11/15 priority date for domestic and international students; for winter admission, 1/15 priority date for domestic students, 1/1 priority date for international students; for spring admission, 3/1 for domestic and international students; for summer admission, 6/1 for domestic students. Application fee: $130. Electronic applications accepted. *Expenses:* $1,397 per credit. *Financial support:* In 2016–17, 78 students received support. Career-related internships or fieldwork, institutionally sponsored loans, scholarships/grants, and unspecified assistantships available. Support available to part-time students. Financial award application deadline: 6/30; financial award applicants required to submit FAFSA. *Unit head:* Dr. Donna Rapaccioli, Dean, 212-636-6165, Fax: 212-307-1779, E-mail: rapaccioli@fordham.edu. *Application contact:* Lawrence Murray, Senior Assistant Dean of Graduate Admissions and Advising, 212-636-6200, Fax: 212-636-7076,
E-mail: admissionsgb@fordham.edu. Website: http://www.fordham.edu/gabelli

Georgia State University, J. Mack Robinson College of Business, Department of Managerial Sciences, Atlanta, GA 30302-3083. Offers business analysis (MBA, MS); entrepreneurship (MBA); human resources management (MBA, MS); operations management (MBA, MS); organization behavior/human resource management (PhD); organization management (MBA); organizational change (MS); strategic management (PhD). *Accreditation:* AACSB. *Program availability:* Part-time, evening/weekend. *Faculty:* 25 full-time (11 women). *Students:* 30 full-time (20 women), 10 part-time (4 women); includes 14 minority (11 Black or African American, non-Hispanic/Latino; 1 Asian, non-Hispanic/Latino; 1 Hispanic/Latino; 1 Two or more races, non-Hispanic/Latino), 12 international. Average age 31. 79 applicants, 30% accepted, 13 enrolled. In 2016, 23 master's, 2 doctorates awarded. *Degree requirements:* For doctorate, comprehensive exam, thesis/dissertation. *Entrance requirements:* For master's, GRE or GMAT, transcripts from all institutions attended, resume, essays; for doctorate, GMAT, three letters of recommendation, personal statement, transcripts from all institutions attended, resume. Additional exam requirements/recommendations for international students: Required—TOEFL (minimum score 610 paper-based; 101 iBT), IELTS (minimum score 7). *Application deadline:* For fall admission, 5/1 priority date for domestic students, 2/1 priority date for international students; for spring admission, 9/15 priority date for domestic students, 4/1 priority date for international students. Applications are processed on a rolling basis. Application fee: $50. Electronic applications accepted. *Expenses:* Tuition, state resident: full-time $6876; part-time $382 per credit hour. Tuition, nonresident: full-time $22,374; part-time $1243 per credit hour. *Required fees:* $2128; $1064 per term. Part-time tuition and fees vary according to course load and program. *Financial support:* Research assistantships, teaching assistantships, scholarships/grants, tuition waivers, and unspecified assistantships available. Financial award applicants required to submit FAFSA. *Faculty research:* Entrepreneurship and innovation; strategy process; workplace interactions, relationships, and processes; leadership and culture; supply chain management. *Unit head:* Dr. Pamela S. Barr, Interim Chair, 404-413-7525, Fax: 404-413-7571. *Application contact:* Toby McChesney, Assistant Dean for Graduate Recruiting and Student Services, 404-413-7167, Fax: 404-413-7162, E-mail: rcbgradadmissions@gsu.edu.
Website: http://mgmt.robinson.gsu.edu/

Georgia State University, J. Mack Robinson College of Business, Institute of International Business, Atlanta, GA 30303. Offers international business (GMBA, MBA, MIB); international business and information technology (MBA); international entrepreneurship (MBA); MIB/MIA. *Program availability:* Part-time, evening/weekend. *Faculty:* 11 full-time (4 women). *Students:* 22 full-time (14 women), 14 part-time (9 women); includes 20 minority (15 Black or African American, non-Hispanic/Latino; 4 Hispanic/Latino; 1 Two or more races, non-Hispanic/Latino), 5 international. Average

age 31. 22 applicants, 27% accepted, 1 enrolled. In 2016, 31 master's awarded. *Entrance requirements:* For master's, GRE or GMAT, transcripts from all institutions attended, resume, essays. Additional exam requirements/recommendations for international students: Required—TOEFL (minimum score 610 paper-based; 101 iBT), IELTS (minimum score 7). *Application deadline:* For fall admission, 5/1 priority date for domestic students, 2/1 priority date for international students; for spring admission, 9/15 priority date for domestic students, 5/1 priority date for international students. Applications are processed on a rolling basis. Application fee: $50. Electronic applications accepted. *Expenses:* Tuition, state resident: full-time $6876; part-time $382 per credit hour. Tuition, nonresident: full-time $22,374; part-time $1243 per credit hour. *Required fees:* $2128; $1064 per term. Part-time tuition and fees vary according to course load and program. *Financial support:* Research assistantships, teaching assistantships, scholarships/grants, tuition waivers (partial), and unspecified assistantships available. Financial award application deadline: 5/1. *Faculty research:* Business challenges in emerging markets (especially in India and China); interorganizational relationships in an international context, such as strategic alliances and global supply chain relations; globalization and entry mode strategy or new (or emerging) multinationals; emerging market development and business environments; cross-cultural effects on business processes and performance. *Unit head:* Dr. Daniel Bello, Professor/Director of the Institute of International Business, 404-413-7275, Fax: 404-413-7276. *Application contact:* Toby McChesney, Assistant Dean for Graduate Recruiting and Student Services, 404-413-7167, Fax: 404-413-7162, E-mail: rcbgradadmissions@gsu.edu. Website: http://iib.gsu.edu/

Grand Canyon University, Colangelo College of Business, Phoenix, AZ 85017-1097. Offers accounting (MBA, MS); business analytics (MS); disaster preparedness and executive fire service leadership (MS); finance (MBA); general management (MBA); health systems management (MBA); information technology management (MS); leadership (MBA, MS); marketing (MBA); organizational leadership and entrepreneurship (MS); project management (MBA); sports business (MBA); strategic human resource management (MBA). *Accreditation:* ACBSP. *Program availability:* Part-time, evening/weekend, online learning. *Faculty:* 8 full-time (3 women), 147 part-time/adjunct (49 women). *Students:* 1 full-time (0 women), 2,121 part-time (1,165 women); includes 341 minority (249 Black or African American, non-Hispanic/Latino; 17 American Indian or Alaska Native, non-Hispanic/Latino; 15 Asian, non-Hispanic/Latino; 29 Hispanic/Latino; 4 Native Hawaiian or other Pacific Islander, non-Hispanic/Latino; 27 Two or more races, non-Hispanic/Latino), 20 international. Average age 38. In 2016, 569 master's awarded. *Entrance requirements:* For master's, equivalent of two years' full-time professional work experience. Additional exam requirements/recommendations for international students: Required—TOEFL (minimum score 575 paper-based; 90 iBT), IELTS (minimum score 7). *Application deadline:* For fall admission, 8/21 for domestic students, 7/2 for international students; for spring admission, 12/24 for domestic students, 11/1 for international students. Applications are processed on a rolling basis. Application fee: $0. Electronic applications accepted. *Financial support:* Federal Work-Study available. Support available to part-time students. Financial award applicants required to submit FAFSA. *Unit head:* Kim Donaldson, Dean, 602-639-6597, E-mail: kdonaldson@gcu.edu. *Application contact:* Matt Tidwell, Enrollment Manager, 602-639-6020, E-mail: mtidwell@gcu.edu.
Website: https://www.gcu.edu/colangelo-college-of-business.php

Harrisburg University of Science and Technology, Program in Information Systems Engineering and Management, Harrisburg, PA 17101. Offers analytics (MS); digital government (MS); digital health (MS); entrepreneurship (MS); information security (MS); software engineering and systems development (MS). *Program availability:* Part-time, evening/weekend. *Faculty:* 9 full-time (0 women), 1 (woman) part-time/adjunct. *Students:* 1,031 full-time (264 women), 35 part-time (10 women); includes 2 minority (1 Black or African American, non-Hispanic/Latino; 1 Asian, non-Hispanic/Latino), 1,060 international. In 2016, 83 master's awarded. *Degree requirements:* For master's, thesis optional. *Entrance requirements:* For master's, baccalaureate degree. Additional exam requirements/recommendations for international students: Required—TOEFL (minimum score 520 paper-based; 80 iBT); Recommended—IELTS (minimum score 6). *Application deadline:* Applications are processed on a rolling basis. Application fee: $0. Electronic applications accepted. *Expenses: Tuition:* Full-time $4800; part-time $800 per semester hour. *Financial support:* In 2016–17, 2 students received support. Teaching assistantships available. Financial award applicants required to submit FAFSA. *Faculty research:* Healthcare Informatics, material analysis, enterprise systems, circuit design, enterprise architectures. *Unit head:* Dr. Amjad Umar, Director and Professor, 717-901-5141, Fax: 717-901-3141, E-mail: aumar@harrisburgu.edu.

Hult International Business School, Graduate Programs, Cambridge, MA 02141. Offers business administration (EMBA); business analytics (MBA, MIB); business statistics (MBS); disruptive innovation (MDI); entrepreneurship (MBA, MIB); family business (MBA, MIB); finance (MBA, MF, MIB); international marketing (MIM); marketing (MBA, MIB); project management (MBA, MIB). MDI and MBS offered in San Francisco; MBA also offered in Boston, San Francisco, Dubai, Shanghai, and New York. *Students:* Average age 31. *Entrance requirements:* For master's, GMAT, 3 years of work experience. Additional exam requirements/recommendations for international students: Required—TOEFL. *Application deadline:* For fall admission, 9/1 priority date for domestic and international students; for winter admission, 11/1 priority date for domestic and international students; for spring admission, 12/1 priority date for domestic and international students; for summer admission, 6/1 for domestic and international students. Applications are processed on a rolling basis. Application fee: $150. Electronic applications accepted. *Expenses:* $75,000 (for MBA); $45,000 (for master's); $85,000 (for executive part-time MBA). *Financial support:* Scholarships/grants and tuition waivers (partial) available. Financial award application deadline: 6/1; financial award applicants required to submit FAFSA. *Application contact:* Boston Admissions Office, 617-746-1990, E-mail: postgraduate@hult.edu. Website: http://www.hult.edu

IGlobal University, Graduate Programs, Vienna, VA 22182. Offers accounting (MBA); data management and analytics (MSIT); entrepreneurship (MBA); finance (MBA); global business management (MBA); health care management (MBA); hospitality and tourism management (MBA); human resources management (MBA); information technology (MBA); information technology systems and management (MSIT); leadership and management (MBA); project management (MBA); public service and administration (MBA); software design and management (MSIT).

Illinois Institute of Technology, Stuart School of Business, Program in Technological Entrepreneurship, Chicago, IL 60616. Offers MTE.

Indiana University–Purdue University Indianapolis, Kelley School of Business, Evening MBA Program, Indianapolis, IN 46202-5151. Offers accounting (MBA); entrepreneurship (MBA); finance (MBA); general administration (MBA); marketing (MBA); supply chain management (MBA); MBA/JD; MBA/MD; MBA/MHA; MBA/MS; MBA/MSA; MBA/MSE. *Program availability:* Part-time-only, evening/weekend, online learning. *Faculty:* 30 full-time (7 women), 4 part-time/adjunct (0 women). *Students:* 294 part-time (46 women); includes 41 minority (11 Black or African American, non-Hispanic/Latino; 22 Asian, non-Hispanic/Latino; 8 Hispanic/Latino), 106 international. Average age 31. 129 applicants, 53% accepted, 61 enrolled. In 2016, 103 degrees awarded. *Entrance requirements:* For master's, GMAT or GRE, 2 years of professional work experience. Additional exam requirements/recommendations for international students: Required—TOEFL or IELTS. *Application deadline:* For fall admission, 6/1 for domestic and international students; for spring admission, 11/1 for domestic and international students. Applications are processed on a rolling basis. Application fee: $60 ($65 for international students). Electronic applications accepted. *Expenses:* $772.34 per credit hour in-state tuition, $1,456.56 per credit hour out-of-state tuition. *Financial support:* Scholarships/grants available. Financial award application deadline: 6/1. *Faculty research:* Entrepreneurship; corporate finance; international business; consumer behavior; supply chain; business law. *Unit head:* Mary Johnson, Associate Director, Evening MBA Program, 317-274-4895, E-mail: mbaindy@iupui.edu. *Application contact:* Kristen Peters, Program Assistant, 317-274-4895, E-mail: mbaindy@iupui.edu.
Website: http://kelley.iupui.edu/evemba

International University in Geneva, Business Programs, Geneva, Switzerland. Offers business administration (MBA, DBA); entrepreneurship (MBA); international business (MIB); international trade (MIT); sales and marketing (MBA). *Accreditation:* ACBSP. *Program availability:* Part-time, evening/weekend. *Degree requirements:* For master's, comprehensive exam. *Entrance requirements:* For master's, GMAT. Additional exam requirements/recommendations for international students: Required—TOEFL. Electronic applications accepted.

The International University of Monaco, Graduate Programs, Monte Carlo, Monaco. Offers entrepreneurship (EMBA, MBA); financial engineering (M Sc); hedge fund and private equity (M Sc); international marketing (EMBA, MBA); international wealth management (M Sc); luxury goods and services (EMBA, M Sc, MBA); wealth and asset management (EMBA, MBA). *Program availability:* Part-time. *Degree requirements:* For master's, comprehensive exam (for some programs), applied research project. *Entrance requirements:* Additional exam requirements/recommendations for international students: Required—TOEFL (minimum score 550 paper-based), IELTS. Electronic applications accepted. *Faculty research:* Gaming, leadership, disintermediation.

James Madison University, The Graduate School, College of Business, Program in Business Administration, Harrisonburg, VA 22807. Offers business (MBA), including executive leadership, information security, innovation. *Accreditation:* AACSB. *Program availability:* Part-time, evening/weekend, blended/hybrid learning. *Faculty:* 31 full-time (8 women), 2 part-time/adjunct (1 woman). *Students:* 20 full-time (9 women), 77 part-time (27 women); includes 21 minority (9 Black or African American, non-Hispanic/Latino; 9 Asian, non-Hispanic/Latino; 2 Hispanic/Latino; 1 Two or more races, non-Hispanic/Latino), 1 international. Average age 30. 62 applicants, 82% accepted, 42 enrolled. In 2016, 45 master's awarded. Application fee: $55. Electronic applications accepted. *Financial support:* In 2016–17, 1 student received support. Federal Work-Study and 1 assistantship (averaging $7911) available. Financial award application deadline: 3/1; financial award applicants required to submit FAFSA. *Unit head:* Dr. Matthew A. Rutherford, Department Head, 540-568-8777, E-mail: rutherma@jmu.edu. *Application contact:* Lynette D. Michael, Director of Graduate Admissions, 540-568-6131 Ext. 6395, Fax: 540-568-7860, E-mail: michaeld@jmu.edu.
Website: http://www.jmu.edu/cob/graduate/mba/index.shtml

Kansas State University, Graduate School, College of Business, Program in Business Administration, Manhattan, KS 66506. Offers data analytics (MBA); finance (MBA); management (MBA); marketing (MBA); technology entrepreneurship (MBA). *Accreditation:* AACSB. *Program availability:* Part-time, 100% online. *Faculty:* 35 full-time (8 women). *Students:* 50 full-time (19 women), 89 part-time (36 women); includes 25 minority (8 Black or African American, non-Hispanic/Latino; 6 Asian, non-Hispanic/Latino; 4 Hispanic/Latino; 7 Two or more races, non-Hispanic/Latino), 17 international. Average age 32. 78 applicants, 90% accepted, 31 enrolled. In 2016, 26 master's, 3 other advanced degrees awarded. *Entrance requirements:* For master's, GMAT (minimum score of 500), minimum undergraduate GPA of 3.0. Additional exam requirements/recommendations for international students: Required—TOEFL (minimum score 550 paper-based; 79 iBT); Recommended—IELTS (minimum score 7). *Application deadline:* For fall admission, 2/1 priority date for domestic and international students; for spring admission, 10/1 priority date for domestic students, 8/1 priority date for international students. Applications are processed on a rolling basis. Application fee: $70 ($80 for international students). Electronic applications accepted. *Expenses:* Contact institution. *Financial support:* In 2016–17, 6 students received support, including 5 research assistantships (averaging $6,400 per year), 6 teaching assistantships with partial tuition reimbursements available (averaging $6,400 per year); institutionally sponsored loans and scholarships/grants also available. Financial award application deadline: 3/1; financial award applicants required to submit FAFSA. *Faculty research:* Organizational citizenship behavior, service marketing, impression management, human resources management, lean manufacturing and supply chain management, financial market behavior and investment management, data analytics, corporate responsibility, technology entrepreneurship. *Unit head:* Dr. Kevin Gwinner, Dean, 785-532-7227, Fax: 785-532-7216, E-mail: kgwinner@ksu.edu. *Application contact:* Dr. Chwen Sheu, Associate Dean for Academic Programs, 785-532-4363, Fax: 785-532-1339, E-mail: gradbusiness@ksu.edu.
Website: http://www.cba.k-state.edu/

Kaplan University, Davenport Campus, School of Business, Davenport, IA 52807. Offers business administration (MBA); change leadership (MS); entrepreneurship (MBA); finance (MBA); health care management (MBA, MS); human resource (MBA); international business (MBA); management (MS); marketing (MBA); project management (MBA, MS); supply chain management and logistics (MBA, MS). *Accreditation:* ACBSP. *Program availability:* Part-time, evening/weekend, online learning. *Entrance requirements:* Additional exam requirements/recommendations for international students: Required—TOEFL (minimum score 550 paper-based; 80 iBT). Electronic applications accepted.

Lamar University, College of Graduate Studies, College of Business, Beaumont, TX 77710. Offers accounting (MBA); experiential business and entrepreneurship (MBA); healthcare administration (MBA); MSA/MBA. *Accreditation:* AACSB. *Program availability:* Part-time, evening/weekend. *Faculty:* 22 full-time (5 women). *Students:* 23 full-time (12 women), 209 part-time (109 women); includes 96 minority (46 Black or African American, non-Hispanic/Latino; 11 Asian, non-Hispanic/Latino; 32 Hispanic/Latino; 7 Two or more races, non-Hispanic/Latino), 33 international. Average age 33. 151 applicants, 99% accepted, 81 enrolled. In 2016, 104 master's awarded. *Degree requirements:* For master's, comprehensive exam (for some programs), thesis optional. *Entrance requirements:* For master's, GMAT. Additional exam requirements/recommendations for international students: Required—TOEFL (minimum score 550 paper-based; 79 iBT), IELTS (minimum score 6.5). *Application deadline:* For fall admission, 8/10 for domestic students, 7/1 for international students; for spring admission, 1/5 for domestic students, 12/1 for international students. Applications are processed on a rolling basis. Application fee: $25 ($50 for international students). Electronic applications accepted. *Expenses:* $8,134 in-state full-time, $5,574 in-state part-time; $15,604 out-of-state full-time, $10,554 out-of-state part-time per year. *Financial support:* Fellowships with tuition reimbursements, research assistantships with partial tuition reimbursements, career-related internships or fieldwork, Federal Work-Study, institutionally sponsored loans, scholarships/grants, and tuition waivers (partial) available. Support available to part-time students. Financial award application

deadline: 4/1; financial award applicants required to submit FAFSA. *Faculty research:* Marketing, finance, quantitative methods, management information systems, legal, environmental. *Unit head:* Dr. Enrique R. Venta, Dean, 409-880-8603, Fax: 409-880-8088, E-mail: henry.venta@lamar.edu. *Application contact:* Deidre Mayer, Interim Director, Admissions and Academic Services, 409-880-8888, Fax: 409-880-7419, E-mail: gradmissions@lamar.edu.
Website: http://business.lamar.edu

Lehigh University, P.C. Rossin College of Engineering and Applied Science, Technical Entrepreneurship Program, Bethlehem, PA 18015. Offers M Eng. *Students:* 23 full-time (3 women); includes 4 minority (1 Black or African American, non-Hispanic/Latino; 1 Asian, non-Hispanic/Latino; 2 Hispanic/Latino), 4 international. Average age 23. 39 applicants, 97% accepted, 23 enrolled. In 2016, 6 master's awarded. *Entrance requirements:* For master's, bachelor's degree. Additional exam requirements/recommendations for international students: Required—TOEFL. *Application deadline:* For fall admission, 1/15 priority date for domestic students. Application fee: $75. Electronic applications accepted. Tuition and fees vary according to program. *Financial support:* Fellowships available. Financial award application deadline: 1/15. *Unit head:* Dr. John Ochs, Director, 610-758-4593, Fax: 610-758-6131, E-mail: jbo0@lehigh.edu. *Application contact:* Jodie L. Johnson, Program Manager, 610-758-4789, Fax: 610-758-6131, E-mail: jlk4@lehigh.edu.
Website: http://www.lehigh.edu/~innovate/

Lenoir-Rhyne University, Graduate Programs, Charles M. Snipes School of Business, Hickory, NC 28601. Offers accounting (MBA); business analytics and information technology (MBA); entrepreneurship (MBA); global business (MBA); healthcare administration (MBA); innovation and change management (MBA); leadership development (MBA). *Accreditation:* ACBSP. *Program availability:* Part-time, evening/weekend, online learning. *Degree requirements:* For master's, capstone course. *Entrance requirements:* For master's, GMAT, GRE, MAT, minimum undergraduate GPA of 2.7, graduate 3.0. Additional exam requirements/recommendations for international students: Required—TOEFL (minimum score 600 paper-based). Electronic applications accepted. *Expenses:* Contact institution.

LIM College, MBA Program, New York, NY 10022-5268. Offers entrepreneurship (MBA); fashion management (MBA). *Accreditation:* ACBSP. *Entrance requirements:* For master's, interview. Additional exam requirements/recommendations for international students: Required—TOEFL (minimum score 550 paper-based; 80 iBT), IELTS (minimum score 6.5).

Lindenwood University, Graduate Programs, Plaster School of Business and Entrepreneurship, St. Charles, MO 63301-1695. Offers accountancy (M Acc); accounting (MBA); business administration (MBA); entrepreneurial studies (MBA); finance (MBA, MS); human resource management (MBA); international business (MBA); leadership (MA); management (MBA); marketing (MBA, MS); nonprofit administration (MA); public administration (MBA); sport management (MA); supply chain management (MBA). *Accreditation:* ACBSP. *Program availability:* Part-time, evening/weekend, 100% online. *Faculty:* 15 full-time (6 women), 25 part-time/adjunct (7 women). *Students:* 197 full-time (97 women), 213 part-time (132 women); includes 81 minority (62 Black or African American, non-Hispanic/Latino; 1 American Indian or Alaska Native, non-Hispanic/Latino; 4 Asian, non-Hispanic/Latino; 9 Hispanic/Latino; 5 Two or more races, non-Hispanic/Latino), 83 international. Average age 31. 279 applicants, 54% accepted, 133 enrolled. In 2016, 269 master's awarded. *Degree requirements:* For master's, comprehensive exam (for some programs), thesis (for some programs), minimum GPA of 3.0. *Entrance requirements:* For master's, interview, minimum undergraduate cumulative GPA of 3.0, letter of recommendation. Additional exam requirements/recommendations for international students: Required—TOEFL (minimum score 550 paper-based; 80 iBT); Recommended—IELTS (minimum score 6.5). *Application deadline:* For fall admission, 8/28 priority date for domestic and international students; for winter admission, 1/8 priority date for domestic and international students; for spring admission, 3/5 for domestic students, 3/5 priority date for international students; for summer admission, 6/4 priority date for domestic and international students. Applications are processed on a rolling basis. Application fee: $30 ($100 for international students). Electronic applications accepted. *Expenses:* Contact institution. *Financial support:* In 2016–17, 256 students received support. Career-related internships or fieldwork, Federal Work-Study, institutionally sponsored loans, scholarships/grants, tuition waivers (partial), and unspecified assistantships available. Financial award application deadline: 6/30; financial award applicants required to submit FAFSA. *Unit head:* Roger Ellis, Dean, School of Business and Entrepreneurship, 636-949-4839, E-mail: rellis@lindenwood.edu. *Application contact:* Tyler Kostich, Director, Evening and Graduate Admissions, 636-949-4138, Fax: 636-949-4109, E-mail: adultadmissions@lindenwood.edu.
Website: http://www.lindenwood.edu/academics/academic-schools/robert-w-plaster-school-of-business-entrepreneurship/

Loyola University Chicago, Quinlan School of Business, MBA Programs, Chicago, IL 60611. Offers accounting (MBA); business administration (EMBA); business ethics (MBA); economics (MBA); entrepreneurship (MBA); finance (MBA); healthcare management (MBA); human resources management (MBA); international business (MBA); management (MBA); marketing (MBA); operation management (MBA); risk management (MBA); supply chain management (MBA). *Program availability:* Part-time, evening/weekend. *Faculty:* 79 full-time (22 women), 10 part-time/adjunct (6 women). *Students:* 309 full-time (151 women), 65 part-time (31 women); includes 82 minority (25 Black or African American, non-Hispanic/Latino; 27 Asian, non-Hispanic/Latino; 27 Hispanic/Latino; 3 Two or more races, non-Hispanic/Latino), 49 international. Average age 30. 371 applicants, 53% accepted, 114 enrolled. In 2016, 216 master's awarded. *Entrance requirements:* For master's, GMAT or GRE, official transcripts, two letters of recommendation, statement of purpose, resume. Additional exam requirements/recommendations for international students: Required—TOEFL (minimum score 90 iBT) or IELTS (minimum score 6.5). *Application deadline:* For fall admission, 7/15 for domestic and international students; for winter admission, 10/1 for domestic and international students; for spring admission, 1/15 for domestic and international students; for summer admission, 4/1 for domestic and international students. Applications are processed on a rolling basis. Application fee: $50. Electronic applications accepted. Application fee is waived when completed online. *Expenses:* $4,488 per course. *Financial support:* In 2016–17, 83 students received support. Federal Work-Study, scholarships/grants, health care benefits, and unspecified assistantships available. Support available to part-time students. *Faculty research:* Social enterprise and responsibility, emerging markets, supply chain management, risk management. *Unit head:* Katherine Acles, Assistant Dean for Graduate Programs, 312-915-6124, Fax: 312-915-7207, E-mail: kacles@luc.edu. *Application contact:* Lauren Griffin, Enrollment Advisor, Quinlan School of Business Graduate Programs, 312-915-6124, Fax: 312-915-7207, E-mail: lgriffin3@luc.edu.

Loyola University New Orleans, Joseph A. Butt, S.J., College of Business, Program in Business Administration, New Orleans, LA 70118-6195. Offers entrepreneurship and marketing innovation (MBA); organizational performance excellence (MBA); JD/MBA; MBA/MPS. *Accreditation:* AACSB. *Program availability:* Part-time, evening/weekend, online learning. *Faculty:* 8 full-time (4 women), 3 part-time/adjunct (0 women). *Students:* 71 full-time (35 women), 13 part-time (9 women); includes 27 minority (14 Black or African American, non-Hispanic/Latino; 1 American Indian or Alaska Native, non-Hispanic/Latino; 3 Asian, non-Hispanic/Latino; 8 Hispanic/Latino; 1 Two or more races, non-Hispanic/Latino), 3 international. Average age 29. 52 applicants, 96% accepted, 28 enrolled. In 2016, 25 master's awarded. *Degree requirements:* For master's, capstone project. *Entrance requirements:* For master's, GMAT or GRE, minimum GPA of 3.0, transcript, resume, 2 letters of recommendation, work experience in field, personal statement. Additional exam requirements/recommendations for international students: Required—TOEFL (minimum score 580 paper-based; 92 iBT). *Application deadline:* For fall admission, 6/15 priority date for domestic students, 5/15 priority date for international students; for spring admission, 11/15 priority date for domestic students, 10/15 priority date for international students. Applications are processed on a rolling basis. Application fee: $50. Electronic applications accepted. *Financial support:* Research assistantships, scholarships/grants, tuition waivers (partial), and unspecified assistantships available. Financial award application deadline: 5/1; financial award applicants required to submit FAFSA. *Faculty research:* Ethics, international business, entrepreneurship, quality management, risk management. *Unit head:* Dr. William B. Locander, Dean, 504-864-7979, Fax: 504-864-7970, E-mail: mba@loyno.edu. *Application contact:* Ashley Francis, Director of Graduate Programs, 504-864-7979, Fax: 504-864-7970,
E-mail: mba@loyno.edu. Website: http://www.business.loyno.edu/mba/programs

Manhattanville College, School of Education, Program in Education Entrepreneurship, Purchase, NY 10577-2132. Offers M Ed. Program offered jointly with the School of Business. *Program availability:* Part-time, evening/weekend. *Degree requirements:* For master's, comprehensive exam (for some programs), thesis (for some programs), student teaching, research seminars, portfolios, internships, writing assessment. *Entrance requirements:* For master's, GRE or MAT, minimum undergraduate GPA of 3.0, 2 letters of recommendation. Additional exam requirements/recommendations for international students: Required—TOEFL (minimum score 85 iBT); Recommended—IELTS. *Application deadline:* For fall admission, 7/1 priority date for domestic and international students; for spring admission, 11/1 priority date for domestic and international students; for summer admission, 4/1 priority date for domestic and international students. Applications are processed on a rolling basis. Application fee: $75. Electronic applications accepted. *Expenses: Tuition:* Full-time $16,470; part-time $915 per credit. *Required fees:* $60 per semester. Part-time tuition and fees vary according to course load and program. *Financial support:* Teaching assistantships, career-related internships or fieldwork, Federal Work-Study, institutionally sponsored loans, scholarships/grants, and unspecified assistantships available. Financial award applicants required to submit FAFSA. *Unit head:* Laurence Krute, Associate Dean, 914-323-5366, E-mail: laurence.krute@mville.edu. *Application contact:* Jeanine Pardey-Levine, Director of Graduate Enrollment Management, 914-323-3208, Fax: 914-694-1732, E-mail: edschool@mville.edu.
Website: http://www.mville.edu/programs/educational-studies-education-entrepreneurship

Marlboro College, Graduate and Professional Studies, Program in Management, Marlboro, VT 05344. Offers collaborative leadership (MS); conscious business (MS); mission driven organizations (MS); project management (MS); social innovation (MS); sustainable food systems (MS). *Program availability:* Part-time, evening/weekend, blended/hybrid learning. *Faculty:* 1 (woman) full-time, 23 part-time/adjunct (14 women). *Students:* 2 full-time (both women), 12 part-time (9 women). Average age 34. 6 applicants, 33% accepted, 2 enrolled. In 2016, 13 master's awarded. *Degree requirements:* For master's, capstone project. *Entrance requirements:* For master's, statement of intent, 2 letters of recommendation. Additional exam requirements/recommendations for international students: Recommended—TOEFL (minimum score 577 paper-based; 90 iBT), IELTS (minimum score 7). *Application deadline:* For fall admission, 8/5 for domestic students; for winter admission, 12/5 for domestic students; for spring admission, 4/5 for domestic students. Applications are processed on a rolling basis. Application fee: $0. Electronic applications accepted. *Expenses:* $765 per credit. *Financial support:* Scholarships/grants available. Financial award applicants required to submit FAFSA. *Unit head:* Tristan Toleno, Degree Chair, 802-258-9200, Fax: 802-258-9201, E-mail: tristant@gradschool.marlboro.edu. *Application contact:* Kelley Barton, Admissions Counselor, 802-258-9209, Fax: 802-258-9201, E-mail: graduateadmissions@marlboro.edu.
Website: https://www.marlboro.edu/academics/graduate/management

Marquette University, Graduate School of Management, Program in Business Administration, Milwaukee, WI 53201-1881. Offers business administration (MBA); economics (MBA); entrepreneurship (Certificate); finance (MBA); human resources (MBA); international business (MBA); management information systems (MBA); marketing (MBA); operations and supply chain management (MBA); sports business (MBA); JD/MBA; MBA/MA; MBA/MSN. *Accreditation:* AACSB. *Program availability:* Part-time, evening/weekend. *Students:* 25 full-time (12 women), 202 part-time (57 women); includes 17 minority (5 Black or African American, non-Hispanic/Latino; 6 Asian, non-Hispanic/Latino; 2 Hispanic/Latino; 1 Native Hawaiian or other Pacific Islander, non-Hispanic/Latino; 3 Two or more races, non-Hispanic/Latino), 7 international. Average age 31. 107 applicants, 87% accepted, 113 enrolled. In 2016, 107 master's, 5 other advanced degrees awarded. *Degree requirements:* For Certificate, business plan. *Entrance requirements:* For master's, GMAT or GRE, letters of recommendation. Additional exam requirements/recommendations for international students: Required—TOEFL (minimum score 550 paper-based; 88 iBT), IELTS (minimum score 6.5), PTE. *Application deadline:* For fall admission, 2/15 for domestic and international students. Applications are processed on a rolling basis. Application fee: $50. Electronic applications accepted. *Financial support:* Fellowships, research assistantships, teaching assistantships, Federal Work-Study, institutionally sponsored loans, scholarships/grants, and tuition waivers (full and partial) available. Support available to part-time students. Financial award application deadline: 2/15. *Faculty research:* Ethics in the professions, services marketing, technology impact on decision-making, mentoring. *Unit head:* Dr. Brian Till, Dean, 414-288-5724. *Application contact:* Dr. Jeanne Simmons, Associate Dean, 414-288-7145.
Website: http://business.marquette.edu/academics/mba

McGill University, Faculty of Graduate and Postdoctoral Studies, Desautels Faculty of Management, Montréal, QC H3A 2T5, Canada. Offers administration (PhD); entrepreneurial studies (MBA); finance (MBA); general management (Post Master's Certificate); information systems (MBA); international business (MBA); international practicing management (MM); management (MBA); management for development (MBA); manufacturing management (MMM); marketing (MBA); operations management (MBA); public accountancy (Diploma); strategic management (MBA); MBA/LL B; MD/MBA. MMM offered jointly with Faculty of Engineering; PhD with Concordia University, HEC Montreal, Université de Montréal, Université du Québec à Montréal.

Mercer University, Graduate Studies, Cecil B. Day Campus, Eugene W. Stetson School of Business and Economics (Atlanta), Atlanta, GA 30341. Offers accounting (M Acc); business analytics (MS); innovation (PMBA), including entrepreneurship; international business (MBA); MBA/M Acc; Pharm D/MBA. *Accreditation:* AACSB. *Program availability:* Part-time, evening/weekend, 100% online, blended/hybrid learning. *Faculty:* 19 full-time (7 women), 7 part-time/adjunct (1 woman). *Students:* 183 full-time

(91 women), 129 part-time (69 women); includes 136 minority (99 Black or African American, non-Hispanic/Latino; 2 American Indian or Alaska Native, non-Hispanic/Latino; 22 Asian, non-Hispanic/Latino; 10 Hispanic/Latino; 3 Two or more races, non-Hispanic/Latino), 43 international. Average age 32. 207 applicants, 77% accepted, 110 enrolled. In 2016, 176 master's awarded. *Entrance requirements:* For master's, GMAT or GRE. Additional exam requirements/recommendations for international students: Required—TOEFL (minimum score 550 paper-based, 80 iBT) or IELTS. *Application deadline:* For fall admission, 6/15 priority date for domestic and international students; for spring admission, 11/1 priority date for domestic and international students; for summer admission, 3/15 priority date for domestic and international students. Applications are processed on a rolling basis. Application fee: $50 ($100 for international students). Electronic applications accepted. *Expenses:* $795 per credit full-time, $727 per credit part-time. *Financial support:* Federal Work-Study available. Financial award application deadline: 5/1; financial award applicants required to submit FAFSA. *Faculty research:* Entrepreneurship, market studies, international business strategy, financial analysis. *Unit head:* Dr. Susan P. Gilbert, Dean, 678-547-6438, Fax: 678-547-6337, E-mail: gilbert_sp@mercer.edu. *Application contact:* Lael Whiteside, Director of Admissions, 678-547-6300, Fax: 678-547-6160, E-mail: whiteside_l@mercer.edu.
Website: http://business.mercer.edu

Mercyhurst University, Graduate Studies, Program in Organizational Leadership, Erie, PA 16546. Offers accounting (MS); higher education administration (MS); human resources (MS); organizational leadership (MS, Certificate); sports leadership (MS); strategy and innovation (MS). *Program availability:* Part-time, evening/weekend. *Degree requirements:* For master's, thesis. *Entrance requirements:* For master's, GRE General Test or MAT, interview, resume, essay, three professional references, transcripts. Additional exam requirements/recommendations for international students: Required—TOEFL (minimum score 80 iBT), IELTS (minimum score 6.5). Electronic applications accepted. *Faculty research:* Leadership training, organizational communication, leadership pedagogy.

Monroe College, King Graduate School, Bronx, NY 10468. Offers accounting (MS); business administration (MBA), including entrepreneurship, finance, general business administration, healthcare management, human resources, information technology, marketing; computer science (MS); criminal justice (MS); hospitality management (MS); public health (MPH), including biostatistics and epidemiology, community health, health administration and leadership. *Program availability:* Online learning. Application fee: $50.
Website: https://www.monroecollege.edu/Degrees/King-Graduate-School/

New York University, Polytechnic School of Engineering, Department of Chemical and Biomolecular Engineering, Major in Biotechnology and Entrepreneurship, New York, NY 10012-1019. Offers MS. *Entrance requirements:* Additional exam requirements/recommendations for international students: Required—TOEFL (minimum score 550 paper-based; 80 iBT); Recommended—IELTS (minimum score 6.5). Electronic applications accepted.

New York University, Polytechnic School of Engineering, Department of Technology Management, New York, NY 10012-1019. Offers construction management (Advanced Certificate); electronic business management (Advanced Certificate); entrepreneurship (Advanced Certificate); human resources management (Advanced Certificate); industrial engineering (MS); information management (Advanced Certificate); management (MS); management of technology (MS); manufacturing engineering (MS); organizational behavior (MS, Advanced Certificate); project management (Advanced Certificate); technology management (MBA, PhD, Advanced Certificate); telecommunications management (Advanced Certificate). *Program availability:* Part-time, evening/weekend. *Degree requirements:* For master's, comprehensive exam (for some programs), thesis (for some programs); for doctorate, comprehensive exam, thesis/dissertation. *Entrance requirements:* For master's, GMAT, minimum B average in undergraduate course work. Additional exam requirements/recommendations for international students: Required—TOEFL (minimum score 550 paper-based; 80 iBT); Recommended—IELTS (minimum score 6.5). Electronic applications accepted. *Faculty research:* Global innovation and research and development strategy, managing emerging technologies, technology and development, service design and innovation, tech entrepreneurship and commercialization, sustainable and clean-tech innovation, impacts of information technology upon individuals, organizations and society.

North Carolina State University, Graduate School, Poole College of Management, Program in Business Administration, Raleigh, NC 27695. Offers biosciences management (MBA); entrepreneurship and technology commercialization (MBA); financial management (MBA); innovation management (MBA); marketing management (MBA); services management (MBA); supply chain management (MBA). *Accreditation:* AACSB. *Program availability:* Part-time. *Degree requirements:* For master's, thesis optional. *Entrance requirements:* For master's, GMAT, interview, 3 letters of recommendation. Additional exam requirements/recommendations for international students: Required—TOEFL (minimum score 600 paper-based; 100 iBT). Electronic applications accepted. *Faculty research:* Manufacturing strategy, Information systems, technology commercialization, managing research and development, historical stock returns.

Northeastern University, D'Amore-McKim School of Business, Boston, MA 02115-5096. Offers accounting (MS); business administration (EMBA, MBA); finance (MS); innovation (MS); international business (MS); international management (MS); taxation (MS); technological entrepreneurship (MS); JD/MBA; LL M/MBA; MBA/MSN; MS/MBA. *Accreditation:* AACSB. *Program availability:* Part-time, evening/weekend, online learning. *Faculty:* 185 full-time (66 women), 57 part-time/adjunct (13 women). *Students:* 379 full-time (180 women), 1,182 part-time (514 women). In 2016, 800 master's awarded. *Entrance requirements:* For master's, GMAT or GRE. Application fee: $75. Electronic applications accepted. *Expenses:* Contact institution. *Financial support:* Scholarships/grants available. Financial award applicants required to submit FAFSA. *Unit head:* Dr. Hugh Courtney, Dean, D'Amore-McKim School of Business. *Application contact:* Evelyn Tate, Director, Graduate Recruitment and Admissions, 617-373-3258, Fax: 617-373-8564, E-mail: e.tate@northeastern.edu.
Website: http://damore-mckim.northeastern.edu/

Northwestern University, The Graduate School, Kellogg School of Management, Management Programs, Evanston, IL 60208. Offers accounting information and management (MBA, PhD); analytical finance (MBA); business administration (MBA); decision sciences (MBA); entrepreneurship and innovation (MBA); finance (MBA, PhD); health enterprise management (MBA); human resources management (MBA); international business (MBA); management and organizations (MBA, PhD); management and organizations and sociology (PhD); management and strategy (MBA); management studies (MS); managerial analytics (MBA); managerial economics (MBA); managerial economics and strategy (PhD); marketing (MBA, PhD); marketing management (MBA); media management (MBA); operations management (MBA, PhD); real estate (MBA); social enterprise at Kellogg (MBA); JD/MBA. *Program availability:* Part-time, evening/weekend. Terminal master's awarded for partial completion of doctoral program. *Degree requirements:* For doctorate, thesis/dissertation, 2 years of coursework, qualifying (field) exam and candidacy, summer research papers and presentations to faculty, proposal defense, final exam/defense. *Entrance requirements:* For master's, GMAT, GRE, interview, 2 letters of recommendation, college transcripts, resume, essays, Kellogg honor code; for doctorate, GMAT, GRE, statement of purpose, transcripts, 2 letters of recommendation, resume, interview. Additional exam requirements/recommendations for international students: Required—TOEFL, IELTS. Electronic applications accepted. *Expenses:* Contact institution. *Faculty research:* Business cycles and international finance, health policy, networks, non-market strategy, consumer psychology.

Notre Dame de Namur University, Division of Academic Affairs, School of Business and Management, Program in Business Administration, Belmont, CA 94002-1908. Offers business administration (MBA); entrepreneurship (MBA); finance (MBA); human resource management (MBA); marketing (MBA); media and promotion (MBA); technology and operations management (MBA). *Accreditation:* ACBSP. *Program availability:* Part-time, evening/weekend. *Entrance requirements:* For master's, minimum GPA of 2.5. Additional exam requirements/recommendations for international students: Required—TOEFL (minimum score 550 paper-based; 79 iBT). Electronic applications accepted.

Notre Dame de Namur University, Division of Academic Affairs, School of Business and Management, Program in Public Administration, Belmont, CA 94002-1908. Offers human resource management (MPA); public administration (MPA); public affairs administration (MPA); social enterprise (MPA). *Program availability:* Part-time, evening/weekend, online learning. *Entrance requirements:* For master's, interview, minimum GPA of 2.5. Additional exam requirements/recommendations for international students: Required—TOEFL (minimum score 550 paper-based; 79 iBT). Electronic applications accepted.

Nova Southeastern University, H. Wayne Huizenga College of Business and Entrepreneurship, Fort Lauderdale, FL 33314-7796. Offers accounting (M Acc); business intelligence/analytics (MBA); entrepreneurship (MBA); finance (MBA); human resource management (MBA); international business (MBA); management (MBA); marketing (MBA); process improvement (MBA); public administration (MPA); real estate development (MS); sport revenue generation (MBA); supply chain management (MBA); taxation (M Tax). *Program availability:* Part-time, evening/weekend, 100% online, blended/hybrid learning. *Faculty:* 65 full-time (26 women), 111 part-time/adjunct (74 women). *Students:* 2,242 full-time (1,400 women), 425 part-time (239 women); includes 1,798 minority (734 Black or African American, non-Hispanic/Latino; 5 American Indian or Alaska Native, non-Hispanic/Latino; 110 Asian, non-Hispanic/Latino; 890 Hispanic/Latino; 2 Native Hawaiian or other Pacific Islander, non-Hispanic/Latino; 57 Two or more races, non-Hispanic/Latino), 255 international. Average age 34. 1,422 applicants, 64% accepted, 672 enrolled. In 2016, 971 master's awarded. *Degree requirements:* For master's, thesis optional. *Entrance requirements:* For master's, GMAT or GRE (depending on undergraduate GPA), official transcripts from all schools attended while in pursuit of bachelor's degree; minimum GPA of 2.5 from regionally-accredited institution. Additional exam requirements/recommendations for international students: Required—TOEFL (minimum score 550 paper-based; 79 iBT), IELTS (minimum score 6), PTE (minimum score 54). *Application deadline:* For fall admission, 8/5 priority date for domestic students, 7/29 priority date for international students; for winter admission, 12/16 priority date for domestic students, 12/9 priority date for international students; for summer admission, 4/21 priority date for domestic and international students. Applications are processed on a rolling basis. Application fee: $50. Electronic applications accepted. *Expenses:* Contact institution. *Financial support:* In 2016–17, 325 students received support. Federal Work-Study and scholarships/grants available. Support available to part-time students. Financial award application deadline: 4/15; financial award applicants required to submit FAFSA. *Faculty research:* Reputation management, call centers, international social capital, corporate earnings guidance, corporate governance. *Unit head:* Dr. J. Preston Jones, Dean, 954-262-5127, E-mail: prestonj@nova.edu. *Application contact:* Zeida Rodriguez, Associate Director of Enrollment Services, 954-262-5163, Fax: 954-262-3822, E-mail: zeida@nova.edu.
Website: http://www.huizenga.nova.edu

Oakland University, Graduate Study and Lifelong Learning, School of Business Administration, Department of Management and Marketing, Rochester, MI 48309-4401. Offers business administration (MBA); entrepreneurship (Certificate); general management (Certificate); human resource management (Certificate); international business (Certificate); management and marketing (EMBA); marketing (Certificate).

Oklahoma State University, Spears School of Business, School of Entrepreneurship, Stillwater, OK 74078. Offers MBA, MS, PhD. *Program availability:* Part-time. *Faculty:* 11 full-time (0 women). *Students:* 9 full-time (3 women), 26 part-time (11 women); includes 7 minority (3 Black or African American, non-Hispanic/Latino; 2 Hispanic/Latino; 2 Two or more races, non-Hispanic/Latino), 4 international. Average age 30. 16 applicants, 69% accepted, 10 enrolled. In 2016, 24 master's, 2 doctorates awarded. *Degree requirements:* For master's, thesis or alternative; for doctorate, comprehensive exam, thesis/dissertation. *Entrance requirements:* For master's and doctorate, GMAT. Additional exam requirements/recommendations for international students: Required—TOEFL (minimum score 550 paper-based; 89 iBT). *Application deadline:* For fall admission, 3/1 priority date for international students; for spring admission, 8/1 priority date for international students. Applications are processed on a rolling basis. Application fee: $40 ($75 for international students). Electronic applications accepted. *Expenses:* Tuition, state resident: full-time $3775; part-time $209.70 per credit hour. Tuition, nonresident: full-time $14,851; part-time $825.05 per credit hour. *Required fees:* $2027; $112.60 per credit hour. Tuition and fees vary according to campus/location. *Financial support:* In 2016–17, 9 research assistantships (averaging $11,957 per year), 12 teaching assistantships (averaging $7,185 per year) were awarded; career-related internships or fieldwork, Federal Work-Study, scholarships/grants, health care benefits, tuition waivers (partial), and unspecified assistantships also available. Support available to part-time students. Financial award application deadline: 3/1; financial award applicants required to submit FAFSA. *Unit head:* Dr. Bruce Barringer, Department Head, 405-744-9702, E-mail: bruce.barringer@okstate.edu.
Website: http://entrepreneurship.okstate.edu/

Oral Roberts University, School of Business, Tulsa, OK 74171. Offers accounting (MBA); entrepreneurship (MBA); finance (MBA); international business (MBA); management (MBA); marketing (MBA); non-profit management (MBA); not for profit management (MNM). *Accreditation:* ACBSP. *Program availability:* Part-time, online learning. *Degree requirements:* For master's, thesis optional. *Entrance requirements:* For master's, minimum cumulative GPA of 3.0. Additional exam requirements/recommendations for international students: Required—TOEFL (minimum score 550 paper-based; 79 iBT). Electronic applications accepted. *Faculty research:* Social media, international business and marketing.

Oregon State University, College of Business, Program in Business Administration, Corvallis, OR 97331. Offers business administration (PhD), including accounting, innovation/commercialization; business analytics (MBA); corporate finance (MBA); innovation management (MBA); organizational leadership (MBA); research thesis (MBA); supply chain and logistics management (MBA). *Program availability:* Part-time, blended/hybrid learning. *Faculty:* 47 full-time (13 women), 10 part-time/adjunct (3 women). *Students:* 132 full-time (58 women), 83 part-time (36 women); includes 24 minority (3 Black or African American, non-Hispanic/Latino; 11 Asian, non-Hispanic/

Latino; 8 Hispanic/Latino; 1 Native Hawaiian or other Pacific Islander, non-Hispanic/Latino; 1 Two or more races, non-Hispanic/Latino), 91 international. Average age 30. 203 applicants, 38% accepted, 67 enrolled. In 2016, 81 master's awarded. *Entrance requirements:* For master's, GMAT. Additional exam requirements/recommendations for international students: Required—TOEFL (minimum score 91 iBT), IELTS (minimum score 7). *Application deadline:* For fall admission, 2/1 priority date for domestic and international students; for winter admission, 9/15 priority date for domestic and international students; for spring admission, 1/1 priority date for domestic and international students. Applications are processed on a rolling basis. Application fee: $75 ($85 for international students). *Expenses:* $19,143 resident full-time tuition, $32,616 non-resident (for MBA). *Financial support:* Application deadline: 1/15. *Unit head:* Dr. David Baldridge, Director for Business Master's Program, 541-737-6062, E-mail: david.baldridge@bus.oregonstate.edu. *Application contact:* E-mail: osumba@bus.oregonstate.edu.
Website: http://business.oregonstate.edu/graduate-programs

Pace University, Lubin School of Business, Program in Management, New York, NY 10038. Offers change management (MBA); entrepreneurial studies (MBA); entrepreneurship (MS); human resource management (MBA, MS); strategic management (MBA, MS). *Program availability:* Part-time, evening/weekend. *Students:* 68 full-time (32 women), 75 part-time (44 women); includes 50 minority (22 Black or African American, non-Hispanic/Latino; 13 Asian, non-Hispanic/Latino; 12 Hispanic/Latino; 3 Two or more races, non-Hispanic/Latino), 47 international. Average age 30. 171 applicants, 60% accepted, 55 enrolled. In 2016, 69 master's awarded. *Entrance requirements:* For master's, GMAT, GRE (GMAT not required for MS with 3 years of HR experience in a management position), undergraduate degree, transcripts from all accredited colleges/universities attended, two letters of recommendation, resume, personal statement. Additional exam requirements/recommendations for international students: Required—TOEFL (minimum score 90 iBT), IELTS (minimum score 7) or PTE (minimum score 61). *Application deadline:* For fall admission, 8/1 priority date for domestic students, 6/1 for international students; for spring admission, 12/1 for domestic students, 10/1 for international students. Applications are processed on a rolling basis. Application fee: $70. Electronic applications accepted. *Expenses: Tuition:* Part-time $1195 per credit. *Required fees:* $260 per semester. Tuition and fees vary according to degree level, campus/location and program. *Financial support:* Research assistantships, career-related internships or fieldwork, and Federal Work-Study available. Support available to part-time students. Financial award application deadline: 2/15; financial award applicants required to submit FAFSA. *Unit head:* Dr. John C. Byrne, Chairperson, 212-618-6581, E-mail: jbyrne@pace.edu. *Application contact:* Susan Ford-Goldschein, Director of Graduate Admissions, 212-346-1531, Fax: 212-346-1585, E-mail: graduateadmission@pace.edu.
Website: http://www.pace.edu/lubin/management-concentration-mba

Penn State Great Valley, Graduate Studies, Management Division, Malvern, PA 19355-1488. Offers business administration (MBA); cyber security (Certificate); data analytics (Certificate); distributed energy and grid modernization (Certificate); finance (M Fin, Certificate); health sector management (Certificate); human resource management (Certificate); information science (MSIS); leadership development (MLD); new ventures and entrepreneurship (Certificate); professional studies in data analytics (MPS); sustainable management practices (Certificate). *Accreditation:* AACSB. *Unit head:* Dr. James A. Nemes, Chancellor, 610-648-3202, Fax: 610-725-5296. *Application contact:* JoAnn Kelly, Director of Admissions, 610-648-3315, Fax: 610-725-5296, E-mail: jek2@psu.edu.
Website: http://greatvalley.psu.edu/academics/masters-degrees/engineering-management

Peru State College, Graduate Programs, Program in Organizational Management, Peru, NE 68421. Offers MS. Program offered online only. *Program availability:* Part-time, online learning. *Degree requirements:* For master's, thesis (for some programs). *Expenses:* Contact institution. *Faculty research:* Emotional intelligence.

Point Loma Nazarene University, Fermanian School of Business, San Diego, CA 92106-2899. Offers general business (MBA); healthcare management (MBA); innovation and entrepreneurship (MBA); organizational leadership (MBA); project management (MBA). *Accreditation:* ACBSP. *Program availability:* Part-time, evening/weekend. *Faculty:* 8 full-time (1 woman), 8 part-time/adjunct (4 women). *Students:* 33 full-time (14 women), 64 part-time (30 women); includes 32 minority (6 Black or African American, non-Hispanic/Latino; 4 Asian, non-Hispanic/Latino; 19 Hispanic/Latino; 3 Two or more races, non-Hispanic/Latino), 7 international. Average age 31. 71 applicants, 79% accepted, 47 enrolled. In 2016, 37 master's awarded. *Entrance requirements:* For master's, GMAT, letters of recommendation, essay, interview. Additional exam requirements/recommendations for international students: Required—TOEFL. *Application deadline:* For fall admission, 7/26 priority date for domestic students; for spring admission, 11/29 priority date for domestic students; for summer admission, 4/2 priority date for domestic students. Applications are processed on a rolling basis. Application fee: $50. Electronic applications accepted. *Expenses:* $825 per credit. *Financial support:* Applicants required to submit FAFSA. *Unit head:* Jamie Ressler, Associate Dean, Graduate Business, 619-849-2721, E-mail: jamieressler@pointloma.edu. *Application contact:* Claire Buckley, Director of Graduate Admission, 866-692-4723, E-mail: gradinfo@pointloma.edu.
Website: http://www.pointloma.edu/discover/graduate-school-san-diego/san-diego-graduate-programs-masters-degree-san-diego/mba

Pontificia Universidad Catolica Madre y Maestra, Graduate School, Faculty of Social and Administrative Sciences, Santiago, Dominican Republic. Offers business administration (MBA), including business development, finance, international business, management skills (M Mgmt, MBA), marketing, operations, strategic cost management, strategy, tourist destination planning and management; law (LL M), including civil law, corporate business law, criminal law, international relations, real estate law; management (M Mgmt), including higher financial management, insurance program administration, management skills (M Mgmt, MBA); psychology (MA), including clinical child and adolescent psychology, forensic psychology; strategic human resources (EMBA).

Post University, Program in Business Administration, Waterbury, CT 06723-2540. Offers accounting (MSA); business administration (MBA); corporate innovation (MBA); entrepreneurship (MBA); finance (MBA); healthcare (MBA); leadership (MBA); marketing (MBA); project management (MBA). *Accreditation:* ACBSP. *Program availability:* Online learning.

Queen's University at Kingston, Queens School of Business, Program in Business Administration, Kingston, ON K7L 3N6, Canada. Offers consulting and project management (MBA); finance (MBA); innovation and entrepreneurship (MBA); marketing (MBA). *Degree requirements:* For master's, thesis optional, research project. *Entrance requirements:* For master's, GMAT, minimum B+ average. Additional exam requirements/recommendations for international students: Required—TOEFL. Electronic applications accepted. *Faculty research:* Management fundamentals, strategic thinking, global business, innovation and change, leadership.

Regent University, Graduate School, School of Business and Leadership, Virginia Beach, VA 23464-9800. Offers business administration (MBA), including accounting, entrepreneurship, finance and investing, general management, healthcare management (MA, MBA), human resource management, innovation management; leadership (Certificate); organizational leadership (MA, PhD), including ecclesial leadership (PhD), entrepreneurial leadership (PhD), future studies (MA), healthcare management (MA, MBA), human resource development (PhD), interdisciplinary studies (MA), international organizations (MA), leadership coaching and mentoring (MA), not-for-profit management (MA), organizational communication (MA), organizational development consulting (MA); strategic leadership (DSL), including global consulting, leadership coaching, strategic foresight. *Program availability:* Part-time, evening/weekend, 100% online, blended/hybrid learning. *Faculty:* 9 full-time (2 women), 28 part-time/adjunct (10 women). *Students:* 100 full-time (56 women), 1,008 part-time (528 women); includes 562 minority (453 Black or African American, non-Hispanic/Latino; 7 American Indian or Alaska Native, non-Hispanic/Latino; 30 Asian, non-Hispanic/Latino; 51 Hispanic/Latino; 1 Native Hawaiian or other Pacific Islander, non-Hispanic/Latino; 20 Two or more races, non-Hispanic/Latino), 76 international. Average age 40. 1,240 applicants, 45% accepted, 352 enrolled. In 2016, 95 master's, 71 doctorates awarded. *Degree requirements:* For master's, thesis or alternative, 3-credit hour culminating experience; for doctorate, thesis/dissertation. *Entrance requirements:* For master's, college transcripts, resume, essay; for doctorate, college transcripts, resume, essay, writing sample; for Certificate, writing sample, resume, transcripts. Additional exam requirements/recommendations for international students: Required—TOEFL (minimum score 577 paper-based). *Application deadline:* For fall admission, 5/1 priority date for domestic students; for spring admission, 10/1 priority date for domestic students. Applications are processed on a rolling basis. Application fee: $50. Electronic applications accepted. *Expenses:* Contact institution. *Financial support:* In 2016–17, 631 students received support. Career-related internships or fieldwork, scholarships/grants, and unspecified assistantships available. Support available to part-time students. *Faculty research:* Servant leadership, global business, team effectiveness, technology utilization, leadership development. *Unit head:* Dr. Doris Gomez, Dean, 757-352-4686, Fax: 757-352-4634, E-mail: dorigom@regent.edu. *Application contact:* Heidi Cece, Assistant Vice President of Enrollment Management, 800-373-5504, Fax: 757-352-4381, E-mail: admissions@regent.edu.
Website: http://www.regent.edu/sbl/

Rensselaer Polytechnic Institute, Graduate School, Lally School of Management, Program in Technology Commercialization and Entrepreneurship, Troy, NY 12180-3590. Offers MS. *Program availability:* Part-time. *Faculty:* 35 full-time (10 women), 7 part-time/adjunct (0 women). *Students:* 5 full-time (1 woman). 11 applicants, 73% accepted, 3 enrolled. *Entrance requirements:* For master's, GMAT or GRE. Additional exam requirements/recommendations for international students: Required—TOEFL (minimum score 570 paper-based; 88 iBT), IELTS (minimum score 6.5), PTE (minimum score 60). *Application deadline:* For fall admission, 1/1 for domestic and international students. Applications are processed on a rolling basis. Application fee: $75. Electronic applications accepted. *Expenses: Tuition:* Full-time $49,520; part-time $2060 per credit hour. *Required fees:* $2617. *Financial support:* Scholarships/grants available. Financial award application deadline: 1/1. *Unit head:* Dr. Gina O'Connor, Associate Dean, 518-276-6842, E-mail: oconng@rpi.edu. *Application contact:* Office of Graduate Admissions, 518-276-6216, E-mail: gradadmissions@rpi.edu.
Website: https://lallyschool.rpi.edu/graduate-programs/ms-tce

Rochester Institute of Technology, Graduate Enrollment Services, Saunders College of Business, Marketing and Management Department, MS Program in Entrepreneurship and Innovative Ventures, Rochester, NY 14623. Offers MS. *Program availability:* Part-time, evening/weekend. *Students:* 17 full-time (6 women), 4 part-time (3 women), 2 international. Average age 29. 41 applicants, 63% accepted, 17 enrolled. *Degree requirements:* For master's, thesis or alternative. *Entrance requirements:* For master's, GMAT or GRE, minimum GPA of 3.0 (recommended). Additional exam requirements/recommendations for international students: Required—TOEFL (minimum score 580 paper-based; 92 iBT), IELTS (minimum score 7), PTE (minimum score 63). *Application deadline:* Applications are processed on a rolling basis. Application fee: $60. Electronic applications accepted. *Expenses:* $1,742 per credit hour. *Financial support:* In 2016–17, 3 students received support. Research assistantships with partial tuition reimbursements available, teaching assistantships with partial tuition reimbursements available, career-related internships or fieldwork, scholarships/grants, and unspecified assistantships available. Support available to part-time students. Financial award applicants required to submit FAFSA. *Faculty research:* Technology management, creativity, and innovation; corporate social responsibility and business ethics; entrepreneurship; leadership; social capital/work relationships; social media and entrepreneurship. *Unit head:* Jenna Lenhardt, Graduate Program Director, 585-475-6916, E-mail: jlenhardt@saunders.rit.edu. *Application contact:* Diane Ellison, Associate Vice President and Director, Graduate Enrollment Services, 585-475-2229, Fax: 585-475-7164, E-mail: gradinfo@rit.edu.
Website: http://saunders.rit.edu/programs/graduate/ms_eiv.php

Rockhurst University, Helzberg School of Management, Kansas City, MO 64110-2561. Offers accounting (MBA); business intelligence (MBA, Certificate); data science (MBA, Certificate); entrepreneurship (MBA); finance (MBA); fundraising leadership (MBA, Certificate); healthcare management (MBA, Certificate); human capital (Certificate); international business (Certificate); management (MBA, Certificate); nonprofit administration (Certificate); organizational development (Certificate); science leadership (Certificate). *Accreditation:* AACSB. *Program availability:* Part-time, evening/weekend. *Entrance requirements:* For master's, GMAT or GRE. Additional exam requirements/recommendations for international students: Required—TOEFL (minimum score 550 paper-based; 79 iBT). Electronic applications accepted. Application fee is waived when completed online. *Faculty research:* Offshoring/outsourcing, systems analysis/synthesis, work teams, multilateral trade, path dependencies/creation.

Rollins College, Crummer Graduate School of Business, Winter Park, FL 32789-4499. Offers business administration (EDBA); entrepreneurship (MBA); finance (MBA); international business (MBA); management (MBA); marketing (MBA); operations and technology management (MBA). *Accreditation:* AACSB. *Program availability:* Part-time, evening/weekend, online learning. *Faculty:* 22 full-time (5 women), 4 part-time/adjunct (3 women). *Students:* 254 full-time (105 women), 83 part-time (36 women); includes 63 minority (15 Black or African American, non-Hispanic/Latino; 9 Asian, non-Hispanic/Latino; 35 Hispanic/Latino; 4 Two or more races, non-Hispanic/Latino), 48 international. Average age 31. 360 applicants, 74% accepted, 207 enrolled. In 2016, 159 master's awarded. *Degree requirements:* For master's, minimum GPA of 2.85; for doctorate, thesis/dissertation, minimum GPA of 3.0. *Entrance requirements:* For master's, GMAT or GRE, official transcripts, two letters of recommendation, essay, current resume/curriculum vitae, interview; for doctorate, official transcripts, two letters of recommendation, essays, current resume/curriculum vitae, interview. Additional exam requirements/recommendations for international students: Required—TOEFL (minimum score 100 iBT) or IELTS (minimum score 7). *Application deadline:* Applications are processed on a rolling basis. Application fee: $50. Electronic applications accepted. *Expenses:* Contact institution. *Financial support:* In 2016–17, 125 students received support. Federal Work-Study and scholarships/grants available. Support available to

part-time students. Financial award applicants required to submit FAFSA. *Faculty research:* Sustainability, world financial markets, international business, market research, strategic marketing. *Unit head:* Deborah Crown, Dean, 407-646-2249, Fax: 407-646-1550, E-mail: dcrown@rollins.edu. *Application contact:* Maralyn E. Graham, Admissions Coordinator, 407-646-2405, Fax: 407-646-1550, E-mail: mbaadmissions@rollins.edu.
Website: http://www.rollins.edu/mba/

Salve Regina University, Program in Business Administration, Newport, RI 02840-4192. Offers cybersecurity issues in business (MBA); entrepreneurial enterprise (MBA); health care administration and management (MBA); social ventures (MBA). *Program availability:* Part-time, evening/weekend, online learning. *Entrance requirements:* For master's, GMAT, GRE General Test, or MAT, 6 undergraduate credits each in accounting, economics, quantitative analysis and calculus or statistics. Additional exam requirements/recommendations for international students: Required—TOEFL (minimum score 600 paper-based; 100 iBT) or IELTS. Electronic applications accepted.

Samford University, Brock School of Business, Birmingham, AL 35229. Offers accounting (M Acc); business administration (MBA); entrepreneurship (MBA); finance (MBA); marketing (MBA); JD/M Acc; JD/MBA; MBA/M Acc; MBA/M Div; MBA/MSEM; MBA/Pharm D. *Accreditation:* AACSB. *Program availability:* Part-time-only, evening/weekend, 100% online, blended/hybrid learning. *Faculty:* 9 full-time (2 women), 3 part-time/adjunct (0 women). *Students:* 87 full-time (33 women), 14 part-time (6 women); includes 10 minority (7 Black or African American, non-Hispanic/Latino; 1 Asian, non-Hispanic/Latino; 1 Hispanic/Latino; 1 Two or more races, non-Hispanic/Latino), 6 international. Average age 28. 148 applicants, 41% accepted, 32 enrolled. In 2016, 63 master's awarded. *Degree requirements:* For master's, capstone course. *Entrance requirements:* For master's, GMAT or GRE. Additional exam requirements/recommendations for international students: Required—TOEFL (minimum score 90 iBT), IELTS (minimum score 6.5). *Application deadline:* For fall admission, 7/1 for domestic and international students; for spring admission, 12/1 for domestic and international students; for summer admission, 4/1 for domestic and international students. Applications are processed on a rolling basis. Application fee: $35. Electronic applications accepted. *Expenses: Tuition:* Full-time $18,530; part-time $789 per credit hour. *Required fees:* $610. Tuition and fees vary according to course load, degree level, program and student level. *Financial support:* In 2016–17, 55 students received support. Career-related internships or fieldwork, institutionally sponsored loans, scholarships/grants, and tuition waivers (partial) available. Support available to part-time students. Financial award application deadline: 3/1; financial award applicants required to submit FAFSA. *Faculty research:* Entrepreneurship, accounting, finance, marketing, economics. *Total annual research expenditures:* $25,000. *Unit head:* Dr. Barbara Cartledge, Assistant Dean, 205-726-2935, Fax: 205-726-2540, E-mail: bhcartle@samford.edu. *Application contact:* Elizabeth Anne Gambrell, Assistant Director of Academic Programs, 205-726-2040, Fax: 205-726-2540, E-mail: eagambre@samford.edu.
Website: http://www.samford.edu/business/

San Diego State University, Graduate and Research Affairs, College of Business Administration, Department of Management, San Diego, CA 92182. Offers entrepreneurship (MS); human resources management (MS); management science (MS). *Program availability:* Part-time, evening/weekend. *Degree requirements:* For master's, thesis or alternative. *Entrance requirements:* For master's, GMAT, resume, letters of reference. Additional exam requirements/recommendations for international students: Required—TOEFL. Electronic applications accepted.

San Francisco State University, Division of Graduate Studies, College of Business, Program in Business Administration, San Francisco, CA 94132-1722. Offers decision sciences/operations research (MBA); ethics and compliance (MBA); finance (MBA); global business and innovation (MBA); healthcare administration (MBA); hospitality and tourism management (MBA); information systems (MBA); leadership (MBA); marketing (MBA); nonprofit and social enterprise leadership (MBA); sustainable business (MBA). *Accreditation:* AACSB. *Program availability:* Part-time, evening/weekend. *Degree requirements:* For master's, thesis, essay test. *Entrance requirements:* For master's, GMAT, minimum GPA of 2.7 in last 60 units. Additional exam requirements/recommendations for international students: Required—TOEFL (minimum score 550 paper-based). *Application deadline:* For fall admission, 5/1 priority date for domestic students, 4/1 for international students; for spring admission, 11/1 for domestic students, 10/15 for international students. Applications are processed on a rolling basis. Application fee: $55. *Expenses:* Tuition, state resident: full-time $6738. Tuition, nonresident: full-time $15,666. *Required fees:* $1012. Tuition and fees vary according to degree level and program. *Financial support:* Application deadline: 3/1. *Unit head:* Dr. Sanjit Sengupta, Faculty Director, 415-817-4366, Fax: 415-817-4340, E-mail: sengupta@sfsu.edu. *Application contact:* Zandra Tan, EMBA Program Coordinator, 415-817-4360, Fax: 415-817-4340, E-mail: zandra13@sfsu.edu.
Website: http://cob.sfsu.edu/graduate-programs/mba

Seton Hall University, Stillman School of Business, Programs in Business Administration, South Orange, NJ 07079-2697. Offers accounting (MBA); entrepreneurship (Certificate); finance (MBA, Certificate); information technology management (MBA); international business (MBA); management (MBA); marketing (MBA); sport management (MBA); supply chain management (MBA, Certificate). *Program availability:* Part-time, evening/weekend. *Degree requirements:* For master's, 20 hours of community service (Social Responsibility Project). *Entrance requirements:* For master's, GMAT or CPA, GRE (waived based on work experience or advanced degree from AACSB institution), MS in business discipline, professional degree (MD, JD, PhD, DVM, DDS, CPA, etc.), minimum undergraduate GPA of 3.0. Additional exam requirements/recommendations for international students: Required—TOEFL (minimum score 607 paper-based; 102 iBT), IELTS (minimum score 6), PTE. Electronic applications accepted. *Expenses:* Contact institution. *Faculty research:* Sport, hedge funds, executive compensation, social media, legal studies.

Seton Hill University, Program in Business Administration, Greensburg, PA 15601. Offers accounting (MBA); entrepreneurship (MBA, Certificate); management (MBA). *Program availability:* Part-time, evening/weekend. *Entrance requirements:* For master's, resume, 3 letters of recommendation, personal statement, transcripts. Additional exam requirements/recommendations for international students: Required—TOEFL (minimum score 600 paper-based; 100 iBT), IELTS (minimum score 6.5). Electronic applications accepted.

Sonoma State University, School of Business and Economics, Rohnert Park, CA 94928-3609. Offers business administration (MBA), including contemporary business issues, global business, leadership and entrepreneurship; executive business administration (MBA); wine business (MBA). *Accreditation:* AACSB. *Program availability:* Part-time, evening/weekend. *Degree requirements:* For master's, thesis or alternative. *Entrance requirements:* For master's, GMAT. Additional exam requirements/recommendations for international students: Required—TOEFL (minimum score 500 paper-based). *Application deadline:* For fall admission, 1/31 priority date for domestic students; for spring admission, 8/31 for domestic students. Applications are processed on a rolling basis. Application fee: $55. *Expenses:* Tuition, state resident: full-time $6738; part-time $3906 per unit. *Required fees:* $1916; $1916 per year. Tuition and fees vary according to course load, degree level and program. *Financial support:* Career-related internships or fieldwork, Federal Work-Study, institutionally sponsored loans, and scholarships/grants available. Support available to part-time students. Financial award application deadline: 3/2; financial award applicants required to submit FAFSA. *Unit head:* Dr. William Silver, Dean, 707-664-2377. *Application contact:* John Stayton, Executive Director, Graduate and Executive Programs, 707-664-3954, E-mail: john.stayton@sonoma.edu.
Website: http://web.sonoma.edu/sbe/

South Carolina State University, College of Graduate and Professional Studies, School of Business, Orangeburg, SC 29117-0001. Offers agribusiness (MBA); entrepreneurship (MBA); general business administration (MBA); healthcare management (MBA). *Program availability:* Part-time, evening/weekend. *Faculty:* 7 full-time (3 women). *Students:* 19 full-time (11 women), 10 part-time (5 women); includes 27 minority (all Black or African American, non-Hispanic/Latino). Average age 27. 17 applicants, 94% accepted, 15 enrolled. In 2016, 6 master's awarded. *Degree requirements:* For master's, comprehensive exam, business plan. *Entrance requirements:* For master's, GMAT, minimum GPA of 2.8. Additional exam requirements/recommendations for international students: Required—TOEFL. *Application deadline:* For fall admission, 6/15 for domestic and international students; for spring admission, 11/1 for domestic and international students. Application fee: $25. Electronic applications accepted. *Expenses:* Tuition, state resident: full-time $8938; part-time $579 per credit hour. Tuition, nonresident: full-time $19,018; part-time $1139 per credit hour. *Required fees:* $1482; $82 per credit hour. *Financial support:* Fellowships, research assistantships, career-related internships or fieldwork, Federal Work-Study, scholarships/grants, and unspecified assistantships available. Financial award application deadline: 6/1. *Unit head:* Dr. Matthew Guah, Chair, 803-516-4834, Fax: 803-536-8078, E-mail: mguah@scsu.edu. *Application contact:* Ellen R. Ricoma, MBA Program Director, 803-533-3777, Fax: 803-516-4651, E-mail: ericoma1@scsu.edu.

Southeastern University, Jannetides College of Business and Entrepreneurial Leadership, Lakeland, FL 33801-6099. Offers executive leadership (MBA); missional leadership (MBA); sport management (MBA). *Accreditation:* ACBSP. *Program availability:* Evening/weekend, online learning. *Entrance requirements:* For master's, GMAT, minimum cumulative GPA of 3.0, writing sample. Electronic applications accepted. *Expenses: Tuition:* Full-time $9450; part-time $6300 per credit. *Required fees:* $500; $250 per semester. One-time fee: $150. Tuition and fees vary according to degree level, campus/location and program. *Unit head:* Lyle L. Bowlin, Dean, 863-667-5118, E-mail: llbowlin@seu.edu.
Website: http://www.seu.edu/business/

Southeast Missouri State University, School of Graduate Studies, Harrison College of Business, Cape Girardeau, MO 63701-4799. Offers accounting (MBA); entrepreneurship (MBA); financial management (MBA); sport management (MBA). *Accreditation:* AACSB. *Program availability:* Part-time, evening/weekend, 100% online. *Faculty:* 27 full-time (7 women), 1 (woman) part-time/adjunct. *Students:* 72 full-time (39 women), 112 part-time (41 women); includes 20 minority (10 Black or African American, non-Hispanic/Latino; 6 Asian, non-Hispanic/Latino; 4 Hispanic/Latino), 64 international. Average age 29. 106 applicants, 70% accepted, 55 enrolled. In 2016, 65 master's awarded. *Degree requirements:* For master's, variable foreign language requirement, comprehensive exam (for some programs), thesis or alternative. *Entrance requirements:* For master's, GMAT or GRE, minimum undergraduate GPA of 2.5, minimum grade of C in prerequisite courses. Additional exam requirements/recommendations for international students: Required—TOEFL (minimum score 550 paper-based; 79 iBT), IELTS (minimum score 6), PTE (minimum score 53). *Application deadline:* For fall admission, 8/1 for domestic students, 6/1 for international students; for spring admission, 11/21 for domestic students, 10/1 for international students; for summer admission, 5/15 for domestic students. Applications are processed on a rolling basis. Application fee: $30 ($40 for international students). Electronic applications accepted. *Expenses:* Tuition, state resident: full-time $3130; part-time $260.80 per credit hour. Tuition, nonresident: full-time $5842; part-time $486.80 per credit hour. *Required fees:* $33.70 per credit hour. *Financial support:* In 2016–17, 61 students received support. Career-related internships or fieldwork, Federal Work-Study, scholarships/grants, traineeships, tuition waivers (full), and unspecified assistantships available. Financial award application deadline: 6/30; financial award applicants required to submit FAFSA. *Faculty research:* Organizational justice, ethics, leadership, corporate finance, generational differences. *Unit head:* Dr. James L. Caldwell, Director, Graduate Business Studies, 573-651-2851, Fax: 573-651-5032, E-mail: jcaldwell@semo.edu. *Application contact:* Gail Amick, Admissions Specialist, 573-651-2590, Fax: 573-651-5936, E-mail: gamick@semo.edu.
Website: http://www.semo.edu/mba

Southern Methodist University, Cox School of Business, MBA Program, Dallas, TX 75275. Offers accounting (MBA, PMBA); business administration (EMBA); finance (MBA); financial statement analysis (PMBA); general business (MBA); information technology and operations management (MBA); management (MBA); marketing (MBA); real estate (MBA); strategy (MBA); strategy and entrepreneurship (MBA); JD/MBA; MA/MBA. *Program availability:* Part-time, evening/weekend. *Entrance requirements:* For master's, GMAT. Additional exam requirements/recommendations for international students: Required—TOEFL. Electronic applications accepted. *Expenses:* Contact institution. *Faculty research:* Corporate finance, financial reporting, modeling consumer decision-making, competition between national brands and store brands, institutional determinants of firms' strategy.

Southern Methodist University, Cox School of Business, Program in Entrepreneurship, Dallas, TX 75275. Offers MS.

Southern New Hampshire University, School of Business, Manchester, NH 03106-1045. Offers accounting (MBA, MS, Graduate Certificate); accounting finance (MS); accounting/auditing (MS); accounting/forensic accounting (MS); accounting/taxation (MS); athletic administration (MBA, Graduate Certificate); business administration (IMBA, MBA, Certificate, Graduate Certificate), including accounting (Certificate), business administration (MBA), business information systems (Graduate Certificate), human resource management (Certificate); corporate social responsibility (MBA); entrepreneurship (MBA); finance (MBA, MS, Graduate Certificate); finance/corporate finance (MS); finance/investments and securities (MS); forensic accounting (MBA); healthcare informatics (MBA); healthcare management (MBA); human resource management (Graduate Certificate); information technology (MS, Graduate Certificate); information technology management (MBA); international business (Graduate Certificate); international business and information technology (Graduate Certificate); international finance (Graduate Certificate); international sport management (Graduate Certificate); justice studies (MBA); leadership of nonprofit organizations (Graduate Certificate); management (MS); marketing (MBA, MS, Graduate Certificate); operations and project management (MS); operations and supply chain management (MBA, Graduate Certificate); organizational leadership (MS); project management (MBA, Graduate Certificate); Six Sigma (MBA); Six Sigma quality (Graduate Certificate); social media marketing (MBA); sport management (MBA, MS, Graduate Certificate); sustainability and environmental compliance (MBA); workplace conflict management

(MBA); MBA/Certificate. *Accreditation:* ACBSP. *Program availability:* Part-time, evening/weekend, online learning. Terminal master's awarded for partial completion of doctoral program. *Degree requirements:* For master's, one foreign language, comprehensive exam (for some programs), thesis or alternative. *Entrance requirements:* For master's, minimum GPA of 2.5. Additional exam requirements/recommendations for international students: Required—TOEFL (minimum score 500 paper-based). Electronic applications accepted.

South University, Graduate Programs, College of Business, Savannah, GA 31406. Offers corrections (MBA); entrepreneurship and small business (MBA); healthcare administration (MBA); hospitality management (MBA); leadership (MS); public administration (MPA); sustainability (MBA).

Stevens Institute of Technology, Graduate School, School of Business, Program in Business Administration, Hoboken, NJ 07030. Offers business intelligence and analytics (MBA); engineering management (MBA); finance (MBA); information systems (MBA); innovation and entrepreneurship (MBA); marketing (MBA); pharmaceutical management (MBA); project management (MBA, Certificate); technology management (MBA); telecommunications management (MBA). *Accreditation:* AACSB. *Program availability:* Part-time, evening/weekend. *Students:* 35 full-time (15 women), 181 part-time (79 women); includes 53 minority (10 Black or African American, non-Hispanic/Latino; 2 American Indian or Alaska Native, non-Hispanic/Latino; 36 Asian, non-Hispanic/Latino; 5 Hispanic/Latino), 30 international. Average age 32. 215 applicants, 53% accepted, 61 enrolled. In 2016, 61 master's awarded. *Degree requirements:* For master's, thesis optional, minimum B average in major field and overall; for Certificate, minimum B average. *Entrance requirements:* Additional exam requirements/recommendations for international students: Required—TOEFL (minimum score 74 iBT), IELTS (minimum score 6). *Application deadline:* For fall admission, 6/1 for domestic students, 4/15 for international students; for spring admission, 11/30 for domestic students, 11/1 for international students. Applications are processed on a rolling basis. Application fee: $65. Electronic applications accepted. *Expenses:* Contact institution. *Financial support:* Fellowships, research assistantships, teaching assistantships, career-related internships or fieldwork, Federal Work-Study, scholarships/grants, and unspecified assistantships available. Financial award application deadline: 2/15; financial award applicants required to submit FAFSA. *Unit head:* Dr. Gregory Prastacos, Dean, 201-216-8366, E-mail: gprastac@stevens.edu. *Application contact:* Graduate Admissions, 888-783-8367, Fax: 888-511-1306, E-mail: graduate@stevens.edu.
Website: https://www.stevens.edu/school-business/masters-programs/mbaemba

Stevens Institute of Technology, Graduate School, School of Business, Program in Information Systems, Hoboken, NJ 07030. Offers computer science (MS); e-commerce (MS); enterprise systems (MS); entrepreneurial information technology (MS); information architecture (MS); information management (MS, Certificate); information security (MS); information technology in financial services industry (MS); information technology in the pharmaceutical industry (MS); information technology outsourcing management (MS); project management (MS, Certificate); software engineering (MS); telecommunications (MS). *Program availability:* Part-time, evening/weekend. *Students:* 280 full-time (100 women), 84 part-time (21 women); includes 23 minority (9 Black or African American, non-Hispanic/Latino; 13 Asian, non-Hispanic/Latino; 1 Hispanic/Latino), 283 international. Average age 26. 925 applicants, 62% accepted, 114 enrolled. In 2016, 212 master's, 32 other advanced degrees awarded. *Degree requirements:* For master's, thesis optional, minimum B average in major field and overall; for Certificate, minimum B average. *Entrance requirements:* Additional exam requirements/recommendations for international students: Required—TOEFL (minimum score 74 iBT), IELTS (minimum score 6). *Application deadline:* For fall admission, 6/1 for domestic students, 4/15 for international students; for spring admission, 11/30 for domestic students, 11/1 for international students. Applications are processed on a rolling basis. Application fee: $65. Electronic applications accepted. *Expenses:* Contact institution. *Financial support:* Fellowships, research assistantships, teaching assistantships, career-related internships or fieldwork, Federal Work-Study, scholarships/grants, and unspecified assistantships available. Financial award application deadline: 2/15; financial award applicants required to submit FAFSA. *Unit head:* Dr. Gregory Prastacos, Dean, 201-216-8366, E-mail: gprastac@stevens.edu. *Application contact:* Graduate Admissions, 888-783-8367, Fax: 888-511-1306, E-mail: graduate@stevens.edu.
Website: https://www.stevens.edu/school-business/masters-programs/information-systems

Stratford University, School of Graduate Studies, Falls Church, VA 22043. Offers accounting (MS); business administration (IMBA, MBA); cyber security (MS); cyber security leadership and policy (MS); digital forensics (MS); enterprise business management (MS); entrepreneurial management (MS); healthcare administration (MS); information systems (MS); international hospitality management (MS); networking and telecommunications (MS); software engineering (MS). *Program availability:* Part-time, evening/weekend, 100% online, blended/hybrid learning. *Students:* 505 full-time (186 women), 172 part-time (88 women); includes 532 minority (165 Black or African American, non-Hispanic/Latino; 18 American Indian or Alaska Native, non-Hispanic/Latino; 324 Asian, non-Hispanic/Latino; 13 Hispanic/Latino; 10 Native Hawaiian or other Pacific Islander, non-Hispanic/Latino; 2 Two or more races, non-Hispanic/Latino). Average age 27. In 2016, 520 master's awarded. *Degree requirements:* For master's, comprehensive exam, capstone project. *Entrance requirements:* For master's, GRE or GMAT, baccalaureate degree. Additional exam requirements/recommendations for international students: Required—TOEFL (minimum score 79 iBT), IELTS (minimum score 6.5), PTE (minimum score 5). *Application deadline:* Applications are processed on a rolling basis. Application fee: $50. Electronic applications accepted. *Expenses: Tuition:* Full-time $4455; part-time $2227.50 per course. One-time fee: $100. *Financial support:* Federal Work-Study and scholarships/grants available. Financial award applicants required to submit FAFSA. *Unit head:* Dr. Richard R. Shurtz, President, 703-539-6890, Fax: 703-539-6960. *Application contact:* Admissions, 800-444-0804, E-mail: fcadmissions@stratford.edu.

Suffolk University, Sawyer Business School, Master of Business Administration Program, Boston, MA 02108-2770. Offers accounting (MBA); entrepreneurship (MBA); executive business administration (EMBA); finance (MBA); global business administration (GMBA); health administration (MBA); international business (MBA); marketing (MBA); nonprofit management (MBA); organizational behavior (MBA); strategic management (MBA); supply chain management (MBA); taxation (MBA); JD/MBA; MBA/MHA; MBA/MSA; MBA/MSF; MBA/MST. *Accreditation:* AACSB. *Program availability:* Part-time, evening/weekend, 100% online. *Faculty:* 17 full-time (6 women), 10 part-time/adjunct (1 woman). *Students:* 137 full-time (70 women), 265 part-time (138 women); includes 78 minority (20 Black or African American, non-Hispanic/Latino; 22 Asian, non-Hispanic/Latino; 31 Hispanic/Latino; 5 Two or more races, non-Hispanic/Latino), 46 international. Average age 30. 416 applicants, 70% accepted, 128 enrolled. In 2016, 165 degrees awarded. *Entrance requirements:* For master's, GMAT, minimum undergraduate GPA of 2.75 (MBA), 5 years of managerial experience (EMBA). Additional exam requirements/recommendations for international students: Required—TOEFL (minimum score 550 paper-based; 80 iBT). *Application deadline:* For fall admission, 3/15 priority date for domestic students, 10/15 priority date for international students; for spring admission, 10/15 priority date for domestic and international students. Applications are processed on a rolling basis. Application fee: $50. Electronic applications accepted. *Expenses: Tuition:* Full-time $41,490; part-time $1383 per credit hour. *Required fees:* $52; $52 per credit hour. Part-time tuition and fees vary according to course load and program. *Financial support:* In 2016–17, 209 students received support, including 176 fellowships (averaging $8,581 per year); career-related internships or fieldwork, Federal Work-Study, institutionally sponsored loans, and scholarships/grants also available. Support available to part-time students. Financial award application deadline: 4/1; financial award applicants required to submit FAFSA. *Faculty research:* Foreign investments; career strategies and boundaryless careers; corporate ethics codes; interest rates, inflation, and growth options; innovation and product development performance. *Unit head:* Jodi Detjen, Director of MBA Programs, 617-573-8306, E-mail: jdetjen@suffolk.edu. *Application contact:* Mara Marzocchi, Associate Director of Graduate Admissions, 617-573-8302, Fax: 617-305-1733, E-mail: grad.admission@suffolk.edu.
Website: http://www.suffolk.edu/mba

Syracuse University, Martin J. Whitman School of Management, Master of Business Administration Program, Syracuse, NY 13244. Offers accounting (MBA); business analytics (MBA); entrepreneurship (MBA); marketing management (MBA); real estate (MBA); supply chain management (MBA); JD/MBA. *Program availability:* Part-time, 100% online. *Students:* 22 full-time (9 women), 495 part-time (147 women); includes 182 minority (81 Black or African American, non-Hispanic/Latino; 3 American Indian or Alaska Native, non-Hispanic/Latino; 42 Asian, non-Hispanic/Latino; 52 Hispanic/Latino; 4 Native Hawaiian or other Pacific Islander, non-Hispanic/Latino), 22 international. Average age 32. 1,086 applicants, 73% accepted, 518 enrolled. In 2016, 84 master's awarded. *Entrance requirements:* For master's, GMAT or GRE, resume, essay, 5-minute video interview, two letters of recommendation, transcripts (unofficial). Additional exam requirements/recommendations for international students: Required—TOEFL (minimum score 100 iBT), IELTS (minimum score 7), PTE (minimum score 68). *Application deadline:* For fall admission, 11/30 for domestic students, 11/30 priority date for international students; for winter admission, 1/1 for domestic students, 1/1 priority date for international students; for spring admission, 2/15 for domestic and international students; for summer admission, 4/19 for domestic students. Application fee: $75. Electronic applications accepted. *Expenses:* Contact institution. *Financial support:* In 2016–17, 22 students received support. Merit scholarships available. Financial award application deadline: 2/15. *Faculty research:* Data analysis, economics of international business, financial markets and institutions, operations management, supply chain management. *Unit head:* Don Harter, Associate Dean, Graduate Programs, 315-443-3502, E-mail: dharter@syr.edu. *Application contact:* Shri Ramakrishnan, Assistant Director, Graduate Recruitment, 315-443-3497, Fax: 315-443-9517, E-mail: busgrad@syr.edu.
Website: http://whitman.syr.edu/ftmba/

Syracuse University, Martin J. Whitman School of Management, MS in Entrepreneurship Program, Syracuse, NY 13244. Offers MS. *Program availability:* Part-time, 100% online. *Students:* 4 full-time (3 women), 2 international. Average age 22. 24 applicants, 38% accepted, 4 enrolled. In 2016, 7 master's awarded. *Entrance requirements:* For master's, GMAT or GRE, resume, essay, one-page business plan, 5-minute video interview, two letters of recommendation, transcripts (unofficial). Additional exam requirements/recommendations for international students: Required—TOEFL (minimum score 100 iBT), IELTS (minimum score 7), PTE (minimum score 68), GMAT or GRE. *Application deadline:* For fall admission, 11/30 for domestic students, 11/30 priority date for international students; for winter admission, 1/1 for domestic students, 1/1 priority date for international students; for spring admission, 2/15 for domestic and international students; for summer admission, 4/19 for domestic students. Application fee: $75. Electronic applications accepted. *Expenses:* Contact institution. *Financial support:* In 2016–17, 4 students received support. Merit scholarships available. Financial award application deadline: 2/15. *Faculty research:* Entrepreneurship, emerging enterprises, financial markets & institutions, competitive strategy, opportunity recognition and ideation. *Unit head:* Dr. Alexander McKelvie, Chair, Department of Entrepreneurship and Emerging Enterprises, 315-443-7252, E-mail: mckelvie@syr.edu. *Application contact:* Shri Ramakrishnan, Assistant Director, Graduate Recruitment, 315-443-3497, Fax: 315-443-9517, E-mail: sramak01@syr.edu.
Website: http://whitman.syr.edu/programs-and-academics/programs/ms/eee/index.aspx

Temple University, Fox School of Business, Doctoral Programs in Business, Philadelphia, PA 19122-6096. Offers accounting (PhD); entrepreneurship (PhD); finance (PhD); international business (PhD); management information systems (PhD); marketing (PhD); risk management and insurance (PhD); statistics (PhD); strategic management (PhD); tourism and sport (PhD). *Accreditation:* AACSB. *Degree requirements:* For doctorate, thesis/dissertation. *Entrance requirements:* For doctorate, GRE General Test, GMAT, minimum GPA of 3.0, master's degree. Additional exam requirements/recommendations for international students: Required—TOEFL (minimum score 600 paper-based; 100 iBT), IELTS (minimum score 7.5). Electronic applications accepted.

Temple University, Fox School of Business, Specialized Master's Programs, Philadelphia, PA 19122-6096. Offers accountancy (MS); actuarial science (MS); finance (MS); financial engineering (MS); human resource management (MS); innovation management and entrepreneurship (MS); marketing (MS); statistics (MS). MS in innovation management and entrepreneurship delivered jointly with College of Engineering. *Accreditation:* AACSB. *Program availability:* Part-time. *Entrance requirements:* For master's, GRE General Test or GMAT, minimum undergraduate GPA of 3.0. Additional exam requirements/recommendations for international students: Required—TOEFL (minimum score 600 paper-based; 100 iBT), IELTS (minimum score 7.5).

Texas A&M University, Mays Business School, Department of Management, College Station, TX 77843. Offers entrepreneurial leadership (MS); human resource management (MS); management (MS). *Faculty:* 30. *Students:* 93 full-time (51 women), 1 part-time (0 women); includes 22 minority (3 Black or African American, non-Hispanic/Latino; 1 American Indian or Alaska Native, non-Hispanic/Latino; 6 Asian, non-Hispanic/Latino; 9 Hispanic/Latino; 3 Two or more races, non-Hispanic/Latino), 5 international. Average age 25. 164 applicants, 29% accepted, 37 enrolled. In 2016, 84 master's awarded. Terminal master's awarded for partial completion of doctoral program. *Degree requirements:* For master's, comprehensive exam. *Entrance requirements:* For master's, GMAT or GRE. Additional exam requirements/recommendations for international students: Required—TOEFL (minimum score 550 paper-based; 80 iBT), IELTS (minimum score 6), PTE (minimum score 53). *Application deadline:* For fall admission, 5/26 for domestic and international students. Applications are processed on a rolling basis. Application fee: $50 ($90 for international students). Electronic applications accepted. *Expenses:* Contact institution. *Financial support:* In 2016–17, 75 students received support, including 2 fellowships with tuition reimbursements available (averaging $6,000 per year), 33 research assistantships with tuition reimbursements available (averaging $3,826 per year), 20 teaching assistantships with tuition reimbursements available (averaging $4,191 per year); career-related internships or fieldwork, institutionally sponsored loans, scholarships/grants, traineeships, health care benefits, tuition waivers (full and partial), and unspecified assistantships also available. Support available to part-time students. Financial award application deadline: 3/15; financial award applicants required to submit FAFSA. *Faculty research:* Strategic and human resource management, business and public policy, organizational behavior, organizational theory. *Unit head:* Dr. Wendy R. Boswell, Head, 979-845-4045, Fax: 979-845-9641, E-mail: wboswell@mays.tamu.edu. *Application contact:* Kristi R. Mora, Senior Academic Advisor II, 979-845-6127, Fax: 979-845-9641, E-mail: kmora@mays.tamu.edu. Website: http://mays.tamu.edu/mgmt/

Tufts University, School of Engineering, The Gordon Institute, Medford, MA 02155. Offers engineering management (MSEM); innovation and management (MS). *Program availability:* Part-time. *Entrance requirements:* Additional exam requirements/recommendations for international students: Required—TOEFL (minimum score 550 paper-based; 80 iBT), IELTS (minimum score 6.5). Electronic applications accepted. *Expenses:* Contact institution. *Faculty research:* Engineering management, engineering leadership.

Tulane University, A. B. Freeman School of Business, New Orleans, LA 70118-5669. Offers accounting (M Acct); analytics (MBA); banking and financial services (M Fin); energy (M Fin, MBA); entrepreneurship (MBA); finance (MBA, PhD); international business (MBA); international management (MBA); strategic management and leadership (MBA); JD/M Acct; JD/MBA; MBA/M Acc; MBA/MA; MBA/MD; MBA/ME; MBA/MPH. *Accreditation:* AACSB. *Program availability:* Part-time, evening/weekend. *Faculty:* 46 full-time (11 women), 36 part-time/adjunct (3 women). *Students:* 488 full-time (240 women), 414 part-time (198 women); includes 81 minority (31 Black or African American, non-Hispanic/Latino; 1 American Indian or Alaska Native, non-Hispanic/Latino; 17 Asian, non-Hispanic/Latino; 29 Hispanic/Latino; 3 Two or more races, non-Hispanic/Latino), 575 international. Average age 27. 2,038 applicants, 71% accepted, 511 enrolled. In 2016, 694 master's, 9 doctorates awarded. Terminal master's awarded for partial completion of doctoral program. *Degree requirements:* For master's, one foreign language, comprehensive exam (for some programs); for doctorate, one foreign language, comprehensive exam, thesis/dissertation. *Entrance requirements:* For master's and doctorate, GMAT or GRE, interview. Additional exam requirements/recommendations for international students: Required—TOEFL or IELTS. *Application deadline:* For fall admission, 11/1 priority date for domestic and international students; for winter admission, 1/6 for domestic and international students; for spring admission, 3/1 priority date for domestic and international students; for summer admission, 5/5 for domestic students. Applications are processed on a rolling basis. Application fee: $125. Electronic applications accepted. *Expenses:* Contact institution. *Financial support:* In 2016–17, 153 students received support. Fellowships with tuition reimbursements available, research assistantships, teaching assistantships, career-related internships or fieldwork, Federal Work-Study, tuition waivers (full and partial), and unspecified assistantships available. Support available to part-time students. Financial award application deadline: 4/15; financial award applicants required to submit FAFSA. *Faculty research:* Corporate finance, managerial accounting and financial reporting, strategic management and leadership, consumer behavior and decision making, organizational behavior and human resource management. *Unit head:* Ira Solomon, PhD, Dean, 504-865-5407, Fax: 504-865-5491, E-mail: businessdean@tulane.edu. *Application contact:* Melissa Booth, Director of Graduate Admissions and Financial Aid, 800-223-5402, E-mail: freeman.admissions@tulane.edu. Website: http://www.freeman.tulane.edu

United States International University–Africa, School of Business Administration, Nairobi, Kenya. Offers business administration (GEMBA); entrepreneurship (MBA); finance (MBA); human resource management (MBA); information technology management (MBA); integrated studies (MBA); international business administration (MBA); management and organizational development (MS); marketing (MBA); organizational development (EMS); strategic management (MBA). *Program availability:* Part-time, evening/weekend. *Degree requirements:* For master's, thesis. *Entrance requirements:* For master's, GMAT, 2 letters of reference, resume. Additional exam requirements/recommendations for international students: Required—TOEFL (minimum score 550 paper-based). *Faculty research:* Marketing in small business enterprises, total quality management in Kenya.

Université Laval, Faculty of Administrative Sciences, Programs in Business Administration, Québec, QC G1K 7P4, Canada. Offers accounting (MBA); agri-food management (MBA); electronic business (MBA, Diploma); factory management and logistics (MBA); finance (MBA); firm management (MBA); geomatic management (MBA); information technology management (MBA); international management (MBA); management (MBA); management accounting (MBA, Diploma); marketing (MBA); modeling and organizational decision (MBA); occupational health and safety management (MBA); pharmacy management (MBA); social and environmental responsibility (MBA); technological entrepreneurship (Diploma). *Accreditation:* AACSB. *Program availability:* Part-time, evening/weekend, online learning. *Entrance requirements:* For master's and Diploma, knowledge of French and English. Electronic applications accepted.

University at Albany, State University of New York, School of Business, MBA Programs, Albany, NY 12222. Offers business administration (MBA); cyber security (MBA); entrepreneurship (MBA); finance (MBA); human resource information systems (MBA); information technology management (MBA); marketing (MBA); JD/MBA. JD/MBA offered with Albany Law School. *Program availability:* Part-time, evening/weekend. *Faculty:* 25 full-time (8 women), 4 part-time/adjunct (1 woman). *Students:* 92 full-time (39 women), 192 part-time (77 women); includes 63 minority (12 Black or African American, non-Hispanic/Latino; 1 American Indian or Alaska Native, non-Hispanic/Latino; 32 Asian, non-Hispanic/Latino; 13 Hispanic/Latino; 5 Two or more races, non-Hispanic/Latino), 27 international. Average age 25. 217 applicants, 73% accepted, 119 enrolled. In 2016, 122 master's awarded. *Degree requirements:* For master's, thesis (for some programs), field or research project. *Entrance requirements:* For master's, GMAT, minimum undergraduate GPA of 3.0; 3 letters of recommendation, resume; statement of goals. Additional exam requirements/recommendations for international students: Required—TOEFL (minimum score 100 iBT); Recommended—IELTS (minimum score 7). *Application deadline:* For fall admission, 4/1 priority date for domestic students, 3/1 for international students; for spring admission, 12/1 for domestic students; for summer admission, 5/1 for domestic students. Applications are processed on a rolling basis. Application fee: $75. Electronic applications accepted. *Expenses:* $16,274 Full-Time MBA per year; $696 Part-Time MBA per credit hour. *Financial support:* In 2016–17, 20 students received support, including 20 fellowships with partial tuition reimbursements available (averaging $6,500 per year); research assistantships, teaching assistantships, and unspecified assistantships also available. Financial award application deadline: 4/1; financial award applicants required to submit FAFSA. *Faculty research:* Cyber security, entrepreneurship, human resource information systems, information technology management, finance, marketing. *Total annual research expenditures:* $136,000. *Unit head:* Dr. Hany A. Shawky, Interim Dean, 518-956-8337, E-mail: hshawky@albany.edu. *Application contact:* Zina Mega Lawrence, Assistant Dean of Graduate Student Services, 518-956-8320, Fax: 518-442-4042, E-mail: zlawrence@albany.edu. Website: http://graduatebusiness.albany.edu/

The University of Alabama in Huntsville, School of Graduate Studies, College of Business Administration, Programs in Business and Management, Huntsville, AL 35899. Offers business analytics (MSMS); federal contracting and procurement management (Certificate); human resource management (MSM); management (MBA), including acquisition management, entrepreneurship, federal contract accounting, finance, human resource management, logistics and supply chain management, marketing, project management; supply chain management (Certificate); technology and innovation management (Certificate). *Accreditation:* AACSB. *Program availability:* Part-time, evening/weekend. *Degree requirements:* For master's, comprehensive exam, thesis or alternative. *Entrance requirements:* For master's, GMAT (minimum score 500), minimum AACSB index of 1080. Additional exam requirements/recommendations for international students: Required—TOEFL (minimum score 550 paper-based; 80 iBT), IELTS (minimum score 6.5). Electronic applications accepted. *Expenses:* Tuition, state resident: full-time $9834; part-time $600 per credit hour. Tuition, nonresident: full-time $21,830; part-time $1325 per credit hour. *Faculty research:* Supply chain management, management of research and development, international marketing and branding, organizational behavior and human resource management, social networks and computational economics.

University of Arkansas at Little Rock, Graduate School, George W. Donaghey College of Engineering and Information Technology, Graduate Certificate in Technology Innovation Program, Little Rock, AR 72204-1099. Offers Graduate Certificate. *Program availability:* Part-time, evening/weekend. *Degree requirements:* For Graduate Certificate, 1 year of full-time study. *Entrance requirements:* For degree, minimum GPA of 2.75 on undergraduate work or 3.0 in the last 60 hours of undergraduate credit. Additional exam requirements/recommendations for international students: Required—TOEFL (minimum score 525 paper-based). Electronic applications accepted. *Faculty research:* Web computing, robotics, text mining, technology foresight, biotechnology.

University of Baltimore, Graduate School, Merrick School of Business, Department of Marketing and Entrepreneurship, Baltimore, MD 21201-5779. Offers innovation management and technology commercialization (MS). *Program availability:* Part-time, evening/weekend. *Entrance requirements:* For master's, GMAT. Additional exam requirements/recommendations for international students: Required—TOEFL (minimum score 550 paper-based). Electronic applications accepted.

University of Bridgeport, School of Business, Bridgeport, CT 06604. Offers accounting (MBA); finance (MBA); general business (MBA); global financial services (MBA); human resource management (MBA); information systems and knowledge management (MBA); international business (MBA); management (MBA); marketing (MBA); operations management (MBA); small business and entrepreneurship (MBA); specialized business (MBA). *Accreditation:* ACBSP. *Program availability:* Part-time, evening/weekend. *Degree requirements:* For master's, thesis optional. *Entrance requirements:* For master's, GMAT. Additional exam requirements/recommendations for international students: Recommended—TOEFL (minimum score 550 paper-based; 80 iBT), IELTS (minimum score 6.5). Electronic applications accepted. *Expenses:* Contact institution.

University of Central Florida, College of Arts and Humanities, School of Visual Arts and Design, Orlando, FL 32816. Offers digital media (MA); emerging media (MFA), including digital media, entrepreneurial digital cinema, studio art and the computer. *Program availability:* Part-time. *Faculty:* 57 full-time (23 women), 15 part-time/adjunct (4 women). *Students:* 26 full-time (12 women), 13 part-time (3 women); includes 7 minority (3 Black or African American, non-Hispanic/Latino; 1 Asian, non-Hispanic/Latino; 3 Hispanic/Latino), 2 international. Average age 31. 49 applicants, 57% accepted, 19 enrolled. In 2016, 7 master's awarded. *Degree requirements:* For master's, comprehensive exam, thesis or alternative. *Entrance requirements:* Additional exam requirements/recommendations for international students: Required—TOEFL. *Application deadline:* For fall admission, 7/1 for domestic students. Application fee: $30. Electronic applications accepted. *Expenses:* Tuition, state resident: part-time $288.16 per credit hour. Tuition, nonresident: part-time $1071.31 per credit hour. *Financial support:* In 2016–17, 15 students received support, including 4 fellowships with partial tuition reimbursements available (averaging $10,000 per year), 2 research assistantships with partial tuition reimbursements available (averaging $3,214 per year), 13 teaching assistantships with partial tuition reimbursements available (averaging $7,570 per year); scholarships/grants and unspecified assistantships also available. Financial award application deadline: 3/1; financial award applicants required to submit FAFSA. *Unit head:* Dr. Rudy McDaniel, Interim Director, 407-823-3145, E-mail: rudy@ucf.edu. *Application contact:* Assistant Director, Graduate Admissions, 407-823-2766, Fax: 407-823-6442, E-mail: gradadmissions@ucf.edu. Website: http://svad.cah.ucf.edu/

University of Central Florida, College of Business Administration, Department of Management, Orlando, FL 32816. Offers entrepreneurship (Graduate Certificate); management (MSM); technology ventures (Graduate Certificate). *Accreditation:* AACSB. *Faculty:* 23 full-time (7 women), 3 part-time/adjunct (1 woman). *Students:* 55 part-time (38 women); includes 24 minority (7 Black or African American, non-Hispanic/Latino; 1 American Indian or Alaska Native, non-Hispanic/Latino; 1 Asian, non-Hispanic/Latino; 12 Hispanic/Latino; 3 Two or more races, non-Hispanic/Latino), 1 international. Average age 33. 19 applicants, 84% accepted, 13 enrolled. In 2016, 30 master's, 13 other advanced degrees awarded. *Degree requirements:* For master's, capstone course. *Entrance requirements:* For master's, GMAT, minimum GPA of 3.0 in last 60 hours. Additional exam requirements/recommendations for international students: Required—TOEFL. *Application deadline:* For fall admission, 7/1 for domestic students; for spring admission, 12/1 for domestic students. Application fee: $30. Electronic applications accepted. *Expenses:* Tuition, state resident: part-time $288.16 per credit hour. Tuition, nonresident: part-time $1071.31 per credit hour. *Financial support:* Fellowships available. Financial award application deadline: 3/1; financial award applicants required to submit FAFSA. *Unit head:* Dr. Stephen Goodman, Chair, 407-823-2675, Fax: 407-823-3725, E-mail: sgoodman@bus.ucf.edu. *Application contact:* Assistant Director, Graduate Admissions, 407-823-2776, Fax: 407-823-6224, E-mail: gradadmissions@ucf.edu.
Website: http://business.ucf.edu/departments-schools/management/

University of Chicago, Booth School of Business, Full-Time MBA Program, Chicago, IL 60637. Offers accounting (MBA); analytic finance (MBA); analytic management (MBA); econometrics and statistics (MBA); economics (MBA); entrepreneurship (MBA); finance (MBA); general management (MBA); health administration and policy (Certificate); international business (MBA); managerial and organizational behavior (MBA); marketing analytics (MBA); marketing management (MBA); operations management (MBA); strategic management (MBA); MBA/AM; MBA/JD; MBA/MA; MBA/MD; MBA/MPP. *Accreditation:* AACSB. *Students:* 1,151 full-time (443 women), 17 part-time (9 women). Terminal master's awarded for partial completion of doctoral program. *Entrance requirements:* For master's, GMAT or GRE, transcripts, resume, 2 letters of recommendation, essay, interview. Additional exam requirements/recommendations for international students: Required—TOEFL (minimum score 600 paper-based; 104 iBT), IELTS (minimum score 7), PTE (minimum score 70). *Application deadline:* For spring admission, 4/1 for domestic and international students. Electronic applications accepted. *Expenses:* Contact institution. *Unit head:* Stacey Kole, Deputy Dean, 773-702-7121. *Application contact:* Full-time MBA Program Admissions, 773-702-7369, Fax: 773-702-9085, E-mail: admissions@chicagobooth.edu.
Website: https://www.chicagobooth.edu/programs/full-time

Entrepreneurship

University of Colorado Denver, Business School, Master of Business Administration Program, Denver, CO 80217. Offers bioinnovation and entrepreneurship (MBA); business intelligence (MBA); business strategy (MBA); business to business marketing (MBA); business to consumer marketing (MBA); change management (MBA); corporate financial management (MBA); enterprise technology management (MBA); entrepreneurship (MBA); health administration (MBA), including financial management, health administration, health information technologies, international health management and policy; human resources management (MBA); international business (MBA); investment management (MBA); managing for sustainability (MBA); sports and entertainment management (MBA). *Accreditation:* AACSB. *Program availability:* Part-time, evening/weekend, 100% online, blended/hybrid learning. *Students:* 544 full-time (210 women), 112 part-time (22 women); includes 99 minority (15 Black or African American, non-Hispanic/Latino; 4 American Indian or Alaska Native, non-Hispanic/Latino; 38 Asian, non-Hispanic/Latino; 36 Hispanic/Latino; 6 Two or more races, non-Hispanic/Latino), 22 international. Average age 32. 335 applicants, 73% accepted, 179 enrolled. In 2016, 251 master's awarded. *Degree requirements:* For master's, 48 semester hours, including 30 of core courses, 3 in international business, and 15 in electives from over 50 other business courses. *Entrance requirements:* For master's, GMAT, resume, official transcripts, essay, two letters of recommendation, financial statements (for international applicants). Additional exam requirements/recommendations for international students: Required—TOEFL (minimum score 560 paper-based; 83 iBT); Recommended—IELTS (minimum score 6.5). *Application deadline:* For fall admission, 4/15 priority date for domestic students, 3/15 priority date for international students; for spring admission, 10/15 priority date for domestic students, 9/15 priority date for international students; for summer admission, 2/15 priority date for domestic students, 1/15 priority date for international students. Applications are processed on a rolling basis. Application fee: $50 ($75 for international students). Electronic applications accepted. *Expenses:* Contact institution. *Financial support:* In 2016–17, 171 students received support. Fellowships, research assistantships, teaching assistantships, Federal Work-Study, institutionally sponsored loans, scholarships/grants, traineeships, and unspecified assistantships available. Financial award application deadline: 4/1; financial award applicants required to submit FAFSA. *Faculty research:* Marketing, management, entrepreneurship, finance, health administration. *Unit head:* Woodrow Eckard, MBA Director, 303-315-8470, E-mail: woody.eckard@ucdenver.edu. *Application contact:* Shelly Townley, Admissions Director, Graduate Programs, 303-315-8202, E-mail: shelly.townley@ucdenver.edu.
Website: http://www.ucdenver.edu/academics/colleges/business/degrees/mba/Pages/MBA.aspx

University of Colorado Denver, Business School, Program in Information Systems, Denver, CO 80217. Offers accounting and information systems audit and control (MS); business intelligence systems (MS); digital health entrepreneurship (MS); enterprise risk management (MS); enterprise technology management (MS); geographic information systems (MS); health information technology (MS); technology innovation and entrepreneurship (MS); Web and mobile computing (MS). *Program availability:* Part-time, evening/weekend, online learning. *Students:* 110 full-time (44 women), 33 part-time (11 women); includes 19 minority (1 Black or African American, non-Hispanic/Latino; 8 Asian, non-Hispanic/Latino; 6 Hispanic/Latino; 4 Two or more races, non-Hispanic/Latino), 79 international. Average age 29. 140 applicants, 71% accepted, 38 enrolled. In 2016, 50 master's awarded. *Degree requirements:* For master's, 30 credit hours. *Entrance requirements:* For master's, GMAT, resume, essay, two letters of recommendation, financial statements (for international applicants). Additional exam requirements/recommendations for international students: Required—TOEFL (minimum score 525 paper-based; 71 iBT); Recommended—IELTS (minimum score 6.5). *Application deadline:* For fall admission, 4/15 priority date for domestic students, 3/15 priority date for international students; for spring admission, 10/15 priority date for domestic students, 9/15 priority date for international students; for summer admission, 2/15 priority date for domestic students, 1/15 priority date for international students. Applications are processed on a rolling basis. Application fee: $50 ($75 for international students). Electronic applications accepted. *Expenses:* Contact institution. *Financial support:* In 2016–17, 24 students received support. Fellowships, research assistantships, teaching assistantships, Federal Work-Study, institutionally sponsored loans, scholarships/grants, and traineeships available. Financial award application deadline: 4/1; financial award applicants required to submit FAFSA. *Faculty research:* Human-computer interaction, expert systems, database management, electronic commerce, object-oriented software development. *Unit head:* Dr. Jahangir Karimi, Director of Information Systems Programs, 303-315-8430, E-mail: jahangir.karimi@ucdenver.edu. *Application contact:* 303-315-8200, E-mail: bschool.admissions@ucdenver.edu.
Website: http://www.ucdenver.edu/academics/colleges/business/degrees/ms/IS/Pages/Information-Systems.aspx

University of Colorado Denver, Business School, Program in Management and Organization, Denver, CO 80217. Offers business strategy (MS); change and innovation (MS); enterprise technology management (MS); entrepreneurship and innovation (MS); global management (MS); leadership (MS); managing for sustainability (MS); managing human resources (MS); sports and entertainment management (MS). *Accreditation:* AACSB. *Program availability:* Part-time, evening/weekend, online learning. *Students:* 20 full-time (13 women), 17 part-time (10 women); includes 6 minority (3 Black or African American, non-Hispanic/Latino; 1 American Indian or Alaska Native, non-Hispanic/Latino; 1 Hispanic/Latino; 1 Two or more races, non-Hispanic/Latino), 6 international. Average age 33. 24 applicants, 58% accepted, 6 enrolled. In 2016, 19 master's awarded. *Degree requirements:* For master's, 30 semester hours (12 of required courses, 12 of management electives, and 6 of free electives). *Entrance requirements:* For master's, GMAT, resume, two letters of recommendation, essay, financial statements (for international applicants). Additional exam requirements/recommendations for international students: Required—TOEFL (minimum score 525 paper-based; 71 iBT); Recommended—IELTS (minimum score 6.5). *Application deadline:* For fall admission, 4/15 priority date for domestic students, 3/15 priority date for international students; for spring admission, 10/15 priority date for domestic students, 9/15 priority date for international students; for summer admission, 2/15 priority date for domestic students, 1/15 priority date for international students. Applications are processed on a rolling basis. Application fee: $50 ($75 for international students). Electronic applications accepted. *Expenses:* Contact institution. *Financial support:* In 2016–17, 7 students received support. Fellowships, research assistantships, teaching assistantships, Federal Work-Study, institutionally sponsored loans, scholarships/grants, and traineeships available. Financial award application deadline: 4/1; financial award applicants required to submit FAFSA. *Faculty research:* Human resource management, management of catastrophe, turnaround strategies. *Unit head:* Dr. Kenneth Bettenhausen, Associate Professor/Director of MS in Management, 303-315-8425, E-mail: kenneth.bettenhausen@ucdenver.edu. *Application contact:* 303-315-8200, E-mail: bschool.admissions@ucdenver.edu.
Website: http://www.ucdenver.edu/academics/colleges/business/degrees/ms/management/Pages/Management.aspx

University of Delaware, Alfred Lerner College of Business and Economics, Department of Economics, Newark, DE 19716. Offers economic education (PhD); economics (MA, MS, PhD); economics for entrepreneurship and educators (MA); MA/MBA. *Program availability:* Part-time. *Degree requirements:* For master's, comprehensive exam, thesis (for some programs), mathematics review exam, research project; for doctorate, comprehensive exam, thesis/dissertation, field exam. *Entrance requirements:* For master's, GMAT or GRE General Test, minimum GPA of 2.5; for doctorate, GRE General Test, minimum GPA of 3.5 in graduate economics course work. Additional exam requirements/recommendations for international students: Required—TOEFL (minimum score 550 paper-based). Electronic applications accepted. *Faculty research:* Applied quantitative economics, industrial organization, resource economics, monetary economics, labor economics.

University of Florida, Graduate School, Warrington College of Business Administration, Hough Graduate School of Business, Department of Finance, Insurance and Real Estate, Gainesville, FL 32611. Offers entrepreneurship (MS); finance (MS, PhD); financial services (Certificate); insurance (PhD); quantitative finance (PhD); real estate (MS); real estate and urban analysis (PhD); JD/MBA; JD/MS. Terminal master's awarded for partial completion of doctoral program. *Degree requirements:* For master's, comprehensive exam, thesis; for doctorate, comprehensive exam, thesis/dissertation. *Entrance requirements:* For master's, GMAT (minimum score of 465) or GRE General Test, minimum GPA of 3.0 for last 60 hours of undergraduate degree, work experience (preferred); for doctorate, GMAT (minimum score of 465) or GRE General Test, minimum GPA of 3.0. Additional exam requirements/recommendations for international students: Required—TOEFL (minimum score 550 paper-based; 80 iBT), IELTS (minimum score 6). Electronic applications accepted. *Faculty research:* Banking, empirical corporate finance, hedge funds.

University of Hawaii at Manoa, Graduate Division, Shidler College of Business, The Pacific Asian Center for Entrepreneurship and E-Business (PACE), Honolulu, HI 96822. Offers entrepreneurship (Graduate Certificate). *Program availability:* Part-time. *Entrance requirements:* Additional exam requirements/recommendations for international students: Required—TOEFL (minimum score 500 paper-based; 61 iBT).

University of Hawaii at Manoa, Graduate Division, Shidler College of Business, Program in Business Administration, Honolulu, HI 96822. Offers Asian business studies (MBA); Chinese business studies (MBA); decision sciences (MBA); entrepreneurship (MBA); finance (MBA); finance and banking (MBA); human resources management (MBA); information management (MBA); information technology (MBA); international business (MBA); Japanese business studies (MBA); marketing (MBA); organizational behavior (MBA); organizational management (MBA); real estate (MBA); student-designed track (MBA). *Accreditation:* AACSB. *Program availability:* Part-time, evening/weekend. *Degree requirements:* For master's, thesis optional. *Entrance requirements:* For master's, GMAT, minimum GPA of 3.0. Additional exam requirements/recommendations for international students: Required—TOEFL (minimum score 600 paper-based; 100 iBT), IELTS (minimum score 7). *Expenses:* Contact institution.

University of Houston–Victoria, School of Business Administration, Victoria, TX 77901-4450. Offers accounting (MBA); economic development and entrepreneurship (MS); finance (GMBA, MBA); general business (MBA); international business (MBA); management (GMBA, MBA); marketing (MBA). *Accreditation:* AACSB. *Program availability:* Part-time, evening/weekend, online learning. *Entrance requirements:* For master's, GMAT. Additional exam requirements/recommendations for international students: Required—TOEFL (minimum score 550 paper-based). Electronic applications accepted. *Faculty research:* Economic development, marketing, finance.

University of Idaho, College of Law, Moscow, ID 83844-2321. Offers business law and entrepreneurship (JD); law (JD); litigation and alternative dispute resolution (JD); Native American law (JD); natural resources and environmental law (JD). *Accreditation:* ABA. *Faculty:* 32 full-time, 11 part-time/adjunct. *Students:* Average age 28. *Entrance requirements:* For doctorate, LSAT, Law School Admission Council Credential Assembly Service (CAS) Report. Additional exam requirements/recommendations for international students: Required—TOEFL. *Application deadline:* For fall admission, 3/15 priority date for domestic students. Applications are processed on a rolling basis. Application fee: $50 ($60 for international students). Electronic applications accepted. *Expenses:* Contact institution. *Financial support:* Career-related internships or fieldwork, Federal Work-Study, and institutionally sponsored loans available. Financial award applicants required to submit FAFSA. *Faculty research:* Transboundary river governance, tribal protection and stewardship, regional water issues, environmental law. *Unit head:* Mark Adams, Dean, 208-885-4977, E-mail: uilaw@uidaho.edu. *Application contact:* Carole Wells, Director of Admissions, 208-885-2300, Fax: 208-885-2252, E-mail: lawadmit@uidaho.edu.
Website: http://www.uidaho.edu/law/

University of Louisville, Graduate School, College of Business, MBA Programs, Louisville, KY 40292-0001. Offers entrepreneurship (MBA); global business (MBA); health sector management (MBA). *Accreditation:* AACSB. *Program availability:* Part-time, evening/weekend. *Students:* 251 full-time (83 women), 9 part-time (0 women); includes 35 minority (10 Black or African American, non-Hispanic/Latino; 1 American Indian or Alaska Native, non-Hispanic/Latino; 11 Asian, non-Hispanic/Latino; 8 Hispanic/Latino; 5 Two or more races, non-Hispanic/Latino), 18 international. Average age 31. 304 applicants, 61% accepted, 159 enrolled. In 2016, 52 master's awarded. *Degree requirements:* For master's, international learning experience. *Entrance requirements:* For master's, GMAT, 2 letters of reference, personal interview, resume, personal statement, college transcript(s). Additional exam requirements/recommendations for international students: Required—TOEFL (minimum score 83 iBT). *Application deadline:* For fall admission, 7/1 for domestic students; for spring admission, 12/1 for domestic students. Applications are processed on a rolling basis. Application fee: $60. *Expenses:* Tuition, state resident: full-time $12,246; part-time $681 per credit hour. Tuition, nonresident: full-time $25,486; part-time $1417 per credit hour. *Required fees:* $196. Tuition and fees vary according to program and reciprocity agreements. *Financial support:* Fellowships with full tuition reimbursements, research assistantships with full tuition reimbursements, health care benefits, and unspecified assistantships available. Financial award application deadline: 3/31; financial award applicants required to submit FAFSA. *Faculty research:* Entrepreneurship, venture capital, retailing/franchising, corporate governance and leadership, supply chain management. *Total annual research expenditures:* $859,000. *Unit head:* Dr. Todd Mooradian, Dean, 502-852-6443, Fax: 502-852-7557, E-mail: todd.mooradian@louisville.edu. *Application contact:* Susan E. Hildebrand, Program Director, 502-852-7257, Fax: 502-852-4901, E-mail: s.hildebrand@louisville.edu.
Website: http://business.louisville.edu/mba

University of Louisville, Graduate School, College of Business, PhD Program in Entrepreneurship, Louisville, KY 40292-0001. Offers PhD. *Faculty:* 4 full-time (1 woman). *Students:* 10 full-time (3 women), 5 international. Average age 36. 5 applicants. *Degree requirements:* For doctorate, comprehensive exam, thesis/dissertation, paper of sufficient quality for journal publication. *Entrance requirements:* For doctorate, GMAT, 3 letters of recommendation, curriculum vitae, personal interview. Additional exam requirements/recommendations for international students: Required—TOEFL (minimum score 83 iBT). *Application deadline:* For fall admission, 12/31 priority date for domestic students, 3/31 for international students. Applications are processed on a rolling basis. Application fee: $60. Electronic applications accepted. *Expenses:* Tuition, state

resident: full-time $12,246; part-time $681 per credit hour. Tuition, nonresident: full-time $25,486; part-time $1417 per credit hour. *Required fees:* $196. Tuition and fees vary according to program and reciprocity agreements. *Financial support:* Fellowships with full tuition reimbursements, research assistantships with full tuition reimbursements, teaching assistantships with full tuition reimbursements, scholarships/grants, health care benefits, and unspecified assistantships available. Financial award application deadline: 3/15; financial award applicants required to submit FAFSA. *Faculty research:* Entrepreneurship, supply chain management, venture capital, retailing/franchising, corporate governance. *Total annual research expenditures:* $133,436. *Unit head:* Dr. Todd Mooradian, Dean, 502-852-6443, Fax: 502-852-7557, E-mail: todd.mooradian@louisville.edu. *Application contact:* Susan E. Hildebrand, Program Director, 502-852-7257, Fax: 502-852-4901, E-mail: s.hildebrand@louisville.edu.
Website: http://business.louisville.edu/entrepreneurshipphd

The University of Manchester, Alliance Manchester Business School, M15 6PB, United Kingdom. Offers accounting and finance (M Sc); business (M Ent); business analysis and strategic management (M Sc); business analytics: operational research and risk analysis (M Sc); business psychology (M Sc); corporate communications and reputation management (M Sc); finance (M Sc); finance and business economics (M Sc); human resource management and industrial relations (M Sc); innovation management and entrepreneurship (M Sc); international business and management (M Sc); international human resource management and comparative industrial relations (M Sc); management (M Sc); marketing (M Sc); operations, project and supply chain management (M Sc); organizational psychology (M Sc); quantitative finance (M Sc). *Entrance requirements:* For master's, UK 2:1 honours degree or overseas equivalent. Additional exam requirements/recommendations for international students: Required—TOEFL (minimum score 100 iBT), IELTS (minimum score 7), PTE. Electronic applications accepted. *Faculty research:* Accounting and finance, management sciences and marketing, people management and organization, innovation management and policy, decision sciences.

University of Massachusetts Amherst, Graduate School, Isenberg School of Management, Program in Management, Amherst, MA 01003. Offers accounting (PhD); business administration (MBA); entrepreneurship (MBA); finance (MBA, PhD); healthcare administration (MBA); hospitality and tourism management (PhD); management science (PhD); marketing (MBA, PhD); organization studies (PhD); sport management (PhD); strategic management (PhD); MBA/MS. *Accreditation:* AACSB. *Program availability:* Part-time, evening/weekend, online learning. Terminal master's awarded for partial completion of doctoral program. *Degree requirements:* For doctorate, comprehensive exam, thesis/dissertation. *Entrance requirements:* For master's and doctorate, GMAT or GRE General Test. Additional exam requirements/recommendations for international students: Required—TOEFL (minimum score 550 paper-based; 80 iBT), IELTS (minimum score 6.5). Electronic applications accepted.

University of Massachusetts Lowell, Manning School of Business, Lowell, MA 01854. Offers business administration (MBA, PhD); healthcare innovation and entrepreneurship (MS). *Accreditation:* AACSB. *Program availability:* Part-time, evening/weekend. *Entrance requirements:* For master's, GMAT.

University of Minnesota, Twin Cities Campus, Carlson School of Management, Doctoral Program in Business Administration, Minneapolis, MN 55455. Offers accounting (PhD); finance (PhD); information and decision sciences (PhD); marketing (PhD); strategic management and entrepreneurship (PhD); supply chain and operations (PhD); work and organizations (PhD). *Faculty:* 101 full-time (32 women). *Students:* 90 full-time (29 women); includes 7 minority (2 Black or African American, non-Hispanic/Latino; 3 Asian, non-Hispanic/Latino; 2 Hispanic/Latino), 64 international. Average age 30. 352 applicants, 7% accepted, 15 enrolled. In 2016, 20 doctorates awarded. *Degree requirements:* For doctorate, comprehensive exam, thesis/dissertation, written and oral preliminary exams, proposal defense, final defense. *Entrance requirements:* For doctorate, GMAT, GRE General Test, minimum undergraduate GPA of 3.0, graduate 3.5 (recommended). Additional exam requirements/recommendations for international students: Required—TOEFL (minimum score 600 paper-based, 100 iBT) or IELTS (minimum score 7.0). *Application deadline:* For fall admission, 12/15 for domestic students, 12/15 priority date for international students. Applications are processed on a rolling basis. Application fee: $75 ($95 for international students). Electronic applications accepted. *Expenses:* Contact institution. *Financial support:* In 2016–17, 80 students received support, including 80 fellowships with full tuition reimbursements available (averaging $13,500 per year), 72 research assistantships with full tuition reimbursements available (averaging $7,371 per year), 72 teaching assistantships with full tuition reimbursements available (averaging $7,371 per year); institutionally sponsored loans, scholarships/grants, health care benefits, unspecified assistantships, and full student service fee waivers also available. Financial award application deadline: 12/15. *Faculty research:* Finance, strategy and entrepreneurship, marketing, information and decision science, operations, accounting, supply chain, human resources and industrial relations, organizational behavior. *Unit head:* Dr. Shawn P. Curley, Director, 612-624-6546, Fax: 612-624-8221, E-mail: curley@umn.edu. *Application contact:* Sandy Herzan, Associate Director, 612-624-0875, Fax: 612-624-8221, E-mail: herza002@umn.edu.
Website: http://carlsonschool.umn.edu/degrees/phd

University of New Brunswick Fredericton, School of Graduate Studies, Faculty of Business Administration, Fredericton, NB E3B 5A3, Canada. Offers business administration (MBA); engineering management (MBA); entrepreneurship (MBA); sports and recreation management (MBA); MBA/LL B. *Program availability:* Part-time. *Degree requirements:* For master's, thesis optional. *Entrance requirements:* For master's, GMAT (minimum score 550), minimum GPA of 3.0; 3-5 years of work experience; 3 letters of reference with at least one academic reference. Additional exam requirements/recommendations for international students: Required—TOEFL (minimum score 580 paper-based; 92 iBT) or IELTS (minimum score 7). Electronic applications accepted. *Faculty research:* Entrepreneurship, finance, law, sport and recreation management, engineering management.

University of New Mexico, Anderson School of Management, Department of Finance, International, Technology and Entrepreneurship, Albuquerque, NM 87131. Offers entrepreneurship (MBA); finance (MBA); international management (MBA); international management in Latin America (MBA); management of technology (MBA). *Program availability:* Part-time, evening/weekend. *Faculty:* 15 full-time (2 women), 5 part-time/adjunct (0 women). In 2016, 41 master's awarded. *Entrance requirements:* For master's, GMAT or GRE, minimum GPA of 3.0 on last 60 hours of coursework; bachelor's degree from regionally-accredited college or university in U.S. or its equivalent in another country. Additional exam requirements/recommendations for international students: Required—TOEFL (minimum score 550 paper-based; 79 iBT), IELTS (minimum score 6.5). *Application deadline:* For fall admission, 4/1 priority date for domestic and international students; for spring admission, 10/1 priority date for domestic and international students. Applications are processed on a rolling basis. Application fee: $50. Electronic applications accepted. *Expenses:* Contact institution. *Financial support:* In 2016–17, 12 fellowships (averaging $15,441 per year), 12 research assistantships with partial tuition reimbursements (averaging $16,707 per year) were awarded; career-related internships or fieldwork, Federal Work-Study, scholarships/grants, and unspecified assistantships also available. Support available to part-time students. Financial award application deadline: 6/1; financial award applicants required to submit FAFSA. *Faculty research:* Corporate finance, investments, management in Latin America, management of technology, entrepreneurship. *Unit head:* Dr. Sul Kassicieh, Chair, 505-277-6471, E-mail: sul@unm.edu. *Application contact:* Lisa Beauchene, Student Recruitment Specialist, 505-277-6471, E-mail: andersonadvising@unm.edu.
Website: https://www.mgt.unm.edu/fite/default.asp?mm=faculty

University of Notre Dame, Mendoza College of Business, Master of Business Administration Program, Notre Dame, IN 46556. Offers business analytics (MBA); business leadership (MBA); consulting (MBA); corporate finance (MBA); innovation and entrepreneurship (MBA); investments (MBA); marketing (MBA). *Accreditation:* AACSB. *Faculty:* 62 full-time (13 women), 26 part-time/adjunct (7 women). *Students:* 304 full-time (78 women); includes 38 minority (10 Black or African American, non-Hispanic/Latino; 7 Asian, non-Hispanic/Latino; 15 Hispanic/Latino; 6 Two or more races, non-Hispanic/Latino), 80 international. Average age 27. 647 applicants, 41% accepted, 121 enrolled. In 2016, 177 master's awarded. *Entrance requirements:* For master's, GMAT or GRE, work experience, essay, four-slide presentation, two recommendations, transcripts from all colleges and/or universities attended, interview. Additional exam requirements/recommendations for international students: Required—TOEFL (minimum score 600 paper-based; 100 iBT), IELTS (minimum score 7), PTE (minimum score 68). *Application deadline:* For fall admission, 11/1 for domestic and international students; for winter admission, 1/10 for domestic and international students; for spring admission, 2/21 for domestic and international students; for summer admission, 3/28 for domestic and international students. Application fee: $175. Electronic applications accepted. *Expenses:* Contact institution. *Financial support:* In 2016–17, 251 students received support, including 243 fellowships (averaging $26,417 per year); career-related internships or fieldwork, Federal Work-Study, institutionally sponsored loans, scholarships/grants, and unspecified assistantships also available. Financial award application deadline: 2/28; financial award applicants required to submit FAFSA. *Faculty research:* Market micro-structure; marketing and public policy; corporate finance and accounting; corporate governance and ethical behavior; high performing organizations. *Unit head:* Dr. Katherine Speiss, Associate Dean, Graduate Business Programs, 574-631-3759, E-mail: spiess.1@nd.edu. *Application contact:* Kristin McAndrew, Director of Admissions, Graduate Business Programs, 574-631-8488, E-mail: kmcadre@nd.edu.
Website: http://mendoza.nd.edu/programs/mba-programs/

University of Oklahoma, Price College of Business, Program in Business Administration, Norman, OK 73019. Offers accounting (PhD); business administration (MBA, PhD); entrepreneurship and economic development (PhD); finance (PhD); management and international business (PhD); management of information systems (PhD); marketing/supply chain (PhD); JD/MBA; MBA/MS. *Accreditation:* AACSB. *Program availability:* Part-time, evening/weekend. *Students:* 122 full-time (27 women), 146 part-time (30 women); includes 36 minority (5 Black or African American, non-Hispanic/Latino; 6 American Indian or Alaska Native, non-Hispanic/Latino; 8 Asian, non-Hispanic/Latino; 11 Hispanic/Latino; 6 Two or more races, non-Hispanic/Latino), 37 international. Average age 30. 261 applicants, 27% accepted, 59 enrolled. In 2016, 127 master's, 5 doctorates awarded. *Degree requirements:* For doctorate, comprehensive exam, thesis/dissertation. *Entrance requirements:* For master's, GMAT or GRE, resume, statement of goals; for doctorate, GMAT or GRE, resume, statement of goals, 3 letters of recommendation. Additional exam requirements/recommendations for international students: Required—TOEFL (minimum score 100 iBT) or IELTS (minimum score 7). *Application deadline:* For fall admission, 11/15 priority date for domestic and international students; for spring admission, 3/15 priority date for domestic and international students; for summer admission, 5/15 for domestic and international students. Application fee: $50 ($100 for international students). Electronic applications accepted. *Expenses:* Contact institution. *Financial support:* In 2016–17, 107 students received support, including 10 fellowships with partial tuition reimbursements available (averaging $3,295 per year); research assistantships with full and partial tuition reimbursements available, teaching assistantships with full and partial tuition reimbursements available, career-related internships or fieldwork, scholarships/grants, health care benefits, and unspecified assistantships also available. Support available to part-time students. Financial award application deadline: 6/1; financial award applicants required to submit FAFSA. *Faculty research:* Energy finance; international accounting; organizational behavior and entrepreneurship; management information systems; supply chain. *Unit head:* Laku Chidambaram, Associate Dean for Academic Programs and Engagement. *Application contact:* Director of MBA Admissions, 405-325-5623.
Website: http://www.ou.edu/content/price/divisions/graduate.html

University of Pennsylvania, Graduate School of Education, Division of Teaching, Learning, and Leadership, Program in Education Entrepreneurship, Philadelphia, PA 19104. Offers MS Ed. *Program availability:* Evening/weekend. *Degree requirements:* For master's, thesis or alternative, capstone project. *Entrance requirements:* For master's, bachelor's degree; at least 3 years of work experience. Additional exam requirements/recommendations for international students: Required—TOEFL, IELTS. *Application deadline:* For summer admission, 2/1 priority date for domestic and international students. Application fee: $75. Electronic applications accepted. *Expenses: Tuition:* Full-time $31,068; part-time $5762 per course. *Required fees:* $3200; $336 per course. Full-time tuition and fees vary according to degree level, program and student level. Part-time tuition and fees vary according to course load, degree level and program. *Financial support:* Scholarships/grants available. *Unit head:* Dr. Jenny Zapf, Director, E-mail: jzapf@upenn.edu. *Application contact:* Ayoung Lee, Administrative Coordinator, 215-573-8149, E-mail: ayoungl@upenn.edu.
Website: http://www.gse.upenn.edu/tll/ee

University of Pennsylvania, School of Engineering and Applied Science, Integrated Product Design Program, Philadelphia, PA 19104. Offers MIPD, MSE. Program offered jointly with the Wharton School and the School of Design. *Program availability:* Part-time. *Students:* 22 full-time (9 women), 11 part-time (4 women); includes 9 minority (2 Black or African American, non-Hispanic/Latino; 4 Asian, non-Hispanic/Latino; 1 Hispanic/Latino; 2 Two or more races, non-Hispanic/Latino), 12 international. Average age 26. 105 applicants, 30% accepted, 20 enrolled. In 2016, 15 master's awarded. *Degree requirements:* For master's, comprehensive exam, thesis optional. *Entrance requirements:* For master's, GRE, portfolio. Additional exam requirements/recommendations for international students: Required—TOEFL (minimum score 100 iBT), IELTS (minimum score 7). *Application deadline:* For fall admission, 3/15 priority date for domestic and international students. Applications are processed on a rolling basis. Application fee: $80. Electronic applications accepted. *Expenses: Tuition:* Full-time $31,068; part-time $5762 per course. *Required fees:* $3200; $336 per course. Full-time tuition and fees vary according to degree level, program and student level. Part-time tuition and fees vary according to course load, degree level and program. *Application contact:* William Fenton, Assistant Director of Graduate Admissions, 215-898-4542, Fax: 215-573-5577, E-mail: gradstudies@seas.upenn.edu.
Website: http://ipd.me.upenn.edu/

University of Portland, Dr. Robert B. Pamplin, Jr. School of Business, Portland, OR 97203-5798. Offers entrepreneurship (MBA); finance (MBA, MS); health care management (MBA); marketing (MBA); nonprofit management (EMBA); operations and technology management (MBA, MS); sustainability (MBA). *Accreditation:* AACSB. *Program availability:* Part-time, evening/weekend. *Entrance requirements:* For master's, GMAT, minimum GPA of 3.0, resume, 2 letters of recommendation. Additional exam requirements/recommendations for international students: Required—TOEFL (minimum score 570 paper-based; 89 iBT), IELTS (minimum score 7). *Expenses:* Contact institution.

University of Rhode Island, Graduate School, College of Business Administration, Kingston, RI 02881. Offers accounting (MS); business administration (PhD), including finance and insurance, marketing, supply chain management; finance (MBA, MS); general business (MBA); health care management (MBA); management (MBA); marketing (MBA); oceanography (MBA); strategic innovation (MBA); supply chain management (MBA); Pharm D/MBA. *Accreditation:* AACSB. *Program availability:* Part-time, evening/weekend. *Faculty:* 57 full-time (24 women). *Students:* 94 full-time (45 women), 166 part-time (84 women); includes 37 minority (6 Black or African American, non-Hispanic/Latino; 1 American Indian or Alaska Native, non-Hispanic/Latino; 22 Asian, non-Hispanic/Latino; 3 Hispanic/Latino; 5 Two or more races, non-Hispanic/Latino), 18 international. In 2016, 124 master's, 4 doctorates awarded. *Degree requirements:* For master's, comprehensive exam (for some programs), thesis optional; for doctorate, comprehensive exam, thesis/dissertation. *Entrance requirements:* For master's, GMAT or GRE, 2 letters of recommendation, resume; for doctorate, GMAT or GRE, 3 letters of recommendation, resume. Additional exam requirements/recommendations for international students: Required—TOEFL. *Application deadline:* For fall admission, 2/1 for domestic and international students. Application fee: $65. Electronic applications accepted. *Expenses:* Tuition, state resident: full-time $11,796; part-time $655 per credit. Tuition, nonresident: full-time $24,206; part-time $1345 per credit. *Required fees:* $1546; $44 per credit. One-time fee: $155 full-time; $35 part-time. *Financial support:* In 2016–17, 17 teaching assistantships with tuition reimbursements (averaging $15,347 per year) were awarded; research assistantships also available. Financial award application deadline: 2/1; financial award applicants required to submit FAFSA. *Unit head:* Dr. Maling Ebrahimpour, Dean, 401-874-4348, Fax: 401-874-4312, E-mail: mebrahimpour@uri.edu. *Application contact:* Lisa Lancellotta, Coordinator, MBA Programs, 401-874-4241, Fax: 401-874-4312, E-mail: mba@uri.edu.
Website: http://www.cba.uri.edu/

See Display on page 161 and Close-Up on page 191.

University of Rochester, Hajim School of Engineering and Applied Sciences, Master of Science in Technical Entrepreneurship and Management Program, Rochester, NY 14642. Offers biomedical engineering (MS); chemical engineering (MS); computer science (MS); electrical and computer engineering (MS); energy and the environment (MS); materials science (MS); mechanical engineering (MS); optics (MS). Program offered in collaboration with the Simon School of Business. *Program availability:* Part-time. *Students:* 42 full-time (13 women), 6 part-time (3 women); includes 7 minority (1 Black or African American, non-Hispanic/Latino; 1 Asian, non-Hispanic/Latino; 4 Hispanic/Latino; 1 Two or more races, non-Hispanic/Latino), 28 international. Average age 24. 245 applicants, 65% accepted, 29 enrolled. In 2016, 31 master's awarded. *Degree requirements:* For master's, comprehensive exam, final exam. *Entrance requirements:* For master's, GRE or GMAT, 3 letters of recommendation; personal statement; official transcript; bachelor's degree (or equivalent for international students) in engineering, science, or mathematics. Additional exam requirements/recommendations for international students: Required—TOEFL (minimum score 600 paper-based; 100 iBT). *Application deadline:* For fall admission, 2/1 for domestic and international students. Application fee: $60. Electronic applications accepted. *Expenses:* $1,800 per credit. *Financial support:* In 2016–17, 45 students received support. Career-related internships or fieldwork and scholarships/grants available. Support available to part-time students. Financial award application deadline: 2/1. *Faculty research:* High efficiency solar cells, macromolecular self-assembly, digital signal processing, memory hierarchy management, molecular and physical mechanisms in cell migration, optical imaging systems. *Unit head:* Duncan T. Moore, Vice Provost for Entrepreneurship, 585-275-5248, Fax: 585-473-6745, E-mail: duncan.moore@rochester.edu. *Application contact:* Andrea Barrett, Executive Director, 585-276-3407, Fax: 585-276-2357, E-mail: andrea.barrett@rochester.edu.
Website: http://www.rochester.edu/team

University of Rochester, Simon Business School, Full-Time Master's Program in Business Administration, Rochester, NY 14627. Offers business systems consulting (MBA); competitive and organizational strategy (MBA); computers and information systems (MBA); corporate accounting (MBA); entrepreneurship (MBA); finance (MBA); health sciences management (MBA); marketing (MBA); operations management (MBA); public accounting (MBA). *Accreditation:* AACSB. *Program availability:* Part-time, evening/weekend. *Faculty:* 66 full-time (13 women), 22 part-time/adjunct (2 women). *Students:* 202 full-time (78 women); includes 50 minority (30 Black or African American, non-Hispanic/Latino; 10 Asian, non-Hispanic/Latino; 9 Hispanic/Latino; 1 Two or more races, non-Hispanic/Latino), 107 international. Average age 27. 915 applicants, 30% accepted, 86 enrolled. In 2016, 110 master's awarded. *Entrance requirements:* For master's, GMAT/GRE. Additional exam requirements/recommendations for international students: Required—TOEFL. *Application deadline:* For fall admission, 10/15 for domestic and international students; for winter admission, 1/5 for domestic and international students; for spring admission, 3/15 for domestic and international students; for summer admission, 5/15 for domestic and international students. Applications are processed on a rolling basis. Application fee: $150. Electronic applications accepted. *Expenses:* Contact institution. *Financial support:* In 2016–17, 190 students received support. Fellowships, research assistantships, teaching assistantships, institutionally sponsored loans, scholarships/grants, and tuition waivers (full and partial) available. Financial award application deadline: 1/5; financial award applicants required to submit FAFSA. *Unit head:* Andrew Ainslie, Dean, 585-275-3316, E-mail: andrew.ainslie@simon.rochester.edu. *Application contact:* Rebekah S. Lewin, Assistant Dean of Admissions and Financial Aid, 585-275-3533, E-mail: admissions@simon.rochester.edu.
Website: http://www.simon.rochester.edu/programs/full-time-mba/index.aspx

University of Rochester, Simon Business School, Part-Time MBA Program, Rochester, NY 14627. Offers business systems consulting (MBA); competitive and organizational strategy (MBA); computers and information systems (MBA); corporate accounting (MBA); entrepreneurship (MBA); finance (MBA); health sciences management (MBA); marketing (MBA); operations management (MBA); public accounting (MBA). *Program availability:* Part-time, evening/weekend. *Faculty:* 66 full-time (13 women), 22 part-time/adjunct (2 women). *Students:* 185 part-time (65 women); includes 29 minority (6 Black or African American, non-Hispanic/Latino; 13 Asian, non-Hispanic/Latino; 8 Hispanic/Latino; 2 Two or more races, non-Hispanic/Latino), 9 international. Average age 32. 33 applicants, 100% accepted, 31 enrolled. In 2016, 70 master's awarded. *Entrance requirements:* For master's, GRE or GMAT. *Application deadline:* For fall admission, 8/1 for domestic students; for spring admission, 2/15 for domestic students. Applications are processed on a rolling basis. Application fee: $150. Electronic applications accepted. *Expenses:* $1,800 per credit hour. *Financial support:* In 2016–17, 75 students received support. Scholarships/grants and tuition waivers (partial) available. Financial award applicants required to submit CSS PROFILE or FAFSA. *Unit head:* Andrew Ainslie, Dean, 585-275-3316, E-mail: andrew.ainslie@simon.rochester.edu. *Application contact:* Molly Mesko, Executive Director, EMBA and Part-Time Programs, 585-275-4277, E-mail: molly.mesko@simon.rochester.edu.
Website: http://www.simon.rochester.edu/programs/ptmba/index.aspx

University of San Francisco, School of Management, Master in Global Entrepreneurial Management Program, San Francisco, CA 94117. Offers MGEM. Program offered jointly with IQS in Barcelona, Spain and Fu Jen Catholic University in Taipei, Taiwan. *Faculty:* 1 full-time (0 women). *Students:* 39 full-time (21 women); includes 6 minority (2 Black or African American, non-Hispanic/Latino; 2 Asian, non-Hispanic/Latino; 1 Hispanic/Latino; 1 Two or more races, non-Hispanic/Latino), 32 international. Average age 24. 78 applicants, 97% accepted, 39 enrolled. In 2016, 37 master's awarded. *Entrance requirements:* For master's, resume, transcripts from each college or university attended, two letters of recommendation, personal statement. Additional exam requirements/recommendations for international students: Required—TOEFL (minimum score 550 paper-based, 79 iBT), IELTS (minimum score 6), or PTE (minimum score 53). *Application deadline:* For fall admission, 5/15 for domestic students. Application fee: $55. Electronic applications accepted. *Expenses: Tuition:* Full-time $23,310; part-time $1295 per credit. Tuition and fees vary according to course load, degree level, campus/location and program. *Financial support:* In 2016–17, 2 students received support. Application deadline: 3/2; applicants required to submit FAFSA. *Unit head:* Dr. Gleb Nikitenko, Director, 415-422-2221, E-mail: management@usfca.edu. *Application contact:* Office of Graduate Recruiting and Admissions, 415-422-2221, Fax: 415-422-6315, E-mail: management@usfca.edu.
Website: http://www.usfca.edu/mgem

University of San Francisco, School of Management, Master of Business Administration Program, San Francisco, CA 94117. Offers entrepreneurship and innovation (MBA); finance (MBA); marketing (MBA); organization development (MBA); DDS/MBA; JD/MBA; MBA/MAPS. *Accreditation:* AACSB. *Program availability:* Part-time, evening/weekend. *Faculty:* 17 full-time (6 women), 5 part-time/adjunct (2 women). *Students:* 146 full-time (70 women), 2 part-time (1 woman); includes 50 minority (5 Black or African American, non-Hispanic/Latino; 27 Asian, non-Hispanic/Latino; 15 Hispanic/Latino; 1 Native Hawaiian or other Pacific Islander, non-Hispanic/Latino; 2 Two or more races, non-Hispanic/Latino), 51 international. Average age 29. 282 applicants, 63% accepted, 70 enrolled. In 2016, 91 master's awarded. *Entrance requirements:* For master's, GMAT or GRE, resume (two years of professional work experience required for part-time students, preferred for full-time), transcripts from each college or university attended, two letters of recommendation, personal statement, interview. Additional exam requirements/recommendations for international students: Required—TOEFL (minimum score 600 paper-based, 100 iBT), IELTS (minimum score 7) or PTE (minimum score 68). *Application deadline:* For fall admission, 6/5 for domestic students, 5/15 for international students; for spring admission, 11/30 for domestic students. Application fee: $55. Electronic applications accepted. *Expenses: Tuition:* Full-time $23,310; part-time $1295 per credit. Tuition and fees vary according to course load, degree level, campus/location and program. *Financial support:* In 2016–17, 60 students received support. Fellowships and scholarships/grants available. Financial award application deadline: 3/2; financial award applicants required to submit FAFSA. *Faculty research:* International financial markets, technology transfer licensing, international marketing, strategic planning. *Total annual research expenditures:* $50,000. *Unit head:* Dr. Frank Fletcher, Director, 415-422-2221, Fax: 415-422-6315, E-mail: management@usfca.edu. *Application contact:* Office of Graduate Recruiting and Admissions, 415-422-2221, Fax: 415-422-6315, E-mail: management@usfca.edu.
Website: http://www.usfca.edu/mba

University of San Francisco, School of Management, Master of Science in Entrepreneurship and Innovation Program, San Francisco, CA 94117-1080. Offers MS. *Application deadline:* For fall admission, 11/15 priority date for domestic students. *Expenses: Tuition:* Full-time $23,310; part-time $1295 per credit. Tuition and fees vary according to course load, degree level, campus/location and program. *Unit head:* Dr. Gleb Nikitenko, Director, 415-422-2151, E-mail: nikitenko@usfca.edu. *Application contact:* Elisabeth Merkel, 415-422-2221, Fax: 415-422-6315, E-mail: management@usfca.edu.
Website: https://www.usfca.edu/management/graduate-programs/entrepreneurship-innovation

University of Sioux Falls, Vucurevich School of Business, Sioux Falls, SD 57105-1699. Offers entrepreneurial leadership (MBA); general management (MBA); health care management (MBA); marketing (MBA). *Program availability:* Part-time, evening/weekend. *Degree requirements:* For master's, project. *Entrance requirements:* For master's, minimum GPA of 3.0. Additional exam requirements/recommendations for international students: Required—TOEFL. *Expenses:* Contact institution.

University of Southern California, Graduate School, Marshall School of Business, Program in Entrepreneurship and Innovation, Los Angeles, CA 90089. Offers MS.

University of South Florida, College of Global Sustainability, Tampa, FL 33620-9951. Offers energy, global, water and sustainable tourism (Graduate Certificate); global sustainability (MA), including building sustainable enterprise, climate change and sustainability, coastal sustainability, entrepreneurship, food sustainability and security, sustainable energy, sustainable tourism, sustainable transportation, water. *Faculty:* 4 full-time (0 women). *Students:* 59 full-time (35 women), 51 part-time (29 women); includes 25 minority (3 Black or African American, non-Hispanic/Latino; 1 American Indian or Alaska Native, non-Hispanic/Latino; 2 Asian, non-Hispanic/Latino; 16 Hispanic/Latino; 3 Two or more races, non-Hispanic/Latino), 30 international. Average age 28. 134 applicants, 59% accepted, 55 enrolled. In 2016, 36 master's awarded. *Degree requirements:* For master's, comprehensive exam (for some programs), thesis or alternative, internship. *Entrance requirements:* For master's, minimum GPA of 3.0 in undergraduate coursework; at least two letters of recommendation (one must be academic); 200-250 word essay on student's background, professional goals, and reasons for seeking degree. Additional exam requirements/recommendations for international students: Required—TOEFL (minimum score 550 paper-based; 79 iBT). *Application deadline:* For fall admission, 6/1 for domestic students, 5/1 for international students; for spring admission, 10/15 for domestic students, 9/15 for international students. Electronic applications accepted. *Expenses:* Tuition, state resident: full-time $7766; part-time $431.43 per credit hour. Tuition, nonresident: full-time $15,789; part-time $877.17 per credit hour. *Required fees:* $37 per term. *Financial support:* In 2016–17, 20 students received support. *Faculty research:* Global sustainability, integrated resource management, systems thinking, green communities, entrepreneurship, ecotourism. *Total annual research expenditures:* $208,988. *Unit head:* Dr. Rafael Perez, Interim Dean, 813-974-9694, E-mail: perez@usf.edu.
Website: http://psgs.usf.edu/

University of South Florida, Innovative Education, Tampa, FL 33620-9951. Offers adult, career and higher education (Graduate Certificate), including college teaching, leadership in developing human resources, leadership in higher education; Africana studies (Graduate Certificate), including diasporas and health disparities, genocide and human rights; aging studies (Graduate Certificate), including gerontology; art research (Graduate Certificate), including museum studies; business foundations (Graduate Certificate); chemical and biomedical engineering (Graduate Certificate), including

materials science and engineering, water, health and sustainability; child and family studies (Graduate Certificate), including positive behavior support; civil and industrial engineering (Graduate Certificate), including transportation systems analysis; community and family health (Graduate Certificate), including maternal and child health, social marketing and public health, violence and injury: prevention and intervention, women's health; criminology (Graduate Certificate), including criminal justice administration; educational measurement and research (Graduate Certificate), including evaluation; English (Graduate Certificate), including comparative literary studies, creative writing, professional and technical communication; entrepreneurship (Graduate Certificate); environmental health (Graduate Certificate), including safety management; epidemiology and biostatistics (Graduate Certificate), including applied biostatistics, biostatistics, concepts and tools of epidemiology, epidemiology, epidemiology of infectious diseases; geography, environment and planning (Graduate Certificate), including community development, environmental policy and management, geographical information systems; geology (Graduate Certificate), including hydrogeology; global health (Graduate Certificate), including disaster management, global health and Latin American and Caribbean studies, global health practice, humanitarian assistance, infection control; government and international affairs (Graduate Certificate), including Cuban studies, globalization studies; health policy and management (Graduate Certificate), including health management and leadership, public health policy and programs; hearing specialist: early intervention (Graduate Certificate); industrial and management systems engineering (Graduate Certificate), including systems engineering, technology management; information studies (Graduate Certificate), including school library media specialist; information systems/decision sciences (Graduate Certificate), including analytics and business intelligence; instructional technology (Graduate Certificate), including distance education, Florida digital/virtual educator, instructional design, multimedia design, Web design; internal medicine, bioethics and medical humanities (Graduate Certificate), including biomedical ethics; Latin American and Caribbean studies (Graduate Certificate); mass communications (Graduate Certificate), including multimedia journalism; mathematics and statistics (Graduate Certificate), including mathematics; medicine (Graduate Certificate), including aging and neuroscience, bioinformatics, biotechnology, brain fitness and memory management, clinical investigation, health informatics, health sciences, integrative weight management, intellectual property, medicine and gender, metabolic and nutritional medicine, metabolic cardiology, pharmacy sciences; national and competitive intelligence (Graduate Certificate); psychological and social foundations (Graduate Certificate), including career counseling, college teaching, diversity in education, mental health counseling, school counseling; public affairs (Graduate Certificate), including nonprofit management, public management, research administration; public health (Graduate Certificate), including environmental health, health equity, public health generalist, translational research in adolescent behavioral health; public health practices (Graduate Certificate), including planning for healthy communities; rehabilitation and mental health counseling (Graduate Certificate), including integrative mental health care, marriage and family therapy, rehabilitation technology; secondary education (Graduate Certificate), including ESOL, foreign language education: culture and content, foreign language education: professional; social work (Graduate Certificate), including geriatric social work/clinical gerontology; special education (Graduate Certificate), including autism spectrum disorder, disabilities education: severe/profound; world languages (Graduate Certificate), including teaching English as a second language (TESL) or foreign language. *Expenses:* Tuition, state resident: full-time $7766; part-time $431.43 per credit hour. Tuition, nonresident: full-time $15,789; part-time $877.17 per credit hour. *Required fees:* $37 per term. *Unit head:* Kathy Barnes, Interdisciplinary Programs Coordinator, 813-974-8031, Fax: 813-974-7061, E-mail: barnesk@usf.edu. *Application contact:* Karen Tylinski, Metro Initiatives, 813-974-9943, Fax: 813-974-7061, E-mail: ktylinsk@usf.edu.
Website: http://www.usf.edu/innovative-education/

University of South Florida, Muma College of Business, Center for Entrepreneurship, Tampa, FL 33620-9951. Offers entrepreneurship and applied technologies (MS). *Program availability:* Part-time, evening/weekend. *Faculty:* 4 full-time (2 women). *Students:* 66 full-time (32 women), 32 part-time (12 women); includes 20 minority (3 Black or African American, non-Hispanic/Latino; 4 Asian, non-Hispanic/Latino; 11 Hispanic/Latino; 2 Two or more races, non-Hispanic/Latino), 46 international. Average age 29. 84 applicants, 64% accepted, 43 enrolled. In 2016, 41 master's awarded. *Degree requirements:* For master's, comprehensive exam, thesis optional. *Entrance requirements:* For master's, GMAT or GRE (preferred), MCAT or LSAT, minimum undergraduate GPA of 3.0 in upper-division course work, two letters of recommendation, letter of interest, statement of purpose, personal interview. Additional exam requirements/recommendations for international students: Required—TOEFL (minimum score 550 paper-based; 79 iBT) or IELTS (minimum score 6.5). *Application deadline:* For fall admission, 6/1 for domestic students, 2/1 for international students; for spring admission, 10/15 for domestic students, 7/1 for international students. Applications are processed on a rolling basis. Application fee: $30. Electronic applications accepted. *Expenses:* Tuition, state resident: full-time $7766; part-time $431.43 per credit hour. Tuition, nonresident: full-time $15,789; part-time $877.17 per credit hour. *Required fees:* $37 per term. *Faculty research:* Underlying success factors which drive the creation, growth and failures of businesses and technologies in the life sciences industry; influences of individual company geographic location, financial parameters, intellectual property, FDA and regulatory compliance, and press coverage on stock performance of over 1000 publicly-traded life sciences companies. *Total annual research expenditures:* $75,781. *Unit head:* Dr. Michael W. Fountain, Director, Center for Entrepreneurship, 813-974-7825, Fax: 813-974-6175, E-mail: fountain@usf.edu. *Application contact:* Dr. Tapas Das, Assistant Director/Professor, 813-974-5585, Fax: 813-974-5953, E-mail: das@usf.edu. Website: http://www.ce.usf.edu/

The University of Tampa, Sykes College of Business, Tampa, FL 33606-1490. Offers accounting (MS); entrepreneurship (MBA); finance (MBA, MS); information systems management (MBA); innovation management (MBA); international business (MBA); marketing (MBA, MS); nonprofit management (MBA). *Accreditation:* AACSB. *Program availability:* Part-time, evening/weekend. *Faculty:* 43 full-time (19 women), 9 part-time/adjunct (3 women). *Students:* 438 full-time (176 women), 126 part-time (57 women); includes 37 minority (22 Black or African American, non-Hispanic/Latino; 11 Asian, non-Hispanic/Latino; 4 Two or more races, non-Hispanic/Latino), 203 international. Average age 28. 1,305 applicants, 39% accepted, 192 enrolled. In 2016, 266 master's awarded. *Degree requirements:* For master's, capstone. *Entrance requirements:* For master's, GMAT or GRE, official transcripts from all colleges and/or universities previously attended, resume, personal statement, letters of recommendation. Additional exam requirements/recommendations for international students: Required—TOEFL (minimum score 577 paper-based, 90 iBT) or IELTS (7.5). *Application deadline:* Applications are processed on a rolling basis. Application fee: $40. Electronic applications accepted. *Expenses:* $588 per credit tuition, $40 per term fees. *Financial support:* In 2016–17, 116 students received support. Career-related internships or fieldwork, scholarships/grants, and unspecified assistantships available. Financial award applicants required to submit FAFSA. *Faculty research:* Job market signaling, on-line shopping behaviors and social media, the Tampa Bay economy, digital literacy, entrepreneurship in small businesses. *Unit head:* Dr. Natasha F. Veltri, Associate Dean, 813-253-6289, E-mail: nveltri@ut.edu. *Application contact:* Chanelle Cox, Staff Assistant, Admissions for Graduate and Continuing Studies, 813-253-6249, E-mail: ccox@ut.edu.
Website: http://www.ut.edu/business/

The University of Texas at Austin, Graduate School, McCombs School of Business, Program in Technology Commercialization, Austin, TX 78712-1111. Offers MS. Twelve-month program, beginning in May, with classes held every other Friday and Saturday. *Program availability:* Evening/weekend, online learning. *Degree requirements:* For master's, year-long global teaming project. *Entrance requirements:* For master's, GRE General Test or GMAT. Additional exam requirements/recommendations for international students: Required—TOEFL (minimum score 550 paper-based; 79 iBT). Electronic applications accepted. *Expenses:* Contact institution. *Faculty research:* Technology transfer; entrepreneurship; commercialization; research, development and innovation.

The University of Texas at Dallas, Naveen Jindal School of Management, Program in Organizations, Strategy and International Management, Richardson, TX 75080. Offers business administration (MBA); executive business administration (EMBA); global leadership (EMBA); healthcare management (MS); healthcare management for physicians (EMBA); innovation and entrepreneurship (MS); international management studies (MS, PhD); management and administrative sciences (MS); management science (PhD); project management (EMBA, MS); systems engineering and management (MS); MS/MBA. *Program availability:* Part-time, evening/weekend. *Faculty:* 29 full-time (7 women), 29 part-time/adjunct (5 women). *Students:* 524 full-time (189 women), 860 part-time (374 women); includes 452 minority (112 Black or African American, non-Hispanic/Latino; 3 American Indian or Alaska Native, non-Hispanic/Latino; 207 Asian, non-Hispanic/Latino; 85 Hispanic/Latino; 45 Two or more races, non-Hispanic/Latino), 317 international. Average age 34. 1,763 applicants, 37% accepted, 420 enrolled. In 2016, 521 master's, 13 doctorates awarded. *Degree requirements:* For doctorate, thesis/dissertation. *Entrance requirements:* For master's and doctorate, GMAT. Additional exam requirements/recommendations for international students: Required—TOEFL (minimum score 550 paper-based). *Application deadline:* For fall admission, 7/15 for domestic students, 5/1 priority date for international students; for spring admission, 11/15 for domestic students, 9/1 priority date for international students. Applications are processed on a rolling basis. Application fee: $50 ($100 for international students). Electronic applications accepted. *Expenses:* Tuition, state resident: full-time $12,418; part-time $690 per semester hour. Tuition, nonresident: full-time $24,150; part-time $1342 per semester hour. Tuition and fees vary according to course load. *Financial support:* In 2016–17, 385 students received support, including 21 research assistantships with partial tuition reimbursements available (averaging $25,698 per year), 68 teaching assistantships with partial tuition reimbursements available (averaging $16,973 per year); Federal Work-Study, institutionally sponsored loans, scholarships/grants, and unspecified assistantships also available. Support available to part-time students. Financial award application deadline: 4/30; financial award applicants required to submit FAFSA. *Faculty research:* International accounting, international trade and finance, economic development, international economics. *Unit head:* Dr. Seung-Hyun Lee, Area Coordinator, 972-883-6267, Fax: 972-883-5977, E-mail: sxl029100@utdallas.edu. *Application contact:* Maria Hasenhuttl, Assistant Area Coordinator, 972-883-5898, Fax: 972-883-5977, E-mail: maria.hasenhuttl@utdallas.edu. Website: http://jindal.utdallas.edu/osim/

University of Washington, Graduate School, Michael G. Foster School of Business, Seattle, WA 98195-3200. Offers auditing and assurance (MP Acc); business administration (MBA, PhD); entrepreneurship (MS); executive business administration (MBA); global executive business administration (MBA); information systems (MSIS); supply chain management (MSSCM); taxation (MP Acc); technology management (MBA); JD/MBA; MBA/MAIS; MBA/MHA. *Accreditation:* AACSB. *Program availability:* Part-time, evening/weekend. Terminal master's awarded for partial completion of doctoral program. *Degree requirements:* For doctorate, comprehensive exam, thesis/dissertation. *Entrance requirements:* For master's and doctorate, GMAT, GRE. Additional exam requirements/recommendations for international students: Required—TOEFL (minimum score 600 paper-based; 100 iBT). Electronic applications accepted. *Expenses:* Contact institution. *Faculty research:* Finance, marketing, organizational behavior, information technology, strategy.

University of Waterloo, Graduate Studies, Faculty of Engineering, Conrad Business, Entrepreneurship and Technology Center, Waterloo, ON N2L 3G1, Canada. Offers MBET. *Entrance requirements:* For master's, honors degree. Additional exam requirements/recommendations for international students: Required—TOEFL (minimum score 90 iBT), IELTS (minimum score 7), PTE (minimum score 63). Electronic applications accepted.

The University of Western Ontario, Richard Ivey School of Business, London, ON N6A 3K7, Canada. Offers business (EMBA, PhD); corporate strategy and leadership elective (MBA); entrepreneurship elective (MBA); finance elective (MBA); health sector stream (MBA); international management elective (MBA); marketing elective (MBA); JD/MBA. *Degree requirements:* For master's, thesis (for some programs); for doctorate, thesis/dissertation. *Entrance requirements:* For master's, GMAT, 2 years of full-time work experience, interview. Additional exam requirements/recommendations for international students: Required—TOEFL (minimum score 100 iBT) or IELTS (minimium score 6). Electronic applications accepted. *Faculty research:* Strategy, organizational behavior, international business, finance, operations management.

Ursuline College, School of Graduate Studies, Program in Business Administration, Pepper Pike, OH 44124-4398. Offers ethical and entrepreneurial leadership (MBA); financial planning and accounting (MBA); health services management (MBA); management (MBA); management and leadership (MBA); marketing and communications management (MBA). *Program availability:* Part-time. *Faculty:* 2 full-time (both women), 1 (woman) part-time/adjunct. *Students:* 27 full-time (25 women), 9 part-time (all women); includes 15 minority (14 Black or African American, non-Hispanic/Latino; 1 Hispanic/Latino), 2 international. Average age 38. 31 applicants, 71% accepted, 18 enrolled. In 2016, 34 master's awarded. *Degree requirements:* For master's, comprehensive exam (for some programs). *Entrance requirements:* For master's, GRE. Additional exam requirements/recommendations for international students: Required—TOEFL (minimum score 500 paper-based) or GRE. Application fee: $25. Electronic applications accepted. *Expenses:* Contact institution. *Financial support:* In 2016–17, 6 students received support. Scholarships/grants available. Financial award applicants required to submit FAFSA. *Faculty research:* Gift economy; sharing economy; cooperative business models; collaborative leadership; corporate social responsibility and the triple bottom line, defined as the three P's: people, planet and profit. *Unit head:* Dr. Nurete Brenner, Executive Director, 440-684-6038, Fax: 440-684-6088, E-mail: nurete.brenner@ursuline.edu. *Application contact:* Melanie Steele, Director of Graduate Admission, 440-646-8146, Fax: 440-684-6138, E-mail: graduateadmissions@ursuline.edu.

Valparaiso University, Graduate School and Continuing Education, College of Business, Valparaiso, IN 46383. Offers business administration (MBA); business intelligence (Certificate); engineering management (Certificate); entrepreneurship (Certificate); finance (Certificate); general business (Certificate); management (Certificate); marketing (Certificate); sustainability (Certificate); JD/MBA; MSN/MBA.

Entrepreneurship

Accreditation: AACSB. *Program availability:* Part-time, evening/weekend, online learning. *Entrance requirements:* For master's, GMAT, GRE, minimum GPA of 3.0. Additional exam requirements/recommendations for international students: Required—TOEFL (minimum score 550 paper-based; 80 iBT), IELTS (minimum score 6). Electronic applications accepted. *Expenses:* Contact institution.

Virginia International University, School of Business, Fairfax, VA 22030. Offers accounting (MBA, MS); entrepreneurship (MBA); executive management (Graduate Certificate); global logistics (MBA); health care management (MBA); hospitality and tourism management (MBA); human resources management (MBA); international business management (MBA); international finance (MBA); marketing management (MBA); mass media and public relations (MBA); project management (MBA, MS). *Program availability:* Part-time, online learning. *Entrance requirements:* For master's and Graduate Certificate, bachelor's degree. Additional exam requirements/recommendations for international students: Required—TOEFL (minimum score 550 paper-based; 80 iBT), IELTS (minimum score 6). Electronic applications accepted.

Walden University, Graduate Programs, School of Management, Minneapolis, MN 55401. Offers accounting (MBA, MS, DBA), including accounting for the professional (MS), accounting with CPA emphasis (MS), self-designed (MS); advanced project management (Graduate Certificate); applied project management (Graduate Certificate); auditing (Graduate Certificate); bridge to business administration (Post-Doctoral Certificate); bridge to management (Post-Doctoral Certificate); business management (Graduate Certificate); communication (MBA); corporate finance (MBA); digital marketing (Graduate Certificate); entrepreneurship (DBA); entrepreneurship and small business (MBA); finance (MS, DBA), including finance for the professional (MS), finance with CFA/investment (MS), finance with CPA emphasis (MS); global supply chain management (DBA); healthcare management (MBA, DBA); human resource management (MBA, MS, Graduate Certificate), including functional human resource management (MS), general program (MS), integrating functional and strategic human resource management (MS), organizational strategy (MS); human resources management (DBA); information systems management (DBA); international business (MBA, DBA); leadership (MBA, MS, DBA, Graduate Certificate), including general program (MS), human resource leadership (MS), leader development (MS), self-designed (MS); management (MS, PhD), including communications (MS), finance (PhD), general program (MS), healthcare management (MS), human resource management (MS), human resources management (PhD), information systems management (PhD), international business (MS), leadership (MS), leadership and organizational change (PhD), marketing (MS), project management (MS), strategy and operations (MS); managerial accounting (Graduate Certificate); marketing (MBA, MS, DBA); project management (MBA, MS, DBA); self-designed (MBA, DBA); social impact management (DBA); technology entrepreneurship (DBA). *Accreditation:* ACBSP. *Program availability:* Part-time, evening/weekend, online only, 100% online. *Degree requirements:* For master's, thesis (for some programs), residency (for EMBA); for doctorate, thesis/dissertation (for some programs), residency. *Entrance requirements:* For master's, bachelor's degree or higher; minimum GPA of 2.5; official transcripts; goal statement (for some programs); access to computer and Internet; for doctorate, master's degree or higher; three years of related professional or academic experience (preferred); minimum GPA of 3.0; goal statement and current resume (for select programs); official transcripts; access to computer and Internet; for other advanced degree, relevant work experience; access to computer and Internet. Additional exam requirements/recommendations for international students: Required—TOEFL (minimum score 550 paper-based, 79 iBT), IELTS (minimum score 6.5), Michigan English Language Assessment Battery (minimum score 82), or PTE (minimum score 53). Electronic applications accepted.

Washington University in St. Louis, School of Medicine, Program in Clinical Investigation, St. Louis, MO 63130-4899. Offers clinical investigation (MS), including bioethics, entrepreneurship, genetics/genomics, translational medicine. *Program availability:* Part-time, evening/weekend. *Degree requirements:* For master's, thesis. *Entrance requirements:* For master's, doctoral-level degree or in process of obtaining doctoral-level degree. Electronic applications accepted. *Faculty research:* Anesthesiology, infectious diseases, neurology, obstetrics and gynecology, orthopedic surgery.

Wayne State University, Mike Ilitch School of Business, Detroit, MI 48202. Offers accounting (MS, Postbaccalaureate Certificate); business (Graduate Certificate); business administration (MBA, PhD); data science (MS), including business analytics; entrepreneurship and innovation (Postbaccalaureate Certificate); finance (MS); information systems management (Postbaccalaureate Certificate); taxation (MST); JD/MBA. Application deadline for PhD is February 15. *Accreditation:* AACSB. *Program availability:* Part-time, evening/weekend. *Faculty:* 32. *Students:* 219 full-time (105 women), 941 part-time (406 women); includes 314 minority (186 Black or African American, non-Hispanic/Latino; 3 American Indian or Alaska Native, non-Hispanic/Latino; 68 Asian, non-Hispanic/Latino; 33 Hispanic/Latino; 24 Two or more races, non-Hispanic/Latino), 88 international. Average age 30. 1,119 applicants, 49% accepted, 329 enrolled. In 2016, 203 master's, 1 doctorate, 3 other advanced degrees awarded. *Degree requirements:* For doctorate, thesis/dissertation. *Entrance requirements:* For master's, GMAT, GRE, LSAT, MCAT, at least three years of relevant work experience that shows increased responsibility, or minimum GPA of 3.0 from AACSB-accredited program or 3.2 from regionally-accredited program, undergraduate degree from accredited institution; undergraduate degree in accounting, business administration, or area of business administration (for MS and MST); for doctorate, GMAT (minimum score of 600), minimum undergraduate GPA of 3.0, 3.5 upper-division or graduate; three letters of recommendation; brief essay; undergraduate degree from accredited institution; personal statement; for other advanced degree, bachelor's degree from accredited institution. Additional exam requirements/recommendations for international students: Required—TOEFL (minimum score 550 paper-based; 79 iBT), Michigan English Language Assessment Battery (minimum score 85); Recommended—IELTS (minimum score 6.5), TWE (minimum score 5.5). *Application deadline:* For fall admission, 7/1 for domestic students, 5/1 priority date for international students; for winter admission, 11/1 for domestic students, 9/1 priority date for international students; for spring admission, 3/1 for domestic students, 1/1 priority date for international students. Applications are processed on a rolling basis. Application fee: $50. Electronic applications accepted. *Expenses:* $18,871 per year resident tuition and fees, $36,065 per year non-resident tuition and fees. *Financial support:* In 2016–17, 174 students received support, including 1 fellowship with tuition reimbursement available (averaging $18,000 per year), 2 research assistantships with tuition reimbursements available (averaging $18,000 per year), 5 teaching assistantships with tuition reimbursements available (averaging $18,000 per year); scholarships/grants, health care benefits, and unspecified assistantships also available. Support available to part-time students. Financial award applicants required to submit FAFSA. *Faculty research:* Executive compensation and stock performance, consumer reactions to pricing strategies, communication across the automotive supply chain, performance of firms in sub-Saharan Africa, implementation issues with ERP software. *Unit head:* Dr. Robert Forsythe, Dean, School of Business Administration, 313-577-4501, E-mail: robert.forsythe@wayne.edu. *Application contact:* Kiantee N. Rupert-Jones, Director, 313-577-4511, Fax: 313-577-9442, E-mail: gradbusiness@wayne.edu.
Website: http://ilitchbusiness.wayne.edu/

West Chester University of Pennsylvania, College of Business and Public Management, School of Business, West Chester, PA 19383. Offers business analytics (Certificate); business education (MBA); entrepreneurship (Certificate); project management (Certificate). *Accreditation:* AACSB. *Program availability:* Part-time, evening/weekend, 100% online. *Faculty:* 13 full-time (6 women), 2 part-time/adjunct (1 woman). *Students:* 44 full-time (23 women), 213 part-time (82 women); includes 37 minority (16 Black or African American, non-Hispanic/Latino; 11 Asian, non-Hispanic/Latino; 9 Hispanic/Latino; 1 Two or more races, non-Hispanic/Latino). Average age 32. 202 applicants, 83% accepted, 126 enrolled. In 2016, 41 master's, 16 other advanced degrees awarded. *Degree requirements:* For master's, minimum GPA of 3.0. *Entrance requirements:* For master's, GMAT or GRE, statement of professional goals, resume, two letters of recommendation, transcripts. Additional exam requirements/recommendations for international students: Required—TOEFL or IELTS. *Application deadline:* For fall admission, 5/15 for international students; for spring admission, 10/15 for international students. Applications are processed on a rolling basis. Application fee: $50. Electronic applications accepted. *Expenses:* Tuition, state resident: full-time $8694; part-time $483 per credit. Tuition, nonresident: full-time $13,050; part-time $725 per credit. *Required fees:* $2399; $119.05 per credit. Tuition and fees vary according to campus/location and program. *Financial support:* Scholarships/grants and unspecified assistantships available. Financial award application deadline: 2/15; financial award applicants required to submit FAFSA. *Unit head:* Dr. Brian Halsey, MBA Director/Graduate Coordinator, 610-425-5000 Ext. 4444, E-mail: mba@wcupa.edu. *Application contact:* Office of Graduate Studies and Extended Education, 610-436-2943, Fax: 610-436-2763, E-mail: gradstudy@wcupa.edu. Website: http://www.wcupa.edu/mba

West Chester University of Pennsylvania, College of Education and Social Work, Department of Professional and Secondary Education, West Chester, PA 19383. Offers education for sustainability (Certificate); educational technology (Certificate); entrepreneurial education (Certificate); transformative education and social change (MS). *Program availability:* Part-time. *Faculty:* 10 full-time (3 women). *Students:* 6 full-time (5 women), 35 part-time (22 women); includes 2 minority (1 Hispanic/Latino; 1 Two or more races, non-Hispanic/Latino). Average age 30. 24 applicants, 88% accepted, 17 enrolled. In 2016, 7 master's, 3 other advanced degrees awarded. *Degree requirements:* For master's, comprehensive exam (for some programs), thesis, 36 credits. *Entrance requirements:* For master's, teaching certification (strongly recommended); for Certificate, minimum GPA of 3.0. Additional exam requirements/recommendations for international students: Required—TOEFL or IELTS. *Application deadline:* For fall admission, 5/15 for international students; for spring admission, 10/15 for international students. Applications are processed on a rolling basis. Application fee: $50. Electronic applications accepted. *Expenses:* Tuition, state resident: full-time $8694; part-time $483 per credit. Tuition, nonresident: full-time $13,050; part-time $725 per credit. *Required fees:* $2399; $119.05 per credit. Tuition and fees vary according to campus/location and program. *Financial support:* Scholarships/grants and unspecified assistantships available. Financial award application deadline: 2/15; financial award applicants required to submit FAFSA. *Faculty research:* Technology integration: preparing our teachers for the twenty-first century, critical pedagogy. *Unit head:* Dr. John Elmore, Chair, 610-436-6934, Fax: 610-436-3102, E-mail: jelmore@wcupa.edu. *Application contact:* Dr. Matthew Kruger-Ross, Graduate Coordinator, 610-436-2106, Fax: 610-436-3102, E-mail: mkruger-ross@wcupa.edu.
Website: http://www.wcupa.edu/education-socialWork/profsecedu/

Western Carolina University, Graduate School, College of Business, Program in Entrepreneurship, Cullowhee, NC 28723. Offers ME. *Program availability:* Part-time, evening/weekend, online learning. *Entrance requirements:* For master's, GMAT or GRE General Test. Additional exam requirements/recommendations for international students: Required—TOEFL (minimum score 550 paper-based; 79 iBT). *Expenses:* Tuition, state resident: full-time $2174. Tuition, nonresident: full-time $7377. *Required fees:* $1442. Part-time tuition and fees vary according to course load.

Wichita State University, Graduate School, Institute for Interdisciplinary Creativity, Wichita, KS 67260. Offers innovation design (MID). *Unit head:* Dr. Jeremy Patterson, Graduate Coordinator, 316-978-3010, E-mail: jeremy.patterson@wichita.edu. *Application contact:* Jordan Oleson, Admissions Coordinator, 316-978-3095, Fax: 316-978-3253, E-mail: jordan.oleson@wichita.edu. Website: http://www.wichita.edu/iic

Wilkes University, College of Graduate and Professional Studies, Jay S. Sidhu School of Business and Leadership, Wilkes-Barre, PA 18766-0002. Offers accounting (MBA); entrepreneurship (MBA); finance (MBA); health care administration (MBA); human resource management (MBA); international business (MBA); operations management (MBA); organizational leadership and development (MBA). *Accreditation:* ACBSP. *Program availability:* Part-time, evening/weekend. *Students:* 35 full-time (17 women), 112 part-time (55 women); includes 17 minority (6 Black or African American, non-Hispanic/Latino; 4 Asian, non-Hispanic/Latino; 5 Hispanic/Latino; 2 Two or more races, non-Hispanic/Latino), 16 international. Average age 31. In 2016, 59 master's awarded. *Entrance requirements:* For master's, GMAT. Additional exam requirements/recommendations for international students: Required—TOEFL (minimum score 550 paper-based; 79 iBT). *Application deadline:* Applications are processed on a rolling basis. Application fee: $45 ($65 for international students). Electronic applications accepted. *Expenses:* Contact institution. *Financial support:* Unspecified assistantships available. Financial award application deadline: 3/1; financial award applicants required to submit FAFSA. *Unit head:* Dr. Abel Adekola, Dean, 570-408-4701, Fax: 570-408-7846, E-mail: abel.adekola@wilkes.edu. *Application contact:* Director of Graduate Enrollment, 570-408-4234, Fax: 570-408-7846.
Website: http://www.wilkes.edu/academics/colleges/sidhu-school-of-business-leadership/index.aspx

Wingate University, Porter B. Byrum School of Business, Wingate, NC 28174. Offers accounting (MAC); corporate innovation (MBA); finance (MBA); general management (MBA); healthcare management (MBA); marketing (MBA); project management (MBA). *Accreditation:* ACBSP. *Program availability:* Part-time, evening/weekend. *Entrance requirements:* For master's, GMAT, work experience, 2 letters of recommendation. *Application deadline:* For fall admission, 8/15 priority date for domestic students; for spring admission, 12/15 priority date for domestic students. Applications are processed on a rolling basis. Application fee: $50. Electronic applications accepted. *Expenses:* Contact institution. *Financial support:* Federal Work-Study and scholarships/grants available. Support available to part-time students. Financial award application deadline: 8/1; financial award applicants required to submit FAFSA. *Faculty research:* Stochastic processes, business ethics, regional economic development, municipal finance, consumer behavior. *Unit head:* Dr. Peter Frank, Dean, 704-233-8148, Fax: 704-233-8146, E-mail: pfrank@wingate.edu. *Application contact:* Mary Maye, Administrative Assistant to the Dean, 704-233-8148, Fax: 704-233-8146.
Website: http://www.wingate.edu/academics/school-of-business

Section 6
Facilities and Entertainment Management

This section contains a directory of institutions offering graduate work in facilities management. Additional information about programs listed in the directory but not augmented by an in-depth entry may be obtained by writing directly to the dean of a graduate school or chair of a department at the address given in the directory.

For programs offering related work, see also in this book *Business Administration and Management.*

CONTENTS

Program Directories

Featured School; Display and Close-Up

See:

Entertainment Management

Berklee College of Music, Berklee Graduate Programs, Boston, MA 02215-3693. Offers contemporary performance (MM), including global jazz, production; global entertainment and music business (MA); music production, technology, and innovation (MM); music therapy (MA); scoring for film, television, and video games (MM). Production; global entertainment and music business; music production, technology, and innovation; and scoring for film, television, and video games programs offered at Valencia, Spain campus. *Program availability:* Part-time, blended/hybrid learning. *Faculty:* 53 full-time (18 women), 39 part-time/adjunct (7 women). *Students:* 159 full-time (51 women), 30 part-time (24 women); includes 35 minority (12 Black or African American, non-Hispanic/Latino; 7 Asian, non-Hispanic/Latino; 12 Hispanic/Latino; 4 Two or more races, non-Hispanic/Latino), 78 international. Average age 26. 774 applicants, 36% accepted, 177 enrolled. In 2016, 137 master's awarded. *Degree requirements:* For master's, thesis, culminating experience project. *Entrance requirements:* Additional exam requirements/recommendations for international students: Required—TOEFL (minimum score 600 paper-based; 100 iBT), IELTS (minimum score 7.5), PTE (minimum score 73). *Application deadline:* For fall admission, 2/1 for domestic and international students. Application fee: $150. Electronic applications accepted. *Expenses:* Contact institution. *Financial support:* In 2016–17, 161 students received support, including 120 fellowships with full and partial tuition reimbursements available (averaging $18,507 per year), 41 research assistantships (averaging $4,220 per year); career-related internships or fieldwork, scholarships/grants, and tuition waivers (full and partial) also available. Support available to part-time students. Financial award application deadline: 2/1; financial award applicants required to submit CSS PROFILE or FAFSA. *Faculty research:* Neuroscience, integrative medicine, music therapy practice, music cognition, ethnomusicology. *Unit head:* Camille Colatosti, PhD, Dean, Institutional Assessment and Graduate Studies, E-mail: ccolatosti@berklee.edu. *Application contact:* Office of Admissions, 617-747-2221, E-mail: admissions@berklee.edu.
Website: https://www.berklee.edu/graduate

California Intercontinental University, Hollywood College of the Entertainment Industry, Irvine, CA 92614. Offers Hollywood and entertainment management (MBA).

California State University, Northridge, Graduate Studies, The Tseng College of Extended Learning, Northridge, CA 91330. Offers business administration (Graduate Certificate); health administration (MPA); health education (MPH); knowledge management (MKM); music industry administration (MA); nonprofit-sector management (Graduate Certificate); public administration (MPA); public sector management and leadership (MPA); social work (MSW); taxation (MS); tourism, hospitality and recreation management (MS). *Faculty:* 55 part-time/adjunct (28 women). *Students:* 1 (woman) full-time, 1 (woman) part-time. Average age 40. *Entrance requirements:* For master's, GRE (if cumulative undergraduate GPA less than 3.0). *Expenses:* Tuition, state resident: full-time $4152. *Unit head:* Joyce Feucht-Haviar, Dean, 866-873-6439.

See Display on page 1665 and Close-Up on page 1687.

Carnegie Mellon University, Heinz College, School of Public Policy and Management, Master of Entertainment Industry Management Program, Pittsburgh, PA 15213-3891. Offers MEIM. *Accreditation:* AACSB. *Entrance requirements:* For master's, GRE or GMAT, college-level course in advanced algebra/pre-calculus; college-level courses in economics and statistics (recommended). Additional exam requirements/recommendations for international students: Required—TOEFL or IELTS.

Columbia College Chicago, Graduate School, Department of Business and Entrepreneurship, Chicago, IL 60605-1996. Offers arts, entertainment and media management (MA), including visual arts management. *Program availability:* Part-time. *Degree requirements:* For master's, thesis, internship. *Entrance requirements:* For master's, GRE (recommended), self-assessment essay, resume, letters of recommendation. Additional exam requirements/recommendations for international students: Required—TOEFL (minimum score 600 paper-based; 100 iBT). Electronic applications accepted. *Expenses:* Contact institution.

Full Sail University, Entertainment Business Master of Science Program - Campus, Winter Park, FL 32792-7437. Offers MS.

Full Sail University, Entertainment Business Master of Science Program - Online, Winter Park, FL 32792-7437. Offers MS. *Program availability:* Online learning. *Entrance requirements:* Additional exam requirements/recommendations for international students: Required—TOEFL (minimum score 550 paper-based; 79 iBT).

Hofstra University, Frank G. Zarb School of Business, Programs in Management and General Business, Hempstead, NY 11549. Offers business administration (MBA), including health services management, management, sports and entertainment management, strategic business management, strategic healthcare management; general management (Advanced Certificate); human resource management (MS, Advanced Certificate). *Program availability:* Part-time, evening/weekend, blended/hybrid learning. *Students:* 140 full-time (67 women), 159 part-time (70 women); includes 100 minority (24 Black or African American, non-Hispanic/Latino; 41 Asian, non-Hispanic/Latino; 32 Hispanic/Latino; 1 Native Hawaiian or other Pacific Islander, non-Hispanic/Latino; 2 Two or more races, non-Hispanic/Latino), 26 international. Average age 33. 354 applicants, 58% accepted, 94 enrolled. In 2016, 84 master's awarded. *Degree requirements:* For master's, thesis optional, capstone course (for MBA), thesis (for MS), minimum GPA of 3.0. *Entrance requirements:* For master's, GMAT/GRE, 2 letters of recommendation, resume, essay. Additional exam requirements/recommendations for international students: Required—TOEFL (minimum score 550 paper-based; 80 iBT); Recommended—IELTS (minimum score 6). *Application deadline:* Applications are processed on a rolling basis. Application fee: $75. Electronic applications accepted. *Expenses:* $1,170 per credit. *Financial support:* In 2016–17, 65 students received support, including 43 fellowships with full and partial tuition reimbursements available (averaging $4,813 per year); research assistantships with full and partial tuition reimbursements available, career-related internships or fieldwork, Federal Work-Study, institutionally sponsored loans, scholarships/grants, tuition waivers (full and partial), and unspecified assistantships also available. Support available to part-time students. Financial award applicants required to submit FAFSA. *Faculty research:* Organizational change; sustainability; entrepreneurial spawning; family business; global supply chain strategies. *Unit head:* Dr. Kaushik Sengupta, Chairperson, 516-463-7825, Fax: 516-463-4834, E-mail: kaushik.sengupta@hofstra.edu. *Application contact:* Sunil Samuel, Assistant Vice President of Admissions, 516-463-4723, Fax: 516-463-4664, E-mail: graduateadmission@hofstra.edu.
Website: http://www.hofstra.edu/business/

New York Institute of Technology, School of Interdisciplinary Studies and Education, Program in Leadership in the Arts and Entertainment Industries, Old Westbury, NY 11568-8000. Offers arts and entertainment leadership (Advanced Certificate); leadership in the arts and entertainment industries (MA). *Program availability:* Part-time, evening/weekend. *Faculty:* 3 full-time (2 women), 1 part-time/adjunct (0 women). *Students:* 3 full-time (all women), 1 (woman) part-time; includes 1 minority (Two or more races, non-Hispanic/Latino), 3 international. Average age 27. 3 applicants, 100% accepted, 2 enrolled. *Degree requirements:* For master's, practicum, capstone seminar. *Entrance requirements:* For master's, bachelor's degree in the arts and/or in-depth knowledge of at least one performing art discipline; demonstration of at least three years of progressively responsible positions in management or an organization in a performing arts industry sector; interview via Skype or phone; resume; personal statement; two letters of recommenadation; for Advanced Certificate, bachelor's degree in the arts and/or in-depth knowledge of at least one performing art discipline; some experience in management; interview via Skype or phone; resume; two letters of recommendation. Additional exam requirements/recommendations for international students: Required—TOEFL (minimum score 79 iBT), IELTS (minimum score 6). *Application deadline:* Applications are processed on a rolling basis. Application fee: $50. Electronic applications accepted. *Expenses:* $1,215 per credit. *Financial support:* Career-related internships or fieldwork, Federal Work-Study, scholarships/grants, tuition waivers (full and partial), and unspecified assistantships available. Support available to part-time students. Financial award application deadline: 3/1; financial award applicants required to submit FAFSA. *Unit head:* David Milch, Program Director, 212-261-1639, E-mail: dmilch@nyit.edu. *Application contact:* Alice Dolitsky, Director, Graduate Admissions, 516-686-7520, Fax: 516-686-1116, E-mail: nyitgrad@nyit.edu.
Website: http://www.nyit.edu/degrees/arts_entertainment_leadership_ma

Point Park University, School of Business, Department of Business, Pittsburgh, PA 15222-1984. Offers business analytics (MBA); health systems management (MBA); international business (MBA); management (MBA); management information systems (MBA); sports, arts and entertainment management (MBA). *Program availability:* Evening/weekend, online learning.

Syracuse University, College of Visual and Performing Arts, MA Program in Audio Arts, Syracuse, NY 13244. Offers audio arts (MA), including audio recording, music industry, music video, radio horizons. Program taught in conjunction with the S.I. Newhouse School of Public Communications. *Entrance requirements:* For master's, resume, sample of work, personal statement, three letters of recommendation. Additional exam requirements/recommendations for international students: Required—TOEFL (minimum score 100 iBT). *Application deadline:* For summer admission, 2/1 priority date for domestic and international students. Application fee: $75. Electronic applications accepted. *Expenses: Tuition:* Full-time $25,974; part-time $1443 per credit hour. *Required fees:* $802; $50 per course. Tuition and fees vary according to course load and program. *Financial support:* Fellowships, teaching assistantships, and scholarships/grants available. Financial award application deadline: 1/1. *Faculty research:* Audio practice, music industry, audio recording, radio horizons, music video. *Unit head:* Prof. Ulf Oesterle, Co-Director, 315-443-3119, E-mail: uoesterl@syr.edu. *Application contact:* Therese West, Information Contact, 315-443-0137, E-mail: admissg@syr.edu.
Website: http://vpa.syr.edu/prospective-students/graduate-students/programs/audio-arts/

Universidad Autonoma de Guadalajara, Graduate Programs, Guadalajara, Mexico. Offers administrative law and justice (LL M); advertising and corporate communications (MA); architecture (M Arch); business (MBA); computational science (MCC); education (Ed M, Ed D); English-Spanish translation (MA); entrepreneurship and management (MBA); integrated management of digital animation (MA); international business (MIB); international corporate law (LL M); internet technologies (MS); manufacturing systems (MMS); occupational health (MS); philosophy (MA, PhD); power electronics (MS); quality systems (MQS); renewable energy (MS); social evaluation of projects (MBA); strategic market research (MBA); tax law (MA); teaching mathematics (MA).

University of Colorado Denver, Business School, Master of Business Administration Program, Denver, CO 80217. Offers bioinnovation and entrepreneurship (MBA); business intelligence (MBA); business strategy (MBA); business to business marketing (MBA); business to consumer marketing (MBA); change management (MBA); corporate financial management (MBA); enterprise technology management (MBA); entrepreneurship (MBA); health administration (MBA), including financial management, health administration, health information technologies, international health management and policy; human resources management (MBA); international business (MBA); investment management (MBA); managing for sustainability (MBA); sports and entertainment management (MBA). *Accreditation:* AACSB. *Program availability:* Part-time, evening/weekend, 100% online, blended/hybrid learning. *Students:* 544 full-time (210 women), 112 part-time (22 women); includes 99 minority (15 Black or African American, non-Hispanic/Latino; 4 American Indian or Alaska Native, non-Hispanic/Latino; 38 Asian, non-Hispanic/Latino; 36 Hispanic/Latino; 6 Two or more races, non-Hispanic/Latino), 22 international. Average age 32. 335 applicants, 73% accepted, 179 enrolled. In 2016, 251 master's awarded. *Degree requirements:* For master's, 48 semester hours, including 30 of core courses, 3 in international business, and 15 in electives from over 50 other business courses. *Entrance requirements:* For master's, GMAT, resume, official transcripts, essay, two letters of recommendation, financial statements (for international applicants). Additional exam requirements/recommendations for international students: Required—TOEFL (minimum score 560 paper-based; 83 iBT); Recommended—IELTS (minimum score 6.5). *Application deadline:* For fall admission, 4/15 priority date for domestic students, 3/15 priority date for international students; for spring admission, 10/15 priority date for domestic students, 9/15 priority date for international students; for summer admission, 2/15 priority date for domestic students, 1/15 priority date for international students. Applications are processed on a rolling basis. Application fee: $50 ($75 for international students). Electronic applications accepted. *Expenses:* Contact institution. *Financial support:* In 2016–17, 171 students received support. Fellowships, research assistantships, teaching assistantships, Federal Work-Study, institutionally sponsored loans, scholarships/grants, traineeships, and unspecified assistantships available. Financial award application deadline: 4/1; financial award applicants required to submit FAFSA. *Faculty research:* Marketing, management, entrepreneurship, finance, health administration. *Unit head:* Woodrow Eckard, MBA Director, 303-315-8470, E-mail: woody.eckard@ucdenver.edu. *Application contact:* Shelly Townley, Admissions Director, Graduate Programs, 303-315-8202, E-mail: shelly.townley@ucdenver.edu.
Website: http://www.ucdenver.edu/academics/colleges/business/degrees/mba/Pages/MBA.aspx

University of Colorado Denver, Business School, Program in Management and Organization, Denver, CO 80217. Offers business strategy (MS); change and innovation (MS); enterprise technology management (MS); entrepreneurship and innovation (MS); global management (MS); leadership (MS); managing for sustainability (MS); managing human resources (MS); sports and entertainment management (MS). *Accreditation:*

AACSB. *Program availability:* Part-time, evening/weekend, online learning. *Students:* 20 full-time (13 women), 17 part-time (10 women); includes 6 minority (3 Black or African American, non-Hispanic/Latino; 1 American Indian or Alaska Native, non-Hispanic/Latino; 1 Hispanic/Latino; 1 Two or more races, non-Hispanic/Latino), 6 international. Average age 33. 24 applicants, 58% accepted, 6 enrolled. In 2016, 19 master's awarded. *Degree requirements:* For master's, 30 semester hours (12 of required courses, 12 of management electives, and 6 of free electives). *Entrance requirements:* For master's, GMAT, resume, two letters of recommendation, essay, financial statements (for international applicants). Additional exam requirements/recommendations for international students: Required—TOEFL (minimum score 525 paper-based; 71 iBT); Recommended—IELTS (minimum score 6.5). *Application deadline:* For fall admission, 4/15 priority date for domestic students, 3/15 priority date for international students; for spring admission, 10/15 priority date for domestic students, 9/15 priority date for international students; for summer admission, 2/15 priority date for domestic students, 1/15 priority date for international students. Applications are processed on a rolling basis. Application fee: $50 ($75 for international students). Electronic applications accepted. *Expenses:* Contact institution. *Financial support:* In 2016–17, 7 students received support. Fellowships, research assistantships, teaching assistantships, Federal Work-Study, institutionally sponsored loans, scholarships/grants, and traineeships available. Financial award application deadline: 4/1; financial award applicants required to submit FAFSA. *Faculty research:* Human resource management, management of catastrophe, turnaround strategies. *Unit head:* Dr. Kenneth Bettenhausen, Associate Professor/Director of MS in Management, 303-315-8425, E-mail: kenneth.bettenhausen@ucdenver.edu. *Application contact:* 303-315-8200, E-mail: bschool.admissions@ucdenver.edu.
Website: http://www.ucdenver.edu/academics/colleges/business/degrees/ms/management/Pages/Management.aspx

University of Colorado Denver, Business School, Program in Marketing, Denver, CO 80217. Offers brand management and marketing communication (MS); global marketing (MS); high-tech and entrepreneurial marketing (MS); marketing for sustainability (MS); marketing research (MS); sports and entertainment marketing (MS). *Program availability:* Part-time, evening/weekend. *Students:* 30 full-time (19 women), 7 part-time (5 women); includes 5 minority (2 Black or African American, non-Hispanic/Latino; 1 Asian, non-Hispanic/Latino; 2 Hispanic/Latino), 12 international. Average age 28. 47 applicants, 62% accepted, 13 enrolled. In 2016, 23 master's awarded. *Degree requirements:* For master's, 30 semester hours (21 of marketing core courses, 9 of marketing electives). *Entrance requirements:* For master's, GMAT, resume, essay, two letters of recommendation, financial statements (for international applicants). Additional exam requirements/recommendations for international students: Required—TOEFL (minimum score 525 paper-based; 71 iBT); Recommended—IELTS (minimum score 6.5). *Application deadline:* For fall admission, 4/15 priority date for domestic students, 3/15 priority date for international students; for spring admission, 10/15 priority date for domestic students, 9/15 priority date for international students; for summer admission, 2/15 priority date for domestic students, 1/15 priority date for international students. Applications are processed on a rolling basis. Application fee: $50 ($75 for international students). Electronic applications accepted. *Expenses:* Contact institution. *Financial support:* In 2016–17, 7 students received support. Fellowships, research assistantships, teaching assistantships, Federal Work-Study, institutionally sponsored loans, scholarships/grants, and traineeships available. Financial award application deadline: 4/1; financial award applicants required to submit FAFSA. *Faculty research:* Marketing issues in the Chinese environment, impact of individual difference and contextual factors on the risk-taking behaviors of managers making new-business creation decisions, attribution theory perspective of conflict between marketers and engineers, organizational identity and identification, international market entry strategies. *Unit head:* Vicki Lane, Director of Marketing Program, 303-315-8468, E-mail: vicki.lane@ucdenver.edu. *Application contact:* 303-315-8200, E-mail: bschool.admissions@ucdenver.edu.
Website: http://www.ucdenver.edu/academics/colleges/business/degrees/ms/marketing/Pages/Marketing.aspx

University of Dallas, Satish and Yasmin Gupta College of Business, Irving, TX 75062-4736. Offers accounting (MBA, MS); business administration (DBA); business analytics (MS); business management (MBA); corporate finance (MBA); cybersecurity (MS); finance (MS); financial services (MBA); global business (MBA, MS); health services management (MBA); human resource management (MBA); information and technology management (MS); information assurance (MBA); information technology (MBA); information technology service management (MBA); marketing management (MBA); organization development (MBA); project management (MBA); sports and entertainment management (MBA); strategic leadership (MBA); supply chain management (MBA). *Accreditation:* AACSB. *Program availability:* Part-time, evening/weekend, online learning. *Entrance requirements:* Additional exam requirements/recommendations for international students: Required—TOEFL. Electronic applications accepted. *Expenses:* Contact institution.

University of Massachusetts Amherst, Graduate School, Interdisciplinary Programs, Dual Degree Programs in Management and Engineering, Amherst, MA 01003. Offers MBA/MIE, MBA/MSEWRE, MSCE/MBA, MSME/MBA. *Program availability:* Part-time. *Entrance requirements:* Additional exam requirements/recommendations for international students: Required—TOEFL (minimum score 600 paper-based; 100 iBT), IELTS (minimum score 7). Electronic applications accepted.

University of South Carolina, The Graduate School, College of Hospitality, Retail, and Sport Management, Department of Sport and Entertainment Management, Columbia, SC 29208. Offers live sport and entertainment events (MS); public assembly facilities management (MS). *Program availability:* Part-time. *Degree requirements:* For master's, comprehensive exam, thesis optional. *Entrance requirements:* For master's, GRE General Test or GMAT (preferred), minimum GPA of 3.0. Additional exam requirements/recommendations for international students: Required—TOEFL (minimum score 570 paper-based; 70 iBT). Electronic applications accepted. *Expenses:* Contact institution. *Faculty research:* Public assembly marketing, operations, box office, booking and scheduling, law/economic impacts.

Valparaiso University, Graduate School and Continuing Education, Program in Arts and Entertainment Administration, Valparaiso, IN 46383. Offers MA. *Program availability:* Part-time, evening/weekend. *Degree requirements:* For master's, internship or research project. *Entrance requirements:* Additional exam requirements/recommendations for international students: Required—TOEFL (minimum score 550 paper-based; 80 iBT), IELTS (minimum score 6). Electronic applications accepted. *Expenses: Tuition:* Full-time $11,070; part-time $615 per credit hour. *Required fees:* $116 per semester. Tuition and fees vary according to course load, degree level and program.

Facilities Management

Cornell University, Graduate School, Graduate Fields of Human Ecology, Field of Design and Environmental Analysis, Ithaca, NY 14853. Offers applied research in human-environment relations (MS); facilities planning and management (MS); housing and design (MS); human factors and ergonomics (MS); human-environment relations (MS); interior design (MA, MPS). *Degree requirements:* For master's, thesis. *Entrance requirements:* For master's, GRE General Test, portfolio or slides of recent work; bachelor's degree in interior design, architecture or related design discipline; 2 letters of recommendation. Additional exam requirements/recommendations for international students: Required—TOEFL (minimum score 600 paper-based; 105 iBT). Electronic applications accepted. *Faculty research:* Facility planning and management, environmental psychology, housing, interior design, ergonomics and human factors.

Indiana University–Purdue University Fort Wayne, College of Engineering, Technology, and Computer Science, Program in Technology, Fort Wayne, IN 46805-1499. Offers facilities/construction management (MS); industrial technology/manufacturing (MS); information technology/advanced computer applications (MS). *Program availability:* Part-time. *Entrance requirements:* For master's, minimum GPA of 3.0. Additional exam requirements/recommendations for international students: Required—TOEFL (minimum score 550 paper-based; 79 iBT), TWE. Electronic applications accepted.

Maastricht School of Management, Graduate Programs, Maastricht, Netherlands. Offers business administration (MBA, DBA, PhD); facility management (Exec MBA); management (M Sc); sustainability (Exec MBA).

Massachusetts Maritime Academy, Program in Facilities Management, Buzzards Bay, MA 02532-1803. Offers MS. *Program availability:* Part-time-only, evening/weekend. *Entrance requirements:* For master's, GRE or GMAT, interview. Electronic applications accepted.

Pratt Institute, School of Architecture, Program in Facilities Management, New York, NY 10011. Offers MS. *Program availability:* Part-time. *Faculty:* 1 (woman) full-time, 5 part-time/adjunct (0 women). *Students:* 16 full-time (7 women), 2 part-time (0 women); includes 8 minority (3 Black or African American, non-Hispanic/Latino; 1 Asian, non-Hispanic/Latino; 3 Hispanic/Latino; 1 Two or more races, non-Hispanic/Latino), 7 international. Average age 29. 24 applicants, 79% accepted, 4 enrolled. In 2016, 10 master's awarded. *Degree requirements:* For master's, thesis. *Entrance requirements:* For master's, writing sample, bachelor's degree, transcripts, letters of recommendation, portfolio. Additional exam requirements/recommendations for international students: Required—TOEFL (minimum score 550 paper-based; 79 iBT). *Application deadline:* For fall admission, 1/5 for domestic and international students; for spring admission, 10/1 for domestic and international students. Application fee: $50 ($90 for international students). Electronic applications accepted. *Expenses:* $29,646 full-time tuition, $1,938 fees. *Financial support:* Career-related internships or fieldwork, Federal Work-Study, institutionally sponsored loans, scholarships/grants, health care benefits, and unspecified assistantships available. Support available to part-time students. Financial award application deadline: 2/1; financial award applicants required to submit FAFSA. *Faculty research:* Benchmarking, organizational studies, resource planning and management, computer-aided facilities management, value analysis. *Unit head:* Regina Ford Cahill, Chairperson, 212-647-7764, E-mail: rcahill8@pratt.edu. *Application contact:* Natalie Capannelli, Director of Graduate Admissions, 718-636-3551, Fax: 718-399-4242, E-mail: ncapanne@pratt.edu.
Website: https://www.pratt.edu/academics/architecture/facilities-management/

Université Laval, Faculty of Administrative Sciences, Programs in Business Administration, Québec, QC G1K 7P4, Canada. Offers accounting (MBA); agri-food management (MBA); electronic business (MBA, Diploma); factory management and logistics (MBA); finance (MBA); firm management (MBA); geomatic management (MBA); information technology management (MBA); international management (MBA); management (MBA); management accounting (MBA, Diploma); marketing (MBA); modeling and organizational decision (MBA); occupational health and safety management (MBA); pharmacy management (MBA); social and environmental responsibility (MBA); technological entrepreneurship (Diploma). *Accreditation:* AACSB. *Program availability:* Part-time, evening/weekend, online learning. *Entrance requirements:* For master's and Diploma, knowledge of French and English. Electronic applications accepted.

University of California, Berkeley, UC Berkeley Extension, Certificate Programs in Engineering, Construction and Facilities Management, Berkeley, CA 94720-1500. Offers construction management (Certificate); HVAC (Certificate); integrated circuit design and techniques (online) (Certificate). *Program availability:* Online learning.

University of New Haven, Graduate School, College of Business, Program in Sport Management, West Haven, CT 06516. Offers collegiate athletic administration (MS); facility management (MS); sport analytics (MS); sport management (Graduate Certificate). *Program availability:* Part-time, evening/weekend. *Students:* 15 full-time (7 women), 9 part-time (2 women); includes 5 minority (3 Black or African American, non-Hispanic/Latino; 1 Hispanic/Latino; 1 Two or more races, non-Hispanic/Latino), 6 international. Average age 25. 26 applicants, 96% accepted, 13 enrolled. In 2016, 12 master's awarded. *Entrance requirements:* For master's, GMAT. Additional exam requirements/recommendations for international students: Required—TOEFL (minimum score 80 iBT), IELTS, PTE. *Application deadline:* Applications are processed on a rolling basis. Application fee: $50. Electronic applications accepted. Application fee is waived when completed online. *Expenses: Tuition:* Full-time $15,660; part-time $870 per credit hour. *Required fees:* $200; $85 per term. Tuition and fees vary according to program. *Financial support:* Research assistantships with partial tuition reimbursements, teaching assistantships with partial tuition reimbursements, career-related internships or fieldwork, Federal Work-Study, scholarships/grants, and unspecified assistantships available. Support available to part-time students. Financial award applicants required to submit FAFSA. *Unit head:* Gil B. Fried, Professor, 203-932-7081, E-mail: gfried@newhaven.edu.
Website: http://www.newhaven.edu/6851/

The University of North Carolina at Charlotte, William States Lee College of Engineering, Department of Engineering Technology and Construction Management, Charlotte, NC 28223-0001. Offers applied energy (Graduate Certificate); applied energy

and electromechanical systems (MS); construction and facilities management (MS); fire protection and administration (MS). *Program availability:* Part-time. *Faculty:* 26 full-time (5 women). *Students:* 46 full-time (8 women), 19 part-time (1 woman); includes 9 minority (4 Black or African American, non-Hispanic/Latino; 2 Asian, non-Hispanic/Latino; 3 Hispanic/Latino), 31 international. Average age 27. 71 applicants, 83% accepted, 24 enrolled. In 2016, 34 master's awarded. *Degree requirements:* For master's, thesis, capstone, or comprehensive exam. *Entrance requirements:* For master's, GRE, minimum undergraduate GPA of 3.0, recommendations, statistics; integral and differential calculus (for students pursuing fire protection concentration or applied energy and electromechanical systems program); for Graduate Certificate, bachelor's degree in engineering, engineering technology, construction management or a closely-related technical or scientific field; undergraduate coursework of at least 3 semesters in engineering analysis or calculus; minimum GPA of 3.0. Additional exam requirements/recommendations for international students: Required—TOEFL (minimum score 523 paper-based, 70 iBT) or IELTS (6.5). *Application deadline:* For fall admission, 3/1 priority date for domestic and international students; for spring admission, 10/1 priority date for domestic and international students. Applications are processed on a rolling basis. Application fee: $75. Electronic applications accepted. *Expenses:* Contact institution. *Financial support:* In 2016–17, 22 students received support, including 22 research assistantships (averaging $8,235 per year); career-related internships or fieldwork, institutionally sponsored loans, scholarships/grants, and unspecified assistantships also available. Support available to part-time students. Financial award application deadline: 3/1; financial award applicants required to submit FAFSA. *Total annual research expenditures:* $1.5 million. *Unit head:* Dr. Anthony Brizendine, Chair, 704-687-5050, E-mail: albrizen@uncc.edu. *Application contact:* Kathy B. Giddings, Director of Graduate Admissions, 704-687-5503, Fax: 704-687-1668, E-mail: gradadm@uncc.edu.
Website: http://et.uncc.edu/

Wentworth Institute of Technology, Master of Science in Facility Management Program, Boston, MA 02115-5998. Offers MS. *Program availability:* Part-time, evening/weekend, online only, 100% online, blended/hybrid learning. *Faculty:* 26 part-time/adjunct (7 women). *Students:* 22 part-time (18 women); includes 4 minority (2 Black or African American, non-Hispanic/Latino; 2 Two or more races, non-Hispanic/Latino). Average age 38. 23 applicants, 83% accepted, 12 enrolled. In 2016, 9 master's awarded. *Degree requirements:* For master's, thesis optional, capstone. *Entrance requirements:* For master's, current resume; two professional recommendation forms from current or former employer; statement of purpose; undergraduate degree in one of the following: architecture, facility management, engineering, construction management, business or interior design; one year of professional experience in technical role and/or technical organization. Additional exam requirements/recommendations for international students: Recommended—TOEFL (minimum score 525 paper-based). *Application deadline:* For fall admission, 8/1 for domestic and international students. Applications are processed on a rolling basis. Application fee: $50. Electronic applications accepted. *Expenses:* Contact institution. *Financial support:* Scholarships/grants available. Support available to part-time students. Financial award application deadline: 8/1; financial award applicants required to submit FAFSA. *Unit head:* Philip Hammond, Director of Graduate Programs, 617-989-4594, Fax: 617-989-4399, E-mail: hammondp1@wit.edu. *Application contact:* Martha Sheehan, Director of Admissions and Marketing, 617-989-4661, Fax: 617-989-4399, E-mail: sheehanm@wit.edu.
Website: http://www.wit.edu/continuinged/programs/facility-mgmt-masters.html

Section 7
Hospitality Management

This section contains a directory of institutions offering graduate work in hospitality management. Additional information about programs listed in the directory may be obtained by writing directly to the dean of a graduate school or chair of a department at the address given in the directory.

For programs offering related work, see also in this book *Business Administration and Management* and *Advertising and Public Relations.*

In the other guides in this series:

Graduate Programs in the Biological/Biomedical Sciences & Health-Related Medical Professions

See *Health Services*

Graduate Programs in the Physical Sciences, Mathematics, Agricultural Sciences, the Environment & Natural Resources

See *Agricultural and Food Sciences (Food Science and Technology)*

CONTENTS

Program Directories

Featured Schools: Displays and Close-Ups

See also:

Hospitality Management

Alabama Agricultural and Mechanical University, School of Graduate Studies, College of Agricultural, Life and Natural Sciences, Department of Family and Consumer Sciences, Huntsville, AL 35811. Offers apparel, merchandising and design (MS); family and consumer sciences (MS); human development and family studies (MS); nutrition and hospitality management (MS). *Program availability:* Part-time, evening/weekend. *Degree requirements:* For master's, comprehensive exam, thesis optional. *Entrance requirements:* For master's, GRE General Test. Additional exam requirements/recommendations for international students: Required—TOEFL (minimum score 500 paper-based; 61 iBT). *Application deadline:* For fall admission, 5/1 for domestic students. Applications are processed on a rolling basis. Application fee: $25. Electronic applications accepted. *Expenses:* Tuition, nonresident: part-time $826 per credit hour. Full-time tuition and fees vary according to course load and program. *Financial support:* Research assistantships with tuition reimbursements, teaching assistantships with tuition reimbursements, career-related internships or fieldwork, Federal Work-Study, and traineeships available. Financial award application deadline: 4/1. *Faculty research:* Food biotechnology, nutrition, food microbiology, food engineering, food chemistry. *Unit head:* Dr. Cynthia Smith, Chair, 256-372-4172, Fax: 256-372-5433, E-mail: cynthia.smith@aamu.edu.
Website: http://www.aamu.edu/academics/alns/consumersciences/

American International College, School of Business, Arts and Sciences, Springfield, MA 01109-3189. Offers accounting and taxation (MS); business administration (MBA); clinical psychology (MA); educational psychology (Ed D); forensic psychology (MS); general psychology (MA, CAGS); management (CAGS); resort and casino management (MBA, CAGS). *Program availability:* Part-time, evening/weekend. *Degree requirements:* For master's, comprehensive exam (for some programs), thesis (for some programs), practicum; for doctorate, comprehensive exam (for some programs), thesis/dissertation; for CAGS, comprehensive exam (for some programs), thesis (for some programs). *Entrance requirements:* For master's, BS or BA; for doctorate, interview. Additional exam requirements/recommendations for international students: Required—TOEFL (minimum score 550 paper-based; 80 iBT). *Expenses: Tuition:* Full-time $7902; part-time $750 per semester hour. *Required fees:* $60; $60 per semester hour. $30 per semester. One-time fee: $100. Tuition and fees vary according to course load, degree level, campus/location and program.

California State Polytechnic University, Pomona, Program in Hospitality Management, Pomona, CA 91768-2557. Offers MS. *Program availability:* Part-time, evening/weekend. *Students:* 12 full-time (10 women), 35 part-time (22 women); includes 14 minority (3 Black or African American, non-Hispanic/Latino; 7 Asian, non-Hispanic/Latino; 2 Hispanic/Latino; 2 Two or more races, non-Hispanic/Latino), 25 international. Average age 29. 17 applicants, 88% accepted, 12 enrolled. In 2016, 19 master's awarded. *Degree requirements:* For master's, thesis or professional paper. *Entrance requirements:* Additional exam requirements/recommendations for international students: Required—TOEFL. *Application deadline:* Applications are processed on a rolling basis. Application fee: $55. Electronic applications accepted. *Expenses:* Contact institution. *Financial support:* Application deadline: 3/2; applicants required to submit FAFSA. *Unit head:* Dr. Neha Singh, Program Director, 909-869-4565, Fax: 909-869-4805, E-mail: nsingh@cpp.edu. *Application contact:* Andrew M. Wright, Director of Admissions, 909-869-3130, Fax: 909-869-4529, E-mail: awright@cpp.edu.
Website: http://www.cpp.edu/~ceu/degree-programs/hospitality-management/index.shtml

California State University, Northridge, Graduate Studies, College of Health and Human Development, Department of Recreation and Tourism Management, Northridge, CA 91330. Offers hospitality and tourism (MS); recreational sport management/campus recreation (MS). *Faculty:* 7 full-time (4 women), 19 part-time/adjunct (8 women). *Students:* 22 full-time (10 women), 13 part-time (10 women); includes 12 minority (1 Black or African American, non-Hispanic/Latino; 7 Hispanic/Latino; 1 Native Hawaiian or other Pacific Islander, non-Hispanic/Latino; 3 Two or more races, non-Hispanic/Latino), 7 international. Average age 29. 57 applicants, 49% accepted, 18 enrolled. *Degree requirements:* For master's, thesis (for some programs). *Entrance requirements:* For master's, GRE (if cumulative undergraduate GPA less than 3.0). Additional exam requirements/recommendations for international students: Required—TOEFL. *Application deadline:* For fall admission, 11/30 for domestic students. Application fee: $55. *Expenses:* Tuition, state resident: full-time $4152. *Financial support:* Application deadline: 3/1. *Unit head:* Dr. Mechelle Best, Chair, 818-677-3202.
Website: http://www.csun.edu/hhd/rtm/

California State University, Northridge, Graduate Studies, The Tseng College of Extended Learning, Northridge, CA 91330. Offers business administration (Graduate Certificate); health administration (MPA); health education (MPH); knowledge management (MKM); music industry administration (MA); nonprofit-sector management (Graduate Certificate); public administration (MPA); public sector management and leadership (MPA); social work (MSW); taxation (MS); tourism, hospitality and recreation management (MS). *Faculty:* 55 part-time/adjunct (28 women). *Students:* 1 (woman) full-time, 1 (woman) part-time. Average age 40. *Entrance requirements:* For master's, GRE (if cumulative undergraduate GPA less than 3.0). *Expenses:* Tuition, state resident: full-time $4152. *Unit head:* Joyce Feucht-Haviar, Dean, 866-873-6439.

See Display on page 1664 and Close-Up on page 1687.

Cornell University, Graduate School, Field of Hotel Administration, Ithaca, NY 14853. Offers hospitality management (MMH); hotel administration (MS, PhD). Terminal master's awarded for partial completion of doctoral program. *Degree requirements:* For master's, thesis (MS); for doctorate, comprehensive exam, thesis/dissertation. *Entrance requirements:* For master's and doctorate, GMAT, 1 academic and 1 employer letter of recommendation, 2 interviews. Additional exam requirements/recommendations for international students: Required—TOEFL (minimum score 600 paper-based). Electronic applications accepted. *Faculty research:* Hospitality finance; property-asset management; real estate; management, strategy, and human resources; organizational communication.

Cornell University, Graduate School, Graduate Fields of Agriculture and Life Sciences, Field of Applied Economics and Management, Ithaca, NY 14853. Offers agricultural finance (MS, PhD); applied econometrics and qualitative analysis (MS, PhD); economics of development (MS, PhD); environmental economics (MS, PhD); environmental management (MPS); farm management and production economics (MS, PhD); marketing and food distribution (MS, PhD); public policy analysis (MS, PhD); resource economics (PhD). *Entrance requirements:* For master's and doctorate, GRE. Additional exam requirements/recommendations for international students: Required—TOEFL.

DePaul University, Kellstadt Graduate School of Business, Chicago, IL 60604. Offers accountancy (M Acc, MS, MSA); applied economics (MBA); banking (MBA); behavioral finance (MBA); brand and product management (MBA); business development (MBA); business information technology (MS); business strategy and decision-making (MBA); computational finance (MS); consumer insights (MBA); corporate finance (MBA); economic policy analysis (MS); entrepreneurship (MBA, MS); finance (MBA, MS); financial analysis (MBA); general business (MBA); health sector management (MBA); hospitality leadership (MBA); hospitality leadership and operational performance (MS); human resource management (MBA); human resources (MS); investment management (MBA); leadership and change management (MBA); management accounting (MBA); marketing (MBA, MS); marketing analysis (MS); marketing strategy and planning (MBA); operations management (MBA); organizational diversity (MBA); real estate (MS); real estate finance and investment (MBA); revenue management (MBA); sports management (MBA); strategic global marketing (MBA); strategy, execution and valuation (MBA); sustainable management (MBA, MS); taxation (MS); wealth management (MS); JD/MBA. *Accreditation:* AACSB. *Program availability:* Part-time, evening/weekend, online learning. *Entrance requirements:* For master's, GMAT, 2 letters of recommendation, resume, essay, official transcripts. Additional exam requirements/recommendations for international students: Required—TOEFL (minimum score 550 paper-based; 80 iBT). Electronic applications accepted. *Expenses:* Contact institution.

Drexel University, Goodwin College of Professional Studies, School of Technology and Professional Studies, Philadelphia, PA 19104-2875. Offers construction management (MS); creativity and innovation (MS); engineering technology (MS); food science (MS); hospitality management (MS); professional studies: creativity studies (MS); professional studies: e-learning leadership (MS); professional studies: homeland security management (MS); project management (MS); property management (MS); sport management (MS). *Program availability:* Part-time, evening/weekend. *Faculty:* 37 full-time (14 women). *Students:* 13 full-time, 462 part-time; includes 133 minority (86 Black or African American, non-Hispanic/Latino; 24 Asian, non-Hispanic/Latino; 23 Hispanic/Latino). In 2016, 88 master's awarded. *Entrance requirements:* Additional exam requirements/recommendations for international students: Required—TOEFL, IELTS. *Application deadline:* For fall admission, 9/1 for domestic students; for winter admission, 12/1 for domestic students; for spring admission, 3/1 for domestic students. Applications are processed on a rolling basis. Application fee: $75. Electronic applications accepted. Application fee is waived when completed online. *Expenses: Tuition:* Full-time $32,184; part-time $1192 per credit hour. *Required fees:* $280. Tuition and fees vary according to campus/location and program. *Financial support:* Applicants required to submit FAFSA. *Unit head:* Dr. William F. Lynch, Dean, 215-895-2159, E-mail: goodwin@drexel.edu. *Application contact:* Matthew Gray, Manager, Recruitment and Enrollment, 215-895-6255, Fax: 215-895-2153, E-mail: mdg67@drexel.edu.
Website: http://drexel.edu/grad/programs/goodwin/

East Carolina University, Graduate School, College of Business, School of Hospitality Leadership, Greenville, NC 27858-4353. Offers hospitality management (MBA). *Students:* 11 full-time (9 women), 5 part-time (4 women); includes 3 minority (all Black or African American, non-Hispanic/Latino). Average age 29. 4 applicants, 75% accepted, 2 enrolled. In 2016, 4 master's awarded. *Unit head:* Dr. Robert O'Halloran, Director, 252-737-1604, E-mail: ohalloranr@ecu.edu. *Application contact:* Dean of Graduate School, 252-328-6012, Fax: 252-328-6071, E-mail: gradschool@ecu.edu.
Website: http://www.ecu.edu/business/shl/

Eastern Michigan University, Graduate School, College of Technology, School of Technology and Professional Services Management, Programs in Hotel and Restaurant Management, Ypsilanti, MI 48197. Offers MS, Graduate Certificate. *Program availability:* Part-time, evening/weekend, online learning. *Students:* 1 (woman) full-time, 4 part-time (2 women); includes 1 minority (Black or African American, non-Hispanic/Latino). Average age 40. 6 applicants, 50% accepted, 2 enrolled. In 2016, 3 master's awarded. *Entrance requirements:* Additional exam requirements/recommendations for international students: Required—TOEFL. *Application deadline:* Applications are processed on a rolling basis. Application fee: $45. *Financial support:* Fellowships, research assistantships with full tuition reimbursements, teaching assistantships with full tuition reimbursements, career-related internships or fieldwork, Federal Work-Study, institutionally sponsored loans, scholarships/grants, tuition waivers (partial), and unspecified assistantships available. Support available to part-time students. Financial award applicants required to submit FAFSA. *Application contact:* Dr. Susan Gregory, Program Coordinator, 734-487-0845, Fax: 734-487-7690, E-mail: susan.gregory@emich.edu.

Ecole Hôtelière de Lausanne, Program in Hospitality Administration, Lausanne, Switzerland. Offers MHA. *Degree requirements:* For master's, project.

ESSEC Business School, Graduate Programs, Paris, France. Offers business administration (PhD); executive business administration (MBA); global business administration (MBA); hospitality management (MBA); international luxury brand management (MBA); management (MSM).

Fairleigh Dickinson University, College at Florham, Anthony J. Petrocelli College of Continuing Studies, International School of Hospitality and Tourism Management, Madison, NJ 07940-1099. Offers hospitality management studies (MS).

Fairleigh Dickinson University, Metropolitan Campus, Anthony J. Petrocelli College of Continuing Studies, International School of Hospitality and Tourism Management, Teaneck, NJ 07666-1914. Offers hospitality management (MS).

Florida International University, Chaplin School of Hospitality and Tourism Management, North Miami, FL 33181-3000. Offers MS. *Program availability:* Part-time, evening/weekend, online learning. *Faculty:* 20 full-time (6 women), 42 part-time/adjunct (13 women). *Students:* 170 full-time (106 women), 99 part-time (76 women); includes 92 minority (23 Black or African American, non-Hispanic/Latino; 5 Asian, non-Hispanic/Latino; 59 Hispanic/Latino; 1 Native Hawaiian or other Pacific Islander, non-Hispanic/Latino; 4 Two or more races, non-Hispanic/Latino), 148 international. Average age 27. 193 applicants, 72% accepted, 85 enrolled. In 2016, 161 master's awarded. *Degree requirements:* For master's, thesis (for some programs). *Entrance requirements:* For master's, minimum GPA of 3.0, 5 years of management experience (for executive track). Additional exam requirements/recommendations for international students: Required—TOEFL (minimum score 550 paper-based; 80 iBT). *Application deadline:* For fall admission, 6/1 for domestic students, 4/1 for international students; for spring admission, 10/1 for domestic students, 9/1 for international students. Applications are processed on a rolling basis. Application fee: $30. Electronic applications accepted. *Expenses:* Tuition, state resident: full-time $8912; part-time $446 per credit hour. Tuition, nonresident: full-time $21,393; part-time $992 per credit hour. *Required fees:* $2185; $195 per semester. Tuition and fees vary according to program. *Financial support:* Institutionally sponsored loans and scholarships/grants available. Financial award application deadline: 3/1; financial award applicants required to submit FAFSA.

Faculty research: Environmental sustainability in hospitality/lodging, casino marketing and management, management philosophy, strategic management and competitive advantage, legal liabilities of hotels and resorts for waterfront amenities. *Unit head:* Dr. Mike Hampton, Dean, 305-919-4018, E-mail: mhampton@fiu.edu. *Application contact:* Nanett Rojas, Manager, Admissions Operations, 305-348-7464, Fax: 305-348-7441, E-mail: gradadm@fiu.edu.
Website: http://hospitality.fiu.edu/

Georgetown University, Graduate School of Arts and Sciences, School of Continuing Studies, Washington, DC 20057. Offers American studies (MALS); Catholic studies (MALS); classical civilizations (MALS); emergency and disaster management (MPS); ethics and the professions (MALS); global strategic communications (MPS); hospitality management (MPS); human resources management (MPS); humanities (MALS); individualized study (MALS); integrated marketing communications (MPS); international affairs (MALS); Islam and Muslim-Christian relations (MALS); journalism (MPS); liberal studies (DLS); literature and society (MALS); medieval and early modern European studies (MALS); public relations and corporate communications (MPS); real estate (MPS); religious studies (MALS); social and public policy (MALS); sports industry management (MPS); systems engineering management (MPS); technology management (MPS); the theory and practice of American democracy (MALS); urban and regional planning (MPS); visual culture (MALS). MPS in systems engineering management offered jointly with Stevens Institute of Technology. *Entrance requirements:* Additional exam requirements/recommendations for international students: Required—TOEFL.

The George Washington University, School of Business, Department of Tourism and Hospitality Management, Washington, DC 20052. Offers destination management (Professional Certificate); event and meeting management (MTA); event management (Professional Certificate); hospitality management (MTA); individualized studies (MTA); sport management (MTA); sustainable tourism destination management (MTA); tourism and hospitality management (MBA). *Program availability:* Part-time, online learning. *Students:* 66 full-time (46 women), 38 part-time (30 women); includes 27 minority (16 Black or African American, non-Hispanic/Latino; 6 Asian, non-Hispanic/Latino; 3 Hispanic/Latino; 2 Two or more races, non-Hispanic/Latino), 44 international. Average age 28. 113 applicants, 76% accepted, 40 enrolled. In 2016, 45 master's awarded. *Degree requirements:* For master's, comprehensive exam, thesis. *Entrance requirements:* For master's, GRE General Test. Additional exam requirements/recommendations for international students: Required—TOEFL. *Application deadline:* For fall admission, 4/1 priority date for domestic students; for spring admission, 10/1 for domestic students. Applications are processed on a rolling basis. Application fee: $75. *Financial support:* In 2016–17, 32 students received support. Fellowships, teaching assistantships, career-related internships or fieldwork, Federal Work-Study, institutionally sponsored loans, and tuition waivers (partial) available. Financial award application deadline: 4/1. *Faculty research:* Tourism policy, tourism impact forecasting, geotourism. *Unit head:* Prof. Lisa Delpy Neirotti, Faculty Director, 202-994-6623, E-mail: delpy@gwu.edu. *Application contact:* Christopher Storer, Executive Director, Graduate Admissions, 202-994-1212, E-mail: gwmba@gwu.edu.
Website: http://business.gwu.edu/tourism/

Glion Institute of Higher Education, Graduate Programs, Glion-sur-Montreux, Switzerland. Offers hospitality organizational training (M Ed); hotel management with leadership (MBA); hotel management with marketing (MBA); international hospitality management (MBA). *Program availability:* Evening/weekend.

Hawai`i Pacific University, College of Business, Program in Business Administration, Honolulu, HI 96813. Offers accounting (MBA); economics (MBA); finance (MBA); hospitality and tourism management (MBA); human resource management (MBA); information systems (MBA); international business (MBA); management (MBA); marketing (MBA); organizational change and development (MBA). *Program availability:* Part-time, evening/weekend, online learning. *Faculty:* 13 full-time (4 women), 1 part-time/adjunct (0 women). *Students:* 106 full-time (47 women), 33 part-time (13 women); includes 66 minority (5 Black or African American, non-Hispanic/Latino; 1 American Indian or Alaska Native, non-Hispanic/Latino; 23 Asian, non-Hispanic/Latino; 11 Hispanic/Latino; 1 Native Hawaiian or other Pacific Islander, non-Hispanic/Latino; 25 Two or more races, non-Hispanic/Latino), 36 international. Average age 33. 77 applicants, 84% accepted, 44 enrolled. In 2016, 78 master's awarded. *Entrance requirements:* For master's, GMAT or GRE. Additional exam requirements/recommendations for international students: Recommended—TOEFL (minimum score 550 paper-based; 80 iBT), IELTS (minimum score 6), TWE (minimum score 5). *Application deadline:* For fall admission, 2/15 priority date for domestic students; for spring admission, 10/15 priority date for domestic students. Applications are processed on a rolling basis. Application fee: $50. Electronic applications accepted. *Expenses: Tuition:* Full-time $17,190; part-time $955 per credit. *Required fees:* $150; $26 per credit. Tuition and fees vary according to course load and program. *Financial support:* In 2016–17, 27 students received support. Research assistantships, career-related internships or fieldwork, Federal Work-Study, scholarships/grants, tuition waivers, and unspecified assistantships available. Financial award application deadline: 3/1; financial award applicants required to submit FAFSA. *Unit head:* Dr. Warren Wee, Associate Dean/Associate Professor of Accounting, 808-544-9325, E-mail: wwee@hpu.edu. *Application contact:* Danny Lam, Assistant Director of Graduate Admissions, 808-544-1135, E-mail: graduate@hpu.edu.
Website: http://www.hpu.edu/CBA/Graduate/MBA/index.html

Husson University, Master of Business Administration Program, Bangor, ME 04401-2999. Offers athletic administration (MBA); biotechnology and innovation (MBA); general business administration (MBA); healthcare management (MBA); hospitality and tourism management (MBA); organizational management (MBA); risk management (MBA). *Program availability:* Part-time, evening/weekend, 100% online, blended/hybrid learning. *Faculty:* 8 full-time (4 women), 20 part-time/adjunct (5 women). *Students:* 81 full-time (47 women), 249 part-time (142 women); includes 32 minority (9 Black or African American, non-Hispanic/Latino; 2 American Indian or Alaska Native, non-Hispanic/Latino; 17 Asian, non-Hispanic/Latino; 3 Hispanic/Latino; 1 Two or more races, non-Hispanic/Latino), 11 international. Average age 34. 199 applicants, 78% accepted, 119 enrolled. In 2016, 109 master's awarded. *Degree requirements:* For master's, comprehensive exam (for some programs), thesis optional. *Entrance requirements:* For master's, minimum GPA of 3.0, letter of recommendation. Additional exam requirements/recommendations for international students: Required—TOEFL (minimum score 550 paper-based; 80 iBT), IELTS (minimum score 6.5). *Application deadline:* Applications are processed on a rolling basis. Application fee: $50. Electronic applications accepted. *Expenses:* $450 per credit; $450 fees per full-time year or $220 part-time. *Financial support:* Career-related internships or fieldwork, Federal Work-Study, scholarships/grants, and unspecified assistantships available. Financial award application deadline: 4/15; financial award applicants required to submit FAFSA. *Unit head:* Prof. Stephanie Shayne, Director, Graduate and Online Programs, 207-404-5632, Fax: 207-992-4987, E-mail: shaynes@husson.edu. *Application contact:* Kristen Card, Director of Graduate Admissions, 207-404-5660, Fax: 207-941-7935, E-mail: cardk@husson.edu.
Website: http://www.husson.edu/college-of-business/school-of-business-and-management/master-of-business-administration-mba/

IGlobal University, Graduate Programs, Vienna, VA 22182. Offers accounting (MBA); data management and analytics (MSIT); entrepreneurship (MBA); finance (MBA); global business management (MBA); health care management (MBA); hospitality and tourism management (MBA); human resources management (MBA); information technology (MBA); information technology systems and management (MSIT); leadership and management (MBA); project management (MBA); public service and administration (MBA); software design and management (MSIT).

Johnson & Wales University, Graduate Studies, MAT Program in Teacher Education, Providence, RI 02903-3703. Offers business education and secondary special education (MAT); culinary arts education (MAT); elementary education and elementary special education (MAT); elementary education and elementary/secondary special education (MAT); elementary education and secondary special education (MAT); food service education (MAT). *Program availability:* Part-time, evening/weekend. *Entrance requirements:* For master's, MAT, minimum GPA of 2.75. Additional exam requirements/recommendations for international students: Required—TOEFL (minimum score 550 paper-based) or IELTS (recommended). *Faculty research:* Secondary education, student teaching, educational reform, evaluation procedures.

Johnson & Wales University, Graduate Studies, MBA Program, Providence, RI 02903-3703. Offers accounting (MBA); business administration (MBA); finance (MBA); hospitality (MBA); human resource management (MBA); information technology (MBA); nonprofit management (MBA); operations and supply chain management (MBA). Program also offered on Denver campus. *Program availability:* Part-time, online learning. *Entrance requirements:* For master's, minimum GPA of 2.75. Additional exam requirements/recommendations for international students: Required—TOEFL (minimum score 550 paper-based); Recommended—IELTS, TWE. *Faculty research:* International banking, global economy, international trade, cultural differences.

Kansas State University, Graduate School, College of Human Ecology, Department of Hospitality Management, Manhattan, KS 66506. Offers hospitality and dietetics administration (MS). *Program availability:* Part-time. *Faculty:* 5 full-time (3 women). *Students:* 2 full-time (1 woman), 2 part-time (1 woman), 2 international. Average age 26. 5 applicants, 40% accepted. In 2016, 4 master's awarded. *Degree requirements:* For master's, comprehensive exam (for some programs), thesis or alternative, residency. *Entrance requirements:* For master's, GRE or GMAT. Additional exam requirements/recommendations for international students: Required—TOEFL (minimum score 550 paper-based; 79 iBT). *Application deadline:* For fall admission, 2/1 priority date for domestic and international students; for spring admission, 8/1 priority date for domestic and international students. Applications are processed on a rolling basis. Application fee: $50 ($75 for international students). Electronic applications accepted. *Expenses:* $402.90 per credit hour, $250 campus privilege fee, $20 per credit course fees. *Financial support:* In 2016–17, 4 students received support, including 1 research assistantship with full tuition reimbursement available (averaging $13,000 per year), 3 teaching assistantships with full tuition reimbursements available (averaging $12,000 per year); scholarships/grants also available. Financial award application deadline: 2/1; financial award applicants required to submit FAFSA. *Faculty research:* Food and beverage management; lodging management; event management; sustainability; customer behaviors; human resource management; food safety in food service operations; gerontology and the hospitality industry; education, training, and career development in hospitality administration. *Total annual research expenditures:* $851,743. *Unit head:* Dr. Kevin Roberts, Interim Head, 785-532-5507, Fax: 785-532-5522, E-mail: kevrob@ksu.edu. *Application contact:* Starla McPheron-Hall, Administrative Specialist, 785-532-5521, Fax: 785-532-5522, E-mail: starla1@ksu.edu.
Website: http://www.he.k-state.edu/hm/

Kansas State University, Graduate School, College of Human Ecology, Doctorate in Human Ecology Program, Manhattan, KS 66506-1407. Offers apparel and textiles (PhD); applied family sciences (PhD); couple and family therapy (PhD); hospitality administration (PhD); kinesiology (PhD); life-span human development (PhD). *Program availability:* Part-time. *Faculty:* 36 full-time (23 women). *Students:* 44 full-time (26 women), 16 part-time (10 women); includes 9 minority (3 Black or African American, non-Hispanic/Latino; 2 Asian, non-Hispanic/Latino; 2 Hispanic/Latino; 2 Two or more races, non-Hispanic/Latino), 18 international. Average age 30. 43 applicants, 35% accepted, 8 enrolled. In 2016, 13 doctorates awarded. *Degree requirements:* For doctorate, thesis/dissertation. *Entrance requirements:* Additional exam requirements/recommendations for international students: Required—TOEFL. *Application deadline:* For fall admission, 2/1 priority date for domestic and international students; for spring admission, 8/1 priority date for domestic and international students. Applications are processed on a rolling basis. Application fee: $50 ($75 for international students). Electronic applications accepted. *Expenses:* Tuition, state resident: full-time $9670. Tuition, nonresident: full-time $21,828. *Required fees:* $862. *Financial support:* In 2016–17, research assistantships with partial tuition reimbursements (averaging $12,000 per year), teaching assistantships with partial tuition reimbursements (averaging $12,000 per year) were awarded. Financial award application deadline: 3/1. *Total annual research expenditures:* $1.8 million. *Unit head:* Dr. John Buckwalter, Dean, 785-532-5500, Fax: 785-532-5504, E-mail: jbb3@ksu.edu. *Application contact:* Dr. Bronwyn Fees, Associate Dean for Academic Affairs, 785-532-5500, Fax: 785-532-5504, E-mail: fees@ksu.edu.

Kent State University, College of Education, Health and Human Services, School of Foundations, Leadership and Administration, Program in Hospitality and Tourism Management, Kent, OH 44242-0001. Offers MS. *Program availability:* Part-time. *Degree requirements:* For master's, thesis optional. *Entrance requirements:* For master's, minimum GPA of 3.0, 3 letters of recommendation, resume, goals statement. Additional exam requirements/recommendations for international students: Required—TOEFL (minimum score 550 paper-based; 80 iBT). Electronic applications accepted. *Expenses:* Tuition, state resident: full-time $10,864; part-time $495 per credit hour. Tuition, nonresident: full-time $18,380; part-time $837 per credit hour. *Faculty research:* Training human service workers, health care services for older adults, early adolescent development, care-giving arrangements with aging families, peace and war.

Lasell College, Graduate and Professional Studies in Management, Newton, MA 02466-2709. Offers business administration (PMBA); elder care management (MSM, Graduate Certificate); hospitality and event management (MSM, Graduate Certificate); human resources management (MSM, Graduate Certificate); management (MSM, Graduate Certificate); marketing (MSM, Graduate Certificate); non-profit management (MSM, Graduate Certificate); project management (MSM, Graduate Certificate). *Accreditation:* ACBSP. *Program availability:* Part-time, evening/weekend, 100% online, blended/hybrid learning. *Faculty:* 3 full-time (2 women), 16 part-time/adjunct (10 women). *Students:* 47 full-time (34 women), 93 part-time (72 women); includes 28 minority (20 Black or African American, non-Hispanic/Latino; 4 Asian, non-Hispanic/Latino; 3 Hispanic/Latino; 1 Two or more races, non-Hispanic/Latino), 24 international. Average age 31. 121 applicants, 55% accepted, 32 enrolled. In 2016, 61 master's, 3 other advanced degrees awarded. *Degree requirements:* For master's, minimum GPA of 3.0; internship or research paper (for MSM). *Entrance requirements:* For master's, one-page personal statement, 2 letters of recommendation, resume, bachelor's degree

transcript; proof of microeconomics and statistics (for PMBA); for Graduate Certificate, bachelor's degree transcript, 2 letters of recommendation, 1-page personal statement, resume. Additional exam requirements/recommendations for international students: Required—TOEFL (minimum score 550 paper-based, 79 iBT) or IELTS (minimum score 6). *Application deadline:* For fall admission, 8/31 priority date for domestic students, 6/30 priority date for international students; for spring admission, 12/31 priority date for domestic students, 10/31 priority date for international students. Applications are processed on a rolling basis. Electronic applications accepted. *Expenses:* $600 per credit. *Financial support:* In 2016–17, 12 students received support. Federal Work-Study, scholarships/grants, and tuition discounts available. Support available to part-time students. Financial award application deadline: 8/31; financial award applicants required to submit FAFSA. *Unit head:* Dr. Joan Dolamore, Dean of Graduate and Professional Studies, 617-243-2485, Fax: 617-243-2450, E-mail: gradinfo@lasell.edu. *Application contact:* Adrienne Franciosi, Director of Graduate Enrollment, 617-243-2214, Fax: 617-243-2450, E-mail: gradinfo@lasell.edu.
Website: http://www.lasell.edu/academics/graduate-and-professional-studies/programs-of-study/master-of-science-in-management.html

Lasell College, Graduate and Professional Studies in Sport Management, Newton, MA 02466. Offers sport hospitality management (MS, Graduate Certificate); sport leadership (MS, Graduate Certificate); sport non-profit management (MS, Graduate Certificate). *Program availability:* Part-time, evening/weekend, online only, 100% online. *Faculty:* 4 full-time (0 women), 3 part-time/adjunct (1 woman). *Students:* 14 full-time (4 women), 30 part-time (10 women); includes 10 minority (9 Black or African American, non-Hispanic/Latino; 1 Hispanic/Latino). Average age 30. 40 applicants, 43% accepted, 9 enrolled. In 2016, 21 master's, 2 other advanced degrees awarded. *Degree requirements:* For master's, minimum GPA of 3.0; internship or thesis. *Entrance requirements:* For master's, one-page personal statement, 2 letters of recommendation, resume, bachelor's degree transcript; for Graduate Certificate, bachelor's degree transcript, 2 letters of recommendation, 1-page personal statement, resume. Additional exam requirements/recommendations for international students: Required—TOEFL (minimum score 550 paper-based, 79 iBT) or IELTS (minimum score 6). *Application deadline:* For fall admission, 8/31 priority date for domestic students, 6/30 priority date for international students; for spring admission, 12/31 priority date for domestic students, 10/31 priority date for international students. Applications are processed on a rolling basis. Electronic applications accepted. *Expenses:* $600 per credit. *Financial support:* In 2016–17, 4 students received support. Federal Work-Study, scholarships/grants, and tuition discounts available. Support available to part-time students. Financial award application deadline: 8/31; financial award applicants required to submit FAFSA. *Faculty research:* How do fans attribute team failure, investigating cross-cultural difference in attribution; sense of ownership as a key predictor of fan loyalty; fans' normative beliefs about sponsorship and sponsors, investigation of new attitudinal variables in sponsorship. *Unit head:* Dr. Joan Dolamore, Dean of Graduate and Professional Studies, 617-243-2485, Fax: 617-243-2450, E-mail: gradinfo@lasell.edu. *Application contact:* Adrienne Franciosi, Director of Graduate Enrollment, 617-243-2214, Fax: 617-243-2450, E-mail: gradinfo@lasell.edu.
Website: http://www.lasell.edu/academics/graduate-and-professional-studies/programs-of-study/master-of-science-in-sport-management.html

Les Roches International School of Hotel Management, Program in Hospitality Management, Bluche, Switzerland. Offers MBA. Available only at Switzerland campus.

Lynn University, College of Business and Management, Boca Raton, FL 33431-5598. Offers business administration (MBA), including aviation management, financial valuation and investment management, hospitality management, human resource management, international business management, marketing, media management, sports management. *Program availability:* Part-time, evening/weekend, 100% online, blended/hybrid learning. *Faculty:* 24 full-time (9 women), 24 part-time/adjunct (4 women). *Students:* 265 full-time (125 women), 182 part-time (96 women); includes 100 minority (41 Black or African American, non-Hispanic/Latino; 11 Asian, non-Hispanic/Latino; 42 Hispanic/Latino; 6 Two or more races, non-Hispanic/Latino), 119 international. Average age 28. 280 applicants, 94% accepted, 181 enrolled. In 2016, 219 master's awarded. *Degree requirements:* For master's, strategic management seminar, simulation capstone. *Entrance requirements:* For master's, bachelor's degree from accredited institution, resume, letter of recommendation, official transcripts, essay/personal statement. Additional exam requirements/recommendations for international students: Required—TOEFL (minimum score 550 paper-based; 80 iBT), IELTS (minimum score 6.5). *Application deadline:* For fall admission, 8/18 for domestic students, 8/4 for international students; for spring admission, 12/15 for domestic students, 12/1 for international students; for summer admission, 4/17 for domestic students, 4/3 for international students. Applications are processed on a rolling basis. Application fee: $45. Electronic applications accepted. *Expenses:* $725 per credit. *Financial support:* In 2016–17, 115 students received support. Career-related internships or fieldwork, Federal Work-Study, scholarships/grants, tuition waivers (full and partial), and unspecified assistantships available. Support available to part-time students. Financial award application deadline: 3/1; financial award applicants required to submit FAFSA. *Faculty research:* Market volatility investing, biometric research, sports legal history, organizational leadership, urban economic development and productivity. *Unit head:* Dr. RT Good, Dean of the College of Business and Management, 561-237-7458, E-mail: rgood@lynn.edu. *Application contact:* Steven Pruitt, Director of Graduate and Undergraduate Evening Admission, 561-237-7834, Fax: 561-237-7100, E-mail: spruitt@lynn.edu.
Website: http://www.lynn.edu/academics/colleges/business-and-management

Marylhurst University, Department of Food Systems and Society, Marylhurst, OR 97036-0261. Offers MS. *Program availability:* Part-time, blended/hybrid learning. *Students:* 21 (20 women); includes 3 minority (1 Black or African American, non-Hispanic/Latino; 1 Hispanic/Latino; 1 Two or more races, non-Hispanic/Latino). Average age 35. *Degree requirements:* For master's, thesis. *Entrance requirements:* For master's, official transcript from regionally-accredited institution, recommendations, statement of intent, writing sample, resume. Additional exam requirements/recommendations for international students: Required—TOEFL (minimum score 550 paper-based; 79 iBT), IELTS (minimum score 6.5), PTE (minimum score 53). *Application deadline:* For fall admission, 3/15 priority date for domestic students. Applications are processed on a rolling basis. Application fee: $0. Electronic applications accepted. *Expenses:* Contact institution. *Financial support:* Career-related internships or fieldwork and scholarships/grants available. Support available to part-time students. Financial award applicants required to submit FAFSA. *Faculty research:* Political economic structures, social justice, food policy, food systems, social change. *Unit head:* Dr. Sean Gillon, Chair, Department of Interdisciplinary and Applied Liberal Arts, 503-534-4037, E-mail: sgillon@marylhurst.edu. *Application contact:* Maruska Lynch, Graduate Admissions Counselor, 503-699-6268, E-mail: admissions@marylhurst.edu.
Website: http://marylhurst.edu/academics/schools-colleges-departments/food-systems-society/ms-food-systems-society/

Michigan State University, The Graduate School, Eli Broad College of Business, The School of Hospitality Business, East Lansing, MI 48224. Offers foodservice business management (MS); hospitality business management (MS). *Degree requirements:* For master's, comprehensive exam, research project. *Entrance requirements:* For master's, GMAT or GRE, minimum GPA of 3.0 in last 2 years of undergraduate course work, resume, 3 letters of recommendation, 2 official transcripts, at least 1 year of professional work experience. Additional exam requirements/recommendations for international students: Required—TOEFL (minimum score 580 paper-based; 87 iBT). Electronic applications accepted. *Faculty research:* Corporate food service management, entrepreneurial and food service management, hospitality business.

Monroe College, King Graduate School, Bronx, NY 10468. Offers accounting (MS); business administration (MBA), including entrepreneurship, finance, general business administration, healthcare management, human resources, information technology, marketing; computer science (MS); criminal justice (MS); hospitality management (MS); public health (MPH), including biostatistics and epidemiology, community health, health administration and leadership. *Program availability:* Online learning. Application fee: $50.
Website: https://www.monroecollege.edu/Degrees/King-Graduate-School/

New York University, School of Continuing and Professional Studies, Tisch Center for Hospitality and Tourism, Program in Hospitality Industry Studies, New York, NY 10012-1019. Offers brand strategy (MS); hospitality industry studies (Advanced Certificate); hotel finance (MS); lodging operations (MS); revenue management (MS). *Program availability:* Part-time, evening/weekend. *Degree requirements:* For master's, thesis. *Entrance requirements:* For master's, GRE or GMAT (only upon request), bachelor's degree, resume with relevant professional work, internship or volunteer experience, two letters of recommendation, statement of purpose. Additional exam requirements/recommendations for international students: Required—TOEFL (minimum score 600 paper-based; 100 iBT), IELTS (minimum score 7). Electronic applications accepted.

New York University, Steinhardt School of Culture, Education, and Human Development, Department of Nutrition, Food Studies, and Public Health, Program in Food Studies, New York, NY 10010. Offers food studies (MA, PhD), including food culture (MA), food systems (MA). *Program availability:* Part-time. *Degree requirements:* For master's, thesis (for some programs); for doctorate, thesis/dissertation. *Entrance requirements:* For doctorate, GRE General Test, interview. Additional exam requirements/recommendations for international students: Required—TOEFL (minimum score 100 iBT). Electronic applications accepted. *Faculty research:* Cultural and social history of food, food systems and agriculture, food and aesthetics, political economy of food.

Oklahoma State University, College of Human Sciences, School of Hotel and Restaurant Administration, Stillwater, OK 74078. Offers MS, PhD. *Faculty:* 14 full-time (8 women), 4 part-time/adjunct (1 woman). *Students:* 10 full-time (6 women), 12 part-time (10 women); includes 7 minority (3 Black or African American, non-Hispanic/Latino; 3 Asian, non-Hispanic/Latino; 1 Hispanic/Latino), 13 international. Average age 30. 9 applicants, 67% accepted, 6 enrolled. In 2016, 5 master's, 6 doctorates awarded. *Degree requirements:* For master's, thesis (for some programs); for doctorate, comprehensive exam, thesis/dissertation. *Entrance requirements:* For master's and doctorate, GRE or GMAT. Additional exam requirements/recommendations for international students: Required—TOEFL (minimum score 550 paper-based; 79 iBT). *Application deadline:* For fall admission, 3/1 priority date for international students; for spring admission, 8/1 priority date for international students. Applications are processed on a rolling basis. Application fee: $40 ($75 for international students). Electronic applications accepted. *Expenses:* Tuition, state resident: full-time $3775; part-time $209.70 per credit hour. Tuition, nonresident: full-time $14,851; part-time $825.05 per credit hour. *Required fees:* $2027; $112.60 per credit hour. Tuition and fees vary according to campus/location. *Financial support:* In 2016–17, 10 research assistantships (averaging $13,429 per year), 16 teaching assistantships (averaging $12,342 per year) were awarded; career-related internships or fieldwork, Federal Work-Study, scholarships/grants, health care benefits, tuition waivers (partial), and unspecified assistantships also available. Support available to part-time students. Financial award application deadline: 3/1; financial award applicants required to submit FAFSA. *Faculty research:* Hotel operations and management, restaurant/food service management, hospitality education, hospitality human resources management, tourism. *Unit head:* Dr. Ben Goh, Director, 405-744-7651, Fax: 405-744-6299, E-mail: ben.goh@okstate.edu. *Application contact:* Dr. Li Miao, Graduate Coordinator, 405-744-1277, Fax: 405-744-6299, E-mail: lm@okstate.edu.
Website: http://humansciences.okstate.edu/hrad/

Penn State University Park, Graduate School, College of Health and Human Development, School of Hospitality Management, University Park, PA 16802. Offers MS, PhD. *Unit head:* Dr. Ann C. Crouter, Dean, 814-865-1420, Fax: 814-865-3282. *Application contact:* Lori Hawn, Director, Graduate Student Services, 814-865-1795, Fax: 814-863-4627, E-mail: l-gswww@lists.psu.edu.
Website: http://hhd.psu.edu/shm

Pontificia Universidad Catolica Madre y Maestra, Graduate School, Faculty of Social and Administrative Sciences, Santiago, Dominican Republic. Offers business administration (MBA), including business development, finance, international business, management skills (M Mgmt, MBA), marketing, operations, strategic cost management, strategy, tourist destination planning and management; law (LL M), including civil law, corporate business law, criminal law, international relations, real estate law; management (M Mgmt), including higher financial management, insurance program administration, management skills (M Mgmt, MBA); psychology (MA), including clinical child and adolescent psychology, forensic psychology; strategic human resources (EMBA).

Purdue University, Graduate School, College of Health and Human Sciences, School of Hospitality and Tourism Management, West Lafayette, IN 47907. Offers MS, PhD. *Program availability:* Online learning. *Faculty:* 17 full-time (6 women), 1 part-time/adjunct (0 women). *Students:* 38 full-time (26 women), 15 part-time (9 women); includes 3 minority (1 Asian, non-Hispanic/Latino; 2 Hispanic/Latino), 43 international. Average age 29. 79 applicants, 61% accepted, 12 enrolled. In 2016, 18 master's, 7 doctorates awarded. *Degree requirements:* For master's, thesis; for doctorate, thesis/dissertation. *Entrance requirements:* For master's, GMAT (minimum score of 550) or GRE General Test (minimum combined verbal and quantitative score of 290 new scoring, minimum of 145 each section, or 1000 with 500 each section, old scoring), minimum GPA of 3.0; for doctorate, GMAT (minimum score of 550) or GRE General Test (minimum combined verbal and quantitative score of 290 new scoring, minimum of 145 each section, or 1000 with 500 each section, old scoring), minimum undergraduate GPA of 3.0; master's degree with minimum GPA of 3.0 or equivalent. Additional exam requirements/recommendations for international students: Required—TOEFL (minimum score 77 iBT), TWE. *Application deadline:* For fall admission, 3/5 priority date for domestic and international students; for spring admission, 9/20 for domestic and international students. Applications are processed on a rolling basis. Application fee: $60 ($75 for international students). Electronic applications accepted. *Financial support:* Research assistantships, teaching assistantships, and career-related internships or fieldwork available. Support available to part-time students. Financial award applicants required to submit FAFSA. *Faculty research:* Human resources, marketing, hotel and restaurant operations, food product and equipment development, tourism development. *Unit head:* Dr. Richard F. Ghiselli, Head, 765-494-2636, E-mail: ghiselli@purdue.edu. *Application*

contact: Ayrielle K. Espinosa, Graduate Contact, 765-494-9811, E-mail: camposm@purdue.edu.
Website: http://www.purdue.edu/hhs/htm/

Rochester Institute of Technology, Graduate Enrollment Services, College of Applied Science and Technology, School of International Hospitality and Service Innovation, MS Program in Hospitality and Tourism Management, Rochester, NY 14623. Offers MS. *Program availability:* Part-time, evening/weekend. *Students:* 6 full-time (1 woman), 5 part-time (3 women); includes 2 minority (both Black or African American, non-Hispanic/Latino), 8 international. Average age 34. 33 applicants, 64% accepted, 2 enrolled. In 2016, 11 master's awarded. *Degree requirements:* For master's, thesis or alternative. *Entrance requirements:* For master's, minimum GPA of 3.0 (recommended). Additional exam requirements/recommendations for international students: Required—TOEFL (minimum score 570 paper-based; 88 iBT), IELTS (minimum score 6.5), PTE (minimum score 61). *Application deadline:* Applications are processed on a rolling basis. Application fee: $60. Electronic applications accepted. *Expenses:* $1,742 per credit hour. *Financial support:* In 2016–17, 14 students received support. Teaching assistantships with partial tuition reimbursements available, career-related internships or fieldwork, scholarships/grants, and unspecified assistantships available. Support available to part-time students. Financial award applicants required to submit FAFSA. *Faculty research:* Service innovation and technology integration, innovative food product development, hospitality employees' occupational health and wellness, tourist behaviors, destination management. *Unit head:* Yu-Chin Hsieh, Department Chair, 585-475-2355, E-mail: yhsieh@rit.edu. *Application contact:* Diane Ellison, Associate Vice President, Graduate Enrollment Services, 585-475-2229, Fax: 585-475-7164, E-mail: gradinfo@rit.edu.
Website: http://www.rit.edu/cast/htm/graduate-program

Rochester Institute of Technology, Graduate Enrollment Services, College of Applied Science and Technology, School of International Hospitality and Service Innovation, MS Program in Service Leadership and Innovation, Rochester, NY 14623. Offers MS. *Program availability:* Part-time, evening/weekend, 100% online. *Students:* 14 full-time (9 women), 35 part-time (23 women); includes 3 minority (1 Black or African American, non-Hispanic/Latino; 2 Hispanic/Latino), 4 international. Average age 31. 55 applicants, 44% accepted, 14 enrolled. In 2016, 5 master's awarded. *Degree requirements:* For master's, thesis or alternative. *Entrance requirements:* For master's, minimum GPA of 3.0 (recommended). Additional exam requirements/recommendations for international students: Required—TOEFL (minimum score 570 paper-based; 88 iBT), IELTS (minimum score 6.5), PTE (minimum score 62). *Application deadline:* Applications are processed on a rolling basis. Application fee: $60. Electronic applications accepted. *Expenses:* $1,742 per credit hour. *Financial support:* In 2016–17, 8 students received support. Teaching assistantships with partial tuition reimbursements available, career-related internships or fieldwork, scholarships/grants, and unspecified assistantships available. Support available to part-time students. Financial award applicants required to submit FAFSA. *Faculty research:* Leadership development, customer service/patient satisfaction, program evaluation, knowledge construction, diversity, individual creativity, healthcare applications. *Unit head:* Dr. Linda Underhill, Department Chair, 585-475-7359, E-mail: lmuism@rit.edu. *Application contact:* Diane Ellison, Associate Vice President, Graduate Enrollment Services, 585-475-2229, Fax: 585-475-7164, E-mail: gradinfo@rit.edu.
Website: http://www.rit.edu/cast/servicesystems/service-leadership-innovation

Roosevelt University, Graduate Division, College of Professional Studies, Program in Hospitality and Tourism Management, Chicago, IL 60605. Offers MS. *Students:* 13 full-time (11 women), 14 part-time (13 women); includes 16 minority (12 Black or African American, non-Hispanic/Latino; 3 Asian, non-Hispanic/Latino; 1 Two or more races, non-Hispanic/Latino), 6 international. Average age 30. 20 applicants, 100% accepted, 9 enrolled. In 2016, 22 master's awarded. *Degree requirements:* For master's, thesis. *Entrance requirements:* For master's, minimum GPA of 2.75, work experience. *Application deadline:* For fall admission, 6/1 priority date for domestic students. Applications are processed on a rolling basis. Application fee: $25 ($35 for international students). *Expenses: Tuition, area resident:* Full-time $19,566; part-time $880 per credit hour. *Required fees:* $175 per semester. One-time fee: $200. Part-time tuition and fees vary according to course load, degree level and program. *Financial support:* Application deadline: 2/15. *Unit head:* Carol Brown, Director, 312-281-3181. *Application contact:* Angela Ryan, Director of Graduate Enrollment, 877-APPLY RU, Fax: 312-281-3356, E-mail: applyru@roosevelt.edu.
Website: https://www.roosevelt.edu/academics/programs/masters-in-hospitality-and-tourism-management-mshtm

Royal Roads University, Graduate Studies, Tourism and Hotel Management Program, Victoria, BC V9B 5Y2, Canada. Offers destination development (Graduate Certificate); international hotel management (MA); sustainable tourism (Graduate Certificate); tourism leadership (Graduate Certificate); tourism management (MA).

San Francisco State University, Division of Graduate Studies, College of Business, Program in Business Administration, San Francisco, CA 94132-1722. Offers decision sciences/operations research (MBA); ethics and compliance (MBA); finance (MBA); global business and innovation (MBA); healthcare administration (MBA); hospitality and tourism management (MBA); information systems (MBA); leadership (MBA); marketing (MBA); nonprofit and social enterprise leadership (MBA); sustainable business (MBA). *Accreditation:* AACSB. *Program availability:* Part-time, evening/weekend. *Degree requirements:* For master's, thesis, essay test. *Entrance requirements:* For master's, GMAT, minimum GPA of 2.7 in last 60 units. Additional exam requirements/recommendations for international students: Required—TOEFL (minimum score 550 paper-based). *Application deadline:* For fall admission, 5/1 priority date for domestic students, 4/1 for international students; for spring admission, 11/1 for domestic students, 10/15 for international students. Applications are processed on a rolling basis. Application fee: $55. *Expenses:* Tuition, state resident: full-time $6738. Tuition, nonresident: full-time $15,666. *Required fees:* $1012. Tuition and fees vary according to degree level and program. *Financial support:* Application deadline: 3/1. *Unit head:* Dr. Sanjit Sengupta, Faculty Director, 415-817-4366, Fax: 415-817-4340, E-mail: sengupta@sfsu.edu. *Application contact:* Zandra Tan, EMBA Program Coordinator, 415-817-4360, Fax: 415-817-4340, E-mail: zandra13@sfsu.edu.
Website: http://cob.sfsu.edu/graduate-programs/mba

Schiller International University, MBA Programs, Florida, Program in International Hotel and Tourism Management, Largo, FL 33771. Offers MBA. *Degree requirements:* For master's, thesis optional. *Entrance requirements:* Additional exam requirements/recommendations for international students: Required—TOEFL (minimum score 550 paper-based).

South University, Graduate Programs, College of Business, Savannah, GA 31406. Offers corrections (MBA); entrepreneurship and small business (MBA); healthcare administration (MBA); hospitality management (MBA); leadership (MS); public administration (MPA); sustainability (MBA).

Stratford University, Program in International Hospitality Management, Baltimore, MD 21202. Offers MS. *Program availability:* Part-time, evening/weekend, online learning.

Stratford University, School of Graduate Studies, Falls Church, VA 22043. Offers accounting (MS); business administration (IMBA, MBA); cyber security (MS); cyber security leadership and policy (MS); digital forensics (MS); enterprise business management (MS); entrepreneurial management (MS); healthcare administration (MS); information systems (MS); international hospitality management (MS); networking and telecommunications (MS); software engineering (MS). *Program availability:* Part-time, evening/weekend, 100% online, blended/hybrid learning. *Students:* 505 full-time (186 women), 172 part-time (88 women); includes 532 minority (165 Black or African American, non-Hispanic/Latino; 18 American Indian or Alaska Native, non-Hispanic/Latino; 324 Asian, non-Hispanic/Latino; 13 Hispanic/Latino; 10 Native Hawaiian or other Pacific Islander, non-Hispanic/Latino; 2 Two or more races, non-Hispanic/Latino). Average age 27. In 2016, 520 master's awarded. *Degree requirements:* For master's, comprehensive exam, capstone project. *Entrance requirements:* For master's, GRE or GMAT, baccalaureate degree. Additional exam requirements/recommendations for international students: Required—TOEFL (minimum score 79 iBT), IELTS (minimum score 6.5), PTE (minimum score 5). *Application deadline:* Applications are processed on a rolling basis. Application fee: $50. Electronic applications accepted. *Expenses: Tuition:* Full-time $4455; part-time $2227.50 per course. One-time fee: $100. *Financial support:* Federal Work-Study and scholarships/grants available. Financial award applicants required to submit FAFSA. *Unit head:* Dr. Richard R. Shurtz, President, 703-539-6890, Fax: 703-539-6960. *Application contact:* Admissions, 800-444-0804, E-mail: fcadmissions@stratford.edu.

Strayer University, Graduate Studies, Washington, DC 20005-2603. Offers accounting (MS); acquisition (MBA); business administration (MBA); communications technology (MS); educational management (M Ed); finance (MBA); health services administration (MHSA); hospitality and tourism management (MBA); human resource management (MBA); information systems (MS), including computer security management, decision support system management, enterprise resource management, network management, software engineering management, systems development management; management (MBA); management information systems (MS); marketing (MBA); professional accounting (MS), including accounting information systems, controllership, taxation; public administration (MPA); supply chain management (MBA); technology in education (M Ed). Programs also offered at campus locations in Birmingham, AL; Chamblee, GA; Cobb County, GA; Morrow, GA; White Marsh, MD; Charleston, SC; Columbia, SC; Greensboro, NC; Greenville, SC; Lexington, KY; Louisville, KY; Nashville, TN; North Raleigh, NC; Washington, DC. *Accreditation:* ACBSP. *Program availability:* Part-time, evening/weekend, online learning. *Degree requirements:* For master's, thesis. *Entrance requirements:* For master's, GMAT, GRE General Test, bachelor's degree from an accredited college or university, minimum undergraduate GPA of 2.75. Electronic applications accepted.

Syracuse University, David B. Falk College of Sport and Human Dynamics, Program in Food Studies, Syracuse, NY 13244. Offers MS, CAS. *Program availability:* Part-time. *Degree requirements:* For master's, thesis or final practicum project. *Entrance requirements:* For master's, GRE, three letters of recommendation, resume, personal statement, official transcripts. *Application deadline:* For fall admission, 2/15 priority date for domestic and international students; for spring admission, 11/15 priority date for domestic and international students. Application fee: $75. Electronic applications accepted. *Expenses: Tuition:* Full-time $25,974; part-time $1443 per credit hour. *Required fees:* $802; $50 per course. Tuition and fees vary according to course load and program. *Financial support:* Fellowships, research assistantships, teaching assistantships, career-related internships or fieldwork, and scholarships/grants available. Financial award application deadline: 1/1. *Faculty research:* Food and nutrition systems and economies, linkages between sustainable agriculture and development, human rights and the right to adequate food and nutrition, food sovereignty, urban-rural food linkages in terms of production for trade and household consumption. *Unit head:* Anne C. Bellows, Director, 315-443-4228, E-mail: acbellow@syr.edu. *Application contact:* Felicia Otero, Director of College Admissions, 315-443-5555, Fax: 315-443-2562, E-mail: falk@syr.edu.
Website: http://falk.syr.edu/FoodStudies/Masters.aspx

Temple University, Fox School of Business, Doctoral Programs in Business, Philadelphia, PA 19122-6096. Offers accounting (PhD); entrepreneurship (PhD); finance (PhD); international business (PhD); management information systems (PhD); marketing (PhD); risk management and insurance (PhD); statistics (PhD); strategic management (PhD); tourism and sport (PhD). *Accreditation:* AACSB. *Degree requirements:* For doctorate, thesis/dissertation. *Entrance requirements:* For doctorate, GRE General Test, GMAT, minimum GPA of 3.0, master's degree. Additional exam requirements/recommendations for international students: Required—TOEFL (minimum score 600 paper-based; 100 iBT), IELTS (minimum score 7.5). Electronic applications accepted.

★ **Temple University,** School of Sport, Tourism and Hospitality Management, Philadelphia, PA 19122-6096. Offers sport business (MS); tourism and hospitality management (MTHM); tourism and sport (PhD); travel and tourism (MS). *Program availability:* Part-time, evening/weekend. *Faculty:* 21 full-time (7 women), 10 part-time/adjunct (3 women). *Students:* 95 full-time (47 women), 32 part-time (16 women); includes 37 minority (27 Black or African American, non-Hispanic/Latino; 6 Hispanic/Latino; 4 Two or more races, non-Hispanic/Latino), 22 international. 152 applicants, 70% accepted, 66 enrolled. In 2016, 31 master's awarded. *Degree requirements:* For master's, thesis optional, internship/project; for doctorate, thesis/dissertation. *Entrance requirements:* For master's, GRE General Test, GMAT, or MAT, bachelor's degree or equivalent with minimum GPA of 3.0, 500-word essay, 2 letters of recommendation, resume; for doctorate, GMAT or GRE. Additional exam requirements/recommendations for international students: Required—TOEFL (minimum score 550 paper-based; 79 iBT), IELTS (minimum score 6.5). *Application deadline:* For fall admission, 3/1 priority date for domestic students, 1/15 priority date for international students; for spring admission, 8/15 priority date for domestic students, 6/30 priority date for international students. Applications are processed on a rolling basis. Application fee: $60. Electronic applications accepted. *Expenses:* Contact institution. *Financial support:* Fellowships with full tuition reimbursements, research assistantships with full tuition reimbursements, and teaching assistantships with full tuition reimbursements available. Financial award application deadline: 3/1; financial award applicants required to submit FAFSA. *Unit head:* Dr. M. Moshe Porat, Dean, 215-204-1836, Fax: 215-204-8705, E-mail: porat@temple.edu. *Application contact:* James Alton, Manager of Graduate Student Services, 215-204-7140, Fax: 215-204-8705, E-mail: jim.alton@temple.edu.
Website: http://sthm.temple.edu/

See Display on next page and Close-Ups on pages 349 and 1651.

Texas Tech University, Graduate School, College of Human Sciences, Department of Hospitality and Retail Management, Lubbock, TX 79409. Offers hospitality administration (PhD); hospitality and retail management (MS). *Program availability:* Part-time, evening/weekend. *Faculty:* 23 full-time (12 women), 1 (woman) part-time/adjunct. *Students:* 32 full-time (12 women), 8 part-time (5 women); includes 5 minority (3 Black or African American, non-Hispanic/Latino; 2 Hispanic/Latino), 16 international. Average age 31. 42 applicants, 43% accepted, 9 enrolled. In 2016, 15 master's, 10 doctorates awarded. Terminal master's awarded for partial completion of doctoral program. *Degree*

requirements: For master's, thesis or alternative; for doctorate, thesis/dissertation. *Entrance requirements:* For master's, GRE, professional experience (restaurant, hotel, and institutional management); for doctorate, GRE General Test. Additional exam requirements/recommendations for international students: Required—TOEFL (minimum score 550 paper-based; 79 iBT), IELTS (minimum score 6.5). *Application deadline:* For fall admission, 6/1 priority date for domestic students, 1/15 priority date for international students; for spring admission, 9/1 priority date for domestic students, 6/15 priority date for international students. Applications are processed on a rolling basis. Application fee: $75. Electronic applications accepted. *Expenses:* $315 per credit hour full-time resident tuition, $723 per credit hour full-time non-resident tuition; $50.50 per credit hour fee plus $608 per term fee. *Financial support:* In 2016–17, 37 students received support, including 36 fellowships (averaging $4,567 per year), 6 research assistantships (averaging $5,705 per year), 23 teaching assistantships (averaging $9,768 per year). Financial award application deadline: 4/15; financial award applicants required to submit FAFSA. *Faculty research:* Cultural intelligence, lodging, emotional intelligence, consumer behavior, beverage. *Total annual research expenditures:* $47,055. *Unit head:* Dr. Shane Blum, Chair, 806-834-8811, Fax: 806-742-3042, E-mail: shane.blum@ttu.edu. *Application contact:* Dr. David Rivera, Jr., Graduate Coordinator, Hospitality and Retail Management, 806-834-8187, Fax: 806-742-3042, E-mail: david.rivera@ttu.edu.
Website: http://www.depts.ttu.edu/hs/hrm/

The University of Alabama, Graduate School, College of Human Environmental Sciences, Department of Human Nutrition and Hospitality Management, Tuscaloosa, AL 35487. Offers MSHES. *Program availability:* Part-time, online only, 100% online. *Faculty:* 13 full-time (11 women). *Students:* 20 full-time (all women), 96 part-time (93 women); includes 8 minority (3 Black or African American, non-Hispanic/Latino; 2 Hispanic/Latino; 3 Two or more races, non-Hispanic/Latino), 1 international. Average age 30. 77 applicants, 66% accepted, 35 enrolled. In 2016, 45 master's awarded. *Degree requirements:* For master's, comprehensive exam, thesis optional. *Entrance requirements:* For master's, minimum GPA of 3.0. Additional exam requirements/recommendations for international students: Required—TOEFL, IELTS. *Application deadline:* For fall admission, 6/1 for domestic students; for spring admission, 11/1 for domestic students; for summer admission, 4/1 for domestic students. Applications are processed on a rolling basis. Application fee: $50 ($60 for international students). Electronic applications accepted. *Expenses:* Tuition, state resident: full-time $10,470. Tuition, nonresident: full-time $26,950. *Financial support:* In 2016–17, 4 students received support, including 2 research assistantships (averaging $8,100 per year), 4 teaching assistantships (averaging $8,100 per year); career-related internships or fieldwork also available. Financial award application deadline: 3/15. *Faculty research:* Maternal and child nutrition, childhood obesity, community nutrition interventions, geriatric nutrition, family eating patterns, food chemistry, phytochemicals, dietary antioxidants. *Total annual research expenditures:* $120,989. *Unit head:* Dr. Jeannine C. Lawrence, Chair/Associate Professor, 205-348-6252, Fax: 205-348-2982, E-mail: jlawrence@ches.ua.edu. *Application contact:* Patrick D. Fuller, Admissions Officer, 205-348-5923, Fax: 205-348-0400, E-mail: patrick.d.fuller@ua.edu.
Website: http://www.nhm.ches.ua.edu/

The University of Alabama, Graduate School, College of Human Environmental Sciences, Program in Human Environmental Science, Tuscaloosa, AL 35487. Offers interactive technology (MS); quality management (MS); restaurant and meeting management (MS); rural community health (MS); sport management (MS). *Program availability:* Part-time, evening/weekend, online learning. *Faculty:* 52 full-time (38 women), 3 part-time/adjunct (2 women). *Students:* 213 full-time (138 women), 392 part-time (278 women); includes 142 minority (105 Black or African American, non-Hispanic/Latino; 3 American Indian or Alaska Native, non-Hispanic/Latino; 4 Asian, non-Hispanic/Latino; 17 Hispanic/Latino; 2 Native Hawaiian or other Pacific Islander, non-Hispanic/Latino; 11 Two or more races, non-Hispanic/Latino), 5 international. Average age 33. 400 applicants, 74% accepted, 232 enrolled. In 2016, 230 master's awarded. *Degree requirements:* For master's, comprehensive exam. *Entrance requirements:* For master's, GRE (for some specializations), minimum GPA of 3.0. Additional exam requirements/recommendations for international students: Required—TOEFL. *Application deadline:* For fall admission, 7/1 for domestic students; for spring admission, 11/1 for domestic students; for summer admission, 4/15 for domestic students. Applications are processed on a rolling basis. Application fee: $50 ($60 for international students). Electronic applications accepted. *Expenses:* Tuition, state resident: full-time $10,470. Tuition, nonresident: full-time $26,950. *Financial support:* In 2016–17, 2 teaching assistantships with full tuition reimbursements were awarded. Financial award application deadline: 7/1. *Faculty research:* Rural health, hospitality management, sport management, interactive technology, consumer quality management, environmental health and safety. *Unit head:* Dr. Milla D. Boschung, Dean, 205-348-6250, Fax: 205-348-1786, E-mail: mboschun@ches.ua.edu. *Application contact:* Dr. Stuart Usdan, Associate Dean, 205-348-6150, Fax: 205-348-3789, E-mail: susdan@ches.ua.edu.
Website: http://www.ches.ua.edu/programs-of-study.html

University of Central Florida, Rosen College of Hospitality Management, Orlando, FL 32816. Offers destination marketing and management (Certificate); event management (Certificate); hospitality and tourism management (MS); hospitality management (PhD). *Program availability:* Part-time. *Faculty:* 63 full-time (28 women), 38 part-time/adjunct (11 women). *Students:* 60 full-time (37 women), 122 part-time (86 women); includes 47 minority (21 Black or African American, non-Hispanic/Latino; 1 American Indian or Alaska Native, non-Hispanic/Latino; 3 Asian, non-Hispanic/Latino; 17 Hispanic/Latino; 5 Two or more races, non-Hispanic/Latino), 20 international. Average age 30. 180 applicants, 62% accepted, 73 enrolled. In 2016, 15 master's, 2 doctorates, 2 other advanced degrees awarded. *Degree requirements:* For master's, thesis or alternative; for doctorate, thesis/dissertation, candidacy exam. *Entrance requirements:* For master's, GMAT or GRE, minimum GPA of 3.0 in last 60 hours; for doctorate, GMAT or GRE. Additional exam requirements/recommendations for international students: Required—TOEFL. *Application deadline:* For fall admission, 7/15 for domestic students; for spring admission, 12/1 for domestic students. Application fee: $30. Electronic applications accepted. *Expenses:* Tuition, state resident: part-time $288.16 per credit hour. Tuition, nonresident: part-time $1071.31 per credit hour. *Financial support:* In 2016–17, 16 students received support, including 2 fellowships with partial tuition reimbursements available (averaging $4,500 per year), 16 teaching assistantships with partial tuition reimbursements available (averaging $13,994 per year); research assistantships also available. Financial award application deadline: 3/1; financial award applicants required to submit FAFSA. *Unit head:* Dr. Abraham C. Pizam, Dean, 407-903-8010, E-mail: abraham.pizam@ucf.edu. *Application contact:* Assistant Director, Graduate Admissions, 407-823-2766, Fax: 407-823-6442, E-mail: gradadmissions@ucf.edu.
Website: http://www.hospitality.ucf.edu/

University of Delaware, Alfred Lerner College of Business and Economics, Program in Hospitality Information Management, Newark, DE 19716. Offers MS. *Entrance requirements:* Additional exam requirements/recommendations for international students: Required—TOEFL (minimum score 550 paper-based). Electronic applications accepted. *Faculty research:* Foodservice, lodging and tourism management.

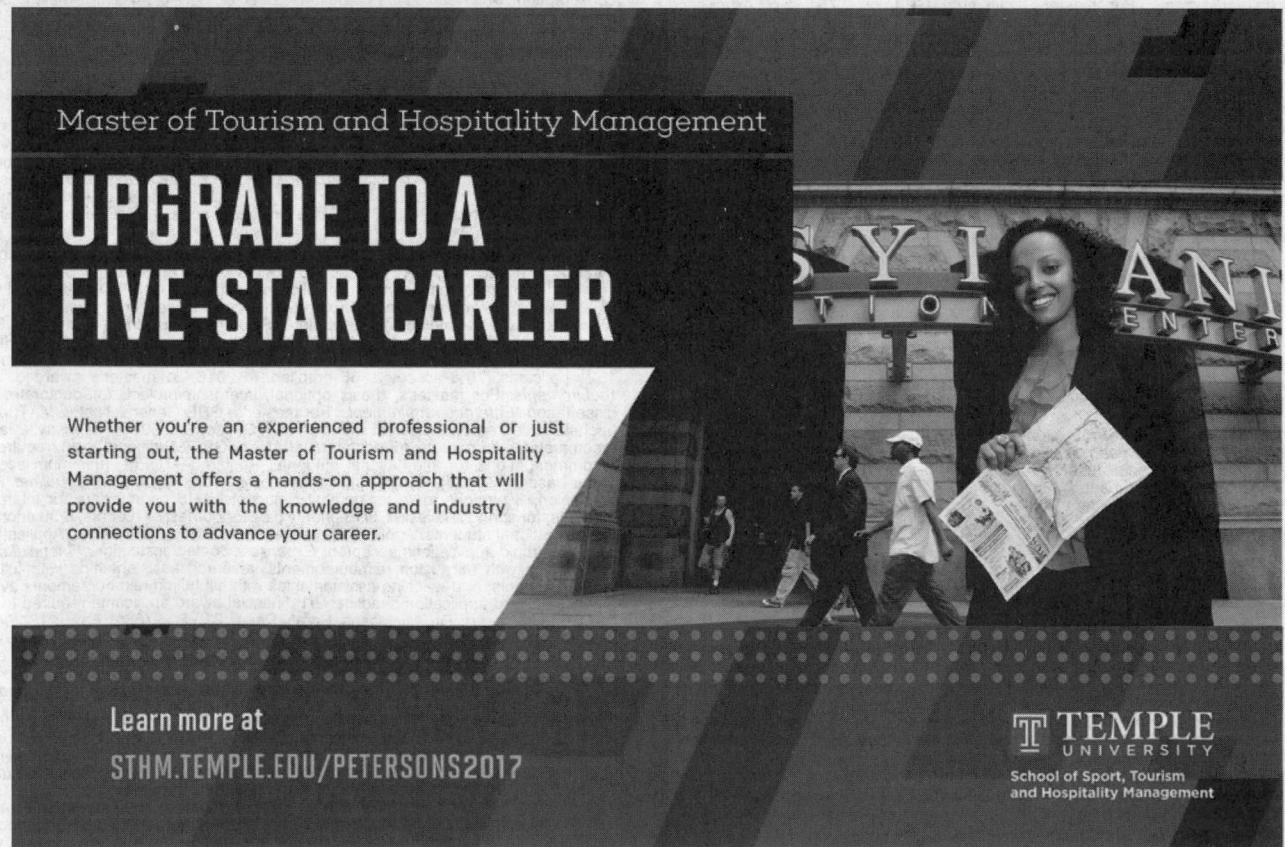

The University of Findlay, Office of Graduate Admissions, Findlay, OH 45840-3653. Offers applied security and analytics (MSAS); athletic training (MAT); business (MBA), including certified management accountant, certified public accountant, health care management, hospitality management; education (MA Ed, Ed D), including children's literature (MA Ed), curriculum and teaching (MA Ed), education (MA Ed), educational administration (MA Ed), human resource development (MA Ed), reading (MA Ed), science education (MA Ed), superintendent (Ed D), teaching (Ed D), technology

(MA Ed); environmental, safety and health management (MSEM); health informatics (MS); occupational therapy (MOT); pharmacy (Pharm D); physical therapy (DPT); physician assistant (MPA); rhetoric and writing (MA); teaching English to speakers of other languages (TESOL) and bilingual education (MA). *Program availability:* Part-time, evening/weekend, 100% online, blended/hybrid learning. *Faculty:* 114 full-time (63 women), 44 part-time/adjunct (18 women). *Students:* 751 full-time (452 women), 573 part-time (323 women); includes 164 minority (82 Black or African American, non-Hispanic/Latino; 1 American Indian or Alaska Native, non-Hispanic/Latino; 27 Asian, non-Hispanic/Latino; 37 Hispanic/Latino; 17 Two or more races, non-Hispanic/Latino), 280 international. Average age 28. 661 applicants, 52% accepted, 288 enrolled. In 2016, 366 master's, 137 doctorates awarded. *Degree requirements:* For master's, comprehensive exam (for some programs), thesis, cumulative project, capstone project; for doctorate, thesis/dissertation. *Entrance requirements:* For master's, GRE (for some programs), bachelor's degree from accredited institution, minimum undergraduate GPA of 3.0 in last 64 hours of course work; for doctorate, MAT, minimum cumulative GPA of 3.0, master's degree. Additional exam requirements/recommendations for international students: Recommended—TOEFL (minimum score 79 iBT), IELTS (minimum score 7). *Application deadline:* For fall admission, 6/15 for international students; for spring admission, 12/1 for international students; for summer admission, 4/1 for international students. Applications are processed on a rolling basis. Electronic applications accepted. *Expenses:* Contact institution. *Financial support:* In 2016–17, 139 students received support, including 15 research assistantships with partial tuition reimbursements available (averaging $7,200 per year), 25 teaching assistantships with partial tuition reimbursements available (averaging $7,200 per year); Federal Work-Study, institutionally sponsored loans, and unspecified assistantships also available. Financial award application deadline: 4/1; financial award applicants required to submit FAFSA. *Unit head:* Christopher M. Harris, Director of Admissions, 419-434-4347, E-mail: harrisc1@findlay.edu. *Application contact:* Madeline Fauser Brennan, Graduate Admissions Counselor, 419-434-4636, Fax: 419-434-4898,
E-mail: fauserbrennan@findlay.edu.
Website: http://www.findlay.edu/admissions/graduate/Pages/default.aspx

University of Guelph, Graduate Studies, College of Management and Economics, MBA Program, Guelph, ON N1G 2W1, Canada. Offers food and agribusiness management (MBA); hospitality and tourism management (MBA). *Program availability:* Part-time, evening/weekend, online learning. *Entrance requirements:* For master's, minimum B-average, minimum of 3 years of relevant work experience. Additional exam requirements/recommendations for international students: Required—TOEFL (minimum score 550 paper-based). Electronic applications accepted. *Faculty research:* Marketing, operations management, business policy, financial management, organizational behavior.

University of Houston, Conrad N. Hilton College of Hotel and Restaurant Management, Houston, TX 77204. Offers hospitality management (MS). *Program availability:* Part-time. *Degree requirements:* For master's, practicum or thesis. *Entrance requirements:* For master's, GMAT or GRE General Test. Additional exam requirements/recommendations for international students: Required—TOEFL (minimum score 100 iBT) or IELTS (minimum score 7). Electronic applications accepted. *Faculty research:* Catering, tourism, hospitality marketing, security and risk management, purchasing and financial information usage.

University of Kentucky, Graduate School, College of Agriculture, Food and Environment, Program in Hospitality and Dietetics Administration, Lexington, KY 40506-0032. Offers MS. *Degree requirements:* For master's, comprehensive exam, thesis optional. *Entrance requirements:* For master's, GRE General Test, minimum undergraduate GPA of 2.75. Additional exam requirements/recommendations for international students: Required—TOEFL (minimum score 550 paper-based). Electronic applications accepted.

University of Massachusetts Amherst, Graduate School, Isenberg School of Management, Program in Management, Amherst, MA 01003. Offers accounting (PhD); business administration (MBA); entrepreneurship (MBA); finance (MBA, PhD); healthcare administration (MBA); hospitality and tourism management (PhD); management science (PhD); marketing (MBA, PhD); organization studies (PhD); sport management (PhD); strategic management (PhD); MBA/MS. *Accreditation:* AACSB. *Program availability:* Part-time, evening/weekend, online learning. Terminal master's awarded for partial completion of doctoral program. *Degree requirements:* For doctorate, comprehensive exam, thesis/dissertation. *Entrance requirements:* For master's and doctorate, GMAT or GRE General Test. Additional exam requirements/recommendations for international students: Required—TOEFL (minimum score 550 paper-based; 80 iBT), IELTS (minimum score 6.5). Electronic applications accepted.

University of Memphis, Graduate School, Kemmons Wilson School of Hospitality and Resort Management, Memphis, TN 38152. Offers hospitality management specialist (Graduate Certificate); sports commerce (MS). *Program availability:* Part-time. *Faculty:* 3 full-time (0 women), 2 part-time/adjunct (0 women). *Students:* 15 full-time (1 woman), 10 part-time (4 women); includes 9 minority (8 Black or African American, non-Hispanic/Latino; 1 Hispanic/Latino), 1 international. Average age 26. 26 applicants, 92% accepted, 21 enrolled. *Degree requirements:* For master's, comprehensive exam, thesis or alternative. *Entrance requirements:* For master's, letters of recommendation, curriculum vitae or resume, statement of goals, minimum undergraduate GPA of 2.5. Additional exam requirements/recommendations for international students: Required—TOEFL (minimum score 550 paper-based; 79 iBT). *Application deadline:* For fall admission, 7/1 for domestic students, 5/1 for international students; for spring admission, 12/1 for domestic students, 9/1 for international students; for summer admission, 5/1 for domestic students, 2/1 for international students. Application fee: $35 ($60 for international students). Electronic applications accepted. *Expenses:* $5,231.50 per semester full-time in-state, $9,623.50 full-time out-of-state. *Financial support:* In 2016–17, 10 research assistantships (averaging $7,200 per year) were awarded; career-related internships or fieldwork, Federal Work-Study, scholarships/grants, and unspecified assistantships also available. Support available to part-time students. Financial award application deadline: 2/1. *Unit head:* Dr. Radesh Palakurthi, Director, 901-678-3430, E-mail: rplkrthi@memphis.edu. *Application contact:* Dr. Timothy Ryan, Coordinator of Graduate Studies, 901-678-5003, E-mail: tdryan@memphis.edu.
Website: http://www.memphis.edu/wilson/programs

University of Missouri, Office of Research and Graduate Studies, College of Agriculture, Food and Natural Resources, Department of Food Science, Columbia, MO 65211. Offers MS, PhD. *Faculty:* 20 full-time (8 women), 1 part-time/adjunct (0 women). *Students:* 16 full-time (10 women), 16 part-time (10 women), 23 international. Average age 28. Terminal master's awarded for partial completion of doctoral program. *Degree requirements:* For doctorate, comprehensive exam, thesis/dissertation. *Entrance requirements:* For master's, GRE General Test (minimum score: Verbal and Quantitative 1000 with neither section below 400, 297 combined under new scoring; Analytical 3.5), minimum GPA of 3.0; BS in food science from accredited university; for doctorate, GRE General Test (minimum score: Verbal and Quantitative 1000 with neither section below 400, Analytical 3.5), minimum GPA of 3.0; BS and MS in food science from accredited university. Additional exam requirements/recommendations for international students: Required—TOEFL (minimum score 550 paper-based; 80 iBT). *Application deadline:* For fall admission, 4/1 priority date for domestic students; for winter admission, 10/31 priority date for domestic students. Application fee: $75 ($90 for international students). Electronic applications accepted. *Expenses:* Tuition, state resident: full-time $6347; part-time $352.60 per credit hour. Tuition, nonresident: full-time $17,379; part-time $965.50 per credit hour. *Required fees:* $1035. Tuition and fees vary according to course load, campus/location and program. *Financial support:* Fellowships, research assistantships with tuition reimbursements, teaching assistantships with tuition reimbursements, institutionally sponsored loans, scholarships/grants, health care benefits, and unspecified assistantships available. Support available to part-time students. *Faculty research:* Food chemistry, food analysis, food microbiology, food engineering and process control, functional foods, meat science and processing technology.
Website: http://foodscience.missouri.edu/graduate/

University of Nevada, Las Vegas, Graduate College, William F. Harrah College of Hotel Administration, Program in Hotel Administration, Las Vegas, NV 89154-6013. Offers MHA, MS, PhD. MHA program also offered in Singapore. *Program availability:* Part-time, evening/weekend, 100% online, blended/hybrid learning. *Faculty:* 16 full-time (5 women), 2 part-time/adjunct (1 woman). *Students:* 33 full-time (15 women), 68 part-time (35 women); includes 30 minority (4 Black or African American, non-Hispanic/Latino; 2 American Indian or Alaska Native, non-Hispanic/Latino; 12 Asian, non-Hispanic/Latino; 4 Hispanic/Latino; 8 Two or more races, non-Hispanic/Latino), 20 international. Average age 34. 92 applicants, 45% accepted, 21 enrolled. In 2016, 36 master's, 7 doctorates awarded. *Degree requirements:* For master's, thesis (for some programs), professional paper, oral examination; for doctorate, comprehensive exam, thesis/dissertation, dissertation defense. *Entrance requirements:* For master's, GRE or GMAT, bachelor's degree with minimum GPA 2.75; minimum of one year of full-time work experience; brief essay; 2 letters of recommendation; for doctorate, GRE or GMAT, master's degree with minimum GPA of 3.0; statement of purpose; 3 letters of recommendation. Additional exam requirements/recommendations for international students: Required—TOEFL (minimum score 550 paper-based; 80 iBT), IELTS (minimum score 7). *Application deadline:* For fall admission, 8/1 for domestic students, 5/1 for international students; for spring admission, 11/15 for domestic students, 10/1 for international students. Application fee: $60 ($95 for international students). Electronic applications accepted. *Expenses:* $269.25 per credit, $792 per 3-credit course; $9,634 per year resident; $23,274 per year non-resident; $7,094 fees non-resident (7 credits or more); $1,307 annual health insurance fee. *Financial support:* In 2016–17, 4 research assistantships with partial tuition reimbursements (averaging $15,890 per year), 24 teaching assistantships with partial tuition reimbursements (averaging $12,500 per year) were awarded; institutionally sponsored loans, scholarships/grants, health care benefits, and unspecified assistantships also available. Financial award application deadline: 3/15. *Faculty research:* Marketing, human resources, financial analysis, tourism, gaming. *Total annual research expenditures:* $753,128. *Unit head:* Dr. Bill Werner, Chair, 702-895-4839, Fax: 702-895-4872, E-mail: william.werner@unlv.edu. *Application contact:* Dr. Christine Bergman, Graduate Coordinator, 702-895-5458, Fax: 702-895-4872, E-mail: christine.bergman@unlv.edu.
Website: http://hotel.unlv.edu

University of New Orleans, Graduate School, College of Business Administration, Lester E. Kabacoff School of Hotel, Restaurant, and Tourism Administration, Program in Hospitality and Tourism Management, New Orleans, LA 70148. Offers MS. *Program availability:* Online learning. *Entrance requirements:* Additional exam requirements/recommendations for international students: Required—TOEFL (minimum score 550 paper-based; 79 iBT).

University of North Texas, Robert B. Toulouse School of Graduate Studies, Denton, TX 76203-5459. Offers accounting (MS); applied anthropology (MA, MS); applied behavior analysis (Certificate); applied geography (MA); applied technology and performance improvement (M Ed, MS); art education (MA); art history (MA); art museum education (Certificate); arts leadership (Certificate); audiology (Au D); behavior analysis (MS); behavioral science (PhD); biochemistry and molecular biology (MS); biology (MA, MS); biomedical engineering (MS); business analysis (MS); chemistry (MS); clinical health psychology (PhD); communication studies (MA, MS); computer engineering (MS); computer science (MS); counseling (M Ed, MS), including clinical mental health counseling (MS), college and university counseling, elementary school counseling, secondary school counseling; creative writing (MA); criminal justice (MS); curriculum and instruction (M Ed); decision sciences (MBA); design (MA, MFA), including fashion design (MFA), innovation studies, interior design (MFA); early childhood studies (MS); economics (MS); educational leadership (M Ed, Ed D); educational psychology (MS, PhD), including family studies (MS), gifted and talented (MS), human development (MS), learning and cognition (MS), research, measurement and evaluation (MS); electrical engineering (MS); emergency management (MPA); engineering technology (MS); English (MA); English as a second language (MA); environmental science (MS); finance (MBA, MS); financial management (MPA); French (MA); health services management (MBA); higher education (M Ed, Ed D); history (MA, MS); hospitality management (MS); human resources management (MPA); information science (MS); information systems (PhD); information technologies (MBA); interdisciplinary studies (MA, MS); international studies (MA); international sustainable tourism (MS); jazz studies (MM); journalism (MA, MJ, Graduate Certificate), including interactive and virtual digital communication (Graduate Certificate), narrative journalism (Graduate Certificate), public relations (Graduate Certificate); kinesiology (MS); linguistics (MA); local government management (MPA); logistics (PhD); logistics and supply chain management (MBA); long-term care, senior housing, and aging services (MA); management (PhD); marketing (MBA); mathematics (MA, MS); mechanical and energy engineering (MS, PhD); music (MA), including ethnomusicology, music theory, musicology, performance; music composition (PhD); music education (MM Ed, PhD); nonprofit management (MPA); operations and supply chain management (MBA); performance (MM, DMA); philosophy (MA); political science (MA); professional and technical communication (MA); radio, television and film (MA, MFA); rehabilitation counseling (Certificate); sociology (MA); Spanish (MA); special education (M Ed); speech-language pathology (MA); strategic management (MBA); studio art (MFA); teaching (M Ed); MBA/MS. *Program availability:* Part-time, evening/weekend, online learning. Terminal master's awarded for partial completion of doctoral program. *Degree requirements:* For master's, variable foreign language requirement, comprehensive exam (for some programs), thesis (for some programs); for doctorate, variable foreign language requirement, comprehensive exam (for some programs), thesis/dissertation; for other advanced degree, variable foreign language requirement, comprehensive exam (for some programs). *Entrance requirements:* For master's and doctorate, GRE, GMAT. Additional exam requirements/recommendations for international students: Required—TOEFL (minimum score 550 paper-based; 79 iBT). Electronic applications accepted.

University of South Carolina, The Graduate School, College of Hospitality, Retail, and Sport Management, School of Hotel, Restaurant and Tourism Management, Columbia, SC 29208. Offers MIHTM. *Entrance requirements:* For master's, GMAT or GRE General Test, minimum GPA of 3.0, 2 letters of recommendation. Electronic applications accepted. *Faculty research:* Corporate strategy and management practices, sustainable tourism, club management, tourism technology, revenue management.

Hospitality Management

University of South Florida Sarasota-Manatee, College of Hospitality and Technology Leadership, Sarasota, FL 34243. Offers hospitality management (MS). *Program availability:* Part-time. *Faculty:* 6 full-time (2 women). *Students:* 14 full-time (10 women), 9 part-time (6 women); includes 6 minority (1 Black or African American, non-Hispanic/Latino; 5 Asian, non-Hispanic/Latino), 1 international. Average age 32. 27 applicants, 22% accepted, 4 enrolled. In 2016, 10 master's awarded. *Degree requirements:* For master's, thesis or professional project. *Entrance requirements:* For master's, GRE or GMAT (taken within last five years) if overall or upper-division GPA is less than 3.0, current resume with employer references which includes at least one of the following: one year of full-time experience in management capacity in hospitality industry or a related industry; minimum of one year of full-time teaching experience in hospitality management program; or three years of consecutive full-time entry level experience. Additional exam requirements/recommendations for international students: Required—TOEFL (minimum score 550 paper-based; 79 iBT), IELTS (minimum score 6.5). *Application deadline:* For fall admission, 3/1 priority date for domestic students, 3/1 for international students; for spring admission, 10/1 priority date for domestic students, 10/1 for international students. Applications are processed on a rolling basis. Application fee: $30. Electronic applications accepted. *Expenses:* Contact institution. *Financial support:* In 2016–17, 1 student received support, including 7 research assistantships with tuition reimbursements available (averaging $7,904 per year); teaching assistantships with tuition reimbursements available, career-related internships or fieldwork, institutionally sponsored loans, health care benefits, and unspecified assistantships also available. Support available to part-time students. Financial award application deadline: 3/1; financial award applicants required to submit FAFSA. *Faculty research:* Technology's impact on hospitality industry, hospitality accounting and cost control, international tourism development, service quality. *Unit head:* Dr. Pat Moreo, Dean, 941-359-4327, E-mail: pmoreo@sar.usf.edu. *Application contact:* Andy Telatovich, Director, Admissions, 941-359-4330, E-mail: atelatovich@sar.usf.edu.
Website: http://www.usfsm.edu/chtl/

The University of Tennessee, Graduate School, College of Education, Health and Human Sciences, Department of Consumer and Industry Services Management, Program in Hotel, Restaurant, and Tourism Management, Knoxville, TN 37996. Offers hospitality management (MS); tourism (MS). *Program availability:* Part-time. *Degree requirements:* For master's, thesis or alternative. *Entrance requirements:* For master's, GRE General Test, minimum GPA of 2.7. Additional exam requirements/recommendations for international students: Required—TOEFL. Electronic applications accepted.

University of the Pacific, College of the Pacific, Program in Food Studies, Stockton, CA 95211-0197. Offers MA. *Students:* 26 full-time (24 women); includes 8 minority (5 Asian, non-Hispanic/Latino; 3 Hispanic/Latino). Average age 35. 33 applicants, 73% accepted, 13 enrolled. *Unit head:* Dr. Polly Adema, Director, 209-946-2434, E-mail: foodstudies@pacific.edu. *Application contact:* Information Contact, 209-946-2261.

Virginia International University, School of Business, Fairfax, VA 22030. Offers accounting (MBA, MS); entrepreneurship (MBA); executive management (Graduate Certificate); global logistics (MBA); health care management (MBA); hospitality and tourism management (MBA); human resources management (MBA); international business management (MBA); international finance (MBA); marketing management (MBA); mass media and public relations (MBA); project management (MBA, MS). *Program availability:* Part-time, online learning. *Entrance requirements:* For master's and Graduate Certificate, bachelor's degree. Additional exam requirements/recommendations for international students: Required—TOEFL (minimum score 550 paper-based; 80 iBT), IELTS (minimum score 6). Electronic applications accepted.

Virginia Polytechnic Institute and State University, Graduate School, Pamplin College of Business, Blacksburg, VA 24061. Offers accounting and information systems (MACIS); business (PhD); business administration (MBA, MS); hospitality and tourism management (MS, PhD). *Faculty:* 126 full-time (38 women), 3 part-time/adjunct (1 woman). *Students:* 255 full-time (101 women), 156 part-time (56 women); includes 95 minority (21 Black or African American, non-Hispanic/Latino; 49 Asian, non-Hispanic/Latino; 13 Hispanic/Latino; 12 Two or more races, non-Hispanic/Latino), 73 international. Average age 33. 310 applicants, 59% accepted, 150 enrolled. In 2016, 167 master's, 8 doctorates awarded. *Degree requirements:* For master's, comprehensive exam (for some programs), thesis (for some programs); for doctorate, comprehensive exam (for some programs), thesis/dissertation (for some programs). *Entrance requirements:* For master's and doctorate, GRE/GMAT. Additional exam requirements/recommendations for international students: Required—TOEFL (minimum score 80 iBT). *Application deadline:* For fall admission, 8/1 for domestic students, 4/1 for international students; for spring admission, 1/1 for domestic students, 9/1 for international students. Applications are processed on a rolling basis. Application fee: $75. Electronic applications accepted. *Expenses:* Tuition, state resident: full-time $12,467; part-time $692.50 per credit hour. Tuition, nonresident: full-time $25,095; part-time $1394.25 per credit hour. *Required fees:* $2669; $491.50 per semester. Tuition and fees vary according to course load, campus/location and program. *Financial support:* In 2016–17, 2 fellowships with full tuition reimbursements (averaging $21,222 per year), 3 research assistantships with full tuition reimbursements (averaging $24,988 per year), 46 teaching assistantships with full tuition reimbursements (averaging $20,054 per year) were awarded. Financial award application deadline: 3/1; financial award applicants required to submit FAFSA. *Total annual research expenditures:* $2.7 million. *Unit head:* Dr. Robert T. Sumichrast, Dean, 540-231-6601, Fax: 540-231-4487, E-mail: busdean@vt.edu. *Application contact:* Kimberly Ridpath, Executive Assistant, 540-231-6601, Fax: 540-231-4487, E-mail: ridpathk@vt.edu. Website: http://www.pamplin.vt.edu/

Widener University, School of Education, Hospitality, and Continuing Studies, Chester, PA 19013-5792. Offers adult education (M Ed); counseling in higher education (M Ed); counselor education (M Ed); early childhood education (M Ed); educational foundations (M Ed); educational leadership (M Ed); educational psychology (M Ed); elementary education (M Ed); English and language arts (M Ed); health education (M Ed); higher education leadership (Ed D); home and school visitor (M Ed); human sexuality (M Ed, PhD); mathematics education (M Ed); middle school education (M Ed); principalship (M Ed); reading and language arts (Ed D); reading education (M Ed); school administration (Ed D); science education (M Ed); social studies education (M Ed); special education (M Ed); technology education (M Ed). *Accreditation:* NCATE. *Program availability:* Part-time, evening/weekend. *Faculty:* 34 full-time (22 women), 37 part-time/adjunct (14 women). *Students:* 97 full-time (64 women), 201 part-time (143 women); includes 56 minority (44 Black or African American, non-Hispanic/Latino; 1 American Indian or Alaska Native, non-Hispanic/Latino; 2 Asian, non-Hispanic/Latino; 8 Hispanic/Latino; 1 Two or more races, non-Hispanic/Latino), 32 international. Average age 39. 139 applicants, 88% accepted. In 2016, 45 master's, 21 doctorates awarded. Terminal master's awarded for partial completion of doctoral program. *Degree requirements:* For doctorate, thesis/dissertation. *Entrance requirements:* For master's, minimum GPA of 2.5; for doctorate, GRE or MAT, minimum GPA of 2.0 (undergraduate), 3.5 (graduate). *Application deadline:* Applications are processed on a rolling basis. Application fee: $25 ($300 for international students). Electronic applications accepted. *Expenses:* Contact institution. *Financial support:* Career-related internships or fieldwork, tuition waivers (full and partial), and unspecified assistantships available. Support available to part-time students. Financial award application deadline: 5/1. *Faculty research:* Reading and cognition, adult education, technology education, educational leadership, special education. *Unit head:* Dr. Shawn Fitzgerald, Dean, 610-499-4294, Fax: 610-499-4623, E-mail: smfitzgerald@widener.edu. *Application contact:* Dr. Roberta Nolan, Director of Graduate Admissions, 610-499-4125, E-mail: rdnolan@widener.edu.
Website: http://www.widener.edu/academics/schools/eics

Travel and Tourism

Arizona State University at the Tempe campus, College of Public Programs, School of Community Resources and Development, Phoenix, AZ 85004-0685. Offers community resources and development (MS, PhD); nonprofit leadership and management (Graduate Certificate); nonprofit studies (MNpS); sustainable tourism (MAS). *Program availability:* Part-time, evening/weekend. Terminal master's awarded for partial completion of doctoral program. *Degree requirements:* For master's, thesis or alternative, interactive Program of Study (iPOS) submitted before completing 50 percent of required credit hours; for doctorate, comprehensive exam, thesis/dissertation, interactive Program of Study (iPOS) submitted before completing 50 percent of required credit hours. *Entrance requirements:* For master's and doctorate, GRE, minimum GPA of 3.0 or equivalent in last 2 years of work leading to bachelor's degree. Additional exam requirements/recommendations for international students: Required—TOEFL, IELTS, or PTE. Electronic applications accepted. *Expenses:* Contact institution.

Boston University, Metropolitan College, Department of Administrative Sciences, Boston, MA 02215. Offers applied business analytics (MS); economic development and tourism management (MSAS); enterprise risk management (MS); financial management (MS); global marketing management (MS); innovation and technology (MSAS); insurance management (MSM); project management (MS); supply chain management (MS). *Accreditation:* AACSB. *Program availability:* Part-time, evening/weekend, online learning. *Faculty:* 15 full-time (3 women), 22 part-time/adjunct (3 women). *Students:* 301 full-time (146 women), 934 part-time (501 women); includes 237 minority (81 Black or African American, non-Hispanic/Latino; 5 American Indian or Alaska Native, non-Hispanic/Latino; 60 Asian, non-Hispanic/Latino; 76 Hispanic/Latino; 1 Native Hawaiian or other Pacific Islander, non-Hispanic/Latino; 14 Two or more races, non-Hispanic/Latino), 514 international. Average age 31. 593 applicants, 69% accepted, 260 enrolled. In 2016, 263 master's awarded. *Degree requirements:* For master's, thesis optional. *Entrance requirements:* For master's, 1 year of work experience, minimum GPA of 3.0. Additional exam requirements/recommendations for international students: Required—TOEFL (minimum score 84 iBT). *Application deadline:* Applications are processed on a rolling basis. Application fee: $80. Electronic applications accepted. *Expenses:* Contact institution. *Financial support:* In 2016–17, 15 students received support, including 14 research assistantships (averaging $8,400 per year); career-related internships or fieldwork, Federal Work-Study, and unspecified assistantships also available. *Faculty research:* International business, innovative process. *Unit head:* Dr. John Sullivan, Chair, 617-353-3016, E-mail: adminsc@bu.edu. *Application contact:* Fiona Niven, Administrative Sciences Department, 617-353-3016, E-mail: adminsc@bu.edu.
Website: http://www.bu.edu/met/academic-community/departments/administrative-sciences/

California State University, Chico, Office of Graduate Studies, College of Communication and Education, Recreation, Hospitality and Parks Management Department, Chico, CA 95929-0722. Offers recreation, parks, and tourism (MS). *Program availability:* Part-time. *Faculty:* 9 full-time (3 women), 9 part-time/adjunct (5 women). *Students:* 6 part-time (3 women). 4 applicants, 100% accepted, 3 enrolled. In 2016, 3 master's awarded. *Degree requirements:* For master's, thesis or project. *Entrance requirements:* For master's, GRE General Test, 3 letters of recommendation, statement of purpose, resume. Additional exam requirements/recommendations for international students: Required—TOEFL (minimum score 550 paper-based; 80 iBT), IELTS (minimum score 6.5), PTE. *Application deadline:* For fall admission, 3/1 priority date for domestic students, 3/1 for international students; for spring admission, 9/15 priority date for domestic students, 9/15 for international students. Application fee: $55. Electronic applications accepted. *Financial support:* Fellowships, career-related internships or fieldwork, scholarships/grants, and traineeships available. Financial award application deadline: 3/1; financial award applicants required to submit FAFSA. *Unit head:* Dr. Morgan Geddie, Chair, 530-898-6408, Fax: 530-898-6557, E-mail: recr@csuchico.edu. *Application contact:* Judy L. Morris, Graduate Admissions Coordinator, 530-898-5416, Fax: 530-898-3342, E-mail: jlmorris@csuchico.edu.
Website: http://www.csuchico.edu/recr/

California State University, East Bay, Office of Graduate Studies, College of Education and Allied Studies, Department of Hospitality, Recreation and Tourism, Hayward, CA 94542-3000. Offers recreation and tourism (MS). *Program availability:* Part-time, evening/weekend, online learning. *Students:* 19 full-time (12 women), 12 part-time (9 women); includes 26 minority (6 Black or African American, non-Hispanic/Latino; 6 Asian, non-Hispanic/Latino; 11 Hispanic/Latino; 1 Native Hawaiian or other Pacific Islander, non-Hispanic/Latino; 2 Two or more races, non-Hispanic/Latino). Average age 34. 15 applicants, 47% accepted, 6 enrolled. In 2016, 11 master's awarded. *Degree requirements:* For master's, thesis optional. *Entrance requirements:* For master's, minimum GPA of 2.75; 2 years' related work experience; 3 letters of recommendation; resume; baccalaureate degree. Additional exam requirements/recommendations for international students: Required—TOEFL (minimum score 550 paper-based). *Application deadline:* For fall admission, 6/30 for domestic and international students. Applications are processed on a rolling basis. Application fee: $55. Electronic applications accepted. *Financial support:* Federal Work-Study, institutionally sponsored loans, and scholarships/grants available. Support available to part-time students. Financial award application deadline: 3/2; financial award applicants required to submit FAFSA. *Faculty research:* Leisure, online vs. face-to-face (F2F) learning, risk management, leadership, tourism consumer behavior. *Unit head:* Dr. Chris

Chamberlain, Chair, 510-885-2101, E-mail: chris.chamberlain@csueastbay.edu. *Application contact:* Dr. Donna Wiley, Interim Associate Vice President for Academic Programs and Graduate Studies, 510-885-3716, Fax: 510-885-4777, E-mail: donna.wiley@csueastbay.edu.

California State University, Fullerton, Graduate Studies, College of Communications, Department of Communications, Fullerton, CA 92834-9480. Offers communications in tourism and entertainment (MA); mass communications research and theory (MA); professional communications (MA). *Program availability:* Part-time. *Degree requirements:* For master's, project or thesis. *Entrance requirements:* For master's, GRE General Test. Application fee: $55. *Expenses:* Tuition, state resident: full-time $3369; part-time $1953 per unit. Tuition, nonresident: full-time $3915; part-time $2499 per unit. Tuition and fees vary according to course load, degree level and program. *Financial support:* Teaching assistantships, career-related internships or fieldwork, Federal Work-Study, institutionally sponsored loans, and scholarships/grants available. Support available to part-time students. Financial award application deadline: 3/1; financial award applicants required to submit FAFSA. *Unit head:* Jason Shepard, Chair, 657-278-5301, E-mail: jshepard@fullerton.edu. *Application contact:* Coordinator, 657-278-3832.

California State University, Northridge, Graduate Studies, College of Health and Human Development, Department of Recreation and Tourism Management, Northridge, CA 91330. Offers hospitality and tourism (MS); recreational sport management/campus recreation (MS). *Faculty:* 7 full-time (4 women), 19 part-time/adjunct (8 women). *Students:* 22 full-time (10 women), 13 part-time (10 women); includes 12 minority (1 Black or African American, non-Hispanic/Latino; 7 Hispanic/Latino; 1 Native Hawaiian or other Pacific Islander, non-Hispanic/Latino; 3 Two or more races, non-Hispanic/Latino), 7 international. Average age 29. 57 applicants, 49% accepted, 18 enrolled. *Degree requirements:* For master's, thesis (for some programs). *Entrance requirements:* For master's, GRE (if cumulative undergraduate GPA less than 3.0). Additional exam requirements/recommendations for international students: Required—TOEFL. *Application deadline:* For fall admission, 11/30 for domestic students. Application fee: $55. *Expenses:* Tuition, state resident: full-time $4152. *Financial support:* Application deadline: 3/1. *Unit head:* Dr. Mechelle Best, Chair, 818-677-3202.
Website: http://www.csun.edu/hhd/rtm/

Clemson University, Graduate School, College of Behavioral, Social and Health Sciences, Department of Parks, Recreation, and Tourism Management, Clemson, SC 29634. Offers international parks and tourism (Certificate); parks, recreation and tourism management (MS, PhD), including recreational therapy (PhD); public administration (MPA); recreational therapy (MS); youth development leadership (MS); youth leadership development (Certificate). *Program availability:* Part-time, evening/weekend, 100% online. *Faculty:* 36 full-time (14 women), 2 part-time/adjunct (0 women). *Students:* 79 full-time (52 women), 159 part-time (100 women); includes 50 minority (36 Black or African American, non-Hispanic/Latino; 2 Asian, non-Hispanic/Latino; 6 Hispanic/Latino; 6 Two or more races, non-Hispanic/Latino), 14 international. Average age 32. 143 applicants, 62% accepted, 71 enrolled. In 2016, 37 master's, 4 doctorates, 38 other advanced degrees awarded. *Degree requirements:* For master's, comprehensive exam (for some programs), thesis (for some programs); for doctorate, comprehensive exam, thesis/dissertation; for Certificate, portfolio. *Entrance requirements:* For master's and doctorate, GRE General Test, unofficial transcripts, letter of intent, letters of reference; for Certificate, letter of recommendation, unofficial transcripts, personal statement, resume. Additional exam requirements/recommendations for international students: Required—TOEFL (minimum score 610 paper-based; 80 iBT), IELTS (minimum score 6.5). *Application deadline:* For fall admission, 1/15 priority date for domestic and international students; for spring admission, 11/15 priority date for domestic and international students. Applications are processed on a rolling basis. Application fee: $80 ($90 for international students). Electronic applications accepted. *Expenses:* $4,264 per semester full-time resident, $8,485 per semester full-time non-resident, $471 per credit hour part-time resident, $942 per credit hour part-time non-resident. *Financial support:* In 2016–17, 83 students received support, including 2 fellowships with partial tuition reimbursements available (averaging $1,750 per year), 4 research assistantships with partial tuition reimbursements available (averaging $9,219 per year), 69 teaching assistantships with partial tuition reimbursements available (averaging $10,425 per year); unspecified assistantships also available. Financial award application deadline: 1/15. *Faculty research:* Human behavior, land use, recreational therapy, sustainability, tourism. *Total annual research expenditures:* $97,805. *Unit head:* Dr. Fran McGuire, Chair, 864-656-3036, Fax: 864-656-2226, E-mail: lefty@clemson.edu. *Application contact:* Dr. Bill Norman, Graduate Coordinator, 864-656-2060, Fax: 864-656-2226, E-mail: wnorman@clemson.edu.
Website: http://www.clemson.edu/hehd/departments/prtm/

Colorado State University, Warner College of Natural Resources, Department of Human Dimensions of Natural Resources, Fort Collins, CO 80523-1480. Offers conservation leadership (MS); human dimensions of natural resources (MS, PhD); tourism management (MTM). *Program availability:* Part-time, 100% online. *Faculty:* 14 full-time (7 women), 1 (woman) part-time/adjunct. *Students:* 63 full-time (42 women), 99 part-time (49 women); includes 19 minority (6 Black or African American, non-Hispanic/Latino; 1 American Indian or Alaska Native, non-Hispanic/Latino; 1 Asian, non-Hispanic/Latino; 8 Hispanic/Latino; 3 Two or more races, non-Hispanic/Latino), 25 international. Average age 29. 125 applicants, 88% accepted, 91 enrolled. In 2016, 55 master's, 4 doctorates awarded. *Degree requirements:* For master's, thesis or alternative; for doctorate, comprehensive exam, thesis/dissertation. *Entrance requirements:* For master's, GRE General Test (minimum combined score of 300), minimum GPA of 3.0, 3 letters of recommendation, statement of interest, official transcripts; for doctorate, GRE General Test (minimum combined score of 300), minimum GPA of 3.0, 3 letters of recommendation, copy of master's thesis or professional paper, interview, statement of interest, official transcripts. Additional exam requirements/recommendations for international students: Required—TOEFL (minimum score 550 paper-based; 80 iBT). *Application deadline:* For fall admission, 2/15 priority date for domestic students, 2/15 for international students. Application fee: $60 ($70 for international students). Electronic applications accepted. *Expenses:* Contact institution. *Financial support:* In 2016–17, 15 students received support, including 4 fellowships (averaging $39,500 per year), 8 research assistantships with full and partial tuition reimbursements available (averaging $22,854 per year), 9 teaching assistantships with full and partial tuition reimbursements available (averaging $13,932 per year); career-related internships or fieldwork, scholarships/grants, and unspecified assistantships also available. Financial award application deadline: 2/15. *Faculty research:* Conservation and sustainable development, environmental communication and governance, human dimensions of wildlife conservation, protected areas, social aspects of wildfire. *Total annual research expenditures:* $1.4 million. *Unit head:* Dr. Michael J. Manfredo, Professor and Department Head, 970-491-6591, Fax: 970-491-2255, E-mail: michael.manfredo@colostate.edu. *Application contact:* Graduate Contact, 970-491-6591, Fax: 970-491-2255, E-mail: wcrnhdnr_info@mail.colostate.edu.
Website: http://warnercnr.colostate.edu/hdnr-home

The George Washington University, School of Business, Department of Tourism and Hospitality Management, Washington, DC 20052. Offers destination management (Professional Certificate); event and meeting management (MTA); event management (Professional Certificate); hospitality management (MTA); individualized studies (MTA); sport management (MTA); sustainable tourism destination management (MTA); tourism and hospitality management (MBA). *Program availability:* Part-time, online learning. *Students:* 66 full-time (46 women), 38 part-time (30 women); includes 27 minority (16 Black or African American, non-Hispanic/Latino; 6 Asian, non-Hispanic/Latino; 3 Hispanic/Latino; 2 Two or more races, non-Hispanic/Latino), 44 international. Average age 28. 113 applicants, 76% accepted, 40 enrolled. In 2016, 45 master's awarded. *Degree requirements:* For master's, comprehensive exam, thesis. *Entrance requirements:* For master's, GRE General Test. Additional exam requirements/recommendations for international students: Required—TOEFL. *Application deadline:* For fall admission, 4/1 priority date for domestic students; for spring admission, 10/1 for domestic students. Applications are processed on a rolling basis. Application fee: $75. *Financial support:* In 2016–17, 32 students received support. Fellowships, teaching assistantships, career-related internships or fieldwork, Federal Work-Study, institutionally sponsored loans, and tuition waivers (partial) available. Financial award application deadline: 4/1. *Faculty research:* Tourism policy, tourism impact forecasting, geotourism. *Unit head:* Prof. Lisa Delpy Neirotti, Faculty Director, 202-994-6623, E-mail: delpy@gwu.edu. *Application contact:* Christopher Storer, Executive Director, Graduate Admissions, 202-994-1212, E-mail: gwmba@gwu.edu.
Website: http://business.gwu.edu/tourism/

IGlobal University, Graduate Programs, Vienna, VA 22182. Offers accounting (MBA); data management and analytics (MSIT); entrepreneurship (MBA); finance (MBA); global business management (MBA); health care management (MBA); hospitality and tourism management (MBA); human resources management (MBA); information technology (MBA); information technology systems and management (MSIT); leadership and management (MBA); project management (MBA); public service and administration (MBA); software design and management (MSIT).

Indiana University Bloomington, School of Public Health, Department of Recreation, Park, and Tourism Studies, Bloomington, IN 47405-7000. Offers leisure behavior (PhD); outdoor recreation (MS); park and public lands management (MS); recreation administration (MS); recreational sports administration (MS); recreational therapy (MS); tourism management (MS). Terminal master's awarded for partial completion of doctoral program. *Degree requirements:* For master's, thesis optional; for doctorate, comprehensive exam, thesis/dissertation. *Entrance requirements:* For master's, GRE General Test, minimum GPA of 2.8; for doctorate, GRE General Test, minimum GPA of 3.0 (undergraduate), 3.5 (graduate). Additional exam requirements/recommendations for international students: Required—TOEFL (minimum score 550 paper-based; 80 iBT). Electronic applications accepted. *Faculty research:* Leisure counseling, gerontology, special populations, planning and development.

Kent State University, College of Education, Health and Human Services, School of Foundations, Leadership and Administration, Program in Hospitality and Tourism Management, Kent, OH 44242-0001. Offers MS. *Program availability:* Part-time. *Degree requirements:* For master's, thesis optional. *Entrance requirements:* For master's, minimum GPA of 3.0, 3 letters of recommendation, resume, goals statement. Additional exam requirements/recommendations for international students: Required—TOEFL (minimum score 550 paper-based; 80 iBT). Electronic applications accepted. *Expenses:* Tuition, state resident: full-time $10,864; part-time $495 per credit hour. Tuition, nonresident: full-time $18,380; part-time $837 per credit hour. *Faculty research:* Training human service workers, health care services for older adults, early adolescent development, care-giving arrangements with aging families, peace and war.

Lasell College, Graduate and Professional Studies in Management, Newton, MA 02466-2709. Offers business administration (PMBA); elder care management (MSM, Graduate Certificate); hospitality and event management (MSM, Graduate Certificate); human resources management (MSM, Graduate Certificate); management (MSM, Graduate Certificate); marketing (MSM, Graduate Certificate); non-profit management (MSM, Graduate Certificate); project management (MSM, Graduate Certificate). *Accreditation:* ACBSP. *Program availability:* Part-time, evening/weekend, 100% online, blended/hybrid learning. *Faculty:* 3 full-time (2 women), 16 part-time/adjunct (10 women). *Students:* 47 full-time (34 women), 93 part-time (72 women); includes 28 minority (20 Black or African American, non-Hispanic/Latino; 4 Asian, non-Hispanic/Latino; 3 Hispanic/Latino; 1 Two or more races, non-Hispanic/Latino), 24 international. Average age 31. 121 applicants, 55% accepted, 32 enrolled. In 2016, 61 master's, 3 other advanced degrees awarded. *Degree requirements:* For master's, minimum GPA of 3.0; internship or research paper (for MSM). *Entrance requirements:* For master's, one-page personal statement, 2 letters of recommendation, resume, bachelor's degree transcript; proof of microeconomics and statistics (for PMBA); for Graduate Certificate, bachelor's degree transcript, 2 letters of recommendation, 1-page personal statement, resume. Additional exam requirements/recommendations for international students: Required—TOEFL (minimum score 550 paper-based, 79 iBT) or IELTS (minimum score 6). *Application deadline:* For fall admission, 8/31 priority date for domestic students, 6/30 priority date for international students; for spring admission, 12/31 priority date for domestic students, 10/31 priority date for international students. Applications are processed on a rolling basis. Electronic applications accepted. *Expenses:* $600 per credit. *Financial support:* In 2016–17, 12 students received support. Federal Work-Study, scholarships/grants, and tuition discounts available. Support available to part-time students. Financial award application deadline: 8/31; financial award applicants required to submit FAFSA. *Unit head:* Dr. Joan Dolamore, Dean of Graduate and Professional Studies, 617-243-2485, Fax: 617-243-2450, E-mail: gradinfo@lasell.edu. *Application contact:* Adrienne Franciosi, Director of Graduate Enrollment, 617-243-2214, Fax: 617-243-2450, E-mail: gradinfo@lasell.edu.
Website: http://www.lasell.edu/academics/graduate-and-professional-studies/programs-of-study/master-of-science-in-management.html

Liberty University, School of Education, Lynchburg, VA 24515. Offers educational leadership (Ed D); gifted education (Certificate); math specialist (M Ed); middle grades (MAT, Certificate); reading specialist (M Ed); school leadership (Certificate); secondary education (MAT); sport management (MS), including administration, outdoor recreation, sport management, tourism. *Accreditation:* NCATE. *Program availability:* Part-time, online learning. *Students:* 1,910 full-time (1,427 women), 4,420 part-time (3,311 women); includes 1,451 minority (1,182 Black or African American, non-Hispanic/Latino; 33 American Indian or Alaska Native, non-Hispanic/Latino; 44 Asian, non-Hispanic/Latino; 46 Hispanic/Latino; 11 Native Hawaiian or other Pacific Islander, non-Hispanic/Latino; 135 Two or more races, non-Hispanic/Latino), 87 international. Average age 37. 5,120 applicants, 44% accepted, 1193 enrolled. In 2016, 1,378 master's, 151 doctorates, 497 other advanced degrees awarded. *Degree requirements:* For doctorate, comprehensive exam, thesis/dissertation. *Entrance requirements:* For master's, GRE General Test or MAT (if taken in or before 1999), 2 letters of recommendation, minimum undergraduate GPA of 3.0, curriculum vitae; for doctorate and Certificate, GRE General Test or MAT (if taken before 1999), minimum master's GPA of 3.0, 3 years of teaching experience. Additional exam requirements/recommendations for international students: Required—TOEFL (minimum score 600 paper-based; 100 iBT). *Application deadline:* For fall admission, 6/1 for domestic students; for spring admission, 11/1 for domestic students. Applications are processed on a rolling basis. Application fee: $50. Electronic applications accepted. *Expenses:* Contact institution. *Financial support:* Federal Work-

Travel and Tourism

Study and tuition waivers (partial) available. *Faculty research:* Self-determination, character education, bibliotherapy, learning styles, distance education. *Unit head:* Dr. Heather Schoffstall, Dean, 434-582-2445, Fax: 434-582-2468, E-mail: awgunter@liberty.edu. *Application contact:* Jay Bridge, Director of Graduate Admissions, 800-424-9595, Fax: 800-628-7977, E-mail: gradadmissions@liberty.edu.
Website: http://www.liberty.edu/academics/education/graduate/

New Mexico State University, College of Agricultural, Consumer and Environmental Sciences, Department of Family and Consumer Sciences, Las Cruces, NM 88003. Offers clothing, textiles, and merchandising (MS); family and child science (MS); family and consumer science education (MS); family and consumer sciences (MS); food science and technology (MS); hotel, restaurant, and tourism management (MS); human nutrition and dietetic sciences (MS). *Program availability:* Part-time. *Faculty:* 9 full-time (6 women), 1 (woman) part-time/adjunct. *Students:* 32 full-time (28 women), 6 part-time (5 women); includes 17 minority (2 Black or African American, non-Hispanic/Latino; 1 American Indian or Alaska Native, non-Hispanic/Latino; 14 Hispanic/Latino), 1 international. Average age 27. 23 applicants, 91% accepted, 15 enrolled. In 2016, 16 master's awarded. *Degree requirements:* For master's, comprehensive exam (for some programs), thesis (for some programs), oral exam. *Entrance requirements:* For master's, GRE, 3 letters of reference from faculty members or employers, resume, letter of interest. Additional exam requirements/recommendations for international students: Required—TOEFL (minimum score 550 paper-based; 79 iBT), IELTS (minimum score 6.5). *Application deadline:* For fall admission, 2/1 priority date for domestic and international students; for spring admission, 10/1 for domestic and international students. Applications are processed on a rolling basis. Application fee: $40 ($50 for international students). Electronic applications accepted. *Expenses:* Tuition, state resident: full-time $4086. Tuition, nonresident: full-time $14,254. *Required fees:* $853. Tuition and fees vary according to course load. *Financial support:* In 2016–17, 27 students received support, including 4 research assistantships (averaging $14,844 per year), 10 teaching assistantships (averaging $10,707 per year); career-related internships or fieldwork, Federal Work-Study, scholarships/grants, traineeships, health care benefits, and unspecified assistantships also available. Support available to part-time students. Financial award application deadline: 3/1. *Faculty research:* Food product analysis, childhood obesity, dietary decision-making, military families, equine assisted psychotherapy. *Total annual research expenditures:* $401,869. *Unit head:* Dr. Esther L. Devall, Department Head, 575-646-1161, Fax: 575-646-1889, E-mail: edevall@nmsu.edu. *Application contact:* Dr. Kourtney Vaillancourt, Graduate Program Contact, 575-646-3383, Fax: 575-646-1889, E-mail: kvaillan@nmsu.edu.
Website: http://aces.nmsu.edu/academics/fcs

New York University, School of Continuing and Professional Studies, Tisch Center for Hospitality and Tourism, Program in Tourism Management, New York, NY 10012-1019. Offers MS, Advanced Certificate. *Program availability:* Part-time, evening/weekend. *Degree requirements:* For master's, thesis. *Entrance requirements:* For master's, GRE or GMAT (only upon request), bachelor's degree, resume with relevant professional work, internship or volunteer experience, two letters of recommendation, statement of purpose. Additional exam requirements/recommendations for international students: Required—TOEFL (minimum score 600 paper-based; 100 iBT), IELTS (minimum score 7). Electronic applications accepted. *Faculty research:* Tourism planning for national parks and protected areas, leadership and organizational behavior issues.

North Carolina State University, Graduate School, College of Natural Resources, Department of Parks, Recreation and Tourism Management, Raleigh, NC 27695. Offers natural resource management (MPRTM, MS); park and recreation management (MPRTM, MS); parks, recreation and tourism management (PhD); recreational sport management (MPRTM, MS); spatial information science (MPRTM, MS); tourism policy and development (MPRTM, MS). *Degree requirements:* For master's, thesis (for some programs); for doctorate, thesis/dissertation. *Entrance requirements:* For master's and doctorate, GRE General Test. Additional exam requirements/recommendations for international students: Required—TOEFL. Electronic applications accepted. *Faculty research:* Tourism policy and development, spatial information systems, natural resource management, recreational sports management, park and recreation management.

Penn State University Park, Graduate School, College of Health and Human Development, Department of Recreation, Park and Tourism Management, University Park, PA 16802. Offers MS, PhD. *Unit head:* Dr. Ann C. Crouter, Dean, 814-865-1420, Fax: 814-865-3282. *Application contact:* Lori Hawn, Director, Graduate Student Services, 814-865-1795, Fax: 814-863-4627, E-mail: l-gswww@lists.psu.edu.
Website: http://hhd.psu.edu/rptm

Pontificia Universidad Catolica Madre y Maestra, Graduate School, Faculty of Social and Administrative Sciences, Santiago, Dominican Republic. Offers business administration (MBA), including business development, finance, international business, management skills (M Mgmt, MBA), marketing, operations, strategic cost management, strategy, tourist destination planning and management; law (LL M), including civil law, corporate business law, criminal law, international relations, real estate law; management (M Mgmt), including higher financial management, insurance program administration, management skills (M Mgmt, MBA); psychology (MA), including clinical child and adolescent psychology, forensic psychology; strategic human resources (EMBA).

Purdue University, Graduate School, College of Health and Human Sciences, School of Hospitality and Tourism Management, West Lafayette, IN 47907. Offers MS, PhD. *Program availability:* Online learning. *Faculty:* 17 full-time (6 women), 1 part-time/adjunct (0 women). *Students:* 38 full-time (26 women), 15 part-time (9 women); includes 3 minority (1 Asian, non-Hispanic/Latino; 2 Hispanic/Latino), 43 international. Average age 29. 79 applicants, 61% accepted, 12 enrolled. In 2016, 18 master's, 7 doctorates awarded. *Degree requirements:* For master's, thesis; for doctorate, thesis/dissertation. *Entrance requirements:* For master's, GMAT (minimum score of 550) or GRE General Test (minimum combined verbal and quantitative score of 290 new scoring, minimum of 145 each section, or 1000 with 500 each section, old scoring), minimum GPA of 3.0; for doctorate, GMAT (minimum score of 550) or GRE General Test (minimum combined verbal and quantitative score of 290 new scoring, minimum of 145 each section, or 1000 with 500 each section, old scoring), minimum undergraduate GPA of 3.0; master's degree with minimum GPA of 3.0 or equivalent. Additional exam requirements/recommendations for international students: Required—TOEFL (minimum score 77 iBT), TWE. *Application deadline:* For fall admission, 3/5 priority date for domestic and international students; for spring admission, 9/20 for domestic and international students. Applications are processed on a rolling basis. Application fee: $60 ($75 for international students). Electronic applications accepted. *Financial support:* Research assistantships, teaching assistantships, and career-related internships or fieldwork available. Support available to part-time students. Financial award applicants required to submit FAFSA. *Faculty research:* Human resources, marketing, hotel and restaurant operations, food product and equipment development, tourism development. *Unit head:* Dr. Richard F. Ghiselli, Head, 765-494-2636, E-mail: ghiselli@purdue.edu. *Application contact:* Ayrielle K. Espinosa, Graduate Contact, 765-494-9811,
E-mail: camposm@purdue.edu.
Website: http://www.purdue.edu/hhs/htm/

Rochester Institute of Technology, Graduate Enrollment Services, College of Applied Science and Technology, School of International Hospitality and Service Innovation, MS Program in Hospitality and Tourism Management, Rochester, NY 14623. Offers MS. *Program availability:* Part-time, evening/weekend. *Students:* 6 full-time (1 woman), 5 part-time (3 women); includes 2 minority (both Black or African American, non-Hispanic/Latino), 8 international. Average age 34. 33 applicants, 64% accepted, 2 enrolled. In 2016, 11 master's awarded. *Degree requirements:* For master's, thesis or alternative. *Entrance requirements:* For master's, minimum GPA of 3.0 (recommended). Additional exam requirements/recommendations for international students: Required—TOEFL (minimum score 570 paper-based; 88 iBT), IELTS (minimum score 6.5), PTE (minimum score 61). *Application deadline:* Applications are processed on a rolling basis. Application fee: $60. Electronic applications accepted. *Expenses:* $1,742 per credit hour. *Financial support:* In 2016–17, 14 students received support. Teaching assistantships with partial tuition reimbursements available, career-related internships or fieldwork, scholarships/grants, and unspecified assistantships available. Support available to part-time students. Financial award applicants required to submit FAFSA. *Faculty research:* Service innovation and technology integration, innovative food product development, hospitality employees' occupational health and wellness, tourist behaviors, destination management. *Unit head:* Yu-Chin Hsieh, Department Chair, 585-475-2355, E-mail: yhsieh@rit.edu. *Application contact:* Diane Ellison, Associate Vice President, Graduate Enrollment Services, 585-475-2229, Fax: 585-475-7164,
E-mail: gradinfo@rit.edu.
Website: http://www.rit.edu/cast/htm/graduate-program

Rochester Institute of Technology, Graduate Enrollment Services, College of Applied Science and Technology, School of International Hospitality and Service Innovation, MS Program in Service Leadership and Innovation, Rochester, NY 14623. Offers MS. *Program availability:* Part-time, evening/weekend, 100% online. *Students:* 14 full-time (9 women), 35 part-time (23 women); includes 3 minority (1 Black or African American, non-Hispanic/Latino; 2 Hispanic/Latino), 4 international. Average age 31. 55 applicants, 44% accepted, 14 enrolled. In 2016, 5 master's awarded. *Degree requirements:* For master's, thesis or alternative. *Entrance requirements:* For master's, minimum GPA of 3.0 (recommended). Additional exam requirements/recommendations for international students: Required—TOEFL (minimum score 570 paper-based; 88 iBT), IELTS (minimum score 6.5), PTE (minimum score 62). *Application deadline:* Applications are processed on a rolling basis. Application fee: $60. Electronic applications accepted. *Expenses:* $1,742 per credit hour. *Financial support:* In 2016–17, 8 students received support. Teaching assistantships with partial tuition reimbursements available, career-related internships or fieldwork, scholarships/grants, and unspecified assistantships available. Support available to part-time students. Financial award applicants required to submit FAFSA. *Faculty research:* Leadership development, customer service/patient satisfaction, program evaluation, knowledge construction, diversity, individual creativity, healthcare applications. *Unit head:* Dr. Linda Underhill, Department Chair, 585-475-7359, E-mail: lmuism@rit.edu. *Application contact:* Diane Ellison, Associate Vice President, Graduate Enrollment Services, 585-475-2229, Fax: 585-475-7164, E-mail: gradinfo@rit.edu.
Website: http://www.rit.edu/cast/servicesystems/service-leadership-innovation

Royal Roads University, Graduate Studies, Tourism and Hotel Management Program, Victoria, BC V9B 5Y2, Canada. Offers destination development (Graduate Certificate); international hotel management (MA); sustainable tourism (Graduate Certificate); tourism leadership (Graduate Certificate); tourism management (MA).

San Francisco State University, Division of Graduate Studies, College of Business, Program in Business Administration, San Francisco, CA 94132-1722. Offers decision sciences/operations research (MBA); ethics and compliance (MBA); finance (MBA); global business and innovation (MBA); healthcare administration (MBA); hospitality and tourism management (MBA); information systems (MBA); leadership (MBA); marketing (MBA); nonprofit and social enterprise leadership (MBA); sustainable business (MBA). *Accreditation:* AACSB. *Program availability:* Part-time, evening/weekend. *Degree requirements:* For master's, thesis, essay test. *Entrance requirements:* For master's, GMAT, minimum GPA of 2.7 in last 60 units. Additional exam requirements/recommendations for international students: Required—TOEFL (minimum score 550 paper-based). *Application deadline:* For fall admission, 5/1 priority date for domestic students, 4/1 for international students; for spring admission, 11/1 for domestic students, 10/15 for international students. Applications are processed on a rolling basis. Application fee: $55. *Expenses:* Tuition, state resident: full-time $6738. Tuition, nonresident: full-time $15,666. *Required fees:* $1012. Tuition and fees vary according to degree level and program. *Financial support:* Application deadline: 3/1. *Unit head:* Dr. Sanjit Sengupta, Faculty Director, 415-817-4366, Fax: 415-817-4340, E-mail: sengupta@sfsu.edu. *Application contact:* Zandra Tan, EMBA Program Coordinator, 415-817-4360, Fax: 415-817-4340, E-mail: zandra13@sfsu.edu.
Website: http://cob.sfsu.edu/graduate-programs/mba

San Francisco State University, Division of Graduate Studies, College of Health and Social Sciences, Department of Recreation, Parks, and Tourism, San Francisco, CA 94132-1722. Offers MS. *Program availability:* Part-time. *Application deadline:* Applications are processed on a rolling basis. *Expenses:* Tuition, state resident: full-time $6738. Tuition, nonresident: full-time $15,666. *Required fees:* $1012. Tuition and fees vary according to degree level and program. *Financial support:* Career-related internships or fieldwork available. *Unit head:* Dr. Erik Rosegard, Chair, 415-338-7529, Fax: 415-338-0543, E-mail: rosegard@sfsu.edu. *Application contact:* Dr. Jackson Wilson, Graduate Coordinator, 415-338-1487, Fax: 415-338-0543,
E-mail: wilsonj@sfsu.edu.
Website: http://recdept.sfsu.edu/graduate

Savannah College of Art and Design, Graduate School, Program in Themed Entertainment Design, Savannah, GA 31402-3146. Offers MFA. *Program availability:* Part-time. *Faculty:* 1 full-time (0 women). *Students:* 21 full-time (14 women), 6 part-time (2 women); includes 2 minority (both Asian, non-Hispanic/Latino), 9 international. Average age 27. 30 applicants, 63% accepted, 11 enrolled. In 2016, 6 master's awarded. *Degree requirements:* For master's, thesis. *Entrance requirements:* For master's, GRE (recommended), portfolio (submitted in digital format), audition or writing submission, resume, statement of purpose, two letters of recommendation. Additional exam requirements/recommendations for international students: Required—TOEFL (minimum score 550 paper-based, 85 iBT), IELTS (minimum score 6.5), or ACTFL. *Application deadline:* For fall admission, 4/1 for domestic and international students. Applications are processed on a rolling basis. Application fee: $40. Electronic applications accepted. *Expenses: Tuition:* Full-time $36,045. Tuition and fees vary according to course load. *Financial support:* Career-related internships or fieldwork, Federal Work-Study, and scholarships/grants available. Financial award application deadline: 4/1; financial award applicants required to submit FAFSA. *Unit head:* Gregory Beck, Chair, Production Design and Themed Entertainment. *Application contact:* Jenny Jaquillard, Executive Director of Admissions, Recruitment and Events, 912-525-5100, Fax: 912-525-5985, E-mail: admission@scad.edu.
Website: http://www.scad.edu/academics/programs/themed-entertainment-design

Schiller International University, MBA Programs, Florida, Program in International Hotel and Tourism Management, Largo, FL 33771. Offers MBA. *Degree requirements:*

For master's, thesis optional. *Entrance requirements:* Additional exam requirements/recommendations for international students: Required—TOEFL (minimum score 550 paper-based).

Strayer University, Graduate Studies, Washington, DC 20005-2603. Offers accounting (MS); acquisition (MBA); business administration (MBA); communications technology (MS); educational management (M Ed); finance (MBA); health services administration (MHSA); hospitality and tourism management (MBA); human resource management (MBA); information systems (MS), including computer security management, decision support system management, enterprise resource management, network management, software engineering management, systems development management; management (MBA); management information systems (MS); marketing (MBA); professional accounting (MS), including accounting information systems, controllership, taxation; public administration (MPA); supply chain management (MBA); technology in education (M Ed). Programs also offered at campus locations in Birmingham, AL; Chamblee, GA; Cobb County, GA; Morrow, GA; White Marsh, MD; Charleston, SC; Columbia, SC; Greensboro, NC; Greenville, SC; Lexington, KY; Louisville, KY; Nashville, TN; North Raleigh, NC; Washington, DC. *Accreditation:* ACBSP. *Program availability:* Part-time, evening/weekend, online learning. *Degree requirements:* For master's, thesis. *Entrance requirements:* For master's, GMAT, GRE General Test, bachelor's degree from an accredited college or university, minimum undergraduate GPA of 2.75. Electronic applications accepted.

Syracuse University, David B. Falk College of Sport and Human Dynamics, MS Program in Sport Venue and Event Management, Syracuse, NY 13244. Offers MS. *Entrance requirements:* For master's, GRE, undergraduate transcripts, three recommendations, resume, personal statement. Additional exam requirements/recommendations for international students: Required—TOEFL (minimum score 100 iBT). *Application deadline:* For fall admission, 2/15 for domestic students; for spring admission, 11/1 priority date for domestic and international students. Application fee: $75. Electronic applications accepted. *Expenses: Tuition:* Full-time $25,974; part-time $1443 per credit hour. *Required fees:* $802; $50 per course. Tuition and fees vary according to course load and program. *Financial support:* Fellowships, research assistantships, teaching assistantships, and career-related internships or fieldwork available. Financial award application deadline: 1/1; financial award applicants required to submit FAFSA. *Faculty research:* Managing and operating sport and entertainment facilities and events, sociology of sport, psychological and social Issues in sport. *Unit head:* Jeff Pauline, Graduate Program Director, 315-443-0364, Fax: 315-443-9811, E-mail: jspaulin@syr.edu. *Application contact:* Felicia Otero, Director of Admissions, 315-443-5555, E-mail: falk@syr.edu.
Website: http://falk.syr.edu/SportManagement/Default.aspx

★ **Temple University,** School of Sport, Tourism and Hospitality Management, Philadelphia, PA 19122-6096. Offers sport business (MS); tourism and hospitality management (MTHM); tourism and sport (PhD); travel and tourism (MS). *Program availability:* Part-time, evening/weekend. *Faculty:* 21 full-time (7 women), 10 part-time/adjunct (3 women). *Students:* 95 full-time (47 women), 32 part-time (16 women); includes 37 minority (27 Black or African American, non-Hispanic/Latino; 6 Hispanic/Latino; 4 Two or more races, non-Hispanic/Latino), 22 international. 152 applicants, 70% accepted, 66 enrolled. In 2016, 31 master's awarded. *Degree requirements:* For master's, thesis optional, internship/project; for doctorate, thesis/dissertation. *Entrance requirements:* For master's, GRE General Test, GMAT, or MAT, bachelor's degree or equivalent with minimum GPA of 3.0, 500-word essay, 2 letters of recommendation, resume; for doctorate, GMAT or GRE. Additional exam requirements/recommendations for international students: Required—TOEFL (minimum score 550 paper-based; 79 iBT), IELTS (minimum score 6.5). *Application deadline:* For fall admission, 3/1 priority date for domestic students, 1/15 priority date for international students; for spring admission, 8/15 priority date for domestic students, 6/30 priority date for international students. Applications are processed on a rolling basis. Application fee: $60. Electronic applications accepted. *Expenses:* Contact institution. *Financial support:* Fellowships with full tuition reimbursements, research assistantships with full tuition reimbursements, and teaching assistantships with full tuition reimbursements available. Financial award application deadline: 3/1; financial award applicants required to submit FAFSA. *Unit head:* Dr. M. Moshe Porat, Dean, 215-204-1836, Fax: 215-204-8705, E-mail: porat@temple.edu. *Application contact:* James Alton, Manager of Graduate Student Services, 215-204-7140, Fax: 215-204-8705, E-mail: jim.alton@temple.edu.
Website: http://sthm.temple.edu/

See Display on page 342 and Close-Ups on pages 349 and 1651.

Tropical Agriculture Research and Higher Education Center, Graduate School, Turrialba, Costa Rica. Offers agribusiness management (MS); agroforestry systems (PhD); development practices (MS); ecological agriculture (MS); environmental socioeconomics (MS); forestry in tropical and subtropical zones (PhD); integrated watershed management (MS); international sustainable tourism (MS); management and conservation of tropical rainforests and biodiversity (MS); tropical agriculture (PhD); tropical agroforestry (MS). *Entrance requirements:* For master's, GRE, 2 years of related professional experience, letters of recommendation; for doctorate, GRE, 4 letters of recommendation, letter of support from employing organization, master's degree in agronomy, biological sciences, forestry, natural resources or related field. Additional exam requirements/recommendations for international students: Required—TOEFL (minimum score 550 paper-based). Electronic applications accepted. *Faculty research:* Biodiversity in fragmented landscapes, ecosystem management, integrated pest management, environmental livestock production, biotechnology carbon balances in diverse land uses.

Université du Québec à Trois-Rivières, Graduate Programs, Program in Leisure, Culture and Tourism Sciences, Trois-Rivières, QC G9A 5H7, Canada. Offers MA, DESS. *Program availability:* Part-time. *Degree requirements:* For master's, thesis optional. *Entrance requirements:* For master's, appropriate bachelor's degree, proficiency in French.

University of Central Florida, Rosen College of Hospitality Management, Orlando, FL 32816. Offers destination marketing and management (Certificate); event management (Certificate); hospitality and tourism management (MS); hospitality management (PhD). *Program availability:* Part-time. *Faculty:* 63 full-time (28 women), 38 part-time/adjunct (11 women). *Students:* 60 full-time (37 women), 122 part-time (86 women); includes 47 minority (21 Black or African American, non-Hispanic/Latino; 1 American Indian or Alaska Native, non-Hispanic/Latino; 3 Asian, non-Hispanic/Latino; 17 Hispanic/Latino; 5 Two or more races, non-Hispanic/Latino), 20 international. Average age 30. 180 applicants, 62% accepted, 73 enrolled. In 2016, 15 master's, 2 doctorates, 2 other advanced degrees awarded. *Degree requirements:* For master's, thesis or alternative; for doctorate, thesis/dissertation, candidacy exam. *Entrance requirements:* For master's, GMAT or GRE, minimum GPA of 3.0 in last 60 hours; for doctorate, GMAT or GRE. Additional exam requirements/recommendations for international students: Required—TOEFL. *Application deadline:* For fall admission, 7/15 for domestic students; for spring admission, 12/1 for domestic students. Application fee: $30. Electronic applications accepted. *Expenses:* Tuition, state resident: part-time $288.16 per credit hour. Tuition, nonresident: part-time $1071.31 per credit hour. *Financial support:* In 2016–17, 16 students received support, including 2 fellowships with partial tuition reimbursements available (averaging $4,500 per year), 16 teaching assistantships with partial tuition reimbursements available (averaging $13,994 per year); research assistantships also available. Financial award application deadline: 3/1; financial award applicants required to submit FAFSA. *Unit head:* Dr. Abraham C. Pizam, Dean, 407-903-8010, E-mail: abraham.pizam@ucf.edu. *Application contact:* Assistant Director, Graduate Admissions, 407-823-2766, Fax: 407-823-6442, E-mail: gradadmissions@ucf.edu.
Website: http://www.hospitality.ucf.edu/

University of Florida, Graduate School, College of Health and Human Performance, Department of Tourism, Recreation and Sport Management, Gainesville, FL 32611. Offers health and human performance (PhD), including historic preservation (MS, PhD), recreation, parks and tourism (MS, PhD), sport management; recreation, parks and tourism (MS), including historic preservation (MS, PhD), natural resource recreation, recreation, parks and tourism (MS, PhD), therapeutic recreation, tourism, tropical conservation and development; sport management (MS), including historic preservation (MS, PhD), tropical conservation and development; JD/MS; MSM/MS. *Degree requirements:* For master's, comprehensive exam (for some programs), thesis (for some programs); for doctorate, comprehensive exam, thesis/dissertation. *Entrance requirements:* For master's and doctorate, GRE General Test, minimum GPA of 3.0. Additional exam requirements/recommendations for international students: Required—TOEFL (minimum score 550 paper-based; 80 iBT), IELTS (minimum score 6). Electronic applications accepted. *Faculty research:* Hospitality, natural resource management, sport management, tourism.

University of Hawaii at Manoa, Graduate Division, School of Travel Industry Management, Honolulu, HI 96822. Offers MS. *Program availability:* Part-time. *Degree requirements:* For master's, thesis optional. *Entrance requirements:* For master's, GRE General Test, minimum GPA of 3.0. Additional exam requirements/recommendations for international students: Required—TOEFL (minimum score 560 paper-based; 83 iBT), IELTS (minimum score 5). Electronic applications accepted. *Faculty research:* Travel information technology, tourism development and policy, transportation management and policy, hospitality management, sustainable tourism development.

University of Massachusetts Amherst, Graduate School, Isenberg School of Management, Program in Management, Amherst, MA 01003. Offers accounting (PhD); business administration (MBA); entrepreneurship (MBA); finance (MBA, PhD); healthcare administration (MBA); hospitality and tourism management (PhD); management science (PhD); marketing (MBA, PhD); organization studies (PhD); sport management (PhD); strategic management (PhD); MBA/MS. *Accreditation:* AACSB. *Program availability:* Part-time, evening/weekend, online learning. Terminal master's awarded for partial completion of doctoral program. *Degree requirements:* For doctorate, comprehensive exam, thesis/dissertation. *Entrance requirements:* For master's and doctorate, GMAT or GRE General Test. Additional exam requirements/recommendations for international students: Required—TOEFL (minimum score 550 paper-based; 80 iBT), IELTS (minimum score 6.5). Electronic applications accepted.

University of Minnesota, Twin Cities Campus, Graduate School, College of Food, Agricultural and Natural Resource Sciences, Program in Natural Resources Science and Management, St. Paul, MN 55108. Offers assessment, monitoring, and geospatial analysis (MS, PhD); economics, policy, management, and society (MS, PhD); forest hydrology and watershed management (MS, PhD); forest products (MS, PhD); forests: biology, ecology, conservation, and management (MS, PhD); natural resources science and management (MS, PhD); paper science and engineering (MS, PhD); recreation resources, tourism, and environmental education (MS, PhD); wildlife ecology and management (MS, PhD). *Program availability:* Part-time. *Faculty:* 71 full-time (28 women), 52 part-time/adjunct (7 women). *Students:* 79 full-time (46 women), 27 part-time (14 women); includes 11 minority (2 Black or African American, non-Hispanic/Latino; 3 American Indian or Alaska Native, non-Hispanic/Latino; 3 Asian, non-Hispanic/Latino; 3 Hispanic/Latino), 9 international. Average age 31. 63 applicants, 57% accepted, 26 enrolled. In 2016, 19 master's, 3 doctorates awarded. Terminal master's awarded for partial completion of doctoral program. *Degree requirements:* For master's, comprehensive exam, thesis (for some programs); for doctorate, comprehensive exam, thesis/dissertation. *Entrance requirements:* For master's and doctorate, GRE General Test. Additional exam requirements/recommendations for international students: Required—TOEFL (minimum score 550 paper-based; 79 iBT), IELTS (minimum score 6.5). *Application deadline:* For fall admission, 12/16 priority date for domestic and international students; for spring admission, 10/15 for domestic and international students. Applications are processed on a rolling basis. Application fee: $75 ($95 for international students). Electronic applications accepted. *Financial support:* In 2016–17, 5 students received support, including fellowships with full tuition reimbursements available (averaging $40,000 per year), research assistantships with full tuition reimbursements available (averaging $40,000 per year), teaching assistantships with full tuition reimbursements available (averaging $40,000 per year); scholarships/grants, health care benefits, and unspecified assistantships also available. *Faculty research:* Forest hydrology, biology, ecology, conservation, and management; recreation resources and environmental education; wildlife ecology; economics, policy, and society; geographic information systems (GIS); forest products and paper science. *Unit head:* Dr. Mae Davenport, Interim Director of Graduate Studies, 612-624-2721, E-mail: mdaven@umn.edu. *Application contact:* Toni Abts, Graduate Program Coordinator, 612-624-7683, Fax: 612-625-5212, E-mail: twheeler@umn.edu.
Website: http://www.nrsm.umn.edu

University of New Orleans, Graduate School, College of Business Administration, Lester E. Kabacoff School of Hotel, Restaurant, and Tourism Administration, Program in Hospitality and Tourism Management, New Orleans, LA 70148. Offers MS. *Program availability:* Online learning. *Entrance requirements:* Additional exam requirements/recommendations for international students: Required—TOEFL (minimum score 550 paper-based; 79 iBT).

University of North Texas, Robert B. Toulouse School of Graduate Studies, Denton, TX 76203-5459. Offers accounting (MS); applied anthropology (MA, MS); applied behavior analysis (Certificate); applied geography (MA); applied technology and performance improvement (M Ed, MS); art education (MA); art history (MA); art museum education (Certificate); arts leadership (Certificate); audiology (Au D); behavior analysis (MS); behavioral science (PhD); biochemistry and molecular biology (MS); biology (MA, MS); biomedical engineering (MS); business analysis (MS); chemistry (MS); clinical health psychology (PhD); communication studies (MA, MS); computer engineering (MS); computer science (MS); counseling (M Ed, MS), including clinical mental health counseling (MS), college and university counseling, elementary school counseling, secondary school counseling; creative writing (MA); criminal justice (MS); curriculum and instruction (M Ed); decision sciences (MBA); design (MA, MFA), including fashion design (MFA), innovation studies, interior design (MFA); early childhood studies (MS); economics (MS); educational leadership (M Ed, Ed D); educational psychology (MS, PhD), including family studies (MS), gifted and talented (MS), human development (MS), learning and cognition (MS), research, measurement and evaluation (MS); electrical engineering (MS); emergency management (MPA); engineering technology (MS); English (MA); English as a second language (MA); environmental science (MS); finance (MBA, MS); financial management (MPA); French (MA); health services management

(MBA); higher education (M Ed, Ed D); history (MA, MS); hospitality management (MS); human resources management (MPA); information science (MS); information systems (PhD); information technologies (MBA); interdisciplinary studies (MA, MS); international studies (MA); international sustainable tourism (MS); jazz studies (MM); journalism (MA, MJ, Graduate Certificate), including interactive and virtual digital communication (Graduate Certificate), narrative journalism (Graduate Certificate), public relations (Graduate Certificate); kinesiology (MS); linguistics (MA); local government management (MPA); logistics (PhD); logistics and supply chain management (MBA); long-term care, senior housing, and aging services (MA); management (PhD); marketing (MBA); mathematics (MA, MS); mechanical and energy engineering (MS, PhD); music (MA), including ethnomusicology, music theory, musicology, performance; music composition (PhD); music education (MM Ed, PhD); nonprofit management (MPA); operations and supply chain management (MBA); performance (MM, DMA); philosophy (MA); political science (MA); professional and technical communication (MA); radio, television and film (MA, MFA); rehabilitation counseling (Certificate); sociology (MA); Spanish (MA); special education (M Ed); speech-language pathology (MA); strategic management (MBA); studio art (MFA); teaching (M Ed); MBA/MS. *Program availability:* Part-time, evening/weekend, online learning. Terminal master's awarded for partial completion of doctoral program. *Degree requirements:* For master's, variable foreign language requirement, comprehensive exam (for some programs), thesis (for some programs); for doctorate, variable foreign language requirement, comprehensive exam (for some programs), thesis/dissertation; for other advanced degree, variable foreign language requirement, comprehensive exam (for some programs). *Entrance requirements:* For master's and doctorate, GRE, GMAT. Additional exam requirements/recommendations for international students: Required—TOEFL (minimum score 550 paper-based; 79 iBT). Electronic applications accepted.

University of South Africa, College of Economic and Management Sciences, Pretoria, South Africa. Offers accounting (D Admin, D Com); accounting science (DA); auditing (D Admin, D Com); business administration (M Tech); business economics (D Admin); business leadership (DBL); business management (D Admin, D Com); economic management analysis (M Tech); economics (D Admin, D Com, PhD); human resource development (M Tech); industrial psychology (D Admin, D Com, PhD); logistics (D Com); marketing (M Tech); public administration (D Admin, D Com, DPA, PhD); public management (M Tech); quantitative management (D Admin, D Com); real estate (M Tech); statistics (D Admin, PhD); tourism management (D Admin, D Com); transport economics (D Admin, D Com).

University of South Carolina, The Graduate School, College of Hospitality, Retail, and Sport Management, School of Hotel, Restaurant and Tourism Management, Columbia, SC 29208. Offers MIHTM. *Entrance requirements:* For master's, GMAT or GRE General Test, minimum GPA of 3.0, 2 letters of recommendation. Electronic applications accepted. *Faculty research:* Corporate strategy and management practices, sustainable tourism, club management, tourism technology, revenue management.

University of South Florida, College of Global Sustainability, Tampa, FL 33620-9951. Offers energy, global, water and sustainable tourism (Graduate Certificate); global sustainability (MA), including building sustainable enterprise, climate change and sustainability, coastal sustainability, entrepreneurship, food sustainability and security, sustainable energy, sustainable tourism, sustainable transportation, water. *Faculty:* 4 full-time (0 women). *Students:* 59 full-time (35 women), 51 part-time (29 women); includes 25 minority (3 Black or African American, non-Hispanic/Latino; 1 American Indian or Alaska Native, non-Hispanic/Latino; 2 Asian, non-Hispanic/Latino; 16 Hispanic/Latino; 3 Two or more races, non-Hispanic/Latino), 30 international. Average age 28. 134 applicants, 59% accepted, 55 enrolled. In 2016, 36 master's awarded. *Degree requirements:* For master's, comprehensive exam (for some programs), thesis or alternative, internship. *Entrance requirements:* For master's, minimum GPA of 3.0 in undergraduate coursework; at least two letters of recommendation (one must be academic); 200-250 word essay on student's background, professional goals, and reasons for seeking degree. Additional exam requirements/recommendations for international students: Required—TOEFL (minimum score 550 paper-based; 79 iBT). *Application deadline:* For fall admission, 6/1 for domestic students, 5/1 for international students; for spring admission, 10/15 for domestic students, 9/15 for international students. Electronic applications accepted. *Expenses:* Tuition, state resident: full-time $7766; part-time $431.43 per credit hour. Tuition, nonresident: full-time $15,789; part-time $877.17 per credit hour. *Required fees:* $37 per term. *Financial support:* In 2016–17, 20 students received support. *Faculty research:* Global sustainability, integrated resource management, systems thinking, green communities, entrepreneurship, ecotourism. *Total annual research expenditures:* $208,988. *Unit head:* Dr. Rafael Perez, Interim Dean, 813-974-9694, E-mail: perez@usf.edu.
Website: http://psgs.usf.edu/

The University of Tennessee, Graduate School, College of Education, Health and Human Sciences, Department of Consumer and Industry Services Management, Program in Hotel, Restaurant, and Tourism Management, Knoxville, TN 37996. Offers hospitality management (MS); tourism (MS). *Program availability:* Part-time. *Degree requirements:* For master's, thesis or alternative. *Entrance requirements:* For master's, GRE General Test, minimum GPA of 2.7. Additional exam requirements/recommendations for international students: Required—TOEFL. Electronic applications accepted.

Virginia Polytechnic Institute and State University, Graduate School, Pamplin College of Business, Blacksburg, VA 24061. Offers accounting and information systems (MACIS); business (PhD); business administration (MBA, MS); hospitality and tourism management (MS, PhD). *Faculty:* 126 full-time (38 women), 3 part-time/adjunct (1 woman). *Students:* 255 full-time (101 women), 156 part-time (56 women); includes 95 minority (21 Black or African American, non-Hispanic/Latino; 49 Asian, non-Hispanic/Latino; 13 Hispanic/Latino; 12 Two or more races, non-Hispanic/Latino), 73 international. Average age 33. 310 applicants, 59% accepted, 150 enrolled. In 2016, 167 master's, 8 doctorates awarded. *Degree requirements:* For master's, comprehensive exam (for some programs), thesis (for some programs); for doctorate, comprehensive exam (for some programs), thesis/dissertation (for some programs). *Entrance requirements:* For master's and doctorate, GRE/GMAT. Additional exam requirements/recommendations for international students: Required—TOEFL (minimum score 80 iBT). *Application deadline:* For fall admission, 8/1 for domestic students, 4/1 for international students; for spring admission, 1/1 for domestic students, 9/1 for international students. Applications are processed on a rolling basis. Application fee: $75. Electronic applications accepted. *Expenses:* Tuition, state resident: full-time $12,467; part-time $692.50 per credit hour. Tuition, nonresident: full-time $25,095; part-time $1394.25 per credit hour. *Required fees:* $2669; $491.50 per semester. Tuition and fees vary according to course load, campus/location and program. *Financial support:* In 2016–17, 2 fellowships with full tuition reimbursements (averaging $21,222 per year), 3 research assistantships with full tuition reimbursements (averaging $24,988 per year), 46 teaching assistantships with full tuition reimbursements (averaging $20,054 per year) were awarded. Financial award application deadline: 3/1; financial award applicants required to submit FAFSA. *Total annual research expenditures:* $2.7 million. *Unit head:* Dr. Robert T. Sumichrast, Dean, 540-231-6601, Fax: 540-231-4487, E-mail: busdean@vt.edu. *Application contact:* Kimberly Ridpath, Executive Assistant, 540-231-6601, Fax: 540-231-4487, E-mail: ridpathk@vt.edu.
Website: http://www.pamplin.vt.edu/

Western Illinois University, School of Graduate Studies, College of Education and Human Services, Department of Recreation, Park, and Tourism Administration, Macomb, IL 61455-1390. Offers MS. *Program availability:* Part-time. *Students:* 24 full-time (13 women), 11 part-time (5 women); includes 6 minority (3 Black or African American, non-Hispanic/Latino; 2 Hispanic/Latino; 1 Two or more races, non-Hispanic/Latino). Average age 27. 20 applicants, 95% accepted, 13 enrolled. In 2016, 17 master's awarded. *Degree requirements:* For master's, thesis or alternative. *Entrance requirements:* Additional exam requirements/recommendations for international students: Required—TOEFL (minimum score 550 paper-based; 80 iBT). *Application deadline:* Applications are processed on a rolling basis. Application fee: $30. Electronic applications accepted. *Financial support:* In 2016–17, 19 students received support. Unspecified assistantships available. Financial award applicants required to submit FAFSA. *Unit head:* Dr. Dan Yoder, Interim Chairperson, 309-298-1967. *Application contact:* Dr. Nancy Parsons, Assistant Director of Graduate Studies, 309-298-1806, Fax: 309-298-2345, E-mail: grad-office@wiu.edu.
Website: http://www.wiu.edu/rpta

TEMPLE UNIVERSITY

Program in Hospitality Management

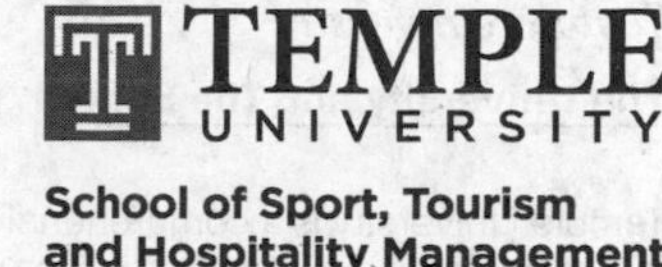

School of Sport, Tourism and Hospitality Management

 For more information, visit http://petersons.to/templeu_hospitalitymgmt

Program of Study

Temple University's School of Sport, Tourism, and Hospitality Management (STHM) offers a Master of Tourism and Hospitality Management (MTHM) degree program that leverages the region's thriving hotel, casino, restaurant, and tourism industries, providing students with exceptional opportunities to engage management and operational theory and apply them to real-world industry cases.

The goal of this master's degree program is to develop advanced professionals in the field of tourism and hospitality management. The program is based not only on the practical application of management techniques, but also on the theoretical foundation that defines the profession. This makes Temple University's program clearly distinct from generic management curricula that do not include an industry-specific core.

Two concentrations allow students wishing to enter the industry, and experienced professionals looking to grow within it, to collaborate with distinguished scholars and industry leaders to become talented managers and executives.

The **Hospitality Operations Management concentration** prepares students who have a degree in an unrelated field, and minimal experience in the hospitality industry, for full-time management roles.

The **Tourism and Hospitality Marketing concentration** allows experienced industry professionals to leverage and apply their operational knowledge of the hospitality sector to the issues impacting consumer preferences and advancements in technology in a competitive and rapidly changing global landscape.

The 36-credit curriculum for this master's degree includes STHM core courses and business courses within the Fox School of Business, as well as a summer internship and a culminating consulting project with a corporate industry partner.

The program may be completed in 18 months, with all courses scheduled after 5 p.m., allowing students to maintain full-time employment or pursue internships and assistantships during regular business hours. Students may do the course work at their own pace, attending classes at any of Temple University's campuses, and designing an individualized graduation plan with an adviser.

Industry-specific career coaching and advising are housed within the school, providing a personalized approach to each students' individual needs.

STHM's Center for Student Professional Development (CSPD) coordinates activities supporting students' career growth. The CSPD staff works with students to provide the latest resources that will help them gain greater insight into their career options. Students who wish to do their internships abroad work closely with the CSPD, which assists with the necessary contacts and supervision.

STHM's Center for Student Services encourages a collaborative relationship between advisers and students, ultimately empowering them to make sound and responsible decisions concerning their education. Students take an active role in the utilization of the services offered by STHM and the university at large, while the academic advisers assist students with their academic and pre-professional needs. This advising unit provides guidance on course sequencing, elective options, registration, financial assistance, scheduling, career planning and academic resources.

Research Facilities

The U.S.-Asia Center for Tourism & Hospitality conducts cutting-edge multidisciplinary research and consultancy specific to the tourism, hospitality, and related industries in the U.S., Asia, and the entire Asia-Pacific region. The Center aims to establish and enhance connections between government, industry, and other public entities in the tourism and hospitality areas. Some of the research areas include: destination marketing, big data analytics, consumer profile analysis, yield and revenue management, and hospitality asset evaluation.

Financial Aid

Teaching and research assistantships and graduate externships within STHM are reserved for students who are capable of teaching undergraduate classes in specialized academic areas or assisting in faculty research. Applications for assistantships and externships are evaluated when a Graduate School application and all appropriate materials are received. Assistantships and externships are available only to admitted students. The evaluation of applicants for these opportunities begins by March and continues until all positions have been filled.

Cost of Study

Temple University is a state-related institution in Pennsylvania. Tuition rates are determined by a student's residency status and program.

The most current information is available online at bursar.temple.edu.

Student Outcomes

The Master of Tourism and Hospitality Management at Temple University has emerged as one of the nation's premier graduate programs for current and future managers within the industry. Graduates of this program become managers and executives in areas including: hotel and resort management, tourism and destination marketing, gaming and casino management, event design and production, venue management, restaurant management, and others.

Location

Philadelphia is a living laboratory for the tourism, hospitality, sport, and recreation industries.

As the United States' fifth-largest city, Philadelphia is a premier destination for visitors from around the world. Home to 13,000 hotel rooms in Center City, over 700 Zagat-rated restaurants, a thriving and growing casino and gaming scene, and the Pennsylvania Convention Center, the city provides countless opportunities for applied learning. Powered by two dynamic destination marketing organizations—Visit Philadelphia and the PHL Convention & Visitors Bureau—Philadelphia attracts thousands of visitors to see and experience attractions like the Liberty Bell, the Philadelphia Museum of Art, and the Philadelphia Zoo.

Temple University

The University and The School

Temple University is a comprehensive public research university located in Philadelphia, Pennsylvania. Nearly 40,000 students from around the globe are enrolled in more than 400 academic degree programs offered at seven campuses in Pennsylvania and three international campuses.

The School of Sport, Tourism and Hospitality Management (STHM) at Temple University is the largest provider of tourism, hospitality, sport, and recreation management programs in the greater Philadelphia region, as well as the area's largest provider of talent for these industries.

Applying

Students with backgrounds from a range of undergraduate majors are welcomed—and encouraged—to apply for admission to the School of Sport, Tourism and Hospitality Management at Temple University. The admission process is comprehensive and takes careful consideration of each applicant's goals and academic aptitude.

Complete details about the admissions process can be found at sthm.temple.edu/petersons2017.

Correspondence and Information

School of Sport, Tourism and Hospitality Management
Speakman Hall 111 (006-68)
1810 N. 13th Street
Philadelphia, Pennsylvania 19122
United States
Phone: 215-204-8701
Fax: 215-204-8705
Website: sthm.temple.edu/petersons2017

The Faculty and Their Research

Dr. Xiang (Robert) Li, Professor, is the author and co-author of over 100 scientific publications, including many in top-tier tourism, business, leisure, and hospitality journals. Li serves on the editorial boards of more than ten journals and book series, including the *Journal of Travel Research*, and *Journal of Leisure Research*. To date, he has been awarded over $1.14 million in research funding. His clients include the United States Department of Commerce/Office of Travel and Tourism Industries (OTTI), China National Tourism Administration (CNTA), the United States Travel Association (UST, formerly TIA), and the National Tour Association (NTA), as well as numerous destination marketing organizations and companies. His research on China and Japan outbound tourism and destination marketing has been cited by a number of American and international media, such as *USA Today*, *Time*, *Las Vegas Sun Times*, *The Globe and Mail, and China Daily*.

Dr. Ceridwyn King, Associate Professor and Chair of the Department of Tourism and Hospitality Management, is an experienced industry consultant and researcher. Prior to becoming an academic, she served as the head of marketing for Conrad Jupiters Hotel and Casino, a 609-room facility with five restaurants, nine bars, and a convention center on the Gold Coast, Australia. She has also held various marketing positions with Starwood Hotels and Resorts and was the founder and principle consultant for Seed–Strategic Marketing Solutions. King's research focuses on service management and marketing, with an emphasis on the internal stakeholder's role in realizing marketing strategies to create competitively sustainable service experiences. To date, she has published 13 peer-reviewed journal articles.

Ira Rosen, Assistant Professor and Director of the Event Leadership Executive Certificate, is a Hall of Fame inductee of the International Festival & Events Association from which he earned the Certified Festivals and Events Executive designation. Rosen's areas of research and expertise include all topics dealing with global event leadership and management, specializing in sponsorship, operations, and risk management.

Michael Sheridan, Assistant Professor, most recently served as director of revenue management for Sofitel Philadelphia, where he was responsible for maximizing revenue for the luxury, four-star hotel through revenue management, inventory control, market-segment pricing, statistical analysis, and demand-stimulating initiatives. From 2005–11, Sheridan served as the hotel program director for the Greater Philadelphia Tourism Marketing Corporation, now known as Visit Philadelphia. During his tenure, he served as a liaison between Philadelphia's tourism-marketing office and the more than 100 hotels in Philadelphia and the suburbs.

A complete listing of STHM faculty and staff can be found at sthm.temple.edu/faculty-and-staff.

Section 8
Human Resources

This section contains a directory of institutions offering graduate work in human resources, followed by in-depth entries submitted by institutions that chose to prepare detailed program descriptions. Additional information about programs listed in the directory but not augmented by an in-depth entry may be obtained by writing directly to the dean of a graduate school or chair of a department at the address given in the directory.

For programs offering related work, see also in this book *Business Administration and Management, Advertising and Public Relations, Hospitality Management, Industrial and Manufacturing Management,* and *Organizational Behavior.* In another guide in this series:

Graduate Programs in the Humanities, Arts & Social Sciences
See *Public, Regional, and Industrial Affairs (Industrial and Labor Relations)*

CONTENTS

Program Directories

Featured Schools: Displays and Close-Ups

See also:

Human Resources Development

Abilene Christian University, Graduate Programs, College of Arts and Sciences, Department of Communication, Program in Organizational Development, Abilene, TX 79699. Offers MS. *Program availability:* Part-time, evening/weekend, online only, 100% online. *Students:* 62 full-time (48 women), 31 part-time (22 women); includes 37 minority (20 Black or African American, non-Hispanic/Latino; 1 American Indian or Alaska Native, non-Hispanic/Latino; 3 Asian, non-Hispanic/Latino; 10 Hispanic/Latino; 3 Two or more races, non-Hispanic/Latino), 1 international. 25 applicants, 92% accepted, 23 enrolled. In 2016, 52 master's awarded. *Degree requirements:* For master's, thesis. *Entrance requirements:* Additional exam requirements/recommendations for international students: Required—TOEFL (minimum score 80 iBT), IELTS (minimum score 6), PTE. *Application deadline:* For fall admission, 8/11 priority date for domestic students; for winter admission, 10/1 priority date for domestic students; for spring admission, 12/15 priority date for domestic students; for summer admission, 4/5 priority date for domestic students. Applications are processed on a rolling basis. Application fee: $50. Electronic applications accepted. *Expenses:* $775 per credit hour. *Financial support:* Scholarships/grants available. Support available to part-time students. Financial award application deadline: 4/1; financial award applicants required to submit FAFSA. *Unit head:* Dr. Jonathan Camp, Graduate Director, 325-674-2136, E-mail: jwc03b@acu.edu. *Application contact:* Corey Patterson, Director of Graduate Admission and Recruiting, 325-674-6566, Fax: 325-674-6717, E-mail: gradinfo@acu.edu.
Website: http://acuonline.acu.edu/

Amberton University, Graduate School, Program in Human Relations and Business, Garland, TX 75041-5595. Offers MS. *Program availability:* Part-time, evening/weekend. *Entrance requirements:* For master's, minimum GPA of 3.0.

Amberton University, Graduate School, Program in Human Resources Training and Development, Garland, TX 75041-5595. Offers MS.

Antioch University Los Angeles, Graduate Programs, Program in Organizational Management, Culver City, CA 90230. Offers human resource development (MA); leadership (MA); organizational development (MA). *Program availability:* Part-time, evening/weekend. *Entrance requirements:* For master's, interview. Additional exam requirements/recommendations for international students: Required—TOEFL. *Faculty research:* Systems thinking and chaos theory, technology and organizational structure, nonprofit management, power and empowerment.

Azusa Pacific University, School of Business and Management, Program in Human and Organizational Development, Azusa, CA 91702-7000. Offers MA. *Program availability:* Part-time, evening/weekend. *Degree requirements:* For master's, comprehensive exam, final project. *Entrance requirements:* For master's, minimum GPA of 3.0.

Barry University, School of Education, Program in Human Resource Development and Administration, Miami Shores, FL 33161-6695. Offers MS. *Program availability:* Part-time, evening/weekend. *Degree requirements:* For master's, comprehensive exam, practicum. *Entrance requirements:* For master's, GRE General Test or MAT, minimum GPA of 3.0. Electronic applications accepted.

Barry University, School of Education, Program in Leadership and Education, Miami Shores, FL 33161-6695. Offers educational technology (PhD); exceptional student education (PhD); higher education administration (PhD); human resource development (PhD); leadership (PhD). *Program availability:* Part-time, evening/weekend. *Degree requirements:* For doctorate, thesis/dissertation. *Entrance requirements:* For doctorate, GRE General Test, minimum GPA of 3.25. Electronic applications accepted.

Bowie State University, Graduate Programs, Program in Human Resource Development, Bowie, MD 20715-9465. Offers MA. *Program availability:* Part-time, evening/weekend. *Degree requirements:* For master's, comprehensive exam, thesis optional, research paper. *Entrance requirements:* For master's, minimum GPA of 2.5. Electronic applications accepted.

California State University, Sacramento, Office of Graduate Studies, College of Business Administration, Sacramento, CA 95819. Offers accountancy (MS); business administration (IMBA, MBA); human resources (MBA); urban land development (MBA). *Accreditation:* AACSB. *Program availability:* Part-time, evening/weekend. *Students:* 138 full-time (68 women), 129 part-time (63 women); includes 211 minority (12 Black or African American, non-Hispanic/Latino; 132 American Indian or Alaska Native, non-Hispanic/Latino; 63 Asian, non-Hispanic/Latino; 4 Native Hawaiian or other Pacific Islander, non-Hispanic/Latino). Average age 34. 198 applicants, 77% accepted, 85 enrolled. In 2016, 168 master's awarded. *Degree requirements:* For master's, thesis or alternative, writing proficiency exam. *Entrance requirements:* For master's, GMAT. Additional exam requirements/recommendations for international students: Required—TOEFL (minimum score 550 paper-based; 80 iBT). *Application deadline:* For fall admission, 2/1 for domestic students, 3/1 for international students; for spring admission, 9/15 for domestic students, 9/30 for international students. Applications are processed on a rolling basis. Application fee: $55. Electronic applications accepted. *Expenses:* $4,302 full-time tuition and fees per semester, $2,796 part-time. *Financial support:* Research assistantships, teaching assistantships, career-related internships or fieldwork, and Federal Work-Study available. Support available to part-time students. Financial award applicants required to submit FAFSA. *Unit head:* Dr. Pierre A. Balthazard, Dean, 916-278-6578, Fax: 916-278-5793, E-mail: cba@csus.edu. *Application contact:* Jose Martinez, Graduate Admissions Supervisor, 916-278-7871, E-mail: martinj@skymail.csus.edu.
Website: http://www.cba.csus.edu

Claremont Graduate University, Graduate Programs, School of Social Science, Policy and Evaluation, Department of Psychology, Claremont, CA 91711-6160. Offers advanced study in evaluation (Certificate); cognitive psychology (MA, PhD); developmental psychology (MA, PhD); evaluation and applied research methods (MA, PhD); health behavior research and evaluation (MA, PhD); human resource development and evaluation (MA); industrial/organizational psychology (MA, PhD); organizational behavior (MA, PhD); organizational psychology (MA, PhD); social psychology (MA, PhD); MBA/PhD. *Program availability:* Part-time. *Faculty:* 19 full-time (9 women), 1 part-time/adjunct (0 women). *Students:* 244 full-time (160 women), 66 part-time (38 women); includes 93 minority (15 Black or African American, non-Hispanic/Latino; 2 American Indian or Alaska Native, non-Hispanic/Latino; 29 Asian, non-Hispanic/Latino; 31 Hispanic/Latino; 2 Native Hawaiian or other Pacific Islander, non-Hispanic/Latino; 14 Two or more races, non-Hispanic/Latino), 41 international. Average age 30. In 2016, 61 master's, 23 doctorates, 5 other advanced degrees awarded. Terminal master's awarded for partial completion of doctoral program. *Entrance requirements:* For master's and doctorate, GRE General Test. Additional exam requirements/recommendations for international students: Required—TOEFL (minimum score 75 iBT). *Application deadline:* For fall admission, 1/15 priority date for domestic and international students. Applications are processed on a rolling basis. Application fee: $80. Electronic applications accepted. *Expenses: Tuition:* Full-time $44,328; part-time $1847 per unit. *Required fees:* $600; $300 per semester. Tuition and fees vary according to course load and program. *Financial support:* Fellowships, research assistantships, teaching assistantships, Federal Work-Study, institutionally sponsored loans, scholarships/grants, and tuition waivers (full and partial) available. Support available to part-time students. Financial award application deadline: 2/15; financial award applicants required to submit FAFSA. *Faculty research:* Social intervention, diversity in organizations, eyewitness memory, aging and cognition, drug policy. *Unit head:* William Crano, Chair, 909-607-3311, E-mail: william.crano@cgu.edu. *Application contact:* Paige Piontkowsky, Senior Assistant Director of Admissions, 909-607-3240, E-mail: paige.piontkowsky@cgu.edu.
Website: https://www.cgu.edu/school/ssspe/programs/?areas_of_study=psychology

Clemson University, Graduate School, College of Education, Clemson, SC 29634-0702. Offers administration and supervision (K-12) (M Ed, Ed S); education and organizational leadership (MS), including athletic leadership; educational leadership (PhD), including P-12; human resource development (MHRD); middle-level education (MAT). *Program availability:* Part-time, evening/weekend, 100% online. *Faculty:* 75 full-time (54 women), 1 part-time/adjunct (0 women). *Students:* 120 full-time (84 women), 309 part-time (206 women); includes 96 minority (68 Black or African American, non-Hispanic/Latino; 1 American Indian or Alaska Native, non-Hispanic/Latino; 3 Asian, non-Hispanic/Latino; 19 Hispanic/Latino; 5 Two or more races, non-Hispanic/Latino), 11 international. Average age 34. 417 applicants, 50% accepted, 133 enrolled. In 2016, 239 master's, 21 doctorates, 59 other advanced degrees awarded. *Degree requirements:* For master's, comprehensive exam (for some programs), thesis (for some programs); for doctorate, comprehensive exam, thesis/dissertation. *Entrance requirements:* For master's, doctorate, and other advanced degree, GRE General Test, unofficial transcripts, letters of recommendation. Additional exam requirements/recommendations for international students: Required—TOEFL (minimum score 80 iBT), IELTS (minimum score 7). *Application deadline:* Applications are processed on a rolling basis. Application fee: $80 ($90 for international students). Electronic applications accepted. *Expenses:* Contact institution. *Financial support:* In 2016–17, 75 students received support, including 22 fellowships with partial tuition reimbursements available (averaging $6,316 per year), 28 research assistantships with partial tuition reimbursements available (averaging $15,399 per year), 5 teaching assistantships with partial tuition reimbursements available (averaging $30,000 per year); unspecified assistantships also available. *Faculty research:* Early literacy and motivation, STEAM education, legal/policy issues in education, leadership, special education interventions/assessment/policy. *Total annual research expenditures:* $2.8 million. *Unit head:* Dr. George Petersen, Dean, 864-656-4444, Fax: 864-656-0311, E-mail: soedean@clemson.edu. *Application contact:* Dr. David Fleming, Graduate Programs Coordinator, 864-656-1881, Fax: 864-656-0311, E-mail: dflemin@clemson.edu.
Website: http://www.clemson.edu/education/

Clemson University, Graduate School, College of Education, Department of Educational and Organizational Leadership Development, Program in Human Resource Development, Greenville, SC 29607. Offers human resource development (MHRD), including intercollegiate athletic leadership. *Program availability:* Part-time, evening/weekend, online only, 100% online. *Faculty:* 3 full-time (2 women), 1 (woman) part-time/adjunct. *Students:* 58 part-time (30 women); includes 22 minority (15 Black or African American, non-Hispanic/Latino; 2 Asian, non-Hispanic/Latino; 4 Hispanic/Latino; 1 Two or more races, non-Hispanic/Latino). Average age 36. 37 applicants, 62% accepted, 20 enrolled. In 2016, 58 master's awarded. *Degree requirements:* For master's, comprehensive exam. *Entrance requirements:* For master's, GRE General Test, unofficial transcripts, personal statement, resume, 2 letters of recommendation. Additional exam requirements/recommendations for international students: Required—TOEFL (minimum score 80 iBT), IELTS (minimum score 7). *Application deadline:* For fall admission, 7/1 priority date for domestic students. Application fee: $80 ($90 for international students). Electronic applications accepted. *Expenses:* $695 per credit hour, $10 per credit hour IT fee, $39 per semester miscellaneous fees. *Financial support:* Application deadline: 7/1. *Faculty research:* Organizational development, human performance improvement, attachment theory, social constructivism, technology-mediated teaching and learning, corporate universities. *Unit head:* Dr. Phillip McGee, Program Coordinator, 864-474-2459, E-mail: pmcgee@clemson.edu. *Application contact:* Alison Search, Student Services Program Coordinator, 864-656-8370, E-mail: alisonp@clemson.edu.
Website: http://www.clemson.edu/education/academics/masters-specialist-programs/masters-education-human-resource-development/index.html

The College of New Rochelle, Graduate School, Division of Human Services, Program in Career Development, New Rochelle, NY 10805-2308. Offers MS, Advanced Certificate. *Program availability:* Part-time. *Degree requirements:* For master's and Advanced Certificate, internship. *Entrance requirements:* For master's, interview, minimum GPA of 3.0, writing sample.

Drexel University, Goodwin College of Professional Studies, School of Education, Philadelphia, PA 19104-2875. Offers applied behavior analysis (MS); creativity and innovation (MS); education improvement and transformation (MS); educational administration (MS); educational leadership and management (Ed D); educational leadership development and learning technologies (PhD); global and international education (MS); higher education (MS); human resources development (MS); learning technologies (MS); mathematics, learning and teaching (MS); special education (MS); teaching, learning and curriculum (MS). *Program availability:* Part-time, evening/weekend, online learning. *Degree requirements:* For doctorate, thesis/dissertation. *Entrance requirements:* For doctorate, GRE or GMAT. Additional exam requirements/recommendations for international students: Required—TOEFL, IELTS. Electronic applications accepted. Application fee is waived when completed online. *Expenses:* Contact institution. *Faculty research:* Leadership development, mathematics education, literacy, autism, educational technology.

See Display on page 660 and Close-Up on page 727.

Florida International University, College of Arts, Sciences, and Education, Department of Leadership and Professional Studies, Miami, FL 33199. Offers adult education and human resource development (MS, Ed D); counseling (MS), including rehabilitation counseling, school counseling; counselor education (MS), including clinical mental health counseling; educational administration and supervision (Ed D); educational leadership (MS, Certificate, Ed S); higher education (Ed D); higher education administration (MS); international and comparative education (MS); recreation and sport management (MS), including recreation and sport management, recreational therapy; school psychology (Ed S); urban education (MS), including instruction in urban

settings, learning technologies, multicultural/bilingual, multicultural/TESOL, urban education. *Program availability:* Part-time, evening/weekend. *Faculty:* 27 full-time (19 women), 38 part-time/adjunct (25 women). *Students:* 253 full-time (191 women), 306 part-time (241 women); includes 444 minority (129 Black or African American, non-Hispanic/Latino; 3 Asian, non-Hispanic/Latino; 304 Hispanic/Latino; 8 Two or more races, non-Hispanic/Latino), 18 international. Average age 31. 366 applicants, 60% accepted, 115 enrolled. In 2016, 193 master's, 8 doctorates awarded. *Degree requirements:* For doctorate, thesis/dissertation. *Entrance requirements:* For master's, minimum GPA of 3.0; for doctorate and other advanced degree, GRE General Test. Additional exam requirements/recommendations for international students: Required—TOEFL (minimum score 550 paper-based; 80 iBT), IELTS (minimum score 6.3). *Application deadline:* For fall admission, 6/1 priority date for domestic students, 4/1 for international students; for winter admission, 10/1 priority date for domestic students, 9/1 for international students; for spring admission, 3/1 priority date for domestic students, 2/1 for international students. Applications are processed on a rolling basis. Application fee: $30. Electronic applications accepted. *Expenses:* Tuition, state resident: full-time $8912; part-time $446 per credit hour. Tuition, nonresident: full-time $21,393; part-time $992 per credit hour. *Required fees:* $2185; $195 per semester. Tuition and fees vary according to program. *Financial support:* Fellowships, research assistantships with tuition reimbursements, teaching assistantships with tuition reimbursements, Federal Work-Study, and tuition waivers (full and partial) available. Support available to part-time students. Financial award applicants required to submit FAFSA. *Unit head:* Dr. Benjamin Baez, Chair, 305-348-3214, Fax: 305-348-1515, E-mail: benjamin.baez@fiu.edu. *Application contact:* Nanett Rojas, Assistant Director, Graduate Admissions, 305-348-7464, Fax: 305-348-7441, E-mail: gradadm@fiu.edu.
Website: http://education.fiu.edu

The George Washington University, Graduate School of Education and Human Development, Department of Human and Organizational Learning, Program in Human Resource Development, Washington, DC 20052. Offers MA. *Program availability:* Part-time, evening/weekend. *Students:* 2 part-time (1 woman), 15 international. Average age 42. In 2016, 19 master's awarded. *Entrance requirements:* For master's, GRE, MAT, or GMAT, two letters of recommendation, statement of purpose, official transcripts, resume. Additional exam requirements/recommendations for international students: Required—TOEFL or IELTS. Electronic applications accepted. *Financial support:* Fellowships available. *Unit head:* Kristin Furio, Program Manager, 202-994-1040, Fax: 202-994-4928, E-mail: hrd@gwu.edu. *Application contact:* Sarah Lang, Director of Graduate Admissions, 202-994-1447, Fax: 202-994-7207, E-mail: slang@gwu.edu.
Website: http://gsehd.gwu.edu/

The George Washington University, Graduate School of Education and Human Development, Department of Human and Organizational Learning, Program in Leadership Development, Washington, DC 20052. Offers Graduate Certificate. *Students:* 13 part-time (10 women); includes 7 minority (2 Black or African American, non-Hispanic/Latino; 4 Asian, non-Hispanic/Latino; 1 Hispanic/Latino). Average age 37. 17 applicants, 94% accepted, 13 enrolled. In 2016, 10 Graduate Certificates awarded. *Degree requirements:* For Graduate Certificate, practicum. *Entrance requirements:* For degree, two letters of recommendation, resume, statement of purpose. Electronic applications accepted. *Unit head:* Michael Feuer, Dean, 202-994-6161, E-mail: mjfeuer@gwu.edu. *Application contact:* Sarah Lang, Director of Graduate Admissions, 202-994-1447, Fax: 202-994-7207, E-mail: slang@gwu.edu.
Website: http://gsehd.gwu.edu/academics/programs/certificates/leadership-development/overview

The George Washington University, Graduate School of Education and Human Development, Department of Human and Organizational Learning, Programs in Human and Organizational Learning, Washington, DC 20052. Offers Ed D, Ed S. *Students:* 42 full-time (23 women), 121 part-time (71 women); includes 60 minority (36 Black or African American, non-Hispanic/Latino; 1 American Indian or Alaska Native, non-Hispanic/Latino; 4 Asian, non-Hispanic/Latino; 12 Hispanic/Latino; 7 Two or more races, non-Hispanic/Latino), 6 international. Average age 46. 71 applicants, 70% accepted, 29 enrolled. In 2016, 15 doctorates, 1 other advanced degree awarded. *Degree requirements:* For doctorate, comprehensive exam, thesis/dissertation; for Ed S, comprehensive exam. *Entrance requirements:* For doctorate, GRE General Test or MAT, interview, minimum GPA of 3.3; for Ed S, GRE General Test or MAT, minimum GPA of 3.3. *Application deadline:* For fall admission, 1/15 priority date for domestic students; for spring admission, 10/1 for domestic students. Applications are processed on a rolling basis. Application fee: $75. *Financial support:* Fellowships, research assistantships, teaching assistantships, career-related internships or fieldwork, Federal Work-Study, and tuition waivers (partial) available. Financial award application deadline: 1/15; financial award applicants required to submit FAFSA. *Faculty research:* Organizational learning, program evaluation. *Unit head:* David Schwandt, Program Manager, 571-553-3770, E-mail: schwandt@gwu.edu. *Application contact:* Sarah Lang, Director of Graduate Admissions, 202-994-1447, E-mail: slang@gwu.edu.
Website: http://gsehd.gwu.edu/

Grantham University, Mark Skousen School of Business, Lenexa, KS 66219. Offers business administration (MBA); business intelligence (MS); human resources management (Certificate); information management (MBA); performance improvement (MS); project management (MBA, Certificate). *Program availability:* Part-time, online only, 100% online. *Faculty:* 1 full-time, 36 part-time/adjunct. *Students:* 73 full-time (37 women), 1,046 part-time (424 women); includes 442 minority (309 Black or African American, non-Hispanic/Latino; 8 American Indian or Alaska Native, non-Hispanic/Latino; 27 Asian, non-Hispanic/Latino; 63 Hispanic/Latino; 7 Native Hawaiian or other Pacific Islander, non-Hispanic/Latino; 28 Two or more races, non-Hispanic/Latino). Average age 40. 1,324 applicants, 95% accepted, 1123 enrolled. In 2016, 331 master's awarded. *Degree requirements:* For master's, capstone project, PMP Prep Exam; for Certificate, comprehensive exam (for some programs), PMP Prep Exam. *Entrance requirements:* For master's, baccalaureate or master's degree with minimum cumulative GPA of 2.5 from institution accredited by agency recognized by U.S. Department of Education or foreign equivalent. Additional exam requirements/recommendations for international students: Required—PTE (minimum score 50), TOEFL (minimum score 530 paper-based, 71 iBT) or IELTS (minimum score 6.5). *Application deadline:* Applications are processed on a rolling basis. Electronic applications accepted. *Expenses:* $325 per credit hour, $45 per 8-week term technology fee. *Financial support:* Scholarships/grants available. Financial award applicants required to submit FAFSA. *Faculty research:* Organizational structures, e-discovery and project management, decision management, resource-based and ethical perspectives, external finance dependence in corporate investments. *Unit head:* Dr. David Marker, Dean, Mark Skousen School of Business, 800-955-2527, E-mail: dmarker@grantham.edu. *Application contact:* Jared Parlette, Vice President of Student Enrollment, 800-955-2527, E-mail: admissions@grantham.edu.
Website: http://www.grantham.edu/colleges-and-schools/school-of-business/

Illinois Institute of Technology, Graduate College, Lewis College of Human Sciences, Department of Psychology, Chicago, IL 60616. Offers clinical psychology (PhD); industrial and organizational psychology (PhD); personnel and human resource development (MS); rehabilitation and mental health counseling (MS); rehabilitation counseling education (PhD). *Accreditation:* APA (one or more programs are accredited); CORE. *Program availability:* Part-time, evening/weekend. Terminal master's awarded for partial completion of doctoral program. *Degree requirements:* For master's, thesis (for some programs); for doctorate, comprehensive exam, thesis/dissertation, minimum of 107 credit hours, 1-year full-time internship. *Entrance requirements:* For master's, GRE General Test (minimum score 298 Quantitative and Verbal, 3.0 Analytical Writing), minimum GPA of 3.0; 3 letters of recommendation; bachelor's degree from accredited institution (for personnel and human resource development); for doctorate, GRE General Test (minimum score 298 Quantitative and Verbal, 3.0 Analytical Writing), bachelor's or master's degree from accredited institution, recommendations. Additional exam requirements/recommendations for international students: Required—TOEFL (minimum score 550 paper-based; 80 iBT). Electronic applications accepted. *Faculty research:* Clinical psychology, rehabilitation and mental health counseling, industrial organizational psychology.

Indiana State University, College of Graduate and Professional Studies, College of Technology, Department of Human Resource Development and Performance Technologies, Terre Haute, IN 47809. Offers career and technical education (MS); human resource development (MS).

Indiana Tech, Program in Business Administration, Fort Wayne, IN 46803-1297. Offers accounting (MBA); health care management (MBA); human resources (MBA); management (MBA); marketing (MBA). *Program availability:* Part-time, evening/weekend, online learning. *Entrance requirements:* For master's, GMAT, bachelor's degree from regionally-accredited university; minimum undergraduate GPA of 2.5; 2 years of significant work experience; 3 letters of recommendation. Electronic applications accepted.

Indiana University of Pennsylvania, School of Graduate Studies and Research, College of Education and Educational Technology, Department of Adult and Community Education, Program in Business/Workforce Development, Indiana, PA 15705. Offers M Ed. *Program availability:* Part-time. *Faculty:* 2 full-time (1 woman). *Students:* 2 full-time (0 women), 8 part-time (2 women), 2 international. Average age 33. 2 applicants, 50% accepted, 1 enrolled. *Degree requirements:* For master's, thesis optional. *Entrance requirements:* For master's, GMAT or GRE. Additional exam requirements/recommendations for international students: Required—TOEFL (minimum score 540 paper-based). *Application deadline:* Applications are processed on a rolling basis. Application fee: $50. Electronic applications accepted. *Expenses:* Tuition, state resident: full-time $8694; part-time $483 per credit. Tuition, nonresident: full-time $13,050; part-time $725 per credit. *Required fees:* $157 per credit. $50 per term. Tuition and fees vary according to course load and program. *Financial support:* In 2016–17, 1 research assistantship with tuition reimbursement (averaging $5,440 per year) was awarded; career-related internships or fieldwork and Federal Work-Study also available. Support available to part-time students. Financial award application deadline: 4/15; financial award applicants required to submit FAFSA. *Unit head:* Dr. Lucinda Willis, Graduate Coordinator, 724-357-4585, E-mail: lucinda.willis@iup.edu.
Website: http://www.iup.edu/ace/grad/default.aspx

Inter American University of Puerto Rico, Metropolitan Campus, Graduate Programs, Program in Human Resources, San Juan, PR 00919-1293. Offers MBA. *Degree requirements:* For master's, comprehensive exam. *Entrance requirements:* For master's, GRE or EXADEP, interview. Electronic applications accepted.

Inter American University of Puerto Rico, San Germán Campus, Graduate Studies Center, Program in Business Administration, San Germán, PR 00683-5008. Offers accounting (MBA); finance (MBA); general business administration (MBA); human resources (MBA, PhD); industrial relations (MBA); information systems (MBA); international and interregional business (PhD); management (MBA); marketing (MBA). *Program availability:* Part-time, evening/weekend. *Degree requirements:* For master's, comprehensive exam. *Entrance requirements:* For master's, GRE General Test or EXADEP, minimum GPA of 3.0.

Iowa State University of Science and Technology, Department of Educational Leadership and Policy Studies, Ames, IA 50011. Offers counselor education (M Ed, MS); educational administration (M Ed, MS); educational leadership (PhD); higher education (M Ed, MS); organizational learning and human resource development (M Ed, MS); research and evaluation (MS); student affairs (MS). *Degree requirements:* For master's, thesis or alternative; for doctorate, thesis/dissertation. *Entrance requirements:* For master's and doctorate, GRE General Test. Additional exam requirements/recommendations for international students: Required—TOEFL (minimum score 560 paper-based; 83 iBT), IELTS (minimum score 6.5). *Application deadline:* For fall admission, 1/1 priority date for domestic and international students. Application fee: $60 ($90 for international students). Electronic applications accepted. *Application contact:* Robyn Goldy, Application Contact, 515-294-1241, Fax: 515-294-4942, E-mail: rgoldy@iastate.edu.
Website: http://www.elps.hs.iastate.edu/

John F. Kennedy University, School of Management, Program in Career Development, Pleasant Hill, CA 94523-4817. Offers career coaching (Certificate); career development (MA, Certificate). *Program availability:* Part-time, evening/weekend. *Degree requirements:* For master's, thesis or alternative. *Entrance requirements:* For master's, interview. Additional exam requirements/recommendations for international students: Required—TOEFL.

Kentucky State University, College of Professional Studies, Frankfort, KY 40601. Offers nursing (DNP); public administration (MPA), including human resource management; special education (MA). *Program availability:* Part-time, evening/weekend, 100% online, blended/hybrid learning. *Faculty:* 6 full-time (3 women), 7 part-time/adjunct (6 women). *Students:* 32 full-time (22 women), 37 part-time (30 women); includes 48 minority (47 Black or African American, non-Hispanic/Latino; 1 Asian, non-Hispanic/Latino). Average age 34. 42 applicants, 79% accepted, 24 enrolled. In 2016, 19 master's awarded. *Degree requirements:* For master's, comprehensive exam, thesis optional; for doctorate, comprehensive exam, thesis/dissertation optional, 180 clinical hours. *Entrance requirements:* For master's, GMAT, GRE, transcript, essay, letters of recommendation; for doctorate, RN license; resume; graduate research and statistics courses (strongly recommended). Additional exam requirements/recommendations for international students: Required—TOEFL (minimum score 525 paper-based). *Application deadline:* For fall admission, 7/1 for domestic students, 4/1 for international students; for spring admission, 11/15 for domestic students, 8/15 for international students; for summer admission, 5/1 for domestic students, 2/1 for international students. Applications are processed on a rolling basis. Application fee: $30 ($100 for international students). Electronic applications accepted. *Expenses:* Tuition, state resident: full-time $7524; part-time $418 per credit hour. Tuition, nonresident: full-time $11,322; part-time $629 per credit hour. Tuition and fees vary according to course load. *Financial support:* In 2016–17, 57 students received support, including 3 research assistantships (averaging $10,083 per year); scholarships/grants, tuition waivers (partial), and unspecified assistantships also available. Financial award application deadline: 4/15; financial award applicants required to submit FAFSA. *Faculty research:* Risk assessment and failure modeling for the public sector implication of property rights on economic development, the social stability of communities, civil peace of nations.

Human Resources Development

Total annual research expenditures: $129,604. *Unit head:* Dr. Candice L. Jackson, Vice President of Academic Affairs, 502-597-6442, E-mail: candice.jackson@kysu.edu. *Application contact:* Dr. James Obielodan, Director of Graduate Studies, 502-597-4723, E-mail: james.obielodan@kysu.edu.
Website: http://kysu.edu/academics/college-of-professional-studies/

La Salle University, School of Business, Program in Human Capital Development, Philadelphia, PA 19141-1199. Offers MS, Certificate. *Program availability:* Part-time, evening/weekend, online only, 100% online. *Faculty:* 3 part-time/adjunct (2 women). *Students:* 1 (woman) full-time, 28 part-time (23 women); includes 16 minority (12 Black or African American, non-Hispanic/Latino; 2 Hispanic/Latino; 2 Two or more races, non-Hispanic/Latino). Average age 38. 7 applicants, 100% accepted, 7 enrolled. In 2016, 8 master's, 1 other advanced degree awarded. *Degree requirements:* For master's, capstone project. *Entrance requirements:* For master's and Certificate, professional resume; 2 letters of recommendation; 500-word essay stating interest in program and goals; baccalaureate degree. Additional exam requirements/recommendations for international students: Required—TOEFL. *Application deadline:* For fall admission, 8/15 priority date for domestic students; for spring admission, 12/15 for domestic students; for summer admission, 4/14 for domestic students. Applications are processed on a rolling basis. Application fee: $35. Electronic applications accepted. Application fee is waived when completed online. *Expenses:* Contact institution. *Financial support:* In 2016–17, 6 students received support. Scholarships/grants and unspecified assistantships available. Support available to part-time students. Financial award application deadline: 8/31; financial award applicants required to submit FAFSA. *Unit head:* Lynnette Clement, Program Director, 215-991-3682, E-mail: clementl@lasalle.edu. *Application contact:* Elizabeth Heenan, Director, Graduate and Adult Enrollment, 215-951-1100, Fax: 215-951-1462, E-mail: heenan@lasalle.edu.
Website: http://www.lasalle.edu/human-capital-development/

Lawrence Technological University, College of Arts and Sciences, Southfield, MI 48075-1058. Offers bioinformatics (Graduate Certificate); computer science (MS), including data science, big data, and data mining, intelligent systems; instructional design, communication, and presentation (Graduate Certificate); instructional technology (Graduate Certificate); premedical studies (Graduate Certificate); technical and professional communication (MS, Graduate Certificate); writing for the digital age (Graduate Certificate). *Program availability:* Part-time, evening/weekend. *Faculty:* 6 full-time (2 women), 10 part-time/adjunct (5 women). *Students:* 37 part-time (18 women); includes 4 minority (1 Black or African American, non-Hispanic/Latino; 1 Asian, non-Hispanic/Latino; 2 Hispanic/Latino), 8 international. Average age 33. 301 applicants, 23% accepted, 9 enrolled. In 2016, 22 master's, 2 other advanced degrees awarded. *Degree requirements:* For master's, thesis (for some programs). *Entrance requirements:* Additional exam requirements/recommendations for international students: Required—TOEFL (minimum score 550 paper-based; 79 iBT), IELTS (minimum score 6.5). *Application deadline:* For fall admission, 5/22 for international students; for spring admission, 10/11 for international students; for summer admission, 2/16 for international students. Applications are processed on a rolling basis. Application fee: $50. Electronic applications accepted. *Expenses: Tuition:* Full-time $14,868; part-time $1062 per credit. *Required fees:* $75 per semester. Tuition and fees vary according to campus/location. *Financial support:* In 2016–17, 9 students received support. Scholarships/grants and tuition reduction available. Financial award application deadline: 4/1; financial award applicants required to submit FAFSA. *Faculty research:* Computer analysis of visual art, psychology of numbers games, neural basis of moral judgement, synthesis of glycosylated warfarin analogs for potential use as antiviral drugs, observation of chemotaxis behavior in c. elegans. *Total annual research expenditures:* $530,625. *Unit head:* Dr. Hsiao-Ping Moore, Dean, 248-204-3500, Fax: 248-204-3518, E-mail: scidean@ltu.edu. *Application contact:* Jane Rohrback, Director of Admissions, 248-204-3160, Fax: 248-204-2228, E-mail: admissions@ltu.edu.

Lincoln Memorial University, Carter and Moyers School of Education, Harrogate, TN 37752-1901. Offers administration and supervision (M Ed, Ed S); counseling and guidance (M Ed); curriculum and instruction (M Ed, Ed D, Ed S); English (M Ed); executive leadership (Ed D); higher education administration (Ed D); human resource development (Ed D); leadership and administration (Ed D). *Program availability:* Part-time, evening/weekend, online learning. *Degree requirements:* For master's, comprehensive exam, thesis optional; for Ed S, comprehensive exam. *Entrance requirements:* For master's, PRAXIS, NTE, GRE, MAT, letters of recommendation; for Ed S, graduate transcripts. Additional exam requirements/recommendations for international students: Recommended—TOEFL. *Faculty research:* Brain compatible teaching and learning; poverty in Appalachia; leadership for change; ethics, moral responsibility and social justice; human and organizational learning.

Louisiana State University and Agricultural & Mechanical College, Graduate School, College of Human Sciences and Education, School of Human Resource Education and Workforce Development, Baton Rouge, LA 70803. Offers agriculture and extension education and youth development (MS, PhD); career and technical education (MS, PhD); comprehensive vocational education (MS, PhD); extension and international education (MS, PhD); human resource and leadership development (MS, PhD); industrial education (MS); vocational agriculture education (MS, PhD); vocational business education (MS); vocational home economics education (MS). *Accreditation:* NCATE.

Marquette University, Graduate School of Management, Program in Human Resources, Milwaukee, WI 53201-1881. Offers MSHR. *Program availability:* Part-time, evening/weekend. *Students:* 14 full-time (8 women), 8 part-time (5 women); includes 3 minority (2 Black or African American, non-Hispanic/Latino; 1 Hispanic/Latino), 12 international. Average age 26. 57 applicants, 81% accepted, 15 enrolled. In 2016, 11 master's awarded. *Entrance requirements:* For master's, GMAT or GRE General Test, letters of recommendation. Additional exam requirements/recommendations for international students: Required—TOEFL (minimum score 550 paper-based; 88 iBT), IELTS (minimum score 6.5), PTE. *Application deadline:* For fall admission, 2/15 for domestic and international students. Applications are processed on a rolling basis. Electronic applications accepted. *Financial support:* Fellowships, research assistantships, teaching assistantships, Federal Work-Study, institutionally sponsored loans, and tuition waivers (full and partial) available. Support available to part-time students. Financial award application deadline: 2/15. *Faculty research:* Diversity, mentoring, executive compensation. *Unit head:* Dr. Brian Till, Dean, 414-288-5724. *Application contact:* Dr. Jeanne Simmons, Associate Professor, 414-288-1458.
Website: http://business.marquette.edu/academics/mshr

McDaniel College, Graduate and Professional Studies, Program in Human Resources Development, Westminster, MD 21157-4390. Offers MS. *Program availability:* Part-time, evening/weekend. *Faculty:* 1 (woman) full-time, 4 part-time/adjunct (2 women). *Students:* 5 full-time (3 women), 15 part-time (9 women); includes 5 minority (4 Black or African American, non-Hispanic/Latino; 1 Asian, non-Hispanic/Latino), 3 international. Average age 31. 9 applicants, 89% accepted. In 2016, 6 master's awarded. *Degree requirements:* For master's, portfolio, internship. *Entrance requirements:* For master's, 3 recommendations; essay. Additional exam requirements/recommendations for international students: Required—TOEFL (minimum score 79 iBT), IELTS (minimum score 6). *Application deadline:* For fall admission, 6/1 priority date for domestic students. Applications are processed on a rolling basis. Application fee: $75. Electronic applications accepted. *Expenses: Tuition:* Full-time $8370; part-time $465 per credit. *Required fees:* $75 per semester. Tuition and fees vary according to course load, program and reciprocity agreements. *Financial support:* Application deadline: 3/1; applicants required to submit FAFSA. *Unit head:* E-mail: gradadms@mcdaniel.edu. *Application contact:* Crystal L. Perry, Assistant Director, Graduate Enrollment Management, 410-857-2516, Fax: 410-857-2515, E-mail: cperry@mcdaniel.edu.

Midwestern State University, Billie Doris McAda Graduate School, West College of Education, Program in Counseling, Wichita Falls, TX 76308. Offers counseling (MA); human resource development (MA); school counseling (M Ed); training and development (MA). *Program availability:* Part-time, evening/weekend. *Degree requirements:* For master's, comprehensive exam, thesis (for some programs). *Entrance requirements:* For master's, GRE General Test, MAT, or GMAT, valid teaching certificate (M Ed). Additional exam requirements/recommendations for international students: Required—TOEFL (minimum score 550 paper-based). Electronic applications accepted. *Faculty research:* Social development of students with disabilities, autism, criminal justice counseling, conflict resolution issues, leadership.

Mississippi State University, College of Education, Department of Instructional Systems and Workforce Development, Mississippi State, MS 39762. Offers distance education (MSIT); instructional design (MSIT); instructional systems and workforce development (MST, PhD); multimedia (MSIT); technology (Ed S). *Faculty:* 12 full-time (8 women). *Students:* 14 full-time (10 women), 53 part-time (44 women); includes 41 minority (39 Black or African American, non-Hispanic/Latino; 1 American Indian or Alaska Native, non-Hispanic/Latino; 1 Two or more races, non-Hispanic/Latino). Average age 38. 17 applicants, 47% accepted, 8 enrolled. In 2016, 6 master's, 3 doctorates, 5 other advanced degrees awarded. *Degree requirements:* For master's, thesis optional, comprehensive oral or written exam; for doctorate, thesis/dissertation, comprehensive oral and written exam; for Ed S, thesis, comprehensive written exam. *Entrance requirements:* For master's, GRE, minimum GPA of 2.75 on undergraduate work, 3.0 graduate; for doctorate, GRE, minimum GPA of 3.4 on graduate work; for Ed S, GRE, minimum GPA of 3.2, master's degree. Additional exam requirements/recommendations for international students: Required—TOEFL (minimum score 550 paper-based; 79 iBT); Recommended—IELTS (minimum score 6.5). *Application deadline:* For fall admission, 7/1 for domestic students, 5/1 for international students; for spring admission, 11/1 for domestic students, 9/1 for international students. Applications are processed on a rolling basis. Application fee: $60. Electronic applications accepted. *Expenses:* Tuition, state resident: full-time $7670; part-time $852.50 per credit hour. Tuition, nonresident: full-time $20,790; part-time $2310.50 per credit hour. Part-time tuition and fees vary according to course load. *Financial support:* In 2016–17, 2 research assistantships with full tuition reimbursements (averaging $13,755 per year), 2 teaching assistantships with full tuition reimbursements (averaging $10,800 per year) were awarded; Federal Work-Study, institutionally sponsored loans, scholarships/grants, and unspecified assistantships also available. Financial award application deadline: 4/1; financial award applicants required to submit FAFSA. *Faculty research:* Computer technology, nontraditional students, interactive video, instructional technology, educational leadership. *Unit head:* Dr. Connie Forde, Professor and Department Head, 662-325-2281, Fax: 662-325-7599, E-mail: cforde@colled.msstate.edu. *Application contact:* Linda Bonner, Senior Admissions Assistant, 662-325-3363, E-mail: lbonner@grad.msstate.edu.
Website: http://www.iswd.msstate.edu

Moravian College, Graduate and Continuing Studies, Business and Management Programs, Bethlehem, PA 18018-6650. Offers accounting (MBA); business analytics (MBA); general management (MBA); health administration (MHA); healthcare management (MBA); human resource management (MBA); leadership (MSHRM); learning and performance management (MSHRM); supply chain management (MBA). *Program availability:* Part-time, evening/weekend. *Faculty:* 4 full-time (1 woman), 9 part-time/adjunct (4 women). *Students:* 14 full-time (7 women), 88 part-time (46 women); includes 17 minority (7 Black or African American, non-Hispanic/Latino; 1 American Indian or Alaska Native, non-Hispanic/Latino; 3 Asian, non-Hispanic/Latino; 6 Hispanic/Latino), 1 international. Average age 33. 25 applicants, 92% accepted, 18 enrolled. In 2016, 11 master's awarded. *Entrance requirements:* For master's, current resume, offical transcripts, 2 letters of recommendation. Additional exam requirements/recommendations for international students: Required—TOEFL (minimum score 550 paper-based), IELTS (minimum score 6.5). *Application deadline:* For fall admission, 8/1 priority date for domestic and international students; for spring admission, 1/1 priority date for domestic and international students; for summer admission, 5/1 priority date for domestic and international students. Applications are processed on a rolling basis. Electronic applications accepted. *Expenses: Tuition:* Full-time $2619. Tuition and fees vary according to course load and program. *Financial support:* Applicants required to submit FAFSA. *Faculty research:* Leadership, change management, human resources. *Unit head:* Dr. Liz Kleintop, Associate Chair of Graduate Business, 610-861-1400, Fax: 610-861-1466, E-mail: mba@moravian.edu. *Application contact:* Kristy Sullivan, Director of Student Recruitment Operations, 610-861-1400, Fax: 610-861-1466, E-mail: graduate@moravian.edu.
Website: https://www.moravian.edu/graduate

National Louis University, College of Management and Business, Chicago, IL 60603. Offers business administration (MBA); human resource management and development (MS); management (MS). *Program availability:* Part-time, evening/weekend. *Entrance requirements:* For master's, college-administered critical thinking and writing skills test, minimum GPA of 3.0, resume, 3 references. Additional exam requirements/recommendations for international students: Required—TOEFL (minimum score 550 paper-based; 79 iBT).

New York University, School of Continuing and Professional Studies, Division of Programs in Business, Program in Leadership and Human Capital Management, New York, NY 10012-1019. Offers benefits and compensation (Advanced Certificate); human resource management (Advanced Certificate); human resource management and development (MS), including global talent management, human resource management, organizational effectiveness; organizational and executive coaching (Advanced Certificate). *Program availability:* Part-time, evening/weekend, online learning. *Degree requirements:* For master's, thesis. *Entrance requirements:* For master's, GRE or GMAT (only upon request), bachelor's degree, resume with relevant professional work, internship or volunteer experience, two letters of recommendation, statement of purpose. Additional exam requirements/recommendations for international students: Required—TOEFL (minimum score 600 paper-based; 100 iBT), IELTS (minimum score 7). Electronic applications accepted.

North Carolina State University, Graduate School, College of Education, Department of Adult and Higher Education, Program in Human Resource Development, Raleigh, NC 27695. Offers MS. *Degree requirements:* For master's, thesis. *Entrance requirements:* For master's, GRE, 3 letters of recommendation, resume.

Northeastern Illinois University, College of Graduate Studies and Research, College of Education, Program in Human Resource Development, Chicago, IL 60625-4699. Offers educational leadership (MA); human resource development (MA). *Program availability:* Part-time, evening/weekend. *Degree requirements:* For master's, comprehensive papers. *Entrance requirements:* For master's, minimum GPA of 2.75, BA in human resource development. Additional exam requirements/recommendations for international students: Required—TOEFL (minimum score 550 paper-based; 79 iBT). Electronic applications accepted. *Faculty research:* Analogics, development of expertise, case-based instruction, action science organizational development, theoretical model building.

Ottawa University, Graduate Studies-Kansas City, Overland Park, KS 66211. Offers business administration (MBA); human resources (MA). *Program availability:* Part-time, evening/weekend, online learning. *Degree requirements:* For master's, thesis or alternative. *Entrance requirements:* For master's, resume, 3 letters of recommendation. Additional exam requirements/recommendations for international students: Required—TOEFL (minimum score 550 paper-based). Electronic applications accepted. *Expenses:* Contact institution.

Penn State Great Valley, Graduate Studies, Management Division, Malvern, PA 19355-1488. Offers business administration (MBA); cyber security (Certificate); data analytics (Certificate); distributed energy and grid modernization (Certificate); finance (M Fin, Certificate); health sector management (Certificate); human resource management (Certificate); information science (MSIS); leadership development (MLD); new ventures and entrepreneurship (Certificate); professional studies in data analytics (MPS); sustainable management practices (Certificate). *Accreditation:* AACSB. *Unit head:* Dr. James A. Nemes, Chancellor, 610-648-3202, Fax: 610-725-5296. *Application contact:* JoAnn Kelly, Director of Admissions, 610-648-3315, Fax: 610-725-5296, E-mail: jek2@psu.edu.
Website: http://greatvalley.psu.edu/academics/masters-degrees/engineering-management

Penn State University Park, Graduate School, College of the Liberal Arts, School of Labor and Employment Relations, University Park, PA 16802. Offers human resources and employment relations (MPS, MS); labor and global workers' rights (MPS). *Unit head:* Dr. Susan Welch, Dean, 814-865-7691, Fax: 814-863-2085. *Application contact:* Lori Hawn, Director, Graduate Student Services, 814-865-1795, Fax: 814-863-4627, E-mail: l-gswww@lists.psu.edu.
Website: http://lser.la.psu.edu/

Pittsburg State University, Graduate School, College of Technology, Department of Technology and Workforce Learning, Program in Human Resource Development, Pittsburg, KS 66762. Offers MS. *Program availability:* Part-time, online only, 100% online. *Students:* 60. In 2016, 32 master's awarded. *Degree requirements:* For master's, thesis or alternative. *Entrance requirements:* Additional exam requirements/recommendations for international students: Required—TOEFL (minimum score 520 paper-based; 68 iBT), IELTS (minimum score 6), PTE (minimum score 47). *Application deadline:* For fall admission, 7/15 for domestic students, 6/1 for international students; for spring admission, 12/15 for domestic students, 10/15 for international students; for summer admission, 5/15 for domestic students, 4/1 for international students. Applications are processed on a rolling basis. Application fee: $35 ($60 for international students). Electronic applications accepted. *Expenses:* Contact institution. *Financial support:* In 2016–17, 1 teaching assistantship with full tuition reimbursement (averaging $5,500 per year) was awarded; career-related internships or fieldwork and Federal Work-Study also available. Financial award application deadline: 2/1; financial award applicants required to submit FAFSA. *Unit head:* Dr. MeLisa Rogers, Program Coordinator, 620-235-4371, E-mail: mrogers@pittstate.edu. *Application contact:* Lisa Allen, Assistant Director of Graduate and Continuing Studies, 620-235-4218, Fax: 620-235-4219, E-mail: lallen@pittstate.edu.
Website: http://www.pittstate.edu/tm/hrd/masters.html

Regent University, Graduate School, School of Business and Leadership, Virginia Beach, VA 23464-9800. Offers business administration (MBA), including accounting, entrepreneurship, finance and investing, general management, healthcare management (MA, MBA), human resource management, innovation management; leadership (Certificate); organizational leadership (MA, PhD), including ecclesial leadership (PhD), entrepreneurial leadership (PhD), future studies (MA), healthcare management (MA, MBA), human resource development (PhD), interdisciplinary studies (MA), international organizations (MA), leadership coaching and mentoring (MA), not-for-profit management (MA), organizational communication (MA), organizational development consulting (MA); strategic leadership (DSL), including global consulting, leadership coaching, strategic foresight. *Program availability:* Part-time, evening/weekend, 100% online, blended/hybrid learning. *Faculty:* 9 full-time (2 women), 28 part-time/adjunct (10 women). *Students:* 100 full-time (56 women), 1,008 part-time (528 women); includes 562 minority (453 Black or African American, non-Hispanic/Latino; 7 American Indian or Alaska Native, non-Hispanic/Latino; 30 Asian, non-Hispanic/Latino; 51 Hispanic/Latino; 1 Native Hawaiian or other Pacific Islander, non-Hispanic/Latino; 20 Two or more races, non-Hispanic/Latino), 76 international. Average age 40. 1,240 applicants, 45% accepted, 352 enrolled. In 2016, 95 master's, 71 doctorates awarded. *Degree requirements:* For master's, thesis or alternative, 3-credit hour culminating experience; for doctorate, thesis/dissertation. *Entrance requirements:* For master's, college transcripts, resume, essay; for doctorate, college transcripts, resume, essay, writing sample; for Certificate, writing sample, resume, transcripts. Additional exam requirements/recommendations for international students: Required—TOEFL (minimum score 577 paper-based). *Application deadline:* For fall admission, 5/1 priority date for domestic students; for spring admission, 10/1 priority date for domestic students. Applications are processed on a rolling basis. Application fee: $50. Electronic applications accepted. *Expenses:* Contact institution. *Financial support:* In 2016–17, 631 students received support. Career-related internships or fieldwork, scholarships/grants, and unspecified assistantships available. Support available to part-time students. *Faculty research:* Servant leadership, global business, team effectiveness, technology utilization, leadership development. *Unit head:* Dr. Doris Gomez, Dean, 757-352-4686, Fax: 757-352-4634, E-mail: dorigom@regent.edu. *Application contact:* Heidi Cece, Assistant Vice President of Enrollment Management, 800-373-5504, Fax: 757-352-4381, E-mail: admissions@regent.edu.
Website: http://www.regent.edu/sbl/

Rochester Institute of Technology, Graduate Enrollment Services, College of Applied Science and Technology, School of International Hospitality and Service Innovation, MS Program in Human Resources Development, Rochester, NY 14623. Offers MS. *Program availability:* Part-time, evening/weekend, 100% online. *Students:* 11 full-time (8 women), 18 part-time (14 women); includes 2 minority (1 Asian, non-Hispanic/Latino; 1 Two or more races, non-Hispanic/Latino), 13 international. Average age 32. 48 applicants, 38% accepted, 9 enrolled. In 2016, 10 master's awarded. *Degree requirements:* For master's, thesis or alternative. *Entrance requirements:* For master's, minimum GPA of 3.0 (recommended). Additional exam requirements/recommendations for international students: Required—TOEFL (minimum score 570 paper-based; 88 iBT), IELTS (minimum score 6.5), PTE (minimum score 62). *Application deadline:* Applications are processed on a rolling basis. Application fee: $60. Electronic applications accepted. *Expenses:* $1,815 per credit hour. *Financial support:* In 2016–17, 12 students received support. Teaching assistantships with partial tuition reimbursements available, career-related internships or fieldwork, scholarships/grants, and unspecified assistantships available. Support available to part-time students. Financial award applicants required to submit FAFSA. *Faculty research:* Diversity recruitment: higher education and corporate America; equity and social justice issues in graduate employability; leadership development. *Unit head:* Dr. Linda Underhill, Director, 585-475-7359, Fax: 585-475-5099, E-mail: lmuism@rit.edu. *Application contact:* Diane Ellison, Associate Vice President, Graduate Enrollment Services, 585-475-2229, Fax: 585-475-7164, E-mail: gradinfo@rit.edu.
Website: http://www.rit.edu/cast/servicesystems/human-resources-development

Rockhurst University, Helzberg School of Management, Kansas City, MO 64110-2561. Offers accounting (MBA); business intelligence (MBA, Certificate); data science (MBA, Certificate); entrepreneurship (MBA); finance (MBA); fundraising leadership (MBA, Certificate); healthcare management (MBA, Certificate); human capital (Certificate); international business (Certificate); management (MBA, Certificate); nonprofit administration (Certificate); organizational development (Certificate); science leadership (Certificate). *Accreditation:* AACSB. *Program availability:* Part-time, evening/weekend. *Entrance requirements:* For master's, GMAT or GRE. Additional exam requirements/recommendations for international students: Required—TOEFL (minimum score 550 paper-based; 79 iBT). Electronic applications accepted. Application fee is waived when completed online. *Faculty research:* Offshoring/outsourcing, systems analysis/synthesis, work teams, multilateral trade, path dependencies/creation.

Rollins College, Hamilton Holt School, Master of Human Resources Program, Winter Park, FL 32789. Offers MHR. *Program availability:* Part-time, evening/weekend. *Faculty:* 4 full-time (0 women), 1 (woman) part-time/adjunct. *Students:* 4 full-time (2 women), 39 part-time (25 women); includes 12 minority (5 Black or African American, non-Hispanic/Latino; 1 American Indian or Alaska Native, non-Hispanic/Latino; 1 Asian, non-Hispanic/Latino; 4 Hispanic/Latino; 1 Two or more races, non-Hispanic/Latino), 4 international. Average age 32. 21 applicants, 81% accepted, 14 enrolled. In 2016, 23 master's awarded. *Degree requirements:* For master's, thesis optional. *Entrance requirements:* For master's, GMAT or GRE, official transcripts, two letters of recommendation, essay, current resume. Additional exam requirements/recommendations for international students: Required—TOEFL (minimum score 550 paper-based; 80 iBT). *Application deadline:* For fall admission, 4/1 for domestic students; for spring admission, 12/1 for domestic students. Application fee: $50. *Expenses:* $639 per credit hour. *Financial support:* Federal Work-Study, scholarships/grants, and unspecified assistantships available. Support available to part-time students. Financial award applicants required to submit FAFSA. *Unit head:* Dr. Donald Rogers, Faculty Director, 407-646-2348, E-mail: drogers@rollins.edu. *Application contact:* Carmen Rasnick, Graduate Coordinator, 407-646-2653, Fax: 407-646-1551, E-mail: crasnick@rollins.edu.
Website: http://www.rollins.edu/holt/graduate/mhr.html

Roosevelt University, Graduate Division, College of Professional Studies, Program in Training and Development, Chicago, IL 60605. Offers MA. *Students:* 11 full-time (10 women), 87 part-time (66 women); includes 55 minority (37 Black or African American, non-Hispanic/Latino; 1 Asian, non-Hispanic/Latino; 14 Hispanic/Latino; 3 Two or more races, non-Hispanic/Latino), 1 international. Average age 41. 31 applicants, 81% accepted, 18 enrolled. In 2016, 34 master's awarded. *Degree requirements:* For master's, thesis. *Entrance requirements:* For master's, minimum GPA of 2.75, relevant work experience. *Application deadline:* For fall admission, 6/1 priority date for domestic students. Applications are processed on a rolling basis. Application fee: $25 ($35 for international students). *Expenses: Tuition, area resident:* Full-time $19,566; part-time $880 per credit hour. *Required fees:* $175 per semester. One-time fee: $200. Part-time tuition and fees vary according to course load, degree level and program. *Financial support:* Application deadline: 2/15. *Unit head:* Tara Hawkins, Director, 847-619-8734. *Application contact:* Angela Ryan, Director of Graduate Enrollment, 877-APPLY RU, Fax: 312-281-3356, E-mail: applyru@roosevelt.edu.
Website: https://www.roosevelt.edu/academics/programs/masters-in-training-and-development-matd

South Dakota State University, Graduate School, College of Education and Human Sciences, Department of Counseling and Human Development, Brookings, SD 57007. Offers counseling and human resource development (M Ed, MS); human sciences (MS). *Accreditation:* ACA (one or more programs are accredited); NCATE. *Program availability:* Part-time, evening/weekend. *Degree requirements:* For master's, comprehensive exam, thesis (for some programs), oral exams. *Entrance requirements:* For master's, minimum GPA of 2.75. Additional exam requirements/recommendations for international students: Required—TOEFL (minimum score 525 paper-based; 71 iBT). *Faculty research:* Rural mental health, family issues, character education, student affairs, solution focused therapy.

Texas A&M University, College of Education and Human Development, Department of Educational Administration and Human Resource Development, College Station, TX 77843. Offers educational administration (M Ed, MS, Ed D, PhD); educational human resource development (MS, PhD). *Program availability:* Part-time. *Students:* 117 full-time (86 women), 273 part-time (171 women); includes 153 minority (49 Black or African American, non-Hispanic/Latino; 13 Asian, non-Hispanic/Latino; 80 Hispanic/Latino; 2 Native Hawaiian or other Pacific Islander, non-Hispanic/Latino; 9 Two or more races, non-Hispanic/Latino), 33 international. Average age 36. 153 applicants, 64% accepted, 84 enrolled. In 2016, 83 master's, 27 doctorates awarded. *Degree requirements:* For master's, thesis optional; for doctorate, thesis/dissertation. *Entrance requirements:* For master's, GRE General Test, writing exam, interview, professional experience; for doctorate, GRE General Test, writing exam, interview/presentation, professional experience. Additional exam requirements/recommendations for international students: Required—TOEFL (minimum score 550 paper-based; 80 iBT), IELTS (minimum score 6), PTE (minimum score 53). *Application deadline:* For fall admission, 12/1 for domestic and international students; for spring admission, 8/15 for domestic and international students. Application fee: $50 ($90 for international students). Electronic applications accepted. *Expenses:* Contact institution. *Financial support:* In 2016–17, 192 students received support, including 5 fellowships with tuition reimbursements available (averaging $8,239 per year), 45 research assistantships with tuition reimbursements available (averaging $5,380 per year), 16 teaching assistantships with tuition reimbursements available (averaging $9,494 per year); career-related internships or fieldwork, institutionally sponsored loans, scholarships/grants, traineeships, health care benefits, tuition waivers (full and partial), and unspecified assistantships also available. Support available to part-time students. Financial award application deadline: 3/15; financial award applicants required to submit FAFSA. *Faculty research:* Higher education administration, public school administration, student affairs. *Unit head:* Dr. Fred M. Nafukho, Head, 979-862-3395, Fax: 979-862-4347, E-mail: fnafukho@tamu.edu. *Application contact:* Joyce Nelson, Director of Academic Advising, 979-845-3017, Fax: 979-862-4347, E-mail: eahradvisor@tamu.edu.
Website: http://eahr.tamu.edu

Towson University, Program in Human Resource Development, Towson, MD 21252-0001. Offers education leadership (MS); general (MS). *Program availability:* Part-time, evening/weekend. *Students:* 13 full-time (all women), 248 part-time (192 women); includes 59 minority (36 Black or African American, non-Hispanic/Latino; 1 American Indian or Alaska Native, non-Hispanic/Latino; 7 Asian, non-Hispanic/Latino; 7 Hispanic/Latino; 8 Two or more races, non-Hispanic/Latino). *Degree requirements:* For master's, comprehensive exam. *Entrance requirements:* For master's, bachelor's degree, 2 letters

of recommendation, minimum GPA of 3.0, essay, resume. Additional exam requirements/recommendations for international students: Required—TOEFL. *Application deadline:* Applications are processed on a rolling basis. Application fee: $45. Electronic applications accepted. *Expenses:* Tuition, state resident: full-time $7580; part-time $379 per unit. Tuition, nonresident: full-time $15,700; part-time $785 per unit. *Required fees:* $2480. *Financial support:* Application deadline: 4/1. *Unit head:* Dr. Abby Mello, Graduate Program Director, 410-704-3364, E-mail: amello@towson.edu. *Application contact:* Coverley Beidleman, Assistant Director of Graduate Admissions, 410-704-2113, Fax: 410-704-3030, E-mail: grads@towson.edu.
Website: http://www.towson.edu/cla/departments/interdisciplinary/grad/hr/

Universidad Central del Este, Graduate School, San Pedro de Macoris, Dominican Republic. Offers environmental engineering (ME); financial management (M Ad); higher education (M Ed), including higher education management, higher education pedagogy; human resources (M Ad). *Entrance requirements:* For master's, letters of recommendation.

Universidad Iberoamericana, Graduate School, Santo Domingo D.N., Dominican Republic. Offers business administration (MBA, PMBA); constitutional law (LL M); dentistry (DMD); educational management (MA); integrated marketing communication (MA); psychopedagogical intervention (M Ed); real estate law (LL M); strategic management of human talent (MM).

University of Arkansas, Graduate School, College of Education and Health Professions, Department of Rehabilitation, Human Resources and Communication Disorders, Fayetteville, AR 72701. Offers adult and lifelong learning (M Ed, Ed D); communication disorders (MS); counseling (MS, PhD, Ed S); higher education (M Ed, Ed D, Ed S); human resource and workforce development education (M Ed, Ed D); rehabilitation (MS, PhD); vocational education (MAT). *Program availability:* Part-time. In 2016, 92 master's, 17 doctorates awarded. *Degree requirements:* For doctorate, thesis/dissertation. *Application deadline:* For fall admission, 4/1 for international students; for spring admission, 10/1 for international students. Applications are processed on a rolling basis. Application fee: $40 ($50 for international students). Electronic applications accepted. *Financial support:* In 2016–17, 55 research assistantships, 3 teaching assistantships were awarded; fellowships with tuition reimbursements, career-related internships or fieldwork, and Federal Work-Study also available. Support available to part-time students. Financial award application deadline: 4/1; financial award applicants required to submit FAFSA. *Unit head:* Dr. Kate Mamiseishvili, Department Chairperson, 479-575-4258, Fax: 479-575-3319, E-mail: kmamisei@uark.edu. *Application contact:* Dr. Brent Williams, Graduate Coordinator, 479-575-4758, E-mail: btwilli@uark.edu.
Website: http://rhrc.uark.edu/

University of Bridgeport, School of Arts and Sciences, Department of Counseling, Bridgeport, CT 06604. Offers clinical mental health counseling (MS); college student personnel (MS); community counseling (MS); human resource development (MS); human service (MS). *Program availability:* Part-time, evening/weekend. *Degree requirements:* For master's, thesis, project. *Entrance requirements:* Additional exam requirements/recommendations for international students: Recommended—TOEFL (minimum score 550 paper-based; 80 iBT), IELTS (minimum score 6.5). Electronic applications accepted. *Expenses:* Contact institution.

University of Houston, College of Technology, Department of Human Development and Consumer Science, Houston, TX 77204. Offers future studies in commerce (MS); human resources development (MS). *Program availability:* Part-time. *Degree requirements:* For master's, project or thesis. *Entrance requirements:* For master's, GMAT, MAT. Additional exam requirements/recommendations for international students: Required—TOEFL (minimum score 550 paper-based; 79 iBT). Electronic applications accepted.

University of Louisville, Graduate School, College of Education and Human Development, Department of Educational Leadership, Evaluation and Organizational Development, Louisville, KY 40292-0001. Offers educational leadership and organizational development (Ed D, PhD), including evaluation (PhD), human resource development (PhD), P-12 administration (PhD), post-secondary administration (PhD), sport administration (PhD); health professions education (Certificate); higher education administration (MA); human resources and organization development (MS), including health professions education, human resource leadership, workplace learning and performance; P-12 educational administration (Ed S), including principalship, supervisor of instruction. *Accreditation:* NCATE. *Program availability:* Part-time, evening/weekend, online learning. *Students:* 278 full-time (65 women), 409 part-time (260 women); includes 202 minority (121 Black or African American, non-Hispanic/Latino; 1 American Indian or Alaska Native, non-Hispanic/Latino; 13 Asian, non-Hispanic/Latino; 44 Hispanic/Latino; 3 Native Hawaiian or other Pacific Islander, non-Hispanic/Latino; 20 Two or more races, non-Hispanic/Latino), 5 international. Average age 36. 233 applicants, 78% accepted, 129 enrolled. In 2016, 58 master's, 4 doctorates, 17 other advanced degrees awarded. Application fee: $60. *Expenses:* Tuition, state resident: full-time $12,246; part-time $681 per credit hour. Tuition, nonresident: full-time $25,486; part-time $1417 per credit hour. *Required fees:* $196. Tuition and fees vary according to program and reciprocity agreements. *Financial support:* Application deadline: 6/1; applicants required to submit FAFSA. *Faculty research:* Urban educational leadership and policy, human resources, organizational development, program evaluation, military education, community partnerships, higher education administration. *Total annual research expenditures:* $256,111. *Unit head:* Dr. Jeffrey Sun, Chair and Professor, 502-852-0618, E-mail: jeffrey.sun@louisville.edu. *Application contact:* Betty Hampton, Director of Graduate Student Services, 502-852-5597, Fax: 502-852-1465, E-mail: edadvise@louisville.edu.
Website: http://louisville.edu/education/departments/eleod

University of Louisville, Graduate School, College of Education and Human Development, Department of Teaching and Learning, Louisville, KY 40292-0001. Offers art education (MAT); autism and applied behavior analysis (Certificate); curriculum and instruction (PhD); early elementary education (MAT); exercise physiology (MS); health and physical education (MAT); health professions education (Certificate); higher education (MA); human resources and organization development (MS); instructional technology (M Ed); interdisciplinary early childhood education (MAT); middle school education (MAT); music education (MAT); secondary education (MAT); special education (MAT); sport administration (MS); teacher leadership (M Ed). *Program availability:* Part-time, evening/weekend. *Students:* 116 full-time (68 women), 158 part-time (112 women); includes 46 minority (24 Black or African American, non-Hispanic/Latino; 8 Asian, non-Hispanic/Latino; 5 Hispanic/Latino; 9 Two or more races, non-Hispanic/Latino), 6 international. Average age 30. 114 applicants, 71% accepted, 57 enrolled. In 2016, 59 master's, 3 doctorates awarded. *Application deadline:* For spring admission, 1/1 priority date for international students. Application fee: $60. *Expenses:* Tuition, state resident: full-time $12,246; part-time $681 per credit hour. Tuition, nonresident: full-time $25,486; part-time $1417 per credit hour. *Required fees:* $196. Tuition and fees vary according to program and reciprocity agreements. *Financial support:* Application deadline: 6/1; applicants required to submit FAFSA. *Faculty research:* STEM teaching and learning; content literacy for English language learners; social justice in teacher education; adolescent literacy; mathematics teacher development. *Total annual research expenditures:* $1.7 million. *Unit head:* Dr. Ann E. Larson, Dean, College of Education and Human Development, 502-852-6411, Fax: 502-852-1464, E-mail: ann@louisville.edu. *Application contact:* Betty Hampton, Director of Graduate Student Services, 502-852-5597, Fax: 502-852-1465, E-mail: edadvise@louisville.edu.
Website: http://louisville.edu/delphi

University of Minnesota, Twin Cities Campus, Graduate School, College of Education and Human Development, Department of Organizational Leadership, Policy and Development, Program in Human Resource Development, Minneapolis, MN 55455-0213. Offers M Ed, MA, Ed D, PhD, Certificate. *Students:* 60 full-time (36 women), 29 part-time (18 women); includes 19 minority (8 Black or African American, non-Hispanic/Latino; 2 American Indian or Alaska Native, non-Hispanic/Latino; 3 Asian, non-Hispanic/Latino; 3 Hispanic/Latino; 3 Two or more races, non-Hispanic/Latino), 30 international. Average age 32. 73 applicants, 79% accepted, 51 enrolled. In 2016, 10 master's, 8 doctorates, 4 other advanced degrees awarded. Application fee: $75 ($95 for international students). *Unit head:* Dr. Heidi Barajas, Chair, 612-625-4823, E-mail: hbarajas@umn.edu. *Application contact:* Dr. Jeremy J. Hernandez, Director of Graduate Studies, 612-626-9377, E-mail: herna220@umn.edu.
Website: http://www.cehd.umn.edu/OLPD/grad-programs/HRD/

University of Nebraska at Omaha, Graduate Studies, College of Arts and Sciences, Department of Psychology, Omaha, NE 68182. Offers applied behavior analysis (Certificate); human resources and training (Certificate); industrial/organizational psychology (MS); psychology (MA, PhD); school psychology (MS, Ed S). *Program availability:* Part-time. *Faculty:* 10 full-time (1 woman). *Students:* 70 full-time (52 women), 49 part-time (33 women); includes 9 minority (2 Asian, non-Hispanic/Latino; 5 Hispanic/Latino; 2 Two or more races, non-Hispanic/Latino), 1 international. Average age 27. 157 applicants, 25% accepted, 38 enrolled. In 2016, 32 master's, 6 doctorates, 10 other advanced degrees awarded. *Degree requirements:* For master's, comprehensive exam, thesis (for some programs); for doctorate, comprehensive exam, thesis/dissertation. *Entrance requirements:* For master's and doctorate, GRE, minimum GPA of 3.0, official transcripts, 3 letters of recommendation, statement of purpose, writing sample, resume. Additional exam requirements/recommendations for international students: Required—TOEFL, IELTS, PTE. *Application deadline:* For fall admission, 1/5 priority date for domestic and international students. Application fee: $45. Electronic applications accepted. *Financial support:* In 2016–17, 50 students received support, including 23 research assistantships with tuition reimbursements available, 27 teaching assistantships with tuition reimbursements available; fellowships with tuition reimbursements available, career-related internships or fieldwork, Federal Work-Study, institutionally sponsored loans, scholarships/grants, health care benefits, tuition waivers (partial), and unspecified assistantships also available. Financial award application deadline: 3/1; financial award applicants required to submit FAFSA. *Unit head:* Dr. Brigette Ryalls, Chairperson, 402-554-2341, E-mail: graduate@unomaha.edu. *Application contact:* Dr. Joseph Brown, Graduate Program Chair, 402-554-2341, E-mail: graduate@unomaha.edu.

University of Nebraska at Omaha, Graduate Studies, College of Business Administration, Program in Business Administration, Omaha, NE 68182. Offers business administration (MBA); business for bioscientists (Certificate); executive business administration (EMBA); human resources and training (Certificate). *Accreditation:* AACSB. *Program availability:* Part-time, evening/weekend. *Faculty:* 9 full-time (3 women). *Students:* 80 full-time (31 women), 207 part-time (78 women); includes 35 minority (6 Black or African American, non-Hispanic/Latino; 1 American Indian or Alaska Native, non-Hispanic/Latino; 11 Asian, non-Hispanic/Latino; 12 Hispanic/Latino; 5 Two or more races, non-Hispanic/Latino), 29 international. Average age 30. 185 applicants, 48% accepted, 78 enrolled. In 2016, 128 master's, 5 other advanced degrees awarded. *Degree requirements:* For master's, thesis (for some programs), capstone course. *Entrance requirements:* For master's, GMAT or GRE, minimum GPA of 3.0, official transcripts, resume; for Certificate, minimum GPA of 3.0, official transcripts, resume, letter of recommendation, statement of purpose. Additional exam requirements/recommendations for international students: Required—TOEFL, IELTS, PTE. *Application deadline:* For fall admission, 7/1 for domestic and international students; for spring admission, 11/1 for domestic and international students; for summer admission, 4/1 for domestic and international students. Applications are processed on a rolling basis. Application fee: $45. Electronic applications accepted. *Financial support:* In 2016–17, 15 students received support, including 9 research assistantships with tuition reimbursements available, 6 teaching assistantships with tuition reimbursements available; Federal Work-Study, institutionally sponsored loans, scholarships/grants, health care benefits, tuition waivers (partial), and unspecified assistantships also available. Support available to part-time students. Financial award application deadline: 3/1; financial award applicants required to submit FAFSA. *Unit head:* Lex Kaczmarek, Graduate Program Chair, 402-554-2341, E-mail: graduate@unomaha.edu.

University of Nebraska at Omaha, Graduate Studies, College of Communication, Fine Arts and Media, School of Communication, Omaha, NE 68182. Offers communication (MA); human resources and training (Certificate); technical communication (Certificate). *Program availability:* Part-time, evening/weekend. *Faculty:* 7 full-time (4 women). *Students:* 6 full-time (4 women), 33 part-time (20 women); includes 9 minority (2 Black or African American, non-Hispanic/Latino; 2 Asian, non-Hispanic/Latino; 2 Hispanic/Latino; 3 Two or more races, non-Hispanic/Latino), 2 international. Average age 31. 14 applicants, 57% accepted, 6 enrolled. In 2016, 11 master's, 5 other advanced degrees awarded. *Degree requirements:* For master's, comprehensive exam, thesis (for some programs). *Entrance requirements:* For master's, minimum GPA of 3.0, 15 undergraduate communication courses, resume, statement of purpose, 3 letters of recommendation. Additional exam requirements/recommendations for international students: Required—TOEFL, IELTS, PTE. *Application deadline:* For fall admission, 3/1 priority date for domestic and international students; for spring admission, 10/1 priority date for domestic and international students. Applications are processed on a rolling basis. Application fee: $45. Electronic applications accepted. *Financial support:* In 2016–17, 13 students received support, including 13 teaching assistantships with tuition reimbursements available; fellowships, research assistantships with tuition reimbursements available, Federal Work-Study, institutionally sponsored loans, scholarships/grants, health care benefits, tuition waivers (partial), and unspecified assistantships also available. Support available to part-time students. Financial award application deadline: 3/1; financial award applicants required to submit FAFSA. *Unit head:* Dr. Hugh Reilly, Director, 402-554-2341, E-mail: graduate@unomaha.edu. *Application contact:* Dr. Adam Tyma, Graduate Program Chair, 402-554-2341, E-mail: graduate@unomaha.edu.

University of Regina, Faculty of Graduate Studies and Research, Faculty of Education, Department of Human Resource Development, Regina, SK S4S 0A2, Canada. Offers MHRD. *Program availability:* Part-time. *Faculty:* 5 full-time (2 women), 20 part-time/adjunct (11 women). *Students:* 8 full-time (3 women), 7 part-time (4 women). 9 applicants, 33% accepted. In 2016, 3 master's awarded. *Degree requirements:* For master's, thesis (for some programs), practicum, project, or thesis. *Entrance requirements:* For master's, 4-year B Ed, two years of teaching or other relevant professional experience. Additional exam requirements/recommendations for international students: Required—TOEFL (minimum score 580 paper-based; 80 iBT),

IELTS (minimum score 6.5), PTE (minimum score 59). *Application deadline:* For fall admission, 2/15 for domestic and international students; for winter admission, 10/15 for domestic and international students; for spring admission, 2/15 for domestic and international students. Application fee: $100. Electronic applications accepted. *Financial support:* Fellowships, teaching assistantships, and scholarships/grants available. Financial award application deadline: 6/15. *Faculty research:* Foundations of adult development, theory and practice of adult education and human resource development, design and assessment of curriculum and instruction, planning and curriculum development, learning and the workplace. *Unit head:* Dr. Ken Montgomery, Associate Dean, Research and Graduate Programs in Education, 306-585-5031, Fax: 306-585-5387, E-mail: ken.montgomery@uregina.ca. *Application contact:* Tania Gates, Graduate Program Coordinator, 306-585-4506, Fax: 306-585-5387, E-mail: edgrad@uregina.ca.
Website: http://www.uregina.ca/education/

The University of Scranton, Panuska College of Professional Studies, Department of Health Administration and Human Resources, Program in Human Resources, Scranton, PA 18510. Offers MS. *Program availability:* Part-time, evening/weekend, 100% online.

University of South Africa, College of Economic and Management Sciences, Pretoria, South Africa. Offers accounting (D Admin, D Com); accounting science (DA); auditing (D Admin, D Com); business administration (M Tech); business economics (D Admin); business leadership (DBL); business management (D Admin, D Com); economic management analysis (M Tech); economics (D Admin, D Com, PhD); human resource development (M Tech); industrial psychology (D Admin, D Com, PhD); logistics (D Com); marketing (M Tech); public administration (D Admin, D Com, DPA, PhD); public management (M Tech); quantitative management (D Admin, D Com); real estate (M Tech); statistics (D Admin, PhD); tourism management (D Admin, D Com); transport economics (D Admin, D Com).

University of South Florida, Innovative Education, Tampa, FL 33620-9951. Offers adult, career and higher education (Graduate Certificate), including college teaching, leadership in developing human resources, leadership in higher education; Africana studies (Graduate Certificate), including diasporas and health disparities, genocide and human rights; aging studies (Graduate Certificate), including gerontology; art research (Graduate Certificate), including museum studies; business foundations (Graduate Certificate); chemical and biomedical engineering (Graduate Certificate), including materials science and engineering, water, health and sustainability; child and family studies (Graduate Certificate), including positive behavior support; civil and industrial engineering (Graduate Certificate), including transportation systems analysis; community and family health (Graduate Certificate), including maternal and child health, social marketing and public health, violence and injury: prevention and intervention, women's health; criminology (Graduate Certificate), including criminal justice administration; educational measurement and research (Graduate Certificate), including evaluation; English (Graduate Certificate), including comparative literary studies, creative writing, professional and technical communication; entrepreneurship (Graduate Certificate); environmental health (Graduate Certificate), including safety management; epidemiology and biostatistics (Graduate Certificate), including applied biostatistics, biostatistics, concepts and tools of epidemiology, epidemiology, epidemiology of infectious diseases; geography, environment and planning (Graduate Certificate), including community development, environmental policy and management, geographical information systems; geology (Graduate Certificate), including hydrogeology; global health (Graduate Certificate), including disaster management, global health and Latin American and Caribbean studies, global health practice, humanitarian assistance, infection control; government and international affairs (Graduate Certificate), including Cuban studies, globalization studies; health policy and management (Graduate Certificate), including health management and leadership, public health policy and programs; hearing specialist: early intervention (Graduate Certificate); industrial and management systems engineering (Graduate Certificate), including systems engineering, technology management; information studies (Graduate Certificate), including school library media specialist; information systems/decision sciences (Graduate Certificate), including analytics and business intelligence; instructional technology (Graduate Certificate), including distance education, Florida digital/virtual educator, instructional design, multimedia design, Web design; internal medicine, bioethics and medical humanities (Graduate Certificate), including biomedical ethics; Latin American and Caribbean studies (Graduate Certificate); mass communications (Graduate Certificate), including multimedia journalism; mathematics and statistics (Graduate Certificate), including mathematics; medicine (Graduate Certificate), including aging and neuroscience, bioinformatics, biotechnology, brain fitness and memory management, clinical investigation, health informatics, health sciences, integrative weight management, intellectual property, medicine and gender, metabolic and nutritional medicine, metabolic cardiology, pharmacy sciences; national and competitive intelligence (Graduate Certificate); psychological and social foundations (Graduate Certificate), including career counseling, college teaching, diversity in education, mental health counseling, school counseling; public affairs (Graduate Certificate), including nonprofit management, public management, research administration; public health (Graduate Certificate), including environmental health, health equity, public health generalist, translational research in adolescent behavioral health; public health practices (Graduate Certificate), including planning for healthy communities; rehabilitation and mental health counseling (Graduate Certificate), including integrative mental health care, marriage and family therapy, rehabilitation technology; secondary education (Graduate Certificate), including ESOL, foreign language education: culture and content, foreign language education: professional; social work (Graduate Certificate), including geriatric social work/clinical gerontology; special education (Graduate Certificate), including autism spectrum disorder, disabilities education: severe/profound; world languages (Graduate Certificate), including teaching English as a second language (TESL) or foreign language. *Expenses:* Tuition, state resident: full-time $7766; part-time $431.43 per credit hour. Tuition, nonresident: full-time $15,789; part-time $877.17 per credit hour. *Required fees:* $37 per term. *Unit head:* Kathy Barnes, Interdisciplinary Programs Coordinator, 813-974-8031, Fax: 813-974-7061, E-mail: barnesk@usf.edu. *Application contact:* Karen Tylinski, Metro Initiatives, 813-974-9943, Fax: 813-974-7061, E-mail: ktylinsk@usf.edu.
Website: http://www.usf.edu/innovative-education/

The University of Tennessee, Graduate School, College of Business Administration, Program in Human Resource Development, Knoxville, TN 37996. Offers teacher licensure (MS); training and development (MS). *Program availability:* Part-time. *Degree requirements:* For master's, thesis. *Entrance requirements:* For master's, GRE General Test, minimum GPA of 2.7. Electronic applications accepted.

The University of Texas at Tyler, College of Business and Technology, Program in Human Resource Development, Tyler, TX 75799-0001. Offers MS, PhD. *Program availability:* Part-time, evening/weekend, online learning. *Degree requirements:* For master's, comprehensive exam. *Entrance requirements:* For master's, GRE General Test or MAT. Additional exam requirements/recommendations for international students: Required—TOEFL. Electronic applications accepted. *Faculty research:* Human resource development.

University of Wisconsin–Milwaukee, Graduate School, College of Letters and Science, Interdepartmental Program in Human Resources and Labor Relations, Milwaukee, WI 53201-0413. Offers human resources and labor relations (MHRLR); international human resources and labor relations (Certificate); mediation and negotiation (Certificate). *Program availability:* Part-time. *Entrance requirements:* For master's, GMAT or GRE General Test. Additional exam requirements/recommendations for international students: Required—TOEFL (minimum score 80 iBT), IELTS (minimum score 6.5). Electronic applications accepted.

University of Wisconsin–Stout, Graduate School, College of Management, Program in Training and Human Resource Development, Menomonie, WI 54751. Offers MS. *Program availability:* Part-time, online learning. *Degree requirements:* For master's, thesis. *Entrance requirements:* For master's, minimum GPA of 2.75. Additional exam requirements/recommendations for international students: Required—TOEFL (minimum score 500 paper-based; 61 iBT). Electronic applications accepted. *Faculty research:* Organizational behavior, performance, learning and performance, strategic planning.

Villanova University, Graduate School of Liberal Arts and Sciences, Department of Human Resource Development, Villanova, PA 19085-1699. Offers MS. *Program availability:* Part-time, evening/weekend, 100% online. *Faculty:* 25. *Students:* 146 full-time (110 women), 166 part-time (122 women); includes 89 minority (45 Black or African American, non-Hispanic/Latino; 1 American Indian or Alaska Native, non-Hispanic/Latino; 7 Asian, non-Hispanic/Latino; 29 Hispanic/Latino; 7 Two or more races, non-Hispanic/Latino), 6 international. Average age 36. 74 applicants, 100% accepted, 65 enrolled. In 2016, 173 master's awarded. *Degree requirements:* For master's, comprehensive exam. *Entrance requirements:* For master's, GRE General Test, minimum GPA of 3.0, statement of goals, resume, 3 letters of recommendation. Additional exam requirements/recommendations for international students: Required—TOEFL. *Application deadline:* For fall admission, 5/1 priority date for international students; for spring admission, 10/15 priority date for international students. Applications are processed on a rolling basis. Application fee: $50. Electronic applications accepted. *Financial support:* Research assistantships, scholarships/grants, and unspecified assistantships available. Financial award applicants required to submit FAFSA. *Unit head:* Dr. Gerarad Brandon, Director, 610-519-8861, E-mail: gerard.brandon@villanova.edu.
Website: http://www.villanova.edu/artsci/hrd/

Virginia Commonwealth University, Graduate School, School of Education, Program in Adult Learning, Richmond, VA 23284-9005. Offers adult literacy (M Ed); human resource development (M Ed); teaching and learning with technology (M Ed). *Accreditation:* NCATE. *Program availability:* Part-time. *Entrance requirements:* For master's, GRE General Test or MAT. Additional exam requirements/recommendations for international students: Required—TOEFL (minimum score 600 paper-based; 100 iBT). *Application deadline:* For fall admission, 3/15 for domestic students; for spring admission, 11/1 for domestic students. Applications are processed on a rolling basis. Application fee: $50. Electronic applications accepted. *Financial support:* Career-related internships or fieldwork and Federal Work-Study available. Financial award application deadline: 3/1; financial award applicants required to submit FAFSA. *Faculty research:* Adult development and learning, program planning and evaluation. *Unit head:* Dr. Leila Christenbury, Interim Department Chair, 804-828-1306, Fax: 804-827-0676, E-mail: lchriste@vcu.edu. *Application contact:* Dr. Robin R. Hurst, Graduate Program Director, 804-828-8021, E-mail: rrhurst@vcu.edu.
Website: http://www.soe.vcu.edu/programs.html#graduate

Waldorf University, Program in Organizational Leadership, Forest City, IA 50436. Offers criminal justice leadership (MA); emergency management leadership (MA); fire/rescue executive leadership (MA); human resource development (MA); public administration (MA); sport management (MA); teacher leader (MA).

Webster University, George Herbert Walker School of Business and Technology, Department of Business, St. Louis, MO 63119-3194. Offers business and organizational security management (MBA); decision support systems (MBA); environmental management (MBA); finance (MBA, MS); forensic accounting (MS); gerontology (MBA); human resources development (MBA); human resources management (MBA); information technology management (MBA); international business (MA, MBA); international relations (MBA); management and leadership (MBA); marketing (MBA); media communications (MBA); procurement and acquisitions management (MBA); Web services (MBA). *Accreditation:* ACBSP. *Program availability:* Part-time, evening/weekend, online learning. *Degree requirements:* For master's, comprehensive exam (for some programs), thesis (for some programs). *Entrance requirements:* Additional exam requirements/recommendations for international students: Required—TOEFL. *Application deadline:* Applications are processed on a rolling basis. Application fee: $35 ($50 for international students). *Expenses: Tuition:* Full-time $21,900; part-time $730 per credit hour. Tuition and fees vary according to campus/location and program. *Financial support:* Federal Work-Study available. Support available to part-time students. Financial award application deadline: 4/1; financial award applicants required to submit FAFSA. *Unit head:* David Porras, Chair, 314-246-8621, E-mail: porrasd@webster.edu. *Application contact:* Sarah Nandor, Director, Graduate and Transfer Admissions, 314-968-7109, E-mail: gadmit@webster.edu.

Webster University, George Herbert Walker School of Business and Technology, Department of Management, St. Louis, MO 63119-3194. Offers business and organizational security management (MA); digital marketing management (Graduate Certificate); government contracting (Graduate Certificate); health administration (MHA); health care management (MA); health services management (MA); human resources development (MA); human resources management (MA); information technology management (MA, MS); management (D Mgt); management and leadership (MA); marketing (MA); nonprofit leadership (MA); nonprofit revenue development (Graduate Certificate); organizational development (Graduate Certificate); procurement and acquisitions management (MA); public administration (MPA); space systems operations management (MS). *Program availability:* Part-time, evening/weekend, online learning. *Degree requirements:* For master's, thesis (for some programs); for doctorate, thesis/dissertation, written exam. *Entrance requirements:* For doctorate, GMAT, 3 years of work experience, MBA. Additional exam requirements/recommendations for international students: Required—TOEFL. *Application deadline:* Applications are processed on a rolling basis. Application fee: $25 ($50 for international students). *Expenses: Tuition:* Full-time $21,900; part-time $730 per credit hour. Tuition and fees vary according to campus/location and program. *Financial support:* Federal Work-Study available. Support available to part-time students. Financial award application deadline: 4/1; financial award applicants required to submit FAFSA. *Unit head:* Barrett Baebler, Chair, 314-246-7940, E-mail: baeblerb@webster.edu. *Application contact:* Sarah Nandor, Director, Graduate and Transfer Admissions, 314-968-7109, E-mail: gadmit@webster.edu.

Western Seminary, Graduate Programs, Program in Ministry and Leadership, Portland, OR 97215-3367. Offers chaplaincy (MA); coaching (MA); Jewish ministry (MA); pastoral care to women (MA); youth ministry (MA). *Degree requirements:* For master's, practicum. *Entrance requirements:* Additional exam requirements/recommendations for international students: Required—TOEFL.

William Woods University, Graduate and Adult Studies, Fulton, MO 65251-1098. Offers administration (M Ed, Ed S); athletic/activities administration (M Ed); curriculum and instruction (M Ed, Ed S); educational leadership (Ed D); equestrian education (M Ed); health management (MBA); human resources (MBA); leadership (MBA); marketing, advertising, and public relations (MBA); teaching and technology (M Ed). *Program availability:* Part-time, evening/weekend. *Degree requirements:* For master's, capstone course (MBA), action research (M Ed); for Ed S, field experience. *Entrance requirements:* Additional exam requirements/recommendations for international students: Required—TOEFL (minimum score 550 paper-based). Electronic applications accepted. *Expenses:* Contact institution.

Xavier University, College of Social Sciences, Health and Education, School of Education, Department of Educational Leadership and Human Resource Development, Cincinnati, OH 45207. Offers educational administration (M Ed); human resource development (MS). *Program availability:* Part-time, evening/weekend. *Degree requirements:* For master's, internship; for doctorate, comprehensive exam, thesis/dissertation. *Entrance requirements:* For master's, GRE or MAT, resume; 2 letters of recommendation; goal statement; official transcript; for doctorate, GRE, GMAT, LSAT or MAT, official transcript; 1,000-word goal statement; resume; 3 letters of recommendation. Additional exam requirements/recommendations for international students: Required—TOEFL (minimum score 550 paper-based; 79 iBT). Electronic applications accepted. Application fee is waived when completed online. *Expenses:* Contact institution.

Human Resources Management

Adelphi University, Robert B. Willumstad School of Business, Certificate Program in Human Resource Management, Garden City, NY 11530-0701. Offers Certificate. *Program availability:* Part-time, evening/weekend. *Students:* 2 part-time (both women); includes 50 minority (all Black or African American, non-Hispanic/Latino). Average age 49. 2 applicants, 100% accepted, 2 enrolled. In 2016, 17 Certificates awarded. *Entrance requirements:* For degree, GMAT or master's degree. Additional exam requirements/recommendations for international students: Required—TOEFL (minimum score 550 paper-based; 80 iBT), IELTS (minimum score 6.5). *Application deadline:* For fall admission, 4/1 for international students; for spring admission, 11/1 for international students. Applications are processed on a rolling basis. Application fee: $50. Electronic applications accepted. *Expenses:* Contact institution. *Financial support:* Career-related internships or fieldwork, Federal Work-Study, tuition waivers, and unspecified assistantships available. Financial award application deadline: 3/1; financial award applicants required to submit FAFSA. *Unit head:* Brian Rothschild, Assistant Dean, 516-877-4670, Fax: 516-877-4607, E-mail: gradbusinquiries@adelphi.edu. *Application contact:* Christine Murphy, Director of Admissions, 516-877-3050, Fax: 516-877-3039, E-mail: graduateadmissions@adelphi.edu.
Website: http://business.adelphi.edu/academics/certificate-programs/advanced-certificate-in-human-resource-management/

Adelphi University, Robert B. Willumstad School of Business, MBA Program, Garden City, NY 11530-0701. Offers accounting (MBA); finance (MBA); health services administration (MBA); human resource management (MBA); management (MBA); management information systems (MBA); marketing (MBA); sport management (MBA). *Accreditation:* AACSB. *Program availability:* Part-time, evening/weekend. *Students:* 172 full-time (74 women), 129 part-time (66 women); includes 30 minority (9 Black or African American, non-Hispanic/Latino; 11 Asian, non-Hispanic/Latino; 9 Hispanic/Latino; 1 Two or more races, non-Hispanic/Latino), 29 international. Average age 32. 4 applicants. In 2016, 130 master's awarded. *Degree requirements:* For master's, capstone course. *Entrance requirements:* For master's, GMAT, 2 letters of recommendation. Additional exam requirements/recommendations for international students: Required—TOEFL (minimum score 550 paper-based; 80 iBT), IELTS (minimum score 6.5). *Application deadline:* For fall admission, 4/1 for international students; for spring admission, 11/1 for international students. Applications are processed on a rolling basis. Application fee: $50. Electronic applications accepted. *Expenses:* Contact institution. *Financial support:* Research assistantships with partial tuition reimbursements, career-related internships or fieldwork, Federal Work-Study, institutionally sponsored loans, scholarships/grants, tuition waivers (partial), and unspecified assistantships available. Financial award application deadline: 3/1; financial award applicants required to submit FAFSA. *Faculty research:* Supply chain management, distribution channels, productivity benchmark analysis, data envelopment analysis, financial portfolio analysis. *Unit head:* Dr. Rakesh Gupta, Associate Dean, 516-877-4629. *Application contact:* Christine Murphy, Director of Admissions, 516-877-3050, Fax: 516-877-3039, E-mail: graduateadmissions@adelphi.edu.
Website: http://business.adelphi.edu/degree-programs/graduate-degree-programs/m-b-a/

Albany State University, College of Arts and Humanities, Albany, GA 31705-2717. Offers criminal justice (MS); English education (M Ed); public administration (MPA), including community and economic development, criminal justice administration, health administration and policy, human resources management, public management, public policy, water resources management and policy; social work (MSW). *Program availability:* Part-time. *Degree requirements:* For master's, comprehensive exam, professional portfolio (for MPA), internship, capstone report. *Entrance requirements:* For master's, GRE, MAT, minimum GPA of 3.0, official transcript, pre-medical record/certificate of immunization, letters of reference. *Application deadline:* For fall admission, 6/1 for domestic students, 5/1 for international students; for spring admission, 11/1 for domestic students, 10/1 for international students. Applications are processed on a rolling basis. Application fee: $20. Electronic applications accepted. *Financial support:* Application deadline: 4/15; applicants required to submit FAFSA. *Faculty research:* HIV prevention for minority students. *Unit head:* Dr. Rani George, Dean, 229-430-1877, Fax: 229-430-4296. *Application contact:* Jeffrey Pierce, II, Graduate Admissions Counselor, 229-430-4646, Fax: 229-430-4105, E-mail: jeffrey.pierce@asurams.edu.
Website: https://www.asurams.edu/Academics/collegeofarthum/

Amberton University, Graduate School, Program in Human Relations and Business, Garland, TX 75041-5595. Offers MS. *Program availability:* Part-time, evening/weekend. *Entrance requirements:* For master's, minimum GPA of 3.0.

American InterContinental University Online, Program in Business Administration, Schaumburg, IL 60173. Offers accounting and finance (MBA); finance (MBA); healthcare management (MBA); human resource management (MBA); international business (MBA); management (MBA); marketing (MBA); operations management (MBA); organizational psychology and development (MBA); project management (MBA). *Accreditation:* ACBSP. *Program availability:* Evening/weekend, online learning. *Entrance requirements:* Additional exam requirements/recommendations for international students: Required—TOEFL (minimum score 550 paper-based). Electronic applications accepted.

American Public University System, AMU/APU Graduate Programs, Charles Town, WV 25414. Offers accounting (MBA, MS); applied business analytics (MBA, MS); criminal justice (MA), including business administration, emergency and disaster management, general (MA, MS); educational leadership (M Ed); emergency and disaster management (MA); entrepreneurship (MBA); environmental policy and management (MS), including environmental planning, environmental sustainability, fish and wildlife management, general (MA, MS), global environmental management; finance (MBA); general (MBA); government contracting and acquisition (MBA); health care administration (MBA); health information management (MS); history (MA), including American history, ancient and classical history, European history, global history, public history; homeland security (MA), including business administration, counterterrorism studies, criminal justice, cyber, emergency management and public health, intelligence studies, transportation security; homeland security resource allocation (MBA); humanities (MA); information technology (MS), including digital forensics, enterprise software development, information assurance and security, IT project management; information technology management (MBA); intelligence studies (MA), including criminal intelligence, cyber, general (MA, MS), homeland security, intelligence analysis, intelligence collection, intelligence management, intelligence operations, terrorism studies; international relations and conflict resolution (MA), including comparative and security issues, conflict resolution, international and transnational security issues, peacekeeping; legal studies (MA); management (MA), including strategic consulting; marketing (MBA); military history (MA), including American military history, American Revolution, civil war, war since 1945, World War II; military studies (MA), including joint warfare, strategic leadership; national security studies (MA), including cyber, general (MA, MS), homeland security, regional security studies, security and intelligence analysis, terrorism studies; nonprofit management (MBA); political science (MA), including American politics and government, comparative government and development, general (MA, MS), international relations, public policy; psychology (MA); public administration (MPA), including disaster management, environmental policy, health policy, human resources, national security, organizational management, security management; public health (MPH); reverse logistics management (MA); security management (MA); space studies (MS), including aerospace science, general (MA, MS), planetary science; sports and health sciences (MS); sports management (MBA); teaching (M Ed), including autism spectrum disorder, curriculum and instruction for elementary teachers, elementary reading, English language learners, instructional leadership, online learning, special education, STEAM (STEM plus the arts); transportation and logistics management (MA). *Program availability:* Part-time, evening/weekend, online only, 100% online. *Faculty:* 401 full-time (228 women), 1,678 part-time/adjunct (781 women). *Students:* 378 full-time (184 women), 8,455 part-time (3,484 women); includes 2,972 minority (1,552 Black or African American, non-Hispanic/Latino; 52 American Indian or Alaska Native, non-Hispanic/Latino; 211 Asian, non-Hispanic/Latino; 791 Hispanic/Latino; 70 Native Hawaiian or other Pacific Islander, non-Hispanic/Latino; 296 Two or more races, non-Hispanic/Latino), 109 international. Average age 37. In 2016, 3,185 master's awarded. *Degree requirements:* For master's, comprehensive exam or practicum. *Entrance requirements:* For master's, official transcript showing earned bachelor's degree from institution accredited by recognized accrediting body. Additional exam requirements/recommendations for international students: Required—TOEFL (minimum score 550 paper-based), IELTS (minimum score 6.5). *Application deadline:* Applications are processed on a rolling basis. Application fee: $0. Electronic applications accepted. *Expenses: Tuition:* Part-time $350 per credit hour. *Required fees:* $50 per course. *Financial support:* Scholarships/grants available. Financial award applicants required to submit FAFSA. *Unit head:* Dr. Karan Powell, President, 877-468-6268, Fax: 304-724-3780. *Application contact:* Terry Grant, Vice President of Enrollment Management, 877-468-6268, Fax: 304-724-3780, E-mail: info@apus.edu.
Website: http://www.apus.edu

American University, School of Professional and Extended Studies, Washington, DC 20016. Offers healthcare management (MS, Graduate Certificate); human resource analytics and management (Graduate Certificate); measurement and evaluation (MS); project monitoring and evaluation (Graduate Certificate); sports analytics and management (MS, Graduate Certificate). *Program availability:* 100% online. *Faculty:* 28 full-time (12 women), 8 part-time/adjunct (4 women). *Students:* 26 part-time (22 women); includes 1 minority (American Indian or Alaska Native, non-Hispanic/Latino), 2 international. Average age 38. 37 applicants, 100% accepted, 22 enrolled. *Entrance requirements:* For master's, statement of purpose, current resume/curriculum vitae, official transcripts from all academic institutions, letters of recommendation. Additional exam requirements/recommendations for international students: Required—TOEFL or IELTS. *Application deadline:* Applications are processed on a rolling basis. Application fee: $55. Electronic applications accepted. *Expenses:* $1,579 per credit; $690 mandatory fees; some programs charge different fee for spring enrollment. *Financial support:* Applicants required to submit FAFSA. *Unit head:* Carola Weil, Dean, 202-885-5990, Fax: 202-895-4960, E-mail: weil@american.edu. *Application contact:* Heather Broberg, Assistant Director for Recruitment and Admission, 202-895-4953, E-mail: broberg@american.edu.
Website: http://www.american.edu/spexs/

American University of Beirut, Graduate Programs, Suliman S. Olayan School of Business, Master in Human Resource Management Program, 11072020, Lebanon. Offers MHRM. *Program availability:* Online learning. *Faculty:* 4 full-time (2 women), 3 part-time/adjunct (1 woman). *Students:* 10 full-time (9 women). Average age 28. 36 applicants, 36% accepted, 10 enrolled. In 2016, 9 master's awarded. Terminal master's awarded for partial completion of doctoral program. *Degree requirements:* For master's, thesis. *Entrance requirements:* Additional exam requirements/recommendations for international students: Required—TOEFL (minimum score 583 paper-based; 97 iBT), IELTS (minimum score 7). *Application deadline:* For fall admission, 2/12 for domestic students; for winter admission, 4/1 for domestic students. Application fee: $80. Electronic applications accepted. *Expenses:* Contact institution. *Financial support:* In 2016–17, 1 research assistantship with tuition reimbursement (averaging $1,300 per year) was awarded; scholarships/grants and unspecified assistantships also available. Financial award application deadline: 6/1. *Application contact:* Maya Naim El-Helou, Director of Graduate Programs, 961-1352700 Ext. 3955, Fax: 961-1750214, E-mail: helou@aub.edu.lb.
Website: http://www.aub.edu.lb/osb/osb_home/program/MHRM/Pages/index.aspx

Anderson University, College of Business, Anderson, SC 29621-4035. Offers business administration (MBA); healthcare leadership (MBA); human resources (MBA); marketing (MBA); supply chain management (MBA). *Accreditation:* ACBSP. *Students:* 7 full-time (0 women), 1 part-time (0 women). *Expenses:* Contact institution. *Financial support:* Tuition waivers available. Financial award application deadline: 3/1; financial award applicants required to submit FAFSA. *Unit head:* Dr. Douglas Goodwin, MBA Director/ Associate Dean, 864-MBA-6000. *Application contact:* Mallory Knight, Graduate Admission Counselor, 864-231-2182, Fax: 864-231-2115, E-mail: malloryknight@andersonuniversity.edu.
Website: http://www.andersonuniversity.edu/business

Argosy University, Schaumburg, Graduate School of Business and Management, Schaumburg, IL 60173-5403. Offers accounting (DBA, Adv C); customized professional concentration (MBA, DBA); finance (MBA, Certificate); fraud examination (MBA); healthcare administration (MBA, Certificate); human resource management (MS); information systems (Adv C, Certificate); information systems management (MBA); international business (MBA, DBA, Adv C, Certificate); management (MBA, MSM, DBA, Adv C, Certificate); marketing (MBA, DBA, Adv C, Certificate); organizational leadership (MS, Ed D); public administration (MBA); sustainable management (MBA).

Ashworth College, Graduate Programs, Norcross, GA 30092. Offers business administration (MBA); criminal justice (MS); health care administration (MBA, MS); human resource management (MBA, MS); international business (MBA); management (MS); marketing (MBA, MS).

Assumption College, Business Studies Program, Worcester, MA 01609-1296. Offers accounting (MBA); business studies (CAGS); finance/economics (MBA); human resources (MBA); international business (MBA); management (MBA); marketing (MBA); nonprofit leadership (MBA). *Program availability:* Part-time, evening/weekend. *Faculty:* 4 full-time (1 woman), 19 part-time/adjunct (6 women). *Students:* 44 full-time (16 women), 97 part-time (47 women); includes 20 minority (8 Black or African American, non-Hispanic/Latino; 5 Asian, non-Hispanic/Latino; 6 Hispanic/Latino; 1 Two or more races, non-Hispanic/Latino), 4 international. Average age 29. 34 applicants, 59% accepted, 16 enrolled. In 2016, 97 master's, 1 other advanced degree awarded. *Degree requirements:* For master's, thesis, capstone. *Entrance requirements:* For master's, bachelor's degree, 3 letters of recommendation, official transcripts, personal statement, current resume; for CAGS, MBA or equivalent degree in a closely related field, 3 letters of recommendation, official transcripts, personal statement, current resume. Additional exam requirements/recommendations for international students: Required—TOEFL (minimum score 540 paper-based; 76 iBT), IELTS (minimum score 6). *Application deadline:* For fall admission, 7/1 priority date for domestic and international students; for spring admission, 12/1 priority date for domestic and international students; for summer admission, 4/1 priority date for domestic and international students. Application fee: $30. Electronic applications accepted. *Expenses: Tuition:* Full-time $11,610; part-time $645 per credit. *Required fees:* $70 per term. Tuition and fees vary according to course load and program. *Financial support:* In 2016–17, 19 students received support. Tuition waivers (full and partial), unspecified assistantships, and institutional discounts available. Financial award applicants required to submit FAFSA. *Faculty research:* Workplace diversity, dynamics of team interaction, utilization of leased employees, experiential learning project on due diligence market for prostheses. *Unit head:* Dr. Robin Frkal, Director, 508-767-7622, E-mail: rafrkal@assumption.edu. *Application contact:* Karen Stoyanoff, Director of Recruitment for Graduate Enrollment, 508-767-7442, Fax: 508-799-4412, E-mail: graduate@assumption.edu.
Website: http://graduate.assumption.edu/mba/assumption-mba

Austin Peay State University, College of Graduate Studies, College of Behavioral and Health Sciences, Department of Professional Studies, Clarksville, TN 37044. Offers human resources leadership (MPS); strategic leadership (MPS); training and development (MPS). *Program availability:* Part-time, online learning. *Faculty:* 3 full-time (all women), 1 (woman) part-time/adjunct. *Students:* 9 full-time (6 women), 25 part-time (20 women); includes 12 minority (8 Black or African American, non-Hispanic/Latino; 3 Hispanic/Latino; 1 Two or more races, non-Hispanic/Latino). Average age 43. 14 applicants, 71% accepted, 7 enrolled. In 2016, 4 master's awarded. *Degree requirements:* For master's, project. *Entrance requirements:* For master's, GRE General Test, minimum GPA of 2.75. Additional exam requirements/recommendations for international students: Required—TOEFL (minimum score 500 paper-based). *Application deadline:* For fall admission, 8/9 priority date for domestic students. Applications are processed on a rolling basis. Application fee: $45 ($50 for international students). Electronic applications accepted. *Expenses:* Tuition, state resident: full-time $8300; part-time $415 per credit hour. Tuition, nonresident: full-time $22,280; part-time $1114 per credit hour. *Required fees:* $1473; $73.65 per credit hour. *Financial support:* Career-related internships or fieldwork, Federal Work-Study, institutionally sponsored loans, scholarships/grants, and unspecified assistantships available. Support available to part-time students. Financial award application deadline: 4/1; financial award applicants required to submit FAFSA. *Unit head:* Dr. Robyn Hulsart, Department Chair, 931-221-1439, E-mail: hulsartr@apsu.edu. *Application contact:* Brad Averitt, Coordinator of Graduate Admissions, 800-859-4723, Fax: 931-221-7641, E-mail: gradadmissions@apsu.edu.
Website: http://www.apsu.edu/apfc/MPS

Averett University, Master of Business Administration Program, Danville, VA 24541-3692. Offers business administration (MBA); human resources management (MBA); leadership (MBA); marketing (MBA). *Program availability:* Part-time, evening/weekend, 100% online, blended/hybrid learning. *Faculty:* 6 full-time (0 women), 21 part-time/ adjunct (6 women). *Students:* 52 full-time (40 women), 215 part-time (117 women); includes 133 minority (110 Black or African American, non-Hispanic/Latino; 5 American Indian or Alaska Native, non-Hispanic/Latino; 9 Asian, non-Hispanic/Latino; 9 Hispanic/ Latino), 6 international. Average age 38. 143 applicants, 78% accepted, 104 enrolled. In 2016, 99 master's awarded. *Degree requirements:* For master's, 41-credit core curriculum, minimum GPA of 3.0 throughout program, no more than 2 grades of C, completion of degree requirements within six years from start of program. *Entrance requirements:* For master's, minimum cumulative GPA of 3.0 over the last 60 semester hours of undergraduate study toward a baccalaureate degree, official transcripts, three years of full-time work experience, three letters of recommendation, current resume. Additional exam requirements/recommendations for international students: Required—TOEFL (minimum score 600 paper-based; 100 iBT). *Application deadline:* Applications are processed on a rolling basis. Electronic applications accepted. *Expenses:* $12,645. *Financial support:* Application deadline: 3/1; applicants required to submit FAFSA. *Unit head:* Dr. Peggy C. Wright, Chair, Business Department, 434-791-7118, E-mail: pwright@averett.edu. *Application contact:* Melissa Anderson, Director of Admissions, Graduate and Professional Studies, 804-729-8285, E-mail: manderson@averett.edu.
Website: http://gps.averett.edu/programs/master-degrees/

Avila University, School of Professional Studies, Kansas City, MO 64145-1698. Offers executive leadership development (MS); fundraising (MA); instructional design and technology (MA, MS); leadership coaching (MS); organizational development (MS); project management (MA); strategic human resources (MS). *Program availability:* Part-time-only, evening/weekend, 100% online, blended/hybrid learning. *Faculty:* 15 part-time/adjunct (9 women). *Students:* 90 full-time (59 women), 47 part-time (40 women); includes 50 minority (38 Black or African American, non-Hispanic/Latino; 1 American Indian or Alaska Native, non-Hispanic/Latino; 3 Asian, non-Hispanic/Latino; 7 Hispanic/ Latino; 1 Two or more races, non-Hispanic/Latino), 6 international. Average age 38. 95 applicants, 58% accepted, 38 enrolled. In 2016, 37 master's awarded. *Degree requirements:* For master's, thesis optional. *Entrance requirements:* For master's, 2 letters of recommendation, minimum GPA of 3.0 during last 60 hours, resume, statement of intent. Additional exam requirements/recommendations for international students: Required—TOEFL (minimum score 550 paper-based; 79 iBT). *Application deadline:* Applications are processed on a rolling basis. Application fee: $0. Electronic applications accepted. *Expenses:* $545 per credit hour. *Financial support:* In 2016–17, 14 students received support. Unspecified assistantships available. Support available to part-time students. Financial award applicants required to submit FAFSA. *Unit head:* Dr. Steve Iliff, Associate Dean/Director, 816-501-3675, Fax: 816-941-4650, E-mail: advantage@avila.edu. *Application contact:* Jessica Burson, Graduate Admission Advisor, 816-501-2482, Fax: 816-941-4650, E-mail: advantage@avila.edu.
Website: https://www.avila.edu/mrk/advantage-3

Azusa Pacific University, School of Business and Management, Azusa, CA 91702-7000. Offers business administration (MBA); diversity for strategic advantage (MA); entrepreneurship (MBA); finance (MBA); human and organizational development (MA); human resources and organizational development (MBA); human resources management (MA); international business (MBA); marketing (MBA); non-profit management (MA); organizational development and change (MA); performance improvement (MA); public administration (MA); strategic management (MBA). *Program availability:* Part-time, evening/weekend. *Degree requirements:* For master's, thesis (for some programs), final project. *Entrance requirements:* For master's, GMAT, minimum GPA of 3.0. Additional exam requirements/recommendations for international students: Required—TOEFL (minimum score 600 paper-based). *Expenses:* Contact institution. *Faculty research:* Gender issues, financial risk, leadership and ethics, marketing strategy.

Baker College Center for Graduate Studies–Online, Graduate Programs, Flint, MI 48507. Offers accounting (MBA); business administration (DBA); finance (MBA); general business (MBA); health care management (MBA); human resources management (MBA); information management (MBA); leadership studies (MBA); management information systems (MSIS); marketing (MBA). *Program availability:* Part-time, evening/ weekend, online learning. *Degree requirements:* For master's, portfolio. *Entrance requirements:* For master's, 3 years of work experience, minimum undergraduate GPA of 2.5, writing sample, 3 letters of recommendation; for doctorate, MBA or acceptable related master's degree from accredited association, 5 years work experience, minimum graduate GPA of 3.25, writing sample, 3 professional references. Additional exam requirements/recommendations for international students: Required—TOEFL (minimum score 550 paper-based). Electronic applications accepted.

Baldwin Wallace University, Graduate Programs, School of Business, Program in Human Resources, Berea, OH 44017-2088. Offers MBA. *Program availability:* Part-time, evening/weekend. *Students:* 12 full-time (9 women), 16 part-time (13 women); includes 8 minority (4 Black or African American, non-Hispanic/Latino; 2 Asian, non-Hispanic/ Latino; 2 Hispanic/Latino). Average age 36. 10 applicants, 80% accepted, 7 enrolled. In 2016, 4 master's awarded. *Degree requirements:* For master's, minimum overall GPA of 3.0. *Entrance requirements:* For master's, GMAT or minimum GPA of 3.0, bachelor's degree in any field, work experience. Additional exam requirements/recommendations for international students: Required—TOEFL (minimum score 550 paper-based; 79 iBT). *Application deadline:* For fall admission, 7/25 priority date for domestic students, 4/30 priority date for international students; for spring admission, 12/15 priority date for domestic students, 9/30 priority date for international students; for summer admission, 4/ 15 priority date for domestic students. Applications are processed on a rolling basis. Application fee: $25. Electronic applications accepted. Application fee is waived when completed online. *Expenses:* $921 per credit hour. *Financial support:* Applicants required to submit FAFSA. *Unit head:* Dale Kramer, Director, 440-826-3331, Fax: 440-826-3331, E-mail: dkramer@bw.edu. *Application contact:* Laura Spencer, Graduate Application Specialist, 440-826-2191, Fax: 440-826-3868, E-mail: lspencer@bw.edu.
Website: http://www.bw.edu/graduate/business/mba/

Barry University, School of Education, Graduate Certificate Programs, Miami Shores, FL 33161-6695. Offers advanced teaching and learning with technology (Certificate); distance education (Certificate); higher education technology integration (Certificate); human resources: not for profit and religious organizations (Certificate); K-12 technology integration (Certificate).

Baruch College of the City University of New York, Zicklin School of Business, Department of Management, New York, NY 10010-5585. Offers entrepreneurship (MBA); management (PhD); operations management (MBA); organizational behavior/ human resources management (MBA); sustainable business (MBA). PhD offered jointly with Graduate School and University Center of the City University of New York. *Program availability:* Part-time, evening/weekend. *Degree requirements:* For doctorate, comprehensive exam, thesis/dissertation. *Entrance requirements:* For master's, GMAT, 2 letters of recommendation, resume, 2 years of work experience; for doctorate, GMAT. Additional exam requirements/recommendations for international students: Required—TOEFL (minimum score 590 paper-based), TWE.

Belhaven University, School of Business, Jackson, MS 39202-1789. Offers business administration (MBA); health administration (MBA, MHA); human resources (MBA, MSL); leadership (MBA); public administration (MPA); sports administration (MBA, MSA). *Program availability:* Part-time, evening/weekend, 100% online. *Faculty:* 16 full-time (3 women), 82 part-time/adjunct (32 women). *Students:* 953 full-time (677 women), 392 part-time (292 women); includes 1,082 minority (1,027 Black or African American, non-Hispanic/Latino; 14 American Indian or Alaska Native, non-Hispanic/Latino; 4 Asian, non-Hispanic/Latino; 20 Hispanic/Latino; 2 Native Hawaiian or other Pacific Islander, non-Hispanic/Latino; 15 Two or more races, non-Hispanic/Latino), 11 international. Average age 35. In 2016, 235 master's awarded. *Degree requirements:* For master's, comprehensive exam (for some programs), thesis (for some programs). *Application deadline:* Applications are processed on a rolling basis. Application fee: $25. Electronic applications accepted. *Expenses:* $535 per credit hour tuition, $75 per course technology fee. *Financial support:* Applicants required to submit FAFSA. *Unit head:* Dr. Ralph Mason, Dean, 601-968-8949, Fax: 601-968-8951, E-mail: cmason@belhaven.edu. *Application contact:* Dr. Audrey Kelleher, Vice President of Adult and Graduate Marketing and Development, 407-804-1424, Fax: 407-620-5210, E-mail: akelleher@belhaven.edu.
Website: http://www.belhaven.edu/campuses/index.htm

Bellevue University, Graduate School, College of Business, Bellevue, NE 68005-3098. Offers acquisition and contract management (MS); business administration (MBA); finance (MS); human capital management (PhD); management (MSM).

Benedictine University, Graduate Programs, Program in Business Administration, Lisle, IL 60532. Offers accounting (MBA); entrepreneurship and managing innovation (MBA); financial management (MBA); health administration (MBA); human resource management (MBA); information systems security (MBA); international business (MBA); management consulting (MBA); management information systems (MBA); marketing management (MBA); operations management and logistics (MBA); organizational leadership (MBA). *Program availability:* Part-time, evening/weekend, online learning. *Faculty:* 4 full-time (2 women), 24 part-time/adjunct (3 women). *Students:* 90 full-time (51 women), 440 part-time (262 women); includes 147 minority (65 Black or African American, non-Hispanic/Latino; 1 American Indian or Alaska Native, non-Hispanic/Latino; 58 Asian, non-Hispanic/Latino; 20 Hispanic/Latino; 3 Native Hawaiian or other Pacific Islander, non-Hispanic/Latino), 2 international. Average age 34. 211 applicants, 89% accepted, 155 enrolled. In 2016, 350 master's awarded. *Entrance requirements:* For master's, GMAT. Additional exam requirements/recommendations for international students: Required—TOEFL (minimum score 550 paper-based). *Application deadline:* For fall admission, 9/1 for domestic students; for winter admission, 12/1 for domestic students; for spring admission, 2/15 for domestic students. Applications are processed on a rolling basis. Application fee: $40. Electronic applications accepted. *Expenses: Tuition:* Full-time $15,600; part-time $650 per hour. *Required fees:* $300. One-time fee: $125 part-time. Tuition and fees vary according to class time, course load, campus/location and program. *Financial support:* Career-related internships or fieldwork and health care benefits available. Support available to part-time students. *Faculty research:* Strategic leadership in professional organizations, sociology of professions, organizational change, social identity theory, applications to change management. *Unit head:* Dr. Sharon Borowicz, Director, 630-829-6219, E-mail: sborowicz@ben.edu. *Application contact:* Kari Gibbons, Director, Admissions, 630-829-6200, Fax: 630-829-6584, E-mail: kgibbons@ben.edu.

Brandman University, School of Business and Professional Studies, Irvine, CA 92618. Offers accounting (MBA); business administration (MBA); e-business strategic management (MBA); entrepreneurship (MBA); finance (MBA); health administration (MBA); human resources (MBA, MS); international business (MBA); marketing (MBA); organizational leadership (MA, MBA, MPA); public administration (MPA). *Expenses: Tuition:* Full-time $14,880; part-time $620 per credit hour. Tuition and fees vary according to degree level and program. *Unit head:* Dr. Glenn Worthington, Dean, 253-861-1024, E-mail: gworthin@brandman.edu.
Website: https://www.brandman.edu/business-professional-studies

Brigham Young University, Graduate Studies, Marriott School of Management, Master of Business Administration Program, Provo, UT 84602. Offers entrepreneurship (MBA); finance (MBA); global supply chain management (MBA); marketing (MBA); strategic human resources (MBA); JD/MBA; MBA/MS. *Accreditation:* AACSB. *Students:* 321 full-time (63 women); includes 16 minority (1 Black or African American, non-Hispanic/Latino; 9 Asian, non-Hispanic/Latino; 6 Hispanic/Latino), 69 international. Average age 31. 397 applicants, 49% accepted, 154 enrolled. In 2016, 146 master's awarded. *Entrance requirements:* For master's, GMAT or GRE, minimum GPA of 3.0 in last 60 hours. Additional exam requirements/recommendations for international students: Required—TOEFL (minimum score 590 paper-based; 94 iBT), IELTS (minimum score 7). *Application deadline:* For fall admission, 5/1 for domestic students, 1/15 for international students. Applications are processed on a rolling basis. Application fee: $50. Electronic applications accepted. *Expenses:* Contact institution. *Financial support:* In 2016–17, 247 students received support. Research assistantships, teaching assistantships, career-related internships or fieldwork, institutionally sponsored loans, and scholarships/grants available. Financial award application deadline: 3/1; financial award applicants required to submit FAFSA. *Faculty research:* Finance, marketing, supply chain management, entrepreneurship, strategic human resources. *Unit head:* Dr. Grant McQueen, Director, 801-422-3500, Fax: 801-422-0513, E-mail: mba@byu.edu. *Application contact:* Yvette Anderson, MBA Program Admissions Director, 801-422-3500, Fax: 801-422-0513, E-mail: mba@byu.edu.
Website: http://mba.byu.edu

Buffalo State College, State University of New York, The Graduate School, Faculty of Applied Science and Education, Department of Educational Foundations, Program in Adult Education, Buffalo, NY 14222-1095. Offers adult education (MS, Certificate); human resources development (Certificate). *Program availability:* Part-time, evening/weekend, online learning. *Degree requirements:* For master's, comprehensive exam. *Entrance requirements:* Additional exam requirements/recommendations for international students: Required—TOEFL (minimum score 550 paper-based).

California Coast University, School of Administration and Management, Santa Ana, CA 92701. Offers business marketing (MBA); health care management (MBA); human resource management (MBA); management (MBA, MS). *Program availability:* Online learning. Electronic applications accepted.

California Intercontinental University, School of Business, Irvine, CA 92614. Offers banking and finance (MBA); entrepreneurship and business management (DBA); global business leadership (DBA); international management and marketing (MBA); organizational management and human resource management (MBA).

California State University, East Bay, Office of Graduate Studies, College of Business and Economics, MBA Program, Option in Human Resources and Organizational Behavior, Hayward, CA 94542-3000. Offers human resources/personnel management (MBA). *Program availability:* Part-time, evening/weekend. *Students:* 11 full-time (9 women), 20 part-time (16 women); includes 20 minority (6 Black or African American, non-Hispanic/Latino; 7 Asian, non-Hispanic/Latino; 3 Hispanic/Latino; 3 Native Hawaiian or other Pacific Islander, non-Hispanic/Latino; 1 Two or more races, non-Hispanic/Latino), 9 international. Average age 32. 30 applicants, 53% accepted, 10 enrolled. In 2016, 4 master's awarded. *Degree requirements:* For master's, comprehensive exam or thesis. *Entrance requirements:* For master's, GMAT, minimum GPA of 2.75. Additional exam requirements/recommendations for international students: Required—TOEFL (minimum score 550 paper-based). *Application deadline:* For fall admission, 6/30 for domestic and international students. Application fee: $55. Electronic applications accepted. *Financial support:* Fellowships, career-related internships or fieldwork, Federal Work-Study, institutionally sponsored loans, and scholarships/grants available. Support available to part-time students. Financial award application deadline: 3/2; financial award applicants required to submit FAFSA. *Unit head:* Dr. Asha Rao, Program Advisor, 510-885-3290, E-mail: asha.rao@csueastbay.edu. *Application contact:* Dr. Donna Wiley, Interim Associate Vice President for Academic Programs and Graduate Studies, 510-885-3716, Fax: 510-885-4777, E-mail: donna.wiley@csueastbay.edu.
Website: http://www20.csueastbay.edu/cbe/mba-options/Human-Resources-Management-Option.html

California State University, Sacramento, Office of Graduate Studies, College of Business Administration, Sacramento, CA 95819. Offers accountancy (MS); business administration (IMBA, MBA); human resources (MBA); urban land development (MBA). *Accreditation:* AACSB. *Program availability:* Part-time, evening/weekend. *Students:* 138 full-time (68 women), 129 part-time (63 women); includes 211 minority (12 Black or African American, non-Hispanic/Latino; 132 American Indian or Alaska Native, non-Hispanic/Latino; 63 Asian, non-Hispanic/Latino; 4 Native Hawaiian or other Pacific Islander, non-Hispanic/Latino). Average age 34. 198 applicants, 77% accepted, 85 enrolled. In 2016, 168 master's awarded. *Degree requirements:* For master's, thesis or alternative, writing proficiency exam. *Entrance requirements:* For master's, GMAT. Additional exam requirements/recommendations for international students: Required—TOEFL (minimum score 550 paper-based; 80 iBT). *Application deadline:* For fall admission, 2/1 for domestic students, 3/1 for international students; for spring admission, 9/15 for domestic students, 9/30 for international students. Applications are processed on a rolling basis. Application fee: $55. Electronic applications accepted. *Expenses:* $4,302 full-time tuition and fees per semester, $2,796 part-time. *Financial support:* Research assistantships, teaching assistantships, career-related internships or fieldwork, and Federal Work-Study available. Support available to part-time students. Financial award applicants required to submit FAFSA. *Unit head:* Dr. Pierre A. Balthazard, Dean, 916-278-6578, Fax: 916-278-5793, E-mail: cba@csus.edu. *Application contact:* Jose Martinez, Graduate Admissions Supervisor, 916-278-7871, E-mail: martinj@skymail.csus.edu.
Website: http://www.cba.csus.edu

Capella University, School of Business and Technology, Doctoral Programs in Business, Minneapolis, MN 55402. Offers accounting (DBA, PhD); business intelligence (DBA); finance (DBA, PhD); general business management (PhD); human resource management (DBA, PhD); leadership (DBA, PhD); management education (PhD); marketing (DBA, PhD); project management (DBA, PhD); strategy and innovation (DBA, PhD). *Accreditation:* ACBSP.

Capella University, School of Business and Technology, Master's Programs in Business, Minneapolis, MN 55402. Offers accounting (MBA); business analysis (MS); business intelligence (MBA); entrepreneurship (MBA); finance (MBA); general business administration (MBA); general human resource management (MS); general leadership (MS); health care management (MBA); human resource management (MBA); marketing (MBA); project management (MBA, MS). *Accreditation:* ACBSP.

Caribbean University, Graduate School, Bayamón, PR 00960-0493. Offers administration and supervision (MA Ed); criminal justice (MA); curriculum and instruction (MA Ed, PhD), including elementary education (MA Ed), English education (MA Ed), history education (MA Ed), mathematics education (MA Ed), primary education (MA Ed), science education (MA Ed), Spanish education (MA Ed); educational technology in instructional systems (MA Ed); gerontology (MSN); human resources (MBA); museology, archiving and art history (MA Ed); neonatal pediatrics (MSN); physical education (MA Ed); special education (MA Ed). *Entrance requirements:* For master's, interview, minimum GPA of 2.5.

Carlow University, College of Leadership and Social Change, MBA Program, Pittsburgh, PA 15213-3165. Offers fraud and forensics (MBA); healthcare management (MBA); human resource management (MBA); leadership and management (MBA); project management (MBA). *Program availability:* Part-time, evening/weekend, 100% online, blended/hybrid learning. *Students:* 87 full-time (65 women), 32 part-time (21 women); includes 31 minority (23 Black or African American, non-Hispanic/Latino; 3 Asian, non-Hispanic/Latino; 2 Hispanic/Latino; 3 Two or more races, non-Hispanic/Latino), 1 international. Average age 33. 54 applicants, 98% accepted, 33 enrolled. In 2016, 29 master's awarded. *Entrance requirements:* For master's, minimum undergraduate GPA of 3.0 (preferred); personal essay; resume; official transcripts; two professional recommendations. Additional exam requirements/recommendations for international students: Required—TOEFL (minimum score 550 paper-based). *Application deadline:* Applications are processed on a rolling basis. Electronic applications accepted. *Expenses: Tuition:* Full-time $11,855; part-time $801 per credit. *Required fees:* $182; $13 per credit. Tuition and fees vary according to course load, degree level and program. *Financial support:* Application deadline: 4/1; applicants required to submit FAFSA. *Unit head:* Dr. Howard Stern, Chair, MBA Program, 412-578-8828, E-mail: hastern@carlow.edu. *Application contact:* 412-578-6059, Fax: 412-578-6321, E-mail: gradstudies@carlow.edu.
Website: http://www.carlow.edu/Business_Administration.aspx

The Catholic University of America, Busch School of Business and Economics, Washington, DC 20064. Offers accounting (MS); business analysis (MSBA); integral economic development management (MA); integral economic development policy (MA); management (MS), including Federal contract management, human resource management, leadership and management, project management, sales management. *Program availability:* Part-time. *Faculty:* 30 full-time (7 women), 30 part-time/adjunct (5 women). *Students:* 60 full-time (32 women), 26 part-time (14 women); includes 26 minority (11 Black or African American, non-Hispanic/Latino; 8 Asian, non-Hispanic/Latino; 5 Hispanic/Latino; 2 Two or more races, non-Hispanic/Latino), 22 international. Average age 29. 121 applicants, 77% accepted, 64 enrolled. In 2016, 48 master's awarded. *Degree requirements:* For master's, comprehensive exam (for some programs). *Entrance requirements:* For master's, GRE General Test, statement of purpose, official copies of academic transcripts, three letters of recommendation. Additional exam requirements/recommendations for international students: Required—TOEFL (minimum score 550 paper-based; 80 iBT). *Application deadline:* For fall admission, 7/15 priority date for domestic students, 7/1 for international students; for spring admission, 11/15 priority date for domestic students, 11/1 for international students. Applications are processed on a rolling basis. Application fee: $55. Electronic applications accepted. *Expenses:* $42,850 per year; $1,170 per credit; $200 per semester part-time fees. *Financial support:* Fellowships, research assistantships, teaching assistantships, Federal Work-Study, scholarships/grants, tuition waivers (full and partial), and unspecified assistantships available. Financial award application deadline: 2/1; financial award applicants required to submit FAFSA. *Faculty research:* Integrity of the marketing process, economics of energy and the environment, emerging markets, social change, international finance and economic development. *Total annual research expenditures:* $3,698. *Unit head:* Dr. William Bowman, Dean, 202-319-5290, Fax: 202-319-4426, E-mail: otey@cua.edu. *Application contact:* Director of Graduate Admissions, 202-319-5057, Fax: 202-319-6533, E-mail: cua-admissions@cua.edu.
Website: http://business.cua.edu/

Central Michigan University, Central Michigan University Global Campus, Program in Administration, Mount Pleasant, MI 48859. Offers acquisitions administration (MSA, Certificate); engineering management administration (MSA, Certificate); general administration (MSA, Certificate); health services administration (MSA, Certificate); human resources administration (MSA, Certificate); information resource management (MSA); information resource management administration (Certificate); international administration (MSA, Certificate); leadership (MSA, Certificate); philanthropy and fundraising administration (MSA, Certificate); public administration (MSA, Certificate); recreation and park administration (MSA); research administration (MSA, Certificate). *Program availability:* Part-time, evening/weekend, online learning. *Faculty:* 21 full-time (5 women), 168 part-time/adjunct (43 women). *Students:* 3,059 (1,741 women); includes 1,392 minority (1,003 Black or African American, non-Hispanic/Latino; 27 American Indian or Alaska Native, non-Hispanic/Latino; 93 Asian, non-Hispanic/Latino; 49 Hispanic/Latino; 10 Native Hawaiian or other Pacific Islander, non-Hispanic/Latino; 210 Two or more races, non-Hispanic/Latino). Average age 38. In 2016, 289 master's awarded. *Entrance requirements:* For master's, minimum GPA of 2.7 in major. *Application deadline:* Applications are processed on a rolling basis. Application fee: $50. Electronic applications accepted. *Financial support:* Scholarships/grants available. Support available to part-time students. Financial award applicants required to submit FAFSA. *Unit head:* Dr. Patricia Chase, Director, 989-774-6525, E-mail: chase1pb@cmich.edu. *Application contact:* 877-268-4636, E-mail: cmuglobal@cmich.edu.

Central Michigan University, Central Michigan University Global Campus, Program in Business Administration, Mount Pleasant, MI 48859. Offers enterprise resource planning (MBA, Certificate); human resource management (MBA); logistics management (MBA, Certificate); marketing (MBA); value-driven organization (MBA). *Program availability:* Part-time, evening/weekend. *Faculty:* 17 full-time (7 women), 3 part-time/adjunct (0 women). *Students:* 189 (82 women); includes 29 minority (17 Black or African American, non-Hispanic/Latino; 2 American Indian or Alaska Native, non-Hispanic/Latino; 3 Asian, non-Hispanic/Latino; 1 Hispanic/Latino; 6 Two or more races, non-Hispanic/Latino). Average age 32. In 2016, 25 master's awarded. *Entrance requirements:* For master's, GMAT. *Financial support:* Scholarships/grants available. Support available to part-time students. *Unit head:* Dr. Debasish Chakraborty, 989-774-3678, E-mail: chakt1d@cmich.edu. *Application contact:* Global Campus Student Services Call Center, 877-268-4636, E-mail: cmuglobal@cmich.edu.

Central Michigan University, College of Graduate Studies, College of Business Administration, MBA Program, Mount Pleasant, MI 48859. Offers accounting (MBA); business economics (MBA); consulting (MBA); finance (MBA); general business (MBA); human resource management (MBA); information systems (MBA); international business (MBA); logistics management (MBA); marketing (MBA); value-driven organization (MBA). *Program availability:* Part-time, evening/weekend, online learning. Electronic applications accepted. *Faculty research:* Accounting, consulting, international business, marketing, information systems.

Central Michigan University, College of Graduate Studies, Interdisciplinary Administration Programs, Mount Pleasant, MI 48859. Offers acquisitions administration (MSA, Graduate Certificate); general administration (MSA, Graduate Certificate); health services administration (MSA, Graduate Certificate); human resource administration (Graduate Certificate); human resources administration (MSA); information resource management (MSA, Graduate Certificate); international administration (MSA, Graduate Certificate); leadership (MSA, Graduate Certificate); public administration (MSA, Graduate Certificate); research administration (Graduate Certificate); sport administration (MSA). *Accreditation:* AACSB. *Program availability:* Part-time, evening/weekend, online learning. *Degree requirements:* For master's, thesis or alternative. *Entrance requirements:* For master's, bachelor's degree with minimum GPA of 2.7. Electronic applications accepted. *Faculty research:* Interdisciplinary studies in acquisitions administration, health services administration, sport administration, recreation and park administration, and international administration.

Charleston Southern University, School of Business, Charleston, SC 29423-8087. Offers accounting (MBA); finance (MBA); general management (MBA); human resource management (MS); leadership (MBA); management information systems (MBA); organizational leadership (MA). *Program availability:* Part-time, evening/weekend. *Degree requirements:* For master's, thesis optional. *Entrance requirements:* For master's, GMAT. Additional exam requirements/recommendations for international students: Required—TOEFL (minimum score 550 paper-based; 79 iBT). *Application deadline:* Applications are processed on a rolling basis. Application fee: $40. *Expenses: Tuition:* Full-time $6000. Tuition and fees vary according to program. *Financial support:* Research assistantships with full tuition reimbursements available. Financial award application deadline: 4/15; financial award applicants required to submit FAFSA. *Unit head:* Dr. David Palmer, Interim Dean, 843-863-7025, Fax: 843-863-7922, E-mail: dpalmer@csuniv.edu. *Application contact:* Dr. Darin L. Gerdes, Director of the MBA Program, 843-863-7814, Fax: 843-863-7922, E-mail: dgerdes@csuniv.edu.
Website: http://www.csuniv.edu/business/

City University of Seattle, Graduate Division, School of Management, Seattle, WA 98121. Offers accounting (Certificate); change leadership (MBA, Certificate); computer systems (MS); finance (Certificate); financial management (MBA); general management (MBA); general management-Europe (MBA); global marketing (MBA); human resources management (Certificate); individualized study (MBA); information security (MS); information systems (MBA); leadership (MA); marketing (MBA, Certificate); project management (MBA, MS, Certificate); sustainable business (Certificate); technology management (MBA, Certificate). *Program availability:* Part-time, evening/weekend, online learning. *Degree requirements:* For master's, comprehensive exam (for some programs), thesis (for some programs). *Entrance requirements:* For master's, baccalaureate degree or equivalent from an accredited or otherwise recognized institution. Additional exam requirements/recommendations for international students: Required—TOEFL (minimum score 567 paper-based; 87 iBT); Recommended—IELTS. Electronic applications accepted.

Claremont Graduate University, Graduate Programs, School of Social Science, Policy and Evaluation, Human Resource Management Program, Claremont, CA 91711-6160. Offers MS. *Program availability:* Part-time, evening/weekend. *Faculty:* 1 full-time (0 women). *Students:* 9 full-time (6 women), 7 part-time (6 women); includes 11 minority (2 Black or African American, non-Hispanic/Latino; 6 Asian, non-Hispanic/Latino; 3 Hispanic/Latino), 2 international. Average age 29. In 2016, 4 master's awarded. *Entrance requirements:* For master's, GMAT or GRE General Test. Additional exam requirements/recommendations for international students: Required—TOEFL (minimum score 75 iBT). *Application deadline:* For fall admission, 1/15 priority date for domestic and international students. Applications are processed on a rolling basis. Application fee: $80. Electronic applications accepted. *Expenses: Tuition:* Full-time $44,328; part-time $1847 per unit. *Required fees:* $600; $300 per semester. Tuition and fees vary according to course load and program. *Financial support:* Fellowships, Federal Work-Study, institutionally sponsored loans, and scholarships/grants available. Support available to part-time students. Financial award application deadline: 2/15; financial award applicants required to submit FAFSA. *Unit head:* Stewart Donaldson, Dean, 909-607-8235, E-mail: stewart.donaldson@cgu.edu. *Application contact:* Paige Piontkowsky, Senior Assistant Director of Admissions, 909-607-3240, E-mail: paige.piontkowsky@cgu.edu.
Website: https://www.cgu.edu/academics/program/human-resource-management/

Clarkson University, School of Business, Master's Program in Business Administration, Potsdam, NY 13099. Offers business administration (MBA); business fundamentals (Advanced Certificate); global supply chain management (Advanced Certificate); human resource management (Advanced Certificate); management and leadership (Advanced Certificate). *Accreditation:* AACSB. *Program availability:* Part-time, evening/weekend, 100% online, blended/hybrid learning. *Faculty:* 53 full-time (12 women), 33 part-time/adjunct (6 women). *Students:* 119 full-time (45 women), 51 part-time (19 women); includes 23 minority (5 Black or African American, non-Hispanic/Latino; 1 American Indian or Alaska Native, non-Hispanic/Latino; 10 Asian, non-Hispanic/Latino; 4 Hispanic/Latino; 3 Two or more races, non-Hispanic/Latino), 14 international. 390 applicants, 39% accepted, 101 enrolled. In 2016, 91 master's, 2 other advanced degrees awarded. *Entrance requirements:* For master's, GRE or GMAT. Additional exam requirements/recommendations for international students: Required—TOEFL (minimum score 550 paper-based, 80 iBT) or IELTS (6.5). *Application deadline:* Applications are processed on a rolling basis. Application fee: $50. Electronic applications accepted. *Expenses: Tuition:* Full-time $23,400; part-time $1300 per credit hour. Tuition and fees vary according to campus/location and program. *Financial support:* Scholarships/grants available. *Unit head:* Dr. Alan Bowman, Senior Associate Dean of Graduate Business Programs, 518-631-9887, E-mail: abowman@clarkson.edu. *Application contact:* Erin Wheeler, Graduate Admissions Contact, 518-631-9910, E-mail: ewheeler@clarkson.edu.

Clayton State University, School of Graduate Studies, College of Business, Program in Business Administration, Morrow, GA 30260-0285. Offers accounting (MBA); human resource leadership (MBA); international business (MBA); sports and entertainment management (MBA); supply chain management (MBA). *Accreditation:* AACSB. *Program availability:* Part-time, evening/weekend. *Degree requirements:* For master's, thesis. *Entrance requirements:* For master's, GMAT, 3 letters of recommendation; statement of purpose; 2 official transcripts. Additional exam requirements/recommendations for international students: Required—TOEFL (minimum score 550 paper-based; 80 iBT). Electronic applications accepted. *Expenses:* Contact institution.

Clemson University, Graduate School, College of Education, Clemson, SC 29634-0702. Offers administration and supervision (K-12) (M Ed, Ed S); education and organizational leadership (MS), including athletic leadership; educational leadership (PhD), including P-12; human resource development (MHRD); middle-level education (MAT). *Program availability:* Part-time, evening/weekend, 100% online. *Faculty:* 75 full-time (54 women), 1 part-time/adjunct (0 women). *Students:* 120 full-time (84 women), 309 part-time (206 women); includes 96 minority (68 Black or African American, non-Hispanic/Latino; 1 American Indian or Alaska Native, non-Hispanic/Latino; 3 Asian, non-Hispanic/Latino; 19 Hispanic/Latino; 5 Two or more races, non-Hispanic/Latino), 11 international. Average age 34. 417 applicants, 50% accepted, 133 enrolled. In 2016, 239 master's, 21 doctorates, 59 other advanced degrees awarded. *Degree requirements:* For master's, comprehensive exam (for some programs), thesis (for some programs); for doctorate, comprehensive exam, thesis/dissertation. *Entrance requirements:* For master's, doctorate, and other advanced degree, GRE General Test, unofficial transcripts, letters of recommendation. Additional exam requirements/recommendations for international students: Required—TOEFL (minimum score 80 iBT), IELTS (minimum score 7). *Application deadline:* Applications are processed on a rolling basis. Application fee: $80 ($90 for international students). Electronic applications accepted. *Expenses:* Contact institution. *Financial support:* In 2016–17, 75 students received support, including 22 fellowships with partial tuition reimbursements available (averaging $6,316 per year), 28 research assistantships with partial tuition reimbursements available (averaging $15,399 per year), 5 teaching assistantships with partial tuition reimbursements available (averaging $30,000 per year); unspecified assistantships also available. *Faculty research:* Early literacy and motivation, STEAM education, legal/policy issues in education, leadership, special education interventions/assessment/policy. *Total annual research expenditures:* $2.8 million. *Unit head:* Dr. George Petersen, Dean, 864-656-4444, Fax: 864-656-0311, E-mail: soedean@clemson.edu. *Application contact:* Dr. David Fleming, Graduate Programs Coordinator, 864-656-1881, Fax: 864-656-0311, E-mail: dflemin@clemson.edu.
Website: http://www.clemson.edu/education/

Cleveland State University, College of Graduate Studies, Monte Ahuja College of Business, Department of Management, Cleveland, OH 44115. Offers health care administration (MBA); labor relations and human resources (MLRHR). *Program availability:* Part-time, evening/weekend. *Faculty:* 6 full-time (3 women), 8 part-time/adjunct (1 woman). *Students:* 7 full-time (5 women), 19 part-time (16 women); includes 10 minority (8 Black or African American, non-Hispanic/Latino; 2 Hispanic/Latino), 3 international. Average age 31. In 2016, 11 master's awarded. *Entrance requirements:* For master's, GMAT or GRE, minimum GPA of 3.0. Additional exam requirements/recommendations for international students: Required—TOEFL (minimum score 550 paper-based; 78 iBT). *Application deadline:* For fall admission, 7/15 for domestic students; for spring admission, 12/15 for domestic students. Applications are processed on a rolling basis. Application fee: $40. Electronic applications accepted. *Expenses:* Tuition, state resident: full-time $9565. Tuition, nonresident: full-time $17,980. Tuition and fees vary according to program. *Financial support:* In 2016–17, 3 students received support. Career-related internships or fieldwork, scholarships/grants, and unspecified assistantships available. Financial award application deadline: 5/1; financial award applicants required to submit FAFSA. *Faculty research:* Employee selection, individual differences, leadership, emotions, interviews. *Unit head:* Dr. Kenneth J. Dunegan, Chairperson, 216-687-4747, Fax: 216-687-4708, E-mail: t.degroot@csuohio.edu. *Application contact:* Lisa Marie Sample, Administrative Assistant, 216-687-4726, Fax: 216-687-6888, E-mail: l.m.sample@csuohio.edu.
Website: https://www.csuohio.edu/business/management/management

College of Saint Elizabeth, Department of Business Administration and Management, Morristown, NJ 07960-6989. Offers human resource management (MS); organizational change (MS). *Program availability:* Part-time. *Degree requirements:* For master's, thesis. *Entrance requirements:* For master's, GRE, GMAT, minimum GPA of 3.25; 2 research projects related to the development design of the action research dissertation study and oral dissertation defense. Additional exam requirements/recommendations for international students: Required—TOEFL (minimum score 550 paper-based; 79 IBT), IELTS (minimum score 6.5). Electronic applications accepted. Application fee is waived when completed online. *Expenses:* Contact institution.

Colorado State University–Global Campus, Graduate Programs, Greenwood Village, CO 80111. Offers criminal justice and law enforcement administration (MS); education leadership (MS); finance (MS); healthcare administration and management (MS); human resource management (MHRM); information technology management (MITM); international management (MS); management (MS); organizational leadership (MS); professional accounting (MPA); project management (MS); teaching and learning (MS). *Accreditation:* ACBSP. *Program availability:* Online learning.

Colorado Technical University Aurora, Programs in Business Administration and Management, Aurora, CO 80014. Offers accounting (MBA); business administration (MBA); business administration and management (EMBA); finance (MBA); human resource management (MBA); marketing (MBA); mediation and dispute resolution (MBA); operations management (MBA); project management (MBA); technology management (MBA). *Program availability:* Part-time, evening/weekend. *Degree requirements:* For master's, thesis or alternative. *Entrance requirements:* For master's, minimum undergraduate GPA of 3.0, resume.

Colorado Technical University Colorado Springs, Graduate Studies, Program in Management, Colorado Springs, CO 80907. Offers accounting (MBA, MSA); business administration (MBA); finance (MBA); human resources management (MBA); logistics/supply chain management (MBA); management (DM); marketing (MBA); mediation and dispute resolution (MBA); operations management (MBA); project management (MBA); technology management (MBA). *Accreditation:* ACBSP. *Program availability:* Part-time, evening/weekend, online learning. *Degree requirements:* For master's, thesis or alternative; for doctorate, thesis/dissertation. *Entrance requirements:* For doctorate, minimum graduate GPA of 3.0, 5 years of related work experience. *Faculty research:* Sexual harassment, performance evaluation, critical thinking.

Columbia College, Master of Business Administration Program, Columbia, MO 65216-0002. Offers accounting (MBA); human resources (MBA). *Program availability:* Part-time, evening/weekend, 100% online, blended/hybrid learning. *Faculty:* 5 full-time (2 women), 39 part-time/adjunct (15 women). *Students:* 76 full-time (51 women), 415 part-time (240 women); includes 109 minority (60 Black or African American, non-Hispanic/Latino; 3 American Indian or Alaska Native, non-Hispanic/Latino; 7 Asian, non-Hispanic/Latino; 25 Hispanic/Latino; 2 Native Hawaiian or other Pacific Islander, non-Hispanic/Latino; 12 Two or more races, non-Hispanic/Latino), 26 international. Average age 36.

121 applicants, 90% accepted, 63 enrolled. In 2016, 194 master's awarded. *Entrance requirements:* For master's, 3 letters of recommendation, minimum cumulative undergraduate GPA of 3.0, resume, goal statement. Additional exam requirements/ recommendations for international students: Required—TOEFL (minimum score 550 paper-based; 79 iBT). *Application deadline:* For fall admission, 8/9 priority date for domestic and international students; for spring admission, 12/27 priority date for domestic and international students. Applications are processed on a rolling basis. Application fee: $55. Electronic applications accepted. *Expenses:* Contact institution. *Financial support:* Federal Work-Study and scholarships/grants available. Financial award application deadline: 3/1; financial award applicants required to submit FAFSA. *Unit head:* Dr. Shanda Traiser, Dean, School of Business Administration, 573-875-7561, Fax: 573-876-4493, E-mail: strasier@ccis.edu. *Application contact:* Stephanie Johnson, Director of Admissions, 573-875-7352, Fax: 573-875-7506, E-mail: sjohnson@ccis.edu.
Website: http://www.ccis.edu/graduate/academics/degrees.asp?MBA

Columbia Southern University, MBA Program, Orange Beach, AL 36561. Offers finance (MBA); health care management (MBA); human resource management (MBA); marketing (MBA); project management (MBA); public administration (MBA). *Program availability:* Part-time, evening/weekend, online learning. *Entrance requirements:* For master's, bachelor's degree from accredited/approved institution. Additional exam requirements/recommendations for international students: Required—TOEFL. Electronic applications accepted.

Columbia University, Graduate School of Business, MBA Program, New York, NY 10027. Offers accounting (MBA); decision, risk, and operations (MBA); entrepreneurship (MBA); finance and economics (MBA); healthcare and pharmaceutical management (MBA); human resource management (MBA); international business (MBA); leadership and ethics (MBA); management (MBA); marketing (MBA); media (MBA); private equity (MBA); real estate (MBA); social enterprise (MBA); value investing (MBA); DDS/MBA; JD/MBA; MBA/MIA; MBA/MPH; MBA/MS; MD/MBA. *Entrance requirements:* For master's, GMAT, 2 letters of recommendation. Additional exam requirements/ recommendations for international students: Required—TOEFL. Electronic applications accepted. *Expenses:* Contact institution. *Faculty research:* Human decision making and behavioral research; real estate market and mortgage defaults; financial crisis and corporate governance; international business; security analysis and accounting.

Columbus State University, Graduate Studies, Turner College of Business, Columbus, GA 31907-5645. Offers applied computer science (MS), including informational assurance, modeling and simulation, software development; business administration (MBA); human resource management (Certificate); information systems security (Certificate); modeling and simulation (Certificate); organizational leadership (MS), including human resource management, leader development, servant leadership; servant leadership (Certificate). *Accreditation:* AACSB. *Program availability:* Part-time, evening/weekend, 100% online, blended/hybrid learning. *Faculty:* 10 full-time (3 women). *Students:* 93 full-time (21 women), 132 part-time (47 women); includes 69 minority (36 Black or African American, non-Hispanic/Latino; 1 American Indian or Alaska Native, non-Hispanic/Latino; 11 Asian, non-Hispanic/Latino; 14 Hispanic/Latino; 7 Two or more races, non-Hispanic/Latino), 35 international. Average age 31. 279 applicants, 44% accepted, 64 enrolled. In 2016, 106 master's awarded. *Entrance requirements:* For master's, GMAT, GRE, minimum undergraduate GPA of 2.75, letters of recommendation. Additional exam requirements/recommendations for international students: Required—TOEFL (minimum score 550 paper-based; 79 iBT). *Application deadline:* For fall admission, 6/30 for domestic students, 5/1 for international students; for spring admission, 11/1 for domestic and international students; for summer admission, 3/1 for domestic and international students. Applications are processed on a rolling basis. Application fee: $50. Electronic applications accepted. *Expenses:* Contact institution. *Financial support:* In 2016–17, 18 students received support, including 16 research assistantships (averaging $3,000 per year); Federal Work-Study also available. Financial award application deadline: 5/1; financial award applicants required to submit FAFSA. *Unit head:* Dr. Linda U. Hadley, Dean, 706-507-8153, Fax: 706-568-2184, E-mail: hadley_linda@columbusstate.edu. *Application contact:* Kristin Williams, Director of International and Graduate Recruitment, 706-507-8848, Fax: 706-568-5091, E-mail: thornton_katie@colstate.edu.
Website: http://turner.columbusstate.edu/

Concordia University, St. Paul, College of Business, St. Paul, MN 55104-5494. Offers business administration (MBA), including cyber-security leadership; business and organizational leadership (MBA); health care management (MBA); human resource management (MA); leadership and management (MA); strategic communication management (MA). *Accreditation:* ACBSP. *Program availability:* Part-time, evening/ weekend, 100% online, blended/hybrid learning. *Faculty:* 12 full-time (4 women), 36 part-time/adjunct (15 women). *Students:* 462 full-time (288 women), 25 part-time (16 women); includes 123 minority (59 Black or African American, non-Hispanic/Latino; 1 American Indian or Alaska Native, non-Hispanic/Latino; 36 Asian, non-Hispanic/Latino; 10 Hispanic/Latino; 1 Native Hawaiian or other Pacific Islander, non-Hispanic/Latino; 16 Two or more races, non-Hispanic/Latino), 28 international. Average age 34. 269 applicants, 73% accepted, 137 enrolled. In 2016, 192 master's awarded. *Degree requirements:* For master's, thesis (for some programs). *Entrance requirements:* For master's, official transcripts from regionally-accredited institution stating the conferral of a bachelor's degree with minimum cumulative GPA of 3.0; personal statement; professional resume. Additional exam requirements/recommendations for international students: Recommended—TOEFL (minimum score 547 paper-based; 78 iBT), IELTS (minimum score 6). *Application deadline:* For fall admission, 8/1 for domestic and international students; for spring admission, 12/1 for domestic and international students; for summer admission, 5/1 for domestic and international students. Applications are processed on a rolling basis. Application fee: $50. Electronic applications accepted. *Expenses:* Contact institution. *Financial support:* In 2016–17, 259 students received support. Scholarships/grants and unspecified assistantships available. Financial award applicants required to submit FAFSA. *Faculty research:* Alternative dispute resolution, franchising, entrepreneurship, applied business ethics, strategic leadership development. *Unit head:* Dr. Kevin Hall, Dean, 651-603-6165, Fax: 651-641-8807, E-mail: khall@csp.edu. *Application contact:* Kimberly Craig, Associate Vice President, Cohort Enrollment Management, 651-603-6223, Fax: 651-603-6320, E-mail: craig@csp.edu.

Concordia University Wisconsin, Graduate Programs, School of Business Administration, MBA Program, Mequon, WI 53097-2402. Offers finance (MBA); health care administration (MBA); human resource management (MBA); international business (MBA); international business-bilingual English/Chinese (MBA); management (MBA); management information systems (MBA); managerial communications (MBA); marketing (MBA); public administration (MBA); risk management (MBA). *Program availability:* Online learning. *Degree requirements:* For master's, comprehensive exam, thesis or alternative. *Entrance requirements:* Additional exam requirements/ recommendations for international students: Required—TOEFL. *Application deadline:* For fall admission, 8/1 priority date for domestic students; for spring admission, 1/15 for domestic students. Applications are processed on a rolling basis. Application fee: $50. *Expenses:* Contact institution. *Financial support:* Application deadline: 8/1. *Unit head:* Dr. David Borst, Director, 262-243-4298, Fax: 262-243-4428, E-mail: david.borst@cuw.edu. *Application contact:* Mary Eberhardt, Graduate Admissions, 262-243-4551, Fax: 262-243-4428, E-mail: mary.eberhardt@cuw.edu.

Cornell University, Graduate School, Graduate Fields of Industrial and Labor Relations, Ithaca, NY 14853. Offers collective bargaining, labor law and labor history (MILR, MPS, MS, PhD); economic and social statistics (MILR); human resource studies (MILR, MPS, MS, PhD); industrial and labor relations problems (MILR, MPS, MS, PhD); international and comparative labor (MILR, MPS, MS, PhD); labor economics (MILR, MPS, MS, PhD); organizational behavior (MILR, MPS, MS, PhD). *Degree requirements:* For master's, thesis (MS); for doctorate, comprehensive exam, thesis/dissertation, teaching experience. *Entrance requirements:* For master's and doctorate, GMAT or GRE General Test, 2 academic recommendations. Additional exam requirements/ recommendations for international students: Required—TOEFL (minimum score 550 paper-based; 77 iBT). Electronic applications accepted. *Expenses:* Contact institution.

Dallas Baptist University, College of Business, Management Program, Dallas, TX 75211-9299. Offers conflict resolution management (MA); general management (MA, MS); health care management (MA); human resource management (MA); organizational communication (MA); performance management (MA); professional sales and management optimization (MA). *Program availability:* Part-time, evening/weekend, 100% online, blended/hybrid learning. *Application deadline:* Applications are processed on a rolling basis. Application fee: $25. Electronic applications accepted. Application fee is waived when completed online. *Expenses: Tuition:* Full-time $15,408; part-time $856 per credit hour. *Required fees:* $400 per semester. Tuition and fees vary according to course load and degree level. *Unit head:* Richard Nassar, Director, 214-333-5280, E-mail: richardn@dbu.edu. *Application contact:* Bobby Soto, Director of Admissions, 214-333-5242, E-mail: graduate@dbu.edu.
Website: http://www.dbu.edu/gsb/ma-in-management

Davenport University, Sneden Graduate School, Grand Rapids, MI 49512. Offers accounting (MBA); business administration (EMBA); finance (MBA); health care management (MBA); human resources (MBA); information assurance (MS); public health (MPH); strategic management (MBA). *Program availability:* Evening/weekend. *Entrance requirements:* For master's, GMAT, minimum undergraduate GPA of 2.75. Additional exam requirements/recommendations for international students: Required—TOEFL. Electronic applications accepted. *Faculty research:* Leadership, management, marketing, organizational culture.

Delaware Valley University, MBA Program, Doylestown, PA 18901-2697. Offers accounting (MBA); entrepreneurship (MBA); finance (MBA); food and agribusiness (MBA); general business (MBA); global executive leadership (MBA); human resource management (MBA); supply chain management (MBA). *Program availability:* Part-time, evening/weekend, online learning. *Entrance requirements:* For master's, minimum undergraduate GPA of 3.0. Electronic applications accepted. *Expenses:* Contact institution.

DePaul University, Kellstadt Graduate School of Business, Chicago, IL 60604. Offers accountancy (M Acc, MS, MSA); applied economics (MBA); banking (MBA); behavioral finance (MBA); brand and product management (MBA); business development (MBA); business information technology (MS); business strategy and decision-making (MBA); computational finance (MS); consumer insights (MBA); corporate finance (MBA); economic policy analysis (MS); entrepreneurship (MBA, MS); finance (MBA, MS); financial analysis (MBA); general business (MBA); health sector management (MBA); hospitality leadership (MBA); hospitality leadership and operational performance (MS); human resource management (MBA); human resources (MS); investment management (MBA); leadership and change management (MBA); management accounting (MBA); marketing (MBA, MS); marketing analysis (MS); marketing strategy and planning (MBA); operations management (MBA); organizational diversity (MBA); real estate (MS); real estate finance and investment (MBA); revenue management (MBA); sports management (MBA); strategic global marketing (MBA); strategy, execution and valuation (MBA); sustainable management (MBA, MS); taxation (MS); wealth management (MS); JD/MBA. *Accreditation:* AACSB. *Program availability:* Part-time, evening/weekend, online learning. *Entrance requirements:* For master's, GMAT, 2 letters of recommendation, resume, essay, official transcripts. Additional exam requirements/recommendations for international students: Required—TOEFL (minimum score 550 paper-based; 80 iBT). Electronic applications accepted. *Expenses:* Contact institution.

DeSales University, Division of Business, Center Valley, PA 18034-9568. Offers accounting (MBA); computer information systems (MBA); finance (MBA); health care systems management (MBA); human resources management (MBA); management (MBA); marketing (MBA); project management (MBA); self-design (MBA); supply chain management (MBA); DNP/MBA; MSN/MBA. *Accreditation:* ACBSP. *Program availability:* Part-time, evening/weekend, 100% online, blended/hybrid learning. *Faculty:* 12 full-time (4 women), 29 part-time/adjunct (5 women). *Students:* 73 full-time (38 women), 323 part-time (163 women); includes 59 minority (16 Black or African American, non-Hispanic/Latino; 23 Asian, non-Hispanic/Latino; 16 Hispanic/Latino; 4 Two or more races, non-Hispanic/Latino). Average age 37. 157 applicants, 87% accepted, 128 enrolled. In 2016, 115 master's awarded. *Entrance requirements:* For master's, GMAT (waived if undergraduate GPA is 3.0 or better), minimum GPA of 3.0 in undergraduate work, literacy in basic software, background or interest in the field of study, personal statement, 2 years of work experience. Additional exam requirements/ recommendations for international students: Required—TOEFL. *Application deadline:* Applications are processed on a rolling basis. Application fee: $50. Electronic applications accepted. *Expenses:* Contact institution. *Financial support:* Applicants required to submit FAFSA. *Faculty research:* Quality improvement, executive development, productivity, cross-cultural managerial differences, leadership. *Unit head:* Dr. David M. Gilfoil, Director, MBA Program, 610-282-1100 Ext. 1828, Fax: 610-282-2869, E-mail: david.gilfoil@desales.edu. *Application contact:* Julia Ferraro, Director of Graduate Admissions, 610-282-1100 Ext. 1768, E-mail: gradadmissions@desales.edu.

DeVry University–Folsom Campus, Graduate Programs, Folsom, CA 95630. Offers accounting (M Acc); accounting and financial management (MAFM); business administration (MBA); curriculum leadership (M Ed); educational leadership (M Ed); educational technology (M Ed); higher education leadership (M Ed); human resource management (MHRM); information systems management (MISM); network and communications management (MNCM); project management (MPM); public administration (MPA).

East Central University, School of Graduate Studies, Department of Human Resources, Ada, OK 74820. Offers administration (MSHR); counseling (MSHR); criminal justice (MSHR); human services (MSHR); rehabilitation counseling (MSHR). *Accreditation:* CORE. *Program availability:* Part-time, evening/weekend. *Degree requirements:* For master's, thesis optional. *Entrance requirements:* For master's, GRE General Test, MAT, minimum GPA of 2.5. Electronic applications accepted.

Eastern Michigan University, Graduate School, College of Business, Department of Management, Program in Human Resources Management and Organizational Development, Ypsilanti, MI 48197. Offers MSHROD. *Program availability:* Part-time, evening/weekend, online learning. *Students:* 13 full-time (10 women), 77 part-time (58 women); includes 29 minority (23 Black or African American, non-Hispanic/Latino; 1

Asian, non-Hispanic/Latino; 4 Hispanic/Latino; 1 Two or more races, non-Hispanic/Latino), 8 international. Average age 30. 38 applicants, 74% accepted, 12 enrolled. In 2016, 75 master's awarded. *Degree requirements:* For master's, thesis optional. *Entrance requirements:* For master's, GMAT. Additional exam requirements/recommendations for international students: Required—TOEFL. *Application deadline:* Applications are processed on a rolling basis. Application fee: $45. *Financial support:* Fellowships, research assistantships with full tuition reimbursements, teaching assistantships with full tuition reimbursements, career-related internships or fieldwork, Federal Work-Study, institutionally sponsored loans, scholarships/grants, tuition waivers (partial), and unspecified assistantships available. Support available to part-time students. Financial award applicants required to submit FAFSA. *Unit head:* Dr. Fraya Wagner-Marsh, Department Head, 734-487-3240, Fax: 734-487-4100, E-mail: fraya.wagner@emich.edu.
Website: http://www.emich.edu/cob/departments_centers/management/mshrod.php

Eastern Michigan University, Graduate School, College of Business, Programs in Business Administration, Ypsilanti, MI 48197. Offers business administration (MBA, Graduate Certificate); computer information systems (Graduate Certificate); e-business (MBA, Graduate Certificate); enterprise business intelligence (MBA); entrepreneurship (MBA, Graduate Certificate); finance (MBA, Graduate Certificate); human resources (MBA); human resources management (Graduate Certificate); information systems (MBA); internal auditing (MBA); international business (MBA, Graduate Certificate); marketing management (Graduate Certificate); nonprofit management (MBA); organizational development (Graduate Certificate); supply chain management (MBA, Graduate Certificate). *Accreditation:* AACSB. *Program availability:* Part-time, online learning. *Students:* 63 full-time (36 women), 320 part-time (186 women); includes 131 minority (76 Black or African American, non-Hispanic/Latino; 5 American Indian or Alaska Native, non-Hispanic/Latino; 16 Asian, non-Hispanic/Latino; 19 Hispanic/Latino; 15 Two or more races, non-Hispanic/Latino), 23 international. Average age 32. 305 applicants, 70% accepted, 124 enrolled. In 2016, 78 master's, 57 other advanced degrees awarded. *Entrance requirements:* For master's, GMAT (minimum score 450), minimum cumulative undergraduate GPA of 2.75. Additional exam requirements/recommendations for international students: Required—TOEFL. *Application deadline:* For fall admission, 5/15 priority date for domestic students, 2/15 priority date for international students; for winter admission, 10/15 priority date for domestic students, 9/1 priority date for international students; for summer admission, 3/15 priority date for domestic students, 3/1 priority date for international students. Applications are processed on a rolling basis. Application fee: $45. *Financial support:* Fellowships, research assistantships with full tuition reimbursements, teaching assistantships with full tuition reimbursements, career-related internships or fieldwork, Federal Work-Study, institutionally sponsored loans, scholarships/grants, tuition waivers (partial), and unspecified assistantships available. Support available to part-time students. Financial award applicants required to submit FAFSA. *Unit head:* K. Michelle Henry, Director, Graduate Business Programs, 734-487-4444, Fax: 734-483-1316, E-mail: cob.graduate@emich.edu.
Website: http://www.emich.edu/cob/mba/

Embry-Riddle Aeronautical University–Worldwide, Department of Decision Sciences, Daytona Beach, FL 32114-3900. Offers aviation and aerospace (MSPM); aviation/aerospace management (MSEM); financial management (MSEM, MSPM); general management (MSPM); global management (MSPM); human resources management (MSPM); information systems (MSPM); leadership (MSEM, MSPM); logistics and supply chain management (MSEM, MSLSCM, MSPM); management (MSEM, MSPM); project management (MSEM); systems engineering (MSEM, MSPM); technical management (MSPM). *Program availability:* Part-time, evening/weekend, 100% online, blended/hybrid learning, EagleVision is a virtual classroom that combines Web video conferencing and a learning management system. EagleVision Classroom (between classrooms), EagleVision Home (faculty and students at home), and a blend of Classroom or Home. *Degree requirements:* For master's, comprehensive exam (for some programs), thesis (for some programs). *Entrance requirements:* Additional exam requirements/recommendations for international students: Required—TOEFL (minimum score 550 paper-based; 79 iBT), IELTS (minimum score 6), TOEFL or IELTS accepted. Electronic applications accepted. *Expenses:* Contact institution.

Embry-Riddle Aeronautical University–Worldwide, Department of Management, Daytona Beach, FL 32114-3900. Offers global management (MS); human resources management (MS); leadership (MS); operations management (MS); project management (MS). *Program availability:* Part-time, evening/weekend, 100% online, blended/hybrid learning, EagleVision is a virtual classroom that combines Web video conferencing and a learning management system. EagleVision Classroom (between classrooms), EagleVision Home (faculty and students at home), and a blend of Classroom or Home. *Entrance requirements:* Additional exam requirements/recommendations for international students: Required—TOEFL (minimum score 550 paper-based; 79 iBT), IELTS (minimum score 6), TOEFL or IELTS accepted. Electronic applications accepted. *Expenses:* Contact institution.

Emmanuel College, Graduate and Professional Programs, Graduate Programs in Human Resource Management, Boston, MA 02115. Offers MS, Graduate Certificate. *Program availability:* Part-time, evening/weekend, blended/hybrid learning. *Faculty:* 9 part-time/adjunct (1 woman). *Students:* 1 (woman) full-time, 37 part-time (28 women); includes 15 minority (7 Black or African American, non-Hispanic/Latino; 1 Asian, non-Hispanic/Latino; 7 Hispanic/Latino). Average age 35. 24 applicants, 38% accepted, 9 enrolled. In 2016, 25 master's, 6 other advanced degrees awarded. *Degree requirements:* For master's, 36 credits. *Entrance requirements:* For master's and Graduate Certificate, transcripts from all regionally-accredited institutions attended (showing proof of bachelor's degree completion), 2 letters of recommendation, essay, resume. Additional exam requirements/recommendations for international students: Required—TOEFL. *Application deadline:* Applications are processed on a rolling basis. Electronic applications accepted. *Expenses:* $13,152 (for Graduate Certificate); $24,112 (for MS). *Financial support:* Application deadline: 2/15; applicants required to submit FAFSA. *Unit head:* Petia Whitmore, Executive Director, Graduate and Professional Programs, 617-732-1740, E-mail: gpp@emmanuel.edu. *Application contact:* Helen Muterperl, Associate Director of Admissions, Graduate and Professional Programs, 617-735-9700, Fax: 617-507-0434, E-mail: gpp@emmanuel.edu.
Website: http://www.emmanuel.edu/graduate-professional-programs/academics/management/human-resource-management.html

Everest University, Department of Business Administration, Tampa, FL 33614. Offers accounting (MBA); human resources (MBA); international business (MBA). *Program availability:* Part-time, evening/weekend. *Degree requirements:* For master's, thesis optional. *Entrance requirements:* For master's, GMAT or GRE General Test, minimum GPA of 3.0.

Everglades University, Graduate Programs, Program in Business Administration, Boca Raton, FL 33431. Offers accounting for managers (MBA); aviation management (MBA); human resource management (MBA); project management (MBA). *Program availability:* Part-time, evening/weekend, 100% online. *Entrance requirements:* For master's, GMAT (minimum score of 400) or GRE (minimum score of 290), bachelor's or graduate degree from college accredited by an agency recognized by the U.S. Department of Education; minimum cumulative GPA of 2.0 at the baccalaureate level, 3.0 at the master's level. Additional exam requirements/recommendations for international students: Recommended—TOEFL (minimum score 500 paper-based). Electronic applications accepted. *Expenses:* Contact institution.

Excelsior College, School of Business and Technology, Albany, NY 12203-5159. Offers business administration (MBA); cybersecurity management (MBA, Graduate Certificate); general business management (MS); health care management (MBA); human performance technology (MBA); human resource management (MS); human resources management (MBA); leadership (MBA, MS); mediation and arbitration (MBA, MS); social media management (MBA); technology management (MBA). *Program availability:* Part-time, evening/weekend, online learning. *Faculty:* 25 part-time/adjunct (9 women). *Students:* 1,801 part-time (487 women); includes 775 minority (424 Black or African American, non-Hispanic/Latino; 5 American Indian or Alaska Native, non-Hispanic/Latino; 58 Asian, non-Hispanic/Latino; 209 Hispanic/Latino; 15 Native Hawaiian or other Pacific Islander, non-Hispanic/Latino; 64 Two or more races, non-Hispanic/Latino), 11 international. Average age 39. In 2016, 288 master's awarded. *Application deadline:* Applications are processed on a rolling basis. Application fee: $50. Electronic applications accepted. *Expenses: Tuition:* Part-time $645 per credit. *Required fees:* $265 per credit. *Financial support:* Scholarships/grants available. *Unit head:* Dr. Lifang Shih, Dean, 888-647-2388. *Application contact:* Admissions, 888-647-2388 Ext. 133, Fax: 518-464-8777, E-mail: admissions@excelsior.edu.

Fairfield University, Dolan School of Business, Fairfield, CT 06824. Offers accounting (MBA, MS, CAS); business analytics (MS); entrepreneurship (MBA); finance (MBA, MS, CAS); general management (MBA, CAS); global management (MBA); human resource management (MBA, CAS); information systems and business analytics (MBA); marketing (MBA, CAS); taxation (MBA, CAS). *Accreditation:* AACSB. *Program availability:* Part-time, evening/weekend. *Faculty:* 20 full-time (6 women), 4 part-time/adjunct (1 woman). *Students:* 106 full-time (41 women), 57 part-time (26 women); includes 18 minority (4 Black or African American, non-Hispanic/Latino; 1 American Indian or Alaska Native, non-Hispanic/Latino; 4 Asian, non-Hispanic/Latino; 7 Hispanic/Latino; 2 Two or more races, non-Hispanic/Latino), 39 international. Average age 26. 136 applicants, 63% accepted, 35 enrolled. In 2016, 90 master's awarded. *Degree requirements:* For master's, capstone course. *Entrance requirements:* For master's, GMAT (minimum score 500), 2 letters of reference, resume, minimum GPA of 3.0. Additional exam requirements/recommendations for international students: Required—TOEFL (minimum score 550 paper-based; 80 iBT) or IELTS (minimum score 6.5). *Application deadline:* For fall admission, 5/15 for international students; for spring admission, 10/15 for international students. Applications are processed on a rolling basis. Application fee: $60. Electronic applications accepted. *Expenses:* $875 per credit hour. *Financial support:* In 2016–17, 33 students received support. Scholarships/grants and unspecified assistantships available. Financial award applicants required to submit FAFSA. *Faculty research:* International finance, leadership and careers, ethics in accounting, emotions in consumer behavior and organizations, data analytics. *Unit head:* Dr. Donald Gibson, Dean, 203-254-4070, Fax: 203-254-4105, E-mail: dgibson@fairfield.edu. *Application contact:* Marianne Gumpper, Director of Graduate and Continuing Studies Admission, 203-254-4184, Fax: 203-254-4073, E-mail: gradadmis@fairfield.edu.
Website: http://fairfield.edu/mba

Fairleigh Dickinson University, College at Florham, Silberman College of Business, Center for Human Resource Management Studies, Program in Human Resource Management, Madison, NJ 07940-1099. Offers MBA, MA/MBA.

Fairleigh Dickinson University, Metropolitan Campus, Silberman College of Business, Center for Human Resources Management Studies, Program in Human Resource Management, Teaneck, NJ 07666-1914. Offers MBA, Certificate.

Fitchburg State University, Division of Graduate and Continuing Education, Program in Business Administration, Fitchburg, MA 01420-2697. Offers accounting (MBA); human resource management (MBA); management (MBA). *Program availability:* Part-time, evening/weekend, online learning. *Entrance requirements:* Additional exam requirements/recommendations for international students: Required—TOEFL (minimum score 550 paper-based; 79 iBT). Electronic applications accepted. *Expenses:* Tuition, state resident: full-time $2871; part-time $1914 per year. Tuition, nonresident: full-time $2871; part-time $1914 per year. *Required fees:* $3828. Tuition and fees vary according to program.

Florida Institute of Technology, Extended Studies Division, Melbourne, FL 32901-6975. Offers acquisition and contract management (MS); aerospace engineering (MS); business administration (MBA, DBA); computer information systems (MS); computer science (MS); electrical engineering (MS); engineering management (MS); human resources management (MS); logistics management (MS), including humanitarian and disaster relief logistics; management (MS), including acquisition and contract management, e-business, human resources management, information systems, logistics management, management, transportation management; material acquisition management (MS); mechanical engineering (MS); operations research (MS); project management (MS), including information systems, operations research; public administration (MPA); quality management (MS); software engineering (MS); space systems (MS); space systems management (MS); supply chain management (MS); systems management (MS), including information systems, operations research; technology management (MS). *Program availability:* Part-time, evening/weekend, online learning. *Faculty:* 10 full-time (3 women), 122 part-time/adjunct (29 women). *Students:* 131 full-time (58 women), 997 part-time (348 women); includes 389 minority (231 Black or African American, non-Hispanic/Latino; 9 American Indian or Alaska Native, non-Hispanic/Latino; 26 Asian, non-Hispanic/Latino; 99 Hispanic/Latino; 3 Native Hawaiian or other Pacific Islander, non-Hispanic/Latino; 21 Two or more races, non-Hispanic/Latino), 53 international. Average age 36. 962 applicants, 48% accepted, 323 enrolled. In 2016, 403 master's awarded. *Degree requirements:* For master's, comprehensive exam (for some programs). *Entrance requirements:* For master's, GMAT or resume showing 8 years of supervised experience, minimum GPA of 3.0, 2 letters of recommendation, resume. Additional exam requirements/recommendations for international students: Required—TOEFL (minimum score 550 paper-based; 79 iBT). *Application deadline:* For fall admission, 4/1 for international students; for spring admission, 9/30 for international students. Applications are processed on a rolling basis. Electronic applications accepted. *Expenses:* Contact institution. *Financial support:* Application deadline: 3/1; applicants required to submit FAFSA. *Unit head:* Dr. Theodore R. Richardson, III, Dean, 321-674-8123, Fax: 321-674-7597, E-mail: trichardson@fit.edu. *Application contact:* Carolyn Farrior, Director of Graduate Admissions, Online Learning and Off-Campus Programs, 321-674-7118, Fax: 321-674-8216, E-mail: cfarrior@fit.edu.
Website: http://es.fit.edu

Florida International University, Chapman Graduate School of Business, Department of Management and International Business, Miami, FL 33199. Offers human resources management (MSHRM); international business (MIB); management and international business (EMBA, IMBA, MBA, PhD). *Program availability:* Part-time, evening/weekend. *Faculty:* 28 full-time (10 women), 30 part-time/adjunct (9 women). *Students:* 1,043 full-time (573 women), 534 part-time (271 women); includes 1,095 minority (211 Black or

African American, non-Hispanic/Latino; 38 Asian, non-Hispanic/Latino; 818 Hispanic/Latino; 2 Native Hawaiian or other Pacific Islander, non-Hispanic/Latino; 26 Two or more races, non-Hispanic/Latino), 231 international. Average age 32. 1,558 applicants, 45% accepted, 530 enrolled. In 2016, 812 master's, 4 doctorates awarded. *Degree requirements:* For doctorate, comprehensive exam, thesis/dissertation. *Entrance requirements:* For master's, GMAT or GRE (depending on program), minimum GPA of 3.0 in upper-level coursework; for doctorate, GMAT or GRE, letter of intent; 3 letters of recommendation; resume. Additional exam requirements/recommendations for international students: Required—TOEFL (minimum score 550 paper-based; 80 iBT) or IELTS (minimum score 6.5). *Application deadline:* For fall admission, 6/1 for domestic students, 4/1 for international students; for spring admission, 10/1 for domestic students, 9/1 for international students. Applications are processed on a rolling basis. Application fee: $30. Electronic applications accepted. *Expenses:* Contact institution. *Financial support:* Institutionally sponsored loans and scholarships/grants available. Financial award application deadline: 3/1; financial award applicants required to submit FAFSA. *Faculty research:* International business, strategy, entrepreneurship, human resource management. *Unit head:* Dr. Willam Newburry, Chair, 305-348-2791, E-mail: newburry@fiu.edu. *Application contact:* Paula Alger, Program Manager, 305-348-7466, E-mail: palger@fiu.edu.

Florida State University, The Graduate School, College of Business, Tallahassee, FL 32306-1110. Offers accounting (M Acc), including assurance and advisory services, generalist, taxation; business administration (MBA, PhD), including accounting (PhD), finance (PhD), management information systems (PhD), marketing (PhD), organizational behavior and human resources (PhD), risk management and insurance (PhD), strategy (PhD); finance (MS); management information systems (MS); risk management and insurance (MS); JD/MBA; MSW/MBA. *Accreditation:* AACSB. *Program availability:* Part-time, 100% online. *Faculty:* 101 full-time (27 women), 4 part-time/adjunct (2 women). *Students:* 272 full-time (127 women), 351 part-time (133 women); includes 141 minority (45 Black or African American, non-Hispanic/Latino; 2 American Indian or Alaska Native, non-Hispanic/Latino; 20 Asian, non-Hispanic/Latino; 59 Hispanic/Latino; 2 Native Hawaiian or other Pacific Islander, non-Hispanic/Latino; 13 Two or more races, non-Hispanic/Latino), 71 international. Average age 30. 688 applicants, 60% accepted, 273 enrolled. In 2016, 231 master's, 12 doctorates awarded. Terminal master's awarded for partial completion of doctoral program. *Degree requirements:* For doctorate, comprehensive exam, thesis/dissertation. *Entrance requirements:* For master's, GMAT, GRE (for all except MS in finance), work experience (MBA, MS); minimum GPA of 3.0, letters of recommendation; for doctorate, GMAT, GRE (for marketing, organizational behavior, risk management and insurance, management information systems, and human resources only), minimum graduate GPA of 3.5, letters of recommendation. Additional exam requirements/recommendations for international students: Required—TOEFL (minimum score 600 paper-based; 85 iBT); Recommended—IELTS (minimum score 6). *Application deadline:* For fall admission, 6/1 for domestic and international students; for spring admission, 10/1 for domestic and international students; for summer admission, 3/1 for domestic and international students. Applications are processed on a rolling basis. Application fee: $30. Electronic applications accepted. *Expenses:* Contact institution. *Financial support:* In 2016–17, 149 students received support, including 9 fellowships (averaging $1,500 per year), 65 research assistantships with full tuition reimbursements available (averaging $20,000 per year), 75 teaching assistantships with full tuition reimbursements available (averaging $20,000 per year); career-related internships or fieldwork, scholarships/grants, health care benefits, tuition waivers (full and partial), and unspecified assistantships also available. Support available to part-time students. Financial award application deadline: 1/1; financial award applicants required to submit FAFSA. *Faculty research:* Business strategy, marketing, finance, accounting, business analytics. *Total annual research expenditures:* $1.4 million. *Unit head:* Dr. Michael Hartline, Dean, 850-644-4405, Fax: 850-644-0915, E-mail: mhartline@business.fsu.edu. *Application contact:* Jennifer Clark, Director, 850-644-6458, E-mail: gradprograms@business.fsu.edu.
Website: http://business.fsu.edu/

Framingham State University, Continuing Education, Program in Human Resource Management, Framingham, MA 01701-9101. Offers MA. *Program availability:* Part-time, evening/weekend.

Franklin Pierce University, Graduate and Professional Studies, Rindge, NH 03461-0060. Offers curriculum and instruction (M Ed); elementary education (MS Ed); emerging network technologies (Graduate Certificate); energy and sustainability studies (MBA, Graduate Certificate); health administration (MBA, Graduate Certificate); human resource management (MBA, Graduate Certificate); information technology (MBA); leadership (MBA); nursing education (MS); nursing leadership (MS); physical therapy (DPT); physician assistant studies (MPAS); special education (M Ed); sports management (MBA). *Accreditation:* APTA. *Program availability:* Part-time, 100% online, blended/hybrid learning. *Faculty:* 47 full-time (36 women), 165 part-time/adjunct (108 women). *Students:* 380 full-time (226 women), 245 part-time (158 women); includes 52 minority (13 Black or African American, non-Hispanic/Latino; 2 American Indian or Alaska Native, non-Hispanic/Latino; 14 Asian, non-Hispanic/Latino; 22 Hispanic/Latino; 1 Native Hawaiian or other Pacific Islander, non-Hispanic/Latino), 13 international. Average age 29. 1,995 applicants, 28% accepted, 267 enrolled. In 2016, 120 master's, 86 doctorates awarded. *Degree requirements:* For master's, concentrated original research projects; student teaching; fieldwork and/or internship; leadership project; PRAXIS I and II (for M Ed); for doctorate, concentrated original research projects, clinical fieldwork and/or internship, leadership project. *Entrance requirements:* For master's, minimum GPA of 2.5, 3 letters of recommendation; competencies in accounting, economics, statistics, and computer skills through life experience or undergraduate coursework (for MBA); certification/e-portfolio, minimum C grade in all education courses (for M Ed); license to practice as RN (for MS); for doctorate, GRE, 80 hours of observation/work in PT settings; completion of anatomy, chemistry, physics, and statistics; minimum GPA of 3.0. Additional exam requirements/recommendations for international students: Required—TOEFL (minimum score 550 paper-based; 61 iBT). *Application deadline:* Applications are processed on a rolling basis. Application fee: $0. Electronic applications accepted. *Expenses: Tuition:* Full-time $15,960; part-time $665 per credit hour. Tuition and fees vary according to program. *Financial support:* Teaching assistantships with tuition reimbursements, career-related internships or fieldwork, and unspecified assistantships available. Support available to part-time students. Financial award applicants required to submit FAFSA. *Faculty research:* Evidence-based practice in sports physical therapy, human resource management in economic crisis, leadership in nursing, innovation in sports facility management, differentiated learning and understanding by design. *Unit head:* Dr. Maria Altobello, Dean, 603-647-3509, Fax: 603-229-4580, E-mail: altobellom@franklinpierce.edu. *Application contact:* Graduate Studies, 800-325-1090, Fax: 603-626-4815, E-mail: cgps@franklinpierce.edu.
Website: http://www.franklinpierce.edu/academics/gradstudies/index.htm

Gannon University, School of Graduate Studies, College of Engineering and Business, Dahlkemper School of Business, Program in Business Administration, Erie, PA 16541-0001. Offers business administration (MBA); finance (MBA); human resources management (MBA); marketing (MBA). *Accreditation:* ACBSP. *Program availability:* Part-time, evening/weekend, 100% online, blended/hybrid learning. *Students:* 43 full-time (17 women), 67 part-time (34 women); includes 7 minority (4 Black or African American, non-Hispanic/Latino; 2 Asian, non-Hispanic/Latino; 1 Hispanic/Latino), 19 international. Average age 30. 160 applicants, 53% accepted, 28 enrolled. In 2016, 60 master's awarded. *Entrance requirements:* For master's, GMAT, bachelor's degree in any discipline from any accredited college or university, resume, transcripts, 3 letters of recommendation. Additional exam requirements/recommendations for international students: Required—TOEFL (minimum score 79 iBT). *Application deadline:* Applications are processed on a rolling basis. Application fee: $25. Electronic applications accepted. Application fee is waived when completed online. *Expenses: Tuition:* Full-time $17,370. *Required fees:* $550. Tuition and fees vary according to course load and program. *Financial support:* Federal Work-Study and unspecified assistantships available. Financial award application deadline: 7/1; financial award applicants required to submit FAFSA. *Unit head:* Dr. Michael Messina, Director, 814-871-5755, Fax: 814-871-7210, E-mail: messina001@gannon.edu. *Application contact:* Bridget Philip, Director of Graduate Admissions, 814-871-7412, E-mail: graduate@gannon.edu.

George Fox University, College of Business, Newberg, OR 97132-2697. Offers accounting (DBA); finance (MBA); management (DBA); management and leadership (MBA); marketing (DBA); organizational strategy (MBA); strategic human resource management (MBA). MBA offered in Newberg, OR and in Portland, OR. *Accreditation:* ACBSP. *Program availability:* Part-time, evening/weekend, online learning. *Degree requirements:* For master's, capstone project; for doctorate, credit-applied research project. *Entrance requirements:* For master's, resume (5 years of professional experience); 3 professional references; interview; financial e-learning course; official transcripts; for doctorate, GRE or GMAT, resume; personal mission statement; academic research writing sample; official transcript from each college/university attended; three professional references. Additional exam requirements/recommendations for international students: Required—TOEFL (minimum score 577 paper-based; 90 iBT) or IELTS (minimum score 7). Electronic applications accepted. *Expenses:* Contact institution.

George Mason University, Schar School of Policy and Government, Program in Organization Development and Knowledge Management, Arlington, VA 22201. Offers MS. *Faculty:* 3 full-time (1 woman), 3 part-time/adjunct (1 woman). *Students:* 12 full-time (10 women), 37 part-time (30 women); includes 21 minority (8 Black or African American, non-Hispanic/Latino; 4 Asian, non-Hispanic/Latino; 7 Hispanic/Latino; 1 Native Hawaiian or other Pacific Islander, non-Hispanic/Latino; 1 Two or more races, non-Hispanic/Latino), 1 international. Average age 35. 39 applicants, 92% accepted, 23 enrolled. In 2016, 26 master's awarded. *Degree requirements:* For master's, thesis or alternative, internship. *Entrance requirements:* For master's, GRE (for students seeking merit-based scholarships), bachelor's degree with minimum GPA of 3.0, current resume, 2 letters of recommendation, expanded goals statement, 2 copies of official transcripts. Additional exam requirements/recommendations for international students: Required—TOEFL (minimum score 575 paper-based; 88 iBT), IELTS (minimum score 6.5), PTE (minimum score 59). *Application deadline:* For fall admission, 6/1 priority date for domestic students, 5/1 priority date for international students; for spring admission, 12/1 priority date for domestic students, 11/1 priority date for international students. Applications are processed on a rolling basis. Application fee: $65 ($80 for international students). Electronic applications accepted. *Expenses:* Contact institution. *Financial support:* Career-related internships or fieldwork, Federal Work-Study, scholarships/grants, unspecified assistantships, and health care benefits (for full-time research or teaching assistantship recipients) available. Financial award application deadline: 3/1; financial award applicants required to submit FAFSA. *Unit head:* Tojo Joseph Thatchenkery, Director, 703-993-3808, Fax: 703-993-8215, E-mail: thatchen@gmu.edu. *Application contact:* Stephanie Ellis, Graduate Admissions Coordinator, 703-993-4478, E-mail: sellis11@gmu.edu.
Website: http://spgia.gmu.edu/programs/graduate-degrees/organization-development-knowledge-management-odkm/

Georgetown University, Graduate School of Arts and Sciences, School of Continuing Studies, Washington, DC 20057. Offers American studies (MALS); Catholic studies (MALS); classical civilizations (MALS); emergency and disaster management (MPS); ethics and the professions (MALS); global strategic communications (MPS); hospitality management (MPS); human resources management (MPS); humanities (MALS); individualized study (MALS); integrated marketing communications (MPS); international affairs (MALS); Islam and Muslim-Christian relations (MALS); journalism (MPS); liberal studies (DLS); literature and society (MALS); medieval and early modern European studies (MALS); public relations and corporate communications (MPS); real estate (MPS); religious studies (MALS); social and public policy (MALS); sports industry management (MPS); systems engineering management (MPS); technology management (MPS); the theory and practice of American democracy (MALS); urban and regional planning (MPS); visual culture (MALS). MPS in systems engineering management offered jointly with Stevens Institute of Technology. *Entrance requirements:* Additional exam requirements/recommendations for international students: Required—TOEFL.

The George Washington University, Columbian College of Arts and Sciences, Department of Organizational Sciences and Communication, Washington, DC 20052. Offers human resources management (MA); non-profit management (Graduate Certificate); organizational management (Graduate Certificate). *Program availability:* Part-time, evening/weekend. *Faculty:* 10 full-time (6 women). *Students:* 46 full-time (25 women), 31 part-time (25 women); includes 27 minority (8 Black or African American, non-Hispanic/Latino; 7 Asian, non-Hispanic/Latino; 5 Hispanic/Latino; 7 Two or more races, non-Hispanic/Latino), 5 international. Average age 28. 133 applicants, 85% accepted, 47 enrolled. In 2016, 35 master's, 21 other advanced degrees awarded. *Degree requirements:* For master's, comprehensive exam. *Entrance requirements:* For master's, GRE General Test, minimum GPA of 3.0; for Graduate Certificate, minimum GPA of 3.0. Additional exam requirements/recommendations for international students: Required—TOEFL (minimum score 500 paper-based; 80 iBT). *Application deadline:* For fall admission, 1/15 priority date for domestic and international students; for spring admission, 10/1 priority date for domestic students, 9/1 priority date for international students. Applications are processed on a rolling basis. Application fee: $75. Electronic applications accepted. *Financial support:* Federal Work-Study and institutionally sponsored loans available. *Unit head:* Dr. Clay Warren, Chair, 202-994-1870, Fax: 202-994-1881, E-mail: claywar@gwu.edu. *Application contact:* Information Contact, 202-994-1880, Fax: 202-994-1881.
Website: http://www.gwu.edu/~orgsci/

Georgia State University, J. Mack Robinson College of Business, Department of Managerial Sciences, Atlanta, GA 30302-3083. Offers business analysis (MBA, MS); entrepreneurship (MBA); human resources management (MBA, MS); operations management (MBA, MS); organization behavior/human resource management (PhD); organization management (MBA); organizational change (MS); strategic management (PhD). *Accreditation:* AACSB. *Program availability:* Part-time, evening/weekend. *Faculty:* 25 full-time (11 women). *Students:* 30 full-time (20 women), 10 part-time (4 women); includes 14 minority (11 Black or African American, non-Hispanic/Latino; 1 Asian, non-Hispanic/Latino; 1 Hispanic/Latino; 1 Two or more races, non-Hispanic/Latino), 12 international. Average age 31. 79 applicants, 30% accepted, 13 enrolled. In

2016, 23 master's, 2 doctorates awarded. *Degree requirements:* For doctorate, comprehensive exam, thesis/dissertation. *Entrance requirements:* For master's, GRE or GMAT, transcripts from all institutions attended, resume, essays; for doctorate, GMAT, three letters of recommendation, personal statement, transcripts from all institutions attended, resume. Additional exam requirements/recommendations for international students: Required—TOEFL (minimum score 610 paper-based; 101 iBT), IELTS (minimum score 7). *Application deadline:* For fall admission, 5/1 priority date for domestic students, 2/1 priority date for international students; for spring admission, 9/15 priority date for domestic students, 4/1 priority date for international students. Applications are processed on a rolling basis. Application fee: $50. Electronic applications accepted. *Expenses:* Tuition, state resident: full-time $6876; part-time $382 per credit hour. Tuition, nonresident: full-time $22,374; part-time $1243 per credit hour. *Required fees:* $2128; $1064 per term. Part-time tuition and fees vary according to course load and program. *Financial support:* Research assistantships, teaching assistantships, scholarships/grants, tuition waivers, and unspecified assistantships available. Financial award applicants required to submit FAFSA. *Faculty research:* Entrepreneurship and innovation; strategy process; workplace interactions, relationships, and processes; leadership and culture; supply chain management. *Unit head:* Dr. Pamela S. Barr, Interim Chair, 404-413-7525, Fax: 404-413-7571. *Application contact:* Toby McChesney, Assistant Dean for Graduate Recruiting and Student Services, 404-413-7167, Fax: 404-413-7162, E-mail: rcbgradadmissions@gsu.edu.
Website: http://mgmt.robinson.gsu.edu/

Golden Gate University, Ageno School of Business, San Francisco, CA 94105-2968. Offers accounting (MBA); business administration (EMBA, MBA, PMBA, DBA); business analytics (MS); finance (MBA, MS, Certificate); financial planning (MS, Certificate); healthcare information systems (Certificate); human resource management (MBA, MS); human resources management (Certificate); information systems (MS); information technology (MBA); information technology management (Certificate); integrated marketing and communications (MS, Certificate); international business (MBA); management (MBA); marketing (MBA, MS, Certificate); operations supply chain management (Certificate); psychology (MA, Certificate); public administration (EMPA); public relations (MS, Certificate); technical market analysis (Certificate); JD/MBA. *Program availability:* Part-time, evening/weekend. *Faculty:* 18 full-time (3 women), 117 part-time/adjunct (44 women). *Students:* 458 full-time (254 women), 664 part-time (331 women); includes 346 minority (75 Black or African American, non-Hispanic/Latino; 2 American Indian or Alaska Native, non-Hispanic/Latino; 132 Asian, non-Hispanic/Latino; 105 Hispanic/Latino; 9 Native Hawaiian or other Pacific Islander, non-Hispanic/Latino; 23 Two or more races, non-Hispanic/Latino), 354 international. Average age 34. 905 applicants, 83% accepted, 165 enrolled. In 2016, 350 master's, 2 doctorates awarded. *Degree requirements:* For doctorate, thesis/dissertation, qualifying examination. *Entrance requirements:* For master's, GMAT (for MBA), minimum GPA of 2.5 (MS). Additional exam requirements/recommendations for international students: Required—TOEFL (minimum score 550 paper-based; 79 iBT). *Application deadline:* For fall admission, 5/15 for domestic and international students; for winter admission, 1/15 for domestic and international students; for spring admission, 9/15 for domestic and international students. Applications are processed on a rolling basis. Application fee: $70 ($110 for international students). Electronic applications accepted. *Expenses:* Contact institution. *Financial support:* In 2016–17, 372 students received support. Career-related internships or fieldwork, Federal Work-Study, institutionally sponsored loans, and scholarships/grants available. Support available to part-time students. Financial award applicants required to submit FAFSA. *Unit head:* Dr. Gordon Swartz, Dean, 415-442-7027, Fax: 415-442-6579, E-mail: gswartz@ggu.edu. *Application contact:* Angela Melero, Enrollment Services, 415-442-7800, Fax: 415-442-7807, E-mail: info@ggu.edu.
Website: http://www.ggu.edu/programs/business-and-management

Goldey-Beacom College, Graduate Program, Wilmington, DE 19808-1999. Offers business administration (MBA); finance (MS); financial management (MBA); health care management (MBA); human resource management (MBA); information technology (MBA); international business management (MBA); major finance (MBA); major taxation (MBA); management (MM); marketing management (MBA); taxation (MBA, MS). *Accreditation:* ACBSP. *Program availability:* Part-time, evening/weekend. *Entrance requirements:* For master's, GMAT, MAT, GRE, minimum GPA of 3.0. Additional exam requirements/recommendations for international students: Required—TOEFL (minimum score 65 iBT); Recommended—IELTS (minimum score 6). Electronic applications accepted.

Grambling State University, School of Graduate Studies and Research, College of Arts and Sciences, Department of Political Science and Public Administration, Grambling, LA 71270. Offers health services administration (MPA); human resource management (MPA); public management (MPA); state and local government (MPA). *Accreditation:* NASPAA. *Program availability:* Part-time. *Degree requirements:* For master's, comprehensive exam (for some programs), thesis optional. *Entrance requirements:* For master's, GRE, minimum GPA of 2.75 on last degree. Additional exam requirements/recommendations for international students: Required—TOEFL (minimum score 500 paper-based; 62 iBT). Electronic applications accepted.

Grand Canyon University, Colangelo College of Business, Phoenix, AZ 85017-1097. Offers accounting (MBA, MS); business analytics (MS); disaster preparedness and executive fire service leadership (MS); finance (MBA); general management (MBA); health systems management (MBA); information technology management (MS); leadership (MBA, MS); marketing (MBA); organizational leadership and entrepreneurship (MS); project management (MBA); sports business (MBA); strategic human resource management (MBA). *Accreditation:* ACBSP. *Program availability:* Part-time, evening/weekend, online learning. *Faculty:* 8 full-time (3 women), 147 part-time/adjunct (49 women). *Students:* 1 full-time (0 women), 2,121 part-time (1,165 women); includes 341 minority (249 Black or African American, non-Hispanic/Latino; 17 American Indian or Alaska Native, non-Hispanic/Latino; 15 Asian, non-Hispanic/Latino; 29 Hispanic/Latino; 4 Native Hawaiian or other Pacific Islander, non-Hispanic/Latino; 27 Two or more races, non-Hispanic/Latino), 20 international. Average age 38. In 2016, 569 master's awarded. *Entrance requirements:* For master's, equivalent of two years' full-time professional work experience. Additional exam requirements/recommendations for international students: Required—TOEFL (minimum score 575 paper-based; 90 iBT), IELTS (minimum score 7). *Application deadline:* For fall admission, 8/21 for domestic students, 7/2 for international students; for spring admission, 12/24 for domestic students, 11/1 for international students. Applications are processed on a rolling basis. Application fee: $0. Electronic applications accepted. *Financial support:* Federal Work-Study available. Support available to part-time students. Financial award applicants required to submit FAFSA. *Unit head:* Kim Donaldson, Dean, 602-639-6597, E-mail: kdonaldson@gcu.edu. *Application contact:* Matt Tidwell, Enrollment Manager, 602-639-6020, E-mail: mtidwell@gcu.edu.
Website: https://www.gcu.edu/colangelo-college-of-business.php

Grantham University, Mark Skousen School of Business, Lenexa, KS 66219. Offers business administration (MBA); business intelligence (MS); human resources management (Certificate); information management (MBA); performance improvement (MS); project management (MBA, Certificate). *Program availability:* Part-time, online only, 100% online. *Faculty:* 1 full-time, 36 part-time/adjunct. *Students:* 73 full-time (37 women), 1,046 part-time (424 women); includes 442 minority (309 Black or African American, non-Hispanic/Latino; 8 American Indian or Alaska Native, non-Hispanic/Latino; 27 Asian, non-Hispanic/Latino; 63 Hispanic/Latino; 7 Native Hawaiian or other Pacific Islander, non-Hispanic/Latino; 28 Two or more races, non-Hispanic/Latino). Average age 40. 1,324 applicants, 95% accepted, 1123 enrolled. In 2016, 331 master's awarded. *Degree requirements:* For master's, capstone project, PMP Prep Exam; for Certificate, comprehensive exam (for some programs), PMP Prep Exam. *Entrance requirements:* For master's, baccalaureate or master's degree with minimum cumulative GPA of 2.5 from institution accredited by agency recognized by U.S. Department of Education or foreign equivalent. Additional exam requirements/recommendations for international students: Required—PTE (minimum score 50), TOEFL (minimum score 530 paper-based, 71 iBT) or IELTS (minimum score 6.5). *Application deadline:* Applications are processed on a rolling basis. Electronic applications accepted. *Expenses:* $325 per credit hour, $45 per 8-week term technology fee. *Financial support:* Scholarships/grants available. Financial award applicants required to submit FAFSA. *Faculty research:* Organizational structures, e-discovery and project management, decision management, resource-based and ethical perspectives, external finance dependence in corporate investments. *Unit head:* Dr. David Marker, Dean, Mark Skousen School of Business, 800-955-2527, E-mail: dmarker@grantham.edu. *Application contact:* Jared Parlette, Vice President of Student Enrollment, 800-955-2527, E-mail: admissions@grantham.edu.
Website: http://www.grantham.edu/colleges-and-schools/school-of-business/

Hawai`i Pacific University, College of Business, Program in Business Administration, Honolulu, HI 96813. Offers accounting (MBA); economics (MBA); finance (MBA); hospitality and tourism management (MBA); human resource management (MBA); information systems (MBA); international business (MBA); management (MBA); marketing (MBA); organizational change and development (MBA). *Program availability:* Part-time, evening/weekend, online learning. *Faculty:* 13 full-time (4 women), 1 part-time/adjunct (0 women). *Students:* 106 full-time (47 women), 33 part-time (13 women); includes 66 minority (5 Black or African American, non-Hispanic/Latino; 1 American Indian or Alaska Native, non-Hispanic/Latino; 23 Asian, non-Hispanic/Latino; 11 Hispanic/Latino; 1 Native Hawaiian or other Pacific Islander, non-Hispanic/Latino; 25 Two or more races, non-Hispanic/Latino), 36 international. Average age 33. 77 applicants, 84% accepted, 44 enrolled. In 2016, 78 master's awarded. *Entrance requirements:* For master's, GMAT or GRE. Additional exam requirements/recommendations for international students: Recommended—TOEFL (minimum score 550 paper-based; 80 iBT), IELTS (minimum score 6), TWE (minimum score 5). *Application deadline:* For fall admission, 2/15 priority date for domestic students; for spring admission, 10/15 priority date for domestic students. Applications are processed on a rolling basis. Application fee: $50. Electronic applications accepted. *Expenses: Tuition:* Full-time $17,190; part-time $955 per credit. *Required fees:* $150; $26 per credit. Tuition and fees vary according to course load and program. *Financial support:* In 2016–17, 27 students received support. Research assistantships, career-related internships or fieldwork, Federal Work-Study, scholarships/grants, tuition waivers, and unspecified assistantships available. Financial award application deadline: 3/1; financial award applicants required to submit FAFSA. *Unit head:* Dr. Warren Wee, Associate Dean/Associate Professor of Accounting, 808-544-9325, E-mail: wwee@hpu.edu. *Application contact:* Danny Lam, Assistant Director of Graduate Admissions, 808-544-1135, E-mail: graduate@hpu.edu.
Website: http://www.hpu.edu/CBA/Graduate/MBA/index.html

Hawai`i Pacific University, College of Business, Program in Human Resource Management, Honolulu, HI 96813. Offers MA. *Program availability:* Part-time, evening/weekend. *Faculty:* 13 full-time (4 women), 1 part-time/adjunct (0 women). *Students:* 12 full-time (6 women), 3 part-time (2 women); includes 7 minority (2 Black or African American, non-Hispanic/Latino; 1 Asian, non-Hispanic/Latino; 1 Hispanic/Latino; 3 Two or more races, non-Hispanic/Latino), 5 international. Average age 35. 16 applicants, 56% accepted, 7 enrolled. In 2016, 15 master's awarded. *Entrance requirements:* Additional exam requirements/recommendations for international students: Recommended—TOEFL (minimum score 550 paper-based; 80 iBT), IELTS (minimum score 6), TWE (minimum score 5). *Application deadline:* For fall admission, 2/15 priority date for domestic students. Applications are processed on a rolling basis. Application fee: $50. Electronic applications accepted. *Expenses: Tuition:* Full-time $17,190; part-time $955 per credit. *Required fees:* $150; $26 per credit. Tuition and fees vary according to course load and program. *Financial support:* In 2016–17, 1 student received support. Research assistantships, career-related internships or fieldwork, Federal Work-Study, scholarships/grants, tuition waivers, and unspecified assistantships available. Financial award application deadline: 3/1; financial award applicants required to submit FAFSA. *Unit head:* Dr. Warren Wee, Associate Dean/Associate Professor of Accounting, 808-544-9325, E-mail: wwee@hpu.edu. *Application contact:* Danny Lam, Assistant Director of Graduate Admissions, 808-544-1135, E-mail: graduate@hpu.edu.
Website: http://www.hpu.edu/CBA/Graduate/MAHRM.html

HEC Montreal, School of Business Administration, Master of Science Programs in Administration, Program in Human Resources Management, Montréal, QC H3T 2A7, Canada. Offers M Sc. All courses are given in English. *Students:* 43 full-time (37 women), 21 part-time (all women). 39 applicants, 77% accepted, 19 enrolled. In 2016, 23 master's awarded. *Degree requirements:* For master's, one foreign language, thesis. *Entrance requirements:* For master's, Test de francais international (TFI) with minimum score of 850 (for those who have never studied in French), BBA, undergraduate degree in another field, degree deemed equivalent by program director and minimum GPA of 3.0 on 4.3 scale. *Application deadline:* For fall admission, 3/15 for domestic and international students; for winter admission, 9/15 for domestic and international students. Application fee: $86 Canadian dollars. Electronic applications accepted. *Expenses: Tuition, area resident:* Part-time $77.80 Canadian dollars per credit. Tuition, state resident: full-time $2797 Canadian dollars; part-time $240.92 Canadian dollars per credit. Tuition, nonresident: full-time $8673 Canadian dollars; part-time $531.43 Canadian dollars per credit. *International tuition:* $19,131 Canadian dollars full-time. *Required fees:* $1699 Canadian dollars; $40.58 Canadian dollars per credit. $67.32 Canadian dollars per term. Tuition and fees vary according to degree level and program. *Financial support:* Research assistantships, teaching assistantships, and scholarships/grants available. Financial award application deadline: 9/2. *Unit head:* Dr. Marie-Helene Jobin, Director, 514-340-6283, E-mail: marie-helene.jobin@hec.ca. *Application contact:* Marianne de Moura, Administrative Director, 514-340-7106, Fax: 514-340-6411, E-mail: marianne.de-moura@hec.ca.
Website: http://www.hec.ca/programmes/maitrises/maitrise-gestion-ressources-humaines/index.html

Herzing University Online, Program in Business Administration, Menomonee Falls, WI 53051. Offers accounting (MBA); business administration (MBA); business management (MBA); healthcare management (MBA); human resources (MBA); marketing (MBA); project management (MBA); technology management (MBA). *Program availability:* Online learning.

Human Resources Management

Hofstra University, Frank G. Zarb School of Business, Programs in Management and General Business, Hempstead, NY 11549. Offers business administration (MBA), including health services management, management, sports and entertainment management, strategic business management, strategic healthcare management; general management (Advanced Certificate); human resource management (MS, Advanced Certificate). *Program availability:* Part-time, evening/weekend, blended/hybrid learning. *Students:* 140 full-time (67 women), 159 part-time (70 women); includes 100 minority (24 Black or African American, non-Hispanic/Latino; 41 Asian, non-Hispanic/Latino; 32 Hispanic/Latino; 1 Native Hawaiian or other Pacific Islander, non-Hispanic/Latino; 2 Two or more races, non-Hispanic/Latino), 26 international. Average age 33. 354 applicants, 58% accepted, 94 enrolled. In 2016, 84 master's awarded. *Degree requirements:* For master's, thesis optional, capstone course (for MBA), thesis (for MS), minimum GPA of 3.0. *Entrance requirements:* For master's, GMAT/GRE, 2 letters of recommendation, resume, essay. Additional exam requirements/recommendations for international students: Required—TOEFL (minimum score 550 paper-based; 80 iBT); Recommended—IELTS (minimum score 6). *Application deadline:* Applications are processed on a rolling basis. Application fee: $75. Electronic applications accepted. *Expenses:* $1,170 per credit. *Financial support:* In 2016–17, 65 students received support, including 43 fellowships with full and partial tuition reimbursements available (averaging $4,813 per year); research assistantships with full and partial tuition reimbursements available, career-related internships or fieldwork, Federal Work-Study, institutionally sponsored loans, scholarships/grants, tuition waivers (full and partial), and unspecified assistantships also available. Support available to part-time students. Financial award applicants required to submit FAFSA. *Faculty research:* Organizational change; sustainability; entrepreneurial spawning; family business; global supply chain strategies. *Unit head:* Dr. Kaushik Sengupta, Chairperson, 516-463-7825, Fax: 516-463-4834, E-mail: kaushik.sengupta@hofstra.edu. *Application contact:* Sunil Samuel, Assistant Vice President of Admissions, 516-463-4723, Fax: 516-463-4664, E-mail: graduateadmission@hofstra.edu.
Website: http://www.hofstra.edu/business/

Holy Family University, Graduate and Professional Programs, School of Business Administration, Philadelphia, PA 19114. Offers accountancy (MS); finance (MBA); health care administration (MBA); human resource management (MBA); information systems management (MBA). *Accreditation:* ACBSP. *Program availability:* Part-time, evening/weekend. *Students:* 140 part-time. 58 applicants, 78% accepted, 42 enrolled. In 2016, 44 master's awarded. *Degree requirements:* For master's, comprehensive exam, thesis optional. *Entrance requirements:* For master's, minimum GPA of 3.0, interview, essay/personal statement, current resume, official transcript of all college or university work. Additional exam requirements/recommendations for international students: Required—TOEFL (minimum score 550 paper-based; 79 iBT), IELTS (minimum score 6), PTE (minimum score 54). *Application deadline:* For fall admission, 7/1 priority date for domestic and international students; for winter admission, 1/1 for domestic students; for spring admission, 11/1 priority date for domestic and international students; for summer admission, 4/1 priority date for domestic and international students. Applications are processed on a rolling basis. Application fee: $25. Electronic applications accepted. *Expenses: Tuition:* Part-time $751 per hour. *Required fees:* $140 per semester. One-time fee: $165 part-time. Part-time tuition and fees vary according to degree level and program. *Financial support:* Available to part-time students. Application deadline: 5/1; applicants required to submit FAFSA. *Unit head:* Dr. Barry Dickinson, Dean, 267-341-3440, Fax: 215-637-5937, E-mail: jdickinson@holyfamily.edu. *Application contact:* Gidget Marie Montelibano, Associate Director of Graduate Admissions, 267-341-3558, Fax: 215-637-1478, E-mail: gmontelibano@holyfamily.edu.
Website: http://www.holyfamily.edu/choosing-holy-family-u/academics/schools-of-study/school-of-business-administration

Hood College, Graduate School, Department of Economics and Business Administration, Frederick, MD 21701-8575. Offers accounting (MBA); finance (MBA); human resource management (MBA); information systems (MBA); marketing (MBA); public management (MBA). *Accreditation:* ACBSP. *Program availability:* Part-time, evening/weekend. *Faculty:* 4 full-time, 8 part-time/adjunct. *Students:* 21 full-time (13 women), 106 part-time (60 women); includes 23 minority (12 Black or African American, non-Hispanic/Latino; 4 Asian, non-Hispanic/Latino; 6 Hispanic/Latino; 1 Two or more races, non-Hispanic/Latino), 15 international. Average age 32. 44 applicants, 91% accepted, 25 enrolled. In 2016, 45 master's awarded. *Degree requirements:* For master's, capstone/final research project. *Entrance requirements:* For master's, minimum GPA of 3.0 (or resume and two letters of recommendation), copy of official transcripts, essay. Additional exam requirements/recommendations for international students: Required—TOEFL (minimum score 575 paper-based; 89 iBT), IELTS (minimum score 6.5). *Application deadline:* For fall admission, 8/15 for domestic students, 8/5 for international students; for spring admission, 12/1 for domestic and international students; for summer admission, 5/1 for domestic students, 4/15 for international students. Applications are processed on a rolling basis. Application fee: $35. Electronic applications accepted. *Expenses:* $525 per credit; $110 comprehensive fee per semester. *Financial support:* Tuition waivers (partial) and unspecified assistantships available. Financial award applicants required to submit FAFSA. *Faculty research:* Corporate strategy and sustainable competitive advantages, business ethics, entrepreneurship, investments management, economic development. *Unit head:* April Boulton, Interim Dean of the Graduate School, 301-696-3600, Fax: 301-696-3597, E-mail: gofurther@hood.edu. *Application contact:* Spencer Berk, Assistant Director of Graduate Admissions, 301-696-3604, E-mail: gofurther@hood.edu.

Houston Baptist University, Archie W. Dunham College of Business, Program in Human Resources Management, Houston, TX 77074-3298. Offers MSHRM. *Program availability:* Part-time, evening/weekend. *Students:* 46 full-time (35 women), 36 part-time (29 women); includes 57 minority (34 Black or African American, non-Hispanic/Latino; 8 Asian, non-Hispanic/Latino; 13 Hispanic/Latino; 2 Two or more races, non-Hispanic/Latino), 10 international. Average age 31. 103 applicants, 45% accepted, 24 enrolled. In 2016, 30 master's awarded. *Entrance requirements:* For master's, minimum GPA of 2.5, essay/personal statement, resume, bachelor's degree conferred transcript. Additional exam requirements/recommendations for international students: Required—TOEFL (minimum score 80 iBT), IELTS (minimum score 6.5). *Application deadline:* For fall admission, 8/1 for domestic students, 6/1 for international students; for spring admission, 1/1 for domestic students, 11/1 for international students; for summer admission, 5/1 for domestic students, 3/1 for international students. Applications are processed on a rolling basis. Application fee: $0 ($100 for international students). Electronic applications accepted. Application fee is waived when completed online. *Expenses:* $2,850 per 3-hour course; $1,275 annual general fee; $1,060 annual technology fee. *Financial support:* In 2016–17, 8 students received support. Federal Work-Study and scholarships/grants available. Support available to part-time students. Financial award application deadline: 4/1; financial award applicants required to submit FAFSA. *Unit head:* Dr. Michael Weeks, Dean, Archie W. Dunham College of Business, 281-649-3014, E-mail: mweeks@hbu.edu. *Application contact:* Laurel Motal, Secretary, 281-649-3306, Fax: 281-649-3436, E-mail: lmotal@hbu.edu.
Website: http://www.hbu.edu/mshrm

Howard University, School of Business, Graduate Programs in Business, Washington, DC 20059-0002. Offers accounting (MBA); entrepreneurship (MBA); finance (MBA); general management (MBA); human resources management (MBA); information systems (MBA); international business (MBA); marketing (MBA); supply chain management (MBA); JD/MBA. *Accreditation:* AACSB. *Program availability:* Part-time, evening/weekend, online learning. *Entrance requirements:* For master's, GMAT, minimum 1 year post undergraduate work experience, resume, 3 letters of recommendation, advanced college algebra. Additional exam requirements/recommendations for international students: Required—TOEFL. *Faculty research:* Marketing research in multi-ethnic populations, U.S. trade policies and international relations, risk management (finance).

IGlobal University, Graduate Programs, Vienna, VA 22182. Offers accounting (MBA); data management and analytics (MSIT); entrepreneurship (MBA); finance (MBA); global business management (MBA); health care management (MBA); hospitality and tourism management (MBA); human resources management (MBA); information technology (MBA); information technology systems and management (MSIT); leadership and management (MBA); project management (MBA); public service and administration (MBA); software design and management (MSIT).

Indiana Tech, Program in Business Administration, Fort Wayne, IN 46803-1297. Offers accounting (MBA); health care management (MBA); human resources (MBA); management (MBA); marketing (MBA). *Program availability:* Part-time, evening/weekend, online learning. *Entrance requirements:* For master's, GMAT, bachelor's degree from regionally-accredited university; minimum undergraduate GPA of 2.5; 2 years of significant work experience; 3 letters of recommendation. Electronic applications accepted.

Indiana University South Bend, Judd Leighton School of Business and Economics, South Bend, IN 46634-7111. Offers accounting (MSA); business (Graduate Certificate); business administration (MBA), including finance, human resource management, marketing; MBA/MSA. *Program availability:* Part-time, evening/weekend. *Faculty:* 17 full-time (2 women), 3 part-time/adjunct (1 woman). *Students:* 28 full-time (18 women), 85 part-time (36 women); includes 10 minority (3 Black or African American, non-Hispanic/Latino; 1 Asian, non-Hispanic/Latino; 5 Hispanic/Latino; 1 Two or more races, non-Hispanic/Latino), 22 international. Average age 32. 57 applicants, 68% accepted, 22 enrolled. In 2016, 67 master's, 7 other advanced degrees awarded. *Entrance requirements:* For master's, GMAT. Additional exam requirements/recommendations for international students: Required—TOEFL (minimum score 550 paper-based; 79 iBT). *Application deadline:* For fall admission, 7/15 priority date for domestic and international students; for spring admission, 11/15 priority date for domestic and international students; for summer admission, 4/1 priority date for domestic and international students. Applications are processed on a rolling basis. Application fee: $40 ($60 for international students). Electronic applications accepted. *Expenses:* $329.79 per credit hour in-state; $739.85 per credit hour out-of-state. *Financial support:* Fellowships, Federal Work-Study, and institutionally sponsored loans available. Support available to part-time students. Financial award application deadline: 7/1; financial award applicants required to submit FAFSA. *Faculty research:* Financial accounting, consumer research, capital budgeting research, business strategy research. *Unit head:* Richard Kolbe, Dean, 574-520-4228, Fax: 574-520-4866, E-mail: rkolbe@iusb.edu. *Application contact:* 574-520-4839, Fax: 574-520-4834, E-mail: graduate@iusb.edu.
Website: https://business.iusb.edu/

Indiana Wesleyan University, College of Adult and Professional Studies, Graduate Studies in Business, Marion, IN 46953. Offers accounting (MBA, Graduate Certificate); applied management (MBA); business administration (MBA); health care (MBA, Graduate Certificate); human resources (MBA, Graduate Certificate); management (MS); organizational leadership (MA). *Program availability:* Part-time, evening/weekend, online learning. *Degree requirements:* For master's, applied business or management project. *Entrance requirements:* For master's, minimum GPA of 2.5, 2 years of related work experience. Additional exam requirements/recommendations for international students: Required—TOEFL (minimum score 550 paper-based). Electronic applications accepted.

Instituto Tecnologico de Santo Domingo, Graduate School, Area of Business, Santo Domingo, Dominican Republic. Offers banking and securities markets (M Mgmt); corporate finance (M Mgmt); human resources management (M Mgmt, Certificate); international trade management (M Mgmt); marketing (M Mgmt); organizational development (M Mgmt); quality and productivity management (Certificate); tax management and planning (M Mgmt); upper management (M Mgmt).

Instituto Tecnologico de Santo Domingo, Graduate School, Area of Engineering, Santo Domingo, Dominican Republic. Offers construction administration (MS, Certificate); data telecommunications (M Eng, MS, Certificate); industrial engineering (M Eng, Certificate); industrial management (M Mgmt); information technology (Certificate); maintenance engineering (M Eng); occupational hazard prevention (M Mgmt); production management (Certificate); quantitative methods (Certificate); sanitary and environmental engineering (M Eng); structural engineering (M Eng); systems engineering and electronic data processing (Certificate); transportation (Certificate).

Instituto Tecnológico y de Estudios Superiores de Monterrey, Campus Cuernavaca, Programs in Business Administration, Temixco, Mexico. Offers finance (MA); human resources management (MA); international business (MA); marketing (MA).

Inter American University of Puerto Rico, Aguadilla Campus, Graduate School, Aguadilla, PR 00605. Offers accounting (MBA); counseling psychology specializing in family (MS); criminal justice (MA); educative management and leadership (MA); elementary education (M Ed); finance (MBA); human resources (MBA); industrial management (MBA); management information systems (MBA); marketing (MBA). *Program availability:* Part-time, evening/weekend. *Degree requirements:* For master's, comprehensive exam. *Entrance requirements:* For master's, EXADEP, 2 letters of recommendation, minimum GPA of 2.5. Electronic applications accepted.

Inter American University of Puerto Rico, Arecibo Campus, Program in Business Administration, Arecibo, PR 00614-4050. Offers accounting (MBA); finance (MBA); human resources (MBA).

Inter American University of Puerto Rico, Bayamón Campus, Graduate School, Bayamón, PR 00957. Offers biology (MS), including environmental sciences and ecology, molecular biotechnology; electrical engineering (ME), including control system, potence system; human resources (MBA); mechanical engineering (ME, MS), including aerospace, energy. *Program availability:* Part-time, evening/weekend. *Faculty:* 12 full-time (5 women), 4 part-time/adjunct (2 women). *Students:* 7 full-time (5 women), 115 part-time (69 women); includes 119 minority (1 Black or African American, non-Hispanic/Latino; 118 Hispanic/Latino). Average age 28. 94 applicants, 72% accepted, 56 enrolled. In 2016, 22 master's awarded. *Degree requirements:* For master's, comprehensive exam, research project. *Entrance requirements:* For master's, EXADEP, GRE General Test, letters of recommendation. *Application deadline:* For fall admission, 7/1 for domestic students, 5/1 priority date for international students; for winter admission, 11/15 priority date for domestic and international students; for spring admission, 2/15 priority date for domestic and international students. Application fee: $31. *Expenses: Tuition:* Part-time $207 per credit. *Required fees:* $328 per semester. *Unit head:* Prof.

Juan F. Martinez, Chancellor, 787-279-1200 Ext. 2295, Fax: 787-279-2205, E-mail: jmartinez@bayamon.inter.edu. *Application contact:* Aurelis Bez, Director of Student Services, 787-279-1912 Ext. 2017, Fax: 787-279-2205, E-mail: abaez@bayamon.inter.edu.

Inter American University of Puerto Rico, Metropolitan Campus, Graduate Programs, Program in Human Resources, San Juan, PR 00919-1293. Offers MBA. *Degree requirements:* For master's, comprehensive exam. *Entrance requirements:* For master's, GRE or EXADEP, interview. Electronic applications accepted.

Inter American University of Puerto Rico, Ponce Campus, Graduate School, Mercedita, PR 00715-1602. Offers accounting (MBA); biology (M Ed); chemistry (M Ed); criminal justice (MA); elementary education (M Ed); English as a Second Language (M Ed); finance (MBA); history (M Ed); human resources (MBA); marketing (MBA); mathematics (M Ed); Spanish (M Ed). *Entrance requirements:* For master's, minimum GPA of 2.5.

Inter American University of Puerto Rico, San Germán Campus, Graduate Studies Center, Program in Business Administration, San Germán, PR 00683-5008. Offers accounting (MBA); finance (MBA); general business administration (MBA); human resources (MBA, PhD); industrial relations (MBA); information systems (MBA); international and interregional business (PhD); management (MBA); marketing (MBA). *Program availability:* Part-time, evening/weekend. *Degree requirements:* For master's, comprehensive exam. *Entrance requirements:* For master's, GRE General Test or EXADEP, minimum GPA of 3.0.

International College of the Cayman Islands, Graduate Program in Management, Newlands, Cayman Islands. Offers business administration (MBA); management (MS), including education, human resources. *Program availability:* Part-time, evening/weekend. *Degree requirements:* For master's, comprehensive exam. *Entrance requirements:* Additional exam requirements/recommendations for international students: Recommended—TOEFL. *Faculty research:* International human resources administration.

Iona College, Hagan School of Business, Department of Management, Business Administration and Health Care Management, New Rochelle, NY 10801-1890. Offers business administration (MBA); health care analytics (AC); health care management (MBA, AC); human resource management (MBA, PMC); long term care services management (AC); management (MBA, PMC). *Program availability:* Part-time, evening/weekend. *Faculty:* 11 full-time (1 woman), 5 part-time/adjunct (3 women). *Students:* 47 full-time (23 women), 69 part-time (39 women); includes 38 minority (13 Black or African American, non-Hispanic/Latino; 5 Asian, non-Hispanic/Latino; 19 Hispanic/Latino; 1 Two or more races, non-Hispanic/Latino), 22 international. Average age 30. 39 applicants, 95% accepted, 19 enrolled. In 2016, 51 master's, 47 other advanced degrees awarded. *Entrance requirements:* For master's, GMAT, 2 letters of recommendation, minimum GPA of 3.0; for other advanced degree, GMAT, minimum GPA of 3.0. Additional exam requirements/recommendations for international students: Required—TOEFL (minimum score 550 paper-based; 80 iBT), IELTS (minimum score 6.5). *Application deadline:* For fall admission, 8/15 priority date for domestic students, 8/1 priority date for international students; for winter admission, 11/15 priority date for domestic students, 11/1 priority date for international students; for spring admission, 2/15 priority date for domestic students, 2/1 priority date for international students; for summer admission, 5/15 priority date for domestic students, 5/1 priority date for international students. Applications are processed on a rolling basis. Application fee: $50. Electronic applications accepted. *Expenses:* Contact institution. *Financial support:* In 2016–17, 44 students received support. Scholarships/grants, tuition waivers (partial), and unspecified assistantships available. Support available to part-time students. Financial award application deadline: 4/15; financial award applicants required to submit FAFSA. *Faculty research:* Information systems, strategic management, corporate values and ethics. *Unit head:* George DeFeis, Chair, 914-633-2631, E-mail: gdefeis@iona.edu. *Application contact:* Katelyn Brunck, Director of MBA Admissions, 914-633-2451, Fax: 914-633-2277, E-mail: kbrunck@iona.edu.
Website: http://www.iona.edu/Academics/Hagan-School-of-Business/Departments/Management-Business-Administration-Health-Car/Graduate-Programs.aspx

Iona College, School of Arts and Science, Department of Psychology, New Rochelle, NY 10801-1890. Offers general-experimental psychology (MA); human resources (Certificate); industrial-organizational psychology (MA); mental health counseling (MA); organizational behavior (Certificate); psychology (MA); school psychology (MA). *Program availability:* Part-time. *Faculty:* 9 full-time (5 women), 6 part-time/adjunct (5 women). *Students:* 61 full-time (42 women), 32 part-time (23 women); includes 40 minority (8 Black or African American, non-Hispanic/Latino; 3 Asian, non-Hispanic/Latino; 28 Hispanic/Latino; 1 Two or more races, non-Hispanic/Latino), 2 international. Average age 25. 91 applicants, 80% accepted, 37 enrolled. In 2016, 18 master's awarded. *Degree requirements:* For master's, thesis (for some programs), literature review (for some programs). *Entrance requirements:* For master's, BA in psychology including 3 credits each in psychology statistics and experimental research methods, or 9 credits in psychology including 3 credits in psychology statistics, 3 credits in psychology research methods and 3 credits of upper-level coursework. Additional exam requirements/recommendations for international students: Required—TOEFL (minimum score 550 paper-based), IELTS (minimum score 6.5). *Application deadline:* For fall admission, 8/15 for domestic students, 5/1 for international students; for spring admission, 1/15 for domestic students, 9/1 for international students. Applications are processed on a rolling basis. Application fee: $50. Electronic applications accepted. *Expenses:* *Tuition:* Full-time $19,692; part-time $1094 per credit. *Required fees:* $245 per term. Tuition and fees vary according to program. *Financial support:* In 2016–17, 49 students received support. Research assistantships with partial tuition reimbursements available, tuition waivers (partial), and unspecified assistantships available. Support available to part-time students. Financial award application deadline: 4/15; financial award applicants required to submit FAFSA. *Faculty research:* Non-suicidal self-injury, trauma response, performance appraisal and evaluation, diversity infusion, assessment and treatment of sexual offenders. *Unit head:* Patricia Oswald, PhD, Chair, 914-633-2374, E-mail: poswald@iona.edu. *Application contact:* Katelyn Brunck, Assistant Director, Graduate Admissions, 914-633-2451, Fax: 914-633-2277, E-mail: kbrunck@iona.edu.
Website: http://www.iona.edu/Academics/School-of-Arts-Science/Departments/Psychology/Graduate-Programs.aspx

James Madison University, The Graduate School, College of Education, Program in Adult Education and Human Resource Development, Harrisonburg, VA 22802. Offers higher education (MS Ed); human resource management (MS Ed); individualized (MS Ed); instructional design (MS Ed); leadership and facilitation (MS Ed); program evaluation and measurement (MS Ed). *Accreditation:* NCATE. *Program availability:* Part-time, evening/weekend. *Students:* 10 full-time (8 women), 11 part-time (10 women); includes 7 minority (4 Black or African American, non-Hispanic/Latino; 1 Hispanic/Latino; 2 Two or more races, non-Hispanic/Latino), 1 international. Average age 30. 23 applicants, 91% accepted, 18 enrolled. In 2016, 17 master's awarded. Application fee: $55. Electronic applications accepted. *Financial support:* In 2016–17, 15 students received support. Teaching assistantships, Federal Work-Study, and 8 assistantships (averaging $7911), 1 athletic assistantship (averaging $9284) available. Financial award application deadline: 3/1; financial award applicants required to submit FAFSA. *Unit head:* Dr. Jane B. Thall, Department Head, 540-568-5531, E-mail: thalljb@jmu.edu. *Application contact:* Lynette D. Michael, Director of Graduate Admissions, 540-568-6131 Ext. 6395, Fax: 540-568-7860, E-mail: michaeld@jmu.edu.

Johnson & Wales University, Graduate Studies, MBA Program, Providence, RI 02903-3703. Offers accounting (MBA); business administration (MBA); finance (MBA); hospitality (MBA); human resource management (MBA); information technology (MBA); nonprofit management (MBA); operations and supply chain management (MBA). Program also offered on Denver campus. *Program availability:* Part-time, online learning. *Entrance requirements:* For master's, minimum GPA of 2.75. Additional exam requirements/recommendations for international students: Required—TOEFL (minimum score 550 paper-based); Recommended—IELTS, TWE. *Faculty research:* International banking, global economy, international trade, cultural differences.

Johnson & Wales University, Graduate Studies, MS Program in Human Resource Management, Providence, RI 02903-3703. Offers MS. *Program availability:* Online learning.

Kaplan University, Davenport Campus, School of Business, Davenport, IA 52807. Offers business administration (MBA); change leadership (MS); entrepreneurship (MBA); finance (MBA); health care management (MBA, MS); human resource (MBA); international business (MBA); management (MS); marketing (MBA); project management (MBA, MS); supply chain management and logistics (MBA, MS). *Accreditation:* ACBSP. *Program availability:* Part-time, evening/weekend, online learning. *Entrance requirements:* Additional exam requirements/recommendations for international students: Required—TOEFL (minimum score 550 paper-based; 80 iBT). Electronic applications accepted.

King University, School of Business and Economics, Bristol, TN 37620-2699. Offers accounting (MBA); finance (MBA); healthcare management (MBA); human resources management (MBA); leadership (MBA); management (MBA); marketing (MBA); project management (MBA). *Program availability:* Part-time, evening/weekend, online learning. *Degree requirements:* For master's, comprehensive exam, thesis optional. *Entrance requirements:* For master's, GMAT, 2 years of work experience. Additional exam requirements/recommendations for international students: Required—TOEFL (minimum score 550 paper-based). Electronic applications accepted. *Faculty research:* International monetary policy.

La Roche College, School of Graduate Studies and Adult Education, Program in Human Resources Management, Pittsburgh, PA 15237-5898. Offers MS, Certificate. *Program availability:* Part-time, evening/weekend. *Faculty:* 1 (woman) full-time, 6 part-time/adjunct (2 women). *Students:* 9 full-time (7 women), 31 part-time (22 women); includes 1 minority (Black or African American, non-Hispanic/Latino), 11 international. Average age 35. In 2016, 12 master's awarded. *Entrance requirements:* For master's, GMAT, GRE or MAT, minimum GPA of 3.0 during previous 2 years, resume, 2 letters of recommendation, interview. Additional exam requirements/recommendations for international students: Recommended—TOEFL (minimum score 550 paper-based). *Application deadline:* For fall admission, 8/15 priority date for domestic students, 8/15 for international students; for spring admission, 12/15 priority date for domestic students, 12/15 for international students. Applications are processed on a rolling basis. Application fee: $50. Electronic applications accepted. *Expenses:* *Tuition:* Full-time $12,600; part-time $700 per credit. *Required fees:* $25 per semester. *Financial support:* Unspecified assistantships available. Financial award application deadline: 3/31; financial award applicants required to submit FAFSA. *Faculty research:* Human resources development. *Unit head:* Dr. Jean Forti, Coordinator, 412-536-1193, Fax: 412-536-1179, E-mail: fortij1@laroche.edu. *Application contact:* Hope Schiffgens, Director of Graduate Studies and Adult Education, 412-536-1266, Fax: 412-536-1283, E-mail: schombh1@laroche.edu.

La Salle University, School of Arts and Sciences, Program in Counseling and Family Therapy, Philadelphia, PA 19141-1199. Offers industrial/organizational management and human resources (MA); marriage and family therapy (MA); pastoral counseling (MA); professional clinical counseling (MA). *Accreditation:* ACA; APA. *Program availability:* Part-time, evening/weekend. *Faculty:* 8 full-time (3 women), 20 part-time/adjunct (13 women). *Students:* 77 full-time (55 women), 180 part-time (147 women); includes 84 minority (44 Black or African American, non-Hispanic/Latino; 5 Asian, non-Hispanic/Latino; 31 Hispanic/Latino; 4 Two or more races, non-Hispanic/Latino), 5 international. Average age 30. 156 applicants, 76% accepted, 48 enrolled. In 2016, 106 master's awarded. *Degree requirements:* For master's, comprehensive exam. *Entrance requirements:* For master's, GRE or MAT (waived for applicants that already possess a master's degree in any field or for applicants that have a cumulative GPA of 3.5 or higher), minimum of 15 hours in psychology, counseling, or marriage and family studies; minimum GPA of 3.0; three letters of recommendation; personal statement; work experience (paid or volunteer). Additional exam requirements/recommendations for international students: Required—TOEFL. *Application deadline:* For fall admission, 8/15 priority date for domestic students, 7/15 for international students; for spring admission, 12/15 priority date for domestic students, 11/15 for international students; for summer admission, 4/15 priority date for domestic students, 3/15 for international students. Applications are processed on a rolling basis. Application fee: $35. Electronic applications accepted. Application fee is waived when completed online. *Expenses:* Contact institution. *Financial support:* In 2016–17, 37 students received support. Scholarships/grants and unspecified assistantships available. Support available to part-time students. Financial award application deadline: 8/31; financial award applicants required to submit FAFSA. *Faculty research:* Cognitive therapy, attribution theory, work habits, single parent families, treatment of addictions. *Unit head:* Dr. Donna A. Tonrey, Director, 215-951-1767, Fax: 215-951-1843, E-mail: psyma@lasalle.edu. *Application contact:* Elizabeth Heenan, Director, Graduate and Adult Enrollment, 215-951-1100, Fax: 215-951-1462, E-mail: heenan@lasalle.edu.
Website: http://www.lasalle.edu/counseling-family-therapy/

La Salle University, School of Business, Master of Business Administration Program, Philadelphia, PA 19141-1199. Offers accounting (MBA, Post-MBA Certificate); business systems and analytics (MBA, Post-MBA Certificate); finance (MBA, Post-MBA Certificate); general business administration (MBA, Post-MBA Certificate); human resource management (MBA, Post-MBA Certificate); management (MBA, Post-MBA Certificate); marketing (Post-MBA Certificate); MBA/MSN. Program also offered in Switzerland. *Accreditation:* AACSB. *Program availability:* Part-time, evening/weekend, online learning. *Faculty:* 19 full-time (6 women), 11 part-time/adjunct (3 women). *Students:* 55 full-time (23 women), 209 part-time (96 women); includes 66 minority (35 Black or African American, non-Hispanic/Latino; 17 Asian, non-Hispanic/Latino; 9 Hispanic/Latino; 5 Two or more races, non-Hispanic/Latino), 17 international. Average age 31. 200 applicants, 59% accepted, 63 enrolled. In 2016, 192 master's, 1 other advanced degree awarded. *Entrance requirements:* For master's, GMAT or GRE, two letters of reference; resume; for Post-MBA Certificate, MBA with minimum GPA of 3.0. Additional exam requirements/recommendations for international students: Required—TOEFL. *Application deadline:* For fall admission, 8/15 priority date for domestic students, 7/15 for international students; for spring admission, 12/15 priority date for domestic students, 11/15 for international students; for summer admission, 4/15 priority date for domestic students, 3/15 for international students. Applications are processed on a rolling basis. Application fee: $35. Electronic applications accepted. Application fee is waived when completed online. *Expenses:* Contact institution. *Financial support:* In 2016–17, 49 students received support. Scholarships/grants available. Support available to part-time students. Financial award application deadline: 8/31; financial award applicants required to submit FAFSA. *Unit head:* Dr. MarySheila McDonald, Interim Dean, 215-951-1040, Fax: 215-951-1886, E-mail: mcdonaldms@lasalle.edu. *Application contact:* Elizabeth Heenan, Director, Graduate and Adult Enrollment, 215-951-1100, Fax: 215-951-1462, E-mail: heenan@lasalle.edu.

Lasell College, Graduate and Professional Studies in Management, Newton, MA 02466-2709. Offers business administration (PMBA); elder care management (MSM, Graduate Certificate); hospitality and event management (MSM, Graduate Certificate); human resources management (MSM, Graduate Certificate); management (MSM, Graduate Certificate); marketing (MSM, Graduate Certificate); non-profit management (MSM, Graduate Certificate); project management (MSM, Graduate Certificate). *Accreditation:* ACBSP. *Program availability:* Part-time, evening/weekend, 100% online, blended/hybrid learning. *Faculty:* 3 full-time (2 women), 16 part-time/adjunct (10 women). *Students:* 47 full-time (34 women), 93 part-time (72 women); includes 28 minority (20 Black or African American, non-Hispanic/Latino; 4 Asian, non-Hispanic/Latino; 3 Hispanic/Latino; 1 Two or more races, non-Hispanic/Latino), 24 international. Average age 31. 121 applicants, 55% accepted, 32 enrolled. In 2016, 61 master's, 3 other advanced degrees awarded. *Degree requirements:* For master's, minimum GPA of 3.0; internship or research paper (for MSM). *Entrance requirements:* For master's, one-page personal statement, 2 letters of recommendation, resume, bachelor's degree transcript; proof of microeconomics and statistics (for PMBA); for Graduate Certificate, bachelor's degree transcript, 2 letters of recommendation, 1-page personal statement, resume. Additional exam requirements/recommendations for international students: Required—TOEFL (minimum score 550 paper-based, 79 iBT) or IELTS (minimum score 6). *Application deadline:* For fall admission, 8/31 priority date for domestic students, 6/30 priority date for international students; for spring admission, 12/31 priority date for domestic students, 10/31 priority date for international students. Applications are processed on a rolling basis. Electronic applications accepted. *Expenses:* $600 per credit. *Financial support:* In 2016–17, 12 students received support. Federal Work-Study, scholarships/grants, and tuition discounts available. Support available to part-time students. Financial award application deadline: 8/31; financial award applicants required to submit FAFSA. *Unit head:* Dr. Joan Dolamore, Dean of Graduate and Professional Studies, 617-243-2485, Fax: 617-243-2450, E-mail: gradinfo@lasell.edu. *Application contact:* Adrienne Franciosi, Director of Graduate Enrollment, 617-243-2214, Fax: 617-243-2450, E-mail: gradinfo@lasell.edu.
Website: http://www.lasell.edu/academics/graduate-and-professional-studies/programs-of-study/master-of-science-in-management.html

La Sierra University, School of Business and Management, Riverside, CA 92515. Offers accounting (MBA); finance (MBA); general management (MBA); human resources management (MBA); leadership, values, and ethics for business and management (Certificate); marketing (MBA). *Degree requirements:* For master's, research project. *Entrance requirements:* For master's, GMAT, minimum GPA of 3.0. Additional exam requirements/recommendations for international students: Required—TOEFL. *Faculty research:* Financial econometrics, institutional assessment and strategic planning, legal issues in management, behavioral finance, content of financial reports.

Lewis University, College of Business, Graduate School of Management, Program in Business Administration, Romeoville, IL 60446. Offers accounting (MBA); custom elective option (MBA); e-business (MBA); finance (MBA); healthcare management (MBA); human resources management (MBA); international business (MBA); management information systems (MBA); marketing (MBA); project management (MBA); technology and operations management (MBA). *Program availability:* Part-time, evening/weekend. *Students:* 145 full-time (72 women), 213 part-time (123 women); includes 101 minority (46 Black or African American, non-Hispanic/Latino; 2 American Indian or Alaska Native, non-Hispanic/Latino; 7 Asian, non-Hispanic/Latino; 41 Hispanic/Latino; 1 Native Hawaiian or other Pacific Islander, non-Hispanic/Latino; 4 Two or more races, non-Hispanic/Latino), 47 international. Average age 31. In 2016, 99 master's awarded. *Degree requirements:* For master's, comprehensive exam. *Entrance requirements:* For master's, interview, bachelor's degree, resume, 2 recommendations. Additional exam requirements/recommendations for international students: Required—TOEFL (minimum score 550 paper-based). *Application deadline:* For fall admission, 8/15 priority date for domestic students, 5/1 priority date for international students; for spring admission, 11/15 priority date for international students. Applications are processed on a rolling basis. Application fee: $40. Electronic applications accepted. *Expenses: Tuition:* Full-time $13,860; part-time $770 per credit hour. *Required fees:* $75 per semester. Tuition and fees vary according to degree level and program. *Financial support:* Career-related internships or fieldwork, Federal Work-Study, scholarships/grants, and unspecified assistantships available. Financial award application deadline: 5/1; financial award applicants required to submit FAFSA. *Unit head:* Dr. Maureen Culleeney, Academic Program Director, 815-838-0500 Ext. 5631, E-mail: culleema@lewisu.edu. *Application contact:* Michele Ryan, Director of Admission, 815-838-0500 Ext. 5384, E-mail: gsm@lewisu.edu.

Lincoln University, Graduate Programs, Philadelphia, PA 19104. Offers counseling (MSC); early childhood education (M Ed), including PreK-4; early childhood education and special education (M Ed); educational leadership (M Ed), including principal certification; finance (MSB); human resources management (MSB); human services (MAHS). *Program availability:* Part-time, evening/weekend. *Faculty:* 11 full-time (5 women), 45 part-time/adjunct (24 women). *Students:* 191 full-time (131 women), 77 part-time (60 women); includes 245 minority (236 Black or African American, non-Hispanic/Latino; 1 American Indian or Alaska Native, non-Hispanic/Latino; 7 Hispanic/Latino; 1 Two or more races, non-Hispanic/Latino), 4 international. Average age 34. 221 applicants, 58% accepted, 55 enrolled. In 2016, 97 master's awarded. *Degree requirements:* For master's, thesis or alternative. *Entrance requirements:* For master's, official academic transcript from accredited institution presenting conferred bachelor's degree. *Application deadline:* For fall admission, 6/1 priority date for domestic and international students. Applications are processed on a rolling basis. Application fee: $50. Electronic applications accepted. *Expenses:* Tuition, state resident: full-time $12,264; part-time $511 per credit hour. Tuition, nonresident: full-time $21,264; part-time $886 per credit hour. *Required fees:* $1344; $56 per credit hour. Tuition and fees vary according to course load. *Financial support:* In 2016–17, 9 students received support. Scholarships/grants available. Financial award application deadline: 8/1; financial award applicants required to submit FAFSA. *Unit head:* Dr. Patricia Joseph, Dean, College of Professional, Graduate and Extended Studies, 484-365-7659, E-mail: joseph@lincoln.edu. *Application contact:* Jernice Lea, Director of Graduate Admissions, 215-590-8231, Fax: 215-387-3859, E-mail: jlea@lincoln.edu.
Website: http://www.lincoln.edu/academics/graduate-programs

Lincoln University, Graduate Studies, Oakland, CA 94612. Offers finance and investments (DBA); finance management (MS); finance management and investments (MBA); general business (MBA); human resource management (MBA, DBA); international business (MBA, MS); management information systems (MBA). *Program availability:* Part-time. *Faculty:* 13 full-time (1 woman), 16 part-time/adjunct (3 women). *Students:* 542 full-time (215 women), 3 part-time (1 woman); includes 10 minority (8 Asian, non-Hispanic/Latino; 1 Hispanic/Latino; 1 Two or more races, non-Hispanic/Latino), 531 international. Average age 26. 800 applicants, 71% accepted, 81 enrolled. In 2016, 109 master's, 1 doctorate awarded. *Degree requirements:* For master's, research project (thesis), internship report, or comprehensive exam; for doctorate, comprehensive exam, thesis/dissertation. *Entrance requirements:* For master's, minimum GPA of 2.7; for doctorate, GMAT (minimum score: 550), GRE (minimum score: 1000), or equivalent test results (waived for master's degree with minimum cumulative GPA of 3.3). Additional exam requirements/recommendations for international students: Required—TOEFL (minimum score 525 paper-based; 71 iBT) or IELTS (minimum score 5.5) for MBA; TOEFL (minimum score 550 paper-based; 79 iBT) or IELTS (minimum score 6) for DBA; Recommended—TOEFL (minimum score 71 iBT), IELTS (minimum score 6), TSE. *Application deadline:* For fall admission, 8/7 for domestic students, 7/14 for international students; for spring admission, 11/30 for domestic students, 10/31 for international students; for summer admission, 5/29 for domestic students, 5/5 for international students. Applications are processed on a rolling basis. Application fee: $75. Electronic applications accepted. *Expenses: Tuition:* Full-time $7920. *Required fees:* $400. Tuition and fees vary according to course level, course load, degree level and program. *Financial support:* Teaching assistantships, career-related internships or fieldwork, and scholarships/grants available. Financial award applicants required to submit FAFSA. *Unit head:* Dr. Marshall Burak, Director of Graduate Programs, 510-628-8016, Fax: 510-628-8012, E-mail: mburak@lincolnuca.edu. *Application contact:* Reenu Shrestha, Assistant to the President, 510-628-8017, Fax: 510-208-2826, E-mail: sreenu@lincolnuca.edu.
Website: http://www.lincolnuca.edu/

Lindenwood University, Graduate Programs, Plaster School of Business and Entrepreneurship, St. Charles, MO 63301-1695. Offers accountancy (M Acc); accounting (MBA); business administration (MBA); entrepreneurial studies (MBA); finance (MBA, MS); human resource management (MBA); international business (MBA); leadership (MA); management (MBA); marketing (MBA, MS); nonprofit administration (MA); public administration (MBA); sport management (MA); supply chain management (MBA). *Accreditation:* ACBSP. *Program availability:* Part-time, evening/weekend, 100% online. *Faculty:* 15 full-time (6 women), 25 part-time/adjunct (7 women). *Students:* 197 full-time (97 women), 213 part-time (132 women); includes 81 minority (62 Black or African American, non-Hispanic/Latino; 1 American Indian or Alaska Native, non-Hispanic/Latino; 4 Asian, non-Hispanic/Latino; 9 Hispanic/Latino; 5 Two or more races, non-Hispanic/Latino), 83 international. Average age 31. 279 applicants, 54% accepted, 133 enrolled. In 2016, 269 master's awarded. *Degree requirements:* For master's, comprehensive exam (for some programs), thesis (for some programs), minimum GPA of 3.0. *Entrance requirements:* For master's, interview, minimum undergraduate cumulative GPA of 3.0, letter of recommendation. Additional exam requirements/recommendations for international students: Required—TOEFL (minimum score 550 paper-based; 80 iBT); Recommended—IELTS (minimum score 6.5). *Application deadline:* For fall admission, 8/28 priority date for domestic and international students; for winter admission, 1/8 priority date for domestic and international students; for spring admission, 3/5 for domestic students, 3/5 priority date for international students; for summer admission, 6/4 priority date for domestic and international students. Applications are processed on a rolling basis. Application fee: $30 ($100 for international students). Electronic applications accepted. *Expenses:* Contact institution. *Financial support:* In 2016–17, 256 students received support. Career-related internships or fieldwork, Federal Work-Study, institutionally sponsored loans, scholarships/grants, tuition waivers (partial), and unspecified assistantships available. Financial award application deadline: 6/30; financial award applicants required to submit FAFSA. *Unit head:* Roger Ellis, Dean, School of Business and Entrepreneurship, 636-949-4839, E-mail: rellis@lindenwood.edu. *Application contact:* Tyler Kostich, Director, Evening and Graduate Admissions, 636-949-4138, Fax: 636-949-4109, E-mail: adultadmissions@lindenwood.edu.
Website: http://www.lindenwood.edu/academics/academic-schools/robert-w-plaster-school-of-business-entrepreneurship/

Lindenwood University, Graduate Programs, School of Accelerated Degree Programs, St. Charles, MO 63301-1695. Offers administration (MSA), including management, marketing, project management; business administration (MBA); communications (MA), including digital and multimedia, media management, promotions, training and development; criminal justice and administration (MS); healthcare administration (MS); human resource management (MS); information technology (Certificate); managing information security (MS); managing information technology (MS); managing virtualization and cloud computing (MS); writing (MFA). *Program availability:* Part-time, evening/weekend, 100% online. *Faculty:* 16 full-time (7 women), 75 part-time/adjunct (27 women). *Students:* 609 full-time (386 women), 179 part-time (121 women); includes 257 minority (202 Black or African American, non-Hispanic/Latino; 4 American Indian or Alaska Native, non-Hispanic/Latino; 5 Asian, non-Hispanic/Latino; 28 Hispanic/Latino; 1 Native Hawaiian or other Pacific Islander, non-Hispanic/Latino; 17 Two or more races, non-Hispanic/Latino), 28 international. Average age 36. 332 applicants, 70% accepted, 205 enrolled. In 2016, 479 master's awarded. *Degree requirements:* For master's, thesis (for some programs), minimum cumulative GPA of 3.0; for Certificate, minimum cumulative GPA of 3.0. *Entrance requirements:* For master's, resume, personal statement, official undergraduate transcript, minimum undergraduate cumulative GPA of 3.0. Additional exam requirements/recommendations for international students: Required—TOEFL (minimum score 550 paper-based; 80 iBT); Recommended—IELTS (minimum score 6.5). *Application deadline:* For fall admission, 9/26 priority date for domestic and international students; for winter admission, 1/3 priority date for domestic and international students; for spring admission, 3/31 priority date for domestic and international students; for summer admission, 7/3 priority date for domestic and international students. Applications are processed on a rolling basis. Application fee: $30 ($100 for international students). Electronic applications accepted. *Expenses: Tuition:* Full-time $15,672; part-time $453 per credit hour. *Required fees:* $205 per semester. Tuition and fees vary according to course level, course load and degree level. *Financial support:* In 2016–17, 467 students received support. Career-related internships or fieldwork, institutionally sponsored loans, scholarships/grants, tuition waivers (partial), and unspecified assistantships available. Financial award application deadline: 6/30; financial award applicants required to submit FAFSA. *Unit head:* Dr. Gina Ganahl, Dean, Accelerated Degree Programs, 636-949-4501, Fax: 636-949-4505, E-mail: gganahl@lindenwood.edu. *Application contact:* Tyler Kostich, Director, Evening and Graduate Admissions, 636-949-4138, Fax: 636-949-4109, E-mail: adultadmissions@lindenwood.edu.
Website: http://www.lindenwood.edu/academics/academic-schools/school-of-accelerated-degree-programs/

Lindenwood University–Belleville, Graduate Programs, Belleville, IL 62226. Offers business administration (MBA); communications (MA), including digital and multimedia, media management, promotions, training and development; counseling (MA); criminal justice administration (MS); education (MA); healthcare administration (MS); human resource management (MS); school administration (MA); teaching (MAT).

Lipscomb University, College of Business, Nashville, TN 37204-3951. Offers accountancy (M Acc); accounting (MBA); business administration (MM); conflict management (MBA); financial services (MBA); health care informatics (MBA); healthcare management (MBA); information security (MBA); leadership (MBA); nonprofit management (MBA); professional accountancy (Certificate); sports management (MBA); strategic human resources (MBA); sustainability (MBA); MBA/MS; Pharm D/MM. *Accreditation:* ACBSP. *Program availability:* Part-time, evening/weekend. *Faculty:* 22 full-time (4 women), 12 part-time/adjunct (4 women). *Students:* 112 full-time (51 women), 69 part-time (34 women); includes 30 minority (17 Black or African American, non-Hispanic/Latino; 3 Asian, non-Hispanic/Latino; 8 Hispanic/Latino; 2 Two or more races, non-Hispanic/Latino), 5 international. Average age 32. 244 applicants, 55% accepted, 54 enrolled. In 2016, 164 master's awarded. *Entrance requirements:* For master's, GMAT, transcripts, interview, 2 references, resume. Additional exam requirements/recommendations for international students: Required—TOEFL (minimum score 570 paper-based). *Application deadline:* For fall admission, 6/15 for domestic students, 2/1 for international students; for winter admission, 6/1 for international students; for spring admission, 11/15 for domestic students. Applications are processed on a rolling basis. Application fee: $50 ($75 for international students). Electronic applications accepted. *Expenses:* $1,150-$1,290 per hour, depending on program. *Financial support:* Career-related internships or fieldwork, scholarships/grants, tuition waivers (partial), and unspecified assistantships available. Support available to part-time students. Financial award application deadline: 7/1; financial award applicants required to submit FAFSA. *Faculty research:* Impact of spirituality on organization commitment, women in corporate leadership, psychological empowerment, training. *Unit head:* Allison Duke, Associate Dean of Graduate Business Programs, 615-966-5732, Fax: 615-966-1818, E-mail: allison.duke@lipscomb.edu. *Application contact:* Karen Risley, Manager, Graduate Business Recruiting, 615-966-5145, E-mail: karen.risley@lipscomb.edu.
Website: http://www.lipscomb.edu/business/Graduate-Programs

London Metropolitan University, Graduate Programs, London, United Kingdom. Offers applied psychology (M Sc); architecture (MA); biomedical science (M Sc); blood science (M Sc); cancer pharmacology (M Sc); computer networking and cyber security (M Sc); computing and information systems (M Sc); conference interpreting (MA); counter-terrorism studies (M Sc); creative, digital and professional writing (MA); crime, violence and prevention (M Sc); criminology (M Sc); curating contemporary art (MA); data analytics (M Sc); digital media (MA); early childhood studies (MA); education (MA, Ed D); financial services law, regulation and compliance (LL M); food science (M Sc); forensic psychology (M Sc); health and social care management and policy (M Sc); human nutrition (M Sc); human resource management (MA); human rights and international conflict (MA); information technology (M Sc); intelligence and security studies (M Sc); international oil, gas and energy law (LL M); international relations (MA); interpreting (MA); learning and teaching in higher education (MA); legal practice (LL M); media and entertainment law (LL M); organizational and consumer psychology (M Sc); psychological therapy (M Sc); psychology of mental health (M Sc); public health (M Sc); public policy and management (MPA); security studies (M Sc); social work (M Sc); spatial planning and urban design (MA); sports therapy (M Sc); supporting older children and young people with dyslexia (MA); teaching languages (MA), including Arabic, English; translation (MA); woman and child abuse (MA).

Long Island University–LIU Brooklyn, School of Business, Public Administration and Information Sciences, Brooklyn, NY 11201-8423. Offers accounting (MBA); accounting (MS); business administration (MBA); computer science (MS); gerontology (Advanced Certificate); health administration (MPA); human resources management (MS); not-for-profit management (Advanced Certificate); public administration (MPA); taxation (MS). *Program availability:* Part-time, evening/weekend, blended/hybrid learning. *Faculty:* 18 full-time (9 women), 32 part-time/adjunct (10 women). *Students:* 275 full-time (150 women), 238 part-time (161 women); includes 281 minority (200 Black or African American, non-Hispanic/Latino; 2 American Indian or Alaska Native, non-Hispanic/Latino; 38 Asian, non-Hispanic/Latino; 36 Hispanic/Latino; 1 Native Hawaiian or other Pacific Islander, non-Hispanic/Latino; 4 Two or more races, non-Hispanic/Latino), 140 international. 796 applicants, 66% accepted, 143 enrolled. In 2016, 185 master's, 17 other advanced degrees awarded. *Entrance requirements:* Additional exam requirements/recommendations for international students: Required—TOEFL (minimum score 527 paper-based; 75 iBT). *Application deadline:* Applications are processed on a rolling basis. Application fee: $50. Electronic applications accepted. *Expenses: Tuition:* Full-time $28,272; part-time $1178 per credit. *Required fees:* $451 per term. Tuition and fees vary according to degree level, program and student level. *Financial support:* In 2016–17, 94 students received support. Career-related internships or fieldwork, Federal Work-Study, institutionally sponsored loans, scholarships/grants, and unspecified assistantships available. Support available to part-time students. Financial award application deadline: 2/15; financial award applicants required to submit FAFSA. *Faculty research:* Corporate social responsibility; executive compensation and corporate governance; combinatorics; secure mobile coding; social equity and justice, particularly among the Latino population; public and healthcare finance. *Unit head:* Dr. Edward Rogoff, Dean, 718-488-1159, E-mail: edward.rogoff@liu.edu. *Application contact:* Gabrielle Gannon, Director of Graduate Admissions, 718-488-1011, Fax: 718-780-6110, E-mail: bkln-admissions@liu.edu.
Website: http://liu.edu/Brooklyn/Academics/School-of-Business-Public-Administration-and-Information-Sciences

Loyola University Chicago, Quinlan School of Business, Master of Science in Human Resources Program, Chicago, IL 60611. Offers MSHR, MBA/MSHR. *Program availability:* Part-time, evening/weekend. *Faculty:* 5 full-time (0 women), 7 part-time/adjunct (5 women). *Students:* 25 full-time (22 women), 7 part-time (5 women); includes 7 minority (3 Black or African American, non-Hispanic/Latino; 1 Asian, non-Hispanic/Latino; 2 Hispanic/Latino; 1 Two or more races, non-Hispanic/Latino), 6 international. Average age 30. 46 applicants, 65% accepted, 13 enrolled. In 2016, 11 master's awarded. *Entrance requirements:* For master's, GMAT or GRE, official transcripts, two letters of recommendation, statement of purpose, resume. Additional exam requirements/recommendations for international students: Required—TOEFL (minimum score 90 iBT) or IELTS (minimum score 6.5). *Application deadline:* For fall admission, 7/15 for domestic and international students; for winter admission, 10/1 for domestic and international students; for spring admission, 1/15 for domestic and international students; for summer admission, 4/1 for domestic and international students. Applications are processed on a rolling basis. Application fee: $50. Electronic applications accepted. Application fee is waived when completed online. *Expenses:* Contact institution. *Financial support:* In 2016–17, 10 students received support. Federal Work-Study, scholarships/grants, health care benefits, and unspecified assistantships available. Support available to part-time students. *Faculty research:* Encouraging innovation with reward programs, alternative dispute resolution, performance appraisal, global human resources, work of Independent contractors. *Unit head:* Dr. Sung Min Kim, Chair, 312-915-7052, E-mail: skim@luc.edu. *Application contact:* Lauren Griffin, Enrollment Advisor, Quinlan School of Business Graduate Programs, 312-915-6124, Fax: 312-915-7207, E-mail: lgriffin3@luc.edu.
Website: http://www.luc.edu/quinlan/mba/masters-degree-in-human-resources/index.shtml

Loyola University Chicago, Quinlan School of Business, MBA Programs, Chicago, IL 60611. Offers accounting (MBA); business administration (EMBA); business ethics (MBA); economics (MBA); entrepreneurship (MBA); finance (MBA); healthcare management (MBA); human resources management (MBA); international business (MBA); management (MBA); marketing (MBA); operation management (MBA); risk management (MBA); supply chain management (MBA). *Program availability:* Part-time, evening/weekend. *Faculty:* 79 full-time (22 women), 10 part-time/adjunct (6 women). *Students:* 309 full-time (151 women), 65 part-time (31 women); includes 82 minority (25 Black or African American, non-Hispanic/Latino; 27 Asian, non-Hispanic/Latino; 27 Hispanic/Latino; 3 Two or more races, non-Hispanic/Latino), 49 international. Average age 30. 371 applicants, 53% accepted, 114 enrolled. In 2016, 216 master's awarded. *Entrance requirements:* For master's, GMAT or GRE, official transcripts, two letters of recommendation, statement of purpose, resume. Additional exam requirements/recommendations for international students: Required—TOEFL (minimum score 90 iBT) or IELTS (minimum score 6.5). *Application deadline:* For fall admission, 7/15 for domestic and international students; for winter admission, 10/1 for domestic and international students; for spring admission, 1/15 for domestic and international students; for summer admission, 4/1 for domestic and international students. Applications are processed on a rolling basis. Application fee: $50. Electronic applications accepted. Application fee is waived when completed online. *Expenses:* $4,488 per course. *Financial support:* In 2016–17, 83 students received support. Federal Work-Study, scholarships/grants, health care benefits, and unspecified assistantships available. Support available to part-time students. *Faculty research:* Social enterprise and responsibility, emerging markets, supply chain management, risk management. *Unit head:* Katherine Acles, Assistant Dean for Graduate Programs, 312-915-6124, Fax: 312-915-7207, E-mail: kacles@luc.edu. *Application contact:* Lauren Griffin, Enrollment Advisor, Quinlan School of Business Graduate Programs, 312-915-6124, Fax: 312-915-7207, E-mail: lgriffin3@luc.edu.

Lynn University, College of Business and Management, Boca Raton, FL 33431-5598. Offers business administration (MBA), including aviation management, financial valuation and investment management, hospitality management, human resource management, international business management, marketing, media management, sports management. *Program availability:* Part-time, evening/weekend, 100% online, blended/hybrid learning. *Faculty:* 24 full-time (9 women), 24 part-time/adjunct (4 women). *Students:* 265 full-time (125 women), 182 part-time (96 women); includes 100 minority (41 Black or African American, non-Hispanic/Latino; 11 Asian, non-Hispanic/Latino; 42 Hispanic/Latino; 6 Two or more races, non-Hispanic/Latino), 119 international. Average age 28. 280 applicants, 94% accepted, 181 enrolled. In 2016, 219 master's awarded. *Degree requirements:* For master's, strategic management seminar, simulation capstone. *Entrance requirements:* For master's, bachelor's degree from accredited institution, resume, letter of recommendation, official transcripts, essay/personal statement. Additional exam requirements/recommendations for international students: Required—TOEFL (minimum score 550 paper-based; 80 iBT), IELTS (minimum score 6.5). *Application deadline:* For fall admission, 8/18 for domestic students, 8/4 for international students; for spring admission, 12/15 for domestic students, 12/1 for international students; for summer admission, 4/17 for domestic students, 4/3 for international students. Applications are processed on a rolling basis. Application fee: $45. Electronic applications accepted. *Expenses:* $725 per credit. *Financial support:* In 2016–17, 115 students received support. Career-related internships or fieldwork, Federal Work-Study, scholarships/grants, tuition waivers (full and partial), and unspecified assistantships available. Support available to part-time students. Financial award application deadline: 3/1; financial award applicants required to submit FAFSA. *Faculty research:* Market volatility investing, biometric research, sports legal history, organizational leadership, urban economic development and productivity. *Unit head:* Dr. RT Good, Dean of the College of Business and Management, 561-237-7458, E-mail: rgood@lynn.edu. *Application contact:* Steven Pruitt, Director of Graduate and Undergraduate Evening Admission, 561-237-7834, Fax: 561-237-7100, E-mail: spruitt@lynn.edu.
Website: http://www.lynn.edu/academics/colleges/business-and-management

Manhattanville College, School of Business, Master of Science in Human Resource Management and Organizational Effectiveness Program, Purchase, NY 10577-2132. Offers human resource management (MS); organizational effectiveness (MS). *Program availability:* Part-time, evening/weekend. *Students:* 24 (21 women); includes 13 minority (5 Black or African American, non-Hispanic/Latino; 2 Asian, non-Hispanic/Latino; 6 Hispanic/Latino). Average age 32. 18 applicants, 39% accepted, 5 enrolled. In 2016, 4 master's awarded. *Degree requirements:* For master's, thesis (for some programs), final project. *Entrance requirements:* For master's, transcripts, 2 letters of recommendation, resume. Additional exam requirements/recommendations for international students: Required—TOEFL (minimum score 563 paper-based; 85 iBT). *Application deadline:* Applications are processed on a rolling basis. Application fee: $75. Electronic applications accepted. *Expenses: Tuition:* Full-time $16,470; part-time $915 per credit. *Required fees:* $60 per semester. Part-time tuition and fees vary according to course load and program. *Financial support:* Federal Work-Study, institutionally sponsored loans, scholarships/grants, and unspecified assistantships available. Financial award applicants required to submit FAFSA. *Faculty research:* Alternative dispute resolution in employment law. *Unit head:* Laura Persky, Graduate Program Director, 914-323-5188, E-mail: laura.persky@mville.edu. *Application contact:* Monika Pottgen, Assistant Director, Recruitment and Admissions, 914-323-5150, E-mail: business@mville.edu.
Website: https://www.mville.edu/programs/ms-human-resource-management

Manhattanville College, School of Business, Master of Science in International Management Program, Purchase, NY 10577-2132. Offers business leadership (MS); finance (MS); human resource management (MS); marketing communication management (MS). *Program availability:* Part-time, evening/weekend. *Students:* 10 (9 women); includes 6 minority (2 Black or African American, non-Hispanic/Latino; 3 Hispanic/Latino; 1 Two or more races, non-Hispanic/Latino). Average age 30. 17 applicants, 35% accepted, 3 enrolled. In 2016, 1 master's awarded. *Degree requirements:* For master's, thesis (for some programs), final project. *Entrance requirements:* For master's, transcripts, 2 letters of recommendation, resume. Additional exam requirements/recommendations for international students: Required—TOEFL (minimum score 563 paper-based; 85 iBT). *Application deadline:* Applications are processed on a rolling basis. Application fee: $75. Electronic applications accepted. *Expenses: Tuition:* Full-time $16,470; part-time $915 per credit. *Required fees:* $60 per semester. Part-time tuition and fees vary according to course load and program. *Financial support:* Federal Work-Study, institutionally sponsored loans, scholarships/grants, and unspecified assistantships available. Financial award applicants required to submit FAFSA. *Faculty research:* Market entry in Cuba, linking strategy and customer satisfaction. *Unit head:* Laura Persky, Graduate Program Director, 914-323-5188, E-mail: laura.persky@mville.edu. *Application contact:* Monika Pottgen, Assistant Director, Recruitment and Admissions, 914-323-5150, E-mail: business@mville.edu.
Website: https://www.mville.edu/programs/ms-international-management

Marquette University, Graduate School of Management, Executive MBA Program, Milwaukee, WI 53201-1881. Offers economics (MBA); finance (MBA); human resources (MBA); international business (MBA); management information systems (MBA); marketing (MBA); operations and supply chain management (MBA); sports business

(MBA). *Accreditation:* AACSB. *Students:* 39 full-time (12 women); includes 7 minority (4 Black or African American, non-Hispanic/Latino; 2 Asian, non-Hispanic/Latino; 1 Hispanic/Latino). Average age 38. 25 applicants, 96% accepted, 29 enrolled. In 2016, 14 master's awarded. *Degree requirements:* For master's, international trip. *Entrance requirements:* For master's, GMAT or GRE, two letters of recommendation, official transcripts from current and previous colleges/universities. Additional exam requirements/recommendations for international students: Required—TOEFL (minimum score 550 paper-based; 88 iBT), IELTS (minimum score 6.5), PTE. *Application deadline:* For fall admission, 2/15 for domestic and international students. Application fee: $50. Electronic applications accepted. *Expenses:* Contact institution. *Financial support:* Application deadline: 2/15. *Faculty research:* International trade and finance, customer relationship management, consumer satisfaction, customer service. *Unit head:* Dr. Brian Till, Dean, 414-288-5724. *Application contact:* Dr. Jeanne Simmons, Associate Dean, 414-288-7145.
Website: http://www.busadm.mu.edu/emba/

Marquette University, Graduate School of Management, Program in Business Administration, Milwaukee, WI 53201-1881. Offers business administration (MBA); economics (MBA); entrepreneurship (Certificate); finance (MBA); human resources (MBA); international business (MBA); management information systems (MBA); marketing (MBA); operations and supply chain management (MBA); sports business (MBA); JD/MBA; MBA/MA; MBA/MSN. *Accreditation:* AACSB. *Program availability:* Part-time, evening/weekend. *Students:* 25 full-time (12 women), 202 part-time (57 women); includes 17 minority (5 Black or African American, non-Hispanic/Latino; 6 Asian, non-Hispanic/Latino; 2 Hispanic/Latino; 1 Native Hawaiian or other Pacific Islander, non-Hispanic/Latino; 3 Two or more races, non-Hispanic/Latino), 7 international. Average age 31. 107 applicants, 87% accepted, 113 enrolled. In 2016, 107 master's, 5 other advanced degrees awarded. *Degree requirements:* For Certificate, business plan. *Entrance requirements:* For master's, GMAT or GRE, letters of recommendation. Additional exam requirements/recommendations for international students: Required—TOEFL (minimum score 550 paper-based; 88 iBT), IELTS (minimum score 6.5), PTE. *Application deadline:* For fall admission, 2/15 for domestic and international students. Applications are processed on a rolling basis. Application fee: $50. Electronic applications accepted. *Financial support:* Fellowships, research assistantships, teaching assistantships, Federal Work-Study, institutionally sponsored loans, scholarships/grants, and tuition waivers (full and partial) available. Support available to part-time students. Financial award application deadline: 2/15. *Faculty research:* Ethics in the professions, services marketing, technology impact on decision-making, mentoring. *Unit head:* Dr. Brian Till, Dean, 414-288-5724. *Application contact:* Dr. Jeanne Simmons, Associate Dean, 414-288-7145.
Website: http://business.marquette.edu/academics/mba

Marquette University, Graduate School of Management, Program in Human Resources, Milwaukee, WI 53201-1881. Offers MSHR. *Program availability:* Part-time, evening/weekend. *Students:* 14 full-time (8 women), 8 part-time (5 women); includes 3 minority (2 Black or African American, non-Hispanic/Latino; 1 Hispanic/Latino), 12 international. Average age 26. 57 applicants, 81% accepted, 15 enrolled. In 2016, 11 master's awarded. *Entrance requirements:* For master's, GMAT or GRE General Test, letters of recommendation. Additional exam requirements/recommendations for international students: Required—TOEFL (minimum score 550 paper-based; 88 iBT), IELTS (minimum score 6.5), PTE. *Application deadline:* For fall admission, 2/15 for domestic and international students. Applications are processed on a rolling basis. Electronic applications accepted. *Financial support:* Fellowships, research assistantships, teaching assistantships, Federal Work-Study, institutionally sponsored loans, and tuition waivers (full and partial) available. Support available to part-time students. Financial award application deadline: 2/15. *Faculty research:* Diversity, mentoring, executive compensation. *Unit head:* Dr. Brian Till, Dean, 414-288-5724. *Application contact:* Dr. Jeanne Simmons, Associate Professor, 414-288-1458.
Website: http://business.marquette.edu/academics/mshr

Marshall University, Academic Affairs Division, College of Business, Program in Human Resource Management, Huntington, WV 25755. Offers MS. *Program availability:* Part-time, evening/weekend. *Degree requirements:* For master's, comprehensive assessment. *Entrance requirements:* For master's, GMAT or GRE General Test.

Marygrove College, Graduate Division, Program in Human Resource Management, Detroit, MI 48221-2599. Offers MA. *Entrance requirements:* For master's, interview, writing sample.

Marymount University, School of Business Administration, Program in Human Resource Management, Arlington, VA 22207-4299. Offers human resource management (MA, Certificate); organization development (Certificate); MBA/MA. *Program availability:* Part-time, evening/weekend. *Faculty:* 8 full-time (3 women), 2 part-time/adjunct (1 woman). *Students:* 11 full-time (8 women), 34 part-time (30 women); includes 22 minority (10 Black or African American, non-Hispanic/Latino; 2 Asian, non-Hispanic/Latino; 8 Hispanic/Latino; 1 Native Hawaiian or other Pacific Islander, non-Hispanic/Latino; 1 Two or more races, non-Hispanic/Latino), 4 international. Average age 31. 26 applicants, 100% accepted, 14 enrolled. In 2016, 14 master's, 5 other advanced degrees awarded. *Degree requirements:* For master's, thesis or alternative. *Entrance requirements:* For master's, GMAT or GRE General Test, resume; for Certificate, resume. Additional exam requirements/recommendations for international students: Required—TOEFL (minimum score 600 paper-based; 96 iBT), IELTS (minimum score 6.5). *Application deadline:* For fall admission, 7/16 priority date for domestic and international students; for spring admission, 11/16 priority date for domestic and international students; for summer admission, 4/16 for domestic and international students. Applications are processed on a rolling basis. Application fee: $40. Electronic applications accepted. *Expenses:* $960 per credit hour. *Financial support:* In 2016–17, 7 students received support, including 2 research assistantships with tuition reimbursements available, 1 teaching assistantship with tuition reimbursement available; career-related internships or fieldwork, Federal Work-Study, scholarships/grants, and unspecified assistantships also available. Support available to part-time students. Financial award applicants required to submit FAFSA. *Unit head:* Dr. Virginia Bianco-Mathis, Chair/Director, 703-284-5957, Fax: 703-527-3830, E-mail: virginia.bianco-mathis@marymount.edu. *Application contact:* Francesca Reed, Director, Graduate Admissions, 703-284-5901, Fax: 703-527-3815, E-mail: grad.admissions@marymount.edu.
Website: http://www.marymount.edu/Academics/School-of-Business-Administration/Graduate-Programs/Human-Resource-Management-(M-A-)

Maryville University of Saint Louis, The John E. Simon School of Business, St. Louis, MO 63141-7299. Offers accounting (MBA, Certificate); business studies (Certificate); cyber security (MBA); cybersecurity (Certificate); financial services (MBA, Certificate); healthcare practice management (MBA, Certificate); human resource management (MBA); information technology (MBA, Certificate); management (MBA, Certificate); management and leadership (MA); marketing (MBA, Certificate); project management (MBA); sport business management (MBA); supply chain management/logistics (MBA). *Accreditation:* ACBSP. *Program availability:* Part-time, evening/weekend, 100% online, blended/hybrid learning. *Faculty:* 7 full-time (3 women), 34 part-time/adjunct (9 women). *Students:* 84 full-time (40 women), 223 part-time (118 women); includes 67 minority (40 Black or African American, non-Hispanic/Latino; 2 American Indian or Alaska Native, non-Hispanic/Latino; 8 Asian, non-Hispanic/Latino; 12 Hispanic/Latino; 1 Native Hawaiian or other Pacific Islander, non-Hispanic/Latino; 4 Two or more races, non-Hispanic/Latino), 15 international. Average age 32. In 2016, 67 master's awarded. *Entrance requirements:* Additional exam requirements/recommendations for international students: Required—TOEFL (minimum score 563 paper-based; 85 iBT). *Application deadline:* Applications are processed on a rolling basis. Electronic applications accepted. *Expenses:* $650 per credit hour. *Financial support:* Career-related internships or fieldwork, Federal Work-Study, tuition waivers (partial), and campus employment available. Financial award application deadline: 3/1; financial award applicants required to submit FAFSA. *Faculty research:* Global business, e-marketing, strategic planning, interpersonal management skills, financial analysis. *Unit head:* Pam Horwitz, Interim Dean, 314-529-9680, Fax: 314-529-9975. *Application contact:* Dustin Loeffler, Director for Graduate Studies in Business, 314-529-9571, Fax: 314-529-9975, E-mail: dloeffler@maryville.edu.
Website: http://www.maryville.edu/bu/business-administration-masters/

McKendree University, Graduate Programs, Master of Business Administration Program, Lebanon, IL 62254-1299. Offers business administration (MBA); human resource management (MBA); international business (MBA). *Program availability:* Part-time, evening/weekend, online learning. *Entrance requirements:* For master's, official transcripts from all institutions attended, essay, minimum GPA of 3.0, three references, resume. Additional exam requirements/recommendations for international students: Required—TOEFL. Electronic applications accepted.

McMaster University, School of Graduate Studies, DeGroote School of Business, Program in Human Resources and Management, Hamilton, ON L8S 4M2, Canada. Offers MBA, PhD. *Program availability:* Part-time. *Degree requirements:* For doctorate, comprehensive exam, thesis/dissertation. *Entrance requirements:* For master's, GMAT; for doctorate, GMAT or GRE, master's degree, minimum B+ average. Additional exam requirements/recommendations for international students: Required—TOEFL (minimum score 580 paper-based). *Faculty research:* Leadership, occupational mental health, work attitudes, human resources recruitment, change and stress management strategies.

Mercy College, School of Business, Program in Human Resource Management, Dobbs Ferry, NY 10522-1189. Offers MS. *Program availability:* Part-time, evening/weekend, 100% online, blended/hybrid learning. *Students:* 36 full-time (29 women), 16 part-time (all women); includes 37 minority (13 Black or African American, non-Hispanic/Latino; 1 American Indian or Alaska Native, non-Hispanic/Latino; 2 Asian, non-Hispanic/Latino; 20 Hispanic/Latino; 1 Two or more races, non-Hispanic/Latino), 4 international. Average age 32. 58 applicants, 79% accepted, 22 enrolled. In 2016, 40 master's awarded. *Entrance requirements:* For master's, interview, two letters of reference, undergraduate transcripts. Additional exam requirements/recommendations for international students: Required—TOEFL (minimum score 600 paper-based; 100 iBT), IELTS (minimum score 8). *Application deadline:* For fall admission, 8/1 for international students. Applications are processed on a rolling basis. Application fee: $40. Electronic applications accepted. *Expenses:* Contact institution. *Financial support:* Career-related internships or fieldwork, Federal Work-Study, scholarships/grants, and unspecified assistantships available. Support available to part-time students. Financial award applicants required to submit FAFSA. *Unit head:* Ed Weis, Dean, School of Business, 914-674-7490, E-mail: eweis@mercy.edu. *Application contact:* Allison Gurdineer, Senior Director of Admissions, 877-637-2946, Fax: 914-674-7382, E-mail: admissions@mercy.edu.
Website: https://www.mercy.edu/degrees-programs/ms-human-resource-management

Mercyhurst University, Graduate Studies, Program in Organizational Leadership, Erie, PA 16546. Offers accounting (MS); higher education administration (MS); human resources (MS); organizational leadership (MS, Certificate); sports leadership (MS); strategy and innovation (MS). *Program availability:* Part-time, evening/weekend. *Degree requirements:* For master's, thesis. *Entrance requirements:* For master's, GRE General Test or MAT, interview, resume, essay, three professional references, transcripts. Additional exam requirements/recommendations for international students: Required—TOEFL (minimum score 80 iBT), IELTS (minimum score 6.5). Electronic applications accepted. *Faculty research:* Leadership training, organizational communication, leadership pedagogy.

Michigan State University, The Graduate School, College of Social Science, School of Labor and Industrial Relations, East Lansing, MI 48824. Offers human resources and labor relations (MLRHR); industrial relations and human resources (PhD). *Entrance requirements:* Additional exam requirements/recommendations for international students: Required—TOEFL.

Michigan State University, The Graduate School, Eli Broad College of Business, Program in Business Administration, East Lansing, MI 48224. Offers finance (MBA); human resource management (MBA); integrative management (MBA); marketing (MBA); supply chain management (MBA). MBA in integrative management is through Weekend MBA Program; other 4 concentrations are through Full-Time MBA Program. *Program availability:* Evening/weekend. *Degree requirements:* For master's, enrichment experience. *Entrance requirements:* For master's, GMAT or GRE, 4-year bachelor's degree; resume; work experience (minimum of 5 years for Weekend MBA); 2-3 personal essays; 2 letters of recommendation; personal interview. Additional exam requirements/recommendations for international students: Required—PTE (minimum score 70), TOEFL (minimum score 100 iBT) or IELTS (minimum score 7) for full-time MBA applicants. Electronic applications accepted. *Expenses:* Contact institution.

Middle Tennessee State University, College of Graduate Studies, University College, Murfreesboro, TN 37132. Offers advanced studies in teaching and learning (M Ed); human resources leadership (MPS); nursing administration (MSN); nursing education (MSN); strategic leadership (MPS); training and development (MPS). *Program availability:* Part-time, evening/weekend, online learning. *Entrance requirements:* Additional exam requirements/recommendations for international students: Required—TOEFL (minimum score 525 paper-based; 71 iBT) or IELTS (minimum score 6).

Millennia Atlantic University, Graduate Programs, Doral, FL 33178. Offers accounting (MBA); business administration (MBA); health information management (MS); human resource management (MA). *Program availability:* Online learning.

Misericordia University, College of Business, Master of Business Administration Program, Dallas, PA 18612-1098. Offers accounting (MBA); healthcare management (MBA); human resources (MBA); management (MBA); sport management (MBA). *Program availability:* Part-time, evening/weekend, online learning. *Entrance requirements:* For master's, GMAT, MAT, GRE (50th percentile or higher), or minimum undergraduate GPA of 3.0, interview. Additional exam requirements/recommendations for international students: Required—TOEFL. Electronic applications accepted. Application fee is waived when completed online.

Misericordia University, College of Business, Program in Organizational Management, Dallas, PA 18612-1098. Offers healthcare management (MS); human resource management (MS); information technology management (MS); management (MS); not-for-profit management (MS). *Program availability:* Part-time, evening/weekend, online learning. *Entrance requirements:* For master's, GRE General Test, MAT (35th percentile or higher), or minimum undergraduate GPA of 3.0. Additional exam requirements/recommendations for international students: Required—TOEFL. Electronic applications accepted. Application fee is waived when completed online. *Expenses:* Contact institution.

Monmouth University, Graduate Studies, Department of Communication, West Long Branch, NJ 07764-1898. Offers corporate and public communication (MA); human resources management and communication (Certificate); public service communication specialist (Certificate); strategic public relations and new media (Certificate). *Program availability:* Part-time, evening/weekend, online learning. *Faculty:* 4 full-time (3 women), 2 part-time/adjunct (both women). *Students:* 11 full-time (9 women), 23 part-time (15 women); includes 8 minority (4 Black or African American, non-Hispanic/Latino; 2 Asian, non-Hispanic/Latino; 2 Hispanic/Latino), 1 international. Average age 27. 27 applicants, 7% accepted, 16 enrolled. In 2016, 8 master's, 2 other advanced degrees awarded. Terminal master's awarded for partial completion of doctoral program. *Degree requirements:* For master's, comprehensive exam (for some programs), thesis (for some programs), project. *Entrance requirements:* For master's, GRE, baccalaureate degree with minimum GPA of 3.0 in major, 2.75 overall; two letters of recommendation; personal essay (750 words or less describing preparation for study and personal objectives); digital or hard copy portfolio of select samples of work including a writing sample; resume. Additional exam requirements/recommendations for international students: Required—TOEFL (minimum score 550 paper-based; 79 iBT), IELTS (minimum score 6), Michigan English Language Assessment Battery (minimum score 77). *Application deadline:* For fall admission, 7/15 priority date for domestic students, 6/1 for international students; for spring admission, 12/1 priority date for domestic students, 11/1 for international students; for summer admission, 5/1 for domestic students. Applications are processed on a rolling basis. Application fee: $50. Electronic applications accepted. *Expenses: Tuition, area resident:* Full-time $19,764; part-time $1098 per credit hour. *Required fees:* $175 per semester. Tuition and fees vary according to program. *Financial support:* In 2016–17, 41 students received support, including 23 fellowships (averaging $2,061 per year), 13 teaching assistantships with full and partial tuition reimbursements available (averaging $5,746 per year); research assistantships, institutionally sponsored loans, scholarships/grants, and unspecified assistantships also available. Support available to part-time students. Financial award application deadline: 2/1; financial award applicants required to submit FAFSA. *Faculty research:* Service-learning, history of television, feminism and the media, executive communication, public relations pedagogy. *Unit head:* Dr. Deanna Shoemaker, Program Director, 732-263-5194, Fax: 732-571-3609, E-mail: dshoemak@monmouth.edu. *Application contact:* Andrea Thompson, Graduate Admission Counselor, 732-571-3452, Fax: 732-263-5123, E-mail: gradadm@monmouth.edu.
Website: http://www.monmouth.edu/cpc

Monroe College, King Graduate School, Bronx, NY 10468. Offers accounting (MS); business administration (MBA), including entrepreneurship, finance, general business administration, healthcare management, human resources, information technology, marketing; computer science (MS); criminal justice (MS); hospitality management (MS); public health (MPH), including biostatistics and epidemiology, community health, health administration and leadership. *Program availability:* Online learning. Application fee: $50.
Website: https://www.monroecollege.edu/Degrees/King-Graduate-School/

Moravian College, Graduate and Continuing Studies, Business and Management Programs, Bethlehem, PA 18018-6650. Offers accounting (MBA); business analytics (MBA); general management (MBA); health administration (MHA); healthcare management (MBA); human resource management (MBA); leadership (MSHRM); learning and performance management (MSHRM); supply chain management (MBA). *Program availability:* Part-time, evening/weekend. *Faculty:* 4 full-time (1 woman), 9 part-time/adjunct (4 women). *Students:* 14 full-time (7 women), 88 part-time (46 women); includes 17 minority (7 Black or African American, non-Hispanic/Latino; 1 American Indian or Alaska Native, non-Hispanic/Latino; 3 Asian, non-Hispanic/Latino; 6 Hispanic/Latino), 1 international. Average age 33. 25 applicants, 92% accepted, 18 enrolled. In 2016, 11 master's awarded. *Entrance requirements:* For master's, current resume, offical transcripts, 2 letters of recommendation. Additional exam requirements/recommendations for international students: Required—TOEFL (minimum score 550 paper-based), IELTS (minimum score 6.5). *Application deadline:* For fall admission, 8/1 priority date for domestic and international students; for spring admission, 1/1 priority date for domestic and international students; for summer admission, 5/1 priority date for domestic and international students. Applications are processed on a rolling basis. Electronic applications accepted. *Expenses: Tuition:* Full-time $2619. Tuition and fees vary according to course load and program. *Financial support:* Applicants required to submit FAFSA. *Faculty research:* Leadership, change management, human resources. *Unit head:* Dr. Liz Kleintop, Associate Chair of Graduate Business, 610-861-1400, Fax: 610-861-1466, E-mail: mba@moravian.edu. *Application contact:* Kristy Sullivan, Director of Student Recruitment Operations, 610-861-1400, Fax: 610-861-1466, E-mail: graduate@moravian.edu.
Website: https://www.moravian.edu/graduate

Mount Ida College, Program in Management, Newton, MA 02459-3310. Offers healthcare management (MSM); human resource management (MSM); interior architecture (MSM); leadership in sport (MSM); management (MSM). *Program availability:* Part-time, evening/weekend, online learning. *Entrance requirements:* For master's, resume, undergraduate transcripts, letters of reference, personal essay. Additional exam requirements/recommendations for international students: Required—TOEFL (minimum score 550 paper-based; 79 iBT); Recommended—IELTS (minimum score 5.5). Electronic applications accepted. *Expenses:* Contact institution.

Mount Mercy University, Program in Business Administration, Cedar Rapids, IA 52402-4797. Offers human resource (MBA); quality management (MBA). *Program availability:* Evening/weekend. *Entrance requirements:* For master's, minimum cumulative GPA of 3.0, 2 letters of recommendation, resume. Additional exam requirements/recommendations for international students: Required—TOEFL (minimum score 570 paper-based; 88 iBT). Electronic applications accepted.

National Louis University, College of Management and Business, Chicago, IL 60603. Offers business administration (MBA); human resource management and development (MS); management (MS). *Program availability:* Part-time, evening/weekend. *Entrance requirements:* For master's, college-administered critical thinking and writing skills test, minimum GPA of 3.0, resume, 3 references. Additional exam requirements/recommendations for international students: Required—TOEFL (minimum score 550 paper-based; 79 iBT).

National University, Academic Affairs, School of Professional Studies, La Jolla, CA 92037-1011. Offers criminal justice (MCJ); digital cinema (MFA); digital journalism (MA); juvenile justice (MS); public administration (MPA), including human resource management. *Program availability:* Part-time, evening/weekend, 100% online, blended/hybrid learning. *Faculty:* 21 full-time (8 women), 35 part-time/adjunct (9 women). *Students:* 280 full-time (155 women), 100 part-time (54 women); includes 226 minority (76 Black or African American, non-Hispanic/Latino; 1 American Indian or Alaska Native, non-Hispanic/Latino; 27 Asian, non-Hispanic/Latino; 102 Hispanic/Latino; 3 Native Hawaiian or other Pacific Islander, non-Hispanic/Latino; 17 Two or more races, non-Hispanic/Latino), 3 international. Average age 37. In 2016, 21 master's awarded. *Degree requirements:* For master's, thesis (for some programs). *Entrance requirements:* For master's, interview, minimum GPA of 2.5. Additional exam requirements/recommendations for international students: Required—TOEFL (minimum score 550 paper-based; 79 iBT), IELTS (minimum score 6). *Application deadline:* Applications are processed on a rolling basis. Application fee: $60 ($65 for international students). Electronic applications accepted. *Financial support:* Career-related internships or fieldwork, institutionally sponsored loans, scholarships/grants, and tuition waivers (partial) available. Support available to part-time students. Financial award application deadline: 6/30; financial award applicants required to submit FAFSA. *Unit head:* School of Professional Studies, 800-628-8648, E-mail: sops@nu.edu. *Application contact:* Brandon Jouganatos, Vice President for Enrollment Services, 800-628-8648, E-mail: advisor@nu.edu.
Website: http://www.nu.edu/OurPrograms/School-of-Professional-Studies.html

Nazareth College of Rochester, Graduate Studies, Department of Business, Program in Human Resource Management, Rochester, NY 14618. Offers MS. *Program availability:* Part-time, evening/weekend. *Students:* 14 full-time (9 women), 63 part-time (43 women); includes 13 minority (8 Black or African American, non-Hispanic/Latino; 4 Asian, non-Hispanic/Latino; 1 Two or more races, non-Hispanic/Latino). Average age 31. 50 applicants, 72% accepted, 29 enrolled. *Entrance requirements:* For master's, minimum GPA of 3.0. Additional exam requirements/recommendations for international students: Required—TOEFL (minimum score 550 paper-based, 79 iBT) or IELTS (6.5). *Application deadline:* For fall admission, 8/1 for domestic students; for spring admission, 11/1 for domestic students. Applications are processed on a rolling basis. Electronic applications accepted. *Expenses: Tuition:* Part-time $880 per credit hour. Part-time tuition and fees vary according to course load, degree level and program. *Financial support:* Unspecified assistantships available. Financial award application deadline: 3/1; financial award applicants required to submit FAFSA. *Unit head:* Albert Cabral, Program Director, 585-389-2395, E-mail: acabral8@naz.edu. *Application contact:* Judith Baker, Director, Transfer and Graduate Admissions, 585-531-1154, Fax: 585-389-2826, E-mail: gradadmissions@naz.edu.

New Mexico Highlands University, Graduate Studies, School of Business, Media and Technology, Las Vegas, NM 87701. Offers business administration (MBA), including human resource management, international business, management; media arts and technology (MA), including media arts and computer science. *Accreditation:* ACBSP. *Degree requirements:* For master's, comprehensive exam, thesis or alternative. *Entrance requirements:* For master's, minimum undergraduate GPA of 3.0. Additional exam requirements/recommendations for international students: Required—TOEFL (minimum score 540 paper-based). *Faculty research:* Real estate valuation, studying expert judgments in complex accounting, decision environments, green marketing, environmentalism, marketing research methodology.

New York Institute of Technology, School of Management, Department of Human Resource Management Studies, Old Westbury, NY 11568-8000. Offers human resource management (Advanced Certificate); human resource management and labor relations (MS). *Program availability:* Part-time, evening/weekend. *Faculty:* 5 full-time (1 woman), 4 part-time/adjunct (1 woman). *Students:* 33 full-time (27 women), 23 part-time (22 women); includes 21 minority (6 Black or African American, non-Hispanic/Latino; 8 Asian, non-Hispanic/Latino; 6 Hispanic/Latino; 1 Native Hawaiian or other Pacific Islander, non-Hispanic/Latino), 20 international. Average age 28. 69 applicants, 71% accepted, 20 enrolled. In 2016, 22 master's, 1 other advanced degree awarded. *Degree requirements:* For master's, seminar and comprehensive exam, or thesis. *Entrance requirements:* For master's and Advanced Certificate, bachelor's degree; minimum undergraduate GPA of 3.0. Additional exam requirements/recommendations for international students: Required—TOEFL (minimum score 79 iBT), IELTS (minimum score 6). *Application deadline:* Applications are processed on a rolling basis. Application fee: $50. Electronic applications accepted. *Expenses:* $1,215 per credit. *Financial support:* Career-related internships or fieldwork, Federal Work-Study, scholarships/grants, tuition waivers (full and partial), and unspecified assistantships available. Support available to part-time students. Financial award application deadline: 3/1; financial award applicants required to submit FAFSA. *Faculty research:* Conflict resolution, adapting human resource practices to the needs of a global workforce, the effect of leadership styles and human resource practices on employee productivity, human resource management practices as a source of competitive advantage. *Unit head:* Dr. Maya Kroumova, Chairperson, 212-261-1667, Fax: 516-686-7425, E-mail: mkroumov@nyit.edu. *Application contact:* Alice Dolitsky, Director, Graduate Admissions, 516-686-7520, Fax: 516-686-1116, E-mail: nyitgrad@nyit.edu.
Website: http://www.nyit.edu/degrees/human_resources_management_labor_relations_ms

New York University, Polytechnic School of Engineering, Department of Technology Management, New York, NY 10012-1019. Offers construction management (Advanced Certificate); electronic business management (Advanced Certificate); entrepreneurship (Advanced Certificate); human resources management (Advanced Certificate); industrial engineering (MS); information management (Advanced Certificate); management (MS); management of technology (MS); manufacturing engineering (MS); organizational behavior (MS, Advanced Certificate); project management (Advanced Certificate); technology management (MBA, PhD, Advanced Certificate); telecommunications management (Advanced Certificate). *Program availability:* Part-time, evening/weekend. *Degree requirements:* For master's, comprehensive exam (for some programs), thesis (for some programs); for doctorate, comprehensive exam, thesis/dissertation. *Entrance requirements:* For master's, GMAT, minimum B average in undergraduate course work. Additional exam requirements/recommendations for international students: Required—TOEFL (minimum score 550 paper-based; 80 iBT); Recommended—IELTS (minimum score 6.5). Electronic applications accepted. *Faculty research:* Global innovation and research and development strategy, managing emerging technologies, technology and development, service design and innovation, tech entrepreneurship and commercialization, sustainable and clean-tech innovation, impacts of information technology upon individuals, organizations and society.

New York University, School of Continuing and Professional Studies, Division of Programs in Business, Program in Leadership and Human Capital Management, New York, NY 10012-1019. Offers benefits and compensation (Advanced Certificate); human resource management (Advanced Certificate); human resource management and development (MS), including global talent management, human resource management, organizational effectiveness; organizational and executive coaching (Advanced Certificate). *Program availability:* Part-time, evening/weekend, online learning. *Degree requirements:* For master's, thesis. *Entrance requirements:* For master's, GRE or GMAT (only upon request), bachelor's degree, resume with relevant professional work, internship or volunteer experience, two letters of recommendation, statement of purpose. Additional exam requirements/recommendations for international students: Required—TOEFL (minimum score 600 paper-based; 100 iBT), IELTS (minimum score 7). Electronic applications accepted.

Niagara University, Graduate Division of Business Administration, Niagara University, NY 14109. Offers accounting (MBA); business administration (MBA); finance (MBA, MS); financial planning (MBA); healthcare administration (MBA, MHA); human

resources (MBA); international business (MBA); marketing (MBA); professional accountancy (MBA); strategic management (MBA); supply chain management (MBA). *Accreditation:* AACSB. *Program availability:* Part-time, evening/weekend. *Students:* 172 full-time (69 women), 65 part-time (36 women); includes 25 minority (4 Black or African American, non-Hispanic/Latino; 7 Asian, non-Hispanic/Latino; 7 Hispanic/Latino; 1 Native Hawaiian or other Pacific Islander, non-Hispanic/Latino; 6 Two or more races, non-Hispanic/Latino), 76 international. Average age 27. In 2016, 107 master's awarded. *Entrance requirements:* For master's, GMAT. Additional exam requirements/recommendations for international students: Required—TOEFL (minimum score 550 paper-based; 79 iBT), IELTS (minimum score 6). *Application deadline:* For fall admission, 8/1 for domestic students; for spring admission, 11/1 for domestic students. Applications are processed on a rolling basis. Electronic applications accepted. *Expenses:* $870 per credit hour. *Financial support:* Fellowships, research assistantships, career-related internships or fieldwork, and Federal Work-Study available. Support available to part-time students. Financial award application deadline: 4/15; financial award applicants required to submit FAFSA. *Faculty research:* Capital flows, Federal Reserve policy, human resource management, public policy, issues in marketing, auctions, economics of information, risk and capital markets, management strategy, consumer behavior, Internet and social media marketing. *Unit head:* Dr. Paul Richardson, MBA Director/Chair of the Marketing Department, 716-286-8169, Fax: 716-286-8206, E-mail: psr@niagara.edu. *Application contact:* Evan Pierce, Associate Director for Graduate Recruitment, 716-286-8769, Fax: 716-286-8170, E-mail: epierce@niagara.edu.
Website: http://mba.niagara.edu

North Carolina Agricultural and Technical State University, School of Graduate Studies, School of Business and Economics, Greensboro, NC 27411. Offers accounting (MBA); business education (MAT); human resources management (MBA); supply chain systems (MBA).

North Central College, School of Graduate and Professional Studies, Program in Business Administration, Naperville, IL 60566-7063. Offers change management (MBA); finance (MBA); human resource management (MBA); management (MBA). *Program availability:* Part-time, evening/weekend. *Faculty:* 15 full-time (9 women), 13 part-time/adjunct (5 women). *Students:* 30 full-time (14 women), 46 part-time (22 women); includes 11 minority (4 Black or African American, non-Hispanic/Latino; 6 Hispanic/Latino; 1 Two or more races, non-Hispanic/Latino), 6 international. Average age 29. 104 applicants, 50% accepted, 31 enrolled. In 2016, 45 master's awarded. *Degree requirements:* For master's, thesis optional, project. *Entrance requirements:* For master's, interview. Additional exam requirements/recommendations for international students: Required—TOEFL (minimum score 550 paper-based; 80 iBT), IELTS (minimum score 6.5). *Application deadline:* For fall admission, 8/15 for domestic students, 7/15 for international students; for winter admission, 12/1 for domestic students, 11/1 for international students; for spring admission, 2/1 for domestic students, 12/1 for international students. Applications are processed on a rolling basis. Application fee: $25. Electronic applications accepted. Application fee is waived when completed online. *Expenses:* Contact institution. *Financial support:* Scholarships/grants available. Support available to part-time students. Financial award applicants required to submit FAFSA. *Unit head:* Dr. Mary Galvan, Chair of Department of Management and Marketing, 630-637-5473, E-mail: mtgalvan@noctrl.edu. *Application contact:* Wendy Kulpinski, Director of Graduate and Continuing Education Admission, 630-637-5808, Fax: 630-637-5844, E-mail: wekulpinski@noctrl.edu.

Northern Michigan University, Office of Graduate Education and Research, College of Health Sciences and Professional Studies, School of Education, Leadership and Public Service, Marquette, MI 49855-5301. Offers administration and supervision (MAE); elementary education (MAE); higher education in student affairs (MA); instruction (MAE); learning disabilities (MAE); public administration (MPA), including criminal justice administration, human resource administration, public administration, public management, state and local government; reading education (MAE), including reading, reading specialist; science education (MS); secondary education (MAE). *Accreditation:* TEAC. *Program availability:* Part-time, online learning. *Degree requirements:* For master's, thesis (for some programs). *Entrance requirements:* For master's, minimum GPA of 3.0. Additional exam requirements/recommendations for international students: Required—TOEFL (minimum score 550 paper-based; 79 iBT), IELTS (minimum score 6.5). Electronic applications accepted.

North Greenville University, T. Walter Brashier Graduate School, Greer, SC 29651. Offers Christian ministry (MCM, D Min); education (M Ed, MAT); financial planning (MBA); human resources (MBA). *Program availability:* Part-time, evening/weekend, online learning. *Degree requirements:* For master's, comprehensive exam (for some programs), thesis or alternative, capstone course. *Entrance requirements:* For master's, minimum GPA of 2.25 overall, 2.5 in major; for doctorate, MAT. Additional exam requirements/recommendations for international students: Required—TOEFL (minimum score 550 paper-based). Electronic applications accepted. *Faculty research:* Organizational behavior, church growth, homiletics, human resources, business strategy.

Northwestern University, The Graduate School, Kellogg School of Management, Management Programs, Evanston, IL 60208. Offers accounting information and management (MBA, PhD); analytical finance (MBA); business administration (MBA); decision sciences (MBA); entrepreneurship and innovation (MBA); finance (MBA, PhD); health enterprise management (MBA); human resources management (MBA); international business (MBA); management and organizations (MBA, PhD); management and organizations and sociology (PhD); management and strategy (MBA); management studies (MS); managerial analytics (MBA); managerial economics (MBA); managerial economics and strategy (PhD); marketing (MBA, PhD); marketing management (MBA); media management (MBA); operations management (MBA, PhD); real estate (MBA); social enterprise at Kellogg (MBA); JD/MBA. *Program availability:* Part-time, evening/weekend. Terminal master's awarded for partial completion of doctoral program. *Degree requirements:* For doctorate, thesis/dissertation, 2 years of coursework, qualifying (field) exam and candidacy, summer research papers and presentations to faculty, proposal defense, final exam/defense. *Entrance requirements:* For master's, GMAT, GRE, interview, 2 letters of recommendation, college transcripts, resume, essays, Kellogg honor code; for doctorate, GMAT, GRE, statement of purpose, transcripts, 2 letters of recommendation, resume, interview. Additional exam requirements/recommendations for international students: Required—TOEFL, IELTS. Electronic applications accepted. *Expenses:* Contact institution. *Faculty research:* Business cycles and international finance, health policy, networks, non-market strategy, consumer psychology.

Northwest Missouri State University, Graduate School, Melvin and Valorie Booth College of Business and Professional Studies, Maryville, MO 64468-6001. Offers agricultural economics (MBA); general management (MBA); human resource management (MBA); marketing (MBA). *Program availability:* Part-time. *Students:* 50 full-time (18 women), 50 part-time (27 women); includes 10 minority (5 Black or African American, non-Hispanic/Latino; 2 Asian, non-Hispanic/Latino; 3 Hispanic/Latino), 16 international. In 2016, 55 master's awarded. *Degree requirements:* For master's, comprehensive exam. *Entrance requirements:* For master's, GMAT, GRE, minimum GPA of 2.5. Additional exam requirements/recommendations for international students: Required—TOEFL (minimum score 550 paper-based). *Application deadline:* For fall admission, 7/1 for domestic and international students; for spring admission, 11/15 for domestic and international students; for summer admission, 4/1 for domestic and international students. Applications are processed on a rolling basis. Application fee: $0 ($50 for international students). Electronic applications accepted. *Expenses:* Tuition, state resident: full-time $3447; part-time $383 per credit hour. Tuition, nonresident: full-time $5724; part-time $636 per credit hour. *Required fees:* $130 per credit hour. *Financial support:* Research assistantships with full tuition reimbursements, teaching assistantships with full tuition reimbursements, career-related internships or fieldwork, and administrative assistantships, tutorial assistantships available. Financial award application deadline: 4/1; financial award applicants required to submit FAFSA. *Unit head:* Dr. Gregory Haddock, Dean of Graduate School, 660-562-1145, Fax: 660-562-1096, E-mail: gradsch@nwmissouri.edu.
Website: http://www.nwmissouri.edu/academics/booth/

Norwich University, College of Graduate and Continuing Studies, Master of Science in Leadership Program, Northfield, VT 05663. Offers leadership (MS), including human resources leadership, leading change management consulting, organizational leadership, public sector/government/military leadership. *Program availability:* Evening/weekend, online only, mostly all online with a week-long residency requirement. *Faculty:* 10 part-time/adjunct (2 women). *Students:* 66 full-time (20 women); includes 13 minority (8 Black or African American, non-Hispanic/Latino; 3 Asian, non-Hispanic/Latino; 1 Hispanic/Latino; 1 Two or more races, non-Hispanic/Latino). Average age 37. 13 applicants, 69% accepted, 6 enrolled. In 2016, 34 master's awarded. *Degree requirements:* For master's, capstone. *Entrance requirements:* For master's, minimum undergraduate GPA of 2.75. Additional exam requirements/recommendations for international students: Required—TOEFL (minimum score 550 paper-based; 80 iBT), IELTS (minimum score 6.5). *Application deadline:* For fall admission, 8/14 for domestic and international students; for winter admission, 11/13 for domestic and international students; for spring admission, 2/13 for domestic and international students; for summer admission, 5/15 for domestic and international students. Electronic applications accepted. *Expenses:* Contact institution. *Financial support:* In 2016–17, 46 students received support. Scholarships/grants available. Financial award application deadline: 8/4; financial award applicants required to submit FAFSA. *Unit head:* Dr. Stacie Morgan, Program Director, 802-485-2866, Fax: 802-485-2533, E-mail: smorgan3@norwich.edu. *Application contact:* Admissions Advisor, 800-460-5597 Ext. 3371, Fax: 802-485-2533, E-mail: msl@online.norwich.edu.
Website: https://online.norwich.edu/degree-programs/masters/master-science-leadership/overview

Notre Dame de Namur University, Division of Academic Affairs, School of Business and Management, Program in Business Administration, Belmont, CA 94002-1908. Offers business administration (MBA); entrepreneurship (MBA); finance (MBA); human resource management (MBA); marketing (MBA); media and promotion (MBA); technology and operations management (MBA). *Accreditation:* ACBSP. *Program availability:* Part-time, evening/weekend. *Entrance requirements:* For master's, minimum GPA of 2.5. Additional exam requirements/recommendations for international students: Required—TOEFL (minimum score 550 paper-based; 79 iBT). Electronic applications accepted.

Notre Dame de Namur University, Division of Academic Affairs, School of Business and Management, Program in Public Administration, Belmont, CA 94002-1908. Offers human resource management (MPA); public administration (MPA); public affairs administration (MPA); social enterprise (MPA). *Program availability:* Part-time, evening/weekend, online learning. *Entrance requirements:* For master's, interview, minimum GPA of 2.5. Additional exam requirements/recommendations for international students: Required—TOEFL (minimum score 550 paper-based; 79 iBT). Electronic applications accepted.

Nova Southeastern University, H. Wayne Huizenga College of Business and Entrepreneurship, Fort Lauderdale, FL 33314-7796. Offers accounting (M Acc); business intelligence/analytics (MBA); entrepreneurship (MBA); finance (MBA); human resource management (MBA); international business (MBA); management (MBA); marketing (MBA); process improvement (MBA); public administration (MPA); real estate development (MS); sport revenue generation (MBA); supply chain management (MBA); taxation (M Tax). *Program availability:* Part-time, evening/weekend, 100% online, blended/hybrid learning. *Faculty:* 65 full-time (26 women), 111 part-time/adjunct (74 women). *Students:* 2,242 full-time (1,400 women), 425 part-time (239 women); includes 1,798 minority (734 Black or African American, non-Hispanic/Latino; 5 American Indian or Alaska Native, non-Hispanic/Latino; 110 Asian, non-Hispanic/Latino; 890 Hispanic/Latino; 2 Native Hawaiian or other Pacific Islander, non-Hispanic/Latino; 57 Two or more races, non-Hispanic/Latino), 255 international. Average age 34. 1,422 applicants, 64% accepted, 672 enrolled. In 2016, 971 master's awarded. *Degree requirements:* For master's, thesis optional. *Entrance requirements:* For master's, GMAT or GRE (depending on undergraduate GPA), official transcripts from all schools attended while in pursuit of bachelor's degree; minimum GPA of 2.5 from regionally-accredited institution. Additional exam requirements/recommendations for international students: Required—TOEFL (minimum score 550 paper-based; 79 iBT), IELTS (minimum score 6), PTE (minimum score 54). *Application deadline:* For fall admission, 8/5 priority date for domestic students, 7/29 priority date for international students; for winter admission, 12/16 priority date for domestic students, 12/9 priority date for international students; for summer admission, 4/21 priority date for domestic and international students. Applications are processed on a rolling basis. Application fee: $50. Electronic applications accepted. *Expenses:* Contact institution. *Financial support:* In 2016–17, 325 students received support. Federal Work-Study and scholarships/grants available. Support available to part-time students. Financial award application deadline: 4/15; financial award applicants required to submit FAFSA. *Faculty research:* Reputation management, call centers, international social capital, corporate earnings guidance, corporate governance. *Unit head:* Dr. J. Preston Jones, Dean, 954-262-5127, E-mail: prestonj@nova.edu. *Application contact:* Zeida Rodriguez, Associate Director of Enrollment Services, 954-262-5163, Fax: 954-262-3822, E-mail: zeida@nova.edu.
Website: http://www.huizenga.nova.edu

Oakland University, Graduate Study and Lifelong Learning, School of Business Administration, Department of Management and Marketing, Rochester, MI 48309-4401. Offers business administration (MBA); entrepreneurship (Certificate); general management (Certificate); human resource management (Certificate); international business (Certificate); management and marketing (EMBA); marketing (Certificate).

Ohio Christian University, Graduate Programs, Circleville, OH 43113-9487. Offers accounting (MBA); business administration (MBA); digital marketing (MBA); finance (MBA); healthcare management (MBA); human resources (MBA); management (MM); organizational leadership (MBA); pastoral care and counseling (MAM); practical theology (MAM).

The Ohio State University, Graduate School, Max M. Fisher College of Business, Program in Human Resource Management, Columbus, OH 43210. Offers human resource management (MHRM, PhD); labor and human resources (PhD). *Program availability:* Part-time. *Faculty:* 21. *Students:* 100 full-time (71 women), 24 part-time (19

women); includes 12 minority (7 Black or African American, non-Hispanic/Latino; 5 Hispanic/Latino), 28 international. Average age 26. In 2016, 44 master's awarded. *Degree requirements:* For doctorate, thesis/dissertation. *Entrance requirements:* For master's and doctorate, GRE General Test or GMAT. Additional exam requirements/recommendations for international students: Required—Michigan English Language Assessment Battery (minimum score 86); Recommended—TOEFL (minimum score 600 paper-based; 100 iBT), IELTS (minimum score 7). *Application deadline:* For fall admission, 11/15 priority date for domestic and international students. Applications are processed on a rolling basis. Application fee: $60 ($70 for international students). Electronic applications accepted. *Financial support:* Fellowships with tuition reimbursements, research assistantships with tuition reimbursements, and teaching assistantships with tuition reimbursements available. *Unit head:* Dr. Bennett J. Tepper, Chair, 614-688-2129, E-mail: tepper.15@osu.edu. *Application contact:* Graduate and Professional Admissions, 614-292-9444, Fax: 614-292-3895, E-mail: gpadmissions@osu.edu.
Website: http://fisher.osu.edu/departments/management-and-hr/

Oklahoma Christian University, Graduate School of Business, Oklahoma City, OK 73136-1100. Offers accounting (M Acc, MBA); financial services (MBA); general business (MBA); health services management (MBA); human resources (MBA); international business (MBA); leadership and organizational development (MBA); marketing (MBA); nonprofit management (MBA); project management (MBA). *Accreditation:* ACBSP. *Program availability:* Part-time, 100% online. *Faculty:* 10 full-time (2 women), 21 part-time/adjunct (2 women). *Students:* 156 full-time (68 women), 137 part-time (73 women). Average age 30. 374 applicants, 213 enrolled. In 2016, 114 master's awarded. *Entrance requirements:* For master's, bachelor's degree. Additional exam requirements/recommendations for international students: Required—TOEFL (minimum score 550 paper-based). Application fee: $25. Electronic applications accepted. *Expenses:* Contact institution. *Unit head:* Dr. Ken Johnson, Chair, 405-425-5567, Fax: 405-425-5585, E-mail: ken.johnson@oc.edu. *Application contact:* Angie Ricketts, Graduate School Admissions Counselor, 405-425-5587, Fax: 405-425-5585, E-mail: angie.ricketts@oc.edu.
Website: http://www.oc.edu/academics/graduate/business/

Ottawa University, Graduate Studies-Arizona, Programs in Business, Ottawa, KS 66067-3399. Offers business administration (MBA); finance (MBA); human resources (MA, MBA); leadership (MBA); marketing (MBA). Programs offered in Mesa, Phoenix, Tempe and West Valley, AZ. *Program availability:* Part-time, evening/weekend, online learning. *Degree requirements:* For master's, thesis or alternative. *Entrance requirements:* For master's, minimum undergraduate GPA of 3.0. Additional exam requirements/recommendations for international students: Required—TOEFL (minimum score 550 paper-based). Electronic applications accepted.

Pace University, Lubin School of Business, Program in Management, New York, NY 10038. Offers change management (MBA); entrepreneurial studies (MBA); entrepreneurship (MS); human resource management (MBA, MS); strategic management (MBA, MS). *Program availability:* Part-time, evening/weekend. *Students:* 68 full-time (32 women), 75 part-time (44 women); includes 50 minority (22 Black or African American, non-Hispanic/Latino; 13 Asian, non-Hispanic/Latino; 12 Hispanic/Latino; 3 Two or more races, non-Hispanic/Latino), 47 international. Average age 30. 171 applicants, 60% accepted, 55 enrolled. In 2016, 69 master's awarded. *Entrance requirements:* For master's, GMAT, GRE (GMAT not required for MS with 3 years of HR experience in a management position), undergraduate degree, transcripts from all accredited colleges/universities attended, two letters of recommendation, resume, personal statement. Additional exam requirements/recommendations for international students: Required—TOEFL (minimum score 90 iBT), IELTS (minimum score 7) or PTE (minimum score 61). *Application deadline:* For fall admission, 8/1 priority date for domestic students, 6/1 for international students; for spring admission, 12/1 for domestic students, 10/1 for international students. Applications are processed on a rolling basis. Application fee: $70. Electronic applications accepted. *Expenses: Tuition:* Part-time $1195 per credit. *Required fees:* $260 per semester. Tuition and fees vary according to degree level, campus/location and program. *Financial support:* Research assistantships, career-related internships or fieldwork, and Federal Work-Study available. Support available to part-time students. Financial award application deadline: 2/15; financial award applicants required to submit FAFSA. *Unit head:* Dr. John C. Byrne, Chairperson, 212-618-6581, E-mail: jbyrne@pace.edu. *Application contact:* Susan Ford-Goldschein, Director of Graduate Admissions, 212-346-1531, Fax: 212-346-1585, E-mail: graduateadmission@pace.edu.
Website: http://www.pace.edu/lubin/management-concentration-mba

Penn State Great Valley, Graduate Studies, Management Division, Malvern, PA 19355-1488. Offers business administration (MBA); cyber security (Certificate); data analytics (Certificate); distributed energy and grid modernization (Certificate); finance (M Fin, Certificate); health sector management (Certificate); human resource management (Certificate); information science (MSIS); leadership development (MLD); new ventures and entrepreneurship (Certificate); professional studies in data analytics (MPS); sustainable management practices (Certificate). *Accreditation:* AACSB. *Unit head:* Dr. James A. Nemes, Chancellor, 610-648-3202, Fax: 610-725-5296. *Application contact:* JoAnn Kelly, Director of Admissions, 610-648-3315, Fax: 610-725-5296, E-mail: jek2@psu.edu.
Website: http://greatvalley.psu.edu/academics/masters-degrees/engineering-management

Penn State Harrisburg, Graduate School, School of Public Affairs, Middletown, PA 17057. Offers criminal justice (MA); health administration (MHA); health administration: long term care (Certificate); homeland security (Certificate); public administration (MPA, PhD); public administration: non-profit administration (Certificate); public budgeting and financial management (Certificate); public sector human resource management (Certificate). *Accreditation:* NASPAA. *Unit head:* Dr. Mukund S. Kulkarni, Chancellor, 717-948-6105, Fax: 717-948-6452. *Application contact:* Robert W. Coffman, Jr., Director of Enrollment Management, Admissions, 717-948-6250, Fax: 717-948-6325, E-mail: hbgadmit@psu.edu.
Website: https://harrisburg.psu.edu/public-affairs

Penn State University Park, Graduate School, College of the Liberal Arts, School of Labor and Employment Relations, University Park, PA 16802. Offers human resources and employment relations (MPS, MS); labor and global workers' rights (MPS). *Unit head:* Dr. Susan Welch, Dean, 814-865-7691, Fax: 814-863-2085. *Application contact:* Lori Hawn, Director, Graduate Student Services, 814-865-1795, Fax: 814-863-4627, E-mail: l-gswww@lists.psu.edu.
Website: http://lser.la.psu.edu/

Pepperdine University, Graziadio School of Business and Management, Full-Time MBA Programs, Malibu, CA 90263. Offers accounting (MS); applied analytics (MS); applied finance (MS); business administration (MBA); global business (MS); human resources (MS); international business administration (MBA); management and leadership (MS); organization development (MS); real estate investment and finance (MS); JD/MBA; MBA/MPP. *Accreditation:* AACSB. *Students:* 472 full-time (239 women), 3 part-time (2 women); includes 424 minority (111 Black or African American, non-Hispanic/Latino; 7 American Indian or Alaska Native, non-Hispanic/Latino; 216 Asian, non-Hispanic/Latino; 88 Hispanic/Latino; 2 Two or more races, non-Hispanic/Latino), 47 international. Average age 25. 1,991 applicants, 59% accepted, 238 enrolled. In 2016, 419 master's awarded. *Entrance requirements:* For master's, GMAT or GRE, two letters of recommendation. Additional exam requirements/recommendations for international students: Required—TOEFL. *Application deadline:* For fall admission, 5/1 for domestic students, 4/1 for international students. Application fee: $75. Electronic applications accepted. *Financial support:* Applicants required to submit FAFSA. *Unit head:* Dr. Michael L. Williams, Associate Dean, 310-506-4112, Fax: 310-506-4126, E-mail: michael.williams@pepperdine.edu.
Website: http://bschool.pepperdine.edu/masters-degree/

Polytechnic University of Puerto Rico, Miami Campus, Graduate School, Miami, FL 33166. Offers accounting (MBA); business administration (MBA); construction management (MEM); environmental management (MEM); finance (MBA); human resources management (MBA); logistics and supply chain management (MBA); management of international enterprises (MBA); manufacturing management (MEM); marketing management (MBA); project management (MBA). *Program availability:* Part-time, evening/weekend, online learning. *Entrance requirements:* For master's, minimum GPA of 3.0. Electronic applications accepted.

Polytechnic University of Puerto Rico, Orlando Campus, Graduate School, Orlando, FL 32825. Offers accounting (MBA); business administration (MBA); construction management (MEM); engineering management (MEM); environmental management (MEM); finance (MBA); human resources management (MBA); management of international enterprises (MBA); management of technology (MBA); manufacturing management (MEM). *Program availability:* Part-time, evening/weekend, online learning. *Entrance requirements:* For master's, minimum GPA of 3.0. Additional exam requirements/recommendations for international students: Recommended—TOEFL. Electronic applications accepted.

Pontifical Catholic University of Puerto Rico, College of Business Administration, Program in Human Resources, Ponce, PR 00717-0777. Offers MBA, Professional Certificate. *Program availability:* Part-time, evening/weekend. *Degree requirements:* For master's, thesis. *Entrance requirements:* For master's, GRE, interview, minimum GPA of 2.75.

Pontificia Universidad Catolica Madre y Maestra, Graduate School, Faculty of Social and Administrative Sciences, Santiago, Dominican Republic. Offers business administration (MBA), including business development, finance, international business, management skills (M Mgmt, MBA), marketing, operations, strategic cost management, strategy, tourist destination planning and management; law (LL M), including civil law, corporate business law, criminal law, international relations, real estate law; management (M Mgmt), including higher financial management, insurance program administration, management skills (M Mgmt, MBA); psychology (MA), including clinical child and adolescent psychology, forensic psychology; strategic human resources (EMBA).

Purdue University, Graduate School, Krannert School of Management, Doctoral Program in Organizational Behavior and Human Resource Management, West Lafayette, IN 47907-2056. Offers PhD. *Degree requirements:* For doctorate, comprehensive exam, thesis/dissertation, dissertation proposal, dissertation defense. *Entrance requirements:* For doctorate, GMAT or GRE, bachelor's degree, two semesters of calculus, one semester each of linear algebra and statistics. Additional exam requirements/recommendations for international students: Required—TOEFL (minimum score 575 paper-based); Recommended—TWE. Electronic applications accepted. *Faculty research:* Human resource management, organizational behavior.

★ **Purdue University,** Graduate School, Krannert School of Management, Master of Science in Human Resource Management Program, West Lafayette, IN 47907. Offers MSHRM. *Faculty:* 129 full-time (28 women), 7 part-time/adjunct (1 woman). *Students:* 50 full-time (33 women); includes 4 minority (2 Black or African American, non-Hispanic/Latino; 1 Asian, non-Hispanic/Latino; 1 Hispanic/Latino), 26 international. Average age 25. 136 applicants, 50% accepted, 25 enrolled. In 2016, 26 master's awarded. *Entrance requirements:* For master's, GMAT or GRE, essays, recommendation letters, work experience/internship, minimum GPA of 3.0, four-year baccalaureate degree. Additional exam requirements/recommendations for international students: Required—TOEFL (minimum score 600 paper-based, 93 iBT), IELTS (minimum score 7.5), or PTE (minimum score 70). *Application deadline:* For fall admission, 11/15 for domestic and international students; for winter admission, 1/15 for domestic and international students; for spring admission, 3/1 for domestic and international students; for summer admission, 5/1 for domestic students. Applications are processed on a rolling basis. Application fee: $60 ($75 for international students). Electronic applications accepted. *Expenses:* Contact institution. *Financial support:* Scholarships/grants and unspecified assistantships available. Financial award applicants required to submit FAFSA. *Faculty research:* Performance periods and the dynamics of the performance-risk relationship, reactions to unfair events in computer-mediated groups: a test of uncertainty management theory, influences on job search self-efficacy of spouses of military personnel; *Faculty publications:* "Cross-Cultural Social Intelligence: An Assessment for Employees Working in Cross-National Contexts", "Will You Trust Your New Boss? The Role of Affective Reactions to Leadership Succession." *Unit head:* Dr. David Hummels, Dean/Professor of Economics, 765-494-4366, E-mail: krannertdean@purdue.edu. *Application contact:* Thomas Bates, Associate Director of Admissions, 765-494-0773, Fax: 765-494-9841, E-mail: krannertmasters@purdue.edu.
Website: http://www.krannert.purdue.edu/masters/programs/mshrm/

See Display on next page and Close-Up on page 389.

Regent's University London, Webster Graduate School, London, United Kingdom. Offers business (MBA); finance (MS); human resources (MA); information technology management (MA); international business (MA); international non-governmental organizations (MA); international relations (MA); management and leadership (MA); marketing (MA). *Program availability:* Part-time.

Regent University, Graduate School, School of Business and Leadership, Virginia Beach, VA 23464-9800. Offers business administration (MBA), including accounting, entrepreneurship, finance and investing, general management, healthcare management (MA, MBA), human resource management, innovation management; leadership (Certificate); organizational leadership (MA, PhD), including ecclesial leadership (PhD), entrepreneurial leadership (PhD), future studies (MA), healthcare management (MA, MBA), human resource development (PhD), interdisciplinary studies (MA), international organizations (MA), leadership coaching and mentoring (MA), not-for-profit management (MA), organizational communication (MA), organizational development consulting (MA); strategic leadership (DSL), including global consulting, leadership coaching, strategic foresight. *Program availability:* Part-time, evening/weekend, 100% online, blended/hybrid learning. *Faculty:* 9 full-time (2 women), 28 part-time/adjunct (10 women). *Students:* 100 full-time (56 women), 1,008 part-time (528 women); includes 562 minority (453 Black or African American, non-Hispanic/Latino; 7 American Indian or Alaska Native, non-Hispanic/Latino; 30 Asian, non-Hispanic/Latino; 51 Hispanic/Latino; 1 Native Hawaiian or other Pacific Islander, non-Hispanic/Latino; 20 Two or more races, non-Hispanic/Latino), 76 international. Average age 40. 1,240 applicants, 45%

accepted, 352 enrolled. In 2016, 95 master's, 71 doctorates awarded. *Degree requirements:* For master's, thesis or alternative, 3-credit hour culminating experience; for doctorate, thesis/dissertation. *Entrance requirements:* For master's, college transcripts, resume, essay; for doctorate, college transcripts, resume, essay, writing sample; for Certificate, writing sample, resume, transcripts. Additional exam requirements/recommendations for international students: Required—TOEFL (minimum score 577 paper-based). *Application deadline:* For fall admission, 5/1 priority date for domestic students; for spring admission, 10/1 priority date for domestic students. Applications are processed on a rolling basis. Application fee: $50. Electronic applications accepted. *Expenses:* Contact institution. *Financial support:* In 2016–17, 631 students received support. Career-related internships or fieldwork, scholarships/grants, and unspecified assistantships available. Support available to part-time students. *Faculty research:* Servant leadership, global business, team effectiveness, technology utilization, leadership development. *Unit head:* Dr. Doris Gomez, Dean, 757-352-4686, Fax: 757-352-4634, E-mail: dorigom@regent.edu. *Application contact:* Heidi Cece, Assistant Vice President of Enrollment Management, 800-373-5504, Fax: 757-352-4381, E-mail: admissions@regent.edu.
Website: http://www.regent.edu/sbl/

Regent University, Graduate School, School of Law, Virginia Beach, VA 23464-9800. Offers American legal studies (LL M); human rights (LL M); law (MA, JD), including business (MA), criminal justice (MA), general legal studies (MA), human resources management (MA), human rights (MA), mediation (MA), national security (MA), non-profit management (MA), regulatory compliance (MA), wealth management and financial planning (MA); JD/MA; JD/MBA. *Accreditation:* ABA. *Program availability:* Part-time, 100% online, blended/hybrid learning. *Faculty:* 20 full-time (6 women), 67 part-time/adjunct (19 women). *Students:* 364 full-time (219 women), 170 part-time (118 women); includes 213 minority (150 Black or African American, non-Hispanic/Latino; 1 American Indian or Alaska Native, non-Hispanic/Latino; 10 Asian, non-Hispanic/Latino; 34 Hispanic/Latino; 1 Native Hawaiian or other Pacific Islander, non-Hispanic/Latino; 17 Two or more races, non-Hispanic/Latino), 87 international. Average age 34. 834 applicants, 45% accepted, 174 enrolled. In 2016, 48 master's, 85 doctorates awarded. *Entrance requirements:* For master's, college transcripts, resume, personal statement; for doctorate, LSAT, minimum undergraduate GPA of 3.0, official transcripts, 2 letters of recommendation, resume, personal statement. Additional exam requirements/recommendations for international students: Required—TOEFL (minimum score 600 paper-based). *Application deadline:* For fall admission, 3/1 for domestic students. Applications are processed on a rolling basis. Application fee: $50. Electronic applications accepted. *Expenses:* $1,140 per credit (for JD); $650 per credit (for MA); $833 per credit (for LL M); $250 technology fee. *Financial support:* In 2016–17, 319 students received support. Career-related internships or fieldwork, scholarships/grants, and unspecified assistantships available. Support available to part-time students. *Faculty research:* Family law, Constitutional law, law and culture, evidence and practice, intellectual property. *Unit head:* Michael Hernandez, Dean, 757-352-4040, Fax: 757-352-4595, E-mail: michher@regent.edu. *Application contact:* Katie Kerley, Director of Law Admissions, 877-267-5072, Fax: 757-352-4139, E-mail: lawschool@regent.edu.
Website: http://www.regent.edu/law/

Regis University, College of Business and Economics, Denver, CO 80221-1099. Offers accounting (MS); executive leadership (Certificate); finance (MS); finance and accounting (MBA); health industry leadership (MBA); human resource management and leadership (MSOL); management (MBA); marketing (MBA); nonprofit leadership (Post-Graduate Certificate); nonprofit management (MNM); nonprofit organizational capacity building (Certificate); operations management (MBA); organizational leadership and management (MSOL); project leadership and management (MS, MSOL); strategic business management (Certificate); strategic human resource integration (Certificate); strategic management (MBA). Programs offered at Colorado Springs Campus, Northwest Denver Campus, Southeast Denver Campus, Fort Collins Campus, Broomfield Campus, Henderson (Nevada) Campus, and Summerlin (Nevada) Campus. *Program availability:* Part-time, evening/weekend, 100% online, blended/hybrid learning. *Faculty:* 15 full-time (5 women), 43 part-time/adjunct (16 women). *Students:* 622 full-time (350 women), 460 part-time (170 women); includes 317 minority (88 Black or African American, non-Hispanic/Latino; 7 American Indian or Alaska Native, non-Hispanic/Latino; 44 Asian, non-Hispanic/Latino; 151 Hispanic/Latino; 1 Native Hawaiian or other Pacific Islander, non-Hispanic/Latino; 26 Two or more races, non-Hispanic/Latino), 44 international. Average age 36. 307 applicants, 73% accepted, 134 enrolled. In 2016, 394 master's awarded. *Degree requirements:* For master's, thesis (for some programs), capstone or final research project. *Entrance requirements:* For master's, official transcript reflecting baccalaureate degree awarded from regionally-accredited college or university, interview, 2 years of full-time related work experience, resume, letters of recommendation. Additional exam requirements/recommendations for international students: Required—TOEFL (minimum score 550 paper-based; 82 iBT). *Application deadline:* For fall admission, 8/15 priority date for domestic students, 8/13 for international students; for winter admission, 10/10 priority date for domestic students, 9/8 for international students; for spring admission, 1/10 priority date for domestic students, 11/17 for international students; for summer admission, 5/1 priority date for domestic students. Applications are processed on a rolling basis. Application fee: $75. Electronic applications accepted. *Expenses:* $780 per credit hour. *Financial support:* Scholarships/grants available. Financial award application deadline: 4/15; financial award applicants required to submit FAFSA. *Faculty research:* Impact of information technology on small business regulation of accounting, international project financing, mineral development, delivery of healthcare to rural indigenous communities. *Unit head:* Dr. Timothy Keane, Academic Dean. *Application contact:* Cate Clark, Director of Admissions, 303-458-4900, Fax: 303-964-5534, E-mail: ruadmissions@regis.edu.
Website: http://www.regis.edu/CBE.aspx

Robert Morris University, School of Business, Moon Township, PA 15108-1189. Offers business administration (MBA); human resource management (MS); taxation (MS); MBA/MS. *Accreditation:* AACSB. *Program availability:* Part-time-only, evening/weekend, 100% online. *Faculty:* 24 full-time (8 women), 4 part-time/adjunct (3 women). *Students:* 148 part-time (64 women); includes 9 minority (3 Black or African American, non-Hispanic/Latino; 6 Asian, non-Hispanic/Latino), 1 international. Average age 27. 147 applicants, 23% accepted, 32 enrolled. In 2016, 96 master's awarded. *Entrance requirements:* For master's, GMAT, letters of recommendation. Additional exam requirements/recommendations for international students: Required—TOEFL (minimum score 550 paper-based; 79 iBT). *Application deadline:* For fall admission, 7/1 priority date for domestic and international students; for spring admission, 11/1 priority date for domestic and international students. Applications are processed on a rolling basis. Application fee: $35. Electronic applications accepted. Application fee is waived when completed online. *Expenses:* $925 per credit. *Financial support:* Institutionally sponsored loans available. Support available to part-time students. Financial award application deadline: 5/1; financial award applicants required to submit FAFSA. *Unit head:* Dr. Michelle L. Patrick, Dean, 412-397-5445, Fax: 412-397-2585, E-mail: patrick@rmu.edu. *Application contact:* E-mail: graduateadmissions@rmu.edu.
Website: http://sbus.rmu.edu

Robert Morris University Illinois, Morris Graduate School of Management, Chicago, IL 60605. Offers accounting (MBA); accounting/finance (MBA); business analytics (MIS); design and media (MM); design management (MM); educational technology (MM); health care administration (MM); higher education administration (MM); human resource management (MBA); information security (MIS); information systems (MBA, MIS); law enforcement administration (MM); management (MBA); management/finance (MBA);

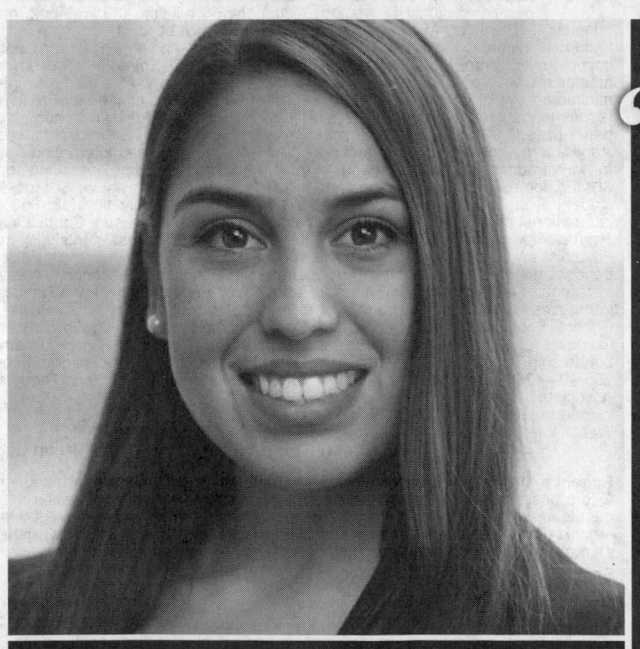

management/human resource management (MBA); mobile computing (MIS); sports administration (MM). *Program availability:* Part-time, evening/weekend. *Faculty:* 4 full-time (1 woman), 25 part-time/adjunct (5 women). *Students:* 196 full-time (98 women), 151 part-time (85 women); includes 200 minority (114 Black or African American, non-Hispanic/Latino; 17 Asian, non-Hispanic/Latino; 67 Hispanic/Latino; 2 Two or more races, non-Hispanic/Latino), 23 international. Average age 33. 174 applicants, 61% accepted, 97 enrolled. In 2016, 190 master's awarded. *Entrance requirements:* For master's, official transcripts and letters of recommendation (for some programs); written personal statement. Additional exam requirements/recommendations for international students: Required—TOEFL (minimum score 550 paper-based). *Application deadline:* Applications are processed on a rolling basis. Application fee: $20 ($100 for international students). Electronic applications accepted. *Expenses: Tuition:* Full-time $16,500; part-time $2750 per course. *Financial support:* In 2016–17, 444 students received support. Federal Work-Study, scholarships/grants, and unspecified assistantships available. Support available to part-time students. Financial award applicants required to submit FAFSA. *Unit head:* Kayed Akkawi, Dean, 312-935-6050, Fax: 312-935-6020, E-mail: kakkawi@robertmorris.edu. *Application contact:* Danielle Naffziger, Vice President of Marketing and Enrollment, 312-935-4812, Fax: 312-935-6020, E-mail: dnaffziger@robertmorris.edu.

Rollins College, Hamilton Holt School, Master of Human Resources Program, Winter Park, FL 32789. Offers MHR. *Program availability:* Part-time, evening/weekend. *Faculty:* 4 full-time (0 women), 1 (woman) part-time/adjunct. *Students:* 4 full-time (2 women), 39 part-time (25 women); includes 12 minority (5 Black or African American, non-Hispanic/Latino; 1 American Indian or Alaska Native, non-Hispanic/Latino; 1 Asian, non-Hispanic/Latino; 4 Hispanic/Latino; 1 Two or more races, non-Hispanic/Latino), 4 international. Average age 32. 21 applicants, 81% accepted, 14 enrolled. In 2016, 23 master's awarded. *Degree requirements:* For master's, thesis optional. *Entrance requirements:* For master's, GMAT or GRE, official transcripts, two letters of recommendation, essay, current resume. Additional exam requirements/recommendations for international students: Required—TOEFL (minimum score 550 paper-based; 80 iBT). *Application deadline:* For fall admission, 4/1 for domestic students; for spring admission, 12/1 for domestic students. Application fee: $50. *Expenses:* $639 per credit hour. *Financial support:* Federal Work-Study, scholarships/grants, and unspecified assistantships available. Support available to part-time students. Financial award applicants required to submit FAFSA. *Unit head:* Dr. Donald Rogers, Faculty Director, 407-646-2348, E-mail: drogers@rollins.edu. *Application contact:* Carmen Rasnick, Graduate Coordinator, 407-646-2653, Fax: 407-646-1551, E-mail: crasnick@rollins.edu.
Website: http://www.rollins.edu/holt/graduate/mhr.html

Roosevelt University, Graduate Division, Walter E. Heller College of Business, Program in Human Resource Management, Chicago, IL 60605. Offers MSHRM. *Students:* 14 full-time (9 women), 56 part-time (47 women); includes 37 minority (16 Black or African American, non-Hispanic/Latino; 4 Asian, non-Hispanic/Latino; 16 Hispanic/Latino; 1 Two or more races, non-Hispanic/Latino), 4 international. Average age 30. 42 applicants, 100% accepted, 20 enrolled. In 2016, 33 master's awarded. Application fee: $40. *Expenses: Tuition, area resident:* Full-time $19,566; part-time $880 per credit hour. *Required fees:* $175 per semester. One-time fee: $200. Part-time tuition and fees vary according to course load, degree level and program. *Unit head:* Ryan Petty, Associate Professor, 312-341-6456. *Application contact:* Angela Ryan, Director of Graduate Enrollment, 877-APPLY RU, Fax: 312-281-3356, E-mail: applyru@roosevelt.edu.
Website: https://www.roosevelt.edu/academics/programs/masters-in-human-resource-management-mshrm

Royal Roads University, Graduate Studies, Applied Leadership and Management Program, Victoria, BC V9B 5Y2, Canada. Offers executive coaching (Graduate Certificate); health systems leadership (Graduate Certificate); project management (Graduate Certificate); public relations management (Graduate Certificate); strategic human resources management (Graduate Certificate).

Royal Roads University, Graduate Studies, Faculty of Management, Victoria, BC V9B 5Y2, Canada. Offers digital technologies management (MBA); executive management (MBA), including global aviation management, knowledge management, leadership; human resources management (MBA). *Program availability:* Online learning. *Degree requirements:* For master's, thesis. *Entrance requirements:* For master's, 5-7 years of related work experience. Additional exam requirements/recommendations for international students: Required—TOEFL (paper-based 570) or IELTS (7) recommended. Electronic applications accepted. *Expenses:* Contact institution. *Faculty research:* Global venture analysis standards; computer assisted venture opportunity screening; teaching philosophies, instructions and methods.

Rutgers University–Newark, Graduate School, Program in Public Administration, Newark, NJ 07102. Offers health care administration (MPA); human resources administration (MPA); public administration (PhD); public management (MPA); public policy analysis (MPA); urban systems and issues (MPA). *Accreditation:* NASPAA (one or more programs are accredited). *Program availability:* Part-time, evening/weekend. *Degree requirements:* For master's, comprehensive exam, thesis or alternative; for doctorate, thesis/dissertation. *Entrance requirements:* For master's, GRE, minimum undergraduate B average; for doctorate, GRE, MPA, minimum B average. Electronic applications accepted. *Faculty research:* Government finance, municipal and state government, public productivity.

Rutgers University–New Brunswick, School of Management and Labor Relations, Program in Human Resource Management, Piscataway, NJ 08854-8097. Offers MHRM. *Program availability:* Part-time, evening/weekend. *Entrance requirements:* For master's, GMAT or GRE General Test, 3 letters of recommendation. Additional exam requirements/recommendations for international students: Required—TOEFL (minimum score 575 paper-based). Electronic applications accepted. *Expenses:* Contact institution. *Faculty research:* Human resource policy and planning, employee ownership and profit sharing, compensation and appraisal of performance, law and public policy, computers and decision making.

Rutgers University–New Brunswick, School of Management and Labor Relations, Program in Industrial Relations and Human Resources, Piscataway, NJ 08854-8097. Offers PhD. *Program availability:* Part-time. *Degree requirements:* For doctorate, comprehensive exam, thesis/dissertation. *Entrance requirements:* For doctorate, GRE or GMAT, 3 letters of recommendation. Additional exam requirements/recommendations for international students: Required—TOEFL (minimum score 575 paper-based; 91 iBT). Electronic applications accepted. *Faculty research:* Strategic human resources, labor relations, organizational change, worker representation.

Sacred Heart University, Graduate Programs, Jack Welch College of Business, Department of Management, Fairfield, CT 06825. Offers administration (MBA); human resource management (MS). *Program availability:* Part-time, evening/weekend. *Faculty:* 9 full-time (4 women), 14 part-time/adjunct (5 women). *Students:* 43 full-time (23 women), 159 part-time (84 women); includes 58 minority (14 Black or African American, non-Hispanic/Latino; 1 American Indian or Alaska Native, non-Hispanic/Latino; 6 Asian, non-Hispanic/Latino; 35 Hispanic/Latino; 2 Two or more races, non-Hispanic/Latino), 13 international. Average age 30. 149 applicants, 72% accepted, 76 enrolled. In 2016, 70 master's awarded. *Degree requirements:* For master's, capstone project. *Entrance requirements:* For master's, GMAT/GRE, bachelor's degree. Additional exam requirements/recommendations for international students: Required—TOEFL (minimum score 570 paper-based, 80 iBT), TWE, or IELTS (6.5); Recommended—TSE. *Application deadline:* Applications are processed on a rolling basis. Application fee: $75. Electronic applications accepted. *Expenses:* $875 per credit. *Financial support:* Applicants required to submit FAFSA. *Unit head:* Michael Carriger, Director of Master's in Human Resource Management Program, 203-396-8252, E-mail: carrigerm@sacredheart.edu. *Application contact:* William Sweeney, Director of Graduate Admissions Operations, 203-365-4827, E-mail: sweeneyw@sacredheart.edu.
Website: http://www.sacredheart.edu/academics/johnfwelchcollegeofbusiness/graduateprogramscertificates/

St. Ambrose University, College of Business, Program in Business Administration, Davenport, IA 52803-2898. Offers business administration (DBA); health care (MBA); human resources (MBA). *Accreditation:* ACBSP. *Program availability:* Part-time, evening/weekend. *Degree requirements:* For master's, comprehensive exam (for some programs), thesis or alternative, capstone seminar; for doctorate, comprehensive exam, thesis/dissertation, oral and written exams. *Entrance requirements:* For master's, GMAT; for doctorate, GMAT, master's degree. Additional exam requirements/recommendations for international students: Required—TOEFL. Electronic applications accepted. *Expenses:* Contact institution.

Saint Francis University, School of Business, Loretto, PA 15940-0600. Offers business administration (MBA); human resource management (MHRM). *Program availability:* Part-time, evening/weekend. *Degree requirements:* For master's, comprehensive exam (for some programs), thesis (for some programs). *Entrance requirements:* For master's, GMAT (waived if undergraduate QPA is 3.3 or above), 2 letters of recommendation, minimum GPA of 2.75, two essays. Additional exam requirements/recommendations for international students: Required—TOEFL (minimum score 550 paper-based; 57 iBT). *Expenses:* Contact institution.

St. Joseph's College, Long Island Campus, Programs in Management, Field in Human Resources Management, Patchogue, NY 11772-2399. Offers MS. *Program availability:* Evening/weekend. *Expenses: Tuition:* Full-time $16,182; part-time $899 per credit. *Required fees:* $440.

St. Joseph's College, New York, Programs in Management, Field in Human Resources Management, Brooklyn, NY 11205-3688. Offers MS. *Program availability:* Part-time, evening/weekend. *Faculty:* 5 part-time/adjunct (4 women). *Students:* 4 full-time (all women), 13 part-time (10 women); includes 11 minority (9 Black or African American, non-Hispanic/Latino; 1 Asian, non-Hispanic/Latino; 1 Hispanic/Latino). Average age 34. 10 applicants, 60% accepted, 4 enrolled. In 2016, 4 master's awarded. *Entrance requirements:* For master's, official transcripts, resume, two letters of reference, verification of employment. Additional exam requirements/recommendations for international students: Required—TOEFL (minimum score 80 iBT). *Application deadline:* Applications are processed on a rolling basis. Application fee: $25. Electronic applications accepted. *Expenses: Tuition:* Full-time $16,182; part-time $899 per credit. *Required fees:* $351. *Financial support:* In 2016–17, 3 students received support. *Unit head:* Charles Pendola, Director and Assistant Professor, 718-687-1297, E-mail: cpendola@sjcny.edu. *Application contact:* John Fitzgerald, Associate Director, Admissions, 718-940-5810, Fax: 718-636-8303, E-mail: jfitzgerald3@sjcny.edu.
Website: https://www.sjcny.edu

Saint Joseph's University, Erivan K. Haub School of Business, MBA Program, Philadelphia, PA 19131-1395. Offers accounting (MBA, Postbaccalaureate Certificate); business intelligence (MBA); finance (MBA); general business (MBA); health and medical services administration (MBA); international business (MBA); international marketing (MBA); managing human capital (MBA); marketing (MBA); DO/MBA. DO/MBA offered jointly with Philadelphia College of Osteopathic Medicine. *Program availability:* Part-time, evening/weekend, 100% online, blended/hybrid learning. *Faculty:* 31 full-time (10 women), 28 part-time/adjunct (7 women). *Students:* 95 full-time (40 women), 348 part-time (137 women); includes 64 minority (29 Black or African American, non-Hispanic/Latino; 17 Asian, non-Hispanic/Latino; 14 Hispanic/Latino; 1 Native Hawaiian or other Pacific Islander, non-Hispanic/Latino; 3 Two or more races, non-Hispanic/Latino), 47 international. Average age 30. 237 applicants, 60% accepted, 76 enrolled. In 2016, 144 master's awarded. *Degree requirements:* For master's and Postbaccalaureate Certificate, minimum GPA of 3.0. *Entrance requirements:* For master's, GMAT or GRE, 2 letters of recommendation, resume, personal statement, official undergraduate and graduate transcripts; for Postbaccalaureate Certificate, official master's-level transcripts. Additional exam requirements/recommendations for international students: Required—TOEFL (minimum score 550 paper-based, 80 iBT), IELTS (minimum score 6.5), or PTE (minimum score 60). *Application deadline:* For fall admission, 7/15 priority date for domestic students, 5/15 priority date for international students; for spring admission, 11/15 priority date for domestic students, 10/15 priority date for international students; for summer admission, 4/15 priority date for domestic students, 2/15 priority date for international students. Applications are processed on a rolling basis. Application fee: $35. Electronic applications accepted. *Expenses:* $1,003 per credit. *Financial support:* In 2016–17, 105 students received support, including 2 research assistantships with partial tuition reimbursements available (averaging $4,000 per year); scholarships/grants and unspecified assistantships also available. Support available to part-time students. Financial award application deadline: 5/1; financial award applicants required to submit FAFSA. *Unit head:* Dr. Patricia Rafferty, Director, 610-660-1318, E-mail: praffert@sju.edu. *Application contact:* Kate Sonstein, Program Manager/Recruiter, 610-660-1693, E-mail: kate.sonstein@sju.edu.
Website: http://www.sju.edu/haubmba

Saint Leo University, Graduate Business Studies, Saint Leo, FL 33574-6665. Offers accounting (M Acc, MBA, Certificate); cybersecurity (MS); health care management (MBA, Certificate); human resource management (MBA, Certificate); information security management (MBA, Certificate); management (MBA, DBA); marketing (MBA, Certificate); marketing research and social media analytics (MBA, Certificate); project management (MBA, Certificate); sport business (MBA); supply chain global integration management (MBA, Certificate). *Accreditation:* ACBSP. *Program availability:* Part-time, evening/weekend, 100% online, blended/hybrid learning. *Faculty:* 53 full-time (18 women), 53 part-time/adjunct (19 women). *Students:* 8 full-time (4 women), 2,001 part-time (1,160 women); includes 928 minority (650 Black or African American, non-Hispanic/Latino; 5 American Indian or Alaska Native, non-Hispanic/Latino; 43 Asian, non-Hispanic/Latino; 193 Hispanic/Latino; 2 Native Hawaiian or other Pacific Islander, non-Hispanic/Latino; 35 Two or more races, non-Hispanic/Latino), 51 international. Average age 37. 922 applicants, 85% accepted, 517 enrolled. In 2016, 874 master's, 17 other advanced degrees awarded. *Degree requirements:* For doctorate, comprehensive exam, thesis/dissertation. *Entrance requirements:* For master's, GMAT (minimum score 500), official transcripts, current resume, 2 professional recommendations, personal statement, bachelor's degree from regionally-accredited university; undergraduate degree in accounting and minimum undergraduate GPA of 3.0 (for M Acc); minimum undergraduate GPA of 3.0 in final 2 years of undergraduate study and 2 years' work experience (for MBA); for doctorate, GMAT (minimum score of 550) if master's GPA is under 3.25, official transcripts, current resume, 2 professional recommendations,

personal statement, master's degree from regionally-accredited university with minimum GPA of 3.25, 3 years' work experience, interview. Additional exam requirements/recommendations for international students: Required—TOEFL (minimum score 550 paper-based; 80 iBT). *Application deadline:* For fall admission, 7/1 priority date for domestic and international students; for spring admission, 11/12 priority date for domestic students, 11/1 for international students. Applications are processed on a rolling basis. Application fee: $80. Electronic applications accepted. *Expenses:* Contact institution. *Financial support:* In 2016–17, 118 students received support. Career-related internships or fieldwork, scholarships/grants, and health care benefits available. Financial award application deadline: 3/1; financial award applicants required to submit FAFSA. *Unit head:* Dr. Lorrie McGovern, Associate Dean, School of Business, 352-588-7869, Fax: 352-588-8912, E-mail: mbaslu@saintleo.edu. *Application contact:* Jennifer Shelley, Senior Associate Director of Graduate Admissions, 800-707-8846, Fax: 352-588-7873, E-mail: grad.admissions@saintleo.edu.
Website: http://www.saintleo.edu/academics/graduate.aspx

Saint Mary's University of Minnesota, Schools of Graduate and Professional Programs, Graduate School of Business and Technology, Human Resource Management Program, Winona, MN 55987-1399. Offers MA. Tuition and fees vary according to degree level and program. *Unit head:* Holly Tapper, Director, 612-238-4547, E-mail: htapper@smumn.edu. *Application contact:* James Callinan, Director of Admissions for Graduate and Professional Programs, 612-728-5185, Fax: 612-728-5121, E-mail: jcallina@smumn.edu.
Website: http://www.smumn.edu/graduate-home/areas-of-study/graduate-school-of-business-technology/ma-in-human-resource-management

Saint Peter's University, Graduate Business Programs, MBA Program, Jersey City, NJ 07306-5997. Offers finance (MBA); health care administration (MBA); human resource management (MBA); international business (MBA); management (MBA); management information systems (MBA); marketing (MBA); risk management (MBA); MBA/MS. *Program availability:* Part-time, evening/weekend. *Entrance requirements:* Additional exam requirements/recommendations for international students: Required—TOEFL. Electronic applications accepted. *Faculty research:* Finance, health care management, human resource management, international business, management, management information systems, marketing, risk management.

St. Thomas University, School of Business, Department of Management, Miami Gardens, FL 33054-6459. Offers accounting (MBA); general management (MSM, Certificate); health management (MBA, MSM, Certificate); human resource management (MBA, MSM, Certificate); international business (MBA, MIB, MSM, Certificate); justice administration (MSM, Certificate); management accounting (MSM, Certificate); public management (MSM, Certificate); sports administration (MS). *Program availability:* Part-time, evening/weekend. *Degree requirements:* For master's, comprehensive exam. *Entrance requirements:* For master's, interview, minimum GPA of 3.0 or GMAT. Additional exam requirements/recommendations for international students: Required—TOEFL (minimum score 550 paper-based; 79 iBT). Electronic applications accepted.

San Diego State University, Graduate and Research Affairs, College of Business Administration, Department of Management, San Diego, CA 92182. Offers entrepreneurship (MS); human resources management (MS); management science (MS). *Program availability:* Part-time, evening/weekend. *Degree requirements:* For master's, thesis or alternative. *Entrance requirements:* For master's, GMAT, resume, letters of reference. Additional exam requirements/recommendations for international students: Required—TOEFL. Electronic applications accepted.

Savannah State University, Master of Public Administration Program, Savannah, GA 31404. Offers city management (MPA); human resources (MPA). *Accreditation:* NASPAA. *Program availability:* Part-time. *Degree requirements:* For master's, comprehensive exam, thesis, public service internship, capstone seminar. *Entrance requirements:* For master's, GRE General Test, GMAT, or MAT, minimum cumulative GPA of 2.5, 3 letters of recommendation, essay, official transcripts, resume, essay of 500-1000 words detailing reasons for pursuing degree. Additional exam requirements/recommendations for international students: Required—TOEFL. Electronic applications accepted. *Expenses:* Contact institution. *Faculty research:* Community development, human resources, leadership, conflict resolution, city management, non-profit management.

Seattle Pacific University, Master of Arts in Management Program, Seattle, WA 98119-1997. Offers faith and business (MA); human resources (MA); social and sustainable management (MA). *Entrance requirements:* For master's, GMAT or GRE (waived with cumulative GPA of 3.3 or above), bachelor's degree from accredited college or university, resume, essay, official transcript.

Southern New Hampshire University, School of Business, Manchester, NH 03106-1045. Offers accounting (MBA, MS, Graduate Certificate); accounting finance (MS); accounting/auditing (MS); accounting/forensic accounting (MS); accounting/taxation (MS); athletic administration (MBA, Graduate Certificate); business administration (IMBA, MBA, Certificate, Graduate Certificate), including accounting (Certificate), business administration (MBA), business information systems (Graduate Certificate), human resource management (Certificate); corporate social responsibility (MBA); entrepreneurship (MBA); finance (MBA, MS, Graduate Certificate); finance/corporate finance (MS); finance/investments and securities (MS); forensic accounting (MBA); healthcare informatics (MBA); healthcare management (MBA); human resource management (Graduate Certificate); information technology (MS, Graduate Certificate); information technology management (MBA); international business (Graduate Certificate); international business and information technology (Graduate Certificate); international finance (Graduate Certificate); international sport management (Graduate Certificate); justice studies (MBA); leadership of nonprofit organizations (Graduate Certificate); management (MS); marketing (MBA, MS, Graduate Certificate); operations and project management (MS); operations and supply chain management (MBA, Graduate Certificate); organizational leadership (MS); project management (MBA, Graduate Certificate); Six Sigma (MBA); Six Sigma quality (Graduate Certificate); social media marketing (MBA); sport management (MBA, MS, Graduate Certificate); sustainability and environmental compliance (MBA); workplace conflict management (MBA); MBA/Certificate. *Accreditation:* ACBSP. *Program availability:* Part-time, evening/weekend, online learning. Terminal master's awarded for partial completion of doctoral program. *Degree requirements:* For master's, one foreign language, comprehensive exam (for some programs), thesis or alternative. *Entrance requirements:* For master's, minimum GPA of 2.5. Additional exam requirements/recommendations for international students: Required—TOEFL (minimum score 500 paper-based). Electronic applications accepted.

State University of New York Polytechnic Institute, Program in Business Administration in Technology Management, Utica, NY 13502. Offers accounting and finance (MBA); business management (MBA); health services management (MBA); human resource management (MBA); marketing management (MBA). *Program availability:* Part-time, online learning. *Degree requirements:* For master's, capstone course. *Entrance requirements:* For master's, GMAT, resume, one letter of reference. Additional exam requirements/recommendations for international students: Required—TOEFL (minimum score 550 paper-based; 79 iBT), IELTS (minimum score 6.5). Electronic applications accepted. *Faculty research:* Technology management, writing schools, leadership, new products.

Stevens Institute of Technology, Graduate School, School of Business, Program in Management, Hoboken, NJ 07030. Offers general management (MS); global innovation management (MS); human resource management (MS); information management (MS); project management (MS); technology commercialization (MS); technology management (MS). *Program availability:* Part-time, evening/weekend. *Students:* 83 full-time (28 women), 82 part-time (36 women); includes 30 minority (6 Black or African American, non-Hispanic/Latino; 1 American Indian or Alaska Native, non-Hispanic/Latino; 21 Asian, non-Hispanic/Latino; 2 Hispanic/Latino), 73 international. Average age 29. 381 applicants, 64% accepted, 53 enrolled. In 2016, 66 master's awarded. *Degree requirements:* For master's, thesis optional, minimum B average in major field and overall. *Entrance requirements:* Additional exam requirements/recommendations for international students: Required—TOEFL (minimum score 74 iBT), IELTS (minimum score 6). *Application deadline:* For fall admission, 6/1 for domestic students, 4/15 for international students; for spring admission, 11/30 for domestic students, 11/1 for international students. Applications are processed on a rolling basis. Application fee: $65. Electronic applications accepted. *Expenses:* Contact institution. *Financial support:* Fellowships, research assistantships, teaching assistantships, career-related internships or fieldwork, Federal Work-Study, scholarships/grants, and unspecified assistantships available. Financial award application deadline: 2/15; financial award applicants required to submit FAFSA. *Unit head:* Brian Rothschild, Director, 201-216-3677, E-mail: brian.rothschild@stevens.edu. *Application contact:* Graduate Admissions, 888-783-8367, Fax: 888-511-1306, E-mail: graduate@stevens.edu.
Website: https://www.stevens.edu/school-business/masters-programs/management

Stony Brook University, State University of New York, Graduate School, College of Business, Program in Business Administration, Stony Brook, NY 11794. Offers accounting (MBA); business administration (MBA); finance (MBA, Certificate); health care management (MBA); innovation, human resources, management, or operations management (MBA); marketing (MBA). *Faculty:* 37 full-time (12 women), 12 part-time/adjunct (4 women). *Students:* 199 full-time (109 women), 139 part-time (64 women); includes 81 minority (19 Black or African American, non-Hispanic/Latino; 41 Asian, non-Hispanic/Latino; 17 Hispanic/Latino; 1 Native Hawaiian or other Pacific Islander, non-Hispanic/Latino; 3 Two or more races, non-Hispanic/Latino), 88 international. Average age 29. 246 applicants, 65% accepted, 91 enrolled. In 2016, 116 master's awarded. *Entrance requirements:* For master's, GMAT, 3 letters of recommendation from current or former employers or professors, transcripts, personal statement, resume. Additional exam requirements/recommendations for international students: Required—TOEFL (minimum score 550 paper-based; 90 iBT), IELTS (minimum score 6.5). *Application deadline:* For fall admission, 5/15 for domestic students, 3/15 for international students; for spring admission, 11/15 for domestic students, 10/15 for international students. Application fee: $100. *Expenses:* Contact institution. *Financial support:* Teaching assistantships available. *Total annual research expenditures:* $5,325. *Unit head:* Dr. Manuel London, Dean, 631-632-7159, E-mail: manuel.london@stonybrook.edu. *Application contact:* Dr. Jadranka Skorin-Kapov, Graduate Program Director, 631-632-7171, Fax: 631-632-8181, E-mail: jadranka.skorin-kapov@stonybrook.edu.

Stony Brook University, State University of New York, School of Professional Development, Stony Brook, NY 11794-443. Offers biology (MAT); chemistry (MAT); coaching (Graduate Certificate); earth science (MAT); educational computing (Graduate Certificate); educational leadership (Advanced Certificate); English (MAT); environmental management (MPS, Graduate Certificate); French (MAT); German (MAT); higher education administration (MA, Certificate); human resource management (MS, Graduate Certificate); industrial management (Graduate Certificate); information systems management (Graduate Certificate); Italian (MAT); liberal studies (MA); mathematics (MAT); operations research (Graduate Certificate); physics (MAT); school district business leadership (Advanced Certificate); social studies (MAT); Spanish (MAT). *Program availability:* Part-time, evening/weekend, online learning. *Faculty:* 4 full-time (3 women), 77 part-time/adjunct (34 women). *Students:* 197 full-time (125 women), 965 part-time (674 women); includes 222 minority (79 Black or African American, non-Hispanic/Latino; 2 American Indian or Alaska Native, non-Hispanic/Latino; 35 Asian, non-Hispanic/Latino; 87 Hispanic/Latino; 1 Native Hawaiian or other Pacific Islander, non-Hispanic/Latino; 18 Two or more races, non-Hispanic/Latino), 5 international. Average age 33. 462 applicants, 87% accepted, 317 enrolled. In 2016, 348 master's, 159 other advanced degrees awarded. *Degree requirements:* For master's, one foreign language, thesis or alternative. *Entrance requirements:* Additional exam requirements/recommendations for international students: Required—TOEFL (minimum score 85 iBT). *Application deadline:* For fall admission, 1/15 for domestic students, 6/1 for international students; for spring admission, 10/1 for domestic and international students. Applications are processed on a rolling basis. Application fee: $100. *Expenses:* Contact institution. *Financial support:* Fellowships, research assistantships, teaching assistantships, and career-related internships or fieldwork available. Support available to part-time students. *Unit head:* Dr. Ken Lindblom, Dean, 631-632-7049, Fax: 631-632-9046, E-mail: kenneth.lindblom@stonybrook.edu. *Application contact:* Melissa Jordan, Assistant Dean, 631-632-7751, E-mail: melissa.jordan@stonybrook.edu.
Website: http://www.stonybrook.edu/spd/

Strayer University, Graduate Studies, Washington, DC 20005-2603. Offers accounting (MS); acquisition (MBA); business administration (MBA); communications technology (MS); educational management (M Ed); finance (MBA); health services administration (MHSA); hospitality and tourism management (MBA); human resource management (MBA); information systems (MS), including computer security management, decision support system management, enterprise resource management, network management, software engineering management, systems development management; management (MBA); management information systems (MS); marketing (MBA); professional accounting (MS), including accounting information systems, controllership, taxation; public administration (MPA); supply chain management (MBA); technology in education (M Ed). Programs also offered at campus locations in Birmingham, AL; Chamblee, GA; Cobb County, GA; Morrow, GA; White Marsh, MD; Charleston, SC; Columbia, SC; Greensboro, NC; Greenville, SC; Lexington, KY; Louisville, KY; Nashville, TN; North Raleigh, NC; Washington, DC. *Accreditation:* ACBSP. *Program availability:* Part-time, evening/weekend, online learning. *Degree requirements:* For master's, thesis. *Entrance requirements:* For master's, GMAT, GRE General Test, bachelor's degree from an accredited college or university, minimum undergraduate GPA of 2.75. Electronic applications accepted.

Tarleton State University, College of Graduate Studies, College of Business Administration, Department of Management, Stephenville, TX 76402. Offers human resources management (MS). *Program availability:* Part-time, evening/weekend, 100% online, blended/hybrid learning. *Faculty:* 8 full-time (0 women), 4 part-time/adjunct (2 women). *Students:* 28 full-time (26 women), 75 part-time (59 women); includes 37 minority (15 Black or African American, non-Hispanic/Latino; 1 Asian, non-Hispanic/Latino; 18 Hispanic/Latino; 3 Two or more races, non-Hispanic/Latino). 41 applicants, 95% accepted, 31 enrolled. In 2016, 4 master's awarded. *Degree requirements:* For master's, comprehensive exam. *Entrance requirements:* For master's, GRE, GMAT, minimum GPA of 3.0. Additional exam requirements/recommendations for international students: Required—TOEFL (minimum score 550 paper-based; 80 iBT). *Application deadline:* For fall admission, 8/15 priority date for domestic students; for spring admission, 1/7 for domestic students. Applications are processed on a rolling basis. Application fee: $45 ($145 for international students). Electronic applications accepted. *Expenses:* $3,672 tuition; $2,437 fees. *Financial support:* Research assistantships, teaching assistantships, Federal Work-Study, scholarships/grants, and unspecified assistantships available. Financial award application deadline: 5/1; financial award applicants required to submit FAFSA. *Unit head:* Dr. Sue Joiner, Department Head, 254-968-9712, E-mail: sjoiner@tarleton.edu. *Application contact:* Information Contact, 254-968-9104, Fax: 254-968-9670, E-mail: gradoffice@tarleton.edu.

Temple University, Fox School of Business, MBA Programs, Philadelphia, PA 19122-6096. Offers accounting (MBA); business management (MBA); financial management (MBA); healthcare and life sciences innovation (MBA); human resource management (MBA); international business (IMBA); IT management (MBA); marketing management (MBA); pharmaceutical management (MBA); strategic management (EMBA, MBA). EMBA offered in Philadelphia, PA and Tokyo, Japan. *Accreditation:* AACSB. *Program availability:* Part-time, evening/weekend, online learning. *Entrance requirements:* For master's, GMAT, minimum undergraduate GPA of 3.0. Additional exam requirements/recommendations for international students: Required—TOEFL (minimum score 600 paper-based; 100 iBT), IELTS (minimum score 7.5).

Temple University, Fox School of Business, Specialized Master's Programs, Philadelphia, PA 19122-6096. Offers accountancy (MS); actuarial science (MS); finance (MS); financial engineering (MS); human resource management (MS); innovation management and entrepreneurship (MS); marketing (MS); statistics (MS). MS in innovation management and entrepreneurship delivered jointly with College of Engineering. *Accreditation:* AACSB. *Program availability:* Part-time. *Entrance requirements:* For master's, GRE General Test or GMAT, minimum undergraduate GPA of 3.0. Additional exam requirements/recommendations for international students: Required—TOEFL (minimum score 600 paper-based; 100 iBT), IELTS (minimum score 7.5).

Tennessee State University, The School of Graduate Studies and Research, College of Public Service, Nashville, TN 37209-1561. Offers human resource management (MPS); public administration (MPA, PhD); social work (MSW); strategic leadership (MPS); training and development (MPS). *Accreditation:* NASPAA (one or more programs are accredited). *Program availability:* Part-time, evening/weekend. *Degree requirements:* For master's, comprehensive exam, thesis optional; for doctorate, comprehensive exam, thesis/dissertation. *Entrance requirements:* For master's, GRE General Test, minimum GPA of 2.5, writing sample; for doctorate, GRE General Test, minimum GPA of 3.25, writing sample. *Faculty research:* Total quality management and process improvement, national health care policy and administration, starting non-profit ventures, public service ethics, state education financing across the U.S. public.

Tennessee Technological University, College of Graduate Studies, College of Business, Cookeville, TN 38505. Offers accounting (MBA); finance (MBA); human resource management (MBA); international business (MBA); management information systems (MBA). *Accreditation:* AACSB. *Program availability:* Part-time, evening/weekend, online learning. *Faculty:* 28 full-time (5 women). *Students:* 45 full-time (22 women), 167 part-time (51 women); includes 18 minority (5 Black or African American, non-Hispanic/Latino; 4 Asian, non-Hispanic/Latino; 4 Hispanic/Latino; 5 Two or more races, non-Hispanic/Latino), 14 international. Average age 25. 173 applicants, 54% accepted, 52 enrolled. In 2016, 78 master's awarded. *Entrance requirements:* For master's, GMAT, GRE. Additional exam requirements/recommendations for international students: Required—TOEFL (minimum score 550 paper-based; 79 iBT), IELTS (minimum score 5.5), PTE (minimum score 53), or TOEIC (Test of English as an International Communication). *Application deadline:* For fall admission, 8/1 for domestic students, 5/1 for international students; for spring admission, 12/1 for domestic students, 10/1 for international students; for summer admission, 5/1 for domestic students, 2/1 for international students. Applications are processed on a rolling basis. Application fee: $35 ($40 for international students). Electronic applications accepted. *Expenses:* Tuition, state resident: full-time $9375; part-time $534 per credit hour. Tuition, nonresident: full-time $22,443; part-time $1260 per credit hour. *Financial support:* In 2016–17, 5 fellowships (averaging $10,000 per year), 1 teaching assistantship (averaging $5,200 per year) were awarded; research assistantships also available. Support available to part-time students. Financial award application deadline: 4/1. *Unit head:* Kate Nicewicz, Director, 931-372-3600, Fax: 931-372-6249, E-mail: knicewicz@tntech.edu. *Application contact:* Shelia K. Kendrick, Coordinator of Graduate Studies, 931-372-3808, Fax: 931-372-3497, E-mail: skendrick@tntech.edu.
Website: http://www.tntech.edu/mba

Tennessee Technological University, College of Graduate Studies, College of Interdisciplinary Studies, School of Professional Studies, Cookeville, TN 38505. Offers human resources leadership (MPS); strategic leadership (MPS); training and development (MPS). *Program availability:* Part-time, evening/weekend, online learning. *Students:* 19 full-time (8 women), 57 part-time (33 women); includes 11 minority (7 Black or African American, non-Hispanic/Latino; 1 Hispanic/Latino; 1 Native Hawaiian or other Pacific Islander, non-Hispanic/Latino; 2 Two or more races, non-Hispanic/Latino). 39 applicants, 64% accepted, 16 enrolled. In 2016, 9 master's awarded. *Degree requirements:* For master's, comprehensive exam, thesis or alternative. *Entrance requirements:* For master's, GRE. Additional exam requirements/recommendations for international students: Required—TOEFL (minimum score 527 paper-based; 71 iBT), IELTS (minimum score 5.5), PTE (minimum score 48), or TOEIC (Test of English as an International Communication). *Application deadline:* For fall admission, 7/1 for domestic students, 5/1 for international students; for spring admission, 11/1 for domestic students, 10/1 for international students; for summer admission, 5/1 for domestic students, 2/1 for international students. Applications are processed on a rolling basis. Application fee: $35 ($40 for international students). Electronic applications accepted. *Expenses:* Tuition, state resident: full-time $9375; part-time $534 per credit hour. Tuition, nonresident: full-time $22,443; part-time $1260 per credit hour. *Financial support:* Application deadline: 4/1. *Unit head:* Dr. Joseph Roberts, Interim Director, School of Professional Studies, 931-372-6223, E-mail: jmroberts@tntech.edu. *Application contact:* Shelia K. Kendrick, Coordinator of Graduate Studies, 931-372-3808, Fax: 931-372-3497, E-mail: skendrick@tntech.edu.
Website: https://www.tntech.edu/is/sps/

Texas A&M University, Mays Business School, Department of Management, College Station, TX 77843. Offers entrepreneurial leadership (MS); human resource management (MS); management (MS). *Faculty:* 30. *Students:* 93 full-time (51 women), 1 part-time (0 women); includes 22 minority (3 Black or African American, non-Hispanic/Latino; 1 American Indian or Alaska Native, non-Hispanic/Latino; 6 Asian, non-Hispanic/Latino; 9 Hispanic/Latino; 3 Two or more races, non-Hispanic/Latino), 5 international. Average age 25. 164 applicants, 29% accepted, 37 enrolled. In 2016, 84 master's awarded. Terminal master's awarded for partial completion of doctoral program. *Degree requirements:* For master's, comprehensive exam. *Entrance requirements:* For master's, GMAT or GRE. Additional exam requirements/recommendations for international students: Required—TOEFL (minimum score 550 paper-based; 80 iBT), IELTS (minimum score 6), PTE (minimum score 53). *Application deadline:* For fall admission, 5/26 for domestic and international students. Applications are processed on a rolling basis. Application fee: $50 ($90 for international students). Electronic applications accepted. *Expenses:* Contact institution. *Financial support:* In 2016–17, 75 students received support, including 2 fellowships with tuition reimbursements available (averaging $6,000 per year), 33 research assistantships with tuition reimbursements available (averaging $3,826 per year), 20 teaching assistantships with tuition reimbursements available (averaging $4,191 per year); career-related internships or fieldwork, institutionally sponsored loans, scholarships/grants, traineeships, health care benefits, tuition waivers (full and partial), and unspecified assistantships also available. Support available to part-time students. Financial award application deadline: 3/15; financial award applicants required to submit FAFSA. *Faculty research:* Strategic and human resource management, business and public policy, organizational behavior, organizational theory. *Unit head:* Dr. Wendy R. Boswell, Head, 979-845-4045, Fax: 979-845-9641, E-mail: wboswell@mays.tamu.edu. *Application contact:* Kristi R. Mora, Senior Academic Advisor II, 979-845-6127, Fax: 979-845-9641, E-mail: kmora@mays.tamu.edu.
Website: http://mays.tamu.edu/mgmt/

Texas A&M University–Central Texas, Graduate Studies and Research, Killeen, TX 76549. Offers accounting (MS); business administration (MBA); clinical mental health counseling (MS); criminal justice (MCJ); curriculum and instruction (M Ed); educational administration (M Ed); educational psychology - experimental psychology (MS); history (MA); human resource management (MS); information systems (MS); liberal studies (MS); management and leadership (MS); marriage and family therapy (MS); mathematics (MS); political science (MA); school counseling (M Ed); school psychology (Ed S).

Texas A&M University–San Antonio, School of Business, San Antonio, TX 78224. Offers business administration (MBA); enterprise resource planning systems (MBA); finance (MBA); healthcare management (MBA); human resources management (MBA); information assurance and security (MBA); international business (MBA); professional accounting (MPA); project management (MBA); supply chain management (MBA). *Program availability:* Part-time, evening/weekend. *Entrance requirements:* For master's, GMAT. Additional exam requirements/recommendations for international students: Required—TOEFL (minimum score 550 paper-based; 80 iBT), IELTS (minimum score 6). Electronic applications accepted.

Texas State University, The Graduate College, Emmett and Miriam McCoy College of Business Administration, Program in Human Resource Management, San Marcos, TX 78666. Offers MS. *Program availability:* Part-time. *Faculty:* 6 full-time (2 women). *Students:* 5 full-time (3 women), 8 part-time (7 women); includes 6 minority (5 Hispanic/Latino; 1 Two or more races, non-Hispanic/Latino), 1 international. Average age 31. 18 applicants, 67% accepted, 6 enrolled. In 2016, 4 master's awarded. *Degree requirements:* For master's, comprehensive exam. *Entrance requirements:* For master's, GMAT or GRE, baccalaureate degree from regionally-accredited university (business administration or a related field preferred); knowledge of business functions (management, marketing, finance, accounting, MIS) through previous course work and/or work experience; 2 letters of recommendation; resume. Additional exam requirements/recommendations for international students: Required—TOEFL (minimum score 550 paper-based; 78 iBT), IELTS (minimum score 6.5). *Application deadline:* For fall admission, 2/1 priority date for domestic and international students; for spring admission, 10/1 for domestic and international students. Application fee: $40 ($90 for international students). Electronic applications accepted. *Expenses:* $4,851 per semester. *Financial support:* In 2016–17, 6 students received support. Research assistantships, teaching assistantships, Federal Work-Study, institutionally sponsored loans, scholarships/grants, health care benefits, and unspecified assistantships available. Support available to part-time students. Financial award application deadline: 3/1; financial award applicants required to submit FAFSA. *Unit head:* Dr. William Chittenden, Graduate Advisor, 512-245-3591, Fax: 512-245-8365, E-mail: wc10@txstate.edu. *Application contact:* Dr. Andrea Golato, Dean of Graduate School, 512-245-2581, Fax: 512-245-8365, E-mail: gradcollege@txstate.edu.
Website: http://graduate.mccoy.txstate.edu/grad_programs/MSHRM.html

Thomas College, Graduate School, Programs in Business, Waterville, ME 04901-5097. Offers business (MBA); computer technology education (MS); education (MS); human resource management (MBA). *Program availability:* Part-time, evening/weekend. *Entrance requirements:* For master's, GMAT, GRE, MAT or minimum GPA of 3.3 in first 3 graduate-level courses. Additional exam requirements/recommendations for international students: Recommended—TOEFL.

Thomas Edison State University, School of Business and Management, Program in Human Resources Management, Trenton, NJ 08608. Offers MSHRM, Graduate Certificate. *Program availability:* Part-time, online learning. *Degree requirements:* For master's, final/capstone project. *Entrance requirements:* For master's, bachelor's degree from a regionally-accredited college or university; minimum 2 letters of recommendation; 3-5 years of related working experience; current resume. Additional exam requirements/recommendations for international students: Required—TOEFL (minimum score 550 paper-based; 79 iBT). Electronic applications accepted.

Tiffin University, Program in Business Administration, Tiffin, OH 44883-2161. Offers finance (MBA); general management (MBA); healthcare administration (MBA); human resource management (MBA); international business (MBA); leadership (MBA); marketing (MBA); non-profit management (MBA); sports management (MBA). *Accreditation:* ACBSP. *Program availability:* Part-time, evening/weekend, online learning. *Students:* 10 full-time (4 women), 497 part-time (240 women); includes 91 minority (67 Black or African American, non-Hispanic/Latino; 1 American Indian or Alaska Native, non-Hispanic/Latino; 5 Asian, non-Hispanic/Latino; 15 Hispanic/Latino; 3 Two or more races, non-Hispanic/Latino), 102 international. Average age 31. 214 applicants, 86% accepted, 146 enrolled. In 2016, 183 master's awarded. *Entrance requirements:* For master's, minimum undergraduate GPA of 2.5, work experience. Additional exam requirements/recommendations for international students: Required—TOEFL (minimum score 550 paper-based; 79 iBT), IELTS. *Application deadline:* For fall admission, 8/15 for domestic students, 8/1 for international students; for spring admission, 1/9 for domestic students, 12/1 for international students. Applications are processed on a rolling basis. Application fee: $50. Electronic applications accepted. Application fee is waived when completed online. *Expenses: Tuition:* Full-time $21,000; part-time $700 per credit hour. *Required fees:* $150. Tuition and fees vary according to program. *Financial support:* Unspecified assistantships available. Support available to part-time students. Financial award application deadline: 7/31; financial award applicants required to submit FAFSA. *Faculty research:* Small business, executive development operations, research and statistical analysis, market research, management information systems. *Unit head:* Dr. Bonnie Tiell, Dean of Graduate Studies, 419-448-3261, Fax: 419-443-5002, E-mail: btiell@tiffin.edu. *Application contact:* Nikki Hintze, Director of Graduate and Distance Education Academic Advising, 800-968-6446 Ext. 3596, Fax: 419-443-5002, E-mail: hintzenm@tiffin.edu.
Website: http://www.tiffin.edu/graduateprograms/

Trident University International, College of Business Administration, Program in Business Administration, Cypress, CA 90630. Offers business administration (PhD);

conflict and negotiation management (MBA); criminal justice administration (MBA); entrepreneurship (MBA); finance (MBA); general management (MBA); government accounting (MBA); human resource management (MBA); information security and digital assurance management (MBA); information technology management (MBA); international business (MBA); logistics management (MBA); marketing (MBA); project management (MBA); public management (MBA); quality management (MBA); strategic leadership (MBA). *Program availability:* Part-time, evening/weekend, online learning. *Degree requirements:* For doctorate, comprehensive exam, thesis/dissertation, defense of dissertation. *Entrance requirements:* For master's, minimum GPA of 2.5 (students with GPA 3.0 or greater may transfer up to 30% of graduate level credits); for doctorate, minimum GPA of 3.4, curriculum vitae, course work in research methods or statistics. Additional exam requirements/recommendations for international students: Required—TOEFL. Electronic applications accepted.

Trinity International University, Trinity Law School, Santa Ana, CA 92705. Offers bioethics (MLS); church and ministry management (MLS); general legal studies (MLS); human resources management (MLS); human rights (MLS); law (JD); nonprofit organizations (MLS). *Program availability:* Part-time, evening/weekend. *Entrance requirements:* For doctorate, LSAT. Additional exam requirements/recommendations for international students: Required—TOEFL (minimum score 580 paper-based). *Application deadline:* For fall admission, 5/1 priority date for domestic and international students; for spring admission, 12/1 priority date for domestic and international students. Applications are processed on a rolling basis. Application fee: $35. *Expenses:* Contact institution. *Financial support:* Scholarships/grants available. Financial award application deadline: 8/15; financial award applicants required to submit FAFSA. *Unit head:* Kevin P. Holsclaw, Academic Dean, 714-836-7160, Fax: 714-796-7190, E-mail: kholscla@tiu.edu. *Application contact:* Doug Eaton, Director of Admissions, 714-796-7103, Fax: 714-796-7190, E-mail: deaton@tiu.edu.
Website: http://www.tls.edu/

Trinity Washington University, School of Business and Graduate Studies, Washington, DC 20017-1094. Offers business administration (MBA); communication (MA); international security studies (MA); organizational management (MSA), including federal program management, human resource management, nonprofit management, organizational development, public and community health. *Program availability:* Part-time, evening/weekend. *Degree requirements:* For master's, thesis (for some programs), capstone project (MSA). *Entrance requirements:* For master's, minimum GPA of 2.5. Additional exam requirements/recommendations for international students: Required—TOEFL (minimum score 550 paper-based).

Troy University, Graduate School, College of Business, Program in Human Resources Management, Troy, AL 36082. Offers MS. *Program availability:* Part-time, evening/weekend. *Faculty:* 7 full-time (1 woman), 1 part-time/adjunct (0 women). *Students:* 66 full-time (52 women), 269 part-time (218 women); includes 151 minority (137 Black or African American, non-Hispanic/Latino; 1 American Indian or Alaska Native, non-Hispanic/Latino; 1 Asian, non-Hispanic/Latino; 7 Hispanic/Latino; 5 Two or more races, non-Hispanic/Latino). Average age 34. 169 applicants, 98% accepted, 67 enrolled. In 2016, 76 master's awarded. *Degree requirements:* For master's, minimum GPA of 3.0; admission to candidacy. *Entrance requirements:* For master's, GRE (minimum score of 900 on old exam or 294 on new exam) or GMAT (minimum score of 500), bachelor's degree; minimum undergraduate GPA of 2.5 or 3.0 on last 30 semester hours, letter of recommendation. Additional exam requirements/recommendations for international students: Required—TOEFL (minimum score 523 paper-based; 70 iBT), IELTS (minimum score 6). *Application deadline:* Applications are processed on a rolling basis. Application fee: $50. Electronic applications accepted. *Expenses:* Tuition, state resident: full-time $7146; part-time $397 per credit hour. Tuition, nonresident: full-time $14,292; part-time $794 per credit hour. *Required fees:* $802; $50 per semester. Tuition and fees vary according to campus/location and program. *Financial support:* Fellowships, career-related internships or fieldwork, and scholarships/grants available. Support available to part-time students. Financial award applicants required to submit FAFSA. *Unit head:* Dr. Bill Heisler, Director, 757-274-0474 Ext. 334, Fax: 241-241-0378, E-mail: wheisler@troy.edu. *Application contact:* Jessica A. Kimbro, Director of Graduate Admissions, 334-670-3178, E-mail: jacord@troy.edu.

Tusculum College, Graduate and Professional Studies, Program in Business Administration, Greeneville, TN 37743-9997. Offers general management (MBA); healthcare administration (MBA); human resources (MBA); nonprofit management (MBA). *Program availability:* Evening/weekend. *Entrance requirements:* For master's, GMAT, GRE, 3 years of work experience, minimum GPA of 2.75. *Expenses: Tuition:* Full-time $7497; part-time $357 per credit hour. *Unit head:* Dr. Michael Dillon, Dean of the School of Business, 423-636-7300 Ext. 5022, E-mail: mdillon@tusculum.edu. *Application contact:* Lindsey Seal, Director of Enrollment, 423-636-7300 Ext. 5006, E-mail: lseal@tusculum.edu.
Website: http://home.tusculum.edu/gps/graduate-degrees/master-business-administration/

United States International University–Africa, School of Business Administration, Nairobi, Kenya. Offers business administration (GEMBA); entrepreneurship (MBA); finance (MBA); human resource management (MBA); information technology management (MBA); integrated studies (MBA); international business administration (MBA); management and organizational development (MS); marketing (MBA); organizational development (EMS); strategic management (MBA). *Program availability:* Part-time, evening/weekend. *Degree requirements:* For master's, thesis. *Entrance requirements:* For master's, GMAT, 2 letters of reference, resume. Additional exam requirements/recommendations for international students: Required—TOEFL (minimum score 550 paper-based). *Faculty research:* Marketing in small business enterprises, total quality management in Kenya.

Universidad del Este, Graduate School, Carolina, PR 00984. Offers accounting (MBA); adult education (M Ed); agribusiness (MBA); criminal justice and criminology (MA); curriculum and instruction - early education (M Ed); curriculum and instruction - elementary (M Ed); curriculum and instruction - English (M Ed); curriculum and instruction - Spanish (M Ed); human resources (MBA); information security management (MBA); information technology and Web business development (MBA); management (MBA); public policy (MPA); social work (MA), including clinical social work; special education (M Ed); strategic leadership (MBA).

Universidad del Turabo, Graduate Programs, School of Business and Entrepreneurship, Program in Human Resources, Gurabo, PR 00778-3030. Offers MBA. *Students:* 41 full-time (28 women), 36 part-time (26 women); all minorities (all Hispanic/Latino). Average age 30. 64 applicants, 53% accepted, 33 enrolled. In 2016, 28 master's awarded. *Entrance requirements:* For master's, GRE, EXADEP or GMAT, interview, essay, official transcript, recommendation letters. *Application deadline:* Applications are processed on a rolling basis. Application fee: $25. Electronic applications accepted. *Financial support:* Institutionally sponsored loans available. Financial award applicants required to submit FAFSA. *Unit head:* Juan Sosa, Dean, 787-743-7979 Ext. 4118, E-mail: negocios_ut@suagm.edu. *Application contact:* Diriee Rodríguez, Admissions Director, 787-743-7979 Ext. 4453, E-mail: admisiones-ut@suagm.edu.
Website: http://ut.suagm.edu/es/negocios

Universidad Metropolitana, School of Business Administration, Program in Human Resources Management, San Juan, PR 00928-1150. Offers MBA. *Program availability:* Part-time.

University at Albany, State University of New York, Nelson A. Rockefeller College of Public Affairs and Policy, Department of Public Administration and Policy, Albany, NY 12222-0001. Offers financial management and public economics (MPA); financial market regulation (MPA); health policy (MPA); healthcare management (MPA); homeland security (MPA); human resources management (MPA); information strategy and management (MPA); local government management (MPA); nonprofit management (MPA); nonprofit management and leadership (Certificate); organizational behavior and theory (MPA, PhD); planning and policy analysis (CAS); policy analysis (MPA); politics and administration (PhD); public finance (PhD); public management (PhD); public policy (PhD); public sector management (Certificate); women and public policy (Certificate); JD/MPA. JD/MPA offered jointly with Albany Law School. *Accreditation:* NASPAA (one or more programs are accredited). *Faculty:* 23 full-time (8 women), 14 part-time/adjunct (7 women). *Students:* 117 full-time (65 women), 95 part-time (46 women); includes 41 minority (12 Black or African American, non-Hispanic/Latino; 8 Asian, non-Hispanic/Latino; 19 Hispanic/Latino; 2 Two or more races, non-Hispanic/Latino), 38 international. 223 applicants, 70% accepted, 81 enrolled. In 2016, 52 master's, 10 doctorates, 16 other advanced degrees awarded. *Degree requirements:* For doctorate, one foreign language, thesis/dissertation. *Entrance requirements:* For doctorate, GRE General Test. Additional exam requirements/recommendations for international students: Required—TOEFL (minimum score 550 paper-based). *Application deadline:* For fall admission, 2/1 priority date for domestic students, 5/1 for international students; for spring admission, 12/1 for domestic students. Applications are processed on a rolling basis. Application fee: $75. Electronic applications accepted. *Expenses:* Tuition, state resident: full-time $10,870; part-time $453 per credit hour. Tuition, nonresident: full-time $22,210; part-time $925 per credit hour. *International tuition:* $21,550 full-time. *Required fees:* $1864; $96 per credit hour. *Financial support:* Application deadline: 2/1. *Total annual research expenditures:* $847,949. *Unit head:* Victor Asal, Chair, 518-591-8729, E-mail: vasal@albany.edu.
Website: http://www.albany.edu/rockefeller/pad.shtml

University at Albany, State University of New York, School of Business, MBA Programs, Albany, NY 12222. Offers business administration (MBA); cyber security (MBA); entrepreneurship (MBA); finance (MBA); human resource information systems (MBA); information technology management (MBA); marketing (MBA); JD/MBA. JD/MBA offered with Albany Law School. *Program availability:* Part-time, evening/weekend. *Faculty:* 25 full-time (8 women), 4 part-time/adjunct (1 woman). *Students:* 92 full-time (39 women), 192 part-time (77 women); includes 63 minority (12 Black or African American, non-Hispanic/Latino; 1 American Indian or Alaska Native, non-Hispanic/Latino; 32 Asian, non-Hispanic/Latino; 13 Hispanic/Latino; 5 Two or more races, non-Hispanic/Latino), 27 international. Average age 25. 217 applicants, 73% accepted, 119 enrolled. In 2016, 122 master's awarded. *Degree requirements:* For master's, thesis (for some programs), field or research project. *Entrance requirements:* For master's, GMAT, minimum undergraduate GPA of 3.0; 3 letters of recommendation; resume; statement of goals. Additional exam requirements/recommendations for international students: Required—TOEFL (minimum score 100 iBT); Recommended—IELTS (minimum score 7). *Application deadline:* For fall admission, 4/1 priority date for domestic students, 3/1 for international students; for spring admission, 12/1 for domestic students; for summer admission, 5/1 for domestic students. Applications are processed on a rolling basis. Application fee: $75. Electronic applications accepted. *Expenses:* $16,274 Full-Time MBA per year; $696 Part-Time MBA per credit hour. *Financial support:* In 2016–17, 20 students received support, including 20 fellowships with partial tuition reimbursements available (averaging $6,500 per year); research assistantships, teaching assistantships, and unspecified assistantships also available. Financial award application deadline: 4/1; financial award applicants required to submit FAFSA. *Faculty research:* Cyber security, entrepreneurship, human resource information systems, information technology management, finance, marketing. *Total annual research expenditures:* $136,000. *Unit head:* Dr. Hany A. Shawky, Interim Dean, 518-956-8337, E-mail: hshawky@albany.edu. *Application contact:* Zina Mega Lawrence, Assistant Dean of Graduate Student Services, 518-956-8320, Fax: 518-442-4042, E-mail: zlawrence@albany.edu.
Website: http://graduatebusiness.albany.edu/

University at Buffalo, the State University of New York, Graduate School, Graduate School of Education, Department of Educational Leadership and Policy, Buffalo, NY 14260. Offers economics and education policy analysis (MA); education studies (Ed M); educational administration (Ed M, Ed D, PhD); educational culture, policy and society (PhD); higher education administration (Ed M, PhD); school building leadership (Certificate); school business and human resource administration (Certificate); school district business leadership (Certificate); school district leadership (Certificate). *Program availability:* Part-time, evening/weekend. *Faculty:* 15 full-time (9 women), 8 part-time/adjunct (6 women). *Students:* 77 full-time (51 women), 122 part-time (76 women); includes 30 minority (23 Black or African American, non-Hispanic/Latino; 4 Asian, non-Hispanic/Latino; 3 Hispanic/Latino), 22 international. Average age 34. 144 applicants, 75% accepted, 63 enrolled. In 2016, 59 master's, 11 doctorates, 29 other advanced degrees awarded. *Degree requirements:* For master's, comprehensive exam (for some programs), thesis optional; for doctorate, comprehensive exam, thesis/dissertation. *Entrance requirements:* For master's, interview, letters of reference; for doctorate, GRE General Test or MAT, writing sample, letters of reference. Additional exam requirements/recommendations for international students: Required—TOEFL (minimum score 550 paper-based; 79 iBT). *Application deadline:* For fall admission, 2/1 priority date for domestic students, 2/1 for international students; for spring admission, 11/15 priority date for domestic students, 10/1 for international students. Applications are processed on a rolling basis. Application fee: $50. Electronic applications accepted. *Financial support:* In 2016–17, 13 fellowships (averaging $6,862 per year), 32 research assistantships with tuition reimbursements (averaging $10,496 per year) were awarded; career-related internships or fieldwork, Federal Work-Study, institutionally sponsored loans, scholarships/grants, health care benefits, tuition waivers (full and partial), and unspecified assistantships also available. Financial award application deadline: 3/15; financial award applicants required to submit FAFSA. *Faculty research:* College access and choice, school leadership preparation and practice, public policy, curriculum and pedagogy, comparative and international education. *Total annual research expenditures:* $435,404. *Unit head:* Dr. Janina C. Brutt-Griffler, Chair, 716-645-2471, Fax: 716-645-2481, E-mail: bruttg@buffalo.edu. *Application contact:* Veronica Kase, Admission Assistant, 716-645-2110, Fax: 716-645-7937, E-mail: vakase@buffalo.edu.
Website: http://gse.buffalo.edu/elp

The University of Alabama in Huntsville, School of Graduate Studies, College of Business Administration, Programs in Business and Management, Huntsville, AL 35899. Offers business analytics (MSMS); federal contracting and procurement management (Certificate); human resource management (MSM); management (MBA), including acquisition management, entrepreneurship, federal contract accounting, finance, human resource management, logistics and supply chain management, marketing, project management; supply chain management (Certificate); technology and innovation management (Certificate). *Accreditation:* AACSB. *Program availability:* Part-time, evening/weekend. *Degree requirements:* For master's, comprehensive exam, thesis or alternative. *Entrance requirements:* For master's, GMAT (minimum score 500), minimum AACSB index of 1080. Additional exam requirements/recommendations for international students: Required—TOEFL (minimum score 550 paper-based; 80 iBT), IELTS (minimum score 6.5). Electronic applications accepted. *Expenses:* Tuition, state resident: full-time $9834; part-time $600 per credit hour. Tuition, nonresident: full-time $21,830; part-time $1325 per credit hour. *Faculty research:* Supply chain management, management of research and development, international marketing and branding, organizational behavior and human resource management, social networks and computational economics.

University of Bridgeport, School of Business, Bridgeport, CT 06604. Offers accounting (MBA); finance (MBA); general business (MBA); global financial services (MBA); human resource management (MBA); information systems and knowledge management (MBA); international business (MBA); management (MBA); marketing (MBA); operations management (MBA); small business and entrepreneurship (MBA); specialized business (MBA). *Accreditation:* ACBSP. *Program availability:* Part-time, evening/weekend. *Degree requirements:* For master's, thesis optional. *Entrance requirements:* For master's, GMAT. Additional exam requirements/recommendations for international students: Recommended—TOEFL (minimum score 550 paper-based; 80 iBT), IELTS (minimum score 6.5). Electronic applications accepted. *Expenses:* Contact institution.

University of California, Berkeley, UC Berkeley Extension, Certificate Programs in Business, Berkeley, CA 94720-1500. Offers accounting (Certificate); business administration (Certificate); finance (Certificate); human resource management (Certificate); management (Certificate); marketing (Certificate); project management (Certificate). *Accreditation:* AACSB. *Program availability:* Online learning.

University of Colorado Denver, Business School, Master of Business Administration Program, Denver, CO 80217. Offers bioinnovation and entrepreneurship (MBA); business intelligence (MBA); business strategy (MBA); business to business marketing (MBA); business to consumer marketing (MBA); change management (MBA); corporate financial management (MBA); enterprise technology management (MBA); entrepreneurship (MBA); health administration (MBA), including financial management, health administration, health information technologies, international health management and policy; human resources management (MBA); international business (MBA); investment management (MBA); managing for sustainability (MBA); sports and entertainment management (MBA). *Accreditation:* AACSB. *Program availability:* Part-time, evening/weekend, 100% online, blended/hybrid learning. *Students:* 544 full-time (210 women), 112 part-time (22 women); includes 99 minority (15 Black or African American, non-Hispanic/Latino; 4 American Indian or Alaska Native, non-Hispanic/Latino; 38 Asian, non-Hispanic/Latino; 36 Hispanic/Latino; 6 Two or more races, non-Hispanic/Latino), 22 international. Average age 32. 335 applicants, 73% accepted, 179 enrolled. In 2016, 251 master's awarded. *Degree requirements:* For master's, 48 semester hours, including 30 of core courses, 3 in international business, and 15 in electives from over 50 other business courses. *Entrance requirements:* For master's, GMAT, resume, official transcripts, essay, two letters of recommendation, financial statements (for international applicants). Additional exam requirements/recommendations for international students: Required—TOEFL (minimum score 560 paper-based; 83 iBT); Recommended—IELTS (minimum score 6.5). *Application deadline:* For fall admission, 4/15 priority date for domestic students, 3/15 priority date for international students; for spring admission, 10/15 priority date for domestic students, 9/15 priority date for international students; for summer admission, 2/15 priority date for domestic students, 1/15 priority date for international students. Applications are processed on a rolling basis. Application fee: $50 ($75 for international students). Electronic applications accepted. *Expenses:* Contact institution. *Financial support:* In 2016–17, 171 students received support. Fellowships, research assistantships, teaching assistantships, Federal Work-Study, institutionally sponsored loans, scholarships/grants, traineeships, and unspecified assistantships available. Financial award application deadline: 4/1; financial award applicants required to submit FAFSA. *Faculty research:* Marketing, management, entrepreneurship, finance, health administration. *Unit head:* Woodrow Eckard, MBA Director, 303-315-8470, E-mail: woody.eckard@ucdenver.edu. *Application contact:* Shelly Townley, Admissions Director, Graduate Programs, 303-315-8202, E-mail: shelly.townley@ucdenver.edu.
Website: http://www.ucdenver.edu/academics/colleges/business/degrees/mba/Pages/MBA.aspx

University of Colorado Denver, Business School, Program in Management and Organization, Denver, CO 80217. Offers business strategy (MS); change and innovation (MS); enterprise technology management (MS); entrepreneurship and innovation (MS); global management (MS); leadership (MS); managing for sustainability (MS); managing human resources (MS); sports and entertainment management (MS). *Accreditation:* AACSB. *Program availability:* Part-time, evening/weekend, online learning. *Students:* 20 full-time (13 women), 17 part-time (10 women); includes 6 minority (3 Black or African American, non-Hispanic/Latino; 1 American Indian or Alaska Native, non-Hispanic/Latino; 1 Hispanic/Latino; 1 Two or more races, non-Hispanic/Latino), 6 international. Average age 33. 24 applicants, 58% accepted, 6 enrolled. In 2016, 19 master's awarded. *Degree requirements:* For master's, 30 semester hours (12 of required courses, 12 of management electives, and 6 of free electives). *Entrance requirements:* For master's, GMAT, resume, two letters of recommendation, essay, financial statements (for international applicants). Additional exam requirements/recommendations for international students: Required—TOEFL (minimum score 525 paper-based; 71 iBT); Recommended—IELTS (minimum score 6.5). *Application deadline:* For fall admission, 4/15 priority date for domestic students, 3/15 priority date for international students; for spring admission, 10/15 priority date for domestic students, 9/15 priority date for international students; for summer admission, 2/15 priority date for domestic students, 1/15 priority date for international students. Applications are processed on a rolling basis. Application fee: $50 ($75 for international students). Electronic applications accepted. *Expenses:* Contact institution. *Financial support:* In 2016–17, 7 students received support. Fellowships, research assistantships, teaching assistantships, Federal Work-Study, institutionally sponsored loans, scholarships/grants, and traineeships available. Financial award application deadline: 4/1; financial award applicants required to submit FAFSA. *Faculty research:* Human resource management, management of catastrophe, turnaround strategies. *Unit head:* Dr. Kenneth Bettenhausen, Associate Professor/Director of MS in Management, 303-315-8425, E-mail: kenneth.bettenhausen@ucdenver.edu. *Application contact:* 303-315-8200, E-mail: bschool.admissions@ucdenver.edu.
Website: http://www.ucdenver.edu/academics/colleges/business/degrees/ms/management/Pages/Management.aspx

University of Connecticut, Graduate School, eCampus, Program in Human Resource Management, Storrs, CT 06269. Offers MS.

University of Dallas, Satish and Yasmin Gupta College of Business, Irving, TX 75062-4736. Offers accounting (MBA, MS); business administration (DBA); business analytics (MS); business management (MBA); corporate finance (MBA); cybersecurity (MS); finance (MS); financial services (MBA); global business (MBA, MS); health services management (MBA); human resource management (MBA); information and technology management (MS); information assurance (MBA); information technology (MBA); information technology service management (MBA); marketing management (MBA); organization development (MBA); project management (MBA); sports and entertainment management (MBA); strategic leadership (MBA); supply chain management (MBA). *Accreditation:* AACSB. *Program availability:* Part-time, evening/weekend, online learning. *Entrance requirements:* Additional exam requirements/recommendations for international students: Required—TOEFL. Electronic applications accepted. *Expenses:* Contact institution.

University of Denver, University College, Denver, CO 80208. Offers arts and culture (MA, Certificate); communication management (MS, Certificate), including translation studies (Certificate), world history and culture (Certificate); environmental policy and management (MS); geographic information systems (MS); global affairs (MA, Certificate), including human capital in organizations (Certificate), philanthropic leadership (Certificate), project management (Certificate), strategic innovation and change (Certificate); healthcare leadership (MS); information communications and technology (MS); leadership and organizations (MS); professional creative writing (MA, Certificate), including emergency planning and response (Certificate), organizational security (Certificate); security management (MS, Certificate); strategic human resources (Certificate). *Program availability:* Part-time, evening/weekend, online learning. *Faculty:* 118 part-time/adjunct (62 women). *Students:* 59 full-time (22 women), 1,285 part-time (750 women); includes 316 minority (111 Black or African American, non-Hispanic/Latino; 8 American Indian or Alaska Native, non-Hispanic/Latino; 39 Asian, non-Hispanic/Latino; 123 Hispanic/Latino; 3 Native Hawaiian or other Pacific Islander, non-Hispanic/Latino; 32 Two or more races, non-Hispanic/Latino), 85 international. Average age 35. 703 applicants, 89% accepted, 390 enrolled. In 2016, 428 master's, 138 other advanced degrees awarded. *Degree requirements:* For master's, capstone project. *Entrance requirements:* For master's, transcripts, two letters of recommendation, personal statement, resume. Additional exam requirements/recommendations for international students: Required—TOEFL (minimum score 550 paper-based; 80 iBT). *Application deadline:* For fall admission, 6/21 priority date for domestic students, 5/1 priority date for international students; for winter admission, 9/14 priority date for domestic students, 9/19 priority date for international students; for spring admission, 1/11 priority date for domestic students, 12/12 priority date for international students; for summer admission, 3/29 priority date for domestic students, 3/6 priority date for international students. Applications are processed on a rolling basis. Application fee: $75. Electronic applications accepted. *Expenses:* $7,236 per year full-time. *Financial support:* In 2016–17, 27 students received support, including 1 teaching assistantship (averaging $1,489 per year). Financial award applicants required to submit FAFSA. *Unit head:* Dr. Michael McGuire, Dean, 303-871-3518, Fax: 303-871-3303, E-mail: mmcguire@du.edu. *Application contact:* Information Contact, 303-871-2291, E-mail: ucoladm@du.edu.
Website: http://universitycollege.du.edu/

University of Florida, Graduate School, Warrington College of Business Administration, Hough Graduate School of Business, Programs in Business Administration, Gainesville, FL 32611. Offers business administration (MA, MS, PhD); competitive strategy (MBA); finance (MBA); global management (MBA); Graham-Buffett security analysis (MBA); human resource management (MBA); information systems and operations management (MBA); international studies (MBA); management (MBA); real estate (MBA); JD/MBA; MBA/MS; MBA/PhD; MBA/Pharm D; MD/MBA. *Accreditation:* AACSB. *Program availability:* Part-time, evening/weekend, online learning. *Degree requirements:* For master's, capstone course. *Entrance requirements:* For master's and doctorate, GMAT (minimum score 465), minimum GPA of 3.0, interview. Additional exam requirements/recommendations for international students: Required—TOEFL (minimum score 550 paper-based; 80 iBT), IELTS (minimum score 6). Electronic applications accepted. *Faculty research:* Accounting, finance, insurance, management, real estate, urban analysis marketing.

University of Hawaii at Manoa, Graduate Division, Shidler College of Business, Program in Business Administration, Honolulu, HI 96822. Offers Asian business studies (MBA); Chinese business studies (MBA); decision sciences (MBA); entrepreneurship (MBA); finance (MBA); finance and banking (MBA); human resources management (MBA); information management (MBA); information technology (MBA); international business (MBA); Japanese business studies (MBA); marketing (MBA); organizational behavior (MBA); organizational management (MBA); real estate (MBA); student-designed track (MBA). *Accreditation:* AACSB. *Program availability:* Part-time, evening/weekend. *Degree requirements:* For master's, thesis optional. *Entrance requirements:* For master's, GMAT, minimum GPA of 3.0. Additional exam requirements/recommendations for international students: Required—TOEFL (minimum score 600 paper-based; 100 iBT), IELTS (minimum score 7). *Expenses:* Contact institution.

University of Hawaii at Manoa, Graduate Division, Shidler College of Business, Program in Human Resources Management, Honolulu, HI 96822. Offers MHRM. *Program availability:* Part-time. *Entrance requirements:* Additional exam requirements/recommendations for international students: Required—TOEFL (minimum score 600 paper-based; 100 iBT), IELTS (minimum score 7). *Expenses:* Contact institution.

University of Houston–Clear Lake, School of Business, Program in Administrative Science, Houston, TX 77058-1002. Offers environmental management (MS); human resource management (MA). *Program availability:* Part-time, evening/weekend. *Degree requirements:* For master's, thesis optional. *Entrance requirements:* For master's, GMAT. Additional exam requirements/recommendations for international students: Required—TOEFL (minimum score 550 paper-based). Electronic applications accepted.

University of Houston–Downtown, Davies College of Business, MBA Program, Houston, TX 77002. Offers finance (MBA); human resource management (MBA); investment management (MBA); leadership (MBA); sales management and business development (MBA); supply chain management (MBA). *Accreditation:* AACSB. *Program availability:* Part-time, evening/weekend. *Faculty:* 33 full-time (12 women), 1 part-time/adjunct (0 women). *Students:* 7 full-time (3 women), 1,037 part-time (565 women); includes 773 minority (361 Black or African American, non-Hispanic/Latino; 2 American Indian or Alaska Native, non-Hispanic/Latino; 132 Asian, non-Hispanic/Latino; 270 Hispanic/Latino), 32 international. Average age 33. 583 applicants, 86% accepted, 409 enrolled. In 2016, 181 master's awarded. *Entrance requirements:* For master's, GMAT, two letters of recommendation from professional references, personal statement, resume. Additional exam requirements/recommendations for international students: Required—TOEFL (minimum score 81 iBT). *Application deadline:* For fall admission, 7/15 for domestic and international students. Application fee: $35 ($60 for international students). Electronic applications accepted. *Expenses:* $428 in-state per credit; $786 non-resident per credit. *Financial support:* Federal Work-Study and scholarships/grants available. Financial award application deadline: 4/1; financial award applicants required to submit FAFSA. *Unit head:* Dr. D. Michael Fields, Dean, Davies College of Business, 713-221-8179, Fax: 713-221-8675, E-mail: fieldsd@uhd.edu. *Application contact:* Ceshia Love, Director of Graduate and International Admissions, 713-221-8093, Fax: 713-223-7408, E-mail: gradadmissions@uhd.edu.
Website: http://mba.uhd.edu/

University of Illinois at Urbana–Champaign, Graduate College, College of Education, Department of Education Policy, Organization, and Leadership, Champaign, IL 61820. Offers educational organization and leadership (Ed M, MS, Ed D, PhD, CAS);

educational policy studies (Ed M, MA, PhD); human resource education (Ed M, MS, Ed D, PhD, CAS). *Program availability:* Part-time, online learning.

University of Illinois at Urbana–Champaign, Graduate College, School of Labor and Employment Relations, Champaign, IL 61820. Offers human resources and industrial relations (MHRIR, PhD); MHRIR/JD; MHRIR/MBA. Terminal master's awarded for partial completion of doctoral program.

The University of Kansas, Graduate Studies, School of Business, Program in Business, Lawrence, KS 66045. Offers accounting (PhD); business and organizational leadership (MS); decision sciences and supply chain management (PhD); finance (PhD); human resources management (PhD); marketing (PhD); organizational behavior (PhD); strategic management (PhD); supply chain management and logistics (MS). *Accreditation:* AACSB. *Program availability:* Part-time. *Students:* 76 full-time (11 women), 170 part-time (83 women); includes 41 minority (15 Black or African American, non-Hispanic/Latino; 3 American Indian or Alaska Native, non-Hispanic/Latino; 6 Asian, non-Hispanic/Latino; 5 Hispanic/Latino; 12 Two or more races, non-Hispanic/Latino), 25 international. Average age 32. 294 applicants, 69% accepted, 152 enrolled. In 2016, 36 master's, 9 doctorates awarded. *Entrance requirements:* For master's, GMAT, official transcript, three letters of recommendation, resume, statement of purpose; for doctorate, GMAT or GRE, official transcript, three letters of recommendation, resume, statement of purpose. Additional exam requirements/recommendations for international students: Required—TOEFL (minimum score 600 paper-based; 100 iBT). *Application deadline:* For fall admission, 1/10 for domestic and international students. Application fee: $65 ($85 for international students). Electronic applications accepted. *Financial support:* Fellowships, research assistantships, teaching assistantships, scholarships/grants, health care benefits, tuition waivers (full), and unspecified assistantships available. Financial award application deadline: 1/10. *Faculty research:* Strategic human resource management, business ethics, organizational theory/behavior, corporate strategy, international business, supply chain management, Bayesian networks, game theory, decision analysis and time/series analysis, pricing, consumer effects, advertising and emotion. *Unit head:* Charly Edmonds, Director, 785-864-3841, E-mail: bschoolphd@ku.edu. *Application contact:* Graduate Admission Contact, 785-864-7500, E-mail: bschoolphd@ku.edu.
Website: http://www.business.ku.edu/

University of La Verne, College of Business and Public Management, Program in Leadership and Management, La Verne, CA 91750-4443. Offers human resource management (Certificate); leadership and management (MS), including human resource management, nonprofit management, organizational development; nonprofit management (Certificate); organizational leadership (Certificate). *Program availability:* Part-time. *Students:* 47 full-time (32 women), 44 part-time (25 women); includes 42 minority (2 Black or African American, non-Hispanic/Latino; 3 Asian, non-Hispanic/Latino; 37 Hispanic/Latino), 14 international. Average age 32. *Degree requirements:* For master's, thesis or research project. *Entrance requirements:* For master's, bachelor's degree, minimum undergraduate GPA of 2.75, 2 letters of recommendation, interview, resume. Additional exam requirements/recommendations for international students: Required—TOEFL (minimum score 550 paper-based). *Application deadline:* Applications are processed on a rolling basis. Application fee: $50. *Expenses: Tuition:* Part-time $795 per credit hour. Tuition and fees vary according to campus/location and program. *Financial support:* Federal Work-Study, institutionally sponsored loans, and scholarships/grants available. Financial award application deadline: 3/2; financial award applicants required to submit FAFSA. *Unit head:* Dr. Kathy Duncan, Program Director, 909-448-4415, E-mail: kduncan2@laverne.edu. *Application contact:* Barbara Cox, Associate Director of Graduate Admissions, 909-448-4004, E-mail: bcox@laverne.edu.
Website: http://laverne.edu/business-and-public-administration/

University of La Verne, Regional and Online Campuses, Graduate Programs, Inland Empire Campus, Ontario, CA 91730. Offers business administration (MBA, MBA-EP), including accounting (MBA), finance (MBA), health services management (MBA-EP), information technology (MBA-EP), international business (MBA), managed care (MBA), management and leadership (MBA-EP), marketing (MBA-EP), supply chain management (MBA); leadership and management (MS), including human resource management, nonprofit management, organizational development. *Program availability:* Part-time, evening/weekend. *Expenses:* Contact institution.

University of Lethbridge, School of Graduate Studies, Lethbridge, AB T1K 3M4, Canada. Offers addictions counseling (M Sc); agricultural biotechnology (M Sc); agricultural studies (M Sc, MA); anthropology (MA); archaeology (M Sc, MA); art (MA, MFA); biochemistry (M Sc); biological sciences (M Sc); biomolecular science (PhD); biosystems and biodiversity (PhD); Canadian studies (MA); chemistry (M Sc); computer science (M Sc); computer science and geographical information science (M Sc); counseling (MC); counseling psychology (M Ed); dramatic arts (MA); earth, space, and physical science (PhD); economics (MA); education (MA, PhD); educational leadership (M Ed); English (MA); environmental science (M Sc); evolution and behavior (PhD); exercise science (M Sc); French (MA); French/German (MA); French/Spanish (MA); general education (M Ed); geography (M Sc, MA); German (MA); health sciences (M Sc); individualized multidisciplinary (M Sc, MA); kinesiology (M Sc, MA); management (M Sc), including accounting, finance, human resource management and labor relations, information systems, international management, marketing, policy and strategy; mathematics (M Sc); music (M Mus, MA); Native American studies (MA); neuroscience (M Sc, PhD); new media (MA, MFA); nursing (M Sc, MN); philosophy (MA); physics (M Sc); political science (MA); psychology (M Sc, MA); religious studies (MA); sociology (MA); theatre and dramatic arts (MFA); theoretical and computational science (PhD); urban and regional studies (MA); women and gender studies (MA). *Program availability:* Part-time, evening/weekend. *Degree requirements:* For master's, thesis (for some programs); for doctorate, comprehensive exam, thesis/dissertation. *Entrance requirements:* For master's, GMAT (for M Sc in management), bachelor's degree in related field, minimum GPA of 3.0 during previous 20 graded semester courses, 2 years' teaching or related experience (M Ed); for doctorate, master's degree, minimum graduate GPA of 3.5. Additional exam requirements/recommendations for international students: Required—TOEFL (minimum score 580 paper-based; 93 iBT). Electronic applications accepted. *Faculty research:* Movement and brain plasticity, gibberellin physiology, photosynthesis, carbon cycling, molecular properties of main-group ring components.

University of Louisville, Graduate School, College of Arts and Sciences, Department of Urban and Public Affairs, Louisville, KY 40208. Offers public administration (MPA), including human resources management, non-profit management, public policy and administration; urban and public affairs (PhD), including urban planning and development, urban policy and administration; urban planning (MUP), including administration of planning organizations, housing and community development, land use and environmental planning, spatial analysis. *Program availability:* Part-time, evening/weekend. *Faculty:* 12 full-time (5 women), 3 part-time/adjunct (1 woman). *Students:* 59 full-time (23 women), 32 part-time (19 women); includes 19 minority (13 Black or African American, non-Hispanic/Latino; 1 Asian, non-Hispanic/Latino; 2 Hispanic/Latino; 3 Two or more races, non-Hispanic/Latino), 5 international. Average age 30. 75 applicants, 65% accepted, 25 enrolled. In 2016, 22 master's, 2 doctorates awarded. Terminal master's awarded for partial completion of doctoral program. *Degree requirements:* For master's, internship; for doctorate, comprehensive exam, thesis/dissertation. *Entrance requirements:* For master's, GRE General Test, minimum GPA of 3.0; for doctorate, GRE General Test, master's degree in appropriate field. Additional exam requirements/recommendations for international students: Required—TOEFL (minimum score 550 paper-based; 79 iBT). *Application deadline:* Applications are processed on a rolling basis. Application fee: $60. *Expenses:* Contact institution. *Financial support:* Fellowships, research assistantships, tuition waivers (full and partial), and unspecified assistantships available. Financial award application deadline: 2/1. *Faculty research:* Urban theory, sustainability, public administration, urban planning, urban management. *Total annual research expenditures:* $240,308. *Unit head:* Dr. David Simpson, Chair, 502-852-8019, Fax: 502-852-4558, E-mail: dave.simpson@louisville.edu. *Application contact:* Libby Leggett, Director, Graduate Admissions, 502-852-3101, Fax: 502-852-4558, E-mail: gradadm@louisville.edu.
Website: http://supa.louisville.edu

University of Louisville, Graduate School, College of Education and Human Development, Department of Educational Leadership, Evaluation and Organizational Development, Louisville, KY 40292-0001. Offers educational leadership and organizational development (Ed D, PhD), including evaluation (PhD), human resource development (PhD), P-12 administration (PhD), post-secondary administration (PhD), sport administration (PhD); health professions education (Certificate); higher education administration (MA); human resources and organization development (MS), including health professions education, human resource leadership, workplace learning and performance; P-12 educational administration (Ed S), including principalship, supervisor of instruction. *Accreditation:* NCATE. *Program availability:* Part-time, evening/weekend, online learning. *Students:* 278 full-time (65 women), 409 part-time (260 women); includes 202 minority (121 Black or African American, non-Hispanic/Latino; 1 American Indian or Alaska Native, non-Hispanic/Latino; 13 Asian, non-Hispanic/Latino; 44 Hispanic/Latino; 3 Native Hawaiian or other Pacific Islander, non-Hispanic/Latino; 20 Two or more races, non-Hispanic/Latino), 5 international. Average age 36. 233 applicants, 78% accepted, 129 enrolled. In 2016, 58 master's, 4 doctorates, 17 other advanced degrees awarded. Application fee: $60. *Expenses:* Tuition, state resident: full-time $12,246; part-time $681 per credit hour. Tuition, nonresident: full-time $25,486; part-time $1417 per credit hour. *Required fees:* $196. Tuition and fees vary according to program and reciprocity agreements. *Financial support:* Application deadline: 6/1; applicants required to submit FAFSA. *Faculty research:* Urban educational leadership and policy, human resources, organizational development, program evaluation, military education, community partnerships, higher education administration. *Total annual research expenditures:* $256,111. *Unit head:* Dr. Jeffrey Sun, Chair and Professor, 502-852-0618, E-mail: jeffrey.sun@louisville.edu. *Application contact:* Betty Hampton, Director of Graduate Student Services, 502-852-5597, Fax: 502-852-1465, E-mail: edadvise@louisville.edu.
Website: http://louisville.edu/education/departments/eleod

University of Louisville, Graduate School, College of Education and Human Development, Department of Teaching and Learning, Louisville, KY 40292-0001. Offers art education (MAT); autism and applied behavior analysis (Certificate); curriculum and instruction (PhD); early elementary education (MAT); exercise physiology (MS); health and physical education (MAT); health professions education (Certificate); higher education (MA); human resources and organization development (MS); instructional technology (M Ed); interdisciplinary early childhood education (MAT); middle school education (MAT); music education (MAT); secondary education (MAT); special education (MAT); sport administration (MS); teacher leadership (M Ed). *Program availability:* Part-time, evening/weekend. *Students:* 116 full-time (68 women), 158 part-time (112 women); includes 46 minority (24 Black or African American, non-Hispanic/Latino; 8 Asian, non-Hispanic/Latino; 5 Hispanic/Latino; 9 Two or more races, non-Hispanic/Latino), 6 international. Average age 30. 114 applicants, 71% accepted, 57 enrolled. In 2016, 59 master's, 3 doctorates awarded. *Application deadline:* For spring admission, 1/1 priority date for international students. Application fee: $60. *Expenses:* Tuition, state resident: full-time $12,246; part-time $681 per credit hour. Tuition, nonresident: full-time $25,486; part-time $1417 per credit hour. *Required fees:* $196. Tuition and fees vary according to program and reciprocity agreements. *Financial support:* Application deadline: 6/1; applicants required to submit FAFSA. *Faculty research:* STEM teaching and learning; content literacy for English language learners; social justice in teacher education; adolescent literacy; mathematics teacher development. *Total annual research expenditures:* $1.7 million. *Unit head:* Dr. Ann E. Larson, Dean, College of Education and Human Development, 502-852-6411, Fax: 502-852-1464, E-mail: ann@louisville.edu. *Application contact:* Betty Hampton, Director of Graduate Student Services, 502-852-5597, Fax: 502-852-1465, E-mail: edadvise@louisville.edu.
Website: http://louisville.edu/delphi

The University of Manchester, Alliance Manchester Business School, M15 6PB, United Kingdom. Offers accounting and finance (M Sc); business (M Ent); business analysis and strategic management (M Sc); business analytics: operational research and risk analysis (M Sc); business psychology (M Sc); corporate communications and reputation management (M Sc); finance (M Sc); finance and business economics (M Sc); human resource management and industrial relations (M Sc); innovation management and entrepreneurship (M Sc); international business and management (M Sc); international human resource management and comparative industrial relations (M Sc); management (M Sc); marketing (M Sc); operations, project and supply chain management (M Sc); organizational psychology (M Sc); quantitative finance (M Sc). *Entrance requirements:* For master's, UK 2:1 honours degree or overseas equivalent. Additional exam requirements/recommendations for international students: Required—TOEFL (minimum score 100 iBT), IELTS (minimum score 7), PTE. Electronic applications accepted. *Faculty research:* Accounting and finance, management sciences and marketing, people management and organization, innovation management and policy, decision sciences.

University of Mary, Gary Tharaldson School of Business, Bismarck, ND 58504-9652. Offers business administration (MBA); energy management (MBA, MS); executive (MBA, MS); health care (MBA, MS); human resource management (MBA); project management (MBA, MPM); virtuous leadership (MBA, MPM, MS). *Program availability:* Part-time, evening/weekend. *Entrance requirements:* For master's, minimum GPA of 2.5. Additional exam requirements/recommendations for international students: Required—TOEFL (minimum score 550 paper-based; 80 iBT). Electronic applications accepted.

University of Memphis, Graduate School, University College, Memphis, TN 38152. Offers human resources (MPS); liberal studies (MALS, Graduate Certificate); strategic leadership (MPS, Graduate Certificate); training and development (MPS). *Program availability:* Part-time, evening/weekend. *Faculty:* 3 full-time (1 woman), 2 part-time/adjunct (0 women). *Students:* 25 full-time (14 women), 98 part-time (71 women); includes 85 minority (76 Black or African American, non-Hispanic/Latino; 1 Asian, non-Hispanic/Latino; 5 Hispanic/Latino; 3 Two or more races, non-Hispanic/Latino), 2 international. Average age 38. 59 applicants, 73% accepted, 29 enrolled. In 2016, 53 master's, 4 other advanced degrees awarded. *Degree requirements:* For master's, comprehensive exam, thesis (for some programs). *Entrance requirements:* For master's,

GRE (for MPS), resume, letters of recommendation, personal essay, interview, minimum undergraduate GPA of 2.75 (for MALS); portfolio in lieu of GRE (for MPS applicants with substantial professional work experience); for Graduate Certificate, essay, letter of recommendation. Additional exam requirements/recommendations for international students: Required—TOEFL (minimum score 550 paper-based; 79 iBT). *Application deadline:* For fall admission, 7/1 for domestic students, 5/1 for international students; for spring admission, 11/1 for domestic students, 9/15 for international students. Applications are processed on a rolling basis. Application fee: $35 ($60 for international students). Electronic applications accepted. *Expenses:* $5,231.50 per semester full-time in-state, $9,623.50 full-time out-of-state. *Financial support:* In 2016–17, 123 students received support, including 2 research assistantships with full tuition reimbursements available (averaging $17,000 per year), 3 teaching assistantships with tuition reimbursements available (averaging $11,334 per year); Federal Work-Study, scholarships/grants, and unspecified assistantships also available. Financial award application deadline: 2/3; financial award applicants required to submit FAFSA. *Faculty research:* Media ethics, history of psychiatry, public relations. *Unit head:* Dr. Dan Lattimore, Dean, 901-678-2991, E-mail: dlattimr@memphis.edu. *Application contact:* Dr. Colin Chapell, Graduate Coordinator, 901-678-4171, Fax: 901-678-2971, E-mail: cbshpell@memphis.edu.
Website: http://www.memphis.edu/univcoll/

University of Minnesota, Twin Cities Campus, Carlson School of Management, Carlson Full-Time MBA Program, Minneapolis, MN 55455. Offers finance (MBA); human resources and industrial relations (MA); information technology (MBA); management (MBA); marketing (MBA); medical industry orientation (MBA); supply chain and operations (MBA); JD/MBA; MBA/MPP; MBA/MSBA; MD/MBA; MHA/MBA; Pharm D/MBA. *Accreditation:* AACSB. *Faculty:* 143 full-time (42 women), 24 part-time/adjunct (6 women). *Students:* 193 full-time (59 women); includes 23 minority (2 Black or African American, non-Hispanic/Latino; 1 American Indian or Alaska Native, non-Hispanic/Latino; 9 Asian, non-Hispanic/Latino; 5 Hispanic/Latino; 1 Native Hawaiian or other Pacific Islander, non-Hispanic/Latino; 5 Two or more races, non-Hispanic/Latino), 31 international. Average age 28. 606 applicants, 45% accepted, 104 enrolled. In 2016, 102 master's awarded. *Entrance requirements:* For master's, GMAT or GRE. Additional exam requirements/recommendations for international students: Required—TOEFL (minimum score 580 paper-based; 84 iBT), IELTS (minimum score 7), PTE. *Application deadline:* For fall admission, 4/1 for domestic students, 2/1 for international students. Application fee: $75. Electronic applications accepted. *Expenses:* $39,378 per year resident tuition and fees; $49,766 per year non-resident tuition and fees; $50,084 per year international tuition and fees. *Financial support:* In 2016–17, 148 students received support, including 148 fellowships with tuition reimbursements available (averaging $21,070 per year); research assistantships with partial tuition reimbursements available, teaching assistantships with partial tuition reimbursements available, career-related internships or fieldwork, Federal Work-Study, institutionally sponsored loans, scholarships/grants, health care benefits, and unspecified assistantships also available. Financial award application deadline: 4/1; financial award applicants required to submit FAFSA. *Faculty research:* Market regulation and asset pricing, social networks and data analytics, consumer behavior, innovation and entrepreneurship, workplace wellbeing and labor relationships. *Total annual research expenditures:* $577,440. *Unit head:* Philip J. Miller, Assistant Dean, MBA Programs and Graduate Business Career Center, 612-625-5555, Fax: 612-625-1012, E-mail: mba@umn.edu. *Application contact:* Linh Gilles, Director of Admissions and Recruiting, 612-625-5555, Fax: 612-625-1012, E-mail: ftmba@umn.edu.
Website: http://www.csom.umn.edu/MBA/full-time/

University of Minnesota, Twin Cities Campus, Carlson School of Management, Master of Arts Program in Human Resources and Industrial Relations, Minneapolis, MN 55455. Offers MA. *Accreditation:* AACSB. *Program availability:* Part-time, evening/weekend. *Faculty:* 16 full-time (9 women), 12 part-time/adjunct (6 women). *Students:* 117 full-time (81 women), 42 part-time (35 women); includes 20 minority (9 Black or African American, non-Hispanic/Latino; 1 American Indian or Alaska Native, non-Hispanic/Latino; 5 Asian, non-Hispanic/Latino; 5 Hispanic/Latino), 56 international. Average age 25. 238 applicants, 52% accepted, 75 enrolled. In 2016, 69 master's awarded. *Degree requirements:* For master's, thesis or alternative, 48 course credits. *Entrance requirements:* For master's, GMAT or GRE General Test, undergraduate degree from accredited institution, course in microeconomics. Additional exam requirements/recommendations for international students: Required—TOEFL (minimum score 550 paper-based; 79 iBT), IELTS (minimum score 6.5). *Application deadline:* For fall admission, 6/15 for domestic and international students; for spring admission, 10/15 for domestic and international students. Applications are processed on a rolling basis. Application fee: $75 ($95 for international students). Electronic applications accepted. *Expenses:* Contact institution. *Financial support:* In 2016–17, 66 students received support, including 57 fellowships (averaging $7,500 per year), 2 research assistantships with partial tuition reimbursements available (averaging $14,500 per year), 7 teaching assistantships with partial tuition reimbursements available (averaging $9,000 per year); Federal Work-Study, institutionally sponsored loans, scholarships/grants, health care benefits, tuition waivers (full and partial), and unspecified assistantships also available. Financial award application deadline: 2/1; financial award applicants required to submit FAFSA. *Faculty research:* Staffing, training, and development; compensation and benefits; organization theory; collective bargaining. *Total annual research expenditures:* $27,000. *Unit head:* Stacy Doepner-Hove, Director, 612-625-8732, Fax: 612-624-8360, E-mail: doepn002@umn.edu. *Application contact:* Amy Danzeisen, Admissions Associate, 612-624-5704, Fax: 612-624-8360, E-mail: hrirgrad@umn.edu.
Website: http://www.csom.umn.edu/chrls/

University of Missouri–St. Louis, College of Business Administration, Program in Business Administration, St. Louis, MO 63121. Offers accounting (MBA); business administration (Certificate); business intelligence (Certificate); cybersecurity (Certificate); digital and social media marketing (Certificate); finance (MBA), human resources management (Certificate); information systems (MBA); international business (MBA); logistics and supply chain management (MBA, PhD, Certificate); management (MBA); marketing (MBA); marketing management (Certificate); operations management (MBA). *Accreditation:* AACSB. *Program availability:* Part-time, evening/weekend. *Faculty:* 32 full-time (10 women), 14 part-time/adjunct (3 women). *Students:* 181 full-time (88 women), 357 part-time (154 women); includes 83 minority (30 Black or African American, non-Hispanic/Latino; 36 Asian, non-Hispanic/Latino; 12 Hispanic/Latino; 2 Native Hawaiian or other Pacific Islander, non-Hispanic/Latino; 3 Two or more races, non-Hispanic/Latino), 100 international. Average age 31. 245 applicants, 83% accepted, 139 enrolled. *Degree requirements:* For doctorate, thesis/dissertation. *Entrance requirements:* For master's, GMAT, 2 letters of recommendation. Additional exam requirements/recommendations for international students: Recommended—TOEFL (minimum score 550 paper-based; 79 iBT), IELTS (minimum score 6.5). *Application deadline:* For fall admission, 7/1 for domestic and international students; for spring admission, 12/1 for domestic and international students. Applications are processed on a rolling basis. Application fee: $50 ($40 for international students). Electronic applications accepted. *Financial support:* Research assistantships with tuition reimbursements, teaching assistantships with tuition reimbursements, career-related internships or fieldwork, Federal Work-Study, and institutionally sponsored loans available. Support available to part-time students. Financial award application deadline: 4/1; financial award applicants required to submit FAFSA. *Faculty research:* Human resources, strategic management, marketing strategy, consumer behavior product development, advertising. *Unit head:* Dr. Thomas H. Eyssell, Associate Dean and Director of Graduate Studies, 314-516-5885, Fax: 314-516-6420, E-mail: mba@umsl.edu. *Application contact:* 314-516-5458, Fax: 314-516-6996, E-mail: gradadm@umsl.edu.

University of Nebraska at Kearney, College of Business and Technology, Department of Business, Kearney, NE 68849-0001. Offers accounting (MBA); generalist (MBA); human resources (MBA); human services (MBA); marketing (MBA). *Accreditation:* AACSB. *Program availability:* Part-time, evening/weekend. *Faculty:* 32 full-time (13 women). *Students:* 11 full-time (5 women), 30 part-time (14 women), 8 international. Average age 39. 13 applicants, 100% accepted, 10 enrolled. In 2016, 6 master's awarded. *Degree requirements:* For master's, thesis optional, capstone course. *Entrance requirements:* For master's, GRE or GMAT (if no significant managerial experience), letters of recommendation, essay, resume. Additional exam requirements/recommendations for international students: Recommended—TOEFL (minimum score 550 paper-based; 79 iBT), IELTS (minimum score 6.5). *Application deadline:* For fall admission, 6/15 for domestic and international students; for spring admission, 10/15 for domestic and international students; for summer admission, 3/15 for domestic and international students. Application fee: $45. Electronic applications accepted. *Expenses:* Tuition, state resident: full-time $4064; part-time $225.75 per credit hour. Tuition, nonresident: full-time $8915; part-time $495.25 per credit hour. *Required fees:* $772; $23 per credit hour. Part-time tuition and fees vary according to course load, campus/location, program and reciprocity agreements. *Financial support:* In 2016–17, 2 research assistantships with full tuition reimbursements (averaging $10,500 per year), 2 teaching assistantships with full tuition reimbursements (averaging $10,500 per year) were awarded; career-related internships or fieldwork, scholarships/grants, health care benefits, and unspecified assistantships also available. Support available to part-time students. Financial award application deadline: 2/28; financial award applicants required to submit FAFSA. *Faculty research:* Small business financial management, employment law, expert systems, international trade and marketing, environmental economics. *Unit head:* Dr. Sri Seshadri, Director, 308-865-8346, Fax: 308-865-8114. *Application contact:* Linda Johnson, Director, Graduate Admissions and Programs, 800-717-7881, Fax: 308-865-8837, E-mail: gradstudies@unk.edu.

University of New Haven, Graduate School, College of Arts and Sciences, Program in Industrial and Organizational Psychology, West Haven, CT 06516. Offers conflict management (MA); industrial organizational psychology (MA); industrial-human resources psychology (MA); organizational development and consultation (MA); psychology of conflict management (Graduate Certificate). *Program availability:* Part-time, evening/weekend. *Students:* 72 full-time (49 women), 18 part-time (12 women); includes 20 minority (10 Black or African American, non-Hispanic/Latino; 1 American Indian or Alaska Native, non-Hispanic/Latino; 6 Asian, non-Hispanic/Latino; 2 Hispanic/Latino; 1 Two or more races, non-Hispanic/Latino), 4 international. Average age 26. 117 applicants, 84% accepted, 34 enrolled. In 2016, 59 master's awarded. *Degree requirements:* For master's, thesis or alternative, internship or practicum. *Entrance requirements:* Additional exam requirements/recommendations for international students: Required—TOEFL (minimum score 80 iBT), IELTS, PTE. *Application deadline:* Applications are processed on a rolling basis. Application fee: $50. Electronic applications accepted. Application fee is waived when completed online. *Expenses:* Contact institution. *Financial support:* Research assistantships with partial tuition reimbursements, teaching assistantships with partial tuition reimbursements, career-related internships or fieldwork, Federal Work-Study, scholarships/grants, and unspecified assistantships available. Support available to part-time students. Financial award applicants required to submit FAFSA. *Unit head:* Dr. Eric Marcus, Coordinator, 203-932-1242, E-mail: emarcus@newhaven.edu. *Application contact:* Michelle Mason, Director of Graduate Enrollment, 203-932-7067.
Website: http://www.newhaven.edu/4730/

University of New Haven, Graduate School, College of Business, Program in Business Administration, West Haven, CT 06516. Offers accounting (MBA), including CPA; business administration (MBA); business intelligence (MBA); business management (Graduate Certificate); business policy and strategic leadership (MBA); finance (MBA), including CFA; global marketing (MBA); human resources management (MBA, Graduate Certificate); sport management (MBA). *Accreditation:* AACSB. *Program availability:* Part-time, evening/weekend. *Students:* 123 full-time (56 women), 74 part-time (29 women); includes 46 minority (24 Black or African American, non-Hispanic/Latino; 8 Asian, non-Hispanic/Latino; 10 Hispanic/Latino; 4 Two or more races, non-Hispanic/Latino), 57 international. Average age 27. In 2016, 100 master's awarded. *Entrance requirements:* For master's, GMAT. Additional exam requirements/recommendations for international students: Required—TOEFL (minimum score 80 iBT), IELTS, PTE. *Application deadline:* Applications are processed on a rolling basis. Application fee: $50. Electronic applications accepted. Application fee is waived when completed online. *Expenses: Tuition:* Full-time $15,660; part-time $870 per credit hour. *Required fees:* $200; $85 per term. Tuition and fees vary according to program. *Financial support:* Research assistantships with partial tuition reimbursements, teaching assistantships with partial tuition reimbursements, career-related internships or fieldwork, Federal Work-Study, scholarships/grants, and unspecified assistantships available. Support available to part-time students. Financial award applicants required to submit FAFSA. *Unit head:* Darell Singleterry, Director, 203-932-1085, E-mail: dsingleterry@newhaven.edu. *Application contact:* Michelle Mason, Director of Graduate Enrollment, 203-932-7067, E-mail: mmason@newhaven.edu.
Website: http://www.newhaven.edu/business/programs/EMBA/

University of New Haven, Graduate School, Henry C. Lee College of Criminal Justice and Forensic Sciences, Program in Public Administration, West Haven, CT 06516. Offers city management (MPA); community-clinical services (MPA); health care management (MPA); long-term health care (MPA); personnel and labor relations (MPA); public administration (MPA, Graduate Certificate); MBA/MPA. *Program availability:* Part-time, evening/weekend. *Students:* 30 full-time (13 women), 15 part-time (8 women); includes 15 minority (12 Black or African American, non-Hispanic/Latino; 1 American Indian or Alaska Native, non-Hispanic/Latino; 1 Asian, non-Hispanic/Latino; 1 Hispanic/Latino), 6 international. Average age 35. 56 applicants, 98% accepted, 25 enrolled. In 2016, 31 master's, 17 other advanced degrees awarded. *Degree requirements:* For master's, thesis or alternative. *Entrance requirements:* Additional exam requirements/recommendations for international students: Required—TOEFL (minimum score 80 iBT), IELTS, PTE. *Application deadline:* Applications are processed on a rolling basis. Application fee: $50. Electronic applications accepted. Application fee is waived when completed online. *Expenses:* Contact institution. *Financial support:* Research assistantships with partial tuition reimbursements, teaching assistantships with partial tuition reimbursements, career-related internships or fieldwork, Federal Work-Study, scholarships/grants, and unspecified assistantships available. Support available to part-time students. Financial award application deadline: 5/1; financial award applicants required to submit FAFSA. *Unit head:* Dr. Cynthia Conrad, Associate Professor, 203-932-7486, E-mail: cconrad@newhaven.edu. *Application contact:* Michelle Mason,

Human Resources Management

Director of Graduate Enrollment, 203-932-7067, E-mail: mmason@newhaven.edu.
Website: http://www.newhaven.edu/6854/

University of New Mexico, Anderson School of Management, Department of Organizational Studies, Albuquerque, NM 87131. Offers organizational behavior and human resources management (MBA); strategic management and policy (MBA). *Program availability:* Part-time, evening/weekend. *Faculty:* 17 full-time (12 women), 6 part-time/adjunct (2 women). In 2016, 26 master's awarded. *Entrance requirements:* For master's, GMAT or GRE, minimum GPA of 3.0 on last 60 hours of coursework; bachelor's degree from regionally-accredited college or university in U.S. or its equivalent in another country. Additional exam requirements/recommendations for international students: Required—TOEFL (minimum score 550 paper-based; 79 iBT), IELTS (minimum score 6.5). *Application deadline:* For fall admission, 4/1 priority date for domestic and international students; for spring admission, 10/1 priority date for domestic and international students. Applications are processed on a rolling basis. Application fee: $50. Electronic applications accepted. *Expenses:* Contact institution. *Financial support:* In 2016–17, 4 fellowships (averaging $24,700 per year), 13 research assistantships with partial tuition reimbursements (averaging $15,345 per year) were awarded; career-related internships or fieldwork, Federal Work-Study, scholarships/grants, and unspecified assistantships also available. Support available to part-time students. Financial award application deadline: 6/1; financial award applicants required to submit FAFSA. *Faculty research:* Business ethics and social corporate responsibility, diversity, human resources, organizational strategy, organizational behavior. *Unit head:* Dr. Michelle Arthur, Chair, 505-277-6471, E-mail: arthurm@unm.edu. *Application contact:* Lisa Beauchene, Student Recruitment Specialist, 505-277-6471, E-mail: andersonadvising@unm.edu.
Website: https://www.mgt.unm.edu/dos/default.asp?mm=faculty

University of Northern Colorado, Graduate School, Monfort College of Business, Greeley, CO 80639. Offers accounting (MA); general business management (MBA); healthcare administration (MBA); human resources management (MBA). *Accreditation:* AACSB. *Unit head:* Donald Gudmundson, Dean, 970-351-2411, E-mail: don.gudmundson@unco.edu. *Application contact:* Linda Sisson, Graduate Student Admission Coordinator, 970-351-1807, Fax: 970-351-2371, E-mail: linda.sisson@unco.edu.
Website: http://mcb.unco.edu/

University of North Florida, Coggin College of Business, MBA Program, Jacksonville, FL 32224. Offers accounting (MBA); construction management (MBA); e-commerce (MBA); economics (MBA); finance (MBA); human resource management (MBA); international business (MBA); logistics (MBA); management applications (MBA). *Accreditation:* AACSB. *Program availability:* Part-time, evening/weekend. *Faculty:* 16 full-time (4 women), 1 (woman) part-time/adjunct. *Students:* 105 full-time (50 women), 162 part-time (68 women); includes 57 minority (14 Black or African American, non-Hispanic/Latino; 1 American Indian or Alaska Native, non-Hispanic/Latino; 17 Asian, non-Hispanic/Latino; 18 Hispanic/Latino; 7 Two or more races, non-Hispanic/Latino), 41 international. Average age 28. 231 applicants, 46% accepted, 84 enrolled. In 2016, 114 master's awarded. *Entrance requirements:* For master's, GMAT or GRE, U.S. bachelor's degree from regionally-accredited university or equivalent foreign degree. Additional exam requirements/recommendations for international students: Required—TOEFL (minimum score 550 paper-based; 79 iBT). *Application deadline:* For fall admission, 8/1 priority date for domestic students, 5/1 for international students; for spring admission, 12/1 priority date for domestic students, 10/1 for international students; for summer admission, 4/29 priority date for domestic students, 2/1 for international students. Application fee: $30. Tuition and fees vary according to course load, campus/location and program. *Financial support:* In 2016–17, 22 students received support, including 1 research assistantship (averaging $2,501 per year); teaching assistantships, Federal Work-Study, and tuition waivers (partial) also available. Support available to part-time students. Financial award application deadline: 4/1; financial award applicants required to submit FAFSA. *Faculty research:* Performance measures, costing, and inventory issues in logistics and supply chain management; inter-organizational systems; international management and marketing practices; e-commerce; organizational learning and socialization processes. *Total annual research expenditures:* $17,654. *Unit head:* Dr. Parvez Ahmed, Graduate Program Director, 904-620-1678, E-mail: pahmed@unf.edu. *Application contact:* Amy Bishop, MSM Advisor, 904-620-2575, Fax: 904-620-2832, E-mail: coggin.students@unf.edu.
Website: http://www.unf.edu/graduateschool/academics/programs/MBA.aspx

University of North Texas, Robert B. Toulouse School of Graduate Studies, Denton, TX 76203-5459. Offers accounting (MS); applied anthropology (MA, MS); applied behavior analysis (Certificate); applied geography (MA); applied technology and performance improvement (M Ed, MS); art education (MA); art history (MA); art museum education (Certificate); arts leadership (Certificate); audiology (Au D); behavior analysis (MS); behavioral science (PhD); biochemistry and molecular biology (MS); biology (MA, MS); biomedical engineering (MS); business analysis (MS); chemistry (MS); clinical health psychology (PhD); communication studies (MA, MS); computer engineering (MS); computer science (MS); counseling (M Ed, MS), including clinical mental health counseling (MS), college and university counseling, elementary school counseling, secondary school counseling; creative writing (MA); criminal justice (MS); curriculum and instruction (M Ed); decision sciences (MBA); design (MA, MFA), including fashion design (MFA), innovation studies, interior design (MFA); early childhood studies (MS); economics (MS); educational leadership (M Ed, Ed D); educational psychology (MS, PhD), including family studies (MS), gifted and talented (MS), human development (MS), learning and cognition (MS), research, measurement and evaluation (MS); electrical engineering (MS); emergency management (MPA); engineering technology (MS); English (MA); English as a second language (MA); environmental science (MS); finance (MBA, MS); financial management (MPA); French (MA); health services management (MBA); higher education (M Ed, Ed D); history (MA, MS); hospitality management (MS); human resources management (MPA); information science (MS); information systems (PhD); information technologies (MBA); interdisciplinary studies (MA, MS); international studies (MA); international sustainable tourism (MS); jazz studies (MM); journalism (MA, MJ, Graduate Certificate), including interactive and virtual digital communication (Graduate Certificate), narrative journalism (Graduate Certificate), public relations (Graduate Certificate); kinesiology (MS); linguistics (MA); local government management (MPA); logistics (PhD); logistics and supply chain management (MBA); long-term care, senior housing, and aging services (MA); management (PhD); marketing (MBA); mathematics (MA, MS); mechanical and energy engineering (MS, PhD); music (MA), including ethnomusicology, music theory, musicology, performance; music composition (PhD); music education (MM Ed, PhD); nonprofit management (MPA); operations and supply chain management (MBA); performance (MM, DMA); philosophy (MA); political science (MA); professional and technical communication (MA); radio, television and film (MA, MFA); rehabilitation counseling (Certificate); sociology (MA); Spanish (MA); special education (M Ed); speech-language pathology (MA); strategic management (MBA); studio art (MFA); teaching (M Ed); MBA/MS. *Program availability:* Part-time, evening/weekend, online learning. Terminal master's awarded for partial completion of doctoral program. *Degree requirements:* For master's, variable foreign language requirement, comprehensive exam (for some programs), thesis (for some programs); for doctorate, variable foreign language requirement, comprehensive exam (for some programs), thesis/dissertation; for other advanced degree, variable foreign language requirement, comprehensive exam (for some programs). *Entrance requirements:* For master's and doctorate, GRE, GMAT. Additional exam requirements/recommendations for international students: Required—TOEFL (minimum score 550 paper-based; 79 iBT). Electronic applications accepted.

University of North Texas at Dallas, Graduate School, Dallas, TX 75241. Offers accounting (MBA); counseling (M Ed, MS); criminal justice (MS); curriculum and instruction (M Ed); educational administration (M Ed); human resources and organizational behavior (MBA); public leadership (MS); strategic management (MBA).

University of Oklahoma, College of Arts and Sciences, Department of Human Relations, Norman, OK 73019. Offers clinical mental health (MHR); helping skills in human relations (Graduate Certificate); human relations (MHR); human resource diversity and development (Graduate Certificate); human resources (MHR); licensed professional counselor (MHR). *Program availability:* Part-time, evening/weekend. *Faculty:* 24 full-time (16 women), 6 part-time/adjunct (3 women). *Students:* 262 full-time (190 women), 397 part-time (260 women); includes 331 minority (161 Black or African American, non-Hispanic/Latino; 23 American Indian or Alaska Native, non-Hispanic/Latino; 25 Asian, non-Hispanic/Latino; 74 Hispanic/Latino; 2 Native Hawaiian or other Pacific Islander, non-Hispanic/Latino; 46 Two or more races, non-Hispanic/Latino), 15 international. Average age 35. 135 applicants, 93% accepted, 89 enrolled. In 2016, 289 master's, 113 other advanced degrees awarded. *Degree requirements:* For master's, comprehensive exam (for some programs), thesis (for some programs), comprehensive exam or thesis; 15 hours in human relations classroom courses. *Entrance requirements:* For degree, minimum GPA of 3.0. Additional exam requirements/recommendations for international students: Required—TOEFL (minimum score 79 iBT) or IELTS (minimum score 6.5). *Application deadline:* For fall admission, 8/21 for domestic and international students; for spring admission, 1/23 for domestic and international students; for summer admission, 6/5 for domestic and international students. Application fee: $50 ($100 for international students). Electronic applications accepted. *Expenses:* Tuition, state resident: full-time $4886; part-time $203.60 per credit hour. Tuition, nonresident: full-time $18,989; part-time $791.20 per credit hour. *Required fees:* $3283; $126.25 per credit hour. $126.50 per semester. *Financial support:* In 2016–17, 148 students received support, including 8 research assistantships with full tuition reimbursements available (averaging $11,124 per year), 5 teaching assistantships with full tuition reimbursements available (averaging $12,199 per year); scholarships/grants also available. Financial award application deadline: 6/1; financial award applicants required to submit FAFSA. *Faculty research:* At-risk youth, strength model, women's health, adolescent addiction and recovery, group psychotherapy. *Unit head:* Dr. Wesley Long, Chair of Department of Human Relations, 405-325-1756, Fax: 405-325-4402, E-mail: wlong@ou.edu. *Application contact:* Lawana Miller, Admissions Coordinator, 405-325-1756, Fax: 405-325-4402, E-mail: lmiller@ou.edu.
Website: http://humanrelations.ou.edu

University of Oklahoma, College of Arts and Sciences, Department of Psychology, Program in Organizational Dynamics, Tulsa, OK 74135. Offers human resource management (MA, Graduate Certificate); project management (MA, Graduate Certificate). *Program availability:* Part-time, evening/weekend. *Students:* 9 full-time (all women), 24 part-time (14 women); includes 6 minority (1 Black or African American, non-Hispanic/Latino; 2 American Indian or Alaska Native, non-Hispanic/Latino; 1 Asian, non-Hispanic/Latino; 2 Hispanic/Latino), 3 international. Average age 34. 13 applicants, 62% accepted, 6 enrolled. In 2016, 6 master's awarded. Terminal master's awarded for partial completion of doctoral program. *Degree requirements:* For master's, comprehensive exam (for some programs), thesis (for some programs), capstone project, comprehensive exam, or thesis; 36 hours of coursework; for Graduate Certificate, 12 hours of coursework from approved list. *Entrance requirements:* For master's, GRE (for students who do not have requisite work experience), current resume showing at least 2 years of relevant work experience; 2 letters of recommendation; statement of career goals; transcripts; for Graduate Certificate, resume showing work experience; 2 letters of recommendation; statement of career goals; transcripts. Additional exam requirements/recommendations for international students: Required—TOEFL (minimum score 79 iBT) or IELTS (minimum score 6.5). *Application deadline:* For fall admission, 5/1 for domestic and international students; for spring admission, 11/1 for domestic and international students; for summer admission, 3/15 for domestic and international students. Application fee: $50 ($100 for international students). Electronic applications accepted. *Expenses:* Tuition, state resident: full-time $4886; part-time $203.60 per credit hour. Tuition, nonresident: full-time $18,989; part-time $791.20 per credit hour. *Required fees:* $3283; $126.25 per credit hour. $126.50 per semester. *Financial support:* In 2016–17, 12 students received support. Research assistantships with full tuition reimbursements available, health care benefits, and unspecified assistantships available. Financial award application deadline: 6/1; financial award applicants required to submit FAFSA. *Faculty research:* Organizational behavior, personality, organizational climate and culture, leadership, ethics. *Unit head:* Dr. Eric Day, Chair, 405-325-4511, Fax: 405-325-4737, E-mail: eday@ou.edu. *Application contact:* Jennifer Kisamore, Associate Professor of Psychology/Graduate Liaison for Organizational Dynamics, 918-660-3603, Fax: 918-660-3383, E-mail: odyn@ou.edu.
Website: http://odyn.ou.edu

University of Phoenix–Atlanta Campus, School of Business, Sandy Springs, GA 30350-4147. Offers accounting (MBA); business administration (MBA); global management (MBA); human resources management (MBA, MM); management (MM); marketing (MBA); public administration (MM). *Accreditation:* ACBSP. *Program availability:* Evening/weekend, online learning. *Degree requirements:* For master's, thesis (for some programs). *Entrance requirements:* For master's, minimum undergraduate GPA of 3.0, 3 years of work experience. Additional exam requirements/recommendations for international students: Required—TOEFL (minimum score 550 paper-based; 79 iBT).

University of Phoenix–Augusta Campus, School of Business, Augusta, GA 30909-4583. Offers accounting (MBA); business administration (MBA); business and management (MBA, MM); global management (MBA); human resources management (MBA, MM); management (MM); marketing (MBA); public administration (MBA, MM). *Accreditation:* ACBSP. *Program availability:* Online learning.

University of Phoenix–Bay Area Campus, School of Business, San Jose, CA 95134-1805. Offers accountancy (MS); accounting (MBA); business administration (MBA, DBA); energy management (MBA); global management (MBA); health care management (MBA); human resource management (MBA); human resources management (MM); management (MM); marketing (MBA); organizational leadership (DM); project management (MBA); public administration (MPA); technology management (MBA). *Accreditation:* ACBSP. *Program availability:* Evening/weekend, online learning. *Degree requirements:* For master's, thesis (for some programs). *Entrance requirements:* For master's, minimum undergraduate GPA of 3.0, 3 years of work experience. Additional exam requirements/recommendations for international students: Required—TOEFL (minimum score 550 paper-based; 79 iBT). Electronic applications accepted.

University of Phoenix–Central Valley Campus, School of Business, Fresno, CA 93720-1552. Offers accounting (MBA); business administration (MBA); global management (MBA); human resources management (MBA, MM); management (MM); marketing (MBA); public administration (MBA, MM). *Accreditation:* ACBSP.

University of Phoenix–Colorado Campus, School of Business, Lone Tree, CO 80124-5453. Offers accountancy (MSA); accounting (MBA); business administration (MBA); e-business (MBA); global management (MBA); human resources management (MBA, MM); management (MM); marketing (MBA); public administration (MBA, MM). *Accreditation:* ACBSP. *Program availability:* Evening/weekend, online learning. *Degree requirements:* For master's, thesis (for some programs). *Entrance requirements:* For master's, minimum undergraduate GPA of 3.0, 3 years work experience. Additional exam requirements/recommendations for international students: Required—TOEFL (minimum score 550 paper-based; 79 iBT). Electronic applications accepted.

University of Phoenix–Colorado Springs Downtown Campus, School of Business, Colorado Springs, CO 80903. Offers accounting (MBA); business administration (MBA); global management (MBA); human resources management (MBA, MM); management (MM); marketing (MBA); public administration (MM). *Program availability:* Evening/weekend. *Degree requirements:* For master's, thesis (for some programs). *Entrance requirements:* For master's, minimum undergraduate GPA of 3.0, 3 years of work experience. Additional exam requirements/recommendations for international students: Required—TOEFL (minimum score 550 paper-based; 79 iBT). Electronic applications accepted.

University of Phoenix–Columbus Georgia Campus, School of Business, Columbus, GA 31909. Offers accounting (MBA); business administration (MBA); global management (MBA); human resources management (MBA, MM); management (MM); marketing (MBA); public administration (MBA). *Accreditation:* ACBSP. *Program availability:* Evening/weekend. *Degree requirements:* For master's, thesis (for some programs). *Entrance requirements:* For master's, minimum undergraduate GPA of 3.0, 3 years of work experience. Additional exam requirements/recommendations for international students: Required—TOEFL (minimum score 550 paper-based; 79 iBT). Electronic applications accepted.

University of Phoenix–Dallas Campus, School of Business, Dallas, TX 75251. Offers accounting (MBA); business administration (MBA); global management (MBA); human resources management (MBA, MM); management (MM); marketing (MBA); public administration (MBA, MM). *Accreditation:* ACBSP. *Program availability:* Evening/weekend, online learning. *Degree requirements:* For master's, thesis (for some programs). *Entrance requirements:* For master's, 3 years of work experience, minimum undergraduate GPA of 3.0. Additional exam requirements/recommendations for international students: Required—TOEFL (minimum score 550 paper-based; 79 iBT). Electronic applications accepted.

University of Phoenix–Hawaii Campus, School of Business, Honolulu, HI 96813-3800. Offers accounting (MBA); business administration (MBA); global management (MBA); human resources management (MBA, MM); management (MM); marketing (MBA); public administration (MBA, MM). *Accreditation:* ACBSP. *Program availability:* Evening/weekend. *Degree requirements:* For master's, thesis (for some programs). *Entrance requirements:* For master's, minimum undergraduate GPA of 3.0, 3 years of work experience. Additional exam requirements/recommendations for international students: Required—TOEFL (minimum score 550 paper-based; 79 iBT). Electronic applications accepted.

University of Phoenix–Houston Campus, School of Business, Houston, TX 77079-2004. Offers accounting (MBA); business administration (MBA); global management (MBA); human resources management (MBA, MM); management (MM); marketing (MBA); public administration (MBA, MM). *Accreditation:* ACBSP. *Program availability:* Evening/weekend, online learning. *Degree requirements:* For master's, thesis (for some programs). *Entrance requirements:* For master's, 3 years of work experience, minimum undergraduate GPA of 3.0. Additional exam requirements/recommendations for international students: Required—TOEFL (minimum score 550 paper-based; 79 iBT). Electronic applications accepted.

University of Phoenix–Jersey City Campus, School of Business, Jersey City, NJ 07310. Offers accounting (MBA); business administration (MBA); global management (MBA); human resources management (MBA, MM); management (MM); marketing (MBA); public administration (MBA, MM). *Accreditation:* ACBSP.

University of Phoenix–Las Vegas Campus, School of Business, Las Vegas, NV 89135. Offers accounting (MBA); business administration (MBA); global management (MBA); human resources management (MBA, MM); management (MM); marketing (MBA); public administration (MM). *Accreditation:* ACBSP. *Program availability:* Evening/weekend, online learning. *Degree requirements:* For master's, thesis (for some programs). *Entrance requirements:* For master's, minimum undergraduate GPA of 3.0, 3 years of work experience. Additional exam requirements/recommendations for international students: Required—TOEFL (minimum score 550 paper-based; 79 iBT). Electronic applications accepted.

University of Phoenix–New Mexico Campus, School of Business, Albuquerque, NM 87113-1570. Offers accounting (MBA); business administration (MBA); global management (MBA); human resources management (MBA, MM); management (MM); marketing (MBA). *Accreditation:* ACBSP. *Program availability:* Evening/weekend. *Degree requirements:* For master's, thesis (for some programs). *Entrance requirements:* For master's, 3 years of work experience, minimum undergraduate GPA of 3.0. Additional exam requirements/recommendations for international students: Required—TOEFL (minimum score 550 paper-based; 79 iBT). Electronic applications accepted.

University of Phoenix–North Florida Campus, School of Business, Jacksonville, FL 32216-0959. Offers accounting (MBA); business administration (MBA); global management (MBA); human resources management (MBA, MM); management (MM); marketing (MBA); public administration (MBA, MM). *Accreditation:* ACBSP. *Program availability:* Evening/weekend. *Degree requirements:* For master's, thesis (for some programs). *Entrance requirements:* For master's, minimum undergraduate GPA of 3.0, 3 years work experience. Additional exam requirements/recommendations for international students: Required—TOEFL (minimum score 550 paper-based; 79 iBT). Electronic applications accepted.

University of Phoenix–Online Campus, School of Business, Phoenix, AZ 85034-7209. Offers accountancy (MS); accounting (MBA, Certificate); business administration (MBA); energy management (MBA); global management (MBA); health care management (MBA); human resource management (MBA, Certificate); human resources management (MM); management (MM); marketing (MBA, Certificate); project management (MBA, Certificate); public administration (MBA, MM); technology management (MBA). *Program availability:* Evening/weekend, online learning. *Entrance requirements:* Additional exam requirements/recommendations for international students: Required—TOEFL, TOEIC (Test of English as an International Communication), Berlitz Online English Proficiency Exam, PTE, or IELTS. Electronic applications accepted. *Expenses:* Contact institution.

University of Phoenix–Phoenix Campus, School of Business, Tempe, AZ 85282-2371. Offers accounting (MBA, MS, Certificate); business administration (MBA); energy management (MBA); global management (MBA); health care management (MBA); human resource management (MBA, Certificate); management (MM); marketing (MBA); project management (MBA); technology management (MBA). *Program availability:* Evening/weekend, online learning. *Entrance requirements:* Additional exam requirements/recommendations for international students: Required—TOEFL, TOEIC (Test of English as an International Communication), Berlitz Online English Proficiency Exam, PTE, or IELTS. Electronic applications accepted. *Expenses:* Contact institution.

University of Phoenix–Sacramento Valley Campus, School of Business, Sacramento, CA 95833-4334. Offers accounting (MBA); business administration (MBA); global management (MBA); human resources management (MBA, MM); management (MM); marketing (MBA); public administration (MBA, MM). *Accreditation:* ACBSP. *Program availability:* Evening/weekend. *Degree requirements:* For master's, thesis (for some programs). *Entrance requirements:* For master's, minimum undergraduate GPA of 3.0, 3 years work experience. Additional exam requirements/recommendations for international students: Required—TOEFL (minimum score 550 paper-based; 79 iBT). Electronic applications accepted.

University of Phoenix–San Antonio Campus, School of Business, San Antonio, TX 78230. Offers accounting (MBA); business administration (MBA); e-business (MBA); global management (MBA); human resources management (MBA, MM); management (MM); marketing (MBA); public administration (MBA, MM). *Accreditation:* ACBSP.

University of Phoenix–San Diego Campus, School of Business, San Diego, CA 92123. Offers accounting (MBA); business administration (MBA); global management (MBA); human resources management (MBA, MM); management (MM); marketing (MBA); public administration (MBA). *Accreditation:* ACBSP. *Program availability:* Evening/weekend. *Degree requirements:* For master's, thesis (for some programs). *Entrance requirements:* For master's, 3 years of work experience, minimum undergraduate GPA of 3.0. Additional exam requirements/recommendations for international students: Required—TOEFL (minimum score 550 paper-based; 79 iBT). Electronic applications accepted.

University of Phoenix–Southern Arizona Campus, School of Business, Tucson, AZ 85711. Offers accountancy (MS); accounting (MBA); business administration (MBA); global management (MBA); human resources management (MBA); management (MM); marketing (MBA). *Accreditation:* ACBSP. *Program availability:* Evening/weekend. *Degree requirements:* For master's, thesis (for some programs). *Entrance requirements:* For master's, minimum undergraduate GPA of 3.0, 3 years of work experience. Additional exam requirements/recommendations for international students: Required—TOEFL (minimum score 550 paper-based; 79 iBT). Electronic applications accepted.

University of Phoenix–Southern California Campus, School of Business, Costa Mesa, CA 92626. Offers accounting (MBA); business administration (MBA); energy management (MBA); global management (MBA); health care management (MBA); human resource management (MBA); management (MM); marketing (MBA); project management (MBA); technology management (MBA). *Program availability:* Evening/weekend, online learning. *Entrance requirements:* Additional exam requirements/recommendations for international students: Required—TOEFL, TOEIC (Test of English as an International Communication), Berlitz Online English Proficiency Exam, PTE, or IELTS. Electronic applications accepted. *Expenses:* Contact institution.

University of Phoenix–South Florida Campus, School of Business, Miramar, FL 33027-4145. Offers accounting (MBA); business administration (MBA); global management (MBA); human resource management (MBA); human resources management (MM); management (MM); marketing (MBA); public administration (MBA, MM). *Accreditation:* ACBSP. *Program availability:* Evening/weekend. *Degree requirements:* For master's, thesis (for some programs). *Entrance requirements:* For master's, minimum undergraduate GPA of 3.0, 3 years work experience. Additional exam requirements/recommendations for international students: Required—TOEFL (minimum score 550 paper-based; 79 iBT). Electronic applications accepted.

University of Phoenix–Utah Campus, School of Business, Salt Lake City, UT 84123-4642. Offers accounting (MBA); business administration (MBA); global management (MBA); human resource management (MBA, MM); management (MM); marketing (MBA); technology management (MBA). *Accreditation:* ACBSP. *Program availability:* Evening/weekend. *Degree requirements:* For master's, thesis (for some programs). *Entrance requirements:* For master's, minimum undergraduate GPA of 3.0, 3 years of work experience. Additional exam requirements/recommendations for international students: Required—TOEFL (minimum score 550 paper-based; 79 iBT). Electronic applications accepted.

University of Phoenix–Washington D.C. Campus, School of Business, Washington, DC 20001. Offers accountancy (MS); business administration (MBA, DBA); human resources management (MM); management (MM); organizational leadership (DM); public administration (MPA). *Accreditation:* ACBSP.

University of Pittsburgh, Katz Graduate School of Business, Doctoral Program in Business Administration, Pittsburgh, PA 15260. Offers accounting (PhD); business analytics and operations (PhD); finance (PhD); information systems and technology management (PhD); marketing (PhD); organizational behavior and human resources (PhD); strategic management (PhD). *Accreditation:* AACSB. *Program availability:* Evening/weekend. *Faculty:* 88 full-time (27 women), 42 part-time/adjunct (15 women). *Students:* 51 full-time (23 women), 1 part-time (0 women); includes 4 minority (1 Black or African American, non-Hispanic/Latino; 2 Asian, non-Hispanic/Latino; 1 Two or more races, non-Hispanic/Latino), 31 international. Average age 31. 344 applicants, 6% accepted, 9 enrolled. In 2016, 5 doctorates awarded. *Degree requirements:* For doctorate, comprehensive exam, thesis/dissertation, student teaching. *Entrance requirements:* For doctorate, GMAT or GRE, 3 recommendations, statement of purpose, transcripts of all previous course work and degrees. Additional exam requirements/recommendations for international students: Required—TOEFL (minimum score 100 iBT) or IELTS (minimum score 7.0). *Application deadline:* For fall admission, 4/1 priority date for domestic students, 2/1 priority date for international students. Applications are processed on a rolling basis. Application fee: $50. Electronic applications accepted. *Expenses:* Contact institution. *Financial support:* In 2016–17, 40 students received support, including 27 research assistantships with full tuition reimbursements available (averaging $26,000 per year), 9 teaching assistantships with full tuition reimbursements available (averaging $26,700 per year); Federal Work-Study, scholarships/grants, health care benefits, and unspecified assistantships also available. Financial award application deadline: 6/1; financial award applicants required to submit FAFSA. *Faculty research:* Accounting systems/financial reporting, corporate finance, shopper marketing/consumer behavior, management information systems, organizational behavior and entrepreneurship. *Total annual research expenditures:* $493,036. *Unit head:* Dr. Arjang A. Assad, Dean, 412-648-1556, Fax: 412-648-1552, E-mail: aassad@katz.pitt.edu. *Application contact:* Dr. Dennis Galletta, Director, 412-648-1699, Fax: 412-648-3633, E-mail: galletta@katz.pitt.edu.
Website: http://www.business.pitt.edu/katz/phd/

See Display on page 160 and Close-Up on page 189.

University of Pittsburgh, Katz Graduate School of Business, Master of Business Administration Programs, Pittsburgh, PA 15260. Offers finance (MBA); information systems (MBA); marketing (MBA); operations (MBA); organizational behavior and human resources (MBA); strategy, environment and organizations (MBA); MBA/JD;

MBA/MSE. *Accreditation:* AACSB. *Program availability:* Part-time, evening/weekend, blended/hybrid learning. *Faculty:* 88 full-time (27 women), 42 part-time/adjunct (15 women). *Students:* 165 full-time (59 women), 330 part-time (103 women); includes 70 minority (29 Black or African American, non-Hispanic/Latino; 20 Asian, non-Hispanic/Latino; 13 Hispanic/Latino; 8 Two or more races, non-Hispanic/Latino), 73 international. Average age 29. 786 applicants, 41% accepted, 179 enrolled. In 2016, 477 master's awarded. *Degree requirements:* For master's, minimum GPA of 3.0. *Entrance requirements:* For master's, GMAT, GRE. Additional exam requirements/recommendations for international students: Required—TOEFL (minimum score 100 iBT) or IELTS (minimum score 7.0). *Application deadline:* For fall admission, 4/1 priority date for domestic students, 2/1 priority date for international students. Application fee: $50. Electronic applications accepted. *Expenses:* Contact institution. *Financial support:* In 2016–17, 110 students received support. Scholarships/grants available. Financial award application deadline: 6/1; financial award applicants required to submit FAFSA. *Faculty research:* Accounting systems/financial reporting, corporate finance, shopper marketing/consumer behavior, management information systems, organizational behavior and entrepreneurship. *Total annual research expenditures:* $493,036. *Unit head:* Dr. Arjang A. Assad, Dean, 412-648-1556, Fax: 412-648-1552, E-mail: aassad@katz.pitt.edu. *Application contact:* Thomas Keller, Director of MBA Admissions, 412-648-1700, Fax: 412-648-1659, E-mail: mba@katz.pitt.edu.
Website: http://www.business.pitt.edu/katz/mba/

See Display on page 160 and Close-Up on page 189.

University of Puerto Rico, Mayagüez Campus, Graduate Studies, College of Business Administration, Mayagüez, PR 00681-9000. Offers business administration (MBA); finance (MBA); human resources (MBA); industrial management (MBA). *Program availability:* Part-time, evening/weekend. *Faculty:* 24 full-time (10 women). *Students:* 37 full-time (24 women), 27 part-time (18 women); includes 60 minority (all Hispanic/Latino). Average age 25. 22 applicants, 68% accepted, 12 enrolled. In 2016, 6 master's awarded. *Degree requirements:* For master's, one foreign language, comprehensive exam, thesis (for some programs). *Entrance requirements:* For master's, GMAT or EXADEP, bachelor's degree with courses in calculus, microeconomics, accounting and statistics. Additional exam requirements/recommendations for international students: Required—TOEFL (minimum score 500 paper-based; 173 iBT), GMAT or EXADEP. *Application deadline:* For fall admission, 2/15 for domestic and international students; for spring admission, 9/15 for domestic and international students. Applications are processed on a rolling basis. Application fee: $25. Electronic applications accepted. *Expenses: Tuition, area resident:* Full-time $2466. *International tuition:* $7166 full-time. *Required fees:* $210. Tuition and fees vary according to course level, campus/location, program and student level. *Financial support:* In 2016–17, 6 students received support, including 5 research assistantships with full and partial tuition reimbursements available (averaging $4,489 per year), 4 teaching assistantships with full and partial tuition reimbursements available (averaging $4,605 per year); unspecified assistantships also available. *Faculty research:* Organizational studies, management, accounting, entrepreneurship, leadership and motivation. *Unit head:* Roberto L. Seijo, PhD, Department Head, 787-832-4040 Ext. 3887, Fax: 787-832-5320, E-mail: roberto.seijo@upr.edu. *Application contact:* Judith Valentín, Administrative Secretary, 787-265-3887, Fax: 787-832-5320, E-mail: grad.adem@uprm.edu.
Website: http://enterprise.uprm.edu/

University of Puerto Rico, Río Piedras Campus, College of Business Administration, San Juan, PR 00931-3300. Offers accounting (MBA); finance (MBA, PhD); general business (MBA); human resources management (MBA); international trade and business (MBA, PhD); marketing (MBA); operations management (MBA); quantitative methods (MBA). *Accreditation:* AACSB. *Program availability:* Part-time. *Degree requirements:* For master's, comprehensive exam, thesis or alternative, research project. *Entrance requirements:* For master's, GMAT or PAEG, minimum GPA of 3.0, letter of recommendation; for doctorate, GMAT, PAEG, minimum GPA of 3.0, master degree. *Faculty research:* Management.

University of Regina, Faculty of Graduate Studies and Research, Kenneth Levene Graduate School of Business, Program in Human Resources Management, Regina, SK S4S 0A2, Canada. Offers MHRM, Master's Certificate. *Program availability:* Part-time. *Faculty:* 43 full-time (15 women), 6 part-time/adjunct (0 women). *Students:* 28 full-time (21 women), 19 part-time (13 women). 65 applicants, 28% accepted. In 2016, 17 master's awarded. *Degree requirements:* For master's, project. *Entrance requirements:* For master's, two years of relevant work experience. Additional exam requirements/recommendations for international students: Required—TOEFL (minimum score 580 paper-based; 80 iBT), IELTS (minimum score 6.5), PTE (minimum score 59). *Application deadline:* Applications are processed on a rolling basis. Application fee: $100. Electronic applications accepted. *Expenses:* Contact institution. *Financial support:* In 2016–17, 2 fellowships (averaging $6,000 per year), 4 teaching assistantships (averaging $2,501 per year) were awarded; career-related internships or fieldwork and scholarships/grants also available. Financial award application deadline: 6/15. *Faculty research:* Human behavior in organizations, labor relations and collective bargaining, organization theory, staffing organizations, human resources systems analysis. *Unit head:* Dr. Andrew Gaudes, Dean, 306-585-4162, Fax: 306-585-5361, E-mail: andrew.gaudes@uregina.ca. *Application contact:* Ronald Camp, Graduate Programs, 306-337-2387, Fax: 306-585-5361, E-mail: ronald.camp@uregina.ca.
Website: http://www.uregina.ca/business/levene/

University of Rhode Island, Graduate School, Schmidt Labor Research Center, Kingston, RI 02881. Offers human resources (MS, Graduate Certificate); labor relations (MS, Graduate Certificate); MS/JD. *Program availability:* Part-time, evening/weekend. *Faculty:* 1 full-time (0 women), 3 part-time/adjunct (2 women). *Students:* 3 full-time (2 women), 30 part-time (24 women); includes 6 minority (4 Black or African American, non-Hispanic/Latino; 1 American Indian or Alaska Native, non-Hispanic/Latino; 1 Hispanic/Latino). In 2016, 5 master's awarded. *Entrance requirements:* For master's, GRE, MAT, GMAT, or LSAT, 2 letters of recommendation. Additional exam requirements/recommendations for international students: Required—TOEFL. *Application deadline:* For fall admission, 7/15 for domestic students, 2/1 for international students; for spring admission, 11/15 for domestic students, 7/15 for international students; for summer admission, 4/15 for domestic students. Application fee: $65. Electronic applications accepted. *Expenses:* Tuition, state resident: full-time $11,796; part-time $655 per credit. Tuition, nonresident: full-time $24,206; part-time $1345 per credit. *Required fees:* $1546; $44 per credit. One-time fee: $155 full-time; $35 part-time. *Financial support:* In 2016–17, 2 teaching assistantships with tuition reimbursements (averaging $17,184 per year) were awarded; institutionally sponsored loans also available. Financial award application deadline: 2/1; financial award applicants required to submit FAFSA. *Unit head:* Dr. Aimee Phelps, Acting Director, 401-874-4693, E-mail: aimee@uri.edu. *Application contact:* Graduate Admission, 401-874-2872, E-mail: gradadm@etal.uri.edu.
Website: http://www.uri.edu/research/lrc/

University of St. Francis, College of Business and Health Administration, School of Business, Joliet, IL 60435-6169. Offers accounting (MBA, Certificate); business analytics (MBA, Certificate); finance (MBA, Certificate); health administration (MBA); human resource management (MBA); logistics (Certificate); management (MBA, MSM); training and development (MBA); transportation and logistics (MBA). *Accreditation:* ACBSP. *Program availability:* Part-time, evening/weekend, 100% online, blended/hybrid learning. *Faculty:* 6 full-time (3 women), 12 part-time/adjunct (6 women). *Students:* 78 full-time (28 women), 110 part-time (62 women); includes 41 minority (22 Black or African American, non-Hispanic/Latino; 3 Asian, non-Hispanic/Latino; 15 Hispanic/Latino; 1 Two or more races, non-Hispanic/Latino), 8 international. Average age 36. 171 applicants, 44% accepted, 58 enrolled. In 2016, 62 master's, 3 other advanced degrees awarded. *Entrance requirements:* For master's, GMAT or 2 years of managerial experience. Additional exam requirements/recommendations for international students: Required—TOEFL (minimum score 550 paper-based; 79 iBT), IELTS (minimum score 6). *Application deadline:* Applications are processed on a rolling basis. Application fee: $30. Electronic applications accepted. Application fee is waived when completed online. *Expenses:* $798 per credit. *Financial support:* In 2016–17, 51 students received support. Career-related internships or fieldwork, scholarships/grants, tuition waivers (partial), and unspecified assistantships available. Support available to part-time students. Financial award applicants required to submit FAFSA. *Unit head:* Dr. Orlando Griego, Dean, 815-740-3395, Fax: 815-740-3537, E-mail: ogriego@stfrancis.edu. *Application contact:* Sandra Sloka, Director of Admissions for Graduate and Degree Completion Programs, 800-735-7500, Fax: 815-740-3431, E-mail: ssloka@stfrancis.edu.
Website: http://www.stfrancis.edu/academics/college-of-business-health-administration/

University of Saint Mary, Graduate Programs, Program in Business Administration, Leavenworth, KS 66048-5082. Offers enterprise risk management (MBA); finance (MBA); general management (MBA); health care management (MBA); human resource management (MBA); marketing and advertising management (MBA). *Program availability:* Part-time, evening/weekend, 100% online, blended/hybrid learning. *Students:* 201 full-time (110 women), 62 part-time (38 women); includes 83 minority (29 Black or African American, non-Hispanic/Latino; 3 American Indian or Alaska Native, non-Hispanic/Latino; 14 Asian, non-Hispanic/Latino; 32 Hispanic/Latino; 1 Native Hawaiian or other Pacific Islander, non-Hispanic/Latino; 4 Two or more races, non-Hispanic/Latino), 7 international. Average age 34. In 2016, 73 master's awarded. *Degree requirements:* For master's, thesis. *Entrance requirements:* For master's, minimum undergraduate GPA of 2.75, official transcripts, two letters of recommendation. *Application deadline:* Applications are processed on a rolling basis. Application fee: $25. Electronic applications accepted. *Expenses:* $595 per hour. *Unit head:* Rick Gunter, Director, 913-319-3007. *Application contact:* Mark Harvey, Program Manager, 913-319-3007, E-mail: mark.harvey@stmary.edu.
Website: http://www.stmary.edu/success/Grad-Program/Master-of-Business-Administration-MBA.aspx

University of South Carolina, The Graduate School, Darla Moore School of Business, Human Resources Program, Columbia, SC 29208. Offers MHR, JD/MHR. *Program availability:* Part-time. *Degree requirements:* For master's, internship. *Entrance requirements:* For master's, GMAT or GRE, minimum GPA of 3.0. Additional exam requirements/recommendations for international students: Required—TOEFL (minimum score 100 iBT); Recommended—IELTS. Electronic applications accepted. *Expenses:* Contact institution. *Faculty research:* Management and compensation, performance appraisal, work values, grievance systems, union formation, group behavior.

The University of South Dakota, Graduate School, College of Arts and Sciences, Program in Administrative Studies, Vermillion, SD 57069. Offers addiction studies (MSA); criminal justice studies (MSA); health services administration (MSA); human resources (MSA); interdisciplinary studies (MSA); long term care administration (MSA); organizational leadership (MSA). *Program availability:* Part-time, evening/weekend, online learning. *Degree requirements:* For master's, thesis or alternative. *Entrance requirements:* For master's, 3 years of work or experience, minimum GPA of 2.7, resume. Additional exam requirements/recommendations for international students: Required—TOEFL (minimum score 550 paper-based; 79 iBT). Electronic applications accepted.

University of Southern Indiana, Graduate Studies, Romain College of Business, Program in Business Administration, Evansville, IN 47712-3590. Offers accounting (MBA); business administration (MBA); data analytics (MBA); engineering management (MBA); health administration (MBA); human resources (MBA). *Accreditation:* AACSB. *Program availability:* Part-time, evening/weekend, 100% online, blended/hybrid learning. *Faculty:* 22 full-time (4 women), 2 part-time/adjunct (0 women). *Students:* 149 full-time (70 women), 64 part-time (29 women); includes 25 minority (17 Black or African American, non-Hispanic/Latino; 1 Asian, non-Hispanic/Latino; 5 Hispanic/Latino; 2 Two or more races, non-Hispanic/Latino), 5 international. Average age 32. In 2016, 36 master's awarded. *Entrance requirements:* For master's, GMAT or GRE, minimum GPA of 2.5, resume, 3 professional references. Additional exam requirements/recommendations for international students: Required—TOEFL (minimum score 550 paper-based; 79 iBT), IELTS (minimum score 6). *Application deadline:* For fall admission, 8/1 for domestic students, 3/1 priority date for international students. Applications are processed on a rolling basis. Application fee: $40. Electronic applications accepted. *Expenses:* Tuition, state resident: full-time $8497. Tuition, nonresident: full-time $16,691. *Required fees:* $500. *Financial support:* In 2016–17, 8 students received support. Federal Work-Study, scholarships/grants, tuition waivers (full and partial), and unspecified assistantships available. Financial award application deadline: 3/1; financial award applicants required to submit FAFSA. *Unit head:* Dr. Jack E. Smothers, Program Director, 812-461-5248, E-mail: jesmothers@usi.edu. *Application contact:* Michelle Simmons, MBA Program Assistant, 812-464-1926, Fax: 812-465-1044, E-mail: masimmons3@usi.edu.
Website: http://www.usi.edu/business/mba

University of South Florida, Muma College of Business, Department of Management, Tampa, FL 33620-9951. Offers management (MS), including human resources. *Accreditation:* AACSB. *Program availability:* Part-time, online learning. *Faculty:* 3 full-time (2 women). *Students:* 22 full-time (5 women), 8 part-time (4 women); includes 1 minority (Black or African American, non-Hispanic/Latino), 23 international. Average age 26. 40 applicants, 38% accepted, 13 enrolled. In 2016, 48 master's awarded. Terminal master's awarded for partial completion of doctoral program. *Degree requirements:* For master's, comprehensive exam, thesis (for some programs). *Entrance requirements:* For master's, GMAT, letters of recommendation, resume, statement of purpose, relevant work experience. Additional exam requirements/recommendations for international students: Required—TOEFL (minimum score 550 paper-based; 79 iBT) or IELTS (minimum score 6.5). *Application deadline:* For fall admission, 6/1 for domestic students, 2/1 for international students; for spring admission, 10/15 for domestic students, 7/1 for international students. Application fee: $30. Electronic applications accepted. *Expenses:* Tuition, state resident: full-time $7766; part-time $431.43 per credit hour. Tuition, nonresident: full-time $15,789; part-time $877.17 per credit hour. *Required fees:* $37 per term. *Financial support:* In 2016–17, 1 student received support, including 1 research assistantship with tuition reimbursement available (averaging $9,002 per year), 3 teaching assistantships with tuition reimbursements available (averaging $9,002 per year); tuition waivers also available. Financial award applicants required to submit FAFSA. *Faculty research:* Leadership and employment relations, time management, personal motivation, crew resource management in aviation, psychology of gambling,

organizational culture, issues of fairness, employment law, marketing strategy/implementation, organizational diversity, ethics, environmentally-friendly business practices, green business, sustainable business plans, institutional theory, social movement theory, diffusion of innovations, stakeholder human resources management, social responsibility. *Unit head:* Dr. Sally Fuller, Interim Department Chair/Associate Professor, 813-974-1766, Fax: 813-905-9964, E-mail: sfuller@usf.edu. *Application contact:* Carrie Fischer, Office Manager, 813-974-1714, Fax: 813-974-9964, E-mail: cfischer1@usf.edu.
Website: http://www.usf.edu/business/graduate/masters/management/

The University of Texas at Arlington, Graduate School, College of Business, Department of Management, Arlington, TX 76019. Offers human resources (MSHRM). *Program availability:* Part-time, evening/weekend. *Degree requirements:* For master's, thesis optional. *Entrance requirements:* For master's, GMAT/GRE. Additional exam requirements/recommendations for international students: Required—TOEFL (minimum score 550 paper-based; 79 iBT). *Application deadline:* For fall admission, 6/5 priority date for domestic students, 4/1 for international students; for spring admission, 10/15 for domestic students, 9/15 for international students. Applications are processed on a rolling basis. Application fee: $40 ($70 for international students). *Financial support:* Teaching assistantships, career-related internships or fieldwork, scholarships/grants, and unspecified assistantships available. Support available to part-time students. Financial award application deadline: 6/1; financial award applicants required to submit FAFSA. *Faculty research:* Compensations, training, diversity, strategic human resources. *Unit head:* Dr. Abdul Rasheed, Chair, 817-272-3412, Fax: 817-272-3122, E-mail: abdul@uta.edu. *Application contact:* Dennis Veit, Graduate Advisor, 817-272-3865, Fax: 817-272-3122, E-mail: dveit@uta.edu.
Website: http://www.management.uta.edu/

University of the Sacred Heart, Graduate Programs, Department of Business Administration, Program in Human Resource Management, San Juan, PR 00914-0383. Offers MBA. *Program availability:* Part-time, evening/weekend. *Degree requirements:* For master's, thesis. *Entrance requirements:* For master's, EXADEP, minimum undergraduate GPA of 2.75, interview.

University of Toronto, School of Graduate Studies, Faculty of Arts and Science, Centre for Industrial Relations and Human Resources, Toronto, ON M5S 1A1, Canada. Offers MIRHR, PhD. *Program availability:* Part-time. *Degree requirements:* For doctorate, thesis/dissertation. *Entrance requirements:* For master's, GRE or GMAT (for applicants who completed degree outside of Canada), minimum B+ in final 2 years of bachelor's degree completion, 2 letters of reference, resume; for doctorate, GRE or GMAT, MIR or equivalent, minimum B+ average, 3 letters of reference, resume. Additional exam requirements/recommendations for international students: Required—TOEFL (minimum score 600 paper-based; 100 iBT), IELTS, TWE (minimum score 5), Michigan English Language Assessment Battery, or COPE. Electronic applications accepted. *Expenses:* Contact institution.

University of Wisconsin–Madison, Graduate School, Wisconsin School of Business, Doctoral Program in Management and Human Resources, Madison, WI 53706-1380. Offers PhD. *Degree requirements:* For doctorate, comprehensive exam, thesis/dissertation. *Entrance requirements:* For doctorate, GMAT or GRE. Additional exam requirements/recommendations for international students: Recommended—TOEFL (minimum score 623 paper-based; 106 iBT), IELTS (minimum score 7.5), TSE. Electronic applications accepted. *Expenses:* Contact institution. *Faculty research:* Employee compensation, performance for work groups, small business management, venture financing, arts industry, entrepreneurship, development economics, corporate finance, work motivation, diversity/discrimination, organizational justice.

University of Wisconsin–Madison, Graduate School, Wisconsin School of Business, Wisconsin Full-Time MBA Program, Madison, WI 53706. Offers applied security analysis (MBA); arts administration (MBA); brand and product management (MBA); corporate finance and investment banking (MBA); marketing research (MBA); operations and technology management (MBA); real estate (MBA); risk management and insurance (MBA); strategic human resource management (MBA); supply chain management (MBA). *Faculty:* 125 full-time (32 women), 48 part-time/adjunct (11 women). *Students:* 197 full-time (73 women); includes 30 minority (11 Black or African American, non-Hispanic/Latino; 9 Asian, non-Hispanic/Latino; 10 Hispanic/Latino), 42 international. Average age 29. 728 applicants, 26% accepted, 99 enrolled. In 2016, 100 master's awarded. *Entrance requirements:* For master's, GMAT or GRE, bachelor's or equivalent degree, 2 years of work experience, essay, letter of recommendation, resume. Additional exam requirements/recommendations for international students: Required—TOEFL (minimum score 100 iBT), IELTS (minimum score 7.5). *Application deadline:* For fall admission, 9/28 for domestic students, 11/1 for international students; for winter admission, 11/2 for domestic students, 12/16 for international students; for spring admission, 1/11 for domestic students, 2/24 for international students; for summer admission, 3/1 for domestic students, 4/14 for international students. Applications are processed on a rolling basis. Application fee: $75 ($81 for international students). Electronic applications accepted. *Expenses:* $7,947 per semester resident tuition, $2,430 fees; $16,082 per semester resident tuition, $2,830 fees. *Financial support:* In 2016–17, 178 students received support, including 8 fellowships with full tuition reimbursements available (averaging $56,413 per year), 23 research assistantships with full tuition reimbursements available (averaging $42,151 per year), 51 teaching assistantships with full tuition reimbursements available (averaging $39,963 per year); scholarships/grants, health care benefits, and unspecified assistantships also available. Financial award application deadline: 4/11. *Faculty research:* Forms of competition and outcomes in dual distribution systems; explaining the accuracy of revised forecasts; supply chain planning for random demand surges; advanced demand information in a multi-product system; the effects of presentation salience and measurement subjectivity on nonprofessional investors' fair value judgments. *Unit head:* Prof. Ella Mae Matsumura, Associate Dean, Full-time MBA Program, 608-262-0731, E-mail: ematsumura@bus.wisc.edu. *Application contact:* Mary Lewitzke, Assistant Director of Admissions and Recruiting, Full-time MBA Program, 608-262-4000, E-mail: mlewitzke@bus.wisc.edu.
Website: http://www.bus.wisc.edu/mba

University of Wisconsin–Platteville, School of Graduate Studies, Distance Learning Center, Platteville, WI 53818-3099. Offers criminal justice (MS); engineering (MS); integrated supply chain management (MS); organizational change leadership (MS); project management (MS). *Program availability:* Part-time, evening/weekend. *Students:* 18 full-time (6 women), 660 part-time (261 women); includes 128 minority (58 Black or African American, non-Hispanic/Latino; 7 American Indian or Alaska Native, non-Hispanic/Latino; 24 Asian, non-Hispanic/Latino; 39 Hispanic/Latino). 205 applicants, 73% accepted, 106 enrolled. In 2016, 157 master's awarded. *Degree requirements:* For master's, thesis or alternative. *Entrance requirements:* Additional exam requirements/recommendations for international students: Required—TOEFL (minimum score 550 paper-based; 79 iBT), IELTS (minimum score 6.5). *Application deadline:* For fall admission, 7/1 priority date for domestic students; for spring admission, 11/1 priority date for domestic students. Applications are processed on a rolling basis. Application fee: $56. Electronic applications accepted. *Expenses:* Contact institution. *Financial support:* Scholarships/grants available. Support available to part-time students. *Unit head:* Dawn Drake, Executive Director, 800-362-5460, Fax: 608-342-1071, E-mail: disted@uwplatt.edu. *Application contact:* 800-362-5460, E-mail: disted@uwplatt.edu.
Website: http://www.uwplatt.edu/disted/

Upper Iowa University, Online Master's Programs, Fayette, IA 52142-1857. Offers accounting (MBA); corporate financial management (MBA); emergency management and homeland security (MPA); general management (MBA); general studies (MPA); government administration (MPA); health and human services (MPA); human resources management (MBA); nonprofit organizational management (MPA); organizational development (MBA); public management (MPA); sport administration (MSA). MBA also available at Madison, WI campus. *Program availability:* Part-time, online learning. *Degree requirements:* For master's, research project. *Entrance requirements:* For master's, GMAT, GRE, or minimum GPA of 2.7 during last 60 hours. Additional exam requirements/recommendations for international students: Required—TOEFL (minimum score 570 paper-based). Electronic applications accepted. *Faculty research:* Total quality management, teams, organization culture and climate, management.

Utah State University, School of Graduate Studies, College of Business, Program in Human Resource Management, Logan, UT 84322. Offers MS. *Program availability:* Part-time, evening/weekend, online learning. *Entrance requirements:* For master's, GMAT or GRE, minimum GPA of 3.0. Additional exam requirements/recommendations for international students: Required—TOEFL. Electronic applications accepted. *Expenses:* Contact institution. *Faculty research:* International human resources, aging workforce.

Virginia International University, School of Business, Fairfax, VA 22030. Offers accounting (MBA, MS); entrepreneurship (MBA); executive management (Graduate Certificate); global logistics (MBA); health care management (MBA); hospitality and tourism management (MBA); human resources management (MBA); international business management (MBA); international finance (MBA); marketing management (MBA); mass media and public relations (MBA); project management (MBA, MS). *Program availability:* Part-time, online learning. *Entrance requirements:* For master's and Graduate Certificate, bachelor's degree. Additional exam requirements/recommendations for international students: Required—TOEFL (minimum score 550 paper-based; 80 iBT), IELTS (minimum score 6). Electronic applications accepted.

Walden University, Graduate Programs, School of Management, Minneapolis, MN 55401. Offers accounting (MBA, MS, DBA), including accounting for the professional (MS), accounting with CPA emphasis (MS), self-designed (MS); advanced project management (Graduate Certificate); applied project management (Graduate Certificate); auditing (Graduate Certificate); bridge to business administration (Post-Doctoral Certificate); bridge to management (Post-Doctoral Certificate); business management (Graduate Certificate); communication (MBA); corporate finance (MBA); digital marketing (Graduate Certificate); entrepreneurship (DBA); entrepreneurship and small business (MBA); finance (MS, DBA), including finance for the professional (MS), finance with CFA/investment (MS), finance with CPA emphasis (MS); global supply chain management (DBA); healthcare management (MBA, DBA); human resource management (MBA, MS, Graduate Certificate), including functional human resource management (MS), general program (MS), integrating functional and strategic human resource management (MS), organizational strategy (MS); human resources management (DBA); information systems management (DBA); international business (MBA, DBA); leadership (MBA, MS, DBA, Graduate Certificate), including general program (MS), human resource leadership (MS), leader development (MS), self-designed (MS); management (MS, PhD), including communications (MS), finance (PhD), general program (MS), healthcare management (MS), human resource management (MS), human resources management (PhD), information systems management (PhD), international business (MS), leadership (MS), leadership and organizational change (PhD), marketing (MS), project management (MS), strategy and operations (MS); managerial accounting (Graduate Certificate); marketing (MBA, MS, DBA); project management (MBA, MS, DBA); self-designed (MBA, DBA); social impact management (DBA); technology entrepreneurship (DBA). *Accreditation:* ACBSP. *Program availability:* Part-time, evening/weekend, online only, 100% online. *Degree requirements:* For master's, thesis (for some programs), residency (for EMBA); for doctorate, thesis/dissertation (for some programs), residency. *Entrance requirements:* For master's, bachelor's degree or higher; minimum GPA of 2.5; official transcripts; goal statement (for some programs); access to computer and Internet; for doctorate, master's degree or higher; three years of related professional or academic experience (preferred); minimum GPA of 3.0; goal statement and current resume (for select programs); official transcripts; access to computer and Internet; for other advanced degree, relevant work experience; access to computer and Internet. Additional exam requirements/recommendations for international students: Required—TOEFL (minimum score 550 paper-based, 79 iBT), IELTS (minimum score 6.5), Michigan English Language Assessment Battery (minimum score 82), or PTE (minimum score 53). Electronic applications accepted.

Walsh College of Accountancy and Business Administration, Graduate Programs, Program in Management, Troy, MI 48083. Offers human resources management (MS); international business (MS); strategic management (MS). *Program availability:* Part-time, evening/weekend. *Faculty:* 12 full-time (6 women), 12 part-time/adjunct (5 women). *Students:* 54 (43 women); includes 20 minority (15 Black or African American, non-Hispanic/Latino; 1 American Indian or Alaska Native, non-Hispanic/Latino; 2 Asian, non-Hispanic/Latino; 1 Hispanic/Latino; 1 Two or more races, non-Hispanic/Latino). Average age 33. 27 applicants, 70% accepted, 13 enrolled. In 2016, 2 master's awarded. *Entrance requirements:* For master's, minimum overall cumulative GPA of 2.75 from all colleges previously attended. Additional exam requirements/recommendations for international students: Required—TOEFL (minimum score 550 paper-based, 79 iBT), IELTS (6.5), Michigan English Language Assessment Battery, or MTELP. *Application deadline:* Applications are processed on a rolling basis. Application fee: $35. Electronic applications accepted. *Expenses:* $740 per credit hour, $125 registration fee per semester. *Financial support:* In 2016–17, 2 students received support. Career-related internships or fieldwork and scholarships/grants available. Financial award application deadline: 6/30; financial award applicants required to submit FAFSA. *Faculty research:* Strategy practice and process, management learning and decision-making, human capital development, global leadership and citizenship, use of systems and complexity theory and management practice. *Unit head:* Dr. Sheila Ronis, Chair, Management, 248-823-1635, Fax: 248-689-0920, E-mail: sronis@walshcollege.edu. *Application contact:* Heather Rigby, Director, Admissions and Academic Advising, 248-823-1610, Fax: 248-689-0938, E-mail: hrigby@walshcollege.edu.

Warner University, School of Business, Lake Wales, FL 33859. Offers accounting (MBA); business administration (MBA); human resource management (MBA); international business (MBA); management (MSMC). *Program availability:* Part-time, evening/weekend, online learning. *Degree requirements:* For master's, comprehensive exam, thesis. *Entrance requirements:* For master's, minimum GPA of 3.0, letters of recommendation (2). Additional exam requirements/recommendations for international students: Required—TOEFL. *Application deadline:* Applications are processed on a rolling basis. Application fee: $50. Electronic applications accepted. *Financial support:* Scholarships/grants available. Financial award applicants required to submit FAFSA.

Human Resources Management

Unit head: Cindy Polston, Program Director, 863-638-7689. *Application contact:* Judianne Steibly, Graduate Academic Advisor, 863-638-3702, Fax: 863-638-4907, E-mail: admissions@warner.edu.

Wayland Baptist University, Graduate Programs, Program in Education, Plainview, TX 79072-6998. Offers education administration (M Ed); education diagnostics (M Ed); education literacy (M Ed); elementary certification (M Ed); English (M Ed); English as a second language (M Ed); higher education administration (M Ed); human resources (M Ed); instructional leadership (M Ed); instructional technology (M Ed); leadership training and development (M Ed); science education (M Ed); secondary certification (M Ed); social studies (M Ed); special education (M Ed); sports administration and management (M Ed). *Program availability:* Part-time, evening/weekend, online learning. *Degree requirements:* For master's, comprehensive exam, capstone course. *Entrance requirements:* For master's, GRE, GMAT or MAT. Additional exam requirements/recommendations for international students: Required—TOEFL (minimum score 500 paper-based; 61 iBT). Electronic applications accepted.

Wayland Baptist University, Graduate Programs, Programs in Business Administration/Management, Plainview, TX 79072-6998. Offers accounting (MBA); general business (MBA); health care administration (MAM, MBA); human resource management (MAM, MBA); international management (MBA); management (MBA, D Mgt); management information systems (MBA); organization management (MAM); project management (MBA). *Program availability:* Part-time, evening/weekend, online learning. *Degree requirements:* For master's, capstone course. *Entrance requirements:* For master's, GMAT, GRE or MAT. Additional exam requirements/recommendations for international students: Required—TOEFL (minimum score 500 paper-based; 61 iBT). Electronic applications accepted.

Waynesburg University, Graduate and Professional Studies, Canonsburg, PA 15370. Offers business (MBA), including energy management, finance, health systems, human resources, leadership, market development; counseling (MA), including addictions counseling, clinical mental health; counselor education and supervision (PhD); criminal investigation (MA); education (M Ed), including autism, curriculum and instruction, educational leadership, online teaching; nursing (MSN), including administration, education, informatics; nursing practice (DNP); special education (M Ed); technology (M Ed); MSN/MBA. *Accreditation:* AACN. *Program availability:* Part-time, evening/weekend. *Degree requirements:* For doctorate, thesis/dissertation. *Entrance requirements:* Additional exam requirements/recommendations for international students: Required—TOEFL. Electronic applications accepted.

Wayne State University, College of Liberal Arts and Sciences, Department of Economics, Detroit, MI 48202. Offers advanced macroeconomics (PhD); econometrics (MA); health economics (MA, PhD); industrial organization (MA, PhD); international economics (MA, PhD); labor and human resources (MA); labor economics (PhD); macroeconomics (MA); microeconomics (MA); JD/MA. *Faculty:* 13. *Students:* 38 full-time (11 women), 7 part-time (3 women); includes 8 minority (5 Black or African American, non-Hispanic/Latino; 1 Asian, non-Hispanic/Latino; 1 Hispanic/Latino; 1 Two or more races, non-Hispanic/Latino), 22 international. Average age 33. 97 applicants, 36% accepted, 8 enrolled. In 2016, 10 master's, 7 doctorates awarded. *Degree requirements:* For master's, comprehensive exam; for doctorate, comprehensive exam, thesis/dissertation, oral examination on research, completion of course work in quantitative methods, final lecture. *Entrance requirements:* For master's, minimum upper-division GPA of 3.0; prior coursework in intermediate microeconomic and macroeconomic theory, statistics, and elementary calculus; for doctorate, GRE, minimum upper-division GPA of 3.0, prior coursework in intermediate microeconomic and macroeconomic theory, statistics, two courses in calculus, three letters of recommendation from officials or teaching staff at institution(s) most recently attended, statement of purpose. Additional exam requirements/recommendations for international students: Required—TOEFL (minimum score 550 paper-based; 79 iBT), TWE (minimum score 5.5), Michigan English Language Assessment Battery (minimum score 85); Recommended—IELTS (minimum score 6.5). *Application deadline:* For fall admission, 5/1 for domestic and international students; for winter admission, 10/1 priority date for domestic students, 9/1 priority date for international students; for spring admission, 1/1 priority date for domestic and international students. Applications are processed on a rolling basis. Application fee: $50. Electronic applications accepted. *Expenses:* $16,503 per year resident tuition and fees, $33,697 per year non-resident tuition and fees. *Financial support:* In 2016–17, 26 students received support, including 2 fellowships with tuition reimbursements available (averaging $16,000 per year), 17 teaching assistantships with tuition reimbursements available (averaging $17,994 per year); research assistantships with tuition reimbursements available, scholarships/grants, health care benefits, and unspecified assistantships also available. Support available to part-time students. Financial award applicants required to submit FAFSA. *Faculty research:* Health economics, international economics, macro economics, urban and labor economics, econometrics. *Unit head:* Dr. Stephen J. Spurr, Professor and Chair, 313-577-3232, Fax: 313-577-9564, E-mail: sspurr@wayne.edu. *Application contact:* Dr. Allen Charles Goodman, Graduate Director, 313-577-3235, Fax: 313-577-9564, E-mail: allen.goodman@wayne.edu.
Website: http://clas.wayne.edu/economics/

Wayne State University, College of Liberal Arts and Sciences, Department of Political Science, Detroit, MI 48202. Offers political science (MA, PhD); public administration (MPA), including economic development policy and management, health and human services policy and management, human and fiscal resource management, nonprofit policy and management, organizational behavior and management, urban and metropolitan policy and management; JD/MA. *Accreditation:* NASPAA. *Faculty:* 20. *Students:* 64 full-time (20 women), 75 part-time (45 women); includes 48 minority (32 Black or African American, non-Hispanic/Latino; 5 Asian, non-Hispanic/Latino; 4 Hispanic/Latino; 7 Two or more races, non-Hispanic/Latino), 7 international. Average age 33. 105 applicants, 50% accepted, 27 enrolled. In 2016, 25 master's, 5 doctorates awarded. *Degree requirements:* For master's, comprehensive exam (for some programs), thesis (for some programs); for doctorate, thesis/dissertation. *Entrance requirements:* For master's, GRE General Test, substantial undergraduate preparation in the social sciences, minimum upper-division undergraduate GPA of 3.0, two letters of recommendation, personal statement; for doctorate, GRE General Test, 3 letters of recommendation; personal statement; interview. Additional exam requirements/recommendations for international students: Required—TOEFL (minimum score 550 paper-based; 79 iBT), TWE (minimum score 5.5), Michigan English Language Assessment Battery (minimum score 85); Recommended—IELTS (minimum score 6.5). *Application deadline:* For fall admission, 5/15 for domestic students, 5/1 priority date for international students; for winter admission, 10/15 for domestic students, 9/1 priority date for international students. Applications are processed on a rolling basis. Application fee: $50. Electronic applications accepted. *Expenses:* $16,503 per year resident tuition and fees, $33,697 per year non-resident tuition and fees. *Financial support:* In 2016–17, 48 students received support, including 3 fellowships with tuition reimbursements available (averaging $17,333 per year), 13 teaching assistantships with tuition reimbursements available (averaging $18,067 per year); research assistantships with tuition reimbursements available, scholarships/grants, health care benefits, and unspecified assistantships also available. Financial award applicants required to submit FAFSA. *Faculty research:* American government and politics, comparative politics, political methodology, political theory, public administration, public law, public policy, world politics/international relations, formal theory/modeling, gender and politics, international law, peace research, political economy, political psychology, politics of developing countries, race, religion, and ethnicity, urban politics. *Unit head:* Dr. Daniel Geller, Professor and Chair, 313-577-6328, E-mail: dgeller@wayne.edu. *Application contact:* Dr. Sharon Lean, Graduate Director, 313-577-2630, E-mail: gradpolisci@wayne.edu.
Website: http://clas.wayne.edu/politicalscience/

Wayne State University, College of Liberal Arts and Sciences, Program in Employment and Labor Relations, Detroit, MI 48202. Offers MA. *Program availability:* Part-time, evening/weekend. *Students:* 4 full-time (3 women), 22 part-time (16 women); includes 14 minority (11 Black or African American, non-Hispanic/Latino; 3 Hispanic/Latino), 2 international. Average age 35. 18 applicants, 56% accepted, 7 enrolled. In 2016, 11 master's awarded. *Entrance requirements:* For master's, GRE or GMAT, personal statement, three letters of recommendation written by former college or university professors and/or current employers, baccalaureate degree from accredited institution, writing sample. Additional exam requirements/recommendations for international students: Required—TOEFL (minimum score 550 paper-based; 79 iBT), IELTS (minimum score 6.5), Michigan English Language Assessment Battery (minimum score 85). *Application deadline:* For fall admission, 6/1 priority date for domestic students, 5/1 priority date for international students; for winter admission, 10/1 priority date for domestic students, 9/1 priority date for international students; for spring admission, 2/1 priority date for domestic students, 1/1 priority date for international students. Application fee: $50. Electronic applications accepted. *Expenses:* $16,503 per year resident tuition and fees, $33,697 per year non-resident tuition and fees. *Financial support:* Scholarships/grants available. Financial award applicants required to submit FAFSA. *Unit head:* Dr. Marick Masters, Director, 313-577-5358, E-mail: marickm@wayne.edu. *Application contact:* Linda Johnson, Academic Services Officer, 313-577-0175, E-mail: ab1232@wayne.edu.
Website: http://clas.wayne.edu/labor/maelr

Webster University, George Herbert Walker School of Business and Technology, Department of Business, St. Louis, MO 63119-3194. Offers business and organizational security management (MBA); decision support systems (MBA); environmental management (MBA); finance (MBA, MS); forensic accounting (MS); gerontology (MBA); human resources development (MBA); human resources management (MBA); information technology management (MBA); international business (MA, MBA); international relations (MBA); management and leadership (MBA); marketing (MBA); media communications (MBA); procurement and acquisitions management (MBA); Web services (MBA). *Accreditation:* ACBSP. *Program availability:* Part-time, evening/weekend, online learning. *Degree requirements:* For master's, comprehensive exam (for some programs), thesis (for some programs). *Entrance requirements:* Additional exam requirements/recommendations for international students: Required—TOEFL. *Application deadline:* Applications are processed on a rolling basis. Application fee: $35 ($50 for international students). *Expenses: Tuition:* Full-time $21,900; part-time $730 per credit hour. Tuition and fees vary according to campus/location and program. *Financial support:* Federal Work-Study available. Support available to part-time students. Financial award application deadline: 4/1; financial award applicants required to submit FAFSA. *Unit head:* David Porras, Chair, 314-246-8621, E-mail: porrasd@webster.edu. *Application contact:* Sarah Nandor, Director, Graduate and Transfer Admissions, 314-968-7109, E-mail: gadmit@webster.edu.

Webster University, George Herbert Walker School of Business and Technology, Department of Management, St. Louis, MO 63119-3194. Offers business and organizational security management (MA); digital marketing management (Graduate Certificate); government contracting (Graduate Certificate); health administration (MHA); health care management (MA); health services management (MA); human resources development (MA); human resources management (MA); information technology management (MA, MS); management (D Mgt); management and leadership (MA); marketing (MA); nonprofit leadership (MA); nonprofit revenue development (Graduate Certificate); organizational development (Graduate Certificate); procurement and acquisitions management (MA); public administration (MPA); space systems operations management (MS). *Program availability:* Part-time, evening/weekend, online learning. *Degree requirements:* For master's, thesis (for some programs); for doctorate, thesis/dissertation, written exam. *Entrance requirements:* For doctorate, GMAT, 3 years of work experience, MBA. Additional exam requirements/recommendations for international students: Required—TOEFL. *Application deadline:* Applications are processed on a rolling basis. Application fee: $25 ($50 for international students). *Expenses: Tuition:* Full-time $21,900; part-time $730 per credit hour. Tuition and fees vary according to campus/location and program. *Financial support:* Federal Work-Study available. Support available to part-time students. Financial award application deadline: 4/1; financial award applicants required to submit FAFSA. *Unit head:* Barrett Baebler, Chair, 314-246-7940, E-mail: baeblerb@webster.edu. *Application contact:* Sarah Nandor, Director, Graduate and Transfer Admissions, 314-968-7109, E-mail: gadmit@webster.edu.

West Chester University of Pennsylvania, College of Business and Public Management, Department of Management, West Chester, PA 19383. Offers human resource management (MS). *Program availability:* Online learning. *Students:* 1 (woman) full-time, 3 part-time (1 woman); includes 1 minority (Hispanic/Latino). Average age 31. *Entrance requirements:* For master's, GMAT or GRE, bachelor's degree or above in any major/field from accredited institution. Additional exam requirements/recommendations for international students: Required—TOEFL or IELTS. *Application deadline:* For fall admission, 5/15 for international students; for spring admission, 10/15 for international students. Applications are processed on a rolling basis. Application fee: $50. Electronic applications accepted. *Expenses:* Tuition, state resident: full-time $8694; part-time $483 per credit. Tuition, nonresident: full-time $13,050; part-time $725 per credit. *Required fees:* $2399; $119.05 per credit. Tuition and fees vary according to campus/location and program. *Financial support:* Scholarships/grants and unspecified assistantships available. Financial award application deadline: 2/15; financial award applicants required to submit FAFSA. *Faculty research:* Organizational behavior, labor law, labor relations. *Unit head:* Dr. Evan Leach, Chair, 610-436-2305, E-mail: eleach@wcupa.edu. *Application contact:* Dr. Susan Fiorentino, Graduate Coordinator, 610-436-2019, E-mail: sfiorentino@wcupa.edu.
Website: http://www.wcupa.edu/business-publicManagement/management/default.aspx

West Chester University of Pennsylvania, College of Business and Public Management, Department of Public Policy and Administration, West Chester, PA 19383. Offers administration (Certificate); human resource management (MPA, Certificate); human resources management (DPA); non profit administration (Certificate); nonprofit administration (MPA); public administration (MPA); public policy and administration (MPA). *Accreditation:* NASPAA. *Program availability:* Part-time, evening/weekend, 100% online. *Faculty:* 6 full-time (4 women), 3 part-time/adjunct (2 women). *Students:* 62 full-time (35 women), 144 part-time (80 women); includes 72 minority (60 Black or African American, non-Hispanic/Latino; 1 American Indian or Alaska Native, non-Hispanic/Latino; 3 Asian, non-Hispanic/Latino; 7 Hispanic/Latino; 1 Two or more races,

non-Hispanic/Latino), 6 international. Average age 33. 133 applicants, 92% accepted, 97 enrolled. In 2016, 58 master's, 1 other advanced degree awarded. *Degree requirements:* For master's, capstone project. *Entrance requirements:* For master's and other advanced degree, statement of professional goals, resume, two letters of reference, academic transcripts. Additional exam requirements/recommendations for international students: Required—TOEFL or IELTS. *Application deadline:* For fall admission, 5/15 for international students; for spring admission, 10/15 for international students. Applications are processed on a rolling basis. Application fee: $50. Electronic applications accepted. *Expenses:* Tuition, state resident: full-time $8694; part-time $483 per credit. Tuition, nonresident: full-time $13,050; part-time $725 per credit. *Required fees:* $2399; $119.05 per credit. Tuition and fees vary according to campus/location and program. *Financial support:* Scholarships/grants and unspecified assistantships available. Financial award application deadline: 2/15; financial award applicants required to submit FAFSA. *Faculty research:* Public policy, economic development, research methodology, public administration, nonprofit administration. *Unit head:* Dr. Allison Turner, Department Chair/Director of MPA Program, 610-436-2438, E-mail: aturner@wcupa.edu. *Application contact:* Dr. Jeremy Phillips, DPA Graduate Coordinator, 610-436-2016, E-mail: jphillips@wcupa.edu.
Website: http://www.wcupa.edu/business-publicManagement/mpa/

Wilfrid Laurier University, Faculty of Graduate and Postdoctoral Studies, School of Business and Economics, Department of Business, Waterloo, ON N2L 3C5, Canada. Offers accounting (PhD); finance (M Fin); financial economics (PhD); marketing (PhD); operations and supply chain management (PhD); organizational behavior and human resource management (M Sc); organizational behaviour and human resource management (PhD); supply chain management (M Sc); technology management (EMTM). *Accreditation:* AACSB. *Program availability:* Part-time, evening/weekend. *Degree requirements:* For master's, thesis optional; for doctorate, comprehensive exam, thesis/dissertation. *Entrance requirements:* For master's, GMAT, 4-year honors degree with minimum B+ average; for doctorate, GMAT, master's degree, minimum B+ average. Additional exam requirements/recommendations for international students: Required—TOEFL (minimum score 89 iBT). Electronic applications accepted. *Faculty research:* Financial economics, management and organizational behavior, operations and supply chain management.

Wilkes University, College of Graduate and Professional Studies, Jay S. Sidhu School of Business and Leadership, Wilkes-Barre, PA 18766-0002. Offers accounting (MBA); entrepreneurship (MBA); finance (MBA); health care administration (MBA); human resource management (MBA); international business (MBA); operations management (MBA); organizational leadership and development (MBA). *Accreditation:* ACBSP. *Program availability:* Part-time, evening/weekend. *Students:* 35 full-time (17 women), 112 part-time (55 women); includes 17 minority (6 Black or African American, non-Hispanic/Latino; 4 Asian, non-Hispanic/Latino; 5 Hispanic/Latino; 2 Two or more races, non-Hispanic/Latino), 16 international. Average age 31. In 2016, 59 master's awarded. *Entrance requirements:* For master's, GMAT. Additional exam requirements/recommendations for international students: Required—TOEFL (minimum score 550 paper-based; 79 iBT). *Application deadline:* Applications are processed on a rolling basis. Application fee: $45 ($65 for international students). Electronic applications accepted. *Expenses:* Contact institution. *Financial support:* Unspecified assistantships available. Financial award application deadline: 3/1; financial award applicants required to submit FAFSA. *Unit head:* Dr. Abel Adekola, Dean, 570-408-4701, Fax: 570-408-7846, E-mail: abel.adekola@wilkes.edu. *Application contact:* Director of Graduate Enrollment, 570-408-4234, Fax: 570-408-7846.
Website: http://www.wilkes.edu/academics/colleges/sidhu-school-of-business-leadership/index.aspx

Wilmington University, College of Business, New Castle, DE 19720-6491. Offers accounting (MBA, MS); business administration (MBA, DBA); environmental stewardship (MBA); finance (MBA); health care administration (MBA, MSM); homeland security (MBA, MSM); human resource management (MSM); management information systems (MBA, MSN); marketing (MSM); marketing management (MBA); military leadership (MSM); organizational leadership (MBA, MSM); public administration (MSM). *Program availability:* Part-time, evening/weekend. *Faculty:* 17 full-time (7 women), 106 part-time/adjunct (46 women). *Students:* 436 full-time (237 women), 1,202 part-time (739 women); includes 594 minority (474 Black or African American, non-Hispanic/Latino; 19 American Indian or Alaska Native, non-Hispanic/Latino; 64 Asian, non-Hispanic/Latino; 30 Hispanic/Latino; 3 Native Hawaiian or other Pacific Islander, non-Hispanic/Latino; 4 Two or more races, non-Hispanic/Latino), 153 international. Average age 35. 814 applicants, 98% accepted, 426 enrolled. In 2016, 594 master's, 23 doctorates awarded. *Entrance requirements:* Additional exam requirements/recommendations for international students: Required—TOEFL (minimum score 500 paper-based). *Application deadline:* Applications are processed on a rolling basis. Application fee: $35. Electronic applications accepted. *Expenses: Tuition:* Full-time $8388; part-time $466 per credit. *Required fees:* $25 per semester. Tuition and fees vary according to degree level. *Financial support:* Applicants required to submit FAFSA. *Unit head:* Dr. Robert W. Rescigno, Dean. *Application contact:* Laura Morris, Director of Admissions, 877-967-5456, E-mail: infocenter@wilmu.edu.
Website: http://www.wilmu.edu/business/

York University, Faculty of Graduate Studies, Faculty of Liberal Arts and Professional Studies, Program in Human Resources Management, Toronto, ON M3J 1P3, Canada. Offers MHRM, PhD. *Program availability:* Part-time. *Degree requirements:* For master's, thesis or alternative. *Entrance requirements:* Additional exam requirements/recommendations for international students: Required—TOEFL (minimum score 600 paper-based). Electronic applications accepted.

PURDUE UNIVERSITY

Krannert School of Management

 For more information, visit http://petersons.to/purduehrm

Programs of Study

Purdue University's Krannert School of Management emphasizes quantitative analysis alongside the qualitative, establishing a strong foundation of business knowledge. Krannert's cohort-based approach and emphasis on the team dynamic simulates a true corporate working environment. Case studies help to develop critical thinking and problem-solving skills that translate to the business world. Krannert's MS in Human Resource Management (MSHRM) program is among the most highly ranked in the nation.

Graduates of the MSHRM program are well-suited to pursue employment opportunities in a variety of industries working domestically and for multinational corporations across the globe. Students learn to develop an organization's talent, lead rapidly changing human resource environments, communicate effectively with other management professionals, and become a business partner on a global stage. Further, through opportunities like Human Capital Consulting Projects, Launching Global Leaders, study abroad, case competitions, and other unique experiences, students gain enriching insights into global business and leadership.

The Krannert School of Management offers two unique MBA programs, a Full-Time MBA as well as a hybrid Weekend MBA. The school also offers a full suite of Master of Science programs in accounting, business analytics and information management, economics, finance, global supply chain management, human resource management, and marketing.

Research and Extension Centers

Students in the Krannert School of Management go beyond theory and actually get down to business. In addition to classrooms, Krannert offers numerous real-world, practical R&D, and business-startup 'ecosystems' to offer an unparalleled learning experience. On campus, this higher-education/private-enterprise merger is where investors, manufacturing partners, entrepreneurs, researchers, professors, alumni, and students work together. By association, Krannert students have access to needs-based opportunities where they receive hands-on experience commercializing, and optimizing in real operational settings, taking the very latest technologies to market.

Human networking and the priceless utility of professional social-skill development are value-add hallmarks of the Krannert School of Management. Students are able to leverage an array of career resources and opportunities that range from leadership coursework and one-on-one coaching, to an alumni network and a full slate of career fairs.

The Krannert School of Management connects to campus and community through its extension centers.

The Business Information and Analytics Center (BIAC) merges two highly regarded areas in the Krannert School—Management Information Systems and Quantitative Methods—to leverage the breadth and depth of its research and corporate collaborations. The Dr. Cornell A. Bell Business Opportunity Program (BOP) was the first program to increase diversity and give all students access to a world-class management education at a major business school. Purdue's Jane Brock-Wilson Women in Management Center supports the leadership development of women from pre-college throughout their careers, while influencing thought and behavior in global business settings. The Purdue University Research Center in Economics (PURCE) conducts research into the effects of government policies in areas such as health care, crime, antitrust, international trade and taxation, to name a few.

For almost three decades, the Dauch Center for the Management of Manufacturing Enterprises (DCMME) and the Global Supply Chain Management Initiative (GSCMI) have been the focal point within Purdue University's Krannert School of Management for promoting education, research and industrial engagement with those interested in operations management, manufacturing management and supply chain management.

Financial Aid

Purdue offers top applicants assistantship opportunities and scholarships, such as the Purdue University MBA Alumnus Scholarship, to help reduce the cost of attending the Krannert School of Management. These merit-based awards do not require any additional application as all applicants are considered.

Graduate Assistantships involve approximately 10 hours of work per week and provide a monthly stipend and significant remission of tuition and fees. (Please note: Graduate Assistantships are only available for MBA and MSHRM applicants)

Many Purdue master's students serve as resident assistants within the Purdue Residence Halls system. All students (first-year, international, and continuing students) are eligible to apply for these positions, which include room and board, a small stipend, partial remission of tuition and fees.

Several forms of need-based financial aid are available, such as Federal Direct Stafford Loans, Federal Graduate Plus Loans, private alternative loans, and additional sources of funding.

Students may also secure graduate assistantships outside of the Krannert School of Management, based upon their special skills and expertise. There are also opportunities for students to find employment outside of the master's programs, working for the University or in the Lafayette/West Lafayette area, although these do not include any type of tuition remission.

Cost of Study

For the 2016–17 academic year, the MSHRM program fee each semester was $11,209 for Indiana residents and $21,092 for nonresidents. All fees are subject to increase based on approval by the Purdue University Board of Trustees. A complete breakdown of tuition and fees for all Krannert School of Management is available at http://www.purdue.edu/bursar/tuition/feerates/2016-2017/graduate/managementhtml#WL_ManagementGrad.

Living and Housing Costs

West Lafayette, Indiana is an inviting community for students and families alike. In 2016, The American Institute for Economic Research ranked West Lafayette/Lafayette, Indiana the tenth-best college town in America. In 2015, *Forbes* ranked West Lafayette/Lafayette second in its rankings of Best Small Cities for Business and Careers. The community is an affordable place to live compared to other university communities across the United States. Purdue offers an off-campus housing resource for students looking to live within the community.

Student Opportunities

Students have access to a full suite of career assistance services provided by the Krannert Professional Development Center (KPDC). Students also have the opportunity to work with entrepreneurs and technology specialists at Purdue's Discovery Park or Burton D. Morgan Center for Entrepreneurship. Purdue is ranked eighth as a producer of start-up talent among U.S. public universities

(Tech.Co) and has the sixth most startups based on university IP among U.S. universities (AUTM U.S. Licensing Survey).

West Lafayette is annually rated among the top college towns in the U.S. (#12 by Business Insider). Purdue's campus is located between Indianapolis and Chicago and offers access to big-city life at a modest cost of living. When combined with tuition rates that have remained static for six straight years, Purdue offers exceptional return on investment for its students. Krannert's Full-Time MBA program has been ranked third by *Bloomberg Businessweek* for highest return on investment (2014).

Purdue has the second-largest international student enrollment among U.S. public institutions and that diversity translates to the Krannert classroom. In its small classroom atmosphere, Krannert students encounter a true cross-continental immersion with classmates from across the globe. In addition, Krannert offers a number of study-abroad opportunities.

Location

West Lafayette/Lafayette is a warm, welcoming community ideally situated between Chicago, Illinois and Indianapolis, Indiana. Home to Purdue University and just over 174,000 residents, the city is known for its diverse community and great quality of life. West Lafayette offers good schools, safe neighborhoods, and excellent public facilities and amenities, including over 40 parks and extensive trail systems. There is a wide spectrum of businesses, including many nationally and internationally known high-tech corporations and institutions.

Other amenities include beautiful turn-of-the-century architecture; a lively downtown with local shopping and restaurants; a sophisticated art scene with galleries and public art; and a full slate of annual festivals throughout the year.

The School and the University

Purdue University's Krannert School of Management provides a vibrant ecosystem for mastering the analytical problem-solving and tech-commercialization skills that move industry forward and change the world.

Krannert is uniquely positioned alongside a globally renowned STEM school, inside a dynamic corporate-partnership R&D community. Operating against that strong science and technology backdrop, Krannert approaches business learning from a research-based, quantitative angle that develops students' analytical skills. Tomorrow's business leaders will be those who speak the language of innovation—who know how to analyze data, develop and statistically justify creative business solutions, and even take new technologies to market.

Krannert School of Management is located on Purdue University's oldest and largest campus with approximately 39,000 students, in West Lafayette, Indiana.

Faculty and Alumni

While part of a Big Ten university, Krannert is proportionately smaller in scale—maintaining a student-professed family feel, a more mutually encouraging atmosphere of competition, and a highly collaborative classroom model that is reflective of the way today's successful business enterprises operate and solve problems.

Krannert students have access to a global and highly engaged alumni network that dramatically enhances learning and career opportunities. The distinguished faculty and alumni serve as student professional mentors. They foster and facilitate career goals, providing students with highly personalized guidance to steer their future careers. Pedagogically, Krannert empowers graduates—emphasizing leadership, professional development, and collaboration to accelerate careers.

Two Krannert faculty members were named to Poets and Quants 2017 Best 40 Under 40 Professors. A complete listing of faculty and their specialties is available at http://www.krannert.purdue.edu/faculty.

Applying

Applications for the Krannert School of Management must be completed using Purdue's Graduate School online application. International applicants must follow a slightly altered application process.

Applications will not be considered until all required materials have been received. This includes submission of a nonrefundable application fee of $60 (U.S. dollars) for domestic applicants and $75 (U.S. dollars) for international applicants, payable online by credit card. Non-degree applicants will not be charged an application fee.

Application deadlines vary by program; specific details can be found online at http://www.krannert.purdue.edu/masters/admissions/application-deadlines/home.php.

Correspondence and Information

Krannert School of Management
Purdue University MBA and M.S. Programs Office
100 South State Street
Rawls Hall, Suite 2020
West Lafayette, Indiana 47907-2056
Phone: 765-494-0773
877-MBA-KRAN (toll-free)
Fax: 765-494-9841
E-mail: gokrannert@purdue.edu
Website: www.krannert.purdue.edu

The director of the Purdue Foundry discusses a business venture with three aspiring entrepreneurs.

Welcome to Purdue University, home of the Krannert School of Management.

Section 9
Industrial and Manufacturing Management

This section contains a directory of institutions offering graduate work in industrial and manufacturing management. Additional information about programs listed in the directory but not augmented by an in-depth entry may be obtained by writing directly to the dean of a graduate school or chair of a department at the address given in the directory.

For programs offering related work, see also in this book *Business Administration and Management* and *Human Resources.* In another guide in this series:

Graduate Programs in the Humanities, Arts & Social Sciences

See *Public, Regional, and Industrial Affairs (Industrial* and *Labor Relations)*

CONTENTS

Program Directory

Featured School: Display and Close-Up

See:

Industrial and Manufacturing Management

American InterContinental University Online, Program in Business Administration, Schaumburg, IL 60173. Offers accounting and finance (MBA); finance (MBA); healthcare management (MBA); human resource management (MBA); international business (MBA); management (MBA); marketing (MBA); operations management (MBA); organizational psychology and development (MBA); project management (MBA). *Accreditation:* ACBSP. *Program availability:* Evening/weekend, online learning. *Entrance requirements:* Additional exam requirements/recommendations for international students: Required—TOEFL (minimum score 550 paper-based). Electronic applications accepted.

Baruch College of the City University of New York, Zicklin School of Business, Department of Management, New York, NY 10010-5585. Offers entrepreneurship (MBA); management (PhD); operations management (MBA); organizational behavior/human resources management (MBA); sustainable business (MBA). PhD offered jointly with Graduate School and University Center of the City University of New York. *Program availability:* Part-time, evening/weekend. *Degree requirements:* For doctorate, comprehensive exam, thesis/dissertation. *Entrance requirements:* For master's, GMAT, 2 letters of recommendation, resume, 2 years of work experience; for doctorate, GMAT. Additional exam requirements/recommendations for international students: Required—TOEFL (minimum score 590 paper-based), TWE.

Bluffton University, Programs in Business, Bluffton, OH 45817. Offers accounting and financial management (MBA); business administration (MBA); health care management (MBA); leadership (MBA); organizational management (MA); production and operations management (MBA). *Program availability:* Evening/weekend, online learning. *Faculty:* 9 full-time (3 women), 12 part-time/adjunct (4 women). *Students:* 55 full-time (34 women), 2 part-time (1 woman); includes 5 minority (1 Black or African American, non-Hispanic/Latino; 2 Asian, non-Hispanic/Latino; 2 Hispanic/Latino), 2 international. Average age 34. 31 applicants, 77% accepted, 22 enrolled. In 2016, 44 master's awarded. *Entrance requirements:* For master's, current resume, official transcript, two recommendation forms, bachelor's degree, minimum GPA of 3.0, four years of professional experience, interview. Additional exam requirements/recommendations for international students: Recommended—TOEFL. *Application deadline:* For fall admission, 7/31 priority date for domestic and international students. Applications are processed on a rolling basis. Application fee: $25. Electronic applications accepted. Application fee is waived when completed online. *Expenses:* $550 per credit. *Financial support:* Scholarships/grants and unspecified assistantships available. Financial award application deadline: 5/1. *Unit head:* Dr. Melissa Green, Director of Graduate Programs in Business, 419-358-3447, E-mail: greenm@bluffton.edu. *Application contact:* Carrie Mast, Administrative Assistant, Graduate Programs in Business, 419-358-3065, E-mail: mastc@bluffton.edu.
Website: http://www.bluffton.edu/grad/

California State University, East Bay, Office of Graduate Studies, College of Business and Economics, MBA Program, Option in Operations and Supply Chain Management, Hayward, CA 94542-3000. Offers MBA. *Degree requirements:* For master's, comprehensive exam or thesis. *Entrance requirements:* For master's, GMAT, minimum GPA of 2.75. Additional exam requirements/recommendations for international students: Required—TOEFL (minimum score 550 paper-based). *Application deadline:* For fall admission, 6/30 for domestic and international students. Application fee: $55. Electronic applications accepted. *Financial support:* Fellowships, career-related internships or fieldwork, Federal Work-Study, institutionally sponsored loans, and scholarships/grants available. Support available to part-time students. Financial award application deadline: 3/1; financial award applicants required to submit FAFSA. *Unit head:* Dr. Zinovy Radovilsky, Program Advisor, 510-885-3290, E-mail: zinovy.radovilsky@csueastbay.edu. *Application contact:* Dr. Donna Wiley, Interim Associate Vice President for Academic Programs and Graduate Studies, 510-885-3716, Fax: 510-885-4777, E-mail: donna.wiley@csueastbay.edu.
Website: http://www.csueastbay.edu/cbe/mba-options/operations-and-supply-chain-management-option.html

Carnegie Mellon University, Carnegie Institute of Technology and School of Design, Program in Product Development, Pittsburgh, PA 15213-3891. Offers MPD. *Entrance requirements:* For master's, GRE General Test, undergraduate degree in engineering, industrial design, or related fields, 3 letters of reference, 2 years of professional experience. Additional exam requirements/recommendations for international students: Required—TOEFL or TSE.

Carnegie Mellon University, College of Fine Arts, School of Design, Pittsburgh, PA 15213-3891. Offers design (MA, D Des, PhD); design for interaction (M Des); design theory (PhD); new product development (PhD); product development (MPD); typography and information design (PhD).

Carnegie Mellon University, Tepper School of Business, Program in Operations Management, Pittsburgh, PA 15213-3891. Offers PhD. *Degree requirements:* For doctorate, thesis/dissertation.

Case Western Reserve University, Weatherhead School of Management, Department of Operations, Cleveland, OH 44106. Offers operations and supply chain management (MSM); operations research (PhD); MBA/MSM. *Program availability:* Part-time. *Degree requirements:* For doctorate, thesis/dissertation. *Entrance requirements:* For master's, GRE General Test; for doctorate, GMAT, GRE General Test. *Expenses: Tuition:* Full-time $42,576; part-time $1774 per credit hour. *Required fees:* $34. Tuition and fees vary according to course load and program. *Faculty research:* Mathematical finance, mathematical programming, scheduling, stochastic optimization, environmental/energy models.

Central Connecticut State University, School of Graduate Studies, School of Engineering, Science and Technology, Department of Manufacturing and Construction Management, New Britain, CT 06050-4010. Offers construction management (MS, Certificate); environmental and occupational safety (Certificate); lean manufacturing and Six Sigma (Certificate); supply chain and logistics (Certificate); technology management (MS). *Program availability:* Part-time, evening/weekend. *Faculty:* 7 full-time (0 women), 3 part-time/adjunct (0 women). *Students:* 23 full-time (6 women), 88 part-time (21 women); includes 29 minority (11 Black or African American, non-Hispanic/Latino; 7 Asian, non-Hispanic/Latino; 10 Hispanic/Latino; 1 Two or more races, non-Hispanic/Latino), 12 international. Average age 34. 79 applicants, 68% accepted, 32 enrolled. In 2016, 43 master's, 4 other advanced degrees awarded. *Degree requirements:* For master's, comprehensive exam, special project; for Certificate, qualifying exam. *Entrance requirements:* For master's, minimum undergraduate GPA of 2.7. Additional exam requirements/recommendations for international students: Required—TOEFL (minimum score 550 paper-based; 79 iBT). *Application deadline:* For fall admission, 8/1 for domestic students, 5/1 for international students; for spring admission, 11/1 for domestic and international students. Applications are processed on a rolling basis. Application fee: $50. Electronic applications accepted. *Expenses: Tuition, area resident:* Full-time $6497; part-time $606 per credit. Tuition, state resident: full-time $9748; part-time $622 per credit. Tuition, nonresident: full-time $18,102; part-time $622 per credit. *Required fees:* $4459; $246 per credit. *Financial support:* In 2016–17, 10 students received support. Career-related internships or fieldwork, Federal Work-Study, scholarships/grants, and unspecified assistantships available. Support available to part-time students. Financial award application deadline: 3/1; financial award applicants required to submit FAFSA. *Faculty research:* All aspects of middle management, technical supervision in the workplace. *Unit head:* Dr. Ravindra Thamma, Chair, 860-832-1830, E-mail: kovelj@ccsu.edu. *Application contact:* Patricia Gardner, Associate Director of Graduate Studies, 860-832-2350, Fax: 860-832-2362.
Website: http://www.ccsu.edu/mcm/

Central Michigan University, College of Graduate Studies, College of Science and Technology, School of Engineering and Technology, Mount Pleasant, MI 48859. Offers industrial management and technology (MA). *Program availability:* Part-time. *Degree requirements:* For master's, thesis or alternative. Electronic applications accepted. *Faculty research:* Computer applications, manufacturing process control, mechanical engineering automation, industrial technology.

Colorado Technical University Aurora, Programs in Business Administration and Management, Aurora, CO 80014. Offers accounting (MBA); business administration (MBA); business administration and management (EMBA); finance (MBA); human resource management (MBA); marketing (MBA); mediation and dispute resolution (MBA); operations management (MBA); project management (MBA); technology management (MBA). *Program availability:* Part-time, evening/weekend. *Degree requirements:* For master's, thesis or alternative. *Entrance requirements:* For master's, minimum undergraduate GPA of 3.0, resume.

Colorado Technical University Colorado Springs, Graduate Studies, Program in Management, Colorado Springs, CO 80907. Offers accounting (MBA, MSA); business administration (MBA); finance (MBA); human resources management (MBA); logistics/supply chain management (MBA); management (DM); marketing (MBA); mediation and dispute resolution (MBA); operations management (MBA); project management (MBA); technology management (MBA). *Accreditation:* ACBSP. *Program availability:* Part-time, evening/weekend, online learning. *Degree requirements:* For master's, thesis or alternative; for doctorate, thesis/dissertation. *Entrance requirements:* For doctorate, minimum graduate GPA of 3.0, 5 years of related work experience. *Faculty research:* Sexual harassment, performance evaluation, critical thinking.

DePaul University, Kellstadt Graduate School of Business, Chicago, IL 60604. Offers accountancy (M Acc, MS, MSA); applied economics (MBA); banking (MBA); behavioral finance (MBA); brand and product management (MBA); business development (MBA); business information technology (MS); business strategy and decision-making (MBA); computational finance (MS); consumer insights (MBA); corporate finance (MBA); economic policy analysis (MS); entrepreneurship (MBA, MS); finance (MBA, MS); financial analysis (MBA); general business (MBA); health sector management (MBA); hospitality leadership (MBA); hospitality leadership and operational performance (MS); human resource management (MBA); human resources (MS); investment management (MBA); leadership and change management (MBA); management accounting (MBA); marketing (MBA, MS); marketing analysis (MS); marketing strategy and planning (MBA); operations management (MBA); organizational diversity (MBA); real estate (MS); real estate finance and investment (MBA); revenue management (MBA); sports management (MBA); strategic global marketing (MBA); strategy, execution and valuation (MBA); sustainable management (MBA, MS); taxation (MS); wealth management (MS); JD/MBA. *Accreditation:* AACSB. *Program availability:* Part-time, evening/weekend, online learning. *Entrance requirements:* For master's, GMAT, 2 letters of recommendation, resume, essay, official transcripts. Additional exam requirements/recommendations for international students: Required—TOEFL (minimum score 550 paper-based; 80 iBT). Electronic applications accepted. *Expenses:* Contact institution.

Duke University, The Fuqua School of Business, The Duke MBA-Daytime Program, Durham, NC 27708-0586. Offers academic excellence in finance (Certificate); business administration (MBA); decision sciences (MBA); energy and environment (MBA); energy finance (MBA); entrepreneurship and innovation (MBA); finance (MBA); financial analysis (MBA); health sector management (Certificate); leadership and ethics (MBA); management (MBA); marketing (MBA); operations management (MBA); social entrepreneurship (MBA); strategy (MBA). *Faculty:* 88 full-time (19 women), 50 part-time/adjunct (9 women). *Students:* 897 full-time (310 women); includes 174 minority (39 Black or African American, non-Hispanic/Latino; 3 American Indian or Alaska Native, non-Hispanic/Latino; 75 Asian, non-Hispanic/Latino; 51 Hispanic/Latino; 1 Native Hawaiian or other Pacific Islander, non-Hispanic/Latino; 5 Two or more races, non-Hispanic/Latino), 343 international. Average age 28. In 2016, 440 master's awarded. *Entrance requirements:* For master's, GMAT or GRE, transcripts, essays, resume, recommendation letters, interview. *Application deadline:* For fall admission, 9/13 for domestic and international students; for winter admission, 10/13 for domestic and international students; for spring admission, 1/4 for domestic and international students; for summer admission, 3/20 for domestic and international students. Application fee: $225. Electronic applications accepted. *Expenses:* $66,717 (first-year tuition and fees). *Financial support:* In 2016–17, 415 students received support. Institutionally sponsored loans and scholarships/grants available. Financial award applicants required to submit FAFSA. *Unit head:* Russ Morgan, Senior Associate Dean for Full-time Programs, 919-660-2931, Fax: 919-684-8742, E-mail: ruskin.morgan@duke.edu. *Application contact:* Sharon Thompson, Assistant Dean, Office of Admissions, 919-660-7705, Fax: 919-681-8026, E-mail: admissions-info@fuqua.duke.edu.
Website: http://www.fuqua.duke.edu/daytime-mba/

Duke University, The Fuqua School of Business, PhD Program, Durham, NC 27708-0586. Offers accounting (PhD); decision sciences (PhD); finance (PhD); management and organizations (PhD); marketing (PhD); operations management (PhD); strategy (PhD). *Faculty:* 100 full-time (19 women). *Students:* 77 full-time (27 women); includes 9 minority (1 Black or African American, non-Hispanic/Latino; 7 Asian, non-Hispanic/Latino; 1 Hispanic/Latino), 46 international. 561 applicants, 7% accepted, 14 enrolled. In 2016, 15 doctorates awarded. *Degree requirements:* For doctorate, thesis/dissertation, major field requirement (exam or major paper, depending upon the area). *Entrance requirements:* For doctorate, GMAT or GRE, transcripts, essays, recommendation letters, statement of purpose. Additional exam requirements/recommendations for international students: Required—TOEFL (minimum score 577 paper-based; 90 iBT), IELTS (minimum score 7). *Application deadline:* For fall admission, 12/31 priority date for domestic and international students. Application fee: $85. Electronic applications accepted. *Expenses:* Contact institution. *Financial support:* In 2016–17, 77 students received support, including 70 fellowships with full tuition reimbursements available (averaging $28,200 per year), 63 research assistantships with full tuition reimbursements available (averaging $7,000 per year); institutionally sponsored loans, scholarships/grants, and tuition waivers (full) also available. Financial award applicants required to submit FAFSA. *Unit head:* William Boulding, Dean, 919-660-7822, Fax: 919-684-8742, E-mail: bb1@duke.edu. *Application contact:* Qi Chen, Director of Graduate Studies, 919-660-7753, Fax: 919-660-7971, E-mail: qc2@duke.edu.

East Carolina University, Graduate School, College of Engineering and Technology, Department of Technology Systems, Greenville, NC 27858-4353. Offers computer network professional (Certificate); information assurance (Certificate); Lean Six Sigma Black Belt (Certificate); network technology (MS), including computer networking management, digital communications technology, information security, Web technologies; occupational safety (MS); technology management (PhD); technology systems (MS), including industrial distribution and logistics, manufacturing systems, performance improvement, quality systems; Website developer (Certificate). *Students:* 23 full-time (1 woman), 199 part-time (55 women); includes 59 minority (39 Black or African American, non-Hispanic/Latino; 3 American Indian or Alaska Native, non-Hispanic/Latino; 4 Asian, non-Hispanic/Latino; 10 Hispanic/Latino; 3 Two or more races, non-Hispanic/Latino), 5 international. Average age 38. 85 applicants, 87% accepted, 61 enrolled. In 2016, 23 master's awarded. *Entrance requirements:* For master's and Certificate, GRE General Test or MAT, minimum GPA of 2.5; for doctorate, GRE General Test, related work experience. *Application deadline:* For fall admission, 6/1 priority date for domestic students. Applications are processed on a rolling basis. Application fee: $50. *Financial support:* Application deadline: 6/1. *Unit head:* Dr. Tijjani Mohammed, Chair, 252-328-9668, E-mail: mohammedt@ecu.edu. *Application contact:* Dean of Graduate School, 252-328-6012, Fax: 252-328-6071, E-mail: gradschool@ecu.edu.

Embry-Riddle Aeronautical University–Worldwide, Department of Management, Daytona Beach, FL 32114-3900. Offers global management (MS); human resources management (MS); leadership (MS); operations management (MS); project management (MS). *Program availability:* Part-time, evening/weekend, 100% online, blended/hybrid learning, EagleVision is a virtual classroom that combines Web video conferencing and a learning management system. EagleVision Classroom (between classrooms), EagleVision Home (faculty and students at home), and a blend of Classroom or Home. *Entrance requirements:* Additional exam requirements/recommendations for international students: Required—TOEFL (minimum score 550 paper-based; 79 iBT), IELTS (minimum score 6), TOEFL or IELTS accepted. Electronic applications accepted. *Expenses:* Contact institution.

Emory University, Goizueta Business School, Full Time MBA Program, Atlanta, GA 30322. Offers accounting (MBA); alternative investments (MBA); business process consulting (MBA); business technology management (MBA); capital markets (MBA); corporate finance (MBA); customer relationship management (MBA); decision analytics (MBA); entrepreneurship (MBA); finance (MBA); global management (MBA); investment banking (MBA); management consulting (MBA); marketing (MBA); marketing analytics (MBA); marketing consulting (MBA); operations management (MBA); organization and management (MBA); product and brand management (MBA); real estate (MBA); social enterprise (MBA); strategy consulting (MBA). *Accreditation:* AACSB. *Faculty:* 72 full-time (17 women), 18 part-time/adjunct (5 women). *Students:* 350 full-time (101 women); includes 77 minority (21 Black or African American, non-Hispanic/Latino; 3 American Indian or Alaska Native, non-Hispanic/Latino; 32 Asian, non-Hispanic/Latino; 15 Hispanic/Latino; 2 Native Hawaiian or other Pacific Islander, non-Hispanic/Latino; 4 Two or more races, non-Hispanic/Latino), 117 international. Average age 29. 1,434 applicants, 31% accepted, 181 enrolled. In 2016, 182 master's awarded. *Degree requirements:* For master's, 1 leadership course; 2 mid-semester module programs; 2 global components. *Entrance requirements:* For master's, GMAT/GRE, essays; recommendation letters; undergraduate degree; interview. Additional exam requirements/recommendations for international students: Required—TOEFL (minimum score 100 iBT), IELTS (minimum score 7), PTE (minimum score 68). *Application deadline:* For fall admission, 10/14 priority date for domestic and international students; for winter admission, 11/11 priority date for domestic and international students; for spring admission, 1/4 priority date for domestic students, 1/4 for international students. Application fee: $150. Electronic applications accepted. *Expenses:* $57,580. *Financial support:* In 2016–17, 289 students received support. Career-related internships or fieldwork, institutionally sponsored loans, and scholarships/grants available. Financial award application deadline: 4/1; financial award applicants required to submit FAFSA. *Faculty research:* Social enterprise; micro vs. large business; mobile health data; mutual fund performance; product evaluation. *Unit head:* Brian Mitchell, Associate Dean, 404-727-4824, Fax: 404-712-9648, E-mail: brian.mitchell@emory.edu. *Application contact:* Julie Barefoot, Associate Dean, 404-727-6311, Fax: 404-727-4612, E-mail: mbaadmissions@emory.edu.
Website: http://www.goizueta.emory.edu

Everglades University, Graduate Programs, Program in Aviation Science, Boca Raton, FL 33431. Offers aviation operations management (MSA); aviation security (MSA); business administration (MSA). *Program availability:* Part-time, evening/weekend, 100% online. *Entrance requirements:* For master's, GMAT (minimum score of 400) or GRE (minimum score of 290), bachelor's or graduate degree from college accredited by an agency recognized by the U.S. Department of Education; minimum cumulative GPA of 2.0 at the baccalaureate level, 3.0 at the master's level. Additional exam requirements/recommendations for international students: Recommended—TOEFL (minimum score 500 paper-based). Electronic applications accepted. *Expenses:* Contact institution.

Georgetown University, Graduate School of Arts and Sciences, Department of Economics, Washington, DC 20057. Offers econometrics (PhD); economic development (PhD); economic theory (PhD); industrial organization (PhD); international macro and finance (PhD); international trade (PhD); labor economics (PhD); macroeconomics (PhD); public economics and political economy (PhD); MA/PhD; MS/MA. *Degree requirements:* For doctorate, comprehensive exam, thesis/dissertation. *Entrance requirements:* For doctorate, GRE General Test. Additional exam requirements/recommendations for international students: Required—TOEFL. *Faculty research:* International economics, economic development.

Harvard University, Harvard Business School, Doctoral Programs in Management, Boston, MA 02163. Offers accounting and management (DBA); business economics (PhD); health policy management (PhD); management (DBA); marketing (DBA); organizational behavior (PhD); science, technology and management (PhD); strategy (DBA); technology and operations management (DBA). *Degree requirements:* For doctorate, comprehensive exam (for some programs), thesis/dissertation. *Entrance requirements:* For doctorate, GRE General Test or GMAT. Additional exam requirements/recommendations for international students: Required—TOEFL.

HEC Montreal, School of Business Administration, Master of Science Programs in Administration, Program in Operations Management, Montréal, QC H3T 2A7, Canada. Offers M Sc. All courses are given in English. *Students:* 25 full-time (11 women), 7 part-time (5 women). 17 applicants, 59% accepted, 8 enrolled. In 2016, 12 master's awarded. *Degree requirements:* For master's, one foreign language, thesis. *Entrance requirements:* For master's, Test de francais international (TFI) with minimum score of 850 (for those who have never studied in French), BBA, undergraduate degree in another field, degree deemed equivalent by program director and minimum GPA of 3.0 on 4.3 scale. *Application deadline:* For fall admission, 3/15 for domestic and international students; for winter admission, 9/15 for domestic and international students. Application fee: $86 Canadian dollars. Electronic applications accepted. *Expenses: Tuition, area resident:* Part-time $77.80 Canadian dollars per credit. Tuition, state resident: full-time $2797 Canadian dollars; part-time $240.92 Canadian dollars per credit. Tuition, nonresident: full-time $8673 Canadian dollars; part-time $531.43 Canadian dollars per credit. *International tuition:* $19,131 Canadian dollars full-time. *Required fees:* $1699 Canadian dollars; $40.58 Canadian dollars per credit. $67.32 Canadian dollars per term. Tuition and fees vary according to degree level and program. *Financial support:* Research assistantships, teaching assistantships, and scholarships/grants available. Financial award application deadline: 9/2. *Unit head:* Dr. Marie-Helene Jobin, Director, 514-340-6283, E-mail: anne.bourhis@hec.ca. *Application contact:* Marianne de Moura, Administrative Director, 514-340-7106, Fax: 514-340-6411, E-mail: marianne.de-moura@hec.ca.
Website: http://www.hec.ca/programmes/maitrises/maitrise-gestion-operations/index.html

Illinois Institute of Technology, Graduate College, School of Applied Technology, Department of Industrial Technology and Management, Wheaton, IL 60819. Offers MAS. *Program availability:* Part-time, evening/weekend, online learning. *Entrance requirements:* For master's, GRE (minimum score 900 verbal and quantitative; 2.5 analytical writing), bachelor's degree with minimum cumulative undergraduate GPA of 3.0 (or its equivalent) from accredited institution. Additional exam requirements/recommendations for international students: Required—TOEFL (minimum score 523 paper-based; 70 iBT); Recommended—IELTS (minimum score 5.5). Electronic applications accepted. *Faculty research:* Industrial logistics, industrial facilities, manufacturing technology, entrepreneurship, energy options.

Instituto Tecnologico de Santo Domingo, Graduate School, Area of Engineering, Santo Domingo, Dominican Republic. Offers construction administration (MS, Certificate); data telecommunications (M Eng, MS, Certificate); industrial engineering (M Eng, Certificate); industrial management (M Mgmt); information technology (Certificate); maintenance engineering (M Eng); occupational hazard prevention (M Mgmt); production management (Certificate); quantitative methods (Certificate); sanitary and environmental engineering (M Eng); structural engineering (M Eng); systems engineering and electronic data processing (Certificate); transportation (Certificate).

Instituto Tecnológico y de Estudios Superiores de Monterrey, Campus Estado de México, Professional and Graduate Division, Estado de Mexico, Mexico. Offers administration of information technologies (MITA); architecture (M Arch); business administration (GMBA, MBA); computer sciences (MCS, PhD); education (M Ed); educational institution administration (MAD); educational technology and innovation (PhD); electronic commerce (MEC); environmental systems (MS); finance (MAF); humanistic studies (MHS); information sciences and knowledge management (MISKM); information systems (MS); manufacturing systems (MS); marketing (MEM); quality systems and productivity (MS); science and materials engineering (PhD); telecommunications management (MTM). *Program availability:* Part-time, online learning. *Degree requirements:* For master's, one foreign language, thesis (for some programs); for doctorate, one foreign language, thesis/dissertation. *Entrance requirements:* For master's, E-PAEP 500, interview; for doctorate, E-PAEP 500, research proposal. Additional exam requirements/recommendations for international students: Required—TOEFL (minimum score 550 paper-based). *Faculty research:* Surface treatments by plasmas, mechanical properties, robotics, graphical computing, mechatronics security protocols.

Instituto Tecnológico y de Estudios Superiores de Monterrey, Campus Irapuato, Graduate Programs, Irapuato, Mexico. Offers administration (MBA); administration of information technology (MAIT); administration of telecommunications (MAT); architecture (M Arch); computer science (MCS); education (M Ed); educational administration (MEA); educational innovation and technology (DEIT); educational technology (MET); electronic commerce (MBA); environmental administration and planning (MEAP); environmental systems (MES); finances (MBA); humanistic studies (MHS); international management for Latin American executives (MIMLAE); library and information science (MLIS); manufacturing quality management (MMQM); marketing research (MBA).

Inter American University of Puerto Rico, Metropolitan Campus, Graduate Programs, Program in Industrial Management, San Juan, PR 00919-1293. Offers MBA. *Degree requirements:* For master's, comprehensive exam. *Entrance requirements:* For master's, GRE or EXADEP, interview. Electronic applications accepted.

Inter American University of Puerto Rico, San Germán Campus, Graduate Studies Center, Program in Business Administration, San Germán, PR 00683-5008. Offers accounting (MBA); finance (MBA); general business administration (MBA); human resources (MBA, PhD); industrial relations (MBA); information systems (MBA); international and interregional business (PhD); management (MBA); marketing (MBA). *Program availability:* Part-time, evening/weekend. *Degree requirements:* For master's, comprehensive exam. *Entrance requirements:* For master's, GRE General Test or EXADEP, minimum GPA of 3.0.

Lawrence Technological University, College of Engineering, Southfield, MI 48075-1058. Offers architectural engineering (MS); automotive engineering (MS); biomedical engineering (MS); civil engineering (MA, MS, PhD), including environmental engineering (MS), geotechnical engineering (MS), structural engineering (MS), transportation engineering (MS), water resource engineering (MS); construction engineering management (MA); electrical and computer engineering (MS); engineering management (MA); engineering technology (MS); fire engineering (MS); industrial engineering (MS), including healthcare; manufacturing systems (ME); mechanical engineering (MS, DE, PhD), including manufacturing (DE), solid mechanics (MS), thermal-fluids (MS); mechatronic systems engineering (MS). *Program availability:* Part-time, evening/weekend. *Faculty:* 24 full-time (5 women), 26 part-time/adjunct (2 women). *Students:* 22 full-time (7 women), 588 part-time (81 women); includes 23 minority (11 Black or African American, non-Hispanic/Latino; 4 Asian, non-Hispanic/Latino; 7 Hispanic/Latino; 1 Two or more races, non-Hispanic/Latino), 469 international. Average age 27. 1,186 applicants, 39% accepted, 99 enrolled. In 2016, 293 master's, 3 doctorates awarded. Terminal master's awarded for partial completion of doctoral program. *Degree requirements:* For master's, thesis optional; for doctorate, comprehensive exam, thesis/dissertation optional. *Entrance requirements:* Additional exam requirements/recommendations for international students: Required—TOEFL (minimum score 550 paper-based; 79 iBT), IELTS (minimum score 6.5). *Application deadline:* For fall admission, 5/22 for international students; for spring admission, 10/11 for international students; for summer admission, 2/16 for international students. Applications are processed on a rolling basis. Application fee: $50. Electronic applications accepted. *Expenses: Tuition:* Full-time $14,868; part-time $1062 per credit. *Required fees:* $75 per semester. Tuition and fees vary according to campus/location. *Financial support:* In 2016–17, 25 students received support, including 5 research assistantships with full tuition reimbursements available; unspecified assistantships also available. Financial award application deadline: 4/1; financial award applicants required to submit FAFSA.

Industrial and Manufacturing Management

Faculty research: Carbon fiber reinforced polymer reinforced concrete structures; low impact storm water management solutions; vehicle battery energy management; wireless communication; entrepreneurial mindset and engineering. *Total annual research expenditures:* $1.7 million. *Unit head:* Dr. Nabil Grace, Dean, 248-204-2500, Fax: 248-204-2509, E-mail: engrdean@ltu.edu. *Application contact:* Jane Rohrback, Director of Admissions, 248-204-3160, Fax: 248-204-2228, E-mail: admissions@ltu.edu.
Website: http://www.ltu.edu/engineering/index.asp

Marquette University, Graduate School of Management, Executive MBA Program, Milwaukee, WI 53201-1881. Offers economics (MBA); finance (MBA); human resources (MBA); international business (MBA); management information systems (MBA); marketing (MBA); operations and supply chain management (MBA); sports business (MBA). *Accreditation:* AACSB. *Students:* 39 full-time (12 women); includes 7 minority (4 Black or African American, non-Hispanic/Latino; 2 Asian, non-Hispanic/Latino; 1 Hispanic/Latino). Average age 38. 25 applicants, 96% accepted, 29 enrolled. In 2016, 14 master's awarded. *Degree requirements:* For master's, international trip. *Entrance requirements:* For master's, GMAT or GRE, two letters of recommendation, official transcripts from current and previous colleges/universities. Additional exam requirements/recommendations for international students: Required—TOEFL (minimum score 550 paper-based; 88 iBT), IELTS (minimum score 6.5), PTE. *Application deadline:* For fall admission, 2/15 for domestic and international students. Application fee: $50. Electronic applications accepted. *Expenses:* Contact institution. *Financial support:* Application deadline: 2/15. *Faculty research:* International trade and finance, customer relationship management, consumer satisfaction, customer service. *Unit head:* Dr. Brian Till, Dean, 414-288-5724. *Application contact:* Dr. Jeanne Simmons, Associate Dean, 414-288-7145.
Website: http://www.busadm.mu.edu/emba/

Marquette University, Graduate School of Management, Program in Business Administration, Milwaukee, WI 53201-1881. Offers business administration (MBA); economics (MBA); entrepreneurship (Certificate); finance (MBA); human resources (MBA); international business (MBA); management information systems (MBA); marketing (MBA); operations and supply chain management (MBA); sports business (MBA); JD/MBA; MBA/MA; MBA/MSN. *Accreditation:* AACSB. *Program availability:* Part-time, evening/weekend. *Students:* 25 full-time (12 women), 202 part-time (57 women); includes 17 minority (5 Black or African American, non-Hispanic/Latino; 6 Asian, non-Hispanic/Latino; 2 Hispanic/Latino; 1 Native Hawaiian or other Pacific Islander, non-Hispanic/Latino; 3 Two or more races, non-Hispanic/Latino), 7 international. Average age 31. 107 applicants, 87% accepted, 113 enrolled. In 2016, 107 master's, 5 other advanced degrees awarded. *Degree requirements:* For Certificate, business plan. *Entrance requirements:* For master's, GMAT or GRE, letters of recommendation. Additional exam requirements/recommendations for international students: Required—TOEFL (minimum score 550 paper-based; 88 iBT), IELTS (minimum score 6.5), PTE. *Application deadline:* For fall admission, 2/15 for domestic and international students. Applications are processed on a rolling basis. Application fee: $50. Electronic applications accepted. *Financial support:* Fellowships, research assistantships, teaching assistantships, Federal Work-Study, institutionally sponsored loans, scholarships/grants, and tuition waivers (full and partial) available. Support available to part-time students. Financial award application deadline: 2/15. *Faculty research:* Ethics in the professions, services marketing, technology impact on decision-making, mentoring. *Unit head:* Dr. Brian Till, Dean, 414-288-5724. *Application contact:* Dr. Jeanne Simmons, Associate Dean, 414-288-7145.
Website: http://business.marquette.edu/academics/mba

McGill University, Faculty of Graduate and Postdoctoral Studies, Desautels Faculty of Management, Montréal, QC H3A 2T5, Canada. Offers administration (PhD); entrepreneurial studies (MBA); finance (MBA); general management (Post Master's Certificate); information systems (MBA); international business (MBA); international practicing management (MM); management (MBA); management for development (MBA); manufacturing management (MMM); marketing (MBA); operations management (MBA); public accountancy (Diploma); strategic management (MBA); MBA/LL B; MD/MBA. MMM offered jointly with Faculty of Engineering; PhD with Concordia University, HEC Montreal, Université de Montréal, Université du Québec à Montréal.

McGill University, Faculty of Graduate and Postdoctoral Studies, Faculty of Engineering, Department of Mechanical Engineering and Desautels Faculty of Management, Master in Manufacturing Management, Montréal, QC H3A 2T5, Canada. Offers MMM.

Milligan College, Area of Business Administration, Milligan College, TN 37682. Offers health sector management (MBA, Graduate Certificate); leadership (MBA, Graduate Certificate); operations management (MBA, Graduate Certificate). *Program availability:* Blended/hybrid learning. *Faculty:* 3 full-time (1 woman), 1 part-time/adjunct (0 women). *Students:* 38 full-time (19 women), 12 part-time (5 women); includes 2 minority (1 Black or African American, non-Hispanic/Latino; 1 Hispanic/Latino). Average age 37. 25 applicants, 100% accepted, 19 enrolled. In 2016, 32 master's awarded. *Degree requirements:* For master's, thesis or alternative. *Entrance requirements:* For master's, GMAT if undergraduate GPA less than 3.0, undergraduate degree and supporting transcripts, relevant full-time work experience, essay/personal statement, professional recommendations. Additional exam requirements/recommendations for international students: Required—TOEFL (minimum score 550 paper-based, 79 iBT) or IELTS (6.5). *Application deadline:* For fall admission, 8/1 for domestic students, 6/1 for international students; for spring admission, 1/15 for domestic students, 12/1 for international students. Applications are processed on a rolling basis. Application fee: $30. Electronic applications accepted. *Expenses:* Contact institution. *Financial support:* Scholarships/grants available. Financial award application deadline: 12/1; financial award applicants required to submit FAFSA. *Faculty research:* International microfinance; economic development in Appalachia; job satisfaction; business ethics; internal migration. *Unit head:* Dr. David Campbell, Area Chair of Business, 423-461-8674, Fax: 423-461-8677, E-mail: dacampbell@milligan.edu. *Application contact:* Rebecca Banton, Graduate Admissions Recruiter, Business Area, 423-461-8662, Fax: 423-461-8789, E-mail: rbbanton@milligan.edu.
Website: http://www.milligan.edu/GPS

Milwaukee School of Engineering, Rader School of Business, Program in New Product Management, Milwaukee, WI 53202-3109. Offers MS. *Program availability:* Part-time, evening/weekend. *Faculty:* 1 (woman) full-time, 1 part-time/adjunct (0 women). *Students:* 6 part-time (0 women); includes 1 minority (Hispanic/Latino). Average age 28. 2 applicants, 50% accepted, 1 enrolled. In 2016, 4 master's awarded. *Degree requirements:* For master's, thesis, thesis defense or capstone project. *Entrance requirements:* For master's, GRE General Test or GMAT if undergraduate GPA less than 2.8, 2 letters of recommendation; BS in engineering, engineering technology, science, business, management or a related field. Additional exam requirements/recommendations for international students: Required—TOEFL (minimum score 90 iBT), IELTS (minimum score 6.5). *Application deadline:* Applications are processed on a rolling basis. Application fee: $0. Electronic applications accepted. *Expenses: Tuition:* Full-time $31,440; part-time $655 per credit. *Financial support:* Career-related internships or fieldwork, institutionally sponsored loans, and scholarships/grants available. Financial award application deadline: 3/15; financial award applicants required to submit FAFSA. *Faculty research:* New product development, product research and design, product development. *Unit head:* Gene Wright, Director, 414-277-2268, Fax: 414-277-2487, E-mail: wright@msoe.edu. *Application contact:* Ian Dahlinghaus, Graduate Admissions Counselor, 414-277-7208, E-mail: dahlinghaus@msoe.edu.
Website: http://www.msoe.edu/community/academics/business/page/1317/new-product-management-overview

Mississippi State University, Bagley College of Engineering, Department of Industrial and Systems Engineering, Mississippi State, MS 39762. Offers human factors and ergonomics (MS); industrial and systems engineering (PhD); industrial systems (MS); management systems (MS); manufacturing systems (MS); operations research (MS). *Program availability:* Part-time, blended/hybrid learning. *Faculty:* 12 full-time (1 woman). *Students:* 25 full-time (5 women), 59 part-time (13 women); includes 18 minority (6 Black or African American, non-Hispanic/Latino; 5 Asian, non-Hispanic/Latino; 6 Hispanic/Latino; 1 Native Hawaiian or other Pacific Islander, non-Hispanic/Latino), 21 international. Average age 35. 72 applicants, 32% accepted, 11 enrolled. In 2016, 11 master's, 7 doctorates awarded. *Degree requirements:* For master's, comprehensive exam (for some programs), thesis optional, comprehensive oral or written exam; for doctorate, comprehensive exam, thesis/dissertation, candidacy exam. *Entrance requirements:* For master's, GRE (for graduates from program not accredited by EAC/ABET), minimum GPA of 3.0 on junior and senior years; for doctorate, GRE (for graduates from program not accredited by EAC/ABET), minimum GPA of 3.5 on master's degree and junior and senior years of BS. Additional exam requirements/recommendations for international students: Required—TOEFL (minimum score 550 paper-based; 79 iBT); Recommended—IELTS (minimum score 6.5). *Application deadline:* For fall admission, 7/1 for domestic students, 5/1 for international students; for spring admission, 11/1 for domestic students, 9/1 for international students. Applications are processed on a rolling basis. Application fee: $60. Electronic applications accepted. *Expenses:* Tuition, state resident: full-time $7670; part-time $852.50 per credit hour. Tuition, nonresident: full-time $20,790; part-time $2310.50 per credit hour. Part-time tuition and fees vary according to course load. *Financial support:* In 2016–17, 12 research assistantships with full tuition reimbursements (averaging $16,360 per year), 3 teaching assistantships with full tuition reimbursements (averaging $17,014 per year) were awarded; Federal Work-Study, institutionally sponsored loans, and unspecified assistantships also available. Financial award application deadline: 4/1; financial award applicants required to submit FAFSA. *Faculty research:* Operations research, ergonomics, production systems, management systems, transportation. *Total annual research expenditures:* $4.4 million. *Unit head:* Dr. John Usher, Professor/Department Head, 662-325-7624, Fax: 662-325-7618, E-mail: usher@ise.msstate.edu. *Application contact:* Doretta Martin, Senior Admissions Assistant, 662-325-9514, E-mail: dmartin@grad.msstate.edu.
Website: http://www.ise.msstate.edu/

Northern Illinois University, Graduate School, College of Engineering and Engineering Technology, Department of Technology, De Kalb, IL 60115-2854. Offers industrial management (MS). *Program availability:* Part-time, evening/weekend. *Faculty:* 14 full-time (1 woman), 1 part-time/adjunct (0 women). *Students:* 4 full-time (1 woman), 19 part-time (4 women); includes 5 minority (1 Black or African American, non-Hispanic/Latino; 2 Hispanic/Latino; 2 Two or more races, non-Hispanic/Latino), 2 international. Average age 33. 17 applicants, 76% accepted, 2 enrolled. In 2016, 15 master's awarded. *Degree requirements:* For master's, thesis optional. *Entrance requirements:* For master's, GRE General Test, minimum GPA of 2.75. Additional exam requirements/recommendations for international students: Required—TOEFL (minimum score 550 paper-based). *Application deadline:* For fall admission, 6/1 for domestic students, 5/1 for international students; for spring admission, 11/1 for domestic students, 10/1 for international students. Applications are processed on a rolling basis. Application fee: $40. Electronic applications accepted. *Financial support:* In 2016–17, 1 research assistantship with full tuition reimbursement, 9 teaching assistantships with full tuition reimbursements were awarded; fellowships with full tuition reimbursements, career-related internships or fieldwork, Federal Work-Study, scholarships/grants, tuition waivers (full), and unspecified assistantships also available. Support available to part-time students. Financial award applicants required to submit FAFSA. *Faculty research:* Digital control, intelligent systems, engineering graphic design, occupational safety, ergonomics. *Unit head:* Dr. Clifford Mirman, Chair, 815-753-1349, Fax: 815-753-3702, E-mail: mirman@ceet.niu.edu. *Application contact:* Graduate School Office, 815-753-0395, E-mail: gradsch@niu.edu.
Website: http://www.niu.edu/tech/

Northwestern University, The Graduate School, Kellogg School of Management, Management Programs, Evanston, IL 60208. Offers accounting information and management (MBA, PhD); analytical finance (MBA); business administration (MBA); decision sciences (MBA); entrepreneurship and innovation (MBA); finance (MBA, PhD); health enterprise management (MBA); human resources management (MBA); international business (MBA); management and organizations (MBA, PhD); management and organizations and sociology (PhD); management and strategy (MBA); management studies (MS); managerial analytics (MBA); managerial economics (MBA); managerial economics and strategy (PhD); marketing (MBA, PhD); marketing management (MBA); media management (MBA); operations management (MBA, PhD); real estate (MBA); social enterprise at Kellogg (MBA); JD/MBA. *Program availability:* Part-time, evening/weekend. Terminal master's awarded for partial completion of doctoral program. *Degree requirements:* For doctorate, thesis/dissertation, 2 years of coursework, qualifying (field) exam and candidacy, summer research papers and presentations to faculty, proposal defense, final exam/defense. *Entrance requirements:* For master's, GMAT, GRE, interview, 2 letters of recommendation, college transcripts, resume, essays, Kellogg honor code; for doctorate, GMAT, GRE, statement of purpose, transcripts, 2 letters of recommendation, resume, interview. Additional exam requirements/recommendations for international students: Required—TOEFL, IELTS. Electronic applications accepted. *Expenses:* Contact institution. *Faculty research:* Business cycles and international finance, health policy, networks, non-market strategy, consumer psychology.

Notre Dame de Namur University, Division of Academic Affairs, School of Business and Management, Program in Business Administration, Belmont, CA 94002-1908. Offers business administration (MBA); entrepreneurship (MBA); finance (MBA); human resource management (MBA); marketing (MBA); media and promotion (MBA); technology and operations management (MBA). *Accreditation:* ACBSP. *Program availability:* Part-time, evening/weekend. *Entrance requirements:* For master's, minimum GPA of 2.5. Additional exam requirements/recommendations for international students: Required—TOEFL (minimum score 550 paper-based; 79 iBT). Electronic applications accepted.

Oakland University, Graduate Study and Lifelong Learning, School of Business Administration, Department of Decision and Information Sciences, Rochester, MI 48309-4401. Offers information technology management (MS); management information systems (Certificate); production and operations management (Certificate).

Penn State Erie, The Behrend College, Graduate School, Erie, PA 16563. Offers accounting (MPAC); business administration (MBA); project management (MPM); quality and manufacturing management (MMM). *Accreditation:* AACSB. *Program*

availability: Part-time. *Students:* 28 full-time (9 women), 118 part-time (31 women); includes 11 minority (5 Black or African American, non-Hispanic/Latino; 2 Asian, non-Hispanic/Latino; 1 Hispanic/Latino; 3 Two or more races, non-Hispanic/Latino), 2 international. Average age 32. 91 applicants, 74% accepted, 55 enrolled. In 2016, 59 master's awarded. *Entrance requirements:* Additional exam requirements/ recommendations for international students: Required—TOEFL (minimum score 550 paper-based; 80 iBT), IELTS. *Application deadline:* Applications are processed on a rolling basis. Application fee: $65. Electronic applications accepted. *Financial support:* Federal Work-Study available. Financial award application deadline: 3/1; financial award applicants required to submit FAFSA. *Unit head:* Dr. Ralph M. Ford, Chancellor, 814-898-6160, Fax: 814-898-6461. *Application contact:* Ann M. Burbules, Assistant Director, Graduate Admissions, 866-374-3378, Fax: 814-898-6044, E-mail: behrend.admissions@psu.edu.
Website: http://behrend.psu.edu/

Polytechnic University of Puerto Rico, Graduate School, Hato Rey, PR 00918. Offers business administration (MBA), including computer information systems, general management, management of information systems, management of international enterprises; civil engineering (ME, MS); computer engineering (ME, MS); computer science (MCS, MS); electrical engineering (ME, MS); engineering management (MEM); environmental management (MEM); landscape architecture (M Land Arch); manufacturing competitiveness (MMC, MS); manufacturing engineering (ME, MS); mechanical engineering (M Mech E). *Program availability:* Part-time, evening/weekend. *Entrance requirements:* For master's, 3 letters of recommendation.

Polytechnic University of Puerto Rico, Miami Campus, Graduate School, Miami, FL 33166. Offers accounting (MBA); business administration (MBA); construction management (MEM); environmental management (MEM); finance (MBA); human resources management (MBA); logistics and supply chain management (MBA); management of international enterprises (MBA); manufacturing management (MEM); marketing management (MBA); project management (MBA). *Program availability:* Part-time, evening/weekend, online learning. *Entrance requirements:* For master's, minimum GPA of 3.0. Electronic applications accepted.

Polytechnic University of Puerto Rico, Orlando Campus, Graduate School, Orlando, FL 32825. Offers accounting (MBA); business administration (MBA); construction management (MEM); engineering management (MEM); environmental management (MEM); finance (MBA); human resources management (MBA); management of international enterprises (MBA); management of technology (MBA); manufacturing management (MEM). *Program availability:* Part-time, evening/weekend, online learning. *Entrance requirements:* For master's, minimum GPA of 3.0. Additional exam requirements/recommendations for international students: Recommended—TOEFL. Electronic applications accepted.

Portland State University, Graduate Studies, Maseeh College of Engineering and Computer Science, Department of Engineering and Technology Management, Portland, OR 97207-0751. Offers engineering and technology management (M Eng); engineering management (MS); manufacturing engineering (ME); manufacturing management (M Eng); systems science/engineering management (PhD); MS/MBA; MS/MS. *Program availability:* Part-time, evening/weekend. *Faculty:* 6 full-time (1 woman), 5 part-time/ adjunct (0 women). *Students:* 53 full-time (19 women), 75 part-time (34 women); includes 18 minority (3 Black or African American, non-Hispanic/Latino; 11 Asian, non-Hispanic/Latino; 3 Hispanic/Latino; 1 Two or more races, non-Hispanic/Latino), 73 international. Average age 36. 76 applicants, 50% accepted, 20 enrolled. In 2016, 34 master's, 4 doctorates awarded. *Degree requirements:* For master's, thesis optional; for doctorate, one foreign language, comprehensive exam, thesis/dissertation, oral and written exams. *Entrance requirements:* For master's, minimum GPA of 2.75 undergraduate or 3.0 graduate (at least 12 credits); minimum 4 years of experience in engineering or related discipline; 3 letters of recommendation; background in probability/ statistics, differential equations, computer programming and linear algebra; for doctorate, GRE General Test (minimum combined score of 1100 for verbal and quantitative), minimum GPA of 3.0 undergraduate, 3.25 graduate. Additional exam requirements/recommendations for international students: Required—TOEFL (minimum score 550 paper-based; 80 iBT). *Application deadline:* For fall admission, 4/1 for domestic students, 3/1 for international students; for winter admission, 9/1 for domestic students, 7/1 for international students; for spring admission, 11/1 for domestic students, 9/1 for international students; for summer admission, 2/1 for domestic students, 12/1 for international students. Application fee: $65. Electronic applications accepted. *Expenses:* Contact institution. *Financial support:* In 2016–17, 7 research assistantships with tuition reimbursements (averaging $2,885 per year), 3 teaching assistantships with tuition reimbursements (averaging $1,176 per year) were awarded; career-related internships or fieldwork, Federal Work-Study, scholarships/grants, and unspecified assistantships also available. Support available to part-time students. Financial award application deadline: 3/1; financial award applicants required to submit FAFSA. *Faculty research:* Scheduling, hierarchical decision modeling, operations research, knowledge-based information systems. *Total annual research expenditures:* $323,951. *Unit head:* Dr. Timothy Anderson, Chair, 503-725-4668, Fax: 503-725-4667, E-mail: tim.anderson@pdx.edu. *Application contact:* Shawn Wall, Department Manager, 503-725-4661, E-mail: shawnw@pdx.edu.
Website: http://www.pdx.edu/engineering-technology-management/

Regis University, College of Business and Economics, Denver, CO 80221-1099. Offers accounting (MS); executive leadership (Certificate); finance (MS); finance and accounting (MBA); health industry leadership (MBA); human resource management and leadership (MSOL); management (MBA); marketing (MBA); nonprofit leadership (Post-Graduate Certificate); nonprofit management (MNM); nonprofit organizational capacity building (Certificate); operations management (MBA); organizational leadership and management (MSOL); project leadership and management (MS, MSOL); strategic business management (Certificate); strategic human resource integration (Certificate); strategic management (MBA). Programs offered at Colorado Springs Campus, Northwest Denver Campus, Southeast Denver Campus, Fort Collins Campus, Broomfield Campus, Henderson (Nevada) Campus, and Summerlin (Nevada) Campus. *Program availability:* Part-time, evening/weekend, 100% online, blended/hybrid learning. *Faculty:* 15 full-time (5 women), 43 part-time/adjunct (16 women). *Students:* 622 full-time (350 women), 460 part-time (170 women); includes 317 minority (88 Black or African American, non-Hispanic/Latino; 7 American Indian or Alaska Native, non-Hispanic/ Latino; 44 Asian, non-Hispanic/Latino; 151 Hispanic/Latino; 1 Native Hawaiian or other Pacific Islander, non-Hispanic/Latino; 26 Two or more races, non-Hispanic/Latino), 44 international. Average age 36. 307 applicants, 73% accepted, 134 enrolled. In 2016, 394 master's awarded. *Degree requirements:* For master's, thesis (for some programs), capstone or final research project. *Entrance requirements:* For master's, official transcript reflecting baccalaureate degree awarded from regionally-accredited college or university, interview, 2 years of full-time related work experience, resume, letters of recommendation. Additional exam requirements/recommendations for international students: Required—TOEFL (minimum score 550 paper-based; 82 iBT). *Application deadline:* For fall admission, 8/15 priority date for domestic students, 8/13 for international students; for winter admission, 10/10 priority date for domestic students, 9/8 for international students; for spring admission, 1/10 priority date for domestic students, 11/17 for international students; for summer admission, 5/1 priority date for domestic students. Applications are processed on a rolling basis. Application fee: $75. Electronic applications accepted. *Expenses:* $780 per credit hour. *Financial support:* Scholarships/grants available. Financial award application deadline: 4/15; financial award applicants required to submit FAFSA. *Faculty research:* Impact of information technology on small business regulation of accounting, international project financing, mineral development, delivery of healthcare to rural indigenous communities. *Unit head:* Dr. Timothy Keane, Academic Dean. *Application contact:* Cate Clark, Director of Admissions, 303-458-4900, Fax: 303-964-5534, E-mail: ruadmissions@regis.edu.
Website: http://www.regis.edu/CBE.aspx

Rochester Institute of Technology, Graduate Enrollment Services, Kate Gleason College of Engineering, Design, Development and Manufacturing Department, MS Program in Manufacturing Leadership, Rochester, NY 14623. Offers MS. *Program availability:* Part-time, evening/weekend, 100% online. *Students:* 23 part-time (2 women); includes 4 minority (1 Black or African American, non-Hispanic/Latino; 1 Asian, non-Hispanic/Latino; 1 Hispanic/Latino; 1 Two or more races, non-Hispanic/Latino). Average age 37. 8 applicants, 75% accepted, 4 enrolled. In 2016, 8 master's awarded. *Degree requirements:* For master's, thesis or alternative, capstone. *Entrance requirements:* For master's, minimum GPA of 3.0 (recommended). Additional exam requirements/recommendations for international students: Required—TOEFL (minimum score 550 paper-based; 79 iBT), IELTS (minimum score 6.5), PTE (minimum score 58). *Application deadline:* Applications are processed on a rolling basis. Application fee: $60. Electronic applications accepted. *Expenses:* $1,742 per credit hour. *Financial support:* Scholarships/grants available. Support available to part-time students. Financial award applicants required to submit FAFSA. *Faculty research:* Lean manufacturing, Lean Six Sigma, modeling and simulation, supply chain management, project management. *Unit head:* Mark Smith, Graduate Program Director, 585-475-7971, Fax: 585-475-4080, E-mail: mml@rit.edu. *Application contact:* Diane Ellison, Associate Vice President, Graduate Enrollment Services, 585-475-2229, Fax: 585-475-7164, E-mail: gradinfo@rit.edu.
Website: https://www.rit.edu/kgcoe/mml/

San Francisco State University, Division of Graduate Studies, College of Business, Program in Business Administration, San Francisco, CA 94132-1722. Offers decision sciences/operations research (MBA); ethics and compliance (MBA); finance (MBA); global business and innovation (MBA); healthcare administration (MBA); hospitality and tourism management (MBA); information systems (MBA); leadership (MBA); marketing (MBA); nonprofit and social enterprise leadership (MBA); sustainable business (MBA). *Accreditation:* AACSB. *Program availability:* Part-time, evening/weekend. *Degree requirements:* For master's, thesis, essay test. *Entrance requirements:* For master's, GMAT, minimum GPA of 2.7 in last 60 units. Additional exam requirements/ recommendations for international students: Required—TOEFL (minimum score 550 paper-based). *Application deadline:* For fall admission, 5/1 priority date for domestic students, 4/1 for international students; for spring admission, 11/1 for domestic students, 10/15 for international students. Applications are processed on a rolling basis. Application fee: $55. *Expenses:* Tuition, state resident: full-time $6738. Tuition, nonresident: full-time $15,666. *Required fees:* $1012. Tuition and fees vary according to degree level and program. *Financial support:* Application deadline: 3/1. *Unit head:* Dr. Sanjit Sengupta, Faculty Director, 415-817-4366, Fax: 415-817-4340, E-mail: sengupta@sfsu.edu. *Application contact:* Zandra Tan, EMBA Program Coordinator, 415-817-4360, Fax: 415-817-4340, E-mail: zandra13@sfsu.edu.
Website: http://cob.sfsu.edu/graduate-programs/mba

Southern New Hampshire University, School of Business, Manchester, NH 03106-1045. Offers accounting (MBA, MS, Graduate Certificate); accounting finance (MS); accounting/auditing (MS); accounting/forensic accounting (MS); accounting/taxation (MS); athletic administration (MBA, Graduate Certificate); business administration (IMBA, MBA, Certificate, Graduate Certificate), including accounting (Certificate), business administration (MBA), business information systems (Graduate Certificate), human resource management (Certificate); corporate social responsibility (MBA); entrepreneurship (MBA); finance (MBA, MS, Graduate Certificate); finance/corporate finance (MS); finance/investments and securities (MS); forensic accounting (MBA); healthcare informatics (MBA); healthcare management (MBA); human resource management (Graduate Certificate); information technology (MS, Graduate Certificate); information technology management (MBA); international business (Graduate Certificate); international business and information technology (Graduate Certificate); international finance (Graduate Certificate); international sport management (Graduate Certificate); justice studies (MBA); leadership of nonprofit organizations (Graduate Certificate); management (MS); marketing (MBA, MS, Graduate Certificate); operations and project management (MS); operations and supply chain management (MBA, Graduate Certificate); organizational leadership (MS); project management (MBA, Graduate Certificate); Six Sigma (MBA); Six Sigma quality (Graduate Certificate); social media marketing (MBA); sport management (MBA, MS, Graduate Certificate); sustainability and environmental compliance (MBA); workplace conflict management (MBA); MBA/Certificate. *Accreditation:* ACBSP. *Program availability:* Part-time, evening/ weekend, online learning. Terminal master's awarded for partial completion of doctoral program. *Degree requirements:* For master's, one foreign language, comprehensive exam (for some programs), thesis or alternative. *Entrance requirements:* For master's, minimum GPA of 2.5. Additional exam requirements/recommendations for international students: Required—TOEFL (minimum score 500 paper-based). Electronic applications accepted.

Stevens Institute of Technology, Graduate School, Charles V. Schaefer Jr. School of Engineering and Science, Department of Mechanical Engineering, Program in Integrated Product Development, Hoboken, NJ 07030. Offers armament engineering (M Eng); computer and electrical engineering (M Eng); manufacturing technologies (M Eng); systems reliability and design (M Eng). *Program availability:* Part-time, evening/weekend. *Students:* 15 applicants. In 2016, 2 master's awarded. *Degree requirements:* For master's, thesis optional, minimum B average in major field and overall. *Entrance requirements:* Additional exam requirements/recommendations for international students: Required—TOEFL (minimum score 74 iBT), IELTS (minimum score 6). *Application deadline:* For fall admission, 6/1 for domestic students, 4/15 for international students; for spring admission, 11/30 for domestic students, 11/1 for international students. Applications are processed on a rolling basis. Application fee: $65. Electronic applications accepted. *Expenses:* Contact institution. *Financial support:* Fellowships, research assistantships, teaching assistantships, career-related internships or fieldwork, Federal Work-Study, scholarships/grants, and unspecified assistantships available. Financial award application deadline: 2/15; financial award applicants required to submit FAFSA. *Unit head:* Dr. Frank Fisher, Interim Department Director, 201-216-8913, Fax: 201-216-8315, E-mail: ffisher@stevens.edu. *Application contact:* Graduate Admissions, 888-783-8367, Fax: 888-511-1306, E-mail: graduate@stevens.edu.

Stony Brook University, State University of New York, Graduate School, College of Business, Program in Business Administration, Stony Brook, NY 11794. Offers accounting (MBA); business administration (MBA); finance (MBA, Certificate); health care management (MBA); innovation, human resources, management, or operations management (MBA); marketing (MBA). *Faculty:* 37 full-time (12 women), 12 part-time/adjunct (4 women). *Students:* 199 full-time (109 women), 139 part-time (64 women); includes 81 minority (19 Black or African American, non-Hispanic/Latino; 41 Asian, non-Hispanic/Latino; 17 Hispanic/Latino; 1 Native Hawaiian or other Pacific Islander, non-Hispanic/Latino; 3 Two or more races, non-Hispanic/Latino), 88 international. Average age 29. 246 applicants, 65% accepted, 91 enrolled. In 2016, 116 master's awarded. *Entrance requirements:* For master's, GMAT, 3 letters of recommendation from current or former employers or professors, transcripts, personal statement, resume. Additional exam requirements/recommendations for international students: Required—TOEFL (minimum score 550 paper-based; 90 iBT), IELTS (minimum score 6.5). *Application deadline:* For fall admission, 5/15 for domestic students, 3/15 for international students; for spring admission, 11/15 for domestic students, 10/15 for international students. Application fee: $100. *Expenses:* Contact institution. *Financial support:* Teaching assistantships available. *Total annual research expenditures:* $5,325. *Unit head:* Dr. Manuel London, Dean, 631-632-7159, E-mail: manuel.london@stonybrook.edu. *Application contact:* Dr. Jadranka Skorin-Kapov, Graduate Program Director, 631-632-7171, Fax: 631-632-8181, E-mail: jadranka.skorin-kapov@stonybrook.edu.

Texas A&M University–Commerce, College of Education and Human Services, Commerce, TX 75429-3011. Offers counseling (MS); curriculum and instruction (M Ed, MS); early childhood education (M Ed, MS); educational administration (M Ed, Ed D); educational psychology (PhD); educational technology leadership (MS); educational technology library science (MS); health, kinesiology and sports studies (MS); higher education (MS, Ed D); organization, learning, and technology (MS); psychology (MS); reading (M Ed, MS); school psychology (SSP); secondary education (M Ed, MS); social work (MSW); special education (M Ed); supervision, curriculum and instruction-elementary education (Ed D). *Program availability:* Part-time, 100% online, blended/hybrid learning. *Faculty:* 88 full-time (52 women), 31 part-time/adjunct (24 women). *Students:* 341 full-time (276 women), 1,495 part-time (1,156 women); includes 762 minority (429 Black or African American, non-Hispanic/Latino; 4 American Indian or Alaska Native, non-Hispanic/Latino; 27 Asian, non-Hispanic/Latino; 247 Hispanic/Latino; 1 Native Hawaiian or other Pacific Islander, non-Hispanic/Latino; 54 Two or more races, non-Hispanic/Latino), 18 international. Average age 37. 1,070 applicants, 54% accepted, 452 enrolled. In 2016, 579 master's, 31 doctorates awarded. *Degree requirements:* For master's, one foreign language, comprehensive exam, thesis optional, departmental qualifying exams (for some programs); for doctorate, comprehensive exam, thesis/dissertation, departmental qualifying exam; for SSP, comprehensive exam, thesis optional. *Entrance requirements:* For master's and doctorate, GRE General Test. Additional exam requirements/recommendations for international students: Required—TOEFL (minimum score 550 paper-based; 79 iBT), IELTS (minimum score 6). *Application deadline:* For fall admission, 6/1 priority date for international students; for spring admission, 10/15 priority date for international students; for summer admission, 3/15 priority date for international students. Applications are processed on a rolling basis. Application fee: $50. Electronic applications accepted. *Expenses:* $2,254 resident; $4,744 non-resident. *Financial support:* In 2016–17, 301 students received support, including 39 research assistantships with partial tuition reimbursements available (averaging $9,000 per year), 17 teaching assistantships with partial tuition reimbursements available (averaging $9,000 per year); career-related internships or fieldwork, Federal Work-Study, institutionally sponsored loans, scholarships/grants, health care benefits, and unspecified assistantships also available. Financial award application deadline: 5/1; financial award applicants required to submit FAFSA. *Faculty research:* Cognitive and bilingual education, positive behavioral intervention, literacy, math readiness. *Total annual research expenditures:* $470,963. *Unit head:* Dr. Timothy Letzring, Dean, 903-886-5181, Fax: 903-886-5905, E-mail: tim.letzring@tamuc.edu. *Application contact:* Jennifer Faunce, Graduate Recruiter, 903-886-5030, Fax: 903-886-5905, E-mail: jennifer.faunce@tamuc.edu.
Website: http://www.tamuc.edu/academics/graduateSchool/programs/education/default.aspx

Texas A&M University–Kingsville, College of Graduate Studies, Frank H. Dotterweich College of Engineering, Department of Industrial Management and Technology, Kingsville, TX 78363. Offers industrial management (MS). *Degree requirements:* For master's, variable foreign language requirement, comprehensive exam, thesis (for some programs). *Entrance requirements:* For master's, GRE, MAT, GMAT. Additional exam requirements/recommendations for international students: Required—TOEFL (minimum score 550 paper-based; 79 iBT). Electronic applications accepted.

Universidad de las Américas Puebla, Division of Graduate Studies, School of Engineering, Program in Industrial Engineering, Puebla, Mexico. Offers industrial engineering (MS); production management (M Adm). *Program availability:* Part-time, evening/weekend. *Degree requirements:* For master's, one foreign language, thesis. *Faculty research:* Textile industry, quality control.

Universidad de las Américas Puebla, Division of Graduate Studies, School of Engineering, Program in Manufacturing Administration, Puebla, Mexico. Offers MS. *Faculty research:* Operations research, construction.

The University of Alabama, Graduate School, Manderson Graduate School of Business, Department of Information Systems, Statistics, and Management Science, Program in Operations Management, Tuscaloosa, AL 35487. Offers MS, PhD. *Accreditation:* AACSB. *Program availability:* Online learning. *Students:* 28 full-time (11 women), 33 part-time (10 women); includes 6 minority (2 Black or African American, non-Hispanic/Latino; 1 Asian, non-Hispanic/Latino; 2 Hispanic/Latino; 1 Two or more races, non-Hispanic/Latino), 12 international. Average age 29. 77 applicants, 60% accepted, 21 enrolled. In 2016, 44 master's, 5 doctorates awarded. Terminal master's awarded for partial completion of doctoral program. *Degree requirements:* For master's, comprehensive exam, business calculus; for doctorate, comprehensive exam, thesis/dissertation. *Entrance requirements:* For master's, GMAT or GRE; for doctorate, GRE or GMAT. Additional exam requirements/recommendations for international students: Required—TOEFL (minimum score 94 iBT), IELTS (minimum score 7). *Application deadline:* For spring admission, 1/10 priority date for domestic and international students. Applications are processed on a rolling basis. Application fee: $50 ($60 for international students). Electronic applications accepted. *Expenses:* Tuition, state resident: full-time $10,470. Tuition, nonresident: full-time $26,950. *Financial support:* In 2016–17, 11 students received support, including 7 teaching assistantships with full tuition reimbursements available (averaging $13,500 per year); scholarships/grants and health care benefits also available. Financial award application deadline: 1/10. *Faculty research:* Supply chain management, inventory, simulation, logistics. *Unit head:* Dr. James Cochran, Interim Department Head, 205-348-8914, E-mail: jocochran@culverhouse.ua.edu. *Application contact:* Sarah Schmidt, Program Assistant, 205-348-8904, E-mail: sschmidt@cba.ua.edu.

University of Arkansas, Graduate School, College of Engineering, Department of Industrial Engineering, Operations Management Program, Fayetteville, AR 72701. Offers MS. *Program availability:* Part-time, evening/weekend, online learning. *Students:* 137 applicants, 94% accepted. In 2016, 214 master's awarded. *Degree requirements:* For master's, thesis optional. *Application deadline:* For fall admission, 4/1 for international students; for spring admission, 10/1 for international students. Applications are processed on a rolling basis. Application fee: $0. Electronic applications accepted. *Financial support:* In 2016–17, 2 research assistantships were awarded; fellowships, teaching assistantships, and institutionally sponsored loans also available. *Unit head:* Dr. Greg Parnell, Departmental Chair, 479-575-7426, E-mail: gparnell@uark.edu. *Application contact:* Dr. Greg Parnell, Director/Chairman, 479-575-3156, Fax: 479-575-8431, E-mail: gparnell@uark.edu.
Website: http://www.msom.uark.edu/

University of Bridgeport, School of Business, Bridgeport, CT 06604. Offers accounting (MBA); finance (MBA); general business (MBA); global financial services (MBA); human resource management (MBA); information systems and knowledge management (MBA); international business (MBA); management (MBA); marketing (MBA); operations management (MBA); small business and entrepreneurship (MBA); specialized business (MBA). *Accreditation:* ACBSP. *Program availability:* Part-time, evening/weekend. *Degree requirements:* For master's, thesis optional. *Entrance requirements:* For master's, GMAT. Additional exam requirements/recommendations for international students: Recommended—TOEFL (minimum score 550 paper-based; 80 iBT), IELTS (minimum score 6.5). Electronic applications accepted. *Expenses:* Contact institution.

University of Central Missouri, The Graduate School, Warrensburg, MO 64093. Offers accountancy (MA); accounting (MBA); applied mathematics (MS); aviation safety (MA); biology (MS); business administration (MBA); career and technical education leadership (MS); college student personnel administration (MS); communication (MA); computer science (MS); counseling (MS); criminal justice (MS); educational leadership (Ed D); educational technology (MS); elementary and early childhood education (MSE); English (MA); environmental studies (MA); finance (MBA); history (MA); human services/educational technology (Ed S); human services/learning resources (Ed S); human services/professional counseling (Ed S); industrial hygiene (MS); industrial management (MS); information systems (MBA); information technology (MS); kinesiology (MS); library science and information services (MS); literacy education (MSE); marketing (MBA); mathematics (MS); music (MA); occupational safety management (MS); psychology (MS); rural family nursing (MS); school administration (MSE); social gerontology (MS); sociology (MA); special education (MSE); speech language pathology (MS); superintendency (Ed S); teaching (MAT); teaching English as a second language (MA); technology (MS); technology management (PhD); theatre (MA). *Program availability:* Part-time, 100% online, blended/hybrid learning. *Degree requirements:* For master's and Ed S, comprehensive exam (for some programs), thesis (for some programs). *Entrance requirements:* Additional exam requirements/recommendations for international students: Required—TOEFL (minimum score 550 paper-based; 79 iBT). Electronic applications accepted.

University of Chicago, Booth School of Business, Full-Time MBA Program, Chicago, IL 60637. Offers accounting (MBA); analytic finance (MBA); analytic management (MBA); econometrics and statistics (MBA); economics (MBA); entrepreneurship (MBA); finance (MBA); general management (MBA); health administration and policy (Certificate); international business (MBA); managerial and organizational behavior (MBA); marketing analytics (MBA); marketing management (MBA); operations management (MBA); strategic management (MBA); MBA/AM; MBA/JD; MBA/MA; MBA/MD; MBA/MPP. *Accreditation:* AACSB. *Students:* 1,151 full-time (443 women), 17 part-time (9 women). Terminal master's awarded for partial completion of doctoral program. *Entrance requirements:* For master's, GMAT or GRE, transcripts, resume, 2 letters of recommendation, essay, interview. Additional exam requirements/recommendations for international students: Required—TOEFL (minimum score 600 paper-based; 104 iBT), IELTS (minimum score 7), PTE (minimum score 70). *Application deadline:* For spring admission, 4/1 for domestic and international students. Electronic applications accepted. *Expenses:* Contact institution. *Unit head:* Stacey Kole, Deputy Dean, 773-702-7121. *Application contact:* Full-time MBA Program Admissions, 773-702-7369, Fax: 773-702-9085, E-mail: admissions@chicagobooth.edu.
Website: https://www.chicagobooth.edu/programs/full-time

University of Cincinnati, Graduate School, Carl H. Lindner College of Business, PhD Programs, Cincinnati, OH 45211. Offers accounting (PhD); economics (PhD); finance (PhD); information systems (PhD); management (PhD); marketing (PhD); operations and business analytics (PhD). *Faculty:* 72 full-time (18 women). *Students:* 37 full-time (19 women); includes 4 minority (1 Black or African American, non-Hispanic/Latino; 3 Asian, non-Hispanic/Latino), 19 international. Average age 30. 92 applicants, 16% accepted, 7 enrolled. In 2016, 4 doctorates awarded. *Degree requirements:* For doctorate, comprehensive exam, thesis/dissertation. *Entrance requirements:* For doctorate, GMAT, GRE, transcripts, essays, resume, letters of recommendation. Additional exam requirements/recommendations for international students: Required—TOEFL (minimum score 600 paper-based; 100 iBT), IELTS (minimum score 7). *Application deadline:* For fall admission, 1/15 for domestic and international students. Application fee: $65 ($70 for international students). Electronic applications accepted. *Expenses:* Contact institution. *Financial support:* In 2016–17, 38 students received support, including 25 research assistantships with tuition reimbursements available (averaging $23,250 per year); scholarships/grants, tuition waivers (full and partial), and unspecified assistantships also available. Financial award application deadline: 1/15; financial award applicants required to submit FAFSA. *Faculty research:* Bayesian Prediction Theory, organizational fairness, consumer insight and market research, EGARCH idiosyncratic volatility and expected stock returns, consumer insight and market research, density estimation from correlated data. *Unit head:* Dr. Suzanne Masterson, Director, 513-556-7125, Fax: 513-556-5499, E-mail: suzanne.masterson@uc.edu. *Application contact:* Angel Elvin, Assistant Director, 513-556-7190, Fax: 513-558-7006, E-mail: angel.elvin@uc.edu.
Website: http://www.business.uc.edu/phd

The University of Manchester, School of Mechanical, Aerospace and Civil Engineering, Manchester, United Kingdom. Offers advanced manufacturing technology (M Ent); aerospace engineering (M Phil, M Sc, PhD); civil engineering (M Phil, M Sc, PhD); environmental engineering (M Phil, PhD); management of projects (M Phil, M Sc, PhD); mechanical engineering (M Phil, M Sc, PhD); mechanical engineering design (M Ent); nuclear engineering (M Phil, D Eng, PhD).

University of Michigan–Flint, School of Management, Program in Business Administration, Flint, MI 48502. Offers accounting (MBA, Post-Master's Certificate); computer information systems (MBA); finance (MBA, Post-Master's Certificate); general business (Graduate Certificate); general business administration (MBA); health care management (MBA); international business (MBA, Post-Master's Certificate); lean manufacturing (MBA); marketing (MBA, Post-Master's Certificate); organizational leadership (MBA, Post-Master's Certificate). *Program availability:* Part-time, evening/weekend, mixed mode programs. *Faculty:* 33 full-time (9 women), 6 part-time/adjunct (1 woman). *Students:* 24 full-time (12 women), 146 part-time (49 women); includes 37 minority (17 Black or African American, non-Hispanic/Latino; 2 American Indian or Alaska Native, non-Hispanic/Latino; 10 Asian, non-Hispanic/Latino; 4 Hispanic/Latino; 1 Native Hawaiian or other Pacific Islander, non-Hispanic/Latino; 3 Two or more races, non-Hispanic/Latino), 17 international. Average age 33. 167 applicants, 47% accepted, 40 enrolled. In 2016, 73 master's, 3 other advanced degrees awarded. *Entrance requirements:* For master's, GMAT or GRE, bachelor's degree in arts, sciences, engineering, or business administration from regionally-accredited college or university with minimum GPA of 3.0; for other advanced degree, bachelor's degree in arts,

sciences, engineering, or business administration from regionally-accredited college or university with minimum GPA of 3.0, college-level math, statistics, or quantitative course (for Graduate Certificate); MBA or equivalent degree from regionally-accredited college or university (for Post Master's Certificate). Additional exam requirements/ recommendations for international students: Required—TOEFL (minimum score 84 iBT), IELTS (minimum score 6.5). *Application deadline:* For fall admission, 8/1 for domestic students, 5/1 for international students; for winter admission, 11/15 for domestic students, 9/1 for international students; for spring admission, 3/15 for domestic students, 1/1 for international students; for summer admission, 5/15 for domestic students. Applications are processed on a rolling basis. Application fee: $55. Electronic applications accepted. *Financial support:* Federal Work-Study, scholarships/grants, and unspecified assistantships available. Support available to part-time students. Financial award application deadline: 3/1; financial award applicants required to submit FAFSA. *Unit head:* Dr. Scott Johnson, Dean, School of Management, 810-762-3164, Fax: 810-237-6685, E-mail: scotjohn@umflint.edu. *Application contact:* Bradley T. Maki, Director of Graduate Admissions, 810-762-3171, E-mail: bmaki@umflint.edu.
Website: http://www.umflint.edu/graduateprograms/business-administration-mba

University of Minnesota, Twin Cities Campus, Carlson School of Management, Carlson Full-Time MBA Program, Minneapolis, MN 55455. Offers finance (MBA); human resources and industrial relations (MA); information technology (MBA); management (MBA); marketing (MBA); medical industry orientation (MBA); supply chain and operations (MBA); JD/MBA; MBA/MPP; MBA/MSBA; MD/MBA; MHA/MBA; Pharm D/ MBA. *Accreditation:* AACSB. *Faculty:* 143 full-time (42 women), 24 part-time/adjunct (6 women). *Students:* 193 full-time (59 women); includes 23 minority (2 Black or African American, non-Hispanic/Latino; 1 American Indian or Alaska Native, non-Hispanic/ Latino; 9 Asian, non-Hispanic/Latino; 5 Hispanic/Latino; 1 Native Hawaiian or other Pacific Islander, non-Hispanic/Latino; 5 Two or more races, non-Hispanic/Latino), 31 international. Average age 28. 606 applicants, 45% accepted, 104 enrolled. In 2016, 102 master's awarded. *Entrance requirements:* For master's, GMAT or GRE. Additional exam requirements/recommendations for international students: Required—TOEFL (minimum score 580 paper-based; 84 iBT), IELTS (minimum score 7), PTE. *Application deadline:* For fall admission, 4/1 for domestic students, 2/1 for international students. Application fee: $75. Electronic applications accepted. *Expenses:* $39,378 per year resident tuition and fees; $49,766 per year non-resident tuition and fees; $50,084 per year international tuition and fees. *Financial support:* In 2016–17, 148 students received support, including 148 fellowships with tuition reimbursements available (averaging $21,070 per year); research assistantships with partial tuition reimbursements available, teaching assistantships with partial tuition reimbursements available, career-related internships or fieldwork, Federal Work-Study, institutionally sponsored loans, scholarships/grants, health care benefits, and unspecified assistantships also available. Financial award application deadline: 4/1; financial award applicants required to submit FAFSA. *Faculty research:* Market regulation and asset pricing, social networks and data analytics, consumer behavior, innovation and entrepreneurship, workplace wellbeing and labor relationships. *Total annual research expenditures:* $577,440. *Unit head:* Philip J. Miller, Assistant Dean, MBA Programs and Graduate Business Career Center, 612-625-5555, Fax: 612-625-1012, E-mail: mba@umn.edu. *Application contact:* Linh Gilles, Director of Admissions and Recruiting, 612-625-5555, Fax: 612-625-1012, E-mail: ftmba@umn.edu.
Website: http://www.csom.umn.edu/MBA/full-time/

University of Missouri–St. Louis, College of Business Administration, Program in Business Administration, St. Louis, MO 63121. Offers accounting (MBA); business administration (Certificate); business intelligence (Certificate); cybersecurity (Certificate); digital and social media marketing (Certificate); finance (MBA); human resources management (Certificate); information systems (MBA); international business (MBA); logistics and supply chain management (MBA, PhD, Certificate); management (MBA); marketing (MBA); marketing management (Certificate); operations management (MBA). *Accreditation:* AACSB. *Program availability:* Part-time, evening/weekend. *Faculty:* 32 full-time (10 women), 14 part-time/adjunct (3 women). *Students:* 181 full-time (88 women), 357 part-time (154 women); includes 83 minority (30 Black or African American, non-Hispanic/Latino; 36 Asian, non-Hispanic/Latino; 12 Hispanic/Latino; 2 Native Hawaiian or other Pacific Islander, non-Hispanic/Latino; 3 Two or more races, non-Hispanic/Latino), 100 international. Average age 31. 245 applicants, 83% accepted, 139 enrolled. *Degree requirements:* For doctorate, thesis/dissertation. *Entrance requirements:* For master's, GMAT, 2 letters of recommendation. Additional exam requirements/recommendations for international students: Recommended—TOEFL (minimum score 550 paper-based; 79 iBT), IELTS (minimum score 6.5). *Application deadline:* For fall admission, 7/1 for domestic and international students; for spring admission, 12/1 for domestic and international students. Applications are processed on a rolling basis. Application fee: $50 ($40 for international students). Electronic applications accepted. *Financial support:* Research assistantships with tuition reimbursements, teaching assistantships with tuition reimbursements, career-related internships or fieldwork, Federal Work-Study, and institutionally sponsored loans available. Support available to part-time students. Financial award application deadline: 4/1; financial award applicants required to submit FAFSA. *Faculty research:* Human resources, strategic management, marketing strategy, consumer behavior product development, advertising. *Unit head:* Dr. Thomas H. Eyssell, Associate Dean and Director of Graduate Studies, 314-516-5885, Fax: 314-516-6420, E-mail: mba@ umsl.edu. *Application contact:* 314-516-5458, Fax: 314-516-6996, E-mail: gradadm@ umsl.edu.

University of New Haven, Graduate School, Tagliatela College of Engineering, Program in Engineering and Operations Management, West Haven, CT 06516. Offers engineering and operations management (MS); engineering management (MS); Lean Six Sigma (Graduate Certificate). *Program availability:* Part-time. *Students:* 32 full-time (8 women), 33 part-time (3 women); includes 6 minority (3 Black or African American, non-Hispanic/Latino; 2 Asian, non-Hispanic/Latino; 1 Hispanic/Latino), 31 international. Average age 30. 141 applicants, 68% accepted, 26 enrolled. In 2016, 58 master's awarded. *Entrance requirements:* Additional exam requirements/recommendations for international students: Required—TOEFL (minimum score 75 iBT), IELTS, PTE (minimum score 50). *Application deadline:* Applications are processed on a rolling basis. Application fee: $50. Electronic applications accepted. Application fee is waived when completed online. *Expenses: Tuition:* Full-time $15,660; part-time $870 per credit hour. *Required fees:* $200; $85 per term. Tuition and fees vary according to program. *Unit head:* Dr. Ali Montazer, Program Director, 203-932-7050, E-mail: amontazer@ newhaven.edu. *Application contact:* Michelle Mason, Director of Graduate Enrollment, 203-932-7067, E-mail: mmason@newhaven.edu.
Website: http://www.newhaven.edu/88389/

The University of North Carolina at Charlotte, College of Computing and Informatics, Program in Computing and Information Systems, Charlotte, NC 28223-0001. Offers computing and information systems (PhD), including bioinformatics, business information systems and operations management, computer science, interdisciplinary, software and information systems. *Faculty:* 3 full-time (0 women). *Students:* 91 full-time (30 women), 23 part-time (3 women); includes 8 minority (2 Black or African American, non-Hispanic/Latino; 4 Asian, non-Hispanic/Latino; 1 Hispanic/Latino; 1 Two or more races, non-Hispanic/Latino), 76 international. Average age 31. 90 applicants, 41% accepted, 18 enrolled. In 2016, 13 doctorates awarded. *Degree requirements:* For doctorate, comprehensive exam, thesis/dissertation. *Entrance requirements:* For doctorate, GRE or GMAT, baccalaureate degree, minimum GPA of 3.0 on courses related to the chosen field of PhD study, essay, reference letters. Additional exam requirements/recommendations for international students: Required—TOEFL (minimum score 523 paper-based, 70 iBT) or IELTS (6.5). *Application deadline:* For fall admission, 2/1 for domestic and international students; for spring admission, 9/1 for domestic and international students. Applications are processed on a rolling basis. Application fee: $75. Electronic applications accepted. *Expenses:* Tuition, state resident: full-time $4252. Tuition, nonresident: full-time $17,423. *Required fees:* $3026. Tuition and fees vary according to course load and program. *Financial support:* Career-related internships or fieldwork, institutionally sponsored loans, scholarships/grants, health care benefits, and unspecified assistantships available. Support available to part-time students. Financial award applicants required to submit FAFSA. *Unit head:* Manuel A. Perez Quinones, Director, 704-687-8553, E-mail: perez.quinones@uncc.edu. *Application contact:* Kathy B. Giddings, Director of Graduate Admissions, 704-687-5503, Fax: 704-687-1668, E-mail: gradadm@uncc.edu.

The University of North Carolina at Charlotte, William States Lee College of Engineering, Department of Systems Engineering and Engineering Management, Charlotte, NC 28223-0001. Offers energy analytics (Graduate Certificate); engineering management (MSEM); Lean Six Sigma (Graduate Certificate); logistics and supply chains (Graduate Certificate); systems analytics (Graduate Certificate). *Program availability:* Part-time, evening/weekend, 100% online, blended/hybrid learning. *Faculty:* 9 full-time (1 woman), 2 part-time/adjunct (1 woman). *Students:* 22 full-time (10 women), 61 part-time (12 women); includes 13 minority (7 Black or African American, non-Hispanic/Latino; 1 Asian, non-Hispanic/Latino; 4 Hispanic/Latino; 1 Two or more races, non-Hispanic/Latino), 29 international. Average age 30. 210 applicants, 56% accepted, 31 enrolled. In 2016, 44 master's, 5 other advanced degrees awarded. *Degree requirements:* For master's, project or thesis. *Entrance requirements:* For master's, GRE or GMAT, bachelor's degree in engineering or a closely-related technical or scientific field, or in business, provided relevant technical course requirements have been met; undergraduate coursework in engineering economics, calculus, or statistics; minimum GPA of 3.0; for Graduate Certificate, bachelor's degree in engineering or closely-related technical or scientific field, or bachelor's degree in business, provided relevant technical course requirements have been met; minimum GPA of 3.0; undergraduate coursework in engineering economics, calculus, and statistics; written description of work experience. Additional exam requirements/recommendations for international students: Required—TOEFL (minimum score 523 paper-based, 70 iBT) or IELTS (6.5). *Application deadline:* For fall admission, 3/1 priority date for domestic and international students; for spring admission, 10/1 priority date for domestic and international students; for summer admission, 4/1 priority date for domestic and international students. Applications are processed on a rolling basis. Application fee: $75. Electronic applications accepted. *Expenses:* Contact institution. *Financial support:* In 2016–17, 2 students received support, including 2 research assistantships (averaging $13,750 per year); career-related internships or fieldwork, institutionally sponsored loans, scholarships/grants, and unspecified assistantships also available. Support available to part-time students. Financial award application deadline: 3/1; financial award applicants required to submit FAFSA. *Total annual research expenditures:* $196,680. *Unit head:* Dr. Simon M. Hsiang, Chair, 704-687-1958, E-mail: shsiang1@uncc.edu. *Application contact:* Kathy B. Giddings, Director of Graduate Admissions, 704-687-5503, Fax: 704-687-1668, E-mail: gradadm@uncc.edu.
Website: http://seem.uncc.edu/

University of North Texas, Robert B. Toulouse School of Graduate Studies, Denton, TX 76203-5459. Offers accounting (MS); applied anthropology (MA, MS); applied behavior analysis (Certificate); applied geography (MA); applied technology and performance improvement (M Ed, MS); art education (MA); art history (MA); art museum education (Certificate); arts leadership (Certificate); audiology (Au D); behavior analysis (MS); behavioral science (PhD); biochemistry and molecular biology (MS); biology (MA, MS); biomedical engineering (MS); business analysis (MS); chemistry (MS); clinical health psychology (PhD); communication studies (MA, MS); computer engineering (MS); computer science (MS); counseling (M Ed, MS), including clinical mental health counseling (MS), college and university counseling, elementary school counseling, secondary school counseling; creative writing (MA); criminal justice (MS); curriculum and instruction (M Ed); decision sciences (MBA); design (MA, MFA), including fashion design (MFA), innovation studies, interior design (MFA); early childhood studies (MS); economics (MS); educational leadership (M Ed, Ed D); educational psychology (MS, PhD), including family studies (MS), gifted and talented (MS), human development (MS), learning and cognition (MS), research, measurement and evaluation (MS); electrical engineering (MS); emergency management (MPA); engineering technology (MS); English (MA); English as a second language (MA); environmental science (MS); finance (MBA, MS); financial management (MPA); French (MA); health services management (MBA); higher education (M Ed, Ed D); history (MA, MS); hospitality management (MS); human resources management (MPA); information science (MS); information systems (PhD); information technologies (MBA); interdisciplinary studies (MA, MS); international studies (MA); international sustainable tourism (MS); jazz studies (MM); journalism (MA, MJ, Graduate Certificate), including interactive and virtual digital communication (Graduate Certificate), narrative journalism (Graduate Certificate), public relations (Graduate Certificate); kinesiology (MS); linguistics (MA); local government management (MPA); logistics (PhD); logistics and supply chain management (MBA); long-term care, senior housing, and aging services (MA); management (PhD); marketing (MBA); mathematics (MA, MS); mechanical and energy engineering (MS, PhD); music (MA), including ethnomusicology, music theory, musicology, performance; music composition (PhD); music education (MM Ed, PhD); nonprofit management (MPA); operations and supply chain management (MBA); performance (MM, DMA); philosophy (MA); political science (MA); professional and technical communication (MA); radio, television and film (MA, MFA), rehabilitation counseling (Certificate); sociology (MA); Spanish (MA); special education (M Ed); speech-language pathology (MA); strategic management (MBA); studio art (MFA); teaching (M Ed); MBA/MS. *Program availability:* Part-time, evening/weekend, online learning. Terminal master's awarded for partial completion of doctoral program. *Degree requirements:* For master's, variable foreign language requirement, comprehensive exam (for some programs), thesis (for some programs); for doctorate, variable foreign language requirement, comprehensive exam (for some programs), thesis/dissertation; for other advanced degree, variable foreign language requirement, comprehensive exam (for some programs). *Entrance requirements:* For master's and doctorate, GRE, GMAT. Additional exam requirements/ recommendations for international students: Required—TOEFL (minimum score 550 paper-based; 79 iBT). Electronic applications accepted.

University of Pittsburgh, Katz Graduate School of Business, Master of Business Administration Programs, Pittsburgh, PA 15260. Offers finance (MBA); information systems (MBA); marketing (MBA); operations (MBA); organizational behavior and human resources (MBA); strategy, environment and organizations (MBA); MBA/JD; MBA/MSE. *Accreditation:* AACSB. *Program availability:* Part-time, evening/weekend, blended/hybrid learning. *Faculty:* 88 full-time (27 women), 42 part-time/adjunct (15 women). *Students:* 165 full-time (59 women), 330 part-time (103 women); includes 70

minority (29 Black or African American, non-Hispanic/Latino; 20 Asian, non-Hispanic/Latino; 13 Hispanic/Latino; 8 Two or more races, non-Hispanic/Latino), 73 international. Average age 29. 786 applicants, 41% accepted, 179 enrolled. In 2016, 477 master's awarded. *Degree requirements:* For master's, minimum GPA of 3.0. *Entrance requirements:* For master's, GMAT, GRE. Additional exam requirements/recommendations for international students: Required—TOEFL (minimum score 100 iBT) or IELTS (minimum score 7.0). *Application deadline:* For fall admission, 4/1 priority date for domestic students, 2/1 priority date for international students. Application fee: $50. Electronic applications accepted. *Expenses:* Contact institution. *Financial support:* In 2016–17, 110 students received support. Scholarships/grants available. Financial award application deadline: 6/1; financial award applicants required to submit FAFSA. *Faculty research:* Accounting systems/financial reporting, corporate finance, shopper marketing/consumer behavior, management information systems, organizational behavior and entrepreneurship. *Total annual research expenditures:* $493,036. *Unit head:* Dr. Arjang A. Assad, Dean, 412-648-1556, Fax: 412-648-1552, E-mail: aassad@katz.pitt.edu. *Application contact:* Thomas Keller, Director of MBA Admissions, 412-648-1700, Fax: 412-648-1659, E-mail: mba@katz.pitt.edu.
Website: http://www.business.pitt.edu/katz/mba/

See Display on page 160 and Close-Up on page 189.

University of Portland, Dr. Robert B. Pamplin, Jr. School of Business, Portland, OR 97203-5798. Offers entrepreneurship (MBA); finance (MBA, MS); health care management (MBA); marketing (MBA); nonprofit management (EMBA); operations and technology management (MBA, MS); sustainability (MBA). *Accreditation:* AACSB. *Program availability:* Part-time, evening/weekend. *Entrance requirements:* For master's, GMAT, minimum GPA of 3.0, resume, 2 letters of recommendation. Additional exam requirements/recommendations for international students: Required—TOEFL (minimum score 570 paper-based; 89 iBT), IELTS (minimum score 7). *Expenses:* Contact institution.

University of Puerto Rico, Mayagüez Campus, Graduate Studies, College of Business Administration, Mayagüez, PR 00681-9000. Offers business administration (MBA); finance (MBA); human resources (MBA); industrial management (MBA). *Program availability:* Part-time, evening/weekend. *Faculty:* 24 full-time (10 women). *Students:* 37 full-time (24 women), 27 part-time (18 women); includes 60 minority (all Hispanic/Latino). Average age 25. 22 applicants, 68% accepted, 12 enrolled. In 2016, 6 master's awarded. *Degree requirements:* For master's, one foreign language, comprehensive exam, thesis (for some programs). *Entrance requirements:* For master's, GMAT or EXADEP, bachelor's degree with courses in calculus, microeconomics, accounting and statistics. Additional exam requirements/recommendations for international students: Required—TOEFL (minimum score 500 paper-based; 173 iBT), GMAT or EXADEP. *Application deadline:* For fall admission, 2/15 for domestic and international students; for spring admission, 9/15 for domestic and international students. Applications are processed on a rolling basis. Application fee: $25. Electronic applications accepted. *Expenses: Tuition, area resident:* Full-time $2466. *International tuition:* $7166 full-time. *Required fees:* $210. Tuition and fees vary according to course level, campus/location, program and student level. *Financial support:* In 2016–17, 6 students received support, including 5 research assistantships with full and partial tuition reimbursements available (averaging $4,489 per year), 4 teaching assistantships with full and partial tuition reimbursements available (averaging $4,605 per year); unspecified assistantships also available. *Faculty research:* Organizational studies, management, accounting, entrepreneurship, leadership and motivation. *Unit head:* Roberto L. Seijo, PhD, Department Head, 787-832-4040 Ext. 3887, Fax: 787-832-5320, E-mail: roberto.seijo@upr.edu. *Application contact:* Judith Valentín, Administrative Secretary, 787-265-3887, Fax: 787-832-5320, E-mail: grad.adem@uprm.edu.
Website: http://enterprise.uprm.edu/

University of Puerto Rico, Río Piedras Campus, College of Business Administration, San Juan, PR 00931-3300. Offers accounting (MBA); finance (MBA, PhD); general business (MBA); human resources management (MBA); international trade and business (MBA, PhD); marketing (MBA); operations management (MBA); quantitative methods (MBA). *Accreditation:* AACSB. *Program availability:* Part-time. *Degree requirements:* For master's, comprehensive exam, thesis or alternative, research project. *Entrance requirements:* For master's, GMAT or PAEG, minimum GPA of 3.0, letter of recommendation; for doctorate, GMAT, PAEG, minimum GPA of 3.0, master degree. *Faculty research:* Management.

University of Rochester, Simon Business School, Doctoral Program in Business Administration, Rochester, NY 14627. Offers accounting (PhD); computer information systems (PhD); finance (PhD); marketing (PhD); operations management (PhD). *Accreditation:* AACSB. *Faculty:* 66 full-time (13 women), 22 part-time/adjunct (2 women). *Students:* 52 full-time (19 women); includes 2 minority (both Asian, non-Hispanic/Latino), 42 international. Average age 29. 210 applicants, 16% accepted, 15 enrolled. In 2016, 6 doctorates awarded. *Degree requirements:* For doctorate, comprehensive exam, thesis/dissertation, qualifying exam. *Entrance requirements:* For doctorate, GMAT or GRE. Additional exam requirements/recommendations for international students: Required—TOEFL. *Application deadline:* For fall admission, 1/5 for domestic and international students. Application fee: $100. Electronic applications accepted. *Expenses:* $1,800 per credit hour. *Financial support:* In 2016–17, 52 students received support. Fellowships, research assistantships, teaching assistantships, and tuition waivers (full) available. Financial award application deadline: 1/5. *Unit head:* Dr. Ron Kaniel, Committee Chair, 585-275-2959. *Application contact:* Sue Harris, PhD Administrator, 585-275-2959, E-mail: phdoffice@simon.rochester.edu.
Website: http://www.simon.rochester.edu/programs/phd/index.aspx

University of Southern Indiana, Graduate Studies, Pott College of Science, Engineering, and Education, Program in Industrial Management, Evansville, IN 47712-3590. Offers MSIM. *Program availability:* Part-time-only, evening/weekend. *Faculty:* 2 full-time (0 women). *Students:* 8 full-time (3 women), 6 part-time (1 woman); includes 3 minority (2 Black or African American, non-Hispanic/Latino; 1 Two or more races, non-Hispanic/Latino), 2 international. Average age 34. In 2016, 4 master's awarded. *Degree requirements:* For master's, project. *Entrance requirements:* For master's, minimum GPA of 2.5, BS in engineering or engineering technology. Additional exam requirements/recommendations for international students: Required—TOEFL (minimum score 550 paper-based; 79 iBT), IELTS (minimum score 6). *Application deadline:* For fall admission, 8/15 priority date for domestic students, 3/1 priority date for international students. Applications are processed on a rolling basis. Application fee: $40. Electronic applications accepted. *Expenses:* Tuition, state resident: full-time $8497. Tuition, nonresident: full-time $16,691. *Required fees:* $500. *Financial support:* Federal Work-Study, scholarships/grants, tuition waivers (full and partial), and unspecified assistantships available. Financial award application deadline: 3/1; financial award applicants required to submit FAFSA. *Unit head:* Dr. Paul A. Kuban, Interim Chair, 812-465-1090, E-mail: pkuban@usi.edu. *Application contact:* Dr. Mayola Rowser, Director, Graduate Studies, 812-465-7015, Fax: 812-464-1956, E-mail: mrowser@usi.edu.
Website: http://www.usi.edu/science/engineering/programs/master-of-science-in-industrial-management

The University of Tennessee, Graduate School, College of Business Administration, Program in Business Administration, Knoxville, TN 37996. Offers accounting (PhD); finance (MBA, PhD); logistics and transportation (MBA, PhD); management (PhD); marketing (MBA, PhD); operations management (MBA); professional business administration (MBA); statistics (PhD); JD/MBA; MS/MBA; Pharm D/MBA. Pharm D/MBA offered jointly with The University of Tennessee Health Science Center. *Accreditation:* AACSB. *Program availability:* Online learning. *Degree requirements:* For master's, thesis or alternative; for doctorate, thesis/dissertation. *Entrance requirements:* For master's and doctorate, GMAT, minimum GPA of 2.7. Additional exam requirements/recommendations for international students: Required—TOEFL. Electronic applications accepted.

The University of Texas at Austin, Graduate School, McCombs School of Business, Department of Information, Risk, and Operations Management, Austin, TX 78712-1111. Offers information management (MBA); information systems (PhD); risk analysis and decision making (PhD); risk management (MBA); supply chain and operations management (MBA, PhD). *Degree requirements:* For doctorate, thesis/dissertation. *Entrance requirements:* For doctorate, GMAT or GRE. Electronic applications accepted. *Faculty research:* Stochastic processing and queuing, discrete nonlinear and large-scale optimization simulation, quality assurance logistics, distributed artificial intelligence, organizational modeling.

The University of Texas at Dallas, Naveen Jindal School of Management, Program in Organizations, Strategy and International Management, Richardson, TX 75080. Offers business administration (MBA); executive business administration (EMBA); global leadership (EMBA); healthcare management (MS); healthcare management for physicians (EMBA); innovation and entrepreneurship (MS); international management studies (MS, PhD); management and administrative sciences (MS); management science (PhD); project management (EMBA, MS); systems engineering and management (MS); MS/MBA. *Program availability:* Part-time, evening/weekend. *Faculty:* 29 full-time (7 women), 29 part-time/adjunct (5 women). *Students:* 524 full-time (189 women), 860 part-time (374 women); includes 452 minority (112 Black or African American, non-Hispanic/Latino; 3 American Indian or Alaska Native, non-Hispanic/Latino; 207 Asian, non-Hispanic/Latino; 85 Hispanic/Latino; 45 Two or more races, non-Hispanic/Latino), 317 international. Average age 34. 1,763 applicants, 37% accepted, 420 enrolled. In 2016, 521 master's, 13 doctorates awarded. *Degree requirements:* For doctorate, thesis/dissertation. *Entrance requirements:* For master's and doctorate, GMAT. Additional exam requirements/recommendations for international students: Required—TOEFL (minimum score 550 paper-based). *Application deadline:* For fall admission, 7/15 for domestic students, 5/1 priority date for international students; for spring admission, 11/15 for domestic students, 9/1 priority date for international students. Applications are processed on a rolling basis. Application fee: $50 ($100 for international students). Electronic applications accepted. *Expenses:* Tuition, state resident: full-time $12,418; part-time $690 per semester hour. Tuition, nonresident: full-time $24,150; part-time $1342 per semester hour. Tuition and fees vary according to course load. *Financial support:* In 2016–17, 385 students received support, including 21 research assistantships with partial tuition reimbursements available (averaging $25,698 per year), 68 teaching assistantships with partial tuition reimbursements available (averaging $16,973 per year); Federal Work-Study, institutionally sponsored loans, scholarships/grants, and unspecified assistantships also available. Support available to part-time students. Financial award application deadline: 4/30; financial award applicants required to submit FAFSA. *Faculty research:* International accounting, international trade and finance, economic development, international economics. *Unit head:* Dr. Seung-Hyun Lee, Area Coordinator, 972-883-6267, Fax: 972-883-5977, E-mail: sxl029100@utdallas.edu. *Application contact:* Maria Hasenhuttl, Assistant Area Coordinator, 972-883-5898, Fax: 972-883-5977, E-mail: maria.hasenhuttl@utdallas.edu.
Website: http://jindal.utdallas.edu/osim/

The University of Texas at Tyler, College of Business and Technology, Program in Industrial Management, Tyler, TX 75799-0001. Offers MS. *Program availability:* Online learning. *Entrance requirements:* For master's, GMAT. Electronic applications accepted.

University of Utah, Graduate School, David Eccles School of Business, Business Administration Program, Salt Lake City, UT 84112. Offers accounting (PhD); business administration (EMBA, MBA, PMBA); finance (PhD); information systems (PhD); marketing (PhD); operations management (PhD); organizational behavior (PhD); strategic management (PhD); MBA/JD; MBA/MHA; MBA/MS. *Program availability:* Part-time, evening/weekend, online learning. *Faculty:* 58 full-time (21 women), 37 part-time/adjunct (7 women). *Students:* 578 full-time (149 women), 89 part-time (28 women); includes 71 minority (1 American Indian or Alaska Native, non-Hispanic/Latino; 17 Asian, non-Hispanic/Latino; 45 Hispanic/Latino; 8 Two or more races, non-Hispanic/Latino), 50 international. Average age 32. 442 applicants, 70% accepted, 226 enrolled. In 2016, 246 master's, 6 doctorates awarded. *Degree requirements:* For doctorate, comprehensive exam, thesis/dissertation. *Entrance requirements:* For master's, GMAT or GRE; for doctorate, GMAT. Additional exam requirements/recommendations for international students: Required—TOEFL (minimum score 600 paper-based; 100 iBT), IELTS (minimum score 7). *Application deadline:* For fall admission, 11/1 priority date for domestic students, 3/1 priority date for international students; for spring admission, 11/1 for domestic and international students. Applications are processed on a rolling basis. Application fee: $55 ($65 for international students). Electronic applications accepted. *Expenses:* Contact institution. *Financial support:* In 2016–17, 53 students received support, including 53 fellowships with partial tuition reimbursements available (averaging $8,600 per year); scholarships/grants and unspecified assistantships also available. Financial award application deadline: 2/1; financial award applicants required to submit FAFSA. *Faculty research:* Corporate finance, strategy services, consumer behavior, financial disclosures, operations. *Unit head:* Kristina Diekmann, Department Chair, 801-581-8524, Fax: 801-581-3380, E-mail: mastersinfo@business.utah.edu. *Application contact:* Christine Harris, Coordinator, 801-581-7785, Fax: 801-585-3962, E-mail: execch@business.utah.edu.
Website: http://www.business.utah.edu/

University of Utah, Graduate School, David Eccles School of Business, Department of Operations and Information Systems, Salt Lake City, UT 84112. Offers information systems (MS, Graduate Certificate), including business intelligence and analytics, IT security, product and process management, software and systems architecture. *Program availability:* Part-time, evening/weekend, 100% online, blended/hybrid learning. *Faculty:* 12 full-time (5 women), 7 part-time/adjunct (0 women). *Students:* 143 full-time (43 women), 107 part-time (28 women); includes 127 minority (1 Black or African American, non-Hispanic/Latino; 120 Asian, non-Hispanic/Latino; 3 Hispanic/Latino; 3 Two or more races, non-Hispanic/Latino), 123 international. Average age 29. 334 applicants, 72% accepted, 127 enrolled. In 2016, 96 master's awarded. *Degree requirements:* For master's, capstone project. *Entrance requirements:* For master's, GMAT/GRE, minimum undergraduate GPA of 3.0, 2 letters of recommendation, personal statement, professional resume. Additional exam requirements/recommendations for international students: Required—TOEFL (minimum score 550 paper-based; 80 iBT), IELTS (minimum score 6.5). *Application deadline:* For fall admission, 7/28 for domestic students, 3/1 for international students; for spring

admission, 12/7 for domestic students, 8/16 for international students. Applications are processed on a rolling basis. Application fee: $55 ($65 for international students). Electronic applications accepted. *Expenses:* Contact institution. *Financial support:* In 2016–17, 75 students received support, including 7 teaching assistantships (averaging $5,000 per year); fellowships with partial tuition reimbursements available, tuition waivers (partial), and unspecified assistantships also available. Financial award application deadline: 3/31; financial award applicants required to submit FAFSA. *Faculty research:* Business intelligence and analytics, software and system architecture, product and process management, IT security, Web and data mining, applications and management of IT in healthcare. *Unit head:* Dr. Bradden Blair, Director of the IS Programs, 801-587-9489, Fax: 801-581-3666, E-mail: b.blair@eccles.utah.edu. *Application contact:* Raven Clissold, Admissions Coordinator, 801-587-5838, Fax: 801-581-3666, E-mail: raven.clissold@eccles.utah.edu.
Website: http://msis.eccles.utah.edu

Wayne State University, College of Liberal Arts and Sciences, Department of Economics, Detroit, MI 48202. Offers advanced macroeconomics (PhD); econometrics (MA); health economics (MA, PhD); industrial organization (MA, PhD); international economics (MA, PhD); labor and human resources (MA); labor economics (PhD); macroeconomics (MA); microeconomics (MA); JD/MA. *Faculty:* 13. *Students:* 38 full-time (11 women), 7 part-time (3 women); includes 8 minority (5 Black or African American, non-Hispanic/Latino; 1 Asian, non-Hispanic/Latino; 1 Hispanic/Latino; 1 Two or more races, non-Hispanic/Latino), 22 international. Average age 33. 97 applicants, 36% accepted, 8 enrolled. In 2016, 10 master's, 7 doctorates awarded. *Degree requirements:* For master's, comprehensive exam; for doctorate, comprehensive exam, thesis/dissertation, oral examination on research, completion of course work in quantitative methods, final lecture. *Entrance requirements:* For master's, minimum upper-division GPA of 3.0; prior coursework in intermediate microeconomic and macroeconomic theory, statistics, and elementary calculus; for doctorate, GRE, minimum upper-division GPA of 3.0, prior coursework in intermediate microeconomic and macroeconomic theory, statistics, two courses in calculus, three letters of recommendation from officials or teaching staff at institution(s) most recently attended, statement of purpose. Additional exam requirements/recommendations for international students: Required—TOEFL (minimum score 550 paper-based; 79 iBT), TWE (minimum score 5.5), Michigan English Language Assessment Battery (minimum score 85); Recommended—IELTS (minimum score 6.5). *Application deadline:* For fall admission, 5/1 for domestic and international students; for winter admission, 10/1 priority date for domestic students, 9/1 priority date for international students; for spring admission, 1/1 priority date for domestic and international students. Applications are processed on a rolling basis. Application fee: $50. Electronic applications accepted. *Expenses:* $16,503 per year resident tuition and fees, $33,697 per year non-resident tuition and fees. *Financial support:* In 2016–17, 26 students received support, including 2 fellowships with tuition reimbursements available (averaging $16,000 per year), 17 teaching assistantships with tuition reimbursements available (averaging $17,994 per year); research assistantships with tuition reimbursements available, scholarships/grants, health care benefits, and unspecified assistantships also available. Support available to part-time students. Financial award applicants required to submit FAFSA. *Faculty research:* Health economics, international economics, macro economics, urban and labor economics, econometrics. *Unit head:* Dr. Stephen J. Spurr, Professor and Chair, 313-577-3232, Fax: 313-577-9564, E-mail: sspurr@wayne.edu. *Application contact:* Dr. Allen Charles Goodman, Graduate Director, 313-577-3235, Fax: 313-577-9564, E-mail: allen.goodman@wayne.edu.
Website: http://clas.wayne.edu/economics/

Wilkes University, College of Graduate and Professional Studies, Jay S. Sidhu School of Business and Leadership, Wilkes-Barre, PA 18766-0002. Offers accounting (MBA); entrepreneurship (MBA); finance (MBA); health care administration (MBA); human resource management (MBA); international business (MBA); operations management (MBA); organizational leadership and development (MBA). *Accreditation:* ACBSP. *Program availability:* Part-time, evening/weekend. *Students:* 35 full-time (17 women), 112 part-time (55 women); includes 17 minority (6 Black or African American, non-Hispanic/Latino; 4 Asian, non-Hispanic/Latino; 5 Hispanic/Latino; 2 Two or more races, non-Hispanic/Latino), 16 international. Average age 31. In 2016, 59 master's awarded. *Entrance requirements:* For master's, GMAT. Additional exam requirements/recommendations for international students: Required—TOEFL (minimum score 550 paper-based; 79 iBT). *Application deadline:* Applications are processed on a rolling basis. Application fee: $45 ($65 for international students). Electronic applications accepted. *Expenses:* Contact institution. *Financial support:* Unspecified assistantships available. Financial award application deadline: 3/1; financial award applicants required to submit FAFSA. *Unit head:* Dr. Abel Adekola, Dean, 570-408-4701, Fax: 570-408-7846, E-mail: abel.adekola@wilkes.edu. *Application contact:* Director of Graduate Enrollment, 570-408-4234, Fax: 570-408-7846.
Website: http://www.wilkes.edu/academics/colleges/sidhu-school-of-business-leadership/index.aspx

Section 10
Insurance and Actuarial Science

This section contains a directory of institutions offering graduate work in insurance and actuarial science. Additional information about programs listed in the directory but not augmented by an in-depth entry may be obtained by writing directly to the dean of a graduate school or chair of a department at the address given in the directory.

For programs offering related work, see also in this book *Business Administration and Management.*

CONTENTS

Program Directories

Actuarial Science

Ball State University, Graduate School, College of Sciences and Humanities, Department of Mathematical Sciences, Program in Actuarial Science, Muncie, IN 47306. Offers MA. *Program availability:* Part-time. *Entrance requirements:* For master's, minimum baccalaureate GPA of 2.75 or 3.0 in latter half of baccalauareate. Additional exam requirements/recommendations for international students: Required—TOEFL (minimum score 550 paper-based; 79 iBT), IELTS (minimum score 6.5). Electronic applications accepted.

Boston University, Metropolitan College, Department of Actuarial Science, Boston, MA 02215. Offers MS. *Program availability:* Part-time, evening/weekend. *Faculty:* 3 full-time (1 woman), 6 part-time/adjunct (1 woman). *Students:* 48 full-time (22 women), 65 part-time (31 women); includes 15 minority (2 Black or African American, non-Hispanic/Latino; 12 Asian, non-Hispanic/Latino; 1 Hispanic/Latino), 76 international. Average age 25. 184 applicants, 75% accepted, 48 enrolled. In 2016, 46 master's awarded. *Entrance requirements:* For master's, prerequisite coursework in calculus. Additional exam requirements/recommendations for international students: Required—TOEFL (minimum score 84 iBT). *Application deadline:* For fall admission, 5/31 priority date for domestic students, 5/15 priority date for international students; for spring admission, 10/31 priority date for domestic students, 10/15 priority date for international students. Applications are processed on a rolling basis. Application fee: $85. Electronic applications accepted. *Expenses:* Contact institution. *Financial support:* In 2016–17, 8 research assistantships with partial tuition reimbursements (averaging $8,400 per year), 6 teaching assistantships (averaging $8,400 per year) were awarded; career-related internships or fieldwork, scholarships/grants, and unspecified assistantships also available. *Faculty research:* Survival models, life contingencies, numerical analysis, operations research, compound interest. *Unit head:* Lois K. Horwitz, Chair, 617-353-8758, Fax: 617-353-8757, E-mail: lhorwitz@bu.edu. *Application contact:* Andrea Cozzi, Administrative Coordinator, 617-353-8758, Fax: 617-353-8757, E-mail: actuary@bu.edu.
Website: http://www.bu.edu/actuary/

California State University, East Bay, Office of Graduate Studies, College of Science, Department of Statistics and Biostatistics, Statistics Program, Hayward, CA 94542-3000. Offers actuarial science (MS); applied statistics (MS); computational statistics (MS); mathematical statistics (MS). *Program availability:* Part-time, evening/weekend. *Students:* 11 full-time (3 women), 76 part-time (38 women); includes 33 minority (2 Black or African American, non-Hispanic/Latino; 25 Asian, non-Hispanic/Latino; 5 Hispanic/Latino; 1 Two or more races, non-Hispanic/Latino), 38 international. Average age 30. 72 applicants, 64% accepted, 24 enrolled. In 2016, 44 master's awarded. *Degree requirements:* For master's, comprehensive exam. *Entrance requirements:* For master's, letters of recommendation, minimum GPA of 3.0, math through lower-division calculus. Additional exam requirements/recommendations for international students: Required—TOEFL (minimum score 550 paper-based). *Application deadline:* For fall admission, 6/30 for domestic and international students. Application fee: $55. Electronic applications accepted. *Financial support:* Fellowships, career-related internships or fieldwork, Federal Work-Study, institutionally sponsored loans, scholarships/grants, and unspecified assistantships available. Support available to part-time students. Financial award application deadline: 3/2; financial award applicants required to submit FAFSA. *Unit head:* Dr. Mitchell Watnik, Chair, 510-885-3435, Fax: 510-885-4714.
Website: http://www20.csueastbay.edu/csci/departments/statistics/

Central Connecticut State University, School of Graduate Studies, School of Engineering, Science and Technology, Department of Mathematical Sciences, New Britain, CT 06050-4010. Offers data mining (MS, Certificate); mathematics (MA, MS), including actuarial science (MA), computer science (MA), statistics (MA); mathematics education leadership (Sixth Year Certificate); mathematics for secondary education (Certificate). *Program availability:* Part-time, evening/weekend, 100% online. *Faculty:* 14 full-time (4 women). *Students:* 8 full-time (5 women), 73 part-time (37 women); includes 17 minority (4 Black or African American, non-Hispanic/Latino; 7 Asian, non-Hispanic/Latino; 4 Hispanic/Latino; 2 Two or more races, non-Hispanic/Latino), 4 international. Average age 37. 44 applicants, 68% accepted, 21 enrolled. In 2016, 23 master's, 1 other advanced degree awarded. *Degree requirements:* For master's, comprehensive exam, thesis or alternative, special project; for other advanced degree, qualifying exam. *Entrance requirements:* For master's, minimum undergraduate GPA of 2.7; for other advanced degree, minimum undergraduate GPA of 3.0, essay, letters of recommendation. Additional exam requirements/recommendations for international students: Required—TOEFL (minimum score 550 paper-based; 79 iBT). *Application deadline:* For fall admission, 5/1 for domestic and international students; for spring admission, 11/1 for domestic and international students. Applications are processed on a rolling basis. Application fee: $50. Electronic applications accepted. *Expenses: Tuition, area resident:* Full-time $6497; part-time $606 per credit. Tuition, state resident: full-time $9748; part-time $622 per credit. Tuition, nonresident: full-time $18,102; part-time $622 per credit. *Required fees:* $4459; $246 per credit. *Financial support:* In 2016–17, 18 students received support. Career-related internships or fieldwork, Federal Work-Study, and scholarships/grants available. Support available to part-time students. Financial award application deadline: 3/1; financial award applicants required to submit FAFSA. *Faculty research:* Statistics, actuarial mathematics, computer systems and engineering, computer programming techniques, operations research. *Unit head:* Dr. Philip Halloran, Chair, 860-832-2835, E-mail: halloranp@ccsu.edu. *Application contact:* Patricia Gardner, Associate Director of Graduate Studies, 860-832-2350, Fax: 860-832-2362.
Website: http://www.ccsu.edu/mathematics/

Columbia University, School of Continuing Education, Program in Actuarial Science, New York, NY 10027. Offers MS. *Program availability:* Part-time. *Degree requirements:* For master's, comprehensive exam. *Entrance requirements:* For master's, minimum GPA of 3.0, knowledge of economics, linear algebra, calculus. Additional exam requirements/recommendations for international students: Required—American Language Program placement test. Electronic applications accepted.

Florida State University, The Graduate School, College of Arts and Sciences, Department of Mathematics, Tallahassee, FL 32306-4510. Offers applied and computational mathematics (MS, PhD); biomathematics (MS, PhD); financial mathematics (MS, PhD), including actuarial science (MS); pure mathematics (MS, PhD). *Program availability:* Part-time. *Faculty:* 34 full-time (4 women). *Students:* 140 full-time (45 women), 8 part-time (0 women); includes 12 minority (1 Black or African American, non-Hispanic/Latino; 2 Asian, non-Hispanic/Latino; 2 Hispanic/Latino; 7 Two or more races, non-Hispanic/Latino), 94 international. 268 applicants, 42% accepted, 39 enrolled. In 2016, 17 master's, 16 doctorates awarded. Terminal master's awarded for partial completion of doctoral program. *Degree requirements:* For master's, comprehensive exam (for some programs), thesis optional; for doctorate, comprehensive exam, thesis/dissertation, candidacy exam (including written qualifying examinations which differ by degree concentration). *Entrance requirements:* For master's and doctorate, GRE General Test, minimum upper-division GPA of 3.0, 4-year bachelor's degree. Additional exam requirements/recommendations for international students: Required—TOEFL (minimum score 550 paper-based; 80 iBT), IELTS (minimum score 6.5). *Application deadline:* For fall admission, 12/15 priority date for domestic and international students. Applications are processed on a rolling basis. Application fee: $30. Electronic applications accepted. *Expenses:* Tuition, state resident: full-time $7263; part-time $403.51 per credit hour. Tuition, nonresident: full-time $18,087; part-time $1004.85 per credit hour. *Required fees:* $1365; $75.81 per credit hour. $20 per semester. Tuition and fees vary according to campus/location. *Financial support:* In 2016–17, 104 students received support, including 2 fellowships with full tuition reimbursements available (averaging $22,600 per year), 10 research assistantships with full tuition reimbursements available (averaging $22,660 per year), 83 teaching assistantships with full tuition reimbursements available (averaging $21,269 per year); career-related internships or fieldwork, institutionally sponsored loans, scholarships/grants, health care benefits, tuition waivers (full and partial), and unspecified assistantships also available. Financial award application deadline: 12/15; financial award applicants required to submit FAFSA. *Faculty research:* Low-dimensional and geometric topology, mathematical modeling in neuroscience, computational stochastics and Monte Carlo methods, mathematical physics, applied analysis. *Total annual research expenditures:* $1.3 million. *Unit head:* Dr. Xiaoming Wang, Chairperson, 850-645-3338, Fax: 850-644-4053, E-mail: wxm@math.fsu.edu. *Application contact:* Kari Aime, Graduate Advisor and Admissions Coordinator, 850-644-2278, Fax: 850-644-4053, E-mail: aime@math.fsu.edu.
Website: http://www.math.fsu.edu/

Georgia State University, J. Mack Robinson College of Business, Department of Risk Management and Insurance, Program in Actuarial Science, Atlanta, GA 30302-3083. Offers MAS. *Program availability:* Part-time, evening/weekend. *Entrance requirements:* For master's, GRE or GMAT, transcripts from all institutions attended, resume, essays. Additional exam requirements/recommendations for international students: Required—TOEFL (minimum score 610 paper-based; 101 iBT), IELTS (minimum score 7). *Application deadline:* For fall admission, 5/1 priority date for domestic students, 2/1 priority date for international students; for spring admission, 9/15 priority date for domestic students, 4/1 priority date for international students. Applications are processed on a rolling basis. Application fee: $50. Electronic applications accepted. *Expenses:* Tuition, state resident: full-time $6876; part-time $382 per credit hour. Tuition, nonresident: full-time $22,374; part-time $1243 per credit hour. *Required fees:* $2128; $1064 per term. Part-time tuition and fees vary according to course load and program. *Financial support:* Research assistantships, scholarships/grants, tuition waivers, and unspecified assistantships available. *Faculty research:* Quantification and pricing of risk, risk modeling, financial methods in insurance, economic theory, enterprise risk management. *Unit head:* Dr. Shaun Wang, Professor/Chair/Director, 404-413-7500, Fax: 404-413-7499. *Application contact:* Toby McChesney, Assistant Dean for Graduate Recruiting and Student Services, 404-413-7167, Fax: 404-413-7162, E-mail: rcbgradadmissions@gsu.edu.
Website: http://rmi.robinson.gsu.edu/academic-programs/mas/

Lock Haven University of Pennsylvania, College of Natural, Behavioral and Health Sciences, Lock Haven, PA 17745-2390. Offers actuarial science (PSM); athletic training (MS); health promotion/education (MHS); healthcare management (MHS); physician assistant (MHS). Program also offered at the Clearfield, Coudersport, and Harrisburg campuses. *Accreditation:* ARC-PA. *Entrance requirements:* For master's, minimum undergraduate GPA of 3.0. Additional exam requirements/recommendations for international students: Required—TOEFL. Electronic applications accepted.

Maryville University of Saint Louis, College of Arts and Sciences, St. Louis, MO 63141-7299. Offers actuarial science (MS); organizational leadership and development (MA); strategic communication and leadership (MA). *Program availability:* Part-time. *Faculty:* 7 full-time (4 women), 10 part-time/adjunct (7 women). *Students:* 37 full-time (16 women), 28 part-time (22 women); includes 10 minority (4 Black or African American, non-Hispanic/Latino; 1 American Indian or Alaska Native, non-Hispanic/Latino; 4 Asian, non-Hispanic/Latino; 1 Two or more races, non-Hispanic/Latino), 22 international. Average age 30. In 2016, 22 master's awarded. *Entrance requirements:* For master's, strong mathematics background, 2 letters of recommendation, and personal statement (MS). Additional exam requirements/recommendations for international students: Required—TOEFL (minimum score 550 paper-based; 80 iBT). *Application deadline:* Applications are processed on a rolling basis. Electronic applications accepted. *Expenses:* $781 per credit hour. *Financial support:* Application deadline: 3/1; applicants required to submit FAFSA. *Unit head:* Cherie Fister, Dean, 314-529-9563, Fax: 314-529-9965, E-mail: cfister@maryville.edu. *Application contact:* Crystal Jacobsmeyer, Assistant Director, Graduate Enrollment Advising, 314-529-9654, Fax: 314-529-9927, E-mail: cjacobsmeyer@maryville.edu.
Website: https://www.maryville.edu/as/

Middle Tennessee State University, College of Graduate Studies, College of Basic and Applied Sciences, Program in Professional Science, Murfreesboro, TN 37132. Offers actuarial sciences (MS); biostatistics (MS); biotechnology (MS); engineering management (MS); health care informatics (MS). *Program availability:* Part-time, evening/weekend, online learning. *Degree requirements:* For master's, comprehensive exam. *Entrance requirements:* For master's, GRE. Additional exam requirements/recommendations for international students: Required—TOEFL (minimum score 525 paper-based; 71 iBT) or IELTS (minimum score 6).

The Ohio State University, Graduate School, College of Arts and Sciences, Division of Natural and Mathematical Sciences, Department of Mathematics, Columbus, OH 43210. Offers actuarial and quantitative risk management (MAQRM); computational sciences (MMS); mathematical biosciences (MMS); mathematics (PhD); mathematics for educators (MMS). *Faculty:* 63. *Students:* 142 full-time (24 women), 1 (woman) part-time; includes 17 minority (7 Asian, non-Hispanic/Latino; 4 Hispanic/Latino; 6 Two or more races, non-Hispanic/Latino), 64 international. Average age 25. In 2016, 32 master's, 12 doctorates awarded. *Degree requirements:* For master's, thesis optional; for doctorate, one foreign language, thesis/dissertation. *Entrance requirements:* For master's, GRE General Test; for doctorate, GRE General Test (recommended), GRE Subject Test (mathematics). Additional exam requirements/recommendations for international students: Required—TOEFL (minimum score 550 paper-based; 79 iBT), Michigan English Language Assessment Battery (minimum score 82); Recommended—IELTS (minimum score 7). *Application deadline:* For fall admission, 12/15 priority date for domestic and international students. Applications are processed on a rolling basis. Application fee: $60 ($70 for international students). Electronic applications accepted. *Financial support:* Fellowships with tuition reimbursements, research assistantships with tuition reimbursements, teaching assistantships with tuition reimbursements, Federal Work-Study, institutionally sponsored loans, and unspecified assistantships

available. Support available to part-time students. *Unit head:* Luis Casian, Chair, 614-292-7173, E-mail: casian.1@osu.edu. *Application contact:* Erin Anthony, Graduate Studies Coordinator, 614-292-6274, Fax: 614-292-1479, E-mail: grad-info@math.osu.edu.
Website: http://www.math.osu.edu/

Oregon State University, College of Science, Program in Mathematics, Corvallis, OR 97331. Offers actuarial science (MA, MS, PhD); algebra (MA, MS, PhD); analysis (MA, MS, PhD); applied mathematics (MA, MS, PhD); computational mathematics (MA, MS, PhD); differential equations (MA, MS, PhD); financial mathematics (MA, MS, PhD); geometry (MA, MS, PhD); mathematics education (MA). *Faculty:* 25 full-time (8 women), 6 part-time/adjunct (2 women). *Students:* 65 full-time (18 women), 4 part-time (1 woman); includes 13 minority (1 Black or African American, non-Hispanic/Latino; 2 Asian, non-Hispanic/Latino; 6 Hispanic/Latino; 4 Two or more races, non-Hispanic/Latino), 16 international. Average age 28. 149 applicants, 30% accepted, 16 enrolled. In 2016, 16 master's, 6 doctorates awarded. Terminal master's awarded for partial completion of doctoral program. *Degree requirements:* For master's, thesis or alternative; for doctorate, thesis/dissertation, qualifying exams. *Entrance requirements:* For master's and doctorate, GRE. Additional exam requirements/recommendations for international students: Required—TOEFL (minimum score 100 iBT). *Application deadline:* For fall admission, 1/15 for domestic and international students. Application fee: $75 ($85 for international students). Electronic applications accepted. *Expenses:* Tuition, state resident: full-time $12,150; part-time $450 per credit. Tuition, nonresident: full-time $21,789; part-time $807 per credit. *Required fees:* $1651; $1507 per credit. One-time fee: $350. Tuition and fees vary according to course load, campus/location and program. *Financial support:* Research assistantships, teaching assistantships, Federal Work-Study, and institutionally sponsored loans available. Support available to part-time students. Financial award application deadline: 1/15. *Unit head:* Dr. Enrique A. Thomann, Professor and Department Head. *Application contact:* Mathematics Advisor, 541-737-4686, E-mail: gradinfo@math.oregonstate.edu.
Website: http://www.math.oregonstate.edu/

Roosevelt University, Graduate Division, College of Arts and Sciences, Department of Math and Actuarial Science, Chicago, IL 60605. Offers mathematics (MS), including mathematical sciences. *Program availability:* Part-time, evening/weekend. *Students:* 8 full-time (4 women), 13 part-time (5 women); includes 8 minority (2 Black or African American, non-Hispanic/Latino; 2 Asian, non-Hispanic/Latino; 4 Hispanic/Latino), 3 international. Average age 29. 25 applicants, 88% accepted, 8 enrolled. In 2016, 12 master's awarded. *Application deadline:* For fall admission, 6/1 priority date for domestic students. Applications are processed on a rolling basis. Application fee: $25 ($35 for international students). *Expenses: Tuition, area resident:* Full-time $19,566; part-time $880 per credit hour. *Required fees:* $175 per semester. One-time fee: $200. Part-time tuition and fees vary according to course load, degree level and program. *Financial support:* Research assistantships, teaching assistantships, career-related internships or fieldwork, and tuition waivers (partial) available. Support available to part-time students. Financial award application deadline: 2/15. *Unit head:* Melanie Pivarski, Chair, 312-341-6763. *Application contact:* Angela Ryan, Director of Graduate Enrollment, 312-341-2420, Fax: 312-281-3356, E-mail: applyru@roosevelt.edu.

St. John's University, The Peter J. Tobin College of Business, School of Risk Management, Insurance and Actuarial Science, Queens, NY 11439. Offers enterprise risk management (MS); management of risk (MS); risk management (MBA). *Program availability:* Online learning. *Degree requirements:* For master's, comprehensive exam (for some programs), thesis optional. *Entrance requirements:* For master's, GMAT or GRE (for MS), 2 letters of recommendation, resume, transcripts, essay. Additional exam requirements/recommendations for international students: Required—TOEFL (minimum score 600 paper-based; 100 iBT), IELTS (minimum score 7). Electronic applications accepted. *Expenses:* Contact institution. *Faculty research:* Insurance company operations and financial analysis, enterprise risk management, risk theory and modeling, credibility theory and actuarial price modeling, international insurance.

Simon Fraser University, Office of Graduate Studies and Postdoctoral Fellows, Faculty of Science, Department of Statistics and Actuarial Science, Burnaby, BC V5A 1S6, Canada. Offers actuarial science (M Sc); statistics (M Sc, PhD). *Faculty:* 21 full-time (8 women). *Students:* 64 full-time (31 women). 194 applicants, 13% accepted, 15 enrolled. In 2016, 5 master's, 5 doctorates awarded. *Degree requirements:* For master's, participation in consulting, project; for doctorate, comprehensive exam, thesis/dissertation. *Entrance requirements:* For master's, minimum GPA of 3.0 (on scale of 4.33) or 3.33 based on last 60 credits of undergraduate courses; for doctorate, minimum GPA of 3.5 (on scale of 4.33). Additional exam requirements/recommendations for international students: Recommended—TOEFL (minimum score 580 paper-based; 93 iBT), IELTS (minimum score 7), TWE (minimum score 5). *Application deadline:* For fall admission, 2/1 for domestic and international students. Application fee: $90 ($125 for international students). Electronic applications accepted. *Financial support:* In 2016–17, 29 students received support, including 25 fellowships (averaging $4,030 per year), teaching assistantships (averaging $5,608 per year); research assistantships, career-related internships or fieldwork, and scholarships/grants also available. *Faculty research:* Biostatistics, experimental design, envirometrics, statistical computing, statistical theory. *Unit head:* Dr. Tim Swartz, Graduate Chair, 778-782-4579, Fax: 778-782-4368, E-mail: stat-grad-chair@sfu.ca. *Application contact:* Kelly Jay, Graduate Secretary, 778-782-3801, Fax: 778-782-4368, E-mail: statgrad@sfu.ca.
Website: http://www.stat.sfu.ca/

Temple University, Fox School of Business, Specialized Master's Programs, Philadelphia, PA 19122-6096. Offers accountancy (MS); actuarial science (MS); finance (MS); financial engineering (MS); human resource management (MS); innovation management and entrepreneurship (MS); marketing (MS); statistics (MS). MS in innovation management and entrepreneurship delivered jointly with College of Engineering. *Accreditation:* AACSB. *Program availability:* Part-time. *Entrance requirements:* For master's, GRE General Test or GMAT, minimum undergraduate GPA of 3.0. Additional exam requirements/recommendations for international students: Required—TOEFL (minimum score 600 paper-based; 100 iBT), IELTS (minimum score 7.5).

Université du Québec à Montréal, Graduate Programs, Program in Actuarial Sciences, Montréal, QC H3C 3P8, Canada. Offers Diploma. *Program availability:* Part-time. *Entrance requirements:* For degree, appropriate bachelor's degree or equivalent and proficiency in French.

University of Illinois at Urbana–Champaign, Graduate College, College of Liberal Arts and Sciences, Department of Mathematics, Champaign, IL 61820. Offers applied mathematics (MS); applied mathematics: actuarial science (MS); mathematics (MS, PhD); teaching of mathematics (MS).

The University of Iowa, Graduate College, College of Liberal Arts and Sciences, Department of Statistics and Actuarial Science, Iowa City, IA 52242-1316. Offers actuarial science (MS); statistics (MS, PhD). *Degree requirements:* For master's, thesis optional, exam; for doctorate, comprehensive exam, thesis/dissertation. *Entrance requirements:* For master's and doctorate, GRE General Test, minimum GPA of 3.0. Additional exam requirements/recommendations for international students: Required—TOEFL (minimum score 550 paper-based; 81 iBT). Electronic applications accepted.

The University of Manchester, School of Mathematics, Manchester, United Kingdom. Offers actuarial science (PhD); applied mathematics (M Phil, PhD); applied numerical computing (M Phil, PhD); financial mathematics (M Phil, PhD); mathematical logic (M Phil); probability (M Phil, PhD); pure mathematics (M Phil, PhD); statistics (M Phil, PhD).

University of Nebraska–Lincoln, Graduate College, College of Business Administration, Interdepartmental Area of Actuarial Science, Lincoln, NE 68588. Offers MS. *Entrance requirements:* For master's, GRE. Additional exam requirements/recommendations for international students: Required—TOEFL (minimum score 550 paper-based). Electronic applications accepted. *Faculty research:* Risk theory, pensions, actuarial finance, decision theory, stochastic calculus.

The University of Texas at Austin, Graduate School, College of Natural Sciences, Department of Mathematics, Austin, TX 78712-1111. Offers MA, PhD. *Entrance requirements:* For master's and doctorate, GRE General Test. Electronic applications accepted.

The University of Texas at Dallas, School of Natural Sciences and Mathematics, Department of Mathematical Sciences, Richardson, TX 75080. Offers actuarial science (MS); mathematics (MS, PhD), including applied mathematics, data science (MS), engineering mathematics (MS), mathematics (MS); statistics (MS, PhD). *Program availability:* Part-time, evening/weekend. *Faculty:* 29 full-time (6 women), 2 part-time/adjunct (0 women). *Students:* 150 full-time (51 women), 31 part-time (12 women); includes 37 minority (8 Black or African American, non-Hispanic/Latino; 19 Asian, non-Hispanic/Latino; 8 Hispanic/Latino; 2 Two or more races, non-Hispanic/Latino), 112 international. Average age 31. 240 applicants, 43% accepted, 56 enrolled. In 2016, 36 master's, 7 doctorates awarded. *Degree requirements:* For master's, thesis optional; for doctorate, thesis/dissertation. *Entrance requirements:* For master's, GRE General Test, minimum GPA of 3.0 in upper-level course work in field; for doctorate, GRE General Test, minimum GPA of 3.5 in upper-level course work in field. Additional exam requirements/recommendations for international students: Required—TOEFL (minimum score 550 paper-based). *Application deadline:* For fall admission, 7/15 for domestic students, 5/1 priority date for international students; for spring admission, 11/15 for domestic students, 9/1 priority date for international students. Applications are processed on a rolling basis. Application fee: $50 ($100 for international students). Electronic applications accepted. *Expenses:* Tuition, state resident: full-time $12,418; part-time $690 per semester hour. Tuition, nonresident: full-time $24,150; part-time $1342 per semester hour. Tuition and fees vary according to course load. *Financial support:* In 2016–17, 114 students received support, including 1 fellowship (averaging $1,000 per year), 12 research assistantships (averaging $23,300 per year), 73 teaching assistantships with partial tuition reimbursements available (averaging $17,100 per year); career-related internships or fieldwork, Federal Work-Study, institutionally sponsored loans, scholarships/grants, and unspecified assistantships also available. Support available to part-time students. Financial award application deadline: 4/30; financial award applicants required to submit FAFSA. *Faculty research:* Sequential analysis, applications in semiconductor manufacturing, medical image analysis, computational anatomy, information theory, probability theory. *Unit head:* Dr. Vladimir Dragovic, Department Head, 972-883-6402, Fax: 972-883-6622, E-mail: mathdepthead@utdallas.edu. *Application contact:* Evangelina Bustamante, Graduate Student Coordinator, 972-883-2161, Fax: 972-883-6622, E-mail: utdmath@utdallas.edu.
Website: http://www.utdallas.edu/math

University of Waterloo, Graduate Studies, Faculty of Mathematics, Department of Statistics and Actuarial Science, Waterloo, ON N2L 3G1, Canada. Offers actuarial science (M Math, MAS, PhD); biostatistics (PhD); statistics (M Math, PhD); statistics-biostatistics (M Math); statistics-computing (M Math); statistics-finance (M Math). *Degree requirements:* For master's, research paper or thesis; for doctorate, comprehensive exam, thesis/dissertation. *Entrance requirements:* For master's, honors degree in field, minimum B+ average; for doctorate, master's degree, minimum B+ average. Additional exam requirements/recommendations for international students: Required—TOEFL, IELTS, PTE. Electronic applications accepted. *Faculty research:* Data analysis, risk theory, inference, stochastic processes, quantitative finance.

University of Wisconsin–Milwaukee, Graduate School, College of Letters and Science, Department of Mathematical Sciences, Milwaukee, WI 53201-0413. Offers mathematics (MS, PhD), including actuarial science, algebra (PhD), applied and computational mathematics (PhD), atmospheric science, foundations of advanced studies (MS), industrial mathematics, probability and statistics (PhD), standard mathematics (MS), statistics (MS), topology (PhD). *Students:* 71 full-time (20 women), 20 part-time (6 women); includes 5 minority (1 Black or African American, non-Hispanic/Latino; 3 Asian, non-Hispanic/Latino; 1 Two or more races, non-Hispanic/Latino), 39 international. Average age 28. 139 applicants, 37% accepted, 36 enrolled. In 2016, 21 master's, 13 doctorates awarded. *Degree requirements:* For master's, comprehensive exam, thesis optional; for doctorate, 2 foreign languages, thesis/dissertation. *Entrance requirements:* Additional exam requirements/recommendations for international students: Required—TOEFL (minimum score 550 paper-based; 79 iBT), IELTS (minimum score 6.5). *Application deadline:* For fall admission, 1/1 priority date for domestic students; for spring admission, 9/1 for domestic students. Applications are processed on a rolling basis. Application fee: $56 ($96 for international students). Electronic applications accepted. *Financial support:* In 2016–17, 23 fellowships, 9 research assistantships, 56 teaching assistantships were awarded; career-related internships or fieldwork, health care benefits, and unspecified assistantships also available. Support available to part-time students. Financial award application deadline: 4/15; financial award applicants required to submit FAFSA. *Faculty research:* Algebra, applied mathematics, atmospheric science, probability and statistics, topology. *Unit head:* Richard Stockbridge, Department Chair, 414-229-4568, E-mail: stockbri@uwm.edu. *Application contact:* General Information Contact, 414-229-4982, Fax: 414-229-6967, E-mail: gradschool@uwm.edu.
Website: http://www.uwm.edu/dept/math/

Insurance

Florida State University, The Graduate School, College of Business, Tallahassee, FL 32306-1110. Offers accounting (M Acc), including assurance and advisory services, generalist, taxation; business administration (MBA, PhD), including accounting (PhD), finance (PhD), management information systems (PhD), marketing (PhD), organizational behavior and human resources (PhD), risk management and insurance (PhD), strategy (PhD); finance (MS); management information systems (MS); risk management and insurance (MS); JD/MBA; MSW/MBA. *Accreditation:* AACSB. *Program availability:* Part-time, 100% online. *Faculty:* 101 full-time (27 women), 4 part-time/adjunct (2 women). *Students:* 272 full-time (127 women), 351 part-time (133 women); includes 141 minority (45 Black or African American, non-Hispanic/Latino; 2 American Indian or Alaska Native, non-Hispanic/Latino; 20 Asian, non-Hispanic/Latino; 59 Hispanic/Latino; 2 Native Hawaiian or other Pacific Islander, non-Hispanic/Latino; 13 Two or more races, non-Hispanic/Latino), 71 international. Average age 30. 688 applicants, 60% accepted, 273 enrolled. In 2016, 231 master's, 12 doctorates awarded. Terminal master's awarded for partial completion of doctoral program. *Degree requirements:* For doctorate, comprehensive exam, thesis/dissertation. *Entrance requirements:* For master's, GMAT, GRE (for all except MS in finance), work experience (MBA, MS); minimum GPA of 3.0, letters of recommendation; for doctorate, GMAT, GRE (for marketing, organizational behavior, risk management and insurance, management information systems, and human resources only), minimum graduate GPA of 3.5, letters of recommendation. Additional exam requirements/recommendations for international students: Required—TOEFL (minimum score 600 paper-based; 85 iBT); Recommended—IELTS (minimum score 6). *Application deadline:* For fall admission, 6/1 for domestic and international students; for spring admission, 10/1 for domestic and international students; for summer admission, 3/1 for domestic and international students. Applications are processed on a rolling basis. Application fee: $30. Electronic applications accepted. *Expenses:* Contact institution. *Financial support:* In 2016–17, 149 students received support, including 9 fellowships (averaging $1,500 per year), 65 research assistantships with full tuition reimbursements available (averaging $20,000 per year), 75 teaching assistantships with full tuition reimbursements available (averaging $20,000 per year); career-related internships or fieldwork, scholarships/grants, health care benefits, tuition waivers (full and partial), and unspecified assistantships also available. Support available to part-time students. Financial award application deadline: 1/1; financial award applicants required to submit FAFSA. *Faculty research:* Business strategy, marketing, finance, accounting, business analytics. *Total annual research expenditures:* $1.4 million. *Unit head:* Dr. Michael Hartline, Dean, 850-644-4405, Fax: 850-644-0915, E-mail: mhartline@business.fsu.edu. *Application contact:* Jennifer Clark, Director, 850-644-6458, E-mail: gradprograms@business.fsu.edu.
Website: http://business.fsu.edu/

Georgia State University, J. Mack Robinson College of Business, Department of Risk Management and Insurance, Program in Risk Management and Insurance, Atlanta, GA 30302-3083. Offers enterprise risk management (MBA, Certificate); financial risk management (MBA); mathematical risk management (MS); risk and insurance (MS); risk management and insurance (MBA, PhD); MAS/MRM. *Program availability:* Part-time, evening/weekend. *Degree requirements:* For doctorate, comprehensive exam, thesis/dissertation. *Entrance requirements:* For master's, GRE or GMAT, transcripts from all institutions attended, resume, essays. Additional exam requirements/recommendations for international students: Required—TOEFL (minimum score 610 paper-based; 101 iBT), IELTS (minimum score 7). *Application deadline:* For fall admission, 5/1 priority date for domestic students, 2/1 priority date for international students; for spring admission, 9/15 priority date for domestic students, 4/1 priority date for international students. Applications are processed on a rolling basis. Application fee: $50. Electronic applications accepted. *Expenses:* Tuition, state resident: full-time $6876; part-time $382 per credit hour. Tuition, nonresident: full-time $22,374; part-time $1243 per credit hour. *Required fees:* $2128; $1064 per term. Part-time tuition and fees vary according to course load and program. *Financial support:* Research assistantships, scholarships/grants, tuition waivers, and unspecified assistantships available. *Faculty research:* Insurance economics, structure and performance of insurance markets, regulation and policy in insurance markets, asset pricing theory, financial econometrics. *Unit head:* Dr. Martin Grace, Professor of Risk Management and Legal Studies/Chair of the Department of Risk Management and Insurance, 404-413-7500, Fax: 404-413-7499. *Application contact:* Toby McChesney, Graduate Recruiting Contact, 404-413-7167, Fax: 404-413-7162, E-mail: rcbgradadmissions@gsu.edu.
Website: http://rmi.robinson.gsu.edu/academic-programs/ms-rmi/

Olivet College, Master of Business Administration in Insurance Program, Olivet, MI 49076-9701. Offers MBA. *Accreditation:* TEAC. *Program availability:* Part-time, online only, 100% online, blended/hybrid learning. *Faculty:* 5 part-time/adjunct (2 women). *Students:* 33 part-time (8 women). Average age 37. In 2016, 7 master's awarded. *Degree requirements:* For master's, thesis optional. *Entrance requirements:* For master's, GMAT or CPCU designation, professional resume, official transcript, two letters of recommendation, 2 years of professional experience in field of insurance or risk management after earning undergraduate degree, minimum undergraduate GPA of 3.0. *Application deadline:* For fall admission, 9/15 for domestic students. Applications are processed on a rolling basis. Application fee: $0. Electronic applications accepted. *Expenses:* $760 per credit hour. *Unit head:* John S. Homer, PhD, MBA Program Director, 269-749-7150, E-mail: jhomer@olivetcollege.edu. *Application contact:* Kelly M. Parker, Associate Director of Graduate Business Programs, 269-749-7626, E-mail: kparker@olivetcollege.edu.
Website: http://www.olivetcollege.edu/graduate

Pontificia Universidad Catolica Madre y Maestra, Graduate School, Faculty of Social and Administrative Sciences, Santiago, Dominican Republic. Offers business administration (MBA), including business development, finance, international business, management skills (M Mgmt, MBA), marketing, operations, strategic cost management, strategy, tourist destination planning and management; law (LL M), including civil law, corporate business law, criminal law, international relations, real estate law; management (M Mgmt), including higher financial management, insurance program administration, management skills (M Mgmt, MBA); psychology (MA), including clinical child and adolescent psychology, forensic psychology; strategic human resources (EMBA).

St. John's University, The Peter J. Tobin College of Business, School of Risk Management, Insurance and Actuarial Science, Queens, NY 11439. Offers enterprise risk management (MS); management of risk (MS); risk management (MBA). *Program availability:* Online learning. *Degree requirements:* For master's, comprehensive exam (for some programs), thesis optional. *Entrance requirements:* For master's, GMAT or GRE (for MS), 2 letters of recommendation, resume, transcripts, essay. Additional exam requirements/recommendations for international students: Required—TOEFL (minimum score 600 paper-based; 100 iBT), IELTS (minimum score 7). Electronic applications accepted. *Expenses:* Contact institution. *Faculty research:* Insurance company operations and financial analysis, enterprise risk management, risk theory and modeling, credibility theory and actuarial price modeling, international insurance.

Temple University, Fox School of Business, Doctoral Programs in Business, Philadelphia, PA 19122-6096. Offers accounting (PhD); entrepreneurship (PhD); finance (PhD); international business (PhD); management information systems (PhD); marketing (PhD); risk management and insurance (PhD); statistics (PhD); strategic management (PhD); tourism and sport (PhD). *Accreditation:* AACSB. *Degree requirements:* For doctorate, thesis/dissertation. *Entrance requirements:* For doctorate, GRE General Test, GMAT, minimum GPA of 3.0, master's degree. Additional exam requirements/recommendations for international students: Required—TOEFL (minimum score 600 paper-based; 100 iBT), IELTS (minimum score 7.5). Electronic applications accepted.

University of Colorado Denver, Business School, Program in Finance, Denver, CO 80217. Offers economics (MS); finance (MS); financial analysis and management (MS); financial and commodities risk management (MS); risk management and insurance (MS); MS/MA; MS/MBA. *Program availability:* Part-time, evening/weekend. *Students:* 59 full-time (19 women), 25 part-time (4 women); includes 11 minority (1 Black or African American, non-Hispanic/Latino; 4 Asian, non-Hispanic/Latino; 5 Hispanic/Latino; 1 Two or more races, non-Hispanic/Latino), 12 international. Average age 31. 85 applicants, 35% accepted, 12 enrolled. In 2016, 45 master's awarded. *Degree requirements:* For master's, 30 semester hours (18 of required core courses, 9 of finance electives, and 3 of free elective). *Entrance requirements:* For master's, GMAT, essay, resume, two letters of recommendation; financial statements (for international students). Additional exam requirements/recommendations for international students: Required—TOEFL (minimum score 537 paper-based; 75 iBT); Recommended—IELTS (minimum score 6.5). *Application deadline:* For fall admission, 4/15 priority date for domestic students, 3/15 priority date for international students; for spring admission, 10/15 priority date for domestic students, 9/15 priority date for international students; for summer admission, 2/15 priority date for domestic students, 1/15 priority date for international students. Applications are processed on a rolling basis. Application fee: $50 ($75 for international students). Electronic applications accepted. *Expenses:* Contact institution. *Financial support:* In 2016–17, 27 students received support. Teaching assistantships, Federal Work-Study, institutionally sponsored loans, scholarships/grants, and traineeships available. Financial award application deadline: 4/1; financial award applicants required to submit FAFSA. *Faculty research:* Corporate governance, debt maturity policies, regulation and financial markets, option management strategies. *Unit head:* Jian Yang, Director of the Finance Program, 303-315-8423, E-mail: jian.yang@ucdenver.edu. *Application contact:* 303-315-8200, E-mail: bschool.admissions@ucdenver.edu.
Website: http://www.ucdenver.edu/academics/colleges/business/degrees/ms/finance/Pages/Finance.aspx

University of Florida, Graduate School, Warrington College of Business Administration, Hough Graduate School of Business, Department of Finance, Insurance and Real Estate, Gainesville, FL 32611. Offers entrepreneurship (MS); finance (MS, PhD); financial services (Certificate); insurance (PhD); quantitative finance (PhD); real estate (MS); real estate and urban analysis (PhD); JD/MBA; JD/MS. Terminal master's awarded for partial completion of doctoral program. *Degree requirements:* For master's, comprehensive exam, thesis; for doctorate, comprehensive exam, thesis/dissertation. *Entrance requirements:* For master's, GMAT (minimum score of 465) or GRE General Test, minimum GPA of 3.0 for last 60 hours of undergraduate degree, work experience (preferred); for doctorate, GMAT (minimum score of 465) or GRE General Test, minimum GPA of 3.0. Additional exam requirements/recommendations for international students: Required—TOEFL (minimum score 550 paper-based; 80 iBT), IELTS (minimum score 6). Electronic applications accepted. *Faculty research:* Banking, empirical corporate finance, hedge funds.

University of Pennsylvania, Wharton School, Insurance and Risk Management Department, Philadelphia, PA 19104. Offers MBA, PhD. *Degree requirements:* For doctorate, thesis/dissertation. *Entrance requirements:* For master's, GMAT; for doctorate, GMAT or GRE. *Expenses: Tuition:* Full-time $31,068; part-time $5762 per course. *Required fees:* $3200; $336 per course. Full-time tuition and fees vary according to degree level, program and student level. Part-time tuition and fees vary according to course load, degree level and program. *Faculty research:* Fair rate of return in insurance economics of pension plans, insurance regulation, malpractice insurance, actuarial science, genetic testing and life insurance.

University of Wisconsin–Madison, Graduate School, Wisconsin School of Business, Doctoral Program in Actuarial Science, Risk Management and Insurance, Madison, WI 53706-1380. Offers PhD. *Degree requirements:* For doctorate, comprehensive exam, thesis/dissertation. *Entrance requirements:* For doctorate, GMAT or GRE General Test. Additional exam requirements/recommendations for international students: Recommended—TOEFL (minimum score 623 paper-based; 106 iBT), IELTS (minimum score 7.5), TSE (minimum score 73). Electronic applications accepted. *Expenses:* Contact institution. *Faculty research:* Actuarial science, regression and business forecasting, panel data, economics of insurance markets, insurance regulation, public economics, behavioral economics, Bayesian methodology related to health insurance, tort reform and government programs, joint and several liability, superfund, predictive modeling, asymmetric information in insurance, psychology and economics, applied microeconomics, insurance markets, risk and decision making.

University of Wisconsin–Madison, Graduate School, Wisconsin School of Business, Wisconsin Full-Time MBA Program, Madison, WI 53706. Offers applied security analysis (MBA); arts administration (MBA); brand and product management (MBA); corporate finance and investment banking (MBA); marketing research (MBA); operations and technology management (MBA); real estate (MBA); risk management and insurance (MBA); strategic human resource management (MBA); supply chain management (MBA). *Faculty:* 125 full-time (32 women), 48 part-time/adjunct (11 women). *Students:* 197 full-time (73 women); includes 30 minority (11 Black or African American, non-Hispanic/Latino; 9 Asian, non-Hispanic/Latino; 10 Hispanic/Latino), 42 international. Average age 29. 728 applicants, 26% accepted, 99 enrolled. In 2016, 100 master's awarded. *Entrance requirements:* For master's, GMAT or GRE, bachelor's or equivalent degree, 2 years of work experience, essay, letter of recommendation, resume. Additional exam requirements/recommendations for international students: Required—TOEFL (minimum score 100 iBT), IELTS (minimum score 7.5). *Application deadline:* For fall admission, 9/28 for domestic students, 11/1 for international students; for winter admission, 11/2 for domestic students, 12/16 for international students; for spring admission, 1/11 for domestic students, 2/24 for international students; for summer admission, 3/1 for domestic students, 4/14 for international students. Applications are

processed on a rolling basis. Application fee: $75 ($81 for international students). Electronic applications accepted. *Expenses:* $7,947 per semester resident tuition, $2,430 fees; $16,082 per semester resident tuition, $2,830 fees. *Financial support:* In 2016–17, 178 students received support, including 8 fellowships with full tuition reimbursements available (averaging $56,413 per year), 23 research assistantships with full tuition reimbursements available (averaging $42,151 per year), 51 teaching assistantships with full tuition reimbursements available (averaging $39,963 per year); scholarships/grants, health care benefits, and unspecified assistantships also available. Financial award application deadline: 4/11. *Faculty research:* Forms of competition and outcomes in dual distribution systems; explaining the accuracy of revised forecasts; supply chain planning for random demand surges; advanced demand information in a multi-product system; the effects of presentation salience and measurement subjectivity on nonprofessional investors' fair value judgments. *Unit head:* Prof. Ella Mae Matsumura, Associate Dean, Full-time MBA Program, 608-262-9731, E-mail: ematsumura@bus.wisc.edu. *Application contact:* Mary Lewitzke, Assistant Director of Admissions and Recruiting, Full-time MBA Program, 608-262-4000, E-mail: mlewitzke@bus.wisc.edu.
Website: http://www.bus.wisc.edu/mba

Western Michigan University Thomas M. Cooley Law School, Graduate Programs, Lansing, MI 48901-3038. Offers administrative law (public law) (JD); business transactions (JD); Canadian law practice (JD); constitutional law/civil rights (public law) (JD); corporate law and finance (LL M); environmental law (public law) (JD); general practice (JD), including solo and small firm; homeland and national security law (LL M); insurance law (LL M); intellectual property (JD); intellectual property law (LL M); international law (JD); litigation (JD); self-directed (LL M, JD); tax law (LL M); taxation (JD); U.S. legal studies for foreign attorneys (LL M); JD/LL M; JD/MBA; JD/MPA; JD/MSW. *Program availability:* Part-time, evening/weekend, 100% online, blended/hybrid learning. *Degree requirements:* For master's, thesis optional; for doctorate, minimum of 3 credits of clinical experience. *Entrance requirements:* For master's, JD or LL B; for doctorate, LSAT. Additional exam requirements/recommendations for international students: Required—TOEFL (for U.S. legal studies for foreign attorneys LL M program); Recommended—TOEFL. Electronic applications accepted. *Faculty research:* Wrongful convictions, civil rights, environmental law, litigation techniques, data mining, intellectual property, practical and skills-based legal education.

Section 11
International Business

This section contains a directory of institutions offering graduate work in international business. Additional information about programs listed in the directory but not augmented by an in-depth entry may be obtained by writing directly to the dean of a graduate school or chair of a department at the address given in the directory.

For programs offering related work, see also in this book *Business Administration and Management, Entrepreneurship, Industrial and Manufacturing Management,* and *Organizational Behavior.* In another guide in this series:

Graduate Programs in the Humanities, Arts & Social Sciences

See *Political Science and International Affairs* and *Public, Regional, and Industrial Affairs*

CONTENTS

Program Directory

Featured School: Display and Close-Up

See:

International Business

American Business & Technology University, Programs in Business Administration, Saint Joseph, MO 64506. Offers business administration (MBA); financial management (MBA); global business management (MBA); information systems management (MBA); marketing and social media (MBA); project and operations management (MBA); public accounting (MBA). *Program availability:* Online learning.

American InterContinental University Atlanta, Program in Global Technology Management, Atlanta, GA 30328. Offers MBA. *Program availability:* Part-time, evening/weekend, online learning. *Entrance requirements:* For master's, interview. Electronic applications accepted. *Faculty research:* E-commerce, service quality leadership, human resources management.

American InterContinental University Online, Program in Business Administration, Schaumburg, IL 60173. Offers accounting and finance (MBA); finance (MBA); healthcare management (MBA); human resource management (MBA); international business (MBA); management (MBA); marketing (MBA); operations management (MBA); organizational psychology and development (MBA); project management (MBA). *Accreditation:* ACBSP. *Program availability:* Evening/weekend, online learning. *Entrance requirements:* Additional exam requirements/recommendations for international students: Required—TOEFL (minimum score 550 paper-based). Electronic applications accepted.

The American University in Dubai, Graduate Programs, Dubai, United Arab Emirates. Offers construction management (MS); education (M Ed); finance (MBA); generalist (MBA); marketing (MBA). *Program availability:* Part-time, evening/weekend. *Degree requirements:* For master's, thesis optional. *Entrance requirements:* For master's, GMAT (for MBA); GRE (for M Ed and MS), minimum undergraduate GPA of 3.0, official transcripts, two reference forms, curriculum vitae/resume, statement of career objectives, work experience. Additional exam requirements/recommendations for international students: Required—TOEFL (minimum score 550 paper-based; 79 iBT). Electronic applications accepted.

The American University of Paris, Graduate Programs, Paris, France. Offers cross-cultural and sustainable business management (MA); cultural translation (MA); global communications (MA); global communications and civil society (MA); international affairs (MA); international affairs, conflict resolution and civil society development (MA); Middle East and Islamic studies (MA); Middle East and Islamic studies and international affairs (MA); public policy and international affairs (MA); public policy and international law (MA). *Degree requirements:* For master's, thesis (for some programs). *Entrance requirements:* For master's, minimum undergraduate GPA of 3.0. Additional exam requirements/recommendations for international students: Recommended—TOEFL, IELTS. Electronic applications accepted.

Anaheim University, Programs in Business Administration, Anaheim, CA 92806-5150. Offers entrepreneurship (ME, DBA); global sustainable management (MBA); international business (MBA, DBA, Certificate, Diploma); management (DBA); sustainable management (DBA, Certificate, Diploma). *Program availability:* Part-time, evening/weekend, online only, 100% online. In 2016, 3 master's, 4 doctorates awarded. *Application deadline:* Applications are processed on a rolling basis. Electronic applications accepted. *Unit head:* Robert Robertson, Dean, Graduate School of Business, 714-772-3330, Fax: 714-772-3331, E-mail: admissions@anaheim.edu.

Argosy University, Atlanta, College of Business, Atlanta, GA 30328. Offers accounting (DBA); corporate compliance (MBA); customized professional concentration (MBA, DBA); finance (MBA); healthcare administration (MBA); information systems (DBA); information systems management (MBA); international business (MBA, DBA); management (MBA, MSM, DBA); marketing (MBA, DBA). *Accreditation:* ACBSP.

Argosy University, Chicago, College of Business, Chicago, IL 60601. Offers accounting (DBA); customized professional concentration (MBA, DBA); finance (MBA); fraud examination (MBA); global business sustainability (DBA); healthcare administration (MBA); information systems (DBA); information systems management (MBA); international business (MBA, DBA); management (MBA, MSM, DBA); marketing (MBA, DBA); organizational leadership (Ed D); public administration (MBA); sustainable management (MBA). *Accreditation:* ACBSP. *Program availability:* Online learning.

Argosy University, Dallas, College of Business, Farmers Branch, TX 75244. Offers accounting (DBA, AGC); corporate compliance (MBA, Graduate Certificate); customized professional concentration (MBA); finance (MBA, Graduate Certificate); fraud examination (MBA, Graduate Certificate); global business sustainability (DBA, AGC); healthcare administration (Graduate Certificate); healthcare management (MBA); information systems (MBA, DBA, AGC); information systems management (Graduate Certificate); international business (MBA, DBA, AGC, Graduate Certificate); management (MBA, DBA, AGC, Graduate Certificate); marketing (MBA, DBA, AGC, Graduate Certificate); public administration (MBA, Graduate Certificate); sustainable management (MBA, Graduate Certificate). *Accreditation:* ACBSP.

Argosy University, Denver, College of Business, Denver, CO 80231. Offers accounting (DBA); corporate compliance (MBA); customized professional concentration (MBA, DBA); finance (MBA); fraud examination (MBA); global business sustainability (DBA); healthcare administration (MBA); information systems (DBA); information systems management (MBA); international business (MBA, DBA); management (MBA, MSM, DBA); marketing (MBA, DBA); organizational leadership (Ed D); public administration (MBA); sustainable management (MBA). *Accreditation:* ACBSP.

Argosy University, Hawai`i, College of Business, Honolulu, HI 96813. Offers accounting (DBA); corporate compliance (MBA); customized professional concentration (MBA, DBA); finance (MBA, Certificate); fraud examination (MBA); global business sustainability (DBA); healthcare administration (MBA, Certificate); information systems (DBA); information systems management (MBA, Certificate); international business (MBA, DBA, Certificate); management (MBA, MSM, DBA); marketing (MBA, DBA, Certificate); organizational leadership (Ed D); public administration (MBA); sustainable management (MBA).

Argosy University, Inland Empire, College of Business, Ontario, CA 91761. Offers accounting (DBA); corporate compliance (MBA); customized professional concentration (MBA, DBA); finance (MBA); fraud examination (MBA); global business sustainability (DBA); healthcare administration (MBA); information systems (DBA); information systems management (MBA); international business (MBA, DBA); management (MBA, MSM, DBA); marketing (MBA, DBA); organizational leadership (Ed D); public administration (MBA); sustainable management (MBA).

Argosy University, Los Angeles, College of Business, Santa Monica, CA 90045. Offers accounting (DBA); corporate compliance (MBA); customized professional concentration (MBA, DBA); finance (MBA); fraud examination (MBA); global business sustainability (DBA); healthcare administration (MBA); information systems (DBA); information systems management (MBA); international business (MBA, DBA); management (MBA, MSM, DBA); marketing (MBA, DBA); organizational leadership (Ed D); public administration (MBA); sustainable management (MBA).

Argosy University, Nashville, College of Business, Nashville, TN 37214. Offers accounting (DBA); customized professional concentration (MBA, DBA); finance (MBA); healthcare administration (MBA); information systems (MBA, DBA); international business (MBA, DBA); management (MBA, MSM, DBA); marketing (MBA, DBA).

Argosy University, Northern Virginia, College of Business, Arlington, VA 22209. Offers accounting (DBA); customized professional concentration (MBA, DBA); finance (MBA); fraud examination (MBA); global business sustainability (DBA); healthcare administration (MBA); information systems (DBA); information systems management (MBA); international business (MBA, DBA, Certificate); management (MBA, MSM, DBA); marketing (MBA, DBA, Certificate); organizational leadership (Ed D); public administration (MBA); sustainable management (MBA).

Argosy University, Orange County, College of Business, Orange, CA 92868. Offers accounting (DBA, Adv C); corporate compliance (MBA); customized professional concentration (MBA, DBA); finance (MBA, Certificate); fraud examination (MBA); global business sustainability (DBA); healthcare administration (MBA, Certificate); information systems (DBA, Adv C, Certificate); information systems management (MBA); international business (MBA, DBA, Adv C, Certificate); management (MBA, MSM, DBA, Adv C); marketing (MBA, DBA, Adv C, Certificate); organizational leadership (Ed D); public administration (MBA, Certificate); sustainable management (MBA).

Argosy University, Phoenix, College of Business, Phoenix, AZ 85021. Offers accounting (DBA); corporate compliance (MBA); customized professional concentration (MBA, DBA); finance (MBA); fraud examination (MBA); global business sustainability (DBA); healthcare administration (MBA); information systems (DBA); information systems management (MBA); international business (MBA, DBA); management (MBA, DBA); marketing (MBA, DBA); public administration (MBA); sustainable management (MBA).

Argosy University, Salt Lake City, College of Business, Draper, UT 84020. Offers accounting (DBA); corporate compliance (MBA); customized professional concentration (MBA, DBA); finance (MBA); fraud examination (MBA); global business sustainability (DBA); healthcare administration (MBA); information systems (DBA); information systems management (MBA); international business (MBA, DBA); management (MBA, DBA); marketing (MBA, DBA); public administration (MBA); sustainable management (MBA).

Argosy University, San Diego, College of Business, San Diego, CA 92108. Offers accounting (DBA); corporate compliance (MBA); customized professional concentration (MBA, DBA); finance (MBA); fraud examination (MBA); global business sustainability (DBA); information systems (DBA); information systems management (MBA); international business (MBA, DBA); management (MBA, MSM, DBA); marketing (MBA, DBA); organizational leadership (Ed D); public administration (MBA).

Argosy University, San Francisco Bay Area, College of Business, Alameda, CA 94501. Offers accounting (DBA); corporate compliance (MBA); customized professional concentration (MBA, DBA); finance (MBA); fraud examination (MBA); global business sustainability (DBA); healthcare administration (MBA); information systems (DBA); information systems management (MBA); international business (MBA, DBA); management (MBA, MSM, DBA); marketing (MBA, DBA); organizational leadership (Ed D); public administration (MBA); sustainable management (MBA).

Argosy University, Sarasota, College of Business, Sarasota, FL 34235. Offers accounting (DBA, Adv C); corporate compliance (MBA, DBA, Certificate); customized professional concentration (MBA, DBA); finance (MBA, Certificate); fraud examination (MBA, Certificate); global business sustainability (DBA, Adv C); healthcare administration (MBA, Certificate); information systems (DBA, Adv C, Certificate); information systems management (MBA); international business (MBA, DBA, Adv C, Certificate); management (MBA, MSM, DBA, Adv C, Certificate); marketing (MBA, DBA, Adv C, Certificate); organizational leadership (Ed D); public administration (MBA, Certificate); sustainable management (MBA, Certificate).

Argosy University, Schaumburg, Graduate School of Business and Management, Schaumburg, IL 60173-5403. Offers accounting (DBA, Adv C); customized professional concentration (MBA, DBA); finance (MBA, Certificate); fraud examination (MBA); healthcare administration (MBA, Certificate); human resource management (MS); information systems (Adv C, Certificate); information systems management (MBA); international business (MBA, DBA, Adv C, Certificate); management (MBA, MSM, DBA, Adv C, Certificate); marketing (MBA, DBA, Adv C, Certificate); organizational leadership (MS, Ed D); public administration (MBA); sustainable management (MBA).

Argosy University, Seattle, College of Business, Seattle, WA 98121. Offers accounting (DBA); corporate compliance (MBA); customized professional concentration (MBA, DBA); finance (MBA); fraud examination (MBA); global business sustainability (DBA); healthcare administration (MBA); information systems (DBA); information systems management (MBA); international business (MBA, DBA); management (MBA, MSM, DBA); marketing (MBA, DBA); organizational leadership (Ed D); public administration (MBA); sustainable management (MBA).

Argosy University, Tampa, College of Business, Tampa, FL 33607. Offers accounting (DBA); corporate compliance (MBA); customized professional concentration (MBA, DBA); finance (MBA); fraud examination (MBA); global business sustainability (DBA); healthcare administration (MBA); information systems (DBA); information systems management (MBA); international business (MBA, DBA); management (MBA, MSM, DBA); marketing (MBA, DBA); organizational leadership (Ed D); public administration (MBA); sustainable management (MBA).

Argosy University, Twin Cities, College of Business, Eagan, MN 55121. Offers accounting (DBA); customized professional concentration (MBA, DBA); finance (MBA); fraud examination (MBA); global business sustainability (DBA); healthcare administration (MBA); information systems (DBA); information systems management (MBA); international business (MBA, DBA); management (MBA, MSM, DBA); marketing (MBA, DBA); organizational leadership (Ed D); public administration (MBA); sustainable management (MBA).

Arizona State University at the Tempe campus, Thunderbird School of Global Management, Tempe, AZ 85287. Offers global affairs and management (MA); global management (MGM). *Accreditation:* AACSB. *Program availability:* Online learning. *Degree requirements:* For master's, one foreign language. *Entrance requirements:* For master's, GMAT. Additional exam requirements/recommendations for international students: Required—TOEFL.

Arizona State University at the Tempe campus, W. P. Carey School of Business, Program in Business Administration, Tempe, AZ 85287-4906. Offers entrepreneurship (MBA); finance (MBA); health sector management (MBA); international business (MBA); leadership (MBA); marketing (MBA); organizational behavior (PhD); strategic management (PhD); supply chain management (MBA, PhD); JD/MBA; MBA/M Acc; MBA/M Arch. *Accreditation:* AACSB. *Program availability:* Part-time, evening/weekend, online learning. Terminal master's awarded for partial completion of doctoral program. *Degree requirements:* For master's, thesis or alternative, internship, interactive Program of Study (iPOS) submitted before completing 50 percent of required credit hours; for doctorate, comprehensive exam, thesis/dissertation, interactive Program of Study (iPOS) submitted before completing 50 percent of required credit hours. *Entrance requirements:* For master's, GMAT, minimum GPA of 3.0 in last 2 years of work leading to bachelor's degree, 2 letters of recommendation, professional resume, official transcripts, 3 essays; for doctorate, GMAT or GRE, minimum GPA of 3.0 in last 2 years of work leading to bachelor's degree, 3 letters of recommendation, resume, personal statement/essay. Additional exam requirements/recommendations for international students: Required—TOEFL (minimum score 550 paper-based; 80 iBT), IELTS (minimum score 6.5). Electronic applications accepted. *Expenses:* Contact institution.

Ashworth College, Graduate Programs, Norcross, GA 30092. Offers business administration (MBA); criminal justice (MS); health care administration (MBA, MS); human resource management (MBA, MS); international business (MBA); management (MS); marketing (MBA, MS).

Assumption College, Business Studies Program, Worcester, MA 01609-1296. Offers accounting (MBA); business studies (CAGS); finance/economics (MBA); human resources (MBA); international business (MBA); management (MBA); marketing (MBA); nonprofit leadership (MBA). *Program availability:* Part-time, evening/weekend. *Faculty:* 4 full-time (1 woman), 19 part-time/adjunct (6 women). *Students:* 44 full-time (16 women), 97 part-time (47 women); includes 20 minority (8 Black or African American, non-Hispanic/Latino; 5 Asian, non-Hispanic/Latino; 6 Hispanic/Latino, 1 Two or more races, non-Hispanic/Latino), 4 international. Average age 29. 34 applicants, 59% accepted, 16 enrolled. In 2016, 97 master's, 1 other advanced degree awarded. *Degree requirements:* For master's, thesis, capstone. *Entrance requirements:* For master's, bachelor's degree, 3 letters of recommendation, official transcripts, personal statement, current resume; for CAGS, MBA or equivalent degree in a closely related field, 3 letters of recommendation, official transcripts, personal statement, current resume. Additional exam requirements/recommendations for international students: Required—TOEFL (minimum score 540 paper-based; 76 iBT), IELTS (minimum score 6). *Application deadline:* For fall admission, 7/1 priority date for domestic and international students; for spring admission, 12/1 priority date for domestic and international students; for summer admission, 4/1 priority date for domestic and international students. Application fee: $30. Electronic applications accepted. *Expenses: Tuition:* Full-time $11,610; part-time $645 per credit. *Required fees:* $70 per term. Tuition and fees vary according to course load and program. *Financial support:* In 2016–17, 19 students received support. Tuition waivers (full and partial), unspecified assistantships, and institutional discounts available. Financial award applicants required to submit FAFSA. *Faculty research:* Workplace diversity, dynamics of team interaction, utilization of leased employees, experiential learning project on due diligence market for prostheses. *Unit head:* Dr. Robin Frkal, Director, 508-767-7622, E-mail: rafrkal@assumption.edu. *Application contact:* Karen Stoyanoff, Director of Recruitment for Graduate Enrollment, 508-767-7442, Fax: 508-799-4412, E-mail: graduate@assumption.edu.
Website: http://graduate.assumption.edu/mba/assumption-mba

Avila University, School of Business, Kansas City, MO 64145-1698. Offers accounting (MBA); finance (MBA); health care administration (MBA); international business (MBA); management (MBA); management information systems (MBA); marketing (MBA). *Program availability:* Part-time, evening/weekend. *Faculty:* 8 full-time (4 women), 4 part-time/adjunct (2 women). *Students:* 58 full-time (22 women), 21 part-time (10 women); includes 20 minority (10 Black or African American, non-Hispanic/Latino; 2 Asian, non-Hispanic/Latino; 5 Hispanic/Latino; 3 Two or more races, non-Hispanic/Latino), 18 international. Average age 30. 75 applicants, 28% accepted, 14 enrolled. In 2016, 40 master's awarded. *Degree requirements:* For master's, comprehensive exam, capstone course. *Entrance requirements:* For master's, GMAT (minimum score 420), minimum GPA of 3.0, interview. Additional exam requirements/recommendations for international students: Required—TOEFL (minimum score 550 paper-based). *Application deadline:* For fall admission, 7/30 priority date for domestic and international students; for winter admission, 11/30 priority date for domestic and international students; for spring admission, 2/28 priority date for domestic and international students; for summer admission, 6/1 priority date for domestic and international students. Applications are processed on a rolling basis. Application fee: $0. Electronic applications accepted. *Expenses:* $628 per credit hour. *Financial support:* In 2016–17, 11 students received support. Career-related internships or fieldwork and scholarships/grants available. Support available to part-time students. Financial award applicants required to submit FAFSA. *Faculty research:* Leadership characteristics, financial hedging, group dynamics. *Unit head:* Dr. Richard Woodall, Dean, 816-501-3720, Fax: 816-501-2463, E-mail: richard.woodall@avila.edu. *Application contact:* Brandon Black, MBA Admission Advisor, 816-501-3601, Fax: 816-501-2463, E-mail: brandon.black@avila.edu.
Website: https://www.avila.edu/mrk/mba

Azusa Pacific University, School of Behavioral and Applied Sciences, Department of Leadership and Organizational Psychology, Program in Global Leadership, Azusa, CA 91702-7000. Offers MA.

Azusa Pacific University, School of Business and Management, Azusa, CA 91702-7000. Offers business administration (MBA); diversity for strategic advantage (MA); entrepreneurship (MBA); finance (MBA); human and organizational development (MA); human resources and organizational development (MBA); human resources management (MA); international business (MBA); marketing (MBA); non-profit management (MA); organizational development and change (MA); performance improvement (MA), public administration (MA); strategic management (MBA). *Program availability:* Part-time, evening/weekend. *Degree requirements:* For master's, thesis (for some programs), final project. *Entrance requirements:* For master's, GMAT, minimum GPA of 3.0. Additional exam requirements/recommendations for international students: Required—TOEFL (minimum score 600 paper-based). *Expenses:* Contact institution. *Faculty research:* Gender issues, financial risk, leadership and ethics, marketing strategy.

Baldwin Wallace University, Graduate Programs, School of Business, Program in International Management, Berea, OH 44017-2088. Offers MBA. *Program availability:* Part-time, evening/weekend. *Students:* 2 full-time (both women), 4 part-time (2 women); includes 2 minority (1 Hispanic/Latino; 1 Two or more races, non-Hispanic/Latino), 1 international. Average age 31. In 2016, 7 master's awarded. *Degree requirements:* For master's, one foreign language, minimum overall GPA of 3.0. *Entrance requirements:* For master's, GMAT or minimum undergraduate GPA of 3.0, interview, work experience, bachelor's degree in any field. Additional exam requirements/recommendations for international students: Required—TOEFL (minimum score 550 paper-based; 79 iBT). *Application deadline:* For fall admission, 7/25 priority date for domestic students, 4/30 priority date for international students; for spring admission, 12/15 priority date for domestic students, 9/30 priority date for international students; for summer admission, 4/15 priority date for domestic students. Applications are processed on a rolling basis. Application fee: $25. Electronic applications accepted. Application fee is waived when completed online. *Expenses:* $921 per credit hour. *Financial support:* Unspecified assistantships available. Financial award applicants required to submit FAFSA. *Faculty research:* International finance, systems approach, international marketing. *Unit head:* Dale Kramer, Director, 440-826-3331, Fax: 440-826-3868, E-mail: dkramer@bw.edu. *Application contact:* Laura Spencer, Graduate Application Specialist, 440-826-2191, Fax: 440-826-3868, E-mail: lspencer@bw.edu.
Website: http://www.bw.edu/graduate/business/mba/

Barry University, Andreas School of Business, Graduate Certificate Programs, Miami Shores, FL 33161-6695. Offers finance (Certificate); health services administration (Certificate); international business (Certificate); management (Certificate); management information systems (Certificate); marketing (Certificate).

Baruch College of the City University of New York, Zicklin School of Business, Department of Marketing and International Business, New York, NY 10010-5585. Offers international business (MBA); marketing (MBA, MS, PhD). PhD offered jointly with Graduate School and University Center of the City University of New York. *Program availability:* Part-time, evening/weekend. *Degree requirements:* For doctorate, comprehensive exam, thesis/dissertation. *Entrance requirements:* For master's, GMAT, 2 letters of recommendation, resume, 2 years of work experience; for doctorate, GMAT. Additional exam requirements/recommendations for international students: Required—TOEFL (minimum score 590 paper-based), TWE (minimum score 5).

Baruch College of the City University of New York, Zicklin School of Business, International Executive MS Programs, New York, NY 10010-5585. Offers entrepreneurship (MS). *Program availability:* Part-time, evening/weekend. *Entrance requirements:* For master's, GMAT, 2 letters of recommendation, resume, 2 years of work experience. Additional exam requirements/recommendations for international students: Required—TOEFL (minimum score 590 paper-based), TWE (minimum score 5).

Benedictine University, Graduate Programs, Program in Business Administration, Lisle, IL 60532. Offers accounting (MBA); entrepreneurship and managing innovation (MBA); financial management (MBA); health administration (MBA); human resource management (MBA); information systems security (MBA); international business (MBA); management consulting (MBA); management information systems (MBA); marketing management (MBA); operations management and logistics (MBA); organizational leadership (MBA). *Program availability:* Part-time, evening/weekend, online learning. *Faculty:* 4 full-time (2 women), 24 part-time/adjunct (3 women). *Students:* 90 full-time (51 women), 440 part-time (262 women); includes 147 minority (65 Black or African American, non-Hispanic/Latino; 1 American Indian or Alaska Native, non-Hispanic/Latino; 58 Asian, non-Hispanic/Latino; 20 Hispanic/Latino; 3 Native Hawaiian or other Pacific Islander, non-Hispanic/Latino), 2 international. Average age 34. 211 applicants, 89% accepted, 155 enrolled. In 2016, 350 master's awarded. *Entrance requirements:* For master's, GMAT. Additional exam requirements/recommendations for international students: Required—TOEFL (minimum score 550 paper-based). *Application deadline:* For fall admission, 9/1 for domestic students; for winter admission, 12/1 for domestic students; for spring admission, 2/15 for domestic students. Applications are processed on a rolling basis. Application fee: $40. Electronic applications accepted. *Expenses: Tuition:* Full-time $15,600; part-time $650 per hour. *Required fees:* $300. One-time fee: $125 part-time. Tuition and fees vary according to class time, course load, campus/location and program. *Financial support:* Career-related internships or fieldwork and health care benefits available. Support available to part-time students. *Faculty research:* Strategic leadership in professional organizations, sociology of professions, organizational change, social identity theory, applications to change management. *Unit head:* Dr. Sharon Borowicz, Director, 630-829-6219, E-mail: sborowicz@ben.edu. *Application contact:* Kari Gibbons, Director, Admissions, 630-829-6200, Fax: 630-829-6584, E-mail: kgibbons@ben.edu.

Boston University, Metropolitan College, Department of Administrative Sciences, Boston, MA 02215. Offers applied business analytics (MS); economic development and tourism management (MSAS); enterprise risk management (MS); financial management (MS); global marketing management (MS); innovation and technology (MSAS); insurance management (MSM); project management (MS); supply chain management (MS). *Accreditation:* AACSB. *Program availability:* Part-time, evening/weekend, online learning. *Faculty:* 15 full-time (3 women), 22 part-time/adjunct (3 women). *Students:* 301 full-time (146 women), 934 part-time (501 women); includes 237 minority (81 Black or African American, non-Hispanic/Latino; 5 American Indian or Alaska Native, non-Hispanic/Latino; 60 Asian, non-Hispanic/Latino; 76 Hispanic/Latino; 1 Native Hawaiian or other Pacific Islander, non-Hispanic/Latino; 14 Two or more races, non-Hispanic/Latino), 514 international. Average age 31. 593 applicants, 69% accepted, 260 enrolled. In 2016, 263 master's awarded. *Degree requirements:* For master's, thesis optional. *Entrance requirements:* For master's, 1 year of work experience, minimum GPA of 3.0. Additional exam requirements/recommendations for international students: Required—TOEFL (minimum score 84 iBT). *Application deadline:* Applications are processed on a rolling basis. Application fee: $80. Electronic applications accepted. *Expenses:* Contact institution. *Financial support:* In 2016–17, 15 students received support, including 14 research assistantships (averaging $8,400 per year); career-related internships or fieldwork, Federal Work-Study, and unspecified assistantships also available. *Faculty research:* International business, innovative process. *Unit head:* Dr. John Sullivan, Chair, 617-353-3016, E-mail: adminsc@bu.edu. *Application contact:* Fiona Niven, Administrative Sciences Department, 617-353-3016, E-mail: adminsc@bu.edu.
Website: http://www.bu.edu/met/academic-community/departments/administrative-sciences/

Brandeis University, International Business School (IBS), Waltham, MA 02454-9110. Offers MA, MBA, MSF, PhD. *Faculty:* 32 full-time (13 women), 27 part-time/adjunct (4 women). *Students:* 387 full-time (174 women), 26 part-time (11 women); includes 270 minority (21 Black or African American, non-Hispanic/Latino; 226 Asian, non-Hispanic/Latino; 23 Hispanic/Latino). Average age 26. 1,383 applicants, 26% accepted, 139 enrolled. In 2016, 171 master's, 3 doctorates awarded. *Degree requirements:* For doctorate, thesis/dissertation. *Entrance requirements:* For master's, minimum two years of full-time work experience (for MBA); for doctorate, GMAT or GRE, writing sample. Additional exam requirements/recommendations for international students: Required—TOEFL (minimum score 600 paper-based, 100 iBT), IELTS (7), or PTE (68). *Application deadline:* For fall admission, 11/1 for domestic and international students; for winter admission, 1/15 for domestic and international students; for spring admission, 3/15 for domestic students, 3/15 priority date for international students; for summer admission, 5/1 for domestic and international students. Application fee: $100. Electronic applications accepted. *Expenses:* Contact institution. *Financial support:* In 2016–17, 176 students received support, including 11 fellowships (averaging $9,545 per year); research assistantships, teaching assistantships, career-related internships or fieldwork, institutionally sponsored loans, scholarships/grants, and health care benefits also available. Financial award application deadline: 1/15. *Faculty research:* Corporate finance, fixed income, monetary policy, business strategy, cross-cultural interaction. *Total annual research expenditures:* $180,337. *Unit head:* Peter Petri, Dean, 781-736-

International Business

2256. *Application contact:* Kelly Sugrue, Director of Admissions, 781-736-2252, Fax: 781-736-2263, E-mail: globaladmissions@brandeis.edu.
Website: http://www.brandeis.edu/global/

Brandman University, School of Business and Professional Studies, Irvine, CA 92618. Offers accounting (MBA); business administration (MBA); e-business strategic management (MBA); entrepreneurship (MBA); finance (MBA); health administration (MBA); human resources (MBA, MS); international business (MBA); marketing (MBA); organizational leadership (MA, MBA, MPA); public administration (MPA). *Expenses: Tuition:* Full-time $14,880; part-time $620 per credit hour. Tuition and fees vary according to degree level and program. *Unit head:* Dr. Glenn Worthington, Dean, 253-861-1024, E-mail: gworthin@brandman.edu.
Website: https://www.brandman.edu/business-professional-studies

Bristol University, Program in Business Administration, Anaheim, CA 92806. Offers business administration (MBA); international business (MBA); marketing (MBA); sports management (MBA). *Degree requirements:* For master's, capstone.

Brooklyn College of the City University of New York, School of Business, Brooklyn, NY 11210-2889. Offers accounting (MS); business administration (MS), including economic analysis, general business, global business and finance. *Program availability:* Part-time, evening/weekend. *Degree requirements:* For master's, comprehensive exam, thesis or alternative. *Entrance requirements:* For master's, GMAT, 2 letters of recommendation. Additional exam requirements/recommendations for international students: Required—TOEFL (minimum score 550 paper-based; 79 iBT). Electronic applications accepted. *Faculty research:* Econometrics, environmental economics, microeconomics, macroeconomics, taxation.

Bryant University, Graduate School of Business, Smithfield, RI 02917. Offers accounting (MPAC); business administration (MBA), including general management, global finance, global supply chain management, international business; business analytics (Graduate Certificate); taxation (MST). *Program availability:* Part-time, evening/weekend. *Faculty:* 16 full-time (3 women), 2 part-time/adjunct (0 women). *Students:* 71 full-time (23 women), 83 part-time (32 women); includes 17 minority (5 Black or African American, non-Hispanic/Latino; 4 Asian, non-Hispanic/Latino; 5 Hispanic/Latino; 3 Two or more races, non-Hispanic/Latino), 17 international. Average age 27. 165 applicants, 57% accepted, 66 enrolled. In 2016, 106 master's, 12 other advanced degrees awarded. *Degree requirements:* For master's, comprehensive exam (for some programs). *Entrance requirements:* For master's, GMAT, resume, recommendation, college transcripts. Additional exam requirements/recommendations for international students: Required—TOEFL (minimum score 580 paper-based; 95 iBT). *Application deadline:* For fall admission, 7/15 for domestic and international students; for spring admission, 11/15 for domestic and international students; for summer admission, 4/15 for domestic and international students. Applications are processed on a rolling basis. Application fee: $80. Electronic applications accepted. *Expenses:* Contact institution. *Financial support:* Research assistantships, scholarships/grants, and unspecified assistantships available. Support available to part-time students. Financial award application deadline: 2/15; financial award applicants required to submit FAFSA. *Faculty research:* International business, public sector auditing, taxation of partnerships, information systems security, financial markets microstructure. *Unit head:* Bjorn Carlsson, Graduate Program Director, 401-232-6707, E-mail: bcarlsson@bryant.edu. *Application contact:* Terri Rogers, Admissions Assistant, 401-232-6230, Fax: 401-232-6494, E-mail: graduateprograms@bryant.edu.
Website: http://gradschool.bryant.edu/business/

Butler University, Lacy School of Business, Indianapolis, IN 46208-3485. Offers finance (MBA); international business (MBA); leadership (MBA); marketing (MBA); professional accounting (MP Acc). *Accreditation:* AACSB. *Program availability:* Part-time. *Faculty:* 18 full-time (6 women), 14 part-time/adjunct (5 women). *Students:* 31 full-time (11 women), 133 part-time (40 women); includes 10 minority (2 Black or African American, non-Hispanic/Latino; 2 Asian, non-Hispanic/Latino; 6 Hispanic/Latino), 2 international. Average age 31. 122 applicants, 68% accepted, 42 enrolled. In 2016, 89 master's awarded. *Entrance requirements:* For master's, GMAT, minimum AACSB index of 950, personal statement, two letters of recommendation, official transcripts, current resume. Additional exam requirements/recommendations for international students: Required—TOEFL (minimum score 550 paper-based; 79 iBT), IELTS (minimum score 6), Michigan English Language Assessment Battery (minimum score of 80). *Application deadline:* For fall admission, 8/1 for domestic and international students; for spring admission, 12/1 for domestic and international students; for summer admission, 4/1 for domestic and international students. Applications are processed on a rolling basis. Application fee: $0. Electronic applications accepted. *Expenses:* $790 per credit hour. *Financial support:* In 2016–17, 15 students received support. Scholarships/grants, tuition waivers (full and partial), and unspecified assistantships available. Financial award application deadline: 7/15; financial award applicants required to submit FAFSA. *Faculty research:* Higher education and pedagogy; ecotourism; healthcare issues and marketing public policy; domestic public policy, international finance and banking, international and management entrepreneurship, organizational management. *Unit head:* Dr. Stephen Standifird, Dean. *Application contact:* Diane Dubord, Graduate Student Service Specialist, 317-940-8107, Fax: 317-940-8250, E-mail: ddubord@butler.edu.
Website: https://www.butler.edu/lacyschool

California Intercontinental University, School of Business, Irvine, CA 92614. Offers banking and finance (MBA); entrepreneurship and business management (DBA); global business leadership (DBA); international management and marketing (MBA); organizational management and human resource management (MBA).

California Lutheran University, Graduate Studies, School of Management, Thousand Oaks, CA 91360-2787. Offers business (IMBA); computer science (MS); econometrics (MBA); economics (MS); entrepreneurship (MBA, Certificate); finance (MBA, Certificate); financial planning (MBA, Certificate); information systems and technology (MS); information technology management (MBA, Certificate); international business (MBA, Certificate); management and organization behavior (MBA); management and organizational behavior (Certificate); marketing (MBA, Certificate); microeconomics (MBA); nonprofit and social enterprise (MBA); public policy and administration (MPPA). *Program availability:* Part-time, evening/weekend, 100% online, blended/hybrid learning. *Faculty:* 25 full-time (10 women), 36 part-time/adjunct (12 women). *Students:* 427 full-time (172 women), 189 part-time (87 women); includes 120 minority (14 Black or African American, non-Hispanic/Latino; 2 American Indian or Alaska Native, non-Hispanic/Latino; 19 Asian, non-Hispanic/Latino; 37 Hispanic/Latino; 48 Two or more races, non-Hispanic/Latino), 338 international. Average age 30. 591 applicants, 64% accepted, 131 enrolled. In 2016, 305 master's awarded. *Entrance requirements:* For master's, GMAT, interview, minimum GPA of 3.0. *Application deadline:* Applications are processed on a rolling basis. Application fee: $50. Electronic applications accepted. *Expenses:* Contact institution. *Unit head:* Dr. Gerhard Apfelthaler, Dean, 805-493-3360. *Application contact:* 805-493-3325, Fax: 805-493-3861, E-mail: clugrad@callutheran.edu.
Website: http://www.callutheran.edu/management/

California State University, East Bay, Office of Graduate Studies, College of Business and Economics, MBA Program, Option in Strategy and International Business, Hayward, CA 94542-3000. Offers MBA. *Program availability:* Part-time, evening/weekend. *Degree requirements:* For master's, comprehensive exam or thesis. *Entrance requirements:* For master's, GMAT, minimum GPA of 2.75. Additional exam requirements/recommendations for international students: Required—TOEFL (minimum score 550 paper-based). *Application deadline:* For fall admission, 6/30 for domestic and international students. Application fee: $55. *Financial support:* Career-related internships or fieldwork, Federal Work-Study, institutionally sponsored loans, and scholarships/grants available. Support available to part-time students. Financial award application deadline: 3/1. *Unit head:* Dr. Yi Jiang-Karnes, Program Advisor, 510-885-3290, E-mail: yi.jiang@csueastbay.edu. *Application contact:* Dr. Donna Wiley, Interim Associate Vice President for Academic Programs and Graduate Studies, 510-885-3716, Fax: 510-885-4777, E-mail: donna.wiley@csueastbay.edu.
Website: http://www.csueastbay.edu/cbe/mba-options/strategy-and-international-business-option.html

California State University, Fullerton, Graduate Studies, College of Business and Economics, Program in Business Administration, Fullerton, CA 92834-9480. Offers business administration (MBA); business analytics (MBA); international business (MBA); organizational leadership (MBA); risk management and insurance (MBA). *Accreditation:* AACSB. *Program availability:* Part-time. *Degree requirements:* For master's, project or thesis. *Entrance requirements:* For master's, GMAT. Application fee: $55. *Expenses:* Tuition, state resident: full-time $3369; part-time $1953 per unit. Tuition, nonresident: full-time $3915; part-time $2499 per unit. Tuition and fees vary according to course load, degree level and program. *Financial support:* Career-related internships or fieldwork, Federal Work-Study, institutionally sponsored loans, and scholarships/grants available. Support available to part-time students. Financial award application deadline: 3/1; financial award applicants required to submit FAFSA. *Unit head:* Shaun Pichler, Director, 657-278-7373, E-mail: spichler@fullerton.edu. *Application contact:* Admissions/Applications, 657-278-2371.

California State University, Los Angeles, Graduate Studies, College of Business and Economics, Department of Marketing, Los Angeles, CA 90032-8530. Offers international business (MBA, MS). *Program availability:* Part-time, evening/weekend. *Degree requirements:* For master's, comprehensive exam (MBA), thesis (MS). *Entrance requirements:* For master's, GMAT, minimum GPA of 2.5 during previous 2 years of course work. Additional exam requirements/recommendations for international students: Required—TOEFL (minimum score 550 paper-based). Electronic applications accepted.

California State University, San Bernardino, Graduate Studies, College of Business and Public Administration, Program in Business Administration, San Bernardino, CA 92407. Offers accounting (MBA); entrepreneurship (MBA); finance (MBA); global business (MBA); information management (MBA); information security (MBA); management (MBA); supply chain management (MBA). *Accreditation:* AACSB. *Program availability:* Part-time, evening/weekend, online learning. *Faculty:* 7 full-time (4 women), 3 part-time/adjunct (2 women). *Students:* 37 full-time (11 women), 141 part-time (51 women); includes 85 minority (16 Black or African American, non-Hispanic/Latino; 1 American Indian or Alaska Native, non-Hispanic/Latino; 20 Asian, non-Hispanic/Latino; 45 Hispanic/Latino; 3 Two or more races, non-Hispanic/Latino), 46 international. 260 applicants, 37% accepted, 34 enrolled. In 2016, 180 master's awarded. *Degree requirements:* For master's, comprehensive exam, thesis. *Entrance requirements:* Additional exam requirements/recommendations for international students: Required—TOEFL. *Application deadline:* For fall admission, 7/16 for domestic students, 7/20 for international students; for winter admission, 10/23 for domestic students, 10/20 for international students; for spring admission, 1/22 for domestic students, 1/20 for international students. Application fee: $55. *Expenses:* Contact institution. *Financial support:* Application deadline: 3/1. *Unit head:* Dr. Lawrence C. Rose, Dean, 909-537-3703, Fax: 909-537-7026, E-mail: lrose@csusb.edu. *Application contact:* Dr. Vipin Gupta, Associate Dean/MBA Director, 909-537-7380, Fax: 909-537-7026, E-mail: vgupta@csusb.edu.
Website: http://mba.csusb.edu/

California University of Management and Sciences, Graduate Programs, Anaheim, CA 92801. Offers business administration (MBA, DBA); computer information systems (MS); economics (MS); international business (MS); sports management (MS).

Canisius College, Graduate Division, Richard J. Wehle School of Business, Department of Management, Buffalo, NY 14208-1098. Offers business administration (MBA); international business (MS). *Accreditation:* AACSB. *Program availability:* Part-time, evening/weekend. *Faculty:* 15 full-time (3 women), 10 part-time/adjunct (2 women). *Students:* 90 full-time (38 women), 123 part-time (43 women); includes 25 minority (12 Black or African American, non-Hispanic/Latino; 1 American Indian or Alaska Native, non-Hispanic/Latino; 6 Asian, non-Hispanic/Latino; 5 Hispanic/Latino; 1 Two or more races, non-Hispanic/Latino), 27 international. Average age 28. 192 applicants, 63% accepted, 91 enrolled. In 2016, 94 master's awarded. *Entrance requirements:* For master's, GMAT, GRE, official transcript from colleges attended, current resume. Additional exam requirements/recommendations for international students: Required—TOEFL (minimum score 550 paper-based, 80 iBT), IELTS (minimum score 6.5), or CAEL (minimum score 70). *Application deadline:* For fall admission, 7/1 priority date for domestic students; for spring admission, 11/1 priority date for domestic students. Applications are processed on a rolling basis. Application fee: $25. Electronic applications accepted. Application fee is waived when completed online. *Expenses: Tuition:* Full-time $14,742. *Required fees:* $724. *Financial support:* Career-related internships or fieldwork, Federal Work-Study, scholarships/grants, tuition waivers (partial), and unspecified assistantships available. Support available to part-time students. Financial award application deadline: 4/30; financial award applicants required to submit FAFSA. *Faculty research:* Global leadership effectiveness, global supply chain management, quality management. *Unit head:* Dr. Gordon W. Meyer, Chair of Management, Entrepreneurship and International Business, 716-888-2634, E-mail: meyerg@canisius.edu. *Application contact:* Kathleen B. Davis, Vice President of Enrollment Management, 716-888-2500, Fax: 716-888-3195, E-mail: daviskb@canisius.edu.
Website: http://www.canisius.edu/graduate/

Central European University, Department of Legal Studies, Budapest, Hungary. Offers comparative Constitutional law (LL M); human rights (LL M, MA); international business law (LL M); juridical sciences (SJD); law and economics (LL M, MA). *Faculty:* 10 full-time (5 women), 15 part-time/adjunct (3 women). *Students:* 89 full-time (43 women). Average age 27. 420 applicants, 27% accepted, 66 enrolled. In 2016, 52 master's, 4 doctorates awarded. Terminal master's awarded for partial completion of doctoral program. *Degree requirements:* For master's, one foreign language, thesis; for doctorate, one foreign language, comprehensive exam, thesis/dissertation. *Entrance requirements:* For master's and doctorate, LSAT. Additional exam requirements/recommendations for international students: Required—TOEFL (minimum score 570 paper-based); Recommended—IELTS (minimum score 6.5). *Application deadline:* For fall admission, 2/4 for domestic and international students. Application fee: $30. Electronic applications accepted. *Expenses:* Contact institution. *Financial support:* Fellowships, career-related internships or fieldwork, institutionally sponsored loans, scholarships/grants, and tuition waivers (full and partial) available. Financial award application deadline: 2/4. *Faculty research:* Institutional, Constitutional and human rights in European Union law;

biomedical law and reproductive rights; data protection law; comparative and international business law and the regulation of business environments;. *Unit head:* Dr. Karoly Bard, Head of Department, 36 1 327-3294, Fax: 361-327-3198, E-mail: legalst@ceu.edu. *Application contact:* Zsuzsanna Jaszberenyi, Department Coordinator, 361-327-3272, Fax: 361-327-3198, E-mail: admissions@ceu.edu.
Website: http://legal.ceu.edu

Central Michigan University, College of Graduate Studies, College of Business Administration, MBA Program, Mount Pleasant, MI 48859. Offers accounting (MBA); business economics (MBA); consulting (MBA); finance (MBA); general business (MBA); human resource management (MBA); information systems (MBA); international business (MBA); logistics management (MBA); marketing (MBA); value-driven organization (MBA). *Program availability:* Part-time, evening/weekend, online learning. Electronic applications accepted. *Faculty research:* Accounting, consulting, international business, marketing, information systems.

Central Michigan University, College of Graduate Studies, Interdisciplinary Administration Programs, Mount Pleasant, MI 48859. Offers acquisitions administration (MSA, Graduate Certificate); general administration (MSA, Graduate Certificate); health services administration (MSA, Graduate Certificate); human resource administration (Graduate Certificate); human resources administration (MSA); information resource management (MSA, Graduate Certificate); international administration (MSA, Graduate Certificate); leadership (MSA, Graduate Certificate); public administration (MSA, Graduate Certificate); research administration (Graduate Certificate); sport administration (MSA). *Accreditation:* AACSB. *Program availability:* Part-time, evening/weekend, online learning. *Degree requirements:* For master's, thesis or alternative. *Entrance requirements:* For master's, bachelor's degree with minimum GPA of 2.7. Electronic applications accepted. *Faculty research:* Interdisciplinary studies in acquisitions administration, health services administration, sport administration, recreation and park administration, and international administration.

Christian Brothers University, School of Business, Memphis, TN 38104-5581. Offers accountancy (M Acc); business (MBA); international business (MIB); project management (Certificate); MBA/MIB. *Program availability:* Part-time, evening/weekend. *Entrance requirements:* For master's, GMAT, GRE. Additional exam requirements/recommendations for international students: Required—TOEFL.

City University of Seattle, Graduate Division, School of Management, Seattle, WA 98121. Offers accounting (Certificate); change leadership (MBA, Certificate); computer systems (MS); finance (Certificate); financial management (MBA); general management (MBA); general management-Europe (MBA); global marketing (MBA); human resources management (Certificate); individualized study (MBA); information security (MS); information systems (MBA); leadership (MA); marketing (MBA, Certificate); project management (MBA, MS, Certificate); sustainable business (Certificate); technology management (MBA, Certificate). *Program availability:* Part-time, evening/weekend, online learning. *Degree requirements:* For master's, comprehensive exam (for some programs), thesis (for some programs). *Entrance requirements:* For master's, baccalaureate degree or equivalent from an accredited or otherwise recognized institution. Additional exam requirements/recommendations for international students: Required—TOEFL (minimum score 567 paper-based; 87 iBT); Recommended—IELTS. Electronic applications accepted.

Clarkson University, School of Business, Master's Program in Business Administration, Potsdam, NY 13699. Offers business administration (MBA); business fundamentals (Advanced Certificate); global supply chain management (Advanced Certificate); human resource management (Advanced Certificate); management and leadership (Advanced Certificate). *Accreditation:* AACSB. *Program availability:* Part-time, evening/weekend, 100% online, blended/hybrid learning. *Faculty:* 53 full-time (12 women), 33 part-time/adjunct (6 women). *Students:* 119 full-time (45 women), 51 part-time (19 women); includes 23 minority (5 Black or African American, non-Hispanic/Latino; 1 American Indian or Alaska Native, non-Hispanic/Latino; 10 Asian, non-Hispanic/Latino; 4 Hispanic/Latino; 3 Two or more races, non-Hispanic/Latino), 14 international. 390 applicants, 39% accepted, 101 enrolled. In 2016, 91 master's, 2 other advanced degrees awarded. *Entrance requirements:* For master's, GRE or GMAT. Additional exam requirements/recommendations for international students: Required—TOEFL (minimum score 550 paper-based, 80 iBT) or IELTS (6.5). *Application deadline:* Applications are processed on a rolling basis. Application fee: $50. Electronic applications accepted. *Expenses: Tuition:* Full-time $23,400; part-time $1300 per credit hour. Tuition and fees vary according to campus/location and program. *Financial support:* Scholarships/grants available. *Unit head:* Dr. Alan Bowman, Senior Associate Dean of Graduate Business Programs, 518-631-9887, E-mail: abowman@clarkson.edu. *Application contact:* Erin Wheeler, Graduate Admissions Contact, 518-631-9910, E-mail: ewheeler@clarkson.edu.

Clayton State University, School of Graduate Studies, College of Business, Program in Business Administration, Morrow, GA 30260-0285. Offers accounting (MBA); human resource leadership (MBA); international business (MBA); sports and entertainment management (MBA); supply chain management (MBA). *Accreditation:* AACSB. *Program availability:* Part-time, evening/weekend. *Degree requirements:* For master's, thesis. *Entrance requirements:* For master's, GMAT, 3 letters of recommendation; statement of purpose; 2 official transcripts. Additional exam requirements/recommendations for international students: Required—TOEFL (minimum score 550 paper-based; 80 iBT). Electronic applications accepted. *Expenses:* Contact institution.

Colorado State University–Global Campus, Graduate Programs, Greenwood Village, CO 80111. Offers criminal justice and law enforcement administration (MS); education leadership (MS); finance (MS); healthcare administration and management (MS); human resource management (MHRM); information technology management (MITM); international management (MS); management (MS); organizational leadership (MS); professional accounting (MPA); project management (MS); teaching and learning (MS). *Accreditation:* ACBSP. *Program availability:* Online learning.

Columbia University, Graduate School of Business, Executive MBA Global Program, New York, NY 10027. Offers EMBA. Program offered jointly with London Business School. *Entrance requirements:* For master's, GMAT, 2 letters of reference, interview, minimum 5 years of work experience, curriculum vitae or resume, employer support. Additional exam requirements/recommendations for international students: Recommended—TOEFL, IELTS. Electronic applications accepted. *Expenses:* Contact institution.

Columbia University, Graduate School of Business, MBA Program, New York, NY 10027. Offers accounting (MBA); decision, risk, and operations (MBA); entrepreneurship (MBA); finance and economics (MBA); healthcare and pharmaceutical management (MBA); human resource management (MBA); international business (MBA); leadership and ethics (MBA); management (MBA); marketing (MBA); media (MBA); private equity (MBA); real estate (MBA); social enterprise (MBA); value investing (MBA); DDS/MBA; JD/MBA; MBA/MIA; MBA/MPH; MBA/MS; MD/MBA. *Entrance requirements:* For master's, GMAT, 2 letters of recommendation. Additional exam requirements/recommendations for international students: Required—TOEFL. Electronic applications accepted. *Expenses:* Contact institution. *Faculty research:* Human decision making and behavioral research; real estate market and mortgage defaults; financial crisis and corporate governance; international business; security analysis and accounting.

Concordia University Wisconsin, Graduate Programs, School of Business Administration, MBA Program, Mequon, WI 53097-2402. Offers finance (MBA); health care administration (MBA); human resource management (MBA); international business (MBA); international business-bilingual English/Chinese (MBA); management (MBA); management information systems (MBA); managerial communications (MBA); marketing (MBA); public administration (MBA); risk management (MBA). *Program availability:* Online learning. *Degree requirements:* For master's, comprehensive exam, thesis or alternative. *Entrance requirements:* Additional exam requirements/recommendations for international students: Required—TOEFL. *Application deadline:* For fall admission, 8/1 priority date for domestic students; for spring admission, 1/15 for domestic students. Applications are processed on a rolling basis. Application fee: $50. *Expenses:* Contact institution. *Financial support:* Application deadline: 8/1. *Unit head:* Dr. David Borst, Director, 262-243-4298, Fax: 262-243-4428, E-mail: david.borst@cuw.edu. *Application contact:* Mary Eberhardt, Graduate Admissions, 262-243-4551, Fax: 262-243-4428, E-mail: mary.eberhardt@cuw.edu.

Copenhagen Business School, Graduate Programs, Copenhagen, Denmark. Offers business administration (Exec MBA, MBA, PhD); business administration and information systems (M Sc); business, language and culture (M Sc); economics and business administration (M Sc); health management (MHM); international business and politics (M Sc); public administration (MPA); shipping and logistics (Exec MBA); technology, market and organization (MBA).

Daemen College, Department of Accounting/Information Systems, Amherst, NY 14226-3592. Offers global business (MS), including accounting, global business, management information systems, marketing. *Program availability:* Part-time, evening/weekend. *Degree requirements:* For master's, minimum GPA of 3.0. *Entrance requirements:* For master's, GMAT if undergraduate GPA is less than 3.0, 2 letters of recommendation; goal statement; transcripts; demonstration of satisfactory oral and written English. Additional exam requirements/recommendations for international students: Required—TOEFL (minimum score 500 paper-based; 63 iBT), IELTS (minimum score 5.5). Electronic applications accepted. *Faculty research:* Internationalization of small business, cultural influences on business practices, international human resource practices.

Dallas Baptist University, College of Business, Business Administration Program, Dallas, TX 75211-9299. Offers accounting (MBA); business communication (MBA); conflict resolution management (MBA); entrepreneurship (MBA); finance (MBA); health care management (MBA); international business (MBA); leading the non-profit organization (MBA); management (MBA); management information systems (MBA); marketing (MBA); project management (MBA); technology and engineering management (MBA). *Accreditation:* ACBSP. *Program availability:* Part-time, evening/weekend, 100% online, blended/hybrid learning. *Application deadline:* Applications are processed on a rolling basis. Application fee: $25. Electronic applications accepted. Application fee is waived when completed online. *Expenses: Tuition:* Full-time $15,408; part-time $856 per credit hour. *Required fees:* $400 per semester. Tuition and fees vary according to course load and degree level. *Unit head:* Dr. Sandra Reid, Chair of Graduate Business Programs, 214-333-5280, E-mail: sandra@dbu.edu. *Application contact:* Bobby Soto, Director of Admissions, 214-333-5242, E-mail: graduate@dbu.edu.
Website: http://www3.dbu.edu/graduate/mba.asp

Dallas Baptist University, Gary Cook School of Leadership, Program in International Studies, Dallas, TX 75211-9299. Offers East Asian studies (MA); European studies (MA); general international studies (MA); global business (MA); international immersion (MA); international ministry (MA); international relations (MA). *Program availability:* Part-time, evening/weekend. *Application deadline:* Applications are processed on a rolling basis. Application fee: $25. Electronic applications accepted. Application fee is waived when completed online. *Expenses: Tuition:* Full-time $15,408; part-time $856 per credit hour. *Required fees:* $400 per semester. Tuition and fees vary according to course load and degree level. *Unit head:* Dr. Brent A. Thomason, Director, 214-333-5236, E-mail: brentt@dbu.edu. *Application contact:* Bobby Soto, Director of Admissions, 214-333-5242, E-mail: graduate@dbu.edu.
Website: http://www4.dbu.edu/leadership/mainternational

Dallas Baptist University, Graduate School of Ministry, Program in Global Leadership, Dallas, TX 75211-9299. Offers church planting (MA); East Asian Studies (MA); English as a second language (MA); general studies (MA); global communication (MA); global studies (MA); international business (MA); leading the nonprofit organization (MA); missions (MA); small group ministry (MA); urban ministry (MA). *Program availability:* Part-time, evening/weekend. *Application deadline:* Applications are processed on a rolling basis. Application fee: $25. Electronic applications accepted. Application fee is waived when completed online. *Expenses: Tuition:* Full-time $15,408; part-time $856 per credit hour. *Required fees:* $400 per semester. Tuition and fees vary according to course load and degree level. *Unit head:* Dr. Bob Garrett, Director, 214-333-5508, E-mail: bobg@dbu.edu. *Application contact:* Bobby Soto, Director of Admissions, 214-333-5242, E-mail: graduate@dbu.edu.
Website: http://www3.dbu.edu/gsom/global-leadership/

Delaware Valley University, MBA Program, Doylestown, PA 18901-2697. Offers accounting (MBA); entrepreneurship (MBA); finance (MBA); food and agribusiness (MBA); general business (MBA); global executive leadership (MBA); human resource management (MBA); supply chain management (MBA). *Program availability:* Part-time, evening/weekend, online learning. *Entrance requirements:* For master's, minimum undergraduate GPA of 3.0. Electronic applications accepted. *Expenses:* Contact institution.

Dominican University of California, Barowsky School of Business, San Rafael, CA 94901-2298. Offers global business (MBA); strategic leadership (MBA), sustainable enterprise (MBA). *Program availability:* Part-time, evening/weekend. *Degree requirements:* For master's, thesis, capstone (for MBA). *Entrance requirements:* For master's, minimum GPA of 3.0. Additional exam requirements/recommendations for international students: Required—TOEFL (minimum score 550 paper-based; 80 iBT), IELTS (minimum score 6.5). Electronic applications accepted. Application fee is waived when completed online. *Expenses:* Contact institution.

Duke University, The Fuqua School of Business, The Duke MBA-Global Executive Program, Durham, NC 27708-0586. Offers business administration (MBA); energy and environment (MBA); entrepreneurship and innovation (MBA); finance (MBA); health sector management (Certificate); marketing (MBA); strategy (MBA). *Faculty:* 88 full-time (19 women), 50 part-time/adjunct (9 women). *Students:* 48 full-time (14 women); includes 18 minority (3 Black or African American, non-Hispanic/Latino; 11 Asian, non-Hispanic/Latino; 4 Hispanic/Latino), 10 international. Average age 39. In 2016, 27 master's awarded. *Entrance requirements:* For master's, transcripts, essays, resume, recommendation letters, letter of company support, interview. *Application deadline:* For fall admission, 10/12 priority date for domestic and international students; for winter admission, 12/7 priority date for domestic and international students; for spring admission, 3/20 priority date for domestic and international students; for summer

admission, 5/31 for domestic and international students. Applications are processed on a rolling basis. Application fee: $225. Electronic applications accepted. *Expenses:* Contact institution. *Financial support:* In 2016–17, 22 students received support. Institutionally sponsored loans and scholarships/grants available. Financial award applicants required to submit FAFSA. *Unit head:* Mohan Venkatachalam, Senior Associate Dean, Executive Programs, 919-660-7859, E-mail: mohan.venkatachalam@duke.edu. *Application contact:* Sharon Thompson, Assistant Dean, Office of Admissions, 919-660-7705, Fax: 919-681-8026, E-mail: admissions-info@fuqua.duke.edu.
Website: http://www.fuqua.duke.edu/programs/duke_mba/global-executive/

Duke University, The Fuqua School of Business, MMS: Duke Kunshan University Program, Durham, NC 27708-0586. Offers MMS. *Faculty:* 88 full-time (19 women), 50 part-time/adjunct (9 women). *Students:* 50 full-time (32 women); includes 2 minority (both Asian, non-Hispanic/Latino), 43 international. Average age 22. In 2016, 24 master's awarded. *Entrance requirements:* For master's, GMAT or GRE, transcripts, essays, resume, recommendation letters, interview. *Application deadline:* For fall admission, 9/13 for domestic and international students; for winter admission, 1/30 for domestic and international students; for spring admission, 3/7 for domestic and international students; for summer admission, 4/4 for domestic and international students. Application fee: $0. Electronic applications accepted. *Financial support:* Applicants required to submit FAFSA. *Unit head:* Patrick Moreton, Associate Dean, 919-660-7741, Fax: 919-681-6244, E-mail: patrick.moreton@dku.edu.cn. *Application contact:* Sharon Thompson, Assistant Dean, Office of Admissions, 919-660-7705, Fax: 919-681-8026, E-mail: mms-dku-info@fuqua.duke.edu.
Website: http://www.fuqua.duke.edu/mms-duke-kunshan/

D'Youville College, Department of Business, Buffalo, NY 14201-1084. Offers business administration (MBA); international business (MS). *Program availability:* Part-time, evening/weekend. *Degree requirements:* For master's, one foreign language, project or thesis. *Entrance requirements:* For master's, minimum GPA of 3.0. Additional exam requirements/recommendations for international students: Required—TOEFL (minimum score 500 paper-based). Electronic applications accepted. *Faculty research:* Assessment, accreditation, supply chain, online learning, adult learning.

Eastern Michigan University, Graduate School, College of Arts and Sciences, Department of World Languages, Program in Language and International Trade, Ypsilanti, MI 48197. Offers MA. *Program availability:* Evening/weekend. In 2016, 1 master's awarded. *Degree requirements:* For master's, one foreign language. *Entrance requirements:* Additional exam requirements/recommendations for international students: Required—TOEFL. *Application deadline:* Applications are processed on a rolling basis. Application fee: $45. *Financial support:* Fellowships, research assistantships with full tuition reimbursements, teaching assistantships with full tuition reimbursements, career-related internships or fieldwork, Federal Work-Study, institutionally sponsored loans, scholarships/grants, tuition waivers (partial), and unspecified assistantships available. Support available to part-time students. Financial award applicants required to submit FAFSA. *Application contact:* Dr. Margrit Zinggeler, Program Advisor, 734-487-1498, Fax: 734-487-3411, E-mail: mzinggele@emich.edu.

Eastern Michigan University, Graduate School, College of Business, Department of Marketing, Ypsilanti, MI 48197. Offers e-business (MBA); integrated marketing communications (MS, Postbaccalaureate Certificate); international business (MBA); marketing management (MBA); supply chain management (MBA). *Program availability:* Part-time, evening/weekend, online learning. *Faculty:* 23 full-time (9 women). *Students:* 15 full-time (11 women), 40 part-time (33 women); includes 14 minority (10 Black or African American, non-Hispanic/Latino; 4 Two or more races, non-Hispanic/Latino). Average age 32. 29 applicants, 72% accepted, 15 enrolled. In 2016, 23 master's, 1 other advanced degree awarded. *Entrance requirements:* For master's, GMAT. Additional exam requirements/recommendations for international students: Required—TOEFL. *Application deadline:* For fall admission, 5/15 priority date for domestic students, 2/15 priority date for international students; for winter admission, 10/15 priority date for domestic students, 9/1 priority date for international students; for summer admission, 3/15 priority date for domestic students, 3/1 priority date for international students. Applications are processed on a rolling basis. Application fee: $45. *Financial support:* Fellowships, research assistantships with full tuition reimbursements, teaching assistantships with full tuition reimbursements, career-related internships or fieldwork, Federal Work-Study, institutionally sponsored loans, scholarships/grants, tuition waivers (partial), and unspecified assistantships available. Support available to part-time students. Financial award applicants required to submit FAFSA. *Unit head:* Dr. Lewis Hershey, Department Head, 734-487-3323, Fax: 734-487-7099, E-mail: lhershe1@emich.edu. *Application contact:* K. Michelle Henry, Director, Graduate Business Programs, 734-487-4444, Fax: 734-483-1316, E-mail: cob.graduate@emich.edu.
Website: http://www.mkt.emich.edu/index.html

Eastern Michigan University, Graduate School, College of Business, Programs in Business Administration, Ypsilanti, MI 48197. Offers business administration (MBA, Graduate Certificate); computer information systems (Graduate Certificate); e-business (MBA, Graduate Certificate); enterprise business intelligence (MBA); entrepreneurship (MBA, Graduate Certificate); finance (MBA, Graduate Certificate); human resources (MBA); human resources management (Graduate Certificate); information systems (MBA); internal auditing (MBA); international business (MBA, Graduate Certificate); marketing management (Graduate Certificate); nonprofit management (MBA); organizational development (Graduate Certificate); supply chain management (MBA, Graduate Certificate). *Accreditation:* AACSB. *Program availability:* Part-time, online learning. *Students:* 63 full-time (36 women), 320 part-time (186 women); includes 131 minority (76 Black or African American, non-Hispanic/Latino; 5 American Indian or Alaska Native, non-Hispanic/Latino; 16 Asian, non-Hispanic/Latino; 19 Hispanic/Latino; 15 Two or more races, non-Hispanic/Latino), 23 international. Average age 32. 305 applicants, 70% accepted, 124 enrolled. In 2016, 78 master's, 57 other advanced degrees awarded. *Entrance requirements:* For master's, GMAT (minimum score 450), minimum cumulative undergraduate GPA of 2.75. Additional exam requirements/recommendations for international students: Required—TOEFL. *Application deadline:* For fall admission, 5/15 priority date for domestic students, 2/15 priority date for international students; for winter admission, 10/15 priority date for domestic students, 9/1 priority date for international students; for summer admission, 3/15 priority date for domestic students, 3/1 priority date for international students. Applications are processed on a rolling basis. Application fee: $45. *Financial support:* Fellowships, research assistantships with full tuition reimbursements, teaching assistantships with full tuition reimbursements, career-related internships or fieldwork, Federal Work-Study, institutionally sponsored loans, scholarships/grants, tuition waivers (partial), and unspecified assistantships available. Support available to part-time students. Financial award applicants required to submit FAFSA. *Unit head:* K. Michelle Henry, Director, Graduate Business Programs, 734-487-4444, Fax: 734-483-1316, E-mail: cob.graduate@emich.edu.
Website: http://www.emich.edu/cob/mba/

Embry-Riddle Aeronautical University–Worldwide, Department of Decision Sciences, Daytona Beach, FL 32114-3900. Offers aviation and aerospace (MSPM); aviation/aerospace management (MSEM); financial management (MSEM, MSPM); general management (MSPM); global management (MSPM); human resources management (MSPM); information systems (MSPM); leadership (MSEM, MSPM); logistics and supply chain management (MSEM, MSLSCM, MSPM); management (MSEM, MSPM); project management (MSEM); systems engineering (MSEM, MSPM); technical management (MSPM). *Program availability:* Part-time, evening/weekend, 100% online, blended/hybrid learning, EagleVision is a virtual classroom that combines Web video conferencing and a learning management system. EagleVision Classroom (between classrooms), EagleVision Home (faculty and students at home), and a blend of Classroom or Home. *Degree requirements:* For master's, comprehensive exam (for some programs), thesis (for some programs). *Entrance requirements:* Additional exam requirements/recommendations for international students: Required—TOEFL (minimum score 550 paper-based; 79 iBT), IELTS (minimum score 6), TOEFL or IELTS accepted. Electronic applications accepted. *Expenses:* Contact institution.

Embry-Riddle Aeronautical University–Worldwide, Department of Management, Daytona Beach, FL 32114-3900. Offers global management (MS); human resources management (MS); leadership (MS); operations management (MS); project management (MS). *Program availability:* Part-time, evening/weekend, 100% online, blended/hybrid learning, EagleVision is a virtual classroom that combines Web video conferencing and a learning management system. EagleVision Classroom (between classrooms), EagleVision Home (faculty and students at home), and a blend of Classroom or Home. *Entrance requirements:* Additional exam requirements/recommendations for international students: Required—TOEFL (minimum score 550 paper-based; 79 iBT), IELTS (minimum score 6), TOEFL or IELTS accepted. Electronic applications accepted. *Expenses:* Contact institution.

Emerson College, Graduate Studies, School of Communication, Department of Marketing Communication, Program in Global Marketing Communication and Advertising, Boston, MA 02116-4624. Offers MA. *Faculty:* 16 full-time (6 women), 5 part-time/adjunct (1 woman). *Students:* 21 full-time (16 women), 1 (woman) part-time; includes 4 minority (3 Hispanic/Latino; 1 Two or more races, non-Hispanic/Latino), 15 international. Average age 25. 43 applicants, 93% accepted, 20 enrolled. In 2016, 31 master's awarded. *Entrance requirements:* For master's, GMAT or GRE General Test. Additional exam requirements/recommendations for international students: Required—TOEFL (minimum score 550 paper-based; 80 iBT), IELTS (minimum score 6.5). *Application deadline:* For fall admission, 3/1 priority date for domestic and international students. Applications are processed on a rolling basis. Application fee: $60 ($75 for international students). Electronic applications accepted. *Financial support:* In 2016–17, 21 students received support, including 21 fellowships with partial tuition reimbursements available (averaging $8,306 per year); research assistantships with partial tuition reimbursements available, Federal Work-Study, scholarships/grants, and unspecified assistantships also available. Financial award application deadline: 3/1; financial award applicants required to submit FAFSA. *Faculty research:* International business, marketing. *Application contact:* Leanda Ferland, Director of Graduate Admission, 617-824-8610, Fax: 617-824-8614, E-mail: gradapp@emerson.edu.
Website: http://www.emerson.edu/academics/departments/marketing-communication/graduate-degrees/global-marketing-communication-advertising

Emory University, Goizueta Business School, Full Time MBA Program, Atlanta, GA 30322. Offers accounting (MBA); alternative investments (MBA); business process consulting (MBA); business technology management (MBA); capital markets (MBA); corporate finance (MBA); customer relationship management (MBA); decision analytics (MBA); entrepreneurship (MBA); finance (MBA); global management (MBA); investment banking (MBA); management consulting (MBA); marketing (MBA); marketing analytics (MBA); marketing consulting (MBA); operations management (MBA); organization and management (MBA); product and brand management (MBA); real estate (MBA); social enterprise (MBA); strategy consulting (MBA). *Accreditation:* AACSB. *Faculty:* 72 full-time (17 women), 18 part-time/adjunct (5 women). *Students:* 350 full-time (101 women); includes 77 minority (21 Black or African American, non-Hispanic/Latino; 3 American Indian or Alaska Native, non-Hispanic/Latino; 32 Asian, non-Hispanic/Latino; 15 Hispanic/Latino; 2 Native Hawaiian or other Pacific Islander, non-Hispanic/Latino; 4 Two or more races, non-Hispanic/Latino), 117 international. Average age 29. 1,434 applicants, 31% accepted, 181 enrolled. In 2016, 182 master's awarded. *Degree requirements:* For master's, 1 leadership course; 2 mid-semester module programs; 2 global components. *Entrance requirements:* For master's, GMAT/GRE, essays; recommendation letters; undergraduate degree; interview. Additional exam requirements/recommendations for international students: Required—TOEFL (minimum score 100 iBT), IELTS (minimum score 7), PTE (minimum score 68). *Application deadline:* For fall admission, 10/14 priority date for domestic and international students; for winter admission, 11/11 priority date for domestic and international students; for spring admission, 1/4 priority date for domestic students, 1/4 for international students. Application fee: $150. Electronic applications accepted. *Expenses:* $57,580. *Financial support:* In 2016–17, 289 students received support. Career-related internships or fieldwork, institutionally sponsored loans, and scholarships/grants available. Financial award application deadline: 4/1; financial award applicants required to submit FAFSA. *Faculty research:* Social enterprise; micro vs. large business; mobile health data; mutual fund performance; product evaluation. *Unit head:* Brian Mitchell, Associate Dean, 404-727-4824, Fax: 404-712-9648, E-mail: brian.mitchell@emory.edu. *Application contact:* Julie Barefoot, Associate Dean, 404-727-6311, Fax: 404-727-4612, E-mail: mbaadmissions@emory.edu.
Website: http://www.goizueta.emory.edu

ESSEC Business School, Graduate Programs, Paris, France. Offers business administration (PhD); executive business administration (MBA); global business administration (MBA); hospitality management (MBA); international luxury brand management (MBA); management (MSM).

Everest University, Department of Business Administration, Tampa, FL 33614. Offers accounting (MBA); human resources (MBA); international business (MBA). *Program availability:* Part-time, evening/weekend. *Degree requirements:* For master's, thesis optional. *Entrance requirements:* For master's, GMAT or GRE General Test, minimum GPA of 3.0.

Fairfield University, Dolan School of Business, Fairfield, CT 06824. Offers accounting (MBA, MS, CAS); business analytics (MS); entrepreneurship (MBA); finance (MBA, MS, CAS); general management (MBA, CAS); global management (MBA); human resource management (MBA, CAS); information systems and business analytics (MBA); marketing (MBA, CAS); taxation (MBA, CAS). *Accreditation:* AACSB. *Program availability:* Part-time, evening/weekend. *Faculty:* 20 full-time (6 women), 4 part-time/adjunct (1 woman). *Students:* 106 full-time (41 women), 57 part-time (26 women); includes 18 minority (4 Black or African American, non-Hispanic/Latino; 1 American Indian or Alaska Native, non-Hispanic/Latino; 4 Asian, non-Hispanic/Latino; 7 Hispanic/Latino; 2 Two or more races, non-Hispanic/Latino), 39 international. Average age 26. 136 applicants, 63% accepted, 35 enrolled. In 2016, 90 master's awarded. *Degree requirements:* For master's, capstone course. *Entrance requirements:* For master's, GMAT (minimum score 500), 2 letters of reference, resume, minimum GPA of 3.0. Additional exam requirements/recommendations for international students: Required—TOEFL (minimum score 550 paper-based; 80 iBT) or IELTS (minimum score 6.5). *Application deadline:* For fall admission, 5/15 for international students; for spring admission, 10/15 for international students. Applications are processed on a rolling

basis. Application fee: $60. Electronic applications accepted. *Expenses:* $875 per credit hour. *Financial support:* In 2016–17, 33 students received support. Scholarships/grants and unspecified assistantships available. Financial award applicants required to submit FAFSA. *Faculty research:* International finance, leadership and careers, ethics in accounting, emotions in consumer behavior and organizations, data analytics. *Unit head:* Dr. Donald Gibson, Dean, 203-254-4070, Fax: 203-254-4105, E-mail: dgibson@fairfield.edu. *Application contact:* Marianne Gumpper, Director of Graduate and Continuing Studies Admission, 203-254-4184, Fax: 203-254-4073, E-mail: gradadmis@fairfield.edu.
Website: http://fairfield.edu/mba

Fairleigh Dickinson University, College at Florham, Silberman College of Business, Department of Economics, Finance, and International Business, Program in International Business, Madison, NJ 07940-1099. Offers MBA, Certificate.

Fairleigh Dickinson University, Metropolitan Campus, Silberman College of Business, Department of Economics, Finance and International Business, Program in International Business, Teaneck, NJ 07666-1914. Offers MBA.

Florida International University, Chapman Graduate School of Business, Department of Management and International Business, Miami, FL 33199. Offers human resources management (MSHRM); international business (MIB); management and international business (EMBA, IMBA, MBA, PhD). *Program availability:* Part-time, evening/weekend. *Faculty:* 28 full-time (10 women), 30 part-time/adjunct (9 women). *Students:* 1,043 full-time (573 women), 534 part-time (271 women); includes 1,095 minority (211 Black or African American, non-Hispanic/Latino; 38 Asian, non-Hispanic/Latino; 818 Hispanic/Latino; 2 Native Hawaiian or other Pacific Islander, non-Hispanic/Latino; 26 Two or more races, non-Hispanic/Latino), 231 international. Average age 32. 1,558 applicants, 45% accepted, 530 enrolled. In 2016, 812 master's, 4 doctorates awarded. *Degree requirements:* For doctorate, comprehensive exam, thesis/dissertation. *Entrance requirements:* For master's, GMAT or GRE (depending on program), minimum GPA of 3.0 in upper-level coursework; for doctorate, GMAT or GRE, letter of intent; 3 letters of recommendation; resume. Additional exam requirements/recommendations for international students: Required—TOEFL (minimum score 550 paper-based; 80 iBT) or IELTS (minimum score 6.5). *Application deadline:* For fall admission, 6/1 for domestic students, 4/1 for international students; for spring admission, 10/1 for domestic students, 9/1 for international students. Applications are processed on a rolling basis. Application fee: $30. Electronic applications accepted. *Expenses:* Contact institution. *Financial support:* Institutionally sponsored loans and scholarships/grants available. Financial award application deadline: 3/1; financial award applicants required to submit FAFSA. *Faculty research:* International business, strategy, entrepreneurship, human resource management. *Unit head:* Dr. Willam Newburry, Chair, 305-348-2791, E-mail: newburry@fiu.edu. *Application contact:* Paula Alger, Program Manager, 305-348-7466, E-mail: palger@fiu.edu.

Florida State University, The Graduate School, College of Human Sciences, Department of Retail, Merchandising and Product Development, Tallahassee, FL 32306. Offers MS. *Program availability:* Part-time. *Faculty:* 6 full-time (5 women). *Students:* 5 full-time (all women), 1 (woman) part-time; includes 4 minority (2 Black or African American, non-Hispanic/Latino; 2 Hispanic/Latino). 8 applicants, 63% accepted, 3 enrolled. In 2016, 2 master's awarded. *Degree requirements:* For master's, thesis optional. *Entrance requirements:* For master's, GRE General Test, minimum upper-division GPA of 3.0. Additional exam requirements/recommendations for international students: Required—TOEFL (minimum score 550 paper-based; 80 iBT). *Application deadline:* For fall admission, 4/1 for domestic and international students; for spring admission, 10/1 for domestic and international students. Applications are processed on a rolling basis. Application fee: $30. Electronic applications accepted. *Expenses:* Tuition, state resident: full-time $7263; part-time $403.51 per credit hour. Tuition, nonresident: full-time $18,087; part-time $1004.85 per credit hour. *Required fees:* $1365; $75.81 per credit hour. $20 per semester. Tuition and fees vary according to campus/location. *Financial support:* In 2016–17, 7 students received support, including 4 research assistantships (averaging $4,329 per year), 8 teaching assistantships with full tuition reimbursements available (averaging $4,615 per year); career-related internships or fieldwork, institutionally sponsored loans, scholarships/grants, and unspecified assistantships also available. Financial award application deadline: 1/15; financial award applicants required to submit FAFSA. *Faculty research:* Global merchandising and product development. *Total annual research expenditures:* $35,875. *Unit head:* Dr. Robert C. Hickner, Interim Department Chair, 850-644-2498, Fax: 850-645-4673, E-mail: rhickner@fsu.edu.
Website: http://humansciences.fsu.edu/departments/retail-merchandising-and-product-development

Franklin University Switzerland, The Taylor Institute for Global Enterprise Management, 6924 Sorengo, Switzerland. Offers international management (MS).

George Mason University, College of Humanities and Social Sciences, Program in Global Affairs, Fairfax, VA 22030. Offers MA. *Faculty:* 18 full-time (8 women), 5 part-time/adjunct (3 women). *Students:* 23 full-time (13 women), 20 part-time (13 women); includes 16 minority (6 Black or African American, non-Hispanic/Latino; 1 Asian, non-Hispanic/Latino; 8 Hispanic/Latino; 1 Two or more races, non-Hispanic/Latino), 4 international. Average age 29. 42 applicants, 93% accepted, 17 enrolled. In 2016, 33 master's awarded. *Degree requirements:* For master's, capstone seminar. *Entrance requirements:* For master's, GRE, expanded goals statement, 2 letters of recommendation, evidence of professional competency in a second language tested through Language Testing International or other means approved by the department. Additional exam requirements/recommendations for international students: Required—TOEFL (minimum score 575 paper-based; 88 iBT), IELTS (minimum score 6.5), PTE (minimum score 59). *Application deadline:* For fall admission, 3/15 for domestic students. Application fee: $75 ($80 for international students). Electronic applications accepted. *Expenses:* Tuition, state resident: full-time $10,628; part-time $443 per credit. Tuition, nonresident: full-time $29,306; part-time $1221 per credit. *Required fees:* $3096; $129 per credit. Tuition and fees vary according to program. *Financial support:* Career-related internships or fieldwork, Federal Work-Study, and scholarships/grants available. Financial award application deadline: 3/1; financial award applicants required to submit FAFSA. *Faculty research:* Social movements, globalization, law and economics, comparative politics, global environmentalism and governance, international business and economic development. *Unit head:* Lisa Breglia, Director, 703-993-9184, Fax: 703-993-1244, E-mail: lbreglia@gmu.edu. *Application contact:* Stephanie Lister, Graduate Coordinator, 703-993-5056, Fax: 703-993-1244, E-mail: slister1@gmu.edu.
Website: http://globalaffairs.gmu.edu

Georgetown University, Graduate School of Arts and Sciences, Department of Economics, Washington, DC 20057. Offers econometrics (PhD); economic development (PhD); economic theory (PhD); industrial organization (PhD); international macro and finance (PhD); international trade (PhD); labor economics (PhD); macroeconomics (PhD); public economics and political economy (PhD); MA/PhD; MS/MA. *Degree requirements:* For doctorate, comprehensive exam, thesis/dissertation. *Entrance requirements:* For doctorate, GRE General Test. Additional exam requirements/recommendations for international students: Required—TOEFL. *Faculty research:* International economics, economic development.

Georgetown University, Law Center, Washington, DC 20001. Offers environmental law (LL M); global health law (LL M); global health law and international institutions (LL M); individualized study (LL M); international business and economic law (LL M); law (JD, SJD); national security law (LL M); securities and financial regulation (LL M); taxation (LL M); JD/LL M; JD/MA; JD/MBA; JD/MPH; JD/PhD. *Accreditation:* ABA. *Program availability:* Part-time, evening/weekend. *Degree requirements:* For master's, thesis; for doctorate, thesis/dissertation (for some programs). *Entrance requirements:* For master's, JD, LL B, or first law degree earned in country of origin; for doctorate, LSAT (for JD). Additional exam requirements/recommendations for international students: Required—TOEFL. *Expenses:* Contact institution. *Faculty research:* Constitutional law, legal history, jurisprudence.

The George Washington University, Elliott School of International Affairs, Program in International Trade and Investment Policy, Washington, DC 20052. Offers MA. *Program availability:* Part-time. *Students:* 30 full-time (12 women), 12 part-time (7 women); includes 15 minority (4 Black or African American, non-Hispanic/Latino; 3 Asian, non-Hispanic/Latino; 7 Hispanic/Latino; 1 Two or more races, non-Hispanic/Latino), 15 international. Average age 28. 61 applicants, 87% accepted, 15 enrolled. In 2016, 19 master's awarded. *Degree requirements:* For master's, one foreign language, capstone project. *Entrance requirements:* For master's, GRE General Test, 2 years of a modern foreign language, 2 semesters of introductory economics. Additional exam requirements/recommendations for international students: Required—TOEFL (minimum score 100 iBT), IELTS (minimum score 7). *Application deadline:* For fall admission, 1/15 priority date for domestic and international students; for spring admission, 10/1 for domestic students. Application fee: $75. Electronic applications accepted. *Financial support:* In 2016–17, 11 students received support. Fellowships with partial tuition reimbursements available, Federal Work-Study, and scholarships/grants available. Financial award application deadline: 1/15. *Unit head:* Prof. Michael Moore, Director, 202-994-5230, E-mail: itip@gwu.edu. *Application contact:* Nicole A. Campbell, Director of Graduate Admissions, 202-994-7050, Fax: 202-994-9537, E-mail: esiagrad@gwu.edu.
Website: http://elliott.gwu.edu/international-trade-investment-policy

The George Washington University, School of Business, Department of International Business, Washington, DC 20052. Offers PhD. *Program availability:* Part-time, evening/weekend. *Degree requirements:* For doctorate, thesis/dissertation. *Entrance requirements:* For doctorate, GMAT or GRE. Additional exam requirements/recommendations for international students: Required—TOEFL. *Application deadline:* For fall admission, 4/1 priority date for domestic students; for spring admission, 10/1 for domestic students. Applications are processed on a rolling basis. Application fee: $75. *Financial support:* Fellowships, teaching assistantships, career-related internships or fieldwork, Federal Work-Study, and institutionally sponsored loans available. Financial award application deadline: 4/1. *Faculty research:* International trade, competitiveness, business management. *Unit head:* Robert Weiner, Chair, 202-994-5981, E-mail: rweiner@gwu.edu. *Application contact:* Christopher Storer, Executive Director, Graduate Admissions, 202-994-1212, E-mail: gwmba@gwu.edu.
Website: http://business.gwu.edu/about-us/departments/department-of-international-business/

Georgia Institute of Technology, Graduate Studies, Scheller College of Business, Program in Business Administration, Atlanta, GA 30332-0001. Offers business administration (MBA); global business (MBA); management of technology (MBA). *Accreditation:* AACSB. *Program availability:* Part-time, evening/weekend. *Entrance requirements:* For master's, GMAT, two essays, three letters of recommendation, transcript from each college/university attended. Additional exam requirements/recommendations for international students: Required—TOEFL (minimum score 600 paper-based; 100 iBT). Electronic applications accepted. *Expenses:* Contact institution.

Georgia State University, J. Mack Robinson College of Business, Institute of International Business, Atlanta, GA 30303. Offers international business (GMBA, MBA, MIB); international business and information technology (MBA); international entrepreneurship (MBA); MIB/MIA. *Program availability:* Part-time, evening/weekend. *Faculty:* 11 full-time (4 women). *Students:* 22 full-time (14 women), 14 part-time (9 women); includes 20 minority (15 Black or African American, non-Hispanic/Latino; 4 Hispanic/Latino; 1 Two or more races, non-Hispanic/Latino), 5 international. Average age 31. 22 applicants, 27% accepted, 1 enrolled. In 2016, 31 master's awarded. *Entrance requirements:* For master's, GRE or GMAT, transcripts from all institutions attended, resume, essays. Additional exam requirements/recommendations for international students: Required—TOEFL (minimum score 610 paper-based; 101 iBT), IELTS (minimum score 7). *Application deadline:* For fall admission, 5/1 priority date for domestic students, 2/1 priority date for international students; for spring admission, 9/15 priority date for domestic students, 5/1 priority date for international students. Applications are processed on a rolling basis. Application fee: $50. Electronic applications accepted. *Expenses:* Tuition, state resident: full-time $6876; part-time $382 per credit hour. Tuition, nonresident: full-time $22,374; part-time $1243 per credit hour. *Required fees:* $2128; $1064 per term. Part-time tuition and fees vary according to course load and program. *Financial support:* Research assistantships, teaching assistantships, scholarships/grants, tuition waivers (partial), and unspecified assistantships available. Financial award application deadline: 5/1. *Faculty research:* Business challenges in emerging markets (especially in India and China); interorganizational relationships in an international context, such as strategic alliances and global supply chain relations; globalization and entry mode strategy or new (or emerging) multinationals; emerging market development and business environments; cross-cultural effects on business processes and performance. *Unit head:* Dr. Daniel Bello, Professor/Director of the Institute of International Business, 404-413-7275, Fax: 404-413-7276. *Application contact:* Toby McChesney, Assistant Dean for Graduate Recruiting and Student Services, 404-413-7167, Fax: 404-413-7162, E-mail: rcbgradadmissions@gsu.edu.
Website: http://iib.gsu.edu/

Golden Gate University, Ageno School of Business, San Francisco, CA 94105-2968. Offers accounting (MBA); business administration (EMBA, MBA, PMBA, DBA); business analytics (MS); finance (MBA, MS, Certificate); financial planning (MS, Certificate); healthcare information systems (Certificate); human resource management (MBA, MS); human resources management (Certificate); information systems (MS); information technology (MBA); information technology management (Certificate); integrated marketing and communications (MS, Certificate); international business (MBA); management (MBA); marketing (MBA, MS, Certificate); operations supply chain management (Certificate); psychology (MA, Certificate); public administration (EMPA); public relations (MS, Certificate); technical market analysis (Certificate); JD/MBA. *Program availability:* Part-time, evening/weekend. *Faculty:* 18 full-time (3 women), 117 part-time/adjunct (44 women). *Students:* 458 full-time (254 women), 664 part-time (331 women); includes 346 minority (75 Black or African American, non-Hispanic/Latino; 2 American Indian or Alaska Native, non-Hispanic/Latino; 132 Asian, non-Hispanic/Latino; 105 Hispanic/Latino; 9 Native Hawaiian or other Pacific Islander, non-Hispanic/Latino; 23 Two or more races, non-Hispanic/Latino), 354 international. Average age 34. 905 applicants, 83% accepted, 165 enrolled. In 2016, 350 master's, 2 doctorates awarded. *Degree requirements:* For doctorate, thesis/dissertation, qualifying examination.

International Business

Entrance requirements: For master's, GMAT (for MBA), minimum GPA of 2.5 (MS). Additional exam requirements/recommendations for international students: Required—TOEFL (minimum score 550 paper-based; 79 iBT). *Application deadline:* For fall admission, 5/15 for domestic and international students; for winter admission, 1/15 for domestic and international students; for spring admission, 9/15 for domestic and international students. Applications are processed on a rolling basis. Application fee: $70 ($110 for international students). Electronic applications accepted. *Expenses:* Contact institution. *Financial support:* In 2016–17, 372 students received support. Career-related internships or fieldwork, Federal Work-Study, institutionally sponsored loans, and scholarships/grants available. Support available to part-time students. Financial award applicants required to submit FAFSA. *Unit head:* Dr. Gordon Swartz, Dean, 415-442-7027, Fax: 415-442-6579, E-mail: gswartz@ggu.edu. *Application contact:* Angela Melero, Enrollment Services, 415-442-7800, Fax: 415-442-7807, E-mail: info@ggu.edu.
Website: http://www.ggu.edu/programs/business-and-management

Goldey-Beacom College, Graduate Program, Wilmington, DE 19808-1999. Offers business administration (MBA); finance (MS); financial management (MBA); health care management (MBA); human resource management (MBA); information technology (MBA); international business management (MBA); major finance (MBA); major taxation (MBA); management (MM); marketing management (MBA); taxation (MBA, MS). *Accreditation:* ACBSP. *Program availability:* Part-time, evening/weekend. *Entrance requirements:* For master's, GMAT, MAT, GRE, minimum GPA of 3.0. Additional exam requirements/recommendations for international students: Required—TOEFL (minimum score 65 iBT); Recommended—IELTS (minimum score 6). Electronic applications accepted.

Hallmark University, School of Business, San Antonio, TX 78230. Offers global management (MBA). *Faculty:* 2 full-time (0 women), 3 part-time/adjunct (1 woman). *Students:* 5 full-time (0 women); includes 2 minority (1 Hispanic/Latino; 1 Two or more races, non-Hispanic/Latino). In 2016, 1 master's awarded. *Degree requirements:* For master's, thesis (for some programs). *Entrance requirements:* For master's, bachelor's degree; minimum undergraduate GPA of 2.5; completion of one course each in college-level statistics, quanitative methods, and calculus or pre-calculus; official undergraduate transcripts; professional resume; personal statement; two letters of recommendation; two 200-word typed essays. Additional exam requirements/recommendations for international students: Required—TOEFL (minimum score 450 paper-based; 45 iBT). *Application deadline:* Applications are processed on a rolling basis. Application fee: $60 ($0 for international students). *Expenses:* Contact institution. *Financial support:* Applicants required to submit FAFSA. *Unit head:* Dr. Darla Kenward, Dean of Academics, 210-690-9000 Ext. 242, Fax: 210-697-8225, E-mail: dkenward@hallmarkuniversity.edu. *Application contact:* Jennifer Sabchez, Director of Admissions, 210-690-9000 Ext. 212, Fax: 210-697-8225, E-mail: jsanchez@hallmarkuniversity.edu.
Website: http://hallmarkuniversity.edu/business/

Harding University, Paul R. Carter College of Business Administration, Searcy, AR 72149-0001. Offers international business (MBA); leadership and organizational management (MBA). *Accreditation:* ACBSP. *Program availability:* Part-time, evening/weekend, 100% online. *Faculty:* 26 part-time/adjunct (6 women). *Students:* 36 full-time (15 women), 86 part-time (35 women); includes 17 minority (7 Black or African American, non-Hispanic/Latino; 5 Asian, non-Hispanic/Latino; 4 Hispanic/Latino; 1 Two or more races, non-Hispanic/Latino), 12 international. Average age 32. 22 applicants, 100% accepted, 22 enrolled. In 2016, 54 master's awarded. *Degree requirements:* For master's, portfolio. *Entrance requirements:* For master's, GMAT (minimum score of 500) or GRE (minimum score of 300), minimum GPA of 3.0, 2 letters of recommendation, resume, 3 essays, all official transcripts. Additional exam requirements/recommendations for international students: Required—TOEFL (minimum score 550 paper-based; 79 iBT). *Application deadline:* For fall admission, 8/1 priority date for domestic and international students; for spring admission, 12/1 priority date for domestic and international students. Applications are processed on a rolling basis. Application fee: $40. Tuition and fees vary according to degree level and program. *Financial support:* Unspecified assistantships available. Financial award application deadline: 7/30; financial award applicants required to submit FAFSA. *Unit head:* Glen Metheny, Director of Graduate Studies, 501-279-5851, Fax: 501-279-4805, E-mail: gmetheny@harding.edu. *Application contact:* Melanie Kiihnl, Recruiting Manager/Director of Marketing, 501-279-4523, Fax: 501-279-4805, E-mail: mba@harding.edu.
Website: http://www.harding.edu/mba

Hawai`i Pacific University, College of Business, Program in Business Administration, Honolulu, HI 96813. Offers accounting (MBA); economics (MBA); finance (MBA); hospitality and tourism management (MBA); human resource management (MBA); information systems (MBA); international business (MBA); management (MBA); marketing (MBA); organizational change and development (MBA). *Program availability:* Part-time, evening/weekend, online learning. *Faculty:* 13 full-time (4 women), 1 part-time/adjunct (0 women). *Students:* 106 full-time (47 women), 33 part-time (13 women); includes 66 minority (5 Black or African American, non-Hispanic/Latino; 1 American Indian or Alaska Native, non-Hispanic/Latino; 23 Asian, non-Hispanic/Latino; 11 Hispanic/Latino; 1 Native Hawaiian or other Pacific Islander, non-Hispanic/Latino; 25 Two or more races, non-Hispanic/Latino), 36 international. Average age 33. 77 applicants, 84% accepted, 44 enrolled. In 2016, 78 master's awarded. *Entrance requirements:* For master's, GMAT or GRE. Additional exam requirements/recommendations for international students: Recommended—TOEFL (minimum score 550 paper-based; 80 iBT), IELTS (minimum score 6), TWE (minimum score 5). *Application deadline:* For fall admission, 2/15 priority date for domestic students; for spring admission, 10/15 priority date for domestic students. Applications are processed on a rolling basis. Application fee: $50. Electronic applications accepted. *Expenses: Tuition:* Full-time $17,190; part-time $955 per credit. *Required fees:* $150; $26 per credit. Tuition and fees vary according to course load and program. *Financial support:* In 2016–17, 27 students received support. Research assistantships, career-related internships or fieldwork, Federal Work-Study, scholarships/grants, tuition waivers, and unspecified assistantships available. Financial award application deadline: 3/1; financial award applicants required to submit FAFSA. *Unit head:* Dr. Warren Wee, Associate Dean/Associate Professor of Accounting, 808-544-9325, E-mail: wwee@hpu.edu. *Application contact:* Danny Lam, Assistant Director of Graduate Admissions, 808-544-1135, E-mail: graduate@hpu.edu.
Website: http://www.hpu.edu/CBA/Graduate/MBA/index.html

HEC Montreal, School of Business Administration, Master of Science Programs in Administration, Program in International Business, Montréal, QC H3T 2A7, Canada. Offers M Sc. All courses are given in English. *Students:* 82 full-time (49 women), 8 part-time (4 women). 84 applicants, 40% accepted, 23 enrolled. In 2016, 25 master's awarded. *Degree requirements:* For master's, one foreign language, thesis. *Entrance requirements:* For master's, Test de francais international (TFI) with minimum score of 850 (for those who have never studied in French), BBA, undergraduate degree in another field, degree deemed equivalent by program director and minimum GPA of 3.0 on 4.3 scale. *Application deadline:* For fall admission, 3/15 for domestic and international students; for winter admission, 9/15 for domestic and international students. Application fee: $86. Electronic applications accepted. *Expenses: Tuition, area resident:* Part-time $77.80 Canadian dollars per credit. Tuition, state resident: full-time $2797 Canadian dollars; part-time $240.92 Canadian dollars per credit. Tuition, nonresident: full-time $8673 Canadian dollars; part-time $531.43 Canadian dollars per credit. *International tuition:* $19,131 Canadian dollars full-time. *Required fees:* $1699 Canadian dollars; $40.58 Canadian dollars per credit. $67.32 Canadian dollars per term. Tuition and fees vary according to degree level and program. *Financial support:* Research assistantships, teaching assistantships, and scholarships/grants available. Financial award application deadline: 9/2. *Unit head:* Dr. Marie-Helene Jobin, Director, 514-340-6283, E-mail: marie-helene.jobin@hec.ca. *Application contact:* Marianne de Moura, Administrative Director, 514-340-7106, Fax: 514-340-6411, E-mail: marianne.de-moura@hec.ca.
Website: http://www.hec.ca/en/programs/masters/master-international-business/index.html

Hofstra University, Frank G. Zarb School of Business, Programs in Marketing and International Business, Hempstead, NY 11549. Offers business administration (MBA), including international business, marketing; international business (Advanced Certificate); marketing (MS, Advanced Certificate); marketing research (MS). *Program availability:* Part-time, evening/weekend, blended/hybrid learning. *Students:* 91 full-time (61 women), 28 part-time (14 women); includes 13 minority (1 Black or African American, non-Hispanic/Latino; 8 Asian, non-Hispanic/Latino; 3 Hispanic/Latino; 1 Two or more races, non-Hispanic/Latino), 84 international. Average age 25. 323 applicants, 67% accepted, 49 enrolled. In 2016, 65 master's awarded. *Degree requirements:* For master's, capstone course (for MBA), thesis (for MS), minimum GPA of 3.0. *Entrance requirements:* For master's, GMAT/GRE, 2 letters of recommendation, resume, essay. Additional exam requirements/recommendations for international students: Required—TOEFL (minimum score 550 paper-based; 80 iBT); Recommended—IELTS (minimum score 6). *Application deadline:* Applications are processed on a rolling basis. Application fee: $75. Electronic applications accepted. *Expenses:* $1,170 per credit. *Financial support:* In 2016–17, 30 students received support, including 24 fellowships with full and partial tuition reimbursements available (averaging $4,896 per year); research assistantships with full and partial tuition reimbursements available, career-related internships or fieldwork, Federal Work-Study, institutionally sponsored loans, scholarships/grants, tuition waivers (full and partial), and unspecified assistantships also available. Support available to part-time students. Financial award applicants required to submit FAFSA. *Faculty research:* Cross-cultural consumer behavior; social, digital, global, and strategic issues in marketing; consumer health/well-being; ethnocentrism and animosity. *Unit head:* Dr. Anil Mathur, Chairperson, 516-463-5346, Fax: 516-463-4834, E-mail: anil.mathur@hofstra.edu. *Application contact:* Sunil Samuel, Assistant Vice President of Admissions, 516-463-4723, Fax: 516-463-4664, E-mail: graduateadmission@hofstra.edu.
Website: http://www.hofstra.edu/business/

Hope International University, School of Graduate and Professional Studies, Program in Business Administration, Fullerton, CA 92831-3138. Offers general management (MBA, MSM); international development (MBA, MSM); marketing management (MBA, MSM); non-profit management (MBA, MSM). *Program availability:* Part-time, online learning. *Degree requirements:* For master's, comprehensive exam (for some programs), thesis (for some programs), project. *Entrance requirements:* For master's, minimum GPA of 3.0; 2 references. Additional exam requirements/recommendations for international students: Required—TOEFL (minimum score 550 paper-based; 86 iBT); Recommended—IELTS (minimum score 6.5). Electronic applications accepted. *Expenses:* Contact institution.

Houston Baptist University, Archie W. Dunham College of Business, Program in International Business, Houston, TX 77074-3298. Offers MIB. *Program availability:* Part-time, evening/weekend. *Students:* 31 full-time (18 women), 16 part-time (12 women); includes 23 minority (12 Black or African American, non-Hispanic/Latino; 2 Asian, non-Hispanic/Latino; 9 Hispanic/Latino), 17 international. Average age 28. 94 applicants, 37% accepted, 18 enrolled. In 2016, 8 master's awarded. *Entrance requirements:* For master's, minimum GPA of 2.5, bachelor's degree conferred transcript, essay/personal statement, resume. Additional exam requirements/recommendations for international students: Required—TOEFL (minimum score 80 iBT), IELTS (minimum score 6.5). *Application deadline:* For fall admission, 8/1 for domestic students, 6/1 for international students; for spring admission, 1/1 for domestic students, 11/1 for international students; for summer admission, 5/1 for domestic students, 3/1 for international students. Applications are processed on a rolling basis. Application fee: $0 ($100 for international students). Electronic applications accepted. Application fee is waived when completed online. *Expenses:* $2,850 per 3-hour course; $1,275 annual general fee; $1,060 annual technology fee. *Financial support:* In 2016–17, 2 students received support. Federal Work-Study and scholarships/grants available. Support available to part-time students. Financial award application deadline: 4/1; financial award applicants required to submit FAFSA. *Unit head:* Dr. Michael Weeks, Dean, Archie W. Dunham College of Business, 281-649-3014, E-mail: mweeks@hbu.edu. *Application contact:* Laurel Motal, Secretary, 281-649-3306, Fax: 281-649-3436, E-mail: lmotal@hbu.edu.
Website: http://www.hbu.edu/MIB

Howard University, School of Business, Graduate Programs in Business, Washington, DC 20059-0002. Offers accounting (MBA); entrepreneurship (MBA); finance (MBA); general management (MBA); human resources management (MBA); information systems (MBA); international business (MBA); marketing (MBA); supply chain management (MBA); JD/MBA. *Accreditation:* AACSB. *Program availability:* Part-time, evening/weekend, online learning. *Entrance requirements:* For master's, GMAT, minimum 1 year post undergraduate work experience, resume, 3 letters of recommendation, advanced college algebra. Additional exam requirements/recommendations for international students: Required—TOEFL. *Faculty research:* Marketing research in multi-ethnic populations, U.S. trade policies and international relations, risk management (finance).

Hult International Business School, Graduate Programs, Cambridge, MA 02141. Offers business administration (EMBA); business analytics (MBA, MIB); business statistics (MBS); disruptive innovation (MDI); entrepreneurship (MBA, MIB); family business (MBA, MIB); finance (MBA, MF, MIB); international marketing (MIM); marketing (MBA, MIB); project management (MBA, MIB). MDI and MBS offered in San Francisco; MBA also offered in Boston, San Francisco, Dubai, Shanghai, and New York. *Students:* Average age 31. *Entrance requirements:* For master's, GMAT, 3 years of work experience. Additional exam requirements/recommendations for international students: Required—TOEFL. *Application deadline:* For fall admission, 9/1 priority date for domestic and international students; for winter admission, 11/1 priority date for domestic and international students; for spring admission, 12/1 priority date for domestic and international students; for summer admission, 6/1 for domestic and international students. Applications are processed on a rolling basis. Application fee: $150. Electronic applications accepted. *Expenses:* $75,000 (for MBA); $45,000 (for master's); $85,000 (for executive part-time MBA). *Financial support:* Scholarships/grants and tuition waivers (partial) available. Financial award application deadline: 6/1; financial award applicants required to submit FAFSA. *Application contact:* Boston Admissions Office, 617-746-1990, E-mail: postgraduate@hult.edu.
Website: http://www.hult.edu

IGlobal University, Graduate Programs, Vienna, VA 22182. Offers accounting (MBA); data management and analytics (MSIT); entrepreneurship (MBA); finance (MBA); global business management (MBA); health care management (MBA); hospitality and tourism management (MBA); human resources management (MBA); information technology (MBA); information technology systems and management (MSIT); leadership and management (MBA); project management (MBA); public service and administration (MBA); software design and management (MSIT).

Indiana Tech, Program in Global Leadership, Fort Wayne, IN 46803-1297. Offers PhD. *Program availability:* Part-time, evening/weekend, online only, 100% online. *Entrance requirements:* For doctorate, GMAT, LSAT, GRE, or MAT, official transcripts of all previous undergraduate and graduate work including evidence of completion of a master's degree at regionally-accredited institution; original essay addressing the candidate's interest in the program and intended goals; current resume including educational record, employment history and relevant accomplishments; interview. Electronic applications accepted.

Instituto Tecnologico de Santo Domingo, Graduate School, Area of Business, Santo Domingo, Dominican Republic. Offers banking and securities markets (M Mgmt); corporate finance (M Mgmt); human resources management (M Mgmt, Certificate); international trade management (M Mgmt); marketing (M Mgmt); organizational development (M Mgmt); quality and productivity management (Certificate); tax management and planning (M Mgmt); upper management (M Mgmt).

Instituto Tecnologico de Santo Domingo, Graduate School, Area of Humanities and Social Sciences, Santo Domingo, Dominican Republic. Offers accounting (Certificate); adult education (Certificate); applied linguistics (MA); economics (MA); education (M Ed); educational psychology (MA, Certificate); gender and development (MA, Certificate); humanistic studies (MA); international marketing management (Certificate); international relations in the Caribbean basin (Certificate); intervention systems in family therapy (MA); linguistic and literary communication (Certificate); pedagogical support (MA); social science education (M Ed); sustainable human development (MA); terminal illness and death psychology (Certificate); youth and adult education (M Ed).

Instituto Tecnológico y de Estudios Superiores de Monterrey, Campus Central de Veracruz, Graduate Programs, Córdoba, Mexico. Offers administration (MA); administration of information technologies (MTI); computer sciences (MCC); education (MEE); educational institution administration (MAD); educational technology (MTE); electronic commerce (MCE); finance (MAF); humanistic studies (MEH); international business for Latin America (MNL); marketing (MMT); science (MCP). *Program availability:* Part-time, evening/weekend, online learning. *Degree requirements:* For master's, thesis (for some programs). *Entrance requirements:* For master's, PAEP College Board. Electronic applications accepted.

Instituto Tecnológico y de Estudios Superiores de Monterrey, Campus Chihuahua, Graduate Programs, Chihuahua, Mexico. Offers computer systems engineering (Ingeniero); electrical engineering (Ingeniero); electromechanical engineering (Ingeniero); electronic engineering (Ingeniero); engineering administration (MEA); industrial engineering (MIE, Ingeniero); international trade (MIT); mechanical engineering (Ingeniero).

Instituto Tecnológico y de Estudios Superiores de Monterrey, Campus Ciudad de México, Virtual University Division, Ciudad de Mexico, Mexico. Offers administration of information technologies (MA); computer sciences (MA); education (MA, PhD); educational technology (MA); environmental engineering (MA); environmental systems (MA); humanistic studies (MA); industrial engineering (MA); international business for Latin America (MA); quality systems (MA); quality systems and productivity (MA). *Program availability:* Part-time, evening/weekend, online learning. *Entrance requirements:* For master's and doctorate, Instituto entrance exam. Additional exam requirements/recommendations for international students: Required—TOEFL.

Instituto Tecnológico y de Estudios Superiores de Monterrey, Campus Cuernavaca, Programs in Business Administration, Temixco, Mexico. Offers finance (MA); human resources management (MA); international business (MA); marketing (MA).

Instituto Tecnológico y de Estudios Superiores de Monterrey, Campus Irapuato, Graduate Programs, Irapuato, Mexico. Offers administration (MBA); administration of information technology (MAIT); administration of telecommunications (MAT); architecture (M Arch); computer science (MCS); education (M Ed); educational administration (MEA); educational innovation and technology (DEIT); educational technology (MET); electronic commerce (MBA); environmental administration and planning (MEAP); environmental systems (MES); finances (MBA); humanistic studies (MHS); international management for Latin American executives (MIMLAE); library and information science (MLIS); manufacturing quality management (MMQM); marketing research (MBA).

Instituto Tecnológico y de Estudios Superiores de Monterrey, Campus Monterrey, Graduate School of Business Administration and Leadership, Program in Business Administration, Monterrey, Mexico. Offers business administration (MA, MBA); finance (M Sc); international business (M Sc); marketing (M Sc). *Program availability:* Part-time. *Degree requirements:* For master's, one foreign language, thesis. *Entrance requirements:* For master's, GMAT. Additional exam requirements/recommendations for international students: Required—TOEFL. *Faculty research:* Technology management, quality management, organizational theory and behavior.

Inter American University of Puerto Rico, Metropolitan Campus, Graduate Programs, Program in International Business, San Juan, PR 00919-1293. Offers international business (MIB); interregional and international business (PhD).

Inter American University of Puerto Rico, San Germán Campus, Graduate Studies Center, Program in Business Administration, San Germán, PR 00683-5008. Offers accounting (MBA); finance (MBA); general business administration (MBA); human resources (MBA, PhD), industrial relations (MBA); information systems (MBA); international and interregional business (PhD); management (MBA); marketing (MBA). *Program availability:* Part-time, evening/weekend. *Degree requirements:* For master's, comprehensive exam. *Entrance requirements:* For master's, GRE General Test or EXADEP, minimum GPA of 3.0.

International University in Geneva, Business Programs, Geneva, Switzerland. Offers business administration (MBA, DBA); entrepreneurship (MBA); international business (MIB); international trade (MIT); sales and marketing (MBA). *Accreditation:* ACBSP. *Program availability:* Part-time, evening/weekend. *Degree requirements:* For master's, comprehensive exam. *Entrance requirements:* For master's, GMAT. Additional exam requirements/recommendations for international students: Required—TOEFL. Electronic applications accepted.

The International University of Monaco, Graduate Programs, Monte Carlo, Monaco. Offers entrepreneurship (EMBA, MBA); financial engineering (M Sc); hedge fund and private equity (M Sc); international marketing (EMBA, MBA); international wealth management (M Sc); luxury goods and services (EMBA, M Sc, MBA); wealth and asset management (EMBA, MBA). *Program availability:* Part-time. *Degree requirements:* For master's, comprehensive exam (for some programs), applied research project. *Entrance requirements:* Additional exam requirements/recommendations for international students: Required—TOEFL (minimum score 550 paper-based), IELTS. Electronic applications accepted. *Faculty research:* Gaming, leadership, disintermediation.

Iona College, Hagan School of Business, Department of Finance, Business Economics and Legal Studies, New Rochelle, NY 10801-1890. Offers finance (MS); financial management (MBA, PMC); financial services (MS); international finance (MS). *Program availability:* Part-time, evening/weekend. *Faculty:* 10 full-time (4 women), 4 part-time/adjunct (1 woman). *Students:* 37 full-time (14 women), 57 part-time (19 women); includes 24 minority (6 Black or African American, non-Hispanic/Latino; 1 American Indian or Alaska Native, non-Hispanic/Latino; 2 Asian, non-Hispanic/Latino; 14 Hispanic/Latino; 1 Native Hawaiian or other Pacific Islander, non-Hispanic/Latino), 23 international. Average age 28. 38 applicants, 100% accepted, 17 enrolled. In 2016, 72 master's awarded. *Entrance requirements:* For master's, GMAT, 2 letters of recommendation, minimum GPA of 3.0; for PMC, minimum GPA of 3.0. Additional exam requirements/recommendations for international students: Required—TOEFL (minimum score 550 paper-based; 80 iBT), IELTS (minimum score 6.5). *Application deadline:* For fall admission, 8/15 priority date for domestic students, 8/1 priority date for international students; for winter admission, 11/15 priority date for domestic students, 11/1 priority date for international students; for spring admission, 2/15 priority date for domestic students, 2/1 priority date for international students; for summer admission, 5/15 priority date for domestic students, 5/1 priority date for international students. Applications are processed on a rolling basis. Application fee: $50. Electronic applications accepted. *Expenses:* Contact institution. *Financial support:* In 2016–17, 40 students received support. Scholarships/grants, tuition waivers (partial), and unspecified assistantships available. Support available to part-time students. Financial award application deadline: 4/15; financial award applicants required to submit FAFSA. *Faculty research:* Options, insurance financing, asset depreciation ranges, international finance, emerging markets. *Unit head:* Dr. John F. Manley, Department Chair, 914-633-2284, E-mail: jmanley@iona.edu. *Application contact:* Katelyn Brunck, Director of MBA Admissions, 914-633-2451, Fax: 914-633-2277, E-mail: kbrunck@iona.edu.
Website: http://www.iona.edu/Academics/Hagan-School-of-Business/Departments/Finance-Business-Economics-Legal-Studies/Graduate-Programs.aspx

Iona College, Hagan School of Business, Department of Marketing and International Business, New Rochelle, NY 10801-1890. Offers international business (AC, PMC); marketing (MBA); sports and entertainment management (AC). *Program availability:* Part-time, evening/weekend. *Faculty:* 2 full-time (1 woman), 3 part-time/adjunct (all women). *Students:* 11 full-time (1 woman), 22 part-time (11 women); includes 9 minority (4 Black or African American, non-Hispanic/Latino; 2 Asian, non-Hispanic/Latino; 3 Hispanic/Latino), 5 international. Average age 25. 19 applicants, 100% accepted, 9 enrolled. In 2016, 22 master's awarded. *Entrance requirements:* For master's, GMAT, 2 letters of recommendation, minimum GPA of 3.0; for other advanced degree, GMAT, minimum GPA of 3.0. Additional exam requirements/recommendations for international students: Required—TOEFL (minimum score 550 paper-based; 80 iBT), IELTS (minimum score 6.5). *Application deadline:* For fall admission, 8/15 priority date for domestic students, 8/1 priority date for international students; for winter admission, 11/15 priority date for domestic students, 11/1 priority date for international students; for spring admission, 2/15 priority date for domestic students, 2/1 priority date for international students; for summer admission, 5/15 for domestic students, 5/1 priority date for international students. Applications are processed on a rolling basis. Application fee: $50. Electronic applications accepted. *Expenses:* Contact institution. *Financial support:* In 2016–17, 13 students received support. Scholarships/grants, tuition waivers (partial), and unspecified assistantships available. Support available to part-time students. Financial award application deadline: 4/15; financial award applicants required to submit FAFSA. *Faculty research:* Business ethics, international retailing, mega-marketing, consumer behavior and consumer confidence. *Unit head:* Dr. Susan G. Rozensher, Department Chair, 914-637-2748, E-mail: srozensher@iona.edu. *Application contact:* Katelyn Brunck, Director of MBA Admissions, 914-633-2451, Fax: 914-633-2277, E-mail: kbrunck@iona.edu.
Website: http://www.iona.edu/Academics/Hagan-School-of-Business/Departments/Marketing/Graduate-Programs.aspx

John Brown University, Soderquist College of Business, Siloam Springs, AR 72761-2121. Offers international business (MBA); leadership and ethics (MBA, MS). *Accreditation:* ACBSP. *Program availability:* Part-time, evening/weekend, online only, 100% online, blended/hybrid learning. *Faculty:* 4 full-time (2 women), 26 part-time/adjunct (7 women). *Students:* 42 full-time (27 women), 246 part-time (129 women); includes 65 minority (25 Black or African American, non-Hispanic/Latino; 7 American Indian or Alaska Native, non-Hispanic/Latino; 6 Asian, non-Hispanic/Latino; 15 Hispanic/Latino; 12 Two or more races, non-Hispanic/Latino), 6 international. Average age 33. 145 applicants, 80% accepted, 88 enrolled. In 2016, 114 master's awarded. *Entrance requirements:* For master's, MAT, GMAT or GRE if undergraduate GPA is less than 3.0, recommendation forms from three people, 200-word essay describing professional plans and reason for seeking acceptance. Additional exam requirements/recommendations for international students: Required—TOEFL (minimum score 550 paper-based; 79 iBT). *Application deadline:* Applications are processed on a rolling basis. Application fee: $35 ($100 for international students). Electronic applications accepted. *Expenses: Tuition:* Full-time $13,000; part-time $6500 per credit hour. Part-time tuition and fees vary according to course load and program. *Financial support:* Fellowships with full tuition reimbursements, scholarships/grants, and unspecified assistantships available. Financial award applicants required to submit FAFSA. *Faculty research:* Ethical leadership. *Unit head:* Kai Togami, Program Director, 479-524-7370, E-mail: ktogami@jbu.edu. *Application contact:* Kent Shaffer, Graduate Business Representative, 479-631-4665, E-mail: kents@jbu.edu.
Website: http://www.jbu.edu/grad/business/

Kaplan University, Davenport Campus, School of Business, Davenport, IA 52807. Offers business administration (MBA); change leadership (MS); entrepreneurship (MBA); finance (MBA); health care management (MBA, MS); human resource (MBA); international business (MBA); management (MS); marketing (MBA); project management (MBA, MS); supply chain management and logistics (MBA, MS). *Accreditation:* ACBSP. *Program availability:* Part-time, evening/weekend, online learning. *Entrance requirements:* Additional exam requirements/recommendations for international students: Required—TOEFL (minimum score 550 paper-based; 80 iBT). Electronic applications accepted.

Kean University, College of Business and Public Management, Program in Global Management, Union, NJ 07083. Offers executive management (MBA); global management (MBA). *Program availability:* Part-time, evening/weekend. *Faculty:* 3 full-time (0 women). *Students:* 57 full-time (34 women), 27 part-time (13 women); includes 42 minority (15 Black or African American, non-Hispanic/Latino; 7 Asian, non-Hispanic/Latino; 20 Hispanic/Latino), 17 international. Average age 32. 95 applicants, 60% accepted, 57 enrolled. In 2016, 30 master's awarded. *Degree requirements:* For master's, one foreign language, internship or consulting project. *Entrance requirements:* For master's, GMAT (minimum score of 500) or GRE (minimum Quantitative and Verbal scores of 152), minimum GPA of 3.0, 2 letters of recommendation, personal essay, resume; 5 years of experience (for executive management option). Additional exam requirements/recommendations for international students: Required—TOEFL (minimum

score 550 paper-based; 79 iBT), IELTS (minimum score 6.5). *Application deadline:* For fall admission, 6/1 for domestic and international students; for spring admission, 12/1 for domestic and international students. Applications are processed on a rolling basis. Application fee: $75. Electronic applications accepted. *Expenses:* Tuition, state resident: full-time $13,156; part-time $640 per credit. Tuition, nonresident: full-time $17,831; part-time $785 per credit. *Required fees:* $3316; $151 per credit. Tuition and fees vary according to course level, course load, degree level and program. *Financial support:* Scholarships/grants and unspecified assistantships available. Financial award applicants required to submit FAFSA. *Unit head:* Dr. Veysel Yucetepe, Program Coordinator, 908-737-4762, E-mail: vyucetep@kean.edu. *Application contact:* Pedro Lopes, Admissions Counselor, 908-737-7100, E-mail: grad-adm@kean.edu.
Website: http://grad.kean.edu/masters-programs/mba-global-management

Keiser University, Doctor of Business Administration Program, Ft. Lauderdale, FL 33309. Offers global business (DBA); global organizational leadership (DBA); marketing (DBA).

Keiser University, Master of Business Administration Program, Ft. Lauderdale, FL 33309. Offers accounting (MBA); health services management (MBA); information security management (MBA); international business (MBA); leadership for managers (MBA); marketing (MBA). All concentrations except information security management also offered in Mandarin; leadership for managers and international business also offered in Spanish. *Program availability:* Part-time, online learning.

Lake Forest Graduate School of Management, The Immersion MBA Program (iMBA), Lake Forest, IL 60045. Offers global business (MBA). *Program availability:* Online learning.

Lake Forest Graduate School of Management, The Leadership MBA Program, Lake Forest, IL 60045. Offers finance (MBA); global business (MBA); healthcare management (MBA); management (MBA); marketing (MBA); organizational behavior (MBA). *Program availability:* Part-time, evening/weekend. *Entrance requirements:* For master's, 4 years of work experience in field, interview, 2 letters of recommendation. Electronic applications accepted.

La Salle University, School of Business, Philadelphia, PA 19141-1199. Offers business administration (MBA, Post-MBA Certificate), including accounting, business systems and analytics, finance, general business administration, human resource management, management, marketing (Post-MBA Certificate); human capital development (MS, Certificate); international business (Post-MBA Certificate); nonprofit leadership (MS); MBA/MSN. *Accreditation:* AACSB. *Program availability:* Part-time, evening/weekend, 100% online, blended/hybrid learning. *Faculty:* 19 full-time (6 women), 20 part-time/adjunct (8 women). *Students:* 57 full-time (25 women), 295 part-time (161 women); includes 95 minority (57 Black or African American, non-Hispanic/Latino; 17 Asian, non-Hispanic/Latino; 15 Hispanic/Latino; 6 Two or more races, non-Hispanic/Latino), 17 international. Average age 32. 232 applicants, 64% accepted, 91 enrolled. In 2016, 201 master's, 2 other advanced degrees awarded. *Entrance requirements:* Additional exam requirements/recommendations for international students: Required—TOEFL. *Application deadline:* For fall admission, 8/15 priority date for domestic students, 7/15 for international students; for spring admission, 12/15 priority date for domestic students, 11/15 for international students; for summer admission, 4/15 priority date for domestic students, 3/15 for international students. Applications are processed on a rolling basis. Application fee: $35. Electronic applications accepted. Application fee is waived when completed online. *Expenses:* Contact institution. *Financial support:* In 2016–17, 63 students received support. Scholarships/grants and unspecified assistantships available. Support available to part-time students. Financial award application deadline: 8/31; financial award applicants required to submit FAFSA. *Unit head:* Dr. MarySheila McDonald, Interim Dean, 215-951-1040, Fax: 215-951-1886, E-mail: mcdonaldms@lasalle.edu. *Application contact:* Elizabeth Heenan, Director, Graduate and Adult Enrollment, 215-951-1100, Fax: 215-951-1462, E-mail: heenan@lasalle.edu.

Lenoir-Rhyne University, Graduate Programs, Charles M. Snipes School of Business, Hickory, NC 28601. Offers accounting (MBA); business analytics and information technology (MBA); entrepreneurship (MBA); global business (MBA); healthcare administration (MBA); innovation and change management (MBA); leadership development (MBA). *Accreditation:* ACBSP. *Program availability:* Part-time, evening/weekend, online learning. *Degree requirements:* For master's, capstone course. *Entrance requirements:* For master's, GMAT, GRE, MAT, minimum undergraduate GPA of 2.7, graduate 3.0. Additional exam requirements/recommendations for international students: Required—TOEFL (minimum score 600 paper-based). Electronic applications accepted. *Expenses:* Contact institution.

Lewis University, College of Business, Graduate School of Management, Program in Business Administration, Romeoville, IL 60446. Offers accounting (MBA); custom elective option (MBA); e-business (MBA); finance (MBA); healthcare management (MBA); human resources management (MBA); international business (MBA); management information systems (MBA); marketing (MBA); project management (MBA); technology and operations management (MBA). *Program availability:* Part-time, evening/weekend. *Students:* 145 full-time (72 women), 213 part-time (123 women); includes 101 minority (46 Black or African American, non-Hispanic/Latino; 2 American Indian or Alaska Native, non-Hispanic/Latino; 7 Asian, non-Hispanic/Latino; 41 Hispanic/Latino; 1 Native Hawaiian or other Pacific Islander, non-Hispanic/Latino; 4 Two or more races, non-Hispanic/Latino), 47 international. Average age 31. In 2016, 99 master's awarded. *Degree requirements:* For master's, comprehensive exam. *Entrance requirements:* For master's, interview, bachelor's degree, resume, 2 recommendations. Additional exam requirements/recommendations for international students: Required—TOEFL (minimum score 550 paper-based). *Application deadline:* For fall admission, 8/15 priority date for domestic students, 5/1 priority date for international students; for spring admission, 11/15 priority date for international students. Applications are processed on a rolling basis. Application fee: $40. Electronic applications accepted. *Expenses: Tuition:* Full-time $13,860; part-time $770 per credit hour. *Required fees:* $75 per semester. Tuition and fees vary according to degree level and program. *Financial support:* Career-related internships or fieldwork, Federal Work-Study, scholarships/grants, and unspecified assistantships available. Financial award application deadline: 5/1; financial award applicants required to submit FAFSA. *Unit head:* Dr. Maureen Culleeney, Academic Program Director, 815-838-0500 Ext. 5631, E-mail: culleema@lewisu.edu. *Application contact:* Michele Ryan, Director of Admission, 815-838-0500 Ext. 5384, E-mail: gsm@lewisu.edu.

Liberty University, School of Business, Lynchburg, VA 24515. Offers accounting (MBA, MS); business administration (MBA); criminal justice (MBA); cyber security (MS); executive leadership (MA); information systems (MS), including information assurance, technology management; international business (MBA, DBA); leadership (DBA); marketing (MBA, MS, DBA), including digital marketing and advertising (MS), project management (MS), public relations (MS), sports marketing and media (MS); project management (MBA, DBA); public administration (MBA); public relations (MBA). *Program availability:* Part-time, online learning. *Students:* 1,458 full-time (807 women), 4,188 part-time (2,041 women); includes 1,372 minority (1,060 Black or African American, non-Hispanic/Latino; 19 American Indian or Alaska Native, non-Hispanic/Latino; 85 Asian, non-Hispanic/Latino; 75 Hispanic/Latino; 10 Native Hawaiian or other Pacific Islander, non-Hispanic/Latino; 123 Two or more races, non-Hispanic/Latino), 124 international. Average age 35. 5,424 applicants, 45% accepted, 1242 enrolled. In 2016, 1,859 master's, 87 other advanced degrees awarded. *Entrance requirements:* For master's, minimum undergraduate GPA of 3.0, 15 hours of upper-level business courses. Additional exam requirements/recommendations for international students: Required—TOEFL (minimum score 600 paper-based; 100 iBT). *Application deadline:* Applications are processed on a rolling basis. Application fee: $50. Electronic applications accepted. *Expenses:* Contact institution. *Financial support:* Applicants required to submit FAFSA. *Unit head:* Dr. Scott Hicks, Dean, 434-592-4808, Fax: 434-582-2366, E-mail: smhicks@liberty.edu. *Application contact:* Jay Bridge, Director of Graduate Admissions, 800-424-9595, Fax: 800-628-7977, E-mail: gradadmissions@liberty.edu.
Website: http://www.liberty.edu/academics/business/index.cfm?PID-149

Lincoln University, Graduate Studies, Oakland, CA 94612. Offers finance and investments (DBA); finance management (MS); finance management and investments (MBA); general business (MBA); human resource management (MBA, DBA); international business (MBA, MS); management information systems (MBA). *Program availability:* Part-time. *Faculty:* 13 full-time (1 woman), 16 part-time/adjunct (3 women). *Students:* 542 full-time (215 women), 3 part-time (1 woman); includes 10 minority (8 Asian, non-Hispanic/Latino; 1 Hispanic/Latino; 1 Two or more races, non-Hispanic/Latino), 531 international. Average age 26. 800 applicants, 71% accepted, 81 enrolled. In 2016, 109 master's, 1 doctorate awarded. *Degree requirements:* For master's, research project (thesis), internship report, or comprehensive exam; for doctorate, comprehensive exam, thesis/dissertation. *Entrance requirements:* For master's, minimum GPA of 2.7; for doctorate, GMAT (minimum score: 550), GRE (minimum score: 1000), or equivalent test results (waived for master's degree with minimum cumulative GPA of 3.3). Additional exam requirements/recommendations for international students: Required—TOEFL (minimum score 525 paper-based; 71 iBT) or IELTS (minimum score 5.5) for MBA; TOEFL (minimum score 550 paper-based; 79 iBT) or IELTS (minimum score 6) for DBA; Recommended—TOEFL (minimum score 71 iBT), IELTS (minimum score 6), TSE. *Application deadline:* For fall admission, 8/7 for domestic students, 7/14 for international students; for spring admission, 11/30 for domestic students, 10/31 for international students; for summer admission, 5/29 for domestic students, 5/5 for international students. Applications are processed on a rolling basis. Application fee: $75. Electronic applications accepted. *Expenses: Tuition:* Full-time $7920. *Required fees:* $400. Tuition and fees vary according to course level, course load, degree level and program. *Financial support:* Teaching assistantships, career-related internships or fieldwork, and scholarships/grants available. Financial award applicants required to submit FAFSA. *Unit head:* Dr. Marshall Burak, Director of Graduate Programs, 510-628-8016, Fax: 510-628-8012, E-mail: mburak@lincolnuca.edu. *Application contact:* Reenu Shrestha, Assistant to the President, 510-628-8017, Fax: 510-208-2826, E-mail: sreenu@lincolnuca.edu.
Website: http://www.lincolnuca.edu/

Lindenwood University, Graduate Programs, Plaster School of Business and Entrepreneurship, St. Charles, MO 63301-1695. Offers accountancy (M Acc); accounting (MBA); business administration (MBA); entrepreneurial studies (MBA); finance (MBA, MS); human resource management (MBA); international business (MBA); leadership (MA); management (MBA); marketing (MBA, MS); nonprofit administration (MA); public administration (MBA); sport management (MA); supply chain management (MBA). *Accreditation:* ACBSP. *Program availability:* Part-time, evening/weekend, 100% online. *Faculty:* 15 full-time (6 women), 25 part-time/adjunct (7 women). *Students:* 197 full-time (97 women), 213 part-time (132 women); includes 81 minority (62 Black or African American, non-Hispanic/Latino; 1 American Indian or Alaska Native, non-Hispanic/Latino; 4 Asian, non-Hispanic/Latino; 9 Hispanic/Latino; 5 Two or more races, non-Hispanic/Latino), 83 international. Average age 31. 279 applicants, 54% accepted, 133 enrolled. In 2016, 269 master's awarded. *Degree requirements:* For master's, comprehensive exam (for some programs), thesis (for some programs), minimum GPA of 3.0. *Entrance requirements:* For master's, interview, minimum undergraduate cumulative GPA of 3.0, letter of recommendation. Additional exam requirements/recommendations for international students: Required—TOEFL (minimum score 550 paper-based; 80 iBT); Recommended—IELTS (minimum score 6.5). *Application deadline:* For fall admission, 8/28 priority date for domestic and international students; for winter admission, 1/8 priority date for domestic and international students; for spring admission, 3/5 for domestic students, 3/5 priority date for international students; for summer admission, 6/4 priority date for domestic and international students. Applications are processed on a rolling basis. Application fee: $30 ($100 for international students). Electronic applications accepted. *Expenses:* Contact institution. *Financial support:* In 2016–17, 256 students received support. Career-related internships or fieldwork, Federal Work-Study, institutionally sponsored loans, scholarships/grants, tuition waivers (partial), and unspecified assistantships available. Financial award application deadline: 6/30; financial award applicants required to submit FAFSA. *Unit head:* Roger Ellis, Dean, School of Business and Entrepreneurship, 636-949-4839, E-mail: rellis@lindenwood.edu. *Application contact:* Tyler Kostich, Director, Evening and Graduate Admissions, 636-949-4138, Fax: 636-949-4109, E-mail: adultadmissions@lindenwood.edu.
Website: http://www.lindenwood.edu/academics/academic-schools/robert-w-plaster-school-of-business-entrepreneurship/

Long Island University–LIU Post, College of Management, Brookville, NY 11548-1300. Offers accountancy (MS); finance (MBA); information systems (MS); international business (MBA); management (MBA); management engineering (MS); marketing (MBA); taxation (MS); technical project management (MS); JD/MBA. *Accreditation:* AACSB. *Program availability:* Part-time, 100% online, blended/hybrid learning. *Faculty:* 35 full-time (12 women), 25 part-time/adjunct (6 women). *Students:* 153 full-time (61 women), 68 part-time (22 women); includes 44 minority (8 Black or African American, non-Hispanic/Latino; 24 Asian, non-Hispanic/Latino; 11 Hispanic/Latino; 1 Two or more races, non-Hispanic/Latino), 79 international. 429 applicants, 58% accepted, 74 enrolled. In 2016, 124 master's awarded. *Degree requirements:* For master's, thesis (for some programs). *Entrance requirements:* For master's, GMAT, GRE, or LSAT. Additional exam requirements/recommendations for international students: Required—PTE, TOEFL (minimum score 550 paper-based, 75 iBT) or IELTS. *Application deadline:* Applications are processed on a rolling basis. Application fee: $50. Electronic applications accepted. *Expenses: Tuition:* Full-time $28,272; part-time $1178 per credit. *Required fees:* $451 per term. Tuition and fees vary according to degree level and program. *Financial support:* In 2016–17, 68 students received support. Career-related internships or fieldwork, Federal Work-Study, institutionally sponsored loans, and scholarships/grants available. Support available to part-time students. Financial award application deadline: 2/15; financial award applicants required to submit FAFSA. *Faculty research:* Finance and sustainability, innovation and intellectual property rights, marketing: data analytics and business intelligence, social networking local and international. *Unit head:* Dr. Robert M. Valli, Dean, 516-299-4192, E-mail: rob.valli@liu.edu. *Application contact:* Carol Zerah, Director of Graduate and International Admissions, 516-299-2900, Fax: 516-299-2137, E-mail: post-enroll@liu.edu.
Website: http://liu.edu/CWPost/Academics/Schools/COM

Loyola University Chicago, Quinlan School of Business, MBA Programs, Chicago, IL 60611. Offers accounting (MBA); business administration (EMBA); business ethics

(MBA); economics (MBA); entrepreneurship (MBA); finance (MBA); healthcare management (MBA); human resources management (MBA); international business (MBA); management (MBA); marketing (MBA); operation management (MBA); risk management (MBA); supply chain management (MBA). *Program availability:* Part-time, evening/weekend. *Faculty:* 79 full-time (22 women), 10 part-time/adjunct (6 women). *Students:* 309 full-time (151 women), 65 part-time (31 women); includes 82 minority (25 Black or African American, non-Hispanic/Latino; 27 Asian, non-Hispanic/Latino; 27 Hispanic/Latino; 3 Two or more races, non-Hispanic/Latino), 49 international. Average age 30. 371 applicants, 53% accepted, 114 enrolled. In 2016, 216 master's awarded. *Entrance requirements:* For master's, GMAT or GRE, official transcripts, two letters of recommendation, statement of purpose, resume. Additional exam requirements/recommendations for international students: Required—TOEFL (minimum score 90 iBT) or IELTS (minimum score 6.5). *Application deadline:* For fall admission, 7/15 for domestic and international students; for winter admission, 10/1 for domestic and international students; for spring admission, 1/15 for domestic and international students; for summer admission, 4/1 for domestic and international students. Applications are processed on a rolling basis. Application fee: $50. Electronic applications accepted. Application fee is waived when completed online. *Expenses:* $4,488 per course. *Financial support:* In 2016–17, 83 students received support. Federal Work-Study, scholarships/grants, health care benefits, and unspecified assistantships available. Support available to part-time students. *Faculty research:* Social enterprise and responsibility, emerging markets, supply chain management, risk management. *Unit head:* Katherine Acles, Assistant Dean for Graduate Programs, 312-915-6124, Fax: 312-915-7207, E-mail: kacles@luc.edu. *Application contact:* Lauren Griffin, Enrollment Advisor, Quinlan School of Business Graduate Programs, 312-915-6124, Fax: 312-915-7207, E-mail: lgriffin3@luc.edu.

Lynn University, College of Business and Management, Boca Raton, FL 33431-5598. Offers business administration (MBA), including aviation management, financial valuation and investment management, hospitality management, human resource management, international business management, marketing, media management, sports management. *Program availability:* Part-time, evening/weekend, 100% online, blended/hybrid learning. *Faculty:* 24 full-time (9 women), 24 part-time/adjunct (4 women). *Students:* 265 full-time (125 women), 182 part-time (96 women); includes 100 minority (41 Black or African American, non-Hispanic/Latino; 11 Asian, non-Hispanic/Latino; 42 Hispanic/Latino; 6 Two or more races, non-Hispanic/Latino), 119 international. Average age 28. 280 applicants, 94% accepted, 181 enrolled. In 2016, 219 master's awarded. *Degree requirements:* For master's, strategic management seminar, simulation capstone. *Entrance requirements:* For master's, bachelor's degree from accredited institution, resume, letter of recommendation, official transcripts, essay/personal statement. Additional exam requirements/recommendations for international students: Required—TOEFL (minimum score 550 paper-based; 80 iBT), IELTS (minimum score 6.5). *Application deadline:* For fall admission, 8/18 for domestic students, 8/4 for international students; for spring admission, 12/15 for domestic students, 12/1 for international students; for summer admission, 4/17 for domestic students, 4/3 for international students. Applications are processed on a rolling basis. Application fee: $45. Electronic applications accepted. *Expenses:* $725 per credit. *Financial support:* In 2016–17, 115 students received support. Career-related internships or fieldwork, Federal Work-Study, scholarships/grants, tuition waivers (full and partial), and unspecified assistantships available. Support available to part-time students. Financial award application deadline: 3/1; financial award applicants required to submit FAFSA. *Faculty research:* Market volatility investing, biometric research, sports legal history, organizational leadership, urban economic development and productivity. *Unit head:* Dr. RT Good, Dean of the College of Business and Management, 561-237-7458, E-mail: rgood@lynn.edu. *Application contact:* Steven Pruitt, Director of Graduate and Undergraduate Evening Admission, 561-237-7834, Fax: 561-237-7100, E-mail: spruitt@lynn.edu.
Website: http://www.lynn.edu/academics/colleges/business-and-management

Madonna University, School of Business, Livonia, MI 48150-1173. Offers business administration (MBA); international business (MSBA); leadership studies (MSBA); leadership studies in criminal justice (MSBA); quality and operations management (MSBA). *Program availability:* Part-time, evening/weekend, online learning. *Degree requirements:* For master's, thesis (for some programs), foreign language proficiency (international business). *Entrance requirements:* For master's, GMAT, GRE General Test, minimum GPA of 3.0. Electronic applications accepted. *Faculty research:* Management, women in management, future studies.

Maine Maritime Academy, Loeb-Sullivan School of International Business and Logistics, Castine, ME 04420. Offers global logistics and maritime management (MS), international logistics management (MS). *Program availability:* Part-time. *Degree requirements:* For master's, capstone course. *Entrance requirements:* For master's, GMAT or GRE, letter of recommendation. Additional exam requirements/recommendations for international students: Required—TOEFL. Application fee is waived when completed online.

Manhattanville College, School of Business, Master of Science in International Management Program, Purchase, NY 10577-2132. Offers business leadership (MS); finance (MS); human resource management (MS); marketing communication management (MS). *Program availability:* Part-time, evening/weekend. *Students:* 10 (9 women); includes 6 minority (2 Black or African American, non-Hispanic/Latino; 3 Hispanic/Latino; 1 Two or more races, non-Hispanic/Latino). Average age 30. 17 applicants, 35% accepted, 3 enrolled. In 2016, 1 master's awarded. *Degree requirements:* For master's, thesis (for some programs), final project. *Entrance requirements:* For master's, transcripts, 2 letters of recommendation, resume. Additional exam requirements/recommendations for international students: Required—TOEFL (minimum score 563 paper-based; 85 iBT). *Application deadline:* Applications are processed on a rolling basis. Application fee: $75. Electronic applications accepted. *Expenses: Tuition:* Full-time $16,470; part-time $915 per credit. *Required fees:* $00 per semester. Part-time tuition and fees vary according to course load and program. *Financial support:* Federal Work-Study, institutionally sponsored loans, scholarships/grants, and unspecified assistantships available. Financial award applicants required to submit FAFSA. *Faculty research:* Market entry in Cuba, linking strategy and customer satisfaction. *Unit head:* Laura Persky, Graduate Program Director, 914-323-5188, E-mail: laura.persky@mville.edu. *Application contact:* Monika Pottgen, Assistant Director, Recruitment and Admissions, 914-323-5150, E-mail: business@mville.edu.
Website: https://www.mville.edu/programs/ms-international-management

Marconi International University, Graduate Programs, Pembroke Pines, FL 33028. Offers business administration (DBA); education leadership (Ed D); education leadership, management and emerging technologies (M Ed); international business administration (IMBA).

Marquette University, Graduate School of Management, Executive MBA Program, Milwaukee, WI 53201-1881. Offers economics (MBA); finance (MBA); human resources (MBA); international business (MBA); management information systems (MBA); marketing (MBA); operations and supply chain management (MBA); sports business (MBA). *Accreditation:* AACSB. *Students:* 39 full-time (12 women); includes 7 minority (4 Black or African American, non-Hispanic/Latino; 2 Asian, non-Hispanic/Latino; 1 Hispanic/Latino). Average age 38. 25 applicants, 96% accepted, 29 enrolled. In 2016, 14 master's awarded. *Degree requirements:* For master's, international trip. *Entrance requirements:* For master's, GMAT or GRE, two letters of recommendation, official transcripts from current and previous colleges/universities. Additional exam requirements/recommendations for international students: Required—TOEFL (minimum score 550 paper-based; 88 iBT), IELTS (minimum score 6.5), PTE. *Application deadline:* For fall admission, 2/15 for domestic and international students. Application fee: $50. Electronic applications accepted. *Expenses:* Contact institution. *Financial support:* Application deadline: 2/15. *Faculty research:* International trade and finance, customer relationship management, consumer satisfaction, customer service. *Unit head:* Dr. Brian Till, Dean, 414-288-5724. *Application contact:* Dr. Jeanne Simmons, Associate Dean, 414-288-7145.
Website: http://www.busadm.mu.edu/emba/

Marquette University, Graduate School of Management, Program in Business Administration, Milwaukee, WI 53201-1881. Offers business administration (MBA); economics (MBA); entrepreneurship (Certificate); finance (MBA); human resources (MBA); international business (MBA); management information systems (MBA); marketing (MBA); operations and supply chain management (MBA); sports business (MBA); JD/MBA; MBA/MA; MBA/MSN. *Accreditation:* AACSB. *Program availability:* Part-time, evening/weekend. *Students:* 25 full-time (12 women), 202 part-time (57 women); includes 17 minority (5 Black or African American, non-Hispanic/Latino; 6 Asian, non-Hispanic/Latino; 2 Hispanic/Latino; 1 Native Hawaiian or other Pacific Islander, non-Hispanic/Latino; 3 Two or more races, non-Hispanic/Latino), 7 international. Average age 31. 107 applicants, 87% accepted, 113 enrolled. In 2016, 107 master's, 5 other advanced degrees awarded. *Degree requirements:* For Certificate, business plan. *Entrance requirements:* For master's, GMAT or GRE, letters of recommendation. Additional exam requirements/recommendations for international students: Required—TOEFL (minimum score 550 paper-based; 88 iBT), IELTS (minimum score 6.5), PTE. *Application deadline:* For fall admission, 2/15 for domestic and international students. Applications are processed on a rolling basis. Application fee: $50. Electronic applications accepted. *Financial support:* Fellowships, research assistantships, teaching assistantships, Federal Work-Study, institutionally sponsored loans, scholarships/grants, and tuition waivers (full and partial) available. Support available to part-time students. Financial award application deadline: 2/15. *Faculty research:* Ethics in the professions, services marketing, technology impact on decision-making, mentoring. *Unit head:* Dr. Brian Till, Dean, 414-288-5724. *Application contact:* Dr. Jeanne Simmons, Associate Dean, 414-288-7145.
Website: http://business.marquette.edu/academics/mba

McGill University, Faculty of Graduate and Postdoctoral Studies, Desautels Faculty of Management, Montréal, QC H3A 2T5, Canada. Offers administration (PhD); entrepreneurial studies (MBA); finance (MBA); general management (Post Master's Certificate); information systems (MBA); international business (MBA); international practicing management (MM); management (MBA); management for development (MBA); manufacturing management (MMM); marketing (MBA); operations management (MBA); public accountancy (Diploma); strategic management (MBA); MBA/LL B; MD/MBA. MMM offered jointly with Faculty of Engineering; PhD with Concordia University, HEC Montreal, Université de Montréal, Université du Québec à Montréal.

McKendree University, Graduate Programs, Master of Business Administration Program, Lebanon, IL 62254-1299. Offers business administration (MBA); human resource management (MBA); international business (MBA). *Program availability:* Part-time, evening/weekend, online learning. *Entrance requirements:* For master's, official transcripts from all institutions attended, essay, minimum GPA of 3.0, three references, resume. Additional exam requirements/recommendations for international students: Required—TOEFL. Electronic applications accepted.

Middlebury Institute of International Studies at Monterey, Graduate School of International Policy and Management, Fisher MBA in Global Impact Management Program, Monterey, CA 93940-2691. Offers corporate risk management and compliance (MBA). *Accreditation:* AACSB. *Degree requirements:* For master's, one foreign language, thesis. *Entrance requirements:* For master's, GMAT, minimum GPA of 3.0, proficiency in a foreign language. Additional exam requirements/recommendations for international students: Required—TOEFL (minimum score 550 paper-based; 80 iBT). Electronic applications accepted. *Expenses: Tuition:* Full-time $38,250; part-time $1820 per credit. *Required fees:* $78 per semester. *Faculty research:* Cross-cultural consumer behavior, foreign direct investment, marketing and entrepreneurial orientation, political risk analysis and area studies, managing international human resources.

Milwaukee School of Engineering, Rader School of Business, Program in Marketing and Export Management, Milwaukee, WI 53202-3109. Offers MS. *Program availability:* Part-time, evening/weekend. *Faculty:* 1 (woman) full-time, 2 part-time/adjunct (0 women). *Students:* 1 (woman) full-time, 2 part-time (0 women), 1 international. Average age 26. 6 applicants, 50% accepted, 2 enrolled. In 2016, 2 master's awarded. *Degree requirements:* For master's, thesis, thesis defense or capstone project. *Entrance requirements:* For master's, GRE or GMAT if undergraduate GPA less than 2.8, 2 letters of recommendation; BS in engineering, engineering technology, science, business, management or a related field. Additional exam requirements/recommendations for international students: Required—TOEFL (minimum score 79 iBT), IELTS (minimum score 6.5). *Application deadline:* Applications are processed on a rolling basis. Application fee: $0. Electronic applications accepted. *Expenses: Tuition:* Full-time $31,440; part-time $655 per credit. *Financial support:* Career-related internships or fieldwork, institutionally sponsored loans, scholarships/grants, and tuition waivers (full) available. Financial award application deadline: 3/15; financial award applicants required to submit FAFSA. *Unit head:* Gene Wright, Director, 414-277-2268, Fax: 414-277-2487, E-mail: wright@msoe.edu. *Application contact:* Ian Dahlinghaus, Graduate Admissions Counselor, 414-277-7208, E-mail: dahlinghaus@msoe.edu.
Website: http://www.msoe.edu/community/academics/business/page/1306/marketing-and-export-management-overview

New Jersey Institute of Technology, Martin Tuchman School of Management, Newark, NJ 07102. Offers business administration (MBA); business data science (PhD); finance for managers (Certificate); international business (MS); management (MS); management essentials (Certificate); management of technology (Certificate). *Accreditation:* AACSB. *Program availability:* Part-time, evening/weekend. *Faculty:* 29 full-time (9 women), 21 part-time/adjunct (3 women). *Students:* 90 full-time (35 women), 147 part-time (53 women); includes 104 minority (30 Black or African American, non-Hispanic/Latino; 30 Asian, non-Hispanic/Latino; 38 Hispanic/Latino; 6 Two or more races, non-Hispanic/Latino), 57 international. Average age 31. 385 applicants, 52% accepted, 80 enrolled. In 2016, 81 master's, 11 other advanced degrees awarded. Terminal master's awarded for partial completion of doctoral program. *Degree requirements:* For master's, thesis optional. *Entrance requirements:* For doctorate, GRE General Test, minimum graduate GPA of 3.5. Additional exam requirements/recommendations for international students: Required—TOEFL (minimum score 550 paper-based; 79 iBT). *Application deadline:* For fall admission, 6/1 priority date for domestic students, 5/1 priority date for international students; for spring admission, 11/15 priority date for domestic and international students. Applications are processed on a rolling basis. Application fee: $75. Electronic applications accepted. *Expenses:* Contact

institution. *Financial support:* In 2016–17, 7 students received support, including 3 research assistantships (averaging $9,088 per year), 4 teaching assistantships (averaging $19,250 per year); fellowships, career-related internships or fieldwork, Federal Work-Study, institutionally sponsored loans, and unspecified assistantships also available. Financial award application deadline: 1/15. *Faculty research:* Manufacturing systems analysis, earnings management, knowledge-based view of the firm, data envelopment analysis, human factors in human/machine systems. *Unit head:* Dr. Reggie Caudill, Interim Dean, 973-596-5856, Fax: 973-596-3074, E-mail: reggie.j.caudill@njit.edu. *Application contact:* Stephen Eck, Director of Admissions, 973-596-3300, Fax: 973-596-3461, E-mail: admissions@njit.edu.
Website: http://management.njit.edu

Newman University, MBA Program, Wichita, KS 67213-2097. Offers finance (MBA); international business (MBA); leadership (MBA); management (MBA); management information technology (MBA). *Program availability:* Part-time. *Degree requirements:* For master's, thesis optional. *Entrance requirements:* For master's, minimum GPA of 3.0; 2 letters of recommendation; course work in algebra, statistics, macroeconomics, and financial accounting. Additional exam requirements/recommendations for international students: Required—TOEFL (minimum score 600 paper-based; 100 iBT). Electronic applications accepted. *Expenses:* Contact institution.

New Mexico Highlands University, Graduate Studies, School of Business, Media and Technology, Las Vegas, NM 87701. Offers business administration (MBA), including human resource management, international business, management; media arts and technology (MA), including media arts and computer science. *Accreditation:* ACBSP. *Degree requirements:* For master's, comprehensive exam, thesis or alternative. *Entrance requirements:* For master's, minimum undergraduate GPA of 3.0. Additional exam requirements/recommendations for international students: Required—TOEFL (minimum score 540 paper-based). *Faculty research:* Real estate valuation, studying expert judgments in complex accounting, decision environments, green marketing, environmentalism, marketing research methodology.

New York University, Graduate School of Arts and Science, Department of Politics, New York, NY 10012-1019. Offers political campaign management (MA); politics (MA, PhD); JD/MA; MBA/MA. *Program availability:* Part-time. Terminal master's awarded for partial completion of doctoral program. *Degree requirements:* For master's, one foreign language, thesis or alternative; for doctorate, 2 foreign languages, comprehensive exam, thesis/dissertation. *Entrance requirements:* For master's and doctorate, GRE General Test. Additional exam requirements/recommendations for international students: Required—TOEFL. *Faculty research:* Comparative politics, democratic theory and practice, rational choice, political economy, international relations.

Niagara University, Graduate Division of Business Administration, Niagara University, NY 14109. Offers accounting (MBA); business administration (MBA); finance (MBA, MS); financial planning (MBA); healthcare administration (MBA, MHA); human resources (MBA); international business (MBA); marketing (MBA); professional accountancy (MBA); strategic management (MBA); supply chain management (MBA). *Accreditation:* AACSB. *Program availability:* Part-time, evening/weekend. *Students:* 172 full-time (69 women), 65 part-time (36 women); includes 25 minority (4 Black or African American, non-Hispanic/Latino; 7 Asian, non-Hispanic/Latino; 7 Hispanic/Latino; 1 Native Hawaiian or other Pacific Islander, non-Hispanic/Latino; 6 Two or more races, non-Hispanic/Latino), 76 international. Average age 27. In 2016, 107 master's awarded. *Entrance requirements:* For master's, GMAT. Additional exam requirements/recommendations for international students: Required—TOEFL (minimum score 550 paper-based; 79 iBT), IELTS (minimum score 6). *Application deadline:* For fall admission, 8/1 for domestic students; for spring admission, 11/1 for domestic students. Applications are processed on a rolling basis. Electronic applications accepted. *Expenses:* $870 per credit hour. *Financial support:* Fellowships, research assistantships, career-related internships or fieldwork, and Federal Work-Study available. Support available to part-time students. Financial award application deadline: 4/15; financial award applicants required to submit FAFSA. *Faculty research:* Capital flows, Federal Reserve policy, human resource management, public policy, issues in marketing, auctions, economics of information, risk and capital markets, management strategy, consumer behavior, Internet and social media marketing. *Unit head:* Dr. Paul Richardson, MBA Director/Chair of the Marketing Department, 716-286-8169, Fax: 716-286-8206, E-mail: psr@niagara.edu. *Application contact:* Evan Pierce, Associate Director for Graduate Recruitment, 716-286-8769, Fax: 716-286-8170, E-mail: epierce@niagara.edu.
Website: http://mba.niagara.edu

Northeastern University, D'Amore-McKim School of Business, Boston, MA 02115-5096. Offers accounting (MS); business administration (EMBA, MBA); finance (MS); innovation (MS); international business (MS); international management (MS); taxation (MS); technological entrepreneurship (MS); JD/MBA; LL M/MBA; MBA/MSN; MS/MBA. *Accreditation:* AACSB. *Program availability:* Part-time, evening/weekend, online learning. *Faculty:* 185 full-time (66 women), 57 part-time/adjunct (13 women). *Students:* 379 full-time (180 women), 1,182 part-time (514 women). In 2016, 800 master's awarded. *Entrance requirements:* For master's, GMAT or GRE. Application fee: $75. Electronic applications accepted. *Expenses:* Contact institution. *Financial support:* Scholarships/grants available. Financial award applicants required to submit FAFSA. *Unit head:* Dr. Hugh Courtney, Dean, D'Amore-McKim School of Business. *Application contact:* Evelyn Tate, Director, Graduate Recruitment and Admissions, 617-373-3258, Fax: 617-373-8564, E-mail: e.tate@northeastern.edu.
Website: http://damore-mckim.northeastern.edu/

Northern Arizona University, Graduate College, NAU-Yuma, Master of Global Business Administration Program, Flagstaff, AZ 86011. Offers MGBA. *Expenses:* Tuition, state resident: full-time $8971; part-time $444 per credit hour. Tuition, nonresident: full-time $20,958; part-time $1164 per credit hour. *Required fees:* $1018; $644 per credit hour. Tuition and fees vary according to course load, campus/location and program.

Northwestern University, The Graduate School, Kellogg School of Management, Management Programs, Evanston, IL 60208. Offers accounting information and management (MBA, PhD); analytical finance (MBA); business administration (MBA); decision sciences (MBA); entrepreneurship and innovation (MBA); finance (MBA, PhD); health enterprise management (MBA); human resources management (MBA); international business (MBA); management and organizations (MBA, PhD); management and organizations and sociology (PhD); management and strategy (MBA); management studies (MS); managerial analytics (MBA); managerial economics (MBA); managerial economics and strategy (PhD); marketing (MBA, PhD); marketing management (MBA); media management (MBA); operations management (MBA, PhD); real estate (MBA); social enterprise at Kellogg (MBA); JD/MBA. *Program availability:* Part-time, evening/weekend. Terminal master's awarded for partial completion of doctoral program. *Degree requirements:* For doctorate, thesis/dissertation, 2 years of coursework, qualifying (field) exam and candidacy, summer research papers and presentations to faculty, proposal defense, final exam/defense. *Entrance requirements:* For master's, GMAT, GRE, interview, 2 letters of recommendation, college transcripts, resume, essays, Kellogg honor code; for doctorate, GMAT, GRE, statement of purpose, transcripts, 2 letters of recommendation, resume, interview. Additional exam requirements/recommendations for international students: Required—TOEFL, IELTS. Electronic applications accepted. *Expenses:* Contact institution. *Faculty research:* Business cycles and international finance, health policy, networks, non-market strategy, consumer psychology.

Northwest University, College of Business, Kirkland, WA 98033. Offers business administration (MBA); international business (MBA); project management (MBA); social entrepreneurship (MBA). *Accreditation:* ACBSP. *Program availability:* Part-time, evening/weekend. *Degree requirements:* For master's, formalized research. *Entrance requirements:* For master's, GMAT. Additional exam requirements/recommendations for international students: Required—TOEFL (minimum score 550 paper-based; 75 iBT). Electronic applications accepted. *Expenses:* Contact institution.

Norwich University, College of Graduate and Continuing Studies, Master of Arts in Diplomacy Program, Northfield, VT 05663. Offers diplomacy (MA), including cyber diplomacy - policy, cyber diplomacy - technical, international commerce, international conflict management, international terrorism. *Program availability:* Evening/weekend, online only, mostly all online with a week-long residency requirement. *Faculty:* 1 full-time (0 women), 20 part-time/adjunct (3 women). *Students:* 154 full-time (49 women); includes 34 minority (18 Black or African American, non-Hispanic/Latino; 1 Asian, non-Hispanic/Latino; 9 Hispanic/Latino; 6 Two or more races, non-Hispanic/Latino), 1 international. Average age 34. 31 applicants, 100% accepted, 25 enrolled. In 2016, 93 master's awarded. *Degree requirements:* For master's, comprehensive exam, thesis optional. *Entrance requirements:* For master's, minimum undergraduate GPA of 2.75. Additional exam requirements/recommendations for international students: Required—TOEFL (minimum score 550 paper-based; 80 iBT), IELTS (minimum score 6.5). *Application deadline:* For fall admission, 8/14 for domestic and international students; for winter admission, 11/13 for domestic and international students; for spring admission, 2/12 for domestic and international students; for summer admission, 6/5 for domestic and international students. Electronic applications accepted. *Expenses:* Contact institution. *Financial support:* In 2016–17, 75 students received support. Scholarships/grants available. Financial award application deadline: 8/4; financial award applicants required to submit FAFSA. *Unit head:* Dr. Lasha Tchantouridze, Program Director, 802-485-2095, Fax: 802-485-2533, E-mail: ltchanto@norwich.edu. *Application contact:* Admissions Advisor, 800-460-5597 Ext. 3378, Fax: 802-485-2533, E-mail: mdy@online.norwich.edu.
Website: https://online.norwich.edu/degree-programs/masters/master-arts-diplomacy/overview

Nova Southeastern University, H. Wayne Huizenga College of Business and Entrepreneurship, Fort Lauderdale, FL 33314-7796. Offers accounting (M Acc); business intelligence/analytics (MBA); entrepreneurship (MBA); finance (MBA); human resource management (MBA); international business (MBA); management (MBA); marketing (MBA); process improvement (MBA); public administration (MPA); real estate development (MS); sport revenue generation (MBA); supply chain management (MBA); taxation (M Tax). *Program availability:* Part-time, evening/weekend, 100% online, blended/hybrid learning. *Faculty:* 65 full-time (26 women), 111 part-time/adjunct (74 women). *Students:* 2,242 full-time (1,400 women), 425 part-time (239 women); includes 1,798 minority (734 Black or African American, non-Hispanic/Latino; 5 American Indian or Alaska Native, non-Hispanic/Latino; 110 Asian, non-Hispanic/Latino; 890 Hispanic/Latino; 2 Native Hawaiian or other Pacific Islander, non-Hispanic/Latino; 57 Two or more races, non-Hispanic/Latino), 255 international. Average age 34. 1,422 applicants, 64% accepted, 672 enrolled. In 2016, 971 master's awarded. *Degree requirements:* For master's, thesis optional. *Entrance requirements:* For master's, GMAT or GRE (depending on undergraduate GPA), official transcripts from all schools attended while in pursuit of bachelor's degree; minimum GPA of 2.5 from regionally-accredited institution. Additional exam requirements/recommendations for international students: Required—TOEFL (minimum score 550 paper-based; 79 iBT), IELTS (minimum score 6), PTE (minimum score 54). *Application deadline:* For fall admission, 8/5 priority date for domestic students, 7/29 priority date for international students; for winter admission, 12/16 priority date for domestic students, 12/9 priority date for international students; for summer admission, 4/21 priority date for domestic and international students. Applications are processed on a rolling basis. Application fee: $50. Electronic applications accepted. *Expenses:* Contact institution. *Financial support:* In 2016–17, 325 students received support. Federal Work-Study and scholarships/grants available. Support available to part-time students. Financial award application deadline: 4/15; financial award applicants required to submit FAFSA. *Faculty research:* Reputation management, call centers, international social capital, corporate earnings guidance, corporate governance. *Unit head:* Dr. J. Preston Jones, Dean, 954-262-5127, E-mail: prestonj@nova.edu. *Application contact:* Zeida Rodriguez, Associate Director of Enrollment Services, 954-262-5163, Fax: 954-262-3822, E-mail: zeida@nova.edu.
Website: http://www.huizenga.nova.edu

Oakland University, Graduate Study and Lifelong Learning, School of Business Administration, Department of Management and Marketing, Rochester, MI 48309-4401. Offers business administration (MBA); entrepreneurship (Certificate); general management (Certificate); human resource management (Certificate); international business (Certificate); management and marketing (EMBA); marketing (Certificate).

Oklahoma Christian University, Graduate School of Business, Oklahoma City, OK 73136-1100. Offers accounting (M Acc, MBA); financial services (MBA); general business (MBA); health services management (MBA); human resources (MBA); international business (MBA); leadership and organizational development (MBA); marketing (MBA); nonprofit management (MBA); project management (MBA). *Accreditation:* ACBSP. *Program availability:* Part-time, 100% online. *Faculty:* 10 full-time (2 women), 21 part-time/adjunct (2 women). *Students:* 156 full-time (68 women), 137 part-time (73 women). Average age 30. 374 applicants, 213 enrolled. In 2016, 114 master's awarded. *Entrance requirements:* For master's, bachelor's degree. Additional exam requirements/recommendations for international students: Required—TOEFL (minimum score 550 paper-based). Application fee: $25. Electronic applications accepted. *Expenses:* Contact institution. *Unit head:* Dr. Ken Johnson, Chair, 405-425-5567, Fax: 405-425-5585, E-mail: ken.johnson@oc.edu. *Application contact:* Angie Ricketts, Graduate School Admissions Counselor, 405-425-5587, Fax: 405-425-5585, E-mail: angie.ricketts@oc.edu.
Website: http://www.oc.edu/academics/graduate/business/

Old Dominion University, Strome College of Business, Program in Maritime Trade and Supply Chain Management, Norfolk, VA 23529. Offers MS. *Program availability:* Part-time, evening/weekend. *Students:* 5 full-time (2 women), 5 part-time (2 women); includes 3 minority (2 Asian, non-Hispanic/Latino; 1 Hispanic/Latino), 2 international. Average age 34. *Degree requirements:* For master's, capstone course. *Entrance requirements:* For master's, GRE or GMAT, bachelor's degree, official transcripts, two letters of recommendation, current resume, statement of professional goals. Additional exam requirements/recommendations for international students: Required—TOEFL (minimum score 550 paper-based; 79 iBT), IELTS (minimum score 6.5). *Application deadline:* For fall admission, 6/1 for domestic students, 4/15 for international students; for spring admission, 11/1 for domestic students, 10/1 for international students. *Expenses:* Tuition, state resident: full-time $8604; part-time $478 per credit hour. Tuition, nonresident: full-time $21,510; part-time $1195 per credit hour. *Required fees:*

$66 per semester. Tuition and fees vary according to campus/location, program and reciprocity agreements. *Financial support:* In 2016–17, 2 students received support. Unspecified assistantships available. *Unit head:* Wayne Talley, Director. *Application contact:* Dr. Ali Ardalan, Associate Dean, 757-683-3520, Fax: 757-683-4076, E-mail: aardalan@odu.edu.

Oral Roberts University, School of Business, Tulsa, OK 74171. Offers accounting (MBA); entrepreneurship (MBA); finance (MBA); international business (MBA); management (MBA); marketing (MBA); non-profit management (MBA); not for profit management (MNM). *Accreditation:* ACBSP. *Program availability:* Part-time, online learning. *Degree requirements:* For master's, thesis optional. *Entrance requirements:* For master's, minimum cumulative GPA of 3.0. Additional exam requirements/recommendations for international students: Required—TOEFL (minimum score 550 paper-based; 79 iBT). Electronic applications accepted. *Faculty research:* Social media, international business and marketing.

Pace University, Lubin School of Business, Advanced Professional Certificate Program, New York, NY 10038. Offers business economics (APC); e-business (APC); financial management (APC); international business (APC); international economics (APC); investment management (APC); marketing (APC); public accounting (APC). *Program availability:* Evening/weekend. *Students:* 1 applicant, 100% accepted, 1 enrolled. *Entrance requirements:* For degree, MBA or MS in business discipline, relevant professional experience. Additional exam requirements/recommendations for international students: Required—TOEFL (minimum score 90 iBT), IELTS (minimum score 7) or PTE (minimum score 61). *Application deadline:* For fall admission, 8/1 priority date for domestic students, 6/1 for international students; for spring admission, 12/1 for domestic students, 10/1 for international students. Applications are processed on a rolling basis. Application fee: $70. Electronic applications accepted. *Expenses: Tuition:* Part-time $1195 per credit. *Required fees:* $260 per semester. Tuition and fees vary according to degree level, campus/location and program. *Unit head:* Dr. Jack Yurkiewicz, Director, 212-618-6567, E-mail: jyurkiewicz@pace.edu. *Application contact:* Susan Ford-Goldschein, Director of Graduate Admissions, 212-346-1531, Fax: 212-346-1585, E-mail: graduateadmission@pace.edu.
Website: http://www.pace.edu/lubin/agc

Pace University, Lubin School of Business, Financial Management Program, New York, NY 10038. Offers financial management (MBA, MS); financial risk management (MS); international finance (MBA); investment management (MBA, MS). *Program availability:* Evening/weekend. *Students:* 130 full-time (49 women), 62 part-time (34 women); includes 33 minority (4 Black or African American, non-Hispanic/Latino; 20 Asian, non-Hispanic/Latino; 6 Hispanic/Latino; 1 Native Hawaiian or other Pacific Islander, non-Hispanic/Latino; 2 Two or more races, non-Hispanic/Latino), 124 international. Average age 26. 397 applicants, 65% accepted, 84 enrolled. In 2016, 166 master's awarded. *Entrance requirements:* For master's, GMAT, GRE (GMAT not required for MS with passing of Level 1 of Chartered Financial Analyst exam or Level 1 of Financial Risk Manager Exam), undergraduate degree, transcripts from all accredited colleges/universities attended, two letters of recommendation, resume, personal statement. Additional exam requirements/recommendations for international students: Required—TOEFL (minimum score 90 iBT), IELTS (minimum score 7) or PTE (minimum score 61). *Application deadline:* For fall admission, 8/1 priority date for domestic students, 6/1 for international students; for spring admission, 12/1 for domestic students, 10/1 for international students. Applications are processed on a rolling basis. Application fee: $70. Electronic applications accepted. *Expenses: Tuition:* Part-time $1195 per credit. *Required fees:* $260 per semester. Tuition and fees vary according to degree level, campus/location and program. *Financial support:* Research assistantships, career-related internships or fieldwork, Federal Work-Study, and tuition waivers (full and partial) available. Support available to part-time students. Financial award application deadline: 2/15; financial award applicants required to submit FAFSA. *Unit head:* Dr. P. V. Viswanath, Chairperson, 212-618-6518, E-mail: pviswanath@pace.edu. *Application contact:* Susan Ford-Goldschein, Director of Graduate Admissions, 212-346-1531, Fax: 212-346-1585, E-mail: graduateadmissions@pace.edu.
Website: http://www.pace.edu/lubin/financial-management-mba

Pace University, Lubin School of Business, International Business Program, New York, NY 10038. Offers MBA. *Program availability:* Evening/weekend. *Students:* 13 full-time (7 women), 5 part-time (3 women); includes 6 minority (1 Black or African American, non-Hispanic/Latino; 1 Asian, non-Hispanic/Latino; 4 Hispanic/Latino), 10 international. Average age 28. 41 applicants, 37% accepted, 4 enrolled. In 2016, 4 master's awarded. *Entrance requirements:* For master's, GMAT, GRE, undergraduate degree, transcripts from all accredited colleges/universities attended, two letters of recommendation, resume, personal statement. Additional exam requirements/recommendations for international students: Required—TOEFL (minimum score 90 iBT), IELTS (minimum score 7) or PTE (minimum score 61). *Application deadline:* For fall admission, 8/1 priority date for domestic students, 6/1 for international students; for spring admission, 12/1 for domestic students, 10/1 for international students. Applications are processed on a rolling basis. Application fee: $70. Electronic applications accepted. *Expenses: Tuition:* Part-time $1195 per credit. *Required fees:* $260 per semester. Tuition and fees vary according to degree level, campus/location and program. *Financial support:* Research assistantships, career-related internships or fieldwork, and Federal Work-Study available. Support available to part-time students. Financial award application deadline: 2/15; financial award applicants required to submit FAFSA. *Unit head:* Lawrence G. Bridwell, Director, 914-773-3391, E-mail: lbridwell@pace.edu. *Application contact:* Susan Ford-Goldschein, Director of Graduate Admissions, 212-346-1531, Fax: 212-346-1585, E-mail: graduateadmission@pace.edu.
Website: http://www.pace.edu/lubin/mba-in-international-business

Pacific States University, College of Business, Los Angeles, CA 90010. Offers accounting (MBA); finance (MBA); international business (MBA, DBA); management of information technology (MBA); real estate management (MBA). *Program availability:* Part-time, evening/weekend, online learning. *Degree requirements:* For doctorate, comprehensive exam, thesis/dissertation. *Entrance requirements:* For master's, minimum undergraduate GPA of 2.5 during last 90 hours of course work. Additional exam requirements/recommendations for international students: Required—TOEFL (minimum score 500 paper-based; 61 iBT), IELTS (minimum score 5.5).

Park University, School of Graduate and Professional Studies, Kansas City, MO 54105. Offers adult education (M Ed); business and government leadership (Graduate Certificate); business, government, and global society (MPA); communication and leadership (MA); creative and life writing (Graduate Certificate); disaster and emergency management (MPA, Graduate Certificate); educational leadership (M Ed); finance (MBA, Graduate Certificate); general business (MBA); global business (Graduate Certificate); healthcare administration (MHA); healthcare services management and leadership (Graduate Certificate); international business (MBA); language and literacy (M Ed), including English for speakers of other languages, special reading teacher/literacy coach; leadership of international healthcare organizations (Graduate Certificate); management information systems (MBA, Graduate Certificate); music performance (ADP, Graduate Certificate), including cello (MM, ADP), piano (MM, ADP), viola (MM, ADP), violin (MM, ADP); nonprofit and community services management (MPA); nonprofit leadership (Graduate Certificate); performance (MM), including cello (MM, ADP), piano (MM, ADP), viola (MM, ADP), violin (MM, ADP); public management (MPA); social work (MSW); teacher leadership (M Ed), including curriculum and assessment, instructional leader. *Program availability:* Part-time, evening/weekend, online learning. *Degree requirements:* For master's, comprehensive exam (for some programs), thesis (for some programs), internship (for some programs); exam (for some programs). *Entrance requirements:* For master's, GRE or GMAT (for some programs), teacher certification (for some M Ed programs), letters of recommendation, essay, resume (for some programs). Additional exam requirements/recommendations for international students: Required—TOEFL (minimum score 550 paper-based; 79 iBT), IELTS (minimum score 6). Electronic applications accepted.

Pepperdine University, Graziadio School of Business and Management, Full-Time MBA Programs, Malibu, CA 90263. Offers accounting (MS); applied analytics (MS); applied finance (MS); business administration (MBA); global business (MS); human resources (MS); international business administration (MBA); management and leadership (MS); organization development (MS); real estate investment and finance (MS); JD/MBA; MBA/MPP. *Accreditation:* AACSB. *Students:* 472 full-time (239 women), 3 part-time (2 women); includes 424 minority (111 Black or African American, non-Hispanic/Latino; 7 American Indian or Alaska Native, non-Hispanic/Latino; 216 Asian, non-Hispanic/Latino; 88 Hispanic/Latino; 2 Two or more races, non-Hispanic/Latino), 47 international. Average age 25. 1,991 applicants, 59% accepted, 238 enrolled. In 2016, 419 master's awarded. *Entrance requirements:* For master's, GMAT or GRE, two letters of recommendation. Additional exam requirements/recommendations for international students: Required—TOEFL. *Application deadline:* For fall admission, 5/1 for domestic students, 4/1 for international students. Application fee: $75. Electronic applications accepted. *Financial support:* Applicants required to submit FAFSA. *Unit head:* Dr. Michael L. Williams, Associate Dean, 310-506-4112, Fax: 310-506-4126, E-mail: michael.williams@pepperdine.edu.
Website: http://bschool.pepperdine.edu/masters-degree/

Pittsburg State University, Graduate School, Kelce College of Business, Department of Management and Marketing, Pittsburg, KS 66762. Offers general administration (MBA); international business (MBA). *Accreditation:* AACSB. *Program availability:* Part-time. *Students:* 50 (24 women). In 2016, 35 master's awarded. *Degree requirements:* For master's, thesis or alternative. *Entrance requirements:* For master's, GMAT or GRE. Additional exam requirements/recommendations for international students: Required—TOEFL (minimum score 550 paper-based; 79 iBT), IELTS (minimum score 6.5), PTE (minimum score 53). *Application deadline:* For fall admission, 7/15 for domestic students, 6/1 for international students; for spring admission, 12/15 for domestic students, 10/15 for international students; for summer admission, 5/15 for domestic students, 4/1 for international students. Applications are processed on a rolling basis. Application fee: $35 ($60 for international students). Electronic applications accepted. *Expenses:* Contact institution. *Financial support:* In 2016–17, 10 teaching assistantships with full tuition reimbursements (averaging $5,500 per year) were awarded; research assistantships, career-related internships or fieldwork, Federal Work-Study, and unspecified assistantships also available. Financial award application deadline: 2/1; financial award applicants required to submit FAFSA. *Faculty research:* Consumer behavior, productions management, forecasting interest rate swaps, strategy management. *Unit head:* Dr. Bienvenido Cortes, MBA Coordinator, 620-235-4594, E-mail: bcortes@pittstate.edu. *Application contact:* Lisa Allen, Assistant Director of Graduate and Continuing Studies, 620-235-4218, Fax: 620-235-4219, E-mail: lallen@pittstate.edu.
Website: http://www.pittstate.edu/mgmkt/

Point Park University, School of Business, Department of Business, Pittsburgh, PA 15222-1984. Offers business analytics (MBA); health systems management (MBA); international business (MBA); management (MBA); management information systems (MBA); sports, arts and entertainment management (MBA). *Program availability:* Evening/weekend, online learning.

Polytechnic University of Puerto Rico, Graduate School, Hato Rey, PR 00918. Offers business administration (MBA), including computer information systems, general management, management of information systems, management of international enterprises; civil engineering (ME, MS); computer engineering (ME, MS); computer science (MCS, MS); electrical engineering (ME, MS); engineering management (MEM); environmental management (MEM); landscape architecture (M Land Arch); manufacturing competitiveness (MMC, MS); manufacturing engineering (ME, MS); mechanical engineering (M Mech E). *Program availability:* Part-time, evening/weekend. *Entrance requirements:* For master's, 3 letters of recommendation.

Polytechnic University of Puerto Rico, Miami Campus, Graduate School, Miami, FL 33166. Offers accounting (MBA); business administration (MBA); construction management (MEM); environmental management (MEM); finance (MBA); human resources management (MBA); logistics and supply chain management (MBA); management of international enterprises (MBA); manufacturing management (MEM); marketing management (MBA); project management (MBA). *Program availability:* Part-time, evening/weekend, online learning. *Entrance requirements:* For master's, minimum GPA of 3.0. Electronic applications accepted.

Polytechnic University of Puerto Rico, Orlando Campus, Graduate School, Orlando, FL 32825. Offers accounting (MBA); business administration (MBA); construction management (MEM); engineering management (MEM); environmental management (MEM); finance (MBA); human resources management (MBA); management of international enterprises (MBA); management of technology (MBA); manufacturing management (MEM). *Program availability:* Part-time, evening/weekend, online learning. *Entrance requirements:* For master's, minimum GPA of 3.0. Additional exam requirements/recommendations for international students: Recommended—TOEFL. Electronic applications accepted.

Pontifical Catholic University of Puerto Rico, College of Business Administration, Program in International Business, Ponce, PR 00717-0777. Offers MBA. *Program availability:* Part-time, evening/weekend. *Entrance requirements:* For master's, GRE, interview, minimum GPA of 2.75.

Pontificia Universidad Catolica Madre y Maestra, Graduate School, Faculty of Social and Administrative Sciences, Santiago, Dominican Republic. Offers business administration (MBA), including business development, finance, international business, management skills (M Mgmt, MBA), marketing, operations, strategic cost management, strategy, tourist destination planning and management; law (LL M), including civil law, corporate business law, criminal law, international relations, real estate law; management (M Mgmt), including higher financial management, insurance program administration, management skills (M Mgmt, MBA); psychology (MA), including clinical child and adolescent psychology, forensic psychology; strategic human resources (EMBA).

Portland State University, Graduate Studies, School of Business Administration, Program in International Management, Portland, OR 97207-0751. Offers MIM. *Program availability:* Part-time, evening/weekend. *Faculty:* 2 full-time (1 woman). *Students:* 56 full-time (31 women), 1 part-time (0 women); includes 10 minority (7 Asian, non-Hispanic/Latino; 3 Two or more races, non-Hispanic/Latino), 34 international. Average age 27. 25 applicants, 76% accepted, 11 enrolled. In 2016, 25 master's awarded.

International Business

Degree requirements: For master's, one foreign language, field study trip to China and Japan, international consulting project. *Entrance requirements:* For master's, GMAT, GRE General Test, minimum GPA of 2.75, resume, 2 letters of recommendation, essay. Additional exam requirements/recommendations for international students: Required—TOEFL (minimum score 550 paper-based; 80 iBT). *Application deadline:* For fall admission, 2/1 priority date for domestic and international students. Applications are processed on a rolling basis. Application fee: $65. Electronic applications accepted. *Expenses:* Contact institution. *Financial support:* Research assistantships with tuition reimbursements, teaching assistantships, career-related internships or fieldwork, Federal Work-Study, and institutionally sponsored loans available. Support available to part-time students. Financial award application deadline: 3/1; financial award applicants required to submit FAFSA. *Unit head:* Talya Bauer, Director, 503-725-5050, E-mail: talyabauer@pdx.edu. *Application contact:* 503-725-8001, E-mail: gradinfo.sba@pdx.edu.
Website: https://www.pdx.edu/sba/master-of-international-management

Providence College, School of Business, Providence, RI 02918. Offers accounting (MBA); finance (MBA); international business (MBA); management (MBA); marketing (MBA). *Accreditation:* AACSB. *Program availability:* Part-time, evening/weekend. *Faculty:* 10 full-time (3 women), 5 part-time/adjunct (2 women). *Students:* 84 full-time (39 women), 66 part-time (23 women); includes 15 minority (6 Black or African American, non-Hispanic/Latino; 1 Asian, non-Hispanic/Latino; 8 Hispanic/Latino), 5 international. Average age 26. 116 applicants, 96% accepted, 94 enrolled. In 2016, 80 master's awarded. *Entrance requirements:* For master's, GMAT. Additional exam requirements/recommendations for international students: Required—TOEFL (minimum score 577 paper-based; 90 iBT). *Application deadline:* For fall admission, 5/1 priority date for domestic and international students; for spring admission, 11/1 priority date for domestic and international students; for summer admission, 3/15 priority date for domestic students, 3/15 for international students. Applications are processed on a rolling basis. Application fee: $55. *Expenses:* Contact institution. *Financial support:* Career-related internships or fieldwork, institutionally sponsored loans, and unspecified assistantships available. Support available to part-time students. Financial award application deadline: 8/1; financial award applicants required to submit FAFSA.
Website: http://www.providence.edu/business/Pages/default.aspx

Purdue University, Graduate School, Krannert School of Management, IMM Global Executive MBA Program, West Lafayette, IN 47907. Offers MBA. *Program availability:* Part-time. *Faculty:* 11 full-time (1 woman), 9 part-time/adjunct (1 woman). *Students:* 39 part-time (14 women); includes 13 minority (8 Black or African American, non-Hispanic/Latino; 4 Asian, non-Hispanic/Latino; 1 Hispanic/Latino), 12 international. Average age 39. 26 applicants, 88% accepted, 19 enrolled. In 2016, 2 master's awarded. *Entrance requirements:* For master's, GMAT, resume (minimum 5 years' work experience), official transcripts, two recommendations, interview. Additional exam requirements/recommendations for international students: Required—TOEFL. *Application deadline:* For spring admission, 1/31 for domestic and international students. Applications are processed on a rolling basis. Application fee: $60 ($75 for international students). Electronic applications accepted. *Expenses:* Contact institution. *Financial support:* In 2016–17, 27 students received support. Scholarships/grants available. Financial award application deadline: 1/31. *Faculty research:* Dimensions of trust, communities of practice and networks, business in Latin America. *Unit head:* Dr. Aldas P. Kriauciunas, Executive Director, 765-496-1860, Fax: 765-494-0862, E-mail: akriauci@purdue.edu. *Application contact:* Nancy Smigiel, Assistant Director of Admissions, 765-494-4580, Fax: 765-494-0862, E-mail: nks@purdue.edu.
Website: http://www.krannert.purdue.edu/executive/emba/IMM-Global-EMBA/home.php

Regent's University London, Webster Graduate School, London, United Kingdom. Offers business (MBA); finance (MS); human resources (MA); information technology management (MA); international business (MA); international non-governmental organizations (MA); international relations (MA); management and leadership (MA); marketing (MA). *Program availability:* Part-time.

Rochester Institute of Technology, Graduate Enrollment Services, Saunders College of Business, Marketing and Management Department, MS Program in Management, Rochester, NY 14623. Offers MS. *Program availability:* Part-time. *Students:* 15 full-time (7 women), 8 part-time (7 women); includes 8 minority (3 Black or African American, non-Hispanic/Latino; 5 Hispanic/Latino), 10 international. Average age 27. 109 applicants, 55% accepted, 15 enrolled. In 2016, 1 master's awarded. *Degree requirements:* For master's, thesis or alternative. *Entrance requirements:* For master's, minimum GPA of 3.0 (recommended). Additional exam requirements/recommendations for international students: Required—TOEFL (minimum score 580 paper-based; 92 iBT), IELTS (minimum score 7), PTE (minimum score 63). *Application deadline:* Applications are processed on a rolling basis. Application fee: $60. Electronic applications accepted. *Expenses:* $1,742 per credit hour. *Financial support:* In 2016–17, 9 students received support. Research assistantships with partial tuition reimbursements available, teaching assistantships with partial tuition reimbursements available, career-related internships or fieldwork, scholarships/grants, and unspecified assistantships available. Support available to part-time students. Financial award applicants required to submit FAFSA. *Faculty research:* Impacts of clinical IT adoption in the U.S. healthcare system; social media and entrepreneurship, cybersecurity. *Unit head:* Jenna Lenhardt, Graduate Program Advisor, 585-475-6916, E-mail: jlenhardt@saunders.rit.edu. *Application contact:* Diane Ellison, Associate Vice President, Graduate Enrollment Services, 585-475-2229, Fax: 585-475-7164, E-mail: gradinfo@rit.edu.
Website: http://saunders.rit.edu/programs/graduate/ms_management.php

Rockhurst University, Helzberg School of Management, Kansas City, MO 64110-2561. Offers accounting (MBA); business intelligence (MBA, Certificate); data science (MBA, Certificate); entrepreneurship (MBA); finance (MBA); fundraising leadership (MBA, Certificate); healthcare management (MBA, Certificate); human capital (Certificate); international business (Certificate); management (MBA, Certificate); nonprofit administration (Certificate); organizational development (Certificate); science leadership (Certificate). *Accreditation:* AACSB. *Program availability:* Part-time, evening/weekend. *Entrance requirements:* For master's, GMAT or GRE. Additional exam requirements/recommendations for international students: Required—TOEFL (minimum score 550 paper-based; 79 iBT). Electronic applications accepted. Application fee is waived when completed online. *Faculty research:* Offshoring/outsourcing, systems analysis/synthesis, work teams, multilateral trade, path dependencies/creation.

Rollins College, Crummer Graduate School of Business, Winter Park, FL 32789-4499. Offers business administration (EDBA); entrepreneurship (MBA); finance (MBA); international business (MBA); management (MBA); marketing (MBA); operations and technology management (MBA). *Accreditation:* AACSB. *Program availability:* Part-time, evening/weekend, online learning. *Faculty:* 22 full-time (5 women), 4 part-time/adjunct (3 women). *Students:* 254 full-time (105 women), 83 part-time (36 women); includes 63 minority (15 Black or African American, non-Hispanic/Latino; 9 Asian, non-Hispanic/Latino; 35 Hispanic/Latino; 4 Two or more races, non-Hispanic/Latino), 48 international. Average age 31. 360 applicants, 74% accepted, 207 enrolled. In 2016, 159 master's awarded. *Degree requirements:* For master's, minimum GPA of 2.85; for doctorate, thesis/dissertation, minimum GPA of 3.0. *Entrance requirements:* For master's, GMAT or GRE, official transcripts, two letters of recommendation, essay, current resume/curriculum vitae, interview; for doctorate, official transcripts, two letters of recommendation, essays, current resume/curriculum vitae, interview. Additional exam requirements/recommendations for international students: Required—TOEFL (minimum score 100 iBT) or IELTS (minimum score 7). *Application deadline:* Applications are processed on a rolling basis. Application fee: $50. Electronic applications accepted. *Expenses:* Contact institution. *Financial support:* In 2016–17, 125 students received support. Federal Work-Study and scholarships/grants available. Support available to part-time students. Financial award applicants required to submit FAFSA. *Faculty research:* Sustainability, world financial markets, international business, market research, strategic marketing. *Unit head:* Deborah Crown, Dean, 407-646-2249, Fax: 407-646-1550, E-mail: dcrown@rollins.edu. *Application contact:* Maralyn E. Graham, Admissions Coordinator, 407-646-2405, Fax: 407-646-1550, E-mail: mbaadmissions@rollins.edu.
Website: http://www.rollins.edu/mba/

Rutgers University–Newark, Graduate School, Program in Management, Newark, NJ 07102. Offers accounting (PhD); accounting information systems (PhD); computer information systems (PhD); finance (PhD); information technology (PhD); international business (PhD); management science (PhD); marketing (PhD); organization management (PhD). Program offered jointly with New Jersey Institute of Technology. *Accreditation:* AACSB. *Degree requirements:* For doctorate, thesis/dissertation, cumulative exams. *Entrance requirements:* For doctorate, GMAT or GRE General Test, minimum undergraduate B average. Additional exam requirements/recommendations for international students: Required—TOEFL. Electronic applications accepted. *Faculty research:* Technology management, leadership and teams, consumer behavior, financial and markets, logistics.

Rutgers University–Newark, Rutgers Business School–Newark and New Brunswick, Doctoral Programs in Management, Newark, NJ 07102. Offers accounting (PhD); accounting information systems (PhD); economics (PhD); finance (PhD); individualized study (PhD); information technology (PhD); international business (PhD); management science (PhD); marketing science (PhD); organizational management (PhD); science, technology and management (PhD); supply chain management (PhD). *Degree requirements:* For doctorate, comprehensive exam, thesis/dissertation. *Entrance requirements:* For doctorate, GRE or GMAT. Additional exam requirements/recommendations for international students: Required—TOEFL (minimum score 550 paper-based; 79 iBT). Electronic applications accepted.

St. John's University, The Peter J. Tobin College of Business, Program in International Business, Queens, NY 11439. Offers MBA. *Program availability:* Part-time, evening/weekend. *Degree requirements:* For master's, comprehensive exam (for some programs), thesis optional. *Entrance requirements:* For master's, GMAT, 2 letters of recommendation, resume, transcripts, essay. Additional exam requirements/recommendations for international students: Required—TOEFL (minimum score 600 paper-based; 100 iBT), IELTS (minimum score 7). Electronic applications accepted. *Expenses:* Contact institution.

Saint Joseph's University, Erivan K. Haub School of Business, MBA Program, Philadelphia, PA 19131-1395. Offers accounting (MBA, Postbaccalaureate Certificate); business intelligence (MBA); finance (MBA); general business (MBA); health and medical services administration (MBA); international business (MBA); international marketing (MBA); managing human capital (MBA); marketing (MBA); DO/MBA. DO/MBA offered jointly with Philadelphia College of Osteopathic Medicine. *Program availability:* Part-time, evening/weekend, 100% online, blended/hybrid learning. *Faculty:* 31 full-time (10 women), 28 part-time/adjunct (7 women). *Students:* 95 full-time (40 women), 348 part-time (137 women); includes 64 minority (29 Black or African American, non-Hispanic/Latino; 17 Asian, non-Hispanic/Latino; 14 Hispanic/Latino; 1 Native Hawaiian or other Pacific Islander, non-Hispanic/Latino; 3 Two or more races, non-Hispanic/Latino), 47 international. Average age 30. 237 applicants, 60% accepted, 76 enrolled. In 2016, 144 master's awarded. *Degree requirements:* For master's and Postbaccalaureate Certificate, minimum GPA of 3.0. *Entrance requirements:* For master's, GMAT or GRE, 2 letters of recommendation, resume, personal statement, official undergraduate and graduate transcripts; for Postbaccalaureate Certificate, official master's-level transcripts. Additional exam requirements/recommendations for international students: Required—TOEFL (minimum score 550 paper-based, 80 iBT), IELTS (minimum score 6.5), or PTE (minimum score 60). *Application deadline:* For fall admission, 7/15 priority date for domestic students, 5/15 priority date for international students; for spring admission, 11/15 priority date for domestic students, 10/15 priority date for international students; for summer admission, 4/15 priority date for domestic students, 2/15 priority date for international students. Applications are processed on a rolling basis. Application fee: $35. Electronic applications accepted. *Expenses:* $1,003 per credit. *Financial support:* In 2016–17, 105 students received support, including 2 research assistantships with partial tuition reimbursements available (averaging $4,000 per year); scholarships/grants and unspecified assistantships also available. Support available to part-time students. Financial award application deadline: 5/1; financial award applicants required to submit FAFSA. *Unit head:* Dr. Patricia Rafferty, Director, 610-660-1318, E-mail: praffert@sju.edu. *Application contact:* Kate Sonstein, Program Manager/Recruiter, 610-660-1693, E-mail: kate.sonstein@sju.edu.
Website: http://www.sju.edu/haubmba

Saint Joseph's University, Erivan K. Haub School of Business, MS Program in International Marketing, Philadelphia, PA 19131-1395. Offers MS. *Program availability:* Part-time, evening/weekend. *Faculty:* 6 full-time (1 woman), 8 part-time/adjunct (2 women). *Students:* 30 full-time (19 women), 7 part-time (5 women); includes 2 minority (1 Hispanic/Latino; 1 Two or more races, non-Hispanic/Latino), 31 international. Average age 25. 76 applicants, 58% accepted, 17 enrolled. In 2016, 21 master's awarded. *Degree requirements:* For master's, minimum GPA of 3.0. *Entrance requirements:* For master's, GMAT or GRE, 2 letters of recommendation, resume, personal statement, official undergraduate and graduate transcripts. Additional exam requirements/recommendations for international students: Required—TOEFL (minimum score 550 paper-based, 80 iBT), IELTS (minimum score 6.5), or PTE (minimum score 60). *Application deadline:* For fall admission, 7/15 priority date for domestic students, 5/15 priority date for international students; for spring admission, 11/15 priority date for domestic students, 10/15 priority date for international students; for summer admission, 4/15 priority date for domestic students. Applications are processed on a rolling basis. Application fee: $35. Electronic applications accepted. *Expenses:* $1,003 per credit. *Financial support:* In 2016–17, 29 students received support, including 1 research assistantship with partial tuition reimbursement available (averaging $8,000 per year); scholarships/grants and unspecified assistantships also available. Support available to part-time students. Financial award application deadline: 5/1; financial award applicants required to submit FAFSA. *Faculty research:* Export marketing, global marketing, international marketing research, new product development, emerging markets, international consumer behavior. *Unit head:* Jeannine Lajeunesse, Director, 610-660-1626, E-mail: jlajeune@sju.edu. *Application contact:* Kate Sonstein, Program Manager/Recruiter, 610-660-1693, E-mail: kate.sonstein@sju.edu.
Website: http://www.sju.edu/academics/hsb/grad/mim/

Saint Louis University, Graduate Education, John Cook School of Business, Boeing Institute of International Business, St. Louis, MO 63103. Offers business administration

(PhD), including international business and marketing; executive international business (EMIB); international business (MBA). *Program availability:* Part-time, evening/weekend. *Degree requirements:* For master's, thesis, study abroad; for doctorate, comprehensive exam, thesis/dissertation. *Entrance requirements:* For master's, GMAT, work experience. Additional exam requirements/recommendations for international students: Required—TOEFL (minimum score 525 paper-based). *Expenses:* Contact institution. *Faculty research:* Foreign direct investment, technology transfer, emerging markets, Asian business, Latin American business.

Saint Mary's University of Minnesota, Schools of Graduate and Professional Programs, Graduate School of Business and Technology, International Business Program, Winona, MN 55987-1399. Offers MA. Tuition and fees vary according to degree level and program. *Unit head:* Dr. Jim Ollhoff, Director, 651-295-2454, E-mail: jollhoff@smumn.edu. *Application contact:* James Callinan, Director of Admissions for Graduate and Professional Programs, 612-728-5185, Fax: 612-728-5121, E-mail: jcallina@smumn.edu.
Website: http://www.smumn.edu/graduate-home/areas-of-study/graduate-school-of-business-technology/ma-in-international-business-twin-cities

Saint Peter's University, Graduate Business Programs, MBA Program, Jersey City, NJ 07306-5997. Offers finance (MBA); health care administration (MBA); human resource management (MBA); international business (MBA); management (MBA); management information systems (MBA); marketing (MBA); risk management (MBA); MBA/MS. *Program availability:* Part-time, evening/weekend. *Entrance requirements:* Additional exam requirements/recommendations for international students: Required—TOEFL. Electronic applications accepted. *Faculty research:* Finance, health care management, human resource management, international business, management, management information systems, marketing, risk management.

St. Thomas University, School of Business, Department of Management, Miami Gardens, FL 33054-6459. Offers accounting (MBA); general management (MSM, Certificate); health management (MBA, MSM, Certificate); human resource management (MBA, MSM, Certificate); international business (MBA, MIB, MSM, Certificate); justice administration (MSM, Certificate); management accounting (MSM, Certificate); public management (MSM, Certificate); sports administration (MS). *Program availability:* Part-time, evening/weekend. *Degree requirements:* For master's, comprehensive exam. *Entrance requirements:* For master's, interview, minimum GPA of 3.0 or GMAT. Additional exam requirements/recommendations for international students: Required—TOEFL (minimum score 550 paper-based; 79 iBT). Electronic applications accepted.

Salem International University, School of Business, Salem, WV 26426-0500. Offers information security (MBA); international business (MBA). *Program availability:* Part-time, online learning. *Entrance requirements:* For master's, minimum undergraduate GPA of 2.5, course work in business, resume. Additional exam requirements/recommendations for international students: Recommended—TOEFL (minimum score 550 paper-based), IELTS (minimum score 6.5). Electronic applications accepted. *Expenses:* Contact institution. *Faculty research:* Organizational behavior strategy, marketing services.

San Francisco State University, Division of Graduate Studies, College of Business, Program in Business Administration, San Francisco, CA 94132-1722. Offers decision sciences/operations research (MBA); ethics and compliance (MBA); finance (MBA); global business and innovation (MBA); healthcare administration (MBA); hospitality and tourism management (MBA); information systems (MBA); leadership (MBA); marketing (MBA); nonprofit and social enterprise leadership (MBA); sustainable business (MBA). *Accreditation:* AACSB. *Program availability:* Part-time, evening/weekend. *Degree requirements:* For master's, thesis, essay test. *Entrance requirements:* For master's, GMAT, minimum GPA of 2.7 in last 60 units. Additional exam requirements/recommendations for international students: Required—TOEFL (minimum score 550 paper-based). *Application deadline:* For fall admission, 5/1 priority date for domestic students, 4/1 for international students; for spring admission, 11/1 for domestic students, 10/15 for international students. Applications are processed on a rolling basis. Application fee: $55. *Expenses:* Tuition, state resident: full-time $6738. Tuition, nonresident: full-time $15,666. *Required fees:* $1012. Tuition and fees vary according to degree level and program. *Financial support:* Application deadline: 3/1. *Unit head:* Dr. Sanjit Sengupta, Faculty Director, 415-817-4366, Fax: 415-817-4340, E-mail: sengupta@sfsu.edu. *Application contact:* Zandra Tan, EMBA Program Coordinator, 415-817-4360, Fax: 415-817-4340, E-mail: zandra13@sfsu.edu.
Website: http://cob.sfsu.edu/graduate-programs/mba

Schiller International University, MBA Program, Madrid, Spain, Madrid, Spain. Offers international business (MBA). *Program availability:* Part-time. *Degree requirements:* For master's, comprehensive exam, thesis optional. *Entrance requirements:* Additional exam requirements/recommendations for international students: Required—TOEFL (minimum score 550 paper-based).

Schiller International University, MBA Program Paris, France, Paris, France. Offers international business (MBA). Bilingual French/English MBA available for native French speakers. *Program availability:* Part-time, evening/weekend, online learning. *Degree requirements:* For master's, comprehensive exam, thesis or alternative. *Entrance requirements:* Additional exam requirements/recommendations for international students: Required—TOEFL (minimum score 550 paper-based).

Schiller International University, MBA Programs, Florida, Program in International Business, Largo, FL 33771. Offers MBA. *Program availability:* Part-time, evening/weekend, online learning. *Degree requirements:* For master's, thesis optional. *Entrance requirements:* Additional exam requirements/recommendations for international students: Required—TOEFL (minimum score 550 paper-based).

Schiller International University, MBA Programs, Heidelberg, Germany, Heidelberg, Germany. Offers international business (MBA, MIM); management of information technology (MBA). *Program availability:* Part-time, evening/weekend. *Degree requirements:* For master's, thesis optional. *Entrance requirements:* Additional exam requirements/recommendations for international students: Required—TOEFL (minimum score 550 paper-based). *Faculty research:* Leadership, international economy, foreign direct investment.

Seton Hall University, Stillman School of Business, Department of International Business, South Orange, NJ 07079-2697. Offers MBA, Certificate. *Program availability:* Part-time, evening/weekend. *Degree requirements:* For master's, 20-hour service project. *Entrance requirements:* For master's, GMAT or GRE (waived based on work experience or advanced degree from AACSB institution), MS in business discipline, professional degree (MD, JD, PhD, DVM, DDS, CPA etc.), minimum undergraduate GPA of 3.0. Additional exam requirements/recommendations for international students: Required—TOEFL (minimum score 607 paper-based; 102 iBT), IELTS (minimum score 6), PTE. Electronic applications accepted. *Expenses:* Contact institution. *Faculty research:* Tariffs, international trade, polish economy, export-led growth, Chinese governance.

Seton Hall University, Stillman School of Business, Programs in Business Administration, South Orange, NJ 07079-2697. Offers accounting (MBA); entrepreneurship (Certificate); finance (MBA, Certificate); information technology management (MBA); international business (MBA); management (MBA); marketing (MBA); sport management (MBA); supply chain management (MBA, Certificate). *Program availability:* Part-time, evening/weekend. *Degree requirements:* For master's, 20 hours of community service (Social Responsibility Project). *Entrance requirements:* For master's, GMAT or CPA, GRE (waived based on work experience or advanced degree from AACSB institution), MS in business discipline, professional degree (MD, JD, PhD, DVM, DDS, CPA, etc.), minimum undergraduate GPA of 3.0. Additional exam requirements/recommendations for international students: Required—TOEFL (minimum score 607 paper-based; 102 iBT), IELTS (minimum score 6), PTE. Electronic applications accepted. *Expenses:* Contact institution. *Faculty research:* Sport, hedge funds, executive compensation, social media, legal studies.

SIT Graduate Institute, Graduate Programs, Master's Programs in Intercultural Service, Leadership, and Management, Brattleboro, VT 05302-0676. Offers intercultural service, leadership, and management (self-designed) (MA); international education (MA); peacebuilding and conflict transformation (MA); sustainable development (MA). *Program availability:* Online learning. *Degree requirements:* For master's, one foreign language, thesis. *Entrance requirements:* For master's, 3 letters of reference. Additional exam requirements/recommendations for international students: Required—TOEFL, IELTS. *Faculty research:* Intercultural communication, conflict resolution, international education, world issues, international affairs.

Sonoma State University, School of Business and Economics, Rohnert Park, CA 94928-3609. Offers business administration (MBA), including contemporary business issues, global business, leadership and entrepreneurship; executive business administration (MBA); wine business (MBA). *Accreditation:* AACSB. *Program availability:* Part-time, evening/weekend. *Degree requirements:* For master's, thesis or alternative. *Entrance requirements:* For master's, GMAT. Additional exam requirements/recommendations for international students: Required—TOEFL (minimum score 500 paper-based). *Application deadline:* For fall admission, 1/31 priority date for domestic students; for spring admission, 8/31 for domestic students. Applications are processed on a rolling basis. Application fee: $55. *Expenses:* Tuition, state resident: full-time $6738; part-time $3906 per unit. *Required fees:* $1916; $1916 per year. Tuition and fees vary according to course load, degree level and program. *Financial support:* Career-related internships or fieldwork, Federal Work-Study, institutionally sponsored loans, and scholarships/grants available. Support available to part-time students. Financial award application deadline: 3/2; financial award applicants required to submit FAFSA. *Unit head:* Dr. William Silver, Dean, 707-664-2377. *Application contact:* John Stayton, Executive Director, Graduate and Executive Programs, 707-664-3954, E-mail: john.stayton@sonoma.edu. Website: http://web.sonoma.edu/sbe/

Southern New Hampshire University, School of Business, Manchester, NH 03106-1045. Offers accounting (MBA, MS, Graduate Certificate); accounting finance (MS); accounting/auditing (MS); accounting/forensic accounting (MS); accounting/taxation (MS); athletic administration (MBA, Graduate Certificate); business administration (IMBA, MBA, Certificate, Graduate Certificate), including accounting (Certificate), business administration (MBA), business information systems (Graduate Certificate), human resource management (Certificate); corporate social responsibility (MBA); entrepreneurship (MBA); finance (MBA, MS, Graduate Certificate); finance/corporate finance (MS); finance/investments and securities (MS); forensic accounting (MBA); healthcare informatics (MBA); healthcare management (MBA); human resource management (Graduate Certificate); information technology (MS, Graduate Certificate); information technology management (MBA); international business (Graduate Certificate); international business and information technology (Graduate Certificate); international finance (Graduate Certificate); international sport management (Graduate Certificate); justice studies (MBA); leadership of nonprofit organizations (Graduate Certificate); management (MS); marketing (MBA, MS, Graduate Certificate); operations and project management (MS); operations and supply chain management (MBA, Graduate Certificate); organizational leadership (MS); project management (MBA, Graduate Certificate); Six Sigma (MBA); Six Sigma quality (Graduate Certificate); social media marketing (MBA); sport management (MBA, MS, Graduate Certificate); sustainability and environmental compliance (MBA); workplace conflict management (MBA); MBA/Certificate. *Accreditation:* ACBSP. *Program availability:* Part-time, evening/weekend, online learning. Terminal master's awarded for partial completion of doctoral program. *Degree requirements:* For master's, one foreign language, comprehensive exam (for some programs), thesis or alternative. *Entrance requirements:* For master's, minimum GPA of 2.5. Additional exam requirements/recommendations for international students: Required—TOEFL (minimum score 500 paper-based). Electronic applications accepted.

Southern Oregon University, Graduate Studies, School of Business, Ashland, OR 97520. Offers accounting (Postbaccalaureate Certificate); business administration (MBA); international management (MIM). *Accreditation:* ACBSP. *Program availability:* Part-time, evening/weekend, online learning. *Faculty:* 18 full-time (6 women), 8 part-time/adjunct (5 women). *Students:* 28 full-time (13 women), 30 part-time (10 women); includes 13 minority (1 Black or African American, non-Hispanic/Latino; 2 Asian, non-Hispanic/Latino; 7 Hispanic/Latino; 3 Two or more races, non-Hispanic/Latino), 19 international. Average age 33. 65 applicants, 49% accepted, 25 enrolled. In 2016, 16 master's awarded. *Degree requirements:* For master's, comprehensive exam. *Entrance requirements:* For master's, GMAT, minimum cumulative GPA of 3.0 in the last 90 quarter credits (60 semester credits) of undergraduate coursework. Additional exam requirements/recommendations for international students: Required—TOEFL (minimum score 540 paper-based; 76 iBT), IELTS (minimum score 6), ELPT (minimum score 964) or ELS (minimum score 112). *Application deadline:* For fall admission, 7/31 priority date for domestic and international students; for winter admission, 11/15 priority date for domestic students, 11/14 priority date for international students; for spring admission, 1/7 priority date for domestic and international students. Applications are processed on a rolling basis. Application fee: $60. Electronic applications accepted. *Expenses:* Tuition, state resident: full-time $10,710; part-time $397 per credit. Tuition, nonresident: full-time $13,419; part-time $497 per credit. *Required fees:* $548. *Financial support:* In 2016–17, 1 student received support, including 1 research assistantship with partial tuition reimbursement available; career-related internships or fieldwork, institutionally sponsored loans, scholarships/grants, and unspecified assistantships also available. *Unit head:* Dr. Mark Siders, Graduate Program Coordinator, 541-552-6709, E-mail: sidersm@sou.edu. *Application contact:* Kelly Moutsatson, Director of Admissions, 541-552-6411, Fax: 541-552-8403, E-mail: admissions@sou.edu.
Website: http://www.sou.edu/business/graduate-programs.html

State University of New York Empire State College, School for Graduate Studies, Program in Business Administration, Saratoga Springs, NY 12866-4391. Offers global leadership (MBA); management (MBA). *Program availability:* Part-time, online learning. *Degree requirements:* For master's, thesis or alternative. *Entrance requirements:* For master's, previous course work in statistics, macroeconomics, microeconomics, and accounting. Additional exam requirements/recommendations for international students: Required—TOEFL (minimum score 600 paper-based). Electronic applications accepted. *Expenses:* Contact institution. *Faculty research:* Corporate strategy, managerial competencies, decision analysis, economics in transition, organizational communication.

International Business

Stevens Institute of Technology, Graduate School, School of Business, Program in Management, Hoboken, NJ 07030. Offers general management (MS); global innovation management (MS); human resource management (MS); information management (MS); project management (MS); technology commercialization (MS); technology management (MS). *Program availability:* Part-time, evening/weekend. *Students:* 83 full-time (28 women), 82 part-time (36 women); includes 30 minority (6 Black or African American, non-Hispanic/Latino; 1 American Indian or Alaska Native, non-Hispanic/Latino; 21 Asian, non-Hispanic/Latino; 2 Hispanic/Latino), 73 international. Average age 29. 381 applicants, 64% accepted, 53 enrolled. In 2016, 66 master's awarded. *Degree requirements:* For master's, thesis optional, minimum B average in major field and overall. *Entrance requirements:* Additional exam requirements/recommendations for international students: Required—TOEFL (minimum score 74 iBT), IELTS (minimum score 6). *Application deadline:* For fall admission, 6/1 for domestic students, 4/15 for international students; for spring admission, 11/30 for domestic students, 11/1 for international students. Applications are processed on a rolling basis. Application fee: $65. Electronic applications accepted. *Expenses:* Contact institution. *Financial support:* Fellowships, research assistantships, teaching assistantships, career-related internships or fieldwork, Federal Work-Study, scholarships/grants, and unspecified assistantships available. Financial award application deadline: 2/15; financial award applicants required to submit FAFSA. *Unit head:* Brian Rothschild, Director, 201-216-3677, E-mail: brian.rothschild@stevens.edu. *Application contact:* Graduate Admissions, 888-783-8367, Fax: 888-511-1306, E-mail: graduate@stevens.edu.
Website: https://www.stevens.edu/school-business/masters-programs/management

Stratford University, School of Graduate Studies, Falls Church, VA 22043. Offers accounting (MS); business administration (IMBA, MBA); cyber security (MS); cyber security leadership and policy (MS); digital forensics (MS); enterprise business management (MS); entrepreneurial management (MS); healthcare administration (MS); information systems (MS); international hospitality management (MS); networking and telecommunications (MS); software engineering (MS). *Program availability:* Part-time, evening/weekend, 100% online, blended/hybrid learning. *Students:* 505 full-time (186 women), 172 part-time (88 women); includes 532 minority (165 Black or African American, non-Hispanic/Latino; 18 American Indian or Alaska Native, non-Hispanic/Latino; 324 Asian, non-Hispanic/Latino; 13 Hispanic/Latino; 10 Native Hawaiian or other Pacific Islander, non-Hispanic/Latino; 2 Two or more races, non-Hispanic/Latino). Average age 27. In 2016, 520 master's awarded. *Degree requirements:* For master's, comprehensive exam, capstone project. *Entrance requirements:* For master's, GRE or GMAT, baccalaureate degree. Additional exam requirements/recommendations for international students: Required—TOEFL (minimum score 79 iBT), IELTS (minimum score 6.5), PTE (minimum score 5). *Application deadline:* Applications are processed on a rolling basis. Application fee: $50. Electronic applications accepted. *Expenses: Tuition:* Full-time $4455; part-time $2227.50 per course. One-time fee: $100. *Financial support:* Federal Work-Study and scholarships/grants available. Financial award applicants required to submit FAFSA. *Unit head:* Dr. Richard R. Shurtz, President, 703-539-6890, Fax: 703-539-6960. *Application contact:* Admissions, 800-444-0804, E-mail: fcadmissions@stratford.edu.

Suffolk University, Sawyer Business School, Master of Business Administration Program, Boston, MA 02108-2770. Offers accounting (MBA); entrepreneurship (MBA); executive business administration (EMBA); finance (MBA); global business administration (GMBA); health administration (MBA); international business (MBA); marketing (MBA); nonprofit management (MBA); organizational behavior (MBA); strategic management (MBA); supply chain management (MBA); taxation (MBA); JD/MBA; MBA/MHA; MBA/MSA; MBA/MSF; MBA/MST. *Accreditation:* AACSB. *Program availability:* Part-time, evening/weekend, 100% online. *Faculty:* 17 full-time (6 women), 10 part-time/adjunct (1 woman). *Students:* 137 full-time (70 women), 265 part-time (138 women); includes 78 minority (20 Black or African American, non-Hispanic/Latino; 22 Asian, non-Hispanic/Latino; 31 Hispanic/Latino; 5 Two or more races, non-Hispanic/Latino), 46 international. Average age 30. 416 applicants, 70% accepted, 128 enrolled. In 2016, 165 degrees awarded. *Entrance requirements:* For master's, GMAT, minimum undergraduate GPA of 2.75 (MBA), 5 years of managerial experience (EMBA). Additional exam requirements/recommendations for international students: Required—TOEFL (minimum score 550 paper-based; 80 iBT). *Application deadline:* For fall admission, 3/15 priority date for domestic students, 10/15 priority date for international students; for spring admission, 10/15 priority date for domestic and international students. Applications are processed on a rolling basis. Application fee: $50. Electronic applications accepted. *Expenses: Tuition:* Full-time $41,490; part-time $1383 per credit hour. *Required fees:* $52; $52 per credit hour. Part-time tuition and fees vary according to course load and program. *Financial support:* In 2016–17, 209 students received support, including 176 fellowships (averaging $8,581 per year); career-related internships or fieldwork, Federal Work-Study, institutionally sponsored loans, and scholarships/grants also available. Support available to part-time students. Financial award application deadline: 4/1; financial award applicants required to submit FAFSA. *Faculty research:* Foreign investments; career strategies and boundaryless careers; corporate ethics codes; interest rates, inflation, and growth options; innovation and product development performance. *Unit head:* Jodi Detjen, Director of MBA Programs, 617-573-8306, E-mail: jdetjen@suffolk.edu. *Application contact:* Mara Marzocchi, Associate Director of Graduate Admissions, 617-573-8302, Fax: 617-305-1733, E-mail: grad.admission@suffolk.edu.
Website: http://www.suffolk.edu/mba

Taylor University, Master of Business Administration Program, Upland, IN 46989-1001. Offers emerging business strategies (MBA); global leadership (MBA). *Program availability:* Part-time.

Temple University, Fox School of Business, Doctoral Programs in Business, Philadelphia, PA 19122-6096. Offers accounting (PhD); entrepreneurship (PhD); finance (PhD); international business (PhD); management information systems (PhD); marketing (PhD); risk management and insurance (PhD); statistics (PhD); strategic management (PhD); tourism and sport (PhD). *Accreditation:* AACSB. *Degree requirements:* For doctorate, thesis/dissertation. *Entrance requirements:* For doctorate, GRE General Test, GMAT, minimum GPA of 3.0, master's degree. Additional exam requirements/recommendations for international students: Required—TOEFL (minimum score 600 paper-based; 100 iBT), IELTS (minimum score 7.5). Electronic applications accepted.

Temple University, Fox School of Business, MBA Programs, Philadelphia, PA 19122-6096. Offers accounting (MBA); business management (MBA); financial management (MBA); healthcare and life sciences innovation (MBA); human resource management (MBA); international business (IMBA); IT management (MBA); marketing management (MBA); pharmaceutical management (MBA); strategic management (EMBA, MBA). EMBA offered in Philadelphia, PA and Tokyo, Japan. *Accreditation:* AACSB. *Program availability:* Part-time, evening/weekend, online learning. *Entrance requirements:* For master's, GMAT, minimum undergraduate GPA of 3.0. Additional exam requirements/recommendations for international students: Required—TOEFL (minimum score 600 paper-based; 100 iBT), IELTS (minimum score 7.5).

Tennessee Technological University, College of Graduate Studies, College of Business, Cookeville, TN 38505. Offers accounting (MBA); finance (MBA); human resource management (MBA); international business (MBA); management information systems (MBA). *Accreditation:* AACSB. *Program availability:* Part-time, evening/weekend, online learning. *Faculty:* 28 full-time (5 women). *Students:* 45 full-time (22 women), 167 part-time (51 women); includes 18 minority (5 Black or African American, non-Hispanic/Latino; 4 Asian, non-Hispanic/Latino; 4 Hispanic/Latino; 5 Two or more races, non-Hispanic/Latino), 14 international. Average age 25. 173 applicants, 54% accepted, 52 enrolled. In 2016, 78 master's awarded. *Entrance requirements:* For master's, GMAT, GRE. Additional exam requirements/recommendations for international students: Required—TOEFL (minimum score 550 paper-based; 79 iBT), IELTS (minimum score 5.5), PTE (minimum score 53), or TOEIC (Test of English as an International Communication). *Application deadline:* For fall admission, 8/1 for domestic students, 5/1 for international students; for spring admission, 12/1 for domestic students, 10/1 for international students; for summer admission, 5/1 for domestic students, 2/1 for international students. Applications are processed on a rolling basis. Application fee: $35 ($40 for international students). Electronic applications accepted. *Expenses:* Tuition, state resident: full-time $9375; part-time $534 per credit hour. Tuition, nonresident: full-time $22,443; part-time $1260 per credit hour. *Financial support:* In 2016–17, 5 fellowships (averaging $10,000 per year), 1 teaching assistantship (averaging $5,200 per year) were awarded; research assistantships also available. Support available to part-time students. Financial award application deadline: 4/1. *Unit head:* Kate Nicewicz, Director, 931-372-3600, Fax: 931-372-6249, E-mail: knicewicz@tntech.edu. *Application contact:* Shelia K. Kendrick, Coordinator of Graduate Studies, 931-372-3808, Fax: 931-372-3497, E-mail: skendrick@tntech.edu.
Website: http://www.tntech.edu/mba

Texas A&M International University, Office of Graduate Studies and Research, A.R. Sanchez, Jr. School of Business, Division of International Business and Technology Studies, Laredo, TX 78041-1900. Offers information systems (MSIS); international business management (MBA, PhD). *Degree requirements:* For master's, thesis (for some programs). *Entrance requirements:* For master's, GMAT or GRE General Test. Additional exam requirements/recommendations for international students: Required—TOEFL (minimum score 550 paper-based; 79 iBT).

Texas A&M University–Corpus Christi, College of Graduate Studies, College of Business, Corpus Christi, TX 78412-5503. Offers accounting (M Acc); business (MBA); finance (MBA); health care administration (MBA); international business (MBA). *Accreditation:* AACSB. *Program availability:* Part-time, evening/weekend, 100% online, blended/hybrid learning. *Faculty:* 31 full-time (11 women), 2 part-time/adjunct (0 women). *Students:* 132 full-time (71 women), 495 part-time (232 women); includes 261 minority (49 Black or African American, non-Hispanic/Latino; 44 Asian, non-Hispanic/Latino; 160 Hispanic/Latino; 8 Two or more races, non-Hispanic/Latino), 111 international. Average age 32. 444 applicants, 55% accepted, 192 enrolled. In 2016, 205 master's awarded. *Degree requirements:* For master's, 30 to 42 hours (for MBA; varies by concentration area, delivery format, and necessity for foundational courses for students with nonbusiness degrees). *Entrance requirements:* For master's, GMAT, GRE. Additional exam requirements/recommendations for international students: Required—TOEFL (minimum score 550 paper-based), IELTS (minimum score 6.5). *Application deadline:* For fall admission, 7/15 priority date for domestic students, 5/1 priority date for international students; for spring admission, 11/15 priority date for domestic students, 9/1 priority date for international students; for summer admission, 4/15 priority date for domestic students, 2/1 priority date for international students. Applications are processed on a rolling basis. Application fee: $50 ($70 for international students). Electronic applications accepted. *Financial support:* Research assistantships, teaching assistantships, career-related internships or fieldwork, Federal Work-Study, institutionally sponsored loans, scholarships/grants, health care benefits, and unspecified assistantships available. Support available to part-time students. Financial award application deadline: 3/15; financial award applicants required to submit FAFSA. *Unit head:* Dr. John Gamble, Dean, 361-825-6045, Fax: 361-825-2725, E-mail: john.gamble@tamucc.edu. *Application contact:* Sharon Polansky, Director, Master's Program, 361-825-3448, Fax: 361-825-2755, E-mail: gradweb@tamucc.edu.
Website: http://cob.tamucc.edu

Texas A&M University–San Antonio, School of Business, San Antonio, TX 78224. Offers business administration (MBA); enterprise resource planning systems (MBA); finance (MBA); healthcare management (MBA); human resources management (MBA); information assurance and security (MBA); international business (MBA); professional accounting (MPA); project management (MBA); supply chain management (MBA). *Program availability:* Part-time, evening/weekend. *Entrance requirements:* For master's, GMAT. Additional exam requirements/recommendations for international students: Required—TOEFL (minimum score 550 paper-based; 80 iBT), IELTS (minimum score 6). Electronic applications accepted.

Tiffin University, Program in Business Administration, Tiffin, OH 44883-2161. Offers finance (MBA); general management (MBA); healthcare administration (MBA); human resource management (MBA); international business (MBA); leadership (MBA); marketing (MBA); non-profit management (MBA); sports management (MBA). *Accreditation:* ACBSP. *Program availability:* Part-time, evening/weekend, online learning. *Students:* 10 full-time (4 women), 497 part-time (240 women); includes 91 minority (67 Black or African American, non-Hispanic/Latino; 1 American Indian or Alaska Native, non-Hispanic/Latino; 5 Asian, non-Hispanic/Latino; 15 Hispanic/Latino; 3 Two or more races, non-Hispanic/Latino), 102 international. Average age 31. 214 applicants, 86% accepted, 146 enrolled. In 2016, 183 master's awarded. *Entrance requirements:* For master's, minimum undergraduate GPA of 2.5, work experience. Additional exam requirements/recommendations for international students: Required—TOEFL (minimum score 550 paper-based; 79 iBT), IELTS. *Application deadline:* For fall admission, 8/15 for domestic students, 8/1 for international students; for spring admission, 1/9 for domestic students, 12/1 for international students. Applications are processed on a rolling basis. Application fee: $50. Electronic applications accepted. Application fee is waived when completed online. *Expenses: Tuition:* Full-time $21,000; part-time $700 per credit hour. *Required fees:* $150. Tuition and fees vary according to program. *Financial support:* Unspecified assistantships available. Support available to part-time students. Financial award application deadline: 7/31; financial award applicants required to submit FAFSA. *Faculty research:* Small business, executive development operations, research and statistical analysis, market research, management information systems. *Unit head:* Dr. Bonnie Tiell, Dean of Graduate Studies, 419-448-3261, Fax: 419-443-5002, E-mail: btiell@tiffin.edu. *Application contact:* Nikki Hintze, Director of Graduate and Distance Education Academic Advising, 800-968-6446 Ext. 3596, Fax: 419-443-5002, E-mail: hintzenm@tiffin.edu.
Website: http://www.tiffin.edu/graduateprograms/

Trident University International, College of Business Administration, Program in Business Administration, Cypress, CA 90630. Offers business administration (PhD); conflict and negotiation management (MBA); criminal justice administration (MBA); entrepreneurship (MBA); finance (MBA); general management (MBA); government accounting (MBA); human resource management (MBA); information security and digital assurance management (MBA); information technology management (MBA); international business (MBA); logistics management (MBA); marketing (MBA); project management (MBA); public management (MBA); quality management (MBA); strategic leadership (MBA). *Program availability:* Part-time, evening/weekend, online learning. *Degree requirements:* For doctorate, comprehensive exam, thesis/dissertation, defense of dissertation. *Entrance requirements:* For master's, minimum GPA of 2.5 (students with GPA 3.0 or greater may transfer up to 30% of graduate level credits); for doctorate, minimum GPA of 3.4, curriculum vitae, course work in research methods or statistics. Additional exam requirements/recommendations for international students: Required—TOEFL. Electronic applications accepted.

Trinity Western University, School of Graduate Studies, Program in Business Administration, Langley, BC V2Y 1Y1, Canada. Offers international business (MBA); management of the growing enterprise (MBA); non-profit and charitable organization management (MBA). *Program availability:* Part-time, online learning. *Degree requirements:* For master's, thesis or alternative, applied project. *Entrance requirements:* For master's, GMAT (minimum score of 550 recommended). Additional exam requirements/recommendations for international students: Required—TOEFL (minimum score 600 paper-based; 100 iBT), IELTS. Electronic applications accepted.

Tufts University, The Fletcher School of Law and Diplomacy, Medford, MA 02155. Offers LL M, MA, MALD, MIB, PhD, DVM/MA, JD/MALD, MALD/MA, MALD/MBA, MALD/MS, MD/MA. *Program availability:* Online learning. *Degree requirements:* For master's, one foreign language, thesis; for doctorate, one foreign language, comprehensive exam, thesis/dissertation, dissertation defense. *Entrance requirements:* For master's and doctorate, GMAT or GRE General Test. Additional exam requirements/recommendations for international students: Required—TOEFL (minimum score 600 paper-based; 100 iBT), IELTS (minimum score 7). Electronic applications accepted. *Expenses:* Contact institution. *Faculty research:* Negotiation and conflict resolution, international organizations, international business and economic law, security studies, development economics.

Tulane University, A. B. Freeman School of Business, New Orleans, LA 70118-5669. Offers accounting (M Acct); analytics (MBA); banking and financial services (M Fin); energy (M Fin, MBA); entrepreneurship (MBA); finance (MBA, PhD); international business (MBA); international management (MBA); strategic management and leadership (MBA); JD/M Acct; JD/MBA; MBA/M Acc; MBA/MA; MBA/MD; MBA/ME; MBA/MPH. *Accreditation:* AACSB. *Program availability:* Part-time, evening/weekend. *Faculty:* 46 full-time (11 women), 36 part-time/adjunct (3 women). *Students:* 488 full-time (240 women), 414 part-time (198 women); includes 81 minority (31 Black or African American, non-Hispanic/Latino; 1 American Indian or Alaska Native, non-Hispanic/Latino; 17 Asian, non-Hispanic/Latino; 29 Hispanic/Latino; 3 Two or more races, non-Hispanic/Latino), 575 international. Average age 27. 2,038 applicants, 71% accepted, 511 enrolled. In 2016, 694 master's, 9 doctorates awarded. Terminal master's awarded for partial completion of doctoral program. *Degree requirements:* For master's, one foreign language, comprehensive exam (for some programs); for doctorate, one foreign language, comprehensive exam, thesis/dissertation. *Entrance requirements:* For master's and doctorate, GMAT or GRE, interview. Additional exam requirements/recommendations for international students: Required—TOEFL or IELTS. *Application deadline:* For fall admission, 11/1 priority date for domestic and international students; for winter admission, 1/6 for domestic and international students; for spring admission, 3/1 priority date for domestic and international students; for summer admission, 5/5 for domestic students. Applications are processed on a rolling basis. Application fee: $125. Electronic applications accepted. *Expenses:* Contact institution. *Financial support:* In 2016–17, 153 students received support. Fellowships with tuition reimbursements available, research assistantships, teaching assistantships, career-related internships or fieldwork, Federal Work-Study, tuition waivers (full and partial), and unspecified assistantships available. Support available to part-time students. Financial award application deadline: 4/15; financial award applicants required to submit FAFSA. *Faculty research:* Corporate finance, managerial accounting and financial reporting, strategic management and leadership, consumer behavior and decision making, organizational behavior and human resource management. *Unit head:* Ira Solomon, PhD, Dean, 504-865-5407, Fax: 504-865-5491, E-mail: businessdean@tulane.edu. *Application contact:* Melissa Booth, Director of Graduate Admissions and Financial Aid, 800-223-5402, E-mail: freeman.admissions@tulane.edu.
Website: http://www.freeman.tulane.edu

United States International University–Africa, School of Business Administration, Nairobi, Kenya. Offers business administration (GEMBA); entrepreneurship (MBA); finance (MBA); human resource management (MBA); information technology management (MBA); integrated studies (MBA); international business administration (MBA); management and organizational development (MS); marketing (MBA); organizational development (EMS); strategic management (MBA). *Program availability:* Part-time, evening/weekend. *Degree requirements:* For master's, thesis. *Entrance requirements:* For master's, GMAT, 2 letters of reference, resume. Additional exam requirements/recommendations for international students: Required—TOEFL (minimum score 550 paper-based). *Faculty research:* Marketing in small business enterprises, total quality management in Kenya.

Universidad Autonoma de Guadalajara, Graduate Programs, Guadalajara, Mexico. Offers administrative law and justice (LL M); advertising and corporate communications (MA); architecture (M Arch); business (MBA); computational science (MCC); education (Ed M, Ed D); English-Spanish translation (MA); entrepreneurship and management (MBA); integrated management of digital animation (MA); international business (MIB); international corporate law (LL M); internet technologies (MS); manufacturing systems (MMS); occupational health (MS); philosophy (MA, PhD); power electronics (MS); quality systems (MQS); renewable energy (MS); social evaluation of projects (MBA); strategic market research (MBA); tax law (MA); teaching mathematics (MA).

Universidad Metropolitana, School of Business Administration, Program in International Business, San Juan, PR 00928-1150. Offers MBA.

Université de Sherbrooke, Faculty of Administration, Program in International Business, Sherbrooke, QC J1K 2R1, Canada. Offers M Sc. *Degree requirements:* For master's, one foreign language, thesis. *Entrance requirements:* For master's, bachelor's degree in related field, minimum GPA of 3.0 (on 4.3 scale). Electronic applications accepted.

Université du Québec, École nationale d'administration publique, Graduate Programs in Public Administration, Program in International Administration, Quebec, QC G1K 9E5, Canada. Offers MAP, Diploma. *Program availability:* Part-time. *Entrance requirements:* For degree, appropriate bachelor's degree, proficiency in French.

Université Laval, Faculty of Administrative Sciences, Programs in Business Administration, Québec, QC G1K 7P4, Canada. Offers accounting (MBA); agri-food management (MBA); electronic business (MBA, Diploma); factory management and logistics (MBA); finance (MBA); firm management (MBA); geomatic management (MBA); information technology management (MBA); international management (MBA); management (MBA); management accounting (MBA, Diploma); marketing (MBA); modeling and organizational decision (MBA); occupational health and safety management (MBA); pharmacy management (MBA); social and environmental responsibility (MBA); technological entrepreneurship (Diploma). *Accreditation:* AACSB. *Program availability:* Part-time, evening/weekend, online learning. *Entrance requirements:* For master's and Diploma, knowledge of French and English. Electronic applications accepted.

University at Buffalo, the State University of New York, Graduate School, College of Arts and Sciences, Department of Geography, Buffalo, NY 14214. Offers earth systems science (MA, MS); economic geography and business geographics (MS); environmental modeling and analysis (MA); geographic information science (MA, MS); geography (MA, PhD); health geography (MS); international trade (MA); urban and regional analysis (MA). *Program availability:* Part-time. *Faculty:* 18 full-time (8 women), 1 part-time/adjunct (0 women). *Students:* 45 full-time (29 women), 51 part-time (15 women); includes 64 minority (1 Black or African American, non-Hispanic/Latino; 61 Asian, non-Hispanic/Latino; 2 Hispanic/Latino), 41 international. Average age 28. 167 applicants, 34% accepted, 28 enrolled. In 2016, 23 master's, 7 doctorates awarded. Terminal master's awarded for partial completion of doctoral program. *Degree requirements:* For master's, thesis (for some programs), project or portfolio; for doctorate, thesis/dissertation. *Entrance requirements:* For master's, GRE General Test, minimum GPA of 2.9; for doctorate, GRE General Test, minimum GPA of 3.0. Additional exam requirements/recommendations for international students: Required—TOEFL (minimum score 550 paper-based; 79 iBT). *Application deadline:* For fall admission, 5/1 priority date for domestic students, 3/10 priority date for international students; for spring admission, 11/1 priority date for domestic students, 9/1 priority date for international students. Applications are processed on a rolling basis. Application fee: $75. Electronic applications accepted. *Expenses:* Contact institution. *Financial support:* In 2016–17, 15 students received support, including 7 fellowships with full tuition reimbursements available (averaging $3,070 per year), 7 research assistantships with full tuition reimbursements available (averaging $14,000 per year), 15 teaching assistantships with full tuition reimbursements available (averaging $14,080 per year); career-related internships or fieldwork, Federal Work-Study, institutionally sponsored loans, traineeships, health care benefits, and unspecified assistantships also available. Financial award application deadline: 1/10. *Faculty research:* International business and world trade, geographic information systems and cartography, transportation, urban and regional analysis, physical and environmental geography. *Total annual research expenditures:* $2.6 million. *Unit head:* Dr. Sean Bennett, Chairman, 716-645-0490, Fax: 716-645-2329, E-mail: seanb@buffalo.edu. *Application contact:* Wendy Zitzka, Graduate Secretary, 716-645-0471, Fax: 716-645-2329, E-mail: wzitzka@buffalo.edu.
Website: http://www.geog.buffalo.edu/

University at Buffalo, the State University of New York, Graduate School, School of Management, Buffalo, NY 14620. Offers accounting (MS); analytics (MBA); business administration (PMBA); consulting (MBA); finance (MBA, MS), including financial risk management (MS), quantitative finance (MS); healthcare (MBA); information assurance (MBA); information systems (MBA); international management (MBA); management (EMBA, PhD); management information systems (MS); marketing (MBA); supply chain and operations (MBA); supply chains and operations management (MS); Au D/MBA; DDS/MBA; JD/MBA; M Arch/MBA; MD/MBA; MPH/MBA; MSW/MBA; Pharm D/MBA. *Accreditation:* AACSB. *Program availability:* Part-time, evening/weekend. *Faculty:* 80 full-time (26 women), 36 part-time/adjunct (6 women). *Students:* 683 full-time (277 women), 196 part-time (63 women); includes 76 minority (23 Black or African American, non-Hispanic/Latino; 1 American Indian or Alaska Native, non-Hispanic/Latino; 48 Asian, non-Hispanic/Latino; 3 Hispanic/Latino; 1 Two or more races, non-Hispanic/Latino), 371 international. Average age 31. 2,451 applicants, 42% accepted, 484 enrolled. In 2016, 515 master's, 10 doctorates awarded. *Degree requirements:* For master's, thesis (for some programs); for doctorate, comprehensive exam, thesis/dissertation. *Entrance requirements:* For master's, GMAT (for MS in accounting, finance); GRE or GMAT (for MBA, PMBA, other MS concentrations), essays, letters of recommendation; for doctorate, GMAT or GRE, essays, writing sample, letters of recommendation. Additional exam requirements/recommendations for international students: Required—TOEFL (minimum score 95 iBT) or IELTS (minimum score 6.5); Recommended—TSE (minimum score 73). *Application deadline:* For fall admission, 10/15 priority date for domestic and international students; for winter admission, 2/1 priority date for domestic and international students; for spring admission, 4/15 for domestic students; for summer admission, 5/15 for domestic students. Application fee: $100. Electronic applications accepted. *Expenses:* Contact institution. *Financial support:* Fellowships with full and partial tuition reimbursements, research assistantships with full and partial tuition reimbursements, teaching assistantships with full and partial tuition reimbursements, career-related internships or fieldwork, Federal Work-Study, institutionally sponsored loans, scholarships/grants, health care benefits, and unspecified assistantships available. Financial award application deadline: 2/15. *Faculty research:* Data analytics, accounting information and corporate finance, consumer behavior, supply chain logistics, leadership and team effectiveness. *Total annual research expenditures:* $1.5 million. *Unit head:* Erin K. O'Brien, Assistant Dean and Director of Graduate Programs, 716-645-3204, Fax: 716-645-2341, E-mail: ekobrien@buffalo.edu. *Application contact:* Meghan Felser, Associate Director of Admissions and Recruiting, 716-645-3204, Fax: 716-645-2341, E-mail: mpwood@buffalo.edu.
Website: http://mgt.buffalo.edu/

The University of Akron, Graduate School, College of Business Administration, Program in International Business, Akron, OH 44325. Offers MBA, JD/MBA. *Program availability:* Part-time, evening/weekend. *Students:* 6 full-time (4 women), 1 part-time (0 women); includes 1 minority (Asian, non-Hispanic/Latino), 3 international. Average age 26. 3 applicants, 100% accepted, 1 enrolled. In 2016, 3 master's awarded. *Entrance requirements:* For master's, GMAT, minimum GPA of 3.0 (preferred), two letters of recommendation, resume, statement of purpose. Additional exam requirements/recommendations for international students: Required—TOEFL (minimum score 550 paper-based; 79 iBT), IELTS (minimum score 6.5). *Application deadline:* For fall admission, 7/15 for domestic and international students; for spring admission, 11/15 for domestic and international students; for summer admission, 4/15 for domestic and international students. Application fee: $45 ($75 for international students). Electronic applications accepted. *Expenses:* Tuition, state resident: full-time $8618; part-time $359 per credit hour. Tuition, nonresident: full-time $17,149; part-time $715 per credit hour. *Required fees:* $1652. *Financial support:* In 2016–17, 2 teaching assistantships with full and partial tuition reimbursements were awarded. *Unit head:* Dr. Terry Daugherty, Interim Chair, 330-972-8304, E-mail: td23@uakron.edu. *Application contact:* Dr. William Hauser, Director of Graduate Business Programs, 330-972-7043, Fax: 330-972-6588, E-mail: whauser@uakron.edu.
Website: http://www.uakron.edu/cba/graduate/programs/mba/internationalbusiness.dot

University of Alberta, Faculty of Graduate Studies and Research, Program in Business Administration, Edmonton, AB T6G 2E1, Canada. Offers international business (MBA); leisure and sport management (MBA); natural resources and energy (MBA); technology commercialization (MBA); MBA/LL B; MBA/M Ag; MBA/M Eng; MBA/ME; MBA/PhD. *Accreditation:* AACSB. *Program availability:* Part-time, evening/weekend. *Degree requirements:* For master's, thesis or alternative. *Entrance requirements:* For master's, GMAT. Additional exam requirements/recommendations for international students: Required—TOEFL (minimum score 600 paper-based). Electronic applications accepted. *Faculty research:* Natural resources and energy/management and policy/family enterprise/international business/healthcare research management.

International Business

University of Baltimore, Graduate School, Merrick School of Business, Department of Management and International Business, Baltimore, MD 21201-5779. Offers global leadership (MS).

University of Bridgeport, School of Business, Bridgeport, CT 06604. Offers accounting (MBA); finance (MBA); general business (MBA); global financial services (MBA); human resource management (MBA); information systems and knowledge management (MBA); international business (MBA); management (MBA); marketing (MBA); operations management (MBA); small business and entrepreneurship (MBA); specialized business (MBA). *Accreditation:* ACBSP. *Program availability:* Part-time, evening/weekend. *Degree requirements:* For master's, thesis optional. *Entrance requirements:* For master's, GMAT. Additional exam requirements/recommendations for international students: Recommended—TOEFL (minimum score 550 paper-based; 80 iBT), IELTS (minimum score 6.5). Electronic applications accepted. *Expenses:* Contact institution.

University of California, Berkeley, UC Berkeley Extension, International Diploma Programs, Berkeley, CA 94720-1500. Offers business administration (Certificate); finance (Certificate); global business management (Certificate); marketing (Certificate); project management (Certificate). *Accreditation:* AACSB.

University of California, San Diego, Graduate Division, School of Global Policy and Strategy, Master of International Affairs Program, La Jolla, CA 92093. Offers international development and nonprofit management (MIA); international economics (MIA); international environmental policy (MIA); international management (MIA); international politics (MIA). Students will choose one of the following country/regional specializations: China, Japan, Korea, Latin America, or Southeast Asia. *Faculty:* 33 full-time (9 women), 20 part-time/adjunct (4 women). *Students:* 300 full-time (150 women). Average age 24. 460 applicants, 120 enrolled. In 2016, 120 master's awarded. *Degree requirements:* For master's, one foreign language. *Entrance requirements:* For master's, GMAT or GRE General Test. Additional exam requirements/recommendations for international students: Required—TOEFL (minimum score 90 iBT), IELTS (minimum score 7). *Application deadline:* For fall admission, 1/15 for domestic and international students. Applications are processed on a rolling basis. Application fee: $90 ($110 for international students). Electronic applications accepted. *Expenses:* Tuition, state resident: full-time $11,220. Tuition, nonresident: full-time $26,322. *Required fees:* $1864. *Financial support:* In 2016–17, 140 students received support, including 60 fellowships with full and partial tuition reimbursements available (averaging $50,000 per year), 15 research assistantships with full tuition reimbursements available (averaging $20,000 per year), 20 teaching assistantships with full tuition reimbursements available (averaging $20,000 per year); career-related internships or fieldwork, scholarships/grants, and unspecified assistantships also available. Financial award application deadline: 1/15. *Unit head:* Sonja Steinbrech, Director of Enrollment, 858-534-7162, E-mail: ssteinbrech@ucsd.edu. *Application contact:* Admissions Representative, 858-534-5914, E-mail: gps-apply@ucsd.edu.
Website: http://gps.ucsd.edu/academics/mia.html

University of Chicago, Booth School of Business, Executive MBA Program Asia (Hong Kong), Hong Kong, IL 60637-1513, Singapore. Offers MBA. *Program availability:* Part-time. *Students:* 5 full-time (1 woman), 143 part-time (24 women). *Entrance requirements:* For master's, letter of company support, letters of recommendation, essays, resume, interview. Electronic applications accepted. *Expenses:* Contact institution. *Unit head:* Associate Dean, Executive MBA Program for Europe and Asia, 852-2533-9520. *Application contact:* Executive MBA Program Asia, 852-2533-9500, E-mail: asia.inquiries@chicagobooth.edu.
Website: http://www.chicagobooth.edu/programs/exec-mba

University of Chicago, Booth School of Business, Executive MBA Program Europe (London), London, IL 60637-1513, United Kingdom. Offers MBA. *Program availability:* Part-time. *Students:* 6 full-time (1 woman), 141 part-time (35 women). *Entrance requirements:* For master's, letter of company support, letters of recommendation, essays, resume, interview. Electronic applications accepted. *Expenses:* Contact institution. *Unit head:* Associate Dean, Executive MBA Program for Europe and Asia, 44 20-7070-2200. *Application contact:* Executive MBA Program Europe, 44 20-7070-2200, Fax: 44 20-7070-2250, E-mail: europe.inquiries@chicagobooth.edu.
Website: http://www.chicagobooth.edu/programs/exec-mba

University of Chicago, Booth School of Business, Executive MBA Program North America, Chicago, IL 60611. Offers MBA. *Program availability:* Part-time. *Students:* 9 full-time (2 women), 167 part-time (41 women). *Entrance requirements:* For master's, letter of company support, letters of recommendation, essays, resume, interview. Electronic applications accepted. *Expenses:* Contact institution. *Unit head:* Associate Dean, Executive MBA and Global Integration, 312-464-8751. *Application contact:* Executive MBA Program North America, 312-464-8750, E-mail: xp@chicagobooth.edu.
Website: http://www.chicagobooth.edu/programs/exec-mba

University of Chicago, Booth School of Business, Full-Time MBA Program, Chicago, IL 60637. Offers accounting (MBA); analytic finance (MBA); analytic management (MBA); econometrics and statistics (MBA); economics (MBA); entrepreneurship (MBA); finance (MBA); general management (MBA); health administration and policy (Certificate); international business (MBA); managerial and organizational behavior (MBA); marketing analytics (MBA); marketing management (MBA); operations management (MBA); strategic management (MBA); MBA/AM; MBA/JD; MBA/MA; MBA/MD; MBA/MPP. *Accreditation:* AACSB. *Students:* 1,151 full-time (443 women), 17 part-time (9 women). Terminal master's awarded for partial completion of doctoral program. *Entrance requirements:* For master's, GMAT or GRE, transcripts, resume, 2 letters of recommendation, essay, interview. Additional exam requirements/recommendations for international students: Required—TOEFL (minimum score 600 paper-based; 104 iBT), IELTS (minimum score 7), PTE (minimum score 70). *Application deadline:* For spring admission, 4/1 for domestic and international students. Electronic applications accepted. *Expenses:* Contact institution. *Unit head:* Stacey Kole, Deputy Dean, 773-702-7121. *Application contact:* Full-time MBA Program Admissions, 773-702-7369, Fax: 773-702-9085, E-mail: admissions@chicagobooth.edu.
Website: https://www.chicagobooth.edu/programs/full-time

University of Colorado Denver, Business School, Master of Business Administration Program, Denver, CO 80217. Offers bioinnovation and entrepreneurship (MBA); business intelligence (MBA); business strategy (MBA); business to business marketing (MBA); business to consumer marketing (MBA); change management (MBA); corporate financial management (MBA); enterprise technology management (MBA); entrepreneurship (MBA); health administration (MBA), including financial management, health administration, health information technologies, international health management and policy; human resources management (MBA); international business (MBA); investment management (MBA); managing for sustainability (MBA); sports and entertainment management (MBA). *Accreditation:* AACSB. *Program availability:* Part-time, evening/weekend, 100% online, blended/hybrid learning. *Students:* 544 full-time (210 women), 112 part-time (22 women); includes 99 minority (15 Black or African American, non-Hispanic/Latino; 4 American Indian or Alaska Native, non-Hispanic/Latino; 38 Asian, non-Hispanic/Latino; 36 Hispanic/Latino; 6 Two or more races, non-Hispanic/Latino), 22 international. Average age 32. 335 applicants, 73% accepted, 179 enrolled. In 2016, 251 master's awarded. *Degree requirements:* For master's, 48 semester hours, including 30 of core courses, 3 in international business, and 15 in electives from over 50 other business courses. *Entrance requirements:* For master's, GMAT, resume, official transcripts, essay, two letters of recommendation, financial statements (for international applicants). Additional exam requirements/recommendations for international students: Required—TOEFL (minimum score 560 paper-based; 83 iBT); Recommended—IELTS (minimum score 6.5). *Application deadline:* For fall admission, 4/15 priority date for domestic students, 3/15 priority date for international students; for spring admission, 10/15 priority date for domestic students, 9/15 priority date for international students; for summer admission, 2/15 priority date for domestic students, 1/15 priority date for international students. Applications are processed on a rolling basis. Application fee: $50 ($75 for international students). Electronic applications accepted. *Expenses:* Contact institution. *Financial support:* In 2016–17, 171 students received support. Fellowships, research assistantships, teaching assistantships, Federal Work-Study, institutionally sponsored loans, scholarships/grants, traineeships, and unspecified assistantships available. Financial award application deadline: 4/1; financial award applicants required to submit FAFSA. *Faculty research:* Marketing, management, entrepreneurship, finance, health administration. *Unit head:* Woodrow Eckard, MBA Director, 303-315-8470, E-mail: woody.eckard@ucdenver.edu. *Application contact:* Shelly Townley, Admissions Director, Graduate Programs, 303-315-8202, E-mail: shelly.townley@ucdenver.edu.
Website: http://www.ucdenver.edu/academics/colleges/business/degrees/mba/Pages/MBA.aspx

University of Colorado Denver, Business School, Program in Global Energy Management, Denver, CO 80217. Offers MS. *Program availability:* Online learning. *Students:* 54 full-time (13 women), 4 part-time (2 women); includes 13 minority (4 Black or African American, non-Hispanic/Latino; 8 Hispanic/Latino; 1 Two or more races, non-Hispanic/Latino), 6 international. Average age 35. 28 applicants, 82% accepted, 16 enrolled. In 2016, 32 master's awarded. *Degree requirements:* For master's, 36 semester credit hours. *Entrance requirements:* For master's, GMAT if less than three years of experience in the energy industry (waived for students already holding a graduate degree), minimum of 5 years' experience in energy industry; resume; letters of recommendation; essays. Additional exam requirements/recommendations for international students: Required—TOEFL (minimum score 525 paper-based; 71 iBT); Recommended—IELTS (minimum score 6). *Application deadline:* For fall admission, 6/1 for domestic and international students; for winter admission, 12/1 for domestic and international students; for spring admission, 12/1 for domestic and international students. Application fee: $50 ($75 for international students). Electronic applications accepted. *Expenses:* Contact institution. *Financial support:* In 2016–17, 6 students received support. Fellowships, research assistantships, teaching assistantships, Federal Work-Study, institutionally sponsored loans, scholarships/grants, and traineeships available. Financial award application deadline: 4/1; financial award applicants required to submit FAFSA. *Unit head:* Jim Marchiori, Executive Director of Global Energy Management, 303-315-8436, E-mail: gem@ucdenver.edu. *Application contact:* Michele Motley, Graduate Advisor, Global Energy Management Program, 303-315-8066, E-mail: michelle.motley@ucdenver.edu.
Website: http://www.ucdenver.edu/academics/colleges/business/degrees/ms/gem/Pages/Overview.aspx

University of Colorado Denver, Business School, Program in International Business, Denver, CO 80217. Offers MSIB. *Program availability:* Part-time, evening/weekend. *Students:* 17 full-time (8 women), 6 part-time (5 women); includes 6 minority (1 Black or African American, non-Hispanic/Latino; 5 Hispanic/Latino), 3 international. Average age 32. 8 applicants, 88% accepted, 3 enrolled. In 2016, 6 master's awarded. *Degree requirements:* For master's, one foreign language, 42 credit hours; thesis, internship or international field study. *Entrance requirements:* For master's, GMAT, resume, essay, two letters of recommendation, financial statements (for international applicants). Additional exam requirements/recommendations for international students: Required—TOEFL (minimum score 525 paper-based; 71 iBT); Recommended—IELTS (minimum score 6.5). *Application deadline:* For fall admission, 4/15 priority date for domestic students, 3/15 priority date for international students; for spring admission, 10/15 priority date for domestic students, 9/15 priority date for international students; for summer admission, 2/15 priority date for domestic students, 1/15 priority date for international students. Applications are processed on a rolling basis. Application fee: $50 ($75 for international students). Electronic applications accepted. *Expenses:* Contact institution. *Financial support:* Fellowships, research assistantships, teaching assistantships, Federal Work-Study, institutionally sponsored loans, scholarships/grants, and traineeships available. Financial award application deadline: 4/1; financial award applicants required to submit FAFSA. *Faculty research:* Foreign direct investment, international business strategies, cross-cultural management, internationalization of research and development, global leadership development. *Unit head:* Dr. Manuel Serapio, Associate Professor/Director of MS in International Business, 303-315-8888, E-mail: manuel.serapio@ucdenver.edu. *Application contact:* 303-315-8200, E-mail: bschool.admissions@ucdenver.edu.
Website: http://www.ucdenver.edu/academics/colleges/business/degrees/ms/ib/Pages/default.aspx

University of Colorado Denver, Business School, Program in Management and Organization, Denver, CO 80217. Offers business strategy (MS); change and innovation (MS); enterprise technology management (MS); entrepreneurship and innovation (MS); global management (MS); leadership (MS); managing for sustainability (MS); managing human resources (MS); sports and entertainment management (MS). *Accreditation:* AACSB. *Program availability:* Part-time, evening/weekend, online learning. *Students:* 20 full-time (13 women), 17 part-time (10 women); includes 6 minority (3 Black or African American, non-Hispanic/Latino; 1 American Indian or Alaska Native, non-Hispanic/Latino; 1 Hispanic/Latino; 1 Two or more races, non-Hispanic/Latino), 6 international. Average age 33. 24 applicants, 58% accepted, 6 enrolled. In 2016, 19 master's awarded. *Degree requirements:* For master's, 30 semester hours (12 of required courses, 12 of management electives, and 6 of free electives). *Entrance requirements:* For master's, GMAT, resume, two letters of recommendation, essay, financial statements (for international applicants). Additional exam requirements/recommendations for international students: Required—TOEFL (minimum score 525 paper-based; 71 iBT); Recommended—IELTS (minimum score 6.5). *Application deadline:* For fall admission, 4/15 priority date for domestic students, 3/15 priority date for international students; for spring admission, 10/15 priority date for domestic students, 9/15 priority date for international students; for summer admission, 2/15 priority date for domestic students, 1/15 priority date for international students. Applications are processed on a rolling basis. Application fee: $50 ($75 for international students). Electronic applications accepted. *Expenses:* Contact institution. *Financial support:* In 2016–17, 7 students received support. Fellowships, research assistantships, teaching assistantships, Federal Work-Study, institutionally sponsored loans, scholarships/grants, and traineeships available. Financial award application deadline: 4/1; financial award applicants required to submit FAFSA. *Faculty research:* Human resource management, management of catastrophe, turnaround strategies. *Unit head:* Dr. Kenneth Bettenhausen, Associate Professor/Director of MS in Management, 303-315-8425, E-mail: kenneth.bettenhausen@ucdenver.edu. *Application contact:* 303-315-8200, E-mail: bschool.admissions@ucdenver.edu.

Website: http://www.ucdenver.edu/academics/colleges/business/degrees/ms/management/Pages/Management.aspx

University of Colorado Denver, Business School, Program in Marketing, Denver, CO 80217. Offers brand management and marketing communication (MS); global marketing (MS); high-tech and entrepreneurial marketing (MS); marketing for sustainability (MS); marketing research (MS); sports and entertainment marketing (MS). *Program availability:* Part-time, evening/weekend. *Students:* 30 full-time (19 women), 7 part-time (5 women); includes 5 minority (2 Black or African American, non-Hispanic/Latino; 1 Asian, non-Hispanic/Latino; 2 Hispanic/Latino), 12 international. Average age 28. 47 applicants, 62% accepted, 13 enrolled. In 2016, 23 master's awarded. *Degree requirements:* For master's, 30 semester hours (21 of marketing core courses, 9 of marketing electives). *Entrance requirements:* For master's, GMAT, resume, essay, two letters of recommendation, financial statements (for international applicants). Additional exam requirements/recommendations for international students: Required—TOEFL (minimum score 525 paper-based; 71 iBT); Recommended—IELTS (minimum score 6.5). *Application deadline:* For fall admission, 4/15 priority date for domestic students, 3/15 priority date for international students; for spring admission, 10/15 priority date for domestic students, 9/15 priority date for international students; for summer admission, 2/15 priority date for domestic students, 1/15 priority date for international students. Applications are processed on a rolling basis. Application fee: $50 ($75 for international students). Electronic applications accepted. *Expenses:* Contact institution. *Financial support:* In 2016–17, 7 students received support. Fellowships, research assistantships, teaching assistantships, Federal Work-Study, institutionally sponsored loans, scholarships/grants, and traineeships available. Financial award application deadline: 4/1; financial award applicants required to submit FAFSA. *Faculty research:* Marketing issues in the Chinese environment, impact of individual difference and contextual factors on the risk-taking behaviors of managers making new-business creation decisions, attribution theory perspective of conflict between marketers and engineers, organizational identity and identification, international market entry strategies. *Unit head:* Vicki Lane, Director of Marketing Program, 303-315-8468, E-mail: vicki.lane@ucdenver.edu. *Application contact:* 303-315-8200, E-mail: bschool.admissions@ucdenver.edu.

Website: http://www.ucdenver.edu/academics/colleges/business/degrees/ms/marketing/Pages/Marketing.aspx

University of Dallas, Satish and Yasmin Gupta College of Business, Irving, TX 75062-4736. Offers accounting (MBA, MS); business administration (DBA); business analytics (MS); business management (MBA); corporate finance (MBA); cybersecurity (MS); finance (MS); financial services (MBA); global business (MBA, MS); health services management (MBA); human resource management (MBA); information and technology management (MS); information assurance (MBA); information technology (MBA); information technology service management (MBA); marketing management (MBA); organization development (MBA); project management (MBA); sports and entertainment management (MBA); strategic leadership (MBA); supply chain management (MBA). *Accreditation:* AACSB. *Program availability:* Part-time, evening/weekend, online learning. *Entrance requirements:* Additional exam requirements/recommendations for international students: Required—TOEFL. Electronic applications accepted. *Expenses:* Contact institution.

University of Florida, Graduate School, Warrington College of Business Administration, Hough Graduate School of Business, Department of Management, Gainesville, FL 32611. Offers health care risk management (MS); international business (MA); management (MS, PhD). *Accreditation:* AACSB. *Program availability:* Online learning. *Degree requirements:* For master's, comprehensive exam, thesis. *Entrance requirements:* For master's, GMAT (minimum score of 465) or GRE General Test, minimum GPA of 3.0. Additional exam requirements/recommendations for international students: Required—TOEFL (minimum score 550 paper-based; 80 iBT), IELTS (minimum score 6). Electronic applications accepted. *Faculty research:* Job attitudes, personality and individual differences, organizational entry and exit, knowledge management, competitive dynamics.

University of Florida, Graduate School, Warrington College of Business Administration, Hough Graduate School of Business, Programs in Business Administration, Gainesville, FL 32611. Offers business administration (MA, MS, PhD); competitive strategy (MBA); finance (MBA); global management (MBA); Graham-Buffett security analysis (MBA); human resource management (MBA); information systems and operations management (MBA); international studies (MBA); management (MBA); real estate (MBA); JD/MBA; MBA/MS; MBA/PhD; MBA/Pharm D; MD/MBA. *Accreditation:* AACSB. *Program availability:* Part-time, evening/weekend, online learning. *Degree requirements:* For master's, capstone course. *Entrance requirements:* For master's and doctorate, GMAT (minimum score 465), minimum GPA of 3.0, interview. Additional exam requirements/recommendations for international students: Required—TOEFL (minimum score 550 paper-based; 80 iBT), IELTS (minimum score 6). Electronic applications accepted. *Faculty research:* Accounting, finance, insurance, management, real estate, urban analysis marketing.

University of Florida, Levin College of Law, Gainesville, FL 32611. Offers comparative law (LL M), including tropical conservation and development; environmental and land use law (LL M); international taxation (LL M); law (JD); taxation (LL M, SJD). *Accreditation:* ABA. *Entrance requirements:* For doctorate, LSAT (for JD). Electronic applications accepted. *Faculty research:* Environmental and land use law, taxation, dispute resolution, family law, Constitutional law.

University of Hawaii at Manoa, Graduate Division, Shidler College of Business, Program in Business Administration, Honolulu, HI 96822. Offers Asian business studies (MBA); Chinese business studies (MBA); decision sciences (MBA); entrepreneurship (MBA); finance (MBA); finance and banking (MBA); human resources management (MBA); information management (MBA); information technology (MBA); international business (MBA); Japanese business studies (MBA); marketing (MBA); organizational behavior (MBA); organizational management (MBA); real estate (MBA); student-designed track (MBA). *Accreditation:* AACSB. *Program availability:* Part-time, evening/weekend. *Degree requirements:* For master's, thesis optional. *Entrance requirements:* For master's, GMAT, minimum GPA of 3.0. Additional exam requirements/recommendations for international students: Required—TOEFL (minimum score 600 paper-based; 100 iBT), IELTS (minimum score 7). *Expenses:* Contact institution.

University of Hawaii at Manoa, Graduate Division, Shidler College of Business, Program in International Management, Honolulu, HI 96822. Offers Asian finance (PhD); global information technology management (PhD); international accounting (PhD); international marketing (PhD); international organization and strategy (PhD). *Program availability:* Part-time. *Degree requirements:* For doctorate, comprehensive exam, thesis/dissertation. *Entrance requirements:* For doctorate, GMAT or GRE General Test, minimum GPA of 3.0. Additional exam requirements/recommendations for international students: Required—TOEFL (minimum score 600 paper-based; 100 iBT), IELTS (minimum score 7). *Expenses:* Contact institution.

University of Houston–Victoria, School of Business Administration, Victoria, TX 77901-4450. Offers accounting (MBA); economic development and entrepreneurship (MS); finance (GMBA, MBA); general business (MBA); international business (MBA); management (GMBA, MBA); marketing (MBA). *Accreditation:* AACSB. *Program availability:* Part-time, evening/weekend, online learning. *Entrance requirements:* For master's, GMAT. Additional exam requirements/recommendations for international students: Required—TOEFL (minimum score 550 paper-based). Electronic applications accepted. *Faculty research:* Economic development, marketing, finance.

University of Kentucky, Graduate School, Patterson School of Diplomacy and International Commerce, Lexington, KY 40506-0027. Offers MA. *Degree requirements:* For master's, one foreign language, comprehensive exam, statistics. *Entrance requirements:* For master's, GRE General Test, minimum undergraduate GPA of 3.0. Additional exam requirements/recommendations for international students: Required—TOEFL (minimum score 550 paper-based; 79 iBT). Electronic applications accepted. *Faculty research:* International relations, foreign and defense policy, cross-cultural negotiation, international science and technology, diplomacy, international economics and development, geopolitical modeling.

University of La Verne, College of Business and Public Management, Graduate Programs in Business Administration, La Verne, CA 91750-4443. Offers accounting (MBA, MBA-EP); finance (MBA, MBA-EP); health services management (MBA); information technology (MBA, MBA-EP); international business (MBA, MBA-EP); management and leadership (MBA, MBA-EP); marketing (MBA, MBA-EP); supply chain management (MBA, MBA-EP). *Program availability:* Part-time, evening/weekend. *Students:* 385 full-time (177 women), 89 part-time (46 women); includes 92 minority (4 Black or African American, non-Hispanic/Latino; 1 American Indian or Alaska Native, non-Hispanic/Latino; 14 Asian, non-Hispanic/Latino; 71 Hispanic/Latino; 1 Native Hawaiian or other Pacific Islander, non-Hispanic/Latino; 1 Two or more races, non-Hispanic/Latino), 319 international. Average age 28. *Entrance requirements:* For master's, GMAT, MAT, or GRE, minimum undergraduate GPA of 3.0, 2 letters of recommendation, resume, statement of purpose. Additional exam requirements/recommendations for international students: Required—TOEFL (minimum score 550 paper-based; 85 iBT). *Application deadline:* Applications are processed on a rolling basis. Application fee: $50. *Expenses: Tuition:* Part-time $795 per credit hour. Tuition and fees vary according to campus/location and program. *Financial support:* Institutionally sponsored loans and scholarships/grants available. Financial award application deadline: 3/2; financial award applicants required to submit FAFSA. *Unit head:* Dr. Abe Helou, Chairperson, 909-448-4455, Fax: 909-392-2704, E-mail: ihelou@laverne.edu. *Application contact:* Rina Lazarian-Chehab, Senior Associate Director of Graduate Admissions, 909-448-4317, Fax: 909-971-2295, E-mail: rlazarian@laverne.edu.

Website: https://laverne.edu/business-and-public-administration/mba-2/

University of La Verne, Regional and Online Campuses, Graduate Programs, Inland Empire Campus, Ontario, CA 91730. Offers business administration (MBA, MBA-EP), including accounting (MBA), finance (MBA), health services management (MBA-EP), information technology (MBA-EP), international business (MBA), managed care (MBA), management and leadership (MBA-EP), marketing (MBA-EP), supply chain management (MBA); leadership and management (MS), including human resource management, nonprofit management, organizational development. *Program availability:* Part-time, evening/weekend. *Expenses:* Contact institution.

University of Lethbridge, School of Graduate Studies, Lethbridge, AB T1K 3M4, Canada. Offers addictions counseling (M Sc); agricultural biotechnology (M Sc); agricultural studies (M Sc, MA); anthropology (MA); archaeology (M Sc, MA); art (MA, MFA); biochemistry (M Sc); biological sciences (M Sc); biomolecular science (PhD); biosystems and biodiversity (PhD); Canadian studies (MA); chemistry (M Sc); computer science (M Sc); computer science and geographical information science (M Sc); counseling (MC); counseling psychology (M Ed); dramatic arts (MA); earth, space, and physical science (PhD); economics (MA); education (MA, PhD); educational leadership (M Ed); English (MA); environmental science (M Sc); evolution and behavior (PhD); exercise science (M Sc); French (MA); French/German (MA); French/Spanish (MA); general education (M Ed); geography (M Sc, MA); German (MA); health sciences (M Sc); individualized multidisciplinary (M Sc, MA); kinesiology (M Sc, MA); management (M Sc), including accounting, finance, human resource management and labor relations, information systems, international management, marketing, policy and strategy; mathematics (M Sc); music (M Mus, MA); Native American studies (MA); neuroscience (M Sc, PhD); new media (MA, MFA); nursing (M Sc, MN); philosophy (MA); physics (M Sc); political science (MA); psychology (M Sc, MA); religious studies (MA); sociology (MA); theatre and dramatic arts (MFA); theoretical and computational science (PhD); urban and regional studies (MA); women and gender studies (MA). *Program availability:* Part-time, evening/weekend. *Degree requirements:* For master's, thesis (for some programs); for doctorate, comprehensive exam, thesis/dissertation. *Entrance requirements:* For master's, GMAT (for M Sc in management), bachelor's degree in related field, minimum GPA of 3.0 during previous 20 graded semester courses, 2 years' teaching or related experience (M Ed); for doctorate, master's degree, minimum graduate GPA of 3.5. Additional exam requirements/recommendations for international students: Required—TOEFL (minimum score 580 paper-based; 93 iBT). Electronic applications accepted. *Faculty research:* Movement and brain plasticity, gibberellin physiology, photosynthesis, carbon cycling, molecular properties of main-group ring components.

University of Louisville, Graduate School, College of Business, MBA Programs, Louisville, KY 40292-0001. Offers entrepreneurship (MBA); global business (MBA); health sector management (MBA). *Accreditation:* AACSB. *Program availability:* Part-time, evening/weekend. *Students:* 251 full-time (83 women), 9 part-time (0 women); includes 35 minority (10 Black or African American, non-Hispanic/Latino; 1 American Indian or Alaska Native, non-Hispanic/Latino; 11 Asian, non-Hispanic/Latino; 8 Hispanic/Latino; 5 Two or more races, non-Hispanic/Latino), 18 international. Average age 31. 304 applicants, 61% accepted, 159 enrolled. In 2016, 52 master's awarded. *Degree requirements:* For master's, international learning experience. *Entrance requirements:* For master's, GMAT, 2 letters of reference, personal interview, resume, personal statement, college transcript(s). Additional exam requirements/recommendations for international students: Required—TOEFL (minimum score 83 iBT). *Application deadline:* For fall admission, 7/1 for domestic students; for spring admission, 12/1 for domestic students. Applications are processed on a rolling basis. Application fee: $60. *Expenses:* Tuition, state resident: full-time $12,246; part-time $681 per credit hour. Tuition, nonresident: full-time $25,486; part-time $1417 per credit hour. *Required fees:* $196. Tuition and fees vary according to program and reciprocity agreements. *Financial support:* Fellowships with full tuition reimbursements, research assistantships with full tuition reimbursements, health care benefits, and unspecified assistantships available. Financial award application deadline: 3/31; financial award applicants required to submit FAFSA. *Faculty research:* Entrepreneurship, venture capital, retailing/franchising, corporate governance and leadership, supply chain management. *Total annual research expenditures:* $859,000. *Unit head:* Dr. Todd Mooradian, Dean, 502-852-6443, Fax: 502-852-7557, E-mail: todd.mooradian@louisville.edu. *Application contact:* Susan E. Hildebrand, Program Director, 502-852-7257, Fax: 502-852-4901,
E-mail: s.hildebrand@louisville.edu. Website: http://business.louisville.edu/mba

The University of Manchester, Alliance Manchester Business School, M15 6PB, United Kingdom. Offers accounting and finance (M Sc); business (M Ent); business analysis and strategic management (M Sc); business analytics: operational research and risk analysis (M Sc); business psychology (M Sc); corporate communications and reputation management (M Sc); finance (M Sc); finance and business economics (M Sc); human resource management and industrial relations (M Sc); innovation management and entrepreneurship (M Sc); international business and management (M Sc); international human resource management and comparative industrial relations (M Sc); management (M Sc); marketing (M Sc); operations, project and supply chain management (M Sc); organizational psychology (M Sc); quantitative finance (M Sc). *Entrance requirements:* For master's, UK 2:1 honours degree or overseas equivalent. Additional exam requirements/recommendations for international students: Required—TOEFL (minimum score 100 iBT), IELTS (minimum score 7), PTE. Electronic applications accepted. *Faculty research:* Accounting and finance, management sciences and marketing, people management and organization, innovation management and policy, decision sciences.

University of Mary Hardin-Baylor, Graduate Studies in Business Administration, Belton, TX 76513. Offers accounting (MBA); information systems management (MBA); international business (MBA); management (MBA). *Program availability:* Part-time, evening/weekend. *Faculty:* 11 full-time (5 women), 6 part-time/adjunct (2 women). *Students:* 21 full-time (12 women), 44 part-time (14 women); includes 23 minority (12 Black or African American, non-Hispanic/Latino; 1 Asian, non-Hispanic/Latino; 10 Hispanic/Latino), 11 international. Average age 29. 96 applicants, 70% accepted, 21 enrolled. In 2016, 22 master's awarded. *Degree requirements:* For master's, comprehensive exam. *Entrance requirements:* For master's, minimum GPA of 3.0, interview. Additional exam requirements/recommendations for international students: Required—TOEFL (minimum score 60 iBT), IELTS (minimum score 4.5). *Application deadline:* For fall admission, 6/1 for domestic students, 4/30 priority date for international students; for spring admission, 11/1 for domestic students, 9/30 priority date for international students. Applications are processed on a rolling basis. Application fee: $35 ($135 for international students). Electronic applications accepted. *Expenses: Tuition:* Full-time $14,940; part-time $830 per credit hour. *Required fees:* $1350; $75 per credit hour. $50 per term. Tuition and fees vary according to course load and degree level. *Financial support:* In 2016–17, 33 students received support. Federal Work-Study, unspecified assistantships, and scholarships for some active duty military personnel available. Financial award applicants required to submit FAFSA. *Faculty research:* Experiential learning, case studies in systems analysis and design, forecasting methodologies, short-selling in the stock market, open educational resources. *Total annual research expenditures:* $17,500. *Unit head:* Dr. Kirk Fischer, Assistant Professor/Director, Graduate Programs in McLane College of Business, 254-295-4655, E-mail: kfischer@umhb.edu. *Application contact:* Sharon Aguilera, Assistant Director, Graduate Admissions, 254-295-4835, Fax: 254-295-5038, E-mail: saguilera@umhb.edu.
Website: http://www.graduate.umhb.edu/mba

University of Massachusetts Boston, College of Management, Program in International Management, Boston, MA 02125-3393. Offers MS. *Students:* 7 full-time (4 women), 6 part-time (3 women); includes 2 minority (1 Black or African American, non-Hispanic/Latino; 1 Asian, non-Hispanic/Latino), 7 international. Average age 29. 17 applicants, 24% accepted, 2 enrolled. In 2016, 3 master's awarded. *Expenses:* Tuition, state resident: full-time $16,863. Tuition, nonresident: full-time $32,913. *Required fees:* $177. *Application contact:* Peggy Roldan Patel, Graduate Admissions Coordinator, 617-287-6400, Fax: 617-287-6236, E-mail: bos.gadm@dpc.umassp.edu.

University of Massachusetts Dartmouth, Graduate School, Charlton College of Business, Program in Business Administration, North Dartmouth, MA 02747-2300. Offers business administration (MBA); business analytics (Postbaccalaureate Certificate); business foundations (Graduate Certificate); international business (Graduate Certificate); management (Postbaccalaureate Certificate); marketing (Postbaccalaureate Certificate); organizational leadership (Graduate Certificate); supply chain management and information systems (Postbaccalaureate Certificate). *Accreditation:* AACSB. *Program availability:* Part-time, 100% online, blended/hybrid learning. *Faculty:* 15 full-time (7 women), 11 part-time/adjunct (4 women). *Students:* 126 full-time (49 women), 178 part-time (100 women); includes 45 minority (10 Black or African American, non-Hispanic/Latino; 1 American Indian or Alaska Native, non-Hispanic/Latino; 16 Asian, non-Hispanic/Latino; 13 Hispanic/Latino; 5 Two or more races, non-Hispanic/Latino), 100 international. Average age 32. 236 applicants, 80% accepted, 132 enrolled. In 2016, 142 master's, 13 other advanced degrees awarded. *Degree requirements:* For master's, thesis or alternative, eportfolio. *Entrance requirements:* For master's, GMAT, statement of purpose (minimum of 300 words), resume, official transcripts, 2 letters of recommendation; for other advanced degree, statement of purpose (minimum of 300 words), resume, official transcripts. Additional exam requirements/recommendations for international students: Required—TOEFL (minimum score 533 paper-based; 72 iBT). *Application deadline:* For fall admission, 7/1 priority date for domestic students, 6/1 priority date for international students; for spring admission, 11/15 priority date for domestic students, 10/15 priority date for international students. Application fee: $60. Electronic applications accepted. *Expenses:* Tuition, state resident: full-time $14,994; part-time $624.75 per credit. Tuition, nonresident: full-time $27,068; part-time $1127.83 per credit. *Required fees:* $405; $25.88 per credit. Tuition and fees vary according to course load and reciprocity agreements. *Financial support:* In 2016–17, 2 research assistantships (averaging $2,667 per year) were awarded; institutionally sponsored loans, scholarships/grants, and unspecified assistantships also available. Support available to part-time students. Financial award application deadline: 3/1; financial award applicants required to submit FAFSA. *Faculty research:* E-commerce, managing diversity, agile manufacturing, green business, activity-based management, build-to-order supply chain management. *Total annual research expenditures:* $413,000. *Unit head:* Melissa Pacheco, Assistant Dean of Graduate Programs, 508-999-8543, Fax: 508-999-8646, E-mail: mpacheco@umassd.edu. *Application contact:* Steven Briggs, Director of Marketing and Recruitment for Graduate Studies, 508-999-8604, Fax: 508-999-8183, E-mail: graduate@umassd.edu.
Website: http://www.umassd.edu/charlton/programs/graduate/mba

University of Michigan–Flint, School of Management, Program in Business Administration, Flint, MI 48502. Offers accounting (MBA, Post-Master's Certificate); computer information systems (MBA); finance (MBA, Post-Master's Certificate); general business (Graduate Certificate); general business administration (MBA); health care management (MBA); international business (MBA, Post-Master's Certificate); lean manufacturing (MBA); marketing (MBA, Post-Master's Certificate); organizational leadership (MBA, Post-Master's Certificate). *Program availability:* Part-time, evening/weekend, mixed mode programs. *Faculty:* 33 full-time (9 women), 6 part-time/adjunct (1 woman). *Students:* 24 full-time (12 women), 146 part-time (49 women); includes 37 minority (17 Black or African American, non-Hispanic/Latino; 2 American Indian or Alaska Native, non-Hispanic/Latino; 10 Asian, non-Hispanic/Latino; 4 Hispanic/Latino; 1 Native Hawaiian or other Pacific Islander, non-Hispanic/Latino; 3 Two or more races, non-Hispanic/Latino), 17 international. Average age 33. 167 applicants, 47% accepted, 40 enrolled. In 2016, 73 master's, 3 other advanced degrees awarded. *Entrance requirements:* For master's, GMAT or GRE, bachelor's degree in arts, sciences, engineering, or business administration from regionally-accredited college or university with minimum GPA of 3.0; for other advanced degree, bachelor's degree in arts, sciences, engineering, or business administration from regionally-accredited college or university with minimum GPA of 3.0, college-level math, statistics, or quantitative course (for Graduate Certificate); MBA or equivalent degree from regionally-accredited college or university (for Post Master's Certificate). Additional exam requirements/recommendations for international students: Required—TOEFL (minimum score 84 iBT), IELTS (minimum score 6.5). *Application deadline:* For fall admission, 8/1 for domestic students, 5/1 for international students; for winter admission, 11/15 for domestic students, 9/1 for international students; for spring admission, 3/15 for domestic students, 1/1 for international students; for summer admission, 5/15 for domestic students. Applications are processed on a rolling basis. Application fee: $55. Electronic applications accepted. *Financial support:* Federal Work-Study, scholarships/grants, and unspecified assistantships available. Support available to part-time students. Financial award application deadline: 3/1; financial award applicants required to submit FAFSA. *Unit head:* Dr. Scott Johnson, Dean, School of Management, 810-762-3164, Fax: 810-237-6685, E-mail: scotjohn@umflint.edu. *Application contact:* Bradley T. Maki, Director of Graduate Admissions, 810-762-3171, E-mail: bmaki@umflint.edu.
Website: http://www.umflint.edu/graduateprograms/business-administration-mba

University of Missouri–St. Louis, College of Business Administration, Program in Business Administration, St. Louis, MO 63121. Offers accounting (MBA); business administration (Certificate); business intelligence (Certificate); cybersecurity (Certificate); digital and social media marketing (Certificate); finance (MBA); human resources management (Certificate); information systems (MBA); international business (MBA); logistics and supply chain management (MBA, PhD, Certificate); management (MBA); marketing (MBA); marketing management (Certificate); operations management (MBA). *Accreditation:* AACSB. *Program availability:* Part-time, evening/weekend. *Faculty:* 32 full-time (10 women), 14 part-time/adjunct (3 women). *Students:* 181 full-time (88 women), 357 part-time (154 women); includes 83 minority (30 Black or African American, non-Hispanic/Latino; 36 Asian, non-Hispanic/Latino; 12 Hispanic/Latino; 2 Native Hawaiian or other Pacific Islander, non-Hispanic/Latino; 3 Two or more races, non-Hispanic/Latino), 100 international. Average age 31. 245 applicants, 83% accepted, 139 enrolled. *Degree requirements:* For doctorate, thesis/dissertation. *Entrance requirements:* For master's, GMAT, 2 letters of recommendation. Additional exam requirements/recommendations for international students: Recommended—TOEFL (minimum score 550 paper-based; 79 iBT), IELTS (minimum score 6.5). *Application deadline:* For fall admission, 7/1 for domestic and international students; for spring admission, 12/1 for domestic and international students. Applications are processed on a rolling basis. Application fee: $50 ($40 for international students). Electronic applications accepted. *Financial support:* Research assistantships with tuition reimbursements, teaching assistantships with tuition reimbursements, career-related internships or fieldwork, Federal Work-Study, and institutionally sponsored loans available. Support available to part-time students. Financial award application deadline: 4/1; financial award applicants required to submit FAFSA. *Faculty research:* Human resources, strategic management, marketing strategy, consumer behavior product development, advertising. *Unit head:* Dr. Thomas H. Eyssell, Associate Dean and Director of Graduate Studies, 314-516-5885, Fax: 314-516-6420, E-mail: mba@umsl.edu. *Application contact:* 314-516-5458, Fax: 314-516-6996, E-mail: gradadm@umsl.edu.

University of New Brunswick Saint John, Faculty of Business, Saint John, NB E2L 4L5, Canada. Offers administration (MBA); electronic commerce (MBA); international business (MBA); natural resource management (MBA). *Program availability:* Part-time. *Entrance requirements:* For master's, GMAT (minimum score of 550) or GRE (minimum 54th percentile), minimum GPA of 3.0. Additional exam requirements/recommendations for international students: Required—TOEFL (minimum score 580 paper-based; 93 iBT), TWE (minimum score 4.5). Electronic applications accepted. *Expenses:* Contact institution. *Faculty research:* International business, project management, innovation and technology management; business use of Weblogs and podcasts to communicate; corporate governance; high-involvement work systems; international competitiveness; supply chain management and logistics.

University of New Haven, Graduate School, College of Business, Program in Business Administration, West Haven, CT 06516. Offers accounting (MBA), including CPA; business administration (MBA); business intelligence (MBA); business management (Graduate Certificate); business policy and strategic leadership (MBA); finance (MBA), including CFA; global marketing (MBA); human resources management (MBA, Graduate Certificate); sport management (MBA). *Accreditation:* AACSB. *Program availability:* Part-time, evening/weekend. *Students:* 123 full-time (56 women), 74 part-time (29 women); includes 46 minority (24 Black or African American, non-Hispanic/Latino; 8 Asian, non-Hispanic/Latino; 10 Hispanic/Latino; 4 Two or more races, non-Hispanic/Latino), 57 international. Average age 27. In 2016, 100 master's awarded. *Entrance requirements:* For master's, GMAT. Additional exam requirements/recommendations for international students: Required—TOEFL (minimum score 80 iBT), IELTS, PTE. *Application deadline:* Applications are processed on a rolling basis. Application fee: $50. Electronic applications accepted. Application fee is waived when completed online. *Expenses: Tuition:* Full-time $15,660; part-time $870 per credit hour. *Required fees:* $200; $85 per term. Tuition and fees vary according to program. *Financial support:* Research assistantships with partial tuition reimbursements, teaching assistantships with partial tuition reimbursements, career-related internships or fieldwork, Federal Work-Study, scholarships/grants, and unspecified assistantships available. Support available to part-time students. Financial award applicants required to submit FAFSA. *Unit head:* Darell Singleterry, Director, 203-932-1085, E-mail: dsingleterry@newhaven.edu. *Application contact:* Michelle Mason, Director of Graduate Enrollment, 203-932-7067, E-mail: mmason@newhaven.edu.
Website: http://www.newhaven.edu/business/programs/EMBA/

University of New Mexico, Anderson School of Management, Department of Finance, International, Technology and Entrepreneurship, Albuquerque, NM 87131. Offers entrepreneurship (MBA); finance (MBA); international management (MBA); international management in Latin America (MBA); management of technology (MBA). *Program availability:* Part-time, evening/weekend. *Faculty:* 15 full-time (2 women), 5 part-time/adjunct (0 women). In 2016, 41 master's awarded. *Entrance requirements:* For master's, GMAT or GRE, minimum GPA of 3.0 on last 60 hours of coursework; bachelor's degree from regionally-accredited college or university in U.S. or its equivalent in another country. Additional exam requirements/recommendations for international students: Required—TOEFL (minimum score 550 paper-based; 79 iBT), IELTS (minimum score 6.5). *Application deadline:* For fall admission, 4/1 priority date for domestic and international students; for spring admission, 10/1 priority date for domestic and international students. Applications are processed on a rolling basis. Application fee: $50. Electronic applications accepted. *Expenses:* Contact institution. *Financial support:* In 2016–17, 12 fellowships (averaging $15,441 per year), 12 research assistantships with partial tuition reimbursements (averaging $16,707 per year) were awarded; career-related internships or fieldwork, Federal Work-Study, scholarships/grants, and unspecified assistantships also available. Support available to part-time students. Financial award application deadline: 6/1; financial award applicants required to submit FAFSA. *Faculty research:* Corporate finance, investments, management in Latin America, management of technology, entrepreneurship. *Unit head:* Dr. Sul Kassicieh,

Chair, 505-277-6471, E-mail: sul@unm.edu. *Application contact:* Lisa Beauchene, Student Recruitment Specialist, 505-277-6471, E-mail: andersonadvising@unm.edu.
Website: https://www.mgt.unm.edu/fite/default.asp?mm=faculty

University of North Alabama, College of Business, Florence, AL 35632-0001. Offers business administration (MBA), including accounting, enterprise resource planning systems, executive, finance, health care management, information systems, international business, project management. *Accreditation:* AACSB; ACBSP. *Program availability:* Part-time, 100% online, blended/hybrid learning. *Faculty:* 24 full-time (2 women), 6 part-time/adjunct (3 women). *Students:* 180 full-time (77 women), 411 part-time (199 women); includes 208 minority (84 Black or African American, non-Hispanic/Latino; 4 American Indian or Alaska Native, non-Hispanic/Latino; 106 Asian, non-Hispanic/Latino; 6 Hispanic/Latino; 8 Two or more races, non-Hispanic/Latino), 37 international. Average age 34. 263 applicants, 84% accepted, 173 enrolled. In 2016, 156 master's awarded. *Entrance requirements:* For master's, GMAT, GRE, minimum GPA of 2.75 in last 60 hours, 2.5 overall (on a 3.0 scale); 27 hours of course work in business and economics. Additional exam requirements/recommendations for international students: Required—TOEFL (minimum score 79 iBT), IELTS (minimum score 6), PTE (minimum score 54). *Application deadline:* Applications are processed on a rolling basis. Application fee: $50 ($100 for international students). Electronic applications accepted. *Expenses:* Tuition, state resident: full-time $2799; part-time $1866 per semester. Tuition, nonresident: full-time $5598; part-time $3732 per semester. *Required fees:* $915; $642 per semester. Tuition and fees vary according to course load. *Financial support:* In 2016–17, 114 students received support. Scholarships/grants available. Financial award application deadline: 2/1; financial award applicants required to submit FAFSA. *Unit head:* Dr. Gregory A. Carnes, Dean, 256-765-4261, Fax: 256-765-4170, E-mail: gacarnes@una.edu. *Application contact:* Hillary N. Coats, Graduate Admissions Coordinator, 256-765-4447, E-mail: graduate@una.edu.
Website: http://www.una.edu/business/

The University of North Carolina Wilmington, Cameron School of Business, Business Administration Program, Wilmington, NC 28403-3297. Offers business administration (MBA); international business administration (MBA). *Accreditation:* AACSB. *Program availability:* Part-time-only. *Faculty:* 41 full-time (11 women). *Students:* 87 full-time (43 women), 45 part-time (18 women); includes 19 minority (7 Black or African American, non-Hispanic/Latino; 1 American Indian or Alaska Native, non-Hispanic/Latino; 4 Asian, non-Hispanic/Latino; 4 Hispanic/Latino; 3 Two or more races, non-Hispanic/Latino), 17 international. Average age 31. 115 applicants, 83% accepted, 75 enrolled. In 2016, 30 master's awarded. *Degree requirements:* For master's, written case analysis, oral competency presentation. *Entrance requirements:* For master's, GMAT or GRE, 2 years of appropriate work experience, 3 letters of recommendation. Additional exam requirements/recommendations for international students: Required—TOEFL (minimum score 79 iBT), IELTS (minimum score 6.5). *Application deadline:* For fall admission, 6/1 for domestic students. Applications are processed on a rolling basis. Application fee: $60. Electronic applications accepted. *Expenses:* Contact institution. *Financial support:* Scholarships/grants and unspecified assistantships available. Financial award application deadline: 3/15; financial award applicants required to submit FAFSA. *Unit head:* Dr. Thom Porter, Interim MBA Director, 910-962-7466, E-mail: portert@uncw.edu. *Application contact:* Candace Wilhelm, Graduate Programs Coordinator, 910-962-3903, Fax: 910-962-2184, E-mail: wilhelmc@uncw.edu.
Website: http://www.csb.uncw.edu/mba/

University of North Florida, Coggin College of Business, MBA Program, Jacksonville, FL 32224. Offers accounting (MBA); construction management (MBA); e-commerce (MBA); economics (MBA); finance (MBA); human resource management (MBA); international business (MBA); logistics (MBA); management applications (MBA). *Accreditation:* AACSB. *Program availability:* Part-time, evening/weekend. *Faculty:* 16 full-time (4 women), 1 (woman) part-time/adjunct. *Students:* 105 full-time (50 women), 162 part-time (68 women); includes 57 minority (14 Black or African American, non-Hispanic/Latino; 1 American Indian or Alaska Native, non-Hispanic/Latino; 17 Asian, non-Hispanic/Latino; 18 Hispanic/Latino; 7 Two or more races, non-Hispanic/Latino), 41 international. Average age 28. 231 applicants, 46% accepted, 84 enrolled. In 2016, 114 master's awarded. *Entrance requirements:* For master's, GMAT or GRE, U.S. bachelor's degree from regionally-accredited university or equivalent foreign degree. Additional exam requirements/recommendations for international students: Required—TOEFL (minimum score 550 paper-based; 79 iBT). *Application deadline:* For fall admission, 8/1 priority date for domestic students, 5/1 for international students; for spring admission, 12/1 priority date for domestic students, 10/1 for international students; for summer admission, 4/29 priority date for domestic students, 2/1 for international students. Application fee: $30. Tuition and fees vary according to course load, campus/location and program. *Financial support:* In 2016–17, 22 students received support, including 1 research assistantship (averaging $2,501 per year); teaching assistantships, Federal Work-Study, and tuition waivers (partial) also available. Support available to part-time students. Financial award application deadline: 4/1; financial award applicants required to submit FAFSA. *Faculty research:* Performance measures, costing, and inventory issues in logistics and supply chain management; inter-organizational systems; international management and marketing practices; e-commerce; organizational learning and socialization processes. *Total annual research expenditures:* $17,654. *Unit head:* Dr. Parvez Ahmed, Graduate Program Director, 904-620-1678, E-mail: pahmed@unf.edu. *Application contact:* Amy Bishop, MSM Advisor, 904-620-2575, Fax: 904-620-2832, E-mail: coggin.students@unf.edu.
Website: http://www.unf.edu/graduateschool/academics/programs/MBA.aspx

University of Oklahoma, Price College of Business, Program in Business Administration, Norman, OK 73019. Offers accounting (PhD); business administration (MBA, PhD); entrepreneurship and economic development (PhD); finance (PhD); management and international business (PhD); management of information systems (PhD); marketing/supply chain (PhD); JD/MBA; MBA/MS. *Accreditation:* AACSB. *Program availability:* Part-time, evening/weekend. *Students:* 122 full-time (27 women), 146 part-time (30 women); includes 36 minority (5 Black or African American, non-Hispanic/Latino; 6 American Indian or Alaska Native, non-Hispanic/Latino; 8 Asian, non-Hispanic/Latino; 11 Hispanic/Latino; 6 Two or more races, non-Hispanic/Latino), 37 international. Average age 30. 261 applicants, 27% accepted, 59 enrolled. In 2016, 127 master's, 5 doctorates awarded. *Degree requirements:* For doctorate, comprehensive exam, thesis/dissertation. *Entrance requirements:* For master's, GMAT or GRE, resume, statement of goals; for doctorate, GMAT or GRE, resume, statement of goals, 3 letters of recommendation. Additional exam requirements/recommendations for international students: Required—TOEFL (minimum score 100 iBT) or IELTS (minimum score 7). *Application deadline:* For fall admission, 11/15 priority date for domestic and international students; for spring admission, 3/15 priority date for domestic and international students; for summer admission, 5/15 for domestic and international students. Application fee: $50 ($100 for international students). Electronic applications accepted. *Expenses:* Contact institution. *Financial support:* In 2016–17, 107 students received support, including 10 fellowships with partial tuition reimbursements available (averaging $3,295 per year); research assistantships with full and partial tuition reimbursements available, teaching assistantships with full and partial tuition reimbursements available, career-related internships or fieldwork, scholarships/grants, health care benefits, and unspecified assistantships also available. Support available to part-time students. Financial award application deadline: 6/1; financial award applicants required to submit FAFSA. *Faculty research:* Energy finance; international accounting; organizational behavior and entrepreneurship; management information systems; supply chain. *Unit head:* Laku Chidambaram, Associate Dean for Academic Programs and Engagement. *Application contact:* Director of MBA Admissions, 405-325-5623.
Website: http://www.ou.edu/content/price/divisions/graduate.html

University of Pennsylvania, School of Arts and Sciences and Wharton School, Joseph H. Lauder Institute of Management and International Studies, Philadelphia, PA 19104. Offers international studies (MA); management and international studies (MBA); MBA/MA. Applications must be made concurrently and separately to the Wharton MBA program. *Degree requirements:* For master's, one foreign language, thesis. *Entrance requirements:* For master's, GMAT or GRE, advanced proficiency in a non-native language (Arabic, Chinese, French, German, Hindi, Japanese, Portuguese, Russian, or Spanish). Additional exam requirements/recommendations for international students: Required—TOEFL. Electronic applications accepted. *Expenses:* Contact institution. *Faculty research:* Finance, marketing, strategy, operations management, multinational management.

University of Phoenix–Atlanta Campus, School of Business, Sandy Springs, GA 30350-4147. Offers accounting (MBA); business administration (MBA); global management (MBA); human resources management (MBA, MM); management (MM); marketing (MBA); public administration (MM). *Accreditation:* ACBSP. *Program availability:* Evening/weekend, online learning. *Degree requirements:* For master's, thesis (for some programs). *Entrance requirements:* For master's, minimum undergraduate GPA of 3.0, 3 years of work experience. Additional exam requirements/recommendations for international students: Required—TOEFL (minimum score 550 paper-based; 79 iBT).

University of Phoenix–Augusta Campus, School of Business, Augusta, GA 30909-4583. Offers accounting (MBA); business administration (MBA); business and management (MBA, MM); global management (MBA); human resources management (MBA, MM); management (MM); marketing (MBA); public administration (MBA, MM). *Accreditation:* ACBSP. *Program availability:* Online learning.

University of Phoenix–Bay Area Campus, School of Business, San Jose, CA 95134-1805. Offers accountancy (MS); accounting (MBA); business administration (MBA, DBA); energy management (MBA); global management (MBA); health care management (MBA); human resource management (MBA); human resources management (MM); management (MM); marketing (MBA); organizational leadership (DM); project management (MBA); public administration (MPA); technology management (MBA). *Accreditation:* ACBSP. *Program availability:* Evening/weekend, online learning. *Degree requirements:* For master's, thesis (for some programs). *Entrance requirements:* For master's, minimum undergraduate GPA of 3.0, 3 years of work experience. Additional exam requirements/recommendations for international students: Required—TOEFL (minimum score 550 paper-based; 79 iBT). Electronic applications accepted.

University of Phoenix–Central Valley Campus, School of Business, Fresno, CA 93720-1552. Offers accounting (MBA); business administration (MBA); global management (MBA); human resources management (MBA, MM); management (MM); marketing (MBA); public administration (MBA, MM). *Accreditation:* ACBSP.

University of Phoenix–Charlotte Campus, School of Business, Charlotte, NC 28273-3409. Offers accounting (MBA); business administration (MBA); global management (MBA). *Accreditation:* ACBSP. *Program availability:* Evening/weekend. *Degree requirements:* For master's, thesis (for some programs). *Entrance requirements:* For master's, minimum undergraduate GPA of 3.0, 3 years work experience. Additional exam requirements/recommendations for international students: Required—TOEFL (minimum score 550 paper-based; 79 iBT). Electronic applications accepted.

University of Phoenix–Colorado Campus, School of Business, Lone Tree, CO 80124-5453. Offers accountancy (MSA); accounting (MBA); business administration (MBA); e-business (MBA); global management (MBA); human resources management (MBA, MM); management (MM); marketing (MBA); public administration (MBA, MM). *Accreditation:* ACBSP. *Program availability:* Evening/weekend, online learning. *Degree requirements:* For master's, thesis (for some programs). *Entrance requirements:* For master's, minimum undergraduate GPA of 3.0, 3 years work experience. Additional exam requirements/recommendations for international students: Required—TOEFL (minimum score 550 paper-based; 79 iBT). Electronic applications accepted.

University of Phoenix–Colorado Springs Downtown Campus, School of Business, Colorado Springs, CO 80903. Offers accounting (MBA); business administration (MBA); global management (MBA); human resources management (MBA, MM); management (MM); marketing (MBA); public administration (MM). *Program availability:* Evening/weekend. *Degree requirements:* For master's, thesis (for some programs). *Entrance requirements:* For master's, minimum undergraduate GPA of 3.0, 3 years of work experience. Additional exam requirements/recommendations for international students: Required—TOEFL (minimum score 550 paper-based; 79 iBT). Electronic applications accepted.

University of Phoenix–Columbus Georgia Campus, School of Business, Columbus, GA 31909. Offers accounting (MBA); business administration (MBA); global management (MBA); human resources management (MBA, MM); management (MM); marketing (MBA); public administration (MBA). *Accreditation:* ACBSP. *Program availability:* Evening/weekend. *Degree requirements:* For master's, thesis (for some programs). *Entrance requirements:* For master's, minimum undergraduate GPA of 3.0, 3 years of work experience. Additional exam requirements/recommendations for international students: Required—TOEFL (minimum score 550 paper-based; 79 iBT). Electronic applications accepted.

University of Phoenix–Dallas Campus, School of Business, Dallas, TX 75251. Offers accounting (MBA); business administration (MBA); global management (MBA); human resources management (MBA, MM); management (MM); marketing (MBA); public administration (MBA, MM). *Accreditation:* ACBSP. *Program availability:* Evening/weekend, online learning. *Degree requirements:* For master's, thesis (for some programs). *Entrance requirements:* For master's, 3 years of work experience, minimum undergraduate GPA of 3.0. Additional exam requirements/recommendations for international students: Required—TOEFL (minimum score 550 paper-based; 79 iBT). Electronic applications accepted.

University of Phoenix–Hawaii Campus, School of Business, Honolulu, HI 96813-3800. Offers accounting (MBA); business administration (MBA); global management (MBA); human resources management (MBA, MM); management (MM); marketing (MBA); public administration (MBA, MM). *Accreditation:* ACBSP. *Program availability:* Evening/weekend. *Degree requirements:* For master's, thesis (for some programs). *Entrance requirements:* For master's, minimum undergraduate GPA of 3.0, 3 years of work experience. Additional exam requirements/recommendations for international students: Required—TOEFL (minimum score 550 paper-based; 79 iBT). Electronic applications accepted.

University of Phoenix–Houston Campus, School of Business, Houston, TX 77079-2004. Offers accounting (MBA); business administration (MBA); global management

(MBA); human resources management (MBA, MM); management (MM); marketing (MBA); public administration (MBA, MM). *Accreditation:* ACBSP. *Program availability:* Evening/weekend, online learning. *Degree requirements:* For master's, thesis (for some programs). *Entrance requirements:* For master's, 3 years of work experience, minimum undergraduate GPA of 3.0. Additional exam requirements/recommendations for international students: Required—TOEFL (minimum score 550 paper-based; 79 iBT). Electronic applications accepted.

University of Phoenix–Jersey City Campus, School of Business, Jersey City, NJ 07310. Offers accounting (MBA); business administration (MBA); global management (MBA); human resources management (MBA, MM); management (MM); marketing (MBA); public administration (MBA, MM). *Accreditation:* ACBSP.

University of Phoenix–Las Vegas Campus, School of Business, Las Vegas, NV 89135. Offers accounting (MBA); business administration (MBA); global management (MBA); human resources management (MBA, MM); management (MM); marketing (MBA); public administration (MM). *Accreditation:* ACBSP. *Program availability:* Evening/weekend, online learning. *Degree requirements:* For master's, thesis (for some programs). *Entrance requirements:* For master's, minimum undergraduate GPA of 3.0, 3 years of work experience. Additional exam requirements/recommendations for international students: Required—TOEFL (minimum score 550 paper-based; 79 iBT). Electronic applications accepted.

University of Phoenix–New Mexico Campus, School of Business, Albuquerque, NM 87113-1570. Offers accounting (MBA); business administration (MBA); global management (MBA); human resources management (MBA, MM); management (MM); marketing (MBA). *Accreditation:* ACBSP. *Program availability:* Evening/weekend. *Degree requirements:* For master's, thesis (for some programs). *Entrance requirements:* For master's, 3 years of work experience, minimum undergraduate GPA of 3.0. Additional exam requirements/recommendations for international students: Required—TOEFL (minimum score 550 paper-based; 79 iBT). Electronic applications accepted.

University of Phoenix–North Florida Campus, School of Business, Jacksonville, FL 32216-0959. Offers accounting (MBA); business administration (MBA); global management (MBA); human resources management (MBA, MM); management (MM); marketing (MBA); public administration (MBA, MM). *Accreditation:* ACBSP. *Program availability:* Evening/weekend. *Degree requirements:* For master's, thesis (for some programs). *Entrance requirements:* For master's, minimum undergraduate GPA of 3.0, 3 years work experience. Additional exam requirements/recommendations for international students: Required—TOEFL (minimum score 550 paper-based; 79 iBT). Electronic applications accepted.

University of Phoenix–Online Campus, School of Business, Phoenix, AZ 85034-7209. Offers accountancy (MS); accounting (MBA, Certificate); business administration (MBA); energy management (MBA); global management (MBA); health care management (MBA); human resource management (MBA, Certificate); human resources management (MM); management (MM); marketing (MBA, Certificate); project management (MBA, Certificate); public administration (MBA, MM); technology management (MBA). *Program availability:* Evening/weekend, online learning. *Entrance requirements:* Additional exam requirements/recommendations for international students: Required—TOEFL, TOEIC (Test of English as an International Communication), Berlitz Online English Proficiency Exam, PTE, or IELTS. Electronic applications accepted. *Expenses:* Contact institution.

University of Phoenix–Phoenix Campus, School of Business, Tempe, AZ 85282-2371. Offers accounting (MBA, MS, Certificate); business administration (MBA); energy management (MBA); global management (MBA); health care management (MBA); human resource management (MBA, Certificate); management (MM); marketing (MBA); project management (MBA); technology management (MBA). *Program availability:* Evening/weekend, online learning. *Entrance requirements:* Additional exam requirements/recommendations for international students: Required—TOEFL, TOEIC (Test of English as an International Communication), Berlitz Online English Proficiency Exam, PTE, or IELTS. Electronic applications accepted. *Expenses:* Contact institution.

University of Phoenix–Sacramento Valley Campus, School of Business, Sacramento, CA 95833-4334. Offers accounting (MBA); business administration (MBA); global management (MBA); human resources management (MBA, MM); management (MM); marketing (MBA); public administration (MBA, MM). *Accreditation:* ACBSP. *Program availability:* Evening/weekend. *Degree requirements:* For master's, thesis (for some programs). *Entrance requirements:* For master's, minimum undergraduate GPA of 3.0, 3 years work experience. Additional exam requirements/recommendations for international students: Required—TOEFL (minimum score 550 paper-based; 79 iBT). Electronic applications accepted.

University of Phoenix–San Antonio Campus, School of Business, San Antonio, TX 78230. Offers accounting (MBA); business administration (MBA); e-business (MBA); global management (MBA); human resources management (MBA, MM); management (MM); marketing (MBA); public administration (MBA, MM). *Accreditation:* ACBSP.

University of Phoenix–San Diego Campus, School of Business, San Diego, CA 92123. Offers accounting (MBA); business administration (MBA); global management (MBA); human resources management (MBA, MM); management (MM); marketing (MBA); public administration (MBA). *Accreditation:* ACBSP. *Program availability:* Evening/weekend. *Degree requirements:* For master's, thesis (for some programs). *Entrance requirements:* For master's, 3 years of work experience, minimum undergraduate GPA of 3.0. Additional exam requirements/recommendations for international students: Required—TOEFL (minimum score 550 paper-based; 79 iBT). Electronic applications accepted.

University of Phoenix–Southern Arizona Campus, School of Business, Tucson, AZ 85711. Offers accountancy (MS); accounting (MBA); business administration (MBA); global management (MBA); human resources management (MBA); management (MM); marketing (MBA). *Accreditation:* ACBSP. *Program availability:* Evening/weekend. *Degree requirements:* For master's, thesis (for some programs). *Entrance requirements:* For master's, minimum undergraduate GPA of 3.0, 3 years of work experience. Additional exam requirements/recommendations for international students: Required—TOEFL (minimum score 550 paper-based; 79 iBT). Electronic applications accepted.

University of Phoenix–Southern California Campus, School of Business, Costa Mesa, CA 92626. Offers accounting (MBA); business administration (MBA); energy management (MBA); global management (MBA); health care management (MBA); human resource management (MBA); management (MM); marketing (MBA); project management (MBA); technology management (MBA). *Program availability:* Evening/weekend, online learning. *Entrance requirements:* Additional exam requirements/recommendations for international students: Required—TOEFL, TOEIC (Test of English as an International Communication), Berlitz Online English Proficiency Exam, PTE, or IELTS. Electronic applications accepted. *Expenses:* Contact institution.

University of Phoenix–South Florida Campus, School of Business, Miramar, FL 33027-4145. Offers accounting (MBA); business administration (MBA); global management (MBA); human resource management (MBA); human resources management (MM); management (MM); marketing (MBA); public administration (MBA, MM). *Accreditation:* ACBSP. *Program availability:* Evening/weekend. *Degree requirements:* For master's, thesis (for some programs). *Entrance requirements:* For master's, minimum undergraduate GPA of 3.0, 3 years work experience. Additional exam requirements/recommendations for international students: Required—TOEFL (minimum score 550 paper-based; 79 iBT). Electronic applications accepted.

University of Phoenix–Utah Campus, School of Business, Salt Lake City, UT 84123-4642. Offers accounting (MBA); business administration (MBA); global management (MBA); human resource management (MBA, MM); management (MM); marketing (MBA); technology management (MBA). *Accreditation:* ACBSP. *Program availability:* Evening/weekend. *Degree requirements:* For master's, thesis (for some programs). *Entrance requirements:* For master's, minimum undergraduate GPA of 3.0, 3 years of work experience. Additional exam requirements/recommendations for international students: Required—TOEFL (minimum score 550 paper-based; 79 iBT). Electronic applications accepted.

University of Pittsburgh, Katz Graduate School of Business, Augsburg Executive Fellows Program, Pittsburgh, PA 15260. Offers Certificate. Students nominated by Augsburg where they earn an MBA. *Faculty:* 88 full-time (27 women), 42 part-time/adjunct (15 women). *Students:* 18 full-time (4 women), all international. Average age 32. 18 applicants, 100% accepted, 18 enrolled. *Entrance requirements:* Additional exam requirements/recommendations for international students: Required—TOEFL (minimum score 100 iBT) or IELTS (minimum score 7.0). *Application deadline:* For fall admission, 2/1 priority date for international students. Application fee: $50. Electronic applications accepted. *Expenses:* Contact institution. *Financial support:* Applicants required to submit FAFSA. *Faculty research:* Accounting systems/financial reporting, corporate finance, shopper marketing/consumer behavior, management information systems, organizational behavior and entrepreneurship. *Total annual research expenditures:* $493,036. *Unit head:* Dr. Arjang A. Assad, Dean, 412-648-1556, Fax: 412-648-1552, E-mail: aassad@katz.pitt.edu. *Application contact:* Thomas Keller, Director of MBA Admissions, 412-648-1700, Fax: 412-648-1659, E-mail: mba@katz.pitt.edu.

University of Pittsburgh, Katz Graduate School of Business, MBA/Master of International Business Dual Degree Program, Pittsburgh, PA 15260. Offers MBA/MIB. *Program availability:* Part-time, evening/weekend. *Faculty:* 88 full-time (27 women), 42 part-time/adjunct (15 women). *Students:* 1 (woman) full-time, 2 part-time (both women); includes 2 minority (both Black or African American, non-Hispanic/Latino). Average age 31. 13 applicants, 8% accepted. *Entrance requirements:* Additional exam requirements/recommendations for international students: Required—TOEFL (minimum score 100 iBT) or IELTS (minimum score 7.0). *Application deadline:* For fall admission, 4/1 priority date for domestic students, 2/1 priority date for international students. Application fee: $50. Electronic applications accepted. Tuition and fees vary according to program. *Financial support:* Scholarships/grants available. Financial award application deadline: 6/1; financial award applicants required to submit FAFSA. *Faculty research:* Accounting systems/financial reporting, corporate finance, shopper marketing/consumer behavior, management information systems, organizational behavior and entrepreneurship. *Total annual research expenditures:* $493,036. *Unit head:* Dr. Arjang A. Assad, Dean, 412-648-1556, Fax: 412-648-1552, E-mail: aassad@katz.pitt.edu. *Application contact:* Thomas Keller, Director of MBA Admissions, 412-648-1700, Fax: 412-648-1659, E-mail: mba@katz.pitt.edu.
Website: http://www.business.pitt.edu/katz/mba/academics/programs/mba-mib.php

See Display on page 160 and Close-Up on page 189.

University of Puerto Rico, Río Piedras Campus, College of Business Administration, San Juan, PR 00931-3300. Offers accounting (MBA); finance (MBA, PhD); general business (MBA); human resources management (MBA); international trade and business (MBA, PhD); marketing (MBA); operations management (MBA); quantitative methods (MBA). *Accreditation:* AACSB. *Program availability:* Part-time. *Degree requirements:* For master's, comprehensive exam, thesis or alternative, research project. *Entrance requirements:* For master's, GMAT or PAEG, minimum GPA of 3.0, letter of recommendation; for doctorate, GMAT, PAEG, minimum GPA of 3.0, master degree. *Faculty research:* Management.

University of Regina, Faculty of Graduate Studies and Research, Kenneth Levene Graduate School of Business, Program in Business Administration, Regina, SK S4S 0A2, Canada. Offers business foundations (PGD); engineering management (MBA); executive business administration (EMBA); international business (MBA); leadership (M Admin); organizational leadership (Master's Certificate); project management (Master's Certificate); public safety management (MBA). *Program availability:* Part-time, evening/weekend. *Faculty:* 43 full-time (15 women), 6 part-time/adjunct (0 women). *Students:* 42 full-time (19 women), 21 part-time (12 women). 65 applicants, 48% accepted. In 2016, 57 master's, 13 other advanced degrees awarded. *Degree requirements:* For master's, project (for some programs). *Entrance requirements:* For master's, GMAT, three years of relevant work experience, four-year undergraduate degree; for other advanced degree, GMAT (for PGD), four-year undergraduate degree and two years of relevant work experience (for Master's Certificate); three years' work experience (for PGD). Additional exam requirements/recommendations for international students: Required—TOEFL (minimum score 580 paper-based; 80 iBT), IELTS (minimum score 6.5), PTE (minimum score 59). *Application deadline:* Applications are processed on a rolling basis. Application fee: $100. Electronic applications accepted. *Expenses:* Contact institution. *Financial support:* In 2016–17, 6 fellowships (averaging $6,000 per year), 7 teaching assistantships (averaging $2,501 per year) were awarded; career-related internships or fieldwork and scholarships/grants also available. Financial award application deadline: 6/15. *Faculty research:* Business policy and strategy, production and operations management, human behavior in organizations, financial management, social issues in business. *Unit head:* Dr. Andrew Gaudes, Dean, 306-585-4162, Fax: 306-585-5361, E-mail: andrew.gaudes@uregina.ca. *Application contact:* Ronald Camp, Graduate Programs, 306-337-2387, Fax: 306-585-5361, E-mail: ronald.camp@uregina.ca.
Website: http://www.uregina.ca/business/levene/

University of St. Thomas, Cameron School of Business, Houston, TX 77006-4696. Offers MBA, MCTM, MIB, MSA, MSF. *Program availability:* Part-time, evening/weekend. *Faculty:* 26 full-time (8 women), 7 part-time/adjunct (2 women). *Students:* 178 full-time (86 women), 222 part-time (127 women); includes 182 minority (38 Black or African American, non-Hispanic/Latino; 36 Asian, non-Hispanic/Latino; 104 Hispanic/Latino; 4 Two or more races, non-Hispanic/Latino), 115 international. Average age 31. 144 applicants, 97% accepted, 72 enrolled. In 2016, 164 master's awarded. *Degree requirements:* For master's, capstone (for some programs), additional course requirements for those sitting for state accountancy exam. *Entrance requirements:* For master's, minimum GPA of 2.5, 3 letters of recommendation. Additional exam requirements/recommendations for international students: Required—TOEFL (minimum score 550 paper-based; 79 iBT), IELTS (minimum score 6.5), PTE (minimum score 53). *Application deadline:* For fall admission, 7/15 for domestic and international students; for winter admission, 7/15 for domestic and international students; for spring admission, 11/15 for domestic students, 10/15 for international students. Applications are processed on a rolling basis. Application fee: $35. Electronic applications accepted. *Expenses: Tuition:* Full-time $20,934; part-time $1163 per credit hour. *Required fees:* $81 per semester. One-time fee: $100. Part-time tuition and fees vary according to course level, course

load, campus/location and program. *Financial support:* In 2016–17, 56 students received support, including research assistantships with partial tuition reimbursements available (averaging $3,000 per year); Federal Work-Study, scholarships/grants, unspecified assistantships, and state work-study, institutional employment also available. Support available to part-time students. Financial award application deadline: 4/15; financial award applicants required to submit FAFSA. *Unit head:* Dr. Beena George, Dean, 713-525-2100, Fax: 713-525-2110, E-mail: cameron@stthom.edu. *Application contact:* Fran Wilson Mayes, Academic Coordinator, 713-525-2100, Fax: 713-525-2110, E-mail: cameron@stthom.edu.
Website: http://www.stthom.edu/Academics/Cameron_School_of_Business/Index.aqf

University of San Diego, School of Business, Program in Global Leadership, San Diego, CA 92110-2492. Offers MS. *Program availability:* Online learning. *Students:* 4 full-time (2 women), 35 part-time (5 women); includes 15 minority (3 Black or African American, non-Hispanic/Latino; 2 Asian, non-Hispanic/Latino; 8 Hispanic/Latino; 1 Native Hawaiian or other Pacific Islander, non-Hispanic/Latino; 1 Two or more races, non-Hispanic/Latino), 2 international. Average age 35. In 2016, 36 master's awarded. *Entrance requirements:* Additional exam requirements/recommendations for international students: Required—TOEFL (minimum score 580 paper-based; 92 iBT), TWE. *Application deadline:* For fall admission, 11/1 priority date for domestic students. Applications are processed on a rolling basis. Application fee: $80. Electronic applications accepted. *Financial support:* In 2016–17, 28 students received support. Career-related internships or fieldwork and scholarships/grants available. Financial award application deadline: 4/1; financial award applicants required to submit FAFSA. *Unit head:* E-mail: msgl@sandiego.edu. *Application contact:* Monica Mahon, Associate Director of Graduate Admissions, 619-260-4524, Fax: 619-260-4158, E-mail: grads@sandiego.edu.
Website: http://www.sandiego.edu/business/programs/ms-global-leadership/

University of San Francisco, School of Law, Master of Law Programs, San Francisco, CA 94117-1080. Offers intellectual property and technology law (LL M); international transactions and comparative law (LL M). *Program availability:* Part-time. *Faculty:* 13 full-time (6 women), 11 part-time/adjunct (2 women). *Students:* 21 full-time (18 women), 65 part-time (31 women); includes 21 minority (3 Black or African American, non-Hispanic/Latino; 13 Asian, non-Hispanic/Latino; 1 Hispanic/Latino; 4 Two or more races, non-Hispanic/Latino), 17 international. Average age 34. 111 applicants, 87% accepted, 46 enrolled. In 2016, 30 master's awarded. *Entrance requirements:* For master's, law degree from U.S. or foreign school (intellectual property and technology law); law degree from foreign school (international transactions and comparative law). Application fee: $60. Electronic applications accepted. *Expenses: Tuition:* Full-time $23,310; part-time $1295 per credit. Tuition and fees vary according to course load, degree level, campus/location and program. *Financial support:* In 2016–17, 28 students received support. Applicants required to submit FAFSA. *Unit head:* Constance De La Vega, Director, 650-728-6658. *Application contact:* Julianne Traylor, Program Assistant, 415-422-6658, E-mail: masterlaws@usfca.edu.
Website: http://www.usfca.edu/law/llm/

University of San Francisco, School of Management, Master in Global Entrepreneurial Management Program, San Francisco, CA 94117. Offers MGEM. Program offered jointly with IQS in Barcelona, Spain and Fu Jen Catholic University in Taipei, Taiwan. *Faculty:* 1 full-time (0 women). *Students:* 39 full-time (21 women); includes 6 minority (2 Black or African American, non-Hispanic/Latino; 2 Asian, non-Hispanic/Latino; 1 Hispanic/Latino; 1 Two or more races, non-Hispanic/Latino), 32 international. Average age 24. 78 applicants, 97% accepted, 39 enrolled. In 2016, 37 master's awarded. *Entrance requirements:* For master's, resume, transcripts from each college or university attended, two letters of recommendation, personal statement. Additional exam requirements/recommendations for international students: Required—TOEFL (minimum score 550 paper-based, 79 iBT), IELTS (minimum score 6), or PTE (minimum score 53). *Application deadline:* For fall admission, 5/15 for domestic students. Application fee: $55. Electronic applications accepted. *Expenses: Tuition:* Full-time $23,310; part-time $1295 per credit. Tuition and fees vary according to course load, degree level, campus/location and program. *Financial support:* In 2016–17, 2 students received support. Application deadline: 3/2; applicants required to submit FAFSA. *Unit head:* Dr. Gleb Nikitenko, Director, 415-422-2221, E-mail: management@usfca.edu. *Application contact:* Office of Graduate Recruiting and Admissions, 415-422-2221, Fax: 415-422-6315, E-mail: management@usfca.edu.
Website: http://www.usfca.edu/mgem

University of Saskatchewan, College of Graduate Studies and Research, Edwards School of Business, Program in Business Administration, Saskatoon, SK S7N 5A2, Canada. Offers agribusiness management (MBA); biotechnology management (MBA); health services management (MBA); indigenous management (MBA); international business management (MBA).

University of Saskatchewan, College of Graduate Studies and Research, School of Public Policy, Saskatoon, SK S7N 5A2, Canada. Offers MIT, MPA, MPP, PhD.

The University of Scranton, Kania School of Management, Program in Business Administration, Scranton, PA 18510. Offers accounting (MBA); finance (MBA); general business administration (MBA); health care management (MBA); international business (MBA); management information systems (MBA); marketing (MBA); operations management (MBA). *Accreditation:* AACSB. *Program availability:* Part-time, evening/weekend, 100% online. *Entrance requirements:* For master's, GMAT (for MBA). *Faculty research:* Financial markets, strategic impact of total quality management, internal accounting controls, consumer preference, information systems and the Internet.

University of South Carolina, The Graduate School, Darla Moore School of Business, International Business Administration Program, Columbia, SC 29208. Offers IMBA. *Degree requirements:* For master's, one foreign language, field consulting project/internship. *Entrance requirements:* For master's, GMAT or GRE, minimum two years of work experience. Additional exam requirements/recommendations for international students: Required—TOEFL (minimum score 100 iBT); Recommended—IELTS. Electronic applications accepted. *Expenses:* Contact institution.

The University of Tampa, Sykes College of Business, Tampa, FL 33606-1490. Offers accounting (MS); entrepreneurship (MBA); finance (MBA, MS); information systems management (MBA); innovation management (MBA); international business (MBA); marketing (MBA, MS); nonprofit management (MBA). *Accreditation:* AACSB. *Program availability:* Part-time, evening/weekend. *Faculty:* 43 full-time (19 women), 9 part-time/adjunct (3 women). *Students:* 438 full-time (176 women), 126 part-time (57 women); includes 37 minority (22 Black or African American, non-Hispanic/Latino; 11 Asian, non-Hispanic/Latino; 4 Two or more races, non-Hispanic/Latino), 203 international. Average age 28. 1,305 applicants, 39% accepted, 192 enrolled. In 2016, 266 master's awarded. *Degree requirements:* For master's, capstone. *Entrance requirements:* For master's, GMAT or GRE, official transcripts from all colleges and/or universities previously attended, resume, personal statement, letters of recommendation. Additional exam requirements/recommendations for international students: Required—TOEFL (minimum score 577 paper-based, 90 iBT) or IELTS (7.5). *Application deadline:* Applications are processed on a rolling basis. Application fee: $40. Electronic applications accepted. *Expenses:* $588 per credit tuition, $40 per term fees. *Financial support:* In 2016–17, 116 students received support. Career-related internships or fieldwork, scholarships/grants, and unspecified assistantships available. Financial award applicants required to submit FAFSA. *Faculty research:* Job market signaling, on-line shopping behaviors and social media, the Tampa Bay economy, digital literacy, entrepreneurship in small businesses. *Unit head:* Dr. Natasha F. Veltri, Associate Dean, 813-253-6289, E-mail: nveltri@ut.edu. *Application contact:* Chanelle Cox, Staff Assistant, Admissions for Graduate and Continuing Studies, 813-253-6249, E-mail: ccox@ut.edu.
Website: http://www.ut.edu/business/

The University of Texas at Dallas, Naveen Jindal School of Management, Program in Organizations, Strategy and International Management, Richardson, TX 75080. Offers business administration (MBA); executive business administration (EMBA); global leadership (EMBA); healthcare management (MS); healthcare management for physicians (EMBA); innovation and entrepreneurship (MS); international management studies (MS, PhD); management and administrative sciences (MS); management science (PhD); project management (EMBA, MS); systems engineering and management (MS); MS/MBA. *Program availability:* Part-time, evening/weekend. *Faculty:* 29 full-time (7 women), 29 part-time/adjunct (5 women). *Students:* 524 full-time (189 women), 860 part-time (374 women); includes 452 minority (112 Black or African American, non-Hispanic/Latino; 3 American Indian or Alaska Native, non-Hispanic/Latino; 207 Asian, non-Hispanic/Latino; 85 Hispanic/Latino; 45 Two or more races, non-Hispanic/Latino), 317 international. Average age 34. 1,763 applicants, 37% accepted, 420 enrolled. In 2016, 521 master's, 13 doctorates awarded. *Degree requirements:* For doctorate, thesis/dissertation. *Entrance requirements:* For master's and doctorate, GMAT. Additional exam requirements/recommendations for international students: Required—TOEFL (minimum score 550 paper-based). *Application deadline:* For fall admission, 7/15 for domestic students, 5/1 priority date for international students; for spring admission, 11/15 for domestic students, 9/1 priority date for international students. Applications are processed on a rolling basis. Application fee: $50 ($100 for international students). Electronic applications accepted. *Expenses:* Tuition, state resident: full-time $12,418; part-time $690 per semester hour. Tuition, nonresident: full-time $24,150; part-time $1342 per semester hour. Tuition and fees vary according to course load. *Financial support:* In 2016–17, 385 students received support, including 21 research assistantships with partial tuition reimbursements available (averaging $25,698 per year), 68 teaching assistantships with partial tuition reimbursements available (averaging $16,973 per year); Federal Work-Study, institutionally sponsored loans, scholarships/grants, and unspecified assistantships also available. Support available to part-time students. Financial award application deadline: 4/30; financial award applicants required to submit FAFSA. *Faculty research:* International accounting, international trade and finance, economic development, international economics. *Unit head:* Dr. Seung-Hyun Lee, Area Coordinator, 972-883-6267, Fax: 972-883-5977, E-mail: sxl029100@utdallas.edu. *Application contact:* Maria Hasenhuttl, Assistant Area Coordinator, 972-883-5898, Fax: 972-883-5977, E-mail: maria.hasenhuttl@utdallas.edu.
Website: http://jindal.utdallas.edu/osim/

The University of Texas at El Paso, Graduate School, College of Business Administration, Programs in Business Administration, El Paso, TX 79968-0001. Offers business administration (MBA, Certificate); international business (PhD). *Accreditation:* AACSB. *Program availability:* Part-time, evening/weekend, online learning. *Degree requirements:* For master's, comprehensive exam. *Entrance requirements:* For master's and doctorate, GMAT. Additional exam requirements/recommendations for international students: Required—TOEFL. Electronic applications accepted. *Faculty research:* Cross-border modeling, human resources, and outsourcing and manufacturing; global information technology transfer; international investments and risk management.

University of the West, Department of Business Administration, Rosemead, CA 91770. Offers business administration (EMBA); computer information systems (MBA); finance (MBA); international business (MBA); nonprofit organization management (MBA). *Program availability:* Part-time, evening/weekend. *Faculty:* 3 full-time (1 woman), 6 part-time/adjunct (2 women). *Students:* 54 full-time (31 women), 14 part-time (3 women); includes 8 minority (4 Asian, non-Hispanic/Latino; 4 Hispanic/Latino), 59 international. Average age 29. *Entrance requirements:* Additional exam requirements/recommendations for international students: Required—TOEFL. *Application deadline:* For fall admission, 6/15 for domestic and international students; for winter admission, 4/1 for domestic and international students; for spring admission, 11/15 for domestic and international students. Applications are processed on a rolling basis. Application fee: $50 ($100 for international students). *Expenses: Tuition:* Full-time $9324; part-time $4662 per year. *Required fees:* $900; $640 per unit. $320 per semester. Tuition and fees vary according to program. *Financial support:* Career-related internships or fieldwork, Federal Work-Study, scholarships/grants, and tuition waivers (partial) available. Financial award applicants required to submit FAFSA. *Unit head:* Dr. Bill Y. Chen, Chair, 626-656-2125, Fax: 626-571-1413, E-mail: billchen@uwest.edu. *Application contact:* Rica Toribio, Director of Enrollment Services, 626-571-8811 Ext. 311, Fax: 626-571-1413, E-mail: ricat@uwest.edu.
Website: http://www.uwest.edu/site/index.php?option=com_content&view=article&id=119&Itemid=162

The University of Toledo, College of Graduate Studies, College of Business and Innovation, Department of Marketing and International Business, Toledo, OH 43606-3390. Offers MBA. *Program availability:* Part-time, evening/weekend. *Entrance requirements:* For master's, GMAT, GRE, or LSAT, minimum GPA of 2.7 for all prior academic work, three letters of recommendation, statement of purpose, transcripts from all prior institutions attended. Additional exam requirements/recommendations for international students: Required—TOEFL (minimum score 550 paper-based; 80 iBT). Electronic applications accepted.

University of Virginia, McIntire School of Commerce, MS Program in Global Commerce, Charlottesville, VA 22903. Offers global commerce (MS); global strategic management (MC); international management (Certificate). *Entrance requirements:* For master's, GMAT. Additional exam requirements/recommendations for international students: Required—TOEFL (minimum score 600 paper-based; 100 iBT), IELTS (minimum score 6.5). *Expenses:* Tuition, state resident: full-time $15,026; part-time $834 per credit hour. Tuition, nonresident: full-time $25,168; part-time $1378 per credit hour. *Required fees:* $2654.

University of Washington, Graduate School, Interdisciplinary Program in Global Trade, Transportation and Logistics Studies, Seattle, WA 98195. Offers Certificate.

University of Washington, Graduate School, Michael G. Foster School of Business, Seattle, WA 98195-3200. Offers auditing and assurance (MP Acc); business administration (MBA, PhD); entrepreneurship (MS); executive business administration (MBA); global executive business administration (MBA); information systems (MSIS); supply chain management (MSSCM); taxation (MP Acc); technology management (MBA); JD/MBA; MBA/MAIS; MBA/MHA. *Accreditation:* AACSB. *Program availability:* Part-time, evening/weekend. Terminal master's awarded for partial completion of doctoral program. *Degree requirements:* For doctorate, comprehensive exam, thesis/dissertation. *Entrance requirements:* For master's and doctorate, GMAT, GRE. Additional exam requirements/recommendations for international students: Required—TOEFL (minimum score 600 paper-based; 100 iBT). Electronic applications accepted.

Expenses: Contact institution. *Faculty research:* Finance, marketing, organizational behavior, information technology, strategy.

The University of Western Ontario, Richard Ivey School of Business, London, ON N6A 3K7, Canada. Offers business (EMBA, PhD); corporate strategy and leadership elective (MBA); entrepreneurship elective (MBA); finance elective (MBA); health sector stream (MBA); international management elective (MBA); marketing elective (MBA); JD/MBA. *Degree requirements:* For master's, thesis (for some programs); for doctorate, thesis/dissertation. *Entrance requirements:* For master's, GMAT, 2 years of full-time work experience, interview. Additional exam requirements/recommendations for international students: Required—TOEFL (minimum score 100 iBT) or IELTS (minimum score 6). Electronic applications accepted. *Faculty research:* Strategy, organizational behavior, international business, finance, operations management.

University of Wisconsin–Milwaukee, Graduate School, College of Letters and Science, Interdepartmental Program in Human Resources and Labor Relations, Milwaukee, WI 53201-0413. Offers human resources and labor relations (MHRLR); international human resources and labor relations (Certificate); mediation and negotiation (Certificate). *Program availability:* Part-time. *Entrance requirements:* For master's, GMAT or GRE General Test. Additional exam requirements/recommendations for international students: Required—TOEFL (minimum score 80 iBT), IELTS (minimum score 6.5). Electronic applications accepted.

University of Wisconsin–Oshkosh, Graduate Studies, College of Business, Program in Global Business Administration, Oshkosh, WI 54901. Offers GMBA. *Degree requirements:* For master's, integrative seminar, study abroad. *Entrance requirements:* For master's, GMAT, GRE, letters of recommendation. Additional exam requirements/recommendations for international students: Required—TOEFL (minimum score 79 iBT).

Vancouver Island University, Master of Business Administration Program, Nanaimo, BC V9R 5S5, Canada. Offers international business (MBA), including finance, marketing. Program offered jointly with University of Hertfordshire. *Accreditation:* ACBSP. *Program availability:* Part-time. *Degree requirements:* For master's, thesis. *Entrance requirements:* Additional exam requirements/recommendations for international students: Required—TOEFL (minimum score 88 iBT), IELTS (minimum score 6.5). Electronic applications accepted. *Expenses:* Contact institution. *Faculty research:* Tourism development, entrepreneurship, organizational development, strategic planning, international business strategy, intercultural team work.

Villanova University, Villanova School of Business, MBA - The Fast Track Program, Villanova, PA 19085. Offers analytics (MBA); cybersecurity (MBA); finance (MBA); healthcare (MBA); international business (MBA); management information systems (MBA); marketing (MBA); real estate (MBA); strategic management (MBA); sustainability (MBA). *Accreditation:* AACSB. *Program availability:* Part-time, evening/weekend. *Faculty:* 108 full-time (39 women), 32 part-time/adjunct (8 women). *Students:* 127 part-time (58 women); includes 18 minority (3 Black or African American, non-Hispanic/Latino; 7 Asian, non-Hispanic/Latino; 6 Hispanic/Latino; 2 Two or more races, non-Hispanic/Latino), 2 international. Average age 30. 88 applicants, 90% accepted, 66 enrolled. In 2016, 75 master's awarded. *Degree requirements:* For master's, minimum GPA of 3.0. *Entrance requirements:* For master's, GMAT or GRE, work experience, 2 letters of recommendation, 2 essays, resume, official transcripts, interview. Additional exam requirements/recommendations for international students: Required—TOEFL (minimum score 550 paper-based; 100 iBT). *Application deadline:* For fall admission, 6/30 for domestic and international students. Application fee: $65. Electronic applications accepted. *Expenses:* Contact institution. *Financial support:* Scholarships/grants available. Financial award application deadline: 6/30; financial award applicants required to submit FAFSA. *Faculty research:* Business analytics; creativity, innovation and entrepreneurship; global leadership; real estate; church management; business ethics; marketing and consumer insights. *Unit head:* Michael L. Capella, Associate Dean of Graduate and Executive Business Programs, 610-519-4336, Fax: 610-519-6273, E-mail: michael.l.capella@villanova.edu. *Application contact:* Kimberly Kane, Manager of Admissions, 610-519-3701, Fax: 610-519-6273, E-mail: kimberly.kane@villanova.edu.
Website: http://www1.villanova.edu/villanova/business/graduate/mba.html

Villanova University, Villanova School of Business, MBA - The Flex Track Program, Villanova, PA 19085. Offers analytics (MBA); finance (MBA); healthcare (MBA); international business (MBA); marketing (MBA); real estate (MBA); strategic management (MBA); JD/MBA. *Accreditation:* AACSB. *Program availability:* Part-time, evening/weekend, online learning. *Faculty:* 108 full-time (39 women), 32 part-time/adjunct (8 women). *Students:* 13 full-time (5 women), 399 part-time (134 women); includes 73 minority (21 Black or African American, non-Hispanic/Latino; 32 Asian, non-Hispanic/Latino; 19 Hispanic/Latino; 1 Two or more races, non-Hispanic/Latino), 11 international. Average age 31. 93 applicants, 94% accepted, 80 enrolled. In 2016, 133 master's awarded. *Degree requirements:* For master's, minimum GPA of 3.0. *Entrance requirements:* For master's, GMAT or GRE, work experience, 2 letters of recommendation, 2 essays, resume, official transcript. Additional exam requirements/recommendations for international students: Required—TOEFL (minimum score 550 paper-based; 100 iBT). *Application deadline:* For fall admission, 6/30 for domestic and international students; for spring admission, 11/15 for domestic and international students; for summer admission, 3/31 for domestic and international students. Applications are processed on a rolling basis. Application fee: $65. Electronic applications accepted. *Expenses:* Contact institution. *Financial support:* In 2016–17, 13 research assistantships with full tuition reimbursements (averaging $13,100 per year) were awarded; scholarships/grants also available. Financial award application deadline: 6/30; financial award applicants required to submit FAFSA. *Faculty research:* Business analytics; creativity, innovation and entrepreneurship; global leadership; real estate; church management; business ethics. *Unit head:* Michael L. Capella, Associate Dean of Graduate and Executive Business Programs, 610-610-4336, Fax: 610-519-6273, E-mail: michael.l.capella@villanova.edu. *Application contact:* Claire Bruno, Director of Recruitment and Enrollment Management, 610-519-4336, Fax: 610-519-6273, E-mail: claire.bruno@villanova.edu.
Website: http://www1.villanova.edu/villanova/business/graduate/mba.html

Virginia International University, School of Business, Fairfax, VA 22030. Offers accounting (MBA, MS); entrepreneurship (MBA); executive management (Graduate Certificate); global logistics (MBA); health care management (MBA); hospitality and tourism management (MBA); human resources management (MBA); international business management (MBA); international finance (MBA); marketing management (MBA); mass media and public relations (MBA); project management (MBA, MS). *Program availability:* Part-time, online learning. *Entrance requirements:* For master's and Graduate Certificate, bachelor's degree. Additional exam requirements/recommendations for international students: Required—TOEFL (minimum score 550 paper-based; 80 iBT), IELTS (minimum score 6). Electronic applications accepted.

Viterbo University, Master of Business Administration Program, La Crosse, WI 54601-4797. Offers general business administration (MBA); health care management (MBA); international business (MBA); leadership (MBA); project management (MBA). *Accreditation:* ACBSP. *Program availability:* Part-time, evening/weekend. *Degree requirements:* For master's, 34 semester credits. *Entrance requirements:* For master's, bachelor's degree, transcripts, minimum undergraduate cumulative GPA of 3.0, 2 letters of reference, 3-5 page essay. Additional exam requirements/recommendations for international students: Recommended—TOEFL (minimum score 550 paper-based). Electronic applications accepted. *Expenses:* Contact institution.

Wagner College, Division of Graduate Studies, Department of Business Administration, Staten Island, NY 10301-4495. Offers accounting (MS); business administration (MBA); finance (MBA); health care administration (MBA); international business (MBA); management (Exec MBA); marketing (MBA). *Accreditation:* ACBSP. *Program availability:* Part-time, evening/weekend. *Faculty:* 8 full-time (3 women), 17 part-time/adjunct (5 women). *Students:* 90 full-time (25 women), 16 part-time (8 women); includes 21 minority (12 Black or African American, non-Hispanic/Latino; 1 American Indian or Alaska Native, non-Hispanic/Latino; 3 Asian, non-Hispanic/Latino; 5 Hispanic/Latino), 5 international. Average age 26. 88 applicants, 85% accepted, 62 enrolled. In 2016, 72 master's awarded. *Degree requirements:* For master's, thesis optional. *Entrance requirements:* For master's, minimum GPA of 2.75, proficiency in computers and math. Additional exam requirements/recommendations for international students: Required—TOEFL (minimum score 550 paper-based; 79 iBT). *Application deadline:* For fall admission, 5/1 priority date for domestic students, 3/1 priority date for international students; for spring admission, 12/1 for domestic students, 11/1 for international students. Applications are processed on a rolling basis. Application fee: $50. Tuition and fees vary according to degree level. *Financial support:* In 2016–17, 93 students received support. Career-related internships or fieldwork, unspecified assistantships, and alumni fellowship grants available. Financial award application deadline: 4/1; financial award applicants required to submit FAFSA. *Unit head:* Dr. Donald Crooks, Director, 718-390-3429, Fax: 718-390-3429, E-mail: dcrooks@wagner.edu. *Application contact:* Patricia Clancy, Assistant Director for Enrollment, 718-420-4464, Fax: 718-390-3105, E-mail: patricia.clancy@wagner.edu.

Walden University, Graduate Programs, School of Management, Minneapolis, MN 55401. Offers accounting (MBA, MS, DBA), including accounting for the professional (MS), accounting with CPA emphasis (MS), self-designed (MS); advanced project management (Graduate Certificate); applied project management (Graduate Certificate); auditing (Graduate Certificate); bridge to business administration (Post-Doctoral Certificate); bridge to management (Post-Doctoral Certificate); business management (Graduate Certificate); communication (MBA); corporate finance (MBA); digital marketing (Graduate Certificate); entrepreneurship (DBA); entrepreneurship and small business (MBA); finance (MS, DBA), including finance for the professional (MS), finance with CFA/investment (MS), finance with CPA emphasis (MS); global supply chain management (DBA); healthcare management (MBA, DBA); human resource management (MBA, MS, Graduate Certificate), including functional human resource management (MS), general program (MS), integrating functional and strategic human resource management (MS), organizational strategy (MS); human resources management (DBA); information systems management (DBA); international business (MBA, DBA); leadership (MBA, MS, DBA, Graduate Certificate), including general program (MS), human resource leadership (MS), leader development (MS), self-designed (MS); management (MS, PhD), including communications (MS), finance (PhD), general program (MS), healthcare management (MS), human resource management (MS), human resources management (PhD), information systems management (PhD), international business (MS), leadership (MS), leadership and organizational change (PhD), marketing (MS), project management (MS), strategy and operations (MS); managerial accounting (Graduate Certificate); marketing (MBA, MS, DBA); project management (MBA, MS, DBA); self-designed (MBA, DBA); social impact management (DBA); technology entrepreneurship (DBA). *Accreditation:* ACBSP. *Program availability:* Part-time, evening/weekend, online only, 100% online. *Degree requirements:* For master's, thesis (for some programs), residency (for EMBA); for doctorate, thesis/dissertation (for some programs), residency. *Entrance requirements:* For master's, bachelor's degree or higher; minimum GPA of 2.5; official transcripts; goal statement (for some programs); access to computer and Internet; for doctorate, master's degree or higher; three years of related professional or academic experience (preferred); minimum GPA of 3.0; goal statement and current resume (for select programs); official transcripts; access to computer and Internet; for other advanced degree, relevant work experience; access to computer and Internet. Additional exam requirements/recommendations for international students: Required—TOEFL (minimum score 550 paper-based, 79 iBT), IELTS (minimum score 6.5), Michigan English Language Assessment Battery (minimum score 82), or PTE (minimum score 53). Electronic applications accepted.

Walsh College of Accountancy and Business Administration, Graduate Programs, Program in Management, Troy, MI 48083. Offers human resources management (MS); international business (MS); strategic management (MS). *Program availability:* Part-time, evening/weekend. *Faculty:* 12 full-time (6 women), 12 part-time/adjunct (5 women). *Students:* 54 (43 women); includes 20 minority (15 Black or African American, non-Hispanic/Latino; 1 American Indian or Alaska Native, non-Hispanic/Latino; 2 Asian, non-Hispanic/Latino; 1 Hispanic/Latino; 1 Two or more races, non-Hispanic/Latino). Average age 33. 27 applicants, 70% accepted, 13 enrolled. In 2016, 2 master's awarded. *Entrance requirements:* For master's, minimum overall cumulative GPA of 2.75 from all colleges previously attended. Additional exam requirements/recommendations for international students: Required—TOEFL (minimum score 550 paper-based, 79 iBT), IELTS (6.5), Michigan English Language Assessment Battery, or MTELP. *Application deadline:* Applications are processed on a rolling basis. Application fee: $35. Electronic applications accepted. *Expenses:* $740 per credit hour, $125 registration fee per semester. *Financial support:* In 2016–17, 2 students received support. Career-related internships or fieldwork and scholarships/grants available. Financial award application deadline: 6/30; financial award applicants required to submit FAFSA. *Faculty research:* Strategy practice and process, management learning and decision-making, human capital development, global leadership and citizenship, use of systems and complexity theory and management practice. *Unit head:* Dr. Sheila Ronis, Chair, Management, 248-823-1635, Fax: 248-689-0920, E-mail: sronis@walshcollege.edu. *Application contact:* Heather Rigby, Director, Admissions and Academic Advising, 248-823-1610, Fax: 248-689-0938, E-mail: hrigby@walshcollege.edu.

Warner University, School of Business, Lake Wales, FL 33859. Offers accounting (MBA); business administration (MBA); human resource management (MBA); international business (MBA); management (MSMC). *Program availability:* Part-time, evening/weekend, online learning. *Degree requirements:* For master's, comprehensive exam, thesis. *Entrance requirements:* For master's, minimum GPA of 3.0, letters of recommendation (2). Additional exam requirements/recommendations for international students: Required—TOEFL. *Application deadline:* Applications are processed on a rolling basis. Application fee: $50. Electronic applications accepted. *Financial support:* Scholarships/grants available. Financial award applicants required to submit FAFSA. *Unit head:* Cindy Polston, Program Director, 863-638-7689. *Application contact:* Judianne Steibly, Graduate Academic Advisor, 863-638-3702, Fax: 863-638-4907, E-mail: admissions@warner.edu.

Wayland Baptist University, Graduate Programs, Programs in Business Administration/Management, Plainview, TX 79072-6998. Offers accounting (MBA); general business (MBA); health care administration (MAM, MBA); human resource management (MAM, MBA); international management (MBA); management (MBA, D Mgt); management information systems (MBA); organization management (MAM); project management (MBA). *Program availability:* Part-time, evening/weekend, online learning. *Degree requirements:* For master's, capstone course. *Entrance requirements:* For master's, GMAT, GRE or MAT. Additional exam requirements/recommendations for international students: Required—TOEFL (minimum score 500 paper-based; 61 iBT). Electronic applications accepted.

Webber International University, Graduate School of Business, Babson Park, FL 33827-0096. Offers accounting (MBA); business (MBA); criminal justice management (MBA); international business (MBA); sport business management (MBA). *Program availability:* Part-time, evening/weekend, 100% online. *Faculty:* 11 full-time (3 women), 1 part-time/adjunct (0 women). *Students:* 44 full-time (21 women), 6 part-time (2 women); includes 11 minority (5 Black or African American, non-Hispanic/Latino; 5 Hispanic/Latino; 1 Two or more races, non-Hispanic/Latino), 11 international. Average age 27. 32 applicants, 69% accepted, 18 enrolled. In 2016, 16 master's awarded. *Degree requirements:* For master's, class trip (for international business); practicum (for criminal justice management). *Entrance requirements:* For master's, three recommendation letters, résumé, essay, official transcripts from all colleges and universities attended. Additional exam requirements/recommendations for international students: Recommended—TOEFL (minimum score 500 paper-based; 61 iBT), IELTS (minimum score 6). *Application deadline:* For fall admission, 7/1 for international students. Applications are processed on a rolling basis. Application fee: $50 ($75 for international students). Electronic applications accepted. *Expenses:* $2,013 tuition per course; $207 technology fee per course (for online courses only). *Financial support:* In 2016–17, 11 students received support. Scholarships/grants and unspecified assistantships available. Financial award application deadline: 8/16; financial award applicants required to submit FAFSA. *Unit head:* Dr. Nikos Orphanoudakis, Dean, 863-638-2910, Fax: 863-638-1591, E-mail: orphanoudakisn@webber.edu. *Application contact:* Lacy Edwards, Admissions Counselor and MBA Coordinator, 863-638-2910, Fax: 863-638-1591, E-mail: admissions@webber.edu.

Webster University, George Herbert Walker School of Business and Technology, Department of Business, St. Louis, MO 63119-3194. Offers business and organizational security management (MBA); decision support systems (MBA); environmental management (MBA); finance (MBA, MS); forensic accounting (MS); gerontology (MBA); human resources development (MBA); human resources management (MBA); information technology management (MBA); international business (MA, MBA); international relations (MBA); management and leadership (MBA); marketing (MBA); media communications (MBA); procurement and acquisitions management (MBA); Web services (MBA). *Accreditation:* ACBSP. *Program availability:* Part-time, evening/weekend, online learning. *Degree requirements:* For master's, comprehensive exam (for some programs), thesis (for some programs). *Entrance requirements:* Additional exam requirements/recommendations for international students: Required—TOEFL. *Application deadline:* Applications are processed on a rolling basis. Application fee: $35 ($50 for international students). *Expenses: Tuition:* Full-time $21,900; part-time $730 per credit hour. Tuition and fees vary according to campus/location and program. *Financial support:* Federal Work-Study available. Support available to part-time students. Financial award application deadline: 4/1; financial award applicants required to submit FAFSA. *Unit head:* David Porras, Chair, 314-246-8621, E-mail: porrasd@webster.edu. *Application contact:* Sarah Nandor, Director, Graduate and Transfer Admissions, 314-968-7109, E-mail: gadmit@webster.edu.

Wilkes University, College of Graduate and Professional Studies, Jay S. Sidhu School of Business and Leadership, Wilkes-Barre, PA 18766-0002. Offers accounting (MBA); entrepreneurship (MBA); finance (MBA); health care administration (MBA); human resource management (MBA); international business (MBA); operations management (MBA); organizational leadership and development (MBA). *Accreditation:* ACBSP. *Program availability:* Part-time, evening/weekend. *Students:* 35 full-time (17 women), 112 part-time (55 women); includes 17 minority (6 Black or African American, non-Hispanic/Latino; 4 Asian, non-Hispanic/Latino; 5 Hispanic/Latino; 2 Two or more races, non-Hispanic/Latino), 16 international. Average age 31. In 2016, 59 master's awarded. *Entrance requirements:* For master's, GMAT. Additional exam requirements/recommendations for international students: Required—TOEFL (minimum score 550 paper-based; 79 iBT). *Application deadline:* Applications are processed on a rolling basis. Application fee: $45 ($65 for international students). Electronic applications accepted. *Expenses:* Contact institution. *Financial support:* Unspecified assistantships available. Financial award application deadline: 3/1; financial award applicants required to submit FAFSA. *Unit head:* Dr. Abel Adekola, Dean, 570-408-4701, Fax: 570-408-7846, E-mail: abel.adekola@wilkes.edu. *Application contact:* Director of Graduate Enrollment, 570-408-4234, Fax: 570-408-7846.
Website: http://www.wilkes.edu/academics/colleges/sidhu-school-of-business-leadership/index.aspx

Xavier University, Williams College of Business, Master of Business Administration Program, Cincinnati, OH 45207. Offers business administration (Exec MBA, MBA); business intelligence (MBA); finance (MBA); health industry (MBA); international business (MBA); marketing (MBA); values-based leadership (MBA); MBA/MHSA; MSN/MBA. *Accreditation:* AACSB. *Program availability:* Part-time, evening/weekend. *Degree requirements:* For master's, capstone course. *Entrance requirements:* For master's, GMAT or GRE, official transcript; resume. Additional exam requirements/recommendations for international students: Required—TOEFL (minimum score 550 paper-based; 79 iBT). Electronic applications accepted. Application fee is waived when completed online. *Expenses:* Contact institution.

York University, Faculty of Graduate Studies, Schulich School of Business, Toronto, ON M3J 1P3, Canada. Offers accounting (M Acc); administration (PhD); business (MBA); business analytics (MBA); finance (MF); international business (IMBA); MBA/JD; MBA/MA; MBA/MFA. *Program availability:* Part-time, evening/weekend. *Degree requirements:* For master's, advanced proficiency in a second language, work term (IMBA); for doctorate, comprehensive exam, thesis/dissertation. *Entrance requirements:* For master's, GMAT or GRE, minimum GPA of 3.0 (3.3 for MF, MBA in business analytics, and IMBA); for doctorate, GMAT or GRE, minimum GPA of 3.3. Additional exam requirements/recommendations for international students: Required—TOEFL (minimum score 600 paper-based; 100 iBT), IELTS (minimum score 7), York English Language Test (minimum score 1); PearsonVUE (minimum score 64). Electronic applications accepted. *Faculty research:* Accounting, finance, marketing, operations management and information systems, organizational studies, strategic management.

Section 12
Management Information Systems

This section contains a directory of institutions offering graduate work in management information systems. Additional information about programs listed in the directory but not augmented by an in-depth entry may be obtained by writing directly to the dean of a graduate school or chair of a department at the address given in the directory.

For programs offering related work, see also in this book *Business Administration and Management*. In another guide in this series:

Graduate Programs in Engineering & Applied Sciences

See *Computer Science and Information Technology* and *Management of Engineering and Technology*

CONTENTS

Program Directory

Featured School: Display and Close-Up

See:

Management Information Systems

Adelphi University, Robert B. Willumstad School of Business, MBA Program, Garden City, NY 11530-0701. Offers accounting (MBA); finance (MBA); health services administration (MBA); human resource management (MBA); management (MBA); management information systems (MBA); marketing (MBA); sport management (MBA). *Accreditation:* AACSB. *Program availability:* Part-time, evening/weekend. *Students:* 172 full-time (74 women), 129 part-time (66 women); includes 30 minority (9 Black or African American, non-Hispanic/Latino; 11 Asian, non-Hispanic/Latino; 9 Hispanic/Latino; 1 Two or more races, non-Hispanic/Latino), 29 international. Average age 32. 4 applicants. In 2016, 130 master's awarded. *Degree requirements:* For master's, capstone course. *Entrance requirements:* For master's, GMAT, 2 letters of recommendation. Additional exam requirements/recommendations for international students: Required—TOEFL (minimum score 550 paper-based; 80 iBT), IELTS (minimum score 6.5). *Application deadline:* For fall admission, 4/1 for international students; for spring admission, 11/1 for international students. Applications are processed on a rolling basis. Application fee: $50. Electronic applications accepted. *Expenses:* Contact institution. *Financial support:* Research assistantships with partial tuition reimbursements, career-related internships or fieldwork, Federal Work-Study, institutionally sponsored loans, scholarships/grants, tuition waivers (partial), and unspecified assistantships available. Financial award application deadline: 3/1; financial award applicants required to submit FAFSA. *Faculty research:* Supply chain management, distribution channels, productivity benchmark analysis, data envelopment analysis, financial portfolio analysis. *Unit head:* Dr. Rakesh Gupta, Associate Dean, 516-877-4629. *Application contact:* Christine Murphy, Director of Admissions, 516-877-3050, Fax: 516-877-3039, E-mail: graduateadmissions@adelphi.edu.
Website: http://business.adelphi.edu/degree-programs/graduate-degree-programs/m-b-a/

Air Force Institute of Technology, Graduate School of Engineering and Management, Department of Systems and Engineering Management, Dayton, OH 45433-7765. Offers cost analysis (MS); environmental and engineering management (MS); environmental engineering science (MS); information resource/systems management (MS). *Accreditation:* ABET. *Program availability:* Part-time. *Degree requirements:* For master's, thesis. *Entrance requirements:* For master's, GRE, GMAT, minimum GPA of 3.0.

American Business & Technology University, Programs in Business Administration, Saint Joseph, MO 64506. Offers business administration (MBA); financial management (MBA); global business management (MBA); information systems management (MBA); marketing and social media (MBA); project and operations management (MBA); public accounting (MBA). *Program availability:* Online learning.

American InterContinental University Atlanta, Program in Information Technology, Atlanta, GA 30328. Offers MIT. *Program availability:* Part-time, evening/weekend. *Degree requirements:* For master's, technical proficiency demonstration. *Entrance requirements:* For master's, Computer Programmer Aptitude Battery Exam, interview. Electronic applications accepted. *Faculty research:* Operating systems, security issues, networks and routing, computer hardware.

American Public University System, AMU/APU Graduate Programs, Charles Town, WV 25414. Offers accounting (MBA, MS); applied business analytics (MBA, MS); criminal justice (MA), including business administration, emergency and disaster management, general (MA, MS); educational leadership (M Ed); emergency and disaster management (MA); entrepreneurship (MBA); environmental policy and management (MS), including environmental planning, environmental sustainability, fish and wildlife management, general (MA, MS), global environmental management; finance (MBA); general (MBA); government contracting and acquisition (MBA); health care administration (MBA); health information management (MS); history (MA), including American history, ancient and classical history, European history, global history, public history; homeland security (MA), including business administration, counterterrorism studies, criminal justice, cyber, emergency management and public health, intelligence studies, transportation security; homeland security resource allocation (MBA); humanities (MA); information technology (MS), including digital forensics, enterprise software development, information assurance and security, IT project management; information technology management (MBA); intelligence studies (MA), including criminal intelligence, cyber, general (MA, MS), homeland security, intelligence analysis, intelligence collection, intelligence management, intelligence operations, terrorism studies; international relations and conflict resolution (MA), including comparative and security issues, conflict resolution, international and transnational security issues, peacekeeping; legal studies (MA); management (MA), including strategic consulting; marketing (MBA); military history (MA), including American military history, American Revolution, civil war, war since 1945, World War II; military studies (MA), including joint warfare, strategic leadership; national security studies (MA), including cyber, general (MA, MS), homeland security, regional security studies, security and intelligence analysis, terrorism studies; nonprofit management (MBA); political science (MA), including American politics and government, comparative government and development, general (MA, MS), international relations, public policy; psychology (MA); public administration (MPA), including disaster management, environmental policy, health policy, human resources, national security, organizational management, security management; public health (MPH); reverse logistics management (MA); security management (MA); space studies (MS), including aerospace science, general (MA, MS), planetary science; sports and health sciences (MS); sports management (MBA); teaching (M Ed), including autism spectrum disorder, curriculum and instruction for elementary teachers, elementary reading, English language learners, instructional leadership, online learning, special education, STEAM (STEM plus the arts); transportation and logistics management (MA). *Program availability:* Part-time, evening/weekend, online only, 100% online. *Faculty:* 401 full-time (228 women), 1,678 part-time/adjunct (781 women). *Students:* 378 full-time (184 women), 8,455 part-time (3,484 women); includes 2,972 minority (1,552 Black or African American, non-Hispanic/Latino; 52 American Indian or Alaska Native, non-Hispanic/Latino; 211 Asian, non-Hispanic/Latino; 791 Hispanic/Latino; 70 Native Hawaiian or other Pacific Islander, non-Hispanic/Latino; 296 Two or more races, non-Hispanic/Latino), 109 international. Average age 37. In 2016, 3,185 master's awarded. *Degree requirements:* For master's, comprehensive exam or practicum. *Entrance requirements:* For master's, official transcript showing earned bachelor's degree from institution accredited by recognized accrediting body. Additional exam requirements/recommendations for international students: Required—TOEFL (minimum score 550 paper-based), IELTS (minimum score 6.5). *Application deadline:* Applications are processed on a rolling basis. Application fee: $0. Electronic applications accepted. *Expenses: Tuition:* Part-time $350 per credit hour. *Required fees:* $50 per course. *Financial support:* Scholarships/grants available. Financial award applicants required to submit FAFSA. *Unit head:* Dr. Karan Powell, President, 877-468-6268, Fax: 304-724-3780. *Application contact:* Terry Grant, Vice President of Enrollment Management, 877-468-6268, Fax: 304-724-3780, E-mail: info@apus.edu.
Website: http://www.apus.edu

American Sentinel University, Graduate Programs, Aurora, CO 80014. Offers business administration (MBA); business intelligence (MS); computer science (MSCS); health information management (MS); healthcare (MBA); information systems (MSIS); nursing (MSN). *Program availability:* Part-time, evening/weekend, online learning. *Entrance requirements:* Additional exam requirements/recommendations for international students: Required—TOEFL (minimum score 600 paper-based). Electronic applications accepted.

American University, Kogod School of Business, Department of Information Technology, Washington, DC 20016-8044. Offers analytics (MS). *Faculty:* 14 full-time (3 women), 17 part-time/adjunct (8 women). *Students:* 71 full-time (28 women), 50 part-time (24 women); includes 56 minority (18 Black or African American, non-Hispanic/Latino; 16 Asian, non-Hispanic/Latino; 14 Hispanic/Latino; 1 Native Hawaiian or other Pacific Islander, non-Hispanic/Latino; 7 Two or more races, non-Hispanic/Latino), 12 international. Average age 31. 134 applicants, 77% accepted, 60 enrolled. *Entrance requirements:* For master's, GMAT. Additional exam requirements/recommendations for international students: Required—TOEFL. Application fee: $100. Electronic applications accepted. *Expenses:* $1,579 per credit tuition; $690 mandatory fees. *Financial support:* Scholarships/grants available. Financial award applicants required to submit FAFSA. *Unit head:* Edward Wasil, Chair, 202-885-1966, E-mail: ewasil@american.edu. *Application contact:* Jason Kennedy, Director of Enrollment Operations, 202-885-1968, E-mail: jkennedy@american.edu.

American University, School of International Service, Washington, DC 20016-8071. Offers comparative and regional studies (Certificate); cross-cultural communication (Certificate); development management (MS); ethics, peace, and global affairs (MA); European studies (Certificate); global environmental policy (MA, Certificate); global information technology (Certificate); international affairs (MA), including comparative and international disability policy, comparative and regional studies, international economic relations, international politics, natural resources and sustainable development, U.S. foreign policy; international arts management (Certificate); international communication (MA, Certificate); international development (MA); international economic policy (Certificate); international economic relations (Certificate); international economics (MA); international media (MA); international peace and conflict resolution (MA, Certificate); international politics (Certificate); international relations (MA, PhD); international service (MIS); peacebuilding (Certificate); social enterprise (MA); the Americas (Certificate); United States foreign policy (Certificate); JD/MA. *Program availability:* Part-time, evening/weekend, 100% online. *Faculty:* 116 full-time (53 women), 57 part-time/adjunct (19 women). *Students:* 575 full-time (360 women), 491 part-time (277 women); includes 287 minority (100 Black or African American, non-Hispanic/Latino; 6 American Indian or Alaska Native, non-Hispanic/Latino; 58 Asian, non-Hispanic/Latino; 92 Hispanic/Latino; 1 Native Hawaiian or other Pacific Islander, non-Hispanic/Latino; 30 Two or more races, non-Hispanic/Latino), 151 international. Average age 29. 1,504 applicants, 84% accepted, 403 enrolled. In 2016, 374 master's, 3 doctorates, 1 other advanced degree awarded. Terminal master's awarded for partial completion of doctoral program. *Degree requirements:* For master's, one foreign language, comprehensive exam, thesis or alternative; for doctorate, one foreign language, comprehensive exam, thesis/dissertation. *Entrance requirements:* For master's, GRE; GMAT or GRE (for MA in social enterprise), transcripts, resume, 2 letters of recommendation, statement of purpose; for doctorate, GRE, transcripts, resume, 3 letters of recommendation, statement of purpose. Additional exam requirements/recommendations for international students: Required—TOEFL (minimum score 600 paper-based, 100 iBT), IELTS (minimum score 7), or PTE (minimum score of 68). Application fee: $55. Electronic applications accepted. *Expenses:* $1,579 per credit tuition; $1,930 mandatory fees. *Financial support:* Research assistantships, teaching assistantships, institutionally sponsored loans, scholarships/grants, and unspecified assistantships available. Financial award application deadline: 1/15; financial award applicants required to submit FAFSA. *Unit head:* Dr. James Goldgeier, Dean, 202-885-1603, Fax: 202-885-2494, E-mail: goldgeier@american.edu. *Application contact:* Jia Jiang, Associate Director, Graduate Education Enrollment, 202-885-1689, Fax: 202-885-1109, E-mail: jiang@american.edu.
Website: http://www.american.edu/sis/

American University of Armenia, Graduate Programs, Yerevan, Armenia. Offers business administration (MBA); computer and information science (MS), including business management, design and manufacturing, energy (ME, MS), industrial engineering and systems management; economics (MS); industrial engineering and systems management (ME), including business, computer aided design/manufacturing, energy (ME, MS), information technology; law (LL M); political science and international affairs (MPSIA); public health (MPH); teaching English as a foreign language (MA). *Program availability:* Part-time, evening/weekend. *Degree requirements:* For master's, thesis (for some programs), capstone/project. *Entrance requirements:* For master's, GRE, GMAT, or LSAT. Additional exam requirements/recommendations for international students: Recommended—TOEFL (minimum score 79 iBT), IELTS (minimum score 6.5). *Faculty research:* Microfinance, finance (rural/development, international, corporate), firm life cycle theory, TESOL, language proficiency testing, public policy, administrative law, economic development, cryptography, artificial intelligence, energy efficiency/renewable energy, computer-aided design/manufacturing, health financing, tuberculosis control, mother/child health, preventive ophthalmology, post-earthquake psychopathological investigations, tobacco control, environmental health risk assessments.

Argosy University, Atlanta, College of Business, Atlanta, GA 30328. Offers accounting (DBA); corporate compliance (MBA); customized professional concentration (MBA, DBA); finance (MBA); healthcare administration (MBA); information systems (DBA); information systems management (MBA); international business (MBA, DBA); management (MBA, MSM, DBA); marketing (MBA, DBA). *Accreditation:* ACBSP.

Argosy University, Chicago, College of Business, Chicago, IL 60601. Offers accounting (DBA); customized professional concentration (MBA, DBA); finance (MBA); fraud examination (MBA); global business sustainability (DBA); healthcare administration (MBA); information systems (DBA); information systems management (MBA); international business (MBA, DBA); management (MBA, MSM, DBA); marketing (MBA, DBA); organizational leadership (Ed D); public administration (MBA); sustainable management (MBA). *Accreditation:* ACBSP. *Program availability:* Online learning.

Argosy University, Dallas, College of Business, Farmers Branch, TX 75244. Offers accounting (DBA, AGC); corporate compliance (MBA, Graduate Certificate); customized professional concentration (MBA); finance (MBA, Graduate Certificate); fraud examination (MBA, Graduate Certificate); global business sustainability (DBA, AGC);

healthcare administration (Graduate Certificate); healthcare management (MBA); information systems (MBA, DBA, AGC); information systems management (Graduate Certificate); international business (MBA, DBA, AGC, Graduate Certificate); management (MBA, DBA, AGC, Graduate Certificate); marketing (MBA, DBA, AGC, Graduate Certificate); public administration (MBA, Graduate Certificate); sustainable management (MBA, Graduate Certificate). *Accreditation:* ACBSP.

Argosy University, Denver, College of Business, Denver, CO 80231. Offers accounting (DBA); corporate compliance (MBA); customized professional concentration (MBA, DBA); finance (MBA); fraud examination (MBA); global business sustainability (DBA); healthcare administration (MBA); information systems (DBA); information systems management (MBA); international business (MBA, DBA); management (MBA, MSM, DBA); marketing (MBA, DBA); organizational leadership (Ed D); public administration (MBA); sustainable management (MBA). *Accreditation:* ACBSP.

Argosy University, Hawai`i, College of Business, Honolulu, HI 96813. Offers accounting (DBA); corporate compliance (MBA); customized professional concentration (MBA, DBA); finance (MBA, Certificate); fraud examination (MBA); global business sustainability (DBA); healthcare administration (MBA, Certificate); information systems (DBA); information systems management (MBA, Certificate); international business (MBA, DBA, Certificate); management (MBA, MSM, DBA); marketing (MBA, DBA, Certificate); organizational leadership (Ed D); public administration (MBA); sustainable management (MBA).

Argosy University, Inland Empire, College of Business, Ontario, CA 91761. Offers accounting (DBA); corporate compliance (MBA); customized professional concentration (MBA, DBA); finance (MBA); fraud examination (MBA); global business sustainability (DBA); healthcare administration (MBA); information systems (DBA); information systems management (MBA); international business (MBA, DBA); management (MBA, MSM, DBA); marketing (MBA, DBA); organizational leadership (Ed D); public administration (MBA); sustainable management (MBA).

Argosy University, Los Angeles, College of Business, Santa Monica, CA 90045. Offers accounting (DBA); corporate compliance (MBA); customized professional concentration (MBA, DBA); finance (MBA); fraud examination (MBA); global business sustainability (DBA); healthcare administration (MBA); information systems (DBA); information systems management (MBA); international business (MBA, DBA); management (MBA, MSM, DBA); marketing (MBA, DBA); organizational leadership (Ed D); public administration (MBA); sustainable management (MBA).

Argosy University, Nashville, College of Business, Nashville, TN 37214. Offers accounting (DBA); customized professional concentration (MBA, DBA); finance (MBA); healthcare administration (MBA); information systems (MBA, DBA); international business (MBA, DBA); management (MBA, MSM, DBA); marketing (MBA, DBA).

Argosy University, Northern Virginia, College of Business, Arlington, VA 22209. Offers accounting (DBA); customized professional concentration (MBA, DBA); finance (MBA); fraud examination (MBA); global business sustainability (DBA); healthcare administration (MBA); information systems (DBA); information systems management (MBA); international business (MBA, DBA, Certificate); management (MBA, MSM, DBA); marketing (MBA, DBA, Certificate); organizational leadership (Ed D); public administration (MBA); sustainable management (MBA).

Argosy University, Orange County, College of Business, Orange, CA 92868. Offers accounting (DBA, Adv C); corporate compliance (MBA); customized professional concentration (MBA, DBA); finance (MBA, Certificate); fraud examination (MBA); global business sustainability (DBA); healthcare administration (MBA, Certificate); information systems (DBA, Adv C, Certificate); information systems management (MBA); international business (MBA, DBA, Adv C, Certificate); management (MBA, MSM, DBA, Adv C); marketing (MBA, DBA, Adv C, Certificate); organizational leadership (Ed D); public administration (MBA, Certificate); sustainable management (MBA).

Argosy University, Phoenix, College of Business, Phoenix, AZ 85021. Offers accounting (DBA); corporate compliance (MBA); customized professional concentration (MBA, DBA); finance (MBA); fraud examination (MBA); global business sustainability (DBA); healthcare administration (MBA); information systems (DBA); information systems management (MBA); international business (MBA, DBA); management (MBA, DBA); marketing (MBA, DBA); public administration (MBA); sustainable management (MBA).

Argosy University, Salt Lake City, College of Business, Draper, UT 84020. Offers accounting (DBA); corporate compliance (MBA); customized professional concentration (MBA, DBA); finance (MBA); fraud examination (MBA); global business sustainability (DBA); healthcare administration (MBA); information systems (DBA); information systems management (MBA); international business (MBA, DBA); management (MBA, DBA); marketing (MBA, DBA); public administration (MBA); sustainable management (MBA).

Argosy University, San Diego, College of Business, San Diego, CA 92108. Offers accounting (DBA); corporate compliance (MBA); customized professional concentration (MBA, DBA); finance (MBA); fraud examination (MBA); global business sustainability (DBA); information systems (DBA); information systems management (MBA); international business (MBA, DBA); management (MBA, MSM, DBA); marketing (MBA, DBA); organizational leadership (Ed D); public administration (MBA).

Argosy University, San Francisco Bay Area, College of Business, Alameda, CA 94501. Offers accounting (DBA); corporate compliance (MBA); customized professional concentration (MBA, DBA); finance (MBA); fraud examination (MBA); global business sustainability (DBA); healthcare administration (MBA); information systems (DBA); information systems management (MBA); international business (MBA, DBA); management (MBA, MSM, DBA); marketing (MBA, DBA); organizational leadership (Ed D); public administration (MBA); sustainable management (MBA).

Argosy University, Sarasota, College of Business, Sarasota, FL 34235. Offers accounting (DBA, Adv C); corporate compliance (MBA, DBA, Certificate); customized professional concentration (MBA, DBA); finance (MBA, Certificate), fraud examination (MBA, Certificate); global business sustainability (DBA, Adv C); healthcare administration (MBA, Certificate); information systems (DBA, Adv C, Certificate); information systems management (MBA); international business (MBA, DBA, Adv C, Certificate); management (MBA, MSM, DBA, Adv C, Certificate); marketing (MBA, DBA, Adv C, Certificate); organizational leadership (Ed D); public administration (MBA, Certificate); sustainable management (MBA, Certificate).

Argosy University, Schaumburg, Graduate School of Business and Management, Schaumburg, IL 60173-5403. Offers accounting (DBA, Adv C); customized professional concentration (MBA, DBA); finance (MBA, Certificate); fraud examination (MBA); healthcare administration (MBA, Certificate); human resource management (MS); information systems (Adv C, Certificate); information systems management (MBA); international business (MBA, DBA, Adv C, Certificate); management (MBA, MSM, DBA, Adv C, Certificate); marketing (MBA, DBA, Adv C, Certificate); organizational leadership (MS, Ed D); public administration (MBA); sustainable management (MBA).

Argosy University, Seattle, College of Business, Seattle, WA 98121. Offers accounting (DBA); corporate compliance (MBA); customized professional concentration (MBA, DBA); finance (MBA); fraud examination (MBA); global business sustainability (DBA); healthcare administration (MBA); information systems (DBA); information systems management (MBA); international business (MBA, DBA); management (MBA, MSM, DBA); marketing (MBA, DBA); organizational leadership (Ed D); public administration (MBA); sustainable management (MBA).

Argosy University, Tampa, College of Business, Tampa, FL 33607. Offers accounting (DBA); corporate compliance (MBA); customized professional concentration (MBA, DBA); finance (MBA); fraud examination (MBA); global business sustainability (DBA); healthcare administration (MBA); information systems (DBA); information systems management (MBA); international business (MBA, DBA); management (MBA, MSM, DBA); marketing (MBA, DBA); organizational leadership (Ed D); public administration (MBA); sustainable management (MBA).

Argosy University, Twin Cities, College of Business, Eagan, MN 55121. Offers accounting (DBA); customized professional concentration (MBA, DBA); finance (MBA); fraud examination (MBA); global business sustainability (DBA); healthcare administration (MBA); information systems (DBA); information systems management (MBA); international business (MBA, DBA); management (MBA, MSM, DBA); marketing (MBA, DBA); organizational leadership (Ed D); public administration (MBA); sustainable management (MBA).

Arizona State University at the Tempe campus, Ira A. Fulton Schools of Engineering, The Polytechnic School, Programs in Technology Management, Mesa, AZ 85212. Offers aviation management and human factors (MS); environmental technology management (MS); global technology and development (MS); graphic information technology (MS); management of technology (MS). *Program availability:* Part-time, evening/weekend, online learning. *Degree requirements:* For master's, thesis or applied project and oral defense; interactive Program of Study (iPOS) submitted before completing 50 percent of required credit hours. *Entrance requirements:* For master's, GRE, minimum GPA of 3.0 or equivalent in last 2 years of work leading to bachelor's degree. Additional exam requirements/recommendations for international students: Required—TOEFL, IELTS, or PTE. Electronic applications accepted. *Faculty research:* Digital imaging, digital publishing, Internet development/e-commerce, information aviation human factors, pilot selection, databases, multimedia, commercial digital photography, digital workflow, computer graphics modeling and animation, information design, sociotechnology, visual and technical literacy, environmental management, quality management, project management, industrial ethics, hazardous materials, environmental chemistry.

Arizona State University at the Tempe campus, W. P. Carey School of Business, Department of Information Systems, Tempe, AZ 85287-4606. Offers business administration (PhD), including information systems; information management (MS); MBA/MS. *Program availability:* Evening/weekend, online learning. Terminal master's awarded for partial completion of doctoral program. *Degree requirements:* For master's, thesis or alternative, applied project, interactive Program of Study (iPOS) submitted before completing 50 percent of required credit hours; for doctorate, comprehensive exam, thesis/dissertation, interactive Program of Study (iPOS) submitted before completing 50 percent of required credit hours. *Entrance requirements:* For master's, 2 years of full-time related work experience, bachelor's degree in related field from accredited university, resume, essay, 2 letters of recommendation, official transcripts; for doctorate, GMAT, MBA, 2 years of full-time related work experience (recommended), bachelor's degree in related field from accredited university, 3 letters of recommendation, resume, personal statement. Additional exam requirements/recommendations for international students: Required—TOEFL (minimum score 550 paper-based; 80 iBT), IELTS (minimum score 6.5). Electronic applications accepted. *Expenses:* Contact institution. *Faculty research:* Strategy and technology, technology investments and firm valuation, Internet e-commerce, IT enablement for emergency preparedness and response, information supply chain, collaborative computing and security/privacy issues for e-health, enterprise information systems and their application to management control systems.

Arkansas State University, Graduate School, College of Business, Department of Computer and Information Technology, State University, AR 72467. Offers business administration education (SCCT); business technology education (SCCT). *Program availability:* Part-time. *Entrance requirements:* Additional exam requirements/recommendations for international students: Required—TOEFL (minimum score 550 paper-based; 79 iBT), IELTS (minimum score 6), PTE (minimum score 56). Electronic applications accepted. *Expenses:* Contact institution.

Aspen University, Programs in Information Management, Denver, CO 80246-1930. Offers information management (MS); information systems (Certificate). *Program availability:* Part-time, evening/weekend, online learning. Electronic applications accepted.

Auburn University at Montgomery, College of Business, Department of Information Systems, Montgomery, AL 36124-4023. Offers information systems management (MS). *Faculty:* 4 full-time (1 woman). *Students:* 11 full-time (2 women), 10 part-time (6 women); includes 8 minority (6 Black or African American, non-Hispanic/Latino; 2 Asian, non-Hispanic/Latino), 5 international. Average age 32. 30 applicants, 70% accepted, 8 enrolled. In 2016, 9 master's awarded. *Degree requirements:* For master's, thesis optional. *Entrance requirements:* For master's, GMAT - College of Business. Additional exam requirements/recommendations for international students: Required—TOEFL (minimum score 500 paper-based; 61 iBT), IELTS (minimum score 5.5), PTE (minimum score 44). *Application deadline:* Applications are processed on a rolling basis. Application fee: $25 ($0 for international students). Electronic applications accepted. *Expenses:* Tuition, state resident: full-time $6462; part-time $359 per credit hour. Tuition, nonresident: full-time $14,526; part-time $807 per credit hour. *Required fees:* $554. *Financial support:* Application deadline: 3/1; applicants required to submit FAFSA. *Unit head:* Dr. David Ang, Head, 334-244-3455, Fax: 334-244-3792, E-mail: dang@aum.edu. *Application contact:* Dr. Joseph Newman, Associate Dean/Graduate Coordinator, 334-244-0905, Fax: 334-244-3792, E-mail: jnewman3@aum.edu.
Website: http://business.aum.edu/academic-programs/undergraduate-programs/information-systems

Avila University, School of Business, Kansas City, MO 64145-1698. Offers accounting (MBA); finance (MBA); health care administration (MBA); international business (MBA); management (MBA); management information systems (MBA); marketing (MBA). *Program availability:* Part-time, evening/weekend. *Faculty:* 8 full-time (4 women), 4 part-time/adjunct (2 women). *Students:* 58 full-time (22 women), 21 part-time (10 women); includes 20 minority (10 Black or African American, non-Hispanic/Latino; 2 Asian, non-Hispanic/Latino; 5 Hispanic/Latino; 3 Two or more races, non-Hispanic/Latino), 18 international. Average age 30. 75 applicants, 28% accepted, 14 enrolled. In 2016, 40 master's awarded. *Degree requirements:* For master's, comprehensive exam, capstone course. *Entrance requirements:* For master's, GMAT (minimum score 420), minimum GPA of 3.0, interview. Additional exam requirements/recommendations for international students: Required—TOEFL (minimum score 550 paper-based). *Application deadline:* For fall admission, 7/30 priority date for domestic and international students; for winter admission, 11/30 priority date for domestic and international students; for spring admission, 2/28 priority date for domestic and international students; for summer

admission, 6/1 priority date for domestic and international students. Applications are processed on a rolling basis. Application fee: $0. Electronic applications accepted. *Expenses:* $628 per credit hour. *Financial support:* In 2016–17, 11 students received support. Career-related internships or fieldwork and scholarships/grants available. Support available to part-time students. Financial award applicants required to submit FAFSA. *Faculty research:* Leadership characteristics, financial hedging, group dynamics. *Unit head:* Dr. Richard Woodall, Dean, 816-501-3720, Fax: 816-501-2463, E-mail: richard.woodall@avila.edu. *Application contact:* Brandon Black, MBA Admission Advisor, 816-501-3601, Fax: 816-501-2463, E-mail: brandon.black@avila.edu.
Website: https://www.avila.edu/mrk/mba

Baker College Center for Graduate Studies–Online, Graduate Programs, Flint, MI 48507. Offers accounting (MBA); business administration (DBA); finance (MBA); general business (MBA); health care management (MBA); human resources management (MBA); information management (MBA); leadership studies (MBA); management information systems (MSIS); marketing (MBA). *Program availability:* Part-time, evening/weekend, online learning. *Degree requirements:* For master's, portfolio. *Entrance requirements:* For master's, 3 years of work experience, minimum undergraduate GPA of 2.5, writing sample, 3 letters of recommendation; for doctorate, MBA or acceptable related master's degree from accredited association, 5 years work experience, minimum graduate GPA of 3.25, writing sample, 3 professional references. Additional exam requirements/recommendations for international students: Required—TOEFL (minimum score 550 paper-based). Electronic applications accepted.

Ball State University, Graduate School, College of Communication, Information, and Media, Center for Information and Communication Sciences, Muncie, IN 47306. Offers information and communication sciences (MS); information and communication technologies (Certificate). *Program availability:* Part-time, 100% online. *Entrance requirements:* For master's, minimum baccalaureate GPA of 2.75 or 3.0 in latter half of baccalaureate, statement of goals. Additional exam requirements/recommendations for international students: Required—TOEFL (minimum score 550 paper-based; 79 iBT), IELTS (minimum score 6.5). Electronic applications accepted.

Ball State University, Graduate School, Miller College of Business, Department of Information Systems and Operations Management, Muncie, IN 47306. Offers business education (MA); information systems security management (Certificate). *Accreditation:* NCATE (one or more programs are accredited). *Program availability:* Part-time, online only, 100% online. *Entrance requirements:* For master's, minimum baccalaureate GPA of 2.75 or 3.0 in latter half of baccalaureate. Additional exam requirements/recommendations for international students: Required—TOEFL (minimum score 550 paper-based; 79 iBT), IELTS (minimum score 6.5). Electronic applications accepted. *Expenses:* Contact institution.

Barry University, Andreas School of Business, Graduate Certificate Programs, Miami Shores, FL 33161-6695. Offers finance (Certificate); health services administration (Certificate); international business (Certificate); management (Certificate); management information systems (Certificate); marketing (Certificate).

Baruch College of the City University of New York, Zicklin School of Business, Department of Statistics and Computer Information Systems, Program in Information Systems, New York, NY 10010-5585. Offers MBA, MS, PhD. *Program availability:* Part-time, evening/weekend. Terminal master's awarded for partial completion of doctoral program. *Degree requirements:* For master's, thesis or alternative; for doctorate, comprehensive exam, thesis/dissertation. *Entrance requirements:* For master's, GMAT, 2 letters of recommendation, resume, 2 years of work experience; for doctorate, GMAT. Additional exam requirements/recommendations for international students: Required—TOEFL (minimum score 590 paper-based), TWE (minimum score 5).

Baylor University, Graduate School, Hankamer School of Business, Department of Information Systems, Waco, TX 76798. Offers information systems (MSIS, PhD); information systems management (MBA); MBA/MSIS. *Faculty:* 12 full-time (4 women). *Students:* 29 full-time (15 women), 2 part-time (1 woman); includes 6 minority (1 Black or African American, non-Hispanic/Latino; 2 Asian, non-Hispanic/Latino; 2 Hispanic/Latino; 1 Two or more races, non-Hispanic/Latino), 17 international. In 2016, 18 master's, 2 doctorates awarded. *Entrance requirements:* For master's, GMAT; for doctorate, GMAT, GRE. Additional exam requirements/recommendations for international students: Required—TOEFL. *Application deadline:* For fall admission, 8/1 for domestic students; for spring admission, 12/1 for domestic students. Applications are processed on a rolling basis. Application fee: $25. *Expenses: Tuition:* Full-time $28,494; part-time $1583 per credit hour. *Required fees:* $167 per credit hour. Tuition and fees vary according to course load and program. *Financial support:* Research assistantships, career-related internships or fieldwork, and Federal Work-Study available. *Faculty research:* Computer personnel, group systems, information technology standards and infrastructure, international information systems, technology and the learning environment. *Unit head:* Dr. Gary Carini, Associate Dean, 254-710-4091, Fax: 254-710-1091, E-mail: gary_carini@baylor.edu. *Application contact:* Laurie Wilson, Director, Graduate Business Programs, 254-710-4163, Fax: 254-710-1066, E-mail: laurie_wilson@baylor.edu.
Website: http://hsb.baylor.edu/isy/

Bay Path University, Program in Communications and Information Management, Longmeadow, MA 01106-2292. Offers MS. *Program availability:* Part-time, evening/weekend, 100% online. *Students:* 12 full-time (8 women), 23 part-time (21 women); includes 10 minority (4 Black or African American, non-Hispanic/Latino; 3 Hispanic/Latino; 1 Native Hawaiian or other Pacific Islander, non-Hispanic/Latino; 2 Two or more races, non-Hispanic/Latino), 4 international. Average age 37. 26 applicants, 92% accepted, 16 enrolled. In 2016, 27 master's awarded. *Degree requirements:* For master's, twelve core courses and four electives (each course is eight weeks long). *Application deadline:* Applications are processed on a rolling basis. Application fee: $45. Electronic applications accepted. Application fee is waived when completed online. *Expenses:* $21,465. *Financial support:* Unspecified assistantships available. Financial award applicants required to submit FAFSA. *Unit head:* Robin Saunders, Program Director, 413-565-1009. *Application contact:* Diane Ranaldi, Dean of Graduate Admissions, 413-565-1332, Fax: 413-565-1250, E-mail: dranaldi@baypath.edu.
Website: http://graduate.baypath.edu/Graduate-Programs/Programs-On-Campus/MS-Programs/Communications-And-Information-Management

Bay Path University, Program in Information Management, Longmeadow, MA 01106-2292. Offers MS. *Program availability:* Part-time, 100% online. *Students:* 1 (woman) full-time, all international. Average age 24. *Application deadline:* Applications are processed on a rolling basis. Application fee: $45. Electronic applications accepted. Application fee is waived when completed online. *Expenses:* $21,465. *Financial support:* Unspecified assistantships available. Financial award applicants required to submit FAFSA. *Unit head:* Robin Saunders, Director, 413-565-1009, E-mail: rsaunders@baypath.edu. *Application contact:* Diane Ranaldi, Dean of Graduate Admissions, 413-565-1332, Fax: 413-565-1250, E-mail: dranaldi@baypath.edu.
Website: http://www.baypath.edu/academics/graduate-programs/information-management-ms/

Bellevue University, Graduate School, College of Information Technology, Bellevue, NE 68005-3098. Offers computer information systems (MS); cybersecurity (MS); management of information systems (MS); project management (MPM).

Benedictine University, Graduate Programs, Program in Business Administration, Lisle, IL 60532. Offers accounting (MBA); entrepreneurship and managing innovation (MBA); financial management (MBA); health administration (MBA); human resource management (MBA); information systems security (MBA); international business (MBA); management consulting (MBA); management information systems (MBA); marketing management (MBA); operations management and logistics (MBA); organizational leadership (MBA). *Program availability:* Part-time, evening/weekend, online learning. *Faculty:* 4 full-time (2 women), 24 part-time/adjunct (3 women). *Students:* 90 full-time (51 women), 440 part-time (262 women); includes 147 minority (65 Black or African American, non-Hispanic/Latino; 1 American Indian or Alaska Native, non-Hispanic/Latino; 58 Asian, non-Hispanic/Latino; 20 Hispanic/Latino; 3 Native Hawaiian or other Pacific Islander, non-Hispanic/Latino), 2 international. Average age 34. 211 applicants, 89% accepted, 155 enrolled. In 2016, 350 master's awarded. *Entrance requirements:* For master's, GMAT. Additional exam requirements/recommendations for international students: Required—TOEFL (minimum score 550 paper-based). *Application deadline:* For fall admission, 9/1 for domestic students; for winter admission, 12/1 for domestic students; for spring admission, 2/15 for domestic students. Applications are processed on a rolling basis. Application fee: $40. Electronic applications accepted. *Expenses: Tuition:* Full-time $15,600; part-time $650 per hour. *Required fees:* $300. One-time fee: $125 part-time. Tuition and fees vary according to class time, course load, campus/location and program. *Financial support:* Career-related internships or fieldwork and health care benefits available. Support available to part-time students. *Faculty research:* Strategic leadership in professional organizations, sociology of professions, organizational change, social identity theory, applications to change management. *Unit head:* Dr. Sharon Borowicz, Director, 630-829-6219, E-mail: sborowicz@ben.edu. *Application contact:* Kari Gibbons, Director, Admissions, 630-829-6200, Fax: 630-829-6584, E-mail: kgibbons@ben.edu.

Benedictine University, Graduate Programs, Program in Management Information Systems, Lisle, IL 60532. Offers MS, MBA/MS, MPH/MS. *Program availability:* Part-time. *Faculty:* 2 full-time (1 woman), 6 part-time/adjunct (1 woman). *Students:* 180 part-time (77 women); includes 2 minority (both Asian, non-Hispanic/Latino), 2 international. Average age 36. 102 applicants, 94% accepted, 84 enrolled. In 2016, 112 master's awarded. *Entrance requirements:* For master's, GMAT. Additional exam requirements/recommendations for international students: Required—TOEFL (minimum score 550 paper-based). *Application deadline:* For fall admission, 9/1 for domestic students; for winter admission, 12/1 for domestic students; for spring admission, 2/15 for domestic students. Applications are processed on a rolling basis. Application fee: $40. Electronic applications accepted. *Expenses: Tuition:* Full-time $15,600; part-time $650 per hour. *Required fees:* $300. One-time fee: $125 part-time. Tuition and fees vary according to class time, course load, campus/location and program. *Financial support:* Career-related internships or fieldwork and health care benefits available. Support available to part-time students. *Faculty research:* Technology management, knowledge management, electronic commerce, information security. *Unit head:* Dr. Barbara Ozog, Director, 630-829-6218, E-mail: bozog@ben.edu. *Application contact:* Kari Gibbons, Associate Vice President, Enrollment Center, 630-829-6200, Fax: 630-829-6584, E-mail: kgibbons@ben.edu.

Boston University, Metropolitan College, Department of Computer Science, Boston, MA 02215. Offers computer information systems (MS), including computer networks, data analytics, database management and business intelligence, health informatics, IT project management, security, Web application development; computer networks (Certificate); computer science (MS); data analytics (Certificate); digital forensics (Certificate); health informatics (Certificate); information technology project management (Certificate); software development (MS); software engineering in health care systems (Certificate); telecommunications (MS), including security. *Program availability:* Part-time, evening/weekend, online learning. *Faculty:* 13 full-time (3 women), 43 part-time/adjunct (3 women). *Students:* 108 full-time (36 women), 1,294 part-time (364 women); includes 428 minority (115 Black or African American, non-Hispanic/Latino; 2 American Indian or Alaska Native, non-Hispanic/Latino; 187 Asian, non-Hispanic/Latino; 98 Hispanic/Latino; 2 Native Hawaiian or other Pacific Islander, non-Hispanic/Latino; 24 Two or more races, non-Hispanic/Latino), 314 international. Average age 33. 463 applicants, 79% accepted, 248 enrolled. In 2016, 311 master's awarded. *Degree requirements:* For master's, thesis optional. *Entrance requirements:* For master's and Certificate, official transcripts from regionally-accredited bachelor's degree program, 3 letters of recommendation, professional resume, personal statement. Additional exam requirements/recommendations for international students: Required—TOEFL (minimum score 84 iBT), IELTS. *Application deadline:* For fall admission, 6/1 priority date for international students; for spring admission, 10/1 priority date for international students. Applications are processed on a rolling basis. Application fee: $85. Electronic applications accepted. *Expenses:* Contact institution. *Financial support:* In 2016–17, 11 research assistantships (averaging $8,400 per year) were awarded; unspecified assistantships also available. Support available to part-time students. Financial award applicants required to submit FAFSA. *Faculty research:* Medical informatics, Web technologies, telecom and networks, security and forensics, software engineering, programming languages, multimedia and artificial intelligence (AI), information systems and IT project management. *Unit head:* Dr. Anatoly Temkin, Chair, 617-353-2566, Fax: 617-353-2367, E-mail: csinfo@bu.edu. *Application contact:* Lesley Moreau, Academic Program Coordinator, 617-353-2566, Fax: 617-353-2367, E-mail: metcs@bu.edu.
Website: http://www.bu.edu/csmet/

Bowie State University, Graduate Programs, Program in Management Information Systems, Bowie, MD 20715-9465. Offers information systems analyst (Certificate); management information systems (MS). *Program availability:* Part-time, evening/weekend. *Degree requirements:* For master's, comprehensive exam, thesis optional, research paper. *Entrance requirements:* For master's, minimum GPA of 2.5. Electronic applications accepted.

Brandeis University, Rabb School of Continuing Studies, Division of Graduate Professional Studies, Master of Science in Technology Management Program, Waltham, MA 02454-9110. Offers MS. *Program availability:* Part-time-only. *Faculty:* 45 part-time/adjunct (16 women). *Students:* 32 part-time (8 women); includes 6 minority (3 Black or African American, non-Hispanic/Latino; 2 Asian, non-Hispanic/Latino; 1 Two or more races, non-Hispanic/Latino). Average age 37. 5 applicants, 100% accepted, 4 enrolled. In 2016, 13 master's awarded. *Entrance requirements:* For master's, four-year bachelor's degree from regionally-accredited U.S. institution or equivalent; official transcript(s) from every college or university attended; resume or curriculum vitae; statement of goals; letter of recommendation. Additional exam requirements/recommendations for international students: Required—TWE (minimum score 4.5), TOEFL (minimum scores: 600 paper-based, 100 iBT), IELTS (7), or PTE (68). *Application deadline:* For fall admission, 6/21 priority date for domestic and international students; for winter admission, 9/13 priority date for domestic and international students; for spring admission, 12/20 priority date for domestic and international students; for summer admission, 3/14 priority date for domestic and international students.

Applications are processed on a rolling basis. Application fee: $50. Electronic applications accepted. *Expenses:* $3,400 per course, $100 graduation fee. *Financial support:* Applicants required to submit FAFSA. *Unit head:* Dr. James La Creta, Chair, 781-736-8787, E-mail: jlacreta@brandeis.edu. *Application contact:* Frances Stearns, Director of Admissions and Recruitment, 781-736-8785, E-mail: fstearns@brandeis.edu.
Website: http://www.brandeis.edu/gps

Broadview University–West Jordan, Graduate Programs, West Jordan, UT 84088. Offers business administration (MBA); health care management (MSM); information technology (MSM); managerial leadership (MSM).

California Intercontinental University, School of Information Technology, Irvine, CA 92614. Offers information systems and enterprise resource management (DBA); information systems and knowledge management (MBA); project and quality management (MBA).

California Lutheran University, Graduate Studies, School of Management, Thousand Oaks, CA 91360-2787. Offers business (IMBA); computer science (MS); econometrics (MBA); economics (MS); entrepreneurship (MBA, Certificate); finance (MBA, Certificate); financial planning (MBA, Certificate); information systems and technology (MS); information technology management (MBA, Certificate); international business (MBA, Certificate); management and organization behavior (MBA); management and organizational behavior (Certificate); marketing (MBA, Certificate); microeconomics (MBA); nonprofit and social enterprise (MBA); public policy and administration (MPPA). *Program availability:* Part-time, evening/weekend, 100% online, blended/hybrid learning. *Faculty:* 25 full-time (10 women), 36 part-time/adjunct (12 women). *Students:* 427 full-time (172 women), 189 part-time (87 women); includes 120 minority (14 Black or African American, non-Hispanic/Latino; 2 American Indian or Alaska Native, non-Hispanic/Latino; 19 Asian, non-Hispanic/Latino; 37 Hispanic/Latino; 48 Two or more races, non-Hispanic/Latino), 338 international. Average age 30. 591 applicants, 64% accepted, 131 enrolled. In 2016, 305 master's awarded. *Entrance requirements:* For master's, GMAT, interview, minimum GPA of 3.0. *Application deadline:* Applications are processed on a rolling basis. Application fee: $50. Electronic applications accepted. *Expenses:* Contact institution. *Unit head:* Dr. Gerhard Apfelthaler, Dean, 805-493-3360. *Application contact:* 805-493-3325, Fax: 805-493-3861, E-mail: clugrad@callutheran.edu.
Website: http://www.callutheran.edu/management/

California State Polytechnic University, Pomona, Master of Science in Business Administration Program, Pomona, CA 91768-2557. Offers information systems auditing (MS). *Accreditation:* AACSB. *Program availability:* Part-time, evening/weekend. *Students:* 6 part-time (1 woman); includes 4 minority (3 Asian, non-Hispanic/Latino; 1 Hispanic/Latino), 1 international. Average age 34. 2 applicants, 100% accepted, 2 enrolled. In 2016, 4 master's awarded. *Entrance requirements:* Additional exam requirements/recommendations for international students: Required—TOEFL. *Application deadline:* Applications are processed on a rolling basis. Application fee: $55. Electronic applications accepted. *Expenses:* Contact institution. *Financial support:* Application deadline: 3/2; applicants required to submit FAFSA. *Unit head:* Dr. Erik Rolland, Dean, 909-869-2400, Fax: 909-869-6799, E-mail: erolland@cpp.edu. *Application contact:* Andrew M. Wright, Director of Admissions, 909-869-3130, Fax: 909-869-4529, E-mail: awright@cpp.edu.
Website: http://www.cpp.edu/~cba/graduate-business-programs/programs/index.shtml

California State University, East Bay, Office of Graduate Studies, College of Business and Economics, MBA Program, Option in Information Technology Management, Hayward, CA 94542-3000. Offers computer information systems (MBA). *Program availability:* Part-time, evening/weekend. *Students:* 1 full-time (0 women), 2 part-time (1 woman), all international. Average age 28. 2 applicants, 100% accepted, 1 enrolled. *Degree requirements:* For master's, comprehensive exam or thesis. *Entrance requirements:* For master's, GMAT, minimum GPA of 2.75. Additional exam requirements/recommendations for international students: Required—TOEFL (minimum score 550 paper-based). *Application deadline:* For fall admission, 6/30 for domestic and international students. Application fee: $55. Electronic applications accepted. *Financial support:* Career-related internships or fieldwork, Federal Work-Study, and institutionally sponsored loans available. Support available to part-time students. Financial award application deadline: 3/2; financial award applicants required to submit FAFSA. *Unit head:* Dr. Hongwei Du, Program Advisor, 510-885-3290, E-mail: hongwei.du@csueastbay.edu. *Application contact:* Dr. Donna Wiley, Interim Associate Vice President for Academic Programs and Graduate Studies, 510-885-3716, Fax: 510-885-4777, E-mail: donna.wiley@csueastbay.edu.
Website: http://www20.csueastbay.edu/cbe/mba-options/Information-Technology-Management-Option.html

California State University, Fullerton, Graduate Studies, College of Business and Economics, Department of Information Systems and Decision Sciences, Fullerton, CA 92834-9480. Offers decision science (MBA); information systems (MBA, MS); information systems and decision sciences (MS); information systems and e-commerce (MS); information technology (MS). *Program availability:* Part-time. *Degree requirements:* For master's, project or thesis. *Entrance requirements:* For master's, GMAT, minimum AACSB index of 950. Application fee: $55. *Expenses:* Tuition, state resident: full-time $3369; part-time $1953 per unit. Tuition, nonresident: full-time $3915; part-time $2499 per unit. Tuition and fees vary according to course load, degree level and program. *Financial support:* Career-related internships or fieldwork, Federal Work-Study, institutionally sponsored loans, and scholarships/grants available. Support available to part-time students. Financial award application deadline: 3/1; financial award applicants required to submit FAFSA. *Unit head:* Dr. Bhushan Kapoor, Chair, 657-278-2221. *Application contact:* Admissions/Applications, 657-278-2371.
Website: http://business.fullerton.edu/isds/

California State University, Los Angeles, Graduate Studies, College of Business and Economics, Department of Information Systems, Los Angeles, CA 90032-8530. Offers management (MS). *Program availability:* Part-time, evening/weekend. *Degree requirements:* For master's, comprehensive exam (MBA), thesis (MS). *Entrance requirements:* For master's, GMAT, minimum GPA of 2.5 during previous 2 years of course work. Additional exam requirements/recommendations for international students: Required—TOEFL (minimum score 550 paper-based). Electronic applications accepted.

California State University, Monterey Bay, College of Science, School of Computing and Design, Seaside, CA 93955-8001. Offers MS, MSMIT. MSMIT offered in conjunction with College of Business. *Degree requirements:* For master's, capstone or thesis. *Entrance requirements:* For master's, GRE, 2 letters of recommendation, minimum GPA of 3.0, technology screening assessment. Additional exam requirements/recommendations for international students: Required—TOEFL (minimum score 550 paper-based; 71 iBT). Electronic applications accepted. *Faculty research:* Electronic commerce, e-learning, knowledge management, international business, business and public policy.

California State University, San Bernardino, Graduate Studies, College of Business and Public Administration, Program in Business Administration, San Bernardino, CA 92407. Offers accounting (MBA); entrepreneurship (MBA); finance (MBA); global business (MBA); information management (MBA); information security (MBA); management (MBA); supply chain management (MBA). *Accreditation:* AACSB. *Program availability:* Part-time, evening/weekend, online learning. *Faculty:* 7 full-time (4 women), 3 part-time/adjunct (2 women). *Students:* 37 full-time (11 women), 141 part-time (51 women); includes 85 minority (16 Black or African American, non-Hispanic/Latino; 1 American Indian or Alaska Native, non-Hispanic/Latino; 20 Asian, non-Hispanic/Latino; 45 Hispanic/Latino; 3 Two or more races, non-Hispanic/Latino), 46 international. 260 applicants, 37% accepted, 34 enrolled. In 2016, 180 master's awarded. *Degree requirements:* For master's, comprehensive exam, thesis. *Entrance requirements:* Additional exam requirements/recommendations for international students: Required—TOEFL. *Application deadline:* For fall admission, 7/16 for domestic students, 7/20 for international students; for winter admission, 10/23 for domestic students, 10/20 for international students; for spring admission, 1/22 for domestic students, 1/20 for international students. Application fee: $55. *Expenses:* Contact institution. *Financial support:* Application deadline: 3/1. *Unit head:* Dr. Lawrence C. Rose, Dean, 909-537-3703, Fax: 909-537-7026, E-mail: lrose@csusb.edu. *Application contact:* Dr. Vipin Gupta, Associate Dean/MBA Director, 909-537-7380, Fax: 909-537-7026, E-mail: vgupta@csusb.edu.
Website: http://mba.csusb.edu/

California University of Management and Sciences, Graduate Programs, Anaheim, CA 92801. Offers business administration (MBA, DBA); computer information systems (MS); economics (MS); international business (MS); sports management (MS).

Capella University, School of Business and Technology, Doctoral Programs in Technology, Minneapolis, MN 55402. Offers general information technology (PhD); global operations and supply chain management (DBA); information assurance and security (PhD); information technology education (PhD); information technology management (DBA, PhD).

Capella University, School of Business and Technology, Master's Programs in Technology, Minneapolis, MN 55402. Offers enterprise software architecture (MS); general information systems and technology management (MS); global operations and supply chain management (MBA); information assurance and security (MS); information technology management (MBA); network management (MS).

Capitol Technology University, Graduate Programs, Laurel, MD 20708-9759. Offers business administration (MBA); computer science (MS); electrical engineering (MS); information and telecommunications systems management (MS); information architecture (MS); network security (MS). *Program availability:* Part-time, evening/weekend, online learning. *Entrance requirements:* For master's, minimum GPA of 3.0. Electronic applications accepted.

Carnegie Mellon University, Heinz College Australia, Master of Science in Information Technology Program (Adelaide, South Australia), Adelaide SA 5000, Australia. Offers MSIT. *Entrance requirements:* For master's, GRE or GMAT, college-level course in advanced algebra/pre-calculus; college-level courses in economics and statistics (recommended). Additional exam requirements/recommendations for international students: Required—TOEFL or IELTS.

Carnegie Mellon University, Heinz College, School of Information Systems and Management, Master of Information Systems Management Program, Pittsburgh, PA 15213-3891. Offers MISM. *Entrance requirements:* For master's, GRE or GMAT, college-level course in advanced algebra/pre-calculus; college-level courses in economics and statistics (recommended). Additional exam requirements/recommendations for international students: Required—TOEFL or IELTS.

Carnegie Mellon University, Heinz College, School of Information Systems and Management, Master of Science in Information Security Policy and Management Program, Pittsburgh, PA 15213-3891. Offers MSISPM. *Entrance requirements:* For master's, GRE or GMAT, college-level course in advanced algebra/pre-calculus; college-level courses in economics and statistics (recommended). Additional exam requirements/recommendations for international students: Required—TOEFL or IELTS.

Carnegie Mellon University, Heinz College, School of Information Systems and Management, Program in Information Technology, Pittsburgh, PA 15213-3891. Offers MSIT.

Carnegie Mellon University, Tepper School of Business, Program in Business Technologies, Pittsburgh, PA 15213-3891. Offers PhD. *Degree requirements:* For doctorate, thesis/dissertation. *Entrance requirements:* For doctorate, GRE General Test.

The Catholic University of America, School of Engineering, Program in Engineering Management, Washington, DC 20064. Offers engineering management (MSE, Certificate), including engineering management and organization (MSE), project and systems engineering management (MSE), technology management (MSE); program management (Certificate); systems engineering and management of information technology (Certificate). *Program availability:* Part-time. *Faculty:* 3 part-time/adjunct (0 women). *Students:* 14 full-time (2 women), 11 part-time (3 women); includes 2 minority (both Two or more races, non-Hispanic/Latino), 20 international. Average age 30. 35 applicants, 54% accepted, 11 enrolled. In 2016, 26 master's awarded. *Degree requirements:* For master's, minimum GPA of 3.0. *Entrance requirements:* For master's and Certificate, statement of purpose, official copies of academic transcripts, two letters of recommendation. Additional exam requirements/recommendations for international students: Required—TOEFL (minimum score 550 paper-based; 80 iBT). *Application deadline:* For fall admission, 7/15 priority date for domestic students, 7/1 for international students; for spring admission, 11/15 priority date for domestic students, 11/1 for international students. Applications are processed on a rolling basis. Application fee: $55. Electronic applications accepted. *Expenses:* $43,380 per year; $1,170 per credit; $200 per semester part-time fees. *Financial support:* Fellowships, research assistantships, teaching assistantships, Federal Work-Study, scholarships/grants, tuition waivers (full and partial), and unspecified assistantships available. Financial award application deadline: 2/1; financial award applicants required to submit FAFSA. *Faculty research:* Engineering management and organization, project and systems engineering management, technology management. *Unit head:* Melvin G. Williams, Jr., Director, 202-319-5191, Fax: 202-319-6860, E-mail: williamsme@cua.edu. *Application contact:* Director of Graduate Admissions, 202-319-5057, Fax: 202-319-6533, E-mail: cua-admissions@cua.edu.
Website: http://engrmgmt.cua.edu/

Central European University, CEU Business School, Budapest, Hungary. Offers business administration (PhD); business analytics (M Sc); executive business administration (EMBA); finance (M Sc); general management (MBA); information technology management (M Sc); international executive (MBA). *Program availability:* Part-time. *Faculty:* 16 full-time (4 women), 15 part-time/adjunct (5 women). *Students:* 73 full-time (29 women), 108 part-time (28 women). Average age 33. 218 applicants, 57% accepted, 69 enrolled. In 2016, 108 master's awarded. *Degree requirements:* For master's, one foreign language; for doctorate, thesis/dissertation or alternative. *Entrance requirements:* For master's, GMAT. Additional exam requirements/recommendations for international students: Required—TOEFL (minimum score 570 paper-based); Recommended—IELTS (minimum score 6.5). *Application deadline:* For fall admission, 2/4 for domestic and international students. Application fee: $30. Electronic applications accepted. *Expenses:* Contact institution. *Financial support:* Scholarships/grants, health care benefits, and tuition waivers (full and partial) available. *Faculty research:* Social

and ethical business, marketing, international business, international trade and investment, management development in Central and East Europe, non-market strategies of emerging-market multinationals, macro and micro analysis of the business environment, international competitive analysis, the transition process from emerging economies to established market economies and its social impact, the regulation of natural monopolies. *Unit head:* Dr. Mel Horwitch, Dean/Managing Director, 36 1 887-5050, E-mail: mhorwitch@ceubusiness.com. *Application contact:* Agnes Schram, Admissions Coordinator, 361-887-5111, E-mail: schrama@business.ceu.edu.
Website: http://business.ceu.hu/

Central Michigan University, Central Michigan University Global Campus, Program in Administration, Mount Pleasant, MI 48859. Offers acquisitions administration (MSA, Certificate); engineering management administration (MSA, Certificate); general administration (MSA, Certificate); health services administration (MSA, Certificate); human resources administration (MSA, Certificate); information resource management (MSA); information resource management administration (Certificate); international administration (MSA, Certificate); leadership (MSA, Certificate); philanthropy and fundraising administration (MSA, Certificate); public administration (MSA, Certificate); recreation and park administration (MSA); research administration (MSA, Certificate). *Program availability:* Part-time, evening/weekend, online learning. *Faculty:* 21 full-time (5 women), 168 part-time/adjunct (43 women). *Students:* 3,059 (1,741 women); includes 1,392 minority (1,003 Black or African American, non-Hispanic/Latino; 27 American Indian or Alaska Native, non-Hispanic/Latino; 93 Asian, non-Hispanic/Latino; 49 Hispanic/Latino; 10 Native Hawaiian or other Pacific Islander, non-Hispanic/Latino; 210 Two or more races, non-Hispanic/Latino). Average age 38. In 2016, 289 master's awarded. *Entrance requirements:* For master's, minimum GPA of 2.7 in major. *Application deadline:* Applications are processed on a rolling basis. Application fee: $50. Electronic applications accepted. *Financial support:* Scholarships/grants available. Support available to part-time students. Financial award applicants required to submit FAFSA. *Unit head:* Dr. Patricia Chase, Director, 989-774-6525, E-mail: chase1pb@cmich.edu. *Application contact:* 877-268-4636, E-mail: cmuglobal@cmich.edu.

Central Michigan University, College of Graduate Studies, College of Business Administration, Department of Business Information Systems, Mount Pleasant, MI 48859. Offers business computing (Graduate Certificate); information systems (MS), including accounting information systems, business informatics, enterprise systems using SAP software, information systems. *Program availability:* Part-time, evening/weekend. *Degree requirements:* For master's, thesis or alternative. Electronic applications accepted. *Faculty research:* Enterprise software, electronic commerce, decision support systems, ethical issues in information systems, information technology management and teaching issues.

Central Michigan University, College of Graduate Studies, College of Business Administration, MBA Program, Mount Pleasant, MI 48859. Offers accounting (MBA); business economics (MBA); consulting (MBA); finance (MBA); general business (MBA); human resource management (MBA); information systems (MBA); international business (MBA); logistics management (MBA); marketing (MBA); value-driven organization (MBA). *Program availability:* Part-time, evening/weekend, online learning. Electronic applications accepted. *Faculty research:* Accounting, consulting, international business, marketing, information systems.

Central Michigan University, College of Graduate Studies, Interdisciplinary Administration Programs, Mount Pleasant, MI 48859. Offers acquisitions administration (MSA, Graduate Certificate); general administration (MSA, Graduate Certificate); health services administration (MSA, Graduate Certificate); human resource administration (Graduate Certificate); human resources administration (MSA); information resource management (MSA, Graduate Certificate); international administration (MSA, Graduate Certificate); leadership (MSA, Graduate Certificate); public administration (MSA, Graduate Certificate); research administration (Graduate Certificate); sport administration (MSA). *Accreditation:* AACSB. *Program availability:* Part-time, evening/weekend, online learning. *Degree requirements:* For master's, thesis or alternative. *Entrance requirements:* For master's, bachelor's degree with minimum GPA of 2.7. Electronic applications accepted. *Faculty research:* Interdisciplinary studies in acquisitions administration, health services administration, sport administration, recreation and park administration, and international administration.

Central Penn College, Graduate Programs, Summerdale, PA 17093-0309. Offers information systems management (MPS); organizational development (MPS). Programs offered in Harrisburg, PA. *Program availability:* Evening/weekend.

Charleston Southern University, School of Business, Charleston, SC 29423-8087. Offers accounting (MBA); finance (MBA); general management (MBA); human resource management (MS); leadership (MBA); management information systems (MBA); organizational leadership (MA). *Program availability:* Part-time, evening/weekend. *Degree requirements:* For master's, thesis optional. *Entrance requirements:* For master's, GMAT. Additional exam requirements/recommendations for international students: Required—TOEFL (minimum score 550 paper-based; 79 iBT). *Application deadline:* Applications are processed on a rolling basis. Application fee: $40. *Expenses: Tuition:* Full-time $6000. Tuition and fees vary according to program. *Financial support:* Research assistantships with full tuition reimbursements available. Financial award application deadline: 4/15; financial award applicants required to submit FAFSA. *Unit head:* Dr. David Palmer, Interim Dean, 843-863-7025, Fax: 843-863-7922, E-mail: dpalmer@csuniv.edu. *Application contact:* Dr. Darin L. Gerdes, Director of the MBA Program, 843-863-7814, Fax: 843-863-7922, E-mail: dgerdes@csuniv.edu.
Website: http://www.csuniv.edu/business/

City College of the City University of New York, Graduate School, Grove School of Engineering, Department of Computer Science, New York, NY 10031-9198. Offers computer science (MS, PhD); information systems (MIS). PhD program offered jointly with Graduate School and University Center of the City University of New York. *Degree requirements:* For master's, thesis optional; for doctorate, one foreign language, comprehensive exam, thesis/dissertation. *Entrance requirements:* For master's and doctorate, GRE General Test. Additional exam requirements/recommendations for international students: Required—TOEFL (minimum score 500 paper-based; 61 iBT). Tuition and fees vary according to course load, degree level and program. *Faculty research:* Complexities of algebraic research, human issues in computer science, scientific computing, super compilers, parallel algorithms.

City University of Seattle, Graduate Division, School of Management, Seattle, WA 98121. Offers accounting (Certificate); change leadership (MBA, Certificate); computer systems (MS); finance (Certificate); financial management (MBA); general management (MBA); general management-Europe (MBA); global marketing (MBA); human resources management (Certificate); individualized study (MBA); information security (MS); information systems (MBA); leadership (MA); marketing (MBA, Certificate); project management (MBA, MS, Certificate); sustainable business (Certificate); technology management (MBA, Certificate). *Program availability:* Part-time, evening/weekend, online learning. *Degree requirements:* For master's, comprehensive exam (for some programs), thesis (for some programs). *Entrance requirements:* For master's, baccalaureate degree or equivalent from an accredited or otherwise recognized institution. Additional exam requirements/recommendations for international students: Required—TOEFL (minimum score 567 paper-based; 87 iBT); Recommended—IELTS. Electronic applications accepted.

Claremont Graduate University, Graduate Programs, Center for Information Systems and Technology, Claremont, CA 91711-6160. Offers cybersecurity and networking (MS); data science and analytics (MS); electronic commerce (PhD); geographic information systems (MS); health informatics (MS); information systems (Certificate); IT strategy and innovation (MS); knowledge management (PhD); systems development (PhD); telecommunications and networking (PhD); MBA/MS. *Program availability:* Part-time. *Faculty:* 8 full-time (1 woman), 1 part-time/adjunct (0 women). *Students:* 60 full-time (18 women), 81 part-time (27 women); includes 34 minority (7 Black or African American, non-Hispanic/Latino; 18 Asian, non-Hispanic/Latino; 7 Hispanic/Latino; 1 Native Hawaiian or other Pacific Islander, non-Hispanic/Latino; 1 Two or more races, non-Hispanic/Latino), 80 international. Average age 35. In 2016, 21 master's, 10 doctorates awarded. *Degree requirements:* For doctorate, comprehensive exam, thesis/dissertation, portfolio. *Entrance requirements:* For master's and doctorate, GMAT, GRE General Test. Additional exam requirements/recommendations for international students: Required—TOEFL (minimum score 75 iBT). *Application deadline:* For fall admission, 2/1 priority date for domestic and international students. Applications are processed on a rolling basis. Application fee: $80. Electronic applications accepted. *Expenses: Tuition:* Full-time $44,328; part-time $1847 per unit. *Required fees:* $600; $300 per semester. Tuition and fees vary according to course load and program. *Financial support:* Fellowships, research assistantships, teaching assistantships, Federal Work-Study, institutionally sponsored loans, and scholarships/grants available. Support available to part-time students. Financial award application deadline: 2/15; financial award applicants required to submit FAFSA. *Faculty research:* Man-machine interaction, organizational aspects of computing, implementation of information systems, information systems practice. *Unit head:* Lorne Olfman, Acting Director, 909-607-3035, E-mail: lorne.olfman@cgu.edu. *Application contact:* Jake Campbell, Senior Assistant Director of Admissions, 909-607-3024, E-mail: jake.campbell@cgu.edu.
Website: https://www.cgu.edu/school/center-for-information-systems-and-technology/

Clark University, Graduate School, Graduate School of Management, Business Administration Program, Worcester, MA 01610-1477. Offers accounting (MBA); finance (MBA); information management and business analytics (MBA); management (MBA); marketing (MBA); social change (MBA); sustainability (MBA). *Accreditation:* AACSB. *Program availability:* Part-time, evening/weekend. *Students:* 91 full-time (48 women), 101 part-time (45 women); includes 22 minority (8 Black or African American, non-Hispanic/Latino; 4 Asian, non-Hispanic/Latino; 9 Hispanic/Latino; 1 Native Hawaiian or other Pacific Islander, non-Hispanic/Latino), 45 international. Average age 31. 225 applicants, 58% accepted, 78 enrolled. In 2016, 113 master's awarded. *Degree requirements:* For master's, thesis optional. *Application deadline:* For fall admission, 6/1 priority date for domestic students; for spring admission, 12/1 priority date for domestic students. Applications are processed on a rolling basis. Application fee: $75. Electronic applications accepted. *Expenses: Tuition:* Full-time $44,050. *Required fees:* $80. Tuition and fees vary according to course load and program. *Financial support:* In 2016–17, research assistantships with partial tuition reimbursements (averaging $4,800 per year), teaching assistantships with partial tuition reimbursements (averaging $4,800 per year) were awarded; fellowships, career-related internships or fieldwork, Federal Work-Study, institutionally sponsored loans, and tuition waivers (partial) also available. Support available to part-time students. Financial award application deadline: 5/31. *Faculty research:* Marketing, accounting, human resource management, management information systems, business finance. *Unit head:* Dr. Catherine Usoff, Dean, 508-793-7543, Fax: 508-793-8822. *Application contact:* Ethan Bernstein, Director of Graduate Admissions, 508-793-7543, E-mail: graduateadmissions@clarku.edu.
Website: http://www.clarku.edu/programs/masters-business-administration

Clemson University, Graduate School, College of Business, Department of Management, Clemson, SC 29634. Offers business administration (PhD), including management information systems, supply chain and operations management; management (MS). *Accreditation:* AACSB. *Faculty:* 17 full-time (3 women). *Students:* 17 full-time (5 women), 2 part-time (1 woman), 13 international. Average age 33. 30 applicants, 7% accepted, 2 enrolled. In 2016, 2 master's, 1 doctorate awarded. Terminal master's awarded for partial completion of doctoral program. *Degree requirements:* For master's, comprehensive exam, thesis optional; for doctorate, comprehensive exam, thesis/dissertation. *Entrance requirements:* For master's and doctorate, GMAT or GRE General Test, unofficial transcripts, two letters of reference, curriculum vitae. Additional exam requirements/recommendations for international students: Required—TOEFL (minimum score 94 iBT), IELTS (minimum score 7), PTE (minimum score 64). *Application deadline:* For fall admission, 1/15 priority date for domestic and international students. Application fee: $80 ($90 for international students). Electronic applications accepted. *Expenses:* $5,617 per semester full-time resident, $11,194 per semester full-time non-resident, $697 per credit hour part-time resident, $1,392 per credit hour part-time non-resident. *Financial support:* In 2016–17, 52 students received support, including 11 fellowships with partial tuition reimbursements available (averaging $3,826 per year), 3 research assistantships with partial tuition reimbursements available (averaging $22,667 per year), 32 teaching assistantships with partial tuition reimbursements available (averaging $25,000 per year); unspecified assistantships also available. Financial award application deadline: 1/15. *Faculty research:* Effective use of information technology in business, manufacturing and service operations strategy, lean operations and quality management, healthcare operations, behavioral market design. *Total annual research expenditures:* $89,179. *Unit head:* Dr. V. Sridharan, Department Chair, 864-656-2624, E-mail: suhas@clemson.edu. *Application contact:* Dr. Janis Miller, Graduate Program Coordinator, 864-656-3757, E-mail: janism@clemson.edu.
Website: https://www.clemson.edu/business/departments/management/

Cleveland State University, College of Graduate Studies, Monte Ahuja College of Business, Doctor of Business Administration Program, Cleveland, OH 44115. Offers information systems (DBA); marketing (DBA). *Accreditation:* AACSB. *Program availability:* Part-time, evening/weekend. *Faculty:* 50 full-time (11 women). *Students:* 8 full-time (5 women), 13 part-time (3 women); includes 4 minority (3 Black or African American, non-Hispanic/Latino; 1 Asian, non-Hispanic/Latino), 3 international. Average age 40. In 2016, 2 doctorates awarded. *Degree requirements:* For doctorate, comprehensive exam, thesis/dissertation, oral dissertation defense. *Entrance requirements:* For doctorate, GMAT, MBA or equivalent. Additional exam requirements/recommendations for international students: Required—TOEFL (minimum score 550 paper-based; 78 iBT). *Application deadline:* For fall admission, 2/1 for domestic and international students. Application fee: $40. Electronic applications accepted. *Expenses:* Tuition, state resident: full-time $9565. Tuition, nonresident: full-time $17,980. Tuition and fees vary according to program. *Financial support:* In 2016–17, 5 research assistantships with full tuition reimbursements (averaging $12,700 per year), 4 teaching assistantships with full tuition reimbursements (averaging $12,700 per year) were awarded; tuition waivers (full) and unspecified assistantships also available. *Faculty research:* Supply chain management, international business, strategic management, risk analysis, consumer behavior. *Unit head:* Dr. Raj Shekhar G. Javalgi, Director, 216-687-3786, Fax: 216-687-9354, E-mail: r.javalgi@csuohio.edu. *Application contact:* Melinda J. Arnold, Administrative Secretary, 216-687-6952, Fax: 216-687-9257, E-mail:

m.arnold@csuohio.edu.
Website: http://www.csuohio.edu/business/academics/mbajuris-doctor

Coastal Carolina University, College of Science, Conway, SC 29528-6054. Offers applied computing and information systems (Certificate); coastal marine and wetland studies (MS); information systems technology (MS); marine science (PhD); sports management (MS). *Program availability:* Part-time, evening/weekend. *Faculty:* 23 full-time (5 women), 1 part-time/adjunct (0 women). *Students:* 41 full-time (14 women), 29 part-time (15 women); includes 7 minority (4 Black or African American, non-Hispanic/Latino; 1 American Indian or Alaska Native, non-Hispanic/Latino; 1 Hispanic/Latino; 1 Two or more races, non-Hispanic/Latino), 6 international. Average age 27. 72 applicants, 57% accepted, 35 enrolled. In 2016, 13 master's awarded. *Degree requirements:* For master's, thesis or internship; for doctorate, comprehensive exam, thesis/dissertation. *Entrance requirements:* For master's, GRE, 3 letters of recommendation, resume, official transcripts, written statement of educational and career goals, baccalaureate degree; for doctorate, GRE, official transcripts; baccalaureate or master's degree; minimum GPA of 3.0 for all collegiate coursework; successful completion of at least two semesters of college-level calculus, physics, and chemistry; 3 letters of recommendation; written statement of educational and career goals; resume; for Certificate, 2 letters of reference, official transcripts, minimum GPA of 3.0 in all computing and information systems courses, documentation of graduation from accredited four-year college or university. Additional exam requirements/recommendations for international students: Required—TOEFL (minimum score 550 paper-based; 79 iBT), IELTS (minimum score 6.5). *Application deadline:* For fall admission, 1/15 priority date for domestic and international students; for spring admission, 11/1 priority date for domestic and international students. Applications are processed on a rolling basis. Application fee: $45. Electronic applications accepted. *Expenses:* Tuition, state resident: full-time $9990; part-time $555 per credit hour. Tuition, nonresident: full-time $18,108; part-time $1006 per credit hour. *Required fees:* $90; $5 per credit hour. *Financial support:* Fellowships, research assistantships, and unspecified assistantships available. Support available to part-time students. Financial award application deadline: 3/1; financial award applicants required to submit FAFSA. *Unit head:* Dr. Michael H. Roberts, Dean, 843-349-2282, Fax: 843-349-2545, E-mail: mroberts@coastal.edu. *Application contact:* Dr. James O. Luken, Associate Provost/Vice-Dean of the Coastal Environment, 843-349-2235, Fax: 843-349-6444, E-mail: joluken@coastal.edu.
Website: http://www.coastal.edu/academics/colleges/science/

College of Charleston, Graduate School, School of Sciences and Mathematics, Program in Computer and Information Sciences, Charleston, SC 29424-0001. Offers MS. Program offered jointly with The Citadel, The Military College of South Carolina. *Program availability:* Part-time, evening/weekend. *Degree requirements:* For master's, thesis optional. *Entrance requirements:* For master's, GRE. Additional exam requirements/recommendations for international students: Required—TOEFL (minimum score 81 iBT). *Application deadline:* For fall admission, 6/1 for domestic students; for spring admission, 11/1 for domestic students. Application fee: $45. Electronic applications accepted. *Financial support:* Research assistantships, Federal Work-Study, scholarships/grants, and unspecified assistantships available. Support available to part-time students. Financial award application deadline: 4/1; financial award applicants required to submit FAFSA. *Unit head:* Aspen Olmsted, Director, 843-953-6600. *Application contact:* Aspen Olmsted, Director, 843-953-6600.

The College of St. Scholastica, Graduate Studies, Department of Computer Information Systems, Duluth, MN 55811-4199. Offers MA, Certificate. *Program availability:* Part-time, online learning. *Degree requirements:* For master's, thesis. *Entrance requirements:* Additional exam requirements/recommendations for international students: Required—TOEFL (minimum score 550 paper-based; 79 iBT). Electronic applications accepted. Application fee is waived when completed online. *Expenses:* Contact institution. *Faculty research:* Organization acceptance of software development methodologies.

Colorado State University, College of Business, Department of Computer Information Systems, Fort Collins, CO 80523-1277. Offers MCIS. *Program availability:* Part-time. *Faculty:* 8 full-time (0 women), 2 part-time/adjunct (0 women). *Students:* 58 full-time (21 women), 175 part-time (55 women); includes 40 minority (8 Black or African American, non-Hispanic/Latino; 1 American Indian or Alaska Native, non-Hispanic/Latino; 15 Asian, non-Hispanic/Latino; 12 Hispanic/Latino; 4 Two or more races, non-Hispanic/Latino), 57 international. Average age 34. 174 applicants, 68% accepted, 81 enrolled. In 2016, 99 master's awarded. *Degree requirements:* For master's, thesis or alternative, project. *Entrance requirements:* For master's, GMAT or GRE, minimum GPA of 3.0, bachelor's degree. Additional exam requirements/recommendations for international students: Required—TOEFL (minimum score 86 iBT); Recommended—IELTS (minimum score 6.5), TSE (minimum score 58). *Application deadline:* For fall admission, 7/1 for domestic students, 5/1 for international students; for spring admission, 12/1 for domestic students, 10/1 for international students. Applications are processed on a rolling basis. Application fee: $60 ($70 for international students). Electronic applications accepted. *Expenses:* Contact institution. *Financial support:* Career-related internships or fieldwork, Federal Work-Study, scholarships/grants, and unspecified assistantships available. Support available to part-time students. Financial award application deadline: 2/1; financial award applicants required to submit FAFSA. *Faculty research:* Database research (SQL, UML, OO); programming research (COBOL, JCL, C, Java, VB); supply chain management; systems development, metrics, modeling and testing; project management. *Total annual research expenditures:* $253,963. *Unit head:* Dr. Jon D. Clark, Chair, 970-491-1618, E-mail: jon.clark@colostate.edu. *Application contact:* Jennifer Ivan, Program Manager, 970-491-1184, E-mail: jennifer.ivan@colostate.edu.
Website: https://biz.colostate.edu/Academics/Graduate-Programs/Master-of-Computer-Information-Systems

Colorado State University–Global Campus, Graduate Programs, Greenwood Village, CO 80111. Offers criminal justice and law enforcement administration (MS); education leadership (MS); finance (MS); healthcare administration and management (MS); human resource management (MHRM); information technology management (MITM); international management (MS); management (MS); organizational leadership (MS); professional accounting (MPA); project management (MS); teaching and learning (MS). *Accreditation:* ACBSP. *Program availability:* Online learning.

Concordia University Wisconsin, Graduate Programs, School of Business Administration, MBA Program, Mequon, WI 53097-2402. Offers finance (MBA); health care administration (MBA); human resource management (MBA); international business (MBA); international business-bilingual English/Chinese (MBA); management (MBA); management information systems (MBA); managerial communications (MBA); marketing (MBA); public administration (MBA); risk management (MBA). *Program availability:* Online learning. *Degree requirements:* For master's, comprehensive exam, thesis or alternative. *Entrance requirements:* Additional exam requirements/recommendations for international students: Required—TOEFL. *Application deadline:* For fall admission, 8/1 priority date for domestic students; for spring admission, 1/15 for domestic students. Applications are processed on a rolling basis. Application fee: $50. *Expenses:* Contact institution. *Financial support:* Application deadline: 8/1. *Unit head:* Dr. David Borst, Director, 262-243-4298, Fax: 262-243-4428, E-mail: david.borst@cuw.edu. *Application contact:* Mary Eberhardt, Graduate Admissions, 262-243-4551, Fax: 262-243-4428, E-mail: mary.eberhardt@cuw.edu.

Copenhagen Business School, Graduate Programs, Copenhagen, Denmark. Offers business administration (Exec MBA, MBA, PhD); business administration and information systems (M Sc); business, language and culture (M Sc); economics and business administration (M Sc); health management (MHM); international business and politics (M Sc); public administration (MPA); shipping and logistics (Exec MBA); technology, market and organization (MBA).

Daemen College, Department of Accounting/Information Systems, Amherst, NY 14226-3592. Offers global business (MS), including accounting, global business, management information systems, marketing. *Program availability:* Part-time, evening/weekend. *Degree requirements:* For master's, minimum GPA of 3.0. *Entrance requirements:* For master's, GMAT if undergraduate GPA is less than 3.0, 2 letters of recommendation; goal statement; transcripts; demonstration of satisfactory oral and written English. Additional exam requirements/recommendations for international students: Required—TOEFL (minimum score 500 paper-based; 63 iBT), IELTS (minimum score 5.5). Electronic applications accepted. *Faculty research:* Internationalization of small business, cultural influences on business practices, international human resource practices.

Dakota State University, College of Business and Information Systems, Madison, SD 57042-1799. Offers analytics (MSA); applied computer science (MSACS); banking security (Graduate Certificate); business analytics (Graduate Certificate); cyber security (D Sc); ethical hacking (Graduate Certificate); general management (MBA); health informatics (MSHI); information assurance and computer security (MSIA); information systems (MSIS, D Sc IS); information technology (Graduate Certificate). *Accreditation:* ACBSP. *Program availability:* Part-time, evening/weekend, 100% online, blended/hybrid learning. *Degree requirements:* For master's, comprehensive exam, thesis optional, examination, integrative project; for doctorate, comprehensive exam, thesis/dissertation, portfolio. *Entrance requirements:* For master's, GRE General Test, demonstration of information systems skills, minimum GPA of 2.7; for doctorate, GRE General Test, demonstration of information systems skills; for Graduate Certificate, GMAT. Additional exam requirements/recommendations for international students: Required—PTE (minimum score 53), TOEFL (minimum score 550 paper-based, 79 iBT) or IELTS (6.5). *Application deadline:* For fall admission, 6/15 for domestic students, 4/15 for international students; for spring admission, 11/15 for domestic students, 9/15 priority date for international students; for summer admission, 4/15 for domestic and international students. Applications are processed on a rolling basis. Application fee: $35. *Expenses:* Contact institution. *Financial support:* Fellowships with partial tuition reimbursements, research assistantships with partial tuition reimbursements, teaching assistantships with partial tuition reimbursements, career-related internships or fieldwork, Federal Work-Study, scholarships/grants, and unspecified assistantships available. Support available to part-time students. Financial award applicants required to submit FAFSA. *Faculty research:* Data mining and analytics, biometrics and information assurance, decision support systems, health informatics, STEM education for K-12 teachers/students and underrepresented populations. *Unit head:* Mark Hawkes, Dean for Graduate Studies and Research, 605-256-5274, E-mail: mark.hawkes@dsu.edu. *Application contact:* Erin Blankespoor, Senior Secretary, Office of Graduate Studies and Research, 605-256-5799, E-mail: erin.blankespoor@dsu.edu.
Website: http://dsu.edu/academics/colleges/college-of-business-and-information-systems

Dalhousie University, Faculty of Management, Centre for Advanced Management Education, Halifax, NS B3H 3J5, Canada. Offers financial services (MBA); information management (MIM); management (MPA); natural resources (MBA). *Program availability:* Part-time, online learning. *Entrance requirements:* For master's, GMAT, minimum GPA of 3.0, resume. Additional exam requirements/recommendations for international students: Required—TOEFL, IELTS, CANTEST, CAEL, or Michigan English Language Assessment Battery. Electronic applications accepted.

Dallas Baptist University, College of Business, Business Administration Program, Dallas, TX 75211-9299. Offers accounting (MBA); business communication (MBA); conflict resolution management (MBA); entrepreneurship (MBA); finance (MBA); health care management (MBA); international business (MBA); leading the non-profit organization (MBA); management (MBA); management information systems (MBA); marketing (MBA); project management (MBA); technology and engineering management (MBA). *Accreditation:* ACBSP. *Program availability:* Part-time, evening/weekend, 100% online, blended/hybrid learning. *Application deadline:* Applications are processed on a rolling basis. Application fee: $25. Electronic applications accepted. Application fee is waived when completed online. *Expenses: Tuition:* Full-time $15,408; part-time $856 per credit hour. *Required fees:* $400 per semester. Tuition and fees vary according to course load and degree level. *Unit head:* Dr. Sandra Reid, Chair of Graduate Business Programs, 214-333-5280, E-mail: sandra@dbu.edu. *Application contact:* Bobby Soto, Director of Admissions, 214-333-5242, E-mail: graduate@dbu.edu.
Website: http://www3.dbu.edu/graduate/mba.asp

Dallas Baptist University, Professional Development Program, Dallas, TX 75211-9299. Offers accounting (MA); church leadership (MA); communication (MA); counseling (MA); criminal justice (MA); English as a second language (MA); finance (MA); higher education (MA); leadership studies (MA); management (MA); management information systems (MA); marketing (MA); missions (MA); professional life coaching (MA); training and development (MA). *Program availability:* Part-time, evening/weekend, 100% online, blended/hybrid learning. *Application deadline:* Applications are processed on a rolling basis. Application fee: $25. Electronic applications accepted. Application fee is waived when completed online. *Expenses: Tuition:* Full-time $15,408; part-time $856 per credit hour. *Required fees:* $400 per semester. Tuition and fees vary according to course load and degree level. *Unit head:* Jared Ingram, Director, 214-333-5584, E-mail: jaredi@dbu.edu. *Application contact:* Bobby Soto, Director of Admissions, 214-333-5242, E-mail: graduate@dbu.edu.
Website: http://www3.dbu.edu/graduate/mapd.asp

DePaul University, College of Computing and Digital Media, Chicago, IL 60604. Offers animation (MA, MFA); business information technology (MS); cinema (MFA); cinema production (MS); computational finance (MS); computer and information sciences (PhD); computer game development (MS); computer information and network security (MS); computer science (MS); e-commerce technology (MS); health informatics (MS); human-computer interaction (MS); information systems (MS); information technology project management (MS); network engineering and management (MS); predictive analytics (MS); screenwriting (MFA); software engineering (MS); JD/MS. *Program availability:* Part-time, evening/weekend, online learning. *Degree requirements:* For master's, thesis (for some programs); for doctorate, comprehensive exam, thesis/dissertation. *Entrance requirements:* For master's, GRE or GMAT (for MS in computational finance only), bachelor's degree, resume (MS in predictive analytics only), IT experience (MS in information technology project management only), portfolio review (all MFA programs and MA in animation); for doctorate, GRE, master's degree in computer science. Additional exam requirements/recommendations for international students: Required—TOEFL (minimum score 590 paper-based; 80 iBT), IELTS (minimum score 6.5), PTE (minimum score 53). Electronic applications accepted. *Expenses:* Contact institution. *Faculty research:* Data mining, computer science, human-computer interaction, security, animation and film.

DePaul University, Kellstadt Graduate School of Business, Chicago, IL 60604. Offers accountancy (M Acc, MS, MSA); applied economics (MBA); banking (MBA); behavioral finance (MBA); brand and product management (MBA); business development (MBA); business information technology (MS); business strategy and decision-making (MBA); computational finance (MS); consumer insights (MBA); corporate finance (MBA); economic policy analysis (MS); entrepreneurship (MBA, MS); finance (MBA, MS); financial analysis (MBA); general business (MBA); health sector management (MBA); hospitality leadership (MBA); hospitality leadership and operational performance (MS); human resource management (MBA); human resources (MS); investment management (MBA); leadership and change management (MBA); management accounting (MBA); marketing (MBA, MS); marketing analysis (MS); marketing strategy and planning (MBA); operations management (MBA); organizational diversity (MBA); real estate (MS); real estate finance and investment (MBA); revenue management (MBA); sports management (MBA); strategic global marketing (MBA); strategy, execution and valuation (MBA); sustainable management (MBA, MS); taxation (MS); wealth management (MS); JD/MBA. *Accreditation:* AACSB. *Program availability:* Part-time, evening/weekend, online learning. *Entrance requirements:* For master's, GMAT, 2 letters of recommendation, resume, essay, official transcripts. Additional exam requirements/recommendations for international students: Required—TOEFL (minimum score 550 paper-based; 80 iBT). Electronic applications accepted. *Expenses:* Contact institution.

DeSales University, Division of Business, Center Valley, PA 18034-9568. Offers accounting (MBA); computer information systems (MBA); finance (MBA); health care systems management (MBA); human resources management (MBA); management (MBA); marketing (MBA); project management (MBA); self-design (MBA); supply chain management (MBA); DNP/MBA; MSN/MBA. *Accreditation:* ACBSP. *Program availability:* Part-time, evening/weekend, 100% online, blended/hybrid learning. *Faculty:* 12 full-time (4 women), 29 part-time/adjunct (5 women). *Students:* 73 full-time (38 women), 323 part-time (163 women); includes 59 minority (16 Black or African American, non-Hispanic/Latino; 23 Asian, non-Hispanic/Latino; 16 Hispanic/Latino; 4 Two or more races, non-Hispanic/Latino). Average age 37. 157 applicants, 87% accepted, 128 enrolled. In 2016, 115 master's awarded. *Entrance requirements:* For master's, GMAT (waived if undergraduate GPA is 3.0 or better), minimum GPA of 3.0 in undergraduate work, literacy in basic software, background or interest in the field of study, personal statement, 2 years of work experience. Additional exam requirements/recommendations for international students: Required—TOEFL. *Application deadline:* Applications are processed on a rolling basis. Application fee: $50. Electronic applications accepted. *Expenses:* Contact institution. *Financial support:* Applicants required to submit FAFSA. *Faculty research:* Quality improvement, executive development, productivity, cross-cultural managerial differences, leadership. *Unit head:* Dr. David M. Gilfoil, Director, MBA Program, 610-282-1100 Ext. 1828, Fax: 610-282-2869, E-mail: david.gilfoil@desales.edu. *Application contact:* Julia Ferraro, Director of Graduate Admissions, 610-282-1100 Ext. 1768, E-mail: gradadmissions@desales.edu.

DeSales University, Division of Science and Mathematics, Center Valley, PA 18034-9568. Offers cyber security (Postbaccalaureate Certificate); data analytics (Postbaccalaureate Certificate); information systems (MS), including cyber security, digital forensics, healthcare information management, project management. *Program availability:* Part-time, evening/weekend, 100% online, blended/hybrid learning. *Faculty:* 1 (woman) full-time, 3 part-time/adjunct (0 women). *Students:* 8 full-time (1 woman), 12 part-time (6 women); includes 1 minority (Asian, non-Hispanic/Latino). Average age 34. 20 applicants, 30% accepted, 6 enrolled. In 2016, 7 master's awarded. *Entrance requirements:* For master's, GRE or GMAT, bachelor's degree in computer-related discipline from accredited college or university, minimum undergraduate GPA of 3.0, personal statement, three letters of recommendation. Additional exam requirements/recommendations for international students: Required—TOEFL. *Application deadline:* Applications are processed on a rolling basis. Application fee: $50. Electronic applications accepted. *Expenses:* Contact institution. *Financial support:* Applicants required to submit FAFSA. *Unit head:* Dr. Patricia Riola, MSIS Director/Assistant Professor of Computer Science, 610-282-1100 Ext. 1647, E-mail: patricia.riola@desales.edu. *Application contact:* Julia Ferraro, Director of Graduate Admissions, 610-282-1100 Ext. 1768, E-mail: gradadmissions@desales.edu.
Website: http://www.desales.edu/home/academics/graduate-studies/programs-of-study/msis---master-of-science-in-information-systems

DeVry University–Folsom Campus, Graduate Programs, Folsom, CA 95630. Offers accounting (M Acc); accounting and financial management (MAFM); business administration (MBA); curriculum leadership (M Ed); educational leadership (M Ed); educational technology (M Ed); higher education leadership (M Ed); human resource management (MHRM); information systems management (MISM); network and communications management (MNCM); project management (MPM); public administration (MPA).

Dominican University, School of Information Studies, River Forest, IL 60305-1099. Offers information management (MSIM); knowledge management (Certificate); library and information science (MLIS, MPS, PhD); special studies (CSS); MBA/MLIS; MLIS/MA. MLIS/M Div offered jointly with McCormick Theological Seminary, MLIS/MA with Loyola University Chicago, MLIS/MM with Northwestern University. *Accreditation:* ALA (one or more programs are accredited). *Program availability:* Part-time, evening/weekend, 100% online, blended/hybrid learning. *Faculty:* 11 full-time (7 women), 8 part-time/adjunct (6 women). *Students:* 79 full-time (66 women), 170 part-time (133 women); includes 46 minority (21 Black or African American, non-Hispanic/Latino; 2 Asian, non-Hispanic/Latino; 20 Hispanic/Latino; 1 Native Hawaiian or other Pacific Islander, non-Hispanic/Latino; 2 Two or more races, non-Hispanic/Latino), 3 international. Average age 33. 121 applicants, 82% accepted, 74 enrolled. In 2016, 113 master's, 3 doctorates awarded. *Degree requirements:* For doctorate, thesis/dissertation. *Entrance requirements:* For master's, minimum GPA of 3.0, GRE General Test, or MAT; for doctorate, MLIS or related MA, minimum GPA of 3.0, GRE General Test, or MAT. Additional exam requirements/recommendations for international students: Required—TOEFL. *Application deadline:* For fall admission, 6/1 priority date for domestic students; for winter admission, 3/1 priority date for domestic students; for spring admission, 10/1 priority date for domestic students. Applications are processed on a rolling basis. Application fee: $25. *Expenses:* $830 per credit hour. *Financial support:* Fellowships, research assistantships, career-related internships or fieldwork, scholarships/grants, and unspecified assistantships available. Support available to part-time students. Financial award application deadline: 4/15; financial award applicants required to submit FAFSA. *Faculty research:* Productivity and the information environment, bibliometrics, library history, subject access, library materials and services for children. *Unit head:* Dr. Kate Marek, Dean and Professor, 708-524-6648, Fax: 708-524-6657, E-mail: kmarek@dom.edu. *Application contact:* Catherine Galarza-Espino, Coordinator of Graduate Marketing and Recruiting, 708-524-6983, E-mail: cgalarza@dom.edu.
Website: http://sois.dom.edu/

Drexel University, College of Computing and Informatics, Department of Information Science, Philadelphia, PA 19104-2875. Offers health informatics (MS); information science (PhD, Post-Master's Certificate, Postbaccalaureate Certificate); information systems (MS); library and information science (MS). *Program availability:* Part-time, evening/weekend, 100% online. *Faculty:* 33 full-time (18 women), 9 part-time/adjunct (3 women). *Students:* 115 full-time (61 women), 281 part-time (184 women); includes 78 minority (29 Black or African American, non-Hispanic/Latino; 16 Asian, non-Hispanic/Latino; 24 Hispanic/Latino; 9 Two or more races, non-Hispanic/Latino), 60 international. Average age 34. 475 applicants, 43% accepted, 102 enrolled. In 2016, 181 master's, 8 doctorates, 20 other advanced degrees awarded. *Degree requirements:* For doctorate, thesis/dissertation. *Entrance requirements:* For master's and doctorate, GRE General Test. Additional exam requirements/recommendations for international students: Required—TOEFL (minimum score 600 paper-based; 100 iBT), IELTS (minimum score 6.5). *Application deadline:* For fall admission, 8/15 for domestic students, 7/15 for international students; for spring admission, 3/1 for domestic students, 2/1 for international students. Applications are processed on a rolling basis. Application fee: $65. Electronic applications accepted. Application fee is waived when completed online. *Expenses: Tuition:* Full-time $32,184; part-time $1192 per credit hour. *Required fees:* $280. Tuition and fees vary according to campus/location and program. *Financial support:* In 2016–17, 82 students received support, including 15 research assistantships with full tuition reimbursements available (averaging $26,670 per year), 9 teaching assistantships with full tuition reimbursements available (averaging $26,750 per year); career-related internships or fieldwork, scholarships/grants, and tuition waivers (partial) also available. Support available to part-time students. Financial award application deadline: 3/1; financial award applicants required to submit FAFSA. *Total annual research expenditures:* $2 million. *Unit head:* Dr. Yi Deng, Dean/Professor, 215-895-2474, Fax: 215-895-2494, E-mail: yd362@drexel.edu. *Application contact:* Matthew Lechtenberg, Director, Recruitment, 215-895-2474, Fax: 215-895-2303, E-mail: cciinfo@drexel.edu.
Website: http://cci.drexel.edu/academics/graduate-programs/ms-in-health-informatics

Duquesne University, Palumbo-Donahue School of Business, Pittsburgh, PA 15282-0001. Offers accounting (M Acc); finance (MBA); information systems management (MSISM); management (MBA, MS); marketing (MBA); sports business (MS); sustainability (MBA); JD/MBA; MBA/M Acc; MBA/MA; MBA/MES; MBA/MHMS; MSISM/MBA; Pharm D/MBA. *Accreditation:* AACSB. *Program availability:* Part-time, evening/weekend, 100% online, minimal on-campus study. *Faculty:* 59 full-time (23 women), 25 part-time/adjunct (6 women). *Students:* 92 full-time (43 women), 176 part-time (71 women); includes 20 minority (9 Black or African American, non-Hispanic/Latino; 8 Asian, non-Hispanic/Latino; 2 Hispanic/Latino; 1 Two or more races, non-Hispanic/Latino), 35 international. Average age 28. 272 applicants, 86% accepted, 137 enrolled. In 2016, 137 master's awarded. *Entrance requirements:* For master's, GMAT or GRE, undergraduate transcripts, 2 letters of recommendation, current resume, personal statement. Additional exam requirements/recommendations for international students: Required—TOEFL (minimum score 577 paper-based; 90 iBT), IELTS (minimum score 7). *Application deadline:* For fall admission, 7/1 priority date for domestic and international students; for spring admission, 12/1 for domestic and international students; for summer admission, 4/1 for domestic and international students. Applications are processed on a rolling basis. Application fee: $0. Electronic applications accepted. *Expenses:* Contact institution. *Financial support:* In 2016–17, 211 students received support, including 12 fellowships with partial tuition reimbursements available (averaging $14,200 per year), 20 research assistantships with partial tuition reimbursements available (averaging $22,212 per year); career-related internships or fieldwork, scholarships/grants, and unspecified assistantships also available. Support available to part-time students. Financial award application deadline: 7/1; financial award applicants required to submit FAFSA. *Faculty research:* Investment management, business ethics, technology management, supply chain management, entrepreneurship. *Unit head:* Dr. Karen Donovan, Associate Dean of Graduate Programs and Executive Education, 412-396-6276, Fax: 412-396-1726, E-mail: donovan6@duq.edu. *Application contact:* Jeff Jewett, Director of Admissions and Enrollment Management, 412-396-6244, Fax: 412-396-1726, E-mail: decrostam@duq.edu.
Website: http://www.duq.edu/business/grad

East Carolina University, Graduate School, College of Engineering and Technology, Department of Technology Systems, Greenville, NC 27858-4353. Offers computer network professional (Certificate); information assurance (Certificate); Lean Six Sigma Black Belt (Certificate); network technology (MS), including computer networking management, digital communications technology, information security, Web technologies; occupational safety (MS); technology management (PhD); technology systems (MS), including industrial distribution and logistics, manufacturing systems, performance improvement, quality systems; Website developer (Certificate). *Students:* 23 full-time (1 woman), 199 part-time (55 women); includes 59 minority (39 Black or African American, non-Hispanic/Latino; 3 American Indian or Alaska Native, non-Hispanic/Latino; 4 Asian, non-Hispanic/Latino; 10 Hispanic/Latino; 3 Two or more races, non-Hispanic/Latino), 5 international. Average age 38. 85 applicants, 87% accepted, 61 enrolled. In 2016, 23 master's awarded. *Entrance requirements:* For master's and Certificate, GRE General Test or MAT, minimum GPA of 2.5; for doctorate, GRE General Test, related work experience. *Application deadline:* For fall admission, 6/1 priority date for domestic students. Applications are processed on a rolling basis. Application fee: $50. *Financial support:* Application deadline: 6/1. *Unit head:* Dr. Tijjani Mohammed, Chair, 252-328-9668, E-mail: mohammedt@ecu.edu. *Application contact:* Dean of Graduate School, 252-328-6012, Fax: 252-328-6071, E-mail: gradschool@ecu.edu.

Eastern Michigan University, Graduate School, College of Business, Department of Computer Information Systems, Ypsilanti, MI 48197. Offers MS. *Program availability:* Part-time, evening/weekend. *Faculty:* 7 full-time (0 women). *Students:* 25 full-time (13 women), 17 part-time (9 women); includes 6 minority (all Asian, non-Hispanic/Latino), 29 international. Average age 28. 52 applicants, 48% accepted, 11 enrolled. In 2016, 37 master's awarded. *Entrance requirements:* Additional exam requirements/recommendations for international students: Required—TOEFL. *Application deadline:* For fall admission, 5/15 priority date for domestic students, 2/15 priority date for international students; for winter admission, 10/15 priority date for domestic students, 9/1 priority date for international students; for summer admission, 3/15 priority date for domestic students, 3/1 priority date for international students. Applications are processed on a rolling basis. Application fee: $45. *Financial support:* Fellowships, research assistantships with full tuition reimbursements, teaching assistantships with full tuition reimbursements, career-related internships or fieldwork, Federal Work-Study, institutionally sponsored loans, scholarships/grants, tuition waivers (partial), and unspecified assistantships available. Support available to part-time students. Financial award applicants required to submit FAFSA. *Unit head:* Dr. David Chou, Interim Department Head, 734-487-2454, Fax: 734-487-1941, E-mail: dchou@emich.edu.
Website: http://www.cis.emich.edu

Eastern Michigan University, Graduate School, College of Business, Programs in Business Administration, Ypsilanti, MI 48197. Offers business administration (MBA, Graduate Certificate); computer information systems (Graduate Certificate); e-business (MBA, Graduate Certificate); enterprise business intelligence (MBA); entrepreneurship

(MBA, Graduate Certificate); finance (MBA, Graduate Certificate); human resources (MBA); human resources management (Graduate Certificate); information systems (MBA); internal auditing (MBA); international business (MBA, Graduate Certificate); marketing management (Graduate Certificate); nonprofit management (MBA); organizational development (Graduate Certificate); supply chain management (MBA, Graduate Certificate). *Accreditation:* AACSB. *Program availability:* Part-time, online learning. *Students:* 63 full-time (36 women), 320 part-time (186 women); includes 131 minority (76 Black or African American, non-Hispanic/Latino; 5 American Indian or Alaska Native, non-Hispanic/Latino; 16 Asian, non-Hispanic/Latino; 19 Hispanic/Latino; 15 Two or more races, non-Hispanic/Latino), 23 international. Average age 32. 305 applicants, 70% accepted, 124 enrolled. In 2016, 78 master's, 57 other advanced degrees awarded. *Entrance requirements:* For master's, GMAT (minimum score 450), minimum cumulative undergraduate GPA of 2.75. Additional exam requirements/recommendations for international students: Required—TOEFL. *Application deadline:* For fall admission, 5/15 priority date for domestic students, 2/15 priority date for international students; for winter admission, 10/15 priority date for domestic students, 9/1 priority date for international students; for summer admission, 3/15 priority date for domestic students, 3/1 priority date for international students. Applications are processed on a rolling basis. Application fee: $45. *Financial support:* Fellowships, research assistantships with full tuition reimbursements, teaching assistantships with full tuition reimbursements, career-related internships or fieldwork, Federal Work-Study, institutionally sponsored loans, scholarships/grants, tuition waivers (partial), and unspecified assistantships available. Support available to part-time students. Financial award applicants required to submit FAFSA. *Unit head:* K. Michelle Henry, Director, Graduate Business Programs, 734-487-4444, Fax: 734-483-1316, E-mail: cob.graduate@emich.edu.
Website: http://www.emich.edu/cob/mba/

Elmhurst College, Graduate Programs, Program in Computer Information Systems, Elmhurst, IL 60126-3296. Offers MS. *Program availability:* Part-time, evening/weekend, online learning. *Faculty:* 1 full-time (0 women), 1 part-time/adjunct (0 women). *Students:* 1 (woman) full-time, 24 part-time (5 women); includes 9 minority (3 Black or African American, non-Hispanic/Latino; 1 Asian, non-Hispanic/Latino; 4 Hispanic/Latino; 1 Two or more races, non-Hispanic/Latino), 7 international. Average age 31. 19 applicants, 37% accepted, 5 enrolled. In 2016, 11 master's awarded. *Entrance requirements:* For master's, 3 recommendations, resume, statement of purpose. Additional exam requirements/recommendations for international students: Required—TOEFL (minimum score 550 paper-based; 79 iBT). *Application deadline:* Applications are processed on a rolling basis. Application fee: $0. Electronic applications accepted. *Expenses:* $775 per semester hour. *Financial support:* In 2016–17, 7 students received support. Scholarships/grants available. Support available to part-time students. Financial award application deadline: 3/1; financial award applicants required to submit FAFSA. *Unit head:* Ali Ghane. *Application contact:* Timothy J. Panfil, Director of Enrollment Management, School for Professional Studies, 630-617-3300 Ext. 3256, Fax: 630-617-6471, E-mail: panfilt@elmhurst.edu.
Website: http://www.elmhurst.edu/cis

Embry-Riddle Aeronautical University–Worldwide, Department of Decision Sciences, Daytona Beach, FL 32114-3900. Offers aviation and aerospace (MSPM); aviation/aerospace management (MSEM); financial management (MSEM, MSPM); general management (MSPM); global management (MSPM); human resources management (MSPM); information systems (MSPM); leadership (MSEM, MSPM); logistics and supply chain management (MSEM, MSLSCM, MSPM); management (MSEM, MSPM); project management (MSEM); systems engineering (MSEM, MSPM); technical management (MSPM). *Program availability:* Part-time, evening/weekend, 100% online, blended/hybrid learning, EagleVision is a virtual classroom that combines Web video conferencing and a learning management system. EagleVision Classroom (between classrooms), EagleVision Home (faculty and students at home), and a blend of Classroom or Home. *Degree requirements:* For master's, comprehensive exam (for some programs), thesis (for some programs). *Entrance requirements:* Additional exam requirements/recommendations for international students: Required—TOEFL (minimum score 550 paper-based; 79 iBT), IELTS (minimum score 6), TOEFL or IELTS accepted. Electronic applications accepted. *Expenses:* Contact institution.

Embry-Riddle Aeronautical University–Worldwide, Department of Technology Management, Daytona Beach, FL 32114-3900. Offers information security and assurance (MS), including information assurance in a global context, information systems security, protecting business intelligence; management information systems (MS), including business intelligence siness and analytics, information security and assurance, information systems project management. *Program availability:* Part-time, evening/weekend, 100% online, blended/hybrid learning, EagleVision is a virtual classroom that combines Web video conferencing and a learning management system. EagleVision Classroom (between classrooms), EagleVision Home (faculty and students at home), and a blend of Classroom or Home. *Entrance requirements:* Additional exam requirements/recommendations for international students: Required—TOEFL (minimum score 550 paper-based; 79 iBT), IELTS (minimum score 6), TOEFL or IELTS accepted. Electronic applications accepted. *Expenses:* Contact institution.

Emory University, Goizueta Business School, Doctoral Program in Business, Atlanta, GA 30322. Offers accounting (PhD); finance (PhD); information systems and operations management (PhD); marketing (PhD); organization and management (PhD). *Faculty:* 59 full-time (16 women). *Students:* 40 full-time (16 women); includes 6 minority (1 Black or African American, non-Hispanic/Latino; 4 Asian, non-Hispanic/Latino; 1 Hispanic/Latino), 26 international. Average age 28. 145 applicants, 9% accepted, 4 enrolled. In 2016, 5 doctorates awarded. *Degree requirements:* For doctorate, comprehensive exam, thesis/dissertation. *Entrance requirements:* For doctorate, GMAT (strongly preferred) or GRE. Additional exam requirements/recommendations for international students: Required—TOEFL (minimum score 600 paper-based; 100 iBT). *Application deadline:* For fall admission, 1/3 priority date for domestic and international students. Application fee: $75. Electronic applications accepted. *Expenses:* $708 fees per year; 100% of tuition covered by scholarship. *Financial support:* In 2016–17, 34 students received support, including 6 fellowships (averaging $3,333 per year); scholarships/grants and health care benefits also available. Financial award application deadline: 1/3. *Faculty research:* Financial and managerial accounting, asset pricing strategy and organizational behavior, information technology marketing analytics and consumer behavior. *Unit head:* Dr. Anand Swaminathan, Associate Dean, Doctoral Program, 404-727-2306, Fax: 404-727-5337, E-mail: anand.swaminathan@emory.edu. *Application contact:* Allison Gilmore, Director of Admissions and Student Services, 404-727-6353, Fax: 404-727-5337, E-mail: allison.gilmore@emory.edu.

Emory University, Goizueta Business School, Full Time MBA Program, Atlanta, GA 30322. Offers accounting (MBA); alternative investments (MBA); business process consulting (MBA); business technology management (MBA); capital markets (MBA); corporate finance (MBA); customer relationship management (MBA); decision analytics (MBA); entrepreneurship (MBA); finance (MBA); global management (MBA); investment banking (MBA); management consulting (MBA); marketing (MBA); marketing analytics (MBA); marketing consulting (MBA); operations management (MBA); organization and management (MBA); product and brand management (MBA); real estate (MBA); social enterprise (MBA); strategy consulting (MBA). *Accreditation:* AACSB. *Faculty:* 72 full-time (17 women), 18 part-time/adjunct (5 women). *Students:* 350 full-time (101 women); includes 77 minority (21 Black or African American, non-Hispanic/Latino; 3 American Indian or Alaska Native, non-Hispanic/Latino; 32 Asian, non-Hispanic/Latino; 15 Hispanic/Latino; 2 Native Hawaiian or other Pacific Islander, non-Hispanic/Latino; 4 Two or more races, non-Hispanic/Latino), 117 international. Average age 29. 1,434 applicants, 31% accepted, 181 enrolled. In 2016, 182 master's awarded. *Degree requirements:* For master's, 1 leadership course; 2 mid-semester module programs; 2 global components. *Entrance requirements:* For master's, GMAT/GRE, essays; recommendation letters; undergraduate degree; interview. Additional exam requirements/recommendations for international students: Required—TOEFL (minimum score 100 iBT), IELTS (minimum score 7), PTE (minimum score 68). *Application deadline:* For fall admission, 10/14 priority date for domestic and international students; for winter admission, 11/11 priority date for domestic and international students; for spring admission, 1/4 priority date for domestic students, 1/4 for international students. Application fee: $150. Electronic applications accepted. *Expenses:* $57,580. *Financial support:* In 2016–17, 289 students received support. Career-related internships or fieldwork, institutionally sponsored loans, and scholarships/grants available. Financial award application deadline: 4/1; financial award applicants required to submit FAFSA. *Faculty research:* Social enterprise; micro vs. large business; mobile health data; mutual fund performance; product evaluation. *Unit head:* Brian Mitchell, Associate Dean, 404-727-4824, Fax: 404-712-9648, E-mail: brian.mitchell@emory.edu. *Application contact:* Julie Barefoot, Associate Dean, 404-727-6311, Fax: 404-727-4612, E-mail: mbaadmissions@emory.edu.
Website: http://www.goizueta.emory.edu

Endicott College, Van Loan School of Graduate and Professional Studies, Program in Information Technology, Beverly, MA 01915-2096. Offers MSIT. *Program availability:* Part-time, evening/weekend. *Faculty:* 1 full-time (0 women), 5 part-time/adjunct (1 woman). *Students:* 7 full-time (3 women), 7 part-time (3 women), 4 international. Average age 33. 3 applicants, 100% accepted, 3 enrolled. In 2016, 6 master's awarded. *Degree requirements:* For master's, thesis. *Entrance requirements:* For master's, GRE or MAT, two letters of recommendation, undergraduate transcript. Additional exam requirements/recommendations for international students: Required—TOEFL. *Application deadline:* Applications are processed on a rolling basis. Application fee: $50. Electronic applications accepted. *Expenses:* Contact institution. *Financial support:* Applicants required to submit FAFSA. *Unit head:* Richard Benedetto, Associate Dean of Graduate School, 978-232-2744, Fax: 978-232-3000, E-mail: rbenedet@endicott.edu. *Application contact:* Ian Menchini, Director, Graduate Enrollment and Advising, 978-232-5292, Fax: 978-232-3000, E-mail: imenchin@endicott.edu.
Website: http://www.endicott.edu/VanLoan/Graduate-Studies/Master-Science/Info-Tech/Classroom.aspx

Fairfield University, Dolan School of Business, Fairfield, CT 06824. Offers accounting (MBA, MS, CAS); business analytics (MS); entrepreneurship (MBA); finance (MBA, MS, CAS); general management (MBA, CAS); global management (MBA); human resource management (MBA, CAS); information systems and business analytics (MBA); marketing (MBA, CAS); taxation (MBA, CAS). *Accreditation:* AACSB. *Program availability:* Part-time, evening/weekend. *Faculty:* 20 full-time (6 women), 4 part-time/adjunct (1 woman). *Students:* 106 full-time (41 women), 57 part-time (26 women); includes 18 minority (4 Black or African American, non-Hispanic/Latino; 1 American Indian or Alaska Native, non-Hispanic/Latino; 4 Asian, non-Hispanic/Latino; 7 Hispanic/Latino; 2 Two or more races, non-Hispanic/Latino), 39 international. Average age 26. 136 applicants, 63% accepted, 35 enrolled. In 2016, 90 master's awarded. *Degree requirements:* For master's, capstone course. *Entrance requirements:* For master's, GMAT (minimum score 500), 2 letters of reference, resume, minimum GPA of 3.0. Additional exam requirements/recommendations for international students: Required—TOEFL (minimum score 550 paper-based; 80 iBT) or IELTS (minimum score 6.5). *Application deadline:* For fall admission, 5/15 for international students; for spring admission, 10/15 for international students. Applications are processed on a rolling basis. Application fee: $60. Electronic applications accepted. *Expenses:* $875 per credit hour. *Financial support:* In 2016–17, 33 students received support. Scholarships/grants and unspecified assistantships available. Financial award applicants required to submit FAFSA. *Faculty research:* International finance, leadership and careers, ethics in accounting, emotions in consumer behavior and organizations, data analytics. *Unit head:* Dr. Donald Gibson, Dean, 203-254-4070, Fax: 203-254-4105, E-mail: dgibson@fairfield.edu. *Application contact:* Marianne Gumpper, Director of Graduate and Continuing Studies Admission, 203-254-4184, Fax: 203-254-4073, E-mail: gradadmis@fairfield.edu.
Website: http://fairfield.edu/mba

Fairleigh Dickinson University, Metropolitan Campus, Silberman College of Business, Departments of Management, Marketing, and Entrepreneurial Studies, Program in Management, Teaneck, NJ 07666-1914. Offers management (MBA); management information systems (Certificate). *Accreditation:* AACSB.

Fairleigh Dickinson University, Metropolitan Campus, University College: Arts, Sciences, and Professional Studies, School of Computer Sciences and Engineering, Program in Management Information Systems, Teaneck, NJ 07666-1914. Offers MS.

Ferris State University, College of Business, Big Rapids, MI 49307. Offers business intelligence (MBA); design and innovation management (MBA); incident response (MBA); information security and intelligence (MS), including business intelligence, incident response, project management; lean systems and leadership (MBA); performance metrics (MBA); project management (MBA); supply chain management and lean logistics (MBA). *Accreditation:* ACBSP. *Program availability:* Part-time, evening/weekend, 100% online, blended/hybrid learning. *Faculty:* 18 full-time (7 women), 6 part-time/adjunct (3 women). *Students:* 25 full-time (11 women), 113 part-time (47 women); includes 12 minority (2 Black or African American, non-Hispanic/Latino; 1 American Indian or Alaska Native, non-Hispanic/Latino; 3 Asian, non-Hispanic/Latino; 3 Hispanic/Latino; 3 Two or more races, non-Hispanic/Latino), 50 international. Average age 31. 128 applicants, 59% accepted, 39 enrolled. In 2016, 94 master's awarded. *Degree requirements:* For master's, comprehensive exam, thesis. *Entrance requirements:* For master's, GRE or GMAT, minimum GPA of 3.0 in junior-/senior-level classes and overall; statement of purpose; 3 letters of reference; resume; transcripts. Additional exam requirements/recommendations for international students: Required—TOEFL (minimum score 500 paper-based; 70 iBT), IELTS (minimum score 6.5). *Application deadline:* For fall admission, 7/1 priority date for domestic students, 6/15 for international students; for winter admission, 11/1 priority date for domestic students, 10/15 for international students; for spring admission, 3/1 priority date for domestic students, 2/15 for international students. Applications are processed on a rolling basis. Application fee: $0 ($30 for international students). Electronic applications accepted. *Expenses:* Contact institution. *Financial support:* Career-related internships or fieldwork, Federal Work-Study, scholarships/grants, and unspecified assistantships available. Support available to part-time students. Financial award application deadline: 3/15; financial award applicants required to submit FAFSA. *Faculty research:* Lifestyle medicine business models, lean systems value chain pptimization, digital forensics/incident response, location-based services, passive data capture and analysis. *Unit*

Management Information Systems

head: Dr. David Nicol, College of Business Dean, 231-591-2168, Fax: 231-591-3521, E-mail: davidnicol@ferris.edu. *Application contact:* Dr. Greg Gogolin, Professor, 231-591-3159, Fax: 231-591-3521, E-mail: greggogolin@ferris.edu.
Website: http://cbgp.ferris.edu/

Florida Agricultural and Mechanical University, Division of Graduate Studies, Research, and Continuing Education, School of Business and Industry, Tallahassee, FL 32307-3200. Offers accounting (MBA); finance (MBA); management information systems (MBA); marketing (MBA). *Accreditation:* ACBSP. *Degree requirements:* For master's, residency. *Entrance requirements:* For master's, GMAT, minimum GPA of 3.0.

Florida Atlantic University, College of Business, Department of Information Technology and Operations Management, Boca Raton, FL 33431-0991. Offers information technology management (MS). *Faculty:* 14 full-time (4 women). *Students:* 12 full-time (6 women), 24 part-time (7 women); includes 18 minority (6 Black or African American, non-Hispanic/Latino; 1 American Indian or Alaska Native, non-Hispanic/Latino; 3 Asian, non-Hispanic/Latino; 7 Hispanic/Latino; 1 Two or more races, non-Hispanic/Latino), 1 international. Average age 31. 33 applicants, 42% accepted, 10 enrolled. In 2016, 10 master's awarded. *Degree requirements:* For master's, thesis optional. *Entrance requirements:* For master's, GMAT, minimum GPA of 3.0. Additional exam requirements/recommendations for international students: Required—TOEFL (minimum score 600 paper-based; 61 iBT), IELTS (minimum score 6). *Application deadline:* For fall admission, 7/1 priority date for domestic students, 2/15 priority date for international students; for spring admission, 4/1 priority date for domestic students, 1/15 priority date for international students. Applications are processed on a rolling basis. Application fee: $30. Electronic applications accepted. *Expenses:* Tuition, state resident: full-time $7392; part-time $369.82 per credit hour. Tuition, nonresident: full-time $19,432; part-time $1024.81 per credit hour. *Financial support:* Research assistantships, teaching assistantships, career-related internships or fieldwork, Federal Work-Study, institutionally sponsored loans, tuition waivers (partial), and unspecified assistantships available. Support available to part-time students. Financial award application deadline: 3/1; financial award applicants required to submit FAFSA. *Unit head:* Dr. Caryn Conley, 561-297-2707, E-mail: cconley8@fau.edu.
Website: http://business.fau.edu/departments/information-technology-operations-management/index.aspx

Florida Institute of Technology, Extended Studies Division, Melbourne, FL 32901-6975. Offers acquisition and contract management (MS); aerospace engineering (MS); business administration (MBA, DBA); computer information systems (MS); computer science (MS); electrical engineering (MS); engineering management (MS); human resources management (MS); logistics management (MS), including humanitarian and disaster relief logistics; management (MS), including acquisition and contract management, e-business, human resources management, information systems, logistics management, management, transportation management; material acquisition management (MS); mechanical engineering (MS); operations research (MS); project management (MS), including information systems, operations research; public administration (MPA); quality management (MS); software engineering (MS); space systems (MS); space systems management (MS); supply chain management (MS); systems management (MS), including information systems, operations research; technology management (MS). *Program availability:* Part-time, evening/weekend, online learning. *Faculty:* 10 full-time (3 women), 122 part-time/adjunct (29 women). *Students:* 131 full-time (58 women), 997 part-time (348 women); includes 389 minority (231 Black or African American, non-Hispanic/Latino; 9 American Indian or Alaska Native, non-Hispanic/Latino; 26 Asian, non-Hispanic/Latino; 99 Hispanic/Latino; 3 Native Hawaiian or other Pacific Islander, non-Hispanic/Latino; 21 Two or more races, non-Hispanic/Latino), 53 international. Average age 36. 962 applicants, 48% accepted, 323 enrolled. In 2016, 403 master's awarded. *Degree requirements:* For master's, comprehensive exam (for some programs). *Entrance requirements:* For master's, GMAT or resume showing 8 years of supervised experience, minimum GPA of 3.0, 2 letters of recommendation, resume. Additional exam requirements/recommendations for international students: Required—TOEFL (minimum score 550 paper-based; 79 iBT). *Application deadline:* For fall admission, 4/1 for international students; for spring admission, 9/30 for international students. Applications are processed on a rolling basis. Electronic applications accepted. *Expenses:* Contact institution. *Financial support:* Application deadline: 3/1; applicants required to submit FAFSA. *Unit head:* Dr. Theodore R. Richardson, III, Dean, 321-674-8123, Fax: 321-674-7597, E-mail: trichardson@fit.edu. *Application contact:* Carolyn Farrior, Director of Graduate Admissions, Online Learning and Off-Campus Programs, 321-674-7118, Fax: 321-674-8216, E-mail: cfarrior@fit.edu.
Website: http://es.fit.edu

Florida International University, Chapman Graduate School of Business, Department of Decision Sciences and Information Systems, Miami, FL 33199. Offers decision sciences and information systems (PhD); health information management systems (MS); systems management (MS). *Program availability:* Part-time, evening/weekend. *Faculty:* 27 full-time (9 women), 10 part-time/adjunct (3 women). *Students:* 81 full-time (26 women), 51 part-time (18 women); includes 78 minority (20 Black or African American, non-Hispanic/Latino; 3 Asian, non-Hispanic/Latino; 52 Hispanic/Latino; 3 Two or more races, non-Hispanic/Latino), 46 international. Average age 31. 372 applicants, 44% accepted, 37 enrolled. In 2016, 77 master's awarded. *Entrance requirements:* For master's, GMAT or GRE, minimum GPA of 3.0 in upper-level coursework; letter of intent; resume. Additional exam requirements/recommendations for international students: Required—TOEFL (minimum score 550 paper-based; 80 iBT) or IELTS. *Application deadline:* For fall admission, 6/1 for domestic students, 4/1 for international students; for spring admission, 10/1 for domestic students, 9/1 for international students. Applications are processed on a rolling basis. Application fee: $30. Electronic applications accepted. *Expenses:* Contact institution. *Financial support:* Institutionally sponsored loans and scholarships/grants available. Financial award application deadline: 3/1; financial award applicants required to submit FAFSA. *Faculty research:* Artificial intelligence, data warehouses, operations management. *Unit head:* Dr. Monica Tremblay, Chair, 305-348-2830, E-mail: tremblay@fiu.edu. *Application contact:* Milza Rosales, Assistant Director of Admissions and Recruiting, Chapman Graduate School of Business, 305-348-7299, E-mail: mrosale@fiu.edu.

Florida International University, College of Engineering and Computing, School of Computing and Information Sciences, Miami, FL 33199. Offers computer science (MS, PhD); cybersecurity (MS); data science (MS); information technology (MS); telecommunications and networking (MS). *Program availability:* Part-time, evening/weekend. *Faculty:* 46 full-time (11 women), 28 part-time/adjunct (5 women). *Students:* 145 full-time (39 women), 109 part-time (16 women); includes 124 minority (14 Black or African American, non-Hispanic/Latino; 1 American Indian or Alaska Native, non-Hispanic/Latino; 10 Asian, non-Hispanic/Latino; 97 Hispanic/Latino; 2 Two or more races, non-Hispanic/Latino), 115 international. Average age 29. 407 applicants, 54% accepted, 78 enrolled. In 2016, 90 master's, 8 doctorates awarded. *Degree requirements:* For master's, thesis or alternative; for doctorate, comprehensive exam, thesis/dissertation. *Entrance requirements:* For master's and doctorate, GRE General Test, 3 letters of recommendation, minimum GPA of 3.0. Additional exam requirements/recommendations for international students: Required—TOEFL (minimum score 550 paper-based; 80 iBT). *Application deadline:* For fall admission, 6/1 for domestic students, 4/1 for international students; for spring admission, 10/1 for domestic students, 9/1 for international students. Applications are processed on a rolling basis. Application fee: $30. Electronic applications accepted. *Expenses:* Tuition, state resident: full-time $8912; part-time $446 per credit hour. Tuition, nonresident: full-time $21,393; part-time $992 per credit hour. *Required fees:* $2185; $195 per semester. Tuition and fees vary according to program. *Financial support:* Research assistantships, teaching assistantships, institutionally sponsored loans, scholarships/grants, and unspecified assistantships available. Financial award application deadline: 3/1; financial award applicants required to submit FAFSA. *Faculty research:* Database systems, software engineering, operating systems, networks. *Unit head:* Dr. S. S. Iyengar, Director, 305-348-3947, E-mail: iyengar@cis.fiu.edu. *Application contact:* Sara-Michelle Lemus, Engineering Admissions Officer, 305-348-1890, E-mail: grad_eng@fiu.edu.

Florida State University, The Graduate School, College of Business, Tallahassee, FL 32306-1110. Offers accounting (M Acc), including assurance and advisory services, generalist, taxation; business administration (MBA, PhD), including accounting (PhD), finance (PhD), management information systems (PhD), marketing (PhD), organizational behavior and human resources (PhD), risk management and insurance (PhD), strategy (PhD); finance (MS); management information systems (MS); risk management and insurance (MS); JD/MBA; MSW/MBA. *Accreditation:* AACSB. *Program availability:* Part-time, 100% online. *Faculty:* 101 full-time (27 women), 4 part-time/adjunct (2 women). *Students:* 272 full-time (127 women), 351 part-time (133 women); includes 141 minority (45 Black or African American, non-Hispanic/Latino; 2 American Indian or Alaska Native, non-Hispanic/Latino; 20 Asian, non-Hispanic/Latino; 59 Hispanic/Latino; 2 Native Hawaiian or other Pacific Islander, non-Hispanic/Latino; 13 Two or more races, non-Hispanic/Latino), 71 international. Average age 30. 688 applicants, 60% accepted, 273 enrolled. In 2016, 231 master's, 12 doctorates awarded. Terminal master's awarded for partial completion of doctoral program. *Degree requirements:* For doctorate, comprehensive exam, thesis/dissertation. *Entrance requirements:* For master's, GMAT, GRE (for all except MS in finance), work experience (MBA, MS); minimum GPA of 3.0, letters of recommendation; for doctorate, GMAT, GRE (for marketing, organizational behavior, risk management and insurance, management information systems, and human resources only), minimum graduate GPA of 3.5, letters of recommendation. Additional exam requirements/recommendations for international students: Required—TOEFL (minimum score 600 paper-based; 85 iBT); Recommended—IELTS (minimum score 6). *Application deadline:* For fall admission, 6/1 for domestic and international students; for spring admission, 10/1 for domestic and international students; for summer admission, 3/1 for domestic and international students. Applications are processed on a rolling basis. Application fee: $30. Electronic applications accepted. *Expenses:* Contact institution. *Financial support:* In 2016–17, 149 students received support, including 9 fellowships (averaging $1,500 per year), 65 research assistantships with full tuition reimbursements available (averaging $20,000 per year), 75 teaching assistantships with full tuition reimbursements available (averaging $20,000 per year); career-related internships or fieldwork, scholarships/grants, health care benefits, tuition waivers (full and partial), and unspecified assistantships also available. Support available to part-time students. Financial award application deadline: 1/1; financial award applicants required to submit FAFSA. *Faculty research:* Business strategy, marketing, finance, accounting, business analytics. *Total annual research expenditures:* $1.4 million. *Unit head:* Dr. Michael Hartline, Dean, 850-644-4405, Fax: 850-644-0915, E-mail: mhartline@business.fsu.edu. *Application contact:* Jennifer Clark, Director, 850-644-6458, E-mail: gradprograms@business.fsu.edu.
Website: http://business.fsu.edu/

Florida State University, The Graduate School, College of Communication and Information, School of Information, Tallahassee, FL 32306-2100. Offers information (MA, MS, PhD, Specialist); information studies (MA, MS, PhD, Specialist); information technology (MS). *Accreditation:* ALA (one or more programs are accredited). *Program availability:* Part-time, evening/weekend, 100% online, blended/hybrid learning. *Faculty:* 27 full-time (13 women), 8 part-time/adjunct (5 women). *Students:* 74 full-time (51 women), 244 part-time (182 women); includes 89 minority (30 Black or African American, non-Hispanic/Latino; 10 Asian, non-Hispanic/Latino; 44 Hispanic/Latino; 5 Two or more races, non-Hispanic/Latino), 10 international. Average age 35. 183 applicants, 70% accepted, 97 enrolled. In 2016, 132 master's, 12 doctorates, 1 other advanced degree awarded. Terminal master's awarded for partial completion of doctoral program. *Degree requirements:* For master's, thesis optional, minimum GPA of 3.0, 36 hours (MSI); 32 hours (MSIT); for doctorate, comprehensive exam, thesis/dissertation, dissertation defense, manuscript clearance, minimum GPA of 3.0; for Specialist, minimum GPA of 3.0; 30 hours. *Entrance requirements:* For master's, GRE (recommended minimum percentile of 50 on each of the verbal and quantitative portions and writing score of 4.0), minimum GPA of 3.0 on last 2 years of baccalaureate degree, resume, statement of goals, two letters of recommendation, official transcripts from every college-level institution attended; for doctorate, GRE (recommended minimum percentile of 50 on each of the verbal and quantitative portions and writing score of 4.0), minimum GPA of 3.0 on last degree program, resume, 3 letters of recommendation, personal/goals statement, writing sample, brief digital video, official transcripts from all college-level institutions attended; for Specialist, GRE (recommended minimum percentile of 50 on each of the verbal and quantitative portions and writing score of 4.0), minimum graduate GPA of 3.2, resume, statement of goals, 2 letters of recommendation, writing sample, official transcripts from every college-level institution attended. Additional exam requirements/recommendations for international students: Required—TOEFL (minimum score 585 paper-based; 94 iBT), IELTS (minimum score 6.5). *Application deadline:* For fall admission, 7/1 for domestic and international students; for spring admission, 11/1 for domestic and international students. Applications are processed on a rolling basis. Application fee: $30. Electronic applications accepted. *Expenses:* Contact institution. *Financial support:* In 2016–17, 192 students received support, including 1 research assistantship with full tuition reimbursement available (averaging $18,578 per year), 18 teaching assistantships with full tuition reimbursements available (averaging $18,578 per year); career-related internships or fieldwork, Federal Work-Study, health care benefits, tuition waivers (full), and 13 assistantships (averaging $17,200); 26 scholarships (averaging $1000) also available. Financial award application deadline: 3/1; financial award applicants required to submit FAFSA. *Faculty research:* Information technology, social informatics, health information, human information behavior, youth services. *Total annual research expenditures:* $3.8 million. *Unit head:* Dr. Lorri Mon, Director/Associate Professor, 850-644-5776, Fax: 850-644-9763, E-mail: lmon@fsu.edu. *Application contact:* Student Services, 850-645-3280, Fax: 850-644-9763, E-mail: ischooladvising@admin.fsu.edu.
Website: http://ischool.cci.fsu.edu

Fordham University, Gabelli School of Business, New York, NY 10023. Offers accounting (MBA, MS); applied statistics and decision-making (MS); business administration (EMBA); business analytics (MS); communications and media management (MBA); electronic business (MBA); entrepreneurship (MBA); finance (MBA); global finance (MS); global sustainability (MBA); healthcare management (MBA); information systems (MBA, MS); investor relations (MS); management (MBA, MS); marketing (MBA); marketing intelligence (MS); media management (MS); nonprofit

leadership (MS); quantitative finance (MS); taxation (MS); JD/MBA; MS/MBA. *Accreditation:* AACSB. *Program availability:* Part-time, evening/weekend. *Faculty:* 132 full-time (44 women), 51 part-time/adjunct (7 women). *Students:* 1,117 full-time (668 women), 553 part-time (282 women); includes 207 minority (44 Black or African American, non-Hispanic/Latino; 92 Asian, non-Hispanic/Latino; 69 Hispanic/Latino; 2 Native Hawaiian or other Pacific Islander, non-Hispanic/Latino), 1,088 international. Average age 27. 4,745 applicants, 46% accepted, 752 enrolled. In 2016, 996 master's awarded. Terminal master's awarded for partial completion of doctoral program. *Degree requirements:* For master's, internships (required for MS in quantitative finance, recommended for MBA). *Entrance requirements:* For master's, GMAT/GRE, 2 letters of recommendation, resume, 2 essays, transcripts. Additional exam requirements/recommendations for international students: Required—TOEFL (minimum score 100 iBT), IELTS (minimum score 7). *Application deadline:* For fall admission, 11/15 priority date for domestic and international students; for winter admission, 1/15 priority date for domestic students, 1/1 priority date for international students; for spring admission, 3/1 for domestic and international students; for summer admission, 6/1 for domestic students. Application fee: $130. Electronic applications accepted. *Expenses:* $1,397 per credit. *Financial support:* In 2016–17, 78 students received support. Career-related internships or fieldwork, institutionally sponsored loans, scholarships/grants, and unspecified assistantships available. Support available to part-time students. Financial award application deadline: 6/30; financial award applicants required to submit FAFSA. *Unit head:* Dr. Donna Rapaccioli, Dean, 212-636-6165, Fax: 212-307-1779, E-mail: rapaccioli@fordham.edu. *Application contact:* Lawrence Murray, Senior Assistant Dean of Graduate Admissions and Advising, 212-636-6200, Fax: 212-636-7076, E-mail: admissionsgb@fordham.edu.
Website: http://www.fordham.edu/gabelli

Franklin Pierce University, Graduate and Professional Studies, Rindge, NH 03461-0060. Offers curriculum and instruction (M Ed); elementary education (MS Ed); emerging network technologies (Graduate Certificate); energy and sustainability studies (MBA, Graduate Certificate); health administration (MBA, Graduate Certificate); human resource management (MBA, Graduate Certificate); information technology (MBA); leadership (MBA); nursing education (MS); nursing leadership (MS); physical therapy (DPT); physician assistant studies (MPAS); special education (M Ed); sports management (MBA). *Accreditation:* APTA. *Program availability:* Part-time, 100% online, blended/hybrid learning. *Faculty:* 47 full-time (36 women), 165 part-time/adjunct (108 women). *Students:* 380 full-time (226 women), 245 part-time (158 women); includes 52 minority (13 Black or African American, non-Hispanic/Latino; 2 American Indian or Alaska Native, non-Hispanic/Latino; 14 Asian, non-Hispanic/Latino; 22 Hispanic/Latino; 1 Native Hawaiian or other Pacific Islander, non-Hispanic/Latino), 13 international. Average age 29. 1,995 applicants, 28% accepted, 267 enrolled. In 2016, 120 master's, 86 doctorates awarded. *Degree requirements:* For master's, concentrated original research projects; student teaching; fieldwork and/or internship; leadership project; PRAXIS I and II (for M Ed); for doctorate, concentrated original research projects, clinical fieldwork and/or internship, leadership project. *Entrance requirements:* For master's, minimum GPA of 2.5, 3 letters of recommendation; competencies in accounting, economics, statistics, and computer skills through life experience or undergraduate coursework (for MBA); certification/e-portfolio, minimum C grade in all education courses (for M Ed); license to practice as RN (for MS); for doctorate, GRE, 80 hours of observation/work in PT settings; completion of anatomy, chemistry, physics, and statistics; minimum GPA of 3.0. Additional exam requirements/recommendations for international students: Required—TOEFL (minimum score 550 paper-based; 61 iBT). *Application deadline:* Applications are processed on a rolling basis. Application fee: $0. Electronic applications accepted. *Expenses: Tuition:* Full-time $15,960; part-time $665 per credit hour. Tuition and fees vary according to program. *Financial support:* Teaching assistantships with tuition reimbursements, career-related internships or fieldwork, and unspecified assistantships available. Support available to part-time students. Financial award applicants required to submit FAFSA. *Faculty research:* Evidence-based practice in sports physical therapy, human resource management in economic crisis, leadership in nursing, innovation in sports facility management, differentiated learning and understanding by design. *Unit head:* Dr. Maria Altobello, Dean, 603-647-3509, Fax: 603-229-4580, E-mail: altobellom@franklinpierce.edu. *Application contact:* Graduate Studies, 800-325-1090, Fax: 603-626-4815, E-mail: cgps@franklinpierce.edu.
Website: http://www.franklinpierce.edu/academics/gradstudies/index.htm

Friends University, Graduate School, Wichita, KS 67213. Offers family therapy (MSFT); global business administration (MBA), including accounting, business law, change management, health care leadership, management information systems, supply chain management and logistics; health care leadership (MHCL); management information systems (MMIS); professional business administration (MBA), including accounting, business law, change management, health care leadership, management information systems, supply chain management and logistics. *Program availability:* Part-time, evening/weekend, online learning. *Degree requirements:* For master's, research project. *Entrance requirements:* For master's, bachelor's degree from accredited institution, official transcripts, interview with program director, letter(s) of recommendation. Additional exam requirements/recommendations for international students: Required—TOEFL (minimum score 560 paper-based). Electronic applications accepted.

George Mason University, School of Business, Program in Management of Secure Information Systems, Fairfax, VA 22030. Offers MS. *Faculty:* 6 full-time (1 woman), 2 part-time/adjunct (0 women). *Students:* 21 full-time (2 women); includes 10 minority (3 Black or African American, non-Hispanic/Latino; 2 Asian, non-Hispanic/Latino; 4 Hispanic/Latino; 1 Native Hawaiian or other Pacific Islander, non-Hispanic/Latino), 1 international. Average age 36. In 2016, 29 master's awarded. *Entrance requirements:* For master's, current resume; official copies of transcripts from all colleges or universities attended; two professional letters of recommendation; goal statement; interview. Additional exam requirements/recommendations for international students: Required—TOEFL (minimum score 650 paper-based; 93 iBT), IELTS, PTE. Application fee: $75 ($80 for international students). Electronic applications accepted. *Expenses:* Tuition, state resident: full-time $10,628; part-time $443 per credit. Tuition, nonresident: full-time $29,306; part-time $1221 per credit. *Required fees:* $3096; $129 per credit. Tuition and fees vary according to program. *Financial support:* In 2016–17, 1 student received support, including 1 teaching assistantship (averaging $12,480 per year); career-related internships or fieldwork, Federal Work-Study, and scholarships/grants also available. Support available to part-time students. Financial award applicants required to submit FAFSA. *Unit head:* Kumar Mehta, Director, 703-993-9412, Fax: 703-993-1809, E-mail: kmehta1@gmu.edu. *Application contact:* Jacky Buchy, Assistant Dean of Graduate Enrollment, 703-993-1856, Fax: 703-993-1778, E-mail: jbuchy@gmu.edu.
Website: http://business.gmu.edu/cyber-security-degree/

The George Washington University, School of Business, Department of Information Systems and Technology Management, Washington, DC 20052. Offers information and decision systems (PhD); information systems (MSIST); information systems development (MSIST); information systems management (MBA); information systems project management (MSIST); management information systems (MSIST); management of science, technology, and innovation (MBA, PhD). Programs also offered in Ashburn and Arlington, VA. *Program availability:* Part-time, evening/weekend, online learning. *Faculty:* 13 full-time (4 women). *Students:* 114 full-time (55 women), 74 part-time (30 women); includes 50 minority (15 Black or African American, non-Hispanic/Latino; 28 Asian, non-Hispanic/Latino; 6 Hispanic/Latino; 1 Two or more races, non-Hispanic/Latino), 103 international. Average age 28. 345 applicants, 66% accepted, 67 enrolled. In 2016, 105 master's awarded. *Entrance requirements:* For master's, GMAT. Additional exam requirements/recommendations for international students: Required—TOEFL. *Application deadline:* For fall admission, 4/1 priority date for domestic students; for spring admission, 10/1 for domestic students. Applications are processed on a rolling basis. Application fee: $75. *Financial support:* In 2016–17, 35 students received support. Fellowships, teaching assistantships, career-related internships or fieldwork, Federal Work-Study, institutionally sponsored loans, and tuition waivers available. Financial award application deadline: 4/1. *Faculty research:* Expert systems, decision support systems. *Unit head:* Richard Donnelly, Chair, 202-994-7155, E-mail: rgd@gwu.edu. *Application contact:* Christopher Storer, Executive Director, Graduate Admissions, 202-994-1212, E-mail: gwmba@gwu.edu.

Georgia College & State University, Graduate School, The J. Whitney Bunting School of Business, Program in Management Information Systems, Milledgeville, GA 31061. Offers MMIS. *Program availability:* Part-time. *Students:* 3 full-time (all women), 23 part-time (6 women); includes 10 minority (5 Black or African American, non-Hispanic/Latino; 4 Asian, non-Hispanic/Latino; 1 Hispanic/Latino), 2 international. Average age 32. 11 applicants, 100% accepted, 10 enrolled. In 2016, 10 master's awarded. *Degree requirements:* For master's, minimum GPA of 3.0, complete program within 7 years of start date. *Entrance requirements:* For master's, GRE or GMAT, transcript, certificate of immunization. *Application deadline:* For fall admission, 7/1 priority date for domestic students; for spring admission, 11/1 priority date for domestic students; for summer admission, 4/1 priority date for domestic students. Applications are processed on a rolling basis. Application fee: $40. Electronic applications accepted. *Expenses:* $288 per credit hour in-state, $1,027 per credit hour out-of-state, $1,990 full-time annual fees. *Financial support:* In 2016–17, 5 students received support. Unspecified assistantships available. Financial award application deadline: 3/1; financial award applicants required to submit FAFSA. *Unit head:* Dr. Dale Young, Dean, School of Business, 478-445-5497, E-mail: dale.young@gcsu.edu. *Application contact:* Lynn Hanson, Director of Graduate Programs, 478-445-5115, E-mail: lynn.hanson@gcsu.edu.
Website: http://www.gcsu.edu/business/graduateprograms/mmis.htm

Georgia Institute of Technology, Graduate Studies, Scheller College of Business, Program in Business Administration, Atlanta, GA 30332-0001. Offers business administration (MBA); global business (MBA); management of technology (MBA). *Accreditation:* AACSB. *Program availability:* Part-time, evening/weekend. *Entrance requirements:* For master's, GMAT, two essays, three letters of recommendation, transcript from each college/university attended. Additional exam requirements/recommendations for international students: Required—TOEFL (minimum score 600 paper-based; 100 iBT). Electronic applications accepted. *Expenses:* Contact institution.

Georgia Southern University, Jack N. Averitt College of Graduate Studies, Allen E. Paulson College of Engineering and Information Technology, Program in Information Technology, Statesboro, GA 30458. Offers MSAE. *Program availability:* Part-time. *Students:* 10 full-time (3 women), 9 part-time (4 women); includes 2 minority (1 Black or African American, non-Hispanic/Latino; 1 Hispanic/Latino), 9 international. Average age 33. In 2016, 4 master's awarded. *Degree requirements:* For master's, comprehensive exam (for some programs), thesis (for some programs). *Entrance requirements:* For master's, GRE. Additional exam requirements/recommendations for international students: Required—TOEFL (minimum score 550 paper-based; 80 iBT), IELTS (minimum score 6). *Application deadline:* For fall admission, 3/1 priority date for domestic and international students; for spring admission, 11/1 priority date for domestic and international students. Application fee: $50. Electronic applications accepted. *Expenses:* Tuition, state resident: full-time $7236; part-time $277 per semester hour. Tuition, nonresident: full-time $27,118; part-time $1105 per semester hour. *Required fees:* $2092. *Financial support:* In 2016–17, 2 students received support. Unspecified assistantships available. Financial award application deadline: 4/20; financial award applicants required to submit FAFSA. *Faculty research:* Electrical systems, information technology, electromagnetics, digital control systems, applied engineering. *Total annual research expenditures:* $22,323. *Unit head:* Dr. Biswanath Samanta, Chair, 912-478-0334, E-mail: bsamanta@georgiasouthern.edu.
Website: http://ceit.georgiasouthern.edu/it/

Georgia Southern University, Jack N. Averitt College of Graduate Studies, College of Business Administration, Enterprise Resources Planning Certificate Program, Statesboro, GA 30458. Offers Graduate Certificate. *Program availability:* Part-time, blended/hybrid learning. *Students:* 7 part-time (6 women); includes 4 minority (all Black or African American, non-Hispanic/Latino). Average age 41. 8 applicants, 88% accepted, 5 enrolled. In 2016, 8 Graduate Certificates awarded. *Entrance requirements:* For degree, bachelor's degree or equivalent with minimum cumulative GPA of 2.7; official copies of all transcripts; resume with three references; personal statement. Additional exam requirements/recommendations for international students: Required—TOEFL (minimum score 550 paper-based), IELTS (minimum score 6). *Application deadline:* For fall admission, 6/15 for domestic students. Application fee: $50. Electronic applications accepted. *Expenses:* Contact institution. *Financial support:* In 2016–17, 15 fellowships with full tuition reimbursements (averaging $7,750 per year), 1 research assistantship with full tuition reimbursement (averaging $7,750 per year), 1 teaching assistantship with full tuition reimbursement (averaging $7,750 per year) were awarded; scholarships/grants and unspecified assistantships also available. Financial award application deadline: 4/20; financial award applicants required to submit FAFSA. *Faculty research:* Enterprise resource planning (ERP) and business intelligence (BI) synergies, cloud-based and on-demand ERP solutions, IT artifact in ERP-centered supply chain information systems, impact of bring your own device (BYOD) policies on deployment of enterprise systems mobile applications, career readiness of SAP University Alliances students for positions in ERP user and consulting firms. *Unit head:* Dr. Camille Rogers, Program Coordinator, 912-478-0194, E-mail: cfrogers@georgiasouthern.edu.
Website: http://coba.georgiasouthern.edu/is/degrees/online-erp-program/

Georgia Southern University, Jack N. Averitt College of Graduate Studies, College of Business Administration, Program in Applied Economics, Statesboro, GA 30460. Offers applied economics (MS); information systems (Graduate Certificate). *Program availability:* Part-time, evening/weekend, blended/hybrid learning. *Students:* 2 full-time (both women), 21 part-time (6 women); includes 4 minority (2 Black or African American, non-Hispanic/Latino; 1 Asian, non-Hispanic/Latino; 1 Hispanic/Latino), 2 international. Average age 36. 20 applicants, 55% accepted, 9 enrolled. In 2016, 19 master's awarded. *Entrance requirements:* For master's, GRE or GMAT, minimum GPA of 3.0. Additional exam requirements/recommendations for international students: Required—TOEFL (minimum score 550 paper-based; 80 iBT), IELTS (minimum score 6). *Application deadline:* For fall admission, 3/1 for domestic and international students; for spring admission, 10/1 priority date for domestic students, 10/1 for international students. Applications are processed on a rolling basis. Application fee: $50. Electronic applications accepted. *Expenses:* Tuition, state resident: full-time $7236; part-time $277 per semester hour. Tuition, nonresident: full-time $27,118; part-time $1105 per

semester hour. *Required fees:* $2092. *Financial support:* Unspecified assistantships available. Financial award application deadline: 4/15; financial award applicants required to submit FAFSA. *Faculty research:* Analytical capabilities in economic development, financial economics, regulatory issues, market analysis, economic development. *Unit head:* Dr. Gordon Smith, Graduate Program Director, 912-478-2357, Fax: 912-478-0710, E-mail: gsmith@georgiasouthern.edu.
Website: http://coba.georgiasouthern.edu/dfe/graduate/master-of-science-in-applied-economics/

Georgia Southwestern State University, School of Computing and Mathematics, Americus, GA 31709-4693. Offers computer information systems (Graduate Certificate); computer science (MS). *Program availability:* Part-time, 100% online, blended/hybrid learning. *Faculty:* 3 full-time (0 women), 1 part-time/adjunct (0 women). *Students:* 7 full-time (0 women), 11 part-time (3 women); includes 5 minority (2 Black or African American, non-Hispanic/Latino; 3 Asian, non-Hispanic/Latino), 8 international. Average age 34. 23 applicants, 57% accepted, 7 enrolled. In 2016, 5 master's, 1 other advanced degree awarded. *Degree requirements:* For master's, thesis optional, minimum cumulative GPA of 3.0; maximum of 6 credit hours with C grade; no courses with D grade; degree must be completed within 7 calendar years from date of initial enrollment in graduate course work; for Graduate Certificate, minimum cumulative GPA of 3.0; maximum of 6 credit hours with C grade; no courses with D grade; degree must be completed within 7 calendar years from date of initial enrollment in graduate course work. *Entrance requirements:* For master's and Graduate Certificate, GRE, bachelor's degree from regionally-accredited college; minimum undergraduate GPA of 2.5 as reported on official final transcripts from all institutions attended; letters of recommendation. Additional exam requirements/recommendations for international students: Required—TOEFL (minimum score 523 paper-based; 69 iBT), IELTS (minimum score 6.5). *Application deadline:* For fall admission, 5/31 for domestic students; for spring admission, 10/15 for domestic students; for summer admission, 3/15 for domestic students. Applications are processed on a rolling basis. Application fee: $25. Electronic applications accepted. *Expenses:* $257 per credit hour for online program courses, plus fees, which vary according to enrolled credit hours. *Financial support:* Application deadline: 6/1; applicants required to submit FAFSA. *Unit head:* Dr. Boris V. Peltsverger, Dean, 229-931-2100. *Application contact:* Whitney Ford, Admissions Specialist, Office of Graduate Admission, 800-338-0082, Fax: 229-931-2983.
Website: https://gsw.edu/Academics/Schools-and-Departments/School-of-Computing-and-Mathematics/index

Georgia State University, J. Mack Robinson College of Business, Department of Computer Information Systems, Atlanta, GA 30302-3083. Offers computer information systems (PhD); health informatics (MBA, MS); information systems (MSIS, Certificate); information systems development and project management (MBA); information systems management (MBA); managing information technology (Exec MS); the wireless organization (MBA). *Program availability:* Part-time, evening/weekend. *Faculty:* 24 full-time (2 women). *Students:* 209 full-time (84 women), 7 part-time (3 women); includes 41 minority (20 Black or African American, non-Hispanic/Latino; 16 Asian, non-Hispanic/Latino; 4 Hispanic/Latino; 1 Two or more races, non-Hispanic/Latino), 158 international. Average age 28. 587 applicants, 56% accepted, 138 enrolled. In 2016, 126 master's, 4 doctorates awarded. *Degree requirements:* For master's, thesis optional; for doctorate, comprehensive exam, thesis/dissertation. *Entrance requirements:* For master's, GRE or GMAT, transcripts from all institutions attended, resume, essays; for doctorate, GRE or GMAT, three letters of recommendation, personal statement, transcripts from all institutions attended, resume. Additional exam requirements/recommendations for international students: Required—TOEFL (minimum score 610 paper-based; 101 iBT), IELTS (minimum score 7). *Application deadline:* For fall admission, 5/1 priority date for domestic students, 2/1 priority date for international students; for spring admission, 9/15 priority date for domestic students, 4/1 priority date for international students. Applications are processed on a rolling basis. Application fee: $50. Electronic applications accepted. *Expenses:* Tuition, state resident: full-time $6876; part-time $382 per credit hour. Tuition, nonresident: full-time $22,374; part-time $1243 per credit hour. *Required fees:* $2128; $1064 per term. Part-time tuition and fees vary according to course load and program. *Financial support:* Research assistantships, teaching assistantships, scholarships/grants, tuition waivers, and unspecified assistantships available. Financial award applicants required to submit FAFSA. *Faculty research:* Process and technological innovation, strategic IT management, intelligent systems, information systems security, software project risk. *Unit head:* Dr. Ephraim R. McLean, Professor/Chair, 404-413-7360, Fax: 404-413-7394. *Application contact:* Toby McChesney, Assistant Dean for Graduate Recruiting and Student Services, 404-413-7167, Fax: 404-413-7167, E-mail: rcbgradadmissions@gsu.edu.
Website: http://cis.robinson.gsu.edu/

Georgia State University, J. Mack Robinson College of Business, Institute of International Business, Atlanta, GA 30303. Offers international business (GMBA, MBA, MIB); international business and information technology (MBA); international entrepreneurship (MBA); MIB/MIA. *Program availability:* Part-time, evening/weekend. *Faculty:* 11 full-time (4 women). *Students:* 22 full-time (14 women), 14 part-time (9 women); includes 20 minority (15 Black or African American, non-Hispanic/Latino; 4 Hispanic/Latino; 1 Two or more races, non-Hispanic/Latino), 5 international. Average age 31. 22 applicants, 27% accepted, 1 enrolled. In 2016, 31 master's awarded. *Entrance requirements:* For master's, GRE or GMAT, transcripts from all institutions attended, resume, essays. Additional exam requirements/recommendations for international students: Required—TOEFL (minimum score 610 paper-based; 101 iBT), IELTS (minimum score 7). *Application deadline:* For fall admission, 5/1 priority date for domestic students, 2/1 priority date for international students; for spring admission, 9/15 priority date for domestic students, 5/1 priority date for international students. Applications are processed on a rolling basis. Application fee: $50. Electronic applications accepted. *Expenses:* Tuition, state resident: full-time $6876; part-time $382 per credit hour. Tuition, nonresident: full-time $22,374; part-time $1243 per credit hour. *Required fees:* $2128; $1064 per term. Part-time tuition and fees vary according to course load and program. *Financial support:* Research assistantships, teaching assistantships, scholarships/grants, tuition waivers (partial), and unspecified assistantships available. Financial award application deadline: 5/1. *Faculty research:* Business challenges in emerging markets (especially in India and China); interorganizational relationships in an international context, such as strategic alliances and global supply chain relations; globalization and entry mode strategy or new (or emerging) multinationals; emerging market development and business environments; cross-cultural effects on business processes and performance. *Unit head:* Dr. Daniel Bello, Professor/Director of the Institute of International Business, 404-413-7275, Fax: 404-413-7276. *Application contact:* Toby McChesney, Assistant Dean for Graduate Recruiting and Student Services, 404-413-7167, Fax: 404-413-7162, E-mail: rcbgradadmissions@gsu.edu.
Website: http://iib.gsu.edu/

Golden Gate University, Ageno School of Business, San Francisco, CA 94105-2968. Offers accounting (MBA); business administration (EMBA, MBA, PMBA, DBA); business analytics (MS); finance (MBA, MS, Certificate); financial planning (MS, Certificate); healthcare information systems (Certificate); human resource management (MBA, MS); human resources management (Certificate); information systems (MS); information technology (MBA); information technology management (Certificate); integrated marketing and communications (MS, Certificate); international business (MBA); management (MBA); marketing (MBA, MS, Certificate); operations supply chain management (Certificate); psychology (MA, Certificate); public administration (EMPA); public relations (MS, Certificate); technical market analysis (Certificate); JD/MBA. *Program availability:* Part-time, evening/weekend. *Faculty:* 18 full-time (3 women), 117 part-time/adjunct (44 women). *Students:* 458 full-time (254 women), 664 part-time (331 women); includes 346 minority (75 Black or African American, non-Hispanic/Latino; 2 American Indian or Alaska Native, non-Hispanic/Latino; 132 Asian, non-Hispanic/Latino; 105 Hispanic/Latino; 9 Native Hawaiian or other Pacific Islander, non-Hispanic/Latino; 23 Two or more races, non-Hispanic/Latino), 354 international. Average age 34. 905 applicants, 83% accepted, 165 enrolled. In 2016, 350 master's, 2 doctorates awarded. *Degree requirements:* For doctorate, thesis/dissertation, qualifying examination. *Entrance requirements:* For master's, GMAT (for MBA), minimum GPA of 2.5 (MS). Additional exam requirements/recommendations for international students: Required—TOEFL (minimum score 550 paper-based; 79 iBT). *Application deadline:* For fall admission, 5/15 for domestic and international students; for winter admission, 1/15 for domestic and international students; for spring admission, 9/15 for domestic and international students. Applications are processed on a rolling basis. Application fee: $70 ($110 for international students). Electronic applications accepted. *Expenses:* Contact institution. *Financial support:* In 2016–17, 372 students received support. Career-related internships or fieldwork, Federal Work-Study, institutionally sponsored loans, and scholarships/grants available. Support available to part-time students. Financial award applicants required to submit FAFSA. *Unit head:* Dr. Gordon Swartz, Dean, 415-442-7027, Fax: 415-442-6579, E-mail: gswartz@ggu.edu. *Application contact:* Angela Melero, Enrollment Services, 415-442-7800, Fax: 415-442-7807, E-mail: info@ggu.edu.
Website: http://www.ggu.edu/programs/business-and-management

Goldey-Beacom College, Graduate Program, Wilmington, DE 19808-1999. Offers business administration (MBA); finance (MS); financial management (MBA); health care management (MBA); human resource management (MBA); information technology (MBA); international business management (MBA); major finance (MBA); major taxation (MBA); management (MM); marketing management (MBA); taxation (MBA, MS). *Accreditation:* ACBSP. *Program availability:* Part-time, evening/weekend. *Entrance requirements:* For master's, GMAT, MAT, GRE, minimum GPA of 3.0. Additional exam requirements/recommendations for international students: Required—TOEFL (minimum score 65 iBT); Recommended—IELTS (minimum score 6). Electronic applications accepted.

Governors State University, College of Business, Program in Management Information Systems, University Park, IL 60484. Offers MS. *Program availability:* Part-time. *Faculty:* 25 full-time (9 women), 30 part-time/adjunct (10 women). *Students:* 19 full-time (6 women), 10 part-time (2 women); includes 6 minority (5 Black or African American, non-Hispanic/Latino; 1 Hispanic/Latino), 21 international. Average age 30. 267 applicants, 28% accepted, 16 enrolled. In 2016, 4 master's awarded. *Entrance requirements:* Additional exam requirements/recommendations for international students: Required—TOEFL (minimum score 550 paper-based; 80 iBT), IELTS. *Application deadline:* For fall admission, 4/1 for domestic students. Application fee: $50. Electronic applications accepted. *Expenses:* $307 per credit hour; $38 per term or $76 per credit hour fees. *Financial support:* Application deadline: 5/1; applicants required to submit FAFSA. *Unit head:* David Green, Chair of Division of Accounting, Finance, Management and Entrepreneurship, 708-534-4967, E-mail: dgreen@govst.edu. *Application contact:* Yakeea Daniels, Assistant Vice President for Enrollment Services/Director of Admission, 708-534-4510, E-mail: ydaniels@govst.edu.

The Graduate Center, City University of New York, Graduate Studies, Program in Business, New York, NY 10016-4039. Offers accounting (PhD); behavioral science (PhD); finance (PhD); management planning systems (PhD). *Degree requirements:* For doctorate, thesis/dissertation. *Entrance requirements:* For doctorate, GMAT, writing sample (15 pages). Additional exam requirements/recommendations for international students: Required—TOEFL. Electronic applications accepted.

Grand Valley State University, Padnos College of Engineering and Computing, School of Computing and Information Systems, Allendale, MI 49401-9403. Offers computer information systems (MS), including databases, distributed systems, management of information systems, object-oriented systems, software engineering. *Program availability:* Part-time, evening/weekend. *Faculty:* 10 full-time (3 women), 1 (woman) part-time/adjunct. *Students:* 28 full-time (3 women), 57 part-time (14 women); includes 11 minority (3 Black or African American, non-Hispanic/Latino; 4 Asian, non-Hispanic/Latino; 3 Hispanic/Latino; 1 Two or more races, non-Hispanic/Latino), 32 international. Average age 30. 97 applicants, 59% accepted, 17 enrolled. In 2016, 36 master's awarded. *Degree requirements:* For master's, capstone course, project, or thesis. *Entrance requirements:* For master's, GMAT or GRE General Test, minimum GPA of 3.0; knowledge of a programming language; coursework or experience in: computer architecture and/or organization, data structures and algorithms, databases, discrete math, networking, operating systems, and software engineering; minimum of 2 letters of recommendation; resume; personal statement. Additional exam requirements/recommendations for international students: Required—TOEFL, Michigan English Language Assessment Battery or completion of ELS 112; Recommended—IELTS. *Application deadline:* For fall admission, 6/1 for international students; for winter admission, 9/1 for international students. Applications are processed on a rolling basis. Application fee: $30. Electronic applications accepted. *Expenses:* $646 per credit hour. *Financial support:* In 2016–17, 11 students received support, including 3 fellowships, 10 research assistantships with full and partial tuition reimbursements available (averaging $8,000 per year). *Faculty research:* Object technology, distributed computing, information systems management database, software engineering. *Unit head:* Dr. Paul Leidig, Director, 616-331-2038, Fax: 616-331-2106, E-mail: leidigp@gvsu.edu. *Application contact:* Dr. D. Robert Adams, Graduate Program Director/Recruiting Contact, 616-331-3885, Fax: 616-331-2106, E-mail: adams@cis.gvsu.edu.
Website: http://www.cis.gvsu.edu/

Grantham University, College of Engineering and Computer Science, Lenexa, KS 66219. Offers information management (MS), including project management; information technology (MS). *Program availability:* Part-time, online only, 100% online. *Faculty:* 12 part-time/adjunct. *Students:* 15 full-time (7 women), 244 part-time (56 women); includes 114 minority (81 Black or African American, non-Hispanic/Latino; 4 American Indian or Alaska Native, non-Hispanic/Latino; 8 Asian, non-Hispanic/Latino; 12 Hispanic/Latino; 9 Two or more races, non-Hispanic/Latino). Average age 40. 293 applicants, 96% accepted, 260 enrolled. In 2016, 78 master's awarded. *Degree requirements:* For master's, comprehensive exam (for information management); capstone (for information technology). *Entrance requirements:* For master's, baccalaureate or master's degree with minimum cumulative GPA of 2.5 from institution accredited by agency recognized by U.S. Department of Education or foreign equivalent. Additional exam requirements/recommendations for international students: Required—PTE (minimum score 50), TOEFL (minimum score 530 paper-based, 71 iBT) or IELTS (minimum score 6.5). *Application deadline:* Applications are processed on a rolling

basis. Electronic applications accepted. *Expenses:* $325 per credit hour, $45 per 8-week term technology fee. *Financial support:* Scholarships/grants available. Financial award applicants required to submit FAFSA. *Unit head:* Dr. Nancy Miller, Dean of the College of Engineering and Computer Sciences, 913-309-4738, Fax: 855-681-5201, E-mail: nmiller@grantham.edu. *Application contact:* Jared Parlette, Vice President of Student Enrollment, 888-947-2684, Fax: 866-908-2360, E-mail: admissions@grantham.edu.
Website: http://www.grantham.edu/engineering-and-computer-science/

Grantham University, Mark Skousen School of Business, Lenexa, KS 66219. Offers business administration (MBA); business intelligence (MS); human resources management (Certificate); information management (MBA); performance improvement (MS); project management (MBA, Certificate). *Program availability:* Part-time, online only, 100% online. *Faculty:* 1 full-time, 36 part-time/adjunct. *Students:* 73 full-time (37 women), 1,046 part-time (424 women); includes 442 minority (309 Black or African American, non-Hispanic/Latino; 8 American Indian or Alaska Native, non-Hispanic/Latino; 27 Asian, non-Hispanic/Latino; 63 Hispanic/Latino; 7 Native Hawaiian or other Pacific Islander, non-Hispanic/Latino; 28 Two or more races, non-Hispanic/Latino). Average age 40. 1,324 applicants, 95% accepted, 1123 enrolled. In 2016, 331 master's awarded. *Degree requirements:* For master's, capstone project, PMP Prep Exam; for Certificate, comprehensive exam (for some programs), PMP Prep Exam. *Entrance requirements:* For master's, baccalaureate or master's degree with minimum cumulative GPA of 2.5 from institution accredited by agency recognized by U.S. Department of Education or foreign equivalent. Additional exam requirements/recommendations for international students: Required—PTE (minimum score 50), TOEFL (minimum score 530 paper-based, 71 iBT) or IELTS (minimum score 6.5). *Application deadline:* Applications are processed on a rolling basis. Electronic applications accepted. *Expenses:* $325 per credit hour, $45 per 8-week term technology fee. *Financial support:* Scholarships/grants available. Financial award applicants required to submit FAFSA. *Faculty research:* Organizational structures, e-discovery and project management, decision management, resource-based and ethical perspectives, external finance dependence in corporate investments. *Unit head:* Dr. David Marker, Dean, Mark Skousen School of Business, 800-955-2527, E-mail: dmarker@grantham.edu. *Application contact:* Jared Parlette, Vice President of Student Enrollment, 800-955-2527, E-mail: admissions@grantham.edu.
Website: http://www.grantham.edu/colleges-and-schools/school-of-business/

Harrisburg University of Science and Technology, Program in Information Systems Engineering and Management, Harrisburg, PA 17101. Offers analytics (MS); digital government (MS); digital health (MS); entrepreneurship (MS); information security (MS); software engineering and systems development (MS). *Program availability:* Part-time, evening/weekend. *Faculty:* 9 full-time (0 women), 1 (woman) part-time/adjunct. *Students:* 1,031 full-time (264 women), 35 part-time (10 women); includes 2 minority (1 Black or African American, non-Hispanic/Latino; 1 Asian, non-Hispanic/Latino), 1,060 international. In 2016, 83 master's awarded. *Degree requirements:* For master's, thesis optional. *Entrance requirements:* For master's, baccalaureate degree. Additional exam requirements/recommendations for international students: Required—TOEFL (minimum score 520 paper-based; 80 iBT); Recommended—IELTS (minimum score 6). *Application deadline:* Applications are processed on a rolling basis. Application fee: $0. Electronic applications accepted. *Expenses: Tuition:* Full-time $4800; part-time $800 per semester hour. *Financial support:* In 2016–17, 2 students received support. Teaching assistantships available. Financial award applicants required to submit FAFSA. *Faculty research:* Healthcare Informatics, material analysis, enterprise systems, circuit design, enterprise architectures. *Unit head:* Dr. Amjad Umar, Director and Professor, 717-901-5141, Fax: 717-901-3141, E-mail: aumar@harrisburgu.edu.

Hawai`i Pacific University, College of Business, Program in Business Administration, Honolulu, HI 96813. Offers accounting (MBA); economics (MBA); finance (MBA); hospitality and tourism management (MBA); human resource management (MBA); information systems (MBA); international business (MBA); management (MBA); marketing (MBA); organizational change and development (MBA). *Program availability:* Part-time, evening/weekend, online learning. *Faculty:* 13 full-time (4 women), 1 part-time/adjunct (0 women). *Students:* 106 full-time (47 women), 33 part-time (13 women); includes 66 minority (5 Black or African American, non-Hispanic/Latino; 1 American Indian or Alaska Native, non-Hispanic/Latino; 23 Asian, non-Hispanic/Latino; 11 Hispanic/Latino; 1 Native Hawaiian or other Pacific Islander, non-Hispanic/Latino; 25 Two or more races, non-Hispanic/Latino), 36 international. Average age 33. 77 applicants, 84% accepted, 44 enrolled. In 2016, 78 master's awarded. *Entrance requirements:* For master's, GMAT or GRE. Additional exam requirements/recommendations for international students: Recommended—TOEFL (minimum score 550 paper-based; 80 iBT), IELTS (minimum score 6), TWE (minimum score 5). *Application deadline:* For fall admission, 2/15 priority date for domestic students; for spring admission, 10/15 priority date for domestic students. Applications are processed on a rolling basis. Application fee: $50. Electronic applications accepted. *Expenses: Tuition:* Full-time $17,190; part-time $955 per credit. *Required fees:* $150; $26 per credit. Tuition and fees vary according to course load and program. *Financial support:* In 2016–17, 27 students received support. Research assistantships, career-related internships or fieldwork, Federal Work-Study, scholarships/grants, tuition waivers, and unspecified assistantships available. Financial award application deadline: 3/1; financial award applicants required to submit FAFSA. *Unit head:* Dr. Warren Wee, Associate Dean/Associate Professor of Accounting, 808-544-9325, E-mail: wwee@hpu.edu. *Application contact:* Danny Lam, Assistant Director of Graduate Admissions, 808-544-1135, E-mail: graduate@hpu.edu.
Website: http://www.hpu.edu/CBA/Graduate/MBA/index.html

Hawai`i Pacific University, College of Business, Program in Information Systems, Honolulu, HI 96813. Offers MSIS. *Program availability:* Part-time, evening/weekend. *Faculty:* 5 full-time (2 women), 5 part-time/adjunct (0 women). *Students:* 16 full-time (4 women), 16 part-time (3 women); includes 17 minority (1 Black or African American, non-Hispanic/Latino; 8 Asian, non-Hispanic/Latino; 1 Hispanic/Latino; 2 Native Hawaiian or other Pacific Islander, non-Hispanic/Latino; 5 Two or more races, non-Hispanic/Latino), 4 international. Average age 33. 26 applicants, 77% accepted, 13 enrolled. In 2016, 33 master's awarded. *Entrance requirements:* For master's, GMAT or GRE. Additional exam requirements/recommendations for international students: Recommended—TOEFL (minimum score 550 paper-based; 80 iBT), IELTS (minimum score 6), TWE (minimum score 5). *Application deadline:* For fall admission, 2/15 priority date for domestic students; for spring admission, 10/15 priority date for domestic students. Applications are processed on a rolling basis. Application fee: $50. Electronic applications accepted. *Expenses: Tuition:* Full-time $17,190; part-time $955 per credit. *Required fees:* $150; $26 per credit. Tuition and fees vary according to course load and program. *Financial support:* Research assistantships, career-related internships or fieldwork, Federal Work-Study, scholarships/grants, tuition waivers, and unspecified assistantships available. Financial award application deadline: 3/1; financial award applicants required to submit FAFSA. *Unit head:* Dr. Lawrence Rowland, Department Chair, 808-544-1468, E-mail: lrowland@hpu.edu. *Application contact:* Danny Lam, Assistant Director of Graduate Admissions, 808-544-1135, E-mail: graduate@hpu.edu.
Website: http://www.hpu.edu/CBA/Graduate/MSIS.html

HEC Montreal, School of Business Administration, Master of Science Programs in Administration, Program in Information Technologies, Montréal, QC H3T 2A7, Canada. Offers M Sc. All courses are given in French. *Students:* 30 full-time (7 women), 12 part-time (1 woman). 26 applicants, 58% accepted, 10 enrolled. In 2016, 14 master's awarded. *Degree requirements:* For master's, one foreign language, thesis. *Entrance requirements:* For master's, Test de francais international (TFI) with minimum score of 850 (for those who have never studied in French), BBA, undergraduate degree in another field, degree deemed equivalent by program director and minimum GPA of 3.0 on 4.3 scale. *Application deadline:* For fall admission, 3/15 for domestic and international students; for winter admission, 9/15 for domestic and international students. Application fee: $86 Canadian dollars. Electronic applications accepted. *Expenses: Tuition, area resident:* Part-time $77.80 Canadian dollars per credit. Tuition, state resident: full-time $2797 Canadian dollars; part-time $240.92 Canadian dollars per credit. Tuition, nonresident: full-time $8673 Canadian dollars; part-time $531.43 Canadian dollars per credit. *International tuition:* $19,131 Canadian dollars full-time. *Required fees:* $1699 Canadian dollars; $40.58 Canadian dollars per credit. $67.32 Canadian dollars per term. Tuition and fees vary according to degree level and program. *Financial support:* Research assistantships, teaching assistantships, and scholarships/grants available. Financial award application deadline: 9/2. *Unit head:* Dr. Marie-Helene Jobin, Director, 514-340-6283, E-mail: marie-helene.jobin@hec.ca. *Application contact:* Marianne de Moura, Administrative Director, 514-340-7106, Fax: 514-340-6411, E-mail: marianne.de-moura@hec.ca.
Website: http://www.hec.ca/programmes/maitrises/maitrise-technologies-information/index.html

Hodges University, Graduate Programs, Naples, FL 34119. Offers accounting (M Acc); business administration (MBA); clinical mental health counseling (MS); health services administration (MS); information systems management (MIS); legal studies (MS); management (MSM). *Program availability:* Part-time, evening/weekend, 100% online, blended/hybrid learning. *Degree requirements:* For master's, comprehensive exam (for some programs), thesis (for some programs). *Entrance requirements:* For master's, essay. Additional exam requirements/recommendations for international students: Recommended—TOEFL. Electronic applications accepted.

Hofstra University, Frank G. Zarb School of Business, Programs in Information Systems, Hempstead, NY 11549. Offers business administration (MBA), including business analytics, information systems, quality management; information systems (MS, Advanced Certificate). *Program availability:* Part-time, evening/weekend, blended/hybrid learning. *Students:* 59 full-time (27 women), 14 part-time (7 women); includes 11 minority (1 Black or African American, non-Hispanic/Latino; 7 Asian, non-Hispanic/Latino; 3 Hispanic/Latino), 50 international. Average age 28. 95 applicants, 56% accepted, 20 enrolled. In 2016, 28 master's awarded. *Degree requirements:* For master's, capstone course (for MBA), thesis (for MS), minimum GPA of 3.0. *Entrance requirements:* For master's, GMAT/GRE, 2 letters of recommendation, resume, essay; for Advanced Certificate, GMAT/GRE, 2 letters of recommendation, resume. Additional exam requirements/recommendations for international students: Required—TOEFL (minimum score 550 paper-based; 80 iBT); Recommended—IELTS (minimum score 6). *Application deadline:* Applications are processed on a rolling basis. Application fee: $75. Electronic applications accepted. *Expenses:* $1,170 per credit. *Financial support:* In 2016–17, 26 students received support, including 26 fellowships with full and partial tuition reimbursements available (averaging $5,034 per year); research assistantships with full and partial tuition reimbursements available, career-related internships or fieldwork, Federal Work-Study, institutionally sponsored loans, scholarships/grants, tuition waivers (full and partial), and unspecified assistantships also available. Support available to part-time students. Financial award applicants required to submit FAFSA. *Faculty research:* Health information systems, healthcare data analytics; text mining and data mining; cybersecurity and digital forensics. *Unit head:* Dr. Hak Kim, Chairperson, 516-463-5716, Fax: 516-463-4834, E-mail: hak.j.kim@hofstra.edu. *Application contact:* Sunil Samuel, Assistant Vice President of Admissions, 516-463-4723, Fax: 516-463-4664, E-mail: graduateadmission@hofstra.edu.
Website: http://www.hofstra.edu/business/

Holy Family University, Graduate and Professional Programs, School of Business Administration, Philadelphia, PA 19114. Offers accountancy (MS); finance (MBA); health care administration (MBA); human resource management (MBA); information systems management (MBA). *Accreditation:* ACBSP. *Program availability:* Part-time, evening/weekend. *Students:* 140 part-time. 58 applicants, 78% accepted, 42 enrolled. In 2016, 44 master's awarded. *Degree requirements:* For master's, comprehensive exam, thesis optional. *Entrance requirements:* For master's, minimum GPA of 3.0, interview, essay/personal statement, current resume, official transcript of all college or university work. Additional exam requirements/recommendations for international students: Required—TOEFL (minimum score 550 paper-based; 79 iBT), IELTS (minimum score 6), PTE (minimum score 54). *Application deadline:* For fall admission, 7/1 priority date for domestic and international students; for winter admission, 1/1 for domestic students; for spring admission, 11/1 priority date for domestic and international students; for summer admission, 4/1 priority date for domestic and international students. Applications are processed on a rolling basis. Application fee: $25. Electronic applications accepted. *Expenses: Tuition:* Part-time $751 per hour. *Required fees:* $140 per semester. One-time fee: $165 part-time. Part-time tuition and fees vary according to degree level and program. *Financial support:* Available to part-time students. Application deadline: 5/1; applicants required to submit FAFSA. *Unit head:* Dr. Barry Dickinson, Dean, 267-341-3440, Fax: 215-637-5937, E-mail: jdickinson@holyfamily.edu. *Application contact:* Gidget Marie Montelibano, Associate Director of Graduate Admissions, 267-341-3558, Fax: 215-637-1478, E-mail: gmontelibano@holyfamily.edu.
Website: http://www.holyfamily.edu/choosing-holy-family-u/academics/schools-of-study/school-of-business-administration

Hood College, Graduate School, Department of Economics and Business Administration, Frederick, MD 21701-8575. Offers accounting (MBA); finance (MBA); human resource management (MBA); information systems (MBA); marketing (MBA); public management (MBA). *Accreditation:* ACBSP. *Program availability:* Part-time, evening/weekend. *Faculty:* 4 full-time, 8 part-time/adjunct. *Students:* 21 full-time (13 women), 106 part-time (60 women); includes 23 minority (12 Black or African American, non-Hispanic/Latino; 4 Asian, non-Hispanic/Latino; 6 Hispanic/Latino; 1 Two or more races, non-Hispanic/Latino), 15 international. Average age 32. 44 applicants, 91% accepted, 25 enrolled. In 2016, 45 master's awarded. *Degree requirements:* For master's, capstone/final research project. *Entrance requirements:* For master's, minimum GPA of 3.0 (or resume and two letters of recommendation), copy of official transcripts, essay. Additional exam requirements/recommendations for international students: Required—TOEFL (minimum score 575 paper-based; 89 iBT), IELTS (minimum score 6.5). *Application deadline:* For fall admission, 8/15 for domestic students, 8/5 for international students; for spring admission, 12/1 for domestic and international students; for summer admission, 5/1 for domestic students, 4/15 for international students. Applications are processed on a rolling basis. Application fee: $35. Electronic applications accepted. *Expenses:* $525 per credit; $110 comprehensive fee per semester. *Financial support:* Tuition waivers (partial) and unspecified assistantships available. Financial award applicants required to submit FAFSA. *Faculty research:* Corporate strategy and sustainable competitive advantages, business ethics, entrepreneurship, investments management, economic development. *Unit head:* April Boulton, Interim Dean of the Graduate School, 301-696-3600, Fax: 301-696-3597, E-mail: gofurther@hood.edu. *Application contact:* Spencer Berk, Assistant Director of Graduate Admissions, 301-696-3604, E-mail: gofurther@hood.edu.

Howard University, School of Business, Graduate Programs in Business, Washington, DC 20059-0002. Offers accounting (MBA); entrepreneurship (MBA); finance (MBA); general management (MBA); human resources management (MBA); information systems (MBA); international business (MBA); marketing (MBA); supply chain management (MBA); JD/MBA. *Accreditation:* AACSB. *Program availability:* Part-time, evening/weekend, online learning. *Entrance requirements:* For master's, GMAT, minimum 1 year post undergraduate work experience, resume, 3 letters of recommendation, advanced college algebra. Additional exam requirements/recommendations for international students: Required—TOEFL. *Faculty research:* Marketing research in multi-ethnic populations, U.S. trade policies and international relations, risk management (finance).

Idaho State University, Office of Graduate Studies, College of Business, Pocatello, ID 83209-8020. Offers business administration (MBA, Postbaccalaureate Certificate); computer information systems (MS, Postbaccalaureate Certificate). *Accreditation:* AACSB. *Program availability:* Part-time. *Degree requirements:* For master's, comprehensive exam, thesis (for some programs), oral exam; for Postbaccalaureate Certificate, comprehensive exam, thesis (for some programs), 6 hours of clerkship. *Entrance requirements:* For master's, GMAT, GRE General Test, minimum GPA of 3.0, resume outlining work experience, 2 letters of reference; for Postbaccalaureate Certificate, GMAT, GRE General Test, minimum upper-level GPA of 3.0, resume of work experience. Additional exam requirements/recommendations for international students: Required—TOEFL (minimum score 550 paper-based; 80 iBT). Electronic applications accepted. *Faculty research:* Information assurance, computer information technology, finance management, marketing.

IGlobal University, Graduate Programs, Vienna, VA 22182. Offers accounting (MBA); data management and analytics (MSIT); entrepreneurship (MBA); finance (MBA); global business management (MBA); health care management (MBA); hospitality and tourism management (MBA); human resources management (MBA); information technology (MBA); information technology systems and management (MSIT); leadership and management (MBA); project management (MBA); public service and administration (MBA); software design and management (MSIT).

Illinois Institute of Technology, Graduate College, College of Science, Department of Computer Science, Chicago, IL 60616. Offers business (MCS); computational intelligence (MCS); computer science (MCS, MS, PhD); cyber-physical systems (MCS); data analytics (MCS); data science (MAS); database systems (MCS); distributed and cloud computing (MCS); education (MCS); finance (MCS); information security and assurance (MCS); networking and communications (MCS); software engineering (MCS); telecommunications and software engineering (MAS); MS/MAS. *Program availability:* Part-time, evening/weekend, online learning. Terminal master's awarded for partial completion of doctoral program. *Degree requirements:* For master's, thesis optional; for doctorate, comprehensive exam, thesis/dissertation. *Entrance requirements:* For master's, GRE General Test with minimum scores of 298 Quantitative and Verbal, 3.0 Analytical Writing (for MS); GRE General Test with minimum scores of 292 Quantitative and Verbal, 2.5 Analytical Writing (for MAS), minimum undergraduate GPA of 3.0; for doctorate, GRE General Test (minimum scores: 304 Quantitative and Verbal, 3.5 Analytical Writing), minimum undergraduate GPA of 3.0. Additional exam requirements/recommendations for international students: Required—TOEFL (minimum score 523 paper-based; 70 iBT). Electronic applications accepted. *Faculty research:* Parallel and distributed processing, high-performance computing, computational linguistics, information retrieval, data mining, grid computing.

Illinois Institute of Technology, Graduate College, Lewis College of Human Sciences, Department of Humanities, Chicago, IL 60616. Offers information architecture (MS); technical communication (PhD); technical communication and information design (MS). *Program availability:* Part-time. *Degree requirements:* For master's, comprehensive exam, thesis or alternative; for doctorate, comprehensive exam, thesis/dissertation. *Entrance requirements:* For master's, GRE General Test (minimum score 144 Quantitative, 153 Verbal, and 4.0 Analytical Writing), minimum undergraduate GPA of 3.0; 2 letters of recommendation from faculty or supervisors; professional statement discussing academic goals; for doctorate, GRE General Test (minimum score 144 Quantitative, 153 Verbal, and 4.0 Analytical Writing), bachelor's or master's degree in a field that, in combination with the 27-credit hour technical core, would provide a solid basis for advanced academic work leading to original research in the field; 3 letters of recommendation from faculty or supervisors; professional statement discussing academic goals. Additional exam requirements/recommendations for international students: Required—TOEFL (minimum score 95 iBT); Recommended—IELTS (minimum score 7). Electronic applications accepted. *Faculty research:* Linguistics, punishment theory, political communication, gender and technology, philosophical and ethical issues in neuroscience.

Illinois Institute of Technology, Graduate College, School of Applied Technology, Department of Information Technology and Management, Wheaton, IL 60189. Offers cyber forensics and security (MAS); information technology and management (MAS). *Program availability:* Part-time, evening/weekend, online learning. *Entrance requirements:* For master's, GRE (minimum score 300 Quantitative and Verbal, 2.5 Analytical Writing), bachelor's degree with minimum cumulative undergraduate GPA of 3.0 (or its equivalent) from accredited institution. Additional exam requirements/recommendations for international students: Required—TOEFL (minimum score 523 paper-based; 70 iBT); Recommended—IELTS (minimum score 5.5). Electronic applications accepted. *Faculty research:* Database design, voice over IP, process engineering, object-oriented programming, computer networking, online design, system administration.

Illinois State University, Graduate School, College of Applied Science and Technology, School of Information Technology, Normal, IL 61790-2200. Offers MS. *Entrance requirements:* For master's, GRE General Test, minimum GPA of 3.0 in last 60 hours; proficiency in COBOL, FORTRAN, Pascal, or P12. *Faculty research:* Graduate practicum training in network support.

Indiana University Bloomington, School of Public and Environmental Affairs, Public Affairs Programs, Bloomington, IN 47405. Offers economic development (MPA); energy (MPA); environmental policy (PhD); environmental policy and natural resource management (MPA); information systems (MPA); international development (MPA); local government management (MPA); nonprofit management (MPA, Certificate); policy analysis (MPA); public budgeting and financial management (Certificate); public finance (PhD); public financial administration (MPA); public management (MPA, PhD, Certificate); public policy analysis (PhD); social entrepreneurship (Certificate); specialized public affairs (MPA); sustainability and sustainable development (MPA); JD/MPA; MPA/MA; MPA/MIS; MPA/MLS; MSES/MPA. *Accreditation:* NASPAA (one or more programs are accredited). *Program availability:* Part-time. *Degree requirements:* For master's, capstone, internship; for doctorate, comprehensive exam, thesis/dissertation. *Entrance requirements:* For master's, GRE General Test or GMAT, official transcripts, 3 letters of recommendation, resume, personal statement; for doctorate, GRE General Test, official transcripts, 3 letters of recommendation, statement of purpose. Additional exam requirements/recommendations for international students: Required—TOEFL (minimum score 600 paper-based; 96 iBT); Recommended—IELTS (minimum score 7). Electronic applications accepted. *Faculty research:* International development, environmental policy and resource management, policy analysis, public finance, public management, urban management, nonprofit management, energy policy, social policy, public finance.

Indiana University Northwest, College of Arts and Sciences, Gary, IN 46408. Offers clinical counseling (MS), including drug and alcohol counseling; community development/urban studies (Graduate Certificate); computer information systems (Graduate Certificate); liberal studies (MLS); race-ethnic studies (Graduate Certificate); women's and gender studies (Graduate Certificate). *Program availability:* Part-time, evening/weekend. *Students:* 4 full-time (all women), 18 part-time (10 women); includes 10 minority (9 Black or African American, non-Hispanic/Latino; 1 Hispanic/Latino). Average age 39. 22 applicants, 77% accepted, 13 enrolled. In 2016, 6 master's awarded. *Entrance requirements:* For master's, GRE (recommended for MS), minimum undergraduate GPA of 3.0, bachelor's degree from accredited university (for MS). *Application deadline:* For fall admission, 7/1 priority date for domestic and international students; for spring admission, 12/1 priority date for domestic and international students. Application fee: $40 ($60 for international students). Electronic applications accepted. *Expenses:* $276.98 per credit hour in-state; $652.54 per credit hour out-of-state. *Financial support:* Applicants required to submit FAFSA. *Unit head:* Mark Hoyert, Dean, E-mail: mhoyert@iun.edu.
Website: http://www.iun.edu/coas/

Instituto Tecnológico y de Estudios Superiores de Monterrey, Campus Central de Veracruz, Graduate Programs, Córdoba, Mexico. Offers administration (MA); administration of information technologies (MTI); computer sciences (MCC); education (MEE); educational institution administration (MAD); educational technology (MTE); electronic commerce (MCE); finance (MAF); humanistic studies (MEH); international business for Latin America (MNL); marketing (MMT); science (MCP). *Program availability:* Part-time, evening/weekend, online learning. *Degree requirements:* For master's, thesis (for some programs). *Entrance requirements:* For master's, PAEP College Board. Electronic applications accepted.

Instituto Tecnológico y de Estudios Superiores de Monterrey, Campus Ciudad de México, Virtual University Division, Ciudad de Mexico, Mexico. Offers administration of information technologies (MA); computer sciences (MA); education (MA, PhD); educational technology (MA); environmental engineering (MA); environmental systems (MA); humanistic studies (MA); industrial engineering (MA); international business for Latin America (MA); quality systems (MA); quality systems and productivity (MA). *Program availability:* Part-time, evening/weekend, online learning. *Entrance requirements:* For master's and doctorate, Instituto entrance exam. Additional exam requirements/recommendations for international students: Required—TOEFL.

Instituto Tecnológico y de Estudios Superiores de Monterrey, Campus Ciudad Juárez, Program in Administration of Information Technology, Ciudad Juárez, Mexico. Offers MAIT.

Instituto Tecnológico y de Estudios Superiores de Monterrey, Campus Ciudad Obregón, Program in Administration of Information Technology, Ciudad Obregón, Mexico. Offers MATI.

Instituto Tecnológico y de Estudios Superiores de Monterrey, Campus Estado de México, Professional and Graduate Division, Estado de Mexico, Mexico. Offers administration of information technologies (MITA); architecture (M Arch); business administration (GMBA, MBA); computer sciences (MCS, PhD); education (M Ed); educational institution administration (MAD); educational technology and innovation (PhD); electronic commerce (MEC); environmental systems (MS); finance (MAF); humanistic studies (MHS); information sciences and knowledge management (MISKM); information systems (MS); manufacturing systems (MS); marketing (MEM); quality systems and productivity (MS); science and materials engineering (PhD); telecommunications management (MTM). *Program availability:* Part-time, online learning. *Degree requirements:* For master's, one foreign language, thesis (for some programs); for doctorate, one foreign language, thesis/dissertation. *Entrance requirements:* For master's, E-PAEP 500, interview; for doctorate, E-PAEP 500, research proposal. Additional exam requirements/recommendations for international students: Required—TOEFL (minimum score 550 paper-based). *Faculty research:* Surface treatments by plasmas, mechanical properties, robotics, graphical computing, mechatronics security protocols.

Instituto Tecnológico y de Estudios Superiores de Monterrey, Campus Irapuato, Graduate Programs, Irapuato, Mexico. Offers administration (MBA); administration of information technology (MAIT); administration of telecommunications (MAT); architecture (M Arch); computer science (MCS); education (M Ed); educational administration (MEA); educational innovation and technology (DEIT); educational technology (MET); electronic commerce (MBA); environmental administration and planning (MEAP); environmental systems (MES); finances (MBA); humanistic studies (MHS); international management for Latin American executives (MIMLAE); library and information science (MLIS); manufacturing quality management (MMQM); marketing research (MBA).

Instituto Tecnológico y de Estudios Superiores de Monterrey, Campus Laguna, Graduate School, Torreón, Mexico. Offers business administration (MBA); industrial engineering (MIE); management information systems (MS). *Program availability:* Part-time. *Entrance requirements:* For master's, GMAT. *Faculty research:* Computer communications from home to the university.

Inter American University of Puerto Rico, Aguadilla Campus, Graduate School, Aguadilla, PR 00605. Offers accounting (MBA); counseling psychology specializing in family (MS); criminal justice (MA); educative management and leadership (MA); elementary education (M Ed); finance (MBA); human resources (MBA); industrial management (MBA); management information systems (MBA); marketing (MBA). *Program availability:* Part-time, evening/weekend. *Degree requirements:* For master's, comprehensive exam. *Entrance requirements:* For master's, EXADEP, 2 letters of recommendation, minimum GPA of 2.5. Electronic applications accepted.

Inter American University of Puerto Rico, Fajardo Campus, Graduate Programs, Fajardo, PR 00738-7003. Offers computer science (MS); educational management and leadership (MA Ed); elementary education (MA Ed); general business (MBA); management information systems (MBA); marketing (MBA); special education (MA Ed).

Inter American University of Puerto Rico, Metropolitan Campus, Graduate Programs, Program in Management Information Systems, San Juan, PR 00919-1293. Offers MBA.

Inter American University of Puerto Rico, San Germán Campus, Graduate Studies Center, Program in Business Administration, San Germán, PR 00683-5008. Offers accounting (MBA); finance (MBA); general business administration (MBA); human resources (MBA, PhD); industrial relations (MBA); information systems (MBA); international and interregional business (PhD); management (MBA); marketing (MBA).

Program availability: Part-time, evening/weekend. *Degree requirements:* For master's, comprehensive exam. *Entrance requirements:* For master's, GRE General Test or EXADEP, minimum GPA of 3.0.

Iowa State University of Science and Technology, Program in Business and Technology, Ames, IA 50011. Offers PhD. *Entrance requirements:* Additional exam requirements/recommendations for international students: Required—TOEFL (minimum score 600 paper-based; 100 iBT), IELTS (minimum score 7). *Application deadline:* For fall admission, 1/15 for domestic students. Application fee: $60 ($90 for international students). Electronic applications accepted. *Application contact:* Debbie Johnson, Application Contact, 515-294-2474, Fax: 515-294-6060, E-mail: dljohns@iastate.edu.
Website: http://www.business.iastate.edu/phd/

Iowa State University of Science and Technology, Program in Information Systems, Ames, IA 50011. Offers information systems (MS). *Degree requirements:* For master's, thesis or alternative. *Entrance requirements:* For master's, GMAT. Additional exam requirements/recommendations for international students: Recommended—TOEFL (minimum score 600 paper-based; 100 iBT), IELTS (minimum score 7). *Application deadline:* For fall admission, 6/1 priority date for domestic students, 3/1 priority date for international students; for spring admission, 11/1 priority date for domestic students, 3/1 priority date for international students. Application fee: $60 ($90 for international students). Electronic applications accepted. *Application contact:* Meleah Cue, Application Contact, 515-294-8118, Fax: 515-294-2446, E-mail: busgrad@iastate.edu.
Website: http://www.business.iastate.edu/masters/msis

James Madison University, The Graduate School, College of Business, Program in Business Administration, Harrisonburg, VA 22807. Offers business (MBA), including executive leadership, information security, innovation. *Accreditation:* AACSB. *Program availability:* Part-time, evening/weekend, blended/hybrid learning. *Faculty:* 31 full-time (8 women), 2 part-time/adjunct (1 woman). *Students:* 20 full-time (9 women), 77 part-time (27 women); includes 21 minority (9 Black or African American, non-Hispanic/Latino; 9 Asian, non-Hispanic/Latino; 2 Hispanic/Latino; 1 Two or more races, non-Hispanic/Latino), 1 international. Average age 30. 62 applicants, 82% accepted, 42 enrolled. In 2016, 45 master's awarded. Application fee: $55. Electronic applications accepted. *Financial support:* In 2016–17, 1 student received support. Federal Work-Study and 1 assistantship (averaging $7911) available. Financial award application deadline: 3/1; financial award applicants required to submit FAFSA. *Unit head:* Dr. Matthew A. Rutherford, Department Head, 540-568-8777, E-mail: rutherma@jmu.edu. *Application contact:* Lynette D. Michael, Director of Graduate Admissions, 540-568-6131 Ext. 6395, Fax: 540-568-7860, E-mail: michaeld@jmu.edu.
Website: http://www.jmu.edu/cob/graduate/mba/index.shtml

Johns Hopkins University, Carey Business School, MS in Information Systems Program, Baltimore, MD 21218. Offers MS. *Program availability:* Part-time, evening/weekend. *Faculty:* 87 full-time (32 women), 51 part-time/adjunct (8 women). *Students:* 68 part-time (28 women); includes 10 minority (2 Black or African American, non-Hispanic/Latino; 7 Asian, non-Hispanic/Latino; 1 Hispanic/Latino), 45 international. Average age 24. 137 applicants, 69% accepted, 40 enrolled. In 2016, 12 master's awarded. *Degree requirements:* For master's, 36 credits. *Entrance requirements:* For master's, GMAT or GRE. Additional exam requirements/recommendations for international students: Required—TOEFL, IELTS. *Application deadline:* For fall admission, 5/1 for domestic and international students. Applications are processed on a rolling basis. Application fee: $100. Electronic applications accepted. *Expenses:* $64,000 (full-time); $1,290 per credit (part-time). *Financial support:* In 2016–17, 7 students received support. Scholarships/grants available. Support available to part-time students. Financial award application deadline: 4/15; financial award applicants required to submit FAFSA. *Faculty research:* Digital innovations in healthcare, digital marketplaces, healthcare information systems, information technology and strategy. *Unit head:* Dr. Kevin Frick, Vice Dean of Education, 410-234-9272, E-mail: kfrick@jhu.edu. *Application contact:* Office of Admissions, 410-234-9220, Fax: 443-529-1554, E-mail: carey.admissions@jhu.edu.
Website: http://carey.jhu.edu/academics/master-of-science/ms-in-information-systems/

Johns Hopkins University, Engineering Program for Professionals, Part-time Program in Information Systems Engineering, Baltimore, MD 21218. Offers MS, Graduate Certificate, Post-Master's Certificate. *Program availability:* Part-time, evening/weekend, 100% online, blended/hybrid learning. *Faculty:* 6 part-time/adjunct (1 woman). *Students:* 6 full-time (2 women), 123 part-time (30 women); includes 32 minority (9 Black or African American, non-Hispanic/Latino; 14 Asian, non-Hispanic/Latino; 6 Hispanic/Latino; 3 Two or more races, non-Hispanic/Latino), 4 international. Average age 31. 61 applicants, 57% accepted, 24 enrolled. In 2016, 35 master's, 1 other advanced degree awarded. *Entrance requirements:* Additional exam requirements/recommendations for international students: Required—TOEFL (minimum score 600 paper-based; 100 iBT). *Application deadline:* Applications are processed on a rolling basis. Application fee: $0. Electronic applications accepted. *Unit head:* Dr. Thomas A. Longstaff, Program Chair, 443-778-9389, E-mail: thomas.longstaff@jhuapl.edu. *Application contact:* Doug Schiller, Admissions Director, 410-516-2300, Fax: 410-579-8049, E-mail: schiller@jhu.edu.
Website: http://www.ep.jhu.edu/

Johnson & Wales University, Graduate Studies, MBA Program, Providence, RI 02903-3703. Offers accounting (MBA); business administration (MBA); finance (MBA); hospitality (MBA); human resource management (MBA); information technology (MBA); nonprofit management (MBA); operations and supply chain management (MBA). Program also offered on Denver campus. *Program availability:* Part-time, online learning. *Entrance requirements:* For master's, minimum GPA of 2.75. Additional exam requirements/recommendations for international students: Required—TOEFL (minimum score 550 paper-based); Recommended—IELTS, TWE. *Faculty research:* International banking, global economy, international trade, cultural differences.

Kaplan University, Davenport Campus, School of Information Technology, Davenport, IA 52807. Offers decision support systems (MS); information security and assurance (MS). *Program availability:* Part-time, evening/weekend, online learning. *Entrance requirements:* Additional exam requirements/recommendations for international students: Required—TOEFL (minimum score 550 paper-based; 80 iBT).

Kean University, College of Natural, Applied and Health Sciences, Program in Computer Information Systems, Union, NJ 07083. Offers MS. *Program availability:* Part-time, 100% online. *Faculty:* 9 full-time (4 women). *Students:* 16 full-time (8 women), 6 part-time (2 women); includes 8 minority (2 Black or African American, non-Hispanic/Latino; 5 Asian, non-Hispanic/Latino; 1 Hispanic/Latino), 12 international. Average age 27. 45 applicants, 27% accepted, 11 enrolled. In 2016, 7 master's awarded. *Entrance requirements:* For master's, baccalaureate degree in computer science or closely-related field from accredited college or university; minimum cumulative GPA of 3.0; official transcripts from all institutions attended; two letters of recommendation; professional resume/curriculum vitae; personal statement. Additional exam requirements/recommendations for international students: Required—TOEFL (minimum score 550 paper-based; 79 iBT), IELTS (minimum score 6.5). *Application deadline:* For fall admission, 6/1 for domestic and international students; for spring admission, 12/1 for domestic and international students. Applications are processed on a rolling basis. Application fee: $75. Electronic applications accepted. *Expenses:* Tuition, state resident: full-time $13,156; part-time $640 per credit. Tuition, nonresident: full-time $17,831; part-time $785 per credit. *Required fees:* $3316; $151 per credit. Tuition and fees vary according to course level, course load, degree level and program. *Financial support:* Scholarships/grants and unspecified assistantships available. Financial award applicants required to submit FAFSA. *Unit head:* Dr. Jing-Chiou Liou, Program Coordinator, 908-737-3803, E-mail: jliou@kean.edu. *Application contact:* Pedro Lopes, Admissions Counselor, 908-737-7100, E-mail: grad-adm@kean.edu.
Website: http://grad.kean.edu/masters-programs/computer-information-systems

Keiser University, MS in Information Technology Leadership Program, Ft. Lauderdale, FL 33309. Offers MS.

Kent State University, College of Business Administration, Doctoral Program in Management Systems, Kent, OH 44242. Offers PhD. *Faculty:* 14 full-time (5 women). *Students:* 11 full-time (8 women); includes 1 minority (Black or African American, non-Hispanic/Latino), 7 international. Average age 33. 12 applicants, 33% accepted, 2 enrolled. *Degree requirements:* For doctorate, comprehensive exam, thesis/dissertation, oral defense. *Entrance requirements:* For doctorate, GMAT or GRE. Additional exam requirements/recommendations for international students: Required—TOEFL (minimum score 600 paper-based; 100 iBT). *Application deadline:* For fall admission, 12/15 for domestic and international students. Application fee: $45 ($70 for international students). Electronic applications accepted. *Expenses:* Tuition, state resident: full-time $10,864; part-time $495 per credit hour. Tuition, nonresident: full-time $18,380; part-time $837 per credit hour. *Financial support:* In 2016–17, 12 students received support, including 12 teaching assistantships with full tuition reimbursements available (averaging $23,000 per year); Federal Work-Study also available. Financial award application deadline: 12/15; financial award applicants required to submit FAFSA. *Unit head:* Dr. O. Felix Offodile, Chair and Professor, 330-672-2750, Fax: 330-672-2953, E-mail: foffodil@kent.edu. *Application contact:* Felecia A. Urbanek, Coordinator, Graduate Programs, 330-672-2282, Fax: 330-672-7303, E-mail: gradbus@kent.edu.
Website: http://www.kent.edu/business/phd

Kent State University, College of Business Administration, Master of Science Program in Business Analytics, Kent, OH 44242-0001. Offers MS. *Program availability:* Part-time, evening/weekend. *Faculty:* 15 full-time (5 women). *Students:* 4 full-time (0 women), 2 part-time (0 women); includes 1 minority (Black or African American, non-Hispanic/Latino), 3 international. Average age 27. 19 applicants, 63% accepted, 6 enrolled. *Entrance requirements:* For master's, GMAT or GRE, official transcripts, resume, statement of goals and objectives, 3 letters of recommendation. Additional exam requirements/recommendations for international students: Required—TOEFL (minimum score 550 paper-based; 80 iBT), IELTS (minimum score 6.5). *Application deadline:* For fall admission, 3/15 for domestic and international students. Applications are processed on a rolling basis. Application fee: $45 ($70 for international students). Electronic applications accepted. *Expenses:* Tuition, state resident: full-time $10,864; part-time $495 per credit hour. Tuition, nonresident: full-time $18,380; part-time $837 per credit hour. *Financial support:* Application deadline: 3/15; applicants required to submit FAFSA. *Unit head:* Dr. O. Felix Offodile, Chair/Professor, 330-672-2750, E-mail: foffodil@kent.edu. *Application contact:* Louise M. Ditchey, Administrative Director, 330-672-2282, Fax: 330-672-7303, E-mail: gradbus@kent.edu.
Website: http://www.kent.edu/business/msba

Lake Erie College, School of Business, Painesville, OH 44077-3389. Offers general management (MBA); health care administration (MBA); information technology management (MBA). *Program availability:* Part-time, evening/weekend. *Entrance requirements:* For master's, GMAT or minimum GPA of 3.0, resume, personal statement. Additional exam requirements/recommendations for international students: Required—TOEFL (minimum score 550 paper-based; 79 iBT), IELTS (minimum score 6), STEP Eiken 1st and pre-1st grade level (for Japanese students). Electronic applications accepted. Application fee is waived when completed online. *Expenses:* Contact institution.

Le Moyne College, Madden School of Business, Syracuse, NY 13214. Offers business administration (MBA); information systems (MS). *Accreditation:* AACSB. *Program availability:* Part-time, evening/weekend. *Faculty:* 9 full-time (2 women), 6 part-time/adjunct (2 women). *Students:* 42 full-time (19 women), 58 part-time (23 women); includes 7 minority (3 Black or African American, non-Hispanic/Latino; 1 Asian, non-Hispanic/Latino; 3 Hispanic/Latino), 1 international. Average age 28. 82 applicants, 88% accepted, 67 enrolled. In 2016, 61 master's awarded. *Degree requirements:* For master's, capstone-level course. *Entrance requirements:* For master's, GMAT or GRE General Test, bachelor's degree with minimum GPA of 3.0, resume, 2 letters of recommendation, personal statement, transcripts, interview. Additional exam requirements/recommendations for international students: Required—TOEFL (minimum score 550 paper-based; 79 iBT); Recommended—IELTS (minimum score 6.5). *Application deadline:* For fall admission, 7/1 priority date for domestic and international students; for spring admission, 11/1 priority date for domestic and international students; for summer admission, 4/1 priority date for domestic and international students. Applications are processed on a rolling basis. Application fee: $0. Electronic applications accepted. *Expenses:* $797 per credit hour. *Financial support:* In 2016–17, 27 students received support. Career-related internships or fieldwork, scholarships/grants, health care benefits, and unspecified assistantships available. Support available to part-time students. Financial award applicants required to submit FAFSA. *Faculty research:* Performance evaluation outcomes assessment, technology outsourcing, international business, systems for Web-based information-seeking, non-profit business practices, business sustainability practices, management/leadership development, operations management optimization applications. *Unit head:* James Joseph, Dean of Madden School of Business, 315-445-4280, Fax: 315-445-4787, E-mail: josepjae@lemoyne.edu. *Application contact:* Kristen P. Richards, Senior Director of Enrollment Management, 315-445-5444, Fax: 315-445-6092, E-mail: trapaskp@lemoyne.edu.
Website: http://www.lemoyne.edu/madden

Lenoir-Rhyne University, Graduate Programs, Charles M. Snipes School of Business, Hickory, NC 28601. Offers accounting (MBA); business analytics and information technology (MBA); entrepreneurship (MBA); global business (MBA); healthcare administration (MBA); innovation and change management (MBA); leadership development (MBA). *Accreditation:* ACBSP. *Program availability:* Part-time, evening/weekend, online learning. *Degree requirements:* For master's, capstone course. *Entrance requirements:* For master's, GMAT, GRE, MAT, minimum undergraduate GPA of 2.7, graduate 3.0. Additional exam requirements/recommendations for international students: Required—TOEFL (minimum score 600 paper-based). Electronic applications accepted. *Expenses:* Contact institution.

Lewis University, College of Business, Graduate School of Management, Program in Business Administration, Romeoville, IL 60446. Offers accounting (MBA); custom elective option (MBA); e-business (MBA); finance (MBA); healthcare management (MBA); human resources management (MBA); international business (MBA); management information systems (MBA); marketing (MBA); project management (MBA); technology and operations management (MBA). *Program availability:* Part-time, evening/weekend. *Students:* 145 full-time (72 women), 213 part-time (123 women); includes 101 minority (46 Black or African American, non-Hispanic/Latino; 2 American Indian or Alaska Native, non-Hispanic/Latino; 7 Asian, non-Hispanic/Latino; 41 Hispanic/

Management Information Systems

Latino; 1 Native Hawaiian or other Pacific Islander, non-Hispanic/Latino; 4 Two or more races, non-Hispanic/Latino), 47 international. Average age 31. In 2016, 99 master's awarded. *Degree requirements:* For master's, comprehensive exam. *Entrance requirements:* For master's, interview, bachelor's degree, resume, 2 recommendations. Additional exam requirements/recommendations for international students: Required—TOEFL (minimum score 550 paper-based). *Application deadline:* For fall admission, 8/15 priority date for domestic students, 5/1 priority date for international students; for spring admission, 11/15 priority date for international students. Applications are processed on a rolling basis. Application fee: $40. Electronic applications accepted. *Expenses: Tuition:* Full-time $13,860; part-time $770 per credit hour. *Required fees:* $75 per semester. Tuition and fees vary according to degree level and program. *Financial support:* Career-related internships or fieldwork, Federal Work-Study, scholarships/grants, and unspecified assistantships available. Financial award application deadline: 5/1; financial award applicants required to submit FAFSA. *Unit head:* Dr. Maureen Culleeney, Academic Program Director, 815-838-0500 Ext. 5631, E-mail: culleema@lewisu.edu. *Application contact:* Michele Ryan, Director of Admission, 815-838-0500 Ext. 5384, E-mail: gsm@lewisu.edu.

Liberty University, School of Business, Lynchburg, VA 24515. Offers accounting (MBA, MS); business administration (MBA); criminal justice (MBA); cyber security (MS); executive leadership (MA); information systems (MS), including information assurance, technology management; international business (MBA, DBA); leadership (DBA); marketing (MBA, MS, DBA), including digital marketing and advertising (MS), project management (MS), public relations (MS), sports marketing and media (MS); project management (MBA, DBA); public administration (MBA); public relations (MBA). *Program availability:* Part-time, online learning. *Students:* 1,458 full-time (807 women), 4,188 part-time (2,041 women); includes 1,372 minority (1,060 Black or African American, non-Hispanic/Latino; 19 American Indian or Alaska Native, non-Hispanic/Latino; 85 Asian, non-Hispanic/Latino; 75 Hispanic/Latino; 10 Native Hawaiian or other Pacific Islander, non-Hispanic/Latino; 123 Two or more races, non-Hispanic/Latino), 124 international. Average age 35. 5,424 applicants, 45% accepted, 1242 enrolled. In 2016, 1,859 master's, 87 other advanced degrees awarded. *Entrance requirements:* For master's, minimum undergraduate GPA of 3.0, 15 hours of upper-level business courses. Additional exam requirements/recommendations for international students: Required—TOEFL (minimum score 600 paper-based; 100 iBT). *Application deadline:* Applications are processed on a rolling basis. Application fee: $50. Electronic applications accepted. *Expenses:* Contact institution. *Financial support:* Applicants required to submit FAFSA. *Unit head:* Dr. Scott Hicks, Dean, 434-592-4808, Fax: 434-582-2366, E-mail: smhicks@liberty.edu. *Application contact:* Jay Bridge, Director of Graduate Admissions, 800-424-9595, Fax: 800-628-7977, E-mail: gradadmissions@liberty.edu.
Website: http://www.liberty.edu/academics/business/index.cfm?PID-149

Lincoln University, Graduate Studies, Oakland, CA 94612. Offers finance and investments (DBA); finance management (MS); finance management and investments (MBA); general business (MBA); human resource management (MBA, DBA); international business (MBA, MS); management information systems (MBA). *Program availability:* Part-time. *Faculty:* 13 full-time (1 woman), 16 part-time/adjunct (3 women). *Students:* 542 full-time (215 women), 3 part-time (1 woman); includes 10 minority (8 Asian, non-Hispanic/Latino; 1 Hispanic/Latino; 1 Two or more races, non-Hispanic/Latino), 531 international. Average age 26. 800 applicants, 71% accepted, 81 enrolled. In 2016, 109 master's, 1 doctorate awarded. *Degree requirements:* For master's, research project (thesis), internship report, or comprehensive exam; for doctorate, comprehensive exam, thesis/dissertation. *Entrance requirements:* For master's, minimum GPA of 2.7; for doctorate, GMAT (minimum score: 550), GRE (minimum score: 1000), or equivalent test results (waived for master's degree with minimum cumulative GPA of 3.3). Additional exam requirements/recommendations for international students: Required—TOEFL (minimum score 525 paper-based; 71 iBT) or IELTS (minimum score 5.5) for MBA; TOEFL (minimum score 550 paper-based; 79 iBT) or IELTS (minimum score 6) for DBA; Recommended—TOEFL (minimum score 71 iBT), IELTS (minimum score 6), TSE. *Application deadline:* For fall admission, 8/7 for domestic students, 7/14 for international students; for spring admission, 11/30 for domestic students, 10/31 for international students; for summer admission, 5/29 for domestic students, 5/5 for international students. Applications are processed on a rolling basis. Application fee: $75. Electronic applications accepted. *Expenses: Tuition:* Full-time $7920. *Required fees:* $400. Tuition and fees vary according to course level, course load, degree level and program. *Financial support:* Teaching assistantships, career-related internships or fieldwork, and scholarships/grants available. Financial award applicants required to submit FAFSA. *Unit head:* Dr. Marshall Burak, Director of Graduate Programs, 510-628-8016, Fax: 510-628-8012, E-mail: mburak@lincolnuca.edu. *Application contact:* Reenu Shrestha, Assistant to the President, 510-628-8017, Fax: 510-208-2826, E-mail: sreenu@lincolnuca.edu.
Website: http://www.lincolnuca.edu/

Lincoln University, Graduate Studies, Jefferson City, MO 65101. Offers business administration (MBA), including accounting, management, management information systems, public administration/policy; elementary teaching (M Ed); environmental science (MS); guidance and counseling (M Ed), including community/agency counseling, elementary school, secondary school; higher education (MA); history (MA); integrated agricultural systems (MS); middle school (M Ed); natural sciences (MS); secondary teaching (M Ed); sociology (MA); sociology/criminal justice (MA). *Program availability:* Part-time, evening/weekend, 100% online, blended/hybrid learning. *Students:* 50 full-time (29 women), 68 part-time (39 women); includes 40 minority (37 Black or African American, non-Hispanic/Latino; 1 Asian, non-Hispanic/Latino; 2 Two or more races, non-Hispanic/Latino), 14 international. Average age 33. 75 applicants, 80% accepted, 34 enrolled. In 2016, 51 master's awarded. *Degree requirements:* For master's, comprehensive exam, thesis optional. *Entrance requirements:* For master's, GRE, MAT or GMAT, minimum GPA of 2.75 overall, 3.0 in courses related to specialization; 3 letters of recommendation; minimum C average in English composition; personal statement of purpose. Additional exam requirements/recommendations for international students: Required—TOEFL (minimum score 500 paper-based; 61 iBT), IELTS (minimum score 5.5), Michigan English Language Assessment Battery (minimum score 80). *Application deadline:* For fall admission, 7/1 priority date for domestic students, 5/1 priority date for international students; for spring admission, 11/1 priority date for domestic students, 10/1 priority date for international students; for summer admission, 6/1 priority date for domestic students. Applications are processed on a rolling basis. Application fee: $30. Electronic applications accepted. *Expenses:* Tuition, state resident: full-time $6840; part-time $5130 per year. Tuition, nonresident: full-time $12,720; part-time $9540 per year. *Required fees:* $852; $811 per unit. Tuition and fees vary according to course load. *Financial support:* In 2016–17, 2 fellowships with tuition reimbursements, 8 research assistantships with tuition reimbursements were awarded; Federal Work-Study, scholarships/grants, and unspecified assistantships also available. Support available to part-time students. Financial award application deadline: 3/1; financial award applicants required to submit FAFSA. *Unit head:* Dr. Rolundus R. Rice, Dean, 573-681-5247, Fax: 573-681-5106, E-mail: gradschool@lincolnu.edu. *Application contact:* Irasema Steck, Administrative Assistant, 573-681-5247, Fax: 573-681-5106, E-mail: gradschool@lincolnu.edu.
Website: http://www.lincolnu.edu/web/graduate-studies/graduate-studies

Lindenwood University, Graduate Programs, School of Accelerated Degree Programs, St. Charles, MO 63301-1695. Offers administration (MSA), including management, marketing, project management; business administration (MBA); communications (MA), including digital and multimedia, media management, promotions, training and development; criminal justice and administration (MS); healthcare administration (MS); human resource management (MS); information technology (Certificate); managing information security (MS); managing information technology (MS); managing virtualization and cloud computing (MS); writing (MFA). *Program availability:* Part-time, evening/weekend, 100% online. *Faculty:* 16 full-time (7 women), 75 part-time/adjunct (27 women). *Students:* 609 full-time (386 women), 179 part-time (121 women); includes 257 minority (202 Black or African American, non-Hispanic/Latino; 4 American Indian or Alaska Native, non-Hispanic/Latino; 5 Asian, non-Hispanic/Latino; 28 Hispanic/Latino; 1 Native Hawaiian or other Pacific Islander, non-Hispanic/Latino; 17 Two or more races, non-Hispanic/Latino), 28 international. Average age 36. 332 applicants, 70% accepted, 205 enrolled. In 2016, 479 master's awarded. *Degree requirements:* For master's, thesis (for some programs), minimum cumulative GPA of 3.0; for Certificate, minimum cumulative GPA of 3.0. *Entrance requirements:* For master's, resume, personal statement, official undergraduate transcript, minimum undergraduate cumulative GPA of 3.0. Additional exam requirements/recommendations for international students: Required—TOEFL (minimum score 550 paper-based; 80 iBT); Recommended—IELTS (minimum score 6.5). *Application deadline:* For fall admission, 9/26 priority date for domestic and international students; for winter admission, 1/3 priority date for domestic and international students; for spring admission, 3/31 priority date for domestic and international students; for summer admission, 7/3 priority date for domestic and international students. Applications are processed on a rolling basis. Application fee: $30 ($100 for international students). Electronic applications accepted. *Expenses: Tuition:* Full-time $15,672; part-time $453 per credit hour. *Required fees:* $205 per semester. Tuition and fees vary according to course level, course load and degree level. *Financial support:* In 2016–17, 467 students received support. Career-related internships or fieldwork, institutionally sponsored loans, scholarships/grants, tuition waivers (partial), and unspecified assistantships available. Financial award application deadline: 6/30; financial award applicants required to submit FAFSA. *Unit head:* Dr. Gina Ganahl, Dean, Accelerated Degree Programs, 636-949-4501, Fax: 636-949-4505, E-mail: gganahl@lindenwood.edu. *Application contact:* Tyler Kostich, Director, Evening and Graduate Admissions, 636-949-4138, Fax: 636-949-4109, E-mail: adultadmissions@lindenwood.edu.
Website: http://www.lindenwood.edu/academics/academic-schools/school-of-accelerated-degree-programs/

Lipscomb University, College of Computing and Technology, Nashville, TN 37204-3951. Offers data science (MS); information technology (MS), including data science, information security, information technology management, software engineering; software engineering (MS). *Program availability:* Part-time, evening/weekend. *Faculty:* 7 full-time (0 women), 6 part-time/adjunct (1 woman). *Students:* 21 full-time (10 women), 10 part-time (3 women); includes 9 minority (5 Black or African American, non-Hispanic/Latino; 4 Asian, non-Hispanic/Latino), 1 international. Average age 34. 47 applicants, 49% accepted, 12 enrolled. In 2016, 26 degrees awarded. *Degree requirements:* For master's, capstone project. *Entrance requirements:* For master's, GRE, 2 references, transcripts, resume, personal statement. Additional exam requirements/recommendations for international students: Required—TOEFL (minimum score 570 paper-based; 80 iBT). *Application deadline:* Applications are processed on a rolling basis. Application fee: $50 ($75 for international students). Electronic applications accepted. *Expenses:* $1,226 per hour. *Financial support:* Scholarships/grants and employer agreements available. Financial award applicants required to submit FAFSA. *Unit head:* Dr. Fortune S. Mhlanga, Dean, 615-966-5073, E-mail: fortune.mhlanga@lipscomb.edu. *Application contact:* Brett Ramsey, Enrollment Management Specialist, 615-966-1193, E-mail: brett.ramsey@lipscomb.edu.
Website: http://www.lipscomb.edu/technology/

London Metropolitan University, Graduate Programs, London, United Kingdom. Offers applied psychology (M Sc); architecture (MA); biomedical science (M Sc); blood science (M Sc); cancer pharmacology (M Sc); computer networking and cyber security (M Sc); computing and information systems (M Sc); conference interpreting (MA); counter-terrorism studies (M Sc); creative, digital and professional writing (MA); crime, violence and prevention (M Sc); criminology (M Sc); curating contemporary art (MA); data analytics (M Sc); digital media (MA); early childhood studies (MA); education (MA, Ed D); financial services law, regulation and compliance (LL M); food science (M Sc); forensic psychology (M Sc); health and social care management and policy (M Sc); human nutrition (M Sc); human resource management (MA); human rights and international conflict (MA); information technology (M Sc); intelligence and security studies (M Sc); international oil, gas and energy law (LL M); international relations (MA); interpreting (MA); learning and teaching in higher education (MA); legal practice (LL M); media and entertainment law (LL M); organizational and consumer psychology (M Sc); psychological therapy (M Sc); psychology of mental health (M Sc); public health (M Sc); public policy and management (MPA); security studies (M Sc); social work (M Sc); spatial planning and urban design (MA); sports therapy (M Sc); supporting older children and young people with dyslexia (MA); teaching languages (MA), including Arabic, English; translation (MA); woman and child abuse (MA).

Long Island University–LIU Post, College of Management, Brookville, NY 11548-1300. Offers accountancy (MS); finance (MBA); information systems (MS); international business (MBA); management (MBA); management engineering (MS); marketing (MBA); taxation (MS); technical project management (MS); JD/MBA. *Accreditation:* AACSB. *Program availability:* Part-time, 100% online, blended/hybrid learning. *Faculty:* 35 full-time (12 women), 25 part-time/adjunct (6 women). *Students:* 153 full-time (61 women), 68 part-time (22 women); includes 44 minority (8 Black or African American, non-Hispanic/Latino; 24 Asian, non-Hispanic/Latino; 11 Hispanic/Latino; 1 Two or more races, non-Hispanic/Latino), 79 international. 429 applicants, 58% accepted, 74 enrolled. In 2016, 124 master's awarded. *Degree requirements:* For master's, thesis (for some programs). *Entrance requirements:* For master's, GMAT, GRE, or LSAT. Additional exam requirements/recommendations for international students: Required—PTE, TOEFL (minimum score 550 paper-based, 75 iBT) or IELTS. *Application deadline:* Applications are processed on a rolling basis. Application fee: $50. Electronic applications accepted. *Expenses: Tuition:* Full-time $28,272; part-time $1178 per credit. *Required fees:* $451 per term. Tuition and fees vary according to degree level and program. *Financial support:* In 2016–17, 68 students received support. Career-related internships or fieldwork, Federal Work-Study, institutionally sponsored loans, and scholarships/grants available. Support available to part-time students. Financial award application deadline: 2/15; financial award applicants required to submit FAFSA. *Faculty research:* Finance and sustainability, innovation and intellectual property rights, marketing: data analytics and business intelligence, social networking local and international. *Unit head:* Dr. Robert M. Valli, Dean, 516-299-4192, E-mail: rob.valli@liu.edu. *Application contact:* Carol Zerah, Director of Graduate and International Admissions, 516-299-2900, Fax: 516-299-2137, E-mail: post-enroll@liu.edu.
Website: http://liu.edu/CWPost/Academics/Schools/COM

Louisiana State University and Agricultural & Mechanical College, Graduate School, E. J. Ourso College of Business, Department of Information Systems and Decision Sciences, Baton Rouge, LA 70803. Offers MS, PhD.

Loyola University Maryland, Graduate Programs, Sellinger School of Business, Professional MBA Program, Baltimore, MD 21210-2699. Offers accounting (MBA); information systems operations management (MBA). *Accreditation:* AACSB. *Program availability:* Part-time, evening/weekend. *Faculty:* 26 full-time (8 women), 13 part-time/adjunct (5 women). *Students:* 59 applicants, 88% accepted, 47 enrolled. In 2016, 125 master's awarded. *Entrance requirements:* For master's, GMAT, resume, essay, official transcripts, professional letter of recommendation. Additional exam requirements/recommendations for international students: Required—TOEFL (minimum score 550 paper-based, 80 iBT) or IELTS (minimum score 7). *Application deadline:* For fall admission, 8/1 for domestic students, 5/1 for international students; for winter admission, 9/1 for international students; for spring admission, 12/1 for domestic students; for summer admission, 5/1 for domestic students. Applications are processed on a rolling basis. Application fee: $60. Electronic applications accepted. *Expenses:* Contact institution. *Financial support:* In 2016–17, 26 students received support. Scholarships/grants available. Financial award application deadline: 4/15; financial award applicants required to submit FAFSA.

Marist College, Graduate Programs, School of Computer Science and Mathematics, Poughkeepsie, NY 12601-1387. Offers computer science/software development (MS); information systems (MS, Adv C); technology management (MS). *Program availability:* Part-time, evening/weekend, online learning. *Entrance requirements:* For master's, resume. Additional exam requirements/recommendations for international students: Required—TOEFL (minimum score 550 paper-based; 80 iBT); Recommended—IELTS (minimum score 6.5). Electronic applications accepted. *Faculty research:* Data quality, artificial intelligence, imaging, analysis of algorithms, distributed systems and applications.

Marquette University, Graduate School of Management, Executive MBA Program, Milwaukee, WI 53201-1881. Offers economics (MBA); finance (MBA); human resources (MBA); international business (MBA); management information systems (MBA); marketing (MBA); operations and supply chain management (MBA); sports business (MBA). *Accreditation:* AACSB. *Students:* 39 full-time (12 women); includes 7 minority (4 Black or African American, non-Hispanic/Latino; 2 Asian, non-Hispanic/Latino; 1 Hispanic/Latino). Average age 38. 25 applicants, 96% accepted, 29 enrolled. In 2016, 14 master's awarded. *Degree requirements:* For master's, international trip. *Entrance requirements:* For master's, GMAT or GRE, two letters of recommendation, official transcripts from current and previous colleges/universities. Additional exam requirements/recommendations for international students: Required—TOEFL (minimum score 550 paper-based; 88 iBT), IELTS (minimum score 6.5), PTE. *Application deadline:* For fall admission, 2/15 for domestic and international students. Application fee: $50. Electronic applications accepted. *Expenses:* Contact institution. *Financial support:* Application deadline: 2/15. *Faculty research:* International trade and finance, customer relationship management, consumer satisfaction, customer service. *Unit head:* Dr. Brian Till, Dean, 414-288-5724. *Application contact:* Dr. Jeanne Simmons, Associate Dean, 414-288-7145.
Website: http://www.busadm.mu.edu/emba/

Marquette University, Graduate School of Management, Program in Business Administration, Milwaukee, WI 53201-1881. Offers business administration (MBA); economics (MBA); entrepreneurship (Certificate); finance (MBA); human resources (MBA); international business (MBA); management information systems (MBA); marketing (MBA); operations and supply chain management (MBA); sports business (MBA); JD/MBA; MBA/MA; MBA/MSN. *Accreditation:* AACSB. *Program availability:* Part-time, evening/weekend. *Students:* 25 full-time (12 women), 202 part-time (57 women); includes 17 minority (5 Black or African American, non-Hispanic/Latino; 6 Asian, non-Hispanic/Latino; 2 Hispanic/Latino; 1 Native Hawaiian or other Pacific Islander, non-Hispanic/Latino; 3 Two or more races, non-Hispanic/Latino), 7 international. Average age 31. 107 applicants, 87% accepted, 113 enrolled. In 2016, 107 master's, 5 other advanced degrees awarded. *Degree requirements:* For Certificate, business plan. *Entrance requirements:* For master's, GMAT or GRE, letters of recommendation. Additional exam requirements/recommendations for international students: Required—TOEFL (minimum score 550 paper-based; 88 iBT), IELTS (minimum score 6.5), PTE. *Application deadline:* For fall admission, 2/15 for domestic and international students. Applications are processed on a rolling basis. Application fee: $50. Electronic applications accepted. *Financial support:* Fellowships, research assistantships, teaching assistantships, Federal Work-Study, institutionally sponsored loans, scholarships/grants, and tuition waivers (full and partial) available. Support available to part-time students. Financial award application deadline: 2/15. *Faculty research:* Ethics in the professions, services marketing, technology impact on decision-making, mentoring. *Unit head:* Dr. Brian Till, Dean, 414-288-5724. *Application contact:* Dr. Jeanne Simmons, Associate Dean, 414-288-7145.
Website: http://business.marquette.edu/academics/mba

Marymount University, School of Business Administration, Program in Information Technology, Arlington, VA 22207-4299. Offers health care informatics (Certificate); information technology (MS, Certificate), including computer security (MS), health care informatics (MS), project management and technology leadership (MS), software engineering (MS); information technology project management and technology leadership (Certificate); MS/MBA; MS/MS. *Program availability:* Part-time, evening/weekend. *Faculty:* 7 full-time (6 women), 7 part-time/adjunct (0 women). *Students:* 39 full-time (23 women), 31 part-time (13 women); includes 24 minority (12 Black or African American, non-Hispanic/Latino; 5 Asian, non-Hispanic/Latino; 6 Hispanic/Latino; 1 Two or more races, non-Hispanic/Latino), 31 international. Average age 30. 67 applicants, 97% accepted, 23 enrolled. In 2016, 29 master's, 12 other advanced degrees awarded. *Degree requirements:* For master's, thesis or alternative. *Entrance requirements:* For master's, resume, bachelor's degree in computer related field or another subject with certificate in computer-related field or related work experience; bachelor's degree in computer science or work in software development (for software engineering track). Additional exam requirements/recommendations for international students: Required—TOEFL (minimum score 600 paper-based; 96 iBT), IELTS (minimum score 6.5). *Application deadline:* For fall admission, 7/16 priority date for domestic and international students; for spring admission, 11/16 priority date for domestic and international students; for summer admission, 4/16 for domestic and international students. Applications are processed on a rolling basis. Application fee: $40. Electronic applications accepted. *Expenses:* $960 per credit hour. *Financial support:* In 2016–17, 5 students received support, including 2 research assistantships with tuition reimbursements available; career-related internships or fieldwork, Federal Work-Study, scholarships/grants, and unspecified assistantships also available. Support available to part-time students. Financial award applicants required to submit FAFSA. *Unit head:* Dr. Diane Murphy, Chair/Director, Information Technology, Management Sciences and Cybersecurity, 703-284-5958, Fax: 703-527-3830, E-mail: diane.murphy@marymount.edu. *Application contact:* Francesca Reed, Director, Graduate Admissions, 703-284-5901, Fax: 703-527-3815, E-mail: grad.admissions@marymount.edu.
Website: http://www.marymount.edu/Academics/School-of-Business-Administration/Graduate-Programs/Information-Technology-(M-S-)

Marywood University, Academic Affairs, Munley College of Liberal Arts and Sciences, School of Business and Global Innovation, Emphasis in Management Information Systems, Scranton, PA 18509-1598. Offers MBA, MS. *Program availability:* Part-time. Electronic applications accepted.

McGill University, Faculty of Graduate and Postdoctoral Studies, Desautels Faculty of Management, Montréal, QC H3A 2T5, Canada. Offers administration (PhD); entrepreneurial studies (MBA); finance (MBA); general management (Post Master's Certificate); information systems (MBA); international business (MBA); international practicing management (MM); management (MBA); management for development (MBA); manufacturing management (MMM); marketing (MBA); operations management (MBA); public accountancy (Diploma); strategic management (MBA); MBA/LL B; MD/MBA. MMM offered jointly with Faculty of Engineering; PhD with Concordia University, HEC Montreal, Université de Montréal, Université du Québec à Montréal.

McMaster University, School of Graduate Studies, DeGroote School of Business, Program in Information Systems, Hamilton, ON L8S 4M2, Canada. Offers PhD. *Program availability:* Part-time. *Degree requirements:* For doctorate, comprehensive exam, thesis/dissertation. *Entrance requirements:* For doctorate, GMAT or GRE General Test, master's degree, minimum B+ average. Additional exam requirements/recommendations for international students: Required—TOEFL (minimum score 580 paper-based). *Faculty research:* Information systems, operations management, web-based decision support systems, web-based agents, financial engineering.

Metropolitan State University, College of Management, St. Paul, MN 55106-5000. Offers business administration (MBA, DBA); database administration (Graduate Certificate); healthcare information technology management (Graduate Certificate); information assurance security (Graduate Certificate); management information systems (MMIS); MIS generalist (Graduate Certificate); MIS systems analysis and design (Graduate Certificate); project management (Graduate Certificate); public and nonprofit administration (MPNA). *Program availability:* Part-time, evening/weekend. *Degree requirements:* For master's, thesis optional, computer language (MMIS). *Entrance requirements:* For master's, GMAT (for MBA), resume. Additional exam requirements/recommendations for international students: Required—TOEFL (minimum score 550 paper-based). Electronic applications accepted. *Faculty research:* Yugoslav economic system, workers' cooperatives, participative management and job enrichment, global business systems.

Michigan State University, The Graduate School, College of Communication Arts and Sciences, Department of Telecommunication, Information Studies, and Media, East Lansing, MI 48824. Offers digital media arts and technology (MA); information and telecommunication management (MA); information, policy and society (MA); serious game design (MA). *Entrance requirements:* Additional exam requirements/recommendations for international students: Required—TOEFL. Electronic applications accepted.

Michigan State University, The Graduate School, Eli Broad College of Business, Department of Accounting and Information Systems, East Lansing, MI 48224. Offers accounting (MS, PhD), including information systems (MS), public and corporate accounting (MS), taxation (MS); business information systems (PhD). *Accreditation:* AACSB. *Degree requirements:* For doctorate, comprehensive exam, thesis/dissertation. *Entrance requirements:* For master's, GMAT (minimum score 550), bachelor's degree in accounting; minimum cumulative GPA of 3.0 at any institution attended and in any junior-/senior-level accounting courses taken; 3 letters of recommendation (at least 1 from faculty); working knowledge of computers including word processing, spreadsheets, networking, and database management system; for doctorate, GMAT (minimum score 600), bachelor's degree; transcripts; 3 letters of recommendation; statement of purpose; resume; on-campus interview; personal qualifications of sound character, perseverance, intellectual curiosity, and interest in scholarly research. Additional exam requirements/recommendations for international students: Required—TOEFL (minimum score 600 paper-based; 100 iBT), IELTS (minimum score 7) accepted for MS only. Electronic applications accepted.

Middle Georgia State University, Office of Graduate Studies, Macon, GA 31206. Offers adult/gerontology acute care nurse practitioner (MSN); information technology (MS), including health informatics, information security and digital forensics, software development. *Entrance requirements:* For master's, GRE. Additional exam requirements/recommendations for international students: Required—TOEFL (minimum score 523 paper-based; 69 iBT). *Expenses:* Contact institution.

Middle Tennessee State University, College of Graduate Studies, Jennings A. Jones College of Business, Department of Computer Information Systems, Murfreesboro, TN 37132. Offers MS. *Program availability:* Part-time, evening/weekend, online learning. *Entrance requirements:* Additional exam requirements/recommendations for international students: Required—TOEFL (minimum score 525 paper-based; 71 iBT) or IELTS (minimum score 6). Electronic applications accepted. *Faculty research:* Safety and security, project management.

Minot State University, Graduate School, Information Systems Program, Minot, ND 58707-0002. Offers MSIS. *Program availability:* Part-time, online learning. *Entrance requirements:* Additional exam requirements/recommendations for international students: Required—TOEFL (minimum score 79 iBT), IELTS (minimum score 6).

Misericordia University, College of Business, Program in Organizational Management, Dallas, PA 18612-1098. Offers healthcare management (MS); human resource management (MS); information technology management (MS); management (MS); not-for-profit management (MS). *Program availability:* Part-time, evening/weekend, online learning. *Entrance requirements:* For master's, GRE General Test, MAT (35th percentile or higher), or minimum undergraduate GPA of 3.0. Additional exam requirements/recommendations for international students: Required—TOEFL. Electronic applications accepted. Application fee is waived when completed online. *Expenses:* Contact institution.

Mississippi State University, Bagley College of Engineering, Department of Industrial and Systems Engineering, Mississippi State, MS 39762. Offers human factors and ergonomics (MS); industrial and systems engineering (PhD); industrial systems (MS); management systems (MS); manufacturing systems (MS); operations research (MS). *Program availability:* Part-time, blended/hybrid learning. *Faculty:* 12 full-time (1 woman). *Students:* 25 full-time (5 women), 59 part-time (13 women); includes 18 minority (6 Black or African American, non-Hispanic/Latino; 5 Asian, non-Hispanic/Latino; 6 Hispanic/Latino; 1 Native Hawaiian or other Pacific Islander, non-Hispanic/Latino), 21 international. Average age 35. 72 applicants, 32% accepted, 11 enrolled. In 2016, 11 master's, 7 doctorates awarded. *Degree requirements:* For master's, comprehensive exam (for some programs), thesis optional, comprehensive oral or written exam; for doctorate, comprehensive exam, thesis/dissertation, candidacy exam. *Entrance requirements:* For master's, GRE (for graduates from program not accredited by EAC/ABET), minimum GPA of 3.0 on junior and senior years; for doctorate, GRE (for graduates from program not accredited by EAC/ABET), minimum GPA of 3.5 on master's degree and junior and senior years of BS. Additional exam requirements/

recommendations for international students: Required—TOEFL (minimum score 550 paper-based; 79 iBT); Recommended—IELTS (minimum score 6.5). *Application deadline:* For fall admission, 7/1 for domestic students, 5/1 for international students; for spring admission, 11/1 for domestic students, 9/1 for international students. Applications are processed on a rolling basis. Application fee: $60. Electronic applications accepted. *Expenses:* Tuition, state resident: full-time $7670; part-time $852.50 per credit hour. Tuition, nonresident: full-time $20,790; part-time $2310.50 per credit hour. Part-time tuition and fees vary according to course load. *Financial support:* In 2016–17, 12 research assistantships with full tuition reimbursements (averaging $16,360 per year), 3 teaching assistantships with full tuition reimbursements (averaging $17,014 per year) were awarded; Federal Work-Study, institutionally sponsored loans, and unspecified assistantships also available. Financial award application deadline: 4/1; financial award applicants required to submit FAFSA. *Faculty research:* Operations research, ergonomics, production systems, management systems, transportation. *Total annual research expenditures:* $4.4 million. *Unit head:* Dr. John Usher, Professor/Department Head, 662-325-7624, Fax: 662-325-7618, E-mail: usher@ise.msstate.edu. *Application contact:* Doretta Martin, Senior Admissions Assistant, 662-325-9514, E-mail: dmartin@grad.msstate.edu.
Website: http://www.ise.msstate.edu/

Mississippi State University, College of Business, Department of Management and Information Systems, Mississippi State, MS 39762. Offers business administration (MBA); information systems (MSIS, PhD); management (PhD); project management (MBA). *Program availability:* Part-time. *Faculty:* 18 full-time (4 women). *Students:* 66 full-time (15 women), 200 part-time (39 women); includes 25 minority (10 Black or African American, non-Hispanic/Latino; 1 American Indian or Alaska Native, non-Hispanic/Latino; 4 Asian, non-Hispanic/Latino; 6 Hispanic/Latino; 4 Two or more races, non-Hispanic/Latino), 20 international. Average age 31. 186 applicants, 39% accepted, 53 enrolled. In 2016, 84 master's, 2 doctorates awarded. *Degree requirements:* For master's, comprehensive exam; for doctorate, comprehensive exam, thesis/dissertation. *Entrance requirements:* For master's, GMAT, minimum GPA of 3.0 in last 60 hours of undergraduate course work; for doctorate, GMAT (minimum score of 550), minimum GPA of 3.25 on all graduate work; BS with minimum GPA of 3.0 cumulative and last 60 hours. Additional exam requirements/recommendations for international students: Required—TOEFL (minimum score 575 paper-based; 84 iBT); Recommended—IELTS (minimum score 7). *Application deadline:* For fall admission, 7/1 for domestic students, 5/1 for international students; for spring admission, 11/1 for domestic students, 9/1 for international students. Applications are processed on a rolling basis. Application fee: $60. Electronic applications accepted. *Expenses:* Tuition, state resident: full-time $7670; part-time $852.50 per credit hour. Tuition, nonresident: full-time $20,790; part-time $2310.50 per credit hour. Part-time tuition and fees vary according to course load. *Financial support:* Career-related internships or fieldwork, Federal Work-Study, institutionally sponsored loans, scholarships/grants, and unspecified assistantships available. Financial award applicants required to submit FAFSA. *Faculty research:* Electronic commerce, management of information technology. *Total annual research expenditures:* $1.3 million. *Unit head:* Dr. James J. Chrisman, Professor and Head, 662-325-1991, Fax: 662-325-8651, E-mail: jchrisman@business.msstate.edu. *Application contact:* Lakan Drinker, Admissions and Enrollment Assistant, 662-325-8951, E-mail: ldrinker@grad.msstate.edu.
Website: http://www.business.msstate.edu/programs/mis/index.php

Missouri State University, Graduate College, College of Business Administration, Department of Computer Information Systems, Springfield, MO 65897. Offers cybersecurity (MS). *Program availability:* Part-time, evening/weekend, online learning. *Faculty:* 12 full-time (2 women), 7 part-time/adjunct (0 women). *Students:* 4 full-time (1 woman), 31 part-time (6 women); includes 6 minority (3 Black or African American, non-Hispanic/Latino; 2 Asian, non-Hispanic/Latino; 1 Two or more races, non-Hispanic/Latino), 3 international. Average age 36. 36 applicants, 50% accepted, 10 enrolled. In 2016, 8 master's awarded. *Degree requirements:* For master's, comprehensive exam (for some programs), thesis optional. *Entrance requirements:* For master's, GMAT, 3 years of work experience in computer information systems, minimum GPA of 2.75 (MS), 9-12 teaching certification (MS Ed). Additional exam requirements/recommendations for international students: Required—TOEFL (minimum score 550 paper-based; 79 iBT), IELTS (minimum score 6). *Application deadline:* For fall admission, 7/20 priority date for domestic students, 5/1 for international students; for spring admission, 12/20 priority date for domestic students, 9/1 for international students; for summer admission, 5/20 priority date for domestic students. Applications are processed on a rolling basis. Application fee: $35 ($50 for international students). Electronic applications accepted. *Expenses:* Contact institution. *Financial support:* Federal Work-Study, institutionally sponsored loans, scholarships/grants, and unspecified assistantships available. Support available to part-time students. Financial award application deadline: 3/31; financial award applicants required to submit FAFSA. *Faculty research:* Information systems development, computer applications, information security. *Unit head:* Josh Davis, Department Head, 417-836-4426, Fax: 417-836-6907, E-mail: joshdavis@missouristate.edu. *Application contact:* Michael Edwards, Coordinator of Graduate Admissions, 417-836-5330, Fax: 417-836-6200, E-mail: michaeledwards@missouristate.edu.
Website: http://cis.missouristate.edu/

Morehead State University, Graduate Programs, College of Business and Public Affairs, Department of Information Systems, Morehead, KY 40351. Offers MSIS. *Entrance requirements:* For master's, GRE, GMAT. Additional exam requirements/recommendations for international students: Required—TOEFL (minimum score 525 paper-based). Electronic applications accepted.

Morehead State University, Graduate Programs, College of Business and Public Affairs, School of Business Administration, Morehead, KY 40351. Offers business administration (MBA); information systems (MSIS); sport management (MA). *Program availability:* Part-time, evening/weekend. *Entrance requirements:* For master's, GRE or GMAT. Additional exam requirements/recommendations for international students: Required—TOEFL (minimum score 500 paper-based). Electronic applications accepted.

Naval Postgraduate School, Departments and Academic Groups, Department of Information Sciences, Monterey, CA 93943. Offers electronic warfare systems engineering (MS); information sciences (PhD); information systems and operations (MS); information technology management (MS); information warfare systems engineering (MS); knowledge superiority (Certificate); remote sensing intelligence (MS); system technology (command, control and communications) (MS). Program open only to commissioned officers of the United States and friendly nations and selected United States federal civilian employees. *Program availability:* Part-time. *Degree requirements:* For master's, thesis (for some programs); for doctorate, thesis/dissertation. *Faculty research:* Designing inter-organisational collectivities for dynamic fit: stability, manoeuvrability and application in disaster relief endeavours; system self-awareness and related methods for Improving the use and understanding of data within DoD; evaluating a macrocognition model of team collaboration using real-world data from the Haiti relief effort; cyber distortion in command and control; performance and QoS in service-based systems.

Naval Postgraduate School, Departments and Academic Groups, Graduate School of Business and Public Policy, Monterey, CA 93943. Offers acquisition and contract management (MBA); business administration (EMBA, MBA); contract management (MS); defense business management (MBA); defense systems analysis (MS), including management; defense systems management (international) (MBA); financial management (MBA); information management (MBA); manpower systems analysis (MS); material logistics support management (MBA); program management (MS); resource planning and management for international defense (MBA); supply chain management (MBA); systems acquisition management (MBA); transportation management (MBA). Program only open to commissioned officers of the United States and friendly nations and selected United States federal civilian employees. *Accreditation:* AACSB; NASPAA. *Program availability:* Part-time, online learning. *Degree requirements:* For master's, thesis (for some programs), terminal project/capstone (for some programs). *Faculty research:* U.S. and European public procurement policies for small and medium-sized enterprises, examining external validity criticisms in the choice of students as subjects in accounting experiment studies, assurance of learning in contract management education, contracting for cloud computing: opportunities and risks, NPS, Apple App Store as a business model supporting U. S. Navy requirements.

New England Institute of Technology, Program in Information Technology, East Greenwich, RI 02818. Offers MS. *Program availability:* Part-time-only, evening/weekend, 100% online, blended/hybrid learning. *Entrance requirements:* Additional exam requirements/recommendations for international students: Required—TOEFL. *Application deadline:* Applications are processed on a rolling basis. Application fee: $25. Electronic applications accepted. *Expenses:* $550 per credit tuition, $50 registration fee, $155 student fee, $100 administrative fee. *Financial support:* Applicants required to submit FAFSA. *Application contact:* Michael Caruso, Director of Admissions, 800-736-7744 Ext. 3411, Fax: 401-886-0868, E-mail: mcaruso@neit.edu.
Website: http://www.neit.edu/Programs/Masters-Degree/Information-Technology

New Jersey Institute of Technology, Ying Wu College of Computing, Newark, NJ 07102. Offers big data management and mining (Certificate); business and information systems (Certificate); computer science (MS, PhD), including bioinformatics (MS), computer science, computing and business (MS), cyber security and privacy (MS), software engineering (MS); data mining (Certificate); information security (Certificate); information systems (MS, PhD), including business and information systems (MS), emergency management and business continuity (MS), information systems; information technology administration and security (MS); IT administration (Certificate); network security and information assurance (Certificate); software engineering analysis/design (Certificate); Web systems development (Certificate). *Program availability:* Part-time, evening/weekend. *Faculty:* 64 full-time (10 women), 38 part-time/adjunct (4 women). *Students:* 818 full-time (241 women), 225 part-time (53 women); includes 162 minority (35 Black or African American, non-Hispanic/Latino; 77 Asian, non-Hispanic/Latino; 41 Hispanic/Latino; 9 Two or more races, non-Hispanic/Latino), 772 international. Average age 27. 2,666 applicants, 51% accepted, 377 enrolled. In 2016, 398 master's, 10 doctorates, 9 other advanced degrees awarded. Terminal master's awarded for partial completion of doctoral program. *Degree requirements:* For master's, thesis optional; for doctorate, thesis/dissertation. *Entrance requirements:* For master's, GRE General Test; for doctorate, GRE General Test, minimum graduate GPA of 3.5. Additional exam requirements/recommendations for international students: Required—TOEFL (minimum score 550 paper-based; 79 iBT). *Application deadline:* For fall admission, 6/1 priority date for domestic students, 5/1 priority date for international students; for spring admission, 11/15 priority date for domestic and international students. Applications are processed on a rolling basis. Application fee: $75. Electronic applications accepted. *Expenses:* Contact institution. *Financial support:* In 2016–17, 57 students received support, including 18 research assistantships (averaging $16,073 per year), 39 teaching assistantships (averaging $20,194 per year); fellowships, career-related internships or fieldwork, Federal Work-Study, institutionally sponsored loans, and unspecified assistantships also available. Financial award application deadline: 1/15. *Faculty research:* Computer systems, communications and networking, artificial intelligence, database engineering, systems analysis, analytics and optimization in crowdsourcing. *Total annual research expenditures:* $3 million. *Unit head:* Dr. Craig Gotsman, Dean, 973-542-5488, Fax: 973-596-5777, E-mail: marek.rusinkiewicz@njit.edu. *Application contact:* Stephen Eck, Director of Admissions, 973-596-3300, Fax: 973-596-3461, E-mail: admissions@njit.edu.
Website: http://computing.njit.edu/

Newman University, MBA Program, Wichita, KS 67213-2097. Offers finance (MBA); international business (MBA); leadership (MBA); management (MBA); management information technology (MBA). *Program availability:* Part-time. *Degree requirements:* For master's, thesis optional. *Entrance requirements:* For master's, minimum GPA of 3.0; 2 letters of recommendation; course work in algebra, statistics, macroeconomics, and financial accounting. Additional exam requirements/recommendations for international students: Required—TOEFL (minimum score 600 paper-based; 100 iBT). Electronic applications accepted. *Expenses:* Contact institution.

New Mexico State University, College of Business, MBA Program, Las Cruces, NM 88003. Offers agribusiness (MBA); finance (MBA); information systems (MBA). *Accreditation:* AACSB. *Program availability:* Part-time-only, evening/weekend, online with required 2-3 day orientation and 2-3 day concluding session in Las Cruces. *Students:* 55 full-time (23 women), 121 part-time (67 women); includes 97 minority (5 Black or African American, non-Hispanic/Latino; 2 American Indian or Alaska Native, non-Hispanic/Latino; 2 Asian, non-Hispanic/Latino; 85 Hispanic/Latino; 3 Two or more races, non-Hispanic/Latino), 10 international. Average age 32. 139 applicants, 62% accepted, 23 enrolled. In 2016, 46 master's awarded. *Degree requirements:* For master's, comprehensive exam, thesis optional. *Entrance requirements:* For master's, GMAT or GRE (depending upon undergraduate or graduate degree institution and GPA), minimum GPA of 3.5 from AACSB international or ACBSP-accredited institution or graduate degree from regionally-accredited U.S. university (without GMAT or GRE). Additional exam requirements/recommendations for international students: Required—TOEFL (minimum score 550 paper-based; 79 iBT), IELTS (minimum score 6.5). *Application deadline:* For fall admission, 7/15 priority date for domestic students, 4/15 priority date for international students; for spring admission, 4/15 priority date for domestic students, 9/15 priority date for international students; for summer admission, 4/15 for domestic students, 1/15 for international students. Applications are processed on a rolling basis. Application fee: $40 ($50 for international students). Electronic applications accepted. *Expenses:* Tuition, state resident: full-time $4086. Tuition, nonresident: full-time $14,254. *Required fees:* $853. Tuition and fees vary according to course load. *Financial support:* In 2016–17, 39 students received support, including 1 fellowship (averaging $4,088 per year); Federal Work-Study, institutionally sponsored loans, scholarships/grants, health care benefits, and unspecified assistantships also available. Financial award application deadline: 3/1. *Unit head:* Dr. Kathleen Brook, Associate Dean, 575-646-5431, Fax: 575-646-6155, E-mail: kbrook@nmsu.edu. *Application contact:* John Shonk, MBA Advisor, 575-646-8003, Fax: 575-646-7977, E-mail: mbaprog@nmsu.edu.
Website: http://business.nmsu.edu/mba

New York University, Leonard N. Stern School of Business, Department of Information, Operations and Management Sciences, New York, NY 10012-1019. Offers information systems (MBA, PhD); operations management (MBA, PhD); statistics (MBA, PhD). *Faculty research:* Knowledge management, economics of information, computer-supported groups and communities financial information systems, data mining and business intelligence.

New York University, Polytechnic School of Engineering, Department of Technology Management, New York, NY 10012-1019. Offers construction management (Advanced Certificate); electronic business management (Advanced Certificate); entrepreneurship (Advanced Certificate); human resources management (Advanced Certificate); industrial engineering (MS); information management (Advanced Certificate); management (MS); management of technology (MS); manufacturing engineering (MS); organizational behavior (MS, Advanced Certificate); project management (Advanced Certificate); technology management (MBA, PhD, Advanced Certificate); telecommunications management (Advanced Certificate). *Program availability:* Part-time, evening/weekend. *Degree requirements:* For master's, comprehensive exam (for some programs), thesis (for some programs); for doctorate, comprehensive exam, thesis/dissertation. *Entrance requirements:* For master's, GMAT, minimum B average in undergraduate course work. Additional exam requirements/recommendations for international students: Required—TOEFL (minimum score 550 paper-based; 80 iBT); Recommended—IELTS (minimum score 6.5). Electronic applications accepted. *Faculty research:* Global innovation and research and development strategy, managing emerging technologies, technology and development, service design and innovation, tech entrepreneurship and commercialization, sustainable and clean-tech innovation, impacts of information technology upon individuals, organizations and society.

New York University, School of Continuing and Professional Studies, Division of Programs in Business, Graduate Programs in Management and Systems, New York, NY 10012-1019. Offers core business competencies (Advanced Certificate); database technologies (MS); enterprise risk management (MS, Advanced Certificate); information technologies (Advanced Certificate); strategy and leadership (MS, Advanced Certificate); systems management (MS). *Program availability:* Part-time, evening/weekend, online learning. *Degree requirements:* For master's, thesis, capstone project. *Entrance requirements:* For master's, GRE or GMAT (only upon request), bachelor's degree, resume with relevant professional work, internship or volunteer experience, two letters of recommendation, statement of purpose. Additional exam requirements/recommendations for international students: Required—TOEFL (minimum score 600 paper-based; 100 iBT), IELTS (minimum score 7). Electronic applications accepted.

North Carolina Agricultural and Technical State University, School of Graduate Studies, School of Technology, Department of Electronics, Computer, and Information Technology, Greensboro, NC 27411. Offers electronics and computer technology (MSIT, MSTM); information technology (MSIT, MSTM).

Northeastern University, College of Computer and Information Science, Boston, MA 02115-5096. Offers computer science (MS, PhD); data science (MS); game science and design (MS); health informatics (MS); information assurance (MS); network science (PhD); personal health informatics (PhD). *Program availability:* Part-time, evening/weekend. *Faculty:* 79 full-time (21 women), 34 part-time/adjunct (7 women). *Students:* 1,064 full-time (306 women), 34 part-time (10 women). In 2016, 322 master's, 8 doctorates awarded. Terminal master's awarded for partial completion of doctoral program. *Degree requirements:* For master's, thesis optional; for doctorate, comprehensive exam, thesis/dissertation. Application fee: $75. Electronic applications accepted. *Expenses:* $1,495 per credit. *Financial support:* Research assistantships, teaching assistantships, scholarships/grants, health care benefits, and unspecified assistantships available. Financial award applicants required to submit FAFSA. *Unit head:* Dr. Carla Brodley, Professor and Dean. *Application contact:* Dr. Rajmohan Rajaraman, Professor/Associate Dean/Director of the Graduate School, 617-373-8493, E-mail: gradschool@ccs.neu.edu.
Website: http://www.ccs.neu.edu/

Northeastern University, College of Engineering, Boston, MA 02115-5096. Offers bioengineering (MS, PhD); chemical engineering (MS, PhD); civil engineering (MS, PhD); computer engineering (PhD); computer systems engineering (MS); electrical and computer engineering (MS); electrical and computer engineering leadership (MS); electrical engineering (PhD); energy systems (MS); engineering and public policy (MS); engineering management (MS, Certificate); environmental engineering (MS); industrial engineering (MS, PhD); information assurance (PhD); information systems (MS); interdisciplinary engineering (PhD); mechanical engineering (PhD); operations research (MS); telecommunication systems management (MS). *Program availability:* Part-time, online learning. *Faculty:* 202 full-time (59 women), 53 part-time/adjunct (9 women). *Students:* 2,982 full-time (954 women), 192 part-time (38 women). In 2016, 851 master's, 74 doctorates awarded. Application fee: $75. Electronic applications accepted. *Expenses:* $1,471 per credit. *Financial support:* Fellowships, research assistantships, teaching assistantships, career-related internships or fieldwork, scholarships/grants, health care benefits, tuition waivers, and unspecified assistantships available. Support available to part-time students. Financial award applicants required to submit FAFSA. *Unit head:* Dr. Nadine Aubry, Dean, College of Engineering. *Application contact:* Jeffery Hengel, Director of Graduate Admissions, 617-373-2711, E-mail: j.hengel@northeastern.edu.
Website: http://www.coe.neu.edu/academics/graduate-school-engineering

Northern Illinois University, Graduate School, College of Business, Department of Operations Management and Information Systems, De Kalb, IL 60115-2854. Offers management information systems (MS). *Program availability:* Part-time. *Degree requirements:* For master's, computer language. *Entrance requirements:* For master's, GMAT, minimum GPA of 2.75. Additional exam requirements/recommendations for international students: Required—TOEFL (minimum score 550 paper-based). Electronic applications accepted. *Faculty research:* Affordability of home ownership, Web portal competition intranet, electronic commerce, corporate-academic alliances.

Northwestern University, School of Professional Studies, Program in Information Systems, Evanston, IL 60208. Offers analytics and business intelligence (MS); database and Internet technologies (MS); information systems (MS); information systems management (MS); information systems security (MS); medical informatics (MS); software project management and development (MS).

Northwest Missouri State University, Graduate School, School of Computer Science and Information Systems, Maryville, MO 64468-6001. Offers applied computer science (MS); information systems (MS); instructional technology (MS). *Program availability:* Part-time. *Degree requirements:* For master's, comprehensive exam. *Entrance requirements:* For master's, GRE General Test, minimum GPA of 3.0. Additional exam requirements/recommendations for international students: Required—TOEFL (minimum score 550 paper-based). *Expenses:* Tuition, state resident: full-time $3447; part-time $383 per credit hour. Tuition, nonresident: full-time $5724; part-time $636 per credit hour. *Required fees:* $130 per credit hour.

Nova Southeastern University, College of Engineering and Computing, Fort Lauderdale, FL 33314-7796. Offers computer science (MS, PhD); information assurance (PhD); information assurance and cybersecurity (MS); information systems (PhD); information technology (MS); management information systems (MS). *Program availability:* Part-time, evening/weekend, blended/hybrid learning. *Faculty:* 18 full-time (4 women), 11 part-time/adjunct (2 women). *Students:* 309 full-time (87 women), 407 part-time (125 women); includes 321 minority (139 Black or African American, non-Hispanic/Latino; 2 American Indian or Alaska Native, non-Hispanic/Latino; 52 Asian, non-Hispanic/Latino; 117 Hispanic/Latino; 11 Two or more races, non-Hispanic/Latino), 160 international. Average age 40. 390 applicants, 74% accepted. In 2016, 188 master's, 53 doctorates awarded. Terminal master's awarded for partial completion of doctoral program. *Degree requirements:* For master's, thesis optional; for doctorate, thesis/dissertation. *Entrance requirements:* For master's, minimum undergraduate GPA of 2.5; 3.0 in major; for doctorate, master's degree, minimum graduate GPA of 3.25. Additional exam requirements/recommendations for international students: Required—TOEFL (minimum score 80 iBT), IELTS (minimum score 6), PTE (minimum score 54). *Application deadline:* Applications are processed on a rolling basis. Application fee: $50. Electronic applications accepted. *Expenses:* $745 per credit hour (for master's); $1,075 per credit hour (for doctoral). *Financial support:* In 2016–17, 43 students received support. Federal Work-Study, scholarships/grants, and traineeships available. Financial award application deadline: 4/15; financial award applicants required to submit FAFSA. *Faculty research:* Artificial intelligence, database management, human-computer interaction, distance education, information assurance and cybersecurity. *Unit head:* Dr. Yong X. Tao, Dean, 954-262-2063, Fax: 954-262-2752, E-mail: ytao@nova.edu. *Application contact:* Nancy Azoulay, Director, Admissions, 954-262-2026, Fax: 954-262-2752, E-mail: azoulayn@nova.edu.
Website: http://scis.nova.edu

Oakland University, Graduate Study and Lifelong Learning, School of Business Administration, Department of Decision and Information Sciences, Rochester, MI 48309-4401. Offers information technology management (MS); management information systems (Certificate); production and operations management (Certificate).

Oakland University, Graduate Study and Lifelong Learning, School of Engineering and Computer Science, Department of Computer Science and Engineering, Rochester, MI 48309-4401. Offers computer science (MS); computer science and informatics (PhD); software engineering and information technology (MS). *Program availability:* Part-time, evening/weekend. *Entrance requirements:* For master's, minimum GPA of 3.0. Electronic applications accepted. *Expenses:* Contact institution.

The Ohio State University, Graduate School, Max M. Fisher College of Business, Department of Accounting and Management Information Systems, Columbus, OH 43210. Offers M Acc, PhD. *Accreditation:* AACSB. *Faculty:* 21. *Students:* 88 full-time (61 women); includes 6 minority (all Two or more races, non-Hispanic/Latino), 43 international. Average age 23. In 2016, 78 master's, 1 doctorate awarded. Terminal master's awarded for partial completion of doctoral program. *Degree requirements:* For doctorate, thesis/dissertation. *Entrance requirements:* For master's, GMAT (minimum score of 550 recommended, 600 preferred) or GRE; for doctorate, GMAT. Additional exam requirements/recommendations for international students: Required—TOEFL (minimum score 600 paper-based; 100 iBT), Michigan English Language Assessment Battery (minimum score 86); Recommended—IELTS (minimum score 7). *Application deadline:* For fall admission, 11/15 priority date for domestic and international students. Applications are processed on a rolling basis. Application fee: $60 ($70 for international students). Electronic applications accepted. *Financial support:* Fellowships with tuition reimbursements, research assistantships with tuition reimbursements, teaching assistantships with tuition reimbursements, career-related internships or fieldwork, Federal Work-Study, and institutionally sponsored loans available. Support available to part-time students. *Faculty research:* Artificial intelligence, protocol analysis, database design in decision-supporting systems. *Unit head:* Dr. Brian Mittendorf, Chair and Professor, 614-292-1720, E-mail: mittendorf.3@osu.edu. *Application contact:* Graduate and Professional Admissions, 614-292-6031, Fax: 614-292-3656, E-mail: gpadmissions@osu.edu.
Website: http://fisher.osu.edu/departments/accounting-and-mis/

Oklahoma State University, Spears School of Business, Department of Management Science and Information Systems, Stillwater, OK 74078. Offers management information systems (MS); management science and information systems (PhD); telecommunications management (MS). *Program availability:* Part-time, online learning. *Faculty:* 21 full-time (1 woman), 5 part-time/adjunct (2 women). *Students:* 95 full-time (20 women), 67 part-time (19 women); includes 14 minority (1 Black or African American, non-Hispanic/Latino; 2 American Indian or Alaska Native, non-Hispanic/Latino; 3 Asian, non-Hispanic/Latino; 4 Hispanic/Latino; 1 Native Hawaiian or other Pacific Islander, non-Hispanic/Latino; 3 Two or more races, non-Hispanic/Latino), 112 international. Average age 28. 779 applicants, 12% accepted, 56 enrolled. In 2016, 89 master's, 1 doctorate awarded. *Degree requirements:* For master's, thesis or alternative; for doctorate, comprehensive exam, thesis/dissertation. *Entrance requirements:* For master's and doctorate, GRE or GMAT. Additional exam requirements/recommendations for international students: Required—TOEFL (minimum score 550 paper-based; 79 iBT). *Application deadline:* For fall admission, 3/1 priority date for international students; for spring admission, 8/1 priority date for international students. Applications are processed on a rolling basis. Application fee: $40 ($75 for international students). Electronic applications accepted. *Expenses:* Tuition, state resident: full-time $3775; part-time $209.70 per credit hour. Tuition, nonresident: full-time $14,851; part-time $825.05 per credit hour. *Required fees:* $2027; $112.60 per credit hour. Tuition and fees vary according to campus/location. *Financial support:* In 2016–17, 2 research assistantships (averaging $5,500 per year), 18 teaching assistantships (averaging $8,542 per year) were awarded; career-related internships or fieldwork, Federal Work-Study, scholarships/grants, health care benefits, tuition waivers (partial), and unspecified assistantships also available. Support available to part-time students. Financial award application deadline: 3/1; financial award applicants required to submit FAFSA. *Unit head:* Dr. Rick Wilson, Department Head, 405-744-3551, Fax: 405-744-5180, E-mail: rick.wilson@okstate.edu. *Application contact:* Dr. Rathin Sarathy, Graduate Coordinator, 405-744-8646, Fax: 405-744-5180, E-mail: rathin.sarathy@okstate.edu.
Website: http://spears.okstate.edu/msis

Old Dominion University, College of Sciences, Program in Computer Science, Norfolk, VA 23529. Offers computer information systems (MS); computer science (MS, PhD). *Program availability:* Part-time, 100% online. *Faculty:* 16 full-time (3 women), 3 part-time/adjunct (0 women). *Students:* 69 full-time (26 women), 52 part-time (6 women); includes 12 minority (6 Black or African American, non-Hispanic/Latino; 2 Asian, non-Hispanic/Latino; 2 Hispanic/Latino; 2 Two or more races, non-Hispanic/Latino), 76 international. Average age 30. 155 applicants, 52% accepted, 30 enrolled. In 2016, 41 master's, 7 doctorates awarded. Terminal master's awarded for partial completion of doctoral program. *Degree requirements:* For master's, comprehensive exam, thesis optional, 34 credit hours; for doctorate, comprehensive exam, thesis/dissertation, 48 credit hours beyond the MS. *Entrance requirements:* For master's, GRE General Test, minimum GPA of 3.0; for doctorate, GRE General Test, MS in computer science. Additional exam requirements/recommendations for international students: Required—TOEFL (minimum score 550 paper-based; 79 iBT), IELTS (minimum score 6.5). *Application deadline:* For fall admission, 6/1 for domestic students, 4/15 for international

students; for spring admission, 11/1 for domestic students, 10/1 for international students; for summer admission, 3/1 for domestic students, 2/1 for international students. Applications are processed on a rolling basis. Application fee: $50. Electronic applications accepted. *Expenses:* Tuition, state resident: full-time $8604; part-time $478 per credit hour. Tuition, nonresident: full-time $21,510; part-time $1195 per credit hour. *Required fees:* $66 per semester. Tuition and fees vary according to campus/location, program and reciprocity agreements. *Financial support:* In 2016–17, 98 students received support, including 5 fellowships with full tuition reimbursements available (averaging $18,000 per year), 27 research assistantships with partial tuition reimbursements available (averaging $16,048 per year), 36 teaching assistantships with partial tuition reimbursements available (averaging $8,570 per year); career-related internships or fieldwork and scholarships/grants also available. Financial award application deadline: 2/15; financial award applicants required to submit FAFSA. *Faculty research:* Machine intelligence and data analytics, web science and digital libraries, networks and mobile computing, bioinformatics, scientific computing. *Total annual research expenditures:* $1.6 million. *Unit head:* Dr. Ravi Mukkamala, Interim Department Chair, 757-683-6001, Fax: 757-683-4900, E-mail: mukka@cs.odu.edu. *Application contact:* Dr. Yaohang Li, Graduate Program Director, 757-683-6001, E-mail: yaohang@cs.odu.edu.
Website: http://www.cs.odu.edu/

Our Lady of the Lake University, School of Business and Leadership, Program in Information Systems and Security, San Antonio, TX 78207-4689. Offers MS. *Program availability:* Part-time, online only, 100% online. *Faculty:* 5 full-time (3 women), 2 part-time/adjunct (0 women). *Students:* 28 full-time (8 women), 15 part-time (5 women); includes 32 minority (2 Black or African American, non-Hispanic/Latino; 1 Asian, non-Hispanic/Latino; 28 Hispanic/Latino; 1 Two or more races, non-Hispanic/Latino). Average age 36. 17 applicants, 65% accepted, 9 enrolled. In 2016, 18 master's awarded. *Entrance requirements:* For master's, GRE or GMAT, official transcripts showing baccalaureate degree from regionally-accredited institution in technical discipline and minimum GPA of 3.0 for cumulative undergraduate work or 3.2 in the major field (technical discipline) of study. Additional exam requirements/recommendations for international students: Required—TOEFL. *Application deadline:* For fall admission, 6/15 for domestic and international students; for spring admission, 11/15 for domestic and international students; for summer admission, 4/15 for domestic and international students. Applications are processed on a rolling basis. Application fee: $40 ($50 for international students). Electronic applications accepted. Application fee is waived when completed online. *Expenses: Tuition:* Full-time $14,796. Tuition and fees vary according to course load, degree level, campus/location and program. *Financial support:* In 2016–17, 14 students received support. Federal Work-Study, scholarships/grants, unspecified assistantships, and tuition discounts available. Support available to part-time students. Financial award application deadline: 5/1; financial award applicants required to submit FAFSA. *Faculty research:* Computer information systems implementation and best practices, computer and network security, cyber security legal issues, information assurance, and information technology education. *Unit head:* Carol Jeffries-Horner, Chair, Computer Information Systems and Security Department, 210-528-6730, E-mail: cjeffries@ollusa.edu. *Application contact:* Office of Graduate Admissions, 210-431-3995, Fax: 210-431-3945, E-mail: gradadm@ollusa.edu.
Website: http://www.ollusa.edu/s/1190/hybrid/default-hybrid-ollu.aspx?sid-1190&gid-1&pgid-7901

Pace University, Lubin School of Business, Information Systems Program, New York, NY 10038. Offers MBA. *Program availability:* Evening/weekend. *Students:* 10 full-time (7 women), 10 part-time (4 women); includes 7 minority (2 Black or African American, non-Hispanic/Latino; 3 Asian, non-Hispanic/Latino; 2 Two or more races, non-Hispanic/Latino), 6 international. Average age 29. 21 applicants, 38% accepted, 3 enrolled. In 2016, 2 master's awarded. *Entrance requirements:* For master's, GMAT, GRE, undergraduate degree, transcripts from all accredited colleges/universities attended, two letters of recommendation, resume, personal statement. Additional exam requirements/recommendations for international students: Required—TOEFL (minimum score 90 iBT), IELTS (minimum score 7) or PTE (minimum score 61). *Application deadline:* For fall admission, 8/1 priority date for domestic students, 6/1 for international students; for spring admission, 12/1 for domestic students, 10/1 for international students. Applications are processed on a rolling basis. Application fee: $70. Electronic applications accepted. *Expenses: Tuition:* Part-time $1195 per credit. *Required fees:* $260 per semester. Tuition and fees vary according to degree level, campus/location and program. *Financial support:* Research assistantships, career-related internships or fieldwork, and Federal Work-Study available. Support available to part-time students. Financial award application deadline: 2/15; financial award applicants required to submit FAFSA. *Unit head:* Dr. Li-Chiou Chen, Chairperson, 914-773-3907, E-mail: lchen@pace.edu. *Application contact:* Susan Ford-Goldschein, Director of Graduate Admissions, 212-346-1531, Fax: 212-346-1585, E-mail: graduateadmission@pace.edu.
Website: http://www.pace.edu/lubin/mba-in-information-systems

Pace University, Seidenberg School of Computer Science and Information Systems, New York, NY 10038. Offers chief information security officer (APC); computer science (MS, PhD); enterprise analytics (MS); information and communication technology strategy and innovation (APC); information systems (MS, APC); Internet technology (MS); professional studies in computing (DPS); secure software and information engineering (APC); security and information assurance (Certificate); software development and engineering (MS, Certificate); telecommunications systems and networks (MS, Certificate). *Program availability:* Part-time, evening/weekend, online only, 100% online, blended/hybrid learning. *Faculty:* 26 full-time (7 women), 7 part-time/adjunct (2 women). *Students:* 537 full-time (175 women), 303 part-time (85 women); includes 192 minority (79 Black or African American, non-Hispanic/Latino; 3 American Indian or Alaska Native, non-Hispanic/Latino; 53 Asian, non-Hispanic/Latino; 49 Hispanic/Latino; 8 Two or more races, non-Hispanic/Latino), 486 international. Average age 32. 599 applicants, 89% accepted, 248 enrolled. In 2016, 180 master's, 19 doctorates, 1 other advanced degree awarded. *Degree requirements:* For master's, thesis or alternative, capstone course; for doctorate, comprehensive exam (for some programs), thesis/dissertation. *Entrance requirements:* For master's, GRE General Test. Additional exam requirements/recommendations for international students: Required—TOEFL (minimum score 78 iBT), IELTS (minimum score 6.5) or PTE (minimum score 52). *Application deadline:* For fall admission, 8/1 priority date for domestic students, 6/1 for international students; for spring admission, 12/1 for domestic students, 10/1 for international students. Applications are processed on a rolling basis. Application fee: $70. Electronic applications accepted. *Expenses:* Contact institution. *Financial support:* In 2016–17, 45 students received support. Research assistantships, career-related internships or fieldwork, scholarships/grants, and unspecified assistantships available. Support available to part-time students. Financial award application deadline: 2/15; financial award applicants required to submit FAFSA. *Faculty research:* Cyber security/digital forensics; mobile app development; big data/enterprise analytics; artificial intelligence; software development. *Total annual research expenditures:* $314,545. *Unit head:* Dr. Jonathan Hill, Dean, Seidenberg School of Computer Science and Information Systems, 212-346-1864, E-mail: jhill@pace.edu. *Application contact:* Susan Ford-Goldschein, Director of Graduate Admissions, 914-422-4283, Fax: 212-346-1585, E-mail: graduateadmission@pace.edu.
Website: http://www.pace.edu/seidenberg

Pacific States University, College of Business, Los Angeles, CA 90010. Offers accounting (MBA); finance (MBA); international business (MBA, DBA); management of information technology (MBA); real estate management (MBA). *Program availability:* Part-time, evening/weekend, online learning. *Degree requirements:* For doctorate, comprehensive exam, thesis/dissertation. *Entrance requirements:* For master's, minimum undergraduate GPA of 2.5 during last 90 hours of course work. Additional exam requirements/recommendations for international students: Required—TOEFL (minimum score 500 paper-based; 61 iBT), IELTS (minimum score 5.5).

Pacific States University, College of Computer Science and Information Systems, Los Angeles, CA 90010. Offers computer science (MS); information systems (MS). *Program availability:* Part-time, evening/weekend. *Entrance requirements:* For master's, bachelor's degree in physics, engineering, computer science, or applied mathematics; minimum undergraduate GPA of 2.5 during last 90 hours of course work. Additional exam requirements/recommendations for international students: Required—TOEFL (minimum score 500 paper-based; 61 iBT), IELTS (minimum score 5.5).

Park University, School of Graduate and Professional Studies, Kansas City, MO 54105. Offers adult education (M Ed); business and government leadership (Graduate Certificate); business, government, and global society (MPA); communication and leadership (MA); creative and life writing (Graduate Certificate); disaster and emergency management (MPA, Graduate Certificate); educational leadership (M Ed); finance (MBA, Graduate Certificate); general business (MBA); global business (Graduate Certificate); healthcare administration (MHA); healthcare services management and leadership (Graduate Certificate); international business (MBA); language and literacy (M Ed), including English for speakers of other languages, special reading teacher/literacy coach; leadership of international healthcare organizations (Graduate Certificate); management information systems (MBA, Graduate Certificate); music performance (ADP, Graduate Certificate), including cello (MM, ADP), piano (MM, ADP), viola (MM, ADP), violin (MM, ADP); nonprofit and community services management (MPA); nonprofit leadership (Graduate Certificate); performance (MM), including cello (MM, ADP), piano (MM, ADP), viola (MM, ADP), violin (MM, ADP); public management (MPA); social work (MSW); teacher leadership (M Ed), including curriculum and assessment, instructional leader. *Program availability:* Part-time, evening/weekend, online learning. *Degree requirements:* For master's, comprehensive exam (for some programs), thesis (for some programs), internship (for some programs); exam (for some programs). *Entrance requirements:* For master's, GRE or GMAT (for some programs), teacher certification (for some M Ed programs), letters of recommendation, essay, resume (for some programs). Additional exam requirements/recommendations for international students: Required—TOEFL (minimum score 550 paper-based; 79 iBT), IELTS (minimum score 6). Electronic applications accepted.

Penn State Harrisburg, Graduate School, School of Business Administration, Middletown, PA 17057. Offers accounting (MPAC, Certificate); business administration (MBA); information systems (MS); operations and supply chain management (Certificate). *Program availability:* Part-time, evening/weekend. *Unit head:* Dr. Mukund S. Kulkarni, Chancellor, 717-948-6105, Fax: 717-948-6452. *Application contact:* Robert W. Coffman, Jr., Director of Enrollment Management, Admissions, 717-948-6250, Fax: 717-948-6325, E-mail: hbgadmit@psu.edu.
Website: https://harrisburg.psu.edu/business-administration/

Penn State University Park, Graduate School, College of Information Sciences and Technology, University Park, PA 16802. Offers enterprise architecture (MPS); information sciences (MPS); information sciences and technology (MS, PhD). *Students:* 108 full-time (41 women), 9 part-time (0 women). Average age 28. 262 applicants, 28% accepted, 38 enrolled. In 2016, 19 master's, 12 doctorates awarded. *Entrance requirements:* Additional exam requirements/recommendations for international students: Required—TOEFL (minimum score 550 paper-based; 80 iBT), IELTS. *Application deadline:* For fall admission, 12/15 for domestic and international students. Applications are processed on a rolling basis. Application fee: $65. Electronic applications accepted. *Financial support:* Fellowships, research assistantships, teaching assistantships, career-related internships or fieldwork, Federal Work-Study, scholarships/grants, traineeships, health care benefits, and unspecified assistantships available. Support available to part-time students. Financial award application deadline: 3/1; financial award applicants required to submit FAFSA. *Unit head:* Dr. Andrew L. Sears, Dean, 814-865-3528, Fax: 814-865-7485. *Application contact:* Lori Hawn, Director, Graduate Student Services, 814-865-1795, Fax: 814-863-4627, E-mail: l-gswww@lists.psu.edu.
Website: http://ist.psu.edu/

Point Park University, School of Business, Department of Business, Pittsburgh, PA 15222-1984. Offers business analytics (MBA); health systems management (MBA); international business (MBA); management (MBA); management information systems (MBA); sports, arts and entertainment management (MBA). *Program availability:* Evening/weekend, online learning.

Polytechnic University of Puerto Rico, Graduate School, Hato Rey, PR 00918. Offers business administration (MBA), including computer information systems, general management, management of information systems, management of international enterprises; civil engineering (ME, MS); computer engineering (ME, MS); computer science (MCS, MS); electrical engineering (ME, MS); engineering management (MEM); environmental management (MEM); landscape architecture (M Land Arch); manufacturing competitiveness (MMC, MS); manufacturing engineering (ME, MS); mechanical engineering (M Mech E). *Program availability:* Part-time, evening/weekend. *Entrance requirements:* For master's, 3 letters of recommendation.

Pontifical Catholic University of Puerto Rico, College of Business Administration, Program in Management Information Systems, Ponce, PR 00717-0777. Offers MBA, Professional Certificate. *Program availability:* Part-time, evening/weekend. *Degree requirements:* For master's, thesis. *Entrance requirements:* For master's, GRE, interview, minimum GPA of 2.75.

Prairie View A&M University, College of Engineering, Prairie View, TX 77446. Offers computer information systems (MSCIS); computer science (MSCS); electrical engineering (MSEE, PhDEE); general engineering (MS Engr). *Program availability:* Part-time, evening/weekend. *Faculty:* 27 full-time (7 women), 2 part-time/adjunct (both women). *Students:* 171 full-time (45 women), 50 part-time (17 women); includes 89 minority (70 Black or African American, non-Hispanic/Latino; 16 Asian, non-Hispanic/Latino; 3 Hispanic/Latino), 115 international. Average age 30. 155 applicants, 94% accepted, 85 enrolled. In 2016, 43 master's, 3 doctorates awarded. *Degree requirements:* For master's, thesis optional; for doctorate, comprehensive exam, thesis/dissertation. *Entrance requirements:* For master's, GRE General Test (minimum score of 900), bachelor's degree in engineering from ABET-accredited institution; for doctorate, minimum GPA of 3.0. Additional exam requirements/recommendations for international students: Required—TOEFL (minimum score 550 paper-based; 79 iBT). *Application deadline:* For fall admission, 5/1 priority date for domestic and international students; for spring admission, 10/1 priority date for domestic students, 9/1 priority date for international students; for summer admission, 3/1 priority date for domestic students,

2/1 priority date for international students. Applications are processed on a rolling basis. Application fee: $50. Electronic applications accepted. *Expenses:* Tuition, state resident: full-time $4362; part-time $273.48 per credit hour. Tuition, nonresident: full-time $12,390; part-time $534.10 per credit hour. *Required fees:* $2782; $178.26 per credit hour. *Financial support:* In 2016–17, 1 fellowship with full tuition reimbursement (averaging $14,000 per year), 33 research assistantships with full and partial tuition reimbursements (averaging $17,260 per year), 3 teaching assistantships with full and partial tuition reimbursements (averaging $15,000 per year) were awarded; career-related internships or fieldwork, institutionally sponsored loans, scholarships/grants, health care benefits, tuition waivers (full), and unspecified assistantships also available. Financial award application deadline: 4/1; financial award applicants required to submit FAFSA. *Faculty research:* Electrical and computer engineering: big data analysis, wireless communications, bioinformatics and computational biology, space radiation; computer science: cloud computing, cyber security; chemical engineering: thermochemical processing of biofuel, photochemical modeling; civil and environmental engineering: environmental sustainability, water resources, structure; mechanical engineering: thermal science, nanocomposites, computational fluid dynamics. *Unit head:* Dr. Kendall T. Harris, Dean, 936-261-9900, Fax: 936-261-9868, E-mail: tharris@pvamu.edu. *Application contact:* Pauline Walker, Administrative Assistant II, Research and Graduate Studies, 936-261-3521, Fax: 936-261-3529, E-mail: gradadmissions@pvamu.edu.

Purdue University, Graduate School, College of Technology, Department of Computer and Information Technology, West Lafayette, IN 47907. Offers MS. *Faculty:* 28 full-time (11 women). *Students:* 52 full-time (29 women), 41 part-time (13 women); includes 10 minority (3 Black or African American, non-Hispanic/Latino; 2 Asian, non-Hispanic/Latino; 2 Hispanic/Latino; 3 Two or more races, non-Hispanic/Latino), 52 international. Average age 30. 157 applicants, 30% accepted, 29 enrolled. In 2016, 32 master's awarded. *Entrance requirements:* For master's, GRE, minimum GPA of 3.0 or equivalent. *Application deadline:* For fall admission, 4/1 for domestic and international students; for spring admission, 10/1 for domestic students, 9/1 for international students; for summer admission, 4/1 for domestic students, 2/15 for international students. Applications are processed on a rolling basis. Application fee: $60 ($75 for international students). Electronic applications accepted. *Unit head:* Jeffrey Whitten, Head, 765-494-2566, E-mail: jwhitten@purdue.edu. *Application contact:* Stacy M. Lane, Graduate Contact, 765-494-4545, E-mail: smlane@purdue.edu.
Website: http://www.tech.purdue.edu/cit/

Radford University, College of Graduate Studies and Research, Program in Data and Information Management, Radford, VA 24142. Offers MS. *Program availability:* Part-time, evening/weekend. *Faculty:* 2 full-time (0 women). *Students:* 3 full-time (1 woman); includes 2 minority (both Asian, non-Hispanic/Latino), 1 international. Average age 27. 5 applicants, 80% accepted, 3 enrolled. *Entrance requirements:* For master's, GRE (minimum scores of 152 on quantitative portion and 148 on verbal portion, or 650 and 420, respectively, under old scoring system), minimum GPA of 3.0 overall from accredited educational institution, three letters of reference from faculty members familiar with academic performance in major coursework or from colleagues or supervisors familiar with work. Additional exam requirements/recommendations for international students: Required—TOEFL (minimum score 567 paper-based). *Application deadline:* Applications are processed on a rolling basis. Application fee: $50. Electronic applications accepted. *Expenses:* Tuition, state resident: full-time $7868; part-time $328 per credit hour. Tuition, nonresident: full-time $16,394; part-time $683 per credit hour. *Required fees:* $3090; $130 per credit hour. Tuition and fees vary according to course load and program. *Financial support:* In 2016–17, 2 students received support, including 1 research assistantship (averaging $11,000 per year); teaching assistantships, scholarships/grants, and unspecified assistantships also available. Support available to part-time students. *Unit head:* Dr. Jeff Pittges, Chair, Department of Information Technology, 540-831-5381, E-mail: jpittges@radford.edu.

Regent's University London, Webster Graduate School, London, United Kingdom. Offers business (MBA); finance (MS); human resources (MA); information technology management (MA); international business (MA); international non-governmental organizations (MA); international relations (MA); management and leadership (MA); marketing (MA). *Program availability:* Part-time.

Regis University, College of Computer and Information Sciences, Denver, CO 80221-1099. Offers agile technologies (Certificate); cybersecurity (Certificate); data science (M Sc); database administration with Oracle (Certificate); database development (Certificate); database technologies (M Sc); enterprise Java software development (Certificate); enterprise resource planning (Certificate); executive information technology (Certificate); health care informatics (Certificate); health care informatics and information management (M Sc); information assurance (M Sc); information assurance policy management (Certificate); information technology management (M Sc); mobile software development (Certificate); software engineering (M Sc, Certificate); software engineering and database technology (M Sc); storage area networks (Certificate); systems engineering (M Sc, Certificate). *Program availability:* Part-time, evening/weekend, 100% online, blended/hybrid learning. *Faculty:* 11 full-time (3 women), 30 part-time/adjunct (10 women). *Students:* 341 full-time (95 women), 318 part-time (98 women); includes 186 minority (56 Black or African American, non-Hispanic/Latino; 2 American Indian or Alaska Native, non-Hispanic/Latino; 48 Asian, non-Hispanic/Latino; 63 Hispanic/Latino; 17 Two or more races, non-Hispanic/Latino), 57 international. Average age 37. 342 applicants, 79% accepted, 174 enrolled. In 2016, 192 master's awarded. *Degree requirements:* For master's, thesis (for some programs), final research project. *Entrance requirements:* For master's, official transcript reflecting baccalaureate degree awarded from regionally-accredited college or university, 2 years of related experience, resume, interview. Additional exam requirements/recommendations for international students: Required—TOEFL (minimum score 550 paper-based; 82 iBT). *Application deadline:* For fall admission, 8/15 priority date for domestic students, 7/13 for international students; for winter admission, 10/10 priority date for domestic students, 9/8 for international students; for spring admission, 1/10 priority date for domestic students, 11/17 for international students; for summer admission, 5/1 priority date for domestic students. Applications are processed on a rolling basis. Application fee: $75. Electronic applications accepted. *Expenses:* $730 per credit hour. *Financial support:* Scholarships/grants available. Financial award application deadline: 4/15; financial award applicants required to submit FAFSA. *Faculty research:* Information policy, knowledge management, software architectures, data science. *Unit head:* Shari Plantz-Masters, Academic Dean. *Application contact:* Cate Clark, Director of Admissions, 303-458-4900, Fax: 303-964-5534, E-mail: ruadmissions@regis.edu.
Website: http://regis.edu/CCIS.aspx

Rensselaer Polytechnic Institute, Graduate School, Lally School of Management, Program in Business Analytics, Troy, NY 12180-3590. Offers MS. *Program availability:* Part-time. *Faculty:* 35 full-time (10 women), 7 part-time/adjunct (0 women). *Students:* 29 full-time (15 women), 6 part-time (5 women). 286 applicants, 25% accepted, 28 enrolled. In 2016, 20 master's awarded. *Entrance requirements:* For master's, GMAT or GRE, essays. Additional exam requirements/recommendations for international students: Required—TOEFL (minimum score 570 paper-based; 88 iBT), IELTS (minimum score 6.5), or PTE (minimum score 60). *Application deadline:* For fall admission, 1/1 for domestic and international students. Applications are processed on a rolling basis. Application fee: $75. Electronic applications accepted. *Expenses: Tuition:* Full-time $49,520; part-time $2060 per credit hour. *Required fees:* $2617. *Financial support:* Scholarships/grants available. Financial award application deadline: 1/1. *Unit head:* Dr. Dorit Nevo, Graduate Program Director, 518-276-2230, E-mail: nevod@rpi.edu. *Application contact:* Office of Graduate Admissions, 518-276-6276, E-mail: gradadmissions@rpi.edu.
Website: http://lallyschool.rpi.edu/academics/ms_ba.html

Rivier University, School of Graduate Studies, Department of Computer Information Systems, Nashua, NH 03060. Offers MS. *Program availability:* Part-time.

Robert Morris University, School of Communications and Information Systems, Moon Township, PA 15108-1189. Offers communication and information systems (MS); cyber security (MS); data analytics (MS); information security and assurance (MS); information systems and communications (D Sc); information systems management (MS); information technology project management (MS); Internet information systems (MS); organizational leadership (MS). *Program availability:* Part-time, evening/weekend, online learning. *Faculty:* 28 full-time (11 women), 6 part-time/adjunct (0 women). *Students:* 269 part-time (110 women); includes 49 minority (29 Black or African American, non-Hispanic/Latino; 10 Asian, non-Hispanic/Latino; 5 Hispanic/Latino; 5 Two or more races, non-Hispanic/Latino), 49 international. Average age 34. 239 applicants, 46% accepted, 83 enrolled. In 2016, 110 master's, 15 doctorates awarded. *Degree requirements:* For doctorate, thesis/dissertation. *Entrance requirements:* For doctorate, employer letter of endorsement, interview. Additional exam requirements/recommendations for international students: Required—TOEFL (minimum score 550 paper-based; 79 iBT). *Application deadline:* For fall admission, 7/1 priority date for domestic and international students; for spring admission, 11/1 priority date for domestic and international students. Applications are processed on a rolling basis. Application fee: $35. Electronic applications accepted. Application fee is waived when completed online. *Expenses:* $870 per credit (for master's degree). *Financial support:* Institutionally sponsored loans available. Support available to part-time students. Financial award application deadline: 5/1. *Unit head:* Ann Marie M. Le Blanc, Dean, 412-397-6433, Fax: 412-397-6469, E-mail: leblanc@rmu.edu. *Application contact:* Kellie L. Laurenzi, Associate Vice President, 412-397-5200, Fax: 412-397-5915, E-mail: graduateadmissions@rmu.edu.
Website: http://www.rmu.edu/web/cms/schools/scis/Pages/default.aspx

Robert Morris University Illinois, Morris Graduate School of Management, Chicago, IL 60605. Offers accounting (MBA); accounting/finance (MBA); business analytics (MIS); design and media (MM); design management (MM); educational technology (MM); health care administration (MM); higher education administration (MM); human resource management (MBA); information security (MIS); information systems (MBA, MIS); law enforcement administration (MM); management (MBA); management/finance (MBA); management/human resource management (MBA); mobile computing (MIS); sports administration (MM). *Program availability:* Part-time, evening/weekend. *Faculty:* 4 full-time (1 woman), 25 part-time/adjunct (5 women). *Students:* 196 full-time (98 women), 151 part-time (85 women); includes 200 minority (114 Black or African American, non-Hispanic/Latino; 17 Asian, non-Hispanic/Latino; 67 Hispanic/Latino; 2 Two or more races, non-Hispanic/Latino), 23 international. Average age 33. 174 applicants, 61% accepted, 97 enrolled. In 2016, 190 master's awarded. *Entrance requirements:* For master's, official transcripts and letters of recommendation (for some programs); written personal statement. Additional exam requirements/recommendations for international students: Required—TOEFL (minimum score 550 paper-based). *Application deadline:* Applications are processed on a rolling basis. Application fee: $20 ($100 for international students). Electronic applications accepted. *Expenses: Tuition:* Full-time $16,500; part-time $2750 per course. *Financial support:* In 2016–17, 444 students received support. Federal Work-Study, scholarships/grants, and unspecified assistantships available. Support available to part-time students. Financial award applicants required to submit FAFSA. *Unit head:* Kayed Akkawi, Dean, 312-935-6050, Fax: 312-935-6020, E-mail: kakkawi@robertmorris.edu. *Application contact:* Danielle Naffziger, Vice President of Marketing and Enrollment, 312-935-4812, Fax: 312-935-6020, E-mail: dnaffziger@robertmorris.edu.

Rochester Institute of Technology, Graduate Enrollment Services, Golisano College of Computing and Information Sciences, Information Science and Technologies Department, Advanced Certificate Program in Networking, Planning and Design, Rochester, NY 14623. Offers Advanced Certificate. *Program availability:* Part-time, evening/weekend, 100% online. *Students:* 4 applicants. In 2016, 1 Advanced Certificate awarded. *Entrance requirements:* For degree, GRE, minimum GPA of 3.0 (recommended). Additional exam requirements/recommendations for international students: Required—TOEFL (minimum score 570 paper-based; 88 iBT), IELTS (minimum score 6.5), PTE (minimum score 61). *Application deadline:* Applications are processed on a rolling basis. Application fee: $60. Electronic applications accepted. *Expenses:* $1,742 per credit hour (classroom), $993 per credit hour (online). *Financial support:* Available to part-time students. Applicants required to submit FAFSA. *Faculty research:* Enterprise network architectures and administration, emerging network technologies, the network design process, and project management. *Unit head:* Qi Yu, Graduate Program Director, 585-475-6929, E-mail: informaticsgrad@rit.edu. *Application contact:* Diane Ellison, Associate Vice President, Graduate Enrollment Services, 585-475-2229, Fax: 585-475-7164, E-mail: gradinfo@rit.edu.
Website: http://www.ist.rit.edu/degrees/graduate/advanced-cert.php

Rose-Hulman Institute of Technology, Faculty of Engineering and Applied Sciences, Department of Electrical and Computer Engineering, Terre Haute, IN 47803-3999. Offers electrical and computer engineering (M Eng); electrical engineering (MS); systems engineering and management (MS). *Program availability:* Part-time. *Faculty:* 18 full-time (2 women), 1 (woman) part-time/adjunct. *Students:* 7 full-time (3 women), 7 part-time (0 women), 12 international. Average age 25. 17 applicants, 65% accepted, 3 enrolled. In 2016, 7 master's awarded. *Degree requirements:* For master's, thesis (for some programs). *Entrance requirements:* For master's, GRE, minimum GPA of 3.0. Additional exam requirements/recommendations for international students: Required—TOEFL (minimum score 580 paper-based; 92 iBT). *Application deadline:* For fall admission, 2/1 priority date for domestic students. Applications are processed on a rolling basis. Application fee: $0. Electronic applications accepted. *Expenses: Tuition:* Full-time $43,122. *Financial support:* In 2016–17, 14 students received support. Fellowships with tuition reimbursements available, research assistantships with tuition reimbursements available, institutionally sponsored loans, scholarships/grants, and tuition waivers (full and partial) available. *Faculty research:* VLSI, power systems, analog electronics, communications, electromagnetics. *Total annual research expenditures:* $84,698. *Unit head:* Dr. Mario Simoni, Chairman, 812-877-8341, Fax: 812-877-8895, E-mail: simoni@rose-hulman.edu. *Application contact:* Dr. Azad Siahmakoun, Associate Dean of the Faculty, 812-877-8400, Fax: 812-877-8061, E-mail: siahmako@rose-hulman.edu.
Website: http://www.rose-hulman.edu/academics/academic-departments/electrical-computer-engineering.aspx

Rutgers University–Newark, Graduate School, Program in Management, Newark, NJ 07102. Offers accounting (PhD); accounting information systems (PhD); computer information systems (PhD); finance (PhD); information technology (PhD); international business (PhD); management science (PhD); marketing (PhD); organization management (PhD). Program offered jointly with New Jersey Institute of Technology. *Accreditation:* AACSB. *Degree requirements:* For doctorate, thesis/dissertation, cumulative exams. *Entrance requirements:* For doctorate, GMAT or GRE General Test, minimum undergraduate B average. Additional exam requirements/recommendations for international students: Required—TOEFL. Electronic applications accepted. *Faculty research:* Technology management, leadership and teams, consumer behavior, financial and markets, logistics.

Rutgers University–Newark, Rutgers Business School–Newark and New Brunswick, Doctoral Programs in Management, Newark, NJ 07102. Offers accounting (PhD); accounting information systems (PhD); economics (PhD); finance (PhD); individualized study (PhD); information technology (PhD); international business (PhD); management science (PhD); marketing science (PhD); organizational management (PhD); science, technology and management (PhD); supply chain management (PhD). *Degree requirements:* For doctorate, comprehensive exam, thesis/dissertation. *Entrance requirements:* For doctorate, GRE or GMAT. Additional exam requirements/recommendations for international students: Required—TOEFL (minimum score 550 paper-based; 79 iBT). Electronic applications accepted.

Rutgers University–Newark, Rutgers Business School–Newark and New Brunswick, Program in Information Technology, Newark, NJ 07102. Offers MIT. *Entrance requirements:* For master's, GMAT. Additional exam requirements/recommendations for international students: Required—TOEFL.

St. John's University, The Peter J. Tobin College of Business, Department of Computer Information Systems and Decision Sciences, Queens, NY 11439. Offers business analytics (MBA). *Program availability:* Part-time, evening/weekend. *Degree requirements:* For master's, comprehensive exam (for some programs), thesis optional. *Entrance requirements:* For master's, GMAT, 2 letters of recommendation, resume, transcripts, essay. Additional exam requirements/recommendations for international students: Required—TOEFL (minimum score 600 paper-based; 100 iBT), IELTS (minimum score 7). Electronic applications accepted. *Expenses:* Contact institution.

Saint Joseph's University, Erivan K. Haub School of Business, MS Program in Business Intelligence and Analytics, Philadelphia, PA 19131-1395. Offers MS. *Program availability:* Part-time, evening/weekend, online learning. *Faculty:* 12 full-time (6 women), 17 part-time/adjunct (3 women). *Students:* 74 full-time (33 women), 224 part-time (94 women); includes 67 minority (33 Black or African American, non-Hispanic/Latino; 24 Asian, non-Hispanic/Latino; 9 Hispanic/Latino; 1 Two or more races, non-Hispanic/Latino), 102 international. Average age 33. 268 applicants, 77% accepted, 97 enrolled. In 2016, 112 master's awarded. *Degree requirements:* For master's, minimum GPA of 3.0. *Entrance requirements:* For master's, GMAT or GRE, 2 letters of recommendation, resume, personal statement, official undergraduate and graduate transcripts. Additional exam requirements/recommendations for international students: Required—TOEFL (minimum score 550 paper-based, 80 iBT), IELTS (minimum score 6.5), or PTE (minimum score 60). *Application deadline:* For fall admission, 7/15 priority date for domestic students, 5/15 priority date for international students; for spring admission, 11/15 priority date for domestic students, 10/15 priority date for international students; for summer admission, 4/15 priority date for domestic students. Applications are processed on a rolling basis. Application fee: $35. Electronic applications accepted. *Expenses:* $1,003 per credit. *Financial support:* In 2016–17, 67 students received support. Scholarships/grants available. Support available to part-time students. Financial award application deadline: 5/1; financial award applicants required to submit FAFSA. *Unit head:* Jeannine Lajeunesse, Director, 610-660-1626, Fax: 610-660-1229, E-mail: jlajeune@sju.edu. *Application contact:* Kate Sonstein, Program Manager/Recruiter, 610-660-1693, E-mail: kate.sonstein@sju.edu.
Website: http://www.sju.edu/hsb/bi/

Saint Peter's University, Graduate Business Programs, MBA Program, Jersey City, NJ 07306-5997. Offers finance (MBA); health care administration (MBA); human resource management (MBA); international business (MBA); management (MBA); management information systems (MBA); marketing (MBA); risk management (MBA); MBA/MS. *Program availability:* Part-time, evening/weekend. *Entrance requirements:* Additional exam requirements/recommendations for international students: Required—TOEFL. Electronic applications accepted. *Faculty research:* Finance, health care management, human resource management, international business, management, management information systems, marketing, risk management.

San Diego State University, Graduate and Research Affairs, College of Business Administration, Department of Management Information Systems, San Diego, CA 92182. Offers information systems (MS). *Program availability:* Evening/weekend. *Degree requirements:* For master's, thesis or alternative. *Entrance requirements:* For master's, GMAT, resume, letters of reference. Additional exam requirements/recommendations for international students: Required—TOEFL. Electronic applications accepted.

San Francisco State University, Division of Graduate Studies, College of Business, Program in Business Administration, San Francisco, CA 94132-1722. Offers decision sciences/operations research (MBA); ethics and compliance (MBA); finance (MBA); global business and innovation (MBA); healthcare administration (MBA); hospitality and tourism management (MBA); information systems (MBA); leadership (MBA); marketing (MBA); nonprofit and social enterprise leadership (MBA); sustainable business (MBA). *Accreditation:* AACSB. *Program availability:* Part-time, evening/weekend. *Degree requirements:* For master's, thesis, essay test. *Entrance requirements:* For master's, GMAT, minimum GPA of 2.7 in last 60 units. Additional exam requirements/recommendations for international students: Required—TOEFL (minimum score 550 paper-based). *Application deadline:* For fall admission, 5/1 priority date for domestic students, 4/1 for international students; for spring admission, 11/1 for domestic students, 10/15 for international students. Applications are processed on a rolling basis. Application fee: $55. *Expenses:* Tuition, state resident: full-time $6738. Tuition, nonresident: full-time $15,666. *Required fees:* $1012. Tuition and fees vary according to degree level and program. *Financial support:* Application deadline: 3/1. *Unit head:* Dr. Sanjit Sengupta, Faculty Director, 415-817-4366, Fax: 415-817-4340, E-mail: sengupta@sfsu.edu. *Application contact:* Zandra Tan, EMBA Program Coordinator, 415-817-4360, Fax: 415-817-4340, E-mail: zandra13@sfsu.edu.
Website: http://cob.sfsu.edu/graduate-programs/mba

Santa Clara University, Leavey School of Business, Santa Clara, CA 95053. Offers business administration (MBA); business analytics (MS); finance (MS); information systems (MS); supply chain management and analytics (MS); JD/MBA. *Accreditation:* AACSB. *Program availability:* Part-time, evening/weekend. *Faculty:* 92 full-time (27 women), 44 part-time/adjunct (18 women). *Students:* 330 full-time (192 women), 323 part-time (136 women); includes 190 minority (7 Black or African American, non-Hispanic/Latino; 140 Asian, non-Hispanic/Latino; 28 Hispanic/Latino; 2 Native Hawaiian or other Pacific Islander, non-Hispanic/Latino; 13 Two or more races, non-Hispanic/Latino), 275 international. Average age 30. 388 applicants, 53% accepted, 107 enrolled. In 2016, 339 master's awarded. *Entrance requirements:* For master's, GMAT or GRE, resume, 2 letters of recommendation, 2 transcripts. Additional exam requirements/recommendations for international students: Required—TOEFL (minimum score 100 iBT) or IELTS (7.0). Application fee: $100 ($150 for international students). Electronic applications accepted. *Expenses:* $1,022 per unit tuition (for MBA); $1,124 per unit tuition (for other master's programs). *Financial support:* Fellowships, research assistantships, teaching assistantships, career-related internships or fieldwork, Federal Work-Study, scholarships/grants, traineeships, health care benefits, tuition waivers, and unspecified assistantships available. Support available to part-time students. Financial award applicants required to submit FAFSA. *Faculty research:* Intellectual property, research and development, international trade. *Unit head:* Caryn Beck-Dudley, Dean. *Application contact:* Taryn Upchurch, Director, Graduate Admissions and Recruitment, 408-551-7858, E-mail: upchurch@scu.edu.
Website: http://www.scu.edu/business/

Schiller International University, MBA Programs, Florida, Program in Information Technology, Largo, FL 33771. Offers MBA. *Entrance requirements:* Additional exam requirements/recommendations for international students: Required—TOEFL.

Schiller International University, MBA Programs, Heidelberg, Germany, Heidelberg, Germany. Offers international business (MBA, MIM); management of information technology (MBA). *Program availability:* Part-time, evening/weekend. *Degree requirements:* For master's, thesis optional. *Entrance requirements:* Additional exam requirements/recommendations for international students: Required—TOEFL (minimum score 550 paper-based). *Faculty research:* Leadership, international economy, foreign direct investment.

Seattle Pacific University, Master of Science in Information Systems Management Program, Seattle, WA 98119-1997. Offers MS. *Program availability:* Part-time. *Entrance requirements:* For master's, GMAT (minimum score of 500 preferred; 25 verbal, 30 quantitative, 4.4 analytical writing); GRE (minimum score of 295 preferred; 150 verbal/450 old scoring, 145 quantitative/525 old scoring), BA, resume as evidence of substantive work experience. Additional exam requirements/recommendations for international students: Required—TOEFL. Electronic applications accepted.

Shepherd University, Hollywood CG School of Digital Arts, Los Angeles, CA 90065. Offers game art and design (MSIT); visual effects and animation (MSIT). *Degree requirements:* For master's, exam, thesis, or portfolio.

Shippensburg University of Pennsylvania, School of Graduate Studies, College of Arts and Sciences, Department of Computer Science and Engineering, Shippensburg, PA 17257-2299. Offers agile software engineering (Certificate); computer science (MS), including computer science, cybersecurity, IT leadership, management information systems, software engineering; IT leadership (Certificate). *Program availability:* Part-time, evening/weekend. *Faculty:* 7 full-time (3 women). *Students:* 16 full-time (8 women), 14 part-time (5 women); includes 3 minority (2 Black or African American, non-Hispanic/Latino; 1 Hispanic/Latino), 21 international. Average age 29. 89 applicants, 49% accepted, 9 enrolled. In 2016, 10 master's awarded. *Entrance requirements:* For master's, GRE (if GPA less than 2.75), professional resume. Additional exam requirements/recommendations for international students: Required—TOEFL (minimum score 70 iBT) or IELTS (minimum score 6). *Application deadline:* For fall admission, 4/30 for international students; for spring admission, 9/30 for international students. Applications are processed on a rolling basis. Application fee: $45. Electronic applications accepted. *Expenses:* Tuition, state resident: part-time $483 per credit. Tuition, nonresident: part-time $725 per credit. *Required fees:* $141 per credit. *Financial support:* In 2016–17, 7 students received support. Career-related internships or fieldwork, scholarships/grants, unspecified assistantships, and resident hall director and student payroll positions available. Support available to part-time students. Financial award application deadline: 3/1; financial award applicants required to submit FAFSA. *Unit head:* Dr. Jeonghwa Lee, Associate Professor and Program Coordinator, 717-477-1178, Fax: 717-477-4002, E-mail: jlee@ship.edu. *Application contact:* Megan N. Luft, Assistant Dean of Graduate Admissions, 717-477-1231, Fax: 717-477-4016, E-mail: mnluft@ship.edu.
Website: http://www.cs.ship.edu/

Shippensburg University of Pennsylvania, School of Graduate Studies, College of Arts and Sciences, Department of Sociology and Anthropology, Shippensburg, PA 17257-2299. Offers organizational development and leadership (MS), including business, higher education structure and policy, historical administration, leadership in society, management information systems, public organizations. *Program availability:* Part-time, evening/weekend. *Faculty:* 4 full-time (3 women). *Students:* 11 full-time (6 women), 29 part-time (18 women); includes 9 minority (7 Black or African American, non-Hispanic/Latino; 1 Hispanic/Latino; 1 Two or more races, non-Hispanic/Latino). Average age 29. 58 applicants, 67% accepted, 21 enrolled. In 2016, 24 master's awarded. *Degree requirements:* For master's, capstone experience including internship. *Entrance requirements:* For master's, interview (if GPA less than 2.75), current resume, personal goals statement. Additional exam requirements/recommendations for international students: Required—TOEFL (minimum score 550 paper-based, 68 iBT) or IELTS (minimum score 6). *Application deadline:* For fall admission, 4/30 for international students; for spring admission, 9/30 for international students. Applications are processed on a rolling basis. Application fee: $45. Electronic applications accepted. *Expenses:* Tuition, state resident: part-time $483 per credit. Tuition, nonresident: part-time $725 per credit. *Required fees:* $141 per credit. *Financial support:* In 2016–17, 9 students received support. Career-related internships or fieldwork, scholarships/grants, unspecified assistantships, and resident hall director and student payroll positions available. Support available to part-time students. Financial award application deadline: 3/1; financial award applicants required to submit FAFSA. *Unit head:* Dr. Barbara J. Denison, Departmental Chair and Program Coordinator, 717-477-1735, Fax: 717-477-4011, E-mail: bjdeni@ship.edu. *Application contact:* Megan N. Luft, Assistant Dean of Graduate Admissions, 717-477-1231, Fax: 717-477-4016, E-mail: mnluft@ship.edu.
Website: http://www.ship.edu/odl/

Shippensburg University of Pennsylvania, School of Graduate Studies, John L. Grove College of Business, Shippensburg, PA 17257-2299. Offers advanced studies in business (Certificate); advanced supply chain and logistics management (Certificate); business administration (MBA), including business administration, finance, healthcare management, management information systems, supply chain management; finance (Certificate); health care management (Certificate); management information systems (Certificate). *Accreditation:* AACSB. *Program availability:* Part-time, evening/weekend, 100% online, blended/hybrid learning. *Faculty:* 23 full-time (4 women), 4 part-time/adjunct (1 woman). *Students:* 58 full-time (17 women), 195 part-time (59 women); includes 26 minority (12 Black or African American, non-Hispanic/Latino; 8 Asian, non-Hispanic/Latino; 5 Hispanic/Latino; 1 Two or more races, non-Hispanic/Latino), 26 international. Average age 32. 224 applicants, 55% accepted, 70 enrolled. In 2016, 101 master's awarded. *Degree requirements:* For master's, thesis optional, practicum. *Entrance requirements:* For master's, GMAT (minimum score 450 if less than 5 years of mid-level experience, including management experience), current resume; relevant work/classroom experience; 500-word statement of purpose; prerequisites of quantitative analysis, computer usage, and oral and written communications; laptop computer. Additional exam requirements/recommendations for international students: Required—TOEFL (minimum score 550 paper-based, 68 iBT) or IELTS (minimum score 6). *Application deadline:* For fall admission, 4/30 for international students; for spring admission, 9/30 for international students. Applications are processed on a rolling basis.

Application fee: $45. Electronic applications accepted. *Expenses:* Tuition, state resident: part-time $483 per credit. Tuition, nonresident: part-time $725 per credit. *Required fees:* $141 per credit. *Financial support:* In 2016–17, 12 students received support. Career-related internships or fieldwork, scholarships/grants, unspecified assistantships, and resident hall director and student payroll positions available. Support available to part-time students. Financial award application deadline: 3/1; financial award applicants required to submit FAFSA. *Unit head:* Dr. John G. Kooti, Dean of the College of Business, 717-477-1435, Fax: 717-477-4003, E-mail: jgkooti@ship.edu. *Application contact:* Megan N. Luft, Associate Dean of Graduate Admissions, 717-477-1231, Fax: 717-477-4016, E-mail: mnluft@ship.edu.
Website: http://www.ship.edu/business

Southeastern Oklahoma State University, School of Arts and Sciences, Durant, OK 74701-0609. Offers biology (MT); computer information systems (MT); occupational safety and health (MT). *Program availability:* Part-time, evening/weekend. *Degree requirements:* For master's, thesis optional. *Entrance requirements:* For master's, minimum GPA of 3.0 in last 60 hours or 2.75 overall. Additional exam requirements/recommendations for international students: Required—TOEFL (minimum score 550 paper-based; 79 iBT). Electronic applications accepted.

Southern Illinois University Edwardsville, Graduate School, School of Business, Department of Computer Management and Information Systems, Edwardsville, IL 62026. Offers MS. *Program availability:* Part-time, evening/weekend. *Degree requirements:* For master's, thesis or alternative, final exam. *Entrance requirements:* For master's, GMAT. Additional exam requirements/recommendations for international students: Required—TOEFL (minimum score 550 paper-based; 79 iBT), IELTS (minimum score 6.5). Electronic applications accepted.

Southern Illinois University Edwardsville, Graduate School, School of Business, Program in Business Administration, Edwardsville, IL 62026. Offers business analytics (MBA); management information systems (MBA); project management (MBA). *Accreditation:* AACSB. *Program availability:* Part-time, evening/weekend. *Degree requirements:* For master's, comprehensive exam. *Entrance requirements:* For master's, GMAT. Additional exam requirements/recommendations for international students: Required—TOEFL (minimum score 550 paper-based; 79 iBT), IELTS (minimum score 6.5). Electronic applications accepted.

Southern Methodist University, Cox School of Business, MBA Program, Dallas, TX 75275. Offers accounting (MBA, PMBA); business administration (EMBA); finance (MBA); financial statement analysis (PMBA); general business (MBA); information technology and operations management (MBA); management (MBA); marketing (MBA); real estate (MBA); strategy (MBA); strategy and entrepreneurship (MBA); JD/MBA; MA/MBA. *Program availability:* Part-time, evening/weekend. *Entrance requirements:* For master's, GMAT. Additional exam requirements/recommendations for international students: Required—TOEFL. Electronic applications accepted. *Expenses:* Contact institution. *Faculty research:* Corporate finance, financial reporting, modeling consumer decision-making, competition between national brands and store brands, institutional determinants of firms' strategy.

Southern New Hampshire University, School of Business, Manchester, NH 03106-1045. Offers accounting (MBA, MS, Graduate Certificate); accounting finance (MS); accounting/auditing (MS); accounting/forensic accounting (MS); accounting/taxation (MS); athletic administration (MBA, Graduate Certificate); business administration (IMBA, MBA, Certificate, Graduate Certificate), including accounting (Certificate), business administration (MBA), business information systems (Graduate Certificate), human resource management (Certificate); corporate social responsibility (MBA); entrepreneurship (MBA); finance (MBA, MS, Graduate Certificate); finance/corporate finance (MS); finance/investments and securities (MS); forensic accounting (MBA); healthcare informatics (MBA); healthcare management (MBA); human resource management (Graduate Certificate); information technology (MS, Graduate Certificate); information technology management (MBA); international business (Graduate Certificate); international business and information technology (Graduate Certificate); international finance (Graduate Certificate); international sport management (Graduate Certificate); justice studies (MBA); leadership of nonprofit organizations (Graduate Certificate); management (MS); marketing (MBA, MS, Graduate Certificate); operations and project management (MS); operations and supply chain management (MBA, Graduate Certificate); organizational leadership (MS); project management (MBA, Graduate Certificate); Six Sigma (MBA); Six Sigma quality (Graduate Certificate), social media marketing (MBA); sport management (MBA, MS, Graduate Certificate); sustainability and environmental compliance (MBA); workplace conflict management (MBA); MBA/Certificate. *Accreditation:* ACBSP. *Program availability:* Part-time, evening/weekend, online learning. Terminal master's awarded for partial completion of doctoral program. *Degree requirements:* For master's, one foreign language, comprehensive exam (for some programs), thesis or alternative. *Entrance requirements:* For master's, minimum GPA of 2.5. Additional exam requirements/recommendations for international students: Required—TOEFL (minimum score 500 paper-based). Electronic applications accepted.

Southern University at New Orleans, School of Graduate Studies, New Orleans, LA 70126-1009. Offers criminal justice (MA); management information systems (MS); museum studies (MA); social work (MSW). *Accreditation:* CSWE. *Program availability:* Part-time, evening/weekend. *Degree requirements:* For master's, thesis. *Entrance requirements:* For master's, GRE/GMAT. Additional exam requirements/recommendations for international students: Required—TOEFL.

South University, Program in Information Systems and Technology, Round Rock, TX 78681. Offers MS.

South University, Program in Information Systems and Technology, Montgomery, AL 36116-1120. Offers MS.

South University, Program in Information Systems and Technology, Tampa, FL 33614. Offers MS.

South University, Program in Information Systems and Technology, Virginia Beach, VA 23452. Offers MS.

South University, Program in Information Systems and Technology, Royal Palm Beach, FL 33411. Offers MS.

Stevens Institute of Technology, Graduate School, School of Business, Doctoral Program in Technology Management, Hoboken, NJ 07030. Offers information management (PhD); technology management (PhD); telecommunications management (PhD). *Program availability:* Part-time, evening/weekend, online learning. *Students:* 10 full-time (3 women), 4 part-time (1 woman); includes 1 minority (American Indian or Alaska Native, non-Hispanic/Latino), 10 international. Average age 30. In 2016, 1 doctorate awarded. *Degree requirements:* For doctorate, comprehensive exam (for some programs), thesis/dissertation. *Entrance requirements:* Additional exam requirements/recommendations for international students: Required—TOEFL (minimum score 74 iBT), IELTS (minimum score 6). *Application deadline:* For fall admission, 6/1 for domestic students, 4/15 for international students; for spring admission, 11/30 for domestic students, 11/1 for international students. Applications are processed on a rolling basis. Application fee: $65. Electronic applications accepted. *Expenses:* Contact institution. *Financial support:* Fellowships, research assistantships, teaching assistantships, career-related internships or fieldwork, Federal Work-Study, scholarships/grants, and unspecified assistantships available. Financial award application deadline: 2/15; financial award applicants required to submit FAFSA. *Unit head:* Dr. Thomas Lechler, Director, 201-216-8174, Fax: 201-216-5385, E-mail: tlechler@stevens.edu. *Application contact:* Graduate Admissions, 888-783-8367, Fax: 888-511-1306, E-mail: graduate@stevens.edu.
Website: https://www.stevens.edu/school-business/phd-business-administration

Stevens Institute of Technology, Graduate School, School of Business, Program in Business Administration, Hoboken, NJ 07030. Offers business intelligence and analytics (MBA); engineering management (MBA); finance (MBA); information systems (MBA); innovation and entrepreneurship (MBA); marketing (MBA); pharmaceutical management (MBA); project management (MBA, Certificate); technology management (MBA); telecommunications management (MBA). *Accreditation:* AACSB. *Program availability:* Part-time, evening/weekend. *Students:* 35 full-time (15 women), 181 part-time (79 women); includes 53 minority (10 Black or African American, non-Hispanic/Latino; 2 American Indian or Alaska Native, non-Hispanic/Latino; 36 Asian, non-Hispanic/Latino; 5 Hispanic/Latino), 30 international. Average age 32. 215 applicants, 53% accepted, 61 enrolled. In 2016, 61 master's awarded. *Degree requirements:* For master's, thesis optional, minimum B average in major field and overall; for Certificate, minimum B average. *Entrance requirements:* Additional exam requirements/recommendations for international students: Required—TOEFL (minimum score 74 iBT), IELTS (minimum score 6). *Application deadline:* For fall admission, 6/1 for domestic students, 4/15 for international students; for spring admission, 11/30 for domestic students, 11/1 for international students. Applications are processed on a rolling basis. Application fee: $65. Electronic applications accepted. *Expenses:* Contact institution. *Financial support:* Fellowships, research assistantships, teaching assistantships, career-related internships or fieldwork, Federal Work-Study, scholarships/grants, and unspecified assistantships available. Financial award application deadline: 2/15; financial award applicants required to submit FAFSA. *Unit head:* Dr. Gregory Prastacos, Dean, 201-216-8366, E-mail: gprastac@stevens.edu. *Application contact:* Graduate Admissions, 888-783-8367, Fax: 888-511-1306, E-mail: graduate@stevens.edu.
Website: https://www.stevens.edu/school-business/masters-programs/mbaemba

Stevens Institute of Technology, Graduate School, School of Business, Program in Information Systems, Hoboken, NJ 07030. Offers computer science (MS); e-commerce (MS); enterprise systems (MS); entrepreneurial information technology (MS); information architecture (MS); information management (MS, Certificate); information security (MS); information technology in financial services industry (MS); information technology in the pharmaceutical industry (MS); information technology outsourcing management (MS); project management (MS, Certificate); software engineering (MS); telecommunications (MS). *Program availability:* Part-time, evening/weekend. *Students:* 280 full-time (100 women), 84 part-time (21 women); includes 23 minority (9 Black or African American, non-Hispanic/Latino; 13 Asian, non-Hispanic/Latino; 1 Hispanic/Latino), 283 international. Average age 26. 925 applicants, 62% accepted, 114 enrolled. In 2016, 212 master's, 32 other advanced degrees awarded. *Degree requirements:* For master's, thesis optional, minimum B average in major field and overall; for Certificate, minimum B average. *Entrance requirements:* Additional exam requirements/recommendations for international students: Required—TOEFL (minimum score 74 iBT), IELTS (minimum score 6). *Application deadline:* For fall admission, 6/1 for domestic students, 4/15 for international students; for spring admission, 11/30 for domestic students, 11/1 for international students. Applications are processed on a rolling basis. Application fee: $65. Electronic applications accepted. *Expenses:* Contact institution. *Financial support:* Fellowships, research assistantships, teaching assistantships, career-related internships or fieldwork, Federal Work-Study, scholarships/grants, and unspecified assistantships available. Financial award application deadline: 2/15; financial award applicants required to submit FAFSA. *Unit head:* Dr. Gregory Prastacos, Dean, 201-216-8366, E-mail: gprastac@stevens.edu. *Application contact:* Graduate Admissions, 888-783-8367, Fax: 888-511-1306, E-mail: graduate@stevens.edu.
Website: https://www.stevens.edu/school-business/masters-programs/information-systems

Stevens Institute of Technology, Graduate School, School of Business, Program in Management, Hoboken, NJ 07030. Offers general management (MS); global innovation management (MS); human resource management (MS); information management (MS); project management (MS); technology commercialization (MS); technology management (MS). *Program availability:* Part-time, evening/weekend. *Students:* 83 full-time (28 women), 82 part-time (36 women); includes 30 minority (6 Black or African American, non-Hispanic/Latino; 1 American Indian or Alaska Native, non-Hispanic/Latino; 21 Asian, non-Hispanic/Latino; 2 Hispanic/Latino), 73 international. Average age 29. 381 applicants, 64% accepted, 53 enrolled. In 2016, 66 master's awarded. *Degree requirements:* For master's, thesis optional, minimum B average in major field and overall. *Entrance requirements:* Additional exam requirements/recommendations for international students: Required—TOEFL (minimum score 74 iBT), IELTS (minimum score 6). *Application deadline:* For fall admission, 6/1 for domestic students, 4/15 for international students; for spring admission, 11/30 for domestic students, 11/1 for international students. Applications are processed on a rolling basis. Application fee: $65. Electronic applications accepted. *Expenses:* Contact institution. *Financial support:* Fellowships, research assistantships, teaching assistantships, career-related internships or fieldwork, Federal Work-Study, scholarships/grants, and unspecified assistantships available. Financial award application deadline: 2/15; financial award applicants required to submit FAFSA. *Unit head:* Brian Rothschild, Director, 201-216-3677, E-mail: brian.rothschild@stevens.edu. *Application contact:* Graduate Admissions, 888-783-8367, Fax: 888-511-1306, E-mail: graduate@stevens.edu.
Website: https://www.stevens.edu/school-business/masters-programs/management

Stony Brook University, State University of New York, Graduate School, College of Engineering and Applied Sciences, Department of Computer Science, Stony Brook, NY 11794-2424. Offers computer science (MS, PhD); information systems (Certificate); information systems engineering (MS); software engineering (Certificate). *Faculty:* 49 full-time (7 women), 3 part-time/adjunct (1 woman). *Students:* 399 full-time (92 women), 113 part-time (27 women); includes 22 minority (17 Asian, non-Hispanic/Latino; 3 Hispanic/Latino; 2 Two or more races, non-Hispanic/Latino), 458 international. Average age 26. 2,225 applicants, 26% accepted, 192 enrolled. In 2016, 198 master's, 18 doctorates awarded. Terminal master's awarded for partial completion of doctoral program. *Degree requirements:* For master's, thesis or alternative; for doctorate, comprehensive exam, thesis/dissertation. *Entrance requirements:* For master's and doctorate, GRE General Test. Additional exam requirements/recommendations for international students: Required—TOEFL (minimum score 90 iBT). *Application deadline:* For fall admission, 1/15 for domestic students; for spring admission, 10/1 for domestic students. Application fee: $100. *Expenses:* Contact institution. *Financial support:* In 2016–17, 1 fellowship, 57 research assistantships, 62 teaching assistantships were awarded. *Faculty research:* Cyber security, computer security, computer software, computer operating systems, computer and information sciences. *Total annual research expenditures:* $7.3 million. *Unit head:* Prof. Arie Kaufman, Chair, 631-632-8441, E-mail: arie.kaufman@stonybrook.edu. *Application contact:* Cynthia Scalzo, Coordinator, 631-

632-1521, E-mail: cscalzo@cs.stonybrook.edu.
Website: http://www.cs.sunysb.edu/

Stony Brook University, State University of New York, School of Professional Development, Stony Brook, NY 11794-443. Offers biology (MAT); chemistry (MAT); coaching (Graduate Certificate); earth science (MAT); educational computing (Graduate Certificate); educational leadership (Advanced Certificate); English (MAT); environmental management (MPS, Graduate Certificate); French (MAT); German (MAT); higher education administration (MA, Certificate); human resource management (MS, Graduate Certificate); industrial management (Graduate Certificate); information systems management (Graduate Certificate); Italian (MAT); liberal studies (MA); mathematics (MAT); operations research (Graduate Certificate); physics (MAT); school district business leadership (Advanced Certificate); social studies (MAT); Spanish (MAT). *Program availability:* Part-time, evening/weekend, online learning. *Faculty:* 4 full-time (3 women), 77 part-time/adjunct (34 women). *Students:* 197 full-time (125 women), 965 part-time (674 women); includes 222 minority (79 Black or African American, non-Hispanic/Latino; 2 American Indian or Alaska Native, non-Hispanic/Latino; 35 Asian, non-Hispanic/Latino; 87 Hispanic/Latino; 1 Native Hawaiian or other Pacific Islander, non-Hispanic/Latino; 18 Two or more races, non-Hispanic/Latino), 5 international. Average age 33. 462 applicants, 87% accepted, 317 enrolled. In 2016, 348 master's, 159 other advanced degrees awarded. *Degree requirements:* For master's, one foreign language, thesis or alternative. *Entrance requirements:* Additional exam requirements/recommendations for international students: Required—TOEFL (minimum score 85 iBT). *Application deadline:* For fall admission, 1/15 for domestic students, 6/1 for international students; for spring admission, 10/1 for domestic and international students. Applications are processed on a rolling basis. Application fee: $100. *Expenses:* Contact institution. *Financial support:* Fellowships, research assistantships, teaching assistantships, and career-related internships or fieldwork available. Support available to part-time students. *Unit head:* Dr. Ken Lindblom, Dean, 631-632-7049, Fax: 631-632-9046, E-mail: kenneth.lindblom@stonybrook.edu. *Application contact:* Melissa Jordan, Assistant Dean, 631-632-7751, E-mail: melissa.jordan@stonybrook.edu.
Website: http://www.stonybrook.edu/spd/

Stratford University, School of Graduate Studies, Falls Church, VA 22043. Offers accounting (MS); business administration (IMBA, MBA); cyber security (MS); cyber security leadership and policy (MS); digital forensics (MS); enterprise business management (MS); entrepreneurial management (MS); healthcare administration (MS); information systems (MS); international hospitality management (MS); networking and telecommunications (MS); software engineering (MS). *Program availability:* Part-time, evening/weekend, 100% online, blended/hybrid learning. *Students:* 505 full-time (186 women), 172 part-time (88 women); includes 532 minority (165 Black or African American, non-Hispanic/Latino; 18 American Indian or Alaska Native, non-Hispanic/Latino; 324 Asian, non-Hispanic/Latino; 13 Hispanic/Latino; 10 Native Hawaiian or other Pacific Islander, non-Hispanic/Latino; 2 Two or more races, non-Hispanic/Latino). Average age 27. In 2016, 520 master's awarded. *Degree requirements:* For master's, comprehensive exam, capstone project. *Entrance requirements:* For master's, GRE or GMAT, baccalaureate degree. Additional exam requirements/recommendations for international students: Required—TOEFL (minimum score 79 iBT), IELTS (minimum score 6.5), PTE (minimum score 5). *Application deadline:* Applications are processed on a rolling basis. Application fee: $50. Electronic applications accepted. *Expenses: Tuition:* Full-time $4455; part-time $2227.50 per course. One-time fee: $100. *Financial support:* Federal Work-Study and scholarships/grants available. Financial award applicants required to submit FAFSA. *Unit head:* Dr. Richard R. Shurtz, President, 703-539-6890, Fax: 703-539-6960. *Application contact:* Admissions, 800-444-0804, E-mail: fcadmissions@stratford.edu.

Strayer University, Graduate Studies, Washington, DC 20005-2603. Offers accounting (MS); acquisition (MBA); business administration (MBA); communications technology (MS); educational management (M Ed); finance (MBA); health services administration (MHSA); hospitality and tourism management (MBA); human resource management (MBA); information systems (MS), including computer security management, decision support system management, enterprise resource management, network management, software engineering management, systems development management; management (MBA); management information systems (MS); marketing (MBA); professional accounting (MS), including accounting information systems, controllership, taxation; public administration (MPA); supply chain management (MBA); technology in education (M Ed). Programs also offered at campus locations in Birmingham, AL; Chamblee, GA; Cobb County, GA; Morrow, GA; White Marsh, MD; Charleston, SC; Columbia, SC; Greensboro, NC; Greenville, SC; Lexington, KY; Louisville, KY; Nashville, TN; North Raleigh, NC; Washington, DC. *Accreditation:* ACBSP. *Program availability:* Part-time, evening/weekend, online learning. *Degree requirements:* For master's, thesis. *Entrance requirements:* For master's, GMAT, GRE General Test, bachelor's degree from an accredited college or university, minimum undergraduate GPA of 2.75. Electronic applications accepted.

Suffolk University, Sawyer Business School, Department of Public Administration, Boston, MA 02108-2770. Offers community health (MPA); information systems, performance management, and big data analytics (MPA); nonprofit management (MPA); state and local government (MPA); JD/MPA; MPA/MS; MPA/MSCJ; MPA/MSMHC; MPA/MSPS. *Accreditation:* NASPAA (one or more programs are accredited). *Program availability:* Part-time, evening/weekend. *Faculty:* 4 full-time (1 woman), 2 part-time/adjunct (both women). *Students:* 26 full-time (13 women), 96 part-time (58 women); includes 42 minority (18 Black or African American, non-Hispanic/Latino; 5 Asian, non-Hispanic/Latino; 18 Hispanic/Latino; 1 Two or more races, non-Hispanic/Latino), 4 international. Average age 34. 133 applicants, 85% accepted, 53 enrolled. In 2016, 47 degrees awarded. *Entrance requirements:* Additional exam requirements/recommendations for international students: Required—TOEFL (minimum score 550 paper-based; 80 iBT). *Application deadline:* For fall admission, 3/15 priority date for domestic and international students; for spring admission, 10/15 priority date for domestic and international students. Applications are processed on a rolling basis. Application fee: $50. Electronic applications accepted. *Expenses: Tuition:* Full-time $41,490; part-time $1383 per credit hour. *Required fees:* $52; $52 per credit hour. Part-time tuition and fees vary according to course load and program. *Financial support:* In 2016–17, 82 students received support, including 78 fellowships (averaging $6,546 per year); career-related internships or fieldwork, Federal Work-Study, institutionally sponsored loans, and scholarships/grants also available. Support available to part-time students. Financial award application deadline: 4/1; financial award applicants required to submit FAFSA. *Faculty research:* Local government, health care, federal policy, mental health, HIV/AIDS. *Unit head:* Brenda Bond, Director/Department Chair, 617-305-1768, E-mail: bbond@suffolk.edu. *Application contact:* Mara Marzocchi, Associate Director of Graduate Admissions, 617-573-8302, Fax: 617-305-1733, E-mail: grad.admission@suffolk.edu.
Website: http://www.suffolk.edu/mpa

Syracuse University, Martin J. Whitman School of Management, PhD Programs, Syracuse, NY 13244. Offers finance (PhD); management information systems (PhD). In 2016, 2 doctorates awarded. *Degree requirements:* For doctorate, comprehensive exam, thesis/dissertation, summer research paper. *Entrance requirements:* For doctorate, GMAT (preferred) or GRE, master's degree (preferred), transcripts, three recommendation letters, personal statement. Additional exam requirements/recommendations for international students: Required—TOEFL (minimum score 600 paper-based; 100 iBT). *Application deadline:* For fall admission, 1/15 for domestic and international students. Application fee: $75. Electronic applications accepted. *Expenses: Tuition:* Full-time $25,974; part-time $1443 per credit hour. *Required fees:* $802; $50 per course. Tuition and fees vary according to course load and program. *Financial support:* Fellowships with full tuition reimbursements, research assistantships with full tuition reimbursements, teaching assistantships with full tuition reimbursements, and scholarships/grants available. *Faculty research:* Marketing models, market microstructure, supply chain, auditing, corporate governance. *Unit head:* Dr. Michel Benaroch, Associate Dean for Research and PhD Programs, 315-443-3492, E-mail: mbenaroc@syr.edu. *Application contact:* Lisa Svegl, Executive Assistant for Development and PhD Programs, 315-443-9141, E-mail: lmsvegl@syr.edu.

Syracuse University, School of Information Studies, CAS Program in Data Science, Syracuse, NY 13244. Offers CAS. *Program availability:* Part-time, evening/weekend, online learning. *Students:* Average age 36. In 2016, 47 CASs awarded. *Entrance requirements:* For degree, resume, personal statement. Additional exam requirements/recommendations for international students: Required—TOEFL (minimum score 100 iBT). *Application deadline:* For fall admission, 1/1 for domestic students, 1/1 priority date for international students; for spring admission, 10/15 for domestic students, 10/15 priority date for international students. Applications are processed on a rolling basis. Application fee: $75. Electronic applications accepted. *Expenses: Tuition:* Full-time $25,974; part-time $1443 per credit hour. *Required fees:* $802; $50 per course. Tuition and fees vary according to course load and program. *Faculty research:* Digital curation, data science education, and information analytics, digital libraries, information assurance. *Unit head:* Carsten Oesterlund, Program Director, 315-443-2911, E-mail: igrad@syr.edu. *Application contact:* Susan Corieri, Director of Enrollment Management, 315-443-2575, E-mail: ischool@syr.edu.
Website: http://ischool.syr.edu/

Syracuse University, School of Information Studies, CAS Program in Information Security Management, Syracuse, NY 13244. Offers CAS. *Program availability:* Part-time, evening/weekend, online learning. *Students:* Average age 26. *Entrance requirements:* For degree, resume, personal statement, official transcripts. Additional exam requirements/recommendations for international students: Required—TOEFL (minimum score 100 iBT). *Application deadline:* For fall admission, 1/1 priority date for domestic and international students; for spring admission, 10/15 priority date for domestic and international students; for summer admission, 2/1 priority date for domestic and international students. Applications are processed on a rolling basis. Application fee: $75. Electronic applications accepted. *Expenses: Tuition:* Full-time $25,974; part-time $1443 per credit hour. *Required fees:* $802; $50 per course. Tuition and fees vary according to course load and program. *Financial support:* Application deadline: 1/1. *Faculty research:* Information security, digital forensics, internet security, risk management, security policy. *Unit head:* Carsten Oesterlund, Program Director, 315-443-2911, E-mail: igrad@syr.edu. *Application contact:* Susan Corieri, Director of Enrollment Management, 315-443-2575, E-mail: ischool@syr.edu.
Website: http://ischool.syr.edu/

Syracuse University, School of Information Studies, MS Program in Enterprise Data Systems, Syracuse, NY 13244. Offers MS. *Program availability:* Part-time, evening/weekend, online learning. *Entrance requirements:* For master's, GRE General Test, official academic credentials, 500-word personal statement, two letters of recommendation, resume or curriculum vitae. Additional exam requirements/recommendations for international students: Required—TOEFL (minimum iBT score 100) or IELTS. *Application deadline:* For fall admission, 6/1 priority date for domestic and international students. Applications are processed on a rolling basis. Application fee: $75. Electronic applications accepted. *Expenses: Tuition:* Full-time $25,974; part-time $1443 per credit hour. *Required fees:* $802; $50 per course. Tuition and fees vary according to course load and program. *Financial support:* Research assistantships, teaching assistantships, career-related internships or fieldwork, and scholarships/grants available. Financial award application deadline: 1/1. *Faculty research:* Information environments, telecommunications and enterprise network management, information architecture. *Unit head:* Carlos Caicedo, Program Director, 315-443-1363, E-mail: ccaicedo@syr.edu. *Application contact:* Susan Corieri, Director of Enrollment Management, 315-443-2575, E-mail: ischool@syr.edu.
Website: http://ischool.syr.edu/

Syracuse University, School of Information Studies, MS Program in Information Management, Syracuse, NY 13244. Offers MS. *Program availability:* Part-time, evening/weekend, online learning. *Entrance requirements:* For master's, GRE General Test, personal statement, two letters of recommendation, resume. Additional exam requirements/recommendations for international students: Required—TOEFL (minimum score 100 iBT). *Application deadline:* For fall admission, 2/1 priority date for domestic and international students; for spring admission, 10/15 priority date for domestic and international students. Applications are processed on a rolling basis. Application fee: $75. Electronic applications accepted. *Expenses: Tuition:* Full-time $25,974; part-time $1443 per credit hour. *Required fees:* $802; $50 per course. Tuition and fees vary according to course load and program. *Financial support:* Fellowships with full tuition reimbursements, research assistantships with partial tuition reimbursements, teaching assistantships with partial tuition reimbursements, and scholarships/grants available. Financial award application deadline: 1/1; financial award applicants required to submit FAFSA. *Faculty research:* Increasing the effectiveness of managers and executives who work with information resources, designing and managing mission-critical information technologies within organizations, developing corporate and government policies to maximize the benefits resulting from the widespread use of these technologies. *Unit head:* Carsten Oesterlund, Program Director, 315-443-2911, Fax: 315-443-6886, E-mail: igrad@syr.edu. *Application contact:* Susan Corieri, Director of Enrollment Management, 315-443-2575, E-mail: ischool@syr.edu.
Website: http://ischool.syr.edu/

Tarleton State University, College of Graduate Studies, College of Business Administration, Department of Marketing and Computer Information Systems, Stephenville, TX 76402. Offers information systems (MS). *Program availability:* Part-time, evening/weekend, 100% online, blended/hybrid learning. *Faculty:* 6 full-time (1 woman). *Students:* 8 full-time (2 women), 40 part-time (14 women); includes 19 minority (4 Black or African American, non-Hispanic/Latino; 1 American Indian or Alaska Native, non-Hispanic/Latino; 6 Asian, non-Hispanic/Latino; 6 Hispanic/Latino; 2 Two or more races, non-Hispanic/Latino). 21 applicants, 95% accepted, 17 enrolled. In 2016, 11 master's awarded. *Degree requirements:* For master's, comprehensive exam. *Entrance requirements:* For master's, GRE, minimum GPA of 3.0. Additional exam requirements/recommendations for international students: Required—TOEFL (minimum score 550 paper-based; 80 iBT). *Application deadline:* For fall admission, 8/15 priority date for domestic students; for spring admission, 1/7 for domestic students. Applications are processed on a rolling basis. Application fee: $45 ($145 for international students). Electronic applications accepted. *Expenses:* $3,672 tuition; $2,437 fees. *Financial support:* Research assistantships and teaching assistantships available. Financial

award application deadline: 5/1; financial award applicants required to submit FAFSA. *Unit head:* Dr. Joseph Schuessler, Department Head, 254-968-9893, E-mail: schuessler@tarleton.edu. *Application contact:* Information Contact, 254-968-9104, Fax: 254-968-9670, E-mail: gradoffice@tarleton.edu.
Website: http://www.tarleton.edu/cis/

Temple University, College of Education, Department of Teaching and Learning, Philadelphia, PA 19122-6096. Offers career and technical education (Ed M), including business, computing, and information technology, industrial education, marketing education; middle grades education (Ed M), including math and language arts, math and science, science and language arts; secondary education (Ed M), including English, math, social studies; teaching English to speakers of other languages (MS Ed); urban education (Ed M). *Program availability:* Part-time, evening/weekend. *Faculty:* 26 full-time (16 women), 74 part-time/adjunct (54 women). *Students:* 204 full-time (139 women), 320 part-time (201 women); includes 112 minority (66 Black or African American, non-Hispanic/Latino; 17 Asian, non-Hispanic/Latino; 18 Hispanic/Latino; 11 Two or more races, non-Hispanic/Latino), 18 international. 300 applicants, 55% accepted, 99 enrolled. In 2016, 93 master's awarded. Terminal master's awarded for partial completion of doctoral program. *Degree requirements:* For master's, thesis or alternative. *Entrance requirements:* Additional exam requirements/recommendations for international students: Required—TOEFL (minimum score 550 paper-based; 79 iBT). *Application deadline:* For fall admission, 4/1 for domestic students, 12/15 for international students; for spring admission, 10/1 for domestic students, 8/1 for international students. Application fee: $60. Electronic applications accepted. *Expenses:* Contact institution. *Financial support:* Fellowships, research assistantships, and teaching assistantships available. Financial award application deadline: 1/15; financial award applicants required to submit FAFSA. *Faculty research:* Workforce development, vocational education, technical education, industrial education, professional development, literacy, classroom management, school communities, curriculum development, instruction, applied linguistics, cross linguistic influence, bilingual education, oral proficiency, multilingualism. *Unit head:* Dr. Christine Woyshner, Chairperson, 215-204-6387, E-mail: christine.woyshner@temple.edu. *Application contact:* Sarah Stapleton, Assistant Director, Academic Operations, 215-204-8220, E-mail: sarah.stapleton@temple.edu.
Website: http://education.temple.edu/tl

Temple University, College of Science and Technology, Department of Computer and Information Sciences, Philadelphia, PA 19122. Offers computational data science (MS); computer and information sciences (PhD), including artificial intelligence, computer and network systems, information systems, software systems; computer science (MS); cyber defense and information assurance (PSM); information science and technology (MS). *Program availability:* Part-time, evening/weekend. *Faculty:* 36 full-time (7 women), 6 part-time/adjunct (1 woman). *Students:* 88 full-time (22 women), 20 part-time (5 women); includes 6 minority (1 Black or African American, non-Hispanic/Latino; 5 Asian, non-Hispanic/Latino), 81 international. 153 applicants, 45% accepted, 34 enrolled. In 2016, 24 master's, 7 doctorates awarded. Terminal master's awarded for partial completion of doctoral program. *Degree requirements:* For doctorate, thesis/dissertation. *Entrance requirements:* For master's and doctorate, GRE General Test, minimum GPA of 3.0. Additional exam requirements/recommendations for international students: Required—TOEFL (minimum score 550 paper-based; 79 iBT). *Application deadline:* For fall admission, 2/1 for domestic students, 12/15 for international students; for spring admission, 8/1 for domestic and international students. Applications are processed on a rolling basis. Application fee: $60. Electronic applications accepted. *Financial support:* Fellowships, research assistantships with tuition reimbursements, teaching assistantships with tuition reimbursements, career-related internships or fieldwork, institutionally sponsored loans, and unspecified assistantships available. Financial award application deadline: 1/15; financial award applicants required to submit FAFSA. *Faculty research:* Artificial intelligence, information systems, software engineering, network-distributed systems. *Unit head:* Chiu Tan, Graduate Program Chair, 215-204-6847, E-mail: cis@temple.edu. *Application contact:* Marilyn Grandshaw, Administrative Coordinator, 215-204-8450, E-mail: marilyng@temple.edu.
Website: https://cis.temple.edu/

Temple University, Fox School of Business, Doctoral Programs in Business, Philadelphia, PA 19122-6096. Offers accounting (PhD); entrepreneurship (PhD); finance (PhD); international business (PhD); management information systems (PhD); marketing (PhD); risk management and insurance (PhD); statistics (PhD); strategic management (PhD); tourism and sport (PhD). *Accreditation:* AACSB. *Degree requirements:* For doctorate, thesis/dissertation. *Entrance requirements:* For doctorate, GRE General Test, GMAT, minimum GPA of 3.0, master's degree. Additional exam requirements/recommendations for international students: Required—TOEFL (minimum score 600 paper-based; 100 iBT), IELTS (minimum score 7.5). Electronic applications accepted.

Tennessee Technological University, College of Graduate Studies, College of Business, Cookeville, TN 38505. Offers accounting (MBA); finance (MBA); human resource management (MBA); international business (MBA); management information systems (MBA). *Accreditation:* AACSB. *Program availability:* Part-time, evening/weekend, online learning. *Faculty:* 28 full-time (5 women). *Students:* 45 full-time (22 women), 167 part-time (51 women); includes 18 minority (5 Black or African American, non-Hispanic/Latino; 4 Asian, non-Hispanic/Latino; 4 Hispanic/Latino; 5 Two or more races, non-Hispanic/Latino), 14 international. Average age 25. 173 applicants, 54% accepted, 52 enrolled. In 2016, 78 master's awarded. *Entrance requirements:* For master's, GMAT, GRE. Additional exam requirements/recommendations for international students: Required—TOEFL (minimum score 550 paper-based; 79 iBT), IELTS (minimum score 5.5), PTE (minimum score 53), or TOEIC (Test of English as an International Communication). *Application deadline:* For fall admission, 8/1 for domestic students, 5/1 for international students; for spring admission, 12/1 for domestic students, 10/1 for international students; for summer admission, 5/1 for domestic students, 2/1 for international students. Applications are processed on a rolling basis. Application fee: $35 ($40 for international students). Electronic applications accepted. *Expenses:* Tuition, state resident: full-time $9375; part-time $534 per credit hour. Tuition, nonresident: full-time $22,443; part-time $1260 per credit hour. *Financial support:* In 2016–17, 5 fellowships (averaging $10,000 per year), 1 teaching assistantship (averaging $5,200 per year) were awarded; research assistantships also available. Support available to part-time students. Financial award application deadline: 4/1. *Unit head:* Kate Nicewicz, Director, 931-372-3600, Fax: 931-372-6249, E-mail: knicewicz@tntech.edu. *Application contact:* Shelia K. Kendrick, Coordinator of Graduate Studies, 931-372-3808, Fax: 931-372-3497, E-mail: skendrick@tntech.edu.
Website: http://www.tntech.edu/mba

Texas A&M International University, Office of Graduate Studies and Research, A.R. Sanchez, Jr. School of Business, Division of International Business and Technology Studies, Laredo, TX 78041-1900. Offers information systems (MSIS); international business management (MBA, PhD). *Degree requirements:* For master's, thesis (for some programs). *Entrance requirements:* For master's, GMAT or GRE General Test. Additional exam requirements/recommendations for international students: Required—TOEFL (minimum score 550 paper-based; 79 iBT).

Texas A&M University, Mays Business School, Department of Information and Operations Management, College Station, TX 77843. Offers management information systems (MS). *Faculty:* 19. *Students:* 275 full-time (102 women), 1 part-time (0 women); includes 17 minority (1 Black or African American, non-Hispanic/Latino; 6 Asian, non-Hispanic/Latino; 8 Hispanic/Latino; 2 Two or more races, non-Hispanic/Latino), 219 international. Average age 26. 510 applicants, 40% accepted, 79 enrolled. In 2016, 156 master's awarded. Terminal master's awarded for partial completion of doctoral program. *Degree requirements:* For master's, comprehensive exam. *Entrance requirements:* For master's, GMAT. Additional exam requirements/recommendations for international students: Required—TOEFL (minimum score 550 paper-based; 80 iBT), IELTS (minimum score 6), PTE (minimum score 53). *Application deadline:* For fall admission, 12/1 priority date for domestic students, 2/15 for international students. Applications are processed on a rolling basis. Application fee: $50 ($90 for international students). Electronic applications accepted. *Expenses:* Contact institution. *Financial support:* In 2016–17, 220 students received support, including 1 fellowship with tuition reimbursement available (averaging $3,000 per year), 45 research assistantships with tuition reimbursements available (averaging $4,186 per year), 34 teaching assistantships with tuition reimbursements available (averaging $5,987 per year); career-related internships or fieldwork, institutionally sponsored loans, scholarships/grants, traineeships, health care benefits, tuition waivers, and unspecified assistantships also available. Support available to part-time students. Financial award application deadline: 3/15; financial award applicants required to submit FAFSA. *Unit head:* Dr. Rich Metters, Head, 979-845-1148, Fax: 979-845-1148, E-mail: rmetters@mays.tamu.edu. *Application contact:* Andre Araujo, Graduate Advisor, 979-845-0809, Fax: 979-845-1148, E-mail: aaraujo@mays.tamu.edu.
Website: http://mays.tamu.edu/info/

Texas A&M University–Central Texas, Graduate Studies and Research, Killeen, TX 76549. Offers accounting (MS); business administration (MBA); clinical mental health counseling (MS); criminal justice (MCJ); curriculum and instruction (M Ed); educational administration (M Ed); educational psychology - experimental psychology (MS); history (MA); human resource management (MS); information systems (MS); liberal studies (MS); management and leadership (MS); marriage and family therapy (MS); mathematics (MS); political science (MA); school counseling (M Ed); school psychology (Ed S).

Texas A&M University–San Antonio, School of Business, San Antonio, TX 78224. Offers business administration (MBA); enterprise resource planning systems (MBA); finance (MBA); healthcare management (MBA); human resources management (MBA); information assurance and security (MBA); international business (MBA); professional accounting (MPA); project management (MBA); supply chain management (MBA). *Program availability:* Part-time, evening/weekend. *Entrance requirements:* For master's, GMAT. Additional exam requirements/recommendations for international students: Required—TOEFL (minimum score 550 paper-based; 80 iBT), IELTS (minimum score 6). Electronic applications accepted.

Texas Southern University, Jesse H. Jones School of Business, Program in Management Information Systems, Houston, TX 77004-4584. Offers MS. Electronic applications accepted.

Texas State University, The Graduate College, Emmett and Miriam McCoy College of Business Administration, Program in Accounting and Information Technology, San Marcos, TX 78666. Offers MS. *Program availability:* Part-time. *Faculty:* 4 full-time (1 woman). *Students:* 11 full-time (5 women), 7 part-time (2 women); includes 5 minority (2 Asian, non-Hispanic/Latino; 3 Hispanic/Latino), 6 international. Average age 35. 16 applicants, 63% accepted, 6 enrolled. In 2016, 5 master's awarded. *Degree requirements:* For master's, comprehensive exam. *Entrance requirements:* For master's, GMAT or GRE, baccalaureate degree from regionally-accredited university; two letters or forms of recommendation from persons best able to assess applicant's ability to succeed in graduate school; essay; resume showing work experience, extracurricular and community activities, and honors and achievements. Additional exam requirements/recommendations for international students: Required—TOEFL (minimum score 550 paper-based; 78 iBT), IELTS (minimum score 6.5). *Application deadline:* For fall admission, 2/1 priority date for domestic and international students; for spring admission, 10/1 for domestic and international students. Application fee: $40 ($90 for international students). Electronic applications accepted. *Expenses:* $4,851 per semester. *Financial support:* In 2016–17, 9 students received support, including 5 teaching assistantships (averaging $13,641 per year); research assistantships, Federal Work-Study, institutionally sponsored loans, scholarships/grants, health care benefits, and unspecified assistantships also available. Support available to part-time students. Financial award application deadline: 3/1; financial award applicants required to submit FAFSA. *Faculty research:* Aerospace MIS evaluation; learning the science of climate change with commuting. *Total annual research expenditures:* $15,531. *Unit head:* Dr. William Chittenden, Graduate Advisor, 512-245-3591, Fax: 512-245-8365, E-mail: wc10@txstate.edu. *Application contact:* Dr. Andrea Golato, Dean of Graduate School, 512-245-2581, Fax: 512-245-8365, E-mail: gradcollege@txstate.edu.
Website: http://mycatalog.txstate.edu/graduate/mccoy-business-administration/accounting/information-technology-ms/

Texas Tech University, Rawls College of Business Administration, Lubbock, TX 79409-2101. Offers accounting (MSA, PhD), including audit/financial reporting (MSA), taxation (MSA); business statistics (MS, PhD); data science (MS); finance (PhD); general business (MBA); healthcare management (MS); information systems and operations management (PhD); management (PhD); marketing (PhD); STEM (MBA); JD/MBA; JD/MSA; MBA/M Arch; MBA/MD; MBA/MS; MBA/Pharm D. *Accreditation:* AACSB; CAHME (one or more programs are accredited). *Program availability:* Evening/weekend. *Faculty:* 74 full-time (13 women). *Students:* 741 full-time (275 women); includes 198 minority (38 Black or African American, non-Hispanic/Latino; 1 American Indian or Alaska Native, non-Hispanic/Latino; 24 Asian, non-Hispanic/Latino; 116 Hispanic/Latino; 1 Native Hawaiian or other Pacific Islander, non-Hispanic/Latino; 18 Two or more races, non-Hispanic/Latino), 95 international. Average age 28. 905 applicants, 48% accepted, 251 enrolled. In 2016, 545 master's, 13 doctorates awarded. *Degree requirements:* For master's, capstone course; for doctorate, comprehensive exam, thesis/dissertation, qualifying exams. *Entrance requirements:* For master's, GMAT, GRE, MCAT, PCAT, LSAT, or DAT, holistic review of academic credentials, resume, essay, letters of recommendation; for doctorate, GMAT, GRE, holistic review of academic credentials, resume, statement of purpose, letters of recommendation. Additional exam requirements/recommendations for international students: Required—TOEFL (minimum score 95 iBT), IELTS. *Application deadline:* For fall admission, 7/1 priority date for domestic students, 1/15 for international students; for spring admission, 12/1 priority date for domestic students, 6/15 for international students; for summer admission, 5/1 for domestic students. Applications are processed on a rolling basis. Application fee: $60. Electronic applications accepted. *Expenses:* $48,000 (MBA for Working Professionals); $20,000 (STEM MBA). *Financial support:* In 2016–17, 157 students received support, including 25 research assistantships (averaging $22,725 per year), 27 teaching assistantships (averaging $22,725 per year); fellowships, career-related internships or fieldwork, Federal Work-Study, scholarships/grants, health care benefits, and unspecified assistantships also available. Financial award application

deadline: 3/1; financial award applicants required to submit FAFSA. *Faculty research:* Governmental and nonprofit accounting, securities and options futures, statistical analysis and design, leadership, consumer behavior. *Unit head:* Dr. Margaret Williams, Dean, 806-742-3188, Fax: 806-742-1092, E-mail: margaret.l.williams@ttu.edu. *Application contact:* Chathry Keaton, Applications Manager, Graduate and Professional Programs, 806-742-3184, Fax: 806-742-3958, E-mail: rawlsgrad@ttu.edu.
Website: http://www.depts.ttu.edu/rawlsbusiness/graduate/

Touro College, Graduate School of Technology, New York, NY 10010. Offers information systems (MS); instructional technology (MS); Web and multimedia design (MA). *Faculty:* 18 part-time/adjunct (6 women). *Students:* 100 full-time (37 women), 122 part-time (59 women); includes 78 minority (31 Black or African American, non-Hispanic/Latino; 1 American Indian or Alaska Native, non-Hispanic/Latino; 25 Asian, non-Hispanic/Latino; 18 Hispanic/Latino; 3 Two or more races, non-Hispanic/Latino), 83 international. Average age 34. *Entrance requirements:* Additional exam requirements/recommendations for international students: Required—TOEFL (minimum score 83 iBT), IELTS (minimum score 6.5), PTE (minimum score 58). *Unit head:* Dr. Issac Herskowitz, Dean of the Graduate School of Technology, 202-463-0400 Ext. 5231, E-mail: issac.herskowitz@touro.edu. *Application contact:* Jack Romano, Program Director, 212-463-0400 Ext. 5462.
Website: http://www.touro.edu/gst/

Towson University, Program in Applied Information Technology, Towson, MD 21252-0001. Offers applied information technology (MS, D Sc); database management systems (Postbaccalaureate Certificate); information security and assurance (Postbaccalaureate Certificate); information systems management (Postbaccalaureate Certificate); Internet applications development (Postbaccalaureate Certificate); networking technologies (Postbaccalaureate Certificate); software engineering (Postbaccalaureate Certificate). *Students:* 135 full-time (50 women), 154 part-time (50 women); includes 119 minority (81 Black or African American, non-Hispanic/Latino; 26 Asian, non-Hispanic/Latino; 4 Hispanic/Latino; 8 Two or more races, non-Hispanic/Latino), 82 international. *Entrance requirements:* For master's and Postbaccalaureate Certificate, bachelor's degree, minimum GPA of 3.0; for doctorate, master's degree in computer science, information systems, information technology, or closely-related area; minimum GPA of 3.0; 2 letters of recommendation; resume. Additional exam requirements/recommendations for international students: Required—TOEFL. *Application deadline:* Applications are processed on a rolling basis. Application fee: $45. Electronic applications accepted. *Expenses:* Tuition, state resident: full-time $7580; part-time $379 per unit. Tuition, nonresident: full-time $15,700; part-time $785 per unit. *Required fees:* $2480. *Unit head:* Dr. Jinjuan Feng, Graduate Program Director, 410-704-3463, E-mail: ait@towson.edu. *Application contact:* Coverley Beidleman, Assistant Director of Graduate Admissions, 410-704-2113, Fax: 410-704-3030, E-mail: grads@towson.edu.
Website: https://www.towson.edu/fcsm/departments/emergingtech/

Trident University International, College of Business Administration, Program in Business Administration, Cypress, CA 90630. Offers business administration (PhD); conflict and negotiation management (MBA); criminal justice administration (MBA); entrepreneurship (MBA); finance (MBA); general management (MBA); government accounting (MBA); human resource management (MBA); information security and digital assurance management (MBA); information technology management (MBA); international business (MBA); logistics management (MBA); marketing (MBA); project management (MBA); public management (MBA); quality management (MBA); strategic leadership (MBA). *Program availability:* Part-time, evening/weekend, online learning. *Degree requirements:* For doctorate, comprehensive exam, thesis/dissertation, defense of dissertation. *Entrance requirements:* For master's, minimum GPA of 2.5 (students with GPA 3.0 or greater may transfer up to 30% of graduate level credits); for doctorate, minimum GPA of 3.4, curriculum vitae, course work in research methods or statistics. Additional exam requirements/recommendations for international students: Required—TOEFL. Electronic applications accepted.

Trident University International, College of Information Systems, Cypress, CA 90630. Offers business intelligence (Certificate); information technology management (MS). *Program availability:* Part-time, evening/weekend, online learning. *Entrance requirements:* For master's, minimum GPA of 2.5 (students with GPA 3.0 or greater may transfer up to 30% of graduate level credits); undergraduate degree completed within the past 5 years. Additional exam requirements/recommendations for international students: Required—TOEFL (minimum score 525 paper-based). Electronic applications accepted.

Troy University, Graduate School, College of Business, Program in Business Administration, Troy, AL 36082. Offers accounting (EMBA, MBA); criminal justice (EMBA); finance (MBA); general management (EMBA, MBA); healthcare management (EMBA); information systems (EMBA, MBA); international economic development (MBA). *Accreditation:* ACBSP. *Program availability:* Part-time, evening/weekend. *Faculty:* 10 full-time (3 women), 2 part-time/adjunct (0 women). *Students:* 44 full-time (23 women), 131 part-time (69 women); includes 58 minority (38 Black or African American, non-Hispanic/Latino; 13 Asian, non-Hispanic/Latino; 4 Hispanic/Latino; 3 Two or more races, non-Hispanic/Latino). Average age 30. 285 applicants, 91% accepted, 22 enrolled. In 2016, 78 master's awarded. *Degree requirements:* For master's, minimum GPA of 3.0, capstone course, research course. *Entrance requirements:* For master's, GMAT (minimum score 500) or GRE (minimum score 900 on old exam or 294 on new exam), bachelor's degree; minimum undergraduate GPA of 2.5 or 3.0 on last 30 semester hours, letter of recommendation. Additional exam requirements/recommendations for international students: Required—TOEFL (minimum score 523 paper-based; 70 iBT), IELTS (minimum score 6). *Application deadline:* Applications are processed on a rolling basis. Application fee: $50. Electronic applications accepted. *Expenses:* Tuition, state resident: full-time $7146; part-time $397 per credit hour. Tuition, nonresident: full-time $14,292; part-time $794 per credit hour. *Required fees:* $802; $50 per semester. Tuition and fees vary according to campus/location and program. *Financial support:* Fellowships, career-related internships or fieldwork, and scholarships/grants available. Support available to part-time students. Financial award applicants required to submit FAFSA. *Unit head:* Dr. Phillip Mixon, MBA Director, 334-670-3140, Fax: 334-670-3708, E-mail: pamixon@troy.edu. *Application contact:* Jessica A. Kimbro, Director of Graduate Admissions, 334-670-3178, E-mail: jacord@troy.edu.

Tuskegee University, Graduate Programs, Andrew F. Brimmer College of Business and Information Science, Tuskegee, AL 36088. Offers information systems and security management (MS). *Degree requirements:* For master's, thesis. *Entrance requirements:* For master's, GRE or GMAT, baccalaureate degree in computer science, management information systems, accounting, finance, management, information technology, or a closely-related field.

United States International University–Africa, School of Business Administration, Nairobi, Kenya. Offers business administration (GEMBA); entrepreneurship (MBA); finance (MBA); human resource management (MBA); information technology management (MBA); integrated studies (MBA); international business administration (MBA); management and organizational development (MS); marketing (MBA); organizational development (EMS); strategic management (MBA). *Program availability:* Part-time, evening/weekend. *Degree requirements:* For master's, thesis. *Entrance requirements:* For master's, GMAT, 2 letters of reference, resume. Additional exam requirements/recommendations for international students: Required—TOEFL (minimum score 550 paper-based). *Faculty research:* Marketing in small business enterprises, total quality management in Kenya.

Universidad del Este, Graduate School, Carolina, PR 00984. Offers accounting (MBA); adult education (M Ed); agribusiness (MBA); criminal justice and criminology (MA); curriculum and instruction - early education (M Ed); curriculum and instruction - elementary (M Ed); curriculum and instruction - English (M Ed); curriculum and instruction - Spanish (M Ed); human resources (MBA); information security management (MBA); information technology and Web business development (MBA); management (MBA); public policy (MPA); social work (MA), including clinical social work; special education (M Ed); strategic leadership (MBA).

Universidad del Turabo, Graduate Programs, School of Business and Entrepreneurship, Program in Management of Information Systems, Gurabo, PR 00778-3030. Offers DBA. *Students:* 5 full-time (1 woman), 23 part-time (7 women); all minorities (all Hispanic/Latino). Average age 42. 32 applicants, 44% accepted, 14 enrolled. In 2016, 4 doctorates awarded. *Entrance requirements:* For doctorate, GRE, EXADEP or GMAT, official transcript, recommendation letters, essay, curriculum vitae, interview. *Application deadline:* Applications are processed on a rolling basis. Application fee: $75. Electronic applications accepted. *Financial support:* Institutionally sponsored loans available. Financial award applicants required to submit FAFSA. *Unit head:* Juan Sosa, Dean, 787-743-7979 Ext. 4118, E-mail: negocios_ut@suagm.edu. *Application contact:* Diriee Rodríguez, Admissions Director, 787-743-7979 Ext. 4553, E-mail: admisiones-ut@suagm.edu.
Website: http://ut.suagm.edu/es/negocios

Universidad Metropolitana, School of Business Administration, Program in Management Information Systems, San Juan, PR 00928-1150. Offers MBA.

Université de Sherbrooke, Faculty of Administration, Program in Governance, Audit and Security of Information Technology, Longueuil, QC J4K0A8, Canada. Offers M Adm. *Program availability:* Part-time, evening/weekend, online learning. *Degree requirements:* For master's, thesis. *Entrance requirements:* For master's, bachelor's degree, related work experience. Electronic applications accepted.

Université de Sherbrooke, Faculty of Administration, Program in Management Information Systems, Sherbrooke, QC J1K 2R1, Canada. Offers M Sc. *Degree requirements:* For master's, one foreign language, thesis. *Entrance requirements:* For master's, bachelor's degree in related field, minimum GPA of 3.0 (on 4.3 scale). Electronic applications accepted. *Faculty research:* Project management in IT, IT governance, business intelligence, IT performance.

Université de Sherbrooke, Faculty of Sciences, Centre de Formation en Technologies de L'information, Sherbrooke, QC J1K 2R1, Canada. Offers M Sc, Diploma. Electronic applications accepted.

Université du Québec à Montréal, Graduate Programs, Program in Management Information Systems, Montréal, QC H3C 3P8, Canada. Offers M Sc, M Sc A. *Program availability:* Part-time. *Entrance requirements:* For master's, appropriate bachelor's degree or equivalent and proficiency in French.

Université Laval, Faculty of Administrative Sciences, Programs in Business Administration, Québec, QC G1K 7P4, Canada. Offers accounting (MBA); agri-food management (MBA); electronic business (MBA, Diploma); factory management and logistics (MBA); finance (MBA); firm management (MBA); geomatic management (MBA); information technology management (MBA); international management (MBA); management (MBA); management accounting (MBA, Diploma); marketing (MBA); modeling and organizational decision (MBA); occupational health and safety management (MBA); pharmacy management (MBA); social and environmental responsibility (MBA); technological entrepreneurship (Diploma). *Accreditation:* AACSB. *Program availability:* Part-time, evening/weekend, online learning. *Entrance requirements:* For master's and Diploma, knowledge of French and English. Electronic applications accepted.

University at Albany, State University of New York, Nelson A. Rockefeller College of Public Affairs and Policy, Department of Public Administration and Policy, Albany, NY 12222-0001. Offers financial management and public economics (MPA); financial market regulation (MPA); health policy (MPA); healthcare management (MPA); homeland security (MPA); human resources management (MPA); information strategy and management (MPA); local government management (MPA); nonprofit management (MPA); nonprofit management and leadership (Certificate); organizational behavior and theory (MPA, PhD); planning and policy analysis (CAS); policy analysis (MPA); politics and administration (PhD); public finance (PhD); public management (PhD); public policy (PhD); public sector management (Certificate); women and public policy (Certificate); JD/MPA. JD/MPA offered jointly with Albany Law School. *Accreditation:* NASPAA (one or more programs are accredited). *Faculty:* 23 full-time (8 women), 14 part-time/adjunct (7 women). *Students:* 117 full-time (65 women), 95 part-time (46 women); includes 41 minority (12 Black or African American, non-Hispanic/Latino; 8 Asian, non-Hispanic/Latino; 19 Hispanic/Latino; 2 Two or more races, non-Hispanic/Latino), 38 international. 223 applicants, 70% accepted, 81 enrolled. In 2016, 52 master's, 10 doctorates, 16 other advanced degrees awarded. *Degree requirements:* For doctorate, one foreign language, thesis/dissertation. *Entrance requirements:* For doctorate, GRE General Test. Additional exam requirements/recommendations for international students: Required—TOEFL (minimum score 550 paper-based). *Application deadline:* For fall admission, 2/1 priority date for domestic students, 5/1 for international students; for spring admission, 12/1 for domestic students. Applications are processed on a rolling basis. Application fee: $75. Electronic applications accepted. *Expenses:* Tuition, state resident: full-time $10,870; part-time $453 per credit hour. Tuition, nonresident: full-time $22,210; part-time $925 per credit hour. *International tuition:* $21,550 full-time. *Required fees:* $1864; $96 per credit hour. *Financial support:* Application deadline: 2/1. *Total annual research expenditures:* $847,949. *Unit head:* Victor Asal, Chair, 518-591-8729, E-mail: vasal@albany.edu.
Website: http://www.albany.edu/rockefeller/pad.shtml

University at Buffalo, the State University of New York, Graduate School, School of Engineering and Applied Sciences, Department of Computer Science and Engineering, Buffalo, NY 14260. Offers computer science and engineering (MS, PhD); information assurance (Certificate). *Program availability:* Part-time. Terminal master's awarded for partial completion of doctoral program. *Degree requirements:* For master's, thesis or alternative; for doctorate, thesis/dissertation, comprehensive qualifying exam. *Entrance requirements:* For master's and doctorate, GRE General Test. Additional exam requirements/recommendations for international students: Required—TOEFL (minimum score 550 paper-based; 79 iBT). Electronic applications accepted. *Faculty research:* Bioinformatics, pattern recognition, computer networks and security, theory and algorithms, databases and data mining.

University at Buffalo, the State University of New York, Graduate School, School of Management, Buffalo, NY 14620. Offers accounting (MS); analytics (MBA); business administration (PMBA); consulting (MBA); finance (MBA, MS), including financial risk management (MS), quantitative finance (MS); healthcare (MBA); information assurance

(MBA); information systems (MBA); international management (MBA); management (EMBA, PhD); management information systems (MS); marketing (MBA); supply chain and operations (MBA); supply chains and operations management (MS); Au D/MBA; DDS/MBA; JD/MBA; M Arch/MBA; MD/MBA; MPH/MBA; MSW/MBA; Pharm D/MBA. *Accreditation:* AACSB. *Program availability:* Part-time, evening/weekend. *Faculty:* 80 full-time (26 women), 36 part-time/adjunct (6 women). *Students:* 683 full-time (277 women), 196 part-time (63 women); includes 76 minority (23 Black or African American, non-Hispanic/Latino; 1 American Indian or Alaska Native, non-Hispanic/Latino; 48 Asian, non-Hispanic/Latino; 3 Hispanic/Latino; 1 Two or more races, non-Hispanic/Latino), 371 international. Average age 31. 2,451 applicants, 42% accepted, 484 enrolled. In 2016, 515 master's, 10 doctorates awarded. *Degree requirements:* For master's, thesis (for some programs); for doctorate, comprehensive exam, thesis/dissertation. *Entrance requirements:* For master's, GMAT (for MS in accounting, finance); GRE or GMAT (for MBA, PMBA, other MS concentrations), essays, letters of recommendation; for doctorate, GMAT or GRE, essays, writing sample, letters of recommendation. Additional exam requirements/recommendations for international students: Required—TOEFL (minimum score 95 iBT) or IELTS (minimum score 6.5); Recommended—TSE (minimum score 73). *Application deadline:* For fall admission, 10/15 priority date for domestic and international students; for winter admission, 2/1 priority date for domestic and international students; for spring admission, 4/15 for domestic students; for summer admission, 5/15 for domestic students. Application fee: $100. Electronic applications accepted. *Expenses:* Contact institution. *Financial support:* Fellowships with full and partial tuition reimbursements, research assistantships with full and partial tuition reimbursements, teaching assistantships with full and partial tuition reimbursements, career-related internships or fieldwork, Federal Work-Study, institutionally sponsored loans, scholarships/grants, health care benefits, and unspecified assistantships available. Financial award application deadline: 2/15. *Faculty research:* Data analytics, accounting information and corporate finance, consumer behavior, supply chain logistics, leadership and team effectiveness. *Total annual research expenditures:* $1.5 million. *Unit head:* Erin K. O'Brien, Assistant Dean and Director of Graduate Programs, 716-645-3204, Fax: 716-645-2341, E-mail: ekobrien@buffalo.edu. *Application contact:* Meghan Felser, Associate Director of Admissions and Recruiting, 716-645-3204, Fax: 716-645-2341, E-mail: mpwood@buffalo.edu.
Website: http://mgt.buffalo.edu/

The University of Akron, Graduate School, College of Business Administration, Department of Management, Program in Information Systems Management, Akron, OH 44325. Offers MSM. *Students:* 78 full-time (48 women), 67 part-time (27 women); includes 5 minority (1 Asian, non-Hispanic/Latino; 3 Hispanic/Latino; 1 Two or more races, non-Hispanic/Latino), 59 international. Average age 26. 57 applicants, 54% accepted, 18 enrolled. In 2016, 36 master's awarded. *Entrance requirements:* For master's, GMAT, undergraduate degree in information systems, minimum GPA of 3.0, two letters of recommendation, statement of purpose, resume. Additional exam requirements/recommendations for international students: Required—TOEFL (minimum score 550 paper-based; 79 iBT), IELTS (minimum score 6.5). *Application deadline:* For fall admission, 7/15 for domestic students, 7/1 for international students; for spring admission, 11/15 for domestic and international students; for summer admission, 4/15 for domestic and international students. Application fee: $45 ($70 for international students). Electronic applications accepted. *Expenses:* Tuition, state resident: full-time $8618; part-time $359 per credit hour. Tuition, nonresident: full-time $17,149; part-time $715 per credit hour. *Required fees:* $1652. *Unit head:* Dr. Steve Ash, Chair, 330-972-6429, E-mail: ash@uakron.edu. *Application contact:* Dr. William Hauser, Director of Graduate Business Programs, 330-972-7043, Fax: 330-972-6588, E-mail: whauser@uakron.edu.
Website: http://www.uakron.edu/cba/graduate/programs/msm/msm-info-systems.dot

The University of Alabama at Birmingham, Collat School of Business, Program in Business Administration, Birmingham, AL 35294. Offers business administration (MBA), including finance, health care management, information technology management, marketing. *Program availability:* Part-time, evening/weekend. *Entrance requirements:* For master's, GMAT. Additional exam requirements/recommendations for international students: Required—TOEFL. Full-time tuition and fees vary according to course load and program.

The University of Alabama at Birmingham, Collat School of Business, Program in Management Information Systems, Birmingham, AL 35294. Offers management information systems (MS), including information security, information technology management, Web and mobile development. *Program availability:* Part-time, online learning. *Entrance requirements:* For master's, GMAT. Additional exam requirements/recommendations for international students: Required—TOEFL. Full-time tuition and fees vary according to course load and program.

The University of Alabama in Huntsville, School of Graduate Studies, College of Business Administration, Program in Accounting, Huntsville, AL 35899. Offers accounting (M Acc), including CPA preparatory with an emphasis in taxation, CPA preparatory with emphasis in assurance and financial reporting, general accounting, information systems audit and control (ISAC). *Accreditation:* AACSB. *Program availability:* Part-time, evening/weekend. *Degree requirements:* For master's, comprehensive exam, thesis or alternative. *Entrance requirements:* For master's, GMAT (minimum score 500), minimum AACSB index of 1080. Additional exam requirements/recommendations for international students: Required—TOEFL (minimum score 550 paper-based; 80 iBT), IELTS (minimum score 6.5). Electronic applications accepted. *Expenses:* Tuition, state resident: full-time $9834; part-time $600 per credit hour. Tuition, nonresident: full-time $21,830; part-time $1325 per credit hour. *Faculty research:* Accounting information systems, managerial accounting, behavioral accounting, state and local taxation, financial accounting.

The University of Alabama in Huntsville, School of Graduate Studies, College of Business Administration, Programs in Information Systems, Huntsville, AL 35899. Offers cybersecurity (MS, Certificate); enterprise resource planning (Certificate); information systems (MSIS); supply chain and logistics management (MS); supply chain management (Certificate). *Program availability:* Part-time, evening/weekend. *Degree requirements:* For master's, comprehensive exam, thesis or alternative. *Entrance requirements:* For master's, GMAT (minimum score 500), minimum AACSB index of 1080. Additional exam requirements/recommendations for international students: Required—TOEFL (minimum score 550 paper-based; 80 iBT), IELTS (minimum score 6.5). Electronic applications accepted. *Expenses:* Tuition, state resident: full-time $9834; part-time $600 per credit hour. Tuition, nonresident: full-time $21,830; part-time $1325 per credit hour. *Faculty research:* Supply chain information systems, information assurance and security, databases and conceptual schema, workflow management, inter-organizational information sharing.

The University of Arizona, Eller College of Management, Department of Management Information Systems, Tucson, AZ 85721. Offers MS, Graduate Certificate. *Degree requirements:* For master's, thesis or alternative. *Entrance requirements:* For master's, GMAT or GRE General Test, 2 letters of recommendation, resume. Additional exam requirements/recommendations for international students: Required—TOEFL (minimum score 550 paper-based; 80 iBT). Electronic applications accepted. *Faculty research:* Group decision support systems, domestic and international computing issues, expert systems, data management and structures.

University of Arkansas, Graduate School, Sam M. Walton College of Business Administration, Department of Information Systems, Fayetteville, AR 72701. Offers MIS. *Program availability:* Part-time, evening/weekend. In 2016, 25 master's awarded. *Entrance requirements:* For master's, GMAT. Application fee: $40 ($50 for international students). *Financial support:* In 2016–17, 18 research assistantships, 7 teaching assistantships were awarded; fellowships with tuition reimbursements also available. Financial award application deadline: 4/1. *Unit head:* Dr. Rajir Sabherwal, Department Head, 479-575-4500, E-mail: rsaberwal@walton.uark.edu.
Website: http://gsb.uark.edu/

University of Arkansas at Little Rock, Graduate School, College of Business, Little Rock, AR 72204-1099. Offers business administration (MBA); business information systems (MS, Graduate Certificate); management (Graduate Certificate). *Accreditation:* AACSB. *Program availability:* Part-time, evening/weekend. *Entrance requirements:* For master's, GMAT, minimum undergraduate GPA of 2.7. Additional exam requirements/recommendations for international students: Required—TOEFL (minimum score 525 paper-based).

University of Baltimore, Graduate School, Merrick School of Business, Department of Accounting, Baltimore, MD 21201-5779. Offers accounting and business advisory services (MS); accounting fundamentals (Graduate Certificate); forensic accounting (Graduate Certificate); taxation (MS). *Program availability:* Part-time, evening/weekend. *Entrance requirements:* For master's, GMAT. Additional exam requirements/recommendations for international students: Required—TOEFL (minimum score 550 paper-based). Electronic applications accepted. *Faculty research:* Health care, accounting and administration, managerial accounting, financial accounting theory, accounting information.

University of Baltimore, Graduate School, Merrick School of Business, Department of Information Systems and Decision Science, Baltimore, MD 21201-5779. Offers accounting and business advisory services (MS).

University of Bridgeport, School of Business, Bridgeport, CT 06604. Offers accounting (MBA); finance (MBA); general business (MBA); global financial services (MBA); human resource management (MBA); information systems and knowledge management (MBA); international business (MBA); management (MBA); marketing (MBA); operations management (MBA); small business and entrepreneurship (MBA); specialized business (MBA). *Accreditation:* ACBSP. *Program availability:* Part-time, evening/weekend. *Degree requirements:* For master's, thesis optional. *Entrance requirements:* For master's, GMAT. Additional exam requirements/recommendations for international students: Recommended—TOEFL (minimum score 550 paper-based; 80 iBT), IELTS (minimum score 6.5). Electronic applications accepted. *Expenses:* Contact institution.

The University of British Columbia, Sauder School of Business, Doctoral Program in Business Administration, Vancouver, BC V6T 1Z2, Canada. Offers accounting (PhD); finance (PhD); management information systems (PhD); management science (PhD); marketing (PhD); organizational behavior (PhD); strategy and business economics (PhD); transportation and logistics (PhD); urban land economics (PhD). *Degree requirements:* For doctorate, comprehensive exam, thesis/dissertation. *Entrance requirements:* For doctorate, GMAT or GRE. Additional exam requirements/recommendations for international students: Required—TOEFL (minimum score 600 paper-based; 100 iBT). *Application deadline:* Applications are processed on a rolling basis. Application fee: $102 Canadian dollars ($165 Canadian dollars for international students). Electronic applications accepted. *Expenses:* $4,802 per year tuition and fees, $8,436 per year international. *Financial support:* Fellowships with full tuition reimbursements, research assistantships with full tuition reimbursements, and teaching assistantships with full tuition reimbursements available. *Application contact:* Elaine Cho, Administrator, PhD and M Sc Programs, 604-822-8366, Fax: 604-822-8755, E-mail: phd.program@sauder.ubc.ca.
Website: http://www.sauder.ubc.ca/Programs/PhD_in_Business_Administration

University of California, Berkeley, Graduate Division, School of Information, Program in Information Management and Systems, Berkeley, CA 94720-1500. Offers MIMS, PhD. *Students:* 114 full-time (53 women); includes 15 minority (13 Asian, non-Hispanic/Latino; 2 Hispanic/Latino), 59 international. 411 applicants, 55 enrolled. In 2016, 48 master's, 1 doctorate awarded. *Application deadline:* For fall admission, 12/1 for domestic students. Application fee: $105 ($125 for international students). Electronic applications accepted. *Financial support:* Fellowships, research assistantships, teaching assistantships, institutionally sponsored loans, health care benefits, and unspecified assistantships available. Financial award applicants required to submit FAFSA. *Unit head:* Prof. AnnaLee Saxenian, Dean, 510-642-1464, E-mail: admissions@ischool.berkeley.edu. *Application contact:* Leticia Sanchez, Student Affairs Officer, 510-642-1464, Fax: 510-642-5814, E-mail: admissions@ischool.berkeley.edu.
Website: https://www.ischool.berkeley.edu

University of California, Berkeley, UC Berkeley Extension, Certificate Programs in Computer Technology and Information Management, Berkeley, CA 94720-1500. Offers information systems and management (Postbaccalaureate Certificate); UNIX/LINUX system administration (Certificate). *Program availability:* Online learning.

University of California, Santa Cruz, Jack Baskin School of Engineering, Department of Technology Management, Santa Cruz, CA 95064. Offers PhD. *Faculty:* 9 full-time (1 woman). *Students:* 9 full-time (5 women), 2 part-time (1 woman), 7 international. 29 applicants, 28% accepted, 4 enrolled. Terminal master's awarded for partial completion of doctoral program. *Degree requirements:* For doctorate, thesis/dissertation, 2 seminars. *Entrance requirements:* For doctorate, GRE General Test; GRE Subject Test preferably in computer science, engineering, physics, or mathematics (highly recommended). Additional exam requirements/recommendations for international students: Required—TOEFL (minimum score 570 paper-based; 89 iBT); Recommended—IELTS (minimum score 8). *Application deadline:* For fall admission, 1/3 for domestic and international students. Application fee: $105 ($125 for international students). Electronic applications accepted. *Financial support:* In 2016–17, 9 students received support, including 5 fellowships (averaging $18,000 per year), 6 research assistantships (averaging $20,043 per year), 15 teaching assistantships (averaging $20,052 per year); institutionally sponsored loans and tuition waivers (full and partial) also available. Financial award application deadline: 1/3; financial award applicants required to submit FAFSA. *Faculty research:* Integration of information systems, technology, and business management. *Unit head:* John Musacchio, Chair, 831-459-1385, E-mail: johnm@soe.ucsc.edu. *Application contact:* Will Suh, Graduate Student Advisor, 831-459-2332, E-mail: bsoe-ga@rt.ucsc.edu.
Website: https://www.soe.ucsc.edu/departments/technology-management

University of Central Missouri, The Graduate School, Warrensburg, MO 64093. Offers accountancy (MA); accounting (MBA); applied mathematics (MS); aviation safety (MA); biology (MS); business administration (MBA); career and technical education leadership (MS); college student personnel administration (MS); communication (MA); computer science (MS); counseling (MS); criminal justice (MS); educational leadership (Ed D); educational technology (MS); elementary and early childhood education (MSE); English (MA); environmental studies (MA); finance (MBA); history (MA); human services/

educational technology (Ed S); human services/learning resources (Ed S); human services/professional counseling (Ed S); industrial hygiene (MS); industrial management (MS); information systems (MBA); information technology (MS); kinesiology (MS); library science and information services (MS); literacy education (MSE); marketing (MBA); mathematics (MS); music (MA); occupational safety management (MS); psychology (MS); rural family nursing (MS); school administration (MSE); social gerontology (MS); sociology (MA); special education (MSE); speech language pathology (MS); superintendency (Ed S); teaching (MAT); teaching English as a second language (MA); technology (MS); technology management (PhD); theatre (MA). *Program availability:* Part-time, 100% online, blended/hybrid learning. *Degree requirements:* For master's and Ed S, comprehensive exam (for some programs), thesis (for some programs). *Entrance requirements:* Additional exam requirements/recommendations for international students: Required—TOEFL (minimum score 550 paper-based; 79 iBT). Electronic applications accepted.

University of Cincinnati, Graduate School, Carl H. Lindner College of Business, MS Program, Cincinnati, OH 45221. Offers accounting (MS); business analytics (MS); finance (MS); information systems (MS); marketing (MS); taxation (MS). *Program availability:* Part-time, evening/weekend. *Faculty:* 74 full-time (17 women), 33 part-time/adjunct (8 women). *Students:* 307 full-time (128 women), 246 part-time (106 women); includes 60 minority (22 Black or African American, non-Hispanic/Latino; 20 Asian, non-Hispanic/Latino; 9 Hispanic/Latino; 1 Native Hawaiian or other Pacific Islander, non-Hispanic/Latino; 8 Two or more races, non-Hispanic/Latino), 321 international. Average age 28. 1,756 applicants, 24% accepted, 351 enrolled. In 2016, 334 master's awarded. *Degree requirements:* For master's, thesis (for some programs). *Entrance requirements:* For master's, GMAT, GRE, resume, transcripts, essays, letters of recommendation. Additional exam requirements/recommendations for international students: Required—TOEFL (minimum score 577 paper-based; 90 iBT), IELTS (minimum score 6.5). *Application deadline:* For fall admission, 8/1 priority date for domestic students, 3/15 for international students; for spring admission, 12/15 for domestic students, 9/15 for international students; for summer admission, 4/15 for domestic and international students. Applications are processed on a rolling basis. Application fee: $65 ($70 for international students). Electronic applications accepted. *Expenses:* Contact institution. *Financial support:* In 2016–17, 251 students received support, including 12 teaching assistantships with tuition reimbursements available (averaging $3,500 per year); scholarships/grants, tuition waivers (full and partial), and unspecified assistantships also available. Financial award application deadline: 2/1; financial award applicants required to submit FAFSA. *Faculty research:* Real estate, empirical pricing, organization information pricing, strategic management, portfolio choice in institutional investment. *Unit head:* Dr. David Szymanski, Dean, 513-556-7001, Fax: 513-556-4891, E-mail: david.szymanski@uc.edu. *Application contact:* Dona Clary, Director, Graduate Programs, 513-556-3546, Fax: 513-558-7006, E-mail: dona.clary@uc.edu.

University of Cincinnati, Graduate School, Carl H. Lindner College of Business, PhD Programs, Cincinnati, OH 45211. Offers accounting (PhD); economics (PhD); finance (PhD); information systems (PhD); management (PhD); marketing (PhD); operations and business analytics (PhD). *Faculty:* 72 full-time (18 women). *Students:* 37 full-time (19 women); includes 4 minority (1 Black or African American, non-Hispanic/Latino; 3 Asian, non-Hispanic/Latino), 19 international. Average age 30. 92 applicants, 16% accepted, 7 enrolled. In 2016, 4 doctorates awarded. *Degree requirements:* For doctorate, comprehensive exam, thesis/dissertation. *Entrance requirements:* For doctorate, GMAT, GRE, transcripts, essays, resume, letters of recommendation. Additional exam requirements/recommendations for international students: Required—TOEFL (minimum score 600 paper-based; 100 iBT), IELTS (minimum score 7). *Application deadline:* For fall admission, 1/15 for domestic and international students. Application fee: $65 ($70 for international students). Electronic applications accepted. *Expenses:* Contact institution. *Financial support:* In 2016–17, 38 students received support, including 25 research assistantships with tuition reimbursements available (averaging $23,250 per year); scholarships/grants, tuition waivers (full and partial), and unspecified assistantships also available. Financial award application deadline: 1/15; financial award applicants required to submit FAFSA. *Faculty research:* Bayesian Prediction Theory, organizational fairness, consumer insight and market research, EGARCH idiosyncratic volatility and expected stock returns, consumer insight and market research, density estimation from correlated data. *Unit head:* Dr. Suzanne Masterson, Director, 513-556-7125, Fax: 513-556-5499, E-mail: suzanne.masterson@uc.edu. *Application contact:* Angel Elvin, Assistant Director, 513-556-7190, Fax: 513-558-7006, E-mail: angel.elvin@uc.edu.
Website: http://www.business.uc.edu/phd

University of Colorado Denver, Business School, Program in Computer Science and Information Systems, Denver, CO 80217. Offers PhD. *Students:* 6 full-time (2 women), 7 part-time (1 woman); includes 1 minority (Black or African American, non-Hispanic/Latino), 7 international. Average age 39. 15 applicants, 13% accepted, 2 enrolled. *Degree requirements:* For doctorate, comprehensive exam, thesis/dissertation. *Entrance requirements:* For doctorate, GMAT or GRE General Test, letters of recommendation, portfolio, essay describing applicant's motivation and initial plan for doctoral study, resume. Additional exam requirements/recommendations for international students: Required—TOEFL (minimum score 525 paper-based; 71 iBT); Recommended—IELTS (minimum score 6.5). *Application deadline:* For fall admission, 3/1 priority date for domestic and international students; for spring admission, 10/15 for domestic students, 10/1 for international students. Applications are processed on a rolling basis. Application fee: $50 ($75 for international students). Electronic applications accepted. *Expenses:* Contact institution. *Financial support:* In 2016–17, 16 students received support. Fellowships, research assistantships, teaching assistantships, Federal Work-Study, institutionally sponsored loans, scholarships/grants, and traineeships available. Financial award application deadline: 4/1; financial award applicants required to submit FAFSA. *Faculty research:* Design science of information systems, information system economics, organizational impacts of information technology, high performance parallel and distributed systems, performance measurement and prediction. *Unit head:* Dr. Michael Mannino, Associate Professor/Co-Director, 303-315-8427, E-mail: michael.mannino@ucdenver.edu. *Application contact:* 303-315-8200, E-mail: bschool.admissions@ucdenver.edu.
Website: http://www.ucdenver.edu/academics/colleges/business/degrees/phd/Pages/default.aspx

University of Colorado Denver, Business School, Program in Information Systems, Denver, CO 80217. Offers accounting and information systems audit and control (MS); business intelligence systems (MS); digital health entrepreneurship (MS); enterprise risk management (MS); enterprise technology management (MS); geographic information systems (MS); health information technology (MS); technology innovation and entrepreneurship (MS); Web and mobile computing (MS). *Program availability:* Part-time, evening/weekend, online learning. *Students:* 110 full-time (44 women), 33 part-time (11 women); includes 19 minority (1 Black or African American, non-Hispanic/Latino; 8 Asian, non-Hispanic/Latino; 6 Hispanic/Latino; 4 Two or more races, non-Hispanic/Latino), 79 international. Average age 29. 140 applicants, 71% accepted, 38 enrolled. In 2016, 50 master's awarded. *Degree requirements:* For master's, 30 credit hours. *Entrance requirements:* For master's, GMAT, resume, essay, two letters of recommendation, financial statements (for international applicants). Additional exam requirements/recommendations for international students: Required—TOEFL (minimum score 525 paper-based; 71 iBT); Recommended—IELTS (minimum score 6.5). *Application deadline:* For fall admission, 4/15 priority date for domestic students, 3/15 priority date for international students; for spring admission, 10/15 priority date for domestic students, 9/15 priority date for international students; for summer admission, 2/15 priority date for domestic students, 1/15 priority date for international students. Applications are processed on a rolling basis. Application fee: $50 ($75 for international students). Electronic applications accepted. *Expenses:* Contact institution. *Financial support:* In 2016–17, 24 students received support. Fellowships, research assistantships, teaching assistantships, Federal Work-Study, institutionally sponsored loans, scholarships/grants, and traineeships available. Financial award application deadline: 4/1; financial award applicants required to submit FAFSA. *Faculty research:* Human-computer interaction, expert systems, database management, electronic commerce, object-oriented software development. *Unit head:* Dr. Jahangir Karimi, Director of Information Systems Programs, 303-315-8430, E-mail: jahangir.karimi@ucdenver.edu. *Application contact:* 303-315-8200, E-mail: bschool.admissions@ucdenver.edu.
Website: http://www.ucdenver.edu/academics/colleges/business/degrees/ms/IS/Pages/Information-Systems.aspx

University of Dallas, Satish and Yasmin Gupta College of Business, Irving, TX 75062-4736. Offers accounting (MBA, MS); business administration (DBA); business analytics (MS); business management (MBA); corporate finance (MBA); cybersecurity (MS); finance (MS); financial services (MBA); global business (MBA, MS); health services management (MBA); human resource management (MBA); information and technology management (MS); information assurance (MBA); information technology (MBA); information technology service management (MBA); marketing management (MBA); organization development (MBA); project management (MBA); sports and entertainment management (MBA); strategic leadership (MBA); supply chain management (MBA). *Accreditation:* AACSB. *Program availability:* Part-time, evening/weekend, online learning. *Entrance requirements:* Additional exam requirements/recommendations for international students: Required—TOEFL. Electronic applications accepted. *Expenses:* Contact institution.

University of Delaware, Alfred Lerner College of Business and Economics, Department of Accounting and Management Information Systems and Department of Electrical and Computer Engineering, Program in Information Systems and Technology Management, Newark, DE 19716. Offers MS. *Program availability:* Part-time, evening/weekend. *Entrance requirements:* For master's, GRE or GMAT, 2 letters of recommendation, resume, minimum GPA of 2.75. Additional exam requirements/recommendations for international students: Required—TOEFL (minimum score 600 paper-based). *Faculty research:* Security, developer trust, XML.

University of Delaware, Alfred Lerner College of Business and Economics, Program in Financial Service Analytics, Newark, DE 19716. Offers PhD. Program admits students every other year.

University of Detroit Mercy, College of Liberal Arts and Education, Detroit, MI 48221. Offers addiction counseling (MA); addiction studies (Certificate); clinical mental health counseling (MA); clinical psychology (MA, PhD); computer and information systems (MS); criminal justice (MA); curriculum and instruction (MA); economics (MA); educational administration (MA); financial economics (MA); industrial/organizational psychology (MA); information assurance (MS); intelligence analysis (MA); liberal studies (MALS); religious studies (MA); school counseling (MA, Certificate); school psychology (Spec); security administration (MS); special education: emotionally impaired/behaviorally disordered (MA); special education: learning disabilities (MA). *Program availability:* Part-time, evening/weekend. *Degree requirements:* For doctorate, departmental qualifying exam. *Faculty research:* Psychology of aging, history of technology, Renaissance humanism, U.S. and Japanese economic relations.

University of Florida, Graduate School, Warrington College of Business Administration, Hough Graduate School of Business, Department of Information Systems and Operations Management, Gainesville, FL 32611. Offers information systems and operations management (PhD); supply chain management (Certificate). Terminal master's awarded for partial completion of doctoral program. *Degree requirements:* For doctorate, thesis/dissertation. *Entrance requirements:* For master's, GMAT or GRE General Test, minimum GPA of 3.0; for doctorate, GMAT (minimum score 650) or GRE General Test, minimum GPA of 3.0. Additional exam requirements/recommendations for international students: Required—TOEFL (minimum score 550 paper-based; 80 iBT), IELTS (minimum score 6). *Faculty research:* Expert systems, nonconvex optimization, manufacturing management, production and operation management, telecommunication.

University of Florida, Graduate School, Warrington College of Business Administration, Hough Graduate School of Business, Programs in Business Administration, Gainesville, FL 32611. Offers business administration (MA, MS, PhD); competitive strategy (MBA); finance (MBA); global management (MBA); Graham-Buffett security analysis (MBA); human resource management (MBA); information systems and operations management (MBA); international studies (MBA); management (MBA); real estate (MBA); JD/MBA; MBA/MS; MBA/PhD; MBA/Pharm D; MD/MBA. *Accreditation:* AACSB. *Program availability:* Part-time, evening/weekend, online learning. *Degree requirements:* For master's, capstone course. *Entrance requirements:* For master's and doctorate, GMAT (minimum score 465), minimum GPA of 3.0, interview. Additional exam requirements/recommendations for international students: Required—TOEFL (minimum score 550 paper-based; 80 iBT), IELTS (minimum score 6). Electronic applications accepted. *Faculty research:* Accounting, finance, insurance, management, real estate, urban analysis marketing.

University of Hawaii at Manoa, Graduate Division, College of Social Sciences, School of Communications, Program in Telecommunication and Information Resource Management, Honolulu, HI 96822. Offers Graduate Certificate. *Program availability:* Part-time. *Entrance requirements:* Additional exam requirements/recommendations for international students: Required—TOEFL (minimum score 500 paper-based; 61 iBT), IELTS (minimum score 5).

University of Hawaii at Manoa, Graduate Division, Shidler College of Business, Program in Accounting, Honolulu, HI 96822. Offers accounting (M Acc); accounting law (M Acc); information systems (M Acc); taxation (M Acc). *Program availability:* Part-time. *Entrance requirements:* For master's, GMAT, bachelor's degree in accounting, minimum GPA of 3.0. Additional exam requirements/recommendations for international students: Required—TOEFL (minimum score 550 paper-based; 79 iBT), IELTS (minimum score 5). *Faculty research:* International accounting, current tax topics, insurance industry financial reporting, behavioral accounting, auditing.

University of Hawaii at Manoa, Graduate Division, Shidler College of Business, Program in Business Administration, Honolulu, HI 96822. Offers Asian business studies (MBA); Chinese business studies (MBA); decision sciences (MBA); entrepreneurship (MBA); finance (MBA); finance and banking (MBA); human resources management (MBA); information management (MBA); information technology (MBA); international business (MBA); Japanese business studies (MBA); marketing (MBA); organizational behavior (MBA); organizational management (MBA); real estate (MBA); student-designed track (MBA). *Accreditation:* AACSB. *Program availability:* Part-time, evening/weekend. *Degree requirements:* For master's, thesis optional. *Entrance requirements:* For master's, GMAT, minimum GPA of 3.0. Additional exam requirements/recommendations for international students: Required—TOEFL (minimum score 600 paper-based; 100 iBT), IELTS (minimum score 7). *Expenses:* Contact institution.

University of Hawaii at Manoa, Graduate Division, Shidler College of Business, Program in International Management, Honolulu, HI 96822. Offers Asian finance (PhD); global information technology management (PhD); international accounting (PhD); international marketing (PhD); international organization and strategy (PhD). *Program availability:* Part-time. *Degree requirements:* For doctorate, comprehensive exam, thesis/dissertation. *Entrance requirements:* For doctorate, GMAT or GRE General Test, minimum GPA of 3.0. Additional exam requirements/recommendations for international students: Required—TOEFL (minimum score 600 paper-based; 100 iBT), IELTS (minimum score 7). *Expenses:* Contact institution.

University of Houston–Clear Lake, School of Business, Program in Management Information Systems, Houston, TX 77058-1002. Offers MS. *Program availability:* Part-time. *Entrance requirements:* For master's, GMAT. Additional exam requirements/recommendations for international students: Required—TOEFL (minimum score 550 paper-based).

University of Houston–Victoria, School of Arts and Sciences, Department of Computer Science, Victoria, TX 77901-4450. Offers computer information systems (MS); computer science (MS). *Program availability:* Part-time, evening/weekend, online learning. *Degree requirements:* For master's, comprehensive exam (for some programs), thesis (for some programs). *Entrance requirements:* For master's, GRE. Additional exam requirements/recommendations for international students: Required—TOEFL (minimum score 550 paper-based).

University of Illinois at Chicago, Liautaud Graduate School of Business, Department of Information and Decision Sciences, Chicago, IL 60607-7128. Offers management information systems (PhD). *Program availability:* Part-time, evening/weekend. *Degree requirements:* For doctorate, thesis/dissertation. *Entrance requirements:* For doctorate, GMAT, minimum GPA of 2.75. Additional exam requirements/recommendations for international students: Required—TOEFL. Electronic applications accepted. *Expenses:* Contact institution. *Faculty research:* Information management/technology and innovation, data and analytics, health informatics, risk management, business statistics and forecasting.

University of Illinois at Springfield, Graduate Programs, College of Business and Management, Program in Management Information Systems, Springfield, IL 62703-5407. Offers MS. *Program availability:* Part-time, evening/weekend, 100% online, blended/hybrid learning. *Faculty:* 9 full-time (2 women), 8 part-time/adjunct (3 women). *Students:* 274 full-time (104 women), 147 part-time (41 women); includes 55 minority (15 Black or African American, non-Hispanic/Latino; 1 American Indian or Alaska Native, non-Hispanic/Latino; 22 Asian, non-Hispanic/Latino; 13 Hispanic/Latino; 4 Two or more races, non-Hispanic/Latino), 289 international. Average age 28. 804 applicants, 36% accepted, 87 enrolled. In 2016, 209 master's awarded. *Degree requirements:* For master's, thesis or alternative, project, closure seminar. *Entrance requirements:* For master's, GMAT or GRE General Test, courses in managerial and financial accounting, production/operations management, statistics, linear algebra or mathematics; competency in a structured, high-level programming language; minimum undergraduate GPA of 2.75. Additional exam requirements/recommendations for international students: Required—TOEFL (minimum score 500 paper-based; 61 iBT). *Application deadline:* Applications are processed on a rolling basis. Application fee: $60 ($75 for international students). Electronic applications accepted. *Expenses:* $369.75 per hour in-state, $715.75 per hour out-of-state, $403 per hour online. *Financial support:* In 2016–17, fellowships with full tuition reimbursements (averaging $9,900 per year), research assistantships with full tuition reimbursements (averaging $9,991 per year), teaching assistantships with full tuition reimbursements (averaging $10,059 per year) were awarded; career-related internships or fieldwork, Federal Work-Study, scholarships/grants, health care benefits, and unspecified assistantships also available. Support available to part-time students. Financial award application deadline: 11/15; financial award applicants required to submit FAFSA. *Unit head:* Dr. Rassule Hadidi, Program Administrator, 217-206-6067, Fax: 217-206-7541, E-mail: rhadi1@uis.edu. *Application contact:* Dr. Cecelia Cornell, Associate Vice Chancellor for Graduate Education, 217-206-7230, E-mail: ccorn1@uis.edu.

University of Illinois at Urbana–Champaign, Graduate College, School of Information Sciences, Champaign, IL 61820. Offers bioinformatics (MS); digital libraries (CAS); information management (MS); library and information science (MS, PhD, CAS). *Accreditation:* ALA (one or more programs are accredited). *Program availability:* Part-time, online learning. *Entrance requirements:* For degree, master's degree in library and information science or related field with minimum GPA of 3.0.

The University of Kansas, Graduate Studies, School of Engineering, Program in Information Technology, Lawrence, KS 66045. Offers MS. *Program availability:* Part-time, evening/weekend. *Students:* 1 (woman) full-time, 19 part-time (2 women); includes 7 minority (4 Black or African American, non-Hispanic/Latino; 3 Asian, non-Hispanic/Latino), 1 international. Average age 35. 35 applicants, 77% accepted, 13 enrolled. In 2016, 8 master's awarded. *Entrance requirements:* For master's, GRE, official transcript, three recommendations, statement of academic objectives, resume. Additional exam requirements/recommendations for international students: Required—TOEFL (minimum score 600 paper-based; 100 iBT), IELTS (minimum score 6). *Application deadline:* For fall admission, 8/1 for domestic and international students; for spring admission, 1/1 for domestic and international students. Application fee: $65 ($85 for international students). Electronic applications accepted. *Faculty research:* Information security and privacy, game theory, graph theory, software process improvement, resilient and survivable networks, object orientation technology. *Unit head:* James Stiles, Associate Chair for Graduate Studies, 785-864-8803, E-mail: jstiles@eecs.ku.edu. *Application contact:* Pam Shadoin, Assistant to Graduate Director, 785-864-4407, Fax: 785-864-3226, E-mail: eecs_graduate@ku.edu.
Website: http://eecs.ku.edu/prospective_students/graduate/masters#information_technology

University of La Verne, College of Business and Public Management, Graduate Programs in Business Administration, La Verne, CA 91750-4443. Offers accounting (MBA, MBA-EP); finance (MBA, MBA-EP); health services management (MBA); information technology (MBA, MBA-EP); international business (MBA, MBA-EP); management and leadership (MBA, MBA-EP); marketing (MBA, MBA-EP); supply chain management (MBA, MBA-EP). *Program availability:* Part-time, evening/weekend. *Students:* 385 full-time (177 women), 89 part-time (46 women); includes 92 minority (4 Black or African American, non-Hispanic/Latino; 1 American Indian or Alaska Native, non Hispanic/Latino; 14 Asian, non-Hispanic/Latino; 71 Hispanic/Latino; 1 Native Hawaiian or other Pacific Islander, non-Hispanic/Latino; 1 Two or more races, non-Hispanic/Latino), 319 international. Average age 28. *Entrance requirements:* For master's, GMAT, MAT, or GRE, minimum undergraduate GPA of 3.0, 2 letters of recommendation, resume, statement of purpose. Additional exam requirements/recommendations for international students: Required—TOEFL (minimum score 550 paper-based; 85 iBT). *Application deadline:* Applications are processed on a rolling basis. Application fee: $50. *Expenses: Tuition:* Part-time $795 per credit hour. Tuition and fees vary according to campus/location and program. *Financial support:* Institutionally sponsored loans and scholarships/grants available. Financial award application deadline: 3/2; financial award applicants required to submit FAFSA. *Unit head:* Dr. Abe Helou, Chairperson, 909-448-4455, Fax: 909-392-2704, E-mail: ihelou@laverne.edu. *Application contact:* Rina Lazarian-Chehab, Senior Associate Director of Graduate Admissions, 909-448-4317, Fax: 909-971-2295, E-mail: rlazarian@laverne.edu.
Website: https://laverne.edu/business-and-public-administration/mba-2/

University of La Verne, Regional and Online Campuses, Graduate Programs, Central Coast/Vandenberg Air Force Base Campuses, La Verne, CA 91750-4443. Offers business administration for experienced professionals (MBA), including health services management, information technology; education (special emphasis) (M Ed); educational counseling (MS); educational leadership (M Ed); multiple subject (elementary) (Credential); preliminary administrative services (Credential); pupil personnel services (Credential); single subject (secondary) (Credential). *Program availability:* Part-time. *Expenses:* Contact institution.

University of La Verne, Regional and Online Campuses, Graduate Programs, Inland Empire Campus, Ontario, CA 91730. Offers business administration (MBA, MBA-EP), including accounting (MBA), finance (MBA), health services management (MBA-EP), information technology (MBA-EP), international business (MBA), managed care (MBA), management and leadership (MBA-EP), marketing (MBA-EP), supply chain management (MBA); leadership and management (MS), including human resource management, nonprofit management, organizational development. *Program availability:* Part-time, evening/weekend. *Expenses:* Contact institution.

University of Lethbridge, School of Graduate Studies, Lethbridge, AB T1K 3M4, Canada. Offers addictions counseling (M Sc); agricultural biotechnology (M Sc); agricultural studies (M Sc, MA); anthropology (MA); archaeology (M Sc, MA); art (MA, MFA); biochemistry (M Sc); biological sciences (M Sc); biomolecular science (PhD); biosystems and biodiversity (PhD); Canadian studies (MA); chemistry (M Sc); computer science (M Sc); computer science and geographical information science (M Sc); counseling (MC); counseling psychology (M Ed); dramatic arts (MA); earth, space, and physical science (PhD); economics (MA); education (MA, PhD); educational leadership (M Ed); English (MA); environmental science (M Sc); evolution and behavior (PhD); exercise science (M Sc); French (MA); French/German (MA); French/Spanish (MA); general education (M Ed); geography (M Sc, MA); German (MA); health sciences (M Sc); individualized multidisciplinary (M Sc, MA); kinesiology (M Sc, MA); management (M Sc), including accounting, finance, human resource management and labor relations, information systems, international management, marketing, policy and strategy; mathematics (M Sc); music (M Mus, MA); Native American studies (MA); neuroscience (M Sc, PhD); new media (MA, MFA); nursing (M Sc, MN); philosophy (MA); physics (M Sc); political science (MA); psychology (M Sc, MA); religious studies (MA); sociology (MA); theatre and dramatic arts (MFA); theoretical and computational science (PhD); urban and regional studies (MA); women and gender studies (MA). *Program availability:* Part-time, evening/weekend. *Degree requirements:* For master's, thesis (for some programs); for doctorate, comprehensive exam, thesis/dissertation. *Entrance requirements:* For master's, GMAT (for M Sc in management), bachelor's degree in related field, minimum GPA of 3.0 during previous 20 graded semester courses, 2 years' teaching or related experience (M Ed); for doctorate, master's degree, minimum graduate GPA of 3.5. Additional exam requirements/recommendations for international students: Required—TOEFL (minimum score 580 paper-based; 93 iBT). Electronic applications accepted. *Faculty research:* Movement and brain plasticity, gibberellin physiology, photosynthesis, carbon cycling, molecular properties of main-group ring components.

University of Management and Technology, Program in Information Technology, Arlington, VA 22209-1609. Offers MS, Advanced Certificate.

University of Mary Hardin-Baylor, Graduate Studies in Business Administration, Belton, TX 76513. Offers accounting (MBA); information systems management (MBA); international business (MBA); management (MBA). *Program availability:* Part-time, evening/weekend. *Faculty:* 11 full-time (5 women), 6 part-time/adjunct (2 women). *Students:* 21 full-time (12 women), 44 part-time (14 women); includes 23 minority (12 Black or African American, non-Hispanic/Latino; 1 Asian, non-Hispanic/Latino; 10 Hispanic/Latino), 11 international. Average age 29. 96 applicants, 70% accepted, 21 enrolled. In 2016, 22 master's awarded. *Degree requirements:* For master's, comprehensive exam. *Entrance requirements:* For master's, minimum GPA of 3.0, interview. Additional exam requirements/recommendations for international students: Required—TOEFL (minimum score 60 iBT), IELTS (minimum score 4.5). *Application deadline:* For fall admission, 6/1 for domestic students, 4/30 priority date for international students; for spring admission, 11/1 for domestic students, 9/30 priority date for international students. Applications are processed on a rolling basis. Application fee: $35 ($135 for international students). Electronic applications accepted. *Expenses: Tuition:* Full-time $14,940; part-time $830 per credit hour. *Required fees:* $1350; $75 per credit hour. $50 per term. Tuition and fees vary according to course load and degree level. *Financial support:* In 2016–17, 33 students received support. Federal Work-Study, unspecified assistantships, and scholarships for some active duty military personnel available. Financial award applicants required to submit FAFSA. *Faculty research:* Experiential learning, case studies in systems analysis and design, forecasting methodologies, short-selling in the stock market, open educational resources. *Total annual research expenditures:* $17,500. *Unit head:* Dr. Kirk Fischer, Assistant Professor/Director, Graduate Programs in McLane College of Business, 254-295-4655, E-mail: kfischer@umhb.edu. *Application contact:* Sharon Aguilera, Assistant Director, Graduate Admissions, 254-295-4835, Fax: 254-295-5038, E-mail: saguilera@umhb.edu.
Website: http://www.graduate.umhb.edu/mba

University of Mary Hardin-Baylor, Graduate Studies in Information Systems, Belton, TX 76513. Offers MS. *Program availability:* Part-time, evening/weekend. *Faculty:* 7 full-time (1 woman), 1 (woman) part-time/adjunct. *Students:* 183 full-time (47 women), 14 part-time (4 women); includes 2 minority (both Hispanic/Latino), 190 international. Average age 24. 623 applicants, 80% accepted, 35 enrolled. In 2016, 174 master's awarded. *Degree requirements:* For master's, comprehensive exam. *Entrance requirements:* For master's, minimum GPA of 3.0, interview. Additional exam requirements/recommendations for international students: Required—TOEFL (minimum score 60 iBT), IELTS (minimum score 4.5). *Application deadline:* For fall admission, 6/1 for domestic students, 4/30 priority date for international students; for spring admission, 11/1 for domestic students, 9/30 priority date for international students. Applications are processed on a rolling basis. Application fee: $35 ($135 for international students). Electronic applications accepted. *Expenses: Tuition:* Full-time $14,940; part-time $830 per credit hour. *Required fees:* $1350; $75 per credit hour. $50 per term. Tuition and fees vary according to course load and degree level. *Financial support:* In 2016–17, 143 students received support. Federal Work-Study, unspecified assistantships, and scholarships for some active duty military personnel available. Support available to part-time students. Financial award applicants required to submit FAFSA. *Faculty research:*

Management Information Systems

Data security in healthcare, information technology impact in supply chain management, impact of technology on Christian faith, entrepreneurial perceptions in China, strategic advantage in information systems. *Total annual research expenditures:* $17,500. *Unit head:* Dr. Kirk Fischer, Associate Dean, Graduate Programs in McLane College of Business, 254-295-4655, E-mail: kfischer@umhb.edu. *Application contact:* Sharon Aguilera, Assistant Director, Graduate Admissions, 254-295-4835, Fax: 254-295-5038, E-mail: saguilera@umhb.edu.
Website: http://www.graduate.umhb.edu/msis

University of Massachusetts Boston, College of Management, Program in Information Technology, Boston, MA 02125-3393. Offers MS. *Students:* 29 full-time (17 women), 13 part-time (7 women); includes 10 minority (2 Black or African American, non-Hispanic/Latino; 7 Asian, non-Hispanic/Latino; 1 Two or more races, non-Hispanic/Latino), 26 international. Average age 28. 48 applicants, 42% accepted, 14 enrolled. In 2016, 20 master's awarded. *Expenses:* Tuition, state resident: full-time $16,863. Tuition, nonresident: full-time $32,913. *Required fees:* $177. *Unit head:* Dr. Jorge Haddock, Dean. *Application contact:* Peggy Roldan Patel, Graduate Admissions Coordinator, 617-287-6400, Fax: 617-287-6236, E-mail: bos.gadm@dpc.umassp.edu.

University of Massachusetts Dartmouth, Graduate School, Charlton College of Business, Program in Business Administration, North Dartmouth, MA 02747-2300. Offers business administration (MBA); business analytics (Postbaccalaureate Certificate); business foundations (Graduate Certificate); international business (Graduate Certificate); management (Postbaccalaureate Certificate); marketing (Postbaccalaureate Certificate); organizational leadership (Graduate Certificate); supply chain management and information systems (Postbaccalaureate Certificate). *Accreditation:* AACSB. *Program availability:* Part-time, 100% online, blended/hybrid learning. *Faculty:* 15 full-time (7 women), 11 part-time/adjunct (4 women). *Students:* 126 full-time (49 women), 178 part-time (100 women); includes 45 minority (10 Black or African American, non-Hispanic/Latino; 1 American Indian or Alaska Native, non-Hispanic/Latino; 16 Asian, non-Hispanic/Latino; 13 Hispanic/Latino; 5 Two or more races, non-Hispanic/Latino), 100 international. Average age 32. 236 applicants, 80% accepted, 132 enrolled. In 2016, 142 master's, 13 other advanced degrees awarded. *Degree requirements:* For master's, thesis or alternative, eportfolio. *Entrance requirements:* For master's, GMAT, statement of purpose (minimum of 300 words), resume, official transcripts, 2 letters of recommendation; for other advanced degree, statement of purpose (minimum of 300 words), resume, official transcripts. Additional exam requirements/recommendations for international students: Required—TOEFL (minimum score 533 paper-based; 72 iBT). *Application deadline:* For fall admission, 7/1 priority date for domestic students, 6/1 priority date for international students; for spring admission, 11/15 priority date for domestic students, 10/15 priority date for international students. Application fee: $60. Electronic applications accepted. *Expenses:* Tuition, state resident: full-time $14,994; part-time $624.75 per credit. Tuition, nonresident: full-time $27,068; part-time $1127.83 per credit. *Required fees:* $405; $25.88 per credit. Tuition and fees vary according to course load and reciprocity agreements. *Financial support:* In 2016–17, 2 research assistantships (averaging $2,667 per year) were awarded; institutionally sponsored loans, scholarships/grants, and unspecified assistantships also available. Support available to part-time students. Financial award application deadline: 3/1; financial award applicants required to submit FAFSA. *Faculty research:* E-commerce, managing diversity, agile manufacturing, green business, activity-based management, build-to-order supply chain management. *Total annual research expenditures:* $413,000. *Unit head:* Melissa Pacheco, Assistant Dean of Graduate Programs, 508-999-8543, Fax: 508-999-8646, E-mail: mpacheco@umassd.edu. *Application contact:* Steven Briggs, Director of Marketing and Recruitment for Graduate Studies, 508-999-8604, Fax: 508-999-8183, E-mail: graduate@umassd.edu.
Website: http://www.umassd.edu/charlton/programs/graduate/mba

University of Memphis, Graduate School, Fogelman College of Business and Economics, Department of Business Information and Technology, Memphis, TN 38152. Offers MS, PhD, Graduate Certificate. *Faculty:* 10 full-time (4 women). *Students:* 14 part-time (6 women); includes 8 minority (4 Black or African American, non-Hispanic/Latino; 3 Asian, non-Hispanic/Latino; 1 Hispanic/Latino), 3 international. 20 applicants, 100% accepted, 8 enrolled. In 2016, 70 other advanced degrees awarded. *Expenses:* Tuition, state resident: full-time $10,463; part-time $9483 per year. Tuition, nonresident: full-time $19,247; part-time $17,291 per year. *Required fees:* $821.50 per semester. Tuition and fees vary according to course load and program. *Financial support:* In 2016–17, 12 research assistantships (averaging $20,500 per year), 1 teaching assistantship (averaging $9,000 per year) were awarded. *Unit head:* Robin Poston, Chair, 901-678-5739, E-mail: rposton@memphis.edu. *Application contact:* Dr. Lloyd Brooks, Associate Dean, 901-678-4620, Fax: 901-678-3759, E-mail: lbrooks@memphis.edu.
Website: http://www.memphis.edu/bitm/

University of Michigan–Dearborn, College of Business, MS Program in Information Systems, Dearborn, MI 48126. Offers MS. *Program availability:* Part-time, evening/weekend. *Faculty:* 33 full-time (14 women), 10 part-time/adjunct (5 women). *Students:* 8 full-time (3 women), 20 part-time (7 women); includes 4 minority (3 Asian, non-Hispanic/Latino; 1 Hispanic/Latino), 17 international. Average age 28. 68 applicants, 40% accepted, 6 enrolled. In 2016, 10 master's awarded. *Entrance requirements:* For master's, GRE or GMAT, equivalent of four-year U.S. bachelor's degree from regionally-accredited institution, undergraduate course in finite math, pre-calculus, or calculus. Additional exam requirements/recommendations for international students: Required—TOEFL (minimum score 560 paper-based; 84 iBT), IELTS (minimum score 6.5). *Application deadline:* For fall admission, 8/1 for domestic students, 5/1 for international students; for winter admission, 12/1 for domestic students, 9/1 for international students; for spring admission, 4/1 for domestic students, 1/1 for international students. Applications are processed on a rolling basis. Application fee: $60. Electronic applications accepted. *Expenses:* Contact institution. *Financial support:* In 2016–17, 16 students received support. Scholarships/grants and non-resident tuition scholarships available. Financial award application deadline: 3/1; financial award applicants required to submit FAFSA. *Faculty research:* Business intelligence, information technology, brand management and new media, management education, operations strategy. *Unit head:* Dr. Michael Kamen, Director, Graduate Programs, 313-593-5460, E-mail: mkamen@umich.edu. *Application contact:* Joan Doherty, Academic Advisor/Counselor, 313-593-5460, Fax: 313-271-9838, E-mail: umd-gradbusiness@umich.edu.
Website: http://umdearborn.edu/cob/ms-information-systems/

University of Michigan–Dearborn, College of Education, Health, and Human Services, Master of Science Program in Health Information Technology, Dearborn, MI 48126. Offers MS. *Program availability:* Part-time, evening/weekend. *Faculty:* 5 full-time (3 women), 2 part-time/adjunct (both women). *Students:* 10 full-time (8 women), 14 part-time (all women); includes 7 minority (2 Black or African American, non-Hispanic/Latino; 4 Asian, non-Hispanic/Latino; 1 Two or more races, non-Hispanic/Latino), 2 international. Average age 30. 26 applicants, 88% accepted, 14 enrolled. In 2016, 2 master's awarded. *Entrance requirements:* Additional exam requirements/recommendations for international students: Required—TOEFL (minimum score 560 paper-based; 84 iBT), IELTS (minimum score 6.5). *Application deadline:* For fall admission, 8/1 for domestic students, 5/1 for international students; for winter admission, 12/1 for domestic students, 9/1 for international students; for spring admission, 4/1 for domestic students, 1/1 for international students. Applications are processed on a rolling basis. Application fee: $60. Electronic applications accepted. *Expenses:* Contact institution. *Financial support:* In 2016–17, 8 students received support. Career-related internships or fieldwork and scholarships/grants available. Financial award application deadline: 3/1; financial award applicants required to submit FAFSA. *Faculty research:* Behavior and new technology, information quality, technology acceptance, healthcare systems, economics of recovery. *Unit head:* Dr. Stein Brunvand, Director, 313-583-6415, E-mail: sbrunvan@umich.edu. *Application contact:* Elizabeth Morden, Program Assistant, 313-593-5090, E-mail: emorden@umich.edu.
Website: http://umdearborn.edu/cehhs/cehhs_m_hit/

University of Michigan–Dearborn, College of Engineering and Computer Science, MS Program in Information Systems and Technology, Dearborn, MI 48128. Offers MS. *Program availability:* Part-time, evening/weekend, 100% online. *Faculty:* 8 full-time (1 woman), 3 part-time/adjunct (0 women). *Students:* 10 full-time (4 women), 38 part-time (15 women); includes 13 minority (5 Black or African American, non-Hispanic/Latino; 7 Asian, non-Hispanic/Latino; 1 Two or more races, non-Hispanic/Latino), 14 international. Average age 34. 38 applicants, 66% accepted, 17 enrolled. In 2016, 16 master's awarded. *Entrance requirements:* For master's, bachelor's degree in engineering, a physical science, computer science, applied mathematics, business administration, or liberal arts with minimum cumulative GPA of 3.0. Additional exam requirements/recommendations for international students: Required—TOEFL (minimum score 560 paper-based; 84 iBT), IELTS (minimum score 6.5). *Application deadline:* For fall admission, 8/1 for domestic students, 5/1 for international students; for winter admission, 12/1 for domestic students, 9/1 for international students; for spring admission, 4/1 for domestic students, 1/1 for international students. Applications are processed on a rolling basis. Application fee: $60. Electronic applications accepted. *Expenses:* Tuition, state resident: full-time $13,118; part-time $2280 per term. Tuition, nonresident: full-time $21,816; part-time $3771 per term. *Required fees:* $866; $658 per unit. $329 per term. Tuition and fees vary according to program. *Financial support:* Scholarships/grants, unspecified assistantships, and non-resident tuition scholarships available. Support available to part-time students. Financial award application deadline: 3/1; financial award applicants required to submit FAFSA. *Faculty research:* Enterprise information systems, data science, information security. *Unit head:* Dr. Armen Zakarian, Chair, 313-593-5361, Fax: 313-593-3692, E-mail: zakarian@umich.edu. *Application contact:* Office of Graduate Studies, 313-583-6321, E-mail: umd-graduatestudies@umich.edu.
Website: https://umdearborn.edu/cecs/departments/industrial-and-manufacturing-systems-engineering/graduate-programs/ms-information-systems-and-technology

University of Michigan–Flint, College of Arts and Sciences, Program in Computer Science and Information Systems, Flint, MI 48502-1950. Offers computer science (MS); information systems (MS), including business information systems, health information systems. *Program availability:* Part-time, evening/weekend, 100% online. *Faculty:* 29 full-time (7 women), 12 part-time/adjunct (7 women). *Students:* 35 full-time (17 women), 91 part-time (24 women); includes 11 minority (3 Black or African American, non-Hispanic/Latino; 2 Asian, non-Hispanic/Latino; 4 Hispanic/Latino; 1 Native Hawaiian or other Pacific Islander, non-Hispanic/Latino; 1 Two or more races, non-Hispanic/Latino), 82 international. Average age 28. 712 applicants, 29% accepted, 29 enrolled. In 2016, 171 master's awarded. *Degree requirements:* For master's, thesis optional. *Entrance requirements:* For master's, BS from regionally-accredited institution in computer science, computer information systems, or computer engineering (preferred); minimum overall undergraduate GPA of 3.0. Additional exam requirements/recommendations for international students: Required—TOEFL (minimum score 84 iBT), IELTS (minimum score 6.5). *Application deadline:* For fall admission, 5/1 for domestic students, 2/1 for international students; for winter admission, 10/1 for domestic students, 8/1 for international students; for spring admission, 3/15 for domestic students, 1/1 for international students; for summer admission, 5/15 for domestic students, 3/1 for international students. Applications are processed on a rolling basis. Application fee: $55. Electronic applications accepted. *Expenses:* Contact institution. *Financial support:* Federal Work-Study, scholarships/grants, and unspecified assistantships available. Support available to part-time students. Financial award application deadline: 3/1; financial award applicants required to submit FAFSA. *Faculty research:* Computer network systems, database management systems, artificial intelligence and controlled systems. *Unit head:* Dr. Jeffrey Livermore, Director, 810-762-3131, Fax: 810-766-6780, E-mail: jefflive@umflint.edu. *Application contact:* Bradley T. Maki, Director of Graduate Admissions, 810-762-3171, Fax: 810-766-6789, E-mail: bmaki@umflint.edu.
Website: http://www.umflint.edu/graduateprograms/computer-science-information-systems-ms

University of Michigan–Flint, School of Management, Program in Business Administration, Flint, MI 48502. Offers accounting (MBA, Post-Master's Certificate); computer information systems (MBA); finance (MBA, Post-Master's Certificate); general business (Graduate Certificate); general business administration (MBA); health care management (MBA); international business (MBA, Post-Master's Certificate); lean manufacturing (MBA); marketing (MBA, Post-Master's Certificate); organizational leadership (MBA, Post-Master's Certificate). *Program availability:* Part-time, evening/weekend, mixed mode programs. *Faculty:* 33 full-time (9 women), 6 part-time/adjunct (1 woman). *Students:* 24 full-time (12 women), 146 part-time (49 women); includes 37 minority (17 Black or African American, non-Hispanic/Latino; 2 American Indian or Alaska Native, non-Hispanic/Latino; 10 Asian, non-Hispanic/Latino; 4 Hispanic/Latino; 1 Native Hawaiian or other Pacific Islander, non-Hispanic/Latino; 3 Two or more races, non-Hispanic/Latino), 17 international. Average age 33. 167 applicants, 47% accepted, 40 enrolled. In 2016, 73 master's, 3 other advanced degrees awarded. *Entrance requirements:* For master's, GMAT or GRE, bachelor's degree in arts, sciences, engineering, or business administration from regionally-accredited college or university with minimum GPA of 3.0; for other advanced degree, bachelor's degree in arts, sciences, engineering, or business administration from regionally-accredited college or university with minimum GPA of 3.0, college-level math, statistics, or quantitative course (for Graduate Certificate); MBA or equivalent degree from regionally-accredited college or university (for Post Master's Certificate). Additional exam requirements/recommendations for international students: Required—TOEFL (minimum score 84 iBT), IELTS (minimum score 6.5). *Application deadline:* For fall admission, 8/1 for domestic students, 5/1 for international students; for winter admission, 11/15 for domestic students, 9/1 for international students; for spring admission, 3/15 for domestic students, 1/1 for international students; for summer admission, 5/15 for domestic students. Applications are processed on a rolling basis. Application fee: $55. Electronic applications accepted. *Financial support:* Federal Work-Study, scholarships/grants, and unspecified assistantships available. Support available to part-time students. Financial award application deadline: 3/1; financial award applicants required to submit FAFSA. *Unit head:* Dr. Scott Johnson, Dean, School of Management, 810-762-3164, Fax: 810-237-6685, E-mail: scotjohn@umflint.edu. *Application contact:* Bradley T. Maki, Director of Graduate Admissions, 810-762-3171, E-mail: bmaki@umflint.edu.
Website: http://www.umflint.edu/graduateprograms/business-administration-mba

University of Minnesota, Twin Cities Campus, Carlson School of Management, Carlson Full-Time MBA Program, Minneapolis, MN 55455. Offers finance (MBA); human

resources and industrial relations (MA); information technology (MBA); management (MBA); marketing (MBA); medical industry orientation (MBA); supply chain and operations (MBA); JD/MBA; MBA/MPP; MBA/MSBA; MD/MBA; MHA/MBA; Pharm D/ MBA. *Accreditation:* AACSB. *Faculty:* 143 full-time (42 women), 24 part-time/adjunct (6 women). *Students:* 193 full-time (59 women); includes 23 minority (2 Black or African American, non-Hispanic/Latino; 1 American Indian or Alaska Native, non-Hispanic/ Latino; 9 Asian, non-Hispanic/Latino; 5 Hispanic/Latino; 1 Native Hawaiian or other Pacific Islander, non-Hispanic/Latino; 5 Two or more races, non-Hispanic/Latino), 31 international. Average age 28. 606 applicants, 45% accepted, 104 enrolled. In 2016, 102 master's awarded. *Entrance requirements:* For master's, GMAT or GRE. Additional exam requirements/recommendations for international students: Required—TOEFL (minimum score 580 paper-based; 84 iBT), IELTS (minimum score 7), PTE. *Application deadline:* For fall admission, 4/1 for domestic students, 2/1 for international students. Application fee: $75. Electronic applications accepted. *Expenses:* $39,378 per year resident tuition and fees; $49,766 per year non-resident tuition and fees; $50,084 per year international tuition and fees. *Financial support:* In 2016–17, 148 students received support, including 148 fellowships with tuition reimbursements available (averaging $21,070 per year); research assistantships with partial tuition reimbursements available, teaching assistantships with partial tuition reimbursements available, career-related internships or fieldwork, Federal Work-Study, institutionally sponsored loans, scholarships/grants, health care benefits, and unspecified assistantships also available. Financial award application deadline: 4/1; financial award applicants required to submit FAFSA. *Faculty research:* Market regulation and asset pricing, social networks and data analytics, consumer behavior, innovation and entrepreneurship, workplace wellbeing and labor relationships. *Total annual research expenditures:* $577,440. *Unit head:* Philip J. Miller, Assistant Dean, MBA Programs and Graduate Business Career Center, 612-625-5555, Fax: 612-625-1012, E-mail: mba@umn.edu. *Application contact:* Linh Gilles, Director of Admissions and Recruiting, 612-625-5555, Fax: 612-625-1012, E-mail: ftmba@umn.edu.
Website: http://www.csom.umn.edu/MBA/full-time/

University of Minnesota, Twin Cities Campus, Carlson School of Management, Carlson Part-Time MBA Program, Minneapolis, MN 55455. Offers finance (MBA); information technology (MBA); management (MBA); marketing (MBA); medical industry orientation (MBA); supply chain and operations (MBA). *Program availability:* Part-time-only, evening/weekend, 100% online, blended/hybrid learning. *Faculty:* 143 full-time (42 women), 26 part-time/adjunct (6 women). *Students:* 1,005 part-time (317 women); includes 110 minority (17 Black or African American, non-Hispanic/Latino; 2 American Indian or Alaska Native, non-Hispanic/Latino; 51 Asian, non-Hispanic/Latino; 19 Hispanic/Latino; 21 Two or more races, non-Hispanic/Latino), 58 international. Average age 28. 251 applicants, 86% accepted, 185 enrolled. In 2016, 336 master's awarded. *Entrance requirements:* For master's, GMAT or GRE. Additional exam requirements/ recommendations for international students: Required—TOEFL (minimum score 580 paper-based; 84 iBT), IELTS (minimum score 7), PTE. *Application deadline:* For fall admission, 5/15 priority date for domestic and international students; for spring admission, 10/15 priority date for domestic and international students. Applications are processed on a rolling basis. Application fee: $75. Electronic applications accepted. *Expenses:* $1,335 per credit. *Financial support:* Applicants required to submit FAFSA. *Faculty research:* Market regulation and asset pricing, social networks and data analytics, consumer behavior, innovation and entrepreneurship, workplace wellbeing and labor relationships. *Total annual research expenditures:* $577,440. *Unit head:* Philip J. Miller, Assistant Dean, MBA Programs and Graduate Business Career Center, 612-624-2039, Fax: 612-625-1012, E-mail: mba@umn.edu. *Application contact:* Linh Gilles, Director of Admissions and Recruiting, 612-625-5555, Fax: 612-625-1012, E-mail: ptmba@umn.edu.
Website: http://www.carlsonschool.umn.edu/ptmba

University of Minnesota, Twin Cities Campus, Carlson School of Management, Doctoral Program in Business Administration, Minneapolis, MN 55455. Offers accounting (PhD); finance (PhD); information and decision sciences (PhD); marketing (PhD); strategic management and entrepreneurship (PhD); supply chain and operations (PhD); work and organizations (PhD). *Faculty:* 101 full-time (32 women). *Students:* 90 full-time (29 women); includes 7 minority (2 Black or African American, non-Hispanic/ Latino; 3 Asian, non-Hispanic/Latino; 2 Hispanic/Latino), 64 international. Average age 30. 352 applicants, 7% accepted, 15 enrolled. In 2016, 20 doctorates awarded. *Degree requirements:* For doctorate, comprehensive exam, thesis/dissertation, written and oral preliminary exams, proposal defense, final defense. *Entrance requirements:* For doctorate, GMAT, GRE General Test, minimum undergraduate GPA of 3.0, graduate 3.5 (recommended). Additional exam requirements/recommendations for international students: Required—TOEFL (minimum score 600 paper-based, 100 iBT) or IELTS (minimum score 7.0). *Application deadline:* For fall admission, 12/15 for domestic students, 12/15 priority date for international students. Applications are processed on a rolling basis. Application fee: $75 ($95 for international students). Electronic applications accepted. *Expenses:* Contact institution. *Financial support:* In 2016–17, 80 students received support, including 80 fellowships with full tuition reimbursements available (averaging $13,500 per year), 72 research assistantships with full tuition reimbursements available (averaging $7,371 per year), 72 teaching assistantships with full tuition reimbursements available (averaging $7,371 per year); institutionally sponsored loans, scholarships/grants, health care benefits, unspecified assistantships, and full student service fee waivers also available. Financial award application deadline: 12/15. *Faculty research:* Finance, strategy and entrepreneurship, marketing, information and decision science, operations, accounting, supply chain, human resources and industrial relations, organizational behavior. *Unit head:* Dr. Shawn P. Curley, Director, 612-624-6546, Fax: 612-624-8221, E-mail: curley@umn.edu. *Application contact:* Sandy Herzan, Associate Director, 612-624-0875, Fax: 612-624-8221, E-mail: herza002@umn.edu.
Website: http://carlsonschool.umn.edu/degrees/phd

University of Mississippi, Graduate School, School of Business Administration, University, MS 38677. Offers business administration (PhD); systems management (MS); JD/MBA. *Accreditation:* AACSB. *Faculty:* 56 full-time (40 women), 9 part-time/ adjunct (4 women). *Students:* 78 full-time (25 women), 111 part-time (20 women); includes 18 minority (3 Black or African American, non-Hispanic/Latino; 5 Asian, non-Hispanic/Latino; 6 Hispanic/Latino; 4 Two or more races, non-Hispanic/Latino), 19 international. Average age 28. In 2016, 83 master's, 6 doctorates awarded. *Degree requirements:* For doctorate, thesis/dissertation. *Entrance requirements:* For master's, GMAT, minimum GPA of 3.0; for doctorate, GMAT. Additional exam requirements/ recommendations for international students: Required—TOEFL. *Application deadline:* For fall admission, 2/1 for domestic students; for spring admission, 10/1 for domestic students. Applications are processed on a rolling basis. Application fee: $40. Electronic applications accepted. *Financial support:* Fellowships, career-related internships or fieldwork, scholarships/grants, tuition waivers (full), and unspecified assistantships available. Financial award application deadline: 3/1; financial award applicants required to submit FAFSA. *Unit head:* Dr. Ken Cyree, Dean, 662-915-5820, Fax: 662-915-5821, E-mail: info@bus.olemiss.edu. *Application contact:* Dr. Christy M. Wyandt, Associate Dean, 662-915-7474, Fax: 662-915-7577, E-mail: cwyandt@olemiss.edu.
Website: http://www.olemissbusiness.com/

University of Missouri–St. Louis, College of Business Administration, Program in Business Administration, St. Louis, MO 63121. Offers accounting (MBA); business administration (Certificate); business intelligence (Certificate); cybersecurity (Certificate); digital and social media marketing (Certificate); finance (MBA); human resources management (Certificate); information systems (MBA); international business (MBA); logistics and supply chain management (MBA, PhD, Certificate); management (MBA); marketing (MBA); marketing management (Certificate); operations management (MBA). *Accreditation:* AACSB. *Program availability:* Part-time, evening/weekend. *Faculty:* 32 full-time (10 women), 14 part-time/adjunct (3 women). *Students:* 181 full-time (88 women), 357 part-time (154 women); includes 83 minority (30 Black or African American, non-Hispanic/Latino; 36 Asian, non-Hispanic/Latino; 12 Hispanic/Latino; 2 Native Hawaiian or other Pacific Islander, non-Hispanic/Latino; 3 Two or more races, non-Hispanic/Latino), 100 international. Average age 31. 245 applicants, 83% accepted, 139 enrolled. *Degree requirements:* For doctorate, thesis/dissertation. *Entrance requirements:* For master's, GMAT, 2 letters of recommendation. Additional exam requirements/recommendations for international students: Recommended—TOEFL (minimum score 550 paper-based; 79 iBT), IELTS (minimum score 6.5). *Application deadline:* For fall admission, 7/1 for domestic and international students; for spring admission, 12/1 for domestic and international students. Applications are processed on a rolling basis. Application fee: $50 ($40 for international students). Electronic applications accepted. *Financial support:* Research assistantships with tuition reimbursements, teaching assistantships with tuition reimbursements, career-related internships or fieldwork, Federal Work-Study, and institutionally sponsored loans available. Support available to part-time students. Financial award application deadline: 4/1; financial award applicants required to submit FAFSA. *Faculty research:* Human resources, strategic management, marketing strategy, consumer behavior product development, advertising. *Unit head:* Dr. Thomas H. Eyssell, Associate Dean and Director of Graduate Studies, 314-516-5885, Fax: 314-516-6420, E-mail: mba@umsl.edu. *Application contact:* 314-516-5458, Fax: 314-516-6996, E-mail: gradadm@umsl.edu.

University of Missouri–St. Louis, College of Business Administration, Program in Information Systems, St. Louis, MO 63121. Offers MS. *Program availability:* Part-time, evening/weekend. *Faculty:* 7 full-time (2 women), 2 part-time/adjunct (0 women). *Entrance requirements:* For master's, GMAT, 2 letters of recommendation. Additional exam requirements/recommendations for international students: Recommended—TOEFL (minimum score 550 paper-based; 79 iBT), IELTS (minimum score 6.5). *Application deadline:* For fall admission, 7/1 priority date for domestic and international students; for spring admission, 12/1 priority date for domestic and international students. Applications are processed on a rolling basis. Application fee: $50 ($40 for international students). Electronic applications accepted. *Financial support:* Career-related internships or fieldwork, Federal Work-Study, and institutionally sponsored loans available. Support available to part-time students. Financial award application deadline: 4/1; financial award applicants required to submit FAFSA. *Faculty research:* International information systems, telecommunications, systems development, information systems sourcing. *Unit head:* Dinesh Mirchandani, Chair, 314-516-7354, Fax: 314-516-6420, E-mail: mirchandanid@umsl.edu. *Application contact:* 314-516-5458, Fax: 314-516-6996, E-mail: gradadm@umsl.edu.

University of Nebraska at Kearney, College of Education, Department of Teacher Education, Kearney, NE 68849-0001. Offers curriculum and instruction (MA Ed), including early childhood education, elementary education, English as a second language, instructional effectiveness, reading/special education, secondary education; instructional technology (MS Ed), including information technology, instructional technology, school librarian; reading PK-12 (MA Ed); special education (MA Ed), including advanced practitioner: assistive technology specialist, advanced practitioner: behavioral interventionist, advanced practitioner: inclusive collaboration specialist, gifted, teacher education. *Program availability:* Part-time, evening/weekend, online only, 100% online. *Faculty:* 18 full-time (13 women). *Students:* 21 full-time (15 women), 296 part-time (240 women); includes 21 minority (3 Black or African American, non-Hispanic/ Latino; 1 Asian, non-Hispanic/Latino; 14 Hispanic/Latino; 1 Native Hawaiian or other Pacific Islander, non-Hispanic/Latino; 2 Two or more races, non-Hispanic/Latino), 1 international. Average age 32. 81 applicants, 100% accepted, 61 enrolled. In 2016, 129 master's awarded. *Degree requirements:* For master's, comprehensive exam, thesis optional. *Entrance requirements:* For master's, portfolio or GRE. Additional exam requirements/recommendations for international students: Recommended—TOEFL (minimum score 550 paper-based; 79 iBT), IELTS (minimum score 6.5). *Application deadline:* For fall admission, 6/15 for domestic students, 5/15 for international students; for spring admission, 10/15 for domestic and international students; for summer admission, 3/15 for domestic and international students. Application fee: $45. Electronic applications accepted. *Expenses:* $285 per credit hour resident tuition, $415 per credit hour non-resident tuition (online). *Financial support:* In 2016–17, 6 students received support, including 6 research assistantships with full tuition reimbursements available (averaging $10,500 per year); career-related internships or fieldwork, scholarships/ grants, health care benefits, and unspecified assistantships also available. Support available to part-time students. Financial award application deadline: 2/28; financial award applicants required to submit FAFSA. *Unit head:* Sarah Bartling, Administrative Assistant, 308-865-8513, E-mail: bartlingseg@unk.edu. *Application contact:* Linda Johnson, Director, Graduate Admissions and Programs, 308-865-8841, Fax: 308-865-8837, E-mail: johnsonli@unk.edu.
Website: http://www.unk.edu/academics/ted/index.php

University of Nebraska at Omaha, Graduate Studies, College of Information Science and Technology, Department of Information Systems and Quantitative Analysis, Omaha, NE 68182. Offers data analytics (Certificate); information assurance (Certificate); information technology (MIT, PhD); management information systems (MS); project management (Certificate); systems analysis and design (Certificate). *Program availability:* Part-time, evening/weekend. *Faculty:* 6 full-time (1 woman). *Students:* 140 full-time (53 women), 102 part-time (29 women); includes 25 minority (9 Black or African American, non-Hispanic/Latino; 7 Asian, non-Hispanic/Latino; 6 Hispanic/Latino; 3 Two or more races, non-Hispanic/Latino), 161 international. Average age 29. 342 applicants, 50% accepted, 68 enrolled. In 2016, 84 master's, 8 doctorates, 54 other advanced degrees awarded. *Degree requirements:* For master's, comprehensive exam, thesis (for some programs); for doctorate, comprehensive exam, thesis/dissertation. *Entrance requirements:* For master's, GRE General Test, minimum GPA of 3.0, 3 letters of recommendation, writing sample, resume, official transcripts; for doctorate, GMAT or GRE General Test, minimum GPA of 3.0, 3 letters of recommendation, writing sample, resume, official transcripts; for Certificate, minimum GPA of 3.0, official transcripts. Additional exam requirements/recommendations for international students: Required—TOEFL, IELTS, PTE. *Application deadline:* For fall admission, 2/15 for domestic and international students; for spring admission, 9/15 for domestic and international students; for summer admission, 4/1 for domestic and international students. Applications are processed on a rolling basis. Application fee: $45. Electronic applications accepted. *Financial support:* In 2016–17, 30 students received support, including 24 research assistantships with tuition reimbursements available, 6 teaching assistantships with tuition reimbursements available; fellowships, career-related internships or fieldwork, Federal Work-Study, scholarships/grants, health care benefits, tuition waivers (partial), and unspecified assistantships also available. Financial award application deadline: 3/1; financial award applicants required to submit FAFSA. *Unit head:* Dr. Peter Wolcott, Chairperson, 402-554-2341, E-mail: graduate@unomaha.edu. *Application contact:* Dr. Martina Greiner, Graduate Program Chair, 402-554-2341, E-mail: graduate@unomaha.edu.

University of Nebraska–Lincoln, Graduate College, College of Agricultural Sciences and Natural Resources, Program in Mechanized Systems Management, Lincoln, NE 68588. Offers MS. *Degree requirements:* For master's, thesis optional. *Entrance requirements:* For master's, GRE General Test. Additional exam requirements/recommendations for international students: Required—TOEFL (minimum score 550 paper-based). Electronic applications accepted. *Faculty research:* Irrigation management, agricultural power and machinery systems, sensors and controls, food/industrial materials handling and processing systems.

University of Nevada, Las Vegas, Graduate College, Lee Business School, Department of Management, Entrepreneurship and Technology, Las Vegas, NV 89154-6034. Offers data analytics (Certificate); data analytics and applied economics (MS); management information systems (MS, Certificate); new venture management (Certificate); MS/MS. *Program availability:* Part-time, evening/weekend. *Faculty:* 11 full-time (1 woman). *Students:* 28 full-time (12 women), 45 part-time (19 women); includes 31 minority (6 Black or African American, non-Hispanic/Latino; 9 Asian, non-Hispanic/Latino; 11 Hispanic/Latino; 5 Two or more races, non-Hispanic/Latino), 21 international. Average age 33. 64 applicants, 81% accepted, 30 enrolled. In 2016, 19 master's, 2 other advanced degrees awarded. *Degree requirements:* For master's, thesis optional. *Entrance requirements:* For master's, GMAT or GRE, bachelor's degree with minimum GPA 3.0; 2 letters of recommendation; for Certificate, GMAT or GRE. Additional exam requirements/recommendations for international students: Required—TOEFL (minimum score 550 paper-based; 80 iBT), IELTS (minimum score 7). *Application deadline:* For fall admission, 8/1 for domestic students, 5/1 for international students; for spring admission, 11/15 for domestic students, 10/1 for international students. Application fee: $60 ($95 for international students). Electronic applications accepted. *Expenses:* $269.25 per credit, $792 per 3-credit course; $9,634 per year resident; $23,274 per year non-resident; $7,094 fees non-resident (7 credits or more); $1,307 annual health insurance fee. *Financial support:* In 2016–17, 5 research assistantships with partial tuition reimbursements (averaging $10,000 per year), 5 teaching assistantships with partial tuition reimbursements (averaging $13,000 per year) were awarded; institutionally sponsored loans, scholarships/grants, health care benefits, and unspecified assistantships also available. Financial award application deadline: 3/15. *Faculty research:* Decision-making, publish or perish, ethical issues in information systems, IT-enabled decision making, business ethics. *Unit head:* Dr. Stoney Alder, Chair/Associate Professor, 702-895-2052, Fax: 702-895-4370, E-mail: stoney.alder@unlv.edu. *Application contact:* Dr. Greg Moody, Graduate Coordinator, 702-895-1365, Fax: 702-895-4370, E-mail: gregory.moody@unlv.edu.
Website: https://www.unlv.edu/met

University of Nevada, Reno, Graduate School, College of Business Administration, Department of Information Systems, Reno, NV 89557. Offers MS. *Degree requirements:* For master's, thesis optional. *Entrance requirements:* For master's, GRE or GMAT, minimum GPA of 2.75. Additional exam requirements/recommendations for international students: Required—TOEFL (minimum score 500 paper-based; 61 iBT), IELTS (minimum score 6). Electronic applications accepted.

University of New Hampshire, Graduate School Manchester Campus, Manchester, NH 03101. Offers business administration (MBA); educational administration and supervision (Ed S); educational studies (M Ed); elementary teacher education (M Ed); information technology (MS); public administration (MPA); public health (MPH, Certificate); secondary teacher education (M Ed, MAT); social work (MSW); substance use disorders (Certificate). *Program availability:* Part-time, evening/weekend. *Degree requirements:* For master's, thesis or alternative. *Entrance requirements:* Additional exam requirements/recommendations for international students: Required—TOEFL (minimum score 550 paper-based; 80 iBT). Electronic applications accepted.

University of New Mexico, Anderson School of Management, Department of Marketing, Information and Decision Sciences, Albuquerque, NM 87131. Offers information assurance (MBA); information systems and assurance (MS); management information systems (MBA); marketing management (MBA); operations management (MBA). *Program availability:* Part-time, evening/weekend. *Faculty:* 17 full-time (3 women), 7 part-time/adjunct (5 women). In 2016, 47 master's awarded. *Entrance requirements:* For master's, GMAT or GRE, minimum GPA of 3.0 on last 60 hours of coursework; bachelor's degree from regionally-accredited college or university in U.S. or its equivalent in another country. Additional exam requirements/recommendations for international students: Required—TOEFL (minimum score 550 paper-based; 79 iBT), IELTS (minimum score 6.5). *Application deadline:* For fall admission, 4/1 priority date for domestic and international students; for spring admission, 10/1 priority date for domestic and international students. Applications are processed on a rolling basis. Application fee: $50. Electronic applications accepted. *Expenses:* Contact institution. *Financial support:* In 2016–17, 8 fellowships (averaging $11,484 per year), 13 research assistantships with partial tuition reimbursements (averaging $9,382 per year) were awarded; career-related internships or fieldwork, Federal Work-Study, scholarships/grants, and unspecified assistantships also available. Support available to part-time students. Financial award application deadline: 6/1; financial award applicants required to submit FAFSA. *Faculty research:* Marketing, operations management, information systems, information assurance. *Unit head:* Dr. Steve Yourstone, Chair, 505-277-6471, E-mail: yourstone@unm.edu. *Application contact:* Lisa Beauchene, Student Recruitment Specialist, 505-277-6471, E-mail: andersonadvising@unm.edu.
Website: https://www.mgt.unm.edu/mids/default.asp?mm=faculty

University of North Alabama, College of Business, Florence, AL 35632-0001. Offers business administration (MBA), including accounting, enterprise resource planning systems, executive, finance, health care management, information systems, international business, project management. *Accreditation:* AACSB; ACBSP. *Program availability:* Part-time, 100% online, blended/hybrid learning. *Faculty:* 24 full-time (2 women), 6 part-time/adjunct (3 women). *Students:* 180 full-time (77 women), 411 part-time (199 women); includes 208 minority (84 Black or African American, non-Hispanic/Latino; 4 American Indian or Alaska Native, non-Hispanic/Latino; 106 Asian, non-Hispanic/Latino; 6 Hispanic/Latino; 8 Two or more races, non-Hispanic/Latino), 37 international. Average age 34. 263 applicants, 84% accepted, 173 enrolled. In 2016, 156 master's awarded. *Entrance requirements:* For master's, GMAT, GRE, minimum GPA of 2.75 in last 60 hours, 2.5 overall (on a 3.0 scale); 27 hours of course work in business and economics. Additional exam requirements/recommendations for international students: Required—TOEFL (minimum score 79 iBT), IELTS (minimum score 6), PTE (minimum score 54). *Application deadline:* Applications are processed on a rolling basis. Application fee: $50 ($100 for international students). Electronic applications accepted. *Expenses:* Tuition, state resident: full-time $2799; part-time $1866 per semester. Tuition, nonresident: full-time $5598; part-time $3732 per semester. *Required fees:* $915; $642 per semester. Tuition and fees vary according to course load. *Financial support:* In 2016–17, 114 students received support. Scholarships/grants available. Financial award application deadline: 2/1; financial award applicants required to submit FAFSA. *Unit head:* Dr. Gregory A. Carnes, Dean, 256-765-4261, Fax: 256-765-4170, E-mail: gacarnes@una.edu. *Application contact:* Hillary N. Coats, Graduate Admissions Coordinator, 256-765-4447, E-mail: graduate@una.edu.
Website: http://www.una.edu/business/

The University of North Carolina at Chapel Hill, Kenan-Flagler Business School, Doctoral Program in Business Administration, Chapel Hill, NC 27599. Offers accounting (PhD); finance (PhD); marketing (PhD); operations management (PhD); organizational behavior (PhD); strategy (PhD). *Accreditation:* AACSB. *Degree requirements:* For doctorate, thesis/dissertation. *Entrance requirements:* For doctorate, GMAT or GRE General Test. Electronic applications accepted. *Expenses:* Contact institution.

The University of North Carolina at Charlotte, College of Computing and Informatics, Department of Software and Information Systems, Charlotte, NC 28223-0001. Offers information security and privacy (Graduate Certificate); information technology (MS); management of information technology (Graduate Certificate); network security (Graduate Certificate); secure software development (Graduate Certificate). *Program availability:* Part-time, evening/weekend. *Faculty:* 15 full-time (6 women), 7 part-time/adjunct (0 women). *Students:* 96 full-time (41 women), 92 part-time (33 women); includes 24 minority (16 Black or African American, non-Hispanic/Latino; 2 Asian, non-Hispanic/Latino; 2 Hispanic/Latino; 4 Two or more races, non-Hispanic/Latino), 144 international. Average age 27. 557 applicants, 38% accepted, 55 enrolled. In 2016, 139 master's, 5 other advanced degrees awarded. *Degree requirements:* For master's, project, internship, or thesis. *Entrance requirements:* For master's, GRE or GMAT, undergraduate or equivalent course work in data structures, object-oriented programming in C++, C#, or Java with minimum GPA of 3.0; for Graduate Certificate, bachelor's degree from accredited institution in computing, mathematical, engineering or business discipline with minimum overall GPA of 2.8, junior/senior 3.0; substantial knowledge of data structures and object-oriented programming in C++, C# or Java. Additional exam requirements/recommendations for international students: Required—TOEFL (minimum score 523 paper-based, 70 iBT) or IELTS (6.5). *Application deadline:* For fall admission, 3/1 for domestic and international students; for spring admission, 10/1 for domestic and international students. Applications are processed on a rolling basis. Application fee: $75. Electronic applications accepted. *Expenses:* Contact institution. *Financial support:* In 2016–17, 62 students received support, including 1 fellowship (averaging $70,000 per year), 28 research assistantships (averaging $9,899 per year), 33 teaching assistantships (averaging $9,193 per year); career-related internships or fieldwork, institutionally sponsored loans, scholarships/grants, and unspecified assistantships also available. Support available to part-time students. Financial award application deadline: 3/1; financial award applicants required to submit FAFSA. *Total annual research expenditures:* $2.8 million. *Unit head:* Dr. Mary Lou Maher, Chair, 704-687-1940, E-mail: mmaher9@uncc.edu. *Application contact:* Kathy B. Giddings, Director of Graduate Admissions, 704-687-5503, Fax: 704-687-1668, E-mail: gradadm@uncc.edu.
Website: http://sis.uncc.edu/

The University of North Carolina at Charlotte, College of Computing and Informatics, Program in Computing and Information Systems, Charlotte, NC 28223-0001. Offers computing and information systems (PhD), including bioinformatics, business information systems and operations management, computer science, interdisciplinary, software and information systems. *Faculty:* 3 full-time (0 women). *Students:* 91 full-time (30 women), 23 part-time (3 women); includes 8 minority (2 Black or African American, non-Hispanic/Latino; 4 Asian, non-Hispanic/Latino; 1 Hispanic/Latino; 1 Two or more races, non-Hispanic/Latino), 76 international. Average age 31. 90 applicants, 41% accepted, 18 enrolled. In 2016, 13 doctorates awarded. *Degree requirements:* For doctorate, comprehensive exam, thesis/dissertation. *Entrance requirements:* For doctorate, GRE or GMAT, baccalaureate degree, minimum GPA of 3.0 on courses related to the chosen field of PhD study, essay, reference letters. Additional exam requirements/recommendations for international students: Required—TOEFL (minimum score 523 paper-based, 70 iBT) or IELTS (6.5). *Application deadline:* For fall admission, 2/1 for domestic and international students; for spring admission, 9/1 for domestic and international students. Applications are processed on a rolling basis. Application fee: $75. Electronic applications accepted. *Expenses:* Tuition, state resident: full-time $4252. Tuition, nonresident: full-time $17,423. *Required fees:* $3026. Tuition and fees vary according to course load and program. *Financial support:* Career-related internships or fieldwork, institutionally sponsored loans, scholarships/grants, health care benefits, and unspecified assistantships available. Support available to part-time students. Financial award applicants required to submit FAFSA. *Unit head:* Manuel A. Perez Quinones, Director, 704-687-8553, E-mail: perez.quinones@uncc.edu. *Application contact:* Kathy B. Giddings, Director of Graduate Admissions, 704-687-5503, Fax: 704-687-1668, E-mail: gradadm@uncc.edu.

The University of North Carolina at Greensboro, Graduate School, Bryan School of Business and Economics, Department of Information Systems and Supply Chain Management, Greensboro, NC 27412-5001. Offers information systems (PhD); information technology (Certificate); information technology and management (MS); supply chain management (Certificate). *Entrance requirements:* For master's, GMAT, GRE General Test. Additional exam requirements/recommendations for international students: Required—TOEFL. Electronic applications accepted.

The University of North Carolina Wilmington, Interdisciplinary Program in Computer Science and Information Systems, Wilmington, NC 28403-3297. Offers MS. *Program availability:* Part-time. *Faculty:* 11 full-time (3 women). *Students:* 13 full-time (3 women), 10 part-time (2 women); includes 3 minority (1 Black or African American, non-Hispanic/Latino; 1 Asian, non-Hispanic/Latino; 1 Hispanic/Latino), 6 international. Average age 28. 22 applicants, 73% accepted, 10 enrolled. In 2016, 10 master's awarded. *Degree requirements:* For master's, thesis or alternative, research project. *Entrance requirements:* For master's, GMAT or GRE, 3 letters of recommendation, resume, statement of interest. Additional exam requirements/recommendations for international students: Required—TOEFL (minimum score 79 iBT), IELTS (minimum score 6.5). *Application deadline:* For fall admission, 6/1 for domestic students; for spring admission, 11/1 for domestic students. Applications are processed on a rolling basis. Application fee: $60. Electronic applications accepted. *Expenses:* Contact institution. *Financial support:* Scholarships/grants and unspecified assistantships available. Financial award application deadline: 3/15; financial award applicants required to submit FAFSA. *Unit head:* Dr. Clayton Ferner, Program Coordinator, 910-962-7552, E-mail: cferner@uncw.edu. *Application contact:* Candace Wilhelm, Graduate Coordinator, 910-962-3903, Fax: 910-962-7457, E-mail: wilhelmc@uncw.edu.
Website: http://csb.uncw.edu/mscsis/

University of North Florida, College of Computing, Engineering, and Construction, School of Computing, Jacksonville, FL 32224. Offers computer science (MS); information systems (MS); software engineering (MS). *Program availability:* Part-time. *Faculty:* 12 full-time (2 women), 1 part-time/adjunct (0 women). *Students:* 13 full-time (5 women), 47 part-time (14 women); includes 14 minority (2 Black or African American, non-Hispanic/Latino; 9 Asian, non-Hispanic/Latino; 1 Hispanic/Latino; 2 Two or more races, non-Hispanic/Latino), 20 international. Average age 30. 62 applicants, 31% accepted, 7 enrolled. In 2016, 3 master's awarded. *Degree requirements:* For master's, thesis. *Entrance requirements:* For master's, GRE General Test, minimum GPA of 3.0 in

last 60 hours of course work. Additional exam requirements/recommendations for international students: Required—TOEFL (minimum score 500 paper-based; 61 iBT). *Application deadline:* For fall admission, 8/1 priority date for domestic students, 5/1 for international students; for spring admission, 12/1 priority date for domestic students, 10/1 for international students; for summer admission, 3/15 priority date for domestic students, 2/1 for international students. Application fee: $30. Electronic applications accepted. Tuition and fees vary according to course load, campus/location and program. *Financial support:* In 2016–17, 4 research assistantships (averaging $2,332 per year) were awarded; teaching assistantships, Federal Work-Study, scholarships/grants, and unspecified assistantships also available. Financial award application deadline: 4/1; financial award applicants required to submit FAFSA. *Total annual research expenditures:* $196,076. *Unit head:* Dr. Sherif Elfayoumy, Director/Professor, 904-620-2985, E-mail: selfayou@unf.edu. *Application contact:* Dr. Amanda Pascale, Director, The Graduate School, 904-620-1360, Fax: 904-620-1362, E-mail: graduateschool@unf.edu.
Website: http://www.unf.edu/ccec/computing/

University of North Texas, Robert B. Toulouse School of Graduate Studies, Denton, TX 76203-5459. Offers accounting (MS); applied anthropology (MA, MS); applied behavior analysis (Certificate); applied geography (MA); applied technology and performance improvement (M Ed, MS); art education (MA); art history (MA); art museum education (Certificate); arts leadership (Certificate); audiology (Au D); behavior analysis (MS); behavioral science (PhD); biochemistry and molecular biology (MS); biology (MA, MS); biomedical engineering (MS); business analysis (MS); chemistry (MS); clinical health psychology (PhD); communication studies (MA, MS); computer engineering (MS); computer science (MS); counseling (M Ed, MS), including clinical mental health counseling (MS), college and university counseling, elementary school counseling, secondary school counseling; creative writing (MA); criminal justice (MS); curriculum and instruction (M Ed); decision sciences (MBA); design (MA, MFA), including fashion design (MFA), innovation studies, interior design (MFA); early childhood studies (MS); economics (MS); educational leadership (M Ed, Ed D); educational psychology (MS, PhD), including family studies (MS), gifted and talented (MS), human development (MS), learning and cognition (MS), research, measurement and evaluation (MS); electrical engineering (MS); emergency management (MPA); engineering technology (MS); English (MA); English as a second language (MA); environmental science (MS); finance (MBA, MS); financial management (MPA); French (MA); health services management (MBA); higher education (M Ed, Ed D); history (MA, MS); hospitality management (MS); human resources management (MPA); information science (MS); information systems (PhD); information technologies (MBA); interdisciplinary studies (MA, MS); international studies (MA); international sustainable tourism (MS); jazz studies (MM); journalism (MA, MJ, Graduate Certificate), including interactive and virtual digital communication (Graduate Certificate), narrative journalism (Graduate Certificate), public relations (Graduate Certificate); kinesiology (MS); linguistics (MA); local government management (MPA); logistics (PhD); logistics and supply chain management (MBA); long-term care, senior housing, and aging services (MA); management (PhD); marketing (MBA); mathematics (MA, MS); mechanical and energy engineering (MS, PhD); music (MA), including ethnomusicology, music theory, musicology, performance; music composition (PhD); music education (MM Ed, PhD); nonprofit management (MPA); operations and supply chain management (MBA); performance (MM, DMA); philosophy (MA); political science (MA); professional and technical communication (MA); radio, television and film (MA, MFA); rehabilitation counseling (Certificate); sociology (MA); Spanish (MA); special education (M Ed); speech-language pathology (MA); strategic management (MBA); studio art (MFA); teaching (M Ed); MBA/MS. *Program availability:* Part-time, evening/weekend, online learning. Terminal master's awarded for partial completion of doctoral program. *Degree requirements:* For master's, variable foreign language requirement, comprehensive exam (for some programs), thesis (for some programs); for doctorate, variable foreign language requirement, comprehensive exam (for some programs), thesis/dissertation; for other advanced degree, variable foreign language requirement, comprehensive exam (for some programs). *Entrance requirements:* For master's and doctorate, GRE, GMAT. Additional exam requirements/recommendations for international students: Required—TOEFL (minimum score 550 paper-based; 79 iBT). Electronic applications accepted.

University of Oklahoma, Price College of Business, Division of Management Information Systems, Norman, OK 73019. Offers MS, Graduate Certificate. *Program availability:* Part-time, evening/weekend. *Faculty:* 11 full-time (6 women). *Students:* 38 full-time (13 women), 15 part-time (2 women); includes 7 minority (1 American Indian or Alaska Native, non-Hispanic/Latino; 1 Asian, non-Hispanic/Latino; 2 Hispanic/Latino; 3 Two or more races, non-Hispanic/Latino), 17 international. Average age 28. 30 applicants, 33% accepted, 9 enrolled. In 2016, 14 master's, 1 other advanced degree awarded. *Degree requirements:* For master's, thesis optional. *Entrance requirements:* For master's and Graduate Certificate, GMAT or GRE, resume, statement of goals, 3 letters of recommendation. Additional exam requirements/recommendations for international students: Required—TOEFL (minimum score 100 iBT) or IELTS (minimum score 7). *Application deadline:* For fall admission, 6/15 for domestic students, 3/1 for international students; for spring admission, 10/1 for domestic students, 8/1 for international students. Applications are processed on a rolling basis. Application fee: $50 ($100 for international students). Electronic applications accepted. *Expenses:* Tuition, state resident: full-time $4886; part-time $203.60 per credit hour. Tuition, nonresident: full-time $18,989; part-time $791.20 per credit hour. *Required fees:* $3283; $126.25 per credit hour. $126.50 per semester. *Financial support:* In 2016–17, 37 students received support, including 6 research assistantships with full tuition reimbursements available (averaging $10,373 per year), 4 teaching assistantships with full tuition reimbursements available (averaging $13,368 per year); career-related internships or fieldwork, scholarships/grants, and unspecified assistantships also available. Support available to part-time students. Financial award application deadline: 6/1; financial award applicants required to submit FAFSA. *Faculty research:* Human-computer interaction and cognition; gamification in training and health; deception detection in IT-mediated contexts; computer-mediated collaboration and communication; meaning in discourse about IT and discourse through IT. *Total annual research expenditures:* $201,333. *Unit head:* Radhika Santhanam, Chair/Director of MIS Division, 405-325-0791, E-mail: radhika@ou.edu. *Application contact:* Jennifer Aragon, Academic Advisor, 405-325-2074, Fax: 405-325-7118, E-mail: jhardman@ou.edu.
Website: http://www.ou.edu/content/price/mis/mis_ms_in_mis.html

University of Oklahoma, Price College of Business, Program in Business Administration, Norman, OK 73019. Offers accounting (PhD); business administration (MBA, PhD); entrepreneurship and economic development (PhD); finance (PhD); management and international business (PhD); management of information systems (PhD); marketing/supply chain (PhD); JD/MBA; MBA/MS. *Accreditation:* AACSB. *Program availability:* Part-time, evening/weekend. *Students:* 122 full-time (27 women), 146 part-time (30 women); includes 36 minority (5 Black or African American, non-Hispanic/Latino; 6 American Indian or Alaska Native, non-Hispanic/Latino; 8 Asian, non-Hispanic/Latino; 11 Hispanic/Latino; 6 Two or more races, non-Hispanic/Latino), 37 international. Average age 30. 261 applicants, 27% accepted, 59 enrolled. In 2016, 127 master's, 5 doctorates awarded. *Degree requirements:* For doctorate, comprehensive exam, thesis/dissertation. *Entrance requirements:* For master's, GMAT or GRE, resume, statement of goals; for doctorate, GMAT or GRE, resume, statement of goals, 3 letters of recommendation. Additional exam requirements/recommendations for international students: Required—TOEFL (minimum score 100 iBT) or IELTS (minimum score 7). *Application deadline:* For fall admission, 11/15 priority date for domestic and international students; for spring admission, 3/15 priority date for domestic and international students; for summer admission, 5/15 for domestic and international students. Application fee: $50 ($100 for international students). Electronic applications accepted. *Expenses:* Contact institution. *Financial support:* In 2016–17, 107 students received support, including 10 fellowships with partial tuition reimbursements available (averaging $3,295 per year); research assistantships with full and partial tuition reimbursements available, teaching assistantships with full and partial tuition reimbursements available, career-related internships or fieldwork, scholarships/grants, health care benefits, and unspecified assistantships also available. Support available to part-time students. Financial award application deadline: 6/1; financial award applicants required to submit FAFSA. *Faculty research:* Energy finance; international accounting; organizational behavior and entrepreneurship; management information systems; supply chain. *Unit head:* Laku Chidambaram, Associate Dean for Academic Programs and Engagement. *Application contact:* Director of MBA Admissions, 405-325-5623.
Website: http://www.ou.edu/content/price/divisions/graduate.html

University of Oregon, Graduate School, Interdisciplinary Program in Applied Information Management, Eugene, OR 97403. Offers MS. *Program availability:* Part-time, online learning. *Degree requirements:* For master's, project. *Entrance requirements:* Additional exam requirements/recommendations for international students: Required—TOEFL. Electronic applications accepted. *Expenses:* Contact institution. *Faculty research:* Business management, information design.

University of Pennsylvania, Wharton School, Operations and Information Management Department, Philadelphia, PA 19104. Offers MBA, PhD. Terminal master's awarded for partial completion of doctoral program. *Degree requirements:* For master's, thesis, preliminary exams; for doctorate, thesis/dissertation, preliminary exams. *Entrance requirements:* For master's, GMAT, GRE; for doctorate, GRE. Electronic applications accepted. *Expenses: Tuition:* Full-time $31,068; part-time $5762 per course. *Required fees:* $3200; $336 per course. Full-time tuition and fees vary according to degree level, program and student level. Part-time tuition and fees vary according to course load, degree level and program. *Faculty research:* Supply chain management, operations research, economics of information systems, risk analysis, electronic commerce.

University of Phoenix–Atlanta Campus, College of Information Systems and Technology, Sandy Springs, GA 30350-4147. Offers information systems (MIS); technology management (MBA). *Program availability:* Evening/weekend. *Degree requirements:* For master's, thesis (for some programs). *Entrance requirements:* For master's, 3 years of work experience, minimum undergraduate GPA of 3.0. Additional exam requirements/recommendations for international students: Required—TOEFL (minimum score 550 paper-based; 79 iBT). Electronic applications accepted.

University of Phoenix–Augusta Campus, College of Information Systems and Technology, Augusta, GA 30909-4583. Offers information systems (MIS); technology management (MBA).

University of Phoenix–Bay Area Campus, College of Information Systems and Technology, San Jose, CA 95134-1805. Offers information systems (MIS); organizational leadership/information systems and technology (DM). *Program availability:* Evening/weekend. *Degree requirements:* For master's, thesis (for some programs). *Entrance requirements:* For master's, minimum undergraduate GPA of 3.0, 3 years of work experience. Additional exam requirements/recommendations for international students: Required—TOEFL (minimum score 550 paper-based; 79 iBT). Electronic applications accepted.

University of Phoenix–Central Valley Campus, College of Information Systems and Technology, Fresno, CA 93720-1552. Offers information systems (MIS); technology management (MBA).

University of Phoenix–Charlotte Campus, College of Information Systems and Technology, Charlotte, NC 28273-3409. Offers information systems (MIS); information systems management (MISM); technology management (MBA). *Program availability:* Evening/weekend. *Degree requirements:* For master's, thesis (for some programs). *Entrance requirements:* For master's, minimum undergraduate GPA of 3.0, 3 years work experience. Additional exam requirements/recommendations for international students: Required—TOEFL (minimum score 550 paper-based; 79 iBT). Electronic applications accepted.

University of Phoenix–Colorado Campus, College of Information Systems and Technology, Lone Tree, CO 80124-5453. Offers e-business (MBA); management (MIS); technology management (MBA). *Program availability:* Evening/weekend, online learning. *Degree requirements:* For master's, thesis (for some programs). *Entrance requirements:* For master's, minimum undergraduate GPA of 3.0, 3 years of work experience. Additional exam requirements/recommendations for international students: Required—TOEFL (minimum score 550 paper-based; 79 iBT). Electronic applications accepted.

University of Phoenix–Colorado Springs Downtown Campus, College of Information Systems and Technology, Colorado Springs, CO 80903. Offers technology management (MBA). *Program availability:* Evening/weekend. *Degree requirements:* For master's, thesis (for some programs). *Entrance requirements:* For master's, minimum undergraduate GPA of 3.0, 3 years of work experience. Additional exam requirements/recommendations for international students: Required—TOEFL (minimum score 550 paper-based; 79 iBT). Electronic applications accepted.

University of Phoenix–Columbus Georgia Campus, College of Information Systems and Technology, Columbus, GA 31909. Offers e-business (MBA); information systems (MIS); technology management (MBA). *Program availability:* Evening/weekend, online learning. *Degree requirements:* For master's, thesis (for some programs). *Entrance requirements:* For master's, minimum undergraduate GPA of 3.0, 3 years of work experience. Additional exam requirements/recommendations for international students: Required—TOEFL (minimum score 550 paper-based; 79 iBT). Electronic applications accepted.

University of Phoenix–Dallas Campus, College of Information Systems and Technology, Dallas, TX 75251. Offers e-business (MBA); information systems (MIS); technology management (MBA). *Program availability:* Evening/weekend. *Degree requirements:* For master's, thesis (for some programs). *Entrance requirements:* For master's, minimum undergraduate GPA of 3.0, 3 years of work experience. Additional exam requirements/recommendations for international students: Required—TOEFL (minimum score 550 paper-based; 79 iBT). Electronic applications accepted.

University of Phoenix–Hawaii Campus, College of Information Systems and Technology, Honolulu, HI 96813-3800. Offers information systems (MIS); technology management (MBA). *Program availability:* Evening/weekend. *Degree requirements:* For master's, thesis (for some programs). *Entrance requirements:* For master's, minimum undergraduate GPA of 3.0, 3 years of work experience. Additional exam requirements/

recommendations for international students: Required—TOEFL (minimum score 550 paper-based; 79 iBT). Electronic applications accepted.

University of Phoenix–Houston Campus, College of Information Systems and Technology, Houston, TX 77079-2004. Offers e-business (MBA); information systems (MIS); technology management (MBA). *Program availability:* Evening/weekend, online learning. *Degree requirements:* For master's, comprehensive exam (for some programs), thesis. *Entrance requirements:* For master's, minimum undergraduate GPA of 3.0, 3 years of work experience. Additional exam requirements/recommendations for international students: Required—TOEFL (minimum score 550 paper-based; 79 iBT). Electronic applications accepted.

University of Phoenix–Jersey City Campus, College of Information Systems and Technology, Jersey City, NJ 07310. Offers information systems (MIS); technology management (MBA). *Program availability:* Online learning.

University of Phoenix–Las Vegas Campus, College of Information Systems and Technology, Las Vegas, NV 89135. Offers information systems (MIS); technology management (MBA). *Program availability:* Evening/weekend. *Degree requirements:* For master's, thesis (for some programs). *Entrance requirements:* For master's, minimum undergraduate GPA of 3.0, 3 years of work experience. Additional exam requirements/recommendations for international students: Required—TOEFL (minimum score 550 paper-based; 79 iBT). Electronic applications accepted.

University of Phoenix–New Mexico Campus, College of Information Systems and Technology, Albuquerque, NM 87113-1570. Offers e-business (MBA); information systems (MS); technology management (MBA). *Program availability:* Evening/weekend. *Degree requirements:* For master's, thesis (for some programs). *Entrance requirements:* For master's, minimum undergraduate GPA of 3.0, 3 years of work experience. Additional exam requirements/recommendations for international students: Required—TOEFL (minimum score 550 paper-based; 79 iBT). Electronic applications accepted.

University of Phoenix–North Florida Campus, College of Information Systems and Technology, Jacksonville, FL 32216-0959. Offers information systems (MIS); management (MIS). *Program availability:* Evening/weekend. *Degree requirements:* For master's, thesis (for some programs). *Entrance requirements:* For master's, minimum undergraduate GPA of 3.0, 3 years work experience. Additional exam requirements/recommendations for international students: Required—TOEFL (minimum score 550 paper-based; 79 iBT). Electronic applications accepted.

University of Phoenix–Online Campus, College of Information Systems and Technology, Phoenix, AZ 85034-7209. Offers MIS. *Program availability:* Evening/weekend, online learning. *Entrance requirements:* Additional exam requirements/recommendations for international students: Required—TOEFL, TOEIC (Test of English as an International Communication), Berlitz Online English Proficiency Exam, PTE, or IELTS. Electronic applications accepted. *Expenses:* Contact institution.

University of Phoenix–Sacramento Valley Campus, College of Information Systems and Technology, Sacramento, CA 95833-4334. Offers management (MIS); technology management (MBA). *Program availability:* Evening/weekend. *Degree requirements:* For master's, thesis (for some programs). *Entrance requirements:* For master's, minimum undergraduate GPA of 3.0, 3 years work experience. Additional exam requirements/recommendations for international students: Required—TOEFL (minimum score 550 paper-based; 79 iBT). Electronic applications accepted.

University of Phoenix–San Antonio Campus, College of Information Systems and Technology, San Antonio, TX 78230. Offers information systems (MIS); technology management (MBA).

University of Phoenix–San Diego Campus, College of Information Systems and Technology, San Diego, CA 92123. Offers management (MIS); technology management (MBA). *Program availability:* Evening/weekend. *Degree requirements:* For master's, thesis (for some programs). *Entrance requirements:* For master's, minimum undergraduate GPA of 3.0, 3 years work experience. Additional exam requirements/recommendations for international students: Required—TOEFL (minimum score 550 paper-based; 79 iBT). Electronic applications accepted.

University of Phoenix–Southern Arizona Campus, College of Information Systems and Technology, Tucson, AZ 85711. Offers information systems (MIS); technology management (MBA). *Program availability:* Evening/weekend. *Degree requirements:* For master's, thesis (for some programs). *Entrance requirements:* For master's, minimum undergraduate GPA of 3.0, 3 years of work experience. Additional exam requirements/recommendations for international students: Required—TOEFL (minimum score 550 paper-based; 79 iBT). Electronic applications accepted.

University of Phoenix–South Florida Campus, College of Information Systems and Technology, Miramar, FL 33027-4145. Offers management (MIS); technology management (MBA). *Program availability:* Evening/weekend. *Degree requirements:* For master's, thesis (for some programs). *Entrance requirements:* For master's, minimum undergraduate GPA of 3.0, 3 years of work experience. Additional exam requirements/recommendations for international students: Required—TOEFL (minimum score 550 paper-based; 79 iBT). Electronic applications accepted.

University of Phoenix–Utah Campus, College of Information Systems and Technology, Salt Lake City, UT 84123-4642. Offers MIS. *Program availability:* Evening/weekend. *Degree requirements:* For master's, thesis (for some programs). *Entrance requirements:* For master's, minimum undergraduate GPA of 2.5, 3 years work experience. Additional exam requirements/recommendations for international students: Required—TOEFL (minimum score 550 paper-based; 79 iBT). Electronic applications accepted.

University of Phoenix–Washington D.C. Campus, College of Information Systems and Technology, Washington, DC 20001. Offers information systems (MIS); organizational leadership/information systems and technology (DM).

University of Pittsburgh, Katz Graduate School of Business, Doctoral Program in Business Administration, Pittsburgh, PA 15260. Offers accounting (PhD); business analytics and operations (PhD); finance (PhD); information systems and technology management (PhD); marketing (PhD); organizational behavior and human resources (PhD); strategic management (PhD). *Accreditation:* AACSB. *Program availability:* Evening/weekend. *Faculty:* 88 full-time (27 women), 42 part-time/adjunct (15 women). *Students:* 51 full-time (23 women), 1 part-time (0 women); includes 4 minority (1 Black or African American, non-Hispanic/Latino; 2 Asian, non-Hispanic/Latino; 1 Two or more races, non-Hispanic/Latino), 31 international. Average age 31. 344 applicants, 6% accepted, 9 enrolled. In 2016, 5 doctorates awarded. *Degree requirements:* For doctorate, comprehensive exam, thesis/dissertation, student teaching. *Entrance requirements:* For doctorate, GMAT or GRE, 3 recommendations, statement of purpose, transcripts of all previous course work and degrees. Additional exam requirements/recommendations for international students: Required—TOEFL (minimum score 100 iBT) or IELTS (minimum score 7.0). *Application deadline:* For fall admission, 4/1 priority date for domestic students, 2/1 priority date for international students. Applications are processed on a rolling basis. Application fee: $50. Electronic applications accepted. *Expenses:* Contact institution. *Financial support:* In 2016–17, 40 students received support, including 27 research assistantships with full tuition reimbursements available (averaging $26,000 per year), 9 teaching assistantships with full tuition reimbursements available (averaging $26,700 per year); Federal Work-Study, scholarships/grants, health care benefits, and unspecified assistantships also available. Financial award application deadline: 6/1; financial award applicants required to submit FAFSA. *Faculty research:* Accounting systems/financial reporting, corporate finance, shopper marketing/consumer behavior, management information systems, organizational behavior and entrepreneurship. *Total annual research expenditures:* $493,036. *Unit head:* Dr. Arjang A. Assad, Dean, 412-648-1556, Fax: 412-648-1552, E-mail: aassad@katz.pitt.edu. *Application contact:* Dr. Dennis Galletta, Director, 412-648-1699, Fax: 412-648-3633, E-mail: galletta@katz.pitt.edu.
Website: http://www.business.pitt.edu/katz/phd/

See Display on page 160 and Close-Up on page 189.

University of Pittsburgh, Katz Graduate School of Business, Master of Business Administration Programs, Pittsburgh, PA 15260. Offers finance (MBA); information systems (MBA); marketing (MBA); operations (MBA); organizational behavior and human resources (MBA); strategy, environment and organizations (MBA); MBA/JD; MBA/MSE. *Accreditation:* AACSB. *Program availability:* Part-time, evening/weekend, blended/hybrid learning. *Faculty:* 88 full-time (27 women), 42 part-time/adjunct (15 women). *Students:* 165 full-time (59 women), 330 part-time (103 women); includes 70 minority (29 Black or African American, non-Hispanic/Latino; 20 Asian, non-Hispanic/Latino; 13 Hispanic/Latino; 8 Two or more races, non-Hispanic/Latino), 73 international. Average age 29. 786 applicants, 41% accepted, 179 enrolled. In 2016, 477 master's awarded. *Degree requirements:* For master's, minimum GPA of 3.0. *Entrance requirements:* For master's, GMAT, GRE. Additional exam requirements/recommendations for international students: Required—TOEFL (minimum score 100 iBT) or IELTS (minimum score 7.0). *Application deadline:* For fall admission, 4/1 priority date for domestic students, 2/1 priority date for international students. Application fee: $50. Electronic applications accepted. *Expenses:* Contact institution. *Financial support:* In 2016–17, 110 students received support. Scholarships/grants available. Financial award application deadline: 6/1; financial award applicants required to submit FAFSA. *Faculty research:* Accounting systems/financial reporting, corporate finance, shopper marketing/consumer behavior, management information systems, organizational behavior and entrepreneurship. *Total annual research expenditures:* $493,036. *Unit head:* Dr. Arjang A. Assad, Dean, 412-648-1556, Fax: 412-648-1552, E-mail: aassad@katz.pitt.edu. *Application contact:* Thomas Keller, Director of MBA Admissions, 412-648-1700, Fax: 412-648-1659, E-mail: mba@katz.pitt.edu.
Website: http://www.business.pitt.edu/katz/mba/

See Display on page 160 and Close-Up on page 189.

University of Pittsburgh, Katz Graduate School of Business, Master of Science in Management Information Systems Program, Pittsburgh, PA 15260. Offers MS. *Faculty:* 88 full-time (27 women), 42 part-time/adjunct (15 women). *Students:* 2 full-time (both women), both international. Average age 25. 49 applicants, 49% accepted, 2 enrolled. In 2016, 5 master's awarded. *Degree requirements:* For master's, minimum GPA of 3.0. *Entrance requirements:* For master's, GMAT, GRE. Additional exam requirements/recommendations for international students: Required—TOEFL (minimum score 100 iBT), IELTS (minimum score 7). *Application deadline:* For fall admission, 7/1 priority date for domestic students, 5/1 priority date for international students. Applications are processed on a rolling basis. Application fee: $50. Electronic applications accepted. *Expenses:* Contact institution. *Financial support:* Scholarships/grants available. Financial award application deadline: 6/1; financial award applicants required to submit FAFSA. *Faculty research:* Accounting systems/financial reporting, corporate finance, shopper marketing/consumer behavior, management information systems, organizational behavior and entrepreneurship. *Total annual research expenditures:* $493,036. *Unit head:* Dr. Arjang A. Assad, Dean, 412-648-1556, Fax: 412-648-1552, E-mail: aassad@katz.pitt.edu. *Application contact:* Thomas Keller, Director of MBA Admissions, 412-648-1700, Fax: 412-648-1659, E-mail: mba@katz.pitt.edu.
Website: http://www.business.pitt.edu/katz/ms-programs/MIS

University of Pittsburgh, Katz Graduate School of Business, MBA/MS in Management of Information Systems Program, Pittsburgh, PA 15260. Offers MBA/MS. *Program availability:* Part-time, evening/weekend. *Faculty:* 88 full-time (27 women), 42 part-time/adjunct (15 women). *Students:* 4 full-time (2 women), 11 part-time (3 women); includes 4 minority (1 Black or African American, non-Hispanic/Latino; 1 Asian, non-Hispanic/Latino; 2 Hispanic/Latino), 1 international. Average age 30. 42 applicants, 21% accepted, 6 enrolled. *Entrance requirements:* Additional exam requirements/recommendations for international students: Required—TOEFL (minimum score 100 iBT) or IELTS (minimum score 7.0). *Application deadline:* For fall admission, 4/1 priority date for domestic students, 2/1 priority date for international students. Application fee: $50. Electronic applications accepted. Tuition and fees vary according to program. *Financial support:* Scholarships/grants available. Financial award application deadline: 6/1; financial award applicants required to submit FAFSA. *Faculty research:* Accounting systems/financial reporting, corporate finance, shopper marketing/consumer behavior, management information systems, organizational behavior and entrepreneurship. *Total annual research expenditures:* $493,036. *Unit head:* Dr. Arjang A. Assad, Dean, 412-648-1556, Fax: 412-648-1552, E-mail: aassad@katz.pitt.edu. *Application contact:* Thomas Keller, Director, MBA Admissions, 412-648-1700, Fax: 412-648-1659, E-mail: mba@katz.pitt.edu.
Website: http://www.business.pitt.edu/katz/mba/academics/programs/mba-mis.php

University of Redlands, School of Business, Redlands, CA 92373-0999. Offers business (MBA); information technology (MS); management (MA). *Program availability:* Evening/weekend. *Entrance requirements:* For master's, minimum GPA of 3.0, 2 letters of recommendation. *Faculty research:* Human resources management, educational leadership, humanities, teacher education.

University of Rochester, Simon Business School, Doctoral Program in Business Administration, Rochester, NY 14627. Offers accounting (PhD); computer information systems (PhD); finance (PhD); marketing (PhD); operations management (PhD). *Accreditation:* AACSB. *Faculty:* 66 full-time (13 women), 22 part-time/adjunct (2 women). *Students:* 52 full-time (19 women); includes 2 minority (both Asian, non-Hispanic/Latino), 42 international. Average age 29. 210 applicants, 16% accepted, 15 enrolled. In 2016, 6 doctorates awarded. *Degree requirements:* For doctorate, comprehensive exam, thesis/dissertation, qualifying exam. *Entrance requirements:* For doctorate, GMAT or GRE. Additional exam requirements/recommendations for international students: Required—TOEFL. *Application deadline:* For fall admission, 1/5 for domestic and international students. Application fee: $100. Electronic applications accepted. *Expenses:* $1,800 per credit hour. *Financial support:* In 2016–17, 52 students received support. Fellowships, research assistantships, teaching assistantships, and tuition waivers (full) available. Financial award application deadline: 1/5. *Unit head:* Dr. Ron Kaniel, Committee Chair, 585-275-2959. *Application contact:* Sue Harris, PhD Administrator, 585-275-2959, E-mail: phdoffice@simon.rochester.edu.
Website: http://www.simon.rochester.edu/programs/phd/index.aspx

University of Rochester, Simon Business School, Full-Time Master's Program in Business Administration, Rochester, NY 14627. Offers business systems consulting (MBA); competitive and organizational strategy (MBA); computers and information

systems (MBA); corporate accounting (MBA); entrepreneurship (MBA); finance (MBA); health sciences management (MBA); marketing (MBA); operations management (MBA); public accounting (MBA). *Accreditation:* AACSB. *Program availability:* Part-time, evening/weekend. *Faculty:* 66 full-time (13 women), 22 part-time/adjunct (2 women). *Students:* 202 full-time (78 women); includes 50 minority (30 Black or African American, non-Hispanic/Latino; 10 Asian, non-Hispanic/Latino; 9 Hispanic/Latino; 1 Two or more races, non-Hispanic/Latino), 107 international. Average age 27. 915 applicants, 30% accepted, 86 enrolled. In 2016, 110 master's awarded. *Entrance requirements:* For master's, GMAT/GRE. Additional exam requirements/recommendations for international students: Required—TOEFL. *Application deadline:* For fall admission, 10/15 for domestic and international students; for winter admission, 1/5 for domestic and international students; for spring admission, 3/15 for domestic and international students; for summer admission, 5/15 for domestic and international students. Applications are processed on a rolling basis. Application fee: $150. Electronic applications accepted. *Expenses:* Contact institution. *Financial support:* In 2016–17, 190 students received support. Fellowships, research assistantships, teaching assistantships, institutionally sponsored loans, scholarships/grants, and tuition waivers (full and partial) available. Financial award application deadline: 1/5; financial award applicants required to submit FAFSA. *Unit head:* Andrew Ainslie, Dean, 585-275-3316, E-mail: andrew.ainslie@simon.rochester.edu. *Application contact:* Rebekah S. Lewin, Assistant Dean of Admissions and Financial Aid, 585-275-3533, E-mail: admissions@simon.rochester.edu.
Website: http://www.simon.rochester.edu/programs/full-time-mba/index.aspx

University of Rochester, Simon Business School, Part-Time MBA Program, Rochester, NY 14627. Offers business systems consulting (MBA); competitive and organizational strategy (MBA); computers and information systems (MBA); corporate accounting (MBA); entrepreneurship (MBA); finance (MBA); health sciences management (MBA); marketing (MBA); operations management (MBA); public accounting (MBA). *Program availability:* Part-time, evening/weekend. *Faculty:* 66 full-time (13 women), 22 part-time/adjunct (2 women). *Students:* 185 part-time (65 women); includes 29 minority (6 Black or African American, non-Hispanic/Latino; 13 Asian, non-Hispanic/Latino; 8 Hispanic/Latino; 2 Two or more races, non-Hispanic/Latino), 9 international. Average age 32. 33 applicants, 100% accepted, 31 enrolled. In 2016, 70 master's awarded. *Entrance requirements:* For master's, GRE or GMAT. *Application deadline:* For fall admission, 8/1 for domestic students; for spring admission, 2/15 for domestic students. Applications are processed on a rolling basis. Application fee: $150. Electronic applications accepted. *Expenses:* $1,800 per credit hour. *Financial support:* In 2016–17, 75 students received support. Scholarships/grants and tuition waivers (partial) available. Financial award applicants required to submit CSS PROFILE or FAFSA. *Unit head:* Andrew Ainslie, Dean, 585-275-3316, E-mail: andrew.ainslie@simon.rochester.edu. *Application contact:* Molly Mesko, Executive Director, EMBA and Part-Time Programs, 585-275-4277, E-mail: molly.mesko@simon.rochester.edu.
Website: http://www.simon.rochester.edu/programs/ptmba/index.aspx

University of San Francisco, School of Management, Master of Science in Information Systems Program, San Francisco, CA 94117. Offers MS. *Program availability:* Part-time, evening/weekend. *Faculty:* 1 (woman) full-time, 3 part-time/adjunct (0 women). *Students:* 45 full-time (14 women), 2 part-time (both women); includes 27 minority (6 Black or African American, non-Hispanic/Latino; 12 Asian, non-Hispanic/Latino; 8 Hispanic/Latino; 1 Two or more races, non-Hispanic/Latino), 4 international. Average age 33. 34 applicants, 85% accepted, 19 enrolled. In 2016, 10 master's awarded. *Degree requirements:* For master's, thesis. *Entrance requirements:* For master's, resume demonstrating minimum of two years of professional work experience, transcripts from each college or university attended, two letters of recommendation, personal statement. Additional exam requirements/recommendations for international students: Required—TOEFL (minimum score 600 paper-based, 100 iBT), IELTS (minimum score 7) or PTE (minimum score 68). *Application deadline:* For fall admission, 6/15 for domestic students, 5/15 for international students. Application fee: $55. Electronic applications accepted. *Expenses: Tuition:* Full-time $23,310; part-time $1295 per credit. Tuition and fees vary according to course load, degree level, campus/location and program. *Financial support:* In 2016–17, 5 students received support. Scholarships/grants available. Financial award application deadline: 3/2; financial award applicants required to submit FAFSA. *Unit head:* Dr. Bill Kolb, Director, 415-422-2221, E-mail: management@usfca.edu. *Application contact:* Office of Graduate Recruiting and Admissions, 415-422-2221, Fax: 415-422-6315, E-mail: management@usfca.edu.
Website: http://www.usfca.edu/msis

The University of Scranton, Kania School of Management, Program in Business Administration, Scranton, PA 18510. Offers accounting (MBA); finance (MBA); general business administration (MBA); health care management (MBA); international business (MBA); management information systems (MBA); marketing (MBA); operations management (MBA). *Accreditation:* AACSB. *Program availability:* Part-time, evening/weekend, 100% online. *Entrance requirements:* For master's, GMAT (for MBA). *Faculty research:* Financial markets, strategic impact of total quality management, internal accounting controls, consumer preference, information systems and the Internet.

University of South Africa, College of Science, Engineering and Technology, Pretoria, South Africa. Offers chemical engineering (M Tech); information technology (M Tech).

University of South Alabama, School of Computing, Mobile, AL 36688. Offers computer science (MS); information systems (MS). *Program availability:* Part-time, evening/weekend. *Faculty:* 18 full-time (2 women). *Students:* 121 full-time (35 women), 21 part-time (6 women); includes 10 minority (2 Black or African American, non-Hispanic/Latino; 4 Asian, non-Hispanic/Latino; 1 Hispanic/Latino; 1 Native Hawaiian or other Pacific Islander, non-Hispanic/Latino; 2 Two or more races, non-Hispanic/Latino), 87 international. Average age 27. 204 applicants, 53% accepted, 29 enrolled. In 2016, 67 master's awarded. *Degree requirements:* For master's, comprehensive exam, project, thesis, or coursework only with additional credit hours earned; for doctorate, comprehensive exam, thesis/dissertation, minimum GPA of 3.0. *Entrance requirements:* For master's, GRE General Test, undergraduate degree, official transcripts, three letters of recommendation, statement of purpose; for doctorate, GRE, master's degree in related discipline, minimum graduate GPA of 3.5, statement of purpose, three letters of recommendation, curriculum vitae, official transcripts. Additional exam requirements/recommendations for international students: Required—TOEFL (minimum score 525 paper-based; 71 iBT). *Application deadline:* For fall admission, 7/15 priority date for domestic students, 6/15 priority date for international students; for spring admission, 12/1 priority date for domestic students, 11/1 priority date for international students; for summer admission, 5/1 priority date for domestic students, 4/1 priority date for international students. Applications are processed on a rolling basis. Application fee: $35. Electronic applications accepted. *Expenses:* Tuition, state resident: full-time $9768; part-time $407 per credit hour. Tuition, nonresident: full-time $19,536; part-time $814 per credit hour. *Financial support:* Fellowships, research assistantships, teaching assistantships, Federal Work-Study, institutionally sponsored loans, scholarships/grants, and unspecified assistantships available. Support available to part-time students. Financial award application deadline: 5/31; financial award applicants required to submit FAFSA. *Faculty research:* Artificial intelligence, big data/data mining, STEM education, visual analytics. *Unit head:* Dr. Alec Yasinsac, Dean, School of Computing, 251-460-6390, Fax: 251-460-7274, E-mail: yasinsac@southalabama.edu. *Application contact:* Dr. Harold Pardue, Director of School of Computing Graduate Studies, 251-460-1600, Fax: 251-460-7274, E-mail: hpardue@southalabama.edu.
Website: http://www.cis.usouthal.edu

University of South Florida, College of Engineering, Department of Industrial and Management Systems Engineering, Tampa, FL 33620-9951. Offers engineering management (MSEM); industrial engineering (MSIE, PhD); information technology (MSIT). *Program availability:* Part-time, online learning. *Faculty:* 13 full-time (3 women). *Students:* 119 full-time (22 women), 85 part-time (19 women); includes 27 minority (4 Black or African American, non-Hispanic/Latino; 7 Asian, non-Hispanic/Latino; 15 Hispanic/Latino; 1 Two or more races, non-Hispanic/Latino), 135 international. Average age 27. 420 applicants, 36% accepted, 50 enrolled. In 2016, 63 master's, 9 doctorates awarded. Terminal master's awarded for partial completion of doctoral program. *Degree requirements:* For master's, comprehensive exam, thesis (for some programs); for doctorate, comprehensive exam, thesis/dissertation, 2 tools of research as specified by dissertation committee. *Entrance requirements:* For master's, GRE General Test, BS in engineering (or equivalent) with minimum GPA of 3.0 in last 60 hours of coursework, letter of recommendation, resume; for doctorate, GRE General Test, minimum GPA of 3.0 in last 60 hours of undergraduate/graduate coursework, three letters of recommendation, statement of purpose, strong background in scientific and engineering principles. Additional exam requirements/recommendations for international students: Required—TOEFL (minimum score 550 paper-based; 79 iBT) or IELTS (minimum score 6.5). *Application deadline:* For fall admission, 2/15 for domestic and international students; for spring admission, 10/15 for domestic students, 9/15 for international students; for summer admission, 2/15 for domestic students, 1/15 for international students. Application fee: $30. Electronic applications accepted. *Expenses:* Tuition, state resident: full-time $7766; part-time $431.43 per credit hour. Tuition, nonresident: full-time $15,789; part-time $877.17 per credit hour. *Required fees:* $37 per term. *Financial support:* In 2016–17, 31 students received support, including 20 research assistantships with partial tuition reimbursements available (averaging $16,748 per year), 11 teaching assistantships with partial tuition reimbursements available (averaging $15,000 per year); tuition waivers (partial) also available. Financial award applicants required to submit FAFSA. *Faculty research:* Healthcare, healthcare systems, public health policies, energy and environment, manufacturing, logistics, transportation. *Total annual research expenditures:* $253,139. *Unit head:* Dr. Tapas K. Das, Professor and Department Chair, 813-974-5585, Fax: 813-974-5953, E-mail: das@usf.edu. *Application contact:* Dr. Alex Savachkin, Associate Professor and Graduate Director, 813-974-5577, Fax: 813-974-5953, E-mail: alexs@usf.edu.
Website: http://imse.eng.usf.edu

University of South Florida, Innovative Education, Tampa, FL 33620-9951. Offers adult, career and higher education (Graduate Certificate), including college teaching, leadership in developing human resources, leadership in higher education; Africana studies (Graduate Certificate), including diasporas and health disparities, genocide and human rights; aging studies (Graduate Certificate), including gerontology; art research (Graduate Certificate), including museum studies; business foundations (Graduate Certificate); chemical and biomedical engineering (Graduate Certificate), including materials science and engineering, water, health and sustainability; child and family studies (Graduate Certificate), including positive behavior support; civil and industrial engineering (Graduate Certificate), including transportation systems analysis; community and family health (Graduate Certificate), including maternal and child health, social marketing and public health, violence and injury: prevention and intervention, women's health; criminology (Graduate Certificate), including criminal justice administration; educational measurement and research (Graduate Certificate), including evaluation; English (Graduate Certificate), including comparative literary studies, creative writing, professional and technical communication; entrepreneurship (Graduate Certificate); environmental health (Graduate Certificate), including safety management; epidemiology and biostatistics (Graduate Certificate), including applied biostatistics, biostatistics, concepts and tools of epidemiology, epidemiology, epidemiology of infectious diseases; geography, environment and planning (Graduate Certificate), including community development, environmental policy and management, geographical information systems; geology (Graduate Certificate), including hydrogeology; global health (Graduate Certificate), including disaster management, global health and Latin American and Caribbean studies, global health practice, humanitarian assistance, infection control; government and international affairs (Graduate Certificate), including Cuban studies, globalization studies; health policy and management (Graduate Certificate), including health management and leadership, public health policy and programs; hearing specialist: early intervention (Graduate Certificate); industrial and management systems engineering (Graduate Certificate), including systems engineering, technology management; information studies (Graduate Certificate), including school library media specialist; information systems/decision sciences (Graduate Certificate), including analytics and business intelligence; instructional technology (Graduate Certificate), including distance education, Florida digital/virtual educator, instructional design, multimedia design, Web design; internal medicine, bioethics and medical humanities (Graduate Certificate), including biomedical ethics; Latin American and Caribbean studies (Graduate Certificate); mass communications (Graduate Certificate), including multimedia journalism; mathematics and statistics (Graduate Certificate), including mathematics; medicine (Graduate Certificate), including aging and neuroscience, bioinformatics, biotechnology, brain fitness and memory management, clinical investigation, health informatics, health sciences, integrative weight management, intellectual property, medicine and gender, metabolic and nutritional medicine, metabolic cardiology, pharmacy sciences; national and competitive intelligence (Graduate Certificate); psychological and social foundations (Graduate Certificate), including career counseling, college teaching, diversity in education, mental health counseling, school counseling; public affairs (Graduate Certificate), including nonprofit management, public management, research administration; public health (Graduate Certificate), including environmental health, health equity, public health generalist, translational research in adolescent behavioral health; public health practices (Graduate Certificate), including planning for healthy communities; rehabilitation and mental health counseling (Graduate Certificate), including integrative mental health care, marriage and family therapy, rehabilitation technology; secondary education (Graduate Certificate), including ESOL, foreign language education: culture and content, foreign language education: professional; social work (Graduate Certificate), including geriatric social work/clinical gerontology; special education (Graduate Certificate), including autism spectrum disorder, disabilities education: severe/profound; world languages (Graduate Certificate), including teaching English as a second language (TESL) or foreign language. *Expenses:* Tuition, state resident: full-time $7766; part-time $431.43 per credit hour. Tuition, nonresident: full-time $15,789; part-time $877.17 per credit hour. *Required fees:* $37 per term. *Unit head:* Kathy Barnes, Interdisciplinary Programs Coordinator, 813-974-8031, Fax: 813-974-7061, E-mail: barnesk@usf.edu. *Application contact:* Karen Tylinski, Metro Initiatives, 813-974-9943, Fax: 813-974-7061, E-mail: ktylinsk@usf.edu.
Website: http://www.usf.edu/innovative-education/

University of South Florida, Muma College of Business, Department of Information Systems and Decision Sciences, Tampa, FL 33620-9951. Offers business

administration (PhD), including information systems; business analytics and information systems (MS), including analytics and business intelligence, information assurance. *Program availability:* Part-time. *Faculty:* 21 full-time (5 women), 1 part-time/adjunct (0 women). *Students:* 149 full-time (54 women), 73 part-time (22 women); includes 13 minority (1 Black or African American, non-Hispanic/Latino; 6 Asian, non-Hispanic/Latino; 5 Hispanic/Latino; 1 Two or more races, non-Hispanic/Latino), 186 international. Average age 27. 1,198 applicants, 44% accepted, 117 enrolled. In 2016, 163 master's awarded. Terminal master's awarded for partial completion of doctoral program. *Degree requirements:* For master's, comprehensive exam, thesis (for some programs), thesis or practicum project; for doctorate, comprehensive exam, thesis/dissertation. *Entrance requirements:* For master's, GMAT or GRE, letters of recommendation, statement of purpose, relevant work experience; for doctorate, GMAT or GRE, letters of recommendation, personal statement, interview. Additional exam requirements/recommendations for international students: Required—TOEFL (minimum score 550 paper-based; 79 iBT) or IELTS (minimum score 6.5). *Application deadline:* For fall admission, 6/1 for domestic students, 2/1 for international students; for spring admission, 10/15 for domestic students, 9/15 for international students. Applications are processed on a rolling basis. Application fee: $30. Electronic applications accepted. *Expenses:* Tuition, state resident: full-time $7766; part-time $431.43 per credit hour. Tuition, nonresident: full-time $15,789; part-time $877.17 per credit hour. *Required fees:* $37 per term. *Financial support:* In 2016–17, 30 students received support, including 8 research assistantships with tuition reimbursements available (averaging $11,972 per year), 22 teaching assistantships with tuition reimbursements available (averaging $9,002 per year); scholarships/grants, health care benefits, and unspecified assistantships also available. Financial award applicants required to submit FAFSA. *Faculty research:* Data mining, business intelligence, bioterrorism surveillance, health informatics/informatics, software engineering, agent-based modeling, distributed systems, statistics, electronic markets, e-commerce, business process improvement, operations management, supply chain, LEAN management, global information systems, organizational impacts of IT, enterprise resource planning, business intelligence, Web and mobile technologies, social networks, information security. *Total annual research expenditures:* $496,876. *Unit head:* Dr. Kaushal Chari, Chair and Professor, 813-974-6768, Fax: 813-974-6749, E-mail: kchari@usf.edu. *Application contact:* Judy Oates, Office Assistant, 813-974-5524, Fax: 813-974-6749, E-mail: joates@usf.edu.
Website: http://business.usf.edu/departments/isds/

The University of Tampa, Sykes College of Business, Tampa, FL 33606-1490. Offers accounting (MS); entrepreneurship (MBA); finance (MBA, MS); information systems management (MBA); innovation management (MBA); international business (MBA); marketing (MBA, MS); nonprofit management (MBA). *Accreditation:* AACSB. *Program availability:* Part-time, evening/weekend. *Faculty:* 43 full-time (19 women), 9 part-time/adjunct (3 women). *Students:* 438 full-time (176 women), 126 part-time (57 women); includes 37 minority (22 Black or African American, non-Hispanic/Latino; 11 Asian, non-Hispanic/Latino; 4 Two or more races, non-Hispanic/Latino), 203 international. Average age 28. 1,305 applicants, 39% accepted, 192 enrolled. In 2016, 266 master's awarded. *Degree requirements:* For master's, capstone. *Entrance requirements:* For master's, GMAT or GRE, official transcripts from all colleges and/or universities previously attended, resume, personal statement, letters of recommendation. Additional exam requirements/recommendations for international students: Required—TOEFL (minimum score 577 paper-based, 90 iBT) or IELTS (7.5). *Application deadline:* Applications are processed on a rolling basis. Application fee: $40. Electronic applications accepted. *Expenses:* $588 per credit tuition, $40 per term fees. *Financial support:* In 2016–17, 116 students received support. Career-related internships or fieldwork, scholarships/grants, and unspecified assistantships available. Financial award applicants required to submit FAFSA. *Faculty research:* Job market signaling, on-line shopping behaviors and social media, the Tampa Bay economy, digital literacy, entrepreneurship in small businesses. *Unit head:* Dr. Natasha F. Veltri, Associate Dean, 813-253-6289, E-mail: nveltri@ut.edu. *Application contact:* Chanelle Cox, Staff Assistant, Admissions for Graduate and Continuing Studies, 813-253-6249, E-mail: ccox@ut.edu.
Website: http://www.ut.edu/business/

The University of Texas at Arlington, Graduate School, College of Business, Department of Information Systems and Operations Management, Arlington, TX 76019. Offers information systems (MS, PhD). *Program availability:* Part-time, evening/weekend. *Degree requirements:* For master's, thesis optional; for doctorate, comprehensive exam, thesis/dissertation. *Entrance requirements:* For master's, GMAT, minimum GPA of 3.0; for doctorate, GMAT/GRE. Additional exam requirements/recommendations for international students: Required—TOEFL (minimum score 550 paper-based; 79 iBT). *Application deadline:* For fall admission, 6/1 for domestic students, 4/1 for international students; for spring admission, 10/15 for domestic students, 9/15 for international students. Applications are processed on a rolling basis. Application fee: $40 ($70 for international students). *Financial support:* Teaching assistantships, career-related internships or fieldwork, scholarships/grants, and unspecified assistantships available. Support available to part-time students. Financial award application deadline: 6/1; financial award applicants required to submit FAFSA. *Faculty research:* Database modeling, strategic issues in information systems, simulations, production operations management. *Unit head:* Dr. Mary Whiteside, Chair. *Application contact:* Dr. Mary Whiteside, Chair.
Website: http://wweb.uta.edu/insyopma

The University of Texas at Austin, Graduate School, McCombs School of Business, Department of Information, Risk, and Operations Management, Austin, TX 78712-1111. Offers information management (MBA); information systems (PhD); risk analysis and decision making (PhD); risk management (MBA); supply chain and operations management (MBA, PhD). *Degree requirements:* For doctorate, thesis/dissertation. *Entrance requirements:* For doctorate, GMAT or GRE. Electronic applications accepted. *Faculty research:* Stochastic processing and queuing, discrete nonlinear and large-scale optimization simulation, quality assurance logistics, distributed artificial intelligence, organizational modeling.

The University of Texas at Dallas, Naveen Jindal School of Management, Program in Information Systems and Operations Management, Richardson, TX 75080. Offers business analytics (MS); information technology and management (MS); supply chain management (MS). *Program availability:* Part-time, evening/weekend. *Faculty:* 19 full-time (0 women), 37 part-time/adjunct (11 women). *Students:* 1,577 full-time (577 women), 457 part-time (189 women); includes 136 minority (21 Black or African American, non-Hispanic/Latino; 83 Asian, non-Hispanic/Latino; 19 Hispanic/Latino; 13 Two or more races, non-Hispanic/Latino), 1,795 international. Average age 27. 3,354 applicants, 66% accepted, 931 enrolled. In 2016, 787 master's awarded. *Degree requirements:* For master's, thesis optional. *Entrance requirements:* For master's, GMAT. Additional exam requirements/recommendations for international students: Required—TOEFL (minimum score 550 paper-based). *Application deadline:* For fall admission, 7/15 for domestic students, 5/1 priority date for international students; for spring admission, 11/15 for domestic students, 9/1 priority date for international students. Applications are processed on a rolling basis. Application fee: $50 ($100 for international students). Electronic applications accepted. *Expenses:* Tuition, state resident: full-time $12,418; part-time $690 per semester hour. Tuition, nonresident: full-time $24,150; part-time $1342 per semester hour. Tuition and fees vary according to course load. *Financial support:* In 2016–17, 473 students received support, including 5 research assistantships with partial tuition reimbursements available (averaging $14,880 per year), 48 teaching assistantships with partial tuition reimbursements available (averaging $10,122 per year); career-related internships or fieldwork, Federal Work-Study, institutionally sponsored loans, scholarships/grants, and unspecified assistantships also available. Support available to part-time students. Financial award application deadline: 4/30; financial award applicants required to submit FAFSA. *Faculty research:* Technology marketing, measuring information work productivity, electronic commerce, decision support systems, data quality. *Unit head:* Dr. Milind Dawande, Area Coordinator, 972-883-2793, E-mail: milind@utdallas.edu. *Application contact:* Dr. Ozalp Ozer, PhD Area Coordinator, 972-883-2316, E-mail: oozer@utdallas.edu.
Website: http://jindal.utdallas.edu/isom/

The University of Texas Rio Grande Valley, College of Engineering and Computer Science, Department of Computer Science, Edinburg, TX 78539. Offers computer science (MS); information technology (MS). *Program availability:* Part-time, evening/weekend, online learning. *Degree requirements:* For master's, final written exam, project. *Entrance requirements:* For master's, GRE General Test, minimum GPA of 3.0 in last 60 hours. Additional exam requirements/recommendations for international students: Required—TOEFL. Tuition and fees vary according to course load and program. *Faculty research:* Artificial intelligence, distributed systems, Internet computing, theoretical computer sciences, information visualization.

University of the Sacred Heart, Graduate Programs, Department of Business Administration, Program in Information Systems Management, San Juan, PR 00914-0383. Offers MBA. *Program availability:* Part-time, evening/weekend. *Degree requirements:* For master's, thesis. *Entrance requirements:* For master's, EXADEP, minimum undergraduate GPA of 2.75, interview.

University of the West, Department of Business Administration, Rosemead, CA 91770. Offers business administration (EMBA); computer information systems (MBA); finance (MBA); international business (MBA); nonprofit organization management (MBA). *Program availability:* Part-time, evening/weekend. *Faculty:* 3 full-time (1 woman), 6 part-time/adjunct (2 women). *Students:* 54 full-time (31 women), 14 part-time (3 women); includes 8 minority (4 Asian, non-Hispanic/Latino; 4 Hispanic/Latino), 59 international. Average age 29. *Entrance requirements:* Additional exam requirements/recommendations for international students: Required—TOEFL. *Application deadline:* For fall admission, 6/15 for domestic and international students; for winter admission, 4/1 for domestic and international students; for spring admission, 11/15 for domestic and international students. Applications are processed on a rolling basis. Application fee: $50 ($100 for international students). *Expenses: Tuition:* Full-time $9324; part-time $4662 per year. *Required fees:* $900; $640 per unit. $320 per semester. Tuition and fees vary according to program. *Financial support:* Career-related internships or fieldwork, Federal Work-Study, scholarships/grants, and tuition waivers (partial) available. Financial award applicants required to submit FAFSA. *Unit head:* Dr. Bill Y. Chen, Chair, 626-656-2125, Fax: 626-571-1413, E-mail: billchen@uwest.edu. *Application contact:* Rica Toribio, Director of Enrollment Services, 626-571-8811 Ext. 311, Fax: 626-571-1413, E-mail: ricat@uwest.edu.
Website: http://www.uwest.edu/site/index.php?option=com_content&view=article&id=119&Itemid=162

University of Utah, Graduate School, David Eccles School of Business, Business Administration Program, Salt Lake City, UT 84112. Offers accounting (PhD); business administration (EMBA, MBA, PMBA); finance (PhD); information systems (PhD); marketing (PhD); operations management (PhD); organizational behavior (PhD); strategic management (PhD); MBA/JD; MBA/MHA; MBA/MS. *Program availability:* Part-time, evening/weekend, online learning. *Faculty:* 58 full-time (21 women), 37 part-time/adjunct (7 women). *Students:* 578 full-time (149 women), 89 part-time (28 women); includes 71 minority (1 American Indian or Alaska Native, non-Hispanic/Latino; 17 Asian, non-Hispanic/Latino; 45 Hispanic/Latino; 8 Two or more races, non-Hispanic/Latino), 50 international. Average age 32. 442 applicants, 70% accepted, 226 enrolled. In 2016, 246 master's, 6 doctorates awarded. *Degree requirements:* For doctorate, comprehensive exam, thesis/dissertation. *Entrance requirements:* For master's, GMAT or GRE; for doctorate, GMAT. Additional exam requirements/recommendations for international students: Required—TOEFL (minimum score 600 paper-based; 100 iBT), IELTS (minimum score 7). *Application deadline:* For fall admission, 11/1 priority date for domestic students, 3/1 priority date for international students; for spring admission, 11/1 for domestic and international students. Applications are processed on a rolling basis. Application fee: $55 ($65 for international students). Electronic applications accepted. *Expenses:* Contact institution. *Financial support:* In 2016–17, 53 students received support, including 53 fellowships with partial tuition reimbursements available (averaging $8,600 per year); scholarships/grants and unspecified assistantships also available. Financial award application deadline: 2/1; financial award applicants required to submit FAFSA. *Faculty research:* Corporate finance, strategy services, consumer behavior, financial disclosures, operations. *Unit head:* Kristina Diekmann, Department Chair, 801-581-8524, Fax: 801-581-3380, E-mail: mastersinfo@business.utah.edu. *Application contact:* Christine Harris, Coordinator, 801-581-7785, Fax: 801-585-3962, E-mail: execch@business.utah.edu.
Website: http://www.business.utah.edu/

University of Utah, Graduate School, David Eccles School of Business, Department of Operations and Information Systems, Salt Lake City, UT 84112. Offers information systems (MS, Graduate Certificate), including business intelligence and analytics, IT security, product and process management, software and systems architecture. *Program availability:* Part-time, evening/weekend, 100% online, blended/hybrid learning. *Faculty:* 12 full-time (5 women), 7 part-time/adjunct (0 women). *Students:* 143 full-time (43 women), 107 part-time (28 women); includes 127 minority (1 Black or African American, non-Hispanic/Latino; 120 Asian, non-Hispanic/Latino; 3 Hispanic/Latino; 3 Two or more races, non-Hispanic/Latino), 123 international. Average age 29. 334 applicants, 72% accepted, 127 enrolled. In 2016, 96 master's awarded. *Degree requirements:* For master's, capstone project. *Entrance requirements:* For master's, GMAT/GRE, minimum undergraduate GPA of 3.0, 2 letters of recommendation, personal statement, professional resume. Additional exam requirements/recommendations for international students: Required—TOEFL (minimum score 550 paper-based; 80 iBT), IELTS (minimum score 6.5). *Application deadline:* For fall admission, 7/28 for domestic students, 3/1 for international students; for spring admission, 12/7 for domestic students, 8/16 for international students. Applications are processed on a rolling basis. Application fee: $55 ($65 for international students). Electronic applications accepted. *Expenses:* Contact institution. *Financial support:* In 2016–17, 75 students received support, including 7 teaching assistantships (averaging $5,000 per year); fellowships with partial tuition reimbursements available, tuition waivers (partial), and unspecified assistantships also available. Financial award application deadline: 3/31; financial award applicants required to submit FAFSA. *Faculty research:* Business intelligence and analytics, software and system architecture, product and process management, IT security, Web and data mining, applications and management of IT in healthcare. *Unit head:* Dr. Bradden Blair, Director of the IS Programs, 801-587-9489, Fax: 801-581-3666, E-mail: b.blair@eccles.utah.edu. *Application contact:* Raven Clissold, Admissions Coordinator, 801-587-5838, Fax: 801-

581-3666, E-mail: raven.clissold@eccles.utah.edu.
Website: http://msis.eccles.utah.edu

University of Washington, Graduate School, Michael G. Foster School of Business, Seattle, WA 98195-3200. Offers auditing and assurance (MP Acc); business administration (MBA, PhD); entrepreneurship (MS); executive business administration (MBA); global executive business administration (MBA); information systems (MSIS); supply chain management (MSSCM); taxation (MP Acc); technology management (MBA); JD/MBA; MBA/MAIS; MBA/MHA. *Accreditation:* AACSB. *Program availability:* Part-time, evening/weekend. Terminal master's awarded for partial completion of doctoral program. *Degree requirements:* For doctorate, comprehensive exam, thesis/dissertation. *Entrance requirements:* For master's and doctorate, GMAT, GRE. Additional exam requirements/recommendations for international students: Required—TOEFL (minimum score 600 paper-based; 100 iBT). Electronic applications accepted. *Expenses:* Contact institution. *Faculty research:* Finance, marketing, organizational behavior, information technology, strategy.

University of Wisconsin–Madison, Graduate School, Wisconsin School of Business, Doctoral Program in Accounting and Information Systems, Madison, WI 53706-1380. Offers PhD. *Accreditation:* AACSB. *Degree requirements:* For doctorate, comprehensive exam, thesis/dissertation. *Entrance requirements:* For doctorate, GMAT or GRE. Additional exam requirements/recommendations for international students: Recommended—TOEFL (minimum score 623 paper-based; 106 iBT), IELTS (minimum score 7.5). Electronic applications accepted. *Expenses:* Contact institution. *Faculty research:* Auditing, financial reporting, economic theory, strategy, computer models, Internal audit and fraud, health care fiscal management, tax reporting, incentives used in nonprofit hospitals, CFO compensation, state and local taxation, audit quality, FASB pronouncements, financial statement analysis.

University of Wisconsin–Madison, Graduate School, Wisconsin School of Business, Doctoral Program in Operations and Information Management, Madison, WI 53706-1380. Offers information systems (PhD); operations management (PhD). *Degree requirements:* For doctorate, comprehensive exam, thesis/dissertation. *Entrance requirements:* For doctorate, GMAT or GRE General Test. Additional exam requirements/recommendations for international students: Recommended—TOEFL (minimum score 623 paper-based; 106 iBT), IELTS (minimum score 7.5), TSE (minimum score 73). Electronic applications accepted. *Expenses:* Contact institution. *Faculty research:* Supply chain management, reorganization of the factory, creating continuous innovation, transportation economics, organizational economics, health care operations management, econometric analysis, forecasting, project management.

Utah State University, School of Graduate Studies, College of Business, Department of Business Information Systems, Logan, UT 84322. Offers business education (MS); business information systems (MS); business information systems and education (Ed D); education (PhD). *Program availability:* Part-time. Terminal master's awarded for partial completion of doctoral program. *Degree requirements:* For master's, thesis optional; for doctorate, thesis/dissertation. *Entrance requirements:* For master's, GMAT, minimum GPA of 3.2; for doctorate, GRE General Test, minimum GPA of 3.0. Additional exam requirements/recommendations for international students: Required—TOEFL. *Faculty research:* Oral and written communication, methods of teaching, CASE tools, object-oriented programming, decision support systems.

Valparaiso University, Graduate School and Continuing Education, Program in Informational Technology, Valparaiso, IN 46383. Offers computing (MS); management (MS). *Program availability:* Part-time, evening/weekend. *Entrance requirements:* For master's, minimum GPA of 3.0; minor or equivalent in computer science, information technology, or a related field. Additional exam requirements/recommendations for international students: Required—TOEFL (minimum score 550 paper-based; 80 iBT), IELTS (minimum score 6). Electronic applications accepted. *Expenses: Tuition:* Full-time $11,070; part-time $615 per credit hour. *Required fees:* $116 per semester. Tuition and fees vary according to course load, degree level and program.

Villanova University, Villanova School of Business, MBA - The Fast Track Program, Villanova, PA 19085. Offers analytics (MBA); cybersecurity (MBA); finance (MBA); healthcare (MBA); international business (MBA); management information systems (MBA); marketing (MBA); real estate (MBA); strategic management (MBA); sustainability (MBA). *Accreditation:* AACSB. *Program availability:* Part-time, evening/weekend. *Faculty:* 108 full-time (39 women), 32 part-time/adjunct (8 women). *Students:* 127 part-time (58 women); includes 18 minority (3 Black or African American, non-Hispanic/Latino; 7 Asian, non-Hispanic/Latino; 6 Hispanic/Latino; 2 Two or more races, non-Hispanic/Latino), 2 international. Average age 30. 88 applicants, 90% accepted, 66 enrolled. In 2016, 75 master's awarded. *Degree requirements:* For master's, minimum GPA of 3.0. *Entrance requirements:* For master's, GMAT or GRE, work experience, 2 letters of recommendation, 2 essays, resume, official transcripts, interview. Additional exam requirements/recommendations for international students: Required—TOEFL (minimum score 550 paper-based; 100 iBT). *Application deadline:* For fall admission, 6/30 for domestic and international students. Application fee: $65. Electronic applications accepted. *Expenses:* Contact institution. *Financial support:* Scholarships/grants available. Financial award application deadline: 6/30; financial award applicants required to submit FAFSA. *Faculty research:* Business analytics; creativity, innovation and entrepreneurship; global leadership; real estate; church management; business ethics; marketing and consumer insights. *Unit head:* Michael L. Capella, Associate Dean of Graduate and Executive Business Programs, 610-519-4336, Fax: 610-519-6273, E-mail: michael.l.capella@villanova.edu. *Application contact:* Kimberly Kane, Manager of Admissions, 610-519-3701, Fax: 610-519-6273, E-mail: kimberly.kane@villanova.edu.
Website: http://www1.villanova.edu/villanova/business/graduate/mba.html

Virginia Commonwealth University, Graduate School, School of Business, Program in Information Systems, Richmond, VA 23284-9005. Offers MS. *Entrance requirements:* For master's, GMAT. Additional exam requirements/recommendations for international students: Required—TOEFL (minimum score 600 paper-based; 100 iBT); Recommended—IELTS (minimum score 6.5). *Application deadline:* For fall admission, 7/1 for domestic students; for spring admission, 11/1 for domestic students. Applications are processed on a rolling basis. Application fee: $50. Electronic applications accepted. *Financial support:* Fellowships, research assistantships, teaching assistantships, Federal Work-Study, institutionally sponsored loans, and tuition waivers (full and partial) available. Financial award application deadline: 3/15; financial award applicants required to submit FAFSA. *Unit head:* Dr. Richard Redmond, Chair, 804-828-1737, Fax: 804-828-3199, E-mail: rtredmon@vcu.edu. *Application contact:* Colleen A. Davis, Graduate Program Director, 804-828-4622, E-mail: androvichcm@vcu.edu.
Website: http://www.business.vcu.edu/graduate.html

Virginia International University, School of Computer Information Systems, Fairfax, VA 22030. Offers business intelligence (Graduate Certificate); business intelligence and data analytics (MIS); computer science (MS), including computer animation and gaming, cybersecurity, data management networking, intelligent systems, software applications development, software engineering; cybersecurity (MIS); data management (MIS); enterprise project management (MIS); health informatics (MIS); information assurance (MIS); information systems (Graduate Certificate); information systems management (MS, Graduate Certificate); information technology (MS); information technology audit and compliance (Graduate Certificate); knowledge management (MIS); software engineering (MS). *Program availability:* Part-time, online learning. *Entrance requirements:* For master's, bachelor's degree. Additional exam requirements/recommendations for international students: Required—TOEFL (minimum score 550 paper-based; 80 iBT), IELTS. Electronic applications accepted.

Virginia Polytechnic Institute and State University, Graduate School, Intercollege, Blacksburg, VA 24061. Offers genetics, bioinformatics and computational biology (PhD); information technology (MIT); macromolecular science and engineering (MS, PhD); translational biology, medicine, and health (PhD). *Students:* 175 full-time (82 women), 763 part-time (279 women); includes 217 minority (71 Black or African American, non-Hispanic/Latino; 1 American Indian or Alaska Native, non-Hispanic/Latino; 77 Asian, non-Hispanic/Latino; 43 Hispanic/Latino; 1 Native Hawaiian or other Pacific Islander, non-Hispanic/Latino; 24 Two or more races, non-Hispanic/Latino), 83 international. Average age 33. 626 applicants, 74% accepted, 373 enrolled. In 2016, 91 master's, 18 doctorates awarded. *Degree requirements:* For master's, comprehensive exam (for some programs), thesis (for some programs); for doctorate, comprehensive exam (for some programs), thesis/dissertation (for some programs). *Entrance requirements:* For master's and doctorate, GRE/GMAT. Additional exam requirements/recommendations for international students: Required—TOEFL (minimum score 80 iBT). *Application deadline:* For fall admission, 8/1 for domestic students, 4/1 for international students; for spring admission, 1/1 for domestic students, 9/1 for international students. Applications are processed on a rolling basis. Application fee: $75. Electronic applications accepted. *Expenses:* Tuition, state resident: full-time $12,467; part-time $692.50 per credit hour. Tuition, nonresident: full-time $25,095; part-time $1394.25 per credit hour. *Required fees:* $2669; $491.50 per semester. Tuition and fees vary according to course load, campus/location and program. *Financial support:* In 2016–17, 100 research assistantships with full tuition reimbursements (averaging $23,321 per year), 10 teaching assistantships with full tuition reimbursements (averaging $20,748 per year) were awarded. Financial award application deadline: 3/1; financial award applicants required to submit FAFSA. *Unit head:* Dr. Karen P. DePauw, Vice President and Dean for Graduate Education, 540-231-7581, Fax: 540-231-1670, E-mail: kpdepauw@vt.edu.
Website: http://www.graduateschool.vt.edu/graduate_catalog/colleges.htm

Virginia Polytechnic Institute and State University, Graduate School, Pamplin College of Business, Blacksburg, VA 24061. Offers accounting and information systems (MACIS); business (PhD); business administration (MBA, MS); hospitality and tourism management (MS, PhD). *Faculty:* 126 full-time (38 women), 3 part-time/adjunct (1 woman). *Students:* 255 full-time (101 women), 156 part-time (56 women); includes 95 minority (21 Black or African American, non-Hispanic/Latino; 49 Asian, non-Hispanic/Latino; 13 Hispanic/Latino; 12 Two or more races, non-Hispanic/Latino), 73 international. Average age 33. 310 applicants, 59% accepted, 150 enrolled. In 2016, 167 master's, 8 doctorates awarded. *Degree requirements:* For master's, comprehensive exam (for some programs), thesis (for some programs); for doctorate, comprehensive exam (for some programs), thesis/dissertation (for some programs). *Entrance requirements:* For master's and doctorate, GRE/GMAT. Additional exam requirements/recommendations for international students: Required—TOEFL (minimum score 80 iBT). *Application deadline:* For fall admission, 8/1 for domestic students, 4/1 for international students; for spring admission, 1/1 for domestic students, 9/1 for international students. Applications are processed on a rolling basis. Application fee: $75. Electronic applications accepted. *Expenses:* Tuition, state resident: full-time $12,467; part-time $692.50 per credit hour. Tuition, nonresident: full-time $25,095; part-time $1394.25 per credit hour. *Required fees:* $2669; $491.50 per semester. Tuition and fees vary according to course load, campus/location and program. *Financial support:* In 2016–17, 2 fellowships with full tuition reimbursements (averaging $21,222 per year), 3 research assistantships with full tuition reimbursements (averaging $24,988 per year), 46 teaching assistantships with full tuition reimbursements (averaging $20,054 per year) were awarded. Financial award application deadline: 3/1; financial award applicants required to submit FAFSA. *Total annual research expenditures:* $2.7 million. *Unit head:* Dr. Robert T. Sumichrast, Dean, 540-231-6601, Fax: 540-231-4487, E-mail: busdean@vt.edu. *Application contact:* Kimberly Ridpath, Executive Assistant, 540-231-6601, Fax: 540-231-4487, E-mail: ridpathk@vt.edu.
Website: http://www.pamplin.vt.edu/

Virginia Polytechnic Institute and State University, VT Online, Blacksburg, VA 24061. Offers advanced transportation systems (Certificate); aerospace engineering (MS); agricultural and life sciences (MSLFS); business information systems (Graduate Certificate); career and technical education (MS); civil engineering (MS); computer engineering (M Eng, MS); decision support systems (Graduate Certificate); eLearning leadership (MA); electrical engineering (M Eng, MS); engineering administration (MEA); environmental engineering (Certificate); environmental politics and policy (Graduate Certificate); environmental sciences and engineering (MS); foundations of political analysis (Graduate Certificate); health product risk management (Graduate Certificate); industrial and systems engineering (MS); information policy and society (Graduate Certificate); information security (Graduate Certificate); information technology (MIT); instructional technology (MA); integrative STEM education (MA Ed); liberal arts (Graduate Certificate); life sciences: health product risk management (MS); natural resources (MNR, Graduate Certificate); networking (Graduate Certificate); nonprofit and nongovernmental organization management (Graduate Certificate); ocean engineering (MS); political science (MA); security studies (Graduate Certificate); software development (Graduate Certificate). *Expenses:* Tuition, state resident: full-time $12,467; part-time $692.50 per credit hour. Tuition, nonresident: full-time $25,095; part-time $1394.25 per credit hour. *Required fees:* $2669; $491.50 per semester. Tuition and fees vary according to course load, campus/location and program.

Walden University, Graduate Programs, School of Information Systems and Technology, Minneapolis, MN 55401. Offers information systems (Graduate Certificate); information systems management (MISM); information technology (MS, DIT), including health informatics (MS), information assurance and cyber security (MS), information systems (MS), software engineering (MS). *Program availability:* Part-time, evening/weekend, online only, 100% online. *Degree requirements:* For doctorate, thesis/dissertation (for some programs), residency. *Entrance requirements:* For master's, bachelor's degree or higher; minimum GPA of 2.5; official transcripts; goal statement (for some programs); access to computer and Internet; for doctorate, master's degree or higher; three years of related professional or academic experience (preferred); minimum GPA of 3.0; goal statement and current resume (for select programs); official transcripts; access to computer and Internet; for Graduate Certificate, relevant work experience; access to computer and Internet. Additional exam requirements/recommendations for international students: Required—TOEFL (minimum score 550 paper-based, 79 iBT), IELTS (minimum score 6.5), Michigan English Language Assessment Battery (minimum score 82), or PTE (minimum score 53). Electronic applications accepted.

Walden University, Graduate Programs, School of Management, Minneapolis, MN 55401. Offers accounting (MBA, MS, DBA), including accounting for the professional (MS), accounting with CPA emphasis (MS), self-designed (MS); advanced project management (Graduate Certificate); applied project management (Graduate Certificate); auditing (Graduate Certificate); bridge to business administration (Post-

Doctoral Certificate); bridge to management (Post-Doctoral Certificate); business management (Graduate Certificate); communication (MBA); corporate finance (MBA); digital marketing (Graduate Certificate); entrepreneurship (DBA); entrepreneurship and small business (MBA); finance (MS, DBA), including finance for the professional (MS), finance with CFA/investment (MS), finance with CPA emphasis (MS); global supply chain management (DBA); healthcare management (MBA, DBA); human resource management (MBA, MS, Graduate Certificate), including functional human resource management (MS), general program (MS), integrating functional and strategic human resource management (MS), organizational strategy (MS); human resources management (DBA); information systems management (DBA); international business (MBA, DBA); leadership (MBA, MS, DBA, Graduate Certificate), including general program (MS), human resource leadership (MS), leader development (MS), self-designed (MS); management (MS, PhD), including communications (MS), finance (PhD), general program (MS), healthcare management (MS), human resource management (MS), human resources management (PhD), information systems management (PhD), international business (MS), leadership (MS), leadership and organizational change (PhD), marketing (MS), project management (MS), strategy and operations (MS); managerial accounting (Graduate Certificate); marketing (MBA, MS, DBA); project management (MBA, MS, DBA); self-designed (MBA, DBA); social impact management (DBA); technology entrepreneurship (DBA). *Accreditation:* ACBSP. *Program availability:* Part-time, evening/weekend, online only, 100% online. *Degree requirements:* For master's, thesis (for some programs), residency (for EMBA); for doctorate, thesis/dissertation (for some programs), residency. *Entrance requirements:* For master's, bachelor's degree or higher; minimum GPA of 2.5; official transcripts; goal statement (for some programs); access to computer and Internet; for doctorate, master's degree or higher; three years of related professional or academic experience (preferred); minimum GPA of 3.0; goal statement and current resume (for select programs); official transcripts; access to computer and Internet; for other advanced degree, relevant work experience; access to computer and Internet. Additional exam requirements/recommendations for international students: Required—TOEFL (minimum score 550 paper-based, 79 iBT), IELTS (minimum score 6.5), Michigan English Language Assessment Battery (minimum score 82), or PTE (minimum score 53). Electronic applications accepted.

Walsh College of Accountancy and Business Administration, Graduate Programs, Program in Information Technology, Troy, MI 48083. Offers cybersecurity (MSIT). *Program availability:* Part-time, evening/weekend. *Faculty:* 1 (woman) full-time, 7 part-time/adjunct (4 women). *Students:* 56 (25 women); includes 14 minority (9 Black or African American, non-Hispanic/Latino; 2 Asian, non-Hispanic/Latino; 1 Hispanic/Latino; 2 Two or more races, non-Hispanic/Latino), 16 international. Average age 34. 34 applicants, 79% accepted, 20 enrolled. In 2016, 4 master's awarded. *Entrance requirements:* For master's, minimum overall cumulative GPA of 2.75 from all colleges previously attended. Additional exam requirements/recommendations for international students: Required—TOEFL (minimum score 550 paper-based, 79 iBT), IELTS (6.5), Michigan English Language Assessment Battery, or MTELP. *Application deadline:* Applications are processed on a rolling basis. Application fee: $35. Electronic applications accepted. *Expenses:* $740 per credit hour, $125 registration fee per semester. *Financial support:* In 2016–17, 6 students received support. Career-related internships or fieldwork and scholarships/grants available. Financial award application deadline: 6/30; financial award applicants required to submit FAFSA. *Faculty research:* Business intelligence, data and decision-making, cyber security, project management, mobile technologies. *Unit head:* Dr. Barbara Ciaramitaro, Chair, Information Technology and Decision Sciences, 248-823-1635, Fax: 248-689-0920, E-mail: bciara2@walshcollege.edu. *Application contact:* Heather Rigby, Director, Admissions and Academic Advising, 248-823-1610, Fax: 248-689-0938, E-mail: hrigby@walshcollege.edu.

Wayland Baptist University, Graduate Programs, Programs in Business Administration/Management, Plainview, TX 79072-6998. Offers accounting (MBA); general business (MBA); health care administration (MAM, MBA); human resource management (MAM, MBA); international management (MBA); management (MBA, D Mgt); management information systems (MBA); organization management (MAM); project management (MBA). *Program availability:* Part-time, evening/weekend, online learning. *Degree requirements:* For master's, capstone course. *Entrance requirements:* For master's, GMAT, GRE or MAT. Additional exam requirements/recommendations for international students: Required—TOEFL (minimum score 500 paper-based; 61 iBT). Electronic applications accepted.

Wayne State University, Mike Ilitch School of Business, Detroit, MI 48202. Offers accounting (MS, Postbaccalaureate Certificate); business (Graduate Certificate); business administration (MBA, PhD); data science (MS), including business analytics; entrepreneurship and innovation (Postbaccalaureate Certificate); finance (MS); information systems management (Postbaccalaureate Certificate); taxation (MST); JD/MBA. Application deadline for PhD is February 15. *Accreditation:* AACSB. *Program availability:* Part-time, evening/weekend. *Faculty:* 32. *Students:* 219 full-time (105 women), 941 part-time (406 women); includes 314 minority (186 Black or African American, non-Hispanic/Latino; 3 American Indian or Alaska Native, non-Hispanic/Latino; 68 Asian, non-Hispanic/Latino; 33 Hispanic/Latino; 24 Two or more races, non-Hispanic/Latino), 88 international. Average age 30. 1,119 applicants, 49% accepted, 329 enrolled. In 2016, 203 master's, 1 doctorate, 3 other advanced degrees awarded. *Degree requirements:* For doctorate, thesis/dissertation. *Entrance requirements:* For master's, GMAT, GRE, LSAT, MCAT, at least three years of relevant work experience that shows increased responsibility, or minimum GPA of 3.0 from AACSB-accredited program or 3.2 from regionally-accredited program, undergraduate degree from accredited institution; undergraduate degree in accounting, business administration, or area of business administration (for MS and MST); for doctorate, GMAT (minimum score of 600), minimum undergraduate GPA of 3.0, 3.5 upper-division or graduate; three letters of recommendation; brief essay; undergraduate degree from accredited institution; personal statement; for other advanced degree, bachelor's degree from accredited institution. Additional exam requirements/recommendations for international students: Required—TOEFL (minimum score 550 paper-based; 79 iBT), Michigan English Language Assessment Battery (minimum score 85); Recommended—IELTS (minimum score 6.5), TWE (minimum score 5.5). *Application deadline:* For fall admission, 7/1 for domestic students, 5/1 priority date for international students; for winter admission, 11/1 for domestic students, 9/1 priority date for international students; for spring admission, 3/1 for domestic students, 1/1 priority date for international students. Applications are processed on a rolling basis. Application fee: $50. Electronic applications accepted. *Expenses:* $18,871 per year resident tuition and fees, $36,065 per year non-resident tuition and fees. *Financial support:* In 2016–17, 174 students received support, including 1 fellowship with tuition reimbursement available (averaging $18,000 per year), 2 research assistantships with tuition reimbursements available (averaging $18,000 per year), 5 teaching assistantships with tuition reimbursements available (averaging $18,000 per year); scholarships/grants, health care benefits, and unspecified assistantships also available. Support available to part-time students. Financial award applicants required to submit FAFSA. *Faculty research:* Executive compensation and stock performance, consumer reactions to pricing strategies, communication across the automotive supply chain, performance of firms in sub-Saharan Africa, implementation issues with ERP software. *Unit head:* Dr. Robert Forsythe, Dean, School of Business Administration, 313-577-4501, E-mail: robert.forsythe@wayne.edu. *Application contact:* Kiantee N. Rupert-Jones, Director, 313-577-4511, Fax: 313-577-9442, E-mail: gradbusiness@wayne.edu.
Website: http://ilitchbusiness.wayne.edu/

Wayne State University, School of Library and Information Science, Detroit, MI 48202. Offers archival administration (Graduate Certificate); information management (Graduate Certificate); library and information science (MLIS, Spec); public library services to children and young adults (Graduate Certificate); MLIS/MA. *Accreditation:* ALA (one or more programs are accredited). *Program availability:* Part-time, evening/weekend, 100% online, blended/hybrid learning. *Faculty:* 11 full-time (7 women), 30 part-time/adjunct (20 women). *Students:* 90 full-time (69 women), 376 part-time (312 women); includes 74 minority (38 Black or African American, non-Hispanic/Latino; 2 American Indian or Alaska Native, non-Hispanic/Latino; 4 Asian, non-Hispanic/Latino; 17 Hispanic/Latino; 2 Native Hawaiian or other Pacific Islander, non-Hispanic/Latino; 11 Two or more races, non-Hispanic/Latino), 3 international. Average age 32. 265 applicants, 73% accepted, 120 enrolled. In 2016, 145 master's, 34 other advanced degrees awarded. *Degree requirements:* For master's and other advanced degree, e-portfolio. *Entrance requirements:* For master's, GRE or MAT (if undergraduate GPA is between 2.5 and 2.99), minimum undergraduate GPA of 3.0 or graduate degree, personal statement, resume or curriculum vitae; for other advanced degree, GRE or MAT (if undergraduate GPA is between 2.5 and 2.99), minimum undergraduate GPA of 3.0 or graduate degree, personal statement, resume or curriculum vitae, MLIS (for specialist certificate). Additional exam requirements/recommendations for international students: Required—TOEFL (minimum score 550 paper-based; 79 iBT); Recommended—IELTS (minimum score 6.5), TWE (minimum score 5.5). *Application deadline:* For fall admission, 7/1 for domestic students, 5/1 priority date for international students; for winter admission, 10/1 priority date for domestic students, 9/1 priority date for international students; for spring admission, 2/1 priority date for domestic students, 1/1 priority date for international students. Applications are processed on a rolling basis. Application fee: $50. Electronic applications accepted. *Expenses:* $18,871 per year resident tuition and fees, $36,065 per year non-resident tuition and fees. *Financial support:* In 2016–17, 107 students received support. Fellowships with tuition reimbursements available, scholarships/grants, health care benefits, and unspecified assistantships available. Support available to part-time students. Financial award applicants required to submit FAFSA. *Faculty research:* Library services, information management issues, digital content management, library/community engagement, archives and preservation. *Unit head:* Dr. Sandra Yee, Dean, 313-577-4059, E-mail: aj0533@wayne.edu. *Application contact:* Academic Services Officer II, 313-577-1825, E-mail: asklis@wayne.edu.
Website: http://slis.wayne.edu/

Webster University, George Herbert Walker School of Business and Technology, Department of Business, St. Louis, MO 63119-3194. Offers business and organizational security management (MBA); decision support systems (MBA); environmental management (MBA); finance (MBA, MS); forensic accounting (MS); gerontology (MBA); human resources development (MBA); human resources management (MBA); information technology management (MBA); international business (MA, MBA); international relations (MBA); management and leadership (MBA); marketing (MBA); media communications (MBA); procurement and acquisitions management (MBA); Web services (MBA). *Accreditation:* ACBSP. *Program availability:* Part-time, evening/weekend, online learning. *Degree requirements:* For master's, comprehensive exam (for some programs), thesis (for some programs). *Entrance requirements:* Additional exam requirements/recommendations for international students: Required—TOEFL. *Application deadline:* Applications are processed on a rolling basis. Application fee: $35 ($50 for international students). *Expenses: Tuition:* Full-time $21,900; part-time $730 per credit hour. Tuition and fees vary according to campus/location and program. *Financial support:* Federal Work-Study available. Support available to part-time students. Financial award application deadline: 4/1; financial award applicants required to submit FAFSA. *Unit head:* David Porras, Chair, 314-246-8621, E-mail: porrasd@webster.edu. *Application contact:* Sarah Nandor, Director, Graduate and Transfer Admissions, 314-968-7109, E-mail: gadmit@webster.edu.

Webster University, George Herbert Walker School of Business and Technology, Department of Management, St. Louis, MO 63119-3194. Offers business and organizational security management (MA); digital marketing management (Graduate Certificate); government contracting (Graduate Certificate); health administration (MHA); health care management (MA); health services management (MA); human resources development (MA); human resources management (MA); information technology management (MA, MS); management (D Mgt); management and leadership (MA); marketing (MA); nonprofit leadership (MA); nonprofit revenue development (Graduate Certificate); organizational development (Graduate Certificate); procurement and acquisitions management (MA); public administration (MPA); space systems operations management (MS). *Program availability:* Part-time, evening/weekend, online learning. *Degree requirements:* For master's, thesis (for some programs); for doctorate, thesis/dissertation, written exam. *Entrance requirements:* For doctorate, GMAT, 3 years of work experience, MBA. Additional exam requirements/recommendations for international students: Required—TOEFL. *Application deadline:* Applications are processed on a rolling basis. Application fee: $25 ($50 for international students). *Expenses: Tuition:* Full-time $21,900; part-time $730 per credit hour. Tuition and fees vary according to campus/location and program. *Financial support:* Federal Work-Study available. Support available to part-time students. Financial award application deadline: 4/1; financial award applicants required to submit FAFSA. *Unit head:* Barrett Baebler, Chair, 314-246-7940, E-mail: baeblerb@webster.edu. *Application contact:* Sarah Nandor, Director, Graduate and Transfer Admissions, 314-968-7109, E-mail: gadmit@webster.edu.

West Chester University of Pennsylvania, College of the Sciences and Mathematics, Department of Computer Science, West Chester, PA 19383. Offers computer science (MS); computer security (information assurance) (Certificate); information systems (Certificate); Web technology (Certificate). *Program availability:* Part-time, evening/weekend. *Faculty:* 10 full-time (3 women). *Students:* 7 full-time (2 women), 29 part-time (10 women); includes 11 minority (5 Black or African American, non-Hispanic/Latino; 5 Asian, non-Hispanic/Latino; 1 Hispanic/Latino), 8 international. Average age 31. 29 applicants, 69% accepted, 12 enrolled. In 2016, 16 master's, 3 other advanced degrees awarded. *Degree requirements:* For master's, thesis optional, 33 credits; for Certificate, 12 credits. *Entrance requirements:* For master's, GRE, two letters of recommendation; for Certificate, BS. Additional exam requirements/recommendations for international students: Required—TOEFL or IELTS. *Application deadline:* For fall admission, 5/15 for international students; for spring admission, 10/15 for international students. Applications are processed on a rolling basis. Application fee: $50. Electronic applications accepted. *Expenses:* Tuition, state resident: full-time $8694; part-time $483 per credit. Tuition, nonresident: full-time $13,050; part-time $725 per credit. *Required fees:* $2399; $119.05 per credit. Tuition and fees vary according to campus/location and program. *Financial support:* Scholarships/grants and unspecified assistantships available. Financial award application deadline: 2/15; financial award applicants required to submit FAFSA. *Faculty research:* Security in mobile ad-hoc networks, intrusion

detection, security and trust in pervasive computing, cloud computing, wireless sensor networks, cloud computing and data mining. *Unit head:* Dr. James Fabrey, Chair, 610-436-2204, E-mail: jfabrey@wcupa.edu. *Application contact:* Dr. Afrand Agah, Graduate Coordinator, 610-430-4419, E-mail: aagah@wcupa.edu.
Website: http://www.cs.wcupa.edu/

Western Governors University, College of Business, Salt Lake City, UT 84107. Offers information technology management (MBA); integrated healthcare management (MS); management and strategy (MBA); strategic leadership (MBA). *Program availability:* Evening/weekend. *Degree requirements:* For master's, capstone project. *Entrance requirements:* For master's, Readiness Assessment, transcripts. Additional exam requirements/recommendations for international students: Required—TOEFL (minimum score 450 paper-based; 80 iBT). Electronic applications accepted.

Wichita State University, Graduate School, W. Frank Barton School of Business, School of Accountancy, Wichita, KS 67260. Offers accounting information systems (M Acc); taxation (M Acc). *Accreditation:* AACSB. *Program availability:* Part-time, evening/weekend. *Unit head:* Dr. Paul D. Harrison, Director, 316-978-3215, Fax: 316-978-3660, E-mail: paul.harrison@wichita.edu. *Application contact:* Jordan Oleson, Admissions Coordinator, 316-978-3095, Fax: 316-978-3253, E-mail: jordan.oleson@wichita.edu.
Website: http://www.wichita.edu/acct

Wilmington University, College of Business, New Castle, DE 19720-6491. Offers accounting (MBA, MS); business administration (MBA, DBA); environmental stewardship (MBA); finance (MBA); health care administration (MBA, MSM); homeland security (MBA, MSM); human resource management (MSM); management information systems (MBA, MSN); marketing (MSM); marketing management (MBA); military leadership (MSM); organizational leadership (MBA, MSM); public administration (MSM). *Program availability:* Part-time, evening/weekend. *Faculty:* 17 full-time (7 women), 106 part-time/adjunct (46 women). *Students:* 436 full-time (237 women), 1,202 part-time (739 women); includes 594 minority (474 Black or African American, non-Hispanic/Latino; 19 American Indian or Alaska Native, non-Hispanic/Latino; 64 Asian, non-Hispanic/Latino; 30 Hispanic/Latino; 3 Native Hawaiian or other Pacific Islander, non-Hispanic/Latino; 4 Two or more races, non-Hispanic/Latino), 153 international. Average age 35. 814 applicants, 98% accepted, 426 enrolled. In 2016, 594 master's, 23 doctorates awarded. *Entrance requirements:* Additional exam requirements/recommendations for international students: Required—TOEFL (minimum score 500 paper-based). *Application deadline:* Applications are processed on a rolling basis. Application fee: $35. Electronic applications accepted. *Expenses: Tuition:* Full-time $8388; part-time $466 per credit. *Required fees:* $25 per semester. Tuition and fees vary according to degree level. *Financial support:* Applicants required to submit FAFSA. *Unit head:* Dr. Robert W. Rescigno, Dean. *Application contact:* Laura Morris, Director of Admissions, 877-967-5456, E-mail: infocenter@wilmu.edu.
Website: http://www.wilmu.edu/business/

Wilmington University, College of Technology, New Castle, DE 19720-6491. Offers geographic information systems (MS); information assurance (MS); information systems technologies (MS); Internet/Web design (MS); management and management information systems (MS). *Program availability:* Part-time, evening/weekend. *Faculty:* 5 full-time (1 woman), 114 part-time/adjunct (31 women). *Students:* 1,316 full-time (321 women), 263 part-time (79 women); includes 71 minority (53 Black or African American, non-Hispanic/Latino; 5 American Indian or Alaska Native, non-Hispanic/Latino; 8 Asian, non-Hispanic/Latino; 4 Hispanic/Latino; 1 Two or more races, non-Hispanic/Latino), 1,437 international. Average age 26. 856 applicants, 100% accepted, 332 enrolled. In 2016, 756 master's awarded. *Entrance requirements:* Additional exam requirements/recommendations for international students: Required—TOEFL (minimum score 500 paper-based). *Application deadline:* Applications are processed on a rolling basis. Application fee: $35. Electronic applications accepted. *Expenses: Tuition:* Full-time $8388; part-time $466 per credit. *Required fees:* $25 per semester. Tuition and fees vary according to degree level. *Unit head:* Dr. Mary Ann K. Westerfield, Dean. *Application contact:* Laura Morris, Director of Admissions, 877-967-5464, E-mail: infocenter@wilmu.edu.
Website: http://www.wilmu.edu/technology/

Winston-Salem State University, Program in Computer Science and Information Technology, Winston-Salem, NC 27110-0003. Offers MS. *Program availability:* Part-time. *Degree requirements:* For master's, thesis optional. *Entrance requirements:* For master's, GRE, resume. Electronic applications accepted. *Faculty research:* Artificial intelligence, network protocols, software engineering.

Worcester Polytechnic Institute, Graduate Studies and Research, Foisie Business School, Worcester, MA 01609-2280. Offers information technology (MS), including information security management; management (Graduate Certificate); marketing and technological innovation (MS); operations design and leadership (MS); technology (MBA, MS). *Accreditation:* AACSB. *Program availability:* Part-time, evening/weekend, 100% online, blended/hybrid learning. *Faculty:* 20 full-time (12 women), 16 part-time/adjunct (1 woman). *Students:* 237 full-time (139 women), 186 part-time (67 women); includes 35 minority (4 Black or African American, non-Hispanic/Latino; 17 Asian, non-Hispanic/Latino; 12 Hispanic/Latino; 2 Two or more races, non-Hispanic/Latino), 221 international. 645 applicants, 62% accepted, 144 enrolled. In 2016, 150 master's awarded. *Degree requirements:* For master's, thesis optional. *Entrance requirements:* For master's, GMAT (MBA); GMAT or GRE General Test (MS), statement of purpose, 3 letters of recommendation, resume; for Graduate Certificate, GMAT or GRE General Test, statement of purpose, 3 letters of recommendation. Additional exam requirements/recommendations for international students: Required—TOEFL (minimum score 563 paper-based; 84 iBT), IELTS (minimum score 7). *Application deadline:* For fall admission, 6/1 priority date for domestic and international students; for spring admission, 11/1 priority date for domestic students, 10/1 priority date for international students. Applications are processed on a rolling basis. Application fee: $70. Electronic applications accepted. *Financial support:* Career-related internships or fieldwork, institutionally sponsored loans, scholarships/grants, and unspecified assistantships available. Financial award application deadline: 6/1; financial award applicants required to submit FAFSA. *Unit head:* Melissa Terrio, Executive Director, 508-831-4665, Fax: 508-831-4665, E-mail: biz@wpi.edu. *Application contact:* Eileen Dagostino, Recruiting Operations Coordinator, 508-831-4665, Fax: 508-831-5720, E-mail: edag@wpi.edu.
Website: https://www.wpi.edu/academics/business

Wright State University, Graduate School, Raj Soin College of Business, Department of Information Systems and Operations Management, Information Systems Program, Dayton, OH 45435. Offers MIS. *Expenses:* Tuition, state resident: full-time $9952; part-time $622 per credit hour. Tuition, nonresident: full-time $16,960; part-time $1060 per credit hour. *Unit head:* Dr. Martin H. Davis, Jr., Director, 937-775-3333. *Application contact:* Michael Evans, Director of MBA Programs, 937-775-2437, Fax: 937-775-3545, E-mail: michael.evans@wright.edu.

Section 13
Management Strategy and Policy

This section contains a directory of institutions offering graduate work in management strategy and policy. Additional information about programs listed in the directory but not augmented by an in-depth entry may be obtained by writing directly to the dean of a graduate school or chair of a department at the address given in the directory.

For programs offering related work, see also in this book *Business Administration and Management.* In another guide in this series:

Graduate Programs in the Humanities, Arts & Social Sciences

See *Public, Regional, and Industrial Affairs (Industrial and Labor Relations)*

CONTENTS

Program Directories

Featured Schools: Displays and Close-Ups

See:

Management Strategy and Policy

Amberton University, Graduate School, Department of Business Administration, Garland, TX 75041-5595. Offers general business (MBA); management (MBA); project management (MBA); strategic leadership (MBA). *Program availability:* Part-time, evening/weekend. *Entrance requirements:* For master's, minimum GPA of 3.0.

American Public University System, AMU/APU Graduate Programs, Charles Town, WV 25414. Offers accounting (MBA, MS); applied business analytics (MBA, MS); criminal justice (MA), including business administration, emergency and disaster management, general (MA, MS); educational leadership (M Ed); emergency and disaster management (MA); entrepreneurship (MBA); environmental policy and management (MS), including environmental planning, environmental sustainability, fish and wildlife management, general (MA, MS), global environmental management; finance (MBA); general (MBA); government contracting and acquisition (MBA); health care administration (MBA); health information management (MS); history (MA), including American history, ancient and classical history, European history, global history, public history; homeland security (MA), including business administration, counterterrorism studies, criminal justice, cyber, emergency management and public health, intelligence studies, transportation security; homeland security resource allocation (MBA); humanities (MA); information technology (MS), including digital forensics, enterprise software development, information assurance and security, IT project management; information technology management (MBA); intelligence studies (MA), including criminal intelligence, cyber, general (MA, MS), homeland security, intelligence analysis, intelligence collection, intelligence management, intelligence operations, terrorism studies; international relations and conflict resolution (MA), including comparative and security issues, conflict resolution, international and transnational security issues, peacekeeping; legal studies (MA); management (MA), including strategic consulting; marketing (MBA); military history (MA), including American military history, American Revolution, civil war, war since 1945, World War II; military studies (MA), including joint warfare, strategic leadership; national security studies (MA), including cyber, general (MA, MS), homeland security, regional security studies, security and intelligence analysis, terrorism studies; nonprofit management (MBA); political science (MA), including American politics and government, comparative government and development, general (MA, MS), international relations, public policy; psychology (MA); public administration (MPA), including disaster management, environmental policy, health policy, human resources, national security, organizational management, security management; public health (MPH); reverse logistics management (MA); security management (MA); space studies (MS), including aerospace science, general (MA, MS), planetary science; sports and health sciences (MS); sports management (MBA); teaching (M Ed), including autism spectrum disorder, curriculum and instruction for elementary teachers, elementary reading, English language learners, instructional leadership, online learning, special education, STEAM (STEM plus the arts); transportation and logistics management (MA). *Program availability:* Part-time, evening/weekend, online only, 100% online. *Faculty:* 401 full-time (228 women), 1,678 part-time/adjunct (781 women). *Students:* 378 full-time (184 women), 8,455 part-time (3,484 women); includes 2,972 minority (1,552 Black or African American, non-Hispanic/Latino; 52 American Indian or Alaska Native, non-Hispanic/Latino; 211 Asian, non-Hispanic/Latino; 791 Hispanic/Latino; 70 Native Hawaiian or other Pacific Islander, non-Hispanic/Latino; 296 Two or more races, non-Hispanic/Latino), 109 international. Average age 37. In 2016, 3,185 master's awarded. *Degree requirements:* For master's, comprehensive exam or practicum. *Entrance requirements:* For master's, official transcript showing earned bachelor's degree from institution accredited by recognized accrediting body. Additional exam requirements/recommendations for international students: Required—TOEFL (minimum score 550 paper-based), IELTS (minimum score 6.5). *Application deadline:* Applications are processed on a rolling basis. Application fee: $0. Electronic applications accepted. *Expenses: Tuition:* Part-time $350 per credit hour. *Required fees:* $50 per course. *Financial support:* Scholarships/grants available. Financial award applicants required to submit FAFSA. *Unit head:* Dr. Karan Powell, President, 877-468-6268, Fax: 304-724-3780. *Application contact:* Terry Grant, Vice President of Enrollment Management, 877-468-6268, Fax: 304-724-3780, E-mail: info@apus.edu.
Website: http://www.apus.edu

Antioch University Midwest, Graduate Programs, Program in Management and Change Leadership, Yellow Springs, OH 45387-1609. Offers MA. *Program availability:* Part-time, evening/weekend, online learning. *Entrance requirements:* For master's, resume, goal statement, interview. *Application deadline:* For fall admission, 9/1 for domestic students; for winter admission, 12/1 for domestic students; for spring admission, 3/10 for domestic students. Applications are processed on a rolling basis. Application fee: $50. Electronic applications accepted. *Expenses:* $799 per credit hour. *Financial support:* Federal Work-Study available. Financial award applicants required to submit FAFSA. *Unit head:* Hays Moulton, Chair, 937-769-1860, Fax: 937-769-1807, E-mail: hmoulton@antioch.edu. *Application contact:* Deena Kent-Hummel, Director of Admissions, 937-769-1816, Fax: 937-769-1804, E-mail: dkent@antioch.edu.
Website: https://www.antioch.edu/midwest/degrees-programs/business-management-leadership/management-and-change-leadership-ma/

Antioch University Santa Barbara, Program in Business Administration, Santa Barbara, CA 93101-1581. Offers non-profit management (MBA); social business (MBA); strategic leadership (MBA).

Arizona State University at the Tempe campus, W. P. Carey School of Business, Program in Business Administration, Tempe, AZ 85287-4906. Offers entrepreneurship (MBA); finance (MBA); health sector management (MBA); international business (MBA); leadership (MBA); marketing (MBA); organizational behavior (PhD); strategic management (PhD); supply chain management (MBA, PhD); JD/MBA; MBA/M Acc; MBA/M Arch. *Accreditation:* AACSB. *Program availability:* Part-time, evening/weekend, online learning. Terminal master's awarded for partial completion of doctoral program. *Degree requirements:* For master's, thesis or alternative, internship, interactive Program of Study (iPOS) submitted before completing 50 percent of required credit hours; for doctorate, comprehensive exam, thesis/dissertation, interactive Program of Study (iPOS) submitted before completing 50 percent of required credit hours. *Entrance requirements:* For master's, GMAT, minimum GPA of 3.0 in last 2 years of work leading to bachelor's degree, 2 letters of recommendation, professional resume, official transcripts, 3 essays; for doctorate, GMAT or GRE, minimum GPA of 3.0 in last 2 years of work leading to bachelor's degree, 3 letters of recommendation, resume, personal statement/essay. Additional exam requirements/recommendations for international students: Required—TOEFL (minimum score 550 paper-based; 80 iBT), IELTS (minimum score 6.5). Electronic applications accepted. *Expenses:* Contact institution.

Austin Peay State University, College of Graduate Studies, College of Behavioral and Health Sciences, Department of Professional Studies, Clarksville, TN 37044. Offers human resources leadership (MPS); strategic leadership (MPS); training and development (MPS). *Program availability:* Part-time, online learning. *Faculty:* 3 full-time (all women), 1 (woman) part-time/adjunct. *Students:* 9 full-time (6 women), 25 part-time (20 women); includes 12 minority (8 Black or African American, non-Hispanic/Latino; 3 Hispanic/Latino; 1 Two or more races, non-Hispanic/Latino). Average age 43. 14 applicants, 71% accepted, 7 enrolled. In 2016, 4 master's awarded. *Degree requirements:* For master's, project. *Entrance requirements:* For master's, GRE General Test, minimum GPA of 2.75. Additional exam requirements/recommendations for international students: Required—TOEFL (minimum score 500 paper-based). *Application deadline:* For fall admission, 8/9 priority date for domestic students. Applications are processed on a rolling basis. Application fee: $45 ($50 for international students). Electronic applications accepted. *Expenses:* Tuition, state resident: full-time $8300; part-time $415 per credit hour. Tuition, nonresident: full-time $22,280; part-time $1114 per credit hour. *Required fees:* $1473; $73.65 per credit hour. *Financial support:* Career-related internships or fieldwork, Federal Work-Study, institutionally sponsored loans, scholarships/grants, and unspecified assistantships available. Support available to part-time students. Financial award application deadline: 4/1; financial award applicants required to submit FAFSA. *Unit head:* Dr. Robyn Hulsart, Department Chair, 931-221-1439, E-mail: hulsartr@apsu.edu. *Application contact:* Brad Averitt, Coordinator of Graduate Admissions, 800-859-4723, Fax: 931-221-7641, E-mail: gradadmissions@apsu.edu.
Website: http://www.apsu.edu/apfc/MPS

Azusa Pacific University, School of Business and Management, Azusa, CA 91702-7000. Offers business administration (MBA); diversity for strategic advantage (MA); entrepreneurship (MBA); finance (MBA); human and organizational development (MA); human resources and organizational development (MBA); human resources management (MA); international business (MBA); marketing (MBA); non-profit management (MA); organizational development and change (MA); performance improvement (MA); public administration (MA); strategic management (MBA). *Program availability:* Part-time, evening/weekend. *Degree requirements:* For master's, thesis (for some programs), final project. *Entrance requirements:* For master's, GMAT, minimum GPA of 3.0. Additional exam requirements/recommendations for international students: Required—TOEFL (minimum score 600 paper-based). *Expenses:* Contact institution. *Faculty research:* Gender issues, financial risk, leadership and ethics, marketing strategy.

Baldwin Wallace University, Graduate Programs, School of Business, Berea, OH 44017-2088. Offers accounting (MBA); analytics (MBA); entrepreneurship (MBA); executive management (MBA); health care (MBA); human resources (MBA); international management (MBA); management (MAM, MBA); sustainability (MBA). *Program availability:* Part-time, evening/weekend, blended/hybrid learning. *Faculty:* 21 full-time (8 women), 23 part-time/adjunct (8 women). *Students:* 200 full-time (84 women), 121 part-time (68 women); includes 61 minority (28 Black or African American, non-Hispanic/Latino; 11 Asian, non-Hispanic/Latino; 17 Hispanic/Latino; 5 Two or more races, non-Hispanic/Latino), 3 international. Average age 34. 131 applicants, 77% accepted, 71 enrolled. In 2016, 168 master's awarded. *Degree requirements:* For master's, minimum overall GPA of 3.0. *Entrance requirements:* For master's, GMAT or minimum GPA of 3.0, bachelor's degree in any field, work experience. Additional exam requirements/recommendations for international students: Required—TOEFL (minimum score 550 paper-based; 79 iBT). *Application deadline:* For fall admission, 7/25 priority date for domestic students, 4/30 priority date for international students; for spring admission, 12/15 priority date for domestic students, 9/30 priority date for international students; for summer admission, 4/15 for domestic students. Applications are processed on a rolling basis. Electronic applications accepted. *Expenses:* Contact institution. *Financial support:* Applicants required to submit FAFSA. *Unit head:* Dale Kramer, MBA Program Director, 440-826-3331, Fax: 440-826-3868, E-mail: dkramer@bw.edu. *Application contact:* Laura Spencer, Graduate Application Specialist, 440-826-2191, Fax: 440-826-3868, E-mail: lspencer@bw.edu.
Website: http://www.bw.edu/graduate/business/

Bay Path University, Program in Leadership and Negotiation, Longmeadow, MA 01106-2292. Offers MS. *Program availability:* Part-time, 100% online, blended/hybrid learning. *Students:* 7 full-time (6 women), 24 part-time (19 women); includes 7 minority (5 Black or African American, non-Hispanic/Latino; 2 Hispanic/Latino). Average age 38. *Entrance requirements:* For master's, minimum GPA of 3.0. *Application deadline:* Applications are processed on a rolling basis. Application fee: $45. Electronic applications accepted. Application fee is waived when completed online. *Expenses:* $20,655. *Financial support:* Unspecified assistantships available. Financial award applicants required to submit FAFSA. *Unit head:* Dr. Joshua Weiss, Director, E-mail: joweiss@baypath.edu. *Application contact:* Diane Ranaldi, Dean of Graduate Admissions, 413-565-1332, Fax: 413-565-1250, E-mail: dranaldi@baypath.edu.
Website: http://graduate.baypath.edu/graduate-programs/programs-online/ms-programs/leadership-and-negotiation

Bellarmine University, School of Continuing and Professional Studies, Louisville, KY 40205. Offers analytics (MSA). *Program availability:* Part-time, evening/weekend. *Faculty:* 1 part-time/adjunct (0 women). *Students:* 25 part-time (3 women); includes 4 minority (1 Black or African American, non-Hispanic/Latino; 1 Asian, non-Hispanic/Latino; 2 Hispanic/Latino). Average age 32. *Entrance requirements:* Additional exam requirements/recommendations for international students: Required—TOEFL (minimum score 550 paper-based; 80 iBT). *Application deadline:* Applications are processed on a rolling basis. Application fee: $40. Electronic applications accepted. *Expenses:* Contact institution. *Unit head:* Dr. Sean Ryan, Vice President of Enrollment Management/Dean of the School of Professional and Continuing Studies, 502-272-8376, E-mail: sryan@bellarmine.edu. *Application contact:* Dr. Sara Pettingill, Dean of Graduate Admission, 502-272-8401, E-mail: spettingill@bellarmine.edu.
Website: http://www.bellarmine.edu/ce/

Bentley University, Graduate School of Business, Graduate Business Certificate Program, Waltham, MA 02452-4705. Offers accounting (GBC); business analytics (GBC); business ethics (GBC); financial planning (GBC); fraud and forensic accounting (GBC); marketing analytics (GBC); taxation (GBC). *Accreditation:* AACSB. *Program availability:* Part-time, evening/weekend. *Faculty:* 71 full-time (25 women), 33 part-time/adjunct (15 women). *Students:* 10 part-time (5 women); includes 2 minority (1 Black or African American, non-Hispanic/Latino; 1 Asian, non-Hispanic/Latino). Average age 39. 12 applicants, 92% accepted, 6 enrolled. In 2016, 118 GBCs awarded. *Entrance requirements:* For degree, GMAT or GRE General Test, current resume; two letters of recommendation; official copies of all university-level transcripts. Additional exam requirements/recommendations for international students: Required—TOEFL (minimum score 600 paper-based; 100 iBT), IELTS (minimum score 7), or PTE. *Application deadline:* Applications are processed on a rolling basis. Application fee: $50. Electronic applications accepted. *Expenses:* $4,225 per course, $160 fee per year. *Financial support:* Scholarships/grants available. Financial award application deadline: 6/1;

financial award applicants required to submit FAFSA. *Unit head:* Dr. Roy A. Wiggins, III, Acting Co-Provost, Dean of Business, 781-891-3166. *Application contact:* Sharon Hill, Senior Assistant Director of Graduate Admissions, 781-891-2108, Fax: 781-891-2464, E-mail: bentleygraduateadmissions@bentley.edu.
Website: http://www.bentley.edu/graduate/special-programs

Black Hills State University, Graduate Studies, Program in Strategic Leadership, Spearfish, SD 57799. Offers MS. *Program availability:* Part-time, evening/weekend. *Entrance requirements:* Additional exam requirements/recommendations for international students: Required—TOEFL (minimum score 500 paper-based; 60 iBT).

Boston University, Metropolitan College, Department of Computer Science, Boston, MA 02215. Offers computer information systems (MS), including computer networks, data analytics, database management and business intelligence, health informatics, IT project management, security, Web application development; computer networks (Certificate); computer science (MS); data analytics (Certificate); digital forensics (Certificate); health informatics (Certificate); information technology project management (Certificate); software development (MS); software engineering in health care systems (Certificate); telecommunications (MS), including security. *Program availability:* Part-time, evening/weekend, online learning. *Faculty:* 13 full-time (3 women), 43 part-time/adjunct (3 women). *Students:* 108 full-time (36 women), 1,294 part-time (364 women); includes 428 minority (115 Black or African American, non-Hispanic/Latino; 2 American Indian or Alaska Native, non-Hispanic/Latino; 187 Asian, non-Hispanic/Latino; 98 Hispanic/Latino; 2 Native Hawaiian or other Pacific Islander, non-Hispanic/Latino; 24 Two or more races, non-Hispanic/Latino), 314 international. Average age 33. 463 applicants, 79% accepted, 248 enrolled. In 2016, 311 master's awarded. *Degree requirements:* For master's, thesis optional. *Entrance requirements:* For master's and Certificate, official transcripts from regionally-accredited bachelor's degree program, 3 letters of recommendation, professional resume, personal statement. Additional exam requirements/recommendations for international students: Required—TOEFL (minimum score 84 iBT), IELTS. *Application deadline:* For fall admission, 6/1 priority date for international students; for spring admission, 10/1 priority date for international students. Applications are processed on a rolling basis. Application fee: $85. Electronic applications accepted. *Expenses:* Contact institution. *Financial support:* In 2016–17, 11 research assistantships (averaging $8,400 per year) were awarded; unspecified assistantships also available. Support available to part-time students. Financial award applicants required to submit FAFSA. *Faculty research:* Medical informatics, Web technologies, telecom and networks, security and forensics, software engineering, programming languages, multimedia and artificial intelligence (AI), information systems and IT project management. *Unit head:* Dr. Anatoly Temkin, Chair, 617-353-2566, Fax: 617-353-2367, E-mail: csinfo@bu.edu. *Application contact:* Lesley Moreau, Academic Program Coordinator, 617-353-2566, Fax: 617-353-2367, E-mail: metcs@bu.edu.
Website: http://www.bu.edu/csmet/

Brandeis University, International Business School (IBS), Master of Science in Finance Program, Waltham, MA 02454-9110. Offers asset management (MSF); corporate finance (MSF); risk management (MSF); transfer pricing and valuation (MSF). *Faculty:* 29 full-time (10 women), 27 part-time/adjunct (3 women). *Students:* 74 full-time (40 women); includes 55 minority (2 Black or African American, non-Hispanic/Latino; 49 Asian, non-Hispanic/Latino; 4 Hispanic/Latino). Average age 22. 663 applicants, 29% accepted, 74 enrolled. In 2016, 50 master's awarded. *Entrance requirements:* For master's, GMAT or GRE. Additional exam requirements/recommendations for international students: Required—TOEFL (minimum score 600 paper-based; 100 iBT), IELTS (minimum score 7), PTE (minimum score 68). *Application deadline:* For fall admission, 11/1 priority date for domestic and international students; for winter admission, 1/15 priority date for domestic and international students; for spring admission, 3/15 priority date for domestic and international students; for summer admission, 5/15 for domestic and international students. Application fee: $55. *Expenses:* Contact institution. *Financial support:* Institutionally sponsored loans and scholarships/grants available. Support available to part-time students. Financial award application deadline: 3/15; financial award applicants required to submit FAFSA. *Faculty research:* Asset management, municipal finance, corporate finance, venture capital, international trade. *Unit head:* Peter Petri, Interim Dean, 781-736-2256. *Application contact:* Kelly Sugrue, Director of Admissions, 781-736-2252, Fax: 781-736-2263, E-mail: admission@lemberg.brandeis.edu.
Website: https://www.brandeis.edu/global/msf

Brandeis University, Rabb School of Continuing Studies, Division of Graduate Professional Studies, Master of Science in Strategic Analytics Program, Waltham, MA 02454-9110. Offers MS. *Program availability:* Part-time-only. *Faculty:* 45 part-time/adjunct (16 women). *Students:* 1 full-time (0 women), 62 part-time (29 women); includes 12 minority (2 Black or African American, non-Hispanic/Latino; 9 Asian, non-Hispanic/Latino; 1 Two or more races, non-Hispanic/Latino). Average age 37. 17 applicants, 100% accepted, 16 enrolled. In 2016, 15 master's awarded. *Entrance requirements:* For master's, four-year bachelor's degree from regionally-accredited U.S. institution or equivalent; official transcript(s) from every college or university attended; resume or curriculum vitae; statement of goals; letter of recommendation. Additional exam requirements/recommendations for international students: Required—TWE (minimum score 4.5), TOEFL (minimum scores: 600 paper-based, 100 iBT), IELTS (7), or PTE (68). *Application deadline:* For fall admission, 6/21 priority date for domestic and international students; for winter admission, 9/13 priority date for domestic and international students; for spring admission, 12/20 priority date for domestic and international students; for summer admission, 3/14 priority date for domestic and international students. Applications are processed on a rolling basis. Application fee: $50. Electronic applications accepted. *Expenses:* $3,400 per course, $100 graduation fee. *Financial support:* Applicants required to submit FAFSA. *Unit head:* Stephen Gentile, Chair, 781-736-8787, E-mail: sagentile@brandeis.edu. *Application contact:* Frances Stearns, Director of Admissions and Recruitment, 781-736-8785, E-mail: fstearns@brandeis.edu.
Website: http://www.brandeis.edu/gps/

Bryant University, Graduate School of Business, Smithfield, RI 02917. Offers accounting (MPAC); business administration (MBA), including general management, global finance, global supply chain management, international business; business analytics (Graduate Certificate); taxation (MST). *Program availability:* Part-time, evening/weekend. *Faculty:* 16 full-time (3 women), 2 part-time/adjunct (0 women). *Students:* 71 full-time (23 women), 83 part-time (32 women); includes 17 minority (5 Black or African American, non-Hispanic/Latino; 4 Asian, non-Hispanic/Latino; 5 Hispanic/Latino; 3 Two or more races, non-Hispanic/Latino), 17 international. Average age 27. 165 applicants, 57% accepted, 66 enrolled. In 2016, 106 master's, 12 other advanced degrees awarded. *Degree requirements:* For master's, comprehensive exam (for some programs). *Entrance requirements:* For master's, GMAT, resume, recommendation, college transcripts. Additional exam requirements/recommendations for international students: Required—TOEFL (minimum score 580 paper-based; 95 iBT). *Application deadline:* For fall admission, 7/15 for domestic and international students; for spring admission, 11/15 for domestic and international students; for summer admission, 4/15 for domestic and international students. Applications are processed on a rolling basis. Application fee: $80. Electronic applications accepted. *Expenses:* Contact institution. *Financial support:* Research assistantships, scholarships/grants, and unspecified assistantships available. Support available to part-time students. Financial award application deadline: 2/15; financial award applicants required to submit FAFSA. *Faculty research:* International business, public sector auditing, taxation of partnerships, information systems security, financial markets microstructure. *Unit head:* Bjorn Carlsson, Graduate Program Director, 401-232-6707, E-mail: bcarlsson@bryant.edu. *Application contact:* Terri Rogers, Admissions Assistant, 401-232-6230, Fax: 401-232-6494, E-mail: graduateprograms@bryant.edu.
Website: http://gradschool.bryant.edu/business/

California Miramar University, Program in Strategic Leadership, San Diego, CA 92108. Offers MS. *Degree requirements:* For master's, capstone project.

California State University, East Bay, Office of Graduate Studies, College of Business and Economics, MBA Program, Option in Strategy and International Business, Hayward, CA 94542-3000. Offers MBA. *Program availability:* Part-time, evening/weekend. *Degree requirements:* For master's, comprehensive exam or thesis. *Entrance requirements:* For master's, GMAT, minimum GPA of 2.75. Additional exam requirements/recommendations for international students: Required—TOEFL (minimum score 550 paper-based). *Application deadline:* For fall admission, 6/30 for domestic and international students. Application fee: $55. *Financial support:* Career-related internships or fieldwork, Federal Work-Study, institutionally sponsored loans, and scholarships/grants available. Support available to part-time students. Financial award application deadline: 3/1. *Unit head:* Dr. Yi Jiang-Karnes, Program Advisor, 510-885-3290, E-mail: yi.jiang@csueastbay.edu. *Application contact:* Dr. Donna Wiley, Interim Associate Vice President for Academic Programs and Graduate Studies, 510-885-3716, Fax: 510-885-4777, E-mail: donna.wiley@csueastbay.edu.
Website: http://www.csueastbay.edu/cbe/mba-options/strategy-and-international-business-option.html

California State University, Fullerton, Graduate Studies, College of Business and Economics, Program in Business Administration, Fullerton, CA 92834-9480. Offers business administration (MBA); business analytics (MBA); international business (MBA); organizational leadership (MBA); risk management and insurance (MBA). *Accreditation:* AACSB. *Program availability:* Part-time. *Degree requirements:* For master's, project or thesis. *Entrance requirements:* For master's, GMAT. Application fee: $55. *Expenses:* Tuition, state resident: full-time $3369; part-time $1953 per unit. Tuition, nonresident: full-time $3915; part-time $2499 per unit. Tuition and fees vary according to course load, degree level and program. *Financial support:* Career-related internships or fieldwork, Federal Work-Study, institutionally sponsored loans, and scholarships/grants available. Support available to part-time students. Financial award application deadline: 3/1; financial award applicants required to submit FAFSA. *Unit head:* Shaun Pichler, Director, 657-278-7373, E-mail: spichler@fullerton.edu. *Application contact:* Admissions/Applications, 657-278-2371.

California University of Pennsylvania, School of Graduate Studies and Research, Eberly College of Science and Technology, Program in Business Administration, California, PA 15419-1394. Offers business administration (MBA); business analytics (MBA); entrepreneurship (MBA); nursing administration and leadership (MBA). *Program availability:* Part-time, evening/weekend. *Degree requirements:* For master's, comprehensive exam. *Entrance requirements:* For master's, minimum GPA of 3.0, official transcripts. Additional exam requirements/recommendations for international students: Required—TOEFL (minimum score 550 paper-based). Electronic applications accepted. *Expenses:* Tuition, state resident: full-time $11,592; part-time $483 per credit. Tuition, nonresident: full-time $17,400; part-time $725 per credit. *Required fees:* $3916. Tuition and fees vary according to course load, degree level, campus/location and reciprocity agreements. *Faculty research:* Economics, applied economics, consumer behavior, technology and business, impact of technology.

Capella University, School of Business and Technology, Doctoral Programs in Business, Minneapolis, MN 55402. Offers accounting (DBA, PhD); business intelligence (DBA); finance (DBA, PhD); general business management (PhD); human resource management (DBA, PhD); leadership (DBA, PhD); management education (PhD); marketing (DBA, PhD); project management (DBA, PhD); strategy and innovation (DBA, PhD). *Accreditation:* ACBSP.

Capella University, School of Business and Technology, Master's Programs in Business, Minneapolis, MN 55402. Offers accounting (MBA); business analysis (MS); business intelligence (MBA); entrepreneurship (MBA); finance (MBA); general business administration (MBA); general human resource management (MS); general leadership (MS); health care management (MBA); human resource management (MBA); marketing (MBA); project management (MBA, MS). *Accreditation:* ACBSP.

Claremont Graduate University, Graduate Programs, Peter F. Drucker and Masatoshi Ito Graduate School of Management, Program in Executive Management, Claremont, CA 91711-6160. Offers advanced management (MS); executive management (EMBA); leadership (Certificate); management (MA, PhD, Certificate); strategy (Certificate). *Accreditation:* AACSB. *Program availability:* Part-time. *Students:* 6 full-time (4 women), 36 part-time (18 women); includes 23 minority (4 Black or African American, non-Hispanic/Latino; 4 Asian, non-Hispanic/Latino; 11 Hispanic/Latino; 2 Native Hawaiian or other Pacific Islander, non-Hispanic/Latino; 2 Two or more races, non-Hispanic/Latino), 4 international. Average age 44. In 2016, 16 master's, 26 other advanced degrees awarded. *Entrance requirements:* Additional exam requirements/recommendations for international students: Required—TOEFL (minimum score 75 iBT). *Application deadline:* For fall admission, 2/1 priority date for domestic and international students. Applications are processed on a rolling basis. Application fee: $80. Electronic applications accepted. *Expenses:* Contact institution. *Financial support:* Federal Work-Study, institutionally sponsored loans, and scholarships/grants available. Support available to part-time students. Financial award application deadline: 2/15; financial award applicants required to submit FAFSA. *Faculty research:* Strategy and leadership, brand management, cost management and control, organizational transformation, general management. *Unit head:* Nola Wanta, Senior Director, Management Programs, 909-607-7262, E-mail: nola.wanta@cgu.edu. *Application contact:* John Lee, Assistant Director of Admissions, 909-607-7811, E-mail: john.lee@cgu.edu.
Website: https://www.cgu.edu/academics/program/executive-mba/

Cleary University, Online Program in Business Administration, Howell, MI 48843. Offers analytics, technology, and innovation (MBA, Graduate Certificate); financial planning (Graduate Certificate); global leadership (MBA, Graduate Certificate); health care leadership (MBA, Graduate Certificate). *Program availability:* Part-time, evening/weekend, online learning. *Faculty:* 13 part-time/adjunct (6 women). *Students:* 92 full-time (47 women), 25 part-time (14 women). *Degree requirements:* For master's, thesis. *Entrance requirements:* For master's, bachelor's degree; minimum GPA of 2.5; professional resume indicating minimum of 2 years of management or related experience; undergraduate degree from accredited college or university with at least 18 quarter hours (or 12 semester hours) of accounting study (for MBA in accounting). Additional exam requirements/recommendations for international students: Required—TOEFL (minimum score 550 paper-based; 79 iBT), Michigan English Language Assessment Battery (minimum score 75). *Application deadline:* For fall admission, 8/15 for domestic students, 7/15 for international students; for spring admission, 4/2 for domestic students, 1/2 for international students. Applications are processed on a rolling basis. Application fee: $50. Electronic applications accepted. *Expenses: Tuition:* Full-time $16,560; part-time $920 per credit hour. *Required fees:* $100 per semester. *Financial support:* Fellowships, Federal Work-Study, and scholarships/grants available. Support available to part-time students. Financial award application deadline: 8/15; financial award applicants required to submit FAFSA. *Unit head:* Dr. Lance B. Lewis, Provost and Chief Academic Officer, 800-686-1883, E-mail: llewis@cleary.edu. *Application contact:* Cassandra Tarnowski, Director of Admissions, 800-686-1883, Fax: 517-338-3336, E-mail: ctarnowski@cleary.edu.

Clemson University, Graduate School, College of Business, Master of Business Administration Program, Greenville, SC 29601. Offers business administration (MBA); business analytics (MBA); entrepreneurship and innovation (MBA). *Accreditation:* AACSB. *Program availability:* Part-time, evening/weekend. *Faculty:* 3 full-time (1 woman), 9 part-time/adjunct (1 woman). *Students:* 146 full-time (57 women), 322 part-time (102 women); includes 81 minority (46 Black or African American, non-Hispanic/Latino; 13 Asian, non-Hispanic/Latino; 17 Hispanic/Latino; 1 Native Hawaiian or other Pacific Islander, non-Hispanic/Latino; 4 Two or more races, non-Hispanic/Latino), 35 international. Average age 31. 226 applicants, 63% accepted, 115 enrolled. In 2016, 165 master's awarded. *Entrance requirements:* For master's, GMAT, resume, unofficial transcripts, personal statement, letters of recommendation. Additional exam requirements/recommendations for international students: Required—TOEFL (minimum score 80 iBT), IELTS (minimum score 6.5). *Application deadline:* For fall admission, 7/15 for domestic students, 4/15 for international students; for spring admission, 12/1 for domestic students. Applications are processed on a rolling basis. Application fee: $80 ($90 for international students). Electronic applications accepted. *Expenses:* $9,761 per semester resident, $15,764 per semester non-resident. *Financial support:* In 2016–17, 38 students received support, including 1 research assistantship with partial tuition reimbursement available (averaging $18,000 per year); unspecified assistantships also available. Financial award application deadline: 7/15. *Unit head:* Dr. Gregory Pickett, Senior Associate Dean, 864-656-3975, Fax: 864-370-8061, E-mail: pgregor@clemson.edu. *Application contact:* Kristin Allen, Director of Admissions, 864-656-8173, Fax: 864-370-8061, E-mail: klallen@clemson.edu.
Website: https://www.clemson.edu/business/departments/mba/

The College of Saint Rose, Graduate Studies, Huether School of Business, Albany, NY 12203-1419. Offers accounting (MS); business administration (MBA); financial planning (Advanced Certificate); organizational leadership and change management (Advanced Certificate); JD/MBA. *Program availability:* Part-time, evening/weekend. *Faculty:* 11 full-time (5 women), 6 part-time/adjunct (2 women). *Students:* 70 full-time (37 women), 67 part-time (29 women); includes 24 minority (17 Black or African American, non-Hispanic/Latino; 1 Asian, non-Hispanic/Latino; 5 Hispanic/Latino; 1 Two or more races, non-Hispanic/Latino), 20 international. Average age 28. 117 applicants, 76% accepted, 33 enrolled. In 2016, 67 master's, 15 other advanced degrees awarded. *Degree requirements:* For master's, comprehensive exam (for some programs), thesis (for some programs); for Advanced Certificate, comprehensive exam (for some programs). *Entrance requirements:* For master's, GMAT, graduate degree, or minimum undergraduate GPA of 3.0. Additional exam requirements/recommendations for international students: Required—TOEFL (minimum score 550 paper-based; 80 iBT), IELTS (minimum score 6), PTE (minimum score 56). *Application deadline:* For fall admission, 4/1 priority date for domestic and international students; for spring admission, 10/15 priority date for domestic and international students; for summer admission, 3/15 priority date for domestic and international students. Applications are processed on a rolling basis. Application fee: $40. Electronic applications accepted. *Expenses: Tuition:* Full-time $14,382; part-time $799 per credit. *Required fees:* $814; $32 per credit. $88 per semester. Tuition and fees vary according to course load. *Financial support:* Career-related internships or fieldwork, scholarships/grants, tuition waivers (partial), and unspecified assistantships available. Support available to part-time students. Financial award application deadline: 4/15. *Faculty research:* Corporate governance, algorithmic trading, organizational attitude, managers having fun. *Unit head:* Gretchen Guenther-Collins, Interim Dean, 518-454-2122, E-mail: guentheg@strose.edu. *Application contact:* Cris Murray, Assistant Vice President for Graduate Recruitment and Enrollment, 518-485-3390, Fax: 518-458-5479, E-mail: grad@strose.edu.
Website: https://www.strose.edu/academics/schools/school-of-business/

Dakota State University, College of Business and Information Systems, Madison, SD 57042-1799. Offers analytics (MSA); applied computer science (MSACS); banking security (Graduate Certificate); business analytics (Graduate Certificate); cyber security (D Sc); ethical hacking (Graduate Certificate); general management (MBA); health informatics (MSHI); information assurance and computer security (MSIA); information systems (MSIS, D Sc IS); information technology (Graduate Certificate). *Accreditation:* ACBSP. *Program availability:* Part-time, evening/weekend, 100% online, blended/hybrid learning. *Degree requirements:* For master's, comprehensive exam, thesis optional, examination, integrative project; for doctorate, comprehensive exam, thesis/dissertation, portfolio. *Entrance requirements:* For master's, GRE General Test, demonstration of information systems skills, minimum GPA of 2.7; for doctorate, GRE General Test, demonstration of information systems skills; for Graduate Certificate, GMAT. Additional exam requirements/recommendations for international students: Required—PTE (minimum score 53), TOEFL (minimum score 550 paper-based, 79 iBT) or IELTS (6.5). *Application deadline:* For fall admission, 6/15 for domestic students, 4/15 for international students; for spring admission, 11/15 for domestic students, 9/15 priority date for international students; for summer admission, 4/15 for domestic and international students. Applications are processed on a rolling basis. Application fee: $35. *Expenses:* Contact institution. *Financial support:* Fellowships with partial tuition reimbursements, research assistantships with partial tuition reimbursements, teaching assistantships with partial tuition reimbursements, career-related internships or fieldwork, Federal Work-Study, scholarships/grants, and unspecified assistantships available. Support available to part-time students. Financial award applicants required to submit FAFSA. *Faculty research:* Data mining and analytics, biometrics and information assurance, decision support systems, health informatics, STEM education for K-12 teachers/students and underrepresented populations. *Unit head:* Mark Hawkes, Dean for Graduate Studies and Research, 605-256-5274, E-mail: mark.hawkes@dsu.edu. *Application contact:* Erin Blankespoor, Senior Secretary, Office of Graduate Studies and Research, 605-256-5799, E-mail: erin.blankespoor@dsu.edu.
Website: http://dsu.edu/academics/colleges/college-of-business-and-information-systems

Davenport University, Sneden Graduate School, Grand Rapids, MI 49512. Offers accounting (MBA); business administration (EMBA); finance (MBA); health care management (MBA); human resources (MBA); information assurance (MS); public health (MPH); strategic management (MBA). *Program availability:* Evening/weekend. *Entrance requirements:* For master's, GMAT, minimum undergraduate GPA of 2.75. Additional exam requirements/recommendations for international students: Required—TOEFL. Electronic applications accepted. *Faculty research:* Leadership, management, marketing, organizational culture.

Defiance College, Program in Business Administration, Defiance, OH 43512-1610. Offers leadership (MBA). *Program availability:* Part-time, evening/weekend. *Degree requirements:* For master's, thesis. *Entrance requirements:* For master's, minimum GPA of 2.5. Additional exam requirements/recommendations for international students: Recommended—TOEFL. *Application deadline:* For fall admission, 8/1 for domestic and international students. Applications are processed on a rolling basis. Application fee: $25. Electronic applications accepted. *Expenses: Tuition:* Part-time $524 per credit hour. *Required fees:* $188 per semester. *Unit head:* Dr. Arif Sultan, Assistant Professor, 419-783-2431, Fax: 419-784-0426, E-mail: asultan@defiance.edu.
Website: http://www.defiance.edu/graduate-programs/mba-home.html

DePaul University, Kellstadt Graduate School of Business, Chicago, IL 60604. Offers accountancy (M Acc, MS, MSA); applied economics (MBA); banking (MBA); behavioral finance (MBA); brand and product management (MBA); business development (MBA); business information technology (MS); business strategy and decision-making (MBA); computational finance (MS); consumer insights (MBA); corporate finance (MBA); economic policy analysis (MS); entrepreneurship (MBA, MS); finance (MBA, MS); financial analysis (MBA); general business (MBA); health sector management (MBA); hospitality leadership (MBA); hospitality leadership and operational performance (MS); human resource management (MBA); human resources (MS); investment management (MBA); leadership and change management (MBA); management accounting (MBA); marketing (MBA, MS); marketing analysis (MS); marketing strategy and planning (MBA); operations management (MBA); organizational diversity (MBA); real estate (MS); real estate finance and investment (MBA); revenue management (MBA); sports management (MBA); strategic global marketing (MBA); strategy, execution and valuation (MBA); sustainable management (MBA, MS); taxation (MS); wealth management (MS); JD/MBA. *Accreditation:* AACSB. *Program availability:* Part-time, evening/weekend, online learning. *Entrance requirements:* For master's, GMAT, 2 letters of recommendation, resume, essay, official transcripts. Additional exam requirements/recommendations for international students: Required—TOEFL (minimum score 550 paper-based; 80 iBT). Electronic applications accepted. *Expenses:* Contact institution.

Dominican University of California, Barowsky School of Business, San Rafael, CA 94901-2298. Offers global business (MBA); strategic leadership (MBA); sustainable enterprise (MBA). *Program availability:* Part-time, evening/weekend. *Degree requirements:* For master's, thesis, capstone (for MBA). *Entrance requirements:* For master's, minimum GPA of 3.0. Additional exam requirements/recommendations for international students: Required—TOEFL (minimum score 550 paper-based; 80 iBT), IELTS (minimum score 6.5). Electronic applications accepted. Application fee is waived when completed online. *Expenses:* Contact institution.

Drexel University, LeBow College of Business, Program in Business Administration, Philadelphia, PA 19104-2875. Offers business administration (MBA, PhD, APC), including accounting (MBA, PhD), decision sciences (PhD), economics (MBA, PhD), finance (MBA, PhD), legal studies (MBA), management (MBA), marketing (MBA, PhD), organizational sciences (PhD), quantitative methods (MBA), strategic management (PhD). *Accreditation:* AACSB. *Program availability:* Part-time, evening/weekend, online learning. *Faculty:* 88 full-time (19 women), 11 part-time/adjunct (2 women). *Students:* 153 full-time (70 women), 388 part-time (168 women); includes 107 minority (31 Black or African American, non-Hispanic/Latino; 1 American Indian or Alaska Native, non-Hispanic/Latino; 48 Asian, non-Hispanic/Latino; 16 Hispanic/Latino; 11 Two or more races, non-Hispanic/Latino), 95 international. Average age 33. In 2016, 174 master's, 8 doctorates, 1 other advanced degree awarded. Terminal master's awarded for partial completion of doctoral program. *Entrance requirements:* For master's, GMAT, minimum GPA of 2.75; for doctorate, GMAT. Additional exam requirements/recommendations for international students: Required—TOEFL. *Application deadline:* For fall admission, 8/21 for domestic students; for spring admission, 3/5 for domestic students. Applications are processed on a rolling basis. Application fee: $50. Electronic applications accepted. *Expenses: Tuition:* Full-time $32,184; part-time $1192 per credit hour. *Required fees:* $280. Tuition and fees vary according to campus/location and program. *Financial support:* Research assistantships, teaching assistantships, career-related internships or fieldwork, and unspecified assistantships available. Financial award application deadline: 2/1. *Faculty research:* Decision support systems, individual and group behavior, operations research, techniques and strategy. *Unit head:* Dr. Thomas Wieckowski, Director of Master's Programs in Business, 215-895-1791, Fax: 215-895-1012. *Application contact:* Director of Graduate Admissions, 215-895-6700, Fax: 215-895-5939, E-mail: enroll@drexel.edu.

Duke University, The Fuqua School of Business, The Duke MBA-Cross Continent Program, Durham, NC 27708-0586. Offers business administration (MBA); energy and environment (MBA); entrepreneurship and innovation (MBA); finance (MBA); health sector management (Certificate); marketing (MBA); strategy (MBA). *Faculty:* 88 full-time (19 women), 50 part-time/adjunct (9 women). *Students:* 214 full-time (74 women); includes 58 minority (13 Black or African American, non-Hispanic/Latino; 35 Asian, non-Hispanic/Latino; 10 Hispanic/Latino), 35 international. Average age 30. In 2016, 105 master's awarded. *Entrance requirements:* For master's, GMAT or GRE, transcripts, essays, resume, recommendation letters, letter of company support, interview. *Application deadline:* For fall admission, 10/12 priority date for domestic and international students; for winter admission, 2/7 priority date for domestic and international students; for spring admission, 5/3 priority date for domestic and international students; for summer admission, 5/31 for domestic and international students. Applications are processed on a rolling basis. Application fee: $225. Electronic applications accepted. *Expenses:* Contact institution. *Financial support:* In 2016–17, 49 students received support. Institutionally sponsored loans and scholarships/grants available. Financial award applicants required to submit FAFSA. *Unit head:* Mohan Venkatachalam, Senior Associate Dean, Executive Programs, 919-660-7859, E-mail: mohan.venkatachalam@duke.edu. *Application contact:* Sharon Thompson, Assistant Dean, Office of Admissions, 919-660-7705, Fax: 919-681-8026, E-mail: admissions-info@fuqua.duke.edu.
Website: http://www.fuqua.duke.edu/programs/duke_mba/cross_continent/

Duke University, The Fuqua School of Business, The Duke MBA-Daytime Program, Durham, NC 27708-0586. Offers academic excellence in finance (Certificate); business administration (MBA); decision sciences (MBA); energy and environment (MBA); energy finance (MBA); entrepreneurship and innovation (MBA); finance (MBA); financial analysis (MBA); health sector management (Certificate); leadership and ethics (MBA); management (MBA); marketing (MBA); operations management (MBA); social entrepreneurship (MBA); strategy (MBA). *Faculty:* 88 full-time (19 women), 50 part-time/adjunct (9 women). *Students:* 897 full-time (310 women); includes 174 minority (39 Black or African American, non-Hispanic/Latino; 3 American Indian or Alaska Native, non-Hispanic/Latino; 75 Asian, non-Hispanic/Latino; 51 Hispanic/Latino; 1 Native Hawaiian or other Pacific Islander, non-Hispanic/Latino; 5 Two or more races, non-Hispanic/Latino), 343 international. Average age 28. In 2016, 440 master's awarded. *Entrance requirements:* For master's, GMAT or GRE, transcripts, essays, resume, recommendation letters, interview. *Application deadline:* For fall admission, 9/13 for domestic and international students; for winter admission, 10/13 for domestic and international students; for spring admission, 1/4 for domestic and international students;

for summer admission, 3/20 for domestic and international students. Application fee: $225. Electronic applications accepted. *Expenses:* $66,717 (first-year tuition and fees). *Financial support:* In 2016–17, 415 students received support. Institutionally sponsored loans and scholarships/grants available. Financial award applicants required to submit FAFSA. *Unit head:* Russ Morgan, Senior Associate Dean for Full-time Programs, 919-660-2931, Fax: 919-684-8742, E-mail: ruskin.morgan@duke.edu. *Application contact:* Sharon Thompson, Assistant Dean, Office of Admissions, 919-660-7705, Fax: 919-681-8026, E-mail: admissions-info@fuqua.duke.edu.
Website: http://www.fuqua.duke.edu/daytime-mba/

Duke University, The Fuqua School of Business, The Duke MBA-Global Executive Program, Durham, NC 27708-0586. Offers business administration (MBA); energy and environment (MBA); entrepreneurship and innovation (MBA); finance (MBA); health sector management (Certificate); marketing (MBA); strategy (MBA). *Faculty:* 88 full-time (19 women), 50 part-time/adjunct (9 women). *Students:* 48 full-time (14 women); includes 18 minority (3 Black or African American, non-Hispanic/Latino; 11 Asian, non-Hispanic/Latino; 4 Hispanic/Latino), 10 international. Average age 39. In 2016, 27 master's awarded. *Entrance requirements:* For master's, transcripts, essays, resume, recommendation letters, letter of company support, interview. *Application deadline:* For fall admission, 10/12 priority date for domestic and international students; for winter admission, 12/7 priority date for domestic and international students; for spring admission, 3/20 priority date for domestic and international students; for summer admission, 5/31 for domestic and international students. Applications are processed on a rolling basis. Application fee: $225. Electronic applications accepted. *Expenses:* Contact institution. *Financial support:* In 2016–17, 22 students received support. Institutionally sponsored loans and scholarships/grants available. Financial award applicants required to submit FAFSA. *Unit head:* Mohan Venkatachalam, Senior Associate Dean, Executive Programs, 919-660-7859, E-mail: mohan.venkatachalam@duke.edu. *Application contact:* Sharon Thompson, Assistant Dean, Office of Admissions, 919-660-7705, Fax: 919-681-8026, E-mail: admissions-info@fuqua.duke.edu.
Website: http://www.fuqua.duke.edu/programs/duke_mba/global-executive/

Duke University, The Fuqua School of Business, The Duke MBA-Weekend Executive Program, Durham, NC 27708-0586. Offers business administration (MBA); energy and environment (MBA); entrepreneurship and innovation (MBA); finance (MBA); health sector management (Certificate); marketing (MBA); strategy (MBA). *Faculty:* 88 full-time (19 women), 50 part-time/adjunct (9 women). *Students:* 190 full-time (43 women); includes 75 minority (11 Black or African American, non-Hispanic/Latino; 3 American Indian or Alaska Native, non-Hispanic/Latino; 48 Asian, non-Hispanic/Latino; 12 Hispanic/Latino; 1 Two or more races, non-Hispanic/Latino), 26 international. Average age 35. In 2016, 87 master's awarded. *Entrance requirements:* For master's, GMAT or GRE, transcripts, essays, resume, recommendation letters, letter of company support, interview. *Application deadline:* For fall admission, 8/30 priority date for domestic and international students; for winter admission, 10/12 priority date for domestic and international students; for spring admission, 2/7 priority date for domestic and international students; for summer admission, 3/20 for domestic and international students. Applications are processed on a rolling basis. Application fee: $225. Electronic applications accepted. *Expenses:* Contact institution. *Financial support:* In 2016–17, 33 students received support. Institutionally sponsored loans and scholarships/grants available. Financial award applicants required to submit FAFSA. *Unit head:* Mohan Venkatachalam, Senior Associate Dean, Executive Programs, 919-660-7859, E-mail: mohan.venkatachalam@duke.edu. *Application contact:* Sharon Thompson, Assistant Dean, Office of Admissions, 919-660-7705, Fax: 919-681-8026, E-mail: admissions-info@fuqua.duke.edu.
Website: http://www.fuqua.duke.edu/programs/duke_mba/weekend_executive/

Duke University, The Fuqua School of Business, Master of Quantitative Management Program, Durham, NC 27708-0586. Offers finance (MQM); forensics (MQM); marketing (MQM); strategy (MQM). *Entrance requirements:* For master's, GMAT/GRE, transcripts, essays, resume, recommendation letters. *Application deadline:* For fall admission, 9/21 for domestic and international students; for winter admission, 11/20 for domestic and international students; for spring admission, 2/16 for domestic and international students; for summer admission, 4/4 for domestic and international students. Application fee: $125. Electronic applications accepted. *Unit head:* Jeremy Petranka, Associate Dean, E-mail: jeremy.petranka@duke.edu. *Application contact:* Sharon Thompson, Assistant Dean, Office of Admissions, 919-660-7705, Fax: 919-681-8026, E-mail: admissions-info@fuqua.duke.edu.
Website: http://www.fuqua.duke.edu/master-quantitative-management/

Duke University, The Fuqua School of Business, PhD Program, Durham, NC 27708-0586. Offers accounting (PhD); decision sciences (PhD); finance (PhD); management and organizations (PhD); marketing (PhD); operations management (PhD); strategy (PhD). *Faculty:* 100 full-time (19 women). *Students:* 77 full-time (27 women); includes 9 minority (1 Black or African American, non-Hispanic/Latino; 7 Asian, non-Hispanic/Latino; 1 Hispanic/Latino), 46 international. 561 applicants, 7% accepted, 14 enrolled. In 2016, 15 doctorates awarded. *Degree requirements:* For doctorate, thesis/dissertation, major field requirement (exam or major paper, depending upon the area). *Entrance requirements:* For doctorate, GMAT or GRE, transcripts, essays, recommendation letters, statement of purpose. Additional exam requirements/recommendations for international students: Required—TOEFL (minimum score 577 paper-based; 90 iBT), IELTS (minimum score 7). *Application deadline:* For fall admission, 12/31 priority date for domestic and international students. Application fee: $85. Electronic applications accepted. *Expenses:* Contact institution. *Financial support:* In 2016–17, 77 students received support, including 70 fellowships with full tuition reimbursements available (averaging $28,200 per year), 63 research assistantships with full tuition reimbursements available (averaging $7,000 per year); institutionally sponsored loans, scholarships/grants, and tuition waivers (full) also available. Financial award applicants required to submit FAFSA. *Unit head:* William Boulding, Dean, 919-660-7822, Fax: 919-684-8742, E-mail: bb1@duke.edu. *Application contact:* Qi Chen, Director of Graduate Studies, 919-660-7753, Fax: 919-660-7971, E-mail: qc2@duke.edu.

Embry-Riddle Aeronautical University–Worldwide, Department of Technology Management, Daytona Beach, FL 32114-3900. Offers information security and assurance (MS), including information assurance in a global context, information systems security, protecting business intelligence; management information systems (MS), including business intelligence siness and analytics, information security and assurance, information systems project management. *Program availability:* Part-time, evening/weekend, 100% online, blended/hybrid learning, EagleVision is a virtual classroom that combines Web video conferencing and a learning management system. EagleVision Classroom (between classrooms), EagleVision Home (faculty and students at home), and a blend of Classroom or Home. *Entrance requirements:* Additional exam requirements/recommendations for international students: Required—TOEFL (minimum score 550 paper-based; 79 iBT), IELTS (minimum score 6), TOEFL or IELTS accepted. Electronic applications accepted. *Expenses:* Contact institution.

Fairfield University, Dolan School of Business, Fairfield, CT 06824. Offers accounting (MBA, MS, CAS); business analytics (MS); entrepreneurship (MBA); finance (MBA, MS, CAS); general management (MBA, CAS); global management (MBA); human resource management (MBA, CAS); information systems and business analytics (MBA); marketing (MBA, CAS); taxation (MBA, CAS). *Accreditation:* AACSB. *Program availability:* Part-time, evening/weekend. *Faculty:* 20 full-time (6 women), 4 part-time/adjunct (1 woman). *Students:* 106 full-time (41 women), 57 part-time (26 women); includes 18 minority (4 Black or African American, non-Hispanic/Latino; 1 American Indian or Alaska Native, non-Hispanic/Latino; 4 Asian, non-Hispanic/Latino; 7 Hispanic/Latino; 2 Two or more races, non-Hispanic/Latino), 39 international. Average age 26. 136 applicants, 63% accepted, 35 enrolled. In 2016, 90 master's awarded. *Degree requirements:* For master's, capstone course. *Entrance requirements:* For master's, GMAT (minimum score 500), 2 letters of reference, resume, minimum GPA of 3.0. Additional exam requirements/recommendations for international students: Required—TOEFL (minimum score 550 paper-based; 80 iBT) or IELTS (minimum score 6.5). *Application deadline:* For fall admission, 5/15 for international students; for spring admission, 10/15 for international students. Applications are processed on a rolling basis. Application fee: $60. Electronic applications accepted. *Expenses:* $875 per credit hour. *Financial support:* In 2016–17, 33 students received support. Scholarships/grants and unspecified assistantships available. Financial award applicants required to submit FAFSA. *Faculty research:* International finance, leadership and careers, ethics in accounting, emotions in consumer behavior and organizations, data analytics. *Unit head:* Dr. Donald Gibson, Dean, 203-254-4070, Fax: 203-254-4105, E-mail: dgibson@fairfield.edu. *Application contact:* Marianne Gumpper, Director of Graduate and Continuing Studies Admission, 203-254-4184, Fax: 203-254-4073, E-mail: gradadmis@fairfield.edu.
Website: http://fairfield.edu/mba

Fisher College, Master of Business Administration Program, Boston, MA 02116-1500. Offers strategic leadership (MBA). *Program availability:* Part-time, evening/weekend, online only, 100% online. *Faculty:* 3 full-time (1 woman), 10 part-time/adjunct (4 women). *Students:* 16 full-time (6 women), 18 part-time (11 women); includes 11 minority (1 Black or African American, non-Hispanic/Latino; 1 American Indian or Alaska Native, non-Hispanic/Latino; 1 Asian, non-Hispanic/Latino; 8 Hispanic/Latino), 5 international. Average age 33. 174 applicants, 17% accepted, 18 enrolled. In 2016, 6 master's awarded. *Degree requirements:* For master's, comprehensive exam. *Entrance requirements:* Additional exam requirements/recommendations for international students: Required—TOEFL (minimum score 80 iBT), IELTS (minimum score 6.5). *Application deadline:* For fall admission, 8/1 for domestic and international students; for winter admission, 11/1 for domestic and international students. Applications are processed on a rolling basis. Electronic applications accepted. *Expenses:* Contact institution. *Financial support:* In 2016–17, 5 students received support. Scholarships/grants and unspecified assistantships available. Financial award applicants required to submit FAFSA. *Faculty research:* Humanistic management, the role of human resources in employee engagement. *Unit head:* Neil Trotta, Dean, 617-236-8867, Fax: 617-236-5462, E-mail: ntrotta@fisher.edu.
Website: http://www.fisher.edu/mba

Florida State University, The Graduate School, College of Business, Tallahassee, FL 32306-1110. Offers accounting (M Acc), including assurance and advisory services, generalist, taxation; business administration (MBA, PhD), including accounting (PhD), finance (PhD), management information systems (PhD), marketing (PhD), organizational behavior and human resources (PhD), risk management and insurance (PhD), strategy (PhD); finance (MS); management information systems (MS); risk management and insurance (MS); JD/MBA; MSW/MBA. *Accreditation:* AACSB. *Program availability:* Part-time, 100% online. *Faculty:* 101 full-time (27 women), 4 part-time/adjunct (2 women). *Students:* 272 full-time (127 women), 351 part-time (133 women); includes 141 minority (45 Black or African American, non-Hispanic/Latino; 2 American Indian or Alaska Native, non-Hispanic/Latino; 20 Asian, non-Hispanic/Latino; 59 Hispanic/Latino; 2 Native Hawaiian or other Pacific Islander, non-Hispanic/Latino; 13 Two or more races, non-Hispanic/Latino), 71 international. Average age 30. 688 applicants, 60% accepted, 273 enrolled. In 2016, 231 master's, 12 doctorates awarded. Terminal master's awarded for partial completion of doctoral program. *Degree requirements:* For doctorate, comprehensive exam, thesis/dissertation. *Entrance requirements:* For master's, GMAT, GRE (for all except MS in finance), work experience (MBA, MS); minimum GPA of 3.0, letters of recommendation; for doctorate, GMAT, GRE (for marketing, organizational behavior, risk management and insurance, management information systems, and human resources only), minimum graduate GPA of 3.5, letters of recommendation. Additional exam requirements/recommendations for international students: Required—TOEFL (minimum score 600 paper-based; 85 iBT); Recommended—IELTS (minimum score 6). *Application deadline:* For fall admission, 6/1 for domestic and international students; for spring admission, 10/1 for domestic and international students; for summer admission, 3/1 for domestic and international students. Applications are processed on a rolling basis. Application fee: $30. Electronic applications accepted. *Expenses:* Contact institution. *Financial support:* In 2016–17, 149 students received support, including 9 fellowships (averaging $1,500 per year), 65 research assistantships with full tuition reimbursements available (averaging $20,000 per year), 75 teaching assistantships with full tuition reimbursements available (averaging $20,000 per year); career-related internships or fieldwork, scholarships/grants, health care benefits, tuition waivers (full and partial), and unspecified assistantships also available. Support available to part-time students. Financial award application deadline: 1/1; financial award applicants required to submit FAFSA. *Faculty research:* Business strategy, marketing, finance, accounting, business analytics. *Total annual research expenditures:* $1.4 million. *Unit head:* Dr. Michael Hartline, Dean, 850-644-4405, Fax: 850-644-0915, E-mail: mhartline@business.fsu.edu. *Application contact:* Jennifer Clark, Director, 850-644-6458, E-mail: gradprograms@business.fsu.edu.
Website: http://business.fsu.edu/

Fordham University, Gabelli School of Business, New York, NY 10023. Offers accounting (MBA, MS); applied statistics and decision-making (MS); business administration (EMBA); business analytics (MS); communications and media management (MBA); electronic business (MBA); entrepreneurship (MBA); finance (MBA); global finance (MS); global sustainability (MBA); healthcare management (MBA); information systems (MBA, MS); investor relations (MS); management (MBA, MS); marketing (MBA); marketing intelligence (MS); media management (MS); nonprofit leadership (MS); quantitative finance (MS); taxation (MS); JD/MBA; MS/MBA. *Accreditation:* AACSB. *Program availability:* Part-time, evening/weekend. *Faculty:* 132 full-time (44 women), 51 part-time/adjunct (7 women). *Students:* 1,117 full-time (668 women), 553 part-time (282 women); includes 207 minority (44 Black or African American, non-Hispanic/Latino; 92 Asian, non-Hispanic/Latino; 69 Hispanic/Latino; 2 Native Hawaiian or other Pacific Islander, non-Hispanic/Latino), 1,088 international. Average age 27. 4,745 applicants, 46% accepted, 752 enrolled. In 2016, 996 master's awarded. Terminal master's awarded for partial completion of doctoral program. *Degree requirements:* For master's, internships (required for MS in quantitative finance, recommended for MBA). *Entrance requirements:* For master's, GMAT/GRE, 2 letters of recommendation, resume, 2 essays, transcripts. Additional exam requirements/recommendations for international students: Required—TOEFL (minimum score 100 iBT), IELTS (minimum score 7). *Application deadline:* For fall admission, 11/15 priority date for domestic and international students; for winter admission, 1/15 priority date for domestic students, 1/1 priority date for international students; for spring admission, 3/1

for domestic and international students; for summer admission, 6/1 for domestic students. Application fee: $130. Electronic applications accepted. *Expenses:* $1,397 per credit. *Financial support:* In 2016–17, 78 students received support. Career-related internships or fieldwork, institutionally sponsored loans, scholarships/grants, and unspecified assistantships available. Support available to part-time students. Financial award application deadline: 6/30; financial award applicants required to submit FAFSA. *Unit head:* Dr. Donna Rapaccioli, Dean, 212-636-6165, Fax: 212-307-1779, E-mail: rapaccioli@fordham.edu. *Application contact:* Lawrence Murray, Senior Assistant Dean of Graduate Admissions and Advising, 212-636-6200, Fax: 212-636-7076, E-mail: admissionsgb@fordham.edu.
Website: http://www.fordham.edu/gabelli

Freed-Hardeman University, Program in Business Administration, Henderson, TN 38340-2399. Offers accounting (MBA); corporate responsibility (MBA); leadership (MBA). *Accreditation:* ACBSP. *Program availability:* Part-time, evening/weekend, online learning. *Entrance requirements:* For master's, GMAT. Additional exam requirements/recommendations for international students: Required—TOEFL (minimum score 500 paper-based).

Friends University, Graduate School, Wichita, KS 67213. Offers family therapy (MSFT); global business administration (MBA), including accounting, business law, change management, health care leadership, management information systems, supply chain management and logistics; health care leadership (MHCL); management information systems (MMIS); professional business administration (MBA), including accounting, business law, change management, health care leadership, management information systems, supply chain management and logistics. *Program availability:* Part-time, evening/weekend, online learning. *Degree requirements:* For master's, research project. *Entrance requirements:* For master's, bachelor's degree from accredited institution, official transcripts, interview with program director, letter(s) of recommendation. Additional exam requirements/recommendations for international students: Required—TOEFL (minimum score 560 paper-based). Electronic applications accepted.

The George Washington University, School of Business, Department of Decision Sciences, Washington, DC 20052. Offers business analytics (MS, Certificate); project management (MS). *Program availability:* Online learning. *Faculty:* 18 full-time (1 woman), 1 part-time/adjunct (0 women). *Students:* 71 full-time (41 women), 125 part-time (53 women); includes 64 minority (30 Black or African American, non-Hispanic/Latino; 19 Asian, non-Hispanic/Latino; 6 Hispanic/Latino; 9 Two or more races, non-Hispanic/Latino), 70 international. Average age 36. 366 applicants, 59% accepted, 73 enrolled. In 2016, 93 master's awarded. Application fee: $75. *Financial support:* Tuition waivers available. *Unit head:* Prof. Refik Soyer, Chair, 202-994-6445, E-mail: soyer@gwu.edu. *Application contact:* Christopher Storer, Executive Director, Graduate Admissions, 202-994-1212, E-mail: gwmba@gwu.edu.
Website: http://business.gwu.edu/decisionsciences/

The George Washington University, School of Business, Department of Strategic Management and Public Policy, Washington, DC 20052. Offers MBA, PhD. *Accreditation:* NASPAA. *Program availability:* Part-time, evening/weekend. *Faculty:* 13 full-time (4 women). *Students:* 178 full-time (71 women), 1 (woman) part-time; includes 34 minority (8 Black or African American, non-Hispanic/Latino; 1 American Indian or Alaska Native, non-Hispanic/Latino; 11 Asian, non-Hispanic/Latino; 9 Hispanic/Latino; 5 Two or more races, non-Hispanic/Latino), 86 international. Average age 29. 522 applicants, 51% accepted, 89 enrolled. In 2016, 93 master's awarded. *Degree requirements:* For doctorate, thesis/dissertation. *Entrance requirements:* For master's, GMAT; for doctorate, GMAT or GRE. Additional exam requirements/recommendations for international students: Required—TOEFL. *Application deadline:* For fall admission, 4/1 priority date for domestic students; for spring admission, 10/1 for domestic students. Applications are processed on a rolling basis. Application fee: $75. *Financial support:* In 2016–17, 1 student received support. Fellowships, teaching assistantships, career-related internships or fieldwork, Federal Work-Study, and institutionally sponsored loans available. Financial award application deadline: 4/1. *Unit head:* Dr. Jennifer Griffin, Chair, 202-994-2536, E-mail: jgriffin@gwu.edu. *Application contact:* Christopher Storer, Executive Director, Graduate Admissions, 202-994-1212, E-mail: gwmba@gwu.edu.
Website: http://business.gwu.edu/smpp/

Georgia State University, J. Mack Robinson College of Business, Department of Managerial Sciences, Atlanta, GA 30302-3083. Offers business analysis (MBA, MS); entrepreneurship (MBA); human resources management (MBA, MS); operations management (MBA, MS); organization behavior/human resource management (PhD); organization management (MBA); organizational change (MS); strategic management (PhD). *Accreditation:* AACSB. *Program availability:* Part-time, evening/weekend. *Faculty:* 25 full-time (11 women). *Students:* 30 full-time (20 women), 10 part-time (4 women); includes 14 minority (11 Black or African American, non-Hispanic/Latino; 1 Asian, non-Hispanic/Latino; 1 Hispanic/Latino; 1 Two or more races, non-Hispanic/Latino), 12 international. Average age 31. 79 applicants, 30% accepted, 13 enrolled. In 2016, 23 master's, 2 doctorates awarded. *Degree requirements:* For doctorate, comprehensive exam, thesis/dissertation. *Entrance requirements:* For master's, GRE or GMAT, transcripts from all institutions attended, resume, essays; for doctorate, GMAT, three letters of recommendation, personal statement, transcripts from all institutions attended, resume. Additional exam requirements/recommendations for international students: Required—TOEFL (minimum score 610 paper-based; 101 iBT), IELTS (minimum score 7). *Application deadline:* For fall admission, 5/1 priority date for domestic students, 2/1 priority date for international students; for spring admission, 9/15 priority date for domestic students, 4/1 priority date for international students. Applications are processed on a rolling basis. Application fee: $50. Electronic applications accepted. *Expenses:* Tuition, state resident: full-time $6876; part-time $382 per credit hour. Tuition, nonresident: full-time $22,374; part-time $1243 per credit hour. *Required fees:* $2128; $1064 per term. Part-time tuition and fees vary according to course load and program. *Financial support:* Research assistantships, teaching assistantships, scholarships/grants, tuition waivers, and unspecified assistantships available. Financial award applicants required to submit FAFSA. *Faculty research:* Entrepreneurship and innovation; strategy process; workplace interactions, relationships, and processes; leadership and culture; supply chain management. *Unit head:* Dr. Pamela S. Barr, Interim Chair, 404-413-7525, Fax: 404-413-7571. *Application contact:* Toby McChesney, Assistant Dean for Graduate Recruiting and Student Services, 404-413-7167, Fax: 404-413-7162, E-mail: rcbgradadmissions@gsu.edu.
Website: http://mgmt.robinson.gsu.edu/

Golden Gate University, Ageno School of Business, San Francisco, CA 94105-2968. Offers accounting (MBA); business administration (EMBA, MBA, PMBA, DBA); business analytics (MS); finance (MBA, MS, Certificate); financial planning (MS, Certificate); healthcare information systems (Certificate); human resource management (MBA, MS); human resources management (Certificate); information systems (MS); information technology (MBA); information technology management (Certificate); integrated marketing and communications (MS, Certificate); international business (MBA); management (MBA); marketing (MBA, MS, Certificate); operations supply chain management (Certificate); psychology (MA, Certificate); public administration (EMPA); public relations (MS, Certificate); technical market analysis (Certificate); JD/MBA. *Program availability:* Part-time, evening/weekend. *Faculty:* 18 full-time (3 women), 117 part-time/adjunct (44 women). *Students:* 458 full-time (254 women), 664 part-time (331 women); includes 346 minority (75 Black or African American, non-Hispanic/Latino; 2 American Indian or Alaska Native, non-Hispanic/Latino; 132 Asian, non-Hispanic/Latino; 105 Hispanic/Latino; 9 Native Hawaiian or other Pacific Islander, non-Hispanic/Latino; 23 Two or more races, non-Hispanic/Latino), 354 international. Average age 34. 905 applicants, 83% accepted, 165 enrolled. In 2016, 350 master's, 2 doctorates awarded. *Degree requirements:* For doctorate, thesis/dissertation, qualifying examination. *Entrance requirements:* For master's, GMAT (for MBA), minimum GPA of 2.5 (MS). Additional exam requirements/recommendations for international students: Required—TOEFL (minimum score 550 paper-based; 79 iBT). *Application deadline:* For fall admission, 5/15 for domestic and international students; for winter admission, 1/15 for domestic and international students; for spring admission, 9/15 for domestic and international students. Applications are processed on a rolling basis. Application fee: $70 ($110 for international students). Electronic applications accepted. *Expenses:* Contact institution. *Financial support:* In 2016–17, 372 students received support. Career-related internships or fieldwork, Federal Work-Study, institutionally sponsored loans, and scholarships/grants available. Support available to part-time students. Financial award applicants required to submit FAFSA. *Unit head:* Dr. Gordon Swartz, Dean, 415-442-7027, Fax: 415-442-6579, E-mail: gswartz@ggu.edu. *Application contact:* Angela Melero, Enrollment Services, 415-442-7800, Fax: 415-442-7807, E-mail: info@ggu.edu.
Website: http://www.ggu.edu/programs/business-and-management

Grantham University, Mark Skousen School of Business, Lenexa, KS 66219. Offers business administration (MBA); business intelligence (MS); human resources management (Certificate); information management (MBA); performance improvement (MS); project management (MBA, Certificate). *Program availability:* Part-time, online only, 100% online. *Faculty:* 1 full-time, 36 part-time/adjunct. *Students:* 73 full-time (37 women), 1,046 part-time (424 women); includes 442 minority (309 Black or African American, non-Hispanic/Latino; 8 American Indian or Alaska Native, non-Hispanic/Latino; 27 Asian, non-Hispanic/Latino; 63 Hispanic/Latino; 7 Native Hawaiian or other Pacific Islander, non-Hispanic/Latino; 28 Two or more races, non-Hispanic/Latino). Average age 40. 1,324 applicants, 95% accepted, 1123 enrolled. In 2016, 331 master's awarded. *Degree requirements:* For master's, capstone project, PMP Prep Exam; for Certificate, comprehensive exam (for some programs), PMP Prep Exam. *Entrance requirements:* For master's, baccalaureate or master's degree with minimum cumulative GPA of 2.5 from institution accredited by agency recognized by U.S. Department of Education or foreign equivalent. Additional exam requirements/recommendations for international students: Required—PTE (minimum score 50), TOEFL (minimum score 530 paper-based, 71 iBT) or IELTS (minimum score 6.5). *Application deadline:* Applications are processed on a rolling basis. Electronic applications accepted. *Expenses:* $325 per credit hour, $45 per 8-week term technology fee. *Financial support:* Scholarships/grants available. Financial award applicants required to submit FAFSA. *Faculty research:* Organizational structures, e-discovery and project management, decision management, resource-based and ethical perspectives, external finance dependence in corporate investments. *Unit head:* Dr. David Marker, Dean, Mark Skousen School of Business, 800-955-2527, E-mail: dmarker@grantham.edu. *Application contact:* Jared Parlette, Vice President of Student Enrollment, 800-955-2527, E-mail: admissions@grantham.edu.
Website: http://www.grantham.edu/colleges-and-schools/school-of-business/

Gwynedd Mercy University, School of Graduate and Professional Studies, Gwynedd Valley, PA 19437-0901. Offers health care administration (MBA); management (MSM); strategic management and leadership (MBA). *Program availability:* Part-time, evening/weekend. *Faculty:* 5 full-time (all women), 22 part-time/adjunct (8 women). *Students:* 73 full-time (48 women); includes 27 minority (20 Black or African American, non-Hispanic/Latino; 2 Asian, non-Hispanic/Latino; 5 Hispanic/Latino). Average age 39. In 2016, 80 master's awarded. *Degree requirements:* For master's, thesis. *Entrance requirements:* For master's, minimum GPA of 3.0. *Application deadline:* Applications are processed on a rolling basis. *Expenses:* *Tuition:* Full-time $14,400; part-time $800 per credit hour. One-time fee: $165. Tuition and fees vary according to degree level and program. *Financial support:* Career-related internships or fieldwork, Federal Work-Study, tuition waivers (full and partial), and unspecified assistantships available. Financial award application deadline: 8/31; financial award applicants required to submit FAFSA. *Unit head:* Dr. Mary Sortino, Dean, 215-646-7300, E-mail: sortino.m@gmercyu.edu. *Application contact:* Information Contact, 800-342-5462, Fax: 215-641-5556.

Harrisburg University of Science and Technology, Program in Information Systems Engineering and Management, Harrisburg, PA 17101. Offers analytics (MS); digital government (MS); digital health (MS); entrepreneurship (MS); information security (MS); software engineering and systems development (MS). *Program availability:* Part-time, evening/weekend. *Faculty:* 9 full-time (0 women), 1 (woman) part-time/adjunct. *Students:* 1,031 full-time (264 women), 35 part-time (10 women); includes 2 minority (1 Black or African American, non-Hispanic/Latino; 1 Asian, non-Hispanic/Latino), 1,060 international. In 2016, 83 master's awarded. *Degree requirements:* For master's, thesis optional. *Entrance requirements:* For master's, baccalaureate degree. Additional exam requirements/recommendations for international students: Required—TOEFL (minimum score 520 paper-based; 80 iBT); Recommended—IELTS (minimum score 6). *Application deadline:* Applications are processed on a rolling basis. Application fee: $0. Electronic applications accepted. *Expenses:* *Tuition:* Full-time $4800; part-time $800 per semester hour. *Financial support:* In 2016–17, 2 students received support. Teaching assistantships available. Financial award applicants required to submit FAFSA. *Faculty research:* Healthcare Informatics, material analysis, enterprise systems, circuit design, enterprise architectures. *Unit head:* Dr. Amjad Umar, Director and Professor, 717-901-5141, Fax: 717-901-3141, E-mail: aumar@harrisburgu.edu.

Harvard University, Harvard Business School, Doctoral Programs in Management, Boston, MA 02163. Offers accounting and management (DBA); business economics (PhD); health policy management (PhD); management (DBA); marketing (DBA); organizational behavior (PhD); science, technology and management (PhD); strategy (DBA); technology and operations management (DBA). *Degree requirements:* For doctorate, comprehensive exam (for some programs), thesis/dissertation. *Entrance requirements:* For doctorate, GRE General Test or GMAT. Additional exam requirements/recommendations for international students: Required—TOEFL.

HEC Montreal, School of Business Administration, Master of Science Programs in Administration, Program in Business Intelligence, Montréal, QC H3T 2A7, Canada. Offers M Sc. All courses are given in French. *Students:* 50 full-time (21 women), 36 part-time (13 women). 46 applicants, 57% accepted, 21 enrolled. In 2016, 14 master's awarded. *Degree requirements:* For master's, one foreign language, thesis. *Entrance requirements:* For master's, Test de francais international (TFI) with minimum score of 850 (for those who have never studied in French), BBA, undergraduate degree in another field, degree deemed equivalent by program director and minimum GPA of 3.0 on 4.3 scale. *Application deadline:* For fall admission, 3/15 for domestic and international students; for winter admission, 9/15 for domestic and international students. Application fee: $86 Canadian dollars. Electronic applications accepted. *Expenses:* *Tuition, area resident:* Part-time $77.80 Canadian dollars per credit. Tuition,

state resident: full-time $2797 Canadian dollars; part-time $240.92 Canadian dollars per credit. Tuition, nonresident: full-time $8673 Canadian dollars; part-time $531.43 Canadian dollars per credit. *International tuition:* $19,131 Canadian dollars full-time. *Required fees:* $1699 Canadian dollars; $40.58 Canadian dollars per credit. $67.32 Canadian dollars per term. Tuition and fees vary according to degree level and program. *Financial support:* Research assistantships, teaching assistantships, and scholarships/grants available. Financial award application deadline: 9/2. *Unit head:* Dr. Marie-Helene Jobin, Director, 514-340-6283, E-mail: marie-helene.jobin@hec.ca. *Application contact:* Marianne de Moura, Administrative Director, 514-340-7106, Fax: 514-340-6411, E-mail: marianne.de-moura@hec.ca.
Website: http://www.hec.ca/programmes/maitrises/maitrise-intelligence-affaires/index.html

HEC Montreal, School of Business Administration, Master of Science Programs in Administration, Program in Strategy, Montréal, QC H3T 2A7, Canada. Offers M Sc. All courses are given in English. *Students:* 75 full-time (34 women), 15 part-time (11 women). 60 applicants, 55% accepted, 20 enrolled. In 2016, 35 master's awarded. *Degree requirements:* For master's, one foreign language, thesis. *Entrance requirements:* For master's, Test de francais international (TFI) with minimum score of 850 (for those who have never studied in French), BBA, undergraduate degree in another field, degree deemed equivalent by program director and minimum GPA of 3.0 on 4.3 scale. *Application deadline:* For fall admission, 3/15 for domestic and international students; for winter admission, 9/15 for domestic and international students. Application fee: $86. Electronic applications accepted. *Expenses: Tuition, area resident:* Part-time $77.80 Canadian dollars per credit. Tuition, state resident: full-time $2797 Canadian dollars; part-time $240.92 Canadian dollars per credit. Tuition, nonresident: full-time $8673 Canadian dollars; part-time $531.43 Canadian dollars per credit. *International tuition:* $19,131 Canadian dollars full-time. *Required fees:* $1699 Canadian dollars; $40.58 Canadian dollars per credit. $67.32 Canadian dollars per term. Tuition and fees vary according to degree level and program. *Financial support:* Research assistantships, teaching assistantships, and scholarships/grants available. Financial award application deadline: 9/2. *Unit head:* Dr. Marie-Helene Jobin, Director, 514-340-6283, E-mail: anne.bourhis@hec.ca. *Application contact:* Marianne de Moura, Administrative Director, 514-340-7106, Fax: 514-340-6411, E-mail: marianne.de-moura@hec.ca.
Website: http://www.hec.ca/programmes/maitrises/maitrise-strategie/index.html

Hofstra University, Frank G. Zarb School of Business, Programs in Information Systems, Hempstead, NY 11549. Offers business administration (MBA), including business analytics, information systems, quality management; information systems (MS, Advanced Certificate). *Program availability:* Part-time, evening/weekend, blended/hybrid learning. *Students:* 59 full-time (27 women), 14 part-time (7 women); includes 11 minority (1 Black or African American, non-Hispanic/Latino; 7 Asian, non-Hispanic/Latino; 3 Hispanic/Latino), 50 international. Average age 28. 95 applicants, 56% accepted, 20 enrolled. In 2016, 28 master's awarded. *Degree requirements:* For master's, capstone course (for MBA), thesis (for MS), minimum GPA of 3.0. *Entrance requirements:* For master's, GMAT/GRE, 2 letters of recommendation, resume, essay; for Advanced Certificate, GMAT/GRE, 2 letters of recommendation, resume. Additional exam requirements/recommendations for international students: Required—TOEFL (minimum score 550 paper-based; 80 iBT); Recommended—IELTS (minimum score 6). *Application deadline:* Applications are processed on a rolling basis. Application fee: $75. Electronic applications accepted. *Expenses:* $1,170 per credit. *Financial support:* In 2016–17, 26 students received support, including 26 fellowships with full and partial tuition reimbursements available (averaging $5,034 per year); research assistantships with full and partial tuition reimbursements available, career-related internships or fieldwork, Federal Work-Study, institutionally sponsored loans, scholarships/grants, tuition waivers (full and partial), and unspecified assistantships also available. Support available to part-time students. Financial award applicants required to submit FAFSA. *Faculty research:* Health information systems, healthcare data analytics; text mining and data mining; cybersecurity and digital forensics. *Unit head:* Dr. Hak Kim, Chairperson, 516-463-5716, Fax: 516-463-4834, E-mail: hak.j.kim@hofstra.edu. *Application contact:* Sunil Samuel, Assistant Vice President of Admissions, 516-463-4723, Fax: 516-463-4664, E-mail: graduateadmission@hofstra.edu.
Website: http://www.hofstra.edu/business/

Hofstra University, Frank G. Zarb School of Business, Programs in Management and General Business, Hempstead, NY 11549. Offers business administration (MBA), including health services management, management, sports and entertainment management, strategic business management, strategic healthcare management; general management (Advanced Certificate); human resource management (MS, Advanced Certificate). *Program availability:* Part-time, evening/weekend, blended/hybrid learning. *Students:* 140 full-time (67 women), 159 part-time (70 women); includes 100 minority (24 Black or African American, non-Hispanic/Latino; 41 Asian, non-Hispanic/Latino; 32 Hispanic/Latino; 1 Native Hawaiian or other Pacific Islander, non-Hispanic/Latino; 2 Two or more races, non-Hispanic/Latino), 26 international. Average age 33. 354 applicants, 58% accepted, 94 enrolled. In 2016, 84 master's awarded. *Degree requirements:* For master's, thesis optional, capstone course (for MBA), thesis (for MS), minimum GPA of 3.0. *Entrance requirements:* For master's, GMAT/GRE, 2 letters of recommendation, resume, essay. Additional exam requirements/recommendations for international students: Required—TOEFL (minimum score 550 paper-based; 80 iBT); Recommended—IELTS (minimum score 6). *Application deadline:* Applications are processed on a rolling basis. Application fee: $75. Electronic applications accepted. *Expenses:* $1,170 per credit. *Financial support:* In 2016–17, 65 students received support, including 43 fellowships with full and partial tuition reimbursements available (averaging $4,813 per year); research assistantships with full and partial tuition reimbursements available, career-related internships or fieldwork, Federal Work-Study, institutionally sponsored loans, scholarships/grants, tuition waivers (full and partial), and unspecified assistantships also available. Support available to part-time students. Financial award applicants required to submit FAFSA. *Faculty research:* Organizational change; sustainability; entrepreneurial spawning; family business; global supply chain strategies. *Unit head:* Dr. Kaushik Sengupta, Chairperson, 516-463-7825, Fax: 516-463-4834, E-mail: kaushik.sengupta@hofstra.edu. *Application contact:* Sunil Samuel, Assistant Vice President of Admissions, 516-463-4723, Fax: 516-463-4664, E-mail: graduateadmission@hofstra.edu.
Website: http://www.hofstra.edu/business/

Hult International Business School, Graduate Programs, Cambridge, MA 02141. Offers business administration (EMBA); business analytics (MBA, MIB); business statistics (MBS); disruptive innovation (MDI); entrepreneurship (MBA, MIB); family business (MBA, MIB); finance (MBA, MF, MIB); international marketing (MIM); marketing (MBA, MIB); project management (MBA, MIB). MDI and MBS offered in San Francisco; MBA also offered in Boston, San Francisco, Dubai, Shanghai, and New York. *Students:* Average age 31. *Entrance requirements:* For master's, GMAT, 3 years of work experience. Additional exam requirements/recommendations for international students: Required—TOEFL. *Application deadline:* For fall admission, 9/1 priority date for domestic and international students; for winter admission, 11/1 priority date for domestic and international students; for spring admission, 12/1 priority date for domestic and international students; for summer admission, 6/1 for domestic and international students. Applications are processed on a rolling basis. Application fee: $150. Electronic applications accepted. *Expenses:* $75,000 (for MBA); $45,000 (for master's); $85,000 (for executive part-time MBA). *Financial support:* Scholarships/grants and tuition waivers (partial) available. Financial award application deadline: 6/1; financial award applicants required to submit FAFSA. *Application contact:* Boston Admissions Office, 617-746-1990, E-mail: postgraduate@hult.edu.
Website: http://www.hult.edu

James Madison University, The Graduate School, College of Business, Program in Strategic Leadership, Harrisonburg, VA 22807. Offers postsecondary analysis and leadership (PhD), including nonprofit and community leadership, organizational science and leadership, postsecondary analysis and leadership. *Program availability:* Part-time, evening/weekend, online learning. *Faculty:* 3 full-time (1 woman). *Students:* 13 full-time (4 women), 25 part-time (10 women); includes 5 minority (all Black or African American, non-Hispanic/Latino), 3 international. Average age 30. 11 applicants, 64% accepted, 7 enrolled. In 2016, 5 doctorates awarded. Application fee: $55. Electronic applications accepted. *Financial support:* In 2016–17, 6 students received support. Fellowships, career-related internships or fieldwork, Federal Work-Study, unspecified assistantships, and 5 doctoral assistantships (stipend varies) available. Financial award application deadline: 3/1; financial award applicants required to submit FAFSA. *Unit head:* Dr. Karen A. Ford, Director of Strategic Leadership Studies, 540-568-7020, Fax: 540-568-7117, E-mail: fordka@jmu.edu. *Application contact:* Lynette D. Michael, Director of Graduate Admissions, 540-568-6131 Ext. 6395, Fax: 540-568-7860, E-mail: michaeld@jmu.edu.
Website: http://www.jmu.edu/leadership/

Lawrence Technological University, College of Management, Southfield, MI 48075-1058. Offers business administration (MBA), including business analytics (MBA, MS), finance, information technology, marketing, project management (MBA, MS); information technology (MS), including business analytics (MBA, MS), information assurance, project management (MBA, MS); project management (Graduate Certificate). *Accreditation:* ACBSP. *Program availability:* Part-time, evening/weekend, 100% online. *Faculty:* 14 full-time (6 women), 10 part-time/adjunct (2 women). *Students:* 7 full-time (3 women), 323 part-time (120 women); includes 60 minority (29 Black or African American, non-Hispanic/Latino; 2 American Indian or Alaska Native, non-Hispanic/Latino; 17 Asian, non-Hispanic/Latino; 8 Hispanic/Latino; 4 Two or more races, non-Hispanic/Latino), 118 international. Average age 33. 275 applicants, 56% accepted, 72 enrolled. In 2016, 167 master's, 12 other advanced degrees awarded. Terminal master's awarded for partial completion of doctoral program. *Degree requirements:* For master's, thesis (for some programs). *Entrance requirements:* Additional exam requirements/recommendations for international students: Required—TOEFL (minimum score 550 paper-based; 79 iBT), IELTS (minimum score 6.5). *Application deadline:* For fall admission, 5/22 for international students; for spring admission, 10/11 for international students; for summer admission, 2/16 for international students. Applications are processed on a rolling basis. Application fee: $50. Electronic applications accepted. *Expenses: Tuition:* Full-time $14,868; part-time $1062 per credit. *Required fees:* $75 per semester. Tuition and fees vary according to campus/location. *Financial support:* In 2016–17, 35 students received support, including 8 research assistantships with partial tuition reimbursements available (averaging $3,250 per year); career-related internships or fieldwork, unspecified assistantships, and corporate tuition incentives also available. Financial award application deadline: 4/1; financial award applicants required to submit FAFSA. *Faculty research:* Cybersecurity; risk management; IT governance; security controls and countermeasures; threat modeling cyber resilience; autonomous cars; natural language processing; text mining; machine learning; reflective leadership; emerging leadership theories and practice; motivational studies; teaching effectiveness strategies; teamwork; organization development; strategic planning; strengths-based and positive organizational scholarship; global leadership; globalization; corporate governance. *Unit head:* Dr. Bahman Mirshab, Dean, 248-204-3050, E-mail: mgtdean@ltu.edu. *Application contact:* Jane Rohrback, Director of Admissions, 248-204-3160, Fax: 248-204-2228, E-mail: admissions@ltu.edu.
Website: http://www.ltu.edu/management/index.asp

Lenoir-Rhyne University, Graduate Programs, Charles M. Snipes School of Business, Hickory, NC 28601. Offers accounting (MBA); business analytics and information technology (MBA); entrepreneurship (MBA); global business (MBA); healthcare administration (MBA); innovation and change management (MBA); leadership development (MBA). *Accreditation:* ACBSP. *Program availability:* Part-time, evening/weekend, online learning. *Degree requirements:* For master's, capstone course. *Entrance requirements:* For master's, GMAT, GRE, MAT, minimum undergraduate GPA of 2.7, graduate 3.0. Additional exam requirements/recommendations for international students: Required—TOEFL (minimum score 600 paper-based). Electronic applications accepted. *Expenses:* Contact institution.

LeTourneau University, Graduate Programs, Longview, TX 75607-7001. Offers business (MBA); counseling (MA), including licensed professional counselor, marriage and family therapy, school counseling; curriculum and instruction (M Ed); educational administration (M Ed); engineering (ME, MS); engineering management (MEM); health care administration (MS); marriage and family therapy (MA); psychology (MA); strategic leadership (MSL); teacher leadership (M Ed); teaching and learning (M Ed). *Program availability:* Part-time, 100% online, blended/hybrid learning. *Faculty:* 24 full-time (7 women), 40 part-time/adjunct (15 women). *Students:* 82 full-time (48 women), 428 part-time (331 women); includes 234 minority (138 Black or African American, non-Hispanic/Latino; 5 American Indian or Alaska Native, non-Hispanic/Latino; 5 Asian, non-Hispanic/Latino; 50 Hispanic/Latino; 36 Two or more races, non-Hispanic/Latino), 15 international. Average age 37. 257 applicants, 60% accepted, 141 enrolled. In 2016, 136 master's awarded. *Degree requirements:* For master's, thesis (for some programs). *Entrance requirements:* Additional exam requirements/recommendations for international students: Required—TOEFL. *Application deadline:* For fall admission, 8/22 for domestic students, 8/29 for international students; for winter admission, 10/10 for domestic students; for spring admission, 1/2 for domestic students, 1/10 for international students; for summer admission, 5/1 for domestic and international students. Applications are processed on a rolling basis. Electronic applications accepted. *Expenses:* $10,890-$18,450 tuition per year (depending on program). *Financial support:* Research assistantships, institutionally sponsored loans, and unspecified assistantships available. Financial award applicants required to submit FAFSA. *Application contact:* Chris Fontaine, Assistant Vice President for Enrollment Services and Global Admissions, 903-233-4312, E-mail: chrisfontaine@letu.edu.
Website: http://www.letu.edu

Manhattanville College, School of Business, Master of Science in Business Leadership Program, Purchase, NY 10577-2132. Offers MS. *Program availability:* Part-time, evening/weekend. *Students:* 11 (4 women); includes 6 minority (1 Black or African American, non-Hispanic/Latino; 1 Asian, non-Hispanic/Latino; 2 Hispanic/Latino; 2 Two or more races, non-Hispanic/Latino). Average age 32. 14 applicants, 29% accepted, 3 enrolled. In 2016, 2 master's awarded. *Degree requirements:* For master's, thesis (for some programs), final project. *Entrance requirements:* For master's, transcripts, 2 letters of recommendation, resume. Additional exam requirements/recommendations for international students: Required—TOEFL (minimum score 563 paper-based; 85 iBT).

Management Strategy and Policy

Application deadline: Applications are processed on a rolling basis. Application fee: $75. Electronic applications accepted. *Expenses: Tuition:* Full-time $16,470; part-time $915 per credit. *Required fees:* $60 per semester. Part-time tuition and fees vary according to course load and program. *Financial support:* Federal Work-Study, institutionally sponsored loans, scholarships/grants, and unspecified assistantships available. Financial award applicants required to submit FAFSA. *Faculty research:* Decision making, analytics, and risk management; insurance standards. *Unit head:* Laura Persky, Graduate Program Director, 914-323-5188, E-mail: laura.persky@mville.edu. *Application contact:* Monika Pottgen, Assistant Director, Recruitment and Admissions, 914-323-5150, E-mail: business@mville.edu.
Website: https://www.mville.edu/programs/ms-business-leadership

McGill University, Faculty of Graduate and Postdoctoral Studies, Desautels Faculty of Management, Montréal, QC H3A 2T5, Canada. Offers administration (PhD); entrepreneurial studies (MBA); finance (MBA); general management (Post Master's Certificate); information systems (MBA); international business (MBA); international practicing management (MM); management (MBA); management for development (MBA); manufacturing management (MMM); marketing (MBA); operations management (MBA); public accountancy (Diploma); strategic management (MBA); MBA/LL B; MD/MBA. MMM offered jointly with Faculty of Engineering; PhD with Concordia University, HEC Montreal, Université de Montréal, Université du Québec à Montréal.

Mercer University, Graduate Studies, Cecil B. Day Campus, Eugene W. Stetson School of Business and Economics (Atlanta), Atlanta, GA 30341. Offers accounting (M Acc); business analytics (MS); innovation (PMBA), including entrepreneurship; international business (MBA); MBA/M Acc; Pharm D/MBA. *Accreditation:* AACSB. *Program availability:* Part-time, evening/weekend, 100% online, blended/hybrid learning. *Faculty:* 19 full-time (7 women), 7 part-time/adjunct (1 woman). *Students:* 183 full-time (91 women), 129 part-time (69 women); includes 136 minority (99 Black or African American, non-Hispanic/Latino; 2 American Indian or Alaska Native, non-Hispanic/Latino; 22 Asian, non-Hispanic/Latino; 10 Hispanic/Latino; 3 Two or more races, non-Hispanic/Latino), 43 international. Average age 32. 207 applicants, 77% accepted, 110 enrolled. In 2016, 176 master's awarded. *Entrance requirements:* For master's, GMAT or GRE. Additional exam requirements/recommendations for international students: Required—TOEFL (minimum score 550 paper-based, 80 iBT) or IELTS. *Application deadline:* For fall admission, 6/15 priority date for domestic and international students; for spring admission, 11/1 priority date for domestic and international students; for summer admission, 3/15 priority date for domestic and international students. Applications are processed on a rolling basis. Application fee: $50 ($100 for international students). Electronic applications accepted. *Expenses:* $795 per credit full-time, $727 per credit part-time. *Financial support:* Federal Work-Study available. Financial award application deadline: 5/1; financial award applicants required to submit FAFSA. *Faculty research:* Entrepreneurship, market studies, international business strategy, financial analysis. *Unit head:* Dr. Susan P. Gilbert, Dean, 678-547-6438, Fax: 678-547-6337, E-mail: gilbert_sp@mercer.edu. *Application contact:* Lael Whiteside, Director of Admissions, 678-547-6300, Fax: 678-547-6160, E-mail: whiteside_l@mercer.edu.
Website: http://business.mercer.edu

Mercyhurst University, Graduate Studies, Program in Organizational Leadership, Erie, PA 16546. Offers accounting (MS); higher education administration (MS); human resources (MS); organizational leadership (MS, Certificate); sports leadership (MS); strategy and innovation (MS). *Program availability:* Part-time, evening/weekend. *Degree requirements:* For master's, thesis. *Entrance requirements:* For master's, GRE General Test or MAT, interview, resume, essay, three professional references, transcripts. Additional exam requirements/recommendations for international students: Required—TOEFL (minimum score 80 iBT), IELTS (minimum score 6.5). Electronic applications accepted. *Faculty research:* Leadership training, organizational communication, leadership pedagogy.

Merrimack College, Girard School of Business, North Andover, MA 01845-5800. Offers accounting (MS); business analytics (MS); management (MS). *Program availability:* Part-time, evening/weekend, 100% online. *Faculty:* 7 full-time, 17 part-time/adjunct. *Students:* 101 full-time (45 women), 35 part-time (13 women); includes 6 minority (2 Asian, non-Hispanic/Latino; 3 Hispanic/Latino; 1 Two or more races, non-Hispanic/Latino), 55 international. Average age 27. 116 applicants, 81% accepted, 53 enrolled. In 2016, 57 master's awarded. *Degree requirements:* For master's, comprehensive exam (for some programs), thesis optional, capstone. *Entrance requirements:* For master's, official college transcripts, resume, personal statement, 2 recommendations. Additional exam requirements/recommendations for international students: Required—TOEFL (minimum score 84 iBT), IELTS (minimum score 6.5), PTE (minimum score 56). *Application deadline:* For fall admission, 8/13 for domestic students, 7/15 for international students; for spring admission, 1/10 for domestic and international students; for summer admission, 5/10 for domestic students, 4/10 for international students. Applications are processed on a rolling basis. Application fee: $0. Electronic applications accepted. *Expenses:* Contact institution. *Financial support:* Career-related internships or fieldwork, scholarships/grants, health care benefits, and unspecified assistantships available. Support available to part-time students. Financial award application deadline: 5/1; financial award applicants required to submit FAFSA. *Application contact:* Jennifer Greenwood, Graduate Admission Counselor, 978-837-3563, E-mail: graduate@merrimack.edu.
Website: http://www.merrimack.edu/academics/graduate/

Messiah College, Program in Business and Leadership, Mechanicsburg, PA 17055. Offers leadership (MBA, Certificate); management (Certificate); strategic leadership (MA). *Program availability:* Online learning.

Michigan State University, The Graduate School, Eli Broad College of Business, Department of Management, East Lansing, MI 48224. Offers management (PhD); management, strategy, and leadership (MS). *Program availability:* Part-time, online learning. *Degree requirements:* For doctorate, comprehensive exam, thesis/dissertation. *Entrance requirements:* For master's, full-time managerial experience in a supervisory role; for doctorate, GMAT or GRE, letters of recommendation, experience in teaching and conducting research, work experience in business contexts, personal essay. Additional exam requirements/recommendations for international students: Required—TOEFL (minimum score 600 paper-based). Electronic applications accepted.

Michigan State University, The Graduate School, Eli Broad College of Business, Program in Business Analytics, East Lansing, MI 48224. Offers MS. Program offered in collaboration with MSU's College of Engineering and College of Natural Science. *Entrance requirements:* For master's, GMAT or GRE, bachelor's degree; minimum cumulative GPA of 3.0 in undergraduate course work and in college-level courses in introductory calculus and statistics; working knowledge of personal computers; knowledge of programming languages; experience in using statistical software program packages; recent laptop computer with MS Office. Additional exam requirements/recommendations for international students: Required—PTE (minimum score 70), TOEFL or IELTS. Electronic applications accepted. *Faculty research:* Artificial intelligence, evolution, and game theory, computational modeling using high performance computing.

Middlebury Institute of International Studies at Monterey, Graduate School of International Policy and Management, Fisher MBA in Global Impact Management Program, Monterey, CA 93940-2691. Offers corporate risk management and compliance (MBA). *Accreditation:* AACSB. *Degree requirements:* For master's, one foreign language, thesis. *Entrance requirements:* For master's, GMAT, minimum GPA of 3.0, proficiency in a foreign language. Additional exam requirements/recommendations for international students: Required—TOEFL (minimum score 550 paper-based; 80 iBT). Electronic applications accepted. *Expenses: Tuition:* Full-time $38,250; part-time $1820 per credit. *Required fees:* $78 per semester. *Faculty research:* Cross-cultural consumer behavior, foreign direct investment, marketing and entrepreneurial orientation, political risk analysis and area studies, managing international human resources.

Middle Tennessee State University, College of Graduate Studies, University College, Murfreesboro, TN 37132. Offers advanced studies in teaching and learning (M Ed); human resources leadership (MPS); nursing administration (MSN); nursing education (MSN); strategic leadership (MPS); training and development (MPS). *Program availability:* Part-time, evening/weekend, online learning. *Entrance requirements:* Additional exam requirements/recommendations for international students: Required—TOEFL (minimum score 525 paper-based; 71 iBT) or IELTS (minimum score 6).

Mount Mercy University, Program in Strategic Leadership, Cedar Rapids, IA 52402-4797. Offers MSL. *Program availability:* Evening/weekend.

Neumann University, Program in Organizational and Strategic Leadership, Aston, PA 19014-1298. Offers MS. *Program availability:* Part-time, evening/weekend, 100% online, blended/hybrid learning. *Faculty:* 9 part-time/adjunct (3 women). *Students:* 5 full-time (3 women), 88 part-time (50 women); includes 27 minority (21 Black or African American, non-Hispanic/Latino; 5 Hispanic/Latino; 1 Two or more races, non-Hispanic/Latino), 1 international. Average age 37. 83 applicants, 75% accepted, 52 enrolled. In 2016, 49 master's awarded. *Degree requirements:* For master's, project. *Entrance requirements:* For master's, official transcripts from all institutions attended, current resume, letter of intent, official letter of recommendation. Additional exam requirements/recommendations for international students: Required—TOEFL (minimum score 70 iBT). *Application deadline:* Applications are processed on a rolling basis. Application fee: $0. Electronic applications accepted. *Expenses:* $615 per credit. *Financial support:* Scholarships/grants and health care benefits available. Support available to part-time students. Financial award application deadline: 3/15; financial award applicants required to submit FAFSA. *Unit head:* Dr. Samuel Lemon, Program Director, Master of Science in Organizational and Strategic Leadership Program, 610-361-5239, Fax: 610-361-5235, E-mail: lemons@neumann.edu. *Application contact:* Janice Sackawicz, Coordinator of Student Services, Division of Continuing Adult and Professional Studies, 610-558-5629, Fax: 610-361-5235, E-mail: CAPS@neumann.edu.

New England College, Program in Management, Henniker, NH 03242-3293. Offers accounting (MSA); healthcare administration (MS); international relations (MA); marketing management (MS); nonprofit leadership (MS); project management (MS); strategic leadership (MS). *Program availability:* Part-time, evening/weekend. *Degree requirements:* For master's, independent research project. Electronic applications accepted.

The New School, Parsons School of Design, Program in Strategic Design and Management, New York, NY 10011. Offers business of design (Advanced Certificate); strategic design management (MS). *Program availability:* Part-time, 100% online. *Faculty:* 41 full-time (18 women), 34 part-time/adjunct (16 women). *Students:* 211 full-time (167 women), 24 part-time (18 women); includes 38 minority (11 Black or African American, non-Hispanic/Latino; 15 Asian, non-Hispanic/Latino; 9 Hispanic/Latino; 3 Two or more races, non-Hispanic/Latino), 148 international. Average age 29. 316 applicants, 67% accepted, 123 enrolled. In 2016, 100 master's, 5 other advanced degrees awarded. *Degree requirements:* For master's, thesis or alternative. *Entrance requirements:* For master's, transcripts, resume, statement of purpose, recommendation letters, essay, interview. Additional exam requirements/recommendations for international students: Required—TOEFL (minimum score 92 iBT), IELTS (minimum score 7), PTE (minimum score 63). *Application deadline:* For fall admission, 1/1 priority date for domestic and international students. Applications are processed on a rolling basis. Application fee: $50. Electronic applications accepted. *Expenses: Tuition:* Full-time $42,610; part-time $1685 per credit. *Required fees:* $276; $138 per semester. Full-time tuition and fees vary according to degree level and program. Part-time tuition and fees vary according to course load and program. *Financial support:* Research assistantships, teaching assistantships, career-related internships or fieldwork, Federal Work-Study, scholarships/grants, and unspecified assistantships available. Support available to part-time students. Financial award application deadline: 2/1; financial award applicants required to submit FAFSA. *Unit head:* Rhea Alexander, Program Chair, E-mail: alexanrc@newschool.edu. *Application contact:* Courtney Malenius, Director of Graduate Admission, 212-229-5150 Ext. 4011, E-mail: maleniuc@newschool.edu.
Website: http://www.newschool.edu/parsons/masters-design-management/

New York University, Leonard N. Stern School of Business, Department of Management and Organizations, New York, NY 10012-1019. Offers management organizations (MBA); organization theory (PhD); organizational behavior (PhD); strategy (PhD). *Faculty research:* Strategic management, managerial cognition, interpersonal processes, conflict and negotiation.

New York University, School of Continuing and Professional Studies, Division of Programs in Business, Graduate Programs in Management and Systems, New York, NY 10012-1019. Offers core business competencies (Advanced Certificate); database technologies (MS); enterprise risk management (MS, Advanced Certificate); information technologies (Advanced Certificate); strategy and leadership (MS, Advanced Certificate); systems management (MS). *Program availability:* Part-time, evening/weekend, online learning. *Degree requirements:* For master's, thesis, capstone project. *Entrance requirements:* For master's, GRE or GMAT (only upon request), bachelor's degree, resume with relevant professional work, internship or volunteer experience, two letters of recommendation, statement of purpose. Additional exam requirements/recommendations for international students: Required—TOEFL (minimum score 600 paper-based; 100 iBT), IELTS (minimum score 7). Electronic applications accepted.

Niagara University, Graduate Division of Business Administration, Niagara University, NY 14109. Offers accounting (MBA); business administration (MBA); finance (MBA, MS); financial planning (MBA); healthcare administration (MBA, MHA); human resources (MBA); international business (MBA); marketing (MBA); professional accountancy (MBA); strategic management (MBA); supply chain management (MBA). *Accreditation:* AACSB. *Program availability:* Part-time, evening/weekend. *Students:* 172 full-time (69 women), 65 part-time (36 women); includes 25 minority (4 Black or African American, non-Hispanic/Latino; 7 Asian, non-Hispanic/Latino; 7 Hispanic/Latino; 1 Native Hawaiian or other Pacific Islander, non-Hispanic/Latino; 6 Two or more races, non-Hispanic/Latino), 76 international. Average age 27. In 2016, 107 master's awarded. *Entrance requirements:* For master's, GMAT. Additional exam requirements/recommendations for international students: Required—TOEFL (minimum score 550 paper-based; 79 iBT), IELTS (minimum score 6). *Application deadline:* For fall admission, 8/1 for domestic students; for spring admission, 11/1 for domestic students. Applications are processed on a rolling basis. Electronic applications accepted.

Expenses: $870 per credit hour. *Financial support:* Fellowships, research assistantships, career-related internships or fieldwork, and Federal Work-Study available. Support available to part-time students. Financial award application deadline: 4/15; financial award applicants required to submit FAFSA. *Faculty research:* Capital flows, Federal Reserve policy, human resource management, public policy, issues in marketing, auctions, economics of information, risk and capital markets, management strategy, consumer behavior, Internet and social media marketing. *Unit head:* Dr. Paul Richardson, MBA Director/Chair of the Marketing Department, 716-286-8169, Fax: 716-286-8206, E-mail: psr@niagara.edu. *Application contact:* Evan Pierce, Associate Director for Graduate Recruitment, 716-286-8769, Fax: 716-286-8170, E-mail: epierce@niagara.edu.
Website: http://mba.niagara.edu

North Central College, School of Graduate and Professional Studies, Program in Business Administration, Naperville, IL 60566-7063. Offers change management (MBA); finance (MBA); human resource management (MBA); management (MBA). *Program availability:* Part-time, evening/weekend. *Faculty:* 15 full-time (9 women), 13 part-time/adjunct (5 women). *Students:* 30 full-time (14 women), 46 part-time (22 women); includes 11 minority (4 Black or African American, non-Hispanic/Latino; 6 Hispanic/Latino; 1 Two or more races, non-Hispanic/Latino), 6 international. Average age 29. 104 applicants, 50% accepted, 31 enrolled. In 2016, 45 master's awarded. *Degree requirements:* For master's, thesis optional, project. *Entrance requirements:* For master's, interview. Additional exam requirements/recommendations for international students: Required—TOEFL (minimum score 550 paper-based; 80 iBT), IELTS (minimum score 6.5). *Application deadline:* For fall admission, 8/15 for domestic students, 7/15 for international students; for winter admission, 12/1 for domestic students, 11/1 for international students; for spring admission, 2/1 for domestic students, 12/1 for international students. Applications are processed on a rolling basis. Application fee: $25. Electronic applications accepted. Application fee is waived when completed online. *Expenses:* Contact institution. *Financial support:* Scholarships/grants available. Support available to part-time students. Financial award applicants required to submit FAFSA. *Unit head:* Dr. Mary Galvan, Chair of Department of Management and Marketing, 630-637-5473, E-mail: mtgalvan@noctrl.edu. *Application contact:* Wendy Kulpinski, Director of Graduate and Continuing Education Admission, 630-637-5808, Fax: 630-637-5844, E-mail: wekulpinski@noctrl.edu.

Northwestern University, The Graduate School, Kellogg School of Management, Department of Management and Strategy, Evanston, IL 60208. Offers PhD.

Northwestern University, The Graduate School, Kellogg School of Management, Department of Managerial Economics and Decision Sciences, Evanston, IL 60208. Offers PhD. Admissions and degree offered through The Graduate School. *Degree requirements:* For doctorate, comprehensive exam, thesis/dissertation. *Entrance requirements:* For doctorate, GMAT or GRE General Test. Additional exam requirements/recommendations for international students: Required—TOEFL. Electronic applications accepted. *Faculty research:* Competitive strategy and organization, managerial economics, decision sciences, game theory, operations management.

Northwestern University, The Graduate School, Kellogg School of Management, Management Programs, Evanston, IL 60208. Offers accounting information and management (MBA, PhD); analytical finance (MBA); business administration (MBA); decision sciences (MBA); entrepreneurship and innovation (MBA); finance (MBA, PhD); health enterprise management (MBA); human resources management (MBA); international business (MBA); management and organizations (MBA, PhD); management and organizations and sociology (PhD); management and strategy (MBA); management studies (MS); managerial analytics (MBA); managerial economics (MBA); managerial economics and strategy (PhD); marketing (MBA, PhD); marketing management (MBA); media management (MBA); operations management (MBA, PhD); real estate (MBA); social enterprise at Kellogg (MBA); JD/MBA. *Program availability:* Part-time, evening/weekend. Terminal master's awarded for partial completion of doctoral program. *Degree requirements:* For doctorate, thesis/dissertation, 2 years of coursework, qualifying (field) exam and candidacy, summer research papers and presentations to faculty, proposal defense, final exam/defense. *Entrance requirements:* For master's, GMAT, GRE, interview, 2 letters of recommendation, college transcripts, resume, essays, Kellogg honor code; for doctorate, GMAT, GRE, statement of purpose, transcripts, 2 letters of recommendation, resume, interview. Additional exam requirements/recommendations for international students: Required—TOEFL, IELTS. Electronic applications accepted. *Expenses:* Contact institution. *Faculty research:* Business cycles and international finance, health policy, networks, non-market strategy, consumer psychology.

Northwestern University, School of Professional Studies, Program in Information Systems, Evanston, IL 60208. Offers analytics and business intelligence (MS); database and Internet technologies (MS); information systems (MS); information systems management (MS); information systems security (MS); medical informatics (MS); software project management and development (MS).

Northwestern University, School of Professional Studies, Program in Predictive Analytics, Evanston, IL 60208. Offers computer-based data mining (MS); marketing analytics (MS); predictive modeling (MS); risk analytics (MS); Web analytics (MS). *Program availability:* Online learning. *Entrance requirements:* For master's, official transcripts, two letters of recommendation, statement of purpose, current resume or curriculum vitae. Additional exam requirements/recommendations for international students: Required—TOEFL (minimum score 600 paper-based; 100 iBT) or IELTS (minimum score 7).

Norwich University, College of Graduate and Continuing Studies, Master of Science in Leadership Program, Northfield, VT 05663. Offers leadership (MS), including human resources leadership, leading change management consulting, organizational leadership, public sector/government/military leadership. *Program availability:* Evening/weekend, online only, mostly all online with a week-long residency requirement. *Faculty:* 10 part-time/adjunct (2 women). *Students:* 66 full-time (20 women); includes 13 minority (8 Black or African American, non-Hispanic/Latino; 3 Asian, non-Hispanic/Latino; 1 Hispanic/Latino; 1 Two or more races, non-Hispanic/Latino). Average age 37. 13 applicants, 69% accepted, 6 enrolled. In 2016, 34 master's awarded. *Degree requirements:* For master's, capstone. *Entrance requirements:* For master's, minimum undergraduate GPA of 2.75. Additional exam requirements/recommendations for international students: Required—TOEFL (minimum score 550 paper-based; 80 iBT), IELTS (minimum score 6.5). *Application deadline:* For fall admission, 8/14 for domestic and international students; for winter admission, 11/13 for domestic and international students; for spring admission, 2/13 for domestic and international students; for summer admission, 5/15 for domestic and international students. Electronic applications accepted. *Expenses:* Contact institution. *Financial support:* In 2016–17, 46 students received support. Scholarships/grants available. Financial award application deadline: 8/4; financial award applicants required to submit FAFSA. *Unit head:* Dr. Stacie Morgan, Program Director, 802-485-2866, Fax: 802-485-2533, E-mail: smorgan3@norwich.edu. *Application contact:* Admissions Advisor, 800-460-5597 Ext. 3371, Fax: 802-485-2533, E-mail: msl@online.norwich.edu.
Website: https://online.norwich.edu/degree-programs/masters/master-science-leadership/overview

Nova Southeastern University, H. Wayne Huizenga College of Business and Entrepreneurship, Fort Lauderdale, FL 33314-7796. Offers accounting (M Acc); business intelligence/analytics (MBA); entrepreneurship (MBA); finance (MBA); human resource management (MBA); international business (MBA); management (MBA); marketing (MBA); process improvement (MBA); public administration (MPA); real estate development (MS); sport revenue generation (MBA); supply chain management (MBA); taxation (M Tax). *Program availability:* Part-time, evening/weekend, 100% online, blended/hybrid learning. *Faculty:* 65 full-time (26 women), 111 part-time/adjunct (74 women). *Students:* 2,242 full-time (1,400 women), 425 part-time (239 women); includes 1,798 minority (734 Black or African American, non-Hispanic/Latino; 5 American Indian or Alaska Native, non-Hispanic/Latino; 110 Asian, non-Hispanic/Latino; 890 Hispanic/Latino; 2 Native Hawaiian or other Pacific Islander, non-Hispanic/Latino; 57 Two or more races, non-Hispanic/Latino), 255 international. Average age 34. 1,422 applicants, 64% accepted, 672 enrolled. In 2016, 971 master's awarded. *Degree requirements:* For master's, thesis optional. *Entrance requirements:* For master's, GMAT or GRE (depending on undergraduate GPA), official transcripts from all schools attended while in pursuit of bachelor's degree; minimum GPA of 2.5 from regionally-accredited institution. Additional exam requirements/recommendations for international students: Required—TOEFL (minimum score 550 paper-based; 79 iBT), IELTS (minimum score 6), PTE (minimum score 54). *Application deadline:* For fall admission, 8/5 priority date for domestic students, 7/29 priority date for international students; for winter admission, 12/16 priority date for domestic students, 12/9 priority date for international students; for summer admission, 4/21 priority date for domestic and international students. Applications are processed on a rolling basis. Application fee: $50. Electronic applications accepted. *Expenses:* Contact institution. *Financial support:* In 2016–17, 325 students received support. Federal Work-Study and scholarships/grants available. Support available to part-time students. Financial award application deadline: 4/15; financial award applicants required to submit FAFSA. *Faculty research:* Reputation management, call centers, international social capital, corporate earnings guidance, corporate governance. *Unit head:* Dr. J. Preston Jones, Dean, 954-262-5127, E-mail: prestonj@nova.edu. *Application contact:* Zeida Rodriguez, Associate Director of Enrollment Services, 954-262-5163, Fax: 954-262-3822, E-mail: zeida@nova.edu.
Website: http://www.huizenga.nova.edu

Ohio Dominican University, Division of Business, Program in Business Administration, Columbus, OH 43219-2099. Offers accounting (MBA); data analytics (MBA); finance (MBA); leadership (MBA); risk management (MBA); sport management (MBA). *Program availability:* Part-time, evening/weekend, 100% online, blended/hybrid learning. *Faculty:* 8 full-time (4 women), 17 part-time/adjunct (3 women). *Students:* 63 full-time (26 women), 112 part-time (59 women); includes 50 minority (29 Black or African American, non-Hispanic/Latino; 2 American Indian or Alaska Native, non-Hispanic/Latino; 6 Asian, non-Hispanic/Latino; 6 Hispanic/Latino; 1 Native Hawaiian or other Pacific Islander, non-Hispanic/Latino; 6 Two or more races, non-Hispanic/Latino), 7 international. Average age 31. 65 applicants, 51% accepted, 26 enrolled. In 2016, 120 master's awarded. *Entrance requirements:* For master's, minimum overall GPA of 3.0 in undergraduate degree from regionally-accredited institution or 2.75 in last 60 semester hours of bachelor's degree. Additional exam requirements/recommendations for international students: Required—TOEFL (minimum score 550 paper-based), IELTS (minimum score 6.5). *Application deadline:* For fall admission, 8/15 for domestic students, 6/10 for international students; for spring admission, 1/4 for domestic students, 11/2 for international students; for summer admission, 5/30 for domestic students. Applications are processed on a rolling basis. Application fee: $25. Electronic applications accepted. *Expenses:* $590 per credit hour; $225 fees per semester. *Financial support:* Applicants required to submit FAFSA. *Unit head:* Dr. Steve Vickner, Director of Master of Business Administration Program, 614-251-4569, E-mail: vickners@ohiodominican.edu. *Application contact:* John W. Naughton, Director for Graduate Admissions, 614-251-4721, Fax: 614-251-6654, E-mail: grad@ohiodominican.edu.
Website: http://www.ohiodominican.edu/academics/graduate/mba

Oklahoma Wesleyan University, Professional Studies Division, Bartlesville, OK 74006-6299. Offers nursing administration (MSN); nursing education (MSN); strategic leadership (MS); theology and apologetics (MA).

Oregon State University, College of Business, Program in Business Administration, Corvallis, OR 97331. Offers business administration (PhD), including accounting, innovation/commercialization; business analytics (MBA); corporate finance (MBA); innovation management (MBA); organizational leadership (MBA); research thesis (MBA); supply chain and logistics management (MBA). *Program availability:* Part-time, blended/hybrid learning. *Faculty:* 47 full-time (13 women), 10 part-time/adjunct (3 women). *Students:* 132 full-time (58 women), 83 part-time (36 women); includes 24 minority (3 Black or African American, non-Hispanic/Latino; 11 Asian, non-Hispanic/Latino; 8 Hispanic/Latino; 1 Native Hawaiian or other Pacific Islander, non-Hispanic/Latino; 1 Two or more races, non-Hispanic/Latino), 91 international. Average age 30. 203 applicants, 38% accepted, 67 enrolled. In 2016, 81 master's awarded. *Entrance requirements:* For master's, GMAT. Additional exam requirements/recommendations for international students: Required—TOEFL (minimum score 91 iBT), IELTS (minimum score 7). *Application deadline:* For fall admission, 2/1 priority date for domestic and international students; for winter admission, 9/15 priority date for domestic and international students; for spring admission, 1/1 priority date for domestic and international students. Applications are processed on a rolling basis. Application fee: $75 ($85 for international students). *Expenses:* $19,143 resident full-time tuition, $32,616 non-resident (for MBA). *Financial support:* Application deadline: 1/15. *Unit head:* Dr. David Baldridge, Director for Business Master's Program, 541-737-6062, E-mail: david.baldridge@bus.oregonstate.edu. *Application contact:* E-mail: osumba@bus.oregonstate.edu.
Website: http://business.oregonstate.edu/graduate-programs

Pace University, Lubin School of Business, Program in Management, New York, NY 10038. Offers change management (MBA); entrepreneurial studies (MBA); entrepreneurship (MS); human resource management (MBA, MS); strategic management (MBA, MS). *Program availability:* Part-time, evening/weekend. *Students:* 68 full-time (32 women), 75 part-time (44 women); includes 50 minority (22 Black or African American, non-Hispanic/Latino; 13 Asian, non-Hispanic/Latino; 12 Hispanic/Latino; 3 Two or more races, non-Hispanic/Latino), 47 international. Average age 30. 171 applicants, 60% accepted, 55 enrolled. In 2016, 69 master's awarded. *Entrance requirements:* For master's, GMAT, GRE (GMAT not required for MS with 3 years of HR experience in a management position), undergraduate degree, transcripts from all accredited colleges/universities attended, two letters of recommendation, resume, personal statement. Additional exam requirements/recommendations for international students: Required—TOEFL (minimum score 90 iBT), IELTS (minimum score 7) or PTE (minimum score 61). *Application deadline:* For fall admission, 8/1 priority date for domestic students, 6/1 for international students; for spring admission, 12/1 for domestic students, 10/1 for international students. Applications are processed on a rolling basis. Application fee: $70. Electronic applications accepted. *Expenses: Tuition:* Part-time $1195 per credit. *Required fees:* $260 per semester. Tuition and fees vary according to

degree level, campus/location and program. *Financial support:* Research assistantships, career-related internships or fieldwork, and Federal Work-Study available. Support available to part-time students. Financial award application deadline: 2/15; financial award applicants required to submit FAFSA. *Unit head:* Dr. John C. Byrne, Chairperson, 212-618-6581, E-mail: jbyrne@pace.edu. *Application contact:* Susan Ford-Goldschein, Director of Graduate Admissions, 212-346-1531, Fax: 212-346-1585, E-mail: graduateadmission@pace.edu.
Website: http://www.pace.edu/lubin/management-concentration-mba

Philadelphia University, School of Business Administration, Program in Business Administration, Philadelphia, PA 19144. Offers general business (MBA); innovation (MBA); management (MBA); marketing (MBA); strategic design (MBA); MBA/MS. *Program availability:* Part-time, evening/weekend, online learning. *Entrance requirements:* For master's, GMAT. Additional exam requirements/recommendations for international students: Required—TOEFL (minimum score 550 paper-based; 79 iBT).

Philadelphia University, School of Business Administration, Program in Strategic Design Business Administration, Philadelphia, PA 19144. Offers MBA. *Program availability:* Evening/weekend.

Pontificia Universidad Catolica Madre y Maestra, Graduate School, Faculty of Social and Administrative Sciences, Santiago, Dominican Republic. Offers business administration (MBA), including business development, finance, international business, management skills (M Mgmt, MBA), marketing, operations, strategic cost management, strategy, tourist destination planning and management; law (LL M), including civil law, corporate business law, criminal law, international relations, real estate law; management (M Mgmt), including higher financial management, insurance program administration, management skills (M Mgmt, MBA); psychology (MA), including clinical child and adolescent psychology, forensic psychology; strategic human resources (EMBA).

Regent University, Graduate School, School of Business and Leadership, Virginia Beach, VA 23464-9800. Offers business administration (MBA), including accounting, entrepreneurship, finance and investing, general management, healthcare management (MA, MBA), human resource management, innovation management; leadership (Certificate); organizational leadership (MA, PhD), including ecclesial leadership (PhD), entrepreneurial leadership (PhD), future studies (MA), healthcare management (MA, MBA), human resource development (PhD), interdisciplinary studies (MA), international organizations (MA), leadership coaching and mentoring (MA), not-for-profit management (MA), organizational communication (MA), organizational development consulting (MA); strategic leadership (DSL), including global consulting, leadership coaching, strategic foresight. *Program availability:* Part-time, evening/weekend, 100% online, blended/hybrid learning. *Faculty:* 9 full-time (2 women), 28 part-time/adjunct (10 women). *Students:* 100 full-time (56 women), 1,008 part-time (528 women); includes 562 minority (453 Black or African American, non-Hispanic/Latino; 7 American Indian or Alaska Native, non-Hispanic/Latino; 30 Asian, non-Hispanic/Latino; 51 Hispanic/Latino; 1 Native Hawaiian or other Pacific Islander, non-Hispanic/Latino; 20 Two or more races, non-Hispanic/Latino), 76 international. Average age 40. 1,240 applicants, 45% accepted, 352 enrolled. In 2016, 95 master's, 71 doctorates awarded. *Degree requirements:* For master's, thesis or alternative, 3-credit hour culminating experience; for doctorate, thesis/dissertation. *Entrance requirements:* For master's, college transcripts, resume, essay; for doctorate, college transcripts, resume, essay, writing sample; for Certificate, writing sample, resume, transcripts. Additional exam requirements/recommendations for international students: Required—TOEFL (minimum score 577 paper-based). *Application deadline:* For fall admission, 5/1 priority date for domestic students; for spring admission, 10/1 priority date for domestic students. Applications are processed on a rolling basis. Application fee: $50. Electronic applications accepted. *Expenses:* Contact institution. *Financial support:* In 2016–17, 631 students received support. Career-related internships or fieldwork, scholarships/grants, and unspecified assistantships available. Support available to part-time students. *Faculty research:* Servant leadership, global business, team effectiveness, technology utilization, leadership development. *Unit head:* Dr. Doris Gomez, Dean, 757-352-4686, Fax: 757-352-4634, E-mail: dorigom@regent.edu. *Application contact:* Heidi Cece, Assistant Vice President of Enrollment Management, 800-373-5504, Fax: 757-352-4381, E-mail: admissions@regent.edu.
Website: http://www.regent.edu/sbl/

Regis University, College of Business and Economics, Denver, CO 80221-1099. Offers accounting (MS); executive leadership (Certificate); finance (MS); finance and accounting (MBA); health industry leadership (MBA); human resource management and leadership (MSOL); management (MBA); marketing (MBA); nonprofit leadership (Post-Graduate Certificate); nonprofit management (MNM); nonprofit organizational capacity building (Certificate); operations management (MBA); organizational leadership and management (MSOL); project leadership and management (MS, MSOL); strategic business management (Certificate); strategic human resource integration (Certificate); strategic management (MBA). Programs offered at Colorado Springs Campus, Northwest Denver Campus, Southeast Denver Campus, Fort Collins Campus, Broomfield Campus, Henderson (Nevada) Campus, and Summerlin (Nevada) Campus. *Program availability:* Part-time, evening/weekend, 100% online, blended/hybrid learning. *Faculty:* 15 full-time (5 women), 43 part-time/adjunct (16 women). *Students:* 622 full-time (350 women), 460 part-time (170 women); includes 317 minority (88 Black or African American, non-Hispanic/Latino; 7 American Indian or Alaska Native, non-Hispanic/Latino; 44 Asian, non-Hispanic/Latino; 151 Hispanic/Latino; 1 Native Hawaiian or other Pacific Islander, non-Hispanic/Latino; 26 Two or more races, non-Hispanic/Latino), 44 international. Average age 36. 307 applicants, 73% accepted, 134 enrolled. In 2016, 394 master's awarded. *Degree requirements:* For master's, thesis (for some programs), capstone or final research project. *Entrance requirements:* For master's, official transcript reflecting baccalaureate degree awarded from regionally-accredited college or university, interview, 2 years of full-time related work experience, resume, letters of recommendation. Additional exam requirements/recommendations for international students: Required—TOEFL (minimum score 550 paper-based; 82 iBT). *Application deadline:* For fall admission, 8/15 priority date for domestic students, 8/13 for international students; for winter admission, 10/10 priority date for domestic students, 9/8 for international students; for spring admission, 1/10 priority date for domestic students, 11/17 for international students; for summer admission, 5/1 priority date for domestic students. Applications are processed on a rolling basis. Application fee: $75. Electronic applications accepted. *Expenses:* $780 per credit hour. *Financial support:* Scholarships/grants available. Financial award application deadline: 4/15; financial award applicants required to submit FAFSA. *Faculty research:* Impact of information technology on small business regulation of accounting, international project financing, mineral development, delivery of healthcare to rural indigenous communities. *Unit head:* Dr. Timothy Keane, Academic Dean. *Application contact:* Cate Clark, Director of Admissions, 303-458-4900, Fax: 303-964-5534, E-mail: ruadmissions@regis.edu.
Website: http://www.regis.edu/CBE.aspx

Robert Morris University Illinois, Morris Graduate School of Management, Chicago, IL 60605. Offers accounting (MBA); accounting/finance (MBA); business analytics (MIS); design and media (MM); design management (MM); educational technology (MM); health care administration (MM); higher education administration (MM); human resource management (MBA); information security (MIS); information systems (MBA, MIS); law enforcement administration (MM); management (MBA); management/finance (MBA); management/human resource management (MBA); mobile computing (MIS); sports administration (MM). *Program availability:* Part-time, evening/weekend. *Faculty:* 4 full-time (1 woman), 25 part-time/adjunct (5 women). *Students:* 196 full-time (98 women), 151 part-time (85 women); includes 200 minority (114 Black or African American, non-Hispanic/Latino; 17 Asian, non-Hispanic/Latino; 67 Hispanic/Latino; 2 Two or more races, non-Hispanic/Latino), 23 international. Average age 33. 174 applicants, 61% accepted, 97 enrolled. In 2016, 190 master's awarded. *Entrance requirements:* For master's, official transcripts and letters of recommendation (for some programs); written personal statement. Additional exam requirements/recommendations for international students: Required—TOEFL (minimum score 550 paper-based). *Application deadline:* Applications are processed on a rolling basis. Application fee: $20 ($100 for international students). Electronic applications accepted. *Expenses: Tuition:* Full-time $16,500; part-time $2750 per course. *Financial support:* In 2016–17, 444 students received support. Federal Work-Study, scholarships/grants, and unspecified assistantships available. Support available to part-time students. Financial award applicants required to submit FAFSA. *Unit head:* Kayed Akkawi, Dean, 312-935-6050, Fax: 312-935-6020, E-mail: kakkawi@robertmorris.edu. *Application contact:* Danielle Naffziger, Vice President of Marketing and Enrollment, 312-935-4812, Fax: 312-935-6020, E-mail: dnaffziger@robertmorris.edu.

Roberts Wesleyan College, Graduate Business Programs, Rochester, NY 14624-1997. Offers strategic leadership (MS); strategic marketing (MS). *Program availability:* Evening/weekend. *Degree requirements:* For master's, thesis or alternative. *Entrance requirements:* For master's, GMAT, minimum GPA of 2.75, verifiable work experience. *Expenses:* Contact institution.

Rockhurst University, Helzberg School of Management, Kansas City, MO 64110-2561. Offers accounting (MBA); business intelligence (MBA, Certificate); data science (MBA, Certificate); entrepreneurship (MBA); finance (MBA); fundraising leadership (MBA, Certificate); healthcare management (MBA, Certificate); human capital (Certificate); international business (Certificate); management (MBA, Certificate); nonprofit administration (Certificate); organizational development (Certificate); science leadership (Certificate). *Accreditation:* AACSB. *Program availability:* Part-time, evening/weekend. *Entrance requirements:* For master's, GMAT or GRE. Additional exam requirements/recommendations for international students: Required—TOEFL (minimum score 550 paper-based; 79 iBT). Electronic applications accepted. Application fee is waived when completed online. *Faculty research:* Offshoring/outsourcing, systems analysis/synthesis, work teams, multilateral trade, path dependencies/creation.

St. John's University, The Peter J. Tobin College of Business, Department of Computer Information Systems and Decision Sciences, Queens, NY 11439. Offers business analytics (MBA). *Program availability:* Part-time, evening/weekend. *Degree requirements:* For master's, comprehensive exam (for some programs), thesis optional. *Entrance requirements:* For master's, GMAT, 2 letters of recommendation, resume, transcripts, essay. Additional exam requirements/recommendations for international students: Required—TOEFL (minimum score 600 paper-based; 100 iBT), IELTS (minimum score 7). Electronic applications accepted. *Expenses:* Contact institution.

Saint Joseph's University, Erivan K. Haub School of Business, MS Program in Business Intelligence and Analytics, Philadelphia, PA 19131-1395. Offers MS. *Program availability:* Part-time, evening/weekend, online learning. *Faculty:* 12 full-time (6 women), 17 part-time/adjunct (3 women). *Students:* 74 full-time (33 women), 224 part-time (94 women); includes 67 minority (33 Black or African American, non-Hispanic/Latino; 24 Asian, non-Hispanic/Latino; 9 Hispanic/Latino; 1 Two or more races, non-Hispanic/Latino), 102 international. Average age 33. 268 applicants, 77% accepted, 97 enrolled. In 2016, 112 master's awarded. *Degree requirements:* For master's, minimum GPA of 3.0. *Entrance requirements:* For master's, GMAT or GRE, 2 letters of recommendation, resume, personal statement, official undergraduate and graduate transcripts. Additional exam requirements/recommendations for international students: Required—TOEFL (minimum score 550 paper-based, 80 iBT), IELTS (minimum score 6.5), or PTE (minimum score 60). *Application deadline:* For fall admission, 7/15 priority date for domestic students, 5/15 priority date for international students; for spring admission, 11/15 priority date for domestic students, 10/15 priority date for international students; for summer admission, 4/15 priority date for domestic students. Applications are processed on a rolling basis. Application fee: $35. Electronic applications accepted. *Expenses:* $1,003 per credit. *Financial support:* In 2016–17, 67 students received support. Scholarships/grants available. Support available to part-time students. Financial award application deadline: 5/1; financial award applicants required to submit FAFSA. *Unit head:* Jeannine Lajeunesse, Director, 610-660-1626, Fax: 610-660-1229, E-mail: jlajeune@sju.edu. *Application contact:* Kate Sonstein, Program Manager/Recruiter, 610-660-1693, E-mail: kate.sonstein@sju.edu.
Website: http://www.sju.edu/hsb/bi/

Saint Joseph's University, Erivan K. Haub School of Business, MS Program in Managing Human Capital, Philadelphia, PA 19131-1395. Offers MS. *Program availability:* Part-time, evening/weekend. *Faculty:* 4 full-time (3 women), 1 (woman) part-time/adjunct. *Students:* 14 part-time (11 women); includes 2 minority (both Black or African American, non-Hispanic/Latino). Average age 38. 15 applicants, 13% accepted, 1 enrolled. In 2016, 7 master's awarded. *Degree requirements:* For master's, minimum GPA of 3.0. *Entrance requirements:* For master's, MAT, GRE, or GMAT, 2 letters of recommendation, resume, personal statement, official undergraduate and graduate transcripts. Additional exam requirements/recommendations for international students: Required—TOEFL (minimum score 550 paper-based, 80 iBT), IELTS (minimum score 6.5), or PTE (minimum score 60). *Application deadline:* For fall admission, 7/15 priority date for domestic students; for spring admission, 11/15 priority date for domestic students. Application fee: $35. *Expenses:* $1,003 per credit. *Financial support:* In 2016–17, 1 student received support. Scholarships/grants available. Support available to part-time students. Financial award application deadline: 5/1; financial award applicants required to submit FAFSA. *Unit head:* Jeannine Lajeunesse, Director, 610-660-1626, E-mail: jlajeune@sju.edu. *Application contact:* Kate Sonstein, Program Manager/Recruiter, 610-660-1693, E-mail: kate.sonstein@sju.edu.
Website: http://sju.edu/majors-programs/graduate-business/master-degrees/managing-human-capital-ms

Saint Mary-of-the-Woods College, Master of Leadership Development Program, Saint Mary of the Woods, IN 47876. Offers not-for-profit leadership (MLD); organizational leadership (MLD). *Program availability:* Part-time, blended/hybrid learning. *Students:* 47 full-time (41 women); includes 4 minority (all Black or African American, non-Hispanic/Latino). Average age 35. *Degree requirements:* For master's, thesis. *Application deadline:* Applications are processed on a rolling basis. Application fee: $0. Electronic applications accepted. *Expenses:* Contact institution. *Financial support:* Scholarships/grants available. *Unit head:* Susan Decker, Director, Master of Leadership Development, 812-535-5206, E-mail: sdecker2@smwc.edu.

Salve Regina University, Holistic Graduate Programs, Newport, RI 02840-4192. Offers expressive and creative arts (CAGS, CGS); holistic counseling (MA); holistic leadership (MA, CAGS, CGS); holistic leadership and change management (CAGS); holistic studies (CGS); substance abuse and treatment (CAGS); substance abuse foundations in holistic studies (CGS). *Program availability:* Part-time, evening/weekend. *Degree requirements:* For master's, internship, project. *Entrance requirements:* For master's, GMAT, GRE General Test, or MAT. Additional exam requirements/recommendations for international students: Required—TOEFL (minimum score 600 paper-based; 100 iBT) or IELTS. Electronic applications accepted.

Salve Regina University, Program in Management, Newport, RI 02840-4192. Offers innovation and strategic management (MS); nonprofit management (CGS). *Program availability:* Part-time, evening/weekend, online learning. *Entrance requirements:* For master's, GMAT, GRE General Test, or MAT. Additional exam requirements/ recommendations for international students: Required—TOEFL (minimum score 600 paper-based; 100 iBT). Electronic applications accepted.

San Jose State University, Graduate Studies and Research, College of Applied Sciences and Arts, San Jose, CA 95192-0001. Offers big data (Certificate); California library media teacher services (Credential); collaborative response to family violence (Certificate); justice studies (MS); kinesiology (MA), including applied sciences and arts (MA, MS), athletic training, exercise physiology, sport management, sport studies; library and information science (MLIS, Certificate); mass communication (MA); nutritional science (MS); occupational therapy (MS); public health (MPH); pupil personnel services (Credential); recreation (MS), including applied sciences and arts (MA, MS), international tourism; social work (MSW); Spanish language counseling (Certificate); strategic management of digital assets and services (Certificate). *Program availability:* Part-time, evening/weekend. Electronic applications accepted.

Southern Illinois University Edwardsville, Graduate School, School of Business, Program in Business Administration, Edwardsville, IL 62026. Offers business analytics (MBA); management information systems (MBA); project management (MBA). *Accreditation:* AACSB. *Program availability:* Part-time, evening/weekend. *Degree requirements:* For master's, comprehensive exam. *Entrance requirements:* For master's, GMAT. Additional exam requirements/recommendations for international students: Required—TOEFL (minimum score 550 paper-based; 79 iBT), IELTS (minimum score 6.5). Electronic applications accepted.

Southern Methodist University, Cox School of Business, MBA Program, Dallas, TX 75275. Offers accounting (MBA, PMBA); business administration (EMBA); finance (MBA); financial statement analysis (PMBA); general business (MBA); information technology and operations management (MBA); management (MBA); marketing (MBA); real estate (MBA); strategy (MBA); strategy and entrepreneurship (MBA); JD/MBA; MA/ MBA. *Program availability:* Part-time, evening/weekend. *Entrance requirements:* For master's, GMAT. Additional exam requirements/recommendations for international students: Required—TOEFL. Electronic applications accepted. *Expenses:* Contact institution. *Faculty research:* Corporate finance, financial reporting, modeling consumer decision-making, competition between national brands and store brands, institutional determinants of firms' strategy.

Stevens Institute of Technology, Graduate School, School of Business, Program in Management, Hoboken, NJ 07030. Offers general management (MS); global innovation management (MS); human resource management (MS); information management (MS); project management (MS); technology commercialization (MS); technology management (MS). *Program availability:* Part-time, evening/weekend. *Students:* 83 full-time (28 women), 82 part-time (36 women); includes 30 minority (6 Black or African American, non-Hispanic/Latino; 1 American Indian or Alaska Native, non-Hispanic/ Latino; 21 Asian, non-Hispanic/Latino; 2 Hispanic/Latino), 73 international. Average age 29. 381 applicants, 64% accepted, 53 enrolled. In 2016, 66 master's awarded. *Degree requirements:* For master's, thesis optional, minimum B average in major field and overall. *Entrance requirements:* Additional exam requirements/recommendations for international students: Required—TOEFL (minimum score 74 iBT), IELTS (minimum score 6). *Application deadline:* For fall admission, 6/1 for domestic students, 4/15 for international students; for spring admission, 11/30 for domestic students, 11/1 for international students. Applications are processed on a rolling basis. Application fee: $65. Electronic applications accepted. *Expenses:* Contact institution. *Financial support:* Fellowships, research assistantships, teaching assistantships, career-related internships or fieldwork, Federal Work-Study, scholarships/grants, and unspecified assistantships available. Financial award application deadline: 2/15; financial award applicants required to submit FAFSA. *Unit head:* Brian Rothschild, Director, 201-216-3677, E-mail: brian.rothschild@stevens.edu. *Application contact:* Graduate Admissions, 888-783-8367, Fax: 888-511-1306, E-mail: graduate@stevens.edu.
Website: https://www.stevens.edu/school-business/masters-programs/management

Suffolk University, Sawyer Business School, Master of Business Administration Program, Boston, MA 02108-2770. Offers accounting (MBA); entrepreneurship (MBA); executive business administration (EMBA); finance (MBA); global business administration (GMBA); health administration (MBA); international business (MBA); marketing (MBA); nonprofit management (MBA); organizational behavior (MBA); strategic management (MBA); supply chain management (MBA); taxation (MBA); JD/ MBA; MBA/MHA; MBA/MSA; MBA/MSF; MBA/MST. *Accreditation:* AACSB. *Program availability:* Part-time, evening/weekend, 100% online. *Faculty:* 17 full-time (6 women), 10 part-time/adjunct (1 woman). *Students:* 137 full-time (70 women), 265 part-time (138 women); includes 78 minority (20 Black or African American, non-Hispanic/Latino; 22 Asian, non-Hispanic/Latino; 31 Hispanic/Latino; 5 Two or more races, non-Hispanic/ Latino), 46 international. Average age 30. 416 applicants, 70% accepted, 128 enrolled. In 2016, 165 degrees awarded. *Entrance requirements:* For master's, GMAT, minimum undergraduate GPA of 2.75 (MBA), 5 years of managerial experience (EMBA). Additional exam requirements/recommendations for international students: Required—TOEFL (minimum score 550 paper-based; 80 iBT). *Application deadline:* For fall admission, 3/15 priority date for domestic students, 10/15 priority date for international students; for spring admission, 10/15 priority date for domestic and international students. Applications are processed on a rolling basis. Application fee: $50. Electronic applications accepted. *Expenses: Tuition:* Full-time $41,490; part-time $1383 per credit hour. *Required fees:* $52; $52 per credit hour. Part-time tuition and fees vary according to course load and program. *Financial support:* In 2016–17, 209 students received support, including 176 fellowships (averaging $8,581 per year); career-related internships or fieldwork, Federal Work-Study, institutionally sponsored loans, and scholarships/grants also available. Support available to part-time students. Financial award application deadline: 4/1; financial award applicants required to submit FAFSA. *Faculty research:* Foreign investments; career strategies and boundaryless careers; corporate ethics codes; interest rates, inflation, and growth options; innovation and product development performance. *Unit head:* Jodi Detjen, Director of MBA Programs, 617-573-8306, E-mail: jdetjen@suffolk.edu. *Application contact:* Mara Marzocchi, Associate Director of Graduate Admissions, 617-573-8302, Fax: 617-305-1733, E-mail: grad.admission@suffolk.edu.
Website: http://www.suffolk.edu/mba

Syracuse University, Martin J. Whitman School of Management, Master of Business Administration Program, Syracuse, NY 13244. Offers accounting (MBA); business analytics (MBA); entrepreneurship (MBA); marketing management (MBA); real estate (MBA); supply chain management (MBA); JD/MBA. *Program availability:* Part-time, 100% online. *Students:* 22 full-time (9 women), 495 part-time (147 women); includes 182 minority (81 Black or African American, non-Hispanic/Latino; 3 American Indian or Alaska Native, non-Hispanic/Latino; 42 Asian, non-Hispanic/Latino; 52 Hispanic/Latino; 4 Native Hawaiian or other Pacific Islander, non-Hispanic/Latino), 22 international. Average age 32. 1,086 applicants, 73% accepted, 518 enrolled. In 2016, 84 master's awarded. *Entrance requirements:* For master's, GMAT or GRE, resume, essay, 5-minute video interview, two letters of recommendation, transcripts (unofficial). Additional exam requirements/recommendations for international students: Required—TOEFL (minimum score 100 iBT), IELTS (minimum score 7), PTE (minimum score 68). *Application deadline:* For fall admission, 11/30 for domestic students, 11/30 priority date for international students; for winter admission, 1/1 for domestic students, 1/1 priority date for international students; for spring admission, 2/15 for domestic and international students; for summer admission, 4/19 for domestic students. Application fee: $75. Electronic applications accepted. *Expenses:* Contact institution. *Financial support:* In 2016–17, 22 students received support. Merit scholarships available. Financial award application deadline: 2/15. *Faculty research:* Data analysis, economics of international business, financial markets and institutions, operations management, supply chain management. *Unit head:* Don Harter, Associate Dean, Graduate Programs, 315-443-3502, E-mail: dharter@syr.edu. *Application contact:* Shri Ramakrishnan, Assistant Director, Graduate Recruitment, 315-443-3497, Fax: 315-443-9517, E-mail: busgrad@ syr.edu.
Website: http://whitman.syr.edu/ftmba/

Taylor University, Master of Business Administration Program, Upland, IN 46989-1001. Offers emerging business strategies (MBA); global leadership (MBA). *Program availability:* Part-time.

Temple University, Fox School of Business, Doctoral Programs in Business, Philadelphia, PA 19122-6096. Offers accounting (PhD); entrepreneurship (PhD); finance (PhD); international business (PhD); management information systems (PhD); marketing (PhD); risk management and insurance (PhD); statistics (PhD); strategic management (PhD); tourism and sport (PhD). *Accreditation:* AACSB. *Degree requirements:* For doctorate, thesis/dissertation. *Entrance requirements:* For doctorate, GRE General Test, GMAT, minimum GPA of 3.0, master's degree. Additional exam requirements/recommendations for international students: Required—TOEFL (minimum score 600 paper-based; 100 iBT), IELTS (minimum score 7.5). Electronic applications accepted.

Tennessee State University, The School of Graduate Studies and Research, College of Public Service, Nashville, TN 37209-1561. Offers human resource management (MPS); public administration (MPA, PhD); social work (MSW); strategic leadership (MPS); training and development (MPS). *Accreditation:* NASPAA (one or more programs are accredited). *Program availability:* Part-time, evening/weekend. *Degree requirements:* For master's, comprehensive exam, thesis optional; for doctorate, comprehensive exam, thesis/dissertation. *Entrance requirements:* For master's, GRE General Test, minimum GPA of 2.5, writing sample; for doctorate, GRE General Test, minimum GPA of 3.25, writing sample. *Faculty research:* Total quality management and process improvement, national health care policy and administration, starting non-profit ventures, public service ethics, state education financing across the U.S. public.

Tennessee Technological University, College of Graduate Studies, College of Interdisciplinary Studies, School of Professional Studies, Cookeville, TN 38505. Offers human resources leadership (MPS); strategic leadership (MPS); training and development (MPS). *Program availability:* Part-time, evening/weekend, online learning. *Students:* 19 full-time (8 women), 57 part-time (33 women); includes 11 minority (7 Black or African American, non-Hispanic/Latino; 1 Hispanic/Latino; 1 Native Hawaiian or other Pacific Islander, non-Hispanic/Latino; 2 Two or more races, non-Hispanic/Latino). 39 applicants, 64% accepted, 16 enrolled. In 2016, 9 master's awarded. *Degree requirements:* For master's, comprehensive exam, thesis or alternative. *Entrance requirements:* For master's, GRE. Additional exam requirements/recommendations for international students: Required—TOEFL (minimum score 527 paper-based; 71 iBT), IELTS (minimum score 5.5), PTE (minimum score 48), or TOEIC (Test of English as an International Communication). *Application deadline:* For fall admission, 7/1 for domestic students, 5/1 for international students; for spring admission, 11/1 for domestic students, 10/1 for international students; for summer admission, 5/1 for domestic students, 2/1 for international students. Applications are processed on a rolling basis. Application fee: $35 ($40 for international students). Electronic applications accepted. *Expenses:* Tuition, state resident: full-time $9375; part-time $534 per credit hour. Tuition, nonresident: full-time $22,443; part-time $1260 per credit hour. *Financial support:* Application deadline: 4/1. *Unit head:* Dr. Joseph Roberts, Interim Director, School of Professional Studies, 931-372-6223, E-mail: jmroberts@tntech.edu. *Application contact:* Shelia K. Kendrick, Coordinator of Graduate Studies, 931-372-3808, Fax: 931-372-3497, E-mail: skendrick@tntech.edu.
Website: https://www.tntech.edu/is/sps/

Tufts University, Graduate School of Arts and Sciences, Graduate Certificate Programs, Program Evaluation Program, Medford, MA 02155. Offers Certificate. *Program availability:* Part-time, evening/weekend. Electronic applications accepted. *Expenses:* Contact institution.

Tulane University, A. B. Freeman School of Business, New Orleans, LA 70118-5669. Offers accounting (M Acct); analytics (MBA); banking and financial services (M Fin); energy (M Fin, MBA); entrepreneurship (MBA); finance (MBA, PhD); international business (MBA); international management (MBA); strategic management and leadership (MBA); JD/M Acct; JD/MBA; MBA/M Acc; MBA/MA; MBA/MD; MBA/ME; MBA/MPH. *Accreditation:* AACSB. *Program availability:* Part-time, evening/weekend. *Faculty:* 46 full-time (11 women), 36 part-time/adjunct (3 women). *Students:* 488 full-time (240 women), 414 part-time (198 women); includes 81 minority (31 Black or African American, non-Hispanic/Latino; 1 American Indian or Alaska Native, non-Hispanic/ Latino; 17 Asian, non-Hispanic/Latino; 29 Hispanic/Latino; 3 Two or more races, non-Hispanic/Latino), 575 international. Average age 27. 2,038 applicants, 71% accepted, 511 enrolled. In 2016, 694 master's, 9 doctorates awarded. Terminal master's awarded for partial completion of doctoral program. *Degree requirements:* For master's, one foreign language, comprehensive exam (for some programs); for doctorate, one foreign language, comprehensive exam, thesis/dissertation. *Entrance requirements:* For master's and doctorate, GMAT or GRE, interview. Additional exam requirements/ recommendations for international students: Required—TOEFL or IELTS. *Application deadline:* For fall admission, 11/1 priority date for domestic and international students; for winter admission, 1/6 for domestic and international students; for spring admission, 3/1 priority date for domestic and international students; for summer admission, 5/5 for domestic students. Applications are processed on a rolling basis. Application fee: $125. Electronic applications accepted. *Expenses:* Contact institution. *Financial support:* In 2016–17, 153 students received support. Fellowships with tuition reimbursements available, research assistantships, teaching assistantships, career-related internships or fieldwork, Federal Work-Study, tuition waivers (full and partial), and unspecified assistantships available. Support available to part-time students. Financial award application deadline: 4/15; financial award applicants required to submit FAFSA. *Faculty research:* Corporate finance, managerial accounting and financial reporting, strategic management and leadership, consumer behavior and decision making, organizational behavior and human resource management. *Unit head:* Ira Solomon, PhD, Dean, 504-865-5407, Fax: 504-865-5491, E-mail: businessdean@tulane.edu. *Application contact:*

Management Strategy and Policy

Melissa Booth, Director of Graduate Admissions and Financial Aid, 800-223-5402, E-mail: freeman.admissions@tulane.edu.
Website: http://www.freeman.tulane.edu

United States International University–Africa, School of Business Administration, Nairobi, Kenya. Offers business administration (GEMBA); entrepreneurship (MBA); finance (MBA); human resource management (MBA); information technology management (MBA); integrated studies (MBA); international business administration (MBA); management and organizational development (MS); marketing (MBA); organizational development (EMS); strategic management (MBA). *Program availability:* Part-time, evening/weekend. *Degree requirements:* For master's, thesis. *Entrance requirements:* For master's, GMAT, 2 letters of reference, resume. Additional exam requirements/recommendations for international students: Required—TOEFL (minimum score 550 paper-based). *Faculty research:* Marketing in small business enterprises, total quality management in Kenya.

Universidad del Este, Graduate School, Carolina, PR 00984. Offers accounting (MBA); adult education (M Ed); agribusiness (MBA); criminal justice and criminology (MA); curriculum and instruction - early education (M Ed); curriculum and instruction - elementary (M Ed); curriculum and instruction - English (M Ed); curriculum and instruction - Spanish (M Ed); human resources (MBA); information security management (MBA); information technology and Web business development (MBA); management (MBA); public policy (MPA); social work (MA), including clinical social work; special education (M Ed); strategic leadership (MBA).

University at Buffalo, the State University of New York, Graduate School, School of Management, Buffalo, NY 14620. Offers accounting (MS); analytics (MBA); business administration (PMBA); consulting (MBA); finance (MBA, MS), including financial risk management (MS), quantitative finance (MS); healthcare (MBA); information assurance (MBA); information systems (MBA); international management (MBA); management (EMBA, PhD); management information systems (MS); marketing (MBA); supply chain and operations (MBA); supply chains and operations management (MS); Au D/MBA; DDS/MBA; JD/MBA; M Arch/MBA; MD/MBA; MPH/MBA; MSW/MBA; Pharm D/MBA. *Accreditation:* AACSB. *Program availability:* Part-time, evening/weekend. *Faculty:* 80 full-time (26 women), 36 part-time/adjunct (6 women). *Students:* 683 full-time (277 women), 196 part-time (63 women); includes 76 minority (23 Black or African American, non-Hispanic/Latino; 1 American Indian or Alaska Native, non-Hispanic/Latino; 48 Asian, non-Hispanic/Latino; 3 Hispanic/Latino; 1 Two or more races, non-Hispanic/Latino), 371 international. Average age 31. 2,451 applicants, 42% accepted, 484 enrolled. In 2016, 515 master's, 10 doctorates awarded. *Degree requirements:* For master's, thesis (for some programs); for doctorate, comprehensive exam, thesis/dissertation. *Entrance requirements:* For master's, GMAT (for MS in accounting, finance); GRE or GMAT (for MBA, PMBA, other MS concentrations), essays, letters of recommendation; for doctorate, GMAT or GRE, essays, writing sample, letters of recommendation. Additional exam requirements/recommendations for international students: Required—TOEFL (minimum score 95 iBT) or IELTS (minimum score 6.5); Recommended—TSE (minimum score 73). *Application deadline:* For fall admission, 10/15 priority date for domestic and international students; for winter admission, 2/1 priority date for domestic and international students; for spring admission, 4/15 for domestic students; for summer admission, 5/15 for domestic students. Application fee: $100. Electronic applications accepted. *Expenses:* Contact institution. *Financial support:* Fellowships with full and partial tuition reimbursements, research assistantships with full and partial tuition reimbursements, teaching assistantships with full and partial tuition reimbursements, career-related internships or fieldwork, Federal Work-Study, institutionally sponsored loans, scholarships/grants, health care benefits, and unspecified assistantships available. Financial award application deadline: 2/15. *Faculty research:* Data analytics, accounting information and corporate finance, consumer behavior, supply chain logistics, leadership and team effectiveness. *Total annual research expenditures:* $1.5 million. *Unit head:* Erin K. O'Brien, Assistant Dean and Director of Graduate Programs, 716-645-3204, Fax: 716-645-2341, E-mail: ekobrien@buffalo.edu. *Application contact:* Meghan Felser, Associate Director of Admissions and Recruiting, 716-645-3204, Fax: 716-645-2341, E-mail: mpwood@buffalo.edu.
Website: http://mgt.buffalo.edu/

The University of Arizona, Eller College of Management, Department of Management and Organizations, Tucson, AZ 85721. Offers MS, PhD. *Program availability:* Evening/weekend. *Entrance requirements:* Additional exam requirements/recommendations for international students: Required—TOEFL (minimum score 550 paper-based; 79 iBT). Electronic applications accepted. *Faculty research:* Organizational behavior, human resources, decision-making, health economics and finance, immigration.

The University of British Columbia, Sauder School of Business, Doctoral Program in Business Administration, Vancouver, BC V6T 1Z2, Canada. Offers accounting (PhD); finance (PhD); management information systems (PhD); management science (PhD); marketing (PhD); organizational behavior (PhD); strategy and business economics (PhD); transportation and logistics (PhD); urban land economics (PhD). *Degree requirements:* For doctorate, comprehensive exam, thesis/dissertation. *Entrance requirements:* For doctorate, GMAT or GRE. Additional exam requirements/recommendations for international students: Required—TOEFL (minimum score 600 paper-based; 100 iBT). *Application deadline:* Applications are processed on a rolling basis. Application fee: $102 Canadian dollars ($165 Canadian dollars for international students). Electronic applications accepted. *Expenses:* $4,802 per year tuition and fees, $8,436 per year international. *Financial support:* Fellowships with full tuition reimbursements, research assistantships with full tuition reimbursements, and teaching assistantships with full tuition reimbursements available. *Application contact:* Elaine Cho, Administrator, PhD and M Sc Programs, 604-822-8366, Fax: 604-822-8755, E-mail: phd.program@sauder.ubc.ca.
Website: http://www.sauder.ubc.ca/Programs/PhD_in_Business_Administration

University of Calgary, Faculty of Graduate Studies, Centre for Military and Strategic Studies, Calgary, AB T2N 1N4, Canada. Offers MSS, PhD. PhD offered in special cases only. *Program availability:* Part-time. *Degree requirements:* For master's, thesis; for doctorate, comprehensive exam, thesis/dissertation. *Entrance requirements:* For master's, minimum GPA of 3.4. Additional exam requirements/recommendations for international students: Recommended—TOEFL (minimum score 550 paper-based). *Faculty research:* Military history, Israeli studies, strategic studies, int'l relations, Arctic security.

University of California, Los Angeles, Graduate Division, UCLA Anderson School of Management, Los Angeles, CA 90095-1481. Offers accounting (PhD); behavioral decision making (PhD); business administration (EMBA, MBA); decisions, operations, and technology management (PhD); finance (PhD); financial engineering (MFE); global economics and management (PhD); management and organizations (PhD); marketing (PhD); strategy and policy (PhD); DDS/MBA; MBA/JD; MBA/MD; MBA/MLAS; MBA/MLIS; MBA/MN; MBA/MPH; MBA/MPP; MBA/MSCS; MBA/MURP. *Accreditation:* AACSB. *Program availability:* Part-time, evening/weekend. *Faculty:* 90 full-time (20 women), 98 part-time/adjunct (19 women). *Students:* 865 full-time (263 women), 1,201 part-time (337 women); includes 710 minority (48 Black or African American, non-Hispanic/Latino; 1 American Indian or Alaska Native, non-Hispanic/Latino; 505 Asian, non-Hispanic/Latino; 88 Hispanic/Latino; 4 Native Hawaiian or other Pacific Islander, non-Hispanic/Latino; 64 Two or more races, non-Hispanic/Latino), 451 international. Average age 31. 5,643 applicants, 26% accepted, 881 enrolled. In 2016, 807 master's, 7 doctorates awarded. *Degree requirements:* For master's, comprehensive exam, field consulting project; internship (for MBA); thesis/dissertation (for MFE); for doctorate, comprehensive exam, thesis/dissertation, oral and written qualifying exams. *Entrance requirements:* For master's, GMAT or GRE, 4-year bachelor's degree or equivalent; 2 letters of recommendation; essays (1 for MBA, 2 for FEMBA and MFE); 4-8 years of full-time work experience (for FEMBA); minimum eight years of work experience with at least three years at management level (for EMBA); for doctorate, GMAT or GRE, bachelor's degree from college or university of fully-recognized standing, minimum B average during junior and senior years of undergraduate years, 3 letters of recommendation, statement of purpose. Additional exam requirements/recommendations for international students: Required—TOEFL (minimum score 560 paper-based; 87 iBT), IELTS (minimum score 7). *Application deadline:* For fall admission, 10/6 priority date for domestic and international students; for winter admission, 1/5 for domestic and international students; for spring admission, 4/12 for domestic and international students. Applications are processed on a rolling basis. Application fee: $200. Electronic applications accepted. *Expenses:* Contact institution. *Financial support:* In 2016–17, 633 students received support, including 455 fellowships (averaging $30,253 per year); research assistantships with partial tuition reimbursements available, teaching assistantships with partial tuition reimbursements available, career-related internships or fieldwork, institutionally sponsored loans, and scholarships/grants also available. Support available to part-time students. *Faculty research:* Finance/global economics, entrepreneurship, accounting, human resources/organizational behavior, marketing, behavioral decision making. *Total annual research expenditures:* $1.1 million. *Unit head:* Dr. Judy D. Olian, Dean/Chair in Management, 310-825-7982, Fax: 310-206-2073, E-mail: judy.olian@anderson.ucla.edu. *Application contact:* Alex Lawrence, Assistant Dean and Director of MBA Admissions, 310-825-6944, Fax: 310-825-8582, E-mail: mba.admissions@anderson.ucla.edu.
Website: http://www.anderson.ucla.edu/

University of California, San Diego, Graduate Division, Rady School of Management, La Jolla, CA 92093. Offers business administration (MBA); business analytics (MS); finance (MF); management (PhD). *Accreditation:* AACSB. *Program availability:* Part-time, evening/weekend. *Faculty:* 28 full-time (5 women), 5 part-time/adjunct (1 woman). *Students:* 433 full-time (183 women), 89 part-time (35 women). 2,021 applicants, 32% accepted, 313 enrolled. In 2016, 152 master's, 5 doctorates awarded. *Degree requirements:* For master's, capstone project; for doctorate, comprehensive exam, thesis/dissertation. *Entrance requirements:* For master's, GMAT (for MBA); GMAT or GRE General Test (for MF); for doctorate, GMAT or GRE General Test. Additional exam requirements/recommendations for international students: Required—TOEFL (minimum score 550 paper-based; 80 iBT), IELTS (minimum score 7). *Application deadline:* Applications are processed on a rolling basis. Application fee: $200. Electronic applications accepted. *Expenses:* Contact institution. *Financial support:* Fellowships, teaching assistantships, and scholarships/grants available. Financial award applicants required to submit FAFSA. *Faculty research:* Innovation technology, operations management, finance, behavioral economics, organizational strategy, marketing, business analytics. *Unit head:* Robert Sullivan, Dean, 858-822-0830, E-mail: rssullivan@ucsd.edu. *Application contact:* Jay Bryant, Director of Graduate Recruitment and Admissions, 858-534-0864, E-mail: radygradadmissions@ucsd.edu.
Website: http://rady.ucsd.edu/

University of Charleston, Master of Science in Strategic Leadership Program, Charleston, WV 25304-1099. Offers MS. *Students:* 136 full-time (35 women), 18 part-time (4 women); includes 25 minority (18 Black or African American, non-Hispanic/Latino; 4 Hispanic/Latino; 1 Native Hawaiian or other Pacific Islander, non-Hispanic/Latino; 2 Two or more races, non-Hispanic/Latino), 1 international. Average age 38. In 2016, 36 master's awarded. *Entrance requirements:* For master's, bachelor's degree from regionally-accredited college or university with minimum GPA of 3.0. *Application deadline:* Applications are processed on a rolling basis. Electronic applications accepted. *Expenses: Tuition:* Full-time $20,602; part-time $425 per credit. *Required fees:* $200. Tuition and fees vary according to course load, campus/location, program and student level. *Unit head:* Dr. John Barnette, Associate Dean of Leadership, 304-720-6688, E-mail: johnbarnette@ucwv.edu. *Application contact:* David Cooper, Admissions Representative, 304-352-0013, E-mail: davidcooper@ucwv.edu.
Website: http://www.ucwv.edu/Academics/Degree-Programs/Graduate-Programs/Master-of-Science-in-Strategic-Leadership/

University of Chicago, Booth School of Business, Full-Time MBA Program, Chicago, IL 60637. Offers accounting (MBA); analytic finance (MBA); analytic management (MBA); econometrics and statistics (MBA); economics (MBA); entrepreneurship (MBA); finance (MBA); general management (MBA); health administration and policy (Certificate); international business (MBA); managerial and organizational behavior (MBA); marketing analytics (MBA); marketing management (MBA); operations management (MBA); strategic management (MBA); MBA/AM; MBA/JD; MBA/MA; MBA/MD; MBA/MPP. *Accreditation:* AACSB. *Students:* 1,151 full-time (443 women), 17 part-time (9 women). Terminal master's awarded for partial completion of doctoral program. *Entrance requirements:* For master's, GMAT or GRE, transcripts, resume, 2 letters of recommendation, essay, interview. Additional exam requirements/recommendations for international students: Required—TOEFL (minimum score 600 paper-based; 104 iBT), IELTS (minimum score 7), PTE (minimum score 70). *Application deadline:* For spring admission, 4/1 for domestic and international students. Electronic applications accepted. *Expenses:* Contact institution. *Unit head:* Stacey Kole, Deputy Dean, 773-702-7121. *Application contact:* Full-time MBA Program Admissions, 773-702-7369, Fax: 773-702-9085, E-mail: admissions@chicagobooth.edu.
Website: https://www.chicagobooth.edu/programs/full-time

University of Colorado Denver, Business School, Master of Business Administration Program, Denver, CO 80217. Offers bioinnovation and entrepreneurship (MBA); business intelligence (MBA); business strategy (MBA); business to business marketing (MBA); business to consumer marketing (MBA); change management (MBA); corporate financial management (MBA); enterprise technology management (MBA); entrepreneurship (MBA); health administration (MBA), including financial management, health administration, health information technologies, international health management and policy; human resources management (MBA); international business (MBA); investment management (MBA); managing for sustainability (MBA); sports and entertainment management (MBA). *Accreditation:* AACSB. *Program availability:* Part-time, evening/weekend, 100% online, blended/hybrid learning. *Students:* 544 full-time (210 women), 112 part-time (22 women); includes 99 minority (15 Black or African American, non-Hispanic/Latino; 4 American Indian or Alaska Native, non-Hispanic/Latino; 38 Asian, non-Hispanic/Latino; 36 Hispanic/Latino; 6 Two or more races, non-Hispanic/Latino), 22 international. Average age 32. 335 applicants, 73% accepted, 179 enrolled. In 2016, 251 master's awarded. *Degree requirements:* For master's, 48 semester hours, including 30 of core courses, 3 in international business, and 15 in electives from over 50 other business courses. *Entrance requirements:* For master's, GMAT, resume, official transcripts, essay, two letters of recommendation, financial statements (for international applicants). Additional exam requirements/recommendations for international students: Required—TOEFL (minimum score 560

paper-based; 83 iBT); Recommended—IELTS (minimum score 6.5). *Application deadline:* For fall admission, 4/15 priority date for domestic students, 3/15 priority date for international students; for spring admission, 10/15 priority date for domestic students, 9/15 priority date for international students; for summer admission, 2/15 priority date for domestic students, 1/15 priority date for international students. Applications are processed on a rolling basis. Application fee: $50 ($75 for international students). Electronic applications accepted. *Expenses:* Contact institution. *Financial support:* In 2016–17, 171 students received support. Fellowships, research assistantships, teaching assistantships, Federal Work-Study, institutionally sponsored loans, scholarships/grants, traineeships, and unspecified assistantships available. Financial award application deadline: 4/1; financial award applicants required to submit FAFSA. *Faculty research:* Marketing, management, entrepreneurship, finance, health administration. *Unit head:* Woodrow Eckard, MBA Director, 303-315-8470, E-mail: woody.eckard@ucdenver.edu. *Application contact:* Shelly Townley, Admissions Director, Graduate Programs, 303-315-8202, E-mail: shelly.townley@ucdenver.edu.
Website: http://www.ucdenver.edu/academics/colleges/business/degrees/mba/Pages/MBA.aspx

University of Colorado Denver, Business School, Program in Management and Organization, Denver, CO 80217. Offers business strategy (MS); change and innovation (MS); enterprise technology management (MS); entrepreneurship and innovation (MS); global management (MS); leadership (MS); managing for sustainability (MS); managing human resources (MS); sports and entertainment management (MS). *Accreditation:* AACSB. *Program availability:* Part-time, evening/weekend, online learning. *Students:* 20 full-time (13 women), 17 part-time (10 women); includes 6 minority (3 Black or African American, non-Hispanic/Latino; 1 American Indian or Alaska Native, non-Hispanic/Latino; 1 Hispanic/Latino; 1 Two or more races, non-Hispanic/Latino), 6 international. Average age 33. 24 applicants, 58% accepted, 6 enrolled. In 2016, 19 master's awarded. *Degree requirements:* For master's, 30 semester hours (12 of required courses, 12 of management electives, and 6 of free electives). *Entrance requirements:* For master's, GMAT, resume, two letters of recommendation, essay, financial statements (for international applicants). Additional exam requirements/recommendations for international students: Required—TOEFL (minimum score 525 paper-based; 71 iBT); Recommended—IELTS (minimum score 6.5). *Application deadline:* For fall admission, 4/15 priority date for domestic students, 3/15 priority date for international students; for spring admission, 10/15 priority date for domestic students, 9/15 priority date for international students; for summer admission, 2/15 priority date for domestic students, 1/15 priority date for international students. Applications are processed on a rolling basis. Application fee: $50 ($75 for international students). Electronic applications accepted. *Expenses:* Contact institution. *Financial support:* In 2016–17, 7 students received support. Fellowships, research assistantships, teaching assistantships, Federal Work-Study, institutionally sponsored loans, scholarships/grants, and traineeships available. Financial award application deadline: 4/1; financial award applicants required to submit FAFSA. *Faculty research:* Human resource management, management of catastrophe, turnaround strategies. *Unit head:* Dr. Kenneth Bettenhausen, Associate Professor/Director of MS in Management, 303-315-8425, E-mail: kenneth.bettenhausen@ucdenver.edu. *Application contact:* 303-315-8200, E-mail: bschool.admissions@ucdenver.edu.
Website: http://www.ucdenver.edu/academics/colleges/business/degrees/ms/management/Pages/Management.aspx

University of Dallas, Satish and Yasmin Gupta College of Business, Irving, TX 75062-4736. Offers accounting (MBA, MS); business administration (DBA); business analytics (MS); business management (MBA); corporate finance (MBA); cybersecurity (MS); finance (MS); financial services (MBA); global business (MBA, MS); health services management (MBA); human resource management (MBA); information and technology management (MS); information assurance (MBA); information technology (MBA); information technology service management (MBA); marketing management (MBA); organization development (MBA); project management (MBA); sports and entertainment management (MBA); strategic leadership (MBA); supply chain management (MBA). *Accreditation:* AACSB. *Program availability:* Part-time, evening/weekend, online learning. *Entrance requirements:* Additional exam requirements/recommendations for international students: Required—TOEFL. Electronic applications accepted. *Expenses:* Contact institution.

University of Denver, Daniels College of Business, Department of Business Information and Analytics, Denver, CO 80208. Offers business analytics (MBA, MS). *Faculty:* 14 full-time (4 women), 10 part-time/adjunct (4 women). *Students:* 36 full-time (21 women), 33 part-time (14 women); includes 10 minority (1 Black or African American, non-Hispanic/Latino; 3 Asian, non-Hispanic/Latino; 3 Hispanic/Latino; 3 Two or more races, non-Hispanic/Latino), 29 international. Average age 28. 109 applicants, 60% accepted, 28 enrolled. In 2016, 30 master's awarded. *Entrance requirements:* For master's, GRE General Test or GMAT, bachelor's degree, transcripts, essays, resume, interview. Additional exam requirements/recommendations for international students: Required—TOEFL (minimum score 570 paper-based; 88 iBT). *Application deadline:* For fall admission, 11/15 priority date for domestic and international students; for spring admission, 10/1 priority date for domestic and international students. Applications are processed on a rolling basis. Application fee: $100. Electronic applications accepted. *Expenses:* $43,458 per year full-time. *Financial support:* In 2016–17, 59 students received support, including 2 teaching assistantships with tuition reimbursements available (averaging $1,488 per year); career-related internships or fieldwork, Federal Work-Study, institutionally sponsored loans, scholarships/grants, and unspecified assistantships also available. Support available to part-time students. Financial award application deadline: 2/15; financial award applicants required to submit FAFSA. *Faculty research:* Information technology strategy, project management, healthcare information systems, distributed knowledge work, complex adaptive systems. *Unit head:* Dr. Andrew Urbaczewski, Associate Professor and Chair, 303-871-4802, Fax: 303-871-2067, E-mail: andrew.urbaczewski@du.edu.
Website: https://daniels.du.edu/business-information-analytics

University of Detroit Mercy, College of Business Administration, Detroit, MI 48221. Offers business administration (MBA); business fundamentals (Certificate); business turnaround management (Certificate); ethical leadership and change management (Certificate); finance (Certificate); forensic accounting (Certificate); JD/MBA; MBA/MHSA. *Program availability:* Part-time, evening/weekend, 100% online, blended/hybrid learning. *Entrance requirements:* For master's, GMAT, resume, letter of recommendation, transcripts; for Certificate, resume, letter of recommendation, transcripts. Electronic applications accepted. Application fee is waived when completed online. *Expenses:* Contact institution. *Faculty research:* Ethics, international finance, trade policy, leadership, information technology.

University of Illinois at Urbana–Champaign, Graduate College, College of Education, Department of Education Policy, Organization, and Leadership, Champaign, IL 61820. Offers educational organization and leadership (Ed M, MS, Ed D, PhD, CAS); educational policy studies (Ed M, MA, PhD); human resource education (Ed M, MS, Ed D, PhD, CAS). *Program availability:* Part-time, online learning.

The University of Kansas, Graduate Studies, School of Business, Program in Business, Lawrence, KS 66045. Offers accounting (PhD); business and organizational leadership (MS); decision sciences and supply chain management (PhD); finance (PhD); human resources management (PhD); marketing (PhD); organizational behavior (PhD); strategic management (PhD); supply chain management and logistics (MS). *Accreditation:* AACSB. *Program availability:* Part-time. *Students:* 76 full-time (11 women), 170 part-time (83 women); includes 41 minority (15 Black or African American, non-Hispanic/Latino; 3 American Indian or Alaska Native, non-Hispanic/Latino; 6 Asian, non-Hispanic/Latino; 5 Hispanic/Latino; 12 Two or more races, non-Hispanic/Latino), 25 international. Average age 32. 294 applicants, 69% accepted, 152 enrolled. In 2016, 36 master's, 9 doctorates awarded. *Entrance requirements:* For master's, GMAT, official transcript, three letters of recommendation, resume, statement of purpose; for doctorate, GMAT or GRE, official transcript, three letters of recommendation, resume, statement of purpose. Additional exam requirements/recommendations for international students: Required—TOEFL (minimum score 600 paper-based; 100 iBT). *Application deadline:* For fall admission, 1/10 for domestic and international students. Application fee: $65 ($85 for international students). Electronic applications accepted. *Financial support:* Fellowships, research assistantships, teaching assistantships, scholarships/grants, health care benefits, tuition waivers (full), and unspecified assistantships available. Financial award application deadline: 1/10. *Faculty research:* Strategic human resource management, business ethics, organizational theory/behavior, corporate strategy, international business, supply chain management, Bayesian networks, game theory, decision analysis and time/series analysis, pricing, consumer effects, advertising and emotion. *Unit head:* Charly Edmonds, Director, 785-864-3841, E-mail: bschoolphd@ku.edu. *Application contact:* Graduate Admission Contact, 785-864-7500, E-mail: bschoolphd@ku.edu.
Website: http://www.business.ku.edu/

University of Lethbridge, School of Graduate Studies, Lethbridge, AB T1K 3M4, Canada. Offers addictions counseling (M Sc); agricultural biotechnology (M Sc); agricultural studies (M Sc, MA); anthropology (MA); archaeology (M Sc, MA); art (MA, MFA); biochemistry (M Sc); biological sciences (M Sc); biomolecular science (PhD); biosystems and biodiversity (PhD); Canadian studies (MA); chemistry (M Sc); computer science (M Sc); computer science and geographical information science (M Sc); counseling (MC); counseling psychology (M Ed); dramatic arts (MA); earth, space, and physical science (PhD); economics (MA); education (MA, PhD); educational leadership (M Ed); English (MA); environmental science (M Sc); evolution and behavior (PhD); exercise science (M Sc); French (MA); French/German (MA); French/Spanish (MA); general education (M Ed); geography (M Sc, MA); German (MA); health sciences (M Sc); individualized multidisciplinary (M Sc, MA); kinesiology (M Sc, MA); management (M Sc), including accounting, finance, human resource management and labor relations, information systems, international management, marketing, policy and strategy; mathematics (M Sc); music (M Mus, MA); Native American studies (MA); neuroscience (M Sc, PhD); new media (MA, MFA); nursing (M Sc, MN); philosophy (MA); physics (M Sc); political science (MA); psychology (M Sc, MA); religious studies (MA); sociology (MA); theatre and dramatic arts (MFA); theoretical and computational science (PhD); urban and regional studies (MA); women and gender studies (MA). *Program availability:* Part-time, evening/weekend. *Degree requirements:* For master's, thesis (for some programs); for doctorate, comprehensive exam, thesis/dissertation. *Entrance requirements:* For master's, GMAT (for M Sc in management), bachelor's degree in related field, minimum GPA of 3.0 during previous 20 graded semester courses, 2 years' teaching or related experience (M Ed); for doctorate, master's degree, minimum graduate GPA of 3.5. Additional exam requirements/recommendations for international students: Required—TOEFL (minimum score 580 paper-based; 93 iBT). Electronic applications accepted. *Faculty research:* Movement and brain plasticity, gibberellin physiology, photosynthesis, carbon cycling, molecular properties of main-group ring components.

The University of Manchester, Alliance Manchester Business School, M15 6PB, United Kingdom. Offers accounting and finance (M Sc); business (M Ent); business analysis and strategic management (M Sc); business analytics: operational research and risk analysis (M Sc); business psychology (M Sc); corporate communications and reputation management (M Sc); finance (M Sc); finance and business economics (M Sc); human resource management and industrial relations (M Sc); innovation management and entrepreneurship (M Sc); international business and management (M Sc); international human resource management and comparative industrial relations (M Sc); management (M Sc); marketing (M Sc); operations, project and supply chain management (M Sc); organizational psychology (M Sc); quantitative finance (M Sc). *Entrance requirements:* For master's, UK 2:1 honours degree or overseas equivalent. Additional exam requirements/recommendations for international students: Required—TOEFL (minimum score 100 iBT), IELTS (minimum score 7), PTE. Electronic applications accepted. *Faculty research:* Accounting and finance, management sciences and marketing, people management and organization, innovation management and policy, decision sciences.

University of Massachusetts Amherst, Graduate School, Isenberg School of Management, Program in Management, Amherst, MA 01003. Offers accounting (PhD); business administration (MBA); entrepreneurship (MBA); finance (MBA, PhD); healthcare administration (MBA); hospitality and tourism management (PhD); management science (PhD); marketing (MBA, PhD); organization studies (PhD); sport management (PhD); strategic management (PhD); MBA/MS. *Accreditation:* AACSB. *Program availability:* Part-time, evening/weekend, online learning. Terminal master's awarded for partial completion of doctoral program. *Degree requirements:* For doctorate, comprehensive exam, thesis/dissertation. *Entrance requirements:* For master's and doctorate, GMAT or GRE General Test. Additional exam requirements/recommendations for international students: Required—TOEFL (minimum score 550 paper-based; 80 iBT), IELTS (minimum score 6.5). Electronic applications accepted.

University of Massachusetts Dartmouth, Graduate School, Charlton College of Business, Program in Business Administration, North Dartmouth, MA 02747-2300. Offers business administration (MBA); business analytics (Postbaccalaureate Certificate); business foundations (Graduate Certificate); international business (Graduate Certificate); management (Postbaccalaureate Certificate); marketing (Postbaccalaureate Certificate); organizational leadership (Graduate Certificate); supply chain management and information systems (Postbaccalaureate Certificate). *Accreditation:* AACSB. *Program availability:* Part-time, 100% online, blended/hybrid learning. *Faculty:* 15 full-time (7 women), 11 part-time/adjunct (4 women). *Students:* 126 full-time (49 women), 178 part-time (100 women); includes 45 minority (10 Black or African American, non-Hispanic/Latino; 1 American Indian or Alaska Native, non-Hispanic/Latino; 16 Asian, non-Hispanic/Latino; 13 Hispanic/Latino; 5 Two or more races, non-Hispanic/Latino), 100 international. Average age 32. 236 applicants, 80% accepted, 132 enrolled. In 2016, 142 master's, 13 other advanced degrees awarded. *Degree requirements:* For master's, thesis or alternative, eportfolio. *Entrance requirements:* For master's, GMAT, statement of purpose (minimum of 300 words), resume, official transcripts, 2 letters of recommendation; for other advanced degree, statement of purpose (minimum of 300 words), resume, official transcripts. Additional exam requirements/recommendations for international students: Required—TOEFL (minimum score 533 paper-based; 72 iBT). *Application deadline:* For fall admission, 7/1 priority date for domestic students, 6/1 priority date for international students; for spring admission, 11/15 priority date for domestic students, 10/15 priority date for international

students. Application fee: $60. Electronic applications accepted. *Expenses:* Tuition, state resident: full-time $14,994; part-time $624.75 per credit. Tuition, nonresident: full-time $27,068; part-time $1127.83 per credit. *Required fees:* $405; $25.88 per credit. Tuition and fees vary according to course load and reciprocity agreements. *Financial support:* In 2016–17, 2 research assistantships (averaging $2,667 per year) were awarded; institutionally sponsored loans, scholarships/grants, and unspecified assistantships also available. Support available to part-time students. Financial award application deadline: 3/1; financial award applicants required to submit FAFSA. *Faculty research:* E-commerce, managing diversity, agile manufacturing, green business, activity-based management, build-to-order supply chain management. *Total annual research expenditures:* $413,000. *Unit head:* Melissa Pacheco, Assistant Dean of Graduate Programs, 508-999-8543, Fax: 508-999-8646, E-mail: mpacheco@umassd.edu. *Application contact:* Steven Briggs, Director of Marketing and Recruitment for Graduate Studies, 508-999-8604, Fax: 508-999-8183, E-mail: graduate@umassd.edu.
Website: http://www.umassd.edu/charlton/programs/graduate/mba

University of Memphis, Graduate School, University College, Memphis, TN 38152. Offers human resources (MPS); liberal studies (MALS, Graduate Certificate); strategic leadership (MPS, Graduate Certificate); training and development (MPS). *Program availability:* Part-time, evening/weekend. *Faculty:* 3 full-time (1 woman), 2 part-time/adjunct (0 women). *Students:* 25 full-time (14 women), 98 part-time (71 women); includes 85 minority (76 Black or African American, non-Hispanic/Latino; 1 Asian, non-Hispanic/Latino; 5 Hispanic/Latino; 3 Two or more races, non-Hispanic/Latino), 2 international. Average age 38. 59 applicants, 73% accepted, 29 enrolled. In 2016, 53 master's, 4 other advanced degrees awarded. *Degree requirements:* For master's, comprehensive exam, thesis (for some programs). *Entrance requirements:* For master's, GRE (for MPS), resume, letters of recommendation, personal essay, interview, minimum undergraduate GPA of 2.75 (for MALS); portfolio in lieu of GRE (for MPS applicants with substantial professional work experience); for Graduate Certificate, essay, letter of recommendation. Additional exam requirements/recommendations for international students: Required—TOEFL (minimum score 550 paper-based; 79 iBT). *Application deadline:* For fall admission, 7/1 for domestic students, 5/1 for international students; for spring admission, 11/1 for domestic students, 9/15 for international students. Applications are processed on a rolling basis. Application fee: $35 ($60 for international students). Electronic applications accepted. *Expenses:* $5,231.50 per semester full-time in-state, $9,623.50 full-time out-of-state. *Financial support:* In 2016–17, 123 students received support, including 2 research assistantships with full tuition reimbursements available (averaging $17,000 per year), 3 teaching assistantships with tuition reimbursements available (averaging $11,334 per year); Federal Work-Study, scholarships/grants, and unspecified assistantships also available. Financial award application deadline: 2/3; financial award applicants required to submit FAFSA. *Faculty research:* Media ethics, history of psychiatry, public relations. *Unit head:* Dr. Dan Lattimore, Dean, 901-678-2991, E-mail: dlattimr@memphis.edu. *Application contact:* Dr. Colin Chapell, Graduate Coordinator, 901-678-4171, Fax: 901-678-2971, E-mail: cbshpell@memphis.edu.
Website: http://www.memphis.edu/univcoll/

University of Michigan–Dearborn, College of Business, MS Program in Business Analytics, Dearborn, MI 48126. Offers MS. *Program availability:* Part-time, evening/weekend. *Faculty:* 33 full-time (14 women), 10 part-time/adjunct (5 women). *Students:* 45 full-time (21 women), 44 part-time (16 women); includes 9 minority (2 Black or African American, non-Hispanic/Latino; 6 Asian, non-Hispanic/Latino; 1 Two or more races, non-Hispanic/Latino), 52 international. Average age 29. 175 applicants, 59% accepted, 46 enrolled. In 2016, 38 master's awarded. *Entrance requirements:* For master's, GMAT or GRE, equivalent of four-year U.S. bachelor's degree from regionally-accredited institution, undergraduate course in finite math, pre-calculus, or calculus. Additional exam requirements/recommendations for international students: Required—TOEFL (minimum score 560 paper-based; 84 iBT), IELTS (minimum score 6.5). *Application deadline:* For fall admission, 8/1 for domestic students, 5/1 for international students; for winter admission, 12/1 for domestic students, 9/1 for international students; for spring admission, 4/1 for domestic students, 1/1 for international students. Applications are processed on a rolling basis. Application fee: $60. Electronic applications accepted. *Expenses:* Contact institution. *Financial support:* In 2016–17, 46 students received support. Scholarships/grants and non-resident tuition scholarships available. Financial award application deadline: 3/1; financial award applicants required to submit FAFSA. *Faculty research:* Business intelligence, information technology, brand management and new media, management education, operations strategy. *Unit head:* Dr. Michael Kamen, Director, Graduate Programs, 313-593-5460, E-mail: mkamen@umich.edu. *Application contact:* Joan Doherty, Academic Advisor/Counselor, 313-593-5460, Fax: 313-271-9838, E-mail: umd-gradbusiness@umich.edu.
Website: http://umdearborn.edu/cob/ms-business-analytics/

University of Minnesota, Twin Cities Campus, Carlson School of Management, Doctoral Program in Business Administration, Minneapolis, MN 55455. Offers accounting (PhD); finance (PhD); information and decision sciences (PhD); marketing (PhD); strategic management and entrepreneurship (PhD); supply chain and operations (PhD); work and organizations (PhD). *Faculty:* 101 full-time (32 women). *Students:* 90 full-time (29 women); includes 7 minority (2 Black or African American, non-Hispanic/Latino; 3 Asian, non-Hispanic/Latino; 2 Hispanic/Latino), 64 international. Average age 30. 352 applicants, 7% accepted, 15 enrolled. In 2016, 20 doctorates awarded. *Degree requirements:* For doctorate, comprehensive exam, thesis/dissertation, written and oral preliminary exams, proposal defense, final defense. *Entrance requirements:* For doctorate, GMAT, GRE General Test, minimum undergraduate GPA of 3.0, graduate 3.5 (recommended). Additional exam requirements/recommendations for international students: Required—TOEFL (minimum score 600 paper-based, 100 iBT) or IELTS (minimum score 7.0). *Application deadline:* For fall admission, 12/15 for domestic students, 12/15 priority date for international students. Applications are processed on a rolling basis. Application fee: $75 ($95 for international students). Electronic applications accepted. *Expenses:* Contact institution. *Financial support:* In 2016–17, 80 students received support, including 80 fellowships with full tuition reimbursements available (averaging $13,500 per year), 72 research assistantships with full tuition reimbursements available (averaging $7,371 per year), 72 teaching assistantships with full tuition reimbursements available (averaging $7,371 per year); institutionally sponsored loans, scholarships/grants, health care benefits, unspecified assistantships, and full student service fee waivers also available. Financial award application deadline: 12/15. *Faculty research:* Finance, strategy and entrepreneurship, marketing, information and decision science, operations, accounting, supply chain, human resources and industrial relations, organizational behavior. *Unit head:* Dr. Shawn P. Curley, Director, 612-624-6546, Fax: 612-624-8221, E-mail: curley@umn.edu. *Application contact:* Sandy Herzan, Associate Director, 612-624-0875, Fax: 612-624-8221, E-mail: herza002@umn.edu.
Website: http://carlsonschool.umn.edu/degrees/phd

University of Missouri–St. Louis, College of Business Administration, Program in Business Administration, St. Louis, MO 63121. Offers accounting (MBA); business administration (Certificate); business intelligence (Certificate); cybersecurity (Certificate); digital and social media marketing (Certificate); finance (MBA); human resources management (Certificate); information systems (MBA); international business (MBA); logistics and supply chain management (MBA, PhD, Certificate); management (MBA); marketing (MBA); marketing management (Certificate); operations management (MBA). *Accreditation:* AACSB. *Program availability:* Part-time, evening/weekend. *Faculty:* 32 full-time (10 women), 14 part-time/adjunct (3 women). *Students:* 181 full-time (88 women), 357 part-time (154 women); includes 83 minority (30 Black or African American, non-Hispanic/Latino; 36 Asian, non-Hispanic/Latino; 12 Hispanic/Latino; 2 Native Hawaiian or other Pacific Islander, non-Hispanic/Latino; 3 Two or more races, non-Hispanic/Latino), 100 international. Average age 31. 245 applicants, 83% accepted, 139 enrolled. *Degree requirements:* For doctorate, thesis/dissertation. *Entrance requirements:* For master's, GMAT, 2 letters of recommendation. Additional exam requirements/recommendations for international students: Recommended—TOEFL (minimum score 550 paper-based; 79 iBT), IELTS (minimum score 6.5). *Application deadline:* For fall admission, 7/1 for domestic and international students; for spring admission, 12/1 for domestic and international students. Applications are processed on a rolling basis. Application fee: $50 ($40 for international students). Electronic applications accepted. *Financial support:* Research assistantships with tuition reimbursements, teaching assistantships with tuition reimbursements, career-related internships or fieldwork, Federal Work-Study, and institutionally sponsored loans available. Support available to part-time students. Financial award application deadline: 4/1; financial award applicants required to submit FAFSA. *Faculty research:* Human resources, strategic management, marketing strategy, consumer behavior product development, advertising. *Unit head:* Dr. Thomas H. Eyssell, Associate Dean and Director of Graduate Studies, 314-516-5885, Fax: 314-516-6420, E-mail: mba@umsl.edu. *Application contact:* 314-516-5458, Fax: 314-516-6996, E-mail: gradadm@umsl.edu.

University of New Haven, Graduate School, College of Business, Program in Business Administration, West Haven, CT 06516. Offers accounting (MBA), including CPA; business administration (MBA); business intelligence (MBA); business management (Graduate Certificate); business policy and strategic leadership (MBA); finance (MBA), including CFA; global marketing (MBA); human resources management (MBA, Graduate Certificate); sport management (MBA). *Accreditation:* AACSB. *Program availability:* Part-time, evening/weekend. *Students:* 123 full-time (56 women), 74 part-time (29 women); includes 46 minority (24 Black or African American, non-Hispanic/Latino; 8 Asian, non-Hispanic/Latino; 10 Hispanic/Latino; 4 Two or more races, non-Hispanic/Latino), 57 international. Average age 27. In 2016, 100 master's awarded. *Entrance requirements:* For master's, GMAT. Additional exam requirements/recommendations for international students: Required—TOEFL (minimum score 80 iBT), IELTS, PTE. *Application deadline:* Applications are processed on a rolling basis. Application fee: $50. Electronic applications accepted. Application fee is waived when completed online. *Expenses: Tuition:* Full-time $15,660; part-time $870 per credit hour. *Required fees:* $200; $85 per term. Tuition and fees vary according to program. *Financial support:* Research assistantships with partial tuition reimbursements, teaching assistantships with partial tuition reimbursements, career-related internships or fieldwork, Federal Work-Study, scholarships/grants, and unspecified assistantships available. Support available to part-time students. Financial award applicants required to submit FAFSA. *Unit head:* Darell Singleterry, Director, 203-932-1085, E-mail: dsingleterry@newhaven.edu. *Application contact:* Michelle Mason, Director of Graduate Enrollment, 203-932-7067, E-mail: mmason@newhaven.edu.
Website: http://www.newhaven.edu/business/programs/EMBA/

University of New Mexico, Anderson School of Management, Department of Marketing, Information and Decision Sciences, Albuquerque, NM 87131. Offers information assurance (MBA); information systems and assurance (MS); management information systems (MBA); marketing management (MBA); operations management (MBA). *Program availability:* Part-time, evening/weekend. *Faculty:* 17 full-time (3 women), 7 part-time/adjunct (5 women). In 2016, 47 master's awarded. *Entrance requirements:* For master's, GMAT or GRE, minimum GPA of 3.0 on last 60 hours of coursework; bachelor's degree from regionally-accredited college or university in U.S. or its equivalent in another country. Additional exam requirements/recommendations for international students: Required—TOEFL (minimum score 550 paper-based; 79 iBT), IELTS (minimum score 6.5). *Application deadline:* For fall admission, 4/1 priority date for domestic and international students; for spring admission, 10/1 priority date for domestic and international students. Applications are processed on a rolling basis. Application fee: $50. Electronic applications accepted. *Expenses:* Contact institution. *Financial support:* In 2016–17, 8 fellowships (averaging $11,484 per year), 13 research assistantships with partial tuition reimbursements (averaging $9,382 per year) were awarded; career-related internships or fieldwork, Federal Work-Study, scholarships/grants, and unspecified assistantships also available. Support available to part-time students. Financial award application deadline: 6/1; financial award applicants required to submit FAFSA. *Faculty research:* Marketing, operations management, information systems, information assurance. *Unit head:* Dr. Steve Yourstone, Chair, 505-277-6471, E-mail: yourstone@unm.edu. *Application contact:* Lisa Beauchene, Student Recruitment Specialist, 505-277-6471, E-mail: andersonadvising@unm.edu.
Website: https://www.mgt.unm.edu/mids/default.asp?mm=faculty

University of New Mexico, Anderson School of Management, Department of Organizational Studies, Albuquerque, NM 87131. Offers organizational behavior and human resources management (MBA); strategic management and policy (MBA). *Program availability:* Part-time, evening/weekend. *Faculty:* 17 full-time (12 women), 6 part-time/adjunct (2 women). In 2016, 26 master's awarded. *Entrance requirements:* For master's, GMAT or GRE, minimum GPA of 3.0 on last 60 hours of coursework; bachelor's degree from regionally-accredited college or university in U.S. or its equivalent in another country. Additional exam requirements/recommendations for international students: Required—TOEFL (minimum score 550 paper-based; 79 iBT), IELTS (minimum score 6.5). *Application deadline:* For fall admission, 4/1 priority date for domestic and international students; for spring admission, 10/1 priority date for domestic and international students. Applications are processed on a rolling basis. Application fee: $50. Electronic applications accepted. *Expenses:* Contact institution. *Financial support:* In 2016–17, 4 fellowships (averaging $24,700 per year), 13 research assistantships with partial tuition reimbursements (averaging $15,345 per year) were awarded; career-related internships or fieldwork, Federal Work-Study, scholarships/grants, and unspecified assistantships also available. Support available to part-time students. Financial award application deadline: 6/1; financial award applicants required to submit FAFSA. *Faculty research:* Business ethics and social corporate responsibility, diversity, human resources, organizational strategy, organizational behavior. *Unit head:* Dr. Michelle Arthur, Chair, 505-277-6471, E-mail: arthurm@unm.edu. *Application contact:* Lisa Beauchene, Student Recruitment Specialist, 505-277-6471, E-mail: andersonadvising@unm.edu.
Website: https://www.mgt.unm.edu/dos/default.asp?mm=faculty

The University of North Carolina at Chapel Hill, Kenan-Flagler Business School, Doctoral Program in Business Administration, Chapel Hill, NC 27599. Offers accounting (PhD); finance (PhD); marketing (PhD); operations management (PhD); organizational behavior (PhD); strategy (PhD). *Accreditation:* AACSB. *Degree requirements:* For doctorate, thesis/dissertation. *Entrance requirements:* For doctorate, GMAT or GRE General Test. Electronic applications accepted. *Expenses:* Contact institution.

University of North Texas, Robert B. Toulouse School of Graduate Studies, Denton, TX 76203-5459. Offers accounting (MS); applied anthropology (MA, MS); applied behavior analysis (Certificate); applied geography (MA); applied technology and performance improvement (M Ed, MS); art education (MA); art history (MA); art museum education (Certificate); arts leadership (Certificate); audiology (Au D); behavior analysis (MS); behavioral science (PhD); biochemistry and molecular biology (MS); biology (MA, MS); biomedical engineering (MS); business analysis (MS); chemistry (MS); clinical health psychology (PhD); communication studies (MA, MS); computer engineering (MS); computer science (MS); counseling (M Ed, MS), including clinical mental health counseling (MS), college and university counseling, elementary school counseling, secondary school counseling; creative writing (MA); criminal justice (MS); curriculum and instruction (M Ed); decision sciences (MBA); design (MA, MFA), including fashion design (MFA), innovation studies, interior design (MFA); early childhood studies (MS); economics (MS); educational leadership (M Ed, Ed D); educational psychology (MS, PhD), including family studies (MS), gifted and talented (MS), human development (MS), learning and cognition (MS), research, measurement and evaluation (MS); electrical engineering (MS); emergency management (MPA); engineering technology (MS); English (MA); English as a second language (MA); environmental science (MS); finance (MBA, MS); financial management (MPA); French (MA); health services management (MBA); higher education (M Ed, Ed D); history (MA, MS); hospitality management (MS); human resources management (MPA); information science (MS); information systems (PhD); information technologies (MBA); interdisciplinary studies (MA, MS); international studies (MA); international sustainable tourism (MS); jazz studies (MM); journalism (MA, MJ, Graduate Certificate), including interactive and virtual digital communication (Graduate Certificate), narrative journalism (Graduate Certificate), public relations (Graduate Certificate); kinesiology (MS); linguistics (MA); local government management (MPA); logistics (PhD); logistics and supply chain management (MBA); long-term care, senior housing, and aging services (MA); management (PhD); marketing (MBA); mathematics (MA, MS); mechanical and energy engineering (MS, PhD); music (MA), including ethnomusicology, music theory, musicology, performance; music composition (PhD); music education (MM Ed, PhD); nonprofit management (MPA); operations and supply chain management (MBA); performance (MM, DMA); philosophy (MA); political science (MA); professional and technical communication (MA); radio, television and film (MA, MFA); rehabilitation counseling (Certificate); sociology (MA); Spanish (MA); special education (M Ed); speech-language pathology (MA); strategic management (MBA); studio art (MFA); teaching (M Ed); MBA/MS. *Program availability:* Part-time, evening/weekend, online learning. Terminal master's awarded for partial completion of doctoral program. *Degree requirements:* For master's, variable foreign language requirement, comprehensive exam (for some programs), thesis (for some programs); for doctorate, variable foreign language requirement, comprehensive exam (for some programs), thesis/dissertation; for other advanced degree, variable foreign language requirement, comprehensive exam (for some programs). *Entrance requirements:* For master's and doctorate, GRE, GMAT. Additional exam requirements/recommendations for international students: Required—TOEFL (minimum score 550 paper-based; 79 iBT). Electronic applications accepted.

University of North Texas at Dallas, Graduate School, Dallas, TX 75241. Offers accounting (MBA); counseling (M Ed, MS); criminal justice (MS); curriculum and instruction (M Ed); educational administration (M Ed); human resources and organizational behavior (MBA); public leadership (MS); strategic management (MBA).

University of Notre Dame, Mendoza College of Business, Master of Business Administration Program, Notre Dame, IN 46556. Offers business analytics (MBA); business leadership (MBA); consulting (MBA); corporate finance (MBA); innovation and entrepreneurship (MBA); investments (MBA); marketing (MBA). *Accreditation:* AACSB. *Faculty:* 62 full-time (13 women), 26 part-time/adjunct (7 women). *Students:* 304 full-time (78 women); includes 38 minority (10 Black or African American, non-Hispanic/Latino; 7 Asian, non-Hispanic/Latino; 15 Hispanic/Latino; 6 Two or more races, non-Hispanic/Latino), 80 international. Average age 27. 647 applicants, 41% accepted, 121 enrolled. In 2016, 177 master's awarded. *Entrance requirements:* For master's, GMAT or GRE, work experience, essay, four-slide presentation, two recommendations, transcripts from all colleges and/or universities attended, interview. Additional exam requirements/recommendations for international students: Required—TOEFL (minimum score 600 paper-based; 100 iBT), IELTS (minimum score 7), PTE (minimum score 68). *Application deadline:* For fall admission, 11/1 for domestic and international students; for winter admission, 1/10 for domestic and international students; for spring admission, 2/21 for domestic and international students; for summer admission, 3/28 for domestic and international students. Application fee: $175. Electronic applications accepted. *Expenses:* Contact institution. *Financial support:* In 2016–17, 251 students received support, including 243 fellowships (averaging $26,417 per year); career-related internships or fieldwork, Federal Work-Study, institutionally sponsored loans, scholarships/grants, and unspecified assistantships also available. Financial award application deadline: 2/28; financial award applicants required to submit FAFSA. *Faculty research:* Market micro-structure; marketing and public policy; corporate finance and accounting; corporate governance and ethical behavior; high performing organizations. *Unit head:* Dr. Katherine Speiss, Associate Dean, Graduate Business Programs, 574-631-3759, E-mail: spiess.1@nd.edu. *Application contact:* Kristin McAndrew, Director of Admissions, Graduate Business Programs, 574-631-8488, E-mail: kmcadre@nd.edu.
Website: http://mendoza.nd.edu/programs/mba-programs/

University of Pittsburgh, Katz Graduate School of Business, Doctoral Program in Business Administration, Pittsburgh, PA 15260. Offers accounting (PhD); business analytics and operations (PhD); finance (PhD); information systems and technology management (PhD); marketing (PhD); organizational behavior and human resources (PhD); strategic management (PhD). *Accreditation:* AACSB. *Program availability:* Evening/weekend. *Faculty:* 88 full-time (27 women), 42 part-time/adjunct (15 women). *Students:* 51 full-time (23 women), 1 part-time (0 women); includes 4 minority (1 Black or African American, non-Hispanic/Latino; 2 Asian, non-Hispanic/Latino; 1 Two or more races, non-Hispanic/Latino), 31 international. Average age 31. 344 applicants, 6% accepted, 9 enrolled. In 2016, 5 doctorates awarded. *Degree requirements:* For doctorate, comprehensive exam, thesis/dissertation, student teaching. *Entrance requirements:* For doctorate, GMAT or GRE, 3 recommendations, statement of purpose, transcripts of all previous course work and degrees. Additional exam requirements/recommendations for international students: Required—TOEFL (minimum score 100 iBT) or IELTS (minimum score 7.0). *Application deadline:* For fall admission, 4/1 priority date for domestic students, 2/1 priority date for international students. Applications are processed on a rolling basis. Application fee: $50. Electronic applications accepted. *Expenses:* Contact institution. *Financial support:* In 2016–17, 40 students received support, including 27 research assistantships with full tuition reimbursements available (averaging $26,000 per year), 9 teaching assistantships with full tuition reimbursements available (averaging $26,700 per year); Federal Work-Study, scholarships/grants, health care benefits, and unspecified assistantships also available. Financial award application deadline: 6/1; financial award applicants required to submit FAFSA. *Faculty research:* Accounting systems/financial reporting, corporate finance, shopper marketing/consumer behavior, management information systems, organizational behavior and entrepreneurship. *Total annual research expenditures:* $493,036. *Unit head:* Dr. Arjang A. Assad, Dean, 412-648-1556, Fax: 412-648-1552, E-mail: aassad@katz.pitt.edu. *Application contact:* Dr. Dennis Galletta, Director, 412-648-1699, Fax: 412-648-3633, E-mail: galletta@katz.pitt.edu.
Website: http://www.business.pitt.edu/katz/phd/

See Display on page 160 and Close-Up on page 189.

University of Pittsburgh, Katz Graduate School of Business, Master of Business Administration Programs, Pittsburgh, PA 15260. Offers finance (MBA); information systems (MBA); marketing (MBA); operations (MBA); organizational behavior and human resources (MBA); strategy, environment and organizations (MBA); MBA/JD; MBA/MSE. *Accreditation:* AACSB. *Program availability:* Part-time, evening/weekend, blended/hybrid learning. *Faculty:* 88 full-time (27 women), 42 part-time/adjunct (15 women). *Students:* 165 full-time (59 women), 330 part-time (103 women); includes 70 minority (29 Black or African American, non-Hispanic/Latino; 20 Asian, non-Hispanic/Latino; 13 Hispanic/Latino; 8 Two or more races, non-Hispanic/Latino), 73 international. Average age 29. 786 applicants, 41% accepted, 179 enrolled. In 2016, 477 master's awarded. *Degree requirements:* For master's, minimum GPA of 3.0. *Entrance requirements:* For master's, GMAT, GRE. Additional exam requirements/recommendations for international students: Required—TOEFL (minimum score 100 iBT) or IELTS (minimum score 7.0). *Application deadline:* For fall admission, 4/1 priority date for domestic students, 2/1 priority date for international students. Application fee: $50. Electronic applications accepted. *Expenses:* Contact institution. *Financial support:* In 2016–17, 110 students received support. Scholarships/grants available. Financial award application deadline: 6/1; financial award applicants required to submit FAFSA. *Faculty research:* Accounting systems/financial reporting, corporate finance, shopper marketing/consumer behavior, management information systems, organizational behavior and entrepreneurship. *Total annual research expenditures:* $493,036. *Unit head:* Dr. Arjang A. Assad, Dean, 412-648-1556, Fax: 412-648-1552, E-mail: aassad@katz.pitt.edu. *Application contact:* Thomas Keller, Director of MBA Admissions, 412-648-1700, Fax: 412-648-1659, E-mail: mba@katz.pitt.edu.
Website: http://www.business.pitt.edu/katz/mba/

See Display on page 160 and Close-Up on page 189.

University of Rhode Island, Graduate School, College of Business Administration, Kingston, RI 02881. Offers accounting (MS); business administration (PhD), including finance and insurance, marketing, supply chain management; finance (MBA, MS); general business (MBA); health care management (MBA); management (MBA); marketing (MBA); oceanography (MBA); strategic innovation (MBA); supply chain management (MBA); Pharm D/MBA. *Accreditation:* AACSB. *Program availability:* Part-time, evening/weekend. *Faculty:* 57 full-time (24 women). *Students:* 94 full-time (45 women), 166 part-time (84 women); includes 37 minority (6 Black or African American, non-Hispanic/Latino; 1 American Indian or Alaska Native, non-Hispanic/Latino; 22 Asian, non-Hispanic/Latino; 3 Hispanic/Latino; 5 Two or more races, non-Hispanic/Latino), 18 international. In 2016, 124 master's, 4 doctorates awarded. *Degree requirements:* For master's, comprehensive exam (for some programs), thesis optional; for doctorate, comprehensive exam, thesis/dissertation. *Entrance requirements:* For master's, GMAT or GRE, 2 letters of recommendation, resume; for doctorate, GMAT or GRE, 3 letters of recommendation, resume. Additional exam requirements/recommendations for international students: Required—TOEFL. *Application deadline:* For fall admission, 2/1 for domestic and international students. Application fee: $65. Electronic applications accepted. *Expenses:* Tuition, state resident: full-time $11,796; part-time $655 per credit. Tuition, nonresident: full-time $24,206; part-time $1345 per credit. *Required fees:* $1546; $44 per credit. One-time fee: $155 full-time; $35 part-time. *Financial support:* In 2016–17, 17 teaching assistantships with tuition reimbursements (averaging $15,347 per year) were awarded; research assistantships also available. Financial award application deadline: 2/1; financial award applicants required to submit FAFSA. *Unit head:* Dr. Maling Ebrahimpour, Dean, 401-874-4348, Fax: 401-874-4312, E-mail: mebrahimpour@uri.edu. *Application contact:* Lisa Lancellotta, Coordinator, MBA Programs, 401-874-4241, Fax: 401-874-4312, E-mail: mba@uri.edu.
Website: http://www.cba.uri.edu/

See Display on page 161 and Close-Up on page 191.

University of Rochester, Simon Business School, Full-Time Master's Program in Business Administration, Rochester, NY 14627. Offers business systems consulting (MBA); competitive and organizational strategy (MBA); computers and information systems (MBA); corporate accounting (MBA); entrepreneurship (MBA); finance (MBA); health sciences management (MBA); marketing (MBA); operations management (MBA); public accounting (MBA). *Accreditation:* AACSB. *Program availability:* Part-time, evening/weekend. *Faculty:* 66 full-time (13 women), 22 part-time/adjunct (2 women). *Students:* 202 full-time (78 women); includes 50 minority (30 Black or African American, non-Hispanic/Latino; 10 Asian, non-Hispanic/Latino; 9 Hispanic/Latino; 1 Two or more races, non-Hispanic/Latino), 107 international. Average age 27. 915 applicants, 30% accepted, 86 enrolled. In 2016, 110 master's awarded. *Entrance requirements:* For master's, GMAT/GRE. Additional exam requirements/recommendations for international students: Required—TOEFL. *Application deadline:* For fall admission, 10/15 for domestic and international students; for winter admission, 1/5 for domestic and international students; for spring admission, 3/15 for domestic and international students; for summer admission, 5/15 for domestic and international students. Applications are processed on a rolling basis. Application fee: $150. Electronic applications accepted. *Expenses:* Contact institution. *Financial support:* In 2016–17, 190 students received support. Fellowships, research assistantships, teaching assistantships, institutionally sponsored loans, scholarships/grants, and tuition waivers (full and partial) available. Financial award application deadline: 1/5; financial award applicants required to submit FAFSA. *Unit head:* Andrew Ainslie, Dean, 585-275-3316, E-mail: andrew.ainslie@simon.rochester.edu. *Application contact:* Rebekah S. Lewin, Assistant Dean of Admissions and Financial Aid, 585-275-3533, E-mail: admissions@simon.rochester.edu.
Website: http://www.simon.rochester.edu/programs/full-time-mba/index.aspx

University of Rochester, Simon Business School, Master of Science Program in Business Analytics, Rochester, NY 14627. Offers MS. *Faculty:* 66 full-time (13 women), 22 part-time/adjunct (2 women). *Students:* 45 full-time (26 women); includes 2 minority (both Asian, non-Hispanic/Latino), 43 international. Average age 24. 463 applicants, 31% accepted, 43 enrolled. In 2016, 5 master's awarded. *Entrance requirements:* For master's, GMAT or GRE. Additional exam requirements/recommendations for international students: Required—TOEFL. *Application deadline:* For fall admission, 10/15 for domestic and international students; for winter admission, 1/5 for domestic and international students; for spring admission, 3/15 for domestic and international students; for summer admission, 5/15 for domestic and international students. Applications are processed on a rolling basis. Application fee: $150. Electronic applications accepted. *Expenses:* Contact institution. *Financial support:* In 2016–17, 37 students received support. Tuition waivers (partial) available. Financial award application deadline: 1/5; financial award applicants required to submit FAFSA. *Unit head:* Andrew Ainslie, Dean, 585-275-3316, E-mail: andrew.ainslie@simon.rochester.edu. *Application contact:* Rebekah S. Lewin, Assistant Dean for Admissions and Financial Aid, 585-275-3533, E-mail: admissions@simon.rochester.edu.

Management Strategy and Policy

Website: http://www.simon.rochester.edu/programs/full-time-ms-in-business-analytics/index.aspx

University of Rochester, Simon Business School, Part-Time MBA Program, Rochester, NY 14627. Offers business systems consulting (MBA); competitive and organizational strategy (MBA); computers and information systems (MBA); corporate accounting (MBA); entrepreneurship (MBA); finance (MBA); health sciences management (MBA); marketing (MBA); operations management (MBA); public accounting (MBA). *Program availability:* Part-time, evening/weekend. *Faculty:* 66 full-time (13 women), 22 part-time/adjunct (2 women). *Students:* 185 part-time (65 women); includes 29 minority (6 Black or African American, non-Hispanic/Latino; 13 Asian, non-Hispanic/Latino; 8 Hispanic/Latino; 2 Two or more races, non-Hispanic/Latino), 9 international. Average age 32. 33 applicants, 100% accepted, 31 enrolled. In 2016, 70 master's awarded. *Entrance requirements:* For master's, GRE or GMAT. *Application deadline:* For fall admission, 8/1 for domestic students; for spring admission, 2/15 for domestic students. Applications are processed on a rolling basis. Application fee: $150. Electronic applications accepted. *Expenses:* $1,800 per credit hour. *Financial support:* In 2016–17, 75 students received support. Scholarships/grants and tuition waivers (partial) available. Financial award applicants required to submit CSS PROFILE or FAFSA. *Unit head:* Andrew Ainslie, Dean, 585-275-3316, E-mail: andrew.ainslie@simon.rochester.edu. *Application contact:* Molly Mesko, Executive Director, EMBA and Part-Time Programs, 585-275-4277, E-mail: molly.mesko@simon.rochester.edu.
Website: http://www.simon.rochester.edu/programs/ptmba/index.aspx

University of St. Francis, College of Business and Health Administration, School of Business, Joliet, IL 60435-6169. Offers accounting (MBA, Certificate); business analytics (MBA, Certificate); finance (MBA, Certificate); health administration (MBA); human resource management (MBA); logistics (Certificate); management (MBA, MSM); training and development (MBA); transportation and logistics (MBA). *Accreditation:* ACBSP. *Program availability:* Part-time, evening/weekend, 100% online, blended/hybrid learning. *Faculty:* 6 full-time (3 women), 12 part-time/adjunct (6 women). *Students:* 78 full-time (28 women), 110 part-time (62 women); includes 41 minority (22 Black or African American, non-Hispanic/Latino; 3 Asian, non-Hispanic/Latino; 15 Hispanic/Latino; 1 Two or more races, non-Hispanic/Latino), 8 international. Average age 36. 171 applicants, 44% accepted, 58 enrolled. In 2016, 62 master's, 3 other advanced degrees awarded. *Entrance requirements:* For master's, GMAT or 2 years of managerial experience. Additional exam requirements/recommendations for international students: Required—TOEFL (minimum score 550 paper-based; 79 iBT), IELTS (minimum score 6). *Application deadline:* Applications are processed on a rolling basis. Application fee: $30. Electronic applications accepted. Application fee is waived when completed online. *Expenses:* $798 per credit. *Financial support:* In 2016–17, 51 students received support. Career-related internships or fieldwork, scholarships/grants, tuition waivers (partial), and unspecified assistantships available. Support available to part-time students. Financial award applicants required to submit FAFSA. *Unit head:* Dr. Orlando Griego, Dean, 815-740-3395, Fax: 815-740-3537, E-mail: ogriego@stfrancis.edu. *Application contact:* Sandra Sloka, Director of Admissions for Graduate and Degree Completion Programs, 800-735-7500, Fax: 815-740-3431, E-mail: ssloka@stfrancis.edu.
Website: http://www.stfrancis.edu/academics/college-of-business-health-administration/

University of South Florida, Innovative Education, Tampa, FL 33620-9951. Offers adult, career and higher education (Graduate Certificate), including college teaching, leadership in developing human resources, leadership in higher education; Africana studies (Graduate Certificate), including diasporas and health disparities, genocide and human rights; aging studies (Graduate Certificate), including gerontology; art research (Graduate Certificate), including museum studies; business foundations (Graduate Certificate); chemical and biomedical engineering (Graduate Certificate), including materials science and engineering, water, health and sustainability; child and family studies (Graduate Certificate), including positive behavior support; civil and industrial engineering (Graduate Certificate), including transportation systems analysis; community and family health (Graduate Certificate), including maternal and child health, social marketing and public health, violence and injury: prevention and intervention, women's health; criminology (Graduate Certificate), including criminal justice administration; educational measurement and research (Graduate Certificate), including evaluation; English (Graduate Certificate), including comparative literary studies, creative writing, professional and technical communication; entrepreneurship (Graduate Certificate); environmental health (Graduate Certificate), including safety management; epidemiology and biostatistics (Graduate Certificate), including applied biostatistics, biostatistics, concepts and tools of epidemiology, epidemiology, epidemiology of infectious diseases; geography, environment and planning (Graduate Certificate), including community development, environmental policy and management, geographical information systems; geology (Graduate Certificate), including hydrogeology; global health (Graduate Certificate), including disaster management, global health and Latin American and Caribbean studies, global health practice, humanitarian assistance, infection control; government and international affairs (Graduate Certificate), including Cuban studies, globalization studies; health policy and management (Graduate Certificate), including health management and leadership, public health policy and programs; hearing specialist: early intervention (Graduate Certificate); industrial and management systems engineering (Graduate Certificate), including systems engineering, technology management; information studies (Graduate Certificate), including school library media specialist; information systems/decision sciences (Graduate Certificate), including analytics and business intelligence; instructional technology (Graduate Certificate), including distance education, Florida digital/virtual educator, instructional design, multimedia design, Web design; internal medicine, bioethics and medical humanities (Graduate Certificate), including biomedical ethics; Latin American and Caribbean studies (Graduate Certificate); mass communications (Graduate Certificate), including multimedia journalism; mathematics and statistics (Graduate Certificate), including mathematics; medicine (Graduate Certificate), including aging and neuroscience, bioinformatics, biotechnology, brain fitness and memory management, clinical investigation, health informatics, health sciences, integrative weight management, intellectual property, medicine and gender, metabolic and nutritional medicine, metabolic cardiology, pharmacy sciences; national and competitive intelligence (Graduate Certificate); psychological and social foundations (Graduate Certificate), including career counseling, college teaching, diversity in education, mental health counseling, school counseling; public affairs (Graduate Certificate), including nonprofit management, public management, research administration; public health (Graduate Certificate), including environmental health, health equity, public health generalist, translational research in adolescent behavioral health; public health practices (Graduate Certificate), including planning for healthy communities; rehabilitation and mental health counseling (Graduate Certificate), including integrative mental health care, marriage and family therapy, rehabilitation technology; secondary education (Graduate Certificate), including ESOL, foreign language education: culture and content, foreign language education: professional; social work (Graduate Certificate), including geriatric social work/clinical gerontology; special education (Graduate Certificate), including autism spectrum disorder, disabilities education: severe/profound; world languages (Graduate Certificate), including teaching English as a second language (TESL) or foreign language. *Expenses:* Tuition, state resident: full-time $7766; part-time $431.43 per credit hour. Tuition, nonresident: full-time $15,789; part-time $877.17 per credit hour. *Required fees:* $37 per term. *Unit head:* Kathy Barnes, Interdisciplinary Programs Coordinator, 813-974-8031, Fax: 813-974-7061, E-mail: barnesk@usf.edu. *Application contact:* Karen Tylinski, Metro Initiatives, 813-974-9943, Fax: 813-974-7061, E-mail: ktylinsk@usf.edu.
Website: http://www.usf.edu/innovative-education/

University of South Florida, Muma College of Business, Department of Information Systems and Decision Sciences, Tampa, FL 33620-9951. Offers business administration (PhD), including information systems; business analytics and information systems (MS), including analytics and business intelligence, information assurance. *Program availability:* Part-time. *Faculty:* 21 full-time (5 women), 1 part-time/adjunct (0 women). *Students:* 149 full-time (54 women), 73 part-time (22 women); includes 13 minority (1 Black or African American, non-Hispanic/Latino; 6 Asian, non-Hispanic/Latino; 5 Hispanic/Latino; 1 Two or more races, non-Hispanic/Latino), 186 international. Average age 27. 1,198 applicants, 44% accepted, 117 enrolled. In 2016, 163 master's awarded. Terminal master's awarded for partial completion of doctoral program. *Degree requirements:* For master's, comprehensive exam, thesis (for some programs), thesis or practicum project; for doctorate, comprehensive exam, thesis/dissertation. *Entrance requirements:* For master's, GMAT or GRE, letters of recommendation, statement of purpose, relevant work experience; for doctorate, GMAT or GRE, letters of recommendation, personal statement, interview. Additional exam requirements/recommendations for international students: Required—TOEFL (minimum score 550 paper-based; 79 iBT) or IELTS (minimum score 6.5). *Application deadline:* For fall admission, 6/1 for domestic students, 2/1 for international students; for spring admission, 10/15 for domestic students, 9/15 for international students. Applications are processed on a rolling basis. Application fee: $30. Electronic applications accepted. *Expenses:* Tuition, state resident: full-time $7766; part-time $431.43 per credit hour. Tuition, nonresident: full-time $15,789; part-time $877.17 per credit hour. *Required fees:* $37 per term. *Financial support:* In 2016–17, 30 students received support, including 8 research assistantships with tuition reimbursements available (averaging $11,972 per year), 22 teaching assistantships with tuition reimbursements available (averaging $9,002 per year); scholarships/grants, health care benefits, and unspecified assistantships also available. Financial award applicants required to submit FAFSA. *Faculty research:* Data mining, business intelligence, bioterrorism surveillance, health informatics/informatics, software engineering, agent-based modeling, distributed systems, statistics, electronic markets, e-commerce, business process improvement, operations management, supply chain, LEAN management, global information systems, organizational impacts of IT, enterprise resource planning, business intelligence, Web and mobile technologies, social networks, information security. *Total annual research expenditures:* $496,876. *Unit head:* Dr. Kaushal Chari, Chair and Professor, 813-974-6768, Fax: 813-974-6749, E-mail: kchari@usf.edu. *Application contact:* Judy Oates, Office Assistant, 813-974-5524, Fax: 813-974-6749, E-mail: joates@usf.edu.
Website: http://business.usf.edu/departments/isds/

The University of Texas at Dallas, Naveen Jindal School of Management, Program in Information Systems and Operations Management, Richardson, TX 75080. Offers business analytics (MS); information technology and management (MS); supply chain management (MS). *Program availability:* Part-time, evening/weekend. *Faculty:* 19 full-time (0 women), 37 part-time/adjunct (11 women). *Students:* 1,577 full-time (577 women), 457 part-time (189 women); includes 136 minority (21 Black or African American, non-Hispanic/Latino; 83 Asian, non-Hispanic/Latino; 19 Hispanic/Latino; 13 Two or more races, non-Hispanic/Latino), 1,795 international. Average age 27. 3,354 applicants, 66% accepted, 931 enrolled. In 2016, 787 master's awarded. *Degree requirements:* For master's, thesis optional. *Entrance requirements:* For master's, GMAT. Additional exam requirements/recommendations for international students: Required—TOEFL (minimum score 550 paper-based). *Application deadline:* For fall admission, 7/15 for domestic students, 5/1 priority date for international students; for spring admission, 11/15 for domestic students, 9/1 priority date for international students. Applications are processed on a rolling basis. Application fee: $50 ($100 for international students). Electronic applications accepted. *Expenses:* Tuition, state resident: full-time $12,418; part-time $690 per semester hour. Tuition, nonresident: full-time $24,150; part-time $1342 per semester hour. Tuition and fees vary according to course load. *Financial support:* In 2016–17, 473 students received support, including 5 research assistantships with partial tuition reimbursements available (averaging $14,880 per year), 48 teaching assistantships with partial tuition reimbursements available (averaging $10,122 per year); career-related internships or fieldwork, Federal Work-Study, institutionally sponsored loans, scholarships/grants, and unspecified assistantships also available. Support available to part-time students. Financial award application deadline: 4/30; financial award applicants required to submit FAFSA. *Faculty research:* Technology marketing, measuring information work productivity, electronic commerce, decision support systems, data quality. *Unit head:* Dr. Milind Dawande, Area Coordinator, 972-883-2793, E-mail: milind@utdallas.edu. *Application contact:* Dr. Ozalp Ozer, PhD Area Coordinator, 972-883-2316, E-mail: oozer@utdallas.edu.
Website: http://jindal.utdallas.edu/isom/

University of Utah, Graduate School, David Eccles School of Business, Business Administration Program, Salt Lake City, UT 84112. Offers accounting (PhD); business administration (EMBA, MBA, PMBA); finance (PhD); information systems (PhD); marketing (PhD); operations management (PhD); organizational behavior (PhD); strategic management (PhD); MBA/JD; MBA/MHA; MBA/MS. *Program availability:* Part-time, evening/weekend, online learning. *Faculty:* 58 full-time (21 women), 37 part-time/adjunct (7 women). *Students:* 578 full-time (149 women), 89 part-time (28 women); includes 71 minority (1 American Indian or Alaska Native, non-Hispanic/Latino; 17 Asian, non-Hispanic/Latino; 45 Hispanic/Latino; 8 Two or more races, non-Hispanic/Latino), 50 international. Average age 32. 442 applicants, 70% accepted, 226 enrolled. In 2016, 246 master's, 6 doctorates awarded. *Degree requirements:* For doctorate, comprehensive exam, thesis/dissertation. *Entrance requirements:* For master's, GMAT or GRE; for doctorate, GMAT. Additional exam requirements/recommendations for international students: Required—TOEFL (minimum score 600 paper-based; 100 iBT), IELTS (minimum score 7). *Application deadline:* For fall admission, 11/1 priority date for domestic students, 3/1 priority date for international students; for spring admission, 11/1 for domestic and international students. Applications are processed on a rolling basis. Application fee: $55 ($65 for international students). Electronic applications accepted. *Expenses:* Contact institution. *Financial support:* In 2016–17, 53 students received support, including 53 fellowships with partial tuition reimbursements available (averaging $8,600 per year); scholarships/grants and unspecified assistantships also available. Financial award application deadline: 2/1; financial award applicants required to submit FAFSA. *Faculty research:* Corporate finance, strategy services, consumer behavior, financial disclosures, operations. *Unit head:* Kristina Diekmann, Department Chair, 801-581-8524, Fax: 801-581-3380, E-mail: mastersinfo@business.utah.edu. *Application contact:* Christine Harris, Coordinator, 801-581-7785, Fax: 801-585-3962, E-mail: execch@business.utah.edu.
Website: http://www.business.utah.edu/

University of Utah, Graduate School, David Eccles School of Business, Department of Operations and Information Systems, Salt Lake City, UT 84112. Offers information systems (MS, Graduate Certificate), including business intelligence and analytics, IT

security, product and process management, software and systems architecture. *Program availability:* Part-time, evening/weekend, 100% online, blended/hybrid learning. *Faculty:* 12 full-time (5 women), 7 part-time/adjunct (0 women). *Students:* 143 full-time (43 women), 107 part-time (28 women); includes 127 minority (1 Black or African American, non-Hispanic/Latino; 120 Asian, non-Hispanic/Latino; 3 Hispanic/Latino; 3 Two or more races, non-Hispanic/Latino), 123 international. Average age 29. 334 applicants, 72% accepted, 127 enrolled. In 2016, 96 master's awarded. *Degree requirements:* For master's, capstone project. *Entrance requirements:* For master's, GMAT/GRE, minimum undergraduate GPA of 3.0, 2 letters of recommendation, personal statement, professional resume. Additional exam requirements/ recommendations for international students: Required—TOEFL (minimum score 550 paper-based; 80 iBT), IELTS (minimum score 6.5). *Application deadline:* For fall admission, 7/28 for domestic students, 3/1 for international students; for spring admission, 12/7 for domestic students, 8/16 for international students. Applications are processed on a rolling basis. Application fee: $55 ($65 for international students). Electronic applications accepted. *Expenses:* Contact institution. *Financial support:* In 2016–17, 75 students received support, including 7 teaching assistantships (averaging $5,000 per year); fellowships with partial tuition reimbursements available, tuition waivers (partial), and unspecified assistantships also available. Financial award application deadline: 3/31; financial award applicants required to submit FAFSA. *Faculty research:* Business intelligence and analytics, software and system architecture, product and process management, IT security, Web and data mining, applications and management of IT in healthcare. *Unit head:* Dr. Bradden Blair, Director of the IS Programs, 801-587-9489, Fax: 801-581-3666, E-mail: b.blair@eccles.utah.edu. *Application contact:* Raven Clissold, Admissions Coordinator, 801-587-5838, Fax: 801-581-3666, E-mail: raven.clissold@eccles.utah.edu.
Website: http://msis.eccles.utah.edu

University of Virginia, McIntire School of Commerce, MS Program in Global Commerce, Charlottesville, VA 22903. Offers global commerce (MS); global strategic management (MS); international management (Certificate). *Entrance requirements:* For master's, GMAT. Additional exam requirements/recommendations for international students: Required—TOEFL (minimum score 600 paper-based; 100 iBT), IELTS (minimum score 6.5). *Expenses:* Tuition, state resident: full-time $15,026; part-time $834 per credit hour. Tuition, nonresident: full-time $25,168; part-time $1378 per credit hour. *Required fees:* $2654.

The University of Western Ontario, Richard Ivey School of Business, London, ON N6A 3K7, Canada. Offers business (EMBA, PhD); corporate strategy and leadership elective (MBA); entrepreneurship elective (MBA); finance elective (MBA); health sector stream (MBA); international management elective (MBA); marketing elective (MBA); JD/ MBA. *Degree requirements:* For master's, thesis (for some programs); for doctorate, thesis/dissertation. *Entrance requirements:* For master's, GMAT, 2 years of full-time work experience, interview. Additional exam requirements/recommendations for international students: Required—TOEFL (minimum score 100 iBT) or IELTS (minimum score 6). Electronic applications accepted. *Faculty research:* Strategy, organizational behavior, international business, finance, operations management.

University of Wisconsin–Madison, Graduate School, College of Engineering, Department of Industrial and Systems Engineering, Madison, WI 53706. Offers industrial engineering (MS, PhD), including human factors and health systems engineering (MS), systems engineering and analytics (MS). *Program availability:* Part-time. *Faculty:* 18 full-time (5 women). *Students:* 94 full-time (37 women), 6 part-time (2 women); includes 2 minority (both Black or African American, non-Hispanic/Latino), 73 international. Average age 26. 463 applicants, 22% accepted, 35 enrolled. In 2016, 28 master's, 13 doctorates awarded. Terminal master's awarded for partial completion of doctoral program. *Degree requirements:* For master's, thesis optional, 30 credits; minimum GPA of 3.0; for doctorate, comprehensive exam, thesis/dissertation, minimum of 32 credits; minimum GPA of 3.0. *Entrance requirements:* For master's and doctorate, GRE General Test, minimum GPA of 3.0, BS in engineering or equivalent, course work in computer programming and statistics. Additional exam requirements/recommendations for international students: Required—TOEFL (minimum score 580 paper-based; 92 iBT), IELTS (minimum score 7). *Application deadline:* For fall admission, 1/1 for domestic and international students; for spring admission, 10/1 for domestic and international students; for summer admission, 2/1 for domestic and international students. Application fee: $75 ($81 for international students). Electronic applications accepted. *Expenses:* $13,157 per year in-state tuition and fees; $26,484 per year out-of-state tuition and fees. *Financial support:* In 2016–17, 50 students received support, including 1 fellowship with full tuition reimbursement available, 30 research assistantships with full tuition reimbursements available, 14 teaching assistantships with full tuition reimbursements available; career-related internships or fieldwork, Federal Work-Study, institutionally sponsored loans, scholarships/grants, traineeships, health care benefits, and unspecified assistantships also available. Financial award application deadline: 12/1; financial award applicants required to submit FAFSA. *Faculty research:* Operations research; human factors and ergonomics; health systems engineering; manufacturing and production systems. *Total annual research expenditures:* $12.5 million. *Unit head:* Dr. Jeff Lindroth, Chair, 608-890-1931, Fax: 608-262-8454, E-mail: linderoth@wisc.edu. *Application contact:* Pam Peterson, Student Services Coordinator, 608-263-4025, Fax: 608-262-8454, E-mail: prpeterson@wisc.edu.
Website: http://www.engr.wisc.edu/department/industrial-systems-engineering/

University of Wisconsin–Milwaukee, Graduate School, Lubar School of Business, MS and Certificate Business Programs, Milwaukee, WI 53201-0413. Offers business analytics (Graduate Certificate); enterprise resource planning (Graduate Certificate); information technology management (MS); investment management (Graduate Certificate); nonprofit management (Graduate Certificate); nonprofit management and leadership (MS); state and local taxation (Graduate Certificate). *Students:* 174 full-time (83 women), 157 part-time (64 women); includes 69 minority (23 Black or African American, non-Hispanic/Latino; 27 Asian, non-Hispanic/Latino; 6 Hispanic/Latino; 13 Two or more races, non-Hispanic/Latino), 65 international. Average age 32. 201 applicants, 56% accepted, 116 enrolled. In 2016, 171 master's, 34 other advanced degrees awarded. *Entrance requirements:* Additional exam requirements/ recommendations for international students: Required—TOEFL (minimum score 550 paper-based; 79 iBT), IELTS (minimum score 6.5). *Application deadline:* Applications are processed on a rolling basis. Application fee: $56 ($96 for international students). Electronic applications accepted. *Financial support:* In 2016–17, 12 teaching assistantships were awarded; fellowships, research assistantships, health care benefits, unspecified assistantships, and project assistantships also available. Financial award applicants required to submit FAFSA. *Application contact:* General Information Contact, 414-229-4982, Fax: 414-229-6967, E-mail: gradschool@uwm.edu.

Valparaiso University, Graduate School and Continuing Education, College of Business, Valparaiso, IN 46383. Offers business administration (MBA); business intelligence (Certificate); engineering management (Certificate); entrepreneurship (Certificate); finance (Certificate); general business (Certificate); management (Certificate); marketing (Certificate); sustainability (Certificate); JD/MBA; MSN/MBA. *Accreditation:* AACSB. *Program availability:* Part-time, evening/weekend, online learning. *Entrance requirements:* For master's, GMAT, GRE, minimum GPA of 3.0. Additional exam requirements/recommendations for international students: Required—TOEFL (minimum score 550 paper-based; 80 iBT), IELTS (minimum score 6). Electronic applications accepted. *Expenses:* Contact institution.

Vanderbilt University, Vanderbilt University Owen Graduate School of Management, Vanderbilt MBA Program, Nashville, TN 37203. Offers accounting (MBA); finance (MBA); general management (MBA); health care (MBA); human and organizational performance (MBA); marketing (MBA); operations (MBA); strategy (MBA); MBA/JD; MBA/M Div; MBA/MD; MBA/MSN; MBA/MTS; MBA/PhD. *Accreditation:* AACSB. *Degree requirements:* For master's, 62 credit hours of coursework; completion of ethics course; minimum GPA of 3.0. *Entrance requirements:* For master's, GMAT (preferred) or GRE, 2 years of work experience (recommended). Additional exam requirements/ recommendations for international students: Required—TOEFL (minimum score 100 iBT). Electronic applications accepted. *Expenses:* Contact institution. *Faculty research:* Accounting and finance, business strategy and economics, marketing, operations management, organization studies.

Villanova University, Villanova School of Business, MBA - The Fast Track Program, Villanova, PA 19085. Offers analytics (MBA); cybersecurity (MBA); finance (MBA); healthcare (MBA); international business (MBA); management information systems (MBA); marketing (MBA); real estate (MBA); strategic management (MBA); sustainability (MBA). *Accreditation:* AACSB. *Program availability:* Part-time, evening/weekend. *Faculty:* 108 full-time (39 women), 32 part-time/adjunct (8 women). *Students:* 127 part-time (58 women); includes 18 minority (3 Black or African American, non-Hispanic/ Latino; 7 Asian, non-Hispanic/Latino; 6 Hispanic/Latino; 2 Two or more races, non-Hispanic/Latino), 2 international. Average age 30. 88 applicants, 90% accepted, 66 enrolled. In 2016, 75 master's awarded. *Degree requirements:* For master's, minimum GPA of 3.0. *Entrance requirements:* For master's, GMAT or GRE, work experience, 2 letters of recommendation, 2 essays, resume, official transcripts, interview. Additional exam requirements/recommendations for international students: Required—TOEFL (minimum score 550 paper-based; 100 iBT). *Application deadline:* For fall admission, 6/ 30 for domestic and international students. Application fee: $65. Electronic applications accepted. *Expenses:* Contact institution. *Financial support:* Scholarships/grants available. Financial award application deadline: 6/30; financial award applicants required to submit FAFSA. *Faculty research:* Business analytics; creativity, innovation and entrepreneurship; global leadership; real estate; church management; business ethics; marketing and consumer insights. *Unit head:* Michael L. Capella, Associate Dean of Graduate and Executive Business Programs, 610-519-4336, Fax: 610-519-6273, E-mail: michael.l.capella@villanova.edu. *Application contact:* Kimberly Kane, Manager of Admissions, 610-519-3701, Fax: 610-519-6273, E-mail: kimberly.kane@ villanova.edu.
Website: http://www1.villanova.edu/villanova/business/graduate/mba.html

Villanova University, Villanova School of Business, MBA - The Flex Track Program, Villanova, PA 19085. Offers analytics (MBA); finance (MBA); healthcare (MBA); international business (MBA); marketing (MBA); real estate (MBA); strategic management (MBA); JD/MBA. *Accreditation:* AACSB. *Program availability:* Part-time, evening/weekend, online learning. *Faculty:* 108 full-time (39 women), 32 part-time/ adjunct (8 women). *Students:* 13 full-time (5 women), 399 part-time (134 women); includes 73 minority (21 Black or African American, non-Hispanic/Latino; 32 Asian, non-Hispanic/Latino; 19 Hispanic/Latino; 1 Two or more races, non-Hispanic/Latino), 11 international. Average age 31. 93 applicants, 94% accepted, 80 enrolled. In 2016, 133 master's awarded. *Degree requirements:* For master's, minimum GPA of 3.0. *Entrance requirements:* For master's, GMAT or GRE, work experience, 2 letters of recommendation, 2 essays, resume, official transcript. Additional exam requirements/ recommendations for international students: Required—TOEFL (minimum score 550 paper-based; 100 iBT). *Application deadline:* For fall admission, 6/30 for domestic and international students; for spring admission, 11/15 for domestic and international students; for summer admission, 3/31 for domestic and international students. Applications are processed on a rolling basis. Application fee: $65. Electronic applications accepted. *Expenses:* Contact institution. *Financial support:* In 2016–17, 13 research assistantships with full tuition reimbursements (averaging $13,100 per year) were awarded; scholarships/grants also available. Financial award application deadline: 6/30; financial award applicants required to submit FAFSA. *Faculty research:* Business analytics; creativity, innovation and entrepreneurship; global leadership; real estate; church management; business ethics. *Unit head:* Michael L. Capella, Associate Dean of Graduate and Executive Business Programs, 610-610-4336, Fax: 610-519-6273, E-mail: michael.l.capella@villanova.edu. *Application contact:* Claire Bruno, Director of Recruitment and Enrollment Management, 610-519-4336, Fax: 610-519-6273, E-mail: claire.bruno@villanova.edu.
Website: http://www1.villanova.edu/villanova/business/graduate/mba.html

Walsh College of Accountancy and Business Administration, Graduate Programs, Program in Management, Troy, MI 48083. Offers human resources management (MS); international business (MS); strategic management (MS). *Program availability:* Part-time, evening/weekend. *Faculty:* 12 full-time (6 women), 12 part-time/adjunct (5 women). *Students:* 54 (43 women); includes 20 minority (15 Black or African American, non-Hispanic/Latino; 1 American Indian or Alaska Native, non-Hispanic/Latino; 2 Asian, non-Hispanic/Latino; 1 Hispanic/Latino; 1 Two or more races, non-Hispanic/Latino). Average age 33. 27 applicants, 70% accepted, 13 enrolled. In 2016, 2 master's awarded. *Entrance requirements:* For master's, minimum overall cumulative GPA of 2.75 from all colleges previously attended. Additional exam requirements/ recommendations for international students: Required—TOEFL (minimum score 550 paper-based, 79 iBT), IELTS (6.5), Michigan English Language Assessment Battery, or MTELP. *Application deadline:* Applications are processed on a rolling basis. Application fee: $35. Electronic applications accepted. *Expenses:* $740 per credit hour, $125 registration fee per semester. *Financial support:* In 2016–17, 2 students received support. Career-related internships or fieldwork and scholarships/grants available. Financial award application deadline: 6/30; financial award applicants required to submit FAFSA. *Faculty research:* Strategy practice and process, management learning and decision-making, human capital development, global leadership and citizenship, use of systems and complexity theory and management practice. *Unit head:* Dr. Sheila Ronis, Chair, Management, 248-823-1635, Fax: 248-689-0920, E-mail: sronis@ walshcollege.edu. *Application contact:* Heather Rigby, Director, Admissions and Academic Advising, 248-823-1610, Fax: 248-689-0938, E-mail: hrigby@ walshcollege.edu.

Wayne State University, College of Engineering, Department of Computer Science, Detroit, MI 48202. Offers computer science (MS, PhD), including bioinformatics (PhD), computational biology (PhD); data science and business analytics (MS). Application deadline for PhD is February 17. *Faculty:* 22. *Students:* 117 full-time (41 women), 37 part-time (11 women); includes 11 minority (1 Black or African American, non-Hispanic/ Latino; 8 Asian, non-Hispanic/Latino; 2 Two or more races, non-Hispanic/Latino), 121 international. Average age 27. 596 applicants, 24% accepted, 29 enrolled. In 2016, 63 master's, 13 doctorates awarded. *Degree requirements:* For master's, thesis (for some programs); for doctorate, thesis/dissertation. *Entrance requirements:* For master's, GRE, minimum GPA of 3.0, three letters of recommendation, adequate preparation in computer science and mathematics courses, personal statement; for doctorate, GRE,

bachelor's or master's degree in computer science or related field; minimum GPA of 3.3 in most recent degree; three letters of recommendation; personal statement; adequate preparation in computer science and mathematics courses. Additional exam requirements/recommendations for international students: Required—TOEFL (minimum score 550 paper-based; 79 iBT), TWE (minimum score 5.5), Michigan English Language Assessment Battery (minimum score 85); Recommended—IELTS (minimum score 6.5). *Application deadline:* For fall admission, 6/1 priority date for domestic students, 5/1 priority date for international students; for winter admission, 10/1 priority date for domestic students, 9/1 priority date for international students; for spring admission, 2/1 priority date for domestic students, 1/2 priority date for international students. Applications are processed on a rolling basis. Application fee: $50. Electronic applications accepted. *Expenses:* $18,871 per year resident tuition and fees, $36,065 per year non-resident tuition and fees. *Financial support:* In 2016–17, 67 students received support, including 4 fellowships with tuition reimbursements available (averaging $17,250 per year), 22 research assistantships with tuition reimbursements available (averaging $22,361 per year), 36 teaching assistantships with tuition reimbursements available (averaging $19,177 per year); scholarships/grants, health care benefits, and unspecified assistantships also available. Financial award applicants required to submit FAFSA. *Faculty research:* Software engineering, databases, bioinformatics, artificial intelligence, networking, distributed and parallel computing, security, graphics, visualizations. *Total annual research expenditures:* $1.5 million. *Unit head:* Dr. Loren Schwiebert, Interim Chair, 313-577-5474, E-mail: loren@wayne.edu. *Application contact:* Eric Scimeca, Graduate Program Director, 313-577-5421, E-mail: eric.scimeca@wayne.edu.
Website: http://engineering.wayne.edu/cs/

Wayne State University, College of Engineering, Department of Industrial and Systems Engineering, Detroit, MI 48202. Offers data science and business analytics (MS); engineering management (MS); industrial engineering (MS, PhD); manufacturing engineering (MS); systems engineering (Certificate). *Faculty:* 10. *Students:* 313 full-time (37 women), 140 part-time (26 women); includes 37 minority (16 Black or African American, non-Hispanic/Latino; 15 Asian, non-Hispanic/Latino; 3 Hispanic/Latino; 3 Two or more races, non-Hispanic/Latino), 340 international. Average age 28. 1,171 applicants, 42% accepted, 105 enrolled. In 2016, 117 master's, 5 doctorates awarded. *Degree requirements:* For master's, thesis (for some programs); for doctorate, thesis/dissertation. *Entrance requirements:* For master's, BS from ABET-accredited institution; for doctorate, MS in industrial engineering or operations research with minimum graduate GPA of 3.5; for Certificate, BS in engineering or other technical field from ABET-accredited institution, full-time work experience as practicing engineer or technical leader. Additional exam requirements/recommendations for international students: Required—TOEFL (minimum score 550 paper-based; 79 iBT), TWE (minimum score 5.5), Michigan English Language Assessment Battery (minimum score 85); Recommended—IELTS (minimum score 6.5). *Application deadline:* For fall admission, 6/1 priority date for domestic students, 5/1 priority date for international students; for winter admission, 10/1 priority date for domestic students, 9/1 priority date for international students; for spring admission, 2/1 priority date for domestic students, 1/1 priority date for international students. Applications are processed on a rolling basis. Application fee: $50. Electronic applications accepted. *Expenses:* $18,871 per year resident tuition and fees, $36,065 per year non-resident tuition and fees. *Financial support:* In 2016–17, 118 students received support, including 2 fellowships with tuition reimbursements available (averaging $16,000 per year), 4 research assistantships with tuition reimbursements available (averaging $18,883 per year), 12 teaching assistantships with tuition reimbursements available (averaging $19,177 per year); scholarships/grants, tuition waivers (full), and unspecified assistantships also available. Financial award applicants required to submit FAFSA. *Faculty research:* Healthcare systems engineering, product design and development, quality and reliability engineering, supply chain management and logistics. *Total annual research expenditures:* $3.2 million. *Unit head:* Dr. Leslie Monplaisir, Associate Professor/Chair, 313-577-3821, Fax: 313-577-8833, E-mail: leslie.monplaisir@wayne.edu. *Application contact:* Eric Scimeca, Graduate Program Coordinator, 313-577-0412, E-mail: eric.scimeca@wayne.edu.
Website: http://engineering.wayne.edu/ise/

Wayne State University, Mike Ilitch School of Business, Detroit, MI 48202. Offers accounting (MS, Postbaccalaureate Certificate); business (Graduate Certificate); business administration (MBA, PhD); data science (MS), including business analytics; entrepreneurship and innovation (Postbaccalaureate Certificate); finance (MS); information systems management (Postbaccalaureate Certificate); taxation (MST); JD/MBA. Application deadline for PhD is February 15. *Accreditation:* AACSB. *Program availability:* Part-time, evening/weekend. *Faculty:* 32. *Students:* 219 full-time (105 women), 941 part-time (406 women); includes 314 minority (186 Black or African American, non-Hispanic/Latino; 3 American Indian or Alaska Native, non-Hispanic/Latino; 68 Asian, non-Hispanic/Latino; 33 Hispanic/Latino; 24 Two or more races, non-Hispanic/Latino), 88 international. Average age 30. 1,119 applicants, 49% accepted, 329 enrolled. In 2016, 203 master's, 1 doctorate, 3 other advanced degrees awarded. *Degree requirements:* For doctorate, thesis/dissertation. *Entrance requirements:* For master's, GMAT, GRE, LSAT, MCAT, at least three years of relevant work experience that shows increased responsibility, or minimum GPA of 3.0 from AACSB-accredited program or 3.2 from regionally-accredited program, undergraduate degree from accredited institution; undergraduate degree in accounting, business administration, or area of business administration (for MS and MST); for doctorate, GMAT (minimum score of 600), minimum undergraduate GPA of 3.0, 3.5 upper-division or graduate; three letters of recommendation; brief essay; undergraduate degree from accredited institution; personal statement; for other advanced degree, bachelor's degree from accredited institution. Additional exam requirements/recommendations for international students: Required—TOEFL (minimum score 550 paper-based; 79 iBT), Michigan English Language Assessment Battery (minimum score 85); Recommended—IELTS (minimum score 6.5), TWE (minimum score 5.5). *Application deadline:* For fall admission, 7/1 for domestic students, 5/1 priority date for international students; for winter admission, 11/1 for domestic students, 9/1 priority date for international students; for spring admission, 3/1 for domestic students, 1/1 priority date for international students. Applications are processed on a rolling basis. Application fee: $50. Electronic applications accepted. *Expenses:* $18,871 per year resident tuition and fees, $36,065 per year non-resident tuition and fees. *Financial support:* In 2016–17, 174 students received support, including 1 fellowship with tuition reimbursement available (averaging $18,000 per year), 2 research assistantships with tuition reimbursements available (averaging $18,000 per year), 5 teaching assistantships with tuition reimbursements available (averaging $18,000 per year); scholarships/grants, health care benefits, and unspecified assistantships also available. Support available to part-time students. Financial award applicants required to submit FAFSA. *Faculty research:* Executive compensation and stock performance, consumer reactions to pricing strategies, communication across the automotive supply chain, performance of firms in sub-Saharan Africa, implementation issues with ERP software. *Unit head:* Dr. Robert Forsythe, Dean, School of Business Administration, 313-577-4501, E-mail: robert.forsythe@wayne.edu. *Application contact:* Kiantee N. Rupert-Jones, Director, 313-577-4511, Fax: 313-577-9442, E-mail: gradbusiness@wayne.edu.
Website: http://ilitchbusiness.wayne.edu/

West Chester University of Pennsylvania, College of Business and Public Management, School of Business, West Chester, PA 19383. Offers business analytics (Certificate); business education (MBA); entrepreneurship (Certificate); project management (Certificate). *Accreditation:* AACSB. *Program availability:* Part-time, evening/weekend, 100% online. *Faculty:* 13 full-time (6 women), 2 part-time/adjunct (1 woman). *Students:* 44 full-time (23 women), 213 part-time (82 women); includes 37 minority (16 Black or African American, non-Hispanic/Latino; 11 Asian, non-Hispanic/Latino; 9 Hispanic/Latino; 1 Two or more races, non-Hispanic/Latino). Average age 32. 202 applicants, 83% accepted, 126 enrolled. In 2016, 41 master's, 16 other advanced degrees awarded. *Degree requirements:* For master's, minimum GPA of 3.0. *Entrance requirements:* For master's, GMAT or GRE, statement of professional goals, resume, two letters of recommendation, transcripts. Additional exam requirements/recommendations for international students: Required—TOEFL or IELTS. *Application deadline:* For fall admission, 5/15 for international students; for spring admission, 10/15 for international students. Applications are processed on a rolling basis. Application fee: $50. Electronic applications accepted. *Expenses:* Tuition, state resident: full-time $8694; part-time $483 per credit. Tuition, nonresident: full-time $13,050; part-time $725 per credit. *Required fees:* $2399; $119.05 per credit. Tuition and fees vary according to campus/location and program. *Financial support:* Scholarships/grants and unspecified assistantships available. Financial award application deadline: 2/15; financial award applicants required to submit FAFSA. *Unit head:* Dr. Brian Halsey, MBA Director/Graduate Coordinator, 610-425-5000 Ext. 4444, E-mail: mba@wcupa.edu. *Application contact:* Office of Graduate Studies and Extended Education, 610-436-2943, Fax: 610-436-2763, E-mail: gradstudy@wcupa.edu.
Website: http://www.wcupa.edu/mba

Western Governors University, College of Business, Salt Lake City, UT 84107. Offers information technology management (MBA); integrated healthcare management (MS); management and strategy (MBA); strategic leadership (MBA). *Program availability:* Evening/weekend. *Degree requirements:* For master's, capstone project. *Entrance requirements:* For master's, Readiness Assessment, transcripts. Additional exam requirements/recommendations for international students: Required—TOEFL (minimum score 450 paper-based; 80 iBT). Electronic applications accepted.

Xavier University, Williams College of Business, Master of Business Administration Program, Cincinnati, OH 45207. Offers business administration (Exec MBA, MBA); business intelligence (MBA); finance (MBA); health industry (MBA); international business (MBA); marketing (MBA); values-based leadership (MBA); MBA/MHSA; MSN/MBA. *Accreditation:* AACSB. *Program availability:* Part-time, evening/weekend. *Degree requirements:* For master's, capstone course. *Entrance requirements:* For master's, GMAT or GRE, official transcript; resume. Additional exam requirements/recommendations for international students: Required—TOEFL (minimum score 550 paper-based; 79 iBT). Electronic applications accepted. Application fee is waived when completed online. *Expenses:* Contact institution.

Sustainability Management

American University, Kogod School of Business, Program in Sustainability Management, Washington, DC 20016. Offers MS. *Students:* 8 full-time (3 women), 16 part-time (11 women); includes 8 minority (2 Black or African American, non-Hispanic/Latino; 1 Asian, non-Hispanic/Latino; 5 Hispanic/Latino), 3 international. Average age 29. 33 applicants, 94% accepted, 15 enrolled. In 2016, 11 master's awarded. *Entrance requirements:* For master's, GMAT/GRE, resume, personal statement, 2 letters of recommendation, transcripts. Additional exam requirements/recommendations for international students: Required—TOEFL (minimum score 100 iBT), IELTS (minimum score 7), PTE (minimum score 68). *Application deadline:* For fall admission, 2/20 priority date for domestic students, 2/20 for international students; for spring admission, 12/10 for domestic students, 11/15 for international students. Application fee: $100. *Expenses:* $1,579 per credit tuition; $690 mandatory fees. *Financial support:* Application deadline: 2/1; applicants required to submit FAFSA. *Application contact:* Jason Kennedy, Associate Director, Graduate Admissions, 202-885-1968, E-mail: jkennedy@american.edu.
Website: http://www.kogod.american.edu

Anaheim University, Programs in Business Administration, Anaheim, CA 92806-5150. Offers entrepreneurship (ME, DBA); global sustainable management (MBA); international business (MBA, DBA, Certificate, Diploma); management (DBA); sustainable management (DBA, Certificate, Diploma). *Program availability:* Part-time, evening/weekend, online only, 100% online. In 2016, 3 master's, 4 doctorates awarded. *Application deadline:* Applications are processed on a rolling basis. Electronic applications accepted. *Unit head:* Robert Robertson, Dean, Graduate School of Business, 714-772-3330, Fax: 714-772-3331, E-mail: admissions@anaheim.edu.

Antioch University New England, Graduate School, Department of Management, Program in Sustainability (Green MBA), Keene, NH 03431-3552. Offers MBA. *Program availability:* Part-time. *Entrance requirements:* For master's, GRE, resume, 3 letters of recommendation. Additional exam requirements/recommendations for international students: Required—TOEFL (minimum score 600 paper-based).

Aquinas College, School of Management, Grand Rapids, MI 49506. Offers marketing management (MM); organizational leadership (MM); sustainable business (MM). *Program availability:* Part-time, evening/weekend. *Entrance requirements:* For master's, GMAT, minimum undergraduate GPA of 2.75, 2 years of work experience. Additional exam requirements/recommendations for international students: Required—TOEFL (minimum score 550 paper-based). *Application deadline:* Applications are processed on a rolling basis. Application fee: $0. *Expenses:* Contact institution. *Financial support:* Scholarships/grants available. Support available to part-time students. Financial award application deadline: 3/15; financial award applicants required to submit FAFSA. *Unit head:* Cynthia G. VanGelderen, Interim Director, 616-632-2922, Fax: 616-732-4489.

Application contact: Lynn Atkins-Rykert, Program Coordinator, 616-632-2925, Fax: 616-732-4489, E-mail: atkinlyn@aquinas.edu.

Argosy University, Chicago, College of Business, Chicago, IL 60601. Offers accounting (DBA); customized professional concentration (MBA, DBA); finance (MBA); fraud examination (MBA); global business sustainability (DBA); healthcare administration (MBA); information systems (DBA); information systems management (MBA); international business (MBA, DBA); management (MBA, MSM, DBA); marketing (MBA, DBA); organizational leadership (Ed D); public administration (MBA); sustainable management (MBA). *Accreditation:* ACBSP. *Program availability:* Online learning.

Argosy University, Dallas, College of Business, Farmers Branch, TX 75244. Offers accounting (DBA, AGC); corporate compliance (MBA, Graduate Certificate); customized professional concentration (MBA); finance (MBA, Graduate Certificate); fraud examination (MBA, Graduate Certificate); global business sustainability (DBA, AGC); healthcare administration (Graduate Certificate); healthcare management (MBA); information systems (MBA, DBA, AGC); information systems management (Graduate Certificate); international business (MBA, DBA, AGC, Graduate Certificate); management (MBA, DBA, AGC, Graduate Certificate); marketing (MBA, DBA, AGC, Graduate Certificate); public administration (MBA, Graduate Certificate); sustainable management (MBA, Graduate Certificate). *Accreditation:* ACBSP.

Argosy University, Denver, College of Business, Denver, CO 80231. Offers accounting (DBA); corporate compliance (MBA); customized professional concentration (MBA, DBA); finance (MBA); fraud examination (MBA); global business sustainability (DBA); healthcare administration (MBA); information systems (DBA); information systems management (MBA); international business (MBA, DBA); management (MBA, MSM, DBA); marketing (MBA, DBA); organizational leadership (Ed D); public administration (MBA); sustainable management (MBA). *Accreditation:* ACBSP.

Argosy University, Hawai`i, College of Business, Honolulu, HI 96813. Offers accounting (DBA); corporate compliance (MBA); customized professional concentration (MBA, DBA); finance (MBA, Certificate); fraud examination (MBA); global business sustainability (DBA); healthcare administration (MBA, Certificate); information systems (DBA); information systems management (MBA, Certificate); international business (MBA, DBA, Certificate); management (MBA, MSM, DBA); marketing (MBA, DBA, Certificate); organizational leadership (Ed D); public administration (MBA); sustainable management (MBA).

Argosy University, Inland Empire, College of Business, Ontario, CA 91761. Offers accounting (DBA); corporate compliance (MBA); customized professional concentration (MBA, DBA); finance (MBA); fraud examination (MBA); global business sustainability (DBA); healthcare administration (MBA); information systems (DBA); information systems management (MBA); international business (MBA, DBA); management (MBA, MSM, DBA); marketing (MBA, DBA); organizational leadership (Ed D); public administration (MBA); sustainable management (MBA).

Argosy University, Los Angeles, College of Business, Santa Monica, CA 90045. Offers accounting (DBA); corporate compliance (MBA); customized professional concentration (MBA, DBA); finance (MBA); fraud examination (MBA); global business sustainability (DBA); healthcare administration (MBA); information systems (DBA); information systems management (MBA); international business (MBA, DBA); management (MBA, MSM, DBA); marketing (MBA, DBA); organizational leadership (Ed D); public administration (MBA); sustainable management (MBA).

Argosy University, Northern Virginia, College of Business, Arlington, VA 22209. Offers accounting (DBA); customized professional concentration (MBA, DBA); finance (MBA); fraud examination (MBA); global business sustainability (DBA); healthcare administration (MBA); information systems (DBA); information systems management (MBA); international business (MBA, DBA, Certificate); management (MBA, MSM, DBA); marketing (MBA, DBA, Certificate); organizational leadership (Ed D); public administration (MBA); sustainable management (MBA).

Argosy University, Orange County, College of Business, Orange, CA 92868. Offers accounting (DBA, Adv C); corporate compliance (MBA); customized professional concentration (MBA, DBA); finance (MBA, Certificate); fraud examination (MBA); global business sustainability (DBA); healthcare administration (MBA, Certificate); information systems (DBA, Adv C, Certificate); information systems management (MBA); international business (MBA, DBA, Adv C, Certificate); management (MBA, MSM, DBA, Adv C); marketing (MBA, DBA, Adv C, Certificate); organizational leadership (Ed D); public administration (MBA, Certificate); sustainable management (MBA).

Argosy University, Phoenix, College of Business, Phoenix, AZ 85021. Offers accounting (DBA); corporate compliance (MBA); customized professional concentration (MBA, DBA); finance (MBA); fraud examination (MBA); global business sustainability (DBA); healthcare administration (MBA); information systems (DBA); information systems management (MBA); international business (MBA, DBA); management (MBA, DBA); marketing (MBA, DBA); public administration (MBA); sustainable management (MBA).

Argosy University, Salt Lake City, College of Business, Draper, UT 84020. Offers accounting (DBA); corporate compliance (MBA); customized professional concentration (MBA, DBA); finance (MBA); fraud examination (MBA); global business sustainability (DBA); healthcare administration (MBA); information systems (DBA); information systems management (MBA); international business (MBA, DBA); management (MBA, DBA); marketing (MBA, DBA); public administration (MBA); sustainable management (MBA).

Argosy University, San Francisco Bay Area, College of Business, Alameda, CA 94501. Offers accounting (DBA); corporate compliance (MBA); customized professional concentration (MBA, DBA); finance (MBA); fraud examination (MBA); global business sustainability (DBA); healthcare administration (MBA); information systems (DBA); information systems management (MBA); international business (MBA, DBA); management (MBA, MSM, DBA); marketing (MBA, DBA); organizational leadership (Ed D); public administration (MBA); sustainable management (MBA).

Argosy University, Sarasota, College of Business, Sarasota, FL 34235. Offers accounting (DBA, Adv C); corporate compliance (MBA, DBA, Certificate); customized professional concentration (MBA, DBA); finance (MBA, Certificate); fraud examination (MBA, Certificate); global business sustainability (DBA, Adv C); healthcare administration (MBA, Certificate); information systems (DBA, Adv C, Certificate); information systems management (MBA); international business (MBA, DBA, Adv C, Certificate); management (MBA, MSM, DBA, Adv C, Certificate); marketing (MBA, DBA, Adv C, Certificate); organizational leadership (Ed D); public administration (MBA, Certificate); sustainable management (MBA, Certificate).

Argosy University, Schaumburg, Graduate School of Business and Management, Schaumburg, IL 60173-5403. Offers accounting (DBA, Adv C); customized professional concentration (MBA, DBA); finance (MBA, Certificate); fraud examination (MBA); healthcare administration (MBA, Certificate); human resource management (MS); information systems (Adv C, Certificate); information systems management (MBA); international business (MBA, DBA, Adv C, Certificate); management (MBA, MSM, DBA, Adv C, Certificate); marketing (MBA, DBA, Adv C, Certificate); organizational leadership (MS, Ed D); public administration (MBA); sustainable management (MBA).

Argosy University, Seattle, College of Business, Seattle, WA 98121. Offers accounting (DBA); corporate compliance (MBA); customized professional concentration (MBA, DBA); finance (MBA); fraud examination (MBA); global business sustainability (DBA); healthcare administration (MBA); information systems (DBA); information systems management (MBA); international business (MBA, DBA); management (MBA, MSM, DBA); marketing (MBA, DBA); organizational leadership (Ed D); public administration (MBA); sustainable management (MBA).

Argosy University, Tampa, College of Business, Tampa, FL 33607. Offers accounting (DBA); corporate compliance (MBA); customized professional concentration (MBA, DBA); finance (MBA); fraud examination (MBA); global business sustainability (DBA); healthcare administration (MBA); information systems (DBA); information systems management (MBA); international business (MBA, DBA); management (MBA, MSM, DBA); marketing (MBA, DBA); organizational leadership (Ed D); public administration (MBA); sustainable management (MBA).

Argosy University, Twin Cities, College of Business, Eagan, MN 55121. Offers accounting (DBA); customized professional concentration (MBA, DBA); finance (MBA); fraud examination (MBA); global business sustainability (DBA); healthcare administration (MBA); information systems (DBA); information systems management (MBA); international business (MBA, DBA); management (MBA, MSM, DBA); marketing (MBA, DBA); organizational leadership (Ed D); public administration (MBA); sustainable management (MBA).

Baldwin Wallace University, Graduate Programs, School of Business, Program in Sustainability, Berea, OH 44017-2088. Offers MBA. *Program availability:* Part-time, evening/weekend. *Students:* 1 (woman) full-time, 3 part-time (all women). Average age 40. 1 applicant. In 2016, 5 master's awarded. *Expenses:* $921 per credit hour. *Financial support:* Applicants required to submit FAFSA. *Unit head:* Ven Ochaya, Director, 440-826-2391, Fax: 440-826-3868, E-mail: vochaya@bw.edu. *Application contact:* Laura Spencer, Graduate Application Specialist, 440-826-2191, Fax: 440-826-3868, E-mail: lspencer@bw.edu.

Bard College, Bard Center for Environmental Policy, Annandale-on-Hudson, NY 12504. Offers climate science and policy (MS, Professional Certificate), including agriculture (MS), ecosystems (MS); environmental policy (MS, Professional Certificate); sustainability (MBA); MS/JD; MS/MAT. *Program availability:* Part-time. *Degree requirements:* For master's, thesis, 4-month, full-time internship. *Entrance requirements:* For master's, GRE, coursework in statistics, chemistry and one other semester of college science; personal statement; curriculum vitae; 3 letters of recommendation; sample of written work. Additional exam requirements/recommendations for international students: Required—TOEFL (minimum score 600 paper-based; 100 iBT). Electronic applications accepted. *Expenses:* Contact institution. *Faculty research:* Climate and agriculture, alternative energy, environmental economics, environmental toxicology, EPA law, sustainable development, international relations, literature and composition, human rights, agronomy, advocacy, leadership.

Baruch College of the City University of New York, Zicklin School of Business, Department of Management, New York, NY 10010-5585. Offers entrepreneurship (MBA); management (PhD); operations management (MBA); organizational behavior/human resources management (MBA); sustainable business (MBA). PhD offered jointly with Graduate School and University Center of the City University of New York. *Program availability:* Part-time, evening/weekend. *Degree requirements:* For doctorate, comprehensive exam, thesis/dissertation. *Entrance requirements:* For master's, GMAT, 2 letters of recommendation, resume, 2 years of work experience; for doctorate, GMAT. Additional exam requirements/recommendations for international students: Required—TOEFL (minimum score 590 paper-based), TWE.

Case Western Reserve University, Weatherhead School of Management, Department of Design and Innovation, Cleveland, OH 44106. Offers designing sustainable systems (PhD). *Program availability:* Part-time, evening/weekend. *Degree requirements:* For doctorate, thesis/dissertation. *Entrance requirements:* For doctorate, GMAT. *Expenses: Tuition:* Full-time $42,576; part-time $1774 per credit hour. *Required fees:* $34. Tuition and fees vary according to course load and program. *Faculty research:* Decision support, business forecasting systems, design and use of information systems, artificial intelligence, executive information systems.

Chatham University, Program in Business Administration, Pittsburgh, PA 15232-2826. Offers business administration (MBA); healthcare management (MBA); sustainability (MBA); women's leadership (MBA). *Program availability:* Part-time, evening/weekend. *Entrance requirements:* For master's, minimum GPA of 3.0, letters of recommendation. Additional exam requirements/recommendations for international students: Required—TOEFL (minimum score 600 paper-based; 100 iBT), IELTS (minimum score 7), TWE. Electronic applications accepted. Application fee is waived when completed online. *Expenses: Tuition:* Full-time $16,254; part-time $903 per credit hour. *Required fees:* $468; $26 per credit hour.

City University of Seattle, Graduate Division, School of Management, Seattle, WA 98121. Offers accounting (Certificate); change leadership (MBA, Certificate); computer systems (MS); finance (Certificate); financial management (MBA); general management (MBA); general management-Europe (MBA); global marketing (MBA); human resources management (Certificate); individualized study (MBA); information security (MS); information systems (MBA); leadership (MA); marketing (MBA, Certificate); project management (MBA, MS, Certificate); sustainable business (Certificate); technology management (MBA, Certificate). *Program availability:* Part-time, evening/weekend, online learning. *Degree requirements:* For master's, comprehensive exam (for some programs), thesis (for some programs). *Entrance requirements:* For master's, baccalaureate degree or equivalent from an accredited or otherwise recognized institution. Additional exam requirements/recommendations for international students: Required—TOEFL (minimum score 567 paper-based; 87 iBT); Recommended—IELTS. Electronic applications accepted.

Clark University, Graduate School, Graduate School of Management, Business Administration Program, Worcester, MA 01610-1477. Offers accounting (MBA); finance (MBA); information management and business analytics (MBA); management (MBA); marketing (MBA); social change (MBA); sustainability (MBA). *Accreditation:* AACSB. *Program availability:* Part-time, evening/weekend. *Students:* 91 full-time (48 women), 101 part-time (45 women); includes 22 minority (8 Black or African American, non-Hispanic/Latino; 4 Asian, non-Hispanic/Latino; 9 Hispanic/Latino; 1 Native Hawaiian or other Pacific Islander, non-Hispanic/Latino), 45 international. Average age 31. 225 applicants, 58% accepted, 78 enrolled. In 2016, 113 master's awarded. *Degree requirements:* For master's, thesis optional. *Application deadline:* For fall admission, 6/1 priority date for domestic students; for spring admission, 12/1 priority date for domestic students. Applications are processed on a rolling basis. Application fee: $75. Electronic applications accepted. *Expenses: Tuition:* Full-time $44,050. *Required fees:* $80. Tuition and fees vary according to course load and program. *Financial support:* In 2016–17, research assistantships with partial tuition reimbursements (averaging $4,800 per year), teaching assistantships with partial tuition reimbursements (averaging $4,800 per year) were awarded; fellowships, career-related internships or fieldwork, Federal Work-Study, institutionally sponsored loans, and tuition waivers (partial) also available. Support available to part-time students. Financial award application deadline: 5/31. *Faculty*

research: Marketing, accounting, human resource management, management information systems, business finance. *Unit head:* Dr. Catherine Usoff, Dean, 508-793-7543, Fax: 508-793-8822. *Application contact:* Ethan Bernstein, Director of Graduate Admissions, 508-793-7543, E-mail: graduateadmissions@clarku.edu.
Website: http://www.clarku.edu/programs/masters-business-administration

Colorado State University, College of Business, Global Social and Sustainable Enterprise MBA Program, Fort Collins, CO 80523-1201. Offers MBA. *Students:* 55 full-time (26 women); includes 3 minority (1 Black or African American, non-Hispanic/Latino; 1 Hispanic/Latino; 1 Two or more races, non-Hispanic/Latino), 22 international. Average age 28. 59 applicants, 78% accepted, 25 enrolled. In 2016, 20 master's awarded. *Degree requirements:* For master's, thesis or alternative, practicum. *Entrance requirements:* For master's, GMAT or GRE, 3 recommendations, current resume, minimum cumulative GPA of 3.0, statement of purpose, official transcripts. Additional exam requirements/recommendations for international students: Required—TOEFL (minimum score 86 iBT); Recommended—IELTS (minimum score 6.5), TSE (minimum score 58). *Application deadline:* For fall admission, 2/1 for domestic and international students. Applications are processed on a rolling basis. Application fee: $60 ($70 for international students). Electronic applications accepted. *Expenses:* Contact institution. *Financial support:* Scholarships/grants and unspecified assistantships available. Financial award application deadline: 2/15; financial award applicants required to submit FAFSA. *Faculty research:* Global social sustainable entrepreneurship; marketing for social sustainable enterprises; supply chain development and management; new venture development for social enterprise; financing, evaluating sustainable enterprise. *Unit head:* Dr. Sanjay Ramchander, Associate Dean of Academic Programs, 970-491-5027, E-mail: gradadmissions@business.colostate.edu. *Application contact:* Kat Ernst, Program Manager, 970-491-5612, E-mail: kat.ernst@colostate.edu.
Website: https://biz.colostate.edu/Academics/Graduate-Programs/Master-of-Business-Administration/Global-Social-Sustainable-Enterprise-MBA

Colorado State University, Warner College of Natural Resources, Department of Ecosystem Science and Sustainability, Fort Collins, CO 80523-1476. Offers greenhouse gas management and accounting (MGMA); watershed science (MS). *Faculty:* 9 full-time (2 women), 3 part-time/adjunct (2 women). *Students:* 14 full-time (8 women), 13 part-time (8 women); includes 5 minority (3 Hispanic/Latino; 2 Two or more races, non-Hispanic/Latino), 2 international. Average age 28. 34 applicants, 47% accepted, 11 enrolled. In 2016, 4 master's awarded. *Degree requirements:* For master's, thesis (for some programs), internship. *Entrance requirements:* For master's, GRE (70th percentile or higher), minimum GPA of 3.0. Additional exam requirements/recommendations for international students: Required—TOEFL (minimum score 550 paper-based; 80 iBT), IELTS (minimum score 6.5). *Application deadline:* For fall admission, 2/1 priority date for domestic and international students. Application fee: $60 ($70 for international students). Electronic applications accepted. *Expenses:* Contact institution. *Financial support:* In 2016–17, 9 students received support, including 1 fellowship (averaging $61,080 per year), 4 research assistantships (averaging $23,138 per year), 7 teaching assistantships (averaging $13,932 per year). *Faculty research:* Watershed/snow/alpine/land use hydrology, geographic information systems and remote sensing, greenhouse gas emissions, climate change, environmental accounting. *Total annual research expenditures:* $2.2 million. *Unit head:* Dr. John Moore, Department Head, 970-491-5589, Fax: 970-491-1965, E-mail: john.moore@colostate.edu. *Application contact:* Nikki Foxley, Graduate Admissions Coordinator, 970-491-5589, Fax: 970-491-1965, E-mail: nikki.foxley@colostate.edu.
Website: http://warnercnr.colostate.edu/departments/ess

Columbia University, School of Continuing Education, Program in Sustainability Management, New York, NY 10027. Offers MS. Program offered in collaboration with Columbia University's Earth Institute. *Program availability:* Part-time. Electronic applications accepted.

DePaul University, Kellstadt Graduate School of Business, Chicago, IL 60604. Offers accountancy (M Acc, MS, MSA); applied economics (MBA); banking (MBA); behavioral finance (MBA); brand and product management (MBA); business development (MBA); business information technology (MS); business strategy and decision-making (MBA); computational finance (MS); consumer insights (MBA); corporate finance (MBA); economic policy analysis (MS); entrepreneurship (MBA, MS); finance (MBA, MS); financial analysis (MBA); general business (MBA); health sector management (MBA); hospitality leadership (MBA); hospitality leadership and operational performance (MS); human resource management (MBA); human resources (MS); investment management (MBA); leadership and change management (MBA); management accounting (MBA); marketing (MBA, MS); marketing analysis (MS); marketing strategy and planning (MBA); operations management (MBA); organizational diversity (MBA); real estate (MS); real estate finance and investment (MBA); revenue management (MBA); sports management (MBA); strategic global marketing (MBA); strategy, execution and valuation (MBA); sustainable management (MBA, MS); taxation (MS); wealth management (MS); JD/MBA. *Accreditation:* AACSB. *Program availability:* Part-time, evening/weekend, online learning. *Entrance requirements:* For master's, GMAT, 2 letters of recommendation, resume, essay, official transcripts. Additional exam requirements/recommendations for international students: Required—TOEFL (minimum score 550 paper-based; 80 iBT). Electronic applications accepted. *Expenses:* Contact institution.

Dominican University of California, Barowsky School of Business, San Rafael, CA 94901-2298. Offers global business (MBA); strategic leadership (MBA); sustainable enterprise (MBA). *Program availability:* Part-time, evening/weekend. *Degree requirements:* For master's, thesis, capstone (for MBA). *Entrance requirements:* For master's, minimum GPA of 3.0. Additional exam requirements/recommendations for international students: Required—TOEFL (minimum score 550 paper-based; 80 iBT), IELTS (minimum score 6.5). Electronic applications accepted. Application fee is waived when completed online. *Expenses:* Contact institution.

Duquesne University, Palumbo-Donahue School of Business, Pittsburgh, PA 15282-0001. Offers accounting (M Acc); finance (MBA); information systems management (MSISM); management (MBA, MS); marketing (MBA); sports business (MS); sustainability (MBA); JD/MBA; MBA/M Acc; MBA/MA; MBA/MES; MBA/MHMS; MSISM/MBA; Pharm D/MBA. *Accreditation:* AACSB. *Program availability:* Part-time, evening/weekend, 100% online, minimal on-campus study. *Faculty:* 59 full-time (23 women), 25 part-time/adjunct (6 women). *Students:* 92 full-time (43 women), 176 part-time (71 women); includes 20 minority (9 Black or African American, non-Hispanic/Latino; 8 Asian, non-Hispanic/Latino; 2 Hispanic/Latino; 1 Two or more races, non-Hispanic/Latino), 35 international. Average age 28. 272 applicants, 86% accepted, 137 enrolled. In 2016, 137 master's awarded. *Entrance requirements:* For master's, GMAT or GRE, undergraduate transcripts, 2 letters of recommendation, current resume, personal statement. Additional exam requirements/recommendations for international students: Required—TOEFL (minimum score 577 paper-based; 90 iBT), IELTS (minimum score 7). *Application deadline:* For fall admission, 7/1 priority date for domestic and international students; for spring admission, 12/1 for domestic and international students; for summer admission, 4/1 for domestic and international students. Applications are processed on a rolling basis. Application fee: $0. Electronic applications accepted. *Expenses:* Contact institution. *Financial support:* In 2016–17, 211 students received support, including 12 fellowships with partial tuition reimbursements available (averaging $14,200 per year), 20 research assistantships with partial tuition reimbursements available (averaging $22,212 per year); career-related internships or fieldwork, scholarships/grants, and unspecified assistantships also available. Support available to part-time students. Financial award application deadline: 7/1; financial award applicants required to submit FAFSA. *Faculty research:* Investment management, business ethics, technology management, supply chain management, entrepreneurship. *Unit head:* Dr. Karen Donovan, Associate Dean of Graduate Programs and Executive Education, 412-396-6276, Fax: 412-396-1726, E-mail: donovan6@duq.edu. *Application contact:* Jeff Jewett, Director of Admissions and Enrollment Management, 412-396-6244, Fax: 412-396-1726, E-mail: decrostam@duq.edu.
Website: http://www.duq.edu/business/grad

Edgewood College, Program in Business, Madison, WI 53711-1997. Offers accountancy (MS); sustainability leadership (MBA). *Accreditation:* ACBSP. *Program availability:* Part-time, evening/weekend. *Students:* 38 full-time (22 women), 109 part-time (61 women); includes 13 minority (2 Black or African American, non-Hispanic/Latino; 4 Asian, non-Hispanic/Latino; 3 Hispanic/Latino; 1 Native Hawaiian or other Pacific Islander, non-Hispanic/Latino; 3 Two or more races, non-Hispanic/Latino), 13 international. Average age 33. In 2016, 50 master's awarded. *Entrance requirements:* For master's, GMAT (minimum score 430), minimum GPA of 2.75, 2 letters of recommendation. Additional exam requirements/recommendations for international students: Required—TOEFL. *Application deadline:* For fall admission, 8/15 for domestic students, 5/1 for international students; for spring admission, 1/8 for domestic students, 11/1 for international students. Applications are processed on a rolling basis. Application fee: $30. Electronic applications accepted. *Expenses: Tuition:* Part-time $898 per credit. Tuition and fees vary according to course load. *Financial support:* Career-related internships or fieldwork and scholarships/grants available. *Unit head:* Dr. Stevie Watson, Dean, 608-663-2224, Fax: 608-663-3291, E-mail: swatson@edgewood.edu. *Application contact:* Joann Eastman, Admissions Counselor, 608-663-3250, Fax: 608-663-2214, E-mail: gps@edgewood.edu.
Website: https://www.edgewood.edu/academics/schools/school-of-business

Edgewood College, Program in Sustainability Leadership, Madison, WI 53711-1997. Offers MA. *Program availability:* Part-time, evening/weekend. *Faculty:* 1 full-time (0 women), 2 part-time/adjunct (1 woman). *Students:* 12 part-time (6 women); includes 2 minority (1 Black or African American, non-Hispanic/Latino; 1 Two or more races, non-Hispanic/Latino), 1 international. Average age 40. 15 applicants, 100% accepted, 14 enrolled. In 2016, 3 master's awarded. *Application deadline:* For fall admission, 7/1 for domestic students. Application fee: $30. *Expenses:* Contact institution. *Financial support:* In 2016–17, 14 students received support. Scholarships/grants available. Support available to part-time students. Financial award application deadline: 5/1; financial award applicants required to submit FAFSA. *Faculty research:* Community development collaborative decision making leadership community well being organizational change. *Unit head:* Dr. Stephan Gilchrist, Director, 608-663-6991, E-mail: sgilchrist@edgewood.edu.
Website: https://www.edgewood.edu/academics/programs/details/social-innovation-and-sustainability-leadership/graduate

Fairleigh Dickinson University, College at Florham, Silberman College of Business, Certificate Program in Managing Sustainability, Madison, NJ 07940-1099. Offers Certificate.

Franklin Pierce University, Graduate and Professional Studies, Rindge, NH 03461-0060. Offers curriculum and instruction (M Ed); elementary education (MS Ed); emerging network technologies (Graduate Certificate); energy and sustainability studies (MBA, Graduate Certificate); health administration (MBA, Graduate Certificate); human resource management (MBA, Graduate Certificate); information technology (MBA); leadership (MBA); nursing education (MS); nursing leadership (MS); physical therapy (DPT); physician assistant studies (MPAS); special education (M Ed); sports management (MBA). *Accreditation:* APTA. *Program availability:* Part-time, 100% online, blended/hybrid learning. *Faculty:* 47 full-time (36 women), 165 part-time/adjunct (108 women). *Students:* 380 full-time (226 women), 245 part-time (158 women); includes 52 minority (13 Black or African American, non-Hispanic/Latino; 2 American Indian or Alaska Native, non-Hispanic/Latino; 14 Asian, non-Hispanic/Latino; 22 Hispanic/Latino; 1 Native Hawaiian or other Pacific Islander, non-Hispanic/Latino), 13 international. Average age 29. 1,995 applicants, 28% accepted, 267 enrolled. In 2016, 120 master's, 86 doctorates awarded. *Degree requirements:* For master's, concentrated original research projects; student teaching; fieldwork and/or internship; leadership project; PRAXIS I and II (for M Ed); for doctorate, concentrated original research projects, clinical fieldwork and/or internship, leadership project. *Entrance requirements:* For master's, minimum GPA of 2.5, 3 letters of recommendation; competencies in accounting, economics, statistics, and computer skills through life experience or undergraduate coursework (for MBA); certification/e-portfolio, minimum C grade in all education courses (for M Ed); license to practice as RN (for MS); for doctorate, GRE, 80 hours of observation/work in PT settings; completion of anatomy, chemistry, physics, and statistics; minimum GPA of 3.0. Additional exam requirements/recommendations for international students: Required—TOEFL (minimum score 550 paper-based; 61 iBT). *Application deadline:* Applications are processed on a rolling basis. Application fee: $0. Electronic applications accepted. *Expenses: Tuition:* Full-time $15,960; part-time $665 per credit hour. Tuition and fees vary according to program. *Financial support:* Teaching assistantships with tuition reimbursements, career-related internships or fieldwork, and unspecified assistantships available. Support available to part-time students. Financial award applicants required to submit FAFSA. *Faculty research:* Evidence-based practice in sports physical therapy, human resource management in economic crisis, leadership in nursing, innovation in sports facility management, differentiated learning and understanding by design. *Unit head:* Dr. Maria Altobello, Dean, 603-647-3509, Fax: 603-229-4580, E-mail: altobellom@franklinpierce.edu. *Application contact:* Graduate Studies, 800-325-1090, Fax: 603-626-4815, E-mail: cgps@franklinpierce.edu.
Website: http://www.franklinpierce.edu/academics/gradstudies/index.htm

Goddard College, Graduate Division, Master of Arts in Social Innovation and Sustainability Program, Plainfield, VT 05667-9432. Offers MA. *Program availability:* Part-time, online learning. *Degree requirements:* For master's, thesis. *Entrance requirements:* For master's, 3 letters of recommendation, relevant prior training or experience, interview. Electronic applications accepted.

Illinois Institute of Technology, Stuart School of Business, Program in Business Administration, Chicago, IL 60661. Offers sustainability (MBA); JD/MBA; M Des/MBA; MBA/MS. *Accreditation:* AACSB. *Program availability:* Part-time, evening/weekend. *Entrance requirements:* For master's, GRE (minimum score 298) or GMAT (500). Additional exam requirements/recommendations for international students: Required—TOEFL (minimum score 600 paper-based; 85 iBT); Recommended—IELTS (minimum score 7). Electronic applications accepted. *Expenses:* Contact institution. *Faculty research:* Global management and marketing strategy, technological innovation, management science, financial management, knowledge management.

Indiana University Bloomington, School of Public and Environmental Affairs, Public Affairs Programs, Bloomington, IN 47405. Offers economic development (MPA); energy (MPA); environmental policy (PhD); environmental policy and natural resource management (MPA); information systems (MPA); international development (MPA); local government management (MPA); nonprofit management (MPA, Certificate); policy analysis (MPA); public budgeting and financial management (Certificate); public finance (PhD); public financial administration (MPA); public management (MPA, PhD, Certificate); public policy analysis (PhD); social entrepreneurship (Certificate); specialized public affairs (MPA); sustainability and sustainable development (MPA); JD/MPA; MPA/MA; MPA/MIS; MPA/MLS; MSES/MPA. *Accreditation:* NASPAA (one or more programs are accredited). *Program availability:* Part-time. *Degree requirements:* For master's, capstone, internship; for doctorate, comprehensive exam, thesis/dissertation. *Entrance requirements:* For master's, GRE General Test or GMAT, official transcripts, 3 letters of recommendation, resume, personal statement; for doctorate, GRE General Test, official transcripts, 3 letters of recommendation, statement of purpose. Additional exam requirements/recommendations for international students: Required—TOEFL (minimum score 600 paper-based; 96 iBT); Recommended—IELTS (minimum score 7). Electronic applications accepted. *Faculty research:* International development, environmental policy and resource management, policy analysis, public finance, public management, urban management, nonprofit management, energy policy, social policy, public finance.

James Madison University, The Graduate School, College of Integrated Science and Engineering, Program in Environmental Management and Sustainability, Harrisonburg, VA 22807. Offers MS. *Faculty:* 37 full-time (13 women), 3 part-time/adjunct (0 women). *Students:* 17 full-time (11 women), 2 part-time (1 woman); includes 3 minority (1 Black or African American, non-Hispanic/Latino; 2 Hispanic/Latino), 3 international. Average age 30. In 2016, 2 master's awarded. Application fee: $55. Electronic applications accepted. *Financial support:* Fellowships, Federal Work-Study, and unspecified assistantships available. Financial award application deadline: 3/1; financial award applicants required to submit FAFSA. *Unit head:* Dr. Eric H. Maslen, Department Head, 540-568-2740, E-mail: masleneh@jmu.edu. *Application contact:* Lynette D. Michael, Director of Graduate Admissions, 540-568-6131 Ext. 6395, Fax: 540-568-7860, E-mail: michaeld@jmu.edu.
Website: http://www.jmu.edu/mems-malta/index.shtml

Lipscomb University, College of Business, Nashville, TN 37204-3951. Offers accountancy (M Acc); accounting (MBA); business administration (MM); conflict management (MBA); financial services (MBA); health care informatics (MBA); healthcare management (MBA); information security (MBA); leadership (MBA); nonprofit management (MBA); professional accountancy (Certificate); sports management (MBA); strategic human resources (MBA); sustainability (MBA); MBA/MS; Pharm D/MM. *Accreditation:* ACBSP. *Program availability:* Part-time, evening/weekend. *Faculty:* 22 full-time (4 women), 12 part-time/adjunct (4 women). *Students:* 112 full-time (51 women), 69 part-time (34 women); includes 30 minority (17 Black or African American, non-Hispanic/Latino; 3 Asian, non-Hispanic/Latino; 8 Hispanic/Latino; 2 Two or more races, non-Hispanic/Latino), 5 international. Average age 32. 244 applicants, 55% accepted, 54 enrolled. In 2016, 164 master's awarded. *Entrance requirements:* For master's, GMAT, transcripts, interview, 2 references, resume. Additional exam requirements/recommendations for international students: Required—TOEFL (minimum score 570 paper-based). *Application deadline:* For fall admission, 6/15 for domestic students, 2/1 for international students; for winter admission, 6/1 for international students; for spring admission, 11/15 for domestic students. Applications are processed on a rolling basis. Application fee: $50 ($75 for international students). Electronic applications accepted. *Expenses:* $1,150-$1,290 per hour, depending on program. *Financial support:* Career-related internships or fieldwork, scholarships/grants, tuition waivers (partial), and unspecified assistantships available. Support available to part-time students. Financial award application deadline: 7/1; financial award applicants required to submit FAFSA. *Faculty research:* Impact of spirituality on organization commitment, women in corporate leadership, psychological empowerment, training. *Unit head:* Allison Duke, Associate Dean of Graduate Business Programs, 615-966-5732, Fax: 615-966-1818, E-mail: allison.duke@lipscomb.edu. *Application contact:* Karen Risley, Manager, Graduate Business Recruiting, 615-966-5145, E-mail: karen.risley@lipscomb.edu.
Website: http://www.lipscomb.edu/business/Graduate-Programs

Maastricht School of Management, Graduate Programs, Maastricht, Netherlands. Offers business administration (MBA, DBA, PhD); facility management (Exec MBA); management (M Sc); sustainability (Exec MBA).

Maharishi University of Management, Graduate Studies, Program in Business Administration, Fairfield, IA 52557. Offers accounting (MBA); management (PhD); sustainability (MBA). *Program availability:* Evening/weekend, online learning. *Degree requirements:* For doctorate, thesis/dissertation. *Entrance requirements:* For master's, GMAT, minimum GPA of 3.0; for doctorate, minimum GPA of 3.0. Additional exam requirements/recommendations for international students: Required—TOEFL. *Faculty research:* Leadership, effects of the group dynamics of consciousness on the economy, innovation, employee development, cooperative strategy.

Michigan Technological University, Graduate School, Interdisciplinary Programs, Houghton, MI 49931. Offers atmospheric sciences (PhD); biochemistry and molecular biology (PhD); computational science and engineering (PhD); data science (MS, Graduate Certificate); engineering (M Eng); environmental engineering (PhD); international profile (Graduate Certificate); nanotechnology (Graduate Certificate); sustainability (Graduate Certificate); sustainable water resources systems (Graduate Certificate). *Program availability:* Part-time. *Faculty:* 122 full-time (26 women), 13 part-time/adjunct. *Students:* 58 full-time (18 women), 17 part-time (5 women); includes 1 minority (Black or African American, non-Hispanic/Latino), 56 international. Average age 28. 395 applicants, 20% accepted, 22 enrolled. In 2016, 3 master's, 7 doctorates, 8 other advanced degrees awarded. Terminal master's awarded for partial completion of doctoral program. *Degree requirements:* For master's, comprehensive exam (for some programs), thesis (for some programs); for doctorate, comprehensive exam, thesis/dissertation. *Entrance requirements:* For master's, doctorate, and Graduate Certificate, GRE, statement of purpose, personal statement, official transcripts, 2-3 letters of recommendation. Additional exam requirements/recommendations for international students: Required—TOEFL or IELTS. *Application deadline:* Applications are processed on a rolling basis. Electronic applications accepted. *Expenses:* Tuition, state resident: full-time $16,290; part-time $905 per credit. Tuition, nonresident: full-time $16,290; part-time $905 per credit. *Required fees:* $248; $124 per term. Tuition and fees vary according to course load and program. *Financial support:* In 2016–17, 54 students received support, including 7 fellowships with tuition reimbursements available (averaging $15,242 per year), 19 research assistantships with tuition reimbursements available (averaging $15,242 per year), 5 teaching assistantships with tuition reimbursements available (averaging $15,242 per year); career-related internships or fieldwork, Federal Work-Study, scholarships/grants, health care benefits, unspecified assistantships, and cooperative program also available. Financial award applicants required to submit FAFSA. *Faculty research:* Big data, atmospheric sciences, bioinformatics and systems biology, molecular dynamics, environmental studies. *Unit head:* Dr. Pushpalathata Murthy, Dean of the Graduate School/Associate Provost for Graduate Education, 906-487-3007, Fax: 906-487-2284, E-mail: ppmurthy@mtu.edu. *Application contact:* Carol T. Wingerson, Administrative Aide, 906-487-2328, Fax: 906-487-2284, E-mail: gradadms@mtu.edu.

The New School, Schools of Public Engagement, Program in Environmental Policy and Sustainability Management, New York, NY 10011. Offers environmental policy and sustainability management (MS); sustainability strategies (Certificate). *Program availability:* Part-time. *Faculty:* 34 full-time (16 women), 7 part-time/adjunct (3 women). *Students:* 38 full-time (28 women), 8 part-time (5 women); includes 14 minority (5 Black or African American, non-Hispanic/Latino; 1 Asian, non-Hispanic/Latino; 4 Hispanic/Latino; 4 Two or more races, non-Hispanic/Latino), 6 international. Average age 28. 79 applicants, 90% accepted, 15 enrolled. In 2016, 31 master's, 5 other advanced degrees awarded. *Degree requirements:* For master's, thesis. *Entrance requirements:* For master's and Certificate, two letters of recommendation, statement of purpose, resume, transcripts. Additional exam requirements/recommendations for international students: Required—TOEFL (minimum score 100 iBT), IELTS (minimum score 7), PTE (minimum score 68). *Application deadline:* For fall admission, 1/15 priority date for domestic and international students; for spring admission, 10/15 priority date for domestic and international students. Applications are processed on a rolling basis. Application fee: $50. Electronic applications accepted. *Expenses:* Contact institution. *Financial support:* Research assistantships, career-related internships or fieldwork, Federal Work-Study, scholarships/grants, and unspecified assistantships available. Support available to part-time students. Financial award application deadline: 2/1; financial award applicants required to submit FAFSA. *Faculty research:* Climate change and cities, corporate sustainability and social responsibility, environmental justice and policy (waste, air quality, etc.), infrastructure economics (transport, water, energy), community based participatory research. *Unit head:* Suzanne Bostwick, Associate Director, 212-229-5400 Ext. 1601, E-mail: suzanneBostwick@newschool.edu. *Application contact:* Sharon Greenidge, Assistant Director of Admission, 212-229-5400 Ext. 1103, E-mail: greenids@newschool.edu.

Oklahoma State University, Graduate College, Stillwater, OK 74078. Offers aerospace security (Graduate Certificate); bioenergy and sustainable technology (Graduate Certificate); business data mining (Graduate Certificate); business sustainability (Graduate Certificate); environmental science (MS); international studies (MS); nonprofit management (Graduate Certificate); teaching English to speakers of other languages (Graduate Certificate); telecommunications management (MS). Programs are interdisciplinary. *Students:* 50 full-time (28 women), 109 part-time (63 women); includes 23 minority (4 Black or African American, non-Hispanic/Latino; 5 American Indian or Alaska Native, non-Hispanic/Latino; 4 Asian, non-Hispanic/Latino; 4 Hispanic/Latino; 6 Two or more races, non-Hispanic/Latino), 58 international. Average age 29. 363 applicants, 81% accepted, 71 enrolled. In 2016, 56 master's, 9 doctorates awarded. *Degree requirements:* For master's, thesis (for some programs); for doctorate, comprehensive exam, thesis/dissertation. *Entrance requirements:* For master's and doctorate, GRE or GMAT. Additional exam requirements/recommendations for international students: Required—TOEFL (minimum score 550 paper-based; 79 iBT). *Application deadline:* For fall admission, 3/1 priority date for domestic and international students; for spring admission, 8/1 priority date for domestic and international students. Applications are processed on a rolling basis. Application fee: $40 ($75 for international students). Electronic applications accepted. *Expenses:* Tuition, state resident: full-time $3775; part-time $209.70 per credit hour. Tuition, nonresident: full-time $14,851; part-time $825.05 per credit hour. *Required fees:* $2027; $112.60 per credit hour. Tuition and fees vary according to campus/location. *Financial support:* Research assistantships, career-related internships or fieldwork, Federal Work-Study, scholarships/grants, health care benefits, tuition waivers (partial), and unspecified assistantships available. Support available to part-time students. Financial award application deadline: 3/1; financial award applicants required to submit FAFSA. *Unit head:* Dr. Sheryl Tucker, Dean, 405-744-6368, Fax: 405-744-0355, E-mail: gradi@okstate.edu. *Application contact:* Dr. Susan Mathew, Assistant Director of Graduate Admissions, 405-744-6368, Fax: 405-744-0355, E-mail: gradi@okstate.edu.
Website: http://gradcollege.okstate.edu/

Oregon State University, College of Forestry, Program in Forest Ecosystems and Society, Corvallis, OR 97331. Offers forest biology (MF); forest, wildlife and landscape ecology (MS, PhD); genetics and physiology (MS, PhD); integrated social and ecological systems (MS, PhD); science of conservation, restoration and sustainable management (MS, PhD); silviculture (MF); social science, policy, and natural resources (MS, PhD); soil-plant-atmosphere continuum (MS, PhD); sustainable recreation and tourism (MS). *Program availability:* Part-time. *Faculty:* 28 full-time (9 women), 7 part-time/adjunct (1 woman). *Students:* 64 full-time (36 women), 3 part-time (1 woman); includes 4 minority (1 Asian, non-Hispanic/Latino; 1 Hispanic/Latino; 2 Two or more races, non-Hispanic/Latino), 13 international. Average age 32. 53 applicants, 40% accepted, 17 enrolled. In 2016, 13 master's, 1 doctorate awarded. *Degree requirements:* For master's, thesis (for some programs); for doctorate, thesis/dissertation. *Entrance requirements:* For master's and doctorate, GRE. Additional exam requirements/recommendations for international students: Required—TOEFL (minimum score 80 iBT), IELTS (minimum score 6.5). *Application deadline:* For fall admission, 8/1 for domestic students, 4/1 for international students; for winter admission, 12/1 for domestic students, 7/1 for international students; for spring admission, 2/1 for domestic students, 10/1 for international students; for summer admission, 5/1 for domestic students, 1/1 for international students. Application fee: $75 ($85 for international students). *Expenses:* Tuition, state resident: full-time $12,150; part-time $450 per credit. Tuition, nonresident: full-time $21,789; part-time $807 per credit. *Required fees:* $1651; $1507 per credit. One-time fee: $350. Tuition and fees vary according to course load, campus/location and program. *Financial support:* Fellowships, research assistantships, career-related internships or fieldwork, Federal Work-Study, and institutionally sponsored loans available. Support available to part-time students. *Faculty research:* Ecosystem structure and function, nutrient cycling, biotechnology, vegetation management, integrated forest protection. *Unit head:* Dr. Troy Hall, Department Head. *Application contact:* Jessica Bagley, Advisor, 541-737-6556, E-mail: jessica.bagley@oregonstate.edu.
Website: http://fes.forestry.oregonstate.edu/

Oregon State University, College of Forestry, Program in Sustainable Forest Management, Corvallis, OR 97331. Offers engineering for sustainable forestry (MF, MS, PhD); forest biometrics and geomatics (MF, MS, PhD); forest operations planning and management (MF, MS, PhD); forest policy analysis and economics (MF, MS, PhD); forest watershed management (MF, MS, PhD); silviculture, fire, and forest health (MF, MS, PhD). *Program availability:* Part-time. *Faculty:* 15 full-time (3 women). *Students:* 44 full-time (10 women), 3 part-time (1 woman); includes 3 minority (all Hispanic/Latino), 12 international. Average age 29. 35 applicants, 63% accepted, 16 enrolled. In 2016, 7 master's, 1 doctorate awarded. *Entrance requirements:* For master's and doctorate, GRE. Additional exam requirements/recommendations for international students: Required—TOEFL (minimum score 80 iBT), IELTS (minimum score 6.5). *Application deadline:* For fall admission, 8/1 for domestic students, 4/1 for international students; for winter admission, 12/1 for domestic students, 7/1 for international students; for spring admission, 2/1 for domestic students, 10/1 for international students; for summer admission, 5/1 for domestic students, 1/1 for international students. Application fee: $75 ($85 for international students). *Expenses:* Tuition, state resident: full-time $12,150; part-time $450 per credit. Tuition, nonresident: full-time $21,789; part-time $807 per credit. *Required fees:* $1651; $1507 per credit. One-time fee: $350. Tuition and fees vary according to course load, campus/location and program. *Unit head:* Dr. Claire

Montgomery, Professor/Department Head. *Application contact:* Madison Dudley, Sustainable Forest Management Graduate Program Coordinator, 541-737-2818, E-mail: madison.dudley@oregonstate.edu.
Website: http://ferm.forestry.oregonstate.edu/academic-programs/graduate-degree

Penn State Great Valley, Graduate Studies, Management Division, Malvern, PA 19355-1488. Offers business administration (MBA); cyber security (Certificate); data analytics (Certificate); distributed energy and grid modernization (Certificate); finance (M Fin, Certificate); health sector management (Certificate); human resource management (Certificate); information science (MSIS); leadership development (MLD); new ventures and entrepreneurship (Certificate); professional studies in data analytics (MPS); sustainable management practices (Certificate). *Accreditation:* AACSB. *Unit head:* Dr. James A. Nemes, Chancellor, 610-648-3202, Fax: 610-725-5296. *Application contact:* JoAnn Kelly, Director of Admissions, 610-648-3315, Fax: 610-725-5296, E-mail: jek2@psu.edu.
Website: http://greatvalley.psu.edu/academics/masters-degrees/engineering-management

Presidio Graduate School, Graduate Programs - San Francisco, San Francisco, CA 94129. Offers MBA, MPA, Certificate, MBA/JD, MBA/MPA. MBA/JD offered in conjunction with the University of California, Hastings College of the Law.

Presidio Graduate School, MBA Programs - Seattle, San Francisco, CA 94129. Offers co-operative management (Certificate); food and agriculture systems (Certificate); sustainable business (MBA); sustainable systems (MBA). *Program availability:* Part-time, evening/weekend, blended/hybrid learning. *Students:* Average age 34. *Entrance requirements:* For master's and Certificate, Quantitative Assessment Summary, GRE, or GMAT, resume, two letters of recommendation, essay, transcripts. Additional exam requirements/recommendations for international students: Required—TOEFL (minimum score 90 iBT), IELTS (minimum score 6.5). *Application deadline:* For fall admission, 6/1 priority date for domestic and international students. Applications are processed on a rolling basis. Application fee: $75. Electronic applications accepted. *Financial support:* Scholarships/grants available. Financial award application deadline: 6/15; financial award applicants required to submit FAFSA. *Unit head:* Steven Crane, Provost, 415-651-6555, E-mail: info@presidio.edu. *Application contact:* Kari Dorth, Director of Admissions, 415-655-8912, E-mail: admissions@presidio.edu.
Website: https://www.presidio.edu/seattle-mbas-overview/

Rochester Institute of Technology, Graduate Enrollment Services, Golisano Institute for Sustainability, Rochester, NY 14623. Offers M Arch, MS, PhD. *Program availability:* Part-time. *Students:* 71 full-time (33 women), 18 part-time (7 women); includes 4 minority (1 Black or African American, non-Hispanic/Latino; 2 Hispanic/Latino; 1 Two or more races, non-Hispanic/Latino), 50 international. Average age 29. 145 applicants, 62% accepted, 21 enrolled. In 2016, 9 master's, 4 doctorates awarded. *Degree requirements:* For master's, comprehensive exam, thesis; for doctorate, comprehensive exam, thesis/dissertation. *Entrance requirements:* For master's and doctorate, GRE, minimum GPA of 3.0 (recommended). Additional exam requirements/recommendations for international students: Required—PTE (minimum score 58), TOEFL (minimum score 550 paper-based, 79 iBT) or IELTS (minimum score 6.5). *Application deadline:* For fall admission, 2/15 priority date for domestic and international students; for spring admission, 12/15 priority date for domestic and international students. Applications are processed on a rolling basis. Application fee: $60. Electronic applications accepted. *Expenses:* $1,742 per credit hour. *Financial support:* In 2016–17, 61 students received support. Research assistantships with tuition reimbursements available, teaching assistantships with tuition reimbursements available, career-related internships or fieldwork, scholarships/grants, unspecified assistantships, and health care benefits (for PhD program only) available. Support available to part-time students. Financial award applicants required to submit FAFSA. *Faculty research:* Environmentally responsive architecture and passive/natural building design and systems; renewable energy; advanced manufacturing technology; built environments; eco-friendly electronics & e-waste; energy generation, storage, and systems; pollution prevention; transportation and interconnected smart city systems. *Unit head:* Dr. Nabil Nasr, Associate Provost and Director, 585-475-5101, E-mail: info@sustainability.rit.edu. *Application contact:* Diane Ellison, Associate Vice President, Graduate Enrollment Services, 585-475-2229, Fax: 585-475-7164, E-mail: gradinfo@rit.edu.
Website: http://www.rit.edu/gis/

San Francisco State University, Division of Graduate Studies, College of Business, Program in Business Administration, San Francisco, CA 94132-1722. Offers decision sciences/operations research (MBA); ethics and compliance (MBA); finance (MBA); global business and innovation (MBA); healthcare administration (MBA); hospitality and tourism management (MBA); information systems (MBA); leadership (MBA); marketing (MBA); nonprofit and social enterprise leadership (MBA); sustainable business (MBA). *Accreditation:* AACSB. *Program availability:* Part-time, evening/weekend. *Degree requirements:* For master's, thesis, essay test. *Entrance requirements:* For master's, GMAT, minimum GPA of 2.7 in last 60 units. Additional exam requirements/recommendations for international students: Required—TOEFL (minimum score 550 paper-based). *Application deadline:* For fall admission, 5/1 priority date for domestic students, 4/1 for international students; for spring admission, 11/1 for domestic students, 10/15 for international students. Applications are processed on a rolling basis. Application fee: $55. *Expenses:* Tuition, state resident: full-time $6738. Tuition, nonresident: full-time $15,666. *Required fees:* $1012. Tuition and fees vary according to degree level and program. *Financial support:* Application deadline: 3/1. *Unit head:* Dr. Sanjit Sengupta, Faculty Director, 415-817-4366, Fax: 415-817-4340, E-mail: sengupta@sfsu.edu. *Application contact:* Zandra Tan, EMBA Program Coordinator, 415-817-4360, Fax: 415-817-4340, E-mail: zandra13@sfsu.edu.
Website: http://cob.sfsu.edu/graduate-programs/mba

Seattle Pacific University, Master of Arts in Management Program, Seattle, WA 98119-1997. Offers faith and business (MA); human resources (MA); social and sustainable management (MA). *Entrance requirements:* For master's, GMAT or GRE (waived with cumulative GPA of 3.3 or above), bachelor's degree from accredited college or university, resume, essay, official transcript.

Seattle Pacific University, Master of Business Administration Program, Seattle, WA 98119-1997. Offers business administration (MBA); social and sustainable enterprise (MBA). *Accreditation:* AACSB. *Program availability:* Part-time. *Entrance requirements:* For master's, GMAT (minimum score of 500 preferred; 25 verbal, 30 quantitative, 4.4 analytical writing); GRE (minimum score of 295 preferred; 150 verbal/450 old scoring, 145 quantitative/525 old scoring), BA, resume as evidence of substantive work experience. Additional exam requirements/recommendations for international students: Required—TOEFL. Electronic applications accepted.

Southern New Hampshire University, School of Business, Manchester, NH 03106-1045. Offers accounting (MBA, MS, Graduate Certificate); accounting finance (MS); accounting/auditing (MS); accounting/forensic accounting (MS); accounting/taxation (MS); athletic administration (MBA, Graduate Certificate); business administration (IMBA, MBA, Certificate, Graduate Certificate), including accounting (Certificate), business administration (MBA), business information systems (Graduate Certificate), human resource management (Certificate); corporate social responsibility (MBA); entrepreneurship (MBA); finance (MBA, MS, Graduate Certificate); finance/corporate finance (MS); finance/investments and securities (MS); forensic accounting (MBA); healthcare informatics (MBA); healthcare management (MBA); human resource management (Graduate Certificate); information technology (MS, Graduate Certificate); information technology management (MBA); international business (Graduate Certificate); international business and information technology (Graduate Certificate); international finance (Graduate Certificate); international sport management (Graduate Certificate); justice studies (MBA); leadership of nonprofit organizations (Graduate Certificate); management (MS); marketing (MBA, MS, Graduate Certificate); operations and project management (MS); operations and supply chain management (MBA, Graduate Certificate); organizational leadership (MS); project management (MBA, Graduate Certificate); Six Sigma (MBA); Six Sigma quality (Graduate Certificate); social media marketing (MBA); sport management (MBA, MS, Graduate Certificate); sustainability and environmental compliance (MBA); workplace conflict management (MBA); MBA/Certificate. *Accreditation:* ACBSP. *Program availability:* Part-time, evening/weekend, online learning. Terminal master's awarded for partial completion of doctoral program. *Degree requirements:* For master's, one foreign language, comprehensive exam (for some programs), thesis or alternative. *Entrance requirements:* For master's, minimum GPA of 2.5. Additional exam requirements/recommendations for international students: Required—TOEFL (minimum score 500 paper-based). Electronic applications accepted.

South University, Graduate Programs, College of Business, Savannah, GA 31406. Offers corrections (MBA); entrepreneurship and small business (MBA); healthcare administration (MBA); hospitality management (MBA); leadership (MS); public administration (MPA); sustainability (MBA).

State University of New York College of Environmental Science and Forestry, Department of Paper and Bioprocess Engineering, Syracuse, NY 13210-2779. Offers biomaterials engineering (MS, PhD); bioprocess engineering (MPS, MS, PhD); bioprocessing (Advanced Certificate); paper science and engineering (MPS, MS, PhD); sustainable engineering management (MPS). *Faculty:* 13 full-time (2 women), 4 part-time/adjunct (0 women). *Students:* 28 full-time (14 women), 3 part-time (2 women); includes 1 minority (Asian, non-Hispanic/Latino), 19 international. Average age 29. 19 applicants, 89% accepted, 6 enrolled. In 2016, 6 master's, 1 doctorate, 4 other advanced degrees awarded. *Degree requirements:* For master's, thesis; for doctorate, comprehensive exam, thesis/dissertation; for Advanced Certificate, 15 credit hours. *Entrance requirements:* For master's and doctorate, GRE General Test, minimum GPA of 3.0; for Advanced Certificate, BS, calculus plus science major. Additional exam requirements/recommendations for international students: Required—TOEFL (minimum score 550 paper-based; 80 iBT), IELTS (minimum score 6). *Application deadline:* For fall admission, 2/1 priority date for domestic and international students; for spring admission, 11/1 priority date for domestic and international students. Applications are processed on a rolling basis. Application fee: $60. *Expenses:* Tuition, state resident: full-time $10,870; part-time $453 per credit. Tuition, nonresident: full-time $22,210; part-time $925 per credit. *Required fees:* $1075; $89.22 per credit. *Financial support:* In 2016–17, 14 students received support. Application deadline: 6/30; applicants required to submit FAFSA. *Faculty research:* Sustainable products and processes, biorefinery, pulping and papermaking, nanocellulose, bioconversions, process control and modeling. *Unit head:* Dr. Gary M. Scott, Chair, 315-470-6501, Fax: 315-470-6945, E-mail: gscott@esf.edu. *Application contact:* Scott Shannon, Associate Provost and Dean, Instruction and Graduate Studies, 315-470-6599, Fax: 315-470-6978, E-mail: esfgrad@esf.edu.
Website: http://www.esf.edu/pbe/

Syracuse University, College of Engineering and Computer Science, Program in Sustainable Enterprise, Syracuse, NY 13244. Offers CAS. *Expenses: Tuition:* Full-time $25,974; part-time $1443 per credit hour. *Required fees:* $802; $50 per course. Tuition and fees vary according to course load and program. *Unit head:* Dr. Sam Salem, Department Chair, Civil and Environmental Engineering and Sustainable Civil Infrastructures, 315-443-3401, E-mail: omsalem@syr.edu. *Application contact:* Kathleen Joyce, Assistant Dean, 315-443-2219, E-mail: topgrads@syr.edu.
Website: http://eng-cs.syr.edu/

The University of British Columbia, Faculty of Forestry, Program in Sustainable Forest Management, Vancouver, BC V6T 1Z1, Canada. Offers MSFM. *Expenses:* Tuition, state resident: full-time $4708 Canadian dollars. Tuition, nonresident: full-time $4708 Canadian dollars. *International tuition:* $8271 Canadian dollars full-time. *Required fees:* $884 Canadian dollars. Tuition and fees vary according to program.

The University of British Columbia, Faculty of Science, Institute for Resources, Environment and Sustainability, Vancouver, BC V6T 1Z4, Canada. Offers M Sc, MA, PhD. *Degree requirements:* For master's, thesis; for doctorate, comprehensive exam, thesis/dissertation. *Entrance requirements:* Additional exam requirements/recommendations for international students: Required—TOEFL. Application fee: $100 Canadian dollars ($162 Canadian dollars for international students). Electronic applications accepted. *Expenses:* $4,802 per year tuition and fees, $8,436 per year international. *Financial support:* Fellowships with partial tuition reimbursements, research assistantships, teaching assistantships, institutionally sponsored loans, scholarships/grants, and unspecified assistantships available. *Faculty research:* Land management, water resources, energy, environmental assessment, risk evaluation. *Application contact:* Lisa Johannesen, Graduate Program Staff, 604-822-9034, Fax: 604-822-9250, E-mail: admissions@ires.ubc.ca.
Website: http://ires.ubc.ca/

University of California, Berkeley, UC Berkeley Extension, Certificate Programs in Sustainability Studies, Berkeley, CA 94720-1500. Offers leadership in sustainability and environmental management (Professional Certificate); solar energy and green building (Professional Certificate); sustainable design (Professional Certificate).

University of Colorado Denver, Business School, Master of Business Administration Program, Denver, CO 80217. Offers bioinnovation and entrepreneurship (MBA); business intelligence (MBA); business strategy (MBA); business to business marketing (MBA); business to consumer marketing (MBA); change management (MBA); corporate financial management (MBA); enterprise technology management (MBA); entrepreneurship (MBA); health administration (MBA), including financial management, health administration, health information technologies, international health management and policy; human resources management (MBA); international business (MBA); investment management (MBA); managing for sustainability (MBA); sports and entertainment management (MBA). *Accreditation:* AACSB. *Program availability:* Part-time, evening/weekend, 100% online, blended/hybrid learning. *Students:* 544 full-time (210 women), 112 part-time (22 women); includes 99 minority (15 Black or African American, non-Hispanic/Latino; 4 American Indian or Alaska Native, non-Hispanic/Latino; 38 Asian, non-Hispanic/Latino; 36 Hispanic/Latino; 6 Two or more races, non-Hispanic/Latino), 22 international. Average age 32. 335 applicants, 73% accepted, 179 enrolled. In 2016, 251 master's awarded. *Degree requirements:* For master's, 48 semester hours, including 30 of core courses, 3 in international business, and 15 in electives from over 50 other business courses. *Entrance requirements:* For master's, GMAT, resume, official transcripts, essay, two letters of recommendation, financial statements (for international applicants). Additional exam requirements/recommendations for international students: Required—TOEFL (minimum score 560

paper-based; 83 iBT); Recommended—IELTS (minimum score 6.5). *Application deadline:* For fall admission, 4/15 priority date for domestic students, 3/15 priority date for international students; for spring admission, 10/15 priority date for domestic students, 9/15 priority date for international students; for summer admission, 2/15 priority date for domestic students, 1/15 priority date for international students. Applications are processed on a rolling basis. Application fee: $50 ($75 for international students). Electronic applications accepted. *Expenses:* Contact institution. *Financial support:* In 2016–17, 171 students received support. Fellowships, research assistantships, teaching assistantships, Federal Work-Study, institutionally sponsored loans, scholarships/grants, traineeships, and unspecified assistantships available. Financial award application deadline: 4/1; financial award applicants required to submit FAFSA. *Faculty research:* Marketing, management, entrepreneurship, finance, health administration. *Unit head:* Woodrow Eckard, MBA Director, 303-315-8470, E-mail: woody.eckard@ucdenver.edu. *Application contact:* Shelly Townley, Admissions Director, Graduate Programs, 303-315-8202, E-mail: shelly.townley@ucdenver.edu.
Website: http://www.ucdenver.edu/academics/colleges/business/degrees/mba/Pages/MBA.aspx

University of Colorado Denver, Business School, Program in Management and Organization, Denver, CO 80217. Offers business strategy (MS); change and innovation (MS); enterprise technology management (MS); entrepreneurship and innovation (MS); global management (MS); leadership (MS); managing for sustainability (MS); managing human resources (MS); sports and entertainment management (MS). *Accreditation:* AACSB. *Program availability:* Part-time, evening/weekend, online learning. *Students:* 20 full-time (13 women), 17 part-time (10 women); includes 6 minority (3 Black or African American, non-Hispanic/Latino; 1 American Indian or Alaska Native, non-Hispanic/Latino; 1 Hispanic/Latino; 1 Two or more races, non-Hispanic/Latino), 6 international. Average age 33. 24 applicants, 58% accepted, 6 enrolled. In 2016, 19 master's awarded. *Degree requirements:* For master's, 30 semester hours (12 of required courses, 12 of management electives, and 6 of free electives). *Entrance requirements:* For master's, GMAT, resume, two letters of recommendation, essay, financial statements (for international applicants). Additional exam requirements/recommendations for international students: Required—TOEFL (minimum score 525 paper-based; 71 iBT); Recommended—IELTS (minimum score 6.5). *Application deadline:* For fall admission, 4/15 priority date for domestic students, 3/15 priority date for international students; for spring admission, 10/15 priority date for domestic students, 9/15 priority date for international students; for summer admission, 2/15 priority date for domestic students, 1/15 priority date for international students. Applications are processed on a rolling basis. Application fee: $50 ($75 for international students). Electronic applications accepted. *Expenses:* Contact institution. *Financial support:* In 2016–17, 7 students received support. Fellowships, research assistantships, teaching assistantships, Federal Work-Study, institutionally sponsored loans, scholarships/grants, and traineeships available. Financial award application deadline: 4/1; financial award applicants required to submit FAFSA. *Faculty research:* Human resource management, management of catastrophe, turnaround strategies. *Unit head:* Dr. Kenneth Bettenhausen, Associate Professor/Director of MS in Management, 303-315-8425, E-mail: kenneth.bettenhausen@ucdenver.edu. *Application contact:* 303-315-8200, E-mail: bschool.admissions@ucdenver.edu.
Website: http://www.ucdenver.edu/academics/colleges/business/degrees/ms/management/Pages/Management.aspx

University of Louisville, School of Interdisciplinary and Graduate Studies, Louisville, KY 40292. Offers interdisciplinary (MA, MS, PhD), including bioethics and medical humanities (MA), bioinformatics (PhD), sustainability (MA, MS), translational bioengineering (PhD), translational neuroscience (PhD). *Program availability:* Part-time. *Students:* 24 full-time (16 women), 8 part-time (4 women); includes 4 minority (1 Asian, non-Hispanic/Latino; 1 Hispanic/Latino; 2 Two or more races, non-Hispanic/Latino), 7 international. Average age 31. 35 applicants, 51% accepted, 12 enrolled. *Degree requirements:* For master's, variable foreign language requirement, comprehensive exam (for some programs), thesis (for some programs); for doctorate, variable foreign language requirement, comprehensive exam, thesis/dissertation. *Entrance requirements:* For master's and doctorate, GRE General Test, 3 letters of recommendation, transcripts from previous post-secondary educational institutions. Additional exam requirements/recommendations for international students: Required—TOEFL (minimum score 550 paper-based; 79 iBT), IELTS (minimum score 6.5). *Application deadline:* For fall admission, 12/1 priority date for domestic and international students; for winter admission, 11/1 for domestic students, 6/1 for international students; for spring admission, 11/1 for domestic students, 6/1 for international students; for summer admission, 4/1 for domestic students, 1/1 for international students. Applications are processed on a rolling basis. Application fee: $65. Electronic applications accepted. *Expenses:* Tuition, state resident: full-time $12,246; part-time $681 per credit hour. Tuition, nonresident: full-time $25,486; part-time $1417 per credit hour. *Required fees:* $196. Tuition and fees vary according to program and reciprocity agreements. *Financial support:* In 2016–17, 120 fellowships with full tuition reimbursements (averaging $20,000 per year) were awarded. Financial award application deadline: 1/15. *Unit head:* Dr. Beth A. Boehm, Dean and Vice Provost for Graduate Affairs, 502-852-6495, E-mail: beth.boehm@louisville.edu. *Application contact:* Dr. Paul DeMarco, Associate Dean, 502-852-6490, E-mail: gradadm@louisville.edu.
Website: http://www.graduate.louisville.edu

University of New Hampshire, Graduate School, College of Liberal Arts, Department of Political Science, Program in Political Science, Durham, NH 03824. Offers political science (MA); sustainability politics and policy (Postbaccalaureate Certificate). *Program availability:* Part-time. *Degree requirements:* For master's, thesis. *Entrance requirements:* For master's, GRE General Test. Additional exam requirements/recommendations for international students: Required—TOEFL (minimum score 550 paper-based; 80 iBT). *Application deadline:* For fall admission, 6/1 priority date for domestic students, 4/1 for international students; for spring admission, 12/1 for domestic students. Applications are processed on a rolling basis. Application fee: $65. Electronic applications accepted. *Financial support:* Fellowships, research assistantships, teaching assistantships, career-related internships or fieldwork, Federal Work-Study, scholarships/grants, and tuition waivers (full and partial) available. Support available to part-time students. Financial award application deadline: 2/15. *Unit head:* Marla Brettschneider, Chair, 603-862-1750. *Application contact:* Michael Cole, Administrative Assistant, 603-862-1750, E-mail: m.cole@unh.edu.
Website: http://cola.unh.edu/political-science/program/political-science-ma

University of Portland, Dr. Robert B. Pamplin, Jr. School of Business, Portland, OR 97203-5798. Offers entrepreneurship (MBA); finance (MBA, MS); health care management (MBA); marketing (MBA); nonprofit management (EMBA); operations and technology management (MBA, MS); sustainability (MBA). *Accreditation:* AACSB. *Program availability:* Part-time, evening/weekend. *Entrance requirements:* For master's, GMAT, minimum GPA of 3.0, resume, 2 letters of recommendation. Additional exam requirements/recommendations for international students: Required—TOEFL (minimum score 570 paper-based; 89 iBT), IELTS (minimum score 7). *Expenses:* Contact institution.

University of Saint Francis, Graduate School, Keith Busse School of Business and Entrepreneurial Leadership, Fort Wayne, IN 46808-3994. Offers business administration (MBA), including sustainability; environmental health (MEH); healthcare administration (MHA); organizational leadership (MOL). *Accreditation:* ACBSP. *Program availability:* Part-time, evening/weekend, online only, 100% online. *Faculty:* 6 full-time (3 women), 13 part-time/adjunct (4 women). *Students:* 77 full-time (51 women), 102 part-time (45 women); includes 40 minority (22 Black or African American, non-Hispanic/Latino; 3 Asian, non-Hispanic/Latino; 12 Hispanic/Latino; 1 Native Hawaiian or other Pacific Islander, non-Hispanic/Latino; 2 Two or more races, non-Hispanic/Latino). Average age 33. 71 applicants, 100% accepted, 46 enrolled. In 2016, 107 master's awarded. *Entrance requirements:* For master's, GMAT if cumulative GPA is below 2.75 with less than five years' professional work experience), minimum undergraduate GPA of 2.75; statement of professional goals; resume. Additional exam requirements/recommendations for international students: Required—TOEFL (minimum score 550 paper-based) or IELTS (minimum score 6.5). *Application deadline:* Applications are processed on a rolling basis. Application fee: $0. Electronic applications accepted. *Expenses:* $475 per credit hour. *Financial support:* Application deadline: 3/10; applicants required to submit FAFSA. *Unit head:* Dr. Karen Palumbo, Director of Virtual Campus Business Programs, 260-399-7700 Ext. 8312, Fax: 260-399-8174, E-mail: kpalumbo@sf.edu. *Application contact:* Kyle Richardson, Enrollment Services Specialist, 260-399-7700 Ext. 6310, Fax: 260-399-8152, E-mail: krichardson@sf.edu.
Website: http://business.sf.edu/graduate/

University of Saskatchewan, College of Graduate Studies and Research, School of Environment and Sustainability, Saskatoon, SK S7N 5A2, Canada. Offers MES.

University of Southern Maine, College of Management and Human Service, School of Business, Portland, ME 04104-9300. Offers accounting (MBA); business administration (MBA); finance (MBA); health management and policy (MBA); sustainability (MBA); JD/MBA; MBA/MSA; MBA/MSN; MS/MBA. *Accreditation:* AACSB. *Program availability:* Part-time, evening/weekend. *Entrance requirements:* For master's, GMAT or GRE, minimum AACSB index of 1100. Additional exam requirements/recommendations for international students: Required—TOEFL (minimum score 550 paper-based; 79 iBT). Electronic applications accepted. *Faculty research:* Economic development, management information systems, real options, system dynamics, simulation.

University of South Florida, College of Global Sustainability, Tampa, FL 33620-9951. Offers energy, global, water and sustainable tourism (Graduate Certificate); global sustainability (MA), including building sustainable enterprise, climate change and sustainability, coastal sustainability, entrepreneurship, food sustainability and security, sustainable energy, sustainable tourism, sustainable transportation, water. *Faculty:* 4 full-time (0 women). *Students:* 59 full-time (35 women), 51 part-time (29 women); includes 25 minority (3 Black or African American, non-Hispanic/Latino; 1 American Indian or Alaska Native, non-Hispanic/Latino; 2 Asian, non-Hispanic/Latino; 16 Hispanic/Latino; 3 Two or more races, non-Hispanic/Latino), 30 international. Average age 28. 134 applicants, 59% accepted, 55 enrolled. In 2016, 36 master's awarded. *Degree requirements:* For master's, comprehensive exam (for some programs), thesis or alternative, internship. *Entrance requirements:* For master's, minimum GPA of 3.0 in undergraduate coursework; at least two letters of recommendation (one must be academic); 200-250 word essay on student's background, professional goals, and reasons for seeking degree. Additional exam requirements/recommendations for international students: Required—TOEFL (minimum score 550 paper-based; 79 iBT). *Application deadline:* For fall admission, 6/1 for domestic students, 5/1 for international students; for spring admission, 10/15 for domestic students, 9/15 for international students. Electronic applications accepted. *Expenses:* Tuition, state resident: full-time $7766; part-time $431.43 per credit hour. Tuition, nonresident: full-time $15,789; part-time $877.17 per credit hour. *Required fees:* $37 per term. *Financial support:* In 2016–17, 20 students received support. *Faculty research:* Global sustainability, integrated resource management, systems thinking, green communities, entrepreneurship, ecotourism. *Total annual research expenditures:* $208,988. *Unit head:* Dr. Rafael Perez, Interim Dean, 813-974-9694, E-mail: perez@usf.edu.
Website: http://psgs.usf.edu/

University of Wisconsin–Green Bay, Graduate Studies, Program in Sustainable Management, Green Bay, WI 54311-7001. Offers MS. Program held jointly with four other University of Wisconsin System campuses: Oshkosh, Parkside, Stout, and Superior. *Program availability:* Part-time, evening/weekend, online only, 100% online. *Faculty:* 1 full-time (0 women). *Students:* 9 full-time (6 women), 44 part-time (20 women); includes 8 minority (1 Black or African American, non-Hispanic/Latino; 3 American Indian or Alaska Native, non-Hispanic/Latino; 2 Hispanic/Latino; 2 Two or more races, non-Hispanic/Latino). Average age 35. 14 applicants, 100% accepted, 10 enrolled. In 2016, 5 master's awarded. *Degree requirements:* For master's, capstone project. *Entrance requirements:* For master's, bachelor's degree from nationally-accredited university with minimum cumulative GPA of 3.0. Additional exam requirements/recommendations for international students: Required—TOEFL. *Application deadline:* Applications are processed on a rolling basis. Application fee: $56. Electronic applications accepted. *Expenses:* Tuition, state resident: full-time $7640; part-time $424 per credit hour. Tuition, nonresident: full-time $16,771; part-time $932 per credit hour. *Required fees:* $1580; $88 per credit hour. Tuition and fees vary according to program and reciprocity agreements. *Financial support:* In 2016–17, 4 students received support. Scholarships/grants available. *Unit head:* Dr. John Katers, Director, 920-465-2278, E-mail: katersj@uwgb.edu. *Application contact:* Mary Valitchka, Graduate Studies Coordinator, 920-465-2123, Fax: 920-465-5043, E-mail: valitchm@uwgb.edu.
Website: http://sustain.wisconsin.edu/degrees-and-certificates/masters/

University of Wisconsin–Stout, Graduate School, College of Management, Program in Sustainable Management, Menomonie, WI 54751. Offers MS. Program offered in collaboration with University of Wisconsin-Parkside, University of Wisconsin-River Falls and University of Wisconisn-Superior. *Program availability:* Online learning.

University of Wisconsin–Superior, Graduate Division, Department of Business and Economics, Superior, WI 54880-4500. Offers sustainable management (MS). Electronic applications accepted.

Valparaiso University, Graduate School and Continuing Education, College of Business, Valparaiso, IN 46383. Offers business administration (MBA); business intelligence (Certificate); engineering management (Certificate); entrepreneurship (Certificate); finance (Certificate); general business (Certificate); management (Certificate); marketing (Certificate); sustainability (Certificate); JD/MBA; MSN/MBA. *Accreditation:* AACSB. *Program availability:* Part-time, evening/weekend, online learning. *Entrance requirements:* For master's, GMAT, GRE, minimum GPA of 3.0. Additional exam requirements/recommendations for international students: Required—TOEFL (minimum score 550 paper-based; 80 iBT), IELTS (minimum score 6). Electronic applications accepted. *Expenses:* Contact institution.

Section 14
Marketing

This section contains a directory of institutions offering graduate work in marketing, followed by an in-depth entry submitted by an institution that chose to prepare a detailed program description. Additional information about programs listed in the directory but not augmented by an in-depth entry may be obtained by writing directly to the dean of a graduate school or chair of a department at the address given in the directory.

For programs offering related work, see also in this book *Advertising and Public Relations, Business Administration and Management*, and *Hospitality Management*. In another guide in this series:

Graduate Programs in the Humanities, Arts & Social Sciences

See *Communication and Media* and *Public, Regional, and Industrial Affairs*

CONTENTS

Program Directories

Featured Schools: Displays and Close-Ups

See also:

Marketing

Adelphi University, Robert B. Willumstad School of Business, MBA Program, Garden City, NY 11530-0701. Offers accounting (MBA); finance (MBA); health services administration (MBA); human resource management (MBA); management (MBA); management information systems (MBA); marketing (MBA); sport management (MBA). *Accreditation:* AACSB. *Program availability:* Part-time, evening/weekend. *Students:* 172 full-time (74 women), 129 part-time (66 women); includes 30 minority (9 Black or African American, non-Hispanic/Latino; 11 Asian, non-Hispanic/Latino; 9 Hispanic/Latino; 1 Two or more races, non-Hispanic/Latino), 29 international. Average age 32. 4 applicants. In 2016, 130 master's awarded. *Degree requirements:* For master's, capstone course. *Entrance requirements:* For master's, GMAT, 2 letters of recommendation. Additional exam requirements/recommendations for international students: Required—TOEFL (minimum score 550 paper-based; 80 iBT), IELTS (minimum score 6.5). *Application deadline:* For fall admission, 4/1 for international students; for spring admission, 11/1 for international students. Applications are processed on a rolling basis. Application fee: $50. Electronic applications accepted. *Expenses:* Contact institution. *Financial support:* Research assistantships with partial tuition reimbursements, career-related internships or fieldwork, Federal Work-Study, institutionally sponsored loans, scholarships/grants, tuition waivers (partial), and unspecified assistantships available. Financial award application deadline: 3/1; financial award applicants required to submit FAFSA. *Faculty research:* Supply chain management, distribution channels, productivity benchmark analysis, data envelopment analysis, financial portfolio analysis. *Unit head:* Dr. Rakesh Gupta, Associate Dean, 516-877-4629. *Application contact:* Christine Murphy, Director of Admissions, 516-877-3050, Fax: 516-877-3039, E-mail: graduateadmissions@adelphi.edu.
Website: http://business.adelphi.edu/degree-programs/graduate-degree-programs/m-b-a/

American Business & Technology University, Programs in Business Administration, Saint Joseph, MO 64506. Offers business administration (MBA); financial management (MBA); global business management (MBA); information systems management (MBA); marketing and social media (MBA); project and operations management (MBA); public accounting (MBA). *Program availability:* Online learning.

American College of Thessaloniki, Department of Business Administration, Pylea, Greece. Offers banking and finance (MBA); entrepreneurship (MBA, Certificate); finance (Certificate); management (MBA, Certificate); marketing (MBA, Certificate). *Program availability:* Part-time, evening/weekend. *Degree requirements:* For master's, thesis. *Entrance requirements:* For master's, bachelor's degree. Additional exam requirements/recommendations for international students: Recommended—TOEFL. Electronic applications accepted.

American InterContinental University Online, Program in Business Administration, Schaumburg, IL 60173. Offers accounting and finance (MBA); finance (MBA); healthcare management (MBA); human resource management (MBA); international business (MBA); management (MBA); marketing (MBA); operations management (MBA); organizational psychology and development (MBA); project management (MBA). *Accreditation:* ACBSP. *Program availability:* Evening/weekend, online learning. *Entrance requirements:* Additional exam requirements/recommendations for international students: Required—TOEFL (minimum score 550 paper-based). Electronic applications accepted.

American Public University System, AMU/APU Graduate Programs, Charles Town, WV 25414. Offers accounting (MBA, MS); applied business analytics (MBA, MS); criminal justice (MA), including business administration, emergency and disaster management, general (MA, MS); educational leadership (M Ed); emergency and disaster management (MA); entrepreneurship (MBA); environmental policy and management (MS), including environmental planning, environmental sustainability, fish and wildlife management, general (MA, MS), global environmental management; finance (MBA); general (MBA); government contracting and acquisition (MBA); health care administration (MBA); health information management (MS); history (MA), including American history, ancient and classical history, European history, global history, public history; homeland security (MA), including business administration, counterterrorism studies, criminal justice, cyber, emergency management and public health, intelligence studies, transportation security; homeland security resource allocation (MBA); humanities (MA); information technology (MS), including digital forensics, enterprise software development, information assurance and security, IT project management; information technology management (MBA); intelligence studies (MA), including criminal intelligence, cyber, general (MA, MS), homeland security, intelligence analysis, intelligence collection, intelligence management, intelligence operations, terrorism studies; international relations and conflict resolution (MA), including comparative and security issues, conflict resolution, international and transnational security issues, peacekeeping; legal studies (MA); management (MA), including strategic consulting; marketing (MBA); military history (MA), including American military history, American Revolution, civil war, war since 1945, World War II; military studies (MA), including joint warfare, strategic leadership; national security studies (MA), including cyber, general (MA, MS), homeland security, regional security studies, security and intelligence analysis, terrorism studies; nonprofit management (MBA); political science (MA), including American politics and government, comparative government and development, general (MA, MS), international relations, public policy; psychology (MA); public administration (MPA), including disaster management, environmental policy, health policy, human resources, national security, organizational management, security management; public health (MPH); reverse logistics management (MA); security management (MA); space studies (MS), including aerospace science, general (MA, MS), planetary science; sports and health sciences (MS); sports management (MBA); teaching (M Ed), including autism spectrum disorder, curriculum and instruction for elementary teachers, elementary reading, English language learners, instructional leadership, online learning, special education, STEAM (STEM plus the arts); transportation and logistics management (MA). *Program availability:* Part-time, evening/weekend, online only, 100% online. *Faculty:* 401 full-time (228 women), 1,678 part-time/adjunct (781 women). *Students:* 378 full-time (184 women), 8,455 part-time (3,484 women); includes 2,972 minority (1,552 Black or African American, non-Hispanic/Latino; 52 American Indian or Alaska Native, non-Hispanic/Latino; 211 Asian, non-Hispanic/Latino; 791 Hispanic/Latino; 70 Native Hawaiian or other Pacific Islander, non-Hispanic/Latino; 296 Two or more races, non-Hispanic/Latino), 109 international. Average age 37. In 2016, 3,185 master's awarded. *Degree requirements:* For master's, comprehensive exam or practicum. *Entrance requirements:* For master's, official transcript showing earned bachelor's degree from institution accredited by recognized accrediting body. Additional exam requirements/recommendations for international students: Required—TOEFL (minimum score 550 paper-based), IELTS (minimum score 6.5). *Application deadline:* Applications are processed on a rolling basis. Application fee: $0. Electronic applications accepted. *Expenses: Tuition:* Part-time $350 per credit hour. *Required fees:* $50 per course. *Financial support:* Scholarships/grants available. Financial award applicants required to submit FAFSA. *Unit head:* Dr. Karan Powell, President, 877-468-6268, Fax: 304-724-3780. *Application contact:* Terry Grant, Vice President of Enrollment Management, 877-468-6268, Fax: 304-724-3780, E-mail: info@apus.edu.
Website: http://www.apus.edu

American University, Kogod School of Business, Department of Marketing, Washington, DC 20016-8044. Offers MS. *Program availability:* Part-time, evening/weekend. *Faculty:* 12 full-time (5 women), 9 part-time/adjunct (2 women). *Students:* 19 full-time (14 women); includes 5 minority (2 Asian, non-Hispanic/Latino; 1 Hispanic/Latino; 2 Two or more races, non-Hispanic/Latino), 4 international. Average age 24. 52 applicants, 58% accepted, 19 enrolled. In 2016, 18 master's awarded. *Entrance requirements:* For master's, GMAT/GRE, resume, personal statement, 2 letters of recommendation, transcripts, interview. Additional exam requirements/recommendations for international students: Required—TOEFL (minimum score 550 paper-based; 100 iBT), IELTS (minimum score 7), PTE (minimum score 68). *Application deadline:* For fall admission, 2/20 priority date for domestic students, 2/20 for international students; for spring admission, 12/10 for domestic students, 11/15 for international students. Application fee: $100. *Expenses:* $1,579 per credit tuition; $690 mandatory fees. *Financial support:* Application deadline: 2/1; applicants required to submit FAFSA. *Faculty research:* Internet marketing, database marketing, consumer behavior, advertising research, public policy in marketing. *Unit head:* Dr. Anusree Mitra, Department Chair, 202-885-1975, Fax: 202-885-2691, E-mail: amitra@american.edu. *Application contact:* Jason Kennedy, Associate Director, Graduate Admissions, 202-885-1968, E-mail: jkennedy@american.edu.
Website: http://www.american.edu/kogod/graduate/index.cfm

The American University in Dubai, Graduate Programs, Dubai, United Arab Emirates. Offers construction management (MS); education (M Ed); finance (MBA); generalist (MBA); marketing (MBA). *Program availability:* Part-time, evening/weekend. *Degree requirements:* For master's, thesis optional. *Entrance requirements:* For master's, GMAT (for MBA); GRE (for M Ed and MS), minimum undergraduate GPA of 3.0, official transcripts, two reference forms, curriculum vitae/resume, statement of career objectives, work experience. Additional exam requirements/recommendations for international students: Required—TOEFL (minimum score 550 paper-based; 79 iBT). Electronic applications accepted.

Anderson University, College of Business, Anderson, SC 29621-4035. Offers business administration (MBA); healthcare leadership (MBA); human resources (MBA); marketing (MBA); supply chain management (MBA). *Accreditation:* ACBSP. *Students:* 7 full-time (0 women), 1 part-time (0 women). *Expenses:* Contact institution. *Financial support:* Tuition waivers available. Financial award application deadline: 3/1; financial award applicants required to submit FAFSA. *Unit head:* Dr. Douglas Goodwin, MBA Director/Associate Dean, 864-MBA-6000. *Application contact:* Mallory Knight, Graduate Admission Counselor, 864-231-2182, Fax: 864-231-2115, E-mail: malloryknight@andersonuniversity.edu.
Website: http://www.andersonuniversity.edu/business

Aquinas College, School of Management, Grand Rapids, MI 49506. Offers marketing management (MM); organizational leadership (MM); sustainable business (MM). *Program availability:* Part-time, evening/weekend. *Entrance requirements:* For master's, GMAT, minimum undergraduate GPA of 2.75, 2 years of work experience. Additional exam requirements/recommendations for international students: Required—TOEFL (minimum score 550 paper-based). *Application deadline:* Applications are processed on a rolling basis. Application fee: $0. *Expenses:* Contact institution. *Financial support:* Scholarships/grants available. Support available to part-time students. Financial award application deadline: 3/15; financial award applicants required to submit FAFSA. *Unit head:* Cynthia G. VanGelderen, Interim Director, 616-632-2922, Fax: 616-732-4489. *Application contact:* Lynn Atkins-Rykert, Program Coordinator, 616-632-2925, Fax: 616-732-4489, E-mail: atkinlyn@aquinas.edu.

Argosy University, Atlanta, College of Business, Atlanta, GA 30328. Offers accounting (DBA); corporate compliance (MBA); customized professional concentration (MBA, DBA); finance (MBA); healthcare administration (MBA); information systems (DBA); information systems management (MBA); international business (MBA, DBA); management (MBA, MSM, DBA); marketing (MBA, DBA). *Accreditation:* ACBSP.

Argosy University, Chicago, College of Business, Chicago, IL 60601. Offers accounting (DBA); customized professional concentration (MBA, DBA); finance (MBA); fraud examination (MBA); global business sustainability (DBA); healthcare administration (MBA); information systems (DBA); information systems management (MBA); international business (MBA, DBA); management (MBA, MSM, DBA); marketing (MBA, DBA); organizational leadership (Ed D); public administration (MBA); sustainable management (MBA). *Accreditation:* ACBSP. *Program availability:* Online learning.

Argosy University, Dallas, College of Business, Farmers Branch, TX 75244. Offers accounting (DBA, AGC); corporate compliance (MBA, Graduate Certificate); customized professional concentration (MBA); finance (MBA, Graduate Certificate); fraud examination (MBA, Graduate Certificate); global business sustainability (DBA, AGC); healthcare administration (Graduate Certificate); healthcare management (MBA); information systems (MBA, DBA, AGC); information systems management (Graduate Certificate); international business (MBA, DBA, AGC, Graduate Certificate); management (MBA, DBA, AGC, Graduate Certificate); marketing (MBA, DBA, AGC, Graduate Certificate); public administration (MBA, Graduate Certificate); sustainable management (MBA, Graduate Certificate). *Accreditation:* ACBSP.

Argosy University, Denver, College of Business, Denver, CO 80231. Offers accounting (DBA); corporate compliance (MBA); customized professional concentration (MBA, DBA); finance (MBA); fraud examination (MBA); global business sustainability (DBA); healthcare administration (MBA); information systems (DBA); information systems management (MBA); international business (MBA, DBA); management (MBA, MSM, DBA); marketing (MBA, DBA); organizational leadership (Ed D); public administration (MBA); sustainable management (MBA). *Accreditation:* ACBSP.

Argosy University, Hawai`i, College of Business, Honolulu, HI 96813. Offers accounting (DBA); corporate compliance (MBA); customized professional concentration (MBA, DBA); finance (MBA, Certificate); fraud examination (MBA); global business sustainability (DBA); healthcare administration (MBA, Certificate); information systems (DBA); information systems management (MBA, Certificate); international business (MBA, DBA, Certificate); management (MBA, MSM, DBA); marketing (MBA, DBA, Certificate); organizational leadership (Ed D); public administration (MBA); sustainable management (MBA).

Argosy University, Inland Empire, College of Business, Ontario, CA 91761. Offers accounting (DBA); corporate compliance (MBA); customized professional concentration

(MBA, DBA); finance (MBA); fraud examination (MBA); global business sustainability (DBA); healthcare administration (MBA); information systems (DBA); information systems management (MBA); international business (MBA, DBA); management (MBA, MSM, DBA); marketing (MBA, DBA); organizational leadership (Ed D); public administration (MBA); sustainable management (MBA).

Argosy University, Los Angeles, College of Business, Santa Monica, CA 90045. Offers accounting (DBA); corporate compliance (MBA); customized professional concentration (MBA, DBA); finance (MBA); fraud examination (MBA); global business sustainability (DBA); healthcare administration (MBA); information systems (DBA); information systems management (MBA); international business (MBA, DBA); management (MBA, MSM, DBA); marketing (MBA, DBA); organizational leadership (Ed D); public administration (MBA); sustainable management (MBA).

Argosy University, Nashville, College of Business, Nashville, TN 37214. Offers accounting (DBA); customized professional concentration (MBA, DBA); finance (MBA); healthcare administration (MBA); information systems (MBA, DBA); international business (MBA, DBA); management (MBA, MSM, DBA); marketing (MBA, DBA).

Argosy University, Northern Virginia, College of Business, Arlington, VA 22209. Offers accounting (DBA); customized professional concentration (MBA, DBA); finance (MBA); fraud examination (MBA); global business sustainability (DBA); healthcare administration (MBA); information systems (DBA); information systems management (MBA); international business (MBA, DBA, Certificate); management (MBA, MSM, DBA); marketing (MBA, DBA, Certificate); organizational leadership (Ed D); public administration (MBA); sustainable management (MBA).

Argosy University, Orange County, College of Business, Orange, CA 92868. Offers accounting (DBA, Adv C); corporate compliance (MBA); customized professional concentration (MBA, DBA); finance (MBA, Certificate); fraud examination (MBA); global business sustainability (DBA); healthcare administration (MBA, Certificate); information systems (DBA, Adv C, Certificate); information systems management (MBA); international business (MBA, DBA, Adv C, Certificate); management (MBA, MSM, DBA, Adv C); marketing (MBA, DBA, Adv C, Certificate); organizational leadership (Ed D); public administration (MBA, Certificate); sustainable management (MBA).

Argosy University, Phoenix, College of Business, Phoenix, AZ 85021. Offers accounting (DBA); corporate compliance (MBA); customized professional concentration (MBA, DBA); finance (MBA); fraud examination (MBA); global business sustainability (DBA); healthcare administration (MBA); information systems (DBA); information systems management (MBA); international business (MBA, DBA); management (MBA, DBA); marketing (MBA, DBA); public administration (MBA); sustainable management (MBA).

Argosy University, Salt Lake City, College of Business, Draper, UT 84020. Offers accounting (DBA); corporate compliance (MBA); customized professional concentration (MBA, DBA); finance (MBA); fraud examination (MBA); global business sustainability (DBA); healthcare administration (MBA); information systems (DBA); information systems management (MBA); international business (MBA, DBA); management (MBA, DBA); marketing (MBA, DBA); public administration (MBA); sustainable management (MBA).

Argosy University, San Diego, College of Business, San Diego, CA 92108. Offers accounting (DBA); corporate compliance (MBA); customized professional concentration (MBA, DBA); finance (MBA); fraud examination (MBA); global business sustainability (DBA); information systems (DBA); information systems management (MBA); international business (MBA, DBA); management (MBA, MSM, DBA); marketing (MBA, DBA); organizational leadership (Ed D); public administration (MBA).

Argosy University, San Francisco Bay Area, College of Business, Alameda, CA 94501. Offers accounting (DBA); corporate compliance (MBA); customized professional concentration (MBA, DBA); finance (MBA); fraud examination (MBA); global business sustainability (DBA); healthcare administration (MBA); information systems (DBA); information systems management (MBA); international business (MBA, DBA); management (MBA, MSM, DBA); marketing (MBA, DBA); organizational leadership (Ed D); public administration (MBA); sustainable management (MBA).

Argosy University, Sarasota, College of Business, Sarasota, FL 34235. Offers accounting (DBA, Adv C); corporate compliance (MBA, DBA, Certificate); customized professional concentration (MBA, DBA); finance (MBA, Certificate); fraud examination (MBA, Certificate); global business sustainability (DBA, Adv C); healthcare administration (MBA, Certificate); information systems (DBA, Adv C, Certificate); information systems management (MBA); international business (MBA, DBA, Adv C, Certificate); management (MBA, MSM, DBA, Adv C, Certificate); marketing (MBA, DBA, Adv C, Certificate); organizational leadership (Ed D); public administration (MBA, Certificate); sustainable management (MBA, Certificate).

Argosy University, Schaumburg, Graduate School of Business and Management, Schaumburg, IL 60173-5403. Offers accounting (DBA, Adv C); customized professional concentration (MBA, DBA); finance (MBA, Certificate); fraud examination (MBA); healthcare administration (MBA, Certificate); human resource management (MS); information systems (Adv C, Certificate); information systems management (MBA); international business (MBA, DBA, Adv C, Certificate); management (MBA, MSM, DBA, Adv C, Certificate); marketing (MBA, DBA, Adv C, Certificate); organizational leadership (MS, Ed D); public administration (MBA); sustainable management (MBA).

Argosy University, Seattle, College of Business, Seattle, WA 98121. Offers accounting (DBA); corporate compliance (MBA); customized professional concentration (MBA, DBA); finance (MBA); fraud examination (MBA); global business sustainability (DBA); healthcare administration (MBA); information systems (DBA); information systems management (MBA); international business (MBA, DBA); management (MBA, MSM, DBA); marketing (MBA, DBA); organizational leadership (Ed D); public administration (MBA); sustainable management (MBA).

Argosy University, Tampa, College of Business, Tampa, FL 33607. Offers accounting (DBA); corporate compliance (MBA); customized professional concentration (MBA, DBA); finance (MBA); fraud examination (MBA); global business sustainability (DBA); healthcare administration (MBA); information systems (DBA); information systems management (MBA); international business (MBA, DBA); management (MBA, MSM, DBA); marketing (MBA, DBA); organizational leadership (Ed D); public administration (MBA); sustainable management (MBA).

Argosy University, Twin Cities, College of Business, Eagan, MN 55121. Offers accounting (DBA); customized professional concentration (MBA, DBA); finance (MBA); fraud examination (MBA); global business sustainability (DBA); healthcare administration (MBA); information systems (DBA); information systems management (MBA); international business (MBA, DBA); management (MBA, MSM, DBA); marketing (MBA, DBA); organizational leadership (Ed D); public administration (MBA); sustainable management (MBA).

Arizona State University at the Tempe campus, W. P. Carey School of Business, Department of Marketing, Tempe, AZ 85287-4106. Offers business administration (PhD), including marketing; real estate development (MRED). *Program availability:* Part-time, evening/weekend, online learning. *Degree requirements:* For master's, thesis or alternative, capstone project, interactive Program of Study (iPOS) submitted before completing 50 percent of required credit hours; for doctorate, comprehensive exam, thesis/dissertation, interactive Program of Study (iPOS) submitted before completing 50 percent of required credit hours. *Entrance requirements:* For master's, GMAT, GRE, or LSAT, minimum GPA of 3.0 in last 2 years of work leading to bachelor's degree, 3 personal references, resume, official transcripts, personal statement; for doctorate, GMAT, minimum GPA of 3.0 in last 2 years of work leading to bachelor's degree, 3 letters of recommendation, personal statement/essay. Additional exam requirements/recommendations for international students: Required—TOEFL (minimum score 550 paper-based; 80 iBT), IELTS (minimum score 6.5). Electronic applications accepted. *Expenses:* Contact institution. *Faculty research:* Service marketing and management, strategic marketing, customer portfolio management, characteristics and skills of high-performing managers, market orientation, market segmentation, consumer behavior, marketing strategy, new product development, management of innovation, social influences on consumption, e-commerce, market research methodology.

Arizona State University at the Tempe campus, W. P. Carey School of Business, Program in Business Administration, Tempe, AZ 85287-4906. Offers entrepreneurship (MBA); finance (MBA); health sector management (MBA); international business (MBA); leadership (MBA); marketing (MBA); organizational behavior (PhD); strategic management (PhD); supply chain management (MBA, PhD); JD/MBA; MBA/M Acc; MBA/M Arch. *Accreditation:* AACSB. *Program availability:* Part-time, evening/weekend, online learning. Terminal master's awarded for partial completion of doctoral program. *Degree requirements:* For master's, thesis or alternative, internship, interactive Program of Study (iPOS) submitted before completing 50 percent of required credit hours; for doctorate, comprehensive exam, thesis/dissertation, interactive Program of Study (iPOS) submitted before completing 50 percent of required credit hours. *Entrance requirements:* For master's, GMAT, minimum GPA of 3.0 in last 2 years of work leading to bachelor's degree, 2 letters of recommendation, professional resume, official transcripts, 3 essays; for doctorate, GMAT or GRE, minimum GPA of 3.0 in last 2 years of work leading to bachelor's degree, 3 letters of recommendation, resume, personal statement/essay. Additional exam requirements/recommendations for international students: Required—TOEFL (minimum score 550 paper-based; 80 iBT), IELTS (minimum score 6.5). Electronic applications accepted. *Expenses:* Contact institution.

Ashworth College, Graduate Programs, Norcross, GA 30092. Offers business administration (MBA); criminal justice (MS); health care administration (MBA, MS); human resource management (MBA, MS); international business (MBA); management (MS); marketing (MBA, MS).

Assumption College, Business Studies Program, Worcester, MA 01609-1296. Offers accounting (MBA); business studies (CAGS); finance/economics (MBA); human resources (MBA); international business (MBA); management (MBA); marketing (MBA); nonprofit leadership (MBA). *Program availability:* Part-time, evening/weekend. *Faculty:* 4 full-time (1 woman), 19 part-time/adjunct (6 women). *Students:* 44 full-time (16 women), 97 part-time (47 women); includes 20 minority (8 Black or African American, non-Hispanic/Latino; 5 Asian, non-Hispanic/Latino; 6 Hispanic/Latino; 1 Two or more races, non-Hispanic/Latino), 4 international. Average age 29. 34 applicants, 59% accepted, 16 enrolled. In 2016, 97 master's, 1 other advanced degree awarded. *Degree requirements:* For master's, thesis, capstone. *Entrance requirements:* For master's, bachelor's degree, 3 letters of recommendation, official transcripts, personal statement, current resume; for CAGS, MBA or equivalent degree in a closely related field, 3 letters of recommendation, official transcripts, personal statement, current resume. Additional exam requirements/recommendations for international students: Required—TOEFL (minimum score 540 paper-based; 76 iBT), IELTS (minimum score 6). *Application deadline:* For fall admission, 7/1 priority date for domestic and international students; for spring admission, 12/1 priority date for domestic and international students; for summer admission, 4/1 priority date for domestic and international students. Application fee: $30. Electronic applications accepted. *Expenses: Tuition:* Full-time $11,610; part-time $645 per credit. *Required fees:* $70 per term. Tuition and fees vary according to course load and program. *Financial support:* In 2016–17, 19 students received support. Tuition waivers (full and partial), unspecified assistantships, and institutional discounts available. Financial award applicants required to submit FAFSA. *Faculty research:* Workplace diversity, dynamics of team interaction, utilization of leased employees, experiential learning project on due diligence market for prostheses. *Unit head:* Dr. Robin Frkal, Director, 508-767-7622, E-mail: rafrkal@assumption.edu. *Application contact:* Karen Stoyanoff, Director of Recruitment for Graduate Enrollment, 508-767-7442, Fax: 508-799-4412, E-mail: graduate@assumption.edu.
Website: http://graduate.assumption.edu/mba/assumption-mba

Averett University, Master of Business Administration Program, Danville, VA 24541-3692. Offers business administration (MBA); human resources management (MBA); leadership (MBA); marketing (MBA). *Program availability:* Part-time, evening/weekend, 100% online, blended/hybrid learning. *Faculty:* 6 full-time (0 women), 21 part-time/adjunct (6 women). *Students:* 52 full-time (40 women), 215 part-time (117 women); includes 133 minority (110 Black or African American, non-Hispanic/Latino; 5 American Indian or Alaska Native, non-Hispanic/Latino; 9 Asian, non-Hispanic/Latino; 9 Hispanic/Latino), 6 international. Average age 38. 143 applicants, 78% accepted, 104 enrolled. In 2016, 99 master's awarded. *Degree requirements:* For master's, 41-credit core curriculum, minimum GPA of 3.0 throughout program, no more than 2 grades of C, completion of degree requirements within six years from start of program. *Entrance requirements:* For master's, minimum cumulative GPA of 3.0 over the last 60 semester hours of undergraduate study toward a baccalaureate degree, official transcripts, three years of full-time work experience, three letters of recommendation, current resume. Additional exam requirements/recommendations for international students: Required—TOEFL (minimum score 600 paper-based; 100 iBT). *Application deadline:* Applications are processed on a rolling basis. Electronic applications accepted. *Expenses:* $12,645. *Financial support:* Application deadline: 3/1; applicants required to submit FAFSA. *Unit head:* Dr. Peggy C. Wright, Chair, Business Department, 434-791-7118, E-mail: pwright@averett.edu. *Application contact:* Melissa Anderson, Director of Admissions, Graduate and Professional Studies, 804-729-8285, E-mail: manderson@averett.edu.
Website: http://gps.averett.edu/programs/master-degrees/

Avila University, School of Business, Kansas City, MO 64145-1698. Offers accounting (MBA); finance (MBA); health care administration (MBA); international business (MBA); management (MBA); management information systems (MBA); marketing (MBA). *Program availability:* Part-time, evening/weekend. *Faculty:* 8 full-time (4 women), 4 part-time/adjunct (2 women). *Students:* 58 full-time (22 women), 21 part-time (10 women); includes 20 minority (10 Black or African American, non-Hispanic/Latino; 2 Asian, non-Hispanic/Latino; 5 Hispanic/Latino; 3 Two or more races, non-Hispanic/Latino), 18 international. Average age 30. 75 applicants, 28% accepted, 14 enrolled. In 2016, 40 master's awarded. *Degree requirements:* For master's, comprehensive exam, capstone course. *Entrance requirements:* For master's, GMAT (minimum score 420), minimum GPA of 3.0, interview. Additional exam requirements/recommendations for international students: Required—TOEFL (minimum score 550 paper-based). *Application deadline:* For fall admission, 7/30 priority date for domestic and international students; for winter admission, 11/30 priority date for domestic and international students; for spring admission, 2/28 priority date for domestic and international students; for summer

admission, 6/1 priority date for domestic and international students. Applications are processed on a rolling basis. Application fee: $0. Electronic applications accepted. *Expenses:* $628 per credit hour. *Financial support:* In 2016–17, 11 students received support. Career-related internships or fieldwork and scholarships/grants available. Support available to part-time students. Financial award applicants required to submit FAFSA. *Faculty research:* Leadership characteristics, financial hedging, group dynamics. *Unit head:* Dr. Richard Woodall, Dean, 816-501-3720, Fax: 816-501-2463, E-mail: richard.woodall@avila.edu. *Application contact:* Brandon Black, MBA Admission Advisor, 816-501-3601, Fax: 816-501-2463, E-mail: brandon.black@avila.edu.
Website: https://www.avila.edu/mrk/mba

Azusa Pacific University, School of Business and Management, Azusa, CA 91702-7000. Offers business administration (MBA); diversity for strategic advantage (MA); entrepreneurship (MBA); finance (MBA); human and organizational development (MA); human resources and organizational development (MBA); human resources management (MA); international business (MBA); marketing (MBA); non-profit management (MA); organizational development and change (MA); performance improvement (MA); public administration (MA); strategic management (MBA). *Program availability:* Part-time, evening/weekend. *Degree requirements:* For master's, thesis (for some programs), final project. *Entrance requirements:* For master's, GMAT, minimum GPA of 3.0. Additional exam requirements/recommendations for international students: Required—TOEFL (minimum score 600 paper-based). *Expenses:* Contact institution. *Faculty research:* Gender issues, financial risk, leadership and ethics, marketing strategy.

Baker College Center for Graduate Studies–Online, Graduate Programs, Flint, MI 48507. Offers accounting (MBA); business administration (DBA); finance (MBA); general business (MBA); health care management (MBA); human resources management (MBA); information management (MBA); leadership studies (MBA); management information systems (MSIS); marketing (MBA). *Program availability:* Part-time, evening/weekend, online learning. *Degree requirements:* For master's, portfolio. *Entrance requirements:* For master's, 3 years of work experience, minimum undergraduate GPA of 2.5, writing sample, 3 letters of recommendation; for doctorate, MBA or acceptable related master's degree from accredited association, 5 years work experience, minimum graduate GPA of 3.25, writing sample, 3 professional references. Additional exam requirements/recommendations for international students: Required—TOEFL (minimum score 550 paper-based). Electronic applications accepted.

Barry University, Andreas School of Business, Graduate Certificate Programs, Miami Shores, FL 33161-6695. Offers finance (Certificate); health services administration (Certificate); international business (Certificate); management (Certificate); management information systems (Certificate); marketing (Certificate).

Baruch College of the City University of New York, Zicklin School of Business, Department of Marketing and International Business, New York, NY 10010-5585. Offers international business (MBA); marketing (MBA, MS, PhD). PhD offered jointly with Graduate School and University Center of the City University of New York. *Program availability:* Part-time, evening/weekend. *Degree requirements:* For doctorate, comprehensive exam, thesis/dissertation. *Entrance requirements:* For master's, GMAT, 2 letters of recommendation, resume, 2 years of work experience; for doctorate, GMAT. Additional exam requirements/recommendations for international students: Required—TOEFL (minimum score 590 paper-based), TWE (minimum score 5).

Bayamón Central University, Graduate Programs, Program in Business Administration, Bayamón, PR 00960-1725. Offers accounting (MBA); finance (MBA); general business (MBA); management (MBA); marketing (MBA). *Program availability:* Part-time, evening/weekend. *Degree requirements:* For master's, comprehensive exam (for some programs). *Entrance requirements:* For master's, EXADEP, bachelor's degree in business or related field.

Benedictine University, Graduate Programs, Program in Business Administration, Lisle, IL 60532. Offers accounting (MBA); entrepreneurship and managing innovation (MBA); financial management (MBA); health administration (MBA); human resource management (MBA); information systems security (MBA); international business (MBA); management consulting (MBA); management information systems (MBA); marketing management (MBA); operations management and logistics (MBA); organizational leadership (MBA). *Program availability:* Part-time, evening/weekend, online learning. *Faculty:* 4 full-time (2 women), 24 part-time/adjunct (3 women). *Students:* 90 full-time (51 women), 440 part-time (262 women); includes 147 minority (65 Black or African American, non-Hispanic/Latino; 1 American Indian or Alaska Native, non-Hispanic/Latino; 58 Asian, non-Hispanic/Latino; 20 Hispanic/Latino; 3 Native Hawaiian or other Pacific Islander, non-Hispanic/Latino), 2 international. Average age 34. 211 applicants, 89% accepted, 155 enrolled. In 2016, 350 master's awarded. *Entrance requirements:* For master's, GMAT. Additional exam requirements/recommendations for international students: Required—TOEFL (minimum score 550 paper-based). *Application deadline:* For fall admission, 9/1 for domestic students; for winter admission, 12/1 for domestic students; for spring admission, 2/15 for domestic students. Applications are processed on a rolling basis. Application fee: $40. Electronic applications accepted. *Expenses: Tuition:* Full-time $15,600; part-time $650 per hour. *Required fees:* $300. One-time fee: $125 part-time. Tuition and fees vary according to class time, course load, campus/location and program. *Financial support:* Career-related internships or fieldwork and health care benefits available. Support available to part-time students. *Faculty research:* Strategic leadership in professional organizations, sociology of professions, organizational change, social identity theory, applications to change management. *Unit head:* Dr. Sharon Borowicz, Director, 630-829-6219, E-mail: sborowicz@ben.edu. *Application contact:* Kari Gibbons, Director, Admissions, 630-829-6200, Fax: 630-829-6584, E-mail: kgibbons@ben.edu.

Bentley University, Graduate School of Business, Program in Marketing Analytics, Waltham, MA 02452-4705. Offers MSMA. *Program availability:* Part-time, evening/weekend. *Faculty:* 71 full-time (25 women), 33 part-time/adjunct (15 women). *Students:* 64 full-time (43 women), 20 part-time (11 women); includes 6 minority (1 Black or African American, non-Hispanic/Latino; 2 Asian, non-Hispanic/Latino; 3 Hispanic/Latino), 60 international. Average age 26. 148 applicants, 72% accepted, 34 enrolled. In 2016, 50 master's awarded. *Entrance requirements:* For master's, GMAT or GRE General Test, current resume; two letters of recommendation; official copies of all university-level transcripts. Additional exam requirements/recommendations for international students: Required—TOEFL (minimum score 600 paper-based; 100 iBT), IELTS (minimum score 7), or PTE. *Application deadline:* Applications are processed on a rolling basis. Application fee: $50. Electronic applications accepted. *Expenses:* $4,225 per course, $480 fee per year. *Financial support:* In 2016–17, 9 students received support. Scholarships/grants available. Financial award application deadline: 6/1; financial award applicants required to submit FAFSA. *Faculty research:* Marketing information processing; blogging and social media; customer lifetime value and customer relationship management; measuring and improving productivity; online consumer behavior. *Unit head:* Dr. Paul D. Berger, Professor, 781-891-2746, E-mail: pberger@bentley.edu. *Application contact:* Sharon Hill, Assistant Dean/Director of Graduate Admissions, 781-891-2108, Fax: 781-891-2464, E-mail: bentleygraduateadmissions@bentley.edu.
Website: http://www.bentley.edu/graduate/ms-programs/masters-in-marketing-analytics

Brandeis University, International Business School (IBS), Master of Business Administration Program, Waltham, MA 02454-9110. Offers corporate finance (MBA); data analytics (MBA); marketing (MBA); real estate (MBA). *Faculty:* 29 full-time (10 women), 27 part-time/adjunct (3 women). *Students:* 65 full-time (25 women). Average age 27. 75 applicants, 59% accepted, 16 enrolled. In 2016, 42 master's awarded. *Entrance requirements:* For master's, GMAT or GRE. Additional exam requirements/recommendations for international students: Required—TOEFL (minimum score 600 paper-based; 100 iBT), IELTS (minimum score 7), PTE (minimum score 68). *Application deadline:* For fall admission, 11/1 priority date for domestic and international students; for winter admission, 1/15 priority date for domestic and international students; for spring admission, 3/15 priority date for domestic and international students; for summer admission, 5/15 for domestic and international students. Application fee: $55. Electronic applications accepted. *Expenses:* Contact institution. *Financial support:* In 2016–17, 80 students received support. Institutionally sponsored loans and scholarships/grants available. Financial award application deadline: 3/15; financial award applicants required to submit FAFSA. *Faculty research:* Strategic alliances, IPO and venture capital financing, real estate, risk management, data analytics. *Unit head:* Peter Petri, Interim Dean, 781-736-2256. *Application contact:* Kelly Sugrue, Director of Admissions, 781-736-2252, Fax: 781-736-2263, E-mail: admission@lemberg.brandeis.edu.

Brandman University, School of Business and Professional Studies, Irvine, CA 92618. Offers accounting (MBA); business administration (MBA); e-business strategic management (MBA); entrepreneurship (MBA); finance (MBA); health administration (MBA); human resources (MBA, MS); international business (MBA); marketing (MBA); organizational leadership (MA, MBA, MPA); public administration (MPA). *Expenses: Tuition:* Full-time $14,880; part-time $620 per credit hour. Tuition and fees vary according to degree level and program. *Unit head:* Dr. Glenn Worthington, Dean, 253-861-1024, E-mail: gworthin@brandman.edu.
Website: https://www.brandman.edu/business-professional-studies

Brigham Young University, Graduate Studies, Marriott School of Management, Master of Business Administration Program, Provo, UT 84602. Offers entrepreneurship (MBA); finance (MBA); global supply chain management (MBA); marketing (MBA); strategic human resources (MBA); JD/MBA; MBA/MS. *Accreditation:* AACSB. *Students:* 321 full-time (63 women); includes 16 minority (1 Black or African American, non-Hispanic/Latino; 9 Asian, non-Hispanic/Latino; 6 Hispanic/Latino), 69 international. Average age 31. 397 applicants, 49% accepted, 154 enrolled. In 2016, 146 master's awarded. *Entrance requirements:* For master's, GMAT or GRE, minimum GPA of 3.0 in last 60 hours. Additional exam requirements/recommendations for international students: Required—TOEFL (minimum score 590 paper-based; 94 iBT), IELTS (minimum score 7). *Application deadline:* For fall admission, 5/1 for domestic students, 1/15 for international students. Applications are processed on a rolling basis. Application fee: $50. Electronic applications accepted. *Expenses:* Contact institution. *Financial support:* In 2016–17, 247 students received support. Research assistantships, teaching assistantships, career-related internships or fieldwork, institutionally sponsored loans, and scholarships/grants available. Financial award application deadline: 3/1; financial award applicants required to submit FAFSA. *Faculty research:* Finance, marketing, supply chain management, entrepreneurship, strategic human resources. *Unit head:* Dr. Grant McQueen, Director, 801-422-3500, Fax: 801-422-0513, E-mail: mba@byu.edu. *Application contact:* Yvette Anderson, MBA Program Admissions Director, 801-422-3500, Fax: 801-422-0513, E-mail: mba@byu.edu.
Website: http://mba.byu.edu

Bristol University, Program in Business Administration, Anaheim, CA 92806. Offers business administration (MBA); international business (MBA); marketing (MBA); sports management (MBA). *Degree requirements:* For master's, capstone.

Butler University, Lacy School of Business, Indianapolis, IN 46208-3485. Offers finance (MBA); international business (MBA); leadership (MBA); marketing (MBA); professional accounting (MP Acc). *Accreditation:* AACSB. *Program availability:* Part-time. *Faculty:* 18 full-time (6 women), 14 part-time/adjunct (5 women). *Students:* 31 full-time (11 women), 133 part-time (40 women); includes 10 minority (2 Black or African American, non-Hispanic/Latino; 2 Asian, non-Hispanic/Latino; 6 Hispanic/Latino), 2 international. Average age 31. 122 applicants, 68% accepted, 42 enrolled. In 2016, 89 master's awarded. *Entrance requirements:* For master's, GMAT, minimum AACSB index of 950, personal statement, two letters of recommendation, official transcripts, current resume. Additional exam requirements/recommendations for international students: Required—TOEFL (minimum score 550 paper-based; 79 iBT), IELTS (minimum score 6), Michigan English Language Assessment Battery (minimum score of 80). *Application deadline:* For fall admission, 8/1 for domestic and international students; for spring admission, 12/1 for domestic and international students; for summer admission, 4/1 for domestic and international students. Applications are processed on a rolling basis. Application fee: $0. Electronic applications accepted. *Expenses:* $790 per credit hour. *Financial support:* In 2016–17, 15 students received support. Scholarships/grants, tuition waivers (full and partial), and unspecified assistantships available. Financial award application deadline: 7/15; financial award applicants required to submit FAFSA. *Faculty research:* Higher education and pedagogy; ecotourism; healthcare issues and marketing public policy; domestic public policy, international finance and banking, international and management entrepreneurship, organizational management. *Unit head:* Dr. Stephen Standifird, Dean. *Application contact:* Diane Dubord, Graduate Student Service Specialist, 317-940-8107, Fax: 317-940-8250, E-mail: ddubord@butler.edu.
Website: https://www.butler.edu/lacyschool

California Coast University, School of Administration and Management, Santa Ana, CA 92701. Offers business marketing (MBA); health care management (MBA); human resource management (MBA); management (MBA, MS). *Program availability:* Online learning. Electronic applications accepted.

California Intercontinental University, School of Business, Irvine, CA 92614. Offers banking and finance (MBA); entrepreneurship and business management (DBA); global business leadership (DBA); international management and marketing (MBA); organizational management and human resource management (MBA).

California Lutheran University, Graduate Studies, School of Management, Thousand Oaks, CA 91360-2787. Offers business (IMBA); computer science (MS); econometrics (MBA); economics (MS); entrepreneurship (MBA, Certificate); finance (MBA, Certificate); financial planning (MBA, Certificate); information systems and technology (MS); information technology management (MBA, Certificate); international business (MBA, Certificate); management and organization behavior (MBA); management and organizational behavior (Certificate); marketing (MBA, Certificate); microeconomics (MBA); nonprofit and social enterprise (MBA); public policy and administration (MPPA). *Program availability:* Part-time, evening/weekend, 100% online, blended/hybrid learning. *Faculty:* 25 full-time (10 women), 36 part-time/adjunct (12 women). *Students:* 427 full-time (172 women), 189 part-time (87 women); includes 120 minority (14 Black or African American, non-Hispanic/Latino; 2 American Indian or Alaska Native, non-Hispanic/Latino; 19 Asian, non-Hispanic/Latino; 37 Hispanic/Latino; 48 Two or more races, non-Hispanic/Latino), 338 international. Average age 30. 591 applicants, 64% accepted, 131 enrolled. In 2016, 305 master's awarded. *Entrance requirements:* For master's, GMAT, interview, minimum GPA of 3.0. *Application deadline:* Applications are processed on a

rolling basis. Application fee: $50. Electronic applications accepted. *Expenses:* Contact institution. *Unit head:* Dr. Gerhard Apfelthaler, Dean, 805-493-3360. *Application contact:* 805-493-3325, Fax: 805-493-3861, E-mail: clugrad@callutheran.edu.
Website: http://www.callutheran.edu/management/

California State University, East Bay, Office of Graduate Studies, College of Business and Economics, MBA Program, Option in Marketing Management, Hayward, CA 94542-3000. Offers marketing (MBA). *Program availability:* Part-time, evening/weekend. *Students:* 5 full-time (4 women), 13 part-time (9 women); includes 8 minority (1 Black or African American, non-Hispanic/Latino; 4 Asian, non-Hispanic/Latino; 3 Hispanic/Latino), 6 international. Average age 31. 40 applicants, 30% accepted, 3 enrolled. In 2016, 3 master's awarded. *Degree requirements:* For master's, comprehensive exam or thesis. *Entrance requirements:* For master's, GMAT, minimum GPA of 2.75. Additional exam requirements/recommendations for international students: Required—TOEFL (minimum score 550 paper-based). *Application deadline:* For fall admission, 6/30 for domestic and international students. Application fee: $55. Electronic applications accepted. *Financial support:* Fellowships, teaching assistantships, career-related internships or fieldwork, Federal Work-Study, institutionally sponsored loans, and scholarships/grants available. Support available to part-time students. Financial award application deadline: 3/1; financial award applicants required to submit FAFSA. *Unit head:* Dr. Lan Wu, Program Advisor, 510-885-3290, E-mail: lan.wu@csueastbay.edu. *Application contact:* Dr. Donna Wiley, Interim Associate Vice President for Academic Programs and Graduate Studies, 510-885-3716, Fax: 510-885-4777, E-mail: donna.wiley@csueastbay.edu.
Website: http://www20.csueastbay.edu/cbe/mba-options/marketing-option.html

California State University, Fullerton, Graduate Studies, College of Business and Economics, Department of Marketing, Fullerton, CA 92834-9480. Offers MBA. *Program availability:* Part-time. *Degree requirements:* For master's, project or thesis. *Entrance requirements:* For master's, GMAT, minimum AACSB index of 950. Application fee: $55. *Expenses:* Tuition, state resident: full-time $3369; part-time $1953 per unit. Tuition, nonresident: full-time $3915; part-time $2499 per unit. Tuition and fees vary according to course load, degree level and program. *Financial support:* Career-related internships or fieldwork, Federal Work-Study, institutionally sponsored loans, and scholarships/grants available. Support available to part-time students. Financial award application deadline: 3/1; financial award applicants required to submit FAFSA. *Unit head:* Dr. Irene Lange, Chair, 657-278-2223. *Application contact:* Admissions/Applications, 657-278-2371.

California State University, Los Angeles, Graduate Studies, College of Business and Economics, Department of Marketing, Los Angeles, CA 90032-8530. Offers international business (MBA, MS). *Program availability:* Part-time, evening/weekend. *Degree requirements:* For master's, comprehensive exam (MBA), thesis (MS). *Entrance requirements:* For master's, GMAT, minimum GPA of 2.5 during previous 2 years of course work. Additional exam requirements/recommendations for international students: Required—TOEFL (minimum score 550 paper-based). Electronic applications accepted.

California State University, San Bernardino, Graduate Studies, College of Arts and Letters, Program in Communication Studies, San Bernardino, CA 92407. Offers communication studies (MA); integrated marketing communication (MA). *Faculty:* 5 full-time (3 women). *Students:* 10 full-time (8 women), 27 part-time (20 women); includes 19 minority (4 Black or African American, non-Hispanic/Latino; 2 Asian, non-Hispanic/Latino; 12 Hispanic/Latino; 1 Two or more races, non-Hispanic/Latino), 3 international. 35 applicants, 60% accepted, 17 enrolled. In 2016, 5 master's awarded. *Degree requirements:* For master's, comprehensive exam. *Entrance requirements:* Additional exam requirements/recommendations for international students: Required—TOEFL. *Application deadline:* For fall admission, 5/15 for domestic students. Application fee: $55. *Expenses:* Tuition, state resident: full-time $7843; part-time $5011.20 per year. Tuition and fees vary according to course load, degree level, program and reciprocity agreements. *Unit head:* Dr. Michael Salvador, Chair, 909-537-5820, Fax: 909-537-7009, E-mail: salvador@csusb.edu. *Application contact:* Dr. Francisca Beer, Dean of Graduate Studies, 909-537-5058, Fax: 909-537-7034, E-mail: fbeer@csusb.edu.

Capella University, School of Business and Technology, Doctoral Programs in Business, Minneapolis, MN 55402. Offers accounting (DBA, PhD); business intelligence (DBA); finance (DBA, PhD); general business management (PhD); human resource management (DBA, PhD); leadership (DBA, PhD); management education (PhD); marketing (DBA, PhD); project management (DBA, PhD); strategy and innovation (DBA, PhD). *Accreditation:* ACBSP.

Capella University, School of Business and Technology, Master's Programs in Business, Minneapolis, MN 55402. Offers accounting (MBA); business analysis (MS); business intelligence (MBA); entrepreneurship (MBA); finance (MBA); general business administration (MBA); general human resource management (MS); general leadership (MS); health care management (MBA); human resource management (MBA); marketing (MBA); project management (MBA, MS). *Accreditation:* ACBSP.

Carnegie Mellon University, Tepper School of Business, Program in Marketing, Pittsburgh, PA 15213-3891. Offers PhD. *Degree requirements:* For doctorate, thesis/dissertation.

Central Michigan University, Central Michigan University Global Campus, Program in Business Administration, Mount Pleasant, MI 48859. Offers enterprise resource planning (MBA, Certificate); human resource management (MBA); logistics management (MBA, Certificate); marketing (MBA); value-driven organization (MBA). *Program availability:* Part-time, evening/weekend. *Faculty:* 17 full-time (7 women), 3 part-time/adjunct (0 women). *Students:* 189 (82 women); includes 29 minority (17 Black or African American, non-Hispanic/Latino; 2 American Indian or Alaska Native, non-Hispanic/Latino; 3 Asian, non-Hispanic/Latino; 1 Hispanic/Latino; 6 Two or more races, non-Hispanic/Latino). Average age 32. In 2016, 25 master's awarded. *Entrance requirements:* For master's, GMAT. *Financial support:* Scholarships/grants available. Support available to part-time students. *Unit head:* Dr. Debasish Chakraborty, 989-774-3678, E-mail: chakt1d@cmich.edu. *Application contact:* Global Campus Student Services Call Center, 877-268-4636, E-mail: cmuglobal@cmich.edu.

Central Michigan University, College of Graduate Studies, College of Business Administration, MBA Program, Mount Pleasant, MI 48859. Offers accounting (MBA); business economics (MBA); consulting (MBA); finance (MBA); general business (MBA); human resource management (MBA); information systems (MBA); international business (MBA); logistics management (MBA); marketing (MBA); value-driven organization (MBA). *Program availability:* Part-time, evening/weekend, online learning. Electronic applications accepted. *Faculty research:* Accounting, consulting, international business, marketing, information systems.

City College of the City University of New York, Graduate School, Division of Humanities and the Arts, Department of Media and Communication Arts, Program in Branding and Integrated Communications, New York, NY 10031. Offers MPS. *Entrance requirements:* Additional exam requirements/recommendations for international students: Required—TOEFL (minimum score 90 iBT). Tuition and fees vary according to course load, degree level and program.

City University of Seattle, Graduate Division, School of Management, Seattle, WA 98121. Offers accounting (Certificate); change leadership (MBA, Certificate); computer systems (MS); finance (Certificate); financial management (MBA); general management (MBA); general management-Europe (MBA); global marketing (MBA); human resources management (Certificate); individualized study (MBA); information security (MS); information systems (MBA); leadership (MA); marketing (MBA, Certificate); project management (MBA, MS, Certificate); sustainable business (Certificate); technology management (MBA, Certificate). *Program availability:* Part-time, evening/weekend, online learning. *Degree requirements:* For master's, comprehensive exam (for some programs), thesis (for some programs). *Entrance requirements:* For master's, baccalaureate degree or equivalent from an accredited or otherwise recognized institution. Additional exam requirements/recommendations for international students: Required—TOEFL (minimum score 567 paper-based; 87 iBT); Recommended—IELTS. Electronic applications accepted.

Clark University, Graduate School, Graduate School of Management, Business Administration Program, Worcester, MA 01610-1477. Offers accounting (MBA); finance (MBA); information management and business analytics (MBA); management (MBA); marketing (MBA); social change (MBA); sustainability (MBA). *Accreditation:* AACSB. *Program availability:* Part-time, evening/weekend. *Students:* 91 full-time (48 women), 101 part-time (45 women); includes 22 minority (8 Black or African American, non-Hispanic/Latino; 4 Asian, non-Hispanic/Latino; 9 Hispanic/Latino; 1 Native Hawaiian or other Pacific Islander, non-Hispanic/Latino), 45 international. Average age 31. 225 applicants, 58% accepted, 78 enrolled. In 2016, 113 master's awarded. *Degree requirements:* For master's, thesis optional. *Application deadline:* For fall admission, 6/1 priority date for domestic students; for spring admission, 12/1 priority date for domestic students. Applications are processed on a rolling basis. Application fee: $75. Electronic applications accepted. *Expenses: Tuition:* Full-time $44,050. *Required fees:* $80. Tuition and fees vary according to course load and program. *Financial support:* In 2016–17, research assistantships with partial tuition reimbursements (averaging $4,800 per year), teaching assistantships with partial tuition reimbursements (averaging $4,800 per year) were awarded; fellowships, career-related internships or fieldwork, Federal Work-Study, institutionally sponsored loans, and tuition waivers (partial) also available. Support available to part-time students. Financial award application deadline: 5/31. *Faculty research:* Marketing, accounting, human resource management, management information systems, business finance. *Unit head:* Dr. Catherine Usoff, Dean, 508-793-7543, Fax: 508-793-8822. *Application contact:* Ethan Bernstein, Director of Graduate Admissions, 508-793-7543, E-mail: graduateadmissions@clarku.edu.
Website: http://www.clarku.edu/programs/masters-business-administration

Cleveland State University, College of Graduate Studies, Monte Ahuja College of Business, Doctor of Business Administration Program, Cleveland, OH 44115. Offers information systems (DBA); marketing (DBA). *Accreditation:* AACSB. *Program availability:* Part-time, evening/weekend. *Faculty:* 50 full-time (11 women). *Students:* 8 full-time (5 women), 13 part-time (3 women); includes 4 minority (3 Black or African American, non-Hispanic/Latino; 1 Asian, non-Hispanic/Latino), 3 international. Average age 40. In 2016, 2 doctorates awarded. *Degree requirements:* For doctorate, comprehensive exam, thesis/dissertation, oral dissertation defense. *Entrance requirements:* For doctorate, GMAT, MBA or equivalent. Additional exam requirements/recommendations for international students: Required—TOEFL (minimum score 550 paper-based; 78 iBT). *Application deadline:* For fall admission, 2/1 for domestic and international students. Application fee: $40. Electronic applications accepted. *Expenses:* Tuition, state resident: full-time $9565. Tuition, nonresident: full-time $17,980. Tuition and fees vary according to program. *Financial support:* In 2016–17, 5 research assistantships with full tuition reimbursements (averaging $12,700 per year), 4 teaching assistantships with full tuition reimbursements (averaging $12,700 per year) were awarded; tuition waivers (full) and unspecified assistantships also available. *Faculty research:* Supply chain management, international business, strategic management, risk analysis, consumer behavior. *Unit head:* Dr. Raj Shekhar G. Javalgi, Director, 216-687-3786, Fax: 216-687-9354, E-mail: r.javalgi@csuohio.edu. *Application contact:* Melinda J. Arnold, Administrative Secretary, 216-687-6952, Fax: 216-687-9257, E-mail: m.arnold@csuohio.edu.
Website: http://www.csuohio.edu/business/academics/mbajuris-doctor

Colorado Technical University Aurora, Programs in Business Administration and Management, Aurora, CO 80014. Offers accounting (MBA); business administration (MBA); business administration and management (EMBA); finance (MBA); human resource management (MBA); marketing (MBA); mediation and dispute resolution (MBA); operations management (MBA); project management (MBA); technology management (MBA). *Program availability:* Part-time, evening/weekend. *Degree requirements:* For master's, thesis or alternative. *Entrance requirements:* For master's, minimum undergraduate GPA of 3.0, resume.

Colorado Technical University Colorado Springs, Graduate Studies, Program in Management, Colorado Springs, CO 80907. Offers accounting (MBA, MSA); business administration (MBA); finance (MBA); human resources management (MBA); logistics/supply chain management (MBA); management (DM); marketing (MBA); mediation and dispute resolution (MBA); operations management (MBA); project management (MBA); technology management (MBA). *Accreditation:* ACBSP. *Program availability:* Part-time, evening/weekend, online learning. *Degree requirements:* For master's, thesis or alternative; for doctorate, thesis/dissertation. *Entrance requirements:* For doctorate, minimum graduate GPA of 3.0, 5 years of related work experience. *Faculty research:* Sexual harassment, performance evaluation, critical thinking.

Columbia Southern University, MBA Program, Orange Beach, AL 36561. Offers finance (MBA); health care management (MBA); human resource management (MBA); marketing (MBA); project management (MBA); public administration (MBA). *Program availability:* Part-time, evening/weekend, online learning. *Entrance requirements:* For master's, bachelor's degree from accredited/approved institution. Additional exam requirements/recommendations for international students: Required—TOEFL. Electronic applications accepted.

Columbia University, Graduate School of Business, Doctoral Program in Business, New York, NY 10027. Offers business (PhD), including accounting, decision, risk, and operations, finance and economics, management, marketing. *Accreditation:* AACSB. *Degree requirements:* For doctorate, comprehensive exam, thesis/dissertation, major field exam, research paper, thesis proposal. *Entrance requirements:* For doctorate, GMAT or GRE (finance), 2 letters of reference, resume. Additional exam requirements/recommendations for international students: Required—TOEFL. Electronic applications accepted. *Expenses:* Contact institution. *Faculty research:* Human decision making and behavioral research; real estate market and mortgage defaults; financial crisis and corporate governance; international business; security analysis and accounting.

Columbia University, Graduate School of Business, MBA Program, New York, NY 10027. Offers accounting (MBA); decision, risk, and operations (MBA); entrepreneurship (MBA); finance and economics (MBA); healthcare and pharmaceutical management (MBA); human resource management (MBA); international business (MBA); leadership and ethics (MBA); management (MBA); marketing (MBA); media (MBA); private equity (MBA); real estate (MBA); social enterprise (MBA); value investing (MBA); DDS/MBA; JD/MBA; MBA/MIA; MBA/MPH; MBA/MS; MD/MBA. *Entrance requirements:* For master's, GMAT, 2 letters of recommendation. Additional exam requirements/recommendations for international students: Required—TOEFL. Electronic applications accepted. *Expenses:* Contact institution. *Faculty research:* Human decision making and behavioral research; real estate market and mortgage defaults; financial crisis and corporate governance; international business; security analysis and accounting.

Concordia University, School of Graduate Studies, John Molson School of Business, Montreal, QC H3H 0A1, Canada. Offers administration (M Sc), including finance, management, marketing; business administration (MBA, PhD, Certificate, Diploma); executive business administration (EMBA); supply chain management (MSCM). PhD program offered jointly with HEC Montreal, McGill University, and Université du Québec à Montréal. *Program availability:* Part-time, evening/weekend. *Degree requirements:* For master's, one foreign language, thesis (for some programs), research project; for doctorate, one foreign language, thesis/dissertation; for other advanced degree, one foreign language. *Entrance requirements:* For master's, GMAT, minimum 2 years of work experience (for MBA); letters of recommendation, bachelor's degree from recognized university with minimum GPA of 3.0, curriculum vitae; for doctorate, GMAT (minimum score of 600), official transcripts, curriculum vitae, 3 letters of reference, statement of purpose; for other advanced degree, minimum GPA of 2.7, 2 letters of reference, statement of purpose, resume. Additional exam requirements/recommendations for international students: Required—TOEFL (minimum score 90 iBT), IELTS (minimum score 7). Electronic applications accepted. *Expenses:* Contact institution. *Faculty research:* General business, capital markets, international business.

Concordia University Wisconsin, Graduate Programs, School of Business Administration, MBA Program, Mequon, WI 53097-2402. Offers finance (MBA); health care administration (MBA); human resource management (MBA); international business (MBA); international business-bilingual English/Chinese (MBA); management (MBA); management information systems (MBA); managerial communications (MBA); marketing (MBA); public administration (MBA); risk management (MBA). *Program availability:* Online learning. *Degree requirements:* For master's, comprehensive exam, thesis or alternative. *Entrance requirements:* Additional exam requirements/recommendations for international students: Required—TOEFL. *Application deadline:* For fall admission, 8/1 priority date for domestic students; for spring admission, 1/15 for domestic students. Applications are processed on a rolling basis. Application fee: $50. *Expenses:* Contact institution. *Financial support:* Application deadline: 8/1. *Unit head:* Dr. David Borst, Director, 262-243-4298, Fax: 262-243-4428, E-mail: david.borst@cuw.edu. *Application contact:* Mary Eberhardt, Graduate Admissions, 262-243-4551, Fax: 262-243-4428, E-mail: mary.eberhardt@cuw.edu.

Cornell University, Graduate School, Graduate Field of Management, Ithaca, NY 14853. Offers accounting (PhD); finance (PhD); marketing (PhD); organizational behavior (PhD); production and operations management (PhD). *Accreditation:* AACSB. *Degree requirements:* For doctorate, comprehensive exam, thesis/dissertation. *Entrance requirements:* For doctorate, GMAT or GRE General Test. Additional exam requirements/recommendations for international students: Required—TOEFL (minimum score 600 paper-based; 77 iBT). Electronic applications accepted. *Expenses:* Contact institution. *Faculty research:* Operations and manufacturing.

Daemen College, Department of Accounting/Information Systems, Amherst, NY 14226-3592. Offers global business (MS), including accounting, global business, management information systems, marketing. *Program availability:* Part-time, evening/weekend. *Degree requirements:* For master's, minimum GPA of 3.0. *Entrance requirements:* For master's, GMAT if undergraduate GPA is less than 3.0, 2 letters of recommendation; goal statement; transcripts; demonstration of satisfactory oral and written English. Additional exam requirements/recommendations for international students: Required—TOEFL (minimum score 500 paper-based; 63 iBT), IELTS (minimum score 5.5). Electronic applications accepted. *Faculty research:* Internationalization of small business, cultural influences on business practices, international human resource practices.

Dallas Baptist University, College of Business, Business Administration Program, Dallas, TX 75211-9299. Offers accounting (MBA); business communication (MBA); conflict resolution management (MBA); entrepreneurship (MBA); finance (MBA); health care management (MBA); international business (MBA); leading the non-profit organization (MBA); management (MBA); management information systems (MBA); marketing (MBA); project management (MBA); technology and engineering management (MBA). *Accreditation:* ACBSP. *Program availability:* Part-time, evening/weekend, 100% online, blended/hybrid learning. *Application deadline:* Applications are processed on a rolling basis. Application fee: $25. Electronic applications accepted. Application fee is waived when completed online. *Expenses: Tuition:* Full-time $15,408; part-time $856 per credit hour. *Required fees:* $400 per semester. Tuition and fees vary according to course load and degree level. *Unit head:* Dr. Sandra Reid, Chair of Graduate Business Programs, 214-333-5280, E-mail: sandra@dbu.edu. *Application contact:* Bobby Soto, Director of Admissions, 214-333-5242, E-mail: graduate@dbu.edu.
Website: http://www3.dbu.edu/graduate/mba.asp

Dallas Baptist University, Professional Development Program, Dallas, TX 75211-9299. Offers accounting (MA); church leadership (MA); communication (MA); counseling (MA); criminal justice (MA); English as a second language (MA); finance (MA); higher education (MA); leadership studies (MA); management (MA); management information systems (MA); marketing (MA); missions (MA); professional life coaching (MA); training and development (MA). *Program availability:* Part-time, evening/weekend, 100% online, blended/hybrid learning. *Application deadline:* Applications are processed on a rolling basis. Application fee: $25. Electronic applications accepted. Application fee is waived when completed online. *Expenses: Tuition:* Full-time $15,408; part-time $856 per credit hour. *Required fees:* $400 per semester. Tuition and fees vary according to course load and degree level. *Unit head:* Jared Ingram, Director, 214-333-5584, E-mail: jaredi@dbu.edu. *Application contact:* Bobby Soto, Director of Admissions, 214-333-5242, E-mail: graduate@dbu.edu.
Website: http://www3.dbu.edu/graduate/mapd.asp

DePaul University, Kellstadt Graduate School of Business, Chicago, IL 60604. Offers accountancy (M Acc, MS, MSA); applied economics (MBA); banking (MBA); behavioral finance (MBA); brand and product management (MBA); business development (MBA); business information technology (MS); business strategy and decision-making (MBA); computational finance (MS); consumer insights (MBA); corporate finance (MBA); economic policy analysis (MS); entrepreneurship (MBA, MS); finance (MBA, MS); financial analysis (MBA); general business (MBA); health sector management (MBA); hospitality leadership (MBA); hospitality leadership and operational performance (MS); human resource management (MBA); human resources (MS); investment management (MBA); leadership and change management (MBA); management accounting (MBA); marketing (MBA, MS); marketing analysis (MS); marketing strategy and planning (MBA); operations management (MBA); organizational diversity (MBA); real estate (MS); real estate finance and investment (MBA); revenue management (MBA); sports management (MBA); strategic global marketing (MBA); strategy, execution and valuation (MBA); sustainable management (MBA, MS); taxation (MS); wealth management (MS); JD/MBA. *Accreditation:* AACSB. *Program availability:* Part-time, evening/weekend, online learning. *Entrance requirements:* For master's, GMAT, 2 letters of recommendation, resume, essay, official transcripts. Additional exam requirements/recommendations for international students: Required—TOEFL (minimum score 550 paper-based; 80 iBT). Electronic applications accepted. *Expenses:* Contact institution.

DEREE - The American College of Greece, Graduate Programs, Athens, Greece. Offers applied psychology (MS); communication (MA); leadership (MS); marketing (MS).

DeSales University, Division of Business, Center Valley, PA 18034-9568. Offers accounting (MBA); computer information systems (MBA); finance (MBA); health care systems management (MBA); human resources management (MBA); management (MBA); marketing (MBA); project management (MBA); self-design (MBA); supply chain management (MBA); DNP/MBA; MSN/MBA. *Accreditation:* ACBSP. *Program availability:* Part-time, evening/weekend, 100% online, blended/hybrid learning. *Faculty:* 12 full-time (4 women), 29 part-time/adjunct (5 women). *Students:* 73 full-time (38 women), 323 part-time (163 women); includes 59 minority (16 Black or African American, non-Hispanic/Latino; 23 Asian, non-Hispanic/Latino; 16 Hispanic/Latino; 4 Two or more races, non-Hispanic/Latino). Average age 37. 157 applicants, 87% accepted, 128 enrolled. In 2016, 115 master's awarded. *Entrance requirements:* For master's, GMAT (waived if undergraduate GPA is 3.0 or better), minimum GPA of 3.0 in undergraduate work, literacy in basic software, background or interest in the field of study, personal statement, 2 years of work experience. Additional exam requirements/recommendations for international students: Required—TOEFL. *Application deadline:* Applications are processed on a rolling basis. Application fee: $50. Electronic applications accepted. *Expenses:* Contact institution. *Financial support:* Applicants required to submit FAFSA. *Faculty research:* Quality improvement, executive development, productivity, cross-cultural managerial differences, leadership. *Unit head:* Dr. David M. Gilfoil, Director, MBA Program, 610-282-1100 Ext. 1828, Fax: 610-282-2869, E-mail: david.gilfoil@desales.edu. *Application contact:* Julia Ferraro, Director of Graduate Admissions, 610-282-1100 Ext. 1768, E-mail: gradadmissions@desales.edu.

Drexel University, LeBow College of Business, Program in Business Administration, Philadelphia, PA 19104-2875. Offers business administration (MBA, PhD, APC), including accounting (MBA, PhD), decision sciences (PhD), economics (MBA, PhD), finance (MBA, PhD), legal studies (MBA), management (MBA), marketing (MBA, PhD), organizational sciences (PhD), quantitative methods (MBA), strategic management (PhD). *Accreditation:* AACSB. *Program availability:* Part-time, evening/weekend, online learning. *Faculty:* 88 full-time (19 women), 11 part-time/adjunct (2 women). *Students:* 153 full-time (70 women), 388 part-time (168 women); includes 107 minority (31 Black or African American, non-Hispanic/Latino; 1 American Indian or Alaska Native, non-Hispanic/Latino; 48 Asian, non-Hispanic/Latino; 16 Hispanic/Latino; 11 Two or more races, non-Hispanic/Latino), 95 international. Average age 33. In 2016, 174 master's, 8 doctorates, 1 other advanced degree awarded. Terminal master's awarded for partial completion of doctoral program. *Entrance requirements:* For master's, GMAT, minimum GPA of 2.75; for doctorate, GMAT. Additional exam requirements/recommendations for international students: Required—TOEFL. *Application deadline:* For fall admission, 8/21 for domestic students; for spring admission, 3/5 for domestic students. Applications are processed on a rolling basis. Application fee: $50. Electronic applications accepted. *Expenses: Tuition:* Full-time $32,184; part-time $1192 per credit hour. *Required fees:* $280. Tuition and fees vary according to campus/location and program. *Financial support:* Research assistantships, teaching assistantships, career-related internships or fieldwork, and unspecified assistantships available. Financial award application deadline: 2/1. *Faculty research:* Decision support systems, individual and group behavior, operations research, techniques and strategy. *Unit head:* Dr. Thomas Wieckowski, Director of Master's Programs in Business, 215-895-1791, Fax: 215-895-1012. *Application contact:* Director of Graduate Admissions, 215-895-6700, Fax: 215-895-5939, E-mail: enroll@drexel.edu.

Duke University, The Fuqua School of Business, The Duke MBA-Cross Continent Program, Durham, NC 27708-0586. Offers business administration (MBA); energy and environment (MBA); entrepreneurship and innovation (MBA); finance (MBA); health sector management (Certificate); marketing (MBA); strategy (MBA). *Faculty:* 88 full-time (19 women), 50 part-time/adjunct (9 women). *Students:* 214 full-time (74 women); includes 58 minority (13 Black or African American, non-Hispanic/Latino; 35 Asian, non-Hispanic/Latino; 10 Hispanic/Latino), 35 international. Average age 30. In 2016, 105 master's awarded. *Entrance requirements:* For master's, GMAT or GRE, transcripts, essays, resume, recommendation letters, letter of company support, interview. *Application deadline:* For fall admission, 10/12 priority date for domestic and international students; for winter admission, 2/7 priority date for domestic and international students; for spring admission, 5/3 priority date for domestic and international students; for summer admission, 5/31 for domestic and international students. Applications are processed on a rolling basis. Application fee: $225. Electronic applications accepted. *Expenses:* Contact institution. *Financial support:* In 2016–17, 49 students received support. Institutionally sponsored loans and scholarships/grants available. Financial award applicants required to submit FAFSA. *Unit head:* Mohan Venkatachalam, Senior Associate Dean, Executive Programs, 919-660-7859, E-mail: mohan.venkatachalam@duke.edu. *Application contact:* Sharon Thompson, Assistant Dean, Office of Admissions, 919-660-7705, Fax: 919-681-8026, E-mail: admissions-info@fuqua.duke.edu.
Website: http://www.fuqua.duke.edu/programs/duke_mba/cross_continent/

Duke University, The Fuqua School of Business, The Duke MBA-Daytime Program, Durham, NC 27708-0586. Offers academic excellence in finance (Certificate); business administration (MBA); decision sciences (MBA); energy and environment (MBA); energy finance (MBA); entrepreneurship and innovation (MBA); finance (MBA); financial analysis (MBA); health sector management (Certificate); leadership and ethics (MBA); management (MBA); marketing (MBA); operations management (MBA); social entrepreneurship (MBA); strategy (MBA). *Faculty:* 88 full-time (19 women), 50 part-time/adjunct (9 women). *Students:* 897 full-time (310 women); includes 174 minority (39 Black or African American, non-Hispanic/Latino; 3 American Indian or Alaska Native, non-Hispanic/Latino; 75 Asian, non-Hispanic/Latino; 51 Hispanic/Latino; 1 Native Hawaiian or other Pacific Islander, non-Hispanic/Latino; 5 Two or more races, non-Hispanic/Latino), 343 international. Average age 28. In 2016, 440 master's awarded. *Entrance requirements:* For master's, GMAT or GRE, transcripts, essays, resume, recommendation letters, interview. *Application deadline:* For fall admission, 9/13 for domestic and international students; for winter admission, 10/13 for domestic and international students; for spring admission, 1/4 for domestic and international students; for summer admission, 3/20 for domestic and international students. Application fee: $225. Electronic applications accepted. *Expenses:* $66,717 (first-year tuition and fees). *Financial support:* In 2016–17, 415 students received support. Institutionally sponsored loans and scholarships/grants available. Financial award applicants required to submit FAFSA. *Unit head:* Russ Morgan, Senior Associate Dean for Full-time Programs, 919-660-2931, Fax: 919-684-8742, E-mail: ruskin.morgan@duke.edu. *Application contact:* Sharon Thompson, Assistant Dean, Office of Admissions, 919-660-7705, Fax: 919-681-8026, E-mail: admissions-info@fuqua.duke.edu.
Website: http://www.fuqua.duke.edu/daytime-mba/

Duke University, The Fuqua School of Business, The Duke MBA-Global Executive Program, Durham, NC 27708-0586. Offers business administration (MBA); energy and environment (MBA); entrepreneurship and innovation (MBA); finance (MBA); health sector management (Certificate); marketing (MBA); strategy (MBA). *Faculty:* 88 full-time

(19 women), 50 part-time/adjunct (9 women). *Students:* 48 full-time (14 women); includes 18 minority (3 Black or African American, non-Hispanic/Latino; 11 Asian, non-Hispanic/Latino; 4 Hispanic/Latino), 10 international. Average age 39. In 2016, 27 master's awarded. *Entrance requirements:* For master's, transcripts, essays, resume, recommendation letters, letter of company support, interview. *Application deadline:* For fall admission, 10/12 priority date for domestic and international students; for winter admission, 12/7 priority date for domestic and international students; for spring admission, 3/20 priority date for domestic and international students; for summer admission, 5/31 for domestic and international students. Applications are processed on a rolling basis. Application fee: $225. Electronic applications accepted. *Expenses:* Contact institution. *Financial support:* In 2016–17, 22 students received support. Institutionally sponsored loans and scholarships/grants available. Financial award applicants required to submit FAFSA. *Unit head:* Mohan Venkatachalam, Senior Associate Dean, Executive Programs, 919-660-7859, E-mail: mohan.venkatachalam@duke.edu. *Application contact:* Sharon Thompson, Assistant Dean, Office of Admissions, 919-660-7705, Fax: 919-681-8026, E-mail: admissions-info@fuqua.duke.edu.
Website: http://www.fuqua.duke.edu/programs/duke_mba/global-executive/

Duke University, The Fuqua School of Business, The Duke MBA-Weekend Executive Program, Durham, NC 27708-0586. Offers business administration (MBA); energy and environment (MBA); entrepreneurship and innovation (MBA); finance (MBA); health sector management (Certificate); marketing (MBA); strategy (MBA). *Faculty:* 88 full-time (19 women), 50 part-time/adjunct (9 women). *Students:* 190 full-time (43 women); includes 75 minority (11 Black or African American, non-Hispanic/Latino; 3 American Indian or Alaska Native, non-Hispanic/Latino; 48 Asian, non-Hispanic/Latino; 12 Hispanic/Latino; 1 Two or more races, non-Hispanic/Latino), 26 international. Average age 35. In 2016, 87 master's awarded. *Entrance requirements:* For master's, GMAT or GRE, transcripts, essays, resume, recommendation letters, letter of company support, interview. *Application deadline:* For fall admission, 8/30 priority date for domestic and international students; for winter admission, 10/12 priority date for domestic and international students; for spring admission, 2/7 priority date for domestic and international students; for summer admission, 3/20 for domestic and international students. Applications are processed on a rolling basis. Application fee: $225. Electronic applications accepted. *Expenses:* Contact institution. *Financial support:* In 2016–17, 33 students received support. Institutionally sponsored loans and scholarships/grants available. Financial award applicants required to submit FAFSA. *Unit head:* Mohan Venkatachalam, Senior Associate Dean, Executive Programs, 919-660-7859, E-mail: mohan.venkatachalam@duke.edu. *Application contact:* Sharon Thompson, Assistant Dean, Office of Admissions, 919-660-7705, Fax: 919-681-8026, E-mail: admissions-info@fuqua.duke.edu.
Website: http://www.fuqua.duke.edu/programs/duke_mba/weekend_executive/

Duke University, The Fuqua School of Business, Master of Quantitative Management Program, Durham, NC 27708-0586. Offers finance (MQM); forensics (MQM); marketing (MQM); strategy (MQM). *Entrance requirements:* For master's, GMAT/GRE, transcripts, essays, resume, recommendation letters. *Application deadline:* For fall admission, 9/21 for domestic and international students; for winter admission, 11/20 for domestic and international students; for spring admission, 2/16 for domestic and international students; for summer admission, 4/4 for domestic and international students. Application fee: $125. Electronic applications accepted. *Unit head:* Jeremy Petranka, Associate Dean, E-mail: jeremy.petranka@duke.edu. *Application contact:* Sharon Thompson, Assistant Dean, Office of Admissions, 919-660-7705, Fax: 919-681-8026, E-mail: admissions-info@fuqua.duke.edu.
Website: http://www.fuqua.duke.edu/master-quantitative-management/

Duke University, The Fuqua School of Business, PhD Program, Durham, NC 27708-0586. Offers accounting (PhD); decision sciences (PhD); finance (PhD); management and organizations (PhD); marketing (PhD); operations management (PhD); strategy (PhD). *Faculty:* 100 full-time (19 women). *Students:* 77 full-time (27 women); includes 9 minority (1 Black or African American, non-Hispanic/Latino; 7 Asian, non-Hispanic/Latino; 1 Hispanic/Latino), 46 international. 561 applicants, 7% accepted, 14 enrolled. In 2016, 15 doctorates awarded. *Degree requirements:* For doctorate, thesis/dissertation, major field requirement (exam or major paper, depending upon the area). *Entrance requirements:* For doctorate, GMAT or GRE, transcripts, essays, recommendation letters, statement of purpose. Additional exam requirements/recommendations for international students: Required—TOEFL (minimum score 577 paper-based; 90 iBT), IELTS (minimum score 7). *Application deadline:* For fall admission, 12/31 priority date for domestic and international students. Application fee: $85. Electronic applications accepted. *Expenses:* Contact institution. *Financial support:* In 2016–17, 77 students received support, including 70 fellowships with full tuition reimbursements available (averaging $28,200 per year), 63 research assistantships with full tuition reimbursements available (averaging $7,000 per year); institutionally sponsored loans, scholarships/grants, and tuition waivers (full) also available. Financial award applicants required to submit FAFSA. *Unit head:* William Boulding, Dean, 919-660-7822, Fax: 919-684-8742, E-mail: bb1@duke.edu. *Application contact:* Qi Chen, Director of Graduate Studies, 919-660-7753, Fax: 919-660-7971, E-mail: qc2@duke.edu.

Duquesne University, Palumbo-Donahue School of Business, Pittsburgh, PA 15282-0001. Offers accounting (M Acc); finance (MBA); information systems management (MSISM); management (MBA, MS); marketing (MBA); sports business (MS); sustainability (MBA); JD/MBA; MBA/M Acc; MBA/MA; MBA/MES; MBA/MHMS; MSISM/MBA; Pharm D/MBA. *Accreditation:* AACSB. *Program availability:* Part-time, evening/weekend, 100% online, minimal on-campus study. *Faculty:* 59 full-time (23 women), 25 part-time/adjunct (6 women). *Students:* 92 full-time (43 women), 176 part-time (71 women); includes 20 minority (9 Black or African American, non-Hispanic/Latino; 8 Asian, non-Hispanic/Latino; 2 Hispanic/Latino; 1 Two or more races, non-Hispanic/Latino), 35 international. Average age 28. 272 applicants, 86% accepted, 137 enrolled. In 2016, 137 master's awarded. *Entrance requirements:* For master's, GMAT or GRE, undergraduate transcripts, 2 letters of recommendation, current resume, personal statement. Additional exam requirements/recommendations for international students: Required—TOEFL (minimum score 577 paper-based; 90 iBT), IELTS (minimum score 7). *Application deadline:* For fall admission, 7/1 priority date for domestic and international students; for spring admission, 12/1 for domestic and international students; for summer admission, 4/1 for domestic and international students. Applications are processed on a rolling basis. Application fee: $0. Electronic applications accepted. *Expenses:* Contact institution. *Financial support:* In 2016–17, 211 students received support, including 12 fellowships with partial tuition reimbursements available (averaging $14,200 per year), 20 research assistantships with partial tuition reimbursements available (averaging $22,212 per year); career-related internships or fieldwork, scholarships/grants, and unspecified assistantships also available. Support available to part-time students. Financial award application deadline: 7/1; financial award applicants required to submit FAFSA. *Faculty research:* Investment management, business ethics, technology management, supply chain management, entrepreneurship. *Unit head:* Dr. Karen Donovan, Associate Dean of Graduate Programs and Executive Education, 412-396-6276, Fax: 412-396-1726, E-mail: donovan6@duq.edu. *Application contact:* Jeff Jewett, Director of Admissions and Enrollment Management, 412-396-6244, Fax: 412-396-1726, E-mail: decrostam@duq.edu.
Website: http://www.duq.edu/business/grad

Eastern Michigan University, Graduate School, Academic and Student Affairs Division, Ypsilanti, MI 48197. Offers individualized studies (MA, MS); integrated marketing communications (MS). *Students:* 2 full-time (both women), 50 part-time (33 women); includes 8 minority (3 Black or African American, non-Hispanic/Latino; 4 Asian, non-Hispanic/Latino; 1 Two or more races, non-Hispanic/Latino), 1 international. 84 applicants, 83% accepted, 31 enrolled. *Entrance requirements:* Additional exam requirements/recommendations for international students: Required—TOEFL. Application fee: $45. *Unit head:* Dr. Wade Tornquist, Interim Dean, 734-487-0042, Fax: 734-487-0050, E-mail: wade.tornquist@emich.edu. *Application contact:* Graduate Admissions, 734-487-2400, Fax: 734-487-6559, E-mail: graduate.admissions@emich.edu.

Eastern Michigan University, Graduate School, College of Business, Department of Marketing, Program in Integrated Marketing Communications, Ypsilanti, MI 48197. Offers MS, Postbaccalaureate Certificate. *Students:* 15 full-time (11 women), 40 part-time (33 women); includes 14 minority (10 Black or African American, non-Hispanic/Latino; 4 Two or more races, non-Hispanic/Latino). Average age 32. 29 applicants, 72% accepted, 15 enrolled. In 2016, 23 master's, 1 other advanced degree awarded. Application fee: $45. *Application contact:* K. Michelle Henry, Director, Graduate Business Programs, 734-487-4444, Fax: 734-478-1316, E-mail: cob.graduate@emich.edu.

Eastern Michigan University, Graduate School, College of Business, Programs in Business Administration, Ypsilanti, MI 48197. Offers business administration (MBA, Graduate Certificate); computer information systems (Graduate Certificate); e-business (MBA, Graduate Certificate); enterprise business intelligence (MBA); entrepreneurship (MBA, Graduate Certificate); finance (MBA, Graduate Certificate); human resources (MBA); human resources management (Graduate Certificate); information systems (MBA); internal auditing (MBA); international business (MBA, Graduate Certificate); marketing management (Graduate Certificate); nonprofit management (MBA); organizational development (Graduate Certificate); supply chain management (MBA, Graduate Certificate). *Accreditation:* AACSB. *Program availability:* Part-time, online learning. *Students:* 63 full-time (36 women), 320 part-time (186 women); includes 131 minority (76 Black or African American, non-Hispanic/Latino; 5 American Indian or Alaska Native, non-Hispanic/Latino; 16 Asian, non-Hispanic/Latino; 19 Hispanic/Latino; 15 Two or more races, non-Hispanic/Latino), 23 international. Average age 32. 305 applicants, 70% accepted, 124 enrolled. In 2016, 78 master's, 57 other advanced degrees awarded. *Entrance requirements:* For master's, GMAT (minimum score 450), minimum cumulative undergraduate GPA of 2.75. Additional exam requirements/recommendations for international students: Required—TOEFL. *Application deadline:* For fall admission, 5/15 priority date for domestic students, 2/15 priority date for international students; for winter admission, 10/15 priority date for domestic students, 9/1 priority date for international students; for summer admission, 3/15 priority date for domestic students, 3/1 priority date for international students. Applications are processed on a rolling basis. Application fee: $45. *Financial support:* Fellowships, research assistantships with full tuition reimbursements, teaching assistantships with full tuition reimbursements, career-related internships or fieldwork, Federal Work-Study, institutionally sponsored loans, scholarships/grants, tuition waivers (partial), and unspecified assistantships available. Support available to part-time students. Financial award applicants required to submit FAFSA. *Unit head:* K. Michelle Henry, Director, Graduate Business Programs, 734-487-4444, Fax: 734-483-1316, E-mail: cob.graduate@emich.edu.
Website: http://www.emich.edu/cob/mba/

East Tennessee State University, School of Graduate Studies, College of Business and Technology, Department of Management and Marketing, Johnson City, TN 37614. Offers business administration (MBA, Postbaccalaureate Certificate); digital marketing (MS); entrepreneurial leadership (Postbaccalaureate Certificate); health care management (Postbaccalaureate Certificate). *Program availability:* Part-time, evening/weekend. *Degree requirements:* For master's, comprehensive exam, capstone. *Entrance requirements:* For master's, GMAT, minimum GPA of 2.5 (for MBA), 3.0 (for MS); for Postbaccalaureate Certificate, minimum GPA of 2.5. Additional exam requirements/recommendations for international students: Required—TOEFL (minimum score 550 paper-based; 79 iBT). Electronic applications accepted. *Faculty research:* Sustainability, healthcare effectiveness, consumer behavior, merchandizing trends, organizational management issues.

Emerson College, Graduate Studies, School of Communication, Department of Marketing Communication, Program in Integrated Marketing Communication, Boston, MA 02116-4624. Offers MA. *Program availability:* Part-time, evening/weekend. *Faculty:* 16 full-time (6 women), 5 part-time/adjunct (1 woman). *Students:* 85 full-time (71 women), 8 part-time (all women); includes 8 minority (4 Black or African American, non-Hispanic/Latino; 1 Asian, non-Hispanic/Latino; 1 Hispanic/Latino; 2 Two or more races, non-Hispanic/Latino), 55 international. Average age 26. 164 applicants, 84% accepted, 43 enrolled. In 2016, 61 master's awarded. *Entrance requirements:* For master's, GMAT or GRE General Test. Additional exam requirements/recommendations for international students: Required—TOEFL (minimum score 550 paper-based; 80 iBT), IELTS (minimum score 6.5). *Application deadline:* For fall admission, 6/1 priority date for domestic students, 5/1 priority date for international students; for spring admission, 11/1 priority date for domestic students. Applications are processed on a rolling basis. Application fee: $60 ($75 for international students). Electronic applications accepted. *Financial support:* In 2016–17, 29 students received support, including 36 fellowships with partial tuition reimbursements available (averaging $8,306 per year); research assistantships with partial tuition reimbursements available, Federal Work-Study, scholarships/grants, and unspecified assistantships also available. Financial award application deadline: 3/1; financial award applicants required to submit FAFSA. *Faculty research:* Marketing, international business. *Application contact:* Leanda Ferland, Director of Graduate Admission, 617-824-8610, Fax: 617-824-8614, E-mail: gradapp@emerson.edu.
Website: http://www.emerson.edu/graduate_admission

Emory University, Goizueta Business School, Doctoral Program in Business, Atlanta, GA 30322. Offers accounting (PhD); finance (PhD); information systems and operations management (PhD); marketing (PhD); organization and management (PhD). *Faculty:* 59 full-time (16 women). *Students:* 40 full-time (16 women); includes 6 minority (1 Black or African American, non-Hispanic/Latino; 4 Asian, non-Hispanic/Latino; 1 Hispanic/Latino), 26 international. Average age 28. 145 applicants, 9% accepted, 4 enrolled. In 2016, 5 doctorates awarded. *Degree requirements:* For doctorate, comprehensive exam, thesis/dissertation. *Entrance requirements:* For doctorate, GMAT (strongly preferred) or GRE. Additional exam requirements/recommendations for international students: Required—TOEFL (minimum score 600 paper-based; 100 iBT). *Application deadline:* For fall admission, 1/3 priority date for domestic and international students. Application fee: $75. Electronic applications accepted. *Expenses:* $708 fees per year; 100% of tuition covered by scholarship. *Financial support:* In 2016–17, 34 students received support, including 6 fellowships (averaging $3,333 per year); scholarships/grants and health care benefits also available. Financial award application deadline: 1/3. *Faculty research:* Financial and managerial accounting, asset pricing strategy and organizational behavior, information technology marketing analytics and consumer behavior. *Unit head:* Dr. Anand Swaminathan, Associate Dean, Doctoral Program, 404-727-2306, Fax: 404-727-5337, E-mail: anand.swaminathan@emory.edu. *Application contact:* Allison Gilmore, Director of Admissions and Student Services, 404-727-6353, Fax: 404-727-5337, E-mail: allison.gilmore@emory.edu.

Emory University, Goizueta Business School, Full Time MBA Program, Atlanta, GA 30322. Offers accounting (MBA); alternative investments (MBA); business process consulting (MBA); business technology management (MBA); capital markets (MBA); corporate finance (MBA); customer relationship management (MBA); decision analytics (MBA); entrepreneurship (MBA); finance (MBA); global management (MBA); investment banking (MBA); management consulting (MBA); marketing (MBA); marketing analytics (MBA); marketing consulting (MBA); operations management (MBA); organization and management (MBA); product and brand management (MBA); real estate (MBA); social enterprise (MBA); strategy consulting (MBA). *Accreditation:* AACSB. *Faculty:* 72 full-time (17 women), 18 part-time/adjunct (5 women). *Students:* 350 full-time (101 women); includes 77 minority (21 Black or African American, non-Hispanic/Latino; 3 American Indian or Alaska Native, non-Hispanic/Latino; 32 Asian, non-Hispanic/Latino; 15 Hispanic/Latino; 2 Native Hawaiian or other Pacific Islander, non-Hispanic/Latino; 4 Two or more races, non-Hispanic/Latino), 117 international. Average age 29. 1,434 applicants, 31% accepted, 181 enrolled. In 2016, 182 master's awarded. *Degree requirements:* For master's, 1 leadership course; 2 mid-semester module programs; 2 global components. *Entrance requirements:* For master's, GMAT/GRE, essays; recommendation letters; undergraduate degree; interview. Additional exam requirements/recommendations for international students: Required—TOEFL (minimum score 100 iBT), IELTS (minimum score 7), PTE (minimum score 68). *Application deadline:* For fall admission, 10/14 priority date for domestic and international students; for winter admission, 11/11 priority date for domestic and international students; for spring admission, 1/4 priority date for domestic students, 1/4 for international students. Application fee: $150. Electronic applications accepted. *Expenses:* $57,580. *Financial support:* In 2016–17, 289 students received support. Career-related internships or fieldwork, institutionally sponsored loans, and scholarships/grants available. Financial award application deadline: 4/1; financial award applicants required to submit FAFSA. *Faculty research:* Social enterprise; micro vs. large business; mobile health data; mutual fund performance; product evaluation. *Unit head:* Brian Mitchell, Associate Dean, 404-727-4824, Fax: 404-712-9648, E-mail: brian.mitchell@emory.edu. *Application contact:* Julie Barefoot, Associate Dean, 404-727-6311, Fax: 404-727-4612, E-mail: mbaadmissions@emory.edu.
Website: http://www.goizueta.emory.edu

Fairfield University, Dolan School of Business, Fairfield, CT 06824. Offers accounting (MBA, MS, CAS); business analytics (MS); entrepreneurship (MBA); finance (MBA, MS, CAS); general management (MBA, CAS); global management (MBA); human resource management (MBA, CAS); information systems and business analytics (MBA); marketing (MBA, CAS); taxation (MBA, CAS). *Accreditation:* AACSB. *Program availability:* Part-time, evening/weekend. *Faculty:* 20 full-time (6 women), 4 part-time/adjunct (1 woman). *Students:* 106 full-time (41 women), 57 part-time (26 women); includes 18 minority (4 Black or African American, non-Hispanic/Latino; 1 American Indian or Alaska Native, non-Hispanic/Latino; 4 Asian, non-Hispanic/Latino; 7 Hispanic/Latino; 2 Two or more races, non-Hispanic/Latino), 39 international. Average age 26. 136 applicants, 63% accepted, 35 enrolled. In 2016, 90 master's awarded. *Degree requirements:* For master's, capstone course. *Entrance requirements:* For master's, GMAT (minimum score 500), 2 letters of reference, resume, minimum GPA of 3.0. Additional exam requirements/recommendations for international students: Required—TOEFL (minimum score 550 paper-based; 80 iBT) or IELTS (minimum score 6.5). *Application deadline:* For fall admission, 5/15 for international students; for spring admission, 10/15 for international students. Applications are processed on a rolling basis. Application fee: $60. Electronic applications accepted. *Expenses:* $875 per credit hour. *Financial support:* In 2016–17, 33 students received support. Scholarships/grants and unspecified assistantships available. Financial award applicants required to submit FAFSA. *Faculty research:* International finance, leadership and careers, ethics in accounting, emotions in consumer behavior and organizations, data analytics. *Unit head:* Dr. Donald Gibson, Dean, 203-254-4070, Fax: 203-254-4105, E-mail: dgibson@fairfield.edu. *Application contact:* Marianne Gumpper, Director of Graduate and Continuing Studies Admission, 203-254-4184, Fax: 203-254-4073, E-mail: gradadmis@fairfield.edu.
Website: http://fairfield.edu/mba

Fairleigh Dickinson University, College at Florham, Silberman College of Business, Departments of Management, Marketing, and Entrepreneurial Studies, Program in Marketing, Madison, NJ 07940-1099. Offers MBA, Certificate. *Entrance requirements:* For master's, GMAT.

Fairleigh Dickinson University, Metropolitan Campus, Silberman College of Business, Departments of Management, Marketing, and Entrepreneurial Studies, Program in Marketing, Teaneck, NJ 07666-1914. Offers MBA, Certificate.

Fashion Institute of Technology, School of Graduate Studies, Program in Cosmetics and Fragrance Marketing and Management, New York, NY 10001-5992. Offers MPS. *Students:* 39. 33 applicants, 61% accepted, 18 enrolled. *Degree requirements:* For master's, capstone seminar. *Entrance requirements:* Additional exam requirements/recommendations for international students: Required—TOEFL (minimum score 550 paper-based). *Application deadline:* For fall admission, 2/15 priority date for domestic and international students. Applications are processed on a rolling basis. Application fee: $50. Electronic applications accepted. *Expenses:* Tuition, state resident: full-time $10,870; part-time $453 per credit. Tuition, nonresident: full-time $22,210; part-time $925 per credit. *Required fees:* $745. *Financial support:* Federal Work-Study and scholarships/grants available. Financial award applicants required to submit FAFSA. *Unit head:* Stephan Kanlian, Chairperson/Professor, 212-217-4306. *Application contact:* Administrative Coordinator, 212-217-4300.
Website: http://www.fitnyc.edu/cfmm/

See Display below and Close-Up on page 533.

Florida Agricultural and Mechanical University, Division of Graduate Studies, Research, and Continuing Education, School of Business and Industry, Tallahassee, FL 32307-3200. Offers accounting (MBA); finance (MBA); management information systems (MBA); marketing (MBA). *Accreditation:* ACBSP. *Degree requirements:* For master's, residency. *Entrance requirements:* For master's, GMAT, minimum GPA of 3.0.

Florida Atlantic University, College of Business, Department of Marketing, Boca Raton, FL 33431-0991. Offers MBA. *Faculty:* 15 full-time (4 women). *Expenses:* Tuition, state resident: full-time $7392; part-time $369.82 per credit hour. Tuition, nonresident: full-time $19,432; part-time $1024.81 per credit hour. *Unit head:* 561-297-2545, E-mail: flexmba@fau.edu.

Florida International University, Chapman Graduate School of Business, Department of Marketing and Logistics, Miami, FL 33199. Offers marketing (MS). *Program availability:* Evening/weekend. *Faculty:* 22 full-time (10 women), 18 part-time/adjunct (8 women). *Students:* 124 full-time (95 women); includes 110 minority (8 Black or African American, non-Hispanic/Latino; 1 Asian, non-Hispanic/Latino; 101 Hispanic/Latino), 10 international. Average age 27. 165 applicants, 54% accepted, 79 enrolled. *Entrance requirements:* For master's, GMAT/GRE or 3 years of work experience, minimum AACSB index of 1000, minimum GPA of 3.0. Application fee: $20. *Expenses:* Tuition, state resident: full-time $8912; part-time $446 per credit hour. Tuition, nonresident: full-time $21,393; part-time $992 per credit hour. *Required fees:* $2185; $195 per semester.

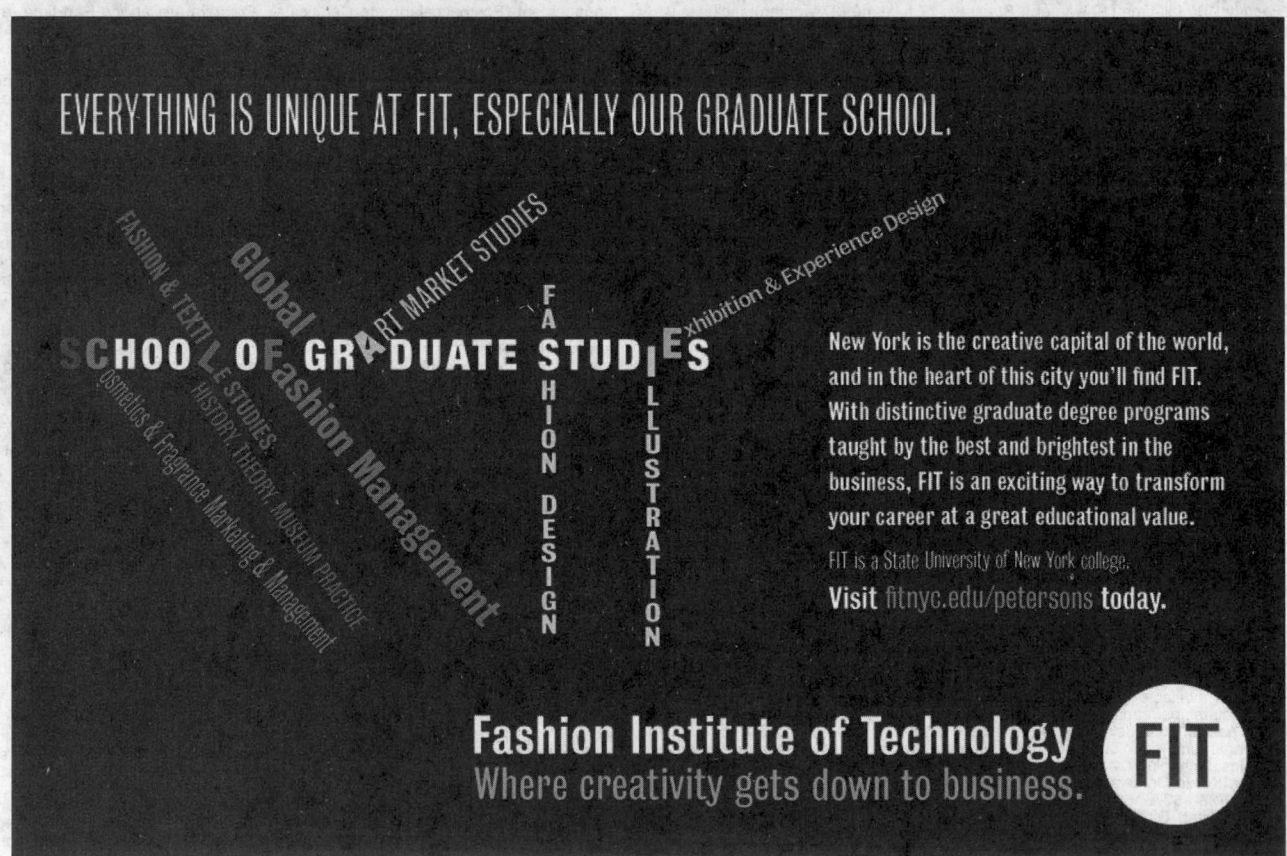

Tuition and fees vary according to program. *Unit head:* Anthony Miyazaki, Chair, 305-348-2571, Fax: 305-348-3792, E-mail: anthony.miyazaki@fiu.edu. *Application contact:* Nanett Rojas, Manager, Admissions Operations, 305-348-7464, Fax: 305-348-7441, E-mail: gradadm@fiu.edu.

Florida National University, Program in Business Administration, Hialeah, FL 33012. Offers finance (MBA); general management (MBA); health services administration (MBA); marketing (MBA); public management and leadership (MBA). *Program availability:* Part-time, blended/hybrid learning. *Degree requirements:* For master's, capstone. *Entrance requirements:* For master's, writing assessment, bachelor's degree from accredited institution; official undergraduate transcripts; minimum undergraduate GPA of 2.5, GMAT (minimum score of 400), or GRE (minimum score of 900); two letters of recommendation. Additional exam requirements/recommendations for international students: Required—TOEFL (minimum score 500 paper-based; 62 iBT), IELTS (minimum score 5.5). *Application deadline:* Applications are processed on a rolling basis. Electronic applications accepted. *Expenses:* Contact institution. *Financial support:* Federal Work-Study, institutionally sponsored loans, scholarships/grants, and tuition waivers available. Financial award applicants required to submit FAFSA. *Unit head:* Dr. Ernesto Gonzalez, Business Department Head, 305-821-3333 Ext. 1070, Fax: 305-362-0595, E-mail: egonzalez@fnu.edu. *Application contact:* Olga Rodriguez, Assistant Campus Dean, 305-821-3333 Ext. 1044, Fax: 305-362-0595, E-mail: orodriguez@fnu.edu.

Florida State University, The Graduate School, College of Business, Tallahassee, FL 32306-1110. Offers accounting (M Acc), including assurance and advisory services, generalist, taxation; business administration (MBA, PhD), including accounting (PhD), finance (PhD), management information systems (PhD), marketing (PhD), organizational behavior and human resources (PhD), risk management and insurance (PhD), strategy (PhD); finance (MS); management information systems (MS); risk management and insurance (MS); JD/MBA; MSW/MBA. *Accreditation:* AACSB. *Program availability:* Part-time, 100% online. *Faculty:* 101 full-time (27 women), 4 part-time/adjunct (2 women). *Students:* 272 full-time (127 women), 351 part-time (133 women); includes 141 minority (45 Black or African American, non-Hispanic/Latino; 2 American Indian or Alaska Native, non-Hispanic/Latino; 20 Asian, non-Hispanic/Latino; 59 Hispanic/Latino; 2 Native Hawaiian or other Pacific Islander, non-Hispanic/Latino; 13 Two or more races, non-Hispanic/Latino), 71 international. Average age 30. 688 applicants, 60% accepted, 273 enrolled. In 2016, 231 master's, 12 doctorates awarded. Terminal master's awarded for partial completion of doctoral program. *Degree requirements:* For doctorate, comprehensive exam, thesis/dissertation. *Entrance requirements:* For master's, GMAT, GRE (for all except MS in finance), work experience (MBA, MS); minimum GPA of 3.0, letters of recommendation; for doctorate, GMAT, GRE (for marketing, organizational behavior, risk management and insurance, management information systems, and human resources only), minimum graduate GPA of 3.5, letters of recommendation. Additional exam requirements/recommendations for international students: Required—TOEFL (minimum score 600 paper-based; 85 iBT); Recommended—IELTS (minimum score 6). *Application deadline:* For fall admission, 6/1 for domestic and international students; for spring admission, 10/1 for domestic and international students; for summer admission, 3/1 for domestic and international students. Applications are processed on a rolling basis. Application fee: $30. Electronic applications accepted. *Expenses:* Contact institution. *Financial support:* In 2016–17, 149 students received support, including 9 fellowships (averaging $1,500 per year), 65 research assistantships with full tuition reimbursements available (averaging $20,000 per year), 75 teaching assistantships with full tuition reimbursements available (averaging $20,000 per year); career-related internships or fieldwork, scholarships/grants, health care benefits, tuition waivers (full and partial), and unspecified assistantships also available. Support available to part-time students. Financial award application deadline: 1/1; financial award applicants required to submit FAFSA. *Faculty research:* Business strategy, marketing, finance, accounting, business analytics. *Total annual research expenditures:* $1.4 million. *Unit head:* Dr. Michael Hartline, Dean, 850-644-4405, Fax: 850-644-0915, E-mail: mhartline@business.fsu.edu. *Application contact:* Jennifer Clark, Director, 850-644-6458, E-mail: gradprograms@business.fsu.edu.
Website: http://business.fsu.edu/

Florida State University, The Graduate School, College of Communication and Information, School of Communication, Tallahassee, FL 32306-2664. Offers communication theory and research (PhD); integrated marketing communication (MA, MS); media and communication studies (MA, MS); public interest media and communication (MA, MS). *Program availability:* Part-time. *Faculty:* 22 full-time (11 women), 2 part-time/adjunct (1 woman). *Students:* 71 full-time (53 women), 72 part-time (46 women); includes 77 minority (20 Black or African American, non-Hispanic/Latino; 36 Asian, non-Hispanic/Latino; 19 Hispanic/Latino; 2 Two or more races, non-Hispanic/Latino). Average age 24. 140 applicants, 57% accepted, 46 enrolled. In 2016, 83 master's, 5 doctorates awarded. *Degree requirements:* For master's, thesis (for some programs); for doctorate, comprehensive exam, thesis/dissertation. *Entrance requirements:* For master's, GRE General Test, minimum GPA of 3.0; for doctorate, GRE General Test, minimum GPA of 3.3 in graduate course work. Additional exam requirements/recommendations for international students: Required—TOEFL (minimum score 600 paper-based; 100 iBT), IELTS (minimum score 7). *Application deadline:* For fall admission, 7/1 priority date for domestic students, 5/1 priority date for international students; for spring admission, 11/1 priority date for domestic and international students; for summer admission, 3/1 priority date for domestic and international students. Applications are processed on a rolling basis. Application fee: $30. Electronic applications accepted. *Expenses:* $479.32 per credit hour in-state, $1,110.72 per credit hour out-of-state. *Financial support:* In 2016–17, 87 students received support, including 17 research assistantships with full tuition reimbursements available (averaging $16,192 per year), 46 teaching assistantships with full tuition reimbursements available (averaging $16,192 per year); fellowships, career-related internships or fieldwork, Federal Work-Study, institutionally sponsored loans, scholarships/grants, health care benefits, tuition waivers (full and partial), and unspecified assistantships also available. Support available to part-time students. Financial award application deadline: 12/15; financial award applicants required to submit FAFSA. *Faculty research:* Communication in the public interest; strategic communication; media and technology; multicultural, intercultural, and international communication. *Total annual research expenditures:* $52,979. *Unit head:* Dr. Gary Heald, Director, 850-644-5034, Fax: 850-644-8642, E-mail: gheald@fsu.edu. *Application contact:* Natashia Hinson-Turner, Graduate Coordinator, 850-644-5034, Fax: 850-644-8642, E-mail: comgradadvising@cci.fsu.edu.
Website: http://www.cci.fsu.edu

Fordham University, Gabelli School of Business, New York, NY 10023. Offers accounting (MBA, MS); applied statistics and decision-making (MS); business administration (EMBA); business analytics (MS); communications and media management (MBA); electronic business (MBA); entrepreneurship (MBA); finance (MBA); global finance (MS); global sustainability (MBA); healthcare management (MBA); information systems (MBA, MS); investor relations (MS); management (MBA, MS); marketing (MBA); marketing intelligence (MS); media management (MS); nonprofit leadership (MS); quantitative finance (MS); taxation (MS); JD/MBA; MS/MBA. *Accreditation:* AACSB. *Program availability:* Part-time, evening/weekend. *Faculty:* 132 full-time (44 women), 51 part-time/adjunct (7 women). *Students:* 1,117 full-time (668 women), 553 part-time (282 women); includes 207 minority (44 Black or African American, non-Hispanic/Latino; 92 Asian, non-Hispanic/Latino; 69 Hispanic/Latino; 2 Native Hawaiian or other Pacific Islander, non-Hispanic/Latino), 1,088 international. Average age 27. 4,745 applicants, 46% accepted, 752 enrolled. In 2016, 996 master's awarded. Terminal master's awarded for partial completion of doctoral program. *Degree requirements:* For master's, internships (required for MS in quantitative finance, recommended for MBA). *Entrance requirements:* For master's, GMAT/GRE, 2 letters of recommendation, resume, 2 essays, transcripts. Additional exam requirements/recommendations for international students: Required—TOEFL (minimum score 100 iBT), IELTS (minimum score 7). *Application deadline:* For fall admission, 11/15 priority date for domestic and international students; for winter admission, 1/15 priority date for domestic students, 1/1 priority date for international students; for spring admission, 3/1 for domestic and international students; for summer admission, 6/1 for domestic students. Application fee: $130. Electronic applications accepted. *Expenses:* $1,397 per credit. *Financial support:* In 2016–17, 78 students received support. Career-related internships or fieldwork, institutionally sponsored loans, scholarships/grants, and unspecified assistantships available. Support available to part-time students. Financial award application deadline: 6/30; financial award applicants required to submit FAFSA. *Unit head:* Dr. Donna Rapaccioli, Dean, 212-636-6165, Fax: 212-307-1779, E-mail: rapaccioli@fordham.edu. *Application contact:* Lawrence Murray, Senior Assistant Dean of Graduate Admissions and Advising, 212-636-6200, Fax: 212-636-7076, E-mail: admissionsgb@fordham.edu.
Website: http://www.fordham.edu/gabelli

Franklin University, Marketing and Communication Program, Columbus, OH 43215-5399. Offers MS. *Program availability:* Part-time, evening/weekend. *Entrance requirements:* For master's, minimum undergraduate GPA of 2.75. Additional exam requirements/recommendations for international students: Required—TOEFL (minimum score 550 paper-based). Electronic applications accepted.

Full Sail University, Internet Marketing Master of Science Program - Online, Winter Park, FL 32792-7437. Offers MS. *Program availability:* Online learning.

Gannon University, School of Graduate Studies, College of Engineering and Business, Dahlkemper School of Business, Program in Business Administration, Erie, PA 16541-0001. Offers business administration (MBA); finance (MBA); human resources management (MBA); marketing (MBA). *Accreditation:* ACBSP. *Program availability:* Part-time, evening/weekend, 100% online, blended/hybrid learning. *Students:* 43 full-time (17 women), 67 part-time (34 women); includes 7 minority (4 Black or African American, non-Hispanic/Latino; 2 Asian, non-Hispanic/Latino; 1 Hispanic/Latino), 19 international. Average age 30. 160 applicants, 53% accepted, 28 enrolled. In 2016, 60 master's awarded. *Entrance requirements:* For master's, GMAT, bachelor's degree in any discipline from any accredited college or university, resume, transcripts, 3 letters of recommendation. Additional exam requirements/recommendations for international students: Required—TOEFL (minimum score 79 iBT). *Application deadline:* Applications are processed on a rolling basis. Application fee: $25. Electronic applications accepted. Application fee is waived when completed online. *Expenses: Tuition:* Full-time $17,370. *Required fees:* $550. Tuition and fees vary according to course load and program. *Financial support:* Federal Work-Study and unspecified assistantships available. Financial award application deadline: 7/1; financial award applicants required to submit FAFSA. *Unit head:* Dr. Michael Messina, Director, 814-871-5755, Fax: 814-871-7210, E-mail: messina001@gannon.edu. *Application contact:* Bridget Philip, Director of Graduate Admissions, 814-871-7412, E-mail: graduate@gannon.edu.

Geneva College, Program in Business Administration, Beaver Falls, PA 15010-3599. Offers business administration (MBA); finance (MBA); marketing (MBA); operations (MBA). *Accreditation:* ACBSP. *Program availability:* Part-time, evening/weekend. *Students:* 22 full-time (6 women), 29 part-time (10 women); includes 4 minority (1 Black or African American, non-Hispanic/Latino; 1 American Indian or Alaska Native, non-Hispanic/Latino; 2 Asian, non-Hispanic/Latino), 1 international. Average age 35. In 2016, 15 master's awarded. *Degree requirements:* For master's, 36 credit hours of course work (30 of which are required of all students). *Entrance requirements:* For master's, GMAT (if college GPA less than 2.5), undergraduate transcript, 2 letters of recommendation, resume, goals statement. Additional exam requirements/recommendations for international students: Required—TOEFL. *Application deadline:* For fall admission, 3/1 priority date for domestic students; for spring admission, 11/1 priority date for domestic students. Applications are processed on a rolling basis. Electronic applications accepted. *Expenses:* $710 per credit. *Financial support:* In 2016–17, 1 student received support. Scholarships/grants available. Financial award application deadline: 8/1; financial award applicants required to submit FAFSA. *Unit head:* Dr. Gary Vander Plaats, Director of the MBA Program, 724-847-6619, E-mail: gpvander@geneva.edu. *Application contact:* Marina Frazier, Director of Graduate Enrollment, 724-847-6697, E-mail: mba@geneva.edu.
Website: http://www.geneva.edu/page/masters_business

George Fox University, College of Business, Newberg, OR 97132-2697. Offers accounting (DBA); finance (MBA); management (DBA); management and leadership (MBA); marketing (DBA); organizational strategy (MBA); strategic human resource management (MBA). MBA offered in Newberg, OR and in Portland, OR. *Accreditation:* ACBSP. *Program availability:* Part-time, evening/weekend, online learning. *Degree requirements:* For master's, capstone project; for doctorate, credit-applied research project. *Entrance requirements:* For master's, resume (5 years of professional experience); 3 professional references; interview; financial e-learning course; official transcripts; for doctorate, GRE or GMAT, resume; personal mission statement; academic research writing sample; official transcript from each college/university attended; three professional references. Additional exam requirements/recommendations for international students: Required—TOEFL (minimum score 577 paper-based; 90 iBT) or IELTS (minimum score 7). Electronic applications accepted. *Expenses:* Contact institution.

The George Washington University, School of Business, Department of Marketing, Washington, DC 20052. Offers MBA, PhD. *Program availability:* Part-time, evening/weekend. *Degree requirements:* For doctorate, thesis/dissertation. *Entrance requirements:* For master's, GMAT; for doctorate, GMAT or GRE. Additional exam requirements/recommendations for international students: Required—TOEFL. *Application deadline:* For fall admission, 4/1 priority date for domestic students; for spring admission, 10/1 for domestic students. Applications are processed on a rolling basis. Application fee: $60. *Financial support:* Fellowships, teaching assistantships, career-related internships or fieldwork, Federal Work-Study, and institutionally sponsored loans available. Financial award application deadline: 4/1. *Faculty research:* Strategic marketing, marketing and public policy, marketing management. *Unit head:* Pradeep Rau, Chairman, 202-994-4989, E-mail: prau@gwu.edu. *Application contact:* Christopher Storer, Executive Director, Graduate Admissions, 202-994-1212, E-mail: gwmba@gwu.edu.
Website: http://business.gwu.edu/marketing/

Georgia State University, J. Mack Robinson College of Business, Department of Marketing, Atlanta, GA 30302-3083. Offers MBA, MS, PhD. *Program availability:* Part-

time, evening/weekend. *Faculty:* 28 full-time (10 women). *Students:* 51 full-time (35 women), 1 part-time (0 women); includes 17 minority (13 Black or African American, non-Hispanic/Latino; 3 Hispanic/Latino; 1 Two or more races, non-Hispanic/Latino), 25 international. Average age 29. 28 applicants, 18% accepted, 4 enrolled. In 2016, 24 master's, 6 doctorates awarded. *Degree requirements:* For doctorate, comprehensive exam, thesis/dissertation. *Entrance requirements:* For master's, GRE or GMAT, transcripts from all institutions attended, resume, essays; for doctorate, GRE or GMAT, three letters of recommendation, personal statement, transcripts from all institutions attended, resume. Additional exam requirements/recommendations for international students: Required—TOEFL (minimum score 610 paper-based; 101 iBT), IELTS (minimum score 7). *Application deadline:* For fall admission, 5/1 priority date for domestic students, 2/1 priority date for international students; for spring admission, 9/15 priority date for domestic students, 4/1 priority date for international students. Applications are processed on a rolling basis. Application fee: $50. Electronic applications accepted. *Expenses:* Tuition, state resident: full-time $6876; part-time $382 per credit hour. Tuition, nonresident: full-time $22,374; part-time $1243 per credit hour. *Required fees:* $2128; $1064 per term. Part-time tuition and fees vary according to course load and program. *Financial support:* Research assistantships, teaching assistantships, scholarships/grants, tuition waivers (partial), and unspecified assistantships available. Financial award applicants required to submit FAFSA. *Faculty research:* Marketing strategy, market in science, brand and customer management, digital and social media marketing, global marketing. *Unit head:* Dr. Naveen Donthu, Professor/Chair of the Department of Marketing, 404-413-7650, Fax: 404-413-7699. *Application contact:* Toby McChesney, Assistant Dean for Graduate Recruiting and Student Services, 404-413-7167, Fax: 404-413-7162, E-mail: rcbgradadmissions@gsu.edu.
Website: http://robinson.gsu.edu/marketing/

Golden Gate University, Ageno School of Business, San Francisco, CA 94105-2968. Offers accounting (MBA); business administration (EMBA, MBA, PMBA, DBA); business analytics (MS); finance (MBA, MS, Certificate); financial planning (MS, Certificate); healthcare information systems (Certificate); human resource management (MBA, MS); human resources management (Certificate); information systems (MS); information technology (MBA); information technology management (Certificate); integrated marketing and communications (MS, Certificate); international business (MBA); management (MBA); marketing (MBA, MS, Certificate); operations supply chain management (Certificate); psychology (MA, Certificate); public administration (EMPA); public relations (MS, Certificate); technical market analysis (Certificate); JD/MBA. *Program availability:* Part-time, evening/weekend. *Faculty:* 18 full-time (3 women), 117 part-time/adjunct (44 women). *Students:* 458 full-time (254 women), 664 part-time (331 women); includes 346 minority (75 Black or African American, non-Hispanic/Latino; 2 American Indian or Alaska Native, non-Hispanic/Latino; 132 Asian, non-Hispanic/Latino; 105 Hispanic/Latino; 9 Native Hawaiian or other Pacific Islander, non-Hispanic/Latino; 23 Two or more races, non-Hispanic/Latino), 354 international. Average age 34. 905 applicants, 83% accepted, 165 enrolled. In 2016, 350 master's, 2 doctorates awarded. *Degree requirements:* For doctorate, thesis/dissertation, qualifying examination. *Entrance requirements:* For master's, GMAT (for MBA), minimum GPA of 2.5 (MS). Additional exam requirements/recommendations for international students: Required—TOEFL (minimum score 550 paper-based; 79 iBT). *Application deadline:* For fall admission, 5/15 for domestic and international students; for winter admission, 1/15 for domestic and international students; for spring admission, 9/15 for domestic and international students. Applications are processed on a rolling basis. Application fee: $70 ($110 for international students). Electronic applications accepted. *Expenses:* Contact institution. *Financial support:* In 2016–17, 372 students received support. Career-related internships or fieldwork, Federal Work-Study, institutionally sponsored loans, and scholarships/grants available. Support available to part-time students. Financial award applicants required to submit FAFSA. *Unit head:* Dr. Gordon Swartz, Dean, 415-442-7027, Fax: 415-442-6579, E-mail: gswartz@ggu.edu. *Application contact:* Angela Melero, Enrollment Services, 415-442-7800, Fax: 415-442-7807, E-mail: info@ggu.edu.
Website: http://www.ggu.edu/programs/business-and-management

Goldey-Beacom College, Graduate Program, Wilmington, DE 19808-1999. Offers business administration (MBA); finance (MS); financial management (MBA); health care management (MBA); human resource management (MBA); information technology (MBA); international business management (MBA); major finance (MBA); major taxation (MBA); management (MM); marketing management (MBA); taxation (MBA, MS). *Accreditation:* ACBSP. *Program availability:* Part-time, evening/weekend. *Entrance requirements:* For master's, GMAT, MAT, GRE, minimum GPA of 3.0. Additional exam requirements/recommendations for international students: Required—TOEFL (minimum score 65 iBT); Recommended—IELTS (minimum score 6). Electronic applications accepted.

Grand Canyon University, Colangelo College of Business, Phoenix, AZ 85017-1097. Offers accounting (MBA, MS); business analytics (MS); disaster preparedness and executive fire service leadership (MS); finance (MBA); general management (MBA); health systems management (MBA); information technology management (MS); leadership (MBA, MS); marketing (MBA); organizational leadership and entrepreneurship (MS); project management (MBA); sports business (MBA); strategic human resource management (MBA). *Accreditation:* ACBSP. *Program availability:* Part-time, evening/weekend, online learning. *Faculty:* 8 full-time (3 women), 147 part-time/adjunct (49 women). *Students:* 1 full-time (0 women), 2,121 part-time (1,165 women); includes 341 minority (249 Black or African American, non-Hispanic/Latino; 17 American Indian or Alaska Native, non-Hispanic/Latino; 15 Asian, non-Hispanic/Latino; 29 Hispanic/Latino; 4 Native Hawaiian or other Pacific Islander, non-Hispanic/Latino; 27 Two or more races, non-Hispanic/Latino), 20 international. Average age 38. In 2016, 569 master's awarded. *Entrance requirements:* For master's, equivalent of two years' full-time professional work experience. Additional exam requirements/recommendations for international students: Required—TOEFL (minimum score 575 paper-based; 90 iBT), IELTS (minimum score 7). *Application deadline:* For fall admission, 8/21 for domestic students, 7/2 for international students; for spring admission, 12/24 for domestic students, 11/1 for international students. Applications are processed on a rolling basis. Application fee: $0. Electronic applications accepted. *Financial support:* Federal Work-Study available. Support available to part-time students. Financial award applicants required to submit FAFSA. *Unit head:* Kim Donaldson, Dean, 602-639-6597, E-mail: kdonaldson@gcu.edu. *Application contact:* Matt Tidwell, Enrollment Manager, 602-639-6020, E-mail: mtidwell@gcu.edu.
Website: https://www.gcu.edu/colangelo-college-of-business.php

Grand Canyon University, College of Doctoral Studies, Phoenix, AZ 85017-1097. Offers data analytics (DBA); general psychology (PhD), including cognition and instruction, industrial and organizational psychology, integrating technology, learning, and psychology, performance psychology; management (DBA); marketing (DBA); organizational leadership (Ed D), including behavioral health, Christian ministry, health care administration, organizational development. *Degree requirements:* For doctorate, comprehensive exam, thesis/dissertation. *Entrance requirements:* For doctorate, minimum GPA of 3.4 on earned advanced degree from regionally-accredited institution; transcripts; goals statement. Application fee: $0. *Unit head:* Michael Berger, Dean, 602-639-7255. *Application contact:* Michael Berger, Dean, 602-639-7255.
Website: https://www.gcu.edu/college-of-doctoral-studies.php

Harvard University, Harvard Business School, Doctoral Programs in Management, Boston, MA 02163. Offers accounting and management (DBA); business economics (PhD); health policy management (PhD); management (DBA); marketing (DBA); organizational behavior (PhD); science, technology and management (PhD); strategy (DBA); technology and operations management (DBA). *Degree requirements:* For doctorate, comprehensive exam (for some programs), thesis/dissertation. *Entrance requirements:* For doctorate, GRE General Test or GMAT. Additional exam requirements/recommendations for international students: Required—TOEFL.

Hawai`i Pacific University, College of Business, Program in Business Administration, Honolulu, HI 96813. Offers accounting (MBA); economics (MBA); finance (MBA); hospitality and tourism management (MBA); human resource management (MBA); information systems (MBA); international business (MBA); management (MBA); marketing (MBA); organizational change and development (MBA). *Program availability:* Part-time, evening/weekend, online learning. *Faculty:* 13 full-time (4 women), 1 part-time/adjunct (0 women). *Students:* 106 full-time (47 women), 33 part-time (13 women); includes 66 minority (5 Black or African American, non-Hispanic/Latino; 1 American Indian or Alaska Native, non-Hispanic/Latino; 23 Asian, non-Hispanic/Latino; 11 Hispanic/Latino; 1 Native Hawaiian or other Pacific Islander, non-Hispanic/Latino; 25 Two or more races, non-Hispanic/Latino), 36 international. Average age 33. 77 applicants, 84% accepted, 44 enrolled. In 2016, 78 master's awarded. *Entrance requirements:* For master's, GMAT or GRE. Additional exam requirements/recommendations for international students: Recommended—TOEFL (minimum score 550 paper-based; 80 iBT), IELTS (minimum score 6), TWE (minimum score 5). *Application deadline:* For fall admission, 2/15 priority date for domestic students; for spring admission, 10/15 priority date for domestic students. Applications are processed on a rolling basis. Application fee: $50. Electronic applications accepted. *Expenses: Tuition:* Full-time $17,190; part-time $955 per credit. *Required fees:* $150; $26 per credit. Tuition and fees vary according to course load and program. *Financial support:* In 2016–17, 27 students received support. Research assistantships, career-related internships or fieldwork, Federal Work-Study, scholarships/grants, tuition waivers, and unspecified assistantships available. Financial award application deadline: 3/1; financial award applicants required to submit FAFSA. *Unit head:* Dr. Warren Wee, Associate Dean/Associate Professor of Accounting, 808-544-9325, E-mail: wwee@hpu.edu. *Application contact:* Danny Lam, Assistant Director of Graduate Admissions, 808-544-1135, E-mail: graduate@hpu.edu.
Website: http://www.hpu.edu/CBA/Graduate/MBA/index.html

HEC Montreal, School of Business Administration, Master of Science Programs in Administration, Program in Marketing, Montréal, QC H3T 2A7, Canada. Offers M Sc. All courses are given in English. *Students:* 89 full-time (69 women), 5 part-time (1 woman). 69 applicants, 54% accepted, 20 enrolled. In 2016, 54 master's awarded. *Degree requirements:* For master's, one foreign language, thesis. *Entrance requirements:* For master's, Test de francais international (TFI) with minimum score of 850 (for those who have never studied in French), BBA, undergraduate degree in another field, degree deemed equivalent by program director and minimum GPA of 3.0 on 4.3 scale. *Application deadline:* For fall admission, 3/15 for domestic and international students; for winter admission, 9/15 for domestic and international students. Application fee: $86 Canadian dollars. Electronic applications accepted. *Expenses: Tuition, area resident:* Part-time $77.80 Canadian dollars per credit. Tuition, state resident: full-time $2797 Canadian dollars; part-time $240.92 Canadian dollars per credit. Tuition, nonresident: full-time $8673 Canadian dollars; part-time $531.43 Canadian dollars per credit. *International tuition:* $19,131 Canadian dollars full-time. *Required fees:* $1699 Canadian dollars; $40.58 Canadian dollars per credit. $67.32 Canadian dollars per term. Tuition and fees vary according to degree level and program. *Financial support:* Research assistantships, teaching assistantships, and scholarships/grants available. Financial award application deadline: 9/2. *Unit head:* Dr. Marie-Helene Jobin, Director, 514-340-6283, E-mail: marie-helene.jobin@hec.ca. *Application contact:* Marianne de Moura, Administrative Director, 514-340-7106, Fax: 514-340-6411, E-mail: marianne.de-moura@hec.ca.
Website: http://www.hec.ca/programmes/maitrises/maitrise-marketing/index.html

Herzing University Online, Program in Business Administration, Menomonee Falls, WI 53051. Offers accounting (MBA); business administration (MBA); business management (MBA); healthcare management (MBA); human resources (MBA); marketing (MBA); project management (MBA); technology management (MBA). *Program availability:* Online learning.

Hofstra University, Frank G. Zarb School of Business, Programs in Marketing and International Business, Hempstead, NY 11549. Offers business administration (MBA), including international business, marketing; international business (Advanced Certificate); marketing (MS, Advanced Certificate); marketing research (MS). *Program availability:* Part-time, evening/weekend, blended/hybrid learning. *Students:* 91 full-time (61 women), 28 part-time (14 women); includes 13 minority (1 Black or African American, non-Hispanic/Latino; 8 Asian, non-Hispanic/Latino; 3 Hispanic/Latino; 1 Two or more races, non-Hispanic/Latino), 84 international. Average age 25. 323 applicants, 67% accepted, 49 enrolled. In 2016, 65 master's awarded. *Degree requirements:* For master's, capstone course (for MBA), thesis (for MS), minimum GPA of 3.0. *Entrance requirements:* For master's, GMAT/GRE, 2 letters of recommendation, resume, essay. Additional exam requirements/recommendations for international students: Required—TOEFL (minimum score 550 paper-based; 80 iBT); Recommended—IELTS (minimum score 6). *Application deadline:* Applications are processed on a rolling basis. Application fee: $75. Electronic applications accepted. *Expenses:* $1,170 per credit. *Financial support:* In 2016–17, 30 students received support, including 24 fellowships with full and partial tuition reimbursements available (averaging $4,896 per year); research assistantships with full and partial tuition reimbursements available, career-related internships or fieldwork, Federal Work-Study, institutionally sponsored loans, scholarships/grants, tuition waivers (full and partial), and unspecified assistantships also available. Support available to part-time students. Financial award applicants required to submit FAFSA. *Faculty research:* Cross-cultural consumer behavior; social, digital, global, and strategic issues in marketing; consumer health/well-being; ethnocentrism and animosity. *Unit head:* Dr. Anil Mathur, Chairperson, 516-463-5346, Fax: 516-463-4834, E-mail: anil.mathur@hofstra.edu. *Application contact:* Sunil Samuel, Assistant Vice President of Admissions, 516-463-4723, Fax: 516-463-4664, E-mail: graduateadmission@hofstra.edu.
Website: http://www.hofstra.edu/business/

Holy Names University, Graduate Division, Department of Business, Oakland, CA 94619-1699. Offers finance (MBA); management and leadership (MBA); marketing (MBA). *Program availability:* Part-time, evening/weekend. *Students:* 17 full-time (11 women), 15 part-time (10 women); includes 22 minority (9 Black or African American, non-Hispanic/Latino; 2 Asian, non-Hispanic/Latino; 10 Hispanic/Latino; 1 Two or more races, non-Hispanic/Latino), 1 international. Average age 31. 31 applicants, 68% accepted, 15 enrolled. In 2016, 9 master's awarded. *Entrance requirements:* For master's, minimum undergraduate GPA of 2.6 overall, 3.0 in major; two recommendations (letter or form) from previous professors or current or previous work

supervisors; 1-3 page personal statement; resume. Additional exam requirements/recommendations for international students: Required—TOEFL (minimum score 550 paper-based; 79 iBT). *Application deadline:* For fall admission, 8/1 priority date for domestic students, 7/15 for international students; for spring admission, 12/1 priority date for domestic students, 12/1 for international students; for summer admission, 5/1 priority date for domestic students, 5/1 for international students. Applications are processed on a rolling basis. Application fee: $65. Electronic applications accepted. Application fee is waived when completed online. *Expenses:* Contact institution. *Financial support:* Career-related internships or fieldwork, Federal Work-Study, scholarships/grants, and unspecified assistantships available. Support available to part-time students. Financial award application deadline: 3/2; financial award applicants required to submit FAFSA. *Faculty research:* Business ethics, sustainable economics, accounting models, cross-cultural management, diversity in organizations. *Unit head:* Russell Jacobus, MBA Program Director, 510-436-1622, E-mail: jacobus@hnu.edu. *Application contact:* 800-430-1321, Fax: 510-436-1325, E-mail: graduateadmissions@hnu.edu.
Website: http://www.hnu.edu

Hood College, Graduate School, Department of Economics and Business Administration, Frederick, MD 21701-8575. Offers accounting (MBA); finance (MBA); human resource management (MBA); information systems (MBA); marketing (MBA); public management (MBA). *Accreditation:* ACBSP. *Program availability:* Part-time, evening/weekend. *Faculty:* 4 full-time, 8 part-time/adjunct. *Students:* 21 full-time (13 women), 106 part-time (60 women); includes 23 minority (12 Black or African American, non-Hispanic/Latino; 4 Asian, non-Hispanic/Latino; 6 Hispanic/Latino; 1 Two or more races, non-Hispanic/Latino), 15 international. Average age 32. 44 applicants, 91% accepted, 25 enrolled. In 2016, 45 master's awarded. *Degree requirements:* For master's, capstone/final research project. *Entrance requirements:* For master's, minimum GPA of 3.0 (or resume and two letters of recommendation), copy of official transcripts, essay. Additional exam requirements/recommendations for international students: Required—TOEFL (minimum score 575 paper-based; 89 iBT), IELTS (minimum score 6.5). *Application deadline:* For fall admission, 8/15 for domestic students, 8/5 for international students; for spring admission, 12/1 for domestic and international students; for summer admission, 5/1 for domestic students, 4/15 for international students. Applications are processed on a rolling basis. Application fee: $35. Electronic applications accepted. *Expenses:* $525 per credit; $110 comprehensive fee per semester. *Financial support:* Tuition waivers (partial) and unspecified assistantships available. Financial award applicants required to submit FAFSA. *Faculty research:* Corporate strategy and sustainable competitive advantages, business ethics, entrepreneurship, investments management, economic development. *Unit head:* April Boulton, Interim Dean of the Graduate School, 301-696-3600, Fax: 301-696-3597, E-mail: gofurther@hood.edu. *Application contact:* Spencer Berk, Assistant Director of Graduate Admissions, 301-696-3604, E-mail: gofurther@hood.edu.

Hope International University, School of Graduate and Professional Studies, Program in Business Administration, Fullerton, CA 92831-3138. Offers general management (MBA, MSM); international development (MBA, MSM); marketing management (MBA, MSM); non-profit management (MBA, MSM). *Program availability:* Part-time, online learning. *Degree requirements:* For master's, comprehensive exam (for some programs), thesis (for some programs), project. *Entrance requirements:* For master's, minimum GPA of 3.0; 2 references. Additional exam requirements/recommendations for international students: Required—TOEFL (minimum score 550 paper-based; 86 iBT); Recommended—IELTS (minimum score 6.5). Electronic applications accepted. *Expenses:* Contact institution.

Howard University, School of Business, Graduate Programs in Business, Washington, DC 20059-0002. Offers accounting (MBA); entrepreneurship (MBA); finance (MBA); general management (MBA); human resources management (MBA); information systems (MBA); international business (MBA); marketing (MBA); supply chain management (MBA); JD/MBA. *Accreditation:* AACSB. *Program availability:* Part-time, evening/weekend, online learning. *Entrance requirements:* For master's, GMAT, minimum 1 year post undergraduate work experience, resume, 3 letters of recommendation, advanced college algebra. Additional exam requirements/recommendations for international students: Required—TOEFL. *Faculty research:* Marketing research in multi-ethnic populations, U.S. trade policies and international relations, risk management (finance).

Hult International Business School, Graduate Programs, Cambridge, MA 02141. Offers business administration (EMBA); business analytics (MBA, MIB); business statistics (MBS); disruptive innovation (MDI); entrepreneurship (MBA, MIB); family business (MBA, MIB); finance (MBA, MF, MIB); international marketing (MIM); marketing (MBA, MID); project management (MBA, MIB). MDI and MBS offered in San Francisco; MBA also offered in Boston, San Francisco, Dubai, Shanghai, and New York. *Students:* Average age 31. *Entrance requirements:* For master's, GMAT, 3 years of work experience. Additional exam requirements/recommendations for international students: Required—TOEFL. *Application deadline:* For fall admission, 9/1 priority date for domestic and international students; for winter admission, 11/1 priority date for domestic and international students; for spring admission, 12/1 priority date for domestic and international students; for summer admission, 6/1 for domestic and international students. Applications are processed on a rolling basis. Application fee: $150. Electronic applications accepted. *Expenses:* $75,000 (for MBA); $45,000 (for master's); $85,000 (for executive part-time MBA). *Financial support:* Scholarships/grants and tuition waivers (partial) available. Financial award application deadline: 6/1; financial award applicants required to submit FAFSA. *Application contact:* Boston Admissions Office, 617-746-1990, E-mail: postgraduate@hult.edu.
Website: http://www.hult.edu

Illinois Institute of Technology, Stuart School of Business, Program in Marketing Analytics and Communication, Chicago, IL 60661. Offers MS, MBA/MS. *Program availability:* Part-time, evening/weekend. *Entrance requirements:* For master's, GRE (minimum score 1000) or GMAT (500). Additional exam requirements/recommendations for international students: Required—TOEFL (minimum score 600 paper-based; 85 iBT); Recommended—IELTS (minimum score 7). Electronic applications accepted. *Expenses:* Contact institution.

Indiana Tech, Program in Business Administration, Fort Wayne, IN 46803-1297. Offers accounting (MBA); health care management (MBA); human resources (MBA); management (MBA); marketing (MBA). *Program availability:* Part-time, evening/weekend, online learning. *Entrance requirements:* For master's, GMAT, bachelor's degree from regionally-accredited university; minimum undergraduate GPA of 2.5; 2 years of significant work experience; 3 letters of recommendation. Electronic applications accepted.

Indiana University–Purdue University Indianapolis, Kelley School of Business, Evening MBA Program, Indianapolis, IN 46202-5151. Offers accounting (MBA); entrepreneurship (MBA); finance (MBA); general administration (MBA); marketing (MBA); supply chain management (MBA); MBA/JD; MBA/MD; MBA/MHA; MBA/MS; MBA/MSA; MBA/MSE. *Program availability:* Part-time-only, evening/weekend, online learning. *Faculty:* 30 full-time (7 women), 4 part-time/adjunct (0 women). *Students:* 294 part-time (46 women); includes 41 minority (11 Black or African American, non-Hispanic/Latino; 22 Asian, non-Hispanic/Latino; 8 Hispanic/Latino), 106 international. Average age 31. 129 applicants, 53% accepted, 61 enrolled. In 2016, 103 degrees awarded. *Entrance requirements:* For master's, GMAT or GRE, 2 years of professional work experience. Additional exam requirements/recommendations for international students: Required—TOEFL or IELTS. *Application deadline:* For fall admission, 6/1 for domestic and international students; for spring admission, 11/1 for domestic and international students. Applications are processed on a rolling basis. Application fee: $60 ($65 for international students). Electronic applications accepted. *Expenses:* $772.34 per credit hour in-state tuition, $1,456.56 per credit hour out-of-state tuition. *Financial support:* Scholarships/grants available. Financial award application deadline: 6/1. *Faculty research:* Entrepreneurship; corporate finance; international business; consumer behavior; supply chain; business law. *Unit head:* Mary Johnson, Associate Director, Evening MBA Program, 317-274-4895, E-mail: mbaindy@iupui.edu. *Application contact:* Kristen Peters, Program Assistant, 317-274-4895, E-mail: mbaindy@iupui.edu.
Website: http://kelley.iupui.edu/evemba

Indiana University South Bend, Judd Leighton School of Business and Economics, South Bend, IN 46634-7111. Offers accounting (MSA); business (Graduate Certificate); business administration (MBA), including finance, human resource management, marketing; MBA/MSA. *Program availability:* Part-time, evening/weekend. *Faculty:* 17 full-time (2 women), 3 part-time/adjunct (1 woman). *Students:* 28 full-time (18 women), 85 part-time (36 women); includes 10 minority (3 Black or African American, non-Hispanic/Latino; 1 Asian, non-Hispanic/Latino; 5 Hispanic/Latino; 1 Two or more races, non-Hispanic/Latino), 22 international. Average age 32. 57 applicants, 68% accepted, 22 enrolled. In 2016, 67 master's, 7 other advanced degrees awarded. *Entrance requirements:* For master's, GMAT. Additional exam requirements/recommendations for international students: Required—TOEFL (minimum score 550 paper-based; 79 iBT). *Application deadline:* For fall admission, 7/15 priority date for domestic and international students; for spring admission, 11/15 priority date for domestic and international students; for summer admission, 4/1 priority date for domestic and international students. Applications are processed on a rolling basis. Application fee: $40 ($60 for international students). Electronic applications accepted. *Expenses:* $329.79 per credit hour in-state; $739.85 per credit hour out-of-state. *Financial support:* Fellowships, Federal Work-Study, and institutionally sponsored loans available. Support available to part-time students. Financial award application deadline: 7/1; financial award applicants required to submit FAFSA. *Faculty research:* Financial accounting, consumer research, capital budgeting research, business strategy research. *Unit head:* Richard Kolbe, Dean, 574-520-4228, Fax: 574-520-4866, E-mail: rkolbe@iusb.edu. *Application contact:* 574-520-4839, Fax: 574-520-4834, E-mail: graduate@iusb.edu.
Website: https://business.iusb.edu/

Instituto Tecnologico de Santo Domingo, Graduate School, Area of Business, Santo Domingo, Dominican Republic. Offers banking and securities markets (M Mgmt); corporate finance (M Mgmt); human resources management (M Mgmt, Certificate); international trade management (M Mgmt); marketing (M Mgmt); organizational development (M Mgmt); quality and productivity management (Certificate); tax management and planning (M Mgmt); upper management (M Mgmt).

Instituto Tecnologico de Santo Domingo, Graduate School, Area of Humanities and Social Sciences, Santo Domingo, Dominican Republic. Offers accounting (Certificate); adult education (Certificate); applied linguistics (MA); economics (MA); education (M Ed); educational psychology (MA, Certificate); gender and development (MA, Certificate); humanistic studies (MA); international marketing management (Certificate); international relations in the Caribbean basin (Certificate); intervention systems in family therapy (MA); linguistic and literary communication (Certificate); pedagogical support (MA); social science education (M Ed); sustainable human development (MA); terminal illness and death psychology (Certificate); youth and adult education (M Ed).

Instituto Tecnológico y de Estudios Superiores de Monterrey, Campus Central de Veracruz, Graduate Programs, Córdoba, Mexico. Offers administration (MA); administration of information technologies (MTI); computer sciences (MCC); education (MEE); educational institution administration (MAD); educational technology (MTE); electronic commerce (MCE); finance (MAF); humanistic studies (MEH); international business for Latin America (MNL); marketing (MMT); science (MCP). *Program availability:* Part-time, evening/weekend, online learning. *Degree requirements:* For master's, thesis (for some programs). *Entrance requirements:* For master's, PAEP College Board. Electronic applications accepted.

Instituto Tecnológico y de Estudios Superiores de Monterrey, Campus Ciudad Obregón, Program in Marketing Technology, Ciudad Obregón, Mexico. Offers MMT.

Instituto Tecnológico y de Estudios Superiores de Monterrey, Campus Cuernavaca, Programs in Business Administration, Temixco, Mexico. Offers finance (MA); human resources management (MA); international business (MA); marketing (MA).

Instituto Tecnológico y de Estudios Superiores de Monterrey, Campus Estado de México, Professional and Graduate Division, Estado de Mexico, Mexico. Offers administration of information technologies (MITA); architecture (M Arch); business administration (GMBA, MBA); computer sciences (MCS, PhD); education (M Ed); educational institution administration (MAD); educational technology and innovation (PhD); electronic commerce (MEC); environmental systems (MS); finance (MAF); humanistic studies (MHS); information sciences and knowledge management (MISKM); information systems (MS); manufacturing systems (MS); marketing (MEM); quality systems and productivity (MS); science and materials engineering (PhD); telecommunications management (MTM). *Program availability:* Part-time, online learning. *Degree requirements:* For master's, one foreign language, thesis (for some programs); for doctorate, one foreign language, thesis/dissertation. *Entrance requirements:* For master's, E-PAEP 500, interview; for doctorate, E-PAEP 500, research proposal. Additional exam requirements/recommendations for international students: Required—TOEFL (minimum score 550 paper-based). *Faculty research:* Surface treatments by plasmas, mechanical properties, robotics, graphical computing, mechatronics security protocols.

Instituto Tecnológico y de Estudios Superiores de Monterrey, Campus Monterrey, Graduate School of Business Administration and Leadership, Program in Business Administration, Monterrey, Mexico. Offers business administration (MA, MBA); finance (M Sc); international business (M Sc); marketing (M Sc). *Program availability:* Part-time. *Degree requirements:* For master's, one foreign language, thesis. *Entrance requirements:* For master's, GMAT. Additional exam requirements/recommendations for international students: Required—TOEFL. *Faculty research:* Technology management, quality management, organizational theory and behavior.

Inter American University of Puerto Rico, Aguadilla Campus, Graduate School, Aguadilla, PR 00605. Offers accounting (MBA); counseling psychology specializing in family (MS); criminal justice (MA); educative management and leadership (MA); elementary education (M Ed); finance (MBA); human resources (MBA); industrial management (MBA); management information systems (MBA); marketing (MBA). *Program availability:* Part-time, evening/weekend. *Degree requirements:* For master's, comprehensive exam. *Entrance requirements:* For master's, EXADEP, 2 letters of recommendation, minimum GPA of 2.5. Electronic applications accepted.

Marketing

Inter American University of Puerto Rico, Fajardo Campus, Graduate Programs, Fajardo, PR 00738-7003. Offers computer science (MS); educational management and leadership (MA Ed); elementary education (MA Ed); general business (MBA); management information systems (MBA); marketing (MBA); special education (MA Ed).

Inter American University of Puerto Rico, Guayama Campus, Department of Business Administration, Guayama, PR 00785. Offers marketing (MBA).

Inter American University of Puerto Rico, Metropolitan Campus, Graduate Programs, Program in Marketing, San Juan, PR 00919-1293. Offers MBA. *Degree requirements:* For master's, comprehensive exam. *Entrance requirements:* For master's, GRE or EXADEP, interview. Electronic applications accepted.

Inter American University of Puerto Rico, Ponce Campus, Graduate School, Mercedita, PR 00715-1602. Offers accounting (MBA); biology (M Ed); chemistry (M Ed); criminal justice (MA); elementary education (M Ed); English as a Second Language (M Ed); finance (MBA); history (M Ed); human resources (MBA); marketing (MBA); mathematics (M Ed); Spanish (M Ed). *Entrance requirements:* For master's, minimum GPA of 2.5.

Inter American University of Puerto Rico, San Germán Campus, Graduate Studies Center, Program in Business Administration, San Germán, PR 00683-5008. Offers accounting (MBA); finance (MBA); general business administration (MBA); human resources (MBA, PhD); industrial relations (MBA); information systems (MBA); international and interregional business (PhD); management (MBA); marketing (MBA). *Program availability:* Part-time, evening/weekend. *Degree requirements:* For master's, comprehensive exam. *Entrance requirements:* For master's, GRE General Test or EXADEP, minimum GPA of 3.0.

International University in Geneva, Business Programs, Geneva, Switzerland. Offers business administration (MBA, DBA); entrepreneurship (MBA); international business (MIB); international trade (MIT); sales and marketing (MBA). *Accreditation:* ACBSP. *Program availability:* Part-time, evening/weekend. *Degree requirements:* For master's, comprehensive exam. *Entrance requirements:* For master's, GMAT. Additional exam requirements/recommendations for international students: Required—TOEFL. Electronic applications accepted.

The International University of Monaco, Graduate Programs, Monte Carlo, Monaco. Offers entrepreneurship (EMBA, MBA); financial engineering (M Sc); hedge fund and private equity (M Sc); international marketing (EMBA, MBA); international wealth management (M Sc); luxury goods and services (EMBA, M Sc, MBA); wealth and asset management (EMBA, MBA). *Program availability:* Part-time. *Degree requirements:* For master's, comprehensive exam (for some programs), applied research project. *Entrance requirements:* Additional exam requirements/recommendations for international students: Required—TOEFL (minimum score 550 paper-based), IELTS. Electronic applications accepted. *Faculty research:* Gaming, leadership, disintermediation.

Iona College, Hagan School of Business, Department of Marketing and International Business, New Rochelle, NY 10801-1890. Offers international business (AC, PMC); marketing (MBA); sports and entertainment management (AC). *Program availability:* Part-time, evening/weekend. *Faculty:* 2 full-time (1 woman), 3 part-time/adjunct (all women). *Students:* 11 full-time (1 woman), 22 part-time (11 women); includes 9 minority (4 Black or African American, non-Hispanic/Latino; 2 Asian, non-Hispanic/Latino; 3 Hispanic/Latino), 5 international. Average age 25. 19 applicants, 100% accepted, 9 enrolled. In 2016, 22 master's awarded. *Entrance requirements:* For master's, GMAT, 2 letters of recommendation, minimum GPA of 3.0; for other advanced degree, GMAT, minimum GPA of 3.0. Additional exam requirements/recommendations for international students: Required—TOEFL (minimum score 550 paper-based; 80 iBT), IELTS (minimum score 6.5). *Application deadline:* For fall admission, 8/15 priority date for domestic students, 8/1 priority date for international students; for winter admission, 11/15 priority date for domestic students, 11/1 priority date for international students; for spring admission, 2/15 priority date for domestic students, 2/1 priority date for international students; for summer admission, 5/15 for domestic students, 5/1 priority date for international students. Applications are processed on a rolling basis. Application fee: $50. Electronic applications accepted. *Expenses:* Contact institution. *Financial support:* In 2016–17, 13 students received support. Scholarships/grants, tuition waivers (partial), and unspecified assistantships available. Support available to part-time students. Financial award application deadline: 4/15; financial award applicants required to submit FAFSA. *Faculty research:* Business ethics, international retailing, mega-marketing, consumer behavior and consumer confidence. *Unit head:* Dr. Susan G. Rozensher, Department Chair, 914-637-2748, E-mail: srozensher@iona.edu. *Application contact:* Katelyn Brunck, Director of MBA Admissions, 914-633-2451, Fax: 914-633-2277, E-mail: kbrunck@iona.edu.
Website: http://www.iona.edu/Academics/Hagan-School-of-Business/Departments/Marketing/Graduate-Programs.aspx

Jacksonville University, Davis College of Business, Accelerated Day-time MBA Program, Jacksonville, FL 32211. Offers accounting and finance (MBA); business administration (MBA); consumer goods and services marketing (MBA); management (MBA); management accounting (MBA). *Faculty:* 13 full-time (3 women), 1 part-time/adjunct (0 women). *Students:* 39 full-time (12 women), 8 part-time (4 women); includes 11 minority (5 Black or African American, non-Hispanic/Latino; 4 Hispanic/Latino; 2 Two or more races, non-Hispanic/Latino), 20 international. Average age 25. 80 applicants, 61% accepted, 33 enrolled. In 2016, 44 master's awarded. *Entrance requirements:* For master's, GMAT or GRE (may be waived for 3.3 or higher undergraduate GPA from AACSB-accredited institution), bachelor's degree from regionally-accredited institution, resume, statement of purpose, 2 letters of recommendation. Additional exam requirements/recommendations for international students: Required—TOEFL (minimum score 500 paper-based; 61 iBT), IELTS (minimum score 6). *Application deadline:* For fall admission, 8/1 priority date for domestic students, 7/15 priority date for international students; for spring admission, 12/1 priority date for domestic students, 11/15 priority date for international students. Application fee: $50. Electronic applications accepted. *Expenses:* $740 per credit hour. *Financial support:* In 2016–17, 7 students received support. Scholarships/grants and unspecified assistantships available. Financial award application deadline: 7/1; financial award applicants required to submit FAFSA. *Faculty research:* Behavioral finance, game theory, regional economic integration, information sabotage, public choice and public finance. *Unit head:* Dr. Douglas Johansen, Associate Dean and Graduate Programs Director, 904-256-7763, Fax: 904-256-7168, E-mail: djohans@ju.edu. *Application contact:* AnnaMaria Murphy, Assistant Director of Graduate Admissions, 904-256-7426, Fax: 904-256-7012, E-mail: mba@ju.edu.

See Display on page 107 and Close-Up on page 179.

Jacksonville University, Davis College of Business, Executive Master of Business Administration Program, Jacksonville, FL 32211. Offers consumer goods and services marketing (MBA); leadership development (MBA). *Accreditation:* AACSB. *Program availability:* Evening/weekend. *Faculty:* 16 full-time (3 women), 1 part-time/adjunct (0 women). *Students:* 28 full-time (10 women), 8 part-time (4 women); includes 5 minority (4 Black or African American, non-Hispanic/Latino; 1 Asian, non-Hispanic/Latino). Average age 41. 19 applicants, 95% accepted, 16 enrolled. In 2016, 10 master's awarded. *Entrance requirements:* For master's, resume, 5-7 years of professional experience, 3 letters of recommendation, corporate letter of support, statement of purpose, interview. Additional exam requirements/recommendations for international students: Required—TOEFL (minimum score 500 paper-based; 61 iBT), IELTS (minimum score 6). *Application deadline:* For fall admission, 9/1 priority date for domestic students, 8/15 priority date for international students. Application fee: $50. Electronic applications accepted. *Expenses:* Contact institution. *Financial support:* In 2016–17, 4 students received support. Scholarships/grants available. Financial award application deadline: 7/1; financial award applicants required to submit FAFSA. *Faculty research:* Data analytics, emerging markets and economic development, high-performing teams, government deficit, learning from corporate failure. *Unit head:* Dr. Douglas Johansen, Associate Dean and Director of Graduate Studies, 904-256-7763, Fax: 904-256-7168, E-mail: djohans@ju.edu. *Application contact:* AnnaMaria Murphy, Assistant Director of Graduate Admissions, 904-256-7426, Fax: 904-256-7012, E-mail: mba@ju.edu.

See Display on page 107 and Close-Up on page 179.

Jacksonville University, Davis College of Business, FLEX Master of Business Administration Program, Jacksonville, FL 32211. Offers accounting and finance (MBA); consumer goods and services marketing (MBA); management accounting (MBA); JD/MBA; MBA/MPP; MSN/MBA. JD/MBA offered jointly with Florida School of Law. *Accreditation:* AACSB. *Program availability:* Part-time, evening/weekend, blended/hybrid learning. *Faculty:* 20 full-time (5 women), 1 part-time/adjunct (0 women). *Students:* 32 full-time (13 women), 71 part-time (29 women); includes 29 minority (11 Black or African American, non-Hispanic/Latino; 1 American Indian or Alaska Native, non-Hispanic/Latino; 6 Asian, non-Hispanic/Latino; 10 Hispanic/Latino; 1 Two or more races, non-Hispanic/Latino), 3 international. Average age 32. 32 applicants, 97% accepted, 27 enrolled. In 2016, 57 master's awarded. *Entrance requirements:* For master's, GMAT or GRE (may be waived for 3.3 or higher undergraduate GPA from AACSB-accredited institution), bachelor's degree from regionally-accredited institution, 3 years of full-time work experience (recommended), resume, statement of purpose, 2 letters of recommendation. Additional exam requirements/recommendations for international students: Required—TOEFL (minimum score 500 paper-based; 61 iBT), IELTS (minimum score 6). *Application deadline:* For fall admission, 8/1 priority date for domestic students, 7/15 priority date for international students; for spring admission, 12/1 priority date for domestic students, 11/15 priority date for international students; for summer admission, 4/1 priority date for domestic students, 3/15 priority date for international students. Applications are processed on a rolling basis. Application fee: $50. Electronic applications accepted. *Expenses:* $740 per credit hour. *Financial support:* In 2016–17, 1 student received support. Scholarships/grants available. Financial award application deadline: 7/1; financial award applicants required to submit FAFSA. *Faculty research:* Downsizing with integrity; impact of YouTube videos; game theory; analysis of effective tax rates; creativity innovation and change. *Unit head:* Dr. Douglas Johansen, Associate Dean and Director of Graduate Studies, 904-256-7763, Fax: 904-256-7168, E-mail: djohans@ju.edu. *Application contact:* AnnaMaria Murphy, Assistant Director of Graduate Admissions, 904-256-7426, Fax: 904-256-7012, E-mail: mba@ju.edu.

See Display on page 107 and Close-Up on page 179.

Johns Hopkins University, Carey Business School, MS in Marketing Program, Baltimore, MD 21218. Offers MS. *Program availability:* Part-time, evening/weekend. *Faculty:* 87 full-time (32 women), 51 part-time/adjunct (8 women). *Students:* 119 full-time (92 women), 21 part-time (19 women); includes 14 minority (2 Black or African American, non-Hispanic/Latino; 6 Asian, non-Hispanic/Latino; 5 Hispanic/Latino; 1 Two or more races, non-Hispanic/Latino), 114 international. Average age 23. 722 applicants, 52% accepted, 124 enrolled. In 2016, 105 master's awarded. *Degree requirements:* For master's, 36 credits. *Entrance requirements:* For master's, GMAT or GRE. Additional exam requirements/recommendations for international students: Required—TOEFL, IELTS. *Application deadline:* For fall admission, 4/3 for domestic and international students. Applications are processed on a rolling basis. Application fee: $100. Electronic applications accepted. *Expenses:* $64,000 (full-time); $1,290 per credit (part-time). *Financial support:* In 2016–17, 22 students received support. Scholarships/grants available. Support available to part-time students. Financial award application deadline: 4/15; financial award applicants required to submit FAFSA. *Faculty research:* Decision making, marketing management, marketing strategy. *Unit head:* Dr. Kevin Frick, Vice Dean of Education, 410-234-9272, E-mail: kfrick@jhu.edu. *Application contact:* Office of Admissions, 410-234-9220, Fax: 443-529-1554, E-mail: carey.admissions@jhu.edu.
Website: http://carey.jhu.edu/academics/master-of-science/ms-in-marketing/

Kansas State University, Graduate School, College of Business, Program in Business Administration, Manhattan, KS 66506. Offers data analytics (MBA); finance (MBA); management (MBA); marketing (MBA); technology entrepreneurship (MBA). *Accreditation:* AACSB. *Program availability:* Part-time, 100% online. *Faculty:* 35 full-time (8 women). *Students:* 50 full-time (19 women), 89 part-time (36 women); includes 25 minority (8 Black or African American, non-Hispanic/Latino; 6 Asian, non-Hispanic/Latino; 4 Hispanic/Latino; 7 Two or more races, non-Hispanic/Latino), 17 international. Average age 32. 78 applicants, 90% accepted, 31 enrolled. In 2016, 26 master's, 3 other advanced degrees awarded. *Entrance requirements:* For master's, GMAT (minimum score of 500), minimum undergraduate GPA of 3.0. Additional exam requirements/recommendations for international students: Required—TOEFL (minimum score 550 paper-based; 79 iBT); Recommended—IELTS (minimum score 7). *Application deadline:* For fall admission, 2/1 priority date for domestic and international students; for spring admission, 10/1 priority date for domestic students, 8/1 priority date for international students. Applications are processed on a rolling basis. Application fee: $70 ($80 for international students). Electronic applications accepted. *Expenses:* Contact institution. *Financial support:* In 2016–17, 6 students received support, including 5 research assistantships (averaging $6,400 per year), 6 teaching assistantships with partial tuition reimbursements available (averaging $6,400 per year); institutionally sponsored loans and scholarships/grants also available. Financial award application deadline: 3/1; financial award applicants required to submit FAFSA. *Faculty research:* Organizational citizenship behavior, service marketing, impression management, human resources management, lean manufacturing and supply chain management, financial market behavior and investment management, data analytics, corporate responsibility, technology entrepreneurship. *Unit head:* Dr. Kevin Gwinner, Dean, 785-532-7227, Fax: 785-532-7216, E-mail: kgwinner@ksu.edu. *Application contact:* Dr. Chwen Sheu, Associate Dean for Academic Programs, 785-532-4363, Fax: 785-532-1339, E-mail: gradbusiness@ksu.edu.
Website: http://www.cba.k-state.edu/

Kaplan University, Davenport Campus, School of Business, Davenport, IA 52807. Offers business administration (MBA); change leadership (MS); entrepreneurship (MBA); finance (MBA); health care management (MBA, MS); human resource (MBA); international business (MBA); management (MS); marketing (MBA); project management (MBA, MS); supply chain management and logistics (MBA, MS). *Accreditation:* ACBSP. *Program availability:* Part-time, evening/weekend, online learning. *Entrance requirements:* Additional exam requirements/recommendations for

international students: Required—TOEFL (minimum score 550 paper-based; 80 iBT). Electronic applications accepted.

Keiser University, Doctor of Business Administration Program, Ft. Lauderdale, FL 33309. Offers global business (DBA); global organizational leadership (DBA); marketing (DBA).

Keiser University, Master of Business Administration Program, Ft. Lauderdale, FL 33309. Offers accounting (MBA); health services management (MBA); information security management (MBA); international business (MBA); leadership for managers (MBA); marketing (MBA). All concentrations except information security management also offered in Mandarin; leadership for managers and international business also offered in Spanish. *Program availability:* Part-time, online learning.

Kent State University, College of Business Administration, Doctoral Program in Marketing, Kent, OH 44242. Offers PhD. *Faculty:* 13 full-time (4 women). *Students:* 10 full-time (5 women), 5 international. Average age 33. 13 applicants, 15% accepted, 2 enrolled. In 2016, 1 doctorate awarded. *Degree requirements:* For doctorate, comprehensive exam, thesis/dissertation, oral defense. *Entrance requirements:* For doctorate, GMAT or GRE. Additional exam requirements/recommendations for international students: Required—TOEFL (minimum score 600 paper-based; 100 iBT). *Application deadline:* For fall admission, 12/15 for domestic and international students. Application fee: $45 ($70 for international students). Electronic applications accepted. *Expenses:* Tuition, state resident: full-time $10,864; part-time $495 per credit hour. Tuition, nonresident: full-time $18,380; part-time $837 per credit hour. *Financial support:* In 2016–17, 12 students received support, including 12 teaching assistantships with full tuition reimbursements available (averaging $23,000 per year); Federal Work-Study also available. Financial award application deadline: 12/15; financial award applicants required to submit FAFSA. *Faculty research:* Advertising effects, satisfaction, international marketing, high-tech marketing, personality and consumer behavior. *Unit head:* Dr. Robert Jewell, Chair and Professor, 330-672-2170, Fax: 330-672-5006, E-mail: rjewell1@kent.edu. *Application contact:* Felecia A. Urbanek, Coordinator, Graduate Programs, 330-672-2282, Fax: 330-672-7303, E-mail: gradbus@kent.edu. Website: http://www.kent.edu/business/phd

King University, School of Business and Economics, Bristol, TN 37620-2699. Offers accounting (MBA); finance (MBA); healthcare management (MBA); human resources management (MBA); leadership (MBA); management (MBA); marketing (MBA); project management (MBA). *Program availability:* Part-time, evening/weekend, online learning. *Degree requirements:* For master's, comprehensive exam, thesis optional. *Entrance requirements:* For master's, GMAT, 2 years of work experience. Additional exam requirements/recommendations for international students: Required—TOEFL (minimum score 550 paper-based). Electronic applications accepted. *Faculty research:* International monetary policy.

Lake Forest Graduate School of Management, The Leadership MBA Program, Lake Forest, IL 60045. Offers finance (MBA); global business (MBA); healthcare management (MBA); management (MBA); marketing (MBA); organizational behavior (MBA). *Program availability:* Part-time, evening/weekend. *Entrance requirements:* For master's, 4 years of work experience in field, interview, 2 letters of recommendation. Electronic applications accepted.

La Salle University, School of Business, Master of Business Administration Program, Philadelphia, PA 19141-1199. Offers accounting (MBA, Post-MBA Certificate); business systems and analytics (MBA, Post-MBA Certificate); finance (MBA, Post-MBA Certificate); general business administration (MBA, Post-MBA Certificate); human resource management (MBA, Post-MBA Certificate); management (MBA, Post-MBA Certificate); marketing (Post-MBA Certificate); MBA/MSN. Program also offered in Switzerland. *Accreditation:* AACSB. *Program availability:* Part-time, evening/weekend, online learning. *Faculty:* 19 full-time (6 women), 11 part-time/adjunct (3 women). *Students:* 55 full-time (23 women), 209 part-time (96 women); includes 66 minority (35 Black or African American, non-Hispanic/Latino; 17 Asian, non-Hispanic/Latino; 9 Hispanic/Latino; 5 Two or more races, non-Hispanic/Latino), 17 international. Average age 31. 200 applicants, 59% accepted, 63 enrolled. In 2016, 192 master's, 1 other advanced degree awarded. *Entrance requirements:* For master's, GMAT or GRE, two letters of reference; resume; for Post-MBA Certificate, MBA with minimum GPA of 3.0. Additional exam requirements/recommendations for international students: Required—TOEFL. *Application deadline:* For fall admission, 8/15 priority date for domestic students, 7/15 for international students; for spring admission, 12/15 priority date for domestic students, 11/15 for international students; for summer admission, 4/15 priority date for domestic students, 3/15 for international students. Applications are processed on a rolling basis. Application fee: $35. Electronic applications accepted. Application fee is waived when completed online. *Expenses:* Contact institution. *Financial support:* In 2016–17, 49 students received support. Scholarships/grants available. Support available to part-time students. Financial award application deadline: 8/31; financial award applicants required to submit FAFSA. *Unit head:* Dr. MarySheila McDonald, Interim Dean, 215-951-1040, Fax: 215-951-1886, E-mail: mcdonaldms@lasalle.edu. *Application contact:* Elizabeth Heenan, Director, Graduate and Adult Enrollment, 215-951-1100, Fax: 215-951-1462, E-mail: heenan@lasalle.edu.

Lasell College, Graduate and Professional Studies in Communication, Newton, MA 02466. Offers health communication (MSC, Graduate Certificate); integrated marketing communication (MSC, Graduate Certificate); public relations (MSC, Graduate Certificate). *Program availability:* Part-time, evening/weekend, 100% online, blended/hybrid learning. *Faculty:* 4 full-time (2 women), 5 part-time/adjunct (2 women). *Students:* 12 full-time (9 women), 38 part-time (28 women); includes 11 minority (8 Black or African American, non-Hispanic/Latino; 1 Asian, non-Hispanic/Latino; 2 Hispanic/Latino), 8 international. Average age 31. 60 applicants, 43% accepted, 13 enrolled. In 2016, 71 master's, 3 other advanced degrees awarded. *Degree requirements:* For master's, comprehensive exam, thesis or alternative, minimum GPA of 3.0; special project or internship. *Entrance requirements:* For master's, one-page personal statement, 2 letters of recommendation, resume, bachelor's degree transcript; for Graduate Certificate, bachelor's degree transcript, 2 letters of recommendation, 1-page personal statement, resume. Additional exam requirements/recommendations for international students: Required—TOEFL (minimum score 550 paper-based, 79 iBT) or IELTS (minimum score 6). *Application deadline:* For fall admission, 8/31 priority date for domestic students, 6/30 priority date for international students; for spring admission, 12/31 priority date for domestic students, 10/31 priority date for international students. Applications are processed on a rolling basis. Electronic applications accepted. *Expenses:* $600 per credit. *Financial support:* In 2016–17, 6 students received support. Federal Work-Study, scholarships/grants, and tuition discounts available. Support available to part-time students. Financial award application deadline: 8/31; financial award applicants required to submit FAFSA. *Faculty research:* Terrorists' use of the internet; refugees' use of cell phones as means of communication in Jordan and Germany; political communication, analysis of the media coverage of the conflict and peace process in northern Ireland; interpersonal communication, strategies to address bullying in online communities, in schools and in the workplace. *Unit head:* Dr. Joan Dolamore, Dean of Graduate and Professional Studies, 617-243-2485, Fax: 617-243-2450, E-mail: gradinfo@lasell.edu. *Application contact:* Adrienne Franciosi, Director of Graduate Enrollment, 617-243-2214, Fax: 617-243-2450, E-mail: gradinfo@lasell.edu.
Website: http://www.lasell.edu/academics/graduate-and-professional-studies/programs-of-study/master-of-science-in-communication.html

Lasell College, Graduate and Professional Studies in Management, Newton, MA 02466-2709. Offers business administration (PMBA); elder care management (MSM, Graduate Certificate); hospitality and event management (MSM, Graduate Certificate); human resources management (MSM, Graduate Certificate); management (MSM, Graduate Certificate); marketing (MSM, Graduate Certificate); non-profit management (MSM, Graduate Certificate); project management (MSM, Graduate Certificate). *Accreditation:* ACBSP. *Program availability:* Part-time, evening/weekend, 100% online, blended/hybrid learning. *Faculty:* 3 full-time (2 women), 16 part-time/adjunct (10 women). *Students:* 47 full-time (34 women), 93 part-time (72 women); includes 28 minority (20 Black or African American, non-Hispanic/Latino; 4 Asian, non-Hispanic/Latino; 3 Hispanic/Latino; 1 Two or more races, non-Hispanic/Latino), 24 international. Average age 31. 121 applicants, 55% accepted, 32 enrolled. In 2016, 61 master's, 3 other advanced degrees awarded. *Degree requirements:* For master's, minimum GPA of 3.0; internship or research paper (for MSM). *Entrance requirements:* For master's, one-page personal statement, 2 letters of recommendation, resume, bachelor's degree transcript; proof of microeconomics and statistics (for PMBA); for Graduate Certificate, bachelor's degree transcript, 2 letters of recommendation, 1-page personal statement, resume. Additional exam requirements/recommendations for international students: Required—TOEFL (minimum score 550 paper-based, 79 iBT) or IELTS (minimum score 6). *Application deadline:* For fall admission, 8/31 priority date for domestic students, 6/30 priority date for international students; for spring admission, 12/31 priority date for domestic students, 10/31 priority date for international students. Applications are processed on a rolling basis. Electronic applications accepted. *Expenses:* $600 per credit. *Financial support:* In 2016–17, 12 students received support. Federal Work-Study, scholarships/grants, and tuition discounts available. Support available to part-time students. Financial award application deadline: 8/31; financial award applicants required to submit FAFSA. *Unit head:* Dr. Joan Dolamore, Dean of Graduate and Professional Studies, 617-243-2485, Fax: 617-243-2450, E-mail: gradinfo@lasell.edu. *Application contact:* Adrienne Franciosi, Director of Graduate Enrollment, 617-243-2214, Fax: 617-243-2450, E-mail: gradinfo@lasell.edu.
Website: http://www.lasell.edu/academics/graduate-and-professional-studies/programs-of-study/master-of-science-in-management.html

La Sierra University, School of Business and Management, Riverside, CA 92515. Offers accounting (MBA); finance (MBA); general management (MBA); human resources management (MBA); leadership, values, and ethics for business and management (Certificate); marketing (MBA). *Degree requirements:* For master's, research project. *Entrance requirements:* For master's, GMAT, minimum GPA of 3.0. Additional exam requirements/recommendations for international students: Required—TOEFL. *Faculty research:* Financial econometrics, institutional assessment and strategic planning, legal issues in management, behavioral finance, content of financial reports.

Lawrence Technological University, College of Management, Southfield, MI 48075-1058. Offers business administration (MBA), including business analytics (MBA, MS), finance, information technology, marketing, project management (MBA, MS); information technology (MS), including business analytics (MBA, MS), information assurance, project management (MBA, MS); project management (Graduate Certificate). *Accreditation:* ACBSP. *Program availability:* Part-time, evening/weekend, 100% online. *Faculty:* 14 full-time (6 women), 10 part-time/adjunct (2 women). *Students:* 7 full-time (3 women), 323 part-time (120 women); includes 60 minority (29 Black or African American, non-Hispanic/Latino; 2 American Indian or Alaska Native, non-Hispanic/Latino; 17 Asian, non-Hispanic/Latino; 8 Hispanic/Latino; 4 Two or more races, non-Hispanic/Latino), 118 international. Average age 33. 275 applicants, 56% accepted, 72 enrolled. In 2016, 167 master's, 12 other advanced degrees awarded. Terminal master's awarded for partial completion of doctoral program. *Degree requirements:* For master's, thesis (for some programs). *Entrance requirements:* Additional exam requirements/recommendations for international students: Required—TOEFL (minimum score 550 paper-based; 79 iBT), IELTS (minimum score 6.5). *Application deadline:* For fall admission, 5/22 for international students; for spring admission, 10/11 for international students; for summer admission, 2/16 for international students. Applications are processed on a rolling basis. Application fee: $50. Electronic applications accepted. *Expenses: Tuition:* Full-time $14,868; part-time $1062 per credit. *Required fees:* $75 per semester. Tuition and fees vary according to campus/location. *Financial support:* In 2016–17, 35 students received support, including 8 research assistantships with partial tuition reimbursements available (averaging $3,250 per year); career-related internships or fieldwork, unspecified assistantships, and corporate tuition incentives also available. Financial award application deadline: 4/1; financial award applicants required to submit FAFSA. *Faculty research:* Cybersecurity; risk management; IT governance; security controls and countermeasures; threat modeling cyber resilience; autonomous cars; natural language processing; text mining; machine learning; reflective leadership; emerging leadership theories and practice; motivational studies; teaching effectiveness strategies; teamwork; organization development; strategic planning; strengths-based and positive organizational scholarship; global leadership; globalization; corporate governance. *Unit head:* Dr. Bahman Mirshab, Dean, 248-204-3050, E-mail: mgtdean@ltu.edu. *Application contact:* Jane Rohrback, Director of Admissions, 248-204-3160, Fax: 248-204-2228, E-mail: admissions@ltu.edu.
Website: http://www.ltu.edu/management/index.asp

Lewis University, College of Business, Graduate School of Management, Program in Business Administration, Romeoville, IL 60446. Offers accounting (MBA); custom elective option (MBA); e-business (MBA); finance (MBA); healthcare management (MBA); human resources management (MBA); international business (MBA); management information systems (MBA); marketing (MBA); project management (MBA); technology and operations management (MBA). *Program availability:* Part-time, evening/weekend. *Students:* 145 full-time (72 women), 213 part-time (123 women); includes 101 minority (46 Black or African American, non-Hispanic/Latino; 2 American Indian or Alaska Native, non-Hispanic/Latino; 7 Asian, non-Hispanic/Latino; 41 Hispanic/Latino; 1 Native Hawaiian or other Pacific Islander, non-Hispanic/Latino; 4 Two or more races, non-Hispanic/Latino), 47 international. Average age 31. In 2016, 99 master's awarded. *Degree requirements:* For master's, comprehensive exam. *Entrance requirements:* For master's, interview, bachelor's degree, resume, 2 recommendations. Additional exam requirements/recommendations for international students: Required—TOEFL (minimum score 550 paper-based). *Application deadline:* For fall admission, 8/15 priority date for domestic students, 5/1 priority date for international students; for spring admission, 11/15 priority date for international students. Applications are processed on a rolling basis. Application fee: $40. Electronic applications accepted. *Expenses: Tuition:* Full-time $13,860; part-time $770 per credit hour. *Required fees:* $75 per semester. Tuition and fees vary according to degree level and program. *Financial support:* Career-related internships or fieldwork, Federal Work-Study, scholarships/grants, and unspecified assistantships available. Financial award application deadline: 5/1; financial award applicants required to submit FAFSA. *Unit head:* Dr. Maureen Culleeney, Academic Program Director, 815-838-0500 Ext. 5631, E-mail: culleema@lewisu.edu. *Application contact:* Michele Ryan, Director of Admission, 815-838-0500 Ext. 5384, E-mail: gsm@lewisu.edu.

Marketing

Liberty University, School of Business, Lynchburg, VA 24515. Offers accounting (MBA, MS); business administration (MBA); criminal justice (MBA); cyber security (MS); executive leadership (MA); information systems (MS), including information assurance, technology management; international business (MBA, DBA); leadership (DBA); marketing (MBA, MS, DBA), including digital marketing and advertising (MS), project management (MS), public relations (MS), sports marketing and media (MS); project management (MBA, DBA); public administration (MBA); public relations (MBA). *Program availability:* Part-time, online learning. *Students:* 1,458 full-time (807 women), 4,188 part-time (2,041 women); includes 1,372 minority (1,060 Black or African American, non-Hispanic/Latino; 19 American Indian or Alaska Native, non-Hispanic/Latino; 85 Asian, non-Hispanic/Latino; 75 Hispanic/Latino; 10 Native Hawaiian or other Pacific Islander, non-Hispanic/Latino; 123 Two or more races, non-Hispanic/Latino), 124 international. Average age 35. 5,424 applicants, 45% accepted, 1242 enrolled. In 2016, 1,859 master's, 87 other advanced degrees awarded. *Entrance requirements:* For master's, minimum undergraduate GPA of 3.0, 15 hours of upper-level business courses. Additional exam requirements/recommendations for international students: Required—TOEFL (minimum score 600 paper-based; 100 iBT). *Application deadline:* Applications are processed on a rolling basis. Application fee: $50. Electronic applications accepted. *Expenses:* Contact institution. *Financial support:* Applicants required to submit FAFSA. *Unit head:* Dr. Scott Hicks, Dean, 434-592-4808, Fax: 434-582-2366, E-mail: smhicks@liberty.edu. *Application contact:* Jay Bridge, Director of Graduate Admissions, 800-424-9595, Fax: 800-628-7977, E-mail: gradadmissions@liberty.edu.
Website: http://www.liberty.edu/academics/business/index.cfm?PID-149

LIM College, MPS Program, New York, NY 10022-5268. Offers fashion marketing (MPS); fashion merchandising and retail management (MPS); visual merchandising (MPS). *Accreditation:* ACBSP.

Lindenwood University, Graduate Programs, Plaster School of Business and Entrepreneurship, St. Charles, MO 63301-1695. Offers accountancy (M Acc); accounting (MBA); business administration (MBA); entrepreneurial studies (MBA); finance (MBA, MS); human resource management (MBA); international business (MBA); leadership (MA); management (MBA); marketing (MBA, MS); nonprofit administration (MA); public administration (MBA); sport management (MA); supply chain management (MBA). *Accreditation:* ACBSP. *Program availability:* Part-time, evening/weekend, 100% online. *Faculty:* 15 full-time (6 women), 25 part-time/adjunct (7 women). *Students:* 197 full-time (97 women), 213 part-time (132 women); includes 81 minority (62 Black or African American, non-Hispanic/Latino; 1 American Indian or Alaska Native, non-Hispanic/Latino; 4 Asian, non-Hispanic/Latino; 9 Hispanic/Latino; 5 Two or more races, non-Hispanic/Latino), 83 international. Average age 31. 279 applicants, 54% accepted, 133 enrolled. In 2016, 269 master's awarded. *Degree requirements:* For master's, comprehensive exam (for some programs), thesis (for some programs), minimum GPA of 3.0. *Entrance requirements:* For master's, interview, minimum undergraduate cumulative GPA of 3.0, letter of recommendation. Additional exam requirements/recommendations for international students: Required—TOEFL (minimum score 550 paper-based; 80 iBT); Recommended—IELTS (minimum score 6.5). *Application deadline:* For fall admission, 8/28 priority date for domestic and international students; for winter admission, 1/8 priority date for domestic and international students; for spring admission, 3/5 for domestic students, 3/5 priority date for international students; for summer admission, 6/4 priority date for domestic and international students. Applications are processed on a rolling basis. Application fee: $30 ($100 for international students). Electronic applications accepted. *Expenses:* Contact institution. *Financial support:* In 2016–17, 256 students received support. Career-related internships or fieldwork, Federal Work-Study, institutionally sponsored loans, scholarships/grants, tuition waivers (partial), and unspecified assistantships available. Financial award application deadline: 6/30; financial award applicants required to submit FAFSA. *Unit head:* Roger Ellis, Dean, School of Business and Entrepreneurship, 636-949-4839, E-mail: rellis@lindenwood.edu. *Application contact:* Tyler Kostich, Director, Evening and Graduate Admissions, 636-949-4138, Fax: 636-949-4109, E-mail: adultadmissions@lindenwood.edu.
Website: http://www.lindenwood.edu/academics/academic-schools/robert-w-plaster-school-of-business-entrepreneurship/

Lindenwood University, Graduate Programs, School of Accelerated Degree Programs, St. Charles, MO 63301-1695. Offers administration (MSA), including management, marketing, project management; business administration (MBA); communications (MA), including digital and multimedia, media management, promotions, training and development; criminal justice and administration (MS); healthcare administration (MS); human resource management (MS); information technology (Certificate); managing information security (MS); managing information technology (MS); managing virtualization and cloud computing (MS); writing (MFA). *Program availability:* Part-time, evening/weekend, 100% online. *Faculty:* 16 full-time (7 women), 75 part-time/adjunct (27 women). *Students:* 609 full-time (386 women), 179 part-time (121 women); includes 257 minority (202 Black or African American, non-Hispanic/Latino; 4 American Indian or Alaska Native, non-Hispanic/Latino; 5 Asian, non-Hispanic/Latino; 28 Hispanic/Latino; 1 Native Hawaiian or other Pacific Islander, non-Hispanic/Latino; 17 Two or more races, non-Hispanic/Latino), 28 international. Average age 36. 332 applicants, 70% accepted, 205 enrolled. In 2016, 479 master's awarded. *Degree requirements:* For master's, thesis (for some programs), minimum cumulative GPA of 3.0; for Certificate, minimum cumulative GPA of 3.0. *Entrance requirements:* For master's, resume, personal statement, official undergraduate transcript, minimum undergraduate cumulative GPA of 3.0. Additional exam requirements/recommendations for international students: Required—TOEFL (minimum score 550 paper-based; 80 iBT); Recommended—IELTS (minimum score 6.5). *Application deadline:* For fall admission, 9/26 priority date for domestic and international students; for winter admission, 1/3 priority date for domestic and international students; for spring admission, 3/31 priority date for domestic and international students; for summer admission, 7/3 priority date for domestic and international students. Applications are processed on a rolling basis. Application fee: $30 ($100 for international students). Electronic applications accepted. *Expenses: Tuition:* Full-time $15,672; part-time $453 per credit hour. *Required fees:* $205 per semester. Tuition and fees vary according to course level, course load and degree level. *Financial support:* In 2016–17, 467 students received support. Career-related internships or fieldwork, institutionally sponsored loans, scholarships/grants, tuition waivers (partial), and unspecified assistantships available. Financial award application deadline: 6/30; financial award applicants required to submit FAFSA. *Unit head:* Dr. Gina Ganahl, Dean, Accelerated Degree Programs, 636-949-4501, Fax: 636-949-4505, E-mail: gganahl@lindenwood.edu. *Application contact:* Tyler Kostich, Director, Evening and Graduate Admissions, 636-949-4138, Fax: 636-949-4109, E-mail: adultadmissions@lindenwood.edu.
Website: http://www.lindenwood.edu/academics/academic-schools/school-of-accelerated-degree-programs/

Long Island University–LIU Post, College of Management, Brookville, NY 11548-1300. Offers accountancy (MS); finance (MBA); information systems (MS); international business (MBA); management (MBA); management engineering (MS); marketing (MBA); taxation (MS); technical project management (MS); JD/MBA. *Accreditation:* AACSB. *Program availability:* Part-time, 100% online, blended/hybrid learning. *Faculty:* 35 full-time (12 women), 25 part-time/adjunct (6 women). *Students:* 153 full-time (61 women), 68 part-time (22 women); includes 44 minority (8 Black or African American, non-Hispanic/Latino; 24 Asian, non-Hispanic/Latino; 11 Hispanic/Latino; 1 Two or more races, non-Hispanic/Latino), 79 international. 429 applicants, 58% accepted, 74 enrolled. In 2016, 124 master's awarded. *Degree requirements:* For master's, thesis (for some programs). *Entrance requirements:* For master's, GMAT, GRE, or LSAT. Additional exam requirements/recommendations for international students: Required—PTE, TOEFL (minimum score 550 paper-based, 75 iBT) or IELTS. *Application deadline:* Applications are processed on a rolling basis. Application fee: $50. Electronic applications accepted. *Expenses: Tuition:* Full-time $28,272; part-time $1178 per credit. *Required fees:* $451 per term. Tuition and fees vary according to degree level and program. *Financial support:* In 2016–17, 68 students received support. Career-related internships or fieldwork, Federal Work-Study, institutionally sponsored loans, and scholarships/grants available. Support available to part-time students. Financial award application deadline: 2/15; financial award applicants required to submit FAFSA. *Faculty research:* Finance and sustainability, innovation and intellectual property rights, marketing: data analytics and business intelligence, social networking local and international. *Unit head:* Dr. Robert M. Valli, Dean, 516-299-4192, E-mail: rob.valli@liu.edu. *Application contact:* Carol Zerah, Director of Graduate and International Admissions, 516-299-2900, Fax: 516-299-2137, E-mail: post-enroll@liu.edu.
Website: http://liu.edu/CWPost/Academics/Schools/COM

Loyola University Chicago, Quinlan School of Business, Master of Science in Integrated Marketing Communications Program, Chicago, IL 60611. Offers MSIMC, MSIMC/MBA. *Program availability:* Part-time, evening/weekend. *Faculty:* 10 full-time (8 women), 6 part-time/adjunct (1 woman). *Students:* 30 full-time (22 women), 3 part-time (all women); includes 2 minority (1 Black or African American, non-Hispanic/Latino; 1 Hispanic/Latino), 24 international. Average age 26. 108 applicants, 60% accepted, 16 enrolled. In 2016, 30 master's awarded. *Entrance requirements:* For master's, GMAT or GRE, official transcripts, two letters of recommendation, statement of purpose, resume. Additional exam requirements/recommendations for international students: Required—TOEFL (minimum score 90 iBT) or IELTS (minimum score 6.5). *Application deadline:* For fall admission, 7/15 for domestic and international students; for winter admission, 10/1 for domestic and international students; for spring admission, 1/15 for domestic and international students; for summer admission, 4/1 for domestic and international students. Applications are processed on a rolling basis. Application fee: $50. Electronic applications accepted. Application fee is waived when completed online. *Expenses:* Contact institution. *Financial support:* In 2016–17, 6 students received support. Federal Work-Study, scholarships/grants, health care benefits, and unspecified assistantships available. Support available to part-time students. *Faculty research:* Brand strategy, consumer behavior, digital/interactive marketing, international marketing. *Unit head:* Dr. Mary Ann McGrath, Chair, 312-915-6136, E-mail: mmcgrat@luc.edu. *Application contact:* Lauren Griffin, Enrollment Advisor, Quinlan School of Business Graduate Programs, 312-915-6124, Fax: 312-915-7207, E-mail: lgriffin3@luc.edu.
Website: http://luc.edu/quinlan/mba/masters-in-marketing/

Loyola University Chicago, Quinlan School of Business, MBA Programs, Chicago, IL 60611. Offers accounting (MBA); business administration (EMBA); business ethics (MBA); economics (MBA); entrepreneurship (MBA); finance (MBA); healthcare management (MBA); human resources management (MBA); international business (MBA); management (MBA); marketing (MBA); operation management (MBA); risk management (MBA); supply chain management (MBA). *Program availability:* Part-time, evening/weekend. *Faculty:* 79 full-time (22 women), 10 part-time/adjunct (6 women). *Students:* 309 full-time (151 women), 65 part-time (31 women); includes 82 minority (25 Black or African American, non-Hispanic/Latino; 27 Asian, non-Hispanic/Latino; 27 Hispanic/Latino; 3 Two or more races, non-Hispanic/Latino), 49 international. Average age 30. 371 applicants, 53% accepted, 114 enrolled. In 2016, 216 master's awarded. *Entrance requirements:* For master's, GMAT or GRE, official transcripts, two letters of recommendation, statement of purpose, resume. Additional exam requirements/recommendations for international students: Required—TOEFL (minimum score 90 iBT) or IELTS (minimum score 6.5). *Application deadline:* For fall admission, 7/15 for domestic and international students; for winter admission, 10/1 for domestic and international students; for spring admission, 1/15 for domestic and international students; for summer admission, 4/1 for domestic and international students. Applications are processed on a rolling basis. Application fee: $50. Electronic applications accepted. Application fee is waived when completed online. *Expenses:* $4,488 per course. *Financial support:* In 2016–17, 83 students received support. Federal Work-Study, scholarships/grants, health care benefits, and unspecified assistantships available. Support available to part-time students. *Faculty research:* Social enterprise and responsibility, emerging markets, supply chain management, risk management. *Unit head:* Katherine Acles, Assistant Dean for Graduate Programs, 312-915-6124, Fax: 312-915-7207, E-mail: kacles@luc.edu. *Application contact:* Lauren Griffin, Enrollment Advisor, Quinlan School of Business Graduate Programs, 312-915-6124, Fax: 312-915-7207, E-mail: lgriffin3@luc.edu.

Loyola University New Orleans, Joseph A. Butt, S.J., College of Business, Program in Business Administration, New Orleans, LA 70118-6195. Offers entrepreneurship and marketing innovation (MBA); organizational performance excellence (MBA); JD/MBA; MBA/MPS. *Accreditation:* AACSB. *Program availability:* Part-time, evening/weekend, online learning. *Faculty:* 8 full-time (4 women), 3 part-time/adjunct (0 women). *Students:* 71 full-time (35 women), 13 part-time (9 women); includes 27 minority (14 Black or African American, non-Hispanic/Latino; 1 American Indian or Alaska Native, non-Hispanic/Latino; 3 Asian, non-Hispanic/Latino; 8 Hispanic/Latino; 1 Two or more races, non-Hispanic/Latino), 3 international. Average age 29. 52 applicants, 96% accepted, 28 enrolled. In 2016, 25 master's awarded. *Degree requirements:* For master's, capstone project. *Entrance requirements:* For master's, GMAT or GRE, minimum GPA of 3.0, transcript, resume, 2 letters of recommendation, work experience in field, personal statement. Additional exam requirements/recommendations for international students: Required—TOEFL (minimum score 580 paper-based; 92 iBT). *Application deadline:* For fall admission, 6/15 priority date for domestic students, 5/15 priority date for international students; for spring admission, 11/15 priority date for domestic students, 10/15 priority date for international students. Applications are processed on a rolling basis. Application fee: $50. Electronic applications accepted. *Financial support:* Research assistantships, scholarships/grants, tuition waivers (partial), and unspecified assistantships available. Financial award application deadline: 5/1; financial award applicants required to submit FAFSA. *Faculty research:* Ethics, international business, entrepreneurship, quality management, risk management. *Unit head:* Dr. William B. Locander, Dean, 504-864-7979, Fax: 504-864-7970, E-mail: mba@loyno.edu. *Application contact:* Ashley Francis, Director of Graduate Programs, 504-864-7979, Fax: 504-864-7970, E-mail: mba@loyno.edu.
Website: http://www.business.loyno.edu/mba/programs

Lynn University, College of Business and Management, Boca Raton, FL 33431-5598. Offers business administration (MBA), including aviation management, financial valuation and investment management, hospitality management, human resource management, international business management, marketing, media management, sports management. *Program availability:* Part-time, evening/weekend, 100% online, blended/hybrid learning. *Faculty:* 24 full-time (9 women), 24 part-time/adjunct (4 women). *Students:* 265 full-time (125 women), 182 part-time (96 women); includes 100

minority (41 Black or African American, non-Hispanic/Latino; 11 Asian, non-Hispanic/Latino; 42 Hispanic/Latino; 6 Two or more races, non-Hispanic/Latino), 119 international. Average age 28. 280 applicants, 94% accepted, 181 enrolled. In 2016, 219 master's awarded. *Degree requirements:* For master's, strategic management seminar, simulation capstone. *Entrance requirements:* For master's, bachelor's degree from accredited institution, resume, letter of recommendation, official transcripts, essay/personal statement. Additional exam requirements/recommendations for international students: Required—TOEFL (minimum score 550 paper-based; 80 iBT), IELTS (minimum score 6.5). *Application deadline:* For fall admission, 8/18 for domestic students, 8/4 for international students; for spring admission, 12/15 for domestic students, 12/1 for international students; for summer admission, 4/17 for domestic students, 4/3 for international students. Applications are processed on a rolling basis. Application fee: $45. Electronic applications accepted. *Expenses:* $725 per credit. *Financial support:* In 2016–17, 115 students received support. Career-related internships or fieldwork, Federal Work-Study, scholarships/grants, tuition waivers (full and partial), and unspecified assistantships available. Support available to part-time students. Financial award application deadline: 3/1; financial award applicants required to submit FAFSA. *Faculty research:* Market volatility investing, biometric research, sports legal history, organizational leadership, urban economic development and productivity. *Unit head:* Dr. RT Good, Dean of the College of Business and Management, 561-237-7458, E-mail: rgood@lynn.edu. *Application contact:* Steven Pruitt, Director of Graduate and Undergraduate Evening Admission, 561-237-7834, Fax: 561-237-7100, E-mail: spruitt@lynn.edu.
Website: http://www.lynn.edu/academics/colleges/business-and-management

Manhattanville College, School of Business, Master of Science in Marketing Communication Management Program, Purchase, NY 10577-2132. Offers MS. *Program availability:* Part-time, evening/weekend. *Students:* 21 (15 women); includes 9 minority (3 Black or African American, non-Hispanic/Latino; 1 Asian, non-Hispanic/Latino; 5 Hispanic/Latino). Average age 29. 28 applicants, 25% accepted, 4 enrolled. In 2016, 5 master's awarded. *Degree requirements:* For master's, thesis (for some programs), final project. *Entrance requirements:* For master's, transcripts, 2 letters of recommendation, resume. Additional exam requirements/recommendations for international students: Required—TOEFL (minimum score 563 paper-based; 85 iBT). *Application deadline:* Applications are processed on a rolling basis. Application fee: $75. Electronic applications accepted. *Expenses: Tuition:* Full-time $16,470; part-time $915 per credit. *Required fees:* $60 per semester. Part-time tuition and fees vary according to course load and program. *Financial support:* Federal Work-Study, institutionally sponsored loans, scholarships/grants, and unspecified assistantships available. Financial award applicants required to submit FAFSA. *Faculty research:* Crisis communications, public relations. *Unit head:* Laura Persky, Graduate Program Director, 914-323-5188, E-mail: laura.persky@mville.edu. *Application contact:* Monika Pottgen, Assistant Director, Recruitment and Admissions, 914-323-5150, E-mail: business@mville.edu.
Website: https://www.mville.edu/programs/ms-marketing-communication-management

Marist College, Graduate Programs, School of Communication and the Arts, Program in Integrated Marketing Communication, Poughkeepsie, NY 12601-1387. Offers MA. *Entrance requirements:* For master's, GRE or GMAT, official undergraduate/graduate transcripts from all institutions attended; current resume; completed recommendation forms for three references; personal statement.

Marquette University, Graduate School of Management, Executive MBA Program, Milwaukee, WI 53201-1881. Offers economics (MBA); finance (MBA); human resources (MBA); international business (MBA); management information systems (MBA); marketing (MBA); operations and supply chain management (MBA); sports business (MBA). *Accreditation:* AACSB. *Students:* 39 full-time (12 women); includes 7 minority (4 Black or African American, non-Hispanic/Latino; 2 Asian, non-Hispanic/Latino; 1 Hispanic/Latino). Average age 38. 25 applicants, 96% accepted, 29 enrolled. In 2016, 14 master's awarded. *Degree requirements:* For master's, international trip. *Entrance requirements:* For master's, GMAT or GRE, two letters of recommendation, official transcripts from current and previous colleges/universities. Additional exam requirements/recommendations for international students: Required—TOEFL (minimum score 550 paper-based; 88 iBT), IELTS (minimum score 6.5), PTE. *Application deadline:* For fall admission, 2/15 for domestic and international students. Application fee: $50. Electronic applications accepted. *Expenses:* Contact institution. *Financial support:* Application deadline: 2/15. *Faculty research:* International trade and finance, customer relationship management, consumer satisfaction, customer service. *Unit head:* Dr. Brian Till, Dean, 414-288-5724. *Application contact:* Dr. Jeanne Simmons, Associate Dean, 414-288-7145.
Website: http://www.busadm.mu.edu/emba/

Marquette University, Graduate School of Management, Program in Business Administration, Milwaukee, WI 53201-1881. Offers business administration (MBA); economics (MBA); entrepreneurship (Certificate); finance (MBA); human resources (MBA); international business (MBA); management information systems (MBA); marketing (MBA); operations and supply chain management (MBA); sports business (MBA); JD/MBA; MBA/MA; MBA/MSN. *Accreditation:* AACSB. *Program availability:* Part-time, evening/weekend. *Students:* 25 full-time (12 women), 202 part-time (57 women); includes 17 minority (5 Black or African American, non-Hispanic/Latino; 6 Asian, non-Hispanic/Latino; 2 Hispanic/Latino; 1 Native Hawaiian or other Pacific Islander, non-Hispanic/Latino; 3 Two or more races, non-Hispanic/Latino), 7 international. Average age 31. 107 applicants, 87% accepted, 113 enrolled. In 2016, 107 master's, 5 other advanced degrees awarded. *Degree requirements:* For Certificate, business plan. *Entrance requirements:* For master's, GMAT or GRE, letters of recommendation. Additional exam requirements/recommendations for international students: Required—TOEFL (minimum score 550 paper-based; 88 iBT), IELTS (minimum score 6.5), PTE. *Application deadline:* For fall admission, 2/15 for domestic and international students. Applications are processed on a rolling basis. Application fee: $50. Electronic applications accepted. *Financial support:* Fellowships, research assistantships, teaching assistantships, Federal Work-Study, institutionally sponsored loans, scholarships/grants, and tuition waivers (full and partial) available. Support available to part-time students. Financial award application deadline: 2/15. *Faculty research:* Ethics in the professions, services marketing, technology impact on decision-making, mentoring. *Unit head:* Dr. Brian Till, Dean, 414-288-5724. *Application contact:* Dr. Jeanne Simmons, Associate Dean, 414-288-7145.
Website: http://business.marquette.edu/academics/mba

Maryville University of Saint Louis, The John E. Simon School of Business, St. Louis, MO 63141-7299. Offers accounting (MBA, Certificate); business studies (Certificate); cyber security (MBA); cybersecurity (Certificate); financial services (MBA, Certificate); healthcare practice management (MBA, Certificate); human resource management (MBA); information technology (MBA, Certificate); management (MBA, Certificate); management and leadership (MA); marketing (MBA, Certificate); project management (MBA); sport business management (MBA); supply chain management/logistics (MBA). *Accreditation:* ACBSP. *Program availability:* Part-time, evening/weekend, 100% online, blended/hybrid learning. *Faculty:* 7 full-time (3 women), 34 part-time/adjunct (9 women). *Students:* 84 full-time (40 women), 223 part-time (118 women); includes 67 minority (40 Black or African American, non-Hispanic/Latino; 2 American Indian or Alaska Native, non-Hispanic/Latino; 8 Asian, non-Hispanic/Latino; 12 Hispanic/Latino; 1 Native Hawaiian or other Pacific Islander, non-Hispanic/Latino; 4 Two or more races, non-Hispanic/Latino), 15 international. Average age 32. In 2016, 67 master's awarded. *Entrance requirements:* Additional exam requirements/recommendations for international students: Required—TOEFL (minimum score 563 paper-based; 85 iBT). *Application deadline:* Applications are processed on a rolling basis. Electronic applications accepted. *Expenses:* $650 per credit hour. *Financial support:* Career-related internships or fieldwork, Federal Work-Study, tuition waivers (partial), and campus employment available. Financial award application deadline: 3/1; financial award applicants required to submit FAFSA. *Faculty research:* Global business, e-marketing, strategic planning, interpersonal management skills, financial analysis. *Unit head:* Pam Horwitz, Interim Dean, 314-529-9680, Fax: 314-529-9975. *Application contact:* Dustin Loeffler, Director for Graduate Studies in Business, 314-529-9571, Fax: 314-529-9975, E-mail: dloeffler@maryville.edu.
Website: http://www.maryville.edu/bu/business-administration-masters/

McGill University, Faculty of Graduate and Postdoctoral Studies, Desautels Faculty of Management, Montréal, QC H3A 2T5, Canada. Offers administration (PhD); entrepreneurial studies (MBA); finance (MBA); general management (Post Master's Certificate); information systems (MBA); international business (MBA); international practicing management (MM); management (MBA); management for development (MBA); manufacturing management (MMM); marketing (MBA); operations management (MBA); public accountancy (Diploma); strategic management (MBA); MBA/LL B; MD/MBA. MMM offered jointly with Faculty of Engineering; PhD with Concordia University, HEC Montreal, Université de Montréal, Université du Québec à Montréal.

Melbourne Business School, Graduate Programs, Carlton, Australia. Offers business administration (Exec MBA, MBA); management (PhD); management science (PhD); marketing (PhD); social impact (Graduate Certificate); JD/MBA.

Michigan State University, The Graduate School, Eli Broad College of Business, Department of Marketing, East Lansing, MI 48224. Offers marketing (PhD); marketing research (MS). *Degree requirements:* For doctorate, comprehensive exam, thesis/dissertation. *Entrance requirements:* For master's, GMAT, bachelor's degree with minimum GPA of 3.0 in last 2 years of undergraduate work; transcripts; 3 letters of recommendation; statement of purpose; resume; working knowledge of computers; basic understanding of accounting, finance, marketing, and the management of people; laptop capable of running Windows software; for doctorate, GMAT (taken within past 5 years), bachelor's degree; letters of recommendation; statement of purpose; previous work experience; personal qualifications of sound character, perseverance, intellectual curiosity, and an interest in scholarly research. Additional exam requirements/recommendations for international students: Required—TOEFL (minimum score 100 iBT), PTE (minimum score 70), IELTS (minimum score 7) accepted for MS only.

Michigan State University, The Graduate School, Eli Broad College of Business, Program in Business Administration, East Lansing, MI 48224. Offers finance (MBA); human resource management (MBA); integrative management (MBA); marketing (MBA); supply chain management (MBA). MBA in integrative management is through Weekend MBA Program; other 4 concentrations are through Full-Time MBA Program. *Program availability:* Evening/weekend. *Degree requirements:* For master's, enrichment experience. *Entrance requirements:* For master's, GMAT or GRE, 4-year bachelor's degree; resume; work experience (minimum of 5 years for Weekend MBA); 2-3 personal essays; 2 letters of recommendation; personal interview. Additional exam requirements/recommendations for international students: Required—PTE (minimum score 70), TOEFL (minimum score 100 iBT) or IELTS (minimum score 7) for full-time MBA applicants. Electronic applications accepted. *Expenses:* Contact institution.

Milwaukee School of Engineering, Rader School of Business, Program in Marketing and Export Management, Milwaukee, WI 53202-3109. Offers MS. *Program availability:* Part-time, evening/weekend. *Faculty:* 1 (woman) full-time, 2 part-time/adjunct (0 women). *Students:* 1 (woman) full-time, 2 part-time (0 women), 1 international. Average age 26. 6 applicants, 50% accepted, 2 enrolled. In 2016, 2 master's awarded. *Degree requirements:* For master's, thesis, thesis defense or capstone project. *Entrance requirements:* For master's, GRE or GMAT if undergraduate GPA less than 2.8, 2 letters of recommendation; BS in engineering, engineering technology, science, business, management or a related field. Additional exam requirements/recommendations for international students: Required—TOEFL (minimum score 79 iBT), IELTS (minimum score 6.5). *Application deadline:* Applications are processed on a rolling basis. Application fee: $0. Electronic applications accepted. *Expenses: Tuition:* Full-time $31,440; part-time $655 per credit. *Financial support:* Career-related internships or fieldwork, institutionally sponsored loans, scholarships/grants, and tuition waivers (full) available. Financial award application deadline: 3/15; financial award applicants required to submit FAFSA. *Unit head:* Gene Wright, Director, 414-277-2268, Fax: 414-277-2487, E-mail: wright@msoe.edu. *Application contact:* Ian Dahlinghaus, Graduate Admissions Counselor, 414-277-7208, E-mail: dahlinghaus@msoe.edu.
Website: http://www.msoe.edu/community/academics/business/page/1306/marketing-and-export-management-overview

Mississippi State University, College of Business, Department of Marketing, Quantitative Analysis and Business Law, Mississippi State, MS 39762. Offers business administration (PhD), including marketing. *Program availability:* Part-time, evening/weekend. *Faculty:* 15 full-time (5 women). *Students:* 6 full-time (4 women), 2 part-time (1 woman); includes 1 minority (Black or African American, non-Hispanic/Latino). Average age 29. 15 applicants, 20% accepted, 2 enrolled. *Degree requirements:* For doctorate, comprehensive exam, thesis/dissertation. *Entrance requirements:* For doctorate, GMAT (taken within last five years with minimum score of 550), minimum GPA of 3.25 on all prior graduate work. Additional exam requirements/recommendations for international students: Required—TOEFL (minimum score 575 paper-based; 84 iBT); Recommended—IELTS (minimum score 6.5). *Application deadline:* For fall admission, 7/1 for domestic students, 5/1 for international students; for spring admission, 11/1 for domestic students, 9/1 for international students. Applications are processed on a rolling basis. Application fee: $60. Electronic applications accepted. *Expenses:* Tuition, state resident: full-time $7670; part-time $852.50 per credit hour. Tuition, nonresident: full-time $20,790; part-time $2310.50 per credit hour. Part-time tuition and fees vary according to course load. *Financial support:* Federal Work-Study, institutionally sponsored loans, and scholarships/grants available. Financial award application deadline: 4/1; financial award applicants required to submit FAFSA. *Unit head:* Dr. Melissa Moore, Department Head, 662-325-8556, Fax: 662-325-7012, E-mail: mlm145@msstate.edu. *Application contact:* Lakan Drinker, Admissions and Enrollment Assistant, 662-325-8951, E-mail: ldrinker@grad.msstate.edu.
Website: http://www.business.msstate.edu/programs/marketing/index.php

Molloy College, Graduate Business Program, Rockville Centre, NY 11571-5002. Offers accounting (MBA); finance (MBA, Advanced Certificate); healthcare (MBA, Advanced Certificate); management (MBA); marketing (MBA, Advanced Certificate); personal financial planning (MBA). *Program availability:* Part-time, evening/weekend. *Faculty:* 6 full-time (3 women), 14 part-time/adjunct (5 women). *Students:* 66 full-time (32 women), 178 part-time (92 women); includes 96 minority (38 Black or African American, non-Hispanic/Latino; 24 Asian, non-Hispanic/Latino; 32 Hispanic/Latino; 1 Native Hawaiian or other Pacific Islander, non-Hispanic/Latino; 1 Two or more races, non-Hispanic/

Latino), 5 international. Average age 40. 198 applicants, 69% accepted, 108 enrolled. In 2016, 55 master's awarded. *Entrance requirements:* Additional exam requirements/recommendations for international students: Required—TOEFL (minimum score 550 paper-based; 79 iBT). *Application deadline:* Applications are processed on a rolling basis. Application fee: $60. Electronic applications accepted. *Expenses: Tuition:* Full-time $19,170; part-time $1065 per credit. *Required fees:* $950; $790 per credit. Tuition and fees vary according to course load. *Financial support:* Applicants required to submit FAFSA. *Faculty research:* Leadership profiles that provide lessons of strength and purpose applicable to business; pedagogy and student learning outcomes for graduate business education; mobilizing social networks for innovation and qualitative analysis of sociocentric (whole) network measures; the ethical considerations of covenants not to compete in employment contracts and the use of liquidated damages clauses in employment contracts. *Unit head:* Dr. Maureen Mackenzie, Dean, Division of Business/Director of Graduate Programs, 516-323-3080, E-mail: mmackenzie@molloy.edu. *Application contact:* Jaclyn Machowicz, Assistant Director for Admissions, 516-323-4010, E-mail: jmachowicz@molloy.edu.
Website: http://www.molloy.edu/academics/graduate-programs/graduate-business

Monmouth University, Graduate Studies, Leon Hess Business School, West Long Branch, NJ 07764-1898. Offers accounting (MBA, Post-Master's Certificate); business administration (MBA); finance (MBA); management (MBA); marketing (MBA); real estate (MBA). *Accreditation:* AACSB. *Program availability:* Part-time, evening/weekend. *Faculty:* 20 full-time (4 women), 8 part-time/adjunct (0 women). *Students:* 76 full-time (37 women), 94 part-time (43 women); includes 17 minority (2 Black or African American, non-Hispanic/Latino; 6 Asian, non-Hispanic/Latino; 6 Hispanic/Latino; 1 Native Hawaiian or other Pacific Islander, non-Hispanic/Latino; 2 Two or more races, non-Hispanic/Latino), 8 international. Average age 30. 105 applicants, 90% accepted, 67 enrolled. In 2016, 93 master's, 1 other advanced degree awarded. *Degree requirements:* For master's, capstone course. *Entrance requirements:* For master's, GMAT or GRE, current resume; essay (500 words or less). Additional exam requirements/recommendations for international students: Required—TOEFL (minimum score 550 paper-based; 79 iBT), IELTS (minimum score 6), Michigan English Language Assessment Battery (minimum score 77) or Certificate of Advanced English (minimum score B2). *Application deadline:* For fall admission, 7/15 priority date for domestic students, 6/1 for international students; for spring admission, 12/1 priority date for domestic students, 11/1 for international students; for summer admission, 5/1 for domestic students. Applications are processed on a rolling basis. Application fee: $50. Electronic applications accepted. *Expenses: Tuition, area resident:* Full-time $19,764; part-time $1098 per credit hour. *Required fees:* $175 per semester. Tuition and fees vary according to program. *Financial support:* In 2016–17, 191 students received support, including 137 fellowships (averaging $2,643 per year), 20 teaching assistantships with full and partial tuition reimbursements available (averaging $10,034 per year); research assistantships, institutionally sponsored loans, scholarships/grants, and unspecified assistantships also available. Support available to part-time students. Financial award application deadline: 2/1; financial award applicants required to submit FAFSA. *Faculty research:* Information technology and marketing, behavioral research in accounting, human resources, management of technology. *Unit head:* Dr. Susan Gupta, MBA Program Director, 732-571-3639, Fax: 732-263-5517, E-mail: sgupta@monmouth.edu. *Application contact:* Laurie Kuhn, Associate Director of Graduate Admission, 732-571-3452, Fax: 732-263-5123, E-mail: gradadm@monmouth.edu.
Website: https://www.monmouth.edu/business-school/leon-hess-business-school.aspx

See Display on page 118 and Close-Up on page 181.

Monroe College, King Graduate School, Bronx, NY 10468. Offers accounting (MS); business administration (MBA), including entrepreneurship, finance, general business administration, healthcare management, human resources, information technology, marketing; computer science (MS); criminal justice (MS); hospitality management (MS); public health (MPH), including biostatistics and epidemiology, community health, health administration and leadership. *Program availability:* Online learning. Application fee: $50.
Website: https://www.monroecollege.edu/Degrees/King-Graduate-School/

National University College, Graduate Programs, Bayamón, PR 00960. Offers digital marketing (MBA); general business (MBA); special education (M Ed).

New England College, Program in Management, Henniker, NH 03242-3293. Offers accounting (MSA); healthcare administration (MS); international relations (MA); marketing management (MS); nonprofit leadership (MS); project management (MS); strategic leadership (MS). *Program availability:* Part-time, evening/weekend. *Degree requirements:* For master's, independent research project. Electronic applications accepted.

New Jersey City University, School of Business, Program in Marketing, Jersey City, NJ 07305-1597. Offers MBA.

New Mexico State University, College of Business, Department of Marketing, Las Cruces, NM 88003. Offers business administration (PhD), including marketing. *Program availability:* Part-time. *Faculty:* 7 full-time (2 women), 1 (woman) part-time/adjunct. *Students:* 10 full-time (6 women), 1 (woman) part-time; includes 3 minority (2 Hispanic/Latino; 1 Two or more races, non-Hispanic/Latino), 4 international. Average age 32. 6 applicants. *Degree requirements:* For doctorate, comprehensive exam, thesis/dissertation. *Entrance requirements:* For doctorate, GMAT or GRE, graduate degree, work experience. Additional exam requirements/recommendations for international students: Required—TOEFL (minimum score 550 paper-based; 79 iBT), IELTS (minimum score 6.5). *Application deadline:* For fall admission, 2/1 for domestic and international students. Application fee: $40 ($50 for international students). Electronic applications accepted. *Expenses:* Tuition, state resident: full-time $4086. Tuition, nonresident: full-time $14,254. *Required fees:* $853. Tuition and fees vary according to course load. *Financial support:* In 2016–17, 10 students received support, including 2 fellowships (averaging $4,088 per year), 10 teaching assistantships (averaging $23,157 per year); career-related internships or fieldwork, Federal Work-Study, scholarships/grants, traineeships, health care benefits, and unspecified assistantships also available. Support available to part-time students. Financial award application deadline: 3/1. *Faculty research:* Consumer behavior, social media marketing, ethics in marketing, advertising, public policy. *Unit head:* Dr. Nancy Orestskin, Department Head, 575-646-3341, Fax: 575-646-1498, E-mail: noretski@nmsu.edu. *Application contact:* Dr. Nancy Oretskin, Coordinator, Marketing PhD Program, 575-646-3341, Fax: 575-646-1498, E-mail: noretski@nmsu.edu.
Website: http://business.nmsu.edu/departments/marketing

New York Institute of Technology, School of Management, Department of Business Administration, Old Westbury, NY 11568-8000. Offers executive (MBA); management (MBA), including finance, marketing, operations and supply chain management; professional accounting (MBA). *Accreditation:* AACSB. *Program availability:* Part-time, evening/weekend. *Faculty:* 25 full-time (4 women), 20 part-time/adjunct (6 women). *Students:* 377 full-time (161 women), 149 part-time (88 women); includes 60 minority (17 Black or African American, non-Hispanic/Latino; 1 American Indian or Alaska Native, non-Hispanic/Latino; 28 Asian, non-Hispanic/Latino; 11 Hispanic/Latino; 2 Native Hawaiian or other Pacific Islander, non-Hispanic/Latino; 1 Two or more races, non-Hispanic/Latino), 446 international. Average age 26. 804 applicants, 68% accepted, 215 enrolled. In 2016, 193 master's awarded. *Entrance requirements:* For master's, bachelor's degree; minimum undergraduate GPA of 3.0. Additional exam requirements/recommendations for international students: Required—TOEFL (minimum score 79 iBT), IELTS (minimum score 6). *Application deadline:* Applications are processed on a rolling basis. Application fee: $50. Electronic applications accepted. *Expenses:* $1,215 per credit. *Financial support:* Career-related internships or fieldwork, Federal Work-Study, scholarships/grants, tuition waivers (full and partial), and unspecified assistantships available. Support available to part-time students. Financial award application deadline: 3/1; financial award applicants required to submit FAFSA. *Faculty research:* Accounting, economics, finance, management, marketing. *Unit head:* Dr. Jess Boronico, Dean, 516-686-7838, E-mail: som@nyit.edu. *Application contact:* Alice Dolitsky, Director, Graduate Admissions, 516-686-7520, Fax: 516-686-1116, E-mail: nyitgrad@nyit.edu.
Website: http://www.nyit.edu/degrees/management_mba

New York University, Leonard N. Stern School of Business, Department of Marketing, New York, NY 10012-1019. Offers entertainment, media and technology (MBA); general marketing (MBA); marketing (PhD); product management (MBA).

New York University, School of Continuing and Professional Studies, Division of Programs in Business, Program in Integrated Marketing, New York, NY 10012-1019. Offers brand management (MS); digital marketing (MS); marketing analytics (MS). *Program availability:* Part-time, evening/weekend. *Degree requirements:* For master's, comprehensive exam, thesis, capstone; writing of complete business plan. *Entrance requirements:* For master's, GRE or GMAT (only upon request), bachelor's degree, resume with relevant professional work, internship or volunteer experience, two letters of recommendation, statement of purpose. Additional exam requirements/recommendations for international students: Required—TOEFL (minimum score 600 paper-based; 100 iBT), IELTS (minimum score 7). Electronic applications accepted. *Faculty research:* Branding, digital marketing, Web analytics, consumer behavior, customer loyalty, campaign planning and management.

New York University, School of Continuing and Professional Studies, Division of Programs in Business, Programs in Marketing and Public Relations, New York, NY 10012-1019. Offers corporate and organizational communication (MS); public relations management (MS). *Program availability:* Part-time, evening/weekend. *Degree requirements:* For master's, thesis. *Entrance requirements:* For master's, GRE or GMAT (only upon request), bachelor's degree, resume with relevant professional work, internship or volunteer experience, two letters of recommendation, statement of purpose. Additional exam requirements/recommendations for international students: Required—TOEFL (minimum score 600 paper-based; 100 iBT), IELTS (minimum score 7). Electronic applications accepted.

New York University, School of Continuing and Professional Studies, Tisch Institute for Sports Management, Media, and Business, New York, NY 10012-1019. Offers global sports media (MS); professional and collegiate sports operations (MS); sports business (Advanced Certificate); sports law (MS); sports marketing and sales (MS). *Program availability:* Part-time, evening/weekend. *Degree requirements:* For master's, thesis. *Entrance requirements:* For master's, GRE or GMAT (only upon request), bachelor's degree, resume with relevant professional work, internship or volunteer experience, two letters of recommendation, statement of purpose. Additional exam requirements/recommendations for international students: Required—TOEFL (minimum score 600 paper-based; 100 iBT), IELTS (minimum score 7). Electronic applications accepted. *Faculty research:* Implications of college football's bowl coalition series from a legal, economic, and academic perspective; social history of sports.

Niagara University, Graduate Division of Business Administration, Niagara University, NY 14109. Offers accounting (MBA); business administration (MBA); finance (MBA, MS); financial planning (MBA); healthcare administration (MBA, MHA); human resources (MBA); international business (MBA); marketing (MBA); professional accountancy (MBA); strategic management (MBA); supply chain management (MBA). *Accreditation:* AACSB. *Program availability:* Part-time, evening/weekend. *Students:* 172 full-time (69 women), 65 part-time (36 women); includes 25 minority (4 Black or African American, non-Hispanic/Latino; 7 Asian, non-Hispanic/Latino; 7 Hispanic/Latino; 1 Native Hawaiian or other Pacific Islander, non-Hispanic/Latino; 6 Two or more races, non-Hispanic/Latino), 76 international. Average age 27. In 2016, 107 master's awarded. *Entrance requirements:* For master's, GMAT. Additional exam requirements/recommendations for international students: Required—TOEFL (minimum score 550 paper-based; 79 iBT), IELTS (minimum score 6). *Application deadline:* For fall admission, 8/1 for domestic students; for spring admission, 11/1 for domestic students. Applications are processed on a rolling basis. Electronic applications accepted. *Expenses:* $870 per credit hour. *Financial support:* Fellowships, research assistantships, career-related internships or fieldwork, and Federal Work-Study available. Support available to part-time students. Financial award application deadline: 4/15; financial award applicants required to submit FAFSA. *Faculty research:* Capital flows, Federal Reserve policy, human resource management, public policy, issues in marketing, auctions, economics of information, risk and capital markets, management strategy, consumer behavior, Internet and social media marketing. *Unit head:* Dr. Paul Richardson, MBA Director/Chair of the Marketing Department, 716-286-8169, Fax: 716-286-8206, E-mail: psr@niagara.edu. *Application contact:* Evan Pierce, Associate Director for Graduate Recruitment, 716-286-8769, Fax: 716-286-8170, E-mail: epierce@niagara.edu.
Website: http://mba.niagara.edu

Northeastern Illinois University, College of Graduate Studies and Research, College of Business and Management, Chicago, IL 60625-4699. Offers accounting (MSA); business administration (MBA); finance (MBA); management (MBA); marketing (MBA). *Program availability:* Part-time, evening/weekend. *Degree requirements:* For master's, thesis optional. *Entrance requirements:* For master's, GMAT, minimum GPA of 2.75. Additional exam requirements/recommendations for international students: Required—TOEFL (minimum score 550 paper-based; 79 iBT). Electronic applications accepted. *Faculty research:* Perception of accountants and non-accountants toward the future of the accounting industry, asynchronous learning outcomes, cost and efficiency of financial markets, impact of deregulation on airline industry, analysis of derivational instruments.

Northwestern University, The Graduate School, Kellogg School of Management, Department of Marketing, Evanston, IL 60208. Offers PhD. Admissions and degree offered through The Graduate School. *Degree requirements:* For doctorate, comprehensive exam, thesis/dissertation. *Entrance requirements:* For doctorate, GMAT or GRE General Test. Additional exam requirements/recommendations for international students: Required—TOEFL. Electronic applications accepted. *Faculty research:* Choice models, database and high-tech marketing, consumer information processing, ethnographic analysis of consumption, psychometric analysis of consumer behavior.

Northwestern University, The Graduate School, Kellogg School of Management, Management Programs, Evanston, IL 60208. Offers accounting information and management (MBA, PhD); analytical finance (MBA); business administration (MBA); decision sciences (MBA); entrepreneurship and innovation (MBA); finance (MBA, PhD);

health enterprise management (MBA); human resources management (MBA); international business (MBA); management and organizations (MBA, PhD); management and organizations and sociology (PhD); management and strategy (MBA); management studies (MS); managerial analytics (MBA); managerial economics (MBA); managerial economics and strategy (PhD); marketing (MBA, PhD); marketing management (MBA); media management (MBA); operations management (MBA, PhD); real estate (MBA); social enterprise at Kellogg (MBA); JD/MBA. *Program availability:* Part-time, evening/weekend. Terminal master's awarded for partial completion of doctoral program. *Degree requirements:* For doctorate, thesis/dissertation, 2 years of coursework, qualifying (field) exam and candidacy, summer research papers and presentations to faculty, proposal defense, final exam/defense. *Entrance requirements:* For master's, GMAT, GRE, interview, 2 letters of recommendation, college transcripts, resume, essays, Kellogg honor code; for doctorate, GMAT, GRE, statement of purpose, transcripts, 2 letters of recommendation, resume, interview. Additional exam requirements/recommendations for international students: Required—TOEFL, IELTS. Electronic applications accepted. *Expenses:* Contact institution. *Faculty research:* Business cycles and international finance, health policy, networks, non-market strategy, consumer psychology.

Northwestern University, Medill School of Journalism, Media, and Integrated Marketing Communications, Integrated Marketing Communications Program, Evanston, IL 60208. Offers brand strategy (MSIMC); content marketing (MSIMC); direct and interactive marketing (MSIMC); marketing analytics (MSIMC); strategic communications (MSIMC). *Program availability:* Part-time. *Entrance requirements:* For master's, GRE General Test or GMAT, full-time work experience (preferred). Additional exam requirements/recommendations for international students: Required—TOEFL. Electronic applications accepted. *Faculty research:* Data mining, business to business marketing, values in advertising, political advertising.

Northwest Missouri State University, Graduate School, Melvin and Valorie Booth College of Business and Professional Studies, Maryville, MO 64468-6001. Offers agricultural economics (MBA); general management (MBA); human resource management (MBA); marketing (MBA). *Program availability:* Part-time. *Students:* 50 full-time (18 women), 50 part-time (27 women); includes 10 minority (5 Black or African American, non-Hispanic/Latino; 2 Asian, non-Hispanic/Latino; 3 Hispanic/Latino), 16 international. In 2016, 55 master's awarded. *Degree requirements:* For master's, comprehensive exam. *Entrance requirements:* For master's, GMAT, GRE, minimum GPA of 2.5. Additional exam requirements/recommendations for international students: Required—TOEFL (minimum score 550 paper-based). *Application deadline:* For fall admission, 7/1 for domestic and international students; for spring admission, 11/15 for domestic and international students; for summer admission, 4/1 for domestic and international students. Applications are processed on a rolling basis. Application fee: $0 ($50 for international students). Electronic applications accepted. *Expenses:* Tuition, state resident: full-time $3447; part-time $383 per credit hour. Tuition, nonresident: full-time $5724; part-time $636 per credit hour. *Required fees:* $130 per credit hour. *Financial support:* Research assistantships with full tuition reimbursements, teaching assistantships with full tuition reimbursements, career-related internships or fieldwork, and administrative assistantships, tutorial assistantships available. Financial award application deadline: 4/1; financial award applicants required to submit FAFSA. *Unit head:* Dr. Gregory Haddock, Dean of Graduate School, 660-562-1145, Fax: 660-562-1096, E-mail: gradsch@nwmissouri.edu.
Website: http://www.nwmissouri.edu/academics/booth/

Notre Dame de Namur University, Division of Academic Affairs, School of Business and Management, Program in Business Administration, Belmont, CA 94002-1908. Offers business administration (MBA); entrepreneurship (MBA); finance (MBA); human resource management (MBA); marketing (MBA); media and promotion (MBA); technology and operations management (MBA). *Accreditation:* ACBSP. *Program availability:* Part-time, evening/weekend. *Entrance requirements:* For master's, minimum GPA of 2.5. Additional exam requirements/recommendations for international students: Required—TOEFL (minimum score 550 paper-based; 79 iBT). Electronic applications accepted.

Nova Southeastern University, H. Wayne Huizenga College of Business and Entrepreneurship, Fort Lauderdale, FL 33314-7796. Offers accounting (M Acc); business intelligence/analytics (MBA); entrepreneurship (MBA); finance (MBA); human resource management (MBA); international business (MBA); management (MBA); marketing (MBA); process improvement (MBA); public administration (MPA); real estate development (MS); sport revenue generation (MBA); supply chain management (MBA); taxation (M Tax). *Program availability:* Part-time, evening/weekend, 100% online, blended/hybrid learning. *Faculty:* 65 full-time (26 women), 111 part-time/adjunct (74 women). *Students:* 2,242 full-time (1,400 women), 425 part-time (239 women); includes 1,798 minority (734 Black or African American, non-Hispanic/Latino; 5 American Indian or Alaska Native, non-Hispanic/Latino; 110 Asian, non-Hispanic/Latino; 890 Hispanic/Latino; 2 Native Hawaiian or other Pacific Islander, non-Hispanic/Latino; 57 Two or more races, non-Hispanic/Latino), 255 international. Average age 34. 1,422 applicants, 64% accepted, 672 enrolled. In 2016, 971 master's awarded. *Degree requirements:* For master's, thesis optional. *Entrance requirements:* For master's, GMAT or GRE (depending on undergraduate GPA), official transcripts from all schools attended while in pursuit of bachelor's degree; minimum GPA of 2.5 from regionally-accredited institution. Additional exam requirements/recommendations for international students: Required—TOEFL (minimum score 550 paper-based; 79 iBT), IELTS (minimum score 6), PTE (minimum score 54). *Application deadline:* For fall admission, 8/5 priority date for domestic students, 7/29 priority date for international students; for winter admission, 12/16 priority date for domestic students, 12/9 priority date for international students; for summer admission, 4/21 priority date for domestic and international students. Applications are processed on a rolling basis. Application fee: $50. Electronic applications accepted. *Expenses:* Contact institution. *Financial support:* In 2016–17, 325 students received support. Federal Work-Study and scholarships/grants available. Support available to part-time students. Financial award application deadline: 4/15; financial award applicants required to submit FAFSA. *Faculty research:* Reputation management, call centers, international social capital, corporate earnings guidance, corporate governance. *Unit head:* Dr. J. Preston Jones, Dean, 954-262-5127, E-mail: prestonj@nova.edu. *Application contact:* Zeida Rodriguez, Associate Director of Enrollment Services, 954-262-5163, Fax: 954-262-3822, E-mail: zeida@nova.edu.
Website: http://www.huizenga.nova.edu

Oakland University, Graduate Study and Lifelong Learning, School of Business Administration, Department of Management and Marketing, Rochester, MI 48309-4401. Offers business administration (MBA); entrepreneurship (Certificate); general management (Certificate); human resource management (Certificate); international business (Certificate); management and marketing (EMBA); marketing (Certificate).

Ohio Christian University, Graduate Programs, Circleville, OH 43113-9487. Offers accounting (MBA); business administration (MBA); digital marketing (MBA); finance (MBA); healthcare management (MBA); human resources (MBA); management (MM); organizational leadership (MBA); pastoral care and counseling (MAM); practical theology (MAM).

Oklahoma Christian University, Graduate School of Business, Oklahoma City, OK 73136-1100. Offers accounting (M Acc, MBA); financial services (MBA); general business (MBA); health services management (MBA); human resources (MBA); international business (MBA); leadership and organizational development (MBA); marketing (MBA); nonprofit management (MBA); project management (MBA). *Accreditation:* ACBSP. *Program availability:* Part-time, 100% online. *Faculty:* 10 full-time (2 women), 21 part-time/adjunct (2 women). *Students:* 156 full-time (68 women), 137 part-time (73 women). Average age 30. 374 applicants, 213 enrolled. In 2016, 114 master's awarded. *Entrance requirements:* For master's, bachelor's degree. Additional exam requirements/recommendations for international students: Required—TOEFL (minimum score 550 paper-based). Application fee: $25. Electronic applications accepted. *Expenses:* Contact institution. *Unit head:* Dr. Ken Johnson, Chair, 405-425-5567, Fax: 405-425-5585, E-mail: ken.johnson@oc.edu. *Application contact:* Angie Ricketts, Graduate School Admissions Counselor, 405-425-5587, Fax: 405-425-5585, E-mail: angie.ricketts@oc.edu.
Website: http://www.oc.edu/academics/graduate/business/

Oklahoma State University, Spears School of Business, Department of Marketing, Stillwater, OK 74078. Offers business administration (PhD), including marketing; marketing (MBA). *Program availability:* Part-time. *Faculty:* 21 full-time (4 women), 7 part-time/adjunct (2 women). *Students:* 68 full-time (25 women), 10 part-time (4 women); includes 4 minority (1 Asian, non-Hispanic/Latino; 1 Hispanic/Latino; 2 Two or more races, non-Hispanic/Latino), 69 international. Average age 27. 149 applicants, 26% accepted, 38 enrolled. In 2016, 2 doctorates awarded. *Degree requirements:* For master's, thesis or alternative; for doctorate, comprehensive exam, thesis/dissertation. *Entrance requirements:* For master's and doctorate, GRE or GMAT. Additional exam requirements/recommendations for international students: Required—TOEFL (minimum score 550 paper-based; 79 iBT). *Application deadline:* For fall admission, 3/1 priority date for international students; for spring admission, 8/1 priority date for international students. Applications are processed on a rolling basis. Application fee: $40 ($75 for international students). Electronic applications accepted. *Expenses:* Tuition, state resident: full-time $3775; part-time $209.70 per credit hour. Tuition, nonresident: full-time $14,851; part-time $825.05 per credit hour. *Required fees:* $2027; $112.60 per credit hour. Tuition and fees vary according to campus/location. *Financial support:* In 2016–17, 17 research assistantships (averaging $10,334 per year), 17 teaching assistantships (averaging $7,271 per year) were awarded; career-related internships or fieldwork, Federal Work-Study, scholarships/grants, health care benefits, tuition waivers (partial), and unspecified assistantships also available. Support available to part-time students. Financial award application deadline: 3/1; financial award applicants required to submit FAFSA. *Faculty research:* Decision-making (consumer, managerial, cross-functional), communication effects, services marketing, public policy and marketing, corporate image. *Unit head:* Dr. Joshua L. Wiener, Department Head, 405-744-5192, Fax: 405-744-5180, E-mail: josh.wiener@okstate.edu. *Application contact:* Dr. Kevin Voss, PhD Coordinator, 405-744-5106, Fax: 405-744-5180, E-mail: kevin.voss@okstate.edu.
Website: http://spears.okstate.edu/marketing

Old Dominion University, Strome College of Business, Doctoral Program in Business Administration, Norfolk, VA 23529. Offers finance (PhD); information technology (PhD); marketing (PhD); strategic management (PhD). *Accreditation:* AACSB. *Faculty:* 29 full-time (6 women). *Students:* 25 full-time (8 women), 23 part-time (5 women); includes 2 minority (both Asian, non-Hispanic/Latino), 38 international. Average age 34. 71 applicants, 17% accepted, 12 enrolled. In 2016, 15 doctorates awarded. *Degree requirements:* For doctorate, comprehensive exam, thesis/dissertation. *Entrance requirements:* For doctorate, GMAT. Additional exam requirements/recommendations for international students: Required—TOEFL (minimum score 550 paper-based; 79 iBT). *Application deadline:* For fall admission, 1/1 priority date for domestic and international students. Application fee: $50. Electronic applications accepted. *Expenses:* Tuition, state resident: full-time $8604; part-time $478 per credit hour. Tuition, nonresident: full-time $21,510; part-time $1195 per credit hour. *Required fees:* $66 per semester. Tuition and fees vary according to campus/location, program and reciprocity agreements. *Financial support:* In 2016–17, 36 students received support, including 15 research assistantships with full tuition reimbursements available (averaging $7,500 per year), 12 teaching assistantships with full tuition reimbursements available (averaging $7,500 per year); scholarships/grants and unspecified assistantships also available. Financial award application deadline: 3/1; financial award applicants required to submit FAFSA. *Faculty research:* International business, buyer behavior, financial markets, strategy, operations research. *Unit head:* Dr. John B. Ford, Graduate Program Director, 757-683-3587, Fax: 757-683-4076, E-mail: jbford@odu.edu. *Application contact:* Katrina Davenport, Program Coordinator, 757-683-5138, Fax: 757-683-4076, E-mail: kdavenpo@odu.edu.
Website: http://www.odu.edu/business/academics/graduate/scb-phd

Oral Roberts University, School of Business, Tulsa, OK 74171. Offers accounting (MBA); entrepreneurship (MBA); finance (MBA); international business (MBA); management (MBA); marketing (MBA); non-profit management (MBA); not for profit management (MNM). *Accreditation:* ACBSP. *Program availability:* Part-time, online learning. *Degree requirements:* For master's, thesis optional. *Entrance requirements:* For master's, minimum cumulative GPA of 3.0. Additional exam requirements/recommendations for international students: Required—TOEFL (minimum score 550 paper-based; 79 iBT). Electronic applications accepted. *Faculty research:* Social media, international business and marketing.

Ottawa University, Graduate Studies-Arizona, Programs in Business, Ottawa, KS 66067-3399. Offers business administration (MBA); finance (MBA); human resources (MA, MBA); leadership (MBA); marketing (MBA). Programs offered in Mesa, Phoenix, Tempe and West Valley, AZ. *Program availability:* Part-time, evening/weekend, online learning. *Degree requirements:* For master's, thesis or alternative. *Entrance requirements:* For master's, minimum undergraduate GPA of 3.0. Additional exam requirements/recommendations for international students: Required—TOEFL (minimum score 550 paper-based). Electronic applications accepted.

Pace University, Lubin School of Business, Advanced Professional Certificate Program, New York, NY 10038. Offers business economics (APC); e-business (APC); financial management (APC); international business (APC); international economics (APC); investment management (APC); marketing (APC); public accounting (APC). *Program availability:* Evening/weekend. *Students:* 1 applicant, 100% accepted, 1 enrolled. *Entrance requirements:* For degree, MBA or MS in business discipline, relevant professional experience. Additional exam requirements/recommendations for international students: Required—TOEFL (minimum score 90 iBT), IELTS (minimum score 7) or PTE (minimum score 61). *Application deadline:* For fall admission, 8/1 priority date for domestic students, 6/1 for international students; for spring admission, 12/1 for domestic students, 10/1 for international students. Applications are processed on a rolling basis. Application fee: $70. Electronic applications accepted. *Expenses: Tuition:* Part-time $1195 per credit. *Required fees:* $260 per semester. Tuition and fees vary according to degree level, campus/location and program. *Unit head:* Dr. Jack Yurkiewicz, Director, 212-618-6567, E-mail: jyurkiewicz@pace.edu. *Application contact:* Susan Ford-Goldschein, Director of Graduate Admissions, 212-346-1531, Fax: 212-

346-1585, E-mail: graduateadmission@pace.edu.
Website: http://www.pace.edu/lubin/agc

Pace University, Lubin School of Business, Doctor of Professional Studies Program, New York, NY 10038. Offers finance (DPS); management (DPS); marketing (DPS). *Program availability:* Part-time. *Students:* 6 full-time (1 woman), 78 part-time (33 women); includes 26 minority (15 Black or African American, non-Hispanic/Latino; 5 Asian, non-Hispanic/Latino; 5 Hispanic/Latino; 1 Two or more races, non-Hispanic/Latino), 3 international. Average age 49. 32 applicants, 75% accepted, 14 enrolled. In 2016, 4 doctorates awarded. *Degree requirements:* For doctorate, thesis/dissertation, oral and written exam. *Entrance requirements:* For doctorate, MBA or similar master's degree, 10 years of experience in business, transcripts from all accredited colleges/universities attended, 4 letters of recommendation, interview. Additional exam requirements/recommendations for international students: Required—TOEFL (minimum score 90 iBT), IELTS (minimum score 7) or PTE (minimum score 61). *Application deadline:* For fall admission, 6/1 priority date for domestic students, 6/1 for international students. Applications are processed on a rolling basis. Application fee: $70. Electronic applications accepted. *Expenses: Tuition:* Part-time $1195 per credit. *Required fees:* $260 per semester. Tuition and fees vary according to degree level, campus/location and program. *Unit head:* Dr. John P. Dory, Director, Doctoral Program in Business, 212-618-6660, E-mail: jdory@pace.edu. *Application contact:* Margaret Hanson, Program Coordinator for Doctoral Programs, 212-618-6660, E-mail: dps.bus@pace.edu.
Website: http://www.pace.edu/lubin/dps/

Pace University, Lubin School of Business, Marketing Program, New York, NY 10038. Offers analytics and customer intelligence (MS); marketing management (MBA); social media and mobile marketing (MS). *Program availability:* Evening/weekend. *Students:* 31 full-time (21 women), 19 part-time (11 women); includes 7 minority (1 Black or African American, non-Hispanic/Latino; 2 Asian, non-Hispanic/Latino; 2 Hispanic/Latino; 2 Two or more races, non-Hispanic/Latino), 31 international. Average age 26. 126 applicants, 56% accepted, 26 enrolled. In 2016, 23 master's awarded. *Entrance requirements:* For master's, GMAT, GRE, undergraduate degree, transcripts from all accredited colleges/universities attended, two letters of recommendation, resume, personal statement. Additional exam requirements/recommendations for international students: Required—TOEFL (minimum score 90 iBT), IELTS (minimum score 7) or PTE (minimum score 61). *Application deadline:* For fall admission, 8/1 priority date for domestic students, 6/1 for international students; for spring admission, 12/1 for domestic students, 10/1 for international students. Applications are processed on a rolling basis. Application fee: $70. Electronic applications accepted. *Expenses: Tuition:* Part-time $1195 per credit. *Required fees:* $260 per semester. Tuition and fees vary according to degree level, campus/location and program. *Financial support:* Research assistantships, career-related internships or fieldwork, and Federal Work-Study available. Support available to part-time students. Financial award application deadline: 2/15; financial award applicants required to submit FAFSA. *Unit head:* Dr. Ipshita Ray, Chairperson, 212-618-6505, E-mail: iray@pace.edu. *Application contact:* Susan Ford-Goldschein, Director of Graduate Admissions, 212-346-1531, Fax: 212-346-1585, E-mail: graduateadmission@pace.edu.
Website: http://www.pace.edu/lubin/mba-in-marketing-management

Philadelphia University, School of Business Administration, Program in Business Administration, Philadelphia, PA 19144. Offers general business (MBA); innovation (MBA); management (MBA); marketing (MBA); strategic design (MBA); MBA/MS. *Program availability:* Part-time, evening/weekend, online learning. *Entrance requirements:* For master's, GMAT. Additional exam requirements/recommendations for international students: Required—TOEFL (minimum score 550 paper-based; 79 iBT).

Polytechnic University of Puerto Rico, Miami Campus, Graduate School, Miami, FL 33166. Offers accounting (MBA); business administration (MBA); construction management (MEM); environmental management (MEM); finance (MBA); human resources management (MBA); logistics and supply chain management (MBA); management of international enterprises (MBA); manufacturing management (MEM); marketing management (MBA); project management (MBA). *Program availability:* Part-time, evening/weekend, online learning. *Entrance requirements:* For master's, minimum GPA of 3.0. Electronic applications accepted.

Pontifical Catholic University of Puerto Rico, College of Business Administration, Program in Marketing, Ponce, PR 00717-0777. Offers MBA. *Program availability:* Part-time, evening/weekend. *Degree requirements:* For master's, thesis. *Entrance requirements:* For master's, GRE, interview, minimum GPA of 2.75.

Pontificia Universidad Catolica Madre y Maestra, Graduate School, Faculty of Social and Administrative Sciences, Santiago, Dominican Republic. Offers business administration (MBA), including business development, finance, international business, management skills (M Mgmt, MBA), marketing, operations, strategic cost management, strategy, tourist destination planning and management; law (LL M), including civil law, corporate business law, criminal law, international relations, real estate law; management (M Mgmt), including higher financial management, insurance program administration, management skills (M Mgmt, MBA); psychology (MA), including clinical child and adolescent psychology, forensic psychology; strategic human resources (EMBA).

Post University, Program in Business Administration, Waterbury, CT 06723-2540. Offers accounting (MSA); business administration (MBA); corporate innovation (MBA); entrepreneurship (MBA); finance (MBA); healthcare (MBA); leadership (MBA); marketing (MBA); project management (MBA). *Accreditation:* ACBSP. *Program availability:* Online learning.

Providence College, School of Business, Providence, RI 02918. Offers accounting (MBA); finance (MBA); international business (MBA); management (MBA); marketing (MBA). *Accreditation:* AACSB. *Program availability:* Part-time, evening/weekend. *Faculty:* 10 full-time (3 women), 5 part-time/adjunct (2 women). *Students:* 84 full-time (39 women), 66 part-time (23 women); includes 15 minority (6 Black or African American, non-Hispanic/Latino; 1 Asian, non-Hispanic/Latino; 8 Hispanic/Latino), 5 international. Average age 26. 116 applicants, 96% accepted, 94 enrolled. In 2016, 80 master's awarded. *Entrance requirements:* For master's, GMAT. Additional exam requirements/recommendations for international students: Required—TOEFL (minimum score 577 paper-based; 90 iBT). *Application deadline:* For fall admission, 5/1 priority date for domestic and international students; for spring admission, 11/1 priority date for domestic and international students; for summer admission, 3/15 priority date for domestic students, 3/15 for international students. Applications are processed on a rolling basis. Application fee: $55. *Expenses:* Contact institution. *Financial support:* Career-related internships or fieldwork, institutionally sponsored loans, and unspecified assistantships available. Support available to part-time students. Financial award application deadline: 8/1; financial award applicants required to submit FAFSA.
Website: http://www.providence.edu/business/Pages/default.aspx

Queen's University at Kingston, Queens School of Business, Program in Business Administration, Kingston, ON K7L 3N6, Canada. Offers consulting and project management (MBA); finance (MBA); innovation and entrepreneurship (MBA); marketing (MBA). *Degree requirements:* For master's, thesis optional, research project. *Entrance requirements:* For master's, GMAT, minimum B+ average. Additional exam requirements/recommendations for international students: Required—TOEFL. Electronic applications accepted. *Faculty research:* Management fundamentals, strategic thinking, global business, innovation and change, leadership.

Regent's University London, Webster Graduate School, London, United Kingdom. Offers business (MBA); finance (MS); human resources (MA); information technology management (MA); international business (MA); international non-governmental organizations (MA); international relations (MA); management and leadership (MA); marketing (MA). *Program availability:* Part-time.

Regis University, College of Business and Economics, Denver, CO 80221-1099. Offers accounting (MS); executive leadership (Certificate); finance (MS); finance and accounting (MBA); health industry leadership (MBA); human resource management and leadership (MSOL); management (MBA); marketing (MBA); nonprofit leadership (Post-Graduate Certificate); nonprofit management (MNM); nonprofit organizational capacity building (Certificate); operations management (MBA); organizational leadership and management (MSOL); project leadership and management (MS, MSOL); strategic business management (Certificate); strategic human resource integration (Certificate); strategic management (MBA). Programs offered at Colorado Springs Campus, Northwest Denver Campus, Southeast Denver Campus, Fort Collins Campus, Broomfield Campus, Henderson (Nevada) Campus, and Summerlin (Nevada) Campus. *Program availability:* Part-time, evening/weekend, 100% online, blended/hybrid learning. *Faculty:* 15 full-time (5 women), 43 part-time/adjunct (16 women). *Students:* 622 full-time (350 women), 460 part-time (170 women); includes 317 minority (88 Black or African American, non-Hispanic/Latino; 7 American Indian or Alaska Native, non-Hispanic/Latino; 44 Asian, non-Hispanic/Latino; 151 Hispanic/Latino; 1 Native Hawaiian or other Pacific Islander, non-Hispanic/Latino; 26 Two or more races, non-Hispanic/Latino), 44 international. Average age 36. 307 applicants, 73% accepted, 134 enrolled. In 2016, 394 master's awarded. *Degree requirements:* For master's, thesis (for some programs), capstone or final research project. *Entrance requirements:* For master's, official transcript reflecting baccalaureate degree awarded from regionally-accredited college or university, interview, 2 years of full-time related work experience, resume, letters of recommendation. Additional exam requirements/recommendations for international students: Required—TOEFL (minimum score 550 paper-based; 82 iBT). *Application deadline:* For fall admission, 8/15 priority date for domestic students, 8/13 for international students; for winter admission, 10/10 priority date for domestic students, 9/8 for international students; for spring admission, 1/10 priority date for domestic students, 11/17 for international students; for summer admission, 5/1 priority date for domestic students. Applications are processed on a rolling basis. Application fee: $75. Electronic applications accepted. *Expenses:* $780 per credit hour. *Financial support:* Scholarships/grants available. Financial award application deadline: 4/15; financial award applicants required to submit FAFSA. *Faculty research:* Impact of information technology on small business regulation of accounting, international project financing, mineral development, delivery of healthcare to rural indigenous communities. *Unit head:* Dr. Timothy Keane, Academic Dean. *Application contact:* Cate Clark, Director of Admissions, 303-458-4900, Fax: 303-964-5534, E-mail: ruadmissions@regis.edu.
Website: http://www.regis.edu/CBE.aspx

Roberts Wesleyan College, Graduate Business Programs, Rochester, NY 14624-1997. Offers strategic leadership (MS); strategic marketing (MS). *Program availability:* Evening/weekend. *Degree requirements:* For master's, thesis or alternative. *Entrance requirements:* For master's, GMAT, minimum GPA of 2.75, verifiable work experience. *Expenses:* Contact institution.

Rollins College, Crummer Graduate School of Business, Winter Park, FL 32789-4499. Offers business administration (EDBA); entrepreneurship (MBA); finance (MBA); international business (MBA); management (MBA); marketing (MBA); operations and technology management (MBA). *Accreditation:* AACSB. *Program availability:* Part-time, evening/weekend, online learning. *Faculty:* 22 full-time (5 women), 4 part-time/adjunct (3 women). *Students:* 254 full-time (105 women), 83 part-time (36 women); includes 63 minority (15 Black or African American, non-Hispanic/Latino; 9 Asian, non-Hispanic/Latino; 35 Hispanic/Latino; 4 Two or more races, non-Hispanic/Latino), 48 international. Average age 31. 360 applicants, 74% accepted, 207 enrolled. In 2016, 159 master's awarded. *Degree requirements:* For master's, minimum GPA of 2.85; for doctorate, thesis/dissertation, minimum GPA of 3.0. *Entrance requirements:* For master's, GMAT or GRE, official transcripts, two letters of recommendation, essay, current resume/curriculum vitae, interview; for doctorate, official transcripts, two letters of recommendation, essays, current resume/curriculum vitae, interview. Additional exam requirements/recommendations for international students: Required—TOEFL (minimum score 100 iBT) or IELTS (minimum score 7). *Application deadline:* Applications are processed on a rolling basis. Application fee: $50. Electronic applications accepted. *Expenses:* Contact institution. *Financial support:* In 2016–17, 125 students received support. Federal Work-Study and scholarships/grants available. Support available to part-time students. Financial award applicants required to submit FAFSA. *Faculty research:* Sustainability, world financial markets, international business, market research, strategic marketing. *Unit head:* Deborah Crown, Dean, 407-646-2249, Fax: 407-646-1550, E-mail: dcrown@rollins.edu. *Application contact:* Maralyn E. Graham, Admissions Coordinator, 407-646-2405, Fax: 407-646-1550, E-mail: mbaadmissions@rollins.edu.
Website: http://www.rollins.edu/mba/

Roosevelt University, Graduate Division, College of Arts and Sciences, Department of Communication, Chicago, IL 60605. Offers integrated marketing communications (MSIMC). *Program availability:* Part-time, evening/weekend. *Students:* 43 full-time (33 women), 35 part-time (28 women); includes 41 minority (27 Black or African American, non-Hispanic/Latino; 5 Asian, non-Hispanic/Latino; 7 Hispanic/Latino; 2 Two or more races, non-Hispanic/Latino), 22 international. Average age 27. 49 applicants, 96% accepted, 26 enrolled. In 2016, 49 master's awarded. *Application deadline:* For fall admission, 6/1 priority date for domestic students. Applications are processed on a rolling basis. Application fee: $25 ($35 for international students). *Expenses: Tuition, area resident:* Full-time $19,566; part-time $880 per credit hour. *Required fees:* $175 per semester. One-time fee: $200. Part-time tuition and fees vary according to course load, degree level and program. *Financial support:* Research assistantships, career-related internships or fieldwork, and Federal Work-Study available. Financial award application deadline: 2/15. *Unit head:* Marian Azzaro, Chair, 312-281-3239. *Application contact:* Angela Ryan, Director of Graduate Enrollment, 312-341-2420, Fax: 312-281-3356, E-mail: applyru@roosevelt.edu.

Rowan University, Graduate School, College of Communication and Creative Arts, Integrated Marketing Communication and New Media Certificate of Graduate Study Program, Glassboro, NJ 08028-1701. Offers CGS. Electronic applications accepted.

Rutgers University–Newark, Graduate School, Program in Management, Newark, NJ 07102. Offers accounting (PhD); accounting information systems (PhD); computer information systems (PhD); finance (PhD); information technology (PhD); international business (PhD); management science (PhD); marketing (PhD); organization management (PhD). Program offered jointly with New Jersey Institute of Technology. *Accreditation:* AACSB. *Degree requirements:* For doctorate, thesis/dissertation, cumulative exams. *Entrance requirements:* For doctorate, GMAT or GRE General Test, minimum undergraduate B average. Additional exam requirements/recommendations for international students: Required—TOEFL. Electronic applications accepted. *Faculty research:* Technology management, leadership and teams, consumer behavior, financial and markets, logistics.

Rutgers University–Newark, Rutgers Business School–Newark and New Brunswick, Doctoral Programs in Management, Newark, NJ 07102. Offers accounting (PhD); accounting information systems (PhD); economics (PhD); finance (PhD); individualized study (PhD); information technology (PhD); international business (PhD); management science (PhD); marketing science (PhD); organizational management (PhD); science, technology and management (PhD); supply chain management (PhD). *Degree requirements:* For doctorate, comprehensive exam, thesis/dissertation. *Entrance requirements:* For doctorate, GRE or GMAT. Additional exam requirements/recommendations for international students: Required—TOEFL (minimum score 550 paper-based; 79 iBT). Electronic applications accepted.

Sacred Heart University, Graduate Programs, Jack Welch College of Business, Department of Marketing, Fairfield, CT 06825. Offers digital marketing (MS); marketing (MBA, Graduate Certificate). *Program availability:* Part-time, evening/weekend. *Faculty:* 3 full-time (1 woman), 2 part-time/adjunct (0 women). *Students:* 15 full-time (12 women), 19 part-time (13 women); includes 8 minority (3 Black or African American, non-Hispanic/Latino; 1 Asian, non-Hispanic/Latino; 4 Hispanic/Latino), 10 international. Average age 29. 26 applicants, 85% accepted, 15 enrolled. In 2016, 7 master's awarded. *Degree requirements:* For master's, capstone project. *Entrance requirements:* For master's, GMAT, bachelor's degree from accredited institution with minimum GPA of 3.0. Additional exam requirements/recommendations for international students: Required—TOEFL (minimum score 570 paper-based, 80 iBT), TWE, or IELTS (6.5); Recommended—TSE. *Application deadline:* Applications are processed on a rolling basis. Application fee: $75. Electronic applications accepted. *Expenses:* $875 per credit. *Financial support:* Unspecified assistantships available. Financial award applicants required to submit FAFSA. *Unit head:* Dr. Anca Micu, Associate Dean/Director of MS in Marketing, 203-371-7813, Fax: 203-365-7538, E-mail: marketing@sacredheart.edu. *Application contact:* William Sweeney, Director of Graduate Admissions Operations, 203-365-4827, E-mail: sweeneyw@sacredheart.edu.
Website: http://www.sacredheart.edu/academics/johnfwelchcollegeofbusiness/graduateprogramscertificates/msindigitalmarketing/

St. Bonaventure University, School of Graduate Studies, Jandoli School of Communication, Program in Integrated Marketing Communications, St. Bonaventure, NY 14778-2284. Offers MA. *Program availability:* Part-time, evening/weekend, 100% online. *Faculty:* 4 full-time (1 woman), 7 part-time/adjunct (6 women). *Students:* 29 full-time (17 women), 20 part-time (16 women); includes 10 minority (4 Black or African American, non-Hispanic/Latino; 5 Hispanic/Latino; 1 Two or more races, non-Hispanic/Latino), 3 international. Average age 28. 60 applicants, 75% accepted, 28 enrolled. In 2016, 24 master's awarded. *Degree requirements:* For master's, campaign project. *Entrance requirements:* For master's, transcripts, essay describing desire to pursue the IMC program. Additional exam requirements/recommendations for international students: Required—TOEFL (minimum score 550 paper-based; 79 iBT). *Application deadline:* For fall admission, 6/5 for domestic students, 2/1 for international students; for spring admission, 10/15 for domestic students, 7/1 for international students. Applications are processed on a rolling basis. Application fee: $0. Electronic applications accepted. *Expenses:* $733 per credit, $100 graduation fee. *Financial support:* Federal Work-Study, scholarships/grants, health care benefits, and unspecified assistantships available. Support available to part-time students. Financial award application deadline: 4/15; financial award applicants required to submit FAFSA. *Faculty research:* Network analysis of internal and external communication networks in organizations, organizational behavior, student engagement in active learning. *Unit head:* Dr. Richard Lee, Director, 716-375-2563, Fax: 716-375-2588, E-mail: rlee@sbu.edu. *Application contact:* Bruce Campbell, Director of Graduate Admissions, 716-375-2429, Fax: 716-375-4015, E-mail: gradsch@sbu.edu.
Website: http://www.sbu.edu/academics/schools/journalism-and-mass-communications/graduate-degrees/ma-integrated-marketing-communications

St. Catherine University, Graduate Programs, Program in Business Administration, St. Paul, MN 55105. Offers healthcare (MBA); integrated marketing communications (MBA); management (MBA). *Program availability:* Part-time, evening/weekend. *Entrance requirements:* For master's, GMAT (if undergraduate GPA is less than 3.0), 2+ years' work or volunteer experience in professional setting(s). Additional exam requirements/recommendations for international students: Required—TOEFL. *Expenses:* Contact institution.

St. John's University, The Peter J. Tobin College of Business, Department of Marketing, Queens, NY 11439. Offers MBA. *Program availability:* Part-time, evening/weekend. *Degree requirements:* For master's, comprehensive exam (for some programs), thesis optional. *Entrance requirements:* For master's, GMAT, 2 letters of recommendation, resume, transcripts, essay. Additional exam requirements/recommendations for international students: Required—TOEFL (minimum score 600 paper-based; 100 iBT), IELTS (minimum score 7). Electronic applications accepted. *Expenses:* Contact institution. *Faculty research:* Global brand management, China's stimulus plan, measuring attitude, marketing in India, consumer decision-making.

Saint Joseph's University, Erivan K. Haub School of Business, Executive Master's in Food Marketing Program, Philadelphia, PA 19131-1395. Offers MBA, MS. *Program availability:* Part-time. *Faculty:* 14 full-time (3 women). *Students:* 2 full-time (1 woman), 38 part-time (24 women); includes 3 minority (2 Black or African American, non-Hispanic/Latino; 1 Two or more races, non-Hispanic/Latino), 1 international. Average age 36. 9 applicants, 56% accepted, 4 enrolled. In 2016, 11 master's awarded. *Degree requirements:* For master's, minimum GPA of 3.0. *Entrance requirements:* For master's, 4 years of industry experience, interview or GMAT/GRE, letter of recommendation, resume, official transcripts, personal statement. Additional exam requirements/recommendations for international students: Required—TOEFL (minimum score 550 paper-based, 80 iBT), IELTS (minimum score 6.5), or PTE (minimum score 60). *Application deadline:* Applications are processed on a rolling basis. Application fee: $0. Electronic applications accepted. *Expenses:* $1,349 per credit. *Financial support:* In 2016–17, 19 students received support. Institutionally sponsored loans and scholarships/grants available. Support available to part-time students. Financial award application deadline: 5/1; financial award applicants required to submit FAFSA. *Faculty research:* Marketing vitamin D, mushrooms, nutrition marketing for specialty groups, transforming food marketing education. *Total annual research expenditures:* $124,447. *Unit head:* Terese W. Waldron, Director, 610-660-3150, Fax: 610-660-3153, E-mail: twaldron@sju.edu. *Application contact:* Kathleen Klarich, Program Manager, 610-660-3155, Fax: 610-660-3160, E-mail: kklarich@sju.edu.
Website: https://www.sju.edu/majors-programs/graduate-business/executive/executive-food-marketing-mba

Saint Joseph's University, Erivan K. Haub School of Business, MBA Program, Philadelphia, PA 19131-1395. Offers accounting (MBA, Postbaccalaureate Certificate); business intelligence (MBA); finance (MBA); general business (MBA); health and medical services administration (MBA); international business (MBA); international marketing (MBA); managing human capital (MBA); marketing (MBA); DO/MBA. DO/MBA offered jointly with Philadelphia College of Osteopathic Medicine. *Program availability:* Part-time, evening/weekend, 100% online, blended/hybrid learning. *Faculty:* 31 full-time (10 women), 28 part-time/adjunct (7 women). *Students:* 95 full-time (40 women), 348 part-time (137 women); includes 64 minority (29 Black or African American, non-Hispanic/Latino; 17 Asian, non-Hispanic/Latino; 14 Hispanic/Latino; 1 Native Hawaiian or other Pacific Islander, non-Hispanic/Latino; 3 Two or more races, non-Hispanic/Latino), 47 international. Average age 30. 237 applicants, 60% accepted, 76 enrolled. In 2016, 144 master's awarded. *Degree requirements:* For master's and Postbaccalaureate Certificate, minimum GPA of 3.0. *Entrance requirements:* For master's, GMAT or GRE, 2 letters of recommendation, resume, personal statement, official undergraduate and graduate transcripts; for Postbaccalaureate Certificate, official master's-level transcripts. Additional exam requirements/recommendations for international students: Required—TOEFL (minimum score 550 paper-based, 80 iBT), IELTS (minimum score 6.5), or PTE (minimum score 60). *Application deadline:* For fall admission, 7/15 priority date for domestic students, 5/15 priority date for international students; for spring admission, 11/15 priority date for domestic students, 10/15 priority date for international students; for summer admission, 4/15 priority date for domestic students, 2/15 priority date for international students. Applications are processed on a rolling basis. Application fee: $35. Electronic applications accepted. *Expenses:* $1,003 per credit. *Financial support:* In 2016–17, 105 students received support, including 2 research assistantships with partial tuition reimbursements available (averaging $4,000 per year); scholarships/grants and unspecified assistantships also available. Support available to part-time students. Financial award application deadline: 5/1; financial award applicants required to submit FAFSA. *Unit head:* Dr. Patricia Rafferty, Director, 610-660-1318, E-mail: praffert@sju.edu. *Application contact:* Kate Sonstein, Program Manager/Recruiter, 610-660-1693, E-mail: kate.sonstein@sju.edu.
Website: http://www.sju.edu/haubmba

Saint Joseph's University, Erivan K. Haub School of Business, MS Program in International Marketing, Philadelphia, PA 19131-1395. Offers MS. *Program availability:* Part-time, evening/weekend. *Faculty:* 6 full-time (1 woman), 8 part-time/adjunct (2 women). *Students:* 30 full-time (19 women), 7 part-time (5 women); includes 2 minority (1 Hispanic/Latino; 1 Two or more races, non-Hispanic/Latino), 31 international. Average age 25. 76 applicants, 58% accepted, 17 enrolled. In 2016, 21 master's awarded. *Degree requirements:* For master's, minimum GPA of 3.0. *Entrance requirements:* For master's, GMAT or GRE, 2 letters of recommendation, resume, personal statement, official undergraduate and graduate transcripts. Additional exam requirements/recommendations for international students: Required—TOEFL (minimum score 550 paper-based, 80 iBT), IELTS (minimum score 6.5), or PTE (minimum score 60). *Application deadline:* For fall admission, 7/15 priority date for domestic students, 5/15 priority date for international students; for spring admission, 11/15 priority date for domestic students, 10/15 priority date for international students; for summer admission, 4/15 priority date for domestic students. Applications are processed on a rolling basis. Application fee: $35. Electronic applications accepted. *Expenses:* $1,003 per credit. *Financial support:* In 2016–17, 29 students received support, including 1 research assistantship with partial tuition reimbursement available (averaging $8,000 per year); scholarships/grants and unspecified assistantships also available. Support available to part-time students. Financial award application deadline: 5/1; financial award applicants required to submit FAFSA. *Faculty research:* Export marketing, global marketing, international marketing research, new product development, emerging markets, international consumer behavior. *Unit head:* Jeannine Lajeunesse, Director, 610-660-1626, E-mail: jlajeune@sju.edu. *Application contact:* Kate Sonstein, Program Manager/Recruiter, 610-660-1693, E-mail: kate.sonstein@sju.edu.
Website: http://www.sju.edu/academics/hsb/grad/mim/

Saint Joseph's University, Erivan K. Haub School of Business, Pharmaceutical and Healthcare Marketing MBA for Executives Program, Philadelphia, PA 19131-1395. Offers MBA, Post Master's Certificate. *Program availability:* Part-time, evening/weekend, 100% online, blended/hybrid learning. *Faculty:* 11 full-time (2 women), 8 part-time/adjunct (1 woman). *Students:* 3 full-time (1 woman), 83 part-time (47 women); includes 27 minority (13 Black or African American, non-Hispanic/Latino; 9 Asian, non-Hispanic/Latino; 4 Hispanic/Latino; 1 Two or more races, non-Hispanic/Latino), 1 international. Average age 40. 20 applicants, 55% accepted, 5 enrolled. In 2016, 43 master's, 1 other advanced degree awarded. *Degree requirements:* For master's and Post Master's Certificate, minimum GPA of 3.0. *Entrance requirements:* For master's, 4 years of industry experience, letter of recommendation, resume, interview, official transcripts; for Post Master's Certificate, MBA, 4 years of industry experience, resume. Additional exam requirements/recommendations for international students: Required—TOEFL (minimum score 550 paper-based, 80 iBT), IELTS (minimum score 6.5), or PTE (minimum score 60). *Application deadline:* For fall admission, 7/15 for domestic students, 4/15 for international students; for spring admission, 11/15 for domestic students, 10/15 for international students. Applications are processed on a rolling basis. Electronic applications accepted. *Expenses:* $1,563 per credit. *Financial support:* In 2016–17, 27 students received support, including research assistantships with partial tuition reimbursements available (averaging $4,000 per year); scholarships/grants and unspecified assistantships also available. Support available to part-time students. Financial award application deadline: 5/1; financial award applicants required to submit FAFSA. *Faculty research:* Pharmaceutical strategy, Internet and pharmaceuticals, pharmaceutical promotion. *Unit head:* Terese W. Waldron, Director, 610-660-3150, Fax: 610-660-5160, E-mail: twaldron@sju.edu. *Application contact:* Jon Dart, Senior Manager, 610-660-3149, Fax: 610-660-3160, E-mail: jdart@sju.edu.
Website: http://www.sju.edu/epharma

Saint Leo University, Graduate Business Studies, Saint Leo, FL 33574-6665. Offers accounting (M Acc, MBA, Certificate); cybersecurity (MS); health care management (MBA, Certificate); human resource management (MBA, Certificate); information security management (MBA, Certificate); management (MBA, DBA); marketing (MBA, Certificate); marketing research and social media analytics (MBA, Certificate); project management (MBA, Certificate); sport business (MBA); supply chain global integration management (MBA, Certificate). *Accreditation:* ACBSP. *Program availability:* Part-time, evening/weekend, 100% online, blended/hybrid learning. *Faculty:* 53 full-time (18 women), 53 part-time/adjunct (19 women). *Students:* 8 full-time (4 women), 2,001 part-time (1,160 women); includes 928 minority (650 Black or African American, non-Hispanic/Latino; 5 American Indian or Alaska Native, non-Hispanic/Latino; 43 Asian, non-Hispanic/Latino; 193 Hispanic/Latino; 2 Native Hawaiian or other Pacific Islander, non-Hispanic/Latino; 35 Two or more races, non-Hispanic/Latino), 51 international. Average age 37. 922 applicants, 85% accepted, 517 enrolled. In 2016, 874 master's, 17 other advanced degrees awarded. *Degree requirements:* For doctorate, comprehensive exam, thesis/dissertation. *Entrance requirements:* For master's, GMAT (minimum score 500), official transcripts, current resume, 2 professional recommendations, personal statement, bachelor's degree from regionally-accredited university; undergraduate degree in accounting and minimum undergraduate GPA of 3.0 (for M Acc); minimum undergraduate GPA of 3.0 in final 2 years of undergraduate study and 2 years' work experience (for MBA); for doctorate, GMAT (minimum score of 550) if master's GPA is under 3.25, official transcripts, current resume, 2 professional recommendations, personal statement, master's degree from regionally-accredited university with minimum GPA of 3.25, 3 years' work experience, interview. Additional exam requirements/recommendations for international students: Required—TOEFL (minimum score 550

paper-based; 80 iBT). *Application deadline:* For fall admission, 7/1 priority date for domestic and international students; for spring admission, 11/12 priority date for domestic students, 11/1 for international students. Applications are processed on a rolling basis. Application fee: $80. Electronic applications accepted. *Expenses:* Contact institution. *Financial support:* In 2016–17, 118 students received support. Career-related internships or fieldwork, scholarships/grants, and health care benefits available. Financial award application deadline: 3/1; financial award applicants required to submit FAFSA. *Unit head:* Dr. Lorrie McGovern, Associate Dean, School of Business, 352-588-7869, Fax: 352-588-8912, E-mail: mbaslu@saintleo.edu. *Application contact:* Jennifer Shelley, Senior Associate Director of Graduate Admissions, 800-707-8846, Fax: 352-588-7873, E-mail: grad.admissions@saintleo.edu.
Website: http://www.saintleo.edu/academics/graduate.aspx

Saint Peter's University, Graduate Business Programs, MBA Program, Jersey City, NJ 07306-5997. Offers finance (MBA); health care administration (MBA); human resource management (MBA); international business (MBA); management (MBA); management information systems (MBA); marketing (MBA); risk management (MBA); MBA/MS. *Program availability:* Part-time, evening/weekend. *Entrance requirements:* Additional exam requirements/recommendations for international students: Required—TOEFL. Electronic applications accepted. *Faculty research:* Finance, health care management, human resource management, international business, management, management information systems, marketing, risk management.

St. Thomas Aquinas College, Division of Business Administration, Sparkill, NY 10976. Offers business administration (MBA); finance (MBA); management (MBA); marketing (MBA). *Program availability:* Part-time, evening/weekend. *Entrance requirements:* For master's, GMAT. Additional exam requirements/recommendations for international students: Required—TOEFL. Electronic applications accepted.

Saint Xavier University, Graduate Studies, Graham School of Management, Chicago, IL 60655-3105. Offers employee health benefits (Certificate); finance (MBA); financial fraud examination and management (MBA, Certificate); financial planning (MBA, Certificate); generalist/individualized (MBA); health administration (MBA); managed care (Certificate); management (MBA); marketing (MBA); project management (MBA, Certificate); MBA/MS. *Accreditation:* AACSB; ACBSP. *Program availability:* Part-time, evening/weekend. *Entrance requirements:* For master's, GMAT, minimum GPA of 3.0, 2 years of work experience. Electronic applications accepted. *Expenses:* Contact institution.

Samford University, Brock School of Business, Birmingham, AL 35229. Offers accounting (M Acc); business administration (MBA); entrepreneurship (MBA); finance (MBA); marketing (MBA); JD/M Acc; JD/MBA; MBA/M Acc; MBA/M Div; MBA/MSEM; MBA/Pharm D. *Accreditation:* AACSB. *Program availability:* Part-time-only, evening/weekend, 100% online, blended/hybrid learning. *Faculty:* 9 full-time (2 women), 3 part-time/adjunct (0 women). *Students:* 87 full-time (33 women), 14 part-time (6 women); includes 10 minority (7 Black or African American, non-Hispanic/Latino; 1 Asian, non-Hispanic/Latino; 1 Hispanic/Latino; 1 Two or more races, non-Hispanic/Latino), 6 international. Average age 28. 148 applicants, 41% accepted, 32 enrolled. In 2016, 63 master's awarded. *Degree requirements:* For master's, capstone course. *Entrance requirements:* For master's, GMAT or GRE. Additional exam requirements/recommendations for international students: Required—TOEFL (minimum score 90 iBT), IELTS (minimum score 6.5). *Application deadline:* For fall admission, 7/1 for domestic and international students; for spring admission, 12/1 for domestic and international students; for summer admission, 4/1 for domestic and international students. Applications are processed on a rolling basis. Application fee: $35. Electronic applications accepted. *Expenses: Tuition:* Full-time $18,530; part-time $789 per credit hour. *Required fees:* $610. Tuition and fees vary according to course load, degree level, program and student level. *Financial support:* In 2016–17, 55 students received support. Career-related internships or fieldwork, institutionally sponsored loans, scholarships/grants, and tuition waivers (partial) available. Support available to part-time students. Financial award application deadline: 3/1; financial award applicants required to submit FAFSA. *Faculty research:* Entrepreneurship, accounting, finance, marketing, economics. *Total annual research expenditures:* $25,000. *Unit head:* Dr. Barbara Cartledge, Assistant Dean, 205-726-2935, Fax: 205-726-2540, E-mail: bhcartle@samford.edu. *Application contact:* Elizabeth Anne Gambrell, Assistant Director of Academic Programs, 205-726-2040, Fax: 205-726-2540, E-mail: eagambre@samford.edu.
Website: http://www.samford.edu/business/

San Diego State University, Graduate and Research Affairs, College of Business Administration, Department of Marketing, San Diego, CA 92182. Offers MS. *Program availability:* Part-time, evening/weekend. *Degree requirements:* For master's, thesis or alternative. *Entrance requirements:* For master's, GMAT, resume, letters of reference. Additional exam requirements/recommendations for international students: Required—TOEFL. Electronic applications accepted.

San Francisco State University, Division of Graduate Studies, College of Business, Program in Business Administration, San Francisco, CA 94132-1722. Offers decision sciences/operations research (MBA); ethics and compliance (MBA); finance (MBA); global business and innovation (MBA); healthcare administration (MBA); hospitality and tourism management (MBA); information systems (MBA); leadership (MBA); marketing (MBA); nonprofit and social enterprise leadership (MBA); sustainable business (MBA). *Accreditation:* AACSB. *Program availability:* Part-time, evening/weekend. *Degree requirements:* For master's, thesis, essay test. *Entrance requirements:* For master's, GMAT, minimum GPA of 2.7 in last 60 units. Additional exam requirements/recommendations for international students: Required—TOEFL (minimum score 550 paper-based). *Application deadline:* For fall admission, 5/1 priority date for domestic students, 4/1 for international students; for spring admission, 11/1 for domestic students, 10/15 for international students. Applications are processed on a rolling basis. Application fee: $55. *Expenses:* Tuition, state resident: full-time $6738. Tuition, nonresident: full-time $15,666. *Required fees:* $1012. Tuition and fees vary according to degree level and program. *Financial support:* Application deadline: 3/1. *Unit head:* Dr. Sanjit Sengupta, Faculty Director, 415-817-4366, Fax: 415-817-4340, E-mail: sengupta@sfsu.edu. *Application contact:* Zandra Tan, EMBA Program Coordinator, 415-817-4360, Fax: 415-817-4340, E-mail: zandra13@sfsu.edu.
Website: http://cob.sfsu.edu/graduate-programs/mba

Seton Hall University, Stillman School of Business, Programs in Business Administration, South Orange, NJ 07079-2697. Offers accounting (MBA); entrepreneurship (Certificate); finance (MBA, Certificate); information technology management (MBA); international business (MBA); management (MBA); marketing (MBA); sport management (MBA); supply chain management (MBA, Certificate). *Program availability:* Part-time, evening/weekend. *Degree requirements:* For master's, 20 hours of community service (Social Responsibility Project). *Entrance requirements:* For master's, GMAT or CPA, GRE (waived based on work experience or advanced degree from AACSB institution), MS in business discipline, professional degree (MD, JD, PhD, DVM, DDS, CPA, etc.), minimum undergraduate GPA of 3.0. Additional exam requirements/recommendations for international students: Required—TOEFL (minimum score 607 paper-based; 102 iBT), IELTS (minimum score 6), PTE. Electronic applications accepted. *Expenses:* Contact institution. *Faculty research:* Sport, hedge funds, executive compensation, social media, legal studies.

Slippery Rock University of Pennsylvania, Graduate Studies (Recruitment), College of Business, School of Business, Slippery Rock, PA 16057-1383. Offers accounting/finance (MBA); general (MBA); marketing/management (MBA). *Program availability:* Part-time, evening/weekend. *Faculty:* 6 full-time (4 women), 1 part-time/adjunct (0 women). *Students:* 16 full-time (9 women), 9 part-time (6 women); includes 1 minority (Black or African American, non-Hispanic/Latino). Average age 29. 109 applicants, 26% accepted, 13 enrolled. In 2016, 26 master's awarded. *Degree requirements:* For master's, comprehensive exam (for some programs), thesis (for some programs). *Entrance requirements:* For master's, minimum cumulative GPA of 3.0, official transcripts, three references. Additional exam requirements/recommendations for international students: Required—TOEFL (minimum score 550 paper-based; 80 iBT). *Application deadline:* For fall admission, 3/1 priority date for domestic students, 5/1 priority date for international students; for spring admission, 10/1 priority date for domestic students, 9/1 priority date for international students. Applications are processed on a rolling basis. Application fee: $25 ($30 for international students). Electronic applications accepted. *Expenses:* $646.50 per credit in-state, $936.80 per credit out-of-state; $581.45 per online credit in-state, $648.65 per online credit out-of-state. *Financial support:* In 2016–17, 5 students received support. Career-related internships or fieldwork, Federal Work-Study, institutionally sponsored loans, scholarships/grants, tuition waivers (partial), and unspecified assistantships available. Support available to part-time students. Financial award application deadline: 5/1; financial award applicants required to submit FAFSA. *Unit head:* Dr. Larry McCarthy, Graduate Coordinator, 724-738-2552, Fax: 724-738-2959, E-mail: larry.mccarthy@sru.edu. *Application contact:* Brandi Weber-Mortimer, Director of Graduate Admissions, 724-738-2051, Fax: 724-738-2146, E-mail: graduate.admissions@sru.edu.
Website: http://www.sru.edu/academics/graduate-programs/mba-master-of-business-administration

Southern Adventist University, School of Business and Management, Collegedale, TN 37315-0370. Offers accounting (MBA); church administration (MSA); church and nonprofit leadership (MBA); financial management (MFM); healthcare administration (MBA); management (MBA); marketing management (MBA); outdoor education (MSA). *Program availability:* Part-time, evening/weekend, online learning. *Entrance requirements:* For master's, GMAT. Additional exam requirements/recommendations for international students: Required—TOEFL (minimum score 600 paper-based; 100 iBT). Electronic applications accepted.

Southern Methodist University, Cox School of Business, MBA Program, Dallas, TX 75275. Offers accounting (MBA, PMBA); business administration (EMBA); finance (MBA); financial statement analysis (PMBA); general business (MBA); information technology and operations management (MBA); management (MBA); marketing (MBA); real estate (MBA); strategy (MBA); strategy and entrepreneurship (MBA); JD/MBA; MA/MBA. *Program availability:* Part-time, evening/weekend. *Entrance requirements:* For master's, GMAT. Additional exam requirements/recommendations for international students: Required—TOEFL. Electronic applications accepted. *Expenses:* Contact institution. *Faculty research:* Corporate finance, financial reporting, modeling consumer decision-making, competition between national brands and store brands, institutional determinants of firms' strategy.

Southern New Hampshire University, School of Business, Manchester, NH 03106-1045. Offers accounting (MBA, MS, Graduate Certificate); accounting finance (MS); accounting/auditing (MS); accounting/forensic accounting (MS); accounting/taxation (MS); athletic administration (MBA, Graduate Certificate); business administration (IMBA, MBA, Certificate, Graduate Certificate), including accounting (Certificate), business administration (MBA), business information systems (Graduate Certificate), human resource management (Certificate); corporate social responsibility (MBA); entrepreneurship (MBA); finance (MBA, MS, Graduate Certificate); finance/corporate finance (MS); finance/investments and securities (MS); forensic accounting (MBA); healthcare informatics (MBA); healthcare management (MBA); human resource management (Graduate Certificate); information technology (MS, Graduate Certificate); information technology management (MBA); international business (Graduate Certificate); international business and information technology (Graduate Certificate); international finance (Graduate Certificate); international sport management (Graduate Certificate); justice studies (MBA); leadership of nonprofit organizations (Graduate Certificate); management (MS); marketing (MBA, MS, Graduate Certificate); operations and project management (MS); operations and supply chain management (MBA, Graduate Certificate); organizational leadership (MS); project management (MBA, Graduate Certificate); Six Sigma (MBA); Six Sigma quality (Graduate Certificate); social media marketing (MBA); sport management (MBA, MS, Graduate Certificate); sustainability and environmental compliance (MBA); workplace conflict management (MBA); MBA/Certificate. *Accreditation:* ACBSP. *Program availability:* Part-time, evening/weekend, online learning. Terminal master's awarded for partial completion of doctoral program. *Degree requirements:* For master's, one foreign language, comprehensive exam (for some programs), thesis or alternative. *Entrance requirements:* For master's, minimum GPA of 2.5. Additional exam requirements/recommendations for international students: Required—TOEFL (minimum score 500 paper-based). Electronic applications accepted.

Southwest Minnesota State University, Department of Business and Public Affairs, Marshall, MN 56258. Offers leadership (MBA); management (MBA); marketing (MBA). *Program availability:* Part-time, evening/weekend, online learning. *Degree requirements:* For master's, thesis. *Entrance requirements:* For master's, GMAT (minimum score: 450). Additional exam requirements/recommendations for international students: Recommended—TOEFL (minimum score 550 paper-based; 79 iBT), IELTS. Electronic applications accepted.

State University of New York Polytechnic Institute, Program in Business Administration in Technology Management, Utica, NY 13502. Offers accounting and finance (MBA); business management (MBA); health services management (MBA); human resource management (MBA); marketing management (MBA). *Program availability:* Part-time, online learning. *Degree requirements:* For master's, capstone course. *Entrance requirements:* For master's, GMAT, resume, one letter of reference. Additional exam requirements/recommendations for international students: Required—TOEFL (minimum score 550 paper-based; 79 iBT), IELTS (minimum score 6.5). Electronic applications accepted. *Faculty research:* Technology management, writing schools, leadership, new products.

Stephen F. Austin State University, Graduate School, College of Business, Program in Business Administration, Nacogdoches, TX 75962. Offers business (MBA); management and marketing (MBA). *Accreditation:* AACSB. *Program availability:* Part-time, evening/weekend. *Degree requirements:* For master's, comprehensive exam. *Entrance requirements:* For master's, GMAT, minimum AACSB index of 1000. Additional exam requirements/recommendations for international students: Required—TOEFL (minimum score 550 paper-based). *Faculty research:* Strategic implications, information search, multinational firms, philosophical guidance.

Stevens Institute of Technology, Graduate School, School of Business, Program in Business Administration, Hoboken, NJ 07030. Offers business intelligence and analytics (MBA); engineering management (MBA); finance (MBA); information systems (MBA); innovation and entrepreneurship (MBA); marketing (MBA); pharmaceutical management (MBA); project management (MBA, Certificate); technology management (MBA); telecommunications management (MBA). *Accreditation:* AACSB. *Program availability:* Part-time, evening/weekend. *Students:* 35 full-time (15 women), 181 part-time (79 women); includes 53 minority (10 Black or African American, non-Hispanic/Latino; 2 American Indian or Alaska Native, non-Hispanic/Latino; 36 Asian, non-Hispanic/Latino; 5 Hispanic/Latino), 30 international. Average age 32. 215 applicants, 53% accepted, 61 enrolled. In 2016, 61 master's awarded. *Degree requirements:* For master's, thesis optional, minimum B average in major field and overall; for Certificate, minimum B average. *Entrance requirements:* Additional exam requirements/recommendations for international students: Required—TOEFL (minimum score 74 iBT), IELTS (minimum score 6). *Application deadline:* For fall admission, 6/1 for domestic students, 4/15 for international students; for spring admission, 11/30 for domestic students, 11/1 for international students. Applications are processed on a rolling basis. Application fee: $65. Electronic applications accepted. *Expenses:* Contact institution. *Financial support:* Fellowships, research assistantships, teaching assistantships, career-related internships or fieldwork, Federal Work-Study, scholarships/grants, and unspecified assistantships available. Financial award application deadline: 2/15; financial award applicants required to submit FAFSA. *Unit head:* Dr. Gregory Prastacos, Dean, 201-216-8366, E-mail: gprastac@stevens.edu. *Application contact:* Graduate Admissions, 888-783-8367, Fax: 888-511-1306, E-mail: graduate@stevens.edu.
Website: https://www.stevens.edu/school-business/masters-programs/mbaemba

Stony Brook University, State University of New York, Graduate School, College of Business, Program in Business Administration, Stony Brook, NY 11794. Offers accounting (MBA); business administration (MBA); finance (MBA, Certificate); health care management (MBA); innovation, human resources, management, or operations management (MBA); marketing (MBA). *Faculty:* 37 full-time (12 women), 12 part-time/adjunct (4 women). *Students:* 199 full-time (109 women), 139 part-time (64 women); includes 81 minority (19 Black or African American, non-Hispanic/Latino; 41 Asian, non-Hispanic/Latino; 17 Hispanic/Latino; 1 Native Hawaiian or other Pacific Islander, non-Hispanic/Latino; 3 Two or more races, non-Hispanic/Latino), 88 international. Average age 29. 246 applicants, 65% accepted, 91 enrolled. In 2016, 116 master's awarded. *Entrance requirements:* For master's, GMAT, 3 letters of recommendation from current or former employers or professors, transcripts, personal statement, resume. Additional exam requirements/recommendations for international students: Required—TOEFL (minimum score 550 paper-based; 90 iBT), IELTS (minimum score 6.5). *Application deadline:* For fall admission, 5/15 for domestic students, 3/15 for international students; for spring admission, 11/15 for domestic students, 10/15 for international students. Application fee: $100. *Expenses:* Contact institution. *Financial support:* Teaching assistantships available. *Total annual research expenditures:* $5,325. *Unit head:* Dr. Manuel London, Dean, 631-632-7159, E-mail: manuel.london@stonybrook.edu. *Application contact:* Dr. Jadranka Skorin-Kapov, Graduate Program Director, 631-632-7171, Fax: 631-632-8181, E-mail: jadranka.skorin-kapov@stonybrook.edu.

Strayer University, Graduate Studies, Washington, DC 20005-2603. Offers accounting (MS); acquisition (MBA); business administration (MBA); communications technology (MS); educational management (M Ed); finance (MBA); health services administration (MHSA); hospitality and tourism management (MBA); human resource management (MBA); information systems (MS), including computer security management, decision support system management, enterprise resource management, network management, software engineering management, systems development management; management (MBA); management information systems (MS); marketing (MBA); professional accounting (MS), including accounting information systems, controllership, taxation; public administration (MPA); supply chain management (MBA); technology in education (M Ed). Programs also offered at campus locations in Birmingham, AL; Chamblee, GA; Cobb County, GA; Morrow, GA; White Marsh, MD; Charleston, SC; Columbia, SC; Greensboro, NC; Greenville, SC; Lexington, KY; Louisville, KY; Nashville, TN; North Raleigh, NC; Washington, DC. *Accreditation:* ACBSP. *Program availability:* Part-time, evening/weekend, online learning. *Degree requirements:* For master's, thesis. *Entrance requirements:* For master's, GMAT, GRE General Test, bachelor's degree from an accredited college or university, minimum undergraduate GPA of 2.75. Electronic applications accepted.

Suffolk University, College of Arts and Sciences, Advertising and Public Relations Department, Boston, MA 02108-2770. Offers communication studies (MAC); integrated marketing communication (MAC); public relations and advertising (MAC). *Program availability:* Part-time, evening/weekend. *Faculty:* 5 full-time (3 women). *Students:* 14 full-time (9 women), 17 part-time (14 women); includes 5 minority (2 Black or African American, non-Hispanic/Latino; 3 Hispanic/Latino), 12 international. Average age 27. 64 applicants, 66% accepted, 15 enrolled. In 2016, 18 master's awarded. *Degree requirements:* For master's, thesis optional. *Entrance requirements:* For master's, GRE General Test, MAT, or GMAT, 2 letters of recommendation, resume. Additional exam requirements/recommendations for international students: Required—TOEFL (minimum score 550 paper-based; 80 iBT). *Application deadline:* For fall admission, 3/15 priority date for domestic and international students; for spring admission, 10/15 priority date for domestic and international students. Applications are processed on a rolling basis. Application fee: $50. Electronic applications accepted. *Expenses:* $27,456 per year full-time tuition, $1,144 per credit hour part-time tuition, $52 per year student activity fee. *Financial support:* In 2016–17, 22 students received support, including 18 fellowships (averaging $9,186 per year); career-related internships or fieldwork, Federal Work-Study, institutionally sponsored loans, and scholarships/grants also available. Support available to part-time students. Financial award application deadline: 4/1; financial award applicants required to submit FAFSA. *Faculty research:* Branding law and management, health care communication, gender roles and violence in video games, new media, political communication. *Unit head:* Robert Rosenthal, Chair, 617-573-8502, E-mail: rrosenthal@suffolk.edu. *Application contact:* Mara Marzocchi, Associate Director of Graduate Admissions, 617-573-8302, Fax: 617-305-1733, E-mail: grad.admission@suffolk.edu.
Website: http://www.suffolk.edu/college/graduate/69298.php

Suffolk University, Sawyer Business School, Master of Business Administration Program, Boston, MA 02108-2770. Offers accounting (MBA); entrepreneurship (MBA); executive business administration (EMBA); finance (MBA); global business administration (GMBA); health administration (MBA); international business (MBA); marketing (MBA); nonprofit management (MBA); organizational behavior (MBA); strategic management (MBA); supply chain management (MBA); taxation (MBA); JD/MBA; MBA/MHA; MBA/MSA; MBA/MSF; MBA/MST. *Accreditation:* AACSB. *Program availability:* Part-time, evening/weekend, 100% online. *Faculty:* 17 full-time (6 women), 10 part-time/adjunct (1 woman). *Students:* 137 full-time (70 women), 265 part-time (138 women); includes 78 minority (20 Black or African American, non-Hispanic/Latino; 22 Asian, non-Hispanic/Latino; 31 Hispanic/Latino; 5 Two or more races, non-Hispanic/Latino), 46 international. Average age 30. 416 applicants, 70% accepted, 128 enrolled. In 2016, 165 degrees awarded. *Entrance requirements:* For master's, GMAT, minimum undergraduate GPA of 2.75 (MBA), 5 years of managerial experience (EMBA). Additional exam requirements/recommendations for international students: Required—TOEFL (minimum score 550 paper-based; 80 iBT). *Application deadline:* For fall admission, 3/15 priority date for domestic students, 10/15 priority date for international students; for spring admission, 10/15 priority date for domestic and international students. Applications are processed on a rolling basis. Application fee: $50. Electronic applications accepted. *Expenses: Tuition:* Full-time $41,490; part-time $1383 per credit hour. *Required fees:* $52; $52 per credit hour. Part-time tuition and fees vary according to course load and program. *Financial support:* In 2016–17, 209 students received support, including 176 fellowships (averaging $8,581 per year); career-related internships or fieldwork, Federal Work-Study, institutionally sponsored loans, and scholarships/grants also available. Support available to part-time students. Financial award application deadline: 4/1; financial award applicants required to submit FAFSA. *Faculty research:* Foreign investments; career strategies and boundaryless careers; corporate ethics codes; interest rates, inflation, and growth options; innovation and product development performance. *Unit head:* Jodi Detjen, Director of MBA Programs, 617-573-8306, E-mail: jdetjen@suffolk.edu. *Application contact:* Mara Marzocchi, Associate Director of Graduate Admissions, 617-573-8302, Fax: 617-305-1733, E-mail: grad.admission@suffolk.edu.
Website: http://www.suffolk.edu/mba

Syracuse University, Martin J. Whitman School of Management, Master of Business Administration Program, Syracuse, NY 13244. Offers accounting (MBA); business analytics (MBA); entrepreneurship (MBA); marketing management (MBA); real estate (MBA); supply chain management (MBA); JD/MBA. *Program availability:* Part-time, 100% online. *Students:* 22 full-time (9 women), 495 part-time (147 women); includes 182 minority (81 Black or African American, non-Hispanic/Latino; 3 American Indian or Alaska Native, non-Hispanic/Latino; 42 Asian, non-Hispanic/Latino; 52 Hispanic/Latino; 4 Native Hawaiian or other Pacific Islander, non-Hispanic/Latino), 22 international. Average age 32. 1,086 applicants, 73% accepted, 518 enrolled. In 2016, 84 master's awarded. *Entrance requirements:* For master's, GMAT or GRE, resume, essay, 5-minute video interview, two letters of recommendation, transcripts (unofficial). Additional exam requirements/recommendations for international students: Required—TOEFL (minimum score 100 iBT), IELTS (minimum score 7), PTE (minimum score 68). *Application deadline:* For fall admission, 11/30 for domestic students, 11/30 priority date for international students; for winter admission, 1/1 for domestic students, 1/1 priority date for international students; for spring admission, 2/15 for domestic and international students; for summer admission, 4/19 for domestic students. Application fee: $75. Electronic applications accepted. *Expenses:* Contact institution. *Financial support:* In 2016–17, 22 students received support. Merit scholarships available. Financial award application deadline: 2/15. *Faculty research:* Data analysis, economics of international business, financial markets and institutions, operations management, supply chain management. *Unit head:* Don Harter, Associate Dean, Graduate Programs, 315-443-3502, E-mail: dharter@syr.edu. *Application contact:* Shri Ramakrishnan, Assistant Director, Graduate Recruitment, 315-443-3497, Fax: 315-443-9517, E-mail: busgrad@syr.edu.
Website: http://whitman.syr.edu/ftmba/

Tarleton State University, College of Graduate Studies, College of Business Administration, Department of Marketing and Computer Information Systems, Stephenville, TX 76402. Offers information systems (MS). *Program availability:* Part-time, evening/weekend, 100% online, blended/hybrid learning. *Faculty:* 6 full-time (1 woman). *Students:* 8 full-time (2 women), 40 part-time (14 women); includes 19 minority (4 Black or African American, non-Hispanic/Latino; 1 American Indian or Alaska Native, non-Hispanic/Latino; 6 Asian, non-Hispanic/Latino; 6 Hispanic/Latino; 2 Two or more races, non-Hispanic/Latino). 21 applicants, 95% accepted, 17 enrolled. In 2016, 11 master's awarded. *Degree requirements:* For master's, comprehensive exam. *Entrance requirements:* For master's, GRE, minimum GPA of 3.0. Additional exam requirements/recommendations for international students: Required—TOEFL (minimum score 550 paper-based; 80 iBT). *Application deadline:* For fall admission, 8/15 priority date for domestic students; for spring admission, 1/7 for domestic students. Applications are processed on a rolling basis. Application fee: $45 ($145 for international students). Electronic applications accepted. *Expenses:* $3,672 tuition; $2,437 fees. *Financial support:* Research assistantships and teaching assistantships available. Financial award application deadline: 5/1; financial award applicants required to submit FAFSA. *Unit head:* Dr. Joseph Schuessler, Department Head, 254-968-9893, E-mail: schuessler@tarleton.edu. *Application contact:* Information Contact, 254-968-9104, Fax: 254-968-9670, E-mail: gradoffice@tarleton.edu.
Website: http://www.tarleton.edu/cis/

Temple University, Fox School of Business, Doctoral Programs in Business, Philadelphia, PA 19122-6096. Offers accounting (PhD); entrepreneurship (PhD); finance (PhD); international business (PhD); management information systems (PhD); marketing (PhD); risk management and insurance (PhD); statistics (PhD); strategic management (PhD); tourism and sport (PhD). *Accreditation:* AACSB. *Degree requirements:* For doctorate, thesis/dissertation. *Entrance requirements:* For doctorate, GRE General Test, GMAT, minimum GPA of 3.0, master's degree. Additional exam requirements/recommendations for international students: Required—TOEFL (minimum score 600 paper-based; 100 iBT), IELTS (minimum score 7.5). Electronic applications accepted.

Temple University, Fox School of Business, MBA Programs, Philadelphia, PA 19122-6096. Offers accounting (MBA); business management (MBA); financial management (MBA); healthcare and life sciences innovation (MBA); human resource management (MBA); international business (IMBA); IT management (MBA); marketing management (MBA); pharmaceutical management (MBA); strategic management (EMBA, MBA). EMBA offered in Philadelphia, PA and Tokyo, Japan. *Accreditation:* AACSB. *Program availability:* Part-time, evening/weekend, online learning. *Entrance requirements:* For master's, GMAT, minimum undergraduate GPA of 3.0. Additional exam requirements/recommendations for international students: Required—TOEFL (minimum score 600 paper-based; 100 iBT), IELTS (minimum score 7.5).

Temple University, Fox School of Business, Specialized Master's Programs, Philadelphia, PA 19122-6096. Offers accountancy (MS); actuarial science (MS); finance (MS); financial engineering (MS); human resource management (MS); innovation management and entrepreneurship (MS); marketing (MS); statistics (MS). MS in innovation management and entrepreneurship delivered jointly with College of Engineering. *Accreditation:* AACSB. *Program availability:* Part-time. *Entrance requirements:* For master's, GRE General Test or GMAT, minimum undergraduate GPA of 3.0. Additional exam requirements/recommendations for international students: Required—TOEFL (minimum score 600 paper-based; 100 iBT), IELTS (minimum score 7.5).

Texas A&M University, Mays Business School, Department of Marketing, College Station, TX 77843. Offers MS. *Faculty:* 15. *Students:* 74 full-time (48 women), 4 part-time (3 women); includes 8 minority (1 Black or African American, non-Hispanic/Latino; 6 Hispanic/Latino; 1 Two or more races, non-Hispanic/Latino), 22 international. Average age 25. 186 applicants, 14% accepted, 20 enrolled. In 2016, 38 master's awarded. Terminal master's awarded for partial completion of doctoral program. *Degree requirements:* For master's, comprehensive exam. *Entrance requirements:* For

master's, GMAT or GRE. Additional exam requirements/recommendations for international students: Required—TOEFL (minimum score 550 paper-based; 80 iBT), IELTS (minimum score 6), PTE (minimum score 53). *Application deadline:* Applications are processed on a rolling basis. Application fee: $50 ($90 for international students). Electronic applications accepted. *Expenses:* Contact institution. *Financial support:* In 2016–17, 58 students received support, including 1 fellowship with tuition reimbursement available (averaging $9,000 per year), 17 research assistantships with tuition reimbursements available (averaging $6,539 per year), 28 teaching assistantships with tuition reimbursements available (averaging $3,736 per year); career-related internships or fieldwork, institutionally sponsored loans, scholarships/grants, traineeships, health care benefits, tuition waivers (full and partial), and unspecified assistantships also available. Support available to part-time students. Financial award application deadline: 3/15; financial award applicants required to submit FAFSA. *Faculty research:* Consumer behavior, innovation and product management, international marketing, marketing management and strategy, services marketing. *Unit head:* Dr. Mark B. Houston, Head, 979-845-7257, E-mail: mhouston@mays.tamu.edu. *Application contact:* Stephen W. McDaniel, Master's Advisor, 979-845-5801, E-mail: smcdaniel@mays.tamu.edu.
Website: http://mays.tamu.edu/mktg/

Texas A&M University–Commerce, College of Business, Commerce, TX 75429-3011. Offers accounting (MSA); business administration (MBA); business analytics (MS); finance (MSF); management (MS); marketing (MS). *Accreditation:* AACSB. *Program availability:* Part-time, evening/weekend, 100% online, blended/hybrid learning. *Faculty:* 48 full-time (17 women), 8 part-time/adjunct (2 women). *Students:* 463 full-time (232 women), 1,109 part-time (539 women); includes 653 minority (280 Black or African American, non-Hispanic/Latino; 7 American Indian or Alaska Native, non-Hispanic/Latino; 131 Asian, non-Hispanic/Latino; 202 Hispanic/Latino; 1 Native Hawaiian or other Pacific Islander, non-Hispanic/Latino; 32 Two or more races, non-Hispanic/Latino), 211 international. Average age 33. 1,021 applicants, 59% accepted, 424 enrolled. In 2016, 617 master's awarded. *Degree requirements:* For master's, comprehensive exam. *Entrance requirements:* For master's, GRE General Test, GMAT, letter of recommendation. Additional exam requirements/recommendations for international students: Required—TOEFL (minimum score 550 paper-based; 79 iBT), IELTS (minimum score 6). *Application deadline:* For fall admission, 5/15 priority date for international students; for spring admission, 10/1 priority date for international students; for summer admission, 2/1 priority date for international students. Applications are processed on a rolling basis. Application fee: $50 ($75 for international students). Electronic applications accepted. *Expenses:* Contact institution. *Financial support:* In 2016–17, 90 students received support, including 20 research assistantships with partial tuition reimbursements available (averaging $8,000 per year); Federal Work-Study, institutionally sponsored loans, scholarships/grants, health care benefits, and unspecified assistantships also available. Financial award application deadline: 5/1; financial award applicants required to submit FAFSA. *Faculty research:* Applied economics emphasis on industries that are important to the region including health, energy and agriculture; finance research on banking, investments, financial institutions and risk management; marketing and big data decisions of product choice behavior and channel behavior of consumers; strategic management and organizational behavior phenomena; International Accounting in Governmental Sectors. *Total annual research expenditures:* $1,920. *Unit head:* Dr. Shanan G. Gibson, Dean of College of Business, 903-886-5191, Fax: 903-886-5650, E-mail: shanan.gibson@tamuc.edu. *Application contact:* Shanna Hoskison, Director, Graduate Advising, 903-886-5190, E-mail: shanna.hoskison@tamuc.edu.
Website: http://www.tamuc.edu/academics/graduateSchool/programs/businessEntrepreneurship/default.aspx

Texas Christian University, Neeley School of Business, Full-time Master's Program in Business Administration and Accelerated MBA, Fort Worth, TX 76129. Offers accounting (MBA); finance (MBA), including corporate finance, investments; marketing (MBA), including marketing management, product and brand management; supply and value chain management (MBA). *Accreditation:* AACSB. *Program availability:* Part-time, evening/weekend. *Faculty:* 60 full-time (17 women), 17 part-time/adjunct (4 women). *Students:* 92 full-time (26 women); includes 14 minority (3 Black or African American, non-Hispanic/Latino; 1 American Indian or Alaska Native, non-Hispanic/Latino; 3 Asian, non-Hispanic/Latino; 7 Hispanic/Latino), 30 international. Average age 28. 205 applicants, 50% accepted, 47 enrolled. In 2016, 43 master's awarded. *Entrance requirements:* For master's, GMAT (preferred); GRE. Additional exam requirements/recommendations for international students: Required—TOEFL (minimum score 100 iBT); Recommended—IELTS (minimum score 7), TSE (minimum score 68). *Application deadline:* For fall admission, 3/1 for domestic and international students; for winter admission, 1/15 for domestic and international students; for spring admission, 11/1 for domestic and international students; for summer admission, 1/15 for domestic and international students. Applications are processed on a rolling basis. Application fee: $100. Electronic applications accepted. Application fee is waived when completed online. *Expenses:* Contact institution. *Financial support:* In 2016–17, 94 students received support. Career-related internships or fieldwork, scholarships/grants, and unspecified assistantships available. Financial award application deadline: 4/1; financial award applicants required to submit FAFSA. *Faculty research:* Emerging financial markets, derivative trading activity, salesforce deployment, examining sales activity, litigation against tax practitioners. *Unit head:* Anne Rooney, Executive Director, Graduate Programs, 817-257-7991, Fax: 817-257-6431, E-mail: mbainfo@tcu.edu. *Application contact:* Peggy Conway, Director, Full-time MBA Admissions, 817-257-7989, Fax: 817-257-6431, E-mail: mbainfo@tcu.edu.
Website: http://www.neeley.tcu.edu/mba

Texas Tech University, Rawls College of Business Administration, Lubbock, TX 79409-2101. Offers accounting (MSA, PhD), including audit/financial reporting (MSA), taxation (MSA); business statistics (MS, PhD); data science (MS); finance (PhD); general business (MBA); healthcare management (MS); information systems and operations management (PhD); management (PhD); marketing (PhD); STEM (MBA); JD/MBA; JD/MSA; MBA/M Arch; MBA/MD; MBA/MS; MBA/Pharm D. *Accreditation:* AACSB; CAHME (one or more programs are accredited). *Program availability:* Evening/weekend. *Faculty:* 74 full-time (13 women). *Students:* 741 full-time (275 women); includes 198 minority (38 Black or African American, non-Hispanic/Latino; 1 American Indian or Alaska Native, non-Hispanic/Latino; 24 Asian, non-Hispanic/Latino; 116 Hispanic/Latino; 1 Native Hawaiian or other Pacific Islander, non-Hispanic/Latino; 18 Two or more races, non-Hispanic/Latino), 95 international. Average age 28. 905 applicants, 48% accepted, 251 enrolled. In 2016, 545 master's, 13 doctorates awarded. *Degree requirements:* For master's, capstone course; for doctorate, comprehensive exam, thesis/dissertation, qualifying exams. *Entrance requirements:* For master's, GMAT, GRE, MCAT, PCAT, LSAT, or DAT, holistic review of academic credentials, resume, essay, letters of recommendation; for doctorate, GMAT, GRE, holistic review of academic credentials, resume, statement of purpose, letters of recommendation. Additional exam requirements/recommendations for international students: Required—TOEFL (minimum score 95 iBT), IELTS. *Application deadline:* For fall admission, 7/1 priority date for domestic students, 1/15 for international students; for spring admission, 12/1 priority date for domestic students, 6/15 for international students; for summer admission, 5/1 for domestic students. Applications are processed on a rolling basis. Application fee: $60. Electronic applications accepted. *Expenses:* $48,000 (MBA for Working Professionals); $20,000 (STEM MBA). *Financial support:* In 2016–17, 157 students received support, including 25 research assistantships (averaging $22,725 per year), 27 teaching assistantships (averaging $22,725 per year); fellowships, career-related internships or fieldwork, Federal Work-Study, scholarships/grants, health care benefits, and unspecified assistantships also available. Financial award application deadline: 3/1; financial award applicants required to submit FAFSA. *Faculty research:* Governmental and nonprofit accounting, securities and options futures, statistical analysis and design, leadership, consumer behavior. *Unit head:* Dr. Margaret Williams, Dean, 806-742-3188, Fax: 806-742-1092, E-mail: margaret.l.williams@ttu.edu. *Application contact:* Chathry Keaton, Applications Manager, Graduate and Professional Programs, 806-742-3184, Fax: 806-742-3958, E-mail: rawlsgrad@ttu.edu.
Website: http://www.depts.ttu.edu/rawlsbusiness/graduate/

Tiffin University, Program in Business Administration, Tiffin, OH 44883-2161. Offers finance (MBA); general management (MBA); healthcare administration (MBA); human resource management (MBA); international business (MBA); leadership (MBA); marketing (MBA); non-profit management (MBA); sports management (MBA). *Accreditation:* ACBSP. *Program availability:* Part-time, evening/weekend, online learning. *Students:* 10 full-time (4 women), 497 part-time (240 women); includes 91 minority (67 Black or African American, non-Hispanic/Latino; 1 American Indian or Alaska Native, non-Hispanic/Latino; 5 Asian, non-Hispanic/Latino; 15 Hispanic/Latino; 3 Two or more races, non-Hispanic/Latino), 102 international. Average age 31. 214 applicants, 86% accepted, 146 enrolled. In 2016, 183 master's awarded. *Entrance requirements:* For master's, minimum undergraduate GPA of 2.5, work experience. Additional exam requirements/recommendations for international students: Required—TOEFL (minimum score 550 paper-based; 79 iBT), IELTS. *Application deadline:* For fall admission, 8/15 for domestic students, 8/1 for international students; for spring admission, 1/9 for domestic students, 12/1 for international students. Applications are processed on a rolling basis. Application fee: $50. Electronic applications accepted. Application fee is waived when completed online. *Expenses: Tuition:* Full-time $21,000; part-time $700 per credit hour. *Required fees:* $150. Tuition and fees vary according to program. *Financial support:* Unspecified assistantships available. Support available to part-time students. Financial award application deadline: 7/31; financial award applicants required to submit FAFSA. *Faculty research:* Small business, executive development operations, research and statistical analysis, market research, management information systems. *Unit head:* Dr. Bonnie Tiell, Dean of Graduate Studies, 419-448-3261, Fax: 419-443-5002, E-mail: btiell@tiffin.edu. *Application contact:* Nikki Hintze, Director of Graduate and Distance Education Academic Advising, 800-968-6446 Ext. 3596, Fax: 419-443-5002, E-mail: hintzenm@tiffin.edu.
Website: http://www.tiffin.edu/graduateprograms/

Trident University International, College of Business Administration, Program in Business Administration, Cypress, CA 90630. Offers business administration (PhD); conflict and negotiation management (MBA); criminal justice administration (MBA); entrepreneurship (MBA); finance (MBA); general management (MBA); government accounting (MBA); human resource management (MBA); information security and digital assurance management (MBA); information technology management (MBA); international business (MBA); logistics management (MBA); marketing (MBA); project management (MBA); public management (MBA); quality management (MBA); strategic leadership (MBA). *Program availability:* Part-time, evening/weekend, online learning. *Degree requirements:* For doctorate, comprehensive exam, thesis/dissertation, defense of dissertation. *Entrance requirements:* For master's, minimum GPA of 2.5 (students with GPA 3.0 or greater may transfer up to 30% of graduate level credits); for doctorate, minimum GPA of 3.4, curriculum vitae, course work in research methods or statistics. Additional exam requirements/recommendations for international students: Required—TOEFL. Electronic applications accepted.

United States International University–Africa, School of Business Administration, Nairobi, Kenya. Offers business administration (GEMBA); entrepreneurship (MBA); finance (MBA); human resource management (MBA); information technology management (MBA); integrated studies (MBA); international business administration (MBA); management and organizational development (MS); marketing (MBA); organizational development (EMS); strategic management (MBA). *Program availability:* Part-time, evening/weekend. *Degree requirements:* For master's, thesis. *Entrance requirements:* For master's, GMAT, 2 letters of reference, resume. Additional exam requirements/recommendations for international students: Required—TOEFL (minimum score 550 paper-based). *Faculty research:* Marketing in small business enterprises, total quality management in Kenya.

Universidad del Turabo, Graduate Programs, School of Business and Entrepreneurship, Program in Marketing, Gurabo, PR 00778-3030. Offers MBA. *Program availability:* Part-time, evening/weekend. *Students:* 8 full-time (7 women), 13 part-time (6 women); all minorities (all Hispanic/Latino). Average age 32. 16 applicants, 38% accepted, 6 enrolled. In 2016, 5 master's awarded. *Entrance requirements:* For master's, GRE, EXADEP or GMAT, interview, essay, official transcript, recommendation letters. *Application deadline:* For fall admission, 8/5 for domestic students. Application fee: $25. Electronic applications accepted. *Financial support:* Institutionally sponsored loans available. Financial award applicants required to submit FAFSA. *Unit head:* Juan Sosa, Dean, 787-743-7979 Ext. 4118, E-mail: negocios_ut@suagm.edu. *Application contact:* Diriee Rodríguez, Admissions Director, 787-743-7979 Ext. 4453, E-mail: admisiones-ut@suagm.edu.
Website: http://ut.suagm.edu/es/negocios

Universidad Iberoamericana, Graduate School, Santo Domingo D.N., Dominican Republic. Offers business administration (MBA, PMBA); constitutional law (LL M); dentistry (DMD); educational management (MA); integrated marketing communication (MA); psychopedagogical intervention (M Ed); real estate law (LL M); strategic management of human talent (MM).

Universidad Metropolitana, School of Business Administration, Program in Marketing, San Juan, PR 00928-1150. Offers MBA. *Program availability:* Part-time. *Degree requirements:* For master's, thesis or alternative. *Entrance requirements:* For master's, GMAT, PAEG, interview. Electronic applications accepted.

Université de Sherbrooke, Faculty of Administration, Program in Marketing, Sherbrooke, QC J1K 2R1, Canada. Offers M Sc. *Degree requirements:* For master's, one foreign language, thesis. *Entrance requirements:* For master's, bachelor's degree in related field, minimum GPA of 3.0 (on 4.3 scale). Electronic applications accepted. *Faculty research:* Consumer behavior, sales force, branding, prices management.

Université Laval, Faculty of Administrative Sciences, Programs in Business Administration, Québec, QC G1K 7P4, Canada. Offers accounting (MBA); agri-food management (MBA); electronic business (MBA, Diploma); factory management and logistics (MBA); finance (MBA); firm management (MBA); geomatic management (MBA); information technology management (MBA); international management (MBA); management (MBA); management accounting (MBA, Diploma); marketing (MBA); modeling and organizational decision (MBA); occupational health and safety management (MBA); pharmacy management (MBA); social and environmental responsibility (MBA); technological entrepreneurship (Diploma). *Accreditation:* AACSB. *Program availability:* Part-time, evening/weekend, online learning. *Entrance requirements:* For master's and Diploma, knowledge of French and English. Electronic applications accepted.

University at Albany, State University of New York, School of Business, MBA Programs, Albany, NY 12222. Offers business administration (MBA); cyber security (MBA); entrepreneurship (MBA); finance (MBA); human resource information systems (MBA); information technology management (MBA); marketing (MBA); JD/MBA. JD/MBA offered with Albany Law School. *Program availability:* Part-time, evening/weekend. *Faculty:* 25 full-time (8 women), 4 part-time/adjunct (1 woman). *Students:* 92 full-time (39 women), 192 part-time (77 women); includes 63 minority (12 Black or African American, non-Hispanic/Latino; 1 American Indian or Alaska Native, non-Hispanic/Latino; 32 Asian, non-Hispanic/Latino; 13 Hispanic/Latino; 5 Two or more races, non-Hispanic/Latino), 27 international. Average age 25. 217 applicants, 73% accepted, 119 enrolled. In 2016, 122 master's awarded. *Degree requirements:* For master's, thesis (for some programs), field or research project. *Entrance requirements:* For master's, GMAT, minimum undergraduate GPA of 3.0; 3 letters of recommendation; resume; statement of goals. Additional exam requirements/recommendations for international students: Required—TOEFL (minimum score 100 iBT); Recommended—IELTS (minimum score 7). *Application deadline:* For fall admission, 4/1 priority date for domestic students, 3/1 for international students; for spring admission, 12/1 for domestic students; for summer admission, 5/1 for domestic students. Applications are processed on a rolling basis. Application fee: $75. Electronic applications accepted. *Expenses:* $16,274 Full-Time MBA per year; $696 Part-Time MBA per credit hour. *Financial support:* In 2016–17, 20 students received support, including 20 fellowships with partial tuition reimbursements available (averaging $6,500 per year); research assistantships, teaching assistantships, and unspecified assistantships also available. Financial award application deadline: 4/1; financial award applicants required to submit FAFSA. *Faculty research:* Cyber security, entrepreneurship, human resource information systems, information technology management, finance, marketing. *Total annual research expenditures:* $136,000. *Unit head:* Dr. Hany A. Shawky, Interim Dean, 518-956-8337, E-mail: hshawky@albany.edu. *Application contact:* Zina Mega Lawrence, Assistant Dean of Graduate Student Services, 518-956-8320, Fax: 518-442-4042, E-mail: zlawrence@albany.edu.
Website: http://graduatebusiness.albany.edu/

University at Buffalo, the State University of New York, Graduate School, School of Management, Buffalo, NY 14620. Offers accounting (MS); analytics (MBA); business administration (PMBA); consulting (MBA); finance (MBA, MS), including financial risk management (MS), quantitative finance (MS); healthcare (MBA); information assurance (MBA); information systems (MBA); international management (MBA); management (EMBA, PhD); management information systems (MS); marketing (MBA); supply chain and operations (MBA); supply chains and operations management (MS); Au D/MBA; DDS/MBA; JD/MBA; M Arch/MBA; MD/MBA; MPH/MBA; MSW/MBA; Pharm D/MBA. *Accreditation:* AACSB. *Program availability:* Part-time, evening/weekend. *Faculty:* 80 full-time (26 women), 36 part-time/adjunct (6 women). *Students:* 683 full-time (277 women), 196 part-time (63 women); includes 76 minority (23 Black or African American, non-Hispanic/Latino; 1 American Indian or Alaska Native, non-Hispanic/Latino; 48 Asian, non-Hispanic/Latino; 3 Hispanic/Latino; 1 Two or more races, non-Hispanic/Latino), 371 international. Average age 31. 2,451 applicants, 42% accepted, 484 enrolled. In 2016, 515 master's, 10 doctorates awarded. *Degree requirements:* For master's, thesis (for some programs); for doctorate, comprehensive exam, thesis/dissertation. *Entrance requirements:* For master's, GMAT (for MS in accounting, finance); GRE or GMAT (for MBA, PMBA, other MS concentrations), essays, letters of recommendation; for doctorate, GMAT or GRE, essays, writing sample, letters of recommendation. Additional exam requirements/recommendations for international students: Required—TOEFL (minimum score 95 iBT) or IELTS (minimum score 6.5); Recommended—TSE (minimum score 73). *Application deadline:* For fall admission, 10/15 priority date for domestic and international students; for winter admission, 2/1 priority date for domestic and international students; for spring admission, 4/15 for domestic students; for summer admission, 5/15 for domestic students. Application fee: $100. Electronic applications accepted. *Expenses:* Contact institution. *Financial support:* Fellowships with full and partial tuition reimbursements, research assistantships with full and partial tuition reimbursements, teaching assistantships with full and partial tuition reimbursements, career-related internships or fieldwork, Federal Work-Study, institutionally sponsored loans, scholarships/grants, health care benefits, and unspecified assistantships available. Financial award application deadline: 2/15. *Faculty research:* Data analytics, accounting information and corporate finance, consumer behavior, supply chain logistics, leadership and team effectiveness. *Total annual research expenditures:* $1.5 million. *Unit head:* Erin K. O'Brien, Assistant Dean and Director of Graduate Programs, 716-645-3204, Fax: 716-645-2341, E-mail: ekobrien@buffalo.edu. *Application contact:* Meghan Felser, Associate Director of Admissions and Recruiting, 716-645-3204, Fax: 716-645-2341, E-mail: mpwood@buffalo.edu.
Website: http://mgt.buffalo.edu/

The University of Akron, Graduate School, College of Business Administration, Department of Marketing, Akron, OH 44325. Offers MBA. *Program availability:* Part-time, evening/weekend. *Faculty:* 9 full-time (2 women), 4 part-time/adjunct (2 women). *Students:* 17 full-time (10 women), 9 part-time (5 women); includes 2 minority (1 Black or African American, non-Hispanic/Latino; 1 Asian, non-Hispanic/Latino), 5 international. Average age 29. 11 applicants, 64% accepted, 2 enrolled. In 2016, 16 master's awarded. *Entrance requirements:* For master's, GMAT, minimum GPA of 3.0 (preferred), two letters of recommendation, resume, statement of purpose. Additional exam requirements/recommendations for international students: Required—TOEFL (minimum score 550 paper-based; 79 iBT), IELTS (minimum score 6.5). *Application deadline:* For fall admission, 7/15 for domestic and international students; for spring admission, 11/15 for domestic and international students; for summer admission, 4/15 for domestic and international students. Application fee: $45 ($75 for international students). Electronic applications accepted. *Expenses:* Tuition, state resident: full-time $8618; part-time $360 per credit hour. Tuition, nonresident: full-time $17,149; part-time $715 per credit hour. *Required fees:* $1652. *Financial support:* In 2016–17, 1 research assistantship with full tuition reimbursement was awarded; unspecified assistantships and instructional support assistantships also available. *Faculty research:* Multi-channel marketing, direct interactive marketing, strategic retailing, marketing strategy and telemarketing. *Total annual research expenditures:* $11,700. *Unit head:* Dr. Terry Daugherty, Chair, 330-972-8304, E-mail: td23@uakron.edu. *Application contact:* Dr. William Hauser, Director of Graduate Business Programs, 330-972-7043, Fax: 330-972-6588, E-mail: whauser@uakron.edu.
Website: http://www.uakron.edu/cba/departments/marketing/

The University of Alabama, Graduate School, Manderson Graduate School of Business, Department of Marketing, Tuscaloosa, AL 35487. Offers MS, PhD. *Accreditation:* AACSB. *Faculty:* 20 full-time (5 women), 2 part-time/adjunct (0 women). *Students:* 64 full-time (30 women), 26 part-time (14 women); includes 15 minority (8 Black or African American, non-Hispanic/Latino; 1 American Indian or Alaska Native, non-Hispanic/Latino; 2 Asian, non-Hispanic/Latino; 2 Hispanic/Latino; 2 Two or more races, non-Hispanic/Latino), 10 international. Average age 27. 145 applicants, 54% accepted, 57 enrolled. In 2016, 63 master's, 2 doctorates awarded. Terminal master's awarded for partial completion of doctoral program. *Degree requirements:* For master's, internship; for doctorate, comprehensive exam, thesis/dissertation. *Entrance requirements:* For master's, GRE or GMAT; for doctorate, GRE or GMAT, minimum GPA of 3.0. Additional exam requirements/recommendations for international students: Required—TOEFL (minimum score 600 paper-based) or IELTS (minimum score 6.5). *Application deadline:* For fall admission, 4/1 priority date for domestic and international students; for spring admission, 2/1 priority date for domestic and international students. Applications are processed on a rolling basis. Application fee: $50 ($60 for international students). Electronic applications accepted. *Expenses:* Tuition, state resident: full-time $10,470. Tuition, nonresident: full-time $26,950. *Financial support:* In 2016–17, 1 fellowship with full tuition reimbursement (averaging $15,000 per year), 5 research assistantships with full tuition reimbursements (averaging $25,000 per year), 5 teaching assistantships with full tuition reimbursements (averaging $25,000 per year) were awarded; scholarships/grants, health care benefits, and unspecified assistantships also available. *Faculty research:* Relationship marketing, consumer behavior, services marketing, professional selling, supply chain management. *Unit head:* Dr. David Mothersbaugh, Department Head, 205-348-2871, E-mail: dmothers@culverhouse.ua.edu. *Application contact:* Courtney Cox, Office Associate II, 205-348-6183, Fax: 205-348-6695, E-mail: crhodes@cba.ua.edu.
Website: http://cba.ua.edu/mkt

The University of Alabama at Birmingham, Collat School of Business, Program in Business Administration, Birmingham, AL 35294. Offers business administration (MBA), including finance, health care management, information technology management, marketing. *Program availability:* Part-time, evening/weekend. *Entrance requirements:* For master's, GMAT. Additional exam requirements/recommendations for international students: Required—TOEFL. Full-time tuition and fees vary according to course load and program.

The University of Alabama in Huntsville, School of Graduate Studies, College of Business Administration, Programs in Business and Management, Huntsville, AL 35899. Offers business analytics (MSMS); federal contracting and procurement management (Certificate); human resource management (MSM); management (MBA), including acquisition management, entrepreneurship, federal contract accounting, finance, human resource management, logistics and supply chain management, marketing, project management; supply chain management (Certificate); technology and innovation management (Certificate). *Accreditation:* AACSB. *Program availability:* Part-time, evening/weekend. *Degree requirements:* For master's, comprehensive exam, thesis or alternative. *Entrance requirements:* For master's, GMAT (minimum score 500), minimum AACSB index of 1080. Additional exam requirements/recommendations for international students: Required—TOEFL (minimum score 550 paper-based; 80 iBT), IELTS (minimum score 6.5). Electronic applications accepted. *Expenses:* Tuition, state resident: full-time $9834; part-time $600 per credit hour. Tuition, nonresident: full-time $21,830; part-time $1325 per credit hour. *Faculty research:* Supply chain management, management of research and development, international marketing and branding, organizational behavior and human resource management, social networks and computational economics.

University of Alberta, Faculty of Graduate Studies and Research, Doctoral Program in Business, Edmonton, AB T6G 2E1, Canada. Offers accounting (PhD); finance (PhD); human resources/industrial relations (PhD); management science (PhD); marketing (PhD); organizational analysis (PhD); MBA/PhD. *Accreditation:* AACSB. *Program availability:* Part-time. *Degree requirements:* For doctorate, comprehensive exam, thesis/dissertation. *Entrance requirements:* For doctorate, GMAT. Additional exam requirements/recommendations for international students: Required—TOEFL (minimum score 550 paper-based). Electronic applications accepted. *Faculty research:* Accounting, capital markets and corporate finance, organizational change and human resource management, marketing, strategic management.

The University of Arizona, Eller College of Management, Department of Marketing, Tucson, AZ 85721. Offers MBA, MS, PhD. *Degree requirements:* For doctorate, comprehensive exam, thesis/dissertation. *Entrance requirements:* For doctorate, GMAT (minimum score 600). Additional exam requirements/recommendations for international students: Required—TOEFL (minimum score 600 paper-based). Electronic applications accepted. *Faculty research:* Consumer behavior, customer relationship management, research methods, brand strategy, public policy.

University of Baltimore, Graduate School, Merrick School of Business, Department of Marketing and Entrepreneurship, Baltimore, MD 21201-5779. Offers innovation management and technology commercialization (MS). *Program availability:* Part-time, evening/weekend. *Entrance requirements:* For master's, GMAT. Additional exam requirements/recommendations for international students: Required—TOEFL (minimum score 550 paper-based). Electronic applications accepted.

University of Bridgeport, School of Business, Bridgeport, CT 06604. Offers accounting (MBA); finance (MBA); general business (MBA); global financial services (MBA); human resource management (MBA); information systems and knowledge management (MBA); international business (MBA); management (MBA); marketing (MBA); operations management (MBA); small business and entrepreneurship (MBA); specialized business (MBA). *Accreditation:* ACBSP. *Program availability:* Part-time, evening/weekend. *Degree requirements:* For master's, thesis optional. *Entrance requirements:* For master's, GMAT. Additional exam requirements/recommendations for international students: Recommended—TOEFL (minimum score 550 paper-based; 80 iBT), IELTS (minimum score 6.5). Electronic applications accepted. *Expenses:* Contact institution.

The University of British Columbia, Sauder School of Business, Doctoral Program in Business Administration, Vancouver, BC V6T 1Z2, Canada. Offers accounting (PhD); finance (PhD); management information systems (PhD); management science (PhD); marketing (PhD); organizational behavior (PhD); strategy and business economics (PhD); transportation and logistics (PhD); urban land economics (PhD). *Degree requirements:* For doctorate, comprehensive exam, thesis/dissertation. *Entrance requirements:* For doctorate, GMAT or GRE. Additional exam requirements/recommendations for international students: Required—TOEFL (minimum score 600 paper-based; 100 iBT). *Application deadline:* Applications are processed on a rolling basis. Application fee: $102 Canadian dollars ($165 Canadian dollars for international students). Electronic applications accepted. *Expenses:* $4,802 per year tuition and fees, $8,436 per year international. *Financial support:* Fellowships with full tuition reimbursements, research assistantships with full tuition reimbursements, and teaching assistantships with full tuition reimbursements available. *Application contact:* Elaine Cho, Administrator, PhD and M Sc Programs, 604-822-8366, Fax: 604-822-8755, E-mail: phd.program@sauder.ubc.ca.
Website: http://www.sauder.ubc.ca/Programs/PhD_in_Business_Administration

University of California, Berkeley, Graduate Division, Haas School of Business, PhD in Business Administration Program, Berkeley, CA 94720-1500. Offers accounting (PhD); business and public policy (PhD); finance (PhD); management of organizations (PhD); marketing (PhD); real estate (PhD). *Accreditation:* AACSB. *Students:* 78 full-time (28 women); includes 34 minority (29 Asian, non-Hispanic/Latino; 5 Hispanic/Latino). Average age 27. *Degree requirements:* For doctorate, comprehensive exam, thesis/dissertation, written preliminary exams, oral qualifying exam. *Entrance requirements:*

Marketing

For doctorate, GMAT or GRE, minimum GPA of 3.0 in undergraduate and graduate coursework. Additional exam requirements/recommendations for international students: Required—TOEFL (minimum score 570 paper-based; 70 iBT), IELTS (minimum score 7). *Application deadline:* For fall admission, 12/1 for domestic and international students. Application fee: $90 ($110 for international students). Electronic applications accepted. *Expenses:* Contact institution. *Financial support:* Fellowships with tuition reimbursements, research assistantships with tuition reimbursements, teaching assistantships with tuition reimbursements, scholarships/grants, health care benefits, tuition waivers (full), unspecified assistantships, and transit passes, travel grants available. Financial award application deadline: 12/10. *Faculty research:* Accounting, business and public policy, entrepreneurship, finance, management of organizations, marketing, operations and information technology management, real estate. *Unit head:* Dr. Nicolae Garleanu, Director, 510-643-6349, Fax: 510-643-4255. *Application contact:* Melissa Hacker, Director, Student Affairs, 510-642-3944, Fax: 510-643-4255, E-mail: melhacker@haas.berkeley.edu.
Website: http://www.haas.berkeley.edu/Phd/

University of California, Berkeley, UC Berkeley Extension, Certificate Programs in Business, Berkeley, CA 94720-1500. Offers accounting (Certificate); business administration (Certificate); finance (Certificate); human resource management (Certificate); management (Certificate); marketing (Certificate); project management (Certificate). *Accreditation:* AACSB. *Program availability:* Online learning.

University of California, Berkeley, UC Berkeley Extension, International Diploma Programs, Berkeley, CA 94720-1500. Offers business administration (Certificate); finance (Certificate); global business management (Certificate); marketing (Certificate); project management (Certificate). *Accreditation:* AACSB.

University of California, Los Angeles, Graduate Division, UCLA Anderson School of Management, Los Angeles, CA 90095-1481. Offers accounting (PhD); behavioral decision making (PhD); business administration (EMBA, MBA); decisions, operations, and technology management (PhD); finance (PhD); financial engineering (MFE); global economics and management (PhD); management and organizations (PhD); marketing (PhD); strategy and policy (PhD); DDS/MBA; MBA/JD; MBA/MD; MBA/MLAS; MBA/MLIS; MBA/MN; MBA/MPH; MBA/MPP; MBA/MSCS; MBA/MURP. *Accreditation:* AACSB. *Program availability:* Part-time, evening/weekend. *Faculty:* 90 full-time (20 women), 98 part-time/adjunct (19 women). *Students:* 865 full-time (263 women), 1,201 part-time (337 women); includes 710 minority (48 Black or African American, non-Hispanic/Latino; 1 American Indian or Alaska Native, non-Hispanic/Latino; 505 Asian, non-Hispanic/Latino; 88 Hispanic/Latino; 4 Native Hawaiian or other Pacific Islander, non-Hispanic/Latino; 64 Two or more races, non-Hispanic/Latino), 451 international. Average age 31. 5,643 applicants, 26% accepted, 881 enrolled. In 2016, 807 master's, 7 doctorates awarded. *Degree requirements:* For master's, comprehensive exam, field consulting project; internship (for MBA); thesis/dissertation (for MFE); for doctorate, comprehensive exam, thesis/dissertation, oral and written qualifying exams. *Entrance requirements:* For master's, GMAT or GRE, 4-year bachelor's degree or equivalent; 2 letters of recommendation; essays (1 for MBA, 2 for FEMBA and MFE); 4-8 years of full-time work experience (for FEMBA); minimum eight years of work experience with at least three years at management level (for EMBA); for doctorate, GMAT or GRE, bachelor's degree from college or university of fully-recognized standing, minimum B average during junior and senior years of undergraduate years, 3 letters of recommendation, statement of purpose. Additional exam requirements/recommendations for international students: Required—TOEFL (minimum score 560 paper-based; 87 iBT), IELTS (minimum score 7). *Application deadline:* For fall admission, 10/6 priority date for domestic and international students; for winter admission, 1/5 for domestic and international students; for spring admission, 4/12 for domestic and international students. Applications are processed on a rolling basis. Application fee: $200. Electronic applications accepted. *Expenses:* Contact institution. *Financial support:* In 2016–17, 633 students received support, including 455 fellowships (averaging $30,253 per year); research assistantships with partial tuition reimbursements available, teaching assistantships with partial tuition reimbursements available, career-related internships or fieldwork, institutionally sponsored loans, and scholarships/grants also available. Support available to part-time students. *Faculty research:* Finance/global economics, entrepreneurship, accounting, human resources/organizational behavior, marketing, behavioral decision making. *Total annual research expenditures:* $1.1 million. *Unit head:* Dr. Judy D. Olian, Dean/Chair in Management, 310-825-7982, Fax: 310-206-2073, E-mail: judy.olian@anderson.ucla.edu. *Application contact:* Alex Lawrence, Assistant Dean and Director of MBA Admissions, 310-825-6944, Fax: 310-825-8582, E-mail: mba.admissions@anderson.ucla.edu.
Website: http://www.anderson.ucla.edu/

University of Central Missouri, The Graduate School, Warrensburg, MO 64093. Offers accountancy (MA); accounting (MBA); applied mathematics (MS); aviation safety (MA); biology (MS); business administration (MBA); career and technical education leadership (MS); college student personnel administration (MS); communication (MA); computer science (MS); counseling (MS); criminal justice (MS); educational leadership (Ed D); educational technology (MS); elementary and early childhood education (MSE); English (MA); environmental studies (MA); finance (MBA); history (MA); human services/educational technology (Ed S); human services/learning resources (Ed S); human services/professional counseling (Ed S); industrial hygiene (MS); industrial management (MS); information systems (MBA); information technology (MS); kinesiology (MS); library science and information services (MS); literacy education (MSE); marketing (MBA); mathematics (MS); music (MA); occupational safety management (MS); psychology (MS); rural family nursing (MS); school administration (MSE); social gerontology (MS); sociology (MA); special education (MSE); speech language pathology (MS); superintendency (Ed S); teaching (MAT); teaching English as a second language (MA); technology (MS); technology management (PhD); theatre (MA). *Program availability:* Part-time, 100% online, blended/hybrid learning. *Degree requirements:* For master's and Ed S, comprehensive exam (for some programs), thesis (for some programs). *Entrance requirements:* Additional exam requirements/recommendations for international students: Required—TOEFL (minimum score 550 paper-based; 79 iBT). Electronic applications accepted.

University of Chicago, Booth School of Business, Full-Time MBA Program, Chicago, IL 60637. Offers accounting (MBA); analytic finance (MBA); analytic management (MBA); econometrics and statistics (MBA); economics (MBA); entrepreneurship (MBA); finance (MBA); general management (MBA); health administration and policy (Certificate); international business (MBA); managerial and organizational behavior (MBA); marketing analytics (MBA); marketing management (MBA); operations management (MBA); strategic management (MBA); MBA/AM; MBA/JD; MBA/MA; MBA/MD; MBA/MPP. *Accreditation:* AACSB. *Students:* 1,151 full-time (443 women), 17 part-time (9 women). Terminal master's awarded for partial completion of doctoral program. *Entrance requirements:* For master's, GMAT or GRE, transcripts, resume, 2 letters of recommendation, essay, interview. Additional exam requirements/recommendations for international students: Required—TOEFL (minimum score 600 paper-based; 104 iBT), IELTS (minimum score 7), PTE (minimum score 70). *Application deadline:* For spring admission, 4/1 for domestic and international students. Electronic applications accepted. *Expenses:* Contact institution. *Unit head:* Stacey Kole, Deputy Dean, 773-702-7121. *Application contact:* Full-time MBA Program Admissions, 773-702-7369, Fax: 773-702-9085, E-mail: admissions@chicagobooth.edu.
Website: https://www.chicagobooth.edu/programs/full-time

University of Cincinnati, Graduate School, Carl H. Lindner College of Business, MS Program, Cincinnati, OH 45221. Offers accounting (MS); business analytics (MS); finance (MS); information systems (MS); marketing (MS); taxation (MS). *Program availability:* Part-time, evening/weekend. *Faculty:* 74 full-time (17 women), 33 part-time/adjunct (8 women). *Students:* 307 full-time (128 women), 246 part-time (106 women); includes 60 minority (22 Black or African American, non-Hispanic/Latino; 20 Asian, non-Hispanic/Latino; 9 Hispanic/Latino; 1 Native Hawaiian or other Pacific Islander, non-Hispanic/Latino; 8 Two or more races, non-Hispanic/Latino), 321 international. Average age 28. 1,756 applicants, 24% accepted, 351 enrolled. In 2016, 334 master's awarded. *Degree requirements:* For master's, thesis (for some programs). *Entrance requirements:* For master's, GMAT, GRE, resume, transcripts, essays, letters of recommendation. Additional exam requirements/recommendations for international students: Required—TOEFL (minimum score 577 paper-based; 90 iBT), IELTS (minimum score 6.5). *Application deadline:* For fall admission, 8/1 priority date for domestic students, 3/15 for international students; for spring admission, 12/15 for domestic students, 9/15 for international students; for summer admission, 4/15 for domestic and international students. Applications are processed on a rolling basis. Application fee: $65 ($70 for international students). Electronic applications accepted. *Expenses:* Contact institution. *Financial support:* In 2016–17, 251 students received support, including 12 teaching assistantships with tuition reimbursements available (averaging $3,500 per year); scholarships/grants, tuition waivers (full and partial), and unspecified assistantships also available. Financial award application deadline: 2/1; financial award applicants required to submit FAFSA. *Faculty research:* Real estate, empirical pricing, organization information pricing, strategic management, portfolio choice in institutional investment. *Unit head:* Dr. David Szymanski, Dean, 513-556-7001, Fax: 513-556-4891, E-mail: david.szymanski@uc.edu. *Application contact:* Dona Clary, Director, Graduate Programs, 513-556-3546, Fax: 513-558-7006, E-mail: dona.clary@uc.edu.

University of Cincinnati, Graduate School, Carl H. Lindner College of Business, PhD Programs, Cincinnati, OH 45211. Offers accounting (PhD); economics (PhD); finance (PhD); information systems (PhD); management (PhD); marketing (PhD); operations and business analytics (PhD). *Faculty:* 72 full-time (18 women). *Students:* 37 full-time (19 women); includes 4 minority (1 Black or African American, non-Hispanic/Latino; 3 Asian, non-Hispanic/Latino), 19 international. Average age 30. 92 applicants, 16% accepted, 7 enrolled. In 2016, 4 doctorates awarded. *Degree requirements:* For doctorate, comprehensive exam, thesis/dissertation. *Entrance requirements:* For doctorate, GMAT, GRE, transcripts, essays, resume, letters of recommendation. Additional exam requirements/recommendations for international students: Required—TOEFL (minimum score 600 paper-based; 100 iBT), IELTS (minimum score 7). *Application deadline:* For fall admission, 1/15 for domestic and international students. Application fee: $65 ($70 for international students). Electronic applications accepted. *Expenses:* Contact institution. *Financial support:* In 2016–17, 38 students received support, including 25 research assistantships with tuition reimbursements available (averaging $23,250 per year); scholarships/grants, tuition waivers (full and partial), and unspecified assistantships also available. Financial award application deadline: 1/15; financial award applicants required to submit FAFSA. *Faculty research:* Bayesian Prediction Theory, organizational fairness, consumer insight and market research, EGARCH idiosyncratic volatility and expected stock returns, consumer insight and market research, density estimation from correlated data. *Unit head:* Dr. Suzanne Masterson, Director, 513-556-7125, Fax: 513-556-5499, E-mail: suzanne.masterson@uc.edu. *Application contact:* Angel Elvin, Assistant Director, 513-556-7190, Fax: 513-558-7006, E-mail: angel.elvin@uc.edu.
Website: http://www.business.uc.edu/phd

University of Colorado Denver, Business School, Master of Business Administration Program, Denver, CO 80217. Offers bioinnovation and entrepreneurship (MBA); business intelligence (MBA); business strategy (MBA); business to business marketing (MBA); business to consumer marketing (MBA); change management (MBA); corporate financial management (MBA); enterprise technology management (MBA); entrepreneurship (MBA); health administration (MBA), including financial management, health administration, health information technologies, international health management and policy; human resources management (MBA); international business (MBA); investment management (MBA); managing for sustainability (MBA); sports and entertainment management (MBA). *Accreditation:* AACSB. *Program availability:* Part-time, evening/weekend, 100% online, blended/hybrid learning. *Students:* 544 full-time (210 women), 112 part-time (22 women); includes 99 minority (15 Black or African American, non-Hispanic/Latino; 4 American Indian or Alaska Native, non-Hispanic/Latino; 38 Asian, non-Hispanic/Latino; 36 Hispanic/Latino; 6 Two or more races, non-Hispanic/Latino), 22 international. Average age 32. 335 applicants, 73% accepted, 179 enrolled. In 2016, 251 master's awarded. *Degree requirements:* For master's, 48 semester hours, including 30 of core courses, 3 in international business, and 15 in electives from over 50 other business courses. *Entrance requirements:* For master's, GMAT, resume, official transcripts, essay, two letters of recommendation, financial statements (for international applicants). Additional exam requirements/recommendations for international students: Required—TOEFL (minimum score 560 paper-based; 83 iBT); Recommended—IELTS (minimum score 6.5). *Application deadline:* For fall admission, 4/15 priority date for domestic students, 3/15 priority date for international students; for spring admission, 10/15 priority date for domestic students, 9/15 priority date for international students; for summer admission, 2/15 priority date for domestic students, 1/15 priority date for international students. Applications are processed on a rolling basis. Application fee: $50 ($75 for international students). Electronic applications accepted. *Expenses:* Contact institution. *Financial support:* In 2016–17, 171 students received support. Fellowships, research assistantships, teaching assistantships, Federal Work-Study, institutionally sponsored loans, scholarships/grants, traineeships, and unspecified assistantships available. Financial award application deadline: 4/1; financial award applicants required to submit FAFSA. *Faculty research:* Marketing, management, entrepreneurship, finance, health administration. *Unit head:* Woodrow Eckard, MBA Director, 303-315-8470, E-mail: woody.eckard@ucdenver.edu. *Application contact:* Shelly Townley, Admissions Director, Graduate Programs, 303-315-8202, E-mail: shelly.townley@ucdenver.edu.
Website: http://www.ucdenver.edu/academics/colleges/business/degrees/mba/Pages/MBA.aspx

University of Colorado Denver, Business School, Program in Marketing, Denver, CO 80217. Offers brand management and marketing communication (MS); global marketing (MS); high-tech and entrepreneurial marketing (MS); marketing for sustainability (MS); marketing research (MS); sports and entertainment marketing (MS). *Program availability:* Part-time, evening/weekend. *Students:* 30 full-time (19 women), 7 part-time (5 women); includes 5 minority (2 Black or African American, non-Hispanic/Latino; 1 Asian, non-Hispanic/Latino; 2 Hispanic/Latino), 12 international. Average age 28. 47 applicants, 62% accepted, 13 enrolled. In 2016, 23 master's awarded. *Degree requirements:* For master's, 30 semester hours (21 of marketing core courses, 9 of marketing electives). *Entrance requirements:* For master's, GMAT, resume, essay, two letters of recommendation, financial statements (for international applicants). Additional

exam requirements/recommendations for international students: Required—TOEFL (minimum score 525 paper-based; 71 iBT); Recommended—IELTS (minimum score 6.5). *Application deadline:* For fall admission, 4/15 priority date for domestic students, 3/15 priority date for international students; for spring admission, 10/15 priority date for domestic students, 9/15 priority date for international students; for summer admission, 2/15 priority date for domestic students, 1/15 priority date for international students. Applications are processed on a rolling basis. Application fee: $50 ($75 for international students). Electronic applications accepted. *Expenses:* Contact institution. *Financial support:* In 2016–17, 7 students received support. Fellowships, research assistantships, teaching assistantships, Federal Work-Study, institutionally sponsored loans, scholarships/grants, and traineeships available. Financial award application deadline: 4/1; financial award applicants required to submit FAFSA. *Faculty research:* Marketing issues in the Chinese environment, impact of individual difference and contextual factors on the risk-taking behaviors of managers making new-business creation decisions, attribution theory perspective of conflict between marketers and engineers, organizational identity and identification, international market entry strategies. *Unit head:* Vicki Lane, Director of Marketing Program, 303-315-8468, E-mail: vicki.lane@ucdenver.edu. *Application contact:* 303-315-8200, E-mail: bschool.admissions@ucdenver.edu.
Website: http://www.ucdenver.edu/academics/colleges/business/degrees/ms/marketing/Pages/Marketing.aspx

University of Connecticut, Graduate School, School of Business, Storrs, CT 06269. Offers accounting (MS, PhD); business administration (MBA, PhD); finance (PhD); health care management and insurance studies (MBA); management (PhD); management consulting (MBA); marketing (PhD); marketing intelligence (MBA). *Accreditation:* AACSB. *Degree requirements:* For master's, comprehensive exam; for doctorate, thesis/dissertation. *Entrance requirements:* For master's and doctorate, GMAT. Additional exam requirements/recommendations for international students: Required—TOEFL (minimum score 550 paper-based). Electronic applications accepted.

University of Dallas, Satish and Yasmin Gupta College of Business, Irving, TX 75062-4736. Offers accounting (MBA, MS); business administration (DBA); business analytics (MS); business management (MBA); corporate finance (MBA); cybersecurity (MS); finance (MS); financial services (MBA); global business (MBA, MS); health services management (MBA); human resource management (MBA); information and technology management (MS); information assurance (MBA); information technology (MBA); information technology service management (MBA); marketing management (MBA); organization development (MBA); project management (MBA); sports and entertainment management (MBA); strategic leadership (MBA); supply chain management (MBA). *Accreditation:* AACSB. *Program availability:* Part-time, evening/weekend, online learning. *Entrance requirements:* Additional exam requirements/recommendations for international students: Required—TOEFL. Electronic applications accepted. *Expenses:* Contact institution.

University of Dayton, School of Business Administration, Dayton, OH 45469. Offers accounting (MBA); cyber security (MBA); finance (MBA); marketing (MBA); JD/MBA. *Accreditation:* AACSB. *Program availability:* Part-time, evening/weekend, blended/hybrid learning. *Faculty:* 23 full-time (5 women), 18 part-time/adjunct (9 women). *Students:* 94 full-time (35 women), 85 part-time (38 women); includes 14 minority (5 Black or African American, non-Hispanic/Latino; 4 Asian, non-Hispanic/Latino; 5 Hispanic/Latino), 26 international. Average age 30. 269 applicants, 31% accepted. In 2016, 93 master's awarded. *Entrance requirements:* For master's, GMAT (minimum score of 500 total, 19 verbal); GRE (minimum score of 149 verbal, 146 quantitative), minimum GPA of 3.0, current resume. Additional exam requirements/recommendations for international students: Required—TOEFL (minimum score 550 paper-based; 80 iBT); Recommended—IELTS (minimum score 6.5). *Application deadline:* Applications are processed on a rolling basis. Application fee: $0 ($50 for international students). Electronic applications accepted. *Expenses:* $970 per credit hour, $25 registration fee per term. *Financial support:* In 2016–17, 7 research assistantships with partial tuition reimbursements (averaging $8,535 per year), 2 teaching assistantships with partial tuition reimbursements (averaging $8,535 per year) were awarded; institutionally sponsored loans, health care benefits, and unspecified assistantships also available. Financial award application deadline: 3/1; financial award applicants required to submit FAFSA. *Faculty research:* Asset pricing, applied microeconomics, financial reporting and auditing, entrepreneurship. *Unit head:* Scott MacDonald, Director, MBA Program, 937-229-3733, Fax: 937-229-3882, E-mail: smacdonald1@udayton.edu. *Application contact:* Mandy Bingaman, MBA Program Manager, 937-229-3733, Fax: 937-229-3882, E-mail: mbingaman1@udayton.edu.
Website: https://www.udayton.edu/business/academics/master_of_business_administration/index.php

University of Denver, Daniels College of Business, Department of Marketing, Denver, CO 80208. Offers MBA, MS. *Program availability:* Part-time, evening/weekend. *Faculty:* 15 full-time (8 women), 5 part-time/adjunct (2 women). *Students:* 34 full-time (23 women), 14 part-time (11 women); includes 14 minority (4 Black or African American, non-Hispanic/Latino; 1 Asian, non-Hispanic/Latino; 8 Hispanic/Latino; 1 Two or more races, non-Hispanic/Latino), 9 international. Average age 25. 184 applicants, 38% accepted, 30 enrolled. In 2016, 30 master's awarded. *Entrance requirements:* For master's, GRE General Test or GMAT, bachelor's degree, transcripts, essays, resume, interview. Additional exam requirements/recommendations for international students: Required—TOEFL (minimum score 570 paper-based; 88 iBT). *Application deadline:* For fall admission, 11/15 priority date for domestic and international students; for spring admission, 10/1 priority date for domestic and international students. Applications are processed on a rolling basis. Application fee: $100. Electronic applications accepted. *Expenses:* $43,458 per year full-time. *Financial support:* In 2016–17, 42 students received support, including 5 teaching assistantships with tuition reimbursements available (averaging $1,940 per year); career-related internships or fieldwork, Federal Work-Study, institutionally sponsored loans, scholarships/grants, and unspecified assistantships also available. Support available to part-time students. Financial award application deadline: 2/15; financial award applicants required to submit FAFSA. *Faculty research:* Consumer behavior, co-creating the customer experience, marketing education and pedagogy, new-product/service innovation, marketing strategy. *Unit head:* Dr. Carol Johnson, Associate Professor and Chair, 303-871-2276, Fax: 303-871-2323, E-mail: carol.johnson@du.edu.
Website: https://daniels.du.edu/marketing

University of Florida, Graduate School, Warrington College of Business Administration, Hough Graduate School of Business, Department of Marketing, Gainesville, FL 32611. Offers MA, MS, PhD. Terminal master's awarded for partial completion of doctoral program. *Degree requirements:* For master's, comprehensive exam, thesis optional; for doctorate, comprehensive exam, thesis/dissertation. *Entrance requirements:* For master's and doctorate, GMAT (minimum score of 465) or GRE General Test, minimum GPA of 3.0. Additional exam requirements/recommendations for international students: Required—TOEFL (minimum score 550 paper-based; 80 iBT), IELTS (minimum score 6). Electronic applications accepted. *Faculty research:* Consumer behavior, decision-making, behavioral decision theory, marketing models, marketing strategy.

University of Hawaii at Manoa, Graduate Division, Shidler College of Business, Program in Business Administration, Honolulu, HI 96822. Offers Asian business studies (MBA); Chinese business studies (MBA); decision sciences (MBA); entrepreneurship (MBA); finance (MBA); finance and banking (MBA); human resources management (MBA); information management (MBA); information technology (MBA); international business (MBA); Japanese business studies (MBA); marketing (MBA); organizational behavior (MBA); organizational management (MBA); real estate (MBA); student-designed track (MBA). *Accreditation:* AACSB. *Program availability:* Part-time, evening/weekend. *Degree requirements:* For master's, thesis optional. *Entrance requirements:* For master's, GMAT, minimum GPA of 3.0. Additional exam requirements/recommendations for international students: Required—TOEFL (minimum score 600 paper-based; 100 iBT), IELTS (minimum score 7). *Expenses:* Contact institution.

University of Hawaii at Manoa, Graduate Division, Shidler College of Business, Program in International Management, Honolulu, HI 96822. Offers Asian finance (PhD); global information technology management (PhD); international accounting (PhD); international marketing (PhD); international organization and strategy (PhD). *Program availability:* Part-time. *Degree requirements:* For doctorate, comprehensive exam, thesis/dissertation. *Entrance requirements:* For doctorate, GMAT or GRE General Test, minimum GPA of 3.0. Additional exam requirements/recommendations for international students: Required—TOEFL (minimum score 600 paper-based; 100 iBT), IELTS (minimum score 7). *Expenses:* Contact institution.

University of Houston, Bauer College of Business, Marketing Program, Houston, TX 77204. Offers PhD. *Program availability:* Part-time, evening/weekend. *Degree requirements:* For doctorate, comprehensive exam, thesis/dissertation. *Entrance requirements:* For doctorate, GMAT or GRE. *Faculty research:* Accountancy and taxation, finance, international business, management.

University of Houston–Victoria, School of Business Administration, Victoria, TX 77901-4450. Offers accounting (MBA); economic development and entrepreneurship (MS); finance (GMBA, MBA); general business (MBA); international business (MBA); management (GMBA, MBA); marketing (MBA). *Accreditation:* AACSB. *Program availability:* Part-time, evening/weekend, online learning. *Entrance requirements:* For master's, GMAT. Additional exam requirements/recommendations for international students: Required—TOEFL (minimum score 550 paper-based). Electronic applications accepted. *Faculty research:* Economic development, marketing, finance.

The University of Iowa, Henry B. Tippie College of Business, Department of Marketing, Iowa City, IA 52242-1316. Offers PhD. *Faculty:* 16 full-time (5 women), 7 part-time/adjunct (0 women). *Students:* 10 full-time (5 women); includes 1 minority (Asian, non-Hispanic/Latino), 8 international. Average age 33. 37 applicants, 30% accepted, 3 enrolled. In 2016, 1 doctorate awarded. *Degree requirements:* For doctorate, comprehensive exam, thesis/dissertation. *Entrance requirements:* Additional exam requirements/recommendations for international students: Required—TOEFL (minimum iBT score 100) or IELTS (minimum score 7.0). *Application deadline:* For fall admission, 1/15 priority date for domestic and international students. Application fee: $60 ($100 for international students). Electronic applications accepted. *Financial support:* In 2016–17, 10 students received support, including 10 fellowships (averaging $4,200 per year), 10 teaching assistantships with full tuition reimbursements available (averaging $18,809 per year); health care benefits and unspecified assistantships also available. Financial award application deadline: 1/15. *Faculty research:* Judgments and decision-making under certainty; consumer behavior: cognitive neuroscience, attitudes and evaluation; hierarchical Bayesian estimation; marketing-finance interface; advertising effects. *Unit head:* Prof. Dhananjay Nayakankuppam, Department Executive Officer, 319-335-1013, Fax: 319-335-1956, E-mail: dhananjay-nayakankuppam@uiowa.edu. *Application contact:* Renea L. Jay, Associate Director, Non-MBA Graduate Programs, 319-335-0830, Fax: 319-335-0860, E-mail: renea-jay@uiowa.edu.
Website: https://tippie.uiowa.edu/marketing

The University of Kansas, Graduate Studies, School of Business, Program in Business, Lawrence, KS 66045. Offers accounting (PhD); business and organizational leadership (MS); decision sciences and supply chain management (PhD); finance (PhD); human resources management (PhD); marketing (PhD); organizational behavior (PhD); strategic management (PhD); supply chain management and logistics (MS). *Accreditation:* AACSB. *Program availability:* Part-time. *Students:* 76 full-time (11 women), 170 part-time (83 women); includes 41 minority (15 Black or African American, non-Hispanic/Latino; 3 American Indian or Alaska Native, non-Hispanic/Latino; 6 Asian, non-Hispanic/Latino; 5 Hispanic/Latino; 12 Two or more races, non-Hispanic/Latino), 25 international. Average age 32. 294 applicants, 69% accepted, 152 enrolled. In 2016, 36 master's, 9 doctorates awarded. *Entrance requirements:* For master's, GMAT, official transcript, three letters of recommendation, resume, statement of purpose; for doctorate, GMAT or GRE, official transcript, three letters of recommendation, resume, statement of purpose. Additional exam requirements/recommendations for international students: Required—TOEFL (minimum score 600 paper-based; 100 iBT). *Application deadline:* For fall admission, 1/10 for domestic and international students. Application fee: $65 ($85 for international students). Electronic applications accepted. *Financial support:* Fellowships, research assistantships, teaching assistantships, scholarships/grants, health care benefits, tuition waivers (full), and unspecified assistantships available. Financial award application deadline: 1/10. *Faculty research:* Strategic human resource management, business ethics, organizational theory/behavior, corporate strategy, international business, supply chain management, Bayesian networks, game theory, decision analysis and time/series analysis, pricing, consumer effects, advertising and emotion. *Unit head:* Charly Edmonds, Director, 785-864-3841, E-mail: bschoolphd@ku.edu. *Application contact:* Graduate Admission Contact, 785-864-7500, E-mail: bschoolphd@ku.edu.
Website: http://www.business.ku.edu/

University of La Verne, College of Business and Public Management, Graduate Programs in Business Administration, La Verne, CA 91750-4443. Offers accounting (MBA, MBA-EP); finance (MBA, MBA-EP); health services management (MBA); information technology (MBA, MBA-EP); international business (MBA, MBA-EP); management and leadership (MBA, MBA-EP); marketing (MBA, MBA-EP); supply chain management (MBA, MBA-EP). *Program availability:* Part-time, evening/weekend. *Students:* 385 full-time (177 women), 89 part-time (46 women); includes 92 minority (4 Black or African American, non-Hispanic/Latino; 1 American Indian or Alaska Native, non-Hispanic/Latino; 14 Asian, non-Hispanic/Latino; 71 Hispanic/Latino; 1 Native Hawaiian or other Pacific Islander, non-Hispanic/Latino; 1 Two or more races, non-Hispanic/Latino), 319 international. Average age 28. *Entrance requirements:* For master's, GMAT, MAT, or GRE, minimum undergraduate GPA of 3.0, 2 letters of recommendation, resume, statement of purpose. Additional exam requirements/recommendations for international students: Required—TOEFL (minimum score 550 paper-based; 85 iBT). *Application deadline:* Applications are processed on a rolling basis. Application fee: $50. *Expenses:* *Tuition:* Part-time $795 per credit hour. Tuition and fees vary according to campus/location and program. *Financial support:* Institutionally sponsored loans and scholarships/grants available. Financial award application deadline: 3/2; financial award applicants required to submit FAFSA. *Unit head:* Dr. Abe Helou, Chairperson, 909-448-4455, Fax: 909-392-2704, E-mail: ihelou@laverne.edu. *Application contact:* Rina Lazarian-Chehab, Senior Associate Director of

Graduate Admissions, 909-448-4317, Fax: 909-971-2295, E-mail: rlazarian@laverne.edu.
Website: https://laverne.edu/business-and-public-administration/mba-2/

University of La Verne, Regional and Online Campuses, Graduate Programs, Inland Empire Campus, Ontario, CA 91730. Offers business administration (MBA, MBA-EP), including accounting (MBA), finance (MBA), health services management (MBA-EP), information technology (MBA-EP), international business (MBA), managed care (MBA), management and leadership (MBA-EP), marketing (MBA-EP), supply chain management (MBA); leadership and management (MS), including human resource management, nonprofit management, organizational development. *Program availability:* Part-time, evening/weekend. *Expenses:* Contact institution.

University of Lethbridge, School of Graduate Studies, Lethbridge, AB T1K 3M4, Canada. Offers addictions counseling (M Sc); agricultural biotechnology (M Sc); agricultural studies (M Sc, MA); anthropology (MA); archaeology (M Sc, MA); art (MA, MFA); biochemistry (M Sc); biological sciences (M Sc); biomolecular science (PhD); biosystems and biodiversity (PhD); Canadian studies (MA); chemistry (M Sc); computer science (M Sc); computer science and geographical information science (M Sc); counseling (MC); counseling psychology (M Ed); dramatic arts (MA); earth, space, and physical science (PhD); economics (MA); education (MA, PhD); educational leadership (M Ed); English (MA); environmental science (M Sc); evolution and behavior (PhD); exercise science (M Sc); French (MA); French/German (MA); French/Spanish (MA); general education (M Ed); geography (M Sc, MA); German (MA); health sciences (M Sc); individualized multidisciplinary (M Sc, MA); kinesiology (M Sc, MA); management (M Sc), including accounting, finance, human resource management and labor relations, information systems, international management, marketing, policy and strategy; mathematics (M Sc); music (M Mus, MA); Native American studies (MA); neuroscience (M Sc, PhD); new media (MA, MFA); nursing (M Sc, MN); philosophy (MA); physics (M Sc); political science (MA); psychology (M Sc, MA); religious studies (MA); sociology (MA); theatre and dramatic arts (MFA); theoretical and computational science (PhD); urban and regional studies (MA); women and gender studies (MA). *Program availability:* Part-time, evening/weekend. *Degree requirements:* For master's, thesis (for some programs); for doctorate, comprehensive exam, thesis/dissertation. *Entrance requirements:* For master's, GMAT (for M Sc in management), bachelor's degree in related field, minimum GPA of 3.0 during previous 20 graded semester courses, 2 years' teaching or related experience (M Ed); for doctorate, master's degree, minimum graduate GPA of 3.5. Additional exam requirements/recommendations for international students: Required—TOEFL (minimum score 580 paper-based; 93 iBT). Electronic applications accepted. *Faculty research:* Movement and brain plasticity, gibberellin physiology, photosynthesis, carbon cycling, molecular properties of main-group ring components.

The University of Manchester, Alliance Manchester Business School, M15 6PB, United Kingdom. Offers accounting and finance (M Sc); business (M Ent); business analysis and strategic management (M Sc); business analytics: operational research and risk analysis (M Sc); business psychology (M Sc); corporate communications and reputation management (M Sc); finance (M Sc); finance and business economics (M Sc); human resource management and industrial relations (M Sc); innovation management and entrepreneurship (M Sc); international business and management (M Sc); international human resource management and comparative industrial relations (M Sc); management (M Sc); marketing (M Sc); operations, project and supply chain management (M Sc); organizational psychology (M Sc); quantitative finance (M Sc). *Entrance requirements:* For master's, UK 2:1 honours degree or overseas equivalent. Additional exam requirements/recommendations for international students: Required—TOEFL (minimum score 100 iBT), IELTS (minimum score 7), PTE. Electronic applications accepted. *Faculty research:* Accounting and finance, management sciences and marketing, people management and organization, innovation management and policy, decision sciences.

University of Massachusetts Amherst, Graduate School, Isenberg School of Management, Program in Management, Amherst, MA 01003. Offers accounting (PhD); business administration (MBA); entrepreneurship (MBA); finance (MBA, PhD); healthcare administration (MBA); hospitality and tourism management (PhD); management science (PhD); marketing (MBA, PhD); organization studies (PhD); sport management (PhD); strategic management (PhD); MBA/MS. *Accreditation:* AACSB. *Program availability:* Part-time, evening/weekend, online learning. Terminal master's awarded for partial completion of doctoral program. *Degree requirements:* For doctorate, comprehensive exam, thesis/dissertation. *Entrance requirements:* For master's and doctorate, GMAT or GRE General Test. Additional exam requirements/recommendations for international students: Required—TOEFL (minimum score 550 paper-based; 80 iBT), IELTS (minimum score 6.5). Electronic applications accepted.

University of Massachusetts Dartmouth, Graduate School, Charlton College of Business, Program in Business Administration, North Dartmouth, MA 02747-2300. Offers business administration (MBA); business analytics (Postbaccalaureate Certificate); business foundations (Graduate Certificate); international business (Graduate Certificate); management (Postbaccalaureate Certificate); marketing (Postbaccalaureate Certificate); organizational leadership (Graduate Certificate); supply chain management and information systems (Postbaccalaureate Certificate). *Accreditation:* AACSB. *Program availability:* Part-time, 100% online, blended/hybrid learning. *Faculty:* 15 full-time (7 women), 11 part-time/adjunct (4 women). *Students:* 126 full-time (49 women), 178 part-time (100 women); includes 45 minority (10 Black or African American, non-Hispanic/Latino; 1 American Indian or Alaska Native, non-Hispanic/Latino; 16 Asian, non-Hispanic/Latino; 13 Hispanic/Latino; 5 Two or more races, non-Hispanic/Latino), 100 international. Average age 32. 236 applicants, 80% accepted, 132 enrolled. In 2016, 142 master's, 13 other advanced degrees awarded. *Degree requirements:* For master's, thesis or alternative, eportfolio. *Entrance requirements:* For master's, GMAT, statement of purpose (minimum of 300 words), resume, official transcripts, 2 letters of recommendation; for other advanced degree, statement of purpose (minimum of 300 words), resume, official transcripts. Additional exam requirements/recommendations for international students: Required—TOEFL (minimum score 533 paper-based; 72 iBT). *Application deadline:* For fall admission, 7/1 priority date for domestic students, 6/1 priority date for international students; for spring admission, 11/15 priority date for domestic students, 10/15 priority date for international students. Application fee: $60. Electronic applications accepted. *Expenses:* Tuition, state resident: full-time $14,994; part-time $624.75 per credit. Tuition, nonresident: full-time $27,068; part-time $1127.83 per credit. *Required fees:* $405; $25.88 per credit. Tuition and fees vary according to course load and reciprocity agreements. *Financial support:* In 2016–17, 2 research assistantships (averaging $2,667 per year) were awarded; institutionally sponsored loans, scholarships/grants, and unspecified assistantships also available. Support available to part-time students. Financial award application deadline: 3/1; financial award applicants required to submit FAFSA. *Faculty research:* E-commerce, managing diversity, agile manufacturing, green business, activity-based management, build-to-order supply chain management. *Total annual research expenditures:* $413,000. *Unit head:* Melissa Pacheco, Assistant Dean of Graduate Programs, 508-999-8543, Fax: 508-999-8646, E-mail: mpacheco@umassd.edu. *Application contact:* Steven Briggs, Director of Marketing and Recruitment for Graduate Studies, 508-999-8604, Fax: 508-999-8183, E-mail: graduate@umassd.edu.
Website: http://www.umassd.edu/charlton/programs/graduate/mba

University of Memphis, Graduate School, Fogelman College of Business and Economics, Program in Business Administration, Memphis, TN 38152. Offers accounting (MBA, PhD); business administration (IMBA); economics (PhD); executive business administration (MBA); finance (PhD); management (PhD); marketing (MS); marketing and supply chain management (PhD); real estate development (MS); JD/MBA. *Accreditation:* AACSB. *Faculty:* 44 full-time (9 women), 5 part-time/adjunct (0 women). *Students:* 167 full-time (64 women), 341 part-time (119 women); includes 154 minority (80 Black or African American, non-Hispanic/Latino; 1 American Indian or Alaska Native, non-Hispanic/Latino; 43 Asian, non-Hispanic/Latino; 12 Hispanic/Latino; 1 Native Hawaiian or other Pacific Islander, non-Hispanic/Latino; 17 Two or more races, non-Hispanic/Latino), 96 international. Average age 33. 306 applicants, 64% accepted, 154 enrolled. In 2016, 273 master's, 7 doctorates awarded. *Degree requirements:* For master's, comprehensive exam; for doctorate, comprehensive exam, thesis/dissertation. *Entrance requirements:* For master's, GMAT, resume; for doctorate, GMAT, interview, minimum GPA of 3.4, resume, letter of recommendation. Additional exam requirements/recommendations for international students: Required—TOEFL (minimum score 550 paper-based). *Application deadline:* For fall admission, 8/1 for domestic students; for spring admission, 12/1 for domestic students. Application fee: $35 ($60 for international students). *Expenses:* Tuition, state resident: full-time $10,463; part-time $9483 per year. Tuition, nonresident: full-time $19,247; part-time $17,291 per year. *Required fees:* $821.50 per semester. Tuition and fees vary according to course load and program. *Financial support:* In 2016–17, 164 students received support. Research assistantships with full tuition reimbursements available, teaching assistantships with full tuition reimbursements available, career-related internships or fieldwork, Federal Work-Study, scholarships/grants, and unspecified assistantships available. Financial award application deadline: 2/15; financial award applicants required to submit FAFSA. *Faculty research:* Competitive business strategy, finance microstructures, supply chain management innovations, health care economics, litigation risks and corporate audits. *Unit head:* Dr. Rajiv Grover, Dean, 901-678-3759, E-mail: rgrover@memphis.edu. *Application contact:* Dr. Carol V. Danehower, Associate Dean, 901-678-5402, Fax: 901-678-3579, E-mail: fcbegp@memphis.edu.
Website: https://web0.memphis.edu/gradcatalog/degreeprog/fcbe/fcbe.php

University of Michigan–Flint, School of Management, Program in Business Administration, Flint, MI 48502. Offers accounting (MBA, Post-Master's Certificate); computer information systems (MBA); finance (MBA, Post-Master's Certificate); general business (Graduate Certificate); general business administration (MBA); health care management (MBA); international business (MBA, Post-Master's Certificate); lean manufacturing (MBA); marketing (MBA, Post-Master's Certificate); organizational leadership (MBA, Post-Master's Certificate). *Program availability:* Part-time, evening/weekend, mixed mode programs. *Faculty:* 33 full-time (9 women), 6 part-time/adjunct (1 woman). *Students:* 24 full-time (12 women), 146 part-time (49 women); includes 37 minority (17 Black or African American, non-Hispanic/Latino; 2 American Indian or Alaska Native, non-Hispanic/Latino; 10 Asian, non-Hispanic/Latino; 4 Hispanic/Latino; 1 Native Hawaiian or other Pacific Islander, non-Hispanic/Latino; 3 Two or more races, non-Hispanic/Latino), 17 international. Average age 33. 167 applicants, 47% accepted, 40 enrolled. In 2016, 73 master's, 3 other advanced degrees awarded. *Entrance requirements:* For master's, GMAT or GRE, bachelor's degree in arts, sciences, engineering, or business administration from regionally-accredited college or university with minimum GPA of 3.0; for other advanced degree, bachelor's degree in arts, sciences, engineering, or business administration from regionally-accredited college or university with minimum GPA of 3.0, college-level math, statistics, or quantitative course (for Graduate Certificate); MBA or equivalent degree from regionally-accredited college or university (for Post Master's Certificate). Additional exam requirements/recommendations for international students: Required—TOEFL (minimum score 84 iBT), IELTS (minimum score 6.5). *Application deadline:* For fall admission, 8/1 for domestic students, 5/1 for international students; for winter admission, 11/15 for domestic students, 9/1 for international students; for spring admission, 3/15 for domestic students, 1/1 for international students; for summer admission, 5/15 for domestic students. Applications are processed on a rolling basis. Application fee: $55. Electronic applications accepted. *Financial support:* Federal Work-Study, scholarships/grants, and unspecified assistantships available. Support available to part-time students. Financial award application deadline: 3/1; financial award applicants required to submit FAFSA. *Unit head:* Dr. Scott Johnson, Dean, School of Management, 810-762-3164, Fax: 810-237-6685, E-mail: scotjohn@umflint.edu. *Application contact:* Bradley T. Maki, Director of Graduate Admissions, 810-762-3171, E-mail: bmaki@umflint.edu.
Website: http://www.umflint.edu/graduateprograms/business-administration-mba

University of Minnesota, Twin Cities Campus, Carlson School of Management, Carlson Full-Time MBA Program, Minneapolis, MN 55455. Offers finance (MBA); human resources and industrial relations (MA); information technology (MBA); management (MBA); marketing (MBA); medical industry orientation (MBA); supply chain and operations (MBA); JD/MBA; MBA/MPP; MBA/MSBA; MD/MBA; MHA/MBA; Pharm D/MBA. *Accreditation:* AACSB. *Faculty:* 143 full-time (42 women), 24 part-time/adjunct (6 women). *Students:* 193 full-time (59 women); includes 23 minority (2 Black or African American, non-Hispanic/Latino; 1 American Indian or Alaska Native, non-Hispanic/Latino; 9 Asian, non-Hispanic/Latino; 5 Hispanic/Latino; 1 Native Hawaiian or other Pacific Islander, non-Hispanic/Latino; 5 Two or more races, non-Hispanic/Latino), 31 international. Average age 28. 606 applicants, 45% accepted, 104 enrolled. In 2016, 102 master's awarded. *Entrance requirements:* For master's, GMAT or GRE. Additional exam requirements/recommendations for international students: Required—TOEFL (minimum score 580 paper-based; 84 iBT), IELTS (minimum score 7), PTE. *Application deadline:* For fall admission, 4/1 for domestic students, 2/1 for international students. Application fee: $75. Electronic applications accepted. *Expenses:* $39,378 per year resident tuition and fees; $49,766 per year non-resident tuition and fees; $50,084 per year international tuition and fees. *Financial support:* In 2016–17, 148 students received support, including 148 fellowships with tuition reimbursements available (averaging $21,070 per year); research assistantships with partial tuition reimbursements available, teaching assistantships with partial tuition reimbursements available, career-related internships or fieldwork, Federal Work-Study, institutionally sponsored loans, scholarships/grants, health care benefits, and unspecified assistantships also available. Financial award application deadline: 4/1; financial award applicants required to submit FAFSA. *Faculty research:* Market regulation and asset pricing, social networks and data analytics, consumer behavior, innovation and entrepreneurship, workplace wellbeing and labor relationships. *Total annual research expenditures:* $577,440. *Unit head:* Philip J. Miller, Assistant Dean, MBA Programs and Graduate Business Career Center, 612-625-5555, Fax: 612-625-1012, E-mail: mba@umn.edu. *Application contact:* Linh Gilles, Director of Admissions and Recruiting, 612-625-5555, Fax: 612-625-1012, E-mail: ftmba@umn.edu.
Website: http://www.csom.umn.edu/MBA/full-time/

University of Minnesota, Twin Cities Campus, Carlson School of Management, Carlson Part-Time MBA Program, Minneapolis, MN 55455. Offers finance (MBA); information technology (MBA); management (MBA); marketing (MBA); medical industry

orientation (MBA); supply chain and operations (MBA). *Program availability:* Part-time-only, evening/weekend, 100% online, blended/hybrid learning. *Faculty:* 143 full-time (42 women), 26 part-time/adjunct (6 women). *Students:* 1,005 part-time (317 women); includes 110 minority (17 Black or African American, non-Hispanic/Latino; 2 American Indian or Alaska Native, non-Hispanic/Latino; 51 Asian, non-Hispanic/Latino; 19 Hispanic/Latino; 21 Two or more races, non-Hispanic/Latino), 58 international. Average age 28. 251 applicants, 86% accepted, 185 enrolled. In 2016, 336 master's awarded. *Entrance requirements:* For master's, GMAT or GRE. Additional exam requirements/recommendations for international students: Required—TOEFL (minimum score 580 paper-based; 84 iBT), IELTS (minimum score 7), PTE. *Application deadline:* For fall admission, 5/15 priority date for domestic and international students; for spring admission, 10/15 priority date for domestic and international students. Applications are processed on a rolling basis. Application fee: $75. Electronic applications accepted. *Expenses:* $1,335 per credit. *Financial support:* Applicants required to submit FAFSA. *Faculty research:* Market regulation and asset pricing, social networks and data analytics, consumer behavior, innovation and entrepreneurship, workplace wellbeing and labor relationships. *Total annual research expenditures:* $577,440. *Unit head:* Philip J. Miller, Assistant Dean, MBA Programs and Graduate Business Career Center, 612-624-2039, Fax: 612-625-1012, E-mail: mba@umn.edu. *Application contact:* Linh Gilles, Director of Admissions and Recruiting, 612-625-5555, Fax: 612-625-1012, E-mail: ptmba@umn.edu.
Website: http://www.carlsonschool.umn.edu/ptmba

University of Minnesota, Twin Cities Campus, Carlson School of Management, Doctoral Program in Business Administration, Minneapolis, MN 55455. Offers accounting (PhD); finance (PhD); information and decision sciences (PhD); marketing (PhD); strategic management and entrepreneurship (PhD); supply chain and operations (PhD); work and organizations (PhD). *Faculty:* 101 full-time (32 women). *Students:* 90 full-time (29 women); includes 7 minority (2 Black or African American, non-Hispanic/Latino; 3 Asian, non-Hispanic/Latino; 2 Hispanic/Latino), 64 international. Average age 30. 352 applicants, 7% accepted, 15 enrolled. In 2016, 20 doctorates awarded. *Degree requirements:* For doctorate, comprehensive exam, thesis/dissertation, written and oral preliminary exams, proposal defense, final defense. *Entrance requirements:* For doctorate, GMAT, GRE General Test, minimum undergraduate GPA of 3.0, graduate 3.5 (recommended). Additional exam requirements/recommendations for international students: Required—TOEFL (minimum score 600 paper-based, 100 iBT) or IELTS (minimum score 7.0). *Application deadline:* For fall admission, 12/15 for domestic students, 12/15 priority date for international students. Applications are processed on a rolling basis. Application fee: $75 ($95 for international students). Electronic applications accepted. *Expenses:* Contact institution. *Financial support:* In 2016–17, 80 students received support, including 80 fellowships with full tuition reimbursements available (averaging $13,500 per year), 72 research assistantships with full tuition reimbursements available (averaging $7,371 per year), 72 teaching assistantships with full tuition reimbursements available (averaging $7,371 per year); institutionally sponsored loans, scholarships/grants, health care benefits, unspecified assistantships, and full student service fee waivers also available. Financial award application deadline: 12/15. *Faculty research:* Finance, strategy and entrepreneurship, marketing, information and decision science, operations, accounting, supply chain, human resources and industrial relations, organizational behavior. *Unit head:* Dr. Shawn P. Curley, Director, 612-624-6546, Fax: 612-624-8221, E-mail: curley@umn.edu. *Application contact:* Sandy Herzan, Associate Director, 612-624-0875, Fax: 612-624-8221, E-mail: herza002@umn.edu.
Website: http://carlsonschool.umn.edu/degrees/phd

University of Missouri, Office of Research and Graduate Studies, Robert J. Trulaske, Sr. College of Business, Program in Business Administration, Columbia, MO 65211. Offers business administration (MBA); executive business administration (MBA); finance (PhD); management (PhD); marketing (PhD); MBA/JD; MBA/MHA; MBA/MSIE. *Accreditation:* AACSB. *Degree requirements:* For doctorate, thesis/dissertation. *Entrance requirements:* For master's and doctorate, GMAT, minimum GPA of 3.0. Additional exam requirements/recommendations for international students: Required—TOEFL (minimum score 500 paper-based; 61 iBT). Electronic applications accepted. *Expenses:* Tuition, state resident: full-time $6347; part-time $352.60 per credit hour. Tuition, nonresident: full-time $17,379; part-time $965.50 per credit hour. *Required fees:* $1035. Tuition and fees vary according to course load, campus/location and program.

University of Missouri–St. Louis, College of Business Administration, Program in Business Administration, St. Louis, MO 63121. Offers accounting (MBA); business administration (Certificate); business intelligence (Certificate); cybersecurity (Certificate); digital and social media marketing (Certificate); finance (MBA); human resources management (Certificate); information systems (MBA); international business (MBA); logistics and supply chain management (MBA, PhD, Certificate); management (MBA); marketing (MBA); marketing management (Certificate); operations management (MBA). *Accreditation:* AACSB. *Program availability:* Part-time, evening/weekend. *Faculty:* 32 full-time (10 women), 14 part-time/adjunct (3 women). *Students:* 181 full-time (88 women), 357 part-time (154 women); includes 83 minority (30 Black or African American, non-Hispanic/Latino; 36 Asian, non-Hispanic/Latino; 12 Hispanic/Latino; 2 Native Hawaiian or other Pacific Islander, non-Hispanic/Latino; 3 Two or more races, non-Hispanic/Latino), 100 international. Average age 31. 245 applicants, 83% accepted, 139 enrolled. *Degree requirements:* For doctorate, thesis/dissertation. *Entrance requirements:* For master's, GMAT, 2 letters of recommendation. Additional exam requirements/recommendations for international students: Recommended—TOEFL (minimum score 550 paper-based; 79 iBT), IELTS (minimum score 6.5). *Application deadline:* For fall admission, 7/1 for domestic and international students; for spring admission, 12/1 for domestic and international students. Applications are processed on a rolling basis. Application fee: $50 ($40 for international students). Electronic applications accepted. *Financial support:* Research assistantships with tuition reimbursements, teaching assistantships with tuition reimbursements, career-related internships or fieldwork, Federal Work-Study, and institutionally sponsored loans available. Support available to part-time students. Financial award application deadline: 4/1; financial award applicants required to submit FAFSA. *Faculty research:* Human resources, strategic management, marketing strategy, consumer behavior product development, advertising. *Unit head:* Dr. Thomas H. Eyssell, Associate Dean and Director of Graduate Studies, 314-516-5885, Fax: 314-516-6420, E-mail: mba@umsl.edu. *Application contact:* 314-516-5458, Fax: 314-516-6996, E-mail: gradadm@umsl.edu.

University of Nebraska at Kearney, College of Business and Technology, Department of Business, Kearney, NE 68849-0001. Offers accounting (MBA); generalist (MBA); human resources (MBA); human services (MBA); marketing (MBA). *Accreditation:* AACSB. *Program availability:* Part-time, evening/weekend. *Faculty:* 32 full-time (13 women). *Students:* 11 full-time (5 women), 30 part-time (14 women), 8 international. Average age 39. 13 applicants, 100% accepted, 10 enrolled. In 2016, 6 master's awarded. *Degree requirements:* For master's, thesis optional, capstone course. *Entrance requirements:* For master's, GRE or GMAT (if no significant managerial experience), letters of recommendation, essay, resume. Additional exam requirements/recommendations for international students: Recommended—TOEFL (minimum score 550 paper-based; 79 iBT), IELTS (minimum score 6.5). *Application deadline:* For fall admission, 6/15 for domestic and international students; for spring admission, 10/15 for domestic and international students; for summer admission, 3/15 for domestic and international students. Application fee: $45. Electronic applications accepted. *Expenses:* Tuition, state resident: full-time $4064; part-time $225.75 per credit hour. Tuition, nonresident: full-time $8915; part-time $495.25 per credit hour. *Required fees:* $772; $23 per credit hour. Part-time tuition and fees vary according to course load, campus/location, program and reciprocity agreements. *Financial support:* In 2016–17, 2 research assistantships with full tuition reimbursements (averaging $10,500 per year), 2 teaching assistantships with full tuition reimbursements (averaging $10,500 per year) were awarded; career-related internships or fieldwork, scholarships/grants, health care benefits, and unspecified assistantships also available. Support available to part-time students. Financial award application deadline: 2/28; financial award applicants required to submit FAFSA. *Faculty research:* Small business financial management, employment law, expert systems, international trade and marketing, environmental economics. *Unit head:* Dr. Sri Seshadri, Director, 308-865-8346, Fax: 308-865-8114. *Application contact:* Linda Johnson, Director, Graduate Admissions and Programs, 800-717-7881, Fax: 308-865-8837, E-mail: gradstudies@unk.edu.

University of Nebraska–Lincoln, Graduate College, College of Arts and Sciences, Department of Communication Studies, Lincoln, NE 68588. Offers instructional communication (MA, PhD); interpersonal communication (MA, PhD); marketing, communication studies, and advertising (MA, PhD); organizational communication (MA, PhD); rhetoric and culture (MA, PhD). *Degree requirements:* For master's, thesis optional; for doctorate, comprehensive exam, thesis/dissertation. *Entrance requirements:* For master's and doctorate, GRE General Test, writing sample. Additional exam requirements/recommendations for international students: Required—TOEFL (minimum score 600 paper-based). Electronic applications accepted. *Faculty research:* Message strategies, gender communication, political communication, organizational communication, instructional communication.

University of Nebraska–Lincoln, Graduate College, College of Business Administration, Interdepartmental Area of Business, Department of Marketing, Lincoln, NE 68588. Offers business (MA, PhD). *Degree requirements:* For doctorate, comprehensive exam, thesis/dissertation. *Entrance requirements:* For master's and doctorate, GMAT. Additional exam requirements/recommendations for international students: Required—TOEFL. Electronic applications accepted. *Faculty research:* Channel information, marketing research methodology, sales management, cross-cultural marketing, impact of new technology.

University of Nebraska–Lincoln, Graduate College, College of Journalism and Mass Communications, Lincoln, NE 68588. Offers marketing, communication and advertising (MA); professional journalism (MA). *Program availability:* Online learning. *Degree requirements:* For master's, thesis. *Entrance requirements:* For master's, samples of work. Additional exam requirements/recommendations for international students: Required—TOEFL (minimum score 600 paper-based). Electronic applications accepted. *Faculty research:* Interactive media and the Internet, community newspapers, children's radio, advertising involvement, telecommunications policy.

University of New Brunswick Fredericton, School of Graduate Studies, Faculty of Forestry and Environmental Management, Fredericton, NB E3B 5A3, Canada. Offers ecological foundations of forest management (PhD); environmental management (MEM); forest engineering (M Sc FE, MFE); forest products marketing (MBA); forest resources (M Sc F, MF, PhD). *Program availability:* Part-time. *Degree requirements:* For master's, thesis; for doctorate, thesis/dissertation. *Entrance requirements:* For master's and doctorate, minimum GPA of 3.0. Additional exam requirements/recommendations for international students: Required—TOEFL (minimum score 550 paper-based; 80 iBT), IELTS (minimum score 7), TWE (minimum score 4). Electronic applications accepted. *Faculty research:* Forest machines, soils, and ecosystems; integrated forest management; forest meteorology; wood engineering; stream ecosystems dynamics; forest and natural resources policy; forest operations planning; wood technology and mechanics; forest road construction and engineering; forest, wildlife, insect, bird, and fire ecology; remote sensing; insect impacts; silviculture; LiDAR analytics; integrated pest management; forest tree genetics; genetic resource conservation and sustainable management.

University of New Haven, Graduate School, College of Business, Program in Business Administration, West Haven, CT 06516. Offers accounting (MBA), including CPA; business administration (MBA); business intelligence (MBA); business management (Graduate Certificate); business policy and strategic leadership (MBA); finance (MBA), including CFA; global marketing (MBA); human resources management (MBA, Graduate Certificate); sport management (MBA). *Accreditation:* AACSB. *Program availability:* Part-time, evening/weekend. *Students:* 123 full-time (56 women), 74 part-time (29 women); includes 46 minority (24 Black or African American, non-Hispanic/Latino; 8 Asian, non-Hispanic/Latino; 10 Hispanic/Latino; 4 Two or more races, non-Hispanic/Latino), 57 international. Average age 27. In 2016, 100 master's awarded. *Entrance requirements:* For master's, GMAT. Additional exam requirements/recommendations for international students: Required—TOEFL (minimum score 80 iBT), IELTS, PTE. *Application deadline:* Applications are processed on a rolling basis. Application fee: $50. Electronic applications accepted. Application fee is waived when completed online. *Expenses: Tuition:* Full-time $15,660; part-time $870 per credit hour. *Required fees:* $200; $85 per term. Tuition and fees vary according to program. *Financial support:* Research assistantships with partial tuition reimbursements, teaching assistantships with partial tuition reimbursements, career-related internships or fieldwork, Federal Work-Study, scholarships/grants, and unspecified assistantships available. Support available to part-time students. Financial award applicants required to submit FAFSA. *Unit head:* Darell Singleterry, Director, 203-932-1085, E-mail: dsingleterry@newhaven.edu. *Application contact:* Michelle Mason, Director of Graduate Enrollment, 203-932-7067, E-mail: mmason@newhaven.edu.
Website: http://www.newhaven.edu/business/programs/EMBA/

University of New Mexico, Anderson School of Management, Department of Marketing, Information and Decision Sciences, Albuquerque, NM 87131. Offers information assurance (MBA); information systems and assurance (MS); management information systems (MBA); marketing management (MBA); operations management (MBA). *Program availability:* Part-time, evening/weekend. *Faculty:* 17 full-time (3 women), 7 part-time/adjunct (5 women). In 2016, 47 master's awarded. *Entrance requirements:* For master's, GMAT or GRE, minimum GPA of 3.0 on last 60 hours of coursework; bachelor's degree from regionally-accredited college or university in U.S. or its equivalent in another country. Additional exam requirements/recommendations for international students: Required—TOEFL (minimum score 550 paper-based; 79 iBT), IELTS (minimum score 6.5). *Application deadline:* For fall admission, 4/1 priority date for domestic and international students; for spring admission, 10/1 priority date for domestic and international students. Applications are processed on a rolling basis. Application fee: $50. Electronic applications accepted. *Expenses:* Contact institution. *Financial support:* In 2016–17, 8 fellowships (averaging $11,484 per year), 13 research assistantships with partial tuition reimbursements (averaging $9,382 per year) were awarded; career-related internships or fieldwork, Federal Work-Study, scholarships/grants, and unspecified assistantships also available. Support available to part-time students. Financial award application deadline: 6/1; financial award applicants required

to submit FAFSA. *Faculty research:* Marketing, operations management, information systems, information assurance. *Unit head:* Dr. Steve Yourstone, Chair, 505-277-6471, E-mail: yourstone@unm.edu. *Application contact:* Lisa Beauchene, Student Recruitment Specialist, 505-277-6471, E-mail: andersonadvising@unm.edu.
Website: https://www.mgt.unm.edu/mids/default.asp?mm=faculty

The University of North Carolina at Chapel Hill, Kenan-Flagler Business School, Doctoral Program in Business Administration, Chapel Hill, NC 27599. Offers accounting (PhD); finance (PhD); marketing (PhD); operations management (PhD); organizational behavior (PhD); strategy (PhD). *Accreditation:* AACSB. *Degree requirements:* For doctorate, thesis/dissertation. *Entrance requirements:* For doctorate, GMAT or GRE General Test. Electronic applications accepted. *Expenses:* Contact institution.

The University of North Carolina at Greensboro, Graduate School, Bryan School of Business and Economics, Department of Consumer, Apparel, and Retail Studies, Greensboro, NC 27412-5001. Offers MS, PhD. *Degree requirements:* For master's, one foreign language; for doctorate, one foreign language, thesis/dissertation. *Entrance requirements:* For master's and doctorate, GRE General Test. Additional exam requirements/recommendations for international students: Required—TOEFL. Electronic applications accepted. *Faculty research:* Impact of phosphate removal, protective clothing for pesticide workers, fabric hand: subjective and objective measurements.

University of North Texas, Robert B. Toulouse School of Graduate Studies, Denton, TX 76203-5459. Offers accounting (MS); applied anthropology (MA, MS); applied behavior analysis (Certificate); applied geography (MA); applied technology and performance improvement (M Ed, MS); art education (MA); art history (MA); art museum education (Certificate); arts leadership (Certificate); audiology (Au D); behavior analysis (MS); behavioral science (PhD); biochemistry and molecular biology (MS); biology (MA, MS); biomedical engineering (MS); business analysis (MS); chemistry (MS); clinical health psychology (PhD); communication studies (MA, MS); computer engineering (MS); computer science (MS); counseling (M Ed, MS), including clinical mental health counseling (MS), college and university counseling, elementary school counseling, secondary school counseling; creative writing (MA); criminal justice (MS); curriculum and instruction (M Ed); decision sciences (MBA); design (MA, MFA), including fashion design (MFA), innovation studies, interior design (MFA); early childhood studies (MS); economics (MS); educational leadership (M Ed, Ed D); educational psychology (MS, PhD), including family studies (MS), gifted and talented (MS), human development (MS), learning and cognition (MS), research, measurement and evaluation (MS); electrical engineering (MS); emergency management (MPA); engineering technology (MS); English (MA); English as a second language (MA); environmental science (MS); finance (MBA, MS); financial management (MPA); French (MA); health services management (MBA); higher education (M Ed, Ed D); history (MA, MS); hospitality management (MS); human resources management (MPA); information science (MS); information systems (PhD); information technologies (MBA); interdisciplinary studies (MA, MS); international studies (MA); international sustainable tourism (MS); jazz studies (MM); journalism (MA, MJ, Graduate Certificate), including interactive and virtual digital communication (Graduate Certificate), narrative journalism (Graduate Certificate), public relations (Graduate Certificate); kinesiology (MS); linguistics (MA); local government management (MPA); logistics (PhD); logistics and supply chain management (MBA); long-term care, senior housing, and aging services (MA); management (PhD); marketing (MBA); mathematics (MA, MS); mechanical and energy engineering (MS, PhD); music (MA), including ethnomusicology, music theory, musicology, performance; music composition (PhD); music education (MM Ed, PhD); nonprofit management (MPA); operations and supply chain management (MBA); performance (MM, DMA); philosophy (MA); political science (MA); professional and technical communication (MA); radio, television and film (MA, MFA); rehabilitation counseling (Certificate); sociology (MA); Spanish (MA); special education (M Ed); speech-language pathology (MA); strategic management (MBA); studio art (MFA); teaching (M Ed); MBA/MS. *Program availability:* Part-time, evening/weekend, online learning. Terminal master's awarded for partial completion of doctoral program. *Degree requirements:* For master's, variable foreign language requirement, comprehensive exam (for some programs), thesis (for some programs); for doctorate, variable foreign language requirement, comprehensive exam (for some programs), thesis/dissertation; for other advanced degree, variable foreign language requirement, comprehensive exam (for some programs). *Entrance requirements:* For master's and doctorate, GRE, GMAT. Additional exam requirements/recommendations for international students: Required—TOEFL (minimum score 550 paper-based; 79 iBT). Electronic applications accepted.

University of Notre Dame, Mendoza College of Business, Master of Business Administration Program, Notre Dame, IN 46556. Offers business analytics (MBA); business leadership (MBA); consulting (MBA); corporate finance (MBA); innovation and entrepreneurship (MBA); investments (MBA); marketing (MBA). *Accreditation:* AACSB. *Faculty:* 62 full-time (13 women), 26 part-time/adjunct (7 women). *Students:* 304 full-time (78 women); includes 38 minority (10 Black or African American, non-Hispanic/Latino; 7 Asian, non-Hispanic/Latino; 15 Hispanic/Latino; 6 Two or more races, non-Hispanic/Latino), 80 international. Average age 27. 647 applicants, 41% accepted, 121 enrolled. In 2016, 177 master's awarded. *Entrance requirements:* For master's, GMAT or GRE, work experience, essay, four-slide presentation, two recommendations, transcripts from all colleges and/or universities attended, interview. Additional exam requirements/recommendations for international students: Required—TOEFL (minimum score 600 paper-based; 100 iBT), IELTS (minimum score 7), PTE (minimum score 68). *Application deadline:* For fall admission, 11/1 for domestic and international students; for winter admission, 1/10 for domestic and international students; for spring admission, 2/21 for domestic and international students; for summer admission, 3/28 for domestic and international students. Application fee: $175. Electronic applications accepted. *Expenses:* Contact institution. *Financial support:* In 2016–17, 251 students received support, including 243 fellowships (averaging $26,417 per year); career-related internships or fieldwork, Federal Work-Study, institutionally sponsored loans, scholarships/grants, and unspecified assistantships also available. Financial award application deadline: 2/28; financial award applicants required to submit FAFSA. *Faculty research:* Market micro-structure; marketing and public policy; corporate finance and accounting; corporate governance and ethical behavior; high performing organizations. *Unit head:* Dr. Katherine Speiss, Associate Dean, Graduate Business Programs, 574-631-3759, E-mail: spiess.1@nd.edu. *Application contact:* Kristin McAndrew, Director of Admissions, Graduate Business Programs, 574-631-8488, E-mail: kmcadre@nd.edu.
Website: http://mendoza.nd.edu/programs/mba-programs/

University of Oklahoma, Price College of Business, Program in Business Administration, Norman, OK 73019. Offers accounting (PhD); business administration (MBA, PhD); entrepreneurship and economic development (PhD); finance (PhD); management and international business (PhD); management of information systems (PhD); marketing/supply chain (PhD); JD/MBA; MBA/MS. *Accreditation:* AACSB. *Program availability:* Part-time, evening/weekend. *Students:* 122 full-time (27 women), 146 part-time (30 women); includes 36 minority (5 Black or African American, non-Hispanic/Latino; 6 American Indian or Alaska Native, non-Hispanic/Latino; 8 Asian, non-Hispanic/Latino; 11 Hispanic/Latino; 6 Two or more races, non-Hispanic/Latino), 37 international. Average age 30. 261 applicants, 27% accepted, 59 enrolled. In 2016, 127 master's, 5 doctorates awarded. *Degree requirements:* For doctorate, comprehensive exam, thesis/dissertation. *Entrance requirements:* For master's, GMAT or GRE, resume, statement of goals; for doctorate, GMAT or GRE, resume, statement of goals, 3 letters of recommendation. Additional exam requirements/recommendations for international students: Required—TOEFL (minimum score 100 iBT) or IELTS (minimum score 7). *Application deadline:* For fall admission, 11/15 priority date for domestic and international students; for spring admission, 3/15 priority date for domestic and international students; for summer admission, 5/15 for domestic and international students. Application fee: $50 ($100 for international students). Electronic applications accepted. *Expenses:* Contact institution. *Financial support:* In 2016–17, 107 students received support, including 10 fellowships with partial tuition reimbursements available (averaging $3,295 per year); research assistantships with full and partial tuition reimbursements available, teaching assistantships with full and partial tuition reimbursements available, career-related internships or fieldwork, scholarships/grants, health care benefits, and unspecified assistantships also available. Support available to part-time students. Financial award application deadline: 6/1; financial award applicants required to submit FAFSA. *Faculty research:* Energy finance; international accounting; organizational behavior and entrepreneurship; management information systems; supply chain. *Unit head:* Laku Chidambaram, Associate Dean for Academic Programs and Engagement. *Application contact:* Director of MBA Admissions, 405-325-5623.
Website: http://www.ou.edu/content/price/divisions/graduate.html

University of Oregon, Graduate School, Charles H. Lundquist College of Business, Department of Marketing, Eugene, OR 97403. Offers PhD. *Program availability:* Part-time. *Degree requirements:* For doctorate, thesis/dissertation, 2 comprehensive exams. *Entrance requirements:* For doctorate, GMAT. Additional exam requirements/recommendations for international students: Required—TOEFL. *Faculty research:* Consumer behavior, marketing research, international marketing, marketing management, price quality.

University of Pennsylvania, Wharton School, Marketing Department, Philadelphia, PA 19104. Offers MBA, PhD. Terminal master's awarded for partial completion of doctoral program. *Degree requirements:* For master's, thesis optional; for doctorate, thesis/dissertation. *Entrance requirements:* For doctorate, GMAT or GRE. *Expenses: Tuition:* Full-time $31,068; part-time $5762 per course. *Required fees:* $3200; $336 per course. Full-time tuition and fees vary according to degree level, program and student level. Part-time tuition and fees vary according to course load, degree level and program. *Faculty research:* Scanner data, consumer preferences, decision-making theory, modeling for marketing and e-business.

University of Phoenix–Atlanta Campus, School of Business, Sandy Springs, GA 30350-4147. Offers accounting (MBA); business administration (MBA); global management (MBA); human resources management (MBA, MM); management (MM); marketing (MBA); public administration (MM). *Accreditation:* ACBSP. *Program availability:* Evening/weekend, online learning. *Degree requirements:* For master's, thesis (for some programs). *Entrance requirements:* For master's, minimum undergraduate GPA of 3.0, 3 years of work experience. Additional exam requirements/recommendations for international students: Required—TOEFL (minimum score 550 paper-based; 79 iBT).

University of Phoenix–Augusta Campus, School of Business, Augusta, GA 30909-4583. Offers accounting (MBA); business administration (MBA); business and management (MBA, MM); global management (MBA); human resources management (MBA, MM); management (MM); marketing (MBA); public administration (MBA, MM). *Accreditation:* ACBSP. *Program availability:* Online learning.

University of Phoenix–Bay Area Campus, School of Business, San Jose, CA 95134-1805. Offers accountancy (MS); accounting (MBA); business administration (MBA, DBA); energy management (MBA); global management (MBA); health care management (MBA); human resource management (MBA); human resources management (MM); management (MM); marketing (MBA); organizational leadership (DM); project management (MBA); public administration (MPA); technology management (MBA). *Accreditation:* ACBSP. *Program availability:* Evening/weekend, online learning. *Degree requirements:* For master's, thesis (for some programs). *Entrance requirements:* For master's, minimum undergraduate GPA of 3.0, 3 years of work experience. Additional exam requirements/recommendations for international students: Required—TOEFL (minimum score 550 paper-based; 79 iBT). Electronic applications accepted.

University of Phoenix–Central Valley Campus, School of Business, Fresno, CA 93720-1552. Offers accounting (MBA); business administration (MBA); global management (MBA); human resources management (MBA, MM); management (MM); marketing (MBA); public administration (MBA, MM). *Accreditation:* ACBSP.

University of Phoenix–Colorado Campus, School of Business, Lone Tree, CO 80124-5453. Offers accountancy (MSA); accounting (MBA); business administration (MBA); e-business (MBA); global management (MBA); human resources management (MBA, MM); management (MM); marketing (MBA); public administration (MBA, MM). *Accreditation:* ACBSP. *Program availability:* Evening/weekend, online learning. *Degree requirements:* For master's, thesis (for some programs). *Entrance requirements:* For master's, minimum undergraduate GPA of 3.0, 3 years work experience. Additional exam requirements/recommendations for international students: Required—TOEFL (minimum score 550 paper-based; 79 iBT). Electronic applications accepted.

University of Phoenix–Colorado Springs Downtown Campus, School of Business, Colorado Springs, CO 80903. Offers accounting (MBA); business administration (MBA); global management (MBA); human resources management (MBA, MM); management (MM); marketing (MBA); public administration (MM). *Program availability:* Evening/weekend. *Degree requirements:* For master's, thesis (for some programs). *Entrance requirements:* For master's, minimum undergraduate GPA of 3.0, 3 years of work experience. Additional exam requirements/recommendations for international students: Required—TOEFL (minimum score 550 paper-based; 79 iBT). Electronic applications accepted.

University of Phoenix–Columbus Georgia Campus, School of Business, Columbus, GA 31909. Offers accounting (MBA); business administration (MBA); global management (MBA); human resources management (MBA, MM); management (MM); marketing (MBA); public administration (MBA). *Accreditation:* ACBSP. *Program availability:* Evening/weekend. *Degree requirements:* For master's, thesis (for some programs). *Entrance requirements:* For master's, minimum undergraduate GPA of 3.0, 3 years of work experience. Additional exam requirements/recommendations for international students: Required—TOEFL (minimum score 550 paper-based; 79 iBT). Electronic applications accepted.

University of Phoenix–Dallas Campus, School of Business, Dallas, TX 75251. Offers accounting (MBA); business administration (MBA); global management (MBA); human resources management (MBA, MM); management (MM); marketing (MBA); public administration (MBA, MM). *Accreditation:* ACBSP. *Program availability:* Evening/weekend, online learning. *Degree requirements:* For master's, thesis (for some programs). *Entrance requirements:* For master's, 3 years of work experience, minimum undergraduate GPA of 3.0. Additional exam requirements/recommendations for

international students: Required—TOEFL (minimum score 550 paper-based; 79 iBT). Electronic applications accepted.

University of Phoenix–Hawaii Campus, School of Business, Honolulu, HI 96813-3800. Offers accounting (MBA); business administration (MBA); global management (MBA); human resources management (MBA, MM); management (MM); marketing (MBA); public administration (MBA, MM). *Accreditation:* ACBSP. *Program availability:* Evening/weekend. *Degree requirements:* For master's, thesis (for some programs). *Entrance requirements:* For master's, minimum undergraduate GPA of 3.0, 3 years of work experience. Additional exam requirements/recommendations for international students: Required—TOEFL (minimum score 550 paper-based; 79 iBT). Electronic applications accepted.

University of Phoenix–Houston Campus, School of Business, Houston, TX 77079-2004. Offers accounting (MBA); business administration (MBA); global management (MBA); human resources management (MBA, MM); management (MM); marketing (MBA); public administration (MBA, MM). *Accreditation:* ACBSP. *Program availability:* Evening/weekend, online learning. *Degree requirements:* For master's, thesis (for some programs). *Entrance requirements:* For master's, 3 years of work experience, minimum undergraduate GPA of 3.0. Additional exam requirements/recommendations for international students: Required—TOEFL (minimum score 550 paper-based; 79 iBT). Electronic applications accepted.

University of Phoenix–Jersey City Campus, School of Business, Jersey City, NJ 07310. Offers accounting (MBA); business administration (MBA); global management (MBA); human resources management (MBA, MM); management (MM); marketing (MBA); public administration (MBA, MM). *Accreditation:* ACBSP.

University of Phoenix–Las Vegas Campus, School of Business, Las Vegas, NV 89135. Offers accounting (MBA); business administration (MBA); global management (MBA); human resources management (MBA, MM); management (MM); marketing (MBA); public administration (MM). *Accreditation:* ACBSP. *Program availability:* Evening/weekend, online learning. *Degree requirements:* For master's, thesis (for some programs). *Entrance requirements:* For master's, minimum undergraduate GPA of 3.0, 3 years of work experience. Additional exam requirements/recommendations for international students: Required—TOEFL (minimum score 550 paper-based; 79 iBT). Electronic applications accepted.

University of Phoenix–New Mexico Campus, School of Business, Albuquerque, NM 87113-1570. Offers accounting (MBA); business administration (MBA); global management (MBA); human resources management (MBA, MM); management (MM); marketing (MBA). *Accreditation:* ACBSP. *Program availability:* Evening/weekend. *Degree requirements:* For master's, thesis (for some programs). *Entrance requirements:* For master's, 3 years of work experience, minimum undergraduate GPA of 3.0. Additional exam requirements/recommendations for international students: Required—TOEFL (minimum score 550 paper-based; 79 iBT). Electronic applications accepted.

University of Phoenix–North Florida Campus, School of Business, Jacksonville, FL 32216-0959. Offers accounting (MBA); business administration (MBA); global management (MBA); human resources management (MBA, MM); management (MM); marketing (MBA); public administration (MBA, MM). *Accreditation:* ACBSP. *Program availability:* Evening/weekend. *Degree requirements:* For master's, thesis (for some programs). *Entrance requirements:* For master's, minimum undergraduate GPA of 3.0, 3 years work experience. Additional exam requirements/recommendations for international students: Required—TOEFL (minimum score 550 paper-based; 79 iBT). Electronic applications accepted.

University of Phoenix–Online Campus, School of Business, Phoenix, AZ 85034-7209. Offers accountancy (MS); accounting (MBA, Certificate); business administration (MBA); energy management (MBA); global management (MBA); health care management (MBA); human resource management (MBA, Certificate); human resources management (MM); management (MM); marketing (MBA, Certificate); project management (MBA, Certificate); public administration (MBA, MM); technology management (MBA). *Program availability:* Evening/weekend, online learning. *Entrance requirements:* Additional exam requirements/recommendations for international students: Required—TOEFL, TOEIC (Test of English as an International Communication), Berlitz Online English Proficiency Exam, PTE, or IELTS. Electronic applications accepted. *Expenses:* Contact institution.

University of Phoenix–Phoenix Campus, School of Business, Tempe, AZ 85282-2371. Offers accounting (MBA, MS, Certificate); business administration (MBA); energy management (MBA); global management (MBA); health care management (MBA); human resource management (MBA, Certificate); management (MM); marketing (MBA); project management (MBA); technology management (MBA). *Program availability:* Evening/weekend, online learning. *Entrance requirements:* Additional exam requirements/recommendations for international students: Required—TOEFL, TOEIC (Test of English as an International Communication), Berlitz Online English Proficiency Exam, PTE, or IELTS. Electronic applications accepted. *Expenses:* Contact institution.

University of Phoenix–Sacramento Valley Campus, School of Business, Sacramento, CA 95833-4334. Offers accounting (MBA); business administration (MBA); global management (MBA); human resources management (MBA, MM); management (MM); marketing (MBA); public administration (MBA, MM). *Accreditation:* ACBSP. *Program availability:* Evening/weekend. *Degree requirements:* For master's, thesis (for some programs). *Entrance requirements:* For master's, minimum undergraduate GPA of 3.0, 3 years work experience. Additional exam requirements/recommendations for international students: Required—TOEFL (minimum score 550 paper-based; 79 iBT). Electronic applications accepted.

University of Phoenix–San Antonio Campus, School of Business, San Antonio, TX 78230. Offers accounting (MBA); business administration (MBA); e-business (MBA); global management (MBA); human resources management (MBA, MM); management (MM); marketing (MBA); public administration (MBA, MM). *Accreditation:* ACBSP.

University of Phoenix–San Diego Campus, School of Business, San Diego, CA 92123. Offers accounting (MBA); business administration (MBA); global management (MBA); human resources management (MBA, MM); management (MM); marketing (MBA); public administration (MBA). *Accreditation:* ACBSP. *Program availability:* Evening/weekend. *Degree requirements:* For master's, thesis (for some programs). *Entrance requirements:* For master's, 3 years of work experience, minimum undergraduate GPA of 3.0. Additional exam requirements/recommendations for international students: Required—TOEFL (minimum score 550 paper-based; 79 iBT). Electronic applications accepted.

University of Phoenix–Southern Arizona Campus, School of Business, Tucson, AZ 85711. Offers accountancy (MS); accounting (MBA); business administration (MBA); global management (MBA); human resource management (MBA); management (MM); marketing (MBA). *Accreditation:* ACBSP. *Program availability:* Evening/weekend. *Degree requirements:* For master's, thesis (for some programs). *Entrance requirements:* For master's, minimum undergraduate GPA of 3.0, 3 years of work experience. Additional exam requirements/recommendations for international students: Required—TOEFL (minimum score 550 paper-based; 79 iBT). Electronic applications accepted.

University of Phoenix–Southern California Campus, School of Business, Costa Mesa, CA 92626. Offers accounting (MBA); business administration (MBA); energy management (MBA); global management (MBA); health care management (MBA); human resource management (MBA); management (MM); marketing (MBA); project management (MBA); technology management (MBA). *Program availability:* Evening/weekend, online learning. *Entrance requirements:* Additional exam requirements/recommendations for international students: Required—TOEFL, TOEIC (Test of English as an International Communication), Berlitz Online English Proficiency Exam, PTE, or IELTS. Electronic applications accepted. *Expenses:* Contact institution.

University of Phoenix–South Florida Campus, School of Business, Miramar, FL 33027-4145. Offers accounting (MBA); business administration (MBA); global management (MBA); human resource management (MBA); human resources management (MM); management (MM); marketing (MBA); public administration (MBA, MM). *Accreditation:* ACBSP. *Program availability:* Evening/weekend. *Degree requirements:* For master's, thesis (for some programs). *Entrance requirements:* For master's, minimum undergraduate GPA of 3.0, 3 years work experience. Additional exam requirements/recommendations for international students: Required—TOEFL (minimum score 550 paper-based; 79 iBT). Electronic applications accepted.

University of Phoenix–Utah Campus, School of Business, Salt Lake City, UT 84123-4642. Offers accounting (MBA); business administration (MBA); global management (MBA); human resource management (MBA, MM); management (MM); marketing (MBA); technology management (MBA). *Accreditation:* ACBSP. *Program availability:* Evening/weekend. *Degree requirements:* For master's, thesis (for some programs). *Entrance requirements:* For master's, minimum undergraduate GPA of 3.0, 3 years of work experience. Additional exam requirements/recommendations for international students: Required—TOEFL (minimum score 550 paper-based; 79 iBT). Electronic applications accepted.

University of Pittsburgh, Katz Graduate School of Business, Doctoral Program in Business Administration, Pittsburgh, PA 15260. Offers accounting (PhD); business analytics and operations (PhD); finance (PhD); information systems and technology management (PhD); marketing (PhD); organizational behavior and human resources (PhD); strategic management (PhD). *Accreditation:* AACSB. *Program availability:* Evening/weekend. *Faculty:* 88 full-time (27 women), 42 part-time/adjunct (15 women). *Students:* 51 full-time (23 women), 1 part-time (0 women); includes 4 minority (1 Black or African American, non-Hispanic/Latino; 2 Asian, non-Hispanic/Latino; 1 Two or more races, non-Hispanic/Latino), 31 international. Average age 31. 344 applicants, 6% accepted, 9 enrolled. In 2016, 5 doctorates awarded. *Degree requirements:* For doctorate, comprehensive exam, thesis/dissertation, student teaching. *Entrance requirements:* For doctorate, GMAT or GRE, 3 recommendations, statement of purpose, transcripts of all previous course work and degrees. Additional exam requirements/recommendations for international students: Required—TOEFL (minimum score 100 iBT) or IELTS (minimum score 7.0). *Application deadline:* For fall admission, 4/1 priority date for domestic students, 2/1 priority date for international students. Applications are processed on a rolling basis. Application fee: $50. Electronic applications accepted. *Expenses:* Contact institution. *Financial support:* In 2016–17, 40 students received support, including 27 research assistantships with full tuition reimbursements available (averaging $26,000 per year), 9 teaching assistantships with full tuition reimbursements available (averaging $26,700 per year); Federal Work-Study, scholarships/grants, health care benefits, and unspecified assistantships also available. Financial award application deadline: 6/1; financial award applicants required to submit FAFSA. *Faculty research:* Accounting systems/financial reporting, corporate finance, shopper marketing/consumer behavior, management information systems, organizational behavior and entrepreneurship. *Total annual research expenditures:* $493,036. *Unit head:* Dr. Arjang A. Assad, Dean, 412-648-1556, Fax: 412-648-1552, E-mail: aassad@katz.pitt.edu. *Application contact:* Dr. Dennis Galletta, Director, 412-648-1699, Fax: 412-648-3633, E-mail: galletta@katz.pitt.edu.
Website: http://www.business.pitt.edu/katz/phd/

See Display on page 160 and Close-Up on page 189.

University of Pittsburgh, Katz Graduate School of Business, Master of Business Administration Programs, Pittsburgh, PA 15260. Offers finance (MBA); information systems (MBA); marketing (MBA); operations (MBA); organizational behavior and human resources (MBA); strategy, environment and organizations (MBA); MBA/JD; MBA/MSE. *Accreditation:* AACSB. *Program availability:* Part-time, evening/weekend, blended/hybrid learning. *Faculty:* 88 full-time (27 women), 42 part-time/adjunct (15 women). *Students:* 165 full-time (59 women), 330 part-time (103 women); includes 70 minority (29 Black or African American, non-Hispanic/Latino; 20 Asian, non-Hispanic/Latino; 13 Hispanic/Latino; 8 Two or more races, non-Hispanic/Latino), 73 international. Average age 29. 786 applicants, 41% accepted, 179 enrolled. In 2016, 477 master's awarded. *Degree requirements:* For master's, minimum GPA of 3.0. *Entrance requirements:* For master's, GMAT, GRE. Additional exam requirements/recommendations for international students: Required—TOEFL (minimum score 100 iBT) or IELTS (minimum score 7.0). *Application deadline:* For fall admission, 4/1 priority date for domestic students, 2/1 priority date for international students. Application fee: $50. Electronic applications accepted. *Expenses:* Contact institution. *Financial support:* In 2016–17, 110 students received support. Scholarships/grants available. Financial award application deadline: 6/1; financial award applicants required to submit FAFSA. *Faculty research:* Accounting systems/financial reporting, corporate finance, shopper marketing/consumer behavior, management information systems, organizational behavior and entrepreneurship. *Total annual research expenditures:* $493,036. *Unit head:* Dr. Arjang A. Assad, Dean, 412-648-1556, Fax: 412-648-1552, E-mail: aassad@katz.pitt.edu. *Application contact:* Thomas Keller, Director of MBA Admissions, 412-648-1700, Fax: 412-648-1659, E-mail: mba@katz.pitt.edu.
Website: http://www.business.pitt.edu/katz/mba/

See Display on page 160 and Close-Up on page 189.

University of Pittsburgh, Katz Graduate School of Business, Master of Science in Customer Insights Program, Pittsburgh, PA 15260. Offers MS. *Program availability:* Part-time, evening/weekend. *Faculty:* 88 full-time (27 women), 42 part-time/adjunct (15 women). *Students:* 9 full-time (all women); includes 2 minority (1 Asian, non-Hispanic/Latino; 1 Two or more races, non-Hispanic/Latino), 5 international. Average age 25. 88 applicants, 44% accepted, 9 enrolled. In 2016, 2 master's awarded. *Degree requirements:* For master's, minimum GPA of 3.0. *Entrance requirements:* For master's, GMAT, GRE. Additional exam requirements/recommendations for international students: Required—TOEFL (minimum score 100 iBT), IELTS (minimum score 7). *Application deadline:* For fall admission, 7/1 priority date for domestic students, 5/1 priority date for international students. Applications are processed on a rolling basis. Application fee: $50. Electronic applications accepted. *Expenses:* Contact institution. *Financial support:* Scholarships/grants available. Financial award application deadline: 6/1; financial award applicants required to submit FAFSA. *Faculty research:* Accounting systems/financial reporting, corporate finance, shopper marketing/consumer behavior, management information systems, organizational behavior and entrepreneurship. *Total annual research expenditures:* $493,036. *Unit head:* Dr. Arjang A. Assad, Dean, 412-648-1556, Fax: 412-648-1552, E-mail: aassad@katz.pitt.edu. *Application contact:*

Thomas Keller, Director of MBA Admissions, 412-648-1700, Fax: 412-648-1659, E-mail: mba@katz.pitt.edu.
Website: http://www.business.pitt.edu/katz/ms-programs/customer-insight

University of Portland, Dr. Robert B. Pamplin, Jr. School of Business, Portland, OR 97203-5798. Offers entrepreneurship (MBA); finance (MBA, MS); health care management (MBA); marketing (MBA); nonprofit management (EMBA); operations and technology management (MBA, MS); sustainability (MBA). *Accreditation:* AACSB. *Program availability:* Part-time, evening/weekend. *Entrance requirements:* For master's, GMAT, minimum GPA of 3.0, resume, 2 letters of recommendation. Additional exam requirements/recommendations for international students: Required—TOEFL (minimum score 570 paper-based; 89 iBT), IELTS (minimum score 7). *Expenses:* Contact institution.

University of Puerto Rico, Río Piedras Campus, College of Business Administration, San Juan, PR 00931-3300. Offers accounting (MBA); finance (MBA, PhD); general business (MBA); human resources management (MBA); international trade and business (MBA, PhD); marketing (MBA); operations management (MBA); quantitative methods (MBA). *Accreditation:* AACSB. *Program availability:* Part-time. *Degree requirements:* For master's, comprehensive exam, thesis or alternative, research project. *Entrance requirements:* For master's, GMAT or PAEG, minimum GPA of 3.0, letter of recommendation; for doctorate, GMAT, PAEG, minimum GPA of 3.0, master degree. *Faculty research:* Management.

University of Rhode Island, Graduate School, College of Business Administration, Kingston, RI 02881. Offers accounting (MS); business administration (PhD), including finance and insurance, marketing, supply chain management; finance (MBA, MS); general business (MBA); health care management (MBA); management (MBA); marketing (MBA); oceanography (MBA); strategic innovation (MBA); supply chain management (MBA); Pharm D/MBA. *Accreditation:* AACSB. *Program availability:* Part-time, evening/weekend. *Faculty:* 57 full-time (24 women). *Students:* 94 full-time (45 women), 166 part-time (84 women); includes 37 minority (6 Black or African American, non-Hispanic/Latino; 1 American Indian or Alaska Native, non-Hispanic/Latino; 22 Asian, non-Hispanic/Latino; 3 Hispanic/Latino; 5 Two or more races, non-Hispanic/Latino), 18 international. In 2016, 124 master's, 4 doctorates awarded. *Degree requirements:* For master's, comprehensive exam (for some programs), thesis optional; for doctorate, comprehensive exam, thesis/dissertation. *Entrance requirements:* For master's, GMAT or GRE, 2 letters of recommendation, resume; for doctorate, GMAT or GRE, 3 letters of recommendation, resume. Additional exam requirements/recommendations for international students: Required—TOEFL. *Application deadline:* For fall admission, 2/1 for domestic and international students. Application fee: $65. Electronic applications accepted. *Expenses:* Tuition, state resident: full-time $11,796; part-time $655 per credit. Tuition, nonresident: full-time $24,206; part-time $1345 per credit. *Required fees:* $1546; $44 per credit. One-time fee: $155 full-time; $35 part-time. *Financial support:* In 2016–17, 17 teaching assistantships with tuition reimbursements (averaging $15,347 per year) were awarded; research assistantships also available. Financial award application deadline: 2/1; financial award applicants required to submit FAFSA. *Unit head:* Dr. Maling Ebrahimpour, Dean, 401-874-4348, Fax: 401-874-4312, E-mail: mebrahimpour@uri.edu. *Application contact:* Lisa Lancellotta, Coordinator, MBA Programs, 401-874-4241, Fax: 401-874-4312, E-mail: mba@uri.edu.
Website: http://www.cba.uri.edu/

See Display on page 161 and Close-Up on page 191.

University of Rochester, Simon Business School, Doctoral Program in Business Administration, Rochester, NY 14627. Offers accounting (PhD); computer information systems (PhD); finance (PhD); marketing (PhD); operations management (PhD). *Accreditation:* AACSB. *Faculty:* 66 full-time (13 women), 22 part-time/adjunct (2 women). *Students:* 52 full-time (19 women); includes 2 minority (both Asian, non-Hispanic/Latino), 42 international. Average age 29. 210 applicants, 16% accepted, 15 enrolled. In 2016, 6 doctorates awarded. *Degree requirements:* For doctorate, comprehensive exam, thesis/dissertation, qualifying exam. *Entrance requirements:* For doctorate, GMAT or GRE. Additional exam requirements/recommendations for international students: Required—TOEFL. *Application deadline:* For fall admission, 1/5 for domestic and international students. Application fee: $100. Electronic applications accepted. *Expenses:* $1,800 per credit hour. *Financial support:* In 2016–17, 52 students received support. Fellowships, research assistantships, teaching assistantships, and tuition waivers (full) available. Financial award application deadline: 1/5. *Unit head:* Dr. Ron Kaniel, Committee Chair, 585-275-2959. *Application contact:* Sue Harris, PhD Administrator, 585-275-2959, E-mail: phdoffice@simon.rochester.edu.
Website: http://www.simon.rochester.edu/programs/phd/index.aspx

University of Rochester, Simon Business School, Full-Time Master's Program in Business Administration, Rochester, NY 14627. Offers business systems consulting (MBA); competitive and organizational strategy (MBA); computers and information systems (MBA); corporate accounting (MBA); entrepreneurship (MBA); finance (MBA); health sciences management (MBA); marketing (MBA); operations management (MBA); public accounting (MBA). *Accreditation:* AACSB. *Program availability:* Part-time, evening/weekend. *Faculty:* 66 full-time (13 women), 22 part-time/adjunct (2 women). *Students:* 202 full-time (78 women); includes 50 minority (30 Black or African American, non-Hispanic/Latino; 10 Asian, non-Hispanic/Latino; 9 Hispanic/Latino; 1 Two or more races, non-Hispanic/Latino), 107 international. Average age 27. 915 applicants, 30% accepted, 86 enrolled. In 2016, 110 master's awarded. *Entrance requirements:* For master's, GMAT/GRE. Additional exam requirements/recommendations for international students: Required—TOEFL. *Application deadline:* For fall admission, 10/15 for domestic and international students; for winter admission, 1/5 for domestic and international students; for spring admission, 3/15 for domestic and international students; for summer admission, 5/15 for domestic and international students. Applications are processed on a rolling basis. Application fee: $150. Electronic applications accepted. *Expenses:* Contact institution. *Financial support:* In 2016–17, 190 students received support. Fellowships, research assistantships, teaching assistantships, institutionally sponsored loans, scholarships/grants, and tuition waivers (full and partial) available. Financial award application deadline: 1/5; financial award applicants required to submit FAFSA. *Unit head:* Andrew Ainslie, Dean, 585-275-3316, E-mail: andrew.ainslie@simon.rochester.edu. *Application contact:* Rebekah S. Lewin, Assistant Dean of Admissions and Financial Aid, 585-275-3533, E-mail: admissions@simon.rochester.edu.
Website: http://www.simon.rochester.edu/programs/full-time-mba/index.aspx

University of Rochester, Simon Business School, Part-Time MBA Program, Rochester, NY 14627. Offers business systems consulting (MBA); competitive and organizational strategy (MBA); computers and information systems (MBA); corporate accounting (MBA); entrepreneurship (MBA); finance (MBA); health sciences management (MBA); marketing (MBA); operations management (MBA); public accounting (MBA). *Program availability:* Part-time, evening/weekend. *Faculty:* 66 full-time (13 women), 22 part-time/adjunct (2 women). *Students:* 185 part-time (65 women); includes 29 minority (6 Black or African American, non-Hispanic/Latino; 13 Asian, non-Hispanic/Latino; 8 Hispanic/Latino; 2 Two or more races, non-Hispanic/Latino), 9 international. Average age 32. 33 applicants, 100% accepted, 31 enrolled. In 2016, 70 master's awarded. *Entrance requirements:* For master's, GRE or GMAT. *Application deadline:* For fall admission, 8/1 for domestic students; for spring admission, 2/15 for domestic students. Applications are processed on a rolling basis. Application fee: $150. Electronic applications accepted. *Expenses:* $1,800 per credit hour. *Financial support:* In 2016–17, 75 students received support. Scholarships/grants and tuition waivers (partial) available. Financial award applicants required to submit CSS PROFILE or FAFSA. *Unit head:* Andrew Ainslie, Dean, 585-275-3316, E-mail: andrew.ainslie@simon.rochester.edu. *Application contact:* Molly Mesko, Executive Director, EMBA and Part-Time Programs, 585-275-4277, E-mail: molly.mesko@simon.rochester.edu.
Website: http://www.simon.rochester.edu/programs/ptmba/index.aspx

University of Saint Mary, Graduate Programs, Program in Business Administration, Leavenworth, KS 66048-5082. Offers enterprise risk management (MBA); finance (MBA); general management (MBA); health care management (MBA); human resource management (MBA); marketing and advertising management (MBA). *Program availability:* Part-time, evening/weekend, 100% online, blended/hybrid learning. *Students:* 201 full-time (110 women), 62 part-time (38 women); includes 83 minority (29 Black or African American, non-Hispanic/Latino; 3 American Indian or Alaska Native, non-Hispanic/Latino; 14 Asian, non-Hispanic/Latino; 32 Hispanic/Latino; 1 Native Hawaiian or other Pacific Islander, non-Hispanic/Latino; 4 Two or more races, non-Hispanic/Latino), 7 international. Average age 34. In 2016, 73 master's awarded. *Degree requirements:* For master's, thesis. *Entrance requirements:* For master's, minimum undergraduate GPA of 2.75, official transcripts, two letters of recommendation. *Application deadline:* Applications are processed on a rolling basis. Application fee: $25. Electronic applications accepted. *Expenses:* $595 per hour. *Unit head:* Rick Gunter, Director, 913-319-3007. *Application contact:* Mark Harvey, Program Manager, 913-319-3007, E-mail: mark.harvey@stmary.edu.
Website: http://www.stmary.edu/success/Grad-Program/Master-of-Business-Administration-MBA.aspx

University of San Francisco, School of Management, Master of Business Administration Program, San Francisco, CA 94117. Offers entrepreneurship and innovation (MBA); finance (MBA); marketing (MBA); organization development (MBA); DDS/MBA; JD/MBA; MBA/MAPS. *Accreditation:* AACSB. *Program availability:* Part-time, evening/weekend. *Faculty:* 17 full-time (6 women), 5 part-time/adjunct (2 women). *Students:* 146 full-time (70 women), 2 part-time (1 woman); includes 50 minority (5 Black or African American, non-Hispanic/Latino; 27 Asian, non-Hispanic/Latino; 15 Hispanic/Latino; 1 Native Hawaiian or other Pacific Islander, non-Hispanic/Latino; 2 Two or more races, non-Hispanic/Latino), 51 international. Average age 29. 282 applicants, 63% accepted, 70 enrolled. In 2016, 91 master's awarded. *Entrance requirements:* For master's, GMAT or GRE, resume (two years of professional work experience required for part-time students, preferred for full-time), transcripts from each college or university attended, two letters of recommendation, personal statement, interview. Additional exam requirements/recommendations for international students: Required—TOEFL (minimum score 600 paper-based, 100 iBT), IELTS (minimum score 7) or PTE (minimum score 68). *Application deadline:* For fall admission, 6/5 for domestic students, 5/15 for international students; for spring admission, 11/30 for domestic students. Application fee: $55. Electronic applications accepted. *Expenses: Tuition:* Full-time $23,310; part-time $1295 per credit. Tuition and fees vary according to course load, degree level, campus/location and program. *Financial support:* In 2016–17, 60 students received support. Fellowships and scholarships/grants available. Financial award application deadline: 3/2; financial award applicants required to submit FAFSA. *Faculty research:* International financial markets, technology transfer licensing, international marketing, strategic planning. *Total annual research expenditures:* $50,000. *Unit head:* Dr. Frank Fletcher, Director, 415-422-2221, Fax: 415-422-6315, E-mail: management@usfca.edu. *Application contact:* Office of Graduate Recruiting and Admissions, 415-422-2221, Fax: 415-422-6315, E-mail: management@usfca.edu.
Website: http://www.usfca.edu/mba

University of Saskatchewan, College of Graduate Studies and Research, Edwards School of Business, Department of Management and Marketing, Saskatoon, SK S7N 5A2, Canada. Offers marketing (M Sc). *Program availability:* Part-time. *Degree requirements:* For master's, thesis. *Entrance requirements:* For master's, GMAT. Additional exam requirements/recommendations for international students: Required—TOEFL.

The University of Scranton, Kania School of Management, Program in Business Administration, Scranton, PA 18510. Offers accounting (MBA); finance (MBA); general business administration (MBA); health care management (MBA); international business (MBA); management information systems (MBA); marketing (MBA); operations management (MBA). *Accreditation:* AACSB. *Program availability:* Part-time, evening/weekend, 100% online. *Entrance requirements:* For master's, GMAT (for MBA). *Faculty research:* Financial markets, strategic impact of total quality management, internal accounting controls, consumer preference, information systems and the Internet.

University of Sioux Falls, Vucurevich School of Business, Sioux Falls, SD 57105-1699. Offers entrepreneurial leadership (MBA); general management (MBA); health care management (MBA); marketing (MBA). *Program availability:* Part-time, evening/weekend. *Degree requirements:* For master's, project. *Entrance requirements:* For master's, minimum GPA of 3.0. Additional exam requirements/recommendations for international students: Required—TOEFL. *Expenses:* Contact institution.

University of South Africa, College of Economic and Management Sciences, Pretoria, South Africa. Offers accounting (D Admin, D Com); accounting science (DA); auditing (D Admin, D Com); business administration (M Tech); business economics (D Admin); business leadership (DBL); business management (D Admin, D Com); economic management analysis (M Tech); economics (D Admin, D Com, PhD); human resource development (M Tech); industrial psychology (D Admin, D Com, PhD); logistics (D Com); marketing (M Tech); public administration (D Admin, D Com, DPA, PhD); public management (M Tech); quantitative management (D Admin, D Com); real estate (M Tech); statistics (D Admin, PhD); tourism management (D Admin, D Com); transport economics (D Admin, D Com).

University of South Florida, Muma College of Business, Department of Marketing, Tampa, FL 33620-9951. Offers business administration (PhD), including marketing; marketing (MSM). *Program availability:* Part-time, evening/weekend. *Faculty:* 13 full-time (2 women). *Students:* 44 full-time (30 women), 15 part-time (9 women); includes 3 minority (2 Asian, non-Hispanic/Latino; 1 Hispanic/Latino), 42 international. Average age 25. 78 applicants, 50% accepted, 14 enrolled. In 2016, 21 master's, 2 doctorates awarded. Terminal master's awarded for partial completion of doctoral program. *Degree requirements:* For master's, comprehensive exam, thesis or alternative; for doctorate, comprehensive exam, thesis/dissertation. *Entrance requirements:* For master's, GMAT or GRE, minimum GPA of 3.0 in upper-division undergraduate and marketing coursework, two letters of recommendation; for doctorate, GMAT or GRE, personal statement, recommendations, interview. Additional exam requirements/recommendations for international students: Required—TOEFL (minimum score 550 paper-based; 79 iBT) or IELTS (minimum score 6.5). *Application deadline:* For fall admission, 1/2 for domestic and international students; for spring admission, 10/15 for domestic students, 7/1 for international students. Applications are processed on a rolling basis. Application fee: $30. Electronic applications accepted. *Expenses:* Tuition, state

resident: full-time $7766; part-time $431.43 per credit hour. Tuition, nonresident: full-time $15,789; part-time $877.17 per credit hour. *Required fees:* $37 per term. *Financial support:* In 2016–17, 4 students received support, including 5 research assistantships (averaging $14,943 per year), 6 teaching assistantships (averaging $11,972 per year); health care benefits and unspecified assistantships also available. *Faculty research:* Branding; consumer behavior; marketing communications' effectiveness; customer satisfaction; customer delight; consumer reactions to new technology, products and services; consumer emotions; brand strategies; communications; advertising effectiveness; green alliances; strategic marketing; international business; international marketing; consumer research; customer service branding; focus group research; market surveys; market research; promotion; services marketing; strategic planning. *Unit head:* Dr. Anand Kumar, Interim Department Chair/Associate Professor, 813-974-6205, Fax: 813-974-6175, E-mail: akumar@usf.edu. *Application contact:* Dr. James Stock, Area Coordinator and Professor, 813-974-6173, Fax: 813-974-6175, E-mail: jstock@usf.edu.
Website: http://business.usf.edu/departments/marketing/

The University of Tampa, Sykes College of Business, Tampa, FL 33606-1490. Offers accounting (MS); entrepreneurship (MBA); finance (MBA, MS); information systems management (MBA); innovation management (MBA); international business (MBA); marketing (MBA, MS); nonprofit management (MBA). *Accreditation:* AACSB. *Program availability:* Part-time, evening/weekend. *Faculty:* 43 full-time (19 women), 9 part-time/adjunct (3 women). *Students:* 438 full-time (176 women), 126 part-time (57 women); includes 37 minority (22 Black or African American, non-Hispanic/Latino; 11 Asian, non-Hispanic/Latino; 4 Two or more races, non-Hispanic/Latino), 203 international. Average age 28. 1,305 applicants, 39% accepted, 192 enrolled. In 2016, 266 master's awarded. *Degree requirements:* For master's, capstone. *Entrance requirements:* For master's, GMAT or GRE, official transcripts from all colleges and/or universities previously attended, resume, personal statement, letters of recommendation. Additional exam requirements/recommendations for international students: Required—TOEFL (minimum score 577 paper-based, 90 iBT) or IELTS (7.5). *Application deadline:* Applications are processed on a rolling basis. Application fee: $40. Electronic applications accepted. *Expenses:* $588 per credit tuition, $40 per term fees. *Financial support:* In 2016–17, 116 students received support. Career-related internships or fieldwork, scholarships/grants, and unspecified assistantships available. Financial award applicants required to submit FAFSA. *Faculty research:* Job market signaling, on-line shopping behaviors and social media, the Tampa Bay economy, digital literacy, entrepreneurship in small businesses. *Unit head:* Dr. Natasha F. Veltri, Associate Dean, 813-253-6289, E-mail: nveltri@ut.edu. *Application contact:* Chanelle Cox, Staff Assistant, Admissions for Graduate and Continuing Studies, 813-253-6249, E-mail: ccox@ut.edu.
Website: http://www.ut.edu/business/

The University of Tennessee, Graduate School, College of Business Administration, Program in Business Administration, Knoxville, TN 37996. Offers accounting (PhD); finance (MBA, PhD); logistics and transportation (MBA, PhD); management (PhD); marketing (MBA, PhD); operations management (MBA); professional business administration (MBA); statistics (PhD); JD/MBA; MS/MBA; Pharm D/MBA. Pharm D/MBA offered jointly with The University of Tennessee Health Science Center. *Accreditation:* AACSB. *Program availability:* Online learning. *Degree requirements:* For master's, thesis or alternative; for doctorate, thesis/dissertation. *Entrance requirements:* For master's and doctorate, GMAT, minimum GPA of 2.7. Additional exam requirements/recommendations for international students: Required—TOEFL. Electronic applications accepted.

The University of Texas at Arlington, Graduate School, College of Business, Department of Marketing, Arlington, TX 76019. Offers marketing (MBA); marketing research (MS). *Program availability:* Part-time, evening/weekend. *Degree requirements:* For master's, thesis optional. *Entrance requirements:* For master's, GMAT, GRE. Additional exam requirements/recommendations for international students: Required—TOEFL (minimum score 550 paper-based; 79 iBT). *Application deadline:* For fall admission, 6/1 for domestic students, 4/1 for international students; for spring admission, 10/15 for domestic students, 9/15 for international students. Applications are processed on a rolling basis. Application fee: $40 ($70 for international students). Electronic applications accepted. *Financial support:* Teaching assistantships, career-related internships or fieldwork, scholarships/grants, and unspecified assistantships available. Support available to part-time students. Financial award application deadline: 6/1; financial award applicants required to submit FAFSA. *Faculty research:* Marketing strategy, marketing research, international marketing. *Unit head:* Dr. Greg Frazier, Interim Chair, 817-272-0264, Fax: 817-272-2854, E-mail: frazier@uta.edu. *Application contact:* Dr. Robert Rogers, MS Program Director, 817-272-2340, Fax: 817-272-2854, E-mail: msmr@uta.edu.
Website: http://wweb.uta.edu/marketing/

The University of Texas at Austin, Graduate School, McCombs School of Business, Department of Marketing, Austin, TX 78712-1111. Offers MBA, MS, PhD. *Degree requirements:* For doctorate, comprehensive exam, thesis/dissertation. *Entrance requirements:* For doctorate, GMAT or GRE. Electronic applications accepted. *Faculty research:* Internet marketing, strategic marketing, buy behavior.

The University of Texas at Dallas, Naveen Jindal School of Management, Program in Marketing, Richardson, TX 75080. Offers marketing (MS); professional sales (MS). *Program availability:* Part-time, evening/weekend. *Faculty:* 13 full-time (3 women), 5 part-time/adjunct (0 women). *Students:* 119 full-time (74 women), 33 part-time (22 women); includes 25 minority (4 Black or African American, non-Hispanic/Latino; 9 Asian, non-Hispanic/Latino; 7 Hispanic/Latino; 5 Two or more races, non-Hispanic/Latino), 101 international. Average age 27. 303 applicants, 50% accepted, 65 enrolled. In 2016, 76 master's awarded. *Degree requirements:* For master's, thesis optional. *Entrance requirements:* For master's, GMAT, minimum GPA of 3.0 in upper-level coursework in field. Additional exam requirements/recommendations for international students: Required—TOEFL (minimum score 550 paper-based). *Application deadline:* For fall admission, 7/15 for domestic students, 5/1 priority date for international students; for spring admission, 11/15 for domestic students, 9/1 priority date for international students. Applications are processed on a rolling basis. Application fee: $50 ($100 for international students). Electronic applications accepted. *Expenses:* Tuition, state resident: full-time $12,418; part-time $690 per semester hour. Tuition, nonresident: full-time $24,150; part-time $1342 per semester hour. Tuition and fees vary according to course load. *Financial support:* In 2016–17, 37 students received support, including 1 fellowship (averaging $1,000 per year), 2 teaching assistantships with partial tuition reimbursements available (averaging $10,050 per year); research assistantships with partial tuition reimbursements available, career-related internships or fieldwork, Federal Work-Study, institutionally sponsored loans, scholarships/grants, and unspecified assistantships also available. Support available to part-time students. Financial award application deadline: 4/30; financial award applicants required to submit FAFSA. *Faculty research:* Inventory control and risk management. *Unit head:* Dr. Nanda Kumar, Area Coordinator, 972-883-6426, E-mail: nkumar@utdallas.edu. *Application contact:* Malissa Cloer, Academic Support Coordinator, 972-883-5974, E-mail: malissa.cloer@utdallas.edu.
Website: http://jindal.utdallas.edu/marketing/

The University of Texas at San Antonio, College of Business, Department of Marketing, San Antonio, TX 78249-0617. Offers marketing (PhD); marketing management (MBA); tourism destination development (MBA). *Program availability:* Part-time, evening/weekend. *Faculty:* 10 full-time (0 women). *Students:* 12 full-time (5 women), 10 part-time (5 women); includes 11 minority (2 Asian, non-Hispanic/Latino; 9 Hispanic/Latino), 7 international. Average age 30. 65 applicants, 22% accepted, 10 enrolled. In 2016, 9 master's, 1 doctorate awarded. *Degree requirements:* For master's, comprehensive exam (for some programs), thesis (for some programs). *Entrance requirements:* For master's, GMAT, minimum GPA of 3.0. Additional exam requirements/recommendations for international students: Required—TOEFL (minimum score 550 paper-based; 79 iBT). *Application deadline:* For fall admission, 7/1 for domestic students, 4/1 for international students; for spring admission, 11/1 for domestic students, 9/1 for international students. Applications are processed on a rolling basis. Application fee: $45 ($80 for international students). Electronic applications accepted. *Financial support:* Career-related internships or fieldwork, Federal Work-Study, scholarships/grants, and unspecified assistantships available. Support available to part-time students. *Faculty research:* Consumer behavior, cross-cultural research, psycholinguistics, pricing, mass media and materialism. *Total annual research expenditures:* $6,693. *Unit head:* Dr. Suman Basuroy, Department Chair, 210-458-6330, E-mail: suman.barusoy@utsa.edu.
Website: http://business.utsa.edu/marketing/

The University of Texas at Tyler, College of Business and Technology, Program in Business Administration, Tyler, TX 75799-0001. Offers cyber security (MBA); engineering management (MBA); general management (MBA); healthcare management (MBA); internal assurance and consulting (MBA); marketing (MBA); oil, gas and energy (MBA); organizational development (MBA); quality management (MBA). *Accreditation:* AACSB. *Program availability:* Part-time, online learning. *Entrance requirements:* Additional exam requirements/recommendations for international students: Required—TOEFL (minimum score 550 paper-based). *Faculty research:* General business, inventory control, institutional markets, service marketing, product distribution, accounting fraud, financial reporting and recognition.

The University of Texas Rio Grande Valley, Robert C. Vackar College of Business and Entrepreneurship, Program in Business Administration, Edinburg, TX 78539. Offers business administration (MBA); finance (PhD); management (PhD); marketing (PhD). *Program availability:* Part-time, evening/weekend, online learning. *Degree requirements:* For master's, thesis optional. *Entrance requirements:* For master's, GMAT, minimum GPA of 3.0. Additional exam requirements/recommendations for international students: Required—TOEFL (minimum score 500 paper-based). Electronic applications accepted. Tuition and fees vary according to course load and program. *Faculty research:* Human resources, border region, entrepreneurship, marketing.

University of the Cumberlands, Graduate Programs in Education, Williamsburg, KY 40769-1372. Offers all grades (P-12) (M Ed); business and marketing (MA Ed, MAT); counselor education and supervision (Ed D); director of pupil personnel (Certificate); director of special education (Certificate); educational administration and supervision (Ed S); educational leadership (Ed D); elementary education (MA Ed, MAT); instructional leadership - principalship (MA Ed); instructional leadership - school principal (Certificate); middle school education (MA Ed, MAT); reading and writing (MA Ed); school counseling (MA Ed); school superintendent (Certificate); secondary education (MA Ed, MAT); special education (MAT); supervisor of instruction (Certificate); teacher leader (MA Ed). *Program availability:* Part-time, evening/weekend, online learning. *Degree requirements:* For master's, comprehensive exam. Electronic applications accepted.

University of the Sacred Heart, Graduate Programs, Department of Business Administration, Program in International Marketing, San Juan, PR 00914-0383. Offers MBA. *Program availability:* Part-time, evening/weekend. *Degree requirements:* For master's, thesis. *Entrance requirements:* For master's, EXADEP, minimum undergraduate GPA of 2.75, interview.

The University of Toledo, College of Graduate Studies, College of Business and Innovation, Department of Marketing and International Business, Toledo, OH 43606-3390. Offers MBA. *Program availability:* Part-time, evening/weekend. *Entrance requirements:* For master's, GMAT, GRE, or LSAT, minimum GPA of 2.7 for all prior academic work, three letters of recommendation, statement of purpose, transcripts from all prior institutions attended. Additional exam requirements/recommendations for international students: Required—TOEFL (minimum score 550 paper-based; 80 iBT). Electronic applications accepted.

University of Utah, Graduate School, David Eccles School of Business, Business Administration Program, Salt Lake City, UT 84112. Offers accounting (PhD); business administration (EMBA, MBA, PMBA); finance (PhD); information systems (PhD); marketing (PhD); operations management (PhD); organizational behavior (PhD); strategic management (PhD); MBA/JD; MBA/MHA; MBA/MS. *Program availability:* Part-time, evening/weekend, online learning. *Faculty:* 58 full-time (21 women), 37 part-time/adjunct (7 women). *Students:* 578 full-time (149 women), 89 part-time (28 women); includes 71 minority (1 American Indian or Alaska Native, non-Hispanic/Latino; 17 Asian, non-Hispanic/Latino; 45 Hispanic/Latino; 8 Two or more races, non-Hispanic/Latino), 50 international. Average age 32. 442 applicants, 70% accepted, 226 enrolled. In 2016, 246 master's, 6 doctorates awarded. *Degree requirements:* For doctorate, comprehensive exam, thesis/dissertation. *Entrance requirements:* For master's, GMAT or GRE; for doctorate, GMAT. Additional exam requirements/recommendations for international students: Required—TOEFL (minimum score 600 paper-based; 100 iBT), IELTS (minimum score 7). *Application deadline:* For fall admission, 11/1 priority date for domestic students, 3/1 priority date for international students; for spring admission, 11/1 for domestic and international students. Applications are processed on a rolling basis. Application fee: $55 ($65 for international students). Electronic applications accepted. *Expenses:* Contact institution. *Financial support:* In 2016–17, 53 students received support, including 53 fellowships with partial tuition reimbursements available (averaging $8,600 per year); scholarships/grants and unspecified assistantships also available. Financial award application deadline: 2/1; financial award applicants required to submit FAFSA. *Faculty research:* Corporate finance, strategy services, consumer behavior, financial disclosures, operations. *Unit head:* Kristina Diekmann, Department Chair, 801-581-8524, Fax: 801-581-3380, E-mail: mastersinfo@business.utah.edu. *Application contact:* Christine Harris, Coordinator, 801-581-7785, Fax: 801-585-3962, E-mail: execch@business.utah.edu.
Website: http://www.business.utah.edu/

University of Virginia, McIntire School of Commerce, Master's Program in Commerce, Charlottesville, VA 22903. Offers business analytics (MSC); finance (MSC); marketing and management (MSC). *Entrance requirements:* For master's, GMAT, 2 letters of recommendation, prerequisite course work in financial accounting, microeconomics, and introduction to statistics. Additional exam requirements/recommendations for international students: Required—TOEFL (minimum score 600 paper-based; 100 iBT), IELTS (minimum score 7.5). Electronic applications accepted. *Expenses:* Contact institution.

Marketing

The University of Western Ontario, Richard Ivey School of Business, London, ON N6A 3K7, Canada. Offers business (EMBA, PhD); corporate strategy and leadership elective (MBA); entrepreneurship elective (MBA); finance elective (MBA); health sector stream (MBA); international management elective (MBA); marketing elective (MBA); JD/MBA. *Degree requirements:* For master's, thesis (for some programs); for doctorate, thesis/dissertation. *Entrance requirements:* For master's, GMAT, 2 years of full-time work experience, interview. Additional exam requirements/recommendations for international students: Required—TOEFL (minimum score 100 iBT) or IELTS (minimum score 6). Electronic applications accepted. *Faculty research:* Strategy, organizational behavior, international business, finance, operations management.

University of Wisconsin–Madison, Graduate School, Wisconsin School of Business, Doctoral Program in Marketing, Madison, WI 53706-1380. Offers PhD. *Degree requirements:* For doctorate, comprehensive exam, thesis/dissertation. *Entrance requirements:* For doctorate, GMAT or GRE. Additional exam requirements/recommendations for international students: Recommended—TOEFL (minimum score 623 paper-based; 106 iBT), IELTS (minimum score 7.5), TSE (minimum score 73). Electronic applications accepted. *Expenses:* Contact institution. *Faculty research:* Marketing strategy, consumer behavior, channels of distribution, advertising, price promotions, behavioral and experimental economics, creativity and design, extensions of research involving the sense of touch, ethics.

University of Wisconsin–Whitewater, School of Graduate Studies, College of Business and Economics, Program in Business and Marketing Education, Whitewater, WI 53190-1790. Offers MS. *Accreditation:* NCATE. *Program availability:* Part-time, evening/weekend, online learning. *Degree requirements:* For master's, thesis or alternative. *Entrance requirements:* For master's, interview, teaching license. Additional exam requirements/recommendations for international students: Required—TOEFL (minimum score 550 paper-based; 80 iBT), IELTS (minimum score 6). Electronic applications accepted.

Ursuline College, School of Graduate Studies, Program in Business Administration, Pepper Pike, OH 44124-4398. Offers ethical and entrepreneurial leadership (MBA); financial planning and accounting (MBA); health services management (MBA); management (MBA); management and leadership (MBA); marketing and communications management (MBA). *Program availability:* Part-time. *Faculty:* 2 full-time (both women), 1 (woman) part-time/adjunct. *Students:* 27 full-time (25 women), 9 part-time (all women); includes 15 minority (14 Black or African American, non-Hispanic/Latino; 1 Hispanic/Latino), 2 international. Average age 38. 31 applicants, 71% accepted, 18 enrolled. In 2016, 34 master's awarded. *Degree requirements:* For master's, comprehensive exam (for some programs). *Entrance requirements:* For master's, GRE. Additional exam requirements/recommendations for international students: Required—TOEFL (minimum score 500 paper-based) or GRE. Application fee: $25. Electronic applications accepted. *Expenses:* Contact institution. *Financial support:* In 2016–17, 6 students received support. Scholarships/grants available. Financial award applicants required to submit FAFSA. *Faculty research:* Gift economy; sharing economy; cooperative business models; collaborative leadership; corporate social responsibility and the triple bottom line, defined as the three P's: people, planet and profit. *Unit head:* Dr. Nurete Brenner, Executive Director, 440-684-6038, Fax: 440-684-6088, E-mail: nurete.brenner@ursuline.edu. *Application contact:* Melanie Steele, Director of Graduate Admission, 440-646-8146, Fax: 440-684-6138, E-mail: graduateadmissions@ursuline.edu.

Valparaiso University, Graduate School and Continuing Education, College of Business, Valparaiso, IN 46383. Offers business administration (MBA); business intelligence (Certificate); engineering management (Certificate); entrepreneurship (Certificate); finance (Certificate); general business (Certificate); management (Certificate); marketing (Certificate); sustainability (Certificate); JD/MBA; MSN/MBA. *Accreditation:* AACSB. *Program availability:* Part-time, evening/weekend, online learning. *Entrance requirements:* For master's, GMAT, GRE, minimum GPA of 3.0. Additional exam requirements/recommendations for international students: Required—TOEFL (minimum score 550 paper-based; 80 iBT), IELTS (minimum score 6). Electronic applications accepted. *Expenses:* Contact institution.

Vancouver Island University, Master of Business Administration Program, Nanaimo, BC V9R 5S5, Canada. Offers international business (MBA), including finance, marketing. Program offered jointly with University of Hertfordshire. *Accreditation:* ACBSP. *Program availability:* Part-time. *Degree requirements:* For master's, thesis. *Entrance requirements:* Additional exam requirements/recommendations for international students: Required—TOEFL (minimum score 88 iBT), IELTS (minimum score 6.5). Electronic applications accepted. *Expenses:* Contact institution. *Faculty research:* Tourism development, entrepreneurship, organizational development, strategic planning, international business strategy, intercultural team work.

Vanderbilt University, Vanderbilt University Owen Graduate School of Management, Master of Marketing Program, Nashville, TN 37240-1001. Offers M Mark. *Entrance requirements:* For master's, GMAT, resume, two essays, two letters of recommendation, interview. Additional exam requirements/recommendations for international students: Required—TOEFL or IELTS. Electronic applications accepted. *Expenses: Tuition:* Part-time $1854 per credit hour.

Vanderbilt University, Vanderbilt University Owen Graduate School of Management, Vanderbilt MBA Program, Nashville, TN 37203. Offers accounting (MBA); finance (MBA); general management (MBA); health care (MBA); human and organizational performance (MBA); marketing (MBA); operations (MBA); strategy (MBA); MBA/JD; MBA/M Div; MBA/MD; MBA/MSN; MBA/MTS; MBA/PhD. *Accreditation:* AACSB. *Degree requirements:* For master's, 62 credit hours of coursework; completion of ethics course; minimum GPA of 3.0. *Entrance requirements:* For master's, GMAT (preferred) or GRE, 2 years of work experience (recommended). Additional exam requirements/recommendations for international students: Required—TOEFL (minimum score 100 iBT). Electronic applications accepted. *Expenses:* Contact institution. *Faculty research:* Accounting and finance, business strategy and economics, marketing, operations management, organization studies.

Villanova University, Villanova School of Business, MBA - The Fast Track Program, Villanova, PA 19085. Offers analytics (MBA); cybersecurity (MBA); finance (MBA); healthcare (MBA); international business (MBA); management information systems (MBA); marketing (MBA); real estate (MBA); strategic management (MBA); sustainability (MBA). *Accreditation:* AACSB. *Program availability:* Part-time, evening/weekend. *Faculty:* 108 full-time (39 women), 32 part-time/adjunct (8 women). *Students:* 127 part-time (58 women); includes 18 minority (3 Black or African American, non-Hispanic/Latino; 7 Asian, non-Hispanic/Latino; 6 Hispanic/Latino; 2 Two or more races, non-Hispanic/Latino), 2 international. Average age 30. 88 applicants, 90% accepted, 66 enrolled. In 2016, 75 master's awarded. *Degree requirements:* For master's, minimum GPA of 3.0. *Entrance requirements:* For master's, GMAT or GRE, work experience, 2 letters of recommendation, 2 essays, resume, official transcripts, interview. Additional exam requirements/recommendations for international students: Required—TOEFL (minimum score 550 paper-based; 100 iBT). *Application deadline:* For fall admission, 6/30 for domestic and international students. Application fee: $65. Electronic applications accepted. *Expenses:* Contact institution. *Financial support:* Scholarships/grants available. Financial award application deadline: 6/30; financial award applicants required to submit FAFSA. *Faculty research:* Business analytics; creativity, innovation and entrepreneurship; global leadership; real estate; church management; business ethics; marketing and consumer insights. *Unit head:* Michael L. Capella, Associate Dean of Graduate and Executive Business Programs, 610-519-4336, Fax: 610-519-6273, E-mail: michael.l.capella@villanova.edu. *Application contact:* Kimberly Kane, Manager of Admissions, 610-519-3701, Fax: 610-519-6273, E-mail: kimberly.kane@villanova.edu.
Website: http://www1.villanova.edu/villanova/business/graduate/mba.html

Villanova University, Villanova School of Business, MBA - The Flex Track Program, Villanova, PA 19085. Offers analytics (MBA); finance (MBA); healthcare (MBA); international business (MBA); marketing (MBA); real estate (MBA); strategic management (MBA); JD/MBA. *Accreditation:* AACSB. *Program availability:* Part-time, evening/weekend, online learning. *Faculty:* 108 full-time (39 women), 32 part-time/adjunct (8 women). *Students:* 13 full-time (5 women), 399 part-time (134 women); includes 73 minority (21 Black or African American, non-Hispanic/Latino; 32 Asian, non-Hispanic/Latino; 19 Hispanic/Latino; 1 Two or more races, non-Hispanic/Latino), 11 international. Average age 31. 93 applicants, 94% accepted, 80 enrolled. In 2016, 133 master's awarded. *Degree requirements:* For master's, minimum GPA of 3.0. *Entrance requirements:* For master's, GMAT or GRE, work experience, 2 letters of recommendation, 2 essays, resume, official transcript. Additional exam requirements/recommendations for international students: Required—TOEFL (minimum score 550 paper-based; 100 iBT). *Application deadline:* For fall admission, 6/30 for domestic and international students; for spring admission, 11/15 for domestic and international students; for summer admission, 3/31 for domestic and international students. Applications are processed on a rolling basis. Application fee: $65. Electronic applications accepted. *Expenses:* Contact institution. *Financial support:* In 2016–17, 13 research assistantships with full tuition reimbursements (averaging $13,100 per year) were awarded; scholarships/grants also available. Financial award application deadline: 6/30; financial award applicants required to submit FAFSA. *Faculty research:* Business analytics; creativity, innovation and entrepreneurship; global leadership; real estate; church management; business ethics. *Unit head:* Michael L. Capella, Associate Dean of Graduate and Executive Business Programs, 610-610-4336, Fax: 610-519-6273, E-mail: michael.l.capella@villanova.edu. *Application contact:* Claire Bruno, Director of Recruitment and Enrollment Management, 610-519-4336, Fax: 610-519-6273, E-mail: claire.bruno@villanova.edu.
Website: http://www1.villanova.edu/villanova/business/graduate/mba.html

Virginia International University, School of Business, Fairfax, VA 22030. Offers accounting (MBA, MS); entrepreneurship (MBA); executive management (Graduate Certificate); global logistics (MBA); health care management (MBA); hospitality and tourism management (MBA); human resources management (MBA); international business management (MBA); international finance (MBA); marketing management (MBA); mass media and public relations (MBA); project management (MBA, MS). *Program availability:* Part-time, online learning. *Entrance requirements:* For master's and Graduate Certificate, bachelor's degree. Additional exam requirements/recommendations for international students: Required—TOEFL (minimum score 550 paper-based; 80 iBT), IELTS (minimum score 6). Electronic applications accepted.

Wagner College, Division of Graduate Studies, Department of Business Administration, Staten Island, NY 10301-4495. Offers accounting (MS); business administration (MBA); finance (MBA); health care administration (MBA); international business (MBA); management (Exec MBA); marketing (MBA). *Accreditation:* ACBSP. *Program availability:* Part-time, evening/weekend. *Faculty:* 8 full-time (3 women), 17 part-time/adjunct (5 women). *Students:* 90 full-time (25 women), 16 part-time (8 women); includes 21 minority (12 Black or African American, non-Hispanic/Latino; 1 American Indian or Alaska Native, non-Hispanic/Latino; 3 Asian, non-Hispanic/Latino; 5 Hispanic/Latino), 5 international. Average age 26. 88 applicants, 85% accepted, 62 enrolled. In 2016, 72 master's awarded. *Degree requirements:* For master's, thesis optional. *Entrance requirements:* For master's, minimum GPA of 2.75, proficiency in computers and math. Additional exam requirements/recommendations for international students: Required—TOEFL (minimum score 550 paper-based; 79 iBT). *Application deadline:* For fall admission, 5/1 priority date for domestic students, 3/1 priority date for international students; for spring admission, 12/1 for domestic students, 11/1 for international students. Applications are processed on a rolling basis. Application fee: $50. Tuition and fees vary according to degree level. *Financial support:* In 2016–17, 93 students received support. Career-related internships or fieldwork, unspecified assistantships, and alumni fellowship grants available. Financial award application deadline: 4/1; financial award applicants required to submit FAFSA. *Unit head:* Dr. Donald Crooks, Director, 718-390-3429, Fax: 718-390-3429, E-mail: dcrooks@wagner.edu. *Application contact:* Patricia Clancy, Assistant Director for Enrollment, 718-420-4464, Fax: 718-390-3105, E-mail: patricia.clancy@wagner.edu.

Walden University, Graduate Programs, School of Management, Minneapolis, MN 55401. Offers accounting (MBA, MS, DBA), including accounting for the professional (MS), accounting with CPA emphasis (MS), self-designed (MS); advanced project management (Graduate Certificate); applied project management (Graduate Certificate); auditing (Graduate Certificate); bridge to business administration (Post-Doctoral Certificate); bridge to management (Post-Doctoral Certificate); business management (Graduate Certificate); communication (MBA); corporate finance (MBA); digital marketing (Graduate Certificate); entrepreneurship (DBA); entrepreneurship and small business (MBA); finance (MS, DBA), including finance for the professional (MS), finance with CFA/investment (MS), finance with CPA emphasis (MS); global supply chain management (DBA); healthcare management (MBA, DBA); human resource management (MBA, MS, Graduate Certificate), including functional human resource management (MS), general program (MS), integrating functional and strategic human resource management (MS), organizational strategy (MS); human resources management (DBA); information systems management (DBA); international business (MBA, DBA); leadership (MBA, MS, DBA, Graduate Certificate), including general program (MS), human resource leadership (MS), leader development (MS), self-designed (MS); management (MS, PhD), including communications (MS), finance (PhD), general program (MS), healthcare management (MS), human resource management (MS), human resources management (PhD), information systems management (PhD), international business (MS), leadership (MS), leadership and organizational change (PhD), marketing (MS), project management (MS), strategy and operations (MS); managerial accounting (Graduate Certificate); marketing (MBA, MS, DBA); project management (MBA, MS, DBA); self-designed (MBA, DBA); social impact management (DBA); technology entrepreneurship (DBA). *Accreditation:* ACBSP. *Program availability:* Part-time, evening/weekend, online only, 100% online. *Degree requirements:* For master's, thesis (for some programs), residency (for EMBA); for doctorate, thesis/dissertation (for some programs), residency. *Entrance requirements:* For master's, bachelor's degree or higher; minimum GPA of 2.5; official transcripts; goal statement (for some programs); access to computer and Internet; for doctorate, master's degree or higher; three years of related professional or academic experience (preferred); minimum GPA of 3.0; goal statement and current resume (for select programs); official transcripts; access to computer and Internet; for other advanced degree, relevant work experience; access to computer and Internet. Additional exam requirements/recommendations for international students: Required—TOEFL (minimum score 550 paper-based, 79 iBT), IELTS (minimum score 6.5), Michigan English Language Assessment Battery (minimum score 82), or PTE (minimum score 53). Electronic applications accepted.

Walsh College of Accountancy and Business Administration, Graduate Programs, Program in Marketing, Troy, MI 48083. Offers MS. *Program availability:* Part-time, evening/weekend. *Faculty:* 7 full-time (4 women), 6 part-time/adjunct (4 women). *Students:* 33 (22 women); includes 10 minority (8 Black or African American, non-Hispanic/Latino; 1 Asian, non-Hispanic/Latino; 1 Hispanic/Latino), 1 international. Average age 31. 20 applicants, 75% accepted, 9 enrolled. In 2016, 1 master's awarded. *Degree requirements:* For master's, internship or project. *Entrance requirements:* For master's, minimum overall cumulative GPA of 2.75 from all colleges previously attended. Additional exam requirements/recommendations for international students: Required—TOEFL (minimum score 550 paper-based, 79 iBT), IELTS (6.5), Michigan English Language Assessment Battery, or MTELP. *Application deadline:* Applications are processed on a rolling basis. Application fee: $35. Electronic applications accepted. *Expenses:* $740 per credit hour, $125 registration fee per semester. *Financial support:* In 2016–17, 2 students received support. Career-related internships or fieldwork and scholarships/grants available. Financial award application deadline: 6/30; financial award applicants required to submit FAFSA. *Faculty research:* Consumer behavior, advertising research, brand management, innovation and strategy, philanthropic initiatives within a value proposition. *Unit head:* Dr. Michael Levens, Chair, Marketing, 248-823-1635, Fax: 248-689-0920, E-mail: mlevens@walshcollege.edu. *Application contact:* Heather Rigby, Director, Admissions and Academic Advising, 248-823-1610, Fax: 248-689-0938, E-mail: hrigby@walshcollege.edu.
Website: http://www.walshcollege.edu/MSMKT

Walsh University, Graduate Programs, MBA Program, North Canton, OH 44720-3396. Offers healthcare management (MBA); management (MBA); marketing (MBA). *Program availability:* Part-time, evening/weekend, online only, 100% online. *Faculty:* 10 full-time (4 women), 22 part-time/adjunct (5 women). *Students:* 37 full-time (14 women), 137 part-time (84 women); includes 21 minority (17 Black or African American, non-Hispanic/Latino; 1 Asian, non-Hispanic/Latino; 2 Hispanic/Latino; 1 Two or more races, non-Hispanic/Latino), 7 international. Average age 35. 66 applicants, 76% accepted, 34 enrolled. In 2016, 66 master's awarded. *Degree requirements:* For master's, capstone course in strategic management. *Entrance requirements:* For master's, GMAT (minimum score of 490), minimum GPA of 3.0. Additional exam requirements/recommendations for international students: Required—TOEFL (minimum score 500 paper-based; 61 iBT). *Application deadline:* For fall admission, 7/15 priority date for domestic students. Applications are processed on a rolling basis. Application fee: $25. Electronic applications accepted. Application fee is waived when completed online. *Expenses:* $665 per credit hour. *Financial support:* In 2016–17, 6 students received support, including 6 research assistantships with partial tuition reimbursements available (averaging $7,395 per year); teaching assistantships and tuition discounts also available. Financial award application deadline: 12/31; financial award applicants required to submit FAFSA. *Faculty research:* Medical tourism, familial influence in financial fitness, pedagogy in finance courses, sociocultural aspects of women entrepreneurs, patient satisfaction. *Unit head:* Dr. Michael Petrochuk, Director of the MBA Program/Associate Professor of Marketing and Healthcare Management, 330-244-4764, Fax: 330-490-7359, E-mail: mpetrochuk@walsh.edu. *Application contact:* Audra Dice, Graduate and Transfer Admissions Counselor, 330-490-7181, Fax: 330-244-4925, E-mail: adice@walsh.edu.
Website: http://www.walsh.edu/mba-program

Webster University, George Herbert Walker School of Business and Technology, Department of Business, St. Louis, MO 63119-3194. Offers business and organizational security management (MBA); decision support systems (MBA); environmental management (MBA); finance (MBA, MS); forensic accounting (MS); gerontology (MBA); human resources development (MBA); human resources management (MBA); information technology management (MBA); international business (MA, MBA); international relations (MBA); management and leadership (MBA); marketing (MBA); media communications (MBA); procurement and acquisitions management (MBA); Web services (MBA). *Accreditation:* ACBSP. *Program availability:* Part-time, evening/weekend, online learning. *Degree requirements:* For master's, comprehensive exam (for some programs), thesis (for some programs). *Entrance requirements:* Additional exam requirements/recommendations for international students: Required—TOEFL. *Application deadline:* Applications are processed on a rolling basis. Application fee: $35 ($50 for international students). *Expenses: Tuition:* Full-time $21,900; part-time $730 per credit hour. Tuition and fees vary according to campus/location and program. *Financial support:* Federal Work-Study available. Support available to part-time students. Financial award application deadline: 4/1; financial award applicants required to submit FAFSA. *Unit head:* David Porras, Chair, 314-246-8621, E-mail: porrasd@webster.edu. *Application contact:* Sarah Nandor, Director, Graduate and Transfer Admissions, 314-968-7109, E-mail: gadmit@webster.edu.

Webster University, George Herbert Walker School of Business and Technology, Department of Management, St. Louis, MO 63119-3194. Offers business and organizational security management (MA); digital marketing management (Graduate Certificate); government contracting (Graduate Certificate); health administration (MHA); health care management (MA); health services management (MA); human resources development (MA); human resources management (MA); information technology management (MA, MS); management (D Mgt); management and leadership (MA); marketing (MA); nonprofit leadership (MA); nonprofit revenue development (Graduate Certificate); organizational development (Graduate Certificate); procurement and acquisitions management (MA); public administration (MPA); space systems operations management (MS). *Program availability:* Part-time, evening/weekend, online learning. *Degree requirements:* For master's, thesis (for some programs); for doctorate, thesis/dissertation, written exam. *Entrance requirements:* For doctorate, GMAT, 3 years of work experience, MBA. Additional exam requirements/recommendations for international students: Required—TOEFL. *Application deadline:* Applications are processed on a rolling basis. Application fee: $25 ($50 for international students). *Expenses: Tuition:* Full-time $21,900; part-time $730 per credit hour. Tuition and fees vary according to campus/location and program. *Financial support:* Federal Work-Study available. Support available to part-time students. Financial award application deadline: 4/1; financial award applicants required to submit FAFSA. *Unit head:* Barrett Baebler, Chair, 314-246-7940, E-mail: baeblerb@webster.edu. *Application contact:* Sarah Nandor, Director, Graduate and Transfer Admissions, 314-968-7109, E-mail: gadmit@webster.edu.

West Virginia University, Reed College of Media, Program in Integrated Marketing Communications, Morgantown, WV 26501. Offers MS, Graduate Certificate. *Program availability:* Part-time, online learning. *Entrance requirements:* For master's, GRE or GMAT (waived with minimum undergraduate GPA of 3.3 or at least 6 years of related professional experience), undergraduate transcript, resume; letters of recommendation (strongly recommended). Additional exam requirements/recommendations for international students: Required—TOEFL.

Wilfrid Laurier University, Faculty of Graduate and Postdoctoral Studies, School of Business and Economics, Department of Business, Waterloo, ON N2L 3C5, Canada. Offers accounting (PhD); finance (M Fin); financial economics (PhD); marketing (PhD); operations and supply chain management (PhD); organizational behavior and human resource management (M Sc); organizational behaviour and human resource management (PhD); supply chain management (M Sc); technology management (EMTM). *Accreditation:* AACSB. *Program availability:* Part-time, evening/weekend. *Degree requirements:* For master's, thesis optional; for doctorate, comprehensive exam, thesis/dissertation. *Entrance requirements:* For master's, GMAT, 4-year honors degree with minimum B+ average; for doctorate, GMAT, master's degree, minimum B+ average. Additional exam requirements/recommendations for international students: Required—TOEFL (minimum score 89 iBT). Electronic applications accepted. *Faculty research:* Financial economics, management and organizational behavior, operations and supply chain management.

William Woods University, Graduate and Adult Studies, Fulton, MO 65251-1098. Offers administration (M Ed, Ed S); athletic/activities administration (M Ed); curriculum and instruction (M Ed, Ed S); educational leadership (Ed D); equestrian education (M Ed); health management (MBA); human resources (MBA); leadership (MBA); marketing, advertising, and public relations (MBA); teaching and technology (M Ed). *Program availability:* Part-time, evening/weekend. *Degree requirements:* For master's, capstone course (MBA), action research (M Ed); for Ed S, field experience. *Entrance requirements:* Additional exam requirements/recommendations for international students: Required—TOEFL (minimum score 550 paper-based). Electronic applications accepted. *Expenses:* Contact institution.

Wilmington University, College of Business, New Castle, DE 19720-6491. Offers accounting (MBA, MS); business administration (MBA, DBA); environmental stewardship (MBA); finance (MBA); health care administration (MBA, MSM); homeland security (MBA, MSM); human resource management (MSM); management information systems (MBA, MSN); marketing (MSM); marketing management (MBA); military leadership (MSM); organizational leadership (MBA, MSM); public administration (MSM). *Program availability:* Part-time, evening/weekend. *Faculty:* 17 full-time (7 women), 106 part-time/adjunct (46 women). *Students:* 436 full-time (237 women), 1,202 part-time (739 women); includes 594 minority (474 Black or African American, non-Hispanic/Latino; 19 American Indian or Alaska Native, non-Hispanic/Latino; 64 Asian, non-Hispanic/Latino; 30 Hispanic/Latino; 3 Native Hawaiian or other Pacific Islander, non-Hispanic/Latino; 4 Two or more races, non-Hispanic/Latino), 153 international. Average age 35. 814 applicants, 98% accepted, 426 enrolled. In 2016, 594 master's, 23 doctorates awarded. *Entrance requirements:* Additional exam requirements/recommendations for international students: Required—TOEFL (minimum score 500 paper-based). *Application deadline:* Applications are processed on a rolling basis. Application fee: $35. Electronic applications accepted. *Expenses: Tuition:* Full-time $8388; part-time $466 per credit. *Required fees:* $25 per semester. Tuition and fees vary according to degree level. *Financial support:* Applicants required to submit FAFSA. *Unit head:* Dr. Robert W. Rescigno, Dean. *Application contact:* Laura Morris, Director of Admissions, 877-967-5456, E-mail: infocenter@wilmu.edu.
Website: http://www.wilmu.edu/business/

Wingate University, Porter B. Byrum School of Business, Wingate, NC 28174. Offers accounting (MAC); corporate innovation (MBA); finance (MBA); general management (MBA); healthcare management (MBA); marketing (MBA); project management (MBA). *Accreditation:* ACBSP. *Program availability:* Part-time, evening/weekend. *Entrance requirements:* For master's, GMAT, work experience, 2 letters of recommendation. *Application deadline:* For fall admission, 8/15 priority date for domestic students; for spring admission, 12/15 priority date for domestic students. Applications are processed on a rolling basis. Application fee: $50. Electronic applications accepted. *Expenses:* Contact institution. *Financial support:* Federal Work-Study and scholarships/grants available. Support available to part-time students. Financial award application deadline: 8/1; financial award applicants required to submit FAFSA. *Faculty research:* Stochastic processes, business ethics, regional economic development, municipal finance, consumer behavior. *Unit head:* Dr. Peter Frank, Dean, 704-233-8148, Fax: 704-233-8146, E-mail: pfrank@wingate.edu. *Application contact:* Mary Maye, Administrative Assistant to the Dean, 704-233-8148, Fax: 704-233-8146.
Website: http://www.wingate.edu/academics/school-of-business

Worcester Polytechnic Institute, Graduate Studies and Research, Foisie Business School, Worcester, MA 01609-2280. Offers information technology (MS), including information security management; management (Graduate Certificate); marketing and technological innovation (MS); operations design and leadership (MS); technology (MBA, MS). *Accreditation:* AACSB. *Program availability:* Part-time, evening/weekend, 100% online, blended/hybrid learning. *Faculty:* 20 full-time (12 women), 16 part-time/adjunct (1 woman). *Students:* 237 full-time (139 women), 186 part-time (67 women); includes 35 minority (4 Black or African American, non-Hispanic/Latino; 17 Asian, non-Hispanic/Latino; 12 Hispanic/Latino; 2 Two or more races, non-Hispanic/Latino), 221 international. 645 applicants, 62% accepted, 144 enrolled. In 2016, 150 master's awarded. *Degree requirements:* For master's, thesis optional. *Entrance requirements:* For master's, GMAT (MBA); GMAT or GRE General Test (MS), statement of purpose, 3 letters of recommendation, resume; for Graduate Certificate, GMAT or GRE General Test, statement of purpose, 3 letters of recommendation. Additional exam requirements/recommendations for international students: Required—TOEFL (minimum score 563 paper-based; 84 iBT), IELTS (minimum score 7). *Application deadline:* For fall admission, 6/1 priority date for domestic and international students; for spring admission, 11/1 priority date for domestic students, 10/1 priority date for international students. Applications are processed on a rolling basis. Application fee: $70. Electronic applications accepted. *Financial support:* Career-related internships or fieldwork, institutionally sponsored loans, scholarships/grants, and unspecified assistantships available. Financial award application deadline: 6/1; financial award applicants required to submit FAFSA. *Unit head:* Melissa Terrio, Executive Director, 508-831-4665, Fax: 508-831-4665, E-mail: biz@wpi.edu. *Application contact:* Eileen Dagostino, Recruiting Operations Coordinator, 508-831-4665, Fax: 508-831-5720, E-mail: edag@wpi.edu.
Website: https://www.wpi.edu/academics/business

Xavier University, Williams College of Business, Master of Business Administration Program, Cincinnati, OH 45207. Offers business administration (Exec MBA, MBA); business intelligence (MBA); finance (MBA); health industry (MBA); international business (MBA); marketing (MBA); values-based leadership (MBA); MBA/MHSA; MSN/MBA. *Accreditation:* AACSB. *Program availability:* Part-time, evening/weekend. *Degree requirements:* For master's, capstone course. *Entrance requirements:* For master's, GMAT or GRE, official transcript; resume. Additional exam requirements/recommendations for international students: Required—TOEFL (minimum score 550 paper-based; 79 iBT). Electronic applications accepted. Application fee is waived when completed online. *Expenses:* Contact institution.

Yale University, Yale School of Management and Graduate School of Arts and Sciences, Doctoral Program in Management, New Haven, CT 06520. Offers accounting (PhD); financial economics (PhD); marketing (PhD); organizations and management (PhD). *Accreditation:* AACSB. *Degree requirements:* For doctorate, comprehensive exam, thesis/dissertation. *Entrance requirements:* For doctorate, GMAT or GRE General

Test. Additional exam requirements/recommendations for international students: Required—TOEFL or IELTS. Electronic applications accepted. *Expenses:* Contact institution. *Faculty research:* Pricing of options and futures, term structure of interest rates, use of accounting numbers in debt contracts, product differentiation, e-commerce and marketing, behavioral finance.

Yeshiva University, Sy Syms School of Business, New York, NY 10016. Offers accounting (MS); business (EMBA); marketing (MS). *Program availability:* Part-time. *Entrance requirements:* For master's, minimum GPA of 3.5 or GMAT.

York College of Pennsylvania, Graham School of Business, York, PA 17403-3651. Offers continuous improvement (MBA); financial management (MBA); health care management (MBA); management (MBA); marketing (MBA); self-designed (MBA). *Accreditation:* ACBSP. *Program availability:* Part-time, evening/weekend. *Faculty:* 11 full-time (3 women), 4 part-time/adjunct (1 woman). *Students:* 2 full-time (1 woman), 68 part-time (31 women); includes 7 minority (2 Black or African American, non-Hispanic/Latino; 1 Asian, non-Hispanic/Latino; 1 Hispanic/Latino; 3 Two or more races, non-Hispanic/Latino). Average age 32. 39 applicants, 79% accepted, 20 enrolled. In 2016, 22 master's awarded. *Degree requirements:* For master's, directed study. *Entrance requirements:* For master's, GMAT. Additional exam requirements/recommendations for international students: Required—TOEFL (minimum score 530 paper-based; 72 iBT), IELTS (minimum score 6). *Application deadline:* For fall admission, 7/15 priority date for domestic students, 5/1 for international students; for spring admission, 11/15 priority date for domestic students, 9/1 for international students; for summer admission, 4/15 priority date for domestic students. Applications are processed on a rolling basis. Application fee: $0. Electronic applications accepted. *Expenses:* $795 per credit. *Financial support:* In 2016–17, 3 students received support. Scholarships/grants available. Financial award applicants required to submit FAFSA. *Unit head:* Nicole Cornell Sadowski, MBA Director, 717-815-1491, Fax: 717-600-3999, E-mail: ncornell@ycp.edu. *Application contact:* MBA Office, 717-815-1491, Fax: 717-600-3999, E-mail: mba@ycp.edu.
Website: http://www.ycp.edu/mba

Youngstown State University, Graduate School, Williamson College of Business Administration, Department of Marketing, Youngstown, OH 44555-0001. Offers MBA. *Program availability:* Part-time, evening/weekend. *Degree requirements:* For master's, thesis optional. *Entrance requirements:* For master's, GMAT, minimum GPA of 2.7. Additional exam requirements/recommendations for international students: Required—TOEFL. *Faculty research:* Media, international marketing, advanced marketing simulations, ethics in business.

Marketing Research

Baldwin Wallace University, Graduate Programs, School of Business, Program in Analytics, Berea, OH 44017-2088. Offers MBA. *Program availability:* Part-time, evening/weekend. *Students:* 6 full-time (2 women), 12 part-time (8 women); includes 5 minority (2 Black or African American, non-Hispanic/Latino; 3 Hispanic/Latino), 1 international. Average age 32. 4 applicants, 100% accepted, 3 enrolled. *Entrance requirements:* For master's, GMAT or minimum GPA of 3.0, bachelor's degree in any field, work experience. Additional exam requirements/recommendations for international students: Required—TOEFL (minimum score 550 paper-based; 79 iBT). *Application deadline:* For fall admission, 7/25 for domestic students; for spring admission, 12/15 for domestic students; for summer admission, 4/15 for domestic students. Applications are processed on a rolling basis. Electronic applications accepted. *Expenses:* $921 per credit hour. *Unit head:* Dale Kramer, MBA Program Director, 440-826-3331, Fax: 440-826-3868, E-mail: dkramer@bw.edu. *Application contact:* Laura Spencer, Graduate Application Specialist, 440-826-2191, Fax: 440-826-3868, E-mail: lspencer@bw.edu.
Website: http://www.bw.edu/graduate/business/mba/

Hofstra University, Frank G. Zarb School of Business, Programs in Marketing and International Business, Hempstead, NY 11549. Offers business administration (MBA), including international business, marketing; international business (Advanced Certificate); marketing (MS, Advanced Certificate); marketing research (MS). *Program availability:* Part-time, evening/weekend, blended/hybrid learning. *Students:* 91 full-time (61 women), 28 part-time (14 women); includes 13 minority (1 Black or African American, non-Hispanic/Latino; 8 Asian, non-Hispanic/Latino; 3 Hispanic/Latino; 1 Two or more races, non-Hispanic/Latino), 84 international. Average age 25. 323 applicants, 67% accepted, 49 enrolled. In 2016, 65 master's awarded. *Degree requirements:* For master's, capstone course (for MBA), thesis (for MS), minimum GPA of 3.0. *Entrance requirements:* For master's, GMAT/GRE, 2 letters of recommendation, resume, essay. Additional exam requirements/recommendations for international students: Required—TOEFL (minimum score 550 paper-based; 80 iBT); Recommended—IELTS (minimum score 6). *Application deadline:* Applications are processed on a rolling basis. Application fee: $75. Electronic applications accepted. *Expenses:* $1,170 per credit. *Financial support:* In 2016–17, 30 students received support, including 24 fellowships with full and partial tuition reimbursements available (averaging $4,896 per year); research assistantships with full and partial tuition reimbursements available, career-related internships or fieldwork, Federal Work-Study, institutionally sponsored loans, scholarships/grants, tuition waivers (full and partial), and unspecified assistantships also available. Support available to part-time students. Financial award applicants required to submit FAFSA. *Faculty research:* Cross-cultural consumer behavior; social, digital, global, and strategic issues in marketing; consumer health/well-being; ethnocentrism and animosity. *Unit head:* Dr. Anil Mathur, Chairperson, 516-463-5346, Fax: 516-463-4834, E-mail: anil.mathur@hofstra.edu. *Application contact:* Sunil Samuel, Assistant Vice President of Admissions, 516-463-4723, Fax: 516-463-4664, E-mail: graduateadmission@hofstra.edu.
Website: http://www.hofstra.edu/business/

Instituto Tecnológico y de Estudios Superiores de Monterrey, Campus Irapuato, Graduate Programs, Irapuato, Mexico. Offers administration (MBA); administration of information technology (MAIT); administration of telecommunications (MAT); architecture (M Arch); computer science (MCS); education (M Ed); educational administration (MEA); educational innovation and technology (DEIT); educational technology (MET); electronic commerce (MBA); environmental administration and planning (MEAP); environmental systems (MES); finances (MBA); humanistic studies (MHS); international management for Latin American executives (MIMLAE); library and information science (MLIS); manufacturing quality management (MMQM); marketing research (MBA).

Marquette University, Graduate School of Management, Department of Economics, Milwaukee, WI 53201-1881. Offers business economics (MSAE); financial economics (MSAE); international economics (MSAE); marketing research (MSAE); real estate economics (MSAE). *Program availability:* Part-time, evening/weekend. *Faculty:* 14 full-time (4 women), 2 part-time/adjunct (both women). *Students:* 14 full-time (2 women), 13 part-time (3 women); includes 5 minority (2 Asian, non-Hispanic/Latino; 3 Hispanic/Latino). Average age 26. 27 applicants, 67% accepted, 27 enrolled. In 2016, 17 master's awarded. *Degree requirements:* For master's, comprehensive exam, professional project. *Entrance requirements:* For master's, GMAT or GRE General Test. Additional exam requirements/recommendations for international students: Required—TOEFL, IELTS, PTE. *Application deadline:* For fall admission, 2/15 for domestic and international students. Applications are processed on a rolling basis. Application fee: $50. Electronic applications accepted. *Financial support:* Fellowships, research assistantships, teaching assistantships, Federal Work-Study, institutionally sponsored loans, scholarships/grants, and tuition waivers (full and partial) available. Support available to part-time students. Financial award application deadline: 2/15. *Faculty research:* Monetary and fiscal policy in open economy, housing and regional migration, political economy of taxation and state/local government. *Unit head:* Dr. Brian Till, Dean, 414-288-5724. *Application contact:* Dr. Jeanne Simmons, Associate Dean, 414-288-7145.
Website: http://business.marquette.edu/academics/msae

Michigan State University, The Graduate School, Eli Broad College of Business, Department of Marketing, East Lansing, MI 48224. Offers marketing (PhD); marketing research (MS). *Degree requirements:* For doctorate, comprehensive exam, thesis/dissertation. *Entrance requirements:* For master's, GMAT, bachelor's degree with minimum GPA of 3.0 in last 2 years of undergraduate work; transcripts; 3 letters of recommendation; statement of purpose; resume; working knowledge of computers; basic understanding of accounting, finance, marketing, and the management of people; laptop capable of running Windows software; for doctorate, GMAT (taken within past 5 years), bachelor's degree; letters of recommendation; statement of purpose; previous work experience; personal qualifications of sound character, perseverance, intellectual curiosity, and an interest in scholarly research. Additional exam requirements/recommendations for international students: Required—TOEFL (minimum score 100 iBT), PTE (minimum score 70), IELTS (minimum score 7) accepted for MS only.

Pacific Lutheran University, School of Business, Master of Science in Market Research Program, Tacoma, WA 98447. Offers MS. *Entrance requirements:* For master's, GRE or GMAT, two references, official transcripts, resume, statement of professional goals and quantitative skills. Additional exam requirements/recommendations for international students: Required—TOEFL (minimum score 88 iBT) or IELTS (minimum score 6.5).

Saint Leo University, Graduate Business Studies, Saint Leo, FL 33574-6665. Offers accounting (M Acc, MBA, Certificate); cybersecurity (MS); health care management (MBA, Certificate); human resource management (MBA, Certificate); information security management (MBA, Certificate); management (MBA, DBA); marketing (MBA, Certificate); marketing research and social media analytics (MBA, Certificate); project management (MBA, Certificate); sport business (MBA); supply chain global integration management (MBA, Certificate). *Accreditation:* ACBSP. *Program availability:* Part-time, evening/weekend, 100% online, blended/hybrid learning. *Faculty:* 53 full-time (18 women), 53 part-time/adjunct (19 women). *Students:* 8 full-time (4 women), 2,001 part-time (1,160 women); includes 928 minority (650 Black or African American, non-Hispanic/Latino; 5 American Indian or Alaska Native, non-Hispanic/Latino; 43 Asian, non-Hispanic/Latino; 193 Hispanic/Latino; 2 Native Hawaiian or other Pacific Islander, non-Hispanic/Latino; 35 Two or more races, non-Hispanic/Latino), 51 international. Average age 37. 922 applicants, 85% accepted, 517 enrolled. In 2016, 874 master's, 17 other advanced degrees awarded. *Degree requirements:* For doctorate, comprehensive exam, thesis/dissertation. *Entrance requirements:* For master's, GMAT (minimum score 500), official transcripts, current resume, 2 professional recommendations, personal statement, bachelor's degree from regionally-accredited university; undergraduate degree in accounting and minimum undergraduate GPA of 3.0 (for M Acc); minimum undergraduate GPA of 3.0 in final 2 years of undergraduate study and 2 years' work experience (for MBA); for doctorate, GMAT (minimum score of 550) if master's GPA is under 3.25, official transcripts, current resume, 2 professional recommendations, personal statement, master's degree from regionally-accredited university with minimum GPA of 3.25, 3 years' work experience, interview. Additional exam requirements/recommendations for international students: Required—TOEFL (minimum score 550 paper-based; 80 iBT). *Application deadline:* For fall admission, 7/1 priority date for domestic and international students; for spring admission, 11/12 priority date for domestic students, 11/1 for international students. Applications are processed on a rolling basis. Application fee: $80. Electronic applications accepted. *Expenses:* Contact institution. *Financial support:* In 2016–17, 118 students received support. Career-related internships or fieldwork, scholarships/grants, and health care benefits available. Financial award application deadline: 3/1; financial award applicants required to submit FAFSA. *Unit head:* Dr. Lorrie McGovern, Associate Dean, School of Business, 352-588-7869, Fax: 352-588-8912, E-mail: mbaslu@saintleo.edu. *Application contact:* Jennifer Shelley, Senior Associate Director of Graduate Admissions, 800-707-8846, Fax: 352-588-7873, E-mail: grad.admissions@saintleo.edu.
Website: http://www.saintleo.edu/academics/graduate.aspx

Southern Illinois University Edwardsville, Graduate School, School of Business, Department of Management and Marketing, Edwardsville, IL 62026. Offers marketing research (MMR). *Program availability:* Part-time, evening/weekend. *Degree requirements:* For master's, comprehensive exam, final exam. *Entrance requirements:* For master's, GMAT. Additional exam requirements/recommendations for international students: Required—TOEFL (minimum score 550 paper-based; 79 iBT), IELTS (minimum score 6.5). Electronic applications accepted.

Towson University, Program in Marketing Intelligence, Towson, MD 21252-0001. Offers MS. *Students:* 11 full-time (7 women), 18 part-time (12 women); includes 9 minority (5 Black or African American, non-Hispanic/Latino; 2 Asian, non-Hispanic/Latino; 1 Hispanic/Latino; 1 Two or more races, non-Hispanic/Latino), 9 international. *Expenses:* Tuition, state resident: full-time $7580; part-time $379 per unit. Tuition, nonresident: full-time $15,700; part-time $785 per unit. *Required fees:* $2480. *Unit head:* Dr. Philippe Duverger, Director, 410-704-3538, E-mail: pduverger@towson.edu. *Application contact:* Coverley Beidleman, Assistant Director of Graduate Admissions, 410-704-2113, Fax: 410-704-3030, E-mail: grads@towson.edu.
Website: http://www.towson.edu/cbe/departments/marketing/grad/

Universidad Autonoma de Guadalajara, Graduate Programs, Guadalajara, Mexico. Offers administrative law and justice (LL M); advertising and corporate communications (MA); architecture (M Arch); business (MBA); computational science (MCC); education (Ed M, Ed D); English-Spanish translation (MA); entrepreneurship and management (MBA); integrated management of digital animation (MA); international business (MIB); international corporate law (LL M); internet technologies (MS); manufacturing systems (MMS); occupational health (MS); philosophy (MA, PhD); power electronics (MS); quality systems (MQS); renewable energy (MS); social evaluation of projects (MBA); strategic market research (MBA); tax law (MA); teaching mathematics (MA).

Universidad de las Americas, A.C., Program in Business Administration, Mexico City, Mexico. Offers finance (MBA); marketing research (MBA); production and quality (MBA).

University of Colorado Denver, Business School, Program in Marketing, Denver, CO 80217. Offers brand management and marketing communication (MS); global marketing (MS); high-tech and entrepreneurial marketing (MS); marketing for sustainability (MS); marketing research (MS); sports and entertainment marketing (MS). *Program availability:* Part-time, evening/weekend. *Students:* 30 full-time (19 women), 7 part-time (5 women); includes 5 minority (2 Black or African American, non-Hispanic/Latino; 1 Asian, non-Hispanic/Latino; 2 Hispanic/Latino), 12 international. Average age 28. 47 applicants, 62% accepted, 13 enrolled. In 2016, 23 master's awarded. *Degree requirements:* For master's, 30 semester hours (21 of marketing core courses, 9 of marketing electives). *Entrance requirements:* For master's, GMAT, resume, essay, two letters of recommendation, financial statements (for international applicants). Additional exam requirements/recommendations for international students: Required—TOEFL (minimum score 525 paper-based; 71 iBT); Recommended—IELTS (minimum score 6.5). *Application deadline:* For fall admission, 4/15 priority date for domestic students, 3/15 priority date for international students; for spring admission, 10/15 priority date for domestic students, 9/15 priority date for international students; for summer admission, 2/15 priority date for domestic students, 1/15 priority date for international students. Applications are processed on a rolling basis. Application fee: $50 ($75 for international students). Electronic applications accepted. *Expenses:* Contact institution. *Financial support:* In 2016–17, 7 students received support. Fellowships, research assistantships, teaching assistantships, Federal Work-Study, institutionally sponsored loans, scholarships/grants, and traineeships available. Financial award application deadline: 4/1; financial award applicants required to submit FAFSA. *Faculty research:* Marketing issues in the Chinese environment, impact of individual difference and contextual factors on the risk-taking behaviors of managers making new-business creation decisions, attribution theory perspective of conflict between marketers and engineers, organizational identity and identification, international market entry strategies. *Unit head:* Vicki Lane, Director of Marketing Program, 303-315-8468, E-mail: vicki.lane@ucdenver.edu. *Application contact:* 303-315-8200, E-mail: bschool.admissions@ucdenver.edu.
Website: http://www.ucdenver.edu/academics/colleges/business/degrees/ms/marketing/Pages/Marketing.aspx

University of Rochester, Simon Business School, Master of Science Program in Marketing Analytics, Rochester, NY 14627. Offers MS. *Faculty:* 66 full-time (13 women), 22 part-time/adjunct (2 women). *Students:* 61 full-time (46 women); includes 1 minority (Asian, non-Hispanic/Latino), 59 international. Average age 23. 564 applicants, 29% accepted, 62 enrolled. In 2016, 38 master's awarded. *Entrance requirements:* For master's, GMAT/GRE. Additional exam requirements/recommendations for international students: Required—TOEFL. *Application deadline:* For fall admission, 10/15 for domestic and international students; for winter admission, 1/5 for domestic and international students; for spring admission, 3/15 for domestic and international students; for summer admission, 5/15 for domestic and international students. Applications are processed on a rolling basis. Application fee: $150. Electronic applications accepted. *Expenses:* Contact institution. *Financial support:* In 2016–17, 38 students received support. Tuition waivers (partial) available. Financial award application deadline: 1/5; financial award applicants required to submit FAFSA. *Unit head:* Andrew Ainslie, Dean, 585-275-3316, E-mail: andrew.ainslie@simon.rochester.edu. *Application contact:* Rebekah S. Lewin, Assistant Dean for Admissions and Financial Aid, 585-275-3533, E-mail: admissions@simon.rochester.edu.
Website: http://www.simon.rochester.edu/programs/full-time-ms-in-marketing-analytics/

The University of Texas at Arlington, Graduate School, College of Business, Department of Marketing, Arlington, TX 76019. Offers marketing (MBA); marketing research (MS). *Program availability:* Part-time, evening/weekend. *Degree requirements:* For master's, thesis optional. *Entrance requirements:* For master's, GMAT, GRE. Additional exam requirements/recommendations for international students: Required—TOEFL (minimum score 550 paper-based; 79 iBT). *Application deadline:* For fall admission, 6/1 for domestic students, 4/1 for international students; for spring admission, 10/15 for domestic students, 9/15 for international students. Applications are processed on a rolling basis. Application fee: $40 ($70 for international students). Electronic applications accepted. *Financial support:* Teaching assistantships, career-related internships or fieldwork, scholarships/grants, and unspecified assistantships available. Support available to part-time students. Financial award application deadline: 6/1; financial award applicants required to submit FAFSA. *Faculty research:* Marketing strategy, marketing research, international marketing. *Unit head:* Dr. Greg Frazier, Interim Chair, 817-272-0264, Fax: 817-272-2854, E-mail: frazier@uta.edu. *Application contact:* Dr. Robert Rogers, MS Program Director, 817-272-2340, Fax: 817-272-2854, E-mail: msmr@uta.edu.
Website: http://wweb.uta.edu/marketing/

University of Wisconsin–Madison, Graduate School, Wisconsin School of Business, Wisconsin Full-Time MBA Program, Madison, WI 53706. Offers applied security analysis (MBA); arts administration (MBA); brand and product management (MBA); corporate finance and investment banking (MBA); marketing research (MBA); operations and technology management (MBA); real estate (MBA); risk management and insurance (MBA); strategic human resource management (MBA); supply chain management (MBA). *Faculty:* 125 full-time (32 women), 48 part-time/adjunct (11 women). *Students:* 197 full-time (73 women); includes 30 minority (11 Black or African American, non-Hispanic/Latino; 9 Asian, non-Hispanic/Latino; 10 Hispanic/Latino), 42 international. Average age 29. 728 applicants, 26% accepted, 99 enrolled. In 2016, 100 master's awarded. *Entrance requirements:* For master's, GMAT or GRE, bachelor's or equivalent degree, 2 years of work experience, essay, letter of recommendation, resume. Additional exam requirements/recommendations for international students: Required—TOEFL (minimum score 100 iBT), IELTS (minimum score 7.5). *Application deadline:* For fall admission, 9/28 for domestic students, 11/1 for international students; for winter admission, 11/2 for domestic students, 12/16 for international students; for spring admission, 1/11 for domestic students, 2/24 for international students; for summer admission, 3/1 for domestic students, 4/14 for international students. Applications are processed on a rolling basis. Application fee: $75 ($81 for international students). Electronic applications accepted. *Expenses:* $7,947 per semester resident tuition, $2,430 fees; $16,082 per semester resident tuition, $2,830 fees. *Financial support:* In 2016–17, 178 students received support, including 8 fellowships with full tuition reimbursements available (averaging $56,413 per year), 23 research assistantships with full tuition reimbursements available (averaging $42,151 per year), 51 teaching assistantships with full tuition reimbursements available (averaging $39,963 per year); scholarships/grants, health care benefits, and unspecified assistantships also available. Financial award application deadline: 4/11. *Faculty research:* Forms of competition and outcomes in dual distribution systems; explaining the accuracy of revised forecasts; supply chain planning for random demand surges; advanced demand information in a multi-product system; the effects of presentation salience and measurement subjectivity on nonprofessional investors' fair value judgments. *Unit head:* Prof. Ella Mae Matsumura, Associate Dean, Full-time MBA Program, 608-262-9731, E-mail: ematsumura@bus.wisc.edu. *Application contact:* Mary Lewitzke, Assistant Director of Admissions and Recruiting, Full-time MBA Program, 608-262-4000, E-mail: mlewitzke@bus.wisc.edu.
Website: http://www.bus.wisc.edu/mba

FASHION INSTITUTE OF TECHNOLOGY

State University of New York

M.P.S. in Cosmetics and Fragrance Marketing and Management

 For more information, visit http://petersons.to/fitfragrancemarketing

Program of Study

The Fashion Institute of Technology (FIT), a State University of New York (SUNY) college of art and design, business, and technology, is home to a mix of innovative achievers, creative thinkers, and industry pioneers. FIT fosters interdisciplinary initiatives, advances research, and provides access to an international network of professionals. With a reputation for excellence, FIT offers its diverse student body access to world-class faculty, dynamic and relevant curricula, and a superior education at an affordable cost. It offers seven programs of graduate study. The programs in Art Market Studies; Exhibition and Experience Design; and Fashion and Textile Studies: History, Theory, Museum Practice lead to the Master of Arts (M.A.) degree. The Illustration and Fashion Design programs lead to the Master of Fine Arts (M.F.A.) degree. The Master of Professional Studies (M.P.S.) degree programs are Cosmetics and Fragrance Marketing and Management, and Global Fashion Management.

Cosmetics and Fragrance Marketing and Management is a 39-credit, part-time M.P.S. program designed to provide industry professionals with intensive training in marketing and leadership skills while helping them build interdisciplinary, global perspectives. The curriculum focuses on building three skill sets that leaders in the cosmetics and fragrance industries have identified as crucial to managerial success: core business skills, such as leadership, corporate finance, supply chain management, and management communication; marketing skills, such as advanced marketing theory, consumer insights, and digital marketing strategy; and technical and creative competencies, such as cosmetics and fragrance product knowledge, retail and creative management, and an intellectual foundation in beauty and fashion culture. An international field study component sends students to Europe and Asia to meet with industry leaders, talk with market research analysts, and visit diverse retail environments to develop a global business and cultural perspective. The program culminates in a capstone seminar with students producing cutting-edge research on leading business topics.

Research Facilities

The School of Graduate Studies is primarily located in the campus's Shirley Goodman Resource Center, which also houses the Gladys Marcus Library and The Museum at FIT. School of Graduate Studies facilities include conference rooms; a fully equipped conservation laboratory; a multipurpose laboratory for conservation projects and the dressing of mannequins; storage facilities for costume and textile materials; a graduate student lounge with computer and printer access; a graduate student library reading room with computers, reference materials, and copies of past classes' qualifying and thesis papers; specialized wireless classrooms; traditional and digital illustration studios; and classrooms equipped with model stands, easels, and drafting tables. The college has the only working cosmetics and fragrance laboratory on a college campus in the United States.

The Gladys Marcus Library houses more than 300,000 volumes of print, nonprint, and digital resources. Specialized holdings include industry reference materials, manufacturers' catalogs, original fashion sketches and scrapbooks, photographs, portfolios of plates, and sample books. The FIT Digital Library provides access to over 90 searchable online databases.

The Museum at FIT houses one of the world's most important collections of clothing and textiles and is the only museum in New York City dedicated to the art of fashion. The permanent collection encompasses more than 50,000 garments and accessories dating from the eighteenth century to the present, with particular strength in twentieth-century fashion, as well as 30,000 textiles and 100,000 textile swatches. Each year, nearly 100,000 visitors are drawn to the museum's award-winning exhibitions and public programs.

Financial Aid

FIT directly administers its institutional grants, scholarships, and loans. Federal funding administered by the college may include Federal Perkins Loans, federally subsidized and unsubsidized Direct Loans for students, Grad PLUS loans, and the Federal Work-Study Program. Priority for institutionally administered funds is given to students enrolled and designated as full-time.

Cost of Study

Tuition for New York State residents is $5,603 per semester, or $467 per credit. Out-of-state residents' tuition is $11,449 per semester, or $954 per credit. Full-time programs adhere to semester tuition rates and part-time graduate programs charge by credit. Tuition and fees are subject to change at the discretion of FIT's Board of Trustees. Additional expenses—for class materials, textbooks, and travel—may apply and vary per program.

Living and Housing Costs

On-campus housing is available to graduate students. Traditional residence hall accommodations (including meal plan) cost from $5,887 to $7,074 per semester. Apartment-style housing options (not including meal plan) cost from $6,299 to $10,495 per semester.

Student Group

Enrollment in the School of Graduate Studies is approximately 200 students per academic year, allowing considerable individualized advisement. Students come to FIT from throughout the country and around the world.

Student Outcomes

Students in the Cosmetics and Fragrance Marketing and Management program maintain full-time employment in the industry while working toward their degree, which provides the basis for advancement to positions of upper-level managerial responsibility.

Fashion Institute of Technology

Location

FIT is located in Manhattan's Chelsea neighborhood, at the heart of the advertising, visual arts, marketing, fashion, business, design, and communications industries. Students are connected to New York City and gain unparalleled exposure to their field through guest lectures, field trips, internships, and sponsored competitions. The location provides access to major museums, galleries, and auction houses as well as dining, entertainment, and shopping options. The campus is near subway, bus, and commuter rail lines.

Applying

Applicants to all School of Graduate Studies programs must hold a baccalaureate degree in an appropriate major from a college or university, with a cumulative GPA of 3.0 or higher. International students from non-English-speaking countries are required to submit minimum TOEFL scores of 550 on the written test, 213 on the computer test, or 80 on the Internet test. Each major has additional, specialized prerequisites for admission; for detailed information, students should visit the School of Graduate Studies on FIT's website.

Domestic and international students use the same application when seeking admission. The deadline for Cosmetics and Fragrance Marketing and Management is March 15. After the deadline date, applicants are considered on a rolling admissions basis. Candidates may apply online at fitnyc.edu/gradstudies.

Correspondence and Information

School of Graduate Studies
Shirley Goodman Resource Center, Room E315
Fashion Institute of Technology
227 West 27 Street
New York, New York 10001-5992
Phone: 212-217-4300
Fax: 212-217-4301
E-mail: gradinfo@fitnyc.edu
Websites: fitnyc.edu/gradstudies
fitnyc.edu/CFMM

THE FACULTY

A partial listing of faculty members is below. Guest lecturers are not included.

Stephan Kanlian, Chairperson; M.P.A., Pennsylvania.
Geb Berry, M.B.A., Duke.
Brooke Carlson, Sc.D., New Haven.
Carly Guerra, M.P.S., Fashion Institute of Technology; M.B.A., Fordham.
Leslie Harris, M.P.S., Fashion Institute of Technology; M.A., London College of Fashion.
Stephanie Kramer, M.P.S., Fashion Institute of Technology.
Mark Polson, M.P.S., Fashion Institute of Technology.
Robert J. Ricci, M.B.A., NYU.
Pamela Vaile, M.B.A., Pace.
Karen Young, B.A., Denver.

Section 15
Nonprofit Management

This section contains a directory of institutions offering graduate work in nonprofit management. Additional information about programs listed in the directory may be obtained by writing directly to the dean of a graduate school or chair of a department at the address given in the directory.

For programs offering related work, see also in this book *Accounting and Finance* and *Business Administration and Management*. In another guide in this series:

Graduate Programs in the Humanities, Arts & Social Sciences
See *Public, Regional, and Industrial Affairs*

CONTENTS

Program Directory

Nonprofit Management

Adler University, Programs in Psychology, Chicago, IL 60602. Offers advanced Adlerian psychotherapy (Certificate); art therapy (MA); clinical mental health counseling (MA); clinical neuropsychology (Certificate); clinical psychology (Psy D); community psychology (MA); counseling and organizational psychology (MA); counseling psychology (MA); counselor education and supervision (PhD); couple and family therapy (DCFT); criminology (MA); emergency management leadership (MA); forensic psychology (MA); marriage and family counseling (MA); marriage and family therapy (Certificate); military psychology (MA); nonprofit management (MA); organizational psychology (MA); police psychology (MA); public policy and administration (MA); rehabilitation counseling (MA); sport and health psychology (MA); substance abuse counseling (Certificate); Psy D/Certificate; Psy D/MACAT; Psy D/MACP; Psy D/MAMFC; Psy D/MASAC. *Accreditation:* APA. *Program availability:* Part-time, evening/weekend, online learning. Terminal master's awarded for partial completion of doctoral program. *Degree requirements:* For master's, thesis or alternative, oral exam, practicum; for doctorate, thesis/dissertation, clinical exam, internship, oral exam, practicum, written qualifying exam. *Entrance requirements:* For master's, 12 semester hours in psychology, minimum GPA of 3.0; for doctorate, 18 semester hours in psychology, minimum GPA of 3.25; for Certificate, appropriate master's or doctoral degree. Additional exam requirements/recommendations for international students: Required—TOEFL (minimum score 550 paper-based; 79 iBT). Electronic applications accepted.

American Jewish University, Graduate School of Nonprofit Management, Program in Business Administration, Bel Air, CA 90077-1599. Offers general nonprofit administration (MBA); Jewish nonprofit administration (MBA). *Program availability:* Part-time, evening/weekend. *Degree requirements:* For master's, thesis, internship. *Entrance requirements:* For master's, GMAT or GRE General Test, interview, minimum undergraduate GPA of 3.0. Additional exam requirements/recommendations for international students: Required—TOEFL (minimum score 550 paper-based).

American Public University System, AMU/APU Graduate Programs, Charles Town, WV 25414. Offers accounting (MBA, MS); applied business analytics (MBA, MS); criminal justice (MA), including business administration, emergency and disaster management, general (MA, MS); educational leadership (M Ed); emergency and disaster management (MA); entrepreneurship (MBA); environmental policy and management (MS), including environmental planning, environmental sustainability, fish and wildlife management, general (MA, MS), global environmental management; finance (MBA); general (MBA); government contracting and acquisition (MBA); health care administration (MBA); health information management (MS); history (MA), including American history, ancient and classical history, European history, global history, public history; homeland security (MA), including business administration, counterterrorism studies, criminal justice, cyber, emergency management and public health, intelligence studies, transportation security; homeland security resource allocation (MBA); humanities (MA); information technology (MS), including digital forensics, enterprise software development, information assurance and security, IT project management; information technology management (MBA); intelligence studies (MA), including criminal intelligence, cyber, general (MA, MS), homeland security, intelligence analysis, intelligence collection, intelligence management, intelligence operations, terrorism studies; international relations and conflict resolution (MA), including comparative and security issues, conflict resolution, international and transnational security issues, peacekeeping; legal studies (MA); management (MA), including strategic consulting; marketing (MBA); military history (MA), including American military history, American Revolution, civil war, war since 1945, World War II; military studies (MA), including joint warfare, strategic leadership; national security studies (MA), including cyber, general (MA, MS), homeland security, regional security studies, security and intelligence analysis, terrorism studies; nonprofit management (MBA); political science (MA), including American politics and government, comparative government and development, general (MA, MS), international relations, public policy; psychology (MA); public administration (MPA), including disaster management, environmental policy, health policy, human resources, national security, organizational management, security management; public health (MPH); reverse logistics management (MA); security management (MA); space studies (MS), including aerospace science, general (MA, MS), planetary science; sports and health sciences (MS); sports management (MBA); teaching (M Ed), including autism spectrum disorder, curriculum and instruction for elementary teachers, elementary reading, English language learners, instructional leadership, online learning, special education, STEAM (STEM plus the arts); transportation and logistics management (MA). *Program availability:* Part-time, evening/weekend, online only, 100% online. *Faculty:* 401 full-time (228 women), 1,678 part-time/adjunct (781 women). *Students:* 378 full-time (184 women), 8,455 part-time (3,484 women); includes 2,972 minority (1,552 Black or African American, non-Hispanic/Latino; 52 American Indian or Alaska Native, non-Hispanic/Latino; 211 Asian, non-Hispanic/Latino; 791 Hispanic/Latino; 70 Native Hawaiian or other Pacific Islander, non-Hispanic/Latino; 296 Two or more races, non-Hispanic/Latino), 109 international. Average age 37. In 2016, 3,185 master's awarded. *Degree requirements:* For master's, comprehensive exam or practicum. *Entrance requirements:* For master's, official transcript showing earned bachelor's degree from institution accredited by recognized accrediting body. Additional exam requirements/recommendations for international students: Required—TOEFL (minimum score 550 paper-based), IELTS (minimum score 6.5). *Application deadline:* Applications are processed on a rolling basis. Application fee: $0. Electronic applications accepted. *Expenses: Tuition:* Part-time $350 per credit hour. *Required fees:* $50 per course. *Financial support:* Scholarships/grants available. Financial award applicants required to submit FAFSA. *Unit head:* Dr. Karan Powell, President, 877-468-6268, Fax: 304-724-3780. *Application contact:* Terry Grant, Vice President of Enrollment Management, 877-468-6268, Fax: 304-724-3780, E-mail: info@apus.edu.
Website: http://www.apus.edu

American University, School of Public Affairs, Department of Public Administration and Policy, Washington, DC 20016-8070. Offers organization development (MSOD, Certificate), including leadership for organizational change (Certificate), organization development (MSOD); public administration (MPA, PhD, Certificate), including nonprofit management (Certificate), public financial management (Certificate), public management (Certificate); public administration and policy (MPAP), including public administration policy; public policy (MPP), including public policy; public policy (Certificate), including public policy analysis; LL M/MPA; MPA/JD; MPP/JD; MPP/LL M. *Program availability:* Part-time, evening/weekend, online learning. *Faculty:* 31 full-time (14 women), 31 part-time/adjunct (7 women). *Students:* 166 full-time (102 women), 306 part-time (193 women); includes 127 minority (76 Black or African American, non-Hispanic/Latino; 4 American Indian or Alaska Native, non-Hispanic/Latino; 27 Asian, non-Hispanic/Latino; 11 Hispanic/Latino; 1 Native Hawaiian or other Pacific Islander, non-Hispanic/Latino; 8 Two or more races, non-Hispanic/Latino), 25 international. Average age 32. 686 applicants, 85% accepted, 190 enrolled. In 2016, 177 master's, 6 doctorates, 6 other advanced degrees awarded. *Degree requirements:* For master's, comprehensive exam; for doctorate, comprehensive exam, thesis/dissertation. *Entrance requirements:* For master's, GRE, statement of purpose, 2 recommendations, resume, transcript; for doctorate, GRE, 3 recommendations, statement of purpose, resume, writing sample, transcript; for Certificate, bachelor's degree. Additional exam requirements/recommendations for international students: Required—TOEFL (minimum score 600 paper-based; 100 iBT), IELTS (minimum score 7), PTE (minimum score 68). *Application deadline:* For fall admission, 2/1 priority date for domestic students, 5/1 for international students; for spring admission, 11/1 for domestic students. Application fee: $55. *Expenses:* $1,579 per credit tuition; $690 mandatory fees. *Financial support:* Research assistantships, teaching assistantships, institutionally sponsored loans, scholarships/grants, and unspecified assistantships available. Financial award application deadline: 2/1; financial award applicants required to submit FAFSA. *Unit head:* Dr. Alison Jacknowitz, Department Chair, 202-885-2137, Fax: 202-885-2347, E-mail: jacknowi@american.edu. *Application contact:* Rosie Walker, Director, Graduate Enrollment and Recruitment, E-mail: rwalker@american.edu.
Website: http://www.american.edu/spa/dpap/

Antioch University Los Angeles, Graduate Programs, Program in Nonprofit Management, Culver City, CA 90230. Offers MA. *Program availability:* Evening/weekend. *Entrance requirements:* For master's, official transcripts, interview. Electronic applications accepted.

Antioch University Santa Barbara, Program in Business Administration, Santa Barbara, CA 93101-1581. Offers non-profit management (MBA); social business (MBA); strategic leadership (MBA).

Arizona State University at the Tempe campus, College of Public Programs, School of Community Resources and Development, Phoenix, AZ 85004-0685. Offers community resources and development (MS, PhD); nonprofit leadership and management (Graduate Certificate); nonprofit studies (MNpS); sustainable tourism (MAS). *Program availability:* Part-time, evening/weekend. Terminal master's awarded for partial completion of doctoral program. *Degree requirements:* For master's, thesis or alternative, interactive Program of Study (iPOS) submitted before completing 50 percent of required credit hours; for doctorate, comprehensive exam, thesis/dissertation, interactive Program of Study (iPOS) submitted before completing 50 percent of required credit hours. *Entrance requirements:* For master's and doctorate, GRE, minimum GPA of 3.0 or equivalent in last 2 years of work leading to bachelor's degree. Additional exam requirements/recommendations for international students: Required—TOEFL, IELTS, or PTE. Electronic applications accepted. *Expenses:* Contact institution.

Arizona State University at the Tempe campus, College of Public Programs, School of Public Affairs, Phoenix, AZ 85004-0687. Offers emergency management and homeland security (MA); program evaluation (MS); public administration (MPA, PhD), including nonprofit administration (MPA), urban management (MPA); public policy (MPP); MPA/MSW. *Accreditation:* NASPAA (one or more programs are accredited). *Program availability:* Part-time, evening/weekend. Terminal master's awarded for partial completion of doctoral program. *Degree requirements:* For master's, thesis or alternative, policy analysis or capstone project; interactive Program of Study (iPOS) submitted before completing 50 percent of required credit hours; for doctorate, comprehensive exam, thesis/dissertation, interactive Program of Study (iPOS) submitted before completing 50 percent of required credit hours. *Entrance requirements:* For master's, GRE, minimum GPA of 3.0 or equivalent in last 2 years of work leading to bachelor's degree; for doctorate, GRE, minimum GPA of 3.0 or equivalent in last 2 years of work leading to bachelor's degree, 3 letters of recommendation, resume, statement of goals, samples of research reports. Additional exam requirements/recommendations for international students: Required—TOEFL (minimum score 600 paper-based; 100 iBT), IELTS (minimum score 6.5). Electronic applications accepted. *Expenses:* Contact institution.

Assumption College, Business Studies Program, Worcester, MA 01609-1296. Offers accounting (MBA); business studies (CAGS); finance/economics (MBA); human resources (MBA); international business (MBA); management (MBA); marketing (MBA); nonprofit leadership (MBA). *Program availability:* Part-time, evening/weekend. *Faculty:* 4 full-time (1 woman), 19 part-time/adjunct (6 women). *Students:* 44 full-time (16 women), 97 part-time (47 women); includes 20 minority (8 Black or African American, non-Hispanic/Latino; 5 Asian, non-Hispanic/Latino; 6 Hispanic/Latino; 1 Two or more races, non-Hispanic/Latino), 4 international. Average age 29. 34 applicants, 59% accepted, 16 enrolled. In 2016, 97 master's, 1 other advanced degree awarded. *Degree requirements:* For master's, thesis, capstone. *Entrance requirements:* For master's, bachelor's degree, 3 letters of recommendation, official transcripts, personal statement, current resume; for CAGS, MBA or equivalent degree in a closely related field, 3 letters of recommendation, official transcripts, personal statement, current resume. Additional exam requirements/recommendations for international students: Required—TOEFL (minimum score 540 paper-based; 76 iBT), IELTS (minimum score 6). *Application deadline:* For fall admission, 7/1 priority date for domestic and international students; for spring admission, 12/1 priority date for domestic and international students; for summer admission, 4/1 priority date for domestic and international students. Application fee: $30. Electronic applications accepted. *Expenses: Tuition:* Full-time $11,610; part-time $645 per credit. *Required fees:* $70 per term. Tuition and fees vary according to course load and program. *Financial support:* In 2016–17, 19 students received support. Tuition waivers (full and partial), unspecified assistantships, and institutional discounts available. Financial award applicants required to submit FAFSA. *Faculty research:* Workplace diversity, dynamics of team interaction, utilization of leased employees, experiential learning project on due diligence market for prostheses. *Unit head:* Dr. Robin Frkal, Director, 508-767-7622, E-mail: rafrkal@assumption.edu. *Application contact:* Karen Stoyanoff, Director of Recruitment for Graduate Enrollment, 508-767-7442, Fax: 508-799-4412, E-mail: graduate@assumption.edu.
Website: http://graduate.assumption.edu/mba/assumption-mba

Azusa Pacific University, School of Business and Management, Azusa, CA 91702-7000. Offers business administration (MBA); diversity for strategic advantage (MA); entrepreneurship (MBA); finance (MBA); human and organizational development (MA); human resources and organizational development (MBA); human resources management (MA); international business (MBA); marketing (MBA); non-profit management (MA); organizational development and change (MA); performance improvement (MA); public administration (MA); strategic management (MBA). *Program availability:* Part-time, evening/weekend. *Degree requirements:* For master's, thesis (for some programs), final project. *Entrance requirements:* For master's, GMAT, minimum GPA of 3.0. Additional exam requirements/recommendations for international students: Required—TOEFL (minimum score 600 paper-based). *Expenses:* Contact institution.

Faculty research: Gender issues, financial risk, leadership and ethics, marketing strategy.

Baruch College of the City University of New York, Austin W. Marxe School of Public and International Affairs, Program in Public Administration, New York, NY 10010-5585. Offers general public administration (MPA); health care policy (MPA); nonprofit administration (MPA); policy analysis and evaluation (MPA); public management (MPA); urban development and sustainability (MPA); MS/MPA. *Accreditation:* NASPAA. *Program availability:* Part-time, evening/weekend. *Degree requirements:* For master's, thesis, capstone. *Entrance requirements:* For master's, GRE General Test. Additional exam requirements/recommendations for international students: Required—TOEFL. Electronic applications accepted. *Expenses:* Contact institution. *Faculty research:* Urbanization, population and poverty in the developing world, housing and community development, labor unions and housing, government-nongovernment relations, immigration policy, social network analysis, cross-sectoral governance, comparative healthcare systems, program evaluation, social welfare policy, health outcomes, educational policy and leadership, transnationalism, infant health, welfare reform, racial/ethnic disparities in health, urban politics, homelessness, race and ethnic relations.

Bay Path University, Program in Nonprofit Management and Philanthropy, Longmeadow, MA 01106-2292. Offers MS. *Program availability:* Part-time, 100% online. *Students:* 7 full-time (6 women), 36 part-time (33 women); includes 12 minority (5 Black or African American, non-Hispanic/Latino; 1 Asian, non-Hispanic/Latino; 3 Hispanic/Latino; 3 Two or more races, non-Hispanic/Latino). Average age 36. 28 applicants, 79% accepted, 20 enrolled. In 2016, 13 master's awarded. *Degree requirements:* For master's, eight courses (24 credits) and four electives (12 credits) for a total of 36 credits; capstone paper. *Application deadline:* Applications are processed on a rolling basis. Application fee: $45. Electronic applications accepted. Application fee is waived when completed online. *Expenses:* $18,225. *Financial support:* Unspecified assistantships available. Financial award applicants required to submit FAFSA. *Unit head:* Silvia de Haas-Phillips, Program Director, E-mail: sdphillips@baypath.edu. *Application contact:* Diane Ranaldi, Dean of Graduate Admissions, 413-565-1332, Fax: 413-565-1250, E-mail: dranaldi@baypath.edu.
Website: http://graduate.baypath.edu/Graduate-Programs/Programs-On-Campus/MS-Programs/Nonprofit-Management-and-Philanthropy

Bay Path University, Program in Strategic Fundraising and Philanthropy, Longmeadow, MA 01106-2292. Offers higher education fundraising (MS); nonprofit fundraising (MS). *Program availability:* Part-time, 100% online. *Students:* 1 full-time (0 women), 15 part-time (14 women); includes 2 minority (both Black or African American, non-Hispanic/Latino). Average age 35. 7 applicants, 71% accepted, 5 enrolled. In 2016, 4 master's awarded. *Degree requirements:* For master's, 36 hours of coursework including portfolio. *Application deadline:* Applications are processed on a rolling basis. Application fee: $45. Electronic applications accepted. Application fee is waived when completed online. *Expenses:* $18,225. *Financial support:* Unspecified assistantships available. Financial award applicants required to submit FAFSA. *Unit head:* Silvia de Haas-Phillips, Program Director, E-mail: sdphillips@baypath.edu. *Application contact:* Diane Ranaldi, Dean of Graduate Admissions, 413-565-1332, Fax: 413-565-1250, E-mail: dranaldi@baypath.edu.
Website: http://graduate.baypath.edu/Graduate-Programs/Programs-On-Campus/MS-Programs/Strategic-Fundraising-and-Philanthropy

Bradley University, The Graduate School, College of Education and Health Sciences, Department of Leadership in Education, Nonprofits and Counseling, Peoria, IL 61625-0002. Offers counseling (MA), including clinical mental health counseling, professional school counseling; leadership in educational administration (MA); nonprofit leadership (MA). *Accreditation:* ACA; NCATE. *Program availability:* Part-time, evening/weekend. *Degree requirements:* For master's, comprehensive exam, thesis optional. *Entrance requirements:* For master's, GRE General Test or MAT, interview, 3 letters of recommendation. Additional exam requirements/recommendations for international students: Required—TOEFL (minimum score 550 paper-based; 79 iBT), IELTS (minimum score 6.5). *Application deadline:* For fall admission, 5/15 priority date for domestic and international students; for spring admission, 10/15 priority date for domestic and international students. Applications are processed on a rolling basis. Application fee: $40 ($50 for international students). Electronic applications accepted. *Expenses: Tuition:* Full-time $7650; part-time $850 per credit. *Required fees:* $50 per credit. One-time fee: $100 full-time. *Financial support:* Research assistantships with full and partial tuition reimbursements, career-related internships or fieldwork, scholarships/grants, tuition waivers (partial), and unspecified assistantships available. Support available to part-time students. Financial award application deadline: 4/1. *Unit head:* Jenny Tripses, Interim Chair, 309-677-3593, E-mail: jtripses@bradley.edu. *Application contact:* Kayla Carroll, Director of International Admissions and Student Services, 309-677-2375, E-mail: klcarroll@fsmail.bradley.edu.
Website: http://www.bradley.edu/academic/departments/lenc/

Brandeis University, The Heller School for Social Policy and Management, Program in Nonprofit Management, Waltham, MA 02454-9110. Offers child, youth, and family management (MBA); health care management (MBA); social impact management (MBA); social policy and management (MBA); sustainable development (MBA); MBA/MA; MBA/MD. MBA/MD program offered in conjunction with Tufts University School of Medicine. *Accreditation:* AACSB. *Program availability:* Part-time. *Degree requirements:* For master's, team consulting project. *Entrance requirements:* For master's, GMAT (preferred) or GRE, 2 letters of recommendation, problem statement analysis, 3-5 years of professional experience. Additional exam requirements/recommendations for international students: Required—TOEFL (minimum score 600 paper-based; 100 iBT). Electronic applications accepted. *Expenses:* Contact institution. *Faculty research:* Health care; children and families; elder and disabled services; social impact management; organizations in the non-profit, for-profit, or public sector.

Brigham Young University, Graduate Studies, Marriott School of Management, Master of Public Administration Program, Provo, UT 84602. Offers federal government (MPA); health care (MPA); local government management (MPA); nonprofit management (MPA); JD/MPA. *Accreditation:* NASPAA. *Students:* 98 full-time (54 women); includes 16 minority (2 Black or African American, non-Hispanic/Latino; 2 Asian, non-Hispanic/Latino; 10 Hispanic/Latino; 2 Native Hawaiian or other Pacific Islander, non-Hispanic/Latino), 20 international. Average age 29. 77 applicants, 81% accepted, 49 enrolled. In 2016, 42 master's awarded. *Entrance requirements:* For master's, GMAT or GRE, minimum GPA of 3.0, MPA Excel prep course. Additional exam requirements/recommendations for international students: Required—TOEFL (minimum score 580 paper-based; 85 iBT). *Application deadline:* For fall admission, 1/15 for domestic and international students. Application fee: $50. Electronic applications accepted. *Expenses:* Contact institution. *Financial support:* In 2016–17, 99 students received support. Research assistantships, teaching assistantships, career-related internships or fieldwork, institutionally sponsored loans, and scholarships/grants available. Financial award application deadline: 4/15; financial award applicants required to submit FAFSA. *Faculty research:* Taxes, budgeting, nonprofit, ethics, decision modeling, work balance, organizational behavior. *Unit head:* Dr. Jeffery Thompson, Director, 801-422-4221, Fax: 801-422-0311, E-mail: mpa@byu.edu. *Application contact:* Catherine Cooper, Associate Director, 801-422-4221, Fax: 801-422-0311, E-mail: mpa@byu.edu.
Website: http://mpa.byu.edu

Cairn University, School of Business, Langhorne, PA 19047-2990. Offers accounting (MBA); business administration (MBA); international entrepreneurship (MBA); nonprofit leadership (MBA); organizational leadership (MSOL, Postbaccalaureate Certificate). *Program availability:* Part-time, evening/weekend, 100% online, blended/hybrid learning. *Faculty:* 3 full-time (0 women), 6 part-time/adjunct (1 woman). *Students:* 7 full-time (5 women), 43 part-time (19 women); includes 20 minority (10 Black or African American, non-Hispanic/Latino; 1 American Indian or Alaska Native, non-Hispanic/Latino; 4 Asian, non-Hispanic/Latino; 3 Hispanic/Latino; 2 Two or more races, non-Hispanic/Latino), 4 international. Average age 36. 17 applicants, 100% accepted, 16 enrolled. In 2016, 16 master's awarded. *Entrance requirements:* Additional exam requirements/recommendations for international students: Required—TOEFL (minimum score 550 paper-based). *Application deadline:* Applications are processed on a rolling basis. Application fee: $25. Electronic applications accepted. Application fee is waived when completed online. *Expenses:* $655 per semester credit. *Financial support:* Scholarships/grants available. Support available to part-time students. Financial award applicants required to submit FAFSA. *Unit head:* Yunn Kang, Dean, School of Business, 215-702-4461, Fax: 215-702-4248, E-mail: ykang@cairn.edu. *Application contact:* Gwen Dorsey, Assistant Director, Graduate Admissions, 800-572-2472, Fax: 215-702-4248, E-mail: gdorsey@cairn.edu.
Website: http://cairn.edu/academics/business

California Baptist University, Program in Leadership and Community Development, Riverside, CA 92504-3206. Offers MA. *Program availability:* Part-time, evening/weekend. *Faculty:* 3 full-time (0 women), 1 part-time/adjunct (0 women). *Students:* 2 full-time (0 women), 1 (woman) part-time; includes 2 minority (both Hispanic/Latino). Average age 24. 3 applicants, 67% accepted, 2 enrolled. *Entrance requirements:* For master's, minimum cumulative GPA of 2.75, three letters of recommendation, current resume, 500-word comprehensive essay. Additional exam requirements/recommendations for international students: Required—TOEFL (minimum score 80 iBT). *Application deadline:* For fall admission, 8/1 priority date for domestic students, 7/1 priority date for international students; for spring admission, 12/1 for domestic students, 11/1 priority date for international students. Applications are processed on a rolling basis. Application fee: $45. Electronic applications accepted. *Expenses:* Contact institution. *Financial support:* In 2016–17, 1 student received support. Applicants required to submit CSS PROFILE or FAFSA. *Faculty research:* Educational leadership, curriculum and instruction, sociology of education, K-12 education, global education. *Unit head:* Dr. John Shoup, Dean, School of Education, 951-343-4205, E-mail: jshoup@calbaptist.edu. *Application contact:* Taylor Neece, Director of Graduate Admissions, 951-343-4871, Fax: 877-228-8877, E-mail: graduateadmissions@calbaptist.edu.
Website: http://www.calbaptist.edu/academics/schools-colleges/school-education/programs/graduate/master-arts-leadership-and-community-development/

California Lutheran University, Graduate Studies, School of Management, Thousand Oaks, CA 91360-2787. Offers business (IMBA); computer science (MS); econometrics (MBA); economics (MS); entrepreneurship (MBA, Certificate); finance (MBA, Certificate); financial planning (MBA, Certificate); information systems and technology (MS); information technology management (MBA, Certificate); international business (MBA, Certificate); management and organization behavior (MBA); management and organizational behavior (Certificate); marketing (MBA, Certificate); microeconomics (MBA); nonprofit and social enterprise (MBA); public policy and administration (MPPA). *Program availability:* Part-time, evening/weekend, 100% online, blended/hybrid learning. *Faculty:* 25 full-time (10 women), 36 part-time/adjunct (12 women). *Students:* 427 full-time (172 women), 189 part-time (87 women); includes 120 minority (14 Black or African American, non-Hispanic/Latino; 2 American Indian or Alaska Native, non-Hispanic/Latino; 19 Asian, non-Hispanic/Latino; 37 Hispanic/Latino; 48 Two or more races, non-Hispanic/Latino), 338 international. Average age 30. 591 applicants, 64% accepted, 131 enrolled. In 2016, 305 master's awarded. *Entrance requirements:* For master's, GMAT, interview, minimum GPA of 3.0. *Application deadline:* Applications are processed on a rolling basis. Application fee: $50. Electronic applications accepted. *Expenses:* Contact institution. *Unit head:* Dr. Gerhard Apfelthaler, Dean, 805-493-3360. *Application contact:* 805-493-3325, Fax: 805-493-3861, E-mail: clugrad@callutheran.edu.
Website: http://www.callutheran.edu/management/

California State University, Northridge, Graduate Studies, The Tseng College of Extended Learning, Program in Nonprofit-Sector Management, Northridge, CA 91330. Offers Graduate Certificate. Offered in collaboration with College of Social and Behavioral Sciences. *Entrance requirements:* For degree, bachelor's degree from accredited college or university with minimum GPA of 2.5 in last 60 semester units or 90 quarter units; at least one year of work experience in the public or non-profit sector. *Expenses:* Tuition, state resident: full-time $4152. *Unit head:* Pat Lyon, Program Manager, 818-677-3332.
Website: http://tsengcollege.csun.edu/programs/NSM

Cambridge College, School of Management, Cambridge, MA 02138-5304. Offers business negotiation and conflict resolution (M Mgt); general business (M Mgt); health care informatics (M Mgt); health care management (M Mgt); leadership in human and organizational dynamics (M Mgt); non-profit and public organization management (M Mgt); small business development (M Mgt); technology management (M Mgt). *Program availability:* Part-time, evening/weekend. *Degree requirements:* For master's, thesis, seminars. *Entrance requirements:* For master's, resume, 2 professional references. Additional exam requirements/recommendations for international students: Required—TOEFL (minimum score 550 paper-based; 79 iBT), Michigan English Language Assessment Battery (minimum score 85); Recommended—IELTS (minimum score 6). Electronic applications accepted. *Expenses:* Contact institution. *Faculty research:* Negotiation, mediation and conflict resolution; leadership; management of diverse organizations; case studies and simulation methodologies for management education, digital as a second language: social networking for digital immigrants, non-profit and public management.

Capella University, School of Public Service Leadership, Doctoral Programs in Healthcare, Minneapolis, MN 55402. Offers criminal justice (PhD); emergency management (PhD); epidemiology (Dr PH); general health administration (DHA); general public administration (DPA); health advocacy and leadership (Dr PH); health care administration (PhD); health care leadership (DHA); health policy advocacy (DHA); multidisciplinary human services (PhD); nonprofit management and leadership (PhD); public safety leadership (PhD); social and community services (PhD).

Carlos Albizu University, Miami Campus, Graduate Programs, Miami, FL 33172-2209. Offers clinical psychology (PhD, Psy D); entrepreneurship (MBA); exceptional student education (MS); human services (PhD); industrial/organizational psychology (MS); marriage and family therapy (MS); mental health counseling (MS); nonprofit management (MBA); organizational management (MBA); psychology (MS); school counseling (MS); speech and language pathology (MS); teaching English for speakers of other languages (MS). *Accreditation:* APA. *Program availability:* Part-time, evening/weekend, 100% online. *Faculty:* 28 full-time (22 women), 31 part-time/adjunct (19 women). *Students:* 475 full-time (396 women), 191 part-time (161 women); includes 560 minority (56 Black or African American, non-Hispanic/Latino; 1 American Indian or

Alaska Native, non-Hispanic/Latino; 4 Asian, non-Hispanic/Latino; 494 Hispanic/Latino; 5 Two or more races, non-Hispanic/Latino), 15 international. Average age 34. 335 applicants, 46% accepted, 122 enrolled. In 2016, 143 master's, 48 doctorates awarded. Terminal master's awarded for partial completion of doctoral program. *Degree requirements:* For master's, comprehensive exam, integrative project (for MBA); research project (for exceptional student education, teaching English as a second language); for doctorate, comprehensive exam, thesis/dissertation, internship, project. *Entrance requirements:* For master's, 3 letters of recommendation, interview, minimum GPA of 3.0, resume, statement of purpose, official transcripts; for doctorate, 3 letters of recommendation, minimum GPA of 3.0, resume, interview, statement of purpose, official transcripts. Additional exam requirements/recommendations for international students: Required—Michigan Test of English Language Proficiency. *Application deadline:* For fall admission, 4/1 priority date for domestic students, 5/1 priority date for international students; for spring admission, 11/1 priority date for domestic students, 9/1 priority date for international students. Applications are processed on a rolling basis. Application fee: $50. Electronic applications accepted. *Expenses:* Contact institution. *Financial support:* In 2016–17, 131 students received support. Federal Work-Study, scholarships/grants, unspecified assistantships, and tuition discounts available. Financial award application deadline: 6/1; financial award applicants required to submit FAFSA. *Faculty research:* Psychotherapy, forensic psychology, neuropsychology, marketing strategy, entrepreneurship, special education, speech-language pathology. *Unit head:* Dr. Etiony Aldarondo, Provost, 305-593-1223 Ext. 3138, Fax: 305-592-7930, E-mail: ealdarondo@albizu.edu. *Application contact:* Sonia Feliciano, Institutional Director of Student Recruitment, 305-593-1223 Ext. 3108, Fax: 305-477-8983, E-mail: sfeliciano@albizu.edu.

Case Western Reserve University, Jack, Joseph and Morton Mandel School of Applied Social Sciences, Cleveland, OH 44106. Offers nonprofit management (MNO); social welfare (PhD); social work (MSSA); JD/MSSA; MSSA/MA; MSSA/MBA; MSSA/MNO. *Accreditation:* CSWE (one or more programs are accredited). *Program availability:* Evening/weekend, online learning. *Degree requirements:* For master's, fieldwork; for doctorate, thesis/dissertation. *Entrance requirements:* For master's, GRE General Test, MAT, or minimum GPA of 2.7; for doctorate, GRE General Test. Additional exam requirements/recommendations for international students: Required—TOEFL (minimum score 557 paper-based, 90 iBT) or IELTS (minimum score 7). Electronic applications accepted. *Expenses:* Contact institution. *Faculty research:* Urban poverty, community social development, substance abuse, health, child welfare, aging, mental health.

Case Western Reserve University, Weatherhead School of Management, Mandel Center for Nonprofit Organizations, Cleveland, OH 44106-7167. Offers MNO, CNM, JD/MNO, MNO/MSSA, MSSA/MNO. *Entrance requirements:* For master's, GMAT or GRE. Additional exam requirements/recommendations for international students: Required—TOEFL. *Expenses:* Contact institution. *Faculty research:* Leadership management of non-profit organizations, strategic alliances, economic analysis of non-profit organizations.

Central Michigan University, Central Michigan University Global Campus, Program in Administration, Mount Pleasant, MI 48859. Offers acquisitions administration (MSA, Certificate); engineering management administration (MSA, Certificate); general administration (MSA, Certificate); health services administration (MSA, Certificate); human resources administration (MSA, Certificate); information resource management (MSA); information resource management administration (Certificate); international administration (MSA, Certificate); leadership (MSA, Certificate); philanthropy and fundraising administration (MSA, Certificate); public administration (MSA, Certificate); recreation and park administration (MSA); research administration (MSA, Certificate). *Program availability:* Part-time, evening/weekend, online learning. *Faculty:* 21 full-time (5 women), 168 part-time/adjunct (43 women). *Students:* 3,059 (1,741 women); includes 1,392 minority (1,003 Black or African American, non-Hispanic/Latino; 27 American Indian or Alaska Native, non-Hispanic/Latino; 93 Asian, non-Hispanic/Latino; 49 Hispanic/Latino; 10 Native Hawaiian or other Pacific Islander, non-Hispanic/Latino; 210 Two or more races, non-Hispanic/Latino). Average age 38. In 2016, 289 master's awarded. *Entrance requirements:* For master's, minimum GPA of 2.7 in major. *Application deadline:* Applications are processed on a rolling basis. Application fee: $50. Electronic applications accepted. *Financial support:* Scholarships/grants available. Support available to part-time students. Financial award applicants required to submit FAFSA. *Unit head:* Dr. Patricia Chase, Director, 989-774-6525, E-mail: chase1pb@cmich.edu. *Application contact:* 877-268-4636, E-mail: cmuglobal@cmich.edu.

Chaminade University of Honolulu, Office of Professional and Continuing Education, Program in Business Administration, Honolulu, HI 96816-1578. Offers accounting (MBA); business (MBA); island business (MBA); not-for-profit (MBA). *Program availability:* Part-time, evening/weekend, 100% online, blended/hybrid learning. *Faculty:* 7 full-time (3 women), 7 part-time/adjunct (2 women). *Students:* 71 full-time (47 women), 40 part-time (23 women); includes 78 minority (4 Black or African American, non-Hispanic/Latino; 1 American Indian or Alaska Native, non-Hispanic/Latino; 37 Asian, non-Hispanic/Latino; 5 Hispanic/Latino; 28 Native Hawaiian or other Pacific Islander, non-Hispanic/Latino; 3 Two or more races, non-Hispanic/Latino). Average age 32. 70 applicants, 96% accepted, 45 enrolled. In 2016, 56 master's awarded. *Entrance requirements:* For master's, minimum GPA of 3.0, resume, two years or more of work experience. Additional exam requirements/recommendations for international students: Required—TOEFL (minimum score 550 paper-based; 79 iBT). *Application deadline:* Applications are processed on a rolling basis. Application fee: $40. Electronic applications accepted. *Expenses:* $820 per credit hour with $93 fee per online course. *Financial support:* Applicants required to submit FAFSA. *Unit head:* Dr. Scott J. Schroeder, Dean, 808-739-4612, Fax: 808-735-4734, E-mail: mba@chaminade.edu. *Application contact:* 808-735-4755, E-mail: gradserv@chaminade.edu.
Website: http://www.chaminade.edu/mba

Clemson University, Graduate School, College of Behavioral, Social and Health Sciences, Program in Public Administration, Clemson, SC 29634. Offers public administration (MPA, Certificate), including emergency management (MPA), homeland defense and security (MPA), local government (MPA), non-profit management (MPA), sustainable development (MPA). *Program availability:* Part-time, evening/weekend, online only, 100% online. *Faculty:* 4 full-time (2 women), 11 part-time/adjunct (5 women). *Students:* 8 full-time (5 women), 54 part-time (30 women); includes 16 minority (13 Black or African American, non-Hispanic/Latino; 2 Hispanic/Latino; 1 Two or more races, non-Hispanic/Latino). Average age 36. 25 applicants, 80% accepted, 18 enrolled. In 2016, 18 master's awarded. *Degree requirements:* For master's, comprehensive exam, thesis or alternative. *Entrance requirements:* For master's, GRE General Test, two letters of recommendation, unofficial transcripts, personal statement of purpose, documentation and explanation of related professional experience, resume. Additional exam requirements/recommendations for international students: Required—TOEFL (minimum score 80 iBT), IELTS (minimum score 6.5). *Application deadline:* For fall admission, 4/1 for domestic students, 3/1 for international students; for spring admission, 11/1 for domestic students, 10/1 for international students. Applications are processed on a rolling basis. Application fee: $80 ($90 for international students). Electronic applications accepted. *Expenses:* $4,264 per semester full-time resident, $8,485 per semester full-time non-resident, $695 per credit hour. *Faculty research:* Economic development, community vitality, entrepreneurship, broadband infrastructure, public health innovations and communities. *Total annual research expenditures:* $11,485. *Unit head:* Dr. Lori Dickes, Program Coordinator, 864-656-7831, E-mail: lorid@clemson.edu.
Website: https://www.clemson.edu/cbshs/departments/mpa/

Cleveland State University, College of Graduate Studies, Maxine Goodman Levin College of Urban Affairs, Program in Environmental Studies, Cleveland, OH 44115. Offers environmental nonprofit management (MAES); environmental planning (MAES); policy and administration (MAES); sustainable economic development (MAES); urban economic development (Certificate); JD/MAES. *Program availability:* Part-time, evening/weekend. *Faculty:* 16 full-time (8 women), 13 part-time/adjunct (5 women). *Students:* 8 full-time (4 women), 3 part-time (1 woman); includes 2 minority (both Black or African American, non-Hispanic/Latino), 1 international. Average age 28. 10 applicants, 100% accepted, 5 enrolled. In 2016, 1 master's awarded. *Degree requirements:* For master's, thesis or alternative, exit project. *Entrance requirements:* For master's, GRE General Test (minimum score: verbal and quantitative combined 40th percentile, analytical writing 4.0), minimum GPA of 3.0. Additional exam requirements/recommendations for international students: Required—TOEFL (minimum score 550 paper-based; 78 iBT), IELTS (6.0), or International Test of English Proficiency (iTEP). *Application deadline:* For fall admission, 7/1 priority date for domestic students, 5/15 for international students; for spring admission, 11/15 for domestic students, 11/1 for international students; for summer admission, 4/1 for domestic students, 3/15 for international students. Applications are processed on a rolling basis. Application fee: $40. Electronic applications accepted. *Expenses:* Contact institution. *Financial support:* In 2016–17, 4 students received support, including research assistantships with tuition reimbursements available (averaging $7,200 per year), 1 teaching assistantship with partial tuition reimbursement available (averaging $2,400 per year); scholarships/grants, tuition waivers (full and partial), and unspecified assistantships also available. Support available to part-time students. Financial award application deadline: 3/1; financial award applicants required to submit FAFSA. *Faculty research:* Environmental policy and administration, environmental planning, geographic information systems (GIS), urban sustainability planning and management, energy policy, land re-use. *Unit head:* Dr. Sanda Kaufman, Professor/Program Director, 216-687-2367, Fax: 216-687-9239, E-mail: s.kaufman@csuohio.edu. *Application contact:* David Arrighi, Graduate Academic Advisor, 216-523-7522, Fax: 216-687-5398, E-mail: d.arrighi@csuohio.edu.
Website: http://urban.csuohio.edu/academics/graduate/maes/

Cleveland State University, College of Graduate Studies, Maxine Goodman Levin College of Urban Affairs, Program in Nonprofit Administration and Leadership, Cleveland, OH 44115. Offers local and urban management (Certificate); nonprofit administration and leadership (MNAL); nonprofit management (Certificate). *Program availability:* Part-time, evening/weekend. *Faculty:* 16 full-time (8 women), 13 part-time/adjunct (5 women). *Students:* 3 full-time (2 women), 18 part-time (13 women); includes 4 minority (2 Black or African American, non-Hispanic/Latino; 2 Hispanic/Latino). Average age 37. 23 applicants, 52% accepted, 3 enrolled. In 2016, 8 master's awarded. *Degree requirements:* For master's, thesis or alternative, capstone course. *Entrance requirements:* For master's, GRE (minimum score: verbal and quantitative combined 40th percentile, analytical writing 4.0), minimum GPA of 3.0. Additional exam requirements/recommendations for international students: Required—TOEFL (minimum score 550 paper-based; 78 iBT), IELTS (6.0), or International Test of English Proficiency (iTEP). *Application deadline:* For fall admission, 7/15 priority date for domestic students, 5/15 for international students; for spring admission, 11/15 for domestic students, 11/1 for international students; for summer admission, 4/1 for domestic students, 3/15 for international students. Applications are processed on a rolling basis. Application fee: $40. Electronic applications accepted. *Expenses:* Contact institution. *Financial support:* In 2016–17, 3 students received support, including 2 research assistantships with full tuition reimbursements available (averaging $7,200 per year), 2 teaching assistantships with partial tuition reimbursements available (averaging $2,400 per year); career-related internships or fieldwork, scholarships/grants, and unspecified assistantships also available. Support available to part-time students. Financial award application deadline: 3/1; financial award applicants required to submit FAFSA. *Faculty research:* Human resource management, volunteerism, performance measurement in nonprofits, government-nonprofit partnerships. *Unit head:* Dr. Mittie Davis Jones, Associate Professor and Department Chairperson, 216-687-3861, Fax: 216-687-9342, E-mail: m.d.jones97@csuohio.edu. *Application contact:* David Arrighi, Graduate Academic Advisor, 216-523-7522, Fax: 216-687-5398, E-mail: urbanprograms@csuohio.edu.
Website: http://urban.csuohio.edu/academics/graduate/mnal/

Cleveland State University, College of Graduate Studies, Maxine Goodman Levin College of Urban Affairs, Program in Public Administration, Cleveland, OH 44115. Offers economic development (MPA); non-profit management (MPA); public management (MPA); JD/MPA. *Accreditation:* NASPAA. *Program availability:* Part-time, evening/weekend. *Faculty:* 16 full-time (8 women), 13 part-time/adjunct (5 women). *Students:* 19 full-time (12 women), 40 part-time (24 women); includes 18 minority (14 Black or African American, non-Hispanic/Latino; 1 Asian, non-Hispanic/Latino; 1 Hispanic/Latino; 2 Two or more races, non-Hispanic/Latino), 4 international. Average age 31. 79 applicants, 77% accepted, 12 enrolled. In 2016, 29 master's awarded. *Degree requirements:* For master's, thesis or alternative, exit project. *Entrance requirements:* For master's, GRE General Test (minimum scores in 40th percentile verbal and quantitative, 4.0 writing), minimum GPA of 3.0. Additional exam requirements/recommendations for international students: Required—TOEFL (minimum score 550 paper-based; 78 iBT), IELTS (6.0), or International Test of English Proficiency (iTEP). *Application deadline:* For fall admission, 7/1 priority date for domestic students, 5/15 for international students; for spring admission, 11/15 for domestic students, 11/1 for international students; for summer admission, 4/1 for domestic students, 3/15 for international students. Applications are processed on a rolling basis. Application fee: $40. Electronic applications accepted. *Expenses:* Contact institution. *Financial support:* In 2016–17, 16 students received support, including 5 research assistantships with full tuition reimbursements available (averaging $7,200 per year), 1 teaching assistantship with partial tuition reimbursement available (averaging $2,400 per year); scholarships/grants, tuition waivers (full and partial), and unspecified assistantships also available. Support available to part-time students. Financial award application deadline: 3/1; financial award applicants required to submit FAFSA. *Faculty research:* City management, nonprofit management, health care administration, public management, economic development. *Unit head:* Dr. Nicholas Zingale, Director, 216-802-3389, Fax: 216-687-9342, E-mail: n.zingale@csuohio.edu. *Application contact:* David Arrighi, Graduate Academic Advisor, 216-523-7522, Fax: 216-687-5398, E-mail: d.arrighi@csuohio.edu.
Website: http://urban.csuohio.edu/academics/graduate/mpa/

The College at Brockport, State University of New York, School of Business and Management, Department of Public Administration, Brockport, NY 14420-2997. Offers arts administration (AGC); nonprofit management (AGC); public administration (MPA), including health care management, nonprofit management, public management. *Accreditation:* NASPAA. *Program availability:* Part-time, evening/weekend. *Faculty:* 5 full-time (3 women), 5 part-time/adjunct (1 woman). *Students:* 59 full-time (41 women), 100 part-time (60 women); includes 32 minority (16 Black or African American, non-

Hispanic/Latino; 5 Asian, non-Hispanic/Latino; 8 Hispanic/Latino; 3 Two or more races, non-Hispanic/Latino), 3 international. 82 applicants, 89% accepted, 53 enrolled. In 2016, 42 master's, 10 other advanced degrees awarded. *Degree requirements:* For master's, thesis or alternative. *Entrance requirements:* For master's, GRE or minimum GPA of 3.0, letters of recommendation, statement of objectives, current resume. Additional exam requirements/recommendations for international students: Required—TOEFL (minimum score 550 paper-based; 79 iBT), IELTS (minimum score 6.5). *Application deadline:* For fall admission, 8/15 priority date for domestic and international students; for spring admission, 1/15 priority date for domestic and international students; for summer admission, 4/15 priority date for domestic and international students. Application fee: $50. Electronic applications accepted. *Expenses:* Contact institution. *Financial support:* In 2016–17, 1 fellowship with full tuition reimbursement (averaging $7,500 per year), 1 teaching assistantship with full tuition reimbursement (averaging $6,000 per year) were awarded; Federal Work-Study, scholarships/grants, and unspecified assistantships also available. Support available to part-time students. Financial award application deadline: 3/15; financial award applicants required to submit FAFSA. *Faculty research:* E-government, performance management, nonprofits and policy implementation, Medicaid and disabilities. *Unit head:* Dr. Celia Watt, Graduate Director, 585-395-5538, Fax: 585-395-2172, E-mail: cwatt@brockport.edu. *Application contact:* Danielle A. Welch, Graduate Admissions Counselor, 585-395-2525, Fax: 585-395-2515.
Website: http://www.brockport.edu/pubadmin

Columbia University, School of Continuing Education, Program in Fundraising Management, New York, NY 10027. Offers MS. *Program availability:* Part-time, evening/weekend. *Degree requirements:* For master's, internship. *Entrance requirements:* For master's, BA with minimum GPA of 3.0. Additional exam requirements/recommendations for international students: Required—American Language Program placement test; Recommended—TOEFL. Electronic applications accepted. *Faculty research:* Fundraising for annual campaigns, capital campaigns, nonprofit financial management, research for fundraising and planned giving.

Corban University, Graduate School, The Corban MBA, Salem, OR 97301-9392. Offers management (MBA); non-profit management (MBA). *Program availability:* Online learning.

Daemen College, Program in Executive Leadership and Change, Amherst, NY 14226-3592. Offers business (MS); health professions (MS); not-for-profit organizations (MS). *Program availability:* Part-time, evening/weekend. *Degree requirements:* For master's, thesis, cohort learning sequence (2 years for weekend cohort; 3 years for weeknight cohort). *Entrance requirements:* For master's, 2 letters of recommendation, interview, goal statement, official transcripts, resume. Additional exam requirements/recommendations for international students: Required—TOEFL (minimum score 500 paper-based; 63 iBT), IELTS (minimum score 5.5). Electronic applications accepted.

Dallas Baptist University, College of Business, Business Administration Program, Dallas, TX 75211-9299. Offers accounting (MBA); business communication (MBA); conflict resolution management (MBA); entrepreneurship (MBA); finance (MBA); health care management (MBA); international business (MBA); leading the non-profit organization (MBA); management (MBA); management information systems (MBA); marketing (MBA); project management (MBA); technology and engineering management (MBA). *Accreditation:* ACBSP. *Program availability:* Part-time, evening/weekend, 100% online, blended/hybrid learning. *Application deadline:* Applications are processed on a rolling basis. Application fee: $25. Electronic applications accepted. Application fee is waived when completed online. *Expenses: Tuition:* Full-time $15,408; part-time $856 per credit hour. *Required fees:* $400 per semester. Tuition and fees vary according to course load and degree level. *Unit head:* Dr. Sandra Reid, Chair of Graduate Business Programs, 214-333-5280, E-mail: sandra@dbu.edu. *Application contact:* Bobby Soto, Director of Admissions, 214-333-5242, E-mail: graduate@dbu.edu.
Website: http://www3.dbu.edu/graduate/mba.asp

Dallas Baptist University, Graduate School of Ministry, Program in Christian Ministry, Dallas, TX 75211-9299. Offers chaplaincy (MA); Christian ministry and education (MA); counseling ministry (MA); family ministry (MA); general ministry (MA); heritage and missions (MA); leading the nonprofit organization (MA); ministry leadership (MA); professional life coaching (MA); urban ministry (MA); worship ministry (MA). *Program availability:* Part-time, evening/weekend, 100% online, blended/hybrid learning. *Application deadline:* Applications are processed on a rolling basis. Application fee: $25. Electronic applications accepted. Application fee is waived when completed online. *Expenses: Tuition:* Full-time $15,408; part-time $856 per credit hour. *Required fees:* $400 per semester. Tuition and fees vary according to course load and degree level. *Unit head:* Dr. Tom Vann, Director, 214-333-5805, E-mail: tomv@dbu.edu. *Application contact:* Bobby Soto, Director of Admissions, 214-333-5242, E-mail: graduate@dbu.edu.
Website: http://www3.dbu.edu/gsom/Christian-Ministry/

Dallas Baptist University, Graduate School of Ministry, Program in Global Leadership, Dallas, TX 75211-9299. Offers church planting (MA); East Asian Studies (MA); English as a second language (MA); general studies (MA); global communication (MA); global studies (MA); international business (MA); leading the nonprofit organization (MA); missions (MA); small group ministry (MA); urban ministry (MA). *Program availability:* Part-time, evening/weekend. *Application deadline:* Applications are processed on a rolling basis. Application fee: $25. Electronic applications accepted. Application fee is waived when completed online. *Expenses: Tuition:* Full-time $15,408; part-time $856 per credit hour. *Required fees:* $400 per semester. Tuition and fees vary according to course load and degree level. *Unit head:* Dr. Bob Garrett, Director, 214-333-5508, E-mail: bobg@dbu.edu. *Application contact:* Bobby Soto, Director of Admissions, 214-333-5242, E-mail: graduate@dbu.edu.
Website: http://www3.dbu.edu/gsom/global-leadership/

DePaul University, College of Liberal Arts and Social Sciences, Chicago, IL 60614. Offers Arabic (MA); Chinese (MA); English (MA); French (MA); German (MA); history (MA); interdisciplinary studies (MA, MS); international public service (MS); international studies (MA); Italian (MA); Japanese (MA); leadership and policy studies (MS); liberal studies (MA); new media studies (MA); nonprofit management (MNM); public administration (MPA); public health (MPH); public service management (MS); social work (MSW); sociology (MA); Spanish (MA); sustainable urban development (MA); women and gender studies (MA); writing and publishing (MA); writing, rhetoric, and discourse (MA); MA/PhD. *Program availability:* Part-time, evening/weekend, online learning. Terminal master's awarded for partial completion of doctoral program. *Degree requirements:* For master's, variable foreign language requirement, comprehensive exam (for some programs), thesis (for some programs). Electronic applications accepted.

Drury University, Master of Nonprofit and Civic Leadership Program, Springfield, MO 65802. Offers MNCL. *Program availability:* Part-time, evening/weekend. *Faculty:* 3 full-time (1 woman), 2 part-time/adjunct (0 women). *Students:* 39 full-time (32 women); includes 4 minority (1 Black or African American, non-Hispanic/Latino; 2 Hispanic/Latino; 1 Two or more races, non-Hispanic/Latino), 2 international. Average age 27. 8 applicants, 88% accepted, 7 enrolled. *Entrance requirements:* For master's, GRE, bachelor's degree, minimum GPA of 3.0. Additional exam requirements/recommendations for international students: Recommended—TOEFL (minimum score 80 iBT), IELTS (minimum score 6.5). *Application deadline:* For fall admission, 8/4 for domestic and international students; for spring admission, 1/6 for domestic and international students; for summer admission, 5/24 for domestic and international students. Applications are processed on a rolling basis. Application fee: $25 ($50 for international students). Electronic applications accepted. *Expenses:* $453 per credit hour, $7 technology fee, $100 graduation fee. *Financial support:* Career-related internships or fieldwork, scholarships/grants, and unspecified assistantships available. Financial award application deadline: 6/30; financial award applicants required to submit FAFSA. *Faculty research:* Nonprofit leadership, organizational change, leadership accountability, digital media, health communication. *Unit head:* Dr. Charles Taylor, Director, 417-873-7391, E-mail: ctaylor@drury.edu.
Website: http://www.drury.edu/master-of-nonprofit-and-civic-leadership

Eastern Mennonite University, Program in Business Administration, Harrisonburg, VA 22802-2462. Offers general management (MBA); health services administration (MBA); non-profit leadership (MBA). *Program availability:* Part-time, evening/weekend. *Degree requirements:* For master's, final capstone course. *Entrance requirements:* For master's, GMAT, minimum GPA of 2.5, 2 years of work experience, 2 letters of reference. Additional exam requirements/recommendations for international students: Required—TOEFL (minimum score 500 paper-based). Electronic applications accepted. *Expenses:* Contact institution. *Faculty research:* Information security, Anabaptist/Mennonite experiences and perspectives, limits of multi-cultural education, international development performance criteria.

Eastern Michigan University, Graduate School, College of Arts and Sciences, Department of Political Science, Programs in Public Administration, Ypsilanti, MI 48197. Offers general public management (Graduate Certificate); local government management (Graduate Certificate); management of public healthcare services (Graduate Certificate); nonprofit management (Graduate Certificate); public administration (MPA); public budget management (Graduate Certificate); public land planning and development management (Graduate Certificate); public personnel management (Graduate Certificate); public policy analysis (Graduate Certificate). *Accreditation:* NASPAA. *Students:* 11 full-time (7 women), 43 part-time (22 women); includes 19 minority (16 Black or African American, non-Hispanic/Latino; 2 Hispanic/Latino; 1 Two or more races, non-Hispanic/Latino). Average age 36. 50 applicants, 64% accepted, 17 enrolled. In 2016, 23 master's, 1 other advanced degree awarded. Application fee: $45. *Application contact:* Dr. Jeffrey L. Bernstein, Program Advisor, 734-487-6970, Fax: 734-487-3340, E-mail: jeffrey.bernstein@emich.edu.
Website: http://www.emich.edu/polisci/

Eastern Michigan University, Graduate School, College of Business, Programs in Business Administration, Ypsilanti, MI 48197. Offers business administration (MBA, Graduate Certificate); computer information systems (Graduate Certificate); e-business (MBA, Graduate Certificate); enterprise business intelligence (MBA); entrepreneurship (MBA, Graduate Certificate); finance (MBA, Graduate Certificate); human resources (MBA); human resources management (Graduate Certificate); information systems (MBA); internal auditing (MBA); international business (MBA, Graduate Certificate); marketing management (Graduate Certificate); nonprofit management (MBA); organizational development (Graduate Certificate); supply chain management (MBA, Graduate Certificate). *Accreditation:* AACSB. *Program availability:* Part-time, online learning. *Students:* 63 full-time (36 women), 320 part-time (186 women); includes 131 minority (76 Black or African American, non-Hispanic/Latino; 5 American Indian or Alaska Native, non-Hispanic/Latino; 16 Asian, non-Hispanic/Latino; 19 Hispanic/Latino; 15 Two or more races, non-Hispanic/Latino), 23 international. Average age 32. 305 applicants, 70% accepted, 124 enrolled. In 2016, 78 master's, 57 other advanced degrees awarded. *Entrance requirements:* For master's, GMAT (minimum score 450), minimum cumulative undergraduate GPA of 2.75. Additional exam requirements/recommendations for international students: Required—TOEFL. *Application deadline:* For fall admission, 5/15 priority date for domestic students, 2/15 priority date for international students; for winter admission, 10/15 priority date for domestic students, 9/1 priority date for international students; for summer admission, 3/15 priority date for domestic students, 3/1 priority date for international students. Applications are processed on a rolling basis. Application fee: $45. *Financial support:* Fellowships, research assistantships with full tuition reimbursements, teaching assistantships with full tuition reimbursements, career-related internships or fieldwork, Federal Work-Study, institutionally sponsored loans, scholarships/grants, tuition waivers (partial), and unspecified assistantships available. Support available to part-time students. Financial award applicants required to submit FAFSA. *Unit head:* K. Michelle Henry, Director, Graduate Business Programs, 734-487-4444, Fax: 734-483-1316, E-mail: cob.graduate@emich.edu.
Website: http://www.emich.edu/cob/mba/

Eastern Michigan University, Graduate School, College of Health and Human Services, Interdisciplinary Program in Non-Profit Management, Ypsilanti, MI 48197. Offers Graduate Certificate. *Unit head:* Dr. Marcia Bombyk, Program Coordinator, 734-487-0393, Fax: 734-487-8536, E-mail: mbombyk@emich.edu.

Eastern University, Program in Organizational Leadership, St. Davids, PA 19087-3696. Offers organizational leadership (PhD), including business, non-profit. *Students:* 74 full-time (42 women); includes 22 minority (17 Black or African American, non-Hispanic/Latino; 3 Asian, non-Hispanic/Latino; 1 Hispanic/Latino; 1 Two or more races, non-Hispanic/Latino), 4 international. Average age 46. In 2016, 8 doctorates awarded. *Application deadline:* Applications are processed on a rolling basis. Electronic applications accepted. *Expenses:* $985 per credit. *Unit head:* Michael Dziedziak, Executive Director of Enrollment, 800-452-0996, E-mail: gpsadmissions@eastern.edu.
Website: http://www.eastern.edu/academics/programs/phd-organizational-leadership/phd-organizational-leadership-0

Eastern University, School of Leadership and Development, St. Davids, PA 19087-3696. Offers economic development (MBA), including international development, urban development (MA, MBA); international development (MA), including global development, urban development (MA, MBA); nonprofit management (MS); organizational leadership (MA); M Div/MBA. *Program availability:* Part-time, evening/weekend, online learning. *Students:* 59 full-time (32 women), 67 part-time (35 women); includes 40 minority (32 Black or African American, non-Hispanic/Latino; 1 Asian, non-Hispanic/Latino; 5 Hispanic/Latino; 2 Two or more races, non-Hispanic/Latino), 22 international. Average age 33. In 2016, 44 master's awarded. *Entrance requirements:* Additional exam requirements/recommendations for international students: Required—TOEFL (minimum score 550 paper-based; 79 iBT). *Application deadline:* Applications are processed on a rolling basis. Application fee: $35. Electronic applications accepted. Application fee is waived when completed online. *Expenses:* $690 per credit. *Faculty research:* Micro-level economic development, China welfare and economic development, macroethics, micro- and macro-level economic development in transitional economics, organizational effectiveness. *Unit head:* Michael Dziedziak, Executive Director of Enrollment, 800-452-0996, E-mail: gpsadmissions@eastern.edu.
Website: http://www.eastern.edu/academics/programs/graduate-programs-leadership-development

Nonprofit Management

East Tennessee State University, School of Graduate Studies, College of Arts and Sciences, Department of Political Science, International Affairs and Public Administration, Johnson City, TN 37614. Offers economic development (Postbaccalaureate Certificate); not-for-profit administration (MPA); planning and development (MPA); public financial management (MPA); urban planning (Postbaccalaureate Certificate). *Program availability:* Part-time. *Degree requirements:* For master's, internship. *Entrance requirements:* For master's, GRE General Test, three letters of recommendation; for Postbaccalaureate Certificate, GRE General Test. Additional exam requirements/recommendations for international students: Required—TOEFL (minimum score 550 paper-based; 79 iBT). Electronic applications accepted. *Faculty research:* Labor issues, presidency, public law in American politics, East Asian politics, European politics, Middle Eastern politics, development in comparative politics, international political economy, international relations, world politics in international affairs.

Fairleigh Dickinson University, Metropolitan Campus, Anthony J. Petrocelli College of Continuing Studies, Public Administration Institute, Teaneck, NJ 07666-1914. Offers public administration (MPA, Certificate); public non-profit management (Certificate).

Fielding Graduate University, Graduate Programs, School of Leadership Studies, Programs in Human and Organizational Development, Santa Barbara, CA 93105-3814. Offers human development (PhD); nonprofit leadership (Certificate); organizational consulting (Certificate); organizational development and change (PhD); organizational development and leadership (MA, Certificate). *Program availability:* Part-time, 100% online, blended/hybrid learning. *Faculty:* 14 full-time (7 women), 33 part-time/adjunct (19 women). *Students:* 221 full-time (163 women), 53 part-time (41 women); includes 75 minority (29 Black or African American, non-Hispanic/Latino; 4 American Indian or Alaska Native, non-Hispanic/Latino; 16 Asian, non-Hispanic/Latino; 17 Hispanic/Latino; 1 Native Hawaiian or other Pacific Islander, non-Hispanic/Latino; 8 Two or more races, non-Hispanic/Latino), 3 international. Average age 49. 66 applicants, 91% accepted, 46 enrolled. In 2016, 30 master's, 39 doctorates, 3 other advanced degrees awarded. *Entrance requirements:* For master's and Certificate, bachelor's or master's degree, resume, statement of purpose, official transcript; for doctorate, bachelor's or master's degree, resume, statement of purpose, reflexive essay, official transcript. *Application deadline:* For fall admission, 7/16 for domestic and international students; for spring admission, 11/1 for domestic and international students; for summer admission, 3/1 for domestic and international students. Application fee: $75. Electronic applications accepted. *Expenses:* Contact institution. *Financial support:* In 2016–17, 10 students received support, including 2 research assistantships (averaging $1,350 per year); scholarships/grants also available. Financial award applicants required to submit FAFSA. *Unit head:* Dr. Dorothy Agger-Gupta, Program Director, E-mail: dotagger@fielding.edu. *Application contact:* Enrollment Coordinator, 800-340-1099 Ext. 4098, Fax: 805-687-9793, E-mail: hodadmission@fielding.edu.
Website: http://www.fielding.edu/our-programs/school-of-leadership-studies/

Florida Atlantic University, College for Design and Social Inquiry, School of Public Administration, Boca Raton, FL 33431-0991. Offers MPA, PhD. *Accreditation:* NASPAA (one or more programs are accredited). *Program availability:* Part-time, evening/weekend. *Faculty:* 10 full-time (2 women). *Students:* 44 full-time (25 women), 110 part-time (60 women); includes 74 minority (43 Black or African American, non-Hispanic/Latino; 3 Asian, non-Hispanic/Latino; 24 Hispanic/Latino; 4 Two or more races, non-Hispanic/Latino), 10 international. Average age 34. 109 applicants, 52% accepted, 32 enrolled. In 2016, 65 master's, 6 doctorates awarded. *Degree requirements:* For master's, thesis optional; for doctorate, comprehensive exam, thesis/dissertation. *Entrance requirements:* For master's, GRE General Test, minimum GPA of 3.0; for doctorate, GRE General Test, faculty reference, scholarly writing samples, letters of recommendation. Additional exam requirements/recommendations for international students: Required—TOEFL (minimum score 500 paper-based; 61 iBT), IELTS (minimum score 6). *Application deadline:* For fall admission, 5/1 priority date for domestic students, 2/15 for international students; for spring admission, 11/1 for domestic students, 7/15 for international students. Applications are processed on a rolling basis. Application fee: $30. *Expenses:* Tuition, state resident: full-time $7392; part-time $369.82 per credit hour. Tuition, nonresident: full-time $19,432; part-time $1024.81 per credit hour. *Financial support:* Fellowships with full tuition reimbursements, research assistantships with partial tuition reimbursements, teaching assistantships with partial tuition reimbursements, career-related internships or fieldwork, Federal Work-Study, institutionally sponsored loans, and tuition waivers (partial) available. Support available to part-time students. Financial award application deadline: 4/1. *Faculty research:* Public finance and budgeting, public management, evaluation, criminal justice, postmodern public administration. *Unit head:* Leslie Leip, 954-924-8818, E-mail: lleip@fau.edu.
Website: http://www.fau.edu/spa/

Fordham University, Gabelli School of Business, New York, NY 10023. Offers accounting (MBA, MS); applied statistics and decision-making (MS); business administration (EMBA); business analytics (MS); communications and media management (MBA); electronic business (MBA); entrepreneurship (MBA); finance (MBA); global finance (MS); global sustainability (MBA); healthcare management (MBA); information systems (MBA, MS); investor relations (MS); management (MBA, MS); marketing (MBA); marketing intelligence (MS); media management (MS); nonprofit leadership (MS); quantitative finance (MS); taxation (MS); JD/MBA; MS/MBA. *Accreditation:* AACSB. *Program availability:* Part-time, evening/weekend. *Faculty:* 132 full-time (44 women), 51 part-time/adjunct (7 women). *Students:* 1,117 full-time (668 women), 553 part-time (282 women); includes 207 minority (44 Black or African American, non-Hispanic/Latino; 92 Asian, non-Hispanic/Latino; 69 Hispanic/Latino; 2 Native Hawaiian or other Pacific Islander, non-Hispanic/Latino), 1,088 international. Average age 27. 4,745 applicants, 46% accepted, 752 enrolled. In 2016, 996 master's awarded. Terminal master's awarded for partial completion of doctoral program. *Degree requirements:* For master's, internships (required for MS in quantitative finance, recommended for MBA). *Entrance requirements:* For master's, GMAT/GRE, 2 letters of recommendation, resume, 2 essays, transcripts. Additional exam requirements/recommendations for international students: Required—TOEFL (minimum score 100 iBT), IELTS (minimum score 7). *Application deadline:* For fall admission, 11/15 priority date for domestic and international students; for winter admission, 1/15 priority date for domestic students, 1/1 priority date for international students; for spring admission, 3/1 for domestic and international students; for summer admission, 6/1 for domestic students. Application fee: $130. Electronic applications accepted. *Expenses:* $1,397 per credit. *Financial support:* In 2016–17, 78 students received support. Career-related internships or fieldwork, institutionally sponsored loans, scholarships/grants, and unspecified assistantships available. Support available to part-time students. Financial award application deadline: 6/30; financial award applicants required to submit FAFSA. *Unit head:* Dr. Donna Rapaccioli, Dean, 212-636-6165, Fax: 212-307-1779, E-mail: rapaccioli@fordham.edu. *Application contact:* Lawrence Murray, Senior Assistant Dean of Graduate Admissions and Advising, 212-636-6200, Fax: 212-636-7076, E-mail: admissionsgb@fordham.edu.
Website: http://www.fordham.edu/gabelli

Fordham University, Graduate School of Social Service, New York, NY 10023. Offers nonprofit leadership (MS); social work (MSW, PhD); JD/MSW. MS jointly sponsored with Graduate School of Business and conducted through the Fordham Center for Nonprofit Leaders. *Accreditation:* CSWE (one or more programs are accredited). *Program availability:* Part-time, evening/weekend, 100% online, blended/hybrid learning. *Faculty:* 48 full-time (36 women), 78 part-time/adjunct (61 women). *Students:* 884 full-time (787 women), 366 part-time (327 women); includes 355 minority (198 Black or African American, non-Hispanic/Latino; 1 American Indian or Alaska Native, non-Hispanic/Latino; 19 Asian, non-Hispanic/Latino; 137 Hispanic/Latino). Average age 32. In 2016, 539 master's, 4 doctorates awarded. *Degree requirements:* For master's, 1200 hours of field placement; for doctorate, comprehensive exam, thesis/dissertation. *Entrance requirements:* For master's, BA in liberal arts; for doctorate, GRE, master's degree in social work or related field. Additional exam requirements/recommendations for international students: Required—TOEFL (minimum score 600 paper-based; 100 iBT), IELTS. *Application deadline:* For fall admission, 2/1 priority date for domestic students; for spring admission, 11/1 priority date for domestic students. Applications are processed on a rolling basis. Application fee: $60. Electronic applications accepted. *Expenses:* Contact institution. *Financial support:* In 2016–17, 838 students received support, including 39 research assistantships with partial tuition reimbursements available (averaging $1,980 per year); fellowships with partial tuition reimbursements available, career-related internships or fieldwork, Federal Work-Study, scholarships/grants, tuition waivers (partial), and unspecified assistantships also available. Support available to part-time students. Financial award application deadline: 2/1. *Faculty research:* Aging, children and family, healthcare, domestic violence, substance abuse. *Unit head:* Dr. Debra McPhee, Dean, 212-636-6616. *Application contact:* Melba Remice, Assistant Dean of Admissions, 212-636-6600, Fax: 212-636-6613, E-mail: gssadmission@fordham.edu.
Website: http://www.fordham.edu/gss/

Geneva College, Program in Leadership Studies, Beaver Falls, PA 15010-3599. Offers business management (MS); ministry leadership (MS); non-profit leadership (MS); organizational management (MS); project management (MS). *Program availability:* Online only, 100% online. *Faculty:* 1 (woman) full-time, 10 part-time/adjunct (3 women). *Students:* 56 full-time (45 women), 9 part-time (6 women); includes 15 minority (12 Black or African American, non-Hispanic/Latino; 1 Asian, non-Hispanic/Latino; 2 Hispanic/Latino). Average age 45. 13 applicants, 77% accepted, 7 enrolled. In 2016, 38 master's awarded. *Degree requirements:* For master's, thesis or alternative, capstone leadership studies project. *Entrance requirements:* For master's, undergraduate degree from regionally-accredited college or university, one to three years of experience in the workplace, minimum GPA of 3.0 (preferred), resume, essay, two recommendations. Additional exam requirements/recommendations for international students: Required—TOEFL. *Application deadline:* For fall admission, 9/21 for domestic students; for spring admission, 2/23 for domestic students; for summer admission, 7/22 for domestic students. Applications are processed on a rolling basis. Electronic applications accepted. *Expenses:* $640 per credit. *Financial support:* In 2016–17, 50 students received support. Scholarships/grants available. Financial award application deadline: 8/1; financial award applicants required to submit FAFSA. *Faculty research:* Servant leadership, leadership essentials. *Unit head:* John D. Gallo, Dean of Graduate, Adult and Online Programs, 800-576-3111, Fax: 724-847-6839, E-mail: msol@geneva.edu. *Application contact:* Lynsey Auell, Graduate Enrollment Representative, 800-576-3111, Fax: 724-847-6839, E-mail: msol@geneva.edu.
Website: http://www.geneva.edu/graduate/leadership-studies/

The George Washington University, Columbian College of Arts and Sciences, Department of Organizational Sciences and Communication, Washington, DC 20052. Offers human resources management (MA); non-profit management (Graduate Certificate); organizational management (Graduate Certificate). *Program availability:* Part-time, evening/weekend. *Faculty:* 10 full-time (6 women). *Students:* 46 full-time (25 women), 31 part-time (25 women); includes 27 minority (8 Black or African American, non-Hispanic/Latino; 7 Asian, non-Hispanic/Latino; 5 Hispanic/Latino; 7 Two or more races, non-Hispanic/Latino), 5 international. Average age 28. 133 applicants, 85% accepted, 47 enrolled. In 2016, 35 master's, 21 other advanced degrees awarded. *Degree requirements:* For master's, comprehensive exam. *Entrance requirements:* For master's, GRE General Test, minimum GPA of 3.0; for Graduate Certificate, minimum GPA of 3.0. Additional exam requirements/recommendations for international students: Required—TOEFL (minimum score 500 paper-based; 80 iBT). *Application deadline:* For fall admission, 1/15 priority date for domestic and international students; for spring admission, 10/1 priority date for domestic students, 9/1 priority date for international students. Applications are processed on a rolling basis. Application fee: $75. Electronic applications accepted. *Financial support:* Federal Work-Study and institutionally sponsored loans available. *Unit head:* Dr. Clay Warren, Chair, 202-994-1870, Fax: 202-994-1881, E-mail: claywar@gwu.edu. *Application contact:* Information Contact, 202-994-1880, Fax: 202-994-1881.
Website: http://www.gwu.edu/~orgsci/

Georgian Court University, School of Business and Digital Media, Lakewood, NJ 08701-2697. Offers business (MBA); business essentials (Certificate); nonprofit management (Certificate). *Program availability:* Part-time, evening/weekend. *Faculty:* 7 full-time (3 women), 11 part-time/adjunct (4 women). *Students:* 29 full-time (22 women), 40 part-time (26 women); includes 22 minority (7 Black or African American, non-Hispanic/Latino; 2 Asian, non-Hispanic/Latino; 9 Hispanic/Latino; 4 Two or more races, non-Hispanic/Latino). Average age 31. 55 applicants, 49% accepted, 13 enrolled. In 2016, 34 master's, 3 other advanced degrees awarded. *Entrance requirements:* For master's, GMAT or CPA exam, 3 letters of recommendation. Additional exam requirements/recommendations for international students: Required—TOEFL (minimum score 550 paper-based). *Application deadline:* For fall admission, 8/15 priority date for domestic students, 5/1 for international students; for spring admission, 1/15 priority date for domestic students, 10/1 for international students. Applications are processed on a rolling basis. Application fee: $40. Electronic applications accepted. *Expenses: Tuition:* Full-time $15,079; part-time $839 per credit. *Required fees:* $968; $496 per credit. Tuition and fees vary according to campus/location and program. *Financial support:* Scholarships/grants, health care benefits, and unspecified assistantships available. Financial award application deadline: 4/15; financial award applicants required to submit FAFSA. *Unit head:* Dr. Janice Warner, Dean, 732-987-2662, Fax: 732-987-2024, E-mail: jwarner@georgian.edu. *Application contact:* Patrick Givens, Director of Graduate and Professional Studies Admissions, 732-987-2736, Fax: 732-987-2000, E-mail: gps@georgian.edu.
Website: http://georgian.edu/academics/school-of-business/

Georgia Southern University, Jack N. Averitt College of Graduate Studies, College of Liberal Arts and Social Sciences, Department of Non-Profit and Public Studies, Program in Public and Nonprofit Management, Statesboro, GA 30458. Offers Graduate Certificate. *Program availability:* Part-time, blended/hybrid learning. *Students:* 4 part-time (3 women); includes 2 minority (both Black or African American, non-Hispanic/Latino). Average age 35. 7 applicants, 71% accepted, 3 enrolled. In 2016, 2 Graduate Certificates awarded. *Entrance requirements:* For degree, GRE, three years of work experience in the public or nonprofit sector, bachelor's degree, minimum cumulative undergraduate GPA of 2.75, three letters of recommendation, statement of career goals

and objectives. Additional exam requirements/recommendations for international students: Required—TOEFL (minimum score 550 paper-based; 80 iBT), IELTS (minimum score 6). *Application deadline:* For fall admission, 3/1 for domestic students; for spring admission, 10/1 for domestic students. Application fee: $50. Electronic applications accepted. *Expenses:* Tuition, state resident: full-time $7236; part-time $277 per semester hour. Tuition, nonresident: full-time $27,118; part-time $1105 per semester hour. *Required fees:* $2092. *Financial support:* In 2016–17, 3 fellowships with full tuition reimbursements (averaging $7,750 per year) were awarded. Financial award application deadline: 4/20; financial award applicants required to submit FAFSA. *Faculty research:* Human resource management, ethics in administration, nonprofit budgeting. *Unit head:* Dr. Trenton Davis, Director, 912-478-5430, Fax: 912-478-8029, E-mail: tjdavis@georgiasouthern.edu.
Website: http://class.georgiasouthern.edu/ipns/online-certificate/

Georgia State University, Andrew Young School of Policy Studies, Department of Public Management and Policy, Atlanta, GA 30303. Offers criminal justice (MPA); disaster management (Certificate); disaster policy (MPA); environmental policy (PhD); health policy (PhD); management and finance (MPA); nonprofit management (MPA, Certificate); nonprofit policy (MPA); planning and economic development (MPP, Certificate); policy analysis and evaluation (MPA), including planning and economic development; public and nonprofit management (PhD); public finance and budgeting (PhD), including science and technology policy, urban and regional economic development; public finance policy (MPA), including social policy; public health (MPA). *Accreditation:* NASPAA (one or more programs are accredited). *Program availability:* Part-time. *Faculty:* 17 full-time (9 women). *Students:* 123 full-time (77 women), 79 part-time (49 women); includes 84 minority (59 Black or African American, non-Hispanic/Latino; 5 Asian, non-Hispanic/Latino; 14 Hispanic/Latino; 6 Two or more races, non-Hispanic/Latino), 34 international. Average age 30. 237 applicants, 60% accepted, 65 enrolled. In 2016, 59 master's, 4 doctorates, 8 other advanced degrees awarded. Terminal master's awarded for partial completion of doctoral program. *Degree requirements:* For master's, thesis optional; for doctorate, comprehensive exam, thesis/dissertation. *Entrance requirements:* For master's and doctorate, GRE. Additional exam requirements/recommendations for international students: Required—TOEFL (minimum score 603 paper-based; 100 iBT) or IELTS (minimum score 7). *Application deadline:* For fall admission, 1/15 for domestic and international students. Application fee: $50. Electronic applications accepted. *Expenses:* Tuition, state resident: full-time $6876; part-time $382 per credit hour. Tuition, nonresident: full-time $22,374; part-time $1243 per credit hour. *Required fees:* $2128; $1064 per term. Part-time tuition and fees vary according to course load and program. *Financial support:* In 2016–17, fellowships (averaging $8,194 per year), research assistantships (averaging $8,068 per year), teaching assistantships (averaging $3,600 per year) were awarded; institutionally sponsored loans, scholarships/grants, health care benefits, and unspecified assistantships also available. Financial award application deadline: 2/1. *Faculty research:* Public budgeting and finance, public management, nonprofit management, performance measurement and management, urban development. *Unit head:* Dr. Carolyn Bourdeaux, Chair and Professor, 404-413-0013, Fax: 404-413-0104, E-mail: cbourdeaux@gsu.edu.
Website: http://aysps.gsu.edu/pmap/

Grand Valley State University, College of Community and Public Service, School of Public, Nonprofit and Health Administration, Program in Philanthropy and Nonprofit Leadership, Allendale, MI 49401-9403. Offers MPNL. *Students:* 13 part-time (12 women); includes 3 minority (1 Black or African American, non-Hispanic/Latino; 2 Two or more races, non-Hispanic/Latino). Average age 38. 9 applicants, 78% accepted, 4 enrolled. In 2016, 1 master's awarded. *Degree requirements:* For master's, capstone. *Entrance requirements:* For master's, 3 years of full-time work experience, 3 letters of reference, 250-750 word essay on career and educational objectives, resume. Additional exam requirements/recommendations for international students: Required—Michigan English Language Assessment Battery; Recommended—TOEFL (minimum score 80 iBT), IELTS (minimum score 6.5). *Application deadline:* For fall admission, 6/1 for domestic students; for winter admission, 11/1 for domestic students; for spring admission, 4/1 for domestic students. Applications are processed on a rolling basis. Electronic applications accepted. *Expenses:* $604 per credit hour. *Financial support:* In 2016–17, 3 students received support, including 2 fellowships, 1 research assistantship with full and partial tuition reimbursement available (averaging $8,000 per year). *Unit head:* Dr. Richard Jelier, Director, 616-331-6575, Fax: 616-331-7120, E-mail: jelierr@gvsu.edu. *Application contact:* Dr. Michelle Wooddell, Graduate Program Director/Recruiting Contact, 616-331-6495, Fax: 616-486-7120, E-mail: wooddelm@gvsu.edu.

Gratz College, Graduate Programs, Program in Nonprofit Management, Melrose Park, PA 19027. Offers MS. *Unit head:* Dr. Jerome Kutnick, Dean for Academic Affairs, 215-635-7300 Ext. 137, Fax: 215-635-7320, E-mail: jkutnick@gratz.edu. *Application contact:* Joanna Boeing Bratton, Director of Admissions, 215-635-7300 Ext. 140, Fax: 215-635-7399, E-mail: admissions@gratz.edu.

Hamline University, School of Business, St. Paul, MN 55104-1284. Offers business administration (MBA); nonprofit management (MNM); public administration (MPA, DPA); MBA/MNM; MBA/MPA; MPA/MNM. *Program availability:* Part-time, evening/weekend, blended/hybrid learning. *Faculty:* 21 full-time (7 women), 25 part-time/adjunct (4 women). *Students:* 272 full-time (137 women), 69 part-time (33 women); includes 76 minority (39 Black or African American, non-Hispanic/Latino; 2 American Indian or Alaska Native, non-Hispanic/Latino; 20 Asian, non-Hispanic/Latino; 10 Hispanic/Latino; 5 Two or more races, non-Hispanic/Latino), 19 international. Average age 34. 166 applicants, 64% accepted, 77 enrolled. In 2016, 191 master's, 3 doctorates awarded. *Degree requirements:* For master's, thesis (for some programs); for doctorate, comprehensive exam, thesis/dissertation. *Entrance requirements:* For master's and doctorate, personal statement, official transcripts, resume or curriculum vitae, letters of recommendation, writing sample. Additional exam requirements/recommendations for international students: Required—TOEFL (minimum score 80 iBT). *Application deadline:* For fall admission, 6/1 for domestic and international students; for spring admission, 11/1 for domestic students, 10/1 for international students; for summer admission, 3/1 for domestic students, 2/1 for international students. Applications are processed on a rolling basis. Application fee: $0 ($100 for international students). Electronic applications accepted. *Expenses:* Contact institution. *Financial support:* Career-related internships or fieldwork, Federal Work-Study, scholarships/grants, and unspecified assistantships available. Support available to part-time students. Financial award applicants required to submit FAFSA. *Faculty research:* Liberal arts-based business programs, experiential learning, organizational process/politics, gender differences, social equity. *Unit head:* Dr. Anne McCarthy, Dean, 651-523-2284, Fax: 651-523-3098, E-mail: hsb@hamline.edu. *Application contact:* Shawn Skoog, Director of Graduate Recruitment and Admission, 651-523-2900, Fax: 651-523-3058, E-mail: gradprog@hamline.edu.
Website: http://www.hamline.edu/business

Hebrew Union College–Jewish Institute of Religion, School of Jewish Nonprofit Management, Los Angeles, CA 90007. Offers MA.

High Point University, Norcross Graduate School, High Point, NC 27268. Offers business administration (MBA); educational leadership (M Ed); elementary education (M Ed); history (MA); nonprofit management (MA); secondary math (M Ed); special education (M Ed); strategic communication (MA); teaching elementary education k-6 (MAT); teaching secondary mathematics 9-12 (MAT). *Accreditation:* NCATE. *Program availability:* Part-time, evening/weekend. *Degree requirements:* For master's, comprehensive exam (for some programs), thesis (for some programs). *Entrance requirements:* For master's, GMAT (MBA), GRE, MAT, minimum GPA of 3.0. Additional exam requirements/recommendations for international students: Required—TOEFL (minimum score 550 paper-based). Electronic applications accepted.

Hope International University, School of Graduate and Professional Studies, Program in Business Administration, Fullerton, CA 92831-3138. Offers general management (MBA, MSM); international development (MBA, MSM); marketing management (MBA, MSM); non-profit management (MBA, MSM). *Program availability:* Part-time, online learning. *Degree requirements:* For master's, comprehensive exam (for some programs), thesis (for some programs), project. *Entrance requirements:* For master's, minimum GPA of 3.0; 2 references. Additional exam requirements/recommendations for international students: Required—TOEFL (minimum score 550 paper-based; 86 iBT); Recommended—IELTS (minimum score 6.5). Electronic applications accepted. *Expenses:* Contact institution.

Indiana University Bloomington, School of Public and Environmental Affairs, Public Affairs Programs, Bloomington, IN 47405. Offers economic development (MPA); energy (MPA); environmental policy (PhD); environmental policy and natural resource management (MPA); information systems (MPA); international development (MPA); local government management (MPA); nonprofit management (MPA, Certificate); policy analysis (MPA); public budgeting and financial management (Certificate); public finance (PhD); public financial administration (MPA); public management (MPA, PhD, Certificate); public policy analysis (PhD); social entrepreneurship (Certificate); specialized public affairs (MPA); sustainability and sustainable development (MPA); JD/MPA; MPA/MA; MPA/MIS; MPA/MLS; MSES/MPA. *Accreditation:* NASPAA (one or more programs are accredited). *Program availability:* Part-time. *Degree requirements:* For master's, capstone, internship; for doctorate, comprehensive exam, thesis/dissertation. *Entrance requirements:* For master's, GRE General Test or GMAT, official transcripts, 3 letters of recommendation, resume, personal statement; for doctorate, GRE General Test, official transcripts, 3 letters of recommendation, statement of purpose. Additional exam requirements/recommendations for international students: Required—TOEFL (minimum score 600 paper-based; 96 iBT); Recommended—IELTS (minimum score 7). Electronic applications accepted. *Faculty research:* International development, environmental policy and resource management, policy analysis, public finance, public management, urban management, nonprofit management, energy policy, social policy, public finance.

Indiana University Bloomington, University Graduate School, College of Arts and Sciences, Robert A. and Sandra S. Borns Jewish Studies Program, Bloomington, IN 47405. Offers Jewish studies (MA), including nonprofit management; Jewish studies and history (MA). *Faculty:* 24 full-time (9 women). *Students:* 7 full-time (3 women), 1 part-time (0 women); includes 1 minority (Hispanic/Latino). Average age 33. 11 applicants, 64% accepted, 6 enrolled. *Degree requirements:* For master's, one foreign language, thesis. *Entrance requirements:* Additional exam requirements/recommendations for international students: Required—TOEFL. *Application deadline:* For fall admission, 1/1 for domestic students, 12/1 for international students. Application fee: $55 ($65 for international students). Electronic applications accepted. *Financial support:* In 2016–17, 16 students received support, including 16 fellowships with full and partial tuition reimbursements available (averaging $17,800 per year); teaching assistantships, scholarships/grants, health care benefits, and grants-in-aid also available. Financial award application deadline: 1/15. *Faculty research:* Jewish studies, religious studies, history, Holocaust study. *Unit head:* Mark Roseman, Director, 812-855-0453, Fax: 812-855-4314, E-mail: marrosem@indiana.edu. *Application contact:* Carolyn Lipson-Walker, Assistant Director, 812-855-0453, Fax: 812-855-4314, E-mail: clipsonw@indiana.edu.
Website: http://www.indiana.edu/~jsp/index.shtml

Indiana University Northwest, School of Public and Environmental Affairs, Gary, IN 46408. Offers criminal justice (MPA); environmental affairs (Graduate Certificate); health services (MPA); nonprofit management (Certificate); public management (MPA, Graduate Certificate). *Accreditation:* NASPAA (one or more programs are accredited). *Program availability:* Part-time. *Faculty:* 5 full-time (3 women). *Students:* 10 full-time (8 women), 39 part-time (28 women); includes 25 minority (18 Black or African American, non-Hispanic/Latino; 7 Hispanic/Latino), 1 international. Average age 37. 31 applicants, 97% accepted, 16 enrolled. In 2016, 13 master's, 9 other advanced degrees awarded. *Entrance requirements:* For master's, GRE General Test (minimum combined verbal and quantitative score of 280), GMAT, or LSAT, letters of recommendation. *Application deadline:* For fall admission, 8/15 priority date for domestic students. Applications are processed on a rolling basis. Application fee: $40 ($60 for international students). Electronic applications accepted. *Financial support:* Career-related internships or fieldwork, Federal Work-Study, and tuition waivers (partial) available. Support available to part-time students. Financial award application deadline: 3/1; financial award applicants required to submit FAFSA. *Faculty research:* Employment in income security policies, evidence in criminal justice, equal employment law, social welfare policy and welfare reform, public finance in developing countries. *Unit head:* Dr. Karl Besel, Assistant Dean and Director, 219-980-6554, Fax: 219-980-6737, E-mail: kbesel@iun.edu.
Website: http://www.iun.edu/spea/index.htm

Indiana University of Pennsylvania, School of Graduate Studies and Research, College of Humanities and Social Sciences, Department of Sociology, Program in Administration and Leadership Studies, Indiana, PA 15705. Offers PhD. *Program availability:* Part-time, evening/weekend. *Faculty:* 13 full-time (9 women). *Students:* 3 full-time (1 woman), 95 part-time (54 women); includes 13 minority (9 Black or African American, non-Hispanic/Latino; 1 American Indian or Alaska Native, non-Hispanic/Latino; 2 Asian, non-Hispanic/Latino; 1 Hispanic/Latino), 5 international. Average age 43. 44 applicants, 43% accepted, 11 enrolled. In 2016, 7 doctorates awarded. *Degree requirements:* For doctorate, comprehensive exam, thesis/dissertation. *Entrance requirements:* For doctorate, GRE, resume, writing sample, 3 letters of recommendation. Additional exam requirements/recommendations for international students: Required—TOEFL (minimum score 540 paper-based). *Application deadline:* For fall admission, 2/15 priority date for domestic students. Applications are processed on a rolling basis. Application fee: $50. Electronic applications accepted. *Expenses:* Contact institution. *Financial support:* In 2016–17, 2 fellowships with full tuition reimbursements (averaging $2,500 per year), 4 research assistantships with tuition reimbursements (averaging $5,764 per year), 1 teaching assistantship with partial tuition reimbursement (averaging $23,305 per year) were awarded; career-related internships or fieldwork, Federal Work-Study, scholarships/grants, and unspecified assistantships also available. Support available to part-time students. Financial award application deadline: 4/15; financial award applicants required to submit FAFSA. *Unit head:* Dr. Robert Millward, Graduate Coordinator, 724-357-5593, E-mail: millward@iup.edu.
Website: http://www.iup.edu/grad/ALS/default.aspx

Indiana University–Purdue University Indianapolis, School of Public and Environmental Affairs, Indianapolis, IN 46202. Offers criminal justice and public safety (MS); homeland security and emergency management (Graduate Certificate); library management (Graduate Certificate); nonprofit management (Graduate Certificate); public affairs (MPA); public management (Graduate Certificate); social entrepreneurship: nonprofit and public benefit organizations (Graduate Certificate); JD/MPA; MLS/NMC; MLS/PMC; MPA/MA. *Accreditation:* CAHME (one or more programs are accredited); NASPAA. *Program availability:* Part-time, evening/weekend, online learning. *Entrance requirements:* For master's, GRE General Test, GMAT or LSAT, minimum GPA of 3.0 (preferred). Additional exam requirements/recommendations for international students: Required—TOEFL (minimum score 93 iBT), IELTS (minimum score 6.5). Electronic applications accepted. *Faculty research:* Nonprofit and public management, public policy, urban policy, sustainability policy, disaster preparedness and recovery, vehicular safety, homicide, offender rehabilitation and re-entry.

Indiana University South Bend, College of Liberal Arts and Sciences, South Bend, IN 46634-7111. Offers advanced computer programming (Graduate Certificate); applied informatics (Graduate Certificate); applied mathematics and computer science (MS); behavior modification (Graduate Certificate); computer applications (Graduate Certificate); computer programming (Graduate Certificate); correctional management and supervision (Graduate Certificate); English (MA); health systems management (Graduate Certificate); international studies (Graduate Certificate); liberal studies (MLS); nonprofit management (Graduate Certificate); paralegal studies (Graduate Certificate); professional writing (Graduate Certificate); public affairs (MPA); public management (Graduate Certificate); social and cultural diversity (Graduate Certificate); strategic sustainability leadership (Graduate Certificate); technology for administration (Graduate Certificate). *Program availability:* Part-time, evening/weekend. *Faculty:* 79 full-time (33 women). *Students:* 31 full-time (11 women), 92 part-time (53 women); includes 28 minority (9 Black or African American, non-Hispanic/Latino; 8 Asian, non-Hispanic/Latino; 5 Hispanic/Latino; 6 Two or more races, non-Hispanic/Latino), 19 international. Average age 38. 51 applicants, 84% accepted, 31 enrolled. In 2016, 30 master's, 6 other advanced degrees awarded. *Degree requirements:* For master's, variable foreign language requirement, thesis (for some programs). *Entrance requirements:* For master's, minimum GPA of 3.0. Additional exam requirements/recommendations for international students: Required—TOEFL (minimum score 550 paper-based; 80 iBT). *Application deadline:* For fall admission, 7/31 priority date for domestic students, 7/1 priority date for international students; for spring admission, 3/31 priority date for domestic students, 11/1 priority date for international students. Applications are processed on a rolling basis. Application fee: $40 ($60 for international students). *Expenses:* $276.98 per credit hour in-state; $652.54 per credit hour out-of-state. *Financial support:* In 2016–17, 5 teaching assistantships were awarded; Federal Work-Study also available. Support available to part-time students. Financial award application deadline: 3/10. *Faculty research:* Artificial intelligence, bioinformatics, English language and literature, creative writing, computer networks. *Total annual research expenditures:* $127,000. *Unit head:* Dr. Elizabeth E. Dunn, Dean, 574-520-4290, E-mail: elizdunn@iusb.edu. *Application contact:* Admissions Counselor, 574-520-4839, Fax: 574-520-4834, E-mail: graduate@iusb.edu.
Website: https://www.iusb.edu/clas/

Iona College, School of Arts and Science, Department of Mass Communication, New Rochelle, NY 10801-1890. Offers non-profit public relations (Certificate); public relations (MA); sports communication and media (MA). *Accreditation:* ACEJMC (one or more programs are accredited). *Program availability:* Part-time, evening/weekend. *Faculty:* 3 full-time (1 woman), 8 part-time/adjunct (4 women). *Students:* 10 full-time (4 women), 28 part-time (22 women); includes 17 minority (10 Black or African American, non-Hispanic/Latino; 7 Hispanic/Latino), 3 international. Average age 27. 19 applicants, 95% accepted, 11 enrolled. In 2016, 19 master's, 6 other advanced degrees awarded. *Degree requirements:* For master's, comprehensive exam (for some programs), thesis or alternative. *Entrance requirements:* For master's, GRE General Test if undergraduate GPA is below 3.0. Additional exam requirements/recommendations for international students: Required—TOEFL (minimum score 550 paper-based; 80 iBT), IELTS (minimum score 6). *Application deadline:* For fall admission, 8/1 for domestic students, 5/1 for international students; for spring admission, 1/1 for domestic students, 9/1 for international students. Applications are processed on a rolling basis. Application fee: $50. Electronic applications accepted. *Expenses:* Contact institution. *Financial support:* In 2016–17, 15 students received support. Scholarships/grants, tuition waivers (partial), and unspecified assistantships available. Support available to part-time students. Financial award application deadline: 4/15; financial award applicants required to submit FAFSA. *Faculty research:* Media ecology, new media, corporate communication, media images, organizational learning in public relations, media law, medicine ethics. *Unit head:* Anthony Kelso, PhD, Chair, 914-633-7795, E-mail: akelso@iona.edu. *Application contact:* Katelyn Brunck, Assistant Director of Graduate Admissions, 914-633-2492, Fax: 914-633-2277, E-mail: kbrunck@iona.edu.
Website: http://www.iona.edu/Academics/School-of-Arts-Science/Departments/Mass-Communication/Graduate-Programs.aspx

James Madison University, The Graduate School, College of Arts and Letters, Program in Public Administration, Harrisonburg, VA 22807. Offers individualized (MPA); public management (MPA), including international stabilization and recovery, management in international non-governmental organizations, nonprofit management, public management. Public and nonprofit management program offered in Roanoke. *Accreditation:* NASPAA. *Program availability:* Part-time. *Students:* 26 full-time (10 women), 19 part-time (8 women); includes 9 minority (6 Black or African American, non-Hispanic/Latino; 1 Hispanic/Latino; 2 Two or more races, non-Hispanic/Latino). Average age 30. 27 applicants, 89% accepted, 12 enrolled. In 2016, 9 master's awarded. Application fee: $55. Electronic applications accepted. *Financial support:* Federal Work-Study and 16 assistantships (averaging $7911) available. Financial award application deadline: 3/1; financial award applicants required to submit FAFSA. *Unit head:* Dr. Charles Blake, Department Head, 540-568-6149, E-mail: blakech@jmu.edu. *Application contact:* Lynette D. Michael, Director of Graduate Admissions, 540-568-6131, Fax: 540-568-7860, E-mail: michaeld@jmu.edu.
Website: http://www.jmu.edu/mpa

James Madison University, The Graduate School, College of Business, Program in Strategic Leadership, Harrisonburg, VA 22807. Offers postsecondary analysis and leadership (PhD), including nonprofit and community leadership, organizational science and leadership, postsecondary analysis and leadership. *Program availability:* Part-time, evening/weekend, online learning. *Faculty:* 3 full-time (1 woman). *Students:* 13 full-time (4 women), 25 part-time (10 women); includes 5 minority (all Black or African American, non-Hispanic/Latino), 3 international. Average age 30. 11 applicants, 64% accepted, 7 enrolled. In 2016, 5 doctorates awarded. Application fee: $55. Electronic applications accepted. *Financial support:* In 2016–17, 6 students received support. Fellowships, career-related internships or fieldwork, Federal Work-Study, unspecified assistantships, and 5 doctoral assistantships (stipend varies) available. Financial award application deadline: 3/1; financial award applicants required to submit FAFSA. *Unit head:* Dr. Karen A. Ford, Director of Strategic Leadership Studies, 540-568-7020, Fax: 540-568-7117, E-mail: fordka@jmu.edu. *Application contact:* Lynette D. Michael, Director of Graduate Admissions, 540-568-6131 Ext. 6395, Fax: 540-568-7860, E-mail: michaeld@jmu.edu.
Website: http://www.jmu.edu/leadership/

John Carroll University, Graduate Studies, Program in Nonprofit Administration, University Heights, OH 44118-4581. Offers MA. *Program availability:* Part-time, evening/weekend. *Degree requirements:* For master's, thesis optional. *Entrance requirements:* For master's, minimum GPA of 3.0, interview. Additional exam requirements/recommendations for international students: Required—TOEFL. *Application deadline:* For fall admission, 7/15 priority date for domestic students; for winter admission, 11/1 priority date for domestic students; for spring admission, 5/1 priority date for domestic students. Applications are processed on a rolling basis. Application fee: $25 ($35 for international students). Electronic applications accepted. *Expenses: Tuition:* Full-time $10,425; part-time $695 per credit hour. One-time fee: $200 full-time. Tuition and fees vary according to course load, campus/location and program. *Financial support:* Research assistantships with full tuition reimbursements and scholarships/grants available. *Unit head:* Dr. Tina Facca, Director, 216-397-1718, Fax: 216-397-1835, E-mail: tfacca@jcu.edu. *Application contact:* Jennifer L. Tucker, Records Management Assistant, 216-397-1925, Fax: 216-397-1835, E-mail: jtucker@jcu.edu.

Johns Hopkins University, Zanvyl Krieger School of Arts and Sciences, Advanced Academic Programs, Program in Government, Washington, DC 20036. Offers global security studies (MA); government (MA); national securities study (Certificate); nonprofit management (Certificate); public management (MA); research administration (MS); MA/MBA. *Program availability:* Part-time, evening/weekend, online learning. *Degree requirements:* For master's, thesis. *Entrance requirements:* For master's, minimum GPA of 3.0. Additional exam requirements/recommendations for international students: Required—TOEFL (minimum score 100 iBT). Electronic applications accepted.

Johnson & Wales University, Graduate Studies, MBA Program, Providence, RI 02903-3703. Offers accounting (MBA); business administration (MBA); finance (MBA); hospitality (MBA); human resource management (MBA); information technology (MBA); nonprofit management (MBA); operations and supply chain management (MBA). Program also offered on Denver campus. *Program availability:* Part-time, online learning. *Entrance requirements:* For master's, minimum GPA of 2.75. Additional exam requirements/recommendations for international students: Required—TOEFL (minimum score 550 paper-based); Recommended—IELTS, TWE. *Faculty research:* International banking, global economy, international trade, cultural differences.

Johnson & Wales University, Graduate Studies, MS Program in Nonprofit Management, Providence, RI 02903-3703. Offers MS. *Program availability:* Online learning.

Johnson University, Graduate and Professional Programs, Knoxville, TN 37998-1001. Offers biblical interpretation (Graduate Certificate); business administration (MBA); Christian ministries (Graduate Certificate); clinical mental health counseling (MA); educational technology (MA); intercultural studies (MA); leadership (MBA); leadership studies (PhD); New Testament (MA); nonprofit management (MBA); school counseling (MA); spiritual formation and leadership (Graduate Certificate); strategic ministry (MA); teacher education (MA). *Program availability:* Part-time, evening/weekend, 100% online, blended/hybrid learning. *Faculty:* 26 full-time (10 women), 32 part-time/adjunct (9 women). *Students:* 126 full-time (46 women), 170 part-time (65 women); includes 33 minority (13 Black or African American, non-Hispanic/Latino; 1 American Indian or Alaska Native, non-Hispanic/Latino; 4 Asian, non-Hispanic/Latino; 8 Hispanic/Latino; 7 Two or more races, non-Hispanic/Latino), 21 international. Average age 35. In 2016, 106 master's, 3 doctorates awarded. *Degree requirements:* For master's, variable foreign language requirement, comprehensive exam, thesis (for some programs), internships; for doctorate, variable foreign language requirement, comprehensive exam, thesis/dissertation, internships. *Entrance requirements:* For master's, PRAXIS (for MA in teacher education); MAT (for counseling); GRE or GMAT (for MBA), interview, 3 references, transcripts, essay, minimum GPA of 2.5 or 3.0 (depending on program); for doctorate, GRE or MAT (taken not less than 5 years prior), interview, 3 references, transcripts, essay, minimum GPA of 3.0; for Graduate Certificate, interview, 3 references, transcripts, essay, minimum GPA of 3.0. Additional exam requirements/recommendations for international students: Required—TOEFL (minimum score 527 paper-based; 71 iBT). *Application deadline:* For fall admission, 7/1 for domestic students; for spring admission, 11/1 for domestic students; for summer admission, 4/1 for domestic students. Application fee: $50. Electronic applications accepted. *Expenses:* Contact institution. *Financial support:* Scholarships/grants available. Financial award application deadline: 4/15; financial award applicants required to submit FAFSA. *Unit head:* Richard Clark, Vice President for External Relations, 865-251-2327, E-mail: rclark@johnsonu.edu. *Application contact:* Lisa Tarwater, Director of Graduate Admissions, 865-251-3400, E-mail: ltarwater@johnsonu.edu.

Kean University, College of Business and Public Management, Program in Public Administration, Union, NJ 07083. Offers health services administration (MPA); non-profit management (MPA); public administration (MPA). *Accreditation:* NASPAA. *Program availability:* Part-time. *Faculty:* 14 full-time (4 women). *Students:* 70 full-time (46 women), 51 part-time (37 women); includes 90 minority (63 Black or African American, non-Hispanic/Latino; 8 Asian, non-Hispanic/Latino; 18 Hispanic/Latino; 1 Two or more races, non-Hispanic/Latino), 4 international. Average age 31. 73 applicants, 42% accepted, 28 enrolled. In 2016, 56 master's awarded. *Degree requirements:* For master's, thesis, internship, research seminar. *Entrance requirements:* For master's, minimum cumulative GPA of 3.0, official transcripts from all institutions attended, two letters of recommendation, personal statement, writing sample, professional resume/curriculum vitae. Additional exam requirements/recommendations for international students: Required—TOEFL (minimum score 550 paper-based; 79 iBT), IELTS (minimum score 6.5). *Application deadline:* For fall admission, 6/1 for domestic and international students; for spring admission, 12/1 for domestic and international students. Applications are processed on a rolling basis. Application fee: $75. Electronic applications accepted. *Expenses:* Tuition, state resident: full-time $13,156; part-time $640 per credit. Tuition, nonresident: full-time $17,831; part-time $785 per credit. *Required fees:* $3316; $151 per credit. Tuition and fees vary according to course level, course load, degree level and program. *Financial support:* Scholarships/grants and unspecified assistantships available. Financial award applicants required to submit FAFSA. *Unit head:* Dr. Patricia Moore, Program Coordinator, 908-737-4314, E-mail: pmoore@kean.edu. *Application contact:* Pedro Lopes, Admissions Counselor, 908-737-7100, E-mail: grad-adm@kean.edu.
Website: http://grad.kean.edu/masters-programs/public-administration

La Salle University, School of Business, Program in Nonprofit Leadership, Philadelphia, PA 19141-1199. Offers MS. *Program availability:* Part-time, evening/weekend, 100% online. *Faculty:* 6 part-time/adjunct (3 women). *Students:* 1 (woman) full-time, 59 part-time (43 women); includes 14 minority (10 Black or African American, non-Hispanic/Latino; 4 Hispanic/Latino). Average age 37. 25 applicants, 92% accepted, 21 enrolled. In 2016, 1 master's awarded. *Degree requirements:* For master's, completion of all required courses within seven-year period; minimum cumulative GPA of 3.0. *Entrance requirements:* For master's, professional resume; personal statement explaining the applicant's interest in and goals for pursuit of this degree; 2 letters of recommendation. Additional exam requirements/recommendations for international students: Required—TOEFL. *Application deadline:* For fall admission, 8/15 priority date for domestic students, 7/15 for international students; for spring admission, 12/15 priority date for domestic students, 11/15 for international students; for summer admission, 4/15

priority date for domestic students, 3/15 for international students. Applications are processed on a rolling basis. Application fee: $35. Electronic applications accepted. Application fee is waived when completed online. *Expenses:* Contact institution. *Financial support:* In 2016–17, 8 students received support. Federal Work-Study, scholarships/grants, and unspecified assistantships available. Support available to part-time students. Financial award application deadline: 8/31; financial award applicants required to submit FAFSA. *Unit head:* Laura Otten, Director, 215-991-3682, Fax: 215-951-1960, E-mail: npl@lasalle.edu. *Application contact:* Lynnette Clement, Online Program Coordinator, Nonprofit Leadership, 215-991-3682, Fax: 215-951-1960, E-mail: clementl@lasalle.edu.
Website: http://www.lasalle.edu/nonprofit-leadership/

Lasell College, Graduate and Professional Studies in Management, Newton, MA 02466-2709. Offers business administration (PMBA); elder care management (MSM, Graduate Certificate); hospitality and event management (MSM, Graduate Certificate); human resources management (MSM, Graduate Certificate); management (MSM, Graduate Certificate); marketing (MSM, Graduate Certificate); non-profit management (MSM, Graduate Certificate); project management (MSM, Graduate Certificate). *Accreditation:* ACBSP. *Program availability:* Part-time, evening/weekend, 100% online, blended/hybrid learning. *Faculty:* 3 full-time (2 women), 16 part-time/adjunct (10 women). *Students:* 47 full-time (34 women), 93 part-time (72 women); includes 28 minority (20 Black or African American, non-Hispanic/Latino; 4 Asian, non-Hispanic/Latino; 3 Hispanic/Latino; 1 Two or more races, non-Hispanic/Latino), 24 international. Average age 31. 121 applicants, 55% accepted, 32 enrolled. In 2016, 61 master's, 3 other advanced degrees awarded. *Degree requirements:* For master's, minimum GPA of 3.0; internship or research paper (for MSM). *Entrance requirements:* For master's, one-page personal statement, 2 letters of recommendation, resume, bachelor's degree transcript; proof of microeconomics and statistics (for PMBA); for Graduate Certificate, bachelor's degree transcript, 2 letters of recommendation, 1-page personal statement, resume. Additional exam requirements/recommendations for international students: Required—TOEFL (minimum score 550 paper-based, 79 iBT) or IELTS (minimum score 6). *Application deadline:* For fall admission, 8/31 priority date for domestic students, 6/30 priority date for international students; for spring admission, 12/31 priority date for domestic students, 10/31 priority date for international students. Applications are processed on a rolling basis. Electronic applications accepted. *Expenses:* $600 per credit. *Financial support:* In 2016–17, 12 students received support. Federal Work-Study, scholarships/grants, and tuition discounts available. Support available to part-time students. Financial award application deadline: 8/31; financial award applicants required to submit FAFSA. *Unit head:* Dr. Joan Dolamore, Dean of Graduate and Professional Studies, 617-243-2485, Fax: 617-243-2450, E-mail: gradinfo@lasell.edu. *Application contact:* Adrienne Franciosi, Director of Graduate Enrollment, 617-243-2214, Fax: 617-243-2450, E-mail: gradinfo@lasell.edu.
Website: http://www.lasell.edu/academics/graduate-and-professional-studies/programs-of-study/master-of-science-in-management.html

Lasell College, Graduate and Professional Studies in Sport Management, Newton, MA 02466. Offers sport hospitality management (MS, Graduate Certificate); sport leadership (MS, Graduate Certificate); sport non-profit management (MS, Graduate Certificate). *Program availability:* Part-time, evening/weekend, online only, 100% online. *Faculty:* 4 full-time (0 women), 3 part-time/adjunct (1 woman). *Students:* 14 full-time (4 women), 30 part-time (10 women); includes 10 minority (9 Black or African American, non-Hispanic/Latino; 1 Hispanic/Latino). Average age 30. 40 applicants, 43% accepted, 9 enrolled. In 2016, 21 master's, 2 other advanced degrees awarded. *Degree requirements:* For master's, minimum GPA of 3.0; internship or thesis. *Entrance requirements:* For master's, one-page personal statement, 2 letters of recommendation, resume, bachelor's degree transcript; for Graduate Certificate, bachelor's degree transcript, 2 letters of recommendation, 1-page personal statement, resume. Additional exam requirements/recommendations for international students: Required—TOEFL (minimum score 550 paper-based, 79 iBT) or IELTS (minimum score 6). *Application deadline:* For fall admission, 8/31 priority date for domestic students, 6/30 priority date for international students; for spring admission, 12/31 priority date for domestic students, 10/31 priority date for international students. Applications are processed on a rolling basis. Electronic applications accepted. *Expenses:* $600 per credit. *Financial support:* In 2016–17, 4 students received support. Federal Work-Study, scholarships/grants, and tuition discounts available. Support available to part-time students. Financial award application deadline: 8/31; financial award applicants required to submit FAFSA. *Faculty research:* How do fans attribute team failure, investigating cross-cultural difference in attribution; sense of ownership as a key predictor of fan loyalty; fans' normative beliefs about sponsorship and sponsors, investigation of new attitudinal variables in sponsorship. *Unit head:* Dr. Joan Dolamore, Dean of Graduate and Professional Studies, 617-243-2485, Fax: 617-243-2450, E-mail: gradinfo@lasell.edu. *Application contact:* Adrienne Franciosi, Director of Graduate Enrollment, 617-243-2214, Fax: 617-243-2450, E-mail: gradinfo@lasell.edu.
Website: http://www.lasell.edu/academics/graduate-and-professional-studies/programs-of-study/master-of-science-in-sport-management.html

Lewis University, College of Arts and Sciences, Program in Organizational Leadership, Romeoville, IL 60446. Offers higher education/student services (MA); non-profit management (MA); organizational management (MA); professional and executive coaching (MA); training and development (MA). *Program availability:* Part-time, evening/weekend, 100% online. *Students:* 15 full-time (12 women), 176 part-time (130 women); includes 75 minority (51 Black or African American, non-Hispanic/Latino; 2 American Indian or Alaska Native, non-Hispanic/Latino; 2 Asian, non-Hispanic/Latino; 16 Hispanic/Latino; 4 Two or more races, non-Hispanic/Latino), 2 international. Average age 36. *Entrance requirements:* For master's, bachelor's degree, at least 24 years of age, minimum of 3 years of work experience, minimum GPA of 3.0, letter of recommendation. Additional exam requirements/recommendations for international students: Required—TOEFL (minimum score 550 paper-based; 80 iBT). *Application deadline:* For fall admission, 5/1 priority date for international students; for spring admission, 11/15 priority date for international students. Applications are processed on a rolling basis. Application fee: $40. Electronic applications accepted. *Expenses: Tuition:* Full-time $13,860; part-time $770 per credit hour. *Required fees:* $75 per semester. Tuition and fees vary according to degree level and program. *Financial support:* Tuition waivers and unspecified assistantships available. Financial award application deadline: 5/1; financial award applicants required to submit FAFSA. *Unit head:* Dr. Keith Lavine, Chair of Organizational Leadership, 815-838-0500, E-mail: lavineke@lewisu.edu. *Application contact:* Nancy Wiksten, Graduate Admission Counselor, 815-836-5628, Fax: 815-836-5578, E-mail: grad@lewisu.edu.

Lindenwood University, Graduate Programs, Plaster School of Business and Entrepreneurship, St. Charles, MO 63301-1695. Offers accountancy (M Acc); accounting (MBA); business administration (MBA); entrepreneurial studies (MBA); finance (MBA, MS); human resource management (MBA); international business (MBA); leadership (MA); management (MBA); marketing (MBA, MS); nonprofit administration (MA); public administration (MBA); sport management (MA); supply chain management (MBA). *Accreditation:* ACBSP. *Program availability:* Part-time, evening/weekend, 100% online. *Faculty:* 15 full-time (6 women), 25 part-time/adjunct (7 women). *Students:* 197 full-time (97 women), 213 part-time (132 women); includes 81 minority (62 Black or African American, non-Hispanic/Latino; 1 American Indian or Alaska Native, non-Hispanic/Latino; 4 Asian, non-Hispanic/Latino; 9 Hispanic/Latino; 5 Two or more races, non-Hispanic/Latino), 83 international. Average age 31. 279 applicants, 54% accepted, 133 enrolled. In 2016, 269 master's awarded. *Degree requirements:* For master's, comprehensive exam (for some programs), thesis (for some programs), minimum GPA of 3.0. *Entrance requirements:* For master's, interview, minimum undergraduate cumulative GPA of 3.0, letter of recommendation. Additional exam requirements/recommendations for international students: Required—TOEFL (minimum score 550 paper-based; 80 iBT); Recommended—IELTS (minimum score 6.5). *Application deadline:* For fall admission, 8/28 priority date for domestic and international students; for winter admission, 1/8 priority date for domestic and international students; for spring admission, 3/5 for domestic students, 3/5 priority date for international students; for summer admission, 6/4 priority date for domestic and international students. Applications are processed on a rolling basis. Application fee: $30 ($100 for international students). Electronic applications accepted. *Expenses:* Contact institution. *Financial support:* In 2016–17, 256 students received support. Career-related internships or fieldwork, Federal Work-Study, institutionally sponsored loans, scholarships/grants, tuition waivers (partial), and unspecified assistantships available. Financial award application deadline: 6/30; financial award applicants required to submit FAFSA. *Unit head:* Roger Ellis, Dean, School of Business and Entrepreneurship, 636-949-4839, E-mail: rellis@lindenwood.edu. *Application contact:* Tyler Kostich, Director, Evening and Graduate Admissions, 636-949-4138, Fax: 636-949-4109, E-mail: adultadmissions@lindenwood.edu.
Website: http://www.lindenwood.edu/academics/academic-schools/robert-w-plaster-school-of-business-entrepreneurship/

Lipscomb University, College of Business, Nashville, TN 37204-3951. Offers accountancy (M Acc); accounting (MBA); business administration (MM); conflict management (MBA); financial services (MBA); health care informatics (MBA); healthcare management (MBA); information security (MBA); leadership (MBA); nonprofit management (MBA); professional accountancy (Certificate); sports management (MBA); strategic human resources (MBA); sustainability (MBA); MBA/MS; Pharm D/MM. *Accreditation:* ACBSP. *Program availability:* Part-time, evening/weekend. *Faculty:* 22 full-time (4 women), 12 part-time/adjunct (4 women). *Students:* 112 full-time (51 women), 69 part-time (34 women); includes 30 minority (17 Black or African American, non-Hispanic/Latino; 3 Asian, non-Hispanic/Latino; 8 Hispanic/Latino; 2 Two or more races, non-Hispanic/Latino), 5 international. Average age 32. 244 applicants, 55% accepted, 54 enrolled. In 2016, 164 master's awarded. *Entrance requirements:* For master's, GMAT, transcripts, interview, 2 references, resume. Additional exam requirements/recommendations for international students: Required—TOEFL (minimum score 570 paper-based). *Application deadline:* For fall admission, 6/15 for domestic students, 2/1 for international students; for winter admission, 6/1 for international students; for spring admission, 11/15 for domestic students. Applications are processed on a rolling basis. Application fee: $50 ($75 for international students). Electronic applications accepted. *Expenses:* $1,150-$1,290 per hour, depending on program. *Financial support:* Career-related internships or fieldwork, scholarships/grants, tuition waivers (partial), and unspecified assistantships available. Support available to part-time students. Financial award application deadline: 7/1; financial award applicants required to submit FAFSA. *Faculty research:* Impact of spirituality on organization commitment, women in corporate leadership, psychological empowerment, training. *Unit head:* Allison Duke, Associate Dean of Graduate Business Programs, 615-966-5732, Fax: 615-966-1818, E-mail: allison.duke@lipscomb.edu. *Application contact:* Karen Risley, Manager, Graduate Business Recruiting, 615-966-5145, E-mail: karen.risley@lipscomb.edu.
Website: http://www.lipscomb.edu/business/Graduate-Programs

Long Island University–LIU Brooklyn, School of Business, Public Administration and Information Sciences, Brooklyn, NY 11201-8423. Offers accounting (MBA); accounting (MS); business administration (MBA); computer science (MS); gerontology (Advanced Certificate); health administration (MPA); human resources management (MS); not-for-profit management (Advanced Certificate); public administration (MPA); taxation (MS). *Program availability:* Part-time, evening/weekend, blended/hybrid learning. *Faculty:* 18 full-time (9 women), 32 part-time/adjunct (10 women). *Students:* 275 full-time (150 women), 238 part-time (161 women); includes 281 minority (200 Black or African American, non-Hispanic/Latino; 2 American Indian or Alaska Native, non-Hispanic/Latino; 38 Asian, non-Hispanic/Latino; 36 Hispanic/Latino; 1 Native Hawaiian or other Pacific Islander, non-Hispanic/Latino; 4 Two or more races, non-Hispanic/Latino), 140 international. 796 applicants, 66% accepted, 143 enrolled. In 2016, 185 master's, 17 other advanced degrees awarded. *Entrance requirements:* Additional exam requirements/recommendations for international students: Required—TOEFL (minimum score 527 paper-based; 75 IBT). *Application deadline:* Applications are processed on a rolling basis. Application fee: $50. Electronic applications accepted. *Expenses: Tuition:* Full-time $28,272; part-time $1178 per credit. *Required fees:* $451 per term. Tuition and fees vary according to degree level, program and student level. *Financial support:* In 2016–17, 94 students received support. Career-related internships or fieldwork, Federal Work-Study, institutionally sponsored loans, scholarships/grants, and unspecified assistantships available. Support available to part-time students. Financial award application deadline: 2/15; financial award applicants required to submit FAFSA. *Faculty research:* Corporate social responsibility; executive compensation and corporate governance; combinatorics; secure mobile coding; social equity and justice, particularly among the Latino population; public and healthcare finance. *Unit head:* Dr. Edward Rogoff, Dean, 718-488-1159, E-mail: edward.rogoff@liu.edu. *Application contact:* Gabrielle Gannon, Director of Graduate Admissions, 718-488-1011, Fax: 718-780-6110, E-mail: bkln-admissions@liu.edu.
Website: http://liu.edu/Brooklyn/Academics/School-of-Business-Public-Administration-and-Information-Sciences

Long Island University–LIU Post, School of Health Professions and Nursing, Brookville, NY 11548-1300. Offers cardiovascular perfusion (MS); clinical lab sciences (MS); clinical laboratory management (MS); dietetic internship (Advanced Certificate); family nurse practitioner (MS, Advanced Certificate); forensic social work (Advanced Certificate); gerontology (Advanced Certificate); health administration (MPA); medical biology (MS); non-profit management (Advanced Certificate); nursing education (MS); nutrition (MS); public administration (MPA); social work (MSW). *Program availability:* Part-time, evening/weekend, blended/hybrid learning. *Faculty:* 27 full-time (20 women), 43 part-time/adjunct (32 women). *Students:* 251 full-time (184 women), 243 part-time (197 women); includes 179 minority (76 Black or African American, non-Hispanic/Latino; 55 Asian, non-Hispanic/Latino; 42 Hispanic/Latino; 1 Native Hawaiian or other Pacific Islander, non-Hispanic/Latino; 5 Two or more races, non-Hispanic/Latino), 79 international. 581 applicants, 67% accepted, 168 enrolled. In 2016, 185 master's, 29 other advanced degrees awarded. *Degree requirements:* For master's, comprehensive exam (for some programs), thesis (for some programs); for Advanced Certificate, comprehensive exam (for some programs). *Entrance requirements:* Additional exam requirements/recommendations for international students: Required—TOEFL (minimum score 550 paper-based, 75 iBT) or IELTS. *Application deadline:* Applications are processed on a rolling basis. Application fee: $50. Electronic applications accepted. *Expenses: Tuition:* Full-time $28,272; part-time $1178 per credit. *Required fees:* $451 per term. Tuition and fees vary according to degree level and program. *Financial*

support: In 2016–17, 5 research assistantships with partial tuition reimbursements (averaging $725 per year), 3 teaching assistantships with partial tuition reimbursements (averaging $800 per year) were awarded; career-related internships or fieldwork, Federal Work-Study, institutionally sponsored loans, scholarships/grants, and unspecified assistantships also available. Support available to part-time students. Financial award application deadline: 2/15; financial award applicants required to submit FAFSA. *Faculty research:* Cancer gene regulation, childhood obesity, host-pathogen Interaction, interprofessional simulation, interstitial cystitis. *Total annual research expenditures:* $35,000. *Unit head:* Dr. Stacy Gropack, Dean, 516-299-2485, Fax: 516-299-2527, E-mail: post-shpn@liu.edu. *Application contact:* Carol Zerah, Director of Graduate Admissions, 516-299-2900, Fax: 516-299-2137, E-mail: post-enroll@liu.edu.
Website: http://liu.edu/post/health

Louisiana State University in Shreveport, College of Arts and Sciences, Program in Nonprofit Administration, Shreveport, LA 71115-2399. Offers MS. *Program availability:* Part-time, evening/weekend, online learning. *Students:* 9 full-time (all women), 44 part-time (38 women); includes 23 minority (18 Black or African American, non-Hispanic/Latino; 1 Asian, non-Hispanic/Latino; 1 Hispanic/Latino; 3 Two or more races, non-Hispanic/Latino). Average age 30. 80 applicants, 93% accepted, 32 enrolled. In 2016, 1 master's awarded. *Degree requirements:* For master's, final project. *Entrance requirements:* For master's, GRE, minimum GPA of 3.0 in last 2 undergraduate years, interview, recommendations. Additional exam requirements/recommendations for international students: Required—TOEFL (minimum score 550 paper-based; 61 iBT). *Application deadline:* For fall admission, 6/30 for domestic and international students; for spring admission, 11/30 for domestic and international students; for summer admission, 4/30 for domestic and international students. Applications are processed on a rolling basis. Application fee: $20 ($30 for international students). Electronic applications accepted. *Expenses:* Tuition, state resident: full-time $5163; part-time $350 per credit hour. Tuition, nonresident: full-time $15,578; part-time $1038 per credit hour. *Required fees:* $63 per credit hour. Tuition and fees vary according to course load and program. *Financial support:* In 2016–17, 2 research assistantships (averaging $3,780 per year) were awarded. Financial award applicants required to submit FAFSA. *Unit head:* Stacey Hargis, Interim Program Director, 318-795-4245, Fax: 318-797-5358, E-mail: stacey.hargis@lsus.edu. *Application contact:* Mary Catherine Harvison, Director of Admissions, 318-797-2400, Fax: 318-797-5286, E-mail: mary.harvison@lsus.edu.

Marymount University, School of Business Administration, Program in Leadership and Management, Arlington, VA 22207-4299. Offers association and nonprofit management (Certificate); leadership and management (MS); management studies (Certificate). *Program availability:* Part-time, evening/weekend. *Faculty:* 1 (woman) full-time. *Students:* 1 (woman) full-time, 13 part-time (8 women); includes 4 minority (2 Black or African American, non-Hispanic/Latino; 1 Asian, non-Hispanic/Latino; 1 Hispanic/Latino). Average age 43. 5 applicants, 100% accepted, 4 enrolled. In 2016, 3 master's, 2 other advanced degrees awarded. *Degree requirements:* For master's, thesis or alternative. *Entrance requirements:* For master's, GMAT or GRE General Test, resume, interview, at least 3 years of managerial experience, essay on a topic provided by School of Business Administration; for Certificate, resume, at least 3 years of managerial experience. Additional exam requirements/recommendations for international students: Required—TOEFL (minimum score 600 paper-based; 96 iBT), IELTS (minimum score 6.5). *Application deadline:* For fall admission, 7/16 priority date for domestic and international students; for spring admission, 11/16 priority date for domestic and international students; for summer admission, 4/16 for domestic and international students. Applications are processed on a rolling basis. Application fee: $40. Electronic applications accepted. *Expenses:* $960 per credit hour. *Financial support:* Research assistantships with tuition reimbursements, career-related internships or fieldwork, Federal Work-Study, scholarships/grants, and unspecified assistantships available. Support available to part-time students. Financial award applicants required to submit FAFSA. *Unit head:* Dr. Lorri Cooper, Chair, Management and Marketing/Director, 703-284-5950, Fax: 703-527-3830, E-mail: lorri.cooper@marymount.edu. *Application contact:* Francesca Reed, Director, Graduate Admissions, 703-284-5901, Fax: 703-527-3815, E-mail: grad.admissions@marymount.edu.
Website: http://www.marymount.edu/Academics/School-of-Business-Administration/Graduate-Programs/Leadership-Management-(M-S-)

Metropolitan State University, College of Management, St. Paul, MN 55106-5000. Offers business administration (MBA, DBA); database administration (Graduate Certificate); healthcare information technology management (Graduate Certificate); information assurance security (Graduate Certificate); management information systems (MMIS); MIS generalist (Graduate Certificate); MIS systems analysis and design (Graduate Certificate); project management (Graduate Certificate); public and nonprofit administration (MPNA). *Program availability:* Part-time, evening/weekend. *Degree requirements:* For master's, thesis optional, computer language (MMIS). *Entrance requirements:* For master's, GMAT (for MBA), resume. Additional exam requirements/recommendations for international students: Required—TOEFL (minimum score 550 paper-based). Electronic applications accepted. *Faculty research:* Yugoslav economic system, workers' cooperatives, participative management and job enrichment, global business systems.

Minnesota State University Mankato, College of Graduate Studies and Research, College of Social and Behavioral Sciences, Department of Urban and Regional Studies, Mankato, MN 56001. Offers local government management (Certificate); non-profit leadership (Certificate); urban and regional studies (MA); urban planning (MA, Certificate). *Students:* 9 full-time (7 women), 12 part-time (4 women). *Degree requirements:* For master's, one foreign language, comprehensive exam, thesis or alternative. *Entrance requirements:* For master's, minimum GPA of 3.0 during previous 2 years, 2 letters of recommendation. Additional exam requirements/recommendations for international students: Required—TOEFL. *Application deadline:* For fall admission, 7/1 priority date for domestic students; for spring admission, 11/1 for domestic students. Applications are processed on a rolling basis. Application fee: $40. Electronic applications accepted. *Financial support:* Fellowships with partial tuition reimbursements, research assistantships with full tuition reimbursements, teaching assistantships with full tuition reimbursements, career-related internships or fieldwork, Federal Work-Study, institutionally sponsored loans, and unspecified assistantships available. Support available to part-time students. Financial award application deadline: 3/15; financial award applicants required to submit FAFSA.
Website: http://sbs.mnsu.edu/ursi/graduate/

Misericordia University, College of Business, Program in Organizational Management, Dallas, PA 18612-1098. Offers healthcare management (MS); human resource management (MS); information technology management (MS); management (MS); not-for-profit management (MS). *Program availability:* Part-time, evening/weekend, online learning. *Entrance requirements:* For master's, GRE General Test, MAT (35th percentile or higher), or minimum undergraduate GPA of 3.0. Additional exam requirements/recommendations for international students: Required—TOEFL. Electronic applications accepted. Application fee is waived when completed online. *Expenses:* Contact institution.

Mount Aloysius College, Program in Business Administration, Cresson, PA 16630-1999. Offers accounting (MBA); health and human services administration (MBA); non-profit management (MBA); project management (MBA). *Program availability:* Part-time, evening/weekend. *Entrance requirements:* Additional exam requirements/recommendations for international students: Required—IELTS (minimum score 5.5); Recommended—TOEFL. *Application deadline:* For fall admission, 8/1 for domestic students; for spring admission, 12/1 for domestic students. Applications are processed on a rolling basis. Application fee: $30. Electronic applications accepted. Application fee is waived when completed online. *Expenses: Tuition:* Full-time $6750; part-time $750 per credit. *Required fees:* $285 per semester. *Financial support:* Unspecified assistantships available. Financial award applicants required to submit FAFSA. *Application contact:* Matthew P. Bodenschatz, Director of Graduate and Continuing Education Admissions, 814-886-6556, Fax: 814-886-6441, E-mail: mbodenschatz@mtaloy.edu.
Website: http://www.mtaloy.edu

New England College, Program in Management, Henniker, NH 03242-3293. Offers accounting (MSA); healthcare administration (MS); international relations (MA); marketing management (MS); nonprofit leadership (MS); project management (MS); strategic leadership (MS). *Program availability:* Part-time, evening/weekend. *Degree requirements:* For master's, independent research project. Electronic applications accepted.

The New School, Schools of Public Engagement, Program in Nonprofit Management, New York, NY 10011. Offers MS. *Program availability:* Part-time, evening/weekend. *Faculty:* 34 full-time (16 women), 8 part-time/adjunct (4 women). *Students:* 31 full-time (27 women), 33 part-time (27 women); includes 27 minority (10 Black or African American, non-Hispanic/Latino; 3 Asian, non-Hispanic/Latino; 12 Hispanic/Latino; 2 Two or more races, non-Hispanic/Latino), 8 international. Average age 29. 45 applicants, 98% accepted, 17 enrolled. In 2016, 34 master's awarded. *Degree requirements:* For master's, capstone project: Paper of Publishable Quality (PPQ), Professional Decision Report (PDR), or thesis. *Entrance requirements:* For master's, two letters of recommendation, statement of purpose, resume, transcripts. Additional exam requirements/recommendations for international students: Required—TOEFL (minimum score 100 iBT), IELTS (minimum score 7), PTE (minimum score 68). *Application deadline:* For fall admission, 1/15 priority date for domestic and international students; for spring admission, 10/15 priority date for domestic and international students. Applications are processed on a rolling basis. Application fee: $50. Electronic applications accepted. *Expenses:* Contact institution. *Financial support:* Research assistantships, teaching assistantships, career-related internships or fieldwork, Federal Work-Study, scholarships/grants, and unspecified assistantships available. Support available to part-time students. Financial award application deadline: 2/1; financial award applicants required to submit FAFSA. *Faculty research:* Economic sustainability of nonprofit organizations; global civil society and nongovernment organizations; philanthropy; social entrepreneurship, innovation and investment; social movements. *Unit head:* Suzanne Bostwick, Chair, 212-229-5400 Ext. 1601, E-mail: bostwics@newschool.edu. *Application contact:* Sharon Greenidge, Assistant Director, 212-229-5400 Ext. 1103, E-mail: greenids@newschool.edu.

New York University, Robert F. Wagner Graduate School of Public Service, Program in Public Administration, New York, NY 10010. Offers public administration (PhD); public and nonprofit management and policy (MPA, Advanced Certificate), including financial management and public finance (MPA), international policy and management (MPA), management for public and nonprofit organizations, public policy analysis, social impact, innovation, and investment (MPA); JD/MPA; MBA/MPA; MPA/MA. *Accreditation:* NASPAA (one or more programs are accredited). *Program availability:* Part-time. *Degree requirements:* For master's, thesis or alternative, capstone end event; for doctorate, one foreign language, comprehensive exam, thesis/dissertation, preliminary qualifying examination. *Entrance requirements:* Additional exam requirements/recommendations for international students: Required—TOEFL (minimum score 100 iBT), IELTS (minimum score 7.5), TWE. Electronic applications accepted. *Expenses:* Contact institution.

New York University, School of Continuing and Professional Studies, The George Heyman Jr. Center for Philanthropy and Fundraising, New York, NY 10012-1019. Offers fundraising and grantmaking (MS). *Program availability:* Part-time, evening/weekend. *Degree requirements:* For master's, thesis, capstone project. *Entrance requirements:* For master's, GRE or GMAT (only upon request), bachelor's degree, resume with relevant professional work, internship or volunteer experience, two letters of recommendation, statement of purpose. Additional exam requirements/recommendations for international students: Required—TOEFL (minimum score 600 paper-based; 100 iBT), IELTS (minimum score 7). Electronic applications accepted.

North Carolina State University, Graduate School, College of Humanities and Social Sciences, School of Public and International Affairs, Raleigh, NC 27695. Offers international studies (MIS); nonprofit management (Certificate); public administration (MPA, PhD). *Accreditation:* NASPAA (one or more programs are accredited). *Program availability:* Part-time, evening/weekend. *Entrance requirements:* For master's, GRE General Test, minimum GPA of 3.0 during previous 2 years. Electronic applications accepted. *Faculty research:* Public sector leadership and ethics, financial management, management systems evaluation, computer applications, service delivery.

Northeastern University, College of Professional Studies, Boston, MA 02115-5096. Offers applied nutrition (MS); college athletics administration (MSL); commerce and economic development (MS); corporate and organizational communication (MS); criminal justice (MS); digital media (MPS); elearning and instructional design (M Ed); elementary education (MAT); geographic information technology (MPS); global studies and international relations (MS); higher education administration (M Ed); homeland security (MA); human services (MS); informatics (MPS); leadership (MS); learning analytics (M Ed); learning and instruction (M Ed); nonprofit management (MS); professional sports administration (MSL); project management (MS); regulatory affairs for drugs, biologics, and medical devices (MS); respiratory care leadership (MS); special education (M Ed); technical communication (MS). *Program availability:* Part-time, evening/weekend, 100% online, blended/hybrid learning. *Faculty:* 82 full-time (51 women), 853 part-time/adjunct (366 women). *Students:* 4,947 part-time (3,076 women). In 2016, 1,456 master's awarded. *Application deadline:* Applications are processed on a rolling basis. Application fee: $0. Electronic applications accepted. *Expenses:* Contact institution. *Financial support:* Applicants required to submit FAFSA. *Unit head:* Dr. Mary Loeffelholz, Interim Dean of the College of Professional Studies.
Website: http://www.cps.neu.edu/

Northern Kentucky University, Office of Graduate Programs, College of Arts and Sciences, Program in Public Administration, Highland Heights, KY 41099. Offers non-profit management (Certificate); public administration (MPA). *Accreditation:* NASPAA. *Program availability:* Part-time. *Degree requirements:* For master's, 39 semester hours, including completion of the capstone course. *Entrance requirements:* For master's, GRE, minimum GPA of 2.5, letters of references, portfolios; for Certificate, minimum GPA of 2.0. Additional exam requirements/recommendations for international students: Required—TOEFL (minimum score 79 iBT); Recommended—IELTS (minimum score 6.5). Electronic applications accepted. *Faculty research:* Nonprofit management, human resource management, urban planning, service-learning, homeland security.

North Park University, School of Business and Nonprofit Management, Chicago, IL 60625-4895. Offers MBA, MHEA, MHRM, MM, MNA. *Program availability:* Part-time, evening/weekend, online learning. *Entrance requirements:* For master's, GMAT, GRE. Additional exam requirements/recommendations for international students: Required—TOEFL. *Expenses:* Contact institution.

Norwich University, College of Graduate and Continuing Studies, Master of Public Administration Program, Northfield, VT 05663. Offers criminal justice and public safety (MPA); fiscal management (MPA); international development and influence (MPA); municipal governance (MPA); nonprofit management (MPA); policy analysis and analytics (MPA); public administration leadership and crisis management (MPA); public works and sustainability (MPA). *Program availability:* Evening/weekend, online only, mostly all online with a week-long residency requirement. *Faculty:* 13 part-time/adjunct (5 women). *Students:* 63 full-time (23 women); includes 9 minority (5 Black or African American, non-Hispanic/Latino; 1 Asian, non-Hispanic/Latino; 1 Hispanic/Latino; 2 Two or more races, non-Hispanic/Latino). Average age 38. 23 applicants, 100% accepted, 15 enrolled. In 2016, 38 master's awarded. *Degree requirements:* For master's, capstone. *Entrance requirements:* For master's, minimum undergraduate GPA of 2.75. Additional exam requirements/recommendations for international students: Required—TOEFL (minimum score 550 paper-based; 80 iBT), IELTS (minimum score 6.5). *Application deadline:* For fall admission, 8/14 for domestic and international students; for winter admission, 11/13 for domestic and international students; for spring admission, 2/12 for domestic and international students; for summer admission, 5/15 for domestic and international students. Electronic applications accepted. *Expenses:* Contact institution. *Financial support:* In 2016–17, 21 students received support. Scholarships/grants available. Financial award application deadline: 8/4; financial award applicants required to submit FAFSA. *Unit head:* Dr. Rosemarie Pelletier, Program Director, 802-485-2767, Fax: 802-485-2533, E-mail: rpellet2@norwich.edu. *Application contact:* Admissions Advisor, 800-460-5597 Ext. 3377, Fax: 802-485-2533, E-mail: mpa@online.norwich.edu.
Website: https://online.norwich.edu/degree-programs/masters/master-public-administration/overview

Notre Dame of Maryland University, Graduate Studies, Program in Nonprofit Management, Baltimore, MD 21210-2476. Offers MA. *Program availability:* Part-time, evening/weekend. *Degree requirements:* For master's, thesis optional. *Entrance requirements:* For master's, minimum GPA of 3.0. Additional exam requirements/recommendations for international students: Required—TOEFL (minimum score 500 paper-based; 61 iBT). Electronic applications accepted.

Oakland University, Graduate Study and Lifelong Learning, College of Arts and Sciences, Department of Political Science, Rochester, MI 48309-4401. Offers local government management (Graduate Certificate); non-profit and organizational management (PMC); public administration (MPA). *Accreditation:* NASPAA. *Program availability:* Part-time, evening/weekend. *Entrance requirements:* For master's, minimum GPA of 3.0. Additional exam requirements/recommendations for international students: Required—TOEFL (minimum score 550 paper-based). Electronic applications accepted.

Oklahoma Christian University, Graduate School of Business, Oklahoma City, OK 73136-1100. Offers accounting (M Acc, MBA); financial services (MBA); general business (MBA); health services management (MBA); human resources (MBA); international business (MBA); leadership and organizational development (MBA); marketing (MBA); nonprofit management (MBA); project management (MBA). *Accreditation:* ACBSP. *Program availability:* Part-time, 100% online. *Faculty:* 10 full-time (2 women), 21 part-time/adjunct (2 women). *Students:* 156 full-time (68 women), 137 part-time (73 women). Average age 30. 374 applicants, 213 enrolled. In 2016, 114 master's awarded. *Entrance requirements:* For master's, bachelor's degree. Additional exam requirements/recommendations for international students: Required—TOEFL (minimum score 550 paper-based). Application fee: $25. Electronic applications accepted. *Expenses:* Contact institution. *Unit head:* Dr. Ken Johnson, Chair, 405-425-5567, Fax: 405-425-5585, E-mail: ken.johnson@oc.edu. *Application contact:* Angie Ricketts, Graduate School Admissions Counselor, 405-425-5587, Fax: 405-425-5585, E-mail: angie.ricketts@oc.edu.
Website: http://www.oc.edu/academics/graduate/business/

Oklahoma State University, Graduate College, Stillwater, OK 74078. Offers aerospace security (Graduate Certificate); bioenergy and sustainable technology (Graduate Certificate); business data mining (Graduate Certificate); business sustainability (Graduate Certificate); environmental science (MS); international studies (MS); non-profit management (Graduate Certificate); teaching English to speakers of other languages (Graduate Certificate); telecommunications management (MS). Programs are interdisciplinary. *Students:* 50 full-time (28 women), 109 part-time (63 women); includes 23 minority (4 Black or African American, non-Hispanic/Latino; 5 American Indian or Alaska Native, non-Hispanic/Latino; 4 Asian, non-Hispanic/Latino; 4 Hispanic/Latino; 6 Two or more races, non-Hispanic/Latino), 58 international. Average age 29. 363 applicants, 81% accepted, 71 enrolled. In 2016, 56 master's, 9 doctorates awarded. *Degree requirements:* For master's, thesis (for some programs); for doctorate, comprehensive exam, thesis/dissertation. *Entrance requirements:* For master's and doctorate, GRE or GMAT. Additional exam requirements/recommendations for international students: Required—TOEFL (minimum score 550 paper-based; 79 iBT). *Application deadline:* For fall admission, 3/1 priority date for domestic and international students; for spring admission, 8/1 priority date for domestic and international students. Applications are processed on a rolling basis. Application fee: $40 ($75 for international students). Electronic applications accepted. *Expenses:* Tuition, state resident: full-time $3775; part-time $209.70 per credit hour. Tuition, nonresident: full-time $14,851; part-time $825.05 per credit hour. *Required fees:* $2027; $112.60 per credit hour. Tuition and fees vary according to campus/location. *Financial support:* Research assistantships, career-related internships or fieldwork, Federal Work-Study, scholarships/grants, health care benefits, tuition waivers (partial), and unspecified assistantships available. Support available to part-time students. Financial award application deadline: 3/1; financial award applicants required to submit FAFSA. *Unit head:* Dr. Sheryl Tucker, Dean, 405-744-6368, Fax: 405-744-0355, E-mail: gradi@okstate.edu. *Application contact:* Dr. Susan Mathew, Assistant Director of Graduate Admissions, 405-744-6368, Fax: 405-744-0355, E-mail: gradi@okstate.edu.
Website: http://gradcollege.okstate.edu/

Oral Roberts University, School of Business, Tulsa, OK 74171. Offers accounting (MBA); entrepreneurship (MBA); finance (MBA); international business (MBA); management (MBA); marketing (MBA); non-profit management (MBA); not for profit management (MNM). *Accreditation:* ACBSP. *Program availability:* Part-time, online learning. *Degree requirements:* For master's, thesis optional. *Entrance requirements:* For master's, minimum cumulative GPA of 3.0. Additional exam requirements/recommendations for international students: Required—TOEFL (minimum score 550 paper-based; 79 iBT). Electronic applications accepted. *Faculty research:* Social media, international business and marketing.

Our Lady of the Lake University, School of Business and Leadership, Program in Nonprofit Management, San Antonio, TX 78207-4689. Offers MS. *Program availability:* Part-time, evening/weekend, online only, 100% online. *Faculty:* 2 full-time (0 women), 2 part-time/adjunct (0 women). *Students:* 33 full-time (26 women); includes 19 minority (7 Black or African American, non-Hispanic/Latino; 10 Hispanic/Latino; 2 Two or more races, non-Hispanic/Latino). Average age 33. 31 applicants, 97% accepted, 20 enrolled. In 2016, 7 master's awarded. *Entrance requirements:* For master's, official transcripts showing minimum cumulative GPA of 2.5, 2 letters of recommendation, resume. Additional exam requirements/recommendations for international students: Required—TOEFL. *Application deadline:* For fall admission, 6/15 for domestic and international students. Application fee: $40 ($50 for international students). Electronic applications accepted. *Expenses:* Contact institution. *Financial support:* In 2016–17, 1 student received support. Federal Work-Study, scholarships/grants, unspecified assistantships, and tuition discounts available. Support available to part-time students. Financial award application deadline: 5/1; financial award applicants required to submit FAFSA. *Unit head:* Dr. Ronald Crowe, Chair of Business Programs, 210-434-6711 Ext. 2713, E-mail: rcrowe@ollusa.edu. *Application contact:* Office of Graduate Admissions, 210-431-3995, Fax: 210-431-3945, E-mail: gradadm@ollusa.edu.
Website: http://www.ollusa.edu/s/1190/hybrid/default-hybrid-ollu.aspx?sid-1190&gid-1&pgid-7921

Pace University, Dyson College of Arts and Sciences, Department of Public Administration, New York, NY 10038. Offers government management (MPA); health care administration (MPA); not-for-profit management (MPA); JD/MPA. *Program availability:* Part-time, evening/weekend. *Faculty:* 6 full-time (4 women), 4 part-time/adjunct (1 woman). *Students:* 65 full-time (43 women), 78 part-time (42 women); includes 62 minority (40 Black or African American, non-Hispanic/Latino; 10 Asian, non-Hispanic/Latino; 11 Hispanic/Latino; 1 Two or more races, non-Hispanic/Latino), 21 international. Average age 30. In 2016, 54 master's awarded. *Degree requirements:* For master's, comprehensive exam, thesis (for some programs), capstone project. *Entrance requirements:* For master's, 2 letters of recommendation, resume, personal statement, official transcripts, essay. Additional exam requirements/recommendations for international students: Required—TOEFL (minimum score 88 iBT), IELTS (minimum score 7) or PTE (minimum score 60). *Application deadline:* For fall admission, 8/1 priority date for domestic students, 6/1 for international students; for spring admission, 12/1 priority date for domestic students, 10/1 for international students. Applications are processed on a rolling basis. Application fee: $70. Electronic applications accepted. *Expenses: Tuition:* Part-time $1195 per credit. *Required fees:* $260 per semester. Tuition and fees vary according to degree level, campus/location and program. *Financial support:* Research assistantships, career-related internships or fieldwork, Federal Work-Study, and tuition waivers (partial) available. Support available to part-time students. Financial award application deadline: 2/15; financial award applicants required to submit FAFSA. *Unit head:* Dr. Hillary Knepper, Chairperson, 914-773-3140, E-mail: hknepper@pace.edu. *Application contact:* Susan Ford-Goldschein, Director of Admissions, 914-422-4283, Fax: 212-346-1585, E-mail: graduateadmission@pace.edu.
Website: http://www.pace.edu/dyson/academic-departments-and-programs/public-admin

Park University, School of Graduate and Professional Studies, Kansas City, MO 54105. Offers adult education (M Ed); business and government leadership (Graduate Certificate); business, government, and global society (MPA); communication and leadership (MA); creative and life writing (Graduate Certificate); disaster and emergency management (MPA, Graduate Certificate); educational leadership (M Ed); finance (MBA, Graduate Certificate); general business (MBA); global business (Graduate Certificate); healthcare administration (MHA); healthcare services management and leadership (Graduate Certificate); international business (MBA); language and literacy (M Ed), including English for speakers of other languages, special reading teacher/literacy coach; leadership of international healthcare organizations (Graduate Certificate); management information systems (MBA, Graduate Certificate); music performance (ADP, Graduate Certificate), including cello (MM, ADP), piano (MM, ADP), viola (MM, ADP), violin (MM, ADP); nonprofit and community services management (MPA); nonprofit leadership (Graduate Certificate); performance (MM), including cello (MM, ADP), piano (MM, ADP), viola (MM, ADP), violin (MM, ADP); public management (MPA); social work (MSW); teacher leadership (M Ed), including curriculum and assessment, instructional leader. *Program availability:* Part-time, evening/weekend, online learning. *Degree requirements:* For master's, comprehensive exam (for some programs), thesis (for some programs), internship (for some programs); exam (for some programs). *Entrance requirements:* For master's, GRE or GMAT (for some programs), teacher certification (for some M Ed programs), letters of recommendation, essay, resume (for some programs). Additional exam requirements/recommendations for international students: Required—TOEFL (minimum score 550 paper-based; 79 iBT), IELTS (minimum score 6). Electronic applications accepted.

Penn State Harrisburg, Graduate School, School of Public Affairs, Middletown, PA 17057. Offers criminal justice (MA); health administration (MHA); health administration: long term care (Certificate); homeland security (Certificate); public administration (MPA, PhD); public administration: non-profit administration (Certificate); public budgeting and financial management (Certificate); public sector human resource management (Certificate). *Accreditation:* NASPAA. *Unit head:* Dr. Mukund S. Kulkarni, Chancellor, 717 948-6105, Fax: 717-948-6452. *Application contact:* Robert W. Coffman, Jr., Director of Enrollment Management, Admissions, 717-948-6250, Fax: 717-948-6325, E-mail: hbgadmit@psu.edu.
Website: https://harrisburg.psu.edu/public-affairs

Post University, Program in Human Services, Waterbury, CT 06723-2540. Offers human services (MS); human services/alcohol and drug counseling (MS); human services/clinical counseling (MS); human services/non-profit management (MS). *Program availability:* Part-time, evening/weekend, online learning.

Regent University, Graduate School, Robertson School of Government, Virginia Beach, VA 23464-9800. Offers government (MA), including American government, healthcare policy and ethics (MA, MPA), international relations, law and public policy, national security studies, political communication, political theory, religion and politics; public administration (MPA), including emergency management and homeland security, federal government, general public administration, healthcare policy and ethics (MA, MPA), law, nonprofit administration and faith-based organizations, public leadership and management, servant leadership. *Program availability:* Part-time, evening/weekend, 100% online, blended/hybrid learning. *Faculty:* 8 full-time (1 woman), 19 part-time/adjunct (3 women). *Students:* 40 full-time (27 women), 119 part-time (69 women); includes 73 minority (47 Black or African American, non-Hispanic/Latino; 3 Asian, non-Hispanic/Latino; 15 Hispanic/Latino; 8 Two or more races, non-Hispanic/Latino), 6 international. Average age 35. 253 applicants, 41% accepted, 70 enrolled. In 2016, 34 master's awarded. *Degree requirements:* For master's, thesis optional, internship. *Entrance requirements:* For master's, GRE General Test or LSAT, personal essay, writing sample, resume, college transcripts. Additional exam requirements/recommendations for international students: Required—TOEFL (minimum score 577 paper-based). *Application deadline:* For fall admission, 5/1 priority date for domestic students; for spring admission, 11/1 priority date for domestic students. Applications are processed on a rolling basis. Application fee: $50. Electronic applications accepted. *Expenses:* $650 per credit (MA/MPA); $250 per semester technology fee. *Financial support:* In 2016–17, 78 students received support. Career-related internships or fieldwork, scholarships/grants, and unspecified assistantships available. Support

available to part-time students. *Faculty research:* International relations and politics, public administration, leadership and ethics, Biblical law, Constitutional law and Supreme Court. *Unit head:* Dr. Eric Patterson, Dean, 757-352-4616, Fax: 757-352-4735, E-mail: epatterson@regent.edu. *Application contact:* Heidi Cece, Assistant Vice President of Enrollment Management, 800-373-5504, Fax: 757-352-4381, E-mail: admissions@regent.edu.
Website: http://www.regent.edu/rsg/

Regent University, Graduate School, School of Business and Leadership, Virginia Beach, VA 23464-9800. Offers business administration (MBA), including accounting, entrepreneurship, finance and investing, general management, healthcare management (MA, MBA), human resource management, innovation management; leadership (Certificate); organizational leadership (MA, PhD), including ecclesial leadership (PhD), entrepreneurial leadership (PhD), future studies (MA), healthcare management (MA, MBA), human resource development (PhD), interdisciplinary studies (MA), international organizations (MA), leadership coaching and mentoring (MA), not-for-profit management (MA), organizational communication (MA), organizational development consulting (MA); strategic leadership (DSL), including global consulting, leadership coaching, strategic foresight. *Program availability:* Part-time, evening/weekend, 100% online, blended/hybrid learning. *Faculty:* 9 full-time (2 women), 28 part-time/adjunct (10 women). *Students:* 100 full-time (56 women), 1,008 part-time (528 women); includes 562 minority (453 Black or African American, non-Hispanic/Latino; 7 American Indian or Alaska Native, non-Hispanic/Latino; 30 Asian, non-Hispanic/Latino; 51 Hispanic/Latino; 1 Native Hawaiian or other Pacific Islander, non-Hispanic/Latino; 20 Two or more races, non-Hispanic/Latino), 76 international. Average age 40. 1,240 applicants, 45% accepted, 352 enrolled. In 2016, 95 master's, 71 doctorates awarded. *Degree requirements:* For master's, thesis or alternative, 3-credit hour culminating experience; for doctorate, thesis/dissertation. *Entrance requirements:* For master's, college transcripts, resume, essay; for doctorate, college transcripts, resume, essay, writing sample; for Certificate, writing sample, resume, transcripts. Additional exam requirements/recommendations for international students: Required—TOEFL (minimum score 577 paper-based). *Application deadline:* For fall admission, 5/1 priority date for domestic students; for spring admission, 10/1 priority date for domestic students. Applications are processed on a rolling basis. Application fee: $50. Electronic applications accepted. *Expenses:* Contact institution. *Financial support:* In 2016–17, 631 students received support. Career-related internships or fieldwork, scholarships/grants, and unspecified assistantships available. Support available to part-time students. *Faculty research:* Servant leadership, global business, team effectiveness, technology utilization, leadership development. *Unit head:* Dr. Doris Gomez, Dean, 757-352-4686, Fax: 757-352-4634, E-mail: dorigom@regent.edu. *Application contact:* Heidi Cece, Assistant Vice President of Enrollment Management, 800-373-5504, Fax: 757-352-4381, E-mail: admissions@regent.edu.
Website: http://www.regent.edu/sbl/

Regent University, Graduate School, School of Law, Virginia Beach, VA 23464-9800. Offers American legal studies (LL M); human rights (LL M); law (MA, JD), including business (MA), criminal justice (MA), general legal studies (MA), human resources management (MA), human rights (MA), mediation (MA), national security (MA), non-profit management (MA), regulatory compliance (MA), wealth management and financial planning (MA); JD/MA; JD/MBA. *Accreditation:* ABA. *Program availability:* Part-time, 100% online, blended/hybrid learning. *Faculty:* 20 full-time (6 women), 67 part-time/adjunct (19 women). *Students:* 364 full-time (219 women), 170 part-time (118 women); includes 213 minority (150 Black or African American, non-Hispanic/Latino; 1 American Indian or Alaska Native, non-Hispanic/Latino; 10 Asian, non-Hispanic/Latino; 34 Hispanic/Latino; 1 Native Hawaiian or other Pacific Islander, non-Hispanic/Latino; 17 Two or more races, non-Hispanic/Latino), 87 international. Average age 34. 834 applicants, 45% accepted, 174 enrolled. In 2016, 48 master's, 85 doctorates awarded. *Entrance requirements:* For master's, college transcripts, resume, personal statement; for doctorate, LSAT, minimum undergraduate GPA of 3.0, official transcripts, 2 letters of recommendation, resume, personal statement. Additional exam requirements/recommendations for international students: Required—TOEFL (minimum score 600 paper-based). *Application deadline:* For fall admission, 3/1 for domestic students. Applications are processed on a rolling basis. Application fee: $50. Electronic applications accepted. *Expenses:* $1,140 per credit (for JD); $650 per credit (for MA); $833 per credit (for LL M); $250 technology fee. *Financial support:* In 2016–17, 319 students received support. Career-related internships or fieldwork, scholarships/grants, and unspecified assistantships available. Support available to part-time students. *Faculty research:* Family law, Constitutional law, law and culture, evidence and practice, intellectual property. *Unit head:* Michael Hernandez, Dean, 757-352-4040, Fax: 757-352-4595, E-mail: michher@regent.edu. *Application contact:* Katie Kerley, Director of Law Admissions, 877-267-5072, Fax: 757-352-4139, E-mail: lawschool@regent.edu.
Website: http://www.regent.edu/law/

Regis University, College of Business and Economics, Denver, CO 80221-1099. Offers accounting (MS); executive leadership (Certificate); finance (MS); finance and accounting (MBA); health industry leadership (MBA); human resource management and leadership (MSOL); management (MBA); marketing (MBA); nonprofit leadership (Post-Graduate Certificate); nonprofit management (MNM); nonprofit organizational capacity building (Certificate); operations management (MBA); organizational leadership and management (MSOL); project leadership and management (MS, MSOL); strategic business management (Certificate); strategic human resource integration (Certificate); strategic management (MBA). Programs offered at Colorado Springs Campus, Northwest Denver Campus, Southeast Denver Campus, Fort Collins Campus, Broomfield Campus, Henderson (Nevada) Campus, and Summerlin (Nevada) Campus. *Program availability:* Part-time, evening/weekend, 100% online, blended/hybrid learning. *Faculty:* 15 full-time (5 women), 43 part-time/adjunct (16 women). *Students:* 622 full-time (350 women), 460 part-time (170 women); includes 317 minority (88 Black or African American, non-Hispanic/Latino; 7 American Indian or Alaska Native, non-Hispanic/Latino; 44 Asian, non-Hispanic/Latino; 151 Hispanic/Latino; 1 Native Hawaiian or other Pacific Islander, non-Hispanic/Latino; 26 Two or more races, non-Hispanic/Latino), 44 international. Average age 36. 307 applicants, 73% accepted, 134 enrolled. In 2016, 394 master's awarded. *Degree requirements:* For master's, thesis (for some programs), capstone or final research project. *Entrance requirements:* For master's, official transcript reflecting baccalaureate degree awarded from regionally-accredited college or university, interview, 2 years of full-time related work experience, resume, letters of recommendation. Additional exam requirements/recommendations for international students: Required—TOEFL (minimum score 550 paper-based; 82 iBT). *Application deadline:* For fall admission, 8/15 priority date for domestic students, 8/13 for international students; for winter admission, 10/10 priority date for domestic students, 9/8 for international students; for spring admission, 1/10 priority date for domestic students, 11/17 for international students; for summer admission, 5/1 priority date for domestic students. Applications are processed on a rolling basis. Application fee: $75. Electronic applications accepted. *Expenses:* $780 per credit hour. *Financial support:* Scholarships/grants available. Financial award application deadline: 4/15; financial award applicants required to submit FAFSA. *Faculty research:* Impact of information technology on small business regulation of accounting, international project financing, mineral development, delivery of healthcare to rural indigenous communities. *Unit head:* Dr. Timothy Keane, Academic Dean. *Application contact:* Cate Clark, Director of Admissions, 303-458-4900, Fax: 303-964-5534, E-mail: ruadmissions@regis.edu.
Website: http://www.regis.edu/CBE.aspx

Rockhurst University, Helzberg School of Management, Kansas City, MO 64110-2561. Offers accounting (MBA); business intelligence (MBA, Certificate); data science (MBA, Certificate); entrepreneurship (MBA); finance (MBA); fundraising leadership (MBA, Certificate); healthcare management (MBA, Certificate); human capital (Certificate); international business (Certificate); management (MBA, Certificate); nonprofit administration (Certificate); organizational development (Certificate); science leadership (Certificate). *Accreditation:* AACSB. *Program availability:* Part-time, evening/weekend. *Entrance requirements:* For master's, GMAT or GRE. Additional exam requirements/recommendations for international students: Required—TOEFL (minimum score 550 paper-based; 79 iBT). Electronic applications accepted. Application fee is waived when completed online. *Faculty research:* Offshoring/outsourcing, systems analysis/synthesis, work teams, multilateral trade, path dependencies/creation.

St. Cloud State University, School of Graduate Studies, College of Social Sciences, Department of Economics, Program in Public and Nonprofit Institutions, St. Cloud, MN 56301-4498. Offers MS. *Program availability:* Part-time. *Degree requirements:* For master's, thesis or alternative. *Entrance requirements:* For master's, GRE General Test, minimum GPA of 2.75. Additional exam requirements/recommendations for international students: Required—Michigan English Language Assessment Battery; Recommended—TOEFL (minimum score 550 paper-based), IELTS (minimum score 6.5). Electronic applications accepted.

Saint Mary-of-the-Woods College, Master of Leadership Development Program, Saint Mary of the Woods, IN 47876. Offers not-for-profit leadership (MLD); organizational leadership (MLD). *Program availability:* Part-time, blended/hybrid learning. *Students:* 47 full-time (41 women); includes 4 minority (all Black or African American, non-Hispanic/Latino). Average age 35. *Degree requirements:* For master's, thesis. *Application deadline:* Applications are processed on a rolling basis. Application fee: $0. Electronic applications accepted. *Expenses:* Contact institution. *Financial support:* Scholarships/grants available. *Unit head:* Susan Decker, Director, Master of Leadership Development, 812-535-5206, E-mail: sdecker2@smwc.edu.

Salve Regina University, Program in Management, Newport, RI 02840-4192. Offers innovation and strategic management (MS); nonprofit management (CGS). *Program availability:* Part-time, evening/weekend, online learning. *Entrance requirements:* For master's, GMAT, GRE General Test, or MAT. Additional exam requirements/recommendations for international students: Required—TOEFL (minimum score 600 paper-based; 100 iBT). Electronic applications accepted.

San Francisco State University, Division of Graduate Studies, College of Business, Program in Business Administration, San Francisco, CA 94132-1722. Offers decision sciences/operations research (MBA); ethics and compliance (MBA); finance (MBA); global business and innovation (MBA); healthcare administration (MBA); hospitality and tourism management (MBA); information systems (MBA); leadership (MBA); marketing (MBA); nonprofit and social enterprise leadership (MBA); sustainable business (MBA). *Accreditation:* AACSB. *Program availability:* Part-time, evening/weekend. *Degree requirements:* For master's, thesis, essay test. *Entrance requirements:* For master's, GMAT, minimum GPA of 2.7 in last 60 units. Additional exam requirements/recommendations for international students: Required—TOEFL (minimum score 550 paper-based). *Application deadline:* For fall admission, 5/1 priority date for domestic students, 4/1 for international students; for spring admission, 11/1 for domestic students, 10/15 for international students. Applications are processed on a rolling basis. Application fee: $55. *Expenses:* Tuition, state resident: full-time $6738. Tuition, nonresident: full-time $15,666. *Required fees:* $1012. Tuition and fees vary according to degree level and program. *Financial support:* Application deadline: 3/1. *Unit head:* Dr. Sanjit Sengupta, Faculty Director, 415-817-4366, Fax: 415-817-4340, E-mail: sengupta@sfsu.edu. *Application contact:* Zandra Tan, EMBA Program Coordinator, 415-817-4360, Fax: 415-817-4340, E-mail: zandra13@sfsu.edu.
Website: http://cob.sfsu.edu/graduate-programs/mba

San Francisco State University, Division of Graduate Studies, College of Health and Social Sciences, Public Administration Program, San Francisco, CA 94132-1722. Offers criminal justice administration (MPA); environmental administration and policy (MPA); gerontology (MPA); nonprofit administration (MPA); public management (MPA); public policy (MPA); urban administration (MPA). *Accreditation:* NASPAA. *Expenses:* Tuition, state resident: full-time $6738. Tuition, nonresident: full-time $15,666. *Required fees:* $1012. Tuition and fees vary according to degree level and program. *Unit head:* Dr. Elizabeth Brown, Director of the School of Public Affairs and Civic Engagement, 415-817-4455, Fax: 415-817-4464, E-mail: mpa@sfsu.edu. *Application contact:* Dr. Jennifer Shea, Graduate Coordinator, 415-817-4462, Fax: 415-817-4464, E-mail: jshea@sfsu.edu.
Website: http://mpa.sfsu.edu/

Seton Hall University, College of Arts and Sciences, Department of Political Science and Public Affairs, South Orange, NJ 07079-2697. Offers nonprofit organization management (Graduate Certificate); public administration (MPA), including health policy and management, nonprofit organization management, public service: leadership, governance, and policy. *Accreditation:* CAHME; NASPAA. *Program availability:* Part-time, evening/weekend. *Degree requirements:* For master's, thesis or alternative, internship or practicum. *Entrance requirements:* Additional exam requirements/recommendations for international students: Required—TOEFL. Electronic applications accepted.

Simmons College, School of Management, Boston, MA 02115. Offers business administration (MBA); health care (MBA); management (MS, MSM), including communications management (MS), non-profit management (MS); MBA/MSW; MS/MA. *Accreditation:* AACSB. *Program availability:* Part-time, evening/weekend. *Faculty:* 14 full-time (10 women), 5 part-time/adjunct (3 women). *Students:* 23 full-time (20 women), 141 part-time (126 women); includes 41 minority (20 Black or African American, non-Hispanic/Latino; 7 Asian, non-Hispanic/Latino; 13 Hispanic/Latino; 1 Two or more races, non-Hispanic/Latino), 7 international. Average age 32. 62 applicants, 74% accepted, 32 enrolled. In 2016, 58 master's awarded. *Entrance requirements:* For master's, GMAT or GRE. Additional exam requirements/recommendations for international students: Required—TOEFL. *Application deadline:* For fall admission, 7/18 priority date for domestic students; for summer admission, 4/24 priority date for domestic students. Applications are processed on a rolling basis. Application fee: $75. Electronic applications accepted. *Expenses:* $1,374 per credit, $4,122 per course, $102 activity fee per semester. *Financial support:* Scholarships/grants and unspecified assistantships available. Financial award applicants required to submit FAFSA. *Faculty research:* Gender and organizations, leadership, health care management. *Unit head:* Patricia Deyton, Associate Dean for Graduate Programs, 617-521-3876.
Website: http://www.simmons.edu/som

Sonoma State University, School of Social Sciences, Department of Political Science, Rohnert Park, CA 94928. Offers administration of nonprofit agencies (Certificate); public administration (MPA). *Program availability:* Part-time, evening/weekend. *Degree requirements:* For master's, thesis or alternative. *Entrance requirements:* For master's,

GRE General Test, minimum GPA of 3.0. Additional exam requirements/ recommendations for international students: Required—TOEFL (minimum score 500 paper-based). *Application deadline:* For fall admission, 11/30 for domestic students; for spring admission, 8/31 for domestic students. Application fee: $55. *Expenses:* Tuition, state resident: full-time $6738; part-time $3906 per unit. *Required fees:* $1916; $1916 per year. Tuition and fees vary according to course load, degree level and program. *Financial support:* Research assistantships, teaching assistantships, career-related internships or fieldwork, and Federal Work-Study available. Support available to part-time students. Financial award application deadline: 3/2; financial award applicants required to submit FAFSA. *Unit head:* Catherine Nelson, Chair, 707-664-2179, E-mail: catherine.nelson@sonoma.edu. *Application contact:* Diane Brown, Graduate Program Coordinator, 707-664-2875, Fax: 707-664-3920, E-mail: diane.brown@sonoma.edu. Website: http://www.sonoma.edu/polisci/

Southern Adventist University, School of Business and Management, Collegedale, TN 37315-0370. Offers accounting (MBA); church administration (MSA); church and nonprofit leadership (MBA); financial management (MFM); healthcare administration (MBA); management (MBA); marketing management (MBA); outdoor education (MSA). *Program availability:* Part-time, evening/weekend, online learning. *Entrance requirements:* For master's, GMAT. Additional exam requirements/recommendations for international students: Required—TOEFL (minimum score 600 paper-based; 100 iBT). Electronic applications accepted.

Southern New Hampshire University, School of Business, Manchester, NH 03106-1045. Offers accounting (MBA, MS, Graduate Certificate); accounting finance (MS); accounting/auditing (MS); accounting/forensic accounting (MS); accounting/taxation (MS); athletic administration (MBA, Graduate Certificate); business administration (IMBA, MBA, Certificate, Graduate Certificate), including accounting (Certificate), business administration (MBA), business information systems (Graduate Certificate), human resource management (Certificate); corporate social responsibility (MBA); entrepreneurship (MBA); finance (MBA, MS, Graduate Certificate); finance/corporate finance (MS); finance/investments and securities (MS); forensic accounting (MBA); healthcare informatics (MBA); healthcare management (MBA); human resource management (Graduate Certificate); information technology (MS, Graduate Certificate); information technology management (MBA); international business (Graduate Certificate); international business and information technology (Graduate Certificate); international finance (Graduate Certificate); international sport management (Graduate Certificate); justice studies (MBA); leadership of nonprofit organizations (Graduate Certificate); management (MS); marketing (MBA, MS, Graduate Certificate); operations and project management (MS); operations and supply chain management (MBA, Graduate Certificate); organizational leadership (MS); project management (MBA, Graduate Certificate); Six Sigma (MBA); Six Sigma quality (Graduate Certificate); social media marketing (MBA); sport management (MBA, MS, Graduate Certificate); sustainability and environmental compliance (MBA); workplace conflict management (MBA); MBA/Certificate. *Accreditation:* ACBSP. *Program availability:* Part-time, evening/ weekend, online learning. Terminal master's awarded for partial completion of doctoral program. *Degree requirements:* For master's, one foreign language, comprehensive exam (for some programs), thesis or alternative. *Entrance requirements:* For master's, minimum GPA of 2.5. Additional exam requirements/recommendations for international students: Required—TOEFL (minimum score 500 paper-based). Electronic applications accepted.

Suffolk University, Sawyer Business School, Department of Public Administration, Boston, MA 02108-2770. Offers community health (MPA); information systems, performance management, and big data analytics (MPA); nonprofit management (MPA); state and local government (MPA); JD/MPA; MPA/MS; MPA/MSCJ; MPA/MSMHC; MPA/MSPS. *Accreditation:* NASPAA (one or more programs are accredited). *Program availability:* Part-time, evening/weekend. *Faculty:* 4 full-time (1 woman), 2 part-time/ adjunct (both women). *Students:* 26 full-time (13 women), 96 part-time (58 women); includes 42 minority (18 Black or African American, non-Hispanic/Latino; 5 Asian, non-Hispanic/Latino; 18 Hispanic/Latino; 1 Two or more races, non-Hispanic/Latino), 4 international. Average age 34. 133 applicants, 85% accepted, 53 enrolled. In 2016, 47 degrees awarded. *Entrance requirements:* Additional exam requirements/ recommendations for international students: Required—TOEFL (minimum score 550 paper-based; 80 iBT). *Application deadline:* For fall admission, 3/15 priority date for domestic and international students; for spring admission, 10/15 priority date for domestic and international students. Applications are processed on a rolling basis. Application fee: $50. Electronic applications accepted. *Expenses: Tuition:* Full-time $41,490; part-time $1383 per credit hour. *Required fees:* $52; $52 per credit hour. Part-time tuition and fees vary according to course load and program. *Financial support:* In 2016–17, 82 students received support, including 78 fellowships (averaging $6,546 per year); career-related internships or fieldwork, Federal Work-Study, institutionally sponsored loans, and scholarships/grants also available. Support available to part-time students. Financial award application deadline: 4/1; financial award applicants required to submit FAFSA. *Faculty research:* Local government, health care, federal policy, mental health, HIV/AIDS. *Unit head:* Brenda Bond, Director/Department Chair, 617-305-1768, E-mail: bbond@suffolk.edu. *Application contact:* Mara Marzocchi, Associate Director of Graduate Admissions, 617-573-8302, Fax: 617-305-1733, E-mail: grad.admission@suffolk.edu.
Website: http://www.suffolk.edu/mpa

Suffolk University, Sawyer Business School, Master of Business Administration Program, Boston, MA 02108-2770. Offers accounting (MBA); entrepreneurship (MBA); executive business administration (EMBA); finance (MBA); global business administration (GMBA); health administration (MBA); international business (MBA); marketing (MBA); nonprofit management (MBA); organizational behavior (MBA); strategic management (MBA); supply chain management (MBA); taxation (MBA); JD/ MBA; MBA/MHA; MBA/MSA; MBA/MSF; MBA/MST. *Accreditation:* AACSB. *Program availability:* Part-time, evening/weekend, 100% online. *Faculty:* 17 full-time (6 women), 10 part-time/adjunct (1 woman). *Students:* 137 full-time (70 women), 265 part-time (138 women); includes 78 minority (20 Black or African American, non-Hispanic/Latino; 22 Asian, non-Hispanic/Latino; 31 Hispanic/Latino; 5 Two or more races, non-Hispanic/ Latino), 46 international. Average age 30. 416 applicants, 70% accepted, 128 enrolled. In 2016, 165 degrees awarded. *Entrance requirements:* For master's, GMAT, minimum undergraduate GPA of 2.75 (MBA), 5 years of managerial experience (EMBA). Additional exam requirements/recommendations for international students: Required—TOEFL (minimum score 550 paper-based; 80 iBT). *Application deadline:* For fall admission, 3/15 priority date for domestic students, 10/15 priority date for international students; for spring admission, 10/15 priority date for domestic and international students. Applications are processed on a rolling basis. Application fee: $50. Electronic applications accepted. *Expenses: Tuition:* Full-time $41,490; part-time $1383 per credit hour. *Required fees:* $52; $52 per credit hour. Part-time tuition and fees vary according to course load and program. *Financial support:* In 2016–17, 209 students received support, including 176 fellowships (averaging $8,581 per year); career-related internships or fieldwork, Federal Work-Study, institutionally sponsored loans, and scholarships/grants also available. Support available to part-time students. Financial award application deadline: 4/1; financial award applicants required to submit FAFSA. *Faculty research:* Foreign investments; career strategies and boundaryless careers; corporate ethics codes; interest rates, inflation, and growth options; innovation and product development performance. *Unit head:* Jodi Detjen, Director of MBA Programs, 617-573-8306, E-mail: jdetjen@suffolk.edu. *Application contact:* Mara Marzocchi, Associate Director of Graduate Admissions, 617-573-8302, Fax: 617-305-1733, E-mail: grad.admission@suffolk.edu.
Website: http://www.suffolk.edu/mba

Texas A&M University, Bush School of Government and Public Service, College Station, TX 77840. Offers homeland security (Certificate); international affairs (MIA, Certificate); national security affairs (Certificate); non-profit management (Certificate); public service and administration (MPSA). *Accreditation:* NASPAA. *Faculty:* 68. *Students:* 324 full-time (165 women), 26 part-time (10 women); includes 89 minority (19 Black or African American, non-Hispanic/Latino; 4 Asian, non-Hispanic/Latino; 58 Hispanic/Latino; 1 Native Hawaiian or other Pacific Islander, non-Hispanic/Latino; 7 Two or more races, non-Hispanic/Latino), 44 international. Average age 27. 261 applicants, 96% accepted, 165 enrolled. In 2016, 164 master's awarded. *Degree requirements:* For master's, summer internship. *Entrance requirements:* For master's, GRE (preferred) or GMAT. Additional exam requirements/recommendations for international students: Required—TOEFL (minimum score 550 paper-based; 80 iBT), IELTS (minimum score 6), PTE (minimum score 53). *Application deadline:* For fall admission, 1/15 for domestic and international students. Application fee: $50 ($90 for international students). Electronic applications accepted. *Expenses:* Contact institution. *Financial support:* In 2016–17, 413 students received support, including 16 fellowships with tuition reimbursements available (averaging $18,236 per year), 61 research assistantships with tuition reimbursements available (averaging $5,904 per year), 1 teaching assistantship (averaging $4,025 per year); career-related internships or fieldwork, institutionally sponsored loans, scholarships/grants, traineeships, health care benefits, tuition waivers (full and partial), and unspecified assistantships also available. Support available to part-time students. Financial award application deadline: 3/15; financial award applicants required to submit FAFSA. *Faculty research:* Public policy, Presidential studies, public leadership, economic policy, social policy. *Unit head:* Dr. Mark Welsh, Dean, 979-862-8007, E-mail: mwelsh@tamu.edu. *Application contact:* Kathryn Meyer, Director of Recruitment and Admissions, 979-458-4767, Fax: 979-845-4155, E-mail: bushschooladmissions@tamu.edu.
Website: http://bush.tamu.edu/

Tiffin University, Program in Business Administration, Tiffin, OH 44883-2161. Offers finance (MBA); general management (MBA); healthcare administration (MBA); human resource management (MBA); international business (MBA); leadership (MBA); marketing (MBA); non-profit management (MBA); sports management (MBA). *Accreditation:* ACBSP. *Program availability:* Part-time, evening/weekend, online learning. *Students:* 10 full-time (4 women), 497 part-time (240 women); includes 91 minority (67 Black or African American, non-Hispanic/Latino; 1 American Indian or Alaska Native, non-Hispanic/Latino; 5 Asian, non-Hispanic/Latino; 15 Hispanic/Latino; 3 Two or more races, non-Hispanic/Latino), 102 international. Average age 31. 214 applicants, 86% accepted, 146 enrolled. In 2016, 183 master's awarded. *Entrance requirements:* For master's, minimum undergraduate GPA of 2.5, work experience. Additional exam requirements/recommendations for international students: Required—TOEFL (minimum score 550 paper-based; 79 iBT), IELTS. *Application deadline:* For fall admission, 8/15 for domestic students, 8/1 for international students; for spring admission, 1/9 for domestic students, 12/1 for international students. Applications are processed on a rolling basis. Application fee: $50. Electronic applications accepted. Application fee is waived when completed online. *Expenses: Tuition:* Full-time $21,000; part-time $700 per credit hour. *Required fees:* $150. Tuition and fees vary according to program. *Financial support:* Unspecified assistantships available. Support available to part-time students. Financial award application deadline: 7/31; financial award applicants required to submit FAFSA. *Faculty research:* Small business, executive development operations, research and statistical analysis, market research, management information systems. *Unit head:* Dr. Bonnie Tiell, Dean of Graduate Studies, 419-448-3261, Fax: 419-443-5002, E-mail: btiell@tiffin.edu. *Application contact:* Nikki Hintze, Director of Graduate and Distance Education Academic Advising, 800-968-6446 Ext. 3596, Fax: 419-443-5002, E-mail: hintzenm@tiffin.edu.
Website: http://www.tiffin.edu/graduateprograms/

Trinity Washington University, School of Business and Graduate Studies, Washington, DC 20017-1094. Offers business administration (MBA); communication (MA); international security studies (MA); organizational management (MSA), including federal program management, human resource management, nonprofit management, organizational development, public and community health. *Program availability:* Part-time, evening/weekend. *Degree requirements:* For master's, thesis (for some programs), capstone project (MSA). *Entrance requirements:* For master's, minimum GPA of 2.5. Additional exam requirements/recommendations for international students: Required—TOEFL (minimum score 550 paper-based).

Trinity Western University, School of Graduate Studies, Program in Business Administration, Langley, BC V2Y 1Y1, Canada. Offers international business (MBA); management of the growing enterprise (MBA); non-profit and charitable organization management (MBA). *Program availability:* Part-time, online learning. *Degree requirements:* For master's, thesis or alternative, applied project. *Entrance requirements:* For master's, GMAT (minimum score of 550 recommended). Additional exam requirements/recommendations for international students: Required—TOEFL (minimum score 600 paper-based; 100 iBT), IELTS. Electronic applications accepted.

Trinity Western University, School of Graduate Studies, Program in Leadership, Langley, BC V2Y 1Y1, Canada. Offers business (MA, Certificate); Christian ministry (MA); education (MA, Certificate); healthcare (MA, Certificate); non-profit (MA, Certificate). *Program availability:* Online learning. *Degree requirements:* For master's, major project. *Entrance requirements:* For master's, minimum GPA of 2.7. Additional exam requirements/recommendations for international students: Required—TOEFL (minimum score 620 paper-based; 105 iBT). Electronic applications accepted. *Expenses:* Contact institution. *Faculty research:* Servant leadership.

Tufts University, Graduate School of Arts and Sciences, Graduate Certificate Programs, Management of Community Organizations Program, Medford, MA 02155. Offers Certificate. *Program availability:* Part-time, evening/weekend. Electronic applications accepted. *Expenses:* Contact institution.

Tusculum College, Graduate and Professional Studies, Program in Business Administration, Greeneville, TN 37743-9997. Offers general management (MBA); healthcare administration (MBA); human resources (MBA); nonprofit management (MBA). *Program availability:* Evening/weekend. *Entrance requirements:* For master's, GMAT, GRE, 3 years of work experience, minimum GPA of 2.75. *Expenses: Tuition:* Full-time $7497; part-time $357 per credit hour. *Unit head:* Dr. Michael Dillon, Dean of the School of Business, 423-636-7300 Ext. 5022, E-mail: mdillon@tusculum.edu. *Application contact:* Lindsey Seal, Director of Enrollment, 423-636-7300 Ext. 5006, E-mail: lseal@tusculum.edu.
Website: http://home.tusculum.edu/gps/graduate-degrees/master-business-administration/

Nonprofit Management

Unification Theological Seminary, Graduate Program, Main Campus, Barrytown, NY 12507. Offers divinity (M Div); ministry (D Min); religious education (MRE), including interfaith peacebuilding (MA, MRE); religious studies (MA), including interfaith peacebuilding (MA, MRE), non-profit leadership, theological studies, unification studies. *Program availability:* Part-time, evening/weekend. *Faculty:* 3 full-time (1 woman), 3 part-time/adjunct (0 women). *Students:* 27 full-time (8 women); includes 15 minority (11 Black or African American, non-Hispanic/Latino; 2 Asian, non-Hispanic/Latino; 1 Hispanic/Latino; 1 Two or more races, non-Hispanic/Latino), 6 international. Average age 50. In 2016, 12 master's, 5 doctorates awarded. *Degree requirements:* For master's, variable foreign language requirement, thesis (for some programs); for doctorate, thesis/dissertation. *Entrance requirements:* For master's, bachelor's degree; for doctorate, M Div or equivalency. Additional exam requirements/recommendations for international students: Required—TOEFL (minimum score 450 paper-based; 45 iBT). *Application deadline:* For fall admission, 3/15 priority date for domestic and international students; for spring admission, 9/15 priority date for domestic and international students. Applications are processed on a rolling basis. Application fee: $30. Electronic applications accepted. *Expenses:* Contact institution. *Financial support:* In 2016–17, 2 students received support. Scholarships/grants available. Financial award application deadline: 6/15; financial award applicants required to submit FAFSA. *Faculty research:* Church leadership, church history, world religions, ecumenism, interfaith peace building, service-learning. *Unit head:* Dr. Kathy Winings, Vice-President for Academic Affairs, 845-752-3000 Ext. 228, Fax: 845-752-3014, E-mail: academics@uts.edu. *Application contact:* Henry Christopher, Director of Admissions, 212-563-6647 Ext. 105, Fax: 845-752-3014, E-mail: h.christopher@uts.edu.
Website: http://www.uts.edu

Unification Theological Seminary, New York Extension Center, New York, NY 10036. Offers divinity (M Div); religious education (MRE), including interfaith peacebuilding (MA, MRE); religious studies (MA), including interfaith peacebuilding (MA, MRE), non-profit leadership, theological studies, unification studies. *Program availability:* Part-time, evening/weekend. *Faculty:* 4 full-time (0 women), 7 part-time/adjunct (1 woman). *Students:* 25 full-time (9 women), 23 part-time (6 women); includes 24 minority (8 Black or African American, non-Hispanic/Latino; 9 Asian, non-Hispanic/Latino; 3 Hispanic/Latino; 4 Two or more races, non-Hispanic/Latino), 14 international. Average age 43. *Degree requirements:* For master's, variable foreign language requirement, thesis (for some programs). *Entrance requirements:* For master's, bachelor's degree. Additional exam requirements/recommendations for international students: Required—TOEFL (minimum score 450 paper-based; 45 iBT). *Application deadline:* For fall admission, 8/15 for domestic students, 3/15 priority date for international students; for spring admission, 1/15 for domestic students, 9/15 priority date for international students. Applications are processed on a rolling basis. Application fee: $30. Electronic applications accepted. *Expenses: Tuition:* Full-time $11,760; part-time $490 per credit. *Required fees:* $320; $250 per credit. $125 per semester. Tuition and fees vary according to degree level. *Financial support:* In 2016–17, 48 students received support. Career-related internships or fieldwork, scholarships/grants, tuition waivers (partial), and on-campus employment (for international students) available. Support available to part-time students. Financial award application deadline: 6/15; financial award applicants required to submit FAFSA. *Faculty research:* Church history, world religions, ecumenism, interfaith peace building, service-learning. *Unit head:* Dr. Kathy Winings, Vice-President for Academic Affairs, 212-563-6647 Ext. 101, Fax: 212-563-6431, E-mail: academics@uts.edu. *Application contact:* Joy Theriot, Recruiter, 212-563-6647 Ext. 110, Fax: 212-563-6431, E-mail: j.theriot@uts.edu.
Website: http://www.uts.edu

University at Albany, State University of New York, Nelson A. Rockefeller College of Public Affairs and Policy, Department of Public Administration and Policy, Albany, NY 12222-0001. Offers financial management and public economics (MPA); financial market regulation (MPA); health policy (MPA); healthcare management (MPA); homeland security (MPA); human resources management (MPA); information strategy and management (MPA); local government management (MPA); nonprofit management (MPA); nonprofit management and leadership (Certificate); organizational behavior and theory (MPA, PhD); planning and policy analysis (CAS); policy analysis (MPA); politics and administration (PhD); public finance (PhD); public management (PhD); public policy (PhD); public sector management (Certificate); women and public policy (Certificate); JD/MPA. JD/MPA offered jointly with Albany Law School. *Accreditation:* NASPAA (one or more programs are accredited). *Faculty:* 23 full-time (8 women), 14 part-time/adjunct (7 women). *Students:* 117 full-time (65 women), 95 part-time (46 women); includes 41 minority (12 Black or African American, non-Hispanic/Latino; 8 Asian, non-Hispanic/Latino; 19 Hispanic/Latino; 2 Two or more races, non-Hispanic/Latino), 38 international. 223 applicants, 70% accepted, 81 enrolled. In 2016, 52 master's, 10 doctorates, 16 other advanced degrees awarded. *Degree requirements:* For doctorate, one foreign language, thesis/dissertation. *Entrance requirements:* For doctorate, GRE General Test. Additional exam requirements/recommendations for international students: Required—TOEFL (minimum score 550 paper-based). *Application deadline:* For fall admission, 2/1 priority date for domestic students, 5/1 for international students; for spring admission, 12/1 for domestic students. Applications are processed on a rolling basis. Application fee: $75. Electronic applications accepted. *Expenses:* Tuition, state resident: full-time $10,870; part-time $453 per credit hour. Tuition, nonresident: full-time $22,210; part-time $925 per credit hour. *International tuition:* $21,550 full-time. *Required fees:* $1864; $96 per credit hour. *Financial support:* Application deadline: 2/1. *Total annual research expenditures:* $847,949. *Unit head:* Victor Asal, Chair, 518-591-8729, E-mail: vasal@albany.edu.
Website: http://www.albany.edu/rockefeller/pad.shtml

University of Arkansas at Little Rock, Graduate School, College of Social Sciences and Communication, Program in Nonprofit Management, Little Rock, AR 72204-1099. Offers Graduate Certificate. *Entrance requirements:* For degree, baccalaureate degree, essay, two letters of reference.

University of California, San Diego, Graduate Division, School of Global Policy and Strategy, Master of International Affairs Program, La Jolla, CA 92093. Offers international development and nonprofit management (MIA); international economics (MIA); international environmental policy (MIA); international management (MIA); international politics (MIA). Students will choose one of the following country/regional specializations: China, Japan, Korea, Latin America, or Southeast Asia. *Faculty:* 33 full-time (9 women), 20 part-time/adjunct (4 women). *Students:* 300 full-time (150 women). Average age 24. 460 applicants, 120 enrolled. In 2016, 120 master's awarded. *Degree requirements:* For master's, one foreign language. *Entrance requirements:* For master's, GMAT or GRE General Test. Additional exam requirements/recommendations for international students: Required—TOEFL (minimum score 90 iBT), IELTS (minimum score 7). *Application deadline:* For fall admission, 1/15 for domestic and international students. Applications are processed on a rolling basis. Application fee: $90 ($110 for international students). Electronic applications accepted. *Expenses:* Tuition, state resident: full-time $11,220. Tuition, nonresident: full-time $26,322. *Required fees:* $1864. *Financial support:* In 2016–17, 140 students received support, including 60 fellowships with full and partial tuition reimbursements available (averaging $50,000 per year), 15 research assistantships with full tuition reimbursements available (averaging $20,000 per year), 20 teaching assistantships with full tuition reimbursements available (averaging $20,000 per year); career-related internships or fieldwork, scholarships/grants, and unspecified assistantships also available. Financial award application deadline: 1/15. *Unit head:* Sonja Steinbrech, Director of Enrollment, 858-534-7162, E-mail: ssteinbrech@ucsd.edu. *Application contact:* Admissions Representative, 858-534-5914, E-mail: gps-apply@ucsd.edu.
Website: http://gps.ucsd.edu/academics/mia.html

University of Central Florida, College of Health and Public Affairs, School of Public Administration, Orlando, FL 32816. Offers emergency management and homeland security (Certificate); fundraising (Certificate); non-profit management (MNM, Certificate); urban and regional planning (MS). *Accreditation:* NASPAA. *Program availability:* Part-time, evening/weekend. *Faculty:* 24 full-time (11 women), 11 part-time/adjunct (6 women). *Students:* 87 full-time (60 women), 257 part-time (190 women); includes 157 minority (83 Black or African American, non-Hispanic/Latino; 1 American Indian or Alaska Native, non-Hispanic/Latino; 9 Asian, non-Hispanic/Latino; 62 Hispanic/Latino; 2 Two or more races, non-Hispanic/Latino), 7 international. Average age 32. 192 applicants, 79% accepted, 108 enrolled. In 2016, 118 master's, 36 other advanced degrees awarded. *Degree requirements:* For master's, comprehensive exam, thesis or alternative, research report. *Entrance requirements:* For master's, GRE General Test. *Application deadline:* For fall admission, 6/15 for domestic students; for spring admission, 11/1 for domestic students. Application fee: $30. Electronic applications accepted. *Expenses:* Tuition, state resident: part-time $288.16 per credit hour. Tuition, nonresident: part-time $1071.31 per credit hour. *Financial support:* In 2016–17, 9 students received support, including 1 fellowship with partial tuition reimbursement available (averaging $4,000 per year), 9 research assistantships with partial tuition reimbursements available (averaging $6,704 per year); career-related internships or fieldwork, Federal Work-Study, institutionally sponsored loans, tuition waivers (partial), and unspecified assistantships also available. Financial award application deadline: 3/1; financial award applicants required to submit FAFSA. *Unit head:* Dr. Naim Kapucu, Director, 407-823-3693, Fax: 407-823-5651, E-mail: naim.kapucu@ucf.edu. *Application contact:* Assistant Director, Graduate Admissions, 407-823-2766, Fax: 407-823-6442, E-mail: gradadmissions@ucf.edu.
Website: https://www.cohpa.ucf.edu/publicadmin/

University of Colorado Denver, School of Public Affairs, Program in Public Affairs and Administration, Denver, CO 80127. Offers public administration (MPA), including domestic violence, emergency management and homeland security, environmental policy, management and law, homeland security and defense, local government, nonprofit management, public administration; public affairs (PhD). *Accreditation:* NASPAA. *Program availability:* Part-time, evening/weekend, online learning. *Students:* 241 full-time (146 women), 135 part-time (86 women); includes 61 minority (15 Black or African American, non-Hispanic/Latino; 1 American Indian or Alaska Native, non-Hispanic/Latino; 10 Asian, non-Hispanic/Latino; 26 Hispanic/Latino; 2 Native Hawaiian or other Pacific Islander, non-Hispanic/Latino; 7 Two or more races, non-Hispanic/Latino), 26 international. Average age 36. 240 applicants, 70% accepted, 91 enrolled. In 2016, 158 master's, 8 doctorates awarded. *Degree requirements:* For master's, thesis or alternative, 36-39 credit hours; for doctorate, comprehensive exam, thesis/dissertation, minimum of 66 semester hours, including at least 30 hours of dissertation. *Entrance requirements:* For master's, GRE, GMAT or LSAT, resume, essay, transcripts, recommendations; for doctorate, GRE, resume, essay, transcripts, recommendations. Additional exam requirements/recommendations for international students: Required—TOEFL (minimum score 550 paper-based; 80 iBT); Recommended—IELTS (minimum score 6.5). *Application deadline:* For fall admission, 2/1 priority date for domestic students, 1/15 priority date for international students; for spring admission, 10/15 priority date for domestic students, 10/1 priority date for international students. Application fee: $50 ($75 for international students). Electronic applications accepted. *Expenses:* Contact institution. *Financial support:* In 2016–17, 92 students received support. Fellowships with partial tuition reimbursements available, research assistantships with partial tuition reimbursements available, teaching assistantships with partial tuition reimbursements available, Federal Work-Study, institutionally sponsored loans, scholarships/grants, traineeships, and unspecified assistantships available. Financial award application deadline: 4/1; financial award applicants required to submit FAFSA. *Faculty research:* Housing, education and the social and economic issues of vulnerable populations; nonprofit governance and management; education finance, effectiveness and reform; P-20 education initiatives; municipal government accountability. *Unit head:* Dr. Christine Martell, Director of MPA Program, 303-315-2716, Fax: 303-315-2229, E-mail: christine.martell@ucdenver.edu. *Application contact:* Dawn Savage, Student Services Coordinator, 303-315-2743, Fax: 303-315-2229, E-mail: dawn.savage@ucdenver.edu.
Website: http://www.ucdenver.edu/academics/colleges/SPA/Academics/programs/PublicAffairsAdmin/Pages/index.aspx

University of Connecticut, Graduate School, College of Liberal Arts and Sciences, Department of Public Policy, Storrs, CT 06269. Offers public administration (MPA, Graduate Certificate), including nonprofit management (Graduate Certificate), public financial management (Graduate Certificate); survey research (MA, Graduate Certificate), including quantitative research methods (Graduate Certificate), survey research (MA); JD/MPA; MPA/MSW. *Degree requirements:* For master's, comprehensive exam. *Entrance requirements:* For master's, GRE General Test. Additional exam requirements/recommendations for international students: Required—TOEFL (minimum score 550 paper-based). Electronic applications accepted.

University of Florida, Graduate School, College of Agricultural and Life Sciences, Department of Family, Youth, and Community Sciences, Gainesville, FL 32611. Offers community studies (MS); family and youth development (MS); family, youth and community sciences (MS); nonprofit organization development (MS). *Program availability:* Part-time, online learning. *Degree requirements:* For master's, comprehensive exam (for some programs), thesis (for some programs). *Entrance requirements:* For master's, GRE General Test, minimum GPA of 3.0. Additional exam requirements/recommendations for international students: Required—TOEFL (minimum score 550 paper-based; 80 iBT), IELTS (minimum score 6). Electronic applications accepted. *Faculty research:* Adolescent risk behaviors, family risk and resilience, family financial management, community-based organizations/interventions, nutrition and wellness.

University of Georgia, School of Social Work, Athens, GA 30602. Offers MA, MSW, PhD, Certificate, MSW/JD. *Accreditation:* CSWE (one or more programs are accredited). *Program availability:* Part-time, evening/weekend. *Degree requirements:* For master's, thesis or alternative; for doctorate, one foreign language, thesis/dissertation. *Entrance requirements:* For master's and doctorate, GRE General Test. *Application deadline:* For fall admission, 7/1 priority date for domestic students, 7/1 for international students; for spring admission, 11/15 for domestic and international students. Applications are processed on a rolling basis. Application fee: $50. Electronic applications accepted. *Financial support:* Fellowships, research assistantships, teaching assistantships, career-related internships or fieldwork, Federal Work-Study, scholarships/grants, tuition waivers (full and partial), and unspecified assistantships available. Support available to part-time students. Financial award application deadline: 2/10; financial award applicants required to submit FAFSA. *Faculty research:* Juvenile

justice, substance abuse, civil rights and social justice, gerontology, social policy. *Unit head:* Dr. Maurice C. Daniels, Dean, 706-542-5424, Fax: 706-542-3282, E-mail: daniels@uga.edu. *Application contact:* Shari Miller, Graduate Coordinator, 706-542-2328, E-mail: semiller@uga.edu.
Website: http://www.ssw.uga.edu/

University of Houston–Downtown, College of Humanities and Social Sciences, Department of Social Sciences, Houston, TX 77002. Offers non-profit management (MA). *Program availability:* Part-time, evening/weekend, online only, 100% online. *Faculty:* 4 full-time (2 women), 2 part-time/adjunct (0 women). *Students:* 20 full-time (16 women), 60 part-time (47 women); includes 57 minority (40 Black or African American, non-Hispanic/Latino; 1 American Indian or Alaska Native, non-Hispanic/Latino; 1 Asian, non-Hispanic/Latino; 15 Hispanic/Latino). Average age 36. 37 applicants, 89% accepted, 30 enrolled. In 2016, 6 master's awarded. *Degree requirements:* For master's, thesis or capstone project, internship which will include capstone assignments. *Entrance requirements:* For master's, GRE, essay, resume, 3 letters of recommendation, transcripts. Additional exam requirements/recommendations for international students: Required—TOEFL (minimum score 550 paper-based; 86 iBT). *Application deadline:* For fall admission, 5/15 for domestic students, 4/1 for international students; for spring admission, 11/15 for domestic and international students. Application fee: $35 ($60 for international students). Electronic applications accepted. *Expenses:* $305.50 in-state, per credit; $663.50 out-of-state, per credit. *Financial support:* Federal Work-Study and scholarships/grants available. Financial award application deadline: 4/1; financial award applicants required to submit FAFSA. *Unit head:* Dr. Jeffery Jackson, Chair, 713-221-2793, Fax: 713-226-5205, E-mail: jacksonjef@uhd.edu. *Application contact:* Ceshia Love, Director of Graduate and International Admissions, 713-221-8093, Fax: 713-223-7408, E-mail: gradadmissions@uhd.edu.
Website: https://www.uhd.edu/academics/humanities/graduate-programs/master-arts-non-profit-management/Pages/ma-index.aspx

University of La Verne, College of Business and Public Management, Master's Program in Public Administration, La Verne, CA 91750-4443. Offers nonprofit (MPA); urban management and affairs (MPA). *Accreditation:* NASPAA. *Program availability:* Part-time. *Students:* 16 full-time (14 women), 44 part-time (25 women); includes 46 minority (1 Asian, non-Hispanic/Latino; 45 Hispanic/Latino), 1 international. Average age 32. *Entrance requirements:* For master's, minimum undergraduate GPA of 3.0, statement of purpose, 2 letters of recommendation, resume. Additional exam requirements/recommendations for international students: Required—TOEFL (minimum score 550 paper-based). *Application deadline:* Applications are processed on a rolling basis. Application fee: $50. *Expenses:* Contact institution. *Financial support:* Institutionally sponsored loans and scholarships/grants available. Financial award application deadline: 3/2; financial award applicants required to submit FAFSA. *Unit head:* Marcia Godwin, Chairperson, 909-448-4103, E-mail: mgodwin@laverne.edu. *Application contact:* Cathy Cook, Associate Director of Graduate Admissions, 909-448-4719, Fax: 909-971-2295, E-mail: ccook2@laverne.edu.
Website: http://laverne.edu/business-and-public-administration/master-of-public-administration/

University of La Verne, College of Business and Public Management, Program in Leadership and Management, La Verne, CA 91750-4443. Offers human resource management (Certificate); leadership and management (MS), including human resource management, nonprofit management, organizational development; nonprofit management (Certificate); organizational leadership (Certificate). *Program availability:* Part-time. *Students:* 47 full-time (32 women), 44 part-time (25 women); includes 42 minority (2 Black or African American, non-Hispanic/Latino; 3 Asian, non-Hispanic/Latino; 37 Hispanic/Latino), 14 international. Average age 32. *Degree requirements:* For master's, thesis or research project. *Entrance requirements:* For master's, bachelor's degree, minimum undergraduate GPA of 2.75, 2 letters of recommendation, interview, resume. Additional exam requirements/recommendations for international students: Required—TOEFL (minimum score 550 paper-based). *Application deadline:* Applications are processed on a rolling basis. Application fee: $50. *Expenses: Tuition:* Part-time $795 per credit hour. Tuition and fees vary according to campus/location and program. *Financial support:* Federal Work-Study, institutionally sponsored loans, and scholarships/grants available. Financial award application deadline: 3/2; financial award applicants required to submit FAFSA. *Unit head:* Dr. Kathy Duncan, Program Director, 909-448-4415, E-mail: kduncan2@laverne.edu. *Application contact:* Barbara Cox, Associate Director of Graduate Admissions, 909-448-4004, E-mail: bcox@laverne.edu.
Website: http://laverne.edu/business-and-public-administration/

University of La Verne, Regional and Online Campuses, Graduate Programs, Inland Empire Campus, Ontario, CA 91730. Offers business administration (MBA, MBA-EP), including accounting (MBA), finance (MBA), health services management (MBA-EP), information technology (MBA-EP), international business (MBA), managed care (MBA), management and leadership (MBA-EP), marketing (MBA-EP), supply chain management (MBA); leadership and management (MS), including human resource management, nonprofit management, organizational development. *Program availability:* Part-time, evening/weekend. *Expenses:* Contact institution.

University of Louisville, Graduate School, College of Arts and Sciences, Department of Urban and Public Affairs, Louisville, KY 40208. Offers public administration (MPA), including human resources management, non-profit management, public policy and administration; urban and public affairs (PhD), including urban planning and development, urban policy and administration; urban planning (MUP), including administration of planning organizations, housing and community development, land use and environmental planning, spatial analysis. *Program availability:* Part-time, evening/weekend. *Faculty:* 12 full-time (5 women), 3 part-time/adjunct (1 woman). *Students:* 59 full-time (23 women), 32 part-time (19 women); includes 19 minority (13 Black or African American, non-Hispanic/Latino; 1 Asian, non-Hispanic/Latino; 2 Hispanic/Latino; 3 Two or more races, non-Hispanic/Latino), 5 international. Average age 30. 75 applicants, 65% accepted, 25 enrolled. In 2016, 22 master's, 2 doctorates awarded. Terminal master's awarded for partial completion of doctoral program. *Degree requirements:* For master's, internship; for doctorate, comprehensive exam, thesis/dissertation. *Entrance requirements:* For master's, GRE General Test, minimum GPA of 3.0; for doctorate, GRE General Test, master's degree in appropriate field. Additional exam requirements/recommendations for international students: Required—TOEFL (minimum score 550 paper-based; 79 iBT). *Application deadline:* Applications are processed on a rolling basis. Application fee: $60. *Expenses:* Contact institution. *Financial support:* Fellowships, research assistantships, tuition waivers (full and partial), and unspecified assistantships available. Financial award application deadline: 2/1. *Faculty research:* Urban theory, sustainability, public administration, urban planning, urban management. *Total annual research expenditures:* $240,308. *Unit head:* Dr. David Simpson, Chair, 502-852-8019, Fax: 502-852-4558, E-mail: dave.simpson@louisville.edu. *Application contact:* Libby Leggett, Director, Graduate Admissions, 502-852-3101, Fax: 502-852-4558, E-mail: gradadm@louisville.edu.
Website: http://supa.louisville.edu

University of Maryland, Baltimore County, The Graduate School, College of Arts, Humanities and Social Sciences, Department of Sociology, Anthropology, and Health Administration and Policy, Baltimore, MD 21250. Offers applied sociology (MA); non-profit sector (Postbaccalaureate Certificate). *Program availability:* Part-time, evening/weekend. *Faculty:* 16 full-time (13 women), 2 part-time/adjunct (0 women). *Students:* 11 full-time (6 women), 17 part-time (11 women); includes 11 minority (4 Black or African American, non-Hispanic/Latino; 3 Asian, non-Hispanic/Latino; 3 Hispanic/Latino; 1 Two or more races, non-Hispanic/Latino). Average age 29. 7 applicants, 86% accepted, 5 enrolled. In 2016, 13 master's awarded. *Degree requirements:* For master's, thesis or alternative. *Entrance requirements:* For master's, minimum GPA of 3.0. Additional exam requirements/recommendations for international students: Required—TOEFL. *Application deadline:* For fall admission, 4/1 priority date for domestic students, 1/1 for international students; for spring admission, 11/15 for domestic students, 9/1 for international students. Application fee: $70. Electronic applications accepted. *Expenses:* Tuition, state resident: full-time $13,294. Tuition, nonresident: full-time $20,286. *Financial support:* In 2016–17, 10 students received support, including 1 research assistantship with tuition reimbursement available, 9 teaching assistantships with tuition reimbursements available; scholarships/grants, health care benefits, unspecified assistantships, and tuition remission also available. *Faculty research:* Sociology of aging; medical sociology; diversity, gender, and culture; research methods. *Unit head:* Dr. J. Kevin Eckert, Department Chair, 410-455-5698, Fax: 410-455-1154, E-mail: eckert@umbc.edu. *Application contact:* Dr. Marina Adler, Graduate Program Director, 410-455-3155, Fax: 410-455-1154, E-mail: adler@umbc.edu.
Website: http://sociology.umbc.edu/

University of Memphis, Graduate School, College of Arts and Sciences, Division of Public and Nonprofit Administration, Memphis, TN 38103. Offers local government management (Graduate Certificate); philanthropy and nonprofit leadership (Graduate Certificate). *Accreditation:* NASPAA. *Program availability:* Part-time, evening/weekend, blended/hybrid learning. *Faculty:* 5 full-time (3 women), 2 part-time/adjunct (1 woman). *Students:* 17 full-time (12 women), 25 part-time (15 women); includes 23 minority (21 Black or African American, non-Hispanic/Latino; 1 Asian, non-Hispanic/Latino; 1 Hispanic/Latino), 1 international. Average age 32. 21 applicants, 90% accepted, 14 enrolled. In 2016, 39 master's, 36 other advanced degrees awarded. *Degree requirements:* For master's, comprehensive exam, thesis or alternative, internship. *Entrance requirements:* For master's, GRE General Test, GMAT, MAT, or LSAT, minimum GPA of 3.0, resume, two references, statement of interest. Additional exam requirements/recommendations for international students: Required—TOEFL. *Application deadline:* For fall admission, 7/1 for domestic students, 5/1 for international students; for spring admission, 12/1 for domestic students, 9/15 for international students; for summer admission, 5/1 for domestic students, 2/1 for international students. Applications are processed on a rolling basis. Application fee: $35 ($60 for international students). Electronic applications accepted. *Expenses:* $5,231.50 per semester full-time in-state, $9,623.50 full-time out-of-state. *Financial support:* In 2016–17, 37 students received support, including 5 fellowships (averaging $9,000 per year); research assistantships with full tuition reimbursements available, career-related internships or fieldwork, Federal Work-Study, scholarships/grants, health care benefits, and unspecified assistantships also available. Support available to part-time students. Financial award application deadline: 2/1; financial award applicants required to submit FAFSA. *Faculty research:* Nonprofit organization governance, local government management, community collaboration, urban problems, accountability. *Unit head:* Dr. Michael Howell-Moroney, Chair, 901-678-3360, Fax: 901-678-2981, E-mail: mhwllmrn@memphis.edu. *Application contact:* Dr. Sharon Wrobel, MPA Coordinator, 901-678-4720, Fax: 901-678-2981, E-mail: swrobel@memphis.edu.
Website: http://www.memphis.edu/padm/

University of Michigan–Flint, Graduate Programs, Program in Public Administration, Flint, MI 48502. Offers administration of non-profit agencies (MPA); criminal justice administration (MPA); educational administration (MPA); general public administration (MPA); healthcare administration (MPA). *Program availability:* Part-time. *Faculty:* 1 full-time (0 women), 3 part-time/adjunct (all women). *Students:* 13 full-time (10 women), 97 part-time (59 women); includes 45 minority (35 Black or African American, non-Hispanic/Latino; 1 Asian, non-Hispanic/Latino; 3 Hispanic/Latino; 1 Native Hawaiian or other Pacific Islander, non-Hispanic/Latino; 5 Two or more races, non-Hispanic/Latino), 5 international. Average age 35. 60 applicants, 78% accepted, 38 enrolled. In 2016, 52 master's awarded. *Degree requirements:* For master's, thesis or alternative, internship. *Entrance requirements:* For master's, bachelor's degree from regionally-accredited institution, minimum overall undergraduate GPA of 3.0. Additional exam requirements/recommendations for international students: Required—TOEFL (minimum score 84 iBT), IELTS (minimum score 6.5). *Application deadline:* For fall admission, 8/1 for domestic students, 5/1 for international students; for winter admission, 11/15 for domestic students, 9/1 for international students; for spring admission, 3/15 for domestic students, 1/1 for international students; for summer admission, 5/15 for domestic students. Applications are processed on a rolling basis. Application fee: $55. Electronic applications accepted. *Expenses:* Contact institution. *Financial support:* Career-related internships or fieldwork, Federal Work-Study, and scholarships/grants available. Support available to part-time students. Financial award application deadline: 3/1; financial award applicants required to submit FAFSA. *Unit head:* Dr. Kathryn Schellenberg, Director, 810-762-3340, E-mail: kathsch@umflint.edu. *Application contact:* Bradley T. Maki, Director of Graduate Admissions, 810-762-3171, Fax: 810-766-6789, E-mail: bmaki@umflint.edu.
Website: http://www.umflint.edu/graduateprograms/public-administration-mpa

University of Missouri, Office of Research and Graduate Studies, Harry S Truman School of Public Affairs, Columbia, MO 65211. Offers grantsmanship (Graduate Certificate); nonprofit management (Graduate Certificate); organizational change (Graduate Certificate); public affairs (MPA, PhD); public management (Graduate Certificate); science and public policy (Graduate Certificate). *Accreditation:* NASPAA. *Faculty:* 10 full-time (7 women), 2 part-time/adjunct (0 women). *Students:* 76 full-time (37 women), 168 part-time (88 women); includes 36 minority (21 Black or African American, non-Hispanic/Latino; 1 American Indian or Alaska Native, non-Hispanic/Latino; 2 Asian, non-Hispanic/Latino; 6 Hispanic/Latino; 6 Two or more races, non-Hispanic/Latino), 24 international. Average age 34. *Entrance requirements:* For master's, GRE General Test, minimum GPA of 3.0. Additional exam requirements/recommendations for international students: Required—TOEFL (minimum score 550 paper-based; 80 iBT), IELTS (minimum score 6.5). *Application deadline:* For fall admission, 2/1 priority date for domestic and international students. Applications are processed on a rolling basis. Application fee: $75 ($90 for international students). Electronic applications accepted. *Expenses:* Tuition, state resident: full-time $6347; part-time $352.60 per credit hour. Tuition, nonresident: full-time $17,379; part-time $965.50 per credit hour. *Required fees:* $1035. Tuition and fees vary according to course load, campus/location and program. *Financial support:* Fellowships, research assistantships, teaching assistantships, institutionally sponsored loans, scholarships/grants, traineeships, health care benefits, and unspecified assistantships available. Support available to part-time students.
Website: http://truman.missouri.edu/

University of Missouri–St. Louis, Graduate School, Program in Public Policy Administration, St. Louis, MO 63121. Offers local government management (MPPA, Certificate); nonprofit management and leadership (MPPA, Certificate); policy and program evaluation (MPPA, Certificate). *Accreditation:* NASPAA. *Program availability:*

Part-time, evening/weekend. *Faculty:* 2 full-time (both women), 6 part-time/adjunct (2 women). *Students:* 10 full-time (5 women), 43 part-time (26 women); includes 14 minority (12 Black or African American, non-Hispanic/Latino; 2 Asian, non-Hispanic/Latino). Average age 33. 28 applicants, 89% accepted, 17 enrolled. *Degree requirements:* For master's, exit project. *Entrance requirements:* For master's, 3 letters of recommendation, personal statement. Additional exam requirements/recommendations for international students: Recommended—TOEFL (minimum score 550 paper-based), IELTS (minimum score 6.5). *Application deadline:* For fall admission, 7/1 priority date for domestic and international students; for spring admission, 12/1 priority date for domestic and international students. Applications are processed on a rolling basis. Application fee: $50 ($40 for international students). Electronic applications accepted. *Financial support:* Research assistantships with tuition reimbursements and career-related internships or fieldwork available. Financial award application deadline: 4/1; financial award applicants required to submit FAFSA. *Faculty research:* Urban policy, public finance, evaluation. *Unit head:* Dr. Deborah Balser, Director, 314-516-5146, Fax: 314-516-5210, E-mail: balserd@umsl.edu. *Application contact:* 314-516-5458, Fax: 314-516-6996, E-mail: gradadm@umsl.edu.
Website: http://www.umsl.edu/gradschool/ppa/

University of Nevada, Las Vegas, Graduate College, Greenspun College of Urban Affairs, School of Public Policy and Leadership, Las Vegas, NV 89154-4030. Offers crisis and emergency management (MS); non-profit management (Certificate); public administration (MPA); public affairs (PhD); public management (Certificate); urban leadership (MA). *Program availability:* Part-time. *Faculty:* 13 full-time (7 women), 10 part-time/adjunct (2 women). *Students:* 76 full-time (43 women), 110 part-time (70 women); includes 81 minority (18 Black or African American, non-Hispanic/Latino; 1 American Indian or Alaska Native, non-Hispanic/Latino; 6 Asian, non-Hispanic/Latino; 38 Hispanic/Latino; 4 Native Hawaiian or other Pacific Islander, non-Hispanic/Latino; 14 Two or more races, non-Hispanic/Latino), 7 international. Average age 36. 70 applicants, 86% accepted, 43 enrolled. In 2016, 70 master's, 9 doctorates, 21 other advanced degrees awarded. *Degree requirements:* For master's, comprehensive exam (for some programs), thesis (for some programs), oral exam; for doctorate, comprehensive exam, thesis/dissertation; for Certificate, portfolio. *Entrance requirements:* For master's, GRE General Test or GMAT, bachelor's degree with minimum GPA 2.75; statement of purpose; 3 letters of recommendation; for doctorate, GRE General Test, master's degree with minimum GPA of 3.5; 3 letters of recommendation; statement of purpose; writing sample; personal interview; for Certificate, bachelor's degree; 2 letters of recommendation; writing sample. Additional exam requirements/recommendations for international students: Required—TOEFL (minimum score 550 paper-based; 80 iBT), IELTS (minimum score 7). *Application deadline:* For fall admission, 6/1 for domestic students, 5/1 for international students; for spring admission, 11/1 for domestic students, 10/1 for international students; for summer admission, 3/1 for domestic students. Application fee: $60 ($95 for international students). Electronic applications accepted. *Expenses:* $269.25 per credit, $792 per 3-credit course; $9,634 per year resident; $23,274 per year non-resident; $7,094 fees non-resident (7 credits or more); $1,307 annual health insurance fee. *Financial support:* In 2016–17, 7 research assistantships with partial tuition reimbursements (averaging $14,200 per year), 14 teaching assistantships with partial tuition reimbursements (averaging $16,411 per year) were awarded; institutionally sponsored loans, scholarships/grants, health care benefits, and unspecified assistantships also available. Financial award application deadline: 3/15. *Faculty research:* Community and organizational resilience; environmental decision-making and management; budgeting and human resource/workforce management; urban design, sustainability, and governance; public and non-profit management, public policy, governance, economic development, and urban planning. *Total annual research expenditures:* $244,881. *Unit head:* Dr. Christopher Stream, Director, 702-895-5120, Fax: 702-895-4436, E-mail: chris.stream@unlv.edu. *Application contact:* Dr. Jessica Word, Graduate Coordinator, 702-895-2684, Fax: 702-895-4436, E-mail: jessica.word@unlv.edu.
Website: https://www.unlv.edu/publicpolicy

The University of North Carolina at Charlotte, College of Liberal Arts and Sciences, Department of Political Science and Public Administration, Charlotte, NC 28223-0001. Offers emergency management (Graduate Certificate); non-profit management (Graduate Certificate); public administration (MPA), including arts administration, emergency management, non-profit management, public budgeting and finance, urban management and policy; public budgeting and finance (Graduate Certificate); urban management and policy (Graduate Certificate). *Accreditation:* NASPAA. *Program availability:* Part-time, evening/weekend. *Faculty:* 19 full-time (10 women), 3 part-time/adjunct (0 women). *Students:* 25 full-time (17 women), 57 part-time (39 women); includes 23 minority (14 Black or African American, non-Hispanic/Latino; 1 American Indian or Alaska Native, non-Hispanic/Latino; 2 Asian, non-Hispanic/Latino; 4 Hispanic/Latino; 2 Two or more races, non-Hispanic/Latino). Average age 30. 55 applicants, 73% accepted, 30 enrolled. In 2016, 31 master's, 12 other advanced degrees awarded. *Degree requirements:* For master's, research project or thesis. *Entrance requirements:* For master's, GRE General Test, bachelor's degree, or its equivalent, from accredited college or university; minimum undergraduate GPA of 3.0; 3 letters of recommendation; statement of purpose; for Graduate Certificate, statement of purpose (1-2 pages in length) explaining applicant's career goals, how the Certificate fits into achieving those goals, and any relevant work experience; official transcripts; letters of recommendation. Additional exam requirements/recommendations for international students: Required—TOEFL (minimum score 523 paper-based, 70 iBT) or IELTS (6.5). *Application deadline:* For fall admission, 8/1 for domestic and international students; for spring admission, 12/1 for domestic and international students. Applications are processed on a rolling basis. Application fee: $75. Electronic applications accepted. *Expenses:* Tuition, state resident: full-time $4252. Tuition, nonresident: full-time $17,423. *Required fees:* $3026. Tuition and fees vary according to course load and program. *Financial support:* In 2016–17, 9 students received support, including 9 research assistantships (averaging $7,117 per year); career-related internships or fieldwork, Federal Work-Study, institutionally sponsored loans, scholarships/grants, and unspecified assistantships also available. Support available to part-time students. Financial award application deadline: 3/1; financial award applicants required to submit FAFSA. *Total annual research expenditures:* $477,651. *Unit head:* Dr. Greg Weeks, Chair, 704-687-7574, E-mail: gbweeks@uncc.edu. *Application contact:* Kathy B. Giddings, Director of Graduate Admissions, 704-687-5503, Fax: 704-687-1668, E-mail: gradadm@uncc.edu.
Website: http://politicalscience.uncc.edu/

The University of North Carolina at Greensboro, Graduate School, College of Arts and Sciences, Department of Political Science, Greensboro, NC 27412-5001. Offers nonprofit management (Certificate); public affairs (MPA); urban and economic development (Certificate). *Accreditation:* NASPAA. *Degree requirements:* For master's, comprehensive exam. *Entrance requirements:* For master's, GRE General Test. Additional exam requirements/recommendations for international students: Required—TOEFL. Electronic applications accepted. *Faculty research:* U.S. Constitution, Canadian parliament, public management, ethical challenge of public service.

University of Northern Iowa, Graduate College, MA Program in Philanthropy and Nonprofit Development, Cedar Falls, IA 50614. Offers MA. *Entrance requirements:* For master's, minimum GPA of 3.0; 3 letters of recommendation; experience in the philanthropy and/or nonprofit areas. Additional exam requirements/recommendations for international students: Required—TOEFL (minimum score 500 paper-based; 61 iBT). Electronic applications accepted.

University of North Florida, College of Arts and Sciences, Department of Political Science and Public Administration, Jacksonville, FL 32224. Offers nonprofit management (Graduate Certificate); public administration (MPA). *Accreditation:* NASPAA. *Program availability:* Part-time. *Faculty:* 13 full-time (5 women). *Students:* 19 full-time (11 women), 40 part-time (19 women); includes 15 minority (9 Black or African American, non-Hispanic/Latino; 1 Asian, non-Hispanic/Latino; 4 Hispanic/Latino; 1 Two or more races, non-Hispanic/Latino), 2 international. Average age 32. 53 applicants, 43% accepted, 17 enrolled. In 2016, 19 master's awarded. *Degree requirements:* For master's, thesis or alternative, internship. *Entrance requirements:* For master's, GRE General Test, minimum GPA of 3.0 in last 60 hours, 2 letters of recommendation, interview. Additional exam requirements/recommendations for international students: Required—TOEFL (minimum score 500 paper-based; 61 iBT). *Application deadline:* For fall admission, 8/1 priority date for domestic students, 5/1 for international students; for spring admission, 12/1 priority date for domestic students, 10/1 for international students; for summer admission, 3/15 priority date for domestic students, 2/1 for international students. Application fee: $30. Electronic applications accepted. Tuition and fees vary according to course load, campus/location and program. *Financial support:* In 2016–17, 7 students received support, including 1 teaching assistantship (averaging $4,590 per year); research assistantships, career-related internships or fieldwork, Federal Work-Study, scholarships/grants, tuition waivers (partial), and unspecified assistantships also available. Financial award application deadline: 4/1; financial award applicants required to submit FAFSA. *Faculty research:* America's usage of the Internet, use of information communication technologies by educators and children. *Total annual research expenditures:* $3,643. *Unit head:* Dr. Matthew T. Corrigan, Chair, 904-620-2997, Fax: 904-620-2979, E-mail: mcorriga@unf.edu. *Application contact:* Dr. Amanda Pascale, Director, The Graduate School, 904-620-1360, Fax: 907-620-1362, E-mail: graduateschool@unf.edu.
Website: http://www.unf.edu/coas/pspa/

University of North Texas, Robert B. Toulouse School of Graduate Studies, Denton, TX 76203-5459. Offers accounting (MS); applied anthropology (MA, MS); applied behavior analysis (Certificate); applied geography (MA); applied technology and performance improvement (M Ed, MS); art education (MA); art history (MA); art museum education (Certificate); arts leadership (Certificate); audiology (Au D); behavior analysis (MS); behavioral science (PhD); biochemistry and molecular biology (MS); biology (MA, MS); biomedical engineering (MS); business analysis (MS); chemistry (MS); clinical health psychology (PhD); communication studies (MA, MS); computer engineering (MS); computer science (MS); counseling (M Ed, MS), including clinical mental health counseling (MS), college and university counseling, elementary school counseling, secondary school counseling; creative writing (MA); criminal justice (MS); curriculum and instruction (M Ed); decision sciences (MBA); design (MA, MFA), including fashion design (MFA), innovation studies, interior design (MFA); early childhood studies (MS); economics (MS); educational leadership (M Ed, Ed D); educational psychology (MS, PhD), including family studies (MS), gifted and talented (MS), human development (MS), learning and cognition (MS), research, measurement and evaluation (MS); electrical engineering (MS); emergency management (MPA); engineering technology (MS); English (MA); English as a second language (MA); environmental science (MS); finance (MBA, MS); financial management (MPA); French (MA); health services management (MBA); higher education (M Ed, Ed D); history (MA, MS); hospitality management (MS); human resources management (MPA); information science (MS); information systems (PhD); information technologies (MBA); interdisciplinary studies (MA, MS); international studies (MA); international sustainable tourism (MS); jazz studies (MM); journalism (MA, MJ, Graduate Certificate), including interactive and virtual digital communication (Graduate Certificate), narrative journalism (Graduate Certificate), public relations (Graduate Certificate); kinesiology (MS); linguistics (MA); local government management (MPA); logistics (PhD); logistics and supply chain management (MBA); long-term care, senior housing, and aging services (MA); management (PhD); marketing (MBA); mathematics (MA, MS); mechanical and energy engineering (MS, PhD); music (MA), including ethnomusicology, music theory, musicology, performance; music composition (PhD); music education (MM Ed, PhD); nonprofit management (MPA); operations and supply chain management (MBA); performance (MM, DMA); philosophy (MA); political science (MA); professional and technical communication (MA); radio, television and film (MA, MFA); rehabilitation counseling (Certificate); sociology (MA); Spanish (MA); special education (M Ed); speech-language pathology (MA); strategic management (MBA); studio art (MFA); teaching (M Ed); MBA/MS. *Program availability:* Part-time, evening/weekend, online learning. Terminal master's awarded for partial completion of doctoral program. *Degree requirements:* For master's, variable foreign language requirement, comprehensive exam (for some programs), thesis (for some programs); for doctorate, variable foreign language requirement, comprehensive exam (for some programs), thesis/dissertation; for other advanced degree, variable foreign language requirement, comprehensive exam (for some programs). *Entrance requirements:* For master's and doctorate, GRE, GMAT. Additional exam requirements/recommendations for international students: Required—TOEFL (minimum score 550 paper-based; 79 iBT). Electronic applications accepted.

University of Notre Dame, Mendoza College of Business, Master in Nonprofit Administration Program, Notre Dame, IN 46556. Offers MNA. *Accreditation:* AACSB. *Program availability:* Part-time-only, blended/hybrid learning. *Faculty:* 14 full-time (4 women), 4 part-time/adjunct (2 women). *Students:* 63 part-time (38 women); includes 8 minority (3 Black or African American, non-Hispanic/Latino; 5 Hispanic/Latino), 7 international. Average age 35. 41 applicants, 90% accepted, 26 enrolled. In 2016, 30 master's awarded. *Degree requirements:* For master's, thesis. *Entrance requirements:* For master's, GRE General Test or GMAT; waiver available to qualifying applicants, minimum of two years' nonprofit work experience. Additional exam requirements/recommendations for international students: Required—TOEFL (minimum score 600 paper-based; 100 iBT), IELTS (minimum score 7). *Application deadline:* Applications are processed on a rolling basis. Application fee: $150. Electronic applications accepted. *Expenses:* $930 per credit hour. *Financial support:* In 2016–17, 41 students received support, including 41 fellowships (averaging $4,374 per year); institutionally sponsored loans, scholarships/grants, and health care benefits also available. Support available to part-time students. Financial award application deadline: 4/30; financial award applicants required to submit FAFSA. *Unit head:* Dr. Angela R. Logan, Interim Director of Nonprofit Professional Development, 574-631-7793, Fax: 574-631-6532, E-mail: alogan2@nd.edu. *Application contact:* Dr. Angela R. Logan, Interim Director of Nonprofit Professional Development, 574-631-7793, Fax: 574-631-6532, E-mail: alogan2@nd.edu.
Website: http://mendoza.nd.edu/programs/specialized-masters/master-of-nonprofit-administration/

University of Oklahoma, College of Arts and Sciences, Department of Political Science, Program in Public Administration, Norman, OK 73019. Offers general (MPA); individualized intensive study (MPA); nonprofit management (MPA). *Program availability:* Part-time, evening/weekend. *Students:* 28 full-time (17 women), 48 part-time (26 women); includes 16 minority (5 Black or African American, non-Hispanic/Latino; 3

American Indian or Alaska Native, non-Hispanic/Latino; 1 Asian, non-Hispanic/Latino; 5 Hispanic/Latino; 2 Two or more races, non-Hispanic/Latino), 1 international. Average age 29. 42 applicants, 88% accepted, 31 enrolled. In 2016, 24 master's awarded. Terminal master's awarded for partial completion of doctoral program. *Degree requirements:* For master's, comprehensive exam, thesis or alternative, 36 hours. *Entrance requirements:* For master's, GRE, statement of purpose, resume, two letters of recommendation. Additional exam requirements/recommendations for international students: Required—TOEFL (minimum score 100 iBT) or IELTS (minimum score 7). *Application deadline:* For fall admission, 4/1 priority date for international students; for spring admission, 9/1 for international students. Applications are processed on a rolling basis. Application fee: $50 ($100 for international students). Electronic applications accepted. *Expenses:* Tuition, state resident: full-time $4886; part-time $203.60 per credit hour. Tuition, nonresident: full-time $18,989; part-time $791.20 per credit hour. *Required fees:* $3283; $126.25 per credit hour. $126.50 per semester. *Financial support:* In 2016–17, 40 students received support. Research assistantships with full tuition reimbursements available, teaching assistantships with full tuition reimbursements available, career-related internships or fieldwork, scholarships/grants, health care benefits, unspecified assistantships, and travel and conference attendance funding available. Financial award application deadline: 6/1; financial award applicants required to submit FAFSA. *Faculty research:* Public and nonprofit management, public policy analysis, program evaluation, public finance and budgeting. *Unit head:* Prof. Keith Gaddie, Chair, 405-325-2061, Fax: 405-325-0718, E-mail: pscgradprog@ou.edu. *Application contact:* Jeff Alexander, Graduate Programs Coordinator, 405-325-1845, Fax: 405-325-0718, E-mail: pscgradprog@ou.edu.
Website: http://psc.ou.edu/mpa

University of Oklahoma, College of Liberal Studies, Norman, OK 73072. Offers administrative leadership (Graduate Certificate); corrections management (Graduate Certificate); criminal justice (MS); government and military leadership (MA); human and health services administration (MA), including human and health services administration, integrated studies; liberal studies (MPS); organizational leadership (MA); restorative justice administration (Graduate Certificate); volunteer and non-profit leadership (MA). *Program availability:* Part-time, online only, 100% online, blended/hybrid learning. *Faculty:* 13 full-time (7 women), 1 part-time/adjunct (0 women). *Students:* 74 full-time (48 women), 598 part-time (289 women); includes 175 minority (45 Black or African American, non-Hispanic/Latino; 39 American Indian or Alaska Native, non-Hispanic/Latino; 8 Asian, non-Hispanic/Latino; 46 Hispanic/Latino; 1 Native Hawaiian or other Pacific Islander, non-Hispanic/Latino; 36 Two or more races, non-Hispanic/Latino), 2 international. Average age 35. 191 applicants, 95% accepted, 120 enrolled. In 2016, 192 master's, 6 other advanced degrees awarded. *Degree requirements:* For master's, comprehensive exam, thesis optional, 33 credit hours; project/internship (for museum studies); for Graduate Certificate, 12 credit hours. *Entrance requirements:* For master's and Graduate Certificate, minimum GPA of 3.0 in last 60 undergraduate hours; statement of goals; resume. Additional exam requirements/recommendations for international students: Required—TOEFL (minimum score 79 iBT) or IELTS (minimum score 6.5). *Application deadline:* For fall admission, 7/1 for domestic and international students; for winter admission, 12/1 for domestic and international students; for spring admission, 5/1 for domestic and international students. Applications are processed on a rolling basis. Application fee: $50 ($100 for international students). Electronic applications accepted. *Expenses:* Tuition, state resident: full-time $4886; part-time $203.60 per credit hour. Tuition, nonresident: full-time $18,989; part-time $791.20 per credit hour. *Required fees:* $3283; $126.25 per credit hour. $126.50 per semester. *Financial support:* In 2016–17, 124 students received support. Career-related internships or fieldwork, institutionally sponsored loans, scholarships/grants, health care benefits, and tuition waivers available. Support available to part-time students. Financial award application deadline: 6/1; financial award applicants required to submit FAFSA. *Faculty research:* Management and leadership; policing and corrections management; neuro-psychology of addiction; disproportionate minority contact; ethnic identity and nationalism. *Unit head:* Dr. Martha L. Banz, Associate Provost for Continuing Education/Interim Dean, College of Liberal Studies, 405-325-1061, Fax: 405-325-7132, E-mail: mlbanz@ou.edu. *Application contact:* Michelle Shults, Academic Advisement Services Coordinator, 405-325-2928, Fax: 405-325-7132, E-mail: mshults@ou.edu.
Website: http://www.ou.edu/cls/html

University of Pennsylvania, School of Arts and Sciences, Fels Institute of Government, Philadelphia, PA 19104. Offers economic development and growth (Certificate); government administration (MGA); nonprofit administration (Certificate); organization dynamics (MS); politics (Certificate); public administration (MPA); public finance (Certificate). *Program availability:* Part-time, evening/weekend. *Students:* 49 full-time (29 women), 65 part-time (35 women); includes 28 minority (13 Black or African American, non-Hispanic/Latino; 6 Asian, non-Hispanic/Latino; 6 Hispanic/Latino; 3 Two or more races, non-Hispanic/Latino), 18 international. Average age 30. 371 applicants, 39% accepted, 71 enrolled. In 2016, 52 master's, 17 other advanced degrees awarded. *Expenses: Tuition:* Full-time $31,068; part-time $5762 per course. *Required fees:* $3200; $336 per course. Full-time tuition and fees vary according to degree level, program and student level. Part-time tuition and fees vary according to course load, degree level and program. *Financial support:* Application deadline: 1/1.
Website: http://www.fels.upenn.edu/

University of Pittsburgh, Graduate School of Public and International Affairs, Master of Public Administration Program, Pittsburgh, PA 15260. Offers energy and environment (MPA); governance and international public management (MPA); policy research and analysis (MPA); public and nonprofit management (MPA); urban affairs and planning (MPA); JD/MPA; MPH/MPA; MSIS/MPA; MSW/MPA. *Accreditation:* NASPAA. *Program availability:* Part-time, evening/weekend. *Faculty:* 34 full-time (12 women), 17 part-time/adjunct (5 women). *Students:* 93 full-time (66 women), 21 part-time (16 women); includes 8 minority (4 Black or African American, non-Hispanic/Latino; 1 Asian, non-Hispanic/Latino; 3 Hispanic/Latino), 61 international. Average age 26. 200 applicants, 81% accepted, 49 enrolled. In 2016, 62 master's awarded. *Degree requirements:* For master's, thesis optional, capstone seminar. *Entrance requirements:* For master's, GRE General Test or GMAT, 2 letters of recommendation, resume, undergraduate transcripts, personal statement. Additional exam requirements/recommendations for international students: Required—TOEFL (minimum score 80 iBT); Recommended—IELTS (minimum score 7). *Application deadline:* For fall admission, 2/1 priority date for domestic students, 1/15 for international students; for spring admission, 11/1 for domestic students, 8/1 for international students. Application fee: $50. Electronic applications accepted. *Expenses:* $22,578 per year in-state; $36,734 per year out-of-state. *Financial support:* In 2016–17, 10 students received support, including 2 research assistantships with full tuition reimbursements available (averaging $14,620 per year); fellowships with full tuition reimbursements available, career-related internships or fieldwork, scholarships/grants, health care benefits, and unspecified assistantships also available. Financial award application deadline: 2/1; financial award applicants required to submit FAFSA. *Faculty research:* Urban affairs and planning, governance and international public management, nonprofit management, policy research and analysis, energy and environmental policy. *Total annual research expenditures:* $1.3 million. *Unit head:* Dr. John T.S. Keeler, Dean, 412-648-7605, Fax: 412-648-2605, E-mail: keeler@pitt.edu. *Application contact:* Dr. Michael T. Rizzi, Director of Student Services, 412-648-7640, Fax: 412-648-7641, E-mail: rizzim@pitt.edu.
Website: http://www.gspia.pitt.edu/

University of Portland, Dr. Robert B. Pamplin, Jr. School of Business, Portland, OR 97203-5798. Offers entrepreneurship (MBA); finance (MBA, MS); health care management (MBA); marketing (MBA); nonprofit management (EMBA); operations and technology management (MBA, MS); sustainability (MBA). *Accreditation:* AACSB. *Program availability:* Part-time, evening/weekend. *Entrance requirements:* For master's, GMAT, minimum GPA of 3.0, resume, 2 letters of recommendation. Additional exam requirements/recommendations for international students: Required—TOEFL (minimum score 570 paper-based; 89 iBT), IELTS (minimum score 7). *Expenses:* Contact institution.

University of San Diego, School of Leadership and Education Sciences, Department of Leadership Studies, San Diego, CA 92110-2492. Offers higher education leadership (MA); leadership studies (MA, PhD, Certificate); nonprofit leadership and management (MA). *Program availability:* Part-time, evening/weekend. *Faculty:* 11 full-time (5 women), 17 part-time/adjunct (9 women). *Students:* 40 full-time (26 women), 219 part-time (149 women); includes 120 minority (28 Black or African American, non-Hispanic/Latino; 15 Asian, non-Hispanic/Latino; 62 Hispanic/Latino; 2 Native Hawaiian or other Pacific Islander, non-Hispanic/Latino; 13 Two or more races, non-Hispanic/Latino), 21 international. Average age 33. 312 applicants, 75% accepted, 110 enrolled. In 2016, 57 master's, 21 doctorates awarded. *Degree requirements:* For master's, thesis (for some programs), international experience; for doctorate, comprehensive exam, thesis/dissertation, international experience. *Entrance requirements:* For master's, GRE (recommended with GPA less than 3.25), minimum GPA of 3.0, interview; for doctorate, GRE (less than 5 years old), master's degree, minimum GPA of 3.5 (recommended), resume. Additional exam requirements/recommendations for international students: Required—TOEFL (minimum score 580 paper-based; 83 iBT), TWE. Application fee: $45. Electronic applications accepted. *Financial support:* In 2016–17, 186 students received support. Career-related internships or fieldwork, Federal Work-Study, institutionally sponsored loans, unspecified assistantships, and stipends available. Support available to part-time students. Financial award application deadline: 4/1; financial award applicants required to submit FAFSA. *Faculty research:* Higher education administration policy and relations, organizational leadership, nonprofits and philanthropy, student affairs leadership. *Unit head:* Dr. Lea Hubbard, Graduate Program Director, 619-260-7818, E-mail: lhubbard@sandiego.edu. *Application contact:* Monica Mahon, Associate Director of Graduate Admissions, 619-260-4524, Fax: 619-260-4158, E-mail: grads@sandiego.edu.
Website: https://www.sandiego.edu/soles/departments/leadership-studies/

University of San Francisco, School of Management, Master of Nonprofit Administration Program, San Francisco, CA 94117. Offers MNA. *Program availability:* Part-time, evening/weekend. *Faculty:* 3 full-time (0 women), 4 part-time/adjunct (2 women). *Students:* 44 full-time (38 women), 4 part-time (3 women); includes 19 minority (2 Black or African American, non-Hispanic/Latino; 2 Asian, non-Hispanic/Latino; 10 Hispanic/Latino; 5 Two or more races, non-Hispanic/Latino), 3 international. Average age 34. 65 applicants, 88% accepted, 31 enrolled. In 2016, 20 master's awarded. *Degree requirements:* For master's, thesis optional. *Entrance requirements:* For master's, resume demonstrating minimum of two years of professional work experience, transcripts from each college or university attended, two letters of recommendation, personal statement. Additional exam requirements/recommendations for international students: Required—TOEFL (minimum score 600 paper-based, 100 iBT), IELTS (minimum score 7) or PTE (minimum score 68). *Application deadline:* For fall admission, 6/15 for domestic students, 5/15 for international students. Application fee: $55. Electronic applications accepted. *Expenses: Tuition:* Full-time $23,310; part-time $1295 per credit. Tuition and fees vary according to course load, degree level, campus/location and program. *Financial support:* In 2016–17, 24 students received support. Scholarships/grants available. Financial award application deadline: 3/2; financial award applicants required to submit FAFSA. *Faculty research:* Philanthropy in ethnic communities. *Unit head:* Dr. Marco Tavanti, Director, 415-422-2221, E-mail: management@usfca.edu. *Application contact:* Office of Graduate Recruiting and Admissions, 415-422-2221, Fax: 415-422-6315, E-mail: management@usfca.edu.
Website: http://www.usfca.edu/mna

University of Southern California, Graduate School, School of Policy, Planning, and Development, Master of Public Administration Program, Los Angeles, CA 90089. Offers nonprofit management and policy (Graduate Certificate); political management (Graduate Certificate); public administration (MPA); public management (Graduate Certificate); MPA/JD; MPA/M Pl; MPA/MA; MPA/MAJCS; MPA/MS; MPA/MSW. *Accreditation:* NASPAA (one or more programs are accredited). *Program availability:* Part-time, evening/weekend, online learning. Terminal master's awarded for partial completion of doctoral program. *Degree requirements:* For master's, capstone, internship. *Entrance requirements:* For master's, GRE, GMAT. Additional exam requirements/recommendations for international students: Required—TOEFL (minimum score 600 paper-based; 100 iBT). Electronic applications accepted. *Faculty research:* Collaborative governance and decision-making, nonprofit management, environmental management, institutional analysis, local government, civic engagement.

University of Southern Indiana, Graduate Studies, College of Liberal Arts, Program in Public Administration, Evansville, IN 47712-3590. Offers nonprofit administration (MPA); public sector administration (MPA). *Program availability:* Part-time, evening/weekend. *Faculty:* 5 full-time (2 women). *Students:* 25 full-time (14 women), 4 part-time (3 women); includes 2 minority (both Black or African American, non-Hispanic/Latino), 4 international. Average age 29. In 2016, 12 master's awarded. *Entrance requirements:* For master's, resume, 2 letters of reference, personal statement, minimum GPA of 3.0. Additional exam requirements/recommendations for international students: Required—TOEFL (minimum score 550 paper-based; 79 iBT), IELTS (minimum score 6). *Application deadline:* For fall admission, 8/15 priority date for domestic students, 3/1 priority date for international students; for spring admission, 1/5 for domestic students, 11/15 for international students. Applications are processed on a rolling basis. Application fee: $40. Electronic applications accepted. *Expenses:* Tuition, state resident: full-time $8497. Tuition, nonresident: full-time $16,691. *Required fees:* $500. *Financial support:* In 2016–17, 4 students received support. Federal Work-Study, scholarships/grants, tuition waivers (full and partial), and unspecified assistantships available. Financial award application deadline: 3/1; financial award applicants required to submit FAFSA. *Unit head:* Dr. Matthew J. Hanka, Director, 812-461-5204, E-mail: mjhanka@usi.edu. *Application contact:* Dr. Mayola Rowser, Director, Graduate Studies, 812-465-7015, E-mail: mrowser@usi.edu.
Website: http://www.usi.edu/liberal-arts/master-of-public-administration

University of South Florida, Innovative Education, Tampa, FL 33620-9951. Offers adult, career and higher education (Graduate Certificate), including college teaching, leadership in developing human resources, leadership in higher education; Africana studies (Graduate Certificate), including diasporas and health disparities, genocide and human rights; aging studies (Graduate Certificate), including gerontology; art research (Graduate Certificate), including museum studies; business foundations (Graduate Certificate); chemical and biomedical engineering (Graduate Certificate), including

materials science and engineering, water, health and sustainability; child and family studies (Graduate Certificate), including positive behavior support; civil and industrial engineering (Graduate Certificate), including transportation systems analysis; community and family health (Graduate Certificate), including maternal and child health, social marketing and public health, violence and injury: prevention and intervention, women's health; criminology (Graduate Certificate), including criminal justice administration; educational measurement and research (Graduate Certificate), including evaluation; English (Graduate Certificate), including comparative literary studies, creative writing, professional and technical communication; entrepreneurship (Graduate Certificate); environmental health (Graduate Certificate), including safety management; epidemiology and biostatistics (Graduate Certificate), including applied biostatistics, biostatistics, concepts and tools of epidemiology, epidemiology, epidemiology of infectious diseases; geography, environment and planning (Graduate Certificate), including community development, environmental policy and management, geographical information systems; geology (Graduate Certificate), including hydrogeology; global health (Graduate Certificate), including disaster management, global health and Latin American and Caribbean studies, global health practice, humanitarian assistance, infection control; government and international affairs (Graduate Certificate), including Cuban studies, globalization studies; health policy and management (Graduate Certificate), including health management and leadership, public health policy and programs; hearing specialist: early intervention (Graduate Certificate); industrial and management systems engineering (Graduate Certificate), including systems engineering, technology management; information studies (Graduate Certificate), including school library media specialist; information systems/decision sciences (Graduate Certificate), including analytics and business intelligence; instructional technology (Graduate Certificate), including distance education, Florida digital/virtual educator, instructional design, multimedia design, Web design; internal medicine, bioethics and medical humanities (Graduate Certificate), including biomedical ethics; Latin American and Caribbean studies (Graduate Certificate); mass communications (Graduate Certificate), including multimedia journalism; mathematics and statistics (Graduate Certificate), including mathematics; medicine (Graduate Certificate), including aging and neuroscience, bioinformatics, biotechnology, brain fitness and memory management, clinical investigation, health informatics, health sciences, integrative weight management, intellectual property, medicine and gender, metabolic and nutritional medicine, metabolic cardiology, pharmacy sciences; national and competitive intelligence (Graduate Certificate); psychological and social foundations (Graduate Certificate), including career counseling, college teaching, diversity in education, mental health counseling, school counseling; public affairs (Graduate Certificate), including nonprofit management, public management, research administration; public health (Graduate Certificate), including environmental health, health equity, public health generalist, translational research in adolescent behavioral health; public health practices (Graduate Certificate), including planning for healthy communities; rehabilitation and mental health counseling (Graduate Certificate), including integrative mental health care, marriage and family therapy, rehabilitation technology; secondary education (Graduate Certificate), including ESOL, foreign language education: culture and content, foreign language education: professional; social work (Graduate Certificate), including geriatric social work/clinical gerontology; special education (Graduate Certificate), including autism spectrum disorder, disabilities education: severe/profound; world languages (Graduate Certificate), including teaching English as a second language (TESL) or foreign language. *Expenses:* Tuition, state resident: full-time $7766; part-time $431.43 per credit hour. Tuition, nonresident: full-time $15,789; part-time $877.17 per credit hour. *Required fees:* $37 per term. *Unit head:* Kathy Barnes, Interdisciplinary Programs Coordinator, 813-974-8031, Fax: 813-974-7061, E-mail: barnesk@usf.edu. *Application contact:* Karen Tylinski, Metro Initiatives, 813-974-9943, Fax: 813-974-7061, E-mail: ktylinsk@usf.edu.
Website: http://www.usf.edu/innovative-education/

The University of Tampa, Sykes College of Business, Tampa, FL 33606-1490. Offers accounting (MS); entrepreneurship (MBA); finance (MBA, MS); information systems management (MBA); innovation management (MBA); international business (MBA); marketing (MBA, MS); nonprofit management (MBA). *Accreditation:* AACSB. *Program availability:* Part-time, evening/weekend. *Faculty:* 43 full-time (19 women), 9 part-time/adjunct (3 women). *Students:* 438 full-time (176 women), 126 part-time (57 women); includes 37 minority (22 Black or African American, non-Hispanic/Latino; 11 Asian, non-Hispanic/Latino; 4 Two or more races, non-Hispanic/Latino), 203 international. Average age 28. 1,305 applicants, 39% accepted, 192 enrolled. In 2016, 266 master's awarded. *Degree requirements:* For master's, capstone. *Entrance requirements:* For master's, GMAT or GRE, official transcripts from all colleges and/or universities previously attended, resume, personal statement, letters of recommendation. Additional exam requirements/recommendations for international students: Required—TOEFL (minimum score 577 paper-based, 90 iBT) or IELTS (7.5). *Application deadline:* Applications are processed on a rolling basis. Application fee: $40. Electronic applications accepted. *Expenses:* $588 per credit tuition, $40 per term fees. *Financial support:* In 2016–17, 116 students received support. Career-related internships or fieldwork, scholarships/grants, and unspecified assistantships available. Financial award applicants required to submit FAFSA. *Faculty research:* Job market signaling, on-line shopping behaviors and social media, the Tampa Bay economy, digital literacy, entrepreneurship in small businesses. *Unit head:* Dr. Natasha F. Veltri, Associate Dean, 813-253-6289, E-mail: nveltri@ut.edu. *Application contact:* Chanelle Cox, Staff Assistant, Admissions for Graduate and Continuing Studies, 813-253-6249, E-mail: ccox@ut.edu.
Website: http://www.ut.edu/business/

The University of Tennessee at Chattanooga, Department of Political Science and Public Service, Chattanooga, TN 37403. Offers local government management (MPA); non profit management (MPA); public administration (MPA); public administration and non-profit management (Postbaccalaureate Certificate). *Program availability:* Part-time, evening/weekend. *Faculty:* 5 full-time (2 women). *Students:* 8 full-time (2 women), 14 part-time (11 women); includes 6 minority (4 Black or African American, non-Hispanic/Latino; 1 Asian, non-Hispanic/Latino; 1 Two or more races, non-Hispanic/Latino). Average age 31. 14 applicants, 86% accepted, 7 enrolled. In 2016, 11 master's awarded. *Degree requirements:* For master's, comprehensive exam, thesis or alternative, internship. *Entrance requirements:* For master's, GRE General Test. Additional exam requirements/recommendations for international students: Required—TOEFL (minimum score 550 paper-based; 79 iBT), IELTS (minimum score 6). *Application deadline:* For fall admission, 6/15 priority date for domestic students, 7/1 for international students; for spring admission, 11/1 priority date for domestic students, 11/1 for international students. Applications are processed on a rolling basis. Application fee: $35 ($40 for international students). Electronic applications accepted. *Expenses:* $9,876 full-time in-state; $25,994 full-time out-of-state; $450 per credit part-time in-state; $1,345 per credit part-time out-of-state. *Financial support:* In 2016–17, 2 research assistantships were awarded; career-related internships or fieldwork, scholarships/grants, and unspecified assistantships also available. Support available to part-time students. Financial award application deadline: 7/1; financial award applicants required to submit FAFSA. *Faculty research:* Organizational cultures and renewal, management theory, public policy, policy analysis, nonprofit organization. *Total annual research expenditures:* $1,700. *Unit head:* Dr. Michelle D. Deardorf, Department Head, 423-425-4231, Fax: 423-425-2373, E-mail: michelle-deardorff@utc.edu. *Application contact:* Dr. Joanne Romagni, Dean of the Graduate School, 423-425-4478, Fax: 423-425-5223, E-mail: joanne-romagni@utc.edu.
Website: http://www.utc.edu/political-science-public-service/

The University of Texas at Dallas, School of Economic, Political and Policy Sciences, Program in Public and Nonprofit Management, Richardson, TX 75080. Offers applied sociology (MS); public affairs (MPA, PhD). *Accreditation:* NASPAA. *Program availability:* Part-time, evening/weekend. *Faculty:* 12 full-time (5 women), 2 part-time/adjunct (0 women). *Students:* 30 full-time (25 women), 89 part-time (55 women); includes 45 minority (17 Black or African American, non-Hispanic/Latino; 6 Asian, non-Hispanic/Latino; 18 Hispanic/Latino; 4 Two or more races, non-Hispanic/Latino), 16 international. Average age 37. 79 applicants, 67% accepted, 45 enrolled. In 2016, 34 master's, 6 doctorates awarded. *Degree requirements:* For master's, internship; for doctorate, thesis/dissertation. *Entrance requirements:* For master's and doctorate, GRE (minimum combined score of 1000 on verbal and quantitative), minimum GPA of 3.0 in upper-level course work in field. Additional exam requirements/recommendations for international students: Required—TOEFL (minimum score 550 paper-based). *Application deadline:* For fall admission, 7/15 for domestic students, 5/1 priority date for international students; for spring admission, 11/15 for domestic students, 9/1 priority date for international students. Applications are processed on a rolling basis. Application fee: $50 ($100 for international students). Electronic applications accepted. *Expenses:* Tuition, state resident: full-time $12,418; part-time $690 per semester hour. Tuition, nonresident: full-time $24,150; part-time $1342 per semester hour. Tuition and fees vary according to course load. *Financial support:* In 2016–17, 46 students received support, including 1 research assistantship with partial tuition reimbursement available (averaging $15,600 per year), 7 teaching assistantships with partial tuition reimbursements available (averaging $13,157 per year); career-related internships or fieldwork, Federal Work-Study, institutionally sponsored loans, and scholarships/grants also available. Support available to part-time students. Financial award application deadline: 4/30; financial award applicants required to submit FAFSA. *Faculty research:* Corporate citizenship and urban problem solving, policy analysis, presidential decision-making, hazardous material safety, emergency management. *Unit head:* Dr. Doug Goodman, Program Head, 972-883-4969, Fax: 972-883-2735, E-mail: doug.goodman@utdallas.edu. *Application contact:* Katie Doctor, Graduate Program Administrator, 972-883-4936, Fax: 972-883-2735, E-mail: kdoctor@utdallas.edu.
Website: http://www.utdallas.edu/epps/public-affairs/

University of the Sacred Heart, Graduate Programs, Program in Nonprofit Organization Administration, San Juan, PR 00914-0383. Offers MBA.

University of the West, Department of Business Administration, Rosemead, CA 91770. Offers business administration (EMBA); computer information systems (MBA); finance (MBA); international business (MBA); nonprofit organization management (MBA). *Program availability:* Part-time, evening/weekend. *Faculty:* 3 full-time (1 woman), 6 part-time/adjunct (2 women). *Students:* 54 full-time (31 women), 14 part-time (3 women); includes 8 minority (4 Asian, non-Hispanic/Latino; 4 Hispanic/Latino), 59 international. Average age 29. *Entrance requirements:* Additional exam requirements/recommendations for international students: Required—TOEFL. *Application deadline:* For fall admission, 6/15 for domestic and international students; for winter admission, 4/1 for domestic and international students; for spring admission, 11/15 for domestic and international students. Applications are processed on a rolling basis. Application fee: $50 ($100 for international students). *Expenses: Tuition:* Full-time $9324; part-time $4662 per year. *Required fees:* $900; $640 per unit. $320 per semester. Tuition and fees vary according to program. *Financial support:* Career-related internships or fieldwork, Federal Work-Study, scholarships/grants, and tuition waivers (partial) available. Financial award applicants required to submit FAFSA. *Unit head:* Dr. Bill Y. Chen, Chair, 626-656-2125, Fax: 626-571-1413, E-mail: billchen@uwest.edu. *Application contact:* Rica Toribio, Director of Enrollment Services, 626-571-8811 Ext. 311, Fax: 626-571-1413, E-mail: ricat@uwest.edu.
Website: http://www.uwest.edu/site/index.php?option=com_content&view=article&id=119&Itemid=162

The University of Toledo, College of Graduate Studies, College of Languages, Literature and Social Sciences, Department of Political Science and Public Administration, Toledo, OH 43606-3390. Offers health care policy and administration (Certificate); management of non-profit organizations (Certificate); municipal administration (Certificate); political science (MA); public administration (MPA); JD/MPA. *Accreditation:* NASPAA. *Program availability:* Part-time. *Degree requirements:* For master's, comprehensive exam (for some programs), thesis. *Entrance requirements:* For master's, GRE General Test, minimum cumulative point-hour ratio of 2.7 (3.0 for MPA) for all previous academic work, three letters of recommendation, statement of purpose, transcripts from all prior institutions attended; for Certificate, minimum cumulative point-hour ratio of 2.7 for all previous academic work, three letters of recommendation, statement of purpose, transcripts from all prior institutions attended. Additional exam requirements/recommendations for international students: Required—TOEFL (minimum score 550 paper-based; 80 iBT). Electronic applications accepted. *Faculty research:* Economic development, health care, Third World, criminal justice, Eastern Europe.

University of West Georgia, College of Social Sciences, Carrollton, GA 30118. Offers criminology (MA); data analysis and evaluation methods (Postbaccalaureate Certificate); European Union studies (Postbaccalaureate Certificate); integrative health systems (Postbaccalaureate Certificate); nonprofit management and community development (Postbaccalaureate Certificate); psychology (MA, PhD), including consciousness and society (PhD); public administration (MPA); public management (Postbaccalaureate Certificate); sociology (MA). *Program availability:* Part-time, evening/weekend, 100% online, blended/hybrid learning. *Faculty:* 45 full-time (21 women). *Students:* 107 full-time (67 women), 73 part-time (46 women); includes 47 minority (39 Black or African American, non-Hispanic/Latino; 4 Asian, non-Hispanic/Latino; 4 Hispanic/Latino), 10 international. Average age 31. 83 applicants, 88% accepted, 60 enrolled. In 2016, 56 master's, 7 doctorates, 5 other advanced degrees awarded. *Entrance requirements:* Additional exam requirements/recommendations for international students: Required—TOEFL (minimum score 523 paper-based; 69 iBT); Recommended—IELTS (minimum score 6.5). *Application deadline:* For fall admission, 7/15 for domestic students, 6/1 for international students; for spring admission, 11/30 for domestic students, 10/15 for international students; for summer admission, 5/15 for domestic students, 3/30 for international students. Applications are processed on a rolling basis. Application fee: $40. Electronic applications accepted. *Expenses:* Tuition, state resident: full-time $5316; part-time $222 per semester hour. Tuition, nonresident: full-time $20,658; part-time $861 per semester hour. *Required fees:* $1962. Tuition and fees vary according to course load, degree level and program. *Financial support:* Fellowships, research assistantships, teaching assistantships, career-related internships or fieldwork, Federal Work-Study, institutionally sponsored loans, scholarships/grants, and unspecified assistantships available. Support available to part-time students. Financial award application deadline: 4/1; financial award applicants required to submit FAFSA. *Unit head:* Dr. N. Jane McCandless, Dean of Social Sciences, 678-839-5170, Fax: 678-839-5171, E-mail: jmccandl@westga.edu. *Application contact:* Dr. Toby Ziglar, Assistant Dean of the Graduate School, 678-839-

1394, Fax: 678-839-1395, E-mail: graduate@westga.edu.
Website: https://www.westga.edu/coss

University of Wisconsin–Milwaukee, Graduate School, College of Letters and Science, Department of Public and Nonprofit Administration, Milwaukee, WI 53201-0413. Offers public administration (MPA), including general public administration, municipal management, non-profit management. *Program availability:* Part-time. *Students:* 12 full-time (8 women), 10 part-time (3 women); includes 3 minority (all Two or more races, non-Hispanic/Latino), 1 international. Average age 33. 16 applicants, 63% accepted, 5 enrolled. In 2016, 11 master's awarded. *Degree requirements:* For master's, thesis or alternative. *Entrance requirements:* For master's, GRE General Test, minimum GPA of 3.0. Additional exam requirements/recommendations for international students: Required—TOEFL (minimum score 550 paper-based; 79 iBT), IELTS (minimum score 6.5). *Application deadline:* For fall admission, 1/1 priority date for domestic students; for spring admission, 9/1 for domestic students. Applications are processed on a rolling basis. Application fee: $56 ($96 for international students). Electronic applications accepted. *Financial support:* In 2016–17, 20 teaching assistantships were awarded; fellowships, research assistantships, career-related internships or fieldwork, health care benefits, and unspecified assistantships also available. Support available to part-time students. Financial award application deadline: 4/15; financial award applicants required to submit FAFSA. *Unit head:* Douglas Ihrke, Department Chair, 414-229-4732, E-mail: dihrke@uwm.edu. *Application contact:* General Information Contact, 414-229-4982, Fax: 414-229-6967, E-mail: gradschool@uwm.edu.
Website: https://uwm.edu/public-nonprofit-administration/

University of Wisconsin–Milwaukee, Graduate School, Helen Bader School of Social Welfare, Department of Social Work, Milwaukee, WI 53201-0413. Offers applied gerontology (Graduate Certificate); nonprofit management (Graduate Certificate); social welfare (PhD); social work (MSW, PhD). *Accreditation:* CSWE. *Program availability:* Part-time. *Students:* 232 full-time (194 women), 84 part-time (69 women); includes 79 minority (43 Black or African American, non-Hispanic/Latino; 1 American Indian or Alaska Native, non-Hispanic/Latino; 6 Asian, non-Hispanic/Latino; 2 Hispanic/Latino; 27 Two or more races, non-Hispanic/Latino), 2 international. Average age 30. 383 applicants, 57% accepted, 129 enrolled. In 2016, 126 master's, 2 doctorates, 6 other advanced degrees awarded. *Degree requirements:* For master's, thesis or alternative. *Entrance requirements:* For doctorate, GRE, bachelor's degree. Additional exam requirements/recommendations for international students: Required—TOEFL (minimum score 550 paper-based; 79 iBT), IELTS (minimum score 6.5). *Application deadline:* For fall admission, 1/1 priority date for domestic students; for spring admission, 9/1 for domestic students. Applications are processed on a rolling basis. Application fee: $56 ($96 for international students). Electronic applications accepted. *Financial support:* Fellowships, research assistantships, teaching assistantships, career-related internships or fieldwork, health care benefits, unspecified assistantships, and project assistantships available. Support available to part-time students. Financial award application deadline: 4/15; financial award applicants required to submit FAFSA. *Application contact:* Deb Padgett, Associate Professor, Social Work, 414-229-6452, E-mail: dpadgett@uwm.edu.
Website: http://uwm.edu/socialwelfare/academics/

University of Wisconsin–Milwaukee, Graduate School, Lubar School of Business, MS and Certificate Business Programs, Milwaukee, WI 53201-0413. Offers business analytics (Graduate Certificate); enterprise resource planning (Graduate Certificate); information technology management (MS); investment management (Graduate Certificate); nonprofit management (Graduate Certificate); nonprofit management and leadership (MS); state and local taxation (Graduate Certificate). *Students:* 174 full-time (83 women), 157 part-time (64 women); includes 69 minority (23 Black or African American, non-Hispanic/Latino; 27 Asian, non-Hispanic/Latino; 6 Hispanic/Latino; 13 Two or more races, non-Hispanic/Latino), 65 international. Average age 32. 281 applicants, 56% accepted, 116 enrolled. In 2016, 171 master's, 34 other advanced degrees awarded. *Entrance requirements:* Additional exam requirements/recommendations for international students: Required—TOEFL (minimum score 550 paper-based; 79 iBT), IELTS (minimum score 6.5). *Application deadline:* Applications are processed on a rolling basis. Application fee: $56 ($96 for international students). Electronic applications accepted. *Financial support:* In 2016–17, 12 teaching assistantships were awarded; fellowships, research assistantships, health care benefits, unspecified assistantships, and project assistantships also available. Financial award applicants required to submit FAFSA. *Application contact:* General Information Contact, 414-229-4982, Fax: 414-229-6967, E-mail: gradschool@uwm.edu.

Upper Iowa University, Online Master's Programs, Fayette, IA 52142-1857. Offers accounting (MBA); corporate financial management (MBA); emergency management and homeland security (MPA); general management (MBA); general studies (MPA); government administration (MPA); health and human services (MPA); human resources management (MBA); nonprofit organizational management (MPA); organizational development (MBA); public management (MPA); sport administration (MSA). MBA also available at Madison, WI campus. *Program availability:* Part-time, online learning. *Degree requirements:* For master's, research project. *Entrance requirements:* For master's, GMAT, GRE, or minimum GPA of 2.7 during last 60 hours. Additional exam requirements/recommendations for international students: Required—TOEFL (minimum score 570 paper-based). Electronic applications accepted. *Faculty research:* Total quality management, teams, organization culture and climate, management.

Villanova University, Graduate School of Liberal Arts and Sciences, Department of Public Administration, Villanova, PA 19085-1699. Offers city management (Certificate); nonprofit management (Certificate); public administration (MPA, Certificate). *Accreditation:* NASPAA. *Program availability:* Part-time, evening/weekend, 100% online. *Faculty:* 26. *Students:* 133 full-time (70 women), 81 part-time (38 women); includes 67 minority (35 Black or African American, non-Hispanic/Latino; 3 American Indian or Alaska Native, non-Hispanic/Latino; 5 Asian, non-Hispanic/Latino; 17 Hispanic/Latino; 1 Native Hawaiian or other Pacific Islander, non Hispanic/Latino; 6 Two or more races, non-Hispanic/Latino), 1 international. Average age 35. 48 applicants, 77% accepted, 26 enrolled. In 2016, 106 master's, 26 other advanced degrees awarded. *Degree requirements:* For master's, comprehensive exam. *Entrance requirements:* For master's, GRE General Test, minimum GPA of 3.0, statement of goals, 3 letters of recommendation. Additional exam requirements/recommendations for international students: Required—TOEFL. *Application deadline:* For fall admission, 5/1 for international students; for spring admission, 10/15 for international students. Applications are processed on a rolling basis. Application fee: $50. Electronic applications accepted. *Financial support:* Career-related internships or fieldwork, scholarships/grants, and unspecified assistantships available. Financial award application deadline: 3/15; financial award applicants required to submit FAFSA. *Unit head:* Dr. Catherine Wilson, Program Director, 610-519-7851.
Website: http://www1.villanova.edu/villanova/artsci/publicadmin.html

Virginia Commonwealth University, Graduate School, College of Humanities and Sciences, Program in Nonprofit Management, Richmond, VA 23284-9005. Offers Graduate Certificate. *Program availability:* Part-time. *Entrance requirements:* Additional exam requirements/recommendations for international students: Required—TOEFL (minimum score 600 paper-based; 100 iBT); Recommended—IELTS (minimum score 6.5). *Application deadline:* Applications are processed on a rolling basis. Application fee: $50. Electronic applications accepted. *Unit head:* Dr. Richard F. Huff, Graduate Program Director, 804-828-9813, E-mail: rrhuff@vcu.edu. *Application contact:* Dr. Nancy B. Stutts, Interim Chair, 804-827-2164, E-mail: nbstutts@vcu.edu.

Virginia Polytechnic Institute and State University, VT Online, Blacksburg, VA 24061. Offers advanced transportation systems (Certificate); aerospace engineering (MS); agricultural and life sciences (MSLFS); business information systems (Graduate Certificate); career and technical education (MS); civil engineering (MS); computer engineering (M Eng, MS); decision support systems (Graduate Certificate); eLearning leadership (MA); electrical engineering (M Eng, MS); engineering administration (MEA); environmental engineering (Certificate); environmental politics and policy (Graduate Certificate); environmental sciences and engineering (MS); foundations of political analysis (Graduate Certificate); health product risk management (Graduate Certificate); industrial and systems engineering (MS); information policy and society (Graduate Certificate); information security (Graduate Certificate); information technology (MIT); instructional technology (MA); integrative STEM education (MA Ed); liberal arts (Graduate Certificate); life sciences: health product risk management (MS); natural resources (MNR, Graduate Certificate); networking (Graduate Certificate); nonprofit and nongovernmental organization management (Graduate Certificate); ocean engineering (MS); political science (MA); security studies (Graduate Certificate); software development (Graduate Certificate). *Expenses:* Tuition, state resident: full-time $12,467; part-time $692.50 per credit hour. Tuition, nonresident: full-time $25,095; part-time $1394.25 per credit hour. *Required fees:* $2669; $491.50 per semester. Tuition and fees vary according to course load, campus/location and program.

Walden University, Graduate Programs, School of Public Policy and Administration, Minneapolis, MN 55401. Offers criminal justice (MPA, MPP, MS, Graduate Certificate), including emergency management (MS, PhD), general program (MS), global leadership (MS, PhD), homeland security and policy coordination (MS, PhD), law and public policy (MS, PhD), policy analysis (MS, PhD), public management and leadership (MS, PhD), self-designed (MS), terrorism, mediation, and peace (MS, PhD); criminal justice and executive management (MS), including global leadership (MS, PhD); criminal justice leadership and executive management (MS), including emergency management (MS, PhD), general program, homeland security and policy coordination (MS, PhD), law and public policy (MS, PhD), policy analysis (MS, PhD), public management and leadership (MS, PhD), self-designed, terrorism, mediation, and peace (MS, PhD); emergency management (MPA, MPP, MS), including criminal justice (MS, PhD), general program (MS), homeland security (MS), public management and leadership (MS, PhD), terrorism and emergency management (MS); general program (MPA, MPP); global leadership (MPA, MPP); government management (Graduate Certificate); health policy (MPA, MPP); homeland security (Graduate Certificate); homeland security and policy coordination (MPA, MPP); international nongovernmental organizations (MPA, MPP); law and public policy (MPA, MPP); local government management for sustainable communities (MPA, MPP); nonprofit management (Graduate Certificate); nonprofit management and leadership (MPA, MPP, MS), including global leadership (MS, PhD), international nongovernmental organization (MS), local government for sustainable communities (MS), self designed (MS); online teaching in higher education (Post-Master's Certificate); policy analysis (MPA); public management and leadership (MPA, MPP, Graduate Certificate); public policy (Graduate Certificate); public policy and administration (PhD), including criminal justice (MS, PhD), emergency management (MS, PhD), global leadership (MS, PhD), health policy, homeland security and policy coordination (MS, PhD), international nongovernmental organizations, law and public policy (MS, PhD), local government management for sustainable communities, nonprofit management and leadership, policy analysis (MS, PhD), public management and leadership (MS, PhD), terrorism, mediation, and peace (MS, PhD); strategic planning and public policy (Graduate Certificate); terrorism, mediation, and peace (MPA, MPP). *Program availability:* Part-time, evening/weekend, online only, 100% online. *Degree requirements:* For doctorate, thesis/dissertation, residency. *Entrance requirements:* For master's, bachelor's degree or higher; minimum GPA of 2.5; official transcripts; goal statement (for some programs); access to computer and Internet; for doctorate, master's degree or higher; three years of related professional or academic experience (preferred); minimum GPA of 3.0; goal statement and current resume (for select programs); official transcripts; access to computer and Internet; for other advanced degree, relevant work experience; access to computer and Internet. Additional exam requirements/recommendations for international students: Required—TOEFL (minimum score 550 paper-based, 79 iBT), IELTS (minimum score 6.5), Michigan English Language Assessment Battery (minimum score 82), or PTE (minimum score 53). Electronic applications accepted.

Walden University, Graduate Programs, School of Social Work and Human Services, Minneapolis, MN 55401. Offers addictions and social work (DSW); advanced clinical practice (MSW); clinical expertise (DSW); criminal justice (DSW); disaster, crisis, and intervention (DSW); family studies and interventions (DSW); human and social services (PhD), including advanced research, community and social services, community intervention and leadership, conflict management, criminal justice, disaster crisis and intervention, family studies and intervention, gerontology, global social services, higher education, human services and nonprofit administration, mental health facilitation; medical social work (DSW); military social work (MSW); policy practice (DSW); social work (PhD), including addictions and social work, clinical expertise, criminal justice, disaster, crisis and intervention, family studies and interventions, medical social work, policy practice, social work administration; social work administration (DSW); social work in healthcare (MSW); social work with children and families (MSW). *Accreditation:* CSWE. *Program availability:* Part-time, evening/weekend, online only, 100% online. *Degree requirements:* For master's, residency (for some programs); for doctorate, thesis/dissertation, residency. *Entrance requirements:* For master's, bachelor's degree or higher; minimum GPA of 2.5; official transcripts; goal statement (for some programs); access to computer and Internet; for doctorate, master's degree or higher; three years of related professional or academic experience (preferred); minimum GPA of 3.0; goal statement and current resume (for select programs); official transcripts; access to computer and Internet. Additional exam requirements/recommendations for international students: Required—TOEFL (minimum score 550 paper-based, 79 iBT), IELTS (minimum score 6.5), Michigan English Language Assessment Battery (minimum score 82), or PTE (minimum score 53). Electronic applications accepted.

Warner Pacific College, Graduate Programs, Portland, OR 97215-4099. Offers human services (MA); not-for-profit leadership (MS); organizational leadership (MS); teaching (MAT). *Program availability:* Part-time, evening/weekend. *Degree requirements:* For master's, thesis or alternative, presentation of defense. *Entrance requirements:* For master's, interview, minimum GPA of 2.5, letters of recommendation. *Faculty research:* New Testament studies, nineteenth-century Wesleyan theology, preaching and church growth, Christian ethics.

Wayne State University, College of Liberal Arts and Sciences, Department of Political Science, Detroit, MI 48202. Offers political science (MA, PhD); public administration (MPA), including economic development policy and management, health and human services policy and management, human and fiscal resource management, nonprofit policy and management, organizational behavior and management, urban and

metropolitan policy and management; JD/MA. *Accreditation:* NASPAA. *Faculty:* 20. *Students:* 64 full-time (20 women), 75 part-time (45 women); includes 48 minority (32 Black or African American, non-Hispanic/Latino; 5 Asian, non-Hispanic/Latino; 4 Hispanic/Latino; 7 Two or more races, non-Hispanic/Latino), 7 international. Average age 33. 105 applicants, 50% accepted, 27 enrolled. In 2016, 25 master's, 5 doctorates awarded. *Degree requirements:* For master's, comprehensive exam (for some programs), thesis (for some programs); for doctorate, thesis/dissertation. *Entrance requirements:* For master's, GRE General Test, substantial undergraduate preparation in the social sciences, minimum upper-division undergraduate GPA of 3.0, two letters of recommendation, personal statement; for doctorate, GRE General Test, 3 letters of recommendation; personal statement; interview. Additional exam requirements/recommendations for international students: Required—TOEFL (minimum score 550 paper-based; 79 iBT), TWE (minimum score 5.5), Michigan English Language Assessment Battery (minimum score 85); Recommended—IELTS (minimum score 6.5). *Application deadline:* For fall admission, 5/15 for domestic students, 5/1 priority date for international students; for winter admission, 10/15 for domestic students, 9/1 priority date for international students. Applications are processed on a rolling basis. Application fee: $50. Electronic applications accepted. *Expenses:* $16,503 per year resident tuition and fees, $33,697 per year non-resident tuition and fees. *Financial support:* In 2016–17, 48 students received support, including 3 fellowships with tuition reimbursements available (averaging $17,333 per year), 13 teaching assistantships with tuition reimbursements available (averaging $18,067 per year); research assistantships with tuition reimbursements available, scholarships/grants, health care benefits, and unspecified assistantships also available. Financial award applicants required to submit FAFSA. *Faculty research:* American government and politics, comparative politics, political methodology, political theory, public administration, public law, public policy, world politics/international relations, formal theory/modeling, gender and politics, international law, peace research, political economy, political psychology, politics of developing countries, race, religion, and ethnicity, urban politics. *Unit head:* Dr. Daniel Geller, Professor and Chair, 313-577-6328, E-mail: dgeller@wayne.edu. *Application contact:* Dr. Sharon Lean, Graduate Director, 313-577-2630, E-mail: gradpolisci@wayne.edu.
Website: http://clas.wayne.edu/politicalscience/

Webster University, George Herbert Walker School of Business and Technology, Department of Management, St. Louis, MO 63119-3194. Offers business and organizational security management (MA); digital marketing management (Graduate Certificate); government contracting (Graduate Certificate); health administration (MHA); health care management (MA); health services management (MA); human resources development (MA); human resources management (MA); information technology management (MA, MS); management (D Mgt); management and leadership (MA); marketing (MA); nonprofit leadership (MA); nonprofit revenue development (Graduate Certificate); organizational development (Graduate Certificate); procurement and acquisitions management (MA); public administration (MPA); space systems operations management (MS). *Program availability:* Part-time, evening/weekend, online learning. *Degree requirements:* For master's, thesis (for some programs); for doctorate, thesis/dissertation, written exam. *Entrance requirements:* For doctorate, GMAT, 3 years of work experience, MBA. Additional exam requirements/recommendations for international students: Required—TOEFL. *Application deadline:* Applications are processed on a rolling basis. Application fee: $25 ($50 for international students). *Expenses: Tuition:* Full-time $21,900; part-time $730 per credit hour. Tuition and fees vary according to campus/location and program. *Financial support:* Federal Work-Study available. Support available to part-time students. Financial award application deadline: 4/1; financial award applicants required to submit FAFSA. *Unit head:* Barrett Baebler, Chair, 314-246-7940, E-mail: baeblerb@webster.edu. *Application contact:* Sarah Nandor, Director, Graduate and Transfer Admissions, 314-968-7109, E-mail: gadmit@webster.edu.

West Chester University of Pennsylvania, College of Business and Public Management, Department of Public Policy and Administration, West Chester, PA 19383. Offers administration (Certificate); human resource management (MPA, Certificate); human resources management (DPA); non profit administration (Certificate); nonprofit administration (MPA); public administration (MPA); public policy and administration (MPA). *Accreditation:* NASPAA. *Program availability:* Part-time, evening/weekend, 100% online. *Faculty:* 6 full-time (4 women), 3 part-time/adjunct (2 women). *Students:* 62 full-time (35 women), 144 part-time (80 women); includes 72 minority (60 Black or African American, non-Hispanic/Latino; 1 American Indian or Alaska Native, non-Hispanic/Latino; 3 Asian, non-Hispanic/Latino; 7 Hispanic/Latino; 1 Two or more races, non-Hispanic/Latino), 6 international. Average age 33. 133 applicants, 92% accepted, 97 enrolled. In 2016, 58 master's, 1 other advanced degree awarded. *Degree requirements:* For master's, capstone project. *Entrance requirements:* For master's and other advanced degree, statement of professional goals, resume, two letters of reference, academic transcripts. Additional exam requirements/recommendations for international students: Required—TOEFL or IELTS. *Application deadline:* For fall admission, 5/15 for international students; for spring admission, 10/15 for international students. Applications are processed on a rolling basis. Application fee: $50. Electronic applications accepted. *Expenses:* Tuition, state resident: full-time $8694; part-time $483 per credit. Tuition, nonresident: full-time $13,050; part-time $725 per credit. *Required fees:* $2399; $119.05 per credit. Tuition and fees vary according to campus/location and program. *Financial support:* Scholarships/grants and unspecified assistantships available. Financial award application deadline: 2/15; financial award applicants required to submit FAFSA. *Faculty research:* Public policy, economic development, research methodology, public administration, nonprofit administration. *Unit head:* Dr. Allison Turner, Department Chair/Director of MPA Program, 610-436-2438, E-mail: aturner@wcupa.edu. *Application contact:* Dr. Jeremy Phillips, DPA Graduate Coordinator, 610-436-2016, E-mail: jphillips@wcupa.edu.
Website: http://www.wcupa.edu/business-publicManagement/mpa/

Western Michigan University, Graduate College, College of Arts and Sciences, School of Public Affairs and Administration, Kalamazoo, MI 49008. Offers health care administration (MPA, Graduate Certificate); nonprofit leadership and administration (Graduate Certificate); public administration (PhD). *Accreditation:* NASPAA (one or more programs are accredited). *Degree requirements:* For doctorate, thesis/dissertation.

Westfield State University, College of Graduate and Continuing Education, Department of Political Science, Westfield, MA 01086. Offers criminal justice administration (MPA); non-profit management (MPA); public management (MPA). *Program availability:* Part-time, evening/weekend. *Faculty:* 2 full-time (1 woman), 4 part-time/adjunct (2 women). *Students:* 13 full-time (6 women), 38 part-time (17 women); includes 11 minority (2 American Indian or Alaska Native, non-Hispanic/Latino; 8 Hispanic/Latino; 1 Two or more races, non-Hispanic/Latino). Average age 29. 16 applicants, 88% accepted, 13 enrolled. In 2016, 17 master's awarded. *Degree requirements:* For master's, comprehensive exam, thesis (for some programs). *Entrance requirements:* For master's, GRE General Test or MAT, minimum undergraduate GPA of 2.8. Additional exam requirements/recommendations for international students: Recommended—TOEFL (minimum score 550 paper-based; 79 iBT). *Application deadline:* For fall admission, 6/30 for domestic students; for spring admission, 10/31 for domestic students; for summer admission, 3/31 for domestic students. Applications are processed on a rolling basis. Application fee: $50. *Expenses:* Tuition, state resident: part-time $318 per semester hour. Tuition, nonresident: part-time $318 per semester hour. *Required fees:* $75 per semester. Tuition and fees vary according to course load and program. *Financial support:* Unspecified assistantships available. Financial award application deadline: 3/1; financial award applicants required to submit FAFSA. *Unit head:* Dr. Hugh Jo, Chair, 413-572-8806, Fax: 413-572-8168, E-mail: hjo@westfield.ma.edu. *Application contact:* Shelly Henrichon, Admissions Coordinator, 413-572-8022, Fax: 413-572-5227, E-mail: mhenrichon@westfield.ma.edu.

Worcester State University, Graduate Studies, Program in Non-Profit Management, Worcester, MA 01602-2597. Offers MS. *Program availability:* Part-time, evening/weekend. *Faculty:* 1 (woman) full-time, 2 part-time/adjunct (1 woman). *Students:* 4 full-time (3 women), 9 part-time (7 women); includes 2 minority (both Black or African American, non-Hispanic/Latino), 3 international. Average age 38. 14 applicants, 57% accepted, 2 enrolled. In 2016, 9 master's awarded. *Degree requirements:* For master's, comprehensive exam (for some programs), thesis. *Entrance requirements:* For master's, GRE General Test or MAT. Additional exam requirements/recommendations for international students: Required—TOEFL (minimum score 550 paper-based; 79 iBT). *Application deadline:* For fall admission, 6/15 for domestic and international students; for spring admission, 11/1 for domestic and international students; for summer admission, 4/1 for domestic and international students. Applications are processed on a rolling basis. Application fee: $50. Electronic applications accepted. *Expenses:* Tuition, state resident: part-time $150 per credit. Tuition, nonresident: part-time $150 per credit. *Financial support:* Career-related internships or fieldwork, scholarships/grants, and unspecified assistantships available. Financial award application deadline: 3/1; financial award applicants required to submit FAFSA. *Unit head:* Dr. Shiko Gathuo, Coordinator, 508-929-8892, Fax: 508-929-8144, E-mail: agathuo@worcester.edu. *Application contact:* Sara Grady, Associate Dean, Graduate Studies and Professional Development, 508-929-8787, Fax: 508-929-8100, E-mail: sara.grady@worcester.edu.

Section 16
Organizational Studies

This section contains a directory of institutions offering graduate work in organizational studies. Additional information about programs listed in the directory but not augmented by an in-depth entry may be obtained by writing directly to the dean of a graduate school or chair of a department at the address given in the directory.

For programs offering related work, see also in this book *Business Administration and Management, Human Resources,* and *Industrial and Manufacturing Management.* In another guide in this series:

Graduate Programs in the Humanities, Arts & Social Sciences

See *Communication and Media* and *Public, Regional, and Industrial Affairs*

CONTENTS

Program Directories

Featured Schools: Displays and Close-Ups

See:

Organizational Behavior

Argosy University, Chicago, Illinois School of Professional Psychology, Doctoral Program in Clinical Psychology, Chicago, IL 60601. Offers child and adolescent psychology (Psy D); client-centered and experiential psychotherapies (Psy D); diversity and multicultural psychology (Psy D); family psychology (Psy D); forensic psychology (Psy D); health psychology (Psy D); neuropsychology (Psy D); organizational consulting (Psy D); psychoanalytic psychology (Psy D); psychology and spirituality (Psy D). *Accreditation:* APA.

Arizona State University at the Tempe campus, W. P. Carey School of Business, Program in Business Administration, Tempe, AZ 85287-4906. Offers entrepreneurship (MBA); finance (MBA); health sector management (MBA); international business (MBA); leadership (MBA); marketing (MBA); organizational behavior (PhD); strategic management (PhD); supply chain management (MBA, PhD); JD/MBA; MBA/M Acc; MBA/M Arch. *Accreditation:* AACSB. *Program availability:* Part-time, evening/weekend, online learning. Terminal master's awarded for partial completion of doctoral program. *Degree requirements:* For master's, thesis or alternative, internship, interactive Program of Study (iPOS) submitted before completing 50 percent of required credit hours; for doctorate, comprehensive exam, thesis/dissertation, interactive Program of Study (iPOS) submitted before completing 50 percent of required credit hours. *Entrance requirements:* For master's, GMAT, minimum GPA of 3.0 in last 2 years of work leading to bachelor's degree, 2 letters of recommendation, professional resume, official transcripts, 3 essays; for doctorate, GMAT or GRE, minimum GPA of 3.0 in last 2 years of work leading to bachelor's degree, 3 letters of recommendation, resume, personal statement/essay. Additional exam requirements/recommendations for international students: Required—TOEFL (minimum score 550 paper-based; 80 iBT), IELTS (minimum score 6.5). Electronic applications accepted. *Expenses:* Contact institution.

A.T. Still University, College of Graduate Health Studies, Kirksville, MO 63501. Offers dental public health (MPH); exercise and sport psychology (Certificate); fundamentals of education (Certificate); geriatric exercise science (Certificate); global health (Certificate); health administration (MHA, DHA); health professions (Ed D); health sciences (DH Sc); kinesiology (MS); leadership and organizational behavior (Certificate); public health (MPH); sports conditioning (Certificate). *Program availability:* Part-time, online only, 100% online, blended/hybrid learning. *Faculty:* 29 full-time (18 women), 89 part-time/adjunct (46 women). *Students:* 505 full-time (319 women), 461 part-time (276 women); includes 337 minority (151 Black or African American, non-Hispanic/Latino; 19 American Indian or Alaska Native, non-Hispanic/Latino; 70 Asian, non-Hispanic/Latino; 89 Hispanic/Latino; 1 Native Hawaiian or other Pacific Islander, non-Hispanic/Latino; 7 Two or more races, non-Hispanic/Latino), 29 international. Average age 37. 366 applicants, 98% accepted, 370 enrolled. In 2016, 113 master's, 94 doctorates, 110 other advanced degrees awarded. *Degree requirements:* For master's, thesis, integrated terminal project, practicum; for doctorate, thesis/dissertation. *Entrance requirements:* For master's, minimum GPA of 2.5, bachelor's degree or equivalent, background check, essay, three references; for doctorate, minimum GPA of 2.5, master's or terminal degree, background check, essay, three references, past experience in relevant field. Additional exam requirements/recommendations for international students: Required—TOEFL (minimum score 550 paper-based; 80 iBT). *Application deadline:* For fall admission, 5/20 for domestic and international students; for winter admission, 9/12 for domestic and international students; for spring admission, 12/12 for domestic and international students; for summer admission, 3/6 for domestic and international students. Applications are processed on a rolling basis. Application fee: $70. Electronic applications accepted. Application fee is waived when completed online. *Expenses:* Contact institution. *Financial support:* Scholarships/grants available. Financial award applicants required to submit FAFSA. *Faculty research:* Public health: influence of availability of comprehensive wellness resources online, student wellness, oral health care needs assessment of community, oral health knowledge and behaviors of Medicaid-eligible pregnant women and mothers of young children in relations to early childhood caries and tooth decay, alcohol use and alcohol related problems among college students. *Unit head:* Dr. Donald Altman, Dean, 660-626-2820, Fax: 660-626-2826, E-mail: daltman@atsu.edu. *Application contact:* Amie Waldemer, Associate Director, Online Admissions, 480-219-6146, E-mail: awaldemer@atsu.edu.
Website: http://www.atsu.edu/college-of-graduate-health-studies

Baruch College of the City University of New York, Zicklin School of Business, Department of Management, New York, NY 10010-5585. Offers entrepreneurship (MBA); management (PhD); operations management (MBA); organizational behavior/human resources management (MBA); sustainable business (MBA). PhD offered jointly with Graduate School and University Center of the City University of New York. *Program availability:* Part-time, evening/weekend. *Degree requirements:* For doctorate, comprehensive exam, thesis/dissertation. *Entrance requirements:* For master's, GMAT, 2 letters of recommendation, resume, 2 years of work experience; for doctorate, GMAT. Additional exam requirements/recommendations for international students: Required—TOEFL (minimum score 590 paper-based), TWE.

Benedictine University, Graduate Programs, Program in Management and Organizational Behavior, Lisle, IL 60532. Offers MS, PhD, MBA/MS, MPH/MS. *Program availability:* Part-time, evening/weekend. *Students:* 38 full-time (21 women), 7 part-time (2 women); includes 6 minority (3 Black or African American, non-Hispanic/Latino; 3 Asian, non-Hispanic/Latino), 3 international. Average age 40. 45 applicants, 96% accepted, 28 enrolled. In 2016, 30 master's, 8 doctorates awarded. *Entrance requirements:* For master's, GMAT. Additional exam requirements/recommendations for international students: Required—TOEFL (minimum score 550 paper-based). *Application deadline:* For fall admission, 9/1 for domestic students; for winter admission, 12/1 for domestic students; for spring admission, 2/15 for domestic students. Applications are processed on a rolling basis. Application fee: $40. Electronic applications accepted. *Expenses: Tuition:* Full-time $15,600; part-time $650 per hour. *Required fees:* $300. One-time fee: $125 part-time. Tuition and fees vary according to class time, course load, campus/location and program. *Financial support:* Career-related internships or fieldwork and health care benefits available. Support available to part-time students. *Faculty research:* Organizational change, transformation, development, learning organizations, career transitions for academics. *Unit head:* Dr. Peter F. Sorensen, Director, 630-829-6220, Fax: 630-960-1126, E-mail: psorensen@ben.edu. *Application contact:* Kari Gibbons, Associate Vice President, Enrollment Center, 630-829-6200, Fax: 630-829-6584, E-mail: kgibbons@ben.edu.

Boston College, Carroll School of Management, Department of Management and Organization, Chestnut Hill, MA 02467-3800. Offers PhD. *Degree requirements:* For doctorate, comprehensive exam, thesis/dissertation, teaching experience. *Entrance requirements:* For doctorate, GMAT or GRE, letters of recommendation, resume, transcripts. Additional exam requirements/recommendations for international students: Required—TOEFL (minimum score 100 iBT), IELTS (minimum score 7.5), or PTE (minimum score 68). Electronic applications accepted. Tuition and fees vary according to program. *Faculty research:* Organizational transformation, mergers and acquisitions, managerial effectiveness, organizational change, organizational structure.

Brooklyn College of the City University of New York, School of Natural and Behavioral Sciences, Department of Psychology, Brooklyn, NY 11210-2889. Offers experimental psychology (MA); industrial and organizational psychology (MA), including human relations, organizational behavior; mental health counseling (MA); psychology (PhD). *Program availability:* Part-time. *Degree requirements:* For master's, comprehensive exam, thesis (for some programs). *Entrance requirements:* For master's, minimum GPA of 3.0, 2 letters of recommendation, essay; for doctorate, GRE. Additional exam requirements/recommendations for international students: Required—TOEFL (minimum score 520 paper-based; 69 iBT). Electronic applications accepted.

California Lutheran University, Graduate Studies, School of Management, Thousand Oaks, CA 91360-2787. Offers business (IMBA); computer science (MS); econometrics (MBA); economics (MS); entrepreneurship (MBA, Certificate); finance (MBA, Certificate); financial planning (MBA, Certificate); information systems and technology (MS); information technology management (MBA, Certificate); international business (MBA, Certificate); management and organization behavior (MBA); management and organizational behavior (Certificate); marketing (MBA, Certificate); microeconomics (MBA); nonprofit and social enterprise (MBA); public policy and administration (MPPA). *Program availability:* Part-time, evening/weekend, 100% online, blended/hybrid learning. *Faculty:* 25 full-time (10 women), 36 part-time/adjunct (12 women). *Students:* 427 full-time (172 women), 189 part-time (87 women); includes 120 minority (14 Black or African American, non-Hispanic/Latino; 2 American Indian or Alaska Native, non-Hispanic/Latino; 19 Asian, non-Hispanic/Latino; 37 Hispanic/Latino; 48 Two or more races, non-Hispanic/Latino), 338 international. Average age 30. 591 applicants, 64% accepted, 131 enrolled. In 2016, 305 master's awarded. *Entrance requirements:* For master's, GMAT, interview, minimum GPA of 3.0. *Application deadline:* Applications are processed on a rolling basis. Application fee: $50. Electronic applications accepted. *Expenses:* Contact institution. *Unit head:* Dr. Gerhard Apfelthaler, Dean, 805-493-3360. *Application contact:* 805-493-3325, Fax: 805-493-3861, E-mail: clugrad@callutheran.edu.
Website: http://www.callutheran.edu/management/

Carnegie Mellon University, Dietrich College of Humanities and Social Sciences, Department of Social and Decision Sciences, Pittsburgh, PA 15213-3891. Offers behavioral decision research (PhD); social and decision science (PhD); strategy, entrepreneurship, and technological change (PhD). Terminal master's awarded for partial completion of doctoral program. *Degree requirements:* For doctorate, comprehensive exam, thesis/dissertation, research paper. *Entrance requirements:* For doctorate, GRE General Test. Additional exam requirements/recommendations for international students: Required—TOEFL. Electronic applications accepted. *Faculty research:* Organization theory, political science, sociology, technology studies.

Carnegie Mellon University, Tepper School of Business, Organizational Behavior and Theory Program, Pittsburgh, PA 15213-3891. Offers PhD. *Degree requirements:* For doctorate, thesis/dissertation. *Entrance requirements:* For doctorate, GMAT or GRE General Test. Additional exam requirements/recommendations for international students: Required—TOEFL. *Faculty research:* Negotiation, organizational learning, interorganizational relations and strategy, group process and performance, communication process and electronic media, group goal setting, uncertainty in organizations, creation and effect of institutions and psychological contracts.

Case Western Reserve University, Weatherhead School of Management, Department of Organizational Behavior, Cleveland, OH 44106. Offers organizational behavior (PhD); positive organization development and change (MS). *Program availability:* Part-time, evening/weekend. *Degree requirements:* For doctorate, thesis/dissertation. *Entrance requirements:* For master's and doctorate, GMAT. *Expenses: Tuition:* Full-time $42,576; part-time $1774 per credit hour. *Required fees:* $34. Tuition and fees vary according to course load and program. *Faculty research:* Social innovation in global management, competency-based learning, life-long learning, organizational theory, organizational change.

Cornell University, Graduate School, Graduate Field of Management, Ithaca, NY 14853. Offers accounting (PhD); finance (PhD); marketing (PhD); organizational behavior (PhD); production and operations management (PhD). *Accreditation:* AACSB. *Degree requirements:* For doctorate, comprehensive exam, thesis/dissertation. *Entrance requirements:* For doctorate, GMAT or GRE General Test. Additional exam requirements/recommendations for international students: Required—TOEFL (minimum score 600 paper-based; 77 iBT). Electronic applications accepted. *Expenses:* Contact institution. *Faculty research:* Operations and manufacturing.

Cornell University, Graduate School, Graduate Fields of Industrial and Labor Relations, Ithaca, NY 14853. Offers collective bargaining, labor law and labor history (MILR, MPS, MS, PhD); economic and social statistics (MILR); human resource studies (MILR, MPS, MS, PhD); industrial and labor relations problems (MILR, MPS, MS, PhD); international and comparative labor (MILR, MPS, MS, PhD); labor economics (MILR, MPS, MS, PhD); organizational behavior (MILR, MPS, MS, PhD). *Degree requirements:* For master's, thesis (MS); for doctorate, comprehensive exam, thesis/dissertation, teaching experience. *Entrance requirements:* For master's and doctorate, GMAT or GRE General Test, 2 academic recommendations. Additional exam requirements/recommendations for international students: Required—TOEFL (minimum score 550 paper-based; 77 iBT). Electronic applications accepted. *Expenses:* Contact institution.

Drexel University, LeBow College of Business, Program in Business Administration, Philadelphia, PA 19104-2875. Offers business administration (MBA, PhD, APC), including accounting (MBA, PhD), decision sciences (PhD), economics (MBA, PhD), finance (MBA, PhD), legal studies (MBA), management (MBA), marketing (MBA, PhD), organizational sciences (PhD), quantitative methods (MBA), strategic management (PhD). *Accreditation:* AACSB. *Program availability:* Part-time, evening/weekend, online learning. *Faculty:* 88 full-time (19 women), 11 part-time/adjunct (2 women). *Students:* 153 full-time (70 women), 388 part-time (168 women); includes 107 minority (31 Black or African American, non-Hispanic/Latino; 1 American Indian or Alaska Native, non-Hispanic/Latino; 48 Asian, non-Hispanic/Latino; 16 Hispanic/Latino; 11 Two or more races, non-Hispanic/Latino), 95 international. Average age 33. In 2016, 174 master's, 8 doctorates, 1 other advanced degree awarded. Terminal master's awarded for partial completion of doctoral program. *Entrance requirements:* For master's, GMAT, minimum GPA of 2.75; for doctorate, GMAT. Additional exam requirements/recommendations for international students: Required—TOEFL. *Application deadline:* For fall admission, 8/21 for domestic students; for spring admission, 3/5 for domestic students. Applications are processed on a rolling basis. Application fee: $50. Electronic applications accepted. *Expenses: Tuition:* Full-time $32,184; part-time $1192 per credit hour. *Required fees:* $280. Tuition and fees vary according to campus/location and program. *Financial support:* Research assistantships, teaching assistantships, career-related internships or fieldwork, and unspecified assistantships available. Financial award application deadline: 2/1. *Faculty research:* Decision support systems, individual and group behavior, operations research, techniques and strategy. *Unit head:* Dr. Thomas Wieckowski, Director of Master's Programs in Business, 215-895-1791, Fax: 215-895-1012. *Application contact:* Director of Graduate Admissions, 215-895-6700, Fax: 215-895-5939, E-mail: enroll@drexel.edu.

Fairleigh Dickinson University, College at Florham, Maxwell Becton College of Arts and Sciences, Department of Psychology, Program in Organizational Behavior, Madison, NJ 07940-1099. Offers organizational behavior (MA); organizational leadership (Certificate).

Florida Institute of Technology, College of Psychology and Liberal Arts, Program in Applied Behavior Analysis and Organizational Behavior Management, Melbourne, FL 32901-6975. Offers MS. *Program availability:* Part-time. *Students:* 22 full-time (18 women), 2 part-time (1 woman); includes 9 minority (3 Asian, non-Hispanic/Latino; 4 Hispanic/Latino; 2 Two or more races, non-Hispanic/Latino). Average age 25. 36 applicants, 39% accepted, 7 enrolled. In 2016, 5 master's awarded. *Degree requirements:* For master's, comprehensive exam, thesis or alternative, minimum of 50 credits, all course grades of B or higher. *Entrance requirements:* For master's, GRE General Test, 3 letters of recommendation, resume, statement of objectives. Additional exam requirements/recommendations for international students: Required—TOEFL (minimum score 550 paper-based; 79 iBT). *Application deadline:* Applications are processed on a rolling basis. Electronic applications accepted. *Expenses: Tuition:* Full-time $22,338; part-time $1241 per credit hour. *Required fees:* $250. Tuition and fees vary according to degree level, campus/location and program. *Unit head:* Dr. David Wilder, Program Chair, 321-674-7516, E-mail: dawilder@fit.edu. *Application contact:* Cheryl A. Brown, Associate Director of Graduate Admissions, 321-674-7581, Fax: 321-723-9468, E-mail: cbrown@fit.edu.
Website: http://cpla.fit.edu/programs.php

Florida Institute of Technology, College of Psychology and Liberal Arts, Program in Organizational Behavior Management, Melbourne, FL 32901-6975. Offers MS. *Students:* 2 full-time (1 woman); includes 1 minority (Asian, non-Hispanic/Latino). Average age 24. 10 applicants, 20% accepted, 2 enrolled. *Degree requirements:* For master's, comprehensive exam, thesis optional, minimum of 42 credit hours, all course grades of B or higher. *Entrance requirements:* For master's, GRE General Test, 3 letters of recommendation, resume, statement of objectives. Additional exam requirements/recommendations for international students: Required—TOEFL (minimum score 550 paper-based; 79 iBT). *Expenses: Tuition:* Full-time $22,338; part-time $1241 per credit hour. *Required fees:* $250. Tuition and fees vary according to degree level, campus/location and program. *Financial support:* Applicants required to submit FAFSA. *Unit head:* Dr. David Wilder, Program Chair, Campus Behavior Analysis Programs, 321-674-7516, E-mail: dawilder@fit.edu. *Application contact:* Cheryl A. Brown, Associate Director of Graduate Admissions, 321-674-7581, Fax: 321-723-9468, E-mail: cbrown@fit.edu.
Website: http://www.fit.edu/programs/

Florida State University, The Graduate School, College of Business, Tallahassee, FL 32306-1110. Offers accounting (M Acc), including assurance and advisory services, generalist, taxation; business administration (MBA, PhD), including accounting (PhD), finance (PhD), management information systems (PhD), marketing (PhD), organizational behavior and human resources (PhD), risk management and insurance (PhD), strategy (PhD); finance (MS); management information systems (MS); risk management and insurance (MS); JD/MBA; MSW/MBA. *Accreditation:* AACSB. *Program availability:* Part-time, 100% online. *Faculty:* 101 full-time (27 women), 4 part-time/adjunct (2 women). *Students:* 272 full-time (127 women), 351 part-time (133 women); includes 141 minority (45 Black or African American, non-Hispanic/Latino; 2 American Indian or Alaska Native, non-Hispanic/Latino; 20 Asian, non-Hispanic/Latino; 59 Hispanic/Latino; 2 Native Hawaiian or other Pacific Islander, non-Hispanic/Latino; 13 Two or more races, non-Hispanic/Latino), 71 international. Average age 30. 688 applicants, 60% accepted, 273 enrolled. In 2016, 231 master's, 12 doctorates awarded. Terminal master's awarded for partial completion of doctoral program. *Degree requirements:* For doctorate, comprehensive exam, thesis/dissertation. *Entrance requirements:* For master's, GMAT, GRE (for all except MS in finance), work experience (MBA, MS); minimum GPA of 3.0, letters of recommendation; for doctorate, GMAT, GRE (for marketing, organizational behavior, risk management and insurance, management information systems, and human resources only), minimum graduate GPA of 3.5, letters of recommendation. Additional exam requirements/recommendations for international students: Required—TOEFL (minimum score 600 paper-based; 85 iBT); Recommended—IELTS (minimum score 6). *Application deadline:* For fall admission, 6/1 for domestic and international students; for spring admission, 10/1 for domestic and international students; for summer admission, 3/1 for domestic and international students. Applications are processed on a rolling basis. Application fee: $30. Electronic applications accepted. *Expenses:* Contact institution. *Financial support:* In 2016–17, 149 students received support, including 9 fellowships (averaging $1,500 per year), 65 research assistantships with full tuition reimbursements available (averaging $20,000 per year), 75 teaching assistantships with full tuition reimbursements available (averaging $20,000 per year); career-related internships or fieldwork, scholarships/grants, health care benefits, tuition waivers (full and partial), and unspecified assistantships also available. Support available to part-time students. Financial award application deadline: 1/1; financial award applicants required to submit FAFSA. *Faculty research:* Business strategy, marketing, finance, accounting, business analytics. *Total annual research expenditures:* $1.4 million. *Unit head:* Dr. Michael Hartline, Dean, 850-644-4405, Fax: 850-644-0915, E-mail: mhartline@business.fsu.edu. *Application contact:* Jennifer Clark, Director, 850-644-6458, E-mail: gradprograms@business.fsu.edu.
Website: http://business.fsu.edu/

The Graduate Center, City University of New York, Graduate Studies, Program in Business, New York, NY 10016-4039. Offers accounting (PhD); behavioral science (PhD); finance (PhD); management planning systems (PhD). *Degree requirements:* For doctorate, thesis/dissertation. *Entrance requirements:* For doctorate, GMAT, writing sample (15 pages). Additional exam requirements/recommendations for international students: Required—TOEFL. Electronic applications accepted.

Harvard University, Graduate School of Arts and Sciences and Doctoral Programs in Management, Committee on Organizational Behavior, Cambridge, MA 02138. Offers PhD. *Entrance requirements:* For doctorate, GRE General Test or GMAT, major in psychology or sociology, course work in statistics or mathematics. Additional exam requirements/recommendations for international students: Required—TOEFL.

Harvard University, Harvard Business School, Doctoral Programs in Management, Boston, MA 02163. Offers accounting and management (DBA); business economics (PhD); health policy management (PhD); management (DBA); marketing (DBA); organizational behavior (PhD); science, technology and management (PhD); strategy (DBA); technology and operations management (DBA). *Degree requirements:* For doctorate, comprehensive exam (for some programs), thesis/dissertation. *Entrance requirements:* For doctorate, GRE General Test or GMAT. Additional exam requirements/recommendations for international students: Required—TOEFL.

International Institute for Restorative Practices, Graduate Programs, Bethlehem, PA 18018. Offers MS, Certificate. *Program availability:* Online learning. *Expenses:* Contact institution.

John Jay College of Criminal Justice of the City University of New York, Graduate Studies, Programs in Criminal Justice, New York, NY 10019. Offers criminal justice (MA, PhD); criminology and deviance (PhD); forensic psychology (PhD); forensic science (PhD); international crime and justice (MA); law and philosophy (PhD); organizational behavior (PhD); public policy (PhD). *Program availability:* Part-time, evening/weekend. Terminal master's awarded for partial completion of doctoral program. *Degree requirements:* For master's, thesis or alternative; for doctorate, one foreign language, thesis/dissertation. *Entrance requirements:* For master's, GRE General Test, minimum B average; for doctorate, GRE General Test. Additional exam requirements/recommendations for international students: Required—TOEFL (minimum score 500 paper-based).

Lake Forest Graduate School of Management, The Leadership MBA Program, Lake Forest, IL 60045. Offers finance (MBA); global business (MBA); healthcare management (MBA); management (MBA); marketing (MBA); organizational behavior (MBA). *Program availability:* Part-time, evening/weekend. *Entrance requirements:* For master's, 4 years of work experience in field, interview, 2 letters of recommendation. Electronic applications accepted.

New York University, Leonard N. Stern School of Business, Department of Management and Organizations, New York, NY 10012-1019. Offers management organizations (MBA); organization theory (PhD); organizational behavior (PhD); strategy (PhD). *Faculty research:* Strategic management, managerial cognition, interpersonal processes, conflict and negotiation.

New York University, Polytechnic School of Engineering, Department of Finance and Risk Engineering, New York, NY 10012-1019. Offers financial engineering (MS, Advanced Certificate), including capital markets (MS), computational finance (MS), financial technology (MS); financial technology management (Advanced Certificate); organizational behavior (Advanced Certificate); risk management (Advanced Certificate); technology management (Advanced Certificate). MS program also offered in Manhattan. *Program availability:* Part-time, evening/weekend. *Degree requirements:* For master's, comprehensive exam (for some programs), thesis (for some programs). *Entrance requirements:* For master's, GMAT, minimum B average in undergraduate course work. Additional exam requirements/recommendations for international students: Required—TOEFL (minimum score 550 paper-based; 80 iBT); Recommended—IELTS (minimum score 6.5). Electronic applications accepted. *Faculty research:* Optimal control theory, general modeling and analysis, risk parity optimality, a new algorithmic approach to entangled political economy.

New York University, Polytechnic School of Engineering, Department of Technology Management, Major in Organizational Behavior, New York, NY 10012-1019. Offers MS. *Program availability:* Part-time, evening/weekend. *Degree requirements:* For master's, comprehensive exam (for some programs), thesis (for some programs). *Entrance requirements:* For master's, GMAT, minimum B average in undergraduate course work. Additional exam requirements/recommendations for international students: Required—TOEFL (minimum score 550 paper-based; 80 iBT); Recommended—IELTS (minimum score 6.5). Electronic applications accepted.

Northwestern University, The Graduate School, School of Education and Social Policy, Program in Learning and Organizational Change, Evanston, IL 60208. Offers MS. *Program availability:* Part-time, evening/weekend, online learning. *Degree requirements:* For master's, thesis, practicum. *Entrance requirements:* For master's, GRE or GMAT (recommended), letters of recommendation. Additional exam requirements/recommendations for international students: Required—TOEFL (minimum score 600 paper-based; 100 iBT); Recommended—IELTS (minimum score 7). Electronic applications accepted. *Faculty research:* Strategic change, learning and performance, workplace learning, leadership development, cognitive design, knowledge management.

Phillips Graduate University, Program in Organizational Management and Consulting, Chatsworth, CA 91311. Offers Psy D. *Program availability:* Evening/weekend. *Degree requirements:* For doctorate, thesis/dissertation. *Entrance requirements:* For doctorate, minimum GPA of 3.0, interview. Electronic applications accepted.

Purdue University, Graduate School, Krannert School of Management, Doctoral Program in Organizational Behavior and Human Resource Management, West Lafayette, IN 47907-2056. Offers PhD. *Degree requirements:* For doctorate, comprehensive exam, thesis/dissertation, dissertation proposal, dissertation defense. *Entrance requirements:* For doctorate, GMAT or GRE, bachelor's degree, two semesters of calculus, one semester each of linear algebra and statistics. Additional exam requirements/recommendations for international students: Required—TOEFL (minimum score 575 paper-based); Recommended—TWE. Electronic applications accepted. *Faculty research:* Human resource management, organizational behavior.

Saybrook University, School of Organizational Leadership and Transformation, San Francisco, CA 94612. Offers MA. Program offered jointly with Bastyr University. *Degree requirements:* For master's, thesis (for some programs), oral exams. *Entrance requirements:* For master's, bachelor's degree from an accredited college or university. *Faculty research:* Cross-functional work teams, communication, management authority, employee influence, systems theory.

Saybrook University, School of Psychology and Interdisciplinary Inquiry, San Francisco, CA 94612. Offers human science (MA, PhD), including consciousness and spirituality, humanistic and transpersonal psychology, integrative health studies, organizational systems, social transformation; organizational systems (MA, PhD), including consciousness and spirituality, humanistic and transpersonal psychology, integrative health studies, leadership of sustainable systems (MA), organizational systems, social transformation; psychology (MA, PhD), including consciousness and spirituality, creativity studies (MA), humanistic and transpersonal psychology, integrative health studies, Jungian studies, marriage and family therapy (MA), organizational systems, social transformation. *Program availability:* Online learning. Terminal master's awarded for partial completion of doctoral program. *Degree requirements:* For master's, thesis or alternative; for doctorate, thesis/dissertation. *Entrance requirements:* Additional exam requirements/recommendations for international students: Required—TOEFL (minimum score 580 paper-based; 93 iBT). Electronic applications accepted. *Faculty research:* Humanistic theory, health studies, organizational systems, consciousness and spirituality, social transformation.

Suffolk University, Sawyer Business School, Master of Business Administration Program, Boston, MA 02108-2770. Offers accounting (MBA); entrepreneurship (MBA); executive business administration (EMBA); finance (MBA); global business administration (GMBA); health administration (MBA); international business (MBA); marketing (MBA); nonprofit management (MBA); organizational behavior (MBA); strategic management (MBA); supply chain management (MBA); taxation (MBA); JD/MBA; MBA/MHA; MBA/MSA; MBA/MSF; MBA/MST. *Accreditation:* AACSB. *Program availability:* Part-time, evening/weekend, 100% online. *Faculty:* 17 full-time (6 women), 10 part-time/adjunct (1 woman). *Students:* 137 full-time (70 women), 265 part-time (138

women); includes 78 minority (20 Black or African American, non-Hispanic/Latino; 22 Asian, non-Hispanic/Latino; 31 Hispanic/Latino; 5 Two or more races, non-Hispanic/Latino), 46 international. Average age 30. 416 applicants, 70% accepted, 128 enrolled. In 2016, 165 degrees awarded. *Entrance requirements:* For master's, GMAT, minimum undergraduate GPA of 2.75 (MBA), 5 years of managerial experience (EMBA). Additional exam requirements/recommendations for international students: Required—TOEFL (minimum score 550 paper-based; 80 iBT). *Application deadline:* For fall admission, 3/15 priority date for domestic students, 10/15 priority date for international students; for spring admission, 10/15 priority date for domestic and international students. Applications are processed on a rolling basis. Application fee: $50. Electronic applications accepted. *Expenses: Tuition:* Full-time $41,490; part-time $1383 per credit hour. *Required fees:* $52; $52 per credit hour. Part-time tuition and fees vary according to course load and program. *Financial support:* In 2016–17, 209 students received support, including 176 fellowships (averaging $8,581 per year); career-related internships or fieldwork, Federal Work-Study, institutionally sponsored loans, and scholarships/grants also available. Support available to part-time students. Financial award application deadline: 4/1; financial award applicants required to submit FAFSA. *Faculty research:* Foreign investments; career strategies and boundaryless careers; corporate ethics codes; interest rates, inflation, and growth options; innovation and product development performance. *Unit head:* Jodi Detjen, Director of MBA Programs, 617-573-8306, E-mail: jdetjen@suffolk.edu. *Application contact:* Mara Marzocchi, Associate Director of Graduate Admissions, 617-573-8302, Fax: 617-305-1733, E-mail: grad.admission@suffolk.edu.
Website: http://www.suffolk.edu/mba

Towson University, Program in Organizational Change, Towson, MD 21252-0001. Offers CAS. *Students:* 86 part-time (68 women); includes 26 minority (21 Black or African American, non-Hispanic/Latino; 2 Asian, non-Hispanic/Latino; 2 Hispanic/Latino; 1 Two or more races, non-Hispanic/Latino). *Entrance requirements:* For degree, minimum 3 years of teaching experience, 2 letters of recommendation, minimum GPA of 3.1, personal statement. *Application deadline:* Applications are processed on a rolling basis. Application fee: $45. Electronic applications accepted. *Expenses:* Tuition, state resident: full-time $7580; part-time $379 per unit. Tuition, nonresident: full-time $15,700; part-time $785 per unit. *Required fees:* $2480. *Unit head:* Carla Finkelstein, Graduate Program Director, 410-704-2974, E-mail: cfinkelstein@towson.edu. *Application contact:* Coverley Beidleman, Assistant Director of Graduate Admissions, 410-704-2113, Fax: 410-704-3030, E-mail: grads@towson.edu.
Website: http://www.towson.edu/coe/departments/leadership/grad/orgchangecas/

Universidad de las Americas, A.C., Program in International Organizations and Institutions, Mexico City, Mexico. Offers MA.

Université de Sherbrooke, Faculty of Administration, Program in Organizational Change and Intervention, Sherbrooke, QC J1K 2R1, Canada. Offers M Sc. *Degree requirements:* For master's, one foreign language, thesis. *Entrance requirements:* For master's, bachelor's degree in related field, minimum GPA of 3.0 (on 4.3 scale). Electronic applications accepted. *Faculty research:* Organizational change, organizational communication, process approaches and qualitative research, organizational behavior.

University at Albany, State University of New York, Nelson A. Rockefeller College of Public Affairs and Policy, Department of Public Administration and Policy, Albany, NY 12222-0001. Offers financial management and public economics (MPA); financial market regulation (MPA); health policy (MPA); healthcare management (MPA); homeland security (MPA); human resources management (MPA); information strategy and management (MPA); local government management (MPA); nonprofit management (MPA); nonprofit management and leadership (Certificate); organizational behavior and theory (MPA, PhD); planning and policy analysis (CAS); policy analysis (MPA); politics and administration (PhD); public finance (PhD); public management (PhD); public policy (PhD); public sector management (Certificate); women and public policy (Certificate); JD/MPA. JD/MPA offered jointly with Albany Law School. *Accreditation:* NASPAA (one or more programs are accredited). *Faculty:* 23 full-time (8 women), 14 part-time/adjunct (7 women). *Students:* 117 full-time (65 women), 95 part-time (46 women); includes 41 minority (12 Black or African American, non-Hispanic/Latino; 8 Asian, non-Hispanic/Latino; 19 Hispanic/Latino; 2 Two or more races, non-Hispanic/Latino), 38 international. 223 applicants, 70% accepted, 81 enrolled. In 2016, 52 master's, 10 doctorates, 16 other advanced degrees awarded. *Degree requirements:* For doctorate, one foreign language, thesis/dissertation. *Entrance requirements:* For doctorate, GRE General Test. Additional exam requirements/recommendations for international students: Required—TOEFL (minimum score 550 paper-based). *Application deadline:* For fall admission, 2/1 priority date for domestic students, 5/1 for international students; for spring admission, 12/1 for domestic students. Applications are processed on a rolling basis. Application fee: $75. Electronic applications accepted. *Expenses:* Tuition, state resident: full-time $10,870; part-time $453 per credit hour. Tuition, nonresident: full-time $22,210; part-time $925 per credit hour. *International tuition:* $21,550 full-time. *Required fees:* $1864; $96 per credit hour. *Financial support:* Application deadline: 2/1. *Total annual research expenditures:* $847,949. *Unit head:* Victor Asal, Chair, 518-591-8729, E-mail: vasal@albany.edu.
Website: http://www.albany.edu/rockefeller/pad.shtml

The University of British Columbia, Sauder School of Business, Doctoral Program in Business Administration, Vancouver, BC V6T 1Z2, Canada. Offers accounting (PhD); finance (PhD); management information systems (PhD); management science (PhD); marketing (PhD); organizational behavior (PhD); strategy and business economics (PhD); transportation and logistics (PhD); urban land economics (PhD). *Degree requirements:* For doctorate, comprehensive exam, thesis/dissertation. *Entrance requirements:* For doctorate, GMAT or GRE. Additional exam requirements/recommendations for international students: Required—TOEFL (minimum score 600 paper-based; 100 iBT). *Application deadline:* Applications are processed on a rolling basis. Application fee: $102 Canadian dollars ($165 Canadian dollars for international students). Electronic applications accepted. *Expenses:* $4,802 per year tuition and fees, $8,436 per year international. *Financial support:* Fellowships with full tuition reimbursements, research assistantships with full tuition reimbursements, and teaching assistantships with full tuition reimbursements available. *Application contact:* Elaine Cho, Administrator, PhD and M Sc Programs, 604-822-8366, Fax: 604-822-8755, E-mail: phd.program@sauder.ubc.ca.
Website: http://www.sauder.ubc.ca/Programs/PhD_in_Business_Administration

University of California, Berkeley, Graduate Division, Haas School of Business, PhD in Business Administration Program, Berkeley, CA 94720-1500. Offers accounting (PhD); business and public policy (PhD); finance (PhD); management of organizations (PhD); marketing (PhD); real estate (PhD). *Accreditation:* AACSB. *Students:* 78 full-time (28 women); includes 34 minority (29 Asian, non-Hispanic/Latino; 5 Hispanic/Latino). Average age 27. *Degree requirements:* For doctorate, comprehensive exam, thesis/dissertation, written preliminary exams, oral qualifying exam. *Entrance requirements:* For doctorate, GMAT or GRE, minimum GPA of 3.0 in undergraduate and graduate coursework. Additional exam requirements/recommendations for international students: Required—TOEFL (minimum score 570 paper-based; 70 iBT), IELTS (minimum score 7). *Application deadline:* For fall admission, 12/1 for domestic and international students. Application fee: $90 ($110 for international students). Electronic applications accepted. *Expenses:* Contact institution. *Financial support:* Fellowships with tuition reimbursements, research assistantships with tuition reimbursements, teaching assistantships with tuition reimbursements, scholarships/grants, health care benefits, tuition waivers (full), unspecified assistantships, and transit passes, travel grants available. Financial award application deadline: 12/10. *Faculty research:* Accounting, business and public policy, entrepreneurship, finance, management of organizations, marketing, operations and information technology management, real estate. *Unit head:* Dr. Nicolae Garleanu, Director, 510-643-6349, Fax: 510-643-4255. *Application contact:* Melissa Hacker, Director, Student Affairs, 510-642-3944, Fax: 510-643-4255, E-mail: melhacker@haas.berkeley.edu.
Website: http://www.haas.berkeley.edu/Phd/

University of Chicago, Booth School of Business, Full-Time MBA Program, Chicago, IL 60637. Offers accounting (MBA); analytic finance (MBA); analytic management (MBA); econometrics and statistics (MBA); economics (MBA); entrepreneurship (MBA); finance (MBA); general management (MBA); health administration and policy (Certificate); international business (MBA); managerial and organizational behavior (MBA); marketing analytics (MBA); marketing management (MBA); operations management (MBA); strategic management (MBA); MBA/AM; MBA/JD; MBA/MA; MBA/MD; MBA/MPP. *Accreditation:* AACSB. *Students:* 1,151 full-time (443 women), 17 part-time (9 women). Terminal master's awarded for partial completion of doctoral program. *Entrance requirements:* For master's, GMAT or GRE, transcripts, resume, 2 letters of recommendation, essay, interview. Additional exam requirements/recommendations for international students: Required—TOEFL (minimum score 600 paper-based; 104 iBT), IELTS (minimum score 7), PTE (minimum score 70). *Application deadline:* For spring admission, 4/1 for domestic and international students. Electronic applications accepted. *Expenses:* Contact institution. *Unit head:* Stacey Kole, Deputy Dean, 773-702-7121. *Application contact:* Full-time MBA Program Admissions, 773-702-7369, Fax: 773-702-9085, E-mail: admissions@chicagobooth.edu.
Website: https://www.chicagobooth.edu/programs/full-time

University of Hartford, College of Arts and Sciences, Department of Psychology, Program in Organizational Behavior, West Hartford, CT 06117-1599. Offers MS. *Program availability:* Part-time, evening/weekend. *Entrance requirements:* Additional exam requirements/recommendations for international students: Required—TOEFL (minimum score 550 paper-based). Electronic applications accepted.

University of Hawaii at Manoa, Graduate Division, Shidler College of Business, Program in Business Administration, Honolulu, HI 96822. Offers Asian business studies (MBA); Chinese business studies (MBA); decision sciences (MBA); entrepreneurship (MBA); finance (MBA); finance and banking (MBA); human resources management (MBA); information management (MBA); information technology (MBA); international business (MBA); Japanese business studies (MBA); marketing (MBA); organizational behavior (MBA); organizational management (MBA); real estate (MBA); student-designed track (MBA). *Accreditation:* AACSB. *Program availability:* Part-time, evening/weekend. *Degree requirements:* For master's, thesis optional. *Entrance requirements:* For master's, GMAT, minimum GPA of 3.0. Additional exam requirements/recommendations for international students: Required—TOEFL (minimum score 600 paper-based; 100 iBT), IELTS (minimum score 7). *Expenses:* Contact institution.

The University of Kansas, Graduate Studies, School of Business, Program in Business, Lawrence, KS 66045. Offers accounting (PhD); business and organizational leadership (MS); decision sciences and supply chain management (PhD); finance (PhD); human resources management (PhD); marketing (PhD); organizational behavior (PhD); strategic management (PhD); supply chain management and logistics (MS). *Accreditation:* AACSB. *Program availability:* Part-time. *Students:* 76 full-time (11 women), 170 part-time (83 women); includes 41 minority (15 Black or African American, non-Hispanic/Latino; 3 American Indian or Alaska Native, non-Hispanic/Latino; 6 Asian, non-Hispanic/Latino; 5 Hispanic/Latino; 12 Two or more races, non-Hispanic/Latino), 25 international. Average age 32. 294 applicants, 69% accepted, 152 enrolled. In 2016, 36 master's, 9 doctorates awarded. *Entrance requirements:* For master's, GMAT, official transcript, three letters of recommendation, resume, statement of purpose; for doctorate, GMAT or GRE, official transcript, three letters of recommendation, resume, statement of purpose. Additional exam requirements/recommendations for international students: Required—TOEFL (minimum score 600 paper-based; 100 iBT). *Application deadline:* For fall admission, 1/10 for domestic and international students. Application fee: $65 ($85 for international students). Electronic applications accepted. *Financial support:* Fellowships, research assistantships, teaching assistantships, scholarships/grants, health care benefits, tuition waivers (full), and unspecified assistantships available. Financial award application deadline: 1/10. *Faculty research:* Strategic human resource management, business ethics, organizational theory/behavior, corporate strategy, international business, supply chain management, Bayesian networks, game theory, decision analysis and time/series analysis, pricing, consumer effects, advertising and emotion. *Unit head:* Charly Edmonds, Director, 785-864-3841, E-mail: bschoolphd@ku.edu. *Application contact:* Graduate Admission Contact, 785-864-7500, E-mail: bschoolphd@ku.edu.
Website: http://www.business.ku.edu/

University of New Mexico, Anderson School of Management, Department of Organizational Studies, Albuquerque, NM 87131. Offers organizational behavior and human resources management (MBA); strategic management and policy (MBA). *Program availability:* Part-time, evening/weekend. *Faculty:* 17 full-time (12 women), 6 part-time/adjunct (2 women). In 2016, 26 master's awarded. *Entrance requirements:* For master's, GMAT or GRE, minimum GPA of 3.0 on last 60 hours of coursework; bachelor's degree from regionally-accredited college or university in U.S. or its equivalent in another country. Additional exam requirements/recommendations for international students: Required—TOEFL (minimum score 550 paper-based; 79 iBT), IELTS (minimum score 6.5). *Application deadline:* For fall admission, 4/1 priority date for domestic and international students; for spring admission, 10/1 priority date for domestic and international students. Applications are processed on a rolling basis. Application fee: $50. Electronic applications accepted. *Expenses:* Contact institution. *Financial support:* In 2016–17, 4 fellowships (averaging $24,700 per year), 13 research assistantships with partial tuition reimbursements (averaging $15,345 per year) were awarded; career-related internships or fieldwork, Federal Work-Study, scholarships/grants, and unspecified assistantships also available. Support available to part-time students. Financial award application deadline: 6/1; financial award applicants required to submit FAFSA. *Faculty research:* Business ethics and social corporate responsibility, diversity, human resources, organizational strategy, organizational behavior. *Unit head:* Dr. Michelle Arthur, Chair, 505-277-6471, E-mail: arthurm@unm.edu. *Application contact:* Lisa Beauchene, Student Recruitment Specialist, 505-277-6471, E-mail: andersonadvising@unm.edu.
Website: https://www.mgt.unm.edu/dos/default.asp?mm=faculty

The University of North Carolina at Chapel Hill, Kenan-Flagler Business School, Doctoral Program in Business Administration, Chapel Hill, NC 27599. Offers accounting (PhD); finance (PhD); marketing (PhD); operations management (PhD); organizational behavior (PhD); strategy (PhD). *Accreditation:* AACSB. *Degree requirements:* For doctorate, thesis/dissertation. *Entrance requirements:* For doctorate, GMAT or GRE General Test. Electronic applications accepted. *Expenses:* Contact institution.

University of North Texas at Dallas, Graduate School, Dallas, TX 75241. Offers accounting (MBA); counseling (M Ed, MS); criminal justice (MS); curriculum and instruction (M Ed); educational administration (M Ed); human resources and organizational behavior (MBA); public leadership (MS); strategic management (MBA).

University of Oklahoma, College of Arts and Sciences, Department of Psychology, Program in Organizational Dynamics, Tulsa, OK 74135. Offers human resource management (MA, Graduate Certificate); project management (MA, Graduate Certificate). *Program availability:* Part-time, evening/weekend. *Students:* 9 full-time (all women), 24 part-time (14 women); includes 6 minority (1 Black or African American, non-Hispanic/Latino; 2 American Indian or Alaska Native, non-Hispanic/Latino; 1 Asian, non-Hispanic/Latino; 2 Hispanic/Latino), 3 international. Average age 34. 13 applicants, 62% accepted, 6 enrolled. In 2016, 6 master's awarded. Terminal master's awarded for partial completion of doctoral program. *Degree requirements:* For master's, comprehensive exam (for some programs), thesis (for some programs), capstone project, comprehensive exam, or thesis; 36 hours of coursework; for Graduate Certificate, 12 hours of coursework from approved list. *Entrance requirements:* For master's, GRE (for students who do not have requisite work experience), current resume showing at least 2 years of relevant work experience; 2 letters of recommendation; statement of career goals; transcripts; for Graduate Certificate, resume showing work experience; 2 letters of recommendation; statement of career goals; transcripts. Additional exam requirements/recommendations for international students: Required—TOEFL (minimum score 79 iBT) or IELTS (minimum score 6.5). *Application deadline:* For fall admission, 5/1 for domestic and international students; for spring admission, 11/1 for domestic and international students; for summer admission, 3/15 for domestic and international students. Application fee: $50 ($100 for international students). Electronic applications accepted. *Expenses:* Tuition, state resident: full-time $4886; part-time $203.60 per credit hour. Tuition, nonresident: full-time $18,989; part-time $791.20 per credit hour. *Required fees:* $3283; $126.25 per credit hour. $126.50 per semester. *Financial support:* In 2016–17, 12 students received support. Research assistantships with full tuition reimbursements available, health care benefits, and unspecified assistantships available. Financial award application deadline: 6/1; financial award applicants required to submit FAFSA. *Faculty research:* Organizational behavior, personality, organizational climate and culture, leadership, ethics. *Unit head:* Dr. Eric Day, Chair, 405-325-4511, Fax: 405-325-4737, E-mail: eday@ou.edu. *Application contact:* Jennifer Kisamore, Associate Professor of Psychology/Graduate Liaison for Organizational Dynamics, 918-660-3603, Fax: 918-660-3383, E-mail: odyn@ou.edu.
Website: http://odyn.ou.edu

University of Pittsburgh, Katz Graduate School of Business, Doctoral Program in Business Administration, Pittsburgh, PA 15260. Offers accounting (PhD); business analytics and operations (PhD); finance (PhD); information systems and technology management (PhD); marketing (PhD); organizational behavior and human resources (PhD); strategic management (PhD). *Accreditation:* AACSB. *Program availability:* Evening/weekend. *Faculty:* 88 full-time (27 women), 42 part-time/adjunct (15 women). *Students:* 51 full-time (23 women), 1 part-time (0 women); includes 4 minority (1 Black or African American, non-Hispanic/Latino; 2 Asian, non-Hispanic/Latino; 1 Two or more races, non-Hispanic/Latino), 31 international. Average age 31. 344 applicants, 6% accepted, 9 enrolled. In 2016, 5 doctorates awarded. *Degree requirements:* For doctorate, comprehensive exam, thesis/dissertation, student teaching. *Entrance requirements:* For doctorate, GMAT or GRE, 3 recommendations, statement of purpose, transcripts of all previous course work and degrees. Additional exam requirements/recommendations for international students: Required—TOEFL (minimum score 100 iBT) or IELTS (minimum score 7.0). *Application deadline:* For fall admission, 4/1 priority date for domestic students, 2/1 priority date for international students. Applications are processed on a rolling basis. Application fee: $50. Electronic applications accepted. *Expenses:* Contact institution. *Financial support:* In 2016–17, 40 students received support, including 27 research assistantships with full tuition reimbursements available (averaging $26,000 per year), 9 teaching assistantships with full tuition reimbursements available (averaging $26,700 per year); Federal Work-Study, scholarships/grants, health care benefits, and unspecified assistantships also available. Financial award application deadline: 6/1; financial award applicants required to submit FAFSA. *Faculty research:* Accounting systems/financial reporting, corporate finance, shopper marketing/consumer behavior, management information systems, organizational behavior and entrepreneurship. *Total annual research expenditures:* $493,036. *Unit head:* Dr. Arjang A. Assad, Dean, 412-648-1556, Fax: 412-648-1552, E-mail: aassad@katz.pitt.edu. *Application contact:* Dr. Dennis Galletta, Director, 412-648-1699, Fax: 412-648-3633, E-mail: galletta@katz.pitt.edu.
Website: http://www.business.pitt.edu/katz/phd/

See Display on page 160 and Close-Up on page 189.

University of Pittsburgh, Katz Graduate School of Business, Master of Business Administration Programs, Pittsburgh, PA 15260. Offers finance (MBA); information systems (MBA); marketing (MBA); operations (MBA); organizational behavior and human resources (MBA); strategy, environment and organizations (MBA); MBA/JD; MBA/MSE. *Accreditation:* AACSB. *Program availability:* Part-time, evening/weekend, blended/hybrid learning. *Faculty:* 88 full-time (27 women), 42 part-time/adjunct (15 women). *Students:* 165 full-time (59 women), 330 part-time (103 women); includes 70 minority (29 Black or African American, non-Hispanic/Latino; 20 Asian, non-Hispanic/Latino; 13 Hispanic/Latino; 8 Two or more races, non-Hispanic/Latino), 73 international. Average age 29. 786 applicants, 41% accepted, 179 enrolled. In 2016, 477 master's awarded. *Degree requirements:* For master's, minimum GPA of 3.0. *Entrance requirements:* For master's, GMAT, GRE. Additional exam requirements/recommendations for international students: Required—TOEFL (minimum score 100 iBT) or IELTS (minimum score 7.0). *Application deadline:* For fall admission, 4/1 priority date for domestic students, 2/1 priority date for international students. Application fee: $50. Electronic applications accepted. *Expenses:* Contact institution. *Financial support:* In 2016–17, 110 students received support. Scholarships/grants available. Financial award application deadline: 6/1; financial award applicants required to submit FAFSA. *Faculty research:* Accounting systems/financial reporting, corporate finance, shopper marketing/consumer behavior, management information systems, organizational behavior and entrepreneurship. *Total annual research expenditures:* $493,036. *Unit head:* Dr. Arjang A. Assad, Dean, 412-648-1556, Fax: 412-648-1552, E-mail: aassad@katz.pitt.edu. *Application contact:* Thomas Keller, Director of MBA Admissions, 412-648-1700, Fax: 412-648-1659, E-mail: mba@katz.pitt.edu.
Website: http://www.business.pitt.edu/katz/mba/

See Display on page 160 and Close-Up on page 189.

The University of Texas at Austin, Graduate School, College of Liberal Arts, Program in Human Dimensions of Organizations, Austin, TX 78712-1111. Offers MA. *Program availability:* Evening/weekend, online learning. *Degree requirements:* For master's, capstone project.

University of Utah, Graduate School, David Eccles School of Business, Business Administration Program, Salt Lake City, UT 84112. Offers accounting (PhD); business administration (EMBA, MBA, PMBA); finance (PhD); information systems (PhD); marketing (PhD); operations management (PhD); organizational behavior (PhD); strategic management (PhD); MBA/JD; MBA/MHA; MBA/MS. *Program availability:* Part-time, evening/weekend, online learning. *Faculty:* 58 full-time (21 women), 37 part-time/adjunct (7 women). *Students:* 578 full-time (149 women), 89 part-time (28 women); includes 71 minority (1 American Indian or Alaska Native, non-Hispanic/Latino; 17 Asian, non-Hispanic/Latino; 45 Hispanic/Latino; 8 Two or more races, non-Hispanic/Latino), 50 international. Average age 32. 442 applicants, 70% accepted, 226 enrolled. In 2016, 246 master's, 6 doctorates awarded. *Degree requirements:* For doctorate, comprehensive exam, thesis/dissertation. *Entrance requirements:* For master's, GMAT or GRE; for doctorate, GMAT. Additional exam requirements/recommendations for international students: Required—TOEFL (minimum score 600 paper-based; 100 iBT), IELTS (minimum score 7). *Application deadline:* For fall admission, 11/1 priority date for domestic students, 3/1 priority date for international students; for spring admission, 11/1 for domestic and international students. Applications are processed on a rolling basis. Application fee: $55 ($65 for international students). Electronic applications accepted. *Expenses:* Contact institution. *Financial support:* In 2016–17, 53 students received support, including 53 fellowships with partial tuition reimbursements available (averaging $8,600 per year); scholarships/grants and unspecified assistantships also available. Financial award application deadline: 2/1; financial award applicants required to submit FAFSA. *Faculty research:* Corporate finance, strategy services, consumer behavior, financial disclosures, operations. *Unit head:* Kristina Diekmann, Department Chair, 801-581-8524, Fax: 801-581-3380, E-mail: mastersinfo@business.utah.edu. *Application contact:* Christine Harris, Coordinator, 801-581-7785, Fax: 801-585-3962, E-mail: execch@business.utah.edu.
Website: http://www.business.utah.edu/

Wayne State University, College of Liberal Arts and Sciences, Department of Political Science, Detroit, MI 48202. Offers political science (MA, PhD); public administration (MPA), including economic development policy and management, health and human services policy and management, human and fiscal resource management, nonprofit policy and management, organizational behavior and management, urban and metropolitan policy and management; JD/MA. *Accreditation:* NASPAA. *Faculty:* 20. *Students:* 64 full-time (20 women), 75 part-time (45 women); includes 48 minority (32 Black or African American, non-Hispanic/Latino; 5 Asian, non-Hispanic/Latino; 4 Hispanic/Latino; 7 Two or more races, non-Hispanic/Latino), 7 international. Average age 33. 105 applicants, 50% accepted, 27 enrolled. In 2016, 25 master's, 5 doctorates awarded. *Degree requirements:* For master's, comprehensive exam (for some programs), thesis (for some programs); for doctorate, thesis/dissertation. *Entrance requirements:* For master's, GRE General Test, substantial undergraduate preparation in the social sciences, minimum upper-division undergraduate GPA of 3.0, two letters of recommendation, personal statement; for doctorate, GRE General Test, 3 letters of recommendation; personal statement; interview. Additional exam requirements/recommendations for international students: Required—TOEFL (minimum score 550 paper-based; 79 iBT), TWE (minimum score 5.5), Michigan English Language Assessment Battery (minimum score 85); Recommended—IELTS (minimum score 6.5). *Application deadline:* For fall admission, 5/15 for domestic students, 5/1 priority date for international students; for winter admission, 10/15 for domestic students, 9/1 priority date for international students. Applications are processed on a rolling basis. Application fee: $50. Electronic applications accepted. *Expenses:* $16,503 per year resident tuition and fees, $33,697 per year non-resident tuition and fees. *Financial support:* In 2016–17, 48 students received support, including 3 fellowships with tuition reimbursements available (averaging $17,333 per year), 13 teaching assistantships with tuition reimbursements available (averaging $18,067 per year); research assistantships with tuition reimbursements available, scholarships/grants, health care benefits, and unspecified assistantships also available. Financial award applicants required to submit FAFSA. *Faculty research:* American government and politics, comparative politics, political methodology, political theory, public administration, public law, public policy, world politics/international relations, formal theory/modeling, gender and politics, international law, peace research, political economy, political psychology, politics of developing countries, race, religion, and ethnicity, urban politics. *Unit head:* Dr. Daniel Geller, Professor and Chair, 313-577-6328, E-mail: dgeller@wayne.edu. *Application contact:* Dr. Sharon Lean, Graduate Director, 313-577-2630, E-mail: gradpolisci@wayne.edu.
Website: http://clas.wayne.edu/politicalscience/

Wilfrid Laurier University, Faculty of Graduate and Postdoctoral Studies, School of Business and Economics, Department of Business, Waterloo, ON N2L 3C5, Canada. Offers accounting (PhD); finance (M Fin); financial economics (PhD); marketing (PhD); operations and supply chain management (PhD); organizational behavior and human resource management (M Sc); organizational behaviour and human resource management (PhD); supply chain management (M Sc); technology management (EMTM). *Accreditation:* AACSB. *Program availability:* Part-time, evening/weekend. *Degree requirements:* For master's, thesis optional; for doctorate, comprehensive exam, thesis/dissertation. *Entrance requirements:* For master's, GMAT, 4-year honors degree with minimum B+ average; for doctorate, GMAT, master's degree, minimum B+ average. Additional exam requirements/recommendations for international students: Required—TOEFL (minimum score 89 iBT). Electronic applications accepted. *Faculty research:* Financial economics, management and organizational behavior, operations and supply chain management.

Organizational Management

Albertus Magnus College, Program in Management and Organizational Leadership, New Haven, CT 06511-1189. Offers MS. *Program availability:* Part-time, evening/weekend, blended/hybrid learning. *Faculty:* 8 full-time (2 women), 5 part-time/adjunct (1 woman). *Students:* 45 full-time (31 women), 13 part-time (9 women); includes 33 minority (19 Black or African American, non-Hispanic/Latino; 3 American Indian or Alaska Native, non-Hispanic/Latino; 10 Hispanic/Latino; 1 Two or more races, non-

Hispanic/Latino). Average age 41. In 2016, 24 master's awarded. *Degree requirements:* For master's, thesis optional, project. *Entrance requirements:* For master's, bachelor's degree from regionally-accredited college or university, minimum GPA of 2.8, three years of professional and/or related experience, official transcripts, essay. Additional exam requirements/recommendations for international students: Recommended—TOEFL (minimum score 550 paper-based; 80 iBT). *Application deadline:* For fall admission, 8/14 for domestic students; for spring admission, 1/15 for domestic students. Applications are processed on a rolling basis. Application fee: $50. Electronic applications accepted. *Expenses:* Contact institution. *Financial support:* Federal Work-Study and unspecified assistantships available. Support available to part-time students. Financial award applicants required to submit FAFSA. *Faculty research:* Quantitative analysis of decision-making, conflict resolution, scientific method, information literacy, leadership management, principles of organizational management, quality management, business ethics, organizational behavior, human resources, international and global business, critical thinking skills in conducting research including developing hypothesis, evaluating research methods, conducting research, analyzing data, interpreting and presenting findings creative thinking skills. *Unit head:* Dr. Howard Fero, Director of Leadership Programs, 203-773-4424, E-mail: hfero@albertus.edu. *Application contact:* Anthony Reich, Director of Admission, Division of Professional and Graduate Studies, 203-773-5032, E-mail: arreich@albertus.edu.
Website: http://www.albertus.edu/graduate-degrees/graduate-degree-programs/management-and-organizational-leadership/

Alvernia University, School of Graduate Studies, Program in Leadership, Reading, PA 19607-1799. Offers PhD. *Degree requirements:* For doctorate, comprehensive exam, thesis/dissertation (for some programs). *Entrance requirements:* For doctorate, GRE, GMAT, or MAT, minimum GPA of 3.3, 3 letters of recommendation, resume, interview.

The American College of Financial Services, Graduate Programs, Bryn Mawr, PA 19010-2105. Offers financial services (MSFS); leadership (MSM). *Program availability:* Part-time, evening/weekend, online learning. Electronic applications accepted. *Faculty research:* Retirement counseling, social security, aging, family composition, inflation.

American Public University System, AMU/APU Graduate Programs, Charles Town, WV 25414. Offers accounting (MBA, MS); applied business analytics (MBA, MS); criminal justice (MA), including business administration, emergency and disaster management, general (MA, MS); educational leadership (M Ed); emergency and disaster management (MA); entrepreneurship (MBA); environmental policy and management (MS), including environmental planning, environmental sustainability, fish and wildlife management, general (MA, MS), global environmental management; finance (MBA); general (MBA); government contracting and acquisition (MBA); health care administration (MBA); health information management (MS); history (MA), including American history, ancient and classical history, European history, global history, public history; homeland security (MA), including business administration, counterterrorism studies, criminal justice, cyber, emergency management and public health, intelligence studies, transportation security; homeland security resource allocation (MBA); humanities (MA); information technology (MS), including digital forensics, enterprise software development, information assurance and security, IT project management; information technology management (MBA); intelligence studies (MA), including criminal intelligence, cyber, general (MA, MS), homeland security, intelligence analysis, intelligence collection, intelligence management, intelligence operations, terrorism studies; international relations and conflict resolution (MA), including comparative and security issues, conflict resolution, international and transnational security issues, peacekeeping; legal studies (MA); management (MA), including strategic consulting; marketing (MBA); military history (MA), including American military history, American Revolution, civil war, war since 1945, World War II; military studies (MA), including joint warfare, strategic leadership; national security studies (MA), including cyber, general (MA, MS), homeland security, regional security studies, security and intelligence analysis, terrorism studies; nonprofit management (MBA); political science (MA), including American politics and government, comparative government and development, general (MA, MS), international relations, public policy; psychology (MA); public administration (MPA), including disaster management, environmental policy, health policy, human resources, national security, organizational management, security management; public health (MPH); reverse logistics management (MA); security management (MA); space studies (MS), including aerospace science, general (MA, MS), planetary science; sports and health sciences (MS); sports management (MBA); teaching (M Ed), including autism spectrum disorder, curriculum and instruction for elementary teachers, elementary reading, English language learners, instructional leadership, online learning, special education, STEAM (STEM plus the arts); transportation and logistics management (MA). *Program availability:* Part-time, evening/weekend, online only, 100% online. *Faculty:* 401 full-time (228 women), 1,678 part-time/adjunct (781 women). *Students:* 378 full-time (184 women), 8,455 part-time (3,484 women); includes 2,972 minority (1,552 Black or African American, non-Hispanic/Latino; 52 American Indian or Alaska Native, non-Hispanic/Latino; 211 Asian, non-Hispanic/Latino; 791 Hispanic/Latino; 70 Native Hawaiian or other Pacific Islander, non-Hispanic/Latino; 296 Two or more races, non-Hispanic/Latino), 109 international. Average age 37. In 2016, 3,185 master's awarded. *Degree requirements:* For master's, comprehensive exam or practicum. *Entrance requirements:* For master's, official transcript showing earned bachelor's degree from institution accredited by recognized accrediting body. Additional exam requirements/recommendations for international students: Required—TOEFL (minimum score 550 paper-based), IELTS (minimum score 6.5). *Application deadline:* Applications are processed on a rolling basis. Application fee: $0. Electronic applications accepted. *Expenses: Tuition:* Part-time $350 per credit hour. *Required fees:* $50 per course. *Financial support:* Scholarships/grants available. Financial award applicants required to submit FAFSA. *Unit head:* Dr. Karan Powell, President, 877-468-6268, Fax: 304-724-3780. *Application contact:* Terry Grant, Vice President of Enrollment Management, 877-468-6268, Fax: 304-724-3780, E-mail: info@apus.edu.
Website: http://www.apus.edu

American University, School of Public Affairs, Department of Public Administration and Policy, Program in Organization Development, Washington, DC 20016-8070. Offers leadership for organizational change (Certificate); organization development (MSOD). *Program availability:* Evening/weekend. *Students:* 7 full-time (all women), 49 part-time (39 women); includes 16 minority (9 Black or African American, non-Hispanic/Latino; 1 American Indian or Alaska Native, non-Hispanic/Latino; 2 Asian, non-Hispanic/Latino; 2 Hispanic/Latino; 2 Two or more races, non-Hispanic/Latino), 2 international. Average age 37. 23 applicants, 87% accepted, 17 enrolled. In 2016, 43 master's awarded. *Degree requirements:* For master's, comprehensive exam. *Entrance requirements:* For master's, GRE, 2 years of related professional experience, 2 recommendations, 2 writing samples, resume/curriculum vitae, list of personal growth workshops and other laboratory trainings attended, interview. Additional exam requirements/recommendations for international students: Required—TOEFL, IELTS (minimum score 7), PTE (minimum score 68). *Application deadline:* For fall admission, 5/1 for domestic students; for spring admission, 11/1 for domestic students. Application fee: $55. *Expenses:* $1,579 per credit tuition; $690 mandatory fees. *Financial support:* Research assistantships, teaching assistantships, institutionally sponsored loans, scholarships/grants, and unspecified assistantships available. Financial award application deadline: 2/1; financial award applicants required to submit FAFSA. *Unit head:* Dr. Alison Jacknowitz, Department Chair, Public Administration and Policy, 202-885-2137, Fax: 202-885-2347, E-mail: jacknowi@american.edu. *Application contact:* Vincent Chapa, Recruitment Specialist, 202-885-6212, E-mail: vchapa@american.edu.
Website: http://www.american.edu/spa/dpap/

Antioch University Los Angeles, Graduate Programs, Program in Organizational Management, Culver City, CA 90230. Offers human resource development (MA); leadership (MA); organizational development (MA). *Program availability:* Part-time, evening/weekend. *Entrance requirements:* For master's, interview. Additional exam requirements/recommendations for international students: Required—TOEFL. *Faculty research:* Systems thinking and chaos theory, technology and organizational structure, nonprofit management, power and empowerment.

Aquinas College, School of Management, Grand Rapids, MI 49506. Offers marketing management (MM); organizational leadership (MM); sustainable business (MM). *Program availability:* Part-time, evening/weekend. *Entrance requirements:* For master's, GMAT, minimum undergraduate GPA of 2.75, 2 years of work experience. Additional exam requirements/recommendations for international students: Required—TOEFL (minimum score 550 paper-based). *Application deadline:* Applications are processed on a rolling basis. Application fee: $0. *Expenses:* Contact institution. *Financial support:* Scholarships/grants available. Support available to part-time students. Financial award application deadline: 3/15; financial award applicants required to submit FAFSA. *Unit head:* Cynthia G. VanGelderen, Interim Director, 616-632-2922, Fax: 616-732-4489. *Application contact:* Lynn Atkins-Rykert, Program Coordinator, 616-632-2925, Fax: 616-732-4489, E-mail: atkinlyn@aquinas.edu.

Argosy University, Chicago, College of Business, Program in Organizational Leadership, Chicago, IL 60601. Offers Ed D.

Argosy University, Denver, College of Business, Denver, CO 80231. Offers accounting (DBA); corporate compliance (MBA); customized professional concentration (MBA, DBA); finance (MBA); fraud examination (MBA); global business sustainability (DBA); healthcare administration (MBA); information systems (DBA); information systems management (MBA); international business (MBA, DBA); management (MBA, MSM, DBA); marketing (MBA, DBA); organizational leadership (Ed D); public administration (MBA); sustainable management (MBA). *Accreditation:* ACBSP.

Argosy University, Hawai`i, College of Business, Program in Organizational Leadership, Honolulu, HI 96813. Offers Ed D.

Argosy University, Inland Empire, College of Business, Ontario, CA 91761. Offers accounting (DBA); corporate compliance (MBA); customized professional concentration (MBA, DBA); finance (MBA); fraud examination (MBA); global business sustainability (DBA); healthcare administration (MBA); information systems (DBA); information systems management (MBA); international business (MBA, DBA); management (MBA, MSM, DBA); marketing (MBA, DBA); organizational leadership (Ed D); public administration (MBA); sustainable management (MBA).

Argosy University, Los Angeles, College of Business, Santa Monica, CA 90045. Offers accounting (DBA); corporate compliance (MBA); customized professional concentration (MBA, DBA); finance (MBA); fraud examination (MBA); global business sustainability (DBA); healthcare administration (MBA); information systems (DBA); information systems management (MBA); international business (MBA, DBA); management (MBA, MSM, DBA); marketing (MBA, DBA); organizational leadership (Ed D); public administration (MBA); sustainable management (MBA).

Argosy University, Northern Virginia, College of Business, Arlington, VA 22209. Offers accounting (DBA); customized professional concentration (MBA, DBA); finance (MBA); fraud examination (MBA); global business sustainability (DBA); healthcare administration (MBA); information systems (DBA); information systems management (MBA); international business (MBA, DBA, Certificate); management (MBA, MSM, DBA); marketing (MBA, DBA, Certificate); organizational leadership (Ed D); public administration (MBA); sustainable management (MBA).

Argosy University, Orange County, College of Business, Program in Organizational Leadership, Orange, CA 92868. Offers Ed D.

Argosy University, San Diego, College of Business, San Diego, CA 92108. Offers accounting (DBA); corporate compliance (MBA); customized professional concentration (MBA, DBA); finance (MBA); fraud examination (MBA); global business sustainability (DBA); information systems (DBA); information systems management (MBA); international business (MBA, DBA); management (MBA, MSM, DBA); marketing (MBA, DBA); organizational leadership (Ed D); public administration (MBA).

Argosy University, San Francisco Bay Area, College of Business, Alameda, CA 94501. Offers accounting (DBA); corporate compliance (MBA); customized professional concentration (MBA, DBA); finance (MBA); fraud examination (MBA); global business sustainability (DBA); healthcare administration (MBA); information systems (DBA); information systems management (MBA); international business (MBA, DBA); management (MBA, MSM, DBA); marketing (MBA, DBA); organizational leadership (Ed D); public administration (MBA); sustainable management (MBA).

Argosy University, Sarasota, College of Business, Sarasota, FL 34235. Offers accounting (DBA, Adv C); corporate compliance (MBA, DBA, Certificate); customized professional concentration (MBA, DBA); finance (MBA, Certificate); fraud examination (MBA, Certificate); global business sustainability (DBA, Adv C); healthcare administration (MBA, Certificate); information systems (DBA, Adv C, Certificate); information systems management (MBA); international business (MBA, DBA, Adv C, Certificate); management (MBA, MSM, DBA, Adv C, Certificate); marketing (MBA, DBA, Adv C, Certificate); organizational leadership (Ed D); public administration (MBA, Certificate); sustainable management (MBA, Certificate).

Argosy University, Schaumburg, Graduate School of Business and Management, Schaumburg, IL 60173-5403. Offers accounting (DBA, Adv C); customized professional concentration (MBA, DBA); finance (MBA, Certificate); fraud examination (MBA); healthcare administration (MBA, Certificate); human resource management (MS); information systems (Adv C, Certificate); information systems management (MBA); international business (MBA, DBA, Adv C, Certificate); management (MBA, MSM, DBA, Adv C, Certificate); marketing (MBA, DBA, Adv C, Certificate); organizational leadership (MS, Ed D); public administration (MBA); sustainable management (MBA).

Argosy University, Seattle, College of Business, Seattle, WA 98121. Offers accounting (DBA); corporate compliance (MBA); customized professional concentration (MBA, DBA); finance (MBA); fraud examination (MBA); global business sustainability (DBA); healthcare administration (MBA); information systems (DBA); information systems management (MBA); international business (MBA, DBA); management (MBA, MSM, DBA); marketing (MBA, DBA); organizational leadership (Ed D); public administration (MBA); sustainable management (MBA).

Argosy University, Tampa, College of Business, Tampa, FL 33607. Offers accounting (DBA); corporate compliance (MBA); customized professional concentration (MBA, DBA); finance (MBA); fraud examination (MBA); global business sustainability (DBA); healthcare administration (MBA); information systems (DBA); information systems management (MBA); international business (MBA, DBA); management (MBA, MSM,

DBA); marketing (MBA, DBA); organizational leadership (Ed D); public administration (MBA); sustainable management (MBA).

Argosy University, Twin Cities, College of Business, Eagan, MN 55121. Offers accounting (DBA); customized professional concentration (MBA, DBA); finance (MBA); fraud examination (MBA); global business sustainability (DBA); healthcare administration (MBA); information systems (DBA); information systems management (MBA); international business (MBA, DBA); management (MBA, MSM, DBA); marketing (MBA, DBA); organizational leadership (Ed D); public administration (MBA); sustainable management (MBA).

Athabasca University, Centre for Interdisciplinary Studies, Athabasca, AB T9S 3A3, Canada. Offers adult education (MA); community studies (MA); cultural studies (MA); educational studies (MA); global change (MA); heritage resource management (Postbaccalaureate Certificate); legislative drafting (Postbaccalaureate Certificate); work, organization, and leadership (MA). *Program availability:* Part-time, evening/weekend, online learning. *Degree requirements:* For master's, project. *Entrance requirements:* Additional exam requirements/recommendations for international students: Required—TOEFL (minimum score 560 paper-based). Electronic applications accepted. *Faculty research:* Women's history, literature and culture studies, sustainable development, labor and education.

Auburn University at Montgomery, College of Public Policy and Justice, Department of Justice and Public Safety, Montgomery, AL 36124-4023. Offers criminal studies (MSJPS); homeland security (MSJPS); homeland security and emergency management (MS); legal studies (MSJPS); organizational leadership (MSJPS). *Program availability:* Part-time, evening/weekend. *Students:* 13 full-time (8 women), 44 part-time (27 women); includes 21 minority (20 Black or African American, non-Hispanic/Latino; 1 Two or more races, non-Hispanic/Latino), 3 international. Average age 32. *Degree requirements:* For master's, comprehensive exam, thesis optional. *Entrance requirements:* For master's, GRE General Test or MAT. *Application deadline:* Applications are processed on a rolling basis. Electronic applications accepted. *Expenses:* Tuition, state resident: full-time $6462; part-time $359 per credit hour. Tuition, nonresident: full-time $14,526; part-time $807 per credit hour. *Required fees:* $554. *Financial support:* Career-related internships or fieldwork and scholarships/grants available. Support available to part-time students. Financial award application deadline: 3/1; financial award applicants required to submit FAFSA. *Faculty research:* Law enforcement, corrections, juvenile justice. *Unit head:* Dr. Ralph Ioimo, Head, 334-244-3691, Fax: 334-244-3244, E-mail: rioimo@aum.edu. *Application contact:* Dr. Ralph Ioimo, Head, 334-244-3691, Fax: 334-244-3244, E-mail: rioimo@aum.edu.
Website: http://cppj.aum.edu/departments/justice-and-public-safety

Augsburg College, Program in Leadership, Minneapolis, MN 55454-1351. Offers MA. *Program availability:* Part-time, evening/weekend. *Degree requirements:* For master's, thesis or alternative. *Entrance requirements:* For master's, MAT, minimum GPA of 3.0. Additional exam requirements/recommendations for international students: Required—TOEFL (minimum score 600 paper-based). *Faculty research:* Soviet leaders, artificial intelligence, homelessness.

Avila University, School of Professional Studies, Kansas City, MO 64145-1698. Offers executive leadership development (MS); fundraising (MA); instructional design and technology (MA, MS); leadership coaching (MS); organizational development (MS); project management (MA); strategic human resources (MS). *Program availability:* Part-time-only, evening/weekend, 100% online, blended/hybrid learning. *Faculty:* 15 part-time/adjunct (9 women). *Students:* 90 full-time (59 women), 47 part-time (40 women); includes 50 minority (38 Black or African American, non-Hispanic/Latino; 1 American Indian or Alaska Native, non-Hispanic/Latino; 3 Asian, non-Hispanic/Latino; 7 Hispanic/Latino; 1 Two or more races, non-Hispanic/Latino), 6 international. Average age 38. 95 applicants, 58% accepted, 38 enrolled. In 2016, 37 master's awarded. *Degree requirements:* For master's, thesis optional. *Entrance requirements:* For master's, 2 letters of recommendation, minimum GPA of 3.0 during last 60 hours, resume, statement of intent. Additional exam requirements/recommendations for international students: Required—TOEFL (minimum score 550 paper-based; 79 iBT). *Application deadline:* Applications are processed on a rolling basis. Application fee: $0. Electronic applications accepted. *Expenses:* $545 per credit hour. *Financial support:* In 2016–17, 14 students received support. Unspecified assistantships available. Support available to part-time students. Financial award applicants required to submit FAFSA. *Unit head:* Dr. Steve Iliff, Associate Dean/Director, 816-501-3675, Fax: 816-941-4650, E-mail: advantage@avila.edu. *Application contact:* Jessica Burson, Graduate Admission Advisor, 816-501-2482, Fax: 816-941-4650, E-mail: advantage@avila.edu.
Website: https://www.avila.edu/mrk/advantage-3

Azusa Pacific University, Center for Adult and Professional Studies, Azusa, CA 91702-7000. Offers leadership and organizational studies (MA). *Program availability:* Online learning.

Azusa Pacific University, School of Behavioral and Applied Sciences, Department of Leadership and Organizational Psychology, Program in Organizational Leadership, Azusa, CA 91702-7000. Offers MA.

Azusa Pacific University, School of Business and Management, Azusa, CA 91702-7000. Offers business administration (MBA); diversity for strategic advantage (MA); entrepreneurship (MBA); finance (MBA); human and organizational development (MA); human resources and organizational development (MBA); human resources management (MA); international business (MBA); marketing (MBA); non-profit management (MA); organizational development and change (MA); performance improvement (MA); public administration (MA); strategic management (MBA). *Program availability:* Part-time, evening/weekend. *Degree requirements:* For master's, thesis (for some programs), final project. *Entrance requirements:* For master's, GMAT, minimum GPA of 3.0. Additional exam requirements/recommendations for international students: Required—TOEFL (minimum score 600 paper-based). *Expenses:* Contact institution. *Faculty research:* Gender issues, financial risk, leadership and ethics, marketing strategy.

Baker University, School of Professional and Graduate Studies, Programs in Business, Baldwin City, KS 66006-0065. Offers MAOL, MBA, MSM, MSSM. Programs also offered in Lee's Summit, MO; Overland Park, KS; Topeka, KS; and Wichita, KS. *Accreditation:* ACBSP. *Program availability:* Part-time, evening/weekend, online learning. *Students:* 116 full-time (63 women), 275 part-time (131 women); includes 86 minority (42 Black or African American, non-Hispanic/Latino; 11 American Indian or Alaska Native, non-Hispanic/Latino; 11 Asian, non-Hispanic/Latino; 18 Hispanic/Latino; 4 Two or more races, non-Hispanic/Latino), 2 international. Average age 34. In 2016, 240 master's awarded. *Entrance requirements:* For master's, 2 years of full-time work experience. Additional exam requirements/recommendations for international students: Required—TOEFL (minimum score 600 paper-based; 100 iBT). *Application deadline:* Applications are processed on a rolling basis. *Financial support:* Applicants required to submit FAFSA. *Unit head:* Dr. Jacob Bucher, Dean of the School of Professional and Graduate Studies, 785-594-8475, E-mail: jacob.bucher@bakeru.edu. *Application contact:* Kelly Belk, Vice President of Enrollment Management, 913-491-4432, E-mail: kelly.belk@learn.bakeru.edu.
Website: https://www.bakeru.edu/spgs/

Bellevue University, Graduate School, College of Professional Studies, Bellevue, NE 68005-3098. Offers instructional design and development (MS); justice administration and criminal management (MS); leadership (MA); organizational performance (MS); public administration (MPA); security management (MS).

Benedictine University, Graduate Programs, Doctoral Program in Values-Driven Leadership, Lisle, IL 60532. Offers DBA, PhD. *Faculty:* 2 full-time (0 women), 2 part-time/adjunct (1 woman). *Students:* 1 (woman) full-time, 19 part-time (10 women), 1 international. *Application deadline:* Applications are processed on a rolling basis. Electronic applications accepted. *Expenses: Tuition:* Full-time $15,600; part-time $650 per hour. *Required fees:* $300. One-time fee: $125 part-time. Tuition and fees vary according to class time, course load, campus/location and program. *Unit head:* Dr. James Ludema, Director, 630-829-6229, E-mail: jludema@ben.edu. *Application contact:* Kari Gibbons, Associate Vice President, Enrollment Center, 630-829-6200, Fax: 630-829-6584, E-mail: kgibbons@ben.edu.
Website: http://www.cvdl.org/education/doctoral-program/

Benedictine University, Graduate Programs, Program in Business Administration, Lisle, IL 60532. Offers accounting (MBA); entrepreneurship and managing innovation (MBA); financial management (MBA); health administration (MBA); human resource management (MBA); information systems security (MBA); international business (MBA); management consulting (MBA); management information systems (MBA); marketing management (MBA); operations management and logistics (MBA); organizational leadership (MBA). *Program availability:* Part-time, evening/weekend, online learning. *Faculty:* 4 full-time (2 women), 24 part-time/adjunct (3 women). *Students:* 90 full-time (51 women), 440 part-time (262 women); includes 147 minority (65 Black or African American, non-Hispanic/Latino; 1 American Indian or Alaska Native, non-Hispanic/Latino; 58 Asian, non-Hispanic/Latino; 20 Hispanic/Latino; 3 Native Hawaiian or other Pacific Islander, non-Hispanic/Latino), 2 international. Average age 34. 211 applicants, 89% accepted, 155 enrolled. In 2016, 350 master's awarded. *Entrance requirements:* For master's, GMAT. Additional exam requirements/recommendations for international students: Required—TOEFL (minimum score 550 paper-based). *Application deadline:* For fall admission, 9/1 for domestic students; for winter admission, 12/1 for domestic students; for spring admission, 2/15 for domestic students. Applications are processed on a rolling basis. Application fee: $40. Electronic applications accepted. *Expenses: Tuition:* Full-time $15,600; part-time $650 per hour. *Required fees:* $300. One-time fee: $125 part-time. Tuition and fees vary according to class time, course load, campus/location and program. *Financial support:* Career-related internships or fieldwork and health care benefits available. Support available to part-time students. *Faculty research:* Strategic leadership in professional organizations, sociology of professions, organizational change, social identity theory, applications to change management. *Unit head:* Dr. Sharon Borowicz, Director, 630-829-6219, E-mail: sborowicz@ben.edu. *Application contact:* Kari Gibbons, Director, Admissions, 630-829-6200, Fax: 630-829-6584, E-mail: kgibbons@ben.edu.

Benedictine University, Graduate Programs, Program in Organization Development, Lisle, IL 60532. Offers PhD. *Program availability:* Evening/weekend. *Students:* 38 full-time (21 women), 7 part-time (2 women); includes 6 minority (3 Black or African American, non-Hispanic/Latino; 3 Asian, non-Hispanic/Latino), 3 international. In 2016, 8 doctorates awarded. *Degree requirements:* For doctorate, thesis/dissertation. *Entrance requirements:* Additional exam requirements/recommendations for international students: Required—TOEFL (minimum score 550 paper-based). *Application deadline:* For fall admission, 9/1 for domestic students; for winter admission, 12/1 for domestic students; for spring admission, 2/15 for domestic students. Application fee: $40. Electronic applications accepted. *Expenses: Tuition:* Full-time $15,600; part-time $650 per hour. *Required fees:* $300. One-time fee: $125 part-time. Tuition and fees vary according to class time, course load, campus/location and program. *Financial support:* Career-related internships or fieldwork and health care benefits available. *Faculty research:* Change management, appreciative inquiry, innovation and organization design, global and international organization development, organization renewal. *Unit head:* Dr. Peter F. Sorensen, Director, 630-829-6220, Fax: 630-960-1126, E-mail: psorensen@ben.edu. *Application contact:* Kari Gibbons, Associate Vice President, Enrollment Center, 630-829-6200, Fax: 630-829-6584, E-mail: kgibbons@ben.edu.

Bethel University, Graduate School, St. Paul, MN 55112-6999. Offers business administration (MBA); classroom management (Certificate); counseling (MA); international baccalaureate teaching and learning (Certificate); K-12 education (MA); leadership (Ed D); leadership foundations (Certificate); nurse educator (MS, Certificate); nurse-midwifery (MS); physician assistant (MS); special education (MA); strategic leadership (MA); teaching (MA). *Program availability:* Part-time, evening/weekend, 100% online, blended/hybrid learning. *Faculty:* 19 full-time (15 women), 57 part-time/adjunct (37 women). *Students:* 674 full-time (466 women), 378 part-time (256 women); includes 188 minority (94 Black or African American, non-Hispanic/Latino; 3 American Indian or Alaska Native, non-Hispanic/Latino; 43 Asian, non-Hispanic/Latino; 31 Hispanic/Latino; 1 Native Hawaiian or other Pacific Islander, non-Hispanic/Latino; 16 Two or more races, non-Hispanic/Latino), 33 international. *Degree requirements:* For master's, comprehensive exam (for some programs), thesis (for some programs); for doctorate, comprehensive exam, thesis/dissertation. *Entrance requirements:* Additional exam requirements/recommendations for international students: Required—TOEFL (minimum score 550 paper-based, 80 iBT) or IELTS. *Application deadline:* Applications are processed on a rolling basis. Application fee: $0. Electronic applications accepted. *Expenses:* Contact institution. *Financial support:* Teaching assistantships, career-related internships or fieldwork, and scholarships/grants available. Support available to part-time students. Financial award applicants required to submit FAFSA. *Unit head:* Dick Crombie, Vice-President/Dean, 651-635-8000, Fax: 651-635-8004, E-mail: gs@bethel.edu. *Application contact:* Director of Admissions, 651-635-8000, Fax: 651-635-8004, E-mail: gs@bethel.edu.
Website: https://www.bethel.edu/graduate/

Bluffton University, Programs in Business, Bluffton, OH 45817. Offers accounting and financial management (MBA); business administration (MBA); health care management (MBA); leadership (MBA); organizational management (MA); production and operations management (MBA). *Program availability:* Evening/weekend, online learning. *Faculty:* 9 full-time (3 women), 12 part-time/adjunct (4 women). *Students:* 55 full-time (34 women), 2 part-time (1 woman); includes 5 minority (1 Black or African American, non-Hispanic/Latino; 2 Asian, non-Hispanic/Latino; 2 Hispanic/Latino), 2 international. Average age 34. 31 applicants, 77% accepted, 22 enrolled. In 2016, 44 master's awarded. *Entrance requirements:* For master's, current resume, official transcript, two recommendation forms, bachelor's degree, minimum GPA of 3.0, four years of professional experience, interview. Additional exam requirements/recommendations for international students: Recommended—TOEFL. *Application deadline:* For fall admission, 7/31 priority date for domestic and international students. Applications are processed on a rolling basis. Application fee: $25. Electronic applications accepted. Application fee is waived when completed online. *Expenses:* $550 per credit. *Financial support:* Scholarships/grants and unspecified assistantships available. Financial award application deadline: 5/1. *Unit head:* Dr. Melissa Green, Director of Graduate Programs in Business, 419-358-3447, E-mail: greenm@bluffton.edu. *Application contact:* Carrie Mast, Administrative

Organizational Management

Assistant, Graduate Programs in Business, 419-358-3065, E-mail: mastc@bluffton.edu. Website: http://www.bluffton.edu/grad/

Boise State University, College of Engineering, Department of Organizational Performance and Workplace Learning, Boise, ID 83725. Offers organizational performance and workplace learning (MS); workplace e-learning and performance support (Graduate Certificate); workplace instructional design (Graduate Certificate); workplace performance improvement (Graduate Certificate). *Program availability:* Part-time, 100% online. *Faculty:* 16. *Students:* 13 full-time (6 women), 158 part-time (100 women); includes 30 minority (14 Black or African American, non-Hispanic/Latino; 4 Asian, non-Hispanic/Latino; 10 Hispanic/Latino; 2 Two or more races, non-Hispanic/Latino), 12 international. Average age 39. 65 applicants, 83% accepted, 37 enrolled. In 2016, 32 master's, 25 other advanced degrees awarded. *Degree requirements:* For master's, thesis optional. *Entrance requirements:* Additional exam requirements/recommendations for international students: Required—TOEFL (minimum score 550 paper-based; 80 iBT), IELTS (minimum score 6). Application fee: $65 ($95 for international students). Electronic applications accepted. *Expenses:* Tuition, state resident: full-time $6058; part-time $358 per credit hour. Tuition, nonresident: full-time $20,108; part-time $608 per credit hour. *Required fees:* $2108. Tuition and fees vary according to program. *Financial support:* In 2016–17, 3 students received support. Scholarships/grants and unspecified assistantships available. Financial award applicants required to submit FAFSA. *Unit head:* Dr. Tony Marker, Department Chair, 208-426-1015, E-mail: anthonymarker@boisestate.edu. *Application contact:* Jo Ann Fenner, Program Coordinator, 208-426-2489, E-mail: jfenner@boisestate.edu.
Website: http://opwl.boisestate.edu/

Boston College, Carroll School of Management, Department of Management and Organization, Chestnut Hill, MA 02467-3800. Offers PhD. *Degree requirements:* For doctorate, comprehensive exam, thesis/dissertation, teaching experience. *Entrance requirements:* For doctorate, GMAT or GRE, letters of recommendation, resume, transcripts. Additional exam requirements/recommendations for international students: Required—TOEFL (minimum score 100 iBT), IELTS (minimum score 7.5), or PTE (minimum score 68). Electronic applications accepted. Tuition and fees vary according to program. *Faculty research:* Organizational transformation, mergers and acquisitions, managerial effectiveness, organizational change, organizational structure.

Boston University, Metropolitan College, Program in Leadership, Boston, MA 02215. Offers MS. Program offered on the Brussels Campus and at military locations in Massachusetts, North Carolina and Virginia. *Faculty:* 2 full-time (0 women), 7 part-time/adjunct (2 women). *Students:* 35 part-time (10 women); includes 3 minority (2 Black or African American, non-Hispanic/Latino; 1 Two or more races, non-Hispanic/Latino). Average age 35. 10 applicants, 100% accepted, 10 enrolled. In 2016, 138 master's awarded. *Application deadline:* Applications are processed on a rolling basis. *Expenses:* Contact institution. *Unit head:* Dr. Tanya Zlateva, Dean, 617-353-3010, Fax: 617-353-6066. *Application contact:* Larry Watson, Director of Military Programs, Virginia and North Carolina, 910-451-5574, E-mail: lwatson@bu.edu.
Website: http://www.bu.edu/met/subject/leadership/

Bowling Green State University, Graduate College, College of Business, Program in Organization Development, Bowling Green, OH 43403. Offers MOD. *Program availability:* Part-time, evening/weekend. *Degree requirements:* For master's, thesis or alternative, internship. *Entrance requirements:* For master's, GMAT or GRE General Test. Additional exam requirements/recommendations for international students: Required—TOEFL. *Application deadline:* Applications are processed on a rolling basis. Application fee: $30. Electronic applications accepted. *Financial support:* Research assistantships with full tuition reimbursements, teaching assistantships with full tuition reimbursements, career-related internships or fieldwork, Federal Work-Study, and unspecified assistantships available. Financial award applicants required to submit FAFSA. *Faculty research:* Charismatic leadership, self-managing work teams, knowledge workers, stress, effects of change processes. *Unit head:* Dr. Janet Hartley, Director, 419-372-8645. *Application contact:* Dr. Angie Stoller, Graduate Coordinator, 419-372-8823.

Brandman University, School of Business and Professional Studies, Irvine, CA 92618. Offers accounting (MBA); business administration (MBA); e-business strategic management (MBA); entrepreneurship (MBA); finance (MBA); health administration (MBA); human resources (MBA, MS); international business (MBA); marketing (MBA); organizational leadership (MA, MBA, MPA); public administration (MPA). *Expenses: Tuition:* Full-time $14,880; part-time $620 per credit hour. Tuition and fees vary according to degree level and program. *Unit head:* Dr. Glenn Worthington, Dean, 253-861-1024, E-mail: gworthin@brandman.edu.
Website: https://www.brandman.edu/business-professional-studies

Brenau University, Sydney O. Smith Graduate School, College of Business and Mass Communication, Gainesville, GA 30501. Offers accounting (MBA); business administration (MBA); healthcare management (MBA); organizational leadership (MS); project management (MBA). *Accreditation:* ACBSP. *Program availability:* Part-time, evening/weekend, online learning. *Degree requirements:* For master's, comprehensive exam (for some programs). *Entrance requirements:* For master's, resume, minimum undergraduate GPA of 2.5. Additional exam requirements/recommendations for international students: Required—TOEFL (minimum score 500 paper-based; 61 iBT); Recommended—IELTS (minimum score 5). Electronic applications accepted. *Expenses:* Contact institution.

Briercrest Seminary, Graduate Programs, Program in Leadership and Management, Caronport, SK S0H 0S0, Canada. Offers organizational leadership (MA). *Program availability:* Part-time. *Degree requirements:* For master's, comprehensive exam, thesis optional. *Entrance requirements:* Additional exam requirements/recommendations for international students: Required—TOEFL (minimum score 550 paper-based).

Cabrini University, Graduate Studies, Radnor, PA 19087. Offers accounting (M Acc); education (M Ed); leadership (MS). *Program availability:* Part-time, evening/weekend. *Degree requirements:* For master's, thesis optional. *Entrance requirements:* For master's, GRE and/or MAT (in some cases), bachelor's degree with minimum GPA of 3.0, one-page personal essay/statement, professional letter of recommendation. Additional exam requirements/recommendations for international students: Required—TOEFL. Electronic applications accepted.

Cairn University, School of Business, Langhorne, PA 19047-2990. Offers accounting (MBA); business administration (MBA); international entrepreneurship (MBA); nonprofit leadership (MBA); organizational leadership (MSOL, Postbaccalaureate Certificate). *Program availability:* Part-time, evening/weekend, 100% online, blended/hybrid learning. *Faculty:* 3 full-time (0 women), 6 part-time/adjunct (1 woman). *Students:* 7 full-time (5 women), 43 part-time (19 women); includes 20 minority (10 Black or African American, non-Hispanic/Latino; 1 American Indian or Alaska Native, non-Hispanic/Latino; 4 Asian, non-Hispanic/Latino; 3 Hispanic/Latino; 2 Two or more races, non-Hispanic/Latino), 4 international. Average age 36. 17 applicants, 100% accepted, 16 enrolled. In 2016, 16 master's awarded. *Entrance requirements:* Additional exam requirements/recommendations for international students: Required—TOEFL (minimum score 550 paper-based). *Application deadline:* Applications are processed on a rolling basis. Application fee: $25. Electronic applications accepted. Application fee is waived when completed online. *Expenses:* $655 per semester credit. *Financial support:* Scholarships/grants available. Support available to part-time students. Financial award applicants required to submit FAFSA. *Unit head:* Yunn Kang, Dean, School of Business, 215-702-4461, Fax: 215-702-4248, E-mail: ykang@cairn.edu. *Application contact:* Gwen Dorsey, Assistant Director, Graduate Admissions, 800-572-2472, Fax: 215-702-4248, E-mail: gdorsey@cairn.edu.
Website: http://cairn.edu/academics/business

California Baptist University, Program in Leadership and Organizational Studies, Riverside, CA 92504-3206. Offers MA. *Program availability:* Part-time, evening/weekend. *Faculty:* 7 full-time (2 women), 3 part-time/adjunct (0 women). *Students:* 17 part-time (11 women); includes 9 minority (1 Black or African American, non-Hispanic/Latino; 6 Hispanic/Latino; 2 Two or more races, non-Hispanic/Latino). Average age 41. 26 applicants, 69% accepted, 15 enrolled. In 2016, 7 master's awarded. *Entrance requirements:* For master's, minimum undergraduate GPA of 2.75; three recommendations; resume; 500-word essay. Additional exam requirements/recommendations for international students: Required—TOEFL (minimum score 80 iBT). *Application deadline:* For fall admission, 8/1 priority date for domestic students, 7/1 for international students; for spring admission, 11/1 priority date for domestic students, 11/1 for international students. Applications are processed on a rolling basis. Application fee: $45. Electronic applications accepted. *Expenses:* Contact institution. *Financial support:* In 2016–17, 7 students received support. Federal Work-Study and scholarships/grants available. Financial award applicants required to submit CSS PROFILE or FAFSA. *Faculty research:* Leadership, educational history, assessment. *Unit head:* Dr. John Shoup, Dean, School of Education, 951-343-4205, E-mail: jshoup@calbaptist.edu. *Application contact:* Dr. Shana Matamala, Associate Dean, School of Education, 951-343-4760, E-mail: smatamala@calbaptist.edu.
Website: http://www.calbaptist.edu/academics/schools-colleges/school-education/programs/graduate/master-arts-leadership-and-organizational-studies

California Baptist University, Program in Organizational Leadership, Riverside, CA 92504-3206. Offers MA. *Program availability:* Part-time, evening/weekend, 100% online. *Faculty:* 9 full-time (2 women), 4 part-time/adjunct (1 woman). *Students:* 58 full-time (47 women), 31 part-time (20 women); includes 54 minority (14 Black or African American, non-Hispanic/Latino; 2 Asian, non-Hispanic/Latino; 31 Hispanic/Latino; 2 Native Hawaiian or other Pacific Islander, non-Hispanic/Latino; 5 Two or more races, non-Hispanic/Latino). Average age 38. 51 applicants, 76% accepted, 32 enrolled. In 2016, 34 master's awarded. *Degree requirements:* For master's, project. *Entrance requirements:* For master's, minimum cumulative GPA of 2.25, current resume, two letters of recommendation, comprehensive 500-word essay. Additional exam requirements/recommendations for international students: Required—TOEFL (minimum score 80 iBT). *Application deadline:* For fall admission, 8/1 priority date for domestic students, 7/1 for international students; for spring admission, 12/1 priority date for domestic students, 11/1 for international students. Applications are processed on a rolling basis. Electronic applications accepted. *Expenses:* Contact institution. *Financial support:* In 2016–17, 36 students received support. Federal Work-Study and scholarships/grants available. Financial award applicants required to submit CSS PROFILE or FAFSA. *Faculty research:* Organizational development, public administration, public service motivation, networked governance, finance. *Unit head:* Dr. David Poole, Vice President, Online and Professional Studies, 951-343-3902, E-mail: dpoole@calbaptist.edu. *Application contact:* Dr. Greg Bowden, Director of Master's in Organizational Leadership, 951-343-5560, E-mail: abowden@calbaptist.edu.
Website: http://www.cbuonline.edu/programs/program/master-of-arts-in-organizational-leadership

California Coast University, School of Education, Santa Ana, CA 92701. Offers administration (M Ed); curriculum and instruction (M Ed); educational administration (Ed D); educational psychology (Ed D); organizational leadership (Ed D). *Program availability:* Online learning.

California College of the Arts, Graduate Programs, MBA in Design Strategy Program, San Francisco, CA 94107. Offers MBA. *Accreditation:* NASAD. *Faculty:* 2 full-time (1 woman), 14 part-time/adjunct (3 women). *Students:* 86 full-time (57 women); includes 23 minority (4 Black or African American, non-Hispanic/Latino; 11 Asian, non-Hispanic/Latino; 7 Hispanic/Latino; 1 Native Hawaiian or other Pacific Islander, non-Hispanic/Latino), 35 international. Average age 30. 141 applicants, 94% accepted, 39 enrolled. In 2016, 54 master's awarded. *Degree requirements:* For master's, thesis. *Entrance requirements:* Additional exam requirements/recommendations for international students: Required—TOEFL, IELTS, or PTE. *Application deadline:* For fall admission, 1/10 for domestic and international students. Applications are processed on a rolling basis. Application fee: $70. Electronic applications accepted. *Expenses:* $1,641 per unit, $49,230 per year tuition; $490 fees. *Financial support:* Federal Work-Study and scholarships/grants available. Financial award application deadline: 7/31; financial award applicants required to submit FAFSA. *Unit head:* Nathan Shedroff, Program Chair, 800-447-1ART, E-mail: nshedroff@cca.edu. *Application contact:* Wes Fanelli, Assistant Director of Graduate Admissions, 415-703-9533, Fax: 415-703-9539, E-mail: wfanelli@cca.edu.

California Intercontinental University, School of Business, Irvine, CA 92614. Offers banking and finance (MBA); entrepreneurship and business management (DBA); global business leadership (DBA); international management and marketing (MBA); organizational management and human resource management (MBA).

California State University, East Bay, Office of Graduate Studies, College of Business and Economics, MBA Program, Option in Human Resources and Organizational Behavior, Hayward, CA 94542-3000. Offers human resources/personnel management (MBA). *Program availability:* Part-time, evening/weekend. *Students:* 11 full-time (9 women), 20 part-time (16 women); includes 20 minority (6 Black or African American, non-Hispanic/Latino; 7 Asian, non-Hispanic/Latino; 3 Hispanic/Latino; 3 Native Hawaiian or other Pacific Islander, non-Hispanic/Latino; 1 Two or more races, non-Hispanic/Latino), 9 international. Average age 32. 30 applicants, 53% accepted, 10 enrolled. In 2016, 4 master's awarded. *Degree requirements:* For master's, comprehensive exam or thesis. *Entrance requirements:* For master's, GMAT, minimum GPA of 2.75. Additional exam requirements/recommendations for international students: Required—TOEFL (minimum score 550 paper-based). *Application deadline:* For fall admission, 6/30 for domestic and international students. Application fee: $55. Electronic applications accepted. *Financial support:* Fellowships, career-related internships or fieldwork, Federal Work-Study, institutionally sponsored loans, and scholarships/grants available. Support available to part-time students. Financial award application deadline: 3/2; financial award applicants required to submit FAFSA. *Unit head:* Dr. Asha Rao, Program Advisor, 510-885-3290, E-mail: asha.rao@csueastbay.edu. *Application contact:* Dr. Donna Wiley, Interim Associate Vice President for Academic Programs and Graduate Studies, 510-885-3716, Fax: 510-885-4777, E-mail: donna.wiley@csueastbay.edu.
Website: http://www20.csueastbay.edu/cbe/mba-options/Human-Resources-Management-Option.html

California State University, Fullerton, Graduate Studies, College of Business and Economics, Program in Business Administration, Fullerton, CA 92834-9480. Offers business administration (MBA); business analytics (MBA); international business (MBA); organizational leadership (MBA); risk management and insurance (MBA). *Accreditation:*

AACSB. *Program availability:* Part-time. *Degree requirements:* For master's, project or thesis. *Entrance requirements:* For master's, GMAT. Application fee: $55. *Expenses:* Tuition, state resident: full-time $3369; part-time $1953 per unit. Tuition, nonresident: full-time $3915; part-time $2499 per unit. Tuition and fees vary according to course load, degree level and program. *Financial support:* Career-related internships or fieldwork, Federal Work-Study, institutionally sponsored loans, and scholarships/grants available. Support available to part-time students. Financial award application deadline: 3/1; financial award applicants required to submit FAFSA. *Unit head:* Shaun Pichler, Director, 657-278-7373, E-mail: spichler@fullerton.edu. *Application contact:* Admissions/Applications, 657-278-2371.

Calvary University, Graduate School and Seminary, Kansas City, MO 64147. Offers Bible and theology (MS); Biblical counseling (MA); education (MS), including administration and leadership, Christian education, curriculum and instruction, elementary education; organization development (MS); pastoral studies (M Div). *Program availability:* Part-time, evening/weekend. *Faculty:* 6 full-time (2 women), 2 part-time/adjunct (1 woman). *Students:* 11 full-time (3 women), 29 part-time (15 women); includes 12 minority (4 Black or African American, non-Hispanic/Latino; 1 American Indian or Alaska Native, non-Hispanic/Latino; 6 Asian, non-Hispanic/Latino; 1 Native Hawaiian or other Pacific Islander, non-Hispanic/Latino). Average age 39. In 2016, 19 master's awarded. *Degree requirements:* For master's, variable foreign language requirement, comprehensive exam, thesis or alternative. *Entrance requirements:* For master's, minimum GPA of 2.5, BA or BS, doctrine agreement. Additional exam requirements/recommendations for international students: Required—TOEFL (minimum score 550 paper-based). *Application deadline:* Applications are processed on a rolling basis. Application fee: $0. Electronic applications accepted. *Expenses: Tuition:* Full-time $7200; part-time $4800 per credit. *Required fees:* $640; $520 per credit. $140 per semester. One-time fee: $100. Tuition and fees vary according to program. *Financial support:* In 2016–17, 8 students received support. Scholarships/grants available. Financial award application deadline: 11/5; financial award applicants required to submit FAFSA. *Unit head:* Dr. Thomas Baurain, Director of Seminary, 816-322-0110 Ext. 1502, Fax: 816-331-4474, E-mail: thomas.baurain@calvary.edu. *Application contact:* Ann Rogers, Admissions Office Assistant, 800-326-3960 Ext. 1321, Fax: 816-331-4474, E-mail: admissions@calvary.edu.
Website: http://www.calvary.edu

Cambridge College, School of Management, Cambridge, MA 02138-5304. Offers business negotiation and conflict resolution (M Mgt); general business (M Mgt); health care informatics (M Mgt); health care management (M Mgt); leadership in human and organizational dynamics (M Mgt); non-profit and public organization management (M Mgt); small business development (M Mgt); technology management (M Mgt). *Program availability:* Part-time, evening/weekend. *Degree requirements:* For master's, thesis, seminars. *Entrance requirements:* For master's, resume, 2 professional references. Additional exam requirements/recommendations for international students: Required—TOEFL (minimum score 550 paper-based; 79 iBT), Michigan English Language Assessment Battery (minimum score 85); Recommended—IELTS (minimum score 6). Electronic applications accepted. *Expenses:* Contact institution. *Faculty research:* Negotiation, mediation and conflict resolution; leadership; management of diverse organizations; case studies and simulation methodologies for management education, digital as a second language: social networking for digital immigrants, non-profit and public management.

Capella University, School of Business and Technology, Doctoral Programs in Business, Minneapolis, MN 55402. Offers accounting (DBA, PhD); business intelligence (DBA); finance (DBA, PhD); general business management (PhD); human resource management (DBA, PhD); leadership (DBA, PhD); management education (PhD); marketing (DBA, PhD); project management (DBA, PhD); strategy and innovation (DBA, PhD). *Accreditation:* ACBSP.

Capella University, School of Business and Technology, Master's Programs in Business, Minneapolis, MN 55402. Offers accounting (MBA); business analysis (MS); business intelligence (MBA); entrepreneurship (MBA); finance (MBA); general business administration (MBA); general human resource management (MS); general leadership (MS); health care management (MBA); human resource management (MBA); marketing (MBA); project management (MBA, MS). *Accreditation:* ACBSP.

Carlos Albizu University, Miami Campus, Graduate Programs, Miami, FL 33172-2209. Offers clinical psychology (PhD, Psy D); entrepreneurship (MBA); exceptional student education (MS); human services (PhD); industrial/organizational psychology (MS); marriage and family therapy (MS); mental health counseling (MS); nonprofit management (MBA); organizational management (MBA); psychology (MS); school counseling (MS); speech and language pathology (MS); teaching English for speakers of other languages (MS). *Accreditation:* APA. *Program availability:* Part-time, evening/weekend, 100% online. *Faculty:* 28 full-time (22 women), 31 part-time/adjunct (19 women). *Students:* 475 full-time (396 women), 191 part-time (161 women); includes 560 minority (56 Black or African American, non-Hispanic/Latino; 1 American Indian or Alaska Native, non-Hispanic/Latino; 4 Asian, non-Hispanic/Latino; 494 Hispanic/Latino; 5 Two or more races, non-Hispanic/Latino), 15 international. Average age 34. 335 applicants, 46% accepted, 122 enrolled. In 2016, 143 master's, 48 doctorates awarded. Terminal master's awarded for partial completion of doctoral program. *Degree requirements:* For master's, comprehensive exam, integrative project (for MBA); research project (for exceptional student education, teaching English as a second language); for doctorate, comprehensive exam, thesis/dissertation, internship, project. *Entrance requirements:* For master's, 3 letters of recommendation, interview, minimum GPA of 3.0, resume, statement of purpose, official transcripts; for doctorate, 3 letters of recommendation, minimum GPA of 3.0, resume, interview, statement of purpose, official transcripts. Additional exam requirements/recommendations for international students: Required—Michigan Test of English Language Proficiency. *Application deadline:* For fall admission, 4/1 priority date for domestic students, 5/1 priority date for international students; for spring admission, 11/1 priority date for domestic students, 9/1 priority date for international students. Applications are processed on a rolling basis. Application fee: $50. Electronic applications accepted. *Expenses:* Contact institution. *Financial support:* In 2016–17, 131 students received support. Federal Work-Study, scholarships/grants, unspecified assistantships, and tuition discounts available. Financial award application deadline: 6/1; financial award applicants required to submit FAFSA. *Faculty research:* Psychotherapy, forensic psychology, neuropsychology, marketing strategy, entrepreneurship, special education, speech-language pathology. *Unit head:* Dr. Etiony Aldarondo, Provost, 305-593-1223 Ext. 3138, Fax: 305-592-7930, E-mail: ealdarondo@albizu.edu. *Application contact:* Sonia Feliciano, Institutional Director of Student Recruitment, 305-593-1223 Ext. 3108, Fax: 305-477-8983, E-mail: sfeliciano@albizu.edu.

Carlow University, College of Leadership and Social Change, Pittsburgh, PA 15213-3165. Offers MBA, MS, Psy D, Certificate. *Program availability:* Part-time, evening/weekend, 100% online, blended/hybrid learning. *Students:* 288 full-time (238 women), 71 part-time (53 women); includes 100 minority (74 Black or African American, non-Hispanic/Latino; 1 American Indian or Alaska Native, non-Hispanic/Latino; 8 Asian, non-Hispanic/Latino; 9 Hispanic/Latino; 8 Two or more races, non-Hispanic/Latino), 2 international. Average age 32. 189 applicants, 89% accepted, 113 enrolled. In 2016, 124 master's, 12 doctorates, 1 other advanced degree awarded. *Degree requirements:* For doctorate, thesis/dissertation, internship. *Entrance requirements:* For master's, personal essay; resume or curriculum vitae; three recommendations; official transcripts; interview; minimum undergraduate GPA of 3.0; for doctorate, GRE, resume or curriculum vitae; personal essay; reflective essay; official transcripts from all previous undergraduate and graduate institutions; three letters of recommendation; master's degree in closely-related field. Additional exam requirements/recommendations for international students: Required—TOEFL (minimum score 550 paper-based). *Application deadline:* For fall admission, 6/15 priority date for domestic and international students; for spring admission, 11/15 priority date for domestic and international students. Applications are processed on a rolling basis. Application fee: $0. Electronic applications accepted. *Expenses:* Contact institution. *Financial support:* Application deadline: 4/1; applicants required to submit FAFSA. *Unit head:* Dr. Allyson M. Lowe, Dean, 412-578-6663, Fax: 412-578-6357, E-mail: amlowe@carlow.edu. *Application contact:* 412-578-6059, Fax: 412-578-6321, E-mail: gradstudies@carlow.edu.
Website: http://www.carlow.edu/College_of_Leadership_and_Social_Change.aspx

Carson-Newman University, Program in Social Entrepreneurship, Jefferson City, TN 37760. Offers MAASJ. *Program availability:* Part-time, evening/weekend, 100% online, blended/hybrid learning. *Degree requirements:* For master's, completion of degree within five years of admissions into program. *Entrance requirements:* For master's, GRE (minimum score of 290), minimum GPA of 3.0. Additional exam requirements/recommendations for international students: Recommended—TOEFL (minimum score 79 iBT), IELTS (minimum score 6.5), TSE (minimum score 53). *Expenses: Tuition:* Full-time $10,142; part-time $461 per credit hour. *Required fees:* $300; $150 per semester. One-time fee: $150.

Central Penn College, Graduate Programs, Summerdale, PA 17093-0309. Offers information systems management (MPS); organizational development (MPS). Programs offered in Harrisburg, PA. *Program availability:* Evening/weekend.

Charleston Southern University, School of Business, Charleston, SC 29423-8087. Offers accounting (MBA); finance (MBA); general management (MBA); human resource management (MS); leadership (MBA); management information systems (MBA); organizational leadership (MA). *Program availability:* Part-time, evening/weekend. *Degree requirements:* For master's, thesis optional. *Entrance requirements:* For master's, GMAT. Additional exam requirements/recommendations for international students: Required—TOEFL (minimum score 550 paper-based; 79 iBT). *Application deadline:* Applications are processed on a rolling basis. Application fee: $40. *Expenses: Tuition:* Full-time $6000. Tuition and fees vary according to program. *Financial support:* Research assistantships with full tuition reimbursements available. Financial award application deadline: 4/15; financial award applicants required to submit FAFSA. *Unit head:* Dr. David Palmer, Interim Dean, 843-863-7025, Fax: 843-863-7922, E-mail: dpalmer@csuniv.edu. *Application contact:* Dr. Darin L. Gerdes, Director of the MBA Program, 843-863-7814, Fax: 843-863-7922, E-mail: dgerdes@csuniv.edu.
Website: http://www.csuniv.edu/business/

The Chicago School of Professional Psychology, Program in Business Psychology, Chicago, IL 60610. Offers business psychology (PhD); industrial and organizational business psychology (Psy D); industrial and organizational psychology (MA); organizational leadership (MA, PhD). *Degree requirements:* For doctorate, thesis/dissertation optional. *Entrance requirements:* For doctorate, GRE. Additional exam requirements/recommendations for international students: Required—TOEFL.

City University of Seattle, Graduate Division, School of Management, Seattle, WA 98121. Offers accounting (Certificate); change leadership (MBA, Certificate); computer systems (MS); finance (Certificate); financial management (MBA); general management (MBA); general management-Europe (MBA); global marketing (MBA); human resources management (Certificate); individualized study (MBA); information security (MS); information systems (MBA); leadership (MA); marketing (MBA, Certificate); project management (MBA, MS, Certificate); sustainable business (Certificate); technology management (MBA, Certificate). *Program availability:* Part-time, evening/weekend, online learning. *Degree requirements:* For master's, comprehensive exam (for some programs), thesis (for some programs). *Entrance requirements:* For master's, baccalaureate degree or equivalent from an accredited or otherwise recognized institution. Additional exam requirements/recommendations for international students: Required—TOEFL (minimum score 567 paper-based; 87 iBT); Recommended—IELTS. Electronic applications accepted.

Clarks Summit University, Baptist Bible Seminary, South Abington Township, PA 18411. Offers Biblical apologetics (MA); church education (M Div, M Min); church planting (M Div, M Min); global ministry (M Div, M Min); leadership in communication (D Min); leadership in counseling and spiritual development (D Min); leadership in global ministry (D Min); leadership in pastoral ministry (D Min); leadership in theological studies (D Min); military chaplaincy (M Div); ministry (PhD); organizational leadership (M Min); outreach pastor (M Div, M Min); pastoral counseling (M Div, M Min); pastoral leadership (M Div, M Min); theology (Th M); worship ministries leadership (M Div, M Min); youth pastor (M Div, M Min). *Program availability:* Part-time, evening/weekend, online learning. Terminal master's awarded for partial completion of doctoral program. *Degree requirements:* For master's, 2 foreign languages, thesis, oral exam (for M Div); for doctorate, 2 foreign languages, comprehensive exam (for some programs), thesis/dissertation, oral exam. *Entrance requirements:* For doctorate, Greek and Hebrew entrance exams (for PhD). Electronic applications accepted.

Clarks Summit University, Graduate Studies, South Abington Township, PA 18411. Offers Bible (MA); counseling (MA, MS); curriculum and instruction (M Ed); educational administration (M Ed); intercultural studies (MA); literature (MA); missions (MA); organizational leadership (MA); reading specialist (M Ed); secondary English/communications (M Ed); social entrepreneurship (MA); worldview studies (MA). MA in missions program available only for Association of Baptists for World Evangelism missionary personnel. *Program availability:* Part-time, evening/weekend, online learning. *Entrance requirements:* Additional exam requirements/recommendations for international students: Required—TOEFL (minimum score 500 paper-based).

Clemson University, Graduate School, College of Education, Clemson, SC 29634-0702. Offers administration and supervision (K-12) (M Ed, Ed S); education and organizational leadership (MS), including athletic leadership; educational leadership (PhD), including P-12; human resource development (MHRD); middle-level education (MAT). *Program availability:* Part-time, evening/weekend, 100% online. *Faculty:* 75 full-time (54 women), 1 part-time/adjunct (0 women). *Students:* 120 full-time (84 women), 309 part-time (206 women); includes 96 minority (68 Black or African American, non-Hispanic/Latino; 1 American Indian or Alaska Native, non-Hispanic/Latino; 3 Asian, non-Hispanic/Latino; 19 Hispanic/Latino; 5 Two or more races, non-Hispanic/Latino), 11 international. Average age 34. 417 applicants, 50% accepted, 133 enrolled. In 2016, 239 master's, 21 doctorates, 59 other advanced degrees awarded. *Degree requirements:* For master's, comprehensive exam (for some programs), thesis (for some programs); for doctorate, comprehensive exam, thesis/dissertation. *Entrance requirements:* For master's, doctorate, and other advanced degree, GRE General Test, unofficial transcripts, letters of recommendation. Additional exam requirements/recommendations for international students: Required—TOEFL (minimum score 80 iBT), IELTS (minimum

score 7). *Application deadline:* Applications are processed on a rolling basis. Application fee: $80 ($90 for international students). Electronic applications accepted. *Expenses:* Contact institution. *Financial support:* In 2016–17, 75 students received support, including 22 fellowships with partial tuition reimbursements available (averaging $6,316 per year), 28 research assistantships with partial tuition reimbursements available (averaging $15,399 per year), 5 teaching assistantships with partial tuition reimbursements available (averaging $30,000 per year); unspecified assistantships also available. *Faculty research:* Early literacy and motivation, STEAM education, legal/policy issues in education, leadership, special education interventions/assessment/policy. *Total annual research expenditures:* $2.8 million. *Unit head:* Dr. George Petersen, Dean, 864-656-4444, Fax: 864-656-0311, E-mail: soedean@clemson.edu. *Application contact:* Dr. David Fleming, Graduate Programs Coordinator, 864-656-1881, Fax: 864-656-0311, E-mail: dflemin@clemson.edu.
Website: http://www.clemson.edu/education/

College of Saint Elizabeth, Department of Business Administration and Management, Morristown, NJ 07960-6989. Offers human resource management (MS); organizational change (MS). *Program availability:* Part-time. *Degree requirements:* For master's, thesis. *Entrance requirements:* For master's, GRE, GMAT, minimum GPA of 3.25; 2 research projects related to the development design of the action research dissertation study and oral dissertation defense. Additional exam requirements/recommendations for international students: Required—TOEFL (minimum score 550 paper-based; 79 iBT), IELTS (minimum score 6.5). Electronic applications accepted. Application fee is waived when completed online. *Expenses:* Contact institution.

College of Saint Mary, Program in Organizational Leadership, Omaha, NE 68106. Offers MOL. *Program availability:* Part-time, evening/weekend. *Entrance requirements:* For master's, resume. Electronic applications accepted.

The College of Saint Rose, Graduate Studies, Huether School of Business, Program in Organizational Leadership and Change Management, Albany, NY 12203-1419. Offers Advanced Certificate. *Program availability:* Part-time, evening/weekend. *Students:* Average age 31. 3 applicants, 33% accepted. In 2016, 5 Advanced Certificates awarded. *Entrance requirements:* Additional exam requirements/recommendations for international students: Required—TOEFL (minimum score 550 paper-based; 80 iBT), IELTS (minimum score 6), PTE (minimum score 56). *Application deadline:* For fall admission, 4/1 priority date for domestic and international students; for spring admission, 10/15 priority date for domestic and international students; for summer admission, 3/15 priority date for domestic and international students. Applications are processed on a rolling basis. Application fee: $40. Electronic applications accepted. *Expenses: Tuition:* Full-time $14,382; part-time $799 per credit. *Required fees:* $814; $32 per credit. $88 per semester. Tuition and fees vary according to course load. *Financial support:* Career-related internships or fieldwork and scholarships/grants available. Support available to part-time students. Financial award application deadline: 4/15. *Unit head:* Michael Mathews, Director, 518-454-5210, E-mail: mathewsk@strose.edu. *Application contact:* Cris Murray, Assistant Vice President for Graduate Recruitment and Enrollment, 518-485-3390, Fax: 518-458-5479, E-mail: grad@strose.edu.
Website: https://www.strose.edu/academics/graduate-programs/graduate-studies/organizational-leadership-and-change-management-certificate/

Colorado State University–Global Campus, Graduate Programs, Greenwood Village, CO 80111. Offers criminal justice and law enforcement administration (MS); education leadership (MS); finance (MS); healthcare administration and management (MS); human resource management (MHRM); information technology management (MITM); international management (MS); management (MS); organizational leadership (MS); professional accounting (MPA); project management (MS); teaching and learning (MS). *Accreditation:* ACBSP. *Program availability:* Online learning.

Columbia Southern University, Program in Organizational Leadership, Orange Beach, AL 36561. Offers MS.

Columbus State University, Graduate Studies, Turner College of Business, Columbus, GA 31907-5645. Offers applied computer science (MS), including informational assurance, modeling and simulation, software development; business administration (MBA); human resource management (Certificate); information systems security (Certificate); modeling and simulation (Certificate); organizational leadership (MS), including human resource management, leader development, servant leadership; servant leadership (Certificate). *Accreditation:* AACSB. *Program availability:* Part-time, evening/weekend, 100% online, blended/hybrid learning. *Faculty:* 10 full-time (3 women). *Students:* 93 full-time (21 women), 132 part-time (47 women); includes 69 minority (36 Black or African American, non-Hispanic/Latino; 1 American Indian or Alaska Native, non-Hispanic/Latino; 11 Asian, non-Hispanic/Latino; 14 Hispanic/Latino; 7 Two or more races, non-Hispanic/Latino), 35 international. Average age 31. 279 applicants, 44% accepted, 64 enrolled. In 2016, 106 master's awarded. *Entrance requirements:* For master's, GMAT, GRE, minimum undergraduate GPA of 2.75, letters of recommendation. Additional exam requirements/recommendations for international students: Required—TOEFL (minimum score 550 paper-based; 79 iBT). *Application deadline:* For fall admission, 6/30 for domestic students, 5/1 for international students; for spring admission, 11/1 for domestic and international students; for summer admission, 3/1 for domestic and international students. Applications are processed on a rolling basis. Application fee: $50. Electronic applications accepted. *Expenses:* Contact institution. *Financial support:* In 2016–17, 18 students received support, including 16 research assistantships (averaging $3,000 per year); Federal Work-Study also available. Financial award application deadline: 5/1; financial award applicants required to submit FAFSA. *Unit head:* Dr. Linda U. Hadley, Dean, 706-507-8153, Fax: 706-568-2184, E-mail: hadley_linda@columbusstate.edu. *Application contact:* Kristin Williams, Director of International and Graduate Recruitment, 706-507-8848, Fax: 706-568-5091, E-mail: thornton_katie@colstate.edu.
Website: http://turner.columbusstate.edu/

Concordia College–New York, Program in Business Leadership, Bronxville, NY 10708-1998. Offers MS. *Degree requirements:* For master's, capstone seminar.

Concordia University, School of Graduate Studies, Faculty of Arts and Science, Department of Applied Human Sciences, Montréal, QC H3G 1M8, Canada. Offers human systems intervention (MA); youth work (Graduate Diploma). *Degree requirements:* For master's, 2-week residential laboratory. *Entrance requirements:* For master's, 1 week residential laboratory, 2 full years of work experience. *Faculty research:* Health promotion, adult learning and transitions, applications of group development and small group leadership, adolescent development, generational issues in immigrant families.

Concordia University Ann Arbor, Graduate Programs, Ann Arbor, MI 48105-2797. Offers curriculum and instruction (MS); educational leadership (MS); organizational leadership and administration (MS). *Program availability:* Part-time, evening/weekend. *Degree requirements:* For master's, thesis. *Entrance requirements:* Additional exam requirements/recommendations for international students: Required—TOEFL (minimum score 80 iBT); Recommended—IELTS (minimum score 6.5). Electronic applications accepted.

Concordia University, St. Paul, College of Business, St. Paul, MN 55104-5494. Offers business administration (MBA), including cyber-security leadership; business and organizational leadership (MBA); health care management (MBA); human resource management (MA); leadership and management (MA); strategic communication management (MA). *Accreditation:* ACBSP. *Program availability:* Part-time, evening/weekend, 100% online, blended/hybrid learning. *Faculty:* 12 full-time (4 women), 36 part-time/adjunct (15 women). *Students:* 462 full-time (288 women), 25 part-time (16 women); includes 123 minority (59 Black or African American, non-Hispanic/Latino; 1 American Indian or Alaska Native, non-Hispanic/Latino; 36 Asian, non-Hispanic/Latino; 10 Hispanic/Latino; 1 Native Hawaiian or other Pacific Islander, non-Hispanic/Latino; 16 Two or more races, non-Hispanic/Latino), 28 international. Average age 34. 269 applicants, 73% accepted, 137 enrolled. In 2016, 192 master's awarded. *Degree requirements:* For master's, thesis (for some programs). *Entrance requirements:* For master's, official transcripts from regionally-accredited institution stating the conferral of a bachelor's degree with minimum cumulative GPA of 3.0; personal statement; professional resume. Additional exam requirements/recommendations for international students: Recommended—TOEFL (minimum score 547 paper-based; 78 iBT), IELTS (minimum score 6). *Application deadline:* For fall admission, 8/1 for domestic and international students; for spring admission, 12/1 for domestic and international students; for summer admission, 5/1 for domestic and international students. Applications are processed on a rolling basis. Application fee: $50. Electronic applications accepted. *Expenses:* Contact institution. *Financial support:* In 2016–17, 259 students received support. Scholarships/grants and unspecified assistantships available. Financial award applicants required to submit FAFSA. *Faculty research:* Alternative dispute resolution, franchising, entrepreneurship, applied business ethics, strategic leadership development. *Unit head:* Dr. Kevin Hall, Dean, 651-603-6165, Fax: 651-641-8807, E-mail: khall@csp.edu. *Application contact:* Kimberly Craig, Associate Vice President, Cohort Enrollment Management, 651-603-6223, Fax: 651-603-6320, E-mail: craig@csp.edu.

Concordia University Wisconsin, Graduate Programs, School of Business Administration, Program in Organizational Leadership Administration, Mequon, WI 53097-2402. Offers MS. *Degree requirements:* For master's, comprehensive exam, thesis or alternative. *Entrance requirements:* Additional exam requirements/recommendations for international students: Required—TOEFL. Application fee: $35 ($125 for international students). *Financial support:* Application deadline: 8/1. *Unit head:* Dr. Kenneth Harris, Jr., Program Director, 262-243-4365, E-mail: kenneth.harris@cuw.edu. *Application contact:* Dr. Kenneth Harris, Jr., Program Director, 262-243-4365, E-mail: kenneth.harris@cuw.edu.

Crandall University, Graduate Programs, Moncton, NB E1C 9L7, Canada. Offers literacy education (M Ed); organizational management (MOM); resource education (M Ed).

Creighton University, Graduate School, Department of Interdisciplinary Studies, MS Program in Organizational Leadership, Omaha, NE 68178-0001. Offers MS. *Program availability:* Part-time, online only, 100% online. *Faculty:* 1 (woman) full-time. *Students:* 3 full-time (2 women), 32 part-time (21 women); includes 5 minority (2 Black or African American, non-Hispanic/Latino; 1 Asian, non-Hispanic/Latino; 2 Hispanic/Latino). Average age 35. 31 applicants, 74% accepted, 16 enrolled. In 2016, 6 master's awarded. *Degree requirements:* For master's, project-based capstone. *Entrance requirements:* For master's, two years of work experience, minimum undergraduate GPA of 3.0, two letters of recommendation, personal statement. Additional exam requirements/recommendations for international students: Required—TOEFL (minimum score 90 iBT), IELTS (minimum score 6.6). *Application deadline:* For fall admission, 7/1 for domestic and international students; for spring admission, 11/1 for domestic and international students; for summer admission, 3/1 for domestic and international students. Applications are processed on a rolling basis. Application fee: $50. Electronic applications accepted. *Expenses:* Contact institution. *Financial support:* Scholarships/grants available. *Unit head:* Dr. Gretchen Oltman, Director, 402-280-3418, Fax: 402-280-2423, E-mail: gretchenoltman@creighton.edu. *Application contact:* Lindsay Johnson, Director of Graduate and Adult Recruitment, 402-280-2703, Fax: 402-280-2423, E-mail: gradschool@creighton.edu.

Dallas Baptist University, College of Business, Management Program, Dallas, TX 75211-9299. Offers conflict resolution management (MA); general management (MA, MS); health care management (MA); human resource management (MA); organizational communication (MA); performance management (MA); professional sales and management optimization (MA). *Program availability:* Part-time, evening/weekend, 100% online, blended/hybrid learning. *Application deadline:* Applications are processed on a rolling basis. Application fee: $25. Electronic applications accepted. Application fee is waived when completed online. *Expenses: Tuition:* Full-time $15,408; part-time $856 per credit hour. *Required fees:* $400 per semester. Tuition and fees vary according to course load and degree level. *Unit head:* Richard Nassar, Director, 214-333-5280, E-mail: richardn@dbu.edu. *Application contact:* Bobby Soto, Director of Admissions, 214-333-5242, E-mail: graduate@dbu.edu.
Website: http://www.dbu.edu/gsb/ma-in-management

Dallas Baptist University, Gary Cook School of Leadership, Program in Educational Leadership, Dallas, TX 75211-9299. Offers educational leadership (Ed D), including educational ministry leadership, general leadership, higher education leadership. *Program availability:* Part-time. *Degree requirements:* For doctorate, thesis/dissertation. *Application deadline:* Applications are processed on a rolling basis. Application fee: $25. Electronic applications accepted. Application fee is waived when completed online. *Expenses: Tuition:* Full-time $15,408; part-time $856 per credit hour. *Required fees:* $400 per semester. Tuition and fees vary according to course load and degree level. *Unit head:* Dr. Ozzie Ingram, Academic Director, 214-333-6875, E-mail: ozzie@dbu.edu. *Application contact:* Bobby Soto, Director of Admissions, 214-333-5242, E-mail: graduate@dbu.edu.
Website: http://www4.dbu.edu/leadership/education-leadership-ed-d

Dallas Baptist University, Gary Cook School of Leadership, Program in Leadership, Dallas, TX 75211-9299. Offers MA. *Program availability:* Part-time, evening/weekend. *Application deadline:* Applications are processed on a rolling basis. Application fee: $25. Electronic applications accepted. Application fee is waived when completed online. *Expenses: Tuition:* Full-time $15,408; part-time $856 per credit hour. *Required fees:* $400 per semester. Tuition and fees vary according to course load and degree level. *Unit head:* David Cook, Director, 214-333-5117, E-mail: davidc@dbu.edu. *Application contact:* Bobby Soto, Director of Admissions, 214-333-5242, E-mail: graduate@dbu.edu.
Website: http://www4.dbu.edu/leadership/maleadership

DePaul University, Kellstadt Graduate School of Business, Chicago, IL 60604. Offers accountancy (M Acc, MS, MSA); applied economics (MBA); banking (MBA); behavioral finance (MBA); brand and product management (MBA); business development (MBA); business information technology (MS); business strategy and decision-making (MBA); computational finance (MS); consumer insights (MBA); corporate finance (MBA); economic policy analysis (MS); entrepreneurship (MBA, MS); finance (MBA, MS); financial analysis (MBA); general business (MBA); health sector management (MBA); hospitality leadership (MBA); hospitality leadership and operational performance (MS);

human resource management (MBA); human resources (MS); investment management (MBA); leadership and change management (MBA); management accounting (MBA); marketing (MBA, MS); marketing analysis (MS); marketing strategy and planning (MBA); operations management (MBA); organizational diversity (MBA); real estate (MS); real estate finance and investment (MBA); revenue management (MBA); sports management (MBA); strategic global marketing (MBA); strategy, execution and valuation (MBA); sustainable management (MBA, MS); taxation (MS); wealth management (MS); JD/MBA. *Accreditation:* AACSB. *Program availability:* Part-time, evening/weekend, online learning. *Entrance requirements:* For master's, GMAT, 2 letters of recommendation, resume, essay, official transcripts. Additional exam requirements/recommendations for international students: Required—TOEFL (minimum score 550 paper-based; 80 iBT). Electronic applications accepted. *Expenses:* Contact institution.

Drury University, Master of Arts in Communication Program, Springfield, MO 65802. Offers integrated marketing communications (MA); organizational leadership and change (MA). *Program availability:* Part-time, evening/weekend. *Faculty:* 3 full-time (1 woman), 2 part-time/adjunct (0 women). *Students:* 39 full-time (32 women); includes 4 minority (1 Black or African American, non-Hispanic/Latino; 2 Hispanic/Latino; 1 Two or more races, non-Hispanic/Latino), 2 international. Average age 27. 8 applicants, 88% accepted, 7 enrolled. In 2016, 8 master's awarded. *Entrance requirements:* For master's, GRE. Additional exam requirements/recommendations for international students: Required—TOEFL (minimum score 80 iBT); Recommended—IELTS (minimum score 6.5). *Application deadline:* For fall admission, 8/4 priority date for domestic and international students; for spring admission, 1/5 priority date for domestic and international students; for summer admission, 5/26 priority date for domestic and international students. Applications are processed on a rolling basis. Application fee: $25 ($50 for international students). Electronic applications accepted. *Expenses:* $453 per credit hour, $7 technology fee, $100 graduation fee. *Financial support:* Career-related internships or fieldwork, scholarships/grants, and unspecified assistantships available. Financial award application deadline: 6/30; financial award applicants required to submit FAFSA. *Faculty research:* Nonprofit leadership, organizational change, leadership accountability, digital media, health communication. *Unit head:* Charles Taylor, Director, Master of Arts in Communication, 417-873-7391, E-mail: ctaylor@drury.edu.
Website: http://www.drury.edu/communication-masters

Duke University, The Fuqua School of Business, The Duke MBA-Daytime Program, Durham, NC 27708-0586. Offers academic excellence in finance (Certificate); business administration (MBA); decision sciences (MBA); energy and environment (MBA); energy finance (MBA); entrepreneurship and innovation (MBA); finance (MBA); financial analysis (MBA); health sector management (Certificate); leadership and ethics (MBA); management (MBA); marketing (MBA); operations management (MBA); social entrepreneurship (MBA); strategy (MBA). *Faculty:* 88 full-time (19 women), 50 part-time/adjunct (9 women). *Students:* 897 full-time (310 women); includes 174 minority (39 Black or African American, non-Hispanic/Latino; 3 American Indian or Alaska Native, non-Hispanic/Latino; 75 Asian, non-Hispanic/Latino; 51 Hispanic/Latino; 1 Native Hawaiian or other Pacific Islander, non-Hispanic/Latino; 5 Two or more races, non-Hispanic/Latino), 343 international. Average age 28. In 2016, 440 master's awarded. *Entrance requirements:* For master's, GMAT or GRE, transcripts, essays, resume, recommendation letters, interview. *Application deadline:* For fall admission, 9/13 for domestic and international students; for winter admission, 10/13 for domestic and international students; for spring admission, 1/4 for domestic and international students; for summer admission, 3/20 for domestic and international students. Application fee: $225. Electronic applications accepted. *Expenses:* $66,717 (first-year tuition and fees). *Financial support:* In 2016–17, 415 students received support. Institutionally sponsored loans and scholarships/grants available. Financial award applicants required to submit FAFSA. *Unit head:* Russ Morgan, Senior Associate Dean for Full-time Programs, 919-660-2931, Fax: 919-684-8742, E-mail: ruskin.morgan@duke.edu. *Application contact:* Sharon Thompson, Assistant Dean, Office of Admissions, 919-660-7705, Fax: 919-681-8026, E-mail: admissions-info@fuqua.duke.edu.
Website: http://www.fuqua.duke.edu/daytime-mba/

Duke University, The Fuqua School of Business, PhD Program, Durham, NC 27708-0586. Offers accounting (PhD); decision sciences (PhD); finance (PhD); management and organizations (PhD); marketing (PhD); operations management (PhD); strategy (PhD). *Faculty:* 100 full-time (19 women). *Students:* 77 full-time (27 women); includes 9 minority (1 Black or African American, non-Hispanic/Latino; 7 Asian, non-Hispanic/Latino; 1 Hispanic/Latino), 46 international. 561 applicants, 7% accepted, 14 enrolled. In 2016, 15 doctorates awarded. *Degree requirements:* For doctorate, thesis/dissertation, major field requirement (exam or major paper, depending upon the area). *Entrance requirements:* For doctorate, GMAT or GRE, transcripts, essays, recommendation letters, statement of purpose. Additional exam requirements/recommendations for international students: Required—TOEFL (minimum score 577 paper-based; 90 iBT), IELTS (minimum score 7). *Application deadline:* For fall admission, 12/31 priority date for domestic and international students. Application fee: $85. Electronic applications accepted. *Expenses:* Contact institution. *Financial support:* In 2016–17, 77 students received support, including 70 fellowships with full tuition reimbursements available (averaging $28,200 per year), 63 research assistantships with full tuition reimbursements available (averaging $7,000 per year); institutionally sponsored loans, scholarships/grants, and tuition waivers (full) also available. Financial award applicants required to submit FAFSA. *Unit head:* William Boulding, Dean, 919-660-7822, Fax: 919-684-8742, E-mail: bb1@duke.edu. *Application contact:* Qi Chen, Director of Graduate Studies, 919-660-7753, Fax: 919-660-7971, E-mail: qc2@duke.edu.

Duquesne University, Graduate School of Liberal Arts, Master of Science in Leadership Program, Pittsburgh, PA 15282-0001. Offers MS. *Program availability:* Part-time, evening/weekend, online only, 100% online. *Students:* 57 full-time (24 women), 78 part-time (37 women); includes 36 minority (30 Black or African American, non-Hispanic/Latino; 2 Asian, non-Hispanic/Latino; 1 Hispanic/Latino; 3 Two or more races, non-Hispanic/Latino), 1 international. Average age 36. 30 applicants, 97% accepted, 21 enrolled. In 2016, 104 master's awarded. *Entrance requirements:* Additional exam requirements/recommendations for international students: Required—TOEFL. *Application deadline:* For fall admission, 8/1 for domestic students; for spring admission, 11/15 priority date for domestic students; for summer admission, 4/15 for domestic students. Applications are processed on a rolling basis. Application fee: $0. Electronic applications accepted. *Expenses: Tuition:* Full-time $22,212; part-time $1234 per credit. Tuition and fees vary according to program. *Financial support:* Available to part-time students. Application deadline: 5/1. *Unit head:* Dr. Magali Michael, Director, 412-396-6389, E-mail: michael@duq.edu. *Application contact:* Linda Rendulic, Assistant to the Dean, 412-396-6400, Fax: 412-396-5265, E-mail: rendulic@duq.edu.
Website: http://duq.edu/academics/schools/liberal-arts/academic-programs/leadership

Eastern Connecticut State University, School of Education and Professional Studies/Graduate Division, Program in Organizational Management, Willimantic, CT 06226-2295. Offers MS. *Program availability:* Part-time, evening/weekend. *Faculty:* 5 full-time (2 women), 2 part-time/adjunct (1 woman). *Students:* 6 full-time (3 women), 27 part-time (16 women); includes 10 minority (4 Black or African American, non-Hispanic/Latino; 2 Asian, non-Hispanic/Latino; 4 Hispanic/Latino). Average age 39. 16 applicants, 69% accepted, 11 enrolled. In 2016, 10 master's awarded. *Degree requirements:* For master's, comprehensive exam or thesis. *Entrance requirements:* For master's, minimum GPA of 2.7, bachelor's degree from accredited institution. Additional exam requirements/recommendations for international students: Required—TOEFL (minimum score 550 paper-based; 79 iBT); Recommended—IELTS (minimum score 6). *Application deadline:* For fall admission, 7/6 priority date for domestic and international students; for spring admission, 11/3 priority date for domestic and international students. Applications are processed on a rolling basis. Application fee: $50. Electronic applications accepted. *Expenses: Tuition, area resident:* Full-time $11,781; part-time $560 per credit. Tuition, state resident: full-time $15,031; part-time $568 per credit. Tuition, nonresident: full-time $24,581; part-time $568 per credit. *Required fees:* $40 per semester. Full-time tuition and fees vary according to course level, course load and reciprocity agreements. *Financial support:* Research assistantships, career-related internships or fieldwork, institutionally sponsored loans, and unspecified assistantships available. Financial award application deadline: 3/1; financial award applicants required to submit FAFSA. *Unit head:* Dr. Elizabeth Scott, Advisor, 860-465-5366, Fax: 860-465-4459, E-mail: scotte@easternct.edu. *Application contact:* Paula Goyette, Graduate Division, School of Education and Professional Studies, 860-465-5292, E-mail: graduateadmissions@easternct.edu.

Eastern Mennonite University, Program in Organizational Leadership, Harrisonburg, VA 22802-2462. Offers MA.

Eastern Michigan University, Graduate School, College of Business, Department of Management, Program in Human Resources Management and Organizational Development, Ypsilanti, MI 48197. Offers MSHROD. *Program availability:* Part-time, evening/weekend, online learning. *Students:* 13 full-time (10 women), 77 part-time (58 women); includes 29 minority (23 Black or African American, non-Hispanic/Latino; 1 Asian, non-Hispanic/Latino; 4 Hispanic/Latino; 1 Two or more races, non-Hispanic/Latino), 8 international. Average age 30. 38 applicants, 74% accepted, 12 enrolled. In 2016, 75 master's awarded. *Degree requirements:* For master's, thesis optional. *Entrance requirements:* For master's, GMAT. Additional exam requirements/recommendations for international students: Required—TOEFL. *Application deadline:* Applications are processed on a rolling basis. Application fee: $45. *Financial support:* Fellowships, research assistantships with full tuition reimbursements, teaching assistantships with full tuition reimbursements, career-related internships or fieldwork, Federal Work-Study, institutionally sponsored loans, scholarships/grants, tuition waivers (partial), and unspecified assistantships available. Support available to part-time students. Financial award applicants required to submit FAFSA. *Unit head:* Dr. Fraya Wagner-Marsh, Department Head, 734-487-3240, Fax: 734-487-4100, E-mail: fraya.wagner@emich.edu.
Website: http://www.emich.edu/cob/departments_centers/management/mshrod.php

Eastern Michigan University, Graduate School, College of Business, Programs in Business Administration, Ypsilanti, MI 48197. Offers business administration (MBA, Graduate Certificate); computer information systems (Graduate Certificate); e-business (MBA, Graduate Certificate); enterprise business intelligence (MBA); entrepreneurship (MBA, Graduate Certificate); finance (MBA, Graduate Certificate); human resources (MBA); human resources management (Graduate Certificate); information systems (MBA); internal auditing (MBA); international business (MBA, Graduate Certificate); marketing management (Graduate Certificate); nonprofit management (MBA); organizational development (Graduate Certificate); supply chain management (MBA, Graduate Certificate). *Accreditation:* AACSB. *Program availability:* Part-time, online learning. *Students:* 63 full-time (36 women), 320 part-time (186 women); includes 131 minority (76 Black or African American, non-Hispanic/Latino; 5 American Indian or Alaska Native, non-Hispanic/Latino; 16 Asian, non-Hispanic/Latino; 19 Hispanic/Latino; 15 Two or more races, non-Hispanic/Latino), 23 international. Average age 32. 305 applicants, 70% accepted, 124 enrolled. In 2016, 78 master's, 57 other advanced degrees awarded. *Entrance requirements:* For master's, GMAT (minimum score 450), minimum cumulative undergraduate GPA of 2.75. Additional exam requirements/recommendations for international students: Required—TOEFL. *Application deadline:* For fall admission, 5/15 priority date for domestic students, 2/15 priority date for international students; for winter admission, 10/15 priority date for domestic students, 9/1 priority date for international students; for summer admission, 3/15 priority date for domestic students, 3/1 priority date for international students. Applications are processed on a rolling basis. Application fee: $45. *Financial support:* Fellowships, research assistantships with full tuition reimbursements, teaching assistantships with full tuition reimbursements, career-related internships or fieldwork, Federal Work-Study, institutionally sponsored loans, scholarships/grants, tuition waivers (partial), and unspecified assistantships available. Support available to part-time students. Financial award applicants required to submit FAFSA. *Unit head:* K. Michelle Henry, Director, Graduate Business Programs, 734-487-4444, Fax: 734-483-1316, E-mail: cob.graduate@emich.edu.
Website: http://www.emich.edu/cob/mba/

Eastern University, Program in Organizational Leadership, St. Davids, PA 19087-3696. Offers organizational leadership (PhD), including business, non-profit. *Students:* 74 full-time (42 women); includes 22 minority (17 Black or African American, non-Hispanic/Latino; 3 Asian, non-Hispanic/Latino; 1 Hispanic/Latino; 1 Two or more races, non-Hispanic/Latino), 4 international. Average age 46. In 2016, 8 doctorates awarded. *Application deadline:* Applications are processed on a rolling basis. Electronic applications accepted. *Expenses:* $985 per credit. *Unit head:* Michael Dziedziak, Executive Director of Enrollment, 800-452-0996, E-mail: gpsadmissions@eastern.edu.
Website: http://www.eastern.edu/academics/programs/phd-organizational-leadership/phd-organizational-leadership-0

Eastern University, School of Leadership and Development, St. Davids, PA 19087-3696. Offers economic development (MBA), including international development, urban development (MA, MBA); international development (MA), including global development, urban development (MA, MBA); nonprofit management (MS); organizational leadership (MA); M Div/MBA. *Program availability:* Part-time, evening/weekend, online learning. *Students:* 59 full-time (32 women), 67 part-time (35 women); includes 40 minority (32 Black or African American, non-Hispanic/Latino; 1 Asian, non-Hispanic/Latino; 5 Hispanic/Latino; 2 Two or more races, non-Hispanic/Latino), 22 international. Average age 33. In 2016, 44 master's awarded. *Entrance requirements:* Additional exam requirements/recommendations for international students: Required—TOEFL (minimum score 550 paper-based; 79 iBT). *Application deadline:* Applications are processed on a rolling basis. Application fee: $35. Electronic applications accepted. Application fee is waived when completed online. *Expenses:* $690 per credit. *Faculty research:* Micro-level economic development, China welfare and economic development, macroethics, micro- and macro-level economic development in transitional economics, organizational effectiveness. *Unit head:* Michael Dziedziak, Executive Director of Enrollment, 800-452-0996, E-mail: gpsadmissions@eastern.edu.
Website: http://www.eastern.edu/academics/programs/graduate-programs-leadership-development

Embry-Riddle Aeronautical University–Worldwide, Department of Organizational Leadership, Daytona Beach, FL 32114-3900. Offers leadership (MS). *Program* *availability:* Part-time, evening/weekend, 100% online, blended/hybrid learning, EagleVision is a virtual classroom that combines Web video conferencing and a learning management system. EagleVision Classroom (between classrooms), EagleVision Home (faculty and students at home), and a blend of Classroom or Home. *Entrance requirements:* Additional exam requirements/recommendations for international students: Required—TOEFL (minimum score 550 paper-based; 79 iBT), IELTS (minimum score 6), TOEFL or IELTS accepted. Electronic applications accepted. *Expenses:* Contact institution.

Emory & Henry College, Graduate Programs, Emory, VA 24327-0947. Offers American history (MA Ed); organizational leadership (MCOL); professional studies (M Ed); reading specialist (MA Ed). *Program availability:* Part-time, evening/weekend. *Entrance requirements:* For master's, GRE or PRAXIS I, recommendations, writing sample. Additional exam requirements/recommendations for international students: Recommended—TOEFL.

Emory University, Goizueta Business School, Doctoral Program in Business, Atlanta, GA 30322. Offers accounting (PhD); finance (PhD); information systems and operations management (PhD); marketing (PhD); organization and management (PhD). *Faculty:* 59 full-time (16 women). *Students:* 40 full-time (16 women); includes 6 minority (1 Black or African American, non-Hispanic/Latino; 4 Asian, non-Hispanic/Latino; 1 Hispanic/Latino), 26 international. Average age 28. 145 applicants, 9% accepted, 4 enrolled. In 2016, 5 doctorates awarded. *Degree requirements:* For doctorate, comprehensive exam, thesis/dissertation. *Entrance requirements:* For doctorate, GMAT (strongly preferred) or GRE. Additional exam requirements/recommendations for international students: Required—TOEFL (minimum score 600 paper-based; 100 iBT). *Application deadline:* For fall admission, 1/3 priority date for domestic and international students. Application fee: $75. Electronic applications accepted. *Expenses:* $708 fees per year; 100% of tuition covered by scholarship. *Financial support:* In 2016–17, 34 students received support, including 6 fellowships (averaging $3,333 per year); scholarships/grants and health care benefits also available. Financial award application deadline: 1/3. *Faculty research:* Financial and managerial accounting, asset pricing strategy and organizational behavior, information technology marketing analytics and consumer behavior. *Unit head:* Dr. Anand Swaminathan, Associate Dean, Doctoral Program, 404-727-2306, Fax: 404-727-5337, E-mail: anand.swaminathan@emory.edu. *Application contact:* Allison Gilmore, Director of Admissions and Student Services, 404-727-6353, Fax: 404-727-5337, E-mail: allison.gilmore@emory.edu.

Emory University, Goizueta Business School, Full Time MBA Program, Atlanta, GA 30322. Offers accounting (MBA); alternative investments (MBA); business process consulting (MBA); business technology management (MBA); capital markets (MBA); corporate finance (MBA); customer relationship management (MBA); decision analytics (MBA); entrepreneurship (MBA); finance (MBA); global management (MBA); investment banking (MBA); management consulting (MBA); marketing (MBA); marketing analytics (MBA); marketing consulting (MBA); operations management (MBA); organization and management (MBA); product and brand management (MBA); real estate (MBA); social enterprise (MBA); strategy consulting (MBA). *Accreditation:* AACSB. *Faculty:* 72 full-time (17 women), 18 part-time/adjunct (5 women). *Students:* 350 full-time (101 women); includes 77 minority (21 Black or African American, non-Hispanic/Latino; 3 American Indian or Alaska Native, non-Hispanic/Latino; 32 Asian, non-Hispanic/Latino; 15 Hispanic/Latino; 2 Native Hawaiian or other Pacific Islander, non-Hispanic/Latino; 4 Two or more races, non-Hispanic/Latino), 117 international. Average age 29. 1,434 applicants, 31% accepted, 181 enrolled. In 2016, 182 master's awarded. *Degree requirements:* For master's, 1 leadership course; 2 mid-semester module programs; 2 global components. *Entrance requirements:* For master's, GMAT/GRE, essays; recommendation letters; undergraduate degree; interview. Additional exam requirements/recommendations for international students: Required—TOEFL (minimum score 100 iBT), IELTS (minimum score 7), PTE (minimum score 68). *Application deadline:* For fall admission, 10/14 priority date for domestic and international students; for winter admission, 11/11 priority date for domestic and international students; for spring admission, 1/4 priority date for domestic students, 1/4 for international students. Application fee: $150. Electronic applications accepted. *Expenses:* $57,580. *Financial support:* In 2016–17, 289 students received support. Career-related internships or fieldwork, institutionally sponsored loans, and scholarships/grants available. Financial award application deadline: 4/1; financial award applicants required to submit FAFSA. *Faculty research:* Social enterprise; micro vs. large business; mobile health data; mutual fund performance; product evaluation. *Unit head:* Brian Mitchell, Associate Dean, 404-727-4824, Fax: 404-712-9648, E-mail: brian.mitchell@emory.edu. *Application contact:* Julie Barefoot, Associate Dean, 404-727-6311, Fax: 404-727-4612, E-mail: mbaadmissions@emory.edu.
Website: http://www.goizueta.emory.edu

Endicott College, Van Loan School of Graduate and Professional Studies, Program in Organizational Management, Beverly, MA 01915-2096. Offers M Ed. *Program availability:* Part-time, evening/weekend, 100% online. *Faculty:* 3 full-time (0 women), 3 part-time/adjunct (2 women). *Students:* 46 full-time (30 women), 3 part-time (2 women); includes 6 minority (3 Black or African American, non-Hispanic/Latino; 1 Asian, non-Hispanic/Latino; 2 Hispanic/Latino). Average age 35. 10 applicants, 100% accepted, 10 enrolled. In 2016, 52 master's awarded. *Degree requirements:* For master's, thesis. *Entrance requirements:* For master's, GRE or MAT, two letters of recommendation, personal interview, 250-500 word essay, official transcripts of undergraduate and graduate course work. Additional exam requirements/recommendations for international students: Required—TOEFL. *Application deadline:* Applications are processed on a rolling basis. Application fee: $50. Electronic applications accepted. *Expenses:* Contact institution. *Financial support:* Applicants required to submit FAFSA. *Unit head:* Richard Weissman, Director, 978-232-2269, Fax: 978-232-3000, E-mail: rweissma@endicott.edu. *Application contact:* Ian Menchini, Director, Graduate Enrollment and Advising, 978-232-5292, Fax: 978-232-3000, E-mail: imenchin@endicott.edu.
Website: http://www.endicott.edu/VanLoan/Graduate-Studies/Master-Education/Organizational-Management.aspx

Evangel University, Organizational Leadership Program, Springfield, MO 65802. Offers MOL. *Program availability:* Part-time, evening/weekend, 100% online, blended/hybrid learning. *Faculty:* 3 full-time (0 women), 5 part-time/adjunct (2 women). *Students:* 32 full-time (17 women), 2 part-time (1 woman); includes 3 minority (1 Black or African American, non-Hispanic/Latino; 1 American Indian or Alaska Native, non-Hispanic/Latino; 1 Asian, non-Hispanic/Latino). Average age 38. 5 applicants, 100% accepted, 5 enrolled. In 2016, 24 master's awarded. *Entrance requirements:* Additional exam requirements/recommendations for international students: Required—TOEFL (minimum score 550 paper-based). *Application deadline:* For fall admission, 7/15 priority date for domestic students, 8/1 for international students; for spring admission, 11/15 priority date for domestic students, 12/1 for international students. Applications are processed on a rolling basis. Application fee: $25. Electronic applications accepted. *Expenses: Tuition:* Part-time $400 per credit hour. *Required fees:* $148 per trimester. One-time fee: $25. Tuition and fees vary according to course load, degree level and program. *Financial support:* In 2016–17, 17 students received support. Scholarships/grants available. Financial award application deadline: 4/1; financial award applicants required to submit FAFSA. *Unit head:* Dr. Duane Praschan, Program Coordinator, 417-865-2815 Ext. 8118, Fax: 417-575-5484, E-mail: praschand@evangel.edu. *Application contact:* Karen Benitez, Admissions Representative, Graduate Studies, 417-865-2815 Ext. 7416, Fax: 417-575-5484, E-mail: benitezk@evangel.edu.
Website: http://www.evangel.edu/academics/graduate-studies/graduate-programs

Excelsior College, School of Health Sciences, Albany, NY 12203-5159. Offers health administration (MS); health care informatics (Certificate); health professions education (MSHS); healthcare informatics (MS); organizational development (MS); public health (MSHS). *Program availability:* Part-time, evening/weekend, online learning. *Faculty:* 5 part-time/adjunct (4 women). *Students:* 307 part-time (240 women); includes 176 minority (101 Black or African American, non-Hispanic/Latino; 2 American Indian or Alaska Native, non-Hispanic/Latino; 17 Asian, non-Hispanic/Latino; 39 Hispanic/Latino; 3 Native Hawaiian or other Pacific Islander, non-Hispanic/Latino; 14 Two or more races, non-Hispanic/Latino), 1 international. Average age 39. In 2016, 21 master's awarded. *Entrance requirements:* For degree, bachelor's degree in applicable field. *Application deadline:* Applications are processed on a rolling basis. Application fee: $50. Electronic applications accepted. *Expenses: Tuition:* Part-time $645 per credit. *Required fees:* $265 per credit. *Financial support:* Scholarships/grants available. *Unit head:* Dr. Laurie Carbo-Porter, Dean, 518-464-8500, Fax: 518-464-8777. *Application contact:* Admissions Counselor, 518-464-8500, Fax: 518-464-8777, E-mail: admissions@excelsior.edu.

Fairleigh Dickinson University, College at Florham, Maxwell Becton College of Arts and Sciences, Department of Psychology, Program in Organizational Behavior, Madison, NJ 07940-1099. Offers organizational behavior (MA); organizational leadership (Certificate).

Fielding Graduate University, Graduate Programs, School of Leadership Studies, Programs in Evidence Based Coaching, Santa Barbara, CA 93105-3814. Offers comprehensive evidence based coaching (Certificate); evidence based coaching for organizational leadership (Certificate). *Program availability:* Part-time, online only, blended/hybrid learning. *Faculty:* 14 part-time/adjunct (9 women). *Students:* 1 full-time (0 women), 34 part-time (30 women); includes 10 minority (6 Black or African American, non-Hispanic/Latino; 4 Hispanic/Latino), 1 international. Average age 49. 16 applicants, 100% accepted, 14 enrolled. In 2016, 47 Certificates awarded. *Entrance requirements:* For degree, bachelor's degree from regionally-accredited U.S. institution or equivalent, resume, official transcript. *Application deadline:* For fall admission, 7/1 for domestic and international students; for spring admission, 11/1 for domestic and international students; for summer admission, 3/1 for domestic and international students. Application fee: $75. Electronic applications accepted. *Expenses:* $720 per credit; $750 per term Skills Training Workshop Fee. *Financial support:* Scholarships/grants available. Financial award applicants required to submit FAFSA. *Unit head:* Francine Campone, Program Faculty Lead, E-mail: fcampone@fielding.edu. *Application contact:* Enrollment Coordinator, 800-340-1099 Ext. 4098, Fax: 805-687-9793, E-mail: hodadmission@fielding.edu.
Website: http://www.fielding.edu/our-programs/school-of-leadership-studies/comprehensive-evidence-based-coaching-certificate/

Florida Institute of Technology, College of Psychology and Liberal Arts, Program in Applied Behavior Analysis and Organizational Behavior Management, Melbourne, FL 32901-6975. Offers MS. *Program availability:* Part-time. *Students:* 22 full-time (18 women), 2 part-time (1 woman); includes 9 minority (3 Asian, non-Hispanic/Latino; 4 Hispanic/Latino; 2 Two or more races, non-Hispanic/Latino). Average age 25. 36 applicants, 39% accepted, 7 enrolled. In 2016, 5 master's awarded. *Degree requirements:* For master's, comprehensive exam, thesis or alternative, minimum of 50 credits, all course grades of B or higher. *Entrance requirements:* For master's, GRE General Test, 3 letters of recommendation, resume, statement of objectives. Additional exam requirements/recommendations for international students: Required—TOEFL (minimum score 550 paper-based; 79 iBT). *Application deadline:* Applications are processed on a rolling basis. Electronic applications accepted. *Expenses: Tuition:* Full-time $22,338; part-time $1241 per credit hour. *Required fees:* $250. Tuition and fees vary according to degree level, campus/location and program. *Unit head:* Dr. David Wilder, Program Chair, 321-674-7516, E-mail: dawilder@fit.edu. *Application contact:* Cheryl A. Brown, Associate Director of Graduate Admissions, 321-674-7581, Fax: 321-723-9468, E-mail: cbrown@fit.edu.
Website: http://cpla.fit.edu/programs.php

Florida Institute of Technology, College of Psychology and Liberal Arts, Program in Organizational Behavior Management, Melbourne, FL 32901-6975. Offers MS. *Students:* 2 full-time (1 woman); includes 1 minority (Asian, non-Hispanic/Latino). Average age 24. 10 applicants, 20% accepted, 2 enrolled. *Degree requirements:* For master's, comprehensive exam, thesis optional, minimum of 42 credit hours, all course grades of B or higher. *Entrance requirements:* For master's, GRE General Test, 3 letters of recommendation, resume, statement of objectives. Additional exam requirements/recommendations for international students: Required—TOEFL (minimum score 550 paper-based; 79 iBT). *Expenses: Tuition:* Full-time $22,338; part-time $1241 per credit hour. *Required fees:* $250. Tuition and fees vary according to degree level, campus/location and program. *Financial support:* Applicants required to submit FAFSA. *Unit head:* Dr. David Wilder, Program Chair, Campus Behavior Analysis Programs, 321-674-7516, E-mail: dawilder@fit.edu. *Application contact:* Cheryl A. Brown, Associate Director of Graduate Admissions, 321-674-7581, Fax: 321-723-9468, E-mail: cbrown@fit.edu.
Website: http://www.fit.edu/programs/

Gannon University, School of Graduate Studies, College of Humanities, Education, and Social Sciences, School of Humanities, Program in Organizational Learning and Leadership, Erie, PA 16541-0001. Offers PhD. *Program availability:* Part-time, evening/weekend. *Students:* 1 (woman) full-time, 65 part-time (37 women); includes 2 minority (1 Asian, non-Hispanic/Latino; 1 Hispanic/Latino), 2 international. Average age 41. 27 applicants, 59% accepted, 10 enrolled. In 2016, 2 doctorates awarded. *Degree requirements:* For doctorate, thesis/dissertation. *Entrance requirements:* For doctorate, GRE, master's or other post-baccalaureate professional graduate-level degree from regionally-accredited institution of higher education with minimum GPA of 3.5; 2 years of post-baccalaureate work experience; 3 letters of recommendation; transcripts; resume; statement of purpose. Additional exam requirements/recommendations for international students: Required—TOEFL (minimum score 79 iBT). *Application deadline:* For spring admission, 2/1 for domestic students. Applications are processed on a rolling basis. Application fee: $25. Electronic applications accepted. Application fee is waived when completed online. *Expenses: Tuition:* Full-time $17,370. *Required fees:* $550. Tuition and fees vary according to course load and program. *Financial support:* Federal Work-Study and unspecified assistantships available. Financial award application deadline: 7/1; financial award applicants required to submit FAFSA. *Unit head:* Dr. Bill Hallock, Director, 814-871-7136, E-mail: hallock002@gannon.edu. *Application contact:* Bridget Philip, Director of Graduate Admissions, 814-871-7412, E-mail: graduate@gannon.edu.

Gardner-Webb University, Graduate School, School of Education, Program in Organizational Leadership, Boiling Springs, NC 28017. Offers Ed D. *Faculty:* 16 full-time (6 women), 35 part-time/adjunct (20 women). *Students:* 48 part-time (26 women); includes 24 minority (23 Black or African American, non-Hispanic/Latino; 1 Asian, non-Hispanic/Latino). Average age 41. 20 applicants, 55% accepted, 10 enrolled. *Degree requirements:* For doctorate, project/practicum. *Entrance requirements:* For doctorate,

MAT or GRE, master's degree with minimum GPA of 3.0, three letters of reference, official transcripts, three years of work experience, personal essay. *Expenses:* Contact institution. *Unit head:* Dr. Alan D. Eury, Dean, 704-406-4402, Fax: 704-406-3921, E-mail: dsimmons@gardner-webb.edu. *Application contact:* Office of Graduate Admissions, 877-498-4723, Fax: 704-406-3895, E-mail: gradinfo@gardner-webb.edu.
Website: http://www.gardner-webb.edu/academic-programs-and-resources/colleges-and-schools/education/schools-and-departments/graduate-programs/doctoral-degrees/

Geneva College, Program in Leadership Studies, Beaver Falls, PA 15010-3599. Offers business management (MS); ministry leadership (MS); non-profit leadership (MS); organizational management (MS); project management (MS). *Program availability:* Online only, 100% online. *Faculty:* 1 (woman) full-time, 10 part-time/adjunct (3 women). *Students:* 56 full-time (45 women), 9 part-time (6 women); includes 15 minority (12 Black or African American, non-Hispanic/Latino; 1 Asian, non-Hispanic/Latino; 2 Hispanic/Latino). Average age 45. 13 applicants, 77% accepted, 7 enrolled. In 2016, 38 master's awarded. *Degree requirements:* For master's, thesis or alternative, capstone leadership studies project. *Entrance requirements:* For master's, undergraduate degree from regionally-accredited college or university, one to three years of experience in the workplace, minimum GPA of 3.0 (preferred), resume, essay, two recommendations. Additional exam requirements/recommendations for international students: Required—TOEFL. *Application deadline:* For fall admission, 9/21 for domestic students; for spring admission, 2/23 for domestic students; for summer admission, 7/22 for domestic students. Applications are processed on a rolling basis. Electronic applications accepted. *Expenses:* $640 per credit. *Financial support:* In 2016–17, 50 students received support. Scholarships/grants available. Financial award application deadline: 8/1; financial award applicants required to submit FAFSA. *Faculty research:* Servant leadership, leadership essentials. *Unit head:* John D. Gallo, Dean of Graduate, Adult and Online Programs, 800-576-3111, Fax: 724-847-6839, E-mail: msol@geneva.edu. *Application contact:* Lynsey Auell, Graduate Enrollment Representative, 800-576-3111, Fax: 724-847-6839, E-mail: msol@geneva.edu.
Website: http://www.geneva.edu/graduate/leadership-studies/

George Fox University, College of Business, Newberg, OR 97132-2697. Offers accounting (DBA); finance (MBA); management (DBA); management and leadership (MBA); marketing (DBA); organizational strategy (MBA); strategic human resource management (MBA). MBA offered in Newberg, OR and in Portland, OR. *Accreditation:* ACBSP. *Program availability:* Part-time, evening/weekend, online learning. *Degree requirements:* For master's, capstone project; for doctorate, credit-applied research project. *Entrance requirements:* For master's, resume (5 years of professional experience); 3 professional references; interview; financial e-learning course; official transcripts; for doctorate, GRE or GMAT, resume; personal mission statement; academic research writing sample; official transcript from each college/university attended; three professional references. Additional exam requirements/recommendations for international students: Required—TOEFL (minimum score 577 paper-based; 90 iBT) or IELTS (minimum score 7). Electronic applications accepted. *Expenses:* Contact institution.

George Mason University, Schar School of Policy and Government, Program in Organization Development and Knowledge Management, Arlington, VA 22201. Offers MS. *Faculty:* 3 full-time (1 woman), 3 part-time/adjunct (1 woman). *Students:* 12 full-time (10 women), 37 part-time (30 women); includes 21 minority (8 Black or African American, non-Hispanic/Latino; 4 Asian, non-Hispanic/Latino; 7 Hispanic/Latino; 1 Native Hawaiian or other Pacific Islander, non-Hispanic/Latino; 1 Two or more races, non-Hispanic/Latino), 1 international. Average age 35. 39 applicants, 92% accepted, 23 enrolled. In 2016, 26 master's awarded. *Degree requirements:* For master's, thesis or alternative, internship. *Entrance requirements:* For master's, GRE (for students seeking merit-based scholarships), bachelor's degree with minimum GPA of 3.0, current resume, 2 letters of recommendation, expanded goals statement, 2 copies of official transcripts. Additional exam requirements/recommendations for international students: Required—TOEFL (minimum score 575 paper-based; 88 iBT), IELTS (minimum score 6.5), PTE (minimum score 59). *Application deadline:* For fall admission, 6/1 priority date for domestic students, 5/1 priority date for international students; for spring admission, 12/1 priority date for domestic students, 11/1 priority date for international students. Applications are processed on a rolling basis. Application fee: $65 ($80 for international students). Electronic applications accepted. *Expenses:* Contact institution. *Financial support:* Career-related internships or fieldwork, Federal Work-Study, scholarships/grants, unspecified assistantships, and health care benefits (for full-time research or teaching assistantship recipients) available. Financial award application deadline: 3/1; financial award applicants required to submit FAFSA. *Unit head:* Tojo Joseph Thatchenkery, Director, 703-993-3808, Fax: 703-993-8215, E-mail: thatchen@gmu.edu. *Application contact:* Stephanie Ellis, Graduate Admissions Coordinator, 703-993-4478, E-mail: sellis11@gmu.edu.
Website: http://spgia.gmu.edu/programs/graduate-degrees/organization-development-knowledge-management-odkm/

The George Washington University, Columbian College of Arts and Sciences, Department of Organizational Sciences and Communication, Washington, DC 20052. Offers human resources management (MA); non-profit management (Graduate Certificate); organizational management (Graduate Certificate). *Program availability:* Part-time, evening/weekend. *Faculty:* 10 full-time (6 women). *Students:* 46 full-time (25 women), 31 part-time (25 women); includes 27 minority (8 Black or African American, non-Hispanic/Latino; 7 Asian, non-Hispanic/Latino; 5 Hispanic/Latino; 7 Two or more races, non-Hispanic/Latino), 5 international. Average age 28. 133 applicants, 85% accepted, 47 enrolled. In 2016, 35 master's, 21 other advanced degrees awarded. *Degree requirements:* For master's, comprehensive exam. *Entrance requirements:* For master's, GRE General Test, minimum GPA of 3.0; for Graduate Certificate, minimum GPA of 3.0. Additional exam requirements/recommendations for international students: Required—TOEFL (minimum score 500 paper-based; 80 iBT). *Application deadline:* For fall admission, 1/15 priority date for domestic and international students; for spring admission, 10/1 priority date for domestic students, 9/1 priority date for international students. Applications are processed on a rolling basis. Application fee: $75. Electronic applications accepted. *Financial support:* Federal Work-Study and institutionally sponsored loans available. *Unit head:* Dr. Clay Warren, Chair, 202-994-1870, Fax: 202-994-1881, E-mail: claywar@gwu.edu. *Application contact:* Information Contact, 202-994-1880, Fax: 202-994-1881.
Website: http://www.gwu.edu/~orgsci/

The George Washington University, Graduate School of Education and Human Development, Department of Human and Organizational Learning, Program in Organizational Learning and Change, Washington, DC 20052. Offers Graduate Certificate. *Students:* 2 part-time (1 woman). Average age 30. 5 applicants, 60% accepted, 2 enrolled. In 2016, 1 Graduate Certificate awarded. *Entrance requirements:* For degree, two letters of recommendation, resume, statement of purpose. *Unit head:* Michael Feuer, Dean, 202-994-6161, E-mail: mjfeuer@gwu.edu. *Application contact:* Sarah Lang, Director of Graduate Admissions, 202-994-1447, Fax: 202-994-7207, E-mail: slang@gwu.edu.
Website: http://gsehd.gwu.edu/programs/organizational-learning-change

Georgia State University, J. Mack Robinson College of Business, Department of Managerial Sciences, Atlanta, GA 30302-3083. Offers business analysis (MBA, MS); entrepreneurship (MBA); human resources management (MBA, MS); operations management (MBA, MS); organization behavior/human resource management (PhD); organization management (MBA); organizational change (MS); strategic management (PhD). *Accreditation:* AACSB. *Program availability:* Part-time, evening/weekend. *Faculty:* 25 full-time (11 women). *Students:* 30 full-time (20 women), 10 part-time (4 women); includes 14 minority (11 Black or African American, non-Hispanic/Latino; 1 Asian, non-Hispanic/Latino; 1 Hispanic/Latino; 1 Two or more races, non-Hispanic/Latino), 12 international. Average age 31. 79 applicants, 30% accepted, 13 enrolled. In 2016, 23 master's, 2 doctorates awarded. *Degree requirements:* For doctorate, comprehensive exam, thesis/dissertation. *Entrance requirements:* For master's, GRE or GMAT, transcripts from all institutions attended, resume, essays; for doctorate, GMAT, three letters of recommendation, personal statement, transcripts from all institutions attended, resume. Additional exam requirements/recommendations for international students: Required—TOEFL (minimum score 610 paper-based; 101 iBT), IELTS (minimum score 7). *Application deadline:* For fall admission, 5/1 priority date for domestic students, 2/1 priority date for international students; for spring admission, 9/15 priority date for domestic students, 4/1 priority date for international students. Applications are processed on a rolling basis. Application fee: $50. Electronic applications accepted. *Expenses:* Tuition, state resident: full-time $6876; part-time $382 per credit hour. Tuition, nonresident: full-time $22,374; part-time $1243 per credit hour. *Required fees:* $2128; $1064 per term. Part-time tuition and fees vary according to course load and program. *Financial support:* Research assistantships, teaching assistantships, scholarships/grants, tuition waivers, and unspecified assistantships available. Financial award applicants required to submit FAFSA. *Faculty research:* Entrepreneurship and innovation; strategy process; workplace interactions, relationships, and processes; leadership and culture; supply chain management. *Unit head:* Dr. Pamela S. Barr, Interim Chair, 404-413-7525, Fax: 404-413-7571. *Application contact:* Toby McChesney, Assistant Dean for Graduate Recruiting and Student Services, 404-413-7167, Fax: 404-413-7162, E-mail: rcbgradadmissions@gsu.edu.
Website: http://mgmt.robinson.gsu.edu/

Gonzaga University, School of Professional Studies, Spokane, WA 99258. Offers communication and leadership (MA); leadership studies (PhD); organizational leadership (MA). *Program availability:* Part-time, evening/weekend, blended/hybrid learning, immersion weekends. *Faculty:* 16 full-time (6 women), 18 part-time/adjunct (6 women). *Students:* 32 full-time (22 women), 574 part-time (343 women); includes 111 minority (33 Black or African American, non-Hispanic/Latino; 8 American Indian or Alaska Native, non-Hispanic/Latino; 11 Asian, non-Hispanic/Latino; 38 Hispanic/Latino; 3 Native Hawaiian or other Pacific Islander, non-Hispanic/Latino; 18 Two or more races, non-Hispanic/Latino), 22 international. Average age 38. 197 applicants, 96% accepted, 156 enrolled. In 2016, 285 master's, 9 doctorates awarded. *Degree requirements:* For master's, leadership seminar; for doctorate, thesis/dissertation. *Entrance requirements:* For master's, MAT or GRE, official transcripts with minimum GPA of 3.0, letter of recommendation, statement of purpose, resume; for doctorate, MAT, GRE, 500-word narrative, short sample of writing, current resume/curriculum vitae, two official transcripts from each college attended, three letters of recommendation, master's degree with minimum GPA of 3.5, interview with department chair and faculty. Additional exam requirements/recommendations for international students: Required—TOEFL (minimum score 88 iBT) or IELTS (minimum score 6.5). *Application deadline:* For fall admission, 7/16 for domestic students; for spring admission, 11/16 for domestic students; for summer admission, 3/16 for domestic students. Applications are processed on a rolling basis. Application fee: $50. Electronic applications accepted. *Expenses:* Contact institution. *Financial support:* In 2016–17, 61 students received support. Scholarships/grants, tuition waivers, and unspecified assistantships available. Support available to part-time students. Financial award applicants required to submit FAFSA. *Unit head:* Dr. Jolanta Weber, Interim Dean, 509-313-6595, E-mail: weberj@gonzaga.edu. *Application contact:* Teresa Crane, Program Specialist, 509-313-6645, E-mail: guonlinestudentservices@gonzaga.edu.
Website: http://www.gonzaga.edu/Academics/Colleges-and-Schools/School-of-Professional-Studies

Graceland University, School of Nursing, Independence, MO 64050-3434. Offers adult and gerontology acute care (MSN, PMC); family nurse practitioner (MSN, PMC); nurse educator (MSN, PMC); organizational leadership (DNP). *Accreditation:* AACN. *Program availability:* Part-time, online learning. *Faculty:* 14 full-time (12 women), 21 part-time/adjunct (20 women). *Students:* 275 full-time (246 women), 313 part-time (273 women); includes 79 minority (25 Black or African American, non-Hispanic/Latino; 4 American Indian or Alaska Native, non-Hispanic/Latino; 12 Asian, non-Hispanic/Latino; 23 Hispanic/Latino; 2 Native Hawaiian or other Pacific Islander, non-Hispanic/Latino; 13 Two or more races, non-Hispanic/Latino), 3 international. 140 applicants, 69% accepted, 69 enrolled. In 2016, 137 master's, 11 doctorates awarded. *Degree requirements:* For master's, comprehensive exam (for some programs), thesis optional, scholarly project; for doctorate, capstone project. *Entrance requirements:* For master's, BSN from nationally-accredited program, RN license, minimum GPA of 3.0, satisfactory criminal background check; for doctorate, MSN from nationally-accredited program, RN license, minimum GPA of 3.2, criminal background check. Additional exam requirements/recommendations for international students: Recommended—TOEFL. *Application deadline:* For fall admission, 6/1 priority date for domestic students; for winter admission, 10/1 priority date for domestic students; for spring admission, 10/1 priority date for domestic students; for summer admission, 2/1 for domestic students. Application fee: $50. Electronic applications accepted. *Expenses:* Contact institution. *Financial support:* Institutionally sponsored loans available. Support available to part-time students. Financial award applicants required to submit FAFSA. *Faculty research:* International nursing, family care-giving, health promotion. *Unit head:* Dr. Claudia D. Horton, Dean, 816-423-4670, Fax: 816-423-4753, E-mail: horton@graceland.edu. *Application contact:* Nick Walker, Admissions Representative, 816-423-4717, Fax: 816-833-2990, E-mail: nowalker@graceland.edu.
Website: http://www.graceland.edu/nursing

Grand Canyon University, Colangelo College of Business, Phoenix, AZ 85017-1097. Offers accounting (MBA, MS); business analytics (MS); disaster preparedness and executive fire service leadership (MS); finance (MBA); general management (MBA); health systems management (MBA); information technology management (MS); leadership (MBA, MS); marketing (MBA); organizational leadership and entrepreneurship (MS); project management (MBA); sports business (MBA); strategic human resource management (MBA). *Accreditation:* ACBSP. *Program availability:* Part-time, evening/weekend, online learning. *Faculty:* 8 full-time (3 women), 147 part-time/adjunct (49 women). *Students:* 1 full-time (0 women), 2,121 part-time (1,165 women); includes 341 minority (249 Black or African American, non-Hispanic/Latino; 17 American Indian or Alaska Native, non-Hispanic/Latino; 15 Asian, non-Hispanic/Latino; 29 Hispanic/Latino; 4 Native Hawaiian or other Pacific Islander, non-Hispanic/Latino; 27 Two or more races, non-Hispanic/Latino), 20 international. Average age 38. In 2016, 569 master's awarded. *Entrance requirements:* For master's, equivalent of two years' full-time professional work experience. Additional exam requirements/recommendations for international students: Required—TOEFL (minimum score 575 paper-based; 90 iBT),

IELTS (minimum score 7). *Application deadline:* For fall admission, 8/21 for domestic students, 7/2 for international students; for spring admission, 12/24 for domestic students, 11/1 for international students. Applications are processed on a rolling basis. Application fee: $0. Electronic applications accepted. *Financial support:* Federal Work-Study available. Support available to part-time students. Financial award applicants required to submit FAFSA. *Unit head:* Kim Donaldson, Dean, 602-639-6597, E-mail: kdonaldson@gcu.edu. *Application contact:* Matt Tidwell, Enrollment Manager, 602-639-6020, E-mail: mtidwell@gcu.edu.
Website: https://www.gcu.edu/colangelo-college-of-business.php

Grand Canyon University, College of Doctoral Studies, Phoenix, AZ 85017-1097. Offers data analytics (DBA); general psychology (PhD), including cognition and instruction, industrial and organizational psychology, integrating technology, learning, and psychology, performance psychology; management (DBA); marketing (DBA); organizational leadership (Ed D), including behavioral health, Christian ministry, health care administration, organizational development. *Degree requirements:* For doctorate, comprehensive exam, thesis/dissertation. *Entrance requirements:* For doctorate, minimum GPA of 3.4 on earned advanced degree from regionally-accredited institution; transcripts; goals statement. Application fee: $0. *Unit head:* Michael Berger, Dean, 602-639-7255. *Application contact:* Michael Berger, Dean, 602-639-7255.
Website: https://www.gcu.edu/college-of-doctoral-studies.php

Grand View University, Graduate Studies, Des Moines, IA 50316-1599. Offers athletic training (MS); clinical nurse leader (MSN, Post Master's Certificate); nursing education (MSN, Post Master's Certificate); organizational leadership (MS); sport management (MS); teacher leadership (M Ed); urban education (M Ed). *Program availability:* Part-time, evening/weekend. *Degree requirements:* For master's, completion of all required coursework in common core and selected track with minimum cumulative GPA of 3.0 and no more than two grades of C. *Entrance requirements:* For master's, GRE, GMAT, or essay, minimum undergraduate GPA of 3.0, professional resume, 3 letters of recommendation, interview. Additional exam requirements/recommendations for international students: Required—TOEFL (minimum score 550 paper-based). Electronic applications accepted.

Granite State College, MS in Leadership Program, Concord, NH 03301. Offers MS. *Program availability:* Part-time, evening/weekend, 100% online, blended/hybrid learning. *Faculty:* 1 (woman) full-time, 7 part-time/adjunct (4 women). *Students:* 25 full-time (11 women), 27 part-time (24 women); includes 1 minority (American Indian or Alaska Native, non-Hispanic/Latino). Average age 40. 11 applicants, 82% accepted, 6 enrolled. In 2016, 4 master's awarded. *Degree requirements:* For master's, capstone. *Entrance requirements:* For master's, bachelor's degree with minimum GPA of 3.0 on last 60 credit hours, 500-1000 word statement of purpose, two letters of professional or academic reference, resume, official transcripts. Additional exam requirements/recommendations for international students: Required—TOEFL (minimum score 80 iBT), IELTS (minimum score 6.5). *Application deadline:* Applications are processed on a rolling basis. Application fee: $0. Electronic applications accepted. *Expenses:* $9,216 full-time in-state, $512 per credit part-time; $9,810 full-time out-of-state, $545 per credit part-time. *Financial support:* Federal Work-Study and National Guard course waivers available. Financial award applicants required to submit FAFSA. *Unit head:* Dr. Johnna Herrick-Phelps, Vice Provost of Academic Affairs, 603-228-3000, E-mail: johnna.herrick-phelps@granite.edu. *Application contact:* Ana Gonzalez, Administrative Assistant, Office of Graduate Studies, 603-822-5433, Fax: 603-513-1387, E-mail: gsc.graduatestudies@granite.edu.
Website: https://www.granite.edu/degree-programs/masters-degrees/leadership/

Harding University, Paul R. Carter College of Business Administration, Searcy, AR 72149-0001. Offers international business (MBA); leadership and organizational management (MBA). *Accreditation:* ACBSP. *Program availability:* Part-time, evening/weekend, 100% online. *Faculty:* 26 part-time/adjunct (6 women). *Students:* 36 full-time (15 women), 86 part-time (35 women); includes 17 minority (7 Black or African American, non-Hispanic/Latino; 5 Asian, non-Hispanic/Latino; 4 Hispanic/Latino; 1 Two or more races, non-Hispanic/Latino), 12 international. Average age 32. 22 applicants, 100% accepted, 22 enrolled. In 2016, 54 master's awarded. *Degree requirements:* For master's, portfolio. *Entrance requirements:* For master's, GMAT (minimum score of 500) or GRE (minimum score of 300), minimum GPA of 3.0, 2 letters of recommendation, resume, 3 essays, all official transcripts. Additional exam requirements/recommendations for international students: Required—TOEFL (minimum score 550 paper-based; 79 iBT). *Application deadline:* For fall admission, 8/1 priority date for domestic and international students; for spring admission, 12/1 priority date for domestic and international students. Applications are processed on a rolling basis. Application fee: $40. Tuition and fees vary according to degree level and program. *Financial support:* Unspecified assistantships available. Financial award application deadline: 7/30; financial award applicants required to submit FAFSA. *Unit head:* Glen Metheny, Director of Graduate Studies, 501-279-5851, Fax: 501-279-4805, E-mail: gmetheny@harding.edu. *Application contact:* Melanie Kiihnl, Recruiting Manager/Director of Marketing, 501-279-4523, Fax: 501-279-4805, E-mail: mba@harding.edu.
Website: http://www.harding.edu/mba

Hawai`i Pacific University, College of Business, Program in Business Administration, Honolulu, HI 96813. Offers accounting (MBA); economics (MBA); finance (MBA); hospitality and tourism management (MBA); human resource management (MBA); information systems (MBA); international business (MBA); management (MBA); marketing (MBA); organizational change and development (MBA). *Program availability:* Part-time, evening/weekend, online learning. *Faculty:* 13 full-time (4 women), 1 part-time/adjunct (0 women). *Students:* 106 full-time (47 women), 33 part-time (13 women); includes 66 minority (5 Black or African American, non-Hispanic/Latino; 1 American Indian or Alaska Native, non-Hispanic/Latino; 23 Asian, non-Hispanic/Latino; 11 Hispanic/Latino; 1 Native Hawaiian or other Pacific Islander, non-Hispanic/Latino; 25 Two or more races, non-Hispanic/Latino), 36 international. Average age 33. 77 applicants, 84% accepted, 44 enrolled. In 2016, 78 master's awarded. *Entrance requirements:* For master's, GMAT or GRE. Additional exam requirements/recommendations for international students: Recommended—TOEFL (minimum score 550 paper-based; 80 iBT), IELTS (minimum score 6), TWE (minimum score 5). *Application deadline:* For fall admission, 2/15 priority date for domestic students; for spring admission, 10/15 priority date for domestic students. Applications are processed on a rolling basis. Application fee: $50. Electronic applications accepted. *Expenses: Tuition:* Full-time $17,190; part-time $955 per credit. *Required fees:* $150; $26 per credit. Tuition and fees vary according to course load and program. *Financial support:* In 2016–17, 27 students received support. Research assistantships, career-related internships or fieldwork, Federal Work-Study, scholarships/grants, tuition waivers, and unspecified assistantships available. Financial award application deadline: 3/1; financial award applicants required to submit FAFSA. *Unit head:* Dr. Warren Wee, Associate Dean/Associate Professor of Accounting, 808-544-9325, E-mail: wwee@hpu.edu. *Application contact:* Danny Lam, Assistant Director of Graduate Admissions, 808-544-1135, E-mail: graduate@hpu.edu.
Website: http://www.hpu.edu/CBA/Graduate/MBA/index.html

Hawai`i Pacific University, College of Business, Program in Organizational Change, Honolulu, HI 96813. Offers MA. *Program availability:* Part-time, evening/weekend, online learning. *Faculty:* 13 full-time (4 women), 1 part-time/adjunct (0 women). *Students:* 15 full-time (8 women), 17 part-time (9 women); includes 15 minority (2 Black or African American, non-Hispanic/Latino; 2 Hispanic/Latino; 1 Native Hawaiian or other Pacific Islander, non-Hispanic/Latino; 10 Two or more races, non-Hispanic/Latino), 9 international. Average age 33. 12 applicants, 100% accepted, 6 enrolled. In 2016, 21 master's awarded. *Entrance requirements:* Additional exam requirements/recommendations for international students: Recommended—TOEFL (minimum score 550 paper-based; 80 iBT), IELTS (minimum score 6), TWE (minimum score 5). *Application deadline:* For fall admission, 2/15 priority date for domestic students; for spring admission, 10/15 priority date for domestic students. Applications are processed on a rolling basis. Application fee: $50. Electronic applications accepted. *Expenses: Tuition:* Full-time $17,190; part-time $955 per credit. *Required fees:* $150; $26 per credit. Tuition and fees vary according to course load and program. *Financial support:* In 2016–17, 2 students received support. Research assistantships, career-related internships or fieldwork, Federal Work-Study, scholarships/grants, tuition waivers, and unspecified assistantships available. Financial award application deadline: 3/1; financial award applicants required to submit FAFSA. *Unit head:* Dr. Warren Wee, Associate Dean/Associate Professor of Accounting, 808-544-9325, E-mail: wwee@hpu.edu. *Application contact:* Danny Lam, Assistant Director of Graduate Admissions, 808-544-1135, E-mail: graduate@hpu.edu.
Website: https://www.hpu.edu/CBA/Graduate/MAODC.html

HEC Montreal, School of Business Administration, Master in Management in Cultural Enterprises Program, Montréal, QC H3T 2A7, Canada. Offers MM. All courses are given in English. *Students:* 14 full-time (13 women), 30 part-time (25 women). 8 applicants, 25% accepted, 2 enrolled. In 2016, 29 master's awarded. *Degree requirements:* For master's, one foreign language. *Entrance requirements:* For master's, bachelor's degree. *Application deadline:* For fall admission, 4/15 for domestic and international students; for winter admission, 9/15 for domestic and international students. Application fee: $86. Electronic applications accepted. *Expenses: Tuition, area resident:* Part-time $77.80 Canadian dollars per credit. Tuition, state resident: full-time $2797 Canadian dollars; part-time $240.92 Canadian dollars per credit. Tuition, nonresident: full-time $8673 Canadian dollars; part-time $531.43 Canadian dollars per credit. *International tuition:* $19,131 Canadian dollars full-time. *Required fees:* $1699 Canadian dollars; $40.58 Canadian dollars per credit. $67.32 Canadian dollars per term. Tuition and fees vary according to degree level and program. *Financial support:* Research assistantships, teaching assistantships, and scholarships/grants available. Financial award application deadline: 9/2. *Unit head:* Renaud Lachance, Director, 514-340-7165, E-mail: renaud.lachance@hec.ca. *Application contact:* Anny Caron, Administrative Director, 514-340-3598, Fax: 514-340-6411, E-mail: joanne.audet@hec.ca.
Website: http://www.hec.ca/programmes/maitrises/maitrise-management-entreprises-culturelles/index.html

HEC Montreal, School of Business Administration, Master of Science Programs in Administration, Program in Management and Social Innovations, Montréal, QC H3T 2A7, Canada. Offers M Sc. All courses are given in English. *Students:* 43 full-time (32 women), 10 part-time (6 women). 27 applicants, 81% accepted, 16 enrolled. In 2016, 5 master's awarded. *Degree requirements:* For master's, one foreign language, thesis. *Entrance requirements:* For master's, Test de francais international (TFI) with minimum score of 850 (for those who have never studied in French), BBA, undergraduate degree in another field, degree deemed equivalent by program director and minimum GPA of 3.0 on 4.3 scale. *Application deadline:* For fall admission, 3/15 for domestic and international students; for winter admission, 9/15 for domestic and international students. Application fee: $86. Electronic applications accepted. *Expenses: Tuition, area resident:* Part-time $77.80 Canadian dollars per credit. Tuition, state resident: full-time $2797 Canadian dollars; part-time $240.92 Canadian dollars per credit. Tuition, nonresident: full-time $8673 Canadian dollars; part-time $531.43 Canadian dollars per credit. *International tuition:* $19,131 Canadian dollars full-time. *Required fees:* $1699 Canadian dollars; $40.58 Canadian dollars per credit. $67.32 Canadian dollars per term. Tuition and fees vary according to degree level and program. *Financial support:* Research assistantships, teaching assistantships, and scholarships/grants available. Financial award application deadline: 9/2. *Unit head:* Dr. Marie-Helene Jobin, Director, 514-340-6283, E-mail: marie-helene.jobin@hec.ca. *Application contact:* Marianne de Moura, Administrative Director, 514-340-7106, Fax: 514-340-6411, E-mail: marianne.de-moura@hec.ca.
Website: http://www.hec.ca/programmes/maitrises/maitrise-gestions-en-contexte-innovations-sociales/index.html

HEC Montreal, School of Business Administration, Master of Science Programs in Administration, Program in Organizational Development, Montréal, QC H3T 2A7, Canada. Offers M Sc. All courses are given in English. *Students:* 49 full-time (40 women), 29 part-time (21 women). 49 applicants, 57% accepted, 13 enrolled. In 2016, 26 master's awarded. *Degree requirements:* For master's, one foreign language, thesis. *Entrance requirements:* For master's, Test de francais international (TFI) with minimum score of 850 (for those who have never studied in French), BBA, undergraduate degree in another field, degree deemed equivalent by program director and minimum GPA of 3.0 on 4.3 scale. *Application deadline:* For fall admission, 3/15 for domestic and international students; for winter admission, 9/15 for domestic and international students. Application fee: $86. Electronic applications accepted. *Expenses: Tuition, area resident:* Part-time $77.80 Canadian dollars per credit. Tuition, state resident: full-time $2797 Canadian dollars; part-time $240.92 Canadian dollars per credit. Tuition, nonresident: full-time $8673 Canadian dollars; part-time $531.43 Canadian dollars per credit. *International tuition:* $19,131 Canadian dollars full-time. *Required fees:* $1699 Canadian dollars; $40.58 Canadian dollars per credit. $67.32 Canadian dollars per term. Tuition and fees vary according to degree level and program. *Financial support:* Research assistantships, teaching assistantships, and scholarships/grants available. Financial award application deadline: 9/2. *Unit head:* Dr. Marie-Helene Jobin, Director, 514-340-6283, E-mail: marie-helene.jobin@hec.ca. *Application contact:* Marianne de Moura, Administrative Director, 514-340-7106, Fax: 514-340-6411, E-mail: marianne.de-moura@hec.ca.
Website: http://www.hec.ca/programmes/maitrises/maitrise-developpement-organisationnel/index.html

Hood College, Graduate School, Program in Organizational Leadership, Frederick, MD 21701-8575. Offers DBA. *Program availability:* Part-time, evening/weekend. *Faculty:* 2 full-time. *Students:* 18 part-time (10 women); includes 4 minority (2 Black or African American, non-Hispanic/Latino; 1 Asian, non-Hispanic/Latino; 1 Two or more races, non-Hispanic/Latino). Average age 46. 31 applicants, 58% accepted, 17 enrolled. *Degree requirements:* For doctorate, research-based capstone project. *Entrance requirements:* For doctorate, master's degree; minimum GPA of 3.25; one course in statistics; resume; two letters of recommendation; two essays; standardized test scores (SLLA, GRE, GMAT, or MAT) or evidence of master's-level culminating research experience. *Application deadline:* For fall admission, 4/15 priority date for domestic and international students. Application fee: $35. Electronic applications accepted. *Expenses:* $995 per credit (DBA); $835 per credit (DOL); $525 comprehensive fee per semester. *Financial support:* Applicants required to submit FAFSA. *Unit head:* Dr. Kathleen C. Bands, Director, 301-696-3818, E-mail: bands@hood.edu. *Application contact:* Spencer

Berk, Assistant Director of Graduate Admissions, 301-696-3600, E-mail: gofurther@hood.edu.

Husson University, Master of Business Administration Program, Bangor, ME 04401-2999. Offers athletic administration (MBA); biotechnology and innovation (MBA); general business administration (MBA); healthcare management (MBA); hospitality and tourism management (MBA); organizational management (MBA); risk management (MBA). *Program availability:* Part-time, evening/weekend, 100% online, blended/hybrid learning. *Faculty:* 8 full-time (4 women), 20 part-time/adjunct (5 women). *Students:* 81 full-time (47 women), 249 part-time (142 women); includes 32 minority (9 Black or African American, non-Hispanic/Latino; 2 American Indian or Alaska Native, non-Hispanic/Latino; 17 Asian, non-Hispanic/Latino; 3 Hispanic/Latino; 1 Two or more races, non-Hispanic/Latino), 11 international. Average age 34. 199 applicants, 78% accepted, 119 enrolled. In 2016, 109 master's awarded. *Degree requirements:* For master's, comprehensive exam (for some programs), thesis optional. *Entrance requirements:* For master's, minimum GPA of 3.0, letter of recommendation. Additional exam requirements/recommendations for international students: Required—TOEFL (minimum score 550 paper-based; 80 iBT), IELTS (minimum score 6.5). *Application deadline:* Applications are processed on a rolling basis. Application fee: $50. Electronic applications accepted. *Expenses:* $450 per credit; $450 fees per full-time year or $220 part-time. *Financial support:* Career-related internships or fieldwork, Federal Work-Study, scholarships/grants, and unspecified assistantships available. Financial award application deadline: 4/15; financial award applicants required to submit FAFSA. *Unit head:* Prof. Stephanie Shayne, Director, Graduate and Online Programs, 207-404-5632, Fax: 207-992-4987, E-mail: shaynes@husson.edu. *Application contact:* Kristen Card, Director of Graduate Admissions, 207-404-5660, Fax: 207-941-7935, E-mail: cardk@husson.edu.
Website: http://www.husson.edu/college-of-business/school-of-business-and-management/master-of-business-administration-mba/

Immaculata University, College of Graduate Studies, Program in Organization Leadership, Immaculata, PA 19345. Offers MA. *Program availability:* Part-time, evening/weekend. *Degree requirements:* For master's, comprehensive exam, thesis optional. *Entrance requirements:* For master's, GMAT, GRE General Test, MAT. Additional exam requirements/recommendations for international students: Required—TOEFL, IELTS. Electronic applications accepted.

Indiana Tech, Program in Organizational Leadership, Fort Wayne, IN 46803-1297. Offers MS. *Program availability:* Part-time, evening/weekend, online only, 100% online. *Entrance requirements:* For master's, minimum GPA of 2.5, bachelor's degree from regionally-accredited university, minimum three years of work experience, three letters of recommendation, essay, current resume. Electronic applications accepted.

Indiana University Bloomington, School of Public and Environmental Affairs, Public Affairs Programs, Bloomington, IN 47405. Offers economic development (MPA); energy (MPA); environmental policy (PhD); environmental policy and natural resource management (MPA); information systems (MPA); international development (MPA); local government management (MPA); nonprofit management (MPA, Certificate); policy analysis (MPA); public budgeting and financial management (Certificate); public finance (PhD); public financial administration (MPA); public management (MPA, PhD, Certificate); public policy analysis (PhD); social entrepreneurship (Certificate); specialized public affairs (MPA); sustainability and sustainable development (MPA); JD/MPA; MPA/MA; MPA/MIS; MPA/MLS; MSES/MPA. *Accreditation:* NASPAA (one or more programs are accredited). *Program availability:* Part-time. *Degree requirements:* For master's, capstone, internship; for doctorate, comprehensive exam, thesis/dissertation. *Entrance requirements:* For master's, GRE General Test or GMAT, official transcripts, 3 letters of recommendation, resume, personal statement; for doctorate, GRE General Test, official transcripts, 3 letters of recommendation, statement of purpose. Additional exam requirements/recommendations for international students: Required—TOEFL (minimum score 600 paper-based; 96 iBT); Recommended—IELTS (minimum score 7). Electronic applications accepted. *Faculty research:* International development, environmental policy and resource management, policy analysis, public finance, public management, urban management, nonprofit management, energy policy, social policy, public finance.

Indiana University–Purdue University Fort Wayne, College of Engineering, Technology, and Computer Science, Department of Organizational Leadership and Supervision, Fort Wayne, IN 46805-1499. Offers human resources (MS); leadership (MS); organizational leadership and supervision (Certificate). *Program availability:* Part-time. *Entrance requirements:* For master's, GRE or GMAT (if undergraduate GPA is below 3.0), current resume, 2 recent letters of recommendation, essay. Additional exam requirements/recommendations for international students: Required—TOEFL (minimum score 550 paper-based; 79 iBT); Recommended—TWE. Electronic applications accepted. *Faculty research:* Replication problem and psychology, virtual leadership.

Indiana University–Purdue University Indianapolis, School of Engineering and Technology, MS in Technology Program, Indianapolis, IN 46202. Offers applied data management and analytics (MS); facilities management (MS); information security and assurance (MS); motorsports (MS); organizational leadership (MS); technical communication (MS). *Program availability:* Online learning.

Indiana University–Purdue University Indianapolis, School of Public and Environmental Affairs, Indianapolis, IN 46202. Offers criminal justice and public safety (MS); homeland security and emergency management (Graduate Certificate); library management (Graduate Certificate); nonprofit management (Graduate Certificate); public affairs (MPA); public management (Graduate Certificate); social entrepreneurship: nonprofit and public benefit organizations (Graduate Certificate); JD/MPA; MLS/NMC; MLS/PMC; MPA/MA. *Accreditation:* CAHME (one or more programs are accredited); NASPAA. *Program availability:* Part-time, evening/weekend, online learning. *Entrance requirements:* For master's, GRE General Test, GMAT or LSAT, minimum GPA of 3.0 (preferred). Additional exam requirements/recommendations for international students: Required—TOEFL (minimum score 93 iBT), IELTS (minimum score 6.5). Electronic applications accepted. *Faculty research:* Nonprofit and public management, public policy, urban policy, sustainability policy, disaster preparedness and recovery, vehicular safety, homicide, offender rehabilitation and re-entry.

Indiana Wesleyan University, College of Adult and Professional Studies, Graduate Studies in Business, Marion, IN 46953. Offers accounting (MBA, Graduate Certificate); applied management (MBA); business administration (MBA); health care (MBA, Graduate Certificate); human resources (MBA, Graduate Certificate); management (MS); organizational leadership (MA). *Program availability:* Part-time, evening/weekend, online learning. *Degree requirements:* For master's, applied business or management project. *Entrance requirements:* For master's, minimum GPA of 2.5, 2 years of related work experience. Additional exam requirements/recommendations for international students: Required—TOEFL (minimum score 550 paper-based). Electronic applications accepted.

Indiana Wesleyan University, College of Adult and Professional Studies, Program in Organizational Leadership, Marion, IN 46953. Offers Ed D. *Program availability:* Part-time, online learning. *Degree requirements:* For doctorate, comprehensive exam, thesis/dissertation, applied field project. *Entrance requirements:* For doctorate, GRE, GMAT. Additional exam requirements/recommendations for international students: Required—TOEFL. *Faculty research:* Organizational leadership as a new structural model for research and teaching, wisdom and its application for leaders, stewardship and its application for leaders, followership and its application for leaders, the importance of a world view in establishing authenticity for leaders.

Instituto Tecnologico de Santo Domingo, Graduate School, Area of Business, Santo Domingo, Dominican Republic. Offers banking and securities markets (M Mgmt); corporate finance (M Mgmt); human resources management (M Mgmt, Certificate); international trade management (M Mgmt); marketing (M Mgmt); organizational development (M Mgmt); quality and productivity management (Certificate); tax management and planning (M Mgmt); upper management (M Mgmt).

Jacksonville University, Davis College of Business, Master of Science in Organizational Leadership Program, Jacksonville, FL 32211. Offers MS. *Program availability:* Part-time-only, evening/weekend, 100% online, blended/hybrid learning. *Faculty:* 2 full-time (both women). *Students:* 1 (woman) full-time, 27 part-time (15 women); includes 4 minority (2 Black or African American, non-Hispanic/Latino; 1 Asian, non-Hispanic/Latino; 1 Hispanic/Latino), 1 international. Average age 32. 19 applicants, 89% accepted, 16 enrolled. In 2016, 7 master's awarded. *Entrance requirements:* For master's, GMAT or GRE (may be waived for 3.0 or higher undergraduate GPA from regionally accredited institution and 3 years' relevant work experience), bachelor's degree from regionally-accredited institution, resume, statement of purpose, 2 letters of recommendation; 3 years of relevant work experience (recommended). Additional exam requirements/recommendations for international students: Required—TOEFL (minimum score 500 paper-based; 61 iBT), IELTS (minimum score 6). *Application deadline:* For fall admission, 8/1 priority date for domestic students, 7/15 priority date for international students; for spring admission, 12/1 priority date for domestic students, 11/15 priority date for international students; for summer admission, 4/1 priority date for domestic students, 3/15 priority date for international students. Applications are processed on a rolling basis. Application fee: $50. Electronic applications accepted. *Expenses:* $740 per credit hour. *Financial support:* Scholarships/grants available. Financial award application deadline: 7/1; financial award applicants required to submit FAFSA. *Faculty research:* Ethics; science of a start-up culture; organizational culture; sustainability. *Unit head:* Dr. Douglas Johansen, Associate Dean and Graduate Programs Director, 904-256-7763, Fax: 904-256-7168, E-mail: djohans@ju.edu. *Application contact:* AnnaMaria Murphy, Assistant Director of Graduate Admissions, 904-256-7426, Fax: 904-256-7012, E-mail: mba@ju.edu.

See Display on page 107 and Close-Up on page 179.

James Madison University, The Graduate School, College of Business, Program in Strategic Leadership, Harrisonburg, VA 22807. Offers postsecondary analysis and leadership (PhD), including nonprofit and community leadership, organizational science and leadership, postsecondary analysis and leadership. *Program availability:* Part-time, evening/weekend, online learning. *Faculty:* 3 full-time (1 woman). *Students:* 13 full-time (4 women), 25 part-time (10 women); includes 5 minority (all Black or African American, non-Hispanic/Latino), 3 international. Average age 30. 11 applicants, 64% accepted, 7 enrolled. In 2016, 5 doctorates awarded. Application fee: $55. Electronic applications accepted. *Financial support:* In 2016–17, 6 students received support. Fellowships, career-related internships or fieldwork, Federal Work-Study, unspecified assistantships, and 5 doctoral assistantships (stipend varies) available. Financial award application deadline: 3/1; financial award applicants required to submit FAFSA. *Unit head:* Dr. Karen A. Ford, Director of Strategic Leadership Studies, 540-568-7020, Fax: 540-568-7117, E-mail: fordka@jmu.edu. *Application contact:* Lynette D. Michael, Director of Graduate Admissions, 540-568-6131 Ext. 6395, Fax: 540-568-7860, E-mail: michaeld@jmu.edu.
Website: http://www.jmu.edu/leadership/

John F. Kennedy University, School of Management, Program in Business Administration, Pleasant Hill, CA 94523-4817. Offers business administration (MBA); organizational leadership (Certificate). *Program availability:* Part-time, evening/weekend. *Degree requirements:* For master's, thesis or alternative. *Entrance requirements:* For master's, interview. Additional exam requirements/recommendations for international students: Required—TOEFL.

Johns Hopkins University, School of Education, Master's Programs in Education, Baltimore, MD 21218. Offers counseling (MS), including clinical mental health counseling, school counseling; education (MS), including educational studies, gifted education, reading, school administration and supervision, technology for educators; elementary education (MAT); health professions (M Ed); intelligence analysis (MS); organizational leadership (MS); secondary education (MAT), including biology, chemistry, earth/space science, English, physics, social studies; special education (MS), including early childhood special education, general special education studies, mild to moderate disabilities, severe disabilities. *Program availability:* Part-time, evening/weekend, 100% online, blended/hybrid learning. *Students:* 345 full-time (265 women), 1,601 part-time (1,245 women); includes 837 minority (392 Black or African American, non-Hispanic/Latino; 7 American Indian or Alaska Native, non-Hispanic/Latino; 141 Asian, non-Hispanic/Latino; 207 Hispanic/Latino; 7 Native Hawaiian or other Pacific Islander, non-Hispanic/Latino; 83 Two or more races, non-Hispanic/Latino), 55 international. Average age 27. 1,352 applicants, 76% accepted, 819 enrolled. In 2016, 642 master's awarded. *Degree requirements:* For master's, comprehensive exam (for some programs), portfolio, capstone project and/or internship; PRAXIS II (subject area assessments) for initial teacher preparation programs that lead to licensure. *Entrance requirements:* For master's, GRE (for full-time programs only); PRAXIS I/core or state-approved alternative (for initial teacher preparation programs that lead to licensure), minimum of bachelor's degree from regionally- or nationally-accredited institution; minimum GPA of 3.0 in all previous programs of study; official transcripts from all post-secondary institutions attended; essay; curriculum vitae/resume; letters of recommendation (3 for full-time programs, 2 for part-time programs); dispositions survey. Additional exam requirements/recommendations for international students: Required—TOEFL (minimum score 600 paper-based; 100 iBT), IELTS (minimum score 7). *Application deadline:* For fall admission, 4/1 priority date for domestic students, 4/1 for international students; for spring admission, 10/1 priority date for domestic students, 10/1 for international students; for summer admission, 2/1 priority date for domestic students, 2/1 for international students. Applications are processed on a rolling basis. Application fee: $80. Electronic applications accepted. *Expenses:* Contact institution. *Financial support:* Application deadline: 4/1; applicants required to submit FAFSA. *Unit head:* Dr. Christopher C. Morphew, Dean. *Application contact:* Elisabeth Woodward, Director of Admissions, 410-516-9796, Fax: 410-516-9817, E-mail: soe.info@jhu.edu.
Website: http://education.jhu.edu

John Wesley University, Graduate Programs, High Point, NC 27265. Offers Christian leadership (D Min); organizational leadership (MBA); theological studies (MTS). *Program availability:* 100% online. *Faculty:* 1 full-time (0 women), 9 part-time/adjunct (3 women). *Students:* 21 full-time (13 women), 3 part-time (all women). *Entrance requirements:* For master's, GMAT or GRE (taken within last five years), bachelor's degree, minimum GPA of 3.0, resume, two letters of recommendation, autobiographical essay, immunizations. Application fee: $50. Electronic applications accepted. *Expenses:*

Tuition: Full-time $3780; part-time $2520 per semester. *Required fees:* $365; $365 per semester. Tuition and fees vary according to degree level. *Application contact:* Rosalie Seitz, Admissions, 336-821-2474, Fax: 336-889-2261, E-mail: admissions@johnwesley.edu.

Judson University, Master of Arts in Organizational Leadership Program, Elgin, IL 60123-1498. Offers MA. *Program availability:* Part-time, evening/weekend, 100% online, blended/hybrid learning. *Faculty:* 4 full-time (2 women), 20 part-time/adjunct (10 women). *Students:* 23 full-time, 14 part-time; includes 13 minority (6 Black or African American, non-Hispanic/Latino; 5 Hispanic/Latino; 2 Two or more races, non-Hispanic/Latino), 2 international. Average age 37. *Degree requirements:* For master's, thesis optional. *Entrance requirements:* For master's, bachelor's degree from regionally-accredited college or university with minimum GPA of 2.5; two letters of reference; professional resume. Additional exam requirements/recommendations for international students: Required—TOEFL (minimum score 550 paper-based). *Application deadline:* For fall admission, 8/1 for domestic students, 7/1 for international students; for spring admission, 3/1 for domestic students, 1/2 for international students. Applications are processed on a rolling basis. Application fee: $35. Electronic applications accepted. *Financial support:* Institutionally sponsored loans and scholarships/grants available. Financial award applicants required to submit FAFSA. *Faculty research:* Leadership, human resource management, public affairs, international marketing. *Unit head:* Dr. Teri Stein, Chair, 847-628-1524, E-mail: tstein@judsonu.edu. *Application contact:* Eric Downs, Enrollment Manager, 847-628-5026, Fax: 847-628-1007, E-mail: eric.downs@info.judsonu.edu.
Website: http://www.judsonu.edu/maol/

Kaplan University, Davenport Campus, School of Business, Davenport, IA 52807. Offers business administration (MBA); change leadership (MS); entrepreneurship (MBA); finance (MBA); health care management (MBA, MS); human resource (MBA); international business (MBA); management (MS); marketing (MBA); project management (MBA, MS); supply chain management and logistics (MBA, MS). *Accreditation:* ACBSP. *Program availability:* Part-time, evening/weekend, online learning. *Entrance requirements:* Additional exam requirements/recommendations for international students: Required—TOEFL (minimum score 550 paper-based; 80 iBT). Electronic applications accepted.

Keiser University, Doctor of Business Administration Program, Ft. Lauderdale, FL 33309. Offers global business (DBA); global organizational leadership (DBA); marketing (DBA).

LaGrange College, Graduate Programs, Program in Organizational Leadership, LaGrange, GA 30240-2999. Offers MA. Program is held on Albany campus. *Program availability:* Evening/weekend. *Entrance requirements:* For master's, GRE or MAT, minimum GPA of 2.5, 3 letters of reference. Additional exam requirements/recommendations for international students: Required—TOEFL (minimum score 500 paper-based; 61 iBT). Electronic applications accepted.

Lenoir-Rhyne University, Graduate Programs, School of Education, Program in Leadership, Hickory, NC 28601. Offers community and nonprofit leadership (MA); general management (MA); higher education leadership (MA); second language community services (MA). *Program availability:* Online learning. *Entrance requirements:* Additional exam requirements/recommendations for international students: Required—TOEFL (minimum score 600 paper-based). Electronic applications accepted. *Expenses:* Contact institution.

Lewis University, College of Arts and Sciences, Program in Organizational Leadership, Romeoville, IL 60446. Offers higher education/student services (MA); non-profit management (MA); organizational management (MA); professional and executive coaching (MA); training and development (MA). *Program availability:* Part-time, evening/weekend, 100% online. *Students:* 15 full-time (12 women), 176 part-time (130 women); includes 75 minority (51 Black or African American, non-Hispanic/Latino; 2 American Indian or Alaska Native, non-Hispanic/Latino; 2 Asian, non-Hispanic/Latino; 16 Hispanic/Latino; 4 Two or more races, non-Hispanic/Latino), 2 international. Average age 36. *Entrance requirements:* For master's, bachelor's degree, at least 24 years of age, minimum of 3 years of work experience, minimum GPA of 3.0, letter of recommendation. Additional exam requirements/recommendations for international students: Required—TOEFL (minimum score 550 paper-based; 80 iBT). *Application deadline:* For fall admission, 5/1 priority date for international students; for spring admission, 11/15 priority date for international students. Applications are processed on a rolling basis. Application fee: $40. Electronic applications accepted. *Expenses: Tuition:* Full-time $13,860; part-time $770 per credit hour. *Required fees:* $75 per semester. Tuition and fees vary according to degree level and program. *Financial support:* Tuition waivers and unspecified assistantships available. Financial award application deadline: 5/1; financial award applicants required to submit FAFSA. *Unit head:* Dr. Keith Lavine, Chair of Organizational Leadership, 815-838-0500, E-mail: lavineke@lewisu.edu. *Application contact:* Nancy Wiksten, Graduate Admission Counselor, 815-836-5628, Fax: 815-836-5578, E-mail: grad@lewisu.edu.

Lincoln Christian University, Graduate Programs, Lincoln, IL 62656-2167. Offers Biblical studies (MA); church history/historical theology (MA); intercultural studies (MA); ministry (MA); organizational leadership (MA); philosophy and apologetics (MA); spiritual formation (MA); theology (MA). MA in spiritual formation offered in Normal, IL. *Program availability:* Online learning. *Faculty:* 22 full-time (6 women), 27 part-time/adjunct (9 women). *Students:* 89 full-time (45 women), 225 part-time (91 women). Average age 39. *Entrance requirements:* For master's, minimum cumulative GPA of 2.5 in undergraduate degree studies. Additional exam requirements/recommendations for international students: Required—TOEFL (minimum score 550 paper-based); Recommended—IELTS (minimum score 6). *Application deadline:* For fall admission, 8/1 for domestic students, 3/1 for international students; for spring admission, 11/15 for domestic students, 11/1 for international students. Application fee: $25 ($50 for international students). Application fee is waived when completed online. *Expenses: Tuition:* Full-time $7812; part-time $5208 per credit hour. *Required fees:* $1000; $1000 per credit hour. One-time fee: $150. Full-time tuition and fees vary according to campus/location and program. *Financial support:* Applicants required to submit FAFSA. *Application contact:* Lindsey Clark, Associate Director of Graduate and Seminary Enrollment, 217-732-3168 Ext. 2398, E-mail: lclark@lincolnchristian.edu.
Website: https://lincolnchristian.edu/academics/programs/masters/

Lipscomb University, Nelson and Sue Andrews Institute for Civic Leadership, Nashville, TN 37204-3951. Offers MA. *Program availability:* Part-time, evening/weekend. *Faculty:* 1 (woman) full-time, 1 (woman) part-time/adjunct. *Students:* 10 full-time (7 women), 15 part-time (10 women); includes 17 minority (15 Black or African American, non-Hispanic/Latino; 2 Two or more races, non-Hispanic/Latino). Average age 37. In 2016, 10 master's awarded. *Degree requirements:* For master's, project, externship. *Entrance requirements:* For master's, GRE, GMAT or MAT, transcripts, 2 references, essay, resume. Additional exam requirements/recommendations for international students: Required—TOEFL (minimum score 570 paper-based; 80 iBT). *Application deadline:* Applications are processed on a rolling basis. Application fee: $50 ($75 for international students). Electronic applications accepted. *Expenses:* $1,312 per hour. *Financial support:* Applicants required to submit FAFSA. *Unit head:* Linda Peek Schacht, Executive Director, 615-966-1341, E-mail: linda.schacht@lipscomb.edu. *Application contact:* Dr. Michelle Steele, Academic Director, 615-966-5181, E-mail: michelle.steele@lipscomb.edu.
Website: http://www.lipscomb.edu/civicleadership

Lipscomb University, Program in Organizational Leadership, Nashville, TN 37204-3951. Offers MPS. *Program availability:* Part-time, online only, blended/hybrid learning. *Faculty:* 2 full-time (both women), 2 part-time/adjunct (1 woman). *Students:* 4 full-time (1 woman), 16 part-time (11 women); includes 2 minority (1 Black or African American, non-Hispanic/Latino; 1 Hispanic/Latino). Average age 42. *Entrance requirements:* For master's, GRE or GMAT, two references, resume, interview. Additional exam requirements/recommendations for international students: Required—TOEFL (minimum score 550 paper-based). *Application deadline:* For fall admission, 8/1 for domestic students. Applications are processed on a rolling basis. Application fee: $50 ($75 for international students). Electronic applications accepted. *Expenses:* $953 per hour. *Unit head:* Dr. Hope Nordstrom, Director, 615-966-1107, E-mail: hope.nordstrom@lipscomb.edu. *Application contact:* Barbara Blackman, Coordinator of Graduate Studies, 615-966-6287, Fax: 615-966-7619, E-mail: graduatestudies@lipscomb.edu.

Lourdes University, Graduate School, Sylvania, OH 43560-2898. Offers business (MBA); leadership (M Ed); nurse anesthesia (MSN); nurse educator (MSN); nurse leader (MSN); organizational leadership (MOL); reading (M Ed); teaching and curriculum (M Ed); theology (MA). *Program availability:* Evening/weekend. *Entrance requirements:* Additional exam requirements/recommendations for international students: Required—TOEFL.

Loyola University New Orleans, Joseph A. Butt, S.J., College of Business, Program in Business Administration, New Orleans, LA 70118-6195. Offers entrepreneurship and marketing innovation (MBA); organizational performance excellence (MBA); JD/MBA; MBA/MPS. *Accreditation:* AACSB. *Program availability:* Part-time, evening/weekend, online learning. *Faculty:* 8 full-time (4 women), 3 part-time/adjunct (0 women). *Students:* 71 full-time (35 women), 13 part-time (9 women); includes 27 minority (14 Black or African American, non-Hispanic/Latino; 1 American Indian or Alaska Native, non-Hispanic/Latino; 3 Asian, non-Hispanic/Latino; 8 Hispanic/Latino; 1 Two or more races, non-Hispanic/Latino), 3 international. Average age 29. 52 applicants, 96% accepted, 28 enrolled. In 2016, 25 master's awarded. *Degree requirements:* For master's, capstone project. *Entrance requirements:* For master's, GMAT or GRE, minimum GPA of 3.0, transcript, resume, 2 letters of recommendation, work experience in field, personal statement. Additional exam requirements/recommendations for international students: Required—TOEFL (minimum score 580 paper-based; 92 iBT). *Application deadline:* For fall admission, 6/15 priority date for domestic students, 5/15 priority date for international students; for spring admission, 11/15 priority date for domestic students, 10/15 priority date for international students. Applications are processed on a rolling basis. Application fee: $50. Electronic applications accepted. *Financial support:* Research assistantships, scholarships/grants, tuition waivers (partial), and unspecified assistantships available. Financial award application deadline: 5/1; financial award applicants required to submit FAFSA. *Faculty research:* Ethics, international business, entrepreneurship, quality management, risk management. *Unit head:* Dr. William B. Locander, Dean, 504-864-7979, Fax: 504-864-7970, E-mail: mba@loyno.edu. *Application contact:* Ashley Francis, Director of Graduate Programs, 504-864-7979, Fax: 504-864-7970, E-mail: mba@loyno.edu.
Website: http://www.business.loyno.edu/mba/programs

Malone University, Graduate Program in Organizational Leadership, Canton, OH 44709. Offers MAOL. *Program availability:* Part-time, evening/weekend. *Entrance requirements:* For master's, minimum GPA of 3.0. Additional exam requirements/recommendations for international students: Required—TOEFL (minimum score 550 paper-based; 79 iBT). *Expenses:* Contact institution. *Faculty research:* Graduates' perceptions of the impact of a Christian higher education.

Manhattan College, Graduate Programs, School of Continuing and Professional Studies, Riverdale, NY 10471. Offers organizational leadership (MS). *Entrance requirements:* For master's, bachelor's degree, minimum cumulative GPA of 2.75, at least three years of work experience. Additional exam requirements/recommendations for international students: Required—TOEFL or IELTS. *Application deadline:* For fall admission, 8/1 for domestic students; for spring admission, 11/15 for domestic students. Electronic applications accepted. *Expenses:* Contact institution. *Unit head:* Cheryl Harrison, Dean, 718-862-7862, E-mail: cheryl.harrison@manhattan.edu. *Application contact:* William Bisset, Vice President for Enrollment Management, 718-862-7199, Fax: 718-862-8019, E-mail: william.bisset@manhattan.edu.
Website: https://manhattan.edu/academics/schools-and-departments/scps/

Manhattanville College, School of Business, Master of Science in Human Resource Management and Organizational Effectiveness Program, Purchase, NY 10577-2132. Offers human resource management (MS); organizational effectiveness (MS). *Program availability:* Part-time, evening/weekend. *Students:* 24 (21 women); includes 13 minority (5 Black or African American, non-Hispanic/Latino; 2 Asian, non-Hispanic/Latino; 6 Hispanic/Latino). Average age 32. 18 applicants, 39% accepted, 5 enrolled. In 2016, 4 master's awarded. *Degree requirements:* For master's, thesis (for some programs), final project. *Entrance requirements:* For master's, transcripts, 2 letters of recommendation, resume. Additional exam requirements/recommendations for international students: Required—TOEFL (minimum score 563 paper-based; 85 iBT). *Application deadline:* Applications are processed on a rolling basis. Application fee: $75. Electronic applications accepted. *Expenses: Tuition:* Full-time $16,470; part-time $915 per credit. *Required fees:* $60 per semester. Part-time tuition and fees vary according to course load and program. *Financial support:* Federal Work-Study, institutionally sponsored loans, scholarships/grants, and unspecified assistantships available. Financial award applicants required to submit FAFSA. *Faculty research:* Alternative dispute resolution in employment law. *Unit head:* Laura Persky, Graduate Program Director, 914-323-5188, E-mail: laura.persky@mville.edu. *Application contact:* Monika Pottgen, Assistant Director, Recruitment and Admissions, 914-323-5150, E-mail: business@mville.edu.
Website: https://www.mville.edu/programs/ms-human-resource-management

Mansfield University of Pennsylvania, Graduate Studies, Program in Organizational Leadership, Mansfield, PA 16933. Offers MA. *Program availability:* Online learning.

Marian University, School of Business and Public Safety, Fond du Lac, WI 54935-4699. Offers organizational leadership (MS). *Program availability:* Part-time, evening/weekend. *Faculty:* 4 part-time/adjunct (2 women). *Students:* 60 part-time (32 women); includes 9 minority (6 Black or African American, non-Hispanic/Latino; 1 Asian, non-Hispanic/Latino; 2 Hispanic/Latino). Average age 36. In 2016, 26 master's awarded. *Degree requirements:* For master's, comprehensive group project. *Entrance requirements:* For master's, 3 years of managerial experience, minimum GPA of 2.75, letters of professional reference. Additional exam requirements/recommendations for international students: Required—TOEFL (minimum score 525 paper-based; 70 iBT). *Application deadline:* Applications are processed on a rolling basis. Application fee: $25. Electronic applications accepted. *Expenses:* Contact institution. *Financial support:* Application deadline: 3/1; applicants required to submit FAFSA. *Faculty research:* Organizational values, statistical decision-making, learning organization, quality planning, customer research. *Unit head:* Dr. Jeffrey G. Reed, Dean, Marian School of Business, 920-923-8759, Fax: 920-923-7167, E-mail: jreed@marianuniversity.edu.

Marlboro College, Graduate and Professional Studies, Program in Business Administration, Brattleboro, VT 05301. Offers collaborative leadership (MBA); conscious business (MBA); mission driven organizations (MBA); project management (MBA); social innovation (MBA); sustainable food systems (MBA). *Program availability:* Part-time, evening/weekend, blended/hybrid learning. *Faculty:* 1 (woman) full-time, 22 part-time/adjunct (13 women). *Students:* 4 full-time (3 women), 13 part-time (11 women); includes 3 minority (1 Hispanic/Latino; 2 Two or more races, non-Hispanic/Latino). Average age 39. 5 applicants, 100% accepted, 3 enrolled. In 2016, 3 master's awarded. *Degree requirements:* For master's, 45 credits including a Master Workshop. *Entrance requirements:* For master's, letter of intent, essay, transcripts, 2 letters of recommendation. *Application deadline:* For fall admission, 7/1 priority date for domestic students; for winter admission, 11/1 priority date for domestic students. Applications are processed on a rolling basis. Application fee: $0. Electronic applications accepted. *Expenses:* $765 per credit. *Financial support:* In 2016–17, 2 students received support. Scholarships/grants available. Financial award applicants required to submit FAFSA. *Unit head:* Tristan Toleno, Degree Chair, 802-258-9200, Fax: 802-258-9201, E-mail: tristant@gradschool.marlboro.edu. *Application contact:* Kelley Barton, Admissions Counselor, 802-258-9209, Fax: 802-258-9201, E-mail: graduateadmissions@marlboro.edu.
Website: https://www.marlboro.edu/academics/graduate/management

Marlboro College, Graduate and Professional Studies, Program in Management, Marlboro, VT 05344. Offers collaborative leadership (MS); conscious business (MS); mission driven organizations (MS); project management (MS); social innovation (MS); sustainable food systems (MS). *Program availability:* Part-time, evening/weekend, blended/hybrid learning. *Faculty:* 1 (woman) full-time, 23 part-time/adjunct (14 women). *Students:* 2 full-time (both women), 12 part-time (9 women). Average age 31. 6 applicants, 33% accepted, 2 enrolled. In 2016, 13 master's awarded. *Degree requirements:* For master's, capstone project. *Entrance requirements:* For master's, statement of intent, 2 letters of recommendation. Additional exam requirements/recommendations for international students: Recommended—TOEFL (minimum score 577 paper-based; 90 iBT), IELTS (minimum score 7). *Application deadline:* For fall admission, 8/5 for domestic students; for winter admission, 12/5 for domestic students; for spring admission, 4/5 for domestic students. Applications are processed on a rolling basis. Application fee: $0. Electronic applications accepted. *Expenses:* $765 per credit. *Financial support:* Scholarships/grants available. Financial award applicants required to submit FAFSA. *Unit head:* Tristan Toleno, Degree Chair, 802-258-9200, Fax: 802-258-9201, E-mail: tristant@gradschool.marlboro.edu. *Application contact:* Kelley Barton, Admissions Counselor, 802-258-9209, Fax: 802-258-9201, E-mail: graduateadmissions@marlboro.edu.
Website: https://www.marlboro.edu/academics/graduate/management

Maryville University of Saint Louis, College of Arts and Sciences, St. Louis, MO 63141-7299. Offers actuarial science (MS); organizational leadership and development (MA); strategic communication and leadership (MA). *Program availability:* Part-time. *Faculty:* 7 full-time (4 women), 10 part-time/adjunct (7 women). *Students:* 37 full-time (16 women), 28 part-time (22 women); includes 10 minority (4 Black or African American, non-Hispanic/Latino; 1 American Indian or Alaska Native, non-Hispanic/Latino; 4 Asian, non-Hispanic/Latino; 1 Two or more races, non-Hispanic/Latino), 22 international. Average age 30. In 2016, 22 master's awarded. *Entrance requirements:* For master's, strong mathematics background, 2 letters of recommendation, and personal statement (MS). Additional exam requirements/recommendations for international students: Required—TOEFL (minimum score 550 paper-based; 80 iBT). *Application deadline:* Applications are processed on a rolling basis. Electronic applications accepted. *Expenses:* $781 per credit hour. *Financial support:* Application deadline: 3/1; applicants required to submit FAFSA. *Unit head:* Cherie Fister, Dean, 314-529-9563, Fax: 314-529-9965, E-mail: cfister@maryville.edu. *Application contact:* Crystal Jacobsmeyer, Assistant Director, Graduate Enrollment Advising, 314-529-9654, Fax: 314-529-9927, E-mail: cjacobsmeyer@maryville.edu.
Website: https://www.maryville.edu/as/

Medaille College, Program in Business Administration - Amherst, Amherst, NY 14221. Offers business administration (MBA); organizational leadership (MA). *Program availability:* Evening/weekend. *Degree requirements:* For master's, thesis or alternative. *Entrance requirements:* For master's, GMAT, minimum undergraduate GPA of 2.7, 3 years of work experience. Additional exam requirements/recommendations for international students: Required—TOEFL (minimum score 550 paper-based). Electronic applications accepted. *Expenses:* Contact institution.

Medaille College, Program in Business Administration - Rochester, Rochester, NY 14623. Offers business administration (MBA); organizational leadership (MA). *Program availability:* Evening/weekend. *Degree requirements:* For master's, thesis or alternative. *Entrance requirements:* For master's, GMAT, 3 years of work experience, minimum undergraduate GPA of 2.7. Additional exam requirements/recommendations for international students: Required—TOEFL (minimum score 550 paper-based). *Expenses:* Contact institution.

Mercer University, Graduate Studies, Cecil B. Day Campus, Penfield College, Atlanta, GA 30341. Offers certified rehabilitation counseling (MS); clinical mental health (MS); counselor education and supervision (PhD); criminal justice and public safety leadership (MS); health informatics (MS); human services (MS), including child and adolescent services, gerontology services; organizational leadership (MS); school counseling (MS). *Program availability:* Part-time, evening/weekend, 100% online, blended/hybrid learning. *Faculty:* 15 full-time (8 women), 22 part-time/adjunct (18 women). *Students:* 168 full-time (136 women), 242 part-time (201 women); includes 231 minority (192 Black or African American, non-Hispanic/Latino; 1 American Indian or Alaska Native, non-Hispanic/Latino; 15 Asian, non-Hispanic/Latino; 10 Hispanic/Latino; 1 Native Hawaiian or other Pacific Islander, non-Hispanic/Latino; 3 Two or more races, non-Hispanic/Latino), 2 international. Average age 32. 300 applicants, 45% accepted, 114 enrolled. In 2016, 92 master's, 8 doctorates awarded. *Degree requirements:* For master's, comprehensive exam (for some programs), thesis (for some programs); for doctorate, thesis/dissertation. *Entrance requirements:* For master's, GRE or MAT, Georgia Professional Standards Commission (GPSC) Certification at the SC-5 level; for doctorate, GRE or MAT. Additional exam requirements/recommendations for international students: Recommended—TOEFL (minimum score 550 paper-based; 80 iBT), IELTS (minimum score 6.5). *Application deadline:* For fall admission, 7/1 priority date for domestic and international students; for spring admission, 11/1 priority date for domestic and international students; for summer admission, 4/1 priority date for domestic and international students. Application fee: $35. Electronic applications accepted. Application fee is waived when completed online. *Expenses:* $588 per credit hour. *Financial support:* In 2016–17, 32 students received support. Federal Work-Study, scholarships/grants, and unspecified assistantships available. Financial award applicants required to submit FAFSA. *Faculty research:* Marriage and families issues, leadership and ethics, cyber-bullying, trauma, narrative counseling and theory. *Total annual research expenditures:* $85,000. *Unit head:* Dr. Priscilla R. Danheiser, Dean, 678-547-6028, Fax: 678-547-6008, E-mail: danheiser_p@mercer.edu.
Website: http://penfield.mercer.edu/programs/graduate-professional/

Mercy College, School of Business, Program in Organizational Leadership, Dobbs Ferry, NY 10522-1189. Offers MS. *Program availability:* Part-time, evening/weekend, 100% online, blended/hybrid learning. *Students:* 50 full-time (36 women), 23 part-time (16 women); includes 53 minority (33 Black or African American, non-Hispanic/Latino; 1 Asian, non-Hispanic/Latino; 17 Hispanic/Latino; 2 Two or more races, non-Hispanic/Latino), 3 international. Average age 32. 61 applicants, 84% accepted, 30 enrolled. In 2016, 11 master's awarded. *Entrance requirements:* For master's, interview by program director, resume, 2 letters of reference. Additional exam requirements/recommendations for international students: Required—TOEFL (minimum score 600 paper-based; 100 iBT), IELTS (minimum score 8). *Application deadline:* For fall admission, 8/1 for international students. Applications are processed on a rolling basis. Application fee: $40. Electronic applications accepted. *Expenses:* Contact institution. *Financial support:* Career-related internships or fieldwork, Federal Work-Study, scholarships/grants, and unspecified assistantships available. Support available to part-time students. Financial award applicants required to submit FAFSA. *Unit head:* Ed Weis, Dean, School of Business, 914-674-7490, E-mail: eweis@mercy.edu. *Application contact:* Allison Gurdineer, Senior Director of Admissions, 877-637-2946, E-mail: admissions@mercy.edu.
Website: https://www.mercy.edu/degrees-programs/ms-organizational-leadership

Mercyhurst University, Graduate Studies, Program in Organizational Leadership, Erie, PA 16546. Offers accounting (MS); higher education administration (MS); human resources (MS); organizational leadership (MS, Certificate); sports leadership (MS); strategy and innovation (MS). *Program availability:* Part-time, evening/weekend. *Degree requirements:* For master's, thesis. *Entrance requirements:* For master's, GRE General Test or MAT, interview, resume, essay, three professional references, transcripts. Additional exam requirements/recommendations for international students: Required—TOEFL (minimum score 80 iBT), IELTS (minimum score 6.5). Electronic applications accepted. *Faculty research:* Leadership training, organizational communication, leadership pedagogy.

Messiah College, Program in Business and Leadership, Mechanicsburg, PA 17055. Offers leadership (MBA, Certificate); management (Certificate); strategic leadership (MA). *Program availability:* Online learning.

Mid-America Christian University, Program in Leadership, Oklahoma City, OK 73170-4504. Offers MA. *Entrance requirements:* For master's, bachelor's degree from a regionally accredited college or university, minimum overall cumulative GPA of 2.75 of bachelor course work. Additional exam requirements/recommendations for international students: Required—TOEFL (minimum score 550 paper-based).

Midway University, Graduate Programs, Midway, KY 40347-1120. Offers education (MAT); leadership (MBA). *Degree requirements:* For master's, capstone course. *Entrance requirements:* For master's, GMAT (for MBA); GRE or PRAXIS I (for MAT), bachelor's degree; interview; minimum GPA of 3.0 (for MBA), 2.75 (for MAT); 3 years of professional work experience (for MBA). Additional exam requirements/recommendations for international students: Required—TOEFL (minimum score 550 paper-based; 80 iBT).

Misericordia University, College of Business, Program in Organizational Management, Dallas, PA 18612-1098. Offers healthcare management (MS); human resource management (MS); information technology management (MS); management (MS); not-for-profit management (MS). *Program availability:* Part-time, evening/weekend, online learning. *Entrance requirements:* For master's, GRE General Test, MAT (35th percentile or higher), or minimum undergraduate GPA of 3.0. Additional exam requirements/recommendations for international students: Required—TOEFL. Electronic applications accepted. Application fee is waived when completed online. *Expenses:* Contact institution.

Mount St. Joseph University, Master of Science in Organizational Leadership Program, Cincinnati, OH 45233-1670. Offers MS. *Program availability:* Part-time, evening/weekend. *Students:* 57 part-time (32 women); includes 11 minority (9 Black or African American, non-Hispanic/Latino; 1 Hispanic/Latino; 1 Two or more races, non-Hispanic/Latino). Average age 43. In 2016, 10 master's awarded. *Degree requirements:* For master's, 36 credit hours. *Entrance requirements:* For master's, minimum GPA of 3.0, interview, 3 years of work experience, 2 letters of reference, resume, letter of intent, essay, official transcript. Additional exam requirements/recommendations for international students: Required—TOEFL (minimum score 560 paper-based; 83 iBT). *Application deadline:* Applications are processed on a rolling basis. Application fee: $50. Electronic applications accepted. *Expenses:* $635 per credit hour. *Financial support:* Applicants required to submit FAFSA. *Faculty research:* Gender and cultural effects on management education, group identity formation, leadership skill development, methods for improving instructional effectiveness, technology-based productivity improvement. *Unit head:* Dr. Anna Goldhahn, Interim Dean, 513-244-4924, Fax: 513-244-4270, E-mail: anna.goldhahn@msj.edu. *Application contact:* Mary Brigham, Assistant Director of Graduate Recruitment, 513-244-4233, Fax: 513-244-4629, E-mail: mary.brigham@msj.edu.
Website: http://www.msj.edu/academics/graduate-programs/master-of-science-in-organizational-leadership-program/

Neumann University, Program in Organizational and Strategic Leadership, Aston, PA 19014-1298. Offers MS. *Program availability:* Part-time, evening/weekend, 100% online, blended/hybrid learning. *Faculty:* 9 part-time/adjunct (3 women). *Students:* 5 full-time (3 women), 88 part-time (50 women); includes 27 minority (21 Black or African American, non-Hispanic/Latino; 5 Hispanic/Latino; 1 Two or more races, non-Hispanic/Latino), 1 international. Average age 37. 83 applicants, 75% accepted, 52 enrolled. In 2016, 49 master's awarded. *Degree requirements:* For master's, project. *Entrance requirements:* For master's, official transcripts from all institutions attended, current resume, letter of intent, official letter of recommendation. Additional exam requirements/recommendations for international students: Required—TOEFL (minimum score 70 iBT). *Application deadline:* Applications are processed on a rolling basis. Application fee: $0. Electronic applications accepted. *Expenses:* $615 per credit. *Financial support:* Scholarships/grants and health care benefits available. Support available to part-time students. Financial award application deadline: 3/15; financial award applicants required to submit FAFSA. *Unit head:* Dr. Samuel Lemon, Program Director, Master of Science in Organizational and Strategic Leadership Program, 610-361-5239, Fax: 610-361-5235, E-mail: lemons@neumann.edu. *Application contact:* Janice Sackawicz, Coordinator of Student Services, Division of Continuing Adult and Professional Studies, 610-558-5629, Fax: 610-361-5235, E-mail: CAPS@neumann.edu.

New Jersey City University, School of Business, Program in Organizational Management and Leadership, Jersey City, NJ 07305-1597. Offers MBA.

Newman University, Master of Science in Education Program, Wichita, KS 67213-2097. Offers building leadership (MS Ed); curriculum and instruction (MS Ed), including English as a second language, reading specialist; organizational leadership (MS Ed). *Accreditation:* NCATE. *Program availability:* Part-time, evening/weekend, online learning. *Degree requirements:* For master's, thesis optional. *Entrance requirements:* For master's, 3 years' full-time teaching experience, minimum GPA of 3.0, writing sample, 2 letters of recommendation, evidence of teaching certification. Additional exam requirements/recommendations for international students: Required—TOEFL (minimum score 600 paper-based; 100 iBT). Electronic applications accepted. *Expenses:* Contact institution. *Faculty research:* Online course design and deliver, staff engagement, classroom action.

Newman University, MBA Program, Wichita, KS 67213-2097. Offers finance (MBA); international business (MBA); leadership (MBA); management (MBA); management information technology (MBA). *Program availability:* Part-time. *Degree requirements:* For master's, thesis optional. *Entrance requirements:* For master's, minimum GPA of 3.0; 2 letters of recommendation; course work in algebra, statistics, macroeconomics, and financial accounting. Additional exam requirements/recommendations for international students: Required—TOEFL (minimum score 600 paper-based; 100 iBT). Electronic applications accepted. *Expenses:* Contact institution.

The New School, Schools of Public Engagement, Program in Organizational Change Management, New York, NY 10011. Offers leadership and change (Graduate Certificate); organizational change management (MS); organizational development (Graduate Certificate). *Program availability:* Part-time, evening/weekend. *Faculty:* 34 full-time (16 women), 8 part-time/adjunct (4 women). *Students:* 23 full-time (19 women), 29 part-time (22 women); includes 21 minority (9 Black or African American, non-Hispanic/Latino; 1 Asian, non-Hispanic/Latino; 10 Hispanic/Latino; 1 Two or more races, non-Hispanic/Latino), 6 international. Average age 33. 40 applicants, 80% accepted, 17 enrolled. In 2016, 18 master's, 14 other advanced degrees awarded. *Degree requirements:* For master's, thesis or alternative, capstone project: Paper of Publishable Quality (PPQ). *Entrance requirements:* For master's, minimum of three years' full-time organizational work experience, two letters of recommendation, statement of purpose, resume, transcripts. Additional exam requirements/recommendations for international students: Required—TOEFL (minimum score 100 iBT), IELTS (minimum score 7), PTE (minimum score 68). *Application deadline:* For fall admission, 1/15 priority date for domestic and international students; for spring admission, 10/15 priority date for domestic and international students. Applications are processed on a rolling basis. Application fee: $50. Electronic applications accepted. *Expenses:* Contact institution. *Financial support:* Research assistantships, career-related internships or fieldwork, Federal Work-Study, scholarships/grants, and unspecified assistantships available. Support available to part-time students. Financial award application deadline: 2/1; financial award applicants required to submit FAFSA. *Faculty research:* Change management, leadership development, leadership transition, organization development consulting, organizational vision. *Unit head:* Suzanne Bostwick, Chair, 212-229-5400 Ext. 1601, E-mail: bostwics@newschool.edu. *Application contact:* Sharon Greenidge, Assistant Director, 212-229-5400 Ext. 1103, E-mail: greenids@newschool.edu.
Website: http://www.newschool.edu/

New York University, Leonard N. Stern School of Business, Department of Management and Organizations, New York, NY 10012-1019. Offers management organizations (MBA); organization theory (PhD); organizational behavior (PhD); strategy (PhD). *Faculty research:* Strategic management, managerial cognition, interpersonal processes, conflict and negotiation.

New York University, School of Continuing and Professional Studies, Division of Programs in Business, Program in Leadership and Human Capital Management, New York, NY 10012-1019. Offers benefits and compensation (Advanced Certificate); human resource management (Advanced Certificate); human resource management and development (MS), including global talent management, human resource management, organizational effectiveness; organizational and executive coaching (Advanced Certificate). *Program availability:* Part-time, evening/weekend, online learning. *Degree requirements:* For master's, thesis. *Entrance requirements:* For master's, GRE or GMAT (only upon request), bachelor's degree, resume with relevant professional work, internship or volunteer experience, two letters of recommendation, statement of purpose. Additional exam requirements/recommendations for international students: Required—TOEFL (minimum score 600 paper-based; 100 iBT), IELTS (minimum score 7). Electronic applications accepted.

Nichols College, Graduate and Professional Studies, Dudley, MA 01571-5000. Offers business administration (MBA); organizational leadership (MSOL). *Program availability:* Part-time, evening/weekend, online learning. *Degree requirements:* For master's, project (for MOL). *Entrance requirements:* For master's, 2 letters of recommendation, current resume, official transcripts, 800-word personal statement. Additional exam requirements/recommendations for international students: Required—TOEFL (minimum score 500 paper-based). Electronic applications accepted.

Northern Kentucky University, Office of Graduate Programs, College of Business, Program in Executive Leadership and Organizational Change, Highland Heights, KY 41099. Offers MS. *Program availability:* Part-time, evening/weekend. *Entrance requirements:* For master's, resume, current career essay, future career objectives essay, personal statement, 3 letters of recommendation with cover forms, transcripts. Additional exam requirements/recommendations for international students: Required—TOEFL (minimum score 79 iBT); Recommended—IELTS (minimum score 6.5). Electronic applications accepted. *Expenses:* Contact institution. *Faculty research:* Leadership assessment and development, teams and conflict management, organizational strategy development and systems thinking, organizational consultation.

Northwestern University, The Graduate School, Kellogg School of Management, Department of Management and Organizations, Evanston, IL 60208. Offers PhD. Admissions and degree offered through The Graduate School. *Degree requirements:* For doctorate, comprehensive exam, thesis/dissertation. *Entrance requirements:* For doctorate, GMAT or GRE General Test. Additional exam requirements/recommendations for international students: Required—TOEFL. Electronic applications accepted. *Faculty research:* Bargaining and negotiation, organizational design, decision-making, organizational change, strategic alliances.

Northwestern University, The Graduate School, Kellogg School of Management, Management Programs, Evanston, IL 60208. Offers accounting information and management (MBA, PhD); analytical finance (MBA); business administration (MBA); decision sciences (MBA); entrepreneurship and innovation (MBA); finance (MBA, PhD); health enterprise management (MBA); human resources management (MBA); international business (MBA); management and organizations (MBA, PhD); management and organizations and sociology (PhD); management and strategy (MBA); management studies (MS); managerial analytics (MBA); managerial economics (MBA); managerial economics and strategy (PhD); marketing (MBA, PhD); marketing management (MBA); media management (MBA); operations management (MBA, PhD); real estate (MBA); social enterprise at Kellogg (MBA); JD/MBA. *Program availability:* Part-time, evening/weekend. Terminal master's awarded for partial completion of doctoral program. *Degree requirements:* For doctorate, thesis/dissertation, 2 years of coursework, qualifying (field) exam and candidacy, summer research papers and presentations to faculty, proposal defense, final exam/defense. *Entrance requirements:* For master's, GMAT, GRE, interview, 2 letters of recommendation, college transcripts, resume, essays, Kellogg honor code; for doctorate, GMAT, GRE, statement of purpose, transcripts, 2 letters of recommendation, resume, interview. Additional exam requirements/recommendations for international students: Required—TOEFL, IELTS. Electronic applications accepted. *Expenses:* Contact institution. *Faculty research:* Business cycles and international finance, health policy, networks, non-market strategy, consumer psychology.

Northwestern University, The Graduate School, School of Education and Social Policy, Program in Learning and Organizational Change, Evanston, IL 60208. Offers MS. *Program availability:* Part-time, evening/weekend, online learning. *Degree requirements:* For master's, thesis, practicum. *Entrance requirements:* For master's, GRE or GMAT (recommended), letters of recommendation. Additional exam requirements/recommendations for international students: Required—TOEFL (minimum score 600 paper-based; 100 iBT); Recommended—IELTS (minimum score 7). Electronic applications accepted. *Faculty research:* Strategic change, learning and performance, workplace learning, leadership development, cognitive design, knowledge management.

Northwest University, College of Business, Kirkland, WA 98033. Offers business administration (MBA); international business (MBA); project management (MBA); social entrepreneurship (MBA). *Accreditation:* ACBSP. *Program availability:* Part-time, evening/weekend. *Degree requirements:* For master's, formalized research. *Entrance requirements:* For master's, GMAT. Additional exam requirements/recommendations for international students: Required—TOEFL (minimum score 550 paper-based; 75 iBT). Electronic applications accepted. *Expenses:* Contact institution.

Norwich University, College of Graduate and Continuing Studies, Master of Business Administration Program, Northfield, VT 05663. Offers construction management (MBA); energy management (MBA); finance (MBA); logistics (MBA); organizational leadership (MBA); project management (MBA); supply chain management (MBA). *Accreditation:* ACBSP. *Program availability:* Evening/weekend, online only, mostly all online with a week-long residency requirement. *Faculty:* 24 part-time/adjunct (5 women). *Students:* 228 full-time (54 women); includes 54 minority (23 Black or African American, non-Hispanic/Latino; 1 American Indian or Alaska Native, non-Hispanic/Latino; 6 Asian, non-Hispanic/Latino; 20 Hispanic/Latino; 1 Native Hawaiian or other Pacific Islander, non-Hispanic/Latino; 3 Two or more races, non-Hispanic/Latino), 2 international. Average age 36. 74 applicants, 100% accepted, 57 enrolled. In 2016, 135 master's awarded. *Degree requirements:* For master's, comprehensive exam. *Entrance requirements:* For master's, minimum undergraduate GPA of 2.75. Additional exam requirements/recommendations for international students: Required—TOEFL (minimum score 550 paper-based; 80 iBT), IELTS (minimum score 6.5). *Application deadline:* For fall admission, 8/14 for domestic and international students; for winter admission, 11/13 for domestic and international students; for spring admission, 2/12 for domestic and international students; for summer admission, 6/5 for domestic and international students. Electronic applications accepted. *Expenses:* Contact institution. *Financial support:* In 2016–17, 113 students received support. Scholarships/grants available. Financial award application deadline: 8/4; financial award applicants required to submit FAFSA. *Unit head:* Dr. Jose Cordova, Program Director, 802-485-2567, Fax: 802-485-2533, E-mail: jcordova@norwich.edu. *Application contact:* Admissions Advisor, 800-460-5597 Ext. 3376, Fax: 802-485-2533, E-mail: mba@online.norwich.edu.
Website: https://online.norwich.edu/degree-programs/masters/master-business-administration/overview

Norwich University, College of Graduate and Continuing Studies, Master of Science in Executive Leadership Program, Northfield, VT 05663. Offers MS. *Program availability:* Evening/weekend, online only, mostly all online with a week-long residency requirement. *Degree requirements:* For master's, capstone. *Entrance requirements:* For master's, minimum of eight years of formal leadership experience, minimum GPA of 2.75. Additional exam requirements/recommendations for international students: Required—TOEFL (minimum score 550 paper-based; 80 iBT), IELTS (minimum score 6.5). *Application deadline:* For fall admission, 8/14 for domestic and international students; for winter admission, 11/13 for domestic and international students; for spring admission, 2/12 for domestic and international students; for summer admission, 6/5 for domestic and international students. Electronic applications accepted. *Expenses:* Contact institution. *Financial support:* Scholarships/grants available. Financial award application deadline: 8/4; financial award applicants required to submit FAFSA. *Unit head:* Dr. Stacie Morgan, Director, 866-684-7237, Fax: 802-485-2533. *Application contact:* Admissions Advisor, 866-684-7237, Fax: 802-485-2533.
Website: https://online.norwich.edu/degree-programs/masters/master-science-executive-leadership/overview

Norwich University, College of Graduate and Continuing Studies, Master of Science in Leadership Program, Northfield, VT 05663. Offers leadership (MS), including human resources leadership, leading change management consulting, organizational leadership, public sector/government/military leadership. *Program availability:* Evening/weekend, online only, mostly all online with a week-long residency requirement. *Faculty:* 10 part-time/adjunct (2 women). *Students:* 66 full-time (20 women); includes 13 minority (8 Black or African American, non-Hispanic/Latino; 3 Asian, non-Hispanic/Latino; 1 Hispanic/Latino; 1 Two or more races, non-Hispanic/Latino). Average age 37. 13 applicants, 69% accepted, 6 enrolled. In 2016, 34 master's awarded. *Degree requirements:* For master's, capstone. *Entrance requirements:* For master's, minimum undergraduate GPA of 2.75. Additional exam requirements/recommendations for international students: Required—TOEFL (minimum score 550 paper-based; 80 iBT), IELTS (minimum score 6.5). *Application deadline:* For fall admission, 8/14 for domestic and international students; for winter admission, 11/13 for domestic and international students; for spring admission, 2/13 for domestic and international students; for summer admission, 5/15 for domestic and international students. Electronic applications accepted. *Expenses:* Contact institution. *Financial support:* In 2016–17, 46 students received support. Scholarships/grants available. Financial award application deadline: 8/4; financial award applicants required to submit FAFSA. *Unit head:* Dr. Stacie Morgan, Program Director, 802-485-2866, Fax: 802-485-2533, E-mail: smorgan3@norwich.edu. *Application contact:* Admissions Advisor, 800-460-5597 Ext. 3371, Fax: 802-485-2533, E-mail: msl@online.norwich.edu.
Website: https://online.norwich.edu/degree-programs/masters/master-science-leadership/overview

Nyack College, School of Business and Leadership, Nyack, NY 10960. Offers business administration (MBA); organizational leadership (MS). *Program availability:* Part-time, evening/weekend, 100% online, blended/hybrid learning. *Students:* 45 full-time (21 women), 20 part-time (15 women); includes 40 minority (26 Black or African American, non-Hispanic/Latino; 1 American Indian or Alaska Native, non-Hispanic/Latino; 4 Asian, non-Hispanic/Latino; 9 Hispanic/Latino), 5 international. Average age 38. In 2016, 40 master's awarded. *Degree requirements:* For master's, thesis (for some programs), capstone project (for MBA). *Entrance requirements:* For master's, GMAT (for MBA only), transcripts, personal goals statement, recommendations, resume, interview. Additional exam requirements/recommendations for international students: Required—TOEFL (minimum score 550 paper-based; 80 iBT), IELTS (minimum score 6.5). *Application deadline:* Applications are processed on a rolling basis. Application fee: $50. Electronic applications accepted. *Expenses:* $700 per credit (for MS); $775 per credit (for MBA). *Financial support:* Scholarships/grants available. Financial award applicants required to submit FAFSA. *Unit head:* Dr. Anita Underwood, Dean, 845-675-4511, Fax: 845-353-5812. *Application contact:* Joseph M. Williams, Graduate Admissions Associate, 800-

541-6891, Fax: 845-348-3912, E-mail: admissions.grad@nyack.edu.
Website: http://www.nyack.edu/sbl

Nyack College, School of Social Work, Nyack, NY 10960. Offers clinical social work practice (MSW); leadership in organizations and communities (MSW). *Program availability:* Part-time, evening/weekend. *Students:* 40 full-time (35 women), 29 part-time (27 women); includes 58 minority (32 Black or African American, non-Hispanic/Latino; 1 American Indian or Alaska Native, non-Hispanic/Latino; 5 Asian, non-Hispanic/Latino; 18 Hispanic/Latino; 2 Two or more races, non-Hispanic/Latino), 1 international. Average age 35. In 2016, 8 master's awarded. *Degree requirements:* For master's, field work. *Entrance requirements:* For master's, official transcripts, academic and professional references, personal statement, essay or case reflection. Additional exam requirements/recommendations for international students: Required—TOEFL (minimum score 550 paper-based; 80 iBT). *Application deadline:* Applications are processed on a rolling basis. Application fee: $45. Electronic applications accepted. *Expenses:* $775 per credit. *Financial support:* Institutionally sponsored loans available. Financial award applicants required to submit FAFSA. *Unit head:* Dr. Janet Furness, Director of MSW Program, 646-378-6169, E-mail: janet.furness@nyack.edu. *Application contact:* Apryll Campbell, Admissions Associate, 646-378-6195, E-mail: admissions.grad@nyack.edu.
Website: https://www.nyack.edu/msw

Oakland University, Graduate Study and Lifelong Learning, School of Education and Human Services, Department of Organizational Leadership, Rochester, MI 48309-4401. Offers educational leadership (M Ed, PhD); higher education (Certificate); school administration (Ed S). *Entrance requirements:* Additional exam requirements/recommendations for international students: Required—TOEFL (minimum score 550 paper-based).

Ohio Christian University, Graduate Programs, Circleville, OH 43113-9487. Offers accounting (MBA); business administration (MBA); digital marketing (MBA); finance (MBA); healthcare management (MBA); human resources (MBA); management (MM); organizational leadership (MBA); pastoral care and counseling (MAM); practical theology (MAM).

Oklahoma Christian University, Graduate School of Business, Oklahoma City, OK 73136-1100. Offers accounting (M Acc, MBA); financial services (MBA); general business (MBA); health services management (MBA); human resources (MBA); international business (MBA); leadership and organizational development (MBA); marketing (MBA); nonprofit management (MBA); project management (MBA). *Accreditation:* ACBSP. *Program availability:* Part-time, 100% online. *Faculty:* 10 full-time (2 women), 21 part-time/adjunct (2 women). *Students:* 156 full-time (68 women), 137 part-time (73 women). Average age 30. 374 applicants, 213 enrolled. In 2016, 114 master's awarded. *Entrance requirements:* For master's, bachelor's degree. Additional exam requirements/recommendations for international students: Required—TOEFL (minimum score 550 paper-based). Application fee: $25. Electronic applications accepted. *Expenses:* Contact institution. *Unit head:* Dr. Ken Johnson, Chair, 405-425-5567, Fax: 405-425-5585, E-mail: ken.johnson@oc.edu. *Application contact:* Angie Ricketts, Graduate School Admissions Counselor, 405-425-5587, Fax: 405-425-5585, E-mail: angie.ricketts@oc.edu.
Website: http://www.oc.edu/academics/graduate/business/

Olivet Nazarene University, Program in Organizational Leadership, Bourbonnais, IL 60914. Offers MOL.

Oregon State University, College of Business, Program in Business Administration, Corvallis, OR 97331. Offers business administration (PhD), including accounting, innovation/commercialization; business analytics (MBA); corporate finance (MBA); innovation management (MBA); organizational leadership (MBA); research thesis (MBA); supply chain and logistics management (MBA). *Program availability:* Part-time, blended/hybrid learning. *Faculty:* 47 full-time (13 women), 10 part-time/adjunct (3 women). *Students:* 132 full-time (58 women), 83 part-time (36 women); includes 24 minority (3 Black or African American, non-Hispanic/Latino; 11 Asian, non-Hispanic/Latino; 8 Hispanic/Latino; 1 Native Hawaiian or other Pacific Islander, non-Hispanic/Latino; 1 Two or more races, non-Hispanic/Latino), 91 international. Average age 30. 203 applicants, 38% accepted, 67 enrolled. In 2016, 81 master's awarded. *Entrance requirements:* For master's, GMAT. Additional exam requirements/recommendations for international students: Required—TOEFL (minimum score 91 iBT), IELTS (minimum score 7). *Application deadline:* For fall admission, 2/1 priority date for domestic and international students; for winter admission, 9/15 priority date for domestic and international students; for spring admission, 1/1 priority date for domestic and international students. Applications are processed on a rolling basis. Application fee: $75 ($85 for international students). *Expenses:* $19,143 resident full-time tuition, $32,616 non-resident (for MBA). *Financial support:* Application deadline: 1/15. *Unit head:* Dr. David Baldridge, Director for Business Master's Program, 541-737-6062, E-mail: david.baldridge@bus.oregonstate.edu. *Application contact:* E-mail: osumba@bus.oregonstate.edu.
Website: http://business.oregonstate.edu/graduate-programs

Our Lady of the Lake University, School of Business and Leadership, Program in Leadership Studies, San Antonio, TX 78207-4689. Offers PhD. *Program availability:* Part-time, evening/weekend. *Faculty:* 9 full-time (6 women), 9 part-time/adjunct (3 women). *Students:* 284 full-time (168 women), 7 part-time (4 women); includes 223 minority (31 Black or African American, non-Hispanic/Latino; 3 Asian, non-Hispanic/Latino; 186 Hispanic/Latino; 1 Native Hawaiian or other Pacific Islander, non-Hispanic/Latino; 2 Two or more races, non-Hispanic/Latino), 1 international. Average age 45. 64 applicants, 81% accepted, 43 enrolled. In 2016, 25 doctorates awarded. *Degree requirements:* For doctorate, comprehensive exam, thesis/dissertation. *Entrance requirements:* For doctorate, GRE or MAT, master's degree with minimum of 36 credit hours in appropriate field from regionally-accredited college or university; minimum GPA of 3.3 in all previous master's degree work (preferred); résumé; personal statement. Additional exam requirements/recommendations for international students: Required—TOEFL. *Application deadline:* For fall admission, 5/15 for domestic and international students. Application fee: $40 ($50 for international students). Electronic applications accepted. Application fee is waived when completed online. *Expenses:* Contact institution. *Financial support:* In 2016–17, 6 students received support. Federal Work-Study, scholarships/grants, unspecified assistantships, and tuition discounts available. Support available to part-time students. Financial award application deadline: 5/1; financial award applicants required to submit FAFSA. *Unit head:* Dr. Esther Gergen, Chair of Leadership Department, 210-434-6711 Ext. 2287, E-mail: esgergen@lake.ollusa.edu. *Application contact:* Office of Graduate Admissions, 210-434-3995, Fax: 210-431-3945, E-mail: gradadm@ollusa.edu.
Website: http://www.ollusa.edu/s/1190/hybrid/default-hybrid-ollu.aspx?sid-1190&gid-1&pgid-7956

Our Lady of the Lake University, School of Business and Leadership, Program in Organizational Leadership, San Antonio, TX 78207-4689. Offers MS. *Program availability:* Part-time, evening/weekend. *Faculty:* 4 full-time (2 women), 13 part-time/adjunct (6 women). *Students:* 62 full-time (40 women), 5 part-time (4 women); includes 58 minority (2 Black or African American, non-Hispanic/Latino; 2 American Indian or Alaska Native, non-Hispanic/Latino; 1 Asian, non-Hispanic/Latino; 52 Hispanic/Latino; 1 Two or more races, non-Hispanic/Latino), 2 international. Average age 35. 38 applicants, 87% accepted, 24 enrolled. In 2016, 23 master's awarded. *Entrance requirements:* For master's, official transcripts showing minimum cumulative GPA of 2.5, 2 letters of recommendation, resume, personal statement. Additional exam requirements/recommendations for international students: Required—TOEFL. *Application deadline:* For fall admission, 6/15 for domestic and international students; for spring admission, 11/15 for domestic and international students. Application fee: $40 ($50 for international students). Electronic applications accepted. *Expenses: Tuition:* Full-time $14,796. Tuition and fees vary according to course load, degree level, campus/location and program. *Financial support:* In 2016–17, 33 students received support. Federal Work-Study, scholarships/grants, unspecified assistantships, and tuition discounts available. Support available to part-time students. Financial award application deadline: 5/1; financial award applicants required to submit FAFSA. *Unit head:* School of Business and Leadership, 210-434-6711 Ext. 2281, E-mail: sbdean@ollusa.edu. *Application contact:* Graduate Admission, 210-431-3995, Fax: 210-431-3945, E-mail: gradadm@ollusa.edu.
Website: http://www.ollusa.edu/s/1190/hybrid/default-hybrid-ollu.aspx?sid-1190&gid-1&pgid-7906

Oxford Graduate School, Graduate Programs, Dayton, TN 37321-6736. Offers family life education (M Litt); integration of religion and society (D Phil); organizational leadership (M Litt). *Faculty:* 10 full-time (2 women), 22 part-time/adjunct (7 women). *Students:* 105 full-time (40 women). *Entrance requirements:* For master's, official transcripts, three letters of recommendation, bachelor's degree or its equivalent, minimum undergraduate GPA of 3.0, minimum of 3 years of professional experience; for doctorate, official transcripts, three letters of recommendation, master's degree with minimum GPA of 3.0, minimum of 5 years of professional experience. *Expenses:* $7,875 per year (for D Phil); $6,000 per year (for M Litt). *Application contact:* Gwen Ballant, Director of Admissions, 423-775-6596, Fax: 423-775-6599, E-mail: oxfordgraduateschool@ogs.edu.

Palm Beach Atlantic University, MacArthur School of Leadership, West Palm Beach, FL 33416-4708. Offers MS. *Program availability:* Part-time, evening/weekend, blended/hybrid learning. *Faculty:* 8 part-time/adjunct (1 woman). *Students:* 59 full-time (40 women), 16 part-time (8 women); includes 49 minority (24 Black or African American, non-Hispanic/Latino; 2 Asian, non-Hispanic/Latino; 18 Hispanic/Latino; 5 Two or more races, non-Hispanic/Latino), 2 international. Average age 39. 27 applicants, 96% accepted, 19 enrolled. In 2016, 37 master's awarded. *Entrance requirements:* For master's, minimum GPA of 3.0; essay. Additional exam requirements/recommendations for international students: Required—TOEFL (minimum score 550 paper-based; 79 iBT). *Application deadline:* Applications are processed on a rolling basis. Application fee: $50. Electronic applications accepted. *Expenses: Tuition:* Full-time $6600; part-time $550 per credit hour. Full-time tuition and fees vary according to degree level, campus/location and program. *Financial support:* Scholarships/grants and employee education grants available. Financial award application deadline: 5/1; financial award applicants required to submit FAFSA. *Faculty research:* Ethics, business strategies, organizational leadership. *Unit head:* Dr. Craig Domeck, Dean, 561-803-2318, E-mail: craig_domeck@pba.edu. *Application contact:* Graduate Admissions, 888-468-6722, E-mail: grad@pba.edu.
Website: http://learn-well.pba.edu/leadership?SectionOverride=55

Peirce College, Program in Organizational Leadership and Management, Philadelphia, PA 19102-4699. Offers MS. *Degree requirements:* For master's, capstone project. *Entrance requirements:* For master's, official transcripts, current resume, statement of intent, two letters of recommendation.

Penn State University Park, Graduate School, Smeal College of Business, University Park, PA 16802. Offers accounting (M Acc); business administration (MBA, MS, PhD); management and organizational leadership (MPS); supply chain management (MPS). *Accreditation:* AACSB. *Students:* 276 full-time (90 women). Average age 30. 1,243 applicants, 26% accepted, 260 enrolled. In 2016, 274 master's, 11 doctorates awarded. *Entrance requirements:* Additional exam requirements/recommendations for international students: Required—TOEFL (minimum score 550 paper-based; 80 iBT), IELTS. *Application deadline:* Applications are processed on a rolling basis. Application fee: $65. Electronic applications accepted. *Financial support:* Fellowships, research assistantships, teaching assistantships, career-related internships or fieldwork, Federal Work-Study, scholarships/grants, traineeships, health care benefits, and unspecified assistantships available. Support available to part-time students. Financial award application deadline: 3/1; financial award applicants required to submit FAFSA. *Unit head:* Dr. Charles H. Whiteman, Dean, 814-863-0448, Fax: 814-865-7064. *Application contact:* Lori Hawn, Director, Graduate Student Services, 814-865-1795, Fax: 814-863-4627, E-mail: l-gswww@lists.psu.edu.
Website: http://smeal.psu.edu/

Pepperdine University, Graduate School of Education and Psychology, Division of Education, Los Angeles, CA 90045. Offers administration and preliminary administrative services (MS); education (MA); educational leadership, administration, and policy (Ed D); global leadership and change (PhD); learning technologies (MA, Ed D); organizational leadership (Ed D); social entrepreneurship and change (MA); teaching (MA); teaching: TESOL (MA). *Program availability:* Part-time, evening/weekend, online learning. *Students:* 262 full-time (169 women), 385 part-time (264 women); includes 286 minority (123 Black or African American, non-Hispanic/Latino; 4 American Indian or Alaska Native, non-Hispanic/Latino; 59 Asian, non-Hispanic/Latino; 77 Hispanic/Latino; 6 Native Hawaiian or other Pacific Islander, non-Hispanic/Latino; 17 Two or more races, non-Hispanic/Latino), 46 international. Average age 38. 372 applicants, 95% accepted, 200 enrolled. In 2016, 142 master's, 66 doctorates awarded. *Degree requirements:* For doctorate, thesis/dissertation. *Entrance requirements:* For master's, GRE General Test; for doctorate, GRE General Test, MAT. Additional exam requirements/recommendations for international students: Required—TOEFL. *Application deadline:* Applications are processed on a rolling basis. Application fee: $55. *Expenses:* $1,165 per unit (for master's); $1,460 per unit (for doctorate). *Financial support:* Research assistantships, teaching assistantships, career-related internships or fieldwork, institutionally sponsored loans, and scholarships/grants available. Support available to part-time students. Financial award application deadline: 7/1; financial award applicants required to submit FAFSA. *Unit head:* Dr. Martine Jago, Associate Dean, Education Division, 310-568-2828, E-mail: martine.jago@pepperdine.edu. *Application contact:* Chris Costa, Director of Enrollment, 310-568-2850, E-mail: chris.costa@pepperdine.edu.
Website: http://gsep.pepperdine.edu/masters-education/

Peru State College, Graduate Programs, Program in Organizational Management, Peru, NE 68421. Offers MS. Program offered online only. *Program availability:* Part-time, online learning. *Degree requirements:* For master's, thesis (for some programs). *Expenses:* Contact institution. *Faculty research:* Emotional intelligence.

Pfeiffer University, Program in Leadership and Organizational Change, Misenheimer, NC 28109-0960. Offers MS, MBA/MS. *Entrance requirements:* For master's, GRE or GMAT.

Organizational Management

Point Loma Nazarene University, Fermanian School of Business, San Diego, CA 92106-2899. Offers general business (MBA); healthcare management (MBA); innovation and entrepreneurship (MBA); organizational leadership (MBA); project management (MBA). *Accreditation:* ACBSP. *Program availability:* Part-time, evening/weekend. *Faculty:* 8 full-time (1 woman), 8 part-time/adjunct (4 women). *Students:* 33 full-time (14 women), 64 part-time (30 women); includes 32 minority (6 Black or African American, non-Hispanic/Latino; 4 Asian, non-Hispanic/Latino; 19 Hispanic/Latino; 3 Two or more races, non-Hispanic/Latino), 7 international. Average age 31. 71 applicants, 79% accepted, 47 enrolled. In 2016, 37 master's awarded. *Entrance requirements:* For master's, GMAT, letters of recommendation, essay, interview. Additional exam requirements/recommendations for international students: Required—TOEFL. *Application deadline:* For fall admission, 7/26 priority date for domestic students; for spring admission, 11/29 priority date for domestic students; for summer admission, 4/2 priority date for domestic students. Applications are processed on a rolling basis. Application fee: $50. Electronic applications accepted. *Expenses:* $825 per credit. *Financial support:* Applicants required to submit FAFSA. *Unit head:* Jamie Ressler, Associate Dean, Graduate Business, 619-849-2721, E-mail: jamieressler@pointloma.edu. *Application contact:* Claire Buckley, Director of Graduate Admission, 866-692-4723, E-mail: gradinfo@pointloma.edu.
Website: http://www.pointloma.edu/discover/graduate-school-san-diego/san-diego-graduate-programs-masters-degree-san-diego/mba

Point Loma Nazarene University, Program in Organizational Leadership, San Diego, CA 92106-2899. Offers MA. *Program availability:* Online learning. *Faculty:* 11 part-time/adjunct (2 women). *Students:* 1 full-time (0 women), 68 part-time (47 women); includes 30 minority (5 Black or African American, non-Hispanic/Latino; 1 American Indian or Alaska Native, non-Hispanic/Latino; 1 Asian, non-Hispanic/Latino; 20 Hispanic/Latino; 3 Two or more races, non-Hispanic/Latino), 1 international. Average age 35. 35 applicants, 94% accepted, 25 enrolled. *Application deadline:* For fall admission, 8/8 priority date for domestic students. *Expenses:* $485 per credit. *Unit head:* Dave Phillips, 619-619-2771, E-mail: davidphillips@pointloma.edu. *Application contact:* Claire Buckley, Director, Graduate Admissions, 866-692-4723, E-mail: gradinfo@pointloma.edu.
Website: http://gps.pointloma.edu/ma-organizational-leadership

Point Park University, School of Business, Department of Management, Pittsburgh, PA 15222-1984. Offers health care administration and management (MS); leadership (MA).

Queens University of Charlotte, McColl School of Business, Charlotte, NC 28274-0002. Offers business administration (EMBA, MBA, PMBA); organization development (MSOD). *Accreditation:* AACSB. *Program availability:* Part-time, evening/weekend, online learning. *Degree requirements:* For master's, capstone course. *Entrance requirements:* For master's, GMAT, minimum GPA of 2.5. Additional exam requirements/recommendations for international students: Required—TOEFL. Electronic applications accepted. *Expenses:* Contact institution.

Quinnipiac University, School of Business and Engineering, Program in Organizational Leadership, Hamden, CT 06518-1940. Offers MS. *Program availability:* Part-time, evening/weekend, online only, 100% online. *Faculty:* 5 full-time (3 women). *Students:* 9 full-time (8 women), 228 part-time (153 women); includes 62 minority (31 Black or African American, non-Hispanic/Latino; 5 Asian, non-Hispanic/Latino; 20 Hispanic/Latino; 6 Two or more races, non-Hispanic/Latino). 96 applicants, 93% accepted, 75 enrolled. In 2016, 83 master's awarded. *Entrance requirements:* For master's, four years of work experience. Additional exam requirements/recommendations for international students: Required—TOEFL (minimum score 575 paper-based; 90 iBT), IELTS (minimum score 6.5). *Application deadline:* For fall admission, 7/30 priority date for domestic students, 4/30 for international students; for spring admission, 12/31 priority date for domestic students, 4/30 for international students; for summer admission, 4/30 priority date for domestic students. Applications are processed on a rolling basis. Application fee: $45. Electronic applications accepted. *Expenses:* Contact institution. *Financial support:* Federal Work-Study and unspecified assistantships available. Financial award application deadline: 6/1; financial award applicants required to submit FAFSA. *Faculty research:* Virtual teams, women and leadership, virtual human resources applications and practices, emotional intelligence and its application in the workplace. *Application contact:* Quinnipiac University Online Admissions, 203-582-3918, Fax: 203-582-3443, E-mail: quonlineadmissions@qu.edu.
Website: https://quonline.quinnipiac.edu/online-programs/online-graduate-programs/ms-in-organizational-leadership/

Regent University, Graduate School, School of Business and Leadership, Virginia Beach, VA 23464-9800. Offers business administration (MBA), including accounting, entrepreneurship, finance and investing, general management, healthcare management (MA, MBA), human resource management, innovation management; leadership (Certificate); organizational leadership (MA, PhD), including ecclesial leadership (PhD), entrepreneurial leadership (PhD), future studies (MA), healthcare management (MA, MBA), human resource development (PhD), interdisciplinary studies (MA), international organizations (MA), leadership coaching and mentoring (MA), not-for-profit management (MA), organizational communication (MA), organizational development consulting (MA); strategic leadership (DSL), including global consulting, leadership coaching, strategic foresight. *Program availability:* Part-time, evening/weekend, 100% online, blended/hybrid learning. *Faculty:* 9 full-time (2 women), 28 part-time/adjunct (10 women). *Students:* 100 full-time (56 women), 1,008 part-time (528 women); includes 562 minority (453 Black or African American, non-Hispanic/Latino; 7 American Indian or Alaska Native, non-Hispanic/Latino; 30 Asian, non-Hispanic/Latino; 51 Hispanic/Latino; 1 Native Hawaiian or other Pacific Islander, non-Hispanic/Latino; 20 Two or more races, non-Hispanic/Latino), 76 international. Average age 40. 1,240 applicants, 45% accepted, 352 enrolled. In 2016, 95 master's, 71 doctorates awarded. *Degree requirements:* For master's, thesis or alternative, 3-credit hour culminating experience; for doctorate, thesis/dissertation. *Entrance requirements:* For master's, college transcripts, resume, essay; for doctorate, college transcripts, resume, essay, writing sample; for Certificate, writing sample, resume, transcripts. Additional exam requirements/recommendations for international students: Required—TOEFL (minimum score 577 paper-based). *Application deadline:* For fall admission, 5/1 priority date for domestic students; for spring admission, 10/1 priority date for domestic students. Applications are processed on a rolling basis. Application fee: $50. Electronic applications accepted. *Expenses:* Contact institution. *Financial support:* In 2016–17, 631 students received support. Career-related internships or fieldwork, scholarships/grants, and unspecified assistantships available. Support available to part-time students. *Faculty research:* Servant leadership, global business, team effectiveness, technology utilization, leadership development. *Unit head:* Dr. Doris Gomez, Dean, 757-352-4686, Fax: 757-352-4634, E-mail: dorigom@regent.edu. *Application contact:* Heidi Cece, Assistant Vice President of Enrollment Management, 800-373-5504, Fax: 757-352-4381, E-mail: admissions@regent.edu.
Website: http://www.regent.edu/sbl/

Regis University, College of Business and Economics, Denver, CO 80221-1099. Offers accounting (MS); executive leadership (Certificate); finance (MS); finance and accounting (MBA); health industry leadership (MBA); human resource management and leadership (MSOL); management (MBA); marketing (MBA); nonprofit leadership (Post-Graduate Certificate); nonprofit management (MNM); nonprofit organizational capacity building (Certificate); operations management (MBA); organizational leadership and management (MSOL); project leadership and management (MS, MSOL); strategic business management (Certificate); strategic human resource integration (Certificate); strategic management (MBA). Programs offered at Colorado Springs Campus, Northwest Denver Campus, Southeast Denver Campus, Fort Collins Campus, Broomfield Campus, Henderson (Nevada) Campus, and Summerlin (Nevada) Campus. *Program availability:* Part-time, evening/weekend, 100% online, blended/hybrid learning. *Faculty:* 15 full-time (5 women), 43 part-time/adjunct (16 women). *Students:* 622 full-time (350 women), 460 part-time (170 women); includes 317 minority (88 Black or African American, non-Hispanic/Latino; 7 American Indian or Alaska Native, non-Hispanic/Latino; 44 Asian, non-Hispanic/Latino; 151 Hispanic/Latino; 1 Native Hawaiian or other Pacific Islander, non-Hispanic/Latino; 26 Two or more races, non-Hispanic/Latino), 44 international. Average age 36. 307 applicants, 73% accepted, 134 enrolled. In 2016, 394 master's awarded. *Degree requirements:* For master's, thesis (for some programs), capstone or final research project. *Entrance requirements:* For master's, official transcript reflecting baccalaureate degree awarded from regionally-accredited college or university, interview, 2 years of full-time related work experience, resume, letters of recommendation. Additional exam requirements/recommendations for international students: Required—TOEFL (minimum score 550 paper-based; 82 iBT). *Application deadline:* For fall admission, 8/15 priority date for domestic students, 8/13 for international students; for winter admission, 10/10 priority date for domestic students, 9/8 for international students; for spring admission, 1/10 priority date for domestic students, 11/17 for international students; for summer admission, 5/1 priority date for domestic students. Applications are processed on a rolling basis. Application fee: $75. Electronic applications accepted. *Expenses:* $780 per credit hour. *Financial support:* Scholarships/grants available. Financial award application deadline: 4/15; financial award applicants required to submit FAFSA. *Faculty research:* Impact of information technology on small business regulation of accounting, international project financing, mineral development, delivery of healthcare to rural indigenous communities. *Unit head:* Dr. Timothy Keane, Academic Dean. *Application contact:* Cate Clark, Director of Admissions, 303-458-4900, Fax: 303-964-5534, E-mail: ruadmissions@regis.edu.
Website: http://www.regis.edu/CBE.aspx

Rider University, Department of Graduate Education, Leadership and Counseling, Program in Organizational Leadership, Lawrenceville, NJ 08648-3001. Offers MA. *Entrance requirements:* For master's, resume.

Robert Morris University, School of Communications and Information Systems, Moon Township, PA 15108-1189. Offers communication and information systems (MS); cyber security (MS); data analytics (MS); information security and assurance (MS); information systems and communications (D Sc); information systems management (MS); information technology project management (MS); Internet information systems (MS); organizational leadership (MS). *Program availability:* Part-time, evening/weekend, online learning. *Faculty:* 28 full-time (11 women), 6 part-time/adjunct (0 women). *Students:* 269 part-time (110 women); includes 49 minority (29 Black or African American, non-Hispanic/Latino; 10 Asian, non-Hispanic/Latino; 5 Hispanic/Latino; 5 Two or more races, non-Hispanic/Latino), 49 international. Average age 34. 239 applicants, 46% accepted, 83 enrolled. In 2016, 110 master's, 15 doctorates awarded. *Degree requirements:* For doctorate, thesis/dissertation. *Entrance requirements:* For doctorate, employer letter of endorsement, interview. Additional exam requirements/recommendations for international students: Required—TOEFL (minimum score 550 paper-based; 79 iBT). *Application deadline:* For fall admission, 7/1 priority date for domestic and international students; for spring admission, 11/1 priority date for domestic and international students. Applications are processed on a rolling basis. Application fee: $35. Electronic applications accepted. Application fee is waived when completed online. *Expenses:* $870 per credit (for master's degree). *Financial support:* Institutionally sponsored loans available. Support available to part-time students. Financial award application deadline: 5/1. *Unit head:* Ann Marie M. Le Blanc, Dean, 412-397-6433, Fax: 412-397-6469, E-mail: leblanc@rmu.edu. *Application contact:* Kellie L. Laurenzi, Associate Vice President, 412-397-5200, Fax: 412-397-5915, E-mail: graduateadmissions@rmu.edu.
Website: http://www.rmu.edu/web/cms/schools/scis/Pages/default.aspx

Rochester Institute of Technology, Graduate Enrollment Services, College of Applied Science and Technology, School of International Hospitality and Service Innovation, Advanced Certificate Program in Organizational Learning, Rochester, NY 14623. Offers Advanced Certificate. *Program availability:* Part-time, evening/weekend, online only, 100% online. *Entrance requirements:* For degree, minimum GPA of 3.0 (recommended). Additional exam requirements/recommendations for international students: Required—TOEFL (minimum score 570 paper-based; 88 iBT), IELTS (minimum score 6.5), PTE (minimum score 62). *Application deadline:* Applications are processed on a rolling basis. Application fee: $60. Electronic applications accepted. *Expenses:* $1,742 per credit hour. *Financial support:* Scholarships/grants available. Support available to part-time students. Financial award applicants required to submit FAFSA. *Unit head:* Dr. Linda Underhill, Department Chair, 585-475-4399, Fax: 585-475-7080, E-mail: cast@rit.edu. *Application contact:* Diane Ellison, Associate Vice President, Graduate Enrollment Services, 585-475-2229, Fax: 585-475-7164, E-mail: gradinfo@rit.edu.
Website: http://www.rit.edu/cast/servicesystems/organizational-learning

Roosevelt University, Graduate Division, College of Education, Program in Instructional Leadership, Chicago, IL 60605. Offers MA. *Students:* 5 full-time (4 women), 63 part-time (39 women); includes 26 minority (19 Black or African American, non-Hispanic/Latino; 1 American Indian or Alaska Native, non-Hispanic/Latino; 3 Asian, non-Hispanic/Latino; 3 Hispanic/Latino). Average age 38. 30 applicants, 100% accepted, 22 enrolled. *Expenses: Tuition, area resident:* Full-time $19,566; part-time $880 per credit hour. *Required fees:* $175 per semester. One-time fee: $200. Part-time tuition and fees vary according to course load, degree level and program. *Unit head:* Roger Chamberlain, Director, 312-281-3196. *Application contact:* Angela Ryan, Director of Graduate Enrollment, 312-341-2420, Fax: 312-281-3356, E-mail: aryan@roosevelt.edu.
Website: https://www.roosevelt.edu/academics/programs/masters-in-instructional-leadership-iled

Rutgers University–Newark, Rutgers Business School–Newark and New Brunswick, Doctoral Programs in Management, Newark, NJ 07102. Offers accounting (PhD); accounting information systems (PhD); economics (PhD); finance (PhD); individualized study (PhD); information technology (PhD); international business (PhD); management science (PhD); marketing science (PhD); organizational management (PhD); science, technology and management (PhD); supply chain management (PhD). *Degree requirements:* For doctorate, comprehensive exam, thesis/dissertation. *Entrance requirements:* For doctorate, GRE or GMAT. Additional exam requirements/recommendations for international students: Required—TOEFL (minimum score 550 paper-based; 79 iBT). Electronic applications accepted.

Sage Graduate School, School of Management, Program in Organization Management, Troy, NY 12180-4115. Offers MS. *Program availability:* Part-time, evening/weekend. *Faculty:* 3 full-time (2 women), 13 part-time/adjunct (4 women). *Students:* 7 full-time (all women), 26 part-time (18 women); includes 7 minority (6 Black or African American, non-Hispanic/Latino; 1 Asian, non-Hispanic/Latino), 2 international. Average age 37. 34 applicants, 47% accepted, 10 enrolled. In 2016, 10 master's

awarded. *Degree requirements:* For master's, capstone seminar. *Entrance requirements:* For master's, minimum GPA of 2.75. Additional exam requirements/ recommendations for international students: Required—TOEFL (minimum score 550 paper-based). *Application deadline:* Applications are processed on a rolling basis. Application fee: $40. Electronic applications accepted. *Expenses: Tuition:* Full-time $12,240; part-time $680 per credit hour. Tuition and fees vary according to degree level and program. *Financial support:* Fellowships, research assistantships, Federal Work-Study, scholarships/grants, tuition waivers (partial), and unspecified assistantships available. Support available to part-time students. Financial award application deadline: 3/1; financial award applicants required to submit FAFSA. *Unit head:* Dr. Kimberly Fredericks, Dean, School of Management, 518-292-1782, Fax: 518-292-1964, E-mail: fredek1@sage.edu. *Application contact:* Wendy D. Diefendorf, Director of Graduate and Adult Admission, 518-244-2443, Fax: 518-244-6880, E-mail: diefew@sage.edu.
Website: http://www.sage.edu/academics/management/programs/organization_management/

St. Ambrose University, College of Business, Program in Organizational Leadership, Davenport, IA 52801. Offers MOL. *Program availability:* Part-time, evening/weekend. *Degree requirements:* For master's, comprehensive exam (for some programs), thesis or alternative, integration projects. *Entrance requirements:* Additional exam requirements/recommendations for international students: Required—TOEFL. Electronic applications accepted. *Expenses:* Contact institution.

St. Catherine University, Graduate Programs, Program in Organizational Leadership, St. Paul, MN 55105. Offers MA. *Program availability:* Part-time, evening/weekend. *Degree requirements:* For master's, thesis. *Entrance requirements:* For master's, GMAT, GRE General Test or MAT, 2 years of work experience, minimum GPA of 3.0. Additional exam requirements/recommendations for international students: Required—TOEFL (minimum score 600 paper-based; 100 iBT). *Expenses:* Contact institution. *Faculty research:* Ethics.

St. Edward's University, Bill Munday School of Business, Program in Leadership and Change, Austin, TX 78704. Offers MS. *Program availability:* Part-time-only, evening/ weekend. *Students:* 6 full-time (4 women), 46 part-time (30 women); includes 31 minority (9 Black or African American, non-Hispanic/Latino; 2 Asian, non-Hispanic/ Latino; 16 Hispanic/Latino; 4 Two or more races, non-Hispanic/Latino), 1 international. Average age 35. 41 applicants, 73% accepted, 20 enrolled. *Degree requirements:* For master's, completion of at least 21 semester hours of the 30 semester hours at St. Edward's University with minimum cumulative GPA of 3.0. *Entrance requirements:* For master's, minimum GPA of 2.75 in final 60 undergraduate semester credit hours of study. Additional exam requirements/recommendations for international students: Required—TOEFL (minimum score 79 iBT), IELTS (minimum score 6). *Application deadline:* For fall admission, 6/1 priority date for domestic and international students; for spring admission, 10/1 priority date for domestic and international students; for summer admission, 3/1 priority date for domestic and international students. Applications are processed on a rolling basis. Application fee: $50. Electronic applications accepted. *Expenses: Tuition:* Full-time $25,092; part-time $1394 per credit hour. *Required fees:* $75 per trimester. Full-time tuition and fees vary according to course load and program. *Unit head:* Dr. Tom Sechrest, Program Director/Associate Professor of Management, 512-637-1954, Fax: 512-428-1217, E-mail: thomasls@stedwards.edu. *Application contact:* Mike Leveriza, Graduate Recruiter, 512-448-8745, Fax: 512-464-8877, E-mail: mleveriz@stedwards.edu.

St. Joseph's College, Long Island Campus, Programs in Management, Field in Organizational Management, Patchogue, NY 11772-2399. Offers MS. *Program availability:* Evening/weekend. *Expenses: Tuition:* Full-time $16,182; part-time $899 per credit. *Required fees:* $440.

St. Joseph's College, New York, Programs in Management, Field in Organizational Management, Brooklyn, NY 11205-3688. Offers MS. *Program availability:* Evening/ weekend. *Faculty:* 5 part-time/adjunct (4 women). *Students:* 3 full-time (1 woman), 4 part-time (3 women); includes 4 minority (2 Black or African American, non-Hispanic/ Latino; 1 Asian, non-Hispanic/Latino; 1 Hispanic/Latino). Average age 40. 3 applicants, 67% accepted, 1 enrolled. In 2016, 1 master's awarded. *Entrance requirements:* For master's, official transcripts, resume, two letters of reference, verification of employment. *Application deadline:* Applications are processed on a rolling basis. Application fee: $25. Electronic applications accepted. *Expenses:* Contact institution. *Financial support:* In 2016–17, 1 student received support. *Unit head:* Charles Pendola, Director and Assistant Professor, 631-687-1297, E-mail: cpendola@sjcny.edu. *Application contact:* John Fitzgerald, Associate Director, Admissions, 718-940-5810, Fax: 718-636-8303, E-mail: jfitzgerald3@sjcny.edu.

Saint Louis University, Graduate Education, College of Education and Public Service, Department of Public Policy Studies, St. Louis, MO 63103. Offers geographic information systems (Certificate); organizational development (Certificate); public administration (MAPA); public policy analysis (PhD); urban affairs (MAUA); urban planning and real estate development (MUPRED). *Program availability:* Part-time. *Degree requirements:* For master's, comprehensive exam (for some programs), thesis (for some programs); for doctorate, comprehensive exam, thesis/dissertation, preliminary exams. *Entrance requirements:* For master's, GMAT, GRE General Test, or LSAT, letters of recommendation, resume; for doctorate, GMAT, GRE General Test, or LSAT, letters of recommendation, resumé, interview, transcripts, goal statement. Additional exam requirements/recommendations for international students: Required—TOEFL (minimum score 525 paper-based). Electronic applications accepted. *Faculty research:* Urban politics, brown fields, e-government, and administration, evaluation research, community development, electronic government and governance.

Saint Mary-of-the-Woods College, Master of Leadership Development Program, Saint Mary of the Woods, IN 47876. Offers not-for-profit leadership (MLD); organizational leadership (MLD). *Program availability:* Part-time, blended/hybrid learning. *Students:* 47 full-time (41 women); includes 4 minority (all Black or African American, non-Hispanic/ Latino). Average age 35. *Degree requirements:* For master's, thesis. *Application deadline:* Applications are processed on a rolling basis. Application fee: $0. Electronic applications accepted. *Expenses:* Contact institution. *Financial support:* Scholarships/ grants available. *Unit head:* Susan Decker, Director, Master of Leadership Development, 812-535-5206, E-mail: sdecker2@smwc.edu.

Saint Mary's College of California, Kalmanovitz School of Education, Leadership Programs, Moraga, CA 94556. Offers coaching and facilitation (MA); organizational leadership and change (MA); peacebuilding and conflict transformation (MA); social justice (MA). *Accreditation:* AACSB. *Program availability:* Part-time, evening/weekend, online learning. *Degree requirements:* For master's, research project. *Entrance requirements:* For master's, letters of recommendation, interview. Electronic applications accepted. *Expenses:* Contact institution. *Faculty research:* Leadership, organizational change, values, adult learning, transformative learning.

Saint Mary's University of Minnesota, Schools of Graduate and Professional Programs, Graduate School of Business and Technology, Organizational Leadership Program, Winona, MN 55987-1399. Offers MA. *Program availability:* Online learning. Tuition and fees vary according to degree level and program. *Unit head:* George Diaz, Director, 612-238-4510, E-mail: gdiaz@smumn.edu. *Application contact:* James Callinan, Director of Admissions for Graduate and Professional Programs, 612-728-5185, Fax: 612-728-5121, E-mail: jcallina@smumn.edu.
Website: http://www.smumn.edu/graduate-home/areas-of-study/graduate-school-of-business-technology/ma-in-organizational-leadership

San Diego Christian College, Graduate Programs, Santee, CA 92071. Offers education (MAT); organization (MSL).

Saybrook University, LIOS MA Residential Programs, Kirkland, WA 98033. Offers leadership and organization development (MA); psychology counseling (MA). *Degree requirements:* For master's, thesis (for some programs), oral exams. *Entrance requirements:* For master's, bachelor's degree from an accredited university or college. Additional exam requirements/recommendations for international students: Recommended—TOEFL, IELTS, TWE.

Saybrook University, School of Organizational Leadership and Transformation, San Francisco, CA 94612. Offers MA. Program offered jointly with Bastyr University. *Degree requirements:* For master's, thesis (for some programs), oral exams. *Entrance requirements:* For master's, bachelor's degree from an accredited college or university. *Faculty research:* Cross-functional work teams, communication, management authority, employee influence, systems theory.

Saybrook University, School of Psychology and Interdisciplinary Inquiry, San Francisco, CA 94612. Offers human science (MA, PhD), including consciousness and spirituality, humanistic and transpersonal psychology, integrative health studies, organizational systems, social transformation; organizational systems (MA, PhD), including consciousness and spirituality, humanistic and transpersonal psychology, integrative health studies, leadership of sustainable systems (MA), organizational systems, social transformation; psychology (MA, PhD), including consciousness and spirituality, creativity studies (MA), humanistic and transpersonal psychology, integrative health studies, Jungian studies, marriage and family therapy (MA), organizational systems, social transformation. *Program availability:* Online learning. Terminal master's awarded for partial completion of doctoral program. *Degree requirements:* For master's, thesis or alternative; for doctorate, thesis/dissertation. *Entrance requirements:* Additional exam requirements/recommendations for international students: Required—TOEFL (minimum score 580 paper-based; 93 iBT). Electronic applications accepted. *Faculty research:* Humanistic theory, health studies, organizational systems, consciousness and spirituality, social transformation.

Seattle University, Albers School of Business and Economics, Center for Leadership Formation, Seattle, WA 98122-1090. Offers leadership (EMBA, Certificate). *Program availability:* Evening/weekend. *Faculty:* 14 full-time (7 women), 4 part-time/adjunct (all women). *Students:* 65 full-time (28 women); includes 14 minority (2 Black or African American, non-Hispanic/Latino; 8 Asian, non-Hispanic/Latino; 3 Hispanic/Latino; 1 Two or more races, non-Hispanic/Latino). Average age 42. 42 applicants, 93% accepted, 34 enrolled. In 2016, 14 master's, 7 other advanced degrees awarded. *Entrance requirements:* For master's, GMAT or three online courses, 7 years of continuous professional experience, undergraduate degree with minimum GPA of 3.0, resume, statement of intent/interest, three letters of recommendation; for Certificate, 7 years of continuous professional experience, undergraduate degree with minimum GPA of 3.0, resume, statement of intent/interest, three letters of recommendation. Additional exam requirements/recommendations for international students: Required—TOEFL (minimum score 580 paper-based; 92 iBT), IELTS (minimum score 7), PTE (minimum score 62). *Application deadline:* Applications are processed on a rolling basis. Application fee: $55. Electronic applications accepted. *Expenses:* Contact institution. *Financial support:* In 2016–17, 15 students received support. Scholarships/grants available. Financial award applicants required to submit FAFSA. *Unit head:* Dr. Marilyn Gist, Associate Dean of Executive Education, 206-296-5413, E-mail: gistm@seattleu.edu. *Application contact:* Sommer Harrison, Manager, Graduate Programs Outreach, 206-296-2529, E-mail: emba@seattleu.edu.
Website: https://www.seattleu.edu/albers/executive/

Shippensburg University of Pennsylvania, School of Graduate Studies, College of Arts and Sciences, Department of Sociology and Anthropology, Shippensburg, PA 17257-2299. Offers organizational development and leadership (MS), including business, higher education structure and policy, historical administration, leadership in society, management information systems, public organizations. *Program availability:* Part-time, evening/weekend. *Faculty:* 4 full-time (3 women). *Students:* 11 full-time (6 women), 29 part-time (18 women); includes 9 minority (7 Black or African American, non-Hispanic/Latino; 1 Hispanic/Latino; 1 Two or more races, non-Hispanic/Latino). Average age 29. 58 applicants, 67% accepted, 21 enrolled. In 2016, 24 master's awarded. *Degree requirements:* For master's, capstone experience including internship. *Entrance requirements:* For master's, interview (if GPA less than 2.75), current resume, personal goals statement. Additional exam requirements/recommendations for international students: Required—TOEFL (minimum score 550 paper-based, 68 iBT) or IELTS (minimum score 6). *Application deadline:* For fall admission, 4/30 for international students; for spring admission, 9/30 for international students. Applications are processed on a rolling basis. Application fee: $45. Electronic applications accepted. *Expenses:* Tuition, state resident: part-time $483 per credit. Tuition, nonresident: part-time $725 per credit. *Required fees:* $141 per credit. *Financial support:* In 2016–17, 9 students received support. Career-related internships or fieldwork, scholarships/grants, unspecified assistantships, and resident hall director and student payroll positions available. Support available to part-time students. Financial award application deadline: 3/1; financial award applicants required to submit FAFSA. *Unit head:* Dr. Barbara J. Denison, Departmental Chair and Program Coordinator, 717-477-1735, Fax: 717-477-4011, E-mail: bjdeni@ship.edu. *Application contact:* Megan N. Luft, Assistant Dean of Graduate Admissions, 717-477-1231, Fax: 717-477-4016, E-mail: mnluft@ship.edu.
Website: http://www.ship.edu/odl/

Siena Heights University, Graduate College, Adrian, MI 49221-1796. Offers clinical mental health counseling (MA); educational leadership (Specialist); leadership (MA), including health care leadership, organizational leadership; teacher education (MA), including early childhood education, early childhood education: Montessori, education leadership: principal, elementary education: reading K-12, leadership: higher education, secondary education: reading K-12, special education: cognitive impairment, special education: learning disabilities. *Program availability:* Part-time, evening/weekend. *Degree requirements:* For master's, thesis, presentation. *Entrance requirements:* For master's, minimum GPA of 3.0, current resume, essay, all post-secondary transcripts, 3 letters of reference, conviction disclosure form; copy of teaching certificate (for some education programs); for Specialist, master's degree, minimum GPA of 3.0, current resume, essay, all post-secondary transcripts, 3 letters of reference, conviction disclosure form; copy of teaching certificate (for some education programs). Electronic applications accepted.

Simpson University, School of Graduate Studies, Redding, CA 96003-8606. Offers counseling psychology (MA); organizational leadership (MA). *Program availability:* Evening/weekend, 100% online, blended/hybrid learning. *Faculty:* 10 part-time/adjunct (8 women). *Students:* 30 full-time (24 women), 9 part-time (7 women); includes 11 minority (1 Black or African American, non-Hispanic/Latino; 2 Asian, non-Hispanic/ Latino; 7 Hispanic/Latino; 1 Two or more races, non-Hispanic/Latino), 1 international.

Organizational Management

Average age 35. In 2016, 17 master's awarded. *Degree requirements:* For master's, thesis optional, portfolio capstone, integrative essay. *Entrance requirements:* For master's, three letters of recommendation, personal statement, resume, transcripts, personal interview, bachelor's degree in psychology or related field with minimum GPA of 3.0 in final 60 credits (for counseling psychology); two references (for organizational leadership). Additional exam requirements/recommendations for international students: Required—TOEFL (minimum score 550 paper-based; 79 iBT). *Application deadline:* For fall admission, 3/1 for domestic and international students; for spring admission, 11/1 for domestic and international students. Application fee: $35. Electronic applications accepted. *Expenses:* $510 per credit. *Financial support:* Applicants required to submit FAFSA. *Faculty research:* Development of executive functioning in young children, cognitive neuropsychology, historical issues in the neurosciences, neurotheology. *Unit head:* Adeline Jackson, Dean, 530-226-4788, E-mail: ajackson@simpsonu.edu. *Application contact:* Stacy Burgess, Director of Admissions for Adult and Graduate Studies, 530-226-4961, E-mail: sburgess@simpsonu.edu.
Website: http://gs.simpsonu.edu/

SIT Graduate Institute, Graduate Programs, Master's Programs in Intercultural Service, Leadership, and Management, Program in Intercultural Service, Leadership, and Management (Self-Designed), Brattleboro, VT 05302-0676. Offers MA.

Southeastern University, College of Education, Lakeland, FL 33801-6099. Offers curriculum and instruction (Ed D); educational leadership (M Ed); elementary education (M Ed); exceptional student education (M Ed); exceptional student education/educational therapy (M Ed); organizational leadership (Ed D); reading education (M Ed); teaching English to speakers of other languages (M Ed). *Expenses: Tuition:* Full-time $9450; part-time $6300 per credit. *Required fees:* $500; $250 per semester. One-time fee: $150. Tuition and fees vary according to degree level, campus/location and program. *Unit head:* Amy N. Bratten, Dean, 863-667-5238, E-mail: anbratten@seu.edu.
Website: http://www.seu.edu/education/

Southern Arkansas University–Magnolia, School of Graduate Studies, Magnolia, AR 71753. Offers agriculture (MS); business administration (MBA), including agri-business, social entrepreneurship, supply chain management; clinical and mental health counseling (MS); computer and information sciences (MS), including cyber security and privacy, data science, information technology; gifted and talented (M Ed), including curriculum and instruction, educational administration and supervision, gifted and talented P-8/7-12, instructional specialist P-4; higher, adult and lifelong education (M Ed); kinesiology (M Ed), including coaching; library media and information specialist (M Ed); public administration (MPA); school counseling K-12 (M Ed); student affairs and college counseling (M Ed); teaching (MAT). *Accreditation:* NCATE. *Program availability:* Part-time, 100% online, blended/hybrid learning. *Faculty:* 36 full-time (19 women), 33 part-time/adjunct (14 women). *Students:* 605 full-time (143 women), 879 part-time (352 women); includes 130 minority (113 Black or African American, non-Hispanic/Latino; 7 American Indian or Alaska Native, non-Hispanic/Latino; 2 Asian, non-Hispanic/Latino; 2 Hispanic/Latino; 6 Two or more races, non-Hispanic/Latino), 1,048 international. Average age 28. 904 applicants, 81% accepted, 262 enrolled. In 2016, 278 master's awarded. *Degree requirements:* For master's, comprehensive exam (for some programs), thesis optional. *Entrance requirements:* For master's, GRE, MAT or GMAT, minimum GPA of 2.5. Additional exam requirements/recommendations for international students: Required—TOEFL (minimum score 550 paper-based), IELTS (minimum score 6). *Application deadline:* For fall admission, 7/20 for domestic students, 7/10 for international students; for spring admission, 12/1 for domestic students, 11/15 for international students; for summer admission, 4/1 for domestic students, 5/1 for international students. Applications are processed on a rolling basis. Application fee: $25 ($50 for international students). Electronic applications accepted. *Expenses:* Tuition, state resident: full-time $2511; part-time $279 per credit hour. Tuition, nonresident: full-time $3726; part-time $414 per credit hour. *Required fees:* $307 per semester. Tuition and fees vary according to course load and program. *Financial support:* Career-related internships or fieldwork, Federal Work-Study, scholarships/grants, tuition waivers (full), and unspecified assistantships available. Financial award applicants required to submit FAFSA. *Faculty research:* Alternative certification for teachers, supervision of instruction, instructional leadership, counseling. *Unit head:* Dr. Kim Bloss, Dean, School of Graduate Studies, 870-235-4150, Fax: 870-235-5227, E-mail: kkbloss@saumag.edu. *Application contact:* Shrijana Malakar, Admissions Specialist, 870-235-4150, Fax: 870-235-5227, E-mail: smalakar@saumag.edu.
Website: http://www.saumag.edu/graduate

Southern New Hampshire University, School of Business, Manchester, NH 03106-1045. Offers accounting (MBA, MS, Graduate Certificate); accounting finance (MS); accounting/auditing (MS); accounting/forensic accounting (MS); accounting/taxation (MS); athletic administration (MBA, Graduate Certificate); business administration (IMBA, MBA, Certificate, Graduate Certificate), including accounting (Certificate), business administration (MBA), business information systems (Graduate Certificate), human resource management (Certificate); corporate social responsibility (MBA); entrepreneurship (MBA); finance (MBA, MS, Graduate Certificate); finance/corporate finance (MS); finance/investments and securities (MS); forensic accounting (MBA); healthcare informatics (MBA); healthcare management (MBA); human resource management (Graduate Certificate); information technology (MS, Graduate Certificate); information technology management (MBA); international business (Graduate Certificate); international business and information technology (Graduate Certificate); international finance (Graduate Certificate); international sport management (Graduate Certificate); justice studies (MBA); leadership of nonprofit organizations (Graduate Certificate); management (MS); marketing (MBA, MS, Graduate Certificate); operations and project management (MS); operations and supply chain management (MBA, Graduate Certificate); organizational leadership (MS); project management (MBA, Graduate Certificate); Six Sigma (MBA); Six Sigma quality (Graduate Certificate); social media marketing (MBA); sport management (MBA, MS, Graduate Certificate); sustainability and environmental compliance (MBA); workplace conflict management (MBA); MBA/Certificate. *Accreditation:* ACBSP. *Program availability:* Part-time, evening/weekend, online learning. Terminal master's awarded for partial completion of doctoral program. *Degree requirements:* For master's, one foreign language, comprehensive exam (for some programs), thesis or alternative. *Entrance requirements:* For master's, minimum GPA of 2.5. Additional exam requirements/recommendations for international students: Required—TOEFL (minimum score 500 paper-based). Electronic applications accepted.

South University, Graduate Programs, College of Business, Program in Leadership, Savannah, GA 31406. Offers MS.

South University, Program in Leadership, Virginia Beach, VA 23452. Offers MS.

South University, Program in Leadership, Columbia, SC 29203. Offers MS.

South University, Program in Leadership, Novi, MI 48377. Offers MS.

Southwest University, MBA Program, Kenner, LA 70062. Offers business administration (MBA); management (MBA); organizational management (MBA).

Southwest University, Program in Organizational Management, Kenner, LA 70062. Offers MA.

State University of New York College at Potsdam, School of Education and Professional Studies, Program in Information and Communication Technology, Potsdam, NY 13676. Offers educational technology specialist (MS Ed); organizational performance, leadership and technology (MS Ed). *Program availability:* Part-time, evening/weekend. *Degree requirements:* For master's, culminating experience. *Entrance requirements:* For master's, minimum GPA of 3.0 in last 60 hours of course work. Additional exam requirements/recommendations for international students: Required—TOEFL (minimum score 550 paper-based; 80 iBT), IELTS (minimum score 6). Electronic applications accepted.

Stockton University, Office of Graduate Studies, Program in Organizational Leadership, Galloway, NJ 08205-9441. Offers Ed D. *Program availability:* Evening/weekend. *Faculty:* 1 full-time (0 women), 1 part-time/adjunct (0 women). *Students:* 1 full-time (0 women), 46 part-time (28 women); includes 17 minority (15 Black or African American, non-Hispanic/Latino; 1 American Indian or Alaska Native, non-Hispanic/Latino; 1 Hispanic/Latino). Average age 44. 39 applicants, 72% accepted, 24 enrolled. *Degree requirements:* For doctorate, thesis/dissertation. *Entrance requirements:* For doctorate, minimum overall GPA of 3.0, three letters of recommendation, essay, resume, official transcripts, personal interview. *Application deadline:* For fall admission, 6/1 for domestic students; for spring admission, 11/16 for domestic students. Application fee: $50. *Expenses:* $832 per credit in-state. *Unit head:* Dr. Joseph Marchetti, Director, 609-652-4642. *Application contact:* Tara Williams, Assistant Director of Enrollment Management, 609-626-3640, Fax: 609-626-6050, E-mail: gradschool@stockton.edu.

Syracuse University, Maxwell School of Citizenship and Public Affairs, CAS Program in Leadership of International and Non-Governmental Organizations, Syracuse, NY 13244. Offers CAS. *Program availability:* Part-time. In 2016, 35 CASs awarded. *Degree requirements:* For CAS, seminar. *Entrance requirements:* For degree, resume, three letters of recommendation, personal statement, official transcripts. Additional exam requirements/recommendations for international students: Required—TOEFL (minimum score 100 iBT). *Application deadline:* For fall admission, 2/1 priority date for domestic and international students; for spring admission, 8/15 priority date for domestic and international students. Applications are processed on a rolling basis. Application fee: $75. Electronic applications accepted. *Expenses: Tuition:* Full-time $25,974; part-time $1443 per credit hour. *Required fees:* $802; $50 per course. Tuition and fees vary according to course load and program. *Financial support:* Application deadline: 1/1. *Faculty research:* Managing nongovernment organizations in transitional and development countries, public budgeting, fundamentals of public policy, humanitarian action. *Unit head:* Steven Lux, Director, Executive Education, 315-443-3759, E-mail: sjlux@maxwell.syr.edu. *Application contact:* Margaret Lane, Assistant Director, Executive Education Programs, 315-443-8708, E-mail: melane02@maxwell.syr.edu.
Website: http://www.maxwell.syr.edu/

Thomas Edison State University, School of Business and Management, Program in Organizational Leadership, Trenton, NJ 08608. Offers Graduate Certificate. *Program availability:* Part-time, online learning. *Entrance requirements:* Additional exam requirements/recommendations for international students: Required—TOEFL (minimum score 550 paper-based; 79 iBT). Electronic applications accepted.

Trevecca Nazarene University, Graduate Business Programs, Nashville, TN 37210-2877. Offers business administration (MBA); management (MSM). *Program availability:* Evening/weekend, online learning. *Faculty:* 8 full-time (1 woman), 8 part-time/adjunct (3 women). *Students:* 168 full-time (108 women), 24 part-time (13 women); includes 98 minority (81 Black or African American, non-Hispanic/Latino; 6 Asian, non-Hispanic/Latino; 8 Hispanic/Latino; 1 Native Hawaiian or other Pacific Islander, non-Hispanic/Latino; 2 Two or more races, non-Hispanic/Latino), 3 international. Average age 32. In 2016, 44 master's awarded. *Entrance requirements:* For master's, minimum GPA of 2.75, resume, official transcript from regionally accredited institution, minimum math grade of C, minimum English composition grade of C. Additional exam requirements/recommendations for international students: Required—TOEFL (minimum score 550 paper-based; 80 iBT). *Application deadline:* Applications are processed on a rolling basis. Application fee: $0. Electronic applications accepted. *Expenses:* $520 per credit hour. *Financial support:* Applicants required to submit FAFSA. *Unit head:* Dr. Rick Mann, Director of Graduate and Professional Programs for School of Business, 615-248-1529, E-mail: management@trevecca.edu. *Application contact:* 615-248-1529, E-mail: sgcsadmissions@trevecca.edu.
Website: http://www.trevecca.edu/mba

Trevecca Nazarene University, Graduate Leadership Programs, Nashville, TN 37210-2877. Offers leadership and professional practice (Ed D); organizational leadership (MOL). *Program availability:* Online learning. *Faculty:* 10 full-time (4 women), 19 part-time/adjunct (6 women). *Students:* 209 full-time (150 women), 220 part-time (159 women); includes 240 minority (209 Black or African American, non-Hispanic/Latino; 1 American Indian or Alaska Native, non-Hispanic/Latino; 2 Asian, non-Hispanic/Latino; 16 Hispanic/Latino; 12 Two or more races, non-Hispanic/Latino), 1 international. Average age 39. In 2016, 32 master's, 43 doctorates awarded. *Degree requirements:* For master's, capstone course; for doctorate, thesis/dissertation, proposal study, symposium presentation. *Entrance requirements:* For master's, minimum GPA of 2.5, official transcript from regionally accredited institution; for doctorate, minimum GPA of 3.4, official transcript from regionally-accredited institution, resume, writing sample, interview, reference forms. Additional exam requirements/recommendations for international students: Required—TOEFL (minimum score 550 paper-based; 80 iBT). *Application deadline:* Applications are processed on a rolling basis. Application fee: $0. Electronic applications accepted. *Expenses:* $395 per credit hour (MOL); $699 per credit hour (Ed D). *Financial support:* Applicants required to submit FAFSA. *Unit head:* Dr. Tom Middendorf, Associate Vice President for Academic Services/Director of Master of Organizational Leadership, 615-248-1529, E-mail: sgcsadmissions@trevecca.edu. *Application contact:* 844-TNU-GRAD, E-mail: sgcsadmissions@trevecca.edu.

Trinity Washington University, School of Business and Graduate Studies, Washington, DC 20017-1094. Offers business administration (MBA); communication (MA); international security studies (MA); organizational management (MSA), including federal program management, human resource management, nonprofit management, organizational development, public and community health. *Program availability:* Part-time, evening/weekend. *Degree requirements:* For master's, thesis (for some programs), capstone project (MSA). *Entrance requirements:* For master's, minimum GPA of 2.5. Additional exam requirements/recommendations for international students: Required—TOEFL (minimum score 550 paper-based).

Trinity Western University, School of Graduate Studies, Program in Leadership, Langley, BC V2Y 1Y1, Canada. Offers business (MA, Certificate); Christian ministry (MA); education (MA, Certificate); healthcare (MA, Certificate); non-profit (MA, Certificate). *Program availability:* Online learning. *Degree requirements:* For master's, major project. *Entrance requirements:* For master's, minimum GPA of 2.7. Additional exam requirements/recommendations for international students: Required—TOEFL (minimum score 620 paper-based; 105 iBT). Electronic applications accepted. *Expenses:* Contact institution. *Faculty research:* Servant leadership.

Union Institute & University, Master of Science Program in Organizational Leadership, Cincinnati, OH 45206-1925. Offers MS. *Program availability:* Part-time, online only,

100% online. *Faculty:* 6 part-time/adjunct (2 women). *Students:* 49 full-time (21 women), 5 part-time (2 women); includes 33 minority (18 Black or African American, non-Hispanic/Latino; 2 American Indian or Alaska Native, non-Hispanic/Latino; 1 Asian, non-Hispanic/Latino; 7 Hispanic/Latino; 2 Native Hawaiian or other Pacific Islander, non-Hispanic/Latino; 3 Two or more races, non-Hispanic/Latino). Average age 40. In 2016, 14 master's awarded. *Degree requirements:* For master's, capstone project. *Entrance requirements:* For master's, recommendations, transcripts, essay. Additional exam requirements/recommendations for international students: Required—TOEFL. *Application deadline:* Applications are processed on a rolling basis. Application fee: $50. Electronic applications accepted. *Expenses:* Contact institution. *Financial support:* Federal Work-Study available. *Faculty research:* Leadership. *Unit head:* Nadine Wheat, Director, E-mail: nadine.wheat@myunion.edu. *Application contact:* Admissions Office, 513-861-6400, E-mail: admissions@myunion.edu.
Website: https://myunion.edu/academics/masters/organizational-leadership/

United States International University–Africa, School of Business Administration, Nairobi, Kenya. Offers business administration (GEMBA); entrepreneurship (MBA); finance (MBA); human resource management (MBA); information technology management (MBA); integrated studies (MBA); international business administration (MBA); management and organizational development (MS); marketing (MBA); organizational development (EMS); strategic management (MBA). *Program availability:* Part-time, evening/weekend. *Degree requirements:* For master's, thesis. *Entrance requirements:* For master's, GMAT, 2 letters of reference, resume. Additional exam requirements/recommendations for international students: Required—TOEFL (minimum score 550 paper-based). *Faculty research:* Marketing in small business enterprises, total quality management in Kenya.

Université Laval, Faculty of Administrative Sciences, Programs in Business Administration, Québec, QC G1K 7P4, Canada. Offers accounting (MBA); agri-food management (MBA); electronic business (MBA, Diploma); factory management and logistics (MBA); finance (MBA); firm management (MBA); geomatic management (MBA); information technology management (MBA); international management (MBA); management (MBA); management accounting (MBA, Diploma); marketing (MBA); modeling and organizational decision (MBA); occupational health and safety management (MBA); pharmacy management (MBA); social and environmental responsibility (MBA); technological entrepreneurship (Diploma). *Accreditation:* AACSB. *Program availability:* Part-time, evening/weekend, online learning. *Entrance requirements:* For master's and Diploma, knowledge of French and English. Electronic applications accepted.

University of Alberta, Faculty of Graduate Studies and Research, Doctoral Program in Business, Edmonton, AB T6G 2E1, Canada. Offers accounting (PhD); finance (PhD); human resources/industrial relations (PhD); management science (PhD); marketing (PhD); organizational analysis (PhD); MBA/PhD. *Accreditation:* AACSB. *Program availability:* Part-time. *Degree requirements:* For doctorate, comprehensive exam, thesis/dissertation. *Entrance requirements:* For doctorate, GMAT. Additional exam requirements/recommendations for international students: Required—TOEFL (minimum score 550 paper-based). Electronic applications accepted. *Faculty research:* Accounting, capital markets and corporate finance, organizational change and human resource management, marketing, strategic management.

The University of Arizona, Eller College of Management, Department of Management and Organizations, Tucson, AZ 85721. Offers MS, PhD. *Program availability:* Evening/weekend. *Entrance requirements:* Additional exam requirements/recommendations for international students: Required—TOEFL (minimum score 550 paper-based; 79 iBT). Electronic applications accepted. *Faculty research:* Organizational behavior, human resources, decision-making, health economics and finance, immigration.

University of Central Arkansas, Graduate School, Interdisciplinary PhD Program in Leadership Studies, Conway, AR 72035-0001. Offers PhD. *Program availability:* Part-time. *Degree requirements:* For doctorate, thesis/dissertation. *Entrance requirements:* For doctorate, GRE. Additional exam requirements/recommendations for international students: Required—TOEFL. Electronic applications accepted.

University of Charleston, Doctor of Executive Leadership Program, Charleston, WV 25304-1099. Offers DEL. *Students:* 86 full-time (30 women), 15 part-time (6 women); includes 17 minority (13 Black or African American, non-Hispanic/Latino; 1 American Indian or Alaska Native, non-Hispanic/Latino; 1 Asian, non-Hispanic/Latino; 2 Hispanic/Latino). Average age 46. In 2016, 2 doctorates awarded. *Entrance requirements:* Additional exam requirements/recommendations for international students: Required—TOEFL. *Application deadline:* Applications are processed on a rolling basis. Electronic applications accepted. *Expenses: Tuition:* Full-time $20,602; part-time $425 per credit. *Required fees:* $200. Tuition and fees vary according to course load, campus/location, program and student level. *Financial support:* Unspecified assistantships available. *Unit head:* Dr. Ruth Wylie, Program Director, E-mail: ruthwylie@ucwv.edu. *Application contact:* David Cooper, Applications Coordinator, 304-352-0013, E-mail: davidcooper@ucwv.edu.
Website: http://www.ucwv.edu/business/DEL/

University of Cincinnati, Graduate School, McMicken College of Arts and Sciences, Center for Organizational Leadership, Cincinnati, OH 45221. Offers MALER. *Program availability:* Part-time, evening/weekend. *Entrance requirements:* For master's, GRE or GMAT. Additional exam requirements/recommendations for international students: Required—TOEFL (minimum score 520 paper-based; 68 iBT). Electronic applications accepted. *Expenses: Tuition, area resident:* Full-time $12,790; part-time $389 per credit hour. Tuition, state resident: full-time $13,290; part-time $419 per credit hour. Tuition, nonresident: full-time $24,532; part-time $976 per credit hour. *International tuition:* $24,832 full-time. *Required fees:* $3958; $140 per credit hour. Tuition and fees vary according to course load, degree level, program and reciprocity agreements. *Faculty research:* Leadership and diversity.

University of Dallas, Satish and Yasmin Gupta College of Business, Irving, TX 75062-4736. Offers accounting (MBA, MS); business administration (DBA); business analytics (MS); business management (MBA); corporate finance (MBA); cybersecurity (MS); finance (MS); financial services (MBA); global business (MBA, MS); health services management (MBA); human resource management (MBA); information and technology management (MS); information assurance (MBA); information technology (MBA); information technology service management (MBA); marketing management (MBA); organization development (MBA); project management (MBA); sports and entertainment management (MBA); strategic leadership (MBA); supply chain management (MBA). *Accreditation:* AACSB. *Program availability:* Part-time, evening/weekend, online learning. *Entrance requirements:* Additional exam requirements/recommendations for international students: Required—TOEFL. Electronic applications accepted. *Expenses:* Contact institution.

University of Denver, University College, Denver, CO 80208. Offers arts and culture (MA, Certificate); communication management (MS, Certificate), including translation studies (Certificate), world history and culture (Certificate); environmental policy and management (MS); geographic information systems (MS); global affairs (MA, Certificate), including human capital in organizations (Certificate), philanthropic leadership (Certificate), project management (Certificate), strategic innovation and change (Certificate); healthcare leadership (MS); information communications and technology (MS); leadership and organizations (MS); professional creative writing (MA, Certificate), including emergency planning and response (Certificate), organizational security (Certificate); security management (MS, Certificate); strategic human resources (Certificate). *Program availability:* Part-time, evening/weekend, online learning. *Faculty:* 118 part-time/adjunct (62 women). *Students:* 59 full-time (22 women), 1,285 part-time (750 women); includes 316 minority (111 Black or African American, non-Hispanic/Latino; 8 American Indian or Alaska Native, non-Hispanic/Latino; 39 Asian, non-Hispanic/Latino; 123 Hispanic/Latino; 3 Native Hawaiian or other Pacific Islander, non-Hispanic/Latino; 32 Two or more races, non-Hispanic/Latino), 85 international. Average age 35. 703 applicants, 89% accepted, 390 enrolled. In 2016, 428 master's, 138 other advanced degrees awarded. *Degree requirements:* For master's, capstone project. *Entrance requirements:* For master's, transcripts, two letters of recommendation, personal statement, resume. Additional exam requirements/recommendations for international students: Required—TOEFL (minimum score 550 paper-based; 80 iBT). *Application deadline:* For fall admission, 6/21 priority date for domestic students, 5/1 priority date for international students; for winter admission, 9/14 priority date for domestic students, 9/19 priority date for international students; for spring admission, 1/11 priority date for domestic students, 12/12 priority date for international students; for summer admission, 3/29 priority date for domestic students, 3/6 priority date for international students. Applications are processed on a rolling basis. Application fee: $75. Electronic applications accepted. *Expenses:* $7,236 per year full-time. *Financial support:* In 2016–17, 27 students received support, including 1 teaching assistantship (averaging $1,489 per year). Financial award applicants required to submit FAFSA. *Unit head:* Dr. Michael McGuire, Dean, 303-871-3518, Fax: 303-871-3303, E-mail: mmcguire@du.edu. *Application contact:* Information Contact, 303-871-2291, E-mail: ucoladm@du.edu.
Website: http://universitycollege.du.edu/

University of Guelph, Graduate Studies, College of Management and Economics, MA (Leadership) Program, Guelph, ON N1G 2W1, Canada. Offers MA. *Program availability:* Part-time, evening/weekend, online learning. *Entrance requirements:* For master's, minimum B-average, minimum 5 years of relevant work experience. Additional exam requirements/recommendations for international students: Required—TOEFL (minimum score 550 paper-based). Electronic applications accepted. *Faculty research:* Theories of leadership, organizational change, ethics in leadership, decision making, politics of organizations.

University of Hawaii at Manoa, Graduate Division, Shidler College of Business, Program in Business Administration, Honolulu, HI 96822. Offers Asian business studies (MBA); Chinese business studies (MBA); decision sciences (MBA); entrepreneurship (MBA); finance (MBA); finance and banking (MBA); human resources management (MBA); information management (MBA); information technology (MBA); international business (MBA); Japanese business studies (MBA); marketing (MBA); organizational behavior (MBA); organizational management (MBA); real estate (MBA); student-designed track (MBA). *Accreditation:* AACSB. *Program availability:* Part-time, evening/weekend. *Degree requirements:* For master's, thesis optional. *Entrance requirements:* For master's, GMAT, minimum GPA of 3.0. Additional exam requirements/recommendations for international students: Required—TOEFL (minimum score 600 paper-based; 100 iBT), IELTS (minimum score 7). *Expenses:* Contact institution.

University of Hawaii at Manoa, Graduate Division, Shidler College of Business, Program in International Management, Honolulu, HI 96822. Offers Asian finance (PhD); global information technology management (PhD); international accounting (PhD); international marketing (PhD); international organization and strategy (PhD). *Program availability:* Part-time. *Degree requirements:* For doctorate, comprehensive exam, thesis/dissertation. *Entrance requirements:* For doctorate, GMAT or GRE General Test, minimum GPA of 3.0. Additional exam requirements/recommendations for international students: Required—TOEFL (minimum score 600 paper-based; 100 iBT), IELTS (minimum score 7). *Expenses:* Contact institution.

The University of Kansas, Graduate Studies, School of Business, Program in Business, Lawrence, KS 66045. Offers accounting (PhD); business and organizational leadership (MS); decision sciences and supply chain management (PhD); finance (PhD); human resources management (PhD); marketing (PhD); organizational behavior (PhD); strategic management (PhD); supply chain management and logistics (MS). *Accreditation:* AACSB. *Program availability:* Part-time. *Students:* 76 full-time (11 women), 170 part-time (83 women); includes 41 minority (15 Black or African American, non-Hispanic/Latino; 3 American Indian or Alaska Native, non-Hispanic/Latino; 6 Asian, non-Hispanic/Latino; 5 Hispanic/Latino; 12 Two or more races, non-Hispanic/Latino), 25 international. Average age 32. 294 applicants, 69% accepted, 152 enrolled. In 2016, 36 master's, 9 doctorates awarded. *Entrance requirements:* For master's, GMAT, official transcript, three letters of recommendation, resume, statement of purpose; for doctorate, GMAT or GRE, official transcript, three letters of recommendation, resume, statement of purpose. Additional exam requirements/recommendations for international students: Required—TOEFL (minimum score 600 paper-based; 100 iBT). *Application deadline:* For fall admission, 1/10 for domestic and international students. Application fee: $65 ($85 for international students). Electronic applications accepted. *Financial support:* Fellowships, research assistantships, teaching assistantships, scholarships/grants, health care benefits, tuition waivers (full), and unspecified assistantships available. Financial award application deadline: 1/10. *Faculty research:* Strategic human resource management, business ethics, organizational theory/behavior, corporate strategy, international business, supply chain management, Bayesian networks, game theory, decision analysis and time/series analysis, pricing, consumer effects, advertising and emotion. *Unit head:* Charly Edmonds, Director, 785-864-3841, E-mail: bschoolphd@ku.edu. *Application contact:* Graduate Admission Contact, 785-864-7500, E-mail: bschoolphd@ku.edu.
Website: http://www.business.ku.edu/

The University of Kansas, University of Kansas Medical Center, School of Nursing, Kansas City, KS 66160. Offers adult/gerontological clinical nurse specialist (PMC); adult/gerontological nurse practitioner (PMC); health care informatics (PMC); health professions educator (PMC); nurse midwife (PMC); nursing (MS, DNP, PhD); organizational leadership (PMC); psychiatric/mental health nurse practitioner (PMC); public health nursing (PMC). *Accreditation:* AACN; ACNM/ACME. *Program availability:* Part-time, 100% online, blended/hybrid learning. *Faculty:* 53. *Students:* 41 full-time (40 women), 270 part-time (244 women); includes 47 minority (15 Black or African American, non-Hispanic/Latino; 2 American Indian or Alaska Native, non-Hispanic/Latino; 9 Asian, non-Hispanic/Latino; 10 Hispanic/Latino; 11 Two or more races, non-Hispanic/Latino), 1 international. Average age 37. 95 applicants, 97% accepted, 67 enrolled. In 2016, 87 master's, 25 doctorates, 9 other advanced degrees awarded. Terminal master's awarded for partial completion of doctoral program. *Degree requirements:* For master's, comprehensive exam, thesis (for some programs), general oral exam; for doctorate, thesis/dissertation or alternative, comprehensive oral exam (for DNP); comprehensive written and oral exam, or three publications (for PhD). *Entrance requirements:* For master's, bachelor's degree in nursing, minimum GPA of 3.0, 1 year of clinical experience, RN license in KS and MO; for doctorate, GRE General Test (for PhD only), bachelor's degree in nursing, minimum GPA of 3.5, RN license in KS and

MO. Additional exam requirements/recommendations for international students: Required—TOEFL. *Application deadline:* For fall admission, 4/1 for domestic and international students; for spring admission, 9/1 for domestic and international students. Application fee: $60. Electronic applications accepted. *Financial support:* In 2016–17, 50 students received support, including 5 research assistantships with tuition reimbursements available (averaging $20,000 per year), 30 teaching assistantships with tuition reimbursements available (averaging $20,000 per year); scholarships/grants and traineeships also available. Financial award application deadline: 3/1; financial award applicants required to submit FAFSA. *Faculty research:* Breastfeeding practices of teen mothers, national database of nursing quality indicators, caregiving of families of patients using technology in the home, simulation in nursing education, diaphragm fatigue. *Total annual research expenditures:* $1.2 million. *Unit head:* Dr. Sally Maliski, Dean, 913-588-1601, Fax: 913-588-1660, E-mail: smaliski@kumc.edu. *Application contact:* Dr. Pamela K. Barnes, Associate Dean, Student Affairs, 913-588-1619, Fax: 913-588-1615, E-mail: pbarnes2@kumc.edu.
Website: http://nursing.kumc.edu

University of La Verne, College of Business and Public Management, Program in Leadership and Management, La Verne, CA 91750-4443. Offers human resource management (Certificate); leadership and management (MS), including human resource management, nonprofit management, organizational development; nonprofit management (Certificate); organizational leadership (Certificate). *Program availability:* Part-time. *Students:* 47 full-time (32 women), 44 part-time (25 women); includes 42 minority (2 Black or African American, non-Hispanic/Latino; 3 Asian, non-Hispanic/Latino; 37 Hispanic/Latino), 14 international. Average age 32. *Degree requirements:* For master's, thesis or research project. *Entrance requirements:* For master's, bachelor's degree, minimum undergraduate GPA of 2.75, 2 letters of recommendation, interview, resume. Additional exam requirements/recommendations for international students: Required—TOEFL (minimum score 550 paper-based). *Application deadline:* Applications are processed on a rolling basis. Application fee: $50. *Expenses: Tuition:* Part-time $795 per credit hour. Tuition and fees vary according to campus/location and program. *Financial support:* Federal Work-Study, institutionally sponsored loans, and scholarships/grants available. Financial award application deadline: 3/2; financial award applicants required to submit FAFSA. *Unit head:* Dr. Kathy Duncan, Program Director, 909-448-4415, E-mail: kduncan2@laverne.edu. *Application contact:* Barbara Cox, Associate Director of Graduate Admissions, 909-448-4004, E-mail: bcox@laverne.edu.
Website: http://laverne.edu/business-and-public-administration/

University of La Verne, LaFetra College of Education, Doctoral Program in Organizational Leadership, La Verne, CA 91750-4443. Offers Ed D. *Program availability:* Part-time. *Students:* 111 full-time (82 women), 56 part-time (29 women); includes 73 minority (15 Black or African American, non-Hispanic/Latino; 6 Asian, non-Hispanic/Latino; 50 Hispanic/Latino; 2 Two or more races, non-Hispanic/Latino), 1 international. Average age 44. *Degree requirements:* For doctorate, thesis/dissertation. *Entrance requirements:* For doctorate, GRE or MAT, minimum graduate GPA of 3.0, resume or curriculum vitae, 2 endorsement forms. Additional exam requirements/recommendations for international students: Required—TOEFL (minimum score 550 paper-based). *Application deadline:* Applications are processed on a rolling basis. Application fee: $75. *Expenses:* Contact institution. *Financial support:* Institutionally sponsored loans and scholarships/grants available. Financial award application deadline: 3/2; financial award applicants required to submit FAFSA. *Unit head:* Dr. Barbara Poling, Professor of Organizational Leadership, 909-448-4380, E-mail: bpoling@laverne.edu. *Application contact:* Christy Ranells, Program and Admission Specialist, 909-448-4644, Fax: 909-971-2295, E-mail: cranells@laverne.edu.
Website: https://sites.laverne.edu/organizational-leadership/

University of La Verne, Regional and Online Campuses, Graduate Programs, Inland Empire Campus, Ontario, CA 91730. Offers business administration (MBA, MBA-EP), including accounting (MBA), finance (MBA), health services management (MBA-EP), information technology (MBA-EP), international business (MBA), managed care (MBA), management and leadership (MBA-EP), marketing (MBA-EP), supply chain management (MBA); leadership and management (MS), including human resource management, nonprofit management, organizational development. *Program availability:* Part-time, evening/weekend. *Expenses:* Contact institution.

University of La Verne, Regional and Online Campuses, Graduate Programs, Kern County Campus, Bakersfield, CA 93301. Offers business administration for experienced professionals (MBA-EP); education (special emphasis) (M Ed); educational counseling (MS); educational leadership (M Ed); health administration (MHA); leadership and management (MS); mild/moderate education specialist (Credential); multiple subject (elementary) (Credential); organizational leadership (Ed D); preliminary administrative services (Credential); single subject (secondary) (Credential); special education studies (MS). *Program availability:* Part-time, evening/weekend. *Expenses:* Contact institution.

University of Maryland Eastern Shore, Graduate Programs, Program in Organizational Leadership, Princess Anne, MD 21853-1299. Offers PhD. *Program availability:* Evening/weekend. *Degree requirements:* For doctorate, comprehensive exam, thesis/dissertation, internship. *Entrance requirements:* For doctorate, interview, writing sample, successful record of employment or career in organization/profession. Additional exam requirements/recommendations for international students: Required—TOEFL (minimum score 80 iBT). Electronic applications accepted.

University of Massachusetts Amherst, Graduate School, Isenberg School of Management, Program in Management, Amherst, MA 01003. Offers accounting (PhD); business administration (MBA); entrepreneurship (MBA); finance (MBA, PhD); healthcare administration (MBA); hospitality and tourism management (PhD); management science (PhD); marketing (MBA, PhD); organization studies (PhD); sport management (PhD); strategic management (PhD); MBA/MS. *Accreditation:* AACSB. *Program availability:* Part-time, evening/weekend, online learning. Terminal master's awarded for partial completion of doctoral program. *Degree requirements:* For doctorate, comprehensive exam, thesis/dissertation. *Entrance requirements:* For master's and doctorate, GMAT or GRE General Test. Additional exam requirements/recommendations for international students: Required—TOEFL (minimum score 550 paper-based; 80 iBT), IELTS (minimum score 6.5). Electronic applications accepted.

University of Massachusetts Dartmouth, Graduate School, Charlton College of Business, Program in Business Administration, North Dartmouth, MA 02747-2300. Offers business administration (MBA); business analytics (Postbaccalaureate Certificate); business foundations (Graduate Certificate); international business (Graduate Certificate); management (Postbaccalaureate Certificate); marketing (Postbaccalaureate Certificate); organizational leadership (Graduate Certificate); supply chain management and information systems (Postbaccalaureate Certificate). *Accreditation:* AACSB. *Program availability:* Part-time, 100% online, blended/hybrid learning. *Faculty:* 15 full-time (7 women), 11 part-time/adjunct (4 women). *Students:* 126 full-time (49 women), 178 part-time (100 women); includes 45 minority (10 Black or African American, non-Hispanic/Latino; 1 American Indian or Alaska Native, non-Hispanic/Latino; 16 Asian, non-Hispanic/Latino; 13 Hispanic/Latino; 5 Two or more races, non-Hispanic/Latino), 100 international. Average age 32. 236 applicants, 80% accepted, 132 enrolled. In 2016, 142 master's, 13 other advanced degrees awarded. *Degree requirements:* For master's, thesis or alternative, eportfolio. *Entrance requirements:* For master's, GMAT, statement of purpose (minimum of 300 words), resume, official transcripts, 2 letters of recommendation; for other advanced degree, statement of purpose (minimum of 300 words), resume, official transcripts. Additional exam requirements/recommendations for international students: Required—TOEFL (minimum score 533 paper-based; 72 iBT). *Application deadline:* For fall admission, 7/1 priority date for domestic students, 6/1 priority date for international students; for spring admission, 11/15 priority date for domestic students, 10/15 priority date for international students. Application fee: $60. Electronic applications accepted. *Expenses:* Tuition, state resident: full-time $14,994; part-time $624.75 per credit. Tuition, nonresident: full-time $27,068; part-time $1127.83 per credit. *Required fees:* $405; $25.88 per credit. Tuition and fees vary according to course load and reciprocity agreements. *Financial support:* In 2016–17, 2 research assistantships (averaging $2,667 per year) were awarded; institutionally sponsored loans, scholarships/grants, and unspecified assistantships also available. Support available to part-time students. Financial award application deadline: 3/1; financial award applicants required to submit FAFSA. *Faculty research:* E-commerce, managing diversity, agile manufacturing, green business, activity-based management, build-to-order supply chain management. *Total annual research expenditures:* $413,000. *Unit head:* Melissa Pacheco, Assistant Dean of Graduate Programs, 508-999-8543, Fax: 508-999-8646, E-mail: mpacheco@umassd.edu. *Application contact:* Steven Briggs, Director of Marketing and Recruitment for Graduate Studies, 508-999-8604, Fax: 508-999-8183, E-mail: graduate@umassd.edu.
Website: http://www.umassd.edu/charlton/programs/graduate/mba

University of Michigan–Flint, School of Management, Program in Business Administration, Flint, MI 48502. Offers accounting (MBA, Post-Master's Certificate); computer information systems (MBA); finance (MBA, Post-Master's Certificate); general business (Graduate Certificate); general business administration (MBA); health care management (MBA); international business (MBA, Post-Master's Certificate); lean manufacturing (MBA); marketing (MBA, Post-Master's Certificate); organizational leadership (MBA, Post-Master's Certificate). *Program availability:* Part-time, evening/weekend, mixed mode programs. *Faculty:* 33 full-time (9 women), 6 part-time/adjunct (1 woman). *Students:* 24 full-time (12 women), 146 part-time (49 women); includes 37 minority (17 Black or African American, non-Hispanic/Latino; 2 American Indian or Alaska Native, non-Hispanic/Latino; 10 Asian, non-Hispanic/Latino; 4 Hispanic/Latino; 1 Native Hawaiian or other Pacific Islander, non-Hispanic/Latino; 3 Two or more races, non-Hispanic/Latino), 17 international. Average age 33. 167 applicants, 47% accepted, 40 enrolled. In 2016, 73 master's, 3 other advanced degrees awarded. *Entrance requirements:* For master's, GMAT or GRE, bachelor's degree in arts, sciences, engineering, or business administration from regionally-accredited college or university with minimum GPA of 3.0; for other advanced degree, bachelor's degree in arts, sciences, engineering, or business administration from regionally-accredited college or university with minimum GPA of 3.0, college-level math, statistics, or quantitative course (for Graduate Certificate); MBA or equivalent degree from regionally-accredited college or university (for Post Master's Certificate). Additional exam requirements/recommendations for international students: Required—TOEFL (minimum score 84 iBT), IELTS (minimum score 6.5). *Application deadline:* For fall admission, 8/1 for domestic students, 5/1 for international students; for winter admission, 11/15 for domestic students, 9/1 for international students; for spring admission, 3/15 for domestic students, 1/1 for international students; for summer admission, 5/15 for domestic students. Applications are processed on a rolling basis. Application fee: $55. Electronic applications accepted. *Financial support:* Federal Work-Study, scholarships/grants, and unspecified assistantships available. Support available to part-time students. Financial award application deadline: 3/1; financial award applicants required to submit FAFSA. *Unit head:* Dr. Scott Johnson, Dean, School of Management, 810-762-3164, Fax: 810-237-6685, E-mail: scotjohn@umflint.edu. *Application contact:* Bradley T. Maki, Director of Graduate Admissions, 810-762-3171, E-mail: bmaki@umflint.edu.
Website: http://www.umflint.edu/graduateprograms/business-administration-mba

University of Missouri, Office of Research and Graduate Studies, Harry S Truman School of Public Affairs, Columbia, MO 65211. Offers grantsmanship (Graduate Certificate); nonprofit management (Graduate Certificate); organizational change (Graduate Certificate); public affairs (MPA, PhD); public management (Graduate Certificate); science and public policy (Graduate Certificate). *Accreditation:* NASPAA. *Faculty:* 10 full-time (7 women), 2 part-time/adjunct (0 women). *Students:* 76 full-time (37 women), 168 part-time (88 women); includes 36 minority (21 Black or African American, non-Hispanic/Latino; 1 American Indian or Alaska Native, non-Hispanic/Latino; 2 Asian, non-Hispanic/Latino; 6 Hispanic/Latino; 6 Two or more races, non-Hispanic/Latino), 24 international. Average age 34. *Entrance requirements:* For master's, GRE General Test, minimum GPA of 3.0. Additional exam requirements/recommendations for international students: Required—TOEFL (minimum score 550 paper-based; 80 iBT), IELTS (minimum score 6.5). *Application deadline:* For fall admission, 2/1 priority date for domestic and international students. Applications are processed on a rolling basis. Application fee: $75 ($90 for international students). Electronic applications accepted. *Expenses:* Tuition, state resident: full-time $6347; part-time $352.60 per credit hour. Tuition, nonresident: full-time $17,379; part-time $965.50 per credit hour. *Required fees:* $1035. Tuition and fees vary according to course load, campus/location and program. *Financial support:* Fellowships, research assistantships, teaching assistantships, institutionally sponsored loans, scholarships/grants, traineeships, health care benefits, and unspecified assistantships available. Support available to part-time students.
Website: http://truman.missouri.edu/

University of Nebraska at Omaha, Graduate Studies, College of Arts and Sciences, Program in Critical and Creative Thinking, Omaha, NE 68182. Offers MA. *Program availability:* Part-time, online learning. *Students:* 2 full-time (1 woman), 30 part-time (21 women); includes 4 minority (3 Black or African American, non-Hispanic/Latino; 1 Asian, non-Hispanic/Latino). Average age 34. 29 applicants, 86% accepted, 18 enrolled. *Entrance requirements:* For master's, undergraduate degree with minimum GPA of 3.0. Additional exam requirements/recommendations for international students: Required—TOEFL, IELTS, or PTE. *Application deadline:* For fall admission, 7/1 priority date for domestic and international students; for spring admission, 11/1 priority date for domestic and international students; for summer admission, 3/1 for domestic and international students. Applications are processed on a rolling basis. Application fee: $45. Electronic applications accepted. *Financial support:* In 2016–17, 1 student received support, including 1 teaching assistantship; fellowships, research assistantships, Federal Work-Study, institutionally sponsored loans, scholarships/grants, health care benefits, tuition waivers, and unspecified assistantships also available. Support available to part-time students. *Unit head:* Joe Price, Coordinator, 402-554-2341, E-mail: graduate@unomaha.edu. *Application contact:* Dr. Joseph Price, Graduate Program Chair, 402-554-2341, E-mail: graduate@unomaha.edu.

University of New Haven, Graduate School, College of Arts and Sciences, Program in Industrial and Organizational Psychology, West Haven, CT 06516. Offers conflict management (MA); industrial organizational psychology (MA); industrial-human resources psychology (MA); organizational development and consultation (MA); psychology of conflict management (Graduate Certificate). *Program availability:* Part-time, evening/weekend. *Students:* 72 full-time (49 women), 18 part-time (12 women);

includes 20 minority (10 Black or African American, non-Hispanic/Latino; 1 American Indian or Alaska Native, non-Hispanic/Latino; 6 Asian, non-Hispanic/Latino; 2 Hispanic/Latino; 1 Two or more races, non-Hispanic/Latino), 4 international. Average age 26. 117 applicants, 84% accepted, 34 enrolled. In 2016, 59 master's awarded. *Degree requirements:* For master's, thesis or alternative, internship or practicum. *Entrance requirements:* Additional exam requirements/recommendations for international students: Required—TOEFL (minimum score 80 iBT), IELTS, PTE. *Application deadline:* Applications are processed on a rolling basis. Application fee: $50. Electronic applications accepted. Application fee is waived when completed online. *Expenses:* Contact institution. *Financial support:* Research assistantships with partial tuition reimbursements, teaching assistantships with partial tuition reimbursements, career-related internships or fieldwork, Federal Work-Study, scholarships/grants, and unspecified assistantships available. Support available to part-time students. Financial award applicants required to submit FAFSA. *Unit head:* Dr. Eric Marcus, Coordinator, 203-932-1242, E-mail: emarcus@newhaven.edu. *Application contact:* Michelle Mason, Director of Graduate Enrollment, 203-932-7067.
Website: http://www.newhaven.edu/4730/

University of New Mexico, Anderson School of Management, Department of Organizational Studies, Albuquerque, NM 87131. Offers organizational behavior and human resources management (MBA); strategic management and policy (MBA). *Program availability:* Part-time, evening/weekend. *Faculty:* 17 full-time (12 women), 6 part-time/adjunct (2 women). In 2016, 26 master's awarded. *Entrance requirements:* For master's, GMAT or GRE, minimum GPA of 3.0 on last 60 hours of coursework; bachelor's degree from regionally-accredited college or university in U.S. or its equivalent in another country. Additional exam requirements/recommendations for international students: Required—TOEFL (minimum score 550 paper-based; 79 iBT), IELTS (minimum score 6.5). *Application deadline:* For fall admission, 4/1 priority date for domestic and international students; for spring admission, 10/1 priority date for domestic and international students. Applications are processed on a rolling basis. Application fee: $50. Electronic applications accepted. *Expenses:* Contact institution. *Financial support:* In 2016–17, 4 fellowships (averaging $24,700 per year), 13 research assistantships with partial tuition reimbursements (averaging $15,345 per year) were awarded; career-related internships or fieldwork, Federal Work-Study, scholarships/grants, and unspecified assistantships also available. Support available to part-time students. Financial award application deadline: 6/1; financial award applicants required to submit FAFSA. *Faculty research:* Business ethics and social corporate responsibility, diversity, human resources, organizational strategy, organizational behavior. *Unit head:* Dr. Michelle Arthur, Chair, 505-277-6471, E-mail: arthurm@unm.edu. *Application contact:* Lisa Beauchene, Student Recruitment Specialist, 505-277-6471, E-mail: andersonadvising@unm.edu.
Website: https://www.mgt.unm.edu/dos/default.asp?mm=faculty

University of Northwestern–St. Paul, Master of Organizational Leadership Program, St. Paul, MN 55113-1598. Offers MOL. *Program availability:* Part-time, evening/weekend, online learning. *Application deadline:* Applications are processed on a rolling basis. Electronic applications accepted. *Application contact:* College of Adult and Graduate Studies Admissions, 651-631-5200, E-mail: gradstudies@unwsp.edu.
Website: https://www.unwsp.edu/web/graduate-studies/master-of-organizational-leadership

University of Oklahoma, College of Liberal Studies, Norman, OK 73072. Offers administrative leadership (Graduate Certificate); corrections management (Graduate Certificate); criminal justice (MS); government and military leadership (MA); human and health services administration (MA), including human and health services administration, integrated studies; liberal studies (MPS); organizational leadership (MA); restorative justice administration (Graduate Certificate); volunteer and non-profit leadership (MA). *Program availability:* Part-time, online only, 100% online, blended/hybrid learning. *Faculty:* 13 full-time (7 women), 1 part-time/adjunct (0 women). *Students:* 74 full-time (48 women), 598 part-time (289 women); includes 175 minority (45 Black or African American, non-Hispanic/Latino; 39 American Indian or Alaska Native, non-Hispanic/Latino; 8 Asian, non-Hispanic/Latino; 46 Hispanic/Latino; 1 Native Hawaiian or other Pacific Islander, non-Hispanic/Latino; 36 Two or more races, non-Hispanic/Latino), 2 international. Average age 35. 191 applicants, 95% accepted, 120 enrolled. In 2016, 192 master's, 6 other advanced degrees awarded. *Degree requirements:* For master's, comprehensive exam, thesis optional, 33 credit hours; project/internship (for museum studies); for Graduate Certificate, 12 credit hours. *Entrance requirements:* For master's and Graduate Certificate, minimum GPA of 3.0 in last 60 undergraduate hours; statement of goals; resume. Additional exam requirements/recommendations for international students: Required—TOEFL (minimum score 79 iBT) or IELTS (minimum score 6.5). *Application deadline:* For fall admission, 7/1 for domestic and international students; for winter admission, 12/1 for domestic and international students; for spring admission, 5/1 for domestic and international students. Applications are processed on a rolling basis. Application fee: $50 ($100 for international students). Electronic applications accepted. *Expenses:* Tuition, state resident: full-time $4886; part-time $203.60 per credit hour. Tuition, nonresident: full-time $18,989; part-time $791.20 per credit hour. *Required fees:* $3283; $126.25 per credit hour. $126.50 per semester. *Financial support:* In 2016–17, 124 students received support. Career-related internships or fieldwork, institutionally sponsored loans, scholarships/grants, health care benefits, and tuition waivers available. Support available to part-time students. Financial award application deadline: 6/1; financial award applicants required to submit FAFSA. *Faculty research:* Management and leadership; policing and corrections management; neuro-psychology of addiction; disproportionate minority contact; ethnic identity and nationalism. *Unit head:* Dr. Martha L. Banz, Associate Provost for Continuing Education/Interim Dean, College of Liberal Studies, 405-325-1061, Fax: 405-325-7132, E-mail: mlbanz@ou.edu. *Application contact:* Michelle Shults, Academic Advisement Services Coordinator, 405-325-2928, Fax: 405-325-7132, E-mail: mshults@ou.edu.
Website: http://www.ou.edu/cls/html

University of Pennsylvania, School of Arts and Sciences, College of Liberal and Professional Studies, Philadelphia, PA 19104. Offers applied geosciences (MSAG); applied positive psychology (MAP); chemical sciences (MCS); environmental studies (MES); individualized study (MLA); liberal arts (M Phil); medical physics (MMP); organization dynamics (M Phil). *Students:* 143 full-time (75 women), 337 part-time (189 women); includes 90 minority (28 Black or African American, non-Hispanic/Latino; 2 American Indian or Alaska Native, non-Hispanic/Latino; 22 Asian, non-Hispanic/Latino; 26 Hispanic/Latino; 12 Two or more races, non-Hispanic/Latino), 66 international. Average age 35. 618 applicants, 51% accepted, 231 enrolled. In 2016, 161 master's awarded. *Expenses: Tuition:* Full-time $31,068; part-time $5762 per course. *Required fees:* $3200; $336 per course. Full-time tuition and fees vary according to degree level, program and student level. Part-time tuition and fees vary according to course load, degree level and program. *Unit head:* Nora Lewis, Vice Dean, Professional and Liberal Education, 215-898-7326, E-mail: nlewis@sas.upenn.edu.
Website: http://www.sas.upenn.edu/lps/graduate

University of Pennsylvania, School of Arts and Sciences, Fels Institute of Government, Philadelphia, PA 19104. Offers economic development and growth (Certificate); government administration (MGA); nonprofit administration (Certificate); organization dynamics (MS); politics (Certificate); public administration (MPA); public finance (Certificate). *Program availability:* Part-time, evening/weekend. *Students:* 49 full-time (29 women), 65 part-time (35 women); includes 28 minority (13 Black or African American, non-Hispanic/Latino; 6 Asian, non-Hispanic/Latino; 6 Hispanic/Latino; 3 Two or more races, non-Hispanic/Latino), 18 international. Average age 30. 371 applicants, 39% accepted, 71 enrolled. In 2016, 52 master's, 17 other advanced degrees awarded. *Expenses: Tuition:* Full-time $31,068; part-time $5762 per course. *Required fees:* $3200; $336 per course. Full-time tuition and fees vary according to degree level, program and student level. Part-time tuition and fees vary according to course load, degree level and program. *Financial support:* Application deadline: 1/1.
Website: http://www.fels.upenn.edu/

University of Phoenix–Bay Area Campus, College of Information Systems and Technology, San Jose, CA 95134-1805. Offers information systems (MIS); organizational leadership/information systems and technology (DM). *Program availability:* Evening/weekend. *Degree requirements:* For master's, thesis (for some programs). *Entrance requirements:* For master's, minimum undergraduate GPA of 3.0, 3 years of work experience. Additional exam requirements/recommendations for international students: Required—TOEFL (minimum score 550 paper-based; 79 iBT). Electronic applications accepted.

University of Phoenix–Bay Area Campus, School of Business, San Jose, CA 95134-1805. Offers accountancy (MS); accounting (MBA); business administration (MBA, DBA); energy management (MBA); global management (MBA); health care management (MBA); human resource management (MBA); human resources management (MM); management (MM); marketing (MBA); organizational leadership (DM); project management (MBA); public administration (MPA); technology management (MBA). *Accreditation:* ACBSP. *Program availability:* Evening/weekend, online learning. *Degree requirements:* For master's, thesis (for some programs). *Entrance requirements:* For master's, minimum undergraduate GPA of 3.0, 3 years of work experience. Additional exam requirements/recommendations for international students: Required—TOEFL (minimum score 550 paper-based; 79 iBT). Electronic applications accepted.

University of Phoenix–Online Campus, School of Advanced Studies, Phoenix, AZ 85034-7209. Offers business administration (DBA); education (Ed S); educational leadership (Ed D), including curriculum and instruction, education technology, educational leadership; health administration (DHA); higher education administration (PhD); industrial/organizational psychology (PhD); nursing (PhD); organizational leadership (DM), including information systems and technology, organizational leadership. *Program availability:* Evening/weekend, online learning. *Degree requirements:* For doctorate, thesis/dissertation. *Entrance requirements:* Additional exam requirements/recommendations for international students: Required—TOEFL, TOEIC (Test of English as an International Communication), Berlitz Online English Proficiency Exam, PTE, or IELTS. Electronic applications accepted. *Expenses:* Contact institution.

University of Phoenix–Washington D.C. Campus, College of Information Systems and Technology, Washington, DC 20001. Offers information systems (MIS); organizational leadership/information systems and technology (DM).

University of Phoenix–Washington D.C. Campus, School of Business, Washington, DC 20001. Offers accountancy (MS); business administration (MBA, DBA); human resources management (MM); management (MM); organizational leadership (DM); public administration (MPA). *Accreditation:* ACBSP.

University of Portland, School of Education, Portland, OR 97203-5798. Offers education (MA, MAT); educational leadership (M Ed); English for speakers of other languages (M Ed); initial administrator licensure (M Ed); neuroeducation (M Ed, Ed D); organizational leadership and development (Ed D); reading (M Ed); school leadership and development (Ed D); special education (M Ed). M Ed also available through the Graduate Outreach Program for teachers residing in the Oregon and Washington state areas. *Accreditation:* NCATE. *Program availability:* Part-time, evening/weekend. *Entrance requirements:* For master's, minimum GPA of 3.0, teaching certificate, letters of recommendation, resume, statement of goals, official transcripts. Additional exam requirements/recommendations for international students: Required—TOEFL (minimum score 550 paper-based; 80 iBT), IELTS (minimum score 7). *Faculty research:* Multicultural education, supervision/leadership.

University of Regina, Faculty of Graduate Studies and Research, Kenneth Levene Graduate School of Business, Program in Business Administration, Regina, SK S4S 0A2, Canada. Offers business foundations (PGD); engineering management (MBA); executive business administration (EMBA); international business (MBA); leadership (M Admin); organizational leadership (Master's Certificate); project management (Master's Certificate); public safety management (MBA). *Program availability:* Part-time, evening/weekend. *Faculty:* 43 full-time (15 women), 6 part-time/adjunct (0 women). *Students:* 42 full-time (19 women), 21 part-time (12 women). 65 applicants, 48% accepted. In 2016, 57 master's, 13 other advanced degrees awarded. *Degree requirements:* For master's, project (for some programs). *Entrance requirements:* For master's, GMAT, three years of relevant work experience, four-year undergraduate degree; for other advanced degree, GMAT (for PGD), four-year undergraduate degree and two years of relevant work experience (for Master's Certificate); three years' work experience (for PGD). Additional exam requirements/recommendations for international students: Required—TOEFL (minimum score 580 paper-based; 80 iBT), IELTS (minimum score 6.5), PTE (minimum score 59). *Application deadline:* Applications are processed on a rolling basis. Application fee: $100. Electronic applications accepted. *Expenses:* Contact institution. *Financial support:* In 2016–17, 6 fellowships (averaging $6,000 per year), 7 teaching assistantships (averaging $2,501 per year) were awarded; career-related internships or fieldwork and scholarships/grants also available. Financial award application deadline: 6/15. *Faculty research:* Business policy and strategy, production and operations management, human behavior in organizations, financial management, social issues in business. *Unit head:* Dr. Andrew Gaudes, Dean, 306-585-4162, Fax: 306-585-5361, E-mail: andrew.gaudes@uregina.ca. *Application contact:* Ronald Camp, Graduate Programs, 306-337-2387, Fax: 306-585-5361, E-mail: ronald.camp@uregina.ca.
Website: http://www.uregina.ca/business/levene/

University of Saint Francis, Graduate School, Keith Busse School of Business and Entrepreneurial Leadership, Fort Wayne, IN 46808-3994. Offers business administration (MBA), including sustainability; environmental health (MEH); healthcare administration (MHA); organizational leadership (MOL). *Accreditation:* ACBSP. *Program availability:* Part-time, evening/weekend, online only, 100% online. *Faculty:* 6 full-time (3 women), 13 part-time/adjunct (4 women). *Students:* 77 full-time (51 women), 102 part-time (45 women); includes 40 minority (22 Black or African American, non-Hispanic/Latino; 3 Asian, non-Hispanic/Latino; 12 Hispanic/Latino; 1 Native Hawaiian or other Pacific Islander, non-Hispanic/Latino; 2 Two or more races, non-Hispanic/Latino). Average age 33. 71 applicants, 100% accepted, 46 enrolled. In 2016, 107 master's awarded. *Entrance requirements:* For master's, GMAT if cumulative GPA is below 2.75 with less than five years' professional work experience), minimum undergraduate GPA of 2.75;

statement of professional goals; resume. Additional exam requirements/recommendations for international students: Required—TOEFL (minimum score 550 paper-based) or IELTS (minimum score 6.5). *Application deadline:* Applications are processed on a rolling basis. Application fee: $0. Electronic applications accepted. *Expenses:* $475 per credit hour. *Financial support:* Application deadline: 3/10; applicants required to submit FAFSA. *Unit head:* Dr. Karen Palumbo, Director of Virtual Campus Business Programs, 260-399-7700 Ext. 8312, Fax: 260-399-8174, E-mail: kpalumbo@sf.edu. *Application contact:* Kyle Richardson, Enrollment Services Specialist, 260-399-7700 Ext. 6310, Fax: 260-399-8152, E-mail: krichardson@sf.edu.
Website: http://business.sf.edu/graduate/

University of St. Thomas, Graduate Studies, College of Education, Leadership and Counseling, Department of Organization Learning and Development, St. Paul, MN 55105-1096. Offers organization development and change (MA, Ed D); public safety and law enforcement leadership (MA). *Program availability:* Part-time, evening/weekend. *Degree requirements:* For master's, practicum; for doctorate, comprehensive exam, thesis/dissertation. *Entrance requirements:* For master's, minimum GPA of 3.0, 2 letters of reference, personal statement, 2-5 years of organization experience; for doctorate, minimum GPA of 3.5, interview, 5-7 years of organization development or leadership experience. Additional exam requirements/recommendations for international students: Required—TOEFL (minimum score 550 paper-based). *Application deadline:* For fall admission, 7/15 priority date for domestic and international students; for spring admission, 12/9 priority date for domestic and international students; for summer admission, 4/3 priority date for domestic students, 4/3 for international students. Applications are processed on a rolling basis. Electronic applications accepted. *Expenses:* Contact institution. *Financial support:* Fellowships, research assistantships, institutionally sponsored loans, and scholarships/grants available. Support available to part-time students. Financial award application deadline: 8/1; financial award applicants required to submit FAFSA. *Faculty research:* Workplace conflict, physician leaders, virtual teams, technology use in schools/workplace, developing masterful practitioners. *Unit head:* Jean Davidson, Chair, 651-962-4387, Fax: 651-962-4169, E-mail: jmdavidson@stthomas.edu. *Application contact:* Liz G. Knight, Program Manager, 651-962-4459, Fax: 651-962-4169, E-mail: egknight@stthomas.edu.

University of San Francisco, School of Management, Master of Business Administration Program, San Francisco, CA 94117. Offers entrepreneurship and innovation (MBA); finance (MBA); marketing (MBA); organization development (MBA); DDS/MBA; JD/MBA; MBA/MAPS. *Accreditation:* AACSB. *Program availability:* Part-time, evening/weekend. *Faculty:* 17 full-time (6 women), 5 part-time/adjunct (2 women). *Students:* 146 full-time (70 women), 2 part-time (1 woman); includes 50 minority (5 Black or African American, non-Hispanic/Latino; 27 Asian, non-Hispanic/Latino; 15 Hispanic/Latino; 1 Native Hawaiian or other Pacific Islander, non-Hispanic/Latino; 2 Two or more races, non-Hispanic/Latino), 51 international. Average age 29. 282 applicants, 63% accepted, 70 enrolled. In 2016, 91 master's awarded. *Entrance requirements:* For master's, GMAT or GRE, resume (two years of professional work experience required for part-time students, preferred for full-time), transcripts from each college or university attended, two letters of recommendation, personal statement, interview. Additional exam requirements/recommendations for international students: Required—TOEFL (minimum score 600 paper-based, 100 iBT), IELTS (minimum score 7) or PTE (minimum score 68). *Application deadline:* For fall admission, 6/5 for domestic students, 5/15 for international students; for spring admission, 11/30 for domestic students. Application fee: $55. Electronic applications accepted. *Expenses: Tuition:* Full-time $23,310; part-time $1295 per credit. Tuition and fees vary according to course load, degree level, campus/location and program. *Financial support:* In 2016–17, 60 students received support. Fellowships and scholarships/grants available. Financial award application deadline: 3/2; financial award applicants required to submit FAFSA. *Faculty research:* International financial markets, technology transfer licensing, international marketing, strategic planning. *Total annual research expenditures:* $50,000. *Unit head:* Dr. Frank Fletcher, Director, 415-422-2221, Fax: 415-422-6315, E-mail: management@usfca.edu. *Application contact:* Office of Graduate Recruiting and Admissions, 415-422-2221, Fax: 415-422-6315, E-mail: management@usfca.edu.
Website: http://www.usfca.edu/mba

University of San Francisco, School of Management, Master of Science in Organization Development Program, San Fransisco, CA 94117. Offers MSOD. *Program availability:* Part-time, evening/weekend. *Faculty:* 5 full-time (1 woman). *Students:* 70 full-time (52 women), 3 part-time (2 women); includes 27 minority (8 Black or African American, non-Hispanic/Latino; 8 Asian, non-Hispanic/Latino; 11 Hispanic/Latino), 2 international. Average age 34. 74 applicants, 77% accepted, 43 enrolled. In 2016, 31 master's awarded. *Degree requirements:* For master's, thesis. *Entrance requirements:* For master's, resume demonstrating minimum of two years of professional work experience, transcripts from each college or university attended, two letters of recommendation, personal statement. Additional exam requirements/recommendations for international students: Required—TOEFL (minimum score 600 paper-based, 100 iBT), IELTS (minimum score 7) or PTE. *Application deadline:* For fall admission, 6/15 for domestic students, 5/15 for international students. Application fee: $55. Electronic applications accepted. *Expenses: Tuition:* Full-time $23,310; part-time $1295 per credit. Tuition and fees vary according to course load, degree level, campus/location and program. *Financial support:* In 2016–17, 16 students received support. Scholarships/grants available. Financial award application deadline: 3/2; financial award applicants required to submit FAFSA. *Unit head:* Dr. Rebekah Dibble, Director, 415-422-2221, E-mail: management@usfca.edu. *Application contact:* Office of Graduate Recruiting and Admissions, 415-422-2221, Fax: 415-422-6315, E-mail: management@usfca.edu.
Website: http://www.usfca.edu/msod

The University of South Dakota, Graduate School, College of Arts and Sciences, Program in Administrative Studies, Vermillion, SD 57069. Offers addiction studies (MSA); criminal justice studies (MSA); health services administration (MSA); human resources (MSA); interdisciplinary studies (MSA); long term care administration (MSA); organizational leadership (MSA). *Program availability:* Part-time, evening/weekend, online learning. *Degree requirements:* For master's, thesis or alternative. *Entrance requirements:* For master's, 3 years of work or experience, minimum GPA of 2.7, resume. Additional exam requirements/recommendations for international students: Required—TOEFL (minimum score 550 paper-based; 79 iBT). Electronic applications accepted.

University of Southern California, Graduate School, School of Policy, Planning, and Development, Executive Master of Leadership Program, Los Angeles, CA 90089. Offers EML. *Program availability:* Part-time, evening/weekend. *Entrance requirements:* Additional exam requirements/recommendations for international students: Required—TOEFL (minimum score 600 paper-based; 100 iBT). Electronic applications accepted. *Expenses:* Contact institution. *Faculty research:* Strategic planning, organizational transformation, strategic management, leadership.

University of Southern Indiana, Graduate Studies, College of Nursing and Health Professions, Program in Nursing, Evansville, IN 47712-3590. Offers adult-gerontology acute care nurse practitioner (MSN, PMC); adult-gerontology clinical nurse specialist (MSN, PMC); adult-gerontology primary care nurse practitioner (MSN, PMC); advanced nursing practice (DNP); family nurse practitioner (MSN, PMC); nursing education (MSN, PMC); nursing management and leadership (MSN, PMC); organizational and systems leadership (DNP); psychiatric mental health nurse practitioner (MSN, PMC). *Accreditation:* AACN. *Program availability:* Part-time, online learning. *Faculty:* 11 full-time (10 women), 3 part-time/adjunct (all women). *Students:* 70 full-time (63 women), 368 part-time (328 women); includes 45 minority (24 Black or African American, non-Hispanic/Latino; 1 American Indian or Alaska Native, non-Hispanic/Latino; 5 Asian, non-Hispanic/Latino; 12 Hispanic/Latino; 3 Two or more races, non-Hispanic/Latino). Average age 36. In 2016, 107 master's, 20 doctorates, 8 other advanced degrees awarded. *Entrance requirements:* For master's, BSN from nationally-accredited school; minimum cumulative GPA of 3.0; satisfactory completion of a course in undergraduate statistics (minimum grade C); one year of full-time experience or 2,000 hours of clinical practice as an RN (recommended); unencumbered U.S. RN license; for doctorate, minimum GPA of 3.0, completion of graduate research course with minimum B grade, unencumbered RN license, resume/curriculum vitae, three professional references, 1-2 page narrative of practice experience and professional goals, Capstone Project Information form. Additional exam requirements/recommendations for international students: Required—TOEFL (minimum score 550 paper-based; 79 iBT), IELTS (minimum score 6). *Application deadline:* For fall admission, 2/1 for domestic students, 1/1 priority date for international students. Applications are processed on a rolling basis. Application fee: $40. Electronic applications accepted. *Expenses:* Contact institution. *Financial support:* Federal Work-Study, scholarships/grants, tuition waivers (full and partial), and unspecified assistantships available. Financial award application deadline: 3/1; financial award applicants required to submit FAFSA. *Unit head:* Dr. Mellisa A. Hall, Chair of the Master of Science in Nursing Program, 812-465-1168, E-mail: mrowser@usi.edu. *Application contact:* Dr. Mayola Rowser, Director, Graduate Studies, 812-465-7015, Fax: 812-464-1956, E-mail: mrowser@usi.edu.
Website: https://www.usi.edu/health/nursing/

The University of Texas at San Antonio, College of Business, Department of Management, San Antonio, TX 78249-0617. Offers management and organization studies (PhD). *Faculty:* 12 full-time (5 women). *Students:* 151 full-time (46 women), 64 part-time (20 women); includes 95 minority (12 Black or African American, non-Hispanic/Latino; 1 American Indian or Alaska Native, non-Hispanic/Latino; 13 Asian, non-Hispanic/Latino; 66 Hispanic/Latino; 3 Two or more races, non-Hispanic/Latino), 11 international. Average age 33. 134 applicants, 77% accepted, 77 enrolled. In 2016, 3 doctorates awarded. Terminal master's awarded for partial completion of doctoral program. *Degree requirements:* For doctorate, comprehensive exam, thesis/dissertation. *Entrance requirements:* For doctorate, GMAT, GRE. Additional exam requirements/recommendations for international students: Required—TOEFL (minimum score 550 paper-based; 79 iBT), IELTS (minimum score 6.5). *Application deadline:* For fall admission, 7/1 for domestic students, 4/1 for international students; for spring admission, 11/1 for domestic students, 9/1 for international students. Application fee: $45 ($80 for international students). Electronic applications accepted. *Financial support:* Application deadline: 3/31. *Total annual research expenditures:* $18,948. *Unit head:* Dr. Robert L. Cardy, Chair, 210-458-4310, E-mail: robert.cardy@utsa.edu. *Application contact:* Caron Kiley, Assistant Director of Graduate Fiscal Services/PhD Program Manager, 210-458-7324, Fax: 210-458-4398, E-mail: caron.kiley@utsa.edu.
Website: http://business.utsa.edu/mgt/

The University of Texas at Tyler, College of Business and Technology, Program in Business Administration, Tyler, TX 75799-0001. Offers cyber security (MBA); engineering management (MBA); general management (MBA); healthcare management (MBA); internal assurance and consulting (MBA); marketing (MBA); oil, gas and energy (MBA); organizational development (MBA); quality management (MBA). *Accreditation:* AACSB. *Program availability:* Part-time, online learning. *Entrance requirements:* Additional exam requirements/recommendations for international students: Required—TOEFL (minimum score 550 paper-based). *Faculty research:* General business, inventory control, institutional markets, service marketing, product distribution, accounting fraud, financial reporting and recognition.

University of Wisconsin–Platteville, School of Graduate Studies, Distance Learning Center, Online Master of Science in Organizational Change Leadership Program, Platteville, WI 53818-3099. Offers MS. *Program availability:* Part-time. *Students:* 1 (woman) full-time, 82 part-time (54 women); includes 14 minority (3 Black or African American, non-Hispanic/Latino; 4 American Indian or Alaska Native, non-Hispanic/Latino; 2 Asian, non-Hispanic/Latino; 5 Hispanic/Latino). 26 applicants, 85% accepted, 15 enrolled. In 2016, 17 master's awarded. *Degree requirements:* For master's, capstone, research paper, or thesis research. *Entrance requirements:* Additional exam requirements/recommendations for international students: Required—TOEFL (minimum score 550 paper-based; 79 iBT), IELTS (minimum score 6.5). *Application deadline:* Applications are processed on a rolling basis. Application fee: $56. Electronic applications accepted. *Unit head:* Dawn Drake, Executive Director, 800-362-5460, Fax: 608-342-1071, E-mail: disted@uwplatt.edu. *Application contact:* 800-362-5460, Fax: 608-342-1071, E-mail: disted@uwplatt.edu.

Upper Iowa University, Online Master's Programs, Fayette, IA 52142-1857. Offers accounting (MBA); corporate financial management (MBA); emergency management and homeland security (MPA); general management (MBA); general studies (MPA); government administration (MPA); health and human services (MPA); human resources management (MBA); nonprofit organizational management (MPA); organizational development (MBA); public management (MPA); sport administration (MSA). MBA also available at Madison, WI campus. *Program availability:* Part-time, online learning. *Degree requirements:* For master's, research project. *Entrance requirements:* For master's, GMAT, GRE, or minimum GPA of 2.7 during last 60 hours. Additional exam requirements/recommendations for international students: Required—TOEFL (minimum score 570 paper-based). Electronic applications accepted. *Faculty research:* Total quality management, teams, organization culture and climate, management.

Vanderbilt University, Peabody College, Department of Leadership, Policy, and Organizations, Nashville, TN 37240-1001. Offers education policy (MPP); educational leadership and policy (Ed D); higher education (M Ed); higher education leadership and policy (Ed D); independent school leadership (M Ed); international education policy and management (M Ed); leadership and organizational performance (M Ed). *Program availability:* Part-time. *Faculty:* 29 full-time (14 women), 21 part-time/adjunct (5 women). *Students:* 166 full-time (124 women), 107 part-time (63 women); includes 50 minority (25 Black or African American, non-Hispanic/Latino; 7 Asian, non-Hispanic/Latino; 9 Hispanic/Latino; 1 Native Hawaiian or other Pacific Islander, non-Hispanic/Latino; 8 Two or more races, non-Hispanic/Latino), 32 international. Average age 29. 543 applicants, 63% accepted, 133 enrolled. In 2016, 109 master's, 22 doctorates awarded. *Degree requirements:* For master's, comprehensive exam, thesis optional; for doctorate, thesis/dissertation, qualifying exams, residency. *Entrance requirements:* For master's and doctorate, GRE General Test. Additional exam requirements/recommendations for international students: Required—TOEFL (minimum score 550 paper-based; 80 iBT). *Application deadline:* For fall admission, 12/31 priority date for domestic and international students; for spring admission, 11/1 priority date for domestic and international students. Applications are processed on a rolling basis. Application fee: $0. Electronic applications accepted. *Expenses: Tuition:* Part-time $1854 per credit hour. *Financial support:* Fellowships with partial tuition reimbursements, research

assistantships with partial tuition reimbursements, teaching assistantships with partial tuition reimbursements, Federal Work-Study, institutionally sponsored loans, scholarships/grants, tuition waivers (partial), and unspecified assistantships available. Support available to part-time students. Financial award application deadline: 1/15; financial award applicants required to submit FAFSA. *Faculty research:* Higher education, educational leadership, education policy, international education, educator effectiveness. *Unit head:* Dr. Ellen B. Goldring, Chair, 615-322-8000, Fax: 615-343-7094, E-mail: ellen.b.goldring@vanderbilt.edu. *Application contact:* Rosie Moody, Educational Coordinator, 615-322-8019, Fax: 615-343-7094, E-mail: rosie.moody@vanderbilt.edu.
Website: http://peabody.vanderbilt.edu/departments/lpo/index.php

Vanderbilt University, Vanderbilt University Owen Graduate School of Management, Vanderbilt MBA Program, Nashville, TN 37203. Offers accounting (MBA); finance (MBA); general management (MBA); health care (MBA); human and organizational performance (MBA); marketing (MBA); operations (MBA); strategy (MBA); MBA/JD; MBA/M Div; MBA/MD; MBA/MSN; MBA/MTS; MBA/PhD. *Accreditation:* AACSB. *Degree requirements:* For master's, 62 credit hours of coursework; completion of ethics course; minimum GPA of 3.0. *Entrance requirements:* For master's, GMAT (preferred) or GRE, 2 years of work experience (recommended). Additional exam requirements/recommendations for international students: Required—TOEFL (minimum score 100 iBT). Electronic applications accepted. *Expenses:* Contact institution. *Faculty research:* Accounting and finance, business strategy and economics, marketing, operations management, organization studies.

Viterbo University, Master of Arts in Servant Leadership Program, La Crosse, WI 54601-4797. Offers ethical leadership in organizations (Certificate); servant leadership (MA). *Program availability:* Part-time, evening/weekend. *Degree requirements:* For master's, 30 credits (15 credits of Servant Leadership core courses and any combination of 15 elective credits). *Entrance requirements:* For master's, letter of reference, statement of goals, baccalaureate degree, transcript, interview. Additional exam requirements/recommendations for international students: Required—TOEFL (minimum score 525 paper-based). Electronic applications accepted. *Expenses:* Contact institution. *Faculty research:* Organizational culture, community building, ethical decision-making, leadership theory and practice.

Walden University, Graduate Programs, School of Management, Minneapolis, MN 55401. Offers accounting (MBA, MS, DBA), including accounting for the professional (MS), accounting with CPA emphasis (MS), self-designed (MS); advanced project management (Graduate Certificate); applied project management (Graduate Certificate); auditing (Graduate Certificate); bridge to business administration (Post-Doctoral Certificate); bridge to management (Post-Doctoral Certificate); business management (Graduate Certificate); communication (MBA); corporate finance (MBA); digital marketing (Graduate Certificate); entrepreneurship (DBA); entrepreneurship and small business (MBA); finance (MS, DBA), including finance for the professional (MS), finance with CFA/investment (MS), finance with CPA emphasis (MS); global supply chain management (DBA); healthcare management (MBA, DBA); human resource management (MBA, MS, Graduate Certificate), including functional human resource management (MS), general program (MS), integrating functional and strategic human resource management (MS), organizational strategy (MS); human resources management (DBA); information systems management (DBA); international business (MBA, DBA); leadership (MBA, MS, DBA, Graduate Certificate), including general program (MS), human resource leadership (MS), leader development (MS), self-designed (MS); management (MS, PhD), including communications (MS), finance (PhD), general program (MS), healthcare management (MS), human resource management (MS), human resources management (PhD), information systems management (PhD), international business (MS), leadership (MS), leadership and organizational change (PhD), marketing (MS), project management (MS), strategy and operations (MS); managerial accounting (Graduate Certificate); marketing (MBA, MS, DBA); project management (MBA, MS, DBA); self-designed (MBA, DBA); social impact management (DBA); technology entrepreneurship (DBA). *Accreditation:* ACBSP. *Program availability:* Part-time, evening/weekend, online only, 100% online. *Degree requirements:* For master's, thesis (for some programs), residency (for EMBA); for doctorate, thesis/dissertation (for some programs), residency. *Entrance requirements:* For master's, bachelor's degree or higher; minimum GPA of 2.5; official transcripts; goal statement (for some programs); access to computer and Internet; for doctorate, master's degree or higher; three years of related professional or academic experience (preferred); minimum GPA of 3.0; goal statement and current resume (for select programs); official transcripts; access to computer and Internet; for other advanced degree, relevant work experience; access to computer and Internet. Additional exam requirements/recommendations for international students: Required—TOEFL (minimum score 550 paper-based, 79 iBT), IELTS (minimum score 6.5), Michigan English Language Assessment Battery (minimum score 82), or PTE (minimum score 53). Electronic applications accepted.

Walden University, Graduate Programs, School of Public Policy and Administration, Minneapolis, MN 55401. Offers criminal justice (MPA, MPP, MS, Graduate Certificate), including emergency management (MS, PhD), general program (MS), global leadership (MS, PhD), homeland security and policy coordination (MS, PhD), law and public policy (MS, PhD), policy analysis (MS, PhD), public management and leadership (MS, PhD), self-designed (MS), terrorism, mediation, and peace (MS, PhD); criminal justice and executive management (MS), including global leadership (MS, PhD); criminal justice leadership and executive management (MS), including emergency management (MS, PhD), general program, homeland security and policy coordination (MS, PhD), law and public policy (MS, PhD), policy analysis (MS, PhD), public management and leadership (MS, PhD), self-designed, terrorism, mediation, and peace (MS, PhD); emergency management (MPA, MPP, MS), including criminal justice (MS, PhD), general program (MS), homeland security (MS), public management and leadership (MS, PhD), terrorism and emergency management (MS); general program (MPA, MPP); global leadership (MPA, MPP); government management (Graduate Certificate); health policy (MPA, MPP); homeland security (Graduate Certificate); homeland security and policy coordination (MPA, MPP); international nongovernmental organizations (MPA, MPP); law and public policy (MPA, MPP); local government management for sustainable communities (MPA, MPP); nonprofit management (Graduate Certificate); nonprofit management and leadership (MPA, MPP, MS), including global leadership (MS, PhD), international nongovernmental organization (MS), local government for sustainable communities (MS), self designed (MS); online teaching in higher education (Post-Master's Certificate); policy analysis (MPA); public management and leadership (MPA, MPP, Graduate Certificate); public policy (Graduate Certificate); public policy and administration (PhD), including criminal justice (MS, PhD), emergency management (MS, PhD), global leadership (MS, PhD), health policy, homeland security and policy coordination (MS, PhD), international nongovernmental organizations, law and public policy (MS, PhD), local government for sustainable communities, nonprofit management and leadership, policy analysis (MS, PhD), public management and leadership (MS, PhD), terrorism, mediation, and peace (MS, PhD); strategic planning and public policy (Graduate Certificate); terrorism, mediation, and peace (MPA, MPP). *Program availability:* Part-time, evening/weekend, online only, 100% online. *Degree requirements:* For doctorate, thesis/dissertation, residency. *Entrance requirements:* For master's, bachelor's degree or higher; minimum GPA of 2.5; official transcripts; goal statement (for some programs); access to computer and Internet; for doctorate, master's degree or higher; three years of related professional or academic experience (preferred); minimum GPA of 3.0; goal statement and current resume (for select programs); official transcripts; access to computer and Internet; for other advanced degree, relevant work experience; access to computer and Internet. Additional exam requirements/recommendations for international students: Required—TOEFL (minimum score 550 paper-based, 79 iBT), IELTS (minimum score 6.5), Michigan English Language Assessment Battery (minimum score 82), or PTE (minimum score 53). Electronic applications accepted.

Waldorf University, Program in Organizational Leadership, Forest City, IA 50436. Offers criminal justice leadership (MA); emergency management leadership (MA); fire/rescue executive leadership (MA); human resource development (MA); public administration (MA); sport management (MA); teacher leader (MA).

Warner Pacific College, Graduate Programs, Portland, OR 97215-4099. Offers human services (MA); not-for-profit leadership (MS); organizational leadership (MS); teaching (MAT). *Program availability:* Part-time, evening/weekend. *Degree requirements:* For master's, thesis or alternative, presentation of defense. *Entrance requirements:* For master's, interview, minimum GPA of 2.5, letters of recommendation. *Faculty research:* New Testament studies, nineteenth-century Wesleyan theology, preaching and church growth, Christian ethics.

Washington University in St. Louis, Olin Business School, Master of Science in Leadership Program, Washington, DC 20036. Offers MS. Program offered in partnership with the Brookings Institution. *Program availability:* Part-time. *Faculty:* 93 full-time (22 women), 46 part-time/adjunct (10 women). *Students:* 80 part-time (30 women); includes 30 minority (17 Black or African American, non-Hispanic/Latino; 1 Asian, non-Hispanic/Latino; 2 Hispanic/Latino; 1 Native Hawaiian or other Pacific Islander, non-Hispanic/Latino; 9 Two or more races, non-Hispanic/Latino). 25 applicants, 100% accepted, 25 enrolled. In 2016, 1 master's awarded. *Degree requirements:* For master's, 30 credit hours: 25 credit hours in the executive pathways courses and 5 credit hours comprised of weeklong residential program and capstone course. *Entrance requirements:* For master's, bachelor's degree. *Application deadline:* Applications are processed on a rolling basis. Application fee: $0. Electronic applications accepted. *Unit head:* Dr. Mark Taylor, Dean, 314-935-5000, E-mail: mark.p.taylor@wustl.edu. *Application contact:* Abby Millar, Information Contact, 202-238-3579, E-mail: amillar@brookings.edu.
Website: http://www.olin.wustl.edu/EN-US/academic-programs/Pages/MS-Leadership.aspx

Wayland Baptist University, Graduate Programs, Programs in Business Administration/Management, Plainview, TX 79072-6998. Offers accounting (MBA); general business (MBA); health care administration (MAM, MBA); human resource management (MAM, MBA); international management (MBA); management (MBA, D Mgt); management information systems (MBA); organization management (MAM); project management (MBA). *Program availability:* Part-time, evening/weekend, online learning. *Degree requirements:* For master's, capstone course. *Entrance requirements:* For master's, GMAT, GRE or MAT. Additional exam requirements/recommendations for international students: Required—TOEFL (minimum score 500 paper-based; 61 iBT). Electronic applications accepted.

Waynesburg University, Graduate and Professional Studies, Canonsburg, PA 15370. Offers business (MBA), including energy management, finance, health systems, human resources, leadership, market development; counseling (MA), including addictions counseling, clinical mental health; counselor education and supervision (PhD); criminal investigation (MA); education (M Ed), including autism, curriculum and instruction, educational leadership, online teaching; nursing (MSN), including administration, education, informatics; nursing practice (DNP); special education (M Ed); technology (M Ed); MSN/MBA. *Accreditation:* AACN. *Program availability:* Part-time, evening/weekend. *Degree requirements:* For doctorate, thesis/dissertation. *Entrance requirements:* Additional exam requirements/recommendations for international students: Required—TOEFL. Electronic applications accepted.

Wayne State College, Department of Health, Human Performance and Sport, Wayne, NE 68787. Offers exercise science (MSE); organizational management (MS), including sport management. *Program availability:* Part-time, evening/weekend. *Degree requirements:* For master's, comprehensive exam, thesis optional. *Entrance requirements:* For master's, GRE General Test, minimum GPA of 3.0. Additional exam requirements/recommendations for international students: Required—TOEFL (minimum score 550 paper-based). Electronic applications accepted.

Wayne State University, College of Liberal Arts and Sciences, Department of Political Science, Detroit, MI 48202. Offers political science (MA, PhD); public administration (MPA), including economic development policy and management, health and human services policy and management, human and fiscal resource management, nonprofit policy and management, organizational behavior and management, urban and metropolitan policy and management; JD/MA. *Accreditation:* NASPAA. *Faculty:* 20. *Students:* 64 full-time (20 women), 75 part-time (45 women); includes 48 minority (32 Black or African American, non-Hispanic/Latino; 5 Asian, non-Hispanic/Latino; 4 Hispanic/Latino; 7 Two or more races, non-Hispanic/Latino), 7 international. Average age 33. 105 applicants, 50% accepted, 27 enrolled. In 2016, 25 master's, 5 doctorates awarded. *Degree requirements:* For master's, comprehensive exam (for some programs), thesis (for some programs); for doctorate, thesis/dissertation. *Entrance requirements:* For master's, GRE General Test, substantial undergraduate preparation in the social sciences, minimum upper-division undergraduate GPA of 3.0, two letters of recommendation, personal statement; for doctorate, GRE General Test, 3 letters of recommendation; personal statement; interview. Additional exam requirements/recommendations for international students: Required—TOEFL (minimum score 550 paper-based; 79 iBT), TWE (minimum score 5.5), Michigan English Language Assessment Battery (minimum score 85); Recommended—IELTS (minimum score 6.5). *Application deadline:* For fall admission, 5/15 for domestic students, 5/1 priority date for international students; for winter admission, 10/15 for domestic students, 9/1 priority date for international students. Applications are processed on a rolling basis. Application fee: $50. Electronic applications accepted. *Expenses:* $16,503 per year resident tuition and fees, $33,697 per year non-resident tuition and fees. *Financial support:* In 2016–17, 48 students received support, including 3 fellowships with tuition reimbursements available (averaging $17,333 per year), 13 teaching assistantships with tuition reimbursements available (averaging $18,067 per year); research assistantships with tuition reimbursements available, scholarships/grants, health care benefits, and unspecified assistantships also available. Financial award applicants required to submit FAFSA. *Faculty research:* American government and politics, comparative politics, political methodology, political theory, public administration, public law, public policy, world politics/international relations, formal theory/modeling, gender and politics, international law, peace research, political economy, political psychology, politics of developing countries, race, religion, and ethnicity, urban politics. *Unit head:* Dr. Daniel Geller, Professor and Chair, 313-577-6328, E-mail: dgeller@wayne.edu. *Application contact:* Dr. Sharon Lean, Graduate Director, 313-577-2630, E-mail: gradpolisci@

wayne.edu.
Website: http://clas.wayne.edu/politicalscience/

Western New England University, College of Business, Program in Organizational Leadership, Springfield, MA 01119. Offers MS. *Program availability:* Part-time, evening/weekend. *Faculty:* 21 full-time (9 women). *Students:* 18 part-time (10 women). Average age 36. 7 applicants, 29% accepted, 1 enrolled. In 2016, 1 master's awarded. *Entrance requirements:* For master's, GMAT, transcript, two letters of recommendation, two essays, resume. Additional exam requirements/recommendations for international students: Required—TOEFL (minimum score 79 iBT). *Application deadline:* Applications are processed on a rolling basis. Application fee: $30. Electronic applications accepted. *Expenses:* Contact institution. *Financial support:* Application deadline: 4/15; applicants required to submit FAFSA. *Unit head:* Dr. Rob Kleine, Dean, 413-782-1395, E-mail: rob.kleine@wne.edu. *Application contact:* Matthew Fox, Director of Admissions for Graduate Students and Adult Learners, 413-782-1410, Fax: 413-782-1777, E-mail: study@wne.edu.
Website: http://www1.wne.edu/academics/graduate/organizational-leadership.cfm

West Liberty University, School of Professional Studies, West Liberty, WV 26074. Offers justice leadership (MPS); organizational leadership (MPS). *Entrance requirements:* For master's, bachelor's degree from accredited institution, minimum GPA of 2.5. *Application deadline:* Applications are processed on a rolling basis. *Expenses:* Tuition, state resident: full-time $7074; part-time $393 per credit. Tuition, nonresident: full-time $11,124; part-time $618 per credit. *Unit head:* Dr. Thomas Michaud, Dean, 304-217-2800, E-mail: tmichaud@westliberty.edu.
Website: http://www.westliberty.edu/highlands/ps/

Wheeling Jesuit University, Department of Social Sciences, Wheeling, WV 26003-6295. Offers MSOL. *Program availability:* Part-time, evening/weekend. *Degree requirements:* For master's, thesis. *Entrance requirements:* For master's, MAT, minimum GPA of 2.75, minimum of three years full-time professional work experience. Additional exam requirements/recommendations for international students: Required—TOEFL (minimum score 600 paper-based; 100 iBT). Electronic applications accepted. Application fee is waived when completed online. *Faculty research:* History, theory and philosophy of leadership; gender roles and leadership; spirituality and leadership.

Wilfrid Laurier University, Faculty of Graduate and Postdoctoral Studies, Lyle S. Hallman Faculty of Social Work, Waterloo, ON N2L 3C5, Canada. Offers Aboriginal studies (MSW); community, policy, planning and organizations (MSW); critical social policy and organizational studies (PhD); individuals, families and groups (MSW); social work practice (individuals, families, groups and communities) (PhD); social work practice: individuals, families, groups and communities (PhD). *Program availability:* Part-time. *Degree requirements:* For master's, thesis optional; for doctorate, thesis/dissertation. *Entrance requirements:* For master's, course work in social science, research methodology, and statistics; honors BA with a minimum B average; for doctorate, master's degree in social work, minimum A- average. Additional exam requirements/recommendations for international students: Required—TOEFL (minimum score 89 iBT). Electronic applications accepted. *Expenses:* Contact institution.

Wilkes University, College of Graduate and Professional Studies, Jay S. Sidhu School of Business and Leadership, Wilkes-Barre, PA 18766-0002. Offers accounting (MBA); entrepreneurship (MBA); finance (MBA); health care administration (MBA); human resource management (MBA); international business (MBA); operations management (MBA); organizational leadership and development (MBA). *Accreditation:* ACBSP. *Program availability:* Part-time, evening/weekend. *Students:* 35 full-time (17 women), 112 part-time (55 women); includes 17 minority (6 Black or African American, non-Hispanic/Latino; 4 Asian, non-Hispanic/Latino; 5 Hispanic/Latino; 2 Two or more races, non-Hispanic/Latino), 16 international. Average age 31. In 2016, 59 master's awarded. *Entrance requirements:* For master's, GMAT. Additional exam requirements/recommendations for international students: Required—TOEFL (minimum score 550 paper-based; 79 iBT). *Application deadline:* Applications are processed on a rolling basis. Application fee: $45 ($65 for international students). Electronic applications accepted. *Expenses:* Contact institution. *Financial support:* Unspecified assistantships available. Financial award application deadline: 3/1; financial award applicants required to submit FAFSA. *Unit head:* Dr. Abel Adekola, Dean, 570-408-4701, Fax: 570-408-7846, E-mail: abel.adekola@wilkes.edu. *Application contact:* Director of Graduate Enrollment, 570-408-4234, Fax: 570-408-7846.
Website: http://www.wilkes.edu/academics/colleges/sidhu-school-of-business-leadership/index.aspx

William Penn University, College for Working Adults, Oskaloosa, IA 52577-1799. Offers business leadership (MBL). *Program availability:* Online learning.

Williamson College, Program in Organizational Leadership, Franklin, TN 37067. Offers MA. *Program availability:* Evening/weekend. *Degree requirements:* For master's, capstone project. *Entrance requirements:* For master's, essay, official transcripts, minimum overall GPA of 2.5.

Wilmington University, College of Business, New Castle, DE 19720-6491. Offers accounting (MBA, MS); business administration (MBA, DBA); environmental stewardship (MBA); finance (MBA); health care administration (MBA, MSM); homeland security (MBA, MSM); human resource management (MSM); management information systems (MBA, MSN); marketing (MSM); marketing management (MBA); military leadership (MSM); organizational leadership (MBA, MSM); public administration (MSM). *Program availability:* Part-time, evening/weekend. *Faculty:* 17 full-time (7 women), 106 part-time/adjunct (46 women). *Students:* 436 full-time (237 women), 1,202 part-time (739 women); includes 594 minority (474 Black or African American, non-Hispanic/Latino; 19 American Indian or Alaska Native, non-Hispanic/Latino; 64 Asian, non-Hispanic/Latino; 30 Hispanic/Latino; 3 Native Hawaiian or other Pacific Islander, non-Hispanic/Latino; 4 Two or more races, non-Hispanic/Latino), 153 international. Average age 35. 814 applicants, 98% accepted, 426 enrolled. In 2016, 594 master's, 23 doctorates awarded. *Entrance requirements:* Additional exam requirements/recommendations for international students: Required—TOEFL (minimum score 500 paper-based). *Application deadline:* Applications are processed on a rolling basis. Application fee: $35. Electronic applications accepted. *Expenses: Tuition:* Full-time $8388; part-time $466 per credit. *Required fees:* $25 per semester. Tuition and fees vary according to degree level. *Financial support:* Applicants required to submit FAFSA. *Unit head:* Dr. Robert W. Rescigno, Dean. *Application contact:* Laura Morris, Director of Admissions, 877-967-5456, E-mail: infocenter@wilmu.edu.
Website: http://www.wilmu.edu/business/

Woodbury University, School of Business, Program in Organizational Leadership, Burbank, CA 91504-1099. Offers MA. *Program availability:* Evening/weekend. *Entrance requirements:* For master's, GRE General Test (if GPA less than 2.5), 3 recommendations, essay, resume, academic transcripts. Additional exam requirements/recommendations for international students: Required—TOEFL (minimum score 550 paper-based; 83 iBT), IELTS (minimum score 6.5).

Worcester Polytechnic Institute, Graduate Studies and Research, Foisie Business School, Worcester, MA 01609-2280. Offers information technology (MS), including information security management; management (Graduate Certificate); marketing and technological innovation (MS); operations design and leadership (MS); technology (MBA, MS). *Accreditation:* AACSB. *Program availability:* Part-time, evening/weekend, 100% online, blended/hybrid learning. *Faculty:* 20 full-time (12 women), 16 part-time/adjunct (1 woman). *Students:* 237 full-time (139 women), 186 part-time (67 women); includes 35 minority (4 Black or African American, non-Hispanic/Latino; 17 Asian, non-Hispanic/Latino; 12 Hispanic/Latino; 2 Two or more races, non-Hispanic/Latino), 221 international. 645 applicants, 62% accepted, 144 enrolled. In 2016, 150 master's awarded. *Degree requirements:* For master's, thesis optional. *Entrance requirements:* For master's, GMAT (MBA); GMAT or GRE General Test (MS), statement of purpose, 3 letters of recommendation, resume; for Graduate Certificate, GMAT or GRE General Test, statement of purpose, 3 letters of recommendation. Additional exam requirements/recommendations for international students: Required—TOEFL (minimum score 563 paper-based; 84 iBT), IELTS (minimum score 7). *Application deadline:* For fall admission, 6/1 priority date for domestic and international students; for spring admission, 11/1 priority date for domestic students, 10/1 priority date for international students. Applications are processed on a rolling basis. Application fee: $70. Electronic applications accepted. *Financial support:* Career-related internships or fieldwork, institutionally sponsored loans, scholarships/grants, and unspecified assistantships available. Financial award application deadline: 6/1; financial award applicants required to submit FAFSA. *Unit head:* Melissa Terrio, Executive Director, 508-831-4665, Fax: 508-831-4665, E-mail: biz@wpi.edu. *Application contact:* Eileen Dagostino, Recruiting Operations Coordinator, 508-831-4665, Fax: 508-831-5720, E-mail: edag@wpi.edu.
Website: https://www.wpi.edu/academics/business

Worcester State University, Graduate Studies, Program in Management, Worcester, MA 01602-2597. Offers accounting (MS); managerial leadership (MS). *Program availability:* Part-time, evening/weekend. *Faculty:* 7 full-time (3 women). *Students:* 9 full-time (5 women), 36 part-time (22 women); includes 11 minority (5 Black or African American, non-Hispanic/Latino; 2 Asian, non-Hispanic/Latino; 3 Hispanic/Latino; 1 Two or more races, non-Hispanic/Latino), 3 international. Average age 32. 44 applicants, 70% accepted, 15 enrolled. In 2016, 10 master's awarded. *Degree requirements:* For master's, comprehensive exam (for some programs), thesis optional. *Entrance requirements:* For master's, GMAT, 3 letters of recommendation from professors and/or supervisors. Additional exam requirements/recommendations for international students: Required—TOEFL (minimum score 550 paper-based; 79 iBT). *Application deadline:* For fall admission, 6/15 for domestic and international students; for spring admission, 11/1 for domestic and international students; for summer admission, 4/1 for domestic and international students. Applications are processed on a rolling basis. Application fee: $50. Electronic applications accepted. *Expenses:* Tuition, state resident: part-time $150 per credit. Tuition, nonresident: part-time $150 per credit. *Financial support:* Career-related internships or fieldwork, scholarships/grants, and unspecified assistantships available. Financial award application deadline: 3/1; financial award applicants required to submit FAFSA. *Unit head:* Dr. Elizabeth Wark, Program Coordinator, 508-929-8743, E-mail: ewark@worcester.edu. *Application contact:* Sara Grady, Associate Dean, Graduate Studies and Professional Development, 508-929-8787, Fax: 508-929-8100, E-mail: sara.grady@worcester.edu.

Yale University, Yale School of Management and Graduate School of Arts and Sciences, Doctoral Program in Management, New Haven, CT 06520. Offers accounting (PhD); financial economics (PhD); marketing (PhD); organizations and management (PhD). *Accreditation:* AACSB. *Degree requirements:* For doctorate, comprehensive exam, thesis/dissertation. *Entrance requirements:* For doctorate, GMAT or GRE General Test. Additional exam requirements/recommendations for international students: Required—TOEFL or IELTS. Electronic applications accepted. *Expenses:* Contact institution. *Faculty research:* Pricing of options and futures, term structure of interest rates, use of accounting numbers in debt contracts, product differentiation, e-commerce and marketing, behavioral finance.

Section 17
Project Management

This section contains a directory of institutions offering graduate work in project management. Additional information about programs listed in the directory but not augmented by an in-depth entry may be obtained by writing directly to the dean of a graduate school or chair of a department at the address given in the directory.

For programs offering related work, see also in this book *Business Administration and Management*.

CONTENTS

Program Directory

Project Management

Amberton University, Graduate School, Department of Business Administration, Garland, TX 75041-5595. Offers general business (MBA); management (MBA); project management (MBA); strategic leadership (MBA). *Program availability:* Part-time, evening/weekend. *Entrance requirements:* For master's, minimum GPA of 3.0.

American Business & Technology University, Programs in Business Administration, Saint Joseph, MO 64506. Offers business administration (MBA); financial management (MBA); global business management (MBA); information systems management (MBA); marketing and social media (MBA); project and operations management (MBA); public accounting (MBA). *Program availability:* Online learning.

American InterContinental University Online, Program in Business Administration, Schaumburg, IL 60173. Offers accounting and finance (MBA); finance (MBA); healthcare management (MBA); human resource management (MBA); international business (MBA); management (MBA); marketing (MBA); operations management (MBA); organizational psychology and development (MBA); project management (MBA). *Accreditation:* ACBSP. *Program availability:* Evening/weekend, online learning. *Entrance requirements:* Additional exam requirements/recommendations for international students: Required—TOEFL (minimum score 550 paper-based). Electronic applications accepted.

American InterContinental University Online, Program in Information Technology, Schaumburg, IL 60173. Offers Internet security (MIT); IT project management (MIT). *Program availability:* Evening/weekend, online learning. *Entrance requirements:* Additional exam requirements/recommendations for international students: Required—TOEFL (minimum score 550 paper-based). Electronic applications accepted.

American Public University System, AMU/APU Graduate Programs, Charles Town, WV 25414. Offers accounting (MBA, MS); applied business analytics (MBA, MS); criminal justice (MA), including business administration, emergency and disaster management, general (MA, MS); educational leadership (M Ed); emergency and disaster management (MA); entrepreneurship (MBA); environmental policy and management (MS), including environmental planning, environmental sustainability, fish and wildlife management, general (MA, MS), global environmental management; finance (MBA); general (MBA); government contracting and acquisition (MBA); health care administration (MBA); health information management (MS); history (MA), including American history, ancient and classical history, European history, global history, public history; homeland security (MA), including business administration, counterterrorism studies, criminal justice, cyber, emergency management and public health, intelligence studies, transportation security; homeland security resource allocation (MBA); humanities (MA); information technology (MS), including digital forensics, enterprise software development, information assurance and security, IT project management; information technology management (MBA); intelligence studies (MA), including criminal intelligence, cyber, general (MA, MS), homeland security, intelligence analysis, intelligence collection, intelligence management, intelligence operations, terrorism studies; international relations and conflict resolution (MA), including comparative and security issues, conflict resolution, international and transnational security issues, peacekeeping; legal studies (MA); management (MA), including strategic consulting; marketing (MBA); military history (MA), including American military history, American Revolution, civil war, war since 1945, World War II; military studies (MA), including joint warfare, strategic leadership; national security studies (MA), including cyber, general (MA, MS), homeland security, regional security studies, security and intelligence analysis, terrorism studies; nonprofit management (MBA); political science (MA), including American politics and government, comparative government and development, general (MA, MS), international relations, public policy; psychology (MA); public administration (MPA), including disaster management, environmental policy, health policy, human resources, national security, organizational management, security management; public health (MPH); reverse logistics management (MA); security management (MA); space studies (MS), including aerospace science, general (MA, MS), planetary science; sports and health sciences (MS); sports management (MBA); teaching (M Ed), including autism spectrum disorder, curriculum and instruction for elementary teachers, elementary reading, English language learners, instructional leadership, online learning, special education, STEAM (STEM plus the arts); transportation and logistics management (MA). *Program availability:* Part-time, evening/weekend, online only, 100% online. *Faculty:* 401 full-time (228 women), 1,678 part-time/adjunct (781 women). *Students:* 378 full-time (184 women), 8,455 part-time (3,484 women); includes 2,972 minority (1,552 Black or African American, non-Hispanic/Latino; 52 American Indian or Alaska Native, non-Hispanic/Latino; 211 Asian, non-Hispanic/Latino; 791 Hispanic/Latino; 70 Native Hawaiian or other Pacific Islander, non-Hispanic/Latino; 296 Two or more races, non-Hispanic/Latino), 109 international. Average age 37. In 2016, 3,185 master's awarded. *Degree requirements:* For master's, comprehensive exam or practicum. *Entrance requirements:* For master's, official transcript showing earned bachelor's degree from institution accredited by recognized accrediting body. Additional exam requirements/recommendations for international students: Required—TOEFL (minimum score 550 paper-based), IELTS (minimum score 6.5). *Application deadline:* Applications are processed on a rolling basis. Application fee: $0. Electronic applications accepted. *Expenses: Tuition:* Part-time $350 per credit hour. *Required fees:* $50 per course. *Financial support:* Scholarships/grants available. Financial award applicants required to submit FAFSA. *Unit head:* Dr. Karan Powell, President, 877-468-6268, Fax: 304-724-3780. *Application contact:* Terry Grant, Vice President of Enrollment Management, 877-468-6268, Fax: 304-724-3780, E-mail: info@apus.edu.
Website: http://www.apus.edu

American University, School of Professional and Extended Studies, Washington, DC 20016. Offers healthcare management (MS, Graduate Certificate); human resource analytics and management (Graduate Certificate); measurement and evaluation (MS); project monitoring and evaluation (Graduate Certificate); sports analytics and management (MS, Graduate Certificate). *Program availability:* 100% online. *Faculty:* 28 full-time (12 women), 8 part-time/adjunct (4 women). *Students:* 26 part-time (22 women); includes 1 minority (American Indian or Alaska Native, non-Hispanic/Latino), 2 international. Average age 38. 37 applicants, 100% accepted, 22 enrolled. *Entrance requirements:* For master's, statement of purpose, current resume/curriculum vitae, official transcripts from all academic institutions, letters of recommendation. Additional exam requirements/recommendations for international students: Required—TOEFL or IELTS. *Application deadline:* Applications are processed on a rolling basis. Application fee: $55. Electronic applications accepted. *Expenses:* $1,579 per credit; $690 mandatory fees; some programs charge different fee for spring enrollment. *Financial support:* Applicants required to submit FAFSA. *Unit head:* Carola Weil, Dean, 202-885-5990, Fax: 202-895-4960, E-mail: weil@american.edu. *Application contact:* Heather Broberg, Assistant Director for Recruitment and Admission, 202-895-4953, E-mail: broberg@american.edu.
Website: http://www.american.edu/spexs/

Aspen University, Program in Business Administration, Denver, CO 80246-1930. Offers business administration (MBA); finance (MBA); information management (MBA); project management (MBA, Certificate). *Program availability:* Part-time, evening/weekend, online learning. *Entrance requirements:* Additional exam requirements/recommendations for international students: Required—TOEFL (minimum score 530 paper-based). Electronic applications accepted.

Athabasca University, Faculty of Business, Edmonton, AB T5L 4W1, Canada. Offers business administration (MBA); information technology management (MBA), including policing concentration; innovative management (DBA); management (GDM); project management (MBA, GDM). *Program availability:* Part-time, evening/weekend, online learning. *Degree requirements:* For master's, thesis or alternative, applied project. *Entrance requirements:* For master's, 3-8 years of managerial experience, 3 years with undergraduate degree, 5 years' managerial experience with professional designation, 8-10 years' management experience (on exception). Electronic applications accepted. *Expenses:* Contact institution. *Faculty research:* Human resources, project management, operations research, information technology management, corporate stewardship, energy management.

Avila University, School of Professional Studies, Kansas City, MO 64145-1698. Offers executive leadership development (MS); fundraising (MA); instructional design and technology (MA, MS); leadership coaching (MS); organizational development (MS); project management (MA); strategic human resources (MS). *Program availability:* Part-time-only, evening/weekend, 100% online, blended/hybrid learning. *Faculty:* 15 part-time/adjunct (9 women). *Students:* 90 full-time (59 women), 47 part-time (40 women); includes 50 minority (38 Black or African American, non-Hispanic/Latino; 1 American Indian or Alaska Native, non-Hispanic/Latino; 3 Asian, non-Hispanic/Latino; 7 Hispanic/Latino; 1 Two or more races, non-Hispanic/Latino), 6 international. Average age 38. 95 applicants, 58% accepted, 38 enrolled. In 2016, 37 master's awarded. *Degree requirements:* For master's, thesis optional. *Entrance requirements:* For master's, 2 letters of recommendation, minimum GPA of 3.0 during last 60 hours, resume, statement of intent. Additional exam requirements/recommendations for international students: Required—TOEFL (minimum score 550 paper-based; 79 iBT). *Application deadline:* Applications are processed on a rolling basis. Application fee: $0. Electronic applications accepted. *Expenses:* $545 per credit hour. *Financial support:* In 2016–17, 14 students received support. Unspecified assistantships available. Support available to part-time students. Financial award applicants required to submit FAFSA. *Unit head:* Dr. Steve Iliff, Associate Dean/Director, 816-501-3675, Fax: 816-941-4650, E-mail: advantage@avila.edu. *Application contact:* Jessica Burson, Graduate Admission Advisor, 816-501-2482, Fax: 816-941-4650, E-mail: advantage@avila.edu.
Website: https://www.avila.edu/mrk/advantage-3

Bellevue University, Graduate School, College of Information Technology, Bellevue, NE 68005-3098. Offers computer information systems (MS); cybersecurity (MS); management of information systems (MS); project management (MPM).

Boston University, Metropolitan College, Department of Administrative Sciences, Boston, MA 02215. Offers applied business analytics (MS); economic development and tourism management (MSAS); enterprise risk management (MS); financial management (MS); global marketing management (MS); innovation and technology (MSAS); insurance management (MSM); project management (MS); supply chain management (MS). *Accreditation:* AACSB. *Program availability:* Part-time, evening/weekend, online learning. *Faculty:* 15 full-time (3 women), 22 part-time/adjunct (3 women). *Students:* 301 full-time (146 women), 934 part-time (501 women); includes 237 minority (81 Black or African American, non-Hispanic/Latino; 5 American Indian or Alaska Native, non-Hispanic/Latino; 60 Asian, non-Hispanic/Latino; 76 Hispanic/Latino; 1 Native Hawaiian or other Pacific Islander, non-Hispanic/Latino; 14 Two or more races, non-Hispanic/Latino), 514 international. Average age 31. 593 applicants, 69% accepted, 260 enrolled. In 2016, 263 master's awarded. *Degree requirements:* For master's, thesis optional. *Entrance requirements:* For master's, 1 year of work experience, minimum GPA of 3.0. Additional exam requirements/recommendations for international students: Required—TOEFL (minimum score 84 iBT). *Application deadline:* Applications are processed on a rolling basis. Application fee: $80. Electronic applications accepted. *Expenses:* Contact institution. *Financial support:* In 2016–17, 15 students received support, including 14 research assistantships (averaging $8,400 per year); career-related internships or fieldwork, Federal Work-Study, and unspecified assistantships also available. *Faculty research:* International business, innovative process. *Unit head:* Dr. John Sullivan, Chair, 617-353-3016, E-mail: adminsc@bu.edu. *Application contact:* Fiona Niven, Administrative Sciences Department, 617-353-3016, E-mail: adminsc@bu.edu.
Website: http://www.bu.edu/met/academic-community/departments/administrative-sciences/

Boston University, Metropolitan College, Department of Computer Science, Boston, MA 02215. Offers computer information systems (MS), including computer networks, data analytics, database management and business intelligence, health informatics, IT project management, security, Web application development; computer networks (Certificate); computer science (MS); data analytics (Certificate); digital forensics (Certificate); health informatics (Certificate); information technology project management (Certificate); software development (MS); software engineering in health care systems (Certificate); telecommunications (MS), including security. *Program availability:* Part-time, evening/weekend, online learning. *Faculty:* 13 full-time (3 women), 43 part-time/adjunct (3 women). *Students:* 108 full-time (36 women), 1,294 part-time (364 women); includes 428 minority (115 Black or African American, non-Hispanic/Latino; 2 American Indian or Alaska Native, non-Hispanic/Latino; 187 Asian, non-Hispanic/Latino; 98 Hispanic/Latino; 2 Native Hawaiian or other Pacific Islander, non-Hispanic/Latino; 24 Two or more races, non-Hispanic/Latino), 314 international. Average age 33. 463 applicants, 79% accepted, 248 enrolled. In 2016, 311 master's awarded. *Degree requirements:* For master's, thesis optional. *Entrance requirements:* For master's and Certificate, official transcripts from regionally-accredited bachelor's degree program, 3 letters of recommendation, professional resume, personal statement. Additional exam requirements/recommendations for international students: Required—TOEFL (minimum score 84 iBT), IELTS. *Application deadline:* For fall admission, 6/1 priority date for international students; for spring admission, 10/1 priority date for international students. Applications are processed on a rolling basis. Application fee: $85. Electronic applications accepted. *Expenses:* Contact institution. *Financial support:* In 2016–17, 11 research assistantships (averaging $8,400 per year) were awarded; unspecified assistantships also available. Support available to part-time students. Financial award applicants required to submit FAFSA. *Faculty research:* Medical informatics, Web technologies, telecom and networks, security and forensics, software engineering, programming languages, multimedia and artificial intelligence (AI), information systems and IT project management. *Unit head:* Dr. Anatoly Temkin, Chair, 617-353-2566, Fax: 617-353-2367, E-mail: csinfo@bu.edu. *Application contact:* Lesley Moreau, Academic

Program Coordinator, 617-353-2566, Fax: 617-353-2367, E-mail: metcs@bu.edu.
Website: http://www.bu.edu/csmet/

Brandeis University, Rabb School of Continuing Studies, Division of Graduate Professional Studies, Master of Science Program in Project and Program Management, Waltham, MA 02454-9110. Offers MS. *Program availability:* Part-time-only. *Faculty:* 45 part-time/adjunct (16 women). *Students:* 2 full-time (both women), 93 part-time (55 women); includes 30 minority (18 Black or African American, non-Hispanic/Latino; 9 Asian, non-Hispanic/Latino; 2 Hispanic/Latino; 1 Two or more races, non-Hispanic/Latino). Average age 37. 18 applicants, 100% accepted, 17 enrolled. In 2016, 24 master's awarded. *Entrance requirements:* For master's, four-year bachelor's degree from regionally-accredited U.S. institution or equivalent; official transcript(s) from every college or university attended; resume or curriculum vitae; statement of goals; letter of recommendation. Additional exam requirements/recommendations for international students: Required—TWE (minimum score 4.5), TOEFL (minimum scores: 600 paper-based, 100 iBT), IELTS (7), or PTE (68). *Application deadline:* For fall admission, 6/21 priority date for domestic and international students; for winter admission, 9/13 priority date for domestic and international students; for spring admission, 12/20 priority date for domestic and international students; for summer admission, 3/14 priority date for domestic and international students. Applications are processed on a rolling basis. Application fee: $50. Electronic applications accepted. *Expenses:* $3,400 per course, $100 graduation fee. *Financial support:* Applicants required to submit FAFSA. *Unit head:* Leanne Bateman, Chair, 781-736-8787, E-mail: lbateman@brandeis.edu. *Application contact:* Frances Stearns, Director of Admissions and Recruitment, 781-736-8785, E-mail: fstearns@brandeis.edu.
Website: http://www.brandeis.edu/gps

Brenau University, Sydney O. Smith Graduate School, College of Business and Mass Communication, Gainesville, GA 30501. Offers accounting (MBA); business administration (MBA); healthcare management (MBA); organizational leadership (MS); project management (MBA). *Accreditation:* ACBSP. *Program availability:* Part-time, evening/weekend, online learning. *Degree requirements:* For master's, comprehensive exam (for some programs). *Entrance requirements:* For master's, resume, minimum undergraduate GPA of 2.5. Additional exam requirements/recommendations for international students: Required—TOEFL (minimum score 500 paper-based; 61 iBT); Recommended—IELTS (minimum score 5). Electronic applications accepted. *Expenses:* Contact institution.

California Intercontinental University, School of Information Technology, Irvine, CA 92614. Offers information systems and enterprise resource management (DBA); information systems and knowledge management (MBA); project and quality management (MBA).

Capella University, School of Business and Technology, Doctoral Programs in Business, Minneapolis, MN 55402. Offers accounting (DBA, PhD); business intelligence (DBA); finance (DBA, PhD); general business management (PhD); human resource management (DBA, PhD); leadership (DBA, PhD); management education (PhD); marketing (DBA, PhD); project management (DBA, PhD); strategy and innovation (DBA, PhD). *Accreditation:* ACBSP.

Capella University, School of Business and Technology, Master's Programs in Business, Minneapolis, MN 55402. Offers accounting (MBA); business analysis (MS); business intelligence (MBA); entrepreneurship (MBA); finance (MBA); general business administration (MBA); general human resource management (MS); general leadership (MS); health care management (MBA); human resource management (MBA); marketing (MBA); project management (MBA, MS). *Accreditation:* ACBSP.

Carlow University, College of Leadership and Social Change, MBA Program, Pittsburgh, PA 15213-3165. Offers fraud and forensics (MBA); healthcare management (MBA); human resource management (MBA); leadership and management (MBA); project management (MBA). *Program availability:* Part-time, evening/weekend, 100% online, blended/hybrid learning. *Students:* 87 full-time (65 women), 32 part-time (21 women); includes 31 minority (23 Black or African American, non-Hispanic/Latino; 3 Asian, non-Hispanic/Latino; 2 Hispanic/Latino; 3 Two or more races, non-Hispanic/Latino), 1 international. Average age 33. 54 applicants, 98% accepted, 33 enrolled. In 2016, 29 master's awarded. *Entrance requirements:* For master's, minimum undergraduate GPA of 3.0 (preferred); personal essay; resume; official transcripts; two professional recommendations. Additional exam requirements/recommendations for international students: Required—TOEFL (minimum score 550 paper-based). *Application deadline:* Applications are processed on a rolling basis. Electronic applications accepted. *Expenses: Tuition:* Full-time $11,855; part-time $801 per credit. *Required fees:* $182; $13 per credit. Tuition and fees vary according to course load, degree level and program. *Financial support:* Application deadline: 4/1; applicants required to submit FAFSA. *Unit head:* Dr. Howard Stern, Chair, MBA Program, 412-578-8828, E-mail: hastern@carlow.edu. *Application contact:* 412-578-6059, Fax: 412-578-6321, E-mail: gradstudies@carlow.edu.
Website: http://www.carlow.edu/Business_Administration.aspx

The Catholic University of America, Busch School of Business and Economics, Washington, DC 20064. Offers accounting (MS); business analysis (MSBA); integral economic development management (MA); integral economic development policy (MA); management (MS), including Federal contract management, human resource management, leadership and management, project management, sales management. *Program availability:* Part-time. *Faculty:* 30 full-time (7 women), 30 part-time/adjunct (5 women). *Students:* 60 full-time (32 women), 26 part-time (14 women); includes 26 minority (11 Black or African American, non-Hispanic/Latino; 8 Asian, non-Hispanic/Latino; 5 Hispanic/Latino; 2 Two or more races, non-Hispanic/Latino), 22 international. Average age 29. 121 applicants, 77% accepted, 64 enrolled. In 2016, 48 master's awarded. *Degree requirements:* For master's, comprehensive exam (for some programs). *Entrance requirements:* For master's, GRE General Test, statement of purpose, official copies of academic transcripts, three letters of recommendation. Additional exam requirements/recommendations for international students: Required—TOEFL (minimum score 550 paper-based; 80 iBT). *Application deadline:* For fall admission, 7/15 priority date for domestic students, 7/1 for international students; for spring admission, 11/15 priority date for domestic students, 11/1 for international students. Applications are processed on a rolling basis. Application fee: $55. Electronic applications accepted. *Expenses:* $42,850 per year; $1,170 per credit; $200 per semester part-time fees. *Financial support:* Fellowships, research assistantships, teaching assistantships, Federal Work-Study, scholarships/grants, tuition waivers (full and partial), and unspecified assistantships available. Financial award application deadline: 2/1; financial award applicants required to submit FAFSA. *Faculty research:* Integrity of the marketing process, economics of energy and the environment, emerging markets, social change, international finance and economic development. *Total annual research expenditures:* $3,698. *Unit head:* Dr. William Bowman, Dean, 202-319-5290, Fax: 202-319-4426, E-mail: otey@cua.edu. *Application contact:* Director of Graduate Admissions, 202-319-5057, Fax: 202-319-6533, E-mail: cua-admissions@cua.edu.
Website: http://business.cua.edu/

The Catholic University of America, School of Engineering, Program in Engineering Management, Washington, DC 20064. Offers engineering management (MSE, Certificate), including engineering management and organization (MSE), project and systems engineering management (MSE), technology management (MSE); program management (Certificate); systems engineering and management of information technology (Certificate). *Program availability:* Part-time. *Faculty:* 3 part-time/adjunct (0 women). *Students:* 14 full-time (2 women), 11 part-time (3 women); includes 2 minority (both Two or more races, non-Hispanic/Latino), 20 international. Average age 30. 35 applicants, 54% accepted, 11 enrolled. In 2016, 26 master's awarded. *Degree requirements:* For master's, minimum GPA of 3.0. *Entrance requirements:* For master's and Certificate, statement of purpose, official copies of academic transcripts, two letters of recommendation. Additional exam requirements/recommendations for international students: Required—TOEFL (minimum score 550 paper-based; 80 iBT). *Application deadline:* For fall admission, 7/15 priority date for domestic students, 7/1 for international students; for spring admission, 11/15 priority date for domestic students, 11/1 for international students. Applications are processed on a rolling basis. Application fee: $55. Electronic applications accepted. *Expenses:* $43,380 per year; $1,170 per credit; $200 per semester part-time fees. *Financial support:* Fellowships, research assistantships, teaching assistantships, Federal Work-Study, scholarships/grants, tuition waivers (full and partial), and unspecified assistantships available. Financial award application deadline: 2/1; financial award applicants required to submit FAFSA. *Faculty research:* Engineering management and organization, project and systems engineering management, technology management. *Unit head:* Melvin G. Williams, Jr., Director, 202-319-5191, Fax: 202-319-6860, E-mail: williamsme@cua.edu. *Application contact:* Director of Graduate Admissions, 202-319-5057, Fax: 202-319-6533, E-mail: cua-admissions@cua.edu.
Website: http://engrmgmt.cua.edu/

Christian Brothers University, School of Business, Memphis, TN 38104-5581. Offers accountancy (M Acc); business (MBA); international business (MIB); project management (Certificate); MBA/MIB. *Program availability:* Part-time, evening/weekend. *Entrance requirements:* For master's, GMAT, GRE. Additional exam requirements/recommendations for international students: Required—TOEFL.

The Citadel, The Military College of South Carolina, Citadel Graduate College, School of Engineering, Department of Engineering Leadership and Program Management, Charleston, SC 29409. Offers project management (MS); systems engineering management (Graduate Certificate); technical program management (Graduate Certificate); technical project management (Graduate Certificate). *Program availability:* Part-time, evening/weekend. *Faculty:* 2 full-time (0 women), 6 part-time/adjunct (0 women). *Students:* 5 full-time (2 women), 85 part-time (37 women); includes 21 minority (10 Black or African American, non-Hispanic/Latino; 1 American Indian or Alaska Native, non-Hispanic/Latino; 2 Asian, non-Hispanic/Latino; 6 Hispanic/Latino; 1 Native Hawaiian or other Pacific Islander, non-Hispanic/Latino; 1 Two or more races, non-Hispanic/Latino), 1 international. 65 applicants, 98% accepted, 38 enrolled. In 2016, 35 master's, 45 other advanced degrees awarded. *Entrance requirements:* For master's, GRE or GMAT, minimum of one year of professional experience or permission from department head; two letters of reference; resume detailing previous work; for Graduate Certificate, one-page letter of intent; resume detailing previous work. Additional exam requirements/recommendations for international students: Required—TOEFL (minimum score 550 paper-based; 79 iBT). *Application deadline:* Applications are processed on a rolling basis. Application fee: $40. Electronic applications accepted. *Expenses:* Tuition, state resident: full-time $5121; part-time $569 per credit hour. Tuition, nonresident: full-time $8613; part-time $957 per credit hour. *Required fees:* $90 per term. *Financial support:* Fellowships and unspecified assistantships available. Support available to part-time students. Financial award application deadline: 7/1; financial award applicants required to submit FAFSA. *Unit head:* Dr. Charles O. Skipper, Department Head, 843-953-9811, E-mail: charles.skipper@citadel.edu. *Application contact:* Dr. Keith Plemmons, Associate Professor, 843-953-7677, E-mail: keith.plemmons@citadel.edu.
Website: http://www.citadel.edu/pmgt/

City University of Seattle, Graduate Division, School of Management, Seattle, WA 98121. Offers accounting (Certificate); change leadership (MBA, Certificate); computer systems (MS); finance (Certificate); financial management (MBA); general management (MBA); general management-Europe (MBA); global marketing (MBA); human resources management (Certificate); individualized study (MBA); information security (MS); information systems (MBA); leadership (MA); marketing (MBA, Certificate); project management (MBA, MS, Certificate); sustainable business (Certificate); technology management (MBA, Certificate). *Program availability:* Part-time, evening/weekend, online learning. *Degree requirements:* For master's, comprehensive exam (for some programs), thesis (for some programs). *Entrance requirements:* For master's, baccalaureate degree or equivalent from an accredited or otherwise recognized institution. Additional exam requirements/recommendations for international students: Required—TOEFL (minimum score 567 paper-based; 87 iBT); Recommended—IELTS. Electronic applications accepted.

Colorado Christian University, Program in Business Administration, Lakewood, CO 80226. Offers corporate training (MBA); information security (MA); leadership (MBA); project management (MBA). *Program availability:* Part-time, evening/weekend, online learning. *Degree requirements:* For master's, thesis optional. *Entrance requirements:* For master's, GMAT, 2 letters of recommendation, resume. Additional exam requirements/recommendations for international students: Required—TOEFL. Electronic applications accepted. *Expenses:* Contact institution.

Colorado State University–Global Campus, Graduate Programs, Greenwood Village, CO 80111. Offers criminal justice and law enforcement administration (MS); education leadership (MS); finance (MS); healthcare administration and management (MS); human resource management (MHRM); information technology management (MITM); international management (MS); management (MS); organizational leadership (MS); professional accounting (MPA); project management (MS); teaching and learning (MS). *Accreditation:* ACBSP. *Program availability:* Online learning.

Colorado Technical University Aurora, Programs in Business Administration and Management, Aurora, CO 80014. Offers accounting (MBA); business administration (MBA); business administration and management (EMBA); finance (MBA); human resource management (MBA); marketing (MBA); mediation and dispute resolution (MBA); operations management (MBA); project management (MBA); technology management (MBA). *Program availability:* Part-time, evening/weekend. *Degree requirements:* For master's, thesis or alternative. *Entrance requirements:* For master's, minimum undergraduate GPA of 3.0, resume.

Colorado Technical University Colorado Springs, Graduate Studies, Program in Management, Colorado Springs, CO 80907. Offers accounting (MBA, MSA); business administration (MBA); finance (MBA); human resources management (MBA); logistics/supply chain management (MBA); management (DM); marketing (MBA); mediation and dispute resolution (MBA); operations management (MBA); project management (MBA); technology management (MBA). *Accreditation:* ACBSP. *Program availability:* Part-time, evening/weekend, online learning. *Degree requirements:* For master's, thesis or alternative; for doctorate, thesis/dissertation. *Entrance requirements:* For doctorate, minimum graduate GPA of 3.0, 5 years of related work experience. *Faculty research:* Sexual harassment, performance evaluation, critical thinking.

Project Management

Dallas Baptist University, College of Business, Business Administration Program, Dallas, TX 75211-9299. Offers accounting (MBA); business communication (MBA); conflict resolution management (MBA); entrepreneurship (MBA); finance (MBA); health care management (MBA); international business (MBA); leading the non-profit organization (MBA); management (MBA); management information systems (MBA); marketing (MBA); project management (MBA); technology and engineering management (MBA). *Accreditation:* ACBSP. *Program availability:* Part-time, evening/weekend, 100% online, blended/hybrid learning. *Application deadline:* Applications are processed on a rolling basis. Application fee: $25. Electronic applications accepted. Application fee is waived when completed online. *Expenses: Tuition:* Full-time $15,408; part-time $856 per credit hour. *Required fees:* $400 per semester. Tuition and fees vary according to course load and degree level. *Unit head:* Dr. Sandra Reid, Chair of Graduate Business Programs, 214-333-5280, E-mail: sandra@dbu.edu. *Application contact:* Bobby Soto, Director of Admissions, 214-333-5242, E-mail: graduate@dbu.edu.
Website: http://www3.dbu.edu/graduate/mba.asp

DeSales University, Division of Business, Center Valley, PA 18034-9568. Offers accounting (MBA); computer information systems (MBA); finance (MBA); health care systems management (MBA); human resources management (MBA); management (MBA); marketing (MBA); project management (MBA); self-design (MBA); supply chain management (MBA); DNP/MBA; MSN/MBA. *Accreditation:* ACBSP. *Program availability:* Part-time, evening/weekend, 100% online, blended/hybrid learning. *Faculty:* 12 full-time (4 women), 29 part-time/adjunct (5 women). *Students:* 73 full-time (38 women), 323 part-time (163 women); includes 59 minority (16 Black or African American, non-Hispanic/Latino; 23 Asian, non-Hispanic/Latino; 16 Hispanic/Latino; 4 Two or more races, non-Hispanic/Latino). Average age 37. 157 applicants, 87% accepted, 128 enrolled. In 2016, 115 master's awarded. *Entrance requirements:* For master's, GMAT (waived if undergraduate GPA is 3.0 or better), minimum GPA of 3.0 in undergraduate work, literacy in basic software, background or interest in the field of study, personal statement, 2 years of work experience. Additional exam requirements/recommendations for international students: Required—TOEFL. *Application deadline:* Applications are processed on a rolling basis. Application fee: $50. Electronic applications accepted. *Expenses:* Contact institution. *Financial support:* Applicants required to submit FAFSA. *Faculty research:* Quality improvement, executive development, productivity, cross-cultural managerial differences, leadership. *Unit head:* Dr. David M. Gilfoil, Director, MBA Program, 610-282-1100 Ext. 1828, Fax: 610-282-2869, E-mail: david.gilfoil@desales.edu. *Application contact:* Julia Ferraro, Director of Graduate Admissions, 610-282-1100 Ext. 1768, E-mail: gradadmissions@desales.edu.

DeSales University, Division of Science and Mathematics, Center Valley, PA 18034-9568. Offers cyber security (Postbaccalaureate Certificate); data analytics (Postbaccalaureate Certificate); information systems (MS), including cyber security, digital forensics, healthcare information management, project management. *Program availability:* Part-time, evening/weekend, 100% online, blended/hybrid learning. *Faculty:* 1 (woman) full-time, 3 part-time/adjunct (0 women). *Students:* 8 full-time (1 woman), 12 part-time (6 women); includes 1 minority (Asian, non-Hispanic/Latino). Average age 34. 20 applicants, 30% accepted, 6 enrolled. In 2016, 7 master's awarded. *Entrance requirements:* For master's, GRE or GMAT, bachelor's degree in computer-related discipline from accredited college or university, minimum undergraduate GPA of 3.0, personal statement, three letters of recommendation. Additional exam requirements/recommendations for international students: Required—TOEFL. *Application deadline:* Applications are processed on a rolling basis. Application fee: $50. Electronic applications accepted. *Expenses:* Contact institution. *Financial support:* Applicants required to submit FAFSA. *Unit head:* Dr. Patricia Riola, MSIS Director/Assistant Professor of Computer Science, 610-282-1100 Ext. 1647, E-mail: patricia.riola@desales.edu. *Application contact:* Julia Ferraro, Director of Graduate Admissions, 610-282-1100 Ext. 1768, E-mail: gradadmissions@desales.edu.
Website: http://www.desales.edu/home/academics/graduate-studies/programs-of-study/msis—-master-of-science-in-information-systems

DeVry University–Folsom Campus, Graduate Programs, Folsom, CA 95630. Offers accounting (M Acc); accounting and financial management (MAFM); business administration (MBA); curriculum leadership (M Ed); educational leadership (M Ed); educational technology (M Ed); higher education leadership (M Ed); human resource management (MHRM); information systems management (MISM); network and communications management (MNCM); project management (MPM); public administration (MPA).

Drexel University, Goodwin College of Professional Studies, School of Technology and Professional Studies, Philadelphia, PA 19104-2875. Offers construction management (MS); creativity and innovation (MS); engineering technology (MS); food science (MS); hospitality management (MS); professional studies: creativity studies (MS); professional studies: e-learning leadership (MS); professional studies: homeland security management (MS); project management (MS); property management (MS); sport management (MS). *Program availability:* Part-time, evening/weekend. *Faculty:* 37 full-time (14 women). *Students:* 13 full-time, 462 part-time; includes 133 minority (86 Black or African American, non-Hispanic/Latino; 24 Asian, non-Hispanic/Latino; 23 Hispanic/Latino). In 2016, 88 master's awarded. *Entrance requirements:* Additional exam requirements/recommendations for international students: Required—TOEFL, IELTS. *Application deadline:* For fall admission, 9/1 for domestic students; for winter admission, 12/1 for domestic students; for spring admission, 3/1 for domestic students. Applications are processed on a rolling basis. Application fee: $75. Electronic applications accepted. Application fee is waived when completed online. *Expenses: Tuition:* Full-time $32,184; part-time $1192 per credit hour. *Required fees:* $280. Tuition and fees vary according to campus/location and program. *Financial support:* Applicants required to submit FAFSA. *Unit head:* Dr. William F. Lynch, Dean, 215-895-2159, E-mail: goodwin@drexel.edu. *Application contact:* Matthew Gray, Manager, Recruitment and Enrollment, 215-895-6255, Fax: 215-895-2153, E-mail: mdg67@drexel.edu.
Website: http://drexel.edu/grad/programs/goodwin/

Elmhurst College, Graduate Programs, Program in Project Management, Elmhurst, IL 60126-3296. Offers MPM. *Program availability:* Part-time, evening/weekend, online learning. *Faculty:* 1 full-time, 1 part-time/adjunct. *Students:* 1 (woman) full-time, 4 part-time (2 women). Average age 39. *Entrance requirements:* For master's, 3 recommendations, resume, statement of purpose. Additional exam requirements/recommendations for international students: Required—TOEFL (minimum score 550 paper-based; 79 iBT). *Application deadline:* Applications are processed on a rolling basis. Application fee: $0. Electronic applications accepted. *Expenses:* $845 per semester hour. *Financial support:* In 2016–17, 5 students received support. Scholarships/grants available. Support available to part-time students. Financial award application deadline: 3/1; financial award applicants required to submit FAFSA. *Unit head:* Dr. Bruce Fischer, Director. *Application contact:* Timothy J. Panfil, Director of Enrollment Management, School for Professional Studies, 630-617-3300 Ext. 3256, Fax: 630-617-6471, E-mail: panfilt@elmhurst.edu.
Website: http://www.elmhurst.edu/master_project_management

Embry-Riddle Aeronautical University–Worldwide, Department of Decision Sciences, Daytona Beach, FL 32114-3900. Offers aviation and aerospace (MSPM); aviation/aerospace management (MSEM); financial management (MSEM, MSPM); general management (MSPM); global management (MSPM); human resources management (MSPM); information systems (MSPM); leadership (MSEM, MSPM); logistics and supply chain management (MSEM, MSLSCM, MSPM); management (MSEM, MSPM); project management (MSEM); systems engineering (MSEM, MSPM); technical management (MSPM). *Program availability:* Part-time, evening/weekend, 100% online, blended/hybrid learning, EagleVision is a virtual classroom that combines Web video conferencing and a learning management system. EagleVision Classroom (between classrooms), EagleVision Home (faculty and students at home), and a blend of Classroom or Home. *Degree requirements:* For master's, comprehensive exam (for some programs), thesis (for some programs). *Entrance requirements:* Additional exam requirements/recommendations for international students: Required—TOEFL (minimum score 550 paper-based; 79 iBT), IELTS (minimum score 6), TOEFL or IELTS accepted. Electronic applications accepted. *Expenses:* Contact institution.

Embry-Riddle Aeronautical University–Worldwide, Department of Management, Daytona Beach, FL 32114-3900. Offers global management (MS); human resources management (MS); leadership (MS); operations management (MS); project management (MS). *Program availability:* Part-time, evening/weekend, 100% online, blended/hybrid learning, EagleVision is a virtual classroom that combines Web video conferencing and a learning management system. EagleVision Classroom (between classrooms), EagleVision Home (faculty and students at home), and a blend of Classroom or Home. *Entrance requirements:* Additional exam requirements/recommendations for international students: Required—TOEFL (minimum score 550 paper-based; 79 iBT), IELTS (minimum score 6), TOEFL or IELTS accepted. Electronic applications accepted. *Expenses:* Contact institution.

Everglades University, Graduate Programs, Program in Business Administration, Boca Raton, FL 33431. Offers accounting for managers (MBA); aviation management (MBA); human resource management (MBA); project management (MBA). *Program availability:* Part-time, evening/weekend, 100% online. *Entrance requirements:* For master's, GMAT (minimum score of 400) or GRE (minimum score of 290), bachelor's or graduate degree from college accredited by an agency recognized by the U.S. Department of Education; minimum cumulative GPA of 2.0 at the baccalaureate level, 3.0 at the master's level. Additional exam requirements/recommendations for international students: Recommended—TOEFL (minimum score 500 paper-based). Electronic applications accepted. *Expenses:* Contact institution.

Ferris State University, College of Business, Big Rapids, MI 49307. Offers business intelligence (MBA); design and innovation management (MBA); incident response (MBA); information security and intelligence (MS), including business intelligence, incident response, project management; lean systems and leadership (MBA); performance metrics (MBA); project management (MBA); supply chain management and lean logistics (MBA). *Accreditation:* ACBSP. *Program availability:* Part-time, evening/weekend, 100% online, blended/hybrid learning. *Faculty:* 18 full-time (7 women), 6 part-time/adjunct (3 women). *Students:* 25 full-time (11 women), 113 part-time (47 women); includes 12 minority (2 Black or African American, non-Hispanic/Latino; 1 American Indian or Alaska Native, non-Hispanic/Latino; 3 Asian, non-Hispanic/Latino; 3 Hispanic/Latino; 3 Two or more races, non-Hispanic/Latino), 50 international. Average age 31. 128 applicants, 59% accepted, 39 enrolled. In 2016, 94 master's awarded. *Degree requirements:* For master's, comprehensive exam, thesis. *Entrance requirements:* For master's, GRE or GMAT, minimum GPA of 3.0 in junior-/senior-level classes and overall; statement of purpose; 3 letters of reference; resume; transcripts. Additional exam requirements/recommendations for international students: Required—TOEFL (minimum score 500 paper-based; 70 iBT), IELTS (minimum score 6.5). *Application deadline:* For fall admission, 7/1 priority date for domestic students, 6/15 for international students; for winter admission, 11/1 priority date for domestic students, 10/15 for international students; for spring admission, 3/1 priority date for domestic students, 2/15 for international students. Applications are processed on a rolling basis. Application fee: $0 ($30 for international students). Electronic applications accepted. *Expenses:* Contact institution. *Financial support:* Career-related internships or fieldwork, Federal Work-Study, scholarships/grants, and unspecified assistantships available. Support available to part-time students. Financial award application deadline: 3/15; financial award applicants required to submit FAFSA. *Faculty research:* Lifestyle medicine business models, lean systems value chain pptimization, digital forensics/incident response, location-based services, passive data capture and analysis. *Unit head:* Dr. David Nicol, College of Business Dean, 231-591-2168, Fax: 231-591-3521, E-mail: davidnicol@ferris.edu. *Application contact:* Dr. Greg Gogolin, Professor, 231-591-3159, Fax: 231-591-3521, E-mail: greggogolin@ferris.edu.
Website: http://cbgp.ferris.edu/

Florida Institute of Technology, Extended Studies Division, Melbourne, FL 32901-6975. Offers acquisition and contract management (MS); aerospace engineering (MS); business administration (MBA, DBA); computer information systems (MS); computer science (MS); electrical engineering (MS); engineering management (MS); human resources management (MS); logistics management (MS), including humanitarian and disaster relief logistics; management (MS), including acquisition and contract management, e-business, human resources management, information systems, logistics management, management, transportation management; material acquisition management (MS); mechanical engineering (MS); operations research (MS); project management (MS), including information systems, operations research; public administration (MPA); quality management (MS); software engineering (MS); space systems (MS); space systems management (MS); supply chain management (MS); systems management (MS), including information systems, operations research; technology management (MS). *Program availability:* Part-time, evening/weekend, online learning. *Faculty:* 10 full-time (3 women), 122 part-time/adjunct (29 women). *Students:* 131 full-time (58 women), 997 part-time (348 women); includes 389 minority (231 Black or African American, non-Hispanic/Latino; 9 American Indian or Alaska Native, non-Hispanic/Latino; 26 Asian, non-Hispanic/Latino; 99 Hispanic/Latino; 3 Native Hawaiian or other Pacific Islander, non-Hispanic/Latino; 21 Two or more races, non-Hispanic/Latino), 53 international. Average age 36. 962 applicants, 48% accepted, 323 enrolled. In 2016, 403 master's awarded. *Degree requirements:* For master's, comprehensive exam (for some programs). *Entrance requirements:* For master's, GMAT or resume showing 8 years of supervised experience, minimum GPA of 3.0, 2 letters of recommendation, resume. Additional exam requirements/recommendations for international students: Required—TOEFL (minimum score 550 paper-based; 79 iBT). *Application deadline:* For fall admission, 4/1 for international students; for spring admission, 9/30 for international students. Applications are processed on a rolling basis. Electronic applications accepted. *Expenses:* Contact institution. *Financial support:* Application deadline: 3/1; applicants required to submit FAFSA. *Unit head:* Dr. Theodore R. Richardson, III, Dean, 321-674-8123, Fax: 321-674-7597, E-mail: trichardson@fit.edu. *Application contact:* Carolyn Farrior, Director of Graduate Admissions, Online Learning and Off-Campus Programs, 321-674-7118, Fax: 321-674-8216, E-mail: cfarrior@fit.edu.
Website: http://es.fit.edu

Geneva College, Program in Leadership Studies, Beaver Falls, PA 15010-3599. Offers business management (MS); ministry leadership (MS); non-profit leadership (MS);

organizational management (MS); project management (MS). *Program availability:* Online only, 100% online. *Faculty:* 1 (woman) full-time, 10 part-time/adjunct (3 women). *Students:* 56 full-time (45 women), 9 part-time (6 women); includes 15 minority (12 Black or African American, non-Hispanic/Latino; 1 Asian, non-Hispanic/Latino; 2 Hispanic/Latino). Average age 45. 13 applicants, 77% accepted, 7 enrolled. In 2016, 38 master's awarded. *Degree requirements:* For master's, thesis or alternative, capstone leadership studies project. *Entrance requirements:* For master's, undergraduate degree from regionally-accredited college or university, one to three years of experience in the workplace, minimum GPA of 3.0 (preferred), resume, essay, two recommendations. Additional exam requirements/recommendations for international students: Required—TOEFL. *Application deadline:* For fall admission, 9/21 for domestic students; for spring admission, 2/23 for domestic students; for summer admission, 7/22 for domestic students. Applications are processed on a rolling basis. Electronic applications accepted. *Expenses:* $640 per credit. *Financial support:* In 2016–17, 50 students received support. Scholarships/grants available. Financial award application deadline: 8/1; financial award applicants required to submit FAFSA. *Faculty research:* Servant leadership, leadership essentials. *Unit head:* John D. Gallo, Dean of Graduate, Adult and Online Programs, 800-576-3111, Fax: 724-847-6839, E-mail: msol@geneva.edu. *Application contact:* Lynsey Auell, Graduate Enrollment Representative, 800-576-3111, Fax: 724-847-6839, E-mail: msol@geneva.edu.
Website: http://www.geneva.edu/graduate/leadership-studies/

George Mason University, Volgenau School of Engineering, Sid and Reva Dewberry Department of Civil, Environmental, and Infrastructure Engineering, Fairfax, VA 22030. Offers construction project management (MS); geotechnical, construction, and structural engineering (M Eng); transportation engineering (PhD). *Faculty:* 14 full-time (6 women), 20 part-time/adjunct (4 women). *Students:* 47 full-time (12 women), 62 part-time (22 women); includes 23 minority (6 Black or African American, non-Hispanic/Latino; 9 Asian, non-Hispanic/Latino; 7 Hispanic/Latino; 1 Native Hawaiian or other Pacific Islander, non-Hispanic/Latino), 38 international. Average age 29. 109 applicants, 77% accepted, 39 enrolled. In 2016, 31 master's, 1 doctorate awarded. *Degree requirements:* For master's, thesis (for some programs), 30 credits, departmental seminars; for doctorate, thesis/dissertation, qualifying exams. *Entrance requirements:* For master's, GRE, photocopy of passport; 2 official college transcripts; resume; official bank statement; proof of financial support; expanded goals statement; self-evaluation form; BS in engineering or other related science; 3 letters of recommendation; for doctorate, GRE (for those who received degree outside of the U.S.), photocopy of passport; 2 official college transcripts; resume; official bank statement; proof of financial support; expanded goals statement; self-evaluation form; baccalaureate degree in engineering or related science; master's degree (preferred); 3 letters of recommendation. Additional exam requirements/recommendations for international students: Required—TOEFL (minimum score 575 paper-based; 88 iBT), IELTS (minimum score 6.5), PTE (minimum score 59). *Application deadline:* For fall admission, 1/15 priority date for domestic students. Application fee: $75 ($80 for international students). Electronic applications accepted. *Expenses:* Contact institution. *Financial support:* In 2016–17, 27 students received support, including 1 fellowship (averaging $10,000 per year), 16 research assistantships with tuition reimbursements available (averaging $20,150 per year), 10 teaching assistantships with tuition reimbursements available (averaging $21,000 per year); career-related internships or fieldwork, Federal Work-Study, scholarships/grants, unspecified assistantships, and health care benefits (for full-time research or teaching assistantship recipients) also available. Support available to part-time students. Financial award application deadline: 3/1; financial award applicants required to submit FAFSA. *Faculty research:* Evolutionary design, infrastructure security, intelligent transportation systems, national transportation networks, water quality modeling. *Total annual research expenditures:* $568,705. *Unit head:* Liza Wilson Durant, Acting Chair, 703-993-1687, Fax: 703-993-9790, E-mail: ldurant2@gmu.edu. *Application contact:* Laura Kosoglu, Director, Graduate Program, 703-993-1675, Fax: 703-993-9790, E-mail: ceiegrad@gmu.edu.
Website: http://civil.gmu.edu/

The George Washington University, School of Business, Department of Decision Sciences, Washington, DC 20052. Offers business analytics (MS, Certificate); project management (MS). *Program availability:* Online learning. *Faculty:* 18 full-time (1 woman), 1 part-time/adjunct (0 women). *Students:* 71 full-time (41 women), 125 part-time (53 women); includes 64 minority (30 Black or African American, non-Hispanic/Latino; 19 Asian, non-Hispanic/Latino; 6 Hispanic/Latino; 9 Two or more races, non-Hispanic/Latino), 70 international. Average age 36. 366 applicants, 59% accepted, 73 enrolled. In 2016, 93 master's awarded. Application fee: $75. *Financial support:* Tuition waivers available. *Unit head:* Prof. Refik Soyer, Chair, 202-994-6445, E-mail: soyer@gwu.edu. *Application contact:* Christopher Storer, Executive Director, Graduate Admissions, 202-994-1212, E-mail: gwmba@gwu.edu.
Website: http://business.gwu.edu/decisionsciences/

The George Washington University, School of Business, Department of Information Systems and Technology Management, Washington, DC 20052. Offers information and decision systems (PhD); information systems (MSIST); information systems development (MSIST); information systems management (MBA); information systems project management (MSIST); management information systems (MSIST); management of science, technology, and innovation (MBA, PhD). Programs also offered in Ashburn and Arlington, VA. *Program availability:* Part-time, evening/weekend, online learning. *Faculty:* 13 full-time (4 women). *Students:* 114 full-time (55 women), 74 part-time (30 women); includes 50 minority (15 Black or African American, non-Hispanic/Latino; 28 Asian, non-Hispanic/Latino; 6 Hispanic/Latino; 1 Two or more races, non-Hispanic/Latino), 103 international. Average age 28. 345 applicants, 66% accepted, 67 enrolled. In 2016, 105 master's awarded. *Entrance requirements:* For master's, GMAT. Additional exam requirements/recommendations for international students: Required—TOEFL. *Application deadline:* For fall admission, 4/1 priority date for domestic students; for spring admission, 10/1 for domestic students. Applications are processed on a rolling basis. Application fee: $75. *Financial support:* In 2016–17, 35 students received support. Fellowships, teaching assistantships, career-related internships or fieldwork, Federal Work-Study, institutionally sponsored loans, and tuition waivers available. Financial award application deadline: 4/1. *Faculty research:* Expert systems, decision support systems. *Unit head:* Richard Donnelly, Chair, 202-994-7155, E-mail: rgd@gwu.edu. *Application contact:* Christopher Storer, Executive Director, Graduate Admissions, 202-994-1212, E-mail: gwmba@gwu.edu.

Grand Canyon University, Colangelo College of Business, Phoenix, AZ 85017-1097. Offers accounting (MBA, MS); business analytics (MS); disaster preparedness and executive fire service leadership (MS); finance (MBA); general management (MBA); health systems management (MBA); information technology management (MS); leadership (MBA, MS); marketing (MBA), organizational leadership and entrepreneurship (MS); project management (MBA); sports business (MBA); strategic human resource management (MBA). *Accreditation:* ACBSP. *Program availability:* Part-time, evening/weekend, online learning. *Faculty:* 8 full-time (3 women), 147 part-time/adjunct (49 women). *Students:* 1 full-time (0 women), 2,121 part-time (1,165 women); includes 341 minority (249 Black or African American, non-Hispanic/Latino; 17 American Indian or Alaska Native, non-Hispanic/Latino; 15 Asian, non-Hispanic/Latino; 29 Hispanic/Latino; 4 Native Hawaiian or other Pacific Islander, non-Hispanic/Latino; 27 Two or more races, non-Hispanic/Latino), 20 international. Average age 38. In 2016, 569 master's awarded. *Entrance requirements:* For master's, equivalent of two years' full-time professional work experience. Additional exam requirements/recommendations for international students: Required—TOEFL (minimum score 575 paper-based; 90 iBT), IELTS (minimum score 7). *Application deadline:* For fall admission, 8/21 for domestic students, 7/2 for international students; for spring admission, 12/24 for domestic students, 11/1 for international students. Applications are processed on a rolling basis. Application fee: $0. Electronic applications accepted. *Financial support:* Federal Work-Study available. Support available to part-time students. Financial award applicants required to submit FAFSA. *Unit head:* Kim Donaldson, Dean, 602-639-6597, E-mail: kdonaldson@gcu.edu. *Application contact:* Matt Tidwell, Enrollment Manager, 602-639-6020, E-mail: mtidwell@gcu.edu.
Website: https://www.gcu.edu/colangelo-college-of-business.php

Granite State College, MS in Project Management Program, Concord, NH 03301. Offers MS. *Program availability:* Part-time, 100% online, blended/hybrid learning. *Faculty:* 1 (woman) full-time, 10 part-time/adjunct (6 women). *Students:* 18 full-time (9 women), 19 part-time (11 women); includes 2 minority (1 American Indian or Alaska Native, non-Hispanic/Latino; 1 Hispanic/Latino). Average age 42. 12 applicants, 92% accepted, 9 enrolled. In 2016, 18 master's awarded. *Degree requirements:* For master's, capstone. *Entrance requirements:* For master's, bachelor's degree with minimum GPA of 3.0 on last 60 credit hours, 500-1000 word statement of purpose, two letters of professional or academic reference, resume, official transcripts. Additional exam requirements/recommendations for international students: Required—TOEFL (minimum score 80 iBT), IELTS (minimum score 6.5). *Application deadline:* Applications are processed on a rolling basis. Application fee: $0. Electronic applications accepted. *Expenses:* $9,216 full-time in-state, $512 per credit part-time; $9,810 full-time out-of-state, $545 per credit part-time. *Financial support:* Federal Work-Study and National Guard course waivers available. Financial award applicants required to submit FAFSA. *Unit head:* Dr. Johnna Herrick-Phelps, Vice Provost for Academic Affairs, 855-228-3000, E-mail: johnna.herrick-phelps@granite.edu. *Application contact:* Ana Gonzalez, Administrative Assistant, Office of Graduate Studies, 603-513-1334, Fax: 603-513-1387, E-mail: gsc.graduatestudies@granite.edu.
Website: https://www.granite.edu/degree-programs/masters-degrees/project-management/

Grantham University, College of Engineering and Computer Science, Lenexa, KS 66219. Offers information management (MS), including project management; information technology (MS). *Program availability:* Part-time, online only, 100% online. *Faculty:* 12 part-time/adjunct. *Students:* 15 full-time (7 women), 244 part-time (56 women); includes 114 minority (81 Black or African American, non-Hispanic/Latino; 4 American Indian or Alaska Native, non-Hispanic/Latino; 8 Asian, non-Hispanic/Latino; 12 Hispanic/Latino; 9 Two or more races, non-Hispanic/Latino). Average age 40. 293 applicants, 96% accepted, 260 enrolled. In 2016, 78 master's awarded. *Degree requirements:* For master's, comprehensive exam (for information management); capstone (for information technology). *Entrance requirements:* For master's, baccalaureate or master's degree with minimum cumulative GPA of 2.5 from institution accredited by agency recognized by U.S. Department of Education or foreign equivalent. Additional exam requirements/recommendations for international students: Required—PTE (minimum score 50), TOEFL (minimum score 530 paper-based, 71 iBT) or IELTS (minimum score 6.5). *Application deadline:* Applications are processed on a rolling basis. Electronic applications accepted. *Expenses:* $325 per credit hour, $45 per 8-week term technology fee. *Financial support:* Scholarships/grants available. Financial award applicants required to submit FAFSA. *Unit head:* Dr. Nancy Miller, Dean of the College of Engineering and Computer Sciences, 913-309-4738, Fax: 855-681-5201, E-mail: nmiller@grantham.edu. *Application contact:* Jared Parlette, Vice President of Student Enrollment, 888-947-2684, Fax: 866-908-2360, E-mail: admissions@grantham.edu.
Website: http://www.grantham.edu/engineering-and-computer-science/

Grantham University, Mark Skousen School of Business, Lenexa, KS 66219. Offers business administration (MBA); business intelligence (MS); human resources management (Certificate); information management (MBA); performance improvement (MS); project management (MBA, Certificate). *Program availability:* Part-time, online only, 100% online. *Faculty:* 1 full-time, 36 part-time/adjunct. *Students:* 73 full-time (37 women), 1,046 part-time (424 women); includes 442 minority (309 Black or African American, non-Hispanic/Latino; 8 American Indian or Alaska Native, non-Hispanic/Latino; 27 Asian, non-Hispanic/Latino; 63 Hispanic/Latino; 7 Native Hawaiian or other Pacific Islander, non-Hispanic/Latino; 28 Two or more races, non-Hispanic/Latino). Average age 40. 1,324 applicants, 95% accepted, 1123 enrolled. In 2016, 331 master's awarded. *Degree requirements:* For master's, capstone project, PMP Prep Exam; for Certificate, comprehensive exam (for some programs), PMP Prep Exam. *Entrance requirements:* For master's, baccalaureate or master's degree with minimum cumulative GPA of 2.5 from institution accredited by agency recognized by U.S. Department of Education or foreign equivalent. Additional exam requirements/recommendations for international students: Required—PTE (minimum score 50), TOEFL (minimum score 530 paper-based, 71 iBT) or IELTS (minimum score 6.5). *Application deadline:* Applications are processed on a rolling basis. Electronic applications accepted. *Expenses:* $325 per credit hour, $45 per 8-week term technology fee. *Financial support:* Scholarships/grants available. Financial award applicants required to submit FAFSA. *Faculty research:* Organizational structures, e-discovery and project management, decision management, resource-based and ethical perspectives, external finance dependence in corporate investments. *Unit head:* Dr. David Marker, Dean, Mark Skousen School of Business, 800-955-2527, E-mail: dmarker@grantham.edu. *Application contact:* Jared Parlette, Vice President of Student Enrollment, 800-955-2527, E-mail: admissions@grantham.edu.
Website: http://www.grantham.edu/colleges-and-schools/school-of-business/

Harrisburg University of Science and Technology, Program in Project Management, Harrisburg, PA 17101. Offers information technology (MS). *Program availability:* Part-time, evening/weekend. *Faculty:* 2 full-time (0 women), 11 part-time/adjunct (1 woman). *Students:* 863 full-time (358 women), 15 part-time (7 women); includes 6 minority (3 Black or African American, non-Hispanic/Latino; 3 Asian, non-Hispanic/Latino), 868 international. In 2016, 17 master's awarded. *Degree requirements:* For master's, thesis optional. *Entrance requirements:* For master's, baccalaureate degree. Additional exam requirements/recommendations for international students: Required—TOEFL (minimum score 520 paper-based; 80 iBT); Recommended—IELTS (minimum score 6). *Application deadline:* Applications are processed on a rolling basis. Application fee: $0. Electronic applications accepted. *Expenses: Tuition:* Full-time $4800; part-time $800 per semester hour. *Financial support:* Applicants required to submit FAFSA. *Faculty research:* Strategic planning, organizational development. *Unit head:* Dr. Thomas Sheives, Program Lead/Associate Professor, 717-901-5158, E-mail: tsheives@harrisburgu.edu.

Herzing University Online, Program in Business Administration, Menomonee Falls, WI 53051. Offers accounting (MBA); business administration (MBA); business management (MBA); healthcare management (MBA); human resources (MBA); marketing (MBA); project management (MBA); technology management (MBA). *Program availability:* Online learning.

Project Management

Hult International Business School, Graduate Programs, Cambridge, MA 02141. Offers business administration (EMBA); business analytics (MBA, MIB); business statistics (MBS); disruptive innovation (MDI); entrepreneurship (MBA, MIB); family business (MBA, MIB); finance (MBA, MF, MIB); international marketing (MIM); marketing (MBA, MIB); project management (MBA, MIB). MDI and MBS offered in San Francisco; MBA also offered in Boston, San Francisco, Dubai, Shanghai, and New York. *Students:* Average age 31. *Entrance requirements:* For master's, GMAT, 3 years of work experience. Additional exam requirements/recommendations for international students: Required—TOEFL. *Application deadline:* For fall admission, 9/1 priority date for domestic and international students; for winter admission, 11/1 priority date for domestic and international students; for spring admission, 12/1 priority date for domestic and international students; for summer admission, 6/1 for domestic and international students. Applications are processed on a rolling basis. Application fee: $150. Electronic applications accepted. *Expenses:* $75,000 (for MBA); $45,000 (for master's); $85,000 (for executive part-time MBA). *Financial support:* Scholarships/grants and tuition waivers (partial) available. Financial award application deadline: 6/1; financial award applicants required to submit FAFSA. *Application contact:* Boston Admissions Office, 617-746-1990, E-mail: postgraduate@hult.edu.
Website: http://www.hult.edu

IGlobal University, Graduate Programs, Vienna, VA 22182. Offers accounting (MBA); data management and analytics (MSIT); entrepreneurship (MBA); finance (MBA); global business management (MBA); health care management (MBA); hospitality and tourism management (MBA); human resources management (MBA); information technology (MBA); information technology systems and management (MSIT); leadership and management (MBA); project management (MBA); public service and administration (MBA); software design and management (MSIT).

Iona College, Hagan School of Business, Department of Information Systems, New Rochelle, NY 10801-1890. Offers accounting and information systems (MS); business continuity and risk management (AC); information systems (MBA, MS, PMC); project management (MS). *Program availability:* Part-time, evening/weekend. *Faculty:* 6 full-time (1 woman), 1 part-time/adjunct (0 women). *Students:* 6 full-time (4 women), 14 part-time (5 women); includes 4 minority (1 Black or African American, non-Hispanic/Latino; 1 American Indian or Alaska Native, non-Hispanic/Latino; 2 Hispanic/Latino), 6 international. Average age 30. 14 applicants, 100% accepted, 6 enrolled. In 2016, 12 master's awarded. *Entrance requirements:* For master's, GMAT, 2 letters of recommendation, minimum GPA of 3.0; for other advanced degree, GMAT, minimum GPA of 3.0. Additional exam requirements/recommendations for international students: Required—TOEFL (minimum score 550 paper-based; 80 iBT), IELTS (minimum score 6.5). *Application deadline:* For fall admission, 8/15 priority date for domestic students, 8/1 priority date for international students; for winter admission, 11/15 priority date for domestic students, 11/1 priority date for international students; for spring admission, 2/15 priority date for domestic students, 2/1 priority date for international students; for summer admission, 5/15 priority date for domestic students, 5/1 priority date for international students. Applications are processed on a rolling basis. Application fee: $50. Electronic applications accepted. *Expenses:* Contact institution. *Financial support:* In 2016–17, 9 students received support. Scholarships/grants, tuition waivers (partial), and unspecified assistantships available. Support available to part-time students. Financial award application deadline: 4/15; financial award applicants required to submit FAFSA. *Faculty research:* Fuzzy sets, risk management, computer security, competence set analysis, investment strategies. *Unit head:* Dr. Shoshana Altschuller, Department Chair, 914-637-7726, E-mail: saltschuller@iona.edu. *Application contact:* Katelyn Brunck, Director of MBA Admissions, 914-633-2451, Fax: 914-633-2277, E-mail: kbrunck@iona.edu.
Website: http://www.iona.edu/Academics/Hagan-School-of-Business/Departments/Information-Systems/Graduate-Programs.aspx

Kaplan University, Davenport Campus, School of Business, Davenport, IA 52807. Offers business administration (MBA); change leadership (MS); entrepreneurship (MBA); finance (MBA); health care management (MBA, MS); human resource (MBA); international business (MBA); management (MS); marketing (MBA); project management (MBA, MS); supply chain management and logistics (MBA, MS). *Accreditation:* ACBSP. *Program availability:* Part-time, evening/weekend, online learning. *Entrance requirements:* Additional exam requirements/recommendations for international students: Required—TOEFL (minimum score 550 paper-based; 80 iBT). Electronic applications accepted.

King University, School of Business and Economics, Bristol, TN 37620-2699. Offers accounting (MBA); finance (MBA); healthcare management (MBA); human resources management (MBA); leadership (MBA); management (MBA); marketing (MBA); project management (MBA). *Program availability:* Part-time, evening/weekend, online learning. *Degree requirements:* For master's, comprehensive exam, thesis optional. *Entrance requirements:* For master's, GMAT, 2 years of work experience. Additional exam requirements/recommendations for international students: Required—TOEFL (minimum score 550 paper-based). Electronic applications accepted. *Faculty research:* International monetary policy.

Lakeland University, Graduate Studies Division, Program in Business Administration, Plymouth, WI 53073. Offers accounting (MBA); finance (MBA); healthcare management (MBA); project management (MBA). *Entrance requirements:* For master's, GMAT. *Expenses:* Contact institution.

Lasell College, Graduate and Professional Studies in Management, Newton, MA 02466-2709. Offers business administration (PMBA); elder care management (MSM, Graduate Certificate); hospitality and event management (MSM, Graduate Certificate); human resources management (MSM, Graduate Certificate); management (MSM, Graduate Certificate); marketing (MSM, Graduate Certificate); non-profit management (MSM, Graduate Certificate); project management (MSM, Graduate Certificate). *Accreditation:* ACBSP. *Program availability:* Part-time, evening/weekend, 100% online, blended/hybrid learning. *Faculty:* 3 full-time (2 women), 16 part-time/adjunct (10 women). *Students:* 47 full-time (34 women), 93 part-time (72 women); includes 28 minority (20 Black or African American, non-Hispanic/Latino; 4 Asian, non-Hispanic/Latino; 3 Hispanic/Latino; 1 Two or more races, non-Hispanic/Latino), 24 international. Average age 31. 121 applicants, 55% accepted, 32 enrolled. In 2016, 61 master's, 3 other advanced degrees awarded. *Degree requirements:* For master's, minimum GPA of 3.0; internship or research paper (for MSM). *Entrance requirements:* For master's, one-page personal statement, 2 letters of recommendation, resume, bachelor's degree transcript; proof of microeconomics and statistics (for PMBA); for Graduate Certificate, bachelor's degree transcript, 2 letters of recommendation, 1-page personal statement, resume. Additional exam requirements/recommendations for international students: Required—TOEFL (minimum score 550 paper-based, 79 iBT) or IELTS (minimum score 6). *Application deadline:* For fall admission, 8/31 priority date for domestic students, 6/30 priority date for international students; for spring admission, 12/31 priority date for domestic students, 10/31 priority date for international students. Applications are processed on a rolling basis. Electronic applications accepted. *Expenses:* $600 per credit. *Financial support:* In 2016–17, 12 students received support. Federal Work-Study, scholarships/grants, and tuition discounts available. Support available to part-time students. Financial award application deadline: 8/31; financial award applicants required to submit FAFSA. *Unit head:* Dr. Joan Dolamore, Dean of Graduate and Professional Studies, 617-243-2485, Fax: 617-243-2450, E-mail: gradinfo@lasell.edu. *Application contact:* Adrienne Franciosi, Director of Graduate Enrollment, 617-243-2214, Fax: 617-243-2450, E-mail: gradinfo@lasell.edu.
Website: http://www.lasell.edu/academics/graduate-and-professional-studies/programs-of-study/master-of-science-in-management.html

Lawrence Technological University, College of Management, Southfield, MI 48075-1058. Offers business administration (MBA), including business analytics (MBA, MS), finance, information technology, marketing, project management (MBA, MS); information technology (MS), including business analytics (MBA, MS), information assurance, project management (MBA, MS); project management (Graduate Certificate). *Accreditation:* ACBSP. *Program availability:* Part-time, evening/weekend, 100% online. *Faculty:* 14 full-time (6 women), 10 part-time/adjunct (2 women). *Students:* 7 full-time (3 women), 323 part-time (120 women); includes 60 minority (29 Black or African American, non-Hispanic/Latino; 2 American Indian or Alaska Native, non-Hispanic/Latino; 17 Asian, non-Hispanic/Latino; 8 Hispanic/Latino; 4 Two or more races, non-Hispanic/Latino), 118 international. Average age 33. 275 applicants, 56% accepted, 72 enrolled. In 2016, 167 master's, 12 other advanced degrees awarded. Terminal master's awarded for partial completion of doctoral program. *Degree requirements:* For master's, thesis (for some programs). *Entrance requirements:* Additional exam requirements/recommendations for international students: Required—TOEFL (minimum score 550 paper-based; 79 iBT), IELTS (minimum score 6.5). *Application deadline:* For fall admission, 5/22 for international students; for spring admission, 10/11 for international students; for summer admission, 2/16 for international students. Applications are processed on a rolling basis. Application fee: $50. Electronic applications accepted. *Expenses: Tuition:* Full-time $14,868; part-time $1062 per credit. *Required fees:* $75 per semester. Tuition and fees vary according to campus/location. *Financial support:* In 2016–17, 35 students received support, including 8 research assistantships with partial tuition reimbursements available (averaging $3,250 per year); career-related internships or fieldwork, unspecified assistantships, and corporate tuition incentives also available. Financial award application deadline: 4/1; financial award applicants required to submit FAFSA. *Faculty research:* Cybersecurity; risk management; IT governance; security controls and countermeasures; threat modeling cyber resilience; autonomous cars; natural language processing; text mining; machine learning; reflective leadership; emerging leadership theories and practice; motivational studies; teaching effectiveness strategies; teamwork; organization development; strategic planning; strengths-based and positive organizational scholarship; global leadership; globalization; corporate governance. *Unit head:* Dr. Bahman Mirshab, Dean, 248-204-3050, E-mail: mgtdean@ltu.edu. *Application contact:* Jane Rohrback, Director of Admissions, 248-204-3160, Fax: 248-204-2228, E-mail: admissions@ltu.edu.
Website: http://www.ltu.edu/management/index.asp

Lehigh University, College of Business and Economics, Department of Management, Bethlehem, PA 18015. Offers business administration (MBA); project management (MBA); MBA/E; MBA/M Ed. *Accreditation:* AACSB. *Program availability:* Part-time, evening/weekend, 100% online. *Faculty:* 10 full-time (2 women), 1 part-time/adjunct (0 women). *Students:* 40 full-time (25 women), 159 part-time (41 women); includes 31 minority (5 Black or African American, non-Hispanic/Latino; 15 Asian, non-Hispanic/Latino; 9 Hispanic/Latino; 2 Two or more races, non-Hispanic/Latino), 20 international. Average age 32. 188 applicants, 69% accepted, 47 enrolled. In 2016, 47 master's awarded. *Entrance requirements:* For master's, GMAT or GRE. Additional exam requirements/recommendations for international students: Required—TOEFL (minimum score 600 paper-based; 94 iBT). *Application deadline:* For fall admission, 7/15 for domestic students, 5/1 for international students; for spring admission, 12/1 for domestic students. Application fee: $75. Electronic applications accepted. Tuition and fees vary according to program. *Financial support:* In 2016–17, 33 students received support, including 10 fellowships (averaging $5,250 per year), 10 teaching assistantships with tuition reimbursements available (averaging $14,200 per year); scholarships/grants, health care benefits, tuition waivers (full and partial), and unspecified assistantships also available. Support available to part-time students. Financial award application deadline: 1/15. *Faculty research:* Information systems, organizational behavior, supply chain management, strategic management, entrepreneurship. *Total annual research expenditures:* $2,418. *Unit head:* Dr. Yuliang Yao, Department Chair, 610-758-6726, Fax: 610-758-6941, E-mail: yuy3@lehigh.edu. *Application contact:* Michael Tarantino, Director of Recruitment and Admissions, 610-758-3418, Fax: 610-758-5283, E-mail: mgt215@lehigh.edu.
Website: http://www4.lehigh.edu/business/academics/depts/management

Lewis University, College of Business, Graduate School of Management, Program in Business Administration, Romeoville, IL 60446. Offers accounting (MBA); custom elective option (MBA); e-business (MBA); finance (MBA); healthcare management (MBA); human resources management (MBA); international business (MBA); management information systems (MBA); marketing (MBA); project management (MBA); technology and operations management (MBA). *Program availability:* Part-time, evening/weekend. *Students:* 145 full-time (72 women), 213 part-time (123 women); includes 101 minority (46 Black or African American, non-Hispanic/Latino; 2 American Indian or Alaska Native, non-Hispanic/Latino; 7 Asian, non-Hispanic/Latino; 41 Hispanic/Latino; 1 Native Hawaiian or other Pacific Islander, non-Hispanic/Latino; 4 Two or more races, non-Hispanic/Latino), 47 international. Average age 31. In 2016, 99 master's awarded. *Degree requirements:* For master's, comprehensive exam. *Entrance requirements:* For master's, interview, bachelor's degree, resume, 2 recommendations. Additional exam requirements/recommendations for international students: Required—TOEFL (minimum score 550 paper-based). *Application deadline:* For fall admission, 8/15 priority date for domestic students, 5/1 priority date for international students; for spring admission, 11/15 priority date for international students. Applications are processed on a rolling basis. Application fee: $40. Electronic applications accepted. *Expenses: Tuition:* Full-time $13,860; part-time $770 per credit hour. *Required fees:* $75 per semester. Tuition and fees vary according to degree level and program. *Financial support:* Career-related internships or fieldwork, Federal Work-Study, scholarships/grants, and unspecified assistantships available. Financial award application deadline: 5/1; financial award applicants required to submit FAFSA. *Unit head:* Dr. Maureen Culleeney, Academic Program Director, 815-838-0500 Ext. 5631, E-mail: culleema@lewisu.edu. *Application contact:* Michele Ryan, Director of Admission, 815-838-0500 Ext. 5384, E-mail: gsm@lewisu.edu.

Lewis University, College of Business, Graduate School of Management, Program in Project Management, Romeoville, IL 60446. Offers MS. *Program availability:* Part-time, evening/weekend, 100% online, blended/hybrid learning. *Students:* 7 full-time (4 women), 23 part-time (6 women); includes 12 minority (4 Black or African American, non-Hispanic/Latino; 2 Asian, non-Hispanic/Latino; 6 Hispanic/Latino), 1 international. Average age 33. *Entrance requirements:* For master's, bachelor's degree, interview, resume, statement of purpose, 2 letters of recommendation, minimum GPA of 2.75. Additional exam requirements/recommendations for international students: Required—TOEFL (minimum score 550 paper-based; 80 iBT). *Application deadline:* For fall admission, 5/1 priority date for international students; for spring admission, 11/15 priority date for international students. Applications are processed on a rolling basis. Application fee: $40. Electronic applications accepted. *Expenses: Tuition:* Full-time $13,860; part-time $770 per credit hour. *Required fees:* $75 per semester. Tuition and fees vary according to degree level and program. *Financial support:* Career-related internships or fieldwork, Federal Work-Study, and unspecified assistantships available. Support available to part-time students. Financial award application deadline: 5/1; financial award applicants required to submit FAFSA. *Unit head:* Rev. Dr. Kevin Spiess, Academic Program Director, 815-838-0500 Ext. 5399, E-mail: spiesske@lewisu.edu. *Application contact:* Michele Ryan, Director of Admission, 815-838-0500 Ext. 5384, E-mail: gsm@lewisu.edu.

Liberty University, School of Business, Lynchburg, VA 24515. Offers accounting (MBA, MS); business administration (MBA); criminal justice (MBA); cyber security (MS); executive leadership (MA); information systems (MS), including information assurance, technology management; international business (MBA, DBA); leadership (DBA); marketing (MBA, MS, DBA), including digital marketing and advertising (MS); project management (MS), public relations (MS), sports marketing and media (MS); project management (MBA, DBA); public administration (MBA); public relations (MBA). *Program availability:* Part-time, online learning. *Students:* 1,458 full-time (807 women), 4,188 part-time (2,041 women); includes 1,372 minority (1,060 Black or African American, non-Hispanic/Latino; 19 American Indian or Alaska Native, non-Hispanic/Latino; 85 Asian, non-Hispanic/Latino; 75 Hispanic/Latino; 10 Native Hawaiian or other Pacific Islander, non-Hispanic/Latino; 123 Two or more races, non-Hispanic/Latino), 124 international. Average age 35. 5,424 applicants, 45% accepted, 1242 enrolled. In 2016, 1,859 master's, 87 other advanced degrees awarded. *Entrance requirements:* For master's, minimum undergraduate GPA of 3.0, 15 hours of upper-level business courses. Additional exam requirements/recommendations for international students: Required—TOEFL (minimum score 600 paper-based; 100 iBT). *Application deadline:* Applications are processed on a rolling basis. Application fee: $50. Electronic applications accepted. *Expenses:* Contact institution. *Financial support:* Applicants required to submit FAFSA. *Unit head:* Dr. Scott Hicks, Dean, 434-592-4808, Fax: 434-582-2366, E-mail: smhicks@liberty.edu. *Application contact:* Jay Bridge, Director of Graduate Admissions, 800-424-9595, Fax: 800-628-7977, E-mail: gradadmissions@liberty.edu.
Website: http://www.liberty.edu/academics/business/index.cfm?PID-149

Lindenwood University, Graduate Programs, School of Accelerated Degree Programs, St. Charles, MO 63301-1695. Offers administration (MSA), including management, marketing, project management; business administration (MBA); communications (MA), including digital and multimedia, media management, promotions, training and development; criminal justice and administration (MS); healthcare administration (MS); human resource management (MS); information technology (Certificate); managing information security (MS); managing information technology (MS); managing virtualization and cloud computing (MS); writing (MFA). *Program availability:* Part-time, evening/weekend, 100% online. *Faculty:* 16 full-time (7 women), 75 part-time/adjunct (27 women). *Students:* 609 full-time (386 women), 179 part-time (121 women); includes 257 minority (202 Black or African American, non-Hispanic/Latino; 4 American Indian or Alaska Native, non-Hispanic/Latino; 5 Asian, non-Hispanic/Latino; 28 Hispanic/Latino; 1 Native Hawaiian or other Pacific Islander, non-Hispanic/Latino; 17 Two or more races, non-Hispanic/Latino), 28 international. Average age 36. 332 applicants, 70% accepted, 205 enrolled. In 2016, 479 master's awarded. *Degree requirements:* For master's, thesis (for some programs), minimum cumulative GPA of 3.0; for Certificate, minimum cumulative GPA of 3.0. *Entrance requirements:* For master's, resume, personal statement, official undergraduate transcript, minimum undergraduate cumulative GPA of 3.0. Additional exam requirements/recommendations for international students: Required—TOEFL (minimum score 550 paper-based; 80 iBT); Recommended—IELTS (minimum score 6.5). *Application deadline:* For fall admission, 9/26 priority date for domestic and international students; for winter admission, 1/3 priority date for domestic and international students; for spring admission, 3/31 priority date for domestic and international students; for summer admission, 7/3 priority date for domestic and international students. Applications are processed on a rolling basis. Application fee: $30 ($100 for international students). Electronic applications accepted. *Expenses: Tuition:* Full-time $15,672; part-time $453 per credit hour. *Required fees:* $205 per semester. Tuition and fees vary according to course level, course load and degree level. *Financial support:* In 2016–17, 467 students received support. Career-related internships or fieldwork, institutionally sponsored loans, scholarships/grants, tuition waivers (partial), and unspecified assistantships available. Financial award application deadline: 6/30; financial award applicants required to submit FAFSA. *Unit head:* Dr. Gina Ganahl, Dean, Accelerated Degree Programs, 636-949-4501, Fax: 636-949-4505, E-mail: gganahl@lindenwood.edu. *Application contact:* Tyler Kostich, Director, Evening and Graduate Admissions, 636-949-4138, Fax: 636-949-4109, E-mail: adultadmissions@lindenwood.edu.
Website: http://www.lindenwood.edu/academics/academic-schools/school-of-accelerated-degree-programs/

Marlboro College, Graduate and Professional Studies, Program in Business Administration, Brattleboro, VT 05301. Offers collaborative leadership (MBA); conscious business (MBA); mission driven organizations (MBA); project management (MBA); social innovation (MBA); sustainable food systems (MBA). *Program availability:* Part-time, evening/weekend, blended/hybrid learning. *Faculty:* 1 (woman) full-time, 22 part-time/adjunct (13 women). *Students:* 4 full-time (3 women), 13 part-time (11 women); includes 3 minority (1 Hispanic/Latino; 2 Two or more races, non-Hispanic/Latino). Average age 39. 5 applicants, 100% accepted, 3 enrolled. In 2016, 3 master's awarded. *Degree requirements:* For master's, 45 credits including a Master Workshop. *Entrance requirements:* For master's, letter of intent, essay, transcripts, 2 letters of recommendation. *Application deadline:* For fall admission, 7/1 priority date for domestic students; for winter admission, 11/1 priority date for domestic students. Applications are processed on a rolling basis. Application fee: $0. Electronic applications accepted. *Expenses:* $765 per credit. *Financial support:* In 2016–17, 2 students received support. Scholarships/grants available. Financial award applicants required to submit FAFSA. *Unit head:* Tristan Toleno, Degree Chair, 802-258-9200, Fax: 802-258-9201, E-mail: tristant@gradschool.marlboro.edu. *Application contact:* Kelley Barton, Admissions Counselor, 802-258-9209, Fax: 802-258-9201, E-mail: graduateadmissions@marlboro.edu.
Website: https://www.marlboro.edu/academics/graduate/management

Marlboro College, Graduate and Professional Studies, Program in Management, Marlboro, VT 05344. Offers collaborative leadership (MS); conscious business (MS); mission driven organizations (MS); project management (MS); social innovation (MS); sustainable food systems (MS). *Program availability:* Part-time, evening/weekend, blended/hybrid learning. *Faculty:* 1 (woman) full-time, 23 part-time/adjunct (14 women). *Students:* 2 full-time (both women), 12 part-time (9 women). Average age 34. 6 applicants, 33% accepted, 2 enrolled. In 2016, 13 master's awarded. *Degree requirements:* For master's, capstone project. *Entrance requirements:* For master's, statement of intent, 2 letters of recommendation. Additional exam requirements/recommendations for international students: Recommended—TOEFL (minimum score 577 paper-based; 90 iBT), IELTS (minimum score 7). *Application deadline:* For fall admission, 8/5 for domestic students; for winter admission, 12/5 for domestic students; for spring admission, 4/5 for domestic students. Applications are processed on a rolling basis. Application fee: $0. Electronic applications accepted. *Expenses:* $765 per credit. *Financial support:* Scholarships/grants available. Financial award applicants required to submit FAFSA. *Unit head:* Tristan Toleno, Degree Chair, 802-258-9200, Fax: 802-258-9201, E-mail: tristant@gradschool.marlboro.edu. *Application contact:* Kelley Barton, Admissions Counselor, 802-258-9209, Fax: 802-258-9201, E-mail: graduateadmissions@marlboro.edu.
Website: https://www.marlboro.edu/academics/graduate/management

Marymount University, School of Business Administration, Program in Information Technology, Arlington, VA 22207-4299. Offers health care informatics (Certificate); information technology (MS, Certificate), including computer security (MS), health care informatics (MS), project management and technology leadership (MS), software engineering (MS); information technology project management and technology leadership (Certificate); MS/MBA; MS/MS. *Program availability:* Part-time, evening/weekend. *Faculty:* 7 full-time (6 women), 7 part-time/adjunct (0 women). *Students:* 39 full-time (23 women), 31 part-time (13 women); includes 24 minority (12 Black or African American, non-Hispanic/Latino; 5 Asian, non-Hispanic/Latino; 6 Hispanic/Latino; 1 Two or more races, non-Hispanic/Latino), 31 international. Average age 30. 67 applicants, 97% accepted, 23 enrolled. In 2016, 29 master's, 12 other advanced degrees awarded. *Degree requirements:* For master's, thesis or alternative. *Entrance requirements:* For master's, resume, bachelor's degree in computer-related field or another subject with certificate in computer-related field or related work experience; bachelor's degree in computer science or work in software development (for software engineering track). Additional exam requirements/recommendations for international students: Required—TOEFL (minimum score 600 paper-based; 96 iBT), IELTS (minimum score 6.5). *Application deadline:* For fall admission, 7/16 priority date for domestic and international students; for spring admission, 11/16 priority date for domestic and international students; for summer admission, 4/16 for domestic and international students. Applications are processed on a rolling basis. Application fee: $40. Electronic applications accepted. *Expenses:* $960 per credit hour. *Financial support:* In 2016–17, 5 students received support, including 2 research assistantships with tuition reimbursements available; career-related internships or fieldwork, Federal Work-Study, scholarships/grants, and unspecified assistantships also available. Support available to part-time students. Financial award applicants required to submit FAFSA. *Unit head:* Dr. Diane Murphy, Chair/Director, Information Technology, Management Sciences and Cybersecurity, 703-284-5958, Fax: 703-527-3830, E-mail: diane.murphy@marymount.edu. *Application contact:* Francesca Reed, Director, Graduate Admissions, 703-284-5901, Fax: 703-527-3815, E-mail: grad.admissions@marymount.edu.
Website: http://www.marymount.edu/Academics/School-of-Business-Administration/Graduate-Programs/Information-Technology-(M-S-)

Maryville University of Saint Louis, The John E. Simon School of Business, St. Louis, MO 63141-7299. Offers accounting (MBA, Certificate); business studies (Certificate); cyber security (MBA); cybersecurity (Certificate); financial services (MBA, Certificate); healthcare practice management (MBA, Certificate); human resource management (MBA); information technology (MBA, Certificate); management (MBA, Certificate); management and leadership (MA); marketing (MBA, Certificate); project management (MBA); sport business management (MBA); supply chain management/logistics (MBA). *Accreditation:* ACBSP. *Program availability:* Part-time, evening/weekend, 100% online, blended/hybrid learning. *Faculty:* 7 full-time (3 women), 34 part-time/adjunct (9 women). *Students:* 84 full-time (40 women), 223 part-time (118 women); includes 67 minority (40 Black or African American, non-Hispanic/Latino; 2 American Indian or Alaska Native, non-Hispanic/Latino; 8 Asian, non-Hispanic/Latino; 12 Hispanic/Latino; 1 Native Hawaiian or other Pacific Islander, non-Hispanic/Latino; 4 Two or more races, non-Hispanic/Latino), 15 international. Average age 32. In 2016, 67 master's awarded. *Entrance requirements:* Additional exam requirements/recommendations for international students: Required—TOEFL (minimum score 563 paper-based; 85 iBT). *Application deadline:* Applications are processed on a rolling basis. Electronic applications accepted. *Expenses:* $650 per credit hour. *Financial support:* Career-related internships or fieldwork, Federal Work-Study, tuition waivers (partial), and campus employment available. Financial award application deadline: 3/1; financial award applicants required to submit FAFSA. *Faculty research:* Global business, e-marketing, strategic planning, interpersonal management skills, financial analysis. *Unit head:* Pam Horwitz, Interim Dean, 314-529-9680, Fax: 314-529-9975. *Application contact:* Dustin Loeffler, Director for Graduate Studies in Business, 314-529-9571, Fax: 314-529-9975, E-mail: dloeffler@maryville.edu.
Website: http://www.maryville.edu/bu/business-administration-masters/

Metropolitan State University, College of Management, St. Paul, MN 55106-5000. Offers business administration (MBA, DBA); database administration (Graduate Certificate); healthcare information technology management (Graduate Certificate); information assurance security (Graduate Certificate); management information systems (MMIS); MIS generalist (Graduate Certificate); MIS systems analysis and design (Graduate Certificate); project management (Graduate Certificate); public and nonprofit administration (MPNA). *Program availability:* Part-time, evening/weekend. *Degree requirements:* For master's, thesis optional, computer language (MMIS). *Entrance requirements:* For master's, GMAT (for MBA), resume. Additional exam requirements/recommendations for international students: Required—TOEFL (minimum score 550 paper-based). Electronic applications accepted. *Faculty research:* Yugoslav economic system, workers' cooperatives, participative management and job enrichment, global business systems.

Mississippi State University, College of Business, Department of Management and Information Systems, Mississippi State, MS 39762. Offers business administration (MBA); information systems (MSIS, PhD); management (PhD); project management (MBA). *Program availability:* Part-time. *Faculty:* 18 full-time (4 women). *Students:* 66 full-time (15 women), 200 part-time (39 women); includes 25 minority (10 Black or African American, non-Hispanic/Latino; 1 American Indian or Alaska Native, non-Hispanic/Latino; 4 Asian, non-Hispanic/Latino; 6 Hispanic/Latino; 4 Two or more races, non-Hispanic/Latino), 20 international. Average age 31. 186 applicants, 39% accepted, 53 enrolled. In 2016, 84 master's, 2 doctorates awarded. *Degree requirements:* For master's, comprehensive exam; for doctorate, comprehensive exam, thesis/dissertation. *Entrance requirements:* For master's, GMAT, minimum GPA of 3.0 in last 60 hours of undergraduate course work; for doctorate, GMAT (minimum score of 550), minimum GPA of 3.25 on all graduate work; BS with minimum GPA of 3.0 cumulative and last 60 hours. Additional exam requirements/recommendations for international students: Required—TOEFL (minimum score 575 paper-based; 84 iBT); Recommended—IELTS (minimum score 7). *Application deadline:* For fall admission, 7/1 for domestic students, 5/1 for international students; for spring admission, 11/1 for domestic students, 9/1 for international students. Applications are processed on a rolling basis. Application fee: $60. Electronic applications accepted. *Expenses:* Tuition, state resident: full-time $7670; part-time $852.50 per credit hour. Tuition, nonresident: full-time $20,790; part-time $2310.50 per credit hour. Part-time tuition and fees vary according to course load. *Financial support:* Career-related internships or fieldwork, Federal Work-Study, institutionally sponsored loans, scholarships/grants, and unspecified assistantships available. Financial award applicants required to submit FAFSA. *Faculty research:* Electronic commerce, management of information technology. *Total annual research expenditures:* $1.3 million. *Unit head:* Dr. James J. Chrisman, Professor and Head, 662-325-1991, Fax: 662-325-8651, E-mail: jchrisman@business.msstate.edu. *Application contact:* Lakan Drinker, Admissions and Enrollment Assistant, 662-325-8951, E-mail:

ldrinker@grad.msstate.edu.
Website: http://www.business.msstate.edu/programs/mis/index.php

Missouri State University, Graduate College, College of Business Administration, Department of Technology and Construction Management, Springfield, MO 65897. Offers project management (MS). *Program availability:* Part-time. *Faculty:* 4 full-time (0 women), 2 part-time/adjunct (1 woman). *Students:* 28 full-time (9 women), 52 part-time (15 women); includes 15 minority (5 Black or African American, non-Hispanic/Latino; 1 Asian, non-Hispanic/Latino; 5 Hispanic/Latino; 4 Two or more races, non-Hispanic/Latino), 14 international. Average age 35. 40 applicants, 48% accepted, 11 enrolled. In 2016, 27 master's awarded. *Degree requirements:* For master's, thesis or alternative. *Entrance requirements:* For master's, GRE or GMAT, minimum GPA of 2.75. Additional exam requirements/recommendations for international students: Required—TOEFL (minimum score 550 paper-based; 79 iBT), IELTS (minimum score 6). *Application deadline:* For fall admission, 7/20 priority date for domestic students, 5/1 for international students; for spring admission, 12/20 priority date for domestic students, 9/1 for international students; for summer admission, 5/20 priority date for domestic students. Applications are processed on a rolling basis. Application fee: $35 ($50 for international students). Electronic applications accepted. *Expenses:* Tuition, state resident: full-time $5830. Tuition, nonresident: full-time $10,708. *Required fees:* $1130. Tuition and fees vary according to class time, course level, course load and program. *Financial support:* Federal Work-Study, institutionally sponsored loans, scholarships/grants, and unspecified assistantships available. Financial award application deadline: 3/31; financial award applicants required to submit FAFSA. *Unit head:* Dr. Richard N. Callahan, Department Head, 417-836-5121, Fax: 417-836-8556, E-mail: indmgt@missouristate.edu. *Application contact:* Michael Edwards, Coordinator of Graduate Admissions, 417-836-5330, Fax: 417-836-6200, E-mail: michaeledwards@missouristate.edu.
Website: http://tcm.missouristate.edu/

Montana Tech of The University of Montana, Project Engineering and Management Program, Butte, MT 59701-8997. Offers MPEM. *Program availability:* Part-time, evening/weekend, online learning. *Faculty:* 1 full-time (0 women), 8 part-time/adjunct (2 women). *Students:* 10 part-time (5 women); includes 2 minority (both Black or African American, non-Hispanic/Latino). Average age 28. 10 applicants, 90% accepted, 5 enrolled. In 2016, 4 master's awarded. *Degree requirements:* For master's, comprehensive exam, final project presentation. *Entrance requirements:* For master's, minimum GPA of 3.0. Additional exam requirements/recommendations for international students: Required—TOEFL (minimum score 550 paper-based; 80 iBT), IELTS (minimum score 7). *Application deadline:* For fall admission, 4/1 priority date for domestic students, 3/1 priority date for international students; for spring admission, 10/1 priority date for domestic students, 8/1 priority date for international students. Applications are processed on a rolling basis. Application fee: $50. Electronic applications accepted. *Expenses:* Tuition, state resident: full-time $2901; part-time $1450.68 per degree program. Tuition, nonresident: full-time $8432; part-time $4215.84 per degree program. *Required fees:* $668; $354 per degree program. Tuition and fees vary according to course load and program. *Financial support:* Application deadline: 4/1; applicants required to submit FAFSA. *Unit head:* Dr. Kumar Ganesan, Director, 406-496-4239, Fax: 406-496-4650, E-mail: kganesan@mtech.edu. *Application contact:* Daniel Stirling, Administrator, Graduate School, 406-496-4304, Fax: 406-496-4710, E-mail: gradschoo@mtech.edu.
Website: https://www.mtech.edu/academics/gradschool/distancelearning/distancelearning-pem.htm

Mount Aloysius College, Program in Business Administration, Cresson, PA 16630-1999. Offers accounting (MBA); health and human services administration (MBA); non-profit management (MBA); project management (MBA). *Program availability:* Part-time, evening/weekend. *Entrance requirements:* Additional exam requirements/recommendations for international students: Required—IELTS (minimum score 5.5); Recommended—TOEFL. *Application deadline:* For fall admission, 8/1 for domestic students; for spring admission, 12/1 for domestic students. Applications are processed on a rolling basis. Application fee: $30. Electronic applications accepted. Application fee is waived when completed online. *Expenses: Tuition:* Full-time $6750; part-time $750 per credit. *Required fees:* $285 per semester. *Financial support:* Unspecified assistantships available. Financial award applicants required to submit FAFSA. *Application contact:* Matthew P. Bodenschatz, Director of Graduate and Continuing Education Admissions, 814-886-6556, Fax: 814-886-6441, E-mail: mbodenschatz@mtaloy.edu.
Website: http://www.mtaloy.edu

New England College, Program in Management, Henniker, NH 03242-3293. Offers accounting (MSA); healthcare administration (MS); international relations (MA); marketing management (MS); nonprofit leadership (MS); project management (MS); strategic leadership (MS). *Program availability:* Part-time, evening/weekend. *Degree requirements:* For master's, independent research project. Electronic applications accepted.

New York University, Polytechnic School of Engineering, Department of Technology Management, New York, NY 10012-1019. Offers construction management (Advanced Certificate); electronic business management (Advanced Certificate); entrepreneurship (Advanced Certificate); human resources management (Advanced Certificate); industrial engineering (MS); information management (Advanced Certificate); management (MS); management of technology (MS); manufacturing engineering (MS); organizational behavior (MS, Advanced Certificate); project management (Advanced Certificate); technology management (MBA, PhD, Advanced Certificate); telecommunications management (Advanced Certificate). *Program availability:* Part-time, evening/weekend. *Degree requirements:* For master's, comprehensive exam (for some programs), thesis (for some programs); for doctorate, comprehensive exam, thesis/dissertation. *Entrance requirements:* For master's, GMAT, minimum B average in undergraduate course work. Additional exam requirements/recommendations for international students: Required—TOEFL (minimum score 550 paper-based; 80 iBT); Recommended—IELTS (minimum score 6.5). Electronic applications accepted. *Faculty research:* Global innovation and research and development strategy, managing emerging technologies, technology and development, service design and innovation, tech entrepreneurship and commercialization, sustainable and clean-tech innovation, impacts of information technology upon individuals, organizations and society.

Northeastern University, College of Professional Studies, Boston, MA 02115-5096. Offers applied nutrition (MS); college athletics administration (MSL); commerce and economic development (MS); corporate and organizational communication (MS); criminal justice (MS); digital media (MPS); elearning and instructional design (M Ed); elementary education (MAT); geographic information technology (MPS); global studies and international relations (MS); higher education administration (M Ed); homeland security (MA); human services (MS); informatics (MPS); leadership (MS); learning analytics (M Ed); learning and instruction (M Ed); nonprofit management (MS); professional sports administration (MSL); project management (MS); regulatory affairs for drugs, biologics, and medical devices (MS); respiratory care leadership (MS); special education (M Ed); technical communication (MS). *Program availability:* Part-time, evening/weekend, 100% online, blended/hybrid learning. *Faculty:* 82 full-time (51 women), 853 part-time/adjunct (366 women). *Students:* 4,947 part-time (3,076 women). In 2016, 1,456 master's awarded. *Application deadline:* Applications are processed on a rolling basis. Application fee: $0. Electronic applications accepted. *Expenses:* Contact institution. *Financial support:* Applicants required to submit FAFSA. *Unit head:* Dr. Mary Loeffelholz, Interim Dean of the College of Professional Studies.
Website: http://www.cps.neu.edu/

Northwestern University, McCormick School of Engineering and Applied Science, Department of Civil and Environmental Engineering, Master of Project Management Program, Evanston, IL 60208. Offers MS. *Program availability:* Part-time, evening/weekend. *Degree requirements:* For master's, capstone report. *Entrance requirements:* Additional exam requirements/recommendations for international students: Required—TOEFL (minimum score 560 paper-based; 83 iBT), IELTS. Electronic applications accepted. *Faculty research:* Construction management, real estate development, sustainability, and transportation management.

Northwestern University, School of Professional Studies, Program in Information Systems, Evanston, IL 60208. Offers analytics and business intelligence (MS); database and Internet technologies (MS); information systems (MS); information systems management (MS); information systems security (MS); medical informatics (MS); software project management and development (MS).

Northwest University, College of Business, Kirkland, WA 98033. Offers business administration (MBA); international business (MBA); project management (MBA); social entrepreneurship (MBA). *Accreditation:* ACBSP. *Program availability:* Part-time, evening/weekend. *Degree requirements:* For master's, formalized research. *Entrance requirements:* For master's, GMAT. Additional exam requirements/recommendations for international students: Required—TOEFL (minimum score 550 paper-based; 75 iBT). Electronic applications accepted. *Expenses:* Contact institution.

Norwich University, College of Graduate and Continuing Studies, Master of Business Administration Program, Northfield, VT 05663. Offers construction management (MBA); energy management (MBA); finance (MBA); logistics (MBA); organizational leadership (MBA); project management (MBA); supply chain management (MBA). *Accreditation:* ACBSP. *Program availability:* Evening/weekend, online only, mostly all online with a week-long residency requirement. *Faculty:* 24 part-time/adjunct (5 women). *Students:* 228 full-time (54 women); includes 54 minority (23 Black or African American, non-Hispanic/Latino; 1 American Indian or Alaska Native, non-Hispanic/Latino; 6 Asian, non-Hispanic/Latino; 20 Hispanic/Latino; 1 Native Hawaiian or other Pacific Islander, non-Hispanic/Latino; 3 Two or more races, non-Hispanic/Latino), 2 international. Average age 36. 74 applicants, 100% accepted, 57 enrolled. In 2016, 135 master's awarded. *Degree requirements:* For master's, comprehensive exam. *Entrance requirements:* For master's, minimum undergraduate GPA of 2.75. Additional exam requirements/recommendations for international students: Required—TOEFL (minimum score 550 paper-based; 80 iBT), IELTS (minimum score 6.5). *Application deadline:* For fall admission, 8/14 for domestic and international students; for winter admission, 11/13 for domestic and international students; for spring admission, 2/12 for domestic and international students; for summer admission, 6/5 for domestic and international students. Electronic applications accepted. *Expenses:* Contact institution. *Financial support:* In 2016–17, 113 students received support. Scholarships/grants available. Financial award application deadline: 8/4; financial award applicants required to submit FAFSA. *Unit head:* Dr. Jose Cordova, Program Director, 802-485-2567, Fax: 802-485-2533, E-mail: jcordova@norwich.edu. *Application contact:* Admissions Advisor, 800-460-5597 Ext. 3376, Fax: 802-485-2533, E-mail: mba@online.norwich.edu.
Website: https://online.norwich.edu/degree-programs/masters/master-business-administration/overview

Norwich University, College of Graduate and Continuing Studies, Master of Science in Information Security and Assurance Program, Northfield, VT 05663. Offers information security and assurance (MS), including computer forensic investigation/incident response team management, critical infrastructure protection and cyber crime, cyber law and international perspectives on cyberspace, project management, vulnerability management. *Program availability:* Evening/weekend, online only, mostly all online with a week-long residency requirement. *Faculty:* 20 part-time/adjunct (3 women). *Students:* 110 full-time (23 women); includes 30 minority (10 Black or African American, non-Hispanic/Latino; 2 American Indian or Alaska Native, non-Hispanic/Latino; 9 Asian, non-Hispanic/Latino; 4 Hispanic/Latino; 5 Two or more races, non-Hispanic/Latino), 1 international. Average age 37. 38 applicants, 97% accepted, 26 enrolled. In 2016, 54 master's awarded. *Entrance requirements:* For master's, minimum undergraduate GPA of 2.75. Additional exam requirements/recommendations for international students: Required—TOEFL (minimum score 550 paper-based; 80 iBT), IELTS (minimum score 6.5). *Application deadline:* For fall admission, 8/14 for domestic and international students; for winter admission, 11/13 for domestic and international students; for spring admission, 2/12 for domestic and international students; for summer admission, 6/5 for domestic and international students. Electronic applications accepted. *Expenses:* Contact institution. *Financial support:* In 2016–17, 52 students received support. Scholarships/grants available. Financial award application deadline: 8/4; financial award applicants required to submit FAFSA. *Unit head:* Dr. Rosemarie Pelletier, Program Director, 802-485-2767, Fax: 802-485-2533, E-mail: rpellet2@norwich.edu. *Application contact:* Admissions Advisor, 800-460-5597 Ext. 3363, Fax: 802-485-2533, E-mail: msisa@online.norwich.edu.
Website: https://online.norwich.edu/degree-programs/masters/master-science-information-security-assurance/overview

Oklahoma Christian University, Graduate School of Business, Oklahoma City, OK 73136-1100. Offers accounting (M Acc, MBA); financial services (MBA); general business (MBA); health services management (MBA); human resources (MBA); international business (MBA); leadership and organizational development (MBA); marketing (MBA); nonprofit management (MBA); project management (MBA). *Accreditation:* ACBSP. *Program availability:* Part-time, 100% online. *Faculty:* 10 full-time (2 women), 21 part-time/adjunct (2 women). *Students:* 156 full-time (68 women), 137 part-time (73 women). Average age 30. 374 applicants, 213 enrolled. In 2016, 114 master's awarded. *Entrance requirements:* For master's, bachelor's degree. Additional exam requirements/recommendations for international students: Required—TOEFL (minimum score 550 paper-based). Application fee: $25. Electronic applications accepted. *Expenses:* Contact institution. *Unit head:* Dr. Ken Johnson, Chair, 405-425-5567, Fax: 405-425-5585, E-mail: ken.johnson@oc.edu. *Application contact:* Angie Ricketts, Graduate School Admissions Counselor, 405-425-5587, Fax: 405-425-5585, E-mail: angie.ricketts@oc.edu.
Website: http://www.oc.edu/academics/graduate/business/

Penn State Erie, The Behrend College, Graduate School, Erie, PA 16563. Offers accounting (MPAC); business administration (MBA); project management (MPM); quality and manufacturing management (MMM). *Accreditation:* AACSB. *Program availability:* Part-time. *Students:* 28 full-time (9 women), 118 part-time (31 women); includes 11 minority (5 Black or African American, non-Hispanic/Latino; 2 Asian, non-Hispanic/Latino; 1 Hispanic/Latino; 3 Two or more races, non-Hispanic/Latino), 2 international. Average age 32. 91 applicants, 74% accepted, 55 enrolled. In 2016, 59 master's awarded. *Entrance requirements:* Additional exam requirements/recommendations for international students: Required—TOEFL (minimum score 550

paper-based; 80 iBT), IELTS. *Application deadline:* Applications are processed on a rolling basis. Application fee: $65. Electronic applications accepted. *Financial support:* Federal Work-Study available. Financial award application deadline: 3/1; financial award applicants required to submit FAFSA. *Unit head:* Dr. Ralph M. Ford, Chancellor, 814-898-6160, Fax: 814-898-6461. *Application contact:* Ann M. Burbules, Assistant Director, Graduate Admissions, 866-374-3378, Fax: 814-898-6044, E-mail: behrend.admissions@psu.edu.
Website: http://behrend.psu.edu/

Point Loma Nazarene University, Fermanian School of Business, San Diego, CA 92106-2899. Offers general business (MBA); healthcare management (MBA); innovation and entrepreneurship (MBA); organizational leadership (MBA); project management (MBA). *Accreditation:* ACBSP. *Program availability:* Part-time, evening/weekend. *Faculty:* 8 full-time (1 woman), 8 part-time/adjunct (4 women). *Students:* 33 full-time (14 women), 64 part-time (30 women); includes 32 minority (6 Black or African American, non-Hispanic/Latino; 4 Asian, non-Hispanic/Latino; 19 Hispanic/Latino; 3 Two or more races, non-Hispanic/Latino), 7 international. Average age 31. 71 applicants, 79% accepted, 47 enrolled. In 2016, 37 master's awarded. *Entrance requirements:* For master's, GMAT, letters of recommendation, essay, interview. Additional exam requirements/recommendations for international students: Required—TOEFL. *Application deadline:* For fall admission, 7/26 priority date for domestic students; for spring admission, 11/29 priority date for domestic students; for summer admission, 4/2 priority date for domestic students. Applications are processed on a rolling basis. Application fee: $50. Electronic applications accepted. *Expenses:* $825 per credit. *Financial support:* Applicants required to submit FAFSA. *Unit head:* Jamie Ressler, Associate Dean, Graduate Business, 619-849-2721, E-mail: jamieressler@pointloma.edu. *Application contact:* Claire Buckley, Director of Graduate Admission, 866-692-4723, E-mail: gradinfo@pointloma.edu.
Website: http://www.pointloma.edu/discover/graduate-school-san-diego/san-diego-graduate-programs-masters-degree-san-diego/mba

Polytechnic University of Puerto Rico, Miami Campus, Graduate School, Miami, FL 33166. Offers accounting (MBA); business administration (MBA); construction management (MEM); environmental management (MEM); finance (MBA); human resources management (MBA); logistics and supply chain management (MBA); management of international enterprises (MBA); manufacturing management (MEM); marketing management (MBA); project management (MBA). *Program availability:* Part-time, evening/weekend, online learning. *Entrance requirements:* For master's, minimum GPA of 3.0. Electronic applications accepted.

Post University, Program in Business Administration, Waterbury, CT 06723-2540. Offers accounting (MSA); business administration (MBA); corporate innovation (MBA); entrepreneurship (MBA); finance (MBA); healthcare (MBA); leadership (MBA); marketing (MBA); project management (MBA). *Accreditation:* ACBSP. *Program availability:* Online learning.

Queen's University at Kingston, Queens School of Business, Program in Business Administration, Kingston, ON K7L 3N6, Canada. Offers consulting and project management (MBA); finance (MBA); innovation and entrepreneurship (MBA); marketing (MBA). *Degree requirements:* For master's, thesis optional, research project. *Entrance requirements:* For master's, GMAT, minimum B+ average. Additional exam requirements/recommendations for international students: Required—TOEFL. Electronic applications accepted. *Faculty research:* Management fundamentals, strategic thinking, global business, innovation and change, leadership.

Regis University, College of Business and Economics, Denver, CO 80221-1099. Offers accounting (MS); executive leadership (Certificate); finance (MS); finance and accounting (MBA); health industry leadership (MBA); human resource management and leadership (MSOL); management (MBA); marketing (MBA); nonprofit leadership (Post-Graduate Certificate); nonprofit management (MNM); nonprofit organizational capacity building (Certificate); operations management (MBA); organizational leadership and management (MSOL); project leadership and management (MS, MSOL); strategic business management (Certificate); strategic human resource integration (Certificate); strategic management (MBA). Programs offered at Colorado Springs Campus, Northwest Denver Campus, Southeast Denver Campus, Fort Collins Campus, Broomfield Campus, Henderson (Nevada) Campus, and Summerlin (Nevada) Campus. *Program availability:* Part-time, evening/weekend, 100% online, blended/hybrid learning. *Faculty:* 15 full-time (5 women), 43 part-time/adjunct (16 women). *Students:* 622 full-time (350 women), 460 part-time (170 women); includes 317 minority (88 Black or African American, non-Hispanic/Latino; 7 American Indian or Alaska Native, non-Hispanic/Latino; 44 Asian, non-Hispanic/Latino; 151 Hispanic/Latino; 1 Native Hawaiian or other Pacific Islander, non-Hispanic/Latino; 26 Two or more races, non-Hispanic/Latino), 44 international. Average age 36. 307 applicants, 73% accepted, 134 enrolled. In 2016, 394 master's awarded. *Degree requirements:* For master's, thesis (for some programs), capstone or final research project. *Entrance requirements:* For master's, official transcript reflecting baccalaureate degree awarded from regionally-accredited college or university, interview, 2 years of full-time related work experience, resume, letters of recommendation. Additional exam requirements/recommendations for international students: Required—TOEFL (minimum score 550 paper-based; 82 iBT). *Application deadline:* For fall admission, 8/15 priority date for domestic students, 8/13 for international students; for winter admission, 10/10 priority date for domestic students, 9/8 for international students; for spring admission, 1/10 priority date for domestic students, 11/17 for international students; for summer admission, 5/1 priority date for domestic students. Applications are processed on a rolling basis. Application fee: $75. Electronic applications accepted. *Expenses:* $780 per credit hour. *Financial support:* Scholarships/grants available. Financial award application deadline: 4/15; financial award applicants required to submit FAFSA. *Faculty research:* Impact of information technology on small business regulation of accounting, international project financing, mineral development, delivery of healthcare to rural indigenous communities. *Unit head:* Dr. Timothy Keane, Academic Dean. *Application contact:* Cate Clark, Director of Admissions, 303-458-4900, Fax: 303-964-5534, E-mail: ruadmissions@regis.edu.
Website: http://www.regis.edu/CBE.aspx

Robert Morris University, School of Communications and Information Systems, Moon Township, PA 15108-1189. Offers communication and information systems (MS); cyber security (MS); data analytics (MS); information security and assurance (MS); information systems and communications (D Sc); information systems management (MS); information technology project management (MS); Internet information systems (MS); organizational leadership (MS). *Program availability:* Part-time, evening/weekend, online learning. *Faculty:* 28 full-time (11 women), 6 part-time/adjunct (0 women). *Students:* 269 part-time (110 women); includes 49 minority (29 Black or African American, non-Hispanic/Latino; 10 Asian, non-Hispanic/Latino; 5 Hispanic/Latino; 5 Two or more races, non-Hispanic/Latino), 49 international. Average age 34. 239 applicants, 46% accepted, 83 enrolled. In 2016, 110 master's, 15 doctorates awarded. *Degree requirements:* For doctorate, thesis/dissertation. *Entrance requirements:* For doctorate, employer letter of endorsement, interview. Additional exam requirements/recommendations for international students: Required—TOEFL (minimum score 550 paper-based; 79 iBT). *Application deadline:* For fall admission, 7/1 priority date for domestic and international students; for spring admission, 11/1 priority date for domestic and international students. Applications are processed on a rolling basis. Application fee: $35. Electronic applications accepted. Application fee is waived when completed online. *Expenses:* $870 per credit (for master's degree). *Financial support:* Institutionally sponsored loans available. Support available to part-time students. Financial award application deadline: 5/1. *Unit head:* Ann Marie M. Le Blanc, Dean, 412-397-6433, Fax: 412-397-6469, E-mail: leblanc@rmu.edu. *Application contact:* Kellie L. Laurenzi, Associate Vice President, 412-397-5200, Fax: 412-397-5915, E-mail: graduateadmissions@rmu.edu.
Website: http://www.rmu.edu/web/cms/schools/scis/Pages/default.aspx

Rochester Institute of Technology, Graduate Enrollment Services, School of Individualized Study, Graduate Programs Department, Advanced Certificate Program in Project Management, Rochester, NY 14623. Offers Advanced Certificate. *Program availability:* Part-time, evening/weekend, 100% online, blended/hybrid learning. *Students:* 1 full-time (0 women), 6 part-time (4 women); includes 2 minority (1 Asian, non-Hispanic/Latino; 1 Hispanic/Latino). Average age 36. 7 applicants, 43% accepted, 3 enrolled. In 2016, 13 Advanced Certificates awarded. *Entrance requirements:* For degree, minimum GPA of 3.0 (recommended). Additional exam requirements/recommendations for international students: Required—TOEFL (minimum score 550 paper-based; 79 iBT), IELTS (minimum score 6.5), PTE (minimum score 58). *Application deadline:* Applications are processed on a rolling basis. Application fee: $60. Electronic applications accepted. *Expenses:* $1,742 per credit hour (classroom), $993 per credit hour (online). *Financial support:* In 2016–17, 2 students received support. Available to part-time students. Applicants required to submit FAFSA. *Faculty research:* Risk management; cross-cultural teams; automation of management process; non-traditional management tools; human performance and emotional intelligence. *Unit head:* Peter Boyd, Graduate Program Director, 585-475-6320, E-mail: plbcms@rit.edu. *Application contact:* Diane Ellison, Associate Vice President, Graduate Enrollment Services, 585-475-2229, Fax: 585-475-7164, E-mail: gradinfo@rit.edu.
Website: http://www.rit.edu/academicaffairs/sois/getting-started/graduate/advanced-certificates

Royal Roads University, Graduate Studies, Applied Leadership and Management Program, Victoria, BC V9B 5Y2, Canada. Offers executive coaching (Graduate Certificate); health systems leadership (Graduate Certificate); project management (Graduate Certificate); public relations management (Graduate Certificate); strategic human resources management (Graduate Certificate).

Saint Leo University, Graduate Business Studies, Saint Leo, FL 33574-6665. Offers accounting (M Acc, MBA, Certificate); cybersecurity (MS); health care management (MBA, Certificate); human resource management (MBA, Certificate); information security management (MBA, Certificate); management (MBA, DBA); marketing (MBA, Certificate); marketing research and social media analytics (MBA, Certificate); project management (MBA, Certificate); sport business (MBA); supply chain global integration management (MBA, Certificate). *Accreditation:* ACBSP. *Program availability:* Part-time, evening/weekend, 100% online, blended/hybrid learning. *Faculty:* 53 full-time (18 women), 53 part-time/adjunct (19 women). *Students:* 8 full-time (4 women), 2,001 part-time (1,160 women); includes 928 minority (650 Black or African American, non-Hispanic/Latino; 5 American Indian or Alaska Native, non-Hispanic/Latino; 43 Asian, non-Hispanic/Latino; 193 Hispanic/Latino; 2 Native Hawaiian or other Pacific Islander, non-Hispanic/Latino; 35 Two or more races, non-Hispanic/Latino), 51 international. Average age 37. 922 applicants, 85% accepted, 517 enrolled. In 2016, 874 master's, 17 other advanced degrees awarded. *Degree requirements:* For doctorate, comprehensive exam, thesis/dissertation. *Entrance requirements:* For master's, GMAT (minimum score 500), official transcripts, current resume, 2 professional recommendations, personal statement, bachelor's degree from regionally-accredited university; undergraduate degree in accounting and minimum undergraduate GPA of 3.0 (for M Acc); minimum undergraduate GPA of 3.0 in final 2 years of undergraduate study and 2 years' work experience (for MBA); for doctorate, GMAT (minimum score of 550) if master's GPA is under 3.25, official transcripts, current resume, 2 professional recommendations, personal statement, master's degree from regionally-accredited university with minimum GPA of 3.25, 3 years' work experience, interview. Additional exam requirements/recommendations for international students: Required—TOEFL (minimum score 550 paper-based; 80 iBT). *Application deadline:* For fall admission, 7/1 priority date for domestic and international students; for spring admission, 11/12 priority date for domestic students, 11/1 for international students. Applications are processed on a rolling basis. Application fee: $80. Electronic applications accepted. *Expenses:* Contact institution. *Financial support:* In 2016–17, 118 students received support. Career-related internships or fieldwork, scholarships/grants, and health care benefits available. Financial award application deadline: 3/1; financial award applicants required to submit FAFSA. *Unit head:* Dr. Lorrie McGovern, Associate Dean, School of Business, 352-588-7869, Fax: 352-588-8912, E-mail: mbaslu@saintleo.edu. *Application contact:* Jennifer Shelley, Senior Associate Director of Graduate Admissions, 800-707-8846, Fax: 352-588-7873, E-mail: grad.admissions@saintleo.edu.
Website: http://www.saintleo.edu/academics/graduate.aspx

Saint Mary's University of Minnesota, Schools of Graduate and Professional Programs, Graduate School of Business and Technology, Project Management Program, Winona, MN 55987-1399. Offers MS, Certificate. *Program availability:* Part-time, evening/weekend, online learning. Tuition and fees vary according to degree level and program. *Unit head:* William Johnson, Director, 612-728-5178, E-mail: wcjohn06@smumn.edu. *Application contact:* James Callinan, Director of Admissions for Graduate and Professional Programs, 612-728-5185, Fax: 612-728-5121, E-mail: jcallina@smumn.edu.
Website: http://www.smumn.edu/graduate-home/areas-of-study/graduate-school-of-business-technology/ms-in-project-management

Saint Xavier University, Graduate Studies, Graham School of Management, Chicago, IL 60655-3105. Offers employee health benefits (Certificate); finance (MBA); financial fraud examination and management (MBA, Certificate); financial planning (MBA, Certificate); generalist/individualized (MBA); health administration (MBA); managed care (Certificate); management (MBA); marketing (MBA); project management (MBA, Certificate); MBA/MS. *Accreditation:* AACSB; ACBSP. *Program availability:* Part-time, evening/weekend. *Entrance requirements:* For master's, GMAT, minimum GPA of 3.0, 2 years of work experience. Electronic applications accepted. *Expenses:* Contact institution.

Sam Houston State University, College of Business Administration, Department of Management and Marketing, Huntsville, TX 77341. Offers project management (MS). *Program availability:* Part-time, online learning. *Entrance requirements:* For master's, GMAT, official transcripts, current resume, essay. Additional exam requirements/recommendations for international students: Required—TOEFL (minimum score 79 iBT), IELTS (minimum score 6.5). Electronic applications accepted.

Southern Illinois University Edwardsville, Graduate School, School of Business, Program in Business Administration, Edwardsville, IL 62026. Offers business analytics (MBA); management information systems (MBA); project management (MBA). *Accreditation:* AACSB. *Program availability:* Part-time, evening/weekend. *Degree requirements:* For master's, comprehensive exam. *Entrance requirements:* For master's, GMAT. Additional exam requirements/recommendations for international students: Required—TOEFL (minimum score 550 paper-based; 79 iBT), IELTS (minimum score 6.5). Electronic applications accepted.

Southern New Hampshire University, School of Business, Manchester, NH 03106-1045. Offers accounting (MBA, MS, Graduate Certificate); accounting finance (MS); accounting/auditing (MS); accounting/forensic accounting (MS); accounting/taxation (MS); athletic administration (MBA, Graduate Certificate); business administration (IMBA, MBA, Certificate, Graduate Certificate), including accounting (Certificate), business administration (MBA), business information systems (Graduate Certificate), human resource management (Certificate); corporate social responsibility (MBA); entrepreneurship (MBA); finance (MBA, MS, Graduate Certificate); finance/corporate finance (MS); finance/investments and securities (MS); forensic accounting (MBA); healthcare informatics (MBA); healthcare management (MBA); human resource management (Graduate Certificate); information technology (MS, Graduate Certificate); information technology management (MBA); international business (Graduate Certificate); international business and information technology (Graduate Certificate); international finance (Graduate Certificate); international sport management (Graduate Certificate); justice studies (MBA); leadership of nonprofit organizations (Graduate Certificate); management (MS); marketing (MBA, MS, Graduate Certificate); operations and project management (MS); operations and supply chain management (MBA, Graduate Certificate); organizational leadership (MS); project management (MBA, Graduate Certificate); Six Sigma (MBA); Six Sigma quality (Graduate Certificate); social media marketing (MBA); sport management (MBA, MS, Graduate Certificate); sustainability and environmental compliance (MBA); workplace conflict management (MBA); MBA/Certificate. *Accreditation:* ACBSP. *Program availability:* Part-time, evening/weekend, online learning. Terminal master's awarded for partial completion of doctoral program. *Degree requirements:* For master's, one foreign language, comprehensive exam (for some programs), thesis or alternative. *Entrance requirements:* For master's, minimum GPA of 2.5. Additional exam requirements/recommendations for international students: Required—TOEFL (minimum score 500 paper-based). Electronic applications accepted.

Stevens Institute of Technology, Graduate School, School of Business, Program in Business Administration, Hoboken, NJ 07030. Offers business intelligence and analytics (MBA); engineering management (MBA); finance (MBA); information systems (MBA); innovation and entrepreneurship (MBA); marketing (MBA); pharmaceutical management (MBA); project management (MBA, Certificate); technology management (MBA); telecommunications management (MBA). *Accreditation:* AACSB. *Program availability:* Part-time, evening/weekend. *Students:* 35 full-time (15 women), 181 part-time (79 women); includes 53 minority (10 Black or African American, non-Hispanic/Latino; 2 American Indian or Alaska Native, non-Hispanic/Latino; 36 Asian, non-Hispanic/Latino; 5 Hispanic/Latino), 30 international. Average age 32. 215 applicants, 53% accepted, 61 enrolled. In 2016, 61 master's awarded. *Degree requirements:* For master's, thesis optional, minimum B average in major field and overall; for Certificate, minimum B average. *Entrance requirements:* Additional exam requirements/recommendations for international students: Required—TOEFL (minimum score 74 iBT), IELTS (minimum score 6). *Application deadline:* For fall admission, 6/1 for domestic students, 4/15 for international students; for spring admission, 11/30 for domestic students, 11/1 for international students. Applications are processed on a rolling basis. Application fee: $65. Electronic applications accepted. *Expenses:* Contact institution. *Financial support:* Fellowships, research assistantships, teaching assistantships, career-related internships or fieldwork, Federal Work-Study, scholarships/grants, and unspecified assistantships available. Financial award application deadline: 2/15; financial award applicants required to submit FAFSA. *Unit head:* Dr. Gregory Prastacos, Dean, 201-216-8366, E-mail: gprastac@stevens.edu. *Application contact:* Graduate Admissions, 888-783-8367, Fax: 888-511-1306, E-mail: graduate@stevens.edu.
Website: https://www.stevens.edu/school-business/masters-programs/mbaemba

Stevens Institute of Technology, Graduate School, School of Business, Program in Information Systems, Hoboken, NJ 07030. Offers computer science (MS); e-commerce (MS); enterprise systems (MS); entrepreneurial information technology (MS); information architecture (MS); information management (MS, Certificate); information security (MS); information technology in financial services industry (MS); information technology in the pharmaceutical industry (MS); information technology outsourcing management (MS); project management (MS, Certificate); software engineering (MS); telecommunications (MS). *Program availability:* Part-time, evening/weekend. *Students:* 280 full-time (100 women), 84 part-time (21 women); includes 23 minority (9 Black or African American, non-Hispanic/Latino; 13 Asian, non-Hispanic/Latino; 1 Hispanic/Latino), 283 international. Average age 26. 925 applicants, 62% accepted, 114 enrolled. In 2016, 212 master's, 32 other advanced degrees awarded. *Degree requirements:* For master's, thesis optional, minimum B average in major field and overall; for Certificate, minimum B average. *Entrance requirements:* Additional exam requirements/recommendations for international students: Required—TOEFL (minimum score 74 iBT), IELTS (minimum score 6). *Application deadline:* For fall admission, 6/1 for domestic students, 4/15 for international students; for spring admission, 11/30 for domestic students, 11/1 for international students. Applications are processed on a rolling basis. Application fee: $65. Electronic applications accepted. *Expenses:* Contact institution. *Financial support:* Fellowships, research assistantships, teaching assistantships, career-related internships or fieldwork, Federal Work-Study, scholarships/grants, and unspecified assistantships available. Financial award application deadline: 2/15; financial award applicants required to submit FAFSA. *Unit head:* Dr. Gregory Prastacos, Dean, 201-216-8366, E-mail: gprastac@stevens.edu. *Application contact:* Graduate Admissions, 888-783-8367, Fax: 888-511-1306, E-mail: graduate@stevens.edu.
Website: https://www.stevens.edu/school-business/masters-programs/information-systems

Stevens Institute of Technology, Graduate School, School of Business, Program in Management, Hoboken, NJ 07030. Offers general management (MS); global innovation management (MS); human resource management (MS); information management (MS); project management (MS); technology commercialization (MS); technology management (MS). *Program availability:* Part-time, evening/weekend. *Students:* 83 full-time (28 women), 82 part-time (36 women); includes 30 minority (6 Black or African American, non-Hispanic/Latino; 1 American Indian or Alaska Native, non-Hispanic/Latino; 21 Asian, non-Hispanic/Latino; 2 Hispanic/Latino), 73 international. Average age 29. 381 applicants, 64% accepted, 53 enrolled. In 2016, 66 master's awarded. *Degree requirements:* For master's, thesis optional, minimum B average in major field and overall. *Entrance requirements:* Additional exam requirements/recommendations for international students: Required—TOEFL (minimum score 74 iBT), IELTS (minimum score 6). *Application deadline:* For fall admission, 6/1 for domestic students, 4/15 for international students; for spring admission, 11/30 for domestic students, 11/1 for international students. Applications are processed on a rolling basis. Application fee: $65. Electronic applications accepted. *Expenses:* Contact institution. *Financial support:* Fellowships, research assistantships, teaching assistantships, career-related internships or fieldwork, Federal Work-Study, scholarships/grants, and unspecified assistantships available. Financial award application deadline: 2/15; financial award applicants required to submit FAFSA. *Unit head:* Brian Rothschild, Director, 201-216-3677, E-mail: brian.rothschild@stevens.edu. *Application contact:* Graduate Admissions, 888-783-8367, Fax: 888-511-1306, E-mail: graduate@stevens.edu.
Website: https://www.stevens.edu/school-business/masters-programs/management

Stevenson University, Program in Healthcare Management, Owings Mills, MD 21117. Offers project management (MS); quality management and patient safety (MS). *Program availability:* Part-time, online only, 100% online. *Faculty:* 1 (woman) full-time, 9 part-time/adjunct (6 women). *Students:* 3 full-time (all women), 22 part-time (20 women); includes 10 minority (8 Black or African American, non-Hispanic/Latino; 1 Asian, non-Hispanic/Latino; 1 Hispanic/Latino). Average age 32. 26 applicants, 54% accepted, 8 enrolled. In 2016, 17 master's awarded. *Degree requirements:* For master's, capstone course. *Entrance requirements:* For master's, official college transcripts from all previous academic work, minimum cumulative GPA of 3.0 in past academic work, minimum grade of B in statistics or an upper-level math and English composition, two professional letters of recommendation with at least one from a current or past supervisor, 250-word personal statement. *Application deadline:* Applications are processed on a rolling basis. Electronic applications accepted. *Expenses:* $670 per credit hour. *Financial support:* Unspecified assistantships available. Financial award applicants required to submit FAFSA. *Unit head:* Sharon Buchbinder, PhD, Coordinator, 443-394-9290, Fax: 443-394-0538, E-mail: sbuchbinder@stevenson.edu. *Application contact:* Amanda Courter, Enrollment Counselor, 443-352-4243, Fax: 443-394-0538, E-mail: acourter@stevenson.edu.
Website: http://www.stevenson.edu

Texas A&M University–San Antonio, School of Business, San Antonio, TX 78224. Offers business administration (MBA); enterprise resource planning systems (MBA); finance (MBA); healthcare management (MBA); human resources management (MBA); information assurance and security (MBA); international business (MBA); professional accounting (MPA); project management (MBA); supply chain management (MBA). *Program availability:* Part-time, evening/weekend. *Entrance requirements:* For master's, GMAT. Additional exam requirements/recommendations for international students: Required—TOEFL (minimum score 550 paper-based; 80 iBT), IELTS (minimum score 6). Electronic applications accepted.

Trident University International, College of Business Administration, Program in Business Administration, Cypress, CA 90630. Offers business administration (PhD); conflict and negotiation management (MBA); criminal justice administration (MBA); entrepreneurship (MBA); finance (MBA); general management (MBA); government accounting (MBA); human resource management (MBA); information security and digital assurance management (MBA); information technology management (MBA); international business (MBA); logistics management (MBA); marketing (MBA); project management (MBA); public management (MBA); quality management (MBA); strategic leadership (MBA). *Program availability:* Part-time, evening/weekend, online learning. *Degree requirements:* For doctorate, comprehensive exam, thesis/dissertation, defense of dissertation. *Entrance requirements:* For master's, minimum GPA of 2.5 (students with GPA 3.0 or greater may transfer up to 30% of graduate level credits); for doctorate, minimum GPA of 3.4, curriculum vitae, course work in research methods or statistics. Additional exam requirements/recommendations for international students: Required—TOEFL. Electronic applications accepted.

Universidad del Turabo, Graduate Programs, School of Business and Entrepreneurship, Program in Project Management, Gurabo, PR 00778-3030. Offers MBA. *Students:* 42 full-time (17 women), 37 part-time (20 women); all minorities (all Hispanic/Latino). Average age 34. 71 applicants, 35% accepted, 23 enrolled. In 2016, 15 master's awarded. *Entrance requirements:* For master's, GRE, EXADEP or GMAT, interview, essay, official transcript, recommendation letters. *Application deadline:* Applications are processed on a rolling basis. Application fee: $25. Electronic applications accepted. *Financial support:* Institutionally sponsored loans available. Financial award applicants required to submit FAFSA. *Unit head:* Juan Sosa, Dean, 787-743-7979 Ext. 4118, E-mail: negocios_ut@suagm.edu. *Application contact:* Diriee Rodríguez, Admissions Director, 787-743-7979 Ext. 4453, E-mail: admisiones-ut@suagm.edu.
Website: http://ut.suagm.edu/es/negocios

Universidad Nacional Pedro Henriquez Urena, Graduate School, Santo Domingo, Dominican Republic. Offers agricultural diversity (MS), including horticultural/fruit production, tropical animal production; conservation of monuments and cultural assets (M Arch); ecology and environment (MS); environmental engineering (MEE); international relations (MA); natural resource management (MS); political science (MA); project optimization (MPM); project feasibility (MPM); project management (MPM); sanitation engineering (ME); science for teachers (MS); tropical Caribbean architecture (M Arch).

Université du Québec à Chicoutimi, Graduate Programs, Program in Project Management, Chicoutimi, QC G7H 2B1, Canada. Offers M Sc. *Program availability:* Part-time. *Entrance requirements:* For master's, appropriate bachelor's degree, proficiency in French.

Université du Québec à Montréal, Graduate Programs, Program in Project Management, Montréal, QC H3C 3P8, Canada. Offers MGP, Diploma. *Program availability:* Part-time. *Entrance requirements:* For master's and Diploma, appropriate bachelor's degree or equivalent, proficiency in French.

Université du Québec à Rimouski, Graduate Programs, Program in Project Management, Rimouski, QC G5L 3A1, Canada. Offers M Sc, Diploma. Programs offered jointly with Université du Québec à Chicoutimi, Université du Québec à Trois-Rivières, Université du Québec en Outaouais, Université du Québec en Abitibi-Témiscamingue, and Université du Québec à Montréal. *Program availability:* Part-time. *Entrance requirements:* For master's, proficiency in French, appropriate bachelor's degree.

Université du Québec en Abitibi-Témiscamingue, Graduate Programs, Program in Project Management, Rouyn-Noranda, QC J9X 5E4, Canada. Offers M Sc, DESS. M Sc offered jointly with Université du Québec à Chicoutimi, Université du Québec à Rimouski, Université du Québec à Trois-Rivières, Université du Québec en Outaouais, and Université du Québec à Montréal. *Program availability:* Part-time. *Entrance requirements:* For master's, appropriate bachelor's degree, proficiency in French.

Université du Québec en Outaouais, Graduate Programs, Program in Project Management, Gatineau, QC J8X 3X7, Canada. Offers M Sc, MA, DESS, Diploma. Programs offered jointly with Universite du Quebec a Chicoutimi, Universite du Quebec a Rimouski, Universite du Quebec a Trois-Rivieres, Universite du Quebec en Abitibi-T'miscamingue, and Universite du Quebec a Montreal. *Program availability:* Part-time, evening/weekend. *Degree requirements:* For master's, thesis (for some programs). *Entrance requirements:* For master's, appropriate bachelor's degree, proficiency in French.

The University of Alabama in Huntsville, School of Graduate Studies, College of Business Administration, Programs in Business and Management, Huntsville, AL 35899. Offers business analytics (MSMS); federal contracting and procurement management (Certificate); human resource management (MSM); management (MBA), including acquisition management, entrepreneurship, federal contract accounting, finance, human resource management, logistics and supply chain management, marketing, project management; supply chain management (Certificate); technology and innovation management (Certificate). *Accreditation:* AACSB. *Program availability:* Part-time, evening/weekend. *Degree requirements:* For master's, comprehensive exam, thesis or alternative. *Entrance requirements:* For master's, GMAT (minimum score 500), minimum AACSB index of 1080. Additional exam requirements/recommendations for international students: Required—TOEFL (minimum score 550 paper-based; 80 iBT), IELTS (minimum score 6.5). Electronic applications accepted. *Expenses:* Tuition, state resident: full-time $9834; part-time $600 per credit hour. Tuition, nonresident: full-time $21,830; part-time $1325 per credit hour. *Faculty research:* Supply chain management, management of research and development, international marketing and branding, organizational behavior and human resource management, social networks and computational economics.

University of Alaska Anchorage, School of Engineering, Program in Project Management, Anchorage, AK 99508. Offers MS. *Program availability:* Part-time, evening/weekend, online learning. *Degree requirements:* For master's, thesis or alternative, case study and research project. *Entrance requirements:* For master's, two years of project management experience. Additional exam requirements/recommendations for international students: Required—TOEFL (minimum score 550 paper-based). *Expenses:* Contact institution.

University of Calgary, Faculty of Graduate Studies, Schulich School of Engineering, Department of Civil Engineering, Calgary, AB T2N 1N4, Canada. Offers avalanche mechanics (M Sc, PhD); civil engineering (M Eng, M Sc, PhD); energy and environment engineering (M Eng, M Sc, PhD); environmental engineering (M Eng, M Sc, PhD); geotechnical engineering (M Eng, M Sc, PhD); materials science (M Eng, M Sc, PhD); project management (M Eng, M Sc, PhD); structures and solid mechanics (M Eng, M Sc, PhD); transportation engineering (M Eng, M Sc, PhD); water resources (M Eng, M Sc, PhD). *Program availability:* Part-time. *Degree requirements:* For master's, thesis; for doctorate, thesis/dissertation, written and oral candidacy exam. *Entrance requirements:* For master's, minimum GPA of 3.0; for doctorate, minimum GPA of 3.5. Additional exam requirements/recommendations for international students: Required—TOEFL (minimum score 580 paper-based; 93 iBT), IELTS (minimum score 7). Electronic applications accepted. *Faculty research:* Geotechnical engineering, energy and environment, transportation, project management, structures and solid mechanics.

University of California, Berkeley, UC Berkeley Extension, Certificate Programs in Business, Berkeley, CA 94720-1500. Offers accounting (Certificate); business administration (Certificate); finance (Certificate); human resource management (Certificate); management (Certificate); marketing (Certificate); project management (Certificate). *Accreditation:* AACSB. *Program availability:* Online learning.

University of California, Berkeley, UC Berkeley Extension, International Diploma Programs, Berkeley, CA 94720-1500. Offers business administration (Certificate); finance (Certificate); global business management (Certificate); marketing (Certificate); project management (Certificate). *Accreditation:* AACSB.

University of Dallas, Satish and Yasmin Gupta College of Business, Irving, TX 75062-4736. Offers accounting (MBA, MS); business administration (DBA); business analytics (MS); business management (MBA); corporate finance (MBA); cybersecurity (MS); finance (MS); financial services (MBA); global business (MBA, MS); health services management (MBA); human resource management (MBA); information and technology management (MS); information assurance (MBA); information technology (MBA); information technology service management (MBA); marketing management (MBA); organization development (MBA); project management (MBA); sports and entertainment management (MBA); strategic leadership (MBA); supply chain management (MBA). *Accreditation:* AACSB. *Program availability:* Part-time, evening/weekend, online learning. *Entrance requirements:* Additional exam requirements/recommendations for international students: Required—TOEFL. Electronic applications accepted. *Expenses:* Contact institution.

University of Denver, University College, Denver, CO 80208. Offers arts and culture (MA, Certificate); communication management (MS, Certificate), including translation studies (Certificate), world history and culture (Certificate); environmental policy and management (MS); geographic information systems (MS); global affairs (MA, Certificate), including human capital in organizations (Certificate), philanthropic leadership (Certificate), project management (Certificate), strategic innovation and change (Certificate); healthcare leadership (MS); information communications and technology (MS); leadership and organizations (MS); professional creative writing (MA, Certificate), including emergency planning and response (Certificate), organizational security (Certificate); security management (MS, Certificate); strategic human resources (Certificate). *Program availability:* Part-time, evening/weekend, online learning. *Faculty:* 118 part-time/adjunct (62 women). *Students:* 59 full-time (22 women), 1,285 part-time (750 women); includes 316 minority (111 Black or African American, non-Hispanic/Latino; 8 American Indian or Alaska Native, non-Hispanic/Latino; 39 Asian, non-Hispanic/Latino; 123 Hispanic/Latino; 3 Native Hawaiian or other Pacific Islander, non-Hispanic/Latino; 32 Two or more races, non-Hispanic/Latino), 85 international. Average age 35. 703 applicants, 89% accepted, 390 enrolled. In 2016, 428 master's, 138 other advanced degrees awarded. *Degree requirements:* For master's, capstone project. *Entrance requirements:* For master's, transcripts, two letters of recommendation, personal statement, resume. Additional exam requirements/recommendations for international students: Required—TOEFL (minimum score 550 paper-based; 80 iBT). *Application deadline:* For fall admission, 6/21 priority date for domestic students, 5/1 priority date for international students; for winter admission, 9/14 priority date for domestic students, 9/19 priority date for international students; for spring admission, 1/11 priority date for domestic students, 12/12 priority date for international students; for summer admission, 3/29 priority date for domestic students, 3/6 priority date for international students. Applications are processed on a rolling basis. Application fee: $75. Electronic applications accepted. *Expenses:* $7,236 per year full-time. *Financial support:* In 2016–17, 27 students received support, including 1 teaching assistantship (averaging $1,489 per year). Financial award applicants required to submit FAFSA. *Unit head:* Dr. Michael McGuire, Dean, 303-871-3518, Fax: 303-871-3303, E-mail: mmcguire@du.edu. *Application contact:* Information Contact, 303-871-2291, E-mail: ucoladm@du.edu.
Website: http://universitycollege.du.edu/

University of Houston, College of Technology, Department of Information and Logistics Technology, Houston, TX 77204. Offers information security (MS); supply chain and logistics technology (MS); technology project management (MS). *Program availability:* Part-time. *Degree requirements:* For master's, project or thesis (most programs). *Entrance requirements:* For master's, GMAT. Additional exam requirements/recommendations for international students: Required—TOEFL (minimum score 550 paper-based; 79 iBT). Electronic applications accepted.

The University of Kansas, Graduate Studies, School of Engineering, Program in Project Management, Overland Park, KS 66213. Offers ME, MS. *Program availability:* Part-time. *Students:* 8 full-time (1 woman), 29 part-time (8 women); includes 8 minority (3 Black or African American, non-Hispanic/Latino; 3 Asian, non-Hispanic/Latino; 2 Two or more races, non-Hispanic/Latino), 2 international. Average age 37. 21 applicants, 67% accepted, 9 enrolled. In 2016, 6 master's awarded. *Entrance requirements:* For master's, undergraduate degree in engineering or closely-related science, minimum undergraduate GPA of 3.0, two years' full-time work experience in engineering or technology-based company (for ME), current resume, official transcript, 3 letters of recommendation. Additional exam requirements/recommendations for international students: Required—TOEFL (minimum score 600 paper-based, 100 iBT) or IELTS (6). Application fee: $65 ($85 for international students). Electronic applications accepted. *Unit head:* Herbert R. Tuttle, Assistant Dean, 913-897-8561, E-mail: htuttle@ku.edu. *Application contact:* Jennifer Keleher-Price, Graduate Admissions Contact, 785-864-8635, E-mail: pmgt@ku.edu.
Website: https://pmgt.ku.edu/ms-pm

University of Management and Technology, Program in Business Administration, Arlington, VA 22209-1609. Offers general management (MBA, DBA); project management (MBA). *Program availability:* Part-time, evening/weekend, online learning. *Degree requirements:* For master's, comprehensive exam; for doctorate, thesis/dissertation. *Entrance requirements:* For master's, 3 recommendations, resume. Additional exam requirements/recommendations for international students: Required—TOEFL (minimum score 530 paper-based; 71 iBT). Electronic applications accepted.

University of Management and Technology, Program in Computer Science, Arlington, VA 22209-1609. Offers computer science (MS); information technology (AC); project management (AC); software engineering (MS). *Program availability:* Part-time, evening/weekend, online learning. *Entrance requirements:* For master's, 3 recommendations, resume. Additional exam requirements/recommendations for international students: Required—TOEFL (minimum score 530 paper-based; 71 iBT). Electronic applications accepted.

University of Management and Technology, Program in Management, Arlington, VA 22209-1609. Offers acquisition management (MS, AC); criminal justice administration (MS); general management (MS); project management (MS, AC). *Program availability:* Part-time, evening/weekend, online learning. *Entrance requirements:* For master's, 3 recommendations, resume. Additional exam requirements/recommendations for international students: Required—TOEFL (minimum score 530 paper-based; 71 iBT). Electronic applications accepted.

The University of Manchester, Alliance Manchester Business School, M15 6PB, United Kingdom. Offers accounting and finance (M Sc); business (M Ent); business analysis and strategic management (M Sc); business analytics: operational research and risk analysis (M Sc); business psychology (M Sc); corporate communications and reputation management (M Sc); finance (M Sc); finance and business economics (M Sc); human resource management and industrial relations (M Sc); innovation management and entrepreneurship (M Sc); international business and management (M Sc); international human resource management and comparative industrial relations (M Sc); management (M Sc); marketing (M Sc); operations, project and supply chain management (M Sc); organizational psychology (M Sc); quantitative finance (M Sc). *Entrance requirements:* For master's, UK 2:1 honours degree or overseas equivalent. Additional exam requirements/recommendations for international students: Required—TOEFL (minimum score 100 iBT), IELTS (minimum score 7), PTE. Electronic applications accepted. *Faculty research:* Accounting and finance, management sciences and marketing, people management and organization, innovation management and policy, decision sciences.

University of Mary, Gary Tharaldson School of Business, Bismarck, ND 58504-9652. Offers business administration (MBA); energy management (MBA, MS); executive (MBA, MS); health care (MBA, MS); human resource management (MBA); project management (MBA, MPM); virtuous leadership (MBA, MPM, MS). *Program availability:* Part-time, evening/weekend. *Entrance requirements:* For master's, minimum GPA of 2.5. Additional exam requirements/recommendations for international students: Required—TOEFL (minimum score 550 paper-based; 80 iBT). Electronic applications accepted.

University of Michigan–Dearborn, College of Engineering and Computer Science, MS Program in Program and Project Management, Dearborn, MI 48128. Offers MS. *Program availability:* Part-time, evening/weekend, 100% online. *Faculty:* 6 full-time (1 woman), 2 part-time/adjunct (1 woman). *Students:* 8 full-time (6 women), 36 part-time (12 women); includes 6 minority (1 American Indian or Alaska Native, non-Hispanic/Latino; 4 Asian, non-Hispanic/Latino; 1 Two or more races, non-Hispanic/Latino), 12 international. Average age 34. 31 applicants, 58% accepted, 11 enrolled. In 2016, 19 master's awarded. *Entrance requirements:* For master's, bachelor's degree in engineering, business, economics, math, computer science, or other physical sciences with minimum undergraduate cumulative GPA of 3.0. Additional exam requirements/recommendations for international students: Required—TOEFL (minimum score 560 paper-based; 84 iBT), IELTS (minimum score 6.5). *Application deadline:* For fall admission, 8/1 for domestic students, 5/1 for international students; for winter admission, 12/1 for domestic students, 9/1 for international students; for spring admission, 4/1 for domestic students, 1/1 for international students. Applications are processed on a rolling basis. Application fee: $60. Electronic applications accepted. *Expenses:* Tuition, state resident: full-time $13,118; part-time $2280 per term. Tuition, nonresident: full-time $21,816; part-time $3771 per term. *Required fees:* $866; $658 per unit. $329 per term. Tuition and fees vary according to program. *Financial support:* Scholarships/grants, unspecified assistantships, and non-resident tuition scholarships available. Support available to part-time students. Financial award application deadline: 3/1; financial award applicants required to submit FAFSA. *Faculty research:* Project management and control, agile project management, project scheduling. *Unit head:* Dr. Armen Zakarian, Chair, 313-593-5361, Fax: 313-593-3692, E-mail: zakarian@umich.edu. *Application contact:* Office of Graduate Studies, 313-583-6321, E-mail: umd-graduatestudies@umich.edu.
Website: https://umdearborn.edu/cecs/departments/industrial-and-manufacturing-systems-engineering/graduate-programs/ms-program-and-project-management

University of Nebraska at Omaha, Graduate Studies, College of Information Science and Technology, Department of Information Systems and Quantitative Analysis, Omaha, NE 68182. Offers data analytics (Certificate); information assurance (Certificate); information technology (MIT, PhD); management information systems (MS); project management (Certificate); systems analysis and design (Certificate). *Program availability:* Part-time, evening/weekend. *Faculty:* 6 full-time (1 woman). *Students:* 140 full-time (53 women), 102 part-time (29 women); includes 25 minority (9 Black or African American, non-Hispanic/Latino; 7 Asian, non-Hispanic/Latino; 6 Hispanic/Latino; 3 Two or more races, non-Hispanic/Latino), 161 international. Average age 29. 342 applicants, 50% accepted, 68 enrolled. In 2016, 84 master's, 8 doctorates, 54 other advanced degrees awarded. *Degree requirements:* For master's, comprehensive exam, thesis (for some programs); for doctorate, comprehensive exam, thesis/dissertation. *Entrance requirements:* For master's, GRE General Test, minimum GPA of 3.0, 3 letters of recommendation, writing sample, resume, official transcripts; for doctorate, GMAT or GRE General Test, minimum GPA of 3.0, 3 letters of recommendation, writing sample, resume, official transcripts; for Certificate, minimum GPA of 3.0, official transcripts. Additional exam requirements/recommendations for international students: Required—TOEFL, IELTS, PTE. *Application deadline:* For fall admission, 2/15 for domestic and international students; for spring admission, 9/15 for domestic and international students; for summer admission, 4/1 for domestic and international students.

Project Management

Applications are processed on a rolling basis. Application fee: $45. Electronic applications accepted. *Financial support:* In 2016–17, 30 students received support, including 24 research assistantships with tuition reimbursements available, 6 teaching assistantships with tuition reimbursements available; fellowships, career-related internships or fieldwork, Federal Work-Study, scholarships/grants, health care benefits, tuition waivers (partial), and unspecified assistantships also available. Financial award application deadline: 3/1; financial award applicants required to submit FAFSA. *Unit head:* Dr. Peter Wolcott, Chairperson, 402-554-2341, E-mail: graduate@unomaha.edu. *Application contact:* Dr. Martina Greiner, Graduate Program Chair, 402-554-2341, E-mail: graduate@unomaha.edu.

University of North Alabama, College of Business, Florence, AL 35632-0001. Offers business administration (MBA), including accounting, enterprise resource planning systems, executive, finance, health care management, information systems, international business, project management. *Accreditation:* AACSB; ACBSP. *Program availability:* Part-time, 100% online, blended/hybrid learning. *Faculty:* 24 full-time (2 women), 6 part-time/adjunct (3 women). *Students:* 180 full-time (77 women), 411 part-time (199 women); includes 208 minority (84 Black or African American, non-Hispanic/Latino; 4 American Indian or Alaska Native, non-Hispanic/Latino; 106 Asian, non-Hispanic/Latino; 6 Hispanic/Latino; 8 Two or more races, non-Hispanic/Latino), 37 international. Average age 34. 263 applicants, 84% accepted, 173 enrolled. In 2016, 156 master's awarded. *Entrance requirements:* For master's, GMAT, GRE, minimum GPA of 2.75 in last 60 hours, 2.5 overall (on a 3.0 scale); 27 hours of course work in business and economics. Additional exam requirements/recommendations for international students: Required—TOEFL (minimum score 79 iBT), IELTS (minimum score 6), PTE (minimum score 54). *Application deadline:* Applications are processed on a rolling basis. Application fee: $50 ($100 for international students). Electronic applications accepted. *Expenses:* Tuition, state resident: full-time $2799; part-time $1866 per semester. Tuition, nonresident: full-time $5598; part-time $3732 per semester. *Required fees:* $915; $642 per semester. Tuition and fees vary according to course load. *Financial support:* In 2016–17, 114 students received support. Scholarships/grants available. Financial award application deadline: 2/1; financial award applicants required to submit FAFSA. *Unit head:* Dr. Gregory A. Carnes, Dean, 256-765-4261, Fax: 256-765-4170, E-mail: gacarnes@una.edu. *Application contact:* Hillary N. Coats, Graduate Admissions Coordinator, 256-765-4447, E-mail: graduate@una.edu.
Website: http://www.una.edu/business/

University of Oklahoma, College of Arts and Sciences, Department of Psychology, Program in Organizational Dynamics, Tulsa, OK 74135. Offers human resource management (MA, Graduate Certificate); project management (MA, Graduate Certificate). *Program availability:* Part-time, evening/weekend. *Students:* 9 full-time (all women), 24 part-time (14 women); includes 6 minority (1 Black or African American, non-Hispanic/Latino; 2 American Indian or Alaska Native, non-Hispanic/Latino; 1 Asian, non-Hispanic/Latino; 2 Hispanic/Latino), 3 international. Average age 34. 13 applicants, 62% accepted, 6 enrolled. In 2016, 6 master's awarded. Terminal master's awarded for partial completion of doctoral program. *Degree requirements:* For master's, comprehensive exam (for some programs), thesis (for some programs), capstone project, comprehensive exam, or thesis; 36 hours of coursework; for Graduate Certificate, 12 hours of coursework from approved list. *Entrance requirements:* For master's, GRE (for students who do not have requisite work experience), current resume showing at least 2 years of relevant work experience; 2 letters of recommendation; statement of career goals; transcripts; for Graduate Certificate, resume showing work experience; 2 letters of recommendation; statement of career goals; transcripts. Additional exam requirements/recommendations for international students: Required—TOEFL (minimum score 79 iBT) or IELTS (minimum score 6.5). *Application deadline:* For fall admission, 5/1 for domestic and international students; for spring admission, 11/1 for domestic and international students; for summer admission, 3/15 for domestic and international students. Application fee: $50 ($100 for international students). Electronic applications accepted. *Expenses:* Tuition, state resident: full-time $4886; part-time $203.60 per credit hour. Tuition, nonresident: full-time $18,989; part-time $791.20 per credit hour. *Required fees:* $3283; $126.25 per credit hour. $126.50 per semester. *Financial support:* In 2016–17, 12 students received support. Research assistantships with full tuition reimbursements available, health care benefits, and unspecified assistantships available. Financial award application deadline: 6/1; financial award applicants required to submit FAFSA. *Faculty research:* Organizational behavior, personality, organizational climate and culture, leadership, ethics. *Unit head:* Dr. Eric Day, Chair, 405-325-4511, Fax: 405-325-4737, E-mail: eday@ou.edu. *Application contact:* Jennifer Kisamore, Associate Professor of Psychology/Graduate Liaison for Organizational Dynamics, 918-660-3603, Fax: 918-660-3383, E-mail: odyn@ou.edu.
Website: http://odyn.ou.edu

University of Ottawa, Faculty of Graduate and Postdoctoral Studies, Faculty of Engineering, Engineering Management Program, Ottawa, ON K1N 6N5, Canada. Offers engineering management (M Eng); information technology (Certificate); project management (Certificate). *Degree requirements:* For master's, thesis or alternative. *Entrance requirements:* For master's and Certificate, honors degree or equivalent, minimum B average. Electronic applications accepted.

University of Phoenix–Bay Area Campus, School of Business, San Jose, CA 95134-1805. Offers accountancy (MS); accounting (MBA); business administration (MBA, DBA); energy management (MBA); global management (MBA); health care management (MBA); human resource management (MBA); human resources management (MM); management (MM); marketing (MBA); organizational leadership (DM); project management (MBA); public administration (MPA); technology management (MBA). *Accreditation:* ACBSP. *Program availability:* Evening/weekend, online learning. *Degree requirements:* For master's, thesis (for some programs). *Entrance requirements:* For master's, minimum undergraduate GPA of 3.0, 3 years of work experience. Additional exam requirements/recommendations for international students: Required—TOEFL (minimum score 550 paper-based; 79 iBT). Electronic applications accepted.

University of Phoenix–Online Campus, School of Business, Phoenix, AZ 85034-7209. Offers accountancy (MS); accounting (MBA, Certificate); business administration (MBA); energy management (MBA); global management (MBA); health care management (MBA); human resource management (MBA, Certificate); human resources management (MM); management (MM); marketing (MBA, Certificate); project management (MBA, Certificate); public administration (MBA, MM); technology management (MBA). *Program availability:* Evening/weekend, online learning. *Entrance requirements:* Additional exam requirements/recommendations for international students: Required—TOEFL, TOEIC (Test of English as an International Communication), Berlitz Online English Proficiency Exam, PTE, or IELTS. Electronic applications accepted. *Expenses:* Contact institution.

University of Phoenix–Phoenix Campus, School of Business, Tempe, AZ 85282-2371. Offers accounting (MBA, MS, Certificate); business administration (MBA); energy management (MBA); global management (MBA); health care management (MBA); human resource management (MBA, Certificate); management (MM); marketing (MBA); project management (MBA); technology management (MBA). *Program availability:* Evening/weekend, online learning. *Entrance requirements:* Additional exam requirements/recommendations for international students: Required—TOEFL, TOEIC (Test of English as an International Communication), Berlitz Online English Proficiency Exam, PTE, or IELTS. Electronic applications accepted. *Expenses:* Contact institution.

University of Phoenix–Southern California Campus, School of Business, Costa Mesa, CA 92626. Offers accounting (MBA); business administration (MBA); energy management (MBA); global management (MBA); health care management (MBA); human resource management (MBA); management (MM); marketing (MBA); project management (MBA); technology management (MBA). *Program availability:* Evening/weekend, online learning. *Entrance requirements:* Additional exam requirements/recommendations for international students: Required—TOEFL, TOEIC (Test of English as an International Communication), Berlitz Online English Proficiency Exam, PTE, or IELTS. Electronic applications accepted. *Expenses:* Contact institution.

University of Regina, Faculty of Graduate Studies and Research, Kenneth Levene Graduate School of Business, Program in Business Administration, Regina, SK S4S 0A2, Canada. Offers business foundations (PGD); engineering management (MBA); executive business administration (EMBA); international business (MBA); leadership (M Admin); organizational leadership (Master's Certificate); project management (Master's Certificate); public safety management (MBA). *Program availability:* Part-time, evening/weekend. *Faculty:* 43 full-time (15 women), 6 part-time/adjunct (0 women). *Students:* 42 full-time (19 women), 21 part-time (12 women). 65 applicants, 48% accepted. In 2016, 57 master's, 13 other advanced degrees awarded. *Degree requirements:* For master's, project (for some programs). *Entrance requirements:* For master's, GMAT, three years of relevant work experience, four-year undergraduate degree; for other advanced degree, GMAT (for PGD), four-year undergraduate degree and two years of relevant work experience (for Master's Certificate); three years' work experience (for PGD). Additional exam requirements/recommendations for international students: Required—TOEFL (minimum score 580 paper-based; 80 iBT), IELTS (minimum score 6.5), PTE (minimum score 59). *Application deadline:* Applications are processed on a rolling basis. Application fee: $100. Electronic applications accepted. *Expenses:* Contact institution. *Financial support:* In 2016–17, 6 fellowships (averaging $6,000 per year), 7 teaching assistantships (averaging $2,501 per year) were awarded; career-related internships or fieldwork and scholarships/grants also available. Financial award application deadline: 6/15. *Faculty research:* Business policy and strategy, production and operations management, human behavior in organizations, financial management, social issues in business. *Unit head:* Dr. Andrew Gaudes, Dean, 306-585-4162, Fax: 306-585-5361, E-mail: andrew.gaudes@uregina.ca. *Application contact:* Ronald Camp, Graduate Programs, 306-337-2387, Fax: 306-585-5361, E-mail: ronald.camp@uregina.ca.
Website: http://www.uregina.ca/business/levene/

The University of Tennessee at Chattanooga, Engineering Management and Technology Program, Chattanooga, TN 37403. Offers construction management (Graduate Certificate); engineering management (MS); fundamentals of engineering management (Graduate Certificate); leadership and ethics (Graduate Certificate); logistics and supply chain management (Graduate Certificate); power systems management (Graduate Certificate); project and technology management (Graduate Certificate); quality management (Graduate Certificate). *Program availability:* 100% online, blended/hybrid learning. *Faculty:* 6 full-time (1 woman). *Students:* 14 full-time (3 women), 49 part-time (11 women); includes 17 minority (10 Black or African American, non-Hispanic/Latino; 2 Asian, non-Hispanic/Latino; 3 Hispanic/Latino; 2 Two or more races, non-Hispanic/Latino), 8 international. Average age 33. 29 applicants, 93% accepted, 15 enrolled. In 2016, 36 master's, 7 other advanced degrees awarded. *Degree requirements:* For master's, thesis. *Entrance requirements:* For master's, GRE General Test, letters of recommendation; minimum undergraduate GPA of 2.7 overall or 3.0 in final two years. Additional exam requirements/recommendations for international students: Required—TOEFL (minimum score 550 paper-based; 79 iBT), IELTS (minimum score 6). *Application deadline:* For fall admission, 6/15 priority date for domestic students, 7/1 for international students; for spring admission, 11/1 priority date for domestic students, 11/1 for international students. Applications are processed on a rolling basis. Application fee: $35 ($40 for international students). Electronic applications accepted. *Expenses:* $9,876 full-time in-state; $25,994 full-time out-of-state; $450 per credit part-time in-state; $1,345 per credit part-time out-of-state. *Financial support:* In 2016–17, 4 research assistantships were awarded; teaching assistantships, career-related internships or fieldwork, scholarships/grants, and unspecified assistantships also available. Support available to part-time students. Financial award application deadline: 7/1; financial award applicants required to submit FAFSA. *Faculty research:* Plant layout design, lean manufacturing, Six Sigma, value management, product development. *Unit head:* Dr. Neslihan Alp, Department Head, 423-425-4032, Fax: 423-425-5818, E-mail: neslihan-alp@utc.edu. *Application contact:* Dr. Joanne Romagni, Dean of the Graduate School, 423-425-4478, Fax: 423-425-5223, E-mail: joanne-romagni@utc.edu.
Website: http://www.utc.edu/college-engineering-computer-science/programs/engineering-management-and-technology/index.php#li03

The University of Texas at Dallas, Naveen Jindal School of Management, Program in Organizations, Strategy and International Management, Richardson, TX 75080. Offers business administration (MBA); executive business administration (EMBA); global leadership (EMBA); healthcare management (MS); healthcare management for physicians (EMBA); innovation and entrepreneurship (MS); international management studies (MS, PhD); management and administrative sciences (MS); management science (PhD); project management (EMBA, MS); systems engineering and management (MS); MS/MBA. *Program availability:* Part-time, evening/weekend. *Faculty:* 29 full-time (7 women), 29 part-time/adjunct (5 women). *Students:* 524 full-time (189 women), 860 part-time (374 women); includes 452 minority (112 Black or African American, non-Hispanic/Latino; 3 American Indian or Alaska Native, non-Hispanic/Latino; 207 Asian, non-Hispanic/Latino; 85 Hispanic/Latino; 45 Two or more races, non-Hispanic/Latino), 317 international. Average age 34. 1,763 applicants, 37% accepted, 420 enrolled. In 2016, 521 master's, 13 doctorates awarded. *Degree requirements:* For doctorate, thesis/dissertation. *Entrance requirements:* For master's and doctorate, GMAT. Additional exam requirements/recommendations for international students: Required—TOEFL (minimum score 550 paper-based). *Application deadline:* For fall admission, 7/15 for domestic students, 5/1 priority date for international students; for spring admission, 11/15 for domestic students, 9/1 priority date for international students. Applications are processed on a rolling basis. Application fee: $50 ($100 for international students). Electronic applications accepted. *Expenses:* Tuition, state resident: full-time $12,418; part-time $690 per semester hour. Tuition, nonresident: full-time $24,150; part-time $1342 per semester hour. Tuition and fees vary according to course load. *Financial support:* In 2016–17, 385 students received support, including 21 research assistantships with partial tuition reimbursements available (averaging $25,698 per year), 68 teaching assistantships with partial tuition reimbursements available (averaging $16,973 per year); Federal Work-Study, institutionally sponsored loans, scholarships/grants, and unspecified assistantships also available. Support available to part-time students. Financial award application deadline: 4/30; financial award applicants required to submit FAFSA. *Faculty research:* International accounting, international trade and finance, economic development, international economics. *Unit head:* Dr. Seung-Hyun Lee, Area Coordinator, 972-883-6267, Fax: 972-883-5977, E-mail: sxl029100@utdallas.edu. *Application contact:* Maria Hasenhuttl, Assistant Area

Coordinator, 972-883-5898, Fax: 972-883-5977, E-mail: maria.hasenhuttl@utdallas.edu.
Website: http://jindal.utdallas.edu/osim/

University of Wisconsin–Platteville, School of Graduate Studies, Distance Learning Center, Online Master of Science in Project Management Program, Platteville, WI 53818-3099. Offers MS. *Program availability:* Part-time. *Students:* 4 full-time (1 woman), 245 part-time (112 women); includes 49 minority (24 Black or African American, non-Hispanic/Latino; 14 Asian, non-Hispanic/Latino; 11 Hispanic/Latino). 74 applicants, 68% accepted, 34 enrolled. In 2016, 68 master's awarded. *Degree requirements:* For master's, thesis or alternative. *Entrance requirements:* Additional exam requirements/recommendations for international students: Required—TOEFL (minimum score 550 paper-based; 79 iBT), IELTS (minimum score 6.5). *Application deadline:* For fall admission, 7/1 priority date for domestic students; for spring admission, 11/1 priority date for domestic students. Applications are processed on a rolling basis. Application fee: $56. Electronic applications accepted. *Unit head:* William Haskins, Coordinator, 608-342-1961, Fax: 608-342-1466, E-mail: disted@uwplatt.edu. *Application contact:* 800-362-5460, Fax: 608-342-1071, E-mail: disted@uwplatt.edu.
Website: http://www.uwplatt.edu/disted/project-management.html

University of Wisconsin–Stout, Graduate School, College of Management, Program in Operations and Supply Management, Menomonie, WI 54751. Offers operations management (MS); project management (MS); quality management (MS); supply chain management (MS).

Virginia International University, School of Business, Fairfax, VA 22030. Offers accounting (MBA, MS); entrepreneurship (MBA); executive management (Graduate Certificate); global logistics (MBA); health care management (MBA); hospitality and tourism management (MBA); human resources management (MBA); international business management (MBA); international finance (MBA); marketing management (MBA); mass media and public relations (MBA); project management (MBA, MS). *Program availability:* Part-time, online learning. *Entrance requirements:* For master's and Graduate Certificate, bachelor's degree. Additional exam requirements/recommendations for international students: Required—TOEFL (minimum score 550 paper-based; 80 iBT), IELTS (minimum score 6). Electronic applications accepted.

Virginia International University, School of Computer Information Systems, Fairfax, VA 22030. Offers business intelligence (Graduate Certificate); business intelligence and data analytics (MIS); computer science (MS), including computer animation and gaming, cybersecurity, data management networking, intelligent systems, software applications development, software engineering; cybersecurity (MIS); data management (MIS); enterprise project management (MIS); health informatics (MIS); information assurance (MIS); information systems (Graduate Certificate); information systems management (MS, Graduate Certificate); information technology (MS); information technology audit and compliance (Graduate Certificate); knowledge management (MIS); software engineering (MS). *Program availability:* Part-time, online learning. *Entrance requirements:* For master's, bachelor's degree. Additional exam requirements/recommendations for international students: Required—TOEFL (minimum score 550 paper-based; 80 iBT), IELTS. Electronic applications accepted.

Viterbo University, Master of Business Administration Program, La Crosse, WI 54601-4797. Offers general business administration (MBA); health care management (MBA); international business (MBA); leadership (MBA); project management (MBA). *Accreditation:* ACBSP. *Program availability:* Part-time, evening/weekend. *Degree requirements:* For master's, 34 semester credits. *Entrance requirements:* For master's, bachelor's degree, transcripts, minimum undergraduate cumulative GPA of 3.0, 2 letters of reference, 3-5 page essay. Additional exam requirements/recommendations for international students: Recommended—TOEFL (minimum score 550 paper-based). Electronic applications accepted. *Expenses:* Contact institution.

Walden University, Graduate Programs, School of Management, Minneapolis, MN 55401. Offers accounting (MBA, MS, DBA), including accounting for the professional (MS), accounting with CPA emphasis (MS), self-designed (MS); advanced project management (Graduate Certificate); applied project management (Graduate Certificate); auditing (Graduate Certificate); bridge to business administration (Post-Doctoral Certificate); bridge to management (Post-Doctoral Certificate); business management (Graduate Certificate); communication (MBA); corporate finance (MBA); digital marketing (Graduate Certificate); entrepreneurship (DBA); entrepreneurship and small business (MBA); finance (MS, DBA), including finance for the professional (MS), finance with CFA/investment (MS), finance with CPA emphasis (MS); global supply chain management (DBA); healthcare management (MBA, DBA); human resource management (MBA, MS, Graduate Certificate), including functional human resource management (MS), general program (MS), integrating functional and strategic human resource management (MS), organizational strategy (MS); human resources management (DBA); information systems management (DBA); international business (MBA, DBA); leadership (MBA, MS, DBA, Graduate Certificate), including general program (MS), human resource leadership (MS), leader development (MS), self-designed (MS); management (MS, PhD), including communications (MS), finance (PhD), general program (MS), healthcare management (MS), human resource management (MS), human resources management (PhD), information systems management (PhD), international business (MS), leadership (MS), leadership and organizational change (PhD), marketing (MS), project management (MS), strategy and operations (MS); managerial accounting (Graduate Certificate); marketing (MBA, MS, DBA); project management (MBA, MS, DBA); self-designed (MBA, DBA); social impact management (DBA); technology entrepreneurship (DBA). *Accreditation:* ACBSP. *Program availability:* Part-time, evening/weekend, online only, 100% online. *Degree requirements:* For master's, thesis (for some programs), residency (for EMBA); for doctorate, thesis/dissertation (for some programs), residency. *Entrance requirements:* For master's, bachelor's degree or higher; minimum GPA of 2.5; official transcripts; goal statement (for some programs); access to computer and Internet; for doctorate, master's degree or higher; three years of related professional or academic experience (preferred); minimum GPA of 3.0; goal statement and current resume (for select programs); official transcripts; access to computer and Internet; for other advanced degree, relevant work experience; access to computer and Internet. Additional exam requirements/recommendations for international students: Required—TOEFL (minimum score 550 paper-based, 79 iBT), IELTS (minimum score 6.5), Michigan English Language Assessment Battery (minimum score 82), or PTE (minimum score 53). Electronic applications accepted.

Wayland Baptist University, Graduate Programs, Programs in Business Administration/Management, Plainview, TX 79072-6998. Offers accounting (MBA); general business (MBA); health care administration (MAM, MBA); human resource management (MAM, MBA); international management (MBA); management (MBA, D Mgt); management information systems (MBA); organization management (MAM); project management (MBA). *Program availability:* Part-time, evening/weekend, online learning. *Degree requirements:* For master's, capstone course. *Entrance requirements:* For master's, GMAT, GRE or MAT. Additional exam requirements/recommendations for international students: Required—TOEFL (minimum score 500 paper-based; 61 iBT). Electronic applications accepted.

West Chester University of Pennsylvania, College of Business and Public Management, School of Business, West Chester, PA 19383. Offers business analytics (Certificate); business education (MBA); entrepreneurship (Certificate); project management (Certificate). *Accreditation:* AACSB. *Program availability:* Part-time, evening/weekend, 100% online. *Faculty:* 13 full-time (6 women), 2 part-time/adjunct (1 woman). *Students:* 44 full-time (23 women), 213 part-time (82 women); includes 37 minority (16 Black or African American, non-Hispanic/Latino; 11 Asian, non-Hispanic/Latino; 9 Hispanic/Latino; 1 Two or more races, non-Hispanic/Latino). Average age 32. 202 applicants, 83% accepted, 126 enrolled. In 2016, 41 master's, 16 other advanced degrees awarded. *Degree requirements:* For master's, minimum GPA of 3.0. *Entrance requirements:* For master's, GMAT or GRE, statement of professional goals, resume, two letters of recommendation, transcripts. Additional exam requirements/recommendations for international students: Required—TOEFL or IELTS. *Application deadline:* For fall admission, 5/15 for international students; for spring admission, 10/15 for international students. Applications are processed on a rolling basis. Application fee: $50. Electronic applications accepted. *Expenses:* Tuition, state resident: full-time $8694; part-time $483 per credit. Tuition, nonresident: full-time $13,050; part-time $725 per credit. *Required fees:* $2399; $119.05 per credit. Tuition and fees vary according to campus/location and program. *Financial support:* Scholarships/grants and unspecified assistantships available. Financial award application deadline: 2/15; financial award applicants required to submit FAFSA. *Unit head:* Dr. Brian Halsey, MBA Director/Graduate Coordinator, 610-425-5000 Ext. 4444, E-mail: mba@wcupa.edu. *Application contact:* Office of Graduate Studies and Extended Education, 610-436-2943, Fax: 610-436-2763, E-mail: gradstudy@wcupa.edu.
Website: http://www.wcupa.edu/mba

Western Carolina University, Graduate School, College of Business, Program in Project Management, Cullowhee, NC 28723. Offers MPM, Graduate Certificate. *Program availability:* Part-time, evening/weekend, online learning. *Entrance requirements:* For master's, GMAT or GRE, work experience in project management, appropriate undergraduate degree with minimum GPA of 3.0, employer recommendation, resume. Additional exam requirements/recommendations for international students: Required—TOEFL (minimum score 550 paper-based; 79 iBT). *Expenses:* Tuition, state resident: full-time $2174. Tuition, nonresident: full-time $7377. *Required fees:* $1442. Part-time tuition and fees vary according to course load.

Wingate University, Porter B. Byrum School of Business, Wingate, NC 28174. Offers accounting (MAC); corporate innovation (MBA); finance (MBA); general management (MBA); healthcare management (MBA); marketing (MBA); project management (MBA). *Accreditation:* ACBSP. *Program availability:* Part-time, evening/weekend. *Entrance requirements:* For master's, GMAT, work experience, 2 letters of recommendation. *Application deadline:* For fall admission, 8/15 priority date for domestic students; for spring admission, 12/15 priority date for domestic students. Applications are processed on a rolling basis. Application fee: $50. Electronic applications accepted. *Expenses:* Contact institution. *Financial support:* Federal Work-Study and scholarships/grants available. Support available to part-time students. Financial award application deadline: 8/1; financial award applicants required to submit FAFSA. *Faculty research:* Stochastic processes, business ethics, regional economic development, municipal finance, consumer behavior. *Unit head:* Dr. Peter Frank, Dean, 704-233-8148, Fax: 704-233-8146, E-mail: pfrank@wingate.edu. *Application contact:* Mary Maye, Administrative Assistant to the Dean, 704-233-8148, Fax: 704-233-8146.
Website: http://www.wingate.edu/academics/school-of-business

Section 18
Quality Management

This section contains a directory of institutions offering graduate work in quality management. Additional information about programs listed in the directory may be obtained by writing directly to the dean of a graduate school or chair of a department at the address given in the directory.

For programs offering related work, see also in this book *Business Administration and Management.*

CONTENTS

Program Directory

Quality Management

California Intercontinental University, School of Information Technology, Irvine, CA 92614. Offers information systems and enterprise resource management (DBA); information systems and knowledge management (MBA); project and quality management (MBA).

California State University, Dominguez Hills, College of Extended and International Education, Program in Quality Assurance, Carson, CA 90747-0001. Offers MS. *Program availability:* Part-time, evening/weekend, 100% online. *Degree requirements:* For master's, thesis. *Entrance requirements:* For master's, minimum GPA of 2.75. Additional exam requirements/recommendations for international students: Required—TOEFL. Electronic applications accepted. *Expenses:* Contact institution. *Faculty research:* Six Sigma, lean thinking, risk management, quality management.

Calumet College of Saint Joseph, Program in Quality Assurance, Whiting, IN 46394-2195. Offers MS.

East Carolina University, Graduate School, College of Engineering and Technology, Department of Technology Systems, Greenville, NC 27858-4353. Offers computer network professional (Certificate); information assurance (Certificate); Lean Six Sigma Black Belt (Certificate); network technology (MS), including computer networking management, digital communications technology, information security, Web technologies; occupational safety (MS); technology management (PhD); technology systems (MS), including industrial distribution and logistics, manufacturing systems, performance improvement, quality systems; Website developer (Certificate). *Students:* 23 full-time (1 woman), 199 part-time (55 women); includes 59 minority (39 Black or African American, non-Hispanic/Latino; 3 American Indian or Alaska Native, non-Hispanic/Latino; 4 Asian, non-Hispanic/Latino; 10 Hispanic/Latino; 3 Two or more races, non-Hispanic/Latino), 5 international. Average age 38. 85 applicants, 87% accepted, 61 enrolled. In 2016, 23 master's awarded. *Entrance requirements:* For master's and Certificate, GRE General Test or MAT, minimum GPA of 2.5; for doctorate, GRE General Test, related work experience. *Application deadline:* For fall admission, 6/1 priority date for domestic students. Applications are processed on a rolling basis. Application fee: $50. *Financial support:* Application deadline: 6/1. *Unit head:* Dr. Tijjani Mohammed, Chair, 252-328-9668, E-mail: mohammedt@ecu.edu. *Application contact:* Dean of Graduate School, 252-328-6012, Fax: 252-328-6071, E-mail: gradschool@ecu.edu.

Eastern Michigan University, Graduate School, College of Technology, School of Engineering Technology, Programs in Quality Management, Ypsilanti, MI 48197. Offers MS, Graduate Certificate. *Program availability:* Part-time, evening/weekend, online learning. *Students:* 2 full-time (1 woman), 47 part-time (17 women); includes 12 minority (8 Black or African American, non-Hispanic/Latino; 1 Asian, non-Hispanic/Latino; 2 Hispanic/Latino; 1 Two or more races, non-Hispanic/Latino), 1 international. Average age 39. 20 applicants, 75% accepted, 9 enrolled. In 2016, 20 master's awarded. *Entrance requirements:* Additional exam requirements/recommendations for international students: Required—TOEFL. *Application deadline:* Applications are processed on a rolling basis. Application fee: $45. *Financial support:* Fellowships, research assistantships with full tuition reimbursements, teaching assistantships with full tuition reimbursements, career-related internships or fieldwork, Federal Work-Study, institutionally sponsored loans, scholarships/grants, tuition waivers (partial), and unspecified assistantships available. Support available to part-time students. Financial award applicants required to submit FAFSA. *Application contact:* Dr. Herman Tang, Program Coordinator, 734-487-2040, Fax: 734-487-8755, E-mail: htang2@emich.edu.

Florida Institute of Technology, Extended Studies Division, Melbourne, FL 32901-6975. Offers acquisition and contract management (MS); aerospace engineering (MS); business administration (MBA, DBA); computer information systems (MS); computer science (MS); electrical engineering (MS); engineering management (MS); human resources management (MS); logistics management (MS), including humanitarian and disaster relief logistics; management (MS), including acquisition and contract management, e-business, human resources management, information systems, logistics management, management, transportation management; material acquisition management (MS); mechanical engineering (MS); operations research (MS); project management (MS), including information systems, operations research; public administration (MPA); quality management (MS); software engineering (MS); space systems (MS); space systems management (MS); supply chain management (MS); systems management (MS), including information systems, operations research; technology management (MS). *Program availability:* Part-time, evening/weekend, online learning. *Faculty:* 10 full-time (3 women), 122 part-time/adjunct (29 women). *Students:* 131 full-time (58 women), 997 part-time (348 women); includes 389 minority (231 Black or African American, non-Hispanic/Latino; 9 American Indian or Alaska Native, non-Hispanic/Latino; 26 Asian, non-Hispanic/Latino; 99 Hispanic/Latino; 3 Native Hawaiian or other Pacific Islander, non-Hispanic/Latino; 21 Two or more races, non-Hispanic/Latino), 53 international. Average age 36. 962 applicants, 48% accepted, 323 enrolled. In 2016, 403 master's awarded. *Degree requirements:* For master's, comprehensive exam (for some programs). *Entrance requirements:* For master's, GMAT or resume showing 8 years of supervised experience, minimum GPA of 3.0, 2 letters of recommendation, resume. Additional exam requirements/recommendations for international students: Required—TOEFL (minimum score 550 paper-based; 79 iBT). *Application deadline:* For fall admission, 4/1 for international students; for spring admission, 9/30 for international students. Applications are processed on a rolling basis. Electronic applications accepted. *Expenses:* Contact institution. *Financial support:* Application deadline: 3/1; applicants required to submit FAFSA. *Unit head:* Dr. Theodore R. Richardson, III, Dean, 321-674-8123, Fax: 321-674-7597, E-mail: trichardson@fit.edu. *Application contact:* Carolyn Farrior, Director of Graduate Admissions, Online Learning and Off-Campus Programs, 321-674-7118, Fax: 321-674-8216, E-mail: cfarrior@fit.edu.
Website: http://es.fit.edu

Hofstra University, Frank G. Zarb School of Business, Programs in Information Systems, Hempstead, NY 11549. Offers business administration (MBA), including business analytics, information systems, quality management; information systems (MS, Advanced Certificate). *Program availability:* Part-time, evening/weekend, blended/hybrid learning. *Students:* 59 full-time (27 women), 14 part-time (7 women); includes 11 minority (1 Black or African American, non-Hispanic/Latino; 7 Asian, non-Hispanic/Latino; 3 Hispanic/Latino), 50 international. Average age 28. 95 applicants, 56% accepted, 20 enrolled. In 2016, 28 master's awarded. *Degree requirements:* For master's, capstone course (for MBA), thesis (for MS), minimum GPA of 3.0. *Entrance requirements:* For master's, GMAT/GRE, 2 letters of recommendation, resume, essay; for Advanced Certificate, GMAT/GRE, 2 letters of recommendation, resume. Additional exam requirements/recommendations for international students: Required—TOEFL (minimum score 550 paper-based; 80 iBT); Recommended—IELTS (minimum score 6). *Application deadline:* Applications are processed on a rolling basis. Application fee: $75. Electronic applications accepted. *Expenses:* $1,170 per credit. *Financial support:* In 2016–17, 26 students received support, including 26 fellowships with full and partial tuition reimbursements available (averaging $5,034 per year); research assistantships with full and partial tuition reimbursements available, career-related internships or fieldwork, Federal Work-Study, institutionally sponsored loans, scholarships/grants, tuition waivers (full and partial), and unspecified assistantships also available. Support available to part-time students. Financial award applicants required to submit FAFSA. *Faculty research:* Health information systems, healthcare data analytics; text mining and data mining; cybersecurity and digital forensics. *Unit head:* Dr. Hak Kim, Chairperson, 516-463-5716, Fax: 516-463-4834, E-mail: hak.j.kim@hofstra.edu. *Application contact:* Sunil Samuel, Assistant Vice President of Admissions, 516-463-4723, Fax: 516-463-4664, E-mail: graduateadmission@hofstra.edu.
Website: http://www.hofstra.edu/business/

Instituto Tecnologico de Santo Domingo, Graduate School, Area of Business, Santo Domingo, Dominican Republic. Offers banking and securities markets (M Mgmt); corporate finance (M Mgmt); human resources management (M Mgmt, Certificate); international trade management (M Mgmt); marketing (M Mgmt); organizational development (M Mgmt); quality and productivity management (Certificate); tax management and planning (M Mgmt); upper management (M Mgmt).

Instituto Tecnológico y de Estudios Superiores de Monterrey, Campus Ciudad de México, Virtual University Division, Ciudad de Mexico, Mexico. Offers administration of information technologies (MA); computer sciences (MA); education (MA, PhD); educational technology (MA); environmental engineering (MA); environmental systems (MA); humanistic studies (MA); industrial engineering (MA); international business for Latin America (MA); quality systems (MA); quality systems and productivity (MA). *Program availability:* Part-time, evening/weekend, online learning. *Entrance requirements:* For master's and doctorate, Instituto entrance exam. Additional exam requirements/recommendations for international students: Required—TOEFL.

Instituto Tecnológico y de Estudios Superiores de Monterrey, Campus Ciudad Juárez, Program in Quality Management, Ciudad Juárez, Mexico. Offers MQM.

Instituto Tecnológico y de Estudios Superiores de Monterrey, Campus Estado de México, Professional and Graduate Division, Estado de Mexico, Mexico. Offers administration of information technologies (MITA); architecture (M Arch); business administration (GMBA, MBA); computer sciences (MCS, PhD); education (M Ed); educational institution administration (MAD); educational technology and innovation (PhD); electronic commerce (MEC); environmental systems (MS); finance (MAF); humanistic studies (MHS); information sciences and knowledge management (MISKM); information systems (MS); manufacturing systems (MS); marketing (MEM); quality systems and productivity (MS); science and materials engineering (PhD); telecommunications management (MTM). *Program availability:* Part-time, online learning. *Degree requirements:* For master's, one foreign language, thesis (for some programs); for doctorate, one foreign language, thesis/dissertation. *Entrance requirements:* For master's, E-PAEP 500, interview; for doctorate, E-PAEP 500, research proposal. Additional exam requirements/recommendations for international students: Required—TOEFL (minimum score 550 paper-based). *Faculty research:* Surface treatments by plasmas, mechanical properties, robotics, graphical computing, mechatronics security protocols.

Instituto Tecnológico y de Estudios Superiores de Monterrey, Campus Irapuato, Graduate Programs, Irapuato, Mexico. Offers administration (MBA); administration of information technology (MAIT); administration of telecommunications (MAT); architecture (M Arch); computer science (MCS); education (M Ed); educational administration (MEA); educational innovation and technology (DEIT); educational technology (MET); electronic commerce (MBA); environmental administration and planning (MEAP); environmental systems (MES); finances (MBA); humanistic studies (MHS); international management for Latin American executives (MIMLAE); library and information science (MLIS); manufacturing quality management (MMQM); marketing research (MBA).

Madonna University, School of Business, Livonia, MI 48150-1173. Offers business administration (MBA); international business (MSBA); leadership studies (MSBA); leadership studies in criminal justice (MSBA); quality and operations management (MSBA). *Program availability:* Part-time, evening/weekend, online learning. *Degree requirements:* For master's, thesis (for some programs), foreign language proficiency (international business). *Entrance requirements:* For master's, GMAT, GRE General Test, minimum GPA of 3.0. Electronic applications accepted. *Faculty research:* Management, women in management, future studies.

Mount Mercy University, Program in Business Administration, Cedar Rapids, IA 52402-4797. Offers human resource (MBA); quality management (MBA). *Program availability:* Evening/weekend. *Entrance requirements:* For master's, minimum cumulative GPA of 3.0, 2 letters of recommendation, resume. Additional exam requirements/recommendations for international students: Required—TOEFL (minimum score 570 paper-based; 88 iBT). Electronic applications accepted.

The National Graduate School of Quality Management, Graduate Programs, Falmouth, MA 02541. Offers homeland security (MS); quality systems management (MS, DBA).

Northwestern University, School of Professional Studies, Program in Regulatory Compliance, Evanston, IL 60208. Offers clinical research (MS); healthcare compliance (MS); quality systems (MS). Offered in partnership with Northwestern Univesity's Clinical and Translational Sciences Institute.

Penn State Erie, The Behrend College, Graduate School, Erie, PA 16563. Offers accounting (MPAC); business administration (MBA); project management (MPM); quality and manufacturing management (MMM). *Accreditation:* AACSB. *Program availability:* Part-time. *Students:* 28 full-time (9 women), 118 part-time (31 women); includes 11 minority (5 Black or African American, non-Hispanic/Latino; 2 Asian, non-Hispanic/Latino; 1 Hispanic/Latino; 3 Two or more races, non-Hispanic/Latino), 2 international. Average age 32. 91 applicants, 74% accepted, 55 enrolled. In 2016, 59 master's awarded. *Entrance requirements:* Additional exam requirements/recommendations for international students: Required—TOEFL (minimum score 550 paper-based; 80 iBT), IELTS. *Application deadline:* Applications are processed on a rolling basis. Application fee: $65. Electronic applications accepted. *Financial support:* Federal Work-Study available. Financial award application deadline: 3/1; financial award applicants required to submit FAFSA. *Unit head:* Dr. Ralph M. Ford, Chancellor, 814-898-6160, Fax: 814-898-6461. *Application contact:* Ann M. Burbules, Assistant Director, Graduate Admissions, 866-374-3378, Fax: 814-898-6044, E-mail:

behrend.admissions@psu.edu.
Website: http://behrend.psu.edu/

Regis College, Program in Regulatory and Clinical Research Management, Weston, MA 02493. Offers MS. *Program availability:* Part-time, evening/weekend, blended/hybrid learning. *Degree requirements:* For master's, thesis optional, internship/field experience. *Entrance requirements:* For master's, GRE or MAT. Additional exam requirements/recommendations for international students: Required—TOEFL; Recommended—IELTS. *Application deadline:* Applications are processed on a rolling basis. Application fee: $65. Electronic applications accepted. *Financial support:* Career-related internships or fieldwork, scholarships/grants, and unspecified assistantships available. Financial award applicants required to submit FAFSA. *Faculty research:* FDA regulatory affairs medical device. *Unit head:* Joni Beshansky, Director, 781-768-7008, E-mail: joni.beshansky@regiscollege.edu.

Rutgers University–New Brunswick, Graduate School-New Brunswick, Program in Statistics, Piscataway, NJ 08854-8097. Offers applied statistics (MS); biostatistics (MS); data mining (MS); quality and productivity management (MS); statistics (MS, PhD). *Program availability:* Part-time. Terminal master's awarded for partial completion of doctoral program. *Degree requirements:* For master's, comprehensive exam, essay, exam, non-thesis essay paper; for doctorate, one foreign language, thesis/dissertation, qualifying oral and written exams. *Entrance requirements:* For master's, GRE General Test; for doctorate, GRE General Test, GRE Subject Test (recommended). Additional exam requirements/recommendations for international students: Required—TOEFL (minimum score 550 paper-based). Electronic applications accepted. *Faculty research:* Probability, decision theory, linear models, multivariate statistics, statistical computing.

Southern New Hampshire University, School of Business, Manchester, NH 03106-1045. Offers accounting (MBA, MS, Graduate Certificate); accounting finance (MS); accounting/auditing (MS); accounting/forensic accounting (MS); accounting/taxation (MS); athletic administration (MBA, Graduate Certificate); business administration (IMBA, MBA, Certificate, Graduate Certificate), including accounting (Certificate), business administration (MBA), business information systems (Graduate Certificate), human resource management (Certificate); corporate social responsibility (MBA); entrepreneurship (MBA); finance (MBA, MS, Graduate Certificate); finance/corporate finance (MS); finance/investments and securities (MS); forensic accounting (MBA); healthcare informatics (MBA); healthcare management (MBA); human resource management (Graduate Certificate); information technology (MS, Graduate Certificate); information technology management (MBA); international business (Graduate Certificate); international business and information technology (Graduate Certificate); international finance (Graduate Certificate); international sport management (Graduate Certificate); justice studies (MBA); leadership of nonprofit organizations (Graduate Certificate); management (MS); marketing (MBA, MS, Graduate Certificate); operations and project management (MS); operations and supply chain management (MBA, Graduate Certificate); organizational leadership (MS); project management (MBA, Graduate Certificate); Six Sigma (MBA); Six Sigma quality (Graduate Certificate); social media marketing (MBA); sport management (MBA, MS, Graduate Certificate); sustainability and environmental compliance (MBA); workplace conflict management (MBA); MBA/Certificate. *Accreditation:* ACBSP. *Program availability:* Part-time, evening/weekend, online learning. Terminal master's awarded for partial completion of doctoral program. *Degree requirements:* For master's, one foreign language, comprehensive exam (for some programs), thesis or alternative. *Entrance requirements:* For master's, minimum GPA of 2.5. Additional exam requirements/recommendations for international students: Required—TOEFL (minimum score 500 paper-based). Electronic applications accepted.

Stevens Institute of Technology, Graduate School, Charles V. Schaefer Jr. School of Engineering and Science, Department of Civil, Environmental, and Ocean Engineering, Program in Construction Management, Hoboken, NJ 07030. Offers construction management (MS, Certificate), including construction accounting/estimating (Certificate), construction engineering (Certificate), construction law/disputes (Certificate), construction/quality management (Certificate). *Program availability:* Part-time, evening/weekend. *Students:* 50 full-time (21 women), 22 part-time (6 women); includes 3 minority (all Black or African American, non-Hispanic/Latino), 49 international. Average age 25. 157 applicants, 72% accepted, 28 enrolled. In 2016, 39 master's, 15 other advanced degrees awarded. *Degree requirements:* For master's, thesis optional, minimum B average in major field and overall; for Certificate, minimum B average. *Entrance requirements:* Additional exam requirements/recommendations for international students: Required—TOEFL (minimum score 74 iBT), IELTS (minimum score 6). *Application deadline:* For fall admission, 6/1 for domestic students, 4/15 for international students; for spring admission, 11/30 for domestic students, 11/1 for international students. Applications are processed on a rolling basis. Application fee: $65. Electronic applications accepted. *Expenses:* Contact institution. *Financial support:* Fellowships, research assistantships, teaching assistantships, career-related internships or fieldwork, Federal Work-Study, scholarships/grants, and unspecified assistantships available. Financial award application deadline: 2/15; financial award applicants required to submit FAFSA. *Unit head:* Dr. Linda Thomas, Director, 201-216-5681, E-mail: lthomas2@stevens.edu. *Application contact:* Graduate Admission, 888-783-8367, Fax: 888-511-1306, E-mail: graduate@stevens.edu.

Stevenson University, Program in Healthcare Management, Owings Mills, MD 21117. Offers project management (MS); quality management and patient safety (MS). *Program availability:* Part-time, online only, 100% online. *Faculty:* 1 (woman) full-time, 9 part-time/adjunct (6 women). *Students:* 3 full-time (all women), 22 part-time (20 women); includes 10 minority (8 Black or African American, non-Hispanic/Latino; 1 Asian, non-Hispanic/Latino; 1 Hispanic/Latino). Average age 32. 26 applicants, 54% accepted, 8 enrolled. In 2016, 17 master's awarded. *Degree requirements:* For master's, capstone course. *Entrance requirements:* For master's, official college transcripts from all previous academic work, minimum cumulative GPA of 3.0 in past academic work, minimum grade of B in statistics or an upper-level math and English composition, two professional letters of recommendation with at least one from a current or past supervisor, 250-word personal statement. *Application deadline:* Applications are processed on a rolling basis. Electronic applications accepted. *Expenses:* $670 per credit hour. *Financial support:* Unspecified assistantships available. Financial award applicants required to submit FAFSA. *Unit head:* Sharon Buchbinder, PhD, Coordinator, 443-394-9290, Fax: 443-394-0538, E-mail: sbuchbinder@stevenson.edu. *Application contact:* Amanda Courter, Enrollment Counselor, 443-352-4243, Fax: 443-394-0538, E-mail: acourter@stevenson.edu.
Website: http://www.stevenson.edu

Trident University International, College of Business Administration, Program in Business Administration, Cypress, CA 90630. Offers business administration (PhD); conflict and negotiation management (MBA); criminal justice administration (MBA); entrepreneurship (MBA); finance (MBA); general management (MBA); government accounting (MBA); human resource management (MBA); information security and digital assurance management (MBA); information technology management (MBA); international business (MBA); logistics management (MBA); marketing (MBA); project management (MBA); public management (MBA); quality management (MBA); strategic leadership (MBA). *Program availability:* Part-time, evening/weekend, online learning. *Degree requirements:* For doctorate, comprehensive exam, thesis/dissertation, defense of dissertation. *Entrance requirements:* For master's, minimum GPA of 2.5 (students with GPA 3.0 or greater may transfer up to 30% of graduate level credits); for doctorate, minimum GPA of 3.4, curriculum vitae, course work in research methods or statistics. Additional exam requirements/recommendations for international students: Required—TOEFL. Electronic applications accepted.

Trident University International, College of Health Sciences, Program in Health Sciences, Cypress, CA 90630. Offers clinical research administration (MS, Certificate); emergency and disaster management (MS, Certificate); environmental health science (Certificate); health care administration (PhD); health care management (MS), including health informatics; health education (MS, Certificate); health informatics (Certificate); health sciences (PhD); international health (MS); international health: educator or researcher option (PhD); international health: practitioner option (PhD); law and expert witness studies (MS, Certificate); public health (MS); quality assurance (Certificate). *Program availability:* Part-time, evening/weekend, online learning. *Degree requirements:* For doctorate, comprehensive exam, thesis/dissertation, defense of dissertation. *Entrance requirements:* For master's, minimum GPA of 2.5 (students with GPA 3.0 or greater may transfer up to 30% of graduate level credits); for doctorate, minimum GPA of 3.4, curriculum vitae, course work in research methods or statistics. Additional exam requirements/recommendations for international students: Required—TOEFL. Electronic applications accepted.

Universidad de las Americas, A.C., Program in Business Administration, Mexico City, Mexico. Offers finance (MBA); marketing research (MBA); production and quality (MBA).

Universidad del Turabo, Graduate Programs, School of Business and Entrepreneurship, Program in Quality Management, Gurabo, PR 00778-3030. Offers MBA. *Students:* 44 full-time (31 women), 22 part-time (15 women); all minorities (all Hispanic/Latino). Average age 34. 43 applicants, 51% accepted, 22 enrolled. In 2016, 20 master's awarded. *Entrance requirements:* For master's, GRE, EXADEP or GMAT, interview, essay, official transcript, recommendation letters. *Application deadline:* Applications are processed on a rolling basis. Application fee: $25. Electronic applications accepted. *Financial support:* Institutionally sponsored loans available. Financial award applicants required to submit FAFSA. *Unit head:* Juan Sosa, Dean, 787-743-7979 Ext. 4118, E-mail: negocios_ut@suagm.edu. *Application contact:* Diriee Rodríguez, Admissions Director, 787-743-7979 Ext. 4453, E-mail: admisiones-ut@suagm.edu.
Website: http://ut.suagm.edu/es/negocios

The University of Alabama, Graduate School, College of Human Environmental Sciences, Program in Human Environmental Science, Tuscaloosa, AL 35487. Offers interactive technology (MS); quality management (MS); restaurant and meeting management (MS); rural community health (MS); sport management (MS). *Program availability:* Part-time, evening/weekend, online learning. *Faculty:* 52 full-time (38 women), 3 part-time/adjunct (2 women). *Students:* 213 full-time (138 women), 392 part-time (278 women); includes 142 minority (105 Black or African American, non-Hispanic/Latino; 3 American Indian or Alaska Native, non-Hispanic/Latino; 4 Asian, non-Hispanic/Latino; 17 Hispanic/Latino; 2 Native Hawaiian or other Pacific Islander, non-Hispanic/Latino; 11 Two or more races, non-Hispanic/Latino), 5 international. Average age 33. 400 applicants, 74% accepted, 232 enrolled. In 2016, 230 master's awarded. *Degree requirements:* For master's, comprehensive exam. *Entrance requirements:* For master's, GRE (for some specializations), minimum GPA of 3.0. Additional exam requirements/recommendations for international students: Required—TOEFL. *Application deadline:* For fall admission, 7/1 for domestic students; for spring admission, 11/1 for domestic students; for summer admission, 4/15 for domestic students. Applications are processed on a rolling basis. Application fee: $50 ($60 for international students). Electronic applications accepted. *Expenses:* Tuition, state resident: full-time $10,470. Tuition, nonresident: full-time $26,950. *Financial support:* In 2016–17, 2 teaching assistantships with full tuition reimbursements were awarded. Financial award application deadline: 7/1. *Faculty research:* Rural health, hospitality management, sport management, interactive technology, consumer quality management, environmental health and safety. *Unit head:* Dr. Milla D. Boschung, Dean, 205-348-6250, Fax: 205-348-1786, E-mail: mboschun@ches.ua.edu. *Application contact:* Dr. Stuart Usdan, Associate Dean, 205-348-6150, Fax: 205-348-3789, E-mail: susdan@ches.ua.edu.
Website: http://www.ches.ua.edu/progr... -of-study.html

University of Massachusetts Boston, College of Advancing and Professional Studies, Program in Critical and Creative Thinking, Boston, MA 02125-3393. Offers MA, Certificate. *Program availability:* Part-time, evening/weekend. *Students:* 6 full-time (4 women), 18 part-time (12 women); includes 7 minority (4 Black or African American, non-Hispanic/Latino; 1 Asian, non-Hispanic/Latino; 2 Hispanic/Latino), 2 international. Average age 38. 12 applicants, 83% accepted, 8 enrolled. In 2016, 8 master's, 9 other advanced degrees awarded. *Degree requirements:* For master's, comprehensive exam, thesis optional, practicum, oral exams. *Entrance requirements:* For master's, GRE General Test or MAT, minimum GPA of 3.0; for Certificate, minimum GPA of 2.75. *Application deadline:* For fall admission, 3/1 for domestic students; for spring admission, 11/1 for domestic students. *Expenses:* Tuition, state resident: full-time $16,863. Tuition, nonresident: full-time $32,913. *Required fees:* $177. *Financial support:* Research assistantships with full tuition reimbursements, teaching assistantships with full tuition reimbursements, career-related internships or fieldwork, Federal Work-Study, and unspecified assistantships available. Support available to part-time students. Financial award application deadline: 3/1; financial award applicants required to submit FAFSA. *Unit head:* Dr. Peter Taylor, Director, 617-287-7636, E-mail: peter.taylor@umb.edu. *Application contact:* Peggy Roldan Patel, Graduate Admissions Coordinator, 617-287-6400, Fax: 617-287-6236, E-mail: bos.gadm@dpc.umassp.edu.

The University of Tennessee at Chattanooga, Engineering Management and Technology Program, Chattanooga, TN 37403. Offers construction management (Graduate Certificate); engineering management (MS); fundamentals of engineering management (Graduate Certificate), leadership and ethics (Graduate Certificate); logistics and supply chain management (Graduate Certificate); power systems management (Graduate Certificate); project and technology management (Graduate Certificate); quality management (Graduate Certificate). *Program availability:* 100% online, blended/hybrid learning. *Faculty:* 6 full-time (1 woman). *Students:* 14 full-time (3 women), 49 part-time (11 women); includes 17 minority (10 Black or African American, non-Hispanic/Latino; 2 Asian, non-Hispanic/Latino; 3 Hispanic/Latino; 2 Two or more races, non-Hispanic/Latino), 8 international. Average age 33. 29 applicants, 93% accepted, 15 enrolled. In 2016, 36 master's, 7 other advanced degrees awarded. *Degree requirements:* For master's, thesis. *Entrance requirements:* For master's, GRE General Test, letters of recommendation; minimum undergraduate GPA of 2.7 overall or 3.0 in final two years. Additional exam requirements/recommendations for international students: Required—TOEFL (minimum score 550 paper-based; 79 iBT), IELTS (minimum score 6). *Application deadline:* For fall admission, 6/15 priority date for domestic students, 7/1 for international students; for spring admission, 11/1 priority date for domestic students, 11/1 for international students. Applications are processed on a rolling basis. Application fee: $35 ($40 for international students). Electronic applications accepted. *Expenses:* $9,876 full-time in-state; $25,994 full-time out-of-state; $450 per credit part-time in-state; $1,345 per credit part-time out-of-state. *Financial support:* In

Quality Management

2016–17, 4 research assistantships were awarded; teaching assistantships, career-related internships or fieldwork, scholarships/grants, and unspecified assistantships also available. Support available to part-time students. Financial award application deadline: 7/1; financial award applicants required to submit FAFSA. *Faculty research:* Plant layout design, lean manufacturing, Six Sigma, value management, product development. *Unit head:* Dr. Neslihan Alp, Department Head, 423-425-4032, Fax: 423-425-5818, E-mail: neslihan-alp@utc.edu. *Application contact:* Dr. Joanne Romagni, Dean of the Graduate School, 423-425-4478, Fax: 423-425-5223, E-mail: joanne-romagni@utc.edu. Website: http://www.utc.edu/college-engineering-computer-science/programs/engineering-management-and-technology/index.php#li03

The University of Texas at Tyler, College of Business and Technology, Program in Business Administration, Tyler, TX 75799-0001. Offers cyber security (MBA); engineering management (MBA); general management (MBA); healthcare management (MBA); internal assurance and consulting (MBA); marketing (MBA); oil, gas and energy (MBA); organizational development (MBA); quality management (MBA). *Accreditation:* AACSB. *Program availability:* Part-time, online learning. *Entrance requirements:* Additional exam requirements/recommendations for international students: Required—TOEFL (minimum score 550 paper-based). *Faculty research:* General business, inventory control, institutional markets, service marketing, product distribution, accounting fraud, financial reporting and recognition.

University of Wisconsin–Stout, Graduate School, College of Management, Program in Operations and Supply Management, Menomonie, WI 54751. Offers operations management (MS); project management (MS); quality management (MS); supply chain management (MS).

Section 19
Quantitative Analysis

This section contains a directory of institutions offering graduate work in quantitative analysis. Additional information about programs listed in the directory may be obtained by writing directly to the dean of a graduate school or chair of a department at the address given in the directory.

For programs offering related work, see also in this book *Business Administration and Management.*

CONTENTS

Program Directory

Quantitative Analysis

Ball State University, Graduate School, Teachers College, Department of Educational Psychology, Program in Quantitative Psychology, Muncie, IN 47306. Offers MS. *Program availability:* Online learning. *Entrance requirements:* For master's, official transcripts, minimum GPA of 2.75. Electronic applications accepted.

Baruch College of the City University of New York, Zicklin School of Business, Department of Operations Research and Quantitative Methods, New York, NY 10010-5585. Offers quantitative methods and modeling (MBA, MS). *Program availability:* Part-time.

Baruch College of the City University of New York, Zicklin School of Business, Department of Statistics and Computer Information Systems, Program in Decision Sciences, New York, NY 10010-5585. Offers MBA. *Program availability:* Part-time, evening/weekend. *Entrance requirements:* For master's, GMAT, 2 letters of recommendation, resume, 2 years of work experience. Additional exam requirements/recommendations for international students: Required—TOEFL (minimum score 590 paper-based), TWE (minimum score 5).

Columbia University, Graduate School of Arts and Sciences, New York, NY 10027. Offers African-American studies (MA); American studies (MA); anthropology (MA, PhD); art history and archaeology (MA, PhD); astronomy (PhD); biological sciences (PhD); biotechnology (MA); chemical physics (PhD); chemistry (PhD); classical studies (MA, PhD); classics (MA, PhD); climate and society (MA); conservation biology (MA); earth and environmental sciences (PhD); East Asia: regional studies (MA); East Asian languages and cultures (MA, PhD); ecology, evolution and environmental biology (MA), including conservation biology; ecology, evolution, and environmental biology (PhD), including ecology and evolutionary biology, evolutionary primatology; economics (MA, PhD); English and comparative literature (MA, PhD); French and Romance philology (MA, PhD); Germanic languages (MA, PhD); global French studies (MA); global thought (MA); Hispanic cultural studies (MA); history (PhD); history and literature (MA); human rights studies (MA); Islamic studies (MA); Italian (MA, PhD); Japanese pedagogy (MA); Jewish studies (MA); Latin America and the Caribbean: regional studies (MA); Latin American and Iberian cultures (PhD); mathematics (MA, PhD), including finance (MA); medieval and Renaissance studies (MA); Middle Eastern, South Asian, and African studies (MA, PhD); modern art: critical and curatorial studies (MA); modern European studies (MA); museum anthropology (MA); music (DMA, PhD); oral history (MA); philosophical foundations of physics (MA); philosophy (MA, PhD); physics (PhD); political science (MA, PhD); psychology (PhD); quantitative methods in the social sciences (MA); religion (MA, PhD); Russia, Eurasia and East Europe: regional studies (MA); Russian translation (MA); Slavic cultures (MA); Slavic languages (MA, PhD); sociology (MA, PhD); South Asian studies (MA); statistics (MA, PhD); theatre (PhD). Dual-degree programs require admission to both Graduate School of Arts and Sciences and another Columbia school. *Program availability:* Part-time. Terminal master's awarded for partial completion of doctoral program. *Degree requirements:* For master's, variable foreign language requirement, comprehensive exam (for some programs), thesis (for some programs); for doctorate, variable foreign language requirement, comprehensive exam (for some programs), thesis/dissertation. *Entrance requirements:* For master's and doctorate, GRE General Test, GRE Subject Test (for some programs). Additional exam requirements/recommendations for international students: Required—TOEFL, IELTS. Electronic applications accepted.

Cornell University, Graduate School, Graduate Fields of Agriculture and Life Sciences, Field of Natural Resources, Ithaca, NY 14853. Offers community-based natural resources management (MS, PhD); conservation biology (MS, PhD); ecosystem biology and biogeochemistry (MPS, MS, PhD); environmental management (MPS); fishery and aquatic science (MPS, MS, PhD); forest science (MPS, MS, PhD); human dimensions of natural resources management (MPS, MS, PhD); policy and institutional analysis (MS, PhD); program development and evaluation (MPS, MS, PhD); quantitative ecology (MS, PhD); wildlife science (MPS, MS, PhD). *Degree requirements:* For master's, thesis (MS), project paper (MPS); for doctorate, comprehensive exam, thesis/dissertation. *Entrance requirements:* For master's and doctorate, GRE General Test, 2 letters of recommendation. Additional exam requirements/recommendations for international students: Required—TOEFL (minimum score 550 paper-based; 77 iBT). Electronic applications accepted. *Faculty research:* Ecosystem-level dynamics, systems modeling, conservation biology/management, resource management's human dimensions, biogeochemistry.

Drexel University, LeBow College of Business, Program in Business Administration, Philadelphia, PA 19104-2875. Offers business administration (MBA, PhD, APC), including accounting (MBA, PhD), decision sciences (PhD), economics (MBA, PhD), finance (MBA, PhD), legal studies (MBA), management (MBA), marketing (MBA, PhD), organizational sciences (PhD), quantitative methods (MBA), strategic management (PhD). *Accreditation:* AACSB. *Program availability:* Part-time, evening/weekend, online learning. *Faculty:* 88 full-time (19 women), 11 part-time/adjunct (2 women). *Students:* 153 full-time (70 women), 388 part-time (168 women); includes 107 minority (31 Black or African American, non-Hispanic/Latino; 1 American Indian or Alaska Native, non-Hispanic/Latino; 48 Asian, non-Hispanic/Latino; 16 Hispanic/Latino; 11 Two or more races, non-Hispanic/Latino), 95 international. Average age 33. In 2016, 174 master's, 8 doctorates, 1 other advanced degree awarded. Terminal master's awarded for partial completion of doctoral program. *Entrance requirements:* For master's, GMAT, minimum GPA of 2.75; for doctorate, GMAT. Additional exam requirements/recommendations for international students: Required—TOEFL. *Application deadline:* For fall admission, 8/21 for domestic students; for spring admission, 3/5 for domestic students. Applications are processed on a rolling basis. Application fee: $50. Electronic applications accepted. *Expenses: Tuition:* Full-time $32,184; part-time $1192 per credit hour. *Required fees:* $280. Tuition and fees vary according to campus/location and program. *Financial support:* Research assistantships, teaching assistantships, career-related internships or fieldwork, and unspecified assistantships available. Financial award application deadline: 2/1. *Faculty research:* Decision support systems, individual and group behavior, operations research, techniques and strategy. *Unit head:* Dr. Thomas Wieckowski, Director of Master's Programs in Business, 215-895-1791, Fax: 215-895-1012. *Application contact:* Director of Graduate Admissions, 215-895-6700, Fax: 215-895-5939, E-mail: enroll@drexel.edu.

Duke University, The Fuqua School of Business, The Duke MBA-Daytime Program, Durham, NC 27708-0586. Offers academic excellence in finance (Certificate); business administration (MBA); decision sciences (MBA); energy and environment (MBA); energy finance (MBA); entrepreneurship and innovation (MBA); finance (MBA); financial analysis (MBA); health sector management (Certificate); leadership and ethics (MBA); management (MBA); marketing (MBA); operations management (MBA); social entrepreneurship (MBA); strategy (MBA). *Faculty:* 88 full-time (19 women), 50 part-time/adjunct (9 women). *Students:* 897 full-time (310 women); includes 174 minority (39 Black or African American, non-Hispanic/Latino; 3 American Indian or Alaska Native, non-Hispanic/Latino; 75 Asian, non-Hispanic/Latino; 51 Hispanic/Latino; 1 Native Hawaiian or other Pacific Islander, non-Hispanic/Latino; 5 Two or more races, non-Hispanic/Latino), 343 international. Average age 28. In 2016, 440 master's awarded. *Entrance requirements:* For master's, GMAT or GRE, transcripts, essays, resume, recommendation letters, interview. *Application deadline:* For fall admission, 9/13 for domestic and international students; for winter admission, 10/13 for domestic and international students; for spring admission, 1/4 for domestic and international students; for summer admission, 3/20 for domestic and international students. Application fee: $225. Electronic applications accepted. *Expenses:* $66,717 (first-year tuition and fees). *Financial support:* In 2016–17, 415 students received support. Institutionally sponsored loans and scholarships/grants available. Financial award applicants required to submit FAFSA. *Unit head:* Russ Morgan, Senior Associate Dean for Full-time Programs, 919-660-2931, Fax: 919-684-8742, E-mail: ruskin.morgan@duke.edu. *Application contact:* Sharon Thompson, Assistant Dean, Office of Admissions, 919-660-7705, Fax: 919-681-8026, E-mail: admissions-info@fuqua.duke.edu.
Website: http://www.fuqua.duke.edu/daytime-mba/

Duke University, The Fuqua School of Business, Master of Quantitative Management Program, Durham, NC 27708-0586. Offers finance (MQM); forensics (MQM); marketing (MQM); strategy (MQM). *Entrance requirements:* For master's, GMAT/GRE, transcripts, essays, resume, recommendation letters. *Application deadline:* For fall admission, 9/21 for domestic and international students; for winter admission, 11/20 for domestic and international students; for spring admission, 2/16 for domestic and international students; for summer admission, 4/4 for domestic and international students. Application fee: $125. Electronic applications accepted. *Unit head:* Jeremy Petranka, Associate Dean, E-mail: jeremy.petranka@duke.edu. *Application contact:* Sharon Thompson, Assistant Dean, Office of Admissions, 919-660-7705, Fax: 919-681-8026, E-mail: admissions-info@fuqua.duke.edu.
Website: http://www.fuqua.duke.edu/master-quantitative-management/

Duke University, The Fuqua School of Business, PhD Program, Durham, NC 27708-0586. Offers accounting (PhD); decision sciences (PhD); finance (PhD); management and organizations (PhD); marketing (PhD); operations management (PhD); strategy (PhD). *Faculty:* 100 full-time (19 women). *Students:* 77 full-time (27 women); includes 9 minority (1 Black or African American, non-Hispanic/Latino; 7 Asian, non-Hispanic/Latino; 1 Hispanic/Latino), 46 international. 561 applicants, 7% accepted, 14 enrolled. In 2016, 15 doctorates awarded. *Degree requirements:* For doctorate, thesis/dissertation, major field requirement (exam or major paper, depending upon the area). *Entrance requirements:* For doctorate, GMAT or GRE, transcripts, essays, recommendation letters, statement of purpose. Additional exam requirements/recommendations for international students: Required—TOEFL (minimum score 577 paper-based; 90 iBT), IELTS (minimum score 7). *Application deadline:* For fall admission, 12/31 priority date for domestic and international students. Application fee: $85. Electronic applications accepted. *Expenses:* Contact institution. *Financial support:* In 2016–17, 77 students received support, including 70 fellowships with full tuition reimbursements available (averaging $28,200 per year), 63 research assistantships with full tuition reimbursements available (averaging $7,000 per year); institutionally sponsored loans, scholarships/grants, and tuition waivers (full) also available. Financial award applicants required to submit FAFSA. *Unit head:* William Boulding, Dean, 919-660-7822, Fax: 919-684-8742, E-mail: bb1@duke.edu. *Application contact:* Qi Chen, Director of Graduate Studies, 919-660-7753, Fax: 919-660-7971, E-mail: qc2@duke.edu.

Fordham University, Gabelli School of Business, New York, NY 10023. Offers accounting (MBA, MS); applied statistics and decision-making (MS); business administration (EMBA); business analytics (MS); communications and media management (MBA); electronic business (MBA); entrepreneurship (MBA); finance (MBA); global finance (MS); global sustainability (MBA); healthcare management (MBA); information systems (MBA, MS); investor relations (MS); management (MBA, MS); marketing (MBA); marketing intelligence (MS); media management (MS); nonprofit leadership (MS); quantitative finance (MS); taxation (MS); JD/MBA; MS/MBA. *Accreditation:* AACSB. *Program availability:* Part-time, evening/weekend. *Faculty:* 132 full-time (44 women), 51 part-time/adjunct (7 women). *Students:* 1,117 full-time (668 women), 553 part-time (282 women); includes 207 minority (44 Black or African American, non-Hispanic/Latino; 92 Asian, non-Hispanic/Latino; 69 Hispanic/Latino; 2 Native Hawaiian or other Pacific Islander, non-Hispanic/Latino), 1,088 international. Average age 27. 4,745 applicants, 46% accepted, 752 enrolled. In 2016, 996 master's awarded. Terminal master's awarded for partial completion of doctoral program. *Degree requirements:* For master's, internships (required for MS in quantitative finance, recommended for MBA). *Entrance requirements:* For master's, GMAT/GRE, 2 letters of recommendation, resume, 2 essays, transcripts. Additional exam requirements/recommendations for international students: Required—TOEFL (minimum score 100 iBT), IELTS (minimum score 7). *Application deadline:* For fall admission, 11/15 priority date for domestic and international students; for winter admission, 1/15 priority date for domestic students, 1/1 priority date for international students; for spring admission, 3/1 for domestic and international students; for summer admission, 6/1 for domestic students. Application fee: $130. Electronic applications accepted. *Expenses:* $1,397 per credit. *Financial support:* In 2016–17, 78 students received support. Career-related internships or fieldwork, institutionally sponsored loans, scholarships/grants, and unspecified assistantships available. Support available to part-time students. Financial award application deadline: 6/30; financial award applicants required to submit FAFSA. *Unit head:* Dr. Donna Rapaccioli, Dean, 212-636-6165, Fax: 212-307-1779, E-mail: rapaccioli@fordham.edu. *Application contact:* Lawrence Murray, Senior Assistant Dean of Graduate Admissions and Advising, 212-636-6200, Fax: 212-636-7076, E-mail: admissionsgb@fordham.edu.
Website: http://www.fordham.edu/gabelli

Hofstra University, Frank G. Zarb School of Business, Programs in Finance, Hempstead, NY 11549. Offers business administration (MBA), including finance; corporate finance (Advanced Certificate); finance (MS), including financial and risk management, investment analysis; investment management (Advanced Certificate); quantitative finance (MS). *Program availability:* Part-time, evening/weekend, blended/hybrid learning. *Students:* 177 full-time (70 women), 47 part-time (9 women); includes 16 minority (6 Black or African American, non-Hispanic/Latino; 6 Asian, non-Hispanic/Latino; 4 Hispanic/Latino), 167 international. Average age 25. 555 applicants, 72% accepted, 93 enrolled. In 2016, 101 master's awarded. *Degree requirements:* For master's, capstone course (for MBA), thesis (for MS), minimum GPA of 3.0. *Entrance requirements:* For master's, GMAT/GRE, 2 letters of recommendation, resume, essay. Additional exam requirements/recommendations for international students: Required—TOEFL (minimum score 550 paper-based; 80 iBT); Recommended—IELTS (minimum score 6). *Application deadline:* Applications are processed on a rolling basis. Application

fee: $75. Electronic applications accepted. *Expenses:* $1,170 per credit. *Financial support:* In 2016–17, 51 students received support, including 43 fellowships with full and partial tuition reimbursements available (averaging $4,829 per year), 1 research assistantship with full and partial tuition reimbursement available (averaging $6,950 per year); career-related internships or fieldwork, Federal Work-Study, institutionally sponsored loans, scholarships/grants, tuition waivers (full and partial), and unspecified assistantships also available. Support available to part-time students. Financial award applicants required to submit FAFSA. *Faculty research:* Individual investors and financial crisis; short-sale constraints and futures trading; social media and sentiment in financial markets; external monitoring of firms; CEO inside debt and insider trading. *Unit head:* Dr. K. G. Viswanathan, Chairperson, 516-463-5699, Fax: 516-463-4834, E-mail: k.g.viswanathan@hofstra.edu. *Application contact:* Sunil Samuel, Assistant Vice President of Admissions, 516-463-4723, Fax: 516-463-4664, E-mail: graduateadmission@hofstra.edu.
Website: http://www.hofstra.edu/business/

Instituto Tecnologico de Santo Domingo, Graduate School, Area of Engineering, Santo Domingo, Dominican Republic. Offers construction administration (MS, Certificate); data telecommunications (M Eng, MS, Certificate); industrial engineering (M Eng, Certificate); industrial management (M Mgmt); information technology (Certificate); maintenance engineering (M Eng); occupational hazard prevention (M Mgmt); production management (Certificate); quantitative methods (Certificate); sanitary and environmental engineering (M Eng); structural engineering (M Eng); systems engineering and electronic data processing (Certificate); transportation (Certificate).

La Salle University, School of Business, Master of Business Administration Program, Philadelphia, PA 19141-1199. Offers accounting (MBA, Post-MBA Certificate); business systems and analytics (MBA, Post-MBA Certificate); finance (MBA, Post-MBA Certificate); general business administration (MBA, Post-MBA Certificate); human resource management (MBA, Post-MBA Certificate); management (MBA, Post-MBA Certificate); marketing (Post-MBA Certificate); MBA/MSN. Program also offered in Switzerland. *Accreditation:* AACSB. *Program availability:* Part-time, evening/weekend, online learning. *Faculty:* 19 full-time (6 women), 11 part-time/adjunct (3 women). *Students:* 55 full-time (23 women), 209 part-time (96 women); includes 66 minority (35 Black or African American, non-Hispanic/Latino; 17 Asian, non-Hispanic/Latino; 9 Hispanic/Latino; 5 Two or more races, non-Hispanic/Latino), 17 international. Average age 31. 200 applicants, 59% accepted, 63 enrolled. In 2016, 192 master's, 1 other advanced degree awarded. *Entrance requirements:* For master's, GMAT or GRE, two letters of reference; resume; for Post-MBA Certificate, MBA with minimum GPA of 3.0. Additional exam requirements/recommendations for international students: Required—TOEFL. *Application deadline:* For fall admission, 8/15 priority date for domestic students, 7/15 for international students; for spring admission, 12/15 priority date for domestic students, 11/15 for international students; for summer admission, 4/15 priority date for domestic students, 3/15 for international students. Applications are processed on a rolling basis. Application fee: $35. Electronic applications accepted. Application fee is waived when completed online. *Expenses:* Contact institution. *Financial support:* In 2016–17, 49 students received support. Scholarships/grants available. Support available to part-time students. Financial award application deadline: 8/31; financial award applicants required to submit FAFSA. *Unit head:* Dr. MarySheila McDonald, Interim Dean, 215-951-1040, Fax: 215-951-1886, E-mail: mcdonaldms@lasalle.edu. *Application contact:* Elizabeth Heenan, Director, Graduate and Adult Enrollment, 215-951-1100, Fax: 215-951-1462, E-mail: heenan@lasalle.edu.

Lehigh University, College of Business and Economics, Department of Finance, Bethlehem, PA 18015. Offers analytical finance (MS). *Faculty:* 4 full-time (0 women). *Students:* 79 full-time (46 women), 1 part-time (0 women); includes 1 minority (Asian, non-Hispanic/Latino), 77 international. Average age 23. 309 applicants, 41% accepted, 40 enrolled. In 2016, 40 master's awarded. *Degree requirements:* For master's, capstone project. *Entrance requirements:* For master's, GMAT or GRE, bachelor's degree from a mathematically rigorous program, minimum GPA of 3.0. Additional exam requirements/recommendations for international students: Required—TOEFL (minimum score 600 paper-based; 94 iBT), IELTS (minimum score 7). *Application deadline:* For fall admission, 7/15 for domestic students, 2/15 for international students. Application fee: $75. Electronic applications accepted. Tuition and fees vary according to program. *Financial support:* Fellowships, research assistantships, teaching assistantships, and health care benefits available. Financial award application deadline: 1/15. *Total annual research expenditures:* $51,538. *Unit head:* Nandu Nayar, Department Chair, 610-758-4161, E-mail: nan2@lehigh.edu. *Application contact:* Michael Tarantino, Director of Recruitment and Admissions, 610-758-3418, Fax: 610-758-5283, E-mail: mgt215@lehigh.edu. Website: http://www4.lehigh.edu/business/academics/depts/finance

Northwestern University, The Graduate School, Kellogg School of Management, Management Programs, Evanston, IL 60208. Offers accounting information and management (MBA, PhD); analytical finance (MBA); business administration (MBA); decision sciences (MBA); entrepreneurship and innovation (MBA); finance (MBA, PhD); health enterprise management (MBA); human resources management (MBA); international business (MBA); management and organizations (MBA, PhD); management and organizations and sociology (PhD); management and strategy (MBA); management studies (MS); managerial analytics (MBA); managerial economics (MBA); managerial economics and strategy (PhD); marketing (MBA, PhD); marketing management (MBA); media management (MBA); operations management (MBA, PhD); real estate (MBA); social enterprise at Kellogg (MBA); JD/MBA. *Program availability:* Part-time, evening/weekend. Terminal master's awarded for partial completion of doctoral program. *Degree requirements:* For doctorate, thesis/dissertation, 2 years of coursework, qualifying (field) exam and candidacy, summer research papers and presentations to faculty, proposal defense, final exam/defense. *Entrance requirements:* For master's, GMAT, GRE, interview, 2 letters of recommendation, college transcripts, resume, essays, Kellogg honor code; for doctorate, GMAT, GRE, statement of purpose, transcripts, 2 letters of recommendation, resume, interview. Additional exam requirements/recommendations for international students: Required—TOEFL, IELTS. Electronic applications accepted. *Expenses:* Contact institution. *Faculty research:* Business cycles and international finance, health policy, networks, non-market strategy, consumer psychology.

Purdue University, Graduate School, College of Agriculture, Department of Forestry and Natural Resources, West Lafayette, IN 47907. Offers fisheries and aquatic sciences (MS, MSF, PhD); forest biology (MS, MSF, PhD); natural resource social science (MS, PhD); natural resources social science (MSF); quantitative ecology (MS, MSF, PhD); wildlife science (MS, MSF, PhD); wood products and wood products manufacturing (MS, MSF, PhD). *Faculty:* 27 full-time (5 women), 1 part-time/adjunct (0 women). *Students:* 61 full-time (35 women), 9 part-time (3 women); includes 5 minority (1 American Indian or Alaska Native, non-Hispanic/Latino; 3 Hispanic/Latino; 1 Two or more races, non-Hispanic/Latino), 16 international. Average age 28. 44 applicants, 34% accepted, 15 enrolled. In 2016, 12 master's, 7 doctorates awarded. *Degree requirements:* For master's, thesis; for doctorate, thesis/dissertation. *Entrance requirements:* For master's and doctorate, GRE General Test (minimum score: verbal 50th percentile; quantitative 50th percentile; analytical writing 4.0), minimum undergraduate GPA of 3.2 or equivalent. Additional exam requirements/recommendations for international students: Required—TOEFL (minimum score 550 paper-based; 77 iBT). *Application deadline:* For fall admission, 1/5 for domestic students, 1/15 for international students; for spring admission, 9/15 for domestic and international students. Applications are processed on a rolling basis. Application fee: $60 ($75 for international students). Electronic applications accepted. *Financial support:* In 2016–17, 10 research assistantships (averaging $15,259 per year) were awarded; fellowships, teaching assistantships, career-related internships or fieldwork, and scholarships/grants also available. Support available to part-time students. Financial award application deadline: 1/5; financial award applicants required to submit FAFSA. *Faculty research:* Wildlife management, forest management, forest ecology, forest soils, limnology. *Unit head:* Robert G. Wagner, Head of the Graduate Program, 765-494-3590, E-mail: rgwagner@purdue.edu. *Application contact:* Christine Hofmeyer, Graduate Contact, 765-494-3572, E-mail: chofmeye@purdue.edu.
Website: https://ag.purdue.edu/fnr

Rutgers University–Newark, School of Public Health, Newark, NJ 07107-1709. Offers clinical epidemiology (Certificate); dental public health (MPH); general public health (Certificate); public policy and oral health services administration (Certificate); quantitative methods (MPH); urban health (MPH); DMD/MPH; MD/MPH; MS/MPH. *Accreditation:* CEPH. *Program availability:* Part-time, evening/weekend. *Degree requirements:* For master's, thesis, internship. *Entrance requirements:* For master's, GRE General Test. Additional exam requirements/recommendations for international students: Required—TOEFL. Electronic applications accepted.

St. John's University, The Peter J. Tobin College of Business, Department of Computer Information Systems and Decision Sciences, Queens, NY 11439. Offers business analytics (MBA). *Program availability:* Part-time, evening/weekend. *Degree requirements:* For master's, comprehensive exam (for some programs), thesis optional. *Entrance requirements:* For master's, GMAT, 2 letters of recommendation, resume, transcripts, essay. Additional exam requirements/recommendations for international students: Required—TOEFL (minimum score 600 paper-based; 100 iBT), IELTS (minimum score 7). Electronic applications accepted. *Expenses:* Contact institution.

San Francisco State University, Division of Graduate Studies, College of Business, Program in Business Administration, San Francisco, CA 94132-1722. Offers decision sciences/operations research (MBA); ethics and compliance (MBA); finance (MBA); global business and innovation (MBA); healthcare administration (MBA); hospitality and tourism management (MBA); information systems (MBA); leadership (MBA); marketing (MBA); nonprofit and social enterprise leadership (MBA); sustainable business (MBA). *Accreditation:* AACSB. *Program availability:* Part-time, evening/weekend. *Degree requirements:* For master's, thesis, essay test. *Entrance requirements:* For master's, GMAT, minimum GPA of 2.7 in last 60 units. Additional exam requirements/recommendations for international students: Required—TOEFL (minimum score 550 paper-based). *Application deadline:* For fall admission, 5/1 priority date for domestic students, 4/1 for international students; for spring admission, 11/1 for domestic students, 10/15 for international students. Applications are processed on a rolling basis. Application fee: $55. *Expenses:* Tuition, state resident: full-time $6738. Tuition, nonresident: full-time $15,666. *Required fees:* $1012. Tuition and fees vary according to degree level and program. *Financial support:* Application deadline: 3/1. *Unit head:* Dr. Sanjit Sengupta, Faculty Director, 415-817-4366, Fax: 415-817-4340, E-mail: sengupta@sfsu.edu. *Application contact:* Zandra Tan, EMBA Program Coordinator, 415-817-4360, Fax: 415-817-4340, E-mail: zandra13@sfsu.edu.
Website: http://cob.sfsu.edu/graduate-programs/mba

University at Buffalo, the State University of New York, Graduate School, School of Management, Buffalo, NY 14620. Offers accounting (MS); analytics (MBA); business administration (PMBA); consulting (MBA); finance (MBA, MS), including financial risk management (MS), quantitative finance (MS); healthcare (MBA); information assurance (MBA); information systems (MBA); international management (MBA); management (EMBA, PhD); management information systems (MS); marketing (MBA); supply chain and operations (MBA); supply chains and operations management (MS); Au D/MBA; DDS/MBA; JD/MBA; M Arch/MBA; MD/MBA; MPH/MBA; MSW/MBA; Pharm D/MBA. *Accreditation:* AACSB. *Program availability:* Part-time, evening/weekend. *Faculty:* 80 full-time (26 women), 36 part-time/adjunct (6 women). *Students:* 683 full-time (277 women), 196 part-time (63 women); includes 76 minority (23 Black or African American, non-Hispanic/Latino; 1 American Indian or Alaska Native, non-Hispanic/Latino; 48 Asian, non-Hispanic/Latino; 3 Hispanic/Latino; 1 Two or more races, non-Hispanic/Latino), 371 international. Average age 31. 2,451 applicants, 42% accepted, 484 enrolled. In 2016, 515 master's, 10 doctorates awarded. *Degree requirements:* For master's, thesis (for some programs); for doctorate, comprehensive exam, thesis/dissertation. *Entrance requirements:* For master's, GMAT (for MS in accounting, finance); GRE or GMAT (for MBA, PMBA, other MS concentrations), essays, letters of recommendation; for doctorate, GMAT or GRE, essays, writing sample, letters of recommendation. Additional exam requirements/recommendations for international students: Required—TOEFL (minimum score 95 iBT) or IELTS (minimum score 6.5); Recommended—TSE (minimum score 73). *Application deadline:* For fall admission, 10/15 priority date for domestic and international students; for winter admission, 2/1 priority date for domestic and international students; for spring admission, 4/15 for domestic students; for summer admission, 5/15 for domestic students. Application fee: $100. Electronic applications accepted. *Expenses:* Contact institution. *Financial support:* Fellowships with full and partial tuition reimbursements, research assistantships with full and partial tuition reimbursements, teaching assistantships with full and partial tuition reimbursements, career-related internships or fieldwork, Federal Work-Study, institutionally sponsored loans, scholarships/grants, health care benefits, and unspecified assistantships available. Financial award application deadline: 2/15. *Faculty research:* Data analytics, accounting information and corporate finance, consumer behavior, supply chain logistics, leadership and team effectiveness. *Total annual research expenditures:* $1.5 million. *Unit head:* Erin K. O'Brien, Assistant Dean and Director of Graduate Programs, 716-645-3204, Fax: 716-645-2341, E-mail: ekobrien@buffalo.edu. *Application contact:* Meghan Felser, Associate Director of Admissions and Recruiting, 716-645-3204, Fax: 716-645-2341, E-mail: mpwood@buffalo.edu.
Website: http://mgt.buffalo.edu/

The University of Alabama at Birmingham, School of Public Health, Program in Public Health, Birmingham, AL 35294. Offers applied epidemiology and pharmacoepidemiology (MSPH); biostatistics (MPH); clinical and translational science (MSPH); environmental health (MPH); environmental health and toxicology (MSPH); epidemiology (MPH); general theory and practice (MPH); health behavior (MPH); health care organization (MPH); health policy quantitative policy analysis (MPH); industrial hygiene (MPH, MSPH); maternal and child health policy (Dr PH); maternal and child health policy and leadership (MPH); occupational health and safety (MPH); outcomes research (MSPH, Dr PH); public health (PhD); public health management (Dr PH); public health preparedness management (MPH). *Accreditation:* CEPH. *Program availability:* Part-time, online learning. *Degree requirements:* For doctorate, comprehensive exam, thesis/dissertation. *Entrance requirements:* For master's and doctorate, GRE. Additional exam requirements/recommendations for international students: Recommended—TOEFL (minimum score 550 paper-based; 79 iBT), IELTS (minimum score 6.5). Electronic applications accepted. Full-time tuition and fees vary according to course load and program.

The University of British Columbia, Faculty of Arts and Faculty of Graduate Studies, Department of Psychology, Vancouver, BC V6T 1Z4, Canada. Offers behavioral neuroscience (MA, PhD); clinical psychology (MA, PhD); cognitive science (MA, PhD); developmental psychology (MA, PhD); health psychology (MA, PhD); quantitative methods (MA, PhD); social/personality psychology (MA, PhD). *Accreditation:* APA (one or more programs are accredited). Terminal master's awarded for partial completion of doctoral program. *Degree requirements:* For master's, thesis; for doctorate, comprehensive exam, thesis/dissertation. *Entrance requirements:* For master's and doctorate, GRE General Test. Additional exam requirements/recommendations for international students: Required—TOEFL. *Application deadline:* Applications are processed on a rolling basis. Application fee: $100 Canadian dollars ($162 Canadian dollars for international students). Electronic applications accepted. *Expenses:* $4,802 per year tuition and fees, $8,436 per year international. *Financial support:* Fellowships, research assistantships, teaching assistantships, career-related internships or fieldwork, Federal Work-Study, institutionally sponsored loans, scholarships/grants, health care benefits, tuition waivers (full and partial), and unspecified assistantships available. Financial award application deadline: 1/1. *Faculty research:* Clinical, developmental, social/personality, cognition, behavioral neuroscience. *Application contact:* Jaclyn Shaw, 604-822-5002, Fax: 604-822-6923, E-mail: gradsec@psych.ubc.ca.
Website: http://psych.ubc.ca/

University of California, Santa Barbara, Graduate Division, College of Letters and Sciences, Division of Mathematics, Life, and Physical Sciences, Department of Geography, Santa Barbara, CA 93106-4060. Offers cognitive science (PhD); geography (MA, PhD); global studies (PhD); quantitative methods in the social sciences (PhD); technology and society (PhD); transportation (PhD); MA/PhD. Terminal master's awarded for partial completion of doctoral program. *Degree requirements:* For master's, comprehensive exam (for some programs), thesis or alternative; for doctorate, comprehensive exam, thesis/dissertation, 1 quarter of teaching assistantship. *Entrance requirements:* For master's and doctorate, GRE (minimum combined verbal and quantitative scores above 1100 in old scoring system or 301 in new scoring system). Additional exam requirements/recommendations for international students: Required—TOEFL (minimum score 550 paper-based; 80 iBT), IELTS (minimum score 7). Electronic applications accepted. *Faculty research:* Earth system science; human environment relations; modeling, measurement, and computation.

University of California, Santa Barbara, Graduate Division, College of Letters and Sciences, Division of Mathematics, Life, and Physical Sciences, Department of Statistics and Applied Probability, Santa Barbara, CA 93106-3110. Offers bioengineering (PhD); financial mathematics and statistics (PhD); quantitative methods in the social sciences (PhD); statistics (MA), including applied statistics, mathematical statistics; statistics and applied probability (PhD); MA/PhD. Terminal master's awarded for partial completion of doctoral program. *Degree requirements:* For master's, comprehensive exam, thesis optional; for doctorate, comprehensive exam, thesis/dissertation. *Entrance requirements:* For master's and doctorate, GRE General Test. Additional exam requirements/recommendations for international students: Required—TOEFL (minimum score 550 paper-based; 80 iBT), IELTS (minimum score 7). Electronic applications accepted. *Faculty research:* Bayesian inference, financial mathematics, stochastic processes, environmental statistics, biostatistical modeling.

University of California, Santa Barbara, Graduate Division, College of Letters and Sciences, Division of Social Sciences, Department of Communication, Santa Barbara, CA 93106-4020. Offers cognitive science (PhD); communication (PhD); feminist studies (PhD); language, interaction and social organization (PhD); quantitative methods in the social sciences (PhD); society and technology (PhD); MA/PhD. Terminal master's awarded for partial completion of doctoral program. *Degree requirements:* For doctorate, comprehensive exam, thesis/dissertation. *Entrance requirements:* For doctorate, GRE. Additional exam requirements/recommendations for international students: Required—TOEFL (minimum score 80 iBT), IELTS (minimum score 7). Electronic applications accepted. *Faculty research:* Interpersonal, intergroup, intercultural, organizational, health, media.

University of California, Santa Barbara, Graduate Division, College of Letters and Sciences, Division of Social Sciences, Department of Sociology, Santa Barbara, CA 93106-9430. Offers interdisciplinary emphasis: Black studies (PhD); interdisciplinary emphasis: environment and society (PhD); interdisciplinary emphasis: feminist studies (PhD); interdisciplinary emphasis: global studies (PhD); interdisciplinary emphasis: language, interaction and social organization (PhD); interdisciplinary emphasis: quantitative methods in the social sciences (PhD); interdisciplinary emphasis: technology and society (PhD); sociology (PhD); MA/PhD. Terminal master's awarded for partial completion of doctoral program. *Degree requirements:* For doctorate, comprehensive exam, thesis/dissertation. *Entrance requirements:* For doctorate, GRE General Test. Additional exam requirements/recommendations for international students: Required—TOEFL (minimum score 550 paper-based; 80 iBT), IELTS (minimum score 7). Electronic applications accepted. *Faculty research:* Gender and sexualities, race/ethnicity, social movements, conversation analysis, global sociology.

University of Cincinnati, Graduate School, Carl H. Lindner College of Business, MS Program, Cincinnati, OH 45221. Offers accounting (MS); business analytics (MS); finance (MS); information systems (MS); marketing (MS); taxation (MS). *Program availability:* Part-time, evening/weekend. *Faculty:* 74 full-time (17 women), 33 part-time/adjunct (8 women). *Students:* 307 full-time (128 women), 246 part-time (106 women); includes 60 minority (22 Black or African American, non-Hispanic/Latino; 20 Asian, non-Hispanic/Latino; 9 Hispanic/Latino; 1 Native Hawaiian or other Pacific Islander, non-Hispanic/Latino; 8 Two or more races, non-Hispanic/Latino), 321 international. Average age 28. 1,756 applicants, 24% accepted, 351 enrolled. In 2016, 334 master's awarded. *Degree requirements:* For master's, thesis (for some programs). *Entrance requirements:* For master's, GMAT, GRE, resume, transcripts, essays, letters of recommendation. Additional exam requirements/recommendations for international students: Required—TOEFL (minimum score 577 paper-based; 90 iBT), IELTS (minimum score 6.5). *Application deadline:* For fall admission, 8/1 priority date for domestic students, 3/15 for international students; for spring admission, 12/15 for domestic students, 9/15 for international students; for summer admission, 4/15 for domestic and international students. Applications are processed on a rolling basis. Application fee: $65 ($70 for international students). Electronic applications accepted. *Expenses:* Contact institution. *Financial support:* In 2016–17, 251 students received support, including 12 teaching assistantships with tuition reimbursements available (averaging $3,500 per year); scholarships/grants, tuition waivers (full and partial), and unspecified assistantships also available. Financial award application deadline: 2/1; financial award applicants required to submit FAFSA. *Faculty research:* Real estate, empirical pricing, organization information pricing, strategic management, portfolio choice in institutional investment. *Unit head:* Dr. David Szymanski, Dean, 513-556-7001, Fax: 513-556-4891, E-mail: david.szymanski@uc.edu. *Application contact:* Dona Clary, Director, Graduate Programs, 513-556-3546, Fax: 513-558-7006, E-mail: dona.clary@uc.edu.

University of Cincinnati, Graduate School, Carl H. Lindner College of Business, PhD Programs, Cincinnati, OH 45211. Offers accounting (PhD); economics (PhD); finance (PhD); information systems (PhD); management (PhD); marketing (PhD); operations and business analytics (PhD). *Faculty:* 72 full-time (18 women). *Students:* 37 full-time (19 women); includes 4 minority (1 Black or African American, non-Hispanic/Latino; 3 Asian, non-Hispanic/Latino), 19 international. Average age 30. 92 applicants, 16% accepted, 7 enrolled. In 2016, 4 doctorates awarded. *Degree requirements:* For doctorate, comprehensive exam, thesis/dissertation. *Entrance requirements:* For doctorate, GMAT, GRE, transcripts, essays, resume, letters of recommendation. Additional exam requirements/recommendations for international students: Required—TOEFL (minimum score 600 paper-based; 100 iBT), IELTS (minimum score 7). *Application deadline:* For fall admission, 1/15 for domestic and international students. Application fee: $65 ($70 for international students). Electronic applications accepted. *Expenses:* Contact institution. *Financial support:* In 2016–17, 38 students received support, including 25 research assistantships with tuition reimbursements available (averaging $23,250 per year); scholarships/grants, tuition waivers (full and partial), and unspecified assistantships also available. Financial award application deadline: 1/15; financial award applicants required to submit FAFSA. *Faculty research:* Bayesian Prediction Theory, organizational fairness, consumer insight and market research, EGARCH idiosyncratic volatility and expected stock returns, consumer insight and market research, density estimation from correlated data. *Unit head:* Dr. Suzanne Masterson, Director, 513-556-7125, Fax: 513-556-5499, E-mail: suzanne.masterson@uc.edu. *Application contact:* Angel Elvin, Assistant Director, 513-556-7190, Fax: 513-558-7006, E-mail: angel.elvin@uc.edu.
Website: http://www.business.uc.edu/phd

University of Colorado Denver, Business School, Program in Decision Sciences, Denver, CO 80217. Offers MS, MS/MBA. *Program availability:* Part-time, evening/weekend. *Students:* 48 full-time (17 women), 15 part-time (4 women); includes 4 minority (3 Asian, non-Hispanic/Latino; 1 Hispanic/Latino), 24 international. Average age 31. 120 applicants, 44% accepted, 21 enrolled. In 2016, 13 master's awarded. *Degree requirements:* For master's, 30 semester hours (18 of required courses and 12 of electives). *Entrance requirements:* For master's, GMAT, essay, resume, two letters of recommendation; financial statements (for international students). Additional exam requirements/recommendations for international students: Required—TOEFL (minimum score 537 paper-based; 75 iBT); Recommended—IELTS (minimum score 6.5). *Application deadline:* For fall admission, 4/15 priority date for domestic students, 3/15 priority date for international students; for spring admission, 10/15 priority date for domestic students, 9/15 priority date for international students; for summer admission, 2/15 priority date for domestic students, 1/15 priority date for international students. Applications are processed on a rolling basis. Application fee: $50 ($75 for international students). Electronic applications accepted. *Expenses:* Contact institution. *Financial support:* In 2016–17, 14 students received support. Fellowships, research assistantships, teaching assistantships, Federal Work-Study, institutionally sponsored loans, scholarships/grants, and traineeships available. Financial award application deadline: 4/1; financial award applicants required to submit FAFSA. *Faculty research:* Quantitative business analysis, quantitative methods and modeling, business intelligence, forecasting, quality and Six Sigma, optimization, project management, data mining, supply chain management. *Unit head:* Deborah Kellogg, Director of Business Analytics Program, 303-315-8435, E-mail: deborah.kellogg@ucdenver.edu. *Application contact:* 303-315-8200, E-mail: bschool.admissions@ucdenver.edu.
Website: http://www.ucdenver.edu/academics/colleges/business/degrees/ms/business-analytics/Pages/default.aspx

University of Connecticut, Graduate School, College of Liberal Arts and Sciences, Department of Public Policy, Field of Survey Research, Storrs, CT 06269. Offers quantitative research methods (Graduate Certificate); survey research (MA). *Degree requirements:* For master's, comprehensive exam. *Entrance requirements:* For master's, GRE General Test. Additional exam requirements/recommendations for international students: Required—TOEFL (minimum score 550 paper-based). Electronic applications accepted.

University of Florida, Graduate School, College of Liberal Arts and Sciences, Department of Mathematics, Gainesville, FL 32611. Offers mathematics (MAT, MS, MST, PhD), including imaging science and technology (PhD), mathematics (PhD), quantitative finance (PhD). *Program availability:* Part-time. Terminal master's awarded for partial completion of doctoral program. *Degree requirements:* For master's, comprehensive exam, thesis optional, first-year exam; for doctorate, one foreign language, comprehensive exam, thesis/dissertation. *Entrance requirements:* For master's and doctorate, GRE General Test, GRE Subject Test (math), minimum GPA of 3.0. Additional exam requirements/recommendations for international students: Required—TOEFL (minimum score 550 paper-based; 80 iBT), IELTS (minimum score 6). Electronic applications accepted. *Faculty research:* Applied mathematics, including imaging, optimization and biomathematics; analysis and probability; combinatorics and number theory; topology and foundations; group theory.

University of Florida, Graduate School, College of Liberal Arts and Sciences, Department of Statistics, Gainesville, FL 32611. Offers quantitative finance (PhD); statistics (M Stat, MS Stat, PhD). *Program availability:* Part-time. Terminal master's awarded for partial completion of doctoral program. *Degree requirements:* For master's, variable foreign language requirement, comprehensive exam, final oral exam; thesis (for MS Stat); for doctorate, comprehensive exam, thesis/dissertation. *Entrance requirements:* For master's and doctorate, GRE General Test, minimum GPA of 3.0. Additional exam requirements/recommendations for international students: Required—TOEFL (minimum score 550 paper-based; 80 iBT), IELTS (minimum score 6). Electronic applications accepted. *Faculty research:* Bayesian statistics, biostatistics, Markov Chain Monte Carlo (MCMC), nonparametric statistics, statistical genetics/genomics.

University of Florida, Graduate School, Warrington College of Business Administration, Hough Graduate School of Business, Department of Finance, Insurance and Real Estate, Gainesville, FL 32611. Offers entrepreneurship (MS); finance (MS, PhD); financial services (Certificate); insurance (PhD); quantitative finance (PhD); real estate (MS); real estate and urban analysis (PhD); JD/MBA; JD/MS. Terminal master's awarded for partial completion of doctoral program. *Degree requirements:* For master's, comprehensive exam, thesis; for doctorate, comprehensive exam, thesis/dissertation. *Entrance requirements:* For master's, GMAT (minimum score of 465) or GRE General Test, minimum GPA of 3.0 for last 60 hours of undergraduate degree, work experience (preferred); for doctorate, GMAT (minimum score of 465) or GRE General Test, minimum GPA of 3.0. Additional exam requirements/recommendations for international students: Required—TOEFL (minimum score 550 paper-based; 80 iBT), IELTS (minimum score 6). Electronic applications accepted. *Faculty research:* Banking, empirical corporate finance, hedge funds.

The University of Iowa, Graduate College, College of Public Health, Department of Biostatistics, Iowa City, IA 52242-1316. Offers biostatistics (MS, PhD, Certificate); quantitative methods (MPH). *Degree requirements:* For master's, thesis optional, exam; for doctorate, comprehensive exam, thesis/dissertation. *Entrance requirements:* For master's and doctorate, GRE General Test, minimum GPA of 3.0. Additional exam requirements/recommendations for international students: Required—TOEFL (minimum score 600 paper-based; 100 iBT). Electronic applications accepted.

University of Maryland, College Park, Academic Affairs, College of Education, Department of Human Development and Quantitative Methodology, College Park, MD 20742. Offers MA, Ed D, PhD. *Entrance requirements:* Additional exam requirements/ recommendations for international students: Required—TOEFL.

University of Minnesota, Twin Cities Campus, College of Science and Engineering, School of Mathematics, Minneapolis, MN 55455-0213. Offers mathematics (MS, PhD); quantitative finance (Certificate). *Program availability:* Part-time. Terminal master's awarded for partial completion of doctoral program. *Degree requirements:* For master's, thesis (for some programs); for doctorate, 2 foreign languages, thesis/dissertation. *Entrance requirements:* For master's, GRE Subject Test (recommended); for doctorate, GRE Subject Test. Additional exam requirements/recommendations for international students: Required—TOEFL. Electronic applications accepted. *Faculty research:* Partial and ordinary differential equations, algebra and number theory, geometry, combinatorics, numerical analysis, probability, financial mathematics.

University of New Mexico, Graduate Studies, College of Arts and Sciences, Program in Psychology, Albuquerque, NM 87131-2039. Offers behavioral neuroscience (PhD); clinical psychology (PhD); cognitive neuroimaging (PhD); developmental psychology (PhD); evolution (PhD); health psychology (PhD); quantitative methodology (PhD). *Accreditation:* APA. *Faculty:* 23 full-time (8 women), 1 part-time/adjunct (0 women). *Students:* 60 full-time (36 women), 16 part-time (10 women); includes 22 minority (2 Black or African American, non-Hispanic/Latino; 2 American Indian or Alaska Native, non-Hispanic/Latino; 3 Asian, non-Hispanic/Latino; 12 Hispanic/Latino; 3 Two or more races, non-Hispanic/Latino), 2 international. Average age 30. 227 applicants, 11% accepted, 16 enrolled. In 2016, 10 doctorates awarded. *Degree requirements:* For doctorate, comprehensive exam, thesis/dissertation. *Entrance requirements:* For doctorate, GRE General Test, GRE Subject Test (psychology), minimum GPA of 3.0. Additional exam requirements/recommendations for international students: Required—TOEFL (minimum score 550 paper-based; 79 iBT), IELTS (minimum score 6.5). *Application deadline:* For fall admission, 12/15 priority date for domestic and international students. Applications are processed on a rolling basis. Application fee: $50. Electronic applications accepted. *Financial support:* Fellowships, research assistantships with tuition reimbursements, teaching assistantships with tuition reimbursements, career-related internships or fieldwork, Federal Work-Study, institutionally sponsored loans, scholarships/grants, health care benefits, tuition waivers (partial), and unspecified assistantships available. Financial award application deadline: 3/1; financial award applicants required to submit FAFSA. *Faculty research:* Addiction, cognition, brain and behavior, developmental, evolutionary, functioning neuroimaging, health psychology, learning and memory, neuroscience. *Total annual research expenditures:* $727,970. *Unit head:* Dr. Jane Ellen Smith, Department Chair, 505-277-4121, Fax: 505-277-1394. *Application contact:* Rikk Murphy, Graduate Program Coordinator, 505-277-5009, Fax: 505-277-1394, E-mail: advising@unm.edu. Website: http://psych.unm.edu

University of North Texas, Robert B. Toulouse School of Graduate Studies, Denton, TX 76203-5459. Offers accounting (MS); applied anthropology (MA, MS); applied behavior analysis (Certificate); applied geography (MA); applied technology and performance improvement (M Ed, MS); art education (MA); art history (MA); art museum education (Certificate); arts leadership (Certificate); audiology (Au D); behavior analysis (MS); behavioral science (PhD); biochemistry and molecular biology (MS); biology (MA, MS); biomedical engineering (MS); business analysis (MS); chemistry (MS); clinical health psychology (PhD); communication studies (MA, MS); computer engineering (MS); computer science (MS); counseling (M Ed, MS), including clinical mental health counseling (MS), college and university counseling, elementary school counseling, secondary school counseling; creative writing (MA); criminal justice (MS); curriculum and instruction (M Ed); decision sciences (MBA); design (MA, MFA), including fashion design (MFA), innovation studies, interior design (MFA); early childhood studies (MS); economics (MS); educational leadership (M Ed, Ed D); educational psychology (MS, PhD), including family studies (MS), gifted and talented (MS), human development (MS), learning and cognition (MS), research, measurement and evaluation (MS); electrical engineering (MS); emergency management (MPA); engineering technology (MS); English (MA); English as a second language (MA); environmental science (MS); finance (MBA, MS); financial management (MPA); French (MA); health services management (MBA); higher education (M Ed, Ed D); history (MA, MS); hospitality management (MS); human resources management (MPA); information science (MS); information systems (PhD); information technologies (MBA); interdisciplinary studies (MA, MS); international studies (MA); international sustainable tourism (MS); jazz studies (MM); journalism (MA, MJ, Graduate Certificate), including interactive and virtual digital communication (Graduate Certificate), narrative journalism (Graduate Certificate), public relations (Graduate Certificate); kinesiology (MS); linguistics (MA); local government management (MPA); logistics (PhD); logistics and supply chain management (MBA); long-term care, senior housing, and aging services (MA); management (PhD); marketing (MBA); mathematics (MA, MS); mechanical and energy engineering (MS, PhD); music (MA), including ethnomusicology, music theory, musicology, performance; music composition (PhD); music education (MM Ed, PhD); nonprofit management (MPA); operations and supply chain management (MBA); performance (MM, DMA); philosophy (MA); political science (MA); professional and technical communication (MA); radio, television and film (MA, MFA); rehabilitation counseling (Certificate); sociology (MA); Spanish (MA); special education (M Ed); speech-language pathology (MA); strategic management (MBA); studio art (MFA); teaching (M Ed); MBA/MS. *Program availability:* Part-time, evening/weekend, online learning. Terminal master's awarded for partial completion of doctoral program. *Degree requirements:* For master's, variable foreign language requirement, comprehensive exam (for some programs), thesis (for some programs); for doctorate, variable foreign language requirement, comprehensive exam (for some programs), thesis/dissertation; for other advanced degree, variable foreign language requirement, comprehensive exam (for some programs). *Entrance requirements:* For master's and doctorate, GRE, GMAT. Additional exam requirements/ recommendations for international students: Required—TOEFL (minimum score 550 paper-based; 79 iBT). Electronic applications accepted.

University of Oregon, Graduate School, Charles H. Lundquist College of Business, Department of Decision Sciences, Eugene, OR 97403. Offers MA, MS. *Entrance requirements:* For master's, GMAT. *Faculty research:* Time-series analysis, production scheduling, nonparametric methods, decision theory.

University of Puerto Rico, Río Piedras Campus, College of Business Administration, San Juan, PR 00931-3300. Offers accounting (MBA); finance (MBA, PhD); general business (MBA); human resources management (MBA); international trade and business (MBA, PhD); marketing (MBA); operations management (MBA); quantitative methods (MBA). *Accreditation:* AACSB. *Program availability:* Part-time. *Degree requirements:* For master's, comprehensive exam, thesis or alternative, research project. *Entrance requirements:* For master's, GMAT or PAEG, minimum GPA of 3.0, letter of recommendation; for doctorate, GMAT, PAEG, minimum GPA of 3.0, master degree. *Faculty research:* Management.

University of South Africa, College of Economic and Management Sciences, Pretoria, South Africa. Offers accounting (D Admin, D Com); accounting science (DA); auditing (D Admin, D Com); business administration (M Tech); business economics (D Admin); business leadership (DBL); business management (D Admin, D Com); economic management analysis (M Tech); economics (D Admin, D Com, PhD); human resource development (M Tech); industrial psychology (D Admin, D Com, PhD); logistics (D Com); marketing (M Tech); public administration (D Admin, D Com, DPA, PhD); public management (M Tech); quantitative management (D Admin, D Com); real estate (M Tech); statistics (D Admin, PhD); tourism management (D Admin, D Com); transport economics (D Admin, D Com).

University of Southern California, Graduate School, Dana and David Dornsife College of Letters, Arts and Sciences, Department of Psychology, Los Angeles, CA 90089. Offers brain and cognitive science (PhD); clinical science (PhD); developmental psychology (PhD); human behavior (MHB); quantitative methods (PhD); social psychology (PhD). *Accreditation:* APA. *Degree requirements:* For doctorate, comprehensive exam, thesis/dissertation, one-year internship (for clinical science students). *Entrance requirements:* For doctorate, GRE. Additional exam requirements/ recommendations for international students: Recommended—TOEFL (minimum score 600 paper-based; 100 iBT). Electronic applications accepted. *Faculty research:* Affective neuroscience; children and families; vision, culture and ethnicity; intergroup relations; aggression and violence; language and reading development; substance abuse.

The University of Texas at Arlington, Graduate School, College of Business, Department of Finance and Real Estate, Arlington, TX 76019. Offers finance (PhD); quantitative finance (MS); real estate (MS). *Program availability:* Part-time, evening/ weekend. *Degree requirements:* For master's, thesis optional; for doctorate, comprehensive exam, thesis/dissertation. *Entrance requirements:* For master's, GMAT/ GRE, minimum GPA of 3.0; for doctorate, GMAT/GRE. Additional exam requirements/ recommendations for international students: Required—TOEFL (minimum score 550 paper-based; 79 iBT). *Application deadline:* For fall admission, 6/1 priority date for domestic students, 4/1 for international students; for spring admission, 10/15 for domestic students, 9/15 for international students. Applications are processed on a rolling basis. Application fee: $40 ($70 for international students). *Financial support:* Teaching assistantships, career-related internships or fieldwork, Federal Work-Study, institutionally sponsored loans, and unspecified assistantships available. Financial award application deadline: 6/1; financial award applicants required to submit FAFSA. *Unit head:* Dr. David Diltz, Chair, 817-272-3705, Fax: 817-272-2252, E-mail: diltz@ uta.edu. *Application contact:* Dr. Fred Forgey, Graduate Advisor, 817-272-0359, Fax: 817-272-2252, E-mail: realestate@uta.edu. Website: http://wweb.uta.edu/finance/

The University of Texas at Austin, Graduate School, College of Education, Department of Educational Psychology, Austin, TX 78712-1111. Offers academic educational psychology (M Ed, MA); counseling psychology (PhD); counselor education (M Ed); human development, culture and learning sciences (PhD); program evaluation (MA); quantitative methods (M Ed, MA, PhD); school psychology (MA, PhD). *Accreditation:* APA (one or more programs are accredited). *Degree requirements:* For master's, thesis optional; for doctorate, thesis/dissertation. *Entrance requirements:* For master's and doctorate, GRE General Test, 3 letters of recommendation. Additional exam requirements/recommendations for international students: Required—TOEFL.

The University of Texas Health Science Center at Houston, MD Anderson UTHealth Graduate School, Houston, TX 77225-0036. Offers biochemistry and cell biology (PhD); biomedical sciences (MS); cancer biology (PhD); genetic counseling (MS); genetics and epigenetics (PhD); immunology (PhD); medical physics (MS, PhD); microbiology and infectious diseases (PhD); neuroscience (PhD); quantitative sciences (PhD); therapeutics and pharmacology (PhD); MD/PhD. Terminal master's awarded for partial completion of doctoral program. *Degree requirements:* For master's, thesis; for doctorate, thesis/dissertation. *Entrance requirements:* For master's and doctorate, GRE General Test. Additional exam requirements/recommendations for international students: Required—TOEFL. Electronic applications accepted. *Faculty research:* Biomedical sciences.

Vanderbilt University, Peabody College, Department of Psychology and Human Development, Nashville, TN 37240-1001. Offers child studies (M Ed); clinical psychological assessment (M Ed); quantitative methods (M Ed). *Accreditation:* APA. *Program availability:* Part-time. *Faculty:* 36 full-time (23 women), 11 part-time/adjunct (8 women). *Students:* 51 full-time (46 women), 6 part-time (4 women); includes 11 minority (4 Black or African American, non-Hispanic/Latino; 1 Asian, non-Hispanic/Latino; 5 Hispanic/Latino; 1 Two or more races, non-Hispanic/Latino), 10 international. Average age 25. 195 applicants, 34% accepted, 33 enrolled. In 2016, 21 master's awarded. *Degree requirements:* For master's, comprehensive exam, thesis optional. *Entrance requirements:* For master's, GRE General Test. Additional exam requirements/ recommendations for international students: Required—TOEFL (minimum score 550 paper-based; 80 iBT). *Application deadline:* For fall admission, 12/31 for domestic and international students; for spring admission, 11/1 for domestic and international students. Applications are processed on a rolling basis. Application fee: $0. Electronic applications accepted. *Expenses: Tuition:* Part-time $1854 per credit hour. *Financial support:* Fellowships with partial tuition reimbursements, research assistantships with partial tuition reimbursements, teaching assistantships with partial tuition reimbursements, Federal Work-Study, institutionally sponsored loans, scholarships/ grants, tuition waivers (partial), and unspecified assistantships available. Financial award application deadline: 1/15; financial award applicants required to submit FAFSA. *Faculty research:* Child clinical psychology and developmental psychopathology; cognitive psychology, language and social development; educational and developmental neuroscience; quantitative methods and evaluation. *Unit head:* Dr. Amy Needham, Chair, 615-322-8141, Fax: 615-343-9494, E-mail: amy.needham@ vanderbilt.edu. *Application contact:* Ally Armstead, Educational Coordinator, 615-343-4963, Fax: 615-343-9494, E-mail: ally.armstead@vanderbilt.edu. Website: http://peabody.vanderbilt.edu/departments/psych/index.php

Virginia Polytechnic Institute and State University, VT Online, Blacksburg, VA 24061. Offers advanced transportation systems (Certificate); aerospace engineering (MS); agricultural and life sciences (MSLFS); business information systems (Graduate Certificate); career and technical education (MS); civil engineering (MS); computer engineering (M Eng, MS); decision support systems (Graduate Certificate); eLearning leadership (MA); electrical engineering (M Eng, MS); engineering administration (MEA); environmental engineering (Certificate); environmental politics and policy (Graduate Certificate); environmental sciences and engineering (MS); foundations of political analysis (Graduate Certificate); health product risk management (Graduate Certificate); industrial and systems engineering (MS); information policy and society (Graduate Certificate); information security (Graduate Certificate); information technology (MIT); instructional technology (MA); integrative STEM education (MA Ed); liberal arts (Graduate Certificate); life sciences: health product risk management (MS); natural resources (MNR, Graduate Certificate); networking (Graduate Certificate); nonprofit and nongovernmental organization management (Graduate Certificate); ocean engineering (MS); political science (MA); security studies (Graduate Certificate); software development (Graduate Certificate). *Expenses:* Tuition, state resident: full-time $12,467; part-time $692.50 per credit hour. Tuition, nonresident: full-time $25,095; part-time $1394.25 per credit hour. *Required fees:* $2669; $491.50 per semester. Tuition and fees vary according to course load, campus/location and program.

Section 20
Real Estate

This section contains a directory of institutions offering graduate work in real estate. Additional information about programs listed in the directory but not augmented by an in-depth entry may be obtained by writing directly to the dean of a graduate school or chair of a department at the address given in the directory.

For programs offering related work, see also in this book *Business Administration and Management.*

CONTENTS

Program Directory

Featured School: Display and Close-Up

See:

Real Estate

American University, Kogod School of Business, Department of Finance, Program in Real Estate, Washington, DC 20016-8044. Offers MS, Certificate. *Program availability:* Part-time, evening/weekend. *Students:* 7 full-time (3 women), 8 part-time (4 women); includes 1 minority (Black or African American, non-Hispanic/Latino), 2 international. Average age 29. 21 applicants, 81% accepted, 6 enrolled. In 2016, 10 master's, 1 other advanced degree awarded. *Entrance requirements:* For master's, GMAT/GRE, resume, personal statement, interview, two letters of recommendation, transcripts. Additional exam requirements/recommendations for international students: Required—TOEFL, IELTS, PTE. *Application deadline:* For fall admission, 2/20 priority date for domestic students, 2/20 for international students; for spring admission, 12/10 priority date for domestic students, 11/15 for international students. Applications are processed on a rolling basis. Application fee: $100. *Expenses:* $1,579 per credit tuition; $690 mandatory fees. *Financial support:* Fellowships, institutionally sponsored loans, and unspecified assistantships available. Financial award application deadline: 2/1; financial award applicants required to submit FAFSA. *Unit head:* Dr. Jeffery Harris, Department Chair, Finance and Real Estate, 202-885-6669, Fax: 202-885-1946, E-mail: jharris@american.edu. *Application contact:* Jason Kennedy, Assistant Director of Admission, 202-885-1968, E-mail: jkennedy@american.edu.
Website: http://www.american.edu/kogod/

Arizona State University at the Tempe campus, W. P. Carey School of Business, Department of Marketing, Tempe, AZ 85287-4106. Offers business administration (PhD), including marketing; real estate development (MRED). *Program availability:* Part-time, evening/weekend, online learning. *Degree requirements:* For master's, thesis or alternative, capstone project, interactive Program of Study (iPOS) submitted before completing 50 percent of required credit hours; for doctorate, comprehensive exam, thesis/dissertation, interactive Program of Study (iPOS) submitted before completing 50 percent of required credit hours. *Entrance requirements:* For master's, GMAT, GRE, or LSAT, minimum GPA of 3.0 in last 2 years of work leading to bachelor's degree, 3 personal references, resume, official transcripts, personal statement; for doctorate, GMAT, minimum GPA of 3.0 in last 2 years of work leading to bachelor's degree, 3 letters of recommendation, personal statement/essay. Additional exam requirements/recommendations for international students: Required—TOEFL (minimum score 550 paper-based; 80 iBT), IELTS (minimum score 6.5). Electronic applications accepted. *Expenses:* Contact institution. *Faculty research:* Service marketing and management, strategic marketing, customer portfolio management, characteristics and skills of high-performing managers, market orientation, market segmentation, consumer behavior, marketing strategy, new product development, management of innovation, social influences on consumption, e-commerce, market research methodology.

Auburn University, Graduate School, Interdepartmental Programs, Program in Real Estate Development, Auburn University, AL 36849. Offers MRED. *Students:* 31 part-time (4 women); includes 9 minority (7 Black or African American, non-Hispanic/Latino; 2 Asian, non-Hispanic/Latino). Average age 38. 25 applicants, 88% accepted, 16 enrolled. In 2016, 21 master's awarded. Application fee: $50 ($60 for international students). *Expenses:* Tuition, state resident: full-time $9072; part-time $504 per credit hour. Tuition, nonresident: full-time $27,216; part-time $1512 per credit hour. *Required fees:* $812 per semester. Tuition and fees vary according to degree level and program. *Unit head:* Joe Collazo, Assistant Director, 334-844-5078, E-mail: mred@business.auburn.edu. *Application contact:* Dr. George Flowers, Dean of the Graduate School, 334-844-2125.
Website: http://mred.auburn.edu/

Baruch College of the City University of New York, Zicklin School of Business, Department of Real Estate, New York, NY 10010-5585. Offers MBA, MS.

Brandeis University, International Business School (IBS), Master of Business Administration Program, Waltham, MA 02454-9110. Offers corporate finance (MBA); data analytics (MBA); marketing (MBA); real estate (MBA). *Faculty:* 29 full-time (10 women), 27 part-time/adjunct (3 women). *Students:* 65 full-time (25 women). Average age 27. 75 applicants, 59% accepted, 16 enrolled. In 2016, 42 master's awarded. *Entrance requirements:* For master's, GMAT or GRE. Additional exam requirements/recommendations for international students: Required—TOEFL (minimum score 600 paper-based; 100 iBT), IELTS (minimum score 7), PTE (minimum score 68). *Application deadline:* For fall admission, 11/1 priority date for domestic and international students; for winter admission, 1/15 priority date for domestic and international students; for spring admission, 3/15 priority date for domestic and international students; for summer admission, 5/15 for domestic and international students. Application fee: $55. Electronic applications accepted. *Expenses:* Contact institution. *Financial support:* In 2016–17, 80 students received support. Institutionally sponsored loans and scholarships/grants available. Financial award application deadline: 3/15; financial award applicants required to submit FAFSA. *Faculty research:* Strategic alliances, IPO and venture capital financing, real estate, risk management, data analytics. *Unit head:* Peter Petri, Interim Dean, 781-736-2256. *Application contact:* Kelly Sugrue, Director of Admissions, 781-736-2252, Fax: 781-736-2263, E-mail: admission@lemberg.brandeis.edu.

California State University, Sacramento, Office of Graduate Studies, College of Business Administration, Sacramento, CA 95819. Offers accountancy (MS); business administration (IMBA, MBA); human resources (MBA); urban land development (MBA). *Accreditation:* AACSB. *Program availability:* Part-time, evening/weekend. *Students:* 138 full-time (68 women), 129 part-time (63 women); includes 211 minority (12 Black or African American, non-Hispanic/Latino; 132 American Indian or Alaska Native, non-Hispanic/Latino; 63 Asian, non-Hispanic/Latino; 4 Native Hawaiian or other Pacific Islander, non-Hispanic/Latino). Average age 34. 198 applicants, 77% accepted, 85 enrolled. In 2016, 168 master's awarded. *Degree requirements:* For master's, thesis or alternative, writing proficiency exam. *Entrance requirements:* For master's, GMAT. Additional exam requirements/recommendations for international students: Required—TOEFL (minimum score 550 paper-based; 80 iBT). *Application deadline:* For fall admission, 2/1 for domestic students, 3/1 for international students; for spring admission, 9/15 for domestic students, 9/30 for international students. Applications are processed on a rolling basis. Application fee: $55. Electronic applications accepted. *Expenses:* $4,302 full-time tuition and fees per semester, $2,796 part-time. *Financial support:* Research assistantships, teaching assistantships, career-related internships or fieldwork, and Federal Work-Study available. Support available to part-time students. Financial award applicants required to submit FAFSA. *Unit head:* Dr. Pierre A. Balthazard, Dean, 916-278-6578, Fax: 916-278-5793, E-mail: cba@csus.edu. *Application contact:* Jose Martinez, Graduate Admissions Supervisor, 916-278-7871, E-mail: martinj@skymail.csus.edu.
Website: http://www.cba.csus.edu

Clemson University, Graduate School, College of Architecture, Arts, and Humanities, Department of City Planning and Real Estate Development and College of Business, Master of Real Estate Development Program, Greenville, SC 29601. Offers MRED. *Faculty:* 4 full-time (0 women), 4 part-time/adjunct (0 women). *Students:* 30 full-time (4 women), 6 international. Average age 26. 2 applicants, 50% accepted. In 2016, 15 master's awarded. *Degree requirements:* For master's, practicum. *Entrance requirements:* For master's, GRE General Test or GMAT, 3 letters of recommendation, resume, personal statement, unofficial transcripts, portfolio for 12-month program. Additional exam requirements/recommendations for international students: Required—TOEFL (minimum score 80 iBT), IELTS (minimum score 6.5). *Application deadline:* For fall admission, 1/15 priority date for domestic and international students. Applications are processed on a rolling basis. Application fee: $80 ($90 for international students). Electronic applications accepted. *Expenses:* Contact institution. *Financial support:* In 2016–17, 6 students received support, including 10 fellowships (averaging $2,650 per year); career-related internships or fieldwork also available. Financial award application deadline: 2/15. *Faculty research:* Real estate education, real estate investment/finance, sustainability, public-private partnership, historic preservation. *Unit head:* Dr. Robert Benedict, Program Director, 864-656-2476, E-mail: benedic@clemson.edu. *Application contact:* Amy Matthews Herrick, Graduate Program Coordinator, 864-656-4257, E-mail: matthe3@clemson.edu.
Website: http://www.clemson.edu/caah/departments/real-estate-development/

Columbia University, Graduate School of Architecture, Planning, and Preservation, Program in Real Estate Development, New York, NY 10027. Offers MS. *Degree requirements:* For master's, thesis. *Entrance requirements:* For master's, GRE General Test.

Columbia University, Graduate School of Business, MBA Program, New York, NY 10027. Offers accounting (MBA); decision, risk, and operations (MBA); entrepreneurship (MBA); finance and economics (MBA); healthcare and pharmaceutical management (MBA); human resource management (MBA); international business (MBA); leadership and ethics (MBA); management (MBA); marketing (MBA); media (MBA); private equity (MBA); real estate (MBA); social enterprise (MBA); value investing (MBA); DDS/MBA; JD/MBA; MBA/MIA; MBA/MPH; MBA/MS; MD/MBA. *Entrance requirements:* For master's, GMAT, 2 letters of recommendation. Additional exam requirements/recommendations for international students: Required—TOEFL. Electronic applications accepted. *Expenses:* Contact institution. *Faculty research:* Human decision making and behavioral research; real estate market and mortgage defaults; financial crisis and corporate governance; international business; security analysis and accounting.

Cornell University, Graduate School, Graduate Fields of Architecture, Art and Planning, Field of Real Estate, Ithaca, NY 14853. Offers MPS. *Degree requirements:* For master's, project paper. *Entrance requirements:* For master's, GMAT, 2 letters of recommendation, resume. Additional exam requirements/recommendations for international students: Required—TOEFL (minimum score 600 paper-based; 77 iBT). Electronic applications accepted. *Faculty research:* Smart growth, economic development, urban redevelopment, development financing, securitization of real estate.

DePaul University, Kellstadt Graduate School of Business, Chicago, IL 60604. Offers accountancy (M Acc, MS, MSA); applied economics (MBA); banking (MBA); behavioral finance (MBA); brand and product management (MBA); business development (MBA); business information technology (MS); business strategy and decision-making (MBA); computational finance (MS); consumer insights (MBA); corporate finance (MBA); economic policy analysis (MS); entrepreneurship (MBA, MS); finance (MBA, MS); financial analysis (MBA); general business (MBA); health sector management (MBA); hospitality leadership (MBA); hospitality leadership and operational performance (MS); human resource management (MBA); human resources (MS); investment management (MBA); leadership and change management (MBA); management accounting (MBA); marketing (MBA, MS); marketing analysis (MS); marketing strategy and planning (MBA); operations management (MBA); organizational diversity (MBA); real estate (MS); real estate finance and investment (MBA); revenue management (MBA); sports management (MBA); strategic global marketing (MBA); strategy, execution and valuation (MBA); sustainable management (MBA, MS); taxation (MS); wealth management (MS); JD/MBA. *Accreditation:* AACSB. *Program availability:* Part-time, evening/weekend, online learning. *Entrance requirements:* For master's, GMAT, 2 letters of recommendation, resume, essay, official transcripts. Additional exam requirements/recommendations for international students: Required—TOEFL (minimum score 550 paper-based; 80 iBT). Electronic applications accepted. *Expenses:* Contact institution.

Drexel University, Goodwin College of Professional Studies, School of Technology and Professional Studies, Philadelphia, PA 19104-2875. Offers construction management (MS); creativity and innovation (MS); engineering technology (MS); food science (MS); hospitality management (MS); professional studies: creativity studies (MS); professional studies: e-learning leadership (MS); professional studies: homeland security management (MS); project management (MS); property management (MS); sport management (MS). *Program availability:* Part-time, evening/weekend. *Faculty:* 37 full-time (14 women). *Students:* 13 full-time, 462 part-time; includes 133 minority (86 Black or African American, non-Hispanic/Latino; 24 Asian, non-Hispanic/Latino; 23 Hispanic/Latino). In 2016, 88 master's awarded. *Entrance requirements:* Additional exam requirements/recommendations for international students: Required—TOEFL, IELTS. *Application deadline:* For fall admission, 9/1 for domestic students; for winter admission, 12/1 for domestic students; for spring admission, 3/1 for domestic students. Applications are processed on a rolling basis. Application fee: $75. Electronic applications accepted. Application fee is waived when completed online. *Expenses: Tuition:* Full-time $32,184; part-time $1192 per credit hour. *Required fees:* $280. Tuition and fees vary according to campus/location and program. *Financial support:* Applicants required to submit FAFSA. *Unit head:* Dr. William F. Lynch, Dean, 215-895-2159, E-mail: goodwin@drexel.edu. *Application contact:* Matthew Gray, Manager, Recruitment and Enrollment, 215-895-6255, Fax: 215-895-2153, E-mail: mdg67@drexel.edu.
Website: http://drexel.edu/grad/programs/goodwin/

Emory University, Goizueta Business School, Full Time MBA Program, Atlanta, GA 30322. Offers accounting (MBA); alternative investments (MBA); business process consulting (MBA); business technology management (MBA); capital markets (MBA); corporate finance (MBA); customer relationship management (MBA); decision analytics (MBA); entrepreneurship (MBA); finance (MBA); global management (MBA); investment banking (MBA); management consulting (MBA); marketing (MBA); marketing analytics (MBA); marketing consulting (MBA); operations management (MBA); organization and management (MBA); product and brand management (MBA); real estate (MBA); social enterprise (MBA); strategy consulting (MBA). *Accreditation:* AACSB. *Faculty:* 72 full-time (17 women), 18 part-time/adjunct (5 women). *Students:* 350 full-time (101 women); includes 77 minority (21 Black or African American, non-Hispanic/Latino; 3 American Indian or Alaska Native, non-Hispanic/Latino; 32 Asian, non-Hispanic/Latino; 15

Hispanic/Latino; 2 Native Hawaiian or other Pacific Islander, non-Hispanic/Latino; 4 Two or more races, non-Hispanic/Latino), 117 international. Average age 29. 1,434 applicants, 31% accepted, 181 enrolled. In 2016, 182 master's awarded. *Degree requirements:* For master's, 1 leadership course; 2 mid-semester module programs; 2 global components. *Entrance requirements:* For master's, GMAT/GRE, essays; recommendation letters; undergraduate degree; interview. Additional exam requirements/recommendations for international students: Required—TOEFL (minimum score 100 iBT), IELTS (minimum score 7), PTE (minimum score 68). *Application deadline:* For fall admission, 10/14 priority date for domestic and international students; for winter admission, 11/11 priority date for domestic and international students; for spring admission, 1/4 priority date for domestic students, 1/4 for international students. Application fee: $150. Electronic applications accepted. *Expenses:* $57,580. *Financial support:* In 2016–17, 289 students received support. Career-related internships or fieldwork, institutionally sponsored loans, and scholarships/grants available. Financial award application deadline: 4/1; financial award applicants required to submit FAFSA. *Faculty research:* Social enterprise; micro vs. large business; mobile health data; mutual fund performance; product evaluation. *Unit head:* Brian Mitchell, Associate Dean, 404-727-4824, Fax: 404-712-9648, E-mail: brian.mitchell@emory.edu. *Application contact:* Julie Barefoot, Associate Dean, 404-727-6311, Fax: 404-727-4612, E-mail: mbaadmissions@emory.edu.
Website: http://www.goizueta.emory.edu

Florida International University, Chapman Graduate School of Business, Hollo School of Real Estate, Miami, FL 33199. Offers international real estate (MS). *Program availability:* Part-time, evening/weekend. *Faculty:* 5 full-time (1 woman), 5 part-time/adjunct (2 women). *Students:* 88 full-time (29 women), 11 part-time (5 women); includes 63 minority (16 Black or African American, non-Hispanic/Latino; 1 Asian, non-Hispanic/Latino; 43 Hispanic/Latino; 3 Two or more races, non-Hispanic/Latino), 11 international. Average age 35. 140 applicants, 56% accepted, 51 enrolled. In 2016, 80 master's awarded. *Entrance requirements:* For master's, GMAT or GRE, letter of intent; resume. Additional exam requirements/recommendations for international students: Required—TOEFL (minimum score 550 paper-based; 80 iBT) or IELTS (minimum score 6.5). *Application deadline:* For fall admission, 4/1 for domestic and international students. Application fee: $30. Electronic applications accepted. *Expenses:* Contact institution. *Financial support:* Institutionally sponsored loans and scholarships/grants available. Financial award application deadline: 3/1; financial award applicants required to submit FAFSA. *Faculty research:* International real estate, real estate investments, commercial real estate. *Unit head:* Eli Beracha, Director, 305-779-7898, E-mail: eli.beracha@fiu.edu. *Application contact:* Isabel Lopez, Associate Director for Academic Support Services, 305-348-4198, E-mail: isabel.lopez@fiu.edu.

Georgetown University, Graduate School of Arts and Sciences, School of Continuing Studies, Washington, DC 20057. Offers American studies (MALS); Catholic studies (MALS); classical civilizations (MALS); emergency and disaster management (MPS); ethics and the professions (MALS); global strategic communications (MPS); hospitality management (MPS); human resources management (MPS); humanities (MALS); individualized study (MALS); integrated marketing communications (MPS); international affairs (MALS); Islam and Muslim-Christian relations (MALS); journalism (MPS); liberal studies (DLS); literature and society (MALS); medieval and early modern European studies (MALS); public relations and corporate communications (MPS); real estate (MPS); religious studies (MALS); social and public policy (MALS); sports industry management (MPS); systems engineering management (MPS); technology management (MPS); the theory and practice of American democracy (MALS); urban and regional planning (MPS); visual culture (MALS). MPS in systems engineering management offered jointly with Stevens Institute of Technology. *Entrance requirements:* Additional exam requirements/recommendations for international students: Required—TOEFL.

The George Washington University, School of Business, Program in Walkable Urban Real Estate Development, Washington, DC 20052. Offers Professional Certificate. *Unit head:* Robert Valero, Executive Director, 202-994-0920, Fax: 202-994-5966, E-mail: rjvalero@gwu.edu. *Application contact:* Christopher Storer, Executive Director, Graduate Admissions, 202-994-1212, E-mail: gwmba@gwu.edu.

Georgia State University, J. Mack Robinson College of Business, Department of Real Estate, Atlanta, GA 30302-3083. Offers hotel real estate (MBA); real estate (MBA, MS, PhD, Certificate). *Program availability:* Part-time, evening/weekend. *Faculty:* 2 full-time (1 woman). *Students:* 24 full-time (6 women); includes 9 minority (7 Black or African American, non-Hispanic/Latino; 1 Asian, non-Hispanic/Latino; 1 Two or more races, non-Hispanic/Latino), 4 international. Average age 33. 33 applicants, 42% accepted, 9 enrolled. In 2016, 21 master's, 3 doctorates awarded. *Degree requirements:* For doctorate, comprehensive exam, thesis/dissertation. *Entrance requirements:* For master's, GRE or GMAT, transcripts from all institutions attended, resume, essays; for doctorate, GRE or GMAT, three letters of recommendation, personal statement, transcripts from all institutions attended, resume. Additional exam requirements/recommendations for international students: Required—TOEFL (minimum score 610 paper-based; 101 iBT), IELTS (minimum score 7). *Application deadline:* For fall admission, 5/1 priority date for domestic students, 2/1 priority date for international students; for spring admission, 9/15 priority date for domestic students, 4/1 priority date for international students. Applications are processed on a rolling basis. Application fee: $50. Electronic applications accepted. *Expenses:* Tuition, state resident: full-time $6876; part-time $382 per credit hour. Tuition, nonresident: full-time $22,374; part-time $1243 per credit hour. *Required fees:* $2128; $1064 per term. Part-time tuition and fees vary according to course load and program. *Financial support:* Research assistantships, teaching assistantships, scholarships/grants, and unspecified assistantships available. *Faculty research:* International real estate investments, corporate real estate, capital formation, consumer behavior applied to real estate, real estate development. *Unit head:* Dr. Gerald D. Gay, Professor of Finance/Interim Chair of the Department of Real Estate, 404-413-7720, Fax: 404-413-7736. *Application contact:* Toby McChesney, Assistant Dean for Graduate Recruiting and Student Services, 404-413-7167, Fax: 404-413-7162, E-mail: rcbgradadmissions@gsu.edu.
Website: http://realestate.robinson.gsu.edu/

Instituto Centroamericano de Administración de Empresas, Graduate Programs, La Garita, Costa Rica. Offers agribusiness management (MIAM); business administration (EMBA); finance (MBA); real estate management (MGREM); sustainable development (MBA); technology (MBA). *Degree requirements:* For master's, comprehensive exam, essay. *Entrance requirements:* For master's, GMAT or GRE General Test, fluency in Spanish, interview, letters of recommendation, minimum 1 year of work experience. Additional exam requirements/recommendations for international students: Recommended—TOEFL. Electronic applications accepted. *Faculty research:* Competitiveness, production.

Johns Hopkins University, Carey Business School, MS in Real Estate and Infrastructure Program, Baltimore, MD 21218. Offers MS. *Program availability:* Part-time, evening/weekend. *Faculty:* 87 full-time (32 women), 51 part-time/adjunct (8 women). *Students:* 28 full-time (9 women), 64 part-time (18 women); includes 15 minority (8 Black or African American, non-Hispanic/Latino; 4 Asian, non-Hispanic/Latino; 3 Hispanic/Latino), 20 international. Average age 24. 114 applicants, 90% accepted, 41 enrolled. In 2016, 57 master's awarded. *Degree requirements:* For master's, 36 credits. *Entrance requirements:* For master's, GMAT or GRE. Additional exam requirements/recommendations for international students: Required—TOEFL, IELTS. *Application deadline:* For fall admission, 5/1 for domestic and international students. Applications are processed on a rolling basis. Application fee: $100. Electronic applications accepted. *Expenses:* $64,000 (full-time); $1,290 per credit (part-time). *Financial support:* In 2016–17, 37 students received support. Scholarships/grants available. Support available to part-time students. Financial award application deadline: 4/15; financial award applicants required to submit FAFSA. *Faculty research:* Real estate markets and investment, retail businesses and product differentiation, spatial competition in cities, structural modeling and estimation. *Unit head:* Dr. Kevin Frick, Vice Dean of Education, 410-234-9272, E-mail: kfrick@jhu.edu. *Application contact:* Office of Admissions, 410-234-9220, Fax: 443-529-1554, E-mail: carey.admissions@jhu.edu.
Website: http://carey.jhu.edu/academics/master-of-science/ms-in-real-estate-infrastructure/

Longwood University, College of Graduate and Professional Studies, College of Business and Economics, Farmville, VA 23909. Offers general business (MBA); real estate (MBA); retail management (MBA). *Accreditation:* AACSB. *Program availability:* Part-time, online only, 100% online. *Degree requirements:* For master's, internship. *Entrance requirements:* For master's, GMAT or GRE, personal essay, 3 recommendations, official transcripts from all colleges and universities attended. Additional exam requirements/recommendations for international students: Required—TOEFL (minimum score 570 paper-based), IELTS (minimum score 6.5). Electronic applications accepted. *Expenses:* Contact institution.

Marquette University, Graduate School of Management, Department of Economics, Milwaukee, WI 53201-1881. Offers business economics (MSAE); financial economics (MSAE); international economics (MSAE); marketing research (MSAE); real estate economics (MSAE). *Program availability:* Part-time, evening/weekend. *Faculty:* 14 full-time (4 women), 2 part-time/adjunct (both women). *Students:* 14 full-time (2 women), 13 part-time (3 women); includes 5 minority (2 Asian, non-Hispanic/Latino; 3 Hispanic/Latino). Average age 26. 27 applicants, 67% accepted, 27 enrolled. In 2016, 17 master's awarded. *Degree requirements:* For master's, comprehensive exam, professional project. *Entrance requirements:* For master's, GMAT or GRE General Test. Additional exam requirements/recommendations for international students: Required—TOEFL, IELTS, PTE. *Application deadline:* For fall admission, 2/15 for domestic and international students. Applications are processed on a rolling basis. Application fee: $50. Electronic applications accepted. *Financial support:* Fellowships, research assistantships, teaching assistantships, Federal Work-Study, institutionally sponsored loans, scholarships/grants, and tuition waivers (full and partial) available. Support available to part-time students. Financial award application deadline: 2/15. *Faculty research:* Monetary and fiscal policy in open economy, housing and regional migration, political economy of taxation and state/local government. *Unit head:* Dr. Brian Till, Dean, 414-288-5724. *Application contact:* Dr. Jeanne Simmons, Associate Dean, 414-288-7145.
Website: http://business.marquette.edu/academics/msae

Marylhurst University, Master of Business Administration Program, Marylhurst, OR 97036-0261. Offers health care management (MBA); real estate (MBA); sustainable business (MBA). *Program availability:* Part-time, evening/weekend, 100% online, blended/hybrid learning. *Students:* 153 (82 women); includes 34 minority (5 Black or African American, non-Hispanic/Latino; 1 American Indian or Alaska Native, non-Hispanic/Latino; 12 Asian, non-Hispanic/Latino; 12 Hispanic/Latino; 4 Two or more races, non-Hispanic/Latino), 1 international. Average age 38. In 2016, 173 master's awarded. *Degree requirements:* For master's, capstone course. *Entrance requirements:* For master's, resume, official transcript from regionally-accredited institution, recommendations, five years of full-time professional experience, statement of intent. Additional exam requirements/recommendations for international students: Required—TOEFL (minimum score 79 iBT), PTE or IELTS (6.5). *Application deadline:* Applications are processed on a rolling basis. Application fee: $0. Electronic applications accepted. *Expenses:* Contact institution. *Financial support:* Career-related internships or fieldwork and scholarships/grants available. Support available to part-time students. Financial award applicants required to submit FAFSA. *Unit head:* Stuart Noble-Goodman, School of Business Director, 503-699-6315, E-mail: snoblegoodman@marylhurst.edu. *Application contact:* Laura Sequeira, Graduate Admissions Counselor, 503-699-6268, E-mail: lsequeira@marylhurst.edu.
Website: http://www.marylhurst.edu/

Massachusetts Institute of Technology, School of Architecture and Planning, Center for Real Estate, Cambridge, MA 02139. Offers real estate development (MSRED). *Faculty:* 3 full-time (0 women), 11 part-time/adjunct (3 women). *Students:* 35 full-time (13 women); includes 5 minority (3 Asian, non-Hispanic/Latino; 1 Hispanic/Latino; 1 Two or more races, non-Hispanic/Latino), 20 international. Average age 32. 125 applicants, 33% accepted, 30 enrolled. In 2016, 26 master's awarded. *Degree requirements:* For master's, thesis. *Entrance requirements:* For master's, GMAT or GRE General Test. Additional exam requirements/recommendations for international students: Required—TOEFL, IELTS. *Application deadline:* For fall admission, 1/15 for domestic and international students. Application fee: $75. Electronic applications accepted. *Expenses: Tuition:* Full-time $46,400; part-time $725 per credit. One-time fee: $312 full-time. Full-time tuition and fees vary according to course load and program. *Financial support:* In 2016–17, 9 students received support, including 12 fellowships (averaging $29,100 per year); research assistantships, teaching assistantships, Federal Work-Study, institutionally sponsored loans, scholarships/grants, traineeships, health care benefits, and unspecified assistantships also available. Support available to part-time students. Financial award application deadline: 5/1; financial award applicants required to submit FAFSA. *Faculty research:* Methods, urban economics, entrepreneurship, strategic planning, housing, leadership development, international housing economics and finance, mortgage securitization, innovation, big data, the local tax implications of inefficient land use, post-war neighborhood decline, the supply of workplace flexibility, LinkedIn economic graph. *Unit head:* Prof. Albert Saiz, Director, 617-253-4373, Fax: 617-258-6991, E-mail: mit-cre@mit.edu. *Application contact:* 617-253-4373, E-mail: msredadmissions@mit.edu.
Website: https://mitcre.mit.edu/

Monmouth University, Graduate Studies, Leon Hess Business School, West Long Branch, NJ 07764-1898. Offers accounting (MBA, Post-Master's Certificate); business administration (MBA); finance (MBA); management (MBA); marketing (MBA); real estate (MBA). *Accreditation:* AACSB. *Program availability:* Part-time, evening/weekend. *Faculty:* 20 full-time (4 women), 8 part-time/adjunct (0 women). *Students:* 76 full-time (37 women), 94 part-time (43 women); includes 17 minority (2 Black or African American, non-Hispanic/Latino; 6 Asian, non-Hispanic/Latino; 6 Hispanic/Latino; 1 Native Hawaiian or other Pacific Islander, non-Hispanic/Latino; 2 Two or more races, non-Hispanic/Latino), 8 international. Average age 30. 105 applicants, 90% accepted, 67 enrolled. In 2016, 93 master's, 1 other advanced degree awarded. *Degree requirements:* For master's, capstone course. *Entrance requirements:* For master's, GMAT or GRE, current resume; essay (500 words or less). Additional exam requirements/recommendations for international students: Required—TOEFL (minimum score 550 paper-based; 79 iBT), IELTS (minimum score 6), Michigan English Language

Assessment Battery (minimum score 77) or Certificate of Advanced English (minimum score B2). *Application deadline:* For fall admission, 7/15 priority date for domestic students, 6/1 for international students; for spring admission, 12/1 priority date for domestic students, 11/1 for international students; for summer admission, 5/1 for domestic students. Applications are processed on a rolling basis. Application fee: $50. Electronic applications accepted. *Expenses: Tuition, area resident:* Full-time $19,764; part-time $1098 per credit hour. *Required fees:* $175 per semester. Tuition and fees vary according to program. *Financial support:* In 2016–17, 191 students received support, including 137 fellowships (averaging $2,643 per year), 20 teaching assistantships with full and partial tuition reimbursements available (averaging $10,034 per year); research assistantships, institutionally sponsored loans, scholarships/grants, and unspecified assistantships also available. Support available to part-time students. Financial award application deadline: 2/1; financial award applicants required to submit FAFSA. *Faculty research:* Information technology and marketing, behavioral research in accounting, human resources, management of technology. *Unit head:* Dr. Susan Gupta, MBA Program Director, 732-571-3639, Fax: 732-263-5517, E-mail: sgupta@monmouth.edu. *Application contact:* Laurie Kuhn, Associate Director of Graduate Admission, 732-571-3452, Fax: 732-263-5123, E-mail: gradadm@monmouth.edu.
Website: https://www.monmouth.edu/business-school/leon-hess-business-school.aspx

See Display on page 118 and Close-Up on page 181.

New York University, School of Continuing and Professional Studies, Schack Institute of Real Estate, Program in Real Estate, New York, NY 10012-1019. Offers finance and investment (MS); real estate (Advanced Certificate); real estate management (MS). *Program availability:* Part-time, evening/weekend. *Degree requirements:* For master's, thesis, capstone. *Entrance requirements:* For master's, GRE or GMAT (only upon request), bachelor's degree, resume with relevant professional work, internship or volunteer experience, two letters of recommendation, statement of purpose. Additional exam requirements/recommendations for international students: Required—TOEFL (minimum score 600 paper-based; 100 iBT), IELTS (minimum score 7). Electronic applications accepted. *Faculty research:* Economics and market cycles, international property rights, comparative metropolitan economies, current market trends.

New York University, School of Continuing and Professional Studies, Schack Institute of Real Estate, Program in Real Estate Development, New York, NY 10012-1019. Offers global real estate (MS); sustainable development (MS); the business of development (MS). *Program availability:* Part-time, evening/weekend. *Degree requirements:* For master's, thesis, capstone project. *Entrance requirements:* For master's, GRE or GMAT (only upon request), bachelor's degree, resume with relevant professional work, internship or volunteer experience, two letters of recommendation, statement of purpose. Additional exam requirements/recommendations for international students: Required—TOEFL (minimum score 600 paper-based; 100 iBT), IELTS (minimum score 7). Electronic applications accepted. *Faculty research:* Valuation, real estate capital markets, regional economics, real estate investment trusts.

Northwestern University, The Graduate School, Kellogg School of Management, Management Programs, Evanston, IL 60208. Offers accounting information and management (MBA, PhD); analytical finance (MBA); business administration (MBA); decision sciences (MBA); entrepreneurship and innovation (MBA); finance (MBA, PhD); health enterprise management (MBA); human resources management (MBA); international business (MBA); management and organizations (MBA, PhD); management and organizations and sociology (PhD); management and strategy (MBA); management studies (MS); managerial analytics (MBA); managerial economics (MBA); managerial economics and strategy (PhD); marketing (MBA, PhD); marketing management (MBA); media management (MBA); operations management (MBA, PhD); real estate (MBA); social enterprise at Kellogg (MBA); JD/MBA. *Program availability:* Part-time, evening/weekend. Terminal master's awarded for partial completion of doctoral program. *Degree requirements:* For doctorate, thesis/dissertation, 2 years of coursework, qualifying (field) exam and candidacy, summer research papers and presentations to faculty, proposal defense, final exam/defense. *Entrance requirements:* For master's, GMAT, GRE, interview, 2 letters of recommendation, college transcripts, resume, essays, Kellogg honor code; for doctorate, GMAT, GRE, statement of purpose, transcripts, 2 letters of recommendation, resume, interview. Additional exam requirements/recommendations for international students: Required—TOEFL, IELTS. Electronic applications accepted. *Expenses:* Contact institution. *Faculty research:* Business cycles and international finance, health policy, networks, non-market strategy, consumer psychology.

Pacific States University, College of Business, Los Angeles, CA 90010. Offers accounting (MBA); finance (MBA); international business (MBA, DBA); management of information technology (MBA); real estate management (MBA). *Program availability:* Part-time, evening/weekend, online learning. *Degree requirements:* For doctorate, comprehensive exam, thesis/dissertation. *Entrance requirements:* For master's, minimum undergraduate GPA of 2.5 during last 90 hours of course work. Additional exam requirements/recommendations for international students: Required—TOEFL (minimum score 500 paper-based; 61 iBT), IELTS (minimum score 5.5).

Philadelphia University, College of Architecture and the Built Environment, Program in Real Estate Development, Philadelphia, PA 19144. Offers MS.

Pontificia Universidad Catolica Madre y Maestra, Graduate School, Faculty of Social and Administrative Sciences, Santiago, Dominican Republic. Offers business administration (MBA), including business development, finance, international business, management skills (M Mgmt, MBA), marketing, operations, strategic cost management, strategy, tourist destination planning and management; law (LL M), including civil law, corporate business law, criminal law, international relations, real estate law; management (M Mgmt), including higher financial management, insurance program administration, management skills (M Mgmt, MBA); psychology (MA), including clinical child and adolescent psychology, forensic psychology; strategic human resources (EMBA).

Portland State University, Graduate Studies, School of Business Administration, Master of Real Estate Development Program, Portland, OR 97207-0751. Offers MRED. *Students:* 21 full-time (7 women), 25 part-time (10 women); includes 6 minority (1 Black or African American, non-Hispanic/Latino; 3 Asian, non-Hispanic/Latino; 2 Hispanic/Latino), 3 international. Average age 32. 37 applicants, 89% accepted, 24 enrolled. In 2016, 21 master's awarded. *Degree requirements:* For master's, real estate development workshop. *Entrance requirements:* For master's, GMAT or GRE, resume, essay, 2 professional references, transcripts. Additional exam requirements/recommendations for international students: Required—TOEFL (minimum score 550 paper-based; 80 iBT). *Application deadline:* For fall admission, 5/1 priority date for domestic and international students; for spring admission, 1/15 priority date for domestic and international students. Application fee: $65. Electronic applications accepted. *Expenses:* Contact institution. *Financial support:* Career-related internships or fieldwork, scholarships/grants, and unspecified assistantships available. *Unit head:* Gerald Mildner, Director, 503-725-5175, E-mail: mildnerg@pdx.edu. *Application contact:* Pam Mitchell, Administrator, 503-725-4733, E-mail: mitchep@pdx.edu.
Website: https://www.pdx.edu/realestate/

Pratt Institute, School of Architecture, Program in Real Estate Practice, Brooklyn, NY 11205-3899. Offers MS. *Program availability:* Part-time, evening/weekend. *Degree requirements:* For master's, thesis optional. *Entrance requirements:* For master's, bachelor's degree in business, architecture, business, construction management, engineering, or interior design; 500-word statement of purpose. Additional exam requirements/recommendations for international students: Required—TOEFL (minimum score 550 paper-based; 79 iBT), IELTS (minimum score 6.5), PTE. *Expenses: Tuition:* Full-time $29,646. *Required fees:* $1938.

Roosevelt University, Graduate Division, Walter E. Heller College of Business, School of Finance and Real Estate, Chicago, IL 60605. Offers commercial real estate development (Certificate); real estate (MS). *Students:* 7 full-time (5 women), 31 part-time (12 women); includes 19 minority (15 Black or African American, non-Hispanic/Latino; 3 Hispanic/Latino; 1 Two or more races, non-Hispanic/Latino), 2 international. Average age 36. 7 applicants, 100% accepted, 4 enrolled. In 2016, 3 master's awarded. Application fee: $40. *Expenses: Tuition, area resident:* Full-time $19,566; part-time $880 per credit hour. *Required fees:* $175 per semester. One-time fee: $200. Part-time tuition and fees vary according to course load, degree level and program. *Unit head:* Henry Silverman, Real Estate Chair, 312-281-3319, Fax: 312-281-3290. *Application contact:* Angela Ryan, Director of Graduate Enrollment, 877-APPLY RU, Fax: 312-281-3356, E-mail: applyru@roosevelt.edu.
Website: https://www.roosevelt.edu/academics/programs/masters-in-real-estate-msre

Rutgers University–Newark, Rutgers Business School–Newark and New Brunswick, Program in Real Estate and Logistics, Newark, NJ 07102. Offers MRE.

San Jose State University, Graduate Studies and Research, College of Social Sciences, San Jose, CA 95192-0001. Offers applications of technology in planning (Certificate); applied anthropology (MA); communication studies (MS); community design and development (Certificate); economics (MA), including applied economics, social sciences; environmental planning (Certificate); geographic information science (Certificate); geography (MA); global citizenship (Certificate); history (MA), including history education, social sciences; Mexican American studies (MA); psychology (MA, MS), including clinical psychology (MS), industrial/organizational psychology (MS), research and experimental psychology (MA); public administration (MA); real estate development (Certificate); social sciences (MPA, MS); sociology (MA); transportation and land use planning (Certificate). *Program availability:* Part-time, evening/weekend. *Entrance requirements:* For master's, minimum GPA of 3.0. Electronic applications accepted.

Southern Methodist University, Cox School of Business, MBA Program, Dallas, TX 75275. Offers accounting (MBA, PMBA); business administration (EMBA); finance (MBA); financial statement analysis (PMBA); general business (MBA); information technology and operations management (MBA); management (MBA); marketing (MBA); real estate (MBA); strategy (MBA); strategy and entrepreneurship (MBA); JD/MBA; MA/MBA. *Program availability:* Part-time, evening/weekend. *Entrance requirements:* For master's, GMAT. Additional exam requirements/recommendations for international students: Required—TOEFL. Electronic applications accepted. *Expenses:* Contact institution. *Faculty research:* Corporate finance, financial reporting, modeling consumer decision-making, competition between national brands and store brands, institutional determinants of firms' strategy.

Syracuse University, Martin J. Whitman School of Management, Master of Business Administration Program, Syracuse, NY 13244. Offers accounting (MBA); business analytics (MBA); entrepreneurship (MBA); marketing management (MBA); real estate (MBA); supply chain management (MBA); JD/MBA. *Program availability:* Part-time, 100% online. *Students:* 22 full-time (9 women), 495 part-time (147 women); includes 182 minority (81 Black or African American, non-Hispanic/Latino; 3 American Indian or Alaska Native, non-Hispanic/Latino; 42 Asian, non-Hispanic/Latino; 52 Hispanic/Latino; 4 Native Hawaiian or other Pacific Islander, non-Hispanic/Latino), 22 international. Average age 32. 1,086 applicants, 73% accepted, 518 enrolled. In 2016, 84 master's awarded. *Entrance requirements:* For master's, GMAT or GRE, resume, essay, 5-minute video interview, two letters of recommendation, transcripts (unofficial). Additional exam requirements/recommendations for international students: Required—TOEFL (minimum score 100 iBT), IELTS (minimum score 7), PTE (minimum score 68). *Application deadline:* For fall admission, 11/30 for domestic students, 11/30 priority date for international students; for winter admission, 1/1 for domestic students, 1/1 priority date for international students; for spring admission, 2/15 for domestic and international students; for summer admission, 4/19 for domestic students. Application fee: $75. Electronic applications accepted. *Expenses:* Contact institution. *Financial support:* In 2016–17, 22 students received support. Merit scholarships available. Financial award application deadline: 2/15. *Faculty research:* Data analysis, economics of international business, financial markets and institutions, operations management, supply chain management. *Unit head:* Don Harter, Associate Dean, Graduate Programs, 315-443-3502, E-mail: dharter@syr.edu. *Application contact:* Shri Ramakrishnan, Assistant Director, Graduate Recruitment, 315-443-3497, Fax: 315-443-9517, E-mail: busgrad@syr.edu.
Website: http://whitman.syr.edu/ftmba/

Texas A&M University, Mays Business School, Department of Finance, College Station, TX 77843. Offers finance (MS); financial management (MFM); land economics and real estate (MRE). *Faculty:* 20. *Students:* 197 full-time (68 women), 21 part-time (3 women); includes 22 minority (8 Asian, non-Hispanic/Latino; 10 Hispanic/Latino; 4 Two or more races, non-Hispanic/Latino), 24 international. Average age 24. 293 applicants, 35% accepted, 76 enrolled. In 2016, 138 master's awarded. Terminal master's awarded for partial completion of doctoral program. *Degree requirements:* For master's, comprehensive exam. *Entrance requirements:* For master's, GMAT or GRE. Additional exam requirements/recommendations for international students: Required—TOEFL (minimum score 550 paper-based; 80 iBT), IELTS (minimum score 6), PTE (minimum score 53). *Application deadline:* For fall admission, 4/7 for domestic students. Applications are processed on a rolling basis. Application fee: $50 ($90 for international students). Electronic applications accepted. *Expenses:* Contact institution. *Financial support:* In 2016–17, 157 students received support, including 9 fellowships with tuition reimbursements available (averaging $3,944 per year), 18 research assistantships with tuition reimbursements available (averaging $5,933 per year), 16 teaching assistantships with tuition reimbursements available (averaging $4,326 per year); career-related internships or fieldwork, institutionally sponsored loans, scholarships/grants, traineeships, health care benefits, tuition waivers (full and partial), and unspecified assistantships also available. Support available to part-time students. Financial award application deadline: 3/15; financial award applicants required to submit FAFSA. *Unit head:* Dr. Sorin Sorescu, Head, 979-458-0380, Fax: 979-845-3884, E-mail: smsorescu@mays.tamu.edu. *Application contact:* Angela G. Degelman, Program Coordinator/Graduate Academic Advisor, 979-845-4858, Fax: 979-845-3884, E-mail: adegelman@mays.tamu.edu.
Website: http://mays.tamu.edu/finc/

Universidad Iberoamericana, Graduate School, Santo Domingo D.N., Dominican Republic. Offers business administration (MBA, PMBA); constitutional law (LL M); dentistry (DMD); educational management (MA); integrated marketing communication

(MA); psychopedagogical intervention (M Ed); real estate law (LL M); strategic management of human talent (MM).

University at Buffalo, the State University of New York, Graduate School, School of Architecture and Planning, Department of Architecture, Buffalo, NY 14214. Offers architecture (M Arch); ecological practices (MS Arch); historic preservation and urban design (MS Arch); inclusive design (MS Arch); real estate development (MS Arch); situated technology (MS Arch); M Arch/MBA; M Arch/MFA; M Arch/MUP. *Faculty:* 32 full-time (11 women), 9 part-time/adjunct (3 women). *Students:* 134 full-time (56 women), 15 part-time (5 women); includes 29 minority (12 Black or African American, non-Hispanic/Latino; 5 Asian, non-Hispanic/Latino; 8 Hispanic/Latino; 4 Two or more races, non-Hispanic/Latino), 27 international. Average age 25. 267 applicants, 34% accepted, 63 enrolled. In 2016, 44 master's awarded. *Degree requirements:* For master's, thesis or alternative, project. *Entrance requirements:* For master's, GRE, portfolio, 3 letters of recommendation, transcripts, 500-word personal statement. Additional exam requirements/recommendations for international students: Required—TOEFL (minimum score 79 iBT), IELTS (minimum score 6.5). *Application deadline:* For fall admission, 1/1 priority date for domestic and international students. Application fee: $75. Electronic applications accepted. *Expenses:* Contact institution. *Financial support:* In 2016–17, 5 students received support, including 5 fellowships with full tuition reimbursements available (averaging $11,040 per year), 2 research assistantships with partial tuition reimbursements available (averaging $13,200 per year), 43 teaching assistantships with partial tuition reimbursements available (averaging $4,337 per year); career-related internships or fieldwork, Federal Work-Study, scholarships/grants, health care benefits, and unspecified assistantships also available. Financial award application deadline: 3/1; financial award applicants required to submit FAFSA. *Faculty research:* Ecological practices, inclusive design, material culture, situated technologies, urban design. *Total annual research expenditures:* $3.8 million. *Unit head:* Prof. Omar Khan, Chair, 716-829-3483 Ext. 105, Fax: 716-829-3256, E-mail: omar.khan@buffalo.edu. *Application contact:* Debra Eggebrecht, Assistant to the Chair, 716-829-3486 Ext. 105, Fax: 716-829-3256, E-mail: dle2@buffalo.edu.
Website: http://www.ap.buffalo.edu/architecture/

University of California, Berkeley, Graduate Division, Haas School of Business, PhD in Business Administration Program, Berkeley, CA 94720-1500. Offers accounting (PhD); business and public policy (PhD); finance (PhD); management of organizations (PhD); marketing (PhD); real estate (PhD). *Accreditation:* AACSB. *Students:* 78 full-time (28 women); includes 34 minority (29 Asian, non-Hispanic/Latino; 5 Hispanic/Latino). Average age 27. *Degree requirements:* For doctorate, comprehensive exam, thesis/dissertation, written preliminary exams, oral qualifying exam. *Entrance requirements:* For doctorate, GMAT or GRE, minimum GPA of 3.0 in undergraduate and graduate coursework. Additional exam requirements/recommendations for international students: Required—TOEFL (minimum score 570 paper-based; 70 iBT), IELTS (minimum score 7). *Application deadline:* For fall admission, 12/1 for domestic and international students. Application fee: $90 ($110 for international students). Electronic applications accepted. *Expenses:* Contact institution. *Financial support:* Fellowships with tuition reimbursements, research assistantships with tuition reimbursements, teaching assistantships with tuition reimbursements, scholarships/grants, health care benefits, tuition waivers (full), unspecified assistantships, and transit passes, travel grants available. Financial award application deadline: 12/10. *Faculty research:* Accounting, business and public policy, entrepreneurship, finance, management of organizations, marketing, operations and information technology management, real estate. *Unit head:* Dr. Nicolae Garleanu, Director, 510-643-6349, Fax: 510-643-4255. *Application contact:* Melissa Hacker, Director, Student Affairs, 510-642-3944, Fax: 510-643-4255, E-mail: melhacker@haas.berkeley.edu.
Website: http://www.haas.berkeley.edu/Phd/

University of Denver, Daniels College of Business, Franklin L. Burns School of Real Estate and Construction Management, Denver, CO 80208. Offers real estate and the built environment (MBA, MS). *Program availability:* Part-time, evening/weekend. *Faculty:* 7 full-time (1 woman), 7 part-time/adjunct (1 woman). *Students:* 19 full-time (1 woman), 68 part-time (19 women); includes 19 minority (2 Black or African American, non-Hispanic/Latino; 4 Asian, non-Hispanic/Latino; 7 Hispanic/Latino; 6 Two or more races, non-Hispanic/Latino), 3 international. Average age 35. 62 applicants, 90% accepted, 39 enrolled. In 2016, 30 master's awarded. *Entrance requirements:* For master's, GRE General Test or GMAT, bachelor's degree, transcripts, essays, resume, interview. Additional exam requirements/recommendations for international students: Required—TOEFL (minimum score 570 paper-based; 88 iBT), TWE. *Application deadline:* For fall admission, 11/15 priority date for domestic and international students; for spring admission, 10/1 priority date for domestic and international students. Applications are processed on a rolling basis. Application fee: $100. Electronic applications accepted. *Expenses:* $43,458 per year full-time. *Financial support:* In 2016–17, 54 students received support, including 2 teaching assistantships with tuition reimbursements available (averaging $1,492 per year); Federal Work-Study, institutionally sponsored loans, scholarships/grants, and unspecified assistantships also available. Support available to part-time students. Financial award application deadline: 2/15; financial award applicants required to submit FAFSA. *Unit head:* Dr. Barbara Jackson, Associate Professor and Director, 303-871-3470, Fax: 303-871-2971, E-mail: barbara.jackson@du.edu.
Website: https://daniels.du.edu/burns-school/

University of Florida, Graduate School, Warrington College of Business Administration, Hough Graduate School of Business, Department of Finance, Insurance and Real Estate, Gainesville, FL 32611. Offers entrepreneurship (MS); finance (MS, PhD); financial services (Certificate); insurance (PhD); quantitative finance (PhD); real estate (MS); real estate and urban analysis (PhD); JD/MBA; JD/MS. Terminal master's awarded for partial completion of doctoral program. *Degree requirements:* For master's, comprehensive exam, thesis; for doctorate, comprehensive exam, thesis/dissertation. *Entrance requirements:* For master's, GMAT (minimum score of 465) or GRE General Test, minimum GPA of 3.0 for last 60 hours of undergraduate degree, work experience (preferred); for doctorate, GMAT (minimum score of 465) or GRE General Test, minimum GPA of 3.0. Additional exam requirements/recommendations for international students: Required—TOEFL (minimum score 550 paper-based; 80 iBT), IELTS (minimum score 6). Electronic applications accepted. *Faculty research:* Banking, empirical corporate finance, hedge funds.

University of Florida, Graduate School, Warrington College of Business Administration, Hough Graduate School of Business, Programs in Business Administration, Gainesville, FL 32611. Offers business administration (MA, MS, PhD); competitive strategy (MBA); finance (MBA); global management (MBA); Graham-Buffett security analysis (MBA); human resource management (MBA); information systems and operations management (MBA); international studies (MBA); management (MBA); real estate (MBA); JD/MBA; MBA/MS; MBA/PhD; MBA/Pharm D; MD/MBA. *Accreditation:* AACSB. *Program availability:* Part-time, evening/weekend, online learning. *Degree requirements:* For master's, capstone course. *Entrance requirements:* For master's and doctorate, GMAT (minimum score 465), minimum GPA of 3.0, interview. Additional exam requirements/recommendations for international students: Required—TOEFL (minimum score 550 paper-based; 80 iBT), IELTS (minimum score 6). Electronic applications accepted. *Faculty research:* Accounting, finance, insurance, management, real estate, urban analysis marketing.

University of Hawaii at Manoa, Graduate Division, Shidler College of Business, Program in Business Administration, Honolulu, HI 96822. Offers Asian business studies (MBA); Chinese business studies (MBA); decision sciences (MBA); entrepreneurship (MBA); finance (MBA); finance and banking (MBA); human resources management (MBA); information management (MBA); information technology (MBA); international business (MBA); Japanese business studies (MBA); marketing (MBA); organizational behavior (MBA); organizational management (MBA); real estate (MBA); student-designed track (MBA). *Accreditation:* AACSB. *Program availability:* Part-time, evening/weekend. *Degree requirements:* For master's, thesis optional. *Entrance requirements:* For master's, GMAT, minimum GPA of 3.0. Additional exam requirements/recommendations for international students: Required—TOEFL (minimum score 600 paper-based; 100 iBT), IELTS (minimum score 7). *Expenses:* Contact institution.

University of Illinois at Chicago, Liautaud Graduate School of Business, Program in Real Estate, Chicago, IL 60607-7128. Offers MA.

University of Maryland, College Park, Academic Affairs, School of Architecture, Planning and Preservation, Program in Real Estate Development, College Park, MD 20742. Offers MRED.

University of Memphis, Graduate School, Fogelman College of Business and Economics, Program in Business Administration, Memphis, TN 38152. Offers accounting (MBA, PhD); business administration (IMBA); economics (PhD); executive business administration (MBA); finance (PhD); management (PhD); marketing (MS); marketing and supply chain management (PhD); real estate development (MS); JD/MBA. *Accreditation:* AACSB. *Faculty:* 44 full-time (9 women), 5 part-time/adjunct (0 women). *Students:* 167 full-time (64 women), 341 part-time (119 women); includes 154 minority (80 Black or African American, non-Hispanic/Latino; 1 American Indian or Alaska Native, non-Hispanic/Latino; 43 Asian, non-Hispanic/Latino; 12 Hispanic/Latino; 1 Native Hawaiian or other Pacific Islander, non-Hispanic/Latino; 17 Two or more races, non-Hispanic/Latino), 96 international. Average age 33. 306 applicants, 64% accepted, 154 enrolled. In 2016, 273 master's, 7 doctorates awarded. *Degree requirements:* For master's, comprehensive exam; for doctorate, comprehensive exam, thesis/dissertation. *Entrance requirements:* For master's, GMAT, resume; for doctorate, GMAT, interview, minimum GPA of 3.4, resume, letter of recommendation. Additional exam requirements/recommendations for international students: Required—TOEFL (minimum score 550 paper-based). *Application deadline:* For fall admission, 8/1 for domestic students; for spring admission, 12/1 for domestic students. Application fee: $35 ($60 for international students). *Expenses:* Tuition, state resident: full-time $10,463; part-time $9483 per year. Tuition, nonresident: full-time $19,247; part-time $17,291 per year. *Required fees:* $821.50 per semester. Tuition and fees vary according to course load and program. *Financial support:* In 2016–17, 164 students received support. Research assistantships with full tuition reimbursements available, teaching assistantships with full tuition reimbursements available, career-related internships or fieldwork, Federal Work-Study, scholarships/grants, and unspecified assistantships available. Financial award application deadline: 2/15; financial award applicants required to submit FAFSA. *Faculty research:* Competitive business strategy, finance microstructures, supply chain management innovations, health care economics, litigation risks and corporate audits. *Unit head:* Dr. Rajiv Grover, Dean, 901-678-3759, E-mail: rgrover@memphis.edu. *Application contact:* Dr. Carol V. Danehower, Associate Dean, 901-678-5402, Fax: 901-678-3579, E-mail: fcbegp@memphis.edu.
Website: https://web0.memphis.edu/gradcatalog/degreeprog/fcbe/fcbe.php

University of Miami, Graduate School, University of Miami School of Law, Coral Gables, FL 33124-8087. Offers entertainment, arts, and sports law (LL M); estate planning (LL M); international arbitration (LL M); international law (LL M), including general international law, inter-American law, U.S. and transnational law for foreign lawyers; law (JD); maritime law (LL M); real estate/property development (LL M); taxation (LL M); taxation of cross-border investment (LL M); JD/LL M; JD/MA; JD/MBA; JD/MBA/LL M; JD/MD; JD/MM; JD/MPA; JD/MPH; JD/MPS; JD/MS Ed; JD/PhD. *Accreditation:* ABA. *Program availability:* Part-time. *Faculty:* 78 full-time (35 women), 98 part-time/adjunct (22 women). *Students:* 995 full-time (464 women), 74 part-time (33 women); includes 457 minority (69 Black or African American, non-Hispanic/Latino; 3 American Indian or Alaska Native, non-Hispanic/Latino; 31 Asian, non-Hispanic/Latino; 323 Hispanic/Latino; 1 Native Hawaiian or other Pacific Islander, non-Hispanic/Latino; 30 Two or more races, non-Hispanic/Latino), 82 international. 2,443 applicants, 55% accepted, 300 enrolled. *Entrance requirements:* For doctorate, LSAT, 2 letters of recommendation. Additional exam requirements/recommendations for international students: Required—TOEFL (minimum score 580 paper-based; 92 iBT), IELTS (minimum score 7). *Application deadline:* For fall admission, 7/31 for domestic and international students. Applications are processed on a rolling basis. Application fee: $60. Electronic applications accepted. *Expenses:* Contact institution. *Financial support:* Fellowships, research assistantships, career-related internships or fieldwork, Federal Work-Study, institutionally sponsored loans, scholarships/grants, and unspecified assistantships available. Financial award application deadline: 3/1; financial award applicants required to submit FAFSA. *Faculty research:* Energy/climate change, international finance, Internet law/law of electronic commerce, race/social justice, art law/cultural heritage law. *Unit head:* Michael Goodnight, Associate Dean of Admissions and Enrollment Management, 305-284-2527, Fax: 305-284-3084, E-mail: mgoodnig@law.miami.edu. *Application contact:* Therese Lambert, Director of Student Recruitment, 305-284-6746, Fax: 305-284-3084, E-mail: tlambert@law.miami.edu.
Website: http://www.law.miami.edu/

The University of North Carolina at Charlotte, Belk College of Business, Interdisciplinary Business Programs, Charlotte, NC 28223-0001. Offers mathematical finance (MS); real estate (MS, Graduate Certificate). *Program availability:* Part-time, evening/weekend. *Faculty:* 10 full-time (4 women), 3 part-time/adjunct (0 women). *Students:* 59 full-time (22 women), 54 part-time (17 women); includes 20 minority (7 Black or African American, non-Hispanic/Latino; 9 Asian, non-Hispanic/Latino; 4 Hispanic/Latino), 44 international. Average age 28. 153 applicants, 75% accepted, 53 enrolled. In 2016, 47 master's, 1 other advanced degree awarded. *Degree requirements:* For master's, comprehensive exam (for some programs). *Entrance requirements:* For master's, GRE or GMAT, baccalaureate degree in related field with minimum GPA of 3.0 overall and in junior and senior years; transcript of all previous academic work; resume; recommendations; for Graduate Certificate, basic proficiency in using spreadsheet computer software, to be demonstrated by past project or certificate from completion of training course in Excel; previous coursework in financial management. Additional exam requirements/recommendations for international students: Required—TOEFL (minimum score 523 paper-based, 70 iBT) or IELTS (6.5). *Application deadline:* For fall admission, 3/1 priority date for domestic and international students; for spring admission, 10/1 priority date for domestic and international students; for summer admission, 4/1 priority date for domestic and international students. Applications are processed on a rolling basis. Application fee: $75. Electronic applications accepted. *Expenses:* Contact institution. *Financial support:* Career-related internships or fieldwork, scholarships/grants, and unspecified assistantships available. Support available to part-time students. Financial award application deadline: 3/1;

financial award applicants required to submit FAFSA. *Unit head:* Dr. Steven Ott, Dean, 704-687-7577, Fax: 704-687-1393, E-mail: cob-dean@uncc.edu. *Application contact:* Kathy B. Giddings, Director of Graduate Admissions, 704-687-5503, Fax: 704-687-1668, E-mail: gradadm@uncc.edu.
Website: http://belkcollege.uncc.edu/

University of Pennsylvania, Wharton School, Real Estate Department, Philadelphia, PA 19104. Offers MBA, PhD. Terminal master's awarded for partial completion of doctoral program. *Degree requirements:* For doctorate, thesis/dissertation. *Entrance requirements:* For master's, GMAT; for doctorate, GRE General Test. *Expenses: Tuition:* Full-time $31,068; part-time $5762 per course. *Required fees:* $3200; $336 per course. Full-time tuition and fees vary according to degree level, program and student level. Part-time tuition and fees vary according to course load, degree level and program. *Faculty research:* Public economics and taxation economics and finance of real estate markets, economics of housing markets, real estate development.

University of San Diego, School of Business, Program in Real Estate, San Diego, CA 92110-2492. Offers MS, MBA/MSRE. *Program availability:* Part-time, evening/weekend. *Students:* 16 full-time (2 women), 5 part-time (0 women); includes 6 minority (2 Black or African American, non-Hispanic/Latino; 3 Hispanic/Latino; 1 Two or more races, non-Hispanic/Latino), 1 international. Average age 30. In 2016, 17 master's awarded. *Degree requirements:* For master's, capstone course. *Entrance requirements:* For master's, GMAT (minimum score of 550), minimum GPA of 3.0. Additional exam requirements/recommendations for international students: Required—TOEFL (minimum score 580 paper-based; 92 iBT), TWE. *Application deadline:* For fall admission, 11/1 priority date for domestic students. Applications are processed on a rolling basis. Application fee: $80. Electronic applications accepted. *Financial support:* In 2016–17, 17 students received support. Research assistantships, career-related internships or fieldwork, Federal Work-Study, institutionally sponsored loans, and scholarships/grants available. Support available to part-time students. Financial award application deadline: 4/1; financial award applicants required to submit FAFSA. *Unit head:* Dr. Charles Tu, Academic Director, Real Estate Program, 619-260-5942, E-mail: tuc@sandiego.edu. *Application contact:* Monica Mahon, Associate Director of Graduate Admissions, 619-260-4524, Fax: 619-260-4158, E-mail: grads@sandiego.edu.
Website: http://www.sandiego.edu/business/programs/ms-real-estate/

University of South Africa, College of Economic and Management Sciences, Pretoria, South Africa. Offers accounting (D Admin, D Com); accounting science (DA); auditing (D Admin, D Com); business administration (M Tech); business economics (D Admin); business leadership (DBL); business management (D Admin, D Com); economic management analysis (M Tech); economics (D Admin, D Com, PhD); human resource development (M Tech); industrial psychology (D Admin, D Com, PhD); logistics (D Com); marketing (M Tech); public administration (D Admin, D Com, DPA, PhD); public management (M Tech); quantitative management (D Admin, D Com); real estate (M Tech); statistics (D Admin, PhD); tourism management (D Admin, D Com); transport economics (D Admin, D Com).

University of Southern California, Graduate School, School of Policy, Planning, and Development, Master of Real Estate Development Program, Los Angeles, CA 90089. Offers MRED, JD/MRED, M Pl/MRED, MBA/MRED. *Program availability:* Part-time. *Degree requirements:* For master's, comprehensive exam. *Entrance requirements:* For master's, GRE, GMAT. Additional exam requirements/recommendations for international students: Required—TOEFL (minimum score 600 paper-based; 100 iBT). Electronic applications accepted. *Expenses:* Contact institution. *Faculty research:* Urban development, urban economics, real estate finance, housing markets.

University of South Florida, Muma College of Business, Department of Finance, Tampa, FL 33620-9951. Offers business administration (PhD), including finance; finance (MS); real estate (MSRE). *Program availability:* Part-time, evening/weekend. *Faculty:* 14 full-time (3 women). *Students:* 80 full-time (32 women), 22 part-time (12 women); includes 5 minority (3 Asian, non-Hispanic/Latino; 2 Hispanic/Latino), 75 international. Average age 26. 117 applicants, 63% accepted, 48 enrolled. In 2016, 43 master's, 2 doctorates awarded. Terminal master's awarded for partial completion of doctoral program. *Degree requirements:* For master's, comprehensive exam, thesis or alternative; for doctorate, comprehensive exam, thesis/dissertation. *Entrance requirements:* For master's, GMAT, minimum undergraduate GPA of 3.0 in upper-division coursework; for doctorate, GMAT or GRE, minimum undergraduate GPA of 3.0 in upper-division coursework, personal statement, recommendations, interview. Additional exam requirements/recommendations for international students: Required—TOEFL (minimum score 550 paper-based; 79 iBT) or IELTS (minimum score 6.5). *Application deadline:* For fall admission, 1/2 for domestic and international students; for spring admission, 10/15 for domestic students, 7/1 for international students; for summer admission, 2/15 for domestic students, 1/1 for international students. Application fee: $30. Electronic applications accepted. *Expenses:* Tuition, state resident: full-time $7766; part-time $431.43 per credit hour. Tuition, nonresident: full-time $15,789; part-time $877.17 per credit hour. *Required fees:* $37 per term. *Financial support:* In 2016–17, 9 students received support, including 8 research assistantships (averaging $14,357 per year), 9 teaching assistantships with tuition reimbursements available (averaging $11,972 per year); scholarships/grants, health care benefits, and unspecified assistantships also available. Financial award application deadline: 6/30. *Faculty research:* International corporate finance, corporate finance, market efficiency, mergers and acquisitions, agency theory, corporate governance, investments, mutual fund industry, mergers and acquisitions, corporate creditworthiness, credit risk issues, empirical asset pricing, financial intermediation, corporate finance theory, public offerings, business strategy. *Unit head:* Dr. Scott Besley, Chairperson and Associate Professor, 813-974-6341, Fax: 813-974-3084, E-mail: sbesley@usf.edu. *Application contact:* Amy Dunkel, Office Manager, Finance Department, 813-974-6294, Fax: 813-974-3084, E-mail: adunkel@usf.edu.
Website: http://business.usf.edu/departments/finance/

The University of Texas at Arlington, Graduate School, College of Business, Department of Finance and Real Estate, Arlington, TX 76019. Offers finance (PhD); quantitative finance (MS); real estate (MS). *Program availability:* Part-time, evening/weekend. *Degree requirements:* For master's, thesis optional; for doctorate, comprehensive exam, thesis/dissertation. *Entrance requirements:* For master's, GMAT/GRE, minimum GPA of 3.0; for doctorate, GMAT/GRE. Additional exam requirements/recommendations for international students: Required—TOEFL (minimum score 550 paper-based; 79 iBT). *Application deadline:* For fall admission, 6/1 priority date for domestic students, 4/1 for international students; for spring admission, 10/15 for domestic students, 9/15 for international students. Applications are processed on a rolling basis. Application fee: $40 ($70 for international students). *Financial support:* Teaching assistantships, career-related internships or fieldwork, Federal Work-Study, institutionally sponsored loans, and unspecified assistantships available. Financial award application deadline: 6/1; financial award applicants required to submit FAFSA. *Unit head:* Dr. David Diltz, Chair, 817-272-3705, Fax: 817-272-2252, E-mail: diltz@uta.edu. *Application contact:* Dr. Fred Forgey, Graduate Advisor, 817-272-0359, Fax: 817-272-2252, E-mail: realestate@uta.edu.
Website: http://wweb.uta.edu/finance/

The University of Texas at Dallas, Naveen Jindal School of Management, Program in Finance and Managerial Economics, Richardson, TX 75080. Offers finance (MS), including corporate finance/investment banking, energy risk management, enterprise risk management, financial analysis, financial risk management, real estate. *Program availability:* Part-time, evening/weekend. *Faculty:* 24 full-time (2 women), 12 part-time/adjunct (5 women). *Students:* 295 full-time (124 women), 56 part-time (37 women); includes 34 minority (3 Black or African American, non-Hispanic/Latino; 21 Asian, non-Hispanic/Latino; 7 Hispanic/Latino; 3 Two or more races, non-Hispanic/Latino), 279 international. Average age 26. 793 applicants, 66% accepted, 157 enrolled. In 2016, 215 master's awarded. *Entrance requirements:* For master's, GMAT or GRE. Additional exam requirements/recommendations for international students: Required—TOEFL (minimum score 550 paper-based). *Application deadline:* For fall admission, 7/15 for domestic students, 5/1 priority date for international students; for spring admission, 11/15 for domestic students, 9/1 priority date for international students. Applications are processed on a rolling basis. Application fee: $50 ($100 for international students). Electronic applications accepted. *Expenses:* Tuition, state resident: full-time $12,418; part-time $690 per semester hour. Tuition, nonresident: full-time $24,150; part-time $1342 per semester hour. Tuition and fees vary according to course load. *Financial support:* In 2016–17, 55 students received support, including 9 teaching assistantships with partial tuition reimbursements available (averaging $10,050 per year); research assistantships with partial tuition reimbursements available, career-related internships or fieldwork, Federal Work-Study, institutionally sponsored loans, scholarships/grants, and unspecified assistantships also available. Support available to part-time students. Financial award application deadline: 4/30; financial award applicants required to submit FAFSA. *Faculty research:* Econometrics, industrial organization, auction theory, file-sharing copyrights and bundling, international financial management, entrepreneurial finance. *Unit head:* Dr. Harold Zhang, Area Coordinator, 972-883-4777, E-mail: harold.zhang@utdallas.edu. *Application contact:* Kristin Spain, Academic Support Coordinator, 972-883-2373, E-mail: kes160430@utdallas.edu.
Website: http://jindal.utdallas.edu/finance

University of Utah, Graduate School, David Eccles School of Business, Master in Real Estate Development Program, Salt Lake City, UT 84112. Offers MRED, MRED/JD, MRED/M Arch, MRED/MCMP. MRED/MArch, MRED/MCMP offered jointly with College of Architecture and Planning; MRED/JD with S.J. Quinney College of Law. *Program availability:* Part-time. *Faculty:* 2 full-time (1 woman), 14 part-time/adjunct (1 woman). *Students:* Average age 26. 31 applicants, 87% accepted, 23 enrolled. In 2016, 26 master's awarded. *Degree requirements:* For master's, professional project. *Entrance requirements:* For master's, GMAT or GRE, minimum undergraduate GPA of 3.0. Additional exam requirements/recommendations for international students: Required—TOEFL (minimum score 90 iBT), IELTS (minimum score 6.5). *Application deadline:* For fall admission, 7/28 for domestic students, 3/1 for international students; for winter admission, 12/7 for domestic students, 9/21 for international students. Applications are processed on a rolling basis. Application fee: $55 ($65 for international students). Electronic applications accepted. *Expenses:* Contact institution. *Financial support:* In 2016–17, 8 students received support, including 8 fellowships with partial tuition reimbursements available (averaging $6,396 per year); scholarships/grants and unspecified assistantships also available. Financial award application deadline: 2/1; financial award applicants required to submit FAFSA. *Unit head:* Danny Wall, Program Director, 801-581-8903, E-mail: danny.wall@eccles.utah.edu. *Application contact:* Regina Mavis, Admissions Coordinator, 801-585-0005, E-mail: regina.mavis@eccles.utah.edu.
Website: http://mred.eccles.utah.edu/

University of Wisconsin–Madison, Graduate School, Wisconsin School of Business, Doctoral Program in Real Estate and Urban Land Economics, Madison, WI 53706-1380. Offers PhD. *Degree requirements:* For doctorate, comprehensive exam, thesis/dissertation. *Entrance requirements:* For doctorate, GMAT or GRE. Additional exam requirements/recommendations for international students: Recommended—TOEFL (minimum score 623 paper-based; 106 iBT), IELTS (minimum score 7.5), TSE (minimum score 73). Electronic applications accepted. *Expenses:* Contact institution. *Faculty research:* Real estate finance, real estate equity investments, zoning restructurings, home ownership, international real estate and public policy, real estate economics.

University of Wisconsin–Madison, Graduate School, Wisconsin School of Business, Wisconsin Full-Time MBA Program, Madison, WI 53706. Offers applied security analysis (MBA); arts administration (MBA); brand and product management (MBA); corporate finance and investment banking (MBA); marketing research (MBA); operations and technology management (MBA); real estate (MBA); risk management and insurance (MBA); strategic human resource management (MBA); supply chain management (MBA). *Faculty:* 125 full-time (32 women), 48 part-time/adjunct (11 women). *Students:* 197 full-time (73 women); includes 30 minority (11 Black or African American, non-Hispanic/Latino; 9 Asian, non-Hispanic/Latino; 10 Hispanic/Latino), 42 international. Average age 29. 728 applicants, 26% accepted, 99 enrolled. In 2016, 100 master's awarded. *Entrance requirements:* For master's, GMAT or GRE, bachelor's or equivalent degree, 2 years of work experience, essay, letter of recommendation, resume. Additional exam requirements/recommendations for international students: Required—TOEFL (minimum score 100 iBT), IELTS (minimum score 7.5). *Application deadline:* For fall admission, 9/28 for domestic students, 11/1 for international students; for winter admission, 11/2 for domestic students, 12/16 for international students; for spring admission, 1/11 for domestic students, 2/24 for international students; for summer admission, 3/1 for domestic students, 4/14 for international students. Applications are processed on a rolling basis. Application fee: $75 ($81 for international students). Electronic applications accepted. *Expenses:* $7,947 per semester resident tuition, $2,430 fees; $16,082 per semester resident tuition, $2,830 fees. *Financial support:* In 2016–17, 178 students received support, including 8 fellowships with full tuition reimbursements available (averaging $56,413 per year), 23 research assistantships with full tuition reimbursements available (averaging $42,151 per year), 51 teaching assistantships with full tuition reimbursements available (averaging $39,963 per year); scholarships/grants, health care benefits, and unspecified assistantships also available. Financial award application deadline: 4/11. *Faculty research:* Forms of competition and outcomes in dual distribution systems; explaining the accuracy of revised forecasts; supply chain planning for random demand surges; advanced demand information in a multi-product system; the effects of presentation salience and measurement subjectivity on nonprofessional investors' fair value judgments. *Unit head:* Prof. Ella Mae Matsumura, Associate Dean, Full-time MBA Program, 608-262-9731, E-mail: ematsumura@bus.wisc.edu. *Application contact:* Mary Lewitzke, Assistant Director of Admissions and Recruiting, Full-time MBA Program, 608-262-4000, E-mail: mlewitzke@bus.wisc.edu.
Website: http://www.bus.wisc.edu/mba

Villanova University, Villanova School of Business, MBA - The Fast Track Program, Villanova, PA 19085. Offers analytics (MBA); cybersecurity (MBA); finance (MBA); healthcare (MBA); international business (MBA); management information systems (MBA); marketing (MBA); real estate (MBA); strategic management (MBA); sustainability (MBA). *Accreditation:* AACSB. *Program availability:* Part-time, evening/weekend. *Faculty:* 108 full-time (39 women), 32 part-time/adjunct (8 women). *Students:* 127 part-

time (58 women); includes 18 minority (3 Black or African American, non-Hispanic/Latino; 7 Asian, non-Hispanic/Latino; 6 Hispanic/Latino; 2 Two or more races, non-Hispanic/Latino), 2 international. Average age 30. 88 applicants, 90% accepted, 66 enrolled. In 2016, 75 master's awarded. *Degree requirements:* For master's, minimum GPA of 3.0. *Entrance requirements:* For master's, GMAT or GRE, work experience, 2 letters of recommendation, 2 essays, resume, official transcripts, interview. Additional exam requirements/recommendations for international students: Required—TOEFL (minimum score 550 paper-based; 100 iBT). *Application deadline:* For fall admission, 6/30 for domestic and international students. Application fee: $65. Electronic applications accepted. *Expenses:* Contact institution. *Financial support:* Scholarships/grants available. Financial award application deadline: 6/30; financial award applicants required to submit FAFSA. *Faculty research:* Business analytics; creativity, innovation and entrepreneurship; global leadership; real estate; church management; business ethics; marketing and consumer insights. *Unit head:* Michael L. Capella, Associate Dean of Graduate and Executive Business Programs, 610-519-4336, Fax: 610-519-6273, E-mail: michael.l.capella@villanova.edu. *Application contact:* Kimberly Kane, Manager of Admissions, 610-519-3701, Fax: 610-519-6273, E-mail: kimberly.kane@villanova.edu.
Website: http://www1.villanova.edu/villanova/business/graduate/mba.html

Villanova University, Villanova School of Business, MBA - The Flex Track Program, Villanova, PA 19085. Offers analytics (MBA); finance (MBA); healthcare (MBA); international business (MBA); marketing (MBA); real estate (MBA); strategic management (MBA); JD/MBA. *Accreditation:* AACSB. *Program availability:* Part-time, evening/weekend, online learning. *Faculty:* 108 full-time (39 women), 32 part-time/adjunct (8 women). *Students:* 13 full-time (5 women), 399 part-time (134 women); includes 73 minority (21 Black or African American, non-Hispanic/Latino; 32 Asian, non-Hispanic/Latino; 19 Hispanic/Latino; 1 Two or more races, non-Hispanic/Latino), 11 international. Average age 31. 93 applicants, 94% accepted, 80 enrolled. In 2016, 133 master's awarded. *Degree requirements:* For master's, minimum GPA of 3.0. *Entrance requirements:* For master's, GMAT or GRE, work experience, 2 letters of recommendation, 2 essays, resume, official transcript. Additional exam requirements/recommendations for international students: Required—TOEFL (minimum score 550 paper-based; 100 iBT). *Application deadline:* For fall admission, 6/30 for domestic and international students; for spring admission, 11/15 for domestic and international students; for summer admission, 3/31 for domestic and international students. Applications are processed on a rolling basis. Application fee: $65. Electronic applications accepted. *Expenses:* Contact institution. *Financial support:* In 2016–17, 13 research assistantships with full tuition reimbursements (averaging $13,100 per year) were awarded; scholarships/grants also available. Financial award application deadline: 6/30; financial award applicants required to submit FAFSA. *Faculty research:* Business analytics; creativity, innovation and entrepreneurship; global leadership; real estate; church management; business ethics. *Unit head:* Michael L. Capella, Associate Dean of Graduate and Executive Business Programs, 610-610-4336, Fax: 610-519-6273, E-mail: michael.l.capella@villanova.edu. *Application contact:* Claire Bruno, Director of Recruitment and Enrollment Management, 610-519-4336, Fax: 610-519-6273, E-mail: claire.bruno@villanova.edu.
Website: http://www1.villanova.edu/villanova/business/graduate/mba.html

Virginia Commonwealth University, Graduate School, School of Business, Program in Real Estate and Urban Land Development, Richmond, VA 23284-9005. Offers Postbaccalaureate Certificate. *Entrance requirements:* Additional exam requirements/recommendations for international students: Required—TOEFL (minimum score 600 paper-based; 100 iBT); Recommended—IELTS (minimum score 6.5). *Application deadline:* For fall admission, 6/1 for domestic students; for winter admission, 11/1 for domestic students. Applications are processed on a rolling basis. Application fee: $50. Electronic applications accepted. *Financial support:* Fellowships, research assistantships, teaching assistantships, Federal Work-Study, institutionally sponsored loans, and tuition waivers (full and partial) available. Financial award application deadline: 3/15; financial award applicants required to submit FAFSA. *Unit head:* Dr. Nanda Rangan, Chair, 804-827-7410, E-mail: nkrangan@vcu.edu. *Application contact:* Colleen A. Davis, Graduate Program Director, 804-828-4622, Fax: 804-828-7174, E-mail: androvichcm@vcu.edu.
Website: http://www.vcu.edu/busweb/gsib/

Section 21
Transportation Management, Logistics, and Supply Chain Management

This section contains a directory of institutions offering graduate work in real estate, followed by an in-depth entry submitted by an institution that chose to prepare a detailed program description. Additional information about programs listed in the directory but not augmented by an in-depth entry may be obtained by writing directly to the dean of a graduate school or chair of a department at the address given in the directory.

For programs offering related work, see also in this book *Business Administration and Management.*

CONTENTS

Program Directories

Featured Schools: Displays and Close-Ups

See also:

Aviation Management

Arizona State University at the Tempe campus, Ira A. Fulton Schools of Engineering, The Polytechnic School, Programs in Technology Management, Mesa, AZ 85212. Offers aviation management and human factors (MS); environmental technology management (MS); global technology and development (MS); graphic information technology (MS); management of technology (MS). *Program availability:* Part-time, evening/weekend, online learning. *Degree requirements:* For master's, thesis or applied project and oral defense; interactive Program of Study (iPOS) submitted before completing 50 percent of required credit hours. *Entrance requirements:* For master's, GRE, minimum GPA of 3.0 or equivalent in last 2 years of work leading to bachelor's degree. Additional exam requirements/recommendations for international students: Required—TOEFL, IELTS, or PTE. Electronic applications accepted. *Faculty research:* Digital imaging, digital publishing, Internet development/e-commerce, information aviation human factors, pilot selection, databases, multimedia, commercial digital photography, digital workflow, computer graphics modeling and animation, information design, sociotechnology, visual and technical literacy, environmental management, quality management, project management, industrial ethics, hazardous materials, environmental chemistry.

Delta State University, Graduate Programs, College of Business, Department of Commercial Aviation, Cleveland, MS 38733-0001. Offers MCA. *Program availability:* Part-time, evening/weekend, online learning. *Degree requirements:* For master's, thesis or alternative. *Entrance requirements:* For master's, GMAT.

★ **Embry-Riddle Aeronautical University–Daytona,** Department of Management, Marketing and Operations, Daytona Beach, FL 32114-3900. Offers airline management (MBA); airport management (MBA); aviation finance (MSAF); aviation management (MBA-AM); aviation system management (MBA); finance (MBA); supply chain management (MBA). *Accreditation:* ACBSP. *Program availability:* Part-time. *Faculty:* 13 full-time (2 women). *Students:* 93 full-time (37 women), 15 part-time (8 women); includes 12 minority (3 Black or African American, non-Hispanic/Latino; 3 Asian, non-Hispanic/Latino; 1 Hispanic/Latino; 5 Two or more races, non-Hispanic/Latino), 71 international. Average age 26. 130 applicants, 39% accepted, 40 enrolled. In 2016, 44 degrees awarded. *Degree requirements:* For master's, thesis (for some programs). *Entrance requirements:* Additional exam requirements/recommendations for international students: Required—TOEFL (minimum score 550 paper-based, 79 iBT) or IELTS (6). *Application deadline:* For fall admission, 3/1 priority date for domestic students; for spring admission, 11/1 priority date for domestic students; for summer admission, 4/1 priority date for domestic students. Applications are processed on a rolling basis. Application fee: $50. Electronic applications accepted. *Expenses: Tuition:* Full-time $16,296; part-time $1358 per credit hour. *Required fees:* $1294; $647 per semester. One-time fee: $100 full-time. Tuition and fees vary according to course load, degree level and program. *Financial support:* Research assistantships, teaching assistantships, career-related internships or fieldwork, scholarships/grants, unspecified assistantships, and on-campus employment available. Financial award application deadline: 3/15; financial award applicants required to submit FAFSA. *Unit head:* Michael J. Williams, PhD, Dean, College of Business/Professor of Management, 386-226-6293, E-mail: michael.williams@erau.edu. *Application contact:* Graduate Admissions, 386-226-6176, E-mail: graduate.admissions@erau.edu.
Website: https://daytonabeach.erau.edu/college-business/index.html

See Display on this page and Close-Up on page 637.

Embry-Riddle Aeronautical University–Worldwide, Department of Business Administration, Daytona Beach, FL 32114-3900. Offers aviation (MBAA). *Program availability:* Part-time, evening/weekend, 100% online, blended/hybrid learning, EagleVision Classroom (between classrooms), EagleVision Home (faculty and students at home), and a blend of Classroom or Home. *Faculty:* 16 full-time (4 women), 64 part-time/adjunct (18 women). *Students:* 368 full-time (81 women), 315 part-time (57 women); includes 173 minority (57 Black or African American, non-Hispanic/Latino; 4 American Indian or Alaska Native, non-Hispanic/Latino; 36 Asian, non-Hispanic/Latino; 35 Hispanic/Latino; 4 Native Hawaiian or other Pacific Islander, non-Hispanic/Latino; 37 Two or more races, non-Hispanic/Latino), 61 international. Average age 35. In 2016, 204 master's awarded. *Degree requirements:* For master's, comprehensive exam. *Entrance requirements:* Additional exam requirements/recommendations for international students: Required—TOEFL (minimum score 550 paper-based, 79 iBT) or IELTS (6). *Application deadline:* Applications are processed on a rolling basis. Application fee: $50. Electronic applications accepted. *Expenses:* $620 per credit (for civilians), $530 per credit (for military). *Financial support:* Career-related internships or fieldwork and scholarships/grants available. Financial award applicants required to submit FAFSA. *Unit head:* Ronald Mau, PhD, Department Chair, E-mail: ronald.mau@erau.edu. *Application contact:* Worldwide Campus, 800-522-6787, E-mail: worldwide@erau.edu.
Website: http://worldwide.erau.edu/degrees-programs/colleges/business/department-of-business-admin/index.html

Florida Institute of Technology, College of Aeronautics, Program in Airport Development and Management, Melbourne, FL 32901-6975. Offers MSA. *Program availability:* Part-time. *Students:* 18 full-time (6 women), 1 part-time (0 women), 18 international. Average age 24. 29 applicants, 59% accepted, 9 enrolled. In 2016, 13 master's awarded. *Degree requirements:* For master's, thesis optional. *Entrance requirements:* For master's, GRE General Test, 3 letters of recommendation, resume, statement of objectives. Additional exam requirements/recommendations for international students: Required—TOEFL (minimum score 550 paper-based; 79 iBT). *Application deadline:* Applications are processed on a rolling basis. Electronic applications accepted. *Expenses: Tuition:* Full-time $22,338; part-time $1241 per credit hour. *Required fees:* $250. Tuition and fees vary according to degree level, campus/location and program. *Financial support:* Applicants required to submit FAFSA. *Unit head:* Dr. Stephen Rice, Chair of Graduate Programs, 321-674-8375, Fax: 321-674-8059, E-mail: srice@fit.edu. *Application contact:* Cheryl A. Brown, Associate Director of Graduate Admissions, 321-674-7581, Fax: 321-723-9468, E-mail: cbrown@fit.edu.
Website: http://coa.fit.edu

Lewis University, College of Arts and Sciences, Program in Aviation and Transportation, Romeoville, IL 60446. Offers administration (MS); safety and security (MS). *Program availability:* Part-time, evening/weekend, 100% online, blended/hybrid learning. *Students:* 30 full-time (7 women), 18 part-time (4 women); includes 10 minority (5 Black or African American, non-Hispanic/Latino; 1 Asian, non-Hispanic/Latino; 2 Hispanic/Latino; 2 Two or more races, non-Hispanic/Latino), 9 international. Average

age 33. *Entrance requirements:* For master's, bachelor's degree, minimum GPA of 3.0, personal statement, 3 letters of recommendation. Additional exam requirements/recommendations for international students: Required—TOEFL (minimum score 550 paper-based; 80 iBT). *Application deadline:* For fall admission, 5/1 priority date for international students; for spring admission, 11/15 priority date for international students. Applications are processed on a rolling basis. Application fee: $40. Electronic applications accepted. *Expenses: Tuition:* Full-time $13,860; part-time $770 per credit hour. *Required fees:* $75 per semester. Tuition and fees vary according to degree level and program. *Financial support:* Application deadline: 5/1; applicants required to submit FAFSA. *Total annual research expenditures:* $30. *Unit head:* Dr. Randal DeMik, Program Chair, 815-838-0500 Ext. 5559, E-mail: demikra@lewisu.edu. *Application contact:* Julie Branchaw, Assistant Director, Graduate and Adult Admission, 815-836-5574, E-mail: branchju@lewisu.edu.

Lynn University, College of Business and Management, Boca Raton, FL 33431-5598. Offers business administration (MBA), including aviation management, financial valuation and investment management, hospitality management, human resource management, international business management, marketing, media management, sports management. *Program availability:* Part-time, evening/weekend, 100% online, blended/hybrid learning. *Faculty:* 24 full-time (9 women), 24 part-time/adjunct (4 women). *Students:* 265 full-time (125 women), 182 part-time (96 women); includes 100 minority (41 Black or African American, non-Hispanic/Latino; 11 Asian, non-Hispanic/Latino; 42 Hispanic/Latino; 6 Two or more races, non-Hispanic/Latino), 119 international. Average age 28. 280 applicants, 94% accepted, 181 enrolled. In 2016, 219 master's awarded. *Degree requirements:* For master's, strategic management seminar, simulation capstone. *Entrance requirements:* For master's, bachelor's degree from accredited institution, resume, letter of recommendation, official transcripts, essay/personal statement. Additional exam requirements/recommendations for international students: Required—TOEFL (minimum score 550 paper-based; 80 iBT), IELTS (minimum score 6.5). *Application deadline:* For fall admission, 8/18 for domestic students, 8/4 for international students; for spring admission, 12/15 for domestic students, 12/1 for international students; for summer admission, 4/17 for domestic students, 4/3 for international students. Applications are processed on a rolling basis. Application fee: $45. Electronic applications accepted. *Expenses:* $725 per credit. *Financial support:* In 2016–17, 115 students received support. Career-related internships or fieldwork, Federal Work-Study, scholarships/grants, tuition waivers (full and partial), and unspecified assistantships available. Support available to part-time students. Financial award application deadline: 3/1; financial award applicants required to submit FAFSA. *Faculty research:* Market volatility investing, biometric research, sports legal history, organizational leadership, urban economic development and productivity. *Unit head:* Dr. RT Good, Dean of the College of Business and Management, 561-237-7458, E-mail: rgood@lynn.edu. *Application contact:* Steven Pruitt, Director of Graduate and Undergraduate Evening Admission, 561-237-7834, Fax: 561-237-7100, E-mail: spruitt@lynn.edu.
Website: http://www.lynn.edu/academics/colleges/business-and-management

Middle Tennessee State University, College of Graduate Studies, College of Basic and Applied Sciences, Department of Aerospace, Program in Aviation Administration, Murfreesboro, TN 37132. Offers MS. *Program availability:* Part-time, evening/weekend, online learning. *Degree requirements:* For master's, comprehensive exam, thesis optional. *Entrance requirements:* For master's, GRE or MAT. Additional exam requirements/recommendations for international students: Required—TOEFL (minimum score 525 paper-based; 71 iBT) or IELTS (minimum score 6).

Purdue University, Graduate School, College of Technology, Department of Aviation Technology, West Lafayette, IN 47907. Offers aviation and aerospace management (MS). *Faculty:* 22 full-time (2 women), 1 (woman) part-time/adjunct. *Students:* 44 full-time (15 women), 37 part-time (6 women); includes 18 minority (2 Black or African American, non-Hispanic/Latino; 7 Asian, non-Hispanic/Latino; 6 Hispanic/Latino; 1 Native Hawaiian or other Pacific Islander, non-Hispanic/Latino; 2 Two or more races, non-Hispanic/Latino), 20 international. Average age 28. 55 applicants, 85% accepted, 28 enrolled. In 2016, 34 master's awarded. *Entrance requirements:* For master's, GRE/GMAT, written and spoken communication skills; general knowledge of aviation industry operations and components; entry-level analytical tools and processes; group activity and interpersonal skills. Additional exam requirements/recommendations for international students: Required—TOEFL (minimum score 550 paper-based; 77 iBT); Recommended—TWE. *Application deadline:* For fall admission, 4/1 for domestic and international students; for spring admission, 10/1 for domestic students, 9/1 for international students; for summer admission, 4/1 for domestic students, 2/15 for international students. Applications are processed on a rolling basis. Application fee: $60 ($75 for international students). Electronic applications accepted. *Unit head:* Dr. John H. Mott, Head, 765-494-2686, E-mail: jhmott@purdue.edu. *Application contact:* Emily Birge, Graduate Contact, 765-494-2884, E-mail: eblrge@purdue.edu.
Website: https://tech.purdue.edu/departments/aviation-technology

Southeastern Oklahoma State University, Department of Aviation Science, Durant, OK 74701-0609. Offers aerospace administration and logistics (MS). *Program availability:* Part-time, evening/weekend. *Entrance requirements:* For master's, minimum GPA of 3.0 in last 60 hours or 2.75 overall. Additional exam requirements/recommendations for international students: Required—TOEFL (minimum score 550 paper-based; 79 iBT). Electronic applications accepted.

Vaughn College of Aeronautics and Technology, Graduate Programs, Flushing, NY 11369. Offers airport management (MS). *Degree requirements:* For master's, project or thesis.

Logistics

Air Force Institute of Technology, Graduate School of Engineering and Management, Department of Operational Sciences, Dayton, OH 45433-7765. Offers logistics management (MS); operations research (MS, PhD); space operations (MS). *Program availability:* Part-time. *Degree requirements:* For master's, thesis; for doctorate, thesis/dissertation. *Entrance requirements:* For doctorate, GRE General Test, minimum GPA of 3.0, U.S. citizenship. *Faculty research:* Optimization, simulation, combat modeling and analysis, reliability and maintainability, resource scheduling.

Albany State University, College of Business, Albany, GA 31705-2717. Offers accounting (MBA); general business administration (MBA); healthcare (MBA); public administration (MBA); supply chain and logistics (MBA). *Accreditation:* ACBSP. *Program availability:* Part-time, evening/weekend. *Degree requirements:* For master's, comprehensive exam, internship, 3 hours of physical education. *Entrance requirements:* For master's, GMAT (minimum score of 450)/GRE (minimum score of 800) for those without earned master's degree or higher, minimum undergraduate GPA of 2.5, 2 letters of reference, official transcript, pre-entrance medical record and certificate of immunization. *Application deadline:* For fall admission, 6/1 for domestic students, 5/1 for international students; for spring admission, 11/1 for domestic students, 10/1 for international students. Applications are processed on a rolling basis. Application fee: $20. Electronic applications accepted. *Financial support:* Application deadline: 4/15; applicants required to submit FAFSA. *Faculty research:* Diversity issues, ancestry, understanding finance through use of technology. *Unit head:* Dr. Alicia Jackson, Dean, 229-430-7009, Fax: 229-430-5119. *Application contact:* Jeffrey Pierce, II, Graduate Counselor, 229-430-4646, Fax: 229-430-4105, E-mail: jeffrey.pierce@asurams.edu.
Website: https://www.asurams.edu/Academics/collegeofbusiness/

American Public University System, AMU/APU Graduate Programs, Charles Town, WV 25414. Offers accounting (MBA, MS); applied business analytics (MBA, MS); criminal justice (MA), including business administration, emergency and disaster management, general (MA, MS); educational leadership (M Ed); emergency and disaster management (MA); entrepreneurship (MBA); environmental policy and management (MS), including environmental planning, environmental sustainability, fish and wildlife management, general (MA, MS), global environmental management; finance (MBA); general (MBA); government contracting and acquisition (MBA); health care administration (MBA); health information management (MS); history (MA), including American history, ancient and classical history, European history, global history, public history; homeland security (MA), including business administration, counterterrorism studies, criminal justice, cyber, emergency management and public health, intelligence studies, transportation security; homeland security resource allocation (MBA); humanities (MA); information technology (MS), including digital forensics, enterprise software development, information assurance and security, IT project management; information technology management (MBA); intelligence studies (MA), including criminal intelligence, cyber, general (MA, MS), homeland security, intelligence analysis, intelligence collection, intelligence management, intelligence operations, terrorism studies; international relations and conflict resolution (MA), including comparative and security issues, conflict resolution, international and transnational security issues, peacekeeping; legal studies (MA); management (MA), including strategic consulting; marketing (MBA); military history (MA), including American military history, American Revolution, civil war, war since 1945, World War II; military studies (MA), including joint warfare, strategic leadership; national security studies (MA), including cyber, general (MA, MS), homeland security, regional security studies, security and intelligence analysis, terrorism studies; nonprofit management (MBA); political science (MA), including American politics and government, comparative government and development, general (MA, MS), international relations, public policy; psychology (MA); public administration (MPA), including disaster management, environmental policy, health policy, human resources, national security, organizational management, security management; public health (MPH); reverse logistics management (MA); security management (MA); space studies (MS), including aerospace science, general (MA, MS), planetary science; sports and health sciences (MS); sports management (MBA); teaching (M Ed), including autism spectrum disorder, curriculum and instruction for elementary teachers, elementary reading, English language learners, instructional leadership, online learning, special education, STEAM (STEM plus the arts); transportation and logistics management (MA). *Program availability:* Part-time, evening/weekend, online only, 100% online. *Faculty:* 401 full-time (228 women), 1,678 part-time/adjunct (781 women). *Students:* 378 full-time (184 women), 8,455 part-time (3,484 women); includes 2,972 minority (1,552 Black or African American, non-Hispanic/Latino; 52 American Indian or Alaska Native, non-Hispanic/Latino; 211 Asian, non-Hispanic/Latino; 791 Hispanic/Latino; 70 Native Hawaiian or other Pacific Islander, non-Hispanic/Latino; 296 Two or more races, non-Hispanic/Latino), 109 international. Average age 37. In 2016, 3,185 master's awarded. *Degree requirements:* For master's, comprehensive exam or practicum. *Entrance requirements:* For master's, official transcript showing earned bachelor's degree from institution accredited by recognized accrediting body. Additional exam requirements/recommendations for international students: Required—TOEFL (minimum score 550 paper-based), IELTS (minimum score 6.5). *Application deadline:* Applications are processed on a rolling basis. Application fee: $0. Electronic applications accepted. *Expenses: Tuition:* Part-time $350 per credit hour. *Required fees:* $50 per course. *Financial support:* Scholarships/grants available. Financial award applicants required to submit FAFSA. *Unit head:* Dr. Karan Powell, President, 877-468-6268, Fax: 304-724-3780. *Application contact:* Terry Grant, Vice President of Enrollment Management, 877-468-6268, Fax: 304-724-3780, E-mail: info@apus.edu.
Website: http://www.apus.edu

Benedictine University, Graduate Programs, Program in Business Administration, Lisle, IL 60532. Offers accounting (MBA); entrepreneurship and managing innovation (MBA); financial management (MBA); health administration (MBA); human resource management (MBA); information systems security (MBA); international business (MBA); management consulting (MBA); management information systems (MBA); marketing management (MBA); operations management and logistics (MBA); organizational leadership (MBA). *Program availability:* Part-time, evening/weekend, online learning. *Faculty:* 4 full-time (2 women), 24 part-time/adjunct (3 women). *Students:* 90 full-time (51 women), 440 part-time (262 women); includes 117 minority (65 Black or African American, non-Hispanic/Latino; 1 American Indian or Alaska Native, non-Hispanic/Latino; 58 Asian, non-Hispanic/Latino; 20 Hispanic/Latino; 3 Native Hawaiian or other Pacific Islander, non-Hispanic/Latino), 2 international. Average age 34. 211 applicants, 89% accepted, 155 enrolled. In 2016, 350 master's awarded. *Entrance requirements:* For master's, GMAT. Additional exam requirements/recommendations for international students: Required—TOEFL (minimum score 550 paper-based). *Application deadline:* For fall admission, 9/1 for domestic students; for winter admission, 12/1 for domestic students; for spring admission, 2/15 for domestic students. Applications are processed on a rolling basis. Application fee: $40. Electronic applications accepted. *Expenses: Tuition:* Full-time $15,600; part-time $650 per hour. *Required fees:* $300. One-time fee: $125 part-time. Tuition and fees vary according to class time, course load, campus/location and program. *Financial support:* Career-related internships or fieldwork and health care benefits available. Support available to part-time students. *Faculty research:* Strategic leadership in professional organizations, sociology of professions, organizational change, social identity theory, applications to change management. *Unit head:* Dr. Sharon Borowicz, Director, 630-829-6219, E-mail: sborowicz@ben.edu. *Application contact:* Kari Gibbons, Director, Admissions, 630-829-6200, Fax: 630-829-6584, E-mail: kgibbons@ben.edu.

Logistics

Case Western Reserve University, School of Graduate Studies, Case School of Engineering, Department of Electrical Engineering and Computer Science, Cleveland, OH 44106. Offers computer engineering (MS, PhD); computing and information sciences (MS, PhD); electrical engineering (MS, PhD); systems and control engineering (MS, PhD). *Program availability:* Part-time, evening/weekend, online only, 100% online. *Faculty:* 32 full-time (3 women). *Students:* 188 full-time (42 women), 14 part-time (3 women); includes 7 minority (1 Black or African American, non-Hispanic/Latino; 5 Asian, non-Hispanic/Latino; 1 Hispanic/Latino), 152 international. In 2016, 25 master's, 26 doctorates awarded. Terminal master's awarded for partial completion of doctoral program. *Degree requirements:* For master's, thesis; for doctorate, thesis/dissertation, qualifying exam, teaching experience. *Entrance requirements:* For master's and doctorate, GRE General Test. Additional exam requirements/recommendations for international students: Required—TOEFL. *Application deadline:* For fall admission, 2/1 for domestic students; for spring admission, 11/1 for domestic students. Applications are processed on a rolling basis. Application fee: $50. *Expenses: Tuition:* Full-time $42,576; part-time $1774 per credit hour. *Required fees:* $34. Tuition and fees vary according to course load and program. *Financial support:* In 2016–17, 1 fellowship with tuition reimbursement, 63 research assistantships with tuition reimbursements, 10 teaching assistantships were awarded; career-related internships or fieldwork, Federal Work-Study, and institutionally sponsored loans also available. Support available to part-time students. Financial award application deadline: 3/1; financial award applicants required to submit FAFSA. *Faculty research:* Micro-/nano-systems; robotics and haptics; applied artificial intelligence; automation; computer-aided design and testing of digital systems. *Total annual research expenditures:* $4.9 million. *Unit head:* Dr. Kenneth Loparo, Department Chair, 216-368-4115, E-mail: kal4@case.edu. *Application contact:* Kimberly Yurchick, Student Affairs Specialist, 216-368-2920, Fax: 216-368-2801, E-mail: ksy4@case.edu.
Website: http://eecs.cwru.edu/

Central Connecticut State University, School of Graduate Studies, School of Engineering, Science and Technology, Department of Manufacturing and Construction Management, New Britain, CT 06050-4010. Offers construction management (MS, Certificate); environmental and occupational safety (Certificate); lean manufacturing and Six Sigma (Certificate); supply chain and logistics (Certificate); technology management (MS). *Program availability:* Part-time, evening/weekend. *Faculty:* 7 full-time (0 women), 3 part-time/adjunct (0 women). *Students:* 23 full-time (6 women), 88 part-time (21 women); includes 29 minority (11 Black or African American, non-Hispanic/Latino; 7 Asian, non-Hispanic/Latino; 10 Hispanic/Latino; 1 Two or more races, non-Hispanic/Latino), 12 international. Average age 34. 79 applicants, 68% accepted, 32 enrolled. In 2016, 43 master's, 4 other advanced degrees awarded. *Degree requirements:* For master's, comprehensive exam, special project; for Certificate, qualifying exam. *Entrance requirements:* For master's, minimum undergraduate GPA of 2.7. Additional exam requirements/recommendations for international students: Required—TOEFL (minimum score 550 paper-based; 79 iBT). *Application deadline:* For fall admission, 8/1 for domestic students, 5/1 for international students; for spring admission, 11/1 for domestic and international students. Applications are processed on a rolling basis. Application fee: $50. Electronic applications accepted. *Expenses: Tuition, area resident:* Full-time $6497; part-time $606 per credit. Tuition, state resident: full-time $9748; part-time $622 per credit. Tuition, nonresident: full-time $18,102; part-time $622 per credit. *Required fees:* $4459; $246 per credit. *Financial support:* In 2016–17, 10 students received support. Career-related internships or fieldwork, Federal Work-Study, scholarships/grants, and unspecified assistantships available. Support available to part-time students. Financial award application deadline: 3/1; financial award applicants required to submit FAFSA. *Faculty research:* All aspects of middle management, technical supervision in the workplace. *Unit head:* Dr. Ravindra Thamma, Chair, 860-832-1830, E-mail: kovelj@ccsu.edu. *Application contact:* Patricia Gardner, Associate Director of Graduate Studies, 860-832-2350, Fax: 860-832-2362.
Website: http://www.ccsu.edu/mcm/

Central Michigan University, Central Michigan University Global Campus, Program in Business Administration, Mount Pleasant, MI 48859. Offers enterprise resource planning (MBA, Certificate); human resource management (MBA); logistics management (MBA, Certificate); marketing (MBA); value-driven organization (MBA). *Program availability:* Part-time, evening/weekend. *Faculty:* 17 full-time (7 women), 3 part-time/adjunct (0 women). *Students:* 189 (82 women); includes 29 minority (17 Black or African American, non-Hispanic/Latino; 2 American Indian or Alaska Native, non-Hispanic/Latino; 3 Asian, non-Hispanic/Latino; 1 Hispanic/Latino; 6 Two or more races, non-Hispanic/Latino). Average age 32. In 2016, 25 master's awarded. *Entrance requirements:* For master's, GMAT. *Financial support:* Scholarships/grants available. Support available to part-time students. *Unit head:* Dr. Debasish Chakraborty, 989-774-3678, E-mail: chakt1d@cmich.edu. *Application contact:* Global Campus Student Services Call Center, 877-268-4636, E-mail: cmuglobal@cmich.edu.

Central Michigan University, College of Graduate Studies, College of Business Administration, MBA Program, Mount Pleasant, MI 48859. Offers accounting (MBA); business economics (MBA); consulting (MBA); finance (MBA); general business (MBA); human resource management (MBA); information systems (MBA); international business (MBA); logistics management (MBA); marketing (MBA); value-driven organization (MBA). *Program availability:* Part-time, evening/weekend, online learning. Electronic applications accepted. *Faculty research:* Accounting, consulting, international business, marketing, information systems.

Colorado Technical University Colorado Springs, Graduate Studies, Program in Management, Colorado Springs, CO 80907. Offers accounting (MBA, MSA); business administration (MBA); finance (MBA); human resources management (MBA); logistics/supply chain management (MBA); management (DM); marketing (MBA); mediation and dispute resolution (MBA); operations management (MBA); project management (MBA); technology management (MBA). *Accreditation:* ACBSP. *Program availability:* Part-time, evening/weekend, online learning. *Degree requirements:* For master's, thesis or alternative; for doctorate, thesis/dissertation. *Entrance requirements:* For doctorate, minimum graduate GPA of 3.0, 5 years of related work experience. *Faculty research:* Sexual harassment, performance evaluation, critical thinking.

Copenhagen Business School, Graduate Programs, Copenhagen, Denmark. Offers business administration (Exec MBA, MBA, PhD); business administration and information systems (M Sc); business, language and culture (M Sc); economics and business administration (M Sc); health management (MHM); international business and politics (M Sc); public administration (MPA); shipping and logistics (Exec MBA); technology, market and organization (MBA).

East Carolina University, Graduate School, College of Engineering and Technology, Department of Technology Systems, Greenville, NC 27858-4353. Offers computer network professional (Certificate); information assurance (Certificate); Lean Six Sigma Black Belt (Certificate); network technology (MS), including computer networking management, digital communications technology, information security, Web technologies; occupational safety (MS); technology management (PhD); technology systems (MS), including industrial distribution and logistics, manufacturing systems, performance improvement, quality systems; Website developer (Certificate). *Students:* 23 full-time (1 woman), 199 part-time (55 women); includes 59 minority (39 Black or African American, non-Hispanic/Latino; 3 American Indian or Alaska Native, non-Hispanic/Latino; 4 Asian, non-Hispanic/Latino; 10 Hispanic/Latino; 3 Two or more races, non-Hispanic/Latino), 5 international. Average age 38. 85 applicants, 87% accepted, 61 enrolled. In 2016, 23 master's awarded. *Entrance requirements:* For master's and Certificate, GRE General Test or MAT, minimum GPA of 2.5; for doctorate, GRE General Test, related work experience. *Application deadline:* For fall admission, 6/1 priority date for domestic students. Applications are processed on a rolling basis. Application fee: $50. *Financial support:* Application deadline: 6/1. *Unit head:* Dr. Tijjani Mohammed, Chair, 252-328-9668, E-mail: mohammedt@ecu.edu. *Application contact:* Dean of Graduate School, 252-328-6012, Fax: 252-328-6071, E-mail: gradschool@ecu.edu.

Embry-Riddle Aeronautical University–Worldwide, Department of Decision Sciences, Daytona Beach, FL 32114-3900. Offers aviation and aerospace (MSPM); aviation/aerospace management (MSEM); financial management (MSEM, MSPM); general management (MSPM); global management (MSPM); human resources management (MSPM); information systems (MSPM); leadership (MSEM, MSPM); logistics and supply chain management (MSEM, MSLSCM, MSPM); management (MSEM, MSPM); project management (MSEM); systems engineering (MSEM, MSPM); technical management (MSPM). *Program availability:* Part-time, evening/weekend, 100% online, blended/hybrid learning, EagleVision is a virtual classroom that combines Web video conferencing and a learning management system. EagleVision Classroom (between classrooms), EagleVision Home (faculty and students at home), and a blend of Classroom or Home. *Degree requirements:* For master's, comprehensive exam (for some programs), thesis (for some programs). *Entrance requirements:* Additional exam requirements/recommendations for international students: Required—TOEFL (minimum score 550 paper-based; 79 iBT), IELTS (minimum score 6), TOEFL or IELTS accepted. Electronic applications accepted. *Expenses:* Contact institution.

Florida Institute of Technology, Extended Studies Division, Melbourne, FL 32901-6975. Offers acquisition and contract management (MS); aerospace engineering (MS); business administration (MBA, DBA); computer information systems (MS); computer science (MS); electrical engineering (MS); engineering management (MS); human resources management (MS); logistics management (MS), including humanitarian and disaster relief logistics; management (MS), including acquisition and contract management, e-business, human resources management, information systems, logistics management, management, transportation management; material acquisition management (MS); mechanical engineering (MS); operations research (MS); project management (MS), including information systems, operations research; public administration (MPA); quality management (MS); software engineering (MS); space systems (MS); space systems management (MS); supply chain management (MS); systems management (MS), including information systems, operations research; technology management (MS). *Program availability:* Part-time, evening/weekend, online learning. *Faculty:* 10 full-time (3 women), 122 part-time/adjunct (29 women). *Students:* 131 full-time (58 women), 997 part-time (348 women); includes 389 minority (231 Black or African American, non-Hispanic/Latino; 9 American Indian or Alaska Native, non-Hispanic/Latino; 26 Asian, non-Hispanic/Latino; 99 Hispanic/Latino; 3 Native Hawaiian or other Pacific Islander, non-Hispanic/Latino; 21 Two or more races, non-Hispanic/Latino), 53 international. Average age 36. 962 applicants, 48% accepted, 323 enrolled. In 2016, 403 master's awarded. *Degree requirements:* For master's, comprehensive exam (for some programs). *Entrance requirements:* For master's, GMAT or resume showing 8 years of supervised experience, minimum GPA of 3.0, 2 letters of recommendation, resume. Additional exam requirements/recommendations for international students: Required—TOEFL (minimum score 550 paper-based; 79 iBT). *Application deadline:* For fall admission, 4/1 for international students; for spring admission, 9/30 for international students. Applications are processed on a rolling basis. Electronic applications accepted. *Expenses:* Contact institution. *Financial support:* Application deadline: 3/1; applicants required to submit FAFSA. *Unit head:* Dr. Theodore R. Richardson, III, Dean, 321-674-8123, Fax: 321-674-7597, E-mail: trichardson@fit.edu. *Application contact:* Carolyn Farrior, Director of Graduate Admissions, Online Learning and Off-Campus Programs, 321-674-7118, Fax: 321-674-8216, E-mail: cfarrior@fit.edu.
Website: http://es.fit.edu

Friends University, Graduate School, Wichita, KS 67213. Offers family therapy (MSFT); global business administration (MBA), including accounting, business law, change management, health care leadership, management information systems, supply chain management and logistics; health care leadership (MHCL); management information systems (MMIS); professional business administration (MBA), including accounting, business law, change management, health care leadership, management information systems, supply chain management and logistics. *Program availability:* Part-time, evening/weekend, online learning. *Degree requirements:* For master's, research project. *Entrance requirements:* For master's, bachelor's degree from accredited institution, official transcripts, interview with program director, letter(s) of recommendation. Additional exam requirements/recommendations for international students: Required—TOEFL (minimum score 560 paper-based). Electronic applications accepted.

George Mason University, Schar School of Policy and Government, Program in Transportation Policy, Operations and Logistics, Arlington, VA 22201. Offers MA, Certificate. *Faculty:* 6 full-time (3 women), 2 part-time/adjunct (0 women). *Students:* 6 full-time (2 women), 27 part-time (7 women); includes 7 minority (3 Black or African American, non-Hispanic/Latino; 3 Hispanic/Latino; 1 Two or more races, non-Hispanic/Latino), 1 international. Average age 34. 13 applicants, 92% accepted, 9 enrolled. In 2016, 12 master's awarded. *Degree requirements:* For master's, thesis or alternative. *Entrance requirements:* For master's, GRE (for students seeking merit-based scholarships), bachelor's degree with minimum GPA of 3.0, current resume, 2 letters of recommendation, expanded goals statement, 2 copies of official transcripts. Additional exam requirements/recommendations for international students: Required—TOEFL (minimum score 575 paper-based; 88 iBT), IELTS (minimum score 6.5), PTE (minimum score 59). *Application deadline:* For fall admission, 2/1 priority date for domestic students. Application fee: $75 ($80 for international students). Electronic applications accepted. *Expenses:* Contact institution. *Financial support:* Career-related internships or fieldwork, Federal Work-Study, and scholarships/grants available. Support available to part-time students. Financial award application deadline: 3/1; financial award applicants required to submit FAFSA. *Unit head:* Laurie Schintler, Director, 703-993-2256, Fax: 703-993-4557, E-mail: lschintl@gmu.edu. *Application contact:* Stephanie Ellis, Graduate Admissions Coordinator, 703-993-4478, E-mail: sellis11@gmu.edu.
Website: http://spgia.gmu.edu/programs/graduate-degrees/transportation-policy-operations-logistics-tpol/

Georgia College & State University, Graduate School, The J. Whitney Bunting School of Business, Logistics Education Center, Milledgeville, GA 31061. Offers MLSCM. *Program availability:* Part-time, evening/weekend. *Students:* 76 part-time (27 women); includes 20 minority (14 Black or African American, non-Hispanic/Latino; 1 Asian, non-Hispanic/Latino; 2 Hispanic/Latino; 1 Native Hawaiian or other Pacific Islander, non-Hispanic/Latino; 2 Two or more races, non-Hispanic/Latino), 2 international. Average age 37. 41 applicants, 88% accepted, 31 enrolled. In 2016, 20 master's awarded.

Degree requirements: For master's, minimum GPA of 3.0, complete program within 7 years. *Entrance requirements:* For master's, GRE or GMAT, transcript, certification of immunization, resume. *Application deadline:* For fall admission, 7/1 priority date for domestic students; for spring admission, 11/1 priority date for domestic students. Applications are processed on a rolling basis. Application fee: $40. Electronic applications accepted. *Expenses:* $338 per credit hour (online); fees vary by hours enrolled. *Financial support:* Application deadline: 3/1; applicants required to submit FAFSA. *Unit head:* Dr. Dale Young, Dean, School of Business, 478-445-5497, Fax: 478-445-5249, E-mail: dale.young@gcsu.edu. *Application contact:* Lynn Hanson, Director of Graduate Programs in Business, 478-445-5115, E-mail: lynn.hanson@gcsu.edu.

Georgia Institute of Technology, Graduate Studies, College of Engineering, H. Milton Stewart School of Industrial and Systems Engineering, Program in International Logistics, Atlanta, GA 30332-0001. Offers MS. *Program availability:* Part-time. *Entrance requirements:* For master's, GRE General Test. Additional exam requirements/recommendations for international students: Required—TOEFL (minimum score 550 paper-based; 79 iBT). Electronic applications accepted. *Expenses:* Contact institution.

Georgia Southern University, Jack N. Averitt College of Graduate Studies, College of Business Administration, Program in Logistics/Supply Chain Management, Statesboro, GA 30458. Offers PhD. *Students:* 6 full-time (1 woman), 3 international. Average age 28. 29 applicants, 17% accepted, 3 enrolled. In 2016, 2 doctorates awarded. *Degree requirements:* For doctorate, comprehensive exam, thesis/dissertation. *Entrance requirements:* For doctorate, GMAT, minimum of three letters of reference; statement of purpose; resume. Additional exam requirements/recommendations for international students: Required—TOEFL (minimum score 550 paper-based; 80 iBT), IELTS (minimum score 6). *Application deadline:* For fall admission, 3/15 priority date for domestic and international students. Application fee: $50. Electronic applications accepted. *Expenses:* Tuition, state resident: full-time $7236; part-time $277 per semester hour. Tuition, nonresident: full-time $27,118; part-time $1105 per semester hour. *Required fees:* $2092. *Financial support:* In 2016–17, 3 research assistantships with full tuition reimbursements (averaging $7,750 per year) were awarded; teaching assistantships, career-related internships or fieldwork, Federal Work-Study, scholarships/grants, traineeships, and unspecified assistantships also available. Support available to part-time students. Financial award application deadline: 4/15; financial award applicants required to submit FAFSA. *Faculty research:* Buyer-supplier relationships, retail supply chain management, military logistics/transportation/supply chain management, strategic sourcing/outsourcing, supply chain metrics, service scheduling, demand and supply planning, supply chain strategy, sustainability, operations and supply management, decision sciences. *Unit head:* Dr. Gordon Smith, Graduate Program Director, 912-478-2357, Fax: 912-478-0292, E-mail: gsmith@georgiasouthern.edu. *Application contact:* E-mail: coba@georgiasouthern.edu.
Website: http://cogs.georgiasouthern.edu/admission/GraduatePrograms/phdlogistics.php

HEC Montreal, School of Business Administration, Master of Science Programs in Administration, Program in International Logistics, Montréal, QC H3T 2A7, Canada. Offers M Sc. Specialization offered in French. *Students:* 24 full-time (14 women), 10 part-time (4 women). 18 applicants, 56% accepted, 7 enrolled. In 2016, 8 master's awarded. *Degree requirements:* For master's, one foreign language, thesis. *Entrance requirements:* For master's, Test de francais international (TFI) with minimum score of 850 (for those who have never studied in French), BBA, undergraduate degree in another field, degree deemed equivalent by program director and minimum GPA of 3.0 on 4.3 scale. *Application deadline:* For fall admission, 3/15 for domestic and international students; for winter admission, 9/15 for domestic and international students. Application fee: $86 Canadian dollars. Electronic applications accepted. *Expenses: Tuition, area resident:* Part-time $77.80 Canadian dollars per credit. Tuition, state resident: full-time $2797 Canadian dollars; part-time $240.92 Canadian dollars per credit. Tuition, nonresident: full-time $8673 Canadian dollars; part-time $531.43 Canadian dollars per credit. *International tuition:* $19,131 Canadian dollars full-time. *Required fees:* $1699 Canadian dollars; $40.58 Canadian dollars per credit. $67.32 Canadian dollars per term. Tuition and fees vary according to degree level and program. *Financial support:* Research assistantships, teaching assistantships, and scholarships/grants available. Financial award application deadline: 9/2. *Unit head:* Dr. Marie-Helene Jobin, Director, 514-340-6283, E-mail: marie-helene.jobin@hec.ca. *Application contact:* Marianne de Moura, Administrative Director, 514-340-7106, Fax: 514-340-6411, E-mail: marianne.de-moura@hec.ca.
Website: http://www.hec.ca/programmes/maitrises/maitrise-logistique-internationale/index.html

Kaplan University, Davenport Campus, School of Business, Davenport, IA 52807. Offers business administration (MBA); change leadership (MS); entrepreneurship (MBA); finance (MBA); health care management (MBA, MS); human resource (MBA); international business (MBA); management (MS); marketing (MBA); project management (MBA, MS); supply chain management and logistics (MBA, MS). *Accreditation:* ACBSP. *Program availability:* Part-time, evening/weekend, online learning. *Entrance requirements:* Additional exam requirements/recommendations for international students: Required—TOEFL (minimum score 550 paper-based; 80 iBT). Electronic applications accepted.

Maryville University of Saint Louis, The John E. Simon School of Business, St. Louis, MO 63141-7299. Offers accounting (MBA, Certificate); business studies (Certificate); cyber security (MBA); cybersecurity (Certificate); financial services (MBA, Certificate); healthcare practice management (MBA, Certificate); human resource management (MBA); information technology (MBA, Certificate); management (MBA, Certificate); management and leadership (MA); marketing (MBA, Certificate); project management (MBA); sport business management (MBA); supply chain management/logistics (MBA). *Accreditation:* ACBSP. *Program availability:* Part-time, evening/weekend, 100% online, blended/hybrid learning. *Faculty:* 7 full-time (3 women), 34 part-time/adjunct (9 women). *Students:* 84 full-time (40 women), 223 part-time (118 women); includes 67 minority (40 Black or African American, non-Hispanic/Latino; 2 American Indian or Alaska Native, non-Hispanic/Latino; 8 Asian, non-Hispanic/Latino; 12 Hispanic/Latino; 1 Native Hawaiian or other Pacific Islander, non-Hispanic/Latino; 4 Two or more races, non-Hispanic/Latino), 15 international. Average age 32. In 2016, 67 master's awarded. *Entrance requirements:* Additional exam requirements/recommendations for international students: Required—TOEFL (minimum score 563 paper-based; 85 iBT). *Application deadline:* Applications are processed on a rolling basis. Electronic applications accepted. *Expenses:* $650 per credit hour. *Financial support:* Career-related internships or fieldwork, Federal Work-Study, tuition waivers (partial), and campus employment available. Financial award application deadline: 3/1; financial award applicants required to submit FAFSA. *Faculty research:* Global business, e-marketing, strategic planning, interpersonal management skills, financial analysis. *Unit head:* Pam Horwitz, Interim Dean, 314-529-9680, Fax: 314-529-9975. *Application contact:* Dustin Loeffler, Director for Graduate Studies in Business, 314-529-9571, Fax: 314-529-9975, E-mail: dloeffler@maryville.edu.
Website: http://www.maryville.edu/bu/business-administration-masters/

Massachusetts Institute of Technology, School of Engineering, Supply Chain Management Program, Cambridge, MA 02139-4307. Offers logistics (M Eng). *Students:* 40 full-time (20 women); includes 5 minority (3 Asian, non-Hispanic/Latino; 1 Hispanic/Latino; 1 Two or more races, non-Hispanic/Latino), 23 international. Average age 28. 188 applicants, 27% accepted, 30 enrolled. In 2016, 37 master's awarded. *Degree requirements:* For master's, thesis. *Entrance requirements:* Additional exam requirements/recommendations for international students: Required—TOEFL, IELTS. Application fee: $75. Electronic applications accepted. *Expenses: Tuition:* Full-time $46,400; part-time $725 per credit. One-time fee: $312 full-time. Full-time tuition and fees vary according to course load and program. *Financial support:* In 2016–17, 40 students received support, including 9 fellowships (averaging $38,400 per year); research assistantships, teaching assistantships, Federal Work-Study, institutionally sponsored loans, scholarships/grants, traineeships, health care benefits, unspecified assistantships, and graduate resident tutors also available. Financial award application deadline: 5/1; financial award applicants required to submit FAFSA. *Faculty research:* Logistics hubs and clusters; supply chain network risk management; urban logistics; carbon efficient supply chains; scenario planning; supply chain strategy alignment; supply chain innovation in emerging markets; supply chain resilience and security. *Unit head:* Prof. Yossi Sheffi, Director, 617-324-6564, Fax: 617-253-7972, E-mail: scm@mit.edu. *Application contact:* Prof. Yossi Sheffi, Director, 617-324-6564, Fax: 617-253-7972, E-mail: scm@mit.edu.
Website: http://scm.mit.edu/

Michigan State University, The Graduate School, Eli Broad College of Business, Department of Supply Chain Management, East Lansing, MI 48224. Offers logistics (PhD); operations and sourcing management (PhD); supply chain management (MS), including logistics management, operations management, rail management, supply management. *Program availability:* Part-time. *Degree requirements:* For master's, field study/research project; for doctorate, comprehensive exam, thesis/dissertation. *Entrance requirements:* For master's, GMAT (taken within past 5 years), bachelor's degree, minimum GPA of 3.0 in junior/senior years, transcripts, at least 2 years of professional supply chain work experience, 3 letters of recommendation, essays, resume; for doctorate, GMAT or GRE, bachelor's or master's degree, transcripts, strong work experience, 3 letters of recommendation, statement of personal goals, interview. Additional exam requirements/recommendations for international students: Required—TOEFL (minimum score 600 paper-based). Electronic applications accepted. *Expenses:* Contact institution.

Naval Postgraduate School, Departments and Academic Groups, Graduate School of Business and Public Policy, Monterey, CA 93943. Offers acquisition and contract management (MBA); business administration (EMBA, MBA); contract management (MS); defense business management (MBA); defense systems analysis (MS), including management; defense systems management (international) (MBA); financial management (MBA); information management (MBA); manpower systems analysis (MS); material logistics support management (MBA); program management (MS); resource planning and management for international defense (MBA); supply chain management (MBA); systems acquisition management (MBA); transportation management (MBA). Program only open to commissioned officers of the United States and friendly nations and selected United States federal civilian employees. *Accreditation:* AACSB; NASPAA. *Program availability:* Part-time, online learning. *Degree requirements:* For master's, thesis (for some programs), terminal project/capstone (for some programs). *Faculty research:* U.S. and European public procurement policies for small and medium-sized enterprises, examining external validity criticisms in the choice of students as subjects in accounting experiment studies, assurance of learning in contract management education, contracting for cloud computing: opportunities and risks, NPS, Apple App Store as a business model supporting U. S. Navy requirements.

North Dakota State University, College of Graduate and Interdisciplinary Studies, Interdisciplinary Program in Transportation and Logistics, Fargo, ND 58102. Offers managerial logistics (MML); transportation and logistics (PhD); transportation and urban systems (MS). *Entrance requirements:* For doctorate, 1 year of calculus, statistics and probability, minimum GPA of 3.0. Additional exam requirements/recommendations for international students: Required—TOEFL (minimum score 550 paper-based; 79 iBT). *Faculty research:* Supply chain optimization, spatial analysis of transportation networks, advanced traffic analysis, transportation demand, railroad/intermodal freight.

Norwich University, College of Graduate and Continuing Studies, Master of Business Administration Program, Northfield, VT 05663. Offers construction management (MBA); energy management (MBA); finance (MBA); logistics (MBA); organizational leadership (MBA); project management (MBA); supply chain management (MBA). *Accreditation:* ACBSP. *Program availability:* Evening/weekend, online only, mostly all online with a week-long residency requirement. *Faculty:* 24 part-time/adjunct (5 women). *Students:* 228 full-time (54 women); includes 54 minority (23 Black or African American, non-Hispanic/Latino; 1 American Indian or Alaska Native, non-Hispanic/Latino; 6 Asian, non-Hispanic/Latino; 20 Hispanic/Latino; 1 Native Hawaiian or other Pacific Islander, non-Hispanic/Latino; 3 Two or more races, non-Hispanic/Latino), 2 international. Average age 36. 74 applicants, 100% accepted, 57 enrolled. In 2016, 135 master's awarded. *Degree requirements:* For master's, comprehensive exam. *Entrance requirements:* For master's, minimum undergraduate GPA of 2.75. Additional exam requirements/recommendations for international students: Required—TOEFL (minimum score 550 paper-based; 80 iBT), IELTS (minimum score 6.5). *Application deadline:* For fall admission, 8/14 for domestic and international students; for winter admission, 11/13 for domestic and international students; for spring admission, 2/12 for domestic and international students; for summer admission, 6/5 for domestic and international students. Electronic applications accepted. *Expenses:* Contact institution. *Financial support:* In 2016–17, 113 students received support. Scholarships/grants available. Financial award application deadline: 8/4; financial award applicants required to submit FAFSA. *Unit head:* Dr. Jose Cordova, Program Director, 802-485-2567, Fax: 802-485-2533, E-mail: jcordova@norwich.edu. *Application contact:* Admissions Advisor, 800-460-5597 Ext. 3376, Fax: 802-485-2533, E-mail: mba@online.norwich.edu.
Website: https://online.norwich.edu/degree-programs/masters/master-business-administration/overview

The Ohio State University, Graduate School, Max M. Fisher College of Business, Program in Business Logistics Engineering, Columbus, OH 43210. Offers MBLE. *Students:* 57 full-time (30 women), 56 international. Average age 24. In 2016, 39 master's awarded. *Entrance requirements:* For master's, GRE or GMAT. Additional exam requirements/recommendations for international students: Required—TOEFL (minimum score 550 paper-based; 79 iBT), Michigan English Language Assessment Battery (minimum score 82); Recommended—IELTS (minimum score 7). *Application deadline:* For fall admission, 12/13 priority date for domestic students, 11/30 priority date for international students. Applications are processed on a rolling basis. Application fee: $60 ($70 for international students). Electronic applications accepted. *Financial support:* Scholarships/grants available. *Unit head:* Steve Denunzio, Program Director, 614-769-3155, E-mail: dununzio.4@osu.edu. *Application contact:* Graduate and Professional Admissions, 614-292-9444, Fax: 614-292-3895, E-mail: gpadmissions@osu.edu.
Website: http://fisher.osu.edu/mble

Polytechnic University of Puerto Rico, Miami Campus, Graduate School, Miami, FL 33166. Offers accounting (MBA); business administration (MBA); construction management (MEM); environmental management (MEM); finance (MBA); human resources management (MBA); logistics and supply chain management (MBA); management of international enterprises (MBA); manufacturing management (MEM); marketing management (MBA); project management (MBA). *Program availability:* Part-time, evening/weekend, online learning. *Entrance requirements:* For master's, minimum GPA of 3.0. Electronic applications accepted.

Pontifical Catholic University of Puerto Rico, College of Business Administration, Program in Maritime Logistics and Transportation, Ponce, PR 00717-0777. Offers Professional Certificate.

Pontificia Universidad Catolica Madre y Maestra, Graduate School, Faculty of Engineering Sciences, Santiago, Dominican Republic. Offers earthquake engineering (ME); logistics management (ME).

Rutgers University–Newark, Rutgers Business School–Newark and New Brunswick, Program in Real Estate and Logistics, Newark, NJ 07102. Offers MRE.

Shippensburg University of Pennsylvania, School of Graduate Studies, John L. Grove College of Business, Shippensburg, PA 17257-2299. Offers advanced studies in business (Certificate); advanced supply chain and logistics management (Certificate); business administration (MBA), including business administration, finance, healthcare management, management information systems, supply chain management; finance (Certificate); health care management (Certificate); management information systems (Certificate). *Accreditation:* AACSB. *Program availability:* Part-time, evening/weekend, 100% online, blended/hybrid learning. *Faculty:* 23 full-time (4 women), 4 part-time/adjunct (1 woman). *Students:* 58 full-time (17 women), 195 part-time (59 women); includes 26 minority (12 Black or African American, non-Hispanic/Latino; 8 Asian, non-Hispanic/Latino; 5 Hispanic/Latino; 1 Two or more races, non-Hispanic/Latino), 26 international. Average age 32. 224 applicants, 55% accepted, 70 enrolled. In 2016, 101 master's awarded. *Degree requirements:* For master's, thesis optional, practicum. *Entrance requirements:* For master's, GMAT (minimum score 450 if less than 5 years of mid-level experience, including management experience), current resume; relevant work/classroom experience; 500-word statement of purpose; prerequisites of quantitative analysis, computer usage, and oral and written communications; laptop computer. Additional exam requirements/recommendations for international students: Required—TOEFL (minimum score 550 paper-based, 68 iBT) or IELTS (minimum score 6). *Application deadline:* For fall admission, 4/30 for international students; for spring admission, 9/30 for international students. Applications are processed on a rolling basis. Application fee: $45. Electronic applications accepted. *Expenses:* Tuition, state resident: part-time $483 per credit. Tuition, nonresident: part-time $725 per credit. *Required fees:* $141 per credit. *Financial support:* In 2016–17, 12 students received support. Career-related internships or fieldwork, scholarships/grants, unspecified assistantships, and resident hall director and student payroll positions available. Support available to part-time students. Financial award application deadline: 3/1; financial award applicants required to submit FAFSA. *Unit head:* Dr. John G. Kooti, Dean of the College of Business, 717-477-1435, Fax: 717-477-4003, E-mail: jgkooti@ship.edu. *Application contact:* Megan N. Luft, Associate Dean of Graduate Admissions, 717-477-1231, Fax: 717-477-4016, E-mail: mnluft@ship.edu.
Website: http://www.ship.edu/business

Stevens Institute of Technology, Graduate School, School of Systems and Enterprises, Program in Systems Design and Operational Effectiveness, Hoboken, NJ 07030. Offers Certificate. *Program availability:* Part-time, evening/weekend. *Students:* 8 part-time (0 women). Average age 34. 2 applicants, 100% accepted, 1 enrolled. In 2016, 4 Certificates awarded. *Degree requirements:* For Certificate, minimum B average. *Entrance requirements:* Additional exam requirements/recommendations for international students: Required—TOEFL (minimum score 74 iBT), IELTS (minimum score 6). *Application deadline:* For fall admission, 6/1 for domestic students, 4/15 for international students; for spring admission, 11/30 for domestic students, 11/1 for international students. Applications are processed on a rolling basis. Application fee: $65. Electronic applications accepted. *Expenses: Tuition:* Full-time $33,328; part-time $1501 per credit. *Required fees:* $1186; $566 per credit. $283 per semester. *Financial support:* Fellowships, research assistantships, teaching assistantships, career-related internships or fieldwork, Federal Work-Study, scholarships/grants, and unspecified assistantships available. Financial award application deadline: 2/15; financial award applicants required to submit FAFSA. *Unit head:* Dr. Dinesh Verma, Dean, 201-216-8645, Fax: 201-216-5541, E-mail: dinesh.verma@stevens.edu. *Application contact:* Graduate Admissions, 888-783-8367, Fax: 888-511-1306, E-mail: graduate@stevens.edu.

Trident University International, College of Business Administration, Program in Business Administration, Cypress, CA 90630. Offers business administration (PhD); conflict and negotiation management (MBA); criminal justice administration (MBA); entrepreneurship (MBA); finance (MBA); general management (MBA); government accounting (MBA); human resource management (MBA); information security and digital assurance management (MBA); information technology management (MBA); international business (MBA); logistics management (MBA); marketing (MBA); project management (MBA); public management (MBA); quality management (MBA); strategic leadership (MBA). *Program availability:* Part-time, evening/weekend, online learning. *Degree requirements:* For doctorate, comprehensive exam, thesis/dissertation, defense of dissertation. *Entrance requirements:* For master's, minimum GPA of 2.5 (students with GPA 3.0 or greater may transfer up to 30% of graduate level credits); for doctorate, minimum GPA of 3.4, curriculum vitae, course work in research methods or statistics. Additional exam requirements/recommendations for international students: Required—TOEFL. Electronic applications accepted.

Universidad del Turabo, Graduate Programs, School of Business and Entrepreneurship, Program in Logistics and Materials Management, Gurabo, PR 00778-3030. Offers MBA. *Program availability:* Part-time, evening/weekend. *Faculty:* 4 full-time (2 women), 21 part-time/adjunct (3 women). *Students:* 11 full-time (8 women), 26 part-time (16 women); all minorities (all Hispanic/Latino). Average age 34. 30 applicants, 47% accepted, 12 enrolled. In 2016, 9 master's awarded. *Entrance requirements:* For master's, GRE, EXADEP or GMAT, interview, essay, official transcript, recommendation letters. *Application deadline:* For fall admission, 8/5 for domestic students. Applications are processed on a rolling basis. Application fee: $25. Electronic applications accepted. *Financial support:* Institutionally sponsored loans available. Financial award applicants required to submit FAFSA. *Unit head:* Juan Sosa, Dean, 787-743-7979 Ext. 4118, E-mail: negocios_ut@suagm.edu. *Application contact:* Diriee Rodríguez, Admissions Director, 787-743-7979 Ext. 4453, E-mail: admisiones-ut@suagm.edu.
Website: http://ut.suagm.edu/es/negocios

University at Buffalo, the State University of New York, Graduate School, School of Management, Buffalo, NY 14620. Offers accounting (MS); analytics (MBA); business administration (PMBA); consulting (MBA); finance (MBA, MS), including financial risk management (MS), quantitative finance (MS); healthcare (MBA); information assurance (MBA); information systems (MBA); international management (MBA); management (EMBA, PhD); management information systems (MS); marketing (MBA); supply chain and operations (MBA); supply chains and operations management (MS); Au D/MBA; DDS/MBA; JD/MBA; M Arch/MBA; MD/MBA; MPH/MBA; MSW/MBA; Pharm D/MBA. *Accreditation:* AACSB. *Program availability:* Part-time, evening/weekend. *Faculty:* 80 full-time (26 women), 36 part-time/adjunct (6 women). *Students:* 683 full-time (277 women), 196 part-time (63 women); includes 76 minority (23 Black or African American, non-Hispanic/Latino; 1 American Indian or Alaska Native, non-Hispanic/Latino; 48 Asian, non-Hispanic/Latino; 3 Hispanic/Latino; 1 Two or more races, non-Hispanic/Latino), 371 international. Average age 31. 2,451 applicants, 42% accepted, 484 enrolled. In 2016, 515 master's, 10 doctorates awarded. *Degree requirements:* For master's, thesis (for some programs); for doctorate, comprehensive exam, thesis/dissertation. *Entrance requirements:* For master's, GMAT (for MS in accounting, finance); GRE or GMAT (for MBA, PMBA, other MS concentrations), essays, letters of recommendation; for doctorate, GMAT or GRE, essays, writing sample, letters of recommendation. Additional exam requirements/recommendations for international students: Required—TOEFL (minimum score 95 iBT) or IELTS (minimum score 6.5); Recommended—TSE (minimum score 73). *Application deadline:* For fall admission, 10/15 priority date for domestic and international students; for winter admission, 2/1 priority date for domestic and international students; for spring admission, 4/15 for domestic students; for summer admission, 5/15 for domestic students. Application fee: $100. Electronic applications accepted. *Expenses:* Contact institution. *Financial support:* Fellowships with full and partial tuition reimbursements, research assistantships with full and partial tuition reimbursements, teaching assistantships with full and partial tuition reimbursements, career-related internships or fieldwork, Federal Work-Study, institutionally sponsored loans, scholarships/grants, health care benefits, and unspecified assistantships available. Financial award application deadline: 2/15. *Faculty research:* Data analytics, accounting information and corporate finance, consumer behavior, supply chain logistics, leadership and team effectiveness. *Total annual research expenditures:* $1.5 million. *Unit head:* Erin K. O'Brien, Assistant Dean and Director of Graduate Programs, 716-645-3204, Fax: 716-645-2341, E-mail: ekobrien@buffalo.edu. *Application contact:* Meghan Felser, Associate Director of Admissions and Recruiting, 716-645-3204, Fax: 716-645-2341, E-mail: mpwood@buffalo.edu.
Website: http://mgt.buffalo.edu/

The University of Alabama in Huntsville, School of Graduate Studies, College of Business Administration, Programs in Business and Management, Huntsville, AL 35899. Offers business analytics (MSMS); federal contracting and procurement management (Certificate); human resource management (MSM); management (MBA), including acquisition management, entrepreneurship, federal contract accounting, finance, human resource management, logistics and supply chain management, marketing, project management; supply chain management (Certificate); technology and innovation management (Certificate). *Accreditation:* AACSB. *Program availability:* Part-time, evening/weekend. *Degree requirements:* For master's, comprehensive exam, thesis or alternative. *Entrance requirements:* For master's, GMAT (minimum score 500), minimum AACSB index of 1080. Additional exam requirements/recommendations for international students: Required—TOEFL (minimum score 550 paper-based; 80 iBT), IELTS (minimum score 6.5). Electronic applications accepted. *Expenses:* Tuition, state resident: full-time $9834; part-time $600 per credit hour. Tuition, nonresident: full-time $21,830; part-time $1325 per credit hour. *Faculty research:* Supply chain management, management of research and development, international marketing and branding, organizational behavior and human resource management, social networks and computational economics.

University of Alaska Anchorage, College of Business and Public Policy, Program in Logistics, Anchorage, AK 99508. Offers global supply chain management (MS); supply chain management (Certificate). *Program availability:* Part-time, evening/weekend, online learning. *Degree requirements:* For master's, thesis or alternative, research project. *Entrance requirements:* Additional exam requirements/recommendations for international students: Required—TOEFL (minimum score 550 paper-based).

University of Dallas, Satish and Yasmin Gupta College of Business, Irving, TX 75062-4736. Offers accounting (MBA, MS); business administration (DBA); business analytics (MS); business management (MBA); corporate finance (MBA); cybersecurity (MS); finance (MS); financial services (MBA); global business (MBA, MS); health services management (MBA); human resource management (MBA); information and technology management (MS); information assurance (MBA); information technology (MBA); information technology service management (MBA); marketing management (MBA); organization development (MBA); project management (MBA); sports and entertainment management (MBA); strategic leadership (MBA); supply chain management (MBA). *Accreditation:* AACSB. *Program availability:* Part-time, evening/weekend, online learning. *Entrance requirements:* Additional exam requirements/recommendations for international students: Required—TOEFL. Electronic applications accepted. *Expenses:* Contact institution.

University of Houston, College of Technology, Department of Information and Logistics Technology, Houston, TX 77204. Offers information security (MS); supply chain and logistics technology (MS); technology project management (MS). *Program availability:* Part-time. *Degree requirements:* For master's, project or thesis (most programs). *Entrance requirements:* For master's, GMAT. Additional exam requirements/recommendations for international students: Required—TOEFL (minimum score 550 paper-based; 79 iBT). Electronic applications accepted.

The University of Kansas, Graduate Studies, School of Business, Program in Business, Lawrence, KS 66045. Offers accounting (PhD); business and organizational leadership (MS); decision sciences and supply chain management (PhD); finance (PhD); human resources management (PhD); marketing (PhD); organizational behavior (PhD); strategic management (PhD); supply chain management and logistics (MS). *Accreditation:* AACSB. *Program availability:* Part-time. *Students:* 76 full-time (11 women), 170 part-time (83 women); includes 41 minority (15 Black or African American, non-Hispanic/Latino; 3 American Indian or Alaska Native, non-Hispanic/Latino; 6 Asian, non-Hispanic/Latino; 5 Hispanic/Latino; 12 Two or more races, non-Hispanic/Latino), 25 international. Average age 32. 294 applicants, 69% accepted, 152 enrolled. In 2016, 36 master's, 9 doctorates awarded. *Entrance requirements:* For master's, GMAT, official transcript, three letters of recommendation, resume, statement of purpose; for doctorate, GMAT or GRE, official transcript, three letters of recommendation, resume, statement of purpose. Additional exam requirements/recommendations for international students: Required—TOEFL (minimum score 600 paper-based; 100 iBT). *Application deadline:* For fall admission, 1/10 for domestic and international students. Application fee: $65 ($85 for international students). Electronic applications accepted. *Financial support:* Fellowships, research assistantships, teaching assistantships, scholarships/grants, health care benefits, tuition waivers (full), and unspecified assistantships available. Financial award application deadline: 1/10. *Faculty research:* Strategic human resource management, business ethics, organizational theory/behavior, corporate strategy, international business, supply chain management, Bayesian networks, game theory, decision analysis and time/series analysis, pricing, consumer effects, advertising and emotion. *Unit head:* Charly Edmonds, Director, 785-864-3841, E-mail: bschoolphd@ku.edu. *Application contact:* Graduate Admission Contact, 785-864-7500, E-mail: bschoolphd@ku.edu.
Website: http://www.business.ku.edu/

University of Louisville, J. B. Speed School of Engineering, Department of Industrial Engineering, Louisville, KY 40292-0001. Offers engineering management (M Eng);

industrial engineering (M Eng, MS, PhD); logistics and distribution (Certificate). *Accreditation:* ABET (one or more programs are accredited). *Program availability:* 100% online. *Faculty:* 7 full-time (4 women), 5 part-time/adjunct (2 women). *Students:* 68 full-time (19 women), 129 part-time (22 women); includes 25 minority (10 Black or African American, non-Hispanic/Latino; 1 American Indian or Alaska Native, non-Hispanic/Latino; 6 Asian, non-Hispanic/Latino; 3 Hispanic/Latino; 5 Two or more races, non-Hispanic/Latino), 86 international. Average age 32. 93 applicants, 44% accepted, 25 enrolled. In 2016, 33 master's, 3 doctorates awarded. *Degree requirements:* For master's and Certificate, thesis optional; for doctorate, comprehensive exam, thesis/dissertation. *Entrance requirements:* For master's and doctorate, GRE General Test, two letters of recommendation, official transcripts. Additional exam requirements/recommendations for international students: Required—TOEFL (minimum score 550 paper-based; 80 iBT), IELTS (minimum score 6.5). *Application deadline:* For fall admission, 5/1 priority date for international students; for spring admission, 11/1 priority date for international students; for summer admission, 3/1 priority date for international students. Applications are processed on a rolling basis. Application fee: $60. Electronic applications accepted. *Expenses:* Tuition, state resident: full-time $12,246; part-time $681 per credit hour. Tuition, nonresident: full-time $25,486; part-time $1417 per credit hour. *Required fees:* $196. Tuition and fees vary according to program and reciprocity agreements. *Financial support:* In 2016–17, 2 fellowships with full tuition reimbursements (averaging $22,000 per year) were awarded; research assistantships with full tuition reimbursements, teaching assistantships with full tuition reimbursements, scholarships/grants, health care benefits, and tuition waivers (full) also available. Financial award application deadline: 1/1; financial award applicants required to submit FAFSA. *Faculty research:* Optimization, computer simulation, logistics and distribution, ergonomics and human factors, advanced manufacturing process. *Total annual research expenditures:* $620,986. *Unit head:* Dr. Suraj M. Alexander, Chair, 502-852-6342, E-mail: usher@louisville.edu. *Application contact:* Lihui Bai, Director of Graduate Studies, 502-852-1416, E-mail: lihui.bai@louisville.edu.
Website: http://www.louisville.edu/speed/industrial/

University of Missouri–St. Louis, College of Business Administration, Program in Business Administration, St. Louis, MO 63121. Offers accounting (MBA); business administration (Certificate); business intelligence (Certificate); cybersecurity (Certificate); digital and social media marketing (Certificate); finance (MBA); human resources management (Certificate); information systems (MBA); international business (MBA); logistics and supply chain management (MBA, PhD, Certificate); management (MBA); marketing (MBA); marketing management (Certificate); operations management (MBA). *Accreditation:* AACSB. *Program availability:* Part-time, evening/weekend. *Faculty:* 32 full-time (10 women), 14 part-time/adjunct (3 women). *Students:* 181 full-time (88 women), 357 part-time (154 women); includes 83 minority (30 Black or African American, non-Hispanic/Latino; 36 Asian, non-Hispanic/Latino; 12 Hispanic/Latino; 2 Native Hawaiian or other Pacific Islander, non-Hispanic/Latino; 3 Two or more races, non-Hispanic/Latino), 100 international. Average age 31. 245 applicants, 83% accepted, 139 enrolled. *Degree requirements:* For doctorate, thesis/dissertation. *Entrance requirements:* For master's, GMAT, 2 letters of recommendation. Additional exam requirements/recommendations for international students: Recommended—TOEFL (minimum score 550 paper-based; 79 iBT), IELTS (minimum score 6.5). *Application deadline:* For fall admission, 7/1 for domestic and international students; for spring admission, 12/1 for domestic and international students. Applications are processed on a rolling basis. Application fee: $50 ($40 for international students). Electronic applications accepted. *Financial support:* Research assistantships with tuition reimbursements, teaching assistantships with tuition reimbursements, career-related internships or fieldwork, Federal Work-Study, and institutionally sponsored loans available. Support available to part-time students. Financial award application deadline: 4/1; financial award applicants required to submit FAFSA. *Faculty research:* Human resources, strategic management, marketing strategy, consumer behavior product development, advertising. *Unit head:* Dr. Thomas H. Eyssell, Associate Dean and Director of Graduate Studies, 314-516-5885, Fax: 314-516-6420, E-mail: mba@umsl.edu. *Application contact:* 314-516-5458, Fax: 314-516-6996, E-mail: gradadm@umsl.edu.

The University of North Carolina at Charlotte, William States Lee College of Engineering, Department of Systems Engineering and Engineering Management, Charlotte, NC 28223-0001. Offers energy analytics (Graduate Certificate); engineering management (MSEM); Lean Six Sigma (Graduate Certificate); logistics and supply chains (Graduate Certificate); systems analytics (Graduate Certificate). *Program availability:* Part-time, evening/weekend, 100% online, blended/hybrid learning. *Faculty:* 9 full-time (1 woman), 2 part-time/adjunct (1 woman). *Students:* 22 full-time (10 women), 61 part-time (12 women); includes 13 minority (7 Black or African American, non-Hispanic/Latino; 1 Asian, non-Hispanic/Latino; 4 Hispanic/Latino; 1 Two or more races, non-Hispanic/Latino), 29 international. Average age 30. 210 applicants, 56% accepted, 31 enrolled. In 2016, 44 master's, 5 other advanced degrees awarded. *Degree requirements:* For master's, project or thesis. *Entrance requirements:* For master's, GRE or GMAT, bachelor's degree in engineering or a closely-related technical or scientific field, or in business, provided relevant technical course requirements have been met; undergraduate coursework in engineering economics, calculus, or statistics; minimum GPA of 3.0; for Graduate Certificate, bachelor's degree in engineering or closely-related technical or scientific field, or bachelor's degree in business, provided relevant technical course requirements have been met; minimum GPA of 3.0; undergraduate coursework in engineering economics, calculus, and statistics; written description of work experience. Additional exam requirements/recommendations for international students: Required—TOEFL (minimum score 523 paper-based, 70 iBT) or IELTS (6.5). *Application deadline:* For fall admission, 3/1 priority date for domestic and international students; for spring admission, 10/1 priority date for domestic and international students; for summer admission, 4/1 priority date for domestic and international students. Applications are processed on a rolling basis. Application fee: $75. Electronic applications accepted. *Expenses:* Contact institution. *Financial support:* In 2016–17, 2 students received support, including 2 research assistantships (averaging $13,750 per year); career-related internships or fieldwork, institutionally sponsored loans, scholarships/grants, and unspecified assistantships also available. Support available to part-time students. Financial award application deadline: 3/1; financial award applicants required to submit FAFSA. *Total annual research expenditures:* $196,680. *Unit head:* Dr. Simon M. Hsiang, Chair, 704-687-1958, E-mail: shsiang1@uncc.edu. *Application contact:* Kathy B. Giddings, Director of Graduate Admissions, 704-687-5503, Fax: 704-687-1668, E-mail: gradadm@uncc.edu.
Website: http://seem.uncc.edu/

University of North Florida, Coggin College of Business, MBA Program, Jacksonville, FL 32224. Offers accounting (MBA); construction management (MBA); e-commerce (MBA); economics (MBA); finance (MBA); human resource management (MBA); international business (MBA); logistics (MBA); management applications (MBA). *Accreditation:* AACSB. *Program availability:* Part-time, evening/weekend. *Faculty:* 16 full-time (4 women), 1 (woman) part-time/adjunct. *Students:* 105 full-time (50 women), 162 part-time (68 women); includes 57 minority (14 Black or African American, non-Hispanic/Latino; 1 American Indian or Alaska Native, non-Hispanic/Latino; 17 Asian, non-Hispanic/Latino; 18 Hispanic/Latino; 7 Two or more races, non-Hispanic/Latino), 41 international. Average age 28. 231 applicants, 46% accepted, 84 enrolled. In 2016, 114 master's awarded. *Entrance requirements:* For master's, GMAT or GRE, U.S. bachelor's degree from regionally-accredited university or equivalent foreign degree. Additional exam requirements/recommendations for international students: Required—TOEFL (minimum score 550 paper-based; 79 iBT). *Application deadline:* For fall admission, 8/1 priority date for domestic students, 5/1 for international students; for spring admission, 12/1 priority date for domestic students, 10/1 for international students; for summer admission, 4/29 priority date for domestic students, 2/1 for international students. Application fee: $30. Tuition and fees vary according to course load, campus/location and program. *Financial support:* In 2016–17, 22 students received support, including 1 research assistantship (averaging $2,501 per year); teaching assistantships, Federal Work-Study, and tuition waivers (partial) also available. Support available to part-time students. Financial award application deadline: 4/1; financial award applicants required to submit FAFSA. *Faculty research:* Performance measures, costing, and inventory issues in logistics and supply chain management; inter-organizational systems; international management and marketing practices; e-commerce; organizational learning and socialization processes. *Total annual research expenditures:* $17,654. *Unit head:* Dr. Parvez Ahmed, Graduate Program Director, 904-620-1678, E-mail: pahmed@unf.edu. *Application contact:* Amy Bishop, MSM Advisor, 904-620-2575, Fax: 904-620-2832, E-mail: coggin.students@unf.edu.
Website: http://www.unf.edu/graduateschool/academics/programs/MBA.aspx

University of North Texas, Robert B. Toulouse School of Graduate Studies, Denton, TX 76203-5459. Offers accounting (MS); applied anthropology (MA, MS); applied behavior analysis (Certificate); applied geography (MA); applied technology and performance improvement (M Ed, MS); art education (MA); art history (MA); art museum education (Certificate); arts leadership (Certificate); audiology (Au D); behavior analysis (MS); behavioral science (PhD); biochemistry and molecular biology (MS); biology (MA, MS); biomedical engineering (MS); business analysis (MS); chemistry (MS); clinical health psychology (PhD); communication studies (MA, MS); computer engineering (MS); computer science (MS); counseling (M Ed, MS), including clinical mental health counseling (MS), college and university counseling, elementary school counseling, secondary school counseling; creative writing (MA); criminal justice (MS); curriculum and instruction (M Ed); decision sciences (MBA); design (MA, MFA), including fashion design (MFA), innovation studies, interior design (MFA); early childhood studies (MS); economics (MS); educational leadership (M Ed, Ed D); educational psychology (MS, PhD), including family studies (MS), gifted and talented (MS), human development (MS), learning and cognition (MS), research, measurement and evaluation (MS); electrical engineering (MS); emergency management (MPA); engineering technology (MS); English (MA); English as a second language (MA); environmental science (MS); finance (MBA, MS); financial management (MPA); French (MA); health services management (MBA); higher education (M Ed, Ed D); history (MA, MS); hospitality management (MS); human resources management (MPA); information science (MS); information systems (PhD); information technologies (MBA); interdisciplinary studies (MA, MS); international studies (MA); international sustainable tourism (MS); jazz studies (MM); journalism (MA, MJ, Graduate Certificate), including interactive and virtual digital communication (Graduate Certificate), narrative journalism (Graduate Certificate), public relations (Graduate Certificate); kinesiology (MS); linguistics (MA); local government management (MPA); logistics (PhD); logistics and supply chain management (MBA); long-term care, senior housing, and aging services (MA); management (PhD); marketing (MBA); mathematics (MA, MS); mechanical and energy engineering (MS, PhD); music (MA), including ethnomusicology, music theory, musicology, performance; music composition (PhD); music education (MM Ed, PhD); nonprofit management (MPA); operations and supply chain management (MBA); performance (MM, DMA); philosophy (MA); political science (MA); professional and technical communication (MA); radio, television and film (MA, MFA); rehabilitation counseling (Certificate); sociology (MA); Spanish (MA); special education (M Ed); speech-language pathology (MA); strategic management (MBA); studio art (MFA); teaching (M Ed); MBA/MS. *Program availability:* Part-time, evening/weekend, online learning. Terminal master's awarded for partial completion of doctoral program. *Degree requirements:* For master's, variable foreign language requirement, comprehensive exam (for some programs), thesis (for some programs); for doctorate, variable foreign language requirement, comprehensive exam (for some programs), thesis/dissertation; for other advanced degree, variable foreign language requirement, comprehensive exam (for some programs). *Entrance requirements:* For master's and doctorate, GRE, GMAT. Additional exam requirements/recommendations for international students: Required—TOEFL (minimum score 550 paper-based; 79 iBT). Electronic applications accepted.

University of St. Francis, College of Business and Health Administration, School of Business, Joliet, IL 60435-6169. Offers accounting (MBA, Certificate); business analytics (MBA, Certificate); finance (MBA, Certificate); health administration (MBA); human resource management (MBA); logistics (Certificate); management (MBA, MSM); training and development (MBA); transportation and logistics (MBA). *Accreditation:* ACBSP. *Program availability:* Part-time, evening/weekend, 100% online, blended/hybrid learning. *Faculty:* 6 full-time (3 women), 12 part-time/adjunct (6 women). *Students:* 78 full-time (28 women), 110 part-time (62 women); includes 41 minority (22 Black or African American, non-Hispanic/Latino; 3 Asian, non-Hispanic/Latino; 15 Hispanic/Latino; 1 Two or more races, non-Hispanic/Latino), 8 international. Average age 36. 171 applicants, 44% accepted, 58 enrolled. In 2016, 62 master's, 3 other advanced degrees awarded. *Entrance requirements:* For master's, GMAT or 2 years of managerial experience. Additional exam requirements/recommendations for international students: Required—TOEFL (minimum score 550 paper-based; 79 iBT), IELTS (minimum score 6). *Application deadline:* Applications are processed on a rolling basis. Application fee: $30. Electronic applications accepted. Application fee is waived when completed online. *Expenses:* $798 per credit. *Financial support:* In 2016–17, 51 students received support. Career-related internships or fieldwork, scholarships/grants, tuition waivers (partial), and unspecified assistantships available. Support available to part-time students. Financial award applicants required to submit FAFSA. *Unit head:* Dr. Orlando Griego, Dean, 815-740-3395, Fax: 815-740-3537, E-mail: ogriego@stfrancis.edu. *Application contact:* Sandra Sloka, Director of Admissions for Graduate and Degree Completion Programs, 800-735-7500, Fax: 815-740-3431, E-mail: ssloka@stfrancis.edu.
Website: http://www.stfrancis.edu/academics/college-of-business-health-administration/

University of South Africa, College of Economic and Management Sciences, Pretoria, South Africa. Offers accounting (D Admin, D Com); accounting science (DA); auditing (D Admin, D Com); business administration (M Tech); business economics (D Admin); business leadership (DBL); business management (D Admin, D Com); economic management analysis (M Tech); economics (D Admin, D Com, PhD); human resource development (M Tech); industrial psychology (D Admin, D Com, PhD); logistics (D Com); marketing (M Tech); public administration (D Admin, D Com, DPA, PhD); public management (M Tech); quantitative management (D Admin, D Com); real estate (M Tech); statistics (D Admin, PhD); tourism management (D Admin, D Com); transport economics (D Admin, D Com).

University of Southern Mississippi, Graduate School, College of Science and Technology, School of Construction, Hattiesburg, MS 39406. Offers logistics, trade and transportation (MS). *Program availability:* Part-time, online learning. *Degree*

requirements: For master's, comprehensive exam, thesis optional. *Entrance requirements:* For master's, GMAT or GRE General Test, minimum GPA of 2.75 in last 60 hours. Additional exam requirements/recommendations for international students: Required—TOEFL, IELTS. *Application deadline:* For fall admission, 3/1 priority date for domestic students, 3/1 for international students. Applications are processed on a rolling basis. Application fee: $60. *Expenses: Tuition, area resident:* Full-time $15,708; part-time $437 per credit hour. *Financial support:* Research assistantships with full tuition reimbursements, teaching assistantships with full tuition reimbursements, career-related internships or fieldwork, Federal Work-Study, scholarships/grants, health care benefits, and unspecified assistantships available. Financial award application deadline: 3/15; financial award applicants required to submit FAFSA. *Faculty research:* Robotics; CAD/CAM; simulation; computer-integrated manufacturing processes; construction scheduling, estimating, and computer systems. *Unit head:* Dr. Erich Connell, Director, 601-266-4895.
Website: http://www.usm.edu/construction

The University of Tennessee, Graduate School, College of Business Administration, Program in Business Administration, Knoxville, TN 37996. Offers accounting (PhD); finance (MBA, PhD); logistics and transportation (MBA, PhD); management (PhD); marketing (MBA, PhD); operations management (MBA); professional business administration (MBA); statistics (PhD); JD/MBA; MS/MBA; Pharm D/MBA. Pharm D/MBA offered jointly with The University of Tennessee Health Science Center. *Accreditation:* AACSB. *Program availability:* Online learning. *Degree requirements:* For master's, thesis or alternative; for doctorate, thesis/dissertation. *Entrance requirements:* For master's and doctorate, GMAT, minimum GPA of 2.7. Additional exam requirements/recommendations for international students: Required—TOEFL. Electronic applications accepted.

The University of Tennessee at Chattanooga, Engineering Management and Technology Program, Chattanooga, TN 37403. Offers construction management (Graduate Certificate); engineering management (MS); fundamentals of engineering management (Graduate Certificate); leadership and ethics (Graduate Certificate); logistics and supply chain management (Graduate Certificate); power systems management (Graduate Certificate); project and technology management (Graduate Certificate); quality management (Graduate Certificate). *Program availability:* 100% online, blended/hybrid learning. *Faculty:* 6 full-time (1 woman). *Students:* 14 full-time (3 women), 49 part-time (11 women); includes 17 minority (10 Black or African American, non-Hispanic/Latino; 2 Asian, non-Hispanic/Latino; 3 Hispanic/Latino; 2 Two or more races, non-Hispanic/Latino), 8 international. Average age 33. 29 applicants, 93% accepted, 15 enrolled. In 2016, 36 master's, 7 other advanced degrees awarded. *Degree requirements:* For master's, thesis. *Entrance requirements:* For master's, GRE General Test, letters of recommendation; minimum undergraduate GPA of 2.7 overall or 3.0 in final two years. Additional exam requirements/recommendations for international students: Required—TOEFL (minimum score 550 paper-based; 79 iBT), IELTS (minimum score 6). *Application deadline:* For fall admission, 6/15 priority date for domestic students, 7/1 for international students; for spring admission, 11/1 priority date for domestic students, 11/1 for international students. Applications are processed on a rolling basis. Application fee: $35 ($40 for international students). Electronic applications accepted. *Expenses:* $9,876 full-time in-state; $25,994 full-time out-of-state; $450 per credit part-time in-state; $1,345 per credit part-time out-of-state. *Financial support:* In 2016–17, 4 research assistantships were awarded; teaching assistantships, career-related internships or fieldwork, scholarships/grants, and unspecified assistantships also available. Support available to part-time students. Financial award application deadline: 7/1; financial award applicants required to submit FAFSA. *Faculty research:* Plant layout design, lean manufacturing, Six Sigma, value management, product development. *Unit head:* Dr. Neslihan Alp, Department Head, 423-425-4032, Fax: 423-425-5818, E-mail: neslihan-alp@utc.edu. *Application contact:* Dr. Joanne Romagni, Dean of the Graduate School, 423-425-4478, Fax: 423-425-5223, E-mail: joanne-romagni@utc.edu.
Website: http://www.utc.edu/college-engineering-computer-science/programs/engineering-management-and-technology/index.php#li03

The University of Texas at Arlington, Graduate School, College of Engineering, Department of Industrial, Manufacturing, and Systems Engineering, Program in Logistics, Arlington, TX 76019. Offers MS. *Degree requirements:* For master's, comprehensive exam, thesis optional. *Entrance requirements:* For master's, GRE, GMAT, minimum GPA of 3.0. Additional exam requirements/recommendations for international students: Required—TOEFL (minimum score 550 paper-based). *Application deadline:* For fall admission, 6/6 for domestic students, 4/4 for international students; for spring admission, 10/15 for domestic students, 9/5 for international students. Application fee: $35 ($50 for international students). *Financial support:* Fellowships, research assistantships, teaching assistantships, career-related internships or fieldwork, Federal Work-Study, institutionally sponsored loans, scholarships/grants, and unspecified assistantships available. Financial award application deadline: 6/1; financial award applicants required to submit FAFSA. *Unit head:* Dr. Donald H. Liles, Chair, 817-272-3092, Fax: 817-272-3406, E-mail: dliles@uta.edu. *Application contact:* Dr. Jamie Rogers, Graduate Advisor, 817-272-2495, Fax: 817-272-3406, E-mail: jrogers@uta.edu.
Website: http://www.ie.uta.edu/

University of Washington, Graduate School, Interdisciplinary Program in Global Trade, Transportation and Logistics Studies, Seattle, WA 98195. Offers Certificate.

Virginia International University, School of Business, Fairfax, VA 22030. Offers accounting (MBA, MS); entrepreneurship (MBA); executive management (Graduate Certificate); global logistics (MBA); health care management (MBA); hospitality and tourism management (MBA); human resources management (MBA); international business management (MBA); international finance (MBA); marketing management (MBA); mass media and public relations (MBA); project management (MBA, MS). *Program availability:* Part-time, online learning. *Entrance requirements:* For master's and Graduate Certificate, bachelor's degree. Additional exam requirements/recommendations for international students: Required—TOEFL (minimum score 550 paper-based; 80 iBT), IELTS (minimum score 6). Electronic applications accepted.

Wright State University, Graduate School, Raj Soin College of Business, Department of Information Systems and Operations Management, Logistics and Supply Chain Management Program, Dayton, OH 45435. Offers MS. *Expenses:* Tuition, state resident: full-time $9952; part-time $622 per credit hour. Tuition, nonresident: full-time $16,960; part-time $1060 per credit hour. *Unit head:* Dr. Andrew W. Lai, Interim Chair, 937-775-2895, Fax: 937-775-3545, E-mail: andrew.lai@wright.edu. *Application contact:* Michael Evans, Director of MBA Programs, 937-775-2437, Fax: 937-775-3545, E-mail: michael.evans@wright.edu.

Supply Chain Management

Adelphi University, Robert B. Willumstad School of Business, Program in Supply Chain Management, Garden City, NY 11530-0701. Offers MS. *Program availability:* Part-time, online learning. *Students:* 2 full-time (0 women), 3 part-time (2 women); includes 1 minority (Asian, non-Hispanic/Latino), 2 international. Average age 33. 11 applicants, 45% accepted, 3 enrolled. *Entrance requirements:* For master's, GMAT, official transcripts, bachelor's degree, 500-word essay, letter of recommendation, resume. Additional exam requirements/recommendations for international students: Required—TOEFL (minimum score 550 paper-based; 80 iBT), IELTS (minimum score 6.5). Application fee: $50. *Expenses:* Contact institution. *Unit head:* Anthony Libertella, Dean, 516-877-4661, E-mail: libertel@adelphi.edu. *Application contact:* Christine Murphy, Director of Admissions, 516-877-3050, Fax: 516-877-3039, E-mail: graduateadmissions@adelphi.edu.
Website: http://business.adelphi.edu/academics/graduate-degree-programs/ms-supply-chain-management/

Albany State University, College of Business, Albany, GA 31705-2717. Offers accounting (MBA); general business administration (MBA); healthcare (MBA); public administration (MBA); supply chain and logistics (MBA). *Accreditation:* ACBSP. *Program availability:* Part-time, evening/weekend. *Degree requirements:* For master's, comprehensive exam, internship, 3 hours of physical education. *Entrance requirements:* For master's, GMAT (minimum score of 450)/GRE (minimum score of 800) for those without earned master's degree or higher, minimum undergraduate GPA of 2.5, 2 letters of reference, official transcript, pre-entrance medical record and certificate of immunization. *Application deadline:* For fall admission, 6/1 for domestic students, 5/1 for international students; for spring admission, 11/1 for domestic students, 10/1 for international students. Applications are processed on a rolling basis. Application fee: $20. Electronic applications accepted. *Financial support:* Application deadline: 4/15; applicants required to submit FAFSA. *Faculty research:* Diversity issues, ancestry, understanding finance through use of technology. *Unit head:* Dr. Alicia Jackson, Dean, 229-430-7009, Fax: 229-430-5119. *Application contact:* Jeffrey Pierce, II, Graduate Counselor, 229-430-4646, Fax: 229-430-4105, E-mail: jeffrey.pierce@asurams.edu.
Website: https://www.asurams.edu/Academics/collegeofbusiness/

American Graduate University, Program in Business Administration, Covina, CA 91724. Offers acquisition and contracting (MBA); supply chain management (MBA). *Program availability:* Part-time, online learning. *Degree requirements:* For master's, thesis. *Entrance requirements:* For master's, undergraduate degree from institution accredited by accrediting agency recognized by the U.S. Department of Education. Additional exam requirements/recommendations for international students: Required—TOEFL. *Application deadline:* Applications are processed on a rolling basis. Application fee: $50. Electronic applications accepted. *Unit head:* Paul McDonald, President, 626-966-4576 Ext. 1006, E-mail: paulmcdonald@agu.edu. *Application contact:* Laurie Mejia, Director of Admissions, 626-966-4576 Ext. 1007, Fax: 626-915-1709, E-mail: lauriemejia@agu.edu.

American Graduate University, Program in Supply Chain Management, Covina, CA 91724. Offers MSCM, Certificate. *Program availability:* Part-time, online learning. *Degree requirements:* For master's, comprehensive exam or project. *Entrance requirements:* For master's, undergraduate degree from institution accredited by accrediting agency recognized by the U.S. Department of Education. Additional exam requirements/recommendations for international students: Required—TOEFL. Application fee: $50. *Unit head:* Paul McDonald, President, 626-966-4576 Ext. 1006, Fax: 626-915-1709, E-mail: paulmcdonald@agu.edu. *Application contact:* Laurie Mejia, Director of Admissions, 626-966-4576 Ext. 1007, Fax: 626-915-1709, E-mail: lauriemejia@agu.edu.
Website: http://www.agu.edu/Acquisition_mgnt/master_supply.html

Anderson University, College of Business, Anderson, SC 29621-4035. Offers business administration (MBA); healthcare leadership (MBA); human resources (MBA); marketing (MBA); supply chain management (MBA). *Accreditation:* ACBSP. *Students:* 7 full-time (0 women), 1 part-time (0 women). *Expenses:* Contact institution. *Financial support:* Tuition waivers available. Financial award application deadline: 3/1; financial award applicants required to submit FAFSA. *Unit head:* Dr. Douglas Goodwin, MBA Director/Associate Dean, 864-MBA-6000. *Application contact:* Mallory Knight, Graduate Admission Counselor, 864-231-2182, Fax: 864-231-2115, E-mail: malloryknight@andersonuniversity.edu.
Website: http://www.andersonuniversity.edu/business

Arizona State University at the Tempe campus, W. P. Carey School of Business, Program in Business Administration, Tempe, AZ 85287-4906. Offers entrepreneurship (MBA); finance (MBA); health sector management (MBA); international business (MBA); leadership (MBA); marketing (MBA); organizational behavior (PhD); strategic management (PhD); supply chain management (MBA, PhD); JD/MBA; MBA/M Acc; MBA/M Arch. *Accreditation:* AACSB. *Program availability:* Part-time, evening/weekend, online learning. Terminal master's awarded for partial completion of doctoral program. *Degree requirements:* For master's, thesis or alternative, internship, interactive Program of Study (iPOS) submitted before completing 50 percent of required credit hours; for doctorate, comprehensive exam, thesis/dissertation, interactive Program of Study (iPOS) submitted before completing 50 percent of required credit hours. *Entrance requirements:* For master's, GMAT, minimum GPA of 3.0 in last 2 years of work leading to bachelor's degree, 2 letters of recommendation, professional resume, official transcripts, 3 essays; for doctorate, GMAT or GRE, minimum GPA of 3.0 in last 2 years of work leading to bachelor's degree, 3 letters of recommendation, resume, personal statement/essay. Additional exam requirements/recommendations for international students: Required—TOEFL (minimum score 550 paper-based; 80 iBT), IELTS (minimum score 6.5). Electronic applications accepted. *Expenses:* Contact institution.

Boston University, Metropolitan College, Department of Administrative Sciences, Boston, MA 02215. Offers applied business analytics (MS); economic development and tourism management (MSAS); enterprise risk management (MS); financial management (MS); global marketing management (MS); innovation and technology (MSAS); insurance management (MSM); project management (MS); supply chain management (MS). *Accreditation:* AACSB. *Program availability:* Part-time, evening/weekend, online learning. *Faculty:* 15 full-time (3 women), 22 part-time/adjunct (3 women). *Students:* 301 full-time (146 women), 934 part-time (501 women); includes 237 minority (81 Black or African American, non-Hispanic/Latino; 5 American Indian or Alaska Native, non-

Hispanic/Latino; 60 Asian, non-Hispanic/Latino; 76 Hispanic/Latino; 1 Native Hawaiian or other Pacific Islander, non-Hispanic/Latino; 14 Two or more races, non-Hispanic/Latino), 514 international. Average age 31. 593 applicants, 69% accepted, 260 enrolled. In 2016, 263 master's awarded. *Degree requirements:* For master's, thesis optional. *Entrance requirements:* For master's, 1 year of work experience, minimum GPA of 3.0. Additional exam requirements/recommendations for international students: Required—TOEFL (minimum score 84 iBT). *Application deadline:* Applications are processed on a rolling basis. Application fee: $80. Electronic applications accepted. *Expenses:* Contact institution. *Financial support:* In 2016–17, 15 students received support, including 14 research assistantships (averaging $8,400 per year); career-related internships or fieldwork, Federal Work-Study, and unspecified assistantships also available. *Faculty research:* International business, innovative process. *Unit head:* Dr. John Sullivan, Chair, 617-353-3016, E-mail: adminsc@bu.edu. *Application contact:* Fiona Niven, Administrative Sciences Department, 617-353-3016, E-mail: adminsc@bu.edu.
Website: http://www.bu.edu/met/academic-community/departments/administrative-sciences/

Brigham Young University, Graduate Studies, Marriott School of Management, Master of Business Administration Program, Provo, UT 84602. Offers entrepreneurship (MBA); finance (MBA); global supply chain management (MBA); marketing (MBA); strategic human resources (MBA); JD/MBA; MBA/MS. *Accreditation:* AACSB. *Students:* 321 full-time (63 women); includes 16 minority (1 Black or African American, non-Hispanic/Latino; 9 Asian, non-Hispanic/Latino; 6 Hispanic/Latino), 69 international. Average age 31. 397 applicants, 49% accepted, 154 enrolled. In 2016, 146 master's awarded. *Entrance requirements:* For master's, GMAT or GRE, minimum GPA of 3.0 in last 60 hours. Additional exam requirements/recommendations for international students: Required—TOEFL (minimum score 590 paper-based; 94 iBT), IELTS (minimum score 7). *Application deadline:* For fall admission, 5/1 for domestic students, 1/15 for international students. Applications are processed on a rolling basis. Application fee: $50. Electronic applications accepted. *Expenses:* Contact institution. *Financial support:* In 2016–17, 247 students received support. Research assistantships, teaching assistantships, career-related internships or fieldwork, institutionally sponsored loans, and scholarships/grants available. Financial award application deadline: 3/1; financial award applicants required to submit FAFSA. *Faculty research:* Finance, marketing, supply chain management, entrepreneurship, strategic human resources. *Unit head:* Dr. Grant McQueen, Director, 801-422-3500, Fax: 801-422-0513, E-mail: mba@byu.edu. *Application contact:* Yvette Anderson, MBA Program Admissions Director, 801-422-3500, Fax: 801-422-0513, E-mail: mba@byu.edu. Website: http://mba.byu.edu

Bryant University, Graduate School of Business, Smithfield, RI 02917. Offers accounting (MPAC); business administration (MBA), including general management, global finance, global supply chain management, international business; business analytics (Graduate Certificate); taxation (MST). *Program availability:* Part-time, evening/weekend. *Faculty:* 16 full-time (3 women), 2 part-time/adjunct (0 women). *Students:* 71 full-time (23 women), 83 part-time (32 women); includes 17 minority (5 Black or African American, non-Hispanic/Latino; 4 Asian, non-Hispanic/Latino; 5 Hispanic/Latino; 3 Two or more races, non-Hispanic/Latino), 17 international. Average age 27. 165 applicants, 57% accepted, 66 enrolled. In 2016, 106 master's, 12 other advanced degrees awarded. *Degree requirements:* For master's, comprehensive exam (for some programs). *Entrance requirements:* For master's, GMAT, resume, recommendation, college transcripts. Additional exam requirements/recommendations for international students: Required—TOEFL (minimum score 580 paper-based; 95 iBT). *Application deadline:* For fall admission, 7/15 for domestic and international students; for spring admission, 11/15 for domestic and international students; for summer admission, 4/15 for domestic and international students. Applications are processed on a rolling basis. Application fee: $80. Electronic applications accepted. *Expenses:* Contact institution. *Financial support:* Research assistantships, scholarships/grants, and unspecified assistantships available. Support available to part-time students. Financial award application deadline: 2/15; financial award applicants required to submit FAFSA. *Faculty research:* International business, public sector auditing, taxation of partnerships, information systems security, financial markets microstructure. *Unit head:* Bjorn Carlsson, Graduate Program Director, 401-232-6707, E-mail: bcarlsson@bryant.edu. *Application contact:* Terri Rogers, Admissions Assistant, 401-232-6230, Fax: 401-232-6494, E-mail: graduateprograms@bryant.edu. Website: http://gradschool.bryant.edu/business/

California State University, East Bay, Office of Graduate Studies, College of Business and Economics, MBA Program, Option in Operations and Supply Chain Management, Hayward, CA 94542-3000. Offers MBA. *Degree requirements:* For master's, comprehensive exam or thesis. *Entrance requirements:* For master's, GMAT, minimum GPA of 2.75. Additional exam requirements/recommendations for international students: Required—TOEFL (minimum score 550 paper-based). *Application deadline:* For fall admission, 6/30 for domestic and international students. Application fee: $55. Electronic applications accepted. *Financial support:* Fellowships, career-related internships or fieldwork, Federal Work-Study, institutionally sponsored loans, and scholarships/grants available. Support available to part-time students. Financial award application deadline: 3/1; financial award applicants required to submit FAFSA. *Unit head:* Dr. Zinovy Radovilsky, Program Advisor, 510-885-3290, E-mail: zinovy.radovilsky@csueastbay.edu. *Application contact:* Dr. Donna Wiley, Interim Associate Vice President for Academic Programs and Graduate Studies, 510-885-3716, Fax: 510-885-4777, E-mail: donna.wiley@csueastbay.edu.
Website: http://www.csueastbay.edu/cbe/mba-options/operations-and-supply-chain-management-option.html

California State University, San Bernardino, Graduate Studies, College of Business and Public Administration, Program in Business Administration, San Bernardino, CA 92407. Offers accounting (MBA); entrepreneurship (MBA); finance (MBA); global business (MBA); information management (MBA); information security (MBA); management (MBA); supply chain management (MBA). *Accreditation:* AACSB. *Program availability:* Part-time, evening/weekend, online learning. *Faculty:* 7 full-time (4 women), 3 part-time/adjunct (2 women). *Students:* 37 full-time (11 women), 141 part-time (51 women); includes 85 minority (16 Black or African American, non-Hispanic/Latino; 1 American Indian or Alaska Native, non-Hispanic/Latino; 20 Asian, non-Hispanic/Latino; 45 Hispanic/Latino; 3 Two or more races, non-Hispanic/Latino), 46 international. 260 applicants, 37% accepted, 34 enrolled. In 2016, 180 master's awarded. *Degree requirements:* For master's, comprehensive exam, thesis. *Entrance requirements:* Additional exam requirements/recommendations for international students: Required—TOEFL. *Application deadline:* For fall admission, 7/16 for domestic students, 7/20 for international students; for winter admission, 10/23 for domestic students, 10/20 for international students; for spring admission, 1/22 for domestic students, 1/20 for international students. Application fee: $55. *Expenses:* Contact institution. *Financial support:* Application deadline: 3/1. *Unit head:* Dr. Lawrence C. Rose, Dean, 909-537-3703, Fax: 909-537-7026, E-mail: lrose@csusb.edu. *Application contact:* Dr. Vipin Gupta, Associate Dean/MBA Director, 909-537-7380, Fax: 909-537-7026, E-mail: vgupta@csusb.edu.
Website: http://mba.csusb.edu/

Capella University, School of Business and Technology, Doctoral Programs in Technology, Minneapolis, MN 55402. Offers general information technology (PhD); global operations and supply chain management (DBA); information assurance and security (PhD); information technology education (PhD); information technology management (DBA, PhD).

Capella University, School of Business and Technology, Master's Programs in Technology, Minneapolis, MN 55402. Offers enterprise software architecture (MS); general information systems and technology management (MS); global operations and supply chain management (MBA); information assurance and security (MS); information technology management (MBA); network management (MS).

Case Western Reserve University, Weatherhead School of Management, Department of Operations, Cleveland, OH 44106. Offers operations and supply chain management (MSM); operations research (PhD); MBA/MSM. *Program availability:* Part-time. *Degree requirements:* For doctorate, thesis/dissertation. *Entrance requirements:* For master's, GRE General Test; for doctorate, GMAT, GRE General Test. *Expenses: Tuition:* Full-time $42,576; part-time $1774 per credit hour. *Required fees:* $34. Tuition and fees vary according to course load and program. *Faculty research:* Mathematical finance, mathematical programming, scheduling, stochastic optimization, environmental/energy models.

Central Connecticut State University, School of Graduate Studies, School of Engineering, Science and Technology, Department of Manufacturing and Construction Management, New Britain, CT 06050-4010. Offers construction management (MS, Certificate); environmental and occupational safety (Certificate); lean manufacturing and Six Sigma (Certificate); supply chain and logistics (Certificate); technology management (MS). *Program availability:* Part-time, evening/weekend. *Faculty:* 7 full-time (0 women), 3 part-time/adjunct (0 women). *Students:* 23 full-time (6 women), 88 part-time (21 women); includes 29 minority (11 Black or African American, non-Hispanic/Latino; 7 Asian, non-Hispanic/Latino; 10 Hispanic/Latino; 1 Two or more races, non-Hispanic/Latino), 12 international. Average age 34. 79 applicants, 68% accepted, 32 enrolled. In 2016, 43 master's, 4 other advanced degrees awarded. *Degree requirements:* For master's, comprehensive exam, special project; for Certificate, qualifying exam. *Entrance requirements:* For master's, minimum undergraduate GPA of 2.7. Additional exam requirements/recommendations for international students: Required—TOEFL (minimum score 550 paper-based; 79 iBT). *Application deadline:* For fall admission, 8/1 for domestic students, 5/1 for international students; for spring admission, 11/1 for domestic and international students. Applications are processed on a rolling basis. Application fee: $50. Electronic applications accepted. *Expenses: Tuition, area resident:* Full-time $6497; part-time $606 per credit. Tuition, state resident: full-time $9748; part-time $622 per credit. Tuition, nonresident: full-time $18,102; part-time $622 per credit. *Required fees:* $4459; $246 per credit. *Financial support:* In 2016–17, 10 students received support. Career-related internships or fieldwork, Federal Work-Study, scholarships/grants, and unspecified assistantships available. Support available to part-time students. Financial award application deadline: 3/1; financial award applicants required to submit FAFSA. *Faculty research:* All aspects of middle management, technical supervision in the workplace. *Unit head:* Dr. Ravindra Thamma, Chair, 860-832-1830, E-mail: kovelj@ccsu.edu. *Application contact:* Patricia Gardner, Associate Director of Graduate Studies, 860-832-2350, Fax: 860-832-2362.
Website: http://www.ccsu.edu/mcm/

Clarkson University, School of Business, Master's Program in Business Administration, Potsdam, NY 13699. Offers business administration (MBA); business fundamentals (Advanced Certificate); global supply chain management (Advanced Certificate); human resource management (Advanced Certificate); management and leadership (Advanced Certificate). *Accreditation:* AACSB. *Program availability:* Part-time, evening/weekend, 100% online, blended/hybrid learning. *Faculty:* 53 full-time (12 women), 33 part-time/adjunct (6 women). *Students:* 119 full-time (45 women), 51 part-time (19 women); includes 23 minority (5 Black or African American, non-Hispanic/Latino; 1 American Indian or Alaska Native, non-Hispanic/Latino; 10 Asian, non-Hispanic/Latino; 4 Hispanic/Latino; 3 Two or more races, non-Hispanic/Latino), 14 international. 390 applicants, 39% accepted, 101 enrolled. In 2016, 91 master's, 2 other advanced degrees awarded. *Entrance requirements:* For master's, GRE or GMAT. Additional exam requirements/recommendations for international students: Required—TOEFL (minimum score 550 paper-based, 80 iBT) or IELTS (6.5). *Application deadline:* Applications are processed on a rolling basis. Application fee: $50. Electronic applications accepted. *Expenses: Tuition:* Full-time $23,400; part-time $1300 per credit hour. Tuition and fees vary according to campus/location and program. *Financial support:* Scholarships/grants available. *Unit head:* Dr. Alan Bowman, Senior Associate Dean of Graduate Business Programs, 518-631-9887, E-mail: abowman@clarkson.edu. *Application contact:* Erin Wheeler, Graduate Admissions Contact, 518-631-9910, E-mail: ewheeler@clarkson.edu.

Clayton State University, School of Graduate Studies, College of Business, Program in Business Administration, Morrow, GA 30260-0285. Offers accounting (MBA); human resource leadership (MBA); international business (MBA); sports and entertainment management (MBA); supply chain management (MBA). *Accreditation:* AACSB. *Program availability:* Part-time, evening/weekend. *Degree requirements:* For master's, thesis. *Entrance requirements:* For master's, GMAT, 3 letters of recommendation; statement of purpose; 2 official transcripts. Additional exam requirements/recommendations for international students: Required—TOEFL (minimum score 550 paper-based; 80 iBT). Electronic applications accepted. *Expenses:* Contact institution.

Clemson University, Graduate School, College of Business, Department of Management, Clemson, SC 29634. Offers business administration (PhD), including management information systems, supply chain and operations management; management (MS). *Accreditation:* AACSB. *Faculty:* 17 full-time (3 women). *Students:* 17 full-time (5 women), 2 part-time (1 woman), 13 international. Average age 33. 30 applicants, 7% accepted, 2 enrolled. In 2016, 2 master's, 1 doctorate awarded. Terminal master's awarded for partial completion of doctoral program. *Degree requirements:* For master's, comprehensive exam, thesis optional; for doctorate, comprehensive exam, thesis/dissertation. *Entrance requirements:* For master's and doctorate, GMAT or GRE General Test, unofficial transcripts, two letters of reference, curriculum vitae. Additional exam requirements/recommendations for international students: Required—TOEFL (minimum score 94 iBT), IELTS (minimum score 7), PTE (minimum score 64). *Application deadline:* For fall admission, 1/15 priority date for domestic and international students. Application fee: $80 ($90 for international students). Electronic applications accepted. *Expenses:* $5,617 per semester full-time resident, $11,194 per semester full-time non-resident, $697 per credit hour part-time resident, $1,392 per credit hour part-time non-resident. *Financial support:* In 2016–17, 52 students received support, including 11 fellowships with partial tuition reimbursements available (averaging $3,826 per year), 3 research assistantships with partial tuition reimbursements available (averaging $22,667 per year), 32 teaching assistantships with partial tuition reimbursements available (averaging $25,000 per year); unspecified assistantships also available. Financial award application deadline: 1/15. *Faculty research:* Effective use of information technology in business, manufacturing and service operations strategy, lean operations and quality management, healthcare operations, behavioral market design. *Total annual research expenditures:* $89,179. *Unit head:* Dr. V. Sridharan, Department

Chair, 864-656-2624, E-mail: suhas@clemson.edu. *Application contact:* Dr. Janis Miller, Graduate Program Coordinator, 864-656-3757, E-mail: janism@clemson.edu.
Website: https://www.clemson.edu/business/departments/management/

Concordia University, School of Graduate Studies, John Molson School of Business, Montreal, QC H3H 0A1, Canada. Offers administration (M Sc), including finance, management, marketing; business administration (MBA, PhD, Certificate, Diploma); executive business administration (EMBA); supply chain management (MSCM). PhD program offered jointly with HEC Montreal, McGill University, and Université du Québec à Montréal. *Program availability:* Part-time, evening/weekend. *Degree requirements:* For master's, one foreign language, thesis (for some programs), research project; for doctorate, one foreign language, thesis/dissertation; for other advanced degree, one foreign language. *Entrance requirements:* For master's, GMAT, minimum 2 years of work experience (for MBA); letters of recommendation, bachelor's degree from recognized university with minimum GPA of 3.0, curriculum vitae; for doctorate, GMAT (minimum score of 600), official transcripts, curriculum vitae, 3 letters of reference, statement of purpose; for other advanced degree, minimum GPA of 2.7, 2 letters of reference, statement of purpose, resume. Additional exam requirements/ recommendations for international students: Required—TOEFL (minimum score 90 iBT), IELTS (minimum score 7). Electronic applications accepted. *Expenses:* Contact institution. *Faculty research:* General business, capital markets, international business.

Delaware Valley University, MBA Program, Doylestown, PA 18901-2697. Offers accounting (MBA); entrepreneurship (MBA); finance (MBA); food and agribusiness (MBA); general business (MBA); global executive leadership (MBA); human resource management (MBA); supply chain management (MBA). *Program availability:* Part-time, evening/weekend, online learning. *Entrance requirements:* For master's, minimum undergraduate GPA of 3.0. Electronic applications accepted. *Expenses:* Contact institution.

DeSales University, Division of Business, Center Valley, PA 18034-9568. Offers accounting (MBA); computer information systems (MBA); finance (MBA); health care systems management (MBA); human resources management (MBA); management (MBA); marketing (MBA); project management (MBA); self-design (MBA); supply chain management (MBA); DNP/MBA; MSN/MBA. *Accreditation:* ACBSP. *Program availability:* Part-time, evening/weekend, 100% online, blended/hybrid learning. *Faculty:* 12 full-time (4 women), 29 part-time/adjunct (5 women). *Students:* 73 full-time (38 women), 323 part-time (163 women); includes 59 minority (16 Black or African American, non-Hispanic/Latino; 23 Asian, non-Hispanic/Latino; 16 Hispanic/Latino; 4 Two or more races, non-Hispanic/Latino). Average age 37. 157 applicants, 87% accepted, 128 enrolled. In 2016, 115 master's awarded. *Entrance requirements:* For master's, GMAT (waived if undergraduate GPA is 3.0 or better), minimum GPA of 3.0 in undergraduate work, literacy in basic software, background or interest in the field of study, personal statement, 2 years of work experience. Additional exam requirements/ recommendations for international students: Required—TOEFL. *Application deadline:* Applications are processed on a rolling basis. Application fee: $50. Electronic applications accepted. *Expenses:* Contact institution. *Financial support:* Applicants required to submit FAFSA. *Faculty research:* Quality improvement, executive development, productivity, cross-cultural managerial differences, leadership. *Unit head:* Dr. David M. Gilfoil, Director, MBA Program, 610-282-1100 Ext. 1828, Fax: 610-282-2869, E-mail: david.gilfoil@desales.edu. *Application contact:* Julia Ferraro, Director of Graduate Admissions, 610-282-1100 Ext. 1768, E-mail: gradadmissions@desales.edu.

Eastern Michigan University, Graduate School, College of Business, Department of Marketing, Ypsilanti, MI 48197. Offers e-business (MBA); integrated marketing communications (MS, Postbaccalaureate Certificate); international business (MBA); marketing management (MBA); supply chain management (MBA). *Program availability:* Part-time, evening/weekend, online learning. *Faculty:* 23 full-time (9 women). *Students:* 15 full-time (11 women), 40 part-time (33 women); includes 14 minority (10 Black or African American, non-Hispanic/Latino; 4 Two or more races, non-Hispanic/Latino). Average age 32. 29 applicants, 72% accepted, 15 enrolled. In 2016, 23 master's, 1 other advanced degree awarded. *Entrance requirements:* For master's, GMAT. Additional exam requirements/recommendations for international students: Required—TOEFL. *Application deadline:* For fall admission, 5/15 priority date for domestic students, 2/15 priority date for international students; for winter admission, 10/15 priority date for domestic students, 9/1 priority date for international students; for summer admission, 3/ 15 priority date for domestic students, 3/1 priority date for international students. Applications are processed on a rolling basis. Application fee: $45. *Financial support:* Fellowships, research assistantships with full tuition reimbursements, teaching assistantships with full tuition reimbursements, career-related internships or fieldwork, Federal Work-Study, institutionally sponsored loans, scholarships/grants, tuition waivers (partial), and unspecified assistantships available. Support available to part-time students. Financial award applicants required to submit FAFSA. *Unit head:* Dr. Lewis Hershey, Department Head, 734-487-3323, Fax: 734-487-7099, E-mail: lhershe1@emich.edu. *Application contact:* K. Michelle Henry, Director, Graduate Business Programs, 734-487-4444, Fax: 734-483-1316, E-mail: cob.graduate@emich.edu.
Website: http://www.mkt.emich.edu/index.html

Eastern Michigan University, Graduate School, College of Business, Programs in Business Administration, Ypsilanti, MI 48197. Offers business administration (MBA, Graduate Certificate); computer information systems (Graduate Certificate); e-business (MBA, Graduate Certificate); enterprise business intelligence (MBA); entrepreneurship (MBA, Graduate Certificate); finance (MBA, Graduate Certificate); human resources (MBA); human resources management (Graduate Certificate); information systems (MBA); internal auditing (MBA); international business (MBA, Graduate Certificate); marketing management (Graduate Certificate); nonprofit management (MBA); organizational development (Graduate Certificate); supply chain management (MBA, Graduate Certificate). *Accreditation:* AACSB. *Program availability:* Part-time, online learning. *Students:* 63 full-time (36 women), 320 part-time (186 women); includes 131 minority (76 Black or African American, non-Hispanic/Latino; 5 American Indian or Alaska Native, non-Hispanic/Latino; 16 Asian, non-Hispanic/Latino; 19 Hispanic/Latino; 15 Two or more races, non-Hispanic/Latino), 23 international. Average age 32. 305 applicants, 70% accepted, 124 enrolled. In 2016, 78 master's, 57 other advanced degrees awarded. *Entrance requirements:* For master's, GMAT (minimum score 450), minimum cumulative undergraduate GPA of 2.75. Additional exam requirements/ recommendations for international students: Required—TOEFL. *Application deadline:* For fall admission, 5/15 priority date for domestic students, 2/15 priority date for international students; for winter admission, 10/15 priority date for domestic students, 9/ 1 priority date for international students; for summer admission, 3/15 priority date for domestic students, 3/1 priority date for international students. Applications are processed on a rolling basis. Application fee: $45. *Financial support:* Fellowships, research assistantships with full tuition reimbursements, teaching assistantships with full tuition reimbursements, career-related internships or fieldwork, Federal Work-Study, institutionally sponsored loans, scholarships/grants, tuition waivers (partial), and unspecified assistantships available. Support available to part-time students. Financial award applicants required to submit FAFSA. *Unit head:* K. Michelle Henry, Director, Graduate Business Programs, 734-487-4444, Fax: 734-483-1316, E-mail: cob.graduate@emich.edu.
Website: http://www.emich.edu/cob/mba/

Elmhurst College, Graduate Programs, Program in Supply Chain Management, Elmhurst, IL 60126-3296. Offers MS. *Program availability:* Part-time, evening/weekend. *Faculty:* 2 full-time (0 women), 4 part-time/adjunct (0 women). *Students:* 34 part-time (9 women); includes 12 minority (3 Black or African American, non-Hispanic/Latino; 7 Asian, non-Hispanic/Latino; 2 Hispanic/Latino), 3 international. Average age 33. 30 applicants, 67% accepted, 17 enrolled. In 2016, 11 master's awarded. *Entrance requirements:* For master's, 3 recommendations, resume, statement of purpose. Additional exam requirements/recommendations for international students: Required—TOEFL (minimum score 550 paper-based; 79 iBT). *Application deadline:* Applications are processed on a rolling basis. Application fee: $0. Electronic applications accepted. *Expenses:* $845 per semester hour. *Financial support:* In 2016–17, 11 students received support. Scholarships/grants available. Support available to part-time students. Financial award application deadline: 3/1; financial award applicants required to submit FAFSA. *Unit head:* Dr. Roby Thomas. *Application contact:* Timothy J. Panfil, Director of Enrollment Management, School for Professional Studies, 630-617-3300 Ext. 3256, Fax: 630-617-6471, E-mail: panfilt@elmhurst.edu.
Website: http://www.elmhurst.edu/scm

Embry-Riddle Aeronautical University–Daytona, Department of Management, Marketing and Operations, Daytona Beach, FL 32114-3900. Offers airline management (MBA); airport management (MBA); aviation finance (MSAF); aviation management (MBA-AM); aviation system management (MBA); finance (MBA); supply chain management (MBA). *Accreditation:* ACBSP. *Program availability:* Part-time. *Faculty:* 13 full-time (2 women). *Students:* 93 full-time (37 women), 15 part-time (8 women); includes 12 minority (3 Black or African American, non-Hispanic/Latino; 3 Asian, non-Hispanic/ Latino; 1 Hispanic/Latino; 5 Two or more races, non-Hispanic/Latino), 71 international. Average age 26. 130 applicants, 39% accepted, 40 enrolled. In 2016, 44 degrees awarded. *Degree requirements:* For master's, thesis (for some programs). *Entrance requirements:* Additional exam requirements/recommendations for international students: Required—TOEFL (minimum score 550 paper-based, 79 iBT) or IELTS (6). *Application deadline:* For fall admission, 3/1 priority date for domestic students; for spring admission, 11/1 priority date for domestic students; for summer admission, 4/1 priority date for domestic students. Applications are processed on a rolling basis. Application fee: $50. Electronic applications accepted. *Expenses: Tuition:* Full-time $16,296; part-time $1358 per credit hour. *Required fees:* $1294; $647 per semester. One-time fee: $100 full-time. Tuition and fees vary according to course load, degree level and program. *Financial support:* Research assistantships, teaching assistantships, career-related internships or fieldwork, scholarships/grants, unspecified assistantships, and on-campus employment available. Financial award application deadline: 3/15; financial award applicants required to submit FAFSA. *Unit head:* Michael J. Williams, PhD, Dean, College of Business/Professor of Management, 386-226-6293, E-mail: michael.williams@erau.edu. *Application contact:* Graduate Admissions, 386-226-6176, E-mail: graduate.admissions@erau.edu.
Website: https://daytonabeach.erau.edu/college-business/index.html

See Display on page 616 and Close-Up on page 637.

Embry-Riddle Aeronautical University–Worldwide, Department of Decision Sciences, Daytona Beach, FL 32114-3900. Offers aviation and aerospace (MSPM); aviation/aerospace management (MSEM); financial management (MSEM, MSPM); general management (MSPM); global management (MSPM); human resources management (MSPM); information systems (MSPM); leadership (MSEM, MSPM); logistics and supply chain management (MSEM, MSLSCM, MSPM); management (MSEM, MSPM); project management (MSEM); systems engineering (MSEM, MSPM); technical management (MSPM). *Program availability:* Part-time, evening/weekend, 100% online, blended/hybrid learning, EagleVision is a virtual classroom that combines Web video conferencing and a learning management system. EagleVision Classroom (between classrooms), EagleVision Home (faculty and students at home), and a blend of Classroom or Home. *Degree requirements:* For master's, comprehensive exam (for some programs), thesis (for some programs). *Entrance requirements:* Additional exam requirements/recommendations for international students: Required—TOEFL (minimum score 550 paper-based; 79 iBT), IELTS (minimum score 6), TOEFL or IELTS accepted. Electronic applications accepted. *Expenses:* Contact institution.

Fairleigh Dickinson University, College at Florham, Silberman College of Business, Program in Supply Chain Management, Madison, NJ 07940-1099. Offers MS. *Entrance requirements:* For master's, GMAT.

Ferris State University, College of Business, Big Rapids, MI 49307. Offers business intelligence (MBA); design and innovation management (MBA); incident response (MBA); information security and intelligence (MS), including business intelligence, incident response, project management; lean systems and leadership (MBA); performance metrics (MBA); project management (MBA); supply chain management and lean logistics (MBA). *Accreditation:* ACBSP. *Program availability:* Part-time, evening/weekend, 100% online, blended/hybrid learning. *Faculty:* 18 full-time (7 women), 6 part-time/adjunct (3 women). *Students:* 25 full-time (11 women), 113 part-time (47 women); includes 12 minority (2 Black or African American, non-Hispanic/ Latino; 1 American Indian or Alaska Native, non-Hispanic/Latino; 3 Asian, non-Hispanic/ Latino; 3 Hispanic/Latino; 3 Two or more races, non-Hispanic/Latino), 50 international. Average age 31. 128 applicants, 59% accepted, 39 enrolled. In 2016, 94 master's awarded. *Degree requirements:* For master's, comprehensive exam, thesis. *Entrance requirements:* For master's, GRE or GMAT, minimum GPA of 3.0 in junior-/senior-level classes and overall; statement of purpose; 3 letters of reference; resume; transcripts. Additional exam requirements/recommendations for international students: Required—TOEFL (minimum score 500 paper-based; 70 iBT), IELTS (minimum score 6.5). *Application deadline:* For fall admission, 7/1 priority date for domestic students, 6/15 for international students; for winter admission, 11/1 priority date for domestic students, 10/ 15 for international students; for spring admission, 3/1 priority date for domestic students, 2/15 for international students. Applications are processed on a rolling basis. Application fee: $0 ($30 for international students). Electronic applications accepted. *Expenses:* Contact institution. *Financial support:* Career-related internships or fieldwork, Federal Work-Study, scholarships/grants, and unspecified assistantships available. Support available to part-time students. Financial award application deadline: 3/15; financial award applicants required to submit FAFSA. *Faculty research:* Lifestyle medicine business models, lean systems value chain pptimization, digital forensics/ incident response, location-based services, passive data capture and analysis. *Unit head:* Dr. David Nicol, College of Business Dean, 231-591-2168, Fax: 231-591-3521, E-mail: davidnicol@ferris.edu. *Application contact:* Dr. Greg Gogolin, Professor, 231-591-3159, Fax: 231-591-3521, E-mail: greggogolin@ferris.edu.
Website: http://cbgp.ferris.edu/

Florida Institute of Technology, Extended Studies Division, Melbourne, FL 32901-6975. Offers acquisition and contract management (MS); aerospace engineering (MS); business administration (MBA, DBA); computer information systems (MS); computer science (MS); electrical engineering (MS); engineering management (MS); human resources management (MS); logistics management (MS), including humanitarian and

disaster relief logistics; management (MS), including acquisition and contract management, e-business, human resources management, information systems, logistics management, management, transportation management; material acquisition management (MS); mechanical engineering (MS); operations research (MS); project management (MS), including information systems, operations research; public administration (MPA); quality management (MS); software engineering (MS); space systems (MS); space systems management (MS); supply chain management (MS); systems management (MS), including information systems, operations research; technology management (MS). *Program availability:* Part-time, evening/weekend, online learning. *Faculty:* 10 full-time (3 women), 122 part-time/adjunct (29 women). *Students:* 131 full-time (58 women), 997 part-time (348 women); includes 389 minority (231 Black or African American, non-Hispanic/Latino; 9 American Indian or Alaska Native, non-Hispanic/Latino; 26 Asian, non-Hispanic/Latino; 99 Hispanic/Latino; 3 Native Hawaiian or other Pacific Islander, non-Hispanic/Latino; 21 Two or more races, non-Hispanic/Latino), 53 international. Average age 36. 962 applicants, 48% accepted, 323 enrolled. In 2016, 403 master's awarded. *Degree requirements:* For master's, comprehensive exam (for some programs). *Entrance requirements:* For master's, GMAT or resume showing 8 years of supervised experience, minimum GPA of 3.0, 2 letters of recommendation, resume. Additional exam requirements/recommendations for international students: Required—TOEFL (minimum score 550 paper-based; 79 iBT). *Application deadline:* For fall admission, 4/1 for international students; for spring admission, 9/30 for international students. Applications are processed on a rolling basis. Electronic applications accepted. *Expenses:* Contact institution. *Financial support:* Application deadline: 3/1; applicants required to submit FAFSA. *Unit head:* Dr. Theodore R. Richardson, III, Dean, 321-674-8123, Fax: 321-674-7597, E-mail: trichardson@fit.edu. *Application contact:* Carolyn Farrior, Director of Graduate Admissions, Online Learning and Off-Campus Programs, 321-674-7118, Fax: 321-674-8216, E-mail: cfarrior@fit.edu.
Website: http://es.fit.edu

Fontbonne University, Graduate Programs, St. Louis, MO 63105-3098. Offers accounting (MBA, MS); art (MA); art (K-12) (MAT); business (MBA); computer science (MS); deaf education (MA); early intervention in deaf education (MA); education (MA), including autism spectrum disorders, curriculum and instruction, diverse learners, early childhood education, reading, special education; elementary education (MAT); family and consumer sciences (MA), including multidisciplinary health communication studies; fine arts (MFA); instructional design and technology (MS); management and leadership (MM); middle school education (MAT); secondary education (MAT); special education (MAT); speech-language pathology (MS); supply chain management (MS); theatre (MA). *Program availability:* Part-time, evening/weekend, online learning. *Faculty:* 32 full-time (24 women), 43 part-time/adjunct (26 women). *Students:* 456 full-time (313 women), 102 part-time (77 women); includes 138 minority (118 Black or African American, non-Hispanic/Latino; 1 American Indian or Alaska Native, non-Hispanic/Latino; 7 Asian, non-Hispanic/Latino; 9 Hispanic/Latino; 3 Two or more races, non-Hispanic/Latino), 37 international. *Degree requirements:* For master's, comprehensive exam (for some programs), thesis (for some programs). *Entrance requirements:* Additional exam requirements/recommendations for international students: Required—TOEFL (minimum score 500 paper-based; 65 iBT). *Application deadline:* For fall admission, 8/1 for international students; for spring admission, 12/1 for international students. Applications are processed on a rolling basis. Application fee: $25 ($30 for international students). Electronic applications accepted. *Expenses: Tuition:* Full-time $8436; part-time $703 per credit hour. *Required fees:* $18 per credit hour. Tuition and fees vary according to course load. *Financial support:* Teaching assistantships with partial tuition reimbursements and scholarships/grants available. Support available to part-time students. Financial award application deadline: 4/1; financial award applicants required to submit FAFSA. *Unit head:* Dr. Carey Adams, Vice President for Academic Affairs, 314-719-3609, E-mail: cadams@fontbonne.edu. *Application contact:* Lauryn Filip, Coordinator, Graduate Admission and Professional Studies, 314-889-4650, E-mail: admissions@fontbonne.edu.
Website: https://www.fontbonne.edu/academics/graduate-programs/

Friends University, Graduate School, Wichita, KS 67213. Offers family therapy (MSFT); global business administration (MBA), including accounting, business law, change management, health care leadership, management information systems, supply chain management and logistics; health care leadership (MHCL); management information systems (MMIS); professional business administration (MBA), including accounting, business law, change management, health care leadership, management information systems, supply chain management and logistics. *Program availability:* Part-time, evening/weekend, online learning. *Degree requirements:* For master's, research project. *Entrance requirements:* For master's, bachelor's degree from accredited institution, official transcripts, interview with program director, letter(s) of recommendation. Additional exam requirements/recommendations for international students: Required—TOEFL (minimum score 560 paper-based). Electronic applications accepted.

Georgia Southern University, Jack N. Averitt College of Graduate Studies, College of Business Administration, Program in Logistics/Supply Chain Management, Statesboro, GA 30458. Offers PhD. *Students:* 6 full-time (1 woman), 3 international. Average age 28. 29 applicants, 17% accepted, 3 enrolled. In 2016, 2 doctorates awarded. *Degree requirements:* For doctorate, comprehensive exam, thesis/dissertation. *Entrance requirements:* For doctorate, GMAT, minimum of three letters of reference; statement of purpose; resume. Additional exam requirements/recommendations for international students: Required—TOEFL (minimum score 550 paper-based; 80 iBT), IELTS (minimum score 6). *Application deadline:* For fall admission, 3/15 priority date for domestic and international students. Application fee: $50. Electronic applications accepted. *Expenses:* Tuition, state resident: full-time $7236; part-time $277 per semester hour. Tuition, nonresident: full-time $27,118; part-time $1105 per semester hour. *Required fees:* $2092. *Financial support:* In 2016–17, 3 research assistantships with full tuition reimbursements (averaging $7,750 per year) were awarded; teaching assistantships, career-related internships or fieldwork, Federal Work-Study, scholarships/grants, traineeships, and unspecified assistantships also available. Support available to part-time students. Financial award application deadline: 4/15; financial award applicants required to submit FAFSA. *Faculty research:* Buyer-supplier relationships, retail supply chain management, military logistics/transportation/supply chain management, strategic sourcing/outsourcing, supply chain metrics, service scheduling, demand and supply planning, supply chain strategy, sustainability, operations and supply management, decision sciences. *Unit head:* Dr. Gordon Smith, Graduate Program Director, 912-478-2357, Fax: 912-478-0292, E-mail: gsmith@georgiasouthern.edu. *Application contact:* E-mail: coba@georgiasouthern.edu.
Website: http://cogs.georgiasouthern.edu/admission/GraduatePrograms/phdlogistics.php

Golden Gate University, Ageno School of Business, San Francisco, CA 94105-2968. Offers accounting (MBA); business administration (EMBA, MBA, PMBA, DBA); business analytics (MS); finance (MBA, MS, Certificate); financial planning (MS, Certificate); healthcare information systems (Certificate); human resource management (MBA, MS); human resources management (Certificate); information systems (MS); information technology (MBA); information technology management (Certificate); integrated marketing and communications (MS, Certificate); international business (MBA); management (MBA); marketing (MBA, MS, Certificate); operations supply chain management (Certificate); psychology (MA, Certificate); public administration (EMPA); public relations (MS, Certificate); technical market analysis (Certificate); JD/MBA. *Program availability:* Part-time, evening/weekend. *Faculty:* 18 full-time (3 women), 117 part-time/adjunct (44 women). *Students:* 458 full-time (254 women), 664 part-time (331 women); includes 346 minority (75 Black or African American, non-Hispanic/Latino; 2 American Indian or Alaska Native, non-Hispanic/Latino; 132 Asian, non-Hispanic/Latino; 105 Hispanic/Latino; 9 Native Hawaiian or other Pacific Islander, non-Hispanic/Latino; 23 Two or more races, non-Hispanic/Latino), 354 international. Average age 34. 905 applicants, 83% accepted, 165 enrolled. In 2016, 350 master's, 2 doctorates awarded. *Degree requirements:* For doctorate, thesis/dissertation, qualifying examination. *Entrance requirements:* For master's, GMAT (for MBA), minimum GPA of 2.5 (MS). Additional exam requirements/recommendations for international students: Required—TOEFL (minimum score 550 paper-based; 79 iBT). *Application deadline:* For fall admission, 5/15 for domestic and international students; for winter admission, 1/15 for domestic and international students; for spring admission, 9/15 for domestic and international students. Applications are processed on a rolling basis. Application fee: $70 ($110 for international students). Electronic applications accepted. *Expenses:* Contact institution. *Financial support:* In 2016–17, 372 students received support. Career-related internships or fieldwork, Federal Work-Study, institutionally sponsored loans, and scholarships/grants available. Support available to part-time students. Financial award applicants required to submit FAFSA. *Unit head:* Dr. Gordon Swartz, Dean, 415-442-7027, Fax: 415-442-6579, E-mail: gswartz@ggu.edu. *Application contact:* Angela Melero, Enrollment Services, 415-442-7800, Fax: 415-442-7807, E-mail: info@ggu.edu.
Website: http://www.ggu.edu/programs/business-and-management

HEC Montreal, School of Business Administration, Graduate Diploma Programs in Administration, Program in Supply Chain Management, Montréal, QC H3T 2A7, Canada. Offers Graduate Diploma. All courses are given in French. *Students:* 14 full-time (6 women), 55 part-time (17 women). 56 applicants, 48% accepted, 20 enrolled. In 2016, 31 Graduate Diplomas awarded. *Degree requirements:* For Graduate Diploma, one foreign language. *Entrance requirements:* For degree, bachelor's degree, two years of working experience, letters of recommendation. *Application deadline:* For fall admission, 4/15 for domestic and international students; for winter admission, 9/15 for domestic and international students. Application fee: $86 Canadian dollars. Electronic applications accepted. *Expenses: Tuition, area resident:* Part-time $77.80 Canadian dollars per credit. Tuition, state resident: full-time $2797 Canadian dollars; part-time $240.92 Canadian dollars per credit. Tuition, nonresident: full-time $8673 Canadian dollars; part-time $531.43 Canadian dollars per credit. *International tuition:* $19,131 Canadian dollars full-time. *Required fees:* $1699 Canadian dollars; $40.58 Canadian dollars per credit. $67.32 Canadian dollars per term. Tuition and fees vary according to degree level and program. *Financial support:* In 2016–17, 814 students received support. Research assistantships, teaching assistantships, and scholarships/grants available. Financial award application deadline: 9/2. *Unit head:* Renaud Lachance, Director, 514-340-7165, E-mail: renaud.lachance@hec.ca. *Application contact:* Anny Caron, Administrative Director, 514-340-3598, Fax: 514-340-6411, E-mail: anny.caron@hec.ca.
Website: http://www.hec.ca/programmes/dess/dess-gestion-chaine-logistique/index.html

HEC Montreal, School of Business Administration, Master of Science Programs in Administration, Program in Global Supply Chain Management, Montréal, QC H3T 2A7, Canada. Offers M Sc. Program offered in English. *Students:* 46 full-time (26 women), 1 part-time (0 women). 44 applicants, 43% accepted, 11 enrolled. In 2016, 1 master's awarded. *Degree requirements:* For master's, one foreign language, thesis. *Entrance requirements:* For master's, BBA, undergraduate degree in another field, degree deemed equivalent by program director and minimum GPA of 3.0 on 4.3 scale. *Application deadline:* For fall admission, 3/15 for domestic and international students; for winter admission, 9/15 for domestic and international students. Application fee: $86. Electronic applications accepted. *Expenses: Tuition, area resident:* Part-time $77.80 Canadian dollars per credit. Tuition, state resident: full-time $2797 Canadian dollars; part-time $240.92 Canadian dollars per credit. Tuition, nonresident: full-time $8673 Canadian dollars; part-time $531.43 Canadian dollars per credit. *International tuition:* $19,131 Canadian dollars full-time. *Required fees:* $1699 Canadian dollars; $40.58 Canadian dollars per credit. $67.32 Canadian dollars per term. Tuition and fees vary according to degree level and program. *Financial support:* Research assistantships, teaching assistantships, and scholarships/grants available. Financial award application deadline: 9/2. *Unit head:* Dr. Marie-Helene Jobin, Director, 514-340-6283, E-mail: marie-helene.jobin@hec.ca. *Application contact:* Marianne de Moura, Administrative Director, 514-340-7106, Fax: 514-340-6411, E-mail: marianne.de-moura@hec.ca.
Website: http://www.hec.ca/en/programs/masters/master-global-supply-chain-management/index.html

Howard University, School of Business, Graduate Programs in Business, Washington, DC 20059-0002. Offers accounting (MBA); entrepreneurship (MBA); finance (MBA); general management (MBA); human resources management (MBA); information systems (MBA); international business (MBA); marketing (MBA); supply chain management (MBA); JD/MBA. *Accreditation:* AACSB. *Program availability:* Part-time, evening/weekend, online learning. *Entrance requirements:* For master's, GMAT, minimum 1 year post undergraduate work experience, resume, 3 letters of recommendation, advanced college algebra. Additional exam requirements/recommendations for international students: Required—TOEFL. *Faculty research:* Marketing research in multi-ethnic populations, U.S. trade policies and international relations, risk management (finance).

Indiana University–Purdue University Indianapolis, Kelley School of Business, Evening MBA Program, Indianapolis, IN 46202-5151. Offers accounting (MBA); entrepreneurship (MBA); finance (MBA); general administration (MBA); marketing (MBA); supply chain management (MBA); MBA/JD; MBA/MD; MBA/MHA; MBA/MS; MBA/MSA; MBA/MSE. *Program availability:* Part-time-only, evening/weekend, online learning. *Faculty:* 30 full-time (7 women), 4 part-time/adjunct (0 women). *Students:* 294 part-time (46 women); includes 41 minority (11 Black or African American, non-Hispanic/Latino; 22 Asian, non-Hispanic/Latino; 8 Hispanic/Latino), 106 international. Average age 31. 129 applicants, 53% accepted, 61 enrolled. In 2016, 103 degrees awarded. *Entrance requirements:* For master's, GMAT or GRE, 2 years of professional work experience. Additional exam requirements/recommendations for international students: Required—TOEFL or IELTS. *Application deadline:* For fall admission, 6/1 for domestic and international students; for spring admission, 11/1 for domestic and international students. Applications are processed on a rolling basis. Application fee: $60 ($65 for international students). Electronic applications accepted. *Expenses:* $772.34 per credit hour in-state tuition, $1,456.56 per credit hour out-of-state tuition. *Financial support:* Scholarships/grants available. Financial award application deadline: 6/1. *Faculty research:* Entrepreneurship; corporate finance; international business; consumer behavior; supply chain; business law. *Unit head:* Mary Johnson, Associate Director, Evening MBA Program, 317-274-4895, E-mail: mbaindy@iupui.edu. *Application contact:*

Supply Chain Management

Kristen Peters, Program Assistant, 317-274-4895, E-mail: mbaindy@iupui.edu.
Website: http://kelley.iupui.edu/evemba

Johnson & Wales University, Graduate Studies, MBA Program, Providence, RI 02903-3703. Offers accounting (MBA); business administration (MBA); finance (MBA); hospitality (MBA); human resource management (MBA); information technology (MBA); nonprofit management (MBA); operations and supply chain management (MBA). Program also offered on Denver campus. *Program availability:* Part-time, online learning. *Entrance requirements:* For master's, minimum GPA of 2.75. Additional exam requirements/recommendations for international students: Required—TOEFL (minimum score 550 paper-based); Recommended—IELTS, TWE. *Faculty research:* International banking, global economy, international trade, cultural differences.

Kaplan University, Davenport Campus, School of Business, Davenport, IA 52807. Offers business administration (MBA); change leadership (MS); entrepreneurship (MBA); finance (MBA); health care management (MBA, MS); human resource (MBA); international business (MBA); management (MS); marketing (MBA); project management (MBA, MS); supply chain management and logistics (MBA, MS). *Accreditation:* ACBSP. *Program availability:* Part-time, evening/weekend, online learning. *Entrance requirements:* Additional exam requirements/recommendations for international students: Required—TOEFL (minimum score 550 paper-based; 80 iBT). Electronic applications accepted.

Lindenwood University, Graduate Programs, Plaster School of Business and Entrepreneurship, St. Charles, MO 63301-1695. Offers accountancy (M Acc); accounting (MBA); business administration (MBA); entrepreneurial studies (MBA); finance (MBA, MS); human resource management (MBA); international business (MBA); leadership (MA); management (MBA); marketing (MBA, MS); nonprofit administration (MA); public administration (MBA); sport management (MA); supply chain management (MBA). *Accreditation:* ACBSP. *Program availability:* Part-time, evening/weekend, 100% online. *Faculty:* 15 full-time (6 women), 25 part-time/adjunct (7 women). *Students:* 197 full-time (97 women), 213 part-time (132 women); includes 81 minority (62 Black or African American, non-Hispanic/Latino; 1 American Indian or Alaska Native, non-Hispanic/Latino; 4 Asian, non-Hispanic/Latino; 9 Hispanic/Latino; 5 Two or more races, non-Hispanic/Latino), 83 international. Average age 31. 279 applicants, 54% accepted, 133 enrolled. In 2016, 269 master's awarded. *Degree requirements:* For master's, comprehensive exam (for some programs), thesis (for some programs), minimum GPA of 3.0. *Entrance requirements:* For master's, interview, minimum undergraduate cumulative GPA of 3.0, letter of recommendation. Additional exam requirements/recommendations for international students: Required—TOEFL (minimum score 550 paper-based; 80 iBT); Recommended—IELTS (minimum score 6.5). *Application deadline:* For fall admission, 8/28 priority date for domestic and international students; for winter admission, 1/8 priority date for domestic and international students; for spring admission, 3/5 for domestic students, 3/5 priority date for international students; for summer admission, 6/4 priority date for domestic and international students. Applications are processed on a rolling basis. Application fee: $30 ($100 for international students). Electronic applications accepted. *Expenses:* Contact institution. *Financial support:* In 2016–17, 256 students received support. Career-related internships or fieldwork, Federal Work-Study, institutionally sponsored loans, scholarships/grants, tuition waivers (partial), and unspecified assistantships available. Financial award application deadline: 6/30; financial award applicants required to submit FAFSA. *Unit head:* Roger Ellis, Dean, School of Business and Entrepreneurship, 636-949-4839, E-mail: rellis@lindenwood.edu. *Application contact:* Tyler Kostich, Director, Evening and Graduate Admissions, 636-949-4138, Fax: 636-949-4109, E-mail: adultadmissions@lindenwood.edu.
Website: http://www.lindenwood.edu/academics/academic-schools/robert-w-plaster-school-of-business-entrepreneurship/

Loyola University Chicago, Quinlan School of Business, Department of Information Systems and Supply Chain Management, Chicago, IL 60611. Offers data warehousing (Certificate); information systems and supply chain management (MSSCM). *Program availability:* Part-time, evening/weekend. *Faculty:* 12 full-time (1 woman), 8 part-time/adjunct (4 women). *Students:* 9 full-time (3 women), 9 part-time (2 women); includes 3 minority (1 Black or African American, non-Hispanic/Latino; 2 Asian, non-Hispanic/Latino), 5 international. Average age 31. 50 applicants, 30% accepted, 7 enrolled. In 2016, 9 master's, 28 Certificates awarded. *Entrance requirements:* For master's, GMAT or GRE, official transcripts, two letters of recommendation, statement of purpose, resume. Additional exam requirements/recommendations for international students: Required—TOEFL (minimum score 90 iBT) or IELTS (minimum score 6.5). *Application deadline:* For fall admission, 7/15 for domestic and international students; for winter admission, 10/1 for domestic and international students; for spring admission, 1/15 for domestic students, 1/14 for international students; for summer admission, 4/1 for domestic and international students. Applications are processed on a rolling basis. Application fee: $50. Electronic applications accepted. Application fee is waived when completed online. *Expenses:* Contact institution. *Financial support:* In 2016–17, 11 students received support. Federal Work-Study, scholarships/grants, health care benefits, and unspecified assistantships available. Support available to part-time students. *Faculty research:* Consistent vehicle routing policies, logistics, operations management. *Unit head:* Dr. Mary Malliaris, Chair, 312-915-7064, E-mail: mmallia@luc.edu. *Application contact:* Lauren Griffin, Enrollment Advisor, Quinlan School of Business Graduate Programs, 312-915-6124, Fax: 312-915-7202, E-mail: lgriffin3@luc.edu.
Website: http://www.luc.edu/quinlan/mba/supply-chain-management-degrees/index.shtml

Loyola University Chicago, Quinlan School of Business, MBA Programs, Chicago, IL 60611. Offers accounting (MBA); business administration (EMBA); business ethics (MBA); economics (MBA); entrepreneurship (MBA); finance (MBA); healthcare management (MBA); human resources management (MBA); international business (MBA); management (MBA); marketing (MBA); operation management (MBA); risk management (MBA); supply chain management (MBA). *Program availability:* Part-time, evening/weekend. *Faculty:* 79 full-time (22 women), 10 part-time/adjunct (6 women). *Students:* 309 full-time (151 women), 65 part-time (31 women); includes 82 minority (25 Black or African American, non-Hispanic/Latino; 27 Asian, non-Hispanic/Latino; 27 Hispanic/Latino; 3 Two or more races, non-Hispanic/Latino), 49 international. Average age 30. 371 applicants, 53% accepted, 114 enrolled. In 2016, 216 master's awarded. *Entrance requirements:* For master's, GMAT or GRE, official transcripts, two letters of recommendation, statement of purpose, resume. Additional exam requirements/recommendations for international students: Required—TOEFL (minimum score 90 iBT) or IELTS (minimum score 6.5). *Application deadline:* For fall admission, 7/15 for domestic and international students; for winter admission, 10/1 for domestic and international students; for spring admission, 1/15 for domestic and international students; for summer admission, 4/1 for domestic and international students. Applications are processed on a rolling basis. Application fee: $50. Electronic applications accepted. Application fee is waived when completed online. *Expenses:* $4,488 per course. *Financial support:* In 2016–17, 83 students received support. Federal Work-Study, scholarships/grants, health care benefits, and unspecified assistantships available. Support available to part-time students. *Faculty research:* Social enterprise and responsibility, emerging markets, supply chain management, risk management. *Unit head:* Katherine Acles, Assistant Dean for Graduate Programs, 312-915-6124, Fax: 312-915-7207, E-mail: kacles@luc.edu. *Application contact:* Lauren Griffin, Enrollment Advisor, Quinlan School of Business Graduate Programs, 312-915-6124, Fax: 312-915-7207, E-mail: lgriffin3@luc.edu.

Maine Maritime Academy, Loeb-Sullivan School of International Business and Logistics, Castine, ME 04420. Offers global logistics and maritime management (MS); international logistics management (MS). *Program availability:* Part-time. *Degree requirements:* For master's, capstone course. *Entrance requirements:* For master's, GMAT or GRE, letter of recommendation. Additional exam requirements/recommendations for international students: Required—TOEFL. Application fee is waived when completed online.

Marquette University, Graduate School of Management, Executive MBA Program, Milwaukee, WI 53201-1881. Offers economics (MBA); finance (MBA); human resources (MBA); international business (MBA); management information systems (MBA); marketing (MBA); operations and supply chain management (MBA); sports business (MBA). *Accreditation:* AACSB. *Students:* 39 full-time (12 women); includes 7 minority (4 Black or African American, non-Hispanic/Latino; 2 Asian, non-Hispanic/Latino; 1 Hispanic/Latino). Average age 38. 25 applicants, 96% accepted, 29 enrolled. In 2016, 14 master's awarded. *Degree requirements:* For master's, international trip. *Entrance requirements:* For master's, GMAT or GRE, two letters of recommendation, official transcripts from current and previous colleges/universities. Additional exam requirements/recommendations for international students: Required—TOEFL (minimum score 550 paper-based; 88 iBT), IELTS (minimum score 6.5), PTE. *Application deadline:* For fall admission, 2/15 for domestic and international students. Application fee: $50. Electronic applications accepted. *Expenses:* Contact institution. *Financial support:* Application deadline: 2/15. *Faculty research:* International trade and finance, customer relationship management, consumer satisfaction, customer service. *Unit head:* Dr. Brian Till, Dean, 414-288-5724. *Application contact:* Dr. Jeanne Simmons, Associate Dean, 414-288-7145.
Website: http://www.busadm.mu.edu/emba/

Marquette University, Graduate School of Management, Program in Business Administration, Milwaukee, WI 53201-1881. Offers business administration (MBA); economics (MBA); entrepreneurship (Certificate); finance (MBA); human resources (MBA); international business (MBA); management information systems (MBA); marketing (MBA); operations and supply chain management (MBA); sports business (MBA); JD/MBA; MBA/MA; MBA/MSN. *Accreditation:* AACSB. *Program availability:* Part-time, evening/weekend. *Students:* 25 full-time (12 women), 202 part-time (57 women); includes 17 minority (5 Black or African American, non-Hispanic/Latino; 6 Asian, non-Hispanic/Latino; 2 Hispanic/Latino; 1 Native Hawaiian or other Pacific Islander, non-Hispanic/Latino; 3 Two or more races, non-Hispanic/Latino), 7 international. Average age 31. 107 applicants, 87% accepted, 113 enrolled. In 2016, 107 master's, 5 other advanced degrees awarded. *Degree requirements:* For Certificate, business plan. *Entrance requirements:* For master's, GMAT or GRE, letters of recommendation. Additional exam requirements/recommendations for international students: Required—TOEFL (minimum score 550 paper-based; 88 iBT), IELTS (minimum score 6.5), PTE. *Application deadline:* For fall admission, 2/15 for domestic and international students. Applications are processed on a rolling basis. Application fee: $50. Electronic applications accepted. *Financial support:* Fellowships, research assistantships, teaching assistantships, Federal Work-Study, institutionally sponsored loans, scholarships/grants, and tuition waivers (full and partial) available. Support available to part-time students. Financial award application deadline: 2/15. *Faculty research:* Ethics in the professions, services marketing, technology impact on decision-making, mentoring. *Unit head:* Dr. Brian Till, Dean, 414-288-5724. *Application contact:* Dr. Jeanne Simmons, Associate Dean, 414-288-7145.
Website: http://business.marquette.edu/academics/mba

Maryville University of Saint Louis, The John E. Simon School of Business, St. Louis, MO 63141-7299. Offers accounting (MBA, Certificate); business studies (Certificate); cyber security (MBA); cybersecurity (Certificate); financial services (MBA, Certificate); healthcare practice management (MBA, Certificate); human resource management (MBA); information technology (MBA, Certificate); management (MBA, Certificate); management and leadership (MA); marketing (MBA, Certificate); project management (MBA); sport business management (MBA); supply chain management/logistics (MBA). *Accreditation:* ACBSP. *Program availability:* Part-time, evening/weekend, 100% online, blended/hybrid learning. *Faculty:* 7 full-time (3 women), 34 part-time/adjunct (9 women). *Students:* 84 full-time (40 women), 223 part-time (118 women); includes 67 minority (40 Black or African American, non-Hispanic/Latino; 2 American Indian or Alaska Native, non-Hispanic/Latino; 8 Asian, non-Hispanic/Latino; 12 Hispanic/Latino; 1 Native Hawaiian or other Pacific Islander, non-Hispanic/Latino; 4 Two or more races, non-Hispanic/Latino), 15 international. Average age 32. In 2016, 67 master's awarded. *Entrance requirements:* Additional exam requirements/recommendations for international students: Required—TOEFL (minimum score 563 paper-based; 85 iBT). *Application deadline:* Applications are processed on a rolling basis. Electronic applications accepted. *Expenses:* $650 per credit hour. *Financial support:* Career-related internships or fieldwork, Federal Work-Study, tuition waivers (partial), and campus employment available. Financial award application deadline: 3/1; financial award applicants required to submit FAFSA. *Faculty research:* Global business, e-marketing, strategic planning, interpersonal management skills, financial analysis. *Unit head:* Pam Horwitz, Interim Dean, 314-529-9680, Fax: 314-529-9975. *Application contact:* Dustin Loeffler, Director for Graduate Studies in Business, 314-529-9571, Fax: 314-529-9975, E-mail: dloeffler@maryville.edu.
Website: http://www.maryville.edu/bu/business-administration-masters/

Michigan State University, The Graduate School, Eli Broad College of Business, Department of Supply Chain Management, East Lansing, MI 48224. Offers logistics (PhD); operations and sourcing management (PhD); supply chain management (MS), including logistics management, operations management, rail management, supply management. *Program availability:* Part-time. *Degree requirements:* For master's, field study/research project; for doctorate, comprehensive exam, thesis/dissertation. *Entrance requirements:* For master's, GMAT (taken within past 5 years), bachelor's degree, minimum GPA of 3.0 in junior/senior years, transcripts, at least 2 years of professional supply chain work experience, 3 letters of recommendation, essays, resume; for doctorate, GMAT or GRE, bachelor's or master's degree, transcripts, strong work experience, 3 letters of recommendation, statement of personal goals, interview. Additional exam requirements/recommendations for international students: Required—TOEFL (minimum score 600 paper-based). Electronic applications accepted. *Expenses:* Contact institution.

Michigan State University, The Graduate School, Eli Broad College of Business, Program in Business Administration, East Lansing, MI 48224. Offers finance (MBA); human resource management (MBA); integrative management (MBA); marketing (MBA); supply chain management (MBA). MBA in integrative management is through Weekend MBA Program; other 4 concentrations are through Full-Time MBA Program. *Program availability:* Evening/weekend. *Degree requirements:* For master's, enrichment experience. *Entrance requirements:* For master's, GMAT or GRE, 4-year bachelor's degree; resume; work experience (minimum of 5 years for Weekend MBA); 2-3 personal essays; 2 letters of recommendation; personal interview. Additional exam requirements/recommendations for international students: Required—PTE (minimum score 70), TOEFL (minimum score 100 iBT) or IELTS (minimum score 7) for full-time MBA applicants. Electronic applications accepted. *Expenses:* Contact institution.

Moravian College, Graduate and Continuing Studies, Business and Management Programs, Bethlehem, PA 18018-6650. Offers accounting (MBA); business analytics (MBA); general management (MBA); health administration (MHA); healthcare management (MBA); human resource management (MBA); leadership (MSHRM); learning and performance management (MSHRM); supply chain management (MBA). *Program availability:* Part-time, evening/weekend. *Faculty:* 4 full-time (1 woman), 9 part-time/adjunct (4 women). *Students:* 14 full-time (7 women), 88 part-time (46 women); includes 17 minority (7 Black or African American, non-Hispanic/Latino; 1 American Indian or Alaska Native, non-Hispanic/Latino; 3 Asian, non-Hispanic/Latino; 6 Hispanic/Latino), 1 international. Average age 33. 25 applicants, 92% accepted, 18 enrolled. In 2016, 11 master's awarded. *Entrance requirements:* For master's, current resume, offical transcripts, 2 letters of recommendation. Additional exam requirements/recommendations for international students: Required—TOEFL (minimum score 550 paper-based), IELTS (minimum score 6.5). *Application deadline:* For fall admission, 8/1 priority date for domestic and international students; for spring admission, 1/1 priority date for domestic and international students; for summer admission, 5/1 priority date for domestic and international students. Applications are processed on a rolling basis. Electronic applications accepted. *Expenses: Tuition:* Full-time $2619. Tuition and fees vary according to course load and program. *Financial support:* Applicants required to submit FAFSA. *Faculty research:* Leadership, change management, human resources. *Unit head:* Dr. Liz Kleintop, Associate Chair of Graduate Business, 610-861-1400, Fax: 610-861-1466, E-mail: mba@moravian.edu. *Application contact:* Kristy Sullivan, Director of Student Recruitment Operations, 610-861-1400, Fax: 610-861-1466, E-mail: graduate@moravian.edu.
Website: https://www.moravian.edu/graduate

Naval Postgraduate School, Departments and Academic Groups, Graduate School of Business and Public Policy, Monterey, CA 93943. Offers acquisition and contract management (MBA); business administration (EMBA, MBA); contract management (MS); defense business management (MBA); defense systems analysis (MS), including management; defense systems management (international) (MBA); financial management (MBA); information management (MBA); manpower systems analysis (MS); material logistics support management (MBA); program management (MS); resource planning and management for international defense (MBA); supply chain management (MBA); systems acquisition management (MBA); transportation management (MBA). Program only open to commissioned officers of the United States and friendly nations and selected United States federal civilian employees. *Accreditation:* AACSB; NASPAA. *Program availability:* Part-time, online learning. *Degree requirements:* For master's, thesis (for some programs), terminal project/capstone (for some programs). *Faculty research:* U.S. and European public procurement policies for small and medium-sized enterprises, examining external validity criticisms in the choice of students as subjects in accounting experiment studies, assurance of learning in contract management education, contracting for cloud computing: opportunities and risks, NPS, Apple App Store as a business model supporting U. S. Navy requirements.

New York Institute of Technology, School of Management, Department of Business Administration, Old Westbury, NY 11568-8000. Offers executive (MBA); management (MBA), including finance, marketing, operations and supply chain management; professional accounting (MBA). *Accreditation:* AACSB. *Program availability:* Part-time, evening/weekend. *Faculty:* 25 full-time (4 women), 20 part-time/adjunct (6 women). *Students:* 377 full-time (161 women), 149 part-time (88 women); includes 60 minority (17 Black or African American, non-Hispanic/Latino; 1 American Indian or Alaska Native, non-Hispanic/Latino; 28 Asian, non-Hispanic/Latino; 11 Hispanic/Latino; 2 Native Hawaiian or other Pacific Islander, non-Hispanic/Latino; 1 Two or more races, non-Hispanic/Latino), 446 international. Average age 26. 804 applicants, 68% accepted, 215 enrolled. In 2016, 193 master's awarded. *Entrance requirements:* For master's, bachelor's degree; minimum undergraduate GPA of 3.0. Additional exam requirements/recommendations for international students: Required—TOEFL (minimum score 79 iBT), IELTS (minimum score 6). *Application deadline:* Applications are processed on a rolling basis. Application fee: $50. Electronic applications accepted. *Expenses:* $1,215 per credit. *Financial support:* Career-related internships or fieldwork, Federal Work-Study, scholarships/grants, tuition waivers (full and partial), and unspecified assistantships available. Support available to part-time students. Financial award application deadline: 3/1; financial award applicants required to submit FAFSA. *Faculty research:* Accounting, economics, finance, management, marketing. *Unit head:* Dr. Jess Boronico, Dean, 516-686-7838, E-mail: som@nyit.edu. *Application contact:* Alice Dolitsky, Director, Graduate Admissions, 516-686-7520, Fax: 516-686-1116, E-mail: nyitgrad@nyit.edu.
Website: http://www.nyit.edu/degrees/management_mba

Niagara University, Graduate Division of Business Administration, Niagara University, NY 14109. Offers accounting (MBA); business administration (MBA); finance (MBA, MS); financial planning (MBA); healthcare administration (MBA, MHA); human resources (MBA); international business (MBA); marketing (MBA); professional accountancy (MBA); strategic management (MBA); supply chain management (MBA). *Accreditation:* AACSB. *Program availability:* Part-time, evening/weekend. *Students:* 172 full-time (69 women), 65 part-time (36 women); includes 25 minority (4 Black or African American, non-Hispanic/Latino; 7 Asian, non-Hispanic/Latino; 7 Hispanic/Latino; 1 Native Hawaiian or other Pacific Islander, non-Hispanic/Latino; 6 Two or more races, non-Hispanic/Latino), 76 international. Average age 27. In 2016, 107 master's awarded. *Entrance requirements:* For master's, GMAT. Additional exam requirements/recommendations for international students: Required—TOEFL (minimum score 550 paper-based; 79 iBT), IELTS (minimum score 6). *Application deadline:* For fall admission, 8/1 for domestic students; for spring admission, 11/1 for domestic students. Applications are processed on a rolling basis. Electronic applications accepted. *Expenses:* $870 per credit hour. *Financial support:* Fellowships, research assistantships, career-related internships or fieldwork, and Federal Work-Study available. Support available to part-time students. Financial award application deadline: 4/15; financial award applicants required to submit FAFSA. *Faculty research:* Capital flows, Federal Reserve policy, human resource management, public policy, issues in marketing, auctions, economics of information, risk and capital markets, management strategy, consumer behavior, Internet and social media marketing. *Unit head:* Dr. Paul Richardson, MBA Director/Chair of the Marketing Department, 716-286-8169, Fax: 716-286-8206, E-mail: psr@niagara.edu. *Application contact:* Evan Pierce, Associate Director for Graduate Recruitment, 716-286-8769, Fax: 716-286-8170, E-mail: epierce@niagara.edu.
Website: http://mba.niagara.edu

North Carolina Agricultural and Technical State University, School of Graduate Studies, School of Business and Economics, Greensboro, NC 27411. Offers accounting (MBA); business education (MAT); human resources management (MBA); supply chain systems (MBA).

North Carolina State University, Graduate School, Poole College of Management, Program in Business Administration, Raleigh, NC 27695. Offers biosciences management (MBA); entrepreneurship and technology commercialization (MBA); financial management (MBA); innovation management (MBA); marketing management (MBA); services management (MBA); supply chain management (MBA). *Accreditation:* AACSB. *Program availability:* Part-time. *Degree requirements:* For master's, thesis optional. *Entrance requirements:* For master's, GMAT, interview, 3 letters of recommendation. Additional exam requirements/recommendations for international students: Required—TOEFL (minimum score 600 paper-based; 100 iBT). Electronic applications accepted. *Faculty research:* Manufacturing strategy, information systems, technology commercialization, managing research and development, historical stock returns.

Norwich University, College of Graduate and Continuing Studies, Master of Business Administration Program, Northfield, VT 05663. Offers construction management (MBA); energy management (MBA); finance (MBA); logistics (MBA); organizational leadership (MBA); project management (MBA); supply chain management (MBA). *Accreditation:* ACBSP. *Program availability:* Evening/weekend, online only, mostly all online with a week-long residency requirement. *Faculty:* 24 part-time/adjunct (5 women). *Students:* 228 full-time (54 women); includes 54 minority (23 Black or African American, non-Hispanic/Latino; 1 American Indian or Alaska Native, non-Hispanic/Latino; 6 Asian, non-Hispanic/Latino; 20 Hispanic/Latino; 1 Native Hawaiian or other Pacific Islander, non-Hispanic/Latino; 3 Two or more races, non-Hispanic/Latino), 2 international. Average age 36. 74 applicants, 100% accepted, 57 enrolled. In 2016, 135 master's awarded. *Degree requirements:* For master's, comprehensive exam. *Entrance requirements:* For master's, minimum undergraduate GPA of 2.75. Additional exam requirements/recommendations for international students: Required—TOEFL (minimum score 550 paper-based; 80 iBT), IELTS (minimum score 6.5). *Application deadline:* For fall admission, 8/14 for domestic and international students; for winter admission, 11/13 for domestic and international students; for spring admission, 2/12 for domestic and international students; for summer admission, 6/5 for domestic and international students. Electronic applications accepted. *Expenses:* Contact institution. *Financial support:* In 2016–17, 113 students received support. Scholarships/grants available. Financial award application deadline: 8/4; financial award applicants required to submit FAFSA. *Unit head:* Dr. Jose Cordova, Program Director, 802-485-2567, Fax: 802-485-2533, E-mail: jcordova@norwich.edu. *Application contact:* Admissions Advisor, 800-460-5597 Ext. 3376, Fax: 802-485-2533, E-mail: mba@online.norwich.edu.
Website: https://online.norwich.edu/degree-programs/masters/master-business-administration/overview

Nova Southeastern University, H. Wayne Huizenga College of Business and Entrepreneurship, Fort Lauderdale, FL 33314-7796. Offers accounting (M Acc); business intelligence/analytics (MBA); entrepreneurship (MBA); finance (MBA); human resource management (MBA); international business (MBA); management (MBA); marketing (MBA); process improvement (MBA); public administration (MPA); real estate development (MS); sport revenue generation (MBA); supply chain management (MBA); taxation (M Tax). *Program availability:* Part-time, evening/weekend, 100% online, blended/hybrid learning. *Faculty:* 65 full-time (26 women), 111 part-time/adjunct (74 women). *Students:* 2,242 full-time (1,400 women), 425 part-time (239 women); includes 1,798 minority (734 Black or African American, non-Hispanic/Latino; 5 American Indian or Alaska Native, non-Hispanic/Latino; 110 Asian, non-Hispanic/Latino; 890 Hispanic/Latino; 2 Native Hawaiian or other Pacific Islander, non-Hispanic/Latino; 57 Two or more races, non-Hispanic/Latino), 255 international. Average age 34. 1,422 applicants, 64% accepted, 672 enrolled. In 2016, 971 master's awarded. *Degree requirements:* For master's, thesis optional. *Entrance requirements:* For master's, GMAT or GRE (depending on undergraduate GPA), official transcripts from all schools attended while in pursuit of bachelor's degree; minimum GPA of 2.5 from regionally-accredited institution. Additional exam requirements/recommendations for international students: Required—TOEFL (minimum score 550 paper-based; 79 iBT), IELTS (minimum score 6), PTE (minimum score 54). *Application deadline:* For fall admission, 8/5 priority date for domestic students, 7/29 priority date for international students; for winter admission, 12/16 priority date for domestic students, 12/9 priority date for international students; for summer admission, 4/21 priority date for domestic and international students. Applications are processed on a rolling basis. Application fee: $50. Electronic applications accepted. *Expenses:* Contact institution. *Financial support:* In 2016–17, 325 students received support. Federal Work-Study and scholarships/grants available. Support available to part-time students. Financial award application deadline: 4/15; financial award applicants required to submit FAFSA. *Faculty research:* Reputation management, call centers, international social capital, corporate earnings guidance, corporate governance. *Unit head:* Dr. J. Preston Jones, Dean, 954-262-5127, E-mail: prestonj@nova.edu. *Application contact:* Zeida Rodriguez, Associate Director of Enrollment Services, 954-262-5163, Fax: 954-262-3822, E-mail: zeida@nova.edu.
Website: http://www.huizenga.nova.edu

Old Dominion University, Strome College of Business, Program in Maritime Trade and Supply Chain Management, Norfolk, VA 23529. Offers MS. *Program availability:* Part-time, evening/weekend. *Students:* 5 full-time (2 women), 5 part-time (2 women); includes 3 minority (2 Asian, non-Hispanic/Latino; 1 Hispanic/Latino), 2 international. Average age 34. *Degree requirements:* For master's, capstone course. *Entrance requirements:* For master's, GRE or GMAT, bachelor's degree, official transcripts, two letters of recommendation, current resume, statement of professional goals. Additional exam requirements/recommendations for international students: Required—TOEFL (minimum score 550 paper-based; 79 iBT), IELTS (minimum score 6.5). *Application deadline:* For fall admission, 6/1 for domestic students, 4/15 for international students; for spring admission, 11/1 for domestic students, 10/1 for international students. *Expenses:* Tuition, state resident: full-time $8604; part-time $478 per credit hour. Tuition, nonresident: full-time $21,510; part-time $1195 per credit hour. *Required fees:* $66 per semester. Tuition and fees vary according to campus/location, program and reciprocity agreements. *Financial support:* In 2016–17, 2 students received support. Unspecified assistantships available. *Unit head:* Wayne Talley, Director. *Application contact:* Dr. Ali Ardalan, Associate Dean, 757-683-3520, Fax: 757-683-4076, E-mail: aardalan@odu.edu.

Oregon State University, College of Business, Program in Business Administration, Corvallis, OR 97331. Offers business administration (PhD), including accounting, innovation/commercialization; business analytics (MBA); corporate finance (MBA); innovation management (MBA); organizational leadership (MBA); research thesis (MBA); supply chain and logistics management (MBA). *Program availability:* Part-time, blended/hybrid learning. *Faculty:* 47 full-time (13 women), 10 part-time/adjunct (3 women). *Students:* 132 full-time (58 women), 83 part-time (36 women); includes 24 minority (3 Black or African American, non-Hispanic/Latino; 11 Asian, non-Hispanic/Latino; 8 Hispanic/Latino; 1 Native Hawaiian or other Pacific Islander, non-Hispanic/Latino; 1 Two or more races, non-Hispanic/Latino), 91 international. Average age 30. 203 applicants, 38% accepted, 67 enrolled. In 2016, 81 master's awarded. *Entrance requirements:* For master's, GMAT. Additional exam requirements/recommendations for international students: Required—TOEFL (minimum score 91 iBT), IELTS (minimum score 7). *Application deadline:* For fall admission, 2/1 priority date for domestic and international students; for winter admission, 9/15 priority date for domestic and international students; for spring admission, 1/1 priority date for domestic and international students. Applications are processed on a rolling basis. Application fee: $75 ($85 for international students). *Expenses:* $19,143 resident full-time tuition, $32,616 non-resident (for MBA). *Financial support:* Application deadline: 1/15. *Unit head:* Dr. David Baldridge, Director for Business Master's Program, 541-737-6062, E-mail: david.baldridge@bus.oregonstate.edu. *Application contact:* E-mail: osumba@bus.oregonstate.edu. Website: http://business.oregonstate.edu/graduate-programs

Penn State Harrisburg, Graduate School, School of Business Administration, Middletown, PA 17057. Offers accounting (MPAC, Certificate); business administration (MBA); information systems (MS); operations and supply chain management (Certificate). *Program availability:* Part-time, evening/weekend. *Unit head:* Dr. Mukund S. Kulkarni, Chancellor, 717-948-6105, Fax: 717-948-6452. *Application contact:* Robert W. Coffman, Jr., Director of Enrollment Management, Admissions, 717-948-6250, Fax: 717-948-6325, E-mail: hbgadmit@psu.edu.
Website: https://harrisburg.psu.edu/business-administration/

Penn State University Park, Graduate School, Smeal College of Business, University Park, PA 16802. Offers accounting (M Acc); business administration (MBA, MS, PhD); management and organizational leadership (MPS); supply chain management (MPS). *Accreditation:* AACSB. *Students:* 276 full-time (90 women). Average age 30. 1,243 applicants, 26% accepted, 260 enrolled. In 2016, 274 master's, 11 doctorates awarded. *Entrance requirements:* Additional exam requirements/recommendations for international students: Required—TOEFL (minimum score 550 paper-based; 80 iBT), IELTS. *Application deadline:* Applications are processed on a rolling basis. Application fee: $65. Electronic applications accepted. *Financial support:* Fellowships, research assistantships, teaching assistantships, career-related internships or fieldwork, Federal Work-Study, scholarships/grants, traineeships, health care benefits, and unspecified assistantships available. Support available to part-time students. Financial award application deadline: 3/1; financial award applicants required to submit FAFSA. *Unit head:* Dr. Charles H. Whiteman, Dean, 814-863-0448, Fax: 814-865-7064. *Application contact:* Lori Hawn, Director, Graduate Student Services, 814-865-1795, Fax: 814-863-4627, E-mail: l-gswww@lists.psu.edu. Website: http://smeal.psu.edu/

Polytechnic University of Puerto Rico, Miami Campus, Graduate School, Miami, FL 33166. Offers accounting (MBA); business administration (MBA); construction management (MEM); environmental management (MEM); finance (MBA); human resources management (MBA); logistics and supply chain management (MBA); management of international enterprises (MBA); manufacturing management (MEM); marketing management (MBA); project management (MBA). *Program availability:* Part-time, evening/weekend, online learning. *Entrance requirements:* For master's, minimum GPA of 3.0. Electronic applications accepted.

Portland State University, Graduate Studies, School of Business Administration, MS in Global Supply Chain Management Program, Portland, OR 97207-0751. Offers MS. *Program availability:* Part-time, online learning. *Students:* 2 full-time (1 woman), 72 part-time (31 women); includes 24 minority (7 Black or African American, non-Hispanic/Latino; 2 American Indian or Alaska Native, non-Hispanic/Latino; 7 Asian, non-Hispanic/Latino; 7 Hispanic/Latino; 1 Two or more races, non-Hispanic/Latino), 6 international. Average age 37. 51 applicants, 76% accepted, 31 enrolled. In 2016, 19 master's awarded. *Entrance requirements:* For master's, GMAT, GRE General Test, minimum undergraduate GPA of 3.0; two academic references; unofficial transcript from each college or university attended. Additional exam requirements/recommendations for international students: Required—TOEFL (minimum score 550 paper-based; 80 iBT). *Application deadline:* For fall admission, 5/1 priority date for domestic and international students; for winter admission, 12/1 for domestic and international students; for spring admission, 1/15 priority date for domestic and international students; for summer admission, 5/1 for domestic and international students. Application fee: $65. Electronic applications accepted. *Expenses:* Contact institution. *Unit head:* Daniel Wong, Academic Director, 503-725-3710, E-mail: dwong@pdx.edu. *Application contact:* Abby Messenger, Recruiting and Admissions Specialist, 503-725-2291, Fax: 503-725-5850, E-mail: a.g.messenger@pdx.edu.
Website: https://www.pdx.edu/sba/ms-in-global-supply-chain-management

Quinnipiac University, School of Business and Engineering, Program in Business Administration, Hamden, CT 06518-1940. Offers chartered financial analyst (MBA); health care management (MBA); supply chain management (MBA); JD/MBA. *Accreditation:* AACSB. *Program availability:* Part-time, evening/weekend, 100% online, blended/hybrid learning. *Faculty:* 29 full-time (8 women), 8 part-time/adjunct (2 women). *Students:* 195 full-time (87 women), 257 part-time (123 women); includes 59 minority (9 Black or African American, non-Hispanic/Latino; 19 Asian, non-Hispanic/Latino; 24 Hispanic/Latino; 7 Two or more races, non-Hispanic/Latino), 23 international. 307 applicants, 79% accepted, 223 enrolled. In 2016, 188 master's awarded. *Entrance requirements:* For master's, GMAT or GRE, minimum GPA of 3.0. Additional exam requirements/recommendations for international students: Required—TOEFL (minimum score 575 paper-based; 90 iBT), IELTS (minimum score 6.5). *Application deadline:* For fall admission, 7/30 priority date for domestic students, 4/30 priority date for international students; for spring admission, 12/15 priority date for domestic students, 9/30 priority date for international students. Applications are processed on a rolling basis. Application fee: $45. Electronic applications accepted. *Expenses:* Contact institution. *Financial support:* Career-related internships or fieldwork, Federal Work-Study, scholarships/grants, and unspecified assistantships available. Financial award application deadline: 6/1; financial award applicants required to submit FAFSA. *Faculty research:* Financial markets and investments, international business, supply chain management, health care management, corporate governance. *Unit head:* Lisa Braiewa, Director of the MBA Program, 800-462-1944, Fax: 203-582-3443, E-mail: graduate@qu.edu. *Application contact:* Office of Graduate Admissions, 800-462-1944, Fax: 203-582-3443, E-mail: graduate@qu.edu.
Website: http://www.qu.edu/mba

Rensselaer Polytechnic Institute, Graduate School, Lally School of Management, Program in Supply Chain Management, Troy, NY 12180-3590. Offers MS, MS/MBA. *Program availability:* Part-time. *Faculty:* 35 full-time (10 women), 7 part-time/adjunct (0 women). *Students:* 14 full-time (9 women). 79 applicants, 41% accepted, 11 enrolled. In 2016, 3 master's awarded. *Entrance requirements:* For master's, GMAT or GRE. Additional exam requirements/recommendations for international students: Required—TOEFL (minimum score 570 paper-based; 88 iBT), IELTS (minimum score 6.8), PTE (minimum score 60). *Application deadline:* For fall admission, 1/1 for domestic and international students. Applications are processed on a rolling basis. Application fee: $75. Electronic applications accepted. *Expenses: Tuition:* Full-time $49,520; part-time $2060 per credit hour. *Required fees:* $2617. *Financial support:* Scholarships/grants available. Financial award application deadline: 1/1. *Unit head:* Dr. Gina O'Connor, Associate Dean, 518-276-6842, E-mail: oconng@rpi.edu. *Application contact:* Office of Graduate Admissions, 518-576-6216, E-mail: gradadmissions@rpi.edu.
Website: https://lallyschool.rpi.edu/graduate-programs/ms-supplychainmanagement

Rutgers University–Newark, Rutgers Business School–Newark and New Brunswick, Doctoral Programs in Management, Newark, NJ 07102. Offers accounting (PhD); accounting information systems (PhD); economics (PhD); finance (PhD); individualized study (PhD); information technology (PhD); international business (PhD); management science (PhD); marketing science (PhD); organizational management (PhD); science, technology and management (PhD); supply chain management (PhD). *Degree requirements:* For doctorate, comprehensive exam, thesis/dissertation. *Entrance requirements:* For doctorate, GRE or GMAT. Additional exam requirements/recommendations for international students: Required—TOEFL (minimum score 550 paper-based; 79 iBT). Electronic applications accepted.

Saint Leo University, Graduate Business Studies, Saint Leo, FL 33574-6665. Offers accounting (M Acc, MBA, Certificate); cybersecurity (MS); health care management (MBA, Certificate); human resource management (MBA, Certificate); information security management (MBA, Certificate); management (MBA, DBA); marketing (MBA, Certificate); marketing research and social media analytics (MBA, Certificate); project management (MBA, Certificate); sport business (MBA); supply chain global integration management (MBA, Certificate). *Accreditation:* ACBSP. *Program availability:* Part-time, evening/weekend, 100% online, blended/hybrid learning. *Faculty:* 53 full-time (18 women), 53 part-time/adjunct (19 women). *Students:* 8 full-time (4 women), 2,001 part-time (1,160 women); includes 928 minority (650 Black or African American, non-Hispanic/Latino; 5 American Indian or Alaska Native, non-Hispanic/Latino; 43 Asian, non-Hispanic/Latino; 193 Hispanic/Latino; 2 Native Hawaiian or other Pacific Islander, non-Hispanic/Latino; 35 Two or more races, non-Hispanic/Latino), 51 international. Average age 37. 922 applicants, 85% accepted, 517 enrolled. In 2016, 874 master's, 17 other advanced degrees awarded. *Degree requirements:* For doctorate, comprehensive exam, thesis/dissertation. *Entrance requirements:* For master's, GMAT (minimum score 500), official transcripts, current resume, 2 professional recommendations, personal statement, bachelor's degree from regionally-accredited university; undergraduate degree in accounting and minimum undergraduate GPA of 3.0 (for M Acc); minimum undergraduate GPA of 3.0 in final 2 years of undergraduate study and 2 years' work experience (for MBA); for doctorate, GMAT (minimum score of 550) if master's GPA is under 3.25, official transcripts, current resume, 2 professional recommendations, personal statement, master's degree from regionally-accredited university with minimum GPA of 3.25, 3 years' work experience, interview. Additional exam requirements/recommendations for international students: Required—TOEFL (minimum score 550 paper-based; 80 iBT). *Application deadline:* For fall admission, 7/1 priority date for domestic and international students; for spring admission, 11/12 priority date for domestic students, 11/1 for international students. Applications are processed on a rolling basis. Application fee: $80. Electronic applications accepted. *Expenses:* Contact institution. *Financial support:* In 2016–17, 118 students received support. Career-related internships or fieldwork, scholarships/grants, and health care benefits available. Financial award application deadline: 3/1; financial award applicants required to submit FAFSA. *Unit head:* Dr. Lorrie McGovern, Associate Dean, School of Business, 352-588-7869, Fax: 352-588-8912, E-mail: mbaslu@saintleo.edu. *Application contact:* Jennifer Shelley, Senior Associate Director of Graduate Admissions, 800-707-8846, Fax: 352-588-7873, E-mail: grad.admissions@saintleo.edu.
Website: http://www.saintleo.edu/academics/graduate.aspx

St. Norbert College, Master of Business Administration Program, De Pere, WI 54115-2099. Offers business (MBA); health care (MBA); supply chain and manufacturing (MBA). *Program availability:* Part-time. *Faculty:* 9 full-time (3 women), 3 part-time/adjunct (0 women). *Students:* 64 part-time (33 women); includes 6 minority (1 American Indian or Alaska Native, non-Hispanic/Latino; 2 Asian, non-Hispanic/Latino; 2 Hispanic/Latino; 1 Two or more races, non-Hispanic/Latino), 1 international. Average age 33. 17 applicants, 100% accepted, 16 enrolled. *Entrance requirements:* For master's, official transcripts, letters of recommendation, professional resume, essay. *Application deadline:* For fall admission, 8/5 for domestic students; for winter admission, 12/16 for domestic students; for spring admission, 3/3 for domestic students; for summer admission, 4/22 for domestic students. Applications are processed on a rolling basis. Application fee: $50. Electronic applications accepted. *Expenses:* $675 per credit tuition. *Financial support:* Federal Work-Study available. Financial award application deadline: 1/1; financial award applicants required to submit FAFSA. *Unit head:* Lisa Gray, Executive Assistant, 920-403-3449, E-mail: lisa.gray@snc.edu. *Application contact:* Brenda Busch, Associate Director of Graduate Recruitment, 920-403-3942, Fax: 920-403-4072, E-mail: brenda.busch@snc.edu.
Website: http://www.snc.edu/mba/

Santa Clara University, Leavey School of Business, Santa Clara, CA 95053. Offers business administration (MBA); business analytics (MS); finance (MS); information systems (MS); supply chain management and analytics (MS); JD/MBA. *Accreditation:* AACSB. *Program availability:* Part-time, evening/weekend. *Faculty:* 92 full-time (27 women), 44 part-time/adjunct (18 women). *Students:* 330 full-time (192 women), 323 part-time (136 women); includes 190 minority (7 Black or African American, non-Hispanic/Latino; 140 Asian, non-Hispanic/Latino; 28 Hispanic/Latino; 2 Native Hawaiian or other Pacific Islander, non-Hispanic/Latino; 13 Two or more races, non-Hispanic/Latino), 275 international. Average age 30. 388 applicants, 53% accepted, 107 enrolled. In 2016, 339 master's awarded. *Entrance requirements:* For master's, GMAT or GRE, resume, 2 letters of recommendation, 2 transcripts. Additional exam requirements/recommendations for international students: Required—TOEFL (minimum score 100 iBT) or IELTS (7.0). Application fee: $100 ($150 for international students). Electronic applications accepted. *Expenses:* $1,022 per unit tuition (for MBA); $1,124 per unit tuition (for other master's programs). *Financial support:* Fellowships, research assistantships, teaching assistantships, career-related internships or fieldwork, Federal Work-Study, scholarships/grants, traineeships, health care benefits, tuition waivers, and unspecified assistantships available. Support available to part-time students. Financial award applicants required to submit FAFSA. *Faculty research:* Intellectual property, research and development, international trade. *Unit head:* Caryn Beck-Dudley, Dean. *Application contact:* Taryn Upchurch, Director, Graduate Admissions and Recruitment, 408-551-7858, E-mail: upchurch@scu.edu.
Website: http://www.scu.edu/business/

Seton Hall University, Stillman School of Business, Programs in Business Administration, South Orange, NJ 07079-2697. Offers accounting (MBA); entrepreneurship (Certificate); finance (MBA, Certificate); information technology management (MBA); international business (MBA); management (MBA); marketing (MBA); sport management (MBA); supply chain management (MBA, Certificate). *Program availability:* Part-time, evening/weekend. *Degree requirements:* For master's, 20 hours of community service (Social Responsibility Project). *Entrance requirements:* For master's, GMAT or CPA, GRE (waived based on work experience or advanced degree from AACSB institution), MS in business discipline, professional degree (MD, JD, PhD, DVM, DDS, CPA, etc.), minimum undergraduate GPA of 3.0. Additional exam requirements/recommendations for international students: Required—TOEFL (minimum score 607 paper-based; 102 iBT), IELTS (minimum score 6), PTE. Electronic applications accepted. *Expenses:* Contact institution. *Faculty research:* Sport, hedge funds, executive compensation, social media, legal studies.

Shippensburg University of Pennsylvania, School of Graduate Studies, John L. Grove College of Business, Shippensburg, PA 17257-2299. Offers advanced studies in business (Certificate); advanced supply chain and logistics management (Certificate); business administration (MBA), including business administration, finance, healthcare management, management information systems, supply chain management; finance (Certificate); health care management (Certificate); management information systems (Certificate). *Accreditation:* AACSB. *Program availability:* Part-time, evening/weekend, 100% online, blended/hybrid learning. *Faculty:* 23 full-time (4 women), 4 part-time/adjunct (1 woman). *Students:* 58 full-time (17 women), 195 part-time (59 women); includes 26 minority (12 Black or African American, non-Hispanic/Latino; 8 Asian, non-Hispanic/Latino; 5 Hispanic/Latino; 1 Two or more races, non-Hispanic/Latino), 26 international. Average age 32. 224 applicants, 55% accepted, 70 enrolled. In 2016, 101 master's awarded. *Degree requirements:* For master's, thesis optional, practicum. *Entrance requirements:* For master's, GMAT (minimum score 450 if less than 5 years of mid-level experience, including management experience), current resume; relevant work/classroom experience; 500-word statement of purpose; prerequisites of quantitative analysis, computer usage, and oral and written communications; laptop computer. Additional exam requirements/recommendations for international students: Required—TOEFL (minimum score 550 paper-based, 68 iBT) or IELTS (minimum score 6). *Application deadline:* For fall admission, 4/30 for international students; for spring admission, 9/30 for international students. Applications are processed on a rolling basis. Application fee: $45. Electronic applications accepted. *Expenses:* Tuition, state resident: part-time $483 per credit. Tuition, nonresident: part-time $725 per credit. *Required fees:* $141 per credit. *Financial support:* In 2016–17, 12 students received support. Career-related internships or fieldwork, scholarships/grants, unspecified assistantships, and resident hall director and student payroll positions available. Support available to part-time students. Financial award application deadline: 3/1; financial award applicants required to submit FAFSA. *Unit head:* Dr. John G. Kooti, Dean of the College of Business, 717-477-1435, Fax: 717-477-4003, E-mail: jgkooti@ship.edu. *Application contact:* Megan N. Luft, Associate Dean of Graduate Admissions, 717-477-1231, Fax: 717-477-4016, E-mail: mnluft@ship.edu.
Website: http://www.ship.edu/business

Southern Arkansas University–Magnolia, School of Graduate Studies, Magnolia, AR 71753. Offers agriculture (MS); business administration (MBA), including agri-business, social entrepreneurship, supply chain management; clinical and mental health counseling (MS); computer and information sciences (MS), including cyber security and privacy, data science, information technology; gifted and talented (M Ed), including curriculum and instruction, educational administration and supervision, gifted and talented P-8/7-12, instructional specialist P-4; higher, adult and lifelong education (M Ed); kinesiology (M Ed), including coaching; library media and information specialist (M Ed); public administration (MPA); school counseling K-12 (M Ed); student affairs and college counseling (M Ed); teaching (MAT). *Accreditation:* NCATE. *Program availability:* Part-time, 100% online, blended/hybrid learning. *Faculty:* 36 full-time (19 women), 33 part-time/adjunct (14 women). *Students:* 605 full-time (143 women), 879 part-time (352 women); includes 130 minority (113 Black or African American, non-Hispanic/Latino; 7 American Indian or Alaska Native, non-Hispanic/Latino; 2 Asian, non-Hispanic/Latino; 2 Hispanic/Latino; 6 Two or more races, non-Hispanic/Latino), 1,048 international. Average age 28. 904 applicants, 81% accepted, 262 enrolled. In 2016, 278 master's awarded. *Degree requirements:* For master's, comprehensive exam (for some programs), thesis optional. *Entrance requirements:* For master's, GRE, MAT or GMAT, minimum GPA of 2.5. Additional exam requirements/recommendations for international students: Required—TOEFL (minimum score 550 paper-based), IELTS (minimum score 6). *Application deadline:* For fall admission, 7/20 for domestic students, 7/10 for international students; for spring admission, 12/1 for domestic students, 11/15 for international students; for summer admission, 4/1 for domestic students, 5/1 for international students. Applications are processed on a rolling basis. Application fee: $25 ($50 for international students). Electronic applications accepted. *Expenses:* Tuition, state resident: full-time $2511; part-time $279 per credit hour. Tuition, nonresident: full-time $3726; part-time $414 per credit hour. *Required fees:* $307 per semester. Tuition and fees vary according to course load and program. *Financial support:* Career-related internships or fieldwork, Federal Work-Study, scholarships/grants, tuition waivers (full), and unspecified assistantships available. Financial award applicants required to submit FAFSA. *Faculty research:* Alternative certification for teachers, supervision of instruction, instructional leadership, counseling. *Unit head:* Dr. Kim Bloss, Dean, School of Graduate Studies, 870-235-4150, Fax: 870-235-5227, E-mail: kkbloss@saumag.edu. *Application contact:* Shrijana Malakar, Admissions Specialist, 870-235-4150, Fax: 870-235-5227, E-mail: smalakar@saumag.edu.
Website: http://www.saumag.edu/graduate

Southern New Hampshire University, School of Business, Manchester, NH 03106-1045. Offers accounting (MBA, MS, Graduate Certificate); accounting finance (MS); accounting/auditing (MS); accounting/forensic accounting (MS); accounting/taxation (MS); athletic administration (MBA, Graduate Certificate); business administration (IMBA, MBA, Certificate, Graduate Certificate), including accounting (Certificate), business administration (MBA), business information systems (Graduate Certificate), human resource management (Certificate); corporate social responsibility (MBA); entrepreneurship (MBA); finance (MBA, MS, Graduate Certificate); finance/corporate finance (MS); finance/investments and securities (MS); forensic accounting (MBA); healthcare informatics (MBA); healthcare management (MBA); human resource management (Graduate Certificate); information technology (MS, Graduate Certificate); information technology management (MBA); international business (Graduate Certificate); international business and information technology (Graduate Certificate); international finance (Graduate Certificate); international sport management (Graduate Certificate); justice studies (MBA); leadership of nonprofit organizations (Graduate Certificate); management (MS); marketing (MBA, MS, Graduate Certificate); operations and project management (MS); operations and supply chain management (MBA, Graduate Certificate); organizational leadership (MS); project management (MBA, Graduate Certificate); Six Sigma (MBA); Six Sigma quality (Graduate Certificate); social media marketing (MBA); sport management (MBA, MS, Graduate Certificate); sustainability and environmental compliance (MBA); workplace conflict management (MBA); MBA/Certificate. *Accreditation:* ACBSP. *Program availability:* Part-time, evening/weekend, online learning. Terminal master's awarded for partial completion of doctoral program. *Degree requirements:* For master's, one foreign language, comprehensive exam (for some programs), thesis or alternative. *Entrance requirements:* For master's, minimum GPA of 2.5. Additional exam requirements/recommendations for international students: Required—TOEFL (minimum score 500 paper-based). Electronic applications accepted.

Strayer University, Graduate Studies, Washington, DC 20005-2603. Offers accounting (MS); acquisition (MBA); business administration (MBA); communications technology (MS); educational management (M Ed); finance (MBA); health services administration (MHSA); hospitality and tourism management (MBA); human resource management (MBA); information systems (MS), including computer security management, decision support system management, enterprise resource management, network management, software engineering management, systems development management; management (MBA); management information systems (MS); marketing (MBA); professional accounting (MS), including accounting information systems, controllership, taxation; public administration (MPA); supply chain management (MBA); technology in education (M Ed). Programs also offered at campus locations in Birmingham, AL; Chamblee, GA; Cobb County, GA; Morrow, GA; White Marsh, MD; Charleston, SC; Columbia, SC; Greensboro, NC; Greenville, SC; Lexington, KY; Louisville, KY; Nashville, TN; North Raleigh, NC; Washington, DC. *Accreditation:* ACBSP. *Program availability:* Part-time, evening/weekend, online learning. *Degree requirements:* For master's, thesis. *Entrance requirements:* For master's, GMAT, GRE General Test, bachelor's degree from an accredited college or university, minimum undergraduate GPA of 2.75. Electronic applications accepted.

Suffolk University, Sawyer Business School, Master of Business Administration Program, Boston, MA 02108-2770. Offers accounting (MBA); entrepreneurship (MBA); executive business administration (EMBA); finance (MBA); global business administration (GMBA); health administration (MBA); international business (MBA); marketing (MBA); nonprofit management (MBA); organizational behavior (MBA); strategic management (MBA); supply chain management (MBA); taxation (MBA); JD/MBA; MBA/MHA; MBA/MSA; MBA/MSF; MBA/MST. *Accreditation:* AACSB. *Program availability:* Part-time, evening/weekend, 100% online. *Faculty:* 17 full-time (6 women), 10 part-time/adjunct (1 woman). *Students:* 137 full-time (70 women), 265 part-time (138 women); includes 78 minority (20 Black or African American, non-Hispanic/Latino; 22 Asian, non-Hispanic/Latino; 31 Hispanic/Latino; 5 Two or more races, non-Hispanic/Latino), 46 international. Average age 30. 416 applicants, 70% accepted, 128 enrolled. In 2016, 165 degrees awarded. *Entrance requirements:* For master's, GMAT, minimum undergraduate GPA of 2.75 (MBA), 5 years of managerial experience (EMBA). Additional exam requirements/recommendations for international students: Required—TOEFL (minimum score 550 paper-based; 80 iBT). *Application deadline:* For fall admission, 3/15 priority date for domestic students, 10/15 priority date for international students; for spring admission, 10/15 priority date for domestic and international students. Applications are processed on a rolling basis. Application fee: $50. Electronic applications accepted. *Expenses: Tuition:* Full-time $41,490; part-time $1383 per credit hour. *Required fees:* $52; $52 per credit hour. Part-time tuition and fees vary according to course load and program. *Financial support:* In 2016–17, 209 students received support, including 176 fellowships (averaging $8,581 per year); career-related internships or fieldwork, Federal Work-Study, institutionally sponsored loans, and scholarships/grants also available. Support available to part-time students. Financial award application deadline: 4/1; financial award applicants required to submit FAFSA. *Faculty research:* Foreign investments; career strategies and boundaryless careers; corporate ethics codes; interest rates, inflation, and growth options; innovation and product development performance. *Unit head:* Jodi Detjen, Director of MBA Programs, 617-573-8306, E-mail: jdetjen@suffolk.edu. *Application contact:* Mara Marzocchi, Associate Director of Graduate Admissions, 617-573-8302, Fax: 617-305-1733, E-mail: grad.admission@suffolk.edu. Website: http://www.suffolk.edu/mba

Syracuse University, Martin J. Whitman School of Management, Master of Business Administration Program, Syracuse, NY 13244. Offers accounting (MBA); business analytics (MBA); entrepreneurship (MBA); marketing management (MBA); real estate (MBA); supply chain management (MBA); JD/MBA. *Program availability:* Part-time, 100% online. *Students:* 22 full-time (9 women), 495 part-time (147 women); includes 182 minority (81 Black or African American, non-Hispanic/Latino; 3 American Indian or Alaska Native, non-Hispanic/Latino; 42 Asian, non-Hispanic/Latino; 52 Hispanic/Latino; 4 Native Hawaiian or other Pacific Islander, non-Hispanic/Latino), 22 international. Average age 32. 1,086 applicants, 73% accepted, 518 enrolled. In 2016, 84 master's awarded. *Entrance requirements:* For master's, GMAT or GRE, resume, essay, 5-minute video interview, two letters of recommendation, transcripts (unofficial). Additional exam requirements/recommendations for international students: Required—TOEFL (minimum score 100 iBT), IELTS (minimum score 7), PTE (minimum score 68). *Application deadline:* For fall admission, 11/30 for domestic students, 11/30 priority date for international students; for winter admission, 1/1 for domestic students, 1/1 priority date for international students; for spring admission, 2/15 for domestic and international students; for summer admission, 4/19 for domestic students. Application fee: $75. Electronic applications accepted. *Expenses:* Contact institution. *Financial support:* In 2016–17, 22 students received support. Merit scholarships available. Financial award application deadline: 2/15. *Faculty research:* Data analysis, economics of international business, financial markets and institutions, operations management, supply chain management. *Unit head:* Don Harter, Associate Dean, Graduate Programs, 315-443-3502, E-mail: dharter@syr.edu. *Application contact:* Shri Ramakrishnan, Assistant Director, Graduate Recruitment, 315-443-3497, Fax: 315-443-9517, E-mail: busgrad@syr.edu.
Website: http://whitman.syr.edu/ftmba/

Syracuse University, Martin J. Whitman School of Management, MS Program in Supply Chain Management, Syracuse, NY 13244. Offers MS. *Students:* 3 full-time (2 women), 2 international. Average age 22. 72 applicants, 36% accepted, 3 enrolled. In 2016, 5 master's awarded. *Entrance requirements:* For master's, GMAT or GRE, resume, essay, 5-minute video interview, two letters of recommendation, transcripts (unofficial). Additional exam requirements/recommendations for international students: Required—TOEFL (minimum score 100 iBT), IELTS (minimum score 7), PTE (minimum score 68), GMAT or GRE. *Application deadline:* For fall admission, 11/30 for domestic students, 11/30 priority date for international students; for winter admission, 1/1 for domestic students, 1/1 priority date for international students; for spring admission, 2/15 for domestic and international students; for summer admission, 4/19 for domestic students. Application fee: $75. Electronic applications accepted. *Expenses:* Contact institution. *Financial support:* In 2016–17, 3 students received support. Merit scholarships available. Financial award application deadline: 2/15. *Faculty research:* Supply chain management, logistics management, management information systems, risk sharing, buyer-seller alliances. *Unit head:* Fred Easton, Director, Operations Management/Professor of Supply Chain Management, 315-443-3463, E-mail: ffeaston@syr.edu. *Application contact:* Shri Ramakrishnan, Assistant Director, Graduate Recruitment, 315-443-3497, Fax: 315-443-9517, E-mail: sramak01@syr.edu.
Website: http://whitman.syr.edu/Academics/Marketing/SupplyChain/

Temple University, College of Science and Technology, Department of Computer and Information Sciences, Philadelphia, PA 19122. Offers computational data science (MS); computer and information sciences (PhD), including artificial intelligence, computer and network systems, information systems, software systems; computer science (MS); cyber defense and information assurance (PSM); information science and technology (MS). *Program availability:* Part-time, evening/weekend. *Faculty:* 36 full-time (7 women), 6 part-time/adjunct (1 woman). *Students:* 88 full-time (22 women), 20 part-time (5 women); includes 6 minority (1 Black or African American, non-Hispanic/Latino; 5 Asian, non-Hispanic/Latino), 81 international. 153 applicants, 45% accepted, 34 enrolled. In 2016, 24 master's, 7 doctorates awarded. Terminal master's awarded for partial completion of doctoral program. *Degree requirements:* For doctorate, thesis/dissertation. *Entrance requirements:* For master's and doctorate, GRE General Test, minimum GPA of 3.0. Additional exam requirements/recommendations for international students: Required—TOEFL (minimum score 550 paper-based; 79 iBT). *Application deadline:* For fall admission, 2/1 for domestic students, 12/15 for international students; for spring admission, 8/1 for domestic and international students. Applications are processed on a

rolling basis. Application fee: $60. Electronic applications accepted. *Financial support:* Fellowships, research assistantships with tuition reimbursements, teaching assistantships with tuition reimbursements, career-related internships or fieldwork, institutionally sponsored loans, and unspecified assistantships available. Financial award application deadline: 1/15; financial award applicants required to submit FAFSA. *Faculty research:* Artificial intelligence, information systems, software engineering, network-distributed systems. *Unit head:* Chiu Tan, Graduate Program Chair, 215-204-6847, E-mail: cis@temple.edu. *Application contact:* Marilyn Grandshaw, Administrative Coordinator, 215-204-8450, E-mail: marilyng@temple.edu.
Website: https://cis.temple.edu/

Texas A&M University–San Antonio, School of Business, San Antonio, TX 78224. Offers business administration (MBA); enterprise resource planning systems (MBA); finance (MBA); healthcare management (MBA); human resources management (MBA); information assurance and security (MBA); international business (MBA); professional accounting (MPA); project management (MBA); supply chain management (MBA). *Program availability:* Part-time, evening/weekend. *Entrance requirements:* For master's, GMAT. Additional exam requirements/recommendations for international students: Required—TOEFL (minimum score 550 paper-based; 80 iBT), IELTS (minimum score 6). Electronic applications accepted.

Texas Christian University, Neeley School of Business, Full-time Master's Program in Business Administration and Accelerated MBA, Fort Worth, TX 76129. Offers accounting (MBA); finance (MBA), including corporate finance, investments; marketing (MBA), including marketing management, product and brand management; supply and value chain management (MBA). *Accreditation:* AACSB. *Program availability:* Part-time, evening/weekend. *Faculty:* 60 full-time (17 women), 17 part-time/adjunct (4 women). *Students:* 92 full-time (26 women); includes 14 minority (3 Black or African American, non-Hispanic/Latino; 1 American Indian or Alaska Native, non-Hispanic/Latino; 3 Asian, non-Hispanic/Latino; 7 Hispanic/Latino), 30 international. Average age 28. 205 applicants, 50% accepted, 47 enrolled. In 2016, 43 master's awarded. *Entrance requirements:* For master's, GMAT (preferred); GRE. Additional exam requirements/recommendations for international students: Required—TOEFL (minimum score 100 iBT); Recommended—IELTS (minimum score 7), TSE (minimum score 68). *Application deadline:* For fall admission, 3/1 for domestic and international students; for winter admission, 1/15 for domestic and international students; for spring admission, 11/1 for domestic and international students; for summer admission, 1/15 for domestic and international students. Applications are processed on a rolling basis. Application fee: $100. Electronic applications accepted. Application fee is waived when completed online. *Expenses:* Contact institution. *Financial support:* In 2016–17, 94 students received support. Career-related internships or fieldwork, scholarships/grants, and unspecified assistantships available. Financial award application deadline: 4/1; financial award applicants required to submit FAFSA. *Faculty research:* Emerging financial markets, derivative trading activity, salesforce deployment, examining sales activity, litigation against tax practitioners. *Unit head:* Anne Rooney, Executive Director, Graduate Programs, 817-257-7991, Fax: 817-257-6431, E-mail: mbainfo@tcu.edu. *Application contact:* Peggy Conway, Director, Full-time MBA Admissions, 817-257-7989, Fax: 817-257-6431, E-mail: mbainfo@tcu.edu.
Website: http://www.neeley.tcu.edu/mba

Towson University, Program in e-Business and Technology Management, Towson, MD 21252-0001. Offers project, program and portfolio management (Postbaccalaureate Certificate); supply chain management (MS, Postbaccalaureate Certificate). *Students:* 2 full-time (1 woman), 22 part-time (8 women); includes 7 minority (3 Black or African American, non-Hispanic/Latino; 1 Asian, non-Hispanic/Latino; 3 Two or more races, non-Hispanic/Latino), 2 international. *Entrance requirements:* For master's and Postbaccalaureate Certificate, GRE or GMAT, bachelor's degree in relevant field and/or three years of post-bachelor's experience working in supply chain related areas; minimum cumulative GPA of 3.0; resume; 2 reference letters. Additional exam requirements/recommendations for international students: Required—TOEFL (minimum score 550 paper-based). *Application deadline:* Applications are processed on a rolling basis. Application fee: $45. Electronic applications accepted. *Expenses:* Tuition, state resident: full-time $7580; part-time $379 per unit. Tuition, nonresident: full-time $15,700; part-time $785 per unit. *Required fees:* $2480. *Unit head:* Dr. Tobin Porterfield, Director, 410-704-3265, E-mail: tporterfield@towson.edu. *Application contact:* Coverley Beidleman, Assistant Director of Graduate Admissions, 410-704-2113, Fax: 410-704-3030, E-mail: grads@towson.edu.
Website: http://www.towson.edu/cbe/departments/ebusiness/grad/

University at Buffalo, the State University of New York, Graduate School, School of Management, Buffalo, NY 14620. Offers accounting (MS); analytics (MBA); business administration (PMBA); consulting (MBA); finance (MBA, MS), including financial risk management (MS), quantitative finance (MS); healthcare (MBA); information assurance (MBA); information systems (MBA); international management (MBA); management (EMBA, PhD); management information systems (MS); marketing (MBA); supply chain and operations (MBA); supply chains and operations management (MS); Au D/MBA; DDS/MBA; JD/MBA; M Arch/MBA; MD/MBA; MPH/MBA; MSW/MBA; Pharm D/MBA. *Accreditation:* AACSB. *Program availability:* Part-time, evening/weekend. *Faculty:* 80 full-time (26 women), 36 part-time/adjunct (6 women). *Students:* 683 full-time (277 women), 196 part-time (63 women); includes 76 minority (23 Black or African American, non-Hispanic/Latino; 1 American Indian or Alaska Native, non-Hispanic/Latino; 48 Asian, non-Hispanic/Latino; 3 Hispanic/Latino; 1 Two or more races, non-Hispanic/Latino), 371 international. Average age 31. 2,451 applicants, 42% accepted, 484 enrolled. In 2016, 515 master's, 10 doctorates awarded. *Degree requirements:* For master's, thesis (for some programs); for doctorate, comprehensive exam, thesis/dissertation. *Entrance requirements:* For master's, GMAT (for MS in accounting, finance); GRE or GMAT (for MBA, PMBA, other MS concentrations), essays, letters of recommendation; for doctorate, GMAT or GRE, essays, writing sample, letters of recommendation. Additional exam requirements/recommendations for international students: Required—TOEFL (minimum score 95 iBT) or IELTS (minimum score 6.5); Recommended—TSE (minimum score 73). *Application deadline:* For fall admission, 10/15 priority date for domestic and international students; for winter admission, 2/1 priority date for domestic and international students; for spring admission, 4/15 for domestic students; for summer admission, 5/15 for domestic students. Application fee: $100. Electronic applications accepted. *Expenses:* Contact institution. *Financial support:* Fellowships with full and partial tuition reimbursements, research assistantships with full and partial tuition reimbursements, teaching assistantships with full and partial tuition reimbursements, career-related internships or fieldwork, Federal Work-Study, institutionally sponsored loans, scholarships/grants, health care benefits, and unspecified assistantships available. Financial award application deadline: 2/15. *Faculty research:* Data analytics, accounting information and corporate finance, consumer behavior, supply chain logistics, leadership and team effectiveness. *Total annual research expenditures:* $1.5 million. *Unit head:* Erin K. O'Brien, Assistant Dean and Director of Graduate Programs, 716-645-3204, Fax: 716-645-2341, E-mail: ekobrien@buffalo.edu. *Application contact:* Meghan Felser, Associate Director of Admissions and Recruiting, 716-645-3204, Fax: 716-645-2341, E-mail: mpwood@buffalo.edu.
Website: http://mgt.buffalo.edu/

The University of Akron, Graduate School, College of Business Administration, Department of Management, Program in Supply Chain Management, Akron, OH 44325. Offers MBA. *Program availability:* Part-time. *Students:* 10 full-time (4 women), 4 part-time (2 women), 9 international. Average age 31. 16 applicants, 69% accepted, 5 enrolled. In 2016, 17 master's awarded. *Entrance requirements:* For master's, GMAT, minimum GPA of 3.0 (preferred), two letters of recommendation, resume, statement of purpose. Additional exam requirements/recommendations for international students: Required—TOEFL (minimum score 550 paper-based; 79 iBT), IELTS (minimum score 6.5). *Application deadline:* For fall admission, 7/15 for domestic and international students; for spring admission, 11/15 for domestic and international students; for summer admission, 4/15 for domestic and international students. Application fee: $45 ($75 for international students). Electronic applications accepted. *Expenses:* Tuition, state resident: full-time $8618; part-time $359 per credit hour. Tuition, nonresident: full-time $17,149; part-time $715 per credit hour. *Required fees:* $1652. *Unit head:* Dr. Steve Ash, Chair, 330-972-6086, E-mail: ash@uakron.edu. *Application contact:* Dr. William Hauser, Director of Graduate Business Programs, 330-972-7043, Fax: 330-972-6588, E-mail: whauser@uakron.edu.
Website: http://www.uakron.edu/cba/graduate/programs/mba/supplychain.dot

The University of Alabama in Huntsville, School of Graduate Studies, College of Business Administration, Programs in Business and Management, Huntsville, AL 35899. Offers business analytics (MSMS); federal contracting and procurement management (Certificate); human resource management (MSM); management (MBA), including acquisition management, entrepreneurship, federal contract accounting, finance, human resource management, logistics and supply chain management, marketing, project management; supply chain management (Certificate); technology and innovation management (Certificate). *Accreditation:* AACSB. *Program availability:* Part-time, evening/weekend. *Degree requirements:* For master's, comprehensive exam, thesis or alternative. *Entrance requirements:* For master's, GMAT (minimum score 500), minimum AACSB index of 1080. Additional exam requirements/recommendations for international students: Required—TOEFL (minimum score 550 paper-based; 80 iBT), IELTS (minimum score 6.5). Electronic applications accepted. *Expenses:* Tuition, state resident: full-time $9834; part-time $600 per credit hour. Tuition, nonresident: full-time $21,830; part-time $1325 per credit hour. *Faculty research:* Supply chain management, management of research and development, international marketing and branding, organizational behavior and human resource management, social networks and computational economics.

The University of Alabama in Huntsville, School of Graduate Studies, College of Business Administration, Programs in Information Systems, Huntsville, AL 35899. Offers cybersecurity (MS, Certificate); enterprise resource planning (Certificate); information systems (MSIS); supply chain and logistics management (MS); supply chain management (Certificate). *Program availability:* Part-time, evening/weekend. *Degree requirements:* For master's, comprehensive exam, thesis or alternative. *Entrance requirements:* For master's, GMAT (minimum score 500), minimum AACSB index of 1080. Additional exam requirements/recommendations for international students: Required—TOEFL (minimum score 550 paper-based; 80 iBT), IELTS (minimum score 6.5). Electronic applications accepted. *Expenses:* Tuition, state resident: full-time $9834; part-time $600 per credit hour. Tuition, nonresident: full-time $21,830; part-time $1325 per credit hour. *Faculty research:* Supply chain information systems, information assurance and security, databases and conceptual schema, workflow management, inter-organizational information sharing.

University of Dallas, Satish and Yasmin Gupta College of Business, Irving, TX 75062-4736. Offers accounting (MBA, MS); business administration (DBA); business analytics (MS); business management (MBA); corporate finance (MBA); cybersecurity (MS); finance (MS); financial services (MBA); global business (MBA, MS); health services management (MBA); human resource management (MBA); information and technology management (MS); information assurance (MBA); information technology (MBA); information technology service management (MBA); marketing management (MBA); organization development (MBA); project management (MBA); sports and entertainment management (MBA); strategic leadership (MBA); supply chain management (MBA). *Accreditation:* AACSB. *Program availability:* Part-time, evening/weekend, online learning. *Entrance requirements:* Additional exam requirements/recommendations for international students: Required—TOEFL. Electronic applications accepted. *Expenses:* Contact institution.

University of Florida, Graduate School, Warrington College of Business Administration, Hough Graduate School of Business, Department of Information Systems and Operations Management, Gainesville, FL 32611. Offers information systems and operations management (PhD); supply chain management (Certificate). Terminal master's awarded for partial completion of doctoral program. *Degree requirements:* For doctorate, thesis/dissertation. *Entrance requirements:* For master's, GMAT or GRE General Test, minimum GPA of 3.0; for doctorate, GMAT (minimum score 650) or GRE General Test, minimum GPA of 3.0. Additional exam requirements/recommendations for international students: Required—TOEFL (minimum score 550 paper-based; 80 iBT), IELTS (minimum score 6). *Faculty research:* Expert systems, nonconvex optimization, manufacturing management, production and operation management, telecommunication.

University of Houston, College of Technology, Department of Information and Logistics Technology, Houston, TX 77204. Offers information security (MS); supply chain and logistics technology (MS); technology project management (MS). *Program availability:* Part-time. *Degree requirements:* For master's, project or thesis (most programs). *Entrance requirements:* For master's, GMAT. Additional exam requirements/recommendations for international students: Required—TOEFL (minimum score 550 paper-based; 79 iBT). Electronic applications accepted.

University of Houston–Downtown, Davies College of Business, MBA Program, Houston, TX 77002. Offers finance (MBA); human resource management (MBA); investment management (MBA); leadership (MBA); sales management and business development (MBA); supply chain management (MBA). *Accreditation:* AACSB. *Program availability:* Part-time, evening/weekend. *Faculty:* 33 full-time (12 women), 1 part-time/adjunct (0 women). *Students:* 7 full-time (3 women), 1,037 part-time (565 women); includes 773 minority (361 Black or African American, non-Hispanic/Latino; 2 American Indian or Alaska Native, non-Hispanic/Latino; 132 Asian, non-Hispanic/Latino; 278 Hispanic/Latino), 32 international. Average age 33. 583 applicants, 86% accepted, 409 enrolled. In 2016, 181 master's awarded. *Entrance requirements:* For master's, GMAT, two letters of recommendation from professional references, personal statement, resume. Additional exam requirements/recommendations for international students: Required—TOEFL (minimum score 81 iBT). *Application deadline:* For fall admission, 7/15 for domestic and international students. Application fee: $35 ($60 for international students). Electronic applications accepted. *Expenses:* $428 in-state per credit; $786 non-resident per credit. *Financial support:* Federal Work-Study and scholarships/grants available. Financial award application deadline: 4/1; financial award applicants required to submit FAFSA. *Unit head:* Dr. D. Michael Fields, Dean, Davies College of Business, 713-221-8179, Fax: 713-221-8675, E-mail: fieldsd@uhd.edu. *Application contact:*

Ceshia Love, Director of Graduate and International Admissions, 713-221-8093, Fax: 713-223-7408, E-mail: gradadmissions@uhd.edu.
Website: http://mba.uhd.edu/

The University of Kansas, Graduate Studies, School of Business, Program in Business, Lawrence, KS 66045. Offers accounting (PhD); business and organizational leadership (MS); decision sciences and supply chain management (PhD); finance (PhD); human resources management (PhD); marketing (PhD); organizational behavior (PhD); strategic management (PhD); supply chain management and logistics (MS). *Accreditation:* AACSB. *Program availability:* Part-time. *Students:* 76 full-time (11 women), 170 part-time (83 women); includes 41 minority (15 Black or African American, non-Hispanic/Latino; 3 American Indian or Alaska Native, non-Hispanic/Latino; 6 Asian, non-Hispanic/Latino; 5 Hispanic/Latino; 12 Two or more races, non-Hispanic/Latino), 25 international. Average age 32. 294 applicants, 69% accepted, 152 enrolled. In 2016, 36 master's, 9 doctorates awarded. *Entrance requirements:* For master's, GMAT, official transcript, three letters of recommendation, resume, statement of purpose; for doctorate, GMAT or GRE, official transcript, three letters of recommendation, resume, statement of purpose. Additional exam requirements/recommendations for international students: Required—TOEFL (minimum score 600 paper-based; 100 iBT). *Application deadline:* For fall admission, 1/10 for domestic and international students. Application fee: $65 ($85 for international students). Electronic applications accepted. *Financial support:* Fellowships, research assistantships, teaching assistantships, scholarships/grants, health care benefits, tuition waivers (full), and unspecified assistantships available. Financial award application deadline: 1/10. *Faculty research:* Strategic human resource management, business ethics, organizational theory/behavior, corporate strategy, international business, supply chain management, Bayesian networks, game theory, decision analysis and time/series analysis, pricing, consumer effects, advertising and emotion. *Unit head:* Charly Edmonds, Director, 785-864-3841, E-mail: bschoolphd@ku.edu. *Application contact:* Graduate Admission Contact, 785-864-7500, E-mail: bschoolphd@ku.edu.
Website: http://www.business.ku.edu/

University of La Verne, College of Business and Public Management, Graduate Programs in Business Administration, La Verne, CA 91750-4443. Offers accounting (MBA, MBA-EP); finance (MBA, MBA-EP); health services management (MBA); information technology (MBA, MBA-EP); international business (MBA, MBA-EP); management and leadership (MBA, MBA-EP); marketing (MBA, MBA-EP); supply chain management (MBA, MBA-EP). *Program availability:* Part-time, evening/weekend. *Students:* 385 full-time (177 women), 89 part-time (46 women); includes 92 minority (4 Black or African American, non-Hispanic/Latino; 1 American Indian or Alaska Native, non-Hispanic/Latino; 14 Asian, non-Hispanic/Latino; 71 Hispanic/Latino; 1 Native Hawaiian or other Pacific Islander, non-Hispanic/Latino; 1 Two or more races, non-Hispanic/Latino), 319 international. Average age 28. *Entrance requirements:* For master's, GMAT, MAT, or GRE, minimum undergraduate GPA of 3.0, 2 letters of recommendation, resume, statement of purpose. Additional exam requirements/recommendations for international students: Required—TOEFL (minimum score 550 paper-based; 85 iBT). *Application deadline:* Applications are processed on a rolling basis. Application fee: $50. *Expenses: Tuition:* Part-time $795 per credit hour. Tuition and fees vary according to campus/location and program. *Financial support:* Institutionally sponsored loans and scholarships/grants available. Financial award application deadline: 3/2; financial award applicants required to submit FAFSA. *Unit head:* Dr. Abe Helou, Chairperson, 909-448-4455, Fax: 909-392-2704, E-mail: ihelou@laverne.edu. *Application contact:* Rina Lazarian-Chehab, Senior Associate Director of Graduate Admissions, 909-448-4317, Fax: 909-971-2295, E-mail: rlazarian@laverne.edu.
Website: https://laverne.edu/business-and-public-administration/mba-2/

University of La Verne, Regional and Online Campuses, Graduate Programs, Inland Empire Campus, Ontario, CA 91730. Offers business administration (MBA, MBA-EP), including accounting (MBA), finance (MBA), health services management (MBA-EP), information technology (MBA-EP), international business (MBA), managed care (MBA), management and leadership (MBA-EP), marketing (MBA-EP), supply chain management (MBA); leadership and management (MS), including human resource management, nonprofit management, organizational development. *Program availability:* Part-time, evening/weekend. *Expenses:* Contact institution.

University of Louisville, J. B. Speed School of Engineering, Department of Industrial Engineering, Louisville, KY 40292-0001. Offers engineering management (M Eng); industrial engineering (M Eng, MS, PhD); logistics and distribution (Certificate). *Accreditation:* ABET (one or more programs are accredited). *Program availability:* 100% online. *Faculty:* 7 full-time (4 women), 5 part-time/adjunct (2 women). *Students:* 68 full-time (19 women), 129 part-time (22 women); includes 25 minority (10 Black or African American, non-Hispanic/Latino; 1 American Indian or Alaska Native, non-Hispanic/Latino; 6 Asian, non-Hispanic/Latino; 3 Hispanic/Latino; 5 Two or more races, non-Hispanic/Latino), 86 international. Average age 32. 93 applicants, 44% accepted, 25 enrolled. In 2016, 33 master's, 3 doctorates awarded. *Degree requirements:* For master's and Certificate, thesis optional; for doctorate, comprehensive exam, thesis/dissertation. *Entrance requirements:* For master's and doctorate, GRE General Test, two letters of recommendation, official transcripts. Additional exam requirements/recommendations for international students: Required—TOEFL (minimum score 550 paper-based; 80 iBT), IELTS (minimum score 6.5). *Application deadline:* For fall admission, 5/1 priority date for international students; for spring admission, 11/1 priority date for international students; for summer admission, 3/1 priority date for international students. Applications are processed on a rolling basis. Application fee: $60. Electronic applications accepted. *Expenses:* Tuition, state resident: full-time $12,246; part-time $681 per credit hour. Tuition, nonresident: full-time $25,486; part-time $1417 per credit hour. *Required fees:* $196. Tuition and fees vary according to program and reciprocity agreements. *Financial support:* In 2016–17, 2 fellowships with full tuition reimbursements (averaging $22,000 per year) were awarded; research assistantships with full tuition reimbursements, teaching assistantships with full tuition reimbursements, scholarships/grants, health care benefits, and tuition waivers (full) also available. Financial award application deadline: 1/1; financial award applicants required to submit FAFSA. *Faculty research:* Optimization, computer simulation, logistics and distribution, ergonomics and human factors, advanced manufacturing process. *Total annual research expenditures:* $620,986. *Unit head:* Dr. Suraj M. Alexander, Chair, 502-852-6342, E-mail: usher@louisville.edu. *Application contact:* Lihui Bai, Director of Graduate Studies, 502-852-1416, E-mail: lihui.bai@louisville.edu.
Website: http://www.louisville.edu/speed/industrial/

The University of Manchester, Alliance Manchester Business School, M15 6PB, United Kingdom. Offers accounting and finance (M Sc); business (M Ent); business analysis and strategic management (M Sc); business analytics: operational research and risk analysis (M Sc); business psychology (M Sc); corporate communications and reputation management (M Sc); finance (M Sc); finance and business economics (M Sc); human resource management and industrial relations (M Sc); innovation management and entrepreneurship (M Sc); international business and management (M Sc); international human resource management and comparative industrial relations (M Sc); management (M Sc); marketing (M Sc); operations, project and supply chain management (M Sc); organizational psychology (M Sc); quantitative finance (M Sc). *Entrance requirements:* For master's, UK 2:1 honours degree or overseas equivalent. Additional exam requirements/recommendations for international students: Required—TOEFL (minimum score 100 iBT), IELTS (minimum score 7), PTE. Electronic applications accepted. *Faculty research:* Accounting and finance, management sciences and marketing, people management and organization, innovation management and policy, decision sciences.

University of Massachusetts Dartmouth, Graduate School, Charlton College of Business, Program in Business Administration, North Dartmouth, MA 02747-2300. Offers business administration (MBA); business analytics (Postbaccalaureate Certificate); business foundations (Graduate Certificate); international business (Graduate Certificate); management (Postbaccalaureate Certificate); marketing (Postbaccalaureate Certificate); organizational leadership (Graduate Certificate); supply chain management and information systems (Postbaccalaureate Certificate). *Accreditation:* AACSB. *Program availability:* Part-time, 100% online, blended/hybrid learning. *Faculty:* 15 full-time (7 women), 11 part-time/adjunct (4 women). *Students:* 126 full-time (49 women), 178 part-time (100 women); includes 45 minority (10 Black or African American, non-Hispanic/Latino; 1 American Indian or Alaska Native, non-Hispanic/Latino; 16 Asian, non-Hispanic/Latino; 13 Hispanic/Latino; 5 Two or more races, non-Hispanic/Latino), 100 international. Average age 32. 236 applicants, 80% accepted, 132 enrolled. In 2016, 142 master's, 13 other advanced degrees awarded. *Degree requirements:* For master's, thesis or alternative, eportfolio. *Entrance requirements:* For master's, GMAT, statement of purpose (minimum of 300 words), resume, official transcripts, 2 letters of recommendation; for other advanced degree, statement of purpose (minimum of 300 words), resume, official transcripts. Additional exam requirements/recommendations for international students: Required—TOEFL (minimum score 533 paper-based; 72 iBT). *Application deadline:* For fall admission, 7/1 priority date for domestic students, 6/1 priority date for international students; for spring admission, 11/15 priority date for domestic students, 10/15 priority date for international students. Application fee: $60. Electronic applications accepted. *Expenses:* Tuition, state resident: full-time $14,994; part-time $624.75 per credit. Tuition, nonresident: full-time $27,068; part-time $1127.83 per credit. *Required fees:* $405; $25.88 per credit. Tuition and fees vary according to course load and reciprocity agreements. *Financial support:* In 2016–17, 2 research assistantships (averaging $2,667 per year) were awarded; institutionally sponsored loans, scholarships/grants, and unspecified assistantships also available. Support available to part-time students. Financial award application deadline: 3/1; financial award applicants required to submit FAFSA. *Faculty research:* E-commerce, managing diversity, agile manufacturing, green business, activity-based management, build-to-order supply chain management. *Total annual research expenditures:* $413,000. *Unit head:* Melissa Pacheco, Assistant Dean of Graduate Programs, 508-999-8543, Fax: 508-999-8646, E-mail: mpacheco@umassd.edu. *Application contact:* Steven Briggs, Director of Marketing and Recruitment for Graduate Studies, 508-999-8604, Fax: 508-999-8183, E-mail: graduate@umassd.edu. Website: http://www.umassd.edu/charlton/programs/graduate/mba

University of Memphis, Graduate School, Fogelman College of Business and Economics, Program in Business Administration, Memphis, TN 38152. Offers accounting (MBA, PhD); business administration (IMBA); economics (PhD); executive business administration (MBA); finance (PhD); management (PhD); marketing (MS); marketing and supply chain management (PhD); real estate development (MS); JD/MBA. *Accreditation:* AACSB. *Faculty:* 44 full-time (9 women), 5 part-time/adjunct (0 women). *Students:* 167 full-time (64 women), 341 part-time (119 women); includes 154 minority (80 Black or African American, non-Hispanic/Latino; 1 American Indian or Alaska Native, non-Hispanic/Latino; 43 Asian, non-Hispanic/Latino; 12 Hispanic/Latino; 1 Native Hawaiian or other Pacific Islander, non-Hispanic/Latino; 17 Two or more races, non-Hispanic/Latino), 96 international. Average age 33. 306 applicants, 64% accepted, 154 enrolled. In 2016, 273 master's, 7 doctorates awarded. *Degree requirements:* For master's, comprehensive exam; for doctorate, comprehensive exam, thesis/dissertation. *Entrance requirements:* For master's, GMAT, resume; for doctorate, GMAT, interview, minimum GPA of 3.4, resume, letter of recommendation. Additional exam requirements/recommendations for international students: Required—TOEFL (minimum score 550 paper-based). *Application deadline:* For fall admission, 8/1 for domestic students; for spring admission, 12/1 for domestic students. Application fee: $35 ($60 for international students). *Expenses:* Tuition, state resident: full-time $10,463; part-time $9483 per year. Tuition, nonresident: full-time $19,247; part-time $17,291 per year. *Required fees:* $821.50 per semester. Tuition and fees vary according to course load and program. *Financial support:* In 2016–17, 164 students received support. Research assistantships with full tuition reimbursements available, teaching assistantships with full tuition reimbursements available, career-related internships or fieldwork, Federal Work-Study, scholarships/grants, and unspecified assistantships available. Financial award application deadline: 2/15; financial award applicants required to submit FAFSA. *Faculty research:* Competitive business strategy, finance microstructures, supply chain management innovations, health care economics, litigation risks and corporate audits. *Unit head:* Dr. Rajiv Grover, Dean, 901-678-3759, E-mail: rgrover@memphis.edu. *Application contact:* Dr. Carol V. Danehower, Associate Dean, 901-678-5402, Fax: 901-678-3579, E-mail: fcbegp@memphis.edu.
Website: https://web0.memphis.edu/gradcatalog/degreeprog/fcbe/fcbe.php

University of Michigan, Ross School of Business, Ann Arbor, MI 48109-1234. Offers accounting (M Acc); business (MBA); business administration (PhD); supply chain management (MSCM); JD/MBA; MBA/M Arch; MBA/M Eng; MBA/MA; MBA/MEM; MBA/MHSA; MBA/MM; MBA/MPP; MBA/MS; MBA/MSE; MBA/MSI; MBA/MSW; MBA/MUP; MD/MBA; MHSA/MBA. *Accreditation:* AACSB. *Program availability:* Part-time, evening/weekend. *Degree requirements:* For doctorate, comprehensive exam, thesis/dissertation, oral defense of dissertation, preliminary exam. *Entrance requirements:* For master's, GMAT or GRE, completion of equivalent of four-year U.S. bachelor's degree, two letters of recommendation, essays, resume; for doctorate, GMAT or GRE. Additional exam requirements/recommendations for international students: Required—TOEFL (minimum score 600 paper-based; 100 iBT). Electronic applications accepted. *Expenses:* Tuition, state resident: full-time $21,466; part-time $1152 per credit hour. Tuition, nonresident: full-time $43,346; part-time $2367 per credit hour. Part-time tuition and fees vary according to course load, degree level and program. *Faculty research:* Finance and accounting, marketing, technology and operations management, corporate strategy, management and organizations.

University of Michigan–Dearborn, College of Business, MS Program in Supply Chain Management, Dearborn, MI 48126. Offers MS. *Program availability:* Part-time, evening/weekend. *Faculty:* 33 full-time (14 women), 10 part-time/adjunct (5 women). *Students:* 10 full-time (6 women), 5 part-time (1 woman), 13 international. Average age 28. 58 applicants, 47% accepted, 9 enrolled. In 2016, 22 master's awarded. *Entrance requirements:* For master's, GRE or GMAT, equivalent of four-year U.S. bachelor's degree from regionally-accredited institution, undergraduate course in finite math, pre-calculus, or calculus. Additional exam requirements/recommendations for international students: Required—TOEFL (minimum score 560 paper-based; 84 iBT), IELTS (minimum score 6.5). *Application deadline:* For fall admission, 8/1 for domestic students, 5/1 for international students; for winter admission, 12/1 for domestic students, 9/1 for international students; for spring admission, 4/1 for domestic students, 1/1 for

international students. Applications are processed on a rolling basis. Application fee: $60. Electronic applications accepted. *Expenses:* Contact institution. *Financial support:* In 2016–17, 12 students received support. Scholarships/grants and non-resident tuition scholarships available. Financial award application deadline: 3/1; financial award applicants required to submit FAFSA. *Faculty research:* Business intelligence, information technology, brand management and new media, management education, operations strategy. *Unit head:* Dr. Michael Kamen, Director, Graduate Programs, 313-593-5460, E-mail: mkamen@umich.edu. *Application contact:* Joan Doherty, Academic Advisor/Counselor, 313-593-5460, Fax: 313-271-9838,
E-mail: umd-gradbusiness@umich.edu.
Website: http://umdearborn.edu/cob/ms-supply-chain/

University of Minnesota, Twin Cities Campus, Carlson School of Management, Carlson Full-Time MBA Program, Minneapolis, MN 55455. Offers finance (MBA); human resources and industrial relations (MA); information technology (MBA); management (MBA); marketing (MBA); medical industry orientation (MBA); supply chain and operations (MBA); JD/MBA; MBA/MPP; MBA/MSBA; MD/MBA; MHA/MBA; Pharm D/MBA. *Accreditation:* AACSB. *Faculty:* 143 full-time (42 women), 24 part-time/adjunct (6 women). *Students:* 193 full-time (59 women); includes 23 minority (2 Black or African American, non-Hispanic/Latino; 1 American Indian or Alaska Native, non-Hispanic/Latino; 9 Asian, non-Hispanic/Latino; 5 Hispanic/Latino; 1 Native Hawaiian or other Pacific Islander, non-Hispanic/Latino; 5 Two or more races, non-Hispanic/Latino), 31 international. Average age 28. 606 applicants, 45% accepted, 104 enrolled. In 2016, 102 master's awarded. *Entrance requirements:* For master's, GMAT or GRE. Additional exam requirements/recommendations for international students: Required—TOEFL (minimum score 580 paper-based; 84 iBT), IELTS (minimum score 7), PTE. *Application deadline:* For fall admission, 4/1 for domestic students, 2/1 for international students. Application fee: $75. Electronic applications accepted. *Expenses:* $39,378 per year resident tuition and fees; $49,766 per year non-resident tuition and fees; $50,084 per year international tuition and fees. *Financial support:* In 2016–17, 148 students received support, including 148 fellowships with tuition reimbursements available (averaging $21,070 per year); research assistantships with partial tuition reimbursements available, teaching assistantships with partial tuition reimbursements available, career-related internships or fieldwork, Federal Work-Study, institutionally sponsored loans, scholarships/grants, health care benefits, and unspecified assistantships also available. Financial award application deadline: 4/1; financial award applicants required to submit FAFSA. *Faculty research:* Market regulation and asset pricing, social networks and data analytics, consumer behavior, innovation and entrepreneurship, workplace wellbeing and labor relationships. *Total annual research expenditures:* $577,440. *Unit head:* Philip J. Miller, Assistant Dean, MBA Programs and Graduate Business Career Center, 612-625-5555, Fax: 612-625-1012, E-mail: mba@umn.edu. *Application contact:* Linh Gilles, Director of Admissions and Recruiting, 612-625-5555, Fax: 612-625-1012, E-mail: ftmba@umn.edu.
Website: http://www.csom.umn.edu/MBA/full-time/

University of Minnesota, Twin Cities Campus, Carlson School of Management, Carlson Part-Time MBA Program, Minneapolis, MN 55455. Offers finance (MBA); information technology (MBA); management (MBA); marketing (MBA); medical industry orientation (MBA); supply chain and operations (MBA). *Program availability:* Part-time-only, evening/weekend, 100% online, blended/hybrid learning. *Faculty:* 143 full-time (42 women), 26 part-time/adjunct (6 women). *Students:* 1,005 part-time (317 women); includes 110 minority (17 Black or African American, non-Hispanic/Latino; 2 American Indian or Alaska Native, non-Hispanic/Latino; 51 Asian, non-Hispanic/Latino; 19 Hispanic/Latino; 21 Two or more races, non-Hispanic/Latino), 58 international. Average age 28. 251 applicants, 86% accepted, 185 enrolled. In 2016, 336 master's awarded. *Entrance requirements:* For master's, GMAT or GRE. Additional exam requirements/recommendations for international students: Required—TOEFL (minimum score 580 paper-based; 84 iBT), IELTS (minimum score 7), PTE. *Application deadline:* For fall admission, 5/15 priority date for domestic and international students; for spring admission, 10/15 priority date for domestic and international students. Applications are processed on a rolling basis. Application fee: $75. Electronic applications accepted. *Expenses:* $1,335 per credit. *Financial support:* Applicants required to submit FAFSA. *Faculty research:* Market regulation and asset pricing, social networks and data analytics, consumer behavior, innovation and entrepreneurship, workplace wellbeing and labor relationships. *Total annual research expenditures:* $577,440. *Unit head:* Philip J. Miller, Assistant Dean, MBA Programs and Graduate Business Career Center, 612-624-2039, Fax: 612-625-1012, E-mail: mba@umn.edu. *Application contact:* Linh Gilles, Director of Admissions and Recruiting, 612-625-5555, Fax: 612-625-1012, E-mail: ptmba@umn.edu.
Website: http://www.carlsonschool.umn.edu/ptmba

University of Minnesota, Twin Cities Campus, Carlson School of Management, Doctoral Program in Business Administration, Minneapolis, MN 55455. Offers accounting (PhD); finance (PhD); information and decision sciences (PhD); marketing (PhD); strategic management and entrepreneurship (PhD); supply chain and operations (PhD); work and organizations (PhD). *Faculty:* 101 full-time (32 women). *Students:* 90 full-time (29 women); includes 7 minority (2 Black or African American, non-Hispanic/Latino; 3 Asian, non-Hispanic/Latino; 2 Hispanic/Latino), 64 international. Average age 30. 352 applicants, 7% accepted, 15 enrolled. In 2016, 20 doctorates awarded. *Degree requirements:* For doctorate, comprehensive exam, thesis/dissertation, written and oral preliminary exams, proposal defense, final defense. *Entrance requirements:* For doctorate, GMAT, GRE General Test, minimum undergraduate GPA of 3.0, graduate 3.5 (recommended). Additional exam requirements/recommendations for international students: Required—TOEFL (minimum score 600 paper-based, 100 iBT) or IELTS (minimum score 7.0). *Application deadline:* For fall admission, 12/15 for domestic students, 12/15 priority date for international students. Applications are processed on a rolling basis. Application fee: $75 ($95 for international students). Electronic applications accepted. *Expenses:* Contact institution. *Financial support:* In 2016–17, 80 students received support, including 80 fellowships with full tuition reimbursements available (averaging $13,500 per year), 72 research assistantships with full tuition reimbursements available (averaging $7,371 per year), 72 teaching assistantships with full tuition reimbursements available (averaging $7,371 per year); institutionally sponsored loans, scholarships/grants, health care benefits, unspecified assistantships, and full student service fee waivers also available. Financial award application deadline: 12/15. *Faculty research:* Finance, strategy and entrepreneurship, marketing, information and decision science, operations, accounting, supply chain, human resources and industrial relations, organizational behavior. *Unit head:* Dr. Shawn P. Curley, Director, 612-624-6546, Fax: 612-624-8221, E-mail: curley@umn.edu. *Application contact:* Sandy Herzan, Associate Director, 612-624-0875, Fax: 612-624-8221, E-mail: herza002@umn.edu.
Website: http://carlsonschool.umn.edu/degrees/phd

University of Missouri–St. Louis, College of Business Administration, Program in Business Administration, St. Louis, MO 63121. Offers accounting (MBA); business administration (Certificate); business intelligence (Certificate); cybersecurity (Certificate); digital and social media marketing (Certificate); finance (MBA); human resources management (Certificate); information systems (MBA); international business (MBA); logistics and supply chain management (MBA, PhD, Certificate); management (MBA); marketing (MBA); marketing management (Certificate); operations management (MBA). *Accreditation:* AACSB. *Program availability:* Part-time, evening/weekend. *Faculty:* 32 full-time (10 women), 14 part-time/adjunct (3 women). *Students:* 181 full-time (88 women), 357 part-time (154 women); includes 83 minority (30 Black or African American, non-Hispanic/Latino; 36 Asian, non-Hispanic/Latino; 12 Hispanic/Latino; 2 Native Hawaiian or other Pacific Islander, non-Hispanic/Latino; 3 Two or more races, non-Hispanic/Latino), 100 international. Average age 31. 245 applicants, 83% accepted, 139 enrolled. *Degree requirements:* For doctorate, thesis/dissertation. *Entrance requirements:* For master's, GMAT, 2 letters of recommendation. Additional exam requirements/recommendations for international students: Recommended—TOEFL (minimum score 550 paper-based; 79 iBT), IELTS (minimum score 6.5). *Application deadline:* For fall admission, 7/1 for domestic and international students; for spring admission, 12/1 for domestic and international students. Applications are processed on a rolling basis. Application fee: $50 ($40 for international students). Electronic applications accepted. *Financial support:* Research assistantships with tuition reimbursements, teaching assistantships with tuition reimbursements, career-related internships or fieldwork, Federal Work-Study, and institutionally sponsored loans available. Support available to part-time students. Financial award application deadline: 4/1; financial award applicants required to submit FAFSA. *Faculty research:* Human resources, strategic management, marketing strategy, consumer behavior product development, advertising. *Unit head:* Dr. Thomas H. Eyssell, Associate Dean and Director of Graduate Studies, 314-516-5885, Fax: 314-516-6420, E-mail: mba@umsl.edu. *Application contact:* 314-516-5458, Fax: 314-516-6996, E-mail: gradadm@umsl.edu.

The University of North Carolina at Charlotte, William States Lee College of Engineering, Department of Systems Engineering and Engineering Management, Charlotte, NC 28223-0001. Offers energy analytics (Graduate Certificate); engineering management (MSEM); Lean Six Sigma (Graduate Certificate); logistics and supply chains (Graduate Certificate); systems analytics (Graduate Certificate). *Program availability:* Part-time, evening/weekend, 100% online, blended/hybrid learning. *Faculty:* 9 full-time (1 woman), 2 part-time/adjunct (1 woman). *Students:* 22 full-time (10 women), 61 part-time (12 women); includes 13 minority (7 Black or African American, non-Hispanic/Latino; 1 Asian, non-Hispanic/Latino; 4 Hispanic/Latino; 1 Two or more races, non-Hispanic/Latino), 29 international. Average age 30. 210 applicants, 56% accepted, 31 enrolled. In 2016, 44 master's, 5 other advanced degrees awarded. *Degree requirements:* For master's, project or thesis. *Entrance requirements:* For master's, GRE or GMAT, bachelor's degree in engineering or a closely-related technical or scientific field, or in business, provided relevant technical course requirements have been met; undergraduate coursework in engineering economics, calculus, or statistics; minimum GPA of 3.0; for Graduate Certificate, bachelor's degree in engineering or closely-related technical or scientific field, or bachelor's degree in business, provided relevant technical course requirements have been met; minimum GPA of 3.0; undergraduate coursework in engineering economics, calculus, and statistics; written description of work experience. Additional exam requirements/recommendations for international students: Required—TOEFL (minimum score 523 paper-based, 70 iBT) or IELTS (6.5). *Application deadline:* For fall admission, 3/1 priority date for domestic and international students; for spring admission, 10/1 priority date for domestic and international students; for summer admission, 4/1 priority date for domestic and international students. Applications are processed on a rolling basis. Application fee: $75. Electronic applications accepted. *Expenses:* Contact institution. *Financial support:* In 2016–17, 2 students received support, including 2 research assistantships (averaging $13,750 per year); career-related internships or fieldwork, institutionally sponsored loans, scholarships/grants, and unspecified assistantships also available. Support available to part-time students. Financial award application deadline: 3/1; financial award applicants required to submit FAFSA. *Total annual research expenditures:* $196,680. *Unit head:* Dr. Simon M. Hsiang, Chair, 704-687-1958, E-mail: shsiang1@uncc.edu. *Application contact:* Kathy B. Giddings, Director of Graduate Admissions, 704-687-5503, Fax: 704-687-1668, E-mail: gradadm@uncc.edu.
Website: http://seem.uncc.edu/

The University of North Carolina at Greensboro, Graduate School, Bryan School of Business and Economics, Department of Information Systems and Supply Chain Management, Greensboro, NC 27412-5001. Offers information systems (PhD); information technology (Certificate); information technology and management (MS); supply chain management (Certificate). *Entrance requirements:* For master's, GMAT, GRE General Test. Additional exam requirements/recommendations for international students: Required—TOEFL. Electronic applications accepted.

University of North Texas, Robert B. Toulouse School of Graduate Studies, Denton, TX 76203-5459. Offers accounting (MS); applied anthropology (MA, MS); applied behavior analysis (Certificate); applied geography (MA); applied technology and performance improvement (M Ed, MS); art education (MA); art history (MA); art museum education (Certificate); arts leadership (Certificate); audiology (Au D); behavior analysis (MS); behavioral science (PhD); biochemistry and molecular biology (MS); biology (MA, MS); biomedical engineering (MS); business analysis (MS); chemistry (MS); clinical health psychology (PhD); communication studies (MA, MS); computer engineering (MS); computer science (MS); counseling (M Ed, MS), including clinical mental health counseling (MS), college and university counseling, elementary school counseling, secondary school counseling; creative writing (MA); criminal justice (MS); curriculum and instruction (M Ed); decision sciences (MBA); design (MA, MFA), including fashion design (MFA), innovation studies, interior design (MFA); early childhood studies (MS); economics (MS); educational leadership (M Ed, Ed D); educational psychology (MS, PhD), including family studies (MS), gifted and talented (MS), human development (MS), learning and cognition (MS), research, measurement and evaluation (MS); electrical engineering (MS); emergency management (MPA); engineering technology (MS); English (MA); English as a second language (MA); environmental science (MS); finance (MBA, MS); financial management (MPA); French (MA); health services management (MBA); higher education (M Ed, Ed D); history (MA, MS); hospitality management (MS); human resources management (MPA); information science (MS); information systems (PhD); information technologies (MBA); interdisciplinary studies (MA, MS); international studies (MA); international sustainable tourism (MS); jazz studies (MM); journalism (MA, MJ, Graduate Certificate), including interactive and virtual digital communication (Graduate Certificate), narrative journalism (Graduate Certificate), public relations (Graduate Certificate); kinesiology (MS); linguistics (MA); local government management (MPA); logistics (PhD); logistics and supply chain management (MBA); long-term care, senior housing, and aging services (MA); management (PhD); marketing (MBA); mathematics (MA, MS); mechanical and energy engineering (MS, PhD); music (MA), including ethnomusicology, music theory, musicology, performance; music composition (PhD); music education (MM Ed, PhD); nonprofit management (MPA); operations and supply chain management (MBA); performance (MM, DMA); philosophy (MA); political science (MA); professional and technical communication (MA); radio, television and film (MA, MFA); rehabilitation counseling (Certificate); sociology (MA); Spanish (MA); special education (M Ed); speech-language pathology (MA); strategic management (MBA); studio art (MFA); teaching (M Ed); MBA/MS. *Program availability:* Part-time, evening/weekend, online learning. Terminal master's awarded for partial completion of doctoral program. *Degree requirements:* For master's, variable foreign language requirement, comprehensive exam (for some programs), thesis (for some programs); for doctorate, variable foreign language requirement, comprehensive exam (for some programs), thesis/dissertation; for other advanced degree, variable foreign language requirement, comprehensive exam (for some programs). *Entrance requirements:* For master's and doctorate, GRE, GMAT. Additional exam requirements/recommendations for international students: Required—TOEFL (minimum score 550 paper-based; 79 iBT). Electronic applications accepted.

University of Oklahoma, Price College of Business, Program in Business Administration, Norman, OK 73019. Offers accounting (PhD); business administration (MBA, PhD); entrepreneurship and economic development (PhD); finance (PhD); management and international business (PhD); management of information systems (PhD); marketing/supply chain (PhD); JD/MBA; MBA/MS. *Accreditation:* AACSB. *Program availability:* Part-time, evening/weekend. *Students:* 122 full-time (27 women), 146 part-time (30 women); includes 36 minority (5 Black or African American, non-Hispanic/Latino; 6 American Indian or Alaska Native, non-Hispanic/Latino; 8 Asian, non-Hispanic/Latino; 11 Hispanic/Latino; 6 Two or more races, non-Hispanic/Latino), 37 international. Average age 30. 261 applicants, 27% accepted, 59 enrolled. In 2016, 127 master's, 5 doctorates awarded. *Degree requirements:* For doctorate, comprehensive exam, thesis/dissertation. *Entrance requirements:* For master's, GMAT or GRE, resume, statement of goals; for doctorate, GMAT or GRE, resume, statement of goals, 3 letters of recommendation. Additional exam requirements/recommendations for international students: Required—TOEFL (minimum score 100 iBT) or IELTS (minimum score 7). *Application deadline:* For fall admission, 11/15 priority date for domestic and international students; for spring admission, 3/15 priority date for domestic and international students; for summer admission, 5/15 for domestic and international students. Application fee: $50 ($100 for international students). Electronic applications accepted. *Expenses:* Contact institution. *Financial support:* In 2016–17, 107 students received support, including 10 fellowships with partial tuition reimbursements available (averaging $3,295 per year); research assistantships with full and partial tuition reimbursements available, teaching assistantships with full and partial tuition reimbursements available, career-related internships or fieldwork, scholarships/grants, health care benefits, and unspecified assistantships also available. Support available to part-time students. Financial award application deadline: 6/1; financial award applicants required to submit FAFSA. *Faculty research:* Energy finance; international accounting; organizational behavior and entrepreneurship; management information systems; supply chain. *Unit head:* Laku Chidambaram, Associate Dean for Academic Programs and Engagement. *Application contact:* Director of MBA Admissions, 405-325-5623.
Website: http://www.ou.edu/content/price/divisions/graduate.html

University of Pittsburgh, Katz Graduate School of Business, Master of Science in Supply Chain Management Program, Pittsburgh, PA 15260. Offers MS. *Faculty:* 88 full-time (27 women), 42 part-time/adjunct (15 women). *Students:* 8 full-time (4 women); includes 1 minority (Asian, non-Hispanic/Latino), 6 international. Average age 25. 82 applicants, 46% accepted, 8 enrolled. In 2016, 1 master's awarded. *Degree requirements:* For master's, minimum GPA of 3.0. *Entrance requirements:* For master's, GMAT, GRE. Additional exam requirements/recommendations for international students: Required—TOEFL (minimum score 100 iBT), IELTS (minimum score 7). *Application deadline:* For fall admission, 7/1 priority date for domestic students, 5/1 priority date for international students. Applications are processed on a rolling basis. Application fee: $50. Electronic applications accepted. *Expenses:* Contact institution. *Financial support:* Scholarships/grants available. Financial award application deadline: 6/1; financial award applicants required to submit FAFSA. *Faculty research:* Accounting systems/financial reporting, corporate finance, shopper marketing/consumer behavior, management information systems, organizational behavior and entrepreneurship. *Total annual research expenditures:* $493,036. *Unit head:* Dr. Arjang A. Assad, Dean, 412-648-1556, Fax: 412-648-1552, E-mail: aassad@katz.pitt.edu. *Application contact:* Thomas Keller, Director of MBA Admissions, 412-648-1700, Fax: 412-648-1659, E-mail: mba@katz.pitt.edu.
Website: http://www.business.pitt.edu/katz/ms-programs/supply-chain

University of Rhode Island, Graduate School, College of Business Administration, Kingston, RI 02881. Offers accounting (MS); business administration (PhD), including finance and insurance, marketing, supply chain management; finance (MBA, MS); general business (MBA); health care management (MBA); management (MBA); marketing (MBA); oceanography (MBA); strategic innovation (MBA); supply chain management (MBA); Pharm D/MBA. *Accreditation:* AACSB. *Program availability:* Part-time, evening/weekend. *Faculty:* 57 full-time (24 women). *Students:* 94 full-time (45 women), 166 part-time (84 women); includes 37 minority (6 Black or African American, non-Hispanic/Latino; 1 American Indian or Alaska Native, non-Hispanic/Latino; 22 Asian, non-Hispanic/Latino; 3 Hispanic/Latino; 5 Two or more races, non-Hispanic/Latino), 18 international. In 2016, 124 master's, 4 doctorates awarded. *Degree requirements:* For master's, comprehensive exam (for some programs), thesis optional; for doctorate, comprehensive exam, thesis/dissertation. *Entrance requirements:* For master's, GMAT or GRE, 2 letters of recommendation, resume; for doctorate, GMAT or GRE, 3 letters of recommendation, resume. Additional exam requirements/recommendations for international students: Required—TOEFL. *Application deadline:* For fall admission, 2/1 for domestic and international students. Application fee: $65. Electronic applications accepted. *Expenses:* Tuition, state resident: full-time $11,796; part-time $655 per credit. Tuition, nonresident: full-time $24,206; part-time $1345 per credit. *Required fees:* $1546; $44 per credit. One-time fee: $155 full-time; $35 part-time. *Financial support:* In 2016–17, 17 teaching assistantships with tuition reimbursements (averaging $15,347 per year) were awarded; research assistantships also available. Financial award application deadline: 2/1; financial award applicants required to submit FAFSA. *Unit head:* Dr. Maling Ebrahimpour, Dean, 401-874-4348, Fax: 401-874-4312, E-mail: mebrahimpour@uri.edu. *Application contact:* Lisa Lancellotta, Coordinator, MBA Programs, 401-874-4241, Fax: 401-874-4312, E-mail: mba@uri.edu.
Website: http://www.cba.uri.edu/

See Display on page 161 and Close-Up on page 191.

University of San Diego, School of Business, Program in Supply Chain Management, San Diego, CA 92110-2492. Offers MS, Certificate. *Program availability:* Part-time, online learning. *Students:* 6 full-time (1 woman), 75 part-time (30 women); includes 35 minority (6 Black or African American, non-Hispanic/Latino; 10 Asian, non-Hispanic/Latino; 17 Hispanic/Latino; 2 Two or more races, non-Hispanic/Latino), 1 international. Average age 33. In 2016, 34 master's awarded. *Degree requirements:* For master's, capstone course. *Entrance requirements:* Additional exam requirements/recommendations for international students: Required—TOEFL (minimum score 580 paper-based; 92 iBT), TWE. *Application deadline:* For fall admission, 11/1 priority date for domestic students. Applications are processed on a rolling basis. Application fee: $80. Electronic applications accepted. *Financial support:* In 2016–17, 7 students received support. Scholarships/grants and tuition waivers available. Financial award application deadline: 4/1; financial award applicants required to submit FAFSA. *Unit head:* Karen Kukta, Program Manager, Supply Chain Management, 619-260-7903, E-mail: kkukta@sandiego.edu. *Application contact:* Monica Mahon, Associate Director of Graduate Admissions, 619-260-4524, Fax: 619-260-4158, E-mail: grads@sandiego.edu.
Website: http://www.sandiego.edu/business/programs/ms-supply-chain-management/

University of Southern California, Graduate School, Viterbi School of Engineering, Daniel J. Epstein Department of Industrial and Systems Engineering, Los Angeles, CA 90089. Offers digital supply chain management (MS); engineering management (MS); engineering technology communication (Graduate Certificate); health systems operations (Graduate Certificate); industrial and systems engineering (MS, PhD, Engr); manufacturing engineering (MS); operations research engineering (MS); optimization and supply chain management (Graduate Certificate); product development engineering (MS); safety systems and security (MS); systems architecting and engineering (MS, Graduate Certificate); systems safety and security (Graduate Certificate); transportation systems (Graduate Certificate); MS/MBA. *Program availability:* Part-time, evening/weekend, online learning. Terminal master's awarded for partial completion of doctoral program. *Degree requirements:* For master's, thesis optional; for doctorate, thesis/dissertation. *Entrance requirements:* For master's and doctorate, GRE General Test. Additional exam requirements/recommendations for international students: Recommended—TOEFL. Electronic applications accepted. *Faculty research:* Health systems, music cognition and retrieval, transportation and logistics, manufacturing and automation, engineering systems design, risk and economic analysis.

The University of Tennessee at Chattanooga, Engineering Management and Technology Program, Chattanooga, TN 37403. Offers construction management (Graduate Certificate); engineering management (MS); fundamentals of engineering management (Graduate Certificate); leadership and ethics (Graduate Certificate); logistics and supply chain management (Graduate Certificate); power systems management (Graduate Certificate); project and technology management (Graduate Certificate); quality management (Graduate Certificate). *Program availability:* 100% online, blended/hybrid learning. *Faculty:* 6 full-time (1 woman). *Students:* 14 full-time (3 women), 49 part-time (11 women); includes 17 minority (10 Black or African American, non-Hispanic/Latino; 2 Asian, non-Hispanic/Latino; 3 Hispanic/Latino; 2 Two or more races, non-Hispanic/Latino), 8 international. Average age 33. 29 applicants, 93% accepted, 15 enrolled. In 2016, 36 master's, 7 other advanced degrees awarded. *Degree requirements:* For master's, thesis. *Entrance requirements:* For master's, GRE General Test, letters of recommendation; minimum undergraduate GPA of 2.7 overall or 3.0 in final two years. Additional exam requirements/recommendations for international students: Required—TOEFL (minimum score 550 paper-based; 79 iBT), IELTS (minimum score 6). *Application deadline:* For fall admission, 6/15 priority date for domestic students, 7/1 for international students; for spring admission, 11/1 priority date for domestic students, 11/1 for international students. Applications are processed on a rolling basis. Application fee: $35 ($40 for international students). Electronic applications accepted. *Expenses:* $9,876 full-time in-state; $25,994 full-time out-of-state; $450 per credit part-time in-state; $1,345 per credit part-time out-of-state. *Financial support:* In 2016–17, 4 research assistantships were awarded; teaching assistantships, career-related internships or fieldwork, scholarships/grants, and unspecified assistantships also available. Support available to part-time students. Financial award application deadline: 7/1; financial award applicants required to submit FAFSA. *Faculty research:* Plant layout design, lean manufacturing, Six Sigma, value management, product development. *Unit head:* Dr. Neslihan Alp, Department Head, 423-425-4032, Fax: 423-425-5818, E-mail: neslihan-alp@utc.edu. *Application contact:* Dr. Joanne Romagni, Dean of the Graduate School, 423-425-4478, Fax: 423-425-5223, E-mail: joanne-romagni@utc.edu.
Website: http://www.utc.edu/college-engineering-computer-science/programs/engineering-management-and-technology/index.php#li03

The University of Texas at Austin, Graduate School, McCombs School of Business, Department of Information, Risk, and Operations Management, Austin, TX 78712-1111. Offers information management (MBA); information systems (PhD); risk analysis and decision making (PhD); risk management (MBA); supply chain and operations management (MBA, PhD). *Degree requirements:* For doctorate, thesis/dissertation. *Entrance requirements:* For doctorate, GMAT or GRE. Electronic applications accepted. *Faculty research:* Stochastic processing and queuing, discrete nonlinear and large-scale optimization simulation, quality assurance logistics, distributed artificial intelligence, organizational modeling.

The University of Texas at Dallas, Naveen Jindal School of Management, Program in Information Systems and Operations Management, Richardson, TX 75080. Offers business analytics (MS); information technology and management (MS); supply chain management (MS). *Program availability:* Part-time, evening/weekend. *Faculty:* 19 full-time (0 women), 37 part-time/adjunct (11 women). *Students:* 1,577 full-time (577 women), 457 part-time (189 women); includes 136 minority (21 Black or African American, non-Hispanic/Latino; 83 Asian, non-Hispanic/Latino; 19 Hispanic/Latino; 13 Two or more races, non-Hispanic/Latino), 1,795 international. Average age 27. 3,354 applicants, 66% accepted, 931 enrolled. In 2016, 787 master's awarded. *Degree requirements:* For master's, thesis optional. *Entrance requirements:* For master's, GMAT. Additional exam requirements/recommendations for international students: Required—TOEFL (minimum score 550 paper-based). *Application deadline:* For fall admission, 7/15 for domestic students, 5/1 priority date for international students; for spring admission, 11/15 for domestic students, 9/1 priority date for international students. Applications are processed on a rolling basis. Application fee: $50 ($100 for international students). Electronic applications accepted. *Expenses:* Tuition, state resident: full-time $12,418; part-time $690 per semester hour. Tuition, nonresident: full-time $24,150; part-time $1342 per semester hour. Tuition and fees vary according to course load. *Financial support:* In 2016–17, 473 students received support, including 5 research assistantships with partial tuition reimbursements available (averaging $14,880 per year), 48 teaching assistantships with partial tuition reimbursements available (averaging $10,122 per year); career-related internships or fieldwork, Federal Work-Study, institutionally sponsored loans, scholarships/grants, and unspecified assistantships also available. Support available to part-time students. Financial award application deadline: 4/30; financial award applicants required to submit FAFSA. *Faculty research:* Technology marketing, measuring information work productivity, electronic commerce, decision support systems, data quality. *Unit head:* Dr. Milind Dawande, Area Coordinator, 972-883-2793, E-mail: milind@utdallas.edu. *Application contact:* Dr. Ozalp Ozer, PhD Area Coordinator, 972-883-2316, E-mail: oozer@utdallas.edu.
Website: http://jindal.utdallas.edu/isom/

University of Washington, Graduate School, Michael G. Foster School of Business, Seattle, WA 98195-3200. Offers auditing and assurance (MP Acc); business administration (MBA, PhD); entrepreneurship (MS); executive business administration (MBA); global executive business administration (MBA); information systems (MSIS); supply chain management (MSSCM); taxation (MP Acc); technology management (MBA); JD/MBA; MBA/MAIS; MBA/MHA. *Accreditation:* AACSB. *Program availability:* Part-time, evening/weekend. Terminal master's awarded for partial completion of doctoral program. *Degree requirements:* For doctorate, comprehensive exam, thesis/dissertation. *Entrance requirements:* For master's and doctorate, GMAT, GRE. Additional exam requirements/recommendations for international students: Required—TOEFL (minimum score 600 paper-based; 100 iBT). Electronic applications accepted. *Expenses:* Contact institution. *Faculty research:* Finance, marketing, organizational behavior, information technology, strategy.

Supply Chain Management

University of Wisconsin–Madison, Graduate School, Wisconsin School of Business, Wisconsin Full-Time MBA Program, Madison, WI 53706. Offers applied security analysis (MBA); arts administration (MBA); brand and product management (MBA); corporate finance and investment banking (MBA); marketing research (MBA); operations and technology management (MBA); real estate (MBA); risk management and insurance (MBA); strategic human resource management (MBA); supply chain management (MBA). *Faculty:* 125 full-time (32 women), 48 part-time/adjunct (11 women). *Students:* 197 full-time (73 women); includes 30 minority (11 Black or African American, non-Hispanic/Latino; 9 Asian, non-Hispanic/Latino; 10 Hispanic/Latino), 42 international. Average age 29. 728 applicants, 26% accepted, 99 enrolled. In 2016, 100 master's awarded. *Entrance requirements:* For master's, GMAT or GRE, bachelor's or equivalent degree, 2 years of work experience, essay, letter of recommendation, resume. Additional exam requirements/recommendations for international students: Required—TOEFL (minimum score 100 iBT), IELTS (minimum score 7.5). *Application deadline:* For fall admission, 9/28 for domestic students, 11/1 for international students; for winter admission, 11/2 for domestic students, 12/16 for international students; for spring admission, 1/11 for domestic students, 2/24 for international students; for summer admission, 3/1 for domestic students, 4/14 for international students. Applications are processed on a rolling basis. Application fee: $75 ($81 for international students). Electronic applications accepted. *Expenses:* $7,947 per semester resident tuition, $2,430 fees; $16,082 per semester resident tuition, $2,830 fees. *Financial support:* In 2016–17, 178 students received support, including 8 fellowships with full tuition reimbursements available (averaging $56,413 per year), 23 research assistantships with full tuition reimbursements available (averaging $42,151 per year), 51 teaching assistantships with full tuition reimbursements available (averaging $39,963 per year); scholarships/grants, health care benefits, and unspecified assistantships also available. Financial award application deadline: 4/11. *Faculty research:* Forms of competition and outcomes in dual distribution systems; explaining the accuracy of revised forecasts; supply chain planning for random demand surges; advanced demand information in a multi-product system; the effects of presentation salience and measurement subjectivity on nonprofessional investors' fair value judgments. *Unit head:* Prof. Ella Mae Matsumura, Associate Dean, Full-time MBA Program, 608-262-9731, E-mail: ematsumura@bus.wisc.edu. *Application contact:* Mary Lewitzke, Assistant Director of Admissions and Recruiting, Full-time MBA Program, 608-262-4000,
E-mail: mlewitzke@bus.wisc.edu.
Website: http://www.bus.wisc.edu/mba

University of Wisconsin–Platteville, School of Graduate Studies, Distance Learning Center, Online Master of Science in Integrated Supply Chain Management Program, Platteville, WI 53818-3099. Offers MS. *Program availability:* Part-time, online learning. *Students:* 3 full-time (1 woman), 84 part-time (19 women); includes 23 minority (11 Black or African American, non-Hispanic/Latino; 1 American Indian or Alaska Native, non-Hispanic/Latino; 4 Asian, non-Hispanic/Latino; 7 Hispanic/Latino). 31 applicants, 77% accepted, 15 enrolled. In 2016, 13 master's awarded. *Entrance requirements:* Additional exam requirements/recommendations for international students: Required—TOEFL (minimum score 550 paper-based; 79 iBT), IELTS (minimum score 6.5). *Application deadline:* Applications are processed on a rolling basis. Application fee: $56. Electronic applications accepted. *Unit head:* Dawn Drake, Executive Director, 800-362-5460, Fax: 608-342-1071, E-mail: disted@uwplatt.edu. *Application contact:* 800-362-5460, Fax: 608-342-1071, E-mail: disted@uwplatt.edu.

University of Wisconsin–Stout, Graduate School, College of Management, Program in Operations and Supply Management, Menomonie, WI 54751. Offers operations management (MS); project management (MS); quality management (MS); supply chain management (MS).

Walden University, Graduate Programs, School of Management, Minneapolis, MN 55401. Offers accounting (MBA, MS, DBA), including accounting for the professional (MS), accounting with CPA emphasis (MS), self-designed (MS); advanced project management (Graduate Certificate); applied project management (Graduate Certificate); auditing (Graduate Certificate); bridge to business administration (Post-Doctoral Certificate); bridge to management (Post-Doctoral Certificate); business management (Graduate Certificate); communication (MBA); corporate finance (MBA); digital marketing (Graduate Certificate); entrepreneurship (DBA); entrepreneurship and small business (MBA); finance (MS, DBA), including finance for the professional (MS), finance with CFA/investment (MS), finance with CPA emphasis (MS); global supply chain management (DBA); healthcare management (MBA, DBA); human resource management (MBA, MS, Graduate Certificate), including functional human resource management (MS), general program (MS), integrating functional and strategic human resource management (MS), organizational strategy (MS); human resources management (DBA); information systems management (DBA); international business (MBA, DBA); leadership (MBA, MS, DBA, Graduate Certificate), including general program (MS), human resource leadership (MS), leader development (MS), self-designed (MS); management (MS, PhD), including communications (MS), finance (PhD), general program (MS), healthcare management (MS), human resource management (MS), human resources management (PhD), information systems management (PhD), international business (MS), leadership (MS), leadership and organizational change (PhD), marketing (MS), project management (MS), strategy and operations (MS); managerial accounting (Graduate Certificate); marketing (MBA, MS, DBA); project management (MBA, MS, DBA); self-designed (MBA, DBA); social impact management (DBA); technology entrepreneurship (DBA). *Accreditation:* ACBSP. *Program availability:* Part-time, evening/weekend, online only, 100% online. *Degree requirements:* For master's, thesis (for some programs), residency (for EMBA); for doctorate, thesis/dissertation (for some programs), residency. *Entrance requirements:* For master's, bachelor's degree or higher; minimum GPA of 2.5; official transcripts; goal statement (for some programs); access to computer and Internet; for doctorate, master's degree or higher; three years of related professional or academic experience (preferred); minimum GPA of 3.0; goal statement and current resume (for select programs); official transcripts; access to computer and Internet; for other advanced degree, relevant work experience; access to computer and Internet. Additional exam requirements/recommendations for international students: Required—TOEFL (minimum score 550 paper-based, 79 iBT), IELTS (minimum score 6.5), Michigan English Language Assessment Battery (minimum score 82), or PTE (minimum score 53). Electronic applications accepted.

Washington University in St. Louis, Olin Business School, Program in Supply Chain Management, St. Louis, MO 63130-4899. Offers MS. *Program availability:* Part-time. *Faculty:* 97 full-time (22 women), 44 part-time/adjunct (13 women). *Students:* 35 full-time (19 women), 2 part-time (1 woman); includes 1 minority (Asian, non-Hispanic/Latino), 33 international. Average age 25. 140 applicants, 24% accepted, 20 enrolled. In 2016, 20 master's awarded. *Entrance requirements:* For master's, GMAT or GRE. Additional exam requirements/recommendations for international students: Required—TOEFL, IELTS. *Application deadline:* For fall admission, 10/3 for domestic students, 2/3 priority date for international students; for winter admission, 12/1 for domestic students; for spring admission, 4/3 for domestic students. Applications are processed on a rolling basis. Application fee: $100. Electronic applications accepted. *Financial support:* Institutionally sponsored loans and scholarships/grants available. Financial award applicants required to submit FAFSA. *Unit head:* Joe Fox, Associate Dean/Director of Specialized Master's Programs, 314-935-6322, Fax: 314-935-4464, E-mail: fox@wustl.edu. *Application contact:* 314-935-7301, E-mail: olingradadmissions@wustl.edu.
Website: http://www.olin.wustl.edu/academicprograms/MSSCM/Pages/default.aspx

Western Illinois University, School of Graduate Studies, College of Business and Technology, Program in Business Administration, Macomb, IL 61455-1390. Offers business administration (MBA, Certificate); supply chain management (Certificate). *Accreditation:* AACSB. *Program availability:* Part-time. *Students:* 37 full-time (17 women), 40 part-time (14 women); includes 6 minority (2 Black or African American, non-Hispanic/Latino; 1 Asian, non-Hispanic/Latino; 3 Hispanic/Latino), 9 international. Average age 31. 63 applicants, 79% accepted, 27 enrolled. In 2016, 42 master's, 6 other advanced degrees awarded. *Degree requirements:* For master's, thesis or alternative. *Entrance requirements:* For master's, GMAT. Additional exam requirements/recommendations for international students: Required—TOEFL (minimum score 550 paper-based; 80 iBT). *Application deadline:* Applications are processed on a rolling basis. Application fee: $30. Electronic applications accepted. *Financial support:* In 2016–17, 13 students received support, including 1 research assistantship with full tuition reimbursement available; unspecified assistantships also available. Financial award applicants required to submit FAFSA. *Unit head:* Dr. Bill Polley, Associate Dean, 309-298-2442. *Application contact:* Dr. Nancy Parsons, Associate Provost and Director of Graduate Studies, 309-298-1806, Fax: 309-298-2345, E-mail: grad-office@wiu.edu.
Website: http://wiu.edu/cbt

Wilfrid Laurier University, Faculty of Graduate and Postdoctoral Studies, School of Business and Economics, Department of Business, Waterloo, ON N2L 3C5, Canada. Offers accounting (PhD); finance (M Fin); financial economics (PhD); marketing (PhD); operations and supply chain management (PhD); organizational behavior and human resource management (M Sc); organizational behaviour and human resource management (PhD); supply chain management (M Sc); technology management (EMTM). *Accreditation:* AACSB. *Program availability:* Part-time, evening/weekend. *Degree requirements:* For master's, thesis optional; for doctorate, comprehensive exam, thesis/dissertation. *Entrance requirements:* For master's, GMAT, 4-year honors degree with minimum B+ average; for doctorate, GMAT, master's degree, minimum B+ average. Additional exam requirements/recommendations for international students: Required—TOEFL (minimum score 89 iBT). Electronic applications accepted. *Faculty research:* Financial economics, management and organizational behavior, operations and supply chain management.

Wright State University, Graduate School, Raj Soin College of Business, Department of Information Systems and Operations Management, Logistics and Supply Chain Management Program, Dayton, OH 45435. Offers MS. *Expenses:* Tuition, state resident: full-time $9952; part-time $622 per credit hour. Tuition, nonresident: full-time $16,960; part-time $1060 per credit hour. *Unit head:* Dr. Andrew W. Lai, Interim Chair, 937-775-2895, Fax: 937-775-3545, E-mail: andrew.lai@wright.edu. *Application contact:* Michael Evans, Director of MBA Programs, 937-775-2437, Fax: 937-775-3545, E-mail: michael.evans@wright.edu.

Transportation Management

American Public University System, AMU/APU Graduate Programs, Charles Town, WV 25414. Offers accounting (MBA, MS); applied business analytics (MBA, MS); criminal justice (MA), including business administration, emergency and disaster management, general (MA, MS); educational leadership (M Ed); emergency and disaster management (MA); entrepreneurship (MBA); environmental policy and management (MS), including environmental planning, environmental sustainability, fish and wildlife management, general (MA, MS), global environmental management; finance (MBA); general (MBA); government contracting and acquisition (MBA); health care administration (MBA); health information management (MS); history (MA), including American history, ancient and classical history, European history, global history, public history; homeland security (MA), including business administration, counterterrorism studies, criminal justice, cyber, emergency management and public health, intelligence studies, transportation security; homeland security resource allocation (MBA); humanities (MA); information technology (MS), including digital forensics, enterprise software development, information assurance and security, IT project management; information technology management (MBA); intelligence studies (MA), including criminal intelligence, cyber, general (MA, MS), homeland security, intelligence analysis, intelligence collection, intelligence management, intelligence operations, terrorism studies; international relations and conflict resolution (MA), including comparative and security issues, conflict resolution, international and transnational security issues, peacekeeping; legal studies (MA); management (MA), including strategic consulting; marketing (MBA); military history (MA), including American military history, American Revolution, civil war, war since 1945, World War II; military studies (MA), including joint warfare, strategic leadership; national security studies (MA), including cyber, general (MA, MS), homeland security, regional security studies, security and intelligence analysis, terrorism studies; nonprofit management (MBA); political science (MA), including American politics and government, comparative government and development, general (MA, MS), international relations, public policy; psychology (MA); public administration (MPA), including disaster management, environmental policy, health policy, human resources, national security, organizational management, security management; public health (MPH); reverse logistics management (MA); security management (MA); space studies (MS), including aerospace science, general (MA, MS), planetary science; sports and health sciences (MS); sports management (MBA); teaching (M Ed), including autism spectrum disorder, curriculum and instruction for elementary teachers, elementary reading, English language learners, instructional leadership, online learning, special education, STEAM (STEM plus the arts); transportation and logistics management (MA). *Program availability:* Part-time, evening/weekend, online only, 100% online. *Faculty:* 401 full-time (228 women), 1,678 part-time/adjunct (781 women). *Students:* 378 full-time (184 women), 8,455 part-time (3,484 women); includes 2,972 minority (1,552 Black or African American, non-Hispanic/Latino;

52 American Indian or Alaska Native, non-Hispanic/Latino; 211 Asian, non-Hispanic/Latino; 791 Hispanic/Latino; 70 Native Hawaiian or other Pacific Islander, non-Hispanic/Latino; 296 Two or more races, non-Hispanic/Latino), 109 international. Average age 37. In 2016, 3,185 master's awarded. *Degree requirements:* For master's, comprehensive exam or practicum. *Entrance requirements:* For master's, official transcript showing earned bachelor's degree from institution accredited by recognized accrediting body. Additional exam requirements/recommendations for international students: Required—TOEFL (minimum score 550 paper-based), IELTS (minimum score 6.5). *Application deadline:* Applications are processed on a rolling basis. Application fee: $0. Electronic applications accepted. *Expenses: Tuition:* Part-time $350 per credit hour. *Required fees:* $50 per course. *Financial support:* Scholarships/grants available. Financial award applicants required to submit FAFSA. *Unit head:* Dr. Karan Powell, President, 877-468-6268, Fax: 304-724-3780. *Application contact:* Terry Grant, Vice President of Enrollment Management, 877-468-6268, Fax: 304-724-3780, E-mail: info@apus.edu.
Website: http://www.apus.edu

California State University Maritime Academy, Graduate Studies, Vallejo, CA 94590. Offers transportation and engineering management (MS), including engineering management, humanitarian disaster management, transportation. *Program availability:* Evening/weekend, online only, 100% online. *Faculty:* 16 part-time/adjunct (2 women). *Students:* 49 full-time (10 women); includes 11 minority (2 Black or African American, non-Hispanic/Latino; 5 Asian, non-Hispanic/Latino; 2 Hispanic/Latino; 2 Native Hawaiian or other Pacific Islander, non-Hispanic/Latino), 1 international. Average age 32. 29 applicants, 93% accepted, 26 enrolled. In 2016, 24 master's awarded. *Degree requirements:* For master's, minimum GPA of 3.0 in 10 required courses including capstone course and project. *Entrance requirements:* For master's, GMAT/GRE (for applicants with fewer than five years of post-baccalaureate professional experience), equivalent of four-year U.S. bachelor's degree with minimum GPA of 2.5 during last two years (60 semester units or 90 quarter units) of coursework in degree program. Additional exam requirements/recommendations for international students: Required—TOEFL (minimum score 550 paper-based). *Application deadline:* Applications are processed on a rolling basis. Application fee: $55. Electronic applications accepted. *Expenses:* Contact institution. *Financial support:* Applicants required to submit FAFSA. *Unit head:* Dr. Jim Burns, Dean, Graduate Studies. *Application contact:* Kathy Arnold, Program Coordinator, 707-654-1271, Fax: 707-654-1158, E-mail: karnold@csum.edu.
Website: http://www.csum.edu/web/industry/graduate-studies

Florida Institute of Technology, Extended Studies Division, Melbourne, FL 32901-6975. Offers acquisition and contract management (MS); aerospace engineering (MS); business administration (MBA, DBA); computer information systems (MS); computer science (MS); electrical engineering (MS); engineering management (MS); human resources management (MS); logistics management (MS), including humanitarian and disaster relief logistics; management (MS), including acquisition and contract management, e-business, human resources management, information systems, logistics management, management, transportation management; material acquisition management (MS); mechanical engineering (MS); operations research (MS); project management (MS), including information systems, operations research; public administration (MPA); quality management (MS); software engineering (MS); space systems (MS); space systems management (MS); supply chain management (MS); systems management (MS), including information systems, operations research; technology management (MS). *Program availability:* Part-time, evening/weekend, online learning. *Faculty:* 10 full-time (3 women), 122 part-time/adjunct (29 women). *Students:* 131 full-time (58 women), 997 part-time (348 women); includes 389 minority (231 Black or African American, non-Hispanic/Latino; 9 American Indian or Alaska Native, non-Hispanic/Latino; 26 Asian, non-Hispanic/Latino; 99 Hispanic/Latino; 3 Native Hawaiian or other Pacific Islander, non-Hispanic/Latino; 21 Two or more races, non-Hispanic/Latino), 53 international. Average age 36. 962 applicants, 48% accepted, 323 enrolled. In 2016, 403 master's awarded. *Degree requirements:* For master's, comprehensive exam (for some programs). *Entrance requirements:* For master's, GMAT or resume showing 8 years of supervised experience, minimum GPA of 3.0, 2 letters of recommendation, resume. Additional exam requirements/recommendations for international students: Required—TOEFL (minimum score 550 paper-based; 79 iBT). *Application deadline:* For fall admission, 4/1 for international students; for spring admission, 9/30 for international students. Applications are processed on a rolling basis. Electronic applications accepted. *Expenses:* Contact institution. *Financial support:* Application deadline: 3/1; applicants required to submit FAFSA. *Unit head:* Dr. Theodore R. Richardson, III, Dean, 321-674-8123, Fax: 321-674-7597, E-mail: trichardson@fit.edu. *Application contact:* Carolyn Farrior, Director of Graduate Admissions, Online Learning and Off-Campus Programs, 321-674-7118, Fax: 321-674-8216, E-mail: cfarrior@fit.edu.
Website: http://es.fit.edu

George Mason University, Schar School of Policy and Government, Program in Transportation Policy, Operations and Logistics, Arlington, VA 22201. Offers MA, Certificate. *Faculty:* 6 full-time (3 women), 2 part-time/adjunct (0 women). *Students:* 6 full-time (2 women), 27 part-time (7 women); includes 7 minority (3 Black or African American, non-Hispanic/Latino; 3 Hispanic/Latino; 1 Two or more races, non-Hispanic/Latino), 1 international. Average age 34. 13 applicants, 92% accepted, 9 enrolled. In 2016, 12 master's awarded. *Degree requirements:* For master's, thesis or alternative. *Entrance requirements:* For master's, GRE (for students seeking merit-based scholarships), bachelor's degree with minimum GPA of 3.0, current resume, 2 letters of recommendation, expanded goals statement, 2 copies of official transcripts. Additional exam requirements/recommendations for international students: Required—TOEFL (minimum score 575 paper-based; 88 iBT), IELTS (minimum score 6.5), PTE (minimum score 59). *Application deadline:* For fall admission, 2/1 priority date for domestic students. Application fee: $75 ($80 for international students). Electronic applications accepted. *Expenses:* Contact institution. *Financial support:* Career-related internships or fieldwork, Federal Work-Study, and scholarships/grants available. Support available to part-time students. Financial award application deadline: 3/1; financial award applicants required to submit FAFSA. *Unit head:* Laurie Schintler, Director, 703-993-2256, Fax: 703-993-4557, E-mail: lschintl@gmu.edu. *Application contact:* Stephanie Ellis, Graduate Admissions Coordinator, 703-993-4478, E-mail: sellis11@gmu.edu.
Website: http://spgia.gmu.edu/programs/graduate-degrees/transportation-policy-operations-logistics-tpol/

Instituto Tecnologico de Santo Domingo, Graduate School, Area of Engineering, Santo Domingo, Dominican Republic. Offers construction administration (MS, Certificate); data telecommunications (M Eng, MS, Certificate); industrial engineering (M Eng, Certificate); industrial management (M Mgmt); information technology (Certificate); maintenance engineering (M Eng); occupational hazard prevention (M Mgmt); production management (Certificate); quantitative methods (Certificate); sanitary and environmental engineering (M Eng); structural engineering (M Eng); systems engineering and electronic data processing (Certificate); transportation (Certificate).

Iowa State University of Science and Technology, Department of Community and Regional Planning, Ames, IA 50011. Offers community and regional planning (MCRP); transportation (MS); M Arch/MCRP; MBA/MCRP; MCRP/MLA; MCRP/MPA. *Accreditation:* ACSP (one or more programs are accredited). *Degree requirements:* For master's, thesis or alternative. *Entrance requirements:* For master's, GRE General Test. Additional exam requirements/recommendations for international students: Required—TOEFL (minimum score 550 paper-based; 79 iBT), IELTS (minimum score 6.5). *Application deadline:* For fall admission, 1/1 priority date for domestic and international students. Applications are processed on a rolling basis. Application fee: $60 ($90 for international students). Electronic applications accepted. *Financial support:* Tuition waivers (partial) available. Financial award applicants required to submit FAFSA. *Faculty research:* Economic development, housing, land use, geographic information systems planning in developing nations, regional and community revitalization, transportation planning in developing countries. *Application contact:* Meredith Foley, Director of Graduate Education, 515-294-0816, Fax: 515-294-2348, E-mail: merfoley@iastate.edu.
Website: http://www.design.iastate.edu/CRP/graduateprograms.php

Iowa State University of Science and Technology, Program in Transportation, Ames, IA 50011. Offers MS. *Entrance requirements:* For master's, GMAT or GRE General Test. Additional exam requirements/recommendations for international students: Required—TOEFL (minimum score 550 paper-based; 82 iBT), IELTS (minimum score 6.5). *Application deadline:* For fall admission, 7/15 priority date for domestic students, 2/15 priority date for international students. Application fee: $60 ($90 for international students). Electronic applications accepted. *Application contact:* Jing Dong, Application Contact, 515-294-3957, Fax: 515-294-0467, E-mail: jingdong@iastate.edu.
Website: http://www.ctre.iastate.edu/mstrans/

Maine Maritime Academy, Loeb-Sullivan School of International Business and Logistics, Castine, ME 04420. Offers global logistics and maritime management (MS); international logistics management (MS). *Program availability:* Part-time. *Degree requirements:* For master's, capstone course. *Entrance requirements:* For master's, GMAT or GRE, letter of recommendation. Additional exam requirements/recommendations for international students: Required—TOEFL. Application fee is waived when completed online.

McGill University, Faculty of Graduate and Postdoctoral Studies, Faculty of Engineering, School of Urban Planning, Montréal, QC H3A 2T5, Canada. Offers environmental planning (MUP); housing (MUP); transportation (MUP); urban design (MUP); urban planning, policy and design (PhD).

Morgan State University, School of Graduate Studies, Clarence M. Mitchell, Jr. School of Engineering, Department of Transportation, Baltimore, MD 21251. Offers MS. *Program availability:* Part-time, evening/weekend. *Degree requirements:* For master's, thesis optional, comprehensive exam or equivalent. *Entrance requirements:* For master's, minimum undergraduate GPA of 2.5. Additional exam requirements/recommendations for international students: Required—TOEFL (minimum score 550 paper-based). *Faculty research:* Distributional impacts of congestion, pricing education and training for intelligent vehicle highway systems.

Naval Postgraduate School, Departments and Academic Groups, Graduate School of Business and Public Policy, Monterey, CA 93943. Offers acquisition and contract management (MBA); business administration (EMBA, MBA); contract management (MS); defense business management (MBA); defense systems analysis (MS), including management; defense systems management (international) (MBA); financial management (MBA); information management (MBA); manpower systems analysis (MS); material logistics support management (MBA); program management (MS); resource planning and management for international defense (MBA); supply chain management (MBA); systems acquisition management (MBA); transportation management (MBA). Program only open to commissioned officers of the United States and friendly nations and selected United States federal civilian employees. *Accreditation:* AACSB; NASPAA. *Program availability:* Part-time, online learning. *Degree requirements:* For master's, thesis (for some programs), terminal project/capstone (for some programs). *Faculty research:* U.S. and European public procurement policies for small and medium-sized enterprises, examining external validity criticisms in the choice of students as subjects in accounting experiment studies, assurance of learning in contract management education, contracting for cloud computing: opportunities and risks, NPS, Apple App Store as a business model supporting U. S. Navy requirements.

New Jersey Institute of Technology, Newark College of Engineering, Newark, NJ 07102. Offers biomedical engineering (MS, PhD); chemical engineering (MS, PhD); computer engineering (MS, PhD); electrical engineering (MS, PhD); engineering management (MS); environmental engineering (PhD); healthcare systems management (MS); industrial engineering (MS, PhD); Internet engineering (MS); manufacturing engineering (MS); mechanical engineering (MS, PhD); occupational safety and health engineering (MS); pharmaceutical bioprocessing (MS); pharmaceutical engineering (MS); pharmaceutical systems management (MS); power and energy systems (MS); telecommunications (MS); transportation (MS, PhD). *Program availability:* Part-time, evening/weekend. *Faculty:* 146 full-time (21 women), 119 part-time/adjunct (10 women). *Students:* 804 full-time (191 women), 550 part-time (129 women); includes 357 minority (82 Black or African American, non-Hispanic/Latino; 1 American Indian or Alaska Native, non-Hispanic/Latino; 138 Asian, non-Hispanic/Latino; 114 Hispanic/Latino; 22 Two or more races, non-Hispanic/Latino), 675 international. Average age 27. 2,959 applicants, 51% accepted, 442 enrolled. In 2016, 595 master's, 29 doctorates awarded. Terminal master's awarded for partial completion of doctoral program. *Degree requirements:* For master's, thesis optional; for doctorate, thesis/dissertation. *Entrance requirements:* For master's, GRE General Test; for doctorate, GRE General Test, minimum graduate GPA of 3.5. Additional exam requirements/recommendations for international students: Required—TOEFL (minimum score 550 paper-based; 79 iBT). *Application deadline:* For fall admission, 6/1 priority date for domestic students, 5/1 priority date for international students; for spring admission, 11/15 priority date for domestic and international students. Applications are processed on a rolling basis. Application fee: $75. Electronic applications accepted. *Expenses:* Contact institution. *Financial support:* In 2016–17, 172 students received support, including 1 fellowship (averaging $1,528 per year), 79 research assistantships (averaging $13,336 per year), 92 teaching assistantships (averaging $20,619 per year); scholarships/grants also available. Financial award application deadline: 1/15. *Faculty research:* Nonlinear signal processing, intelligent medical image analysis, calibration issues in coherent localization, computer-aided design, neural network for tool wear measurement. *Total annual research expenditures:* $11.1 million. *Unit head:* Dr. Moshe Kam, Dean, 973-596-5534, E-mail: moshe.kam@njit.edu. *Application contact:* Stephen Eck, Director of Admissions, 973-596-3300, Fax: 973-596-3461, E-mail: admissions@njit.edu.
Website: http://engineering.njit.edu/

New York University, Polytechnic School of Engineering, Department of Civil and Urban Engineering, Major in Transportation Management, New York, NY 10012-1019. Offers MS. *Program availability:* Part-time, evening/weekend. *Degree requirements:* For master's, comprehensive exam (for some programs), thesis (for some programs). *Entrance requirements:* Additional exam requirements/recommendations for international students: Required—TOEFL (minimum score 550 paper-based; 80 iBT); Recommended—IELTS (minimum score 6.5). Electronic applications accepted.

Transportation Management

North Dakota State University, College of Graduate and Interdisciplinary Studies, Interdisciplinary Program in Transportation and Logistics, Fargo, ND 58102. Offers managerial logistics (MML); transportation and logistics (PhD); transportation and urban systems (MS). *Entrance requirements:* For doctorate, 1 year of calculus, statistics and probability, minimum GPA of 3.0. Additional exam requirements/recommendations for international students: Required—TOEFL (minimum score 550 paper-based; 79 iBT). *Faculty research:* Supply chain optimization, spatial analysis of transportation networks, advanced traffic analysis, transportation demand, railroad/intermodal freight.

Pontifical Catholic University of Puerto Rico, College of Business Administration, Program in Maritime Logistics and Transportation, Ponce, PR 00717-0777. Offers Professional Certificate.

San Jose State University, Graduate Studies and Research, Lucas Graduate School of Business, San Jose, CA 95192-0001. Offers accountancy (MS); business administration (MBA); taxation (MS); transportation management (MS). *Program availability:* Part-time, evening/weekend, online learning. *Degree requirements:* For master's, comprehensive exam, thesis or alternative. *Entrance requirements:* For master's, GMAT, minimum GPA of 3.0. Electronic applications accepted.

State University of New York Maritime College, Program in International Transportation Management, Throggs Neck, NY 10465-4198. Offers MS. *Program availability:* Part-time, evening/weekend. *Degree requirements:* For master's, thesis. *Entrance requirements:* For master's, minimum GPA of 2.5. Additional exam requirements/recommendations for international students: Required—TOEFL. *Faculty research:* Ports, intermodal, shipping, logistics, port tax.

Temple University, Tyler School of Art, Department of Planning and Community Development, Ambler, PA 19122. Offers city and regional planning (MS); sustainable community planning (Graduate Certificate); transportation planning (Graduate Certificate). *Accreditation:* ACSP. *Program availability:* Part-time, evening/weekend. *Entrance requirements:* For master's, GRE or GMAT, 2 letters of recommendation, minimum undergraduate GPA of 3.0, statement of goals. Additional exam requirements/recommendations for international students: Required—TOEFL (minimum score 550 paper-based; 79 iBT). *Faculty research:* Regional environmental planning, collaboration, management community development through sustainable food systems, storm water management and floodplain mapping, land use policy innovations, community planning for aging.

Texas A&M University, Galveston Campus, Department of Maritime Administration, College Station, TX 77843. Offers maritime administration and logistics (MMAL). *Program availability:* Part-time, evening/weekend. *Students:* 59 full-time (16 women), 19 part-time (3 women); includes 7 minority (6 Hispanic/Latino; 1 Two or more races, non-Hispanic/Latino), 4 international. Average age 29. 30 applicants, 77% accepted, 21 enrolled. In 2016, 14 master's awarded. *Degree requirements:* For master's, comprehensive exam (for some programs), thesis (for some programs). *Entrance requirements:* For master's, GMAT, coursework in statistics, microeconomics, organizational behavior, financial and managerial accounting, management information systems. Additional exam requirements/recommendations for international students: Required—TOEFL (minimum score 550 paper-based; 80 iBT), IELTS (minimum score 6). *Application deadline:* For fall admission, 5/1 for domestic and international students; for spring admission, 10/15 for domestic students, 10/1 for international students. Application fee: $50 ($90 for international students). Electronic applications accepted. *Expenses:* Contact institution. *Financial support:* In 2016–17, 43 students received support, including 4 research assistantships (averaging $4,942 per year), 15 teaching assistantships (averaging $12,033 per year); scholarships/grants and unspecified assistantships also available. Financial award application deadline: 3/15; financial award applicants required to submit FAFSA. *Faculty research:* International trade, inland waterways management, brokerage and chartering, organizational behavior, transportation economics, port and terminal management. *Unit head:* Dr. Joan P. Mileski, Professor/Chair of Maritime Administration, 409-740-4978, E-mail: mileskij@tamug.edu. *Application contact:* Nicole Kinslow, Director of Graduate Studies, 409-740-4937, Fax: 409-740-4754, E-mail: kinslown@tamug.edu.
Website: http://www.tamug.edu/mara/

Texas Southern University, School of Science and Technology, Program in Transportation, Planning and Management, Houston, TX 77004-4584. Offers MS. *Program availability:* Part-time, evening/weekend. *Degree requirements:* For master's, comprehensive exam, thesis optional. *Entrance requirements:* For master's, GRE General Test, minimum GPA of 2.5. Additional exam requirements/recommendations for international students: Required—TOEFL. Electronic applications accepted. *Faculty research:* Highway traffic operations, transportation and policy planning, air quality in transportation, transportation modeling.

The University of British Columbia, Sauder School of Business, Doctoral Program in Business Administration, Vancouver, BC V6T 1Z2, Canada. Offers accounting (PhD); finance (PhD); management information systems (PhD); management science (PhD); marketing (PhD); organizational behavior (PhD); strategy and business economics (PhD); transportation and logistics (PhD); urban land economics (PhD). *Degree requirements:* For doctorate, comprehensive exam, thesis/dissertation. *Entrance requirements:* For doctorate, GMAT or GRE. Additional exam requirements/recommendations for international students: Required—TOEFL (minimum score 600 paper-based; 100 iBT). *Application deadline:* Applications are processed on a rolling basis. Application fee: $102 Canadian dollars ($165 Canadian dollars for international students). Electronic applications accepted. *Expenses:* $4,802 per year tuition and fees, $8,436 per year international. *Financial support:* Fellowships with full tuition reimbursements, research assistantships with full tuition reimbursements, and teaching assistantships with full tuition reimbursements available. *Application contact:* Elaine Cho, Administrator, PhD and M Sc Programs, 604-822-8366, Fax: 604-822-8755, E-mail: phd.program@sauder.ubc.ca.
Website: http://www.sauder.ubc.ca/Programs/PhD_in_Business_Administration

University of California, Davis, College of Engineering, Graduate Group in Transportation Technology and Policy, Davis, CA 95616. Offers MS, PhD. Terminal master's awarded for partial completion of doctoral program. *Degree requirements:* For master's, comprehensive exam (for some programs), thesis (for some programs); for doctorate, thesis/dissertation. *Entrance requirements:* For master's, GRE General Test, minimum GPA of 3.0; for doctorate, GRE General Test, minimum GPA of 3.5. Additional exam requirements/recommendations for international students: Required—TOEFL (minimum score 550 paper-based). Electronic applications accepted.

University of California, Santa Barbara, Graduate Division, College of Letters and Sciences, Division of Mathematics, Life, and Physical Sciences, Department of Geography, Santa Barbara, CA 93106-4060. Offers cognitive science (PhD); geography (MA, PhD); global studies (PhD); quantitative methods in the social sciences (PhD); technology and society (PhD); transportation (PhD); MA/PhD. Terminal master's awarded for partial completion of doctoral program. *Degree requirements:* For master's, comprehensive exam (for some programs), thesis or alternative; for doctorate, comprehensive exam, thesis/dissertation, 1 quarter of teaching assistantship. *Entrance requirements:* For master's and doctorate, GRE (minimum combined verbal and quantitative scores above 1100 in old scoring system or 301 in new scoring system). Additional exam requirements/recommendations for international students: Required—TOEFL (minimum score 550 paper-based; 80 iBT), IELTS (minimum score 7). Electronic applications accepted. *Faculty research:* Earth system science; human environment relations; modeling, measurement, and computation.

University of Hawaii at Manoa, Graduate Division, College of Social Sciences, Department of Urban and Regional Planning, Honolulu, HI 96822. Offers community planning (MURP); disaster management and humanitarian assistance (Graduate Certificate); environmental planning and sustainability (MURP); international development planning (MURP); land use, transportation and infrastructure planning (MURP); planning studies (Graduate Certificate); urban and regional planning (PhD, Graduate Certificate). *Accreditation:* ACSP. *Program availability:* Part-time. *Entrance requirements:* For master's, GRE General Test, minimum GPA of 3.0; for doctorate, GRE General Test. Additional exam requirements/recommendations for international students: Required—TOEFL (minimum score 500 paper-based; 61 iBT), IELTS (minimum score 5).

University of New Orleans, Graduate School, College of Liberal Arts, Department of Planning and Urban Studies, Program in Transportation, New Orleans, LA 70148. Offers MS. *Program availability:* Online learning.

The University of Tennessee, Graduate School, College of Business Administration, Program in Business Administration, Knoxville, TN 37996. Offers accounting (PhD); finance (MBA, PhD); logistics and transportation (MBA, PhD); management (PhD); marketing (MBA, PhD); operations management (MBA); professional business administration (MBA); statistics (PhD); JD/MBA; MS/MBA; Pharm D/MBA. Pharm D/MBA offered jointly with The University of Tennessee Health Science Center. *Accreditation:* AACSB. *Program availability:* Online learning. *Degree requirements:* For master's, thesis or alternative; for doctorate, thesis/dissertation. *Entrance requirements:* For master's and doctorate, GMAT, minimum GPA of 2.7. Additional exam requirements/recommendations for international students: Required—TOEFL. Electronic applications accepted.

University of Washington, Graduate School, Interdisciplinary Program in Global Trade, Transportation and Logistics Studies, Seattle, WA 98195. Offers Certificate.

EMBRY-RIDDLE AERONAUTICAL UNIVERSITY

College of Business–Daytona Beach

EMBRY-RIDDLE
Aeronautical University
DAYTONA BEACH, FLORIDA
COLLEGE OF BUSINESS

Programs of Study

The Embry-Riddle College of Business on the Daytona Beach campus provides graduates with two degree options for students seeking a cutting-edge management or finance education in an aviation/aerospace context. With the choice of the Master of Business Administration (M.B.A.) or the Master of Science in Aviation Finance (M.S.A.F.), the College offers students seeking a career in the aviation, airport, or aerospace industries programs designed to meet the needs of industry. Professional managers who have earned their graduate degree at Embry-Riddle Aeronautical University (ERAU) understand the imperatives of change, globalization, technological innovation, and increasingly sophisticated and demanding customers that mark the financial, strategic, and operational environments of today's airlines, airports, and aerospace firms. Both the M.B.A. and M.S.A.F. are offered as full-time residential programs. The M.B.A. curriculum combines a strong traditional business core with specializations in airport management, airline management, finance, aviation human resources, and aviation system management. The M.S.A.F. program stresses pragmatic solutions to the financial and economic problems that arise in the aviation/aerospace industry as a result of the need to finance large capital expenditures occurring in an international marketplace with changing regulations and challenging economic conditions. The M.S.A.F. program is recognized by the CFA Institute. Students in the M.S.A.F. program can obtain an International Society for Transport Aircraft Trading (ISTAT) U diploma and experience a state-of-the-art curriculum developed with industry input in the field of aviation finance. One hundred percent of the 2015–16 M.S.A.F. program graduates are currently employed.

Both degree programs consist of 33 credit hours. The M.B.A. consists of 21 hours of core curriculum and 12 hours of specified electives. Three hours of elective credit may be awarded for an internship, which is strongly advised for all students. The M.S.A.F. consists of a 12-hour core curriculum and 18 hours of advanced finance and economic courses with the option of a concluding internship or research project. The employer-supported Business Eagles program is open to all students and provides special access to development and placement activities. Both the M.B.A. and M.S.A.F. programs can usually be completed in sixteen to twenty-four months based on how the student progresses through the curriculum and whether an internship is taken.

Research Facilities

A collection of networked servers and PCs provide the faculty and students with the latest advances in data mining and computational facilities. Through classes, students have access to SABRE products for airline scheduling scenarios along with extensive and diverse aviation databases utilized for ongoing research projects. Students are also introduced to the latest financial modeling software. Dedicated facilities provide the opportunity to work with the Total Airspace and Airport Modeler (TAMM) and in the Applied Aviation Simulation and Optimization labs. The multimodal transportation lab enables students to explore the viability of each transportation mode within the overall logistics and supply chain developed. Efforts are underway to develop a finance lab.

Financial Aid

Scholarships are awarded to outstanding graduate students during the admissions process. Graduate assistantships are also available on a limited and competitive basis. Students may apply for financial aid by calling 800-943-6279 (toll-free). All graduate programs are approved for U.S. Veterans Administration education benefits.

Cost of Study

In 2016–17 tuition costs for the M.B.A. and M.S.A.F. programs are $1,358 per credit hour. The estimated cost of books and supplies is $1,400 per semester; there are also mandatory University fees estimated at $1,394 for domestic students and $1,594 for international students for the academic year. Additional details are available at http://daytonabeach.erau.edu/admissions/estimated-costs/index.html.

Living and Housing Costs

On-campus housing is available on a limited basis to graduate students on the Daytona Beach campus, with an estimated cost of $5,413 per semester for room and board. Single students who share rent and utility expenses can expect off-campus room, board, and living expenses of $5,500 per semester.

Student Group

ERAU's graduate programs on the Daytona Beach campus currently enroll approximately 600 students. The students possess various cultural origins—many are from other countries, 25 percent are women, and 23 percent are members of U.S. minority groups. The graduate programs in the College of Business attract students with diverse academic backgrounds and common scholastic abilities that enrich the program. The majority of incoming students have business degrees, although all degrees are welcomed with many engineers, air science, and aviation management students from other universities continuing their air transport studies at ERAU. The average age of incoming students is 28.

Student Outcomes

In addition to contacts gained from internships with leading airlines, airports, and aerospace firms, the College of Business conducts placement activities for its graduates. Years of research and consulting have allowed the faculty to cultivate contacts within the aviation industry, and this network provides job opportunities for graduates. The Career Services Office sponsors an annual industry Career Expo, which attracts more than 100 major companies such as Boeing, Federal Express, Delta, and United Airlines. In addition, the Career Resource Center offers corporate profiles, job postings, and development information. The office also assists with resume development and interview preparation.

Location

The Daytona Beach, Florida campus is located next to the Daytona Beach International Airport, the world-famous Daytona International Speedway, and 10 minutes from Daytona's beaches. The campus is an hour's drive from Orlando and destinations such as Disney World, EPCOT, Universal Studios, SeaWorld, and other Florida attractions such as the Kennedy Space Center and St. Augustine.

The University

Since its founding in 1926, Embry-Riddle Aeronautical University has built a reputation for high-quality education within the field of aviation and has become a world leader in aerospace higher education. The University is comprised of the eastern campus in Daytona Beach, Florida; the western campus in Prescott, Arizona; and the WorldWide Campus, with off-campus programs.

Embry-Riddle Aeronautical University

Applying

A desired minimum bachelor degree cumulative GPA of 3.0 (4.0 scale) and a minimum score of 550 on the GMAT are the requirements for full admission consideration for the M.B.A. program. For the M.S.A.F. program a GPA of 3.0 (4.0 scale) and GRE General Test scores of 305 or above are required. The ability to apply test scores from either the GMAT or GRE exam to the preferred degree program is available. Applications not meeting these qualifications may be considered for conditional admission with enhanced student oversight as an applicant matriculates into the program. Applications are accepted on a rolling basis and should be completed sixty days prior to the start of a semester for U.S. citizens, resident aliens, and international students. For international applicants the required minimum IELTS score is 6.0, or a TOEFL score of 550 or 79 on the TOFEL-IBT.

Correspondence and Information

Office of International and Graduate Admissions
Embry-Riddle Aeronautical University
600 South Clyde Morris Boulevard
Daytona Beach, Florida 32114-3900
United States
Phone: 386-226-6176 (outside the United States)
800-388-3728 (toll-free within the United States)
Fax: 386-226-7070
E-mail: graduate.admissions@erau.edu
Website: http://www.embryriddle.edu/graduate

THE FACULTY

The College of Business (COB) faculty takes pride in bringing relevant, real-world problems, issues, and experiences into the classrooms. Faculty members give a high priority to preparing students for the leadership roles they will eventually assume. The faculty members accomplish this not only by excellence in teaching but also by advising students on research and consulting projects. Many members of the faculty serve as consultants to a variety of industries, and the diverse backgrounds of the faculty members provide a rich, multicultural experience, with an emphasis on global standards and practices.

In addition, the Embry-Riddle faculty members are the go-to references for print and broadcast journalists on questions of aviation. When the question concerns aviation business, the savvy journalist calls the experts at the Embry-Riddle College of Business. For issues such as airline mergers, acquisitions, bankruptcies, or the general state of the aviation business, members of the COB faculty have provided information to scores of journalists for countless articles and broadcasts. Such is the reputation of the faculty of the College of Business. The College of Business offers short courses taught by its renowned faculty in aircraft appraisal, revenue management, and aircraft financing and leasing to industry professionals.

On the subject of aviation business, Embry-Riddle faculty members have written some of the leading textbooks in the field and worked as external experts, such as the following COB professors.

Ahmed Abdelghany, Ph.D., Associate Professor. *Modeling Applications in the Airline Industry.*

Massoud Bazargan, Ph.D., Professor, *Airline Operations and Scheduling.*

Vedapuri Raghavan, Ph.D., Christine and Lou Seno Distinguished Professor, Finance. *A Study of Corporate Bond Market in India: Theoretical and policy Implications, Reserve Bank of India (India's Central Bank),* DRG Report.

Dawna Rhoades, Ph.D., Professor. *Evolution of International Aviation: Phoenix Rising.*

Bijan Vasigh, Ph.D., Professor. *Introduction to Air Transport Economics, From Theory to Applications: Foundations of Airline Finance,* and *Airline Finance.*

The other faculty members of the College whom students may have as instructors in the graduate programs are:

Hari P. Adhikari, Ph.D., Assistant Professor, Finance.
Scott Ambrose, Ph.D., Assistant Professor, Marketing.
Anke Arnaud, Ph.D., Associate Professor, Organizational Behavior.
Farshid Azadian, Ph.D., Assistant Professor, Logistics.
Michael Bowers, Ph.D., Professor of Entrepreneurship and Marketing
Tamilla Curtis, Ph.D., Associate Professor, Marketing.
Jayendra Gokhale, Ph.D., Assistant Professor, Economics.
Vitaly Guzhva, Ph.D., Professor, Finance.
Lee Hays, D.B.A., Assistant Professor, Management.
John Ledgerwood, CPA, MSA, Associate Professor, Accounting.
John Longshore, Ph.D., Assistant Professor, Management.
Thomas Tacker, Ph.D., Professor, Economics. Co-author of *Introduction to Air Transport Economics, From Theory to Applications.*
Janet Tinoco, Ph.D., Associate Professor, Marketing and Management.
Blaise Waguespack, Ph.D., Professor, Marketing.
Michael J. Williams, Ph.D., Dean, Professor, Management Information Systems.
Chunyan Yu, Ph.D., Professor of Transport Management.
Bert Zarb, D.B.A., CPA, Professor, Accounting.
Li Zou, Ph.D., Associate Professor, Marketing.

The recently opened College of Business building on the Daytona Beach campus, part of a major infrastructure program bringing new academic and student facilities across the campus.

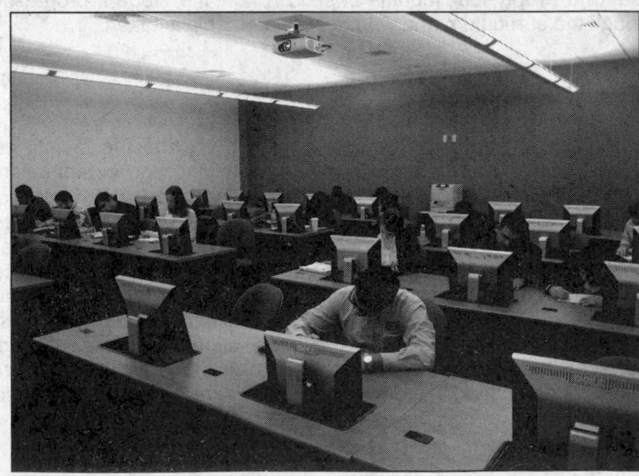

Students in the ISTAT U program.

ACADEMIC AND PROFESSIONAL PROGRAMS IN EDUCATION

Section 22
Education

This section contains a directory of institutions offering graduate work in education, followed by in-depth entries submitted by institutions that chose to prepare detailed program descriptions. Additional information about programs listed in the directory but not augmented by an in-depth entry may be obtained by writing directly to the dean of a graduate school or chair of a department at the address given in the directory.

For programs offering related work, see also in this book *Administration, Instruction, and Theory; Instructional Levels; Leisure Studies and Recreation; Physical Education and Kinesiology; Special Focus;* and *Subject Areas.* In other guides in this series:

Graduate Programs in the Humanities, Arts & Social Sciences
See *Psychology and Counseling (School Psychology)*

Graduate Programs in the Biological/Biomedical Sciences and Health-Related Medical Professions
See *Health-Related Professions*

CONTENTS

Program Directory

Featured Schools: Displays and Close-Ups

Education—General

Abilene Christian University, Graduate Programs, College of Education and Human Services, Abilene, TX 79699. Offers M Ed, MS, Certificate. *Accreditation:* TEAC. *Faculty:* 3 full-time (all women), 26 part-time/adjunct (16 women). *Students:* 137 full-time (124 women), 19 part-time (14 women); includes 39 minority (8 Black or African American, non-Hispanic/Latino; 1 American Indian or Alaska Native, non-Hispanic/Latino; 26 Hispanic/Latino; 4 Two or more races, non-Hispanic/Latino), 2 international. 439 applicants, 38% accepted, 93 enrolled. In 2016, 83 master's, 10 other advanced degrees awarded. *Degree requirements:* For master's, comprehensive exam (for some programs), thesis (for some programs), practicum. *Entrance requirements:* For master's, GRE. Additional exam requirements/recommendations for international students: Required—TOEFL (minimum score 80 iBT), IELTS (minimum score 6), PTE. *Application deadline:* For fall admission, 8/15 priority date for domestic students; for winter admission, 10/1 priority date for domestic students; for spring admission, 12/15 priority date for domestic students; for summer admission, 4/15 for domestic students. Applications are processed on a rolling basis. Application fee: $50. Electronic applications accepted. *Expenses: Tuition:* Full-time $19,890; part-time $1105 per credit hour. Tuition and fees vary according to course load and program. *Financial support:* In 2016–17, 61 students received support. Career-related internships or fieldwork and scholarships/grants available. Financial award application deadline: 4/1; financial award applicants required to submit FAFSA. *Unit head:* Dr. Donnie Snider, Dean, 325-674-2700, Fax: 325-674-3707, E-mail: cehs@acu.edu. *Application contact:* Corey Patterson, Director of Graduate Admission and Recruiting, 325-674-6566, Fax: 325-674-6717, E-mail: gradinfo@acu.edu.
Website: http://www.acu.edu/community/cehs.html

Acacia University, American Graduate School of Education, Tempe, AZ 85284. Offers educational administration (M Ed); elementary education (MA); English as a second language (M Ed); secondary education (MA); special education (M Ed).

Acadia University, Faculty of Professional Studies, Inter-University Doctoral Program in Educational Studies, Wolfville, NS B4P 2R6, Canada. Offers PhD. Program offered jointly with Mount Saint Vincent University and St. Francis Xavier University. *Degree requirements:* For doctorate, thesis/dissertation, comprehensive research/scholarly portfolio.

Acadia University, Faculty of Professional Studies, School of Education, Wolfville, NS B4P 2R6, Canada. Offers counseling (M Ed); curriculum studies (M Ed), including cultural and media studies, learning and technology, science, math and technology; inclusive education (M Ed); leadership (M Ed). *Degree requirements:* For master's, thesis optional. *Entrance requirements:* For master's, B Ed or the equivalent, 2 years of teaching or related experience. Additional exam requirements/recommendations for international students: Required—TOEFL (minimum score 580 paper-based; 93 iBT), IELTS (minimum score 6.5).

Adams State University, The Graduate School, Department of Teacher Education, Alamosa, CO 81101. Offers education (MA); special education (MA). *Program availability:* Part-time, online learning. *Degree requirements:* For master's, qualifying exam. *Entrance requirements:* For master's, GRE General Test or MAT, minimum undergraduate GPA of 3.0.

Adelphi University, Ruth S. Ammon School of Education, Garden City, NY 11530-0701. Offers MA, MS, DA, Certificate. *Accreditation:* NCATE. *Program availability:* Part-time, evening/weekend. *Faculty:* 63 full-time (41 women), 101 part-time/adjunct (67 women). *Students:* 448 full-time (378 women), 270 part-time (168 women); includes 29 minority (8 Black or African American, non-Hispanic/Latino; 4 Asian, non-Hispanic/Latino; 15 Hispanic/Latino; 2 Two or more races, non-Hispanic/Latino), 4 international. Average age 27. 1,329 applicants, 47% accepted, 252 enrolled. In 2016, 334 master's, 5 doctorates, 82 other advanced degrees awarded. *Degree requirements:* For doctorate, one foreign language, comprehensive exam, thesis/dissertation. *Entrance requirements:* For master's, resume, letters of recommendation, minimum cumulative GPA of 2.75; for doctorate, GRE General Test, 3 letters of recommendation, interview. Additional exam requirements/recommendations for international students: Required—TOEFL (minimum score 550 paper-based; 80 iBT), IELTS (minimum score 6.5). *Application deadline:* For fall admission, 4/1 for international students; for spring admission, 11/1 for international students. Applications are processed on a rolling basis. Application fee: $50. Electronic applications accepted. *Expenses:* Contact institution. *Financial support:* In 2016–17, 95 teaching assistantships with full and partial tuition reimbursements (averaging $11,059 per year) were awarded; fellowships, research assistantships, career-related internships or fieldwork, Federal Work-Study, scholarships/grants, traineeships, tuition waivers (full and partial), unspecified assistantships, and tuition remission for employees also available. Support available to part-time students. Financial award application deadline: 2/15; financial award applicants required to submit FAFSA. *Faculty research:* Multicultural and gender issues, psychometric assessment, quantitative research methods. *Unit head:* Dr. Jane Ashdown, Dean, 516-877-4065, E-mail: jashdown@adelphi.edu. *Application contact:* Christine Murphy, Director of Admissions, 516-877-3050, Fax: 516-877-3039, E-mail: graduateadmissions@adelphi.edu.
Website: http://education.adelphi.edu/

Alabama Agricultural and Mechanical University, School of Graduate Studies, College of Education, Humanities, and Behavioral Sciences, Huntsville, AL 35811. Offers M Ed, MS, MS Ed, PhD, Ed S. *Accreditation:* NCATE. *Program availability:* Part-time, evening/weekend. *Degree requirements:* For master's, comprehensive exam. *Entrance requirements:* For master's, GRE General Test. Additional exam requirements/recommendations for international students: Required—TOEFL (minimum score 500 paper-based; 61 iBT). *Application deadline:* For fall admission, 5/1 for domestic students. Applications are processed on a rolling basis. Application fee: $25. Electronic applications accepted. *Expenses:* Tuition, nonresident: part-time $826 per credit hour. Full-time tuition and fees vary according to course load and program. *Financial support:* Fellowships, research assistantships, career-related internships or fieldwork, Federal Work-Study, institutionally sponsored loans, and traineeships available. Support available to part-time students. Financial award application deadline: 4/1. *Faculty research:* Speech defects, aging, blindness, multicultural education, learning styles. *Unit head:* Dr. Rodney Whittle, Interim Dean, 256-372-5500.

Alabama State University, College of Education, Montgomery, AL 36101-0271. Offers M Ed, MS, Ed D, Ed S. *Accreditation:* NCATE. *Program availability:* Part-time. *Faculty:* 7 full-time (4 women), 7 part-time/adjunct (4 women). *Students:* 93 full-time (65 women), 221 part-time (168 women); includes 300 minority (297 Black or African American, non-Hispanic/Latino; 3 Two or more races, non-Hispanic/Latino), 3 international. Average age 35. 156 applicants, 55% accepted, 43 enrolled. In 2016, 65 master's, 19 doctorates, 10 other advanced degrees awarded. *Degree requirements:* For master's, comprehensive exam; for doctorate, thesis/dissertation; for Ed S, comprehensive exam, thesis. *Entrance requirements:* For master's, GRE General Test, MAT, writing competency test; for Ed S, writing competency test, GRE, MAT. Additional exam requirements/recommendations for international students: Required—TOEFL (minimum score 500 paper-based). *Application deadline:* For fall admission, 4/15 for domestic and international students; for spring admission, 11/15 for domestic and international students; for summer admission, 3/15 for domestic and international students. Applications are processed on a rolling basis. Application fee: $25. Electronic applications accepted. *Expenses:* Tuition, state resident: full-time $3087; part-time $2744 per credit. Tuition, nonresident: full-time $6174; part-time $5488 per credit. *Required fees:* $2284; $1142 per credit. $571 per semester. Tuition and fees vary according to class time, course level, course load, degree level, program and student level. *Financial support:* In 2016–17, 4 students received support. Research assistantships and unspecified assistantships available. Financial award application deadline: 6/30; financial award applicants required to submit FAFSA. *Faculty research:* Whole language instruction, African-American children's literature. *Unit head:* Dr. Doris Screws, Interim Dean, 334-229-4250, E-mail: dscrews@alasu.edu. *Application contact:* Dr. William Person, Dean of Graduate Studies, 334-229-4274, Fax: 334-229-4928, E-mail: wperson@alasu.edu.
Website: http://www.alasu.edu/Education/

Alaska Pacific University, Graduate Programs, Education Department, Program in Teaching, Anchorage, AK 99508-4672. Offers teaching (K-8) (MAT). *Degree requirements:* For master's, research project. *Entrance requirements:* For master's, GRE or MAT, PRAXIS, minimum GPA of 3.0.

Albany State University, College of Education, Albany, GA 31705-2717. Offers early childhood education (M Ed); educational leadership (Ed S); health and physical education (M Ed); middle grades education (M Ed); school counseling (M Ed); special education (M Ed). *Accreditation:* NCATE. *Program availability:* Part-time, evening/weekend, online learning. *Degree requirements:* For master's, comprehensive exam, internship, GACE Content Exam. *Entrance requirements:* For master's, GRE or MAT. *Application deadline:* For fall admission, 6/1 for domestic students, 5/1 for international students; for spring admission, 11/1 for domestic students, 10/1 for international students. Applications are processed on a rolling basis. Application fee: $20. Electronic applications accepted. *Financial support:* Scholarships/grants available. Financial award application deadline: 4/15; financial award applicants required to submit FAFSA. *Faculty research:* GACE preparation, STEM (science, technology, engineering, and mathematics), technology education, special education, professional teacher development, health implications liberation philosophy, NET-Q, learning community, disabled or at-risk students. *Unit head:* Dr. Rhonda C. Porter, Interim Dean, 229-430-1718, Fax: 229-430-4993. *Application contact:* Jeffrey Pierce, II, Graduate Admissions Counselor, 229-430-4646, Fax: 229-430-4105, E-mail: jeffrey.pierce@asurams.edu.
Website: https://www.asurams.edu/Academics/collegeofeducation/

Albertus Magnus College, Master of Science in Education Program, New Haven, CT 06511-1189. Offers MS Ed. *Program availability:* Part-time, evening/weekend, blended/hybrid learning. *Faculty:* 3 full-time (1 woman), 9 part-time/adjunct (4 women). *Students:* 5 full-time (3 women), 1 part-time (0 women); includes 2 minority (1 Black or African American, non-Hispanic/Latino; 1 Hispanic/Latino). Average age 28. In 2016, 7 master's awarded. *Degree requirements:* For master's, thesis, capstone. *Entrance requirements:* For master's, bachelor's degree, official transcripts of all undergraduate work, three letters of recommendation, resume, essay, valid Connecticut initial teacher certificate (preferred). Additional exam requirements/recommendations for international students: Recommended—TOEFL (minimum score 550 paper-based; 80 iBT). *Application deadline:* For fall admission, 8/15 for domestic students; for spring admission, 1/15 for domestic students. Application fee: $50. *Expenses:* Contact institution. *Financial support:* Federal Work-Study and unspecified assistantships available. Support available to part-time students. Financial award applicants required to submit FAFSA. *Faculty research:* Assessment, learning theory, educational leadership, differentiated instruction, multiculturalism. *Unit head:* Dr. Joan Venditto, Director, Education Programs, 203-773-8087, Fax: 203-773-4422, E-mail: jvenditto@albertus.edu. *Application contact:* Anthony Reich, Director of Admission, Division of Professional and Graduate Studies, 203-773-5032, E-mail: arreich@albertus.edu.
Website: http://www.albertus.edu/masters-degrees/education/

Albright College, Graduate Division, Reading, PA 19612-5234. Offers early childhood education (MS); elementary education (MS); English as a second language (MA); general education (MA); special education (MS). *Program availability:* Part-time, evening/weekend. *Degree requirements:* For master's, thesis. *Entrance requirements:* For master's, GRE General Test or MAT, minimum undergraduate GPA of 3.0, 2 letters of recommendation, interview. Additional exam requirements/recommendations for international students: Recommended—TOEFL (minimum score 525 paper-based). Electronic applications accepted.

Alcorn State University, School of Graduate Studies, School of Psychology and Education, Lorman, MS 39096-7500. Offers agricultural education (MS Ed); elementary education (MS Ed, Ed S); guidance and counseling (MS Ed); industrial education (MS Ed); secondary education (MS Ed), including health and physical education; special education (MS Ed). *Accreditation:* NCATE. *Degree requirements:* For master's, thesis optional.

Alfred University, Graduate School, Division of Education, Alfred, NY 14802-1205. Offers college student development (MS Ed); literacy (MS Ed). *Accreditation:* TEAC. *Program availability:* Part-time. *Faculty:* 4 full-time (3 women), 3 part-time/adjunct (2 women). *Students:* 50 full-time (38 women), 245 part-time (195 women); includes 169 minority (91 Black or African American, non-Hispanic/Latino; 2 American Indian or Alaska Native, non-Hispanic/Latino; 7 Asian, non-Hispanic/Latino; 69 Hispanic/Latino). Average age 34. In 2016, 21 master's awarded. *Entrance requirements:* For master's, Liberal Arts and Sciences Test (LAST), Assessment of Teaching Skills (written) (ATS-W), Content Specialty Test (CST). Additional exam requirements/recommendations for international students: Required—TOEFL (minimum score 590 paper-based; 90 iBT), IELTS (minimum score 6.5). *Application deadline:* For fall admission, 8/1 for domestic students, 3/15 for international students; for spring admission, 12/1 for domestic students, 10/1 for international students. Applications are processed on a rolling basis. Application fee: $60. Electronic applications accepted. *Expenses: Tuition:* Full-time $38,020; part-time $810 per credit. *Required fees:* $970; $82 per semester. *Financial support:* Research assistantships with partial tuition reimbursements, tuition waivers (partial), and unspecified assistantships available. Financial award applicants required to submit FAFSA. *Unit head:* Kevin Curtin, Program Director, 607-871-2699. *Application contact:* Sara Love, Coordinator of Graduate Admissions, 607-871-2115, Fax: 607-871-2198, E-mail: gradinquiry@alfred.edu.
Website: http://www.alfred.edu/gradschool/education/

Alliant International University–Los Angeles, Shirley M. Hufstedler School of Education, TeachersCHOICE Preparation Programs, Alhambra, CA 91803. Offers MA, Credential. *Program availability:* Part-time. *Entrance requirements:* For master's, CBEST, CSET, interview; offer of employment as a teacher of record in a California school; minimum GPA of 2.5; 2 letters of recommendation. Additional exam requirements/recommendations for international students: Required—TOEFL (minimum score 550 paper-based). *Faculty research:* Multicultural and bilingual education pedagogy, teacher training pedagogy, curriculum development, instructional strategies.

Alliant International University–Sacramento, Shirley M. Hufstedler School of Education, TeachersCHOICE Preparation Programs, Sacramento, CA 95833. Offers MA, Credential. *Entrance requirements:* For master's, CBEST, CSET, interview; offer of employment as a teacher of record in a California school; minimum GPA of 3.0; 2 letters of recommendation. Electronic applications accepted. *Faculty research:* Innovative teacher education, educational leadership, cross-cultural education.

Alliant International University–San Diego, Shirley M. Hufstedler School of Education, Teacher Education Programs, San Diego, CA 92131. Offers preliminary single subject (Credential); professional clear multiple subject (Credential); professional clear single subject (Credential); teacher education (MA). *Program availability:* Part-time, evening/weekend. *Entrance requirements:* For degree, California Basic Educational Skills Test, minimum GPA of 2.5. Additional exam requirements/recommendations for international students: Required—TOEFL (minimum score 550 paper-based; 80 iBT), TWE (minimum score 5). Electronic applications accepted. *Faculty research:* Curriculum and instructional planning.

Alliant International University–San Francisco, Shirley M. Hufstedler School of Education, Teacher Education Programs, San Francisco, CA 94133. Offers auditory oral education (Certificate); CLAD (Certificate); education specialist: mild/moderate disabilities (Credential); preliminary multiple subject (Credential); preliminary single subject (Credential); professional clear multiple subject (Credential); professional clear single subject (Credential); special education (MA); teaching (MA); TESOL (Certificate). *Program availability:* Part-time, evening/weekend. *Degree requirements:* For master's, thesis. *Entrance requirements:* For degree, California Basic Educational Skills Test, minimum GPA of 2.5. Additional exam requirements/recommendations for international students: Required—TOEFL (minimum score 550 paper-based), TWE (minimum score 5). Electronic applications accepted. *Faculty research:* Curriculum development, first year teachers, cross-cultural issues in teaching, biliteracy.

Alvernia University, School of Graduate Studies, Program in Education, Reading, PA 19607-1799. Offers urban education (M Ed). *Program availability:* Part-time, evening/weekend. *Degree requirements:* For master's, thesis optional. *Entrance requirements:* For master's, GRE or MAT (alumni excluded). Electronic applications accepted.

Alverno College, School of Education, Milwaukee, WI 53234-3922. Offers adaptive education (MA); administrative leadership (MA); adult education and organizational development (MA); adult educational and instructional design (MA); adult educational and instructional technology (MA); global connections in the humanities (MA); instructional leadership (MA); instructional technology for K-12 settings (MA); professional development (MA); reading education (MA); reading education with adaptive education (MA); science education (MA); special education (MA); teaching in alternative schools (MA). *Accreditation:* NCATE. *Program availability:* Part-time, evening/weekend. *Faculty:* 4 full-time (3 women), 23 part-time/adjunct (17 women). *Students:* 58 full-time (57 women), 62 part-time (54 women); includes 32 minority (22 Black or African American, non-Hispanic/Latino; 2 Asian, non-Hispanic/Latino; 8 Hispanic/Latino), 1 international. Average age 39. 77 applicants, 99% accepted, 61 enrolled. In 2016, 85 master's awarded. *Degree requirements:* For master's, presentation/defense of proposal, conference presentation of inquiry projects. *Entrance requirements:* For master's, bachelor's degree in related field, communication samples from work setting, 3 letters of recommendation. Additional exam requirements/recommendations for international students: Required—TOEFL. *Application deadline:* For fall admission, 7/15 priority date for domestic and international students; for spring admission, 12/15 priority date for domestic and international students. Applications are processed on a rolling basis. Application fee: $0. Electronic applications accepted. *Expenses:* Contact institution. *Financial support:* In 2016–17, 17 students received support. Federal Work-Study and scholarships/grants available. Support available to part-time students. Financial award applicants required to submit FAFSA. *Faculty research:* Student self-assessment, self-reflection, integration of curriculum, identifying needs of students in strategic situations and designing appropriate classroom strategies. *Unit head:* Dr. Desiree Pointer Mace, Associate Dean, Graduate Program, 414-382-6345, Fax: 414-382-6332, E-mail: desiree.pointer-mace@alverno.edu. *Application contact:* Katie Kipp, Graduate Admissions Counselor, 414-382-6045, Fax: 414-382-6354, E-mail: katie.kipp@alverno.edu.

American College of Education, Graduate Programs, Indianapolis, IN 46204. Offers curriculum and instruction (M Ed), including bilingual, ESL; educational leadership (M Ed); educational technology (M Ed).

American InterContinental University Online, Program in Education, Schaumburg, IL 60173. Offers curriculum and instruction (M Ed); educational assessment and evaluation (M Ed); instructional technology (M Ed); leadership of educational organizations (M Ed). *Accreditation:* TEAC. *Program availability:* Evening/weekend, online learning. *Entrance requirements:* Additional exam requirements/recommendations for international students: Required—TOEFL (minimum score 550 paper-based). Electronic applications accepted.

American International College, Low Residency Programs, Springfield, MA 01109-3189. Offers counseling psychology (MA); educational leadership and supervision (Ed D); individual and institutional development (Ed D); professional counseling and supervision (Ed D); psychology (Ed D); teaching and learning (Ed D). *Expenses: Tuition:* Full-time $7902; part-time $750 per semester hour. *Required fees:* $60; $60 per semester hour. $30 per semester. One-time fee: $100. Tuition and fees vary according to course load, degree level, campus/location and program. *Application contact:* Kerry Barnes, Director of Graduate Admissions, 413-205-3703, Fax: 413-205-3051, E-mail: kerry.barnes@aic.edu.

American International College, School of Education, Springfield, MA 01109-3189. Offers early childhood education (M Ed, CAGS); elementary education (M Ed, CAGS); middle education/secondary education (M Ed, CAGS); moderate disabilities (M Ed, CAGS); reading specialist (M Ed, CAGS); school adjustment counseling (MAEP, CAGS); school guidance counseling (MAEP, CAGS); school leadership (M Ed, CAGS). *Program availability:* Evening/weekend. *Faculty:* 1 (woman) full-time, 90 part-time/adjunct (63 women). *Students:* 1,194 full-time (970 women), 118 part-time (83 women); includes 108 minority (15 Black or African American, non-Hispanic/Latino; 4 American Indian or Alaska Native, non-Hispanic/Latino; 12 Asian, non-Hispanic/Latino; 55 Hispanic/Latino; 2 Native Hawaiian or other Pacific Islander, non-Hispanic/Latino; 20 Two or more races, non-Hispanic/Latino). Average age 34. 517 applicants, 417 enrolled. In 2016, 879 master's, 194 CAGSs awarded. Terminal master's awarded for partial completion of doctoral program. *Degree requirements:* For master's, comprehensive exam (for some programs), thesis (for some programs), practicum/culminating experience; for CAGS, practicum/culminating experience. *Entrance requirements:* For master's, Communication and Literacy portion of the Massachusetts Tests for Education Licensure, graduate of accredited four-year college with minimum B- average in undergraduate course work; for CAGS, M Ed or master's degree in field related to licensure from accredited institution. *Application deadline:* Applications are processed on a rolling basis. Application fee: $50. Electronic applications accepted. *Expenses:* $439 per credit. *Financial support:* Applicants required to submit FAFSA. *Unit head:* Sylvia Mason, Dean, 413-205-1743, Fax: 413-205-3943, E-mail: sylvia.mason@aic.edu. *Application contact:* Kerry Barnes, Dean of Graduate Admissions, 413-205-3703, Fax: 413-205-3051, E-mail: kerry.barnes@aic.edu.
Website: http://www.aic.edu/school-of-education/

American Jewish University, Graduate School of Education, Program in Education, Bel Air, CA 90077-1599. Offers MA Ed. *Degree requirements:* For master's, one foreign language. *Entrance requirements:* For master's, GRE General Test, interview, minimum GPA of 3.0. Additional exam requirements/recommendations for international students: Required—TOEFL. *Faculty research:* Philosophy of education, curriculum development, teacher training.

American Jewish University, Graduate School of Education, Program in Education for Working Professionals, Bel Air, CA 90077-1599. Offers MA Ed. *Degree requirements:* For master's, comprehensive exam, internships. *Entrance requirements:* For master's, GRE General Test, interview. Additional exam requirements/recommendations for international students: Required—TOEFL.

American University, School of Education, Washington, DC 20016-8030. Offers M Ed, MA, MAT, Certificate, M Ed/MPA, M Ed/MPP, MAT/MA. *Accreditation:* NCATE. *Program availability:* Part-time, evening/weekend. *Faculty:* 14 full-time (11 women), 27 part-time/adjunct (18 women). *Students:* 79 full-time (68 women), 91 part-time (72 women); includes 59 minority (32 Black or African American, non-Hispanic/Latino; 11 Asian, non-Hispanic/Latino; 11 Hispanic/Latino; 5 Two or more races, non-Hispanic/Latino), 7 international. Average age 28. 211 applicants, 89% accepted, 77 enrolled. In 2016, 139 master's, 10 other advanced degrees awarded. *Degree requirements:* For master's, comprehensive exam, thesis or alternative. *Entrance requirements:* For master's, bachelor's degree, statement of purpose, transcripts, 2 letters of recommendation. Additional exam requirements/recommendations for international students: Required—TOEFL (minimum score 100 iBT), IELTS (minimum score 7), PTE (minimum score 68). *Application deadline:* Applications are processed on a rolling basis. Application fee: $55. Electronic applications accepted. *Expenses:* $1,579 per credit tuition; $690 mandatory fees. *Financial support:* Research assistantships, teaching assistantships, institutionally sponsored loans, scholarships/grants, and unspecified assistantships available. Financial award application deadline: 2/1; financial award applicants required to submit FAFSA. *Unit head:* Cheryl Holcomb-McCoy, Dean, 202-885-3720, E-mail: educate@american.edu. *Application contact:* Brittney Cosby, Graduate Programs Coordinator, 202-885-8201, E-mail: bcosby@american.edu.
Website: http://www.american.edu/cas/seth/

The American University in Cairo, Graduate School of Education, Cairo, Egypt. Offers educational leadership (MA); international and comparative education (MA). *Program availability:* Part-time, evening/weekend. *Faculty:* 8 full-time (7 women). *Students:* 6 full-time (5 women), 75 part-time (64 women). Average age 33. 60 applicants, 68% accepted, 27 enrolled. In 2016, 14 master's awarded. *Degree requirements:* For master's, thesis. *Entrance requirements:* Additional exam requirements/recommendations for international students: Required—TOEFL (minimum score 450 paper-based; 45 iBT), IELTS (minimum score 5). *Application deadline:* For fall admission, 2/1 priority date for domestic and international students; for spring admission, 10/15 priority date for domestic and international students. Applications are processed on a rolling basis. Application fee: $80. Electronic applications accepted. *Expenses:* Contact institution. *Financial support:* Fellowships with partial tuition reimbursements, teaching assistantships, career-related internships or fieldwork, scholarships/grants, tuition waivers (partial), and unspecified assistantships available. Financial award application deadline: 3/10. *Faculty research:* Educational reform. *Unit head:* Dr. Ted Purinton, Dean, 20-2-2615-1490, E-mail: tedpurinton@aucegypt.edu. *Application contact:* Maha Hegazi, Director for Graduate Admissions, 20-2-2615-1462, E-mail: mahahegazi@aucegypt.edu.
Website: http://www.aucegypt.edu/GSE/Pages/default.aspx

The American University in Dubai, Graduate Programs, Dubai, United Arab Emirates. Offers construction management (MS); education (M Ed); finance (MBA); generalist (MBA); marketing (MBA). *Program availability:* Part-time, evening/weekend. *Degree requirements:* For master's, thesis optional. *Entrance requirements:* For master's, GMAT (for MBA); GRE (for M Ed and MS), minimum undergraduate GPA of 3.0, official transcripts, two reference forms, curriculum vitae/resume, statement of career objectives, work experience. Additional exam requirements/recommendations for international students: Required—TOEFL (minimum score 550 paper-based; 79 iBT). Electronic applications accepted.

American University of Beirut, Graduate Programs, Faculty of Arts and Sciences, Beirut, Lebanon. Offers anthropology (MA); Arab and Middle Eastern history (PhD); Arabic language and literature (MA, PhD); archaeology (MA); art history and curating (MA); biology (MS); cell and molecular biology (PhD); chemistry (MS); clinical psychology (MA); computational sciences (MS); computer science (MS); economics (MA); education (MA); English language (MA); English literature (MA); environmental policy planning (MS); financial economics (MAFE); geology (MS); history (MA); Islamic studies (MA); mathematics (MS); media studies (MA); Middle Eastern studies (MA); physics (MS); political studies (MA); psychology (MA); public administration (MA); public policy and international affairs (MA); sociology (MA); statistics (MA, MS); theoretical physics (PhD); transnational American studies (MA). *Program availability:* Part-time. *Faculty:* 133 full-time (42 women), 6 part-time/adjunct (2 women). *Students:* 240 full-time (172 women), 227 part-time (166 women). Average age 27. 286 applicants, 67% accepted, 108 enrolled. In 2016, 60 master's, 3 doctorates awarded. Terminal master's awarded for partial completion of doctoral program. *Degree requirements:* For master's, one foreign language, comprehensive exam, thesis (for some programs); for doctorate, one foreign language, comprehensive exam, thesis/dissertation. *Entrance requirements:* For master's, GRE (for some MA, MS programs), letters of recommendation; for doctorate, GRE, letters of recommendation. Additional exam requirements/recommendations for international students: Required—TOEFL (minimum score 600 paper-based; 97 iBT), IELTS (minimum score 7). *Application deadline:* For fall admission, 4/3 for domestic students; for winter admission, 11/3 for domestic students. Application fee: $50. Electronic applications accepted. *Expenses:* Contact institution. *Financial support:* In 2016–17, 4 fellowships (averaging $11,200 per year), 18 research assistantships (averaging $5,400 per year) were awarded; teaching assistantships, career-related internships or fieldwork, Federal Work-Study, institutionally sponsored loans, scholarships/grants, traineeships, health care benefits, tuition waivers (full), and unspecified assistantships also available. Support available to part-time students. *Faculty research:* Development economics, spatial econometrics, health economics, labor economics, energy economics, hydrogeology, geophysics, petrophysics, structural geology, mineralogy, petrology, geochemistry, multilingualism, comparative/world literature, translation studies, book histories/ cultures, biocatalysis, molecular recognition, photocatalysis, photophysical and biophysical chemistry, probe chemistry,

machine learning, data science. *Unit head:* Dr. Nadia Maria El Cheikh, Dean, Faculty of Arts and Sciences, 961-1374374 Ext. 3800, Fax: 961-1744461, E-mail: nmcheikh@aub.edu.lb. *Application contact:* Dr. Salim Kanaan, Director, Admissions Office, 961-1350000 Ext. 2590, Fax: 961-1750775, E-mail: sk00@aub.edu.lb.
Website: http://www.aub.edu.lb/fas/

American University of Puerto Rico, Program in Education, Bayamon, PR 00960-2037. Offers art education (M Ed); elementary education 4-6 (M Ed); elementary education K-3 (M Ed); general science education (M Ed); physical education (M Ed); special education (M Ed). *Program availability:* Part-time, evening/weekend. *Faculty:* 17 part-time/adjunct (7 women). *Students:* 22 full-time (18 women), 54 part-time (42 women); all minorities (all Hispanic/Latino). Average age 33. 22 applicants, 86% accepted, 19 enrolled. In 2016, 53 master's awarded. *Entrance requirements:* For master's, EXADEP, GRE, or MAT, 2 letters of recommendation, minimum GPA of 2.5. *Application deadline:* For fall admission, 8/1 for domestic students; for winter admission, 10/18 for domestic students; for spring admission, 3/15 for domestic students. Applications are processed on a rolling basis. Application fee: $25. *Financial support:* In 2016–17, 79 students received support, including 76 fellowships (averaging $400 per year), 55 teaching assistantships (averaging $1,741 per year). Financial award applicants required to submit FAFSA. *Unit head:* Prof. Bolivar Ramirez-Carlo, III, Dean of Faculty, 787-620-2040 Ext. 2010, Fax: 787-620-2958, E-mail: bramirez@aupr.edu. *Application contact:* Keren I. Llanos-Figueroa, Information Contact, 787-620-2040 Ext. 2021, Fax: 787-785-7377, E-mail: oficnaadmisiones@aupr.edu.

Anderson University, College of Education, Anderson, SC 29621-4035. Offers administration and supervision (M Ed); education (M Ed); elementary education (MAT). *Accreditation:* NCATE. *Program availability:* 100% online. *Expenses:* Contact institution. *Financial support:* Tuition waivers available. Financial award application deadline: 3/1; financial award applicants required to submit FAFSA. *Unit head:* Dr. Mark Butler, Dean, 864-231-2042. *Application contact:* Mallory Knight, Graduate Admission Counselor, 864-231-2182, Fax: 864-231-2115, E-mail: malloryknight@andersonuniversity.edu.
Website: https://www.andersonuniversity.edu/education

Anderson University, School of Education, Anderson, IN 46012-3495. Offers M Ed. *Accreditation:* NCATE.

Andrews University, School of Graduate Studies, School of Education, Berrien Springs, MI 49104. Offers MA, MAT, MS, Ed D, PhD, Ed S. *Accreditation:* NCATE. *Program availability:* Part-time. *Faculty:* 21 full-time (9 women), 5 part-time/adjunct (2 women). *Students:* 127 full-time (82 women), 76 part-time (49 women); includes 74 minority (42 Black or African American, non-Hispanic/Latino; 3 Asian, non-Hispanic/Latino; 26 Hispanic/Latino; 3 Two or more races, non-Hispanic/Latino), 42 international. Average age 41. In 2016, 39 master's, 17 doctorates, 2 other advanced degrees awarded. Terminal master's awarded for partial completion of doctoral program. *Degree requirements:* For doctorate, thesis/dissertation. *Entrance requirements:* For master's, GRE Subject Test. Additional exam requirements/recommendations for international students: Required—TOEFL (minimum score 550 paper-based). *Application deadline:* Applications are processed on a rolling basis. Application fee: $40. *Financial support:* Fellowships, research assistantships, teaching assistantships, career-related internships or fieldwork, Federal Work-Study, institutionally sponsored loans, and tuition waivers (partial) available. Support available to part-time students. *Faculty research:* Church planting, bilingual education, leadership development, exercise education. *Unit head:* Dr. Robson Marinho, Dean, 269-471-3464. *Application contact:* Justina Clayburn, Supervisor of Graduate Admission, 800-253-2874, Fax: 269-471-6321, E-mail: graduate@andrews.edu.

Anna Maria College, Graduate Division, Program in Education, Paxton, MA 01612. Offers early childhood education (M Ed); education (CAGS); elementary education (M Ed); English language arts (M Ed); visual arts (M Ed). *Program availability:* Part-time, evening/weekend. *Entrance requirements:* For master's, bachelor's degree in liberal arts or sciences, minimum GPA of 3.0. Additional exam requirements/recommendations for international students: Required—TOEFL (minimum score 500 paper-based). Electronic applications accepted.

Antioch University Los Angeles, Graduate Programs, Program in Education, Culver City, CA 90230. Offers MA. *Program availability:* Evening/weekend. *Entrance requirements:* Additional exam requirements/recommendations for international students: Required—TOEFL.

Antioch University Midwest, Graduate Programs, School of Education, Yellow Springs, OH 45387-1609. Offers conflict management (M Ed); dyslexia (M Ed); early childhood education (M Ed); educational leadership (M Ed); intervention specialist, mild to moderate (M Ed); middle childhood education (M Ed); trauma informed education (M Ed). *Accreditation:* NCATE. *Program availability:* Part-time, evening/weekend. *Degree requirements:* For master's, thesis or alternative. *Entrance requirements:* For master's, resume, goal statement, interview. *Application deadline:* For fall admission, 9/7 for domestic students; for winter admission, 12/10 for domestic students; for spring admission, 3/10 for domestic students. Applications are processed on a rolling basis. Application fee: $50. Electronic applications accepted. *Expenses:* $675 per credit hour. *Financial support:* Federal Work-Study available. Financial award applicants required to submit FAFSA. *Unit head:* Dr. Marian Glancy, Director, 937-769-1880, Fax: 937-769-1805, E-mail: mglancy@antioch.edu. *Application contact:* Deena Kent-Hummel, Director of Admissions, 937-769-1823, Fax: 937-769-1804, E-mail: dkent@antioch.edu.
Website: https://www.antioch.edu/midwest/degrees-programs/education-degree/

Antioch University New England, Graduate School, Department of Education, Keene, NH 03431-3552. Offers integrated learning (M Ed), including elementary and early childhood education, elementary education (M Ed, Certificate); teaching (M Ed, PMC), including foundations of education (M Ed), principal certification (PMC); Waldorf teacher training (M Ed, Certificate), including elementary education, foundations of education (M Ed). *Degree requirements:* For master's, thesis (for some programs), internship. *Entrance requirements:* Additional exam requirements/recommendations for international students: Required—TOEFL (minimum score 550 paper-based). Electronic applications accepted. *Expenses:* Contact institution. *Faculty research:* Classroom and school restructuring, problem-based learning, Waldorf collaborative leadership, ecological literacy.

Antioch University Santa Barbara, Program in Education/Teacher Credentialing, Santa Barbara, CA 93101-1581. Offers M Ed, MA. *Program availability:* Part-time. *Entrance requirements:* Additional exam requirements/recommendations for international students: Required—TOEFL (minimum score 550 paper-based). Electronic applications accepted.

Antioch University Seattle, Graduate Programs, Program in Education, Seattle, WA 98121-1814. Offers adult education (MA); drama therapy (MA); individualized studies (MA); leadership in edible education (MA); teaching (MAT); urban environmental education (MA). *Program availability:* Part-time, evening/weekend. *Degree requirements:* For master's, comprehensive exam (for some programs), thesis. *Entrance requirements:* For master's, WEST-B, WEST-E, current resume, transcripts of undergraduate degree and coursework (or for highest degree completed), two letters of recommendation, proof of fingerprinting and background check, moral character with fitness statement of understanding, documentation of 40 hours' experience in school classroom(s). *Application deadline:* Applications are processed on a rolling basis. *Expenses:* Contact institution. *Financial support:* Research assistantships, Federal Work-Study, scholarships/grants, and unspecified assistantships available. Financial award application deadline: 6/15. *Faculty research:* Visual thinking and science education, K-8 equity and engaged pedagogy in science education, K-12 inquiry-based mathematics education, education in prisons and other institutions of confinement. *Unit head:* Ed Mikel, Interim Dean, 206-268-4617, E-mail: emikel@antioch.edu. *Application contact:* Eileen Knight, Recruitment and Admissions Director, 206-268-4200, E-mail: eknight@antioch.edu.
Website: https://www.antioch.edu/seattle/degrees-programs/education-degrees/

Aquinas College, School of Education, Nashville, TN 37205-2005. Offers elementary education (MAT); secondary education (MAT); teaching and learning (M Ed). *Unit head:* Sr. Mary Anne Zuberbueler, OP, Dean, 615-297-7545 Ext. 282, Fax: 615-279-3892, E-mail: srmanne@aquinascollege.edu.

Aquinas College, School of Education, Grand Rapids, MI 49506. Offers M Ed, MAT. *Accreditation:* TEAC. *Program availability:* Part-time, evening/weekend. *Degree requirements:* For master's, teaching project; action research. *Entrance requirements:* For master's, Michigan Basic Skills Test, minimum undergraduate GPA of 3.0, teaching certificate. Additional exam requirements/recommendations for international students: Required—TOEFL (minimum score 550 paper-based). *Application deadline:* Applications are processed on a rolling basis. Application fee: $0. *Expenses:* Contact institution. *Financial support:* Scholarships/grants available. Support available to part-time students. Financial award application deadline: 3/15. *Unit head:* Dr. Susan English, Dean, 616-632-2800, Fax: 616-732-4465, E-mail: englisus@aquinas.edu. *Application contact:* Administrative Assistant, 616-632-2440.
Website: http://www.aquinas.edu/education/

Arcadia University, School of Education, Glenside, PA 19038-3295. Offers art education (M Ed); computer education (CAS); curriculum (CAS); curriculum studies (M Ed); early childhood education (M Ed), including individualized, master teacher, research in child development; educational leadership (M Ed, Ed D, CAS); elementary education (M Ed); English education (MA Ed); environmental education (MA Ed); instructional technology (M Ed); language arts (M Ed); library science (M Ed); mathematics education (M Ed, MA Ed); music education (MA Ed); psychology (MA Ed); reading (M Ed, CAS); science education (M Ed, CAS); secondary education (M Ed, CAS); special education (M Ed, Ed D, CAS); theater arts (MA Ed); written communication (MA Ed). *Accreditation:* NASAD. *Program availability:* Part-time, evening/weekend, online learning. *Faculty:* 19 full-time (13 women), 3 part-time/adjunct (all women). *Students:* 22 full-time (16 women), 356 part-time (284 women); includes 84 minority (55 Black or African American, non-Hispanic/Latino; 2 American Indian or Alaska Native, non-Hispanic/Latino; 13 Asian, non-Hispanic/Latino; 11 Hispanic/Latino; 3 Two or more races, non-Hispanic/Latino), 4 international. Average age 34. 145 applicants, 73% accepted, 80 enrolled. In 2016, 95 master's, 11 doctorates awarded. *Application deadline:* Applications are processed on a rolling basis. Application fee: $50. Electronic applications accepted. *Expenses:* Contact institution. *Financial support:* Career-related internships or fieldwork, tuition waivers (partial), and unspecified assistantships available. *Unit head:* John T Groves, Interim Dean of the School of Education, 215-572-2940. *Application contact:* 215-572-2925, Fax: 215-572-2126, E-mail: grad@arcadia.edu.

Argosy University, Atlanta, College of Education, Atlanta, GA 30328. Offers educational leadership (MAEd, Ed D, Ed S), including higher education administration (Ed D), K-12 education (Ed D); teaching and learning (MAEd, Ed D, Ed S), including education technology (Ed D), higher education (Ed D), K-12 education (Ed D).

Argosy University, Chicago, College of Education, Chicago, IL 60601. Offers adult education and training (MA Ed); community college executive leadership (Ed D); educational leadership (MA Ed, Ed D, Ed S), including district leadership (Ed D), higher education administration (Ed D), K-12 education (Ed D); instructional leadership (Ed D, Ed S), including higher education (Ed D), K-12 education (Ed D). *Program availability:* Online learning.

Argosy University, Dallas, College of Education, Farmers Branch, TX 75244. Offers educational administration (MA Ed); educational leadership (Ed D); higher and postsecondary education (MA Ed); instructional leadership (MA Ed); school psychology (MA).

Argosy University, Denver, College of Education, Denver, CO 80231. Offers community college executive leadership (Ed D); educational leadership (MA Ed, Ed D), including higher education (Ed D), K-12 education (Ed D); instructional leadership (MA Ed, Ed D), including higher education administration (Ed D), K-12 education (Ed D).

Argosy University, Hawai`i, College of Education, Honolulu, HI 96813. Offers adult education and training (MAEd); educational leadership (Ed D), including higher education administration, K-12 education; instructional leadership (Ed D), including higher education, K-12 education; school psychology (MA).

Argosy University, Inland Empire, College of Education, Ontario, CA 91761. Offers community college executive leadership (Ed D); educational leadership (MA Ed, Ed D), including higher education administration (Ed D), K-12 education (Ed D); instructional leadership (MA Ed, Ed D), including higher education (Ed D), K-12 education (Ed D), multiple subject teacher preparation (MA Ed), single subject teacher preparation (MA Ed).

Argosy University, Los Angeles, College of Education, Santa Monica, CA 90045. Offers community college executive leadership (Ed D); educational leadership (MA Ed, Ed D), including higher education administration (Ed D), K-12 education (Ed D); instructional leadership (MA Ed, Ed D), including higher education (Ed D), K-12 education (Ed D), multiple subject teacher preparation (MA Ed), single subject teacher preparation (MA Ed).

Argosy University, Nashville, College of Education, Nashville, TN 37214. Offers MA Ed, Ed D, Ed S.

Argosy University, Northern Virginia, College of Education, Arlington, VA 22209. Offers community college executive leadership (Ed D); educational leadership (MA Ed, Ed D, Ed S), including higher education administration (Ed D), K-12 education (Ed D); instructional leadership (MA Ed, Ed D, Ed S), including higher education (Ed D), K-12 education (Ed D).

Argosy University, Orange County, College of Education, Orange, CA 92868. Offers community college executive leadership (Ed D); educational leadership (MA Ed, Ed D), including higher education administration (Ed D), K-12 education (Ed D); instructional leadership (MA Ed, Ed D), including education technology (Ed D), higher education (Ed D), K-12 education (Ed D), multiple subject teacher preparation (MA Ed), single subject teacher preparation (MA Ed).

Argosy University, Phoenix, College of Education, Phoenix, AZ 85021. Offers adult education and training (MA Ed); advanced educational administration (Ed D, Ed S); community college executive leadership (Ed D); educational administration (MA Ed); educational leadership (MA Ed, Ed D, Ed S), including education technology (Ed D), higher education administration (Ed D), K-12 education (Ed D); higher and postsecondary education (MA Ed); initial educational administration (Ed D, Ed S); school psychology (MA); teaching and learning (MA Ed, Ed D, Ed S), including education technology (Ed D), higher education (Ed D), K-12 education (Ed D).

Argosy University, Salt Lake City, College of Education, Draper, UT 84020. Offers educational leadership (MA Ed, Ed D).

Argosy University, San Diego, College of Education, San Diego, CA 92108. Offers community college executive leadership (Ed D); educational leadership (MA Ed, Ed D), including higher education administration (Ed D), K-12 education (Ed D); instructional leadership (MA Ed, Ed D), including higher education (Ed D), K-12 education (Ed D).

Argosy University, San Francisco Bay Area, College of Education, Alameda, CA 94501. Offers community college executive leadership (Ed D); educational leadership (MA Ed, Ed D), including education technology (Ed D), higher education administration (Ed D), K-12 education (Ed D); instructional leadership (MA Ed, Ed D), including education technology (Ed D), higher education (Ed D), K-12 education (Ed D), multiple subject teacher preparation (MA Ed), single subject teacher preparation (MA Ed).

Argosy University, Sarasota, College of Education, Sarasota, FL 34235. Offers community college executive leadership (Ed D); educational leadership (MA Ed, Ed D, Ed S), including higher education administration (Ed D), K-12 education (Ed D); school counseling (MA, Ed S); school psychology (MA); teaching and learning (MA Ed, Ed D, Ed S), including education technology (Ed D), higher education (Ed D), K-12 education (Ed D).

Argosy University, Seattle, College of Education, Seattle, WA 98121. Offers adult education and training (MA Ed); community college executive leadership (Ed D); educational leadership (MA Ed, Ed D), including higher education administration (Ed D), K-12 education (Ed D); higher and postsecondary education (MA Ed); instructional leadership (MA Ed, Ed D), including education technology (Ed D), higher education (Ed D), K-12 education (Ed D).

Argosy University, Tampa, College of Education, Tampa, FL 33607. Offers community college executive leadership (Ed D); educational leadership (MA Ed, Ed D, Ed S), including higher education administration (Ed D), K-12 education (Ed D); school counseling (MA); teaching and learning (MA Ed, Ed D, Ed S), including higher education (Ed D), K-12 education (Ed D).

Argosy University, Twin Cities, College of Education, Eagan, MN 55121. Offers advanced educational administration (Ed D, Ed S); educational leadership (MA Ed, Ed D, Ed S), including higher education administration (Ed D), K-12 education (Ed D); higher and postsecondary education (MA Ed); initial educational administration (Ed D, Ed S); instructional leadership (MA Ed, Ed D, Ed S), including education technology (Ed D), higher education (Ed D), K-12 education (Ed D).

Arizona State University at the Tempe campus, Mary Lou Fulton Teachers College, Phoenix, AZ 85069. Offers M Ed, MA, MC, MPE, Ed D, PhD, Graduate Certificate. *Program availability:* Part-time, evening/weekend, online learning. *Degree requirements:* For master's, comprehensive exam (for some programs), thesis (for some programs), interactive Program of Study (iPOS) submitted before completing 50 percent of required credit hours; for doctorate, comprehensive exam, thesis/dissertation, interactive Program of Study (iPOS) submitted before completing 50 percent of required credit hours. *Entrance requirements:* For master's and doctorate, GRE General Test or GMAT, minimum GPA of 3.0 or equivalent in last 2 years of work leading to bachelor's degree. Additional exam requirements/recommendations for international students: Required—TOEFL, IELTS, or PTE. Electronic applications accepted. *Expenses:* Contact institution.

Arkansas State University, Graduate School, College of Education and Behavioral Science, State University, AR 72467. Offers MAT, MRC, MS, MSE, Ed D, Ed S, Graduate Certificate, SCCT. *Accreditation:* NCATE. *Program availability:* Part-time, online learning. *Degree requirements:* For master's and other advanced degree, comprehensive exam, thesis or alternative; for doctorate, comprehensive exam, thesis/dissertation. *Entrance requirements:* For master's, GRE General Test or MAT, appropriate bachelor's degree, interview, letters of reference, official transcripts, immunization records; for doctorate, GRE General Test or MAT, interview, master's degree, letters of reference, official transcript, personal statement, immunization records, writing sample; for other advanced degree, GRE General Test, MAT, interview, master's degree, letters of reference, official transcript, 3 years of teaching experience, teaching license, immunization records. Additional exam requirements/recommendations for international students: Required—TOEFL (minimum score 550 paper-based; 79 iBT), IELTS (minimum score 6), PTE (minimum score 56). Electronic applications accepted.

Arkansas Tech University, College of Education, Russellville, AR 72801. Offers college student personnel (MS); educational leadership (M Ed, Ed S); elementary education (M Ed); instructional improvement (M Ed); instructional technology (M Ed); school counseling and leadership (M Ed); school leadership (Ed D); strength and conditioning studies (MS); teaching (MAT); teaching, learning, and leadership (M Ed). *Accreditation:* NCATE. *Program availability:* Part-time, evening/weekend, online learning. *Students:* 72 full-time (43 women), 371 part-time (283 women); includes 108 minority (80 Black or African American, non-Hispanic/Latino; 1 American Indian or Alaska Native, non-Hispanic/Latino; 4 Asian, non-Hispanic/Latino; 13 Hispanic/Latino; 10 Two or more races, non-Hispanic/Latino), 6 international. Average age 33. In 2016, 181 master's, 1 other advanced degree awarded. *Degree requirements:* For master's, comprehensive exam, thesis optional, action research project. *Entrance requirements:* Additional exam requirements/recommendations for international students: Required—TOEFL (minimum score 550 paper-based; 79 iBT), IELTS (minimum score 6.5). *Application deadline:* For fall admission, 3/1 priority date for domestic students, 5/1 priority date for international students; for spring admission, 10/1 priority date for domestic and international students. Applications are processed on a rolling basis. Application fee: $25 ($75 for international students). Electronic applications accepted. *Expenses:* Tuition, state resident: full-time $4932; part-time $274 per credit hour. Tuition, nonresident: full-time $9864; part-time $548 per credit hour. *Required fees:* $513 per semester. Tuition and fees vary according to course load. *Financial support:* In 2016–17, research assistantships with full tuition reimbursements (averaging $4,800 per year), teaching assistantships with full tuition reimbursements (averaging $4,800 per year) were awarded; career-related internships or fieldwork, Federal Work-Study, scholarships/grants, health care benefits, and unspecified assistantships also available. Support available to part-time students. Financial award application deadline: 4/15; financial award applicants required to submit FAFSA. *Unit head:* Dr. Mary Gunter, Dean, 479-964-3217, E-mail: mgunter@atu.edu.
Website: http://www.atu.edu/education/

Arlington Baptist College, Program in Education, Arlington, TX 76012-3425. Offers curriculum and instruction (M Ed); educational leadership (M Ed). *Degree requirements:* For master's, professional portfolio; internship (for educational leadership). *Entrance requirements:* For master's, bachelor's degree from accredited college or university with minimum GPA of 3.0, minimum of 12 hours in Bible; minimum of three years' classroom teaching experience in an accredited K-12 public or private school (for educational leadership only).

Armstrong State University, School of Graduate Studies, Department of Childhood and Exceptional Student Education, Savannah, GA 31419-1997. Offers early childhood education (M Ed, MAT); reading (Certificate); special education (M Ed, MAT); special education transition specialist (Certificate). *Accreditation:* NCATE. *Program availability:* Part-time, evening/weekend. *Faculty:* 14 full-time (12 women), 1 (woman) part-time/adjunct. *Students:* 10 full-time (9 women), 199 part-time (177 women); includes 67 minority (55 Black or African American, non-Hispanic/Latino; 1 Asian, non-Hispanic/Latino; 5 Hispanic/Latino; 6 Two or more races, non-Hispanic/Latino). Average age 34. 131 applicants, 42% accepted, 45 enrolled. In 2016, 72 master's, 24 other advanced degrees awarded. *Degree requirements:* For master's, portfolio. *Entrance requirements:* For master's, MAT, Georgia Assessment for the Certification of Educators. Additional exam requirements/recommendations for international students: Required—TOEFL (minimum score 523 paper-based; 70 iBT). *Application deadline:* For fall admission, 7/1 priority date for domestic students, 5/1 priority date for international students; for spring admission, 11/15 priority date for domestic students, 9/15 priority date for international students; for summer admission, 4/15 priority date for domestic students, 9/15 for international students. Applications are processed on a rolling basis. Application fee: $30. Electronic applications accepted. *Expenses:* Tuition, state resident: full-time $1781; part-time $161.93 per credit hour. Tuition, nonresident: full-time $6482; part-time $589.27 per credit hour. *Required fees:* $1224 per unit. $612 per semester. Tuition and fees vary according to course load, campus/location and program. *Financial support:* In 2016–17, research assistantships with full tuition reimbursements (averaging $5,000 per year) were awarded; career-related internships or fieldwork, Federal Work-Study, and scholarships/grants also available. Support available to part-time students. Financial award application deadline: 3/15; financial award applicants required to submit FAFSA. *Faculty research:* Literacy, instructional design, poetry, working with local schools. *Unit head:* Dr. John Hobe, Department Head, 912-344-2619, Fax: 912-344-3443, E-mail: john.hobe@armstrong.edu. *Application contact:* McKenzie Peterman, Assistant Director of Graduate Admissions, 912-344-2503, Fax: 912-344-3417, E-mail: graduate@armstrong.edu.
Website: https://www.armstrong.edu/academic-departments/education-ceed

Ashland University, Dwight Schar College of Education, Ashland, OH 44805-3702. Offers M Ed, Ed D. *Accreditation:* NCATE. *Program availability:* Part-time, evening/weekend. *Degree requirements:* For master's, thesis optional, capstone project; for doctorate, comprehensive exam, thesis/dissertation. *Entrance requirements:* For master's, GRE General Test or MAT, teaching certificate, minimum GPA of 2.75; for doctorate, GRE, master's degree, minimum GPA of 3.3, writing sample, letters of recommendation. Additional exam requirements/recommendations for international students: Required—TOEFL. *Application deadline:* For fall admission, 8/27 for domestic students; for spring admission, 1/14 for domestic students. Applications are processed on a rolling basis. Application fee: $30. *Financial support:* Teaching assistantships with partial tuition reimbursements and scholarships/grants available. Financial award application deadline: 4/15. *Faculty research:* Teacher performance, administrative performance, collaborative learning groups, talent development, environmental education. *Unit head:* Dr. James P. Van Keuren, Dean, 419-289-5377, E-mail: jvankeu1@ashland.edu. *Application contact:* Dr. Linda Billman, Associate Dean, 419-289-5369, Fax: 419-289-5331, E-mail: lbillman@ashland.edu.

Athabasca University, Centre for Distance Education, Athabasca, AB T9S 3A3, Canada. Offers distance education (MDE, Ed D); distance education technology (Advanced Diploma). *Program availability:* Part-time, online learning. *Degree requirements:* For master's, thesis optional. *Entrance requirements:* For master's, 3- or 4-year baccalaureate degree. Electronic applications accepted. *Expenses:* Contact institution. *Faculty research:* Role development, interaction, educational technology, and communities of practice in distance education; instructional design.

Athabasca University, Centre for Interdisciplinary Studies, Athabasca, AB T9S 3A3, Canada. Offers adult education (MA); community studies (MA); cultural studies (MA); educational studies (MA); global change (MA); heritage resource management (Postbaccalaureate Certificate); legislative drafting (Postbaccalaureate Certificate); work, organization, and leadership (MA). *Program availability:* Part-time, evening/weekend, online learning. *Degree requirements:* For master's, project. *Entrance requirements:* Additional exam requirements/recommendations for international students: Required—TOEFL (minimum score 560 paper-based). Electronic applications accepted. *Faculty research:* Women's history, literature and culture studies, sustainable development, labor and education.

Auburn University, Graduate School, College of Education, Auburn University, AL 36849. Offers M Ed, MS, Ed D, PhD, Ed S, Graduate Certificate. *Accreditation:* NCATE. *Program availability:* Part-time. *Faculty:* 97 full-time (60 women), 12 part-time/adjunct (7 women). *Students:* 457 full-time (321 women), 515 part-time (344 women); includes 273 minority (209 Black or African American, non-Hispanic/Latino; 4 American Indian or Alaska Native, non-Hispanic/Latino; 8 Asian, non-Hispanic/Latino; 33 Hispanic/Latino; 2 Native Hawaiian or other Pacific Islander, non-Hispanic/Latino; 17 Two or more races, non-Hispanic/Latino), 37 international. Average age 33. 726 applicants, 55% accepted, 256 enrolled. In 2016, 251 master's, 71 doctorates, 65 other advanced degrees awarded. *Degree requirements:* For master's, thesis (for some programs); for doctorate, thesis/dissertation. *Entrance requirements:* For master's, doctorate, and other advanced degree, GRE General Test. Application fee: $50 ($60 for international students). Electronic applications accepted. *Expenses:* Tuition, state resident: full-time $9072; part-time $504 per credit hour. Tuition, nonresident: full-time $27,216; part-time $1512 per credit hour. *Required fees:* $812 per semester. Tuition and fees vary according to degree level and program. *Financial support:* Fellowships, research assistantships, teaching assistantships, career-related internships or fieldwork, and Federal Work-Study available. Support available to part-time students. Financial award application deadline: 3/15; financial award applicants required to submit FAFSA. *Faculty research:* Dropout phenomena, high school students and substance use and abuse. *Unit head:* Dr. Betty Lou Whitford, Dean, 334-844-4446. *Application contact:* Dr. George Flowers, Dean of the Graduate School, 334-844-2125.
Website: http://www.education.auburn.edu/

Auburn University at Montgomery, College of Education, Montgomery, AL 36124-4023. Offers M Ed, Ed S. *Accreditation:* NCATE. *Program availability:* Part-time, evening/weekend. *Faculty:* 25 full-time (15 women), 11 part-time/adjunct (9 women). *Students:* 80 full-time (63 women), 170 part-time (141 women); includes 72 minority (68 Black or African American, non-Hispanic/Latino; 2 Asian, non-Hispanic/Latino; 1 Hispanic/Latino; 1 Two or more races, non-Hispanic/Latino), 3 international. Average age 33. *Degree requirements:* For master's and Ed S, comprehensive exam. *Entrance requirements:* For master's, GRE General Test or MAT, BS in teaching, certification; for Ed S, GRE General Test or MAT, certification. Additional exam requirements/recommendations for international students: Recommended—TOEFL (minimum score 500 paper-based; 61 iBT), IELTS (minimum score 5.5), TSE (minimum score 44). *Application deadline:* Applications are processed on a rolling basis. Electronic applications accepted. *Expenses:* Tuition, state resident: full-time $6462; part-time $359 per credit hour. Tuition, nonresident: full-time $14,526; part-time $807 per credit hour. *Required fees:* $554. *Financial support:* In 2016–17, 5 teaching assistantships were awarded; career-related internships or fieldwork and scholarships/grants also available.

Support available to part-time students. Financial award application deadline: 3/1; financial award applicants required to submit FAFSA. *Unit head:* Dr. Sheila Austin, Dean, 334-244-3425, Fax: 334-244-3102, E-mail: saustin1@aum.edu. *Application contact:* Dr. Rhonda Morton, Associate Dean/Graduate Coordinator, 334-224-3287, Fax: 334-244-3978, E-mail: rmorton@aum.edu.
Website: http://www.education.aum.edu/

Augsburg College, Program in Education, Minneapolis, MN 55454-1351. Offers MAE. *Accreditation:* NCATE. *Program availability:* Part-time, evening/weekend. *Degree requirements:* For master's, comprehensive exam, final project. *Entrance requirements:* For master's, minimum GPA of 3.0. Additional exam requirements/recommendations for international students: Required—TOEFL (minimum score 600 paper-based). Electronic applications accepted.

Augustana University, MA in Education Program, Sioux Falls, SD 57197. Offers instructional strategies (MA); reading (MA); special populations (MA); STEM (MA); technology (MA). *Accreditation:* NCATE. *Program availability:* Part-time, evening/weekend, online only, 100% online. *Degree requirements:* For master's, thesis. *Entrance requirements:* For master's, appropriate bachelor's degree, minimum GPA of 3.0, teaching certificate. Additional exam requirements/recommendations for international students: Required—TOEFL (minimum score 550 paper-based). *Application deadline:* For fall admission, 8/1 for domestic and international students; for spring admission, 11/1 for domestic and international students; for summer admission, 4/1 for domestic and international students. Applications are processed on a rolling basis. Application fee: $50. Electronic applications accepted. *Expenses:* Contact institution. *Financial support:* Application deadline: 3/1; applicants required to submit FAFSA. *Unit head:* Dr. Laurie Daily, Chair, 605-274-5211, E-mail: laurie.daily@augie.edu. *Application contact:* Jody Nitz, Graduate Coordinator, 605-274-4043, Fax: 605-274-4450, E-mail: graduate@augie.edu.
Website: http://www.augie.edu/master-arts-education

Aurora University, School of Education and Human Performance, Aurora, IL 60506-4892. Offers bilingual-ESL education (MA); educational leadership (MA); educational technology (MA); leadership in administration (Ed D); leadership in adult learning and higher education (Ed D); leadership in curriculum and instruction (Ed D); reading instruction (MA); special education (MA). *Accreditation:* NCATE. *Program availability:* Part-time, evening/weekend. *Faculty:* 22 full-time (12 women), 46 part-time/adjunct (27 women). *Students:* 36 full-time (30 women), 559 part-time (372 women); includes 68 minority (27 Black or African American, non-Hispanic/Latino; 1 American Indian or Alaska Native, non-Hispanic/Latino; 6 Asian, non-Hispanic/Latino; 29 Hispanic/Latino; 2 Native Hawaiian or other Pacific Islander, non-Hispanic/Latino; 3 Two or more races, non-Hispanic/Latino). Average age 37. 126 applicants, 98% accepted, 72 enrolled. In 2016, 178 master's, 27 doctorates awarded. *Degree requirements:* For master's, student teaching; for doctorate, comprehensive exam, thesis/dissertation. *Entrance requirements:* For master's, 2 years of teaching experience, valid teaching certificate; for doctorate, appropriate master's degree, two references, curriculum vitae, personal statement, professional project, reflective essay. Additional exam requirements/recommendations for international students: Required—TOEFL (minimum score 550 paper-based; 79 iBT). *Application deadline:* For fall admission, 6/1 for international students; for spring admission, 10/1 for international students. Applications are processed on a rolling basis. Application fee: $0. Electronic applications accepted. *Expenses:* Contact institution. *Financial support:* In 2016–17, 10 students received support. Federal Work-Study, scholarships/grants, and unspecified assistantships available. Support available to part-time students. Financial award applicants required to submit FAFSA. *Unit head:* Dr. Jen Buckley, Executive Director of the School of Education and Human Performance, 630-844-1542, Fax: 630-844-6155, E-mail: jbuckley@aurora.edu. *Application contact:* Elizabeth Botica, Graduate Education Recruiter, 630-947-8918, E-mail: ebotica@aurora.edu.
Website: http://aurora.edu/education

Austin College, Austin Teacher Program, Sherman, TX 75090-4400. Offers MAT. *Program availability:* Part-time. *Faculty:* 5 full-time (4 women), 1 (woman) part-time/adjunct. *Students:* 13 full-time (10 women), 3 part-time (2 women); includes 4 minority (1 Black or African American, non-Hispanic/Latino; 2 Hispanic/Latino; 1 Two or more races, non-Hispanic/Latino), 1 international. Average age 23. In 2016, 16 master's awarded. *Degree requirements:* For master's, one foreign language, thesis or alternative. *Entrance requirements:* For master's, Texas Academic Skills Program Test. *Application deadline:* For fall admission, 5/1 priority date for domestic students; for spring admission, 1/15 priority date for domestic students. Applications are processed on a rolling basis. Application fee: $35. Electronic applications accepted. *Expenses:* Tuition: Part-time $5285 per course. *Financial support:* Career-related internships or fieldwork, Federal Work-Study, scholarships/grants, and unspecified assistantships available. Support available to part-time students. Financial award application deadline: 4/1; financial award applicants required to submit FAFSA. *Unit head:* Julia Shahid, Department Chair, 903-813-2457, E-mail: jshahid@austincollege.edu. *Application contact:* Nikki Christensen, 903-813-2327, E-mail: nchristensen@austincollege.edu.
Website: http://www.austincollege.edu/academics/atp/

Austin Peay State University, College of Graduate Studies, College of Education, Clarksville, TN 37044. Offers MA Ed, MAT, Ed S. *Accreditation:* NCATE. *Program availability:* Part-time, evening/weekend, online learning. *Faculty:* 19 full-time (12 women), 5 part-time/adjunct (4 women). *Students:* 66 full-time (42 women), 156 part-time (132 women); includes 44 minority (24 Black or African American, non-Hispanic/Latino; 2 Asian, non-Hispanic/Latino; 11 Hispanic/Latino; 7 Two or more races, non-Hispanic/Latino), 2 international. Average age 35. 78 applicants, 82% accepted, 47 enrolled. In 2016, 87 master's, 9 other advanced degrees awarded. *Degree requirements:* For master's, comprehensive exam, thesis optional. *Entrance requirements:* For master's, GRE General Test, MAT, 3 letters of recommendation, minimum undergraduate GPA of 2.75; for Ed S, GRE General Test, master's degree, minimum graduate GPA of 3.0, 3 letters of recommendation. Additional exam requirements/recommendations for international students: Required—TOEFL (minimum score 500 paper-based). *Application deadline:* For fall admission, 8/9 priority date for domestic students. Applications are processed on a rolling basis. Application fee: $45 ($50 for international students). Electronic applications accepted. *Expenses:* Tuition, state resident: full-time $8300; part-time $415 per credit hour. Tuition, nonresident: full-time $22,280; part-time $1114 per credit hour. *Required fees:* $1473; $73.65 per credit hour. *Financial support:* Research assistantships with full tuition reimbursements, career-related internships or fieldwork, Federal Work-Study, institutionally sponsored loans, scholarships/grants, and unspecified assistantships available. Support available to part-time students. Financial award application deadline: 4/1; financial award applicants required to submit FAFSA. *Unit head:* Dr. Carlette Hardin, Director, 931-221-7696, Fax: 931-221-1292, E-mail: hardinc@apsu.edu. *Application contact:* Brad Averitt, Coordinator of Graduate Admissions, 800-859-4723, Fax: 931-221-7641, E-mail: gradadmissions@apsu.edu.
Website: http://www.apsu.edu/educ/

Averett University, Master in Education Program, Danville, VA 24541-3692. Offers administration and supervision (M Ed); curriculum and instruction (M Ed); special education with endorsement (M Ed); special education with licensure (M Ed). Program offered on Danville Campus only. *Program availability:* Part-time, online only, 100% online. *Faculty:* 1 full-time (0 women), 15 part-time/adjunct (12 women). *Students:* 26 full-time (22 women), 98 part-time (73 women); includes 39 minority (34 Black or African American, non-Hispanic/Latino; 3 American Indian or Alaska Native, non-Hispanic/Latino; 2 Hispanic/Latino). Average age 36. 109 applicants, 54% accepted, 56 enrolled. In 2016, 19 master's awarded. *Degree requirements:* For master's, 30-credit core curriculum, minimum GPA of 3.0 throughout program, completion of degree requirements within six years from start of program. *Entrance requirements:* For master's, PRAXIS I, GRE, or MAT; writing proficiency test, minimum cumulative GPA of 3.0 over the last 60 hours of undergraduate study toward a baccalaureate degree, three letters of recommendation, Virginia teaching license (or eligibility). Additional exam requirements/recommendations for international students: Required—TOEFL (minimum score 600 paper-based; 100 iBT). *Application deadline:* Applications are processed on a rolling basis. Electronic applications accepted. *Expenses:* $9,600. *Financial support:* Application deadline: 3/1; applicants required to submit FAFSA. *Faculty research:* Digital story telling for instruction and assessment; online collaborative tools; digital field trips with Google Earth; teacher preparation in special education in Kenya, Malawi, Zambia, and Zimbabwe; self-efficacy of regular education teachers regarding inclusion of special education students in their classrooms. *Total annual research expenditures:* $5,000. *Unit head:* Dr. Sue Davis, Education Chair, 434-791-5741, Fax: 434-791-5020, E-mail: suedavis@averett.edu.
Website: http://gps.averett.edu/online/education/

Avila University, School of Education, Kansas City, MO 64145-1698. Offers English language learners (Advanced Certificate); international advocacy and leadership (MA, Certificate); literacy (MA); special reading (Advanced Certificate); teaching and learning (MA); TESL (MA). *Program availability:* Part-time, evening/weekend, online learning. *Faculty:* 6 full-time (5 women), 11 part-time/adjunct (6 women). *Students:* 65 full-time (50 women), 23 part-time (17 women); includes 12 minority (8 Black or African American, non-Hispanic/Latino; 2 Asian, non-Hispanic/Latino; 1 Hispanic/Latino; 1 Two or more races, non-Hispanic/Latino), 3 international. Average age 34. 135 applicants, 44% accepted, 33 enrolled. In 2016, 29 master's awarded. *Entrance requirements:* For master's, minimum GPA of 3.0, writing sample, recommendation, interview; for other advanced degree, foreign language. Additional exam requirements/recommendations for international students: Required—TOEFL (minimum score 580 paper-based; 92 iBT). *Application deadline:* Applications are processed on a rolling basis. Electronic applications accepted. *Expenses:* $483 per credit hour. *Financial support:* In 2016–17, 6 students received support. Unspecified assistantships available. Financial award applicants required to submit FAFSA. *Unit head:* Dr. Stacy Keith, Director of Graduate Education, 816-501-2446, Fax: 816-501-2915, E-mail: stacy.keith@avila.edu. *Application contact:* Cory Roup, Graduate Education Enrollment and Academic Advisor, 816-501-2464, E-mail: cory.roup@avila.edu.
Website: https://www.avila.edu/academics/graduate-studies/grad-education

Azusa Pacific University, School of Education, Azusa, CA 91702-7000. Offers M Ed, MA, MA Ed, Ed D, Credential. *Program availability:* Part-time, evening/weekend. *Degree requirements:* For doctorate, oral defense of dissertation, qualifying exam. *Entrance requirements:* For master's, minimum GPA of 3.0; for doctorate, GRE General Test or MAT, 5 years of experience, writing sample. Additional exam requirements/recommendations for international students: Required—TOEFL.

Baker University, School of Education, Baldwin City, KS 66006-0065. Offers MA Ed, MSSE, MSSL, MST, Ed D. Master's-level programs also offered in Wichita, KS. *Accreditation:* NCATE; TEAC. *Program availability:* Part-time, evening/weekend, 100% online. *Students:* 16 full-time (10 women), 375 part-time (276 women); includes 45 minority (19 Black or African American, non-Hispanic/Latino; 7 American Indian or Alaska Native, non-Hispanic/Latino; 3 Asian, non-Hispanic/Latino; 11 Hispanic/Latino; 1 Native Hawaiian or other Pacific Islander, non-Hispanic/Latino; 4 Two or more races, non-Hispanic/Latino). Average age 36. In 2016, 187 master's, 43 doctorates awarded. *Degree requirements:* For master's, portfolio of learning; for doctorate, thesis/dissertation, portfolio of learning. *Entrance requirements:* For master's, one year of full-time work experience, teaching certificate; for doctorate, interview. Additional exam requirements/recommendations for international students: Required—TOEFL (minimum score 600 paper-based; 100 iBT). *Application deadline:* Applications are processed on a rolling basis. Electronic applications accepted. *Expenses:* Contact institution. *Financial support:* Applicants required to submit FAFSA. *Unit head:* Dr. Marc Childress, Dean of the School of Education, 913-344-1235, E-mail: marcus.childress@bakeru.edu. *Application contact:* Linda Reynolds, Director of Graduate Education Enrollment, 913-344-6037, E-mail: linda.reynolds@bakeru.edu.
Website: https://www.bakeru.edu/SOE/

Baldwin Wallace University, Graduate Programs, School of Education, Berea, OH 44017-2088. Offers leadership in higher education (MA Ed); literacy (MA Ed); mild/moderate educational needs (MA Ed); school leadership (MA Ed); technology leadership (MA Ed). *Accreditation:* NCATE. *Program availability:* Part-time, evening/weekend, 100% online, blended/hybrid learning. *Faculty:* 7 full-time (3 women), 9 part-time/adjunct (1 woman). *Students:* 126 full-time (99 women), 82 part-time (59 women); includes 20 minority (12 Black or African American, non-Hispanic/Latino; 1 Asian, non-Hispanic/Latino; 3 Hispanic/Latino; 4 Two or more races, non-Hispanic/Latino). Average age 32. 123 applicants, 50% accepted, 49 enrolled. In 2016, 54 master's awarded. *Degree requirements:* For master's, comprehensive exam, capstone, practica or portfolio. *Entrance requirements:* For master's, bachelor's degree in field, MAT or minimum GPA of 3.0, teaching license (for all but technology program). Additional exam requirements/recommendations for international students: Required—TOEFL (minimum score 550 paper-based; 79 iBT). *Application deadline:* For fall admission, 8/15 priority date for domestic students; for spring admission, 12/15 priority date for domestic students. Applications are processed on a rolling basis. Application fee: $25. Electronic applications accepted. Application fee is waived when completed online. *Expenses:* $721 per credit hour. *Financial support:* Career-related internships or fieldwork available. Financial award applicants required to submit FAFSA. *Faculty research:* Literacy, technology and literacy, diversity in education, assessment, special education, research methodology, leadership, and organization. *Unit head:* Dr. Karen Kaye, Dean, 440-826-2168, Fax: 440-826-3779, E-mail: kkaye@bw.edu. *Application contact:* Winifred W. Gerhardt, Director of Transfer, Adult and Graduate Admission, 440-826-2222, Fax: 440-826-3830, E-mail: admission@bw.edu.
Website: http://www.bw.edu/academics/master-of-arts-in-education

Ball State University, Graduate School, Teachers College, Muncie, IN 47306. Offers MA, MAE, MS, Ed D, PhD, Certificate, Ed S. *Accreditation:* NCATE. *Program availability:* Part-time, evening/weekend, 100% online, blended/hybrid learning. Terminal master's awarded for partial completion of doctoral program. *Degree requirements:* For doctorate, comprehensive exam, thesis/dissertation; for other advanced degree, comprehensive exam, thesis. *Entrance requirements:* For master's, minimum baccalaureate GPA of 2.75 or 3.0 in latter half of baccalauareate; for doctorate, GRE General Test, minimum graduate GPA of 3.2; for other advanced degree, GRE General Test. Additional exam requirements/recommendations for international students: Required—TOEFL (minimum score 550 paper-based; 79 iBT), IELTS (minimum score 6.5). Electronic applications accepted.

Bank Street College of Education, Graduate School, New York, NY 10025. Offers Ed M, MS, MS Ed. *Degree requirements:* For master's, thesis. *Entrance requirements:* For master's, interview, essays. Additional exam requirements/recommendations for international students: Required—TOEFL (minimum score 600 paper-based; 100 iBT), IELTS (minimum score 7). Electronic applications accepted. *Faculty research:* Understanding developmental variations in inclusive classrooms, urban teacher education and technology, learner-centered education, improving teacher preparation.

Bard College, Master of Arts in Teaching Program, Annandale-on-Hudson, NY 12504. Offers secondary education (MAT), including biology, history, literature, mathematics, Spanish; MS/MAT. *Program availability:* Part-time. *Degree requirements:* For master's, year-long teaching residencies in area middle and high schools. *Entrance requirements:* For master's, GRE General Test, resume, 3 letters of recommendation, personal statement, official transcripts. Additional exam requirements/recommendations for international students: Required—TOEFL. *Application deadline:* For winter admission, 1/30 priority date for domestic students; for spring admission, 4/27 for domestic students, 4/30 for international students. Applications are processed on a rolling basis. Application fee: $65. Electronic applications accepted. Application fee is waived when completed online. *Financial support:* Fellowships, institutionally sponsored loans, and scholarships/grants available. Support available to part-time students. Financial award application deadline: 4/28; financial award applicants required to submit FAFSA. *Unit head:* Derek Furr, Director, 845-758-7136, Fax: 845-758-7149, E-mail: mat@bard.edu. *Application contact:* Cecilia Maple, Assistant Director for Admission and Student Affairs, 845-758-7145, E-mail: mat@bard.edu.
Website: http://www.bard.edu/mat/ny

Barry University, School of Education, Miami Shores, FL 33161-6695. Offers MS, Ed D, PhD, Certificate, Ed S. *Program availability:* Part-time, evening/weekend, online learning. *Degree requirements:* For master's, comprehensive exam; for doctorate, thesis/dissertation. *Entrance requirements:* For master's, GRE General Test or MAT, minimum GPA of 3.0; for doctorate, GRE General Test, minimum GPA of 3.25; for other advanced degree, GRE General Test, minimum GPA of 3.0. Additional exam requirements/recommendations for international students: Required—TOEFL (minimum score 550 paper-based). Electronic applications accepted.

Bayamón Central University, Graduate Programs, Program in Education, Bayamón, PR 00960-1725. Offers administration and supervision (MA Ed); commercial education (MA Ed); elementary education (K–3) (MA Ed); family counseling (Graduate Certificate); guidance and counseling (MA Ed); pre-elementary teacher (MA Ed); rehabilitation counseling (MA Ed); special education (MA Ed), including attention deficit disorder, education of the autistic, learning disabilities. *Program availability:* Part-time, evening/weekend. *Degree requirements:* For master's, comprehensive exam. *Entrance requirements:* For master's, EXADEP, bachelor's degree in education or related field.

Baylor University, Graduate School, School of Education, Waco, TX 76798. Offers MA, MPH, MS Ed, Ed D, PhD, Ed S. *Accreditation:* NCATE. *Program availability:* Part-time, online learning. *Faculty:* 44 full-time (20 women). *Students:* 133 full-time (90 women), 41 part-time (28 women); includes 38 minority (15 Black or African American, non-Hispanic/Latino; 3 Asian, non-Hispanic/Latino; 12 Hispanic/Latino; 1 Native Hawaiian or other Pacific Islander, non-Hispanic/Latino; 7 Two or more races, non-Hispanic/Latino), 5 international. 248 applicants, 35% accepted, 28 enrolled. In 2016, 60 master's, 13 doctorates, 7 other advanced degrees awarded. *Degree requirements:* For master's, thesis; for doctorate, thesis/dissertation. *Entrance requirements:* Additional exam requirements/recommendations for international students: Required—TOEFL. *Application deadline:* Applications are processed on a rolling basis. Application fee: $25. Electronic applications accepted. *Expenses: Tuition:* Full-time $28,494; part-time $1583 per credit hour. *Required fees:* $167 per credit hour. Tuition and fees vary according to course load and program. *Financial support:* In 2016–17, 181 students received support, including 38 research assistantships (averaging $12,050 per year), 68 teaching assistantships (averaging $12,050 per year); career-related internships or fieldwork, Federal Work-Study, institutionally sponsored loans, scholarships/grants, and tuition waivers (partial) also available. Financial award applicants required to submit FAFSA. *Unit head:* Dr. Jon Engelhardt, Dean, 254-710-3111, Fax: 254-710-3987. *Application contact:* Julie Baker, Administrative Assistant, 254-710-3050, Fax: 254-710-3870, E-mail: julie_baker@baylor.edu.
Website: http://www.baylor.edu/soe/

Belhaven University, School of Education, Jackson, MS 39202-1789. Offers educational technology (M Ed); elementary education (M Ed, MAT); reading literacy (M Ed); secondary education (M Ed, MAT). *Program availability:* Part-time, evening/weekend, 100% online, blended/hybrid learning. *Faculty:* 36 full-time (27 women), 9 part-time/adjunct (6 women). *Students:* 319 full-time (270 women), 403 part-time (318 women); includes 502 minority (486 Black or African American, non-Hispanic/Latino; 2 Asian, non-Hispanic/Latino; 3 Hispanic/Latino; 11 Two or more races, non-Hispanic/Latino). Average age 35. In 2016, 78 master's awarded. *Degree requirements:* For master's, comprehensive exam, portfolio. *Entrance requirements:* For master's, PRAXIS I and II, minimum GPA of 2.8. *Application deadline:* Applications are processed on a rolling basis. Application fee: $25. Electronic applications accepted. *Expenses:* $495 per credit hour plus $75 technology fee per course. *Financial support:* Applicants required to submit FAFSA. *Unit head:* Dr. David Hand, Dean, 601-965-7020, E-mail: dhand@belhaven.edu. *Application contact:* Sean Kirnan, Assistant Vice President for Adult and Graduate Enrollment and Student Services, 601-968-8727, Fax: 601-968-5953, E-mail: gradadmission@belhaven.edu.
Website: http://graduateed.belhaven.edu

Bellarmine University, Annsley Frazier Thornton School of Education, Louisville, KY 40205. Offers education and district leadership (Ed D); education and social change (PhD); elementary education (MA Ed, MAT); leadership in higher education (PhD); learning and behavior disorders (MA Ed, MAT); middle grades education (MA Ed, MAT); principalship (Ed S); reading and writing (MA Ed); secondary education (MAT); teacher leadership (MA Ed). *Accreditation:* NCATE. *Program availability:* Part-time, evening/weekend. *Faculty:* 15 full-time (7 women), 44 part-time/adjunct (36 women). *Students:* 39 full-time (28 women), 211 part-time (164 women); includes 46 minority (35 Black or African American, non-Hispanic/Latino; 3 Asian, non-Hispanic/Latino; 5 Hispanic/Latino; 3 Two or more races, non-Hispanic/Latino). Average age 34. In 2016, 66 master's, 3 doctorates, 43 other advanced degrees awarded. *Degree requirements:* For master's, thesis (for some programs); for doctorate, thesis/dissertation. *Entrance requirements:* For master's, GRE, baccalaureate degree from accredited institution; minimum cumulative GPA of 2.75; recommendations from employers, supervisors, or professors attesting to applicant's potential as graduate student; statement of intent to pursue graduate degree; for doctorate, GRE, minimum GPA of 3.5 in all graduate coursework; baccalaureate and master's degrees in education or fields directly relevant to education; three letters of recommendation; two essays (no more than 1,000 words each); interview. Additional exam requirements/recommendations for international students: Required—TOEFL (minimum score 550 paper-based, 68 iBT), IELTS (minimum score 6), or Michigan English Language Assessment Battery. *Application deadline:* For fall admission, 8/1 priority date for domestic and international students; for spring admission, 12/1 priority date for domestic and international students; for summer admission, 4/10 priority date for domestic and international students. Applications are processed on a rolling basis. Application fee: $40. Electronic applications accepted. Tuition and fees vary according to program. *Financial support:* Scholarships/grants available. Financial award applicants required to submit FAFSA. *Faculty research:* Literacy, service-learning, dispositions, educational technology, special education. *Unit head:* Dr. Robert Cooter, Dean, 502-272-8191, Fax: 502-272-8189, E-mail: rcooter@bellarmine.edu. *Application contact:* Sarah Shumway Schuble, Senior Graduate Recruiter, 502-272-8271, Fax: 502-272-8002, E-mail: sshumway@bellarmine.edu.
Website: http://www.bellarmine.edu/education/graduate

Bemidji State University, School of Graduate Studies, Bemidji, MN 56601. Offers biology (MS); education (MS); English (MA, MS); environmental studies (MS); mathematics (MS); mathematics (elementary and middle level education) (MS); special education (M Sp Ed). *Program availability:* Part-time, online learning. *Degree requirements:* For master's, comprehensive exam, thesis (for some programs). *Entrance requirements:* For master's, GRE; GMAT, letters of recommendation, letters of interest. Additional exam requirements/recommendations for international students: Required—TOEFL (minimum score 550 paper-based; 80 iBT). Electronic applications accepted. *Expenses:* Contact institution. *Faculty research:* Human performance, sport, and health: physical education teacher education, continuum models, spiritual health, intellectual health, resiliency, health priorities; psychology: health psychology, college student drinking behavior, micro-aggressions, infant cognition, false memories, leadership assessment; biology: structure and dynamics of forest communities, aquatic and riverine ecology, interaction between animal populations and aquatic environments, cellular motility.

Benedictine College, Master of Arts in Education Program, Atchison, KS 66002-1499. Offers MA. *Program availability:* Part-time, evening/weekend. In 2016, 3 master's awarded. *Entrance requirements:* For master's, minimum GPA of 3.0 in last two years (60 hours) of college course work from accredited institutions, official transcripts, bachelor's degree, teacher certification/licensure, resume, essay. Additional exam requirements/recommendations for international students: Recommended—TOEFL, IELTS. *Application deadline:* Applications are processed on a rolling basis. Application fee: $50. Electronic applications accepted. Application fee is waived when completed online. *Expenses:* Contact institution. *Financial support:* Unspecified assistantships available. Financial award applicants required to submit FAFSA. *Application contact:* Dr. Cheryl Reding, Director, Graduate Programs in Education, 913-360-7384, E-mail: creding@benedictine.edu.

Benedictine University, Graduate Programs, Program in Education, Lisle, IL 60532. Offers curriculum and instruction and collaborative teaching (M Ed); elementary education (MA Ed); leadership and administration (M Ed); reading and literacy (M Ed); secondary education (MA Ed); special education (MA Ed). *Program availability:* Part-time, evening/weekend. *Students:* 17 full-time (16 women), 30 part-time (26 women); includes 2 minority (both Black or African American, non-Hispanic/Latino). 21 applicants, 62% accepted, 8 enrolled. In 2016, 68 master's awarded. *Degree requirements:* For master's, comprehensive exam, thesis (for some programs). *Entrance requirements:* For master's, GRE or MAT. Additional exam requirements/recommendations for international students: Required—TOEFL (minimum score 550 paper-based). *Application deadline:* For fall admission, 9/1 for domestic students; for winter admission, 12/1 for domestic students; for spring admission, 2/15 for domestic students. Applications are processed on a rolling basis. Application fee: $40. Electronic applications accepted. *Expenses:* Contact institution. *Financial support:* Career-related internships or fieldwork and health care benefits available. Support available to part-time students. *Unit head:* MeShelda Jackson, Director, 630-829-6282, E-mail: mjackson@ben.edu. *Application contact:* Kari Gibbons, Associate Vice President, Enrollment Center, 630-829-6200, Fax: 630-829-6584, E-mail: kgibbons@ben.edu.

Berry College, Graduate Programs, Graduate Programs in Education, Mount Berry, GA 30149-0159. Offers curriculum and instruction (M Ed, Ed S); early childhood education (M Ed, MAT); educational leadership (Ed S); middle-grades education and reading (M Ed, MAT), including middle grades education (MAT), middle-grades education (M Ed), reading (M Ed); secondary education (MAT). *Accreditation:* NCATE. *Program availability:* Part-time. *Faculty:* 2 full-time (0 women), 11 part-time/adjunct (8 women). *Students:* 34 full-time (27 women), 44 part-time (32 women); includes 21 minority (17 Black or African American, non-Hispanic/Latino; 4 Hispanic/Latino). Average age 40. In 2016, 6 master's, 76 other advanced degrees awarded. *Degree requirements:* For master's and Ed S, thesis, portfolio, oral exams. *Entrance requirements:* For master's, GRE General Test or MAT, minimum GPA of 2.5; for Ed S, M Ed from NCATE-accredited school, minimum GPA of 3.25. Additional exam requirements/recommendations for international students: Required—TOEFL (minimum score 550 paper-based). *Application deadline:* For fall admission, 7/21 for domestic students, 5/1 for international students; for spring admission, 12/1 for domestic students, 10/1 for international students. Applications are processed on a rolling basis. Application fee: $25 ($30 for international students). *Expenses:* Contact institution. *Financial support:* In 2016–17, 4 students received support. Research assistantships with full tuition reimbursements available, scholarships/grants, tuition waivers (partial), and unspecified assistantships available. Support available to part-time students. Financial award application deadline: 3/1; financial award applicants required to submit FAFSA. *Faculty research:* Focus on faculty research, school readiness, literacy, K-12 hiring, education policy, arts education. *Total annual research expenditures:* $11,064. *Unit head:* Dr. Jacqueline McDowell, Dean, Charter School of Education and Human Sciences, 706-236-1717, Fax: 706-238-5827, E-mail: jmcdowell@berry.edu. *Application contact:* Brett Kennedy, Assistant Vice President of Enrollment Management, 706-236-2215, Fax: 706-290-2178, E-mail: admissions@berry.edu.
Website: http://www.berry.edu/academics/education/graduate/

Bethany College, Master of Arts in Teaching Program, Bethany, WV 26032. Offers MAT. *Program availability:* Part-time. *Degree requirements:* For master's, thesis. *Entrance requirements:* For master's, baccalaureate degree from accredited U.S. college/university or international equivalent; minimum undergraduate GPA of 2.75. Additional exam requirements/recommendations for international students: Required—TOEFL (minimum score 500 paper-based; 90 iBT); Recommended—IELTS (minimum score 7). *Application deadline:* Applications are processed on a rolling basis. Application fee: $0. Electronic applications accepted. *Financial support:* Unspecified assistantships available. Financial award applicants required to submit FAFSA. *Unit head:* Dr. Edward Shephard, MAT Program Director, 304-829-7176, E-mail: eshephard@bethanywv.edu. *Application contact:* Mollie Cecere, Vice President for Enrollment Management, 304-829-7611, E-mail: mcecere@bethanywv.edu.
Website: http://www.bethanywv.edu/academics/graduate-mat/

Bethel College, Adult and Graduate Programs, Program in Education, Mishawaka, IN 46545-5591. Offers M Ed, MAT. *Accreditation:* NCATE; TEAC. *Program availability:* Part-time. *Faculty:* 10 part-time/adjunct (6 women). *Students:* 22 full-time (18 women), 64 part-time (42 women); includes 9 minority (5 Black or African American, non-Hispanic/Latino; 3 Hispanic/Latino; 1 Two or more races, non-Hispanic/Latino). Average age 35. 61 applicants, 56% accepted, 31 enrolled. In 2016, 15 master's awarded. *Entrance requirements:* Additional exam requirements/recommendations for international students: Required—TOEFL (minimum score 540 paper-based). *Application deadline:* For fall admission, 5/1 for international students; for spring admission, 10/1 for international students. Applications are processed on a rolling basis. Application fee: $0. Electronic applications accepted. *Expenses: Tuition:* Full-time $6750; part-time $3375 per credit hour. *Required fees:* $75 per semester. Tuition and fees vary according to course load and program. *Financial support:* Career-related internships or fieldwork available. Financial award applicants required to submit FAFSA. *Unit head:* Dr. Kristina Cerling, Director, 574-807-7347, E-mail: kristina.cerling@gmail.com.

Bethel University, Graduate School, St. Paul, MN 55112-6999. Offers business administration (MBA); classroom management (Certificate); counseling (MA); international baccalaureate teaching and learning (Certificate); K-12 education (MA); leadership (Ed D); leadership foundations (Certificate); nurse educator (MS, Certificate); nurse-midwifery (MS); physician assistant (MS); special education (MA); strategic leadership (MA); teaching (MA). *Program availability:* Part-time, evening/weekend, 100% online, blended/hybrid learning. *Faculty:* 19 full-time (15 women), 57 part-time/adjunct (37 women). *Students:* 674 full-time (466 women), 378 part-time (256 women); includes 188 minority (94 Black or African American, non-Hispanic/Latino; 3 American Indian or Alaska Native, non-Hispanic/Latino; 43 Asian, non-Hispanic/Latino; 31 Hispanic/Latino; 1 Native Hawaiian or other Pacific Islander, non-Hispanic/Latino; 16 Two or more races, non-Hispanic/Latino), 33 international. *Degree requirements:* For master's, comprehensive exam (for some programs), thesis (for some programs); for doctorate, comprehensive exam, thesis/dissertation. *Entrance requirements:* Additional exam requirements/recommendations for international students: Required—TOEFL (minimum score 550 paper-based, 80 iBT) or IELTS. *Application deadline:* Applications are processed on a rolling basis. Application fee: $0. Electronic applications accepted. *Expenses:* Contact institution. *Financial support:* Teaching assistantships, career-related internships or fieldwork, and scholarships/grants available. Support available to part-time students. Financial award applicants required to submit FAFSA. *Unit head:* Dick Crombie, Vice-President/Dean, 651-635-8000, Fax: 651-635-8004, E-mail: gs@bethel.edu. *Application contact:* Director of Admissions, 651-635-8000, Fax: 651-635-8004, E-mail: gs@bethel.edu.
Website: https://www.bethel.edu/graduate/

Binghamton University, State University of New York, Graduate School, Graduate School of Education, Binghamton, NY 13902-6000. Offers MAT, MS, MS Ed, Ed D, Certificate. *Accreditation:* TEAC. *Program availability:* Part-time, evening/weekend. *Faculty:* 18 full-time (12 women), 24 part-time/adjunct (20 women). *Students:* 103 full-time (75 women), 130 part-time (101 women); includes 21 minority (7 Black or African American, non-Hispanic/Latino; 2 American Indian or Alaska Native, non-Hispanic/Latino; 3 Asian, non-Hispanic/Latino; 7 Hispanic/Latino; 2 Two or more races, non-Hispanic/Latino), 5 international. Average age 32. 139 applicants, 86% accepted, 77 enrolled. In 2016, 79 master's, 4 doctorates, 9 other advanced degrees awarded. *Degree requirements:* For doctorate, thesis/dissertation. *Entrance requirements:* For master's, GRE General Test, teaching certification; for doctorate, GRE General Test, writing sample. Additional exam requirements/recommendations for international students: Required—TOEFL (minimum score 550 paper-based; 80 iBT). Application fee: $75. Electronic applications accepted. *Financial support:* In 2016–17, 21 students received support, including 2 fellowships with full tuition reimbursements available (averaging $10,000 per year), 3 teaching assistantships with full tuition reimbursements available (averaging $15,500 per year); research assistantships, career-related internships or fieldwork, Federal Work-Study, institutionally sponsored loans, scholarships/grants, health care benefits, tuition waivers (full and partial), and unspecified assistantships also available. Financial award applicants required to submit FAFSA. *Unit head:* Dr. Susan Strehle, Dean, 607-777-7329, E-mail: sstrehle@binghamton.edu. *Application contact:* Ben Balkaya, Assistant Dean and Director, 607-777-2151, Fax: 607-777-2501, E-mail: balkaya@binghamton.edu.
Website: http://www.binghamton.edu/gse/

Biola University, School of Education, La Mirada, CA 90639-0001. Offers curriculum and instruction (Certificate); early childhood (MA Ed, MAT); multiple subject (MAT); single subject (MAT); special education (MA Ed, MAT, Certificate). *Program availability:* Part-time, evening/weekend, online learning. *Entrance requirements:* For master's, CBEST, CSET, GRE (waived if cumulative GPA is 3.5 or above or if CBEST and all CSET subtests are passed). Additional exam requirements/recommendations for international students: Required—TOEFL (minimum score 100 iBT). Electronic applications accepted. *Faculty research:* Early childhood education, elementary education, special education, curriculum development, teacher preparation.

Bishop's University, School of Education, Sherbrooke, QC J1M 1Z7, Canada. Offers advanced studies in education (Diploma); education (M Ed, MA); teaching English as a second language (Certificate). *Program availability:* Part-time, online learning. *Degree requirements:* For master's, thesis (for some programs). *Entrance requirements:* For master's, teaching license, 2 years of teaching experience. *Faculty research:* Integration of special needs students, multigrade classes/small schools, leadership in organizational development, second language acquisition.

Bloomsburg University of Pennsylvania, School of Graduate Studies, College of Education, Bloomsburg, PA 17815-1301. Offers M Ed, MS, Certificate. *Accreditation:* NCATE. *Program availability:* Part-time. *Faculty:* 26 full-time (13 women), 4 part-time/adjunct (all women). *Students:* 106 full-time (67 women), 128 part-time (97 women); includes 26 minority (10 Black or African American, non-Hispanic/Latino; 5 Asian, non-Hispanic/Latino; 5 Hispanic/Latino; 1 Native Hawaiian or other Pacific Islander, non-Hispanic/Latino; 5 Two or more races, non-Hispanic/Latino), 1 international. Average age 28. 181 applicants, 66% accepted, 98 enrolled. In 2016, 86 master's awarded. *Degree requirements:* For master's, thesis optional. *Entrance requirements:* For master's, minimum QPA of 3.0. Additional exam requirements/recommendations for international students: Required—TOEFL, IELTS. Application fee: $35 ($60 for international students). Electronic applications accepted. *Expenses:* Tuition, state resident: full-time $9660; part-time $483 per credit. Tuition, nonresident: full-time $14,500; part-time $725 per credit. *Required fees:* $2410; $107 per credit. $75 per term. Tuition and fees vary according to course load, degree level and program. *Financial support:* Federal Work-Study and unspecified assistantships available. *Unit head:* Dr. Ingrid Everett, College of Education Graduate Program Coordinator, 570-389-5120, Fax: 570-389-3030, E-mail: ieverett@bloomu.edu. *Application contact:* Jennifer Kessler, Administrative Assistant, 570-389-4015, Fax: 570-389-3054, E-mail: jkessler@bloomu.edu.
Website: http://www.bloomu.edu/coe

Bluefield College, School of Education, Bluefield, VA 24605-1799. Offers MA Ed. *Accreditation:* TEAC. *Program availability:* Part-time, online only, 100% online. *Faculty:* 2 full-time (1 woman), 2 part-time/adjunct (1 woman). *Students:* 10 full-time (6 women), 3 part-time (all women); includes 2 minority (1 Black or African American, non-Hispanic/Latino; 1 Two or more races, non-Hispanic/Latino). Average age 32. 13 applicants, 23% accepted, 3 enrolled. In 2016, 7 master's awarded. *Degree requirements:* For master's, action research project. *Entrance requirements:* For master's, GRE, MAT or PRAXIS, bachelor's degree from regionally-accredited institution of higher education, minimum GPA of 2.75 in all college work, two letters of recommendation, Pre-Self-Assessment of Professional Temperament and Performance. Additional exam requirements/recommendations for international students: Required—TOEFL. *Application deadline:* Applications are processed on a rolling basis. Application fee: $0. Electronic applications accepted. *Expenses:* $460 per credit hour. *Financial support:* Applicants required to submit FAFSA. *Unit head:* Dr. Donna Hardy Watson, Dean, 276-326-4475, E-mail: dwatson@bluefield.edu.
Website: http://www.bluefield.edu/masters-in-education-degree/

Bluffton University, Programs in Education, Bluffton, OH 45817. Offers faith-based education (MA Ed); intervention specialist (MA Ed); leadership (MA Ed); reading (MA Ed). *Accreditation:* NCATE. *Program availability:* Part-time. *Faculty:* 6 full-time (3 women), 1 part-time/adjunct (0 women). *Students:* 9 full-time (all women); 10 part-time (9 women); includes 1 minority (Black or African American, non-Hispanic/Latino). Average age 34. 14 applicants, 50% accepted, 6 enrolled. In 2016, 1 master's awarded. *Degree requirements:* For master's, action research project, public presentation. *Entrance requirements:* For master's, PRAXIS I, bachelor's degree, minimum GPA of 3.0. Additional exam requirements/recommendations for international students: Required—TOEFL. *Application deadline:* For fall admission, 8/15 priority date for domestic students, 6/15 priority date for international students; for spring admission, 12/15 priority date for domestic students, 9/15 priority date for international students. Applications are processed on a rolling basis. Application fee: $25. Electronic applications accepted. Application fee is waived when completed online. *Expenses:* $453 per credit. *Financial support:* Health care benefits available. Support available to part-time students. Financial award application deadline: 9/15; financial award applicants required to submit FAFSA. *Faculty research:* Mentoring. *Unit head:* Dr. Gayle M. Trollinger, Director of Graduate Programs in Education, 419-358-3341, E-mail: trollingerg@bluffton.edu. *Application contact:* Nancey Schortgen, Program Representative, 419-358-3202, Fax: 419-358-3399, E-mail: schortgenn@bluffton.edu.
Website: http://www.bluffton.edu/grad/

Boise State University, College of Education, Boise, ID 83725-1700. Offers M Ed, MA, MET, MPE, MS, MS Ed, Ed D, Ed S, Graduate Certificate. *Accreditation:* NCATE. *Program availability:* Part-time, 100% online, blended/hybrid learning. *Faculty:* 106. *Students:* 131 full-time (106 women), 762 part-time (486 women); includes 88 minority (13 Black or African American, non-Hispanic/Latino; 4 American Indian or Alaska Native, non-Hispanic/Latino; 19 Asian, non-Hispanic/Latino; 46 Hispanic/Latino; 4 Native Hawaiian or other Pacific Islander, non-Hispanic/Latino; 2 Two or more races, non-Hispanic/Latino), 32 international. Average age 37. 399 applicants, 61% accepted, 146 enrolled. In 2016, 234 master's, 12 doctorates awarded. Terminal master's awarded for partial completion of doctoral program. *Degree requirements:* For master's, thesis (for some programs); for doctorate, thesis/dissertation. *Entrance requirements:* For master's, minimum GPA of 3.0; for doctorate, GRE General Test, minimum GPA of 3.0. Additional exam requirements/recommendations for international students: Required—TOEFL (minimum score 550 paper-based; 80 iBT), IELTS (minimum score 6). Application fee: $65 ($95 for international students). Electronic applications accepted. *Expenses:* Tuition, state resident: full-time $6058; part-time $358 per credit hour. Tuition, nonresident: full-time $20,108; part-time $608 per credit hour. *Required fees:* $2108. Tuition and fees vary according to program. *Financial support:* In 2016–17, 36 students received support, including 1 teaching assistantship (averaging $2,148 per year); scholarships/grants and unspecified assistantships also available. Financial award applicants required to submit FAFSA. *Unit head:* Dr. Rich Osguthorpe, Dean, 208-426-1611, E-mail: richardosguthorpe@boisestate.edu.
Website: http://education.boisestate.edu/

Boston College, Lynch School of Education, Chestnut Hill, MA 02467. Offers M Ed, MA, MAT, MS, MST, Ed D, PhD, CAES, JD/M Ed, JD/MA, M Ed/MA, MA/MA, MBA/MA. *Accreditation:* TEAC. *Program availability:* Part-time, evening/weekend. *Faculty:* 62 full-time (37 women). *Students:* 345 full-time (277 women), 422 part-time (318 women); includes 157 minority (50 Black or African American, non-Hispanic/Latino; 36 Asian, non-Hispanic/Latino; 50 Hispanic/Latino; 1 Native Hawaiian or other Pacific Islander, non-Hispanic/Latino; 20 Two or more races, non-Hispanic/Latino), 103 international. Average age 28. 1,385 applicants, 58% accepted, 322 enrolled. In 2016, 375 master's, 56 doctorates, 7 other advanced degrees awarded. Terminal master's awarded for partial completion of doctoral program. *Degree requirements:* For master's, comprehensive exam; for doctorate, comprehensive exam, thesis/dissertation. *Entrance requirements:* For master's, GRE, letters of recommendation, transcripts, personal statement, resume; for doctorate, GRE, letters of recommendation, transcripts, writing sample, personal statement, resume. Additional exam requirements/recommendations for international students: Required—TOEFL (minimum score 100 iBT). *Application deadline:* For fall admission, 12/1 priority date for domestic and international students; for spring admission, 11/1 for domestic and international students. Application fee: $65. Electronic applications accepted. Tuition and fees vary according to program. *Financial support:* Fellowships with tuition reimbursements, research assistantships with tuition reimbursements, teaching assistantships with tuition reimbursements, career-related internships or fieldwork, Federal Work-Study, scholarships/grants, traineeships, health care benefits, tuition waivers (partial), and unspecified assistantships available. Support available to part-time students. Financial award applicants required to submit FAFSA. *Unit head:* Dr. Stanton Wortham, Dean, 617-552-4200, Fax: 617-552-0812. *Application contact:* Jamie Grenon, Associate Dean for Graduate Admissions and Financial Aid, 617-552-4214, Fax: 617-552-0398, E-mail: grenonj@bc.edu.
Website: http://www.bc.edu/schools/lsoe

Boston University, School of Education, Boston, MA 02215. Offers Ed M, MAT, Ed D, PhD, CAGS. *Program availability:* Part-time, evening/weekend. *Students:* 293 full-time (222 women), 492 part-time (361 women); includes 186 minority (60 Black or African American, non-Hispanic/Latino; 46 Asian, non-Hispanic/Latino; 62 Hispanic/Latino; 1 Native Hawaiian or other Pacific Islander, non-Hispanic/Latino; 17 Two or more races, non-Hispanic/Latino), 78 international. Average age 28. 1,039 applicants, 64% accepted, 292 enrolled. In 2016, 276 master's, 19 doctorates, 13 other advanced degrees awarded. Terminal master's awarded for partial completion of doctoral program. *Degree requirements:* For master's, thesis (for some programs); for doctorate, comprehensive exam, thesis/dissertation; for CAGS, comprehensive exam. *Entrance requirements:* For master's, GRE or MAT (for Ed M in counseling); for doctorate, GRE General Test; for CAGS, GRE General Test or MAT. Additional exam requirements/recommendations for international students: Required—TOEFL (minimum score 84 iBT), IELTS. *Application deadline:* For fall admission, 1/15 priority date for domestic and international students; for spring admission, 9/15 priority date for domestic and international students. Applications are processed on a rolling basis. Application fee: $95. Electronic applications accepted. *Financial support:* Fellowships with full tuition reimbursements, research assistantships, teaching assistantships with partial tuition reimbursements, career-related internships or fieldwork, Federal Work-Study, and scholarships/grants available. Support available to part-time students. Financial award applicants required to submit FAFSA. *Faculty research:* Deaf studies, social emotional learning, civic engagement and education, STEM education, pre-college educational pipelines. *Total annual research expenditures:* $3.7 million. *Unit head:* Dr. Hardin Coleman, Dean, 617-353-3213. *Application contact:* Katharine Nelson, Director of Graduate Student Services, 617-353-4237, E-mail: sedgrad@bu.edu.
Website: http://www.bu.edu/sed

Bowie State University, Graduate Programs, Program in Teaching, Bowie, MD 20715-9465. Offers MAT. *Accreditation:* NCATE. *Program availability:* Part-time, evening/weekend. *Entrance requirements:* For master's, PRAXIS I. Electronic applications accepted.

Bradley University, The Graduate School, College of Education and Health Sciences, Peoria, IL 61625-0002. Offers MA, MSN, DNP, DPT, Certificate. *Accreditation:* NCATE. *Program availability:* Part-time, evening/weekend. *Degree requirements:* For master's, comprehensive exam, thesis optional. *Entrance requirements:* For master's, GRE General Test or MAT, letters of recommendation; for doctorate, GRE, letters of recommendation. Additional exam requirements/recommendations for international students: Required—TOEFL (minimum score 550 paper-based; 79 iBT), IELTS (minimum score 6.5). *Application deadline:* For fall admission, 5/15 priority date for domestic students, 5/15 for international students; for spring admission, 10/15 priority date for domestic students, 10/15 for international students. Applications are processed on a rolling basis. Application fee: $40 ($50 for international students). Electronic applications accepted. *Expenses: Tuition:* Full-time $7650; part-time $850 per credit. *Required fees:* $50 per credit. One-time fee: $100 full-time. *Financial support:* Research assistantships with full and partial tuition reimbursements, career-related internships or fieldwork, institutionally sponsored loans, scholarships/grants, tuition waivers (partial), and unspecified assistantships available. Support available to part-time students. Financial award application deadline: 4/1. *Faculty research:* Health care, professional nurse traineeship, gifted education. *Unit head:* Dr. Joan Sattler, Dean, 309-677-3181, E-mail: jls@bradley.edu. *Application contact:* Kayla Carroll, Director of International Admissions and Student Services, 309-677-2375, E-mail: klcarroll@fsmail.bradley.edu.
Website: http://www.bradley.edu/academic/colleges/ehs/

Brandman University, School of Education, Irvine, CA 92618. Offers education (MA); elementary education (MAT); organizational leadership (Ed D); school counseling (MA); secondary education (MAT); special education (MA). *Expenses: Tuition:* Full-time $14,880; part-time $620 per credit hour. Tuition and fees vary according to degree level and program. *Unit head:* Dr. Christine G. Zeppos, Dean, 949-341-9948, E-mail: zeppos@brandman.edu.
Website: http://www.brandman.edu/education/

Brandon University, Faculty of Education, Brandon, MB R7A 6A9, Canada. Offers curriculum and instruction (M Ed, Diploma); educational administration (M Ed, Diploma); guidance and counseling (M Ed, Diploma); special education (M Ed, Diploma). *Degree requirements:* For master's, thesis. *Entrance requirements:* For master's, minimum GPA of 3.0, teaching certificate or equivalent. Additional exam requirements/recommendations for international students: Required—TOEFL. *Faculty research:* Comparative education, environmental studies, parent/school council.

Brenau University, Sydney O. Smith Graduate School, College of Education, Gainesville, GA 30501. Offers early childhood (Ed S); early childhood education (M Ed, MAT); middle grades (Ed S); middle grades education (M Ed, MAT); secondary education (MAT); special education (M Ed, MAT). *Accreditation:* NCATE. *Program availability:* Part-time, evening/weekend, online learning. *Degree requirements:* For master's, thesis optional, comprehensive exam or applied research project, effective portfolio; for Ed S, thesis, applied research project. *Entrance requirements:* For master's, GRE, MAT, interview, minimum GPA of 3.0, 3 references, writing samples; for Ed S, GRE, MAT, master's degree, minimum GPA of 3.0, writing sample, letters of reference. Additional exam requirements/recommendations for international students: Required—TOEFL (minimum score 500 paper-based; 61 iBT); Recommended—IELTS (minimum score 5). Electronic applications accepted. *Expenses:* Contact institution.

Bridgewater State University, College of Graduate Studies, College of Education and Allied Studies, Bridgewater, MA 02325. Offers M Ed, MAT, MS, CAGS. *Accreditation:* NCATE. *Program availability:* Part-time, evening/weekend. *Degree requirements:* For CAGS, comprehensive exam. *Entrance requirements:* For master's, GRE General Test or Massachusetts Test for Educator Licensure; for CAGS, master's degree. Additional exam requirements/recommendations for international students: Required—TOEFL.

Brigham Young University, Graduate Studies, David O. McKay School of Education, Provo, UT 84602. Offers M Ed, MA, MS, Ed D, PhD, Ed S. *Accreditation:* TEAC. *Program availability:* Part-time, evening/weekend. *Faculty:* 71 full-time (24 women), 10 part-time/adjunct (3 women). *Students:* 189 full-time (102 women), 115 part-time (81 women); includes 28 minority (1 Black or African American, non-Hispanic/Latino; 2 American Indian or Alaska Native, non-Hispanic/Latino; 7 Asian, non-Hispanic/Latino; 8 Hispanic/Latino; 8 Native Hawaiian or other Pacific Islander, non-Hispanic/Latino; 2 Two or more races, non-Hispanic/Latino), 8 international. Average age 34. 337 applicants, 42% accepted, 123 enrolled. In 2016, 83 master's, 29 doctorates, 14 other advanced degrees awarded. *Degree requirements:* For master's, comprehensive exam, thesis; for doctorate, comprehensive exam, thesis/dissertation; for Ed S, comprehensive exam (for some programs). *Entrance requirements:* For master's, GRE, MAT, LSAT, minimum GPA of 3.25, minimum 1 year of teaching experience, letters of recommendation; for doctorate, GRE, MAT, LSAT, minimum GPA of 3.0 in last 60 hours of undergraduate coursework. Additional exam requirements/recommendations for international students: Required—TOEFL (minimum score 580 paper-based; 85 iBT) or IELTS (minimum score 7). *Application deadline:* For fall admission, 2/1 for domestic and international students; for winter admission, 2/1 for domestic and international students; for spring admission, 1/15 for domestic and international students; for summer admission, 3/1 for domestic and international students. Application fee: $50. Electronic applications accepted. *Expenses: Tuition:* Full-time $6680; part-time $393 per credit. Tuition and fees vary according to course load, program and student's religious affiliation. *Financial support:* In 2016–17, 118 students received support, including 108 research assistantships with tuition reimbursements available (averaging $6,525 per year), 30 teaching assistantships with tuition reimbursements available (averaging $4,893 per year); fellowships, career-related internships or fieldwork, institutionally sponsored loans, scholarships/grants, tuition waivers (partial), and unspecified assistantships also available. Support available to part-time students. Financial award application deadline: 3/15; financial award applicants required to submit FAFSA. *Unit head:* Dr. Mary Anne Prater, Dean, 801-422-1592, Fax: 801-422-0200, E-mail: prater@byu.edu. *Application contact:* Brandan Beerli, Director, Education Student Services, 801-422-9199, Fax: 801-422-0195.
Website: http://education.byu.edu/

Brock University, Faculty of Graduate Studies, Faculty of Education, St. Catharines, ON L2S 3A1, Canada. Offers M Ed, PhD. *Program availability:* Part-time, evening/weekend. *Degree requirements:* For master's, thesis optional; for doctorate, thesis/dissertation. *Entrance requirements:* For master's, 1 year of teaching experience, honors degree; for doctorate, master's degree. Additional exam requirements/recommendations for international students: Required—TOEFL (minimum score 550 paper-based; 80 iBT), IELTS (minimum score 6.5), TWE (minimum score 4). Electronic applications accepted. *Expenses:* Contact institution. *Faculty research:* International and comparative education, early childhood education, educational leadership, adult education.

Brooklyn College of the City University of New York, School of Education, Brooklyn, NY 11210-2889. Offers MA, MAT, MS Ed, AC. *Accreditation:* NCATE. *Program availability:* Part-time, evening/weekend. *Entrance requirements:* For master's, GRE, GMAT, MAT (depending on program). Additional exam requirements/recommendations for international students: Required—TOEFL or IELTS. Electronic applications accepted.

Brown University, Graduate School, Department of Education, Providence, RI 02912. Offers teaching (MAT), including elementary education, English, history/social studies, science, secondary education; urban education policy (AM). *Degree requirements:* For master's, student teaching, portfolio. *Entrance requirements:* For master's, GRE General Test, letters of recommendation, interview. Additional exam requirements/recommendations for international students: Recommended—TOEFL.

Bucknell University, Graduate Studies, College of Arts and Sciences, Department of Education, Lewisburg, PA 17837. Offers college student personnel (MS Ed). *Program availability:* Part-time. *Degree requirements:* For master's, comprehensive exam (for some programs), thesis or alternative. *Entrance requirements:* For master's, GRE General Test, minimum GPA of 3.0. Additional exam requirements/recommendations for international students: Required—TOEFL (minimum score 600 paper-based). *Application deadline:* For fall admission, 2/1 priority date for domestic students, 1/1 priority date for international students. Application fee: $25. *Expenses: Tuition:* Part-time $5475 per course. *Financial support:* Fellowships with full and partial tuition reimbursements, scholarships/grants, and tuition waivers (full and partial) available. Financial award application deadline: 2/1. *Unit head:* Dr. Joe Murray, Head, 717-577-1324. *Application contact:* Gretchen H. Fegley, Coordinator, 570-577-3655, Fax: 570-577-3760, E-mail: gfegley@bucknell.edu.
Website: http://www.bucknell.edu/education

Buena Vista University, School of Education, Storm Lake, IA 50588. Offers curriculum and instruction (M Ed), including effective teaching, TESL; school guidance and counseling (MS Ed). Program offered in summer only. *Program availability:* Part-time, evening/weekend, online learning. *Degree requirements:* For master's, thesis, fieldwork/practicum, capstone portfolio. *Entrance requirements:* For master's, Analytical Writing Assessment (in-house), minimum undergraduate GPA of 2.75. Electronic applications accepted. *Faculty research:* Reading, curriculum, educational psychology, special education.

Butler University, College of Education, Indianapolis, IN 46208-3485. Offers alternative special education licensure (Certificate); educational administration (MS); effective teaching and leadership (MS); international baccalaureate teaching and learning (Certificate); licensed mental health counselor (Certificate); school counseling (MS); teachers of the visually impaired (Certificate). *Accreditation:* ACA; NCATE. *Program availability:* Part-time. *Faculty:* 13 full-time (10 women), 5 part-time/adjunct (4 women). *Students:* 9 full-time (7 women), 119 part-time (85 women); includes 14 minority (10 Black or African American, non-Hispanic/Latino; 1 Asian, non-Hispanic/Latino; 2 Hispanic/Latino; 1 Two or more races, non-Hispanic/Latino). Average age 32. 79 applicants, 76% accepted, 63 enrolled. In 2016, 42 master's, 30 other advanced degrees awarded. *Entrance requirements:* For master's, GRE (minimum score 291) or MAT (minimum score 396) unless undergraduate GPA is a 3.0 or higher, two letters of recommendation, transcripts, interview, professional resume. Additional exam requirements/recommendations for international students: Required—TOEFL (minimum score 550 paper-based; 79 iBT), IELTS (minimum score 6). *Application deadline:* For fall admission, 2/1 for domestic and international students; for spring admission, 11/1 for domestic and international students; for summer admission, 4/1 for domestic and international students. Applications are processed on a rolling basis. Application fee: $0. Electronic applications accepted. *Expenses:* Contact institution. *Financial support:* In 2016–17, 60 students received support. Scholarships/grants and unspecified assistantships available. Financial award application deadline: 7/15; financial award applicants required to submit FAFSA. *Faculty research:* Principals role in school improvement, leadership and school climate, retention of teachers in special education, the neuro-diversity brain, school counseling intervention. *Unit head:* Dr. Ena Shelley, Dean, 317-940-9752, Fax: 317-940-6481. *Application contact:* Diane Dubord, Graduate Student Services Specialist, 317-940-8100, Fax: 317-940-8250, E-mail: ddubord@butler.edu.
Website: https://www.butler.edu/coe/graduate-programs

Cabrini University, Graduate Studies, Radnor, PA 19087. Offers accounting (M Acc); education (M Ed); leadership (MS). *Program availability:* Part-time, evening/weekend. *Degree requirements:* For master's, thesis optional. *Entrance requirements:* For master's, GRE and/or MAT (in some cases), bachelor's degree with minimum GPA of 3.0, one-page personal essay/statement, professional letter of recommendation. Additional exam requirements/recommendations for international students: Required—TOEFL. Electronic applications accepted.

Cairn University, School of Education, Langhorne, PA 19047-2990. Offers applied behavior analysis (MS Sp Ed, Certificate); educational leadership and administration (MS El); instruction (MS Sp Ed); teacher education (MS Ed). *Program availability:* Part-time, evening/weekend, 100% online, blended/hybrid learning. *Faculty:* 2 full-time (both women), 4 part-time/adjunct (3 women). *Students:* 3 full-time (2 women), 89 part-time (62 women); includes 18 minority (10 Black or African American, non-Hispanic/Latino; 6 Asian, non-Hispanic/Latino; 2 Hispanic/Latino), 21 international. Average age 38. 35 applicants, 100% accepted, 25 enrolled. In 2016, 17 master's awarded. *Entrance requirements:* Additional exam requirements/recommendations for international students: Required—TOEFL (minimum score 550 paper-based). *Application deadline:* Applications are processed on a rolling basis. Application fee: $25. Electronic applications accepted. Application fee is waived when completed online. *Expenses:* $655 per semester credit. *Financial support:* Scholarships/grants available. Support available to part-time students. Financial award applicants required to submit FAFSA. *Unit head:* Joseph Beeson, Interim Dean, 215-702-4498, E-mail: teacher.ed@cairn.edu. *Application contact:* Abigail Simon, Enrollment Counselor, Graduate Education, 800-572-2472, Fax: 215-702-4248, E-mail: asimon@cairn.edu.
Website: http://www.cairn.edu/academics/education

Caldwell University, Graduate Studies, Division of Education, Caldwell, NJ 07006-6195. Offers curriculum and instruction (MA); education (Ed D, Postbaccalaureate Certificate); educational administration (MA); learning disabilities teacher-consultant (Post-Master's Certificate); literacy instruction (MA); principal (Post-Master's Certificate); reading specialist (Post-Master's Certificate); special education (MA), including special education, teaching of students with disabilities, teaching of students with disabilities and learning disabilities teacher-consultant; superintendent (Post-Master's Certificate); supervisor (Post-Master's Certificate). *Program availability:* Part-time, evening/weekend. *Degree requirements:* For master's, comprehensive exam (for some programs). *Entrance requirements:* For master's, PRAXIS, 3 years of work experience, prior teaching certification. Additional exam requirements/recommendations for international students: Required—TOEFL (minimum score 580 paper-based). Electronic applications accepted. *Faculty research:* Curriculum and instruction, secondary education, special education, education and technology.

California Baptist University, Program in Education, Riverside, CA 92504-3206. Offers educational leadership (MS); educational leadership for faith-based institutions (MS); educational leadership for public institutions (MS); educational technology (MS);

instructional computer applications (MS); international education (MS); leadership and adult learning (MS); leadership and organizational studies (MS); online teaching and learning (MS); reading (MS); science education (MA); special education in mild/moderate disabilities (MS); special education in moderate/severe disabilities (MS); teacher leadership (MS); teaching (MS); teaching and learning (MS). *Program availability:* Part-time, evening/weekend, 100% online, blended/hybrid learning. *Faculty:* 20 full-time (8 women), 11 part-time/adjunct (7 women). *Students:* 191 full-time (148 women), 234 part-time (178 women); includes 194 minority (23 Black or African American, non-Hispanic/Latino; 5 American Indian or Alaska Native, non-Hispanic/Latino; 15 Asian, non-Hispanic/Latino; 131 Hispanic/Latino; 4 Native Hawaiian or other Pacific Islander, non-Hispanic/Latino; 16 Two or more races, non-Hispanic/Latino), 2 international. Average age 31. 277 applicants, 61% accepted, 150 enrolled. In 2016, 280 master's awarded. *Degree requirements:* For master's, comprehensive exam, project, or thesis. *Entrance requirements:* For master's, minimum undergraduate GPA of 2.75; 500-word essay; three letters of recommendation; two prerequisite courses completed with minimum C grade. Additional exam requirements/recommendations for international students: Required—TOEFL (minimum score 80 iBT). *Application deadline:* For fall admission, 8/1 priority date for domestic students, 7/1 for international students; for spring admission, 12/1 priority date for domestic students, 11/1 for international students. Applications are processed on a rolling basis. Application fee: $45. Electronic applications accepted. *Expenses:* Contact institution. *Financial support:* In 2016–17, 162 students received support. Federal Work-Study and scholarships/grants available. Financial award applicants required to submit CSS PROFILE or FAFSA. *Faculty research:* Leadership development, complexity theory, faith and learning, special education, social and philosophical contexts of education. *Unit head:* Dr. John Shoup, Dean, School of Education, 951-343-4516, E-mail: jshoup@calbaptist.edu.
Website: http://www.calbaptist.edu/mastersined/

California Coast University, School of Education, Santa Ana, CA 92701. Offers administration (M Ed); curriculum and instruction (M Ed); educational administration (Ed D); educational psychology (Ed D); organizational leadership (Ed D). *Program availability:* Online learning.

California Lutheran University, Graduate Studies, Graduate School of Education, Thousand Oaks, CA 91360-2787. Offers counseling and guidance (MS), including college student personnel, counseling and guidance; educational leadership (MA, Ed D), including educational leadership (K-12) (Ed D), higher education leadership (Ed D); special education (MS); teacher leadership (M Ed); teaching (M Ed). *Accreditation:* NCATE. *Program availability:* Part-time, evening/weekend. *Faculty:* 23 full-time (17 women), 39 part-time/adjunct (26 women). *Students:* 518 full-time (411 women), 79 part-time (67 women); includes 252 minority (12 Black or African American, non-Hispanic/Latino; 3 American Indian or Alaska Native, non-Hispanic/Latino; 17 Asian, non-Hispanic/Latino; 108 Hispanic/Latino; 1 Native Hawaiian or other Pacific Islander, non-Hispanic/Latino; 111 Two or more races, non-Hispanic/Latino), 14 international. Average age 35. 319 applicants, 74% accepted, 192 enrolled. In 2016, 93 master's, 13 doctorates awarded. *Degree requirements:* For master's, comprehensive exam or thesis; for doctorate, thesis/dissertation. *Entrance requirements:* For master's, GRE General Test, interview, minimum GPA of 3.0. *Application deadline:* For fall admission, 7/1 priority date for domestic students; for spring admission, 11/1 priority date for domestic students; for summer admission, 4/1 priority date for domestic students. Applications are processed on a rolling basis. Application fee: $50. Electronic applications accepted. *Unit head:* Dr. Michael Hillis, Dean, 805-493-3421. *Application contact:* 805-493-3325, Fax: 805-493-3861, E-mail: clugrad@callutheran.edu.

California Polytechnic State University, San Luis Obispo, College of Science and Mathematics, School of Education, San Luis Obispo, CA 93407. Offers MA. *Accreditation:* NCATE. *Program availability:* Part-time, evening/weekend. *Faculty:* 8 full-time (6 women), 14 part-time/adjunct (6 women). *Students:* 82 full-time (63 women), 21 part-time (17 women); includes 30 minority (1 Black or African American, non-Hispanic/Latino; 1 American Indian or Alaska Native, non-Hispanic/Latino; 2 Asian, non-Hispanic/Latino; 22 Hispanic/Latino; 4 Two or more races, non-Hispanic/Latino), 1 international. Average age 31. 202 applicants, 49% accepted, 87 enrolled. In 2016, 63 master's awarded. *Degree requirements:* For master's, comprehensive exam (for some programs), thesis (for some programs). *Entrance requirements:* Additional exam requirements/recommendations for international students: Required—TOEFL (minimum score 80 iBT). *Application deadline:* For fall admission, 4/1 for domestic students, 3/1 for international students. Applications are processed on a rolling basis. Application fee: $55. Electronic applications accepted. *Expenses:* Tuition, state resident: full-time $6738; part-time $3906 per year. Tuition, nonresident: full-time $15,666; part-time $8370 per year. *Required fees:* $3603; $3141 per unit. $1047 per term. *Financial support:* Fellowships, research assistantships, career-related internships or fieldwork, Federal Work-Study, and institutionally sponsored loans available. Support available to part-time students. Financial award application deadline: 3/2; financial award applicants required to submit FAFSA. *Faculty research:* Rural school counseling, partner school effectiveness, college student affairs, special education, educational leadership and administration. *Unit head:* Dr. Kevin Taylor, Director, 805-756-1503, E-mail: jktaylor@calpoly.edu. *Application contact:* E-mail: soe@calpoly.edu.
Website: http://soe.calpoly.edu/

California State University, Dominguez Hills, College of Education, Carson, CA 90747-0001. Offers MA, MS. *Accreditation:* NCATE. *Program availability:* Part-time, evening/weekend. *Degree requirements:* For master's, comprehensive exam, thesis or alternative. *Entrance requirements:* For master's, minimum GPA of 2.75. Additional exam requirements/recommendations for international students: Required—TOEFL. *Faculty research:* Science education, literacy, language acquisition, math, social adjustment.

California State University, East Bay, Office of Graduate Studies, College of Education and Allied Studies, Department of Teacher Education, Hayward, CA 94542-3000. Offers education (MS), including curriculum, early childhood education, educational technology and leadership, reading instruction. *Program availability:* Online learning. *Students:* 55 full-time (43 women), 21 part-time (15 women); includes 34 minority (5 Black or African American, non-Hispanic/Latino; 1 American Indian or Alaska Native, non-Hispanic/Latino; 14 Asian, non-Hispanic/Latino; 10 Hispanic/Latino; 1 Native Hawaiian or other Pacific Islander, non-Hispanic/Latino; 3 Two or more races, non-Hispanic/Latino), 6 international. Average age 33. 65 applicants, 91% accepted, 11 enrolled. In 2016, 67 master's awarded. *Degree requirements:* For master's, project or thesis. *Entrance requirements:* For master's, minimum GPA of 3.0 in field, 2.5 overall; teaching experience; baccalaureate degree; 3 letters of recommendation. Additional exam requirements/recommendations for international students: Required—TOEFL (minimum score 550 paper-based), IELTS. *Application deadline:* For fall admission, 6/30 for domestic and international students. Application fee: $55. Electronic applications accepted. *Financial support:* Career-related internships or fieldwork, Federal Work-Study, and institutionally sponsored loans available. Support available to part-time students. Financial award application deadline: 3/2; financial award applicants required to submit FAFSA. *Faculty research:* Online, pedagogy, writing, learning, teaching. *Unit head:* Dr. Eric Engdahl, Chair, 510-885-4599, E-mail: eric.engdahl@csueastbay.edu. *Application contact:* Prof. Valerie Helgren-Lempesis, Education Graduate Advisor, 510-885-3006, Fax: 510-885-4632, E-mail: valerie.helgren-lempesis@csueastbay.edu.
Website: http://www20.csueastbay.edu/ceas/departments/ted/index.html

California State University, Fresno, Division of Research and Graduate Studies, Kremen School of Education and Human Development, Fresno, CA 93740-8027. Offers MA, MS, Ed D. *Accreditation:* NCATE. *Program availability:* Part-time, evening/weekend. *Degree requirements:* For master's, thesis or alternative; for doctorate, thesis/dissertation. *Entrance requirements:* For master's, GRE General Test, MAT; for doctorate, GRE or MAT, minimum GPA of 3.2, master's degree. Additional exam requirements/recommendations for international students: Required—TOEFL. *Application deadline:* For fall admission, 5/1 for domestic and international students; for spring admission, 10/1 for domestic and international students. Applications are processed on a rolling basis. Application fee: $55. Electronic applications accepted. *Financial support:* Career-related internships or fieldwork, Federal Work-Study, scholarships/grants, and research awards available. Support available to part-time students. Financial award application deadline: 3/1; financial award applicants required to submit FAFSA. *Faculty research:* Adult community education, parenting, gifted and talented curriculum and instruction, peer mediation and conflict resolution. *Unit head:* Dr. Paul Beare, Dean, 559-278-0210, Fax: 559-278-0113, E-mail: pbeare@csufresno.edu. *Application contact:* Administrative Assistant, 559-278-2448, Fax: 559-278-4658.
Website: http://www.fresnostate.edu/kremen/

California State University, Long Beach, Graduate Studies, College of Education, Long Beach, CA 90840. Offers MA, MS, Ed D. *Accreditation:* NCATE. *Program availability:* Part-time, evening/weekend. *Entrance requirements:* For master's, GRE General Test, minimum GPA of 2.75. *Application deadline:* For fall admission, 3/1 for domestic students. Applications are processed on a rolling basis. Application fee: $55. Electronic applications accepted. *Financial support:* Federal Work-Study, institutionally sponsored loans, and scholarships/grants available. Financial award application deadline: 3/2. *Faculty research:* K-16 educational reform and partnership, gender issues related to teaching and learning, urban education (poverty, diversity, language), assessment and standards-based education. *Unit head:* Shireen Pavri, Dean, 562-985-4513, Fax: 562-985-4951.

California State University, Los Angeles, Graduate Studies, Charter College of Education, Los Angeles, CA 90032-8530. Offers MA, MS, Ed D, PhD, Graduate Certificate. *Accreditation:* NCATE. *Program availability:* Part-time, evening/weekend. *Degree requirements:* For doctorate, thesis/dissertation. *Entrance requirements:* For master's, minimum GPA of 2.75 in last 90 units of course work, teaching certificate; for doctorate, GRE General Test, master's degree; minimum undergraduate GPA of 3.0, graduate 3.5. Additional exam requirements/recommendations for international students: Required—TOEFL (minimum score 500 paper-based). Electronic applications accepted.

California State University, Monterey Bay, College of Education, Seaside, CA 93955-8001. Offers MAE. *Accreditation:* NCATE. *Program availability:* Part-time, evening/weekend. *Degree requirements:* For master's, one foreign language, thesis, 2 years of teaching experience. *Entrance requirements:* For master's, recommendations. Additional exam requirements/recommendations for international students: Required—TOEFL (minimum score 550 paper-based; 71 iBT). Electronic applications accepted. *Faculty research:* Multicultural education, linguistic diversity, behavior analysis.

California State University, Northridge, Graduate Studies, Michael D. Eisner College of Education, Northridge, CA 91330. Offers MA, MA Ed, MS, Ed D. *Accreditation:* NCATE. *Program availability:* Part-time, evening/weekend. *Faculty:* 65 full-time (46 women), 176 part-time/adjunct (104 women). *Students:* 368 full-time (291 women), 465 part-time (371 women); includes 430 minority (27 Black or African American, non-Hispanic/Latino; 1 American Indian or Alaska Native, non-Hispanic/Latino; 49 Asian, non-Hispanic/Latino; 321 Hispanic/Latino; 1 Native Hawaiian or other Pacific Islander, non-Hispanic/Latino; 31 Two or more races, non-Hispanic/Latino), 26 international. Average age 33. 740 applicants, 53% accepted, 319 enrolled. *Entrance requirements:* Additional exam requirements/recommendations for international students: Required—TOEFL. *Application deadline:* For fall admission, 11/30 for domestic students. Application fee: $55. *Expenses:* Tuition, state resident: full-time $4152. *Financial support:* Fellowships, career-related internships or fieldwork, Federal Work-Study, institutionally sponsored loans, scholarships/grants, and tuition waivers (partial) available. Support available to part-time students. Financial award application deadline: 3/1. *Faculty research:* Federal teacher center support, bilingual teacher training. *Unit head:* Dr. Michael E. Spagna, Dean, 818-677-2590.
Website: http://www.csun.edu/eisner-education

California State University, Sacramento, Office of Graduate Studies, College of Education, Sacramento, CA 95819. Offers MA, MS, Ed D. *Program availability:* Part-time. *Students:* 429 full-time (297 women), 179 part-time (102 women); includes 368 minority (41 Black or African American, non-Hispanic/Latino; 3 American Indian or Alaska Native, non-Hispanic/Latino; 176 Asian, non-Hispanic/Latino; 142 Hispanic/Latino; 6 Native Hawaiian or other Pacific Islander, non-Hispanic/Latino). Average age 32. 540 applicants, 80% accepted, 250 enrolled. In 2016, 107 master's, 7 doctorates awarded. *Degree requirements:* For master's, thesis or alternative, writing proficiency exam. *Entrance requirements:* Additional exam requirements/recommendations for international students: Required—TOEFL (minimum score 550 paper-based; 80 iBT). *Application deadline:* Applications are processed on a rolling basis. Application fee: $55. Electronic applications accepted. Tuition and fees vary according to degree level and program. *Financial support:* Research assistantships, teaching assistantships, career-related internships or fieldwork, and Federal Work-Study available. Support available to part-time students. Financial award application deadline: 3/1; financial award applicants required to submit FAFSA. *Unit head:* Dr. Alexander Sidorkin, Dean, 916-278-6639, E-mail: sidorkin@csus.edu. *Application contact:* Jose Martinez, Graduate Admissions Supervisor, 916-278-7871, E-mail: martinj@skymail.csus.edu.
Website: http://www.edweb.csus.edu

California State University, San Bernardino, Graduate Studies, College of Education, Program in Education, San Bernardino, CA 92407. Offers MA. *Faculty:* 11 full-time (7 women), 5 part-time/adjunct (2 women). *Students:* 108 full-time (75 women), 198 part-time (136 women); includes 139 minority (18 Black or African American, non-Hispanic/Latino; 10 Asian, non-Hispanic/Latino; 101 Hispanic/Latino; 10 Two or more races, non-Hispanic/Latino), 47 international. 193 applicants, 81% accepted, 105 enrolled. In 2016, 183 master's awarded. *Degree requirements:* For master's, comprehensive exam (for some programs), thesis (for some programs). *Entrance requirements:* Additional exam requirements/recommendations for international students: Required—TOEFL. *Application deadline:* For fall admission, 7/16 for domestic students. Application fee: $55. *Expenses:* Tuition, state resident: full-time $7843; part-time $5011.20 per year. Tuition and fees vary according to course load, degree level, program and reciprocity agreements. *Unit head:* Dr. Jay Fiene, Dean, 909-537-5600, Fax: 909-537-7510, E-mail: jfiene@csusb.edu. *Application contact:* Dr. Francisca Beer, Dean of Graduate Studies, 909-537-5058, E-mail: fbeer@csusb.edu.

California State University, San Marcos, College of Education, Health and Human Services, School of Education, San Marcos, CA 92096-0001. Offers educational administration (MA); educational leadership (Ed D); general education (MA); literacy education (MA); special education (MA). *Accreditation:* NCATE (one or more programs are accredited). *Program availability:* Part-time, evening/weekend. *Degree requirements:* For master's, thesis. *Entrance requirements:* For master's, minimum GPA of 3.0, teaching credentials, 1 year of teaching experience. *Expenses:* Tuition, state resident: full-time $6738. Tuition, nonresident: full-time $13,434. *Required fees:* $1906. Tuition and fees vary according to campus/location and program. *Faculty research:* Multicultural literature, art as knowledge, poetry and second language acquisition, restructuring K–12 education and improving the training of K–8 science teachers.

California State University, Stanislaus, College of Education, Turlock, CA 95382. Offers MA, Ed D, Graduate Certificate. *Accreditation:* NCATE. *Program availability:* Part-time, evening/weekend. *Degree requirements:* For master's, thesis. *Entrance requirements:* For master's, MAT, minimum GPA of 3.0. Additional exam requirements/recommendations for international students: Required—TOEFL (minimum score 550 paper-based).

California University of Pennsylvania, School of Graduate Studies and Research, College of Education and Human Services, California, PA 15419-1394. Offers M Ed, MAT, MS, MSW. *Accreditation:* NCATE. *Program availability:* Part-time, evening/weekend, online learning. *Degree requirements:* For master's, comprehensive exam, thesis optional. *Entrance requirements:* For master's, PRAXIS, MAT, minimum GPA of 3.0. Additional exam requirements/recommendations for international students: Required—TOEFL (minimum score 550 paper-based; 80 iBT). Electronic applications accepted. *Expenses:* Tuition, state resident: full-time $11,592; part-time $483 per credit. Tuition, nonresident: full-time $17,400; part-time $725 per credit. *Required fees:* $3916. Tuition and fees vary according to course load, degree level, campus/location and reciprocity agreements. *Faculty research:* Autism counseling, injury and education, early childhood education, National Board certification.

Calvary University, Graduate School and Seminary, Kansas City, MO 64147. Offers Bible and theology (MS); Biblical counseling (MA); education (MS), including administration and leadership, Christian education, curriculum and instruction, elementary education; organization development (MS); pastoral studies (M Div). *Program availability:* Part-time, evening/weekend. *Faculty:* 6 full-time (2 women), 2 part-time/adjunct (1 woman). *Students:* 11 full-time (3 women), 29 part-time (15 women); includes 12 minority (4 Black or African American, non-Hispanic/Latino; 1 American Indian or Alaska Native, non-Hispanic/Latino; 6 Asian, non-Hispanic/Latino; 1 Native Hawaiian or other Pacific Islander, non-Hispanic/Latino). Average age 39. In 2016, 19 master's awarded. *Degree requirements:* For master's, variable foreign language requirement, comprehensive exam, thesis or alternative. *Entrance requirements:* For master's, minimum GPA of 2.5, BA or BS, doctrine agreement. Additional exam requirements/recommendations for international students: Required—TOEFL (minimum score 550 paper-based). *Application deadline:* Applications are processed on a rolling basis. Application fee: $0. Electronic applications accepted. *Expenses: Tuition:* Full-time $7200; part-time $4800 per credit. *Required fees:* $640; $520 per credit. $140 per semester. One-time fee: $100. Tuition and fees vary according to program. *Financial support:* In 2016–17, 8 students received support. Scholarships/grants available. Financial award application deadline: 11/5; financial award applicants required to submit FAFSA. *Unit head:* Dr. Thomas Baurain, Director of Seminary, 816-322-0110 Ext. 1502, Fax: 816-331-4474, E-mail: thomas.baurain@calvary.edu. *Application contact:* Ann Rogers, Admissions Office Assistant, 800-326-3960 Ext. 1321, Fax: 816-331-4474, E-mail: admissions@calvary.edu.
Website: http://www.calvary.edu

Calvin College, Graduate Programs in Education, Grand Rapids, MI 49546-4388. Offers curriculum and instruction (M Ed). *Accreditation:* TEAC. *Program availability:* Part-time. *Faculty:* 12 full-time (5 women). *Students:* 4 full-time (3 women), 120 part-time (80 women); includes 13 minority (3 Black or African American, non-Hispanic/Latino; 4 Asian, non-Hispanic/Latino; 1 Hispanic/Latino; 5 Two or more races, non-Hispanic/Latino), 15 international. Average age 29. 24 applicants, 100% accepted, 24 enrolled. In 2016, 23 master's awarded. *Degree requirements:* For master's, thesis or seminar. *Entrance requirements:* For master's, teaching certificate. Additional exam requirements/recommendations for international students: Required—TOEFL (minimum score 550 paper-based; 80 iBT). *Application deadline:* For fall admission, 8/1 priority date for domestic students, 5/1 priority date for international students; for spring admission, 1/1 priority date for domestic students, 12/1 priority date for international students; for summer admission, 5/18 for domestic students. Applications are processed on a rolling basis. Application fee: $0. Electronic applications accepted. *Expenses:* Contact institution. *Financial support:* Federal Work-Study, scholarships/grants, and tuition waivers (full and partial) available. Financial award application deadline: 4/3; financial award applicants required to submit FAFSA. *Faculty research:* Literacy, racialized gender and gendered identity, teacher learning, learning disabilities identification, leadership. *Unit head:* Dr. David Smith, Graduate Program Director, 616-526-6158, Fax: 616-526-6505, E-mail: dsmith@calvin.edu. *Application contact:* Cindi Hoekstra, Program Manager, 616-526-6158, Fax: 616-526-6505, E-mail: choekstr@calvin.edu.
Website: http://www.calvin.edu/academic/graduate_studies

Cambridge College, School of Education, Cambridge, MA 02138-5304. Offers autism specialist (M Ed); autism/behavior analyst (M Ed); behavior analyst (Post-Master's Certificate); behavioral management (M Ed); early childhood teacher (M Ed); education specialist in curriculum and instruction (CAGS); educational leadership (Ed D); elementary teacher (M Ed); English as a second language (M Ed, Certificate); general science (M Ed); health education (Post-Master's Certificate); health/family and consumer sciences (M Ed); history (M Ed); individualized (M Ed); information technology literacy (M Ed); instructional technology (M Ed); interdisciplinary studies (M Ed); library teacher (M Ed); literacy education (M Ed); mathematics (M Ed); mathematics specialist (Certificate); middle school mathematics and science (M Ed); school administration (M Ed, CAGS); school guidance counselor (M Ed); school nurse education (M Ed); school social worker/school adjustment counselor (M Ed); special education administrator (CAGS); special education/moderate disabilities (M Ed); teaching skills and methodologies (M Ed). *Program availability:* Part-time, evening/weekend, online learning. *Degree requirements:* For master's, thesis, internship/practicum (licensure program only); for doctorate, thesis/dissertation; for other advanced degree, thesis. *Entrance requirements:* For master's, interview, resume, documentation of licensure, 2 professional references; for doctorate, official transcripts, interview, resume, documentation of licensure (if any), written personal statement/essay, portfolio of scholarly and professional work, qualifying assessment, 2 professional references, health insurance, immunizations form; for other advanced degree, official transcripts, interview, resume, documentation of licensure (if any), written personal statement/essay, 2 professional references, health insurance, immunizations form. Additional exam requirements/recommendations for international students: Required—TOEFL (minimum score 550 paper-based; 79 iBT), Michigan English Language Assessment Battery (minimum score 85); Recommended—IELTS (minimum score 6). Electronic applications accepted. *Expenses:* Contact institution. *Faculty research:* Adult education, accelerated learning, mathematics education, brain compatible learning, special education and law.

Cameron University, Office of Graduate Studies, Program in Education, Lawton, OK 73505-6377. Offers M Ed. *Accreditation:* NCATE. *Program availability:* Part-time, evening/weekend. *Degree requirements:* For master's, portfolio. *Entrance requirements:* Additional exam requirements/recommendations for international students: Required—TOEFL (minimum score 550 paper-based). Electronic applications accepted. *Faculty research:* Motivation, computer learning, special education mathematics, inquiry-based learning.

Cameron University, Office of Graduate Studies, Program in Teaching, Lawton, OK 73505-6377. Offers MAT. *Accreditation:* NCATE. *Degree requirements:* For master's, portfolio. *Entrance requirements:* Additional exam requirements/recommendations for international students: Required—TOEFL (minimum score 550 paper-based). Electronic applications accepted. *Faculty research:* Teacher retention/attrition, teacher education.

Campbellsville University, School of Education, Campbellsville, KY 42718-2799. Offers special education (MASE). *Accreditation:* NCATE. *Program availability:* Part-time, evening/weekend, 100% online, blended/hybrid learning. *Faculty:* 13 full-time (11 women), 12 part-time/adjunct (7 women). *Students:* 36 full-time (29 women), 163 part-time (128 women); includes 16 minority (14 Black or African American, non-Hispanic/Latino; 1 Hispanic/Latino; 1 Two or more races, non-Hispanic/Latino). Average age 35. 173 applicants, 58% accepted, 87 enrolled. In 2016, 58 master's awarded. *Degree requirements:* For master's, thesis, research paper. *Entrance requirements:* For master's, GRE or PRAXIS, minimum undergraduate GPA of 2.75, teaching certificate, professional growth plan, letters of recommendation, interview. Additional exam requirements/recommendations for international students: Recommended—TOEFL (minimum score 550 paper-based; 79 iBT), IELTS (minimum score 6). *Application deadline:* Applications are processed on a rolling basis. Application fee: $25. Electronic applications accepted. Application fee is waived when completed online. *Expenses:* $399 per credit hour. *Financial support:* Applicants required to submit FAFSA. *Faculty research:* Professional development, curriculum development, school governance, assessment, special education. *Unit head:* Dr. Beverly Ennis, Dean, 270-789-5344, Fax: 270-789-5206, E-mail: bcennis@campbellsville.edu. *Application contact:* Monica Bamwine, Assistant Director of Graduate Admissions, 270-789-5221, Fax: 270-789-5071, E-mail: mkbamwine@campbellsville.edu.

Campbell University, Graduate and Professional Programs, School of Education, Buies Creek, NC 27506. Offers elementary education (M Ed); interdisciplinary studies (M Ed); middle grades education (M Ed); physical education (M Ed); school administration (MSA); school counseling (M Ed); secondary education (M Ed). *Accreditation:* NCATE. *Program availability:* Part-time, evening/weekend. *Degree requirements:* For master's, comprehensive exam. *Entrance requirements:* For master's, GRE General Test, minimum GPA of 2.7. *Faculty research:* Spiritual values and wellness issues in counseling, stress and professional burnout among counselors, thinking strategies, leadership, adaptive technology.

Canisius College, Graduate Division, School of Education and Human Services, Buffalo, NY 14208-1098. Offers MS, MS Ed, MSA, Certificate. *Program availability:* Part-time, evening/weekend, 100% online, blended/hybrid learning. *Faculty:* 28 full-time (18 women), 60 part-time/adjunct (37 women). *Students:* 314 full-time (217 women), 442 part-time (298 women); includes 103 minority (58 Black or African American, non-Hispanic/Latino; 3 American Indian or Alaska Native, non-Hispanic/Latino; 7 Asian, non-Hispanic/Latino; 24 Hispanic/Latino; 11 Two or more races, non-Hispanic/Latino), 16 international. Average age 29. 490 applicants, 86% accepted, 315 enrolled. In 2016, 455 master's awarded. *Degree requirements:* For master's, thesis (for some programs). *Entrance requirements:* For master's, GRE (if cumulative GPA less than 2.7), transcripts, BA from accredited institution. Additional exam requirements/recommendations for international students: Required—TOEFL (minimum score 550 paper-based, 79 iBT), IELTS (minimum score 6.5), or CAEL (minimum score 70). *Application deadline:* Applications are processed on a rolling basis. Application fee: $25. Electronic applications accepted. Application fee is waived when completed online. *Expenses: Tuition:* Full-time $14,742. *Required fees:* $724. *Financial support:* Career-related internships or fieldwork, Federal Work-Study, scholarships/grants, tuition waivers (partial), and unspecified assistantships available. Support available to part-time students. Financial award application deadline: 4/30; financial award applicants required to submit FAFSA. *Faculty research:* Asperger's disease, autism, culturally congruent pedagogy in physical education, family as faculty, impact of trauma on adults, information processing and perceptual styles of athletes, integrating digital technologies in the classroom, long term psych-social impact on police officers, private higher education, qualities of effective coaches, reading strategies, student perceptions of online courses, teaching effectiveness, teaching methods, tutorial experiences in modern math. *Unit head:* Dr. Jeffrey R. Lindauer, Dean, 716-888-3294, Fax: 716-888-3164, E-mail: lindauej@canisius.edu. *Application contact:* Kathleen B. Davis, Vice President of Enrollment Management, 716-888-2500, Fax: 716-888-3195, E-mail: daviskb@canisius.edu.
Website: http://www.canisius.edu/graduate/

Capella University, School of Education, Doctoral Programs in Education, Minneapolis, MN 55402. Offers curriculum and instruction (PhD); educational leadership and management (Ed D); instructional design for online learning (PhD); K-12 studies in education (PhD); leadership for higher education (PhD); leadership in educational administration (PhD); postsecondary and adult education (PhD); professional studies in education (PhD); reading and literacy (Ed D); special education leadership (PhD); training and performance improvement (PhD).

Capella University, School of Education, Master's Programs in Education, Minneapolis, MN 55402. Offers adult education (MS); curriculum and instruction (MS); early childhood education (MS); enrollment management (MS); higher education leadership and management (MS); instructional design for online learning (MS); integrative studies (MS); K-12 studies in education (MS); leadership in educational administration (MS); reading and literacy (MS); special education teaching (MS).

Cardinal Stritch University, College of Education and Leadership, Milwaukee, WI 53217-3985. Offers MA, MS, Ed D, PhD. *Accreditation:* NCATE. *Program availability:* Part-time, evening/weekend, 100% online. *Students:* 106 full-time (87 women), 499 part-time (334 women); includes 147 minority (89 Black or African American, non-Hispanic/Latino; 6 American Indian or Alaska Native, non-Hispanic/Latino; 8 Asian, non-Hispanic/Latino; 33 Hispanic/Latino; 2 Native Hawaiian or other Pacific Islander, non-Hispanic/Latino; 9 Two or more races, non-Hispanic/Latino), 17 international. Average age 36. 344 applicants, 100% accepted, 137 enrolled. In 2016, 155 master's, 42 doctorates awarded. *Degree requirements:* For master's, comprehensive exam, thesis (for some programs); for doctorate, thesis/dissertation, practica/field experience. *Entrance requirements:* For doctorate, minimum GPA of 3.5 in master's coursework, portfolio, interview, 3 letters of recommendation. Additional exam requirements/recommendations for international students: Required—TOEFL (minimum score 79 iBT), IELTS (minimum score 6.5). *Application deadline:* For fall admission, 7/15 priority date for domestic students; for spring admission, 12/15 priority date for domestic students. Applications are processed on a rolling basis. Electronic applications accepted. *Expenses: Tuition:* Full-time $11,890; part-time $765 per credit hour. Tuition and fees vary according to class time, course load, degree level, program and student's religious affiliation. *Financial support:* Fellowships, research assistantships with partial tuition reimbursements, career-related internships or fieldwork, Federal Work-Study, and scholarships/grants available. Financial award applicants required to submit FAFSA. *Unit head:* Dr. Freda Russell, Dean, 414-410-4735, E-mail: frrussell@stritch.edu. *Application contact:* Graduate Admissions, 800-347-8822 Ext. 4042, E-mail: admissions@stritch.edu.

Caribbean University, Graduate School, Bayamón, PR 00960-0493. Offers administration and supervision (MA Ed); criminal justice (MA); curriculum and instruction (MA Ed, PhD), including elementary education (MA Ed), English education (MA Ed), history education (MA Ed), mathematics education (MA Ed), primary education (MA Ed), science education (MA Ed), Spanish education (MA Ed); educational technology in instructional systems (MA Ed); gerontology (MSN); human resources (MBA); museology, archiving and art history (MA Ed); neonatal pediatrics (MSN); physical education (MA Ed); special education (MA Ed). *Entrance requirements:* For master's, interview, minimum GPA of 2.5.

Carlow University, College of Learning and Innovation, Pittsburgh, PA 15213-3165. Offers M Ed, MFA, MS, Graduate Certificate. *Program availability:* Part-time, evening/weekend, 100% online, blended/hybrid learning, low-residency. *Students:* 79 full-time (72 women), 49 part-time (43 women); includes 17 minority (10 Black or African American, non-Hispanic/Latino; 1 American Indian or Alaska Native, non-Hispanic/Latino; 1 Hispanic/Latino; 5 Two or more races, non-Hispanic/Latino). Average age 34. 51 applicants, 86% accepted, 28 enrolled. In 2016, 26 master's, 3 other advanced degrees awarded. *Entrance requirements:* For master's, personal essay (two for MFA); resume or curriculum vitae; two recommendations; official transcripts; interview; minimum undergraduate GPA of 3.0; for Graduate Certificate, personal essay; resume or curriculum vitae; two recommendations; official transcripts; interview; minimum undergraduate GPA of 3.0. Additional exam requirements/recommendations for international students: Required—TOEFL (minimum score 550 paper-based). *Application deadline:* Applications are processed on a rolling basis. Application fee: $0. Electronic applications accepted. *Expenses:* Contact institution. *Financial support:* Application deadline: 4/1; applicants required to submit FAFSA. *Unit head:* Dr. Matthew Gordley, Dean, 412-578-6262, E-mail: megordley@carlow.edu.
Website: http://www.carlow.edu/College_of_Learning_and_Innovation.aspx

Carroll University, Graduate Programs in Education, Waukesha, WI 53186-5593. Offers adult and continuing education (M Ed); educational leadership (MS); pk-12 (M Ed). *Program availability:* Part-time, evening/weekend. *Faculty:* 7 full-time (5 women), 14 part-time/adjunct (all women). *Students:* 11 full-time (10 women), 163 part-time (125 women); includes 11 minority (3 Black or African American, non-Hispanic/Latino; 3 American Indian or Alaska Native, non-Hispanic/Latino; 2 Asian, non-Hispanic/Latino; 3 Hispanic/Latino), 1 international. Average age 34. 96 applicants, 38% accepted, 18 enrolled. In 2016, 43 master's awarded. *Degree requirements:* For master's, thesis. *Entrance requirements:* For master's, minimum undergraduate GPA of 2.5 in related field. Additional exam requirements/recommendations for international students: Required—TOEFL. *Application deadline:* For fall admission, 8/15 priority date for domestic students. Applications are processed on a rolling basis. Application fee: $0. Electronic applications accepted. *Expenses: Tuition:* Full-time $10,548; part-time $586 per credit. *Required fees:* $520 per semester. Tuition and fees vary according to course load, degree level and program. *Financial support:* Available to part-time students. Application deadline: 3/15; applicants required to submit FAFSA. *Faculty research:* Qualitative research methods, whole language approaches to teaching, the writing process, multicultural education, gifted/talented learners. *Unit head:* Dr. Kathrine Kramer, Director of Graduate Studies, 262-650-4917, E-mail: kkramer@carrollu.edu. *Application contact:* Lori Aliota, Graduate Admission Counselor, 262-524-7226, E-mail: laliota@carrollu.edu.
Website: http://www.carrollu.edu/gradprograms/education/default.asp

Carson-Newman University, Graduate Program in Education, Jefferson City, TN 37760. Offers curriculum and instruction (M Ed); educational leadership (M Ed); elementary education (MAT); school counseling (MS); secondary education (MAT); teaching English as a second language (MATESL). *Accreditation:* NCATE. *Program availability:* Part-time, evening/weekend, 100% online, blended/hybrid learning. *Degree requirements:* For master's, thesis or alternative. *Entrance requirements:* For master's, PRAXIS II or GRE with minimum score of 290 on the verbal and quantitative components (for MAT), minimum GPA of 3.0 in major, 2.5 overall. Additional exam requirements/recommendations for international students: Recommended—TOEFL (minimum score 79 iBT), IELTS (minimum score 6.5), TSE (minimum score 53). *Expenses: Tuition:* Full-time $10,142; part-time $461 per credit hour. *Required fees:* $300; $150 per semester. One-time fee: $150.

Carthage College, Division of Teacher Education, Kenosha, WI 53140. Offers classroom guidance and counseling (M Ed); creative arts (M Ed); gifted and talented children (M Ed); language arts (M Ed); modern language (M Ed); natural sciences (M Ed); reading (M Ed, Certificate); social sciences (M Ed); teacher leadership (M Ed). *Program availability:* Part-time, evening/weekend. *Degree requirements:* For master's, thesis optional. *Entrance requirements:* For master's, MAT, minimum B average, letters of reference.

Castleton University, Division of Graduate Studies, Department of Education, Castleton, VT 05735. Offers curriculum and instruction (MA Ed); educational leadership (MA Ed, CAGS); language arts and reading (MA Ed, CAGS); special education (MA Ed, CAGS). *Program availability:* Part-time, evening/weekend. *Degree requirements:* For master's, thesis or alternative; for CAGS, publishable paper. *Entrance requirements:* For master's, GRE General Test, MAT, interview, minimum undergraduate GPA of 3.0; for CAGS, educational research, master's degree, minimum undergraduate GPA of 3.0. *Faculty research:* Assessment, narrative.

The Catholic University of America, School of Arts and Sciences, Department of Education, Washington, DC 20064. Offers Catholic school leadership (MA); education (Certificate); secondary education (MA); special education (MA), including early childhood, non-categorical. *Accreditation:* NCATE. *Program availability:* Part-time. *Faculty:* 8 full-time (7 women), 2 part-time/adjunct (both women). *Students:* 7 full-time (6 women), 21 part-time (13 women); includes 5 minority (2 Black or African American, non-Hispanic/Latino; 3 Hispanic/Latino), 3 international. Average age 38. 22 applicants, 45% accepted, 3 enrolled. In 2016, 14 master's awarded. *Degree requirements:* For master's, comprehensive exam, thesis or alternative; for Certificate, action research project. *Entrance requirements:* For master's, GRE General Test or MAT, statement of purpose, official copies of academic transcripts, three letters of recommendation, interview; for Certificate, PRAXIS I, statement of purpose, official copies of academic transcripts, three letters of recommendation, interview. Additional exam requirements/recommendations for international students: Required—TOEFL (minimum score 550 paper-based; 80 iBT). *Application deadline:* For fall admission, 7/15 priority date for domestic students, 7/1 for international students; for spring admission, 11/15 priority date for domestic students, 11/1 for international students. Applications are processed on a rolling basis. Application fee: $55. Electronic applications accepted. *Expenses:* $42,850 per year; $1,170 per credit; $200 per semester part-time fees. *Financial support:* Fellowships, research assistantships, teaching assistantships, Federal Work-Study, scholarships/grants, tuition waivers (full and partial), and unspecified assistantships available. Financial award application deadline: 2/1; financial award applicants required to submit FAFSA. *Faculty research:* Special education, early childhood education, educational psychology, Catholic school administration, leadership and policy studies, counseling, curriculum and instruction. *Total annual research expenditures:* $54,518. *Unit head:* Dr. John Convey, Chair, 202-319-5810, Fax: 202-319-5815, E-mail: convey@cua.edu. *Application contact:* Director of Graduate Admissions, 202-319-5057, Fax: 202-319-6533, E-mail: cua-admissions@cua.edu.
Website: http://education.cua.edu/

Cedar Crest College, Department of Education, Allentown, PA 18104-6196. Offers M Ed. *Program availability:* Part-time, evening/weekend. *Faculty:* 4 full-time (all women), 5 part-time/adjunct (4 women). *Students:* 11 full-time (9 women), 68 part-time (63 women); includes 10 minority (3 Black or African American, non-Hispanic/Latino; 2 American Indian or Alaska Native, non-Hispanic/Latino; 1 Asian, non-Hispanic/Latino; 4 Hispanic/Latino). Average age 34. In 2016, 18 master's awarded. *Entrance requirements:* Additional exam requirements/recommendations for international students: Required—TOEFL. *Application deadline:* For fall admission, 8/7 priority date for domestic and international students; for winter admission, 11/7 priority date for domestic and international students; for spring admission, 1/8 priority date for domestic and international students. Applications are processed on a rolling basis. Electronic applications accepted. *Expenses:* $483 per credit. *Financial support:* In 2016–17, 60 students received support. Available to part-time students. Applicants required to submit FAFSA. *Faculty research:* Science education, reading, history of Pennsylvania, math education. *Unit head:* Dr. Jill Purdy, Graduate Program Director, 610-606-4666 Ext. 3419, E-mail: jepurdy@cedarcrest.edu. *Application contact:* Mary Ellen Hickes, Director of School of Adult and Graduate Education, 610-606-4666, E-mail: sage@cedarcrest.edu.

Cedarville University, Graduate Programs, Cedarville, OH 45314. Offers business administration (MBA); curriculum (M Ed); educational administration (M Ed); family nurse practitioner (MSN); global health ministries (MSN); instruction (M Ed); ministry (M Min); pharmacy (Pharm D). *Program availability:* Part-time, evening/weekend, online learning. *Degree requirements:* For master's, thesis. *Entrance requirements:* For master's, GRE, 2 professional recommendations; for doctorate, PCAT, professional recommendation from a practicing pharmacist or current employer/supervisor, resume, essay, interview. Additional exam requirements/recommendations for international students: Required—TOEFL (minimum score 550 paper-based; 80 iBT). Electronic applications accepted. *Expenses:* Contact institution.

Centenary College of Louisiana, Graduate Programs, Department of Education, Shreveport, LA 71104. Offers elementary education (MAT); secondary education (MAT). *Program availability:* Part-time, evening/weekend. *Faculty:* 2 full-time (1 woman), 3 part-time/adjunct (all women). *Students:* 1 (woman) full-time, 47 part-time (30 women). In 2016, 25 master's awarded. *Degree requirements:* For master's, comprehensive exam. *Entrance requirements:* For master's, PRAXIS I and II (for MAT), undergraduate degree, minimum GPA of 2.5. *Application deadline:* For fall admission, 7/1 for domestic and international students; for spring admission, 11/1 for domestic and international students; for summer admission, 4/1 for domestic and international students. Application fee: $50. *Expenses:* Contact institution. *Financial support:* Unspecified assistantships available. *Faculty research:* Teachers as advocates for teachers, portfolio assessment, disabled readers. *Unit head:* Dr. Dominic Salinas, Director, 318-869-5225, Fax: 318-869-5795, E-mail: dsalinas@centenary.edu. *Application contact:* Lori Payne, Administrative Assistant, 318-869-5223, Fax: 318-869-5795, E-mail: lpayne@centenary.edu.

Centenary University, Program in Education, Hackettstown, NJ 07840-2100. Offers education practice (M Ed); educational leadership (MA, Ed D); instructional leadership (MA); reading (M Ed); special education (MA). *Accreditation:* TEAC. *Program availability:* Part-time, evening/weekend, online learning. *Degree requirements:* For master's, thesis. *Entrance requirements:* For master's, interview, minimum undergraduate GPA of 2.8.

Central Connecticut State University, School of Graduate Studies, School of Education and Professional Studies, New Britain, CT 06050-4010. Offers MAT, MS, Ed D, AC, Certificate, Sixth Year Certificate. *Accreditation:* NCATE. *Program availability:* Part-time, evening/weekend. *Faculty:* 45 full-time (21 women), 52 part-time/adjunct (38 women). *Students:* 229 full-time (172 women), 789 part-time (608 women); includes 183 minority (75 Black or African American, non-Hispanic/Latino; 12 Asian, non-Hispanic/Latino; 76 Hispanic/Latino; 1 Native Hawaiian or other Pacific Islander, non-Hispanic/Latino; 19 Two or more races, non-Hispanic/Latino), 2 international. Average age 33. 403 applicants, 73% accepted, 212 enrolled. In 2016, 289 master's, 5 doctorates, 124 other advanced degrees awarded. *Degree requirements:* For master's, comprehensive exam, thesis or alternative; for doctorate, thesis/dissertation; for other advanced degree, qualifying exam. *Entrance requirements:* For master's, minimum undergraduate GPA of 2.7; for doctorate, GRE. Additional exam requirements/recommendations for international students: Required—TOEFL (minimum score 550 paper-based; 79 iBT). *Application deadline:* For fall admission, 6/1 for domestic students, 5/1 for international students; for spring admission, 11/1 for domestic and international students. Applications are processed on a rolling basis. Application fee: $50. Electronic applications accepted. *Expenses: Tuition, area resident:* Full-time $6497; part-time $606 per credit. Tuition, state resident: full-time $9748; part-time $622 per credit. Tuition, nonresident: full-time $18,102; part-time $622 per credit. *Required fees:* $4459; $246 per credit. *Financial support:* In 2016–17, 67 students received support. Career-related internships or fieldwork, Federal Work-Study, scholarships/grants, and unspecified assistantships available. Support available to part-time students. Financial award application deadline: 3/1; financial award applicants required to submit FAFSA. *Unit head:* Dr. Michael Alfano, Dean, 860-832-2101, E-mail: malfano@ccsu.edu. *Application contact:* Patricia Gardner, Associate Director of Graduate Studies, 860-832-2350, Fax: 860-832-2362.
Website: http://www.ccsu.edu/seps/

Central Methodist University, College of Graduate and Extended Studies, Fayette, MO 65248-1198. Offers clinical counseling (MS); clinical nurse leader (MSN); education (M Ed); music education (MME); nurse educator (MSN). *Program availability:* Part-time, evening/weekend, online learning. *Degree requirements:* For master's, thesis. *Entrance requirements:* For master's, GRE General Test, minimum GPA of 2.75. Electronic applications accepted.

Central Michigan University, Central Michigan University Global Campus, Program in Education, Mount Pleasant, MI 48859. Offers college teaching (Graduate Certificate); community college (MA); curriculum and instruction (MA); educational technology (MA, DET); reading and literacy K-12 (MA); school principalship (MA), including charter school leadership; training and development (MA). *Accreditation:* TEAC. *Program availability:* Part-time, evening/weekend. *Faculty:* 24 full-time (14 women), 24 part-time/adjunct (8 women). *Students:* 888 (620 women); includes 225 minority (142 Black or African American, non-Hispanic/Latino; 8 American Indian or Alaska Native, non-Hispanic/Latino; 16 Asian, non-Hispanic/Latino; 13 Hispanic/Latino; 46 Two or more races, non-Hispanic/Latino). Average age 37. In 2016, 76 master's awarded. *Entrance requirements:* For master's, minimum GPA of 2.7 in major. Additional exam requirements/recommendations for international students: Required—TOEFL. *Application deadline:* Applications are processed on a rolling basis. Application fee: $50.

Electronic applications accepted. *Financial support:* Scholarships/grants available. Support available to part-time students. *Unit head:* Kaleb Patrick, Director, 989-774-3144, E-mail: patri1kg@cmich.edu. *Application contact:* 877-268-4636, E-mail: cmuglobal@cmich.edu.

Central Michigan University, College of Graduate Studies, College of Education and Human Services, Mount Pleasant, MI 48859. Offers MA, MS, Ed D, Ed S, Graduate Certificate. *Accreditation:* TEAC. *Program availability:* Part-time, evening/weekend. *Degree requirements:* For master's and other advanced degree, thesis or alternative; for doctorate, thesis/dissertation. Electronic applications accepted.

Central Washington University, Graduate Studies and Research, College of Education and Professional Studies, Department of Language, Literacy and Special Education, Ellensburg, WA 98926. Offers reading education (M Ed); special education (M Ed). *Program availability:* Part-time. *Degree requirements:* For master's, thesis or alternative. *Entrance requirements:* For master's, minimum GPA of 3.0. Additional exam requirements/recommendations for international students: Required—TOEFL (minimum score 550 paper-based; 79 iBT), IELTS (minimum score 6.5). Electronic applications accepted.

Chadron State College, School of Professional and Graduate Studies, Department of Education, Chadron, NE 69337. Offers business (MA Ed); community counseling (MA Ed); educational administration (MS Ed, Sp Ed); elementary education (MS Ed); history (MA Ed); language and literature (MA Ed); secondary administration (MS Ed); secondary education (MS Ed). *Accreditation:* NCATE. *Program availability:* Part-time, evening/weekend, online learning. *Degree requirements:* For master's, thesis optional. *Entrance requirements:* For master's, GRE General Test, GRE Writing Test, minimum GPA of 2.75 or 12 graduate hours at CSC with minimum GPA of 3.25. Additional exam requirements/recommendations for international students: Required—TOEFL. Electronic applications accepted. *Faculty research:* Rural education, technology, mental health.

Chaminade University of Honolulu, Office of Professional and Continuing Education, Program in Education, Honolulu, HI 96816-1578. Offers child development (M Ed); early childhood education (MAT); educational leadership (M Ed); elementary education (MAT); instructional leadership (M Ed); Montessori (M Ed); secondary education (MAT); special education (MAT). *Program availability:* Part-time, evening/weekend, 100% online, blended/hybrid learning. *Faculty:* 7 full-time (4 women), 8 part-time/adjunct (6 women). *Students:* 98 full-time (80 women), 82 part-time (62 women); includes 110 minority (6 Black or African American, non-Hispanic/Latino; 2 American Indian or Alaska Native, non-Hispanic/Latino; 51 Asian, non-Hispanic/Latino; 9 Hispanic/Latino; 41 Native Hawaiian or other Pacific Islander, non-Hispanic/Latino; 1 Two or more races, non-Hispanic/Latino), 1 international. Average age 35. 38 applicants, 100% accepted, 29 enrolled. In 2016, 79 master's awarded. *Degree requirements:* For master's, thesis or alternative. *Entrance requirements:* For master's, PRAXIS (for MAT), minimum GPA of 2.75 (for M Ed), 3.0 (for MAT); 2 letters of recommendation, resume, writing sample (for MAT). Additional exam requirements/recommendations for international students: Required—TOEFL (minimum score 550 paper-based; 79 iBT). *Application deadline:* Applications are processed on a rolling basis. Application fee: $40. Electronic applications accepted. *Expenses:* $740 per credit hour plus $93 fee per online course. *Financial support:* Applicants required to submit FAFSA. *Unit head:* Dr. Dale Fryxell, Interim Dean, 808-739-4684, Fax: 808-739-4607, E-mail: edu-advising@chaminade.edu. *Application contact:* 808-735-4755, E-mail: gradserv@chaminade.edu.
Website: http://www.chaminade.edu/education

Chapman University, College of Educational Studies, Orange, CA 92866. Offers counseling (MA), including school counseling (MA, Credential); education (PhD), including cultural and curricular studies, disability studies, leadership studies, school psychology (PhD, Credential); educational psychology (MA); leadership development (MA); multiple subjects (Credential), including Spanish/English bilingual; pupil personnel services (Credential), including school counseling (MA, Credential), school psychology (PhD, Credential); school psychology (Ed S); single subject (Credential); special education (MA, Credential), including mild/moderate (Credential), moderate/severe (Credential); teaching (MA), including elementary education, secondary education, secondary music education. *Accreditation:* TEAC. *Program availability:* Part-time, evening/weekend. *Faculty:* 29 full-time (14 women), 36 part-time/adjunct (28 women). *Students:* 186 full-time (148 women), 186 part-time (134 women); includes 144 minority (9 Black or African American, non-Hispanic/Latino; 39 Asian, non-Hispanic/Latino; 78 Hispanic/Latino; 2 Native Hawaiian or other Pacific Islander, non-Hispanic/Latino; 16 Two or more races, non-Hispanic/Latino), 8 international. Average age 29. 143 applicants, 63% accepted, 64 enrolled. In 2016, 111 master's, 24 doctorates awarded. *Degree requirements:* For doctorate, thesis/dissertation. *Entrance requirements:* Additional exam requirements/recommendations for international students: Required—TOEFL (minimum score 550 paper-based, 80 iBT), IELTS (6.5), PTE Academic (53), or CAE. *Application deadline:* Applications are processed on a rolling basis. Application fee: $60. Electronic applications accepted. *Expenses:* Contact institution. *Financial support:* Fellowships and scholarships/grants available. Financial award application deadline: 3/2; financial award applicants required to submit FAFSA. *Unit head:* Dr. Margaret Grogan, Dean, 714-516-5968, E-mail: grogan@chapman.edu. *Application contact:* Sara Simon, Graduate Admission Counselor, 714-997-6770, E-mail: simon@chapman.edu.
Website: http://www.chapman.edu/CES/

Charleston Southern University, School of Education, Charleston, SC 29423-8087. Offers elementary administration and supervision (M Ed); elementary education (M Ed); secondary administration and supervision (M Ed). *Accreditation:* NCATE. *Program availability:* Part-time, evening/weekend. *Degree requirements:* For master's, thesis optional. *Entrance requirements:* For master's, GRE or MAT. Additional exam requirements/recommendations for international students: Required—TOEFL (minimum score 550 paper-based; 79 iBT). *Application deadline:* Applications are processed on a rolling basis. Application fee: $40. *Expenses:* Contact institution. *Financial support:* Research assistantships with full tuition reimbursements, career-related internships or fieldwork, and Federal Work-Study available. Financial award application deadline: 4/15; financial award applicants required to submit FAFSA. *Unit head:* Dr. Melanie G. Reynolds-Murphy, Interim Dean, 843-863-7765, Fax: 843-863-7784, E-mail: mmurphy@csuniv.edu. *Application contact:* Dr. Melanie G. Reynolds-Murphy, Interim Dean, 843-863-7765, Fax: 843-863-7784, E-mail: mmurphy@csuniv.edu.
Website: http://www.csuniv.edu/education/

Chatham University, Program in Education, Pittsburgh, PA 15232-2826. Offers early childhood education (MAT); elementary education (MAT); environmental education (K-12) (MAT); secondary art (MAT); secondary biology education (MAT); secondary chemistry education (MAT); secondary English education (MAT); secondary math education (MAT); secondary physics education (MAT); secondary social studies education (MAT); special education (MAT). *Degree requirements:* For master's, thesis, teaching experience. *Entrance requirements:* For master's, minimum GPA of 3.0, sample of written work, recommendation letters. Additional exam requirements/recommendations for international students: Required—TOEFL (minimum score 600 paper-based; 100 iBT), IELTS (minimum score 7), TWE. Electronic applications accepted. Application fee is waived when completed online. *Expenses: Tuition:* Full-time $16,254; part-time $903 per credit hour. *Required fees:* $468; $26 per credit hour. *Faculty research:* Gifted education, environmental education, technology in education, writing as learning, class size and achievement.

Chestnut Hill College, School of Graduate Studies, Department of Education, Philadelphia, PA 19118-2693. Offers early education (M Ed), including early education; educational leadership (M Ed); elementary/middle education (M Ed); reading (M Ed), including reading specialist; secondary education (M Ed); special education (M Ed), including special education. *Program availability:* Part-time, evening/weekend. *Degree requirements:* For master's, thesis optional. *Entrance requirements:* For master's, PRAXIS I or proof of teaching certification, letters of recommendation, writing sample, 6 graduate credits with minimum B grade if undergraduate GPA less than 3.0. Additional exam requirements/recommendations for international students: Required—TOEFL (minimum score 500 paper-based), IELTS (minimum score 6.0), or TWE (minimum score 22). Electronic applications accepted. *Expenses:* Contact institution. *Faculty research:* Culturally responsive pedagogy, gender issues, autism, inclusive education, mentoring and induction programs.

Cheyney University of Pennsylvania, Graduate Programs, Cheyney, PA 19319. Offers M Ed, MPA, Certificate. *Program availability:* Part-time, evening/weekend. *Degree requirements:* For master's and Certificate, thesis or alternative. *Entrance requirements:* For master's and Certificate, GRE General Test, MAT, minimum GPA of 2.75. Electronic applications accepted. *Faculty research:* Teacher motivation, critical thinking.

Chicago State University, School of Graduate and Professional Studies, College of Education, Chicago, IL 60628. Offers M Ed, MA, MAT, MS Ed, Ed D. *Accreditation:* NCATE. *Program availability:* Part-time. *Degree requirements:* For master's, thesis optional. *Entrance requirements:* For master's, minimum GPA of 2.75.

Chowan University, School of Graduate Studies, Murfreesboro, NC 27855. Offers education (M Ed). *Entrance requirements:* For master's, official transcripts, three letters of recommendation, personal statement, current teacher license. Additional exam requirements/recommendations for international students: Required—TOEFL. Electronic applications accepted.

Christian Brothers University, School of Arts, Memphis, TN 38104-5581. Offers Catholic studies (MACS); educational leadership (MSEL); teacher-leadership (M Ed); teaching (MAT). *Program availability:* Part-time, evening/weekend. *Entrance requirements:* For master's, GRE, GMAT, PRAXIS II. *Expenses:* Contact institution.

Christopher Newport University, Graduate Studies, Department of Teacher Preparation, Newport News, VA 23606-3072. Offers MAT. *Faculty:* 18 full-time (9 women), 13 part-time/adjunct (11 women). *Students:* 67 full-time (57 women), 3 part-time (2 women); includes 12 minority (2 Black or African American, non-Hispanic/Latino; 4 Hispanic/Latino; 6 Two or more races, non-Hispanic/Latino). Average age 23. 78 applicants, 85% accepted, 60 enrolled. In 2016, 67 master's awarded. *Degree requirements:* For master's, comprehensive exam, thesis or alternative. *Entrance requirements:* For master's, PRAXIS II/Virginia Communication and Literacy Assessment (VCLA)/PRAXIS (core mathematics), minimum GPA of 3.0. Additional exam requirements/recommendations for international students: Required—TOEFL (minimum score 580 paper-based; 92 iBT), IELTS (minimum score 7). *Application deadline:* For fall admission, 4/1 for international students; for spring admission, 10/15 for domestic students, 10/1 for international students; for summer admission, 12/1 for domestic and international students. Applications are processed on a rolling basis. Application fee: $65. Electronic applications accepted. *Expenses:* Tuition, state resident: full-time $6660; part-time $370 per credit hour. Tuition, nonresident: full-time $15,138; part-time $841 per credit hour. *Required fees:* $3906; $217 per credit hour. Tuition and fees vary according to course load. *Financial support:* In 2016–17, 3 students received support. Unspecified assistantships available. Financial award application deadline: 3/1; financial award applicants required to submit FAFSA. *Faculty research:* Early literacy development, instructional innovations, professional teaching standards, multicultural issues, aesthetic education. *Total annual research expenditures:* $11,900. *Unit head:* Dr. Jean Filetti, Director, 757-594-7388, Fax: 757-594-7803, E-mail: filetti@cnu.edu. *Application contact:* Lyn Sawyer, Associate Director, Graduate Admissions, 757-594-7544, Fax: 757-594-7649, E-mail: gradstdy@cnu.edu.

The Citadel, The Military College of South Carolina, Citadel Graduate College, Zucker Family School of Education, Charleston, SC 29409. Offers elementary/secondary school administration and supervision (M Ed); elementary/secondary school counseling (M Ed); interdisciplinary STEM education (M Ed); literacy education (M Ed, Graduate Certificate); middle grades (MAT), including English, mathematics, science, social studies; physical education (grades K-12) (MAT); school superintendency (Ed S); secondary education (MAT), including biology, English, mathematics, social studies; student affairs (Graduate Certificate); student affairs and college counseling (M Ed). *Accreditation:* NCATE. *Program availability:* Part-time, evening/weekend, 100% online, blended/hybrid learning. *Faculty:* 9 full-time (4 women), 9 part-time/adjunct (5 women). *Students:* 70 full-time (58 women), 249 part-time (200 women); includes 87 minority (70 Black or African American, non-Hispanic/Latino; 1 Asian, non-Hispanic/Latino; 9 Hispanic/Latino; 7 Two or more races, non-Hispanic/Latino), 2 international. 146 applicants, 98% accepted, 105 enrolled. In 2016, 85 master's, 7 other advanced degrees awarded. *Degree requirements:* For master's, comprehensive exam (for some programs). *Entrance requirements:* For master's, GRE (minimum combined verbal and quantitative score of 290) or MAT (minimum score 396). Additional exam requirements/recommendations for international students: Required—TOEFL (minimum score 550 paper-based; 79 iBT). *Application deadline:* Applications are processed on a rolling basis. Application fee: $40. Electronic applications accepted. *Expenses:* Tuition, state resident: full-time $5121; part-time $569 per credit hour. Tuition, nonresident: full-time $8613; part-time $957 per credit hour. *Required fees:* $90 per term. *Financial support:* Fellowships and unspecified assistantships available. Support available to part-time students. Financial award application deadline: 7/1; financial award applicants required to submit FAFSA. *Unit head:* Dr. Larry G. Daniel, Dean, 843-953-5097, E-mail: ldaniel@citadel.edu. *Application contact:* Dr. Tammy J. Graham, Associate Professor, 843-953-6854, E-mail: tammy.graham@citadel.edu.
Website: http://www.citadel.edu/root/education-graduate-programs

City College of the City University of New York, Graduate School, School of Education, New York, NY 10031-9198. Offers MA, MS, MS Ed, AC. *Accreditation:* NCATE. *Program availability:* Part-time, evening/weekend. *Entrance requirements:* For master's, Liberal Arts and Sciences Test (LAST), Content Specialty Test (CST). Additional exam requirements/recommendations for international students: Required—TOEFL. Tuition and fees vary according to course load, degree level and program.

City University of Seattle, Graduate Division, Albright School of Education, Seattle, WA 98121. Offers administrator certification (Certificate); curriculum and instruction (M Ed); elementary education (MIT); guidance and counseling (M Ed); leadership (M Ed); reading and literacy (M Ed); school counseling (M Ed); special education (MIT); superintendent certification (Certificate). *Program availability:* Part-time, evening/weekend, online learning. *Degree requirements:* For master's, comprehensive exam (for some programs), thesis (for some programs). *Entrance requirements:* For master's, baccalaureate degree or equivalent from an accredited or otherwise recognized institution. Additional exam requirements/recommendations for international students: Required—TOEFL (minimum score 567 paper-based; 87 iBT); Recommended—IELTS. Electronic applications accepted. *Expenses:* Contact institution.

Claremont Graduate University, Graduate Programs, School of Educational Studies, Claremont, CA 91711-6160. Offers Africana education (Certificate); education and policy (MA, PhD); higher education/student affairs (MA, PhD); human development (MA, PhD); public school administration (MA, PhD); quantitative evaluation (MA, PhD); special education (MA, PhD); teacher education (MA); teaching and learning (MA, PhD); urban leadership (PhD); MBA/PhD. PhD program offered jointly with San Diego State University. *Program availability:* Part-time. *Faculty:* 14 full-time (9 women), 1 part-time/adjunct (0 women). *Students:* 195 full-time (143 women), 196 part-time (137 women); includes 217 minority (43 Black or African American, non-Hispanic/Latino; 4 American Indian or Alaska Native, non-Hispanic/Latino; 32 Asian, non-Hispanic/Latino; 117 Hispanic/Latino; 2 Native Hawaiian or other Pacific Islander, non-Hispanic/Latino; 19 Two or more races, non-Hispanic/Latino), 14 international. Average age 38. In 2016, 48 master's, 39 doctorates, 7 other advanced degrees awarded. Terminal master's awarded for partial completion of doctoral program. *Entrance requirements:* For master's and doctorate, GRE General Test. Additional exam requirements/recommendations for international students: Required—TOEFL (minimum score 75 iBT). *Application deadline:* For fall admission, 3/1 priority date for domestic and international students. Applications are processed on a rolling basis. Application fee: $80. Electronic applications accepted. *Expenses: Tuition:* Full-time $44,328; part-time $1847 per unit. *Required fees:* $600; $300 per semester. Tuition and fees vary according to course load and program. *Financial support:* Fellowships, research assistantships, Federal Work-Study, institutionally sponsored loans, and scholarships/grants available. Support available to part-time students. Financial award application deadline: 2/15; financial award applicants required to submit FAFSA. *Faculty research:* Education administration, K-12 and higher education, multicultural education, education policy, diversity in higher education, faculty issues. *Unit head:* Allen Omoto, Dean, 909-607-3786, E-mail: allen.omoto@cgu.edu. *Application contact:* Rachel Camacho, Senior Assistant Director of Admission, 909-607-9418, E-mail: camacho@cgu.edu.
Website: https://www.cgu.edu/school/school-of-educational-studies/

Clarion University of Pennsylvania, Office of Transfer, Adult and Graduate Admissions, Master of Education Program, Clarion, PA 16214. Offers curriculum and instruction (M Ed); early childhood (M Ed); math education (M Ed); reading (M Ed); science education (M Ed); special education (M Ed); technology (M Ed). *Accreditation:* NCATE. *Program availability:* Part-time, evening/weekend, 100% online, blended/hybrid learning. *Faculty:* 12 full-time (8 women), 5 part-time/adjunct (all women). *Students:* 17 full-time (15 women), 97 part-time (78 women); includes 1 minority (Two or more races, non-Hispanic/Latino). Average age 29. 76 applicants, 99% accepted, 48 enrolled. In 2016, 34 master's awarded. *Degree requirements:* For master's, comprehensive exam, thesis, or portfolio. *Entrance requirements:* For master's, minimum QPA of 3.0. Additional exam requirements/recommendations for international students: Required—TOEFL (minimum score 550 paper-based; 80 iBT), IELTS (minimum score 7). *Application deadline:* For fall admission, 8/1 for domestic students, 4/15 for international students; for spring admission, 8/1 for domestic students, 9/15 for international students. Applications are processed on a rolling basis. Application fee: $40. Electronic applications accepted. *Expenses:* $632.35 per credit. *Financial support:* Career-related internships or fieldwork, Federal Work-Study, scholarships/grants, and unspecified assistantships available. Support available to part-time students. Financial award application deadline: 3/1; financial award applicants required to submit FAFSA. *Unit head:* Dr. John McCullough, Chair, Department of Education, 814-393-2104, Fax: 814-393-2446, E-mail: gradstudies@clarion.edu. *Application contact:* Dana Bearer, Associate Director for Transfer, Adult, and Graduate Programs, 814-393-2337, Fax: 814-393-2722, E-mail: gradstudies@clarion.edu.

Clark Atlanta University, School of Education, Atlanta, GA 30314. Offers MA, MAT, Ed D, Ed S. *Accreditation:* NCATE. *Program availability:* Part-time, evening/weekend. *Faculty:* 10 full-time (6 women), 11 part-time/adjunct (8 women). *Students:* 85 full-time (49 women), 49 part-time (29 women); includes 101 minority (99 Black or African American, non-Hispanic/Latino; 1 Asian, non-Hispanic/Latino; 1 Hispanic/Latino), 16 international. Average age 33. 63 applicants, 86% accepted, 25 enrolled. In 2016, 36 master's, 12 doctorates, 2 other advanced degrees awarded. *Degree requirements:* For master's, comprehensive exam; for doctorate, comprehensive exam, thesis/dissertation. *Entrance requirements:* For master's, GRE General Test, minimum undergraduate GPA of 2.6; for doctorate, GRE General Test, minimum graduate GPA of 3.0. Additional exam requirements/recommendations for international students: Required—TOEFL (minimum score 500 paper-based; 61 iBT). *Application deadline:* For fall admission, 4/1 for domestic and international students; for spring admission, 11/1 for domestic and international students. Applications are processed on a rolling basis. Application fee: $40 ($55 for international students). Electronic applications accepted. *Expenses: Tuition:* Full-time $15,498; part-time $861 per credit hour. *Required fees:* $1326; $1326 per credit hour. Tuition and fees vary according to course load. *Financial support:* Career-related internships or fieldwork, Federal Work-Study, scholarships/grants, and unspecified assistantships available. Support available to part-time students. Financial award application deadline: 4/30; financial award applicants required to submit FAFSA. *Unit head:* Dr. Moses C. Norman, Dean, 404-880-8495, E-mail: mnorman@cau.edu. *Application contact:* Graduate Program Admissions, 404-880-8483, E-mail: graduateadmissions@cau.edu.

Clarke University, Program in Education, Dubuque, IA 52001-3198. Offers instructional leadership (MAE). *Program availability:* Part-time, 100% online, blended/hybrid learning. *Faculty:* 6 full-time (all women), 1 (woman) part-time/adjunct. *Students:* 6 full-time (all women), 13 part-time (all women); includes 2 minority (1 Hispanic/Latino; 1 Two or more races, non-Hispanic/Latino). Average age 26. 17 applicants, 82% accepted, 10 enrolled. In 2016, 16 master's awarded. *Degree requirements:* For master's, thesis optional. *Entrance requirements:* For master's, official transcripts documenting completion of undergraduate degree from accredited college or university, copy of teaching certificates and licenses, two recommendation forms, statement of goals and career plans, minimum GPA of 2.75. Additional exam requirements/recommendations for international students: Required—TOEFL (minimum score 550 paper-based, 80 iBT) or IELTS (6.5). *Application deadline:* Applications are processed on a rolling basis. Application fee: $35. Electronic applications accepted. *Expenses:* $500 per credit. *Financial support:* Applicants required to submit FAFSA. *Unit head:* Dr. Paula Schmidt, Director of Graduate Education, 563-588-6573, E-mail: paula.schmidt@clarke.edu. *Application contact:* Kimberly Roush, Director of Admission, Graduate and Adult Programs, 563-588-6539, Fax: 563-552-7994, E-mail: graduate@clarke.edu.

Clarkson University, Program in Education, Schenectady, NY 12308. Offers adolescence education 7-12 (MAT); technology education K-12 (MAT). *Accreditation:* TEAC. *Faculty:* 8 full-time (all women), 31 part-time/adjunct (17 women). *Students:* 38 full-time (23 women), 2 part-time (0 women); includes 6 minority (3 Asian, non-Hispanic/Latino; 2 Hispanic/Latino; 1 Two or more races, non-Hispanic/Latino), 7 international. 39 applicants, 79% accepted, 26 enrolled. In 2016, 15 master's awarded. *Degree requirements:* For master's, thesis (for some programs), thesis or project. *Entrance requirements:* For master's, GRE, minimum undergraduate GPA of 3.0. Additional exam requirements/recommendations for international students: Required—TOEFL (minimum score 550 paper-based, 80 iBT) or IELTS (6.5). *Application deadline:* Applications are processed on a rolling basis. Application fee: $50. Electronic applications accepted. *Expenses:* $900 per credit. *Financial support:* Scholarships/grants available. *Unit head:* Dr. Catherine Snyder, Chair of Education, 518-631-9870, E-mail: csnyder@clarkson.edu. *Application contact:* Dan Capogna, Graduate Admissions Contact, 518-631-9910, E-mail: graduate@clarkson.edu.
Website: http://graduate.clarkson.edu

Clark University, Graduate School, Adam Institute for Urban Teaching and School Practice, Worcester, MA 01610-1477. Offers MAT. *Faculty:* 9 full-time (6 women), 5 part-time/adjunct (3 women). *Students:* 24 full-time (18 women), 6 part-time (4 women); includes 8 minority (1 Black or African American, non-Hispanic/Latino; 3 Asian, non-Hispanic/Latino; 3 Hispanic/Latino; 1 Two or more races, non-Hispanic/Latino). Average age 26. 48 applicants, 69% accepted, 29 enrolled. In 2016, 29 master's awarded. *Degree requirements:* For master's, thesis or alternative, oral exam. *Entrance requirements:* For master's, GRE General Test, minimum GPA of 3.0, professional experience. Additional exam requirements/recommendations for international students: Required—TOEFL. *Application deadline:* For fall admission, 1/15 priority date for domestic students. Applications are processed on a rolling basis. Application fee: $75. *Expenses: Tuition:* Full-time $44,050. *Required fees:* $80. Tuition and fees vary according to course load and program. *Financial support:* Fellowships with tuition reimbursements, research assistantships with tuition reimbursements, teaching assistantships with tuition reimbursements, institutionally sponsored loans, and tuition waivers (partial) available. Financial award application deadline: 5/1. *Faculty research:* Developmental learning, instructional theory, educational program management, special education, urban education. *Total annual research expenditures:* $420,632. *Unit head:* Dr. Thomas Del Prete, Director, 508-793-7197. *Application contact:* Andrea Allen, Program Administrator, 508-793-7685, E-mail: aallen@clarku.edu.
Website: http://www.clarku.edu/education/adam-institute/

Clayton State University, School of Graduate Studies, College of Arts and Sciences, Program in Education, Morrow, GA 30260-0285. Offers biology (MAT); English (MAT); history (MAT); mathematics (MAT). *Accreditation:* NCATE. *Entrance requirements:* For master's, GRE, GACE, 2 official copies of transcripts, 3 recommendation letters, statement of purpose. Additional exam requirements/recommendations for international students: Required—TOEFL (minimum score 550 paper-based). Electronic applications accepted. *Expenses:* Tuition, state resident: full-time $3528; part-time $196 per credit hour. Tuition, nonresident: full-time $13,176; part-time $732 per credit hour. *Required fees:* $1454; $1454 per credit hour. $727 per semester. Tuition and fees vary according to campus/location and program.

Clemson University, Graduate School, College of Education, Clemson, SC 29634-0702. Offers administration and supervision (K-12) (M Ed, Ed S); education and organizational leadership (MS), including athletic leadership; educational leadership (PhD), including P-12; human resource development (MHRD); middle-level education (MAT). *Program availability:* Part-time, evening/weekend, 100% online. *Faculty:* 75 full-time (54 women), 1 part-time/adjunct (0 women). *Students:* 120 full-time (84 women), 309 part-time (206 women); includes 96 minority (68 Black or African American, non-Hispanic/Latino; 1 American Indian or Alaska Native, non-Hispanic/Latino; 3 Asian, non-Hispanic/Latino; 19 Hispanic/Latino; 5 Two or more races, non-Hispanic/Latino), 11 international. Average age 34. 417 applicants, 50% accepted, 133 enrolled. In 2016, 239 master's, 21 doctorates, 59 other advanced degrees awarded. *Degree requirements:* For master's, comprehensive exam (for some programs), thesis (for some programs); for doctorate, comprehensive exam, thesis/dissertation. *Entrance requirements:* For master's, doctorate, and other advanced degree, GRE General Test, unofficial transcripts, letters of recommendation. Additional exam requirements/recommendations for international students: Required—TOEFL (minimum score 80 iBT), IELTS (minimum score 7). *Application deadline:* Applications are processed on a rolling basis. Application fee: $80 ($90 for international students). Electronic applications accepted. *Expenses:* Contact institution. *Financial support:* In 2016–17, 75 students received support, including 22 fellowships with partial tuition reimbursements available (averaging $6,316 per year), 28 research assistantships with partial tuition reimbursements available (averaging $15,399 per year), 5 teaching assistantships with partial tuition reimbursements available (averaging $30,000 per year); unspecified assistantships also available. *Faculty research:* Early literacy and motivation, STEAM education, legal/policy issues in education, leadership, special education interventions/assessment/policy. *Total annual research expenditures:* $2.8 million. *Unit head:* Dr. George Petersen, Dean, 864-656-4444, Fax: 864-656-0311, E-mail: soedean@clemson.edu. *Application contact:* Dr. David Fleming, Graduate Programs Coordinator, 864-656-1881, Fax: 864-656-0311, E-mail: dflemin@clemson.edu.
Website: http://www.clemson.edu/education/

Cleveland State University, College of Graduate Studies, College of Education and Human Services, Cleveland, OH 44115. Offers M Ed, MPH, PhD, Certificate, Ed S. *Accreditation:* NCATE. *Program availability:* Part-time, evening/weekend, 100% online, blended/hybrid learning. *Faculty:* 86 full-time (60 women), 106 part-time/adjunct (81 women). *Students:* 253 full-time (188 women), 751 part-time (576 women); includes 320 minority (249 Black or African American, non-Hispanic/Latino; 2 American Indian or Alaska Native, non-Hispanic/Latino; 8 Asian, non-Hispanic/Latino; 41 Hispanic/Latino; 1 Native Hawaiian or other Pacific Islander, non-Hispanic/Latino; 19 Two or more races, non-Hispanic/Latino), 65 international. Average age 34. 487 applicants, 58% accepted, 178 enrolled. In 2016, 314 master's, 20 doctorates awarded. *Degree requirements:* For master's, comprehensive exam (for some programs), thesis optional; for doctorate, one foreign language, comprehensive exam, thesis/dissertation; for other advanced degree, comprehensive exam (for some programs), thesis optional, internship. *Entrance requirements:* For master's, GRE General Test or MAT, minimum undergraduate GPA of 2.75, 3.0 if undergraduate degree is 6 or more years old; for doctorate, GRE General Test, master's degree, minimum graduate GPA of 3.25; for other advanced degree, GRE General Test or MAT, master's degree, minimum graduate GPA of 3.0. Additional exam requirements/recommendations for international students: Required—TOEFL (minimum score 550 paper-based; 78 iBT). *Application deadline:* For fall admission, 7/1 priority date for domestic students, 5/15 for international students; for spring admission, 11/15 priority date for domestic students, 11/1 for international students; for summer admission, 4/1 for domestic students, 3/15 for international students. Applications are processed on a rolling basis. Application fee: $30. Electronic applications accepted. *Expenses:* Tuition, state resident: full-time $9565. Tuition, nonresident: full-time $17,980. Tuition and fees vary according to program. *Financial support:* In 2016–17, 64 students received support, including 38 research assistantships with full tuition reimbursements available (averaging $6,960 per year), 2 teaching assistantships with full tuition reimbursements available (averaging $7,800 per year); career-related internships or fieldwork, Federal Work-Study, scholarships/grants, tuition waivers (partial), and unspecified assistantships also available. Support available to part-time students. Financial award application deadline: 8/1; financial award applicants required to submit FAFSA. *Faculty research:* Adult learning and development, counseling theory and practice, equity issues in education (race, ethnicity, gender, socioeconomics), health care and health education, population nursing, urban educational leadership, curriculum and instruction. *Total annual research expenditures:* $7.5 million. *Unit head:*

Dr. Sajit Zachariah, Dean, 216-523-7143, Fax: 216-687-5415, E-mail: sajit.zachariah@csuohio.edu. *Application contact:* Patricia Sokolowski, Office Coordinator/Assistant to the Dean, 216-523-7143, Fax: 216-687-5415, E-mail: p.sokolowski@csuohio.edu.
Website: http://www.csuohio.edu/cehs/

Coastal Carolina University, Spadoni College of Education, Conway, SC 29528-6054. Offers education (MAT); educational leadership (M Ed, Ed S); English for speakers of other languages (Certificate); instructional technology (M Ed, Ed S); learning and teaching (M Ed); online teaching and training (Certificate); special education (M Ed). *Accreditation:* NCATE. *Program availability:* Part-time, evening/weekend. *Faculty:* 16 full-time (8 women), 12 part-time/adjunct (7 women). *Students:* 74 full-time (48 women), 340 part-time (271 women); includes 78 minority (70 Black or African American, non-Hispanic/Latino; 1 American Indian or Alaska Native, non-Hispanic/Latino; 2 Asian, non-Hispanic/Latino; 4 Hispanic/Latino; 1 Two or more races, non-Hispanic/Latino), 2 international. Average age 33. 298 applicants, 93% accepted, 213 enrolled. In 2016, 167 master's, 8 other advanced degrees awarded. *Degree requirements:* For master's and other advanced degree, comprehensive exam. *Entrance requirements:* For master's, GRE, GMAT, 2 letters of recommendation, evidence of teacher certification, official transcripts; for other advanced degree, official transcripts, minimum of 3 years' teaching experience, statement of interest in the program, 3 letters of reference, master's degree in educational leadership or related field with minimum overall GPA of 3.0. Additional exam requirements/recommendations for international students: Required—TOEFL (minimum score 550 paper-based; 79 iBT), IELTS (minimum score 6.5). *Application deadline:* For fall admission, 7/1 priority date for domestic and international students; for spring admission, 11/1 priority date for domestic and international students; for summer admission, 3/1 priority date for domestic and international students. Applications are processed on a rolling basis. Application fee: $45. Electronic applications accepted. *Expenses:* Tuition, state resident: full-time $9990; part-time $555 per credit hour. Tuition, nonresident: full-time $18,108; part-time $1006 per credit hour. *Required fees:* $90; $5 per credit hour. *Financial support:* Fellowships, research assistantships, and unspecified assistantships available. Support available to part-time students. Financial award application deadline: 3/1; financial award applicants required to submit FAFSA. *Unit head:* Dr. Edward Jadallah, Dean, 843-349-2773, Fax: 843-349-2106, E-mail: ejadalla@coastal.edu. *Application contact:* Dr. James O. Luken, Associate Provost/Vice-Dean of the Coastal Environment, 843-349-2235, Fax: 843-349-6444, E-mail: joluken@coastal.edu.
Website: http://www.coastal.edu/education/

The College at Brockport, State University of New York, School of Education, Health, and Human Services, Department of Education and Human Development, Brockport, NY 14420-2997. Offers adolescence education (MS Ed), including adolescence biology education, adolescence chemistry education, adolescence earth science education, adolescence English education, adolescence mathematics education, adolescence physics education, adolescence social studies education; bilingual education (MS Ed, AGC); childhood curriculum specialist (MS Ed); inclusive generalist education (MS Ed, AGC, Advanced Certificate), including biology (MS Ed, AGC), chemistry (MS Ed), English (MS Ed, Advanced Certificate), mathematics (MS Ed, Advanced Certificate), science (MS Ed, Advanced Certificate), social studies (MS Ed, Advanced Certificate); literacy education B-12 (MS Ed). *Accreditation:* NCATE. *Faculty:* 14 full-time (9 women), 12 part-time/adjunct (11 women). *Students:* 56 full-time (36 women), 168 part-time (130 women); includes 16 minority (5 Black or African American, non-Hispanic/Latino; 3 Asian, non-Hispanic/Latino; 4 Hispanic/Latino; 4 Two or more races, non-Hispanic/Latino). 93 applicants, 78% accepted, 62 enrolled. In 2016, 74 master's, 1 AGC awarded. *Degree requirements:* For master's, thesis or alternative. *Entrance requirements:* For master's, minimum GPA of 3.0, letters of recommendation, interview (for some programs); statement of objectives, current resume. Additional exam requirements/recommendations for international students: Required—TOEFL (minimum score 550 paper-based; 79 iBT), IELTS (minimum score 6.5). *Application deadline:* For fall admission, 3/15 priority date for domestic and international students; for spring admission, 10/15 priority date for domestic and international students; for summer admission, 3/15 priority date for domestic and international students. Application fee: $80. Electronic applications accepted. *Expenses:* Contact institution. *Financial support:* In 2016–17, 1 fellowship with full tuition reimbursement (averaging $7,500 per year), 1 teaching assistantship with full tuition reimbursement (averaging $6,000 per year) were awarded; Federal Work-Study, scholarships/grants, and unspecified assistantships also available. Support available to part-time students. Financial award application deadline: 3/15; financial award applicants required to submit FAFSA. *Faculty research:* Educational assessment, literacy education, inclusive education, teacher preparation, qualitative methodology. *Unit head:* Dr. Sue Robb, Chairperson, 585-395-5550, Fax: 585-395-2172, E-mail: srobb@brockport.edu. *Application contact:* Anne Walton, Coordinator of Certification and Graduate Advisement, 585-395-2326, Fax: 585-395-2172, E-mail: awalton@brockport.edu.
Website: http://www.brockport.edu/ehd/

College of Charleston, Graduate School, School of Education, Health, and Human Performance, Charleston, SC 29424-0001. Offers M Ed, MAT, Certificate. *Accreditation:* NCATE. *Program availability:* Part-time, evening/weekend. *Degree requirements:* For master's, thesis or alternative, written qualifying exam, student teaching experience (MAT). *Entrance requirements:* For master's, teaching certificate (M Ed). Additional exam requirements/recommendations for international students: Required—TOEFL (minimum score 81 iBT). *Application deadline:* For fall admission, 4/1 for domestic students; for spring admission, 11/1 for domestic students. Applications are processed on a rolling basis. Application fee: $45. Electronic applications accepted. *Financial support:* Research assistantships, teaching assistantships, career-related internships or fieldwork, Federal Work-Study, scholarships/grants, and unspecified assistantships available. Support available to part-time students. Financial award application deadline: 4/1; financial award applicants required to submit FAFSA. *Faculty research:* Computer-assisted instruction, higher education, faculty development, teaching study skills to college students. *Unit head:* Dr. Frances Welch, Dean, 843-953-5613, Fax: 843-953-5407, E-mail: welchf@cofc.edu. *Application contact:* Susan Hallatt, Director of Graduate Admissions, 843-953-5614, Fax: 843-953-1434, E-mail: hallatts@cofc.edu.
Website: http://www.cofc.edu/schoolofeducation/

The College of Idaho, Department of Education, Caldwell, ID 83605. Offers curriculum and instruction (M Ed); teaching (MAT). *Degree requirements:* For master's, thesis. *Entrance requirements:* For master's, GRE, portfolio, minimum undergraduate GPA of 3.0, interview. *Faculty research:* Discourse analysis, at-risk youth, children's literature, research design, program evaluation.

College of Mount Saint Vincent, School of Professional and Graduate Studies, Department of Teacher Education, Riverdale, NY 10471-1093. Offers instructional technology and global perspectives (Certificate); middle level education (Certificate); multicultural studies (Certificate); teaching English to speakers of other languages (MS Ed); urban and multicultural education (MS Ed). *Accreditation:* TEAC. *Program availability:* Part-time. *Degree requirements:* For master's, comprehensive exam. *Entrance requirements:* For master's, interview, New York teaching certificate. Additional exam requirements/recommendations for international students: Required—TOEFL.

The College of New Jersey, Office of Graduate and Advancing Education, School of Education, Ewing, NJ 08628. Offers M Ed, MA, MAT, Certificate, Ed S. *Accreditation:* NCATE. *Program availability:* Part-time, evening/weekend. *Degree requirements:* For master's, comprehensive exam. *Entrance requirements:* For master's, GRE, minimum GPA of 3.0 in field or 2.75 overall; for other advanced degree, previous master's degree or higher. Additional exam requirements/recommendations for international students: Required—TOEFL. Electronic applications accepted.

The College of New Rochelle, Graduate School, Division of Education, New Rochelle, NY 10805-2308. Offers art education (MS); childhood education/early childhood education (MS Ed), including childhood education, early childhood education; educational leadership (MS, Advanced Certificate, Advanced Diploma), including school building leader (MS, Advanced Certificate), school district leader (MS, Advanced Diploma); gifted education (Certificate); literacy education (MS Ed); multilingual/multicultural education (MS Ed, Certificate), including bilingual education (Certificate), multilingual/multicultural education (Certificate), teaching English to speakers of other languages; special education (MS Ed). *Program availability:* Part-time, evening/weekend. *Degree requirements:* For master's, comprehensive exam (for some programs), thesis (for some programs). *Entrance requirements:* For master's, interview; minimum GPA of 3.0 in field, 2.7 overall. Electronic applications accepted.

College of Saint Elizabeth, Department of Educational Leadership, Morristown, NJ 07960-6989. Offers assistive technology (Certificate); education (MA); educational leadership (MA, Ed D). *Program availability:* Part-time. *Degree requirements:* For master's, thesis or alternative; for doctorate, thesis/dissertation. *Entrance requirements:* For master's, GRE, GMAT, baccalaureate degree with minimum GPA of 2.75, standard teaching certificate, three years of exemplary certified teaching experience, writing sample, two letters of recommendation from school(s) of employment, personal interview (for educational leadership); for doctorate, GRE, MA in educational leadership or related field; leadership experience including certification as principal and/or supervisor; letter of recommendation from college/university professor attesting to candidate's ability to perform a high level of academic work in the program; for Certificate, MA in education; certification; baccalaureate degree with minimum GPA of 2.75; personal written statement; two letters of recommendation; official transcripts from all colleges attended. Additional exam requirements/recommendations for international students: Required—TOEFL (minimum score 550 paper-based; 79 iBT), IELTS (minimum score 6.5). Electronic applications accepted. Application fee is waived when completed online. *Expenses:* Contact institution.

College of St. Joseph, Graduate Programs, Division of Education, Rutland, VT 05701-3899. Offers elementary education (M Ed); general education (M Ed); reading (M Ed); secondary education (M Ed), including English, social studies; special education (M Ed). *Program availability:* Part-time, evening/weekend. *Degree requirements:* For master's, comprehensive exam. *Entrance requirements:* For master's, PRAXIS I, essay; two letters of reference from academic or professional sources; official transcripts of all graduate and undergraduate study. Additional exam requirements/recommendations for international students: Required—TOEFL (minimum score 550 paper-based). *Application deadline:* Applications are processed on a rolling basis. Application fee: $35. Electronic applications accepted. *Expenses: Tuition:* Full-time $13,800; part-time $560 per credit. *Required fees:* $75 per semester. Full-time tuition and fees vary according to course load. *Financial support:* Career-related internships or fieldwork, Federal Work-Study, and unspecified assistantships available. Support available to part-time students. Financial award application deadline: 3/1. *Faculty research:* Co-teaching, Response to Intervention (RTI). *Unit head:* Dr. Maria Bove, Chair, 802-773-5900 Ext. 3243, Fax: 802-776-5258, E-mail: mbove@csj.edu. *Application contact:* Alan Young, Dean of Admissions, 802-773-5900 Ext. 3227, Fax: 802-776-5310, E-mail: alanyoung@csj.edu.
Website: http://www.csj.edu/

College of Saint Mary, Program in Teaching, Omaha, NE 68106. Offers MAT. *Program availability:* Evening/weekend. *Entrance requirements:* For master's, Pre-Professional Skills Tests (PPST), minimum cumulative GPA of 2.5, background check.

The College of Saint Rose, Graduate Studies, Thelma P. Lally School of Education, Albany, NY 12203-1419. Offers MS, MS Ed, Advanced Certificate, Certificate. *Accreditation:* NCATE. *Program availability:* Part-time, evening/weekend, 100% online. *Faculty:* 42 full-time (24 women), 60 part-time/adjunct (36 women). *Students:* 398 full-time (337 women), 923 part-time (731 women); includes 385 minority (186 Black or African American, non-Hispanic/Latino; 4 American Indian or Alaska Native, non-Hispanic/Latino; 37 Asian, non-Hispanic/Latino; 142 Hispanic/Latino; 1 Native Hawaiian or other Pacific Islander, non-Hispanic/Latino; 15 Two or more races, non-Hispanic/Latino), 21 international. Average age 33. 1,023 applicants, 62% accepted, 487 enrolled. In 2016, 347 master's, 610 other advanced degrees awarded. *Degree requirements:* For master's, comprehensive exam (for some programs), thesis (for some programs), capstone project. *Entrance requirements:* For master's, minimum undergraduate GPA of 3.0. Additional exam requirements/recommendations for international students: Required—TOEFL (minimum score 550 paper-based; 80 iBT), IELTS (minimum score 6), PTE (minimum score 56). *Application deadline:* For fall admission, 4/1 priority date for domestic and international students; for spring admission, 10/15 priority date for domestic and international students; for summer admission, 3/15 priority date for domestic and international students. Applications are processed on a rolling basis. Application fee: $40. Electronic applications accepted. *Expenses: Tuition:* Full-time $14,382; part-time $799 per credit. *Required fees:* $814; $32 per credit. $88 per semester. Tuition and fees vary according to course load. *Financial support:* Career-related internships or fieldwork, scholarships/grants, tuition waivers (partial), and unspecified assistantships available. Support available to part-time students. Financial award application deadline: 4/15. *Unit head:* Dr. Margaret McLane, Dean, 518-454-2147. *Application contact:* Cris Murray, Assistant Vice President for Graduate Recruitment and Enrollment, 518-454-5136, Fax: 518-458-5479, E-mail: grad@strose.edu.
Website: https://www.strose.edu/academics/schools/school-of-education/

The College of St. Scholastica, Graduate Studies, Department of Education, Duluth, MN 55811-4199. Offers M Ed, MS, Certificate. *Accreditation:* TEAC. *Program availability:* Part-time, evening/weekend, online learning. *Entrance requirements:* Additional exam requirements/recommendations for international students: Required—TOEFL (minimum score 550 paper-based; 79 iBT). Electronic applications accepted.

College of Staten Island of the City University of New York, Graduate Programs, School of Education, Staten Island, NY 10314-6600. Offers MS Ed, Advanced Certificate, Post-Master's Certificate. *Accreditation:* NCATE. *Faculty:* 25 full-time, 40 part-time/adjunct. *Students:* 32 full-time, 414 part-time. Average age 30. In 2016, 117 master's, 26 Advanced Certificates awarded. *Expenses:* Tuition, state resident: full-time $10,130; part-time $425 per credit. Tuition, nonresident: full-time $18,720; part-time $780 per credit. *Required fees:* $181.10 per semester. Tuition and fees vary according to program. *Unit head:* Dr. Kenneth Gold, 718-982-3737, Fax: 718-982-3743, E-mail: kenneth.gold@csi.cuny.edu. *Application contact:* Sasha Spence, Associate Director for Graduate Admissions, 718-982-2019, Fax: 718-982-2500, E-mail: sasha.spence@csi.cuny.edu.
Website: http://csivc.csi.cuny.edu/education/files

Education—General

★ **The College of William and Mary,** School of Education, Williamsburg, VA 23187-8795. Offers M Ed, MA Ed, Ed D, PhD, Ed S. *Accreditation:* NCATE. *Program availability:* Part-time, evening/weekend. *Faculty:* 54 full-time (31 women), 84 part-time/adjunct (57 women). *Students:* 201 full-time (147 women), 167 part-time (118 women); includes 80 minority (43 Black or African American, non-Hispanic/Latino; 1 American Indian or Alaska Native, non-Hispanic/Latino; 7 Asian, non-Hispanic/Latino; 19 Hispanic/Latino; 10 Two or more races, non-Hispanic/Latino), 9 international. Average age 33. 432 applicants, 65% accepted, 167 enrolled. In 2016, 127 master's, 30 doctorates, 12 other advanced degrees awarded. *Degree requirements:* For master's, project; for doctorate, comprehensive exam, thesis/dissertation; for Ed S, internship. *Entrance requirements:* For master's, GRE, MAT, PRAXIS Core Academic Skills for Educators, minimum GPA of 2.5; for doctorate, GRE or MAT, minimum GPA of 3.5; for Ed S, GRE, minimum GPA of 3.0. Additional exam requirements/recommendations for international students: Required—TOEFL (minimum score 100 iBT), IELTS (minimum score 7). *Application deadline:* For fall admission, 1/15 for domestic and international students; for spring admission, 10/1 for domestic and international students. Application fee: $50. Electronic applications accepted. *Expenses:* $14,258 per year in-state full-time, $275 per credit in-state part-time; $30,500 per year out-of-state full-time, $1,200 per credit out-of-state part-time. *Financial support:* In 2016–17, 140 students received support, including 1 fellowship with full tuition reimbursement available (averaging $20,000 per year), 96 research assistantships (averaging $17,926 per year); career-related internships or fieldwork, scholarships/grants, and unspecified assistantships also available. Financial award application deadline: 1/15; financial award applicants required to submit FAFSA. *Faculty research:* Gifted education, curriculum and instruction, technology and education, leadership, classroom assessment. *Total annual research expenditures:* $6.6 million. *Unit head:* Dr. Spencer G. Niles, Dean, 757-221-2317, E-mail: sgniles@wm.edu. *Application contact:* Dorothy Smith Osborne, Assistant Dean for Academic Programs and Student Services, 757-221-2317, E-mail: dsosbo@wm.edu.
Website: http://education.wm.edu

See Display on this page and Close-Up on page 725.

Colorado Christian University, Program in Curriculum and Instruction, Lakewood, CO 80226. Offers corporate education (MACI); early childhood educator (MACI); elementary educator (MACI); instructional technology (MACI); master educator (MACI); online course developer (MACI); online teaching and learning (MACI); special education generalist (MACI). *Program availability:* Part-time, evening/weekend. *Degree requirements:* For master's, thesis optional, practicum. *Entrance requirements:* For master's, interviews, letters of recommendation. Additional exam requirements/recommendations for international students: Required—TOEFL. Electronic applications accepted. *Expenses:* Contact institution.

The Colorado College, Education Department, Colorado Springs, CO 80903-3294. Offers elementary education (MAT), including elementary school teaching; secondary education (MAT), including art teaching (K-12), English teaching, foreign language teaching, mathematics teaching, music teaching, science teaching, social studies teaching; teaching (MAT), including arts and humanities, integrated natural sciences, liberal arts, Southwest studies. *Degree requirements:* For master's, thesis, internship. Electronic applications accepted. *Faculty research:* Geology, environmental resources, urban education, educational psychology, arts integration in the classroom, literacy/early childhood.

Colorado Mesa University, Center for Teacher Education, Grand Junction, CO 81501-3122. Offers educational leadership (MAEd); English for speakers of other languages (MAEd); exceptional learner/special education (MAEd); teacher education (Graduate Certificate); teacher leader (MAEd). *Accreditation:* NCATE. *Program availability:* Part-time. *Faculty:* 6 full-time (5 women), 12 part-time/adjunct (6 women). *Students:* 18 full-time (13 women), 35 part-time (28 women); includes 4 minority (1 American Indian or Alaska Native, non-Hispanic/Latino; 3 Hispanic/Latino), 1 international. Average age 34. 28 applicants, 25% accepted, 6 enrolled. In 2016, 26 master's, 36 other advanced degrees awarded. *Degree requirements:* For master's, comprehensive exam (for some programs), capstone presentation. *Entrance requirements:* For master's, 3 professional letters of recommendation, Colorado teaching license, minimum baccalaureate GPA of 3.0; for Graduate Certificate, minimum baccalaureate GPA of 3.0. Additional exam requirements/recommendations for international students: Required—TOEFL (minimum score 550 paper-based). *Application deadline:* For fall admission, 6/1 priority date for domestic and international students; for spring admission, 11/1 priority date for domestic and international students; for summer admission, 3/1 priority date for domestic and international students. Applications are processed on a rolling basis. Application fee: $50. Electronic applications accepted. *Expenses:* $406.43 per credit hour resident tuition and fees, $1,092.43 per credit hour non-resident tuition and fees. *Financial support:* In 2016–17, 2 students received support. Scholarships/grants available. Financial award applicants required to submit FAFSA. *Faculty research:* K-8 STEM instruction, special education inclusion, elementary math literacy, secondary literacy, elementary/early childhood education literacy. *Unit head:* Dr. Blake Bickham, Department Head, 970-248-1729, E-mail: bbickham@coloradomesa.edu. *Application contact:* Mary Kienietz, Administrative Assistant, 970-248-1786, E-mail: mkieniet@coloradomesa.edu. Website: http://coloradomesa.edu/teachered/index.html

Colorado State University, College of Health and Human Sciences, School of Education, Fort Collins, CO 80523-1588. Offers adult education and training (M Ed); counseling and career development (M Ed); education sciences (PhD); higher education leadership (PhD); organization learning, performance, and change (PhD); organizational learning, performance, and change (M Ed); student affairs in higher education (MS); teaching and learning (M Ed), including principal licensure, teacher licensure. *Accreditation:* ACA; TEAC. *Program availability:* Part-time, online only, 100% online, blended/hybrid learning, face-to-face off-campus courses. *Faculty:* 29 full-time (21 women), 23 part-time/adjunct (11 women). *Students:* 80 full-time (56 women), 541 part-time (353 women); includes 142 minority (26 Black or African American, non-Hispanic/Latino; 2 American Indian or Alaska Native, non-Hispanic/Latino; 22 Asian, non-Hispanic/Latino; 71 Hispanic/Latino; 21 Two or more races, non-Hispanic/Latino), 18 international. Average age 37. 483 applicants, 31% accepted, 137 enrolled. In 2016, 183 master's, 33 doctorates awarded. *Degree requirements:* For master's, thesis optional, professional portfolio; for doctorate, comprehensive exam, thesis/dissertation. *Entrance requirements:* For master's, bachelor's degree; minimum GPA of 3.0 in last degree earned; for doctorate, GRE or GMAT (depending upon specialization), master's degree; minimum GPA of 3.0 in last degree earned. Additional exam requirements/recommendations for international students: Required—TOEFL (minimum score 550 paper-based; 80 iBT), IELTS (minimum score 6.5), PTE (minimum score 58). *Application deadline:* Applications are processed on a rolling basis. Application fee: $60 ($70 for international students). Electronic applications accepted. *Expenses:* Contact institution. *Financial support:* In 2016–17, 3 students received support, including 7 research assistantships with full tuition reimbursements available (averaging $11,749 per year), 5 teaching assistantships with full tuition reimbursements available (averaging $15,886 per year); fellowships with full tuition reimbursements available, scholarships/grants, and unspecified assistantships also available. Financial award application

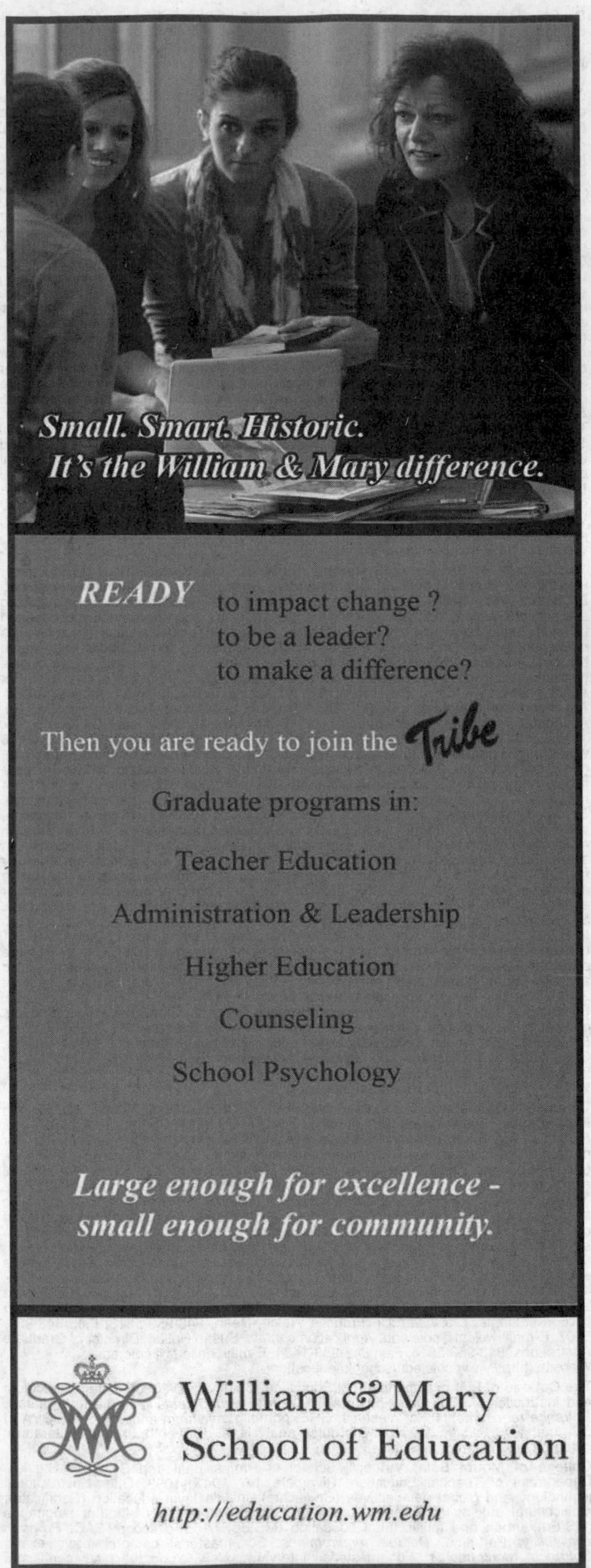
Small. Smart. Historic.
It's the William & Mary difference.
READY
to impact change ?
to be a leader?
to make a difference?
Then you are ready to join the Tribe
Graduate programs in:
Teacher Education
Administration & Leadership
Higher Education
Counseling
School Psychology
Large enough for excellence -
small enough for community.
William & Mary
School of Education
http://education.wm.edu

deadline: 3/1; financial award applicants required to submit FAFSA. *Faculty research:* Higher education leadership; research methods; human resource development; K-16 education; diversity, equity, and inclusion. *Total annual research expenditures:* $499,898. *Unit head:* Dr. Louise Jennings, Co-Director, 970-491-6317, Fax: 970-491-1317, E-mail: louise.jennings@colostate.edu. *Application contact:* Kelli Clark, Graduate Programs Coordinator, 970-491-2093, Fax: 970-491-1317, E-mail: kelli.clark@colostate.edu.
Website: http://www.soe.chhs.colostate.edu/

Colorado State University–Global Campus, Graduate Programs, Greenwood Village, CO 80111. Offers criminal justice and law enforcement administration (MS); education leadership (MS); finance (MS); healthcare administration and management (MS); human resource management (MHRM); information technology management (MITM); international management (MS); management (MS); organizational leadership (MS); professional accounting (MPA); project management (MS); teaching and learning (MS). *Accreditation:* ACBSP. *Program availability:* Online learning.

Colorado State University–Pueblo, College of Education, Engineering and Professional Studies, Education Program, Pueblo, CO 81001-4901. Offers art education (M Ed); foreign language education (M Ed); health and physical education (M Ed); instructional technology (M Ed); linguistically diverse education (M Ed); music education (M Ed); special education (M Ed). *Accreditation:* TEAC. *Program availability:* Part-time. *Degree requirements:* For master's, portfolio. *Entrance requirements:* For master's, 3 recommendations, teaching license. Additional exam requirements/recommendations for international students: Required—TOEFL (minimum score 500 paper-based). Electronic applications accepted. *Faculty research:* Portfolio assessment, math education, science education.

Columbia College, Graduate Programs, Education Division, Columbia, SC 29203-5998. Offers divergent learning (M Ed); higher education administration (M Ed). *Accreditation:* NCATE. *Program availability:* Part-time, evening/weekend, online learning. *Degree requirements:* For master's, thesis. *Entrance requirements:* For master's, GRE General Test, MAT, 2 recommendations, current South Carolina teaching certificate, minimum GPA of 3.2. Electronic applications accepted. *Expenses:* Contact institution.

Columbia College, Master of Arts in Teaching Program, Columbia, MO 65216-0002. Offers MAT. *Program availability:* Part-time, evening/weekend, 100% online, blended/hybrid learning. *Faculty:* 6 full-time (4 women), 18 part-time/adjunct (14 women). *Students:* 14 full-time (11 women), 86 part-time (66 women); includes 20 minority (7 Black or African American, non-Hispanic/Latino; 1 American Indian or Alaska Native, non-Hispanic/Latino; 2 Asian, non-Hispanic/Latino; 7 Hispanic/Latino; 3 Two or more races, non-Hispanic/Latino), 2 international. Average age 35. 58 applicants, 86% accepted, 40 enrolled. In 2016, 45 master's awarded. *Entrance requirements:* For master's, 3 letters of recommendation, minimum cumulative undergraduate GPA of 3.0, resume, goal statement. Additional exam requirements/recommendations for international students: Required—TOEFL (minimum score 500 paper-based; 61 iBT). *Application deadline:* For fall admission, 8/9 priority date for domestic and international students; for spring admission, 12/27 priority date for domestic and international students. Applications are processed on a rolling basis. Application fee: $55. Electronic applications accepted. *Expenses:* Contact institution. *Financial support:* In 2016–17, 1 student received support. Career-related internships or fieldwork, Federal Work-Study, and scholarships/grants available. Financial award application deadline: 3/15; financial award applicants required to submit FAFSA. *Unit head:* Dr. Kristi Clevenger, Graduate Program Coordinator, 573-875-7590, Fax: 573-876-4493, E-mail: kclevenger@ccis.edu. *Application contact:* Stephanie Johnson, Director of Admissions, 573-875-7352, Fax: 573-875-7506, E-mail: sjohnson@ccis.edu.
Website: http://www.ccis.edu/graduate/academics/degrees.asp?MAT

Columbia International University, Columbia Graduate School, Columbia, SC 29230-3122. Offers Bible teaching (MABT); counseling (MACN); early childhood and elementary education (MAT); educational administration (M Ed); educational leadership (PhD); instruction and learning (M Ed); teaching English as a foreign language (Certificate); teaching English as a foreign language and intercultural studies (MATF). *Program availability:* Part-time, evening/weekend, online learning. *Degree requirements:* For master's, internships, professional project. *Entrance requirements:* For master's, MAT; GRE (for some programs), minimum GPA of 2.7. Additional exam requirements/recommendations for international students: Required—TOEFL. Electronic applications accepted.

Columbus State University, Graduate Studies, College of Education and Health Professions, Columbus, GA 31907-5645. Offers M Ed, MAT, MS, MSN, Ed D, Ed S. *Accreditation:* ACA (one or more programs are accredited); NCATE. *Program availability:* Part-time, evening/weekend, 100% online, blended/hybrid learning. *Faculty:* 43 full-time (24 women), 45 part-time/adjunct (31 women). *Students:* 365 full-time (260 women), 597 part-time (476 women); includes 483 minority (428 Black or African American, non-Hispanic/Latino; 2 American Indian or Alaska Native, non-Hispanic/Latino; 12 Asian, non-Hispanic/Latino; 23 Hispanic/Latino; 18 Two or more races, non-Hispanic/Latino), 6 international. Average age 37. 748 applicants, 53% accepted, 283 enrolled. In 2016, 162 master's, 7 doctorates, 139 other advanced degrees awarded. *Degree requirements:* For master's, thesis, exit exam; for doctorate, thesis/dissertation; for Ed S, thesis or alternative. *Entrance requirements:* For master's, GRE General Test, minimum undergraduate GPA of 2.75; for doctorate, GRE General Test, minimum graduate GPA of 3.5, four years of professional service; for Ed S, GRE General Test, minimum undergraduate GPA of 2.75, graduate 3.0. Additional exam requirements/recommendations for international students: Required—TOEFL (minimum score 550 paper-based; 79 iBT). *Application deadline:* For fall admission, 6/30 for domestic students, 5/1 for international students; for spring admission, 11/1 for domestic and international students; for summer admission, 3/1 for domestic and international students. Applications are processed on a rolling basis. Application fee: $50. Electronic applications accepted. *Expenses:* Tuition, state resident: full-time $4804; part-time $2412 per semester hour. Tuition, nonresident: full-time $19,218; part-time $9612 per semester hour. *Required fees:* $1850; $1850 per semester hour. Tuition and fees vary according to program. *Financial support:* In 2016–17, 113 students received support, including 25 research assistantships with partial tuition reimbursements available (averaging $3,000 per year); career-related internships or fieldwork, Federal Work-Study, institutionally sponsored loans, scholarships/grants, tuition waivers (partial), and unspecified assistantships also available. Support available to part-time students. Financial award application deadline: 5/1; financial award applicants required to submit FAFSA. *Unit head:* Dr. Deirdre Greer, Dean, 706-507-8505, Fax: 706-569-3134, E-mail: greer_deirdre@columbusstate.edu. *Application contact:* Kristin Williams, Director of International and Graduate Recruitment, 706-507-8848, Fax: 706-568-5091, E-mail: williams_kristin@columbusstate.edu.
Website: http://coehp.columbusstate.edu/

Concordia College, Program in Education, Moorhead, MN 56562. Offers world language instruction (M Ed). *Degree requirements:* For master's, thesis/seminar. *Entrance requirements:* For master's, 2 professional references, 1 personal reference.

Concordia University, College of Education, Portland, OR 97211-6099. Offers career and technical education (M Ed); curriculum and instruction (M Ed), including adolescent literacy, career and technical education, e-learning/technology education, early childhood education, English for speakers of other languages, English language development, environmental education, mathematics, methods and curriculum, reading, science, teacher leadership, the inclusive classroom; early childhood (MAT); education leadership (Ed D); educational administration (M Ed); elementary education (MAT); secondary education (MAT); special education (M Ed); teacher leadership (Ed D). *Program availability:* Part-time, online learning. *Degree requirements:* For master's, comprehensive exam, work samples/portfolio. *Entrance requirements:* For master's, California Basic Educational Skills Test or PRAXIS I, minimum undergraduate GPA of 2.8, graduate 3.0; 2 letters of recommendation. Additional exam requirements/recommendations for international students: Required—TOEFL (minimum score 525 paper-based). Electronic applications accepted. *Faculty research:* Learner-centered classroom, brain-based learning, future of online learning.

Concordia University, School of Graduate Studies, Faculty of Arts and Science, Department of Education, Montréal, QC H3G 1M8, Canada. Offers adult education (Certificate, Diploma); applied linguistics (MA, Certificate), including applied linguistics (MA), teaching English as a second language (Certificate); child studies (MA); educational studies (MA); educational technology (MA); instructional technology (Diploma). *Degree requirements:* For master's, one foreign language, thesis optional.

Concordia University Chicago, College of Education, Program in Teaching, River Forest, IL 60305-1499. Offers early childhood education (MAT); elementary education (MAT); secondary education (MAT). *Degree requirements:* For master's, thesis or alternative. *Entrance requirements:* For master's, minimum GPA of 2.9. Additional exam requirements/recommendations for international students: Required—TOEFL (minimum score 550 paper-based). Electronic applications accepted.

Concordia University Irvine, School of Education, Irvine, CA 92612-3299. Offers curriculum and instruction (MA); education and preliminary teaching credential (M Ed); educational administration and preliminary administrative services credential (MA); educational technology (MA); school counseling with pupil personnel services credential (MA). *Program availability:* Part-time, evening/weekend, online learning. *Degree requirements:* For master's, action research project. *Entrance requirements:* For master's, California Basic Educational Skills Test, California Subject Examinations for Teachers (M Ed and MA in educational administration and preliminary administrative services credential), official college transcript(s), signed statement of intent, two references, copy of credential. Additional exam requirements/recommendations for international students: Required—TOEFL. Electronic applications accepted. *Expenses:* Contact institution.

Concordia University, Nebraska, Graduate Programs in Education, Seward, NE 68434-1556. Offers M Ed, MPE, MS. *Accreditation:* NCATE. *Program availability:* Part-time, evening/weekend. *Degree requirements:* For master's, comprehensive exam, thesis or alternative. *Entrance requirements:* For master's, GRE, MAT, or NTE, minimum GPA of 3.0, BS in education or equivalent. Additional exam requirements/recommendations for international students: Required—TOEFL. Electronic applications accepted.

Concordia University, St. Paul, College of Education, St. Paul, MN 55104-5494. Offers classroom instruction (MA Ed), including K-12 reading; differentiated instruction (MA Ed); education (Ed D); educational leadership (MA Ed); educational technology (MA Ed); K-12 principal licensure (Ed S); special education (MA Ed, Certificate), including autism spectrum disorder (MA Ed), emotional and behavioral disorders (MA Ed), learning disabilities (MA Ed); superintendent (Ed S); teaching (MAT). *Accreditation:* NCATE. *Program availability:* Part-time, evening/weekend, 100% online, blended/hybrid learning. *Faculty:* 9 full-time (5 women), 88 part-time/adjunct (52 women). *Students:* 994 full-time (745 women), 40 part-time (34 women); includes 118 minority (40 Black or African American, non-Hispanic/Latino; 7 American Indian or Alaska Native, non-Hispanic/Latino; 33 Asian, non-Hispanic/Latino; 20 Hispanic/Latino; 18 Two or more races, non-Hispanic/Latino), 15 international. Average age 34. 549 applicants, 82% accepted, 372 enrolled. In 2016, 399 master's, 108 other advanced degrees awarded. *Degree requirements:* For master's, thesis (for some programs); for doctorate, thesis/dissertation, capstone projects; for other advanced degree, e-folio review of competencies. *Entrance requirements:* For master's, official transcripts from regionally-accredited institution stating the conferral of a bachelor's degree with minimum cumulative GPA of 3.0; personal statement; professional resume; practitioner in field through work or volunteerism; resume; for doctorate, minimum master's or specialist degree GPA of 3.25; transcript; writing sample; three letters of recommendation; current resume; on-campus interview; for other advanced degree, at least three years of teaching experience; master's degree; valid MN teaching license; writing sample; two letters of recommendation; resume. Additional exam requirements/recommendations for international students: Recommended—TOEFL (minimum score 547 paper-based; 78 iBT), IELTS (minimum score 6). *Application deadline:* For fall admission, 8/1 for domestic and international students; for spring admission, 12/1 for domestic and international students; for summer admission, 5/1 for domestic and international students. Applications are processed on a rolling basis. Application fee: $50. Electronic applications accepted. *Expenses:* Contact institution. *Financial support:* In 2016–17, 112 students received support. Scholarships/grants and unspecified assistantships available. Financial award applicants required to submit FAFSA. *Faculty research:* Differentiated instruction in K-12 educational settings; educational leadership; effective online pedagogy in higher education; equine-assisted learning; faculty development in higher education. *Unit head:* Lonn Maly, Dean, 651-641-8203, E-mail: maly@csp.edu. *Application contact:* Kimberly Craig, Associate Vice President, Cohort Enrollment Management, 651-603-6223, Fax: 651-603-6320, E-mail: craig@csp.edu.

Concordia University Texas, College of Education, Austin, TX 78726. Offers M Ed. *Program availability:* Part-time, evening/weekend. *Degree requirements:* For master's, thesis (for some programs), portfolio presentation.

Concordia University Wisconsin, Graduate Programs, Department of Education, Mequon, WI 53097-2402. Offers art education (MS Ed); early childhood (MS Ed); educational administration (MS Ed); environmental education (MS Ed); family studies (MS Ed); literacy (MS Ed); school counseling (MS Ed); special education (MS Ed). *Program availability:* Part-time, evening/weekend, online learning. *Degree requirements:* For master's, comprehensive exam, thesis or alternative. *Entrance requirements:* For master's, minimum GPA of 3.0, teaching license. Additional exam requirements/recommendations for international students: Required—TOEFL. Application fee: $35. *Financial support:* Career-related internships or fieldwork and tuition waivers (partial) available. Financial award application deadline: 8/1. *Faculty research:* Motivation, developmental learning, learning styles. *Unit head:* Dr. James Juergensen, Director, 262-243-4214, E-mail: james.juergensen@cuw.edu. *Application contact:* Graduate Admissions, 262-243-4248, Fax: 262-243-4428.

Concord University, Graduate Studies, Athens, WV 24712-1000. Offers educational leadership and supervision (M Ed); health promotion (MA); reading specialist (M Ed); social work (MSW); special education (M Ed); teaching (MAT). *Program availability:* Part-time, evening/weekend, online learning. *Faculty:* 16 full-time (10 women), 7 part-time/adjunct (4 women). *Students:* 129 full-time (105 women), 220 part-time (169 women); includes 28 minority (26 Black or African American, non-Hispanic/Latino; 1 American Indian or Alaska Native, non-Hispanic/Latino; 1 Hispanic/Latino), 2 international. *Degree requirements:* For master's, thesis (for some programs). *Entrance requirements:* For master's, GRE or MAT, baccalaureate degree with minimum GPA of 2.5 from regionally-accredited institution; teaching license; 2 letters of recommendation; completed disposition assessment form. *Application deadline:* Applications are processed on a rolling basis. Application fee: $30. Electronic applications accepted. *Expenses:* Tuition, state resident: full-time $3800; part-time $2539 per semester. Tuition, nonresident: full-time $6627; part-time $4416 per semester. Tuition and fees vary according to course load. *Financial support:* Tuition waivers and unspecified assistantships available. Financial award applicants required to submit FAFSA. *Unit head:* Dr. Cheryl Barnes, Director, 304-384-6306, E-mail: cbarnes@concord.edu. *Application contact:* Debra Moore, Special Events Assistant, 304-384-5113, E-mail: dlm@concord.edu. Website: http://www.concord.edu/graduate

Converse College, School of Education and Graduate Studies, Spartanburg, SC 29302. Offers M Ed, M Mus, MAT, MFA, MLA, MMFT, Ed S. *Accreditation:* NASAD; NCATE. *Program availability:* Part-time, evening/weekend. *Entrance requirements:* For master's, PRAXIS II (for M Ed), minimum GPA of 2.75; for Ed S, GRE or MAT, minimum GPA of 3.0. *Application deadline:* For fall admission, 8/1 for domestic and international students; for winter admission, 11/15 for domestic and international students; for spring admission, 1/15 for domestic and international students. Applications are processed on a rolling basis. Application fee: $40. Electronic applications accepted. *Expenses: Tuition:* Full-time $3600; part-time $400 per credit hour. *Required fees:* $70 per term. *Financial support:* Research assistantships, career-related internships or fieldwork, and scholarships/grants available. Support available to part-time students. Financial award applicants required to submit FAFSA. *Faculty research:* Motivation, classroom management, predictors of success in classroom teaching, sex equity in public education, gifted research. *Application contact:* 864-596-9404, E-mail: graduate@converse.edu.

Coppin State University, Division of Graduate Studies, Division of Education, Department of Curriculum and Instruction, Program in Teaching, Baltimore, MD 21216-3698. Offers teacher education (MAT). *Program availability:* Part-time, evening/weekend, online learning. *Degree requirements:* For master's, thesis, exit portfolio. *Entrance requirements:* For master's, GRE, resume, references.

Corban University, Graduate School, Education Program, Salem, OR 97301-9392. Offers MS Ed.

Cornell University, Graduate School, Graduate Fields of Agriculture and Life Sciences, Field of Education, Ithaca, NY 14853. Offers adult and extension education (MPS, MS, PhD); learning, teaching, and social policy (MPS, MS, PhD); mathematics 7-12 (MS). Terminal master's awarded for partial completion of doctoral program. *Degree requirements:* For master's, thesis (MS); for doctorate, comprehensive exam, thesis/dissertation. *Entrance requirements:* For master's and doctorate, GRE General Test, sample of written work (recommended), 2 letters of recommendation. Additional exam requirements/recommendations for international students: Required—TOEFL (minimum score 550 paper-based; 77 iBT). Electronic applications accepted. *Faculty research:* Moral development and professional ethics, public issues education and community development, socio/political issues in public education, teacher education and curriculum in agricultural science and mathematics, extension research.

Cornerstone University, Graduate Programs, Grand Rapids, MI 49525-5897. Offers business administration (MBA); education (MA Ed); management (MSM); teaching English to speakers of other languages (MA, Graduate Certificate). Programs also offered at Holland, Kalamazoo, and Troy, MI campuses. *Program availability:* Part-time, online learning. *Degree requirements:* For master's, comprehensive exam (for some programs), thesis (for some programs). *Entrance requirements:* For master's, minimum GPA of 2.5, 2 letters of reference. Additional exam requirements/recommendations for international students: Required—TOEFL (minimum score 575 paper-based). Electronic applications accepted.

Covenant College, Program in Education, Lookout Mountain, GA 30750. Offers M Ed, MAT. *Program availability:* Part-time. *Degree requirements:* For master's, comprehensive exam, special project. *Entrance requirements:* For master's, GRE General Test, 2 professional recommendations, minimum GPA of 3.0, writing sample.

Crandall University, Graduate Programs, Moncton, NB E1C 9L7, Canada. Offers literacy education (M Ed); organizational management (MOM); resource education (M Ed).

Creighton University, Graduate School, College of Arts and Sciences, Department of Education, Omaha, NE 68178-0001. Offers educational leadership (MS), including elementary school administration, secondary school administration, teacher leadership; school counseling and preventive mental health (MS), including elementary school guidance, secondary school guidance; teaching (M Ed), including elementary teaching, secondary teaching. *Accreditation:* NCATE. *Program availability:* Part-time, 100% online, blended/hybrid learning. *Faculty:* 10 full-time (5 women). *Students:* 26 full-time (21 women), 151 part-time (109 women); includes 11 minority (4 Black or African American, non-Hispanic/Latino; 1 American Indian or Alaska Native, non-Hispanic/Latino; 1 Asian, non-Hispanic/Latino; 4 Hispanic/Latino; 1 Two or more races, non-Hispanic/Latino). Average age 33. 20 applicants, 85% accepted, 17 enrolled. In 2016, 40 master's awarded. *Degree requirements:* For master's, comprehensive exam (for some programs), portfolio. *Entrance requirements:* For master's, GRE General Test, PPST, 3 letters of recommendation, writing samples, resume. Additional exam requirements/recommendations for international students: Required—TOEFL (minimum score 90 iBT). *Application deadline:* For fall admission, 7/1 priority date for domestic students, 3/1 priority date for international students; for winter admission, 12/1 for domestic students, 7/1 for international students; for spring admission, 4/1 for domestic students, 10/1 for international students; for summer admission, 3/1 for domestic and international students. Applications are processed on a rolling basis. Application fee: $50. Electronic applications accepted. *Expenses: Tuition:* Full-time $14,400; part-time $800 per credit hour. *Required fees:* $158 per semester. Tuition and fees vary according to course load, campus/location, program, reciprocity agreements and student's religious affiliation. *Financial support:* Scholarships/grants and tuition waivers (partial) available. Support available to part-time students. Financial award applicants required to submit FAFSA. *Unit head:* Dr. Timothy Cook, Chair, 402-280-2561, E-mail: timothycook@creighton.edu. *Application contact:* Lindsay Johnson, Director of Graduate and Adult Recruitment, 402-280-2703, Fax: 402-280-2423, E-mail: gradschool@creighton.edu.

Cumberland University, Program in Education, Lebanon, TN 37087. Offers MAE. *Accreditation:* NCATE. *Program availability:* Part-time, evening/weekend, online learning. *Degree requirements:* For master's, comprehensive exam. *Entrance requirements:* For master's, GRE General Test, MAT, or NTE, 3 letters of recommendation. Additional exam requirements/recommendations for international students: Required—TOEFL (minimum score 500 paper-based).

Curry College, Graduate Studies, Program in Education, Milton, MA 02186-9984. Offers elementary education (M Ed); foundations (non-license) (M Ed); reading (M Ed, Certificate); special education (M Ed). *Program availability:* Part-time, evening/weekend. *Degree requirements:* For master's, project or thesis. *Entrance requirements:* For master's, interview, recommendations, resume, written statement. Additional exam requirements/recommendations for international students: Required—TOEFL (minimum score 550 paper-based; 80 iBT). *Expenses:* Contact institution. *Faculty research:* Classroom trauma, therapeutic writing, inclusionary practices.

Daemen College, Education Department, Amherst, NY 14226-3592. Offers adolescence education (MS); childhood education (MS); childhood special education (MS); childhood special-alternative certification (MS); early childhood special-alternative certification (MS). *Accreditation:* TEAC. *Program availability:* Part-time. *Degree requirements:* For master's, thesis optional, research thesis in lieu of comprehensive exam; completion of degree within 5 years. *Entrance requirements:* For master's, 2 letters of recommendation (professional and character), proof of initial certificate of license for professional programs, resume. Additional exam requirements/recommendations for international students: Required—TOEFL (minimum score 500 paper-based; 63 iBT), IELTS (minimum score 5.5). Electronic applications accepted. *Faculty research:* Transition for students with disabilities, early childhood special education, traumatic brain injury (TBI), reading assessment.

Dakota State University, College of Education, Madison, SD 57042-1799. Offers educational technology (MSET). *Accreditation:* NCATE. *Program availability:* Part-time-only, evening/weekend, online only, 100% online. *Degree requirements:* For master's, thesis, portfolio. *Entrance requirements:* For master's, GRE General Test, demonstration of technology skills, minimum GPA of 2.7. *Application deadline:* For fall admission, 6/15 for domestic students; for spring admission, 11/15 for domestic students; for summer admission, 4/15 for domestic students. Applications are processed on a rolling basis. Application fee: $35. *Expenses:* Tuition, state resident: full-time $7310. Tuition, nonresident: full-time $13,824. *Required fees:* $930. Tuition and fees vary according to program and reciprocity agreements. *Financial support:* Fellowships with partial tuition reimbursements, career-related internships or fieldwork, Federal Work-Study, scholarships/grants, unspecified assistantships, and administrative assistantships available. Support available to part-time students. Financial award applicants required to submit FAFSA. *Faculty research:* Educational technology evaluation, computer-supported collaborative learning, cognitive theory and visual representation of the effects of ubiquitous wireless computing on student learning and productivity, accessible learning, pedagogies for exceptional children. *Unit head:* Dr. Crystal Pauli, Dean, 605-256-5799. *Application contact:* Mark Hawkes, Dean of Graduate Studies and Research/Academic Coordinator, 605-256-5274, Fax: 605-256-5093, E-mail: mark.hawkes@dsu.edu. Website: http://dsu.edu/graduate-students/mset

Dakota Wesleyan University, Program in Education, Mitchell, SD 57301-4398. Offers curriculum and instruction (MA Ed); educational policy and administration (MA Ed); preK-12 principal certification (MA Ed); secondary certification (MA Ed). *Program availability:* Part-time, evening/weekend. *Degree requirements:* For master's, comprehensive exam, thesis optional, electronic portfolio. *Entrance requirements:* For master's, minimum GPA of 2.7, elementary statistics course, statement of purpose, official transcripts, resume, three letters of recommendation. Additional exam requirements/recommendations for international students: Required—TOEFL (minimum score 500 paper-based), IELTS (minimum score 6.5). Electronic applications accepted. *Faculty research:* Math, political policy, technology in the classroom.

Dallas Baptist University, Dorothy M. Bush College of Education, Teaching Program, Dallas, TX 75211-9299. Offers distance learning (MAT); early childhood through grade 6 certification (MAT); early childhood-12 (MAT); elementary (MAT); English as a second language (MAT); Montessori (MAT); multisensory (MAT); secondary (MAT). *Program availability:* Part-time, evening/weekend, 100% online, blended/hybrid learning. *Application deadline:* Applications are processed on a rolling basis. Application fee: $25. Electronic applications accepted. Application fee is waived when completed online. *Expenses: Tuition:* Full-time $15,408; part-time $856 per credit hour. *Required fees:* $400 per semester. Tuition and fees vary according to course load and degree level. *Unit head:* Dr. Carolyn Spain, Director, 214-333-5217, E-mail: carolyns@dbu.edu. *Application contact:* Bobby Soto, Director of Admissions, 214-333-5242, E-mail: graduate@dbu.edu. Website: http://www3.dbu.edu/graduate/mat.asp

Defiance College, Program in Education, Defiance, OH 43512-1610. Offers education (MAE); sport coaching (MAE). *Program availability:* Part-time. *Degree requirements:* For master's, thesis (for some programs). *Entrance requirements:* For master's, teaching certificate. *Application deadline:* For fall admission, 8/1 for domestic students. Applications are processed on a rolling basis. Application fee: $25. *Expenses: Tuition:* Part-time $524 per credit hour. *Required fees:* $188 per semester. *Unit head:* Dr. Jo Ann Burkhardt, Professor, 419-783-2315, Fax: 419-784-0426, E-mail: jburkhardt@defiance.edu. *Application contact:* Teresa Watkins, Administrative Assistant, 419-783-2323, Fax: 419-784-0426, E-mail: twatkins@defiance.edu. Website: http://www.defiance.edu/graduate-programs/mae-home.html

Delaware State University, Graduate Programs, College of Education, Health and Public Policy, Dover, DE 19901-2277. Offers MA, MS, MSW, Ed D. *Accreditation:* NCATE. *Program availability:* Part-time, evening/weekend. *Degree requirements:* For master's, comprehensive exam, thesis optional. *Entrance requirements:* For master's, GRE General Test, minimum GPA of 3.0 in major, 2.75 overall. Additional exam requirements/recommendations for international students: Required—TOEFL (minimum score 500 paper-based). Electronic applications accepted.

Delta State University, Graduate Programs, College of Education, Cleveland, MS 38733-0001. Offers M Ed, MAT, MS, Ed D, Ed S. *Accreditation:* NCATE. *Program availability:* Part-time, evening/weekend. *Degree requirements:* For master's, thesis optional; for doctorate, thesis/dissertation. *Entrance requirements:* For doctorate, GRE General Test; for Ed S, master's degree, teaching certificate.

DePaul University, College of Education, Chicago, IL 60614. Offers bilingual bicultural education (M Ed, MA); counseling (M Ed, MA), including clinical mental health counseling, college student development, school counseling; curriculum studies (M Ed, MA, Ed D); early childhood education (M Ed, MA, Ed D); educating adults (MA); educational leadership (M Ed, MA, Ed D), including administration and supervision (M Ed, MA), principal preparation (M Ed, MA); elementary education (MA); mathematics education (MA); mathematics for teaching (MS); middle school mathematics education (MS); reading specialist (M Ed, MA); secondary education (M Ed); social and cultural foundations in education (MA); special education (M Ed, MA); world languages education (M Ed, MA). *Program availability:* Part-time, evening/weekend, online learning. *Degree requirements:* For doctorate, thesis/dissertation. Electronic applications accepted.

DePaul University, School for New Learning, Chicago, IL 60604. Offers applied professional studies (MA); applied technology (MS); educating adults (MA). *Program availability:* Part-time, evening/weekend. *Degree requirements:* For master's, thesis or alternative. Electronic applications accepted.

DeSales University, Division of Liberal Arts and Social Sciences, Center Valley, PA 18034-9568. Offers criminal justice (MCJ); digital forensics (MCJ, Postbaccalaureate Certificate); education (M Ed), including instructional technology, secondary education, special education, teaching English to speakers of other languages; investigative forensics (MCJ, Postbaccalaureate Certificate). *Program availability:* Part-time, 100% online, blended/hybrid learning. *Faculty:* 5 full-time (3 women), 20 part-time/adjunct (13 women). *Students:* 55 full-time (36 women), 100 part-time (64 women); includes 25 minority (5 Black or African American, non-Hispanic/Latino; 14 Hispanic/Latino; 6 Two or more races, non-Hispanic/Latino). Average age 33. 145 applicants, 80% accepted, 103 enrolled. In 2016, 36 master's awarded. *Entrance requirements:* For master's, bachelor's degree from accredited institution, minimum undergraduate GPA of 3.0, personal statement showing potential of graduate work, three letters of recommendation, professional goal statement. Additional exam requirements/ recommendations for international students: Required—TOEFL. *Application deadline:* Applications are processed on a rolling basis. Application fee: $50. Electronic applications accepted. *Expenses: Tuition:* Part-time $815 per credit hour. Tuition and fees vary according to degree level and program. *Financial support:* Applicants required to submit FAFSA. *Unit head:* Dr. Brain Kane, Division Head of Liberal Arts and Social Studies, 610-282-1100 Ext. 1274, E-mail: brian.kane@desales.edu. *Application contact:* Julia Ferraro, Director of Graduate Admissions, 610-282-1100 Ext. 1768, E-mail: gradadmissions@desales.edu.

Doane University, Program in Education, Crete, NE 68333-2430. Offers curriculum and instruction (M Ed); educational leadership (M Ed). *Accreditation:* NCATE. *Program availability:* Part-time, evening/weekend. *Faculty:* 10 full-time (7 women), 66 part-time/ adjunct (50 women). *Students:* 224 full-time (167 women), 488 part-time (388 women); includes 22 minority (9 Black or African American, non-Hispanic/Latino; 2 American Indian or Alaska Native, non-Hispanic/Latino; 1 Asian, non-Hispanic/Latino; 7 Hispanic/ Latino; 1 Native Hawaiian or other Pacific Islander, non-Hispanic/Latino; 2 Two or more races, non-Hispanic/Latino), 1 international. Average age 34. In 2016, 257 master's awarded. *Degree requirements:* For master's, thesis. *Entrance requirements:* For master's, minimum GPA of 2.5. Additional exam requirements/recommendations for international students: Required—TOEFL. *Application deadline:* Applications are processed on a rolling basis. Electronic applications accepted. *Expenses:* Contact institution. *Financial support:* Applicants required to submit FAFSA. *Unit head:* Dr. Lyn C. Forester, Dean, 402-826-8604, Fax: 402-826-8278. *Application contact:* Wilma Daddario, Assistant Dean, 402-464-1223, Fax: 402-466-4228, E-mail: wdaddario@ doane.edu. Website: http://www.doane.edu/masters-degrees

Dominican College, Division of Teacher Education, Orangeburg, NY 10962-1210. Offers education/teaching of individuals with multiple disabilities (MS Ed). *Program availability:* Part-time, evening/weekend, online learning. *Faculty:* 6 full-time (4 women), 4 part-time/ adjunct (all women). *Students:* 3 full-time (all women), 53 part-time (41 women); includes 13 minority (3 Black or African American, non-Hispanic/Latino; 10 Hispanic/Latino). In 2016, 28 master's awarded. *Degree requirements:* For master's, comprehensive exam (for some programs), thesis. *Entrance requirements:* For master's, 3 letters of recommendation (written by former or current work supervisors or instructors), interview. Additional exam requirements/recommendations for international students: Required—TOEFL (minimum score 90 iBT). *Application deadline:* Applications are processed on a rolling basis. *Expenses: Tuition:* Part-time $900 per credit. One-time fee: $200 full-time. *Financial support:* Application deadline: 2/1; applicants required to submit FAFSA. *Unit head:* Dr. Mike Kelly, Director, 845-848-4090, Fax: 845-359-7802, E-mail: mike.kelly@ dc.edu. *Application contact:* Christina Lifshey, Assistant Director of Graduate Admissions, 845-848-7908 Ext. 15, Fax: 845-365-3150, E-mail: admissions@dc.edu.

Dominican University, School of Education, River Forest, IL 60305-1099. Offers early childhood education (MS); education (MAT); elementary education (MA Ed); English as a second language (MA Ed); reading (MA Ed); special education (MS). *Accreditation:* NCATE. *Program availability:* Part-time, evening/weekend, 100% online, blended/hybrid learning. *Faculty:* 12 full-time (8 women), 64 part-time/adjunct (57 women). *Students:* 13 full-time (all women), 500 part-time (385 women); includes 88 minority (40 Black or African American, non-Hispanic/Latino; 3 American Indian or Alaska Native, non-Hispanic/Latino; 18 Asian, non-Hispanic/Latino; 11 Hispanic/Latino; 2 Native Hawaiian or other Pacific Islander, non-Hispanic/Latino; 14 Two or more races, non-Hispanic/ Latino), 1 international. Average age 32. 162 applicants, 96% accepted, 104 enrolled. In 2016, 200 master's awarded. *Entrance requirements:* For master's, Illinois Test of Basic Skills. Additional exam requirements/recommendations for international students: Required—TOEFL (minimum score 550 paper-based; 79 iBT). *Application deadline:* Applications are processed on a rolling basis. Application fee: $25. *Expenses:* $550 per credit hour. *Financial support:* Career-related internships or fieldwork, scholarships/ grants, tuition waivers (partial), and unspecified assistantships available. Support available to part-time students. Financial award application deadline: 8/15; financial award applicants required to submit FAFSA. *Faculty research:* Governance of private education institutions, reading and language arts, inclusion, organizational planning, leadership and vision. *Unit head:* Dr. Colleen Reardon, Interim Executive Director, School of Education, 708-524-6643, Fax: 708-524-6665, E-mail: creardon@dom.edu. *Application contact:* Keven Hansen, Coordinator of Recruitment and Admissions, 708-524-6921, Fax: 708-524-6665, E-mail: educate@dom.edu.
Website: http://educate.dom.edu/

Dominican University of California, School of Education and Counseling Psychology, San Rafael, CA 94901-2298. Offers MFT, MS. *Program availability:* Part-time, evening/ weekend. *Degree requirements:* For master's, thesis (for some programs). *Entrance requirements:* Additional exam requirements/recommendations for international students: Required—TOEFL (minimum score 550 paper-based; 80 iBT), IELTS (minimum score 6.5). Electronic applications accepted. Application fee is waived when completed online. *Expenses: Tuition:* Full-time $11,400; part-time $950 per credit. *Required fees:* $300 per credit. Tuition and fees vary according to course load and program.

Dordt College, Program in Education, Sioux Center, IA 51250-1697. Offers M Ed. *Program availability:* Part-time, online learning. *Degree requirements:* For master's, comprehensive exam, thesis. *Entrance requirements:* For master's, GRE or MAT. Additional exam requirements/recommendations for international students: Required—TOEFL. Electronic applications accepted.

Drake University, School of Education, Des Moines, IA 50311-4516. Offers MAT, MS, MSE, MST, Ed D, PhD, Ed S. *Program availability:* Part-time, evening/weekend. *Faculty:* 24 full-time (11 women), 48 part-time/adjunct (37 women). *Students:* 80 full-time (65 women), 582 part-time (436 women); includes 42 minority (19 Black or African American, non-Hispanic/Latino; 1 American Indian or Alaska Native, non-Hispanic/ Latino; 4 Asian, non-Hispanic/Latino; 10 Hispanic/Latino; 8 Two or more races, non-Hispanic/Latino), 2 international. Average age 33. 328 applicants, 87% accepted, 219 enrolled. In 2016, 190 master's, 4 doctorates, 8 other advanced degrees awarded. *Degree requirements:* For master's and Ed S, comprehensive exam, internships (for some programs); for doctorate, comprehensive exam, thesis/dissertation, internships (for some programs). *Entrance requirements:* For master's, GRE General Test, MAT, or Drake Writing Assessment, resume, 2 letters of recommendation; for doctorate, GRE General Test or MAT, master's degree, 3 letters of recommendation; for Ed S, GRE General Test or MAT. Additional exam requirements/recommendations for international students: Required—TOEFL (minimum score 550 paper-based). *Application deadline:* For fall admission, 7/1 priority date for domestic students, 6/1 priority date for international students; for spring admission, 11/1 priority date for domestic students, 10/ 1 priority date for international students. Applications are processed on a rolling basis. Application fee: $25. Electronic applications accepted. *Expenses:* Contact institution. *Financial support:* In 2016–17, 14 research assistantships were awarded; career-related internships or fieldwork and unspecified assistantships also available. Support available to part-time students. *Faculty research:* Counseling and rehabilitation, behavioral supports, inquiry-based science methods, teacher quality enhancement. *Unit head:* Dr. Janet McMahill, Dean, 515-271-3829, E-mail: janet.mcmahill@drake.edu.

★ **Drexel University,** Goodwin College of Professional Studies, School of Education, Philadelphia, PA 19104-2875. Offers applied behavior analysis (MS); creativity and innovation (MS); education improvement and transformation (MS); educational administration (MS); educational leadership and management (Ed D); educational leadership development and learning technologies (PhD); global and international education (MS); higher education (MS); human resources development (MS); learning technologies (MS); mathematics, learning and teaching (MS); special education (MS); teaching, learning and curriculum (MS). *Program availability:* Part-time, evening/weekend, online learning. *Degree requirements:* For doctorate, thesis/dissertation. *Entrance requirements:* For doctorate, GRE or GMAT. Additional exam requirements/recommendations for international students: Required—TOEFL, IELTS. Electronic applications accepted. Application fee is waived when completed online. *Expenses:* Contact institution. *Faculty research:* Leadership development, mathematics education, literacy, autism, educational technology.

See Display on next page and Close-Up on page 727.

Drury University, Master in Education Program, Springfield, MO 5802. Offers curriculum and instruction (M Ed), including elementary, middle school, secondary; gifted education (M Ed); instructional leadership (M Ed); instructional technology (M Ed); integrated learning (M Ed); online teaching (M Ed); special education (M Ed); special reading (M Ed). *Accreditation:* NCATE. *Program availability:* Part-time, evening/ weekend, 100% online, blended/hybrid learning. *Students:* 146 full-time (111 women); includes 6 minority (1 Asian, non-Hispanic/Latino; 3 Hispanic/Latino; 2 Two or more races, non-Hispanic/Latino), 1 international. Average age 34. 42 applicants, 74% accepted. In 2016, 74 master's awarded. *Entrance requirements:* For master's, GRE, bachelor's degree with minimum GPA of 2.75. Additional exam requirements/ recommendations for international students: Recommended—TOEFL (minimum score 80 iBT), IELTS (minimum score 6.5). *Application deadline:* For fall admission, 8/4 priority date for domestic and international students; for spring admission, 1/5 priority date for domestic and international students; for summer admission, 5/26 priority date for domestic and international students. Applications are processed on a rolling basis. Application fee: $25 ($50 for international students). Electronic applications accepted. *Expenses:* $352 tuition per credit hour; $7 per credit hour technology fee; $100 graduation fee; $59 portfolio fee (one-time). *Financial support:* In 2016–17, 20 students received support. Career-related internships or fieldwork, scholarships/grants, tuition waivers (partial), and unspecified assistantships available. Financial award application deadline: 6/30; financial award applicants required to submit FAFSA. *Faculty research:* Gifted students, instructional technology, autism, diversity and social justice. *Unit head:* Dr. Asikaa Cosgrove, Director, Master in Education, 417-873-7806, E-mail: acosgrov@ drury.edu. Website: http://www.drury.edu/education-masters

Duke University, Graduate School, Program in Teaching, Durham, NC 27708. Offers MAT. *Accreditation:* NCATE. *Entrance requirements:* For master's, GRE General Test. Additional exam requirements/recommendations for international students: Required—TOEFL (minimum score 577 paper-based; 90 iBT) or IELTS (minimum score 7). Electronic applications accepted.

Duquesne University, School of Education, Pittsburgh, PA 15282-0001. Offers MS Ed, Ed D, PhD, Psy D, CAGS, Post-Master's Certificate. *Accreditation:* NCATE. *Program availability:* Part-time, evening/weekend, 100% online, blended/hybrid learning. *Faculty:* 52 full-time (31 women), 83 part-time/adjunct (63 women). *Students:* 482 full-time (355 women), 46 part-time (35 women); includes 79 minority (47 Black or African American, non-Hispanic/Latino; 8 Asian, non-Hispanic/Latino; 9 Hispanic/Latino; 15 Two or more races, non-Hispanic/Latino), 51 international. Average age 31. 453 applicants, 79% accepted, 174 enrolled. In 2016, 175 master's, 40 doctorates, 2 other advanced degrees awarded. *Degree requirements:* For master's, comprehensive exam (for some programs); for doctorate, comprehensive exam (for some programs), thesis/dissertation (for some programs); for other advanced degree, comprehensive exam (for some programs), thesis (for some programs). *Entrance requirements:* For master's, letters of recommendation, essay, personal statement, interview, bachelor's degree; for doctorate, GRE, letters of recommendation, essay, personal statement, interview, master's degree; for other advanced degree, GRE, letters of recommendation, essay, personal statement, interview, bachelor's/master's degree. Additional exam requirements/recommendations for international students: Required—TOEFL (minimum score 550 paper-based), IELTS (minimum score 7). *Application deadline:* For fall admission, 3/1 for domestic students; for spring admission, 9/1 for domestic students. Applications are processed on a rolling basis. Application fee: $0. Electronic applications accepted. *Expenses: Tuition:* Full-time $22,212; part-time $1234 per credit. Tuition and fees vary according to program. *Financial support:* Research assistantships, teaching assistantships with tuition reimbursements, career-related internships or fieldwork, Federal Work-Study, institutionally sponsored loans, and tuition waivers available. Support available to part-time students. *Unit head:* Dr. Cindy Walker, Dean, 412-396-6102, Fax: 412-396-5585. *Application contact:* Michael Dolinger, Director of Student and Academic Services, 412-396-6647, Fax: 412-396-5585, E-mail: dolingerm@duq.edu.
Website: http://www.duq.edu/academics/schools/education

D'Youville College, Department of Education, Buffalo, NY 14201-1084. Offers educational leadership (Ed D); elementary education (MS Ed); secondary education (MS Ed); special education (MS Ed). *Program availability:* Part-time, evening/weekend. *Degree requirements:* For master's, one foreign language, comprehensive exam, project or thesis. *Entrance requirements:* For master's, GRE (if GPA less than 2.75), minimum GPA of 3.0. Additional exam requirements/recommendations for international students: Required—TOEFL (minimum score 500 paper-based). Electronic applications accepted. *Faculty research:* Developmental disabilities, multiculturalism, early childhood education.

Earlham College, Graduate Programs, Richmond, IN 47374-4095. Offers M Ed, MAT. *Entrance requirements:* For master's, GRE, PRAXIS I, PRAXIS II.

East Carolina University, Graduate School, College of Education, Greenville, NC 27858-4353. Offers MA, MA Ed, MAT, MLS, MS, MSA, Ed D, Certificate, Ed S. *Accreditation:* NCATE. *Program availability:* Part-time, evening/weekend, online learning. *Students:* 155 full-time (126 women), 1,088 part-time (880 women); includes 259 minority (178 Black or African American, non-Hispanic/Latino; 18 American Indian or Alaska Native, non-Hispanic/Latino; 10 Asian, non-Hispanic/Latino; 39 Hispanic/ Latino; 14 Two or more races, non-Hispanic/Latino), 8 international. Average age 37. 656 applicants, 95% accepted, 512 enrolled. In 2016, 206 master's, 13 doctorates, 4 other advanced degrees awarded. *Degree requirements:* For master's, comprehensive exam, thesis optional; for doctorate, thesis/dissertation. *Entrance requirements:* For master's, GRE or MAT, bachelor's degree in related field, minimum GPA of 2.5; for doctorate, GRE or MAT, interview, minimum GPA of 3.5. Additional exam requirements/ recommendations for international students: Required—TOEFL. *Application deadline:*

For fall admission, 6/1 priority date for domestic students. Applications are processed on a rolling basis. Application fee: $50. *Financial support:* Research assistantships with partial tuition reimbursements, teaching assistantships with partial tuition reimbursements, and Federal Work-Study available. Support available to part-time students. Financial award application deadline: 6/1. *Unit head:* Dr. Linda Ann Patriarca, Dean, 252-328-1000, Fax: 252-328-4219, E-mail: patriarcal@ecu.edu. *Application contact:* Dean of Graduate School, 252-328-6012, Fax: 252-328-6071, E-mail: gradschool@ecu.edu.
Website: http://www.ecu.edu/cs-educ/

East Central University, School of Graduate Studies, Department of Education, Ada, OK 74820. Offers M Ed. *Accreditation:* NCATE. *Program availability:* Part-time, evening/weekend. *Entrance requirements:* For master's, minimum GPA of 2.5. Electronic applications accepted.

Eastern Connecticut State University, School of Education and Professional Studies/Graduate Division, Willimantic, CT 06226-2295. Offers MS. *Accreditation:* NCATE. *Program availability:* Part-time, evening/weekend. *Faculty:* 20 full-time (11 women), 24 part-time/adjunct (17 women). *Students:* 69 full-time (45 women), 127 part-time (84 women); includes 38 minority (10 Black or African American, non-Hispanic/Latino; 1 American Indian or Alaska Native, non-Hispanic/Latino; 14 Asian, non-Hispanic/Latino; 11 Hispanic/Latino; 1 Native Hawaiian or other Pacific Islander, non-Hispanic/Latino; 1 Two or more races, non-Hispanic/Latino), 6 international. Average age 34. 105 applicants, 69% accepted, 55 enrolled. In 2016, 64 master's awarded. *Degree requirements:* For master's, comprehensive exam, thesis optional. *Entrance requirements:* For master's, PRAXIS I and II, GMAT or GRE, minimum GPA of 2.7. Additional exam requirements/recommendations for international students: Required—TOEFL (minimum score 550 paper-based; 79 iBT); Recommended—IELTS (minimum score 6). *Application deadline:* For fall admission, 7/6 priority date for domestic and international students; for spring admission, 11/3 priority date for domestic and international students; for summer admission, 4/5 priority date for domestic and international students. Applications are processed on a rolling basis. Application fee: $50. Electronic applications accepted. *Expenses: Tuition, area resident:* Full-time $11,781; part-time $560 per credit. Tuition, state resident: full-time $15,031; part-time $568 per credit. Tuition, nonresident: full-time $24,581; part-time $568 per credit. *Required fees:* $40 per semester. Full-time tuition and fees vary according to course level, course load and reciprocity agreements. *Financial support:* Research assistantships, teaching assistantships, career-related internships or fieldwork, scholarships/grants, and unspecified assistantships available. Financial award application deadline: 3/1; financial award applicants required to submit FAFSA. *Unit head:* Dr. Jacob Easley, II, Dean, 860-465-5293, Fax: 860-465-4538, E-mail: easleyj@easternct.edu. *Application contact:* Paula Goyette, Secretary II, 860-465-5292, Fax: 860-465-4538, E-mail: graduateadmissions@easternct.edu.

Eastern Illinois University, Graduate School, College of Education and Professional Studies, Charleston, IL 61920. Offers MS, MS Ed, Ed S. *Accreditation:* NCATE. *Program availability:* Part-time, evening/weekend. *Degree requirements:* For master's and Ed S, comprehensive exam (for some programs), thesis (for some programs). *Entrance requirements:* For master's and Ed S, GMAT or GRE. Additional exam requirements/recommendations for international students: Required—TOEFL (minimum score 500 paper-based; 61 iBT), IELTS (minimum score 6). Electronic applications accepted.

Eastern Kentucky University, The Graduate School, College of Education, Richmond, KY 40475-3102. Offers MA, MA Ed, MAT. *Accreditation:* NCATE. *Program availability:* Part-time, online learning. *Entrance requirements:* For master's, GRE General Test, minimum GPA of 2.5. *Faculty research:* Dispositions to teach, technology in education, distance learning.

Eastern Mennonite University, Program in Education, Harrisonburg, VA 22802-2462. Offers MA. *Accreditation:* NCATE. *Program availability:* Part-time. *Degree requirements:* For master's, portfolio, research projects. *Entrance requirements:* For master's, 1 year of teaching experience, interview, minimum undergraduate GPA of 2.75. Additional exam requirements/recommendations for international students: Required—TOEFL (minimum score 550 paper-based). Electronic applications accepted. *Expenses:* Contact institution. *Faculty research:* Effective literacy instruction for middle school English language learners, beginning teacher's emotional experiences, constructivist learning environments, restorative discipline.

Eastern Michigan University, Graduate School, College of Education, Ypsilanti, MI 48197. Offers M Ed, MA, Ed D, PhD, Graduate Certificate, Post Master's Certificate, SPA. *Accreditation:* NCATE. *Program availability:* Part-time, evening/weekend, online learning. *Faculty:* 72 full-time (49 women). *Students:* 179 full-time (159 women), 722 part-time (553 women); includes 193 minority (131 Black or African American, non-Hispanic/Latino; 4 American Indian or Alaska Native, non-Hispanic/Latino; 14 Asian, non-Hispanic/Latino; 27 Hispanic/Latino; 17 Two or more races, non-Hispanic/Latino), 20 international. Average age 34. 682 applicants, 57% accepted, 182 enrolled. In 2016, 268 master's, 29 doctorates, 48 other advanced degrees awarded. *Degree requirements:* For doctorate, thesis/dissertation. *Entrance requirements:* For master's, GRE; for doctorate, GRE General Test. Additional exam requirements/recommendations for international students: Required—TOEFL. *Application deadline:* Applications are processed on a rolling basis. Application fee: $45. *Financial support:* Fellowships, research assistantships with full tuition reimbursements, teaching assistantships with full tuition reimbursements, career-related internships or fieldwork, Federal Work-Study, institutionally sponsored loans, scholarships/grants, tuition waivers (partial), and unspecified assistantships available. Support available to part-time students. Financial award applicants required to submit FAFSA. *Unit head:* Dr. Michael Sayler, Dean, 734-487-1414, Fax: 734-484-6471, E-mail: msayler@emich.edu.
Website: http://www.emich.edu/coe/

Eastern Nazarene College, Adult and Graduate Studies, Division of Teacher Education, Quincy, MA 02170. Offers administration (M Ed); early childhood education (M Ed, Certificate); elementary education (M Ed, Certificate); English as a second language (Certificate); instructional enrichment and development (Certificate); middle school education (M Ed, Certificate); moderate special needs education (Certificate); principal (Certificate); program development and supervision (Certificate); secondary education (M Ed, Certificate); special education administrator (Certificate); special needs (M Ed); supervisor (Certificate); teacher of reading (M Ed, Certificate). M Ed also available through weekend program for administration, special needs, and teacher of reading only. *Program availability:* Part-time, evening/weekend. *Entrance requirements:* Additional exam requirements/recommendations for international students: Required—TOEFL (minimum score 550 paper-based).

Eastern New Mexico University, Graduate School, College of Education and Technology, Department of Educational Studies, Portales, NM 88130. Offers counseling (MA); education (M Ed), including educational administration, secondary education; school counseling (M Ed); special education (M Sp Ed), including early childhood special education, general. *Accreditation:* NCATE. *Program availability:* Part-time, evening/weekend, online learning. *Degree requirements:* For master's, comprehensive exam, thesis optional. *Entrance requirements:* For master's, minimum GPA of 3.0, letter of recommendation, photocopy of teaching license, writing assessment, Level II teaching license (for M Ed in educational administration). Additional exam requirements/

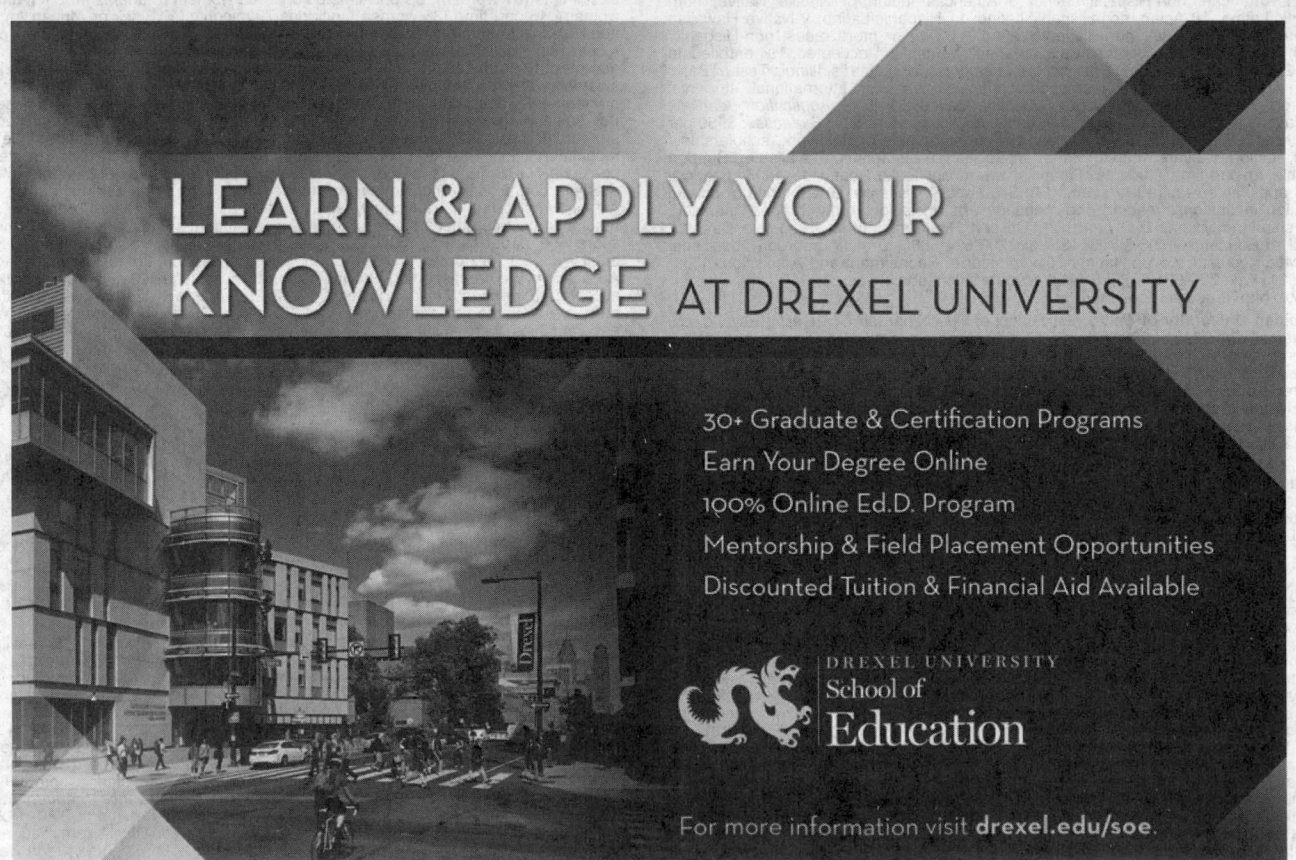

recommendations for international students: Required—TOEFL (minimum score 550 paper-based; 79 iBT), IELTS (minimum score 6). Electronic applications accepted.

Eastern Oregon University, Master of Arts in Teaching Program, La Grande, OR 97850-2899. Offers elementary education (MAT); secondary education (MAT). *Program availability:* Online learning. *Faculty:* 9 full-time (6 women), 5 part-time/adjunct (2 women). *Students:* 43 full-time (31 women), 1 (woman) part-time; includes 8 minority (1 Black or African American, non-Hispanic/Latino; 1 American Indian or Alaska Native, non-Hispanic/Latino; 2 Asian, non-Hispanic/Latino; 4 Hispanic/Latino). Average age 31. In 2016, 40 master's awarded. *Degree requirements:* For master's, thesis. *Entrance requirements:* For master's, NTE. *Application deadline:* For fall admission, 1/1 priority date for domestic students. Applications are processed on a rolling basis. Application fee: $50. Electronic applications accepted. *Expenses:* $353.50 per credit plus campus fees for portion of degree delivered on-campus. *Financial support:* In 2016–17, 13 students received support. Federal Work-Study, scholarships/grants, and tuition waivers (full and partial) available. Support available to part-time students. *Unit head:* Dr. Danny Ray Mielke, Dean of College of Business and Education, 541-962-3399, Fax: 541-962-3701, E-mail: dmeilke@eou.edu. *Application contact:* Janet Frye, Administrative Support, MAT/MS Graduate Admission, 541-962-3772, Fax: 541-962-3701, E-mail: jfrye@eou.edu.

Eastern Oregon University, Master of Science Program, La Grande, OR 97850-2899. Offers MS. *Program availability:* Part-time, online only, 100% online. *Faculty:* 11 full-time (8 women), 6 part-time/adjunct (4 women). *Students:* 9 full-time (8 women), 56 part-time (48 women); includes 6 minority (2 Asian, non-Hispanic/Latino; 3 Hispanic/Latino; 1 Two or more races, non-Hispanic/Latino), 1 international. Average age 37. In 2016, 21 master's awarded. *Degree requirements:* For master's, thesis. *Entrance requirements:* For master's, minimum GPA of 3.0 on last 60 quarter hours completed of undergraduate upper-division coursework or 15 quarter hours of approved graduate-level coursework; two letters of professional reference attesting to applicant's ability to be successful; essay. *Application deadline:* Applications are processed on a rolling basis. Electronic applications accepted. *Expenses:* Tuition, state resident: full-time $11,808; part-time $328 per credit. Tuition, nonresident: full-time $14,886; part-time $413.50 per credit. *Required fees:* $312 per quarter. One-time fee: $120. Tuition and fees vary according to course load, campus/location and program. *Financial support:* In 2016–17, 8 students received support. Federal Work-Study, scholarships/grants, and tuition waivers (full and partial) available. Support available to part-time students. *Unit head:* Dr. Danny Ray Mielke, Coordinator, 541-962-3349, Fax: 541-962-3701, E-mail: danny.mielke@eou.edu. *Application contact:* College of Business and Education, 541-962-3772, Fax: 541-962 3701, E-mail: ed@eou.edu.

Eastern University, Loeb School of Education, St. Davids, PA 19087-3696. Offers ESL program specialist (K-12) (Certificate); general supervisor (PreK-12) (Certificate); health and physical education (K-12) (Certificate); middle level (4-8) (Certificate); multicultural education (M Ed); organizational leadership with education (PhD); Pre K-4 (Certificate); Pre K-4 with special education (Certificate); reading (M Ed); reading specialist (K-12) (Certificate); reading supervisor (K-12) (Certificate); school health supervisor (Certificate); school nurse (K-12) (Certificate); secondary biology education (7-12) (Certificate); secondary chemistry education (7-12) (Certificate); secondary communication education (7-12) (Certificate); secondary education (7-12) (Certificate); secondary English education (7-12) (Certificate); secondary math education (7-12) (Certificate); secondary social studies education (7-12) (Certificate); special education (M Ed); special education (7-12) (Certificate); special education (Pre K-8) (Certificate); special education supervisor (N-12) (Certificate); TESOL (M Ed); world language (Certificate), including French, Spanish. *Program availability:* Part-time, evening/weekend, online learning. *Students:* 41 full-time (32 women), 89 part-time (68 women); includes 54 minority (38 Black or African American, non-Hispanic/Latino; 3 Asian, non-Hispanic/Latino; 11 Hispanic/Latino; 2 Two or more races, non-Hispanic/Latino), 2 international. Average age 37. In 2016, 64 master's awarded. *Entrance requirements:* Additional exam requirements/recommendations for international students: Required—TOEFL. *Application deadline:* Applications are processed on a rolling basis. Application fee: $35. Electronic applications accepted. Application fee is waived when completed online. *Expenses:* $690 per credit. *Unit head:* Michael Dziedziak, Executive Director of Enrollment, 800-452-0996, E-mail: gpsadmissions@eastern.edu.
Website: http://www.eastern.edu/academics/programs/loeb-school-education-0

Eastern Washington University, Graduate Studies, College of Arts, Letters and Education, Department of Education, Cheney, WA 99004-2431. Offers adult education (M Ed); curriculum development (M Ed); early childhood education (M Ed); education (M Ed); educational foundations (M Ed); elementary teaching (M Ed); literacy (M Ed); secondary teaching (M Ed); teaching K-8 (M Ed). *Program availability:* Part-time. *Faculty:* 18 full-time (12 women), 8 part-time/adjunct (4 women). *Students:* 33 full-time (26 women), 18 part-time (15 women); includes 7 minority (2 American Indian or Alaska Native, non-Hispanic/Latino; 2 Asian, non-Hispanic/Latino; 3 Hispanic/Latino), 1 international. Average age 34. 26 applicants, 73% accepted, 14 enrolled. In 2016, 39 master's awarded. *Degree requirements:* For master's, comprehensive exam. *Entrance requirements:* For master's, minimum GPA of 3.0. Additional exam requirements/recommendations for international students: Required—TOEFL (minimum score 580 paper-based; 92 iBT), IELTS (minimum score 7), PTE (minimum score 63). *Application deadline:* For fall admission, 4/1 priority date for domestic students; for spring admission, 1/15 for domestic students. Applications are processed on a rolling basis. Application fee: $75. Electronic applications accepted. *Expenses:* Tuition, state resident: full-time $11,000; part-time $5500 per credit. Tuition, nonresident: full-time $24,000; part-time $12,000 per credit. *Required fees:* $1300. One-time fee: $50 full-time. Part-time tuition and fees vary according to course load, campus/location and program. *Financial support:* In 2016–17, teaching assistantships with partial tuition reimbursements (averaging $10,000 per year) were awarded; career-related internships or fieldwork, Federal Work-Study, institutionally sponsored loans, scholarships/grants, health care benefits, tuition waivers (partial), and unspecified assistantships also available. Support available to part-time students. Financial award application deadline: 2/1; financial award applicants required to submit FAFSA. *Unit head:* Dr. Tara Haskins, Education Department Chair/Associate Professor of Literacy, 509-359-2831, E-mail: thaskins@ewu.edu. *Application contact:* Dr. Robin Showalter, Graduate Program Coordinator, 509-359-6492, E-mail: rshowalter@ewu.edu.
Website: http://www.ewu.edu/CALE/Programs/Education.xml

East Stroudsburg University of Pennsylvania, Graduate and Extended Studies, College of Education, East Stroudsburg, PA 18301-2999. Offers M Ed, Ed D. *Program availability:* Part-time, evening/weekend, online learning. *Students:* 27 full-time (16 women), 205 part-time (155 women); includes 25 minority (9 Black or African American, non-Hispanic/Latino; 13 Hispanic/Latino; 3 Two or more races, non-Hispanic/Latino), 1 international. *Degree requirements:* For master's, comprehensive exam, thesis (for some programs). *Entrance requirements:* Additional exam requirements/recommendations for international students: Recommended—TOEFL (minimum score 560 paper-based; 83 iBT), IELTS. *Application deadline:* For fall admission, 7/31 priority date for domestic students, 6/30 priority date for international students; for spring admission, 11/30 for domestic students, 10/31 for international students. Applications are processed on a rolling basis. Application fee: $50. Electronic applications accepted. *Expenses:* Tuition, state resident: full-time $8694; part-time $5796 per year. Tuition, nonresident: full-time $13,050; part-time $8700 per year. *Required fees:* $2550; $1690 per unit. $845 per semester. Tuition and fees vary according to course load, campus/location and program. *Financial support:* Research assistantships with tuition reimbursements, career-related internships or fieldwork, Federal Work-Study, and unspecified assistantships available. Support available to part-time students. Financial award application deadline: 3/1; financial award applicants required to submit FAFSA. *Unit head:* Dr. Terry Barry, Dean, 570-422-3377, Fax: 570-422-3506, E-mail: tbarry1@esu.edu. *Application contact:* Kevin Quintero, Associate Director, Graduate and Extended Studies, 570-422-3890, Fax: 570-422-3711, E-mail: kquintero@esu.edu.

East Tennessee State University, School of Graduate Studies, College of Education, Johnson City, TN 37614. Offers M Ed, MA, MAT, Ed D, PhD, Ed S, Post-Master's Certificate, Postbaccalaureate Certificate. *Accreditation:* NCATE. *Entrance requirements:* Additional exam requirements/recommendations for international students: Required—TOEFL (minimum score 550 paper-based; 79 iBT).

East Texas Baptist University, Master of Education Program, Marshall, TX 75670-1498. Offers college and university leadership (M Ed); curriculum and instruction (M Ed); principal certification (M Ed); sports and exercise leadership (M Ed); teacher certification (M Ed). *Program availability:* Part-time, evening/weekend. *Faculty:* 3 full-time (1 woman), 3 part-time/adjunct (all women). *Students:* 33 part-time (19 women); includes 14 minority (10 Black or African American, non-Hispanic/Latino; 4 Hispanic/Latino), 1 international. Average age 29. 53 applicants, 51% accepted, 25 enrolled. In 2016, 20 master's awarded. *Entrance requirements:* Additional exam requirements/recommendations for international students: Recommended—TOEFL (minimum score 550 paper-based; 79 iBT). *Application deadline:* For fall admission, 8/17 for domestic students; for spring admission, 1/10 for domestic students; for summer admission, 5/2 for domestic students. Applications are processed on a rolling basis. Application fee: $50. Electronic applications accepted. *Expenses:* $700 per credit hour tuition; $150 per semester fees (6 or more hours enrolled); $75 per semester fees (1-5 hours enrolled). *Financial support:* In 2016–17, 14 students received support. Federal Work-Study, unspecified assistantships, and staff grants available. Financial award applicants required to submit FAFSA. *Unit head:* Dr. PJ Winters, Director, 903-923-2276, Fax: 903-935-4318, E-mail: med@etbu.edu. *Application contact:* Den Murley, Director of Graduate Admissions, 903-923-2079, Fax: 903-934-8115, E-mail: dmurley@etbu.edu.
Website: https://www.etbu.edu/education/master-education/

Edgewood College, Program in Education, Madison, WI 53711-1997. Offers adult learning (MA Ed); director of special education and pupil services (Certificate); education (MA Ed); teaching and learning (MA Ed). *Accreditation:* NCATE (one or more programs are accredited). *Program availability:* Part-time, evening/weekend. *Faculty:* 13 full-time (9 women), 15 part-time/adjunct (10 women). *Students:* 137 full-time (91 women), 215 part-time (150 women); includes 51 minority (23 Black or African American, non-Hispanic/Latino; 3 American Indian or Alaska Native, non-Hispanic/Latino; 5 Asian, non-Hispanic/Latino; 17 Hispanic/Latino; 3 Two or more races, non-Hispanic/Latino), 18 international. Average age 37. In 2016, 74 master's, 18 doctorates awarded. *Degree requirements:* For master's, practicum, research project; for doctorate, comprehensive exam, thesis/dissertation. *Entrance requirements:* For master's, minimum GPA of 2.75, 2 letters of recommendation, personal statement; for doctorate, resume, letter of intent, 2 letters of recommendation, interview, writing sample. Additional exam requirements/recommendations for international students: Required—TOEFL (minimum score 525 paper-based; 72 iBT). *Application deadline:* For fall admission, 8/15 for domestic students, 5/1 for international students; for spring admission, 1/8 for domestic students, 11/1 for international students. Applications are processed on a rolling basis. Application fee: $30. Electronic applications accepted. *Expenses: Tuition:* Part-time $898 per credit. Tuition and fees vary according to course load. *Financial support:* Applicants required to submit FAFSA. *Faculty research:* Urban high schools, transgender students, literacy pedagogy, funds of knowledge, English language learners. *Unit head:* Dr. Timothy D. Slekar, Dean, E-mail: tslekar@edgewood.edu. *Application contact:* Joann Eastman, Admissions Counselor, 608-663-3250, Fax: 608-663-2214, E-mail: gps@edgewood.edu.
Website: https://www.edgewood.edu/academics/schools/school-of-education

Elizabeth City State University, School of Education and Psychology, Elizabeth City, NC 27909-7806. Offers M Ed, MSA. *Program availability:* Part-time, evening/weekend. *Degree requirements:* For master's, comprehensive exam (for some programs), thesis. Electronic applications accepted.

Elms College, Division of Education, Chicopee, MA 01013-2839. Offers early childhood education (MAT); education (M Ed, CAGS); elementary education (MAT); English as a second language (MAT); reading (MAT); secondary education (MAT), including biology education, English education, Spanish education; special education (MAT). *Program availability:* Part-time, evening/weekend. *Faculty:* 5 full-time (all women), 7 part-time/adjunct (6 women). *Students:* 6 full-time (all women), 136 part-time (111 women); includes 6 minority (1 Asian, non-Hispanic/Latino; 5 Hispanic/Latino). Average age 33. 27 applicants, 89% accepted, 20 enrolled. In 2016, 47 master's, 3 other advanced degrees awarded. *Degree requirements:* For master's, thesis (for some programs). *Entrance requirements:* For master's, Massachusetts Educators Certification Test, minimum GPA of 3.0; for CAGS, master's degree in education. Additional exam requirements/recommendations for international students: Required—TOEFL. *Application deadline:* For fall admission, 7/1 priority date for domestic students; for spring admission, 11/1 priority date for domestic students. Applications are processed on a rolling basis. Application fee: $30. *Expenses: Tuition:* Full-time $13,392. *Required fees:* $200. *Financial support:* In 2016–17, 2 teaching assistantships with partial tuition reimbursements were awarded; tuition waivers (partial) also available. Support available to part-time students. Financial award applicants required to submit FAFSA. *Unit head:* Dr. Mary Janeczek, Chair, Division of Education, 413-594-2761, Fax: 413-592-4871, E-mail: janeczeke@elms.edu. *Application contact:* Dr. Elizabeth Teahan Hukowicz, Dean, School of Graduate and Professional Studies, 413-265-2360, Fax: 413-265-2459, E-mail: hukowicze@elms.edu.

Elon University, Program in Education, Elon, NC 27244-2010. Offers elementary education (M Ed); gifted education (M Ed); special education (M Ed). *Accreditation:* NCATE. *Program availability:* Part-time. *Faculty:* 9 full-time (7 women), 2 part-time/adjunct (both women). *Students:* 17 part-time (all women); includes 7 minority (3 Black or African American, non-Hispanic/Latino; 1 American Indian or Alaska Native, non-Hispanic/Latino; 2 Hispanic/Latino; 1 Two or more races, non-Hispanic/Latino). Average age 33. 24 applicants, 50% accepted, 8 enrolled. In 2016, 24 master's awarded. *Entrance requirements:* For master's, GRE, MAT. Additional exam requirements/recommendations for international students: Required—TOEFL (minimum score 550 paper-based; 79 iBT). *Application deadline:* For fall admission, 5/1 for domestic students. Applications are processed on a rolling basis. Application fee: $50. Electronic applications accepted. *Financial support:* Federal Work-Study and scholarships/grants available. Support available to part-time students. Financial award application deadline: 6/1; financial award applicants required to submit FAFSA. *Faculty research:* Teaching reading to low-achieving second and third graders, pre- and post-student teaching attitudes, children's writing, whole language methodology, critical creative thinking. *Unit head:* Dr. Ann Bullock, Dean of the School of Education/Professor, 336-278-5900,

E-mail: abullock9@elon.edu. *Application contact:* Art Fadde, Director of Graduate Admissions, 800-334-8448 Ext. 3, Fax: 336-278-7699, E-mail: afadde@elon.edu.
Website: http://www.elon.edu/med

Embry-Riddle Aeronautical University–Worldwide, Department of Aeronautics, Graduate Studies, Daytona Beach, FL 32114-3900. Offers aeronautics (MSA); aeronautics and design (MS); aviation maintenance (MAM); aviation/aerospace management (MS); education (MS); human factors (MS, MSHFS), including aerospace (MSHFS), systems engineering (MSHFS); occupational safety management (MS); operations (MS); safety/emergency response (MS); small unmanned aircraft system (SUAS) operation (MS); space systems (MS); unmanned aerospace systems (MS). *Program availability:* Part-time, evening/weekend, 100% online, blended/hybrid learning, EagleVision Classroom (between classrooms), EagleVision Home (faculty and students at home), and a blend of Classroom or Home. *Faculty:* 34 full-time (9 women), 146 part-time/adjunct (20 women). *Students:* 865 full-time (156 women), 998 part-time (163 women); includes 434 minority (179 Black or African American, non-Hispanic/Latino; 7 American Indian or Alaska Native, non-Hispanic/Latino; 65 Asian, non-Hispanic/Latino; 71 Hispanic/Latino; 4 Native Hawaiian or other Pacific Islander, non-Hispanic/Latino; 108 Two or more races, non-Hispanic/Latino), 128 international. Average age 37. In 2016, 572 master's awarded. *Degree requirements:* For master's, comprehensive exam (for some programs), thesis (for some programs), thesis or capstone project. *Entrance requirements:* For master's, GRE (for MSHFS). Additional exam requirements/recommendations for international students: Required—TOEFL (minimum score 550 paper-based, 79 iBT) or IELTS (6). *Application deadline:* Applications are processed on a rolling basis. Application fee: $50. Electronic applications accepted. *Expenses:* $620 per credit (for civilians), $530 per credit (for military). *Financial support:* Career-related internships or fieldwork and scholarships/grants available. Financial award applicants required to submit FAFSA. *Faculty research:* Aerodynamics statistical design and educational development. *Unit head:* Ian R. McAndrew, PhD, Department Chair, E-mail: ian.mcandrew@erau.edu. *Application contact:* Worldwide Campus, 800-522-6787, E-mail: worldwide@erau.edu.
Website: http://worldwide.erau.edu/colleges/aeronautics/department-aeronautics-graduate-studies/

Emmanuel College, Graduate and Professional Programs, Graduate Programs in Education, Boston, MA 02115. Offers M Ed. *Program availability:* Part-time, evening/weekend. *Faculty:* 1 (woman) full-time, 5 part-time/adjunct (all women). *Students:* 7 full-time (5 women), 9 part-time (7 women); includes 5 minority (1 Black or African American, non-Hispanic/Latino; 1 Asian, non-Hispanic/Latino; 2 Hispanic/Latino; 1 Two or more races, non-Hispanic/Latino). Average age 28. 15 applicants, 33% accepted, 2 enrolled. In 2016, 12 master's awarded. *Degree requirements:* For master's, 36 credits, including 6-credit practicum. *Entrance requirements:* For master's, transcripts from all regionally-accredited institutions attended (showing proof of bachelor's degree completion), 2 letters of recommendation, essay, resume. Additional exam requirements/recommendations for international students: Required—TOEFL. *Application deadline:* Applications are processed on a rolling basis. Electronic applications accepted. *Expenses:* Contact institution. *Financial support:* Application deadline: 2/15; applicants required to submit FAFSA. *Unit head:* Petia Whitmore, Executive Director, Graduate and Professional Programs, 617-732-1740, E-mail: gpp@emmanuel.edu. *Application contact:* Helen Muterperl, Associate Director of Admissions, Graduate and Professional Programs, 617-735-9700, Fax: 617-507-0434, E-mail: gpp@emmanuel.edu.
Website: http://www.emmanuel.edu/graduate-professional-programs/academics/education.html

Emory & Henry College, Graduate Programs, Emory, VA 24327-0947. Offers American history (MA Ed); organizational leadership (MCOL); professional studies (M Ed); reading specialist (MA Ed). *Program availability:* Part-time, evening/weekend. *Entrance requirements:* For master's, GRE or PRAXIS I, recommendations, writing sample. Additional exam requirements/recommendations for international students: Recommended—TOEFL.

Emory University, Laney Graduate School, Division of Educational Studies, Atlanta, GA 30322-1100. Offers educational studies (MA, PhD); middle grades teaching (MAT); secondary teaching (MAT). *Accreditation:* NCATE. Terminal master's awarded for partial completion of doctoral program. *Degree requirements:* For master's, thesis; for doctorate, comprehensive exam, thesis/dissertation. *Entrance requirements:* For master's and doctorate, GRE General Test, minimum GPA of 3.0. Additional exam requirements/recommendations for international students: Required—TOEFL. Electronic applications accepted. *Faculty research:* Educational policy, educational measurement, urban and multicultural education, mathematics and science education, comparative education.

Emporia State University, Program in Teaching, Emporia, KS 66801-5415. Offers M Ed. *Program availability:* Part-time, online learning. *Faculty:* 10 full-time (3 women). *Students:* 9 full-time (7 women), 16 part-time (8 women); includes 4 minority (1 Black or African American, non-Hispanic/Latino; 3 Hispanic/Latino). 15 applicants, 100% accepted, 4 enrolled. In 2016, 16 master's awarded. *Entrance requirements:* For master's, GRE or MAT, minimum GPA of 2.5 on last 60 undergraduate hours; two personal references. Application fee: $40. *Expenses:* Tuition, state resident: full-time $5922; part-time $246.75 per credit hour. Tuition, nonresident: full-time $18,414; part-time $767.25 per credit hour. *Required fees:* $1884; $78.50 per credit hour. *Unit head:* Dr. Daniel Stiffler, Chair, 620-341-5776, E-mail: dstiffle@emporia.edu. *Application contact:* Mary Sewell, Admissions Coordinator, 800-950-GRAD, Fax: 620-341-5909, E-mail: msewell@emporia.edu.

Evangel University, Department of Education, Springfield, MO 65802. Offers curriculum and instruction (M Ed); educational leadership (M Ed); literacy (M Ed); secondary teaching (M Ed). *Accreditation:* NCATE. *Program availability:* Part-time, evening/weekend, 100% online, blended/hybrid learning. *Faculty:* 3 full-time (2 women), 4 part-time/adjunct (2 women). *Students:* 2 full-time (1 woman), 33 part-time (29 women); includes 1 minority (Asian, non-Hispanic/Latino). Average age 30. 10 applicants, 90% accepted, 9 enrolled. In 2016, 28 master's awarded. *Degree requirements:* For master's, comprehensive exam, thesis optional. *Entrance requirements:* For master's, PRAXIS II (preferred) or GRE, minimum undergraduate GPA of 3.0. Additional exam requirements/recommendations for international students: Required—TOEFL (minimum score 550 paper-based). *Application deadline:* For fall admission, 7/15 priority date for domestic students, 8/1 for international students; for spring admission, 11/15 priority date for domestic students, 12/1 for international students. Applications are processed on a rolling basis. Application fee: $25. Electronic applications accepted. Application fee is waived when completed online. *Expenses: Tuition:* Part-time $400 per credit hour. *Required fees:* $148 per trimester. One-time fee: $25. Tuition and fees vary according to course load, degree level and program. *Financial support:* In 2016–17, 11 students received support. Scholarships/grants and unspecified assistantships available. Financial award application deadline: 4/1; financial award applicants required to submit FAFSA. *Unit head:* Dr. Susan Langston, Program Coordinator, 417-865-2815 Ext. 8552, E-mail: langstons@evangel.edu. *Application contact:* Karen Benitez, Admissions Representative, Graduate Studies, 417-865-2815 Ext. 7416, Fax: 417-575-5484, E-mail: benitezk@evangel.edu.
Website: http://www.evangel.edu/academics/graduate-studies/graduate-programs

The Evergreen State College, Graduate Programs, Program in Teaching, Olympia, WA 98505. Offers MIT. *Faculty:* 4 full-time (all women), 2 part-time/adjunct (both women). *Students:* 47 full-time (30 women); includes 12 minority (2 Black or African American, non-Hispanic/Latino; 2 American Indian or Alaska Native, non-Hispanic/Latino; 1 Asian, non-Hispanic/Latino; 3 Hispanic/Latino; 4 Two or more races, non-Hispanic/Latino). Average age 27. 49 applicants, 94% accepted, 31 enrolled. In 2016, 30 master's awarded. *Degree requirements:* For master's, project, 20-week teaching internship. *Entrance requirements:* For master's, Washington Educator Skills Test-Basic (WEST-B), Washington Educator Skills Test-Endorsements, minimum undergraduate GPA of 3.0 for last 90 quarter hours; official transcript; resume; 3 letters of recommendation; personal statement; thesis-based essay. Additional exam requirements/recommendations for international students: Required—TOEFL (minimum score 600 paper-based; 100 iBT). *Application deadline:* For fall admission, 4/3 priority date for domestic and international students. Applications are processed on a rolling basis. Application fee: $50. Electronic applications accepted. *Expenses:* Contact institution. *Financial support:* In 2016–17, 52 students received support, including 15 fellowships with partial tuition reimbursements available (averaging $678 per year); career-related internships or fieldwork, institutionally sponsored loans, scholarships/grants, and tuition waivers (partial) also available. Financial award application deadline: 2/1; financial award applicants required to submit FAFSA. *Faculty research:* Mathematics teacher education, education, teacher education, urban education, elementary, social and personality psychology, children's and adolescent literature, language acquisition, developmental psychology, multicultural education, qualitative research, critical pedagogy, feminist theory. *Unit head:* Dr. Patrick Naughton, Director, 360-867-6909, E-mail: naughtonp@evergreen.edu. *Application contact:* Maggie Foran, Associate Director, 360-867-6559, Fax: 360-867-6575, E-mail: foranm@evergreen.edu.
Website: http://www.evergreen.edu/mit/

Fairfield University, Graduate School of Education and Allied Professions, Fairfield, CT 06824. Offers applied behavior analysis (ATC); applied psychology (MA); clinical mental health counseling (MA, CAS); educational technology (MA); elementary education (MA, CAS); family studies (MA); integration of spirituality and religion in counseling (ATC); marriage and family therapy (MA); reading and language development (Sixth Year Certificate); school counseling (MA, CAS); school psychology (MA, CAS); school-based marriage and family therapy (ATC); secondary education (MA); special education (MA, CAS); substance abuse counseling (ATC); teaching (Certificate); teaching and foundations (MA, CAS); TESOL, world languages, and bilingual education (MA, CAS). *Accreditation:* NCATE. *Program availability:* Part-time, evening/weekend. *Faculty:* 19 full-time (15 women), 38 part-time/adjunct (26 women). *Students:* 153 full-time (132 women), 302 part-time (252 women); includes 97 minority (24 Black or African American, non-Hispanic/Latino; 12 Asian, non-Hispanic/Latino; 55 Hispanic/Latino; 6 Two or more races, non-Hispanic/Latino), 6 international. Average age 32. 283 applicants, 61% accepted, 97 enrolled. In 2016, 130 master's awarded. *Degree requirements:* For master's, comprehensive exam. *Entrance requirements:* For master's, minimum GPA of 3.0, 2 recommendations, resume. Additional exam requirements/recommendations for international students: Required—TOEFL (minimum score 550 paper-based; 84 iBT) or IELTS (minimum score 7.5). *Application deadline:* For fall admission, 2/15 for international students; for spring admission, 10/1 for international students. Application fee: $60. Electronic applications accepted. *Expenses:* $725 per credit hour. *Financial support:* In 2016–17, 42 students received support. Career-related internships or fieldwork and unspecified assistantships available. Support available to part-time students. Financial award applicants required to submit FAFSA. *Faculty research:* Reading and literacy, writing, social justice and inequality in education, addictions and mental health issues, therapeutic relationships and clinical supervision. *Unit head:* Dr. Robert D. Hannafin, Dean, 203-254-4250, Fax: 203-254-4241, E-mail: rhannafin@fairfield.edu. *Application contact:* Marianne Gumpper, Director of Graduate Admission, 203-254-4184, Fax: 203-254-4073, E-mail: gradadmis@fairfield.edu.
Website: http://www.fairfield.edu/gseap

Fairleigh Dickinson University, College at Florham, Maxwell Becton College of Arts and Sciences, Department of English, Communication and Philosophy, Program in Creative Writing and Literature for Educators, Madison, NJ 07940-1099. Offers MA.

Fairleigh Dickinson University, College at Florham, University College: Arts, Sciences, and Professional Studies, Peter Sammartino School of Education, Madison, NJ 07940-1099. Offers education for certified teachers (MA, Certificate); educational leadership (MA); instructional technology (Certificate); literacy/reading (Certificate); teaching (MAT).

Fairleigh Dickinson University, Metropolitan Campus, University College: Arts, Sciences, and Professional Studies, Peter Sammartino School of Education, Teaneck, NJ 07666-1914. Offers dyslexia specialist (Certificate); education for certified teachers (MA); educational leadership (MA); instructional technology (Certificate); learning disabilities (MA); literacy/reading (Certificate); multilingual education (MA); teacher of the handicapped (Certificate); teaching (MAT). *Accreditation:* TEAC. *Program availability:* Part-time. *Degree requirements:* For master's, research project (MAT).

Fairmont State University, Programs in Education, Fairmont, WV 26554. Offers digital media, new literacies and learning (M Ed); education (MAT); exercise science, fitness and wellness (M Ed); professional studies (M Ed); reading (M Ed); special education (M Ed). *Accreditation:* NCATE. *Program availability:* Part-time, evening/weekend, 100% online. *Faculty:* 18 full-time (11 women), 5 part-time/adjunct (3 women). *Students:* 62 full-time (52 women), 102 part-time (82 women); includes 6 minority (2 Black or African American, non-Hispanic/Latino; 1 American Indian or Alaska Native, non-Hispanic/Latino; 1 Hispanic/Latino; 2 Two or more races, non-Hispanic/Latino). Average age 33. 68 applicants, 84% accepted, 47 enrolled. In 2016, 44 degrees awarded. *Entrance requirements:* For master's, GRE. Additional exam requirements/recommendations for international students: Required—TOEFL (minimum score 80 iBT), IELTS (minimum score 6.5). *Application deadline:* For fall admission, 5/1 for domestic and international students. Applications are processed on a rolling basis. Application fee: $40. Electronic applications accepted. *Expenses:* Tuition, state resident: full-time $7504; part-time $405 per credit hour. Tuition, nonresident: full-time $16,060; part-time $880 per credit hour. Part-time tuition and fees vary according to course load. *Financial support:* In 2016–17, 20 students received support. Research assistantships, teaching assistantships, scholarships/grants, and unspecified assistantships available. Financial award applicants required to submit FAFSA. *Unit head:* Dr. Carolyn Crislip-Tacy, Interim Dean, School of Education, 304-367-4143, Fax: 304-367-4599, E-mail: carolyn.crislip-tacy@fairmontstate.edu. *Application contact:* Jack Kirby, Director of Graduate Studies, 304-367-4101, E-mail: jack.kirby@fairmontstate.edu.
Website: http://www.fairmontstate.edu/graduatestudies/

Faulkner University, College of Education, Montgomery, AL 36109-3398. Offers M Ed.

Felician University, Program in Education, Lodi, NJ 07644-2117. Offers education (MA); educational leadership (principal/supervision) (MA); educational supervision (PMC); principal (PMC). *Accreditation:* TEAC. *Program availability:* Part-time, evening/

weekend. *Faculty:* 2 full-time (1 woman), 7 part-time/adjunct (2 women). *Students:* 4 full-time (3 women), 65 part-time (60 women); includes 19 minority (9 Black or African American, non-Hispanic/Latino; 2 Asian, non-Hispanic/Latino; 8 Hispanic/Latino), 1 international. Average age 36. 36 applicants, 78% accepted, 16 enrolled. In 2016, 18 master's, 11 other advanced degrees awarded. *Degree requirements:* For master's and PMC, presentation. *Entrance requirements:* For master's, PRAXIS Core (Reading/Writing/Math), minimum GPA of 3.0, two professional letters of recommendation, personal statement, personal interview. Additional exam requirements/recommendations for international students: Required—TOEFL (minimum score 650 paper-based; 79 iBT), IELTS (minimum score 6.5). *Application deadline:* Applications are processed on a rolling basis. Application fee: $40. Electronic applications accepted. Application fee is waived when completed online. *Expenses:* $790 per credit, $290 comprehensive fees, $165 mandatory fees. *Financial support:* Federal Work-Study and scholarships/grants available. Financial award applicants required to submit FAFSA. *Faculty research:* Educational leadership, administration, supervision, curriculum. *Unit head:* Dr. Rose Rudnitski, Dean and Professor, School of Education, 201-559-3551, E-mail: rudnitskir@felician.edu. *Application contact:* Michael Szarek, Assistant Vice-President, Graduate Admissions, 201-559-1450, E-mail: szarekm@felician.edu.

Ferris State University, College of Education and Human Services, School of Education, Big Rapids, MI 49307. Offers curriculum and instruction (M Ed), including special education, subject area; educational leadership (MS); instructor (MSCTE); post-secondary administration (MSCTE); training and development (MSCTE). *Program availability:* Part-time, evening/weekend, blended/hybrid learning. *Faculty:* 7 full-time (4 women), 9 part-time/adjunct (6 women). *Students:* 3 full-time (1 woman), 62 part-time (34 women); includes 8 minority (3 Black or African American, non-Hispanic/Latino; 1 Hispanic/Latino; 4 Two or more races, non-Hispanic/Latino), 9 international. Average age 37. 24 applicants, 71% accepted, 10 enrolled. In 2016, 36 master's awarded. *Degree requirements:* For master's, thesis, research paper or project. *Entrance requirements:* For master's, minimum undergraduate GPA of 3.0. Additional exam requirements/recommendations for international students: Required—TOEFL (minimum score 500 paper-based, 79 iBT) or IELTS. *Application deadline:* For fall admission, 7/1 priority date for domestic and international students; for spring admission, 11/1 priority date for domestic and international students; for summer admission, 3/1 priority date for domestic and international students. Applications are processed on a rolling basis. Application fee: $30. Electronic applications accepted. Application fee is waived when completed online. Tuition and fees vary according to degree level and program. *Financial support:* Career-related internships or fieldwork and scholarships/grants available. Support available to part-time students. Financial award applicants required to submit FAFSA. *Faculty research:* Suicide prevention, reading, women in education, special needs, administration. *Unit head:* Arrick L. Jackson, Dean, 231-591-2702, Fax: 231-591-2043, E-mail: arrickJackson@ferris.edu. *Application contact:* Liza Ing, Graduate Program Coordinator, 231-591-5362, Fax: 231-591-2043, E-mail: lizaIng@ferris.edu.
Website: http://www.ferris.edu/education/education/

Fielding Graduate University, Graduate Programs, School of Leadership Studies, Programs in Education, Santa Barbara, CA 93105-3814. Offers digital teaching and learning (MA); educational administration (Certificate); leadership for change (Ed D). *Program availability:* 100% online, blended/hybrid learning. *Faculty:* 7 full-time (5 women), 15 part-time/adjunct (11 women). *Students:* 93 full-time (65 women), 5 part-time (3 women); includes 56 minority (30 Black or African American, non-Hispanic/Latino; 4 American Indian or Alaska Native, non-Hispanic/Latino; 2 Asian, non-Hispanic/Latino; 12 Hispanic/Latino; 8 Two or more races, non-Hispanic/Latino), 1 international. Average age 50. 19 applicants, 95% accepted, 12 enrolled. In 2016, 5 master's, 27 doctorates awarded. *Degree requirements:* For doctorate, thesis/dissertation. *Entrance requirements:* For master's, bachelor's degree from regionally-accredited U.S. institution or equivalent, resume, statement of purpose, official transcript; for doctorate, bachelor's or master's degree from regionally-accredited U.S. institution or equivalent, resume, statement of purpose, reflexive essay, official transcript; for Certificate, bachelor's degree from regionally-accredited U.S. institution or equivalent, resume, statement of purpose, 3 letters of recommendation, official transcript, copy of professional license. *Application deadline:* For fall admission, 7/15 for domestic and international students; for spring admission, 11/1 for domestic and international students; for summer admission, 3/1 for domestic and international students. Application fee: $75. Electronic applications accepted. *Expenses:* $8,275 per term (for Ed D); $3,500 per term (for MA). *Financial support:* In 2016–17, 9 students received support. Scholarships/grants available. Financial award applicants required to submit FAFSA. *Unit head:* Dr. Barbara Mink, Program Director, E-mail: bmink@fielding.edu. *Application contact:* Enrollment Coordinator, 800-340-1099 Ext. 4098, Fax: 805-687-9793, E-mail: admissions@fielding.edu.
Website: http://www.fielding.edu/our-programs/school-of-leadership-studies/

Florida Agricultural and Mechanical University, Division of Graduate Studies, Research, and Continuing Education, College of Education, Tallahassee, FL 32307-3200. Offers M Ed, MBE, MS, MS Ed, PhD. *Accreditation:* NCATE. *Program availability:* Part-time, evening/weekend. *Degree requirements:* For master's, thesis (for some programs); for doctorate, thesis/dissertation. *Entrance requirements:* For master's, GRE General Test, minimum GPA of 3.0. Additional exam requirements/recommendations for international students: Required—TOEFL.

Florida Atlantic University, College of Education, Boca Raton, FL 33431-0991. Offers M Ed, MA, MS, Ed D, PhD, Ed S. *Accreditation:* NCATE. *Program availability:* Part-time, evening/weekend. *Faculty:* 85 full-time (49 women), 28 part-time/adjunct (15 women). *Students:* 316 full-time (234 women), 501 part-time (372 women); includes 319 minority (170 Black or African American, non-Hispanic/Latino; 17 Asian, non-Hispanic/Latino; 110 Hispanic/Latino; 1 Native Hawaiian or other Pacific Islander, non-Hispanic/Latino; 21 Two or more races, non-Hispanic/Latino), 19 international. Average age 33. 974 applicants, 34% accepted, 237 enrolled. In 2016, 207 master's, 42 doctorates, 13 other advanced degrees awarded. *Degree requirements:* For doctorate, comprehensive exam, thesis/dissertation; for Ed S, departmental qualifying exam. *Entrance requirements:* For master's, doctorate, and Ed S, GRE General Test. Additional exam requirements/recommendations for international students: Required—TOEFL (minimum score 500 paper-based; 61 iBT), IELTS (minimum score 6). *Application deadline:* For fall admission, 5/1 for domestic students. Applications are processed on a rolling basis. Application fee: $30. Electronic applications accepted. *Expenses:* Tuition, state resident: full-time $7392; part-time $369.82 per credit hour. Tuition, nonresident: full-time $19,432; part-time $1024.81 per credit hour. *Financial support:* Fellowships with partial tuition reimbursements, research assistantships with partial tuition reimbursements, teaching assistantships with partial tuition reimbursements, career-related internships or fieldwork, Federal Work-Study, and unspecified assistantships available. *Faculty research:* Marriage and family counseling, multicultural education, self-directed learning, assessment, reading. *Unit head:* Dr. Valerie Bristor, 561-297-3357, E-mail: bristor@fau.edu.
Website: http://www.coe.fau.edu/

Florida Gulf Coast University, College of Education, Fort Myers, FL 33965-6565. Offers M Ed, MA. *Program availability:* Part-time, evening/weekend, online learning. *Faculty:* 26 full-time (18 women), 44 part-time/adjunct (32 women). *Students:* 11 full-time (2 women), 114 part-time (94 women); includes 49 minority (19 Black or African American, non-Hispanic/Latino; 4 Asian, non-Hispanic/Latino; 24 Hispanic/Latino; 2 Two or more races, non-Hispanic/Latino), 2 international. Average age 33. 109 applicants, 81% accepted, 65 enrolled. In 2016, 52 master's awarded. *Entrance requirements:* For master's, GRE General Test, MAT, minimum GPA of 3.0. Additional exam requirements/recommendations for international students: Required—TOEFL (minimum score 550 paper-based). *Application deadline:* For fall admission, 7/1 priority date for domestic students; for spring admission, 10/15 for domestic students. Applications are processed on a rolling basis. Application fee: $30. Electronic applications accepted. *Expenses:* Tuition, state resident: full-time $6721. Tuition, nonresident: full-time $28,170. *Required fees:* $1987. Tuition and fees vary according to course load and degree level. *Financial support:* In 2016–17, 9 students received support. Application deadline: 3/1; applicants required to submit FAFSA. *Faculty research:* Inclusion, emergent literacy, pre-service and in-service teacher education, education policy. *Total annual research expenditures:* $859,751. *Unit head:* Dr. Eunny Hyun, Dean, 239-590-7791, Fax: 239-590-7801, E-mail: ehyun@fgcu.edu. *Application contact:* Shannon Acosta, Graduate Studies Admissions, 239-590-7027, Fax: 239-590-7843, E-mail: sacosta@fgcu.edu.
Website: http://coe.fgcu.edu/

Florida Institute of Technology, College of Science, Program in Teaching, Melbourne, FL 32901-6975. Offers MAT. *Students:* 2 full-time (1 woman), 1 (woman) part-time; includes 1 minority (Hispanic/Latino), 1 international. Average age 29. 5 applicants, 20% accepted. In 2016, 1 master's awarded. *Degree requirements:* For master's, comprehensive exam, minimum GPA of 3.0, field experience. *Entrance requirements:* For master's, appropriate bachelor's degree, resume, statement of objectives. Additional exam requirements/recommendations for international students: Required—TOEFL (minimum score 550 paper-based; 79 iBT). *Application deadline:* Applications are processed on a rolling basis. Electronic applications accepted. *Expenses: Tuition:* Full-time $22,338; part-time $1241 per credit hour. *Required fees:* $250. Tuition and fees vary according to degree level, campus/location and program. *Financial support:* Applicants required to submit FAFSA. *Unit head:* Dr. Kastro Hamed, Department Head, 321-674-7206, E-mail: khamed@fit.edu. *Application contact:* Cheryl A. Brown, Associate Director of Graduate Admissions, 321-674-7581, Fax: 321-723-9468, E-mail: cbrown@fit.edu.
Website: http://cos.fit.edu/education/

Florida Memorial University, School of Education, Miami-Dade, FL 33054. Offers elementary education (MS); exceptional student education (MS); reading (MS). *Degree requirements:* For master's, comprehensive exam or thesis, field and clinical experiences, exit exam. *Entrance requirements:* For master's, GRE, CLAST, PRAXIS I, baccalaureate or graduate degree with minimum GPA of 3.0 in last 60 hours, 3 recommendations. Additional exam requirements/recommendations for international students: Recommended—TOEFL.

Florida Southern College, Programs in Teaching, Lakeland, FL 33801-5698. Offers collaborative teaching and learning (M Ed); educational leadership (M Ed, Ed D); teaching (MAT). *Program availability:* Part-time, evening/weekend. *Faculty:* 7 full-time (3 women), 8 part-time/adjunct (5 women). *Students:* 49 full-time (40 women), 31 part-time (19 women); includes 19 minority (9 Black or African American, non-Hispanic/Latino; 1 American Indian or Alaska Native, non-Hispanic/Latino; 7 Hispanic/Latino; 1 Native Hawaiian or other Pacific Islander, non-Hispanic/Latino; 1 Two or more races, non-Hispanic/Latino), 2 international. Average age 40. 133 applicants, 54% accepted, 50 enrolled. In 2016, 1 master's awarded. *Degree requirements:* For master's, comprehensive exam (for some programs), thesis (for some programs), FICE General Knowledge test and professional education exam (for MAT), eligibility for the Florida Professional Teacher Certificate (for M Ed); for doctorate, thesis/dissertation. *Entrance requirements:* For master's, Florida Teacher Certification exam (for MAT), letter of reference, resume, personal statement. Additional exam requirements/recommendations for international students: Required—TOEFL (minimum score 550 paper-based; 79 iBT), IELTS (minimum score 6.5). *Application deadline:* For fall admission, 8/1 for domestic and international students; for winter admission, 4/1 for domestic and international students; for spring admission, 12/1 for domestic and international students. Applications are processed on a rolling basis. Application fee: $30. Electronic applications accepted. *Expenses:* $410 per credit hour tuition, $100 per term fees. *Financial support:* In 2016–17, 3 students received support. Scholarships/grants available. Support available to part-time students. Financial award applicants required to submit FAFSA. *Unit head:* Dr. Tracey Tedder, Dean, 863-680-4177, Fax: 863-680-4102, E-mail: ttedder@flsouthern.edu. *Application contact:* Kathy Connelly, Evening Program Assistant Director, 863-680-4205, Fax: 863-680-3872, E-mail: kconnelly@flsouthern.edu.

Florida State University, The Graduate School, College of Education, Tallahassee, FL 32306. Offers MS, Ed D, PhD, Certificate, Ed S, MS/Ed S. *Accreditation:* NCATE. *Program availability:* Part-time, evening/weekend, blended/hybrid learning, asynchronous, minimal on-campus study. *Faculty:* 99 full-time (67 women), 54 part-time/adjunct (35 women). *Students:* 611 full-time (394 women), 425 part-time (294 women); includes 252 minority (117 Black or African American, non-Hispanic/Latino; 4 American Indian or Alaska Native, non-Hispanic/Latino; 6 Asian, non-Hispanic/Latino; 95 Hispanic/Latino; 30 Two or more races, non-Hispanic/Latino), 209 international. Average age 32. 1,042 applicants, 52% accepted, 295 enrolled. In 2016, 312 master's, 66 doctorates, 52 other advanced degrees awarded. Terminal master's awarded for partial completion of doctoral program. *Degree requirements:* For master's and other advanced degree, comprehensive exam, thesis optional; for doctorate, comprehensive exam, thesis/dissertation, diagnostic exam, preliminary exam, prospectus defense, dissertation defense. *Entrance requirements:* For master's, doctorate, and other advanced degree, GRE General Test, minimum upper-division GPA of 3.0. Additional exam requirements/recommendations for international students: Required—TOEFL (minimum score 550 paper-based, 80 iBT), IELTS (minimum score 6.5), Michigan English Language Assessment Battery (minimum score 77), or PTE (minimum score 55). Application fee: $30. Electronic applications accepted. *Expenses:* Tuition, state resident: full-time $7263; part-time $403.51 per credit hour. Tuition, nonresident: full-time $18,087; part-time $1004.85 per credit hour. *Required fees:* $1365; $75.81 per credit hour. $20 per semester. Tuition and fees vary according to campus/location. *Financial support:* In 2016–17, 313 students received support, including 22 fellowships with tuition reimbursements available, 254 research assistantships with tuition reimbursements available, 278 teaching assistantships with tuition reimbursements available; scholarships/grants, tuition waivers (full and partial), and unspecified assistantships also available. Financial award application deadline: 1/15; financial award applicants required to submit FAFSA. *Faculty research:* Sport management and administration, educational psychology, instructional systems, teacher education, educational leadership and policy. *Total annual research expenditures:* $13.3 million. *Unit head:* Marcy P. Driscoll, Dean, 850-644-6885, Fax: 850-644-2725, E-mail: mdriscoll@fsu.edu. *Application contact:* Jennie H. Kroeger, Assistant Director, Office of Communication and Recruitment, 850-644-6885, Fax: 850-644-2725, E-mail: jennie.kroeger@fsu.edu.
Website: http://education.fsu.edu

Education—General

Fontbonne University, Graduate Programs, St. Louis, MO 63105-3098. Offers accounting (MBA, MS); art (MA); art (K-12) (MAT); business (MBA); computer science (MS); deaf education (MA); early intervention in deaf education (MA); education (MA), including autism spectrum disorders, curriculum and instruction, diverse learners, early childhood education, reading, special education; elementary education (MAT); family and consumer sciences (MA), including multidisciplinary health communication studies; fine arts (MFA); instructional design and technology (MS); management and leadership (MM); middle school education (MAT); secondary education (MAT); special education (MAT); speech-language pathology (MS); supply chain management (MS); theatre (MA). *Program availability:* Part-time, evening/weekend, online learning. *Faculty:* 32 full-time (24 women), 43 part-time/adjunct (26 women). *Students:* 456 full-time (313 women), 102 part-time (77 women); includes 138 minority (118 Black or African American, non-Hispanic/Latino; 1 American Indian or Alaska Native, non-Hispanic/Latino; 7 Asian, non-Hispanic/Latino; 9 Hispanic/Latino; 3 Two or more races, non-Hispanic/Latino), 37 international. *Degree requirements:* For master's, comprehensive exam (for some programs), thesis (for some programs). *Entrance requirements:* Additional exam requirements/recommendations for international students: Required—TOEFL (minimum score 500 paper-based; 65 iBT). *Application deadline:* For fall admission, 8/1 for international students; for spring admission, 12/1 for international students. Applications are processed on a rolling basis. Application fee: $25 ($30 for international students). Electronic applications accepted. *Expenses: Tuition:* Full-time $8436; part-time $703 per credit hour. *Required fees:* $18 per credit hour. Tuition and fees vary according to course load. *Financial support:* Teaching assistantships with partial tuition reimbursements and scholarships/grants available. Support available to part-time students. Financial award application deadline: 4/1; financial award applicants required to submit FAFSA. *Unit head:* Dr. Carey Adams, Vice President for Academic Affairs, 314-719-3609, E-mail: cadams@fontbonne.edu. *Application contact:* Lauryn Filip, Coordinator, Graduate Admission and Professional Studies, 314-889-4650, E-mail: admissions@fontbonne.edu.
Website: https://www.fontbonne.edu/academics/graduate-programs/

Fordham University, Graduate School of Education, New York, NY 10023. Offers MSE, MST, Ed D, PhD, Adv C. *Accreditation:* NCATE. *Program availability:* Part-time, evening/weekend. Terminal master's awarded for partial completion of doctoral program. *Degree requirements:* For master's and Adv C, comprehensive exam (for some programs); for doctorate, comprehensive exam (for some programs), thesis/dissertation. *Entrance requirements:* For master's and Adv C, minimum GPA of 3.0; for doctorate, GRE or MAT. Additional exam requirements/recommendations for international students: Required—TOEFL (minimum score 577 paper-based, 90 iBT) or IELTS (minimum score 7.0). Electronic applications accepted. *Expenses:* Contact institution.

Fort Hays State University, Graduate School, College of Education, Hays, KS 67601-4099. Offers MS, MSE, Ed S. *Accreditation:* NCATE. *Program availability:* Part-time. *Degree requirements:* For master's, comprehensive exam, thesis or alternative. *Entrance requirements:* Additional exam requirements/recommendations for international students: Required—TOEFL (minimum score 550 paper-based). Electronic applications accepted.

Franciscan University of Steubenville, Graduate Programs, Department of Education, Steubenville, OH 43952-1763. Offers administration (MS Ed); teaching (MS Ed). *Accreditation:* NCATE. *Program availability:* Part-time, evening/weekend, online learning. *Degree requirements:* For master's, project. *Entrance requirements:* For master's, minimum undergraduate GPA of 2.5 or written exam. Additional exam requirements/recommendations for international students: Required—TOEFL. Electronic applications accepted. Application fee is waived when completed online. *Expenses:* Contact institution.

Francis Marion University, Graduate Programs, School of Education, Florence, SC 29502-0547. Offers learning disabilities (M Ed, MAT). *Accreditation:* NCATE. *Program availability:* Part-time. *Degree requirements:* For master's, comprehensive exam (for some programs), thesis (for some programs), supervised internship (for MAT). *Entrance requirements:* For master's, GRE General Test, MAT, NTE, or PRAXIS II, official transcripts; two letters of recommendation. Additional exam requirements/recommendations for international students: Required—TOEFL (minimum score 550 paper-based; 79 iBT). *Expenses:* Tuition, state resident: full-time $10,100; part-time $505 per credit hour. Tuition, nonresident: full-time $20,196; part-time $1009.80 per credit hour. *Required fees:* $14.80 per credit hour. $73 per semester. Tuition and fees vary according to course load and program. *Faculty research:* Identification and alternate assessment of at-risk students.

Freed-Hardeman University, Program in Education, Henderson, TN 38340-2399. Offers curriculum and instruction (M Ed); school counseling (M Ed), including administration and supervision, special education; school leadership (Ed S). *Accreditation:* NCATE. *Program availability:* Part-time, evening/weekend. *Degree requirements:* For master's, comprehensive exam, thesis optional; for Ed S, thesis. *Entrance requirements:* For master's, GRE General Test or NTE; for Ed S, 3 years of teaching experience. Additional exam requirements/recommendations for international students: Required—TOEFL (minimum score 500 paper-based).

Fresno Pacific University, Graduate Programs, School of Education, Fresno, CA 93702-4709. Offers MA, MA Ed, Certificate. *Program availability:* Part-time, evening/weekend. *Degree requirements:* For master's, thesis (for some programs). *Entrance requirements:* For master's, interview; GMAT, GRE, MAT, or 6 units of course work with a faculty recommendation. Additional exam requirements/recommendations for international students: Required—TOEFL (minimum score 550 paper-based). Electronic applications accepted.

Frostburg State University, Graduate School, College of Education, Frostburg, MD 21532-1099. Offers M Ed, MAT, MS. *Accreditation:* NCATE. *Program availability:* Part-time, evening/weekend. *Entrance requirements:* Additional exam requirements/recommendations for international students: Required—TOEFL. Electronic applications accepted.

Furman University, Graduate Division, Department of Education, Greenville, SC 29613. Offers curriculum and instruction (MA); early childhood education (MA); educational leadership (Ed S); English as a second language (MA); literacy (MA); school leadership (MA); special education (MA). *Accreditation:* NCATE. *Program availability:* Part-time, online learning. *Degree requirements:* For master's, comprehensive exam (for some programs), thesis or alternative. *Entrance requirements:* For master's, PRAXIS II. *Faculty research:* Literacy, pedagogy and practice, social justice, advanced leadership, achievement in high poverty schools.

Gallaudet University, The Graduate School, Washington, DC 20002-3625. Offers American Sign Language/English bilingual early childhood deaf education: birth to 5 (Certificate); audiology (Au D); clinical psychology (PhD); deaf and hard of hearing infants, toddlers, and their families (Certificate); deaf education (MA, Ed S); deaf history (Certificate); deaf studies (Certificate); educating deaf students with disabilities (Certificate); education: teacher preparation (MA), including deaf education, early childhood education and deaf education, elementary education and deaf education, secondary education and deaf education; educational neuroscience (PhD); hearing, speech and language sciences (MS, PhD); international development (MA); interpretation (MA, PhD), including combined interpreting practice and research (MA), interpreting research (MA); linguistics (MA, PhD); mental health counseling (MA); peer mentoring (Certificate); public administration (MPA); school counseling (MA); school psychology (Psy S); sign language teaching (MA); social work (MSW); speech-language pathology (MS). *Program availability:* Part-time. *Students:* 297 full-time (231 women), 129 part-time (97 women); includes 105 minority (35 Black or African American, non-Hispanic/Latino; 20 Asian, non-Hispanic/Latino; 39 Hispanic/Latino; 11 Two or more races, non-Hispanic/Latino), 22 international. Average age 30. 471 applicants, 52% accepted, 147 enrolled. In 2016, 138 master's, 25 doctorates, 14 other advanced degrees awarded. Terminal master's awarded for partial completion of doctoral program. *Degree requirements:* For master's, comprehensive exam (for some programs), thesis optional; for doctorate, comprehensive exam, thesis/dissertation. *Entrance requirements:* For master's and doctorate, GRE General Test or MAT, letters of recommendation, interviews, goals statement, American Sign Language proficiency interview, written English competency. Additional exam requirements/recommendations for international students: Required—TOEFL. *Application deadline:* For fall admission, 2/15 for domestic students. Applications are processed on a rolling basis. Application fee: $75. Electronic applications accepted. *Expenses: Tuition:* Full-time $17,100; part-time $950 per credit hour. *Required fees:* $3725; $276 per semester. *Financial support:* Fellowships, research assistantships, teaching assistantships, career-related internships or fieldwork, Federal Work-Study, scholarships/grants, tuition waivers (partial), and unspecified assistantships available. Support available to part-time students. Financial award application deadline: 7/1; financial award applicants required to submit FAFSA. *Faculty research:* Signing math dictionaries, telecommunications access, cancer genetics, linguistics, visual language and visual learning, integrated quantum materials, deaf legal discourse, advance recruitment and retention in geosciences. *Unit head:* Dr. Gaurav Mathur, Dean, Graduate School and Continuing Studies, 202-250-2380, Fax: 202-651-5027, E-mail: gaurav.mathur@gallaudet.edu. *Application contact:* Wednesday Luria, Coordinator of Prospective Graduate Student Services, 202-651-5400, Fax: 202-651-5295, E-mail: graduate.school@gallaudet.edu.

Gannon University, School of Graduate Studies, College of Humanities, Education, and Social Sciences, School of Education, Erie, PA 16541-0001. Offers curriculum and instruction (M Ed); curriculum supervisor (Certificate); English as a second language (Certificate); principal certification (Certificate); reading (M Ed); reading specialist (Certificate); superintendent letter of eligibility (Certificate). *Program availability:* Part-time, evening/weekend, 100% online. *Faculty:* 7 full-time (6 women), 13 part-time/adjunct (9 women). *Students:* 7 full-time (all women), 133 part-time (107 women); includes 5 minority (1 Black or African American, non-Hispanic/Latino; 1 American Indian or Alaska Native, non-Hispanic/Latino; 1 Asian, non-Hispanic/Latino; 2 Hispanic/Latino). Average age 33. 124 applicants, 88% accepted, 91 enrolled. In 2016, 70 master's, 24 Certificates awarded. *Degree requirements:* For master's, thesis (for some programs), portfolio project. *Entrance requirements:* For master's, GRE, bachelor's degree from accredited institution, letters of recommendation, transcripts, teaching certificate (for some programs), minimum GPA of 3.0; for Certificate, GRE, master's degree (for some programs), teaching certificate, minimum GPA of 3.0, experience in field (for some programs). Additional exam requirements/recommendations for international students: Required—TOEFL (minimum score 79 iBT). *Application deadline:* Applications are processed on a rolling basis. Application fee: $25. Electronic applications accepted. Application fee is waived when completed online. *Expenses:* Contact institution. *Financial support:* Federal Work-Study available. Financial award application deadline: 7/1; financial award applicants required to submit FAFSA. *Application contact:* Bridget Philip, Director of Graduate Admissions, 814-871-7412, E-mail: graduate@gannon.edu.

Gardner-Webb University, Graduate School, School of Education, Boiling Springs, NC 28017. Offers curriculum and instruction (Ed D); educational leadership (Ed D); executive leadership studies (MA, Ed S); organizational leadership (Ed D); school administration (MA). *Accreditation:* NCATE. *Program availability:* Part-time, evening/weekend. *Faculty:* 16 full-time (6 women), 35 part-time/adjunct (20 women). *Students:* 10 full-time (7 women), 690 part-time (527 women); includes 286 minority (262 Black or African American, non-Hispanic/Latino; 5 American Indian or Alaska Native, non-Hispanic/Latino; 6 Asian, non-Hispanic/Latino; 11 Hispanic/Latino; 2 Two or more races, non-Hispanic/Latino), 1 international. Average age 37. 428 applicants, 52% accepted, 180 enrolled. In 2016, 163 master's, 51 doctorates awarded. *Degree requirements:* For master's, comprehensive exam. *Entrance requirements:* For master's, GRE General Test or NTE, PRAXIS, minimum GPA of 2.5. *Application deadline:* For fall admission, 8/1 priority date for domestic students. Applications are processed on a rolling basis. Electronic applications accepted. *Expenses:* Contact institution. *Financial support:* Unspecified assistantships available. *Unit head:* Dr. Alan D. Eury, Dean, 704-406-4402, Fax: 704-406-3921, E-mail: dsimmons@gardner-webb.edu. *Application contact:* Office of Graduate Admissions, 877-498-4723, Fax: 704-406-3895, E-mail: gradinfo@gardner-webb.edu.

Geneva College, Master of Arts in Higher Education Program, Beaver Falls, PA 15010-3599. Offers campus ministry (MA); college teaching (MA); educational leadership (MA); student affairs administration (MA). *Program availability:* Part-time, evening/weekend, blended/hybrid learning. *Faculty:* 2 full-time (0 women), 11 part-time/adjunct (4 women). *Students:* 49 full-time (30 women), 7 part-time (2 women); includes 6 minority (3 Black or African American, non-Hispanic/Latino; 1 Hispanic/Latino; 2 Two or more races, non-Hispanic/Latino), 1 international. Average age 26. 47 applicants, 74% accepted, 23 enrolled. In 2016, 23 master's awarded. *Degree requirements:* For master's, 36 hours (27 in core courses) including a capstone research project. *Entrance requirements:* For master's, minimum GPA of 3.0, writing sample, 3 letters of recommendation, essay on motivation for participation in the program. Additional exam requirements/recommendations for international students: Required—TOEFL. *Application deadline:* For fall admission, 9/1 priority date for domestic students; for winter admission, 1/2 priority date for domestic students; for spring admission, 3/11 priority date for domestic students. Applications are processed on a rolling basis. Electronic applications accepted. *Expenses:* $655 per credit. *Financial support:* In 2016–17, 37 students received support. Unspecified assistantships available. Financial award application deadline: 8/1; financial award applicants required to submit FAFSA. *Faculty research:* Learning theories, church-related higher education, organizational culture, sexual assault and transgender students at Christian colleges, emerging technology in higher education. *Unit head:* Dr. Keith Martel, Program Director, 724-847-6884, Fax: 724-847-6107, E-mail: hed@geneva.edu. *Application contact:* Jerryn S. Carson, Program Coordinator, 724-847-6510, Fax: 724-847-6696, E-mail: hed@geneva.edu.
Website: http://www.geneva.edu/page/higher_ed

George Fox University, College of Education, Newberg, OR 97132-2697. Offers M Ed, MA, MAT, Ed D, Certificate, Ed S.

George Mason University, College of Education and Human Development, Fairfax, VA 22030. Offers M Ed, MS, PhD, Certificate. *Accreditation:* NCATE. *Program availability:* Part-time, evening/weekend, online learning. *Faculty:* 167 full-time (118 women), 193 part-time/adjunct (132 women). *Students:* 455 full-time (369 women), 2,127 part-time (1,746 women); includes 719 minority (282 Black or African American, non-Hispanic/

Latino; 9 American Indian or Alaska Native, non-Hispanic/Latino; 168 Asian, non-Hispanic/Latino; 204 Hispanic/Latino; 4 Native Hawaiian or other Pacific Islander, non-Hispanic/Latino; 52 Two or more races, non-Hispanic/Latino), 62 international. Average age 34. 1,231 applicants, 88% accepted, 762 enrolled. In 2016, 692 master's, 45 doctorates, 198 other advanced degrees awarded. *Degree requirements:* For doctorate, comprehensive exam, final project, internship. *Entrance requirements:* For master's, PRAXIS Core, GRE, or MAT (depending on program), minimum GPA of 3.0 in last 60 hours of course work, goals statement, interview or writing sample; for doctorate, GRE, appropriate master's degree, transcripts, resume, interview, 3 letters of recommendation, goals statement; 3 years of experience in educational, community, and human development settings (depending on program). Additional exam requirements/recommendations for international students: Required—TOEFL (minimum score 575 paper-based; 88 iBT), IELTS (minimum score 6.5), PTE (minimum score 59). Application fee: $75 ($80 for international students). Electronic applications accepted. *Expenses:* Tuition, state resident: full-time $10,628; part-time $443 per credit. Tuition, nonresident: full-time $29,306; part-time $1221 per credit. *Required fees:* $3096; $129 per credit. Tuition and fees vary according to program. *Financial support:* In 2016–17, 104 students received support, including 13 fellowships (averaging $8,748 per year), 77 research assistantships with tuition reimbursements available (averaging $13,507 per year), 36 teaching assistantships with tuition reimbursements available (averaging $7,243 per year); career-related internships or fieldwork, Federal Work-Study, scholarships/grants, unspecified assistantships, and health care benefits (for full-time research or teaching assistantship recipients) also available. Support available to part-time students. Financial award application deadline: 3/1; financial award applicants required to submit FAFSA. *Faculty research:* Special education/human disabilities, mathematics/science/technology education, education leadership, school/community/agency/higher education, counseling and administration. *Total annual research expenditures:* $16.8 million. *Unit head:* Mark Ginsberg, Dean, 703-993-2004, Fax: 703-993-2001, E-mail: mginsber@gmu.edu. *Application contact:* Nicole Mariam, Graduate Admissions Coordinator, 703-993-3832, Fax: 703-993-2020, E-mail: nwhite5@gmu.edu.
Website: http://cehd.gmu.edu/

Georgetown College, Department of Education, Georgetown, KY 40324-1696. Offers reading and writing (MA Ed); special education (MA Ed); teaching (MA Ed). *Accreditation:* NCATE. *Program availability:* Part-time. *Degree requirements:* For master's, portfolio. *Entrance requirements:* For master's, teaching certificate, minimum GPA of 2.7 or GRE General Test.

The George Washington University, Graduate School of Education and Human Development, Washington, DC 20052. Offers M Ed, MA, MA Ed, MA Ed/HD, MAT, Ed D, PhD, Certificate, Ed S, Graduate Certificate, Teaching Certificate. *Accreditation:* NCATE. *Program availability:* Part-time, evening/weekend, online learning. *Faculty:* 83 full-time (50 women). *Students:* 418 full-time (332 women), 1,082 part-time (828 women); includes 564 minority (326 Black or African American, non-Hispanic/Latino; 6 American Indian or Alaska Native, non-Hispanic/Latino; 79 Asian, non-Hispanic/Latino; 108 Hispanic/Latino; 2 Native Hawaiian or other Pacific Islander, non-Hispanic/Latino; 43 Two or more races, non-Hispanic/Latino), 103 international. Average age 36. 1,654 applicants, 71% accepted, 669 enrolled. In 2016, 376 master's, 69 doctorates, 115 other advanced degrees awarded. *Degree requirements:* For master's and other advanced degree, comprehensive exam; for doctorate, comprehensive exam, thesis/dissertation. *Entrance requirements:* For master's, GRE General Test or MAT, minimum GPA of 2.75; for doctorate, GRE General Test or MAT, interview, minimum GPA of 3.3; for other advanced degree, GRE General Test or MAT, minimum GPA of 3.3. *Application deadline:* For fall admission, 1/15 priority date for domestic students; for spring admission, 10/1 for domestic students. Applications are processed on a rolling basis. Application fee: $75. Electronic applications accepted. *Financial support:* In 2016–17, 279 students received support. Fellowships with tuition reimbursements available, research assistantships with tuition reimbursements available, teaching assistantships with tuition reimbursements available, career-related internships or fieldwork, Federal Work-Study, and tuition waivers (full and partial) available. Support available to part-time students. Financial award application deadline: 1/15. *Faculty research:* Policy, special education, bilingual education, counseling, human resource development. *Total annual research expenditures:* $4.6 million. *Unit head:* Michael Feuer, Dean, 202-994-6161, Fax: 202-994-7207, E-mail: mjfeuer@gwu.edu. *Application contact:* Sarah Lang, Director of Graduate Admissions, 202-994-1447, Fax: 202-994-7207, E-mail: slang@gwu.edu.
Website: http://gsehd.gwu.edu/

Georgia College & State University, Graduate School, The John H. Lounsbury College of Education, Milledgeville, GA 31061. Offers M Ed, MAT, Ed S. *Accreditation:* NCATE. *Program availability:* Part-time, 100% online, blended/hybrid learning. *Students:* 140 full-time (98 women), 144 part-time (111 women); includes 115 minority (101 Black or African American, non-Hispanic/Latino; 2 Asian, non-Hispanic/Latino; 5 Hispanic/Latino; 7 Two or more races, non-Hispanic/Latino). Average age 35. 87 applicants, 100% accepted, 66 enrolled. In 2016, 108 master's, 82 other advanced degrees awarded. *Degree requirements:* For master's, comprehensive exam, minimum GPA of 3.0, complete program within 6 years; for Ed S, comprehensive exam, minimum GPA of 3.0, complete program within 4 years. *Entrance requirements:* For master's, on-site writing assessment, GRE General Test taken within six years (minimum scores 1,000 verbal and quantitative combined if taken before August 1, 2011, 305 if taken on or after August 1, 2011), or MAT (minimum score 400), 2 professional recommendations, transcripts, proof of immunization, minimum GPA of 2.75; for Ed S, on-site writing assessment, GRE General Test taken within six years (minimum scores 1,000 verbal and quantitative combined if taken before August 1, 2011; 305 if taken on or after August 1, 2011), or MAT, minimum GPA of 3.25, Georgia teaching certificate, 2 years of teaching experience, transcript, 2 professional recommendations, verification of immunization. *Application deadline:* For fall admission, 7/1 priority date for domestic students; for spring admission, 11/1 priority date for domestic students; for summer admission, 4/1 priority date for domestic students. Applications are processed on a rolling basis. Application fee: $40. Electronic applications accepted. *Expenses:* $288 per credit hour in-state tuition; $1,027 per credit hour out-of-state; fees vary by hours enrolled. *Financial support:* In 2016–17, 9 students received support. Unspecified assistantships available. Support available to part-time students. Financial award application deadline: 3/1; financial award applicants required to submit FAFSA. *Unit head:* Dr. Joseph Peters, Dean, College of Education, 478-445-2518, Fax: 478-445-6582, E-mail: joseph.peters@gcsu.edu. *Application contact:* Shanda Brand, Graduate Admissions Advisor, 478-445-1383, Fax: 478-445-6582, E-mail: shanda.brand@gcsu.edu.
Website: http://www.gcsu.edu/education/graduate/index.htm

Georgian Court University, School of Education, Lakewood, NJ 08701-2697. Offers administration and leadership (MA); autism spectrum disorders (Certificate); education (MA); instructional technology (Certificate). *Accreditation:* TEAC. *Program availability:* Part-time, evening/weekend. *Faculty:* 14 full-time (8 women), 31 part-time/adjunct (18 women). *Students:* 66 full-time (55 women), 376 part-time (312 women); includes 92 minority (44 Black or African American, non-Hispanic/Latino; 1 American Indian or Alaska Native, non-Hispanic/Latino; 8 Asian, non-Hispanic/Latino; 34 Hispanic/Latino; 5 Two or more races, non-Hispanic/Latino). Average age 34. 409 applicants, 62% accepted, 174 enrolled. In 2016, 95 master's, 1 other advanced degree awarded. *Degree requirements:* For master's, comprehensive exam (for some programs), thesis (for some programs). *Entrance requirements:* For master's, GRE, GMAT or NTE/PRAXIS, 3 letters of recommendation. Additional exam requirements/recommendations for international students: Required—TOEFL (minimum score 550 paper-based). *Application deadline:* For fall admission, 8/15 priority date for domestic students, 5/1 for international students; for spring admission, 1/15 priority date for domestic students, 10/1 for international students. Applications are processed on a rolling basis. Application fee: $40. Electronic applications accepted. *Expenses: Tuition:* Full-time $15,079; part-time $839 per credit. *Required fees:* $968; $496 per credit. Tuition and fees vary according to campus/location and program. *Financial support:* Scholarships/grants, health care benefits, and unspecified assistantships available. Financial award application deadline: 4/15; financial award applicants required to submit FAFSA. *Unit head:* Dr. Lynn DeCapua, Dean, 732-987-2729, E-mail: ldecapua@georgian.edu. *Application contact:* Patrick Givens, Director of Graduate and Professional Studies Admissions, 732-987-2736, Fax: 732-987-2000, E-mail: gps@georgian.edu.
Website: http://georgian.edu/academics/school-of-education/

Georgia Southern University, Jack N. Averitt College of Graduate Studies, College of Education, Statesboro, GA 30460. Offers M Ed, MAT, Ed D, Ed S. *Accreditation:* NCATE. *Program availability:* Part-time, evening/weekend, blended/hybrid learning. *Faculty:* 80 full-time (55 women), 21 part-time/adjunct (11 women). *Students:* 322 full-time (271 women), 900 part-time (713 women); includes 374 minority (314 Black or African American, non-Hispanic/Latino; 1 American Indian or Alaska Native, non-Hispanic/Latino; 4 Asian, non-Hispanic/Latino; 36 Hispanic/Latino; 19 Two or more races, non-Hispanic/Latino), 7 international. Average age 33. 385 applicants, 88% accepted, 216 enrolled. In 2016, 334 master's, 30 doctorates, 55 other advanced degrees awarded. *Degree requirements:* For master's, comprehensive exam (for some programs), portfolio or assessments; for doctorate, comprehensive exam, thesis/dissertation, exams; for Ed S, assessments. *Entrance requirements:* For master's, GRE General Test or MAT, minimum GPA of 2.5; for doctorate, GRE General Test or MAT, minimum GPA of 3.5, letters of reference, writing sample; for Ed S, GRE General Test or MAT, minimum graduate GPA of 3.25. Additional exam requirements/recommendations for international students: Required—TOEFL (minimum score 550 paper-based; 80 iBT), IELTS (minimum score 6). *Application deadline:* For fall admission, 3/1 priority date for domestic and international students; for spring admission, 10/1 priority date for domestic students, 10/1 for international students. Applications are processed on a rolling basis. Application fee: $50. Electronic applications accepted. *Expenses:* Tuition, state resident: full-time $7236; part-time $277 per semester hour. Tuition, nonresident: full-time $27,118; part-time $1105 per semester hour. *Required fees:* $2092. *Financial support:* In 2016–17, 103 students received support, including 1 teaching assistantship with full tuition reimbursement available (averaging $7,750 per year); research assistantships with partial tuition reimbursements available, career-related internships or fieldwork, Federal Work-Study, scholarships/grants, tuition waivers (full), unspecified assistantships, and doctoral stipends also available. Support available to part-time students. Financial award application deadline: 4/15; financial award applicants required to submit FAFSA. *Faculty research:* Teacher preparation, literacy education, curriculum issues, technology-enhanced teaching and learning, school reform, assessment of teaching and learning, educational leadership, educational technology, educational psychology, educational counseling. *Total annual research expenditures:* $97,282. *Unit head:* Dr. Thomas Koballa, Dean, 912-478-5648, Fax: 912-478-5093, E-mail: tkoballa@georgiasouthern.edu.
Website: http://coe.georgiasouthern.edu/

Georgia Southwestern State University, School of Education, Americus, GA 31709-4693. Offers early childhood education (M Ed, Ed S); middle grades education (Ed S); middle grades language arts (M Ed); middle grades mathematics (M Ed); special education (M Ed). *Accreditation:* NCATE. *Faculty:* 13 full-time (8 women), 7 part-time/adjunct (6 women). *Students:* 209 full-time (199 women), 6 part-time (all women); includes 52 minority (45 Black or African American, non-Hispanic/Latino; 6 Hispanic/Latino; 1 Two or more races, non-Hispanic/Latino). Average age 33. In 2016, 57 master's awarded. *Degree requirements:* For master's, minimum cumulative GPA of 3.0; for Ed S, minimum GPA of 3.25 in all courses with no grade less than a B; degree must be completed within 7 calendar years from date of initial enrollment in graduate work. *Entrance requirements:* For master's, undergraduate degree from accredited institution; professional Georgia Teaching Certificate or eligibility; minimum undergraduate GPA of 2.75 as reported on official final transcripts from all accredited institutions attended; 2 confidential Administrative Recommendation Forms; for Ed S, master's degree from accredited college or university; professional Georgia Teaching Certificate or eligibility; minimum graduate GPA of 3.0 as reported on official final graduate transcripts from all accredited institutions attended; 2 confidential Administrative Recommendation Forms. *Application deadline:* For summer admission, 4/15 for domestic students. Application fee: $25. Electronic applications accepted. *Expenses:* $257 per credit hour for online program courses, plus fees, which vary according to enrolled credit hours. *Financial support:* Application deadline: 6/1; applicants required to submit FAFSA. *Unit head:* Dr. Rachel Abbott, Dean, 229-931-2145. *Application contact:* Whitney Ford, Admissions Specialist, Office of Graduate Admissions, 800-338-0082, Fax: 229-931-2983.
Website: https://gsw.edu/Academics/Schools-and-Departments/School-of-Education/index

Georgia State University, College of Education and Human Development, Atlanta, GA 30302-3083. Offers M Ed, MAT, MS, Ed D, PhD, Ed S. *Accreditation:* NCATE. *Program availability:* Part-time, evening/weekend, online learning. *Faculty:* 148 full-time (98 women). *Students:* 785 full-time (573 women), 395 part-time (270 women); includes 521 minority (371 Black or African American, non-Hispanic/Latino; 1 American Indian or Alaska Native, non-Hispanic/Latino; 39 Asian, non-Hispanic/Latino; 74 Hispanic/Latino; 36 Two or more races, non-Hispanic/Latino), 44 international. Average age 32. 1,113 applicants, 34% accepted, 280 enrolled. In 2016, 366 master's, 65 doctorates, 28 other advanced degrees awarded. Terminal master's awarded for partial completion of doctoral program. *Degree requirements:* For master's, comprehensive exam (for some programs), thesis (for some programs), minimum GPA of 3.0; for doctorate, comprehensive exam, thesis/dissertation, minimum GPA of 3.5; for Ed S, thesis or alternative, minimum GPA of 3.0. *Entrance requirements:* For master's, GRE, MAT (for some programs), minimum GPA of 2.5 on all undergraduate work attempted in which letter grades were awarded; for doctorate, GRE, MAT (for some programs), minimum GPA of 3.3 on all graduate coursework for which letter grades were awarded (for PhD); for Ed S, GRE, MAT (for some programs), graduate degree from regionally-accredited college or university unless specified otherwise by the program with minimum GPA of 3.25 on all graduate coursework for which letter grades were awarded. Additional exam requirements/recommendations for international students: Required—TOEFL (minimum score 550 paper-based; 79 iBT) or IELTS (minimum score 6.5). Application fee: $50. Electronic applications accepted. *Expenses:* Tuition, state resident: full-time $6876; part-time $382 per credit hour. Tuition, nonresident: full-time $22,374; part-time $1243 per credit hour. *Required fees:* $2128; $1064 per term. Part-time tuition and fees vary according to course load and program. *Financial support:* In 2016–17, fellowships with full tuition reimbursements (averaging $25,000 per year), research assistantships with tuition reimbursements (averaging $4,867 per year), teaching assistantships with tuition

reimbursements (averaging $4,683 per year) were awarded; career-related internships or fieldwork, Federal Work-Study, scholarships/grants, tuition waivers (partial), and unspecified assistantships also available. Support available to part-time students. Financial award applicants required to submit FAFSA. *Faculty research:* Literacy: early, middle-secondary, adult and deaf/hard of hearing; teacher professional development, evaluation and urban education; STEM teacher education; health, physical activity and exercise science; school safety and counseling. *Unit head:* Dr. Paul A. Alberto, Interim Dean, 404-413-8100, Fax: 404-413-8103, E-mail: palberto@gsu.edu. *Application contact:* Nancy Keita, Director, Office of Academic Assistance and Graduate Admissions, 404-413-8001, E-mail: nkeita@gsu.edu.
Website: http://education.gsu.edu/main/

Goddard College, Graduate Division, Master of Arts in Education Program, Plainfield, VT 05667-9432. Offers community education (MA); teacher licensure (MA). *Program availability:* Part-time, online learning. *Degree requirements:* For master's, thesis. *Entrance requirements:* For master's, PRAXIS, 3 letters of recommendation, statement of purpose, interview. Electronic applications accepted. *Faculty research:* Democratic curriculum leadership, service-learning and academic achievement, middle grades curriculum, community education, dual language.

Gonzaga University, School of Education, Spokane, WA 99258. Offers clinical mental health counseling (MA); elementary education (MIT); leadership and administration (MA); marriage and family counseling (MA); school counseling (MA); secondary education (MIT); special education (M Ed, MIT); sport and athletic administration (MA). *Accreditation:* NCATE. *Program availability:* Part-time, evening/weekend, 100% online. *Faculty:* 22 full-time (17 women), 38 part-time/adjunct (22 women). *Students:* 104 full-time (73 women), 275 part-time (184 women); includes 31 minority (5 Black or African American, non-Hispanic/Latino; 1 American Indian or Alaska Native, non-Hispanic/Latino; 3 Asian, non-Hispanic/Latino; 18 Hispanic/Latino; 4 Two or more races, non-Hispanic/Latino), 163 international. Average age 32. 419 applicants, 67% accepted, 165 enrolled. In 2016, 39 master's awarded. *Degree requirements:* For master's, comprehensive exam. *Entrance requirements:* For master's, GRE, MAT, and/or Washington Educators Skills Test-Basic (WEST-B), official transcripts from all colleges or universities attended, interview, two letters of recommendation, resume, essay, minimum GPA of 3.0. Additional exam requirements/recommendations for international students: Required—TOEFL (minimum score 580 paper-based, 88 iBT) or IELTS (minimum score 6.5). *Application deadline:* Applications are processed on a rolling basis. Application fee: $50. Electronic applications accepted. *Expenses:* Contact institution. *Financial support:* In 2016–17, 28 students received support. Scholarships/grants and tuition waivers available. Support available to part-time students. Financial award applicants required to submit FAFSA. *Unit head:* Dr. Vincent Alfonso, Dean, 509-313-3594, Fax: 509-313-5821, E-mail: alfonso@gonzaga.edu. *Application contact:* Luke Cairney, Graduate Admissions Program Specialist, 509-313-3821, E-mail: cairney@gonzaga.edu.
Website: http://www.gonzaga.edu/Academics/Colleges-and-Schools/School-of-Education

Gordon College, Graduate Education Program, Wenham, MA 01984-1899. Offers early childhood (M Ed); educational leadership (M Ed, Ed S); elementary education (M Ed); English as a second language (M Ed, Ed S); math specialist (M Ed); mathematics specialist (Ed S); middle school education (M Ed); moderate disabilities (M Ed); Montessori education (M Ed); reading (M Ed, Ed S); secondary education (M Ed). *Program availability:* Part-time, evening/weekend. *Faculty:* 17 full-time (9 women), 41 part-time/adjunct (34 women). *Students:* 81 full-time (61 women), 109 part-time (87 women); includes 28 minority (2 Black or African American, non-Hispanic/Latino; 11 Asian, non-Hispanic/Latino; 13 Hispanic/Latino; 2 Two or more races, non-Hispanic/Latino), 12 international. Average age 34. 190 applicants, 100% accepted, 141 enrolled. In 2016, 110 master's, 16 Ed Ss awarded. *Degree requirements:* For master's, action research or clinical experience (for most programs); for Ed S, action research or clinical experience (for some programs). *Entrance requirements:* For master's, minimum undergraduate GPA of 3.0; 2 official undergraduate transcripts; professional resume; 3 recommendation letters (one professional reference, one academic reference, one personal reference); 500-700 word statement of purpose; for Ed S, minimum master's GPA of 3.3; 2 official transcripts from undergraduate and graduate schools; professional resume; 3 recommendation letters (one professional reference, one academic reference, one personal reference); 500-700 word statement of purpose. Additional exam requirements/recommendations for international students: Required—TOEFL (minimum score 550 paper-based, 80 iBT) or IELTS (minimum score 6.5). *Application deadline:* Applications are processed on a rolling basis. Application fee: $75. *Expenses:* $325 per credit tuition, $75 per term fee. *Financial support:* Applicants required to submit FAFSA. *Faculty research:* Reading, early childhood development, English language learners, universal design for learning. *Unit head:* Dr. Janet Arndt, Director of Graduate Studies, 978-867-4355, Fax: 978-867-4663. *Application contact:* Julie Lenocker, Program Administrator, 978-867-4322, Fax: 978-867-4663, E-mail: graduate-education@gordon.edu.
Website: http://www.gordon.edu/graduate

Goucher College, Graduate Programs in Education, Baltimore, MD 21204-2794. Offers at-risk and diverse learners (M Ed, Certificate); athletic program leadership and administration (M Ed, Certificate); elementary and special education (MAT); elementary education (MAT); literacy strategies for content learning (M Ed, Certificate); middle school (M Ed, Certificate); Montessori studies (M Ed); reading instruction (M Ed, Certificate); school improvement leadership (M Ed, Certificate); school mediation (M Ed, Certificate); secondary and special education (MAT); secondary education (MAT); special education (MAT), including elementary education, secondary education; special education for certified teachers (M Ed, Certificate); teacher as leader in technology (M Ed, Certificate). *Program availability:* Part-time, evening/weekend. *Faculty:* 3 full-time (all women), 52 part-time/adjunct (40 women). *Students:* 29 full-time (20 women), 285 part-time (217 women); includes 54 minority (41 Black or African American, non-Hispanic/Latino; 3 Asian, non-Hispanic/Latino; 7 Hispanic/Latino; 3 Two or more races, non-Hispanic/Latino), 1 international. Average age 34. 85 applicants, 100% accepted, 61 enrolled. In 2016, 207 master's awarded. *Degree requirements:* For master's, thesis (M Ed), final presentation (MAT). *Entrance requirements:* For master's, minimum GPA of 3.0. Additional exam requirements/recommendations for international students: Required—TOEFL (minimum score 560 paper-based). *Application deadline:* For fall admission, 9/1 for domestic students; for spring admission, 1/15 for domestic students. Applications are processed on a rolling basis. Application fee: $75. Electronic applications accepted. *Expenses:* Contact institution. *Financial support:* Career-related internships or fieldwork and unspecified assistantships available. Support available to part-time students. Financial award application deadline: 4/15; financial award applicants required to submit FAFSA. *Faculty research:* Urban education, middle school, school improvement, teacher education, at-risk student achievement. *Unit head:* Dr. Phyllis Sunshine, Assistant Provost, 410-337-6047, Fax: 410-337-6394, E-mail: psunshin@goucher.edu. *Application contact:* Shelby Hillers, Admissions Coordinator, 410-337-6200, Fax: 410-337-6085, E-mail: shelby.hillers@goucher.edu.
Website: http://www.goucher.edu/graduate-programs/graduate-programs-in-education

Governors State University, College of Education, Program in Education, University Park, IL 60484. Offers MA. *Program availability:* Part-time. *Faculty:* 47 full-time (31 women), 49 part-time/adjunct (39 women). *Students:* 2 full-time (both women), 31 part-time (26 women); includes 12 minority (6 Black or African American, non-Hispanic/Latino; 6 Hispanic/Latino), 1 international. Average age 39. 40 applicants, 55% accepted, 20 enrolled. In 2016, 9 master's awarded. *Entrance requirements:* Additional exam requirements/recommendations for international students: Required—TOEFL (minimum score 550 paper-based; 80 iBT), IELTS. *Application deadline:* For fall admission, 4/1 for domestic students. Application fee: $50. Electronic applications accepted. *Expenses:* $307 per credit hour; $38 per term or $76 per credit hour fees. *Financial support:* Application deadline: 5/1; applicants required to submit FAFSA. *Unit head:* Timothy Harrington, Chair, Division of Education, 708-534-4361, E-mail: tharrington2@govst.edu. *Application contact:* Yakeea Daniels, Assistant Vice President for Enrollment Services/Director of Admission, 708-534-4510, E-mail: ydaniels@govst.edu.

Graceland University, Gleazer School of Education, Independence, MO 64050. Offers curriculum and instruction (M Ed); differentiated instruction (M Ed); instructional leadership (M Ed); literacy and instruction (M Ed); management in the inclusive classroom (M Ed); special education (M Ed); technology integration (M Ed). *Accreditation:* NCATE. *Program availability:* Part-time, evening/weekend, online learning. *Faculty:* 2 full-time (both women), 9 part-time/adjunct (5 women). *Students:* 115 full-time (96 women), 20 part-time (17 women); includes 10 minority (5 Black or African American, non-Hispanic/Latino; 1 Asian, non-Hispanic/Latino; 1 Hispanic/Latino; 1 Native Hawaiian or other Pacific Islander, non-Hispanic/Latino; 2 Two or more races, non-Hispanic/Latino), 2 international. 155 applicants, 61% accepted, 85 enrolled. In 2016, 61 master's awarded. *Degree requirements:* For master's, action research project. *Entrance requirements:* For master's, minimum GPA of 3.0, teaching certificate, current teaching contract. Additional exam requirements/recommendations for international students: Required—TOEFL. *Application deadline:* For fall admission, 10/1 for domestic students; for winter admission, 11/15 for domestic students; for spring admission, 2/15 priority date for domestic students; for summer admission, 6/1 for domestic students. Applications are processed on a rolling basis. Application fee: $50. Electronic applications accepted. *Expenses:* Contact institution. *Financial support:* Institutionally sponsored loans and scholarships/grants available. Financial award application deadline: 12/15; financial award applicants required to submit FAFSA. *Faculty research:* Literacy, technology, faculty mentoring, adult literacy, e-learning, online teaching. *Unit head:* Dr. Lee Bash, Interim Dean, 641-784-5072, E-mail: bash@graceland.edu. *Application contact:* Jeanette Calipetro, Admissions Representative, 816-423-4716, Fax: 816-833-2990, E-mail: jcali1@graceland.edu.
Website: http://www.graceland.edu/education

Grambling State University, School of Graduate Studies and Research, College of Education, Grambling, LA 71245. Offers M Ed, MAT, MS, Ed D, PMC. *Accreditation:* NCATE. *Program availability:* Part-time, evening/weekend. *Degree requirements:* For master's, comprehensive exam, thesis (for some programs); for doctorate, comprehensive exam, thesis/dissertation. *Entrance requirements:* For master's, GRE; for doctorate, GRE (minimum score 1000, 500 on Verbal), master's degree, minimum GPA of 3.0 on last degree. Additional exam requirements/recommendations for international students: Required—TOEFL (minimum score 500 paper-based; 62 iBT). Electronic applications accepted.

Grand Canyon University, College of Education, Phoenix, AZ 85017-1097. Offers autism spectrum disorders (MA); curriculum and instruction (MA); early childhood education (M Ed); educational administration (M Ed); educational leadership (M Ed); elementary education (M Ed); gifted education (MA); instructional technology (MS); K-12 leadership (Ed S); reading (MA); secondary education (M Ed); secondary humanities education (M Ed); secondary STEM education (M Ed); special education (M Ed); teaching and learning (Ed D); teaching English to speakers of other languages (MA). *Program availability:* Part-time, evening/weekend, online learning. *Degree requirements:* For master's, publishable research paper (M Ed), e-portfolio. *Entrance requirements:* For master's, undergraduate degree from accredited, GCU-approved college, university, or program with minimum GPA 2.8. Additional exam requirements/recommendations for international students: Required—TOEFL (minimum score 550 paper-based; 79 iBT), IELTS (minimum score 6). *Application deadline:* For fall admission, 8/21 for domestic students, 7/2 for international students; for spring admission, 12/24 for domestic students, 11/1 for international students. Applications are processed on a rolling basis. Application fee: $100. Electronic applications accepted. *Financial support:* Federal Work-Study available. Support available to part-time students. Financial award applicants required to submit FAFSA. *Unit head:* Dr. Kimberly L. LaPrade, Dean, 602-639-6360, E-mail: kimberly.laprade@gcu.edu. *Application contact:* Dr. Kimberly L. LaPrade, Dean, 602-639-6360, E-mail: kimberly.laprade@gcu.edu.
Website: https://www.gcu.edu/college-of-education.php

Grand Valley State University, College of Education, Programs in General Education, Allendale, MI 49401-9403. Offers adult and higher education (M Ed); early childhood education (M Ed); educational differentiation (M Ed); educational leadership (M Ed); educational technology integration (M Ed); elementary education (M Ed); middle level education (M Ed); school library media services (M Ed); secondary level education (M Ed); teaching English to speakers of other languages (M Ed). *Program availability:* Part-time, evening/weekend, 100% online, blended/hybrid learning. *Students:* 28 part-time (20 women); includes 6 minority (4 Black or African American, non-Hispanic/Latino; 1 American Indian or Alaska Native, non-Hispanic/Latino; 1 Hispanic/Latino). Average age 42. In 2016, 17 master's awarded. *Degree requirements:* For master's, project or thesis. *Entrance requirements:* For master's, GRE General Test or minimum GPA of 3.0, last 60 credits from regionally-accredited college/university, 3 letters of recommendation. Additional exam requirements/recommendations for international students: Required—TOEFL (minimum score 550 paper-based, 80 iBT), IELTS (6.5), or Michigan English Language Assessment Battery. *Application deadline:* Applications are processed on a rolling basis. Application fee: $30. Electronic applications accepted. *Expenses:* $628 per credit hour. *Financial support:* In 2016–17, 2 students received support. Career-related internships or fieldwork, Federal Work-Study, scholarships/grants, and unspecified assistantships available. *Faculty research:* Effectiveness of technology in education, parental involvement, effective teaching, effective schools research. *Unit head:* Dr. Doug Busman, Graduate Program Director, 616-331-6250, E-mail: busmando@gvsu.edu. *Application contact:* Thomas Owens, Director, Student Information and Services Center, 616-331-6282, Fax: 616-331-6217, E-mail: owenst@gvsu.edu.
Website: http://www.gvsu.edu/coe/

Gratz College, Graduate Programs, Program in Education, Melrose Park, PA 19027. Offers MA. *Program availability:* Part-time. *Degree requirements:* For master's, one foreign language, project. *Entrance requirements:* For master's, teaching certificate. *Application deadline:* Applications are processed on a rolling basis. Application fee: $50. *Financial support:* Application deadline: 4/1. *Unit head:* Director, 215-635-7300. *Application contact:* Roz Weinstein, Admissions Coordinator, 215-635-7300 Ext. 129, Fax: 215-635-7320, E-mail: rweinstein@gratz.edu.
Website: https://www.gratz.edu/academics/education-ma

Greensboro College, Program in Education, Greensboro, NC 27401-1875. Offers elementary education (M Ed); special education (M Ed). *Program availability:* Part-time, evening/weekend. *Degree requirements:* For master's, thesis. *Entrance requirements:* For master's, GRE, teacher license, 2 years of teaching experience, 2 letters of recommendation. Additional exam requirements/recommendations for international students: Required—TOEFL (minimum score 550 paper-based). Electronic applications accepted.

Greenville College, Program in Education, Greenville, IL 62246-0159. Offers education (MAT); elementary education (MAE); secondary education (MAE). *Degree requirements:* For master's, thesis (for some programs). *Entrance requirements:* For master's, GRE, Illinois Basic Skills Test, teacher certification. Electronic applications accepted.

Gwynedd Mercy University, School of Education, Gwynedd Valley, PA 19437-0901. Offers educational administration (MS); master teacher (MS); school counseling (MS); special education (MS). *Program availability:* Part-time, evening/weekend, 100% online. *Faculty:* 8 full-time (5 women), 38 part-time/adjunct (24 women). *Students:* 466 full-time (355 women); includes 93 minority (66 Black or African American, non-Hispanic/Latino; 12 Asian, non-Hispanic/Latino; 15 Hispanic/Latino). Average age 36. 127 applicants, 18% accepted, 9 enrolled. In 2016, 86 master's awarded. *Degree requirements:* For master's, thesis, internship, practicum. *Entrance requirements:* For master's, GRE or MAT; PRAXIS I, minimum GPA of 3.0. *Application deadline:* Applications are processed on a rolling basis. *Expenses: Tuition:* Full-time $14,400; part-time $800 per credit hour. One-time fee: $165. Tuition and fees vary according to degree level and program. *Financial support:* In 2016–17, 2 research assistantships were awarded; career-related internships or fieldwork, Federal Work-Study, institutionally sponsored loans, tuition waivers (full and partial), and unspecified assistantships also available. Financial award applicants required to submit FAFSA. *Faculty research:* Learning and the brain, reading literacy, ethics and moral judgment, leadership, teaching and multicultural education. *Unit head:* Dr. Heather Pfleger, Dean, 215-646-7300 Ext. 21581, E-mail: pfleger.h@gmercyu.edu. *Application contact:* Graduate Program Coordinator, 877-499-6333, E-mail: graduate@gmercyu.edu.
Website: https://www.gmercyu.edu/academics/graduate-education-programs

Hamline University, School of Education, St. Paul, MN 55104-1284. Offers education (MA Ed, Ed D); English as a second language (MA); literacy education (MA); natural science and environmental education (MA Ed); teaching (MAT); teaching English to speakers of other languages (MA). *Accreditation:* NCATE (one or more programs are accredited). *Program availability:* Part-time, evening/weekend, 100% online, blended/hybrid learning. *Faculty:* 29 full-time (23 women), 90 part-time/adjunct (70 women). *Students:* 277 full-time (201 women), 762 part-time (601 women); includes 122 minority (29 Black or African American, non-Hispanic/Latino; 1 American Indian or Alaska Native, non-Hispanic/Latino; 43 Asian, non-Hispanic/Latino; 29 Hispanic/Latino; 20 Two or more races, non-Hispanic/Latino), 12 international. Average age 34. 408 applicants, 77% accepted, 230 enrolled. In 2016, 279 master's, 14 doctorates awarded. *Degree requirements:* For master's, thesis (for some programs), thesis or capstone project; for doctorate, comprehensive exam, thesis/dissertation. *Entrance requirements:* For master's, official transcripts, essay, letters of recommendation, minimum GPA of 3.0 from bachelor's work; resume and/or writing samples (for some programs); for doctorate, personal statement, master's degree with minimum GPA of 3.0, letters of recommendation, writing sample. Additional exam requirements/recommendations for international students: Required—TOEFL. *Application deadline:* For fall admission, 6/1 for domestic and international students; for spring admission, 11/1 for domestic and international students; for summer admission, 3/1 for domestic and international students. Applications are processed on a rolling basis. Application fee: $0 ($100 for international students). Electronic applications accepted. *Expenses:* $466-$721 per credit. *Financial support:* Career-related internships or fieldwork, Federal Work-Study, and scholarships/grants available. Support available to part-time students. Financial award applicants required to submit FAFSA. *Faculty research:* Adult basic education, service-learning, teacher dispositions, diversity, technology. *Unit head:* Dr. Nancy Sorenson, Dean, 651-523-2600, Fax: 651-523-2489, E-mail: education@hamline.edu. *Application contact:* Shawn Skoog, Director of Graduate Recruitment and Admission, 651-523-2900, Fax: 651-523-3058, E-mail: gradprog@hamline.edu.
Website: http://www.hamline.edu/education

Hampton University, School of Education and Human Development, Hampton, VA 23668. Offers MA, MS, MT, PhD, Ed S. *Accreditation:* NCATE. *Program availability:* Part-time, evening/weekend. *Faculty:* 18 full-time (11 women), 2 part-time/adjunct (both women). *Students:* 81 full-time (60 women), 80 part-time (44 women); includes 148 minority (all Black or African American, non-Hispanic/Latino), 2 international. Average age 33. 107 applicants, 59% accepted, 51 enrolled. In 2016, 54 master's, 12 doctorates awarded. *Degree requirements:* For master's, comprehensive exam, thesis (for some programs); for doctorate, comprehensive exam, thesis/dissertation. *Entrance requirements:* For master's, GRE General Test, PRAXIS; for doctorate, GRE General Test, GMAT. Additional exam requirements/recommendations for international students: Required—TOEFL (minimum score 525 paper-based) or IELTS (6.5). *Application deadline:* For fall admission, 6/1 priority date for domestic students, 4/1 priority date for international students; for winter admission, 9/1 priority date for international students; for spring admission, 11/1 for domestic students; for summer admission, 4/15 for domestic students, 2/1 priority date for international students. Applications are processed on a rolling basis. Application fee: $35. Electronic applications accepted. *Expenses: Tuition:* Full-time $10,776; part-time $548 per credit hour. *Required fees:* $35; $35 per credit hour. Tuition and fees vary according to course load and program. *Financial support:* Fellowships, research assistantships, teaching assistantships, career-related internships or fieldwork, Federal Work-Study, institutionally sponsored loans, and scholarships/grants available. Support available to part-time students. Financial award application deadline: 5/1; financial award applicants required to submit FAFSA. *Unit head:* Dr. Linda Malone-Colon, Dean, 757-727-5400. *Application contact:* Dr. Michelle Penn-Marshall, Director, Graduate Programs, 757-727-5454, E-mail: hugrad@hamptonu.edu.
Website: http://edhd.hamptonu.edu/

Hannibal-LaGrange University, Program in Education, Hannibal, MO 63401-1999. Offers literacy (MS Ed); teaching and learning (MS Ed). *Program availability:* Part-time, evening/weekend. *Degree requirements:* For master's, thesis, portfolio, documenting of program outcomes, public sharing of research. *Entrance requirements:* For master's, copy of current teaching certificate; minimum GPA of 2.75. *Faculty research:* Reading assessment, reading remediation, handwriting instruction, early childhood intervention.

Harding University, Cannon-Clary College of Education, Searcy, AR 72149-0001. Offers advanced studies in teaching and learning (M Ed); art (MSE); behavioral science (MSE); counseling (MS, Ed S); early childhood special education (M Ed, MSE); education (MSE); educational leadership (M Ed, Ed S); elementary education (M Ed); English (MSE); French (MSE); history/social science (MSE); kinesiology (MSE); math (MSE); reading (M Ed); secondary education (M Ed); Spanish (MSE); teaching (MAT); teaching English as a second language (MSE). *Accreditation:* NCATE. *Program availability:* Part-time, evening/weekend. *Faculty:* 22 full-time (9 women), 51 part-time/adjunct (37 women). *Students:* 130 full-time (94 women), 321 part-time (234 women); includes 83 minority (50 Black or African American, non-Hispanic/Latino; 4 American Indian or Alaska Native, non-Hispanic/Latino; 6 Asian, non-Hispanic/Latino; 13 Hispanic/Latino; 10 Two or more races, non-Hispanic/Latino), 11 international. Average age 35. 125 applicants, 88% accepted, 110 enrolled. In 2016, 124 master's, 27 other advanced degrees awarded. *Degree requirements:* For master's, comprehensive exam (for some programs), thesis optional, portfolio(s); for Ed S, comprehensive exam, portfolio, project. *Entrance requirements:* For master's, GRE, MAT, PRAXIS; for Ed S, MAT or GRE. Additional exam requirements/recommendations for international students: Required—TOEFL (minimum score 550 paper-based; 79 iBT). *Application deadline:* For fall admission, 8/1 for domestic and international students; for spring admission, 1/1 for domestic and international students. Applications are processed on a rolling basis. Application fee: $35. Tuition and fees vary according to degree level and program. *Financial support:* In 2016–17, 31 students received support. Unspecified assistantships available. *Faculty research:* Reading, comprehension, school violence, educational technology, behavior, college choice, differentiated instruction, brain-based teaching. *Unit head:* Dr. Clara Carroll, Chair, 501-279-4501, Fax: 501-279-4083, E-mail: ccarroll@harding.edu. *Application contact:* Information Contact, 501-279-4315, E-mail: gradstudiesedu@harding.edu.
Website: http://www.harding.edu/education

Hardin-Simmons University, Graduate School, Irvin School of Education, Abilene, TX 79698-0001. Offers M Ed, Ed D. *Program availability:* Part-time. *Faculty:* 16 full-time (8 women), 6 part-time/adjunct (3 women). *Students:* 29 full-time (20 women), 96 part-time (73 women); includes 27 minority (14 Black or African American, non-Hispanic/Latino; 12 Hispanic/Latino; 1 Two or more races, non-Hispanic/Latino), 4 international. Average age 36. In 2016, 31 master's, 3 doctorates awarded. *Degree requirements:* For master's, comprehensive exam. *Entrance requirements:* For master's, minimum undergraduate GPA of 3.0 in major, 2.7 overall. Additional exam requirements/recommendations for international students: Required—TOEFL (minimum score 550 paper-based; 75 iBT). *Application deadline:* For fall admission, 8/15 priority date for domestic students, 4/1 for international students; for spring admission, 1/5 priority date for domestic students, 9/1 for international students. Applications are processed on a rolling basis. Application fee: $50. Electronic applications accepted. *Expenses: Tuition:* Full-time $12,510; part-time $695 per credit hour. *Required fees:* $325; $110 per semester. *Financial support:* In 2016–17, 71 students received support, including 14 fellowships (averaging $3,125 per year); career-related internships or fieldwork, scholarships/grants, and coaching assistantships also available. Support available to part-time students. Financial award application deadline: 6/30; financial award applicants required to submit FAFSA. *Unit head:* Dr. Perry Kay Brown, Dean, 325-670-1021, Fax: 325-670-5859, E-mail: pkbrown@hsutx.edu. *Application contact:* Dr. Nancy Kucinski, Dean of Graduate Studies, 325-670-1298, Fax: 325-670-1564, E-mail: gradoff@hsutx.edu.
Website: http://www.hsutx.edu/academics/irvin

Harrison Middleton University, Graduate Program, Tempe, AZ 85282. Offers education (MA, Ed D); humanities (MA); imaginative literature (MA); interdisciplinary studies (DA); jurisprudence (MA); natural science (MA); philosophy and religion (MA); social science (MA). *Program availability:* Part-time, evening/weekend, online learning. *Degree requirements:* For master's and doctorate, capstone project. *Entrance requirements:* For master's, interview; for doctorate, 2 academic letters of reference, interview, essay. Additional exam requirements/recommendations for international students: Required—TOEFL (minimum score 550 paper-based; 80 iBT). Electronic applications accepted. *Faculty research:* Japanese animation, educational leadership, war art, John Muir's wilderness.

Harvard University, Harvard Graduate School of Education, Cambridge, MA 02138. Offers Ed M, Ed L D, PhD. *Program availability:* Part-time. *Degree requirements:* For doctorate, thesis/dissertation (for some programs), capstone project or thesis (for Ed.L.D.). *Entrance requirements:* For master's, GRE General Test, statement of purpose, 3 letters of recommendation, resume, official transcripts; for doctorate, GRE General Test or GMAT (for Ed.L.D. only), statement of purpose, 3 letters of recommendation, resume, official transcripts, 2 short essay questions (for Ed.L.D. only). Additional exam requirements/recommendations for international students: Required—TOEFL (minimum score 613 paper-based; 104 iBT), TWE (minimum score 5). Electronic applications accepted. *Expenses:* Contact institution. *Faculty research:* Learning and development, educational leadership and organizations, education policy analysis.

Hastings College, Department of Teacher Education, Hastings, NE 68901. Offers MAT. *Accreditation:* NCATE. *Program availability:* Part-time. *Degree requirements:* For master's, comprehensive exam, thesis, or oral teaching presentation; digital portfolio. *Entrance requirements:* For master's, minimum GPA of 2.5, 2 letters of reference, interview. Additional exam requirements/recommendations for international students: Required—TOEFL. Electronic applications accepted. *Faculty research:* Assessments, performance competencies.

Hebrew College, Shoolman Graduate School of Jewish Education, Newton Centre, MA 02459. Offers early childhood Jewish education (Certificate); Jewish day school education (Certificate); Jewish education (MJ Ed); Jewish family education (Certificate); Jewish special education (Certificate); Jewish youth education, informal education and camping (Certificate). *Program availability:* Part-time, evening/weekend, online learning. *Degree requirements:* For master's, one foreign language. *Entrance requirements:* For master's, GRE, interview. Additional exam requirements/recommendations for international students: Required—TOEFL.

Hebrew Union College–Jewish Institute of Religion, School of Education, New York, NY 10012-1186. Offers MARE. *Program availability:* Part-time. *Degree requirements:* For master's, one foreign language, thesis. *Entrance requirements:* For master's, GRE, minimum 2 years of college-level Hebrew.

Heidelberg University, Master of Arts in Education Program, Tiffin, OH 44883-2462. Offers MAE. *Accreditation:* NCATE. *Program availability:* Part-time, evening/weekend. In 2016, 13 master's awarded. *Degree requirements:* For master's, thesis or alternative, internship, practicum. *Entrance requirements:* For master's, bachelor's degree with minimum cumulative GPA of 2.75, 3 recommendations. Additional exam requirements/recommendations for international students: Required—TOEFL (minimum score 550 paper-based, 79 iBT) or IELTS (minimum score 6.5). *Application deadline:* Applications are processed on a rolling basis. Application fee: $0. Electronic applications accepted. *Expenses:* $510 per semester hour. *Financial support:* Applicants required to submit FAFSA. *Unit head:* Dr. Karen Jones, Associate Dean and Director of the School of Education, 419-448-2130, E-mail: kjones9@heidelberg.edu. *Application contact:* Katie Slosser, Graduate Admissions Coordinator, 419-448-2602, Fax: 419-448-2565, E-mail: kslosser@heidelberg.edu.
Website: https://www.heidelberg.edu/academics/programs/master-education

Henderson State University, Graduate Studies, Teachers College, Arkadelphia, AR 71999-0001. Offers MAT, MS, MSE, Ed S, Graduate Certificate. *Accreditation:* NCATE. *Program availability:* Part-time, 100% online. *Faculty:* 20 full-time (11 women), 6 part-time/adjunct (4 women). *Students:* 67 full-time (46 women), 306 part-time (218 women); includes 106 minority (86 Black or African American, non-Hispanic/Latino; 3 American Indian or Alaska Native, non-Hispanic/Latino; 1 Asian, non-Hispanic/Latino; 8 Hispanic/

Latino; 8 Two or more races, non-Hispanic/Latino), 4 international. Average age 32. 79 applicants, 97% accepted, 77 enrolled. In 2016, 95 master's, 9 other advanced degrees awarded. *Entrance requirements:* For master's, GRE General Test or MAT, minimum GPA of 2.7, teacher certification. Additional exam requirements/recommendations for international students: Required—TOEFL (minimum score 600 paper-based); Recommended—IELTS (minimum score 6.5). *Application deadline:* For fall admission, 8/1 priority date for domestic students, 6/30 priority date for international students; for spring admission, 1/1 priority date for domestic students, 11/30 priority date for international students. Applications are processed on a rolling basis. Application fee: $25 ($75 for international students). *Expenses:* Tuition, state resident: full-time $6288; part-time $3144 per credit hour. Tuition, nonresident: full-time $12,888; part-time $6444 per credit hour. *Required fees:* $1429; $1024 per credit hour. Tuition and fees vary according to course load and student level. *Financial support:* In 2016–17, 7 teaching assistantships with partial tuition reimbursements (averaging $4,000 per year) were awarded; scholarships/grants and unspecified assistantships also available. Financial award application deadline: 4/15; financial award applicants required to submit FAFSA. *Unit head:* Dr. Celya Taylor, Dean, 870-230-5363, Fax: 870-230-5455, E-mail: taylorc@hsu.edu. *Application contact:* Dr. Ken Taylor, Graduate Dean, 870-230-5126, Fax: 870-230-5479, E-mail: taylorke@hsu.edu.
Website: http://www.hsu.edu/Academics/TeachersCollege/index.html

Heritage University, Graduate Programs in Education, Toppenish, WA 98948-9599. Offers counseling (M Ed); educational administration (M Ed); professional studies (M Ed), including bilingual education/ESL, biology, English and literature, reading/literacy, special education; teaching (MIT). *Program availability:* Part-time, evening/weekend. *Degree requirements:* For master's, comprehensive exam, thesis (for some programs). *Entrance requirements:* For master's, interview, letters of recommendation, teaching certificate. Additional exam requirements/recommendations for international students: Recommended—TOEFL (minimum score 550 paper-based).

High Point University, Norcross Graduate School, High Point, NC 27268. Offers business administration (MBA); educational leadership (M Ed); elementary education (M Ed); history (MA); nonprofit management (MA); secondary math (M Ed); special education (M Ed); strategic communication (MA); teaching elementary education k-6 (MAT); teaching secondary mathematics 9-12 (MAT). *Accreditation:* NCATE. *Program availability:* Part-time, evening/weekend. *Degree requirements:* For master's, comprehensive exam (for some programs), thesis (for some programs). *Entrance requirements:* For master's, GMAT (MBA), GRE, MAT, minimum GPA of 3.0. Additional exam requirements/recommendations for international students: Required—TOEFL (minimum score 550 paper-based). Electronic applications accepted.

Hofstra University, School of Education, Hempstead, NY 11549. Offers MA, MS, MS Ed, Ed D, PhD, Advanced Certificate. *Accreditation:* TEAC. *Program availability:* Part-time, evening/weekend, 100% online, blended/hybrid learning. *Students:* 288 full-time (212 women), 403 part-time (293 women); includes 157 minority (65 Black or African American, non-Hispanic/Latino; 2 American Indian or Alaska Native, non-Hispanic/Latino; 23 Asian, non-Hispanic/Latino; 65 Hispanic/Latino; 1 Native Hawaiian or other Pacific Islander, non-Hispanic/Latino; 1 Two or more races, non-Hispanic/Latino), 26 international. Average age 31. 505 applicants, 87% accepted, 268 enrolled. In 2016, 186 master's, 17 doctorates, 78 other advanced degrees awarded. *Degree requirements:* For master's, variable foreign language requirement, comprehensive exam (for some programs), thesis (for some programs), capstone, minimum GPA of 3.0, electronic portfolio, student teaching, practicum, internship, seminars, field work, curriculum project, clinical hours; for doctorate, variable foreign language requirement, comprehensive exam (for some programs), thesis/dissertation, qualifying hearing; for Advanced Certificate, comprehensive exam (for some programs), thesis optional, electronic portfolio, fieldwork, internship, state exams, exit project. *Entrance requirements:* For master's, GRE, MAT, letters of recommendation, interview, portfolio, resume, essay, certification; for doctorate, GRE, 3 letters of recommendation, essay, interview, 2 years' full-time teaching. Additional exam requirements/recommendations for international students: Required—TOEFL (minimum score 550 paper-based; 80 iBT). *Application deadline:* Applications are processed on a rolling basis. Application fee: $75. Electronic applications accepted. *Expenses: Tuition:* Full-time $1240. *Required fees:* $970. Tuition and fees vary according to program. *Financial support:* In 2016–17, 367 students received support, including 165 fellowships with full and partial tuition reimbursements available (averaging $4,323 per year), 17 research assistantships with full and partial tuition reimbursements available (averaging $6,661 per year); Federal Work-Study, institutionally sponsored loans, scholarships/grants, traineeships, tuition waivers (full and partial), and unspecified assistantships also available. Support available to part-time students. Financial award applicants required to submit FAFSA. *Faculty research:* Minority student persistence and resilience, bilingual leadership in K-12 settings, charter school development, administrative management of curriculum, K-20 policy implications for leadership, social justice in pedagogy, analysis of pre-service teachers' edTPA lesson plan videos, reading flow, eye movement miscue analysis, writing evaluation, corporate-driven reforms and privatization/impact on teachers and students. *Total annual research expenditures:* $387,434. *Unit head:* Dr. Karin Spencer, Senior Associate Dean, 516-463-5742, E-mail: karin.j.spencer@hofstra.edu. *Application contact:* Sunil Samuel, Assistant Vice President of Admissions, 516-463-4723, Fax: 516-463-4664, E-mail: graduateadmission@hofstra.edu.
Website: http://www.hofstra.edu/education/

Hollins University, Graduate Programs, Program in Teaching, Roanoke, VA 24020. Offers MAT. *Accreditation:* TEAC. *Program availability:* Part-time, evening/weekend. *Degree requirements:* For master's, thesis. *Entrance requirements:* For master's, PRAXIS I, three letters of recommendation, bachelor's degree, official transcripts with minimum GPA of 2.5, personal statement. Additional exam requirements/recommendations for international students: Required—TOEFL (minimum score 550 paper-based; 80 iBT), IELTS (minimum score 6.5). *Application deadline:* For fall admission, 8/1 for domestic and international students; for spring admission, 12/1 for domestic and international students; for summer admission, 5/1 for domestic and international students. Applications are processed on a rolling basis. Application fee: $40. Electronic applications accepted. *Expenses:* $395 per credit hour. *Financial support:* Federal Work-Study and scholarships/grants available. Support available to part-time students. Financial award application deadline: 7/15; financial award applicants required to submit FAFSA. *Faculty research:* Television violence and its effect on the developing brain, phonological/phonemic awareness, technology in the classroom. *Unit head:* Lorraine Lange, Director, 540-362-7460, Fax: 540-362-6288, E-mail: hugrad@hollins.edu. *Application contact:* Donna Martin, Administrative Assistant, 540-362-7460, Fax: 540-362-6288, E-mail: dmartin@hollins.edu.
Website: http://www.hollins.edu/academics/graduate-degrees/teaching/

Holy Family University, Division of Academic Affairs, Philadelphia, PA 19114. Offers accountancy (MS); business administration (MBA); counseling psychology (MS); criminal justice (MA); education (M Ed); educational leadership (Ed D); nursing (MS). *Accreditation:* ACBSP. *Program availability:* Part-time, evening/weekend. *Faculty:* 28 full-time (19 women), 66 part-time/adjunct (36 women). *Students:* 329 full-time (281 women), 458 part-time (327 women); includes 153 minority (83 Black or African American, non-Hispanic/Latino; 1 American Indian or Alaska Native, non-Hispanic/Latino; 27 Asian, non-Hispanic/Latino; 41 Hispanic/Latino; 1 Native Hawaiian or other Pacific Islander, non-Hispanic/Latino), 4 international. Average age 34. 467 applicants, 69% accepted, 262 enrolled. In 2016, 6 master's, 2 doctorates awarded. *Degree requirements:* For master's, comprehensive exam, thesis or alternative; for doctorate, comprehensive exam, thesis/dissertation. *Entrance requirements:* For master's, minimum GPA of 3.0, interview, essay/professional statement, 2 recommendations, current resume, official transcripts of college or university work. Additional exam requirements/recommendations for international students: Required—TOEFL (minimum score 550 paper-based; 79 iBT), IELTS (minimum score 6). *Application deadline:* For fall admission, 7/1 priority date for domestic and international students; for spring admission, 11/1 priority date for domestic and international students; for summer admission, 4/1 priority date for domestic and international students. Applications are processed on a rolling basis. Application fee: $25. Electronic applications accepted. *Expenses:* $9,292 per year. *Financial support:* Available to part-time students. Applicants required to submit FAFSA. *Unit head:* Dr. Michael Markowitz, Vice President of Academic Affairs, 267-341-3286, E-mail: mmarkowitz@holyfamily.edu. *Application contact:* Don Reinmold, Director of Graduate Admissions, 267-341-5001 Ext. 3230, Fax: 215-633-0558, E-mail: dreinmold@holyfamily.edu.

Holy Family University, Graduate and Professional Programs, School of Education, Philadelphia, PA 19114. Offers education (M Ed, Ed D), including early elementary education (PreK-Grade 4) (M Ed), education leadership (M Ed), educational leadership and professional studies (Ed D), general education (M Ed), reading specialist (M Ed), special education (M Ed), TESOL and literacy (M Ed). *Accreditation:* TEAC. *Program availability:* Part-time, evening/weekend. *Students:* 65 full-time, 35 part-time. 87 applicants, 66% accepted, 36 enrolled. In 2016, 29 master's awarded. *Degree requirements:* For master's, comprehensive exam, thesis optional; for doctorate, comprehensive exam, thesis/dissertation. *Entrance requirements:* For master's, GRE or MAT (if GPA is below 3.0), interview, minimum GPA of 3.0, essay/personal statement, 2 letters of recommendation, official transcripts of all college or university work; for doctorate, GRE or MAT (taken within 5 years of application), minimum GPA of 3.5, 3 letters of recommendation, official transcripts of all college or university work, current resume, essay/personal statement, writing sample, interview. Additional exam requirements/recommendations for international students: Required—TOEFL (minimum score 550 paper-based; 79 iBT), IELTS (minimum score 6), or PTE (minimum score 54). *Application deadline:* For fall admission, 7/1 priority date for domestic and international students; for winter admission, 1/1 for domestic students; for spring admission, 11/1 priority date for domestic and international students; for summer admission, 4/1 priority date for domestic and international students. Applications are processed on a rolling basis. Application fee: $25. Electronic applications accepted. *Expenses: Tuition:* Part-time $751 per hour. *Required fees:* $140 per semester. One-time fee: $165 part-time. Part-time tuition and fees vary according to degree level and program. *Financial support:* Research assistantships with partial tuition reimbursements available. Support available to part-time students. Financial award application deadline: 2/15; financial award applicants required to submit FAFSA. *Unit head:* Dr. Kevin Zook, Dean, 267-341-3565, Fax: 215-824-2438, E-mail: kzook@holyfamily.edu. *Application contact:* Donald Reimold, Director of Graduate Admissions, 267-341-5001, Fax: 215-637-1478, E-mail: dreimold@holyfamily.edu.
Website: http://www.holyfamily.edu/choosing-holy-family-u/academics/school-of-education

Holy Names University, Graduate Division, Department of Education, Oakland, CA 94619-1699. Offers educational therapy (Certificate); mild/moderate disabilities (Ed S); multiple subject teaching (Credential); single subject teaching (Credential); urban education: educational therapy (M Ed); urban education: K-12 education (M Ed); urban education: special education (M Ed). *Program availability:* Part-time. *Students:* 18 full-time (11 women), 111 part-time (79 women); includes 74 minority (37 Black or African American, non-Hispanic/Latino; 1 American Indian or Alaska Native, non-Hispanic/Latino; 10 Asian, non-Hispanic/Latino; 24 Hispanic/Latino; 1 Native Hawaiian or other Pacific Islander, non-Hispanic/Latino; 1 Two or more races, non-Hispanic/Latino), 3 international. Average age 35. 62 applicants, 81% accepted, 39 enrolled. In 2016, 11 master's, 33 Certificates awarded. *Degree requirements:* For master's, comprehensive exam, research paper, thesis or project. *Entrance requirements:* For master's, minimum undergraduate GPA of 2.6 overall, 3.0 in major; personal statement; two recommendations; interview. Additional exam requirements/recommendations for international students: Required—TOEFL (minimum score 550 paper-based; 79 iBT). *Application deadline:* For fall admission, 8/1 priority date for domestic students, 7/15 for international students; for spring admission, 12/1 priority date for domestic students, 12/1 for international students; for summer admission, 5/1 priority date for domestic students, 5/1 for international students. Applications are processed on a rolling basis. Application fee: $65. Electronic applications accepted. Application fee is waived when completed online. *Expenses: Tuition:* Full-time $17,532; part-time $974 per credit hour. *Required fees:* $500; $250 per credit hour. *Financial support:* Career-related internships or fieldwork, Federal Work-Study, scholarships/grants, and unspecified assistantships available. Support available to part-time students. Financial award application deadline: 3/2; financial award applicants required to submit FAFSA. *Faculty research:* Cognitive development, language development, learning handicaps. *Unit head:* Dr. Kimberly Mayfield, Chair, 510-436-1396, Fax: 510-436-1325, E-mail: mayfield@hnu.edu. *Application contact:* Graduate Admission, 800-430-1321, Fax: 510-436-1325, E-mail: graduateadmissions@hnu.edu.
Website: http://www.hnu.edu/academics/graduatePrograms/education.html

Hood College, Graduate School, Department of Education, Frederick, MD 21701-8575. Offers curriculum and instruction (MS), including elementary education, elementary science and mathematics education, secondary education, special education; educational leadership (MS); reading specialization (MS); STEM education (Certificate). *Accreditation:* NCATE. *Program availability:* Part-time-only, evening/weekend. *Faculty:* 3 full-time, 37 part-time/adjunct. *Students:* 1 (woman) full-time, 357 part-time (283 women); includes 71 minority (41 Black or African American, non-Hispanic/Latino; 6 Asian, non-Hispanic/Latino; 15 Hispanic/Latino; 9 Two or more races, non-Hispanic/Latino). Average age 33. 96 applicants, 95% accepted, 83 enrolled. In 2016, 47 master's awarded. *Degree requirements:* For master's, action research project, portfolio (for reading specialization); for Certificate, STEM capstone activity. *Entrance requirements:* For master's, minimum GPA of 2.75, teaching certification, writing sample during interview, letter of recommendation from principal (for educational leadership program only). Additional exam requirements/recommendations for international students: Required—TOEFL (minimum score 575 paper-based; 89 iBT), IELTS (minimum score 6.5). *Application deadline:* For fall admission, 8/15 priority date for domestic students, 8/5 for international students; for spring admission, 12/1 priority date for domestic students, 12/1 for international students; for summer admission, 5/1 priority date for domestic students, 4/15 for international students. Applications are processed on a rolling basis. Application fee: $35. Electronic applications accepted. *Expenses:* $450 per credit; $105 comprehensive fee per semester. *Financial support:* Tuition waivers (partial) and unspecified assistantships available. Financial award applicants required to submit FAFSA. *Faculty research:* Leadership, action research, brain research, learning styles. *Unit head:* April Boulton, Interim Dean of the Graduate School, E-mail: gofurther@hood.edu. *Application contact:* Jan Marcus, Assistant Director of Graduate

Admissions, 301-696-3600, E-mail: gofurther@hood.edu.
Website: http://www.hood.edu/academics/education/index.html

Hope International University, School of Graduate and Professional Studies, Program in Education, Fullerton, CA 92831-3138. Offers education administration (MA); elementary education (ME); secondary education (ME). *Program availability:* Part-time, evening/weekend. *Degree requirements:* For master's, comprehensive exam (for some programs), thesis. *Entrance requirements:* For master's, minimum GPA of 3.0, 2 references. Additional exam requirements/recommendations for international students: Required—TOEFL (minimum score 550 paper-based; 86 iBT); Recommended—IELTS (minimum score 6.5). Electronic applications accepted. *Expenses:* Contact institution. *Faculty research:* Distance education.

Houston Baptist University, College of Education and Behavioral Sciences, Programs in Education, Houston, TX 77074-3298. Offers bilingual education (M Ed); counselor education (M Ed); curriculum and instruction (M Ed); educational administration (M Ed); educational diagnostician (M Ed); executive educational leadership (Ed D); reading education (M Ed). *Program availability:* Part-time, evening/weekend, 100% online, blended/hybrid learning. *Students:* 45 full-time (35 women), 158 part-time (136 women); includes 141 minority (87 Black or African American, non-Hispanic/Latino; 1 American Indian or Alaska Native, non-Hispanic/Latino; 5 Asian, non-Hispanic/Latino; 47 Hispanic/Latino; 1 Two or more races, non-Hispanic/Latino), 3 international. Average age 34. 320 applicants, 30% accepted, 61 enrolled. In 2016, 121 degrees awarded. *Degree requirements:* For master's, comprehensive exam; for doctorate, thesis/dissertation. *Entrance requirements:* For master's, minimum GPA of 2.75, two recommendations, resume, bachelor's degree conferred transcript; interview (for non-certified teachers); for doctorate, GRE, 3 letters of recommendation. Additional exam requirements/recommendations for international students: Required—TOEFL (minimum score 80 iBT), IELTS (minimum score 6.5). *Application deadline:* For fall admission, 8/1 for domestic students, 6/1 for international students; for spring admission, 1/1 for domestic students, 11/1 for international students; for summer admission, 5/1 for domestic students, 3/1 for international students. Applications are processed on a rolling basis. Application fee: $0 ($100 for international students). Electronic applications accepted. Application fee is waived when completed online. *Expenses:* $1,650 per 3-hour course; $1,275 annual general fee; $1,060 annual technology fee. *Financial support:* In 2016–17, 2 students received support. Research assistantships, teaching assistantships, Federal Work-Study, and scholarships/grants available. Support available to part-time students. Financial award application deadline: 4/1; financial award applicants required to submit FAFSA. *Faculty research:* Autism and inclusion, integrating technology into instruction, school change and leadership trust. *Unit head:* Dr. Charlotte Fontenot, Director, Graduate Programs, 281-649-3078, Fax: 281-649-3361, E-mail: cfontenot@hbu.edu. *Application contact:* Kristy Wright, Administrative Assistant for Graduate Programs, 281-649-3094, Fax: 281-649-3361, E-mail: kwright@hbu.edu.
Website: http://www.hbu.edu/MED

Howard University, School of Education, Washington, DC 20059. Offers M Ed, Ed D, PhD, CAGS. *Accreditation:* NCATE. *Degree requirements:* For master's, comprehensive exam, expository writing exam, practicum, PRAXIS II; for doctorate, one foreign language, comprehensive exam, thesis/dissertation, expository writing exam, internship. *Entrance requirements:* For master's, PRAXIS I or GRE General Test (for curriculum and instruction students only), minimum GPA of 2.7; for doctorate, GRE General Test, minimum GPA of 3.4. Additional exam requirements/recommendations for international students: Required—TOEFL (minimum score 550 paper-based; 79 iBT). Electronic applications accepted. *Faculty research:* Policy affecting education for African-Americans; information technology use in underserved school populations; increasing literacy skills for public school students; violence intervention and prevention; successes, problems, and needs of disabled African-Americans.

Humboldt State University, Academic Programs, College of Professional Studies, School of Education, Arcata, CA 95521-8299. Offers MA. *Program availability:* Part-time, evening/weekend, online only, 100% online, blended/hybrid learning. *Degree requirements:* For master's, thesis or alternative. *Entrance requirements:* For master's, minimum GPA of 3.0, 3 letters of recommendation. Additional exam requirements/recommendations for international students: Required—TOEFL (minimum score 500 paper-based). Electronic applications accepted. *Expenses:* Tuition, state resident: full-time $6738; part-time $1953 per semester. Tuition, nonresident: full-time $13,434; part-time $3813 per semester. *Required fees:* $1738; $653 per semester. Tuition and fees vary according to program.

Hunter College of the City University of New York, Graduate School, School of Education, New York, NY 10065-5085. Offers MA, MS, MS Ed, Ed D, AC. *Accreditation:* NCATE. *Program availability:* Part-time, evening/weekend. *Faculty:* 66 full-time (46 women), 221 part-time/adjunct (175 women). *Students:* 359 full-time (294 women), 2,554 part-time (2,089 women); includes 1,320 minority (355 Black or African American, non-Hispanic/Latino; 4 American Indian or Alaska Native, non-Hispanic/Latino; 250 Asian, non-Hispanic/Latino; 668 Hispanic/Latino; 3 Native Hawaiian or other Pacific Islander, non-Hispanic/Latino; 40 Two or more races, non-Hispanic/Latino), 75 international. Average age 31. 1,848 applicants, 73% accepted, 892 enrolled. In 2016, 879 master's, 214 other advanced degrees awarded. *Degree requirements:* For master's, comprehensive exam (for some programs), thesis (for some programs), minimum overall GPA of 3.0; portfolio review; for doctorate, thesis/dissertation; for AC, comprehensive exam (for some programs), minimum overall GPA of 3.0; portfolio review; valid and appropriate NY state certification. *Entrance requirements:* For master's, GRE (for teacher preparation programs), transcript review requiring BA with minimum GPA of 3.0; personal statement, letters of recommendation and/or writing sample; for doctorate, GRE (for teacher preparation programs), official transcripts; letters of recommendation; essay; resume; minimum GPA of 3.5 in a master's program; interview; for AC, GRE (for teacher preparation programs), transcript review requiring minimum B average in graduate course work; teaching certificate; minimum 3 years of full-time teaching experience; personal statement, letters of recommendation and/or writing sample. Additional exam requirements/recommendations for international students: Required—TOEFL. *Application deadline:* For fall admission, 3/15 for domestic students, 2/1 for international students; for spring admission, 10/15 for domestic students, 9/1 for international students. Applications are processed on a rolling basis. Application fee: $125. Electronic applications accepted. *Financial support:* Application deadline: 6/30; applicants required to submit FAFSA. *Faculty research:* Multicultural and multiracial urban education; mentoring new teachers; mathematics and science education; bilingual, bi-cultural, and special education. *Unit head:* Dr. Michael Middleton, Dean, 212-772-4622, E-mail: mm5378@hunter.cuny.edu. *Application contact:* Milena Solo, Director for Graduate Admissions, 212-772-4482, E-mail: milena.solo@hunter.cuny.edu.
Website: http://www.hunter.cuny.edu/school-of-education/programs/graduate

Huntington University, Graduate School, Huntington, IN 46750-1299. Offers counseling (MA), including licensed mental health counselor; early adolescent education (M Ed); education (M Ed); global missions leadership (MA); global youth ministry (MA); TESOL education (M Ed); youth ministry leadership (MA). *Program availability:* Part-time, online learning. *Degree requirements:* For master's, comprehensive exam (for some programs), thesis (for some programs). *Entrance requirements:* For master's, GRE (for counseling and education students only); for doctorate, GRE (for occupational therapy students). Additional exam requirements/recommendations for international students: Required—TOEFL (minimum score 85 iBT), IELTS (minimum score 6.5). Electronic applications accepted. *Faculty research:* Leadership, educational technology trends, evangelism, youth ministry, mental health.

Idaho State University, Office of Graduate Studies, College of Education, Pocatello, ID 83209-8059. Offers M Ed, MPE, Ed D, PhD, 5th Year Certificate, 6th Year Certificate, Ed S. *Accreditation:* NCATE. *Program availability:* Part-time. *Degree requirements:* For master's, comprehensive exam, thesis optional, oral exam, written exam; for doctorate, comprehensive exam, thesis/dissertation, written exam; for other advanced degree, comprehensive exam, oral exam, written exam, practicum or field project. *Entrance requirements:* For master's, GRE General Test or MAT, minimum undergraduate GPA of 3.0, interview, bachelor's degree or equivalent; for doctorate, GRE General Test or MAT, minimum undergraduate GPA of 3.0, 3.5 graduate; departmental interview; current curriculum vitae, computer skill competency checklist; for other advanced degree, GRE General Test, minimum graduate GPA of 3.0, master's degree, letter from supervisor attesting to school administration potential. Additional exam requirements/recommendations for international students: Required—TOEFL (minimum score 550 paper-based; 80 iBT). Electronic applications accepted. *Faculty research:* School reform, inclusion, students at risk, teacher education standards, teaching cases, education leadership.

Illinois College, Program in Education, Jacksonville, IL 62650-2299. Offers MA Ed. *Program availability:* Part-time-only, evening/weekend. *Faculty:* 8 part-time/adjunct (3 women). *Students:* 2 part-time (both women). Average age 39. *Degree requirements:* For master's, action research capstone experience. *Application deadline:* For fall admission, 5/31 priority date for domestic students. Applications are processed on a rolling basis. Application fee: $0. Electronic applications accepted. *Expenses:* $6,540. *Financial support:* In 2016–17, 2 students received support. Applicants required to submit FAFSA. *Unit head:* Dr. Daniel Meyer, Assistant Professor of Education, 217-291-1609, E-mail: daniel.meyer@mail.ic.edu. *Application contact:* Evan Wilson, Director of Admission, 217-245-3030, E-mail: evan.wilson@mail.ic.edu.
Website: http://www.ic.edu/masters

Illinois State University, Graduate School, College of Education, Normal, IL 61790-2200. Offers MS, MS Ed, Ed D, PhD, Certificate. *Accreditation:* NCATE. *Program availability:* Part-time. *Degree requirements:* For doctorate, thesis/dissertation, 2 terms of residency. *Entrance requirements:* For master's and doctorate, GRE General Test.

Indiana State University, College of Graduate and Professional Studies, Bayh College of Education, Terre Haute, IN 47809. Offers M Ed, MS, PhD, Ed S, MA/MS. *Accreditation:* NCATE. *Program availability:* Part-time, evening/weekend. *Degree requirements:* For doctorate, thesis/dissertation. *Entrance requirements:* For master's, minimum undergraduate GPA of 2.5; for doctorate, GRE General Test; for Ed S, GRE General Test, minimum graduate GPA of 3.25. Electronic applications accepted.

Indiana University Bloomington, School of Education, Bloomington, IN 47405-1006. Offers MS, Ed D, PhD, Ed S, Graduate Certificate. *Accreditation:* NCATE. *Program availability:* Part-time, 100% online, blended/hybrid learning. *Students:* 717 full-time (502 women), 308 part-time (213 women); includes 182 minority (86 Black or African American, non-Hispanic/Latino; 1 American Indian or Alaska Native, non-Hispanic/Latino; 33 Asian, non-Hispanic/Latino; 43 Hispanic/Latino; 1 Native Hawaiian or other Pacific Islander, non-Hispanic/Latino; 18 Two or more races, non-Hispanic/Latino), 205 international. Average age 34. 907 applicants, 46% accepted, 166 enrolled. In 2016, 225 master's, 79 doctorates, 50 other advanced degrees awarded. Terminal master's awarded for partial completion of doctoral program. *Degree requirements:* For master's, thesis optional; for doctorate, comprehensive exam, thesis/dissertation; for other advanced degree, comprehensive exam (for some programs), thesis (for some programs), comprehensive exam or project. *Entrance requirements:* For master's and other advanced degree, GRE General Test, minimum GPA of 3.0 (recommended), 3 letters of recommendation; for doctorate, GRE General Test, minimum GPA of 3.0, 3 letters of recommendation. Additional exam requirements/recommendations for international students: Required—TOEFL (minimum score 550 paper-based; 79 iBT). *Application deadline:* For fall admission, 1/15 priority date for domestic students, 12/1 priority date for international students; for spring admission, 11/1 priority date for domestic students, 9/1 priority date for international students. Application fee: $60 ($65 for international students). Electronic applications accepted. *Financial support:* Fellowships with full and partial tuition reimbursements, research assistantships with tuition reimbursements, teaching assistantships with tuition reimbursements, Federal Work-Study, scholarships/grants, tuition waivers (full and partial), and unspecified assistantships available. Financial award application deadline: 3/1; financial award applicants required to submit FAFSA. *Unit head:* Dr. Terrence C. Mason, Dean, 812-856-8504, E-mail: educate@indiana.edu. *Application contact:* Christy Richards, Admissions Coordinator, 812-856-8504, Fax: 812-856-8505, E-mail: richarcj@indiana.edu.
Website: http://education.indiana.edu/

Indiana University East, School of Education, Richmond, IN 47374-1289. Offers MS Ed. *Accreditation:* NCATE. *Entrance requirements:* For master's, 3 letters of recommendation, interview.

Indiana University Northwest, School of Education, Gary, IN 46408. Offers educational leadership (MS Ed); elementary education (MS Ed); K-12 online teaching (Graduate Certificate); secondary education (MS Ed). *Accreditation:* NCATE. *Program availability:* Part-time, evening/weekend. *Faculty:* 10 full-time (5 women), 2 part-time/adjunct (both women). *Students:* 11 full-time (8 women), 67 part-time (47 women); includes 32 minority (25 Black or African American, non-Hispanic/Latino; 7 Hispanic/Latino). Average age 38. 24 applicants, 96% accepted, 14 enrolled. In 2016, 22 master's awarded. *Entrance requirements:* For master's, GRE General Test or MAT, minimum GPA of 3.0. *Application deadline:* For fall admission, 7/15 priority date for domestic students; for spring admission, 11/15 for domestic students. Application fee: $40 ($60 for international students). Electronic applications accepted. *Expenses:* $276.98 per credit hour in-state; $652.54 per credit hour out-of-state. *Financial support:* Applicants required to submit FAFSA. *Unit head:* Dr. Charles Hobsen, Interim Dean, 219-980-6903, Fax: 219-680-4208, E-mail: chobson@iun.edu. *Application contact:* Kelly Zieba, Director of Enrollment Management, Finance, and Operations, 219-980-6879, Fax: 219-980-4208, E-mail: kmzieba@iun.edu.
Website: http://www.iun.edu/education/degrees/masters.htm

Indiana University of Pennsylvania, School of Graduate Studies and Research, College of Education and Educational Technology, Indiana, PA 15705. Offers M Ed, MA, MS, D Ed, PhD, Certificate. *Accreditation:* NCATE. *Program availability:* Part-time, evening/weekend. *Faculty:* 62 full-time (38 women), 12 part-time/adjunct (9 women). *Students:* 282 full-time (223 women), 419 part-time (279 women); includes 76 minority (44 Black or African American, non-Hispanic/Latino; 2 Asian, non-Hispanic/Latino; 14 Hispanic/Latino; 16 Two or more races, non-Hispanic/Latino), 31 international. Average age 33. 895 applicants, 53% accepted, 234 enrolled. In 2016, 174 master's, 45 doctorates, 10 other advanced degrees awarded. Terminal master's awarded for partial completion of doctoral program. *Degree requirements:* For master's, thesis optional; for

doctorate, comprehensive exam, thesis/dissertation. *Entrance requirements:* For master's and doctorate, 2 letters of recommendation. Additional exam requirements/recommendations for international students: Required—TOEFL (minimum score 540 paper-based; 76 iBT). *Application deadline:* Applications are processed on a rolling basis. Application fee: $50. Electronic applications accepted. *Expenses:* Tuition, state resident: full-time $8694; part-time $483 per credit. Tuition, nonresident: full-time $13,050; part-time $725 per credit. *Required fees:* $157 per credit. $50 per term. Tuition and fees vary according to course load and program. *Financial support:* In 2016–17, 22 fellowships (averaging $919 per year), 135 research assistantships with tuition reimbursements (averaging $4,373 per year), 8 teaching assistantships with tuition reimbursements (averaging $18,450 per year) were awarded; career-related internships or fieldwork, Federal Work-Study, scholarships/grants, and unspecified assistantships also available. Support available to part-time students. Financial award application deadline: 4/15; financial award applicants required to submit FAFSA. *Unit head:* Dr. Lara Luetkehans, Dean, 724-357-2480, Fax: 724-357-5595. *Application contact:* Paula Stossel, Assistant Dean for Administration, 724-357-4511, Fax: 724-357-4862, E-mail: graduate-admissions@iup.edu.
Website: http://www.iup.edu/education

Indiana University–Purdue University Fort Wayne, College of Education and Public Policy, Fort Wayne, IN 46805-1499. Offers MPM, MS Ed, Certificate. *Accreditation:* NCATE. *Program availability:* Part-time. *Entrance requirements:* For master's, minimum GPA of 2.5, 3 professional letters of recommendation. Additional exam requirements/recommendations for international students: Required—TOEFL (minimum score 550 paper-based; 79 iBT). *Faculty research:* Alcoholism and sobriety, international faculty perceptions.

Indiana University–Purdue University Indianapolis, School of Education, Indianapolis, IN 46202-5155. Offers curriculum and instruction (MS); early childhood (MS); educational leadership (MS, Certificate); English as a second language (Certificate); kindergarten (Certificate); language education (MS); reading (Certificate); school counseling (MS); special education (MS, Certificate). *Program availability:* Part-time, evening/weekend. *Faculty:* 35 full-time (27 women), 56 part-time/adjunct (42 women). *Students:* 125 full-time (86 women), 181 part-time (139 women); includes 106 minority (78 Black or African American, non-Hispanic/Latino; 9 Asian, non-Hispanic/Latino; 12 Hispanic/Latino; 7 Two or more races, non-Hispanic/Latino), 3 international. Average age 32. 73 applicants, 93% accepted, 68 enrolled. In 2016, 73 master's awarded. Terminal master's awarded for partial completion of doctoral program. *Degree requirements:* For master's, thesis optional. *Entrance requirements:* For master's, GRE General Test, minimum GPA of 2.5; for Certificate, official transcripts. Additional exam requirements/recommendations for international students: Required—TOEFL (minimum score 60 iBT), IELTS (minimum score 5.5). *Application deadline:* For fall admission, 5/1 for domestic students; for spring admission, 11/1 for domestic students. Application fee: $60 ($65 for international students). Electronic applications accepted. *Expenses:* $1,262 tuition, $213 general fee. *Financial support:* Applicants required to submit FAFSA. *Faculty research:* Educational policies and school leaders' responses to these; issues of intersectionality in the experiences of African American lesbian, gay, and bisexual students attending historically black colleges and universities and those who belong to black Greek-letter organizations; students' experiential knowledge and their evolving disciplinary-specific literacy and understanding; innovative program development; urban ESL teacher preparation; target-based instructional coaching. *Total annual research expenditures:* $2.1 million. *Unit head:* Dr. Robin Hughes, Executive Associate Dean, 317-274-6817, E-mail: roblhugh@iupui.edu. *Application contact:* Ky Shaw, Graduate Admissions Coordinator, 317-278-6778, E-mail: kycshaw@iupui.edu.
Website: http://education.iupui.edu/

Indiana University South Bend, School of Education, South Bend, IN 46634-7111. Offers addiction counseling (MS Ed); alcohol and drug counseling (Graduate Certificate); clinical mental health counseling (MS Ed); educational leadership (MS Ed); elementary education (MS Ed); marriage, couple, and family counseling (MS Ed); school counseling (MS Ed); secondary education (MS Ed); special education (MAT, MS Ed), including intense intervention (MS Ed), mild intervention (MS Ed). *Accreditation:* NCATE. *Program availability:* Part-time, evening/weekend. *Faculty:* 21 full-time (11 women), 9 part-time/adjunct (3 women). *Students:* 26 full-time (19 women), 104 part-time (80 women); includes 22 minority (13 Black or African American, non-Hispanic/Latino; 5 Hispanic/Latino; 4 Two or more races, non-Hispanic/Latino). Average age 35. 51 applicants, 69% accepted, 22 enrolled. In 2016, 31 master's, 2 other advanced degrees awarded. *Degree requirements:* For master's, thesis or alternative, exit project. *Entrance requirements:* For master's, letters of recommendation, GRE or minimum GPA of 3.0. Additional exam requirements/recommendations for international students: Required—TOEFL. *Application deadline:* For fall admission, 7/1 for domestic students; for spring admission, 11/1 for domestic students. Applications are processed on a rolling basis. Application fee: $40 ($60 for international students). Electronic applications accepted. *Expenses:* $276.98 per credit hour in-state; $652.54 per credit hour out-of-state. *Financial support:* Career-related internships or fieldwork available. Support available to part-time students. Financial award application deadline: 3/1; financial award applicants required to submit FAFSA. *Faculty research:* Professional dispositions, early childhood literacy, online learning, program assessments, problem-based learning. *Unit head:* Dr. Marvin Lynn, Dean, 574-520-4339, E-mail: lynnm@iusb.edu. *Application contact:* Yvonne Walker, Student Services Representative, 574-520-4185, E-mail: ydwalker@iusb.edu.
Website: https://www.iusb.edu/education/index.php

Indiana University Southeast, School of Education, New Albany, IN 47150. Offers counselor education (MS Ed); elementary education (MS Ed); secondary education (MS Ed). *Accreditation:* NCATE. *Program availability:* Part-time, evening/weekend. *Students:* 13 full-time (10 women), 190 part-time (150 women); includes 29 minority (21 Black or African American, non-Hispanic/Latino; 5 Hispanic/Latino; 3 Two or more races, non-Hispanic/Latino). Average age 33. 61 applicants, 84% accepted, 43 enrolled. In 2016, 70 master's awarded. *Entrance requirements:* For master's, minimum undergraduate GPA of 2.5, graduate 3.0. *Application deadline:* Applications are processed on a rolling basis. Application fee: $40 ($60 for international students). Electronic applications accepted. *Financial support:* Career-related internships or fieldwork, Federal Work-Study, and institutionally sponsored loans available. Support available to part-time students. Financial award applicants required to submit FAFSA. *Faculty research:* Learning styles, technology, constructivism, group process, innovative math strategies. *Unit head:* Dr. Faye Marsha Camahalan, Director of Graduate Studies, 812-941-2136, Fax: 812-941-2667, E-mail: fcamahal@ius.edu. *Application contact:* Admissions Counselor, 812-941-2212, Fax: 812-941-2595, E-mail: admissions@ius.edu.
Website: http://www.ius.edu/education/graduate-programs/

Institute for Christian Studies, Graduate Programs, Toronto, ON M5T 1R4, Canada. Offers education (M Phil F, PhD); history of philosophy (M Phil F, PhD); philosophical aesthetics (M Phil F, PhD); philosophy of religion (M Phil F, PhD); political theory (M Phil F, PhD); systematic philosophy (M Phil F, PhD); theology (M Phil F, PhD); worldview studies (MWS). *Program availability:* Part-time, online learning. *Degree requirements:* For master's, one foreign language, thesis; for doctorate, 2 foreign languages, thesis/dissertation. *Entrance requirements:* For master's and doctorate, philosophy background. Additional exam requirements/recommendations for international students: Required—TOEFL (minimum score 600 paper-based). *Faculty research:* Human rights, anthropology of self, medieval discourse, gender and body, post-modern thought; biblical hermeneutics, creational aesthetics, ecumenism, epistemology, political theory and public policy, relational psychotherapy.

Instituto Tecnologico de Santo Domingo, Graduate School, Area of Humanities and Social Sciences, Santo Domingo, Dominican Republic. Offers accounting (Certificate); adult education (Certificate); applied linguistics (MA); economics (MA); education (M Ed); educational psychology (MA, Certificate); gender and development (MA, Certificate); humanistic studies (MA); international marketing management (Certificate); international relations in the Caribbean basin (Certificate); intervention systems in family therapy (MA); linguistic and literary communication (Certificate); pedagogical support (MA); social science education (M Ed); sustainable human development (MA); terminal illness and death psychology (Certificate); youth and adult education (M Ed).

Instituto Tecnológico y de Estudios Superiores de Monterrey, Campus Central de Veracruz, Graduate Programs, Córdoba, Mexico. Offers administration (MA); administration of information technologies (MTI); computer sciences (MCC); education (MEE); educational institution administration (MAD); educational technology (MTE); electronic commerce (MCE); finance (MAF); humanistic studies (MEH); international business for Latin America (MNL); marketing (MMT); science (MCP). *Program availability:* Part-time, evening/weekend, online learning. *Degree requirements:* For master's, thesis (for some programs). *Entrance requirements:* For master's, PAEP College Board. Electronic applications accepted.

Instituto Tecnológico y de Estudios Superiores de Monterrey, Campus Ciudad de México, Virtual University Division, Ciudad de Mexico, Mexico. Offers administration of information technologies (MA); computer sciences (MA); education (MA, PhD); educational technology (MA); environmental engineering (MA); environmental systems (MA); humanistic studies (MA); industrial engineering (MA); international business for Latin America (MA); quality systems (MA); quality systems and productivity (MA). *Program availability:* Part-time, evening/weekend, online learning. *Entrance requirements:* For master's and doctorate, Instituto entrance exam. Additional exam requirements/recommendations for international students: Required—TOEFL.

Instituto Tecnológico y de Estudios Superiores de Monterrey, Campus Ciudad Juárez, Program in Education, Ciudad Juárez, Mexico. Offers M Ed.

Instituto Tecnológico y de Estudios Superiores de Monterrey, Campus Ciudad Obregón, Programs in Education, Ciudad Obregón, Mexico. Offers cognitive development (ME); communications (ME); mathematics (ME).

Instituto Tecnológico y de Estudios Superiores de Monterrey, Campus Estado de México, Professional and Graduate Division, Estado de Mexico, Mexico. Offers administration of information technologies (MITA); architecture (M Arch); business administration (GMBA, MBA); computer sciences (MCS, PhD); education (M Ed); educational institution administration (MAD); educational technology and innovation (PhD); electronic commerce (MEC); environmental systems (MS); finance (MAF); humanistic studies (MHS); information sciences and knowledge management (MISKM); information systems (MS); manufacturing systems (MS); marketing (MEM); quality systems and productivity (MS); science and materials engineering (PhD); telecommunications management (MTM). *Program availability:* Part-time, online learning. *Degree requirements:* For master's, one foreign language, thesis (for some programs); for doctorate, one foreign language, thesis/dissertation. *Entrance requirements:* For master's, E-PAEP 500, interview; for doctorate, E-PAEP 500, research proposal. Additional exam requirements/recommendations for international students: Required—TOEFL (minimum score 550 paper-based). *Faculty research:* Surface treatments by plasmas, mechanical properties, robotics, graphical computing, mechatronics security protocols.

Instituto Tecnológico y de Estudios Superiores de Monterrey, Campus Irapuato, Graduate Programs, Irapuato, Mexico. Offers administration (MBA); administration of information technology (MAIT); administration of telecommunications (MAT); architecture (M Arch); computer science (MCS); education (M Ed); educational administration (MEA); educational innovation and technology (DEIT); educational technology (MET); electronic commerce (MBA); environmental administration and planning (MEAP); environmental systems (MES); finances (MBA); humanistic studies (MHS); international management for Latin American executives (MIMLAE); library and information science (MLIS); manufacturing quality management (MMQM); marketing research (MBA).

Instituto Tecnológico y de Estudios Superiores de Monterrey, Campus Sonora Norte, Program in Education, Hermosillo, Mexico. Offers MA. *Entrance requirements:* For master's, MAT.

Inter American University of Puerto Rico, Arecibo Campus, Programs in Education, Arecibo, PR 00614-4050. Offers administration and educational supervision (MA Ed); counseling and guidance (MA Ed); curriculum and teaching (MA Ed), including biology education, English as a second language, history education, math education, Spanish; elementary education (MA Ed). *Accreditation:* TEAC. *Degree requirements:* For master's, comprehensive exam, thesis optional. *Entrance requirements:* For master's, GRE, EXADEP, bachelor's degree in education or teaching license (administration and supervision) or courses in education and psychology (counseling and guidance), minimum GPA of 2.5 in last 60 credits.

Inter American University of Puerto Rico, Barranquitas Campus, Program in Education, Barranquitas, PR 00794. Offers curriculum and teaching (M Ed), including biology education, English as a second language, history education, mathematics education, Spanish; educational leadership and management (MA); elementary education (M Ed); information and library service technology (M Ed); special education (MA). *Accreditation:* TEAC. *Degree requirements:* For master's, comprehensive exam, thesis optional. *Entrance requirements:* For master's, EXADEP, letter of recommendation. Electronic applications accepted.

Inter American University of Puerto Rico, Metropolitan Campus, Graduate Programs, Program in Education, San Juan, PR 00919-1293. Offers curriculum and instruction (Ed D); educational administration (Ed D); guidance and counseling (MA, Ed D); special education administration (Ed D). *Accreditation:* TEAC. *Degree requirements:* For doctorate, comprehensive exam, thesis/dissertation. *Entrance requirements:* For doctorate, GRE, MAT, or EXADEP. Electronic applications accepted.

International Baptist College and Seminary, Program in Education, Chandler, AZ 85286. Offers M Ed. *Degree requirements:* For master's, research paper/thesis. *Entrance requirements:* For master's, letter of recommendation.

Iona College, School of Arts and Science, Department of Education, New Rochelle, NY 10801-1890. Offers adolescence education: biology (MS Ed, MST); adolescence education: English (MS Ed); adolescence education: mathematics (MST); adolescence education: social studies (MS Ed, MST); adolescence education: Spanish (MS Ed); adolescence special education 5-12 (MST); childhood and special education (MST); early childhood and childhood (MST); educational leadership (MS Ed). *Accreditation:* NCATE. *Program availability:* Part-time, evening/weekend. *Faculty:* 7 full-time (6

women), 4 part-time/adjunct (2 women). *Students:* 27 full-time (19 women), 27 part-time (18 women); includes 18 minority (4 Black or African American, non-Hispanic/Latino; 1 Asian, non-Hispanic/Latino; 12 Hispanic/Latino; 1 Two or more races, non-Hispanic/Latino). Average age 26. 6 applicants, 67% accepted, 3 enrolled. In 2016, 25 master's awarded. *Degree requirements:* For master's, thesis or alternative. *Entrance requirements:* For master's, minimum GPA of 3.0, NY State teaching certificate and bachelor's degree (for MS Ed). Additional exam requirements/recommendations for international students: Required—TOEFL (minimum score 550 paper-based; 80 iBT), IELTS (minimum score 6.5). *Application deadline:* For fall admission, 8/1 priority date for domestic students, 5/1 priority date for international students; for spring admission, 1/1 priority date for domestic students, 9/1 priority date for international students. Applications are processed on a rolling basis. Application fee: $50. Electronic applications accepted. *Expenses: Tuition:* Full-time $19,692; part-time $1094 per credit. *Required fees:* $245 per term. Tuition and fees vary according to program. *Financial support:* In 2016–17, 3 students received support. Unspecified assistantships available. Support available to part-time students. Financial award application deadline: 4/15; financial award applicants required to submit FAFSA. *Faculty research:* Engaging teacher educators in scientific process, cross-national comparisons of mathematics teaching, questioning strategies in the classroom, research methods, literacy development. *Unit head:* Margaret Smith, PhD, Chair, 914-633-2210, Fax: 914-633-2608, E-mail: msmith@iona.edu. *Application contact:* Richard McMahon, Coordinator, Graduate School of Education, 914-633-2552, E-mail: rmcmahon@iona.edu.
Website: http://www.iona.edu/Academics/School-of-Arts-Science/Departments/Education/Graduate-Programs.aspx

Iowa State University of Science and Technology, Department of Education, Ames, IA 50011. Offers curriculum and instructional technology (M Ed, MS, PhD); elementary education (M Ed, MS); historical, philosophical, and comparative studies in education (M Ed, MS); special education (M Ed, MS, PhD). *Degree requirements:* For master's, thesis or alternative; for doctorate, thesis/dissertation. *Entrance requirements:* For master's and doctorate, GRE General Test. Additional exam requirements/recommendations for international students: Required—TOEFL (minimum score 560 paper-based; 83 iBT), IELTS (minimum score 6.5). *Application deadline:* For fall admission, 1/1 priority date for domestic and international students; for spring admission, 9/1 for domestic and international students. Application fee: $60 ($90 for international students). Electronic applications accepted. *Application contact:* Robyn Goldy, Application Contact, 515-294-1241, Fax: 515-294-4942, E-mail: rgoldy@iastate.edu.
Website: http://www.ci.hs.iastate.edu

Jackson State University, Graduate School, College of Education and Human Development, Jackson, MS 39217. Offers MS, MS Ed, Ed D, PhD, Ed S. *Accreditation:* NCATE. *Program availability:* Part-time, evening/weekend, 100% online, blended/hybrid learning. *Faculty:* 43 full-time (25 women), 9 part-time/adjunct (2 women). *Students:* 262 full-time (208 women), 669 part-time (526 women); includes 863 minority (853 Black or African American, non-Hispanic/Latino; 2 American Indian or Alaska Native, non-Hispanic/Latino; 4 Hispanic/Latino; 1 Native Hawaiian or other Pacific Islander, non-Hispanic/Latino; 3 Two or more races, non-Hispanic/Latino), 23 international. Average age 33. 1,687 applicants, 26% accepted, 269 enrolled. In 2016, 127 master's, 37 doctorates, 13 other advanced degrees awarded. Terminal master's awarded for partial completion of doctoral program. *Degree requirements:* For master's, comprehensive exam; for doctorate, comprehensive exam, thesis/dissertation. *Entrance requirements:* For master's, GRE General Test; for doctorate, MAT, teaching experience. Additional exam requirements/recommendations for international students: Required—TOEFL (minimum score 520 paper-based; 67 iBT). *Application deadline:* For fall admission, 3/1 priority date for domestic students, 3/1 for international students; for spring admission, 10/1 for domestic and international students. Applications are processed on a rolling basis. Application fee: $25. Electronic applications accepted. *Expenses:* Contact institution. *Financial support:* Teaching assistantships, career-related internships or fieldwork, Federal Work-Study, scholarships/grants, and unspecified assistantships available. Support available to part-time students. Financial award application deadline: 3/1; financial award applicants required to submit FAFSA. *Unit head:* Dr. Daniel Watkins, Interim Dean, 601-979-2433, E-mail: daniel.watkins@jsums.edu. *Application contact:* Dr. Milliard Bingham, Associate Interim Dean, 601-979-1750, Fax: 601-979-3419, E-mail: millard.j.bingham@jsums.edu.
Website: http://www.jsums.edu/education/

Jacksonville State University, College of Graduate Studies and Continuing Education, College of Education and Professional Studies, Jacksonville, AL 36265-1602. Offers MS, MS Ed, Ed S. *Accreditation:* NCATE. *Program availability:* Part-time, evening/weekend, 100% online, blended/hybrid learning. *Faculty:* 41 full-time (24 women), 15 part-time/adjunct (8 women). *Students:* 142 full-time (109 women), 359 part-time (243 women); includes 95 minority (90 Black or African American, non-Hispanic/Latino; 3 American Indian or Alaska Native, non-Hispanic/Latino; 2 Hispanic/Latino), 9 international. Average age 33. 319 applicants, 66% accepted, 150 enrolled. In 2016, 181 master's, 37 other advanced degrees awarded. *Degree requirements:* For master's, comprehensive exam, thesis (for some programs). *Entrance requirements:* For master's, GRE General Test or MAT. Additional exam requirements/recommendations for international students: Required—TOEFL (minimum score 500 paper-based; 61 iBT). *Application deadline:* Applications are processed on a rolling basis. Application fee: $35. Electronic applications accepted. *Financial support:* In 2016–17, 92 students received support. Available to part-time students. Application deadline: 4/1; applicants required to submit FAFSA. *Unit head:* Dr. John Hammett, Dean, 256-782-8212, E-mail: jhammett@jsu.edu. *Application contact:* Dr. Jean Pugliese, Associate Dean, 256-782-8278, Fax: 256-782-5321, E-mail: pugliese@jsu.edu.
Website: http://www.jsu.edu/edprof/

John Brown University, Graduate Education Programs, Siloam Springs, AR 72761-2121. Offers curriculum and instruction (M Ed); secondary education (MAT). *Program availability:* Part-time, evening/weekend. *Faculty:* 1 (woman) full-time, 5 part-time/adjunct (3 women). *Students:* 17 part-time (8 women). Average age 32. 11 applicants, 64% accepted, 5 enrolled. In 2016, 7 master's awarded. *Entrance requirements:* For master's, GRE (minimum score of 300). Additional exam requirements/recommendations for international students: Required—TOEFL (minimum score 550 paper-based; 79 iBT). *Application deadline:* Applications are processed on a rolling basis. Application fee: $35 ($100 for international students). Electronic applications accepted. *Expenses: Tuition:* Full-time $13,000; part-time $6500 per credit hour. Part-time tuition and fees vary according to course load and program. *Financial support:* Scholarships/grants and unspecified assistantships available. *Unit head:* Dr. Connie Matchell, Graduate Program Director, 479-524-9500, E-mail: cmatchell@jbu.edu. *Application contact:* Mark Bjornsen, Graduate Education Representative, 479-631-4665, E-mail: mbjornsen@jbu.edu.
Website: http://www.jbu.edu/grad/education/

John F. Kennedy University, School of Education and Liberal Arts, Department of Education, Pleasant Hill, CA 94523-4817. Offers MAT. *Program availability:* Part-time, evening/weekend. *Degree requirements:* For master's, thesis. *Entrance requirements:* For master's, California Basic Educational Skills Test, NTE, interview. Additional exam requirements/recommendations for international students: Required—TOEFL.

Johns Hopkins University, School of Education, Baltimore, MD 21218. Offers M Ed, MAT, MS, Ed D, PhD, Advanced Certificate, Graduate Certificate, Post-Master's Certificate. *Accreditation:* NCATE. *Program availability:* Part-time, evening/weekend, 100% online, blended/hybrid learning. *Faculty:* 104 full-time (79 women), 224 part-time/adjunct (166 women). *Students:* 371 full-time (283 women), 2,008 part-time (1,557 women); includes 965 minority (456 Black or African American, non-Hispanic/Latino; 9 American Indian or Alaska Native, non-Hispanic/Latino; 158 Asian, non-Hispanic/Latino; 240 Hispanic/Latino; 7 Native Hawaiian or other Pacific Islander, non-Hispanic/Latino; 95 Two or more races, non-Hispanic/Latino), 79 international. Average age 29. 2,008 applicants, 66% accepted, 1044 enrolled. In 2016, 642 master's, 11 doctorates, 167 other advanced degrees awarded. *Degree requirements:* For master's, comprehensive exam (for some programs), portfolio, capstone project and/or internship; PRAXIS II (subject area assessments) for initial teacher preparation programs that lead to licensure; for doctorate, comprehensive exam, thesis/dissertation. *Entrance requirements:* For master's, GRE (for full-time programs only); PRAXIS I/core or state-approved alternative (for initial teacher preparation programs that lead to licensure), minimum of bachelor's degree from regionally- or nationally-accredited institution; minimum GPA of 3.0 in all previous programs of study; official transcripts from all post-secondary institutions attended; essay; curriculum vitae/resume; letters of recommendation (3 for full-time programs, 2 for part-time programs); dispositions survey; for doctorate, GRE (for PhD only), master's degree from regionally- or nationally-accredited institution; minimum GPA of 3.0 in previous undergraduate and graduate studies (for Ed D only); official transcripts from all post-secondary institutions attended; three letters of recommendation; curriculum vitae/resume; personal statement; dispositions survey; for other advanced degree, minimum of bachelor's degree from regionally- or nationally-accredited institution (master's degree for some programs); minimum GPA of 3.0 in all previous programs of study; official transcripts from all post-secondary institutions attended; essay; curriculum vitae/resume; two letters of recommendation; dispositions survey. Additional exam requirements/recommendations for international students: Required—TOEFL (minimum score 600 paper-based; 100 iBT), IELTS (minimum score 7). *Application deadline:* For fall admission, 4/1 priority date for domestic students, 4/1 for international students; for spring admission, 10/1 priority date for domestic students, 10/1 for international students; for summer admission, 2/1 priority date for domestic students, 2/1 for international students. Applications are processed on a rolling basis. Application fee: $80. Electronic applications accepted. *Expenses:* Contact institution. *Financial support:* In 2016–17, 206 students received support, including 23 fellowships (averaging $25,500 per year); research assistantships, teaching assistantships, Federal Work-Study, and scholarships/grants also available. Support available to part-time students. Financial award application deadline: 4/1; financial award applicants required to submit FAFSA. *Faculty research:* Comprehensive school reform, dropout prevention, evidence-based decision making in education, neuro-education, entrepreneurial leadership. *Total annual research expenditures:* $42.8 million. *Unit head:* Dr. Christopher C. Morphew, Dean. *Application contact:* Elisabeth Woodward, Director of Admissions, 410-516-9796, Fax: 410-516-9817, E-mail: soe.info@jhu.edu.
Website: http://education.jhu.edu

Johnson & Wales University, Graduate Studies, MAT Program in Teacher Education, Providence, RI 02903-3703. Offers business education and secondary special education (MAT); culinary arts education (MAT); elementary education and elementary special education (MAT); elementary education and elementary/secondary special education (MAT); elementary education and secondary special education (MAT); food service education (MAT). *Program availability:* Part-time, evening/weekend. *Entrance requirements:* For master's, MAT, minimum GPA of 2.75. Additional exam requirements/recommendations for international students: Required—TOEFL (minimum score 550 paper-based) or IELTS (recommended). *Faculty research:* Secondary education, student teaching, educational reform, evaluation procedures.

Johnson & Wales University, M Ed Program in Teaching and Learning, Providence, RI 02903-3703. Offers M Ed. *Program availability:* Evening/weekend. *Entrance requirements:* For master's, bachelor's degree with minimum GPA of 2.75 from accredited institution of higher education, valid teaching license. Additional exam requirements/recommendations for international students: Required—TOEFL (minimum score 80 iBT), TOEFL (minimum score 550 paper-based) or Michigan English Language Assessment Battery (minimum score 77).

Johnson State College, Program in Education, Johnson, VT 05656. Offers applied behavior analysis (MA Ed); curriculum and instruction (MA Ed); foundations of education (MA Ed); special education (MA Ed). *Program availability:* Part-time. *Degree requirements:* For master's, thesis or alternative, exit interview. *Entrance requirements:* For master's, interview. Additional exam requirements/recommendations for international students: Required—TOEFL. *Application deadline:* For fall admission, 5/1 for domestic students, 2/1 for international students. Applications are processed on a rolling basis. Electronic applications accepted. *Expenses:* Tuition, state resident: part-time $555 per credit. Tuition, nonresident: part-time $800 per credit. *Financial support:* Scholarships/grants and unspecified assistantships available. Financial award application deadline: 3/1; financial award applicants required to submit FAFSA. *Unit head:* Dr. Kathleen Brinegar, Chair, Department of Education, 802-635-1472, Fax: 802-635-1465, E-mail: kathleen.brinegar@jsc.edu. *Application contact:* Catherine H. Higley, Administrative Assistant, 800-635-2356 Ext. 1244, Fax: 802-635-1248, E-mail: catherine.higley@jsc.edu.
Website: http://www.jsc.edu/academics/education/majors-and-minors/master-of-arts-in-education/

Johnson University, Graduate and Professional Programs, Knoxville, TN 37998-1001. Offers biblical interpretation (Graduate Certificate); business administration (MBA); Christian ministries (Graduate Certificate); clinical mental health counseling (MA); educational technology (MA); intercultural studies (MA); leadership (MBA); leadership studies (PhD); New Testament (MA); nonprofit management (MBA); school counseling (MA); spiritual formation and leadership (Graduate Certificate); strategic ministry (MA); teacher education (MA). *Program availability:* Part-time, evening/weekend, 100% online, blended/hybrid learning. *Faculty:* 26 full-time (10 women), 32 part-time/adjunct (9 women). *Students:* 126 full-time (46 women), 170 part-time (65 women); includes 33 minority (13 Black or African American, non-Hispanic/Latino; 1 American Indian or Alaska Native, non-Hispanic/Latino; 4 Asian, non-Hispanic/Latino; 8 Hispanic/Latino; 7 Two or more races, non-Hispanic/Latino), 21 international. Average age 35. In 2016, 106 master's, 3 doctorates awarded. *Degree requirements:* For master's, variable foreign language requirement, comprehensive exam, thesis (for some programs), internships; for doctorate, variable foreign language requirement, comprehensive exam, thesis/dissertation, internships. *Entrance requirements:* For master's, PRAXIS (for MA in teacher education); MAT (for counseling); GRE or GMAT (for MBA), interview, 3 references, transcripts, essay, minimum GPA of 2.5 or 3.0 (depending on program); for doctorate, GRE or MAT (taken not less than 5 years prior), interview, 3 references, transcripts, essay, minimum GPA of 3.0; for Graduate Certificate, interview, 3 references, transcripts, essay, minimum GPA of 3.0. Additional exam requirements/

recommendations for international students: Required—TOEFL (minimum score 527 paper-based; 71 iBT). *Application deadline:* For fall admission, 7/1 for domestic students; for spring admission, 11/1 for domestic students; for summer admission, 4/1 for domestic students. Application fee: $50. Electronic applications accepted. *Expenses:* Contact institution. *Financial support:* Scholarships/grants available. Financial award application deadline: 4/15; financial award applicants required to submit FAFSA. *Unit head:* Richard Clark, Vice President for External Relations, 865-251-2327, E-mail: rclark@johnsonu.edu. *Application contact:* Lisa Tarwater, Director of Graduate Admissions, 865-251-3400, E-mail: ltarwater@johnsonu.edu.

Kansas State University, Graduate School, College of Education, Manhattan, KS 66506. Offers MS, Ed D, PhD, Certificate. *Accreditation:* NCATE. *Program availability:* Part-time, evening/weekend, online learning. *Faculty:* 43 full-time (28 women), 14 part-time/adjunct (7 women). *Students:* 209 full-time (123 women), 646 part-time (452 women); includes 169 minority (62 Black or African American, non-Hispanic/Latino; 10 American Indian or Alaska Native, non-Hispanic/Latino; 13 Asian, non-Hispanic/Latino; 60 Hispanic/Latino; 3 Native Hawaiian or other Pacific Islander, non-Hispanic/Latino; 21 Two or more races, non-Hispanic/Latino), 27 international. Average age 36. 439 applicants, 84% accepted, 258 enrolled. In 2016, 305 master's, 18 doctorates, 81 other advanced degrees awarded. Terminal master's awarded for partial completion of doctoral program. *Degree requirements:* For master's, thesis or alternative, oral or comprehensive exam; for doctorate, thesis/dissertation, residency. *Entrance requirements:* For master's and doctorate, GRE or MAT. Additional exam requirements/recommendations for international students: Required—GRE General Test or TOEFL. *Application deadline:* For fall admission, 2/1 priority date for domestic and international students; for spring admission, 8/1 priority date for domestic and international students. Applications are processed on a rolling basis. Application fee: $50 ($75 for international students). Electronic applications accepted. *Expenses:* Tuition, state resident: full-time $9670. Tuition, nonresident: full-time $21,828. *Required fees:* $862. *Financial support:* In 2016–17, 10 research assistantships (averaging $14,458 per year), 16 teaching assistantships with full tuition reimbursements (averaging $13,015 per year) were awarded; career-related internships or fieldwork, Federal Work-Study, institutionally sponsored loans, and scholarships/grants also available. Support available to part-time students. Financial award application deadline: 3/1; financial award applicants required to submit FAFSA. *Faculty research:* Teacher preparation, program evaluation, science education, ESL-bilingual education, rural issues in education. *Total annual research expenditures:* $6.1 million. *Unit head:* Dr. Debbie Mercer, Dean, 785-532-5525, Fax: 785-532-7304, E-mail: edcoll@ksu.edu. *Application contact:* Dr. Linda P. Thurston, Associate Dean for Research and Graduate Studies, 785-532-5765, E-mail: coegrads@ksu.edu.
Website: http://coe.k-state.edu/

Kaplan University, Davenport Campus, School of Teacher Education, Davenport, IA 52807. Offers education (M Ed); secondary education (M Ed); teaching and learning (MA); teaching literacy and language: grades 6-12 (MA); teaching literacy and language: grades K-6 (MA); teaching mathematics: grades 6-8 (MA); teaching mathematics: grades 9-12 (MA); teaching mathematics: grades K-5 (MA); teaching science: grades 6-12 (MA); teaching science: grades K-6 (MA); teaching students with special needs (MA); teaching with technology (MA). *Program availability:* Part-time, evening/weekend, online learning. *Entrance requirements:* Additional exam requirements/recommendations for international students: Required—TOEFL (minimum score 550 paper-based; 80 iBT).

Kean University, College of Education, Union, NJ 07083. Offers MA, MS. *Accreditation:* NCATE. *Program availability:* Part-time. *Faculty:* 46 full-time (29 women). *Students:* 30 full-time (21 women), 145 part-time (115 women); includes 72 minority (14 Black or African American, non-Hispanic/Latino; 14 Asian, non-Hispanic/Latino; 43 Hispanic/Latino; 1 Two or more races, non-Hispanic/Latino), 2 international. Average age 33. 272 applicants, 55% accepted, 151 enrolled. In 2016, 91 master's awarded. *Degree requirements:* For master's, comprehensive exam, thesis, practicum, portfolio, field experience. *Entrance requirements:* Additional exam requirements/recommendations for international students: Required—TOEFL (minimum score 550 paper-based; 79 iBT), IELTS (minimum score 6.5). *Application deadline:* For fall admission, 6/1 for domestic and international students; for spring admission, 12/1 for domestic and international students. Applications are processed on a rolling basis. Application fee: $75. Electronic applications accepted. *Expenses:* Tuition, state resident: full-time $13,156; part-time $640 per credit. Tuition, nonresident: full-time $17,831; part-time $785 per credit. *Required fees:* $3316; $151 per credit. Tuition and fees vary according to course level, course load, degree level and program. *Financial support:* Scholarships/grants and unspecified assistantships available. Financial award applicants required to submit FAFSA. *Unit head:* Dr. Anthony Pitmann, Acting Dean, 908-737-3750, Fax: 908-737-3760, E-mail: polirsts@kean.edu. *Application contact:* Brittany Gerstenhaber, Admissions Counselor, 908-737-7100, E-mail: grad-adm@kean.edu.
Website: http://www.kean.edu/KU/College-of-Education

Keene State College, School of Professional and Graduate Studies, Keene, NH 03435. Offers curriculum and instruction (M Ed); education leadership (PMC); educational leadership (M Ed); safety and occupational health applied science (MS); school counselor (M Ed, PMC); special education (M Ed). *Accreditation:* NCATE. *Program availability:* Part-time, evening/weekend. *Faculty:* 9 full-time (4 women), 8 part-time/adjunct (3 women). *Students:* 24 full-time (17 women), 66 part-time (38 women); includes 3 minority (1 Black or African American, non-Hispanic/Latino; 1 Hispanic/Latino; 1 Two or more races, non-Hispanic/Latino), 1 international. Average age 33. 24 applicants, 100% accepted, 24 enrolled. In 2016, 26 master's, 1 other advanced degree awarded. *Degree requirements:* For master's, thesis (for some programs). *Entrance requirements:* For master's, PRAXIS I, 3 references; official transcripts; minimum GPA of 2.5; interview; essay; teacher/educator certificate; work/internship experience. Additional exam requirements/recommendations for international students: Required—TOEFL (minimum score 550 paper-based; 61 iBT). *Application deadline:* For fall admission, 4/1 for domestic and international students; for spring admission, 11/1 for domestic and international students; for summer admission, 3/1 for domestic and international students. Applications are processed on a rolling basis. Application fee: $50. Electronic applications accepted. *Expenses:* Tuition, state resident: full-time $9180; part-time $510 per credit. Tuition, nonresident: full-time $10,080; part-time $560 per credit. *Required fees:* $1908; $106 per credit. Tuition and fees vary according to course load. *Financial support:* In 2016–17, 27 students received support. Career-related internships or fieldwork, Federal Work-Study, institutionally sponsored loans, scholarships/grants, and unspecified assistantships available. Support available to part-time students. Financial award application deadline: 3/1; financial award applicants required to submit FAFSA. *Unit head:* Dr. Karrie Kalich, Dean of Professional and Graduate Studies, 603-358-2885, E-mail: kkalich@keene.edu. *Application contact:* Peter Tandy, Assistant Director for Graduate Studies, 603-358-2332, E-mail: kscgraduatestudies@keene.edu.
Website: http://www.keene.edu/academics/graduate/

Keiser University, Master of Science in Education Program, Ft. Lauderdale, FL 33309. Offers allied health teaching and leadership (MS Ed); career college administration (MS Ed); leadership (MS Ed); online teaching and learning (MS Ed); teaching and learning (MS Ed). *Program availability:* Part-time, online learning.

Kennesaw State University, Leland and Clarice C. Bagwell College of Education, Kennesaw, GA 30144. Offers M Ed, MAT, Ed D, Ed S. *Accreditation:* NCATE. *Program availability:* Part-time. *Degree requirements:* For master's, thesis or alternative. *Entrance requirements:* For master's, GRE General Test, minimum GPA of 2.75, renewable teaching certificate. Additional exam requirements/recommendations for international students: Required—TOEFL (minimum score 550 paper-based; 80 iBT), IELTS (minimum score 6.5). Electronic applications accepted.

Kent State University, College of Education, Health and Human Services, Kent, OH 44242-0001. Offers M Ed, MA, MAT, MS, Au D, PhD, Ed S. *Accreditation:* NCATE. *Program availability:* Part-time, evening/weekend, online learning. *Degree requirements:* For master's, thesis (for some programs); for doctorate, comprehensive exam, thesis/dissertation. *Entrance requirements:* For doctorate and Ed S, GRE General Test. Additional exam requirements/recommendations for international students: Required—TOEFL (minimum score 550 paper-based; 80 iBT). Electronic applications accepted. *Expenses:* Tuition, state resident: full-time $10,864; part-time $495 per credit hour. Tuition, nonresident: full-time $18,380; part-time $837 per credit hour.

Kent State University at Stark, Graduate School of Education, Health and Human Services, Canton, OH 44720-7599. Offers curriculum and instruction studies (M Ed, MA).

King's College, Program in Education, Wilkes-Barre, PA 18711-0801. Offers M Ed. *Accreditation:* NCATE. *Program availability:* Part-time, evening/weekend. *Degree requirements:* For master's, thesis. *Entrance requirements:* Additional exam requirements/recommendations for international students: Required—TOEFL (minimum score 600 paper-based).

Kutztown University of Pennsylvania, College of Education, Kutztown, PA 19530-0730. Offers M Ed, MA, MLS, MS. *Accreditation:* NCATE. *Program availability:* Part-time, evening/weekend. *Faculty:* 25 full-time (17 women), 3 part-time/adjunct (1 woman). *Students:* 168 full-time (139 women), 348 part-time (277 women); includes 51 minority (19 Black or African American, non-Hispanic/Latino; 5 Asian, non-Hispanic/Latino; 22 Hispanic/Latino; 5 Two or more races, non-Hispanic/Latino), 1 international. Average age 30. 373 applicants, 88% accepted, 187 enrolled. In 2016, 161 master's awarded. *Degree requirements:* For master's, comprehensive exam. *Entrance requirements:* For master's, GRE. Additional exam requirements/recommendations for international students: Required—TOEFL (minimum score 550 paper-based, 79 iBT) or IELTS (minimum score 6.5). *Application deadline:* For fall admission, 8/1 for domestic and international students; for spring admission, 12/1 for domestic and international students. Application fee: $35. Electronic applications accepted. *Expenses:* Tuition, state resident: full-time $4347; part-time $483 per credit. Tuition, nonresident: full-time $6525; part-time $725 per credit. *Required fees:* $88 per credit. One-time fee: $50 full-time. *Financial support:* Career-related internships or fieldwork, Federal Work-Study, scholarships/grants, and unspecified assistantships available. Financial award application deadline: 3/1; financial award applicants required to submit FAFSA. *Unit head:* Dr. Kenneth Teitelbaum, Dean, 610-683-4253, Fax: 610-683-4255, E-mail: teitelba@kutztown.edu.
Website: http://www.kutztown.edu/Education

LaGrange College, Graduate Programs, Department of Education, LaGrange, GA 30240-2999. Offers curriculum and instruction (M Ed, Ed S); middle grades (MAT); secondary education (MAT). *Program availability:* Part-time, evening/weekend. *Degree requirements:* For master's, comprehensive exam. *Entrance requirements:* For master's, GRE, MAT, minimum GPA of 2.5. Additional exam requirements/recommendations for international students: Required—TOEFL (minimum score 550 paper-based).

Lake Erie College, School of Education and Professional Studies, Painesville, OH 44077-3389. Offers M Ed. *Accreditation:* TEAC. *Program availability:* Part-time, evening/weekend. *Degree requirements:* For master's, comprehensive exam (for some programs), thesis optional, applied research project. *Entrance requirements:* For master's, GRE General Test (minimum score of 440 verbal or 500 quantitative) or minimum GPA of 2.75, bachelor's degree from accredited 4-year institution; references; essay. Additional exam requirements/recommendations for international students: Required—TOEFL (minimum score 550 paper-based; 79 iBT), IELTS (minimum score 6), STEP Eiken 1st and pre-1st grade level (for Japanese students). Electronic applications accepted. Application fee is waived when completed online. *Expenses:* Contact institution.

Lake Forest College, Master of Arts in Teaching Program, Lake Forest, IL 60045. Offers elementary education (MAT); K-12 French (MAT); K-12 music (MAT); K-12 Spanish (MAT); K-12 visual art (MAT); secondary biology (MAT); secondary chemistry (MAT); secondary English (MAT); secondary history (MAT); secondary mathematics (MAT). *Degree requirements:* For master's, comprehensive exam, portfolio. *Entrance requirements:* For master's, GRE.

Lakehead University, Graduate Studies, Faculty of Education, Thunder Bay, ON P7B 5E1, Canada. Offers educational studies (PhD); gerontology (M Ed); women's studies (M Ed). *Program availability:* Part-time, evening/weekend. *Degree requirements:* For master's, project or thesis. *Entrance requirements:* For master's, minimum B average. Additional exam requirements/recommendations for international students: Required—TOEFL. *Faculty research:* Art education, AIDS education, language arts education, gerontology, women's studies.

Lakeland University, Graduate Studies Division, Program in Education, Plymouth, WI 53073. Offers M Ed. *Accreditation:* TEAC. *Degree requirements:* For master's, thesis. *Expenses:* Contact institution.

Lamar University, College of Graduate Studies, College of Education and Human Development, Beaumont, TX 77710. Offers M Ed, MS, Ed D, Certificate. *Accreditation:* NCATE. *Program availability:* Part-time, evening/weekend, online learning. *Faculty:* 72 full-time (51 women), 29 part-time/adjunct (17 women). *Students:* 95 full-time (65 women), 4,039 part-time (3,122 women); includes 1,731 minority (829 Black or African American, non-Hispanic/Latino; 14 American Indian or Alaska Native, non-Hispanic/Latino; 56 Asian, non-Hispanic/Latino; 754 Hispanic/Latino; 3 Native Hawaiian or other Pacific Islander, non-Hispanic/Latino; 75 Two or more races, non-Hispanic/Latino), 18 international. Average age 37. 1,904 applicants, 93% accepted, 1051 enrolled. In 2016, 1,849 master's, 82 doctorates, 17 other advanced degrees awarded. *Degree requirements:* For master's, comprehensive exam, thesis optional; for doctorate, comprehensive exam, thesis/dissertation. *Entrance requirements:* For master's, GRE General Test, minimum GPA of 2.5; for doctorate, GRE, interview. Additional exam requirements/recommendations for international students: Required—TOEFL (minimum score 550 paper-based; 79 iBT), IELTS (minimum score 6.5). *Application deadline:* For fall admission, 8/10 for domestic students, 7/1 for international students; for spring admission, 1/5 for domestic students, 12/1 for international students. Applications are processed on a rolling basis. Application fee: $25 ($50 for international students). Electronic applications accepted. *Expenses:* $8,134 in-state full-time, $5,574 in-state part-time; $15,604 out-of-state full-time, $10,554 out-of-state part-time per year. *Financial support:* Fellowships, research assistantships, teaching assistantships, career-related internships or fieldwork, Federal Work-Study, institutionally sponsored loans, and scholarships/grants available. Support available to part-time students.

Financial award application deadline: 4/1; financial award applicants required to submit FAFSA. *Faculty research:* School dropouts, suicide prevention in public school students, school climate and gifted performance, teacher evaluation. *Unit head:* Dr. Robert Spina, Dean, 409-880-8661. *Application contact:* Deidre Mayer, Interim Director, Admissions and Academic Services, 409-880-8888, Fax: 409-880-7419, E-mail: gradmissions@lamar.edu.
Website: http://education.lamar.edu

Lander University, Graduate Studies, Greenwood, SC 29649-2099. Offers clinical nurse leader (MSN); emergency management (MS); Montessori education (M Ed); teaching and learning (M Ed). *Accreditation:* NCATE. *Program availability:* Part-time, online learning. *Degree requirements:* For master's, comprehensive exam, thesis or alternative. *Entrance requirements:* For master's, GRE General Test. Additional exam requirements/recommendations for international students: Required—TOEFL (minimum score 550 paper-based). Electronic applications accepted.

Langston University, School of Education and Behavioral Sciences, Langston, OK 73050. Offers bilingual/multicultural (M Ed); elementary education (M Ed); English as a second language (M Ed); rehabilitation counseling (M Sc); urban education (M Ed). *Accreditation:* CORE; NCATE (one or more programs are accredited). *Program availability:* Part-time. *Degree requirements:* For master's, comprehensive exam, thesis optional. *Entrance requirements:* For master's, GRE, writing skills test, minimum GPA of 2.5, 3 letters of recommendation. Additional exam requirements/recommendations for international students: Required—TOEFL, TWE. *Faculty research:* Bilingual/multicultural education, financing post-secondary education.

La Salle University, School of Arts and Sciences, Program in Education, Philadelphia, PA 19141-1199. Offers autism spectrum disorders (MA, Certificate); bilingual/bicultural studies (MA); classroom management (MA); dual early childhood and special education (MA); dual middle-level science and math and special education (MA); education (MA); English (MA); English as a second language (Certificate); history (MA); instructional coach (Certificate); instructional leadership (MA); reading specialist (MA, Certificate); secondary education (MA); special education (MA, Certificate). *Program availability:* Part-time, evening/weekend. *Faculty:* 5 full-time (4 women), 12 part-time/adjunct (8 women). *Students:* 10 full-time (all women), 98 part-time (74 women); includes 28 minority (13 Black or African American, non-Hispanic/Latino; 1 American Indian or Alaska Native, non-Hispanic/Latino; 1 Asian, non-Hispanic/Latino; 10 Hispanic/Latino; 3 Two or more races, non-Hispanic/Latino). Average age 34. 128 applicants, 84% accepted, 69 enrolled. In 2016, 53 master's awarded. *Degree requirements:* For master's, comprehensive exam. *Entrance requirements:* For master's, MAT or GRE, 2 letters of recommendation; for Certificate, GMAT or GRE, 2 letters of recommendation. Additional exam requirements/recommendations for international students: Required—TOEFL. *Application deadline:* For fall admission, 8/15 priority date for domestic students, 7/15 for international students; for spring admission, 12/15 priority date for domestic students, 11/15 for international students; for summer admission, 4/15 priority date for domestic students, 3/15 for international students. Applications are processed on a rolling basis. Application fee: $35. Electronic applications accepted. Application fee is waived when completed online. *Expenses:* Contact institution. *Financial support:* In 2016–17, 27 students received support. Scholarships/grants available. Support available to part-time students. Financial award application deadline: 8/31; financial award applicants required to submit FAFSA. *Unit head:* Dr. Greer Richardson, Director, 215-951-1806, Fax: 215-951-1843, E-mail: graded@lasalle.edu. *Application contact:* Elizabeth Heenan, Director, Graduate and Adult Enrollment, 215-951-1100, Fax: 215-951-1462, E-mail: heenan@lasalle.edu.
Website: http://www.lasalle.edu/grad-education-programs/

Lasell College, Graduate and Professional Studies in Education, Newton, MA 02466. Offers elementary education (M Ed); special education (M Ed), including moderate disabilities. *Program availability:* Part-time-only, evening/weekend, blended/hybrid learning. *Faculty:* 3 full-time (all women), 6 part-time/adjunct (5 women). *Students:* 4 full-time (3 women), 45 part-time (40 women); includes 2 minority (1 Hispanic/Latino; 1 Two or more races, non-Hispanic/Latino). Average age 28. 31 applicants, 58% accepted, 9 enrolled. In 2016, 12 master's awarded. *Degree requirements:* For master's, minimum GPA of 3.0; practicum. *Entrance requirements:* For master's, Massachusetts Tests for Educator Licensure (MTEL) Curriculum and Literacy foundations of reading and writing subtest, one-page personal statement, 2 letters of recommendation, resume, bachelor's degree transcript. Additional exam requirements/recommendations for international students: Required—TOEFL (minimum score 550 paper-based, 79 iBT) or IELTS (minimum score 6). *Application deadline:* For fall admission, 8/31 priority date for domestic students, 6/30 priority date for international students; for spring admission, 12/31 priority date for domestic students, 10/31 priority date for international students. Applications are processed on a rolling basis. Electronic applications accepted. *Expenses:* $600 per credit. *Financial support:* In 2016–17, 13 students received support. Federal Work-Study, scholarships/grants, and tuition discounts available. Support available to part-time students. Financial award application deadline: 8/31; financial award applicants required to submit FAFSA. *Faculty research:* Inclusion, English language learners, literacy, and urban education; teacher inquiry; universal design for learning, deaf-blindness, and visual impairments; social and emotional learning; educational law, applied behavior analysis, and classroom management. *Unit head:* Dr. Joan Dolamore, Dean of Graduate and Professional Studies, 617-243-2485, Fax: 617-243-2450, E-mail: gradinfo@lasell.edu. *Application contact:* Adrienne Franciosi, Director of Graduate Enrollment, 617-243-2214, Fax: 617-243-2450, E-mail: gradinfo@lasell.edu.
Website: http://www.lasell.edu/academics/graduate-and-professional-studies/programs-of-study/master-of-education.html

La Sierra University, School of Education, Riverside, CA 92515. Offers MA, MAT, Ed D, Ed S. *Program availability:* Part-time, evening/weekend. Terminal master's awarded for partial completion of doctoral program. *Degree requirements:* For doctorate, thesis/dissertation; for Ed S, thesis optional. *Entrance requirements:* For master's, minimum GPA of 3.0; for doctorate, GRE General Test, GRE Subject Test, minimum GPA of 3.3; for Ed S, minimum GPA of 3.3.

Lee University, Program in Education, Cleveland, TN 37320-3450. Offers art (MAT); curriculum and instruction (M Ed, Ed S); early childhood (MAT); educational leadership (M Ed, Ed S); elementary education (MAT); English and math (MAT); English and science (MAT); English and social studies (MAT); higher education administration (MS); history (MAT); history and economics (MAT); math and science (MAT); math and social studies (MAT); middle grades (MAT); science and social studies (MASW); secondary education (MAT); Spanish (MAT); special education (M Ed, MAT); TESOL (MAT). *Accreditation:* NCATE. *Program availability:* Part-time. *Faculty:* 13 full-time (6 women), 9 part-time/adjunct (4 women). *Students:* 35 full-time (27 women), 50 part-time (32 women); includes 12 minority (5 Black or African American, non-Hispanic/Latino; 5 Hispanic/Latino; 2 Two or more races, non-Hispanic/Latino), 4 international. Average age 30. 43 applicants, 79% accepted, 28 enrolled. In 2016, 42 master's, 6 other advanced degrees awarded. *Degree requirements:* For master's, variable foreign language requirement, thesis optional, internship. *Entrance requirements:* For master's, MAT or GRE General Test, minimum undergraduate GPA of 2.75, 3 letters of recommendation, interview, writing sample, official transcripts, background check; for Ed S, minimum undergraduate and master's GPA of 2.75, official transcripts for undergraduate and master's degrees. Additional exam requirements/recommendations for international students: Required—TOEFL (minimum score 61 iBT). *Application deadline:* For fall admission, 6/1 priority date for domestic and international students; for spring admission, 11/1 priority date for domestic and international students; for summer admission, 4/1 priority date for domestic and international students. Applications are processed on a rolling basis. Application fee: $25. Electronic applications accepted. *Expenses: Tuition:* Full-time $11,367; part-time $632 per credit hour. *Required fees:* $35 per term. One-time fee: $25. Tuition and fees vary according to program. *Financial support:* In 2016–17, 42 students received support. Career-related internships or fieldwork, Federal Work-Study, institutionally sponsored loans, scholarships/grants, and unspecified assistantships available. Financial award application deadline: 3/1; financial award applicants required to submit FAFSA. *Unit head:* Dr. William Kamm, Director, 423-614-8544, E-mail: wkamm@leeuniversity.edu. *Application contact:* Crystal Keeter, Graduate Education Secretary, 423-614-8544, E-mail: ckeeter@leeuniversity.edu.
Website: http://www.leeuniversity.edu/academics/graduate/education

Lehigh University, College of Education, Bethlehem, PA 18015. Offers M Ed, MA, MS, Ed D, PhD, Certificate, Ed S, Graduate Certificate, M Ed/MA, MBA/M Ed. *Program availability:* Part-time, evening/weekend, 100% online, blended/hybrid learning. *Faculty:* 36 full-time (22 women), 23 part-time/adjunct (16 women). *Students:* 159 full-time (137 women), 291 part-time (212 women); includes 50 minority (13 Black or African American, non-Hispanic/Latino; 12 Asian, non-Hispanic/Latino; 22 Hispanic/Latino; 1 Native Hawaiian or other Pacific Islander, non-Hispanic/Latino; 2 Two or more races, non-Hispanic/Latino), 43 international. Average age 32. 496 applicants, 55% accepted, 74 enrolled. In 2016, 138 master's, 18 doctorates, 5 other advanced degrees awarded. Terminal master's awarded for partial completion of doctoral program. *Degree requirements:* For master's, thesis (for some programs), internship; for doctorate, comprehensive exam, thesis/dissertation, internship. *Entrance requirements:* For master's, essay, transcripts, 2 recommendation letters; for doctorate, GRE and/or MAT. Additional exam requirements/recommendations for international students: Required—TOEFL (minimum score 600 paper-based; 93 iBT). *Application deadline:* For fall admission, 1/1 for domestic and international students; for spring admission, 11/1 for domestic and international students; for summer admission, 5/1 for domestic and international students. Application fee: $65. Electronic applications accepted. *Expenses:* $565 per credit. *Financial support:* In 2016–17, 162 students received support, including 3 fellowships with tuition reimbursements available (averaging $21,556 per year), 47 research assistantships with tuition reimbursements available (averaging $12,882 per year); teaching assistantships, career-related internships or fieldwork, institutionally sponsored loans, scholarships/grants, tuition waivers (partial), and unspecified assistantships also available. Financial award application deadline: 3/1. *Faculty research:* Urban educational leadership, special education, instructional technology, school and counseling psychology, international education. *Unit head:* Dr. Gary M. Sasso, Dean, 610-758-3221, Fax: 610-758-6223, E-mail: gary.sasso@lehigh.edu. *Application contact:* Donna M. Johnson, Manager of Admissions and Recruitment, 610-758-3231, Fax: 610-758-6223, E-mail: dmj4@lehigh.edu.
Website: http://coe.lehigh.edu

Lehman College of the City University of New York, School of Education, Bronx, NY 10468-1589. Offers MA, MS Ed. *Accreditation:* NCATE. *Program availability:* Part-time, evening/weekend.

Le Moyne College, Department of Education, Syracuse, NY 13214. Offers adolescent education (MS Ed, MST); adolescent education/special education (MS Ed, MST); adolescent English (MST), including grades 7-12; adolescent English/special education (MST), including grades 7-12; adolescent foreign language (MST), including grades 7-12; adolescent history (MST), including grades 7-12; childhood education (MS Ed); childhood education/special education (MS Ed); elementary education (MS Ed); general education (MS Ed); inclusive childhood education (MST); literacy education (MS Ed), including birth to grade 6, grades 5-12; school building leader (MS Ed); school building leadership (CAS); school district business leader (MS Ed, CAS); school district leader (MS Ed); school district leadership (CAS); secondary education (MS Ed); special education (MS Ed); teaching English to speakers of other languages (MS Ed); urban studies (MS Ed). *Accreditation:* TEAC. *Program availability:* Part-time, evening/weekend. *Faculty:* 8 full-time (5 women), 20 part-time/adjunct (12 women). *Students:* 66 full-time (40 women), 155 part-time (117 women); includes 13 minority (4 Black or African American, non-Hispanic/Latino; 2 American Indian or Alaska Native, non-Hispanic/Latino; 2 Asian, non-Hispanic/Latino; 5 Hispanic/Latino), 3 international. Average age 30. 74 applicants, 99% accepted, 66 enrolled. In 2016, 81 master's, 53 CASs awarded. *Degree requirements:* For master's, thesis. *Entrance requirements:* For master's, bachelor's degree with minimum undergraduate GPA of 3.0, 2 letters of recommendation, transcripts. Additional exam requirements/recommendations for international students: Required—TOEFL (minimum score 550 paper-based; 79 iBT); Recommended—IELTS (minimum score 6.5). *Application deadline:* For fall admission, 4/1 priority date for domestic and international students; for spring admission, 10/1 priority date for domestic and international students; for summer admission, 3/1 priority date for domestic and international students. Applications are processed on a rolling basis. Application fee: $50. Electronic applications accepted. *Expenses:* $700 per credit hour. *Financial support:* In 2016–17, 21 students received support. Career-related internships or fieldwork, scholarships/grants, and health care benefits available. Support available to part-time students. Financial award applicants required to submit FAFSA. *Faculty research:* Minority teachers, special education, multiculturalism, literacy, technology, media literacy learning, autism, school district organization, service-learning, higher level problem solving, teacher leadership. *Unit head:* Dr. Stephen C. Fleury, Chair, Department of Education, 315-445-4376, Fax: 315-445-4744, E-mail: fleurysc@lemoyne.edu. *Application contact:* Kristen P. Richards, Senior Director of Enrollment Management, 315-445-5444, Fax: 315-445-6092, E-mail: trapaskp@lemoyne.edu.
Website: http://www.lemoyne.edu/education

Lenoir-Rhyne University, Graduate Programs, School of Education, Hickory, NC 28601. Offers MA, MAT, MS. *Accreditation:* NCATE. *Program availability:* Part-time, evening/weekend, online learning. *Degree requirements:* For master's, comprehensive exam, thesis optional. *Entrance requirements:* Additional exam requirements/recommendations for international students: Required—TOEFL. Electronic applications accepted. *Expenses:* Contact institution.

Lesley University, Graduate School of Education, Cambridge, MA 02138-2790. Offers arts, community, and education (M Ed); autism studies (Certificate); curriculum and instruction (M Ed, CAGS); early childhood education (M Ed); ecological teaching and learning (MS); educational studies (PhD), including adult learning, educational leadership, individually designed; elementary education (M Ed); emergent technologies for educators (Certificate); ESLArts: language learning through the arts (M Ed); high school education (M Ed); individually designed (M Ed); integrated teaching through the arts (M Ed); literacy for K-8 classroom teachers (M Ed); mathematics education (M Ed); middle school education (M Ed); moderate disabilities (M Ed); online learning (Certificate); reading (CAGS); science in education (M Ed); severe disabilities (M Ed); special needs (CAGS); specialist teacher of reading (M Ed); teacher of visual art (M Ed);

technology in education (M Ed, CAGS). *Accreditation:* TEAC. *Program availability:* Part-time, evening/weekend, online learning. *Degree requirements:* For master's, practicum; for doctorate, thesis/dissertation. *Entrance requirements:* For master's, Massachusetts Tests for Educator Licensure (MTEL), transcripts, statement of purpose, recommendations; interview (for special education); for doctorate, GRE General Test, transcripts, statement of purpose, recommendations, interview, master's degree, resume; for other advanced degree, interview, master's degree. Additional exam requirements/recommendations for international students: Required—TOEFL (minimum score 550 paper-based; 80 iBT). Electronic applications accepted. *Faculty research:* Assessment in literacy, mathematics and science; autism spectrum disorders; instructional technology and online learning; multicultural education and English language learners.

Lewis University, College of Education, Romeoville, IL 60446. Offers M Ed, MA, Ed D. *Accreditation:* NCATE. *Program availability:* Part-time, evening/weekend. *Students:* 38 full-time (25 women), 187 part-time (135 women); includes 54 minority (26 Black or African American, non-Hispanic/Latino; 1 Asian, non-Hispanic/Latino; 26 Hispanic/Latino; 1 Two or more races, non-Hispanic/Latino), 11 international. *Degree requirements:* For master's, thesis optional, departmental qualifying exam; for doctorate, thesis/dissertation. *Entrance requirements:* For master's, writing exam, minimum GPA of 2.75, 3 letters of recommendation, interview. Additional exam requirements/recommendations for international students: Required—TOEFL (minimum score 550 paper-based; 80 iBT). *Application deadline:* For fall admission, 5/1 priority date for international students; for spring admission, 11/15 priority date for international students. Applications are processed on a rolling basis. Application fee: $40. Electronic applications accepted. *Expenses: Tuition:* Full-time $13,860; part-time $770 per credit hour. *Required fees:* $75 per semester. Tuition and fees vary according to degree level and program. *Financial support:* Career-related internships or fieldwork, Federal Work-Study, scholarships/grants, tuition waivers (partial), and unspecified assistantships available. Financial award application deadline: 5/1; financial award applicants required to submit FAFSA. *Total annual research expenditures:* $34. *Unit head:* Dr. Pamela Jessee, Dean, 815-836-5316, E-mail: jesseepa@lewisu.edu. *Application contact:* Linda Campbell, Graduate Admission Counselor, 815-836-5704, Fax: 815-836-5578, E-mail: campbeli@lewisu.edu.

Liberty University, School of Education, Lynchburg, VA 24515. Offers educational leadership (Ed D); gifted education (Certificate); math specialist (M Ed); middle grades (MAT, Certificate); reading specialist (M Ed); school leadership (Certificate); secondary education (MAT); sport management (MS), including administration, outdoor recreation, sport management, tourism. *Accreditation:* NCATE. *Program availability:* Part-time, online learning. *Students:* 1,910 full-time (1,427 women), 4,420 part-time (3,311 women); includes 1,451 minority (1,182 Black or African American, non-Hispanic/Latino; 33 American Indian or Alaska Native, non-Hispanic/Latino; 44 Asian, non-Hispanic/Latino; 46 Hispanic/Latino; 11 Native Hawaiian or other Pacific Islander, non-Hispanic/Latino; 135 Two or more races, non-Hispanic/Latino), 87 international. Average age 37. 5,120 applicants, 44% accepted, 1193 enrolled. In 2016, 1,378 master's, 151 doctorates, 497 other advanced degrees awarded. *Degree requirements:* For doctorate, comprehensive exam, thesis/dissertation. *Entrance requirements:* For master's, GRE General Test or MAT (if taken in or before 1999), 2 letters of recommendation, minimum undergraduate GPA of 3.0, curriculum vitae; for doctorate and Certificate, GRE General Test or MAT (if taken before 1999), minimum master's GPA of 3.0, 3 years of teaching experience. Additional exam requirements/recommendations for international students: Required—TOEFL (minimum score 600 paper-based; 100 iBT). *Application deadline:* For fall admission, 6/1 for domestic students; for spring admission, 11/1 for domestic students. Applications are processed on a rolling basis. Application fee: $50. Electronic applications accepted. *Expenses:* Contact institution. *Financial support:* Federal Work-Study and tuition waivers (partial) available. *Faculty research:* Self-determination, character education, bibliotherapy, learning styles, distance education. *Unit head:* Dr. Heather Schoffstall, Dean, 434-582-2445, Fax: 434-582-2468, E-mail: awgunter@liberty.edu. *Application contact:* Jay Bridge, Director of Graduate Admissions, 800-424-9595, Fax: 800-628-7977, E-mail: gradadmissions@liberty.edu.
Website: http://www.liberty.edu/academics/education/graduate/

Lincoln Memorial University, Carter and Moyers School of Education, Harrogate, TN 37752-1901. Offers administration and supervision (M Ed, Ed S); counseling and guidance (M Ed); curriculum and instruction (M Ed, Ed D, Ed S); English (M Ed); executive leadership (Ed D); higher education administration (Ed D); human resource development (Ed D); leadership and administration (Ed D). *Program availability:* Part-time, evening/weekend, online learning. *Degree requirements:* For master's, comprehensive exam, thesis optional; for Ed S, comprehensive exam. *Entrance requirements:* For master's, PRAXIS, NTE, GRE, MAT, letters of recommendation; for Ed S, graduate transcripts. Additional exam requirements/recommendations for international students: Recommended—TOEFL. *Faculty research:* Brain compatible teaching and learning; poverty in Appalachia; leadership for change; ethics, moral responsibility and social justice; human and organizational learning.

Lindenwood University, Graduate Programs, School of Education, St. Charles, MO 63301-1695. Offers education (MA), including autism spectrum disorders, character education, early intervention in autism and sensory impairment, gifted, technology; educational administration (MA, Ed D, Ed S); English to speakers of other languages (MA); instructional leadership (Ed D, Ed S); library media (MA); professional counseling (MA); school administration (MA, Ed S); school counseling (MA); teaching (MA). *Program availability:* Part-time, evening/weekend, 100% online, blended/hybrid learning. *Faculty:* 39 full-time (27 women), 210 part-time/adjunct (136 women). *Students:* 292 full-time (227 women), 1,580 part-time (1,203 women); includes 404 minority (333 Black or African American, non-Hispanic/Latino; 4 American Indian or Alaska Native, non-Hispanic/Latino; 10 Asian, non-Hispanic/Latino; 36 Hispanic/Latino; 1 Native Hawaiian or other Pacific Islander, non-Hispanic/Latino; 20 Two or more races, non-Hispanic/Latino), 20 international. Average age 36. 558 applicants, 72% accepted, 353 enrolled. In 2016, 491 master's, 72 doctorates, 111 other advanced degrees awarded. *Degree requirements:* For master's, thesis (for some programs), minimum GPA of 3.0; for doctorate, thesis/dissertation, minimum GPA of 3.0; for Ed S, comprehensive exam, project, minimum GPA of 3.0. *Entrance requirements:* For master's, interview, minimum undergraduate cumulative GPA of 3.0, writing sample, letter of recommendation; for doctorate, GRE, minimum graduate GPA of 3.4, resume, interview, writing sample, 4 letters of recommendation; for Ed S, master's degree in education, relevant work experience. Additional exam requirements/recommendations for international students: Required—TOEFL (minimum score 550 paper-based; 80 iBT); Recommended—IELTS (minimum score 6.5). *Application deadline:* For fall admission, 8/28 priority date for domestic and international students; for spring admission, 1/8 priority date for domestic and international students; for summer admission, 6/5 priority date for domestic and international students. Applications are processed on a rolling basis. Application fee: $30 ($100 for international students). Electronic applications accepted. *Expenses: Tuition:* Full-time $15,672; part-time $453 per credit hour. *Required fees:* $205 per semester. Tuition and fees vary according to course level, course load and degree level. *Financial support:* In 2016–17, 334 students received support. Career-related internships or fieldwork, Federal Work-Study, institutionally sponsored loans, scholarships/grants, tuition waivers (partial), and unspecified assistantships available. Financial award application deadline: 6/30; financial award applicants required to submit FAFSA. *Unit head:* Dr. Cynthia Bice, Dean, School of Education, 636-949-4618, Fax: 636-949-4197, E-mail: cbice@lindenwood.edu. *Application contact:* Tyler Kostich, Director, Evening and Graduate Admissions, 636-949-4138, Fax: 636-949-4109, E-mail: adultadmissions@lindenwood.edu.
Website: http://www.lindenwood.edu/academics/academic-schools/school-of-education/

Lindenwood University–Belleville, Graduate Programs, Belleville, IL 62226. Offers business administration (MBA); communications (MA), including digital and multimedia, media management, promotions, training and development; counseling (MA); criminal justice administration (MS); education (MA); healthcare administration (MS); human resource management (MS); school administration (MA); teaching (MAT).

Lipscomb University, College of Education, Nashville, TN 37204-3951. Offers applied behavior analysis (MS, Certificate); educational leadership (M Ed, Ed S); English language learning (M Ed, Ed S); instructional coaching (M Ed, Certificate, Ed S); instructional practice (M Ed); learning organizations and strategic change (Ed D); literacy coaching (Certificate); reading specialty (M Ed, Ed S); special education (M Ed); teaching, learning, and leading (M Ed); technology integration (M Ed, Ed S); technology integration specialist (Certificate). *Accreditation:* NCATE. *Program availability:* Part-time, evening/weekend, 100% online. *Faculty:* 21 full-time (15 women), 38 part-time/adjunct (26 women). *Students:* 111 full-time (80 women), 345 part-time (292 women); includes 104 minority (70 Black or African American, non-Hispanic/Latino; 1 American Indian or Alaska Native, non-Hispanic/Latino; 3 Asian, non-Hispanic/Latino; 20 Hispanic/Latino; 10 Two or more races, non-Hispanic/Latino), 1 international. Average age 33. In 2016, 201 master's, 36 doctorates, 86 other advanced degrees awarded. *Degree requirements:* For master's, comprehensive exam, portfolio, research project and presentation; for doctorate, practical capstone project in experiential setting. *Entrance requirements:* For master's, MAT (minimum score 31) or GRE General Test (minimum score 294), 2 reference letters, goals statement, writing sample, interview; for doctorate, MAT or GRE General Test, 3 reference letters, artifact of demonstrated academic excellence, written personal statements, interview. Additional exam requirements/recommendations for international students: Required—TOEFL (minimum score 570 paper-based; 80 iBT). *Application deadline:* For fall admission, 8/29 priority date for domestic students; for spring admission, 1/15 priority date for domestic students. Applications are processed on a rolling basis. Application fee: $50 ($75 for international students). Electronic applications accepted. *Expenses:* $934 per hour; $570 per hour (Teach for America). *Financial support:* Scholarships/grants, unspecified assistantships, and partnerships with local school districts available. Financial award applicants required to submit FAFSA. *Faculty research:* Facilitative learning styles, leadership, student assessment, interactive multimedia inclusion, learning organizations and strategic change. *Unit head:* Dr. Deborah Boyd, Director of Graduate Studies, 615-966-6263, E-mail: deborah.boyd@lipscomb.edu. *Application contact:* Amanda Logsdon, Director of Enrollment and Outreach, 615-966-7199, E-mail: amanda.logsdon@lipscomb.edu.
Website: http://www.lipscomb.edu/education/graduate-programs

Lock Haven University of Pennsylvania, College of Liberal Arts and Education, Lock Haven, PA 17745-2390. Offers alternative education (M Ed); educational leadership (M Ed); teaching and learning (M Ed). *Accreditation:* NCATE. *Program availability:* Part-time, evening/weekend, online learning. *Degree requirements:* For master's, thesis. *Entrance requirements:* For master's, minimum undergraduate GPA of 3.0. Additional exam requirements/recommendations for international students: Required—TOEFL. Electronic applications accepted.

London Metropolitan University, Graduate Programs, London, United Kingdom. Offers applied psychology (M Sc); architecture (MA); biomedical science (M Sc); blood science (M Sc); cancer pharmacology (M Sc); computer networking and cyber security (M Sc); computing and information systems (M Sc); conference interpreting (MA); counter-terrorism studies (M Sc); creative, digital and professional writing (MA); crime, violence and prevention (M Sc); criminology (M Sc); curating contemporary art (MA); data analytics (M Sc); digital media (MA); early childhood studies (MA); education (MA, Ed D); financial services law, regulation and compliance (LL M); food science (M Sc); forensic psychology (M Sc); health and social care management and policy (M Sc); human nutrition (M Sc); human resource management (MA); human rights and international conflict (MA); information technology (M Sc); intelligence and security studies (M Sc); international oil, gas and energy law (LL M); international relations (MA); interpreting (MA); learning and teaching in higher education (MA); legal practice (LL M); media and entertainment law (LL M); organizational and consumer psychology (M Sc); psychological therapy (M Sc); psychology of mental health (M Sc); public health (M Sc); public policy and management (MPA); security studies (M Sc); social work (M Sc); spatial planning and urban design (MA); sports therapy (M Sc); supporting older children and young people with dyslexia (MA); teaching languages (MA), including Arabic, English; translation (MA); woman and child abuse (MA).

Long Island University–LIU Brooklyn, School of Education, Brooklyn, NY 11201-8423. Offers adolescence urban education (MS Ed); applied behavior analysis (Advanced Certificate); bilingual education (Advanced Certificate); bilingual school counselor (MS Ed, Advanced Certificate); childhood urban education (MS Ed); childhood/early childhood urban education (MS Ed); early childhood urban education (MS Ed, Advanced Certificate); educational leadership (Advanced Certificate); marriage and family therapy (MS, Advanced Certificate); mental health counseling (MS, Advanced Certificate); school building district leader (Advanced Certificate); school counselor (MS Ed, Advanced Certificate); school psychologist (MS Ed); teaching urban children/adolescents with disabilities (MS Ed); TESOL (MS Ed). *Accreditation:* TEAC. *Program availability:* Part-time, evening/weekend. *Faculty:* 23 full-time (17 women), 44 part-time/adjunct (32 women). *Students:* 161 full-time (144 women), 594 part-time (461 women); includes 493 minority (229 Black or African American, non-Hispanic/Latino; 1 American Indian or Alaska Native, non-Hispanic/Latino; 30 Asian, non-Hispanic/Latino; 218 Hispanic/Latino; 2 Native Hawaiian or other Pacific Islander, non-Hispanic/Latino; 13 Two or more races, non-Hispanic/Latino), 9 international. 513 applicants, 73% accepted, 272 enrolled. In 2016, 262 master's, 18 other advanced degrees awarded. *Degree requirements:* For master's, thesis optional, electronic portfolio. *Entrance requirements:* For master's, GRE (for MS Ed). Additional exam requirements/recommendations for international students: Required—TOEFL (minimum score 527 paper-based; 75 iBT). *Application deadline:* Applications are processed on a rolling basis. Application fee: $50. Electronic applications accepted. *Expenses: Tuition:* Full-time $28,272; part-time $1178 per credit. *Required fees:* $451 per term. Tuition and fees vary according to degree level, program and student level. *Financial support:* In 2016–17, 81 students received support. Career-related internships or fieldwork, Federal Work-Study, institutionally sponsored loans, scholarships/grants, and unspecified assistantships available. Support available to part-time students. Financial award application deadline: 2/15; financial award applicants required to submit FAFSA. *Faculty research:* Technology in education, teaching civics and sustainability, biliteracy and dual language instruction, diversity in organizations and leadership, counseling diverse couples and families. *Unit head:* Dr. Amy Ginsberg, Dean, 718-246-6308, E-mail: amy.ginsberg@liu.edu. *Application contact:* Gabrielle Gannon, Director of Graduate

Admissions, 718-488-1011, Fax: 718-780-6110, E-mail: bkln-admissions@liu.edu.
Website: http://www.liu.edu/Brooklyn/Academics/School-of-Education

Long Island University–LIU Post, College of Education, Information and Technology, Brookville, NY 11548-1300. Offers adolescence education (MS); adolescence education 7-12 (MS); archives and records management (AC); art education (MS); childhood education (MS); childhood teaching literacy B-6 (MS); childhood/special education (MS); clinical mental health counseling (MS, AC); early childhood education (MS); early childhood education/childhood education (MS); educational leadership (AC); educational technology (MS); information studies (PhD); interdisciplinary educational studies (Ed D); middle childhood education (MS); music education (MS); school counselor (MS); special education (MS Ed); speech-language pathology (MA); students with disabilities, 7-12 generalist (AC); TESOL (MA). *Accreditation:* TEAC. *Program availability:* Part-time, 100% online, blended/hybrid learning. *Faculty:* 55 full-time (35 women), 104 part-time/adjunct (57 women). *Students:* 464 full-time (390 women), 740 part-time (580 women); includes 265 minority (99 Black or African American, non-Hispanic/Latino; 45 Asian, non-Hispanic/Latino; 113 Hispanic/Latino; 1 Native Hawaiian or other Pacific Islander, non-Hispanic/Latino; 7 Two or more races, non-Hispanic/Latino), 33 international. 928 applicants, 76% accepted, 406 enrolled. In 2016, 334 master's, 10 doctorates, 137 other advanced degrees awarded. Terminal master's awarded for partial completion of doctoral program. *Degree requirements:* For master's, variable foreign language requirement, comprehensive exam (for some programs), thesis optional; for doctorate, comprehensive exam, thesis/dissertation. *Entrance requirements:* For master's and AC, GRE. Additional exam requirements/recommendations for international students: Required—PTE, TOEFL (minimum score 550 paper-based, 75 iBT) or IELTS. *Application deadline:* Applications are processed on a rolling basis. Application fee: $50. Electronic applications accepted. *Expenses: Tuition:* Full-time $28,272; part-time $1178 per credit. *Required fees:* $451 per term. Tuition and fees vary according to degree level and program. *Financial support:* Career-related internships or fieldwork, Federal Work-Study, institutionally sponsored loans, scholarships/grants, tuition waivers (partial), and unspecified assistantships available. Support available to part-time students. Financial award application deadline: 2/15; financial award applicants required to submit FAFSA. *Faculty research:* English language learners, early childhood literacy development through play, sleep, social justice through education, using a structured protocol for discussing bad news. *Total annual research expenditures:* $575,000. *Unit head:* Dr. Albert Inserra, Dean, 516-299-2210, E-mail: albert.inserra@liu.edu. *Application contact:* Carol Zerah, Director of Graduate Admissions, 516-299-2900, Fax: 516-299-2137, E-mail: post-enroll@liu.edu.
Website: http://liu.edu/CWPost/Academics/College-of-Education-Information-and-Technology

Longwood University, College of Graduate and Professional Studies, College of Education and Human Services, Farmville, VA 23909. Offers education (MS), including algebra and middle school mathematics, counselor education, elementary and middle school mathematics, elementary education, elementary education initial licensure, health and physical education, special education general curriculum, special education initial licensure; reading, literacy and learning (M Ed); school librarianship (M Ed); social work and communication sciences and disorders (MS), including communication sciences and disorders. *Accreditation:* NCATE. *Program availability:* Part-time, evening/weekend. *Degree requirements:* For master's, comprehensive exam (for some programs), thesis optional, professional portfolio, internship, clinical experience, or practicum. *Entrance requirements:* For master's, PRAXIS I (for initial teaching licensure programs); GRE (for some programs), bachelor's degree from regionally-accredited institution, 2 recommendations (3 for some programs), minimum 500-word personal essay, official transcripts, minimum GPA of 2.75, valid teaching license (for some programs). Additional exam requirements/recommendations for international students: Required—TOEFL (minimum score 570 paper-based), IELTS (minimum score 6.5). Electronic applications accepted. *Expenses:* Contact institution.

Louisiana College, Graduate Programs, Pineville, LA 71359-0001. Offers teaching (MAT).

Louisiana State University and Agricultural & Mechanical College, Graduate School, College of Human Sciences and Education, Baton Rouge, LA 70803. Offers M Ed, MA, MAT, MLIS, MS, MSW, PhD, Ed S. *Accreditation:* NCATE.

Louisiana State University in Shreveport, College of Business, Education, and Human Development, Program in Education, Shreveport, LA 71115-2399. Offers curriculum and instruction (M Ed); leadership (M Ed); leadership studies (Ed D). *Accreditation:* NCATE. *Program availability:* Part-time. *Students:* 5 full-time (all women), 236 part-time (198 women); includes 110 minority (92 Black or African American, non-Hispanic/Latino; 6 Asian, non-Hispanic/Latino; 6 Hispanic/Latino; 6 Two or more races, non-Hispanic/Latino). Average age 36. 148 applicants, 95% accepted, 39 enrolled. In 2016, 61 master's awarded. *Degree requirements:* For master's, orally-presented project, 200-hour internship (educational leadership). *Entrance requirements:* For master's, GRE, minimum GPA of 2.5; teacher certification; recommendations and interview (for educational leadership). Additional exam requirements/recommendations for international students: Required—TOEFL (minimum score 550 paper-based; 61 iBT). *Application deadline:* For fall admission, 6/30 for domestic and international students; for spring admission, 11/30 for domestic and international students; for summer admission, 4/30 for domestic and international students. Applications are processed on a rolling basis. Application fee: $20 ($30 for international students). Electronic applications accepted. *Expenses:* Tuition, state resident: full-time $5163; part-time $350 per credit hour. Tuition, nonresident: full-time $15,578; part-time $1038 per credit hour. *Required fees:* $63 per credit hour. Tuition and fees vary according to course load and program. *Financial support:* In 2016–17, 5 research assistantships (averaging $2,150 per year) were awarded. *Unit head:* Dr. Pat Doerr, Coordinator, 318-797-5033, Fax: 318-798-4144, E-mail: pat.doerr@lsus.edu. *Application contact:* Mary Catherine Harvison, Director of Admissions, 318-797-2400, Fax: 318-797-5286, E-mail: mary.harvison@lsus.edu.

Louisiana Tech University, Graduate School, College of Education, Ruston, LA 71272. Offers M Ed, MA, MS, Ed D, PhD. *Accreditation:* NCATE. *Program availability:* Part-time. *Degree requirements:* For doctorate, thesis/dissertation. *Entrance requirements:* For master's and doctorate, GRE General Test. *Application deadline:* For fall admission, 7/29 for domestic students; for spring admission, 2/3 for domestic students. Application fee: $20 ($30 for international students). *Financial support:* Fellowships, research assistantships, teaching assistantships, and career-related internships or fieldwork available. Financial award application deadline: 2/1. *Unit head:* Don Schillinger, Dean, 318-257-3712. *Application contact:* Dr. Cathy Stockton, Associate Dean of Graduate Studies, 318-257-3229, Fax: 318-257-2379, E-mail: cstock@latech.edu.
Website: http://education.latech.edu/

Loyola Marymount University, School of Education, Los Angeles, CA 90045-2659. Offers MA, Ed D. *Accreditation:* NCATE. *Students:* 64 full-time (37 women), 112 part-time (61 women). *Unit head:* Dr. Shane P. Martin, Dean, 310-338-7301, E-mail: smartin@lmu.edu. *Application contact:* Chake H. Kouyoumjian, Associate Dean of Graduate Studies, 310-338-2721, E-mail: ckouyoum@lmu.edu.
Website: http://soe.lmu.edu

Loyola University Chicago, School of Education, Chicago, IL 60660. Offers M Ed, MA, Ed D, PhD, Certificate, Ed S. *Accreditation:* NCATE. *Program availability:* Part-time, evening/weekend, blended/hybrid learning. *Faculty:* 59 full-time (40 women), 71 part-time/adjunct (48 women). *Students:* 430 full-time (329 women), 211 part-time (167 women); includes 242 minority (101 Black or African American, non-Hispanic/Latino; 1 American Indian or Alaska Native, non-Hispanic/Latino; 30 Asian, non-Hispanic/Latino; 88 Hispanic/Latino; 1 Native Hawaiian or other Pacific Islander, non-Hispanic/Latino; 21 Two or more races, non-Hispanic/Latino), 22 international. Average age 30. 718 applicants, 62% accepted, 280 enrolled. In 2016, 145 master's, 45 doctorates, 9 other advanced degrees awarded. *Degree requirements:* For master's, comprehensive exam (for some programs), thesis (for some programs); for doctorate, comprehensive exam, thesis/dissertation; for other advanced degree, comprehensive exam. *Entrance requirements:* For master's, minimum GPA of 3.0, 3 letters of recommendation, resume, transcripts; for doctorate, GRE, interview, minimum GPA of 3.0, 3 letters of recommendation, resume; for other advanced degree, GRE, interview, minimum GPA of 3.0, letters of recommendation, resume, transcripts. Additional exam requirements/recommendations for international students: Required—TOEFL (minimum score 550 paper-based; 79 iBT). Application fee: $50. Electronic applications accepted. Application fee is waived when completed online. *Expenses:* $949 per hour; $2,847 per course; $8,541-$11,388 per semester plus fees $432 per semester and $225 the first semester. *Financial support:* In 2016–17, 392 students received support, including 132 fellowships with partial tuition reimbursements available, 87 research assistantships with full tuition reimbursements available (averaging $14,000 per year), 96 teaching assistantships (averaging $4,000 per year); career-related internships or fieldwork, Federal Work-Study, institutionally sponsored loans, scholarships/grants, traineeships, health care benefits, and unspecified assistantships also available. Support available to part-time students. Financial award application deadline: 2/1; financial award applicants required to submit FAFSA. *Faculty research:* Policy studies, historical foundations, teacher education, research methodologies, comparative education. *Total annual research expenditures:* $2.5 million. *Unit head:* Dr. David Slavsky, Interim Dean, 312-915-6992, Fax: 312-915-6980, E-mail: dslavsk@luc.edu. *Application contact:* Thomas Ott, Information Contact, 312-915-8907, E-mail: tott@luc.edu.
Website: http://www.luc.edu/education

Loyola University Maryland, Graduate Programs, School of Education, Baltimore, MD 21210-2699. Offers M Ed, MA, MAT, CAS. *Accreditation:* NCATE. *Program availability:* Part-time, evening/weekend. *Faculty:* 34 full-time (22 women), 30 part-time/adjunct (24 women). *Students:* 126 full-time (110 women), 618 part-time (516 women); includes 247 minority (165 Black or African American, non-Hispanic/Latino; 1 American Indian or Alaska Native, non-Hispanic/Latino; 22 Asian, non-Hispanic/Latino; 36 Hispanic/Latino; 2 Native Hawaiian or other Pacific Islander, non-Hispanic/Latino; 21 Two or more races, non-Hispanic/Latino), 7 international. Average age 31. 549 applicants, 66% accepted, 171 enrolled. In 2016, 275 master's awarded. *Degree requirements:* For master's, thesis. *Entrance requirements:* Additional exam requirements/recommendations for international students: Required—TOEFL (minimum score 550 paper-based), IELTS (minimum score 7). *Application deadline:* For fall admission, 6/15 for domestic students. Applications are processed on a rolling basis. Application fee: $60. Electronic applications accepted. *Expenses:* Contact institution. *Financial support:* In 2016–17, 30 students received support. Research assistantships, scholarships/grants, and unspecified assistantships available. Financial award application deadline: 4/15; financial award applicants required to submit FAFSA. *Unit head:* Dr. Joshua Smith, Dean, School of Education, 410-617-5343. *Application contact:* Mechelle Palmer, Senior Associate Director of Graduate Admission, 410-617-7741, E-mail: mjpalmer@loyola.edu.
Website: http://www.loyola.edu/education/

Loyola University New Orleans, College of Arts and Sciences, Master of Arts in Teaching Program, New Orleans, LA 70118-6195. Offers MAT. *Program availability:* Part-time. *Faculty:* 1 (woman) full-time, 2 part-time/adjunct (1 woman). *Students:* 9 part-time (5 women); includes 5 minority (2 Black or African American, non-Hispanic/Latino; 1 American Indian or Alaska Native, non-Hispanic/Latino; 1 Asian, non-Hispanic/Latino; 1 Hispanic/Latino). Average age 30. 10 applicants, 100% accepted, 9 enrolled. *Application deadline:* Applications are processed on a rolling basis. Electronic applications accepted. *Expenses:* Contact institution. *Financial support:* Applicants required to submit FAFSA. *Unit head:* Dr. Glenda Hembree, Office of Teacher Education, E-mail: gghembre@loyno.edu. *Application contact:* 800-4LOYOLA, Fax: 504-865-3383, E-mail: admit@loyno.edu.
Website: http://cas.loyno.edu/teacher-education/mat

Lyndon State College, Graduate Programs in Education, Lyndonville, VT 05851-0919. Offers education (M Ed), including curriculum and instruction, reading specialist, special education, teaching and counseling; natural sciences (MST), including science education. *Program availability:* Part-time, evening/weekend. *Degree requirements:* For master's, exam or major field project. *Entrance requirements:* Additional exam requirements/recommendations for international students: Recommended—TOEFL (minimum score 500 paper-based). *Faculty research:* Impaired reading, cognitive style, counseling relationship.

Lynn University, Donald E. and Helen L. Ross College of Education, Boca Raton, FL 33431-5598. Offers educational leadership (M Ed, Ed D), including K-12 (Ed D); exceptional student education (M Ed), including school administration K-12. *Program availability:* Part-time, evening/weekend, online learning. *Faculty:* 5 full-time (4 women), 8 part-time/adjunct (all women). *Students:* 85 full-time (63 women), 10 part-time (6 women); includes 27 minority (19 Black or African American, non-Hispanic/Latino; 7 Hispanic/Latino; 1 Two or more races, non-Hispanic/Latino), 4 international. Average age 36. 17 applicants, 94% accepted, 11 enrolled. In 2016, 24 master's, 22 doctorates awarded. *Degree requirements:* For master's, comprehensive exam, thesis (for some programs); for doctorate, thesis/dissertation, mid-program review. *Entrance requirements:* For master's, bachelor's degree from accredited institution, letter of recommendation, statement of professional goals, official transcripts; for doctorate, master's degree from accredited institution, resume, 2 letters of recommendation, professional practice statement, official transcripts. Additional exam requirements/recommendations for international students: Required—TOEFL (minimum score 550 paper-based; 80 iBT), IELTS (minimum score 6.5). *Application deadline:* For fall admission, 8/18 for domestic students, 8/4 for international students; for spring admission, 12/15 for domestic students, 12/1 for international students; for summer admission, 4/17 for domestic students, 4/3 for international students. Applications are processed on a rolling basis. Application fee: $45. Electronic applications accepted. *Expenses:* $850 per credit hour, $44,200 per year tuition and fees (for Ed D); $725 per credit hour, $29,000 per year tuition and fees (for master's). *Financial support:* In 2016–17, 74 students received support. Career-related internships or fieldwork, Federal Work-Study, scholarships/grants, tuition waivers (partial), and unspecified assistantships available. Support available to part-time students. Financial award application deadline: 3/1; financial award applicants required to submit FAFSA. *Unit head:* Dr. Kathleen Weigel, Dean, College of Education, 561-237-7441, E-mail: kweigel@lynn.edu. *Application contact:* Steven Pruitt, Director of Graduate and Undergraduate Evening Admission, 561-237-7834, Fax: 561-237-7100, E-mail: spruitt@lynn.edu.
Website: http://www.lynn.edu/academics/colleges/education

Madonna University, Programs in Education, Livonia, MI 48150-1173. Offers Catholic school leadership (MSA); educational leadership (MSA); learning disabilities (MAT); literacy education (MAT); teaching and learning (MAT). *Accreditation:* NCATE. *Program availability:* Part-time, evening/weekend. *Degree requirements:* For master's, thesis or alternative. Electronic applications accepted.

Malone University, Graduate Program in Education, Canton, OH 44709. Offers curriculum and instruction (MA); curriculum, instruction, and professional development (MA); educational leadership (principal license) (MA); intervention specialist (MA). *Accreditation:* NCATE. *Program availability:* Part-time, evening/weekend. *Degree requirements:* For master's, research project. *Entrance requirements:* For master's, minimum GPA of 3.0, teaching license. Additional exam requirements/recommendations for international students: Required—TOEFL (minimum score 550 paper-based; 79 iBT). *Faculty research:* Educational leadership styles: Jesus as master teacher, assessment accommodations for English language learners, preparing culturally proficient teachers, using naturally occurring text in the classroom to meet the syntactic needs of students with learning disabilities, using tablet instructional technology to meet the needs of students with disabilities.

Manhattan College, Graduate Programs, School of Education and Health, Riverdale, NY 10471. Offers MA, MS, MS Ed, Advanced Certificate, Certificate, Professional Diploma. *Accreditation:* TEAC. *Program availability:* Part-time, evening/weekend, online learning. *Faculty:* 8 full-time (6 women), 35 part-time/adjunct (20 women). *Students:* 140 full-time (124 women), 139 part-time (111 women). 218 applicants, 81% accepted, 145 enrolled. In 2016, 75 master's, 24 other advanced degrees awarded. *Degree requirements:* For master's and other advanced degree, thesis, internship. *Entrance requirements:* For master's and other advanced degree, minimum GPA of 3.0. Additional exam requirements/recommendations for international students: Required—TOEFL. *Application deadline:* For fall admission, 8/10 priority date for domestic students, 4/10 for international students; for spring admission, 1/7 priority date for domestic students, 8/1 for international students. Applications are processed on a rolling basis. Application fee: $60. *Financial support:* In 2016–17, 1 research assistantship was awarded; scholarships/grants and tuition waivers (partial) also available. Financial award application deadline: 2/1. *Faculty research:* Leadership, assessment, professional development, school improvement. *Unit head:* Dr. Remigia Kushner, Program Director, 718-862-7473, Fax: 718-862-7816, E-mail: sr.remigia.kushner@manhattan.edu. *Application contact:* William Bisset, Vice President for Enrollment, 718-862-7199, Fax: 718-862-8019, E-mail: william.bisset@manhattan.edu.
Website: http://manhattan.edu/academics/education

Manhattanville College, School of Education, Purchase, NY 10577-2132. Offers M Ed, MAT, MPS, Ed D, Advanced Certificate, PD. *Accreditation:* NCATE. *Program availability:* Part-time, evening/weekend. *Faculty:* 23 full-time (15 women), 67 part-time/adjunct (39 women). *Students:* 137 full-time (92 women), 741 part-time (537 women); includes 100 minority (32 Black or African American, non-Hispanic/Latino; 2 American Indian or Alaska Native, non-Hispanic/Latino; 11 Asian, non-Hispanic/Latino; 55 Hispanic/Latino). Average age 33. 315 applicants, 64% accepted, 161 enrolled. In 2016, 192 master's, 8 doctorates, 13 other advanced degrees awarded. *Degree requirements:* For master's, comprehensive exam (for some programs), thesis (for some programs), student teaching, research seminars, portfolios, internships, writing assessment; for doctorate, comprehensive exam (for some programs), thesis/dissertation. *Entrance requirements:* For master's, GRE or MAT, minimum undergraduate GPA of 3.0, 2 letters of recommendation; for doctorate, GRE or MAT, minimum GPA of 3.0, 2 letters of recommendation, interview, writing sample, resume. Additional exam requirements/recommendations for international students: Required—TOEFL (minimum score 85 iBT); Recommended—IELTS. *Application deadline:* For fall admission, 7/1 priority date for domestic and international students; for spring admission, 11/1 priority date for domestic and international students; for summer admission, 4/1 priority date for domestic and international students. Applications are processed on a rolling basis. Application fee: $75. Electronic applications accepted. *Expenses: Tuition:* Full-time $16,470; part-time $915 per credit. *Required fees:* $60 per semester. Part-time tuition and fees vary according to course load and program. *Financial support:* Teaching assistantships, career-related internships or fieldwork, Federal Work-Study, institutionally sponsored loans, scholarships/grants, and unspecified assistantships available. Financial award applicants required to submit FAFSA. *Unit head:* Dr. Shelley Wepner, Dean, 914-323-3153, Fax: 914-323-5493, E-mail: shelley.wepner@mville.edu. *Application contact:* Jeanine Pardey-Levine, Director of Graduate Enrollment Management, 914-323-3208, Fax: 914-694-1732, E-mail: edschool@mville.edu.
Website: http://www.mville.edu/academics/school-education

See Display below and Close-Up on page 729.

Mansfield University of Pennsylvania, Graduate Studies, Department of Education and Special Education, Mansfield, PA 16933. Offers elementary education (M Ed); secondary education (MS); special education (M Ed). *Accreditation:* NCATE (one or more programs are accredited). *Program availability:* Part-time, evening/weekend, online learning. *Degree requirements:* For master's, comprehensive exam, thesis optional. *Entrance requirements:* For master's, minimum GPA of 3.0. Additional exam requirements/recommendations for international students: Required—TOEFL (minimum score 550 paper-based). Electronic applications accepted.

Maranatha Baptist University, Program in Teaching and Learning, Watertown, WI 53094. Offers M Ed. *Program availability:* Part-time, evening/weekend, 100% online. *Expenses:* $180 per credit hour. *Financial support:* Scholarships/grants, tuition waivers (full and partial), and unspecified assistantships available. Support available to part-time students. Financial award applicants required to submit FAFSA. *Unit head:* David Handyside, Director of the School of Education, 920-261-6987, Fax: 920-261-9109, E-mail: david.handyside@mbu.edu. *Application contact:* Dr. Jim Harrison, Director of Admissions, 920-206-2327, Fax: 920-261-9109, E-mail: admissions@mbu.edu.
Website: http://www.mbu.edu/med/

Marian University, School of Education, Fond du Lac, WI 54935-4699. Offers curriculum and instruction leadership (PhD); educational administration (PhD); educational leadership (MAE); educational technology (MAE); leadership studies (PhD); special education (MAE); teacher education (MAE). *Accreditation:* NCATE. *Program availability:* Part-time, evening/weekend, online learning. *Faculty:* 11 full-time (7 women), 14 part-time/adjunct (8 women). *Students:* 13 full-time (9 women), 179 part-time (113 women); includes 16 minority (6 Black or African American, non-Hispanic/Latino; 3 American Indian or Alaska Native, non-Hispanic/Latino; 2 Asian, non-Hispanic/Latino; 3 Hispanic/Latino; 2 Two or more races, non-Hispanic/Latino). Average age 39. In 2016, 72 master's, 8 doctorates awarded. *Degree requirements:* For master's, exam, field-based experience project, portfolio; for doctorate, comprehensive exam, thesis/dissertation, field-based experience. *Entrance requirements:* For master's, minimum GPA of 3.0, BA in education or related field, teaching license; for doctorate, GRE, MAT, resume, 2 writing samples, interview. Additional exam requirements/recommendations for international students: Required—TOEFL (minimum score 525 paper-based; 70 iBT). *Application deadline:* Applications are processed on a rolling basis. Application fee: $50. *Expenses: Tuition:* Full-time $5130; part-time $570 per credit hour. *Financial support:* In 2016–17, 3 students received support. Federal Work-Study available. Support available to part-time students. Financial award application deadline: 3/1; financial award applicants required to submit FAFSA. *Faculty research:* At-risk youth, multicultural issues, values in education, teaching/learning strategies. *Unit head:* Dr. Kelly Chaney, Dean, 920-923-8610, Fax: 920-923-7663, E-mail: kachaney01@marianuniversity.edu.
Website: https://www.marianuniversity.edu/academic-programs/graduate-studies/

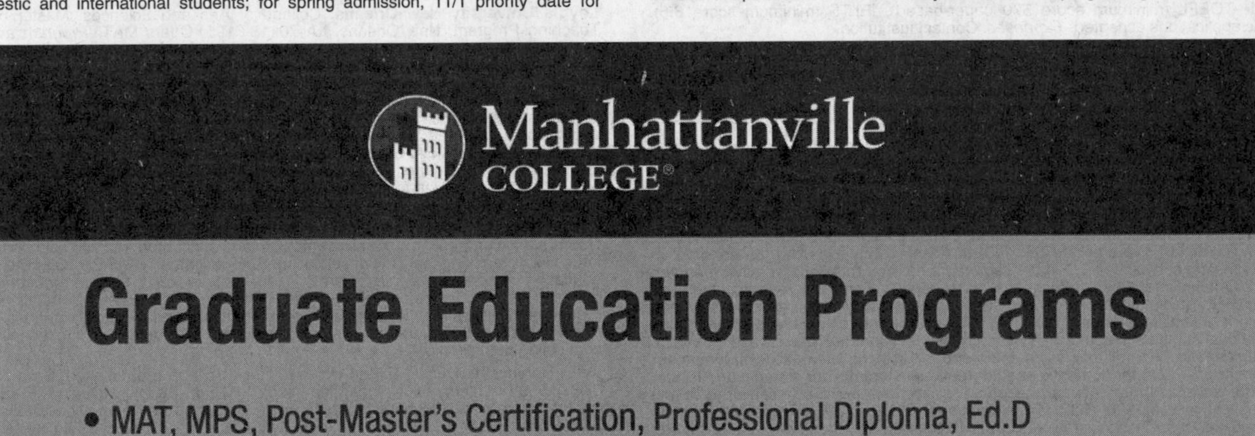

Marist College, Graduate Programs, School of Social and Behavioral Sciences, Poughkeepsie, NY 12601-1387. Offers education (M Ed, MA); mental health counseling (MA); school psychology (MA, Adv C). *Program availability:* Part-time, evening/weekend. *Degree requirements:* For master's, thesis optional. *Entrance requirements:* For master's, GRE General Test, letters of recommendation, minimum undergraduate GPA of 3.0, interview. Additional exam requirements/recommendations for international students: Required—TOEFL (minimum score 550 paper-based; 80 iBT); Recommended—IELTS (minimum score 6.5). Electronic applications accepted. *Faculty research:* AIDS prevention, educational intervention, humanistic counseling research, aging and development, neuroimaging.

Marlboro College, Graduate and Professional Studies, Program in Teaching with Technology, Marlboro, VT 05344. Offers educational technology (Certificate); teaching with technology (MAT). *Program availability:* Part-time, evening/weekend, blended/hybrid learning. *Faculty:* 1 full-time (0 women), 8 part-time/adjunct (5 women). *Students:* 6 full-time (3 women), 13 part-time (5 women); includes 3 minority (1 Black or African American, non-Hispanic/Latino; 2 Two or more races, non-Hispanic/Latino). Average age 44. 8 applicants, 88% accepted, 7 enrolled. In 2016, 5 master's awarded. *Degree requirements:* For master's, 36 credits including capstone project. *Entrance requirements:* For master's, statement of intent, 2 letters of recommendation, transcripts. *Application deadline:* For fall admission, 7/1 priority date for domestic students; for winter admission, 11/1 priority date for domestic students; for spring admission, 3/1 priority date for domestic students. Applications are processed on a rolling basis. Application fee: $0. Electronic applications accepted. *Expenses:* $765 per credit. *Financial support:* In 2016–17, 2 students received support. Scholarships/grants available. Financial award application deadline: 8/5; financial award applicants required to submit FAFSA. *Unit head:* Caleb Clark, Degree Chair, 802-258-9207, Fax: 802-258-9201, E-mail: cclark@gradschool.marlboro.edu. *Application contact:* Don Parker, Admissions Assistant, 802-451-7505, Fax: 802-258-9201, E-mail: graduateadmissions@marlboro.edu.
Website: https://www.marlboro.edu/academics/graduate/mat

Marquette University, Graduate School, College of Education, Milwaukee, WI 53201-1881. Offers M Ed, MA, MS, PhD, Certificate. *Accreditation:* NCATE. *Program availability:* Part-time. *Faculty:* 23 full-time (17 women), 33 part-time/adjunct (26 women). *Students:* 100 full-time (76 women), 116 part-time (76 women); includes 40 minority (13 Black or African American, non-Hispanic/Latino; 1 American Indian or Alaska Native, non-Hispanic/Latino; 9 Asian, non-Hispanic/Latino; 13 Hispanic/Latino; 4 Two or more races, non-Hispanic/Latino), 3 international. Average age 29. 218 applicants, 67% accepted, 99 enrolled. In 2016, 71 master's, 2 doctorates, 3 other advanced degrees awarded. Terminal master's awarded for partial completion of doctoral program. *Degree requirements:* For master's, comprehensive exam, thesis (for some programs); for doctorate, thesis/dissertation, qualifying exam. *Entrance requirements:* For master's, GRE General Test or MAT, official transcripts from all current and previous colleges/universities except Marquette, three letters of recommendation, statement of purpose; for doctorate, GRE General Test, MAT, sample of written work, official transcripts from all current and previous colleges/universities except Marquette, three letters of recommendation, statement of purpose, resume/curriculum vitae; for Certificate, GRE General Test or MAT, master's degree. Additional exam requirements/recommendations for international students: Required—TOEFL (minimum score 530 paper-based). *Application deadline:* For fall admission, 1/15 for domestic and international students. *Expenses:* Contact institution. *Financial support:* Fellowships, research assistantships, scholarships/grants, health care benefits, tuition waivers (partial), and unspecified assistantships available. Support available to part-time students. Financial award application deadline: 2/15. *Faculty research:* Parenting, psychology of motivation, reading assessment, socialization of educational administrators, education philosophy of Cardinal Newman. *Total annual research expenditures:* $13,358.
Website: http://www.marquette.edu/education/

Marshall University, Academic Affairs Division, College of Education and Professional Development, Huntington, WV 25755. Offers MA, MAT, MS, Ed D, Certificate, Ed S, Graduate Certificate. *Accreditation:* NCATE. *Program availability:* Part-time, evening/weekend. *Degree requirements:* For master's, thesis optional, comprehensive or oral assessment. *Entrance requirements:* Additional exam requirements/recommendations for international students: Required—TOEFL. Electronic applications accepted.

Martin Luther College, Graduate Studies, New Ulm, MN 56073. Offers early childhood director (MS Ed Admin); educational technology (MS Ed); instruction (MS Ed); leadership (MS Ed); principal (MS Ed Admin); special education (MS Ed). *Program availability:* Part-time, evening/weekend. *Faculty:* 9 full-time (1 woman), 21 part-time/adjunct (10 women). *Students:* 1 (woman) full-time, 77 part-time (30 women); includes 2 minority (1 Asian, non-Hispanic/Latino; 1 Two or more races, non-Hispanic/Latino), 4 international. Average age 37. 6 applicants, 100% accepted, 6 enrolled. In 2016, 15 master's awarded. *Degree requirements:* For master's, capstone project or comprehensive exam. *Entrance requirements:* For master's, undergraduate degree in education from an accredited college or university, minimum undergraduate GPA of 3.0. Additional exam requirements/recommendations for international students: Required—TOEFL (minimum score 550 paper-based; 80 iBT); Recommended—IELTS (minimum score 6.5). *Application deadline:* Applications are processed on a rolling basis. Application fee: $35. Electronic applications accepted. *Expenses:* $11,220 tuition, $140 graduation fee. *Financial support:* In 2016–17, 2 students received support. Scholarships/grants available. Financial award application deadline: 9/1. *Faculty research:* Principal effectiveness, principal support, cognitive load in math instruction, reading strategies in multigrade classrooms, mentor provided professional development for new teachers. *Unit head:* John E. Meyer, Director of Graduate Studies, 507-354-8221 Ext. 398, E-mail: meyerjd@mlc-wels.edu.
Website: https://mlc-wels.edu/graduate-studies/

Mary Baldwin University, Graduate Studies, Program in Teaching, Staunton, VA 24401-3610. Offers elementary education (MAT); middle grades education (MAT). *Accreditation:* TEAC.

Marygrove College, Graduate Division, Program in the Art of Teaching, Detroit, MI 48221-2599. Offers MAT. *Accreditation:* TEAC. *Program availability:* Online learning. *Degree requirements:* For master's, portfolio. *Entrance requirements:* For master's, MAT, interview, minimum undergraduate GPA of 3.0, teaching certificate.

Marylhurst University, Department of Education, Marylhurst, OR 97036-0261. Offers education (M Ed); teaching (MA). *Program availability:* Part-time. *Students:* 46 (39 women); includes 10 minority (1 Asian, non-Hispanic/Latino; 5 Hispanic/Latino; 4 Two or more races, non-Hispanic/Latino), 1 international. Average age 35. In 2016, 21 master's awarded. *Degree requirements:* For master's, comprehensive exam. *Entrance requirements:* For master's, PRAXIS I or CBEST (for MA), official transcript from regionally-accredited institution, recommendations, personal statement of intent, essay or writing sample, fingerprint verification; copy of current teaching license (for M Ed). Additional exam requirements/recommendations for international students: Required—TOEFL (minimum score 79 iBT), IELTS (minimum score 6.5). *Application deadline:* Applications are processed on a rolling basis. Application fee: $0. Electronic applications accepted. *Expenses:* Contact institution. *Financial support:* Career-related internships or fieldwork and scholarships/grants available. Support available to part-time students. Financial award applicants required to submit FAFSA. *Faculty research:* ESOL, reading education. *Unit head:* Dr. Jan Carpenter, Chair, 503-675-3975, E-mail: jcarpenter@marylhurst.edu. *Application contact:* Maruska Lynch, Graduate Admissions Counselor, 800-699-6322, E-mail: admissions@marylhurst.edu.
Website: https://www.marylhurst.edu

Marymount University, School of Education and Human Services, Program in Education, Arlington, VA 22207-4299. Offers elementary education (M Ed); English as a second language (M Ed); professional studies (M Ed); secondary education (M Ed); special education: general curriculum (M Ed). *Accreditation:* NCATE. *Program availability:* Part-time, evening/weekend. *Faculty:* 28 full-time (all women), 8 part-time/adjunct (5 women). *Students:* 42 full-time (33 women), 94 part-time (72 women); includes 25 minority (6 Black or African American, non-Hispanic/Latino; 6 Asian, non-Hispanic/Latino; 8 Hispanic/Latino; 5 Two or more races, non-Hispanic/Latino), 12 international. Average age 32. 32 applicants, 100% accepted, 24 enrolled. In 2016, 79 master's awarded. *Degree requirements:* For master's, thesis or alternative, capstone/internship. *Entrance requirements:* For master's, GRE or MAT and PRAXIS I or SAT/ACT and Virginia Communication and Literacy Assessment (VCLA), 2 letters of recommendation, resume, interview, minimum undergraduate GPA of 2.75 or 3.25 in the last 60 hours. Additional exam requirements/recommendations for international students: Required—TOEFL (minimum score 600 paper-based; 96 iBT), IELTS (minimum score 6.5). *Application deadline:* Applications are processed on a rolling basis. Application fee: $40. Electronic applications accepted. *Expenses:* $690 per credit hour. *Financial support:* In 2016–17, 6 students received support, including 2 teaching assistantships with tuition reimbursements available; career-related internships or fieldwork, Federal Work-Study, scholarships/grants, and unspecified assistantships also available. Support available to part-time students. Financial award applicants required to submit FAFSA. *Unit head:* Dr. Lisa Turissini, Chair, Education, 703-526-1668, Fax: 703-284-1631, E-mail: lisa.turissini@marymount.edu. *Application contact:* Francesca Reed, Director, Graduate Admissions, 703-284-5901, Fax: 703-527-3815, E-mail: grad.admissions@marymount.edu.
Website: http://www.marymount.edu/Academics/School-of-Education-Human-Services/Graduate-Programs/Education-(M-Ed-)

Maryville University of Saint Louis, School of Education, St. Louis, MO 63141-7299. Offers early childhood education (MA Ed); educational leadership (Ed D); educational leadership: principal certification (MA Ed); elementary education (MA Ed); gifted education (MA Ed); higher education leadership (Ed D); literacy specialist (MA Ed); middle grades education (MA Ed); secondary teaching and inquiry (MA Ed); teacher as leader (MA Ed); teacher leadership (Ed D). *Accreditation:* NCATE. *Program availability:* Part-time, evening/weekend. *Faculty:* 17 full-time (11 women), 21 part-time/adjunct (17 women). *Students:* 12 full-time (11 women), 297 part-time (208 women); includes 92 minority (79 Black or African American, non-Hispanic/Latino; 4 Asian, non-Hispanic/Latino; 4 Hispanic/Latino; 5 Two or more races, non-Hispanic/Latino), 4 international. Average age 38. In 2016, 32 master's, 61 doctorates awarded. *Degree requirements:* For master's, thesis, project. *Entrance requirements:* For master's, minimum cumulative GPA of 3.0, 3 professional recommendations, essays, interview with program faculty; for doctorate, minimum GPA of 3.0, 3 professional recommendations, essay, interview, on-site writing sample. Additional exam requirements/recommendations for international students: Required—TOEFL (minimum score 550 paper-based). *Application deadline:* Applications are processed on a rolling basis. Electronic applications accepted. *Expenses:* $879 per credit (for Ed D); $781 per credit (for master's). *Financial support:* Career-related internships or fieldwork, Federal Work-Study, tuition waivers (partial), and professional educator discounts available. Financial award application deadline: 3/1; financial award applicants required to submit FAFSA. *Faculty research:* Collaboration with public schools, pre-service program development, mathematics, diversity, literacy. *Unit head:* Dr. Cathy Bear, Dean, 314-529-9692, Fax: 314-529-9921, E-mail: cbear@maryville.edu. *Application contact:* Stacey Ruffin, Coordinator of Clinical Experiences and Graduate Programs, 314-529-9542, Fax: 314-529-9921, E-mail: teachered@maryville.edu.
Website: http://www.maryville.edu/ed/graduate-programs/

Marywood University, Academic Affairs, Reap College of Education and Human Development, Department of Education, Scranton, PA 18509-1598. Offers early childhood intervention (MS), including birth to age 9; higher education administration (MS); instructional leadership (M Ed); PK-4 education (MAT); reading education (MS); school leadership (MS); secondary/K-12 education (MAT); special education (MS); special education administration and supervision (MS). *Accreditation:* NCATE. *Program availability:* Part-time. Electronic applications accepted.

Massachusetts College of Liberal Arts, Graduate Programs, North Adams, MA 01247-4100. Offers business (MBA); educational administration (M Ed); educational leadership (CAGS); instruction and curriculum (M Ed); instructional technology (M Ed); physical education and health (M Ed); reading (M Ed); special education (M Ed). *Program availability:* Part-time, evening/weekend. *Degree requirements:* For master's, thesis. *Entrance requirements:* For master's, writing sample.

McGill University, Faculty of Graduate and Postdoctoral Studies, Faculty of Education, Department of Integrated Studies in Education, Montréal, QC H3A 2T5, Canada. Offers culture and values in education (MA, PhD); curriculum studies (MA); educational leadership (MA, Certificate); educational studies (PhD); integrated studies in education (M Ed); second language education (MA, PhD).

McKendree University, Graduate Programs, Programs in Education, Lebanon, IL 62254-1299. Offers curriculum design and instruction (Ed D, Ed S); educational administration and leadership (MA Ed); educational studies (MA Ed); higher education administrative services (MA Ed); music education (MA Ed); reading (MA Ed); special education (MA Ed); teacher leadership (MA Ed); teaching certification (MA Ed). *Accreditation:* NCATE. *Program availability:* Part-time, evening/weekend, online learning. *Entrance requirements:* For master's, official transcripts from all institutions previously attended, minimum GPA of 3.0, resume, references; for doctorate, GRE (within the past 5 years), master's degree in education and Ed S, or the equivalent, from regionally-accredited institution; official transcripts from all institutions previously attended; curriculum vitae/resume; essay/personal statement; two years of teaching/professional experience; for Ed S, GRE (within the past 5 years), master's degree in education from regionally-accredited institution of higher education; official transcripts from all institutions previously attended; curriculum vitae/resume; essay/personal statement; two years of teaching/professional experience. Additional exam requirements/recommendations for international students: Required—TOEFL. Electronic applications accepted.

McNeese State University, Doré School of Graduate Studies, Burton College of Education, Office of Student Teaching and Professional Education Services, Program in Multiple Levels Grades K-12, Lake Charles, LA 70609. Offers Postbaccalaureate Certificate. *Entrance requirements:* For degree, PRAXIS, 2 letters of recommendation, autobiography.

McPherson College, Program in Education, McPherson, KS 67460-1402. Offers M Ed. *Degree requirements:* For master's, project.

Education—General

Medaille College, Program in Education, Buffalo, NY 14214-2695. Offers adolescent education (MS Ed); curriculum and instruction (MS Ed); education preparation (MS Ed); literacy (MS Ed); special education (MS). *Accreditation:* TEAC. *Program availability:* Part-time, evening/weekend. *Degree requirements:* For master's, comprehensive exam (for some programs), thesis or alternative. *Entrance requirements:* For master's, minimum undergraduate GPA of 2.7. Additional exam requirements/recommendations for international students: Required—TOEFL (minimum score 550 paper-based). Electronic applications accepted. *Faculty research:* Curriculum planning, truancy, tracking minority students, curriculum design, mentoring students.

Memorial University of Newfoundland, School of Graduate Studies, Faculty of Education, St. John's, NL A1C 5S7, Canada. Offers counseling psychology (M Ed); curriculum, teaching, and learning studies (M Ed); education (PhD); educational leadership studies (M Ed, Graduate Diploma); information technology (M Ed); post-secondary studies (M Ed, Diploma), including health professional education (Diploma). *Program availability:* Part-time. *Degree requirements:* For master's, thesis optional, internship, paper folio, project; for doctorate, comprehensive exam, thesis/dissertation, thesis seminar, oral defense of thesis. *Entrance requirements:* For master's, undergraduate degree with at least 2nd class standing, 1-2 years of work experience; for doctorate, minimum A average in graduate course work, MA in education, 2 years of professional experience; for other advanced degree, 2nd class degree, 2 years of work experience with adult learners, appropriate academic qualifications and work experience in a health-related field. Electronic applications accepted. *Faculty research:* Critical thinking, literacy, cognitive studies and counseling, educational change, technology in instruction.

Mercer University, Graduate Studies, Cecil B. Day Campus, Tift College of Education (Atlanta), Macon, GA 31207. Offers curriculum and instruction (PhD); early childhood education (M Ed, MAT, Ed S); educational leadership (PhD), including higher education leadership, P-12 school leadership; educational leadership P-12 (M Ed, Ed S); higher education leadership (M Ed); independent and charter school leadership (M Ed); middle grades education (M Ed, MAT); reading specialist (M Ed); secondary education (M Ed, MAT); teacher leadership (Ed S). *Accreditation:* NCATE. *Program availability:* Part-time, evening/weekend. *Faculty:* 28 full-time (15 women), 30 part-time/adjunct (27 women). *Students:* 177 full-time (150 women), 324 part-time (264 women); includes 288 minority (256 Black or African American, non-Hispanic/Latino; 1 American Indian or Alaska Native, non-Hispanic/Latino; 7 Asian, non-Hispanic/Latino; 17 Hispanic/Latino; 1 Native Hawaiian or other Pacific Islander, non-Hispanic/Latino; 6 Two or more races, non-Hispanic/Latino), 1 international. Average age 35. In 2016, 173 master's, 34 doctorates, 54 other advanced degrees awarded. *Degree requirements:* For master's and Ed S, research project; for doctorate, comprehensive exam, thesis/dissertation. *Entrance requirements:* For master's, GRE or MAT, minimum undergraduate GPA of 2.75; for doctorate, GRE; for Ed S, GRE or MAT, minimum GPA of 3.25; 3 years of certified teaching experience (for educational leadership and teacher leadership). Additional exam requirements/recommendations for international students: Required—TOEFL (minimum score 80 iBT). *Application deadline:* For fall admission, 8/1 for domestic and international students; for spring admission, 12/1 for domestic and international students; for summer admission, 5/1 for domestic and international students. Applications are processed on a rolling basis. Application fee: $25 ($50 for international students). Electronic applications accepted. *Expenses:* $590 per credit, $1,770 per course (for M Ed); $595 per credit, $1,785 per course (for MAT); $615 per credit, $1,845 per course (for Ed S); $717 per credit, $2,151 per course (for PhD); $150 per semester technology fee. *Financial support:* Federal Work-Study and unspecified assistantships available. Support available to part-time students. Financial award application deadline: 5/1; financial award applicants required to submit FAFSA. *Faculty research:* Educational technology, multicultural and minority issues in education, educational leadership (P-12 and higher education), school discipline and school bullying, standards-based mathematics education. *Unit head:* Dr. James Barta, Dean, 478-301-5355, Fax: 478-301-2280, E-mail: barta_jj@mercer.edu. *Application contact:* Renee Slaton, Associate Director of Graduate Admissions, 678-547-6084, Fax: 678-547-6055, E-mail: mercereducation@mercer.edu.
Website: http://education.mercer.edu/

Mercer University, Graduate Studies, Macon Campus, Tift College of Education (Macon), Macon, GA 31207. Offers early childhood education (M Ed, Ed S); educational leadership (M Ed, PhD, Ed S), including higher education (PhD), P-12; higher education leadership (M Ed); teacher leadership (Ed S). *Accreditation:* NCATE. *Program availability:* Part-time, evening/weekend, 100% online, blended/hybrid learning. *Faculty:* 14 full-time (11 women), 1 part-time/adjunct (0 women). *Students:* 61 full-time (39 women), 39 part-time (30 women); includes 39 minority (34 Black or African American, non-Hispanic/Latino; 1 Asian, non-Hispanic/Latino; 2 Hispanic/Latino; 1 Native Hawaiian or other Pacific Islander, non-Hispanic/Latino; 1 Two or more races, non-Hispanic/Latino), 3 international. Average age 33. In 2016, 23 master's, 13 doctorates awarded. *Degree requirements:* For master's, research project report; for doctorate, comprehensive exam, thesis/dissertation. *Entrance requirements:* For master's, GRE or MAT, minimum GPA of 2.75; for doctorate, GRE, minimum GPA of 3.5; interview; writing sample; 3 recommendations; for Ed S, GRE or MAT, minimum GPA of 3.5 (for teacher leadership), 3.0 (for educational leadership). Additional exam requirements/recommendations for international students: Required—TOEFL (minimum score 80 iBT). *Application deadline:* For fall admission, 8/1 for domestic and international students; for spring admission, 12/1 for domestic and international students. Applications are processed on a rolling basis. Application fee: $35. Electronic applications accepted. *Expenses:* Contact institution. *Financial support:* Federal Work-Study, institutionally sponsored loans, and unspecified assistantships available. Support available to part-time students. Financial award application deadline: 5/1; financial award applicants required to submit FAFSA. *Faculty research:* Teacher effectiveness, specific learning disabilities, inclusion. *Unit head:* Dr. James Barta, Dean, 478-301-5397, Fax: 478-301-2280, E-mail: barta_jj@mercer.edu. *Application contact:* Tracey M. Wofford, Associate Director of Admissions, 678-547-6422, Fax: 678-547-6367, E-mail: wofford_tm@mercer.edu.
Website: http://education.mercer.edu/

Mercy College, School of Education, Dobbs Ferry, NY 10522-1189. Offers MS, Advanced Certificate. *Program availability:* Part-time, evening/weekend, 100% online, blended/hybrid learning. *Students:* 329 full-time (300 women), 714 part-time (598 women); includes 489 minority (215 Black or African American, non-Hispanic/Latino; 8 American Indian or Alaska Native, non-Hispanic/Latino; 21 Asian, non-Hispanic/Latino; 233 Hispanic/Latino; 1 Native Hawaiian or other Pacific Islander, non-Hispanic/Latino; 11 Two or more races, non-Hispanic/Latino). Average age 32. 344 applicants, 40% accepted, 76 enrolled. In 2016, 476 master's, 38 other advanced degrees awarded. *Degree requirements:* For master's, comprehensive exam (for some programs), thesis (for some programs). *Entrance requirements:* For master's, GRE, resume, undergraduate transcript. Additional exam requirements/recommendations for international students: Required—TOEFL (minimum score 600 paper-based; 100 iBT), IELTS (minimum score 8). *Application deadline:* For fall admission, 8/1 for international students. Applications are processed on a rolling basis. Application fee: $40. Electronic applications accepted. *Expenses: Tuition:* Full-time $15,156; part-time $842 per credit hour. *Required fees:* $620; $155 per term. Tuition and fees vary according to course load and program. *Financial support:* Career-related internships or fieldwork, Federal Work-Study, scholarships/grants, and unspecified assistantships available. Support available to part-time students. Financial award applicants required to submit FAFSA. *Unit head:* Dean for the School of Education, 914-674-7350. *Application contact:* Allison Gurdineer, Senior Director of Admissions, 877-637-2946, Fax: 914-674-7382, E-mail: admissions@mercy.edu.
Website: https://www.mercy.edu/education/

Meredith College, School of Education, Health and Human Sciences, Raleigh, NC 27607-5298. Offers academically and intellectually gifted (M Ed); curriculum instruction specialist (M Ed); elementary education (M Ed, MAT); English as a second language (M Ed, MAT); health and physical education (MAT); nutrition, health and human performance (MS, Postbaccalaureate Certificate), including dietetic internship (Postbaccalaureate Certificate), nutrition (MS); reading (M Ed); special education (MAT). *Accreditation:* NCATE. *Program availability:* Part-time, evening/weekend. *Degree requirements:* For master's, thesis optional. *Entrance requirements:* For master's, GRE General Test or MAT, minimum GPA of 2.5, teaching license, recommendations. Additional exam requirements/recommendations for international students: Required—TOEFL. Electronic applications accepted. *Expenses:* Contact institution.

Merrimack College, School of Education and Social Policy, North Andover, MA 01845-5800. Offers community engagement (M Ed), including community organizations, higher education, K-12 education; criminology and criminal justice (MS); curriculum and instruction (M Ed); early childhood education (M Ed); educational leadership (CAGS), including instructional leadership; elementary education (M Ed); English as a second language (PreK-6) (M Ed); high school education (M Ed); higher education (M Ed), including leadership and organizational development, student affairs; middle school education (M Ed); moderate disabilities (PreK-8) (M Ed); school counseling (M Ed). *Program availability:* Part-time, evening/weekend, 100% online courses with immersion events and in-classroom practicum close to home. *Faculty:* 17 full-time, 34 part-time/adjunct. *Students:* 204 full-time (172 women), 83 part-time (67 women); includes 32 minority (4 Black or African American, non-Hispanic/Latino; 2 Asian, non-Hispanic/Latino; 23 Hispanic/Latino; 3 Two or more races, non-Hispanic/Latino), 1 international. Average age 27. 261 applicants, 89% accepted, 200 enrolled. In 2016, 153 master's, 2 other advanced degrees awarded. *Degree requirements:* For master's, practicum, portfolio, and state test (for licensure track); capstone (for higher education, curriculum and instruction, and community engagement tracks). *Entrance requirements:* For master's, Massachusetts Teacher Education Licensure (MTEL), official transcripts from other colleges, resume, personal statement, 2 letters of recommendation. Additional exam requirements/recommendations for international students: Required—TOEFL (minimum score 84 iBT), IELTS (minimum score 6.5), PTE (minimum score 56). *Application deadline:* For fall admission, 8/14 for domestic students, 7/14 for international students; for spring admission, 1/10 for domestic students, 12/10 for international students; for summer admission, 5/10 for domestic students, 4/10 for international students. Applications are processed on a rolling basis. Application fee: $0. Electronic applications accepted. *Expenses:* Contact institution. *Financial support:* Fellowships with full tuition reimbursements, career-related internships or fieldwork, scholarships/grants, and health care benefits available. Support available to part-time students. Financial award application deadline: 5/1; financial award applicants required to submit FAFSA. *Faculty research:* Feminist praxis in higher education, transgender student agency and belonging, campus sexual violence prevention, the scholarship of engagement; community engagement; service learning; diversity education; community-university partnerships, college going behaviors and indicators of success for inner city youth, strategies to increase students pursuit and success in STEM higher education, effective workforce development for displaced or under employed individuals, police reform, e.g. surveillance. *Application contact:* Alyssa Frey, Graduate Admissions Counselor, 978-837-3563, E-mail: freya@merrimack.edu.
Website: http://www.merrimack.edu/academics/graduate/education/

Metropolitan State University of Denver, School of Education, Denver, CO 80204. Offers elementary education (MAT); special education (MAT). *Faculty:* 20 full-time (16 women), 1 part-time/adjunct (0 women). *Students:* 115 full-time (90 women), 14 part-time (11 women); includes 23 minority (7 Black or African American, non-Hispanic/Latino; 2 American Indian or Alaska Native, non-Hispanic/Latino; 1 Asian, non-Hispanic/Latino; 9 Hispanic/Latino; 4 Two or more races, non-Hispanic/Latino). Average age 32. In 2016, 59 master's awarded. *Application deadline:* For fall admission, 2/1 for domestic and international students; for spring admission, 10/1 for domestic and international students; for summer admission, 2/1 for domestic and international students. Application fee: $50. *Expenses:* $6,429.60 for full-time residents, $8,881.20 for full-time non-residents; $357.20 per credit hour for part-time residents, $493.40 per credit hour for part-time non-residents. *Unit head:* Kathy Heyl, Interim Dean, 303-556-2978, E-mail: heyl@msudenver.edu. *Application contact:* Ellen Sunbury, Graduate Admissions Coordinator, 303-556-6228, E-mail: esunbury@msudenver.edu.
Website: http://www.msudenver.edu/scops/

Miami University, College of Education, Health and Society, Oxford, OH 45056. Offers M Ed, MA, MAT, MS, Ed D, PhD, Ed S. *Accreditation:* NCATE. *Expenses:* Tuition, state resident: full-time $12,890; part-time $564 per credit hour. Tuition, nonresident: full-time $29,604; part-time $1260 per credit hour. *Required fees:* $638. Part-time tuition and fees vary according to course load and program. *Unit head:* Dr. Michael Dantley, Dean, 513-529-6317, E-mail: ehs@miamioh.edu. *Application contact:* Graduate Admission Coordinator, 513-529-3734, E-mail: applygrad@miamioh.edu.
Website: http://www.MiamiOH.edu/eap/

Michigan State University, The Graduate School, College of Education, East Lansing, MI 48824. Offers MA, MS, PhD, Ed S. *Accreditation:* TEAC. *Entrance requirements:* Additional exam requirements/recommendations for international students: Required—TOEFL. Electronic applications accepted.

MidAmerica Nazarene University, Professional and Graduate Studies in Education, Olathe, KS 66062-1899. Offers ESOL (M Ed); reading specialist (M Ed); technology enhanced teaching (M Ed). *Accreditation:* NCATE. *Program availability:* Part-time, evening/weekend, online only, 100% online. *Faculty:* 5 full-time (3 women), 12 part-time/adjunct (7 women). *Students:* 22 full-time (16 women), 43 part-time (38 women); includes 6 minority (3 Black or African American, non-Hispanic/Latino; 1 Asian, non-Hispanic/Latino; 2 Two or more races, non-Hispanic/Latino). Average age 32. 18 applicants, 22% accepted, 2 enrolled. In 2016, 41 master's awarded. *Entrance requirements:* For master's, bachelor's degree from an accredited college or university, minimum undergraduate GPA of 3.0, valid teaching license. Additional exam requirements/recommendations for international students: Required—TOEFL (minimum score 81 iBT), IELTS (minimum score 6). *Application deadline:* For fall admission, 8/6 for domestic students; for spring admission, 12/15 for domestic students; for summer admission, 5/7 for domestic students. Applications are processed on a rolling basis. Electronic applications accepted. *Expenses:* Contact institution. *Financial support:* Scholarships/grants available. Financial award applicants required to submit FAFSA. *Unit head:* Dr. Ramona Stowe, Chair, 913-971-3524, Fax: 913-971-3407, E-mail: rsstowe@mnu.edu. *Application contact:* Glenna Murray, Administrative Assistant, 913-

971-3292, Fax: 913-971-3002, E-mail: gkmurray@mnu.edu.
Website: http://www.mnu.edu/education.html

Middle Tennessee State University, College of Graduate Studies, College of Education, Murfreesboro, TN 37132. Offers M Ed, PhD, Ed S. *Accreditation:* NCATE. *Program availability:* Part-time, evening/weekend, online learning. *Degree requirements:* For master's, comprehensive exam, thesis (for some programs); for doctorate, comprehensive exam, thesis/dissertation; for Ed S, comprehensive exam, thesis or alternative. *Entrance requirements:* For master's, doctorate, and Ed S, GRE, MAT, current teaching license or PRAXIS. Additional exam requirements/recommendations for international students: Required—TOEFL (minimum score 525 paper-based; 71 iBT) or IELTS (minimum score 6). Electronic applications accepted.

Midway University, Graduate Programs, Midway, KY 40347-1120. Offers education (MAT); leadership (MBA). *Degree requirements:* For master's, capstone course. *Entrance requirements:* For master's, GMAT (for MBA); GRE or PRAXIS I (for MAT), bachelor's degree; interview; minimum GPA of 3.0 (for MBA), 2.75 (for MAT); 3 years of professional work experience (for MBA). Additional exam requirements/recommendations for international students: Required—TOEFL (minimum score 550 paper-based; 80 iBT).

Midwestern State University, Billie Doris McAda Graduate School, West College of Education, Wichita Falls, TX 76308. Offers M Ed, MA. *Program availability:* Part-time, evening/weekend. *Degree requirements:* For master's, comprehensive exam, thesis (for some programs). *Entrance requirements:* For master's, GRE General Test or MAT. Additional exam requirements/recommendations for international students: Required—TOEFL (minimum score 550 paper-based). Electronic applications accepted. *Faculty research:* Assessment, reading education, vocabulary instruction, current role of the principal, educational research methodology.

Millersville University of Pennsylvania, College of Graduate Studies and Adult Learning, College of Education and Human Services, Millersville, PA 17551-0302. Offers M Ed, MS, MSW, DSW, Ed D, Post-Master's Certificate, Postbaccalaureate Certificate. *Accreditation:* NCATE. *Program availability:* Part-time, 100% online, blended/hybrid learning. *Faculty:* 60 full-time (38 women), 2 part-time/adjunct (both women). *Students:* 121 full-time (104 women), 369 part-time (300 women); includes 62 minority (26 Black or African American, non-Hispanic/Latino; 2 American Indian or Alaska Native, non-Hispanic/Latino; 4 Asian, non-Hispanic/Latino; 25 Hispanic/Latino; 5 Two or more races, non-Hispanic/Latino), 2 international. Average age 30. 272 applicants, 88% accepted, 150 enrolled. In 2016, 167 master's awarded. *Degree requirements:* For master's, comprehensive exam (for some programs), thesis (for some programs). *Entrance requirements:* For master's, GRE; MAT, teacher certificate. Additional exam requirements/recommendations for international students: Required—TOEFL (minimum score 600 paper-based), IELTS (minimum score 6). Application fee: $40. Electronic applications accepted. *Expenses:* $483 per credit resident tuition; $725 per credit non-resident tuition. *Financial support:* In 2016–17, 80 students received support. Unspecified assistantships available. Financial award application deadline: 3/15; financial award applicants required to submit FAFSA. *Unit head:* Dr. George Drake, Dean, 717-871-7333, E-mail: george.drake@millersville.edu. *Application contact:* Dr. Victor S. DeSantis, Dean of College of Graduate Studies and Adult Learning/Associate Provost for Civic and Community Engagement, 717-871-7619, Fax: 717-871-7954, E-mail: victor.desantis@millersville.edu.
Website: http://www.millersville.edu/education/

Milligan College, Area of Education, Milligan College, TN 37682. Offers combined preK-3/K-5 education (M Ed); educational leadership (Ed D, Ed S); K-5 education (M Ed); middle grades education (M Ed); preK-3 education (M Ed); preK-3 special education (M Ed); secondary education (M Ed). *Accreditation:* NCATE. *Program availability:* Part-time. *Faculty:* 5 full-time (3 women), 3 part-time/adjunct (1 woman). *Students:* 26 full-time (19 women), 20 part-time (10 women); includes 2 minority (1 Black or African American, non-Hispanic/Latino; 1 Hispanic/Latino), 2 international. Average age 28. 16 applicants, 81% accepted, 11 enrolled. In 2016, 19 master's awarded. *Degree requirements:* For master's, thesis, portfolio, research project; for doctorate, thesis/dissertation, portfolio, research project. *Entrance requirements:* For master's, MAT, GRE General Test, ACT, SAT, or PRAXIS, undergraduate degree and supporting transcripts, professional recommendations, interview; for doctorate, MAT or GRE, master's degree and supporting transcripts, demonstrated scholastic ability, recognized leadership role within education, professional recommendations, essay/personal statement, portfolio (professional development plan, evidence of ability, knowledge and qualities), interview. Additional exam requirements/recommendations for international students: Required—TOEFL (minimum score 550 paper-based, 79 iBT) or IELTS (6.5). *Application deadline:* For fall admission, 8/1 priority date for domestic students, 6/1 for international students; for spring admission, 11/15 priority date for domestic students, 12/1 for international students; for summer admission, 4/1 for domestic students. Applications are processed on a rolling basis. Application fee: $30. Electronic applications accepted. *Expenses:* $360 per hour tuition (for M Ed); $475 per hour tuition (for Ed D and Ed S); $325 per semester tech/activity fees. *Financial support:* Scholarships/grants available. Financial award application deadline: 12/1; financial award applicants required to submit FAFSA. *Faculty research:* Assessment; school mental health; literacy; technology; educator preparation. *Unit head:* Dr. Angela Hilton-Prillhart, Area Chair of Education, 423-461-8769, Fax: 423-461-3103, E-mail: anhilton-prillhart@milligan.edu. *Application contact:* Melissa Dillow, Graduate Admissions Recruiter, Education, 423-461-8306, Fax: 423-461-8982, E-mail: msdillow@milligan.edu.
Website: http://www.Milligan.edu/GPS

Mills College, Graduate Studies, School of Education, Oakland, CA 94613-1000. Offers MA, Ed D, Certificate. *Program availability:* Part-time, evening/weekend. *Faculty:* 11 full-time (9 women), 13 part-time/adjunct (10 women). *Students:* 131 full-time (116 women), 49 part-time (36 women); includes 85 minority (25 Black or African American, non-Hispanic/Latino; 1 American Indian or Alaska Native, non-Hispanic/Latino; 16 Asian, non-Hispanic/Latino; 33 Hispanic/Latino; 10 Two or more races, non-Hispanic/Latino), 7 international. Average age 31. 231 applicants, 84% accepted, 99 enrolled. In 2016, 31 master's, 15 doctorates, 71 other advanced degrees awarded. Terminal master's awarded for partial completion of doctoral program. *Degree requirements:* For master's, comprehensive exam, thesis (for some programs); for doctorate, thesis/dissertation. *Entrance requirements:* For master's, statement of purpose, official transcript, 3 recommendations. Additional exam requirements/recommendations for international students: Required—TOEFL (minimum score 550 paper-based; 80 iBT) or IELTS (minimum score 6). *Application deadline:* For fall admission, 12/31 priority date for domestic students, 12/15 for international students; for spring admission, 11/1 priority date for domestic students, 10/1 for international students. Applications are processed on a rolling basis. Application fee: $50. Electronic applications accepted. *Expenses:* Contact institution. *Financial support:* In 2016–17, 205 students received support, including 177 fellowships with tuition reimbursements available (averaging $7,171 per year), 28 teaching assistantships with tuition reimbursements available (averaging $3,700 per year); career-related internships or fieldwork and scholarships/grants also available. Support available to part-time students. Financial award application deadline: 2/1; financial award applicants required to submit FAFSA. *Faculty research:* Early childhood education, teacher preparation, educational leadership. *Total annual research expenditures:* $3 million. *Unit head:* Dr. Diane Ketelle, Department Head, 510-430-3190, Fax: 510-430-2159, E-mail: dketelle@mills.edu. *Application contact:* Robynne Lofton, Director of Admissions, 510-430-3295, Fax: 510-430-2159, E-mail: grad-admission@mills.edu.
Website: http://www.mills.edu/education

Minnesota State University Mankato, College of Graduate Studies and Research, College of Education, Mankato, MN 56001. Offers MAT, MS, Ed D, Certificate. *Accreditation:* NCATE. *Program availability:* Part-time, evening/weekend. *Students:* 153 full-time (121 women), 289 part-time (183 women). *Degree requirements:* For master's, comprehensive exam, thesis or alternative; for Certificate, thesis. *Entrance requirements:* For master's, GRE or MAT, minimum GPA of 3.0 during previous 2 years; for Certificate, minimum GPA of 3.0. Additional exam requirements/recommendations for international students: Required—TOEFL. *Application deadline:* Applications are processed on a rolling basis. Application fee: $40. Electronic applications accepted. *Financial support:* Fellowships with partial tuition reimbursements, research assistantships with full tuition reimbursements, teaching assistantships with full tuition reimbursements, career-related internships or fieldwork, Federal Work-Study, institutionally sponsored loans, and unspecified assistantships available. Support available to part-time students. Financial award application deadline: 3/15; financial award applicants required to submit FAFSA. *Unit head:* Dr. Jean Haar, Dean, 507-389-5445.
Website: http://ed.mnsu.edu/

Minnesota State University Moorhead, Graduate Studies, College of Education and Human Services, Moorhead, MN 56563. Offers counseling and student affairs (MS); curriculum and instruction (MS); educational leadership (MS, Ed S); special education (MS); speech-language pathology (MS). *Accreditation:* NCATE. *Program availability:* Part-time, 100% online, blended/hybrid learning. *Students:* 133 full-time (116 women), 363 part-time (274 women). Average age 32. 273 applicants, 49% accepted. In 2016, 114 master's awarded. *Degree requirements:* For master's, comprehensive exam (for some programs), thesis. *Entrance requirements:* For master's, GRE, essay, letter of intent, letters of reference, teaching license, teaching verification. Additional exam requirements/recommendations for international students: Required—TOEFL (minimum score 550 paper-based). *Application deadline:* For fall admission, 4/15 priority date for domestic students; for spring admission, 11/1 priority date for domestic students. Applications are processed on a rolling basis. Application fee: $20. Electronic applications accepted. *Expenses:* Tuition, state resident: full-time $9000; part-time $4500 per credit. Tuition, nonresident: full-time $18,000; part-time $9000 per credit. *Required fees:* $942; $39.25 per credit. One-time fee: $90 full-time. Full-time tuition and fees vary according to course load, degree level, program and reciprocity agreements. *Financial support:* Federal Work-Study and unspecified assistantships available. Financial award application deadline: 10/1; financial award applicants required to submit FAFSA. *Unit head:* Dr. Ok-Hee Lee, Dean, 218-477-2095, E-mail: okheelee@mnstate.edu. *Application contact:* Karla Wenger, Office Manager, 218-477-2344, Fax: 218-477-2482, E-mail: wengerk@mnstate.edu.
Website: http://www.mnstate.edu/cehs/

Misericordia University, College of Health Sciences and Education, Program in Education, Dallas, PA 18612-1098. Offers instructional technology (MS); reading specialist (MS); special education (MS). *Program availability:* Part-time, evening/weekend. *Entrance requirements:* For master's, minimum undergraduate GPA of 3.0. Additional exam requirements/recommendations for international students: Required—TOEFL. Electronic applications accepted.

Mississippi College, Graduate School, School of Education, Clinton, MS 39058. Offers M Ed, MS, Ed D, Ed S. *Accreditation:* NCATE. *Program availability:* Part-time, evening/weekend, online learning. *Degree requirements:* For master's, comprehensive exam, thesis optional. *Entrance requirements:* For master's, GRE or NTE, minimum GPA of 2.5, Class A Certificate (for some programs); for Ed S, NTE, minimum GPA of 3.0. Additional exam requirements/recommendations for international students: Recommended—TOEFL, IELTS. Electronic applications accepted.

Mississippi State University, College of Agriculture and Life Sciences, School of Human Sciences, Mississippi State, MS 39762. Offers agriculture and extension education (MS, PhD), including agriculture and extension education (PhD), leadership (MS), teaching (MS); human development and family studies (MS, PhD). *Accreditation:* NCATE (one or more programs are accredited). *Program availability:* Part-time. *Faculty:* 23 full-time (13 women), 1 part-time/adjunct (0 women). *Students:* 35 full-time (25 women), 61 part-time (45 women); includes 19 minority (15 Black or African American, non-Hispanic/Latino; 2 Hispanic/Latino; 2 Two or more races, non-Hispanic/Latino), 5 international. Average age 35. 22 applicants, 73% accepted, 12 enrolled. In 2016, 8 master's, 4 doctorates awarded. *Degree requirements:* For master's, thesis optional, comprehensive oral or written exam. *Entrance requirements:* For master's, GRE, minimum GPA of 2.75 in last 4 semesters of course work; for doctorate, minimum GPA of 3.0 on prior graduate work. Additional exam requirements/recommendations for international students: Required—TOEFL (minimum score 477 paper-based; 53 iBT); Recommended—IELTS (minimum score 4.5). *Application deadline:* For fall admission, 7/1 for domestic students, 5/1 for international students; for spring admission, 11/1 for domestic students, 9/1 for international students. Applications are processed on a rolling basis. Application fee: $60. Electronic applications accepted. *Expenses:* Tuition, state resident: full-time $7670; part-time $852.50 per credit hour. Tuition, nonresident: full-time $20,790; part-time $2310.50 per credit hour. Part-time tuition and fees vary according to course load. *Financial support:* Federal Work-Study, institutionally sponsored loans, and unspecified assistantships available. Financial award application deadline: 4/1; financial award applicants required to submit FAFSA. *Faculty research:* Animal welfare, agro science, information technology, learning styles, problem solving. *Unit head:* Dr. Michael Newman, Director and Professor, 662-325-2950, E-mail: mnewman@humansci.msstate.edu. *Application contact:* Marina Hunt, Admissions and Enrollment Assistant, 662-325-5188, E-mail: mhunt@grad.msstate.edu.
Website: http://www.humansci.msstate.edu

Mississippi State University, College of Education, Mississippi State, MS 39762. Offers MAT, MS, MSIT, MST, PhD, Ed S. *Accreditation:* NCATE. *Program availability:* Part-time, evening/weekend, online learning. *Faculty:* 99 full-time (53 women), 4 part-time/adjunct (3 women). *Students:* 267 full-time (163 women), 455 part-time (333 women); includes 246 minority (215 Black or African American, non-Hispanic/Latino; 4 American Indian or Alaska Native, non-Hispanic/Latino; 6 Asian, non-Hispanic/Latino; 9 Hispanic/Latino; 1 Native Hawaiian or other Pacific Islander, non-Hispanic/Latino; 11 Two or more races, non-Hispanic/Latino), 16 international. Average age 33. 401 applicants, 59% accepted, 189 enrolled. In 2016, 180 master's, 27 doctorates, 24 other advanced degrees awarded. Terminal master's awarded for partial completion of doctoral program. *Degree requirements:* For master's, thesis optional, comprehensive oral or written exam; for doctorate, thesis/dissertation; for Ed S, thesis or alternative, final written or oral exam. *Entrance requirements:* For master's, doctorate, and Ed S, GRE. Additional exam requirements/recommendations for international students: Required—TOEFL (minimum score 550 paper-based; 79 iBT); Recommended—IELTS (minimum score 6.5). *Application deadline:* For fall admission, 7/1 for domestic students,

5/1 for international students; for spring admission, 11/1 for domestic students, 9/1 for international students. Applications are processed on a rolling basis. Application fee: $60. Electronic applications accepted. *Expenses:* Tuition, state resident: full-time $7670; part-time $852.50 per credit hour. Tuition, nonresident: full-time $20,790; part-time $2310.50 per credit hour. Part-time tuition and fees vary according to course load. *Financial support:* In 2016–17, 13 research assistantships (averaging $12,017 per year), 28 teaching assistantships (averaging $9,736 per year) were awarded; career-related internships or fieldwork, Federal Work-Study, institutionally sponsored loans, scholarships/grants, and unspecified assistantships also available. Financial award application deadline: 4/1; financial award applicants required to submit FAFSA. *Faculty research:* Leadership behavior, creativity measures, early childhood education, employability of the blind, quality indicators of professional educators. *Total annual research expenditures:* $2.5 million. *Unit head:* Dr. Richard Blackbourn, Dean, 662-325-3717, Fax: 662-325-8784, E-mail: rlb277@msstate.edu. *Application contact:* Linda Bonner, Senior Admissions Assistant, 662-325-3363, E-mail: lbonner@grad.msstate.edu.
Website: http://www.educ.msstate.edu/

Mississippi University for Women, Graduate School, College of Education and Human Sciences, Columbus, MS 39701-9998. Offers differentiated instruction (M Ed); educational leadership (M Ed); gifted studies (M Ed); reading/literacy (M Ed); teaching (MAT). *Accreditation:* ASHA; NCATE. *Program availability:* Part-time. *Degree requirements:* For master's, comprehensive exam, thesis optional. *Entrance requirements:* For master's, GRE General Test or NTE (M Ed in gifted education or MS in speech/language pathology), MAT (M Ed in instructional management), minimum QPA of 3.0.

Mississippi Valley State University, College of Education, Itta Bena, MS 38941-1400. Offers MAT, MS. *Accreditation:* NCATE. *Program availability:* Part-time, evening/weekend. *Faculty:* 7 full-time (6 women), 2 part-time/adjunct (both women). *Students:* 6 full-time (4 women), 132 part-time (89 women); includes 133 minority (132 Black or African American, non-Hispanic/Latino; 1 Asian, non-Hispanic/Latino). Average age 34. In 2016, 17 master's awarded. *Degree requirements:* For master's, comprehensive exam, thesis (for some programs). *Entrance requirements:* Additional exam requirements/recommendations for international students: Required—TOEFL (minimum score 525 paper-based). *Application deadline:* Applications are processed on a rolling basis. Application fee: $0. *Expenses:* Contact institution. *Financial support:* Institutionally sponsored loans available. Financial award application deadline: 8/1; financial award applicants required to submit FAFSA. *Unit head:* Dr. Chukwuma Ahanonu, Chair, 601-254-3619. *Application contact:* Office of Admissions, 601-254-3344.

Missouri Baptist University, Graduate Programs, St. Louis, MO 63141-8660. Offers business administration (MBA); Christian ministries (MACM); counseling (MAC); education (MSE); education administration (MEA); educational leadership (MSE, Ed S); teaching (MAT).

Missouri Southern State University, Program in Teaching, Joplin, MO 64801-1595. Offers MAT. Program offered jointly with Missouri State University. *Accreditation:* NCATE. *Degree requirements:* For master's, research seminar.

Molloy College, Graduate Education Program, Rockville Centre, NY 11571-5002. Offers adolescent education in biology (MS Ed); adolescent special education (Advanced Certificate); bilingual extension (Advanced Certificate); childhood education (MS Ed); childhood special education (Advanced Certificate); early childhood education (MS Ed); educational technology (MS Ed); English (MS Ed); mathematics (MS Ed); social studies (MS Ed); Spanish (MS Ed); special education on both childhood and adolescent levels (MS Ed); teaching English to speakers of other languages (TESOL) in grades Pre-K to 12 (MS Ed); TESOL (Advanced Certificate). *Accreditation:* NCATE. *Program availability:* Part-time, evening/weekend. *Faculty:* 17 full-time (16 women), 23 part-time/adjunct (19 women). *Students:* 95 full-time (75 women), 221 part-time (177 women); includes 59 minority (14 Black or African American, non-Hispanic/Latino; 6 Asian, non-Hispanic/Latino; 38 Hispanic/Latino; 1 Two or more races, non-Hispanic/Latino), 1 international. Average age 42. 214 applicants, 66% accepted, 125 enrolled. In 2016, 95 master's, 4 Advanced Certificates awarded. *Entrance requirements:* Additional exam requirements/recommendations for international students: Required—TOEFL (minimum score 550 paper-based; 79 iBT). *Application deadline:* Applications are processed on a rolling basis. Application fee: $60. Electronic applications accepted. *Expenses: Tuition:* Full-time $19,170; part-time $1065 per credit. *Required fees:* $950; $790 per credit. Tuition and fees vary according to course load. *Financial support:* Applicants required to submit FAFSA. *Faculty research:* ESL - general education teacher collaboration; special education; school desegregation; American intellectual and social history; families and schools. *Unit head:* Joanne O'Brien, Associate Dean/Director, 516-323-3116, E-mail: jobrien@molloy.edu. *Application contact:* Jaclyn Machowicz, Assistant Director for Admissions, 516-323-4010, E-mail: jmachowicz@molloy.edu.

Montana State University, The Graduate School, College of Education, Health, and Human Development, Department of Education, Bozeman, MT 59717. Offers adult and higher education (Ed D); curriculum and instruction (M Ed, Ed D), including professional educator (M Ed), technology education (M Ed); education (M Ed), including adult and higher education, educational leadership, school counseling; educational leadership (Ed D, Ed S). *Accreditation:* TEAC. *Program availability:* Part-time, online learning. *Degree requirements:* For master's, comprehensive exam; for doctorate, comprehensive exam, thesis/dissertation. *Entrance requirements:* For master's, GRE, 3 letters of reference, essays, BA transcripts; for doctorate, GRE, MAT, 3 letters of reference, essay, BA and M Ed transcripts; for Ed S, PRAXIS. Additional exam requirements/recommendations for international students: Required—TOEFL (minimum score 550 paper-based). Electronic applications accepted. *Faculty research:* Critical literacy; standards-based education; school Improvement, organizational change, leadership in rural education, leadership in Indian education; student Learning; multicultural/culturally responsive education for social justice Native American indigenous education, community-centered education teacher preparation.

Montana State University Billings, College of Education, Billings, MT 59101. Offers M Ed, MS Sp Ed, Certificate. *Accreditation:* NCATE. *Program availability:* Part-time, 100% online, blended/hybrid learning. *Faculty:* 16 full-time (11 women), 1 (woman) part-time/adjunct. *Students:* 158. *Degree requirements:* For master's, thesis optional. *Entrance requirements:* For master's, GRE General Test, minimum GPA of 3.0. Additional exam requirements/recommendations for international students: Required—TOEFL (minimum score 79 iBT), IELTS (minimum score 6.5). *Application deadline:* For fall admission, 7/15 for international students; for spring admission, 12/1 for international students. Applications are processed on a rolling basis. Application fee: $40. Electronic applications accepted. *Expenses:* Tuition, state resident: full-time $5265; part-time $3436 per year. Tuition, nonresident: full-time $14,030; part-time $9280 per year. *International tuition:* $19,295 full-time. Tuition and fees vary according to degree level, campus/location and program. *Financial support:* In 2016–17, research assistantships with partial tuition reimbursements (averaging $2,500 per year), teaching assistantships with partial tuition reimbursements (averaging $2,500 per year) were awarded; career-related internships or fieldwork, Federal Work-Study, institutionally sponsored loans, scholarships/grants, tuition waivers (partial), and unspecified assistantships also available. Support available to part-time students. Financial award application deadline: 5/1; financial award applicants required to submit FAFSA. *Faculty research:* Social studies education, science education. *Unit head:* Dr. Mary Susan Fishbaugh, Dean, 406-657-2285, Fax: 406-657-2299, E-mail: mfishbaugh@msubillings.edu. *Application contact:* David M. Sullivan, Graduate Studies Counselor, 406-657-2053, Fax: 406-657-2299, E-mail: dsullivan@msubillings.edu.
Website: http://www.msubillings.edu/coe/

Montana State University–Northern, Graduate Programs, Havre, MT 59501-7751. Offers counselor education (M Ed); instruction and learning (MS Ed). *Program availability:* Part-time, evening/weekend, online learning. *Degree requirements:* For master's, comprehensive exam, oral exams or thesis. *Entrance requirements:* For master's, GRE General Test or MAT, minimum GPA of 3.0. *Application deadline:* For fall admission, 9/20 priority date for domestic students. Applications are processed on a rolling basis. Application fee: $30. Electronic applications accepted. *Financial support:* Research assistantships with partial tuition reimbursements, teaching assistantships with partial tuition reimbursements, career-related internships or fieldwork, Federal Work-Study, institutionally sponsored loans, and unspecified assistantships available. Support available to part-time students. Financial award application deadline: 4/1; financial award applicants required to submit FAFSA. *Unit head:* Larry Strizich, Interim Provost, 406-265-3726, Fax: 406-265-3530, E-mail: strizich@msun.edu. *Application contact:* Robert Kurtz, Program Advisor, 406-265-3700.
Website: http://www.msun.edu/academics/grad/

Montclair State University, The Graduate School, College of Education and Human Services, Montclair, NJ 07043-1624. Offers M Ed, MA, MAT, MPH, MS, Ed D, PhD, Certificate, Post Master's Certificate, Postbaccalaureate Certificate. *Accreditation:* NCATE. *Program availability:* Part-time, evening/weekend. *Degree requirements:* For master's, comprehensive exam (for some programs), thesis (for some programs); for doctorate, comprehensive exam, thesis/dissertation. *Entrance requirements:* For master's, GRE, GMAT, MAT, 2 letters of recommendation; for doctorate, GRE General Test, 3 letters of recommendation. Additional exam requirements/recommendations for international students: Required—TOEFL (minimum score 83 iBT) or IELTS. Electronic applications accepted. *Expenses:* Tuition, state resident: part-time $553 per credit. Tuition, nonresident: part-time $854 per credit. *Required fees:* $91 per credit. Tuition and fees vary according to program. *Faculty research:* Key factors in the preparation of teachers for urban schools, factors affecting upper extremity motion patterns and injuries, implementation fidelity of instructional interventions, data-based decision-making in educational contexts, nutrition and physical activity of the aging population in the U. S.

Moravian College, Graduate and Continuing Studies, Education Programs, Bethlehem, PA 18018-6650. Offers curriculum and instruction (M Ed); education (MAT). *Program availability:* Part-time, evening/weekend. *Faculty:* 7 full-time (4 women), 17 part-time/adjunct (12 women). *Students:* 1 (woman) full-time, 91 part-time (71 women); includes 7 minority (1 Asian, non-Hispanic/Latino; 5 Hispanic/Latino; 1 Two or more races, non-Hispanic/Latino). Average age 35. 15 applicants, 80% accepted, 11 enrolled. In 2016, 17 master's awarded. *Degree requirements:* For master's, thesis. *Entrance requirements:* For master's, state teacher certification. *Application deadline:* For fall admission, 8/1 priority date for domestic and international students; for spring admission, 1/1 priority date for domestic and international students; for summer admission, 5/1 priority date for domestic and international students. Applications are processed on a rolling basis. Electronic applications accepted. *Expenses:* Contact institution. *Financial support:* Applicants required to submit FAFSA. *Faculty research:* Teacher action research, youth participatory research, practitioner inquiry, science education, deaf and hard of hearing education. *Unit head:* Dr. Joseph Shosh, Director, 610-861-1400, Fax: 610-861-1466, E-mail: shoshj@moravian.edu. *Application contact:* 610-861-1400, Fax: 610-861-1466, E-mail: graduate@moravian.edu.

Morehead State University, Graduate Programs, College of Education, Morehead, KY 40351. Offers MA, MA Ed, MAT, Ed S. *Accreditation:* NCATE. *Program availability:* Part-time, evening/weekend. *Degree requirements:* For master's, comprehensive exam, thesis or alternative; for Ed S, thesis. *Entrance requirements:* For master's, GRE General Test or PRAXIS, minimum overall undergraduate GPA of 2.5; for Ed S, GRE General Test, interview, master's degree, minimum GPA of 3.5, work experience. Additional exam requirements/recommendations for international students: Required—TOEFL (minimum score 500 paper-based). Electronic applications accepted. *Faculty research:* Regional economic development, computer applications for school administrators, effectiveness of teacher interns, perceptual processes, alcoholism.

Morgan State University, School of Graduate Studies, School of Education and Urban Studies, Baltimore, MD 21251. Offers MA, MAT, MS, Ed D, PhD. *Program availability:* Part-time. *Degree requirements:* For master's, comprehensive exam; for doctorate, comprehensive exam, thesis/dissertation. *Entrance requirements:* For doctorate, GRE General Test or MAT. Additional exam requirements/recommendations for international students: Required—TOEFL (minimum score 550 paper-based). *Faculty research:* Multicultural education, cooperative learning, psychology of cognition.

Morningside College, Graduate Division, Sharon Walker School of Education, Sioux City, IA 51106. Offers professional educator (MAT); special education (MAT), including instructional strategist: mild/moderate (7-12), instructional strategist: mild/moderate (K-6), K-12 instructional strategist: behavior disorders/learning disabilities, K-12 instructional strategist: mental disabilities. *Program availability:* Part-time, evening/weekend, online only, 100% online. *Faculty:* 4 full-time (1 woman), 108 part-time/adjunct (80 women). *Students:* 23 full-time (20 women), 1,468 part-time (1,191 women); includes 51 minority (5 Black or African American, non-Hispanic/Latino; 4 American Indian or Alaska Native, non-Hispanic/Latino; 9 Asian, non-Hispanic/Latino; 27 Hispanic/Latino; 1 Native Hawaiian or other Pacific Islander, non-Hispanic/Latino; 5 Two or more races, non-Hispanic/Latino), 1 international. Average age 35. In 2016, 316 master's awarded. *Entrance requirements:* For master's, MAT, writing sample. *Application deadline:* Applications are processed on a rolling basis. Application fee: $15. Electronic applications accepted. Application fee is waived when completed online. *Expenses:* $240 per credit hour. *Financial support:* Institutionally sponsored loans and tuition waivers (partial) available. Support available to part-time students. *Unit head:* Barbara Chambers, Director, 712-274-5465, Fax: 712-274-5488, E-mail: chambersb@morningside.edu. *Application contact:* Tracy Sursely, Student Records Enrollment Coordinator, 712-274-5576, Fax: 712-274-5101, E-mail: surselyt@morningside.edu.

Mount Mary University, Graduate Programs, Programs in Education, Milwaukee, WI 53222-4597. Offers professional development (MA). *Program availability:* Part-time, evening/weekend. *Faculty:* 1 (woman) full-time, 9 part-time/adjunct (8 women). *Students:* 32 full-time (27 women), 22 part-time (17 women); includes 13 minority (2 Black or African American, non-Hispanic/Latino; 1 Asian, non-Hispanic/Latino; 7 Hispanic/Latino; 3 Two or more races, non-Hispanic/Latino). Average age 34. 7 applicants, 43% accepted, 2 enrolled. In 2016, 5 master's awarded. *Degree requirements:* For master's, action research project. *Entrance requirements:* For master's, minimum GPA of 2.75, teaching license. Additional exam requirements/recommendations for international students: Required—TOEFL (minimum score 550 paper-based; 80 iBT); Recommended—IELTS (minimum score 6.5). *Application*

deadline: For fall admission, 8/1 for domestic and international students; for spring admission, 12/1 for domestic and international students; for summer admission, 5/1 for domestic and international students. Applications are processed on a rolling basis. Application fee: $45. Electronic applications accepted. *Expenses:* Contact institution. *Financial support:* Federal Work-Study available. Support available to part-time students. Financial award application deadline: 5/1; financial award applicants required to submit FAFSA. *Faculty research:* Staff development, writing across the curriculum, effective schools, critical thinking skills, mathematics education. *Unit head:* Dr. Deb Dosemagen, Graduate Program Director, 414-930-3160, E-mail: dosemagd@mtmary.edu. *Application contact:* Kirk Heller de Messer, Director, Graduate Admissions, 414-930-3221, E-mail: hellerk@mtmary.edu.
Website: http://www.mtmary.edu/majors-programs/graduate/education/index.html

Mount Mercy University, Program in Education, Cedar Rapids, IA 52402-4797. Offers reading (MA Ed); special education (MA Ed); teacher leadership (MA Ed). *Entrance requirements:* For master's, minimum cumulative GPA of 3.0, 2 letters of recommendation, resume, valid teaching license. Additional exam requirements/recommendations for international students: Required—TOEFL (minimum score 570 paper-based; 88 iBT). Electronic applications accepted.

Mount St. Joseph University, Graduate Education Program, Cincinnati, OH 45233-1670. Offers adolescent to young adult education (MA); dyslexia (Certificate); inclusive early childhood education (MA); middle childhood education (MA); multicultural special education (MA); reading science (MA). *Accreditation:* TEAC. *Program availability:* Part-time, evening/weekend, online learning. *Faculty:* 7 full-time (5 women), 12 part-time/adjunct (10 women). *Students:* 44 full-time (33 women), 112 part-time (104 women); includes 16 minority (15 Black or African American, non-Hispanic/Latino; 1 Two or more races, non-Hispanic/Latino). Average age 34. In 2016, 60 master's awarded. *Degree requirements:* For master's, comprehensive exam, thesis, research project, student teaching, clinical and field-based experiences. *Entrance requirements:* For master's, GRE (if GPA is below 3.0), letter of intent, 2 referrals, background check, interview, resume, minimum undergraduate GPA of 3.0. Additional exam requirements/recommendations for international students: Required—TOEFL (minimum score 560 paper-based; 83 iBT). *Application deadline:* Applications are processed on a rolling basis. Application fee: $50. Electronic applications accepted. *Expenses:* $580 per credit hour. *Financial support:* Applicants required to submit FAFSA. *Faculty research:* Foreign and second language learning problems/reading disabilities, multicultural/bilingual special education, science education, pedagogical content knowledge, early childhood, response to intervention. *Unit head:* Dr. Laura Saylor, Dean, 513-244-3263, E-mail: laura.saylor@msj.edu. *Application contact:* Mary Brigham, Assistant Director of Graduate Recruitment, 513-244-4233, Fax: 513-244-4629, E-mail: mary.brigham@msj.edu.
Website: http://www.msj.edu/academics/graduate-programs/master-of-arts-initial-teacher-licensure-programs/

Mount Saint Mary College, Division of Education, Newburgh, NY 12550-3494. Offers adolescence and special education (MS Ed); childhood education (MS Ed); literacy education (MS Ed); middle school (7-9) (MS Ed). *Accreditation:* NCATE. *Program availability:* Part-time, evening/weekend. *Faculty:* 12 full-time (10 women), 3 part-time/adjunct (all women). *Students:* 27 full-time (19 women), 78 part-time (59 women); includes 12 minority (1 Black or African American, non-Hispanic/Latino; 1 Asian, non-Hispanic/Latino; 7 Hispanic/Latino; 3 Two or more races, non-Hispanic/Latino). Average age 28. 30 applicants, 100% accepted, 16 enrolled. In 2016, 62 master's awarded. *Entrance requirements:* Additional exam requirements/recommendations for international students: Required—TOEFL (minimum score 80 iBT). *Application deadline:* Applications are processed on a rolling basis. Application fee: $45. Electronic applications accepted. Application fee is waived when completed online. *Expenses: Tuition:* Full-time $13,914; part-time $773 per credit. *Required fees:* $82 per semester. *Financial support:* In 2016–17, 18 students received support. Unspecified assistantships available. Financial award application deadline: 4/15; financial award applicants required to submit FAFSA. *Faculty research:* Learning and teaching styles, computers in special education, language development. *Unit head:* Dr. Monica Merritt, Graduate Coordinator, 845-569-3430, Fax: 845-569-3535, E-mail: monica.merritt@msmc.edu. *Application contact:* Lisa Gallina, Director of Admissions for Graduate Programs and Adult Degree Completion, 845-569-3166, Fax: 845-569-3450, E-mail: lisa.gallina@msmc.edu.
Website: http://www.msmc.edu/Academics/Graduate_Programs/Master_of_Science_in_Education

Mount Saint Mary's University, Graduate Division, Los Angeles, CA 90049. Offers business administration (MBA); counseling psychology (MS); creative writing (MFA); education (MS, Certificate); film and television (MFA); health policy and management (MS); humanities (MA); nursing (MSN, Certificate); physical therapy (DPT); religious studies (MA). *Program availability:* Part-time, evening/weekend. *Faculty:* 50 full-time (35 women), 116 part-time/adjunct (81 women). *Students:* 670 full-time (518 women), 147 part-time (116 women); includes 414 minority (73 Black or African American, non-Hispanic/Latino; 4 American Indian or Alaska Native, non-Hispanic/Latino; 60 Asian, non-Hispanic/Latino; 259 Hispanic/Latino; 7 Native Hawaiian or other Pacific Islander, non-Hispanic/Latino; 11 Two or more races, non-Hispanic/Latino), 4 international. Average age 32. 1,398 applicants, 21% accepted, 242 enrolled. In 2016, 170 master's, 28 doctorates, 35 other advanced degrees awarded. *Entrance requirements:* Additional exam requirements/recommendations for international students: Required—TOEFL. *Application deadline:* For fall admission, 6/30 priority date for domestic and international students; for spring admission, 10/30 priority date for domestic and international students; for summer admission, 3/30 priority date for domestic and international students. Applications are processed on a rolling basis. Application fee: $50. Electronic applications accepted. *Expenses: Tuition:* Full-time $9983; part-time $829 per unit. One-time fee: $135. Tuition and fees vary according to degree level and program. *Financial support:* Career-related internships or fieldwork, Federal Work-Study, institutionally sponsored loans, and tuition waivers (full and partial) available. Support available to part-time students. Financial award application deadline: 3/15; financial award applicants required to submit FAFSA. *Unit head:* Albert Ramos, Director of Graduate Admissions, 213-477-2800, E-mail: gradprograms@msmu.edu. *Application contact:* Shawn Peters, Graduate Admission Counselor, 213-477-2676, E-mail: gradprograms@msmu.edu.
Website: http://www.msmu.edu/graduate-programs/

Mount St. Mary's University, Program in Education, Emmitsburg, MD 21727-7799. Offers M Ed, MAT. *Accreditation:* NCATE. *Faculty:* 5 full-time (4 women), 7 part-time/adjunct (all women). *Students:* 18 full-time (13 women), 78 part-time (57 women); includes 7 minority (2 Black or African American, non-Hispanic/Latino; 2 American Indian or Alaska Native, non-Hispanic/Latino; 1 Asian, non-Hispanic/Latino; 1 Hispanic/Latino; 1 Two or more races, non-Hispanic/Latino), 3 international. Average age 32. In 2016, 15 master's awarded. *Degree requirements:* For master's, thesis (for some programs), exit portfolio/presentation. *Entrance requirements:* For master's, PRAXIS I and II. Additional exam requirements/recommendations for international students: Required—TOEFL (minimum score 550 paper-based; 83 iBT). *Application deadline:* Applications are processed on a rolling basis. Electronic applications accepted. *Expenses:* $500 per credit hour. *Financial support:* Unspecified assistantships available. Financial award applicants required to submit FAFSA. *Unit head:* Dr. Barbara Martin-Palmer, Dean of School of Education and Human Services, 301-447-5371, Fax: 301-447-5250, E-mail: palmer@msmary.edu.
Website: http://msmary.edu/School_of_education_and_human_services/Graduate_programs/

Mount Saint Vincent University, Graduate Programs, Faculty of Education, Halifax, NS B3M 2J6, Canada. Offers adult education (M Ed, MA Ed, MA-R); curriculum studies (M Ed, MA Ed, MA-R), including education of young adolescents, general studies, teaching English as a second language; educational foundations (M Ed, MA Ed, MA-R); educational psychology (M Ed, MA Ed, MA-R), including education of the blind or visually impaired (M Ed, MA Ed), education of the deaf or hard of hearing (M Ed, MA Ed), educational psychology (MA-R), human relations (M Ed, MA Ed); elementary education (M Ed, MA Ed, MA-R); literacy education (M Ed, MA Ed, MA-R); school psychology (MASP). *Program availability:* Part-time, evening/weekend, online learning. *Degree requirements:* For master's, thesis (for some programs), practicum. *Entrance requirements:* For master's, bachelor's degree in related field. Electronic applications accepted.

Mount Vernon Nazarene University, Department of Education, Mount Vernon, OH 43050-9500. Offers education (MA Ed); professional educator's license (MA Ed). *Accreditation:* NCATE. *Program availability:* Part-time, evening/weekend. *Degree requirements:* For master's, project.

Multnomah University, Graduate Programs, Portland, OR 97220-5898. Offers counseling (MA); global development and justice (MA); teaching (MA); TESOL (MA). *Program availability:* Part-time, evening/weekend. *Faculty:* 6 full-time (4 women), 16 part-time/adjunct (10 women). *Students:* 120 full-time (80 women), 31 part-time (23 women); includes 35 minority (15 Black or African American, non-Hispanic/Latino; 2 Asian, non-Hispanic/Latino; 9 Hispanic/Latino; 1 Native Hawaiian or other Pacific Islander, non-Hispanic/Latino; 8 Two or more races, non-Hispanic/Latino), 3 international. Average age 30. 69 applicants, 55% accepted, 24 enrolled. In 2016, 55 degrees awarded. *Degree requirements:* For master's, variable foreign language requirement, comprehensive exam (for some programs), thesis (for some programs). *Entrance requirements:* For master's, CBEST or WEST-B (for MAT), interview; references (4 for teaching); writing sample (for counseling). Additional exam requirements/recommendations for international students: Required—TOEFL (minimum score 550 paper-based). *Application deadline:* For fall admission, 8/1 for domestic students, 12/1 for international students; for spring admission, 12/1 for domestic and international students. Application fee: $40. Electronic applications accepted. *Expenses: Tuition:* Full-time $10,000; part-time $6000 per semester. *Required fees:* $230; $120 per semester. Tuition and fees vary according to course load, degree level and program. *Financial support:* Career-related internships or fieldwork and scholarships/grants available. Support available to part-time students. Financial award application deadline: 7/1; financial award applicants required to submit FAFSA. *Unit head:* Dr. Daniel Scalberg, Academic Dean, 503-251-6441, E-mail: dscalberg@multnomah.edu. *Application contact:* Mindy Kate Hasenkamp, Director of Admissions, 503-251-6483, Fax: 503-254-1268, E-mail: admiss@multnomah.edu.

Murray State University, College of Education, Murray, KY 42071. Offers MA Ed, MS, Ed D, PhD, Ed S. PhD, Ed D offered jointly with University of Kentucky. *Accreditation:* NCATE. *Program availability:* Part-time.

Muskingum University, Graduate Programs in Education, New Concord, OH 43762. Offers MAE, MAT. *Accreditation:* NCATE. *Program availability:* Part-time. *Entrance requirements:* For master's, minimum GPA of 2.7, teaching license. *Faculty research:* Brain behavior relationships, school partnerships, staff development, school law, proficiency testing, multi-age groupings.

Naropa University, Graduate Programs, Program in Contemplative Education, Boulder, CO 80302-6697. Offers MA. *Program availability:* Part-time, blended/hybrid learning. *Faculty:* 1 full-time (0 women), 5 part-time/adjunct (4 women). *Students:* 18 part-time (13 women); includes 2 minority (1 American Indian or Alaska Native, non-Hispanic/Latino; 1 Two or more races, non-Hispanic/Latino), 2 international. Average age 33. 14 applicants, 93% accepted, 9 enrolled. In 2016, 10 master's awarded. *Degree requirements:* For master's, thesis. *Entrance requirements:* For master's, 2 letters of recommendation; transcripts; resume/curriculum vitae with pertinent academic, employment and volunteer activity; statement of interest. Additional exam requirements/recommendations for international students: Required—TOEFL (minimum score 550 paper-based; 80 iBT). *Application deadline:* For fall admission, 1/15 priority date for domestic and international students. Applications are processed on a rolling basis. Application fee: $60. Electronic applications accepted. *Expenses:* $18,530 for first year. *Financial support:* In 2016–17, 9 students received support. Fellowships with full tuition reimbursements available, research assistantships with partial tuition reimbursements available, teaching assistantships with partial tuition reimbursements available, career-related internships or fieldwork, Federal Work-Study, scholarships/grants, tuition waivers (partial), and unspecified assistantships available. Support available to part-time students. Financial award application deadline: 3/1; financial award applicants required to submit FAFSA. *Unit head:* Barbara Catbagan, Chair, 303-245-4834, E-mail: bcatbagan@naropa.edu. *Application contact:* Office of Admissions, 303-546-3572, Fax: 303-546-3583, E-mail: admissions@naropa.edu.
Website: http://www.naropa.edu/academics/masters/contemplative-education/index.php

National Louis University, National College of Education, Chicago, IL 60603. Offers administration and supervision (M Ed, Ed D, CAS, Ed S); curriculum and instruction (M Ed, MS Ed, CAS); early childhood administration (M Ed, CAS); early childhood education (M Ed, MAT, MS Ed, CAS); education (Ed D); educational psychology/human learning and development (M Ed, MS Ed, CAS, Ed S); elementary education (MAT); interdisciplinary curriculum and instruction (M Ed); mathematics education (M Ed, MS Ed, CAS); middle grades education (MAT); reading and language (M Ed, MS Ed, CAS); school psychology (M Ed, Ed S); science education (M Ed, MS Ed, CAS); secondary education (MAT); special education (M Ed, MAT, CAS); technology in education (M Ed, CAS). *Accreditation:* NCATE. *Program availability:* Part-time, evening/weekend. *Degree requirements:* For doctorate, comprehensive exam, thesis/dissertation. *Entrance requirements:* For master's, MAT or GRE, minimum GPA of 3.0; for doctorate, GRE General Test, minimum GPA of 3.25, interview, resume, writing sample, 4 recommendations. Additional exam requirements/recommendations for international students: Required—TOEFL (minimum score 550 paper-based; 79 iBT).

National University, Academic Affairs, School of Education, La Jolla, CA 92037-1011. Offers e-teaching and learning (Certificate); educational administration (MS). *Program availability:* Part-time, evening/weekend, 100% online, blended/hybrid learning. *Faculty:* 74 full-time (48 women), 422 part-time/adjunct (260 women). *Students:* 3,376 full-time (2,418 women), 2,410 part-time (1,641 women); includes 2,652 minority (357 Black or African American, non-Hispanic/Latino; 29 American Indian or Alaska Native, non-Hispanic/Latino; 337 Asian, non-Hispanic/Latino; 1,680 Hispanic/Latino; 45 Native Hawaiian or other Pacific Islander, non-Hispanic/Latino; 204 Two or more races, non-Hispanic/Latino). Average age 33. In 2016, 1,456 master's awarded. *Degree requirements:* For master's, thesis (for some programs). *Entrance requirements:* For

master's, interview, minimum GPA of 2.5. Additional exam requirements/recommendations for international students: Required—TOEFL (minimum score 550 paper-based; 79 iBT), IELTS (minimum score 6). *Application deadline:* Applications are processed on a rolling basis. Application fee: $60 ($65 for international students). Electronic applications accepted. *Financial support:* Career-related internships or fieldwork, institutionally sponsored loans, scholarships/grants, and tuition waivers (partial) available. Support available to part-time students. Financial award application deadline: 6/30. *Faculty research:* Teacher education, special education, educational effectiveness, teaching abroad, school counseling. *Unit head:* School of Education, 800-628-8648, E-mail: soe@nu.edu. *Application contact:* Brandon Jouganatos, Vice President for Enrollment Services, 800-628-8648, E-mail: advisor@nu.edu.
Website: http://www.nu.edu/OurPrograms/SchoolOfEducation.html

Nazareth College of Rochester, Graduate Studies, Department of Education, Rochester, NY 14618. Offers educational technology (MS Ed); inclusive adolescence education (MS Ed); inclusive childhood education (MS Ed); inclusive early childhood education (MS Ed); literacy education (MS Ed); teaching English to speakers of other languages (MS Ed). *Accreditation:* TEAC. *Program availability:* Part-time, evening/weekend. *Students:* 56 full-time (49 women), 99 part-time (84 women); includes 17 minority (12 Black or African American, non-Hispanic/Latino; 1 American Indian or Alaska Native, non-Hispanic/Latino; 2 Asian, non-Hispanic/Latino; 2 Two or more races, non-Hispanic/Latino). Average age 28. 138 applicants, 85% accepted, 70 enrolled. *Entrance requirements:* For master's, GRE or MAT (for education programs), minimum GPA of 3.0. Additional exam requirements/recommendations for international students: Required—TOEFL (minimum score 550 paper-based, 79 iBT) or IELTS (6.5). *Application deadline:* For fall admission, 4/1 priority date for domestic students; for spring admission, 10/1 priority date for domestic students. Applications are processed on a rolling basis. Electronic applications accepted. *Expenses: Tuition:* Part-time $880 per credit hour. Part-time tuition and fees vary according to course load, degree level and program. *Financial support:* Scholarships/grants and unspecified assistantships available. Financial award application deadline: 3/1; financial award applicants required to submit FAFSA. *Unit head:* Dr. Kathleen M. DaBoll-Lavoie, Dean, School of Education, 585-389-2618. *Application contact:* Judith Baker, Director, Transfer and Graduate Admissions, 585-531-1154, Fax: 585-389-2826, E-mail: gradadmissions@naz.edu.

Neumann University, Graduate Program in Education, Aston, PA 19014-1298. Offers education (MS), including administrative (principal K-12), autism, early elementary education, secondary education, special education. *Program availability:* Part-time, evening/weekend, 100% online, blended/hybrid learning. *Faculty:* 6 full-time (5 women), 18 part-time/adjunct (7 women). *Students:* 80 full-time (64 women), 108 part-time (91 women); includes 40 minority (30 Black or African American, non-Hispanic/Latino; 6 Hispanic/Latino; 4 Two or more races, non-Hispanic/Latino), 1 international. Average age 34. 152 applicants, 67% accepted, 82 enrolled. In 2016, 42 master's awarded. *Entrance requirements:* For master's, official transcripts from all institutions attended, letter of intent, three professional references, copy of any teaching certifications. Additional exam requirements/recommendations for international students: Required—TOEFL (minimum score 70 iBT). *Application deadline:* Applications are processed on a rolling basis. Application fee: $0. Electronic applications accepted. *Expenses:* $700 per credit on-campus tuition; $480 per credit online or off-campus tuition; additional $320 for student teaching course. *Financial support:* Scholarships/grants and health care benefits available. Support available to part-time students. Financial award application deadline: 3/15; financial award applicants required to submit FAFSA. *Unit head:* Dr. Stephanie Smith-Budhai, Director of Graduate Education, 610-358-4249, E-mail: budhais@neumann.edu. *Application contact:* Dr. Erika Davis, Director of Adult and Graduate Admissions, 800-9-NEUMANN Ext. 5208, Fax: 610-361-2548, E-mail: GradAdultAdmiss@neumann.edu.
Website: https://www.neumann.edu/academics/grad/education/index.asp

New England College, Program in Education, Henniker, NH 03242-3293. Offers higher education administration (MS, Ed D); K-12 leadership (Ed D); literacy and language arts (M Ed); meeting the needs of all learners/special education (M Ed); teacher leadership/school reform (M Ed). *Program availability:* Part-time, evening/weekend.

New Jersey City University, Debra Cannon Partridge Wolfe College of Education, Jersey City, NJ 07305-1597. Offers MA, MAT, Ed D. *Program availability:* Part-time, evening/weekend. *Entrance requirements:* Additional exam requirements/recommendations for international students: Required—TOEFL (minimum score 79 iBT).

Newman University, Master of Science in Education Program, Wichita, KS 67213-2097. Offers building leadership (MS Ed); curriculum and instruction (MS Ed), including English as a second language, reading specialist; organizational leadership (MS Ed). *Accreditation:* NCATE. *Program availability:* Part-time, evening/weekend, online learning. *Degree requirements:* For master's, thesis optional. *Entrance requirements:* For master's, 3 years' full-time teaching experience, minimum GPA of 3.0, writing sample, 2 letters of recommendation, evidence of teaching certification. Additional exam requirements/recommendations for international students: Required—TOEFL (minimum score 600 paper-based; 100 iBT). Electronic applications accepted. *Expenses:* Contact institution. *Faculty research:* Online course design and deliver, staff engagement, classroom action.

New Mexico Highlands University, Graduate Studies, School of Education, Las Vegas, NM 87701. Offers curriculum and instruction (MA); educational leadership (MA); professional counseling (MA); special education (MA). *Accreditation:* NCATE. *Program availability:* Part-time. *Degree requirements:* For master's, comprehensive exam, thesis or alternative. *Entrance requirements:* For master's, minimum undergraduate GPA of 3.0. Additional exam requirements/recommendations for international students: Required—TOEFL (minimum score 540 paper-based). *Faculty research:* Middle school curriculum, integrated computer applications for pre-service classroom teachers, adolescent literacy, narrative cognitive modes in New Mexico multicultural setting, math and math education.

New Mexico State University, College of Education, Las Cruces, NM 88003. Offers MA, MAT, Ed D, PhD, Ed S, Graduate Certificate. *Accreditation:* NCATE. *Program availability:* Part-time, evening/weekend, blended/hybrid learning. *Faculty:* 66 full-time (46 women), 16 part-time/adjunct (10 women). *Students:* 268 full-time (204 women), 412 part-time (307 women); includes 404 minority (23 Black or African American, non-Hispanic/Latino; 12 American Indian or Alaska Native, non-Hispanic/Latino; 18 Asian, non-Hispanic/Latino; 338 Hispanic/Latino; 1 Native Hawaiian or other Pacific Islander, non-Hispanic/Latino; 12 Two or more races, non-Hispanic/Latino), 44 international. Average age 36. 445 applicants, 40% accepted, 127 enrolled. In 2016, 171 master's, 32 doctorates, 18 other advanced degrees awarded. *Degree requirements:* For doctorate, comprehensive exam, thesis/dissertation. *Entrance requirements:* Additional exam requirements/recommendations for international students: Required—TOEFL (minimum score 550 paper-based; 79 iBT), IELTS (minimum score 6.5). *Application deadline:* Applications are processed on a rolling basis. Application fee: $40 ($50 for international students). Electronic applications accepted. *Expenses:* Tuition, state resident: full-time $4086. Tuition, nonresident: full-time $14,254. *Required fees:* $853. Tuition and fees vary according to course load. *Financial support:* In 2016–17, 233 students received support, including 8 fellowships (averaging $4,085 per year), 17 research assistantships (averaging $13,906 per year), 63 teaching assistantships (averaging $13,051 per year); career-related internships or fieldwork, Federal Work-Study, scholarships/grants, traineeships, health care benefits, and unspecified assistantships also available. Support available to part-time students. Financial award application deadline: 3/1. *Faculty research:* Bilingual special education, early childhood education/Head Start, leadership in border settings, exercise physiology, school-based mental health. *Total annual research expenditures:* $835,681. *Unit head:* Dr. Donald Pope Davis, Dean, 575-646-5858, Fax: 575-646-6032, E-mail: dpd@nmsu.edu. *Application contact:* Dr. David Rutledge, Graduate Education Advising, 575-646-5411, Fax: 575-646-6032, E-mail: rutledge@nmsu.edu.
Website: http://education.nmsu.edu/

New York Institute of Technology, School of Interdisciplinary Studies and Education, Old Westbury, NY 11568-8000. Offers MA, MS, Advanced Certificate, Advanced Diploma. *Accreditation:* NCATE. *Program availability:* Part-time, evening/weekend, 100% online, blended/hybrid learning. *Faculty:* 12 full-time (7 women), 19 part-time/adjunct (11 women). *Students:* 58 full-time (48 women), 284 part-time (210 women); includes 95 minority (33 Black or African American, non-Hispanic/Latino; 1 American Indian or Alaska Native, non-Hispanic/Latino; 13 Asian, non-Hispanic/Latino; 42 Hispanic/Latino; 6 Two or more races, non-Hispanic/Latino), 4 international. Average age 33. 247 applicants, 74% accepted, 135 enrolled. In 2016, 76 master's, 13 other advanced degrees awarded. *Entrance requirements:* Additional exam requirements/recommendations for international students: Required—TOEFL (minimum score 79 iBT), IELTS (minimum score 6). *Application deadline:* Applications are processed on a rolling basis. Application fee: $50. Electronic applications accepted. *Expenses:* $1,215 per credit. *Financial support:* Career-related internships or fieldwork, Federal Work-Study, scholarships/grants, tuition waivers (full and partial), and unspecified assistantships available. Support available to part-time students. Financial award application deadline: 3/1; financial award applicants required to submit FAFSA. *Unit head:* Dr. Jess Boronico, Interim Dean, 516-686-7403, E-mail: soeinfo@nyit.edu. *Application contact:* Alice Dolitsky, Director, Graduate Admissions, 516-686-7520, Fax: 516-686-1116, E-mail: nyitgrad@nyit.edu.
Website: http://www.nyit.edu/interdisciplinary

New York University, Steinhardt School of Culture, Education, and Human Development, New York, NY 10003. Offers MA, MFA, MM, MPH, MS, DPS, DPT, Ed D, PhD, Advanced Certificate, Post Master's Certificate, Postbaccalaureate Certificate, Advanced Certificate/MPH, MA/Advanced Certificate, MA/MA, MA/MS, MLIS/MA. *Accreditation:* TEAC. *Program availability:* Part-time. *Degree requirements:* For master's, thesis (for some programs); for doctorate, comprehensive exam (for some programs), thesis/dissertation. *Entrance requirements:* For doctorate, GRE General Test, interview. Additional exam requirements/recommendations for international students: Required—TOEFL (minimum score 100 iBT). Electronic applications accepted. *Expenses:* Contact institution. *Faculty research:* Equity, urban adolescents, arts in education, globalization, multivariate analysis, psychometrics.

Niagara University, Graduate Division of Education, Niagara University, NY 14109. Offers educational leadership (MS Ed, Certificate), including school building leader (MS Ed), school district business leader (Certificate), school district leader; literacy instruction (MS Ed); mental health counseling (MS, Certificate); school counseling (MS Ed, Certificate); school psychology (MS); teacher education (MS, MS Ed, Certificate), including early childhood and childhood education (MS Ed, Certificate), early childhood special education (MS), middle and adolescence education (Certificate), special education (MS Ed), special education (grades 1-6) (Certificate), special education (grades 7-12) (Certificate), teaching English to speakers of other languages (TESOL) (Certificate). *Accreditation:* NCATE (one or more programs are accredited). *Program availability:* Part-time, evening/weekend. *Students:* 239 full-time (195 women), 302 part-time (234 women); includes 53 minority (26 Black or African American, non-Hispanic/Latino; 1 American Indian or Alaska Native, non-Hispanic/Latino; 3 Asian, non-Hispanic/Latino; 15 Hispanic/Latino; 8 Two or more races, non-Hispanic/Latino), 79 international. Average age 31. In 2016, 159 master's, 35 other advanced degrees awarded. *Entrance requirements:* For master's, GRE General Test or MAT. Additional exam requirements/recommendations for international students: Required—TOEFL (minimum score 550 paper-based; 79 iBT), IELTS (minimum score 6). *Application deadline:* For fall admission, 8/1 for domestic students. Applications are processed on a rolling basis. Application fee: $30. *Expenses:* Contact institution. *Financial support:* Research assistantships with tuition reimbursements, teaching assistantships with tuition reimbursements, career-related internships or fieldwork, Federal Work-Study, scholarships/grants, and unspecified assistantships available. Financial award application deadline: 4/15; financial award applicants required to submit FAFSA. *Faculty research:* Instructional supervision, appraisal and evaluation, career opportunities. *Unit head:* Dr. Chandra Foote, Dean, College of Education, 716-286-8549, Fax: 716-286-8561, E-mail: cjf@niagara.edu. *Application contact:* Evan Pierce, Associate Director for Graduate Recruitment, 716-286-8769, Fax: 716-286-8170, E-mail: epierce@niagara.edu.
Website: http://www.niagara.edu/advance/

Nicholls State University, Graduate Studies, College of Education, Department of Teacher Education, Thibodaux, LA 70310. Offers curriculum and instruction (M Ed); educational leadership (M Ed); elementary education (MAT); human performance education (MAT); middle school education (MAT); secondary education (MAT). *Accreditation:* NCATE. *Program availability:* Part-time, evening/weekend, online learning. *Degree requirements:* For master's, comprehensive exam, portfolio. *Entrance requirements:* For master's, GRE General Test, teaching license. Electronic applications accepted.

Nipissing University, Faculty of Education, North Bay, ON P1B 8L7, Canada. Offers M Ed, Certificate. *Program availability:* Part-time, evening/weekend. *Degree requirements:* For master's, comprehensive exam (for some programs), thesis (for some programs). *Entrance requirements:* For master's, 1 year of experience, letters of recommendation, minimum undergraduate GPA of 3.0. Additional exam requirements/recommendations for international students: Required—TOEFL (minimum score 600 paper-based), IELTS (minimum score 7), TWE (minimum score 5).

Norfolk State University, School of Graduate Studies, School of Education, Norfolk, VA 23504. Offers MA, MAT. *Accreditation:* NCATE. *Program availability:* Part-time. *Degree requirements:* For master's, comprehensive exam. *Entrance requirements:* For master's, PRAXIS, GRE/GMAT, interview, teacher license. *Faculty research:* Urban, pre-elementary, and special education.

North Carolina Agricultural and Technical State University, School of Graduate Studies, School of Education, Greensboro, NC 27411. Offers MA Ed, MAT, MS. *Accreditation:* NCATE. *Program availability:* Part-time, evening/weekend. *Degree requirements:* For master's, comprehensive exam, qualifying exam. *Entrance requirements:* For master's, GRE General Test.

North Carolina Central University, School of Education, Durham, NC 27707-3129. Offers M Ed, MA, MSA. *Accreditation:* NCATE. *Program availability:* Part-time, evening/weekend. *Degree requirements:* For master's, comprehensive exam, thesis or alternative. *Entrance requirements:* For master's, minimum GPA of 3.0 in major, 2.5 overall. Additional exam requirements/recommendations for international students: Required—TOEFL.

North Carolina State University, Graduate School, College of Education, Raleigh, NC 27695. Offers M Ed, MS, MS Ed, MSA, Ed D, PhD, Certificate. *Accreditation:* NCATE. *Program availability:* Part-time. *Degree requirements:* For doctorate, thesis/dissertation. *Entrance requirements:* For master's, doctorate, and Certificate, GRE General Test or MAT, minimum GPA of 3.0 in major. Electronic applications accepted. *Faculty research:* Moral/ethical development, financial policy analysis, middle years education, adult education.

North Central College, School of Graduate and Professional Studies, Department of Education, Naperville, IL 60566-7063. Offers MA Ed. *Program availability:* Part-time, evening/weekend. *Faculty:* 8 full-time (5 women), 2 part-time/adjunct (1 woman). *Students:* 9 full-time (6 women), 59 part-time (44 women); includes 14 minority (2 Black or African American, non-Hispanic/Latino; 3 Asian, non-Hispanic/Latino; 7 Hispanic/Latino; 1 Native Hawaiian or other Pacific Islander, non-Hispanic/Latino; 1 Two or more races, non-Hispanic/Latino). Average age 31. 65 applicants, 43% accepted, 23 enrolled. In 2016, 13 master's awarded. *Degree requirements:* For master's, thesis optional, clinical practicum, project. *Entrance requirements:* For master's, interview. Additional exam requirements/recommendations for international students: Required—TOEFL (minimum score 550 paper-based; 80 iBT), IELTS (minimum score 6.5). *Application deadline:* For fall admission, 8/15 for domestic students; for winter admission, 12/1 for domestic students; for spring admission, 2/1 for domestic students. Applications are processed on a rolling basis. Application fee: $25. Electronic applications accepted. Application fee is waived when completed online. *Expenses:* Contact institution. *Financial support:* Available to part-time students. Applicants required to submit FAFSA. *Unit head:* Dr. Maureen Kincaid, Education Department Chair, 630-637-5750, Fax: 630-637-5844, E-mail: mkincaid@noctrl.edu. *Application contact:* Wendy Kulpinski, Director of Graduate and Professional Studies Admission, 630-637-5808, Fax: 630-637-5844, E-mail: wekulpinski@noctrl.edu.

Northcentral University, Graduate Studies, San Diego, CA 92106. Offers business (MBA, DBA, PhD, Postbaccalaureate Certificate); education (M Ed, Ed D, PhD, Ed S, Post-Master's Certificate, Postbaccalaureate Certificate); marriage and family therapy (MA, DMFT, PhD, Post-Master's Certificate, Postbaccalaureate Certificate); psychology (MA, PhD, Post-Master's Certificate, Postbaccalaureate Certificate). *Program availability:* Part-time, evening/weekend, online only, 100% online. *Faculty:* 98 full-time (63 women), 385 part-time/adjunct (203 women). *Students:* 5,036 full-time (3,291 women), 5,747 part-time (3,977 women); includes 3,777 minority (2,550 Black or African American, non-Hispanic/Latino; 76 American Indian or Alaska Native, non-Hispanic/Latino; 192 Asian, non-Hispanic/Latino; 603 Hispanic/Latino; 39 Native Hawaiian or other Pacific Islander, non-Hispanic/Latino; 317 Two or more races, non-Hispanic/Latino). Average age 45. In 2016, 799 master's, 399 doctorates, 230 other advanced degrees awarded. *Degree requirements:* For doctorate, comprehensive exam, thesis/dissertation. *Entrance requirements:* For master's, bachelor's degree from regionally- or nationally-accredited institution, current resume or curriculum vitae, statement of intent, interview, and background check (for marriage and family therapy); for doctorate, post-baccalaureate master's degree and/or doctoral degree from nationally- or regionally-accredited academic institution; for other advanced degree, bachelor's-level or higher degree from accredited institution or university (for Post-Baccalaureate Certificate); master's and/or doctoral degree from regionally- or nationally-accredited academic institution (for Post-Master's Certificate). Additional exam requirements/recommendations for international students: Required—TOEFL (minimum score 550 paper-based; 79 iBT), IELTS (minimum score 6.5), PTE (minimum score 53). *Application deadline:* Applications are processed on a rolling basis. Application fee: $0. Electronic applications accepted. *Expenses: Tuition:* Full-time $16,821; part-time $935 per credit hour. One-time fee: $350. Tuition and fees vary according to degree level and program. *Financial support:* Scholarships/grants available. *Faculty research:* Business management, curriculum and instruction, educational leadership, health psychology, organizational behavior. *Unit head:* Dr. David Harpool, Acting Provost, 888-327-2877 Ext. 8181, E-mail: provost@ncu.edu. *Application contact:* Ken Boutelle, Vice President, Enrollment Services, 888-628-4979, E-mail: enrollmentservices@ncu.edu.

North Dakota State University, College of Graduate and Interdisciplinary Studies, College of Human Development and Education, School of Education, Fargo, ND 58102. Offers agricultural education (M Ed, MS), including agricultural education; counselor education (M Ed, MS, PhD), including clinical mental health counseling (M Ed, MS), counselor education and supervision (PhD), school counseling (M Ed, MS); curriculum and instruction (M Ed, MS); education (PhD); educational leadership (M Ed, MS, Ed S); family and consumer sciences education (M Ed, MS); history education (M Ed, MS); institutional analysis (Ed D); mathematics education (M Ed, MS); music education (M Ed, MS); occupational and adult education (Ed D); science education (M Ed, MS). *Accreditation:* NCATE. *Program availability:* Part-time, evening/weekend, online learning. *Degree requirements:* For master's, comprehensive exam; for doctorate, thesis/dissertation; for Ed S, thesis. *Entrance requirements:* For degree, GRE General Test, master's degree, minimum GPA of 3.25. Additional exam requirements/recommendations for international students: Required—TOEFL.

Northeastern Illinois University, College of Graduate Studies and Research, College of Education, Chicago, IL 60625-4699. Offers MA, MAT, MS, MSI. *Program availability:* Part-time, evening/weekend. *Degree requirements:* For master's, comprehensive exam (for some programs), thesis (for some programs). *Entrance requirements:* For master's, minimum GPA of 2.75. Additional exam requirements/recommendations for international students: Required—TOEFL (minimum score 550 paper-based; 79 iBT). Electronic applications accepted. *Faculty research:* Leadership, problem-based learning strategies, school improvement, bilingual education, use of technology.

Northeastern State University, College of Education, Tahlequah, OK 74464-2399. Offers M Ed, MS, MS Ed. *Accreditation:* NCATE. *Program availability:* Part-time, evening/weekend. *Faculty:* 43 full-time (28 women). *Students:* 145 full-time (112 women), 336 part-time (285 women); includes 193 minority (17 Black or African American, non-Hispanic/Latino; 89 American Indian or Alaska Native, non-Hispanic/Latino; 8 Asian, non-Hispanic/Latino; 10 Hispanic/Latino; 69 Two or more races, non-Hispanic/Latino), 6 international. Average age 34. In 2016, 167 master's awarded. *Degree requirements:* For master's, thesis. *Entrance requirements:* For master's, GRE or MAT. Additional exam requirements/recommendations for international students: Required—TOEFL. *Application deadline:* For fall admission, 6/1 priority date for domestic students. Applications are processed on a rolling basis. Application fee: $25. Electronic applications accepted. *Expenses:* Tuition, state resident: full-time $2816; part-time $216.60 per credit hour. Tuition, nonresident: full-time $6365; part-time $489.60 per credit hour. *Required fees:* $37.40 per credit hour. *Financial support:* Teaching assistantships, career-related internships or fieldwork, and Federal Work-Study available. Financial award application deadline: 3/1. *Unit head:* Dr. Deborah Landry, Dean of the College of Education, 918-444-3700, E-mail: landryd@nsuok.edu. *Application contact:* Josh McCollum, Graduate Coordinator, 918-444-2093, E-mail: mccolluj@nsuok.edu.
Website: http://academics.nsuok.edu/education/EducationHome.aspx

Northern Arizona University, Graduate College, College of Education, Flagstaff, AZ 86011. Offers M Ed, MA, Ed D, PhD, Certificate, Ed S. *Accreditation:* NCATE. *Program availability:* Part-time, evening/weekend, online learning. *Degree requirements:* For master's, comprehensive exam, thesis (for some programs); for doctorate, comprehensive exam, thesis/dissertation. *Entrance requirements:* For master's, minimum GPA of 3.0; for doctorate, GRE or MAT. Additional exam requirements/recommendations for international students: Required—TOEFL (minimum score 550 paper-based; 80 iBT), IELTS (minimum score 7). Electronic applications accepted. *Expenses:* Tuition, state resident: full-time $8971; part-time $444 per credit hour. Tuition, nonresident: full-time $20,958; part-time $1164 per credit hour. *Required fees:* $1018; $644 per credit hour. Tuition and fees vary according to course load, campus/location and program.

Northern Illinois University, Graduate School, College of Education, De Kalb, IL 60115-2854. Offers MS, MS Ed, Ed D, Ed S. *Accreditation:* NCATE. *Program availability:* Part-time, evening/weekend, online learning. *Faculty:* 110 full-time (66 women), 5 part-time/adjunct (3 women). *Students:* 320 full-time (193 women), 882 part-time (637 women); includes 275 minority (122 Black or African American, non-Hispanic/Latino; 2 American Indian or Alaska Native, non-Hispanic/Latino; 27 Asian, non-Hispanic/Latino; 90 Hispanic/Latino; 34 Two or more races, non-Hispanic/Latino), 66 international. Average age 35. 544 applicants, 67% accepted, 195 enrolled. In 2016, 331 master's, 69 doctorates, 17 other advanced degrees awarded. Terminal master's awarded for partial completion of doctoral program. *Degree requirements:* For master's and Ed S, comprehensive exam, thesis optional; for doctorate, thesis/dissertation, candidacy exam, dissertation defense. *Entrance requirements:* For master's, GRE General Test or MAT, minimum GPA of 2.75; for doctorate, GRE General Test or MAT, minimum GPA of 2.75 (undergraduate), 3.2 (graduate); for Ed S, GRE General Test, master's degree; minimum undergraduate GPA of 2.75, graduate 3.2. Additional exam requirements/recommendations for international students: Required—TOEFL (minimum score 550 paper-based). *Application deadline:* For fall admission, 6/1 for domestic students, 5/1 for international students; for spring admission, 11/1 for domestic students, 10/1 for international students. Applications are processed on a rolling basis. Application fee: $40. Electronic applications accepted. *Financial support:* Fellowships with full tuition reimbursements, research assistantships with full tuition reimbursements, teaching assistantships with full tuition reimbursements, career-related internships or fieldwork, Federal Work-Study, scholarships/grants, tuition waivers (full), and staff assistantships available. Support available to part-time students. Financial award applicants required to submit FAFSA. *Unit head:* Laurie Elish-Piper, Dean, 815-753-1949, Fax: 851-753-2100. *Application contact:* Graduate School Office, 815-753-0395, E-mail: gradsch@niu.edu.
Website: http://www.cedu.niu.edu/

Northern Kentucky University, Office of Graduate Programs, College of Education and Human Services, Highland Heights, KY 41099. Offers MA, MAT, MS, MSW, Ed D, Certificate, Ed S. *Accreditation:* NCATE. *Program availability:* Part-time, evening/weekend. *Degree requirements:* For master's, comprehensive exam (for some programs), thesis (for some programs). *Entrance requirements:* For master's, GRE. Additional exam requirements/recommendations for international students: Required—TOEFL (minimum score 550 paper-based; 79 iBT); Recommended—IELTS (minimum score 6.5). Electronic applications accepted.

Northern Michigan University, Office of Graduate Education and Research, College of Health Sciences and Professional Studies, School of Education, Leadership and Public Service, Marquette, MI 49855-5301. Offers administration and supervision (MAE); elementary education (MAE); higher education in student affairs (MA); instruction (MAE); learning disabilities (MAE); public administration (MPA), including criminal justice administration, human resource administration, public administration, public management, state and local government; reading education (MAE), including reading, reading specialist; science education (MS); secondary education (MAE). *Accreditation:* TEAC. *Program availability:* Part-time, online learning. *Degree requirements:* For master's, thesis (for some programs). *Entrance requirements:* For master's, minimum GPA of 3.0. Additional exam requirements/recommendations for international students: Required—TOEFL (minimum score 550 paper-based; 79 iBT), IELTS (minimum score 6.5). Electronic applications accepted.

Northern State University, MS Ed Program in Educational Studies, Aberdeen, SD 57401-7198. Offers MS Ed. *Program availability:* Part-time, online learning. *Degree requirements:* For master's, comprehensive exam, thesis optional. *Entrance requirements:* For master's, minimum GPA of 2.75. Additional exam requirements/recommendations for international students: Required—TOEFL (minimum score 550 paper-based; 78 iBT), IELTS (minimum score 6). Electronic applications accepted.

North Greenville University, T. Walter Brashier Graduate School, Greer, SC 29651. Offers Christian ministry (MCM, D Min); education (M Ed, MAT); financial planning (MBA); human resources (MBA). *Program availability:* Part-time, evening/weekend, online learning. *Degree requirements:* For master's, comprehensive exam (for some programs), thesis or alternative, capstone course. *Entrance requirements:* For master's, minimum GPA of 2.25 overall, 2.5 in major; for doctorate, MAT. Additional exam requirements/recommendations for international students: Required—TOEFL (minimum score 550 paper-based). Electronic applications accepted. *Faculty research:* Organizational behavior, church growth, homiletics, human resources, business strategy.

North Park University, School of Education, Chicago, IL 60625-4895. Offers MA. *Degree requirements:* For master's, thesis. *Entrance requirements:* For master's, GRE General Test. *Faculty research:* Teacher leadership, research design, teacher education.

Northwest Christian University, School of Education and Counseling, Eugene, OR 97401-3745. Offers clinical mental health counseling (MA); elementary teaching (MAT); English for speakers of other languages (ESOL) (MAT); school counseling (MA); secondary teaching (MAT). *Program availability:* Part-time, evening/weekend, online learning. *Faculty:* 9 full-time (5 women), 21 part-time/adjunct (14 women). *Students:* 87 full-time (64 women), 52 part-time (40 women); includes 22 minority (5 Black or African American, non-Hispanic/Latino; 2 American Indian or Alaska Native, non-Hispanic/Latino; 2 Asian, non-Hispanic/Latino; 7 Hispanic/Latino; 2 Native Hawaiian or other Pacific Islander, non-Hispanic/Latino; 4 Two or more races, non-Hispanic/Latino). Average age 36. In 2016, 76 master's awarded. *Degree requirements:* For master's, thesis (for some programs). *Entrance requirements:* For master's, MAT, minimum undergraduate GPA of 3.0, interview, 2-3 page statement of purpose, two letters of recommendation, resume, background check. Additional exam requirements/recommendations for international students: Required—TOEFL (minimum score 550 paper-based; 80 iBT). *Application deadline:* Applications are processed on a rolling basis. Electronic applications accepted. *Expenses:* Contact institution. *Unit head:* Gene James, Dean of Counseling, 541-684-7261, Fax: 541-684-7310, E-mail: gjames@nwcu.edu. *Application contact:* Billy Dorsch, Admission Counselor for Graduate Studies, 541-684-7279, Fax: 541-349-5281, E-mail: wdorsch@nwcu.edu.

Education—General

Northwestern College, Program in Education, Orange City, IA 51041-1996. Offers early childhood (M Ed); master teacher (M Ed); teacher leadership (M Ed, Graduate Certificate). *Program availability:* Online learning.

Northwestern Oklahoma State University, School of Professional Studies, Alva, OK 73717-2799. Offers adult education management and administration (M Ed); counseling psychology (MCP); curriculum and instruction (M Ed); educational leadership (M Ed); elementary education (M Ed); reading specialist (M Ed); school counseling (M Ed); secondary education (M Ed). *Accreditation:* NCATE (one or more programs are accredited). *Program availability:* Part-time. *Degree requirements:* For master's, comprehensive exam (for some programs), thesis optional, portfolio. *Entrance requirements:* For master's, GRE General Test or MAT, minimum GPA of 2.75.

Northwestern State University of Louisiana, Graduate Studies and Research, College of Education and Human Development, Natchitoches, LA 71497. Offers M Ed, MA, MAT, Ed S. *Accreditation:* NCATE. *Degree requirements:* For master's, comprehensive exam, thesis (for some programs); for Ed S, comprehensive exam, thesis. *Entrance requirements:* For master's, GRE General Test, GRE Subject Test, minimum undergraduate GPA of 2.5; for Ed S, GRE General Test. Additional exam requirements/recommendations for international students: Required—TOEFL. Electronic applications accepted. *Faculty research:* Teacher-parent-child-friendly physical activities for young children, Net generation and social media, positive emotion and multimedia learning, the effects of Web-based mathematics resources on the motivation and achievement of high school students with learning disabilities, educational leadership.

★ **Northwestern University,** The Graduate School, School of Education and Social Policy, Evanston, IL 60208. Offers education (MS), including elementary teaching, secondary teaching, teacher leadership; human development and social policy (PhD); learning and organizational change (MS); learning sciences (MA, PhD). MA and PhD admissions and degrees offered through The Graduate School. *Program availability:* Part-time, evening/weekend. *Degree requirements:* For doctorate, comprehensive exam, thesis/dissertation. *Entrance requirements:* For master's and doctorate, GRE General Test. Electronic applications accepted. *Expenses:* Contact institution. *Faculty research:* Technology, curriculum design, welfare, education reform, learning.

See Display below and Close-Up on page 731.

Northwest Missouri State University, Graduate School, School of Education, Maryville, MO 64468-6001. Offers early childhood education (MS Ed); education leadership (MS Ed), including elementary, K-12, secondary; educational leadership (Ed S), including elementary school principalship, secondary school principalship, superintendency; educational leadership and policy analysis (Ed D); elementary education (MS Ed); elementary mathematics (MS Ed); higher education leadership (MS); middle school education (MS Ed); reading (MS Ed); special education (MS Ed); teacher leadership (MS Ed); teaching English language learners (MS Ed). *Accreditation:* NCATE. *Program availability:* Part-time. *Students:* 15 full-time (11 women), 150 part-time (103 women). In 2016, 46 master's awarded. *Degree requirements:* For master's, comprehensive exam; for Ed S, comprehensive exam, thesis. *Entrance requirements:* For master's, GRE General Test, writing sample; for Ed S, minimum graduate GPA of 3.25. Additional exam requirements/recommendations for international students: Required—TOEFL (minimum score 550 paper-based). *Application deadline:* For fall admission, 7/1 for domestic and international students; for spring admission, 11/15 for domestic and international students. Applications are processed on a rolling basis. Application fee: $0 ($50 for international students). Electronic applications accepted. *Expenses:* Tuition, state resident: full-time $3447; part-time $383 per credit hour. Tuition, nonresident: full-time $5724; part-time $636 per credit hour. *Required fees:* $130 per credit hour. *Financial support:* Research assistantships with full tuition reimbursements, teaching assistantships with full tuition reimbursements, and unspecified assistantships available. Financial award application deadline: 4/1; financial award applicants required to submit FAFSA. *Faculty research:* Great books of educational administration. *Unit head:* Dr. Tim Wall, Dean, 660-562-1179, E-mail: timwall@nwmissouri.edu.
Website: http://www.nwmissouri.edu/academics/ed/

Northwest Nazarene University, Graduate Education Program, Nampa, ID 83686-5897. Offers curriculum and instruction (M Ed); educational leadership (M Ed, Ed D, PhD, Ed S), including building administrator (M Ed, Ed S), director of special education (Ed S), leadership and organizational development (Ed S), superintendent (Ed S). *Accreditation:* ACA (one or more programs are accredited); NCATE. *Program availability:* Part-time, online only, 100% online, 2-week face-to-face residency (for doctoral programs). *Faculty:* 4 full-time (3 women), 17 part-time/adjunct (6 women). *Students:* 112 full-time (72 women), 73 part-time (36 women); includes 19 minority (3 Black or African American, non-Hispanic/Latino; 2 Asian, non-Hispanic/Latino; 6 Hispanic/Latino; 1 Native Hawaiian or other Pacific Islander, non-Hispanic/Latino; 7 Two or more races, non-Hispanic/Latino), 5 international. Average age 39. 96 applicants, 72% accepted, 67 enrolled. In 2016, 59 master's, 13 doctorates, 33 other advanced degrees awarded. *Degree requirements:* For master's, comprehensive exam (for some programs), action research project; for doctorate, thesis/dissertation; for Ed S, comprehensive exam, research project. *Entrance requirements:* For master's, minimum undergraduate GPA of 3.0 overall or during final 30 semester credits, undergraduate degree, valid teaching certificate; for doctorate, Ed S or equivalent, minimum GPA of 3.5; for Ed S, undergraduate degree, valid teaching certificate. Additional exam requirements/recommendations for international students: Recommended—TOEFL. *Application deadline:* Applications are processed on a rolling basis. Application fee: $50. Electronic applications accepted. *Expenses:* Contact institution. *Financial support:* In 2016–17, research assistantships (averaging $5,000 per year) were awarded. Financial award application deadline: 1/15; financial award applicants required to submit FAFSA. *Faculty research:* Action research, cooperative learning, accountability, institutional accreditation. *Unit head:* Dr. Heidi Curtis, Chair, 208-467-8250, E-mail: hlcurtis@nnu.edu. *Application contact:* Charlene Brown, Admissions Counselor, 208-467-8492, Fax: 208-467-8384, E-mail: gradeducationinfo@nnu.edu.
Website: http://www.nnu.edu/graded/

Northwest University, School of Education, Kirkland, WA 98033. Offers education (M Ed); teaching (MIT). *Program availability:* Part-time, evening/weekend. *Degree requirements:* For master's, action research project. *Entrance requirements:* For master's, Washington Educator Skills Test-Basic (WEST-B)/Washington Educator Skills Test-Endorsements (WEST-E), minimum GPA of 3.3. Additional exam requirements/recommendations for international students: Recommended—TOEFL. Electronic applications accepted. *Expenses:* Contact institution.

Notre Dame de Namur University, Division of Academic Affairs, School of Education and Leadership, Program in Education, Belmont, CA 94002-1908. Offers curriculum and instruction (MA). *Program availability:* Part-time, evening/weekend. *Degree requirements:* For master's, thesis (for some programs). *Entrance requirements:* For master's, CBEST, CSET, valid teaching credential or substantial teaching experience. Additional exam requirements/recommendations for international students: Required—TOEFL (minimum score 550 paper-based; 79 iBT). Electronic applications accepted.

Notre Dame of Maryland University, Graduate Studies, Program in Teaching, Baltimore, MD 21210-2476. Offers MA. *Accreditation:* NCATE. *Entrance requirements:* For master's, Watson-Glaser Critical Thinking Appraisal, writing test, grammar test, interview. Additional exam requirements/recommendations for international students:

Required—TOEFL (minimum score 500 paper-based; 61 iBT). Electronic applications accepted.

Nova Southeastern University, Abraham S. Fischler College of Education, Fort Lauderdale, FL 33314. Offers education (MS, Ed D, PhD, Ed S); instructional technology and distance education (MS); teaching and learning (MA). *Accreditation:* NCATE. *Program availability:* Part-time, evening/weekend, 100% online, blended/hybrid learning. *Faculty:* 94 full-time (58 women), 204 part-time/adjunct (145 women). *Students:* 1,841 full-time (1,435 women), 1,705 part-time (1,336 women); includes 2,584 minority (1,389 Black or African American, non-Hispanic/Latino; 8 American Indian or Alaska Native, non-Hispanic/Latino; 44 Asian, non-Hispanic/Latino; 1,078 Hispanic/Latino; 2 Native Hawaiian or other Pacific Islander, non-Hispanic/Latino; 63 Two or more races, non-Hispanic/Latino), 26 international. Average age 41. 1,753 applicants, 47% accepted, 581 enrolled. In 2016, 654 master's, 387 doctorates, 119 other advanced degrees awarded. *Degree requirements:* For master's, practicum, internship; for doctorate, thesis/dissertation; for Ed S, thesis, practicum, internship. *Entrance requirements:* For master's, MAT or GRE (for some programs), CLAST, PRAXIS I, CBEST, General Knowledge Test, teaching certification, minimum GPA of 2.5, verification of teaching, BS; for doctorate, MAT or GRE, master's degree, minimum cumulative GPA of 3.0; for Ed S, MAT or GRE, master's degree, teaching certificate, minimum GPA of 3.0. Additional exam requirements/recommendations for international students: Recommended—TOEFL (minimum score 550 paper-based; 79 iBT), IELTS (minimum score 6). *Application deadline:* Applications are processed on a rolling basis. Application fee: $50. Electronic applications accepted. *Expenses:* Contact institution. *Financial support:* In 2016–17, 67 students received support. Career-related internships or fieldwork and Federal Work-Study available. Support available to part-time students. Financial award application deadline: 4/15; financial award applicants required to submit FAFSA. *Faculty research:* STEM education, educational technology, principal training, quality of life. *Total annual research expenditures:* $50,000. *Unit head:* Dr. Kim Durham, Interim Dean, 954-262-8731, Fax: 954-262-3894, E-mail: durham@nova.edu. *Application contact:* Adriana Garay, Executive Director for Marketing, Recruitment and Admissions, 800-986-3223 Ext. 8500, E-mail: fserecruit@nova.edu.
Website: http://www.fischlerschool.nova.edu/

Oakland City University, School of Education, Oakland City, IN 47660-1099. Offers educational leadership (Ed D); teaching (MA). *Accreditation:* NCATE. Terminal master's awarded for partial completion of doctoral program. *Degree requirements:* For master's, thesis; for doctorate, comprehensive exam, thesis/dissertation. *Entrance requirements:* For master's, MAT, minimum GPA of 3.0, interview, resume, letters of recommendation; for doctorate, MAT, GRE, minimum GPA of 3.2, interview, resume, letters of recommendation. *Expenses:* Contact institution. *Faculty research:* Assessment, cultural diversity, teacher education, education leadership.

Oakland University, Graduate Study and Lifelong Learning, School of Education and Human Services, Rochester, MI 48309-4401. Offers M Ed, MA, MAT, PhD, Certificate, Ed S, Graduate Certificate, PMC. *Accreditation:* TEAC. *Program availability:* Part-time, evening/weekend. *Degree requirements:* For doctorate, thesis/dissertation. *Entrance requirements:* For master's and doctorate, minimum GPA of 3.0. Additional exam requirements/recommendations for international students: Required—TOEFL (minimum score 550 paper-based). Electronic applications accepted.

Ohio Dominican University, Division of Education, Columbus, OH 43219-2099. Offers curriculum and instruction (M Ed); educational leadership (M Ed); teaching English to speakers of other languages (MA). *Accreditation:* NCATE. *Program availability:* Part-time, evening/weekend, 100% online, blended/hybrid learning. *Faculty:* 7 full-time (4 women), 8 part-time/adjunct (1 woman). *Students:* 10 full-time (9 women), 111 part-time (87 women); includes 14 minority (6 Black or African American, non-Hispanic/Latino; 2 Asian, non-Hispanic/Latino; 4 Hispanic/Latino; 2 Two or more races, non-Hispanic/Latino), 5 international. Average age 32. 49 applicants, 67% accepted, 30 enrolled. *Entrance requirements:* For master's, minimum undergraduate GPA of 3.0, teaching certificate/license, teaching experience, 2 letters of recommendation, currently teaching or access to academic classroom. Additional exam requirements/recommendations for international students: Required—TOEFL (minimum score 550 paper-based), IELTS (minimum score 6.5). *Application deadline:* For fall admission, 8/15 for domestic students, 6/10 for international students; for spring admission, 1/4 for domestic students, 11/2 for international students; for summer admission, 5/30 for domestic students. Applications are processed on a rolling basis. Application fee: $25. Electronic applications accepted. *Expenses:* Contact institution. *Financial support:* Tuition waivers and tuition discount for Diocesan teachers available. Financial award applicants required to submit FAFSA. *Unit head:* Dr. JoAnn Hohenbrink, Chair, 614-251-4759, E-mail: hohenbrj@ohiodominican.edu. *Application contact:* John W. Naughton, Director for Graduate Admissions, 614-251-4721, Fax: 614-251-6654, E-mail: grad@ohiodominican.edu.
Website: http://www.ohiodominican.edu/academics/graduate/master-of-education

The Ohio State University, Graduate School, College of Education and Human Ecology, Columbus, OH 43210. Offers M Ed, MA, MS, PhD, Ed S. *Accreditation:* NCATE. *Faculty:* 144. *Students:* 810 full-time (545 women), 239 part-time (175 women); includes 171 minority (82 Black or African American, non-Hispanic/Latino; 29 Asian, non-Hispanic/Latino; 38 Hispanic/Latino; 22 Two or more races, non-Hispanic/Latino), 202 international. Average age 31. In 2016, 281 master's, 72 doctorates, 7 other advanced degrees awarded. Terminal master's awarded for partial completion of doctoral program. *Degree requirements:* For master's, comprehensive exam (for some programs), thesis optional; for doctorate, comprehensive exam, thesis/dissertation. *Entrance requirements:* For master's and doctorate, GRE or GMAT. Additional exam requirements/recommendations for international students: Required—TOEFL (minimum score 550 paper-based; 79 iBT), Michigan English Language Assessment Battery (minimum score 82); Recommended—IELTS (minimum score 7). *Application deadline:* Applications are processed on a rolling basis. Application fee: $60 ($70 for international students). Electronic applications accepted. *Financial support:* Fellowships with tuition reimbursements, research assistantships with tuition reimbursements, teaching assistantships with tuition reimbursements, career-related internships or fieldwork, Federal Work-Study, institutionally sponsored loans, scholarships/grants, traineeships, health care benefits, and unspecified assistantships available. Support available to part-time students. *Faculty research:* Math and science education; teaching professional development; issues related to urban education; health, well-being, and sports; literacy education. *Unit head:* Dr. Cheryl Achterberg, Dean, 614-292-2461, Fax: 614-292-8052, E-mail: achterberg.1@osu.edu. *Application contact:* Graduate and Professional Admissions, 614-292-9444, Fax: 614-292-3895, E-mail: gpadmissions@osu.edu.
Website: http://ehe.osu.edu/

The Ohio State University at Marion, Graduate Programs, Marion, OH 43302-5695. Offers education (MA), including teaching and learning. *Program availability:* Part-time. *Faculty:* 38. *Degree requirements:* For master's, comprehensive exam (for some programs), thesis (for some programs). *Entrance requirements:* For master's, GRE, minimum undergraduate GPA of 3.0. Additional exam requirements/recommendations for international students: Required—TOEFL (minimum score 550 paper-based, 79 iBT), IELTS (minimum score 7) or Michigan English Language Assessment Battery (minimum score 82). *Application deadline:* Applications are processed on a rolling basis. Application fee: $60 ($70 for international students). Electronic applications accepted. *Financial support:* Application deadline: 2/15; applicants required to submit FAFSA. *Unit head:* Dr. Gregory S. Rose, Dean/Director, 740-725-6218, E-mail: rose.9@osu.edu. *Application contact:* Graduate and Professional Admissions, 614-292-9444, Fax: 614-292-3895, E-mail: gpadmissions@osu.edu.

The Ohio State University–Mansfield Campus, Graduate Programs, Mansfield, OH 44906-1599. Offers education (MA); social work (MSW). *Program availability:* Part-time. *Faculty:* 40. *Students:* 3 (all women). *Degree requirements:* For master's, comprehensive exam (for some programs), thesis (for some programs). *Entrance requirements:* For master's, GRE, minimum GPA of 3.0. Additional exam requirements/recommendations for international students: Required—TOEFL (minimum 550 paper-based, 79 iBT), IELTS (minimum score 7) or Michigan English Language Assessment Battery (minimum score 82). *Application deadline:* For fall admission, 4/1 for domestic students, 3/1 for international students; for spring admission, 10/15 for domestic and international students. Applications are processed on a rolling basis. Application fee: $60 ($70 for international students). Electronic applications accepted. *Financial support:* Teaching assistantships with full tuition reimbursements, Federal Work-Study, and scholarships/grants available. Support available to part-time students. Financial award application deadline: 2/15; financial award applicants required to submit FAFSA. *Application contact:* Graduate and Professional Admissions, 614-292-9444, Fax: 614-292-3895, E-mail: gpadmissions@osu.edu.

The Ohio State University–Newark Campus, Graduate Programs, Newark, OH 43055-1797. Offers education - teaching and learning (MA); social work (MSW). *Program availability:* Part-time. *Faculty:* 51. *Students:* 15 (all women); includes 2 minority (1 Black or African American, non-Hispanic/Latino; 1 Hispanic/Latino). Average age 32. Terminal master's awarded for partial completion of doctoral program. *Degree requirements:* For master's, comprehensive exam (for some programs), thesis (for some programs). *Entrance requirements:* For master's, GRE, minimum GPA of 3.0. Additional exam requirements/recommendations for international students: Required—TOEFL (minimum score 550 paper-based; 79 iBT), IELTS (minimum score 7), or Michigan English Language Assessment Battery (minimum score 82). *Application deadline:* For fall admission, 3/1 for domestic and international students. Applications are processed on a rolling basis. Application fee: $60 ($70 for international students). Electronic applications accepted. *Financial support:* Application deadline: 2/15. *Unit head:* Dr. William L. MacDonald, Dean/Director, 740-366-9333 Ext. 330, E-mail: macdonald.24@osu.edu. *Application contact:* Graduate and Professional Admissions, 614-292-9444, Fax: 614-292-3985, E-mail: gpadmissions@osu.edu.

Ohio University, Graduate College, Gladys W. and David H. Patton College of Education and Human Services, Athens, OH 45701-2979. Offers M Ed, MS, MSA, Ed D, PhD. *Accreditation:* NCATE. *Program availability:* Part-time, evening/weekend. *Degree requirements:* For master's, comprehensive exam (for some programs), thesis or alternative; for doctorate, comprehensive exam, thesis/dissertation. *Entrance requirements:* For master's, GRE General Test or MAT; for doctorate, GRE General Test, MAT, master's degree. Additional exam requirements/recommendations for international students: Required—TOEFL (minimum score 550 paper-based; 80 iBT) or IELTS (minimum score 6.5). *Application deadline:* Applications are processed on a rolling basis. Application fee: $50 ($55 for international students). Electronic applications accepted. *Financial support:* Research assistantships with full and partial tuition reimbursements, teaching assistantships with full and partial tuition reimbursements, Federal Work-Study, institutionally sponsored loans, tuition waivers (full and partial), and unspecified assistantships available. Financial award application deadline: 3/15. *Faculty research:* School improvement, partnerships, literacy, rural education. *Unit head:* Dr. Renee A. Middleton, Dean, 740-593-4403, E-mail: middletonr@ohio.edu. *Application contact:* Floyd J. Doney, Director of Student Affairs, 740-593-4400, Fax: 740-593-9310, E-mail: doney@ohio.edu.
Website: http://www.cehs.ohio.edu/

Ohio Valley University, School of Graduate Education, Vienna, WV 26105-8000. Offers curriculum and instruction (M Ed). *Program availability:* Online learning. *Entrance requirements:* For master's, 2 letters of recommendation, official transcripts from all previous institutions, essay, bachelor's degree.

Oklahoma State University, College of Education, Stillwater, OK 74078. Offers MS, Ed D, PhD, Ed S. *Accreditation:* NCATE. *Program availability:* Part-time, online learning. *Faculty:* 95 full-time (67 women), 73 part-time/adjunct (40 women). *Students:* 264 full-time (182 women), 543 part-time (347 women); includes 216 minority (56 Black or African American, non-Hispanic/Latino; 38 American Indian or Alaska Native, non-Hispanic/Latino; 12 Asian, non-Hispanic/Latino; 52 Hispanic/Latino; 1 Native Hawaiian or other Pacific Islander, non-Hispanic/Latino; 57 Two or more races, non-Hispanic/Latino), 25 international. Average age 35. 312 applicants, 59% accepted, 163 enrolled. In 2016, 170 master's, 55 doctorates awarded. *Degree requirements:* For master's, thesis or alternative; for doctorate, comprehensive exam, thesis/dissertation. *Entrance requirements:* For master's and doctorate, GRE or GMAT. Additional exam requirements/recommendations for international students: Required—TOEFL (minimum score 550 paper-based; 79 iBT). *Application deadline:* For fall admission, 3/1 priority date for domestic and international students; for spring admission, 8/1 priority date for domestic and international students. Applications are processed on a rolling basis. Application fee: $40 ($75 for international students). Electronic applications accepted. *Expenses:* Tuition, state resident: full-time $3775; part-time $209.70 per credit hour. Tuition, nonresident: full-time $14,851; part-time $825.05 per credit hour. *Required fees:* $2027; $112.60 per credit hour. Tuition and fees vary according to campus/location. *Financial support:* In 2016–17, 56 research assistantships (averaging $9,206 per year), 78 teaching assistantships (averaging $11,175 per year) were awarded; career-related internships or fieldwork, Federal Work-Study, scholarships/grants, health care benefits, tuition waivers (partial), and unspecified assistantships also available. Support available to part-time students. Financial award application deadline: 3/1; financial award applicants required to submit FAFSA. *Unit head:* Dr. Robert Davis, Interim Dean, 405-744-6350, Fax: 405-744-6350, E-mail: robert.davis@okstate.edu.
Website: http://education.okstate.edu/

Old Dominion University, Darden College of Education, Norfolk, VA 23529. Offers MS, MS Ed, PhD, Ed S, Postbaccalaureate Certificate. *Program availability:* Part-time, evening/weekend, 100% online, blended/hybrid learning. *Faculty:* 94 full-time (55 women), 62 part-time/adjunct (40 women). *Students:* 529 full-time (427 women), 794 part-time (599 women); includes 378 minority (251 Black or African American, non-Hispanic/Latino; 4 American Indian or Alaska Native, non-Hispanic/Latino; 21 Asian, non-Hispanic/Latino; 60 Hispanic/Latino; 42 Two or more races, non-Hispanic/Latino), 28 international. Average age 34. 808 applicants, 58% accepted, 309 enrolled. In 2016, 420 master's, 53 doctorates, 56 other advanced degrees awarded. *Degree requirements:* For master's, thesis (for some programs), exam; for doctorate, comprehensive exam, thesis/dissertation; for other advanced degree, comprehensive exam. *Entrance requirements:* For doctorate, GRE General Test, master's degree, minimum GPA of 3.25; for other advanced degree, GRE General Test or MAT. Additional exam requirements/recommendations for international students: Required—TOEFL (minimum score 550 paper-based). *Application deadline:* For fall admission, 6/1 priority date for domestic and international students; for spring admission, 11/1 priority

date for domestic and international students. Applications are processed on a rolling basis. Application fee: $50. Electronic applications accepted. *Expenses:* Tuition, state resident: full-time $8604; part-time $478 per credit hour. Tuition, nonresident: full-time $21,510; part-time $1195 per credit hour. *Required fees:* $66 per semester. Tuition and fees vary according to campus/location, program and reciprocity agreements. *Financial support:* In 2016–17, 141 students received support, including 4 fellowships with tuition reimbursements available (averaging $15,000 per year), 60 research assistantships with tuition reimbursements available (averaging $15,000 per year), 72 teaching assistantships with tuition reimbursements available (averaging $15,000 per year); career-related internships or fieldwork, Federal Work-Study, institutionally sponsored loans, scholarships/grants, tuition waivers (partial), and unspecified assistantships also available. Support available to part-time students. Financial award application deadline: 2/15; financial award applicants required to submit CSS PROFILE or FAFSA. *Faculty research:* Effective urban teaching practices, curriculum theory, clinical practices, special education, instructional technology. *Total annual research expenditures:* $11.9 million. *Unit head:* Dr. Jane S. Bray, Dean, 757-683-3938, Fax: 757-683-5083, E-mail: jsbray@odu.edu. *Application contact:* William Heffelfinger, Director of Graduate Admissions, 757-683-5554, Fax: 757-683-3255, E-mail: gradadmit@odu.edu.
Website: http://education.odu.edu/

Olivet Nazarene University, Graduate School, Division of Education, Bourbonnais, IL 60914. Offers curriculum and instruction (MAE); elementary education (MAT); library information specialist (MAE); reading specialist (MAE); school leadership (MAE); secondary education (MAT). *Accreditation:* NCATE. *Program availability:* Evening/weekend. *Degree requirements:* For master's, thesis or alternative.

Open University, Graduate Programs, Milton Keynes, United Kingdom. Offers business (MBA); education (M Ed); engineering (M Eng); history (MA); music (MA); philosophy (MA).

Oral Roberts University, School of Education, Tulsa, OK 74171. Offers Christian school administration (K-12) (MA Ed, Ed D); Christian school curriculum development (MA Ed); college and higher education administration (Ed D); public school administration (K-12) (MA Ed, Ed D); public school teaching (MA Ed). *Accreditation:* NCATE. *Program availability:* Part-time, online learning. *Degree requirements:* For master's, comprehensive exam, thesis optional; for doctorate, comprehensive exam, thesis/dissertation. *Entrance requirements:* For master's, GRE General Test or MAT, minimum GPA of 3.0; for doctorate, minimum GPA of 3.0. Additional exam requirements/recommendations for international students: Required—TOEFL (minimum score 500 paper-based). *Expenses:* Contact institution. *Faculty research:* Teacher effectiveness, college success in high achieving African-Americans, professional development practices.

Oregon State University, College of Education, Program in Education, Corvallis, OR 97331. Offers advanced science and mathematics education (Ed M); agricultural education (PhD); education (Ed D); free-choice learning (Ed M); language equity and educational policy (PhD); mathematics education (MS); pre-K-12 English to speakers of other languages (ESOL) (Ed M); science education (MS); science/mathematics education (PhD); social justice in education (Ed M). *Program availability:* Part-time, 100% online, blended/hybrid learning. *Faculty:* 9 full-time (8 women), 6 part-time/adjunct (2 women). *Students:* 14 full-time (8 women), 76 part-time (53 women); includes 25 minority (6 Black or African American, non-Hispanic/Latino; 2 American Indian or Alaska Native, non-Hispanic/Latino; 5 Asian, non-Hispanic/Latino; 10 Hispanic/Latino; 2 Two or more races, non-Hispanic/Latino), 3 international. Average age 38. 72 applicants, 69% accepted, 40 enrolled. In 2016, 14 master's, 21 doctorates awarded. Terminal master's awarded for partial completion of doctoral program. *Degree requirements:* For master's, variable foreign language requirement, thesis (for some programs); for doctorate, variable foreign language requirement, thesis/dissertation. *Entrance requirements:* Additional exam requirements/recommendations for international students: Required—TOEFL (minimum score 575 paper-based). Application fee: $75 ($85 for international students). *Expenses:* Tuition, state resident: full-time $12,150; part-time $450 per credit. Tuition, nonresident: full-time $21,789; part-time $807 per credit. *Required fees:* $1651; $1507 per credit. One-time fee: $350. Tuition and fees vary according to course load, campus/location and program. *Financial support:* Fellowships, research assistantships, teaching assistantships, career-related internships or fieldwork, Federal Work-Study, and institutionally sponsored loans available. Support available to part-time students. *Faculty research:* School administration, educational foundations, research methodology, education policy development, higher education administration. *Unit head:* Dr. Larry Flick, Dean. *Application contact:* E-mail: askcoed@oregonstate.edu.

Oregon State University, College of Education, Program in Teaching, Corvallis, OR 97331. Offers clinically based elementary education (MAT); elementary education (MAT); language arts (MAT); mathematics (MAT); music education (MAT); science (MAT); social studies (MAT). *Program availability:* Part-time, blended/hybrid learning. *Faculty:* 17 full-time (8 women), 2 part-time/adjunct (both women). *Students:* 57 full-time (39 women), 22 part-time (18 women); includes 11 minority (2 Hispanic/Latino; 1 Native Hawaiian or other Pacific Islander, non-Hispanic/Latino; 8 Two or more races, non-Hispanic/Latino). Average age 29. 131 applicants, 76% accepted, 76 enrolled. In 2016, 92 master's awarded. *Entrance requirements:* For master's, CBEST. Additional exam requirements/recommendations for international students: Required—TOEFL (minimum score 575 paper-based). *Application deadline:* For fall admission, 12/1 for domestic students. Application fee: $60. *Expenses:* Contact institution. *Unit head:* Dr. Larry Flick, Dean. *Application contact:* E-mail: askcoed@oregonstate.edu.
Website: http://education.oregonstate.edu/mat

Oregon State University–Cascades, Program in Education, Bend, OR 97701. Offers MAT.

Ottawa University, Graduate Studies-Arizona, Program in Education, Ottawa, KS 66067-3399. Offers community college counseling (MA); curriculum and instruction (MA); early childhood (MA); education intervention (MA); education leadership (MA); education technology (MA); Montessori early childhood education (MA); Montessori elementary education (MA); professional development (MA); school guidance counseling (MA); special education - cross categorical (MA). Programs offered in Mesa, Phoenix, Tempe and West Valley, AZ. *Accreditation:* NCATE. *Program availability:* Part-time. *Degree requirements:* For master's, thesis or alternative. *Entrance requirements:* For master's, minimum undergraduate GPA of 3.0, copy of current state certification or teaching license. Additional exam requirements/recommendations for international students: Required—TOEFL (minimum score 550 paper-based). Electronic applications accepted. *Expenses:* Contact institution.

Otterbein University, Department of Education, Westerville, OH 43081. Offers MAE, MAT. *Accreditation:* NCATE. *Degree requirements:* For master's, capstone project. *Entrance requirements:* For master's, 2 reference forms, essay, interview. Additional exam requirements/recommendations for international students: Required—TOEFL (minimum score 550 paper-based; 79 iBT). *Faculty research:* Computer technology middle level education, assessment, teacher leadership, multicultural education.

Our Lady of the Lake University, School of Professional Studies, San Antonio, TX 78207-4689. Offers communication and learning disorders (MA), including communication disorders; counseling psychology (Psy D); curriculum and instruction (M Ed), including integrated science teaching; psychology (MS), including family, couple, and individual psychotherapy, school psychology; school counseling (M Ed); social work (MSW); sociology (MA). *Program availability:* Part-time, evening/weekend, 100% online, blended/hybrid learning. *Faculty:* 36 full-time (30 women), 73 part-time/adjunct (54 women). *Students:* 1,059 full-time (950 women), 59 part-time (51 women); includes 713 minority (253 Black or African American, non-Hispanic/Latino; 8 American Indian or Alaska Native, non-Hispanic/Latino; 9 Asian, non-Hispanic/Latino; 426 Hispanic/Latino; 3 Native Hawaiian or other Pacific Islander, non-Hispanic/Latino; 14 Two or more races, non-Hispanic/Latino), 1 international. Average age 34. 565 applicants, 66% accepted, 226 enrolled. In 2016, 251 master's, 9 doctorates awarded. *Degree requirements:* For master's, comprehensive exam (for some programs); for doctorate, comprehensive exam, thesis/dissertation, internship, qualifying exam. *Entrance requirements:* For doctorate, GRE General Test, GRE Subject Test (psychology), master's degree in psychology or closely-related discipline of at least 45 hours from regionally-accredited institution; minimum cumulative GPA of 3.5 in the master's program; criminal background check; 3 letters of recommendation; pertinent professional experience; personal statement. Additional exam requirements/recommendations for international students: Required—TOEFL. Application fee: $40 ($50 for international students). Electronic applications accepted. Application fee is waived when completed online. *Expenses: Tuition:* Full-time $14,796. Tuition and fees vary according to course load, degree level, campus/location and program. *Financial support:* In 2016–17, 111 students received support. Research assistantships, teaching assistantships, Federal Work-Study, scholarships/grants, unspecified assistantships, and tuition discounts available. Support available to part-time students. Financial award application deadline: 5/1; financial award applicants required to submit FAFSA. *Faculty research:* Culturally and linguistically diverse persons within various professional contexts, research, service-learning, student-centeredness, clinical experiences. *Unit head:* Dr. Marcheta Evans, Dean, 210-431-4140, E-mail: sps@ollusa.edu. *Application contact:* Graduate Admissions, 210-431-3995 Ext. 2314, Fax: 210-431-3945, E-mail: gradadm@lake.ollusa.edu.
Website: http://www.ollusa.edu/s/1190/hybrid/hw-hybrid-ollu.aspx?sid-1190&gid-1&pgid-7761

Pace University, School of Education, New York, NY 10038. Offers adolescent education (MST), including biology, business education, chemistry, earth science, English, foreign languages, mathematics, physics, social studies, visual arts; childhood education (MST); early childhood development, learning and intervention (MST); educational technology studies (MS); inclusive adolescent education (MST), including biology, business education, chemistry, earth science, English, foreign languages, mathematics, physics, social studies, visual arts; integrated instruction for educational technology (Certificate); integrated instruction for literacy and technology (Certificate); literacy (MS Ed); special education (MS Ed). *Accreditation:* NCATE. *Program availability:* Part-time, evening/weekend, blended/hybrid learning. *Faculty:* 19 full-time (13 women), 86 part-time/adjunct (49 women). *Students:* 115 full-time (97 women), 543 part-time (381 women); includes 280 minority (137 Black or African American, non-Hispanic/Latino; 1 American Indian or Alaska Native, non-Hispanic/Latino; 40 Asian, non-Hispanic/Latino; 87 Hispanic/Latino; 15 Two or more races, non-Hispanic/Latino), 13 international. Average age 30. 181 applicants, 78% accepted, 72 enrolled. In 2016, 193 master's, 9 other advanced degrees awarded. *Degree requirements:* For master's, certification exams. *Entrance requirements:* For master's, GRE, interview, teaching certificate (except for MST). Additional exam requirements/recommendations for international students: Required—TOEFL (minimum score 88 iBT), IELTS or PTE. *Application deadline:* For fall admission, 8/1 priority date for domestic students, 6/1 for international students; for spring admission, 12/1 priority date for domestic students, 10/1 for international students. Applications are processed on a rolling basis. Application fee: $70. Electronic applications accepted. *Expenses:* Contact institution. *Financial support:* In 2016–17, 17 students received support, including 17 research assistantships with partial tuition reimbursements available (averaging $6,020 per year); career-related internships or fieldwork and Federal Work-Study also available. Financial award application deadline: 9/1; financial award applicants required to submit FAFSA. *Faculty research:* STEM education, TESOL, teacher education, special education, language and literary development. *Total annual research expenditures:* $290,153. *Unit head:* Dr. Xiao-Lei Wang, Dean, School of Education, 914-773-3876, E-mail: xwang@pace.edu. *Application contact:* Susan Ford-Goldschein, Director of Graduate Admissions, 212-346-1531, Fax: 212-346-1585, E-mail: graduateadmission@pace.edu.
Website: http://www.pace.edu/school-of-education

Pacific Lutheran University, School of Education and Kinesiology, Tacoma, WA 98447. Offers MAE. *Accreditation:* NCATE. *Program availability:* Part-time, evening/weekend. *Degree requirements:* For master's, comprehensive exam, thesis optional. *Entrance requirements:* For master's, WEST-B or WEST-B Exemption, interview. Additional exam requirements/recommendations for international students: Required—TOEFL (minimum score 550 paper-based; 88 iBT). Electronic applications accepted. *Expenses:* Contact institution.

Pacific Oaks College, Graduate School, Program in Education, Pasadena, CA 91103. Offers preliminary education specialist (MA); preliminary multiple subject (MA). *Program availability:* Online learning. *Degree requirements:* For master's, practicum. *Entrance requirements:* For master's, bachelor's degree from accredited college or university.

Pacific Union College, Education Department, Angwin, CA 94508-9707. Offers education (M Ed); elementary teaching (MAT); secondary teaching (MAT). *Program availability:* Part-time. *Faculty:* 3 full-time (1 woman), 1 (woman) part-time/adjunct. *Students:* 1 (woman) full-time, 5 part-time (3 women); includes 1 minority (Hispanic/Latino). Average age 41. In 2016, 1 master's awarded. *Degree requirements:* For master's, thesis, action research project, field experiences. *Entrance requirements:* For master's, GRE General Test, two interviews, teaching credential, letters of recommendation, essay. *Application deadline:* For summer admission, 6/1 for domestic students. Applications are processed on a rolling basis. Application fee: $0. *Expenses: Tuition:* Part-time $405 per quarter hour. *Required fees:* $210 per quarter. Tuition and fees vary according to student's religious affiliation. *Financial support:* Scholarships/grants available. Support available to part-time students. *Unit head:* Prof. Thomas Lee, Department Chair, 707-965-6646, Fax: 707-965-6645, E-mail: tdlee@puc.edu. *Application contact:* Cherith Mundy, Credential Analyst, 707-965-6643, Fax: 707-965-6645, E-mail: teachingcredentials@puc.edu.
Website: http://www.puc.edu/academics/departments/education/

Pacific University, College of Education, Forest Grove, OR 97116-1797. Offers early childhood education (MAT); education (MAE); elementary education (MAT); ESOL (MAT); high school education (MAT); middle school education (MAT); special education (MAT); speech-language pathology (MS); STEM education (MAT); talented and gifted (M Ed); visual function in learning (M Ed). *Accreditation:* NCATE. *Program availability:* Part-time, evening/weekend. *Degree requirements:* For master's, research project. *Entrance requirements:* For master's, California Basic Educational Skills Test, PRAXIS II, minimum undergraduate GPA of 2.75, 3.0 graduate. Additional exam requirements/recommendations for international students: Required—TOEFL. Electronic applications accepted. *Expenses:* Contact institution. *Faculty research:* Defining a culturally competent classroom, technology in the k-12 classroom, Socratic seminars, social studies education.

Palm Beach Atlantic University, School of Education and Behavioral Studies, West Palm Beach, FL 33416-4708. Offers counseling psychology (MS), including addictions/mental health, general counseling, marriage and family therapy, mental health counseling, school guidance counseling. *Program availability:* Part-time, evening/weekend. *Faculty:* 8 full-time (2 women), 17 part-time/adjunct (13 women). *Students:* 243 full-time (206 women), 29 part-time (24 women); includes 147 minority (67 Black or African American, non-Hispanic/Latino; 4 Asian, non-Hispanic/Latino; 60 Hispanic/Latino; 1 Native Hawaiian or other Pacific Islander, non-Hispanic/Latino; 15 Two or more races, non-Hispanic/Latino), 6 international. Average age 35. 81 applicants, 89% accepted, 53 enrolled. In 2016, 122 master's awarded. *Entrance requirements:* For master's, GRE or MAT, minimum GPA of 3.0; essay. Additional exam requirements/recommendations for international students: Required—TOEFL (minimum score 550 paper-based; 79 iBT). *Application deadline:* Applications are processed on a rolling basis. Application fee: $50. Electronic applications accepted. *Expenses: Tuition:* Full-time $6600; part-time $550 per credit hour. Full-time tuition and fees vary according to degree level, campus/location and program. *Financial support:* In 2016–17, 11 students received support. Career-related internships or fieldwork, scholarships/grants, and employee education grants available. Financial award application deadline: 5/1; financial award applicants required to submit FAFSA. *Faculty research:* Group dynamics, phenomenology, spirituality, multicultural psychology. *Unit head:* Dr. Gene Sale, Program Director, 561-803-2352. *Application contact:* Graduate Admissions, 888-468-6722, E-mail: grad@pba.edu.
Website: http://www.pba.edu/graduate-counseling-program

Park University, School of Graduate and Professional Studies, Kansas City, MO 54105. Offers adult education (M Ed); business and government leadership (Graduate Certificate); business, government, and global society (MPA); communication and leadership (MA); creative and life writing (Graduate Certificate); disaster and emergency management (MPA, Graduate Certificate); educational leadership (M Ed); finance (MBA, Graduate Certificate); general business (MBA); global business (Graduate Certificate); healthcare administration (MHA); healthcare services management and leadership (Graduate Certificate); international business (MBA); language and literacy (M Ed), including English for speakers of other languages, special reading teacher/literacy coach; leadership of international healthcare organizations (Graduate Certificate); management information systems (MBA, Graduate Certificate); music performance (ADP, Graduate Certificate), including cello (MM, ADP), piano (MM, ADP), viola (MM, ADP), violin (MM, ADP); nonprofit and community services management (MPA); nonprofit leadership (Graduate Certificate); performance (MM), including cello (MM, ADP), piano (MM, ADP), viola (MM, ADP), violin (MM, ADP); public management (MPA); social work (MSW); teacher leadership (M Ed), including curriculum and assessment, instructional leader. *Program availability:* Part-time, evening/weekend, online learning. *Degree requirements:* For master's, comprehensive exam (for some programs), thesis (for some programs), internship (for some programs); exam (for some programs). *Entrance requirements:* For master's, GRE or GMAT (for some programs), teacher certification (for some M Ed programs), letters of recommendation, essay, resume (for some programs). Additional exam requirements/recommendations for international students: Required—TOEFL (minimum score 550 paper-based; 79 iBT), IELTS (minimum score 6). Electronic applications accepted.

Penn State Harrisburg, Graduate School, School of Behavioral Sciences and Education, Middletown, PA 17057. Offers adult education in the health and medical professions (Certificate); applied behavior analysis (MA); applied clinical psychology (MA); applied psychological research (MA); community psychology and social change (MA); English as a second language (ESL) program specialist and leadership (Certificate); folklore and ethnography (Certificate); health education (M Ed); lifelong learning and adult education (M Ed, D Ed); literacy education (M Ed); literacy leadership (Certificate); psychology: applications in clinical psychology (Certificate); psychology: health psychology (Certificate); teaching and curriculum (M Ed); training and development (M Ed, Certificate). *Program availability:* Part-time, evening/weekend. *Unit head:* Dr. Mukund S. Kulkarni, Chancellor, 717-948-6105, Fax: 717-948-6452. *Application contact:* Robert W. Coffman, Jr., Director of Enrollment Management, Recruitment and Admissions, 717-948-6250, Fax: 717-948-6325, E-mail: hbgadmit@psu.edu.
Website: https://harrisburg.psu.edu/behavioral-sciences-and-education/

Penn State University Park, Graduate School, College of Education, University Park, PA 16802. Offers M Ed, MA, MPS, MS, D Ed, PhD, Certificate. *Accreditation:* NCATE. *Students:* 476 full-time (346 women), 221 part-time (130 women). Average age 33. 714 applicants, 42% accepted, 167 enrolled. In 2016, 160 master's, 85 doctorates awarded. *Entrance requirements:* Additional exam requirements/recommendations for international students: Required—TOEFL (minimum score 550 paper-based; 80 iBT), IELTS. *Application deadline:* Applications are processed on a rolling basis. Application fee: $65. Electronic applications accepted. *Financial support:* Fellowships, research assistantships, teaching assistantships, career-related internships or fieldwork, Federal Work-Study, scholarships/grants, traineeships, health care benefits, and unspecified assistantships available. Support available to part-time students. Financial award application deadline: 3/1; financial award applicants required to submit FAFSA. *Unit head:* Dr. David H. Monk, Dean, 814-865-2523, Fax: 814-865-0555. *Application contact:* Lori Hawn, Director, Graduate Student Services, 814-865-1795, Fax: 814-863-4627, E-mail: l-gswww@lists.psu.edu.
Website: http://ed.psu.edu/

Penn State York, Graduate School, York, PA 17403. Offers ESL specialist (Certificate); teaching and curriculum (M Ed). *Students:* 6 part-time (all women). Average age 33. 3 applicants, 33% accepted, 1 enrolled. *Unit head:* Dr. Regina Vasilatos-Younken, Vice Provost for Graduate Education/Dean, Graduate School, 814-865-2516, Fax: 814-863-4627. *Application contact:* Lori Hawn, Director, Graduate Student Services, 814-865-1795, Fax: 814-863-4627, E-mail: l-gswww@lists.psu.edu.
Website: http://www.gradschool.psu.edu/

Peru State College, Graduate Programs, Program in Education, Peru, NE 68421. Offers curriculum and instruction (MS Ed). *Accreditation:* NCATE. *Program availability:* Part-time. *Degree requirements:* For master's, comprehensive exam (for some programs), thesis optional.

Piedmont College, School of Education, Demorest, GA 30535. Offers art education (MAT); curriculum and instruction (Ed S); early childhood education (MA, MAT); instructional technology (MAT); middle grades education (MA, MAT); music education (MAT); secondary education (MA, MAT); special education (MA, MAT). *Program availability:* Part-time, evening/weekend. *Students:* 290 full-time (217 women), 614 part-time (508 women); includes 131 minority (97 Black or African American, non-Hispanic/Latino; 4 American Indian or Alaska Native, non-Hispanic/Latino; 5 Asian, non-Hispanic/Latino; 11 Hispanic/Latino; 6 Native Hawaiian or other Pacific Islander, non-Hispanic/Latino; 8 Two or more races, non-Hispanic/Latino), 6 international. Average age 37. 257 applicants, 64% accepted, 160 enrolled. In 2016, 288 master's, 243 other advanced degrees awarded. *Degree requirements:* For master's, thesis, field experience in the classroom teaching. *Entrance requirements:* For master's, GRE General Test, MAT, minimum undergraduate GPA of 2.5; for Ed S, minimum graduate GPA of 3.5, valid teaching certificate. Additional exam requirements/recommendations for international students: Required—TOEFL (minimum score 550 paper-based). *Application deadline:* For fall admission, 7/15 for domestic students; for spring admission, 12/1 for domestic students. Applications are processed on a rolling basis. Electronic applications accepted. *Expenses: Tuition:* Full-time $8910. *Financial support:* Career-related internships or fieldwork, Federal Work-Study, and unspecified assistantships available. Support available to part-time students. Financial award applicants required to submit FAFSA. *Unit head:* Dr. Don Gnecco, Dean, 706-778-3000 Ext. 1201, Fax: 706-776-9608, E-mail: dgnecco@piedmont.edu. *Application contact:* Kathleen Anderson, Director of Graduate Enrollment Management, 706-778-8500 Ext. 1181, Fax: 706-778-0150, E-mail: kanderson@piedmont.edu.

Pittsburg State University, Graduate School, College of Education, Pittsburg, KS 66762. Offers MS, Ed S. *Accreditation:* NCATE. *Program availability:* Part-time, 100% online, blended/hybrid learning. *Students:* 550 (409 women); includes 61 minority (17 Black or African American, non-Hispanic/Latino; 12 American Indian or Alaska Native, non-Hispanic/Latino; 2 Asian, non-Hispanic/Latino; 16 Hispanic/Latino; 14 Two or more races, non-Hispanic/Latino), 8 international. In 2016, 266 master's, 13 other advanced degrees awarded. Terminal master's awarded for partial completion of doctoral program. *Degree requirements:* For master's, thesis or alternative. *Entrance requirements:* For master's, GRE. Additional exam requirements/recommendations for international students: Required—TOEFL (minimum score 520 paper-based; 68 iBT), IELTS (minimum score 6), PTE (minimum score 47). *Application deadline:* For fall admission, 6/1 for international students; for spring admission, 10/15 for international students; for summer admission, 4/1 for international students. Applications are processed on a rolling basis. Application fee: $35 ($60 for international students). Electronic applications accepted. *Expenses:* Contact institution. *Financial support:* In 2016–17, 25 teaching assistantships with full tuition reimbursements (averaging $5,500 per year) were awarded; career-related internships or fieldwork, Federal Work-Study, and unspecified assistantships also available. Financial award application deadline: 2/1; financial award applicants required to submit FAFSA. *Unit head:* Dr. Jan Smith, Interim Dean, 620-235-4518, Fax: 620-235-4520, E-mail: jsmith@pittstate.edu. *Application contact:* Lisa Allen, Assistant Director of Graduate and Continuing Studies, 620-235-4223, Fax: 620-235-4219, E-mail: lallen@pittstate.edu.
Website: http://www.pittstate.edu/edsc/

Plymouth State University, College of Graduate Studies, Graduate Studies in Education, Certificate of Advanced Graduate Studies Programs, Plymouth, NH 03264-1595. Offers clinical mental health counseling (CAGS); educational leadership (CAGS); higher education (CAGS); school psychology (CAGS). *Program availability:* Part-time, evening/weekend.

Point Loma Nazarene University, School of Education, Program in Teaching, San Diego, CA 92106-2899. Offers education specialist mild to moderate (MAT); education specialist moderate to severe (MAT); multiple subject (MAT); single subject (MAT). *Program availability:* Part-time, evening/weekend. *Students:* 202 full-time (156 women), 213 part-time (159 women); includes 175 minority (16 Black or African American, non-Hispanic/Latino; 2 American Indian or Alaska Native, non-Hispanic/Latino; 10 Asian, non-Hispanic/Latino; 123 Hispanic/Latino; 2 Native Hawaiian or other Pacific Islander, non-Hispanic/Latino; 22 Two or more races, non-Hispanic/Latino). Average age 30. 134 applicants, 84% accepted, 92 enrolled. In 2016, 45 master's awarded. *Entrance requirements:* For master's, letters of recommendation, essay, interview. *Application deadline:* For fall admission, 8/4 priority date for domestic students; for spring admission, 12/8 priority date for domestic students; for summer admission, 4/13 priority date for domestic students. Applications are processed on a rolling basis. Application fee: $50. Electronic applications accepted. *Expenses:* $610 per credit (for San Diego campus), $595 per credit (for Bakersfield campus). *Financial support:* Career-related internships or fieldwork, scholarships/grants, and unspecified assistantships available. Financial award applicants required to submit FAFSA. *Faculty research:* Teaching preparation, the lives of teachers, co-teaching, teacher dispositions. *Unit head:* Jill Hamilton Bunch, Associate Dean, Bakersfield Regional Center, 661-321-3483, E-mail: jillhamilton-bunch@pointloma.edu. *Application contact:* Claire Buckley, Director of Graduate Admission, 866-692-4723, E-mail: gradinfo@pointloma.edu.
Website: http://gps.pointloma.edu/ma-teaching

Point Park University, School of Arts and Sciences, Department of Education, Pittsburgh, PA 15222-1984. Offers curriculum and instruction (MA); educational administration (MA); special education (M Ed); teaching and leadership (M Ed). *Program availability:* Part-time, evening/weekend. *Degree requirements:* For master's, comprehensive exam (for some programs), thesis or alternative. *Entrance requirements:* For master's, minimum GPA of 3.0, resume, 2 letters of recommendation. Additional exam requirements/recommendations for international students: Required—TOEFL. Electronic applications accepted.

Pontifical Catholic University of Puerto Rico, College of Education, Ponce, PR 00717-0777. Offers M Ed, MA Ed, MRE, PhD. *Accreditation:* TEAC. *Program availability:* Part-time, evening/weekend. *Degree requirements:* For master's, comprehensive exam, thesis (for some programs). *Entrance requirements:* For master's, GRE General Test, 2 letters of recommendation, interview, minimum GPA of 2.75; for doctorate, EXADEP, GRE or MAT, 3 letters of recommendation. *Faculty research:* Teaching English as a second language, learning styles, leadership styles.

Portland State University, Graduate Studies, School of Education, Portland, OR 97207-0751. Offers M Ed, MA, MAT, MS, MST, Ed D. *Accreditation:* NCATE. *Program availability:* Part-time, evening/weekend. *Faculty:* 67 full-time (44 women), 94 part-time/adjunct (69 women). *Students:* 480 full-time (342 women), 756 part-time (590 women); includes 311 minority (29 Black or African American, non-Hispanic/Latino; 22 American Indian or Alaska Native, non-Hispanic/Latino; 54 Asian, non-Hispanic/Latino; 150 Hispanic/Latino; 6 Native Hawaiian or other Pacific Islander, non-Hispanic/Latino; 50 Two or more races, non-Hispanic/Latino), 38 international. Average age 36. 455 applicants, 51% accepted, 205 enrolled. In 2016, 412 master's, 16 doctorates awarded. *Degree requirements:* For master's, variable foreign language requirement, comprehensive exam (for some programs), thesis (for some programs); for doctorate, variable foreign language requirement, comprehensive exam, thesis/dissertation. *Entrance requirements:* Additional exam requirements/recommendations for international students: Required—TOEFL (minimum score 550 paper-based; 80 iBT). *Application deadline:* For fall admission, 4/1 for domestic and international students; for winter admission, 9/1 for domestic and international students; for spring admission, 11/1 for domestic and international students. Application fee: $65. Electronic applications accepted. *Expenses:* Contact institution. *Financial support:* In 2016–17, 6 research assistantships with tuition reimbursements (averaging $7,366 per year), 5 teaching assistantships with tuition reimbursements (averaging $5,621 per year) were awarded; career-related internships or fieldwork, Federal Work-Study, institutionally sponsored loans, scholarships/grants, and unspecified assistantships also available. Support available to part-time students. Financial award application deadline: 3/1; financial award applicants required to submit FAFSA. *Total annual research expenditures:* $6.1 million. *Unit head:* Dr. Randy Hitz, Dean, 503-725-4697, Fax: 503-725-5399, E-mail:

hitz@pdx.edu. *Application contact:* Information Contact, 503-725-4619, Fax: 503-725-5599, E-mail: gseinfo@pdx.edu.
Website: http://www.pdx.edu/education/

Post University, Program in Education, Waterbury, CT 06723-2540. Offers education (M Ed); higher education administration (M Ed); instructional design and technology (M Ed); online teaching (M Ed); teaching and learning (M Ed); TESOL (teaching English to speakers of other languages) (M Ed). *Program availability:* Online learning.

Prairie View A&M University, College of Education, Prairie View, TX 77446. Offers M Ed, MA, MA Ed, MS, MS Ed, PhD. *Accreditation:* NCATE. *Program availability:* Part-time, evening/weekend, blended/hybrid learning. *Faculty:* 24 full-time (13 women), 11 part-time/adjunct (9 women). *Students:* 150 full-time (119 women), 351 part-time (273 women); includes 468 minority (442 Black or African American, non-Hispanic/Latino; 2 American Indian or Alaska Native, non-Hispanic/Latino; 1 Asian, non-Hispanic/Latino; 19 Hispanic/Latino; 4 Two or more races, non-Hispanic/Latino), 8 international. Average age 39. 329 applicants, 85% accepted, 213 enrolled. In 2016, 146 master's, 6 doctorates awarded. *Degree requirements:* For master's, comprehensive exam, thesis optional, minimum GPA of 3.0; for doctorate, comprehensive exam, thesis/dissertation. *Entrance requirements:* For master's, GRE, 3 letters of reference, minimum undergraduate GPA of 2.75; for doctorate, GRE General Test, 3 letters of reference, minimum undergraduate GPA of 3.0, essay. Additional exam requirements/recommendations for international students: Required—TOEFL (minimum score 550 paper-based; 79 iBT). *Application deadline:* For fall admission, 5/1 priority date for domestic and international students; for spring admission, 10/1 priority date for domestic students, 9/1 priority date for international students; for summer admission, 3/1 priority date for domestic students, 2/1 priority date for international students. Applications are processed on a rolling basis. Application fee: $50. Electronic applications accepted. *Expenses:* Tuition, state resident: full-time $4362; part-time $273.48 per credit hour. Tuition, nonresident: full-time $12,390; part-time $534.10 per credit hour. *Required fees:* $2782; $178.26 per credit hour. *Financial support:* Career-related internships or fieldwork, institutionally sponsored loans, scholarships/grants, and unspecified assistantships available. Support available to part-time students. Financial award application deadline: 4/1; financial award applicants required to submit FAFSA. *Faculty research:* Mentoring, assessment, humanistic education, diversity, literacy education, recruitment, student retention, school collaboration, leadership skills, structural equations. *Unit head:* Dr. Phyllis Metcalf-Turner, Dean, 936-261-3600, Fax: 936-261-3621, E-mail: pmmetcalf@pvamu.edu. *Application contact:* Pauline Walker, Administrative Assistant II, Research and Graduate Studies, 936-261-3521, Fax: 936-261-3529, E-mail: gradadmissions@pvamu.edu.

Prescott College, Graduate Programs, Program in Education, Prescott, AZ 86301. Offers early childhood education (MA); early childhood special education (MA); education (MA); elementary education (MA); environmental education leadership and administration (MA); equine-assisted learning (MA); school guidance counseling (MA); secondary education (MA); special education: learning disabilities (MA); special education: mental retardation (MA); special education: serious emotional disabilities (MA); student-directed independent study (MA); sustainability education (PhD). *Program availability:* Part-time, online learning. *Faculty:* 3 full-time (all women). *Students:* 9 full-time (8 women), 30 part-time (20 women); includes 11 minority (3 Black or African American, non-Hispanic/Latino; 2 American Indian or Alaska Native, non-Hispanic/Latino; 6 Hispanic/Latino). Average age 36. 66 applicants, 82% accepted, 32 enrolled. In 2016, 12 master's, 8 doctorates awarded. *Degree requirements:* For master's, thesis, fieldwork or internship, practicum; for doctorate, thesis/dissertation. *Entrance requirements:* For master's, 2 letters of recommendation, resume; for doctorate, 3 letters of recommendation, resume, official transcripts, personal statement, program proposal. Additional exam requirements/recommendations for international students: Required—TOEFL (minimum score 500 paper-based). *Application deadline:* For fall admission, 4/15 priority date for domestic and international students; for spring admission, 9/15 priority date for domestic and international students. Applications are processed on a rolling basis. Application fee: $40. Electronic applications accepted. *Expenses: Tuition:* Full-time $19,680. One-time fee: $260 part-time. *Financial support:* Fellowships, research assistantships, teaching assistantships, career-related internships or fieldwork, Federal Work-Study, institutionally sponsored loans, scholarships/grants, traineeships, health care benefits, tuition waivers, and unspecified assistantships available. Support available to part-time students. Financial award applicants required to submit FAFSA. *Unit head:* Bob Ellis, 928-350-2217, E-mail: bellis@prescott.edu. *Application contact:* Melanie Lefever, Assistant Director, Limited-residency Programs, 928-350-2106, Fax: 928-776-5242, E-mail: mlefever@prescott.edu.

Purdue University, Graduate School, College of Education, West Lafayette, IN 47907. Offers MS, MS Ed, PhD, Ed S. *Accreditation:* NCATE. *Program availability:* Part-time, evening/weekend. *Faculty:* 70 full-time (51 women), 2 part-time/adjunct (1 woman). *Students:* 156 full-time (110 women), 530 part-time (370 women); includes 114 minority (41 Black or African American, non-Hispanic/Latino; 3 American Indian or Alaska Native, non-Hispanic/Latino; 18 Asian, non-Hispanic/Latino; 38 Hispanic/Latino; 1 Native Hawaiian or other Pacific Islander, non-Hispanic/Latino; 13 Two or more races, non-Hispanic/Latino), 97 international. Average age 34. 377 applicants, 64% accepted, 151 enrolled. In 2016, 40 master's, 145 doctorates, 6 other advanced degrees awarded. *Degree requirements:* For master's, thesis optional; for doctorate, thesis/dissertation, oral and written exams; for Ed S, oral presentation, project. *Entrance requirements:* For master's, GRE General Test (if undergraduate GPA is below 3.0), minimum undergraduate GPA of 3.0 or equivalent; for doctorate, GRE General Test (minimum combined verbal and quantitative score of 1000, 300 for new scoring), minimum undergraduate GPA of 3.0 or equivalent; master's degree with minimum GPA of 3.0 or equivalent; for Ed S, GRE General Test (minimum combined verbal and quantitative score of 1000, 300 for new scoring), minimum undergraduate GPA of 3.0 or equivalent; master's degree. Additional exam requirements/recommendations for international students: Required—TOEFL (minimum score 550 paper-based; 77 iBT); Recommended—TWE. *Application deadline:* For fall admission, 12/15 for domestic students, 3/1 for international students; for spring admission, 9/15 for domestic students, 8/1 for international students. Application fee: $60 ($75 for international students). Electronic applications accepted. *Financial support:* Fellowships with full tuition reimbursements, research assistantships with full tuition reimbursements, teaching assistantships with full tuition reimbursements, career-related internships or fieldwork, and tuition waivers (full) available. Support available to part-time students. Financial award application deadline: 3/1; financial award applicants required to submit FAFSA. *Unit head:* Dr. M. Smith, Dean, 765-494-2604, Fax: 765-494-0136, E-mail: gradinfo@purdue.edu. *Application contact:* Graduate School Admissions, 765-494-2600, Fax: 765-494-0136, E-mail: gradinfo@purdue.edu.
Website: http://www.education.purdue.edu/

Purdue University Northwest, Graduate Studies Office, School of Education, Hammond, IN 46323-2094. Offers counseling (MS Ed), including human services, mental health counseling, school counseling; educational administration (MS Ed); instructional technology (MS Ed); special education (MS Ed). *Accreditation:* NCATE. *Entrance requirements:* Additional exam requirements/recommendations for international students: Required—TOEFL.

Queens College of the City University of New York, Division of Education, Queens, NY 11367-1597. Offers MA, MAT, MS Ed, AC. *Accreditation:* NCATE. *Program availability:* Part-time, evening/weekend. *Faculty:* 67 full-time (47 women), 123 part-time/adjunct (80 women). *Students:* 266 full-time (225 women), 1,189 part-time (943 women); includes 645 minority (121 Black or African American, non-Hispanic/Latino; 4 American Indian or Alaska Native, non-Hispanic/Latino; 182 Asian, non-Hispanic/Latino; 312 Hispanic/Latino; 1 Native Hawaiian or other Pacific Islander, non-Hispanic/Latino; 25 Two or more races, non-Hispanic/Latino), 26 international. Average age 29. 1,069 applicants, 68% accepted, 540 enrolled. In 2016, 425 master's, 130 other advanced degrees awarded. *Degree requirements:* For master's, comprehensive exam (for some programs), thesis (for some programs), research project. *Entrance requirements:* For master's, minimum GPA of 3.0. Additional exam requirements/recommendations for international students: Required—TOEFL, IELTS. *Application deadline:* For fall admission, 4/1 for domestic students; for spring admission, 11/1 for domestic students. Applications are processed on a rolling basis. Application fee: $125. Electronic applications accepted. *Expenses:* Tuition, state resident: full-time $5065; part-time $425 per credit. Tuition, nonresident: part-time $780 per credit. *Required fees:* $522; $397 per credit. Part-time tuition and fees vary according to course load and program. *Financial support:* Career-related internships or fieldwork available. Financial award application deadline: 4/1; financial award applicants required to submit FAFSA. *Unit head:* Dr. Craig Michaels, Dean, 718-997-5220, E-mail: craig.michaels@qc.cuny.edu.

Queen's University at Kingston, School of Graduate Studies, Faculty of Education, Kingston, ON K7L 3N6, Canada. Offers M Ed, PhD. *Program availability:* Part-time. *Degree requirements:* For master's, thesis optional; for doctorate, comprehensive exam, thesis/dissertation. *Entrance requirements:* Additional exam requirements/recommendations for international students: Required—TOEFL (minimum score 580 paper-based); Recommended—TWE (minimum score 4). *Faculty research:* Literacy, assessment and evaluation, special needs, mathematics, science and technology education.

Queens University of Charlotte, Wayland H. Cato, Jr. School of Education, Charlotte, NC 28274-0002. Offers educational leadership (MA); K-6 (MAT); literacy K-12 (M Ed). *Accreditation:* NCATE. *Program availability:* Part-time, evening/weekend, online learning. *Degree requirements:* For master's, comprehensive exam. *Entrance requirements:* For master's, GRE General Test. *Expenses:* Contact institution.

Quincy University, Master of Science in Education Programs, Quincy, IL 62301-2699. Offers curriculum and instruction (MS Ed), including bilingual/English as a second language; leadership (MS Ed); reading education (MS Ed); special education (MS Ed); teacher leader (MS Ed). *Program availability:* Part-time, evening/weekend, online learning. *Degree requirements:* For master's, comprehensive exam (for some programs), thesis optional. *Entrance requirements:* For master's, MAT or GRE. Additional exam requirements/recommendations for international students: Required—TOEFL (minimum score 550 paper-based; 79 iBT). Electronic applications accepted. Application fee is waived when completed online.

Quinnipiac University, School of Education, Hamden, CT 06518-1940. Offers MAT, MS, Diploma. *Accreditation:* NCATE. *Faculty:* 11 full-time (7 women), 35 part-time/adjunct (21 women). *Students:* 93 full-time (77 women), 145 part-time (113 women); includes 21 minority (3 Black or African American, non-Hispanic/Latino; 1 American Indian or Alaska Native, non-Hispanic/Latino; 1 Asian, non-Hispanic/Latino; 11 Hispanic/Latino; 5 Two or more races, non-Hispanic/Latino). 149 applicants, 93% accepted, 123 enrolled. In 2016, 81 master's, 23 other advanced degrees awarded. *Application deadline:* Applications are processed on a rolling basis. Application fee: $45. Electronic applications accepted. *Expenses: Tuition:* Part-time $985 per credit. *Required fees:* $40 per credit. $150 per semester. Tuition and fees vary according to program. *Financial support:* Career-related internships or fieldwork, Federal Work-Study, and unspecified assistantships available. Financial award application deadline: 6/1; financial award applicants required to submit FAFSA. *Faculty research:* Equity and excellence in education, school leadership.
Website: http://www.qu.edu/gradeducation

Randolph College, Programs in Education, Lynchburg, VA 24503. Offers curriculum and instruction (MAT); special education-learning disabilities (M Ed, MAT). *Accreditation:* TEAC. *Entrance requirements:* For master's, minimum GPA of 3.0 in prerequisite education coursework, 2.7 in major or field of interest (MAT); teaching license (M Ed); 2 recommendations; interview.

Regent University, Graduate School, School of Education, Virginia Beach, VA 23464-9800. Offers adult education (Ed D, PhD, Ed S); advanced educational leadership (Ed D, PhD, Ed S); career switcher (M Ed); character education (Ed D, PhD, Ed S); Christian education leadership (Ed D, PhD, Ed S); Christian school administration (M Ed); curriculum and instruction (M Ed), including adult education, Christian school, gifted and talented education, STEM education, teacher leader; educational leadership (M Ed); educational psychology (Ed D, PhD, Ed S); educational technology and online learning (Ed D, PhD, Ed S); elementary education (M Ed); exceptional education executive leadership (Ed D, PhD, Ed S); higher education (Ed D, PhD, Ed S); higher education leadership and management (Ed D, PhD, Ed S); individualized degree plan (M Ed); K-12 school leadership (Ed D, PhD, Ed S); K-12 special education (M Ed); K-8 leadership in mathematics education (M Ed); leadership in mathematics education (Ed S); reading specialist (M Ed); special education (Ed D, PhD, Ed S); student affairs (M Ed); TESOL (M Ed), including adult education - collegiate, K-12. *Accreditation:* TEAC. *Program availability:* Part-time, evening/weekend, 100% online, blended/hybrid learning. *Faculty:* 22 full-time (10 women), 42 part-time/adjunct (31 women). *Students:* 89 full-time (62 women), 1,035 part-time (823 women); includes 466 minority (381 Black or African American, non-Hispanic/Latino; 3 American Indian or Alaska Native, non-Hispanic/Latino; 19 Asian, non-Hispanic/Latino; 50 Hispanic/Latino; 13 Two or more races, non-Hispanic/Latino), 11 international. Average age 39. 976 applicants, 59% accepted, 449 enrolled. In 2016, 241 master's, 22 doctorates, 4 other advanced degrees awarded. *Degree requirements:* For master's, thesis or alternative; for doctorate, comprehensive exam, thesis/dissertation. *Entrance requirements:* For master's, Virginia Communication and Literacy Assessment (VCLA), PRAXIS, college transcripts, writing sample, interview; for doctorate, GRE, writing sample, resume, transcripts, interview. Additional exam requirements/recommendations for international students: Required—TOEFL (minimum score 577 paper-based). *Application deadline:* For fall admission, 4/1 priority date for domestic students; for spring admission, 10/15 priority date for domestic students. Applications are processed on a rolling basis. Application fee: $50. Electronic applications accepted. *Expenses:* Contact institution. *Financial support:* In 2016–17, 622 students received support, including 1 fellowship (averaging $5,000 per year); career-related internships or fieldwork, scholarships/grants, and unspecified assistantships also available. Support available to part-time students. *Faculty research:* Christian school administration, curriculum and instruction, educational technology and online learning, higher education, special education. *Unit head:* Dr. Donald Finn, Dean, 757-352-4278, Fax: 757-352-4318, E-mail: dfinn@regent.edu. *Application contact:* Heidi Cece, Assistant Vice President of Enrollment Management, 800-373-5504, Fax: 757-352-4381, E-mail: admissions@regent.edu.
Website: http://www.regent.edu/soe/

Regis College, Department of Education, Weston, MA 02493. Offers elementary teacher (MAT); higher education leadership (Ed D); reading (MAT); special education (MAT). *Program availability:* Part-time, evening/weekend, blended/hybrid learning. *Degree requirements:* For master's, thesis. *Entrance requirements:* For master's, GRE or MAT. Additional exam requirements/recommendations for international students: Required—TOEFL; Recommended—IELTS. *Application deadline:* Applications are processed on a rolling basis. Application fee: $50. Electronic applications accepted. *Financial support:* Federal Work-Study, scholarships/grants, and unspecified assistantships available. Financial award applicants required to submit FAFSA. *Unit head:* Dr. Priscilla Boerger, Department Chair/Graduate Program Director, 781-768-7422, E-mail: priscilla.boerger@regiscollege.edu.

Regis University, Regis College, Denver, CO 80221-1099. Offers biomedical sciences (MS); developmental practice (MDP); education (MA); environmental biology (MS). *Accreditation:* TEAC. *Program availability:* Part-time. *Faculty:* 2 full-time (1 woman), 22 part-time/adjunct (12 women). *Students:* 109 full-time (64 women), 15 part-time (13 women); includes 29 minority (7 Black or African American, non-Hispanic/Latino; 8 Asian, non-Hispanic/Latino; 7 Hispanic/Latino; 7 Two or more races, non-Hispanic/Latino), 25 international. Average age 30. 390 applicants, 71% accepted, 45 enrolled. In 2016, 29 master's awarded. *Degree requirements:* For master's, thesis (for some programs), capstone presentation. *Entrance requirements:* For master's, official transcript reflecting baccalaureate degree awarded from U.S.-based regionally-accredited college or university. Additional exam requirements/recommendations for international students: Required—TOEFL (minimum score 550 paper-based; 82 iBT). *Application deadline:* For fall admission, 5/15 priority date for domestic students, 4/1 priority date for international students; for spring admission, 12/15 priority date for domestic students. Applications are processed on a rolling basis. Application fee: $75. Electronic applications accepted. *Expenses:* $810 per credit hour. *Financial support:* Federal Work-Study and scholarships/grants available. Financial award application deadline: 4/15; financial award applicants required to submit FAFSA. *Unit head:* Dr. Thomas Bowie, Academic Dean. *Application contact:* Sarah Engel, Director of Admissions, 303-458-4900, Fax: 303-964-5534, E-mail: ruadmissions@regis.edu.
Website: http://www.regis.edu/RC.aspx

Reinhardt University, Price School of Education, Waleska, GA 30183-2981. Offers M Ed, MAT. *Program availability:* Part-time, evening/weekend, online learning. *Degree requirements:* For master's, comprehensive exam. *Entrance requirements:* For master's, GACE, background check. Additional exam requirements/recommendations for international students: Required—TOEFL. *Application deadline:* For fall admission, 5/7 for domestic and international students. Applications are processed on a rolling basis. Application fee: $25. Electronic applications accepted. *Expenses: Tuition:* Part-time $475 per credit hour. *Required fees:* $100 per semester. Part-time tuition and fees vary according to program. *Financial support:* Application deadline: 5/1; applicants required to submit FAFSA. *Unit head:* Dr. Nancy Marsh, Interim Dean, 770-720-5657, Fax: 770-720-9173, E-mail: njm@reinhardt.edu. *Application contact:* Dr. Nancy Marsh, Interim Dean, 770-720-5657, Fax: 770-720-9173, E-mail: njm@reinhardt.edu.

Relay Graduate School of Education, Graduate Programs, New York, NY 10011. Offers MAT. Program also offered at Chicago, Delaware, Houston, Memphis, New Orleans, and Newark campuses. *Program availability:* Online learning.

Rhode Island College, School of Graduate Studies, Feinstein School of Education and Human Development, Program in Education, Providence, RI 02908-1991. Offers PhD. Program offered jointly with University of Rhode Island. *Accreditation:* NCATE. *Program availability:* Part-time, evening/weekend. *Faculty:* 8 part-time/adjunct (5 women). *Students:* 2 full-time (1 woman), 51 part-time (29 women); includes 10 minority (3 Black or African American, non-Hispanic/Latino; 6 Asian, non-Hispanic/Latino; 1 Hispanic/Latino). Average age 41. In 2016, 3 doctorates awarded. *Degree requirements:* For doctorate, comprehensive exam, thesis/dissertation. *Entrance requirements:* For doctorate, GRE, two official transcripts from all colleges and universities attended, 3 letters of recommendation, personal statement, professional resume. Additional exam requirements/recommendations for international students: Recommended—TOEFL (minimum score 550 paper-based; 79 iBT). *Application deadline:* For fall admission, 1/29 for domestic students. Applications are processed on a rolling basis. Application fee: $65. Electronic applications accepted. *Expenses:* Tuition, state resident: full-time $8928; part-time $372 per credit. Tuition, nonresident: full-time $17,376; part-time $724 per credit. *Required fees:* $604; $22 per credit. One-time fee: $74. *Financial support:* Health care benefits available. Support available to part-time students. Financial award application deadline: 5/15; financial award applicants required to submit FAFSA. *Unit head:* Dr. Janet Johnson, Co-Director, 401-456-8701. *Application contact:* Graduate Studies, 401-456-8700.
Website: http://www.ric.edu/feinsteinschooleducationhumandevelopment/jointPHD.php

Rice University, Graduate Programs, Programs in Education Certification, Houston, TX 77251-1892. Offers MAT. *Entrance requirements:* For master's, GRE General Test, minimum GPA of 3.0. Additional exam requirements/recommendations for international students: Required—TOEFL (minimum score 600 paper-based; 90 iBT). Electronic applications accepted. *Faculty research:* Assessment, integration of math and science.

Rider University, Department of Graduate Education, Leadership and Counseling, Lawrenceville, NJ 08648-3001. Offers counseling services (MA, Certificate, Ed S), including counseling services (MA, Ed S), director of school counseling (Certificate), school counseling services (Certificate); curriculum, instruction and supervision (MA, Certificate), including curriculum, instruction and supervision (MA), supervisor (Certificate); educational administration (MA, Certificate), including educational administration (MA), principal (Certificate), school administrator (Certificate); organizational leadership (MA); reading/language arts (MA, Certificate), including reading specialist (Certificate), reading/language arts (MA); school psychology (Certificate, Ed S); special education (MA, Certificate), including alternative route in special education (Certificate), special education (MA), teacher of students with disabilities (Certificate), teacher of the handicapped (Certificate); teacher certification (Certificate), including business education, elementary education, English as a second language, English education, mathematics education, preschool to grade 3, science education, social studies education, world languages; teaching (MA). *Accreditation:* NCATE. *Program availability:* Part-time, evening/weekend. *Degree requirements:* For master's, comprehensive exam (for some programs), thesis or alternative, internship, portfolios; for other advanced degree, internship, professional portfolio. *Entrance requirements:* For master's, GRE (counseling, school psychology), MAT, interview, resume, letters of recommendation; for other advanced degree, PRAXIS. Additional exam requirements/recommendations for international students: Required—TOEFL (minimum score 550 paper-based). Electronic applications accepted. *Faculty research:* Gifted students, self-esteem, hope and mental health, conflicts in group work, cultural diversity and counseling assessment of special needs in children.

Rivier University, School of Graduate Studies, Department of Education, Nashua, NH 03060. Offers curriculum and instruction (M Ed); early childhood education (M Ed); educational administration (M Ed); educational studies (M Ed); elementary education (M Ed); elementary education and general special education (M Ed); emotional and behavioral disorders (M Ed); general social education (M Ed); leadership and learning (Ed D, CAGS); learning disabilities (M Ed); learning disabilities and reading (M Ed); mental health counseling (MA); reading (M Ed); school counseling (M Ed). *Program availability:* Part-time, evening/weekend. *Degree requirements:* For master's, comprehensive exam (for some programs), internships. *Entrance requirements:* For master's, GRE General Test or MAT.

Robert Morris University, School of Education and Social Sciences, Moon Township, PA 15108-1189. Offers business education (MS); counseling psychology (MS); education (Postbaccalaureate Certificate); higher education (MS); instructional leadership (MS), including education; instructional management and leadership (PhD); literacy (MS); special education (MS). *Accreditation:* TEAC. *Program availability:* Part-time, evening/weekend, online learning. *Faculty:* 17 full-time (9 women), 4 part-time/adjunct (3 women). *Students:* 154 part-time (104 women); includes 18 minority (11 Black or African American, non-Hispanic/Latino; 2 Hispanic/Latino; 5 Two or more races, non-Hispanic/Latino), 1 international. Average age 26. 69 applicants, 26% accepted, 18 enrolled. In 2016, 40 master's, 15 doctorates awarded. *Degree requirements:* For doctorate, thesis/dissertation. *Entrance requirements:* Additional exam requirements/recommendations for international students: Required—TOEFL (minimum score 550 paper-based; 79 iBT). *Application deadline:* For fall admission, 7/1 priority date for domestic and international students; for spring admission, 11/1 priority date for domestic and international students. Applications are processed on a rolling basis. Application fee: $35. Electronic applications accepted. *Expenses:* $840 per credit (for master's degree). *Unit head:* Dr. Mary Ann Rafoth, Dean, 412-397-6020, Fax: 412-397-6044, E-mail: rafoth@rmu.edu.
Website: http://www.rmu.edu/web/cms/schools/sess/

Roberts Wesleyan College, Graduate Teacher Education Programs, Rochester, NY 14624-1997. Offers adolescence and special education (M Ed); childhood and special education (M Ed); literacy education (M Ed); special education (M Ed). *Program availability:* Part-time, evening/weekend. *Degree requirements:* For master's, thesis. Electronic applications accepted.

Rockford University, Graduate Studies, Department of Education, Rockford, IL 61108-2393. Offers early childhood education (MAT); elementary education (MAT); instructional strategies (MAT); reading (MAT); secondary education (MAT); special education (MAT). *Program availability:* Part-time, evening/weekend. *Degree requirements:* For master's, thesis optional, professional portfolio (for instructional strategies program). *Entrance requirements:* For master's, GRE General Test, basic skills test (for students seeking certification), 3 letters of recommendation. Additional exam requirements/recommendations for international students: Required—TOEFL (minimum score 550 paper-based; 79 iBT). *Application deadline:* Applications are processed on a rolling basis. Application fee: $50. Electronic applications accepted. *Expenses: Tuition:* Part-time $710 per credit. *Required fees:* $50 per semester. *Financial support:* Scholarships/grants and unspecified assistantships available. Support available to part-time students. Financial award application deadline: 3/1; financial award applicants required to submit FAFSA. *Unit head:* Dr. Christopher McCullough, Chair, 815-394-5071, Fax: 815-394-5249, E-mail: cmccullough@rockford.edu. *Application contact:* Michele Mehren, Assistant Director, Office of Graduate Studies, 815-226-4040, Fax: 815-394-3706, E-mail: mmehren@rockford.edu.
Website: https://www.rockford.edu/academics/departments/education/

Rockhurst University, College of Health and Human Services, Program in Education, Kansas City, MO 64110-2561. Offers M Ed. *Accreditation:* TEAC. *Program availability:* Part-time, evening/weekend. *Entrance requirements:* For master's, minimum GPA of 2.5, 2 letters of recommendation. Additional exam requirements/recommendations for international students: Required—TOEFL (minimum score 550 paper-based; 79 iBT). Electronic applications accepted. Application fee is waived when completed online. *Expenses:* Contact institution. *Faculty research:* English language learners, urban literacy, online discussions, character education, teaching K-12 students about math and literacy.

Roger Williams University, School of Education, Bristol, RI 02809. Offers literacy education (MA). *Program availability:* Part-time, evening/weekend. *Faculty:* 1 (woman) full-time, 2 part-time/adjunct (1 woman). *Students:* 7 full-time (all women), 10 part-time (all women); includes 1 minority (Hispanic/Latino). Average age 34. 4 applicants, 100% accepted, 2 enrolled. In 2016, 3 master's awarded. *Entrance requirements:* For master's, resume, 2 letters of recommendation, college transcript, letter of intent, verification of active teaching license. Additional exam requirements/recommendations for international students: Required—TOEFL (minimum score 85 iBT), IELTS (minimum score 6.5). *Application deadline:* Applications are processed on a rolling basis. Application fee: $50. Electronic applications accepted. Application fee is waived when completed online. *Expenses:* $552 per credit hour. *Financial support:* Application deadline: 4/1; applicants required to submit FAFSA. *Unit head:* Robert McKenna, Interim Dean of School of Education, 401-254-3715, Fax: 401-254-3710, E-mail: rmckenna@rwu.edu. *Application contact:* Marcus Hanscom, Director of Graduate Admissions, 401-254-3345, Fax: 401-254-3557, E-mail: gradadmit@rwu.edu.
Website: http://www.rwu.edu/academics/schools/sed/

Rollins College, Hamilton Holt School, Graduate Education Programs, Winter Park, FL 32789-4499. Offers elementary education (M Ed, MAT). *Program availability:* Part-time, evening/weekend. *Faculty:* 4 full-time (2 women), 1 part-time/adjunct (0 women). *Students:* 5 full-time (4 women), 10 part-time (6 women); includes 3 minority (1 Black or African American, non-Hispanic/Latino; 2 American Indian or Alaska Native, non-Hispanic/Latino). Average age 34. 10 applicants, 70% accepted, 7 enrolled. In 2016, 5 master's awarded. *Degree requirements:* For master's, comprehensive exam, Professional Education Test (PED) and Subject Area Examination (SAE) of the Florida Teacher Certification Examinations (FTCE), successful review of the Expanded Teacher Education Portfolio (ETEP). *Entrance requirements:* For master's, General Knowledge Test of the Florida Teacher Certification Examination (FTCE), official transcripts, letter(s) of recommendation, essay. Additional exam requirements/recommendations for international students: Required—TOEFL (minimum score 550 paper-based; 80 iBT). *Application deadline:* For fall admission, 8/11 for domestic students; for spring admission, 12/10 for domestic students. Applications are processed on a rolling basis. Application fee: $50. *Expenses:* $525 per credit hour. *Financial support:* In 2016–17, 5 students received support. Federal Work-Study, scholarships/grants, and unspecified assistantships available. Support available to part-time students. Financial award applicants required to submit FAFSA. *Unit head:* Dr. Scott J. Hewit, Faculty Director, 407-646-2300, E-mail: shewit@rollins.edu. *Application contact:* 407-646-1568, Fax: 407-975-6430.

Roosevelt University, Graduate Division, College of Education, Chicago, IL 60605. Offers MA. *Accreditation:* ACA; NCATE. *Program availability:* Part-time, evening/weekend. *Students:* 79 full-time (62 women), 178 part-time (135 women); includes 92 minority (55 Black or African American, non-Hispanic/Latino; 1 American Indian or Alaska Native, non-Hispanic/Latino; 7 Asian, non-Hispanic/Latino; 25 Hispanic/Latino; 4 Two or more races, non-Hispanic/Latino), 4 international. Average age 32. 176 applicants, 97% accepted, 74 enrolled. In 2016, 99 master's awarded. *Application deadline:* For fall admission, 6/1 priority date for domestic students. Applications are processed on a rolling basis. Application fee: $25 ($35 for international students). *Expenses: Tuition, area resident:* Full-time $19,566; part-time $880 per credit hour. *Required fees:* $175 per semester. One-time fee: $200. Part-time tuition and fees vary

according to course load, degree level and program. *Financial support:* Federal Work-Study available. Support available to part-time students. Financial award application deadline: 2/15. *Unit head:* George Olson, Interim Dean, 312-341-3700. *Application contact:* Angela Ryan, Director of Graduate Enrollment, 312-341-2420, Fax: 312-281-3356, E-mail: aryan@roosevelt.edu.
Website: https://www.roosevelt.edu/colleges/education

Rosemont College, Schools of Graduate and Professional Studies, Graduate Education PreK-4 Program, Rosemont, PA 19010-1699. Offers elementary certification (MA); PreK-4 (MA). *Program availability:* Part-time, evening/weekend. *Degree requirements:* For master's, thesis optional. *Entrance requirements:* For master's, minimum college GPA of 3.0, 3 letters of recommendation. Additional exam requirements/recommendations for international students: Required—TOEFL. Electronic applications accepted. Application fee is waived when completed online.

Rowan University, Graduate School, College of Education, Glassboro, NJ 08028-1701. Offers M Ed, MA, MST, Ed D, CAGS, CGS, Ed S, Postbaccalaureate Certificate. *Accreditation:* NCATE. *Program availability:* Part-time, evening/weekend. *Degree requirements:* For master's, comprehensive exam, thesis; for doctorate, thesis/dissertation. *Entrance requirements:* For master's, GRE General Test, PRAXIS I, PRAXIS II; for doctorate, GRE, master's degree. Additional exam requirements/recommendations for international students: Required—TOEFL. Electronic applications accepted.

Rudolf Steiner College, Waldorf Teacher Education Programs, Fair Oaks, CA 95628-6811. Offers early childhood education (MA); elementary education (MA).

Rutgers University–New Brunswick, Graduate School of Education, New Brunswick, NJ 08901. Offers Ed M, Ed D, PhD. *Accreditation:* TEAC. *Program availability:* Part-time, evening/weekend. Terminal master's awarded for partial completion of doctoral program. *Degree requirements:* For master's, comprehensive exam (for some programs); for doctorate, thesis/dissertation. *Entrance requirements:* For master's and doctorate, GRE General Test. Additional exam requirements/recommendations for international students: Required—TOEFL (minimum score 575 paper-based; 83 iBT). Electronic applications accepted.

Sacred Heart University, Graduate Programs, Isabelle Farrington College of Education, Fairfield, CT 06825. Offers MAT, CAS, Professional Certificate. *Accreditation:* NCATE. *Program availability:* Part-time, evening/weekend. *Faculty:* 21 full-time (10 women), 28 part-time/adjunct (14 women). *Students:* 203 full-time (155 women), 510 part-time (398 women); includes 98 minority (30 Black or African American, non-Hispanic/Latino; 1 American Indian or Alaska Native, non-Hispanic/Latino; 12 Asian, non-Hispanic/Latino; 50 Hispanic/Latino; 5 Two or more races, non-Hispanic/Latino). Average age 34. 306 applicants, 97% accepted, 263 enrolled. In 2016, 241 master's, 91 other advanced degrees awarded. *Degree requirements:* For master's, comprehensive exam (for some programs), thesis (for some programs). *Entrance requirements:* For master's, PRAXIS, minimum GPA of 2.68; for other advanced degree, CT teacher certification. Additional exam requirements/recommendations for international students: Required—TOEFL (minimum score 570 paper-based, 80 iBT), TWE, or IELTS (6.5); Recommended—TSE. *Application deadline:* Applications are processed on a rolling basis. Application fee: $75. Electronic applications accepted. *Expenses:* Contact institution. *Financial support:* Teaching assistantships with partial tuition reimbursements and unspecified assistantships available. Financial award applicants required to submit FAFSA. *Faculty research:* Reading education, learning theory, teacher preparation, education of underachievers. *Unit head:* Dr. Jim Carl, Dean, 203-396-8454, Fax: 203-365-7513, E-mail: carlj@sacredheart.edu. *Application contact:* William Sweeney, Director of Graduate Admissions Operations, 203-365-4827, E-mail: sweeneyw@sacredheart.edu.
Website: http://www.sacredheart.edu/academics/isabellefarringtoncollegeofeducation/

Sage Graduate School, Esteves School of Education, Troy, NY 12180-4115. Offers MS, MS Ed, Ed D, Post Master's Certificate. *Accreditation:* NCATE. *Program availability:* Part-time, evening/weekend. *Faculty:* 17 full-time (13 women), 18 part-time/adjunct (12 women). *Students:* 121 full-time (107 women), 289 part-time (215 women); includes 115 minority (55 Black or African American, non-Hispanic/Latino; 1 American Indian or Alaska Native, non-Hispanic/Latino; 15 Asian, non-Hispanic/Latino; 35 Hispanic/Latino; 9 Two or more races, non-Hispanic/Latino). Average age 33. 475 applicants, 45% accepted, 142 enrolled. In 2016, 135 master's, 26 doctorates, 16 other advanced degrees awarded. *Entrance requirements:* Additional exam requirements/recommendations for international students: Required—TOEFL (minimum score 550 paper-based). *Application deadline:* Applications are processed on a rolling basis. Application fee: $40. Electronic applications accepted. *Expenses: Tuition:* Full-time $12,240; part-time $680 per credit hour. Tuition and fees vary according to degree level and program. *Financial support:* Fellowships, research assistantships, Federal Work-Study, scholarships/grants, tuition waivers (partial), and unspecified assistantships available. Support available to part-time students. Financial award application deadline: 3/1; financial award applicants required to submit FAFSA. *Faculty research:* Literacy development in at-risk children, effective behavior strategies for class instruction. *Unit head:* Dr. John Pelizza, Interim Dean, Esteves School of Education, 518-244-2051, Fax: 518-244-2334, E-mail: pelizj@sage.edu. *Application contact:* Wendy D. Diefendorf, Director of Graduate and Adult Admission, 518-244-2443, Fax: 518-244-6880, E-mail: diefew@sage.edu.

Saginaw Valley State University, College of Education, University Center, MI 48710. Offers M Ed, MA, MAT, Ed S. *Accreditation:* NCATE. *Program availability:* Part-time, evening/weekend, online learning. *Faculty:* 12 full-time (9 women), 23 part-time/adjunct (17 women). *Students:* 15 full-time (12 women), 233 part-time (188 women); includes 17 minority (8 Black or African American, non-Hispanic/Latino; 6 Hispanic/Latino; 3 Two or more races, non-Hispanic/Latino), 5 international. Average age 34. 83 applicants, 89% accepted, 47 enrolled. In 2016, 143 master's, 24 other advanced degrees awarded. *Entrance requirements:* For master's, minimum GPA of 3.0, teaching certificate. Additional exam requirements/recommendations for international students: Required—TOEFL (minimum score 550 paper-based; 79 iBT). *Application deadline:* For fall admission, 7/15 for international students; for winter admission, 11/15 for international students; for spring admission, 4/15 for international students. Applications are processed on a rolling basis. Application fee: $30 ($90 for international students). Electronic applications accepted. *Expenses:* Tuition, state resident: full-time $9652; part-time $536 per credit hour. Tuition, nonresident: full-time $12,259; part-time $1022 per credit hour. *Required fees:* $263; $14.60 per credit hour. Tuition and fees vary according to degree level. *Financial support:* Federal Work-Study and scholarships/grants available. Support available to part-time students. Financial award applicants required to submit FAFSA. *Unit head:* Dr. Craig Douglas, Dean, 989-964-4057, Fax: 989-964-4563, E-mail: coeconnect@svsu.edu. *Application contact:* Jenna Briggs, Director, Graduate and International Admissions, 989-964-6096, Fax: 989-964-2788, E-mail: gradadm@svsu.edu.
Website: http://www.svsu.edu/collegeofeducation

St. Ambrose University, College of Education and Health Sciences, Program in Education, Davenport, IA 52803-2898. Offers special education (M Ed); teaching (M Ed). *Accreditation:* TEAC. *Program availability:* Part-time, evening/weekend, online learning. *Degree requirements:* For master's, comprehensive exam. *Entrance requirements:* For master's, GRE General Test or MAT, minimum GPA of 2.75. Additional exam requirements/recommendations for international students: Required—TOEFL. Electronic applications accepted. *Faculty research:* Disabilities and postsecondary career avenues, self-determination.

St. Bonaventure University, School of Graduate Studies, School of Education, St. Bonaventure, NY 14778-2284. Offers MS Ed, Adv C. *Accreditation:* NCATE. *Program availability:* Part-time, evening/weekend. *Faculty:* 12 full-time (8 women), 16 part-time/adjunct (13 women). *Students:* 90 full-time (70 women), 83 part-time (63 women); includes 11 minority (5 Black or African American, non-Hispanic/Latino; 2 Hispanic/Latino; 4 Two or more races, non-Hispanic/Latino), 2 international. Average age 29. 99 applicants, 76% accepted, 54 enrolled. In 2016, 55 master's, 12 Adv Cs awarded. *Degree requirements:* For master's and Adv C, comprehensive exam, thesis optional, student teaching, electronic portfolio, internship, practicum. *Entrance requirements:* Additional exam requirements/recommendations for international students: Required—TOEFL (minimum score 550 paper-based; 79 iBT). *Application deadline:* For fall admission, 6/15 priority date for domestic students, 2/1 priority date for international students; for spring admission, 11/15 priority date for domestic students, 7/1 priority date for international students. Applications are processed on a rolling basis. Application fee: $0. Electronic applications accepted. *Expenses:* $733 per credit, $100 graduation fee. *Financial support:* Career-related internships or fieldwork, Federal Work-Study, scholarships/grants, health care benefits, and unspecified assistantships available. Support available to part-time students. Financial award application deadline: 4/15; financial award applicants required to submit FAFSA. *Faculty research:* Critical and media literacy, gifted education, global competence, cyberbullying. *Unit head:* Dr. Nancy Casey, Interim Dean, 716-375-2394, Fax: 716-375-2360, E-mail: jezimmer@sbu.edu. *Application contact:* Bruce Campbell, Director of Graduate Admissions, 716-375-2429, Fax: 716-375-4015, E-mail: gradsch@sbu.edu.

St. Catherine University, Graduate Programs, Program in Education–Curriculum and Instruction, St. Paul, MN 55105. Offers MA. *Program availability:* Part-time, evening/weekend, online learning. *Degree requirements:* For master's, thesis. *Entrance requirements:* For master's, current teaching license, classroom experience, minimum GPA of 3.0. Additional exam requirements/recommendations for international students: Required—Michigan English Language Assessment Battery or TOEFL (minimum score 600 paper-based; 100 iBT). *Expenses:* Contact institution.

St. Catherine University, Graduate Programs, Program in Education - Initial Licensure, St. Paul, MN 55105. Offers MA. *Program availability:* Part-time, evening/weekend. *Expenses:* Contact institution.

St. Cloud State University, School of Graduate Studies, School of Education, St. Cloud, MN 56301-4498. Offers MS, Ed D. *Accreditation:* NCATE. *Program availability:* Part-time, evening/weekend, online learning. *Degree requirements:* For master's, comprehensive exam (for some programs), thesis or alternative; for doctorate, comprehensive exam, thesis/dissertation. *Entrance requirements:* For master's, GRE General Test (for some programs), minimum GPA of 2.75; for doctorate, GRE. Additional exam requirements/recommendations for international students: Required—Michigan English Language Assessment Battery; Recommended—TOEFL (minimum score 550 paper-based), IELTS (minimum score 6.5).

St. Edward's University, School of Education, Austin, TX 78704. Offers counseling (MA); education (Certificate). *Program availability:* Part-time, evening/weekend. *Degree requirements:* For master's, completion of required 60 hrs of coursework with a cumulative GPA of 3.0. *Entrance requirements:* For master's, GRE General Test, minimum GPA of 3.0 in last 60 hours or 2.75 overall. Additional exam requirements/recommendations for international students: Required—TOEFL (minimum score 79 iBT), IELTS (minimum score 6). Electronic applications accepted. *Expenses: Tuition:* Full-time $25,092; part-time $1394 per credit hour. *Required fees:* $75 per trimester. Full-time tuition and fees vary according to course load and program.

Saint Francis University, Graduate Education Program, Loretto, PA 15940-0600. Offers education (M Ed); leadership (M Ed); reading (M Ed). *Program availability:* Part-time, 100% online, blended/hybrid learning. *Degree requirements:* For master's, comprehensive exam, thesis optional. *Entrance requirements:* For master's, GRE or MAT (if undergraduate GPA less than 3.0). Additional exam requirements/recommendations for international students: Required—TOEFL (minimum score 550 paper-based; 75 iBT), IELTS (minimum score 6.5), International Test of English Proficiency (minimum score 4). *Expenses:* Contact institution.

St. Francis Xavier University, Graduate Studies, Graduate Studies in Education, Antigonish, NS B2G 2W5, Canada. Offers curriculum and instruction (M Ed); educational administration and leadership (M Ed). *Program availability:* Part-time, online learning. *Degree requirements:* For master's, thesis. *Entrance requirements:* For master's, minimum undergraduate B average, 2 years of teaching experience. *Application deadline:* For fall admission, 2/15 for domestic and international students. Application fee: $40. *Expenses: Tuition:* Full-time $9060 Canadian dollars; part-time $725 Canadian dollars per credit. *Required fees:* $789 Canadian dollars; $78.84 Canadian dollars per credit. Tuition and fees vary according to course load, degree level and program. *Financial support:* Teaching assistantships available. *Faculty research:* Inclusive education, qualitative research. *Unit head:* Dr. Robert E. White, Chair, 902-867-3420, Fax: 902-867-3887, E-mail: rwhite@stfx.ca. *Application contact:* Colleen Jones, Assistant, 902-867-3906, Fax: 902-867-5154, E-mail: med@stfx.ca.

St. John Fisher College, Ralph C. Wilson Jr. School of Education, Rochester, NY 14618-3597. Offers MS, MS Ed, Ed D, Certificate. *Accreditation:* NCATE. *Program availability:* Part-time, evening/weekend. *Faculty:* 26 full-time (20 women), 12 part-time/adjunct (11 women). *Students:* 168 full-time (121 women), 89 part-time (67 women); includes 87 minority (62 Black or African American, non-Hispanic/Latino; 3 American Indian or Alaska Native, non-Hispanic/Latino; 2 Asian, non-Hispanic/Latino; 16 Hispanic/Latino; 4 Two or more races, non-Hispanic/Latino). Average age 37. 168 applicants, 71% accepted, 90 enrolled. In 2016, 61 master's, 41 doctorates awarded. *Degree requirements:* For doctorate, thesis/dissertation. *Entrance requirements:* For master's and doctorate, 2 letters of recommendation, current resume. Additional exam requirements/recommendations for international students: Required—TOEFL (minimum score 575 paper-based; 80 iBT). *Application deadline:* Applications are processed on a rolling basis. Application fee: $30. Electronic applications accepted. *Expenses:* Contact institution. *Financial support:* Scholarships/grants available. Financial award applicants required to submit FAFSA. *Unit head:* Dr. Michael Wischnowski, Dean, 585-385-7361, E-mail: mwischnowski@sjfc.edu. *Application contact:* Michelle Gosier, Associate Director of Transfer and Graduate Admissions, 585-385-8064, E-mail: mgosier@sjfc.edu.
Website: https://www.sjfc.edu/schools/school-of-education/

St. John's University, The School of Education, Queens, NY 11439. Offers MS Ed, Ed D, PhD, Adv C, Certificate. *Accreditation:* TEAC. *Program availability:* Part-time, evening/weekend, online learning. *Degree requirements:* For master's, comprehensive exam (for some programs), thesis (for some programs), residency; for doctorate, comprehensive exam, thesis/dissertation. *Entrance requirements:* For master's, 2 letters of recommendation, official transcript, minimum GPA of 3.0, personal statement, resume; for doctorate, GRE General Test, MAT (for PhD in literacy), interview, writing sample, 2 years of teaching experience, resume (for PhD in literacy only), personal statement, minimum master's GPA of 3.2; for other advanced degree, 2 letters of recommendation, master's degree from accredited college or university. Additional exam requirements/recommendations for international students: Required—TOEFL (minimum score 600 paper-based; 100 iBT), IELTS (minimum score 7). Electronic applications accepted. *Faculty research:* Results of school partnerships, effective means of working with recent immigrant populations, results of graduates who participated in programs leading to alternative certification routes, resolution of issues surrounding middle schools, identifying means of supporting children at both ends of the academic continuum.

St. Joseph's College, New York, Programs in Education, Brooklyn, NY 11205-3688. Offers educational leadership (MA); literacy and cognition (MA); special education (MA), including severe and multiple disabilities. *Faculty:* 2 part-time/adjunct (both women). *Students:* 34 part-time (29 women); includes 6 minority (1 Black or African American, non-Hispanic/Latino; 5 Hispanic/Latino). Average age 23. 37 applicants, 70% accepted, 18 enrolled. In 2016, 22 master's awarded. *Entrance requirements:* For master's, GRE, PRAXIS or MAT, official transcripts, two letters of recommendation, resume, copy of teaching certification. Additional exam requirements/recommendations for international students: Required—TOEFL (minimum score 80 iBT). *Application deadline:* Applications are processed on a rolling basis. Application fee: $25. Electronic applications accepted. *Expenses:* Contact institution. *Financial support:* In 2016–17, 30 students received support. *Unit head:* Sr. Nancy Gilchriest, Professor/Department Chair, 631-687-1472, E-mail: ngilchriest@sjcny.edu.
Website: http://www.sjcny.edu

Saint Joseph's College of Maine, Master of Science in Education Program, Standish, ME 04084. Offers adult education and training (MS Ed); Catholic school leadership (MS Ed); health care educator (MS Ed); school educator (MS Ed). Program available by correspondence. *Program availability:* Part-time, online learning. Electronic applications accepted.

Saint Joseph's University, College of Arts and Sciences, Graduate Programs in Education, Philadelphia, PA 19131-1395. Offers curriculum supervisor (Certificate); educational leadership (MS, Ed D); elementary education (MS, Certificate); elementary/middle school education (Certificate); instructional technology (MS, Certificate); organizational development and leadership (MS); principal (Certificate); professional education (MS); reading specialist (MS, Certificate); reading supervisor (Certificate); secondary education (MS, Certificate); special education (MS); special education 7-12 (Certificate); special education PK-8 (Certificate); superintendent's letter of eligibility (Certificate); supervisor of special education (Certificate); teacher of the deaf and hard of hearing (Certificate). *Program availability:* Part-time, evening/weekend, blended/hybrid learning. *Faculty:* 26 full-time (21 women), 74 part-time/adjunct (45 women). *Students:* 107 full-time (88 women), 826 part-time (622 women); includes 170 minority (115 Black or African American, non-Hispanic/Latino; 2 American Indian or Alaska Native, non-Hispanic/Latino; 11 Asian, non-Hispanic/Latino; 31 Hispanic/Latino; 1 Native Hawaiian or other Pacific Islander, non-Hispanic/Latino; 10 Two or more races, non-Hispanic/Latino), 18 international. Average age 33. 338 applicants, 76% accepted, 173 enrolled. In 2016, 419 master's, 16 doctorates, 24 other advanced degrees awarded. *Degree requirements:* For master's, thesis or alternative; for doctorate, comprehensive exam, thesis/dissertation. *Entrance requirements:* For master's, 2 letters of recommendation, minimum GPA of 3.0, official transcripts, personal statement; for doctorate, GRE, master's degree from accredited institution, minimum graduate GPA of 3.5, computer competence, interview with program director. Additional exam requirements/recommendations for international students: Required—TOEFL (minimum score 550 paper-based; 80 iBT), IELTS (minimum score 6.5), PTE (minimum score 60). *Application deadline:* For fall admission, 7/15 for international students; for spring admission, 11/1 for international students. Applications are processed on a rolling basis. Application fee: $35. Electronic applications accepted. *Expenses:* $750 per credit, $100 education fee, $360 online organization development and leadership residency fee. *Financial support:* In 2016–17, 25 students received support. Unspecified assistantships available. Financial award application deadline: 5/1; financial award applicants required to submit FAFSA. *Faculty research:* Factors predicting early mathematics skills for low income children, early child care and development, preschool quality, parent communication and home-school collaboration issues, education of terminally ill children, preparing literacy teachers for urban schools. *Total annual research expenditures:* $18,118. *Unit head:* Dr. John Vacca, Associate Dean, Education, 610-660-3131, E-mail: gradcas@sju.edu. *Application contact:* Graduate Admissions, College of Arts and Sciences, 610-660-3131, E-mail: gradcas@sju.edu.
Website: http://sju.edu/int/academics/cas/grad/education/index.html

St. Lawrence University, Department of Education, Canton, NY 13617. Offers counseling and human development (M Ed, MS, CAS), including mental health counseling (MS), school counseling (M Ed, CAS); educational leadership (M Ed, CAS), including combined school building leadership/school district leadership (CAS), educational leadership (M Ed), school building leadership (M Ed), school district leadership (CAS); general studies in education (M Ed). *Accreditation:* TEAC. *Program availability:* Part-time, evening/weekend. *Degree requirements:* For master's, thesis optional. *Entrance requirements:* For master's, GRE General Test. *Faculty research:* Defense mechanisms, conflict negotiations and mediation, teacher education policy.

Saint Leo University, Graduate Studies in Education, Saint Leo, FL 33574-6665. Offers educational leadership (M Ed), including Catholic school administration; exceptional student education (M Ed); instructional design (MS, Certificate); instructional leadership (M Ed); reading (M Ed, Certificate); school leadership (Ed S). *Program availability:* Part-time, evening/weekend, online learning. *Faculty:* 11 full-time (10 women), 22 part-time/adjunct (15 women). *Students:* 424 part-time (335 women); includes 94 minority (54 Black or African American, non-Hispanic/Latino; 2 Asian, non-Hispanic/Latino; 32 Hispanic/Latino; 6 Two or more races, non-Hispanic/Latino), 1 international. Average age 37. 260 applicants, 76% accepted, 107 enrolled. In 2016, 166 master's, 6 other advanced degrees awarded. *Degree requirements:* For master's, appropriate State of Florida certification tests. *Entrance requirements:* For master's, GRE (minimum score of 1000), MAT (minimum score of 410), or minimum undergraduate GPA of 3.0 in final 2 years, official transcripts, current resumé, 2 professional recommendations, personal statement, bachelor's degree from regionally-accredited university, valid professional teaching certificate; for other advanced degree, valid professional teaching certificate (for Ed S). Additional exam requirements/recommendations for international students: Required—TOEFL (minimum score 550 paper-based; 80 iBT). *Application deadline:* For fall admission, 7/1 priority date for domestic students, 7/1 for international students; for winter admission, 7/1 for international students; for spring admission, 11/1 priority date for domestic students. Applications are processed on a rolling basis. Application fee: $80. Electronic applications accepted. *Expenses:* $465 per semester hour (for MS); $480 per semester hour (for M Ed); $670 per semester hour (for Ed S). *Financial support:* In 2016–17, 17 students received support. Career-related internships or fieldwork, scholarships/grants, and health care benefits available. Financial award application deadline: 3/1; financial award applicants required to submit FAFSA. *Faculty research:* Student achievement in literacy, leadership, instructional technology. *Unit head:* Dr. Fern Aefsky, Director of Graduate Studies in Education, 352-588-8309, Fax: 352-588-8861, E-mail: kara.winkler@saintleo.edu. *Application contact:* Jennifer Shelley, Senior Associate Director of Graduate Admissions, 800-707-8846, Fax: 352-588-7873, E-mail: grad.admissions@saintleo.edu.
Website: http://www.saintleo.edu/academics/graduate.aspx

Saint Louis University, Graduate Education, College of Education and Public Service, Department of Educational Studies, St. Louis, MO 63103. Offers curriculum and instruction (MA, Ed D, PhD); educational foundations (MA, Ed D, PhD); special education (MA); teaching (MAT). *Accreditation:* NCATE. *Program availability:* Part-time. *Degree requirements:* For master's, comprehensive exam; for doctorate, comprehensive exam, thesis/dissertation, preliminary oral and written exams. *Entrance requirements:* For master's, GRE General Test or MAT, letters of recommendation, resume; for doctorate, GRE General Test, letters of recommendation, resumé, goal statement, transcripts. Additional exam requirements/recommendations for international students: Required—TOEFL (minimum score 525 paper-based). Electronic applications accepted. *Faculty research:* Teacher preparation, multicultural issues, children with special needs, qualitative research in education, inclusion.

Saint Martin's University, Office of Graduate Studies, College of Education, Lacey, WA 98503. Offers M Ed, MIT. *Accreditation:* TEAC. *Program availability:* Part-time, evening/weekend. *Faculty:* 10 full-time (7 women), 12 part-time/adjunct (8 women). *Students:* 50 full-time (29 women), 14 part-time (11 women); includes 14 minority (2 Black or African American, non-Hispanic/Latino; 1 American Indian or Alaska Native, non-Hispanic/Latino; 9 Hispanic/Latino; 2 Two or more races, non-Hispanic/Latino). Average age 33. 31 applicants, 61% accepted, 13 enrolled. In 2016, 30 master's awarded. *Degree requirements:* For master's, comprehensive exam (for some programs), thesis or alternative, project or comprehensives. *Entrance requirements:* For master's, GRE General Test or MAT, three letters of recommendation; curriculum vitae. Additional exam requirements/recommendations for international students: Required—TOEFL (minimum score 550 paper-based; 79 iBT); Recommended—IELTS (minimum score 6.5). *Application deadline:* For fall admission, 4/1 priority date for domestic and international students; for spring admission, 11/1 priority date for domestic and international students. Applications are processed on a rolling basis. Application fee: $50. Electronic applications accepted. *Expenses: Tuition:* Full-time $13,800; part-time $1150 per credit hour. *Required fees:* $720; $60 per credit hour. Tuition and fees vary according to course level and program. *Financial support:* Career-related internships or fieldwork, Federal Work-Study, institutionally sponsored loans, and unspecified assistantships available. Support available to part-time students. Financial award application deadline: 3/1; financial award applicants required to submit FAFSA. *Faculty research:* Reader's theatre and reader/writer workshops, curriculum and assessment integration, gender and equity, classroom evaluations, organizational leadership. *Unit head:* Dr. Kathleen M. Boyle, College of Education and Counseling Psychology, 360-438-4333, Fax: 360-438-4486, E-mail: kboyle@stmartin.edu. *Application contact:* Casey Caronna, Administrative Assistant, 360-412-6128, E-mail: ccaronna@stmartin.edu.
Website: https://www.stmartin.edu/directory/office-graduate-studies

Saint Mary's College of California, Kalmanovitz School of Education, Moraga, CA 94575. Offers M Ed, MA, MA Ed, Ed D, Credential. *Program availability:* Part-time, evening/weekend. *Degree requirements:* For master's, thesis or alternative; for doctorate, thesis/dissertation. *Entrance requirements:* For master's, interview, minimum GPA of 3.0; for doctorate, GRE or MAT, interview, MA, minimum GPA of 3.0. *Expenses:* Contact institution. *Faculty research:* Teacher effectiveness, school-based management, multicultural teaching, language and literacy development.

St. Mary's College of Maryland, Department of Educational Studies, St. Mary's City, MD 20686-3001. Offers MAT. *Degree requirements:* For master's, internship, electronic portfolio, research projects, PRAXIS II. *Entrance requirements:* For master's, SAT, ACT, GRE or PRAXIS, 2 letters of recommendation, minimum GPA of 3.0. Additional exam requirements/recommendations for international students: Required—TOEFL. Electronic applications accepted. *Expenses:* Contact institution. *Faculty research:* Supporting English language learners across the curriculum, supporting women and minorities in math and science, instructional technology, multicultural young adult literature, educating teachers to be advocates for equity and social justice.

Saint Mary's University of Minnesota, Schools of Graduate and Professional Programs, Graduate School of Education, Education Program, Winona, MN 55987-1399. Offers culturally responsive teaching (Certificate); education (MA); gifted inclusive education (Certificate). Tuition and fees vary according to degree level and program. *Unit head:* Lynn Albee, Director, 612-728-5179, Fax: 612-728-5128, E-mail: lalbee@smumn.edu. *Application contact:* James Callinan, Director of Admissions for Graduate and Professional Programs, 612-728-5185, Fax: 612-728-5121, E-mail: jcallina@smumn.edu.
Website: http://www.smumn.edu/graduate-home/areas-of-study/graduate-school-of-education/ma-in-education

Saint Mary's University of Minnesota, Schools of Graduate and Professional Programs, Graduate School of Education, Education-Wisconsin Program, Winona, MN 55987-1399. Offers MA. Tuition and fees vary according to degree level and program. *Unit head:* Dr. Lynda Sullivan, Director, 877-442-4020, E-mail: lsulliva@smumn.edu. *Application contact:* James Callinan, Director of Admissions for Graduate and Professional Programs, 612-728-5185, Fax: 612-728-5121, E-mail: jcallina@smumn.edu.
Website: http://www.smumn.edu/graduate-home/areas-of-study/graduate-school-of-education/ma-in-education-wisconsin

Saint Mary's University of Minnesota, Schools of Graduate and Professional Programs, Graduate School of Education, Teaching and Learning Program, Winona, MN 55987-1399. Offers M Ed. Tuition and fees vary according to degree level and program. *Unit head:* Tracy Lysne, Program Director, 612-238-4520, E-mail: tlysne@smumn.edu. *Application contact:* James Callinan, Director of Admissions for Graduate and Professional Programs, 612-728-5185, Fax: 612-728-5121, E-mail: jcallina@smumn.edu.
Website: http://www.smumn.edu/graduate-home/areas-of-study/graduate-school-of-education/med-in-teaching-learning

Saint Michael's College, Graduate Programs, Program in Education, Colchester, VT 05439. Offers arts in education (CAGS); literacy (M Ed); school leadership (CAGS); special education (M Ed). *Program availability:* Part-time, evening/weekend. *Students:* 5 full-time (4 women), 239 part-time (199 women); includes 9 minority (2 Black or African American, non-Hispanic/Latino; 1 American Indian or Alaska Native, non-Hispanic/Latino; 1 Asian, non-Hispanic/Latino; 4 Hispanic/Latino; 1 Two or more races, non-Hispanic/Latino), 1 international. Average age 36. In 2016, 31 master's awarded. *Degree requirements:* For master's, thesis. *Entrance requirements:* For master's, minimum GPA of 3.0, official transcripts, essay, interview. *Application deadline:* Applications are processed on a rolling basis. Application fee: $50. Electronic applications accepted. *Expenses: Tuition:* Full-time $10,620; part-time $590 per credit. Part-time tuition and fees vary according to course load and program. *Financial support:* Fellowships with partial tuition reimbursements and scholarships/grants available. Support available to part-time students. Financial award applicants required to submit

Education—General

FAFSA. *Faculty research:* Integrative curriculum, moral and spiritual dimensions of education, learning styles, multiple intelligences, integrating technology into the curriculum. *Unit head:* Jonathan Silverman, Department Chair, 802-654-2306, Fax: 802-654-2664, E-mail: jsilverman@smcvt.edu. *Application contact:* Lindsay A. Damici, Marketing Communications Manager, 802-654-2556, Fax: 802-654-2732.
Website: http://www.smcvt.edu/graduate-programs/academic-programs/education.aspx

Saint Peter's University, Graduate Programs in Education, Jersey City, NJ 07306-5997. Offers director of school counseling services (Certificate); educational leadership (MA Ed, Ed D); higher education (Ed D); middle school mathematics (Certificate); professional/associate counselor (Certificate); reading (MA Ed); school business administrator (Certificate); school counseling (MA, Certificate); special education (MA Ed, Certificate), including applied behavioral analysis (MA Ed), literacy (MA Ed), teacher of students with disabilities (Certificate); teaching (MA Ed, Certificate), including 6-8 middle school education, K-12 secondary education, K-5 elementary education. *Accreditation:* TEAC. *Program availability:* Part-time, evening/weekend. *Degree requirements:* For master's, comprehensive exam; for doctorate, comprehensive exam, thesis/dissertation. *Entrance requirements:* For master's and doctorate, GRE or MAT. Additional exam requirements/recommendations for international students: Required—TOEFL. Electronic applications accepted.

St. Thomas Aquinas College, Division of Teacher Education, Sparkill, NY 10976. Offers adolescence education (MST); childhood and special education (MST); childhood education (MST); educational leadership (MS Ed); reading (MS Ed, PMC); special education (MS Ed, PMC); teaching (MS Ed), including elementary education, middle school education, secondary education. *Accreditation:* NCATE. *Program availability:* Part-time, evening/weekend. *Degree requirements:* For master's, comprehensive exam, comprehensive professional portfolio; for PMC, action research project. *Entrance requirements:* For master's, New York State Qualifying Exam, GRE General Test or minimum GPA of 3.0, teaching certificate; for PMC, GRE General Test or minimum GPA of 3.0. Electronic applications accepted. *Faculty research:* Computer applications in education, adolescent special education students, literacy development, inclusive practices for special education students.

St. Thomas University, School of Leadership Studies, Institute for Education, Miami Gardens, FL 33054-6459. Offers earth/space science (Certificate); educational administration (MS, Certificate); educational leadership (Ed D); elementary education (MS); ESOL (Certificate); gifted education (Certificate); instructional technology (MS, Certificate); professional/studies (Certificate); reading (MS, Certificate); special education (MS). *Program availability:* Part-time, evening/weekend. *Degree requirements:* For master's, comprehensive exam; for doctorate, comprehensive exam, thesis/dissertation. *Entrance requirements:* For master's, interview, minimum GPA of 3.0 or GRE; for doctorate, GRE or MAT. Additional exam requirements/recommendations for international students: Required—TOEFL (minimum score 550 paper-based; 79 iBT). Electronic applications accepted.

Saint Vincent College, Program in Education, Latrobe, PA 15650-2690. Offers curriculum and instruction (MS); instructional design and technology (MS); school administration and supervision (MS); special education (MS). *Program availability:* Part-time, evening/weekend. *Degree requirements:* For master's, comprehensive exam. *Entrance requirements:* For master's, GRE (if undergraduate GPA less than 3.0). Additional exam requirements/recommendations for international students: Required—TOEFL (minimum score 550 paper-based). *Faculty research:* Assessment and instructional technology.

Saint Xavier University, Graduate Studies, School of Education, Chicago, IL 60655-3105. Offers counseling (MA); curriculum and instruction (MA); early childhood education (MA); educational administration (MA); elementary education (MA); individualized studies (MA), including educational technology, English as a second language (ESL), ISTEM (integrative science, technology, engineering, and math), science education (MA); music education (MA); reading (MA); secondary education (MA); Spanish education (MA); special education (MA); teaching and leadership (MA). *Accreditation:* NCATE. *Program availability:* Part-time, evening/weekend. *Degree requirements:* For master's, thesis or project. *Entrance requirements:* For master's, minimum GPA of 3.0. *Expenses:* Contact institution.

Salem College, Department of Education, Winston-Salem, NC 27101. Offers art education (MAT); elementary education (M Ed, MAT); language and literacy (M Ed); middle school education (MAT); school counseling (M Ed); second language studies (MAT); secondary education (MAT); special education (M Ed, MAT). *Accreditation:* NCATE. *Program availability:* Part-time, evening/weekend, online learning. *Degree requirements:* For master's, practicum (MAT), project (M Ed), oral and written comprehensive exams. *Entrance requirements:* For master's, minimum GPA of 2.5. *Faculty research:* Content area reading strategies, literacy development, brain compatible instruction.

Salem International University, School of Education, Salem, WV 26426-0500. Offers curriculum and instruction (M Ed); educational leadership (M Ed). *Program availability:* Part-time, evening/weekend, online learning. *Degree requirements:* For master's, comprehensive exam (for some programs), thesis (for some programs). *Entrance requirements:* For master's, GRE, MAT, NTE, 3 letters of recommendation. Additional exam requirements/recommendations for international students: Required—TOEFL (minimum score 550 paper-based). Electronic applications accepted. *Expenses:* Contact institution. *Faculty research:* Improved classroom effectiveness.

Samford University, Orlean Beeson School of Education, Birmingham, AL 35229. Offers education (Ed D, Certificate); educational leadership: policy, organizations, leadership (MSE); elementary education (MS Ed); gifted certification (MSE); instructional design and technology (MSE); instructional leadership (MSE, Ed S); K-12 collaborative special education (MSE); teacher leader (Ed S). *Accreditation:* NCATE. *Program availability:* Part-time, evening/weekend, 100% online, blended/hybrid learning. *Faculty:* 15 full-time (9 women), 17 part-time/adjunct (12 women). *Students:* 219 full-time (161 women), 86 part-time (55 women); includes 97 minority (86 Black or African American, non-Hispanic/Latino; 5 American Indian or Alaska Native, non-Hispanic/Latino; 1 Asian, non-Hispanic/Latino; 1 Hispanic/Latino; 4 Two or more races, non-Hispanic/Latino), 2 international. Average age 38. 244 applicants, 52% accepted, 112 enrolled. In 2016, 84 master's, 22 doctorates, 12 Certificates awarded. *Degree requirements:* For master's, comprehensive exam (for some programs); for doctorate, comprehensive exam, thesis/dissertation; for other advanced degree, comprehensive exam. *Entrance requirements:* For master's, GRE or MAT; Alabama Educator Certification Testing Program (AECTP), transcripts, essays, recommendations; for doctorate, professional resume, recommendations, transcripts, interview, essays; for other advanced degree, recommendations, transcripts. Additional exam requirements/recommendations for international students: Required—TOEFL (minimum score 90 iBT), IELTS (minimum score 6.5). *Application deadline:* For fall admission, 7/15 for domestic students, 7/1 for international students; for spring admission, 11/15 for domestic and international students; for summer admission, 4/15 for domestic and international students. Application fee: $35. Electronic applications accepted. *Expenses: Tuition:* Full-time $18,530; part-time $789 per credit hour. *Required fees:* $610. Tuition and fees vary according to course load, degree level, program and student level. *Financial support:* In 2016–17, 246 students received support. Scholarships/grants available. Financial award application deadline: 3/1; financial award applicants required to submit FAFSA. *Faculty research:* Standards-based grading in K-12 schools, effective school principal leadership, effective educational leadership preparation programs, teacher/administrator shortages and job retention, instructional strategies to maximize student learning. *Total annual research expenditures:* $254,360. *Unit head:* Dr. Jean Box, Dean, 205-726-2565, Fax: 205-726-4233, E-mail: jabox@samford.edu. *Application contact:* Brooke Karr, Graduate Admissions Coordinator, 205-729-2783, Fax: 205-726-4233, E-mail: kbgilrea@samford.edu.
Website: http://www.samford.edu/education/

Sam Houston State University, College of Education, Huntsville, TX 77341. Offers M Ed, MA, MLS, Ed D, PhD. *Accreditation:* NCATE. *Program availability:* Part-time, evening/weekend, online learning. *Degree requirements:* For master's, comprehensive exam (for some programs), thesis optional, portfolio, internship; for doctorate, comprehensive exam (for some programs), thesis/dissertation. *Entrance requirements:* For master's, GRE General Test, references, essay, face-to-face interview, personal statement, resume; for doctorate, GRE General Test, on-site interview, on-site professional presentation, on-site writing prompt, personal statement, five references, master's degree, resume. Additional exam requirements/recommendations for international students: Required—TOEFL (minimum score 550 paper-based; 79 iBT), IELTS (minimum score 6.5). Electronic applications accepted.

San Diego Christian College, Graduate Programs, Santee, CA 92071. Offers education (MAT); organization (MSL).

San Diego State University, Graduate and Research Affairs, College of Education, San Diego, CA 92182. Offers MA, MS, Ed D, PhD. *Accreditation:* NCATE. *Program availability:* Part-time, evening/weekend. *Degree requirements:* For master's, thesis optional; for doctorate, thesis/dissertation. *Entrance requirements:* For master's, GRE General Test, letters of reference; for doctorate, GRE General Test, 3 letters of reference, resumé. Additional exam requirements/recommendations for international students: Required—TOEFL. Electronic applications accepted. *Faculty research:* Special education, rehabilitation counseling, educational psychology.

San Francisco State University, Division of Graduate Studies, College of Education, San Francisco, CA 94132-1722. Offers MA, MS, Ed D, PhD, AC, Certificate, Credential. *Accreditation:* NCATE. *Expenses:* Tuition, state resident: full-time $6738. Tuition, nonresident: full-time $15,666. *Required fees:* $1012. Tuition and fees vary according to degree level and program. *Unit head:* Dr. Nancy Robinson, Interim Dean, 415-338-2687, Fax: 415-338-7019, E-mail: nancyr@sfsu.edu. *Application contact:* Victoria Narkewicz, Executive Assistant, 415-338-2687, Fax: 415-338-7019, E-mail: toria@sfsu.edu.
Website: http://gcoe.sfsu.edu/

San Jose State University, Graduate Studies and Research, Connie L. Lurie College of Education, San Jose, CA 95192-0001. Offers child and adolescent development (MA); common core mathematics (K-8) (Certificate, Credential); education (MA, Credential), including counseling and student personnel (MA), speech pathology (MA); educational leadership (MA, Ed D, Credential), including administration and supervision (MA), higher education (MA), preliminary administrative services (Credential), professional administrative services (Credential); elementary education (MA), including curriculum and instruction; K-12 school counseling (Credential); K-12 school counseling internship (Credential); school child welfare attendance (Credential); single subject (Credential). *Accreditation:* NCATE. *Program availability:* Evening/weekend. Electronic applications accepted.

Santa Clara University, School of Education and Counseling Psychology, Santa Clara, CA 95053. Offers Catholic school teaching (MA); counseling (MA); counseling psychology (MA); educational leadership (MA); interdisciplinary education (MA); teaching multiple subjects (MA); teaching single subjects (MA). *Program availability:* Part-time, evening/weekend. *Faculty:* 32 full-time (22 women), 40 part-time/adjunct (25 women). *Students:* 265 full-time (213 women), 333 part-time (270 women); includes 282 minority (16 Black or African American, non-Hispanic/Latino; 1 American Indian or Alaska Native, non-Hispanic/Latino; 78 Asian, non-Hispanic/Latino; 156 Hispanic/Latino; 31 Two or more races, non-Hispanic/Latino), 46 international. Average age 30. 266 applicants, 74% accepted, 126 enrolled. In 2016, 253 master's awarded. *Entrance requirements:* For master's, transcript, letters of recommendation, statement of purpose, resume. Additional exam requirements/recommendations for international students: Required—TOEFL (minimum score 90 iBT) or IELTS (6.5). *Application deadline:* Applications are processed on a rolling basis. Application fee: $50. Electronic applications accepted. *Expenses:* $581 per unit. *Financial support:* Fellowships, research assistantships, teaching assistantships, career-related internships or fieldwork, Federal Work-Study, scholarships/grants, traineeships, health care benefits, and tuition waivers available. Support available to part-time students. Financial award applicants required to submit FAFSA. *Unit head:* Dr. Sabrina Zirkel, Dean, 408-551-3074, Fax: 408-554-4367, E-mail: szirkel@scu.edu. *Application contact:* Victoria Rodriguez, Graduate Admissions Advisor, 408-554-4723, E-mail: v1rodriguez@scu.edu.
Website: http://www.scu.edu/ecp/

Sarah Lawrence College, Graduate Studies, Program in the Art of Teaching, Bronxville, NY 10708-5999. Offers MS Ed. *Program availability:* Part-time. *Degree requirements:* For master's, thesis, fieldwork, oral presentation. *Entrance requirements:* For master's, minimum B average in undergraduate coursework. Additional exam requirements/recommendations for international students: Required—TOEFL (minimum score 600 paper-based). Electronic applications accepted. *Expenses:* Contact institution.

Schreiner University, Department of Education, Kerrville, TX 78028-5697. Offers education (M Ed); principal (Certificate). *Program availability:* Part-time, evening/weekend, online learning. *Entrance requirements:* For master's, GRE (waived if undergraduate cumulative GPA is 3.0 or above), 3 references; transcripts; interview. Additional exam requirements/recommendations for international students: Required—TOEFL. Electronic applications accepted.

Seattle Pacific University, Doctoral Program in Education, Seattle, WA 98119-1997. Offers Ed D, PhD. *Accreditation:* NCATE. *Degree requirements:* For doctorate, comprehensive exam, thesis/dissertation. *Entrance requirements:* For doctorate, GRE, MAT. *Expenses:* Contact institution. *Faculty research:* International education, curriculum and instruction, values and morals, school reform.

Seattle University, College of Education, Seattle, WA 98122-1090. Offers M Ed, MA, MIT, Ed D, Certificate, Ed S, Post-Master's Certificate. *Accreditation:* NCATE. *Program availability:* Part-time, evening/weekend. *Faculty:* 27 full-time (13 women), 17 part-time/adjunct (14 women). *Students:* 196 full-time (144 women), 300 part-time (221 women); includes 165 minority (24 Black or African American, non-Hispanic/Latino; 7 American Indian or Alaska Native, non-Hispanic/Latino; 46 Asian, non-Hispanic/Latino; 61 Hispanic/Latino; 1 Native Hawaiian or other Pacific Islander, non-Hispanic/Latino; 26 Two or more races, non-Hispanic/Latino), 17 international. Average age 32. 487 applicants, 50% accepted, 141 enrolled. In 2016, 184 master's, 19 doctorates, 48 other advanced degrees awarded. *Degree requirements:* For master's and other advanced degree, comprehensive exam; for doctorate, comprehensive exam, thesis/dissertation. *Entrance requirements:* For doctorate, GRE General Test, MAT, interview, MA,

minimum GPA of 3.5, 3 years of related experience. Additional exam requirements/ recommendations for international students: Required—TOEFL. *Application deadline:* Applications are processed on a rolling basis. Application fee: $55. Electronic applications accepted. *Expenses:* Contact institution. *Financial support:* In 2016–17, 89 students received support. Career-related internships or fieldwork, Federal Work-Study, scholarships/grants, and unspecified assistantships available. Support available to part-time students. Financial award applicants required to submit FAFSA. *Faculty research:* Service-learning, learning and technology, assessment models of professional education, alternative delivery systems. *Unit head:* Dr. Deanna Sands, Dean, 206-296-5758, E-mail: sandsd@seattleu.edu. *Application contact:* Janet Shandley, Director of Graduate Admissions, 206-296-5900, Fax: 206-298-5656, E-mail: grad_admissions@seattleu.edu.
Website: http://www.seattleu.edu/soe/

Seton Hall University, College of Education and Human Services, South Orange, NJ 07079-2697. Offers MA, MS, Ed D, Exec Ed D, PhD, Ed S. *Accreditation:* NCATE. *Program availability:* Part-time, evening/weekend, 100% online, blended/hybrid learning. *Faculty:* 45 full-time (24 women), 71 part-time/adjunct (38 women). *Students:* 72 full-time (53 women), 989 part-time (589 women); includes 319 minority (181 Black or African American, non-Hispanic/Latino; 3 American Indian or Alaska Native, non-Hispanic/Latino; 22 Asian, non-Hispanic/Latino; 106 Hispanic/Latino; 2 Native Hawaiian or other Pacific Islander, non-Hispanic/Latino; 5 Two or more races, non-Hispanic/Latino), 23 international. Average age 33. 539 applicants, 61% accepted, 221 enrolled. In 2016, 327 master's, 57 doctorates, 136 other advanced degrees awarded. *Degree requirements:* For master's, comprehensive exam (for some programs), internship; for doctorate, comprehensive exam, thesis/dissertation, internship. *Entrance requirements:* For master's, GRE or MAT, PRAXIS, letters of recommendation, interview, personal statement, curriculum vitae, transcript; for doctorate, GRE, interview, letters of recommendation, personal statement, curriculum vitae, transcript; for Ed S, GRE or MAT, PRAXIS, interview, letters of recommendation, personal statement, curriculum vitae, transcript. Additional exam requirements/recommendations for international students: Required—TOEFL. *Application deadline:* Applications are processed on a rolling basis. Application fee: $75. Electronic applications accepted. *Expenses:* Contact institution. *Financial support:* In 2016–17, 30 students received support. Fellowships, research assistantships, career-related internships or fieldwork, institutionally sponsored loans, and unspecified assistantships available. Financial award application deadline: 2/1; financial award applicants required to submit FAFSA. *Faculty research:* Integration of technology, education leadership, educational media, special education, school district management. *Total annual research expenditures:* $30,000. *Unit head:* Dr. Maureen D. Gillette, Dean, 973-761-9025, E-mail: maureen.gillette@shu.edu. *Application contact:* Dr. Joseph J. Martinelli, Associate Dean for Academic Affairs, 973-275-2733, Fax: 973-275-2187, E-mail: joseph.martinelli@shu.edu.
Website: http://education.shu.edu/

Shawnee State University, Program in Curriculum and Instruction, Portsmouth, OH 45662. Offers M Ed. *Accreditation:* NCATE.

Shenandoah University, School of Education and Human Development, Winchester, VA 22601-5195. Offers administrative leadership (D Ed); educational administration (MSE); emphasis in teaching (MSE); health and physical education (Certificate); individual focus (MSE); literacy education (MS); middle school teacher education (Certificate); organizational leadership (MS, D Prof); secondary school teacher education (Certificate); special education (MSE). *Accreditation:* TEAC. *Program availability:* Part-time, evening/weekend. *Faculty:* 9 full-time (7 women), 43 part-time/adjunct (33 women). *Students:* 31 full-time (25 women), 236 part-time (160 women); includes 39 minority (19 Black or African American, non-Hispanic/Latino; 1 American Indian or Alaska Native, non-Hispanic/Latino; 10 Asian, non-Hispanic/Latino; 7 Hispanic/Latino; 1 Native Hawaiian or other Pacific Islander, non-Hispanic/Latino; 1 Two or more races, non-Hispanic/Latino), 4 international. Average age 37. 90 applicants, 97% accepted, 56 enrolled. In 2016, 113 master's, 13 doctorates, 38 other advanced degrees awarded. *Degree requirements:* For master's, comprehensive exam (for some programs), thesis (for some programs); for doctorate, comprehensive exam, thesis/dissertation. *Entrance requirements:* For degree, PRAXIS Academic Core, SAT/ACT, PRAXIS Academic Core Math, or VCLA, three letters of recommendation, writing sample, undergraduate degree. Additional exam requirements/recommendations for international students: Required—TOEFL (minimum score 550 paper-based; 79 iBT), IELTS (minimum score 6.5). *Application deadline:* For fall admission, 5/1 priority date for domestic students, 5/1 for international students; for spring admission, 10/15 priority date for domestic students, 10/15 for international students; for summer admission, 3/15 priority date for domestic students, 3/15 for international students. Application fee: $30. Electronic applications accepted. *Expenses:* Contact institution. *Financial support:* In 2016–17, 18 students received support. Scholarships/grants and unspecified assistantships available. Financial award applicants required to submit FAFSA. *Faculty research:* Exploring helplessness and anxiety in learning statistics, facilitating effective classroom group work, expert-novice dynamics in teaching, K-12 policy implementation and change, adult education, family-school-community relations, mentoring of first-year school principals. *Total annual research expenditures:* $2,000. *Unit head:* Dennis William Kellison, PhD, Director, 540-535-7324, Fax: 540-665-4726, E-mail: dkelliso@su.edu. *Application contact:* Andrew Woodall, Executive Director of Recruitment and Admissions, 540-665-4581, Fax: 540-665-4627, E-mail: admit@su.edu.
Website: http://www.su.edu/education/

Shippensburg University of Pennsylvania, School of Graduate Studies, College of Education and Human Services, Shippensburg, PA 17257-2299. Offers M Ed, MAT, MS, MSW, Ed D, Certificate. *Accreditation:* NCATE. *Program availability:* Part-time, evening/weekend, blended/hybrid learning. *Faculty:* 45 full-time (21 women), 24 part-time/adjunct (18 women). *Students:* 169 full-time (139 women), 297 part-time (209 women); includes 64 minority (38 Black or African American, non-Hispanic/Latino; 4 Asian, non-Hispanic/Latino; 16 Hispanic/Latino; 6 Two or more races, non-Hispanic/Latino), 20 international. Average age 30. 422 applicants, 61% accepted, 202 enrolled. In 2016, 144 master's awarded. *Entrance requirements:* Additional exam requirements/recommendations for international students: Required—TOEFL (minimum score 550 paper-based, 68 iBT) or IELTS (minimum score 6). *Application deadline:* For fall admission, 4/30 for international students; for spring admission, 9/30 for international students. Applications are processed on a rolling basis. Application fee: $45. Electronic applications accepted. *Expenses:* Tuition, state resident: part-time $483 per credit. Tuition, nonresident: part-time $725 per credit. *Required fees:* $141 per credit. *Financial support:* In 2016–17, 81 students received support. Career-related internships or fieldwork, scholarships/grants, unspecified assistantships, and resident hall director and student payroll positions available. Support available to part-time students. Financial award application deadline: 3/1; financial award applicants required to submit FAFSA. *Unit head:* Dr. James R. Johnson, Dean of the College of Education and Human Services, 717-477-1373, Fax: 717-477-4012, E-mail: jrjohnson@ship.edu. *Application contact:* Megan N. Luft, Assistant Dean of Graduate Admissions, 717-477-1231, Fax: 717-477-4016, E-mail: mnluft@ship.edu.
Website: http://www.ship.edu/COEHS/

Siena Heights University, Graduate College, Adrian, MI 49221-1796. Offers clinical mental health counseling (MA); educational leadership (Specialist); leadership (MA), including health care leadership, organizational leadership; teacher education (MA), including early childhood education, early childhood education: Montessori, education leadership: principal, elementary education: reading K-12, leadership: higher education, secondary education: reading K-12, special education: cognitive impairment, special education: learning disabilities. *Program availability:* Part-time, evening/weekend. *Degree requirements:* For master's, thesis, presentation. *Entrance requirements:* For master's, minimum GPA of 3.0, current resume, essay, all post-secondary transcripts, 3 letters of reference, conviction disclosure form; copy of teaching certificate (for some education programs); for Specialist, master's degree, minimum GPA of 3.0, current resume, essay, all post-secondary transcripts, 3 letters of reference, conviction disclosure form; copy of teaching certificate (for some education programs). Electronic applications accepted.

Sierra Nevada College, Teacher Education Program, Incline Village, NV 89451. Offers advanced teaching and leadership (M Ed); elementary education (MAT); secondary education (MAT). *Program availability:* Part-time, evening/weekend, online learning. *Degree requirements:* For master's, comprehensive exam, thesis, PRAXIS I and II. *Entrance requirements:* For master's, 2 letters of recommendation, minimum GPA of 3.0. Electronic applications accepted.

Silver Lake College of the Holy Family, Graduate School, Graduate Education Program, Manitowoc, WI 54220-9319. Offers administrative leadership (MA Ed); teacher leadership (MA Ed). *Program availability:* Part-time, evening/weekend, blended/hybrid learning. *Faculty:* 2 full-time (both women), 4 part-time/adjunct (2 women). *Students:* 16 full-time (8 women), 10 part-time (8 women); includes 2 minority (both Black or African American, non-Hispanic/Latino). Average age 38. In 2016, 18 master's awarded. *Degree requirements:* For master's, comprehensive exam, thesis or alternative, capstone culminating project, comprehensive portfolio, or public presentation of project. *Entrance requirements:* For master's, ACT (preferred) or SAT, minimum undergraduate GPA of 3.0. Additional exam requirements/recommendations for international students: Required—TOEFL (minimum score 550 paper-based; 89 iBT). *Application deadline:* For fall admission, 8/1 for domestic and international students; for spring admission, 12/1 for domestic and international students. Applications are processed on a rolling basis. Application fee: $50. Electronic applications accepted. *Expenses:* $540 per credit; $220 comprehensive fee. *Financial support:* Federal Work-Study, scholarships/grants, and unspecified assistantships available. Support available to part-time students. Financial award application deadline: 6/1; financial award applicants required to submit FAFSA. *Faculty research:* Student development; school administration. *Unit head:* Nancy Sim, Director of Graduate Education Programs, 920-686-6117, Fax: 920-686-6322, E-mail: nancy.sim@sl.edu. *Application contact:* Jamie A. Grant, Executive Director of Enrollment Management, 920-686-6175, Fax: 920-686-6322, E-mail: jamie.grant@sl.edu.
Website: http://www.sl.edu/future-students/graduate-programs/degrees-offered/master-of-arts-in-education

Simmons College, School of Social Work, Boston, MA 02115. Offers behavior analysis (MS, PhD, Ed S); education (MS Ed); social work (MSW, PhD); special education (MS Ed), including moderate and severe disabilities; teaching (MAT), including elementary education; MSW/MBA. *Accreditation:* CSWE (one or more programs are accredited). *Program availability:* Part-time, 100% online. *Faculty:* 37 full-time (28 women), 62 part-time/adjunct (44 women). *Students:* 797 full-time (705 women), 951 part-time (829 women); includes 420 minority (200 Black or African American, non-Hispanic/Latino; 5 American Indian or Alaska Native, non-Hispanic/Latino; 46 Asian, non-Hispanic/Latino; 122 Hispanic/Latino; 4 Native Hawaiian or other Pacific Islander, non-Hispanic/Latino; 43 Two or more races, non-Hispanic/Latino), 13 international. Average age 31. 1,356 applicants, 78% accepted, 592 enrolled. In 2016, 342 master's, 2 doctorates, 1 other advanced degree awarded. Terminal master's awarded for partial completion of doctoral program. *Degree requirements:* For master's, thesis (for some programs); for doctorate, comprehensive exam (for some programs), thesis/dissertation (for some programs). *Entrance requirements:* For master's, GRE, MAT, Massachusetts Tests for Education Licensure (for different programs); for doctorate, GRE, BCBA Analyst Exam. Additional exam requirements/recommendations for international students: Required—TOEFL (minimum score 600 paper-based; 100 iBT). *Application deadline:* For fall admission, 8/1 for domestic students; for spring admission, 12/15 for domestic students; for summer admission, 5/1 for domestic students. Applications are processed on a rolling basis. Application fee: $35. Electronic applications accepted. *Expenses:* $1,010 per credit; $52 activity fee per semester. *Financial support:* In 2016–17, 12 fellowships with partial tuition reimbursements were awarded; scholarships/grants and unspecified assistantships also available. Support available to part-time students. *Unit head:* Dr. Cheryl Parks, Dean, 617-521-3293, E-mail: cheryl.parks@simmons.edu. *Application contact:* Carlos D. Frontado, Director of Admissions, 617-521-3920, Fax: 617-521-3980, E-mail: ssw@simmons.edu.
Website: http://www.simmons.edu/ssw/

Simon Fraser University, Office of Graduate Studies and Postdoctoral Fellows, Faculty of Education, Burnaby, BC V5A 1S6, Canada. Offers M Ed, M Sc, MA, Ed D, PhD, Graduate Diploma. *Faculty:* 70 full-time (44 women). *Students:* 712 full-time (528 women), 361 part-time (303 women). 880 applicants, 41% accepted, 225 enrolled. In 2016, 245 master's, 29 doctorates, 42 other advanced degrees awarded. *Degree requirements:* For doctorate, thesis/dissertation. *Entrance requirements:* Additional exam requirements/recommendations for international students: Recommended—TOEFL (minimum score 580 paper-based; 93 iBT), IELTS (minimum score 7), TWE (minimum score 5). Application fee: $90 ($125 for international students). Electronic applications accepted. *Financial support:* In 2016–17, 70 students received support, including 30 fellowships (averaging $6,500 per year), teaching assistantships (averaging $5,608 per year); research assistantships, career-related internships or fieldwork, and scholarships/grants also available. Support available to part-time students. *Unit head:* Dr. Shawn Bullock, Graduate Chair, 778-782-4102. *Application contact:* Kim Peterson, Administrative Assistant, 778-782-9488, Fax: 778-782-4320, E-mail: educadgs@sfu.ca.
Website: http://www.sfu.ca/education.html

Simpson College, Department of Education, Indianola, IA 50125-1297. Offers secondary education (MAT). *Degree requirements:* For master's, PRAXIS II, electronic portfolio. *Entrance requirements:* For master's, bachelor's degree; minimum cumulative GPA of 2.75, 3.0 in major; 3 letters of recommendation.

Simpson University, School of Education, Redding, CA 96003-8606. Offers education (MA), including curriculum, education leadership; education and preliminary administrative services credential (MA); education and preliminary teaching credential (MA); teaching (MA). *Program availability:* Part-time, evening/weekend. *Faculty:* 4 full-time (1 woman), 9 part-time/adjunct (3 women). *Students:* 8 full-time (7 women), 10 part-time (7 women); includes 1 minority (Two or more races, non-Hispanic/Latino), 1 international. Average age 37. In 2016, 16 master's awarded. *Degree requirements:* For master's, thesis optional. *Entrance requirements:* For master's, statement of purpose, 2 professional references, professional essay, interview. Additional exam requirements/recommendations for international students: Required—TOEFL (minimum score 550 paper-based). *Application deadline:* Applications are processed on a rolling basis.

Application fee: $35. Electronic applications accepted. *Expenses:* $420 per credit. *Financial support:* Scholarships/grants available. Financial award application deadline: 7/15; financial award applicants required to submit FAFSA. *Unit head:* Dr. Craig Cook, Dean of Education, 530-226-4188, Fax: 530-226-4872, E-mail: ccook@simpsonu.edu. *Application contact:* Stacy Burgess, Director of Admissions for Adult and Graduate Studies, 530-226-4961, E-mail: sburgess@simpsonu.edu.

Sinte Gleska University, Graduate Education Program, Mission, SD 57555. Offers elementary education (M Ed). *Program availability:* Part-time, evening/weekend. *Degree requirements:* For master's, thesis. *Entrance requirements:* For master's, 2 years of experience in elementary education, minimum GPA of 2.5, South Dakota elementary education certification. *Faculty research:* American Indian graduate education, teaching of Native American students.

Slippery Rock University of Pennsylvania, Graduate Studies (Recruitment), College of Education, Slippery Rock, PA 16057-1383. Offers M Ed, MA, MS, Ed D. *Accreditation:* NCATE. *Program availability:* Part-time, evening/weekend, 100% online. *Faculty:* 39 full-time (24 women), 2 part-time/adjunct (1 woman). *Students:* 198 full-time (137 women), 466 part-time (396 women); includes 26 minority (13 Black or African American, non-Hispanic/Latino; 1 Asian, non-Hispanic/Latino; 7 Hispanic/Latino; 5 Two or more races, non-Hispanic/Latino), 1 international. Average age 30. 552 applicants, 73% accepted, 248 enrolled. In 2016, 283 master's awarded. *Degree requirements:* For master's, comprehensive exam (for some programs), thesis (for some programs), internship (depending on program). *Entrance requirements:* For master's, GRE General Test or MAT (depending on program), official transcripts, minimum GPA of 2.75 (depending on program). Additional exam requirements/recommendations for international students: Required—TOEFL (minimum score 550 paper-based; 80 iBT). *Application deadline:* For fall admission, 3/1 priority date for domestic students, 5/1 priority date for international students; for spring admission, 10/1 priority date for domestic students, 9/1 priority date for international students. Applications are processed on a rolling basis. Application fee: $25 ($30 for international students). Electronic applications accepted. *Expenses:* $646.50 per credit in-state, $936.80 per credit out-of-state; $581.45 per online credit in-state, $648.65 per online credit out-of-state. *Financial support:* In 2016–17, 88 students received support. Career-related internships or fieldwork, Federal Work-Study, institutionally sponsored loans, scholarships/grants, tuition waivers (partial), and unspecified assistantships available. Support available to part-time students. Financial award application deadline: 5/1; financial award applicants required to submit FAFSA. *Unit head:* Dr. A. Keith Dils, Dean, 724-738-2007, Fax: 724-738-2880, E-mail: keith.dils@sru.edu. *Application contact:* Brandi Weber-Mortimer, Director of Graduate Admissions, 724-738-2051, Fax: 724-738-2146, E-mail: graduate.admissions@sru.edu.
Website: http://www.sru.edu/academics/colleges-and-departments/coe

Smith College, Graduate and Special Programs, Department of Education and Child Study, Northampton, MA 01063. Offers elementary education (MAT); middle school education (MAT); secondary education (MAT), including secondary education. *Program availability:* Part-time. *Students:* 14 full-time (10 women), 3 part-time (2 women); includes 1 minority (Two or more races, non-Hispanic/Latino). Average age 27. 36 applicants, 78% accepted, 14 enrolled. In 2016, 21 master's awarded. *Entrance requirements:* Additional exam requirements/recommendations for international students: Required—TOEFL (minimum score 595 paper-based; 97 iBT), IELTS. *Application deadline:* For fall admission, 4/1 for domestic students, 1/15 for international students; for spring admission, 12/1 for domestic students. Application fee: $60. *Expenses: Tuition:* Full-time $34,560; part-time $1440 per credit. Tuition and fees vary according to course load and program. *Financial support:* In 2016–17, 16 students received support, including 6 fellowships with full tuition reimbursements available; scholarships/grants also available. Support available to part-time students. Financial award application deadline: 4/1; financial award applicants required to submit CSS PROFILE or FAFSA. *Unit head:* Alan Rudnitsky, Chair, 413-585-3261, Fax: 413-585-3268, E-mail: arudnits@smith.edu. *Application contact:* Ruth Morgan, Program Assistant, 413-585-3050, Fax: 413-585-3054, E-mail: gradstdy@smith.edu.
Website: http://www.smith.edu/education

Sonoma State University, School of Education, Rohnert Park, CA 94928-3609. Offers administrative services (Credential); curriculum, teaching, and learning (MA); early childhood education (MA); education specialist (Credential); educational leadership (MA); multiple subject (Credential); reading and literacy (MA, Credential); single subject (Credential); special education (MA). *Accreditation:* NCATE. *Program availability:* Part-time, evening/weekend. *Degree requirements:* For master's, thesis or alternative. *Entrance requirements:* For master's, minimum GPA of 2.5. Additional exam requirements/recommendations for international students: Required—TOEFL (minimum score 500 paper-based). Application fee: $55. *Expenses:* Tuition, state resident: full-time $6738; part-time $3906 per unit. *Required fees:* $1916; $1916 per year. Tuition and fees vary according to course load, degree level and program. *Financial support:* Fellowships, research assistantships, career-related internships or fieldwork, and Federal Work-Study available. Support available to part-time students. Financial award application deadline: 3/2; financial award applicants required to submit FAFSA. *Unit head:* Dr. Carlos Ayala, Dean, 707-664-4412, E-mail: carlos.ayala@sonoma.edu. *Application contact:* Dr. Jennifer Mahdavi, Coordinator of Graduate Studies, 707-664-3311, E-mail: jennifer.mahdavi@sonoma.edu.
Website: http://www.sonoma.edu/education/

South Carolina State University, College of Graduate and Professional Studies, Department of Education, Orangeburg, SC 29117-0001. Offers early childhood education (MAT); education (M Ed); elementary education (M Ed, MAT); English (MAT); general science/biology (MAT); mathematics (MAT); secondary education (M Ed), including biology education, business education, counselor education, English education, home economics education, industrial education, mathematics education, science education, social studies education; special education (M Ed), including emotionally handicapped, learning disabilities, mentally handicapped. *Accreditation:* NCATE. *Program availability:* Part-time, evening/weekend. *Faculty:* 12 full-time (8 women), 3 part-time/adjunct (1 woman). *Students:* 28 full-time (20 women), 20 part-time (17 women); includes 45 minority (44 Black or African American, non-Hispanic/Latino; 1 Two or more races, non-Hispanic/Latino). Average age 31. 22 applicants, 100% accepted, 16 enrolled. In 2016, 9 master's awarded. *Degree requirements:* For master's, thesis optional, departmental qualifying exam. *Entrance requirements:* For master's, GRE General Test, NTE, interview, teaching certificate. *Application deadline:* For fall admission, 6/15 priority date for domestic students, 6/15 for international students; for spring admission, 11/1 for domestic and international students. Application fee: $25. Electronic applications accepted. *Expenses:* Tuition, state resident: full-time $8938; part-time $579 per credit hour. Tuition, nonresident: full-time $19,018; part-time $1139 per credit hour. *Required fees:* $1482; $82 per credit hour. *Financial support:* Fellowships, career-related internships or fieldwork, Federal Work-Study, and scholarships/grants available. Financial award application deadline: 6/1. *Unit head:* Dr. Charlie Spell, Interim Chair, Department of Education, 803-536-8963, Fax: 803-516-4568, E-mail: cspell@scsu.edu. *Application contact:* Curtis Foskey, Coordinator of Graduate Studies, 803-536-8419, Fax: 803-536-8812, E-mail: cfoskey@scsu.edu.

South Dakota State University, Graduate School, College of Education and Human Sciences, Brookings, SD 57007. Offers M Ed, MFCS, MS, PhD. *Degree requirements:* For master's, thesis, oral exam. *Entrance requirements:* Additional exam requirements/recommendations for international students: Required—TOEFL.

Southeastern Louisiana University, College of Education, Hammond, LA 70402. Offers M Ed, MAT, Ed D. *Accreditation:* NCATE. *Program availability:* Part-time. *Faculty:* 22 full-time (19 women), 3 part-time/adjunct (1 woman). *Students:* 10 full-time (all women), 162 part-time (136 women); includes 58 minority (51 Black or African American, non-Hispanic/Latino; 5 Hispanic/Latino; 2 Two or more races, non-Hispanic/Latino), 1 international. Average age 37. 94 applicants, 65% accepted, 28 enrolled. In 2016, 103 master's, 2 doctorates awarded. *Degree requirements:* For master's, comprehensive exam (for some programs), thesis optional; for doctorate, thesis/dissertation. *Entrance requirements:* Additional exam requirements/recommendations for international students: Required—TOEFL (minimum score 500 paper-based; 61 iBT), IELTS (minimum score 5.5). *Application deadline:* For fall admission, 7/15 priority date for domestic students, 6/1 priority date for international students; for spring admission, 12/1 priority date for domestic students, 10/1 priority date for international students. Applications are processed on a rolling basis. Application fee: $20 ($30 for international students). Electronic applications accepted. *Expenses:* Tuition, state resident: full-time $6540; part-time $465 per credit hour. Tuition, nonresident: full-time $19,017; part-time $1158 per credit hour. *Required fees:* $1829. *Financial support:* In 2016–17, 21 students received support. Research assistantships, teaching assistantships, career-related internships or fieldwork, Federal Work-Study, institutionally sponsored loans, scholarships/grants, and unspecified assistantships available. Support available to part-time students. Financial award application deadline: 5/1; financial award applicants required to submit FAFSA. *Faculty research:* School effectiveness, using data to drive instruction, change leadership, dyslexia, struggling at risk readers. *Unit head:* Dr. Shirley Jacob, Interim Dean, 985-549-2217, Fax: 985-549-2070, E-mail: shirly.jacob@southeastern.edu. *Application contact:* Amanda Harper, Graduate Admissions Analyst, 985-549-5620, Fax: 985-549-5632, E-mail: admissions@southeastern.edu.
Website: http://www.southeastern.edu/acad_research/colleges/edu_hd/index.html

Southeastern Oklahoma State University, School of Education, Durant, OK 74701-0609. Offers math specialist (M Ed); reading specialist (M Ed); school administration (M Ed); school counseling (M Ed). *Accreditation:* NCATE. *Program availability:* Part-time, evening/weekend. *Degree requirements:* For master's, comprehensive exam, thesis optional, portfolio (M Ed). *Entrance requirements:* For master's, GRE General Test (for school counseling), minimum GPA of 3.0 in last 60 hours or 2.75 overall. Additional exam requirements/recommendations for international students: Required—TOEFL (minimum score 550 paper-based; 79 iBT). Electronic applications accepted.

Southeastern University, College of Education, Lakeland, FL 33801-6099. Offers curriculum and instruction (Ed D); educational leadership (M Ed); elementary education (M Ed); exceptional student education (M Ed); exceptional student education/educational therapy (M Ed); organizational leadership (Ed D); reading education (M Ed); teaching English to speakers of other languages (M Ed). *Expenses: Tuition:* Full-time $9450; part-time $6300 per credit. *Required fees:* $500; $250 per semester. One-time fee: $150. Tuition and fees vary according to degree level, campus/location and program. *Unit head:* Amy N. Bratten, Dean, 863-667-5238, E-mail: anbratten@seu.edu.
Website: http://www.seu.edu/education/

Southern Adventist University, School of Education and Psychology, Collegedale, TN 37315-0370. Offers clinical mental health counseling (MS); inclusive education (MS Ed); instructional leadership (MS Ed); literacy education (MS Ed); outdoor teacher education (MS Ed); school counseling (MS). *Accreditation:* NCATE. *Program availability:* Part-time, evening/weekend. *Degree requirements:* For master's, comprehensive exam (for some programs), thesis optional, position paper (MS), portfolio (MS Ed in outdoor teacher education). *Entrance requirements:* For master's, interview (MS); 9 semester hours of upper-division course work in psychology or related field, including 1 course in psychology research or statistics; 9 semester hours of education (MS Ed). Additional exam requirements/recommendations for international students: Required—TOEFL (minimum score 600 paper-based; 100 iBT). Electronic applications accepted.

Southern Arkansas University–Magnolia, School of Graduate Studies, Magnolia, AR 71753. Offers agriculture (MS); business administration (MBA), including agri-business, social entrepreneurship, supply chain management; clinical and mental health counseling (MS); computer and information sciences (MS), including cyber security and privacy, data science, information technology; gifted and talented (M Ed), including curriculum and instruction, educational administration and supervision, gifted and talented P-8/7-12, instructional specialist P-4; higher, adult and lifelong education (M Ed); kinesiology (M Ed), including coaching; library media and information specialist (M Ed); public administration (MPA); school counseling K-12 (M Ed); student affairs and college counseling (M Ed); teaching (MAT). *Accreditation:* NCATE. *Program availability:* Part-time, 100% online, blended/hybrid learning. *Faculty:* 36 full-time (19 women), 33 part-time/adjunct (14 women). *Students:* 605 full-time (143 women), 879 part-time (352 women); includes 130 minority (113 Black or African American, non-Hispanic/Latino; 7 American Indian or Alaska Native, non-Hispanic/Latino; 2 Asian, non-Hispanic/Latino; 2 Hispanic/Latino; 6 Two or more races, non-Hispanic/Latino), 1,048 international. Average age 28. 904 applicants, 81% accepted, 262 enrolled. In 2016, 278 master's awarded. *Degree requirements:* For master's, comprehensive exam (for some programs), thesis optional. *Entrance requirements:* For master's, GRE, MAT or GMAT, minimum GPA of 2.5. Additional exam requirements/recommendations for international students: Required—TOEFL (minimum score 550 paper-based), IELTS (minimum score 6). *Application deadline:* For fall admission, 7/20 for domestic students, 7/10 for international students; for spring admission, 12/1 for domestic students, 11/15 for international students; for summer admission, 4/1 for domestic students, 5/1 for international students. Applications are processed on a rolling basis. Application fee: $25 ($50 for international students). Electronic applications accepted. *Expenses:* Tuition, state resident: full-time $2511; part-time $279 per credit hour. Tuition, nonresident: full-time $3726; part-time $414 per credit hour. *Required fees:* $307 per semester. Tuition and fees vary according to course load and program. *Financial support:* Career-related internships or fieldwork, Federal Work-Study, scholarships/grants, tuition waivers (full), and unspecified assistantships available. Financial award applicants required to submit FAFSA. *Faculty research:* Alternative certification for teachers, supervision of instruction, instructional leadership, counseling. *Unit head:* Dr. Kim Bloss, Dean, School of Graduate Studies, 870-235-4150, Fax: 870-235-5227, E-mail: kkbloss@saumag.edu. *Application contact:* Shrijana Malakar, Admissions Specialist, 870-235-4150, Fax: 870-235-5227, E-mail: smalakar@saumag.edu.
Website: http://www.saumag.edu/graduate

Southern Connecticut State University, School of Graduate Studies, School of Education, New Haven, CT 06515-1355. Offers MLS, MS, MS Ed, Ed D, Diploma. *Accreditation:* NCATE. *Program availability:* Part-time. *Faculty:* 40 full-time (27 women), 22 part-time/adjunct (17 women). *Students:* 190 full-time (159 women), 440 part-time (336 women); includes 83 minority (45 Black or African American, non-Hispanic/Latino; 1 American Indian or Alaska Native, non-Hispanic/Latino; 5 Asian, non-Hispanic/Latino; 27 Hispanic/Latino; 5 Two or more races, non-Hispanic/Latino), 4 international. Average age 32. 644 applicants, 48% accepted, 245 enrolled. In 2016, 232 master's, 15 doctorates, 203 other advanced degrees awarded. *Degree requirements:* For doctorate, comprehensive exam, thesis/dissertation. *Entrance requirements:* For degree, master's degree. Application fee: $50. Electronic applications accepted. *Expenses:* Tuition, state resident: full-time $6497; part-time $519 per credit hour. Tuition, nonresident: full-time $18,102; part-time $535 per credit hour. *Required fees:* $4722; $55 per semester. Tuition and fees vary according to program. *Financial support:* Career-related internships or fieldwork, scholarships/grants, and unspecified assistantships available. Financial award application deadline: 4/15; financial award applicants required to submit FAFSA. *Unit head:* Dr. Stephen Hegedus, Dean, 203-392-5900, E-mail: hegeduss1@southernct.edu. *Application contact:* Lisa Galvin, Director of Graduate Admissions, 203-392-5240, Fax: 203-392-5235, E-mail: galvinl1@southernct.edu.

Southern Illinois University Carbondale, Graduate School, College of Education and Human Services, Carbondale, IL 62901-4701. Offers MPH, MS, MS Ed, MSW, PhD, JD/MSW. *Accreditation:* NCATE. *Program availability:* Part-time. Terminal master's awarded for partial completion of doctoral program. *Degree requirements:* For doctorate, thesis/dissertation. *Entrance requirements:* For master's, minimum GPA of 2.7. Additional exam requirements/recommendations for international students: Required—TOEFL (minimum score 550 paper-based; 80 iBT). Electronic applications accepted. *Faculty research:* Safety education, community health, curriculum development, gifted, effective schools.

Southern Illinois University Edwardsville, Graduate School, School of Education, Health, and Human Behavior, Edwardsville, IL 62062. Offers MA, MS, MS Ed, Ed D, Ed S, Post-Master's Certificate, Postbaccalaureate Certificate, SD. *Accreditation:* NCATE. *Program availability:* Part-time, evening/weekend. *Degree requirements:* For master's, comprehensive exam (for some programs), thesis (for some programs), final exam, portfolio. *Entrance requirements:* For master's, GRE. Additional exam requirements/recommendations for international students: Required—TOEFL (minimum score 550 paper-based; 79 iBT), IELTS (minimum score 6.5). Electronic applications accepted.

Southern Methodist University, Annette Caldwell Simmons School of Education and Human Development, Department of Teaching and Learning, Dallas, TX 75275. Offers bilingual/ESL education (MBE); education (M Ed, PhD); gifted education (MBE); reading and writing (M Ed); special education (M Ed). *Program availability:* Part-time, evening/weekend. Terminal master's awarded for partial completion of doctoral program. *Degree requirements:* For master's, comprehensive exam, minimum GPA of 3.0; for doctorate, thesis/dissertation, qualifying exams, major area paper, evidence of teaching competency, dissemination of research (e.g., conference presentation), professional portfolio. *Entrance requirements:* For master's, minimum GPA of 3.0 or GRE, 3 letters of recommendation; for doctorate, GRE, minimum GPA of 3.3, 3 years of full-time teaching, 3 letters of recommendation, interview. Additional exam requirements/recommendations for international students: Required—TOEFL. Electronic applications accepted. *Faculty research:* Reading intervention, mathematics intervention, bilingual education, new literacies.

Southern New Hampshire University, School of Education, Manchester, NH 03106-1045. Offers business education (M Ed); child development (M Ed); curriculum and instruction (M Ed), including education leadership, reading, special education, technology integration; education (M Ed); educational leadership (M Ed, Ed D); educational studies (M Ed); elementary education (M Ed); English (MAT); English for speakers of other languages (M Ed); reading and writing specialist (M Ed); school business administration (Certificate); secondary education (M Ed); special education (M Ed); technology integration specialist (M Ed). *Program availability:* Part-time, evening/weekend, online learning. *Degree requirements:* For master's, comprehensive exam (for some programs), thesis or alternative. *Entrance requirements:* For master's, PRAXIS I, minimum GPA of 2.75. Additional exam requirements/recommendations for international students: Required—TOEFL (minimum score 550 paper-based). Electronic applications accepted. *Expenses:* Contact institution.

Southern Oregon University, Graduate Studies, School of Education, Ashland, OR 97520. Offers elementary education (MA Ed, MS Ed), including classroom teacher, early childhood, handicapped learner, reading, supervision; secondary education (MA Ed, MS Ed), including classroom teacher, handicapped learner, reading, supervision; teaching (MAT). *Program availability:* Online learning. *Faculty:* 15 full-time (10 women), 27 part-time/adjunct (21 women). *Students:* 116 full-time (82 women), 86 part-time (68 women); includes 22 minority (1 American Indian or Alaska Native, non-Hispanic/Latino; 4 Asian, non-Hispanic/Latino; 8 Hispanic/Latino; 9 Two or more races, non-Hispanic/Latino). Average age 34. 81 applicants, 80% accepted, 49 enrolled. In 2016, 107 master's awarded. *Degree requirements:* For master's, thesis optional. *Entrance requirements:* For master's, GRE General Test, minimum cumulative GPA of 3.0 in the last 90 quarter credits (60 semester credits) of undergraduate coursework. Additional exam requirements/recommendations for international students: Required—TOEFL (minimum score 540 paper-based; 76 iBT), IELTS (minimum score 6), ELPT (minimum score 964) or ELS (minimum score 112). *Application deadline:* For fall admission, 7/31 priority date for domestic and international students; for winter admission, 11/15 priority date for domestic and international students; for spring admission, 1/7 priority date for domestic and international students. Applications are processed on a rolling basis. Application fee: $60. Electronic applications accepted. *Expenses:* Tuition, state resident: full-time $10,719; part-time $397 per credit. Tuition, nonresident: full-time $13,419; part-time $497 per credit. *Required fees:* $548. *Financial support:* In 2016–17, 2 students received support. Career-related internships or fieldwork, institutionally sponsored loans, scholarships/grants, and unspecified assistantships available. *Unit head:* Dr. Gerry McCain, Graduate Program Coordinator, 541-552-6934, E-mail: mccaing@sou.edu. *Application contact:* Kelly Moutsatson, Director of Admissions, 541-552-6411, Fax: 541-552-8403, E-mail: admissions@sou.edu.
Website: http://www.sou.edu/education/

Southern University and Agricultural and Mechanical College, Graduate School, College of Education, Baton Rouge, LA 70813. Offers M Ed, MA, MS, PhD. *Accreditation:* NCATE. *Degree requirements:* For master's, comprehensive exam, thesis optional. *Entrance requirements:* For master's and doctorate, GRE General Test. Additional exam requirements/recommendations for international students: Required—TOEFL (minimum score 525 paper-based).

Southern Utah University, Program in Education, Cedar City, UT 84720-2498. Offers M Ed, Certificate. *Accreditation:* TEAC. *Program availability:* Part-time, 100% online. *Faculty:* 12 full-time (6 women), 28 part-time/adjunct (10 women). *Students:* 5 full-time (all women), 431 part-time (313 women); includes 25 minority (4 Black or African American, non-Hispanic/Latino; 2 American Indian or Alaska Native, non-Hispanic/Latino; 8 Asian, non-Hispanic/Latino; 8 Hispanic/Latino; 3 Native Hawaiian or other Pacific Islander, non-Hispanic/Latino). Average age 39. 85 applicants, 92% accepted, 64 enrolled. In 2016, 119 master's awarded. *Entrance requirements:* For master's, GRE (if GPA is less than 3.25). Additional exam requirements/recommendations for international students: Required—TOEFL (minimum score 550 paper-based, 79 iBT) or IELTS (minimum score 6). *Application deadline:* For fall admission, 7/15 for domestic and international students; for spring admission, 11/15 for domestic and international students; for summer admission, 4/15 for domestic and international students. Applications are processed on a rolling basis. Application fee: $60 ($65 for international students). Electronic applications accepted. *Expenses:* $6,034 per year resident or online full-time; $18,332 per year on campus non-resident full-time. *Financial support:* Tuition waivers (partial) available. *Unit head:* Dr. Bart Reynolds, Department Chair, 435-865-8125, Fax: 435-865-8485, E-mail: reynolds@suu.edu. *Application contact:* Tamara Lovell, Program Specialist, 435-865-8759, Fax: 435-865-8485, E-mail: tamaralovell@suu.edu.
Website: http://www.suu.edu/ed/

Southern Wesleyan University, Program in Education, Central, SC 29630-1020. Offers M Ed. Program also offered at Greenville, S. C. site. *Accreditation:* NCATE. *Program availability:* Evening/weekend. *Entrance requirements:* For master's, GRE General Test or MAT, 1 year teaching experience, minimum undergraduate GPA of 3.0, teacher certification. Additional exam requirements/recommendations for international students: Required—TOEFL (minimum score 500 paper-based).

Southwest Baptist University, Program in Education, Bolivar, MO 65613-2597. Offers education (MS); educational administration (MS, Ed S). *Program availability:* Part-time. *Degree requirements:* For master's, comprehensive exam, thesis optional, 6-hour residency; for Ed S, comprehensive exam, 5-hour residency. *Entrance requirements:* For master's, GRE or PRAXIS II, interviews, minimum GPA of 2.75; for Ed S, master's degree. Additional exam requirements/recommendations for international students: Required—TOEFL (minimum score 550 paper-based). *Faculty research:* At-risk programs, principal retention, mentoring beginning principals.

Southwestern Adventist University, Education Department, Keene, TX 76059. Offers curriculum and instruction with reading emphasis (M Ed); educational leadership (M Ed). *Program availability:* Part-time, evening/weekend. *Degree requirements:* For master's, thesis or alternative, professional paper. *Entrance requirements:* For master's, GRE General Test.

Southwestern Assemblies of God University, Thomas F. Harrison School of Graduate Studies, Program in Education, Waxahachie, TX 75165-5735. Offers Christian school administration (MS); curriculum development (MS); early education administration (M Ed); middle and secondary education (M Ed). *Degree requirements:* For master's, comprehensive written and oral exams. *Entrance requirements:* For master's, GRE General Test, minimum GPA of 2.5. Electronic applications accepted.

Southwestern College, Education Programs, Winfield, KS 67156-2499. Offers curriculum and instruction (M Ed); early childhood education (M Ed); educational leadership (Ed D); special education (M Ed), including adaptive, functional; teaching (MA). *Accreditation:* NCATE. *Program availability:* Part-time, evening/weekend, 100% online, blended/hybrid learning. *Faculty:* 7 full-time (5 women), 15 part-time/adjunct (12 women). *Students:* 27 full-time (18 women), 102 part-time (77 women); includes 17 minority (8 Black or African American, non-Hispanic/Latino; 1 American Indian or Alaska Native, non-Hispanic/Latino; 1 Asian, non-Hispanic/Latino; 6 Hispanic/Latino; 1 Native Hawaiian or other Pacific Islander, non-Hispanic/Latino), 32 international. Average age 38. 36 applicants, 64% accepted, 16 enrolled. In 2016, 71 master's, 10 doctorates awarded. *Degree requirements:* For master's, practicum, portfolio; for doctorate, thesis/dissertation, professional portfolio. *Entrance requirements:* For master's, baccalaureate degree, minimum GPA of 3.0, valid teaching certificate (for special education); for doctorate, GRE if no master's degree, baccalaureate degree with minimum GPA of 3.25 and current teaching experience, or master's degree with minimum GPA of 3.5. Additional exam requirements/recommendations for international students: Required—TOEFL (minimum score 550 paper-based; 80 iBT). *Application deadline:* Applications are processed on a rolling basis. Application fee: $40. Electronic applications accepted. *Expenses:* $550 per credit; $485 per credit (online); $580 per credit (doctorate program). *Financial support:* In 2016–17, 8 students received support. Scholarships/grants available. Financial award applicants required to submit FAFSA. *Unit head:* Dana Thomson, Director of Education Operations, 800-846-1543 Ext. 6253, Fax: 620-229-6253, E-mail: dana.thomson@sckans.edu. *Application contact:* Dennis Russell, Director of Admissions and Student Services, 888-684-5335 Ext. 3372, Fax: 888-684-5218, E-mail: dennis.russell@sckans.edu.
Website: http://www.sckans.edu/graduate/education-med/

Southwestern Oklahoma State University, College of Professional and Graduate Studies, School of Behavioral Sciences and Education, Weatherford, OK 73096-3098. Offers community counseling (M Ed); early childhood education (M Ed); educational administration (M Ed); elementary education (M Ed); health sciences and microbiology (M Ed); kinesiology (M Ed); parks and recreation management (M Ed); school counseling (M Ed); school psychology (MS); school psychometry (M Ed); secondary education (M Ed); special education (M Ed). *Accreditation:* NCATE. *Program availability:* Part-time, evening/weekend, online learning. *Degree requirements:* For master's, exam. *Entrance requirements:* For master's, GRE General Test or minimum undergraduate GPA of 3.0. Additional exam requirements/recommendations for international students: Required—TOEFL.

Southwest Minnesota State University, Department of Education, Marshall, MN 56258. Offers ESL (MS); math (MS); reading (MS); special education (MS), including developmental disabilities, early childhood education, emotional behavioral disorders, learning disabilities; teaching, learning and leadership (MS). *Program availability:* Part-time, evening/weekend, online learning. *Entrance requirements:* Additional exam requirements/recommendations for international students: Required—TOEFL or IELTS; Recommended—TOEFL (minimum score 550 paper-based; 80 iBT), IELTS.

Spalding University, Graduate Studies, College of Education, Louisville, KY 40203-2188. Offers M Ed, MA, MAT, Ed D. *Accreditation:* NCATE. *Program availability:* Part-time, evening/weekend. *Faculty:* 24 full-time (17 women), 12 part-time/adjunct (4 women). *Students:* 123 full-time (92 women), 57 part-time (42 women); includes 67 minority (58 Black or African American, non-Hispanic/Latino; 1 Asian, non-Hispanic/Latino; 5 Hispanic/Latino; 3 Two or more races, non-Hispanic/Latino). Average age 38. 86 applicants, 59% accepted, 51 enrolled. In 2016, 49 master's, 8 doctorates awarded. *Degree requirements:* For doctorate, comprehensive exam, thesis/dissertation. *Entrance requirements:* For master's, GRE, GMAT, or MAT, transcripts, interview, letters of recommendation. Additional exam requirements/recommendations for international students: Required—TOEFL (minimum score 535 paper-based). *Application deadline:* Applications are processed on a rolling basis. Application fee: $30. Electronic applications accepted. Application fee is waived when completed online. *Expenses:* Contact institution. *Financial support:* In 2016–17, 125 students received support. Tuition waivers and unspecified assistantships available. Financial award applicants required to submit FAFSA. *Faculty research:* School leadership, assessment of student learning, classroom management. *Unit head:* Dr. Chris Walsh, Associate Dean, 502-873-4272, E-mail: cwalsh@spalding.edu. *Application contact:* Valerie Anderson, Administrative Assistant, 502-873-4260, E-mail: vanderson@spalding.edu.

Spring Arbor University, School of Education, Spring Arbor, MI 49283-9799. Offers education (MAE); reading (MAR); special education (MSE). *Accreditation:* TEAC. *Program availability:* Part-time, evening/weekend, online learning. *Degree requirements:* For master's, thesis. *Entrance requirements:* For master's, official transcripts from all institutions attended, including evidence of an earned bachelor's degree from regionally-accredited college or university with minimum cumulative GPA of 3.0 for the last two years of the bachelor's degree; two professional letters of recommendation. Additional exam requirements/recommendations for international students: Required—TOEFL (minimum score 600 paper-based). Electronic applications accepted.

Springfield College, Graduate Programs, Programs in Education, Springfield, MA 01109-3797. Offers educational studies (M Ed); school guidance counseling (M Ed); secondary education (M Ed); special education (M Ed). *Program availability:* Part-time, evening/weekend. *Entrance requirements:* Additional exam requirements/recommendations for international students: Required—TOEFL (minimum score 550 paper-based); Recommended—IELTS (minimum score 6). Electronic applications accepted. *Expenses: Tuition:* Full-time $29,640; part-time $988 per credit. *Required fees:* $195.

Spring Hill College, Graduate Programs, Program in Education, Mobile, AL 36608-1791. Offers early childhood education (MAT, MS Ed); educational theory (MS Ed); elementary education (MAT, MS Ed); secondary education (MAT, MS Ed). *Program availability:* Part-time. *Faculty:* 3 full-time (all women). *Students:* 3 full-time (all women), 7 part-time (5 women); includes 1 minority (Black or African American, non-Hispanic/Latino). Average age 26. In 2016, 10 master's awarded. *Degree requirements:* For master's, comprehensive exam, completion of program within 6 calendar years of entrance into graduate studies at Spring Hill; documentation of course field assignments (MS) or completion of internship (MAT). *Entrance requirements:* For master's, GRE, MAT, or PRAXIS (varies by program), bachelor's degree with minimum undergraduate GPA of 3.0; class B certificate (for MS); minimum number of hours in specific fields (for MAT). Additional exam requirements/recommendations for international students: Required—TOEFL (minimum score 550 paper-based; 80 iBT), IELTS (minimum score 6.5), CPE or CAE (minimum score C), Michigan English Language Assessment Battery (minimum score 90). *Application deadline:* For fall admission, 8/1 priority date for domestic and international students; for spring admission, 12/1 priority date for domestic and international students. Applications are processed on a rolling basis. Application fee: $25 ($35 for international students). Electronic applications accepted. *Expenses:* Contact institution. *Financial support:* Applicants required to submit FAFSA. *Unit head:* Dr. Lori P. Aultman, Chair of Education, 251-380-3473, Fax: 251-460-2184, E-mail: laultman@shc.edu. *Application contact:* Robert Stewart, Vice President of Enrollment, 251-380-3030, Fax: 251-460-2186, E-mail: rstewart@shc.edu.
Website: http://ug.shc.edu/graduate-degrees/master-science-education/

Stanford University, Graduate School of Education, Stanford, CA 94305-2004. Offers MA, MAE, PhD, MA/JD, MA/MBA, MPP/MA. *Accreditation:* NCATE. *Degree requirements:* For doctorate, thesis/dissertation. *Entrance requirements:* For master's and doctorate, GRE General Test. Electronic applications accepted. *Expenses: Tuition:* Full-time $47,331. *Required fees:* $609.

State University of New York at Fredonia, College of Education, Fredonia, NY 14063. Offers curriculum and instruction (MS Ed); literacy education (MS Ed), including birth-grade 12, grades 5-12; TESOL (MS Ed). *Accreditation:* NCATE. *Program availability:* Part-time. *Faculty:* 21 full-time (17 women), 11 part-time/adjunct (9 women). *Students:* 39 full-time (32 women), 54 part-time (33 women); includes 8 minority (1 Black or African American, non-Hispanic/Latino; 4 Asian, non-Hispanic/Latino; 2 Hispanic/Latino; 1 Two or more races, non-Hispanic/Latino). Average age 29. 60 applicants, 97% accepted, 39 enrolled. In 2016, 56 master's awarded. *Degree requirements:* For master's, thesis. *Entrance requirements:* For master's, GRE, minimum undergraduate GPA of 3.0. Additional exam requirements/recommendations for international students: Required—TOEFL (minimum score 79 iBT), IELTS (minimum score 6.5). *Application deadline:* For fall admission, 4/1 priority date for domestic and international students; for spring admission, 11/1 priority date for domestic students, 11/1 for international students. Applications are processed on a rolling basis. Application fee: $75. Electronic applications accepted. *Expenses:* Tuition, state resident: full-time $10,370; part-time $453 per credit. Tuition, nonresident: full-time $20,190; part-time $925 per credit. *Required fees:* $1619; $67.30 per credit hour. $403.80 per semester. *Financial support:* In 2016–17, 4 teaching assistantships with full and partial tuition reimbursements (averaging $7,075 per year) were awarded. Financial award application deadline: 3/15; financial award applicants required to submit FAFSA. *Faculty research:* Positive behavioral intervention and support (PBIS), place-based science education, peer support for education, primary source material for social studies education, policies and practices in learning English language. *Unit head:* Dr. Christine Givner, Dean, 716-673-3311, E-mail: christine.givner@fredonia.edu. *Application contact:* Wendy S. Dunst, Interim Graduate Recruitment and Admissions Associate, 716-673-3808, Fax: 716-673-3712, E-mail: wendy.dunst@fredonia.edu.
Website: http://www.fredonia.edu/coe/

State University of New York at New Paltz, Graduate School, School of Education, New Paltz, NY 12561. Offers MAT, MPS, MS Ed, MST, AC, CAS. *Accreditation:* NCATE. *Program availability:* Part-time, evening/weekend. *Students:* 131 full-time (95 women), 269 part-time (217 women); includes 77 minority (14 Black or African American, non-Hispanic/Latino; 1 American Indian or Alaska Native, non-Hispanic/Latino; 6 Asian, non-Hispanic/Latino; 50 Hispanic/Latino; 6 Two or more races, non-Hispanic/Latino). 132 applicants, 79% accepted, 73 enrolled. In 2016, 177 master's, 29 other advanced degrees awarded. *Degree requirements:* For master's, comprehensive exam (for some programs), portfolio. *Entrance requirements:* For master's, GRE, MAT, minimum GPA of 3.0, New York State Teaching Certificate; for other advanced degree, minimum GPA of 3.0. Additional exam requirements/recommendations for international students: Required—TOEFL (minimum score 550 paper-based; 80 iBT), IELTS (minimum score 6.5). *Application deadline:* For fall admission, 3/1 for domestic and international students; for spring admission, 10/1 for domestic and international students. Application fee: $50. Electronic applications accepted. *Financial support:* Scholarships/grants available. Financial award application deadline: 8/1. *Faculty research:* Kindergarten readiness, translation learning experiences, assessment in mathematics education, long and short term outcomes of delayed school entry, parental involvement in children's education. *Unit head:* Dr. Michael Rosenberg, Dean, 845-257-2800, E-mail: schoolofed@newpaltz.edu. *Application contact:* Vika Shock, Director of Graduate Admissions, 845-257-3285, Fax: 845-257-3284, E-mail: gradschool@newpaltz.edu. Website: http://www.newpaltz.edu/schoolofed/

State University of New York at Oswego, Graduate Studies, School of Education, Oswego, NY 13126. Offers MAT, MS, MS Ed, MST, CAS, MS/CAS. *Accreditation:* NCATE. *Program availability:* Part-time. *Degree requirements:* For master's, comprehensive exam (for some programs), thesis optional. *Entrance requirements:* For degree, GRE General Test, interview, MA or MS, minimum GPA of 3.0. Additional exam requirements/recommendations for international students: Required—TOEFL (minimum score 560 paper-based).

State University of New York College at Cortland, Graduate Studies, School of Education, Cortland, NY 13045. Offers MS Ed, MST, CAS. *Accreditation:* NCATE. *Program availability:* Part-time, evening/weekend. *Entrance requirements:* Additional exam requirements/recommendations for international students: Required—TOEFL.

State University of New York College at Geneseo, Graduate Studies, School of Education, Geneseo, NY 14454-1401. Offers MS Ed. *Accreditation:* NCATE. *Program availability:* Part-time. *Faculty:* 8 full-time (5 women), 2 part-time/adjunct (both women). *Students:* 16 full-time (15 women), 46 part-time (36 women); includes 8 minority (3 Black or African American, non-Hispanic/Latino; 1 American Indian or Alaska Native, non-Hispanic/Latino; 2 Asian, non-Hispanic/Latino; 2 Hispanic/Latino). Average age 26. 28 applicants, 50% accepted, 11 enrolled. In 2016, 40 master's awarded. *Degree requirements:* For master's, thesis optional. *Entrance requirements:* For master's, initial certification to teach in New York state. *Application deadline:* For fall admission, 4/1 priority date for domestic students; for spring admission, 11/1 for domestic students. Applications are processed on a rolling basis. Application fee: $50. Electronic applications accepted. *Expenses:* Tuition, state resident: full-time $10,870; part-time $453 per credit. Tuition, nonresident: full-time $22,210; part-time $925 per credit. *Required fees:* $865; $35.85 per credit hour. *Financial support:* In 2016–17, 9 students received support, including 9 research assistantships with full tuition reimbursements available (averaging $8,823 per year); fellowships, career-related internships or fieldwork, scholarships/grants, health care benefits, tuition waivers (full), and unspecified assistantships also available. Support available to part-time students. Financial award application deadline: 4/1; financial award applicants required to submit FAFSA. *Unit head:* Dr. Anjoo Sikka, Dean of School of Education, 585-245-5151, Fax: 585-245-5220, E-mail: sikka@geneseo.edu. *Application contact:* Michael R. George, Graduate Enrollment Coordinator, 585-245-5148, Fax: 585-245-5550, E-mail: georgem@geneseo.edu. Website: http://www.geneseo.edu/education/grad_programs

State University of New York College at Old Westbury, School of Education, Old Westbury, NY 11568-0210. Offers biology (MAT, MS); chemistry (MAT, MS); English language arts (MAT, MS); math (MAT, MS); social studies (MAT, MS); Spanish (MAT, MS). *Program availability:* Part-time, evening/weekend. *Faculty:* 17 full-time (9 women), 5 part-time/adjunct (2 women). *Students:* 46 full-time (19 women), 26 part-time (17 women); includes 20 minority (1 Black or African American, non-Hispanic/Latino; 4 Asian, non-Hispanic/Latino; 15 Hispanic/Latino). Average age 30. 35 applicants, 77% accepted, 23 enrolled. In 2016, 25 master's awarded. *Entrance requirements:* For master's, Liberal Arts and Sciences Test, undergraduate degree with at least 30 semester hours of appropriate coursework as defined by the respective discipline; minimum cumulative undergraduate GPA of 3.0; two letters of recommendation (one from an academic source); essay. Additional exam requirements/recommendations for international students: Required—TOEFL (minimum score 550 paper-based); Recommended—IELTS. Application fee: $50. *Expenses:* Tuition, state resident: full-time $10,870; part-time $453 per credit. Tuition, nonresident: full-time $22,210; part-time $925 per credit. *Required fees:* $24.35 per credit. $76 per semester. Tuition and fees vary according to course load. *Financial support:* Applicants required to submit FAFSA. *Unit head:* Dr. Nancy Brown, Dean, School of Education, 516-876-3275, E-mail: brownn@oldwestbury.edu. *Application contact:* Philip D'Angelo, Graduate Admissions Office, 516-876-3073, E-mail: enroll@oldwestbury.edu.

State University of New York College at Oneonta, Graduate Programs, Division of Education, Oneonta, NY 13820-4015. Offers educational psychology, counseling and special education (MS Ed, CAS), including school counselor K-12, special education (MS Ed); elementary education and reading (MS Ed), including childhood education, literacy education. *Accreditation:* NCATE. *Program availability:* Part-time, evening/weekend. *Entrance requirements:* For master's, GRE General Test. *Application deadline:* For fall admission, 3/25 priority date for domestic students; for spring admission, 10/1 priority date for domestic students. Applications are processed on a rolling basis. Application fee: $50. *Unit head:* Dr. Jan Bowers, Dean, 607-436-2541, Fax: 607-436-2554. *Application contact:* Patrick J. Mente, Director of Graduate Studies, 607-436-2523, Fax: 607-436-3084, E-mail: gradstudies@oneonta.edu.
Website: https://www.oneonta.edu/academics/ed/

State University of New York Empire State College, School for Graduate Studies, Programs in Education, Saratoga Springs, NY 12866-4391. Offers adult learning (MA); learning and emerging technologies (MA); teaching (MAT); teaching and learning (M Ed). *Program availability:* Online learning.

Stephen F. Austin State University, Graduate School, College of Education, Nacogdoches, TX 75962. Offers M Ed, MA, MS, Ed D. *Accreditation:* NCATE. *Program availability:* Part-time, evening/weekend. *Degree requirements:* For master's, comprehensive exam; for doctorate, thesis/dissertation. *Entrance requirements:* For master's, GRE General Test; for doctorate, GRE General Test, interview, writing sample. Additional exam requirements/recommendations for international students: Required—TOEFL.

Stetson University, College of Arts and Sciences, Division of Education, DeLand, FL 32723. Offers counselor education (MS), including marriage, couple and family counseling, mental health counseling, school counseling; teacher education (M Ed), including educating for social justice, educational leadership. *Accreditation:* NCATE (one or more programs are accredited). *Program availability:* Part-time, evening/weekend. *Faculty:* 12 full-time (8 women), 8 part-time/adjunct (7 women). *Students:* 190 full-time (160 women), 17 part-time (13 women); includes 56 minority (20 Black or African American, non-Hispanic/Latino; 1 Asian, non-Hispanic/Latino; 30 Hispanic/Latino; 5 Two or more races, non-Hispanic/Latino), 3 international. Average age 32. 145 applicants, 81% accepted, 98 enrolled. In 2016, 47 master's awarded. *Entrance requirements:* For master's, GRE or MAT. *Application deadline:* For fall admission, 8/1 priority date for domestic students; for spring admission, 1/1 priority date for domestic students; for summer admission, 5/1 priority date for domestic students. Applications are processed on a rolling basis. Application fee: $50. Electronic applications accepted. *Expenses:* $886 per credit hour. *Financial support:* In 2016–17, 119 students received support. Career-related internships or fieldwork, Federal Work-Study, institutionally sponsored loans, scholarships/grants, unspecified assistantships, and tuition waivers for staff and dependents available. Support available to part-time students. *Faculty research:* School leadership succession planning; restorative practices in schools; literacy and art teacher evaluation and support in place of personnel appraisal; mission-driven leadership. *Unit head:* Dr. Karen Ryan, Dean, 386-822-7515. *Application contact:* Jamie Vanderlip, Senior Associate Director of Graduate Admissions, 386-822-7100, Fax: 386-822-7112, E-mail: jlvander@stetson.edu.

Stevenson University, Master of Arts in Teaching Program, Stevenson, MD 21153. Offers secondary biology (MAT); secondary chemistry (MAT); secondary mathematics (MAT). *Program availability:* Part-time, blended/hybrid learning. *Faculty:* 3 part-time/adjunct (all women). *Students:* 17 part-time (10 women); includes 3 minority (2 Black or African American, non-Hispanic/Latino; 1 Asian, non-Hispanic/Latino). Average age 29. 13 applicants, 85% accepted, 10 enrolled. In 2016, 8 master's awarded. *Degree requirements:* For master's, internship, portfolio, action research project. *Entrance requirements:* For master's, PRAXIS, GRE, SAT, or ACT, official transcripts from each college or university attended verifying completion of baccalaureate degree in a science or math discipline from regionally-accredited institution. *Application deadline:* Applications are processed on a rolling basis. Electronic applications accepted. *Expenses:* $475 per credit hour. *Financial support:* Unspecified assistantships available. Financial award applicants required to submit FAFSA. *Unit head:* Anne P. Davis, Associate Dean of Teacher Education. *Application contact:* Amanda Courter, Senior Enrollment Counselor, 443-352-4243, Fax: 443-352-4440,
E-mail: acourter@stevenson.edu.
Website: http://www.stevenson.edu/graduate-professional-studies/graduate-programs/master-of-arts-in-teaching/

Stockton University, Office of Graduate Studies, Program in Education, Galloway, NJ 08205-9441. Offers MA. *Accreditation:* TEAC. *Program availability:* Part-time, evening/weekend. *Faculty:* 6 full-time (all women), 9 part-time/adjunct (7 women). *Students:* 18 full-time (all women), 173 part-time (153 women); includes 26 minority (8 Black or African American, non-Hispanic/Latino; 1 American Indian or Alaska Native, non-Hispanic/Latino; 2 Asian, non-Hispanic/Latino; 11 Hispanic/Latino; 4 Two or more races, non-Hispanic/Latino). Average age 35. 118 applicants, 73% accepted, 67 enrolled. In 2016, 23 master's awarded. *Degree requirements:* For master's, comprehensive exam (for some programs), project. *Entrance requirements:* For master's, GRE, MAT, minimum GPA of 2.75, teaching certificate. *Application deadline:* For fall admission, 7/1 for domestic students; for spring admission, 12/1 for domestic students. Applications are processed on a rolling basis. Application fee: $50. Electronic applications accepted. *Expenses:* $772 per credit in-state. *Financial support:* Fellowships, research assistantships with partial tuition reimbursements, career-related internships or fieldwork, Federal Work-Study, scholarships/grants, and unspecified assistantships available. Support available to part-time students. Financial award application deadline: 3/1; financial award applicants required to submit FAFSA. *Faculty research:* Curriculum instruction, math, science, special education, language arts, literacy. *Unit head:* Dr. Kim LeBak, Program Director, 609-626-3640, E-mail: gradschool@stockton.edu. *Application contact:* Tara Williams, Assistant Director of Graduate Enrollment Management, 609-626-3640, Fax: 609-626-6050, E-mail: gradschool@stockton.edu.

Strayer University, Graduate Studies, Washington, DC 20005-2603. Offers accounting (MS); acquisition (MBA); business administration (MBA); communications technology (MS); educational management (M Ed); finance (MBA); health services administration (MHSA); hospitality and tourism management (MBA); human resource management (MBA); information systems (MS), including computer security management, decision support system management, enterprise resource management, network management, software engineering management, systems development management; management (MBA); management information systems (MS); marketing (MBA); professional accounting (MS), including accounting information systems, controllership, taxation; public administration (MPA); supply chain management (MBA); technology in education (M Ed). Programs also offered at campus locations in Birmingham, AL; Chamblee, GA; Cobb County, GA; Morrow, GA; White Marsh, MD; Charleston, SC; Columbia, SC; Greensboro, NC; Greenville, SC; Lexington, KY; Louisville, KY; Nashville, TN; North Raleigh, NC; Washington, DC. *Accreditation:* ACBSP. *Program availability:* Part-time, evening/weekend, online learning. *Degree requirements:* For master's, thesis. *Entrance requirements:* For master's, GMAT, GRE General Test, bachelor's degree from an accredited college or university, minimum undergraduate GPA of 2.75. Electronic applications accepted.

Sul Ross State University, College of Professional Studies, Department of Education, Alpine, TX 79832. Offers counseling (M Ed); educational diagnostics (M Ed); reading specialist (M Ed, Certificate), including master reading teacher (Certificate), Texas reading specialist (M Ed); school administration (M Ed). *Program availability:* Part-time, evening/weekend. *Degree requirements:* For master's, thesis optional. *Entrance requirements:* For master's, GMAT or GRE General Test, minimum GPA of 2.5 in last 60 hours of undergraduate work. *Faculty research:* Critical thinking skills, adolescent eating disorders, reading-based study skills, cross-cultural adaptations, educational leadership.

Sul Ross State University, Rio Grande College of Sul Ross State University, Alpine, TX 79832. Offers business administration (MBA); teacher education (M Ed), including bilingual education, counseling, educational diagnostics, elementary education, general education, reading, school administration, secondary education. *Program availability:* Part-time, evening/weekend, online learning. *Degree requirements:* For master's, comprehensive exam, thesis optional, minimum GPA of 3.0. *Entrance requirements:* For master's, GMAT or GRE General Test, minimum GPA of 2.5 in last 60 hours of undergraduate work. Additional exam requirements/recommendations for international students: Required—TOEFL.

Sweet Briar College, Department of Education, Sweet Briar, VA 24595. Offers M Ed, MAT. *Program availability:* Part-time. *Degree requirements:* For master's, comprehensive exam (for some programs), thesis. *Entrance requirements:* For master's, PRAXIS I and II; Virginia Communication and Literacy Assessment, Virginia Reading Assessment (MAT); GRE (M Ed), current teaching license (M Ed). Additional exam requirements/recommendations for international students: Required—TOEFL (minimum score 550 paper-based; 79 iBT), IELTS (minimum score 6.5). Electronic applications accepted. *Faculty research:* Differentiation of K-12 student achievement, mentoring and teacher retention, teaching science by inquiry.

Syracuse University, School of Education, Syracuse, NY 13244. Offers M Mus, MM, MS, Ed D, PhD, CAS, Ed D/PhD. *Accreditation:* NCATE. *Program availability:* Part-time. *Faculty:* 50 full-time (28 women), 50 part-time/adjunct (35 women). *Students:* 342 full-time (246 women), 216 part-time (143 women); includes 134 minority (62 Black or African American, non-Hispanic/Latino; 8 American Indian or Alaska Native, non-Hispanic/Latino; 15 Asian, non-Hispanic/Latino; 36 Hispanic/Latino; 1 Native Hawaiian or other Pacific Islander, non-Hispanic/Latino; 12 Two or more races, non-Hispanic/Latino), 77 international. Average age 33. 486 applicants, 61% accepted, 137 enrolled. In 2016, 161 master's, 31 doctorates, 34 other advanced degrees awarded. *Degree requirements:* For master's, thesis or alternative; for doctorate, comprehensive exam, thesis/dissertation; for CAS, thesis. *Entrance requirements:* For master's, GRE (for some programs), baccalaureate degree from regionally-accredited college/university; for doctorate, GRE, master's degree. Additional exam requirements/recommendations for international students: Required—TOEFL (minimum score 100 iBT). *Application deadline:* Applications are processed on a rolling basis. Application fee: $75. Electronic applications accepted. *Expenses: Tuition:* Full-time $25,974; part-time $1443 per credit hour. *Required fees:* $802; $50 per course. Tuition and fees vary according to course load and program. *Financial support:* Fellowships with full tuition reimbursements, research assistantships with tuition reimbursements, teaching assistantships with tuition reimbursements, career-related internships or fieldwork, institutionally sponsored loans, scholarships/grants, health care benefits, tuition waivers (partial), and unspecified assistantships available. Financial award application deadline: 1/15; financial award applicants required to submit FAFSA. *Faculty research:* Literacy education, inclusive education, communication sciences and disorders, facilitated communication, school sustainability. *Unit head:* Dr. Joanna Masingila, Dean, 315-443-4751, E-mail: jomasing@syr.edu. *Application contact:* Speranza Migliore, Graduate Recruiter, School of Education, 315-443-2505, E-mail: gradrcrt@syr.edu.
Website: http://soeweb.syr.edu/

Taft University System, The Boyer Graduate School of Education, Denver, CO 80246. Offers M Ed.

Tarleton State University, College of Graduate Studies, College of Education, Stephenville, TX 76402. Offers M Ed, MS, Ed D, Certificate. *Program availability:* Part-time, evening/weekend, online learning. *Faculty:* 35 full-time (21 women), 22 part-time/adjunct (16 women). *Students:* 67 full-time (40 women), 502 part-time (376 women); includes 158 minority (73 Black or African American, non-Hispanic/Latino; 5 American Indian or Alaska Native, non-Hispanic/Latino; 2 Asian, non-Hispanic/Latino; 68 Hispanic/Latino; 10 Two or more races, non-Hispanic/Latino), 3 international. Average age 36. 135 applicants, 96% accepted, 80 enrolled. In 2016, 146 master's, 15 doctorates awarded. *Degree requirements:* For master's, comprehensive exam, thesis (for some programs); for doctorate, thesis/dissertation. *Entrance requirements:* For master's, GRE General Test, minimum GPA of 3.0; for doctorate, GRE, 4 letters of reference, leadership portfolio. Additional exam requirements/recommendations for international students: Required—TOEFL (minimum score 550 paper-based; 80 iBT). *Application deadline:* For fall admission, 8/15 priority date for domestic students; for spring admission, 1/7 for domestic students. Applications are processed on a rolling basis. Application fee: $45 ($130 for international students). Electronic applications accepted. *Expenses:* $3,672 tuition; $2,437 fees. *Financial support:* Research assistantships, teaching assistantships with partial tuition reimbursements, career-related internships or fieldwork, Federal Work-Study, institutionally sponsored loans, and tuition waivers (partial) available. Support available to part-time students. Financial award application deadline: 5/1; financial award applicants required to submit FAFSA. *Unit head:* Dr. Jordan Barkley, Dean, 254-968-9088, Fax: 254-968-9525, E-mail: jbarkley@tarleton.edu. *Application contact:* Wendy Weiss, Information Contact, 254-968-9104, Fax: 254-968-9670, E-mail: weiss@tarleton.edu.
Website: http://www.tarleton.edu/coe/index.html

Teachers College, Columbia University, Department of International and Transcultural Studies, New York, NY 10027-6696. Offers anthropology and education (MA, Ed D, PhD); applied anthropology (PhD); comparative and international education (MA, Ed D, PhD); international educational development (Ed M, MA, Ed D, PhD). *Program availability:* Part-time. *Students:* 151 full-time (128 women), 119 part-time (95 women); includes 83 minority (17 Black or African American, non-Hispanic/Latino; 32 Asian, non-Hispanic/Latino; 23 Hispanic/Latino; 11 Two or more races, non-Hispanic/Latino), 97 international. 422 applicants, 67% accepted, 138 enrolled. *Degree requirements:* For doctorate, thesis/dissertation. *Expenses: Tuition:* Full-time $36,288; part-time $1512 per credit. *Required fees:* $438 per semester. One-time fee: $510 full-time. Full-time tuition and fees vary according to course load. *Unit head:* Prof. Herve Varenne, Chair, 212-678-3190, E-mail: varenne@tc.columbia.edu. *Application contact:* David Estrella, Director of Admission, 212-678-3305, E-mail: estrella@tc.columbia.edu.

Teachers College, Columbia University, Department of Mathematics, Science and Technology, New York, NY 10027-6696. Offers biology 7-12 (MA); chemistry 7-12 (MA); communication and education (MA, Ed D); computing in education (MA); earth science 7-12 (MA); instructional technology and media (Ed M, MA, Ed D); mathematics education (Ed M, MA, Ed D, Ed DCT, PhD); physics 7-12 (MA); science and dental education (MA); science education (Ed M, MS, Ed DCT, PhD); supervisor/teacher of science education (MA); technology specialist (MA). *Program availability:* Part-time, evening/weekend, online learning. *Students:* 195 full-time (133 women), 222 part-time (139 women); includes 152 minority (44 Black or African American, non-Hispanic/Latino; 66 Asian, non-Hispanic/Latino; 32 Hispanic/Latino; 10 Two or more races, non-Hispanic/Latino), 106 international. 368 applicants, 65% accepted, 123 enrolled. Terminal master's awarded for partial completion of doctoral program. *Degree requirements:* For doctorate, thesis/dissertation. *Expenses: Tuition:* Full-time $36,288; part-time $1512 per credit. *Required fees:* $438 per semester. One-time fee: $510 full-time. Full-time tuition and fees vary according to course load. *Unit head:* Dr. O. Roger Anderson, Chair, 212-678-3405, Fax: 212-678-8129, E-mail: ora@ldeo.columbia.edu. *Application contact:* David Estrella, Director of Admission, 212-678-3305, E-mail: estrella@tc.columbia.edu.
Website: http://www.tc.columbia.edu/mathematics-science-and-technology/

Temple University, College of Education, Philadelphia, PA 19122-6096. Offers Ed M, MS Ed, Ed D, PhD, Ed S. *Accreditation:* TEAC. *Program availability:* Part-time, evening/weekend. *Faculty:* 56 full-time (31 women), 101 part-time/adjunct (67 women). *Students:* 490 full-time (354 women), 496 part-time (326 women); includes 261 minority (162 Black or African American, non-Hispanic/Latino; 2 American Indian or Alaska Native, non-Hispanic/Latino; 38 Asian, non-Hispanic/Latino; 38 Hispanic/Latino; 21 Two or more races, non-Hispanic/Latino), 43 international. 822 applicants, 59% accepted, 281 enrolled. In 2016, 220 master's, 63 doctorates, 63 other advanced degrees awarded. *Degree requirements:* For doctorate, thesis/dissertation. *Entrance requirements:* Additional exam requirements/recommendations for international students: Required—TOEFL. *Application deadline:* For fall admission, 4/1 for domestic students, 1/1 for international students; for spring admission, 10/1 for domestic students, 7/3 for international students. Applications are processed on a rolling basis. Application fee: $60. Electronic applications accepted. *Expenses:* Contact institution. *Financial support:* Research assistantships with full tuition reimbursements, teaching assistantships with full tuition reimbursements, career-related internships or fieldwork, Federal Work-Study, scholarships/grants, health care benefits, and unspecified assistantships available. Financial award application deadline: 1/15; financial award applicants required to submit FAFSA. *Faculty research:* Curriculum development, instruction, technology, learning, educational achievement. *Unit head:* Dr. Gregory Anderson, Dean, 215-204-8017, Fax: 215-204-5622, E-mail: coedean@temple.edu. *Application contact:* Elizabeth Jung, Enrollment Management, 215-204-5634, E-mail: educate@temple.edu.
Website: http://education.temple.edu/

Tennessee State University, The School of Graduate Studies and Research, College of Education, Nashville, TN 37209-1561. Offers M Ed, MA Ed, MS, Ed D, PhD, Ed S. *Accreditation:* NCATE. *Program availability:* Part-time, evening/weekend. *Degree requirements:* For doctorate, thesis/dissertation. *Entrance requirements:* For doctorate, minimum GPA of 3.25. *Faculty research:* Class size, biobehavioral research, equity, dropout rate, K–12 teachers: first 5 years of employment.

Tennessee Technological University, College of Graduate Studies, College of Education, Cookeville, TN 38505. Offers M Ed, MA, PhD, Ed S. *Accreditation:* NCATE. *Program availability:* Part-time, evening/weekend. *Faculty:* 58 full-time (16 women). *Students:* 121 full-time (84 women), 244 part-time (178 women); includes 40 minority (21 Black or African American, non-Hispanic/Latino; 1 American Indian or Alaska Native, non-Hispanic/Latino; 1 Asian, non-Hispanic/Latino; 7 Hispanic/Latino; 10 Two or more races, non-Hispanic/Latino), 7 international. Average age 27. 226 applicants, 61% accepted, 104 enrolled. In 2016, 114 master's, 5 doctorates, 27 other advanced degrees awarded. *Degree requirements:* For master's and Ed S, comprehensive exam, thesis or alternative; for doctorate, comprehensive exam, thesis/dissertation. *Entrance requirements:* For master's, GRE or MAT; for doctorate, GRE; for Ed S, MAT or GRE. Additional exam requirements/recommendations for international students: Required—TOEFL (minimum score 527 paper-based; 71 iBT), IELTS (minimum score 5.5), PTE (minimum score 48), TOEIC (Test of English as an International Communication). *Application deadline:* For fall admission, 8/1 for domestic students, 5/1 for international students; for spring admission, 12/1 for domestic students, 10/1 for international students; for summer admission, 5/1 for domestic students, 2/1 for international students. Applications are processed on a rolling basis. Application fee: $35 ($40 for international students). Electronic applications accepted. *Expenses:* Tuition, state resident: full-time $9375; part-time $534 per credit hour. Tuition, nonresident: full-time $22,443; part-time $1260 per credit hour. *Financial support:* In 2016–17, 42 fellowships (averaging $8,000 per year), 12 research assistantships (averaging $8,566 per year), 24 teaching assistantships (averaging $4,483 per year) were awarded; career-related internships or fieldwork also available. Support available to part-time students. Financial award application deadline: 4/1. *Faculty research:* Teacher evaluation. *Unit head:* Dr. Jennifer Shank, Dean, 931-372-3124, Fax: 931-372-6319, E-mail: jshank@tntech.edu.

Education—General

Application contact: Shelia K. Kendrick, Coordinator of Graduate Studies, 931-372-3808, Fax: 931-372-3497, E-mail: skendrick@tntech.edu.

Texas A&M International University, Office of Graduate Studies and Research, College of Education, Laredo, TX 78041-1900. Offers MS, MS Ed. *Program availability:* Part-time, evening/weekend. *Degree requirements:* For master's, thesis (for some programs). *Entrance requirements:* For master's, GRE General Test. Additional exam requirements/recommendations for international students: Required—TOEFL (minimum score 550 paper-based; 79 iBT).

Texas A&M University, College of Education and Human Development, College Station, TX 77843. Offers M Ed, MS, Ed D, PhD. *Program availability:* Part-time, evening/weekend, blended/hybrid learning. *Faculty:* 179. *Students:* 680 full-time (486 women), 955 part-time (691 women); includes 529 minority (169 Black or African American, non-Hispanic/Latino; 1 American Indian or Alaska Native, non-Hispanic/Latino; 53 Asian, non-Hispanic/Latino; 276 Hispanic/Latino; 3 Native Hawaiian or other Pacific Islander, non-Hispanic/Latino; 27 Two or more races, non-Hispanic/Latino), 170 international. Average age 33. 634 applicants, 66% accepted, 287 enrolled. In 2016, 413 master's, 104 doctorates awarded. *Degree requirements:* For doctorate, thesis/dissertation. *Entrance requirements:* For master's and doctorate, GRE General Test. Additional exam requirements/recommendations for international students: Required—TOEFL (minimum score 550 paper-based; 80 iBT), IELTS (minimum score 6), PTE (minimum score 53). *Application deadline:* Applications are processed on a rolling basis. Application fee: $50 ($90 for international students). Electronic applications accepted. *Expenses:* Contact institution. *Financial support:* In 2016–17, 785 students received support, including 18 fellowships with tuition reimbursements available (averaging $11,766 per year), 231 research assistantships with tuition reimbursements available (averaging $5,798 per year), 137 teaching assistantships with tuition reimbursements available (averaging $9,224 per year); career-related internships or fieldwork, institutionally sponsored loans, scholarships/grants, traineeships, health care benefits, tuition waivers (full and partial), and unspecified assistantships also available. Support available to part-time students. Financial award application deadline: 3/15; financial award applicants required to submit FAFSA. *Unit head:* Dr. Joyce Alexander, Professor and Dean, 979-862-6649, E-mail: joycemalexander@tamu.edu. *Application contact:* Dr. George Cunningham, Professor and Associate Dean for Academic Affairs, 979-845-5311, E-mail: gbcunningham@tamu.edu.
Website: http://education.tamu.edu/

Texas A&M University–Commerce, College of Education and Human Services, Commerce, TX 75429-3011. Offers counseling (MS); curriculum and instruction (M Ed, MS); early childhood education (M Ed, MS); educational administration (M Ed, Ed D); educational psychology (PhD); educational technology leadership (MS); educational technology library science (MS); health, kinesiology and sports studies (MS); higher education (MS, Ed D); organization, learning, and technology (MS); psychology (MS); reading (M Ed, MS); school psychology (SSP); secondary education (M Ed, MS); social work (MSW); special education (M Ed); supervision, curriculum and instruction-elementary education (Ed D). *Program availability:* Part-time, 100% online, blended/hybrid learning. *Faculty:* 88 full-time (52 women), 31 part-time/adjunct (24 women). *Students:* 341 full-time (276 women), 1,495 part-time (1,156 women); includes 762 minority (429 Black or African American, non-Hispanic/Latino; 4 American Indian or Alaska Native, non-Hispanic/Latino; 27 Asian, non-Hispanic/Latino; 247 Hispanic/Latino; 1 Native Hawaiian or other Pacific Islander, non-Hispanic/Latino; 54 Two or more races, non-Hispanic/Latino), 18 international. Average age 37. 1,070 applicants, 54% accepted, 452 enrolled. In 2016, 579 master's, 31 doctorates awarded. *Degree requirements:* For master's, one foreign language, comprehensive exam, thesis optional, departmental qualifying exams (for some programs); for doctorate, comprehensive exam, thesis/dissertation, departmental qualifying exam; for SSP, comprehensive exam, thesis optional. *Entrance requirements:* For master's and doctorate, GRE General Test. Additional exam requirements/recommendations for international students: Required—TOEFL (minimum score 550 paper-based; 79 iBT), IELTS (minimum score 6). *Application deadline:* For fall admission, 6/1 priority date for international students; for spring admission, 10/15 priority date for international students; for summer admission, 3/15 priority date for international students. Applications are processed on a rolling basis. Application fee: $50. Electronic applications accepted. *Expenses:* $2,254 resident; $4,744 non-resident. *Financial support:* In 2016–17, 301 students received support, including 39 research assistantships with partial tuition reimbursements available (averaging $9,000 per year), 17 teaching assistantships with partial tuition reimbursements available (averaging $9,000 per year); career-related internships or fieldwork, Federal Work-Study, institutionally sponsored loans, scholarships/grants, health care benefits, and unspecified assistantships also available. Financial award application deadline: 5/1; financial award applicants required to submit FAFSA. *Faculty research:* Cognitive and bilingual education, positive behavioral intervention, literacy, math readiness. *Total annual research expenditures:* $470,963. *Unit head:* Dr. Timothy Letzring, Dean, 903-886-5181, Fax: 903-886-5905, E-mail: tim.letzring@tamuc.edu. *Application contact:* Jennifer Faunce, Graduate Recruiter, 903-886-5030, Fax: 903-886-5905, E-mail: jennifer.faunce@tamuc.edu.
Website: http://www.tamuc.edu/academics/graduateSchool/programs/education/default.aspx

Texas A&M University–Corpus Christi, College of Graduate Studies, College of Education, Corpus Christi, TX 78412-5503. Offers counseling (MS), including counseling; counselor education (PhD); curriculum and instruction (MS, PhD); early childhood education (MS); educational administration (MS); educational leadership (Ed D); elementary education (MS); instructional design and educational technology (MS); kinesiology (MS); reading (MS); secondary education (MS); special education (MS). *Program availability:* Part-time, evening/weekend, online learning. *Faculty:* 50 full-time (29 women), 29 part-time/adjunct (18 women). *Students:* 158 full-time (130 women), 344 part-time (281 women); includes 288 minority (28 Black or African American, non-Hispanic/Latino; 2 American Indian or Alaska Native, non-Hispanic/Latino; 8 Asian, non-Hispanic/Latino; 246 Hispanic/Latino; 4 Two or more races, non-Hispanic/Latino), 22 international. Average age 35. 273 applicants, 60% accepted, 142 enrolled. In 2016, 67 master's, 13 doctorates awarded. *Degree requirements:* For master's, comprehensive exam, capstone; for doctorate, thesis/dissertation. *Entrance requirements:* For master's, GRE General Test, essay (300 words); for doctorate, GRE, essay, resume, 3-4 reference forms. *Application deadline:* For fall admission, 7/15 priority date for domestic students, 5/1 priority date for international students; for spring admission, 11/15 priority date for domestic students, 9/1 priority date for international students. Applications are processed on a rolling basis. Application fee: $50 ($70 for international students). Electronic applications accepted. *Financial support:* Research assistantships, teaching assistantships, career-related internships or fieldwork, Federal Work-Study, institutionally sponsored loans, scholarships/grants, health care benefits, and unspecified assistantships available. Support available to part-time students. Financial award application deadline: 3/15; financial award applicants required to submit FAFSA. *Unit head:* Dr. Arthur Hernandez, Dean, 361-825-2660, E-mail: art.hernandez@tamucc.edu. *Application contact:* Graduate Admissions Coordinator, 361-825-2177, Fax: 361-825-2755, E-mail: gradweb@tamucc.edu.
Website: http://education.tamucc.edu/

Texas A&M University–Kingsville, College of Graduate Studies, College of Education and Human Performance, Kingsville, TX 78363. Offers M Ed, MA, MS, Ed D, Certificate. *Program availability:* 100% online, blended/hybrid learning. *Entrance requirements:* Additional exam requirements/recommendations for international students: Required—TOEFL (minimum score 550 paper-based; 79 iBT); Recommended—IELTS. Electronic applications accepted.

Texas A&M University–Texarkana, Graduate Studies and Research, College of Education and Liberal Arts, Texarkana, TX 75505-5518. Offers adult education (MS); curriculum and instruction (M Ed); education (MS); educational administration (M Ed); English (MA); instructional technology (MS); interdisciplinary studies (MA, MS); special education (MS). *Program availability:* Part-time, evening/weekend. *Degree requirements:* For master's, comprehensive exam (for some programs), thesis optional. *Entrance requirements:* For master's, minimum GPA of 2.5 on last 60 hours of bachelor's degree. Additional exam requirements/recommendations for international students: Required—TOEFL. Electronic applications accepted.

Texas Christian University, College of Education, Fort Worth, TX 76129. Offers M Ed, Ed D, PhD, Certificate, MBA/Ed D. *Program availability:* Part-time, evening/weekend. *Faculty:* 29 full-time (21 women), 8 part-time/adjunct (5 women). *Students:* 189 full-time (151 women), 31 part-time (18 women); includes 72 minority (18 Black or African American, non-Hispanic/Latino; 7 Asian, non-Hispanic/Latino; 42 Hispanic/Latino; 1 Native Hawaiian or other Pacific Islander, non-Hispanic/Latino; 4 Two or more races, non-Hispanic/Latino), 8 international. Average age 32. 141 applicants, 72% accepted, 79 enrolled. In 2016, 54 master's, 5 doctorates awarded. *Degree requirements:* For master's, comprehensive exam (for some programs), thesis (for some programs); for doctorate, comprehensive exam, thesis/dissertation. *Entrance requirements:* For master's and doctorate, GRE General Test. Additional exam requirements/recommendations for international students: Required—TOEFL (minimum score 550 paper-based; 80 iBT), IELTS (minimum score 6.5). *Application deadline:* For fall admission, 2/1 for domestic and international students; for spring admission, 11/16 for domestic and international students; for summer admission, 2/1 for domestic and international students. Application fee: $60. Electronic applications accepted. *Expenses: Tuition:* Full-time $26,640; part-time $1480 per credit hour. *Required fees:* $48. Tuition and fees vary according to program. *Financial support:* In 2016–17, 164 students received support, including 14 research assistantships with full tuition reimbursements available (averaging $18,166 per year), 38 teaching assistantships with full tuition reimbursements available (averaging $15,875 per year); career-related internships or fieldwork, scholarships/grants, health care benefits, and unspecified assistantships also available. Support available to part-time students. Financial award application deadline: 2/1; financial award applicants required to submit FAFSA. *Unit head:* Dr. Jan Lacina, Associate Dean, 817-257-6786, Fax: 817-257-7466, E-mail: j.lacina@tcu.edu. *Application contact:* Lori Kimball, Administrative Program Specialist, 817-257-7661, Fax: 817-257-7466, E-mail: l.kimball@tcu.edu.
Website: http://coe.tcu.edu/graduate-overview/

Texas Southern University, College of Education, Houston, TX 77004-4584. Offers M Ed, MS, Ed D. *Program availability:* Part-time, evening/weekend. *Degree requirements:* For master's, comprehensive exam; for doctorate, comprehensive exam, thesis/dissertation. *Entrance requirements:* For master's, GRE General Test, minimum GPA of 2.5; for doctorate, GRE General Test or MAT, master's degree, minimum B+ average. Additional exam requirements/recommendations for international students: Required—TOEFL. Electronic applications accepted.

Texas State University, The Graduate College, College of Education, San Marcos, TX 78666. Offers M Ed, MA, MS, MSRLS, Ed D, PhD, SSP. *Program availability:* Part-time, evening/weekend. *Faculty:* 123 full-time (79 women), 51 part-time/adjunct (37 women). *Students:* 569 full-time (440 women), 573 part-time (423 women); includes 464 minority (84 Black or African American, non-Hispanic/Latino; 1 American Indian or Alaska Native, non-Hispanic/Latino; 29 Asian, non-Hispanic/Latino; 320 Hispanic/Latino; 30 Two or more races, non-Hispanic/Latino), 26 international. Average age 32. 764 applicants, 64% accepted, 304 enrolled. In 2016, 384 master's, 19 doctorates awarded. *Degree requirements:* For master's, comprehensive exam, thesis (for some programs); for doctorate, comprehensive exam, thesis/dissertation. *Entrance requirements:* For master's, GRE (for some programs), baccalaureate degree from regionally-accredited institution; letters of recommendation, statement of purpose, resume, and/or interview (for some programs); for doctorate, GRE, baccalaureate and master's degrees from regionally-accredited institution; letters of recommendation, statement of purpose, resume, and/or interview (for some programs). Additional exam requirements/recommendations for international students: Required—TOEFL (minimum score 550 paper-based; 78 iBT). *Application deadline:* For fall admission, 1/15 priority date for domestic and international students; for spring admission, 10/1 priority date for domestic and international students. Applications are processed on a rolling basis. Application fee: $40 ($90 for international students). Electronic applications accepted. *Expenses:* $4,851 per semester. *Financial support:* In 2016–17, 624 students received support, including 64 research assistantships (averaging $18,495 per year), 73 teaching assistantships (averaging $15,290 per year); fellowships, career-related internships or fieldwork, Federal Work-Study, institutionally sponsored loans, and scholarships/grants also available. Support available to part-time students. Financial award application deadline: 3/1; financial award applicants required to submit FAFSA. *Faculty research:* Teaching STEM subjects, using psychology and education to reach bilinguals, increasing college readiness and creating a college-going culture, interactive visualization in conceptualizing calculus, product efficacy research study design-developmental English and composition, responsive interaction parent training (RIPT) overview, effects of neuromuscular electrical stimulation frequency on metabolic markers, community youth development, evaluation of teacher preparation in Texas. *Total annual research expenditures:* $5.1 million. *Unit head:* Dr. Stan Carpenter, Dean, 512-245-2150, Fax: 512-245-3158, E-mail: sc33@txstate.edu. *Application contact:* Dr. Andrea Golato, Dean of Graduate School, 512-245-2581, Fax: 512-245-8365, E-mail: gradcollege@txstate.edu.
Website: http://www.education.txstate.edu/

Texas Tech University, Graduate School, College of Education, Lubbock, TX 79409-1071. Offers M Ed, MS, Ed D, PhD. *Accreditation:* NCATE. *Program availability:* Part-time, evening/weekend. *Faculty:* 83 full-time (46 women), 4 part-time/adjunct (3 women). *Students:* 365 full-time (270 women), 893 part-time (673 women); includes 417 minority (117 Black or African American, non-Hispanic/Latino; 6 American Indian or Alaska Native, non-Hispanic/Latino; 15 Asian, non-Hispanic/Latino; 247 Hispanic/Latino; 32 Two or more races, non-Hispanic/Latino), 92 international. Average age 36. 840 applicants, 56% accepted, 363 enrolled. In 2016, 191 master's, 75 doctorates awarded. Terminal master's awarded for partial completion of doctoral program. *Degree requirements:* For master's, comprehensive exam (for some programs), thesis or alternative; for doctorate, thesis/dissertation. *Entrance requirements:* For master's and doctorate, GRE General Test. Additional exam requirements/recommendations for international students: Required—TOEFL (minimum score 550 paper-based; 79 iBT). *Application deadline:* For fall admission, 6/1 priority date for domestic students, 1/15 priority date for international students; for spring admission, 9/1 priority date for domestic students, 6/15 priority date for international students. Applications are processed on a

rolling basis. Application fee: $75. Electronic applications accepted. *Expenses:* $285 per credit hour full-time resident tuition, $693 per credit hour full-time non-resident tuition; $50.50 per credit hour fee plus $608 per term fee. *Financial support:* In 2016–17, 511 students received support, including 494 fellowships (averaging $3,521 per year), 108 research assistantships (averaging $11,570 per year), 10 teaching assistantships (averaging $9,227 per year); career-related internships or fieldwork, Federal Work-Study, institutionally sponsored loans, scholarships/grants, traineeships, health care benefits, and unspecified assistantships also available. Support available to part-time students. Financial award application deadline: 2/15; financial award applicants required to submit FAFSA. *Faculty research:* Multicultural foundations of education, teacher education, psychological processes of teaching and learning, teaching populations with special needs, institutional technology, teacher preparation and educator quality, STEM education, blended and personalized learning using technology, autism and educational interventions around autism, partnerships for education and school reform. *Total annual research expenditures:* $8.1 million. *Unit head:* Dr. Scott Ridley, Dean, 806-834-1431, Fax: 806-742-2179, E-mail: scott.ridley@ttu.edu. *Application contact:* Brianna Sanchez, Coordinator, 806-834-2353, Fax: 806-742-2179, E-mail: brianna.sanchez@ttu.edu.
Website: http://www.educ.ttu.edu/

Texas Wesleyan University, Graduate Programs, Programs in Education, Fort Worth, TX 76105. Offers education (M Ed, Ed D); marriage and family therapy (MSMFT, PhD); professional counseling (MA); school counseling (MS). *Program availability:* Part-time, evening/weekend. *Faculty:* 18 full-time (9 women), 10 part-time/adjunct (5 women). *Students:* 23 full-time (18 women), 217 part-time (190 women); includes 121 minority (61 Black or African American, non-Hispanic/Latino; 3 American Indian or Alaska Native, non-Hispanic/Latino; 2 Asian, non-Hispanic/Latino; 47 Hispanic/Latino; 8 Two or more races, non-Hispanic/Latino), 9 international. Average age 36. 194 applicants, 70% accepted, 118 enrolled. In 2016, 52 master's, 8 doctorates awarded. *Degree requirements:* For master's, comprehensive exam (for some programs); for doctorate, thesis/dissertation. *Entrance requirements:* For master's and doctorate, GRE General Test. Additional exam requirements/recommendations for international students: Required—TOEFL (minimum score 550 paper-based; 79 iBT), IELTS (minimum score 6.5). *Application deadline:* Applications are processed on a rolling basis. Application fee: $64. Electronic applications accepted. *Expenses:* Contact institution. *Financial support:* Career-related internships or fieldwork, Federal Work-Study, scholarships/grants, and tuition waivers (full and partial) available. Support available to part-time students. Financial award application deadline: 3/15; financial award applicants required to submit FAFSA. *Faculty research:* Teacher effectiveness, bilingual education, analytic teaching. *Unit head:* Dr. Carlos Martinez, Dean, School of Education, 817-531-4940, Fax: 817-531-4943. *Application contact:* Amy Orcutt, Interim Director of Graduate Admissions, 817-531-4288, Fax: 817-531-4261, E-mail: arorcutt@txwes.edu.
Website: https://txwes.edu/academics/school-of-education/

Texas Woman's University, Graduate School, College of Professional Education, Denton, TX 76204. Offers M Ed, MA, MAT, MLS, MS, PhD. *Program availability:* Part-time, evening/weekend. *Faculty:* 62 full-time (48 women), 50 part-time/adjunct (41 women). *Students:* 277 full-time (264 women), 885 part-time (825 women); includes 436 minority (156 Black or African American, non-Hispanic/Latino; 7 American Indian or Alaska Native, non-Hispanic/Latino; 27 Asian, non-Hispanic/Latino; 219 Hispanic/Latino; 27 Two or more races, non-Hispanic/Latino), 14 international. Average age 35. 429 applicants, 61% accepted, 206 enrolled. In 2016, 376 master's, 13 doctorates awarded. Terminal master's awarded for partial completion of doctoral program. *Degree requirements:* For master's, comprehensive exam (for some programs), thesis (for some programs); for doctorate, comprehensive exam, thesis/dissertation. *Entrance requirements:* For master's and doctorate, minimum GPA of 3.0. Additional exam requirements/recommendations for international students: Required—TOEFL (minimum score 550 paper-based; 79 iBT). *Application deadline:* For fall admission, 7/1 priority date for domestic students, 3/1 for international students; for spring admission, 12/1 priority date for domestic students, 7/1 for international students. Applications are processed on a rolling basis. Application fee: $50 ($75 for international students). Electronic applications accepted. *Expenses:* Tuition, state resident: full-time $9046; part-time $251 per credit hour. Tuition, nonresident: full-time $22,922; part-time $614 per credit hour. *International tuition:* $23,046 full-time. *Required fees:* $2690; $1285 per credit hour. One-time fee: $50. Tuition and fees vary according to course level, course load, program and reciprocity agreements. *Financial support:* In 2016–17, 332 students received support, including 40 research assistantships (averaging $12,164 per year), 8 teaching assistantships (averaging $12,164 per year); career-related internships or fieldwork, Federal Work-Study, institutionally sponsored loans, scholarships/grants, traineeships, health care benefits, and unspecified assistantships also available. Support available to part-time students. Financial award application deadline: 3/1; financial award applicants required to submit FAFSA. *Total annual research expenditures:* $254,752. *Unit head:* Dr. Jerry Whitworth, Interim Dean, 940-898-2202, Fax: 940-898-2209, E-mail: cope@twu.edu. *Application contact:* Dr. Samuel Wheeler, Assistant Director of Admissions, 940-898-3188, Fax: 940-898-3081, E-mail: wheelersr@twu.edu.
Website: http://www.twu.edu/college-professional-education/

Thomas More College, Program in Teaching, Crestview Hills, KY 41017-3495. Offers MAT. *Program availability:* Part-time. *Degree requirements:* For master's, comprehensive exam. *Entrance requirements:* For master's, GRE (minimum scores: verbal 450, quantitative 490, and analytical 4.0) or PPST (minimum scores: math 174, reading 176, and writing 174), minimum undergraduate content GPA of 2.75, interview. Additional exam requirements/recommendations for international students: Required—TOEFL (minimum score 600 paper-based; 100 iBT). Electronic applications accepted. *Expenses:* Contact institution.

Thomas University, Department of Education, Thomasville, GA 31792-7499. Offers M Ed. *Program availability:* Part-time. *Entrance requirements:* For master's, resume, 3 academic/professional references. Additional exam requirements/recommendations for international students: Required—TOEFL (minimum score 600 paper-based). Electronic applications accepted.

Thompson Rivers University, Program in Education, Kamloops, BC V2C 0C8, Canada. Offers M Ed. *Program availability:* Part-time. *Entrance requirements:* For master's, 2 letters of reference, minimum GPA of 3.0 in final 2 years of undergraduate degree.

Tiffin University, Program in Education, Tiffin, OH 44883-2161. Offers educational technology management (M Ed); higher education administration (M Ed). *Program availability:* Part-time, evening/weekend, online only, 100% online, blended/hybrid learning. *Students:* 99 part-time (75 women); includes 26 minority (20 Black or African American, non-Hispanic/Latino; 1 Asian, non-Hispanic/Latino; 4 Hispanic/Latino; 1 Two or more races, non-Hispanic/Latino). Average age 32. 31 applicants, 90% accepted, 24 enrolled. In 2016, 45 master's awarded. *Entrance requirements:* Additional exam requirements/recommendations for international students: Required—TOEFL. *Application deadline:* Applications are processed on a rolling basis. Electronic applications accepted. *Expenses:* Contact institution. *Financial support:* Unspecified assistantships available. *Application contact:* Nikki Hintze, Director of Graduate Admissions and Student Services, 800-968-6446 Ext. 3445, Fax: 419-443-5002, E-mail: hintzenm@tiffin.edu.

Touro College, Graduate School of Education, New York, NY 10010. Offers education and special education (MS); education biology (MS); instructional technology (MS); mathematics education (MS); school leadership (MS); teaching English to speakers of other languages (MS); teaching literacy (MS). *Accreditation:* TEAC. *Program availability:* Part-time, evening/weekend, online learning. *Faculty:* 52 full-time (34 women), 199 part-time/adjunct (136 women). *Students:* 578 full-time (483 women), 1,932 part-time (1,626 women); includes 749 minority (318 Black or African American, non-Hispanic/Latino; 5 American Indian or Alaska Native, non-Hispanic/Latino; 108 Asian, non-Hispanic/Latino; 288 Hispanic/Latino; 2 Native Hawaiian or other Pacific Islander, non-Hispanic/Latino; 28 Two or more races, non-Hispanic/Latino), 17 international. Average age 32. 1,422 applicants, 50% accepted, 675 enrolled. In 2016, 6 master's awarded. *Entrance requirements:* Additional exam requirements/recommendations for international students: Required—TOEFL (minimum score 83 iBT), IELTS (minimum score 6.5). *Application deadline:* For fall admission, 8/26 for domestic students, 7/15 for international students; for spring admission, 12/31 for domestic students, 12/15 for international students. Applications are processed on a rolling basis. Application fee: $50. *Financial support:* Federal Work-Study available. Financial award applicants required to submit FAFSA. *Faculty research:* Equity assistance, language development, scholarly communications, Latin American studies and cultural sensitivity, behavior management techniques and strategies in special education. *Unit head:* Dr. Arnold Spinner, Dean, 212-463-0400 Ext. 5561, Fax: 212-462-4889, E-mail: aspinner@touro.edu. *Application contact:* Luna Feliciano, Admissions, 212-463-0400.

Touro University California, Graduate Programs, Vallejo, CA 94592. Offers education (MA); medical health sciences (MS); osteopathic medicine (DO); pharmacy (Pharm D); public health (MPH). *Accreditation:* AOsA; ARC-PA. *Program availability:* Part-time, evening/weekend. *Degree requirements:* For master's, comprehensive exam, thesis; for doctorate, comprehensive exam. *Entrance requirements:* For doctorate, BS/BA. Electronic applications accepted. *Faculty research:* Cancer, heart disease.

Towson University, Program in Teaching, Towson, MD 21252-0001. Offers MAT. *Students:* 93 full-time (67 women), 75 part-time (53 women); includes 25 minority (10 Black or African American, non-Hispanic/Latino; 1 American Indian or Alaska Native, non-Hispanic/Latino; 8 Asian, non-Hispanic/Latino; 3 Hispanic/Latino; 3 Two or more races, non-Hispanic/Latino), 2 international. *Entrance requirements:* For master's, ACT, GRE, PRAXIS I or SAT, 2 letters of reference, resume, minimum GPA of 3.0, essay. *Application deadline:* For fall admission, 6/15 for domestic and international students; for spring admission, 10/15 for domestic and international students. Applications are processed on a rolling basis. Application fee: $45. Electronic applications accepted. *Expenses:* Tuition, state resident: full-time $7580; part-time $379 per unit. Tuition, nonresident: full-time $15,700; part-time $785 per unit. *Required fees:* $2480. *Financial support:* Application deadline: 4/1. *Unit head:* Dr. Marie Heath, Graduate Program Director, 410-704-4935, E-mail: mheath@towson.edu. *Application contact:* Coverley Beidleman, Assistant Director of Graduate Admissions, 410-704-2113, Fax: 410-704-3030, E-mail: grads@towson.edu.
Website: http://www.towson.edu/coe/departments/teaching/index.html

Trevecca Nazarene University, Graduate Education Program, Nashville, TN 37210-2877. Offers accountability and instructional leadership (Ed S); curriculum and instruction for Christian school educators (M Ed); curriculum and instruction K-12 (M Ed); educational leadership (M Ed); English second language (M Ed); library and information science (MLI Sc); special education: visual impairments (M Ed); teaching (MAT), including teaching 6-12, teaching K-5. *Accreditation:* NCATE. *Program availability:* Part-time, evening/weekend, online learning. *Faculty:* 5 full-time (3 women), 18 part-time/adjunct (12 women). *Students:* 80 full-time (64 women), 16 part-time (13 women); includes 19 minority (17 Black or African American, non-Hispanic/Latino; 2 Hispanic/Latino). Average age 35. In 2016, 68 master's, 7 other advanced degrees awarded. *Degree requirements:* For master's, comprehensive exam, exit assessment/e-portfolio. *Entrance requirements:* For master's, GRE (minimum score of 290) or MAT (minimum score of 378); PRAXIS (for MAT), minimum GPA of 3.0, official transcript from regionally-accredited institution, at least 3 years' successful teaching experience (for M Ed in educational leadership major). Additional exam requirements/recommendations for international students: Required—TOEFL (minimum score 550 paper-based). *Application deadline:* Applications are processed on a rolling basis. Electronic applications accepted. *Expenses:* Contact institution. *Financial support:* Applicants required to submit FAFSA. *Unit head:* Dr. Suzie Harris, Dean, School of Education/Director of Graduate Education Programs, 615-248-1201, Fax: 615-248-1597, E-mail: admissions_ged@trevecca.edu. *Application contact:* 844-TNU-GRAD, E-mail: sgcsadmissions@trevecca.edu.
Website: http://www.trevecca.edu/soe

Trident University International, College of Education, Cypress, CA 90630. Offers MA Ed, PhD. *Program availability:* Part-time, evening/weekend, online learning. *Degree requirements:* For doctorate, comprehensive exam, thesis/dissertation, defense of dissertation. *Entrance requirements:* For master's, minimum GPA of 2.5 (students with GPA 3.0 or greater may transfer up to 30% of graduate level credits); for doctorate, minimum GPA of 3.4, curriculum vitae, course work in research methods or statistics. Additional exam requirements/recommendations for international students: Required—TOEFL (minimum score 525 paper-based). Electronic applications accepted.

Trinity International University, Trinity Graduate School, Deerfield, IL 60015-1284. Offers athletic training (MA); bioethics (MA); counseling psychology (MA); diverse learning (M Ed); leadership (MA); teaching (MA). *Program availability:* Part-time, evening/weekend, online learning. *Degree requirements:* For master's, comprehensive exam. *Entrance requirements:* For master's, GRE General Test or MAT, minimum undergraduate GPA of 3.0. Additional exam requirements/recommendations for international students: Required—TOEFL (minimum score 580 paper-based), TWE (minimum score 4). *Application deadline:* For fall admission, 8/1 priority date for domestic students, 5/1 for international students; for spring admission, 12/1 priority date for domestic students, 12/1 for international students. Applications are processed on a rolling basis. Application fee: $25. Electronic applications accepted. *Expenses: Tuition:* Full-time $19,898. *Required fees:* $200. *Financial support:* Career-related internships or fieldwork, Federal Work-Study, institutionally sponsored loans, and tuition waivers (partial) available. Support available to part-time students. Financial award application deadline: 4/1; financial award applicants required to submit FAFSA. *Unit head:* Dr. Thomas Cornman, Dean, 847-317-7001, Fax: 847-317-4786. *Application contact:* Blaise Brankatelli, Director of Graduate Admissions, 847-317-8000, Fax: 847-317-8097, E-mail: gradadmissions@tiu.edu.
Website: https://graduate.tiu.edu/

Trinity University, Department of Education, San Antonio, TX 78212-7200. Offers school leadership (M Ed); school psychology (MA); teaching (MAT). *Accreditation:* NCATE. *Program availability:* Part-time, evening/weekend. *Expenses: Tuition:* Full-time $38,974. *Required fees:* $586.

Trinity Washington University, School of Education, Washington, DC 20017-1094. Offers clinical mental health counseling (MA); early childhood education (MAT);

educating for change (M Ed); educational administration (MSA); elementary education (MAT); reading (M Ed); school counseling (MA); secondary education (MAT), including English, social studies; special education (MAT). *Accreditation:* NCATE. *Program availability:* Part-time, evening/weekend. *Degree requirements:* For master's, thesis (for some programs), capstone project(s). *Entrance requirements:* For master's, PRAXIS I, minimum GPA of 2.8. Additional exam requirements/recommendations for international students: Required—TOEFL (minimum score 550 paper-based). *Faculty research:* Technology, literacy, special education, organizations, inclusion models.

Troy University, Graduate School, College of Education, Troy, AL 36082. Offers MS, MS Ed, Ed S. *Accreditation:* NCATE. *Program availability:* Part-time, evening/weekend. *Faculty:* 89 full-time (43 women), 46 part-time/adjunct (30 women). *Students:* 165 full-time (136 women), 372 part-time (298 women); includes 252 minority (221 Black or African American, non-Hispanic/Latino; 3 American Indian or Alaska Native, non-Hispanic/Latino; 2 Asian, non-Hispanic/Latino; 11 Hispanic/Latino; 15 Two or more races, non-Hispanic/Latino). Average age 34. 491 applicants, 198% accepted, 136 enrolled. In 2016, 474 master's, 11 other advanced degrees awarded. *Degree requirements:* For master's, comprehensive exam, thesis. *Entrance requirements:* For master's, GRE (minimum score of 850 on old exam or 290 on new exam), GMAT (minimum score of 380), or MAT (minimum score of 385), bachelor's degree; minimum undergraduate GPA of 2.5 or 3.0 on last 30 semester hours, letter of recommendation; for Ed S, GRE (minimum score of 850 on old exam or 290 on new exam), GMAT (minimum score of 380), or MAT (minimum score of 385), Alabama Class A certificate or equivalent, minimum graduate GPA of 3.0. Additional exam requirements/recommendations for international students: Required—TOEFL (minimum score 523 paper-based; 70 iBT), IELTS (minimum score 6). *Application deadline:* For fall admission, 1/1 for domestic students, 6/1 for international students; for spring admission, 10/15 for international students. Applications are processed on a rolling basis. Application fee: $50. Electronic applications accepted. *Expenses:* Tuition, state resident: full-time $7146; part-time $397 per credit hour. Tuition, nonresident: full-time $14,292; part-time $794 per credit hour. *Required fees:* $802; $50 per semester. Tuition and fees vary according to campus/location and program. *Financial support:* Fellowships, career-related internships or fieldwork, and scholarships/grants available. Support available to part-time students. Financial award applicants required to submit FAFSA. *Unit head:* Dr. Royce Dasinger, Dean, 334-670-3365, Fax: 334-670-3474, E-mail: rdasinger@troy.edu. *Application contact:* Jessica A. Kimbro, Director of Graduate Admissions, 334-670-3178, E-mail: jacord@troy.edu.

Truman State University, Graduate School, School of Health Sciences and Education, Program in Education, Kirksville, MO 63501-4221. Offers MAE. *Accreditation:* NCATE. *Students:* 252 full-time (214 women), 5 part-time (3 women); includes 6 minority (2 Asian, non-Hispanic/Latino; 1 Hispanic/Latino; 3 Two or more races, non-Hispanic/Latino). Average age 23. 36 applicants, 83% accepted, 29 enrolled. In 2016, 217 master's awarded. *Degree requirements:* For master's, comprehensive exam, thesis or alternative. *Entrance requirements:* For master's, GRE, minimum GPA of 2.75. Additional exam requirements/recommendations for international students: Required—TOEFL (minimum score 550 paper-based). *Application deadline:* For fall admission, 2/1 for domestic and international students; for spring admission, 9/1 for domestic and international students; for summer admission, 4/1 for domestic and international students. Application fee: $40. Electronic applications accepted. *Expenses:* Tuition, state resident: full-time $6300; part-time $350 per credit hour. Tuition, nonresident: full-time $10,818; part-time $601 per credit hour. Tuition and fees vary according to course load and program. *Financial support:* Fellowships, research assistantships with tuition reimbursements, teaching assistantships with tuition reimbursements, and career-related internships or fieldwork available. *Unit head:* Dr. Pete Kelly, Director, 660-785-4386, E-mail: pkelly@truman.edu. *Application contact:* Stephanie Rudolph, Graduate Office Secretary, 660-785-4109, Fax: 660-785-7460, E-mail: sdunn@truman.edu.

Tufts University, Graduate School of Arts and Sciences, Department of Education, Medford, MA 02155. Offers art education (MAT); education (MA, MAT, MS, PhD), including educational studies (MA), elementary education (MAT), middle and secondary education (MAT), museum education (MA), secondary education (MA), STEM education (MS, PhD); school psychology (MA, Ed S). *Program availability:* Part-time. *Students:* 109 full-time (84 women), 15 part-time (12 women); includes 25 minority (7 Black or African American, non-Hispanic/Latino; 10 Asian, non-Hispanic/Latino; 7 Hispanic/Latino; 1 Two or more races, non-Hispanic/Latino), 7 international. Average age 27. 197 applicants, 57% accepted, 65 enrolled. In 2016, 55 master's, 14 other advanced degrees awarded. *Degree requirements:* For master's, thesis optional; for doctorate, thesis/dissertation. *Entrance requirements:* For master's and doctorate, GRE General Test. Additional exam requirements/recommendations for international students: Required—TOEFL (minimum score 550 paper-based; 80 iBT), IELTS (minimum score 6.5). *Application deadline:* For fall admission, 1/2 for domestic and international students; for spring admission, 10/15 for domestic and international students. Applications are processed on a rolling basis. Application fee: $85. Electronic applications accepted. *Expenses:* Contact institution. *Financial support:* Teaching assistantships, Federal Work-Study, scholarships/grants, and tuition waivers (full and partial) available. Support available to part-time students. Financial award application deadline: 1/2. *Unit head:* Dr. Sabina Vaught, Graduate Program Director. *Application contact:* Office of Graduate Admissions, 617-627-3395, E-mail: gradadmissions@tufts.edu.
Website: http://www.ase.tufts.edu/education/

Tusculum College, Graduate and Professional Studies, Program in Teaching, Greeneville, TN 37743-9997. Offers MAT. *Program availability:* Evening/weekend. *Entrance requirements:* For master's, PRAXIS I, GRE, MAT, minimum GPA of 3.0. *Expenses:* *Tuition:* Full-time $7497; part-time $357 per credit hour. *Unit head:* Dr. Tricia Hunsader, Dean, School of Education, 423-636-7300 Ext. 5693, E-mail: thunsader@tusculum.edu. *Application contact:* Lindsey Seal, Director of Enrollment, 423-636-7300 Ext. 5006, E-mail: lseal@tusculum.edu.
Website: http://home.tusculum.edu/gps/graduate-degrees/master-arts-teaching/

Union College, Graduate Programs, Department of Education, Barbourville, KY 40906-1499. Offers elementary education (MA); health and physical education (MA); middle grades (MA); music education (MA); principalship (MA); reading specialist (MA); secondary education (MA); special education (MA). *Degree requirements:* For master's, thesis optional. *Entrance requirements:* For master's, GRE General Test, NTE.

Union Institute & University, PhD Program in Interdisciplinary Studies, Cincinnati, OH 45206-1925. Offers education studies (PhD), including Martin Luther King studies. Program requires participation in brief on-campus residencies twice each year (January and July). *Program availability:* Part-time, online only, blended/hybrid learning. *Faculty:* 9 full-time (5 women), 16 part-time/adjunct (7 women). *Students:* 122 full-time (76 women), 19 part-time (14 women); includes 76 minority (58 Black or African American, non-Hispanic/Latino; 4 American Indian or Alaska Native, non-Hispanic/Latino; 2 Asian, non-Hispanic/Latino; 8 Hispanic/Latino; 3 Native Hawaiian or other Pacific Islander, non-Hispanic/Latino; 1 Two or more races, non-Hispanic/Latino). Average age 46. In 2016, 22 doctorates awarded. *Degree requirements:* For doctorate, comprehensive exam, thesis/dissertation. *Entrance requirements:* For doctorate, master's degree, three letters of recommendation, statement of purpose. Additional exam requirements/recommendations for international students: Required—TOEFL. *Application deadline:* Applications are processed on a rolling basis. Application fee: $50. Electronic applications accepted. *Expenses:* Contact institution. *Financial support:* Federal Work-Study and scholarships/grants available. Financial award application deadline: 5/1; financial award applicants required to submit FAFSA. *Faculty research:* Social responsibility, ethical leadership, Martin Luther King studies. *Unit head:* Dr. Michael Raffanti, Dean, 513-861-6400, E-mail: michael.raffanti@myunion.edu. *Application contact:* Admissions Counselor, 800-486-3116.
Website: https://myunion.edu/academics/doctoral/

Union University, School of Education, Jackson, TN 38305-3697. Offers education (M Ed, MA Ed); education administration generalist (Ed S); educational leadership (Ed D); educational supervision (Ed S); higher education (Ed D). M Ed also available at Germantown campus. *Accreditation:* NCATE. *Program availability:* Part-time, evening/weekend, online learning. *Degree requirements:* For master's, thesis (for some programs), capstone research course (for MA Ed); performance exhibition (for M Ed); for doctorate, comprehensive exam, thesis/dissertation; for Ed S, thesis or alternative. *Entrance requirements:* For master's, MAT, PRAXIS II or GRE, minimum GPA of 3.0, teaching license (for M Ed only), writing sample; for doctorate, GRE, minimum graduate GPA of 3.2, writing sample; for Ed S, PRAXIS II, minimum graduate GPA of 3.2, writing sample. Additional exam requirements/recommendations for international students: Required—TOEFL (minimum score 560 paper-based; 80 iBT). Electronic applications accepted. *Expenses:* Contact institution. *Faculty research:* Mathematics education, brain compatible learning, transformational teaching, cognitive strategy development, instructional technology.

Universidad Autonoma de Guadalajara, Graduate Programs, Guadalajara, Mexico. Offers administrative law and justice (LL M); advertising and corporate communications (MA); architecture (M Arch); business (MBA); computational science (MCC); education (Ed M, Ed D); English-Spanish translation (MA); entrepreneurship and management (MBA); integrated management of digital animation (MA); international business (MIB); international corporate law (LL M); internet technologies (MS); manufacturing systems (MMS); occupational health (MS); philosophy (MA, PhD); power electronics (MS); quality systems (MQS); renewable energy (MS); social evaluation of projects (MBA); strategic market research (MBA); tax law (MA); teaching mathematics (MA).

Universidad de las Americas, A.C., Program in Education, Mexico City, Mexico. Offers M Ed. *Entrance requirements:* For master's, 2 years of professional experience; undergraduate degree in early childhood education, human communication, psychology, science of education, special education or related fields.

Universidad de las Américas Puebla, Division of Graduate Studies, School of Social Sciences, Program in Education, Puebla, Mexico. Offers MA. *Program availability:* Part-time, evening/weekend. *Degree requirements:* For master's, one foreign language, thesis. *Faculty research:* Curriculum development, curriculum evaluation, instructional technology, critical thinking.

Universidad del Turabo, Graduate Programs, Programs in Education, Gurabo, PR 00778-3030. Offers M Ed, MPHE, D Ed. *Program availability:* Part-time, evening/weekend. *Students:* 231 full-time (168 women), 345 part-time (246 women); all minorities (all Hispanic/Latino). Average age 38. 393 applicants, 63% accepted, 205 enrolled. In 2016, 132 master's, 17 doctorates awarded. *Degree requirements:* For master's, thesis (for some programs). *Entrance requirements:* For master's, GRE, EXADEP, GMAT, interview, official transcript, essay, recommendation letter; for doctorate, GRE, EXADEP, GMAT, official transcript, recommendation letters, essay, curriculum vitae, interview. *Application deadline:* Applications are processed on a rolling basis. Application fee: $25. Electronic applications accepted. *Financial support:* Institutionally sponsored loans available. Financial award applicants required to submit FAFSA. *Unit head:* Israel Rodriguez, 787-743-7979 Ext. 4126. *Application contact:* Diriee Rodríguez, Admission's Director, 787-743-7979 Ext. 4453, E-mail: admisiones-ut@suagm.edu.
Website: http://ut.suagm.edu/es/educacion

Universidad Metropolitana, School of Education, San Juan, PR 00928-1150. Offers administration and supervision (M Ed); curriculum and teaching (M Ed); educational administration and supervision (M Ed); managing recreation and sports services (M Ed); pre-school centers administration (M Ed); special education (M Ed); teaching of physical education (M Ed), including teaching of adult physical education, teaching of elementary physical education, teaching of secondary physical education. *Program availability:* Part-time, evening/weekend. *Degree requirements:* For master's, thesis or alternative. Electronic applications accepted.

Université de Moncton, Faculty of Education, Graduate Studies in Education, Moncton, NB E1A 3E9, Canada. Offers educational psychology (M Ed, MA Ed); guidance (M Ed, MA Ed); school administration (M Ed, MA Ed); teaching (M Ed, MA Ed). *Program availability:* Part-time. *Degree requirements:* For master's, proficiency in English and French. *Entrance requirements:* For master's, minimum GPA of 3.0. *Faculty research:* Guidance, ethnolinguistic vitality, children's rights, ecological education, entrepreneurship.

Université de Montréal, Faculty of Education, Montréal, QC H3C 3J7, Canada. Offers M Ed, MA, PhD, DESS. *Program availability:* Part-time, evening/weekend. *Degree requirements:* For doctorate, thesis/dissertation, general exam. Electronic applications accepted.

Université de Saint-Boniface, Department of Education, Saint-Boniface, MB R2H 0H7, Canada. Offers M Ed.

Université de Sherbrooke, Faculty of Education, Sherbrooke, QC J1K 2R1, Canada. Offers M Ed, MA, Diploma. *Program availability:* Part-time, evening/weekend. *Degree requirements:* For master's, thesis. *Faculty research:* Career education, teaching, professional instruction.

Université du Québec à Chicoutimi, Graduate Programs, Program in Education, Chicoutimi, QC G7H 2B1, Canada. Offers M Ed, MA, PhD. PhD offered jointly with Université du Québec à Rimouski, Université du Québec à Trois-Rivières, Université du Québec èn Outaouais, Université du Québec en Abitibi-Témiscamingue. and Université du Québec à Montréal. *Program availability:* Part-time. *Degree requirements:* For doctorate, thesis/dissertation. *Entrance requirements:* For master's, appropriate bachelor's degree, proficiency in French; for doctorate, appropriate master's degree, proficiency in French.

Université du Québec à Montréal, Graduate Programs, Program in Education, Montréal, QC H3C 3P8, Canada. Offers education (M Ed, MA, PhD); education of the environmental sciences (Diploma). PhD offered jointly with Université du Québec à Chicoutimi, Université du Québec à Rimouski, Université du Québec à Trois-Rivières, Université du Québec en Outaouais, and Université du Québec en Abitibi-Témiscamingue. *Program availability:* Part-time. *Degree requirements:* For master's, thesis (for some programs); for doctorate, thesis/dissertation. *Entrance requirements:* For master's and Diploma, appropriate bachelor's degree or equivalent, proficiency in French; for doctorate, appropriate master's degree or equivalent, proficiency in French.

Université du Québec à Rimouski, Graduate Programs, Program in Education, Rimouski, QC G5L 3A1, Canada. Offers M Ed, MA, PhD, Diploma. M Ed and MA offered jointly with Université du Québec en Outaouais and Université du Québec en Abitibi-Témiscamingue; PhD with Université du Québec à Chicoutimi, Université du Québec à Trois-Rivières, Université du Québec en Outaouais, and Université du Québec en Abitibi-Témiscamingue. *Program availability:* Part-time. *Degree requirements:* For master's, thesis optional; for doctorate, thesis/dissertation. *Entrance requirements:* For master's, appropriate bachelor's degree, proficiency in French; for doctorate, appropriate master's degree, proficiency in French.

Université du Québec à Trois-Rivières, Graduate Programs, Program in Education, Trois-Rivières, QC G9A 5H7, Canada. Offers M Ed, PhD. *Program availability:* Part-time. *Degree requirements:* For master's, research report. *Entrance requirements:* For master's, appropriate bachelor's degree, proficiency in French.

Université du Québec en Abitibi-Témiscamingue, Graduate Programs, Program in Education, Rouyn-Noranda, QC J9X 5E4, Canada. Offers M Ed, MA, PhD, DESS. M Ed and MA offered jointly with Université du Québec à Rimouski and Université du Québec en Outaouais; PhD with Université du Québec à Chicoutimi, Université du Québec à Rimouski, Université du Québec à Trois-Rivières, Université du Québec en Outaouais, and Université du Québec à Montréal. *Program availability:* Part-time. *Degree requirements:* For master's, thesis optional; for doctorate, thesis/dissertation. *Entrance requirements:* For master's, appropriate bachelor's degree, proficiency in French; for doctorate, appropriate master's degree, proficiency in French.

Université du Québec en Outaouais, Graduate Programs, Program in Education, Gatineau, QC J8X 3X7, Canada. Offers M Ed, MA, PhD, DESS, Diploma. *Program availability:* Part-time. *Degree requirements:* For master's, thesis optional; for doctorate, thesis/dissertation. *Entrance requirements:* For master's, appropriate bachelor's degree, proficiency in French; for doctorate, appropriate master's degree, proficiency in French.

Université Laval, Faculty of Education, Québec, QC G1K 7P4, Canada. Offers MA, PhD, Diploma. *Program availability:* Part-time. *Degree requirements:* For doctorate, comprehensive exam, thesis/dissertation. Electronic applications accepted.

Université Sainte-Anne, Program in Education, Church Point, NS B0W 1M0, Canada. Offers M Ed. *Program availability:* Part-time.

University at Albany, State University of New York, School of Education, Albany, NY 12222-0001. Offers MS, PhD, Psy D, CAS. *Accreditation:* TEAC. *Program availability:* Part-time, evening/weekend, 100% online, blended/hybrid learning. *Faculty:* 38 full-time (20 women), 46 part-time/adjunct (36 women). *Students:* 327 full-time (247 women), 577 part-time (439 women); includes 125 minority (44 Black or African American, non-Hispanic/Latino; 1 American Indian or Alaska Native, non-Hispanic/Latino; 23 Asian, non-Hispanic/Latino; 45 Hispanic/Latino; 12 Two or more races, non-Hispanic/Latino), 66 international. Average age 31. 457 applicants, 63% accepted, 325 enrolled. In 2016, 283 master's, 35 doctorates, 36 other advanced degrees awarded. *Degree requirements:* For doctorate, thesis/dissertation. *Entrance requirements:* For doctorate, GRE General Test. Additional exam requirements/recommendations for international students: Required—TOEFL (minimum score 550 paper-based). Application fee: $75. Electronic applications accepted. *Expenses:* Tuition, state resident: full-time $10,870; part-time $453 per credit hour. Tuition, nonresident: full-time $22,210; part-time $925 per credit hour. *International tuition:* $21,550 full-time. *Required fees:* $1864; $96 per credit hour. *Financial support:* Fellowships, career-related internships or fieldwork, and Federal Work-Study available. *Total annual research expenditures:* $3.3 million. *Unit head:* Robert Bangert-Drowns, Dean, 518-442-4988, E-mail: rbangert-drowns@albany.edu.
Website: http://www.albany.edu/education/

University at Buffalo, the State University of New York, Graduate School, Graduate School of Education, Buffalo, NY 14260. Offers Ed M, MA, MS, Ed D, PhD, Advanced Certificate, Certificate, Certificate/Ed M. *Accreditation:* TEAC. *Program availability:* Part-time, 100% online. *Faculty:* 80 full-time (47 women), 136 part-time/adjunct (106 women). *Students:* 470 full-time (362 women), 718 part-time (517 women); includes 116 minority (76 Black or African American, non-Hispanic/Latino; 7 American Indian or Alaska Native, non-Hispanic/Latino; 26 Asian, non-Hispanic/Latino; 7 Hispanic/Latino), 113 international. Average age 33. 894 applicants, 74% accepted, 417 enrolled. In 2016, 339 master's, 45 doctorates, 101 other advanced degrees awarded. Terminal master's awarded for partial completion of doctoral program. *Degree requirements:* For master's, comprehensive exam; for doctorate, thesis/dissertation. *Entrance requirements:* For master's, GRE General Test; for doctorate, GRE, MAT. Additional exam requirements/recommendations for international students: Required—TOEFL (minimum score 79 iBT), PTE. *Application deadline:* Applications are processed on a rolling basis. Application fee: $50. Electronic applications accepted. *Financial support:* In 2016–17, 96 fellowships (averaging $5,091 per year), 110 research assistantships with tuition reimbursements (averaging $10,240 per year) were awarded; teaching assistantships, Federal Work-Study, institutionally sponsored loans, scholarships/grants, tuition waivers (full and partial), and unspecified assistantships also available. Support available to part-time students. Financial award applicants required to submit FAFSA. *Faculty research:* Early childhood mathematics education, finance and management of higher education, curricular policy, practice and reform, student behavior in small classes, psychological measurement and assessment. *Total annual research expenditures:* $3.5 million. *Unit head:* Dr. Jaekyung Lee, Dean, 716-645-6640, Fax: 716-645-2479, E-mail: gse-info@buffalo.edu. *Application contact:* Dr. Radhika Suresh, Assistant Dean for Enrollment Management, 716-645-2110, Fax: 716-645-7937, E-mail: gse-info@buffalo.edu.
Website: http://www.gse.buffalo.edu/

The University of Akron, Graduate School, College of Education, Akron, OH 44325. Offers MA, MS. *Accreditation:* NCATE. *Program availability:* Part-time. *Faculty:* 25 full-time (18 women), 60 part-time/adjunct (41 women). *Students:* 84 full-time (51 women), 192 part-time (149 women); includes 41 minority (27 Black or African American, non-Hispanic/Latino; 1 American Indian or Alaska Native, non-Hispanic/Latino; 2 Asian, non-Hispanic/Latino; 3 Hispanic/Latino; 8 Two or more races, non-Hispanic/Latino), 22 international. Average age 33. 98 applicants, 79% accepted, 71 enrolled. In 2016, 163 master's awarded. Terminal master's awarded for partial completion of doctoral program. *Degree requirements:* For master's, comprehensive exam, thesis optional. *Entrance requirements:* For master's, GRE, letters of recommendation, resume, statement of purpose. Additional exam requirements/recommendations for international students: Required—TOEFL (minimum score 550 paper-based; 79 iBT), IELTS (minimum score 6.5). *Application deadline:* Applications are processed on a rolling basis. Application fee: $45 ($70 for international students). Electronic applications accepted. *Expenses:* Tuition, state resident: full-time $8618; part-time $359 per credit hour. Tuition, nonresident: full-time $17,149; part-time $715 per credit hour. *Required fees:* $1652. *Financial support:* In 2016–17, 6 teaching assistantships with full tuition reimbursements were awarded; instructional support assistantships, administrative assistantships also available. *Faculty research:* History, philosophy of education, ethnographic research in education, case study methodology in education, multiple linear regression. *Total annual research expenditures:* $288,213. *Unit head:* Dr. Susan Clark, Interim Dean, 330-972-7780, E-mail: sclark1@uakron.edu. *Application contact:* Kelly Chaff, College Program Specialist, 330-972-7028, E-mail: klchaff@uakron.edu.
Website: http://www.uakron.edu/education/

The University of Alabama at Birmingham, School of Education, Birmingham, AL 35294. Offers MA, MA Ed, Ed D, PhD, Ed S. *Accreditation:* NCATE. *Program availability:* Part-time, evening/weekend, online learning. *Degree requirements:* For master's, thesis optional; for doctorate, thesis/dissertation; for Ed S, comprehensive exam, thesis optional. *Entrance requirements:* For master's, GRE General Test, MAT, or NTE, minimum GPA of 3.0; for doctorate, GRE General Test, MAT, minimum GPA of 3.25; for Ed S, GRE General Test, MAT, minimum GPA of 3.0, master's degree. Electronic applications accepted. Full-time tuition and fees vary according to course load and program.

The University of Alabama in Huntsville, School of Graduate Studies, College of Education, Huntsville, AL 35899. Offers autism spectrum disorders (M Ed, Graduate Certificate); biology (MAT); chemistry (MAT); differentiated instruction in elementary education (M Ed); English language arts (MAT); English speakers of other languages (M Ed, MAT); history (MAT); mathematics (MAT); physics (MAT); reading education (M Ed); secondary education (M Ed). *Expenses:* Tuition, state resident: full-time $9834; part-time $600 per credit hour. Tuition, nonresident: full-time $21,830; part-time $1325 per credit hour.

University of Alaska Anchorage, College of Education, Anchorage, AK 99508. Offers M Ed, Certificate. *Accreditation:* NCATE. *Program availability:* Part-time. *Degree requirements:* For master's, comprehensive exam, thesis or alternative, portfolio. *Entrance requirements:* For master's, interview, minimum GPA of 3.0. Additional exam requirements/recommendations for international students: Required—TOEFL (minimum score 550 paper-based).

University of Alaska Fairbanks, School of Education, Fairbanks, AK 99775. Offers M Ed, Graduate Certificate. *Accreditation:* NCATE. *Program availability:* 100% online, blended/hybrid learning. *Faculty:* 16 full-time (11 women), 2 part-time/adjunct (1 woman). *Students:* 46 full-time (31 women), 127 part-time (105 women); includes 22 minority (8 American Indian or Alaska Native, non-Hispanic/Latino; 5 Hispanic/Latino; 9 Two or more races, non-Hispanic/Latino), 3 international. Average age 37. 74 applicants, 58% accepted, 39 enrolled. In 2016, 41 master's, 21 other advanced degrees awarded. *Degree requirements:* For master's, comprehensive exam, oral defense of project or thesis, student teaching. *Entrance requirements:* For master's and Graduate Certificate, bachelor's degree from accredited institution with minimum cumulative undergraduate and major GPA of 3.0. Additional exam requirements/recommendations for international students: Required—TOEFL (minimum score 550 paper-based; 79 iBT), IELTS (minimum score 6.5). *Application deadline:* For fall admission, 2/15 for domestic and international students; for spring admission, 10/1 for domestic students, 8/1 for international students. Application fee: $60. Electronic applications accepted. *Expenses:* Tuition, state resident: full-time $7992; part-time $444 per credit. Tuition, nonresident: full-time $16,326; part-time $907 per credit. *Required fees:* $39 per credit. $322 per semester. Tuition and fees vary according to course level, course load, campus/location, program and reciprocity agreements. *Financial support:* In 2016–17, 1 research assistantship with full tuition reimbursement (averaging $5,251 per year), 1 teaching assistantship with full tuition reimbursement (averaging $4,247 per year) were awarded; fellowships with full tuition reimbursements, career-related internships or fieldwork, Federal Work-Study, scholarships/grants, health care benefits, and unspecified assistantships also available. Support available to part-time students. Financial award application deadline: 6/1; financial award applicants required to submit FAFSA. *Faculty research:* Native ways of knowing, classroom research in methods of literacy instruction, multiple intelligence theory, geometry concept development, mathematics and science curriculum development. *Total annual research expenditures:* $203,000. *Unit head:* Steve Atwater, Interim Dean, 907-474-7341, Fax: 907-474-5451, E-mail: uaf-soe-school@alaska.edu. *Application contact:* Mary Kreta, Director of Admissions, 907-474-7500, Fax: 907-474-7097, E-mail: admissions@uaf.edu.
Website: http://www.uaf.edu/soe/

University of Alaska Southeast, Graduate Programs, Program in Education, Juneau, AK 99801. Offers educational leadership (M Ed); elementary education (MAT); learning design and technology (M Ed); mathematics education (M Ed); reading specialist (M Ed); secondary education (MAT); special education (M Ed, MAT). *Accreditation:* NCATE. *Program availability:* Part-time, evening/weekend, online learning. *Degree requirements:* For master's, comprehensive exam or project, portfolio. *Entrance requirements:* For master's, PRAXIS, minimum GPA of 3.0, writing sample, letters of recommendation. *Application deadline:* For fall admission, 3/8 for domestic students. Applications are processed on a rolling basis. Application fee: $60. Electronic applications accepted. *Expenses:* Tuition, state resident: part-time $466 per credit. Tuition, nonresident: part-time $979 per credit. *Required fees:* $19 per credit. Part-time tuition and fees vary according to course level, campus/location and reciprocity agreements. *Financial support:* Federal Work-Study, scholarships/grants, and tuition waivers (full and partial) available. Support available to part-time students. Financial award applicants required to submit FAFSA. *Faculty research:* Applied classroom research, culturally responsive practices, action research, teaching effectiveness. *Unit head:* Dr. Larry Harris, Dean, 907-796-6551, Fax: 907-796-6550, E-mail: larry.harris@uas.alaska.edu. *Application contact:* Susan A. Stuck, Administrative Assistant, 866-465-6424, Fax: 866-465-5159, E-mail: jnsas@uas.alaska.edu.

The University of Arizona, College of Education, Tucson, AZ 85721. Offers M Ed, MA, MS, Ed D, PhD, Certificate, Ed S. *Program availability:* Part-time, online learning. Terminal master's awarded for partial completion of doctoral program. *Degree requirements:* For master's, comprehensive exam, thesis (for some programs); for doctorate, comprehensive exam, thesis/dissertation. *Entrance requirements:* For doctorate, GRE. Additional exam requirements/recommendations for international students: Required—TOEFL (minimum score 550 paper-based; 79 iBT). Electronic applications accepted. *Faculty research:* Teacher effectiveness, pupil achievement, learning skills, program evaluation, instructional method effects.

University of Arkansas, Graduate School, College of Education and Health Professions, Fayetteville, AR 72701. Offers M Ed, MAT, MAT, MS, MSN, Ed D, PhD, Ed S. *Accreditation:* NCATE. In 2016, 399 master's, 43 doctorates awarded. *Degree requirements:* For doctorate, thesis/dissertation. *Application deadline:* For fall admission, 4/1 for international students; for spring admission, 10/1 for international students. Applications are processed on a rolling basis. Application fee: $40 ($50 for international students). Electronic applications accepted. *Financial support:* In 2016–17, 110 research assistantships, 15 teaching assistantships were awarded; fellowships with tuition reimbursements, career-related internships or fieldwork, and Federal Work-Study also available. Support available to part-time students. Financial award application deadline: 4/1; financial award applicants required to submit FAFSA. *Unit head:* Dr. Michael T. Miller, Dean, 479-575-3208, Fax: 479-575-3119, E-mail: mtmille@uark.edu. *Application contact:* Graduate Admissions, 479-575-6246, Fax: 479-575-5908, E-mail: gradinfo@uark.edu.
Website: http://coehp.uark.edu/

University of Arkansas at Little Rock, Graduate School, College of Education and Health Professions, Little Rock, AR 72204-1099. Offers M Ed, MA, MS, MSW, Ed D, Ed S, Graduate Certificate. *Accreditation:* CORE; NCATE (one or more programs are accredited). *Program availability:* Part-time, evening/weekend. *Degree requirements:* For doctorate, comprehensive exam, oral defense of dissertation, residency; for other advanced degree, comprehensive exam. *Entrance requirements:* For master's, minimum GPA of 2.75; for doctorate, GRE General Test or MAT, minimum graduate GPA of 3.0, teaching certificate, work experience; for other advanced degree, GRE General Test or MAT, teaching certificate.

University of Arkansas at Monticello, School of Education, Monticello, AR 71656. Offers education (M Ed, MAT); educational leadership (M Ed). *Accreditation:* NCATE. *Program availability:* Part-time, evening/weekend, online learning. *Degree requirements:* For master's, comprehensive exam. *Entrance requirements:* For master's, minimum GPA of 3.0. Additional exam requirements/recommendations for international students: Required—TOEFL (minimum score 550 paper-based). Electronic applications accepted.

University of Arkansas at Pine Bluff, School of Education, Pine Bluff, AR 71601-2799. Offers elementary education (M Ed); secondary education (M Ed), including English education, mathematics education, science education, social studies education; teaching (MAT). *Accreditation:* NCATE. *Program availability:* Part-time, evening/weekend. *Degree requirements:* For master's, comprehensive exam. *Entrance requirements:* For master's, GRE, minimum GPA of 2.75, NTE or Standard Arkansas Teaching Certificate. Application fee: $25. *Expenses:* Tuition, state resident: full-time $4776. Tuition, nonresident: full-time $10,824. *Required fees:* $1612. Tuition and fees vary according to course load. *Financial support:* Research assistantships with full and partial tuition reimbursements, teaching assistantships with full and partial tuition reimbursements, institutionally sponsored loans, and scholarships/grants available. Support available to part-time students. *Faculty research:* Teacher certification, accreditation, assessment, standards, portfolio development, rehabilitation, technology. *Unit head:* Dr. George Herts, Dean, 870-575-8000, E-mail: johnson_c@uapb.edu.
Website: http://www.uapb.edu/academics/school_of_education.aspx

University of Bridgeport, School of Education, Department of Education, Bridgeport, CT 06604. Offers education (MS); educational management (Ed D, Diploma), including intermediate administrator or supervisor (Diploma), leadership (Ed D); elementary education (MS, Diploma), including early childhood education, elementary education; middle school education (MS); music education (MS); remedial reading and language arts (Diploma); secondary education (MS, Diploma), including computer specialist (Diploma), international education (Diploma), reading specialist, secondary education. *Program availability:* Part-time, evening/weekend. *Degree requirements:* For master's, final exam, final project, or thesis; for doctorate, comprehensive exam, thesis/dissertation; for Diploma, thesis or alternative, final project. *Entrance requirements:* For master's, minimum undergraduate QPA of 2.67; for doctorate, GRE, MAT; for Diploma, GRE General Test or MAT, minimum graduate QPA of 3.0. Additional exam requirements/recommendations for international students: Recommended—TOEFL (minimum score 550 paper-based; 80 iBT), IELTS (minimum score 6.5). Electronic applications accepted. *Expenses:* Contact institution.

The University of British Columbia, Faculty of Education, Vancouver, BC V6T1Z4, Canada. Offers M Ed, M Kin, M Sc, MA, MET, MHPCTL, Ed D, PhD, Diploma. *Program availability:* Part-time, evening/weekend, online learning. Terminal master's awarded for partial completion of doctoral program. *Degree requirements:* For master's, thesis (for some programs); for doctorate, comprehensive exam, thesis/dissertation. *Entrance requirements:* Additional exam requirements/recommendations for international students: Required—TOEFL. Application fee: $102 Canadian dollars ($165 Canadian dollars for international students). Electronic applications accepted. *Expenses:* Contact institution. *Financial support:* In 2016–17, 200 students received support. Fellowships with full and partial tuition reimbursements available, research assistantships with full and partial tuition reimbursements available, teaching assistantships with full and partial tuition reimbursements available, career-related internships or fieldwork, Federal Work-Study, institutionally sponsored loans, scholarships/grants, and unspecified assistantships available. *Faculty research:* Curriculum and pedagogy; school counseling psychology; educational administration; human kinetics; language and literacy education. *Unit head:* Dr. Blye Frank, Dean, 604-822-2221, Fax: 604-822-8971.
Website: http://educ.ubc.ca/

University of California, Berkeley, Graduate Division, School of Education, Berkeley, CA 94720-1500. Offers MA, PhD, MA/Credential, PhD/Credential, PhD/MA. *Students:* 323 full-time (239 women); includes 137 minority (31 Black or African American, non-Hispanic/Latino; 2 American Indian or Alaska Native, non-Hispanic/Latino; 46 Asian, non-Hispanic/Latino; 58 Hispanic/Latino), 34 international. Average age 34. 676 applicants, 91 enrolled. In 2016, 105 master's, 38 doctorates awarded. Terminal master's awarded for partial completion of doctoral program. *Degree requirements:* For master's, exam or thesis; for doctorate, thesis/dissertation, oral qualifying exam (PhD). *Entrance requirements:* For master's and doctorate, GRE General Test, minimum undergraduate GPA of 3.0 during last 2 years, 3 letters of recommendation. *Application deadline:* For fall admission, 12/16 for domestic students. Application fee: $105 ($125 for international students). Electronic applications accepted. *Financial support:* Fellowships, research assistantships, teaching assistantships, career-related internships or fieldwork, institutionally sponsored loans, health care benefits, and unspecified assistantships available. *Faculty research:* Cognition and development; language, literacy and culture. *Unit head:* Prof. Prudence L. Carter, Dean, 510-642-3726, E-mail: gsedean@berkeley.edu. *Application contact:* 510-642-5345, E-mail: gse_info@berkeley.edu.
Website: https://gse.berkeley.edu

University of California, Berkeley, UC Berkeley Extension, Certificate Programs in Education, Berkeley, CA 94720-1500. Offers college admissions and career planning (Certificate); teaching English as a second language (Certificate).

University of California, Davis, Graduate Studies, Graduate Group in Education, Davis, CA 95616. Offers education (MA, Ed D); instructional studies (PhD); psychological studies (PhD); sociocultural studies (PhD). Ed D offered jointly with California State University, Fresno. Terminal master's awarded for partial completion of doctoral program. *Degree requirements:* For master's, comprehensive exam (for some programs), thesis (for some programs); for doctorate, thesis/dissertation. *Entrance requirements:* For master's and doctorate, GRE. Additional exam requirements/recommendations for international students: Required—TOEFL (minimum score 550 paper-based). Electronic applications accepted. *Faculty research:* Language and literacy, mathematics education, science education, teacher development, school psychology.

University of California, Irvine, School of Education, Irvine, CA 92697. Offers educational administration (Ed D); educational administration and leadership (Ed D); elementary and secondary education (MAT). *Program availability:* Part-time, evening/weekend. *Students:* 189 full-time (139 women), 1 part-time (0 women); includes 101 minority (44 Asian, non-Hispanic/Latino; 40 Hispanic/Latino; 1 Native Hawaiian or other Pacific Islander, non-Hispanic/Latino; 16 Two or more races, non-Hispanic/Latino), 16 international. Average age 27. 456 applicants, 54% accepted, 131 enrolled. In 2016, 139 master's, 16 doctorates awarded. *Degree requirements:* For doctorate, thesis/dissertation. *Entrance requirements:* For master's, GRE, minimum GPA of 3.0; for doctorate, GRE General Test, minimum GPA of 3.0. Additional exam requirements/recommendations for international students: Required—TOEFL (minimum score 550 paper-based). *Application deadline:* For fall admission, 1/2 priority date for domestic students, 1/2 for international students. Application fee: $105 ($125 for international students). Electronic applications accepted. *Financial support:* Fellowships, research assistantships with full tuition reimbursements, institutionally sponsored loans, traineeships, health care benefits, and unspecified assistantships available. Financial award application deadline: 3/1; financial award applicants required to submit FAFSA. *Faculty research:* Education technology, learning theory, social theory, cultural diversity, postmodernism. *Unit head:* Richard Arum, Dean, 949-824-2534, E-mail: richard.arum@uci.edu. *Application contact:* Denise Earley, Assistant Director of Student Affairs, 949-824-4022, E-mail: denise.earley@uci.edu.
Website: http://education.uci.edu/

University of California, Los Angeles, Graduate Division, Graduate School of Education and Information Studies, Department of Education, Los Angeles, CA 90095. Offers M Ed, MA, Ed D, PhD. *Program availability:* Evening/weekend. *Degree requirements:* For master's, comprehensive exam; for doctorate, thesis/dissertation, oral and written qualifying exams. *Entrance requirements:* For master's, GRE General Test, minimum GPA of 3.0; for doctorate, GRE General Test, minimum undergraduate GPA of 3.0. Additional exam requirements/recommendations for international students: Required—TOEFL (minimum score 560 paper-based; 87 iBT). Electronic applications accepted.

University of California, Riverside, Graduate Division, Graduate School of Education, Riverside, CA 92521-0102. Offers autism (M Ed); diversity and equity (M Ed); education specialist (Credential); education, society, and culture (MA, PhD); educational psychology (MA, PhD); general education (M Ed); higher education administration and policy (M Ed, PhD); multiple subject (Credential); reading (M Ed); school psychology (PhD); single subject (Credential); special education (M Ed, MA, PhD); TESOL (M Ed). Terminal master's awarded for partial completion of doctoral program. *Degree requirements:* For master's, thesis optional, comprehensive exams or thesis (MA), case study or analytical report (M Ed); for doctorate, thesis/dissertation, written and oral qualifying exams, college teaching practicum. *Entrance requirements:* For master's, GRE General Test (for MA); CBEST and CSET (for M Ed in general education only), UCR Extension TESOL certificate (for M Ed with TESOL emphasis only); for doctorate, GRE General Test, writing sample; for Credential, CBEST, CSET. Additional exam requirements/recommendations for international students: Required—TOEFL (minimum score 550 paper-based; 80 iBT), IELTS (minimum score 7). Electronic applications accepted. *Expenses:* Tuition, state resident: full-time $16,666. Tuition, nonresident: full-time $31,768. *Required fees:* $11,055.54 per quarter. $3685.18 per quarter. Tuition and fees vary according to campus/location and program. *Faculty research:* Responsiveness to intervention, faculty core, response to intervention of English language learners, advanced modeling techniques, study on social capital, trust, and motivation.

University of California, San Diego, Graduate Division, Program in Education Studies, La Jolla, CA 92093. Offers education (M Ed, PhD); educational leadership (Ed D); teaching and learning (MA, Ed D), including bilingual education (MA), curriculum design (MA). Ed D offered jointly with California State University, San Marcos. *Students:* 89 full-time (59 women), 52 part-time (38 women). 228 applicants, 52% accepted, 74 enrolled. In 2016, 68 master's, 6 doctorates awarded. *Degree requirements:* For master's, thesis (for some programs), student teaching; for doctorate, comprehensive exam, thesis/dissertation. *Entrance requirements:* For master's, GRE General Test; CBEST and appropriate CSET exam (for select tracks), current teaching or educational assignment (for select tracks); for doctorate, GRE General Test, current teaching or educational assignment (for select tracks). Additional exam requirements/recommendations for international students: Required—TOEFL (minimum score 550 paper-based; 80 iBT), IELTS (minimum score 7). *Application deadline:* For fall admission, 12/1 for domestic students. Application fee: $105 ($125 for international students). Electronic applications accepted. *Expenses:* Tuition, state resident: full-time $11,220. Tuition, nonresident: full-time $26,322. *Required fees:* $1864. *Financial support:* Fellowships, career-related internships or fieldwork, and scholarships/grants available. Financial award applicants required to submit FAFSA. *Faculty research:* Language, culture and literacy development of deaf/hard of hearing children; equity issues in education; educational reform; evaluation, assessment, and research methodologies; distributed learning. *Unit head:* Alan J. Daly, Chair, 858-822-6472, E-mail: ajdaly@ucsd.edu. *Application contact:* Giselle Van Luit, Graduate Coordinator, 858-534-2958, E-mail: edsinfo@ucsd.edu.

University of California, Santa Barbara, Graduate Division, Gevirtz Graduate School of Education, Santa Barbara, CA 93106-9490. Offers counseling, clinical and school psychology (MA, PhD, Credential), including clinical psychology (PhD), counseling psychology (MA, PhD), pupil personnel services (Credential), school psychology (PhD); education (MA, PhD); teacher education (M Ed, Credential), including multiple subject teaching (Credential), single subject teaching (Credential), special education (Credential), teaching (M Ed); MA/PhD. *Accreditation:* APA (one or more programs are accredited). Terminal master's awarded for partial completion of doctoral program. *Degree requirements:* For master's, comprehensive exam (for some programs), thesis (for some programs); for doctorate, comprehensive exam (for some programs), thesis/dissertation. *Entrance requirements:* For master's and doctorate, GRE; for Credential, GRE or MAT, CSET, CBEST. Additional exam requirements/recommendations for international students: Required—TOEFL (minimum score 550 paper-based; 80 iBT), IELTS (minimum score 7). Electronic applications accepted. *Faculty research:* Needs of diverse students, school accountability and leadership, school violence, language learning and literacy, science/math education.

University of California, Santa Cruz, Division of Graduate Studies, Division of Social Sciences, Department of Education, Santa Cruz, CA 95064. Offers MA, PhD. Terminal master's awarded for partial completion of doctoral program. *Degree requirements:* For master's, thesis; for doctorate, thesis/dissertation. *Entrance requirements:* Additional exam requirements/recommendations for international students: Required—TOEFL (minimum score 550 paper-based; 83 iBT); Recommended—IELTS (minimum score 8). Electronic applications accepted. *Faculty research:* Bilingual/multicultural education, special education, curriculum and instruction, child development, gaps in the learning opportunities of underserved students, discovery of more effective practices.

University of Central Arkansas, Graduate School, College of Education, Conway, AR 72035-0001. Offers MAT, MS, MSE, Ed S, Graduate Certificate, PMC. *Accreditation:* NCATE. *Program availability:* Part-time, evening/weekend, online learning. Terminal master's awarded for partial completion of doctoral program. *Degree requirements:* For master's, comprehensive exam, thesis optional, portfolio. *Entrance requirements:* For master's, GRE General Test, minimum GPA of 2.7. Additional exam requirements/recommendations for international students: Required—TOEFL (minimum score 550 paper-based; 80 iBT). Electronic applications accepted.

University of Central Arkansas, Graduate School, College of Education, Department of Teaching and Learning, Graduate Program in Teaching, Conway, AR 72035-0001. Offers MAT. *Program availability:* Part-time, online learning. *Degree requirements:* For master's, comprehensive exam, thesis optional. *Entrance requirements:* For master's, GRE General Test, minimum GPA of 2.7. Additional exam requirements/recommendations for international students: Required—TOEFL (minimum score 550 paper-based). Electronic applications accepted.

University of Central Arkansas, Graduate School, College of Education, Department of Teaching and Learning, Program in Advanced Studies of Teaching and Learning, Conway, AR 72035-0001. Offers MSE. *Program availability:* Evening/weekend, online learning. *Entrance requirements:* For master's, GRE General Test, minimum GPA of 2.7. Additional exam requirements/recommendations for international students: Required—TOEFL (minimum score 550 paper-based). Electronic applications accepted.

University of Central Florida, College of Education and Human Performance, Department of Child, Family and Community Sciences, Orlando, FL 32816. Offers early childhood development and education (MS); exceptional student education (M Ed, MA, Certificate), including autism spectrum disorders (Certificate), exceptional student education (M Ed), exceptional student education K-12 (MA), intervention specialist (Certificate), pre-kindergarten disabilities (Certificate), severe or profound disabilities (Certificate), special education (Certificate). *Program availability:* Part-time, evening/weekend. *Faculty:* 34 full-time (22 women), 40 part-time/adjunct (31 women). *Students:* 75 full-time (47 women), 187 part-time (153 women); includes 89 minority (26 Black or African American, non-Hispanic/Latino; 1 American Indian or Alaska Native, non-Hispanic/Latino; 6 Asian, non-Hispanic/Latino; 55 Hispanic/Latino; 1 Two or more races, non-Hispanic/Latino), 3 international. Average age 32. 205 applicants, 67% accepted, 86 enrolled. In 2016, 87 master's, 64 other advanced degrees awarded. *Degree requirements:* For master's, thesis or alternative, research project; for Certificate, thesis or alternative. *Entrance requirements:* For master's, GRE General Test; for Certificate, GRE General Test, minimum GPA of 3.0. Additional exam requirements/recommendations for international students: Required—TOEFL. *Application deadline:* For fall admission, 7/15 for domestic students; for spring admission, 11/15 for domestic students. Application fee: $30. Electronic applications accepted. *Expenses:* Tuition, state resident: part-time $288.16 per credit hour. Tuition, nonresident: part-time $1071.31 per credit hour. *Financial support:* In 2016–17, 5 students received support, including 6 research assistantships with partial tuition reimbursements available (averaging $5,881 per year), 2 teaching assistantships with partial tuition reimbursements available (averaging $9,252 per year); fellowships, career-related internships or fieldwork, Federal Work-Study, institutionally sponsored loans, and unspecified assistantships also available. Financial award application deadline: 3/1; financial award applicants required to submit FAFSA. *Unit head:* Dr. Glenn Lambie, Chair, 407-823-6106, E-mail: glenn.lambie@ucf.edu. *Application contact:* Assistant Director, Graduate Admissions, 407-823-2766, Fax: 407-823-6442, E-mail: gradadmissions@ucf.edu.
Website: http://education.ucf.edu/cfcs/

University of Central Missouri, The Graduate School, Warrensburg, MO 64093. Offers accountancy (MA); accounting (MBA); applied mathematics (MS); aviation safety (MA); biology (MS); business administration (MBA); career and technical education leadership (MS); college student personnel administration (MS); communication (MA); computer science (MS); counseling (MS); criminal justice (MS); educational leadership (Ed D); educational technology (MS); elementary and early childhood education (MSE); English (MA); environmental studies (MA); finance (MBA); history (MA); human services/educational technology (Ed S); human services/learning resources (Ed S); human services/professional counseling (Ed S); industrial hygiene (MS); industrial management (MS); information systems (MBA); information technology (MS); kinesiology (MS); library science and information services (MS); literacy education (MSE); marketing (MBA); mathematics (MS); music (MA); occupational safety management (MS); psychology (MS); rural family nursing (MS); school administration (MSE); social gerontology (MS); sociology (MA); special education (MSE); speech language pathology (MS); superintendency (Ed S); teaching (MAT); teaching English as a second language (MA); technology (MS); technology management (PhD); theatre (MA). *Program availability:* Part-time, 100% online, blended/hybrid learning. *Degree requirements:* For master's and Ed S, comprehensive exam (for some programs), thesis (for some programs). *Entrance requirements:* Additional exam requirements/recommendations for international students: Required—TOEFL (minimum score 550 paper-based; 79 iBT). Electronic applications accepted.

University of Central Oklahoma, The Jackson College of Graduate Studies, College of Education and Professional Studies, Edmond, OK 73034-5209. Offers M Ed, MA, MS. *Accreditation:* NCATE. *Program availability:* Part-time. *Degree requirements:* For master's, comprehensive exam (for some programs), thesis (for some programs). *Entrance requirements:* For master's, GRE. Additional exam requirements/recommendations for international students: Required—TOEFL (minimum score 550 paper-based; 79 iBT), IELTS (minimum score 6.5). Electronic applications accepted.

University of Cincinnati, Graduate School, College of Education, Criminal Justice, and Human Services, Cincinnati, OH 45221. Offers M Ed, MA, MS, Ed D, PhD, CAGS, Certificate, Ed S. *Accreditation:* NCATE. *Program availability:* Part-time, online learning. *Degree requirements:* For master's, comprehensive exam (for some programs), thesis (for some programs); for doctorate, comprehensive exam, thesis/dissertation. *Entrance requirements:* For master's and doctorate, GRE. Additional exam requirements/recommendations for international students: Required—TOEFL (minimum score 550 paper-based), OEPT 3. Electronic applications accepted. *Expenses: Tuition, area resident:* Full-time $12,790; part-time $389 per credit hour. Tuition, state resident: full-time $13,290; part-time $419 per credit hour. Tuition, nonresident: full-time $24,532; part-time $976 per credit hour. *International tuition:* $24,832 full-time. *Required fees:* $3958; $140 per credit hour. Tuition and fees vary according to course load, degree level, program and reciprocity agreements. *Faculty research:* Alcohol and drug prevention, family-based prevention, criminal justice, literacy, urban education.

University of Colorado Boulder, Graduate School, School of Education, Boulder, CO 80309. Offers MA, PhD. *Accreditation:* NCATE. *Faculty:* 34 full-time (20 women). *Students:* 144 full-time (99 women), 181 part-time (155 women); includes 102 minority (13 Black or African American, non-Hispanic/Latino; 1 American Indian or Alaska Native, non-Hispanic/Latino; 7 Asian, non-Hispanic/Latino; 72 Hispanic/Latino; 2 Native Hawaiian or other Pacific Islander, non-Hispanic/Latino; 7 Two or more races, non-Hispanic/Latino), 6 international. Average age 33. 345 applicants, 53% accepted, 58 enrolled. In 2016, 93 master's, 19 doctorates awarded. Terminal master's awarded for partial completion of doctoral program. *Degree requirements:* For master's, comprehensive exam, thesis or alternative; for doctorate, one foreign language, comprehensive exam, thesis/dissertation. *Entrance requirements:* For master's, GRE General Test or MAT, minimum undergraduate GPA of 2.75; for doctorate, GRE General Test. *Application deadline:* For fall admission, 2/1 for domestic students, 12/1 for international students; for spring admission, 9/1 for domestic and international students. Application fee: $60 ($80 for international students). Electronic applications accepted. Application fee is waived when completed online. *Financial support:* In 2016–17, 438 students received support, including 115 fellowships (averaging $3,501 per year), 78 research assistantships with full and partial tuition reimbursements available (averaging $33,196 per year), 33 teaching assistantships with full and partial tuition reimbursements available (averaging $20,617 per year); institutionally sponsored loans, scholarships/grants, health care benefits, and unspecified assistantships also available. Financial award applicants required to submit FAFSA. *Faculty research:* Teacher education, minority education, educational reform, literacy, classroom instruction. *Total annual research expenditures:* $8.2 million.
Website: http://www.colorado.edu/education/

University of Colorado Colorado Springs, College of Education, Colorado Springs, CO 80918. Offers counseling and human services (MA); curriculum and instruction (MA); educational leadership (MA); educational leadership, research and policy (PhD); special education (MA); teaching English to speakers of other languages (MA). *Accreditation:* ACA; NCATE. *Program availability:* Part-time, evening/weekend, 100% online, blended/hybrid learning. *Faculty:* 26 full-time (18 women), 33 part-time/adjunct (21 women). *Students:* 136 full-time (94 women), 264 part-time (177 women); includes 99 minority (17 Black or African American, non-Hispanic/Latino; 1 American Indian or Alaska Native, non-Hispanic/Latino; 8 Asian, non-Hispanic/Latino; 55 Hispanic/Latino; 18 Two or more races, non-Hispanic/Latino), 9 international. Average age 35. 152 applicants, 89% accepted, 88 enrolled. In 2016, 161 master's, 11 doctorates awarded. *Degree requirements:* For master's, comprehensive exam, thesis or alternative, microcomputer proficiency; for doctorate, comprehensive exam, thesis/dissertation, research lab. *Entrance requirements:* For master's and doctorate, GRE General Test. Additional exam requirements/recommendations for international students: Recommended—TOEFL (minimum score 550 paper-based; 80 iBT), IELTS (minimum score 6). *Application deadline:* For fall admission, 2/1 priority date for domestic students, 2/1 for international students; for spring admission, 10/15 for domestic students, 10/1 for international students. Applications are processed on a rolling basis. Application fee: $60 ($100 for international students). Electronic applications accepted. *Expenses:* Contact institution. *Financial support:* In 2016–17, 108 students received support. Career-related internships or fieldwork, Federal Work-Study, scholarships/grants, and unspecified assistantships available. Support available to part-time students. Financial award application deadline: 3/1; financial award applicants required to submit FAFSA. *Faculty research:* Linguistically diverse education (LDE), educational policy, evidence-based reading and writing instruction, relational and social aggression, positive behavior supports, inclusive schooling, K-12 education policy. *Total annual research expenditures:* $272,136. *Unit head:* Dr. Valerie Martin Conley, Dean, 719-255-4133, E-mail: vmconley@uccs.edu. *Application contact:* The College of Education Student Resource Office, 719-255-4996, E-mail: education@uccs.edu.
Website: http://www.uccs.edu/coe

University of Colorado Denver, School of Education and Human Development, Denver, CO 80217. Offers MA, MS Ed, Ed D, PhD, Psy D, Ed S. *Accreditation:* NCATE. *Program availability:* Part-time, evening/weekend, online learning. *Faculty:* 72 full-time (44 women), 82 part-time/adjunct (63 women). *Students:* 867 full-time (691 women), 447 part-time (369 women); includes 251 minority (47 Black or African American, non-Hispanic/Latino; 4 American Indian or Alaska Native, non-Hispanic/Latino; 26 Asian, non-Hispanic/Latino; 145 Hispanic/Latino; 2 Native Hawaiian or other Pacific Islander, non-Hispanic/Latino; 27 Two or more races, non-Hispanic/Latino), 20 international. Average age 34. 519 applicants, 59% accepted, 215 enrolled. In 2016, 479 master's, 23 doctorates, 18 other advanced degrees awarded. *Degree requirements:* For master's and Ed S, comprehensive exam (for some programs); for doctorate, comprehensive exam, thesis/dissertation. *Entrance requirements:* Additional exam requirements/recommendations for international students: Required—TOEFL (minimum score 537 paper-based; 75 iBT); Recommended—IELTS (minimum score 6.5). Application fee: $50 ($75 for international students). Electronic applications accepted. *Expenses:* Contact institution. *Financial support:* In 2016–17, 272 students received support. Fellowships, research assistantships, teaching assistantships, Federal Work-Study, institutionally sponsored loans, scholarships/grants, and traineeships available. Financial award application deadline: 4/1; financial award applicants required to submit FAFSA. *Faculty research:* Educational equity: race, class, culture, power and privilege; analytic approaches to educational program effectiveness and measuring student learning; early childhood special education/early intervention policies; recruiting and retention of African-American teachers; secondary and postsecondary institutions; accountability systems to improve public education. *Total annual research expenditures:* $5.5 million. *Unit head:* Rebecca Kantor, Dean, 303-315-6343, E-mail: rebecca.kantor@ucdenver.edu. *Application contact:* Student Services Center, 303-315-6300, Fax: 303-315-6311, E-mail: education@ucdenver.edu.
Website: http://www.ucdenver.edu/academics/colleges/SchoolOfEducation/Pages/home.aspx

University of Connecticut, Graduate School, Neag School of Education, Storrs, CT 06269. Offers MA, PhD. *Accreditation:* NCATE. Terminal master's awarded for partial completion of doctoral program. *Degree requirements:* For master's, comprehensive exam, thesis or alternative; for doctorate, thesis/dissertation. *Entrance requirements:* For doctorate, GRE General Test. Additional exam requirements/recommendations for international students: Required—TOEFL (minimum score 550 paper-based). Electronic applications accepted.

University of Delaware, College of Education and Human Development, School of Education, Newark, DE 19716. Offers education (PhD); educational leadership (Ed D); higher education (M Ed); instruction (MI); reading (M Ed); school leadership (M Ed); school psychology (MA, Ed S); teaching English as a second language (TESL) (MA). *Accreditation:* NCATE. *Program availability:* Part-time, evening/weekend. Terminal master's awarded for partial completion of doctoral program. *Degree requirements:* For master's, comprehensive exam (for some programs), thesis (for some programs); for doctorate, comprehensive exam (for some programs), thesis/dissertation. *Entrance requirements:* For master's and doctorate, GRE, 3 letters of recommendation. Additional exam requirements/recommendations for international students: Required—TOEFL (minimum score 600 paper-based). Electronic applications accepted. *Faculty research:* Teacher education; curriculum theory and development; community based education models, educational leadership.

University of Denver, Morgridge College of Education, Denver, CO 80208. Offers child, family and school psychology (MA, PhD, Ed S); counseling psychology (MA, PhD); curriculum and instruction (MA, Ed D, PhD); curriculum instruction and teaching (Certificate); early childhood special education (MA, Certificate); educational leadership and policy studies (MA, Ed D, PhD, Certificate); higher education (Ed D, PhD); library and information science (MLIS); research methods and statistics (MA, PhD). *Accreditation:* ALA; APA (one or more programs are accredited). *Program availability:* Part-time, evening/weekend, online learning. *Faculty:* 39 full-time (29 women), 60 part-time/adjunct (42 women). *Students:* 498 full-time (392 women), 362 part-time (282 women); includes 223 minority (63 Black or African American, non-Hispanic/Latino; 6 American Indian or Alaska Native, non-Hispanic/Latino; 20 Asian, non-Hispanic/Latino; 102 Hispanic/Latino; 1 Native Hawaiian or other Pacific Islander, non-Hispanic/Latino; 31 Two or more races, non-Hispanic/Latino), 40 international. Average age 32. 1,027 applicants, 69% accepted, 386 enrolled. In 2016, 252 master's, 36 doctorates, 141 other advanced degrees awarded. Terminal master's awarded for partial completion of doctoral program. *Degree requirements:* For master's, comprehensive exam; for doctorate, 2 foreign languages, comprehensive exam, thesis/dissertation. *Entrance requirements:* For master's and doctorate, GRE General Test or GMAT. Additional exam requirements/recommendations for international students: Required—TOEFL (minimum score 550 paper-based; 80 iBT). *Application deadline:* Applications are processed on a rolling basis. Application fee: $65. Electronic applications accepted. *Expenses:* $29,022

per year full-time. *Financial support:* In 2016–17, 697 students received support, including 37 research assistantships with tuition reimbursements available (averaging $11,209 per year), 66 teaching assistantships with tuition reimbursements available (averaging $3,742 per year); career-related internships or fieldwork, Federal Work-Study, institutionally sponsored loans, scholarships/grants, and unspecified assistantships also available. Support available to part-time students. Financial award application deadline: 2/15; financial award applicants required to submit FAFSA. *Faculty research:* Early childhood education, access and equity, educational leadership, family and school partnerships, neurodevelopmental disorders. *Total annual research expenditures:* $3.3 million. *Unit head:* Dr. Karen Riley, Dean, 303-871-3665, Fax: 303-871-4456, E-mail: karen.riley@du.edu. *Application contact:* Jodi Dye, Director of Admissions, 303-871-2510, Fax: 303-871-4456, E-mail: jodi.dye@du.edu.
Website: http://morgridge.du.edu

The University of Findlay, Office of Graduate Admissions, Findlay, OH 45840-3653. Offers applied security and analytics (MSAS); athletic training (MAT); business (MBA), including certified management accountant, certified public accountant, health care management, hospitality management; education (MA Ed, Ed D), including children's literature (MA Ed), curriculum and teaching (MA Ed), education (MA Ed), educational administration (MA Ed), human resource development (MA Ed), reading (MA Ed), science education (MA Ed), superintendent (Ed D), teaching (Ed D), technology (MA Ed); environmental, safety and health management (MSEM); health informatics (MS); occupational therapy (MOT); pharmacy (Pharm D); physical therapy (DPT); physician assistant (MPA); rhetoric and writing (MA); teaching English to speakers of other languages (TESOL) and bilingual education (MA). *Program availability:* Part-time, evening/weekend, 100% online, blended/hybrid learning. *Faculty:* 114 full-time (63 women), 44 part-time/adjunct (18 women). *Students:* 751 full-time (452 women), 573 part-time (323 women); includes 164 minority (82 Black or African American, non-Hispanic/Latino; 1 American Indian or Alaska Native, non-Hispanic/Latino; 27 Asian, non-Hispanic/Latino; 37 Hispanic/Latino; 17 Two or more races, non-Hispanic/Latino), 280 international. Average age 28. 661 applicants, 52% accepted, 288 enrolled. In 2016, 366 master's, 137 doctorates awarded. *Degree requirements:* For master's, comprehensive exam (for some programs), thesis, cumulative project, capstone project; for doctorate, thesis/dissertation. *Entrance requirements:* For master's, GRE (for some programs), bachelor's degree from accredited institution, minimum undergraduate GPA of 3.0 in last 64 hours of course work; for doctorate, MAT, minimum cumulative GPA of 3.0, master's degree. Additional exam requirements/recommendations for international students: Recommended—TOEFL (minimum score 79 iBT), IELTS (minimum score 7). *Application deadline:* For fall admission, 6/15 for international students; for spring admission, 12/1 for international students; for summer admission, 4/1 for international students. Applications are processed on a rolling basis. Electronic applications accepted. *Expenses:* Contact institution. *Financial support:* In 2016–17, 139 students received support, including 15 research assistantships with partial tuition reimbursements available (averaging $7,200 per year), 25 teaching assistantships with partial tuition reimbursements available (averaging $7,200 per year); Federal Work-Study, institutionally sponsored loans, and unspecified assistantships also available. Financial award application deadline: 4/1; financial award applicants required to submit FAFSA. *Unit head:* Christopher M. Harris, Director of Admissions, 419-434-4347, E-mail: harrisc1@findlay.edu. *Application contact:* Madeline Fauser Brennan, Graduate Admissions Counselor, 419-434-4636, Fax: 419-434-4898, E-mail: fauserbrennan@findlay.edu. Website: http://www.findlay.edu/admissions/graduate/Pages/default.aspx

University of Florida, Graduate School, College of Education, Gainesville, FL 32611. Offers M Ed, MAE, Ed D, PhD, Ed S, PhD/JD. *Accreditation:* NCATE. *Program availability:* Part-time, evening/weekend, online learning. Terminal master's awarded for partial completion of doctoral program. *Degree requirements:* For master's, comprehensive exam (for some programs), thesis (for some programs); for doctorate, comprehensive exam (for some programs), thesis/dissertation (for some programs), capstone project. *Entrance requirements:* For master's and doctorate, GRE General Test, minimum GPA of 3.0; for Ed S, GRE General Test. Additional exam requirements/recommendations for international students: Required—TOEFL (minimum score 550 paper-based; 80 iBT), IELTS (minimum score 6). Electronic applications accepted. *Faculty research:* Early childhood, teacher education, educator professional development, learning and intervention sciences, educational leadership and policy.

University of Georgia, College of Education, Athens, GA 30602. Offers M Ed, MA, MA Ed, MAT, MS, Ed D, PhD, Ed S. *Accreditation:* NCATE. *Degree requirements:* For doctorate, thesis/dissertation. *Entrance requirements:* For doctorate, GRE General Test. *Application deadline:* For fall admission, 7/1 priority date for domestic students; for spring admission, 11/15 for domestic students. Application fee: $50. Electronic applications accepted. *Financial support:* Fellowships, research assistantships, teaching assistantships, and unspecified assistantships available. *Unit head:* Dr. Arthur M. Horne, Interim Dean, 706-542-6446, Fax: 706-542-0360, E-mail: ahorne@uga.edu.
Website: http://www.coe.uga.edu/

University of Guam, Office of Graduate Studies, School of Education, Mangilao, GU 96923. Offers M Ed, MA. *Accreditation:* NCATE. *Program availability:* Part-time. *Degree requirements:* For master's, comprehensive oral and written exams. *Entrance requirements:* For master's, GRE General Test. Additional exam requirements/recommendations for international students: Required—TOEFL. *Faculty research:* Multicultural issues, computerized student advising.

University of Hartford, College of Education, Nursing, and Health Professions, West Hartford, CT 06117-1599. Offers M Ed, MS, MSN, MSPT, DPT, Ed D, CAGS, Sixth Year Certificate. *Accreditation:* NCATE. *Program availability:* Part-time, evening/weekend. *Degree requirements:* For doctorate, thesis/dissertation; for other advanced degree, comprehensive exam or research project. *Entrance requirements:* For doctorate, MAT. Additional exam requirements/recommendations for international students: Required—TOEFL (minimum score 550 paper-based). Electronic applications accepted. *Expenses:* Contact institution.

University of Hawaii at Hilo, Program in Education, Hilo, HI 96720-4091. Offers M Ed. *Program availability:* Part-time, evening/weekend. *Entrance requirements:* Additional exam requirements/recommendations for international students: Required—TOEFL, IELTS. Electronic applications accepted.

University of Hawaii at Hilo, Program in Teaching, Hilo, HI 96720-4091. Offers MA. *Entrance requirements:* Additional exam requirements/recommendations for international students: Required—TOEFL, IELTS. Electronic applications accepted.

University of Hawaii at Manoa, Graduate Division, College of Education, Honolulu, HI 96822. Offers M Ed, M Ed T, MS, Ed D, PhD, Graduate Certificate. *Accreditation:* NCATE. *Program availability:* Part-time, evening/weekend. *Entrance requirements:* Additional exam requirements/recommendations for international students: Required—TOEFL or IELTS.

University of Holy Cross, Program in Education and Counseling, New Orleans, LA 70131-7399. Offers administration and supervision (M Ed); curriculum and instruction (M Ed); marriage and family counseling (MA); school counseling (M Ed, MA). *Accreditation:* ACA; NCATE. *Program availability:* Part-time, evening/weekend. *Degree requirements:* For master's, thesis. *Entrance requirements:* For master's, GRE General Test, minimum GPA of 2.7.

University of Houston, College of Education, Houston, TX 77204. Offers M Ed, Ed D, PhD. *Accreditation:* NCATE. *Program availability:* Part-time. *Degree requirements:* For master's, comprehensive exam or thesis; for doctorate, comprehensive exam, thesis/dissertation. *Entrance requirements:* For master's, GRE General Test, transcripts, 3 letters of recommendation, curriculum vita, goal statement; for doctorate, GRE General Test, transcripts, 3 letters of recommendation, curriculum vita, goal statement, writing sample, interview. Additional exam requirements/recommendations for international students: Required—TOEFL (minimum score 550 paper-based). Electronic applications accepted.

University of Houston–Clear Lake, School of Education, Houston, TX 77058-1002. Offers MS, Ed D. *Accreditation:* NCATE. *Program availability:* Part-time, evening/weekend. *Degree requirements:* For master's, thesis optional; for doctorate, comprehensive exam, thesis/dissertation. *Entrance requirements:* For master's, GRE or minimum GPA of 3.0 in last 60 hours; for doctorate, GRE, master's degree, letters of reference. Additional exam requirements/recommendations for international students: Required—TOEFL (minimum score 550 paper-based). Electronic applications accepted.

University of Houston–Victoria, School of Education, Health Professions and Human Development, Victoria, TX 77901-4450. Offers administration and supervision (M Ed); adult and higher education (M Ed); counselor education (M Ed); curriculum and instruction (M Ed); educational technology (M Ed); special education (M Ed). *Program availability:* Part-time, evening/weekend, online learning. *Degree requirements:* For master's, comprehensive exam, project or thesis. *Entrance requirements:* For master's, GRE General Test. Additional exam requirements/recommendations for international students: Required—TOEFL. Electronic applications accepted. *Faculty research:* Reading and language arts education, evaluation and diagnosis of special children's abilities.

University of Idaho, College of Graduate Studies, College of Education, Moscow, ID 83844. Offers M Ed, MS, MSAT, DAT, Ed D, PhD, Ed S. *Accreditation:* NCATE. *Faculty:* 52 full-time (26 women), 14 part-time/adjunct (9 women). *Students:* 162 full-time (103 women), 258 part-time (154 women). Average age 37. In 2016, 116 master's, 13 doctorates, 27 other advanced degrees awarded. *Degree requirements:* For doctorate, thesis/dissertation. *Entrance requirements:* For master's, minimum GPA of 3.0. Additional exam requirements/recommendations for international students: Required—TOEFL. *Application deadline:* For fall admission, 8/1 for domestic students; for spring admission, 12/15 for domestic students. Applications are processed on a rolling basis. Application fee: $60. Electronic applications accepted. *Expenses:* Tuition, state resident: full-time $6460; part-time $414 per credit hour. Tuition, nonresident: full-time $21,268; part-time $1237 per credit hour. *Required fees:* $2070; $60 per credit hour. Full-time tuition and fees vary according to course load and reciprocity agreements. *Financial support:* Teaching assistantships and Federal Work-Study available. Support available to part-time students. Financial award applicants required to submit FAFSA. *Faculty research:* Technology integration, curricular development for cooperative environments, increasing science literacy, best practices for online pedagogy. *Unit head:* Dr. Alison Carr-Chellman, Dean, 208-885-6772, E-mail: coe@uidaho.edu. *Application contact:* Sean Scoggin, Graduate Recruitment Coordinator, 208-885-4001, Fax: 208-885-4406, E-mail: graduateadmissions@uidaho.edu.
Website: http://www.uidaho.edu/ed/

University of Illinois at Chicago, College of Education, Chicago, IL 60607-7128. Offers M Ed, Ed D, PhD. *Program availability:* Part-time, evening/weekend. Terminal master's awarded for partial completion of doctoral program. *Degree requirements:* For doctorate, thesis/dissertation. *Entrance requirements:* For master's, minimum GPA of 2.75; for doctorate, GRE General Test, minimum GPA of 2.75. Additional exam requirements/recommendations for international students: Required—TOEFL. Electronic applications accepted. *Faculty research:* Teaching and learning, program design, school and classroom organization with emphasis on urban settings.

University of Illinois at Springfield, Graduate Programs, College of Education and Human Services, Springfield, IL 62703-5407. Offers MA, CAS, Certificate, Graduate Certificate. *Program availability:* Part-time, evening/weekend, 100% online, blended/hybrid learning. *Faculty:* 15 full-time (10 women), 12 part-time/adjunct (9 women). *Students:* 72 full-time (62 women), 211 part-time (148 women); includes 58 minority (44 Black or African American, non-Hispanic/Latino; 1 American Indian or Alaska Native, non-Hispanic/Latino; 10 Hispanic/Latino; 3 Two or more races, non-Hispanic/Latino), 3 international. Average age 34. 141 applicants, 52% accepted, 56 enrolled. In 2016, 81 master's, 7 other advanced degrees awarded. *Entrance requirements:* Additional exam requirements/recommendations for international students: Required—TOEFL (minimum score 500 paper-based; 61 iBT). *Application deadline:* Applications are processed on a rolling basis. Application fee: $60 ($75 for international students). Electronic applications accepted. *Expenses:* Tuition, state resident: part-time $329 per credit hour. Tuition, nonresident: part-time $675 per credit hour. *Financial support:* In 2016–17, fellowships with full tuition reimbursements (averaging $9,900 per year), research assistantships with full tuition reimbursements (averaging $9,991 per year), teaching assistantships with full tuition reimbursements (averaging $10,059 per year) were awarded; career-related internships or fieldwork, Federal Work-Study, scholarships/grants, health care benefits, and unspecified assistantships also available. Support available to part-time students. Financial award application deadline: 11/15; financial award applicants required to submit FAFSA. *Unit head:* Dr. Hanfu Mi, Dean, 217-206-6784, Fax: 217-206-6775, E-mail: hmi2@uis.edu. *Application contact:* Dr. Cecelia Cornell, Associate Vice Chancellor for Graduate Education, 217-206-7230, E-mail: ccorn1@uis.edu.

University of Illinois at Urbana–Champaign, Graduate College, College of Education, Champaign, IL 61820. Offers Ed M, MA, MS, Ed D, PhD, CAS. *Program availability:* Part-time, online learning.

University of Indianapolis, Graduate Programs, School of Education, Indianapolis, IN 46227-3697. Offers art education (MAT); biology (MAT); chemistry (MAT); curriculum and instruction (MA); earth sciences (MAT); education (MA, MAT); educational leadership (MA); elementary education (MA); English (MAT); French (MAT); math (MAT); physical education (MAT); physics (MAT); secondary education (MA), including art education, education, English education, social studies education; social studies (MAT); Spanish (MAT). *Accreditation:* NCATE. *Program availability:* Part-time, evening/weekend. *Entrance requirements:* For master's, GRE Subject Test, PRAXIS I, minimum GPA of 2.5, 3 letters of recommendation, interview. Additional exam requirements/recommendations for international students: Required—TOEFL (minimum score 550 paper-based). *Faculty research:* Assessment of teacher education, perceptions of prospective teachers by parents.

The University of Iowa, Graduate College, College of Education, Iowa City, IA 52242-1316. Offers MA, MAT, MM, PhD, Ed S. *Degree requirements:* For master's and Ed S, exam; for doctorate, comprehensive exam, thesis/dissertation. *Entrance requirements:* For master's, doctorate, and Ed S, GRE General Test, minimum GPA of 3.0. Additional exam requirements/recommendations for international students: Required—TOEFL (minimum score 550 paper-based; 81 iBT). Electronic applications accepted. *Faculty research:* Computer-assisted instrumentation, testing and measurement, instructional design.

University of Jamestown, Program in Education, Jamestown, ND 58405. Offers curriculum and instruction (M Ed). *Degree requirements:* For master's, thesis or project.

The University of Kansas, Graduate Studies, School of Education, Lawrence, KS 66045-3101. Offers MA, MS, MS Ed, MSE, Ed D, PhD, Certificate, Ed S. *Accreditation:* NCATE. *Program availability:* Part-time, online learning. *Students:* 546 full-time (364 women), 821 part-time (662 women); includes 207 minority (75 Black or African American, non-Hispanic/Latino; 14 American Indian or Alaska Native, non-Hispanic/Latino; 26 Asian, non-Hispanic/Latino; 35 Hispanic/Latino; 57 Two or more races, non-Hispanic/Latino), 107 international. Average age 33. 948 applicants, 72% accepted, 490 enrolled. In 2016, 214 master's, 55 doctorates, 40 other advanced degrees awarded. *Entrance requirements:* For master's and other advanced degree, minimum GPA of 3.0; for doctorate, GRE General Test. Additional exam requirements/recommendations for international students: Required—TOEFL or IELTS. Application fee: $65 ($85 for international students). Electronic applications accepted. *Financial support:* Fellowships, research assistantships, teaching assistantships, career-related internships or fieldwork, scholarships/grants, and unspecified assistantships available. Financial award application deadline: 2/1. *Unit head:* Dr. Rick J. Ginsberg, Dean, 785-864-3726, E-mail: ginsberg@ku.edu. *Application contact:* Kim Huggett, Graduate Student Services Manager, 785-864-4510, E-mail: khuggett@ku.edu.
Website: http://www.soe.ku.edu/

University of Kentucky, Graduate School, College of Education, Lexington, KY 40506-0032. Offers M Ed, MA Ed, MRC, MS, MS Ed, Ed D, PhD, Ed S. *Accreditation:* NCATE. *Program availability:* Part-time, evening/weekend. Terminal master's awarded for partial completion of doctoral program. *Degree requirements:* For master's and Ed S, comprehensive exam; for doctorate, comprehensive exam, thesis/dissertation. *Entrance requirements:* For master's, GRE General Test, minimum undergraduate GPA of 2.75; for doctorate, GRE General Test, minimum graduate GPA of 3.0; for Ed S, GRE General Test. Additional exam requirements/recommendations for international students: Required—TOEFL (minimum score 550 paper-based). Electronic applications accepted.

University of La Verne, LaFetra College of Education, Credential Program in Teacher Education, La Verne, CA 91750-4443. Offers multiple subject (Credential); single subject (Credential); teaching (Credential). *Accreditation:* NCATE. *Program availability:* Part-time. *Students:* 40 full-time (26 women), 139 part-time (101 women); includes 104 minority (8 Black or African American, non-Hispanic/Latino; 1 American Indian or Alaska Native, non-Hispanic/Latino; 8 Asian, non-Hispanic/Latino; 82 Hispanic/Latino; 1 Native Hawaiian or other Pacific Islander, non-Hispanic/Latino; 4 Two or more races, non-Hispanic/Latino), 1 international. Average age 32. *Entrance requirements:* For degree, California Basic Educational Skills Test, minimum GPA of 3.0, interview, writing sample. Additional exam requirements/recommendations for international students: Required—TOEFL (minimum score 550 paper-based). *Application deadline:* Applications are processed on a rolling basis. Application fee: $50. *Expenses:* Contact institution. *Financial support:* Federal Work-Study, institutionally sponsored loans, and scholarships/grants available. Financial award application deadline: 3/2; financial award applicants required to submit FAFSA. *Unit head:* Dr. Jessica Decker, 909-448-4582, E-mail: jdecker@laverne.edu. *Application contact:* Christy Ranells, Associate Director of Graduate Admission, 909-448-4644, Fax: 909-971-2295, E-mail: cranells@laverne.edu.
Website: http://laverne.edu/education/

University of La Verne, LaFetra College of Education, Master's Program in Education, La Verne, CA 91750-4443. Offers advanced teaching skills (M Ed); education (M Ed); educational leadership (M Ed); special emphasis (M Ed). *Accreditation:* NCATE. *Program availability:* Part-time. *Students:* 37 full-time (31 women), 107 part-time (83 women); includes 74 minority (6 Black or African American, non-Hispanic/Latino; 1 American Indian or Alaska Native, non-Hispanic/Latino; 3 Asian, non-Hispanic/Latino; 62 Hispanic/Latino; 2 Two or more races, non-Hispanic/Latino). Average age 31. *Degree requirements:* For master's, thesis optional. *Entrance requirements:* For master's, California Basic Educational Skills Test, interview, writing sample, minimum GPA of 3.0, 3 letters of recommendation. Additional exam requirements/recommendations for international students: Required—TOEFL (minimum score 550 paper-based). *Application deadline:* Applications are processed on a rolling basis. Application fee: $50. *Expenses:* Contact institution. *Financial support:* Institutionally sponsored loans and scholarships/grants available. Financial award application deadline: 3/2; financial award applicants required to submit FAFSA. *Unit head:* Dr. Jessica Decker, Chair, 909-448-4582, E-mail: jdecker@laverne.edu. *Application contact:* Christy Ranells, Program and Admission Specialist, 909-448-4644, Fax: 909-392-2744, E-mail: cranells@laverne.edu.
Website: http://www.laverne.edu/education/

University of La Verne, Regional and Online Campuses, Graduate Credential Program in Education, California Statewide Campus, La Verne, CA 91750-4443. Offers administration services (preliminary) (Credential); education specialist: mild/moderate (Credential); English (Certificate); multiple subject teaching (Credential); pupil personnel services: school counseling (Credential); single subject teaching (Credential); special education (MS); special emphasis (M Ed). *Accreditation:* NCATE. *Program availability:* Part-time. *Entrance requirements:* For degree, California Basic Educational Skills Test, minimum undergraduate GPA of 2.75, 3 letters of recommendation, interview. *Expenses:* Contact institution.

University of La Verne, Regional and Online Campuses, Graduate Programs, Central Coast/Vandenberg Air Force Base Campuses, La Verne, CA 91750-4443. Offers business administration for experienced professionals (MBA), including health services management, information technology; education (special emphasis) (M Ed); educational counseling (MS); educational leadership (M Ed); multiple subject (elementary) (Credential); preliminary administrative services (Credential); pupil personnel services (Credential); single subject (secondary) (Credential). *Program availability:* Part-time. *Expenses:* Contact institution.

University of La Verne, Regional and Online Campuses, Master's Programs in Education, California Statewide Campus, La Verne, CA 91750-4443. Offers administration services (preliminary) (Credential); education specialist: mild/moderate (Credential); educational counseling (MS); educational leadership (M Ed); multiple subject teaching (Credential); pupil personnel services: school counseling (Credential); single subject teaching (Credential); special education studies (MS); special emphasis (M Ed). *Accreditation:* NCATE. *Entrance requirements:* For master's, California Basic Educational Skills Test, 3 letters of recommendation, teaching credential. *Expenses:* Contact institution.

University of Lethbridge, School of Graduate Studies, Lethbridge, AB T1K 3M4, Canada. Offers addictions counseling (M Sc); agricultural biotechnology (M Sc); agricultural studies (M Sc, MA); anthropology (MA); archaeology (M Sc, MA); art (MA, MFA); biochemistry (M Sc); biological sciences (M Sc); biomolecular science (PhD); biosystems and biodiversity (PhD); Canadian studies (MA); chemistry (M Sc); computer science (M Sc); computer science and geographical information science (M Sc); counseling (MC); counseling psychology (M Ed); dramatic arts (MA); earth, space, and physical science (PhD); economics (MA); education (MA, PhD); educational leadership (M Ed); English (MA); environmental science (M Sc); evolution and behavior (PhD); exercise science (M Sc); French (MA); French/German (MA); French/Spanish (MA); general education (M Ed); geography (M Sc, MA); German (MA); health sciences (M Sc); individualized multidisciplinary (M Sc, MA); kinesiology (M Sc, MA); management (M Sc), including accounting, finance, human resource management and labor relations, information systems, international management, marketing, policy and strategy; mathematics (M Sc); music (M Mus, MA); Native American studies (MA); neuroscience (M Sc, PhD); new media (MA, MFA); nursing (M Sc, MN); philosophy (MA); physics (M Sc); political science (MA); psychology (M Sc, MA); religious studies (MA); sociology (MA); theatre and dramatic arts (MFA); theoretical and computational science (PhD); urban and regional studies (MA); women and gender studies (MA). *Program availability:* Part-time, evening/weekend. *Degree requirements:* For master's, thesis (for some programs); for doctorate, comprehensive exam, thesis/dissertation. *Entrance requirements:* For master's, GMAT (for M Sc in management), bachelor's degree in related field, minimum GPA of 3.0 during previous 20 graded semester courses, 2 years' teaching or related experience (M Ed); for doctorate, master's degree, minimum graduate GPA of 3.5. Additional exam requirements/recommendations for international students: Required—TOEFL (minimum score 580 paper-based; 93 iBT). Electronic applications accepted. *Faculty research:* Movement and brain plasticity, gibberellin physiology, photosynthesis, carbon cycling, molecular properties of main-group ring components.

University of Louisiana at Lafayette, College of Education, Lafayette, LA 70504. Offers M Ed, Ed D. *Accreditation:* NCATE. *Program availability:* Part-time. *Degree requirements:* For master's, thesis or alternative. *Entrance requirements:* For master's, GRE General Test, teaching certificate. Additional exam requirements/recommendations for international students: Required—TOEFL (minimum score 550 paper-based). Electronic applications accepted.

University of Louisiana at Monroe, Graduate School, College of Arts, Education, and Sciences, School of Education, Monroe, LA 71209-0001. Offers curriculum and instruction (M Ed, Ed D), including art education (M Ed), biology education (M Ed), chemistry education (M Ed), curriculum and instruction (Ed D), early childhood education (M Ed), earth science education (M Ed), educational leadership (M Ed), elementary education (1-5) (M Ed), English as a second language (M Ed), English education (M Ed), family and consumer education (M Ed), French education (M Ed), history education (M Ed), math education (M Ed), middle school education (M Ed), music education (M Ed), reading education (K-12) (M Ed), Spanish education (M Ed), special education - academically gifted (M Ed), special education - early intervention (M Ed), special education - educational diagnostician (M Ed), special education - mild/moderate disabilities (M Ed), speech education (M Ed); elementary education (MAT); secondary education (MAT); special education (MAT). *Accreditation:* NCATE. *Program availability:* Part-time, evening/weekend, online learning. *Faculty:* 8 full-time (4 women), 4 part-time/adjunct (3 women). *Students:* 34 full-time (27 women), 136 part-time (109 women); includes 55 minority (43 Black or African American, non-Hispanic/Latino; 1 American Indian or Alaska Native, non-Hispanic/Latino; 2 Asian, non-Hispanic/Latino; 5 Hispanic/Latino; 4 Two or more races, non-Hispanic/Latino). Average age 35. 170 applicants, 48% accepted, 39 enrolled. In 2016, 37 master's, 5 doctorates awarded. *Degree requirements:* For master's, thesis; for doctorate, comprehensive exam, thesis/dissertation. *Entrance requirements:* For master's, GRE General Test, PRAXIS, minimum GPA of 2.5; for doctorate, GRE General Test, minimum undergraduate GPA of 2.75, 3.25 graduate; 3 letters of recommendation; interview. Additional exam requirements/recommendations for international students: Required—TOEFL (minimum score 500 paper-based; 61 iBT). *Application deadline:* For fall admission, 8/24 priority date for domestic students, 7/1 for international students; for winter admission, 12/14 priority date for domestic students; for spring admission, 1/19 for domestic students, 11/1 for international students. Applications are processed on a rolling basis. Application fee: $20 ($30 for international students). Electronic applications accepted. *Expenses:* Tuition, state resident: full-time $6489. Tuition, nonresident: full-time $18,589. *Required fees:* $8984. Tuition and fees vary according to course level, course load, degree level and program. *Financial support:* Research assistantships, career-related internships or fieldwork, Federal Work-Study, and unspecified assistantships available. Financial award application deadline: 4/1; financial award applicants required to submit FAFSA. *Unit head:* Dr. Dorothy Schween, Director, 318-342-1266, E-mail: schween@ulm.edu.
Website: http://www.ulm.edu/education/index.html

University of Louisville, Graduate School, College of Education and Human Development, Louisville, KY 40292-0001. Offers M Ed, MA, MAT, MS, Ed D, PhD, Certificate, Ed S. *Accreditation:* NCATE. *Program availability:* Part-time, evening/weekend, 100% online, blended/hybrid learning. *Faculty:* 100 full-time (66 women), 115 part-time/adjunct (72 women). *Students:* 582 full-time (267 women), 625 part-time (414 women); includes 306 minority (185 Black or African American, non-Hispanic/Latino; 2 American Indian or Alaska Native, non-Hispanic/Latino; 25 Asian, non-Hispanic/Latino; 57 Hispanic/Latino; 3 Native Hawaiian or other Pacific Islander, non-Hispanic/Latino; 34 Two or more races, non-Hispanic/Latino), 14 international. Average age 33. 627 applicants, 67% accepted, 282 enrolled. In 2016, 180 master's, 8 doctorates, 17 other advanced degrees awarded. Terminal master's awarded for partial completion of doctoral program. *Degree requirements:* For master's, comprehensive exam (for some programs), thesis optional; for doctorate, comprehensive exam (for some programs), thesis/dissertation. *Entrance requirements:* For master's, GRE (for most programs); PRAXIS (for educator preparation programs), professional statement, recommendation letters, resume, transcripts; for doctorate and other advanced degree, GRE, professional statement, recommendation letters, resume, transcripts. Additional exam requirements/recommendations for international students: Required—TOEFL (minimum score 550 paper-based; 79 iBT); Recommended—IELTS (minimum score 6.5). *Application deadline:* For fall admission, 6/1 priority date for domestic students; for spring admission, 10/1 priority date for domestic students; for summer admission, 3/1 priority date for domestic students. Application fee: $60. *Expenses:* Tuition, state resident: full-time $12,246; part-time $681 per credit hour. Tuition, nonresident: full-time $25,486; part-time $1417 per credit hour. *Required fees:* $196. Tuition and fees vary according to program and reciprocity agreements. *Financial support:* In 2016–17, 3 fellowships with full tuition reimbursements (averaging $20,694 per year), 31 research assistantships with full tuition reimbursements (averaging $20,694 per year), 7 teaching assistantships with full tuition reimbursements (averaging $20,694 per year) were awarded; Federal Work-Study, scholarships/grants, health care benefits, and unspecified assistantships also available. Financial award application deadline: 3/1; financial award applicants required to submit FAFSA. *Faculty research:* Teacher preparation and P-12 school partnerships, behavioral and psychological intervention and supports in P-20 settings, teacher capacities in effective STEM instruction and assessment, understanding workplace systems and cultures, Health and sport sciences. *Total annual research expenditures:* $4.4 million. *Unit head:* Dr. Elisabeth A. Larson, Dean, College of Education and Human Development, 502-852-6411, Fax: 502-852-1464, E-mail: ann.larson@louisville.edu. *Application contact:* Betty Hampton, Director, Graduate Student Services, 502-852-0411, Fax: 502-852-1465, E-mail: betty.hampton@louisville.edu.
Website: http://www.louisville.edu/education

Education—General

University of Maine, Graduate School, College of Education and Human Development, Orono, ME 04469. Offers M Ed, MA, MAT, MS, Ed D, PhD, CAS, CGS. *Accreditation:* NCATE. *Program availability:* Part-time, evening/weekend. *Faculty:* 36 full-time (21 women), 40 part-time/adjunct (30 women). *Students:* 150 full-time (118 women), 269 part-time (225 women); includes 24 minority (3 Black or African American, non-Hispanic/Latino; 10 American Indian or Alaska Native, non-Hispanic/Latino; 7 Hispanic/Latino; 1 Native Hawaiian or other Pacific Islander, non-Hispanic/Latino; 3 Two or more races, non-Hispanic/Latino), 7 international. Average age 37. 235 applicants, 94% accepted, 168 enrolled. In 2016, 85 master's, 4 doctorates, 58 other advanced degrees awarded. Terminal master's awarded for partial completion of doctoral program. *Degree requirements:* For master's, thesis (for some programs); for doctorate, comprehensive exam, thesis/dissertation. *Entrance requirements:* For master's, GRE General Test, MAT; for doctorate, GRE General Test; for other advanced degree, MA, M Ed, or MS. Additional exam requirements/recommendations for international students: Required—TOEFL (minimum score 550 paper-based; 80 iBT), IELTS (minimum score 6.5). *Application deadline:* For fall admission, 1/15 priority date for domestic students. Applications are processed on a rolling basis. Application fee: $65. Electronic applications accepted. *Expenses:* Tuition, state resident: full-time $7524; part-time $2508 per credit. Tuition, nonresident: full-time $24,498; part-time $8166 per credit. *Required fees:* $1148; $571 per credit. *Financial support:* In 2016–17, 51 students received support, including 19 teaching assistantships with full tuition reimbursements available (averaging $14,600 per year); fellowships, career-related internships or fieldwork, Federal Work-Study, institutionally sponsored loans, scholarships/grants, and unspecified assistantships also available. Support available to part-time students. Financial award application deadline: 3/1. *Faculty research:* Student hazing and hazing prevention epidemiology and birth defects prevention theories of science thinking and learning using writing to improve performance in athletics rural poverty and education. *Total annual research expenditures:* $5 million. *Unit head:* Dr. Timothy Reagan, Dean, 207-581-2441, Fax: 207-581-2423. *Application contact:* Scott G. Delcourt, Senior Associate Dean of the Graduate School, 207-581-3291, Fax: 207-581-3232, E-mail: graduate@maine.edu. Website: http://umaine.edu/edhd/

University of Maine at Farmington, Graduate Programs in Education, Farmington, ME 04938. Offers early childhood education (MS Ed); educational leadership (MS Ed); instructional technology (M Ed). M Ed offered in collaboration with University of Maine and University of Southern Maine. *Accreditation:* NCATE. *Program availability:* Part-time-only, evening/weekend, 100% online, blended/hybrid learning. *Faculty:* 7 full-time (6 women), 6 part-time/adjunct (3 women). *Students:* 90 part-time (76 women). Average age 36. 30 applicants, 100% accepted, 29 enrolled. In 2016, 14 master's awarded. *Degree requirements:* For master's, thesis, capstone project (for educational leadership). *Entrance requirements:* For master's, baccalaureate degree from accredited institution, valid teaching certificate or professional experience in education. Additional exam requirements/recommendations for international students: Required—TOEFL. *Application deadline:* For fall admission, 8/10 for domestic students; for spring admission, 1/5 for domestic students; for summer admission, 4/10 for domestic students. Applications are processed on a rolling basis. Application fee: $60. Electronic applications accepted. *Expenses:* Contact institution. *Financial support:* Applicants required to submit FAFSA. *Faculty research:* Teacher leadership, school improvement strategies, technology integration. *Unit head:* Dr. Johanna Prince, Director of Graduate Programs in Education, 207-778-7066, E-mail: gradstudies@maine.edu. *Application contact:* Valerie Soucie, Administrative Specialist, 207-778-7502, Fax: 207-778-8134, E-mail: gradstudies@maine.edu.
Website: http://www2.umf.maine.edu/gradstudies/

The University of Manchester, School of Education, Manchester, United Kingdom. Offers counseling (D Couns); counseling psychology (D Couns); education (M Phil, Ed D, PhD); educational and child psychology (Ed D); educational psychology (Ed D).

University of Manitoba, Faculty of Graduate Studies, College Universitaire de Saint Boniface, Education Program–Saint-Boniface, Winnipeg, MB R3T 2N2, Canada. Offers M Ed.

University of Manitoba, Faculty of Graduate Studies, Faculty of Education, Winnipeg, MB R3T 2N2, Canada. Offers M Ed, PhD. *Degree requirements:* For master's, thesis or alternative.

University of Mary, Liffrig Family School of Education and Behavioral Sciences, Department of Education, Bismarck, ND 58504-9652. Offers curriculum, instruction and assessment (M Ed); education (Ed D); elementary administration (M Ed); reading (M Ed); secondary administration (M Ed); special education strategist (M Ed). *Program availability:* Part-time. *Degree requirements:* For master's, portfolio or thesis. *Entrance requirements:* For master's, interview, letters of reference, minimum GPA of 2.5. Additional exam requirements/recommendations for international students: Required—TOEFL (minimum score 500 paper-based; 71 iBT). Electronic applications accepted.

University of Mary Hardin-Baylor, Graduate Studies in Education, Belton, TX 76513. Offers curriculum and instruction (M Ed); educational administration (M Ed, Ed D), including higher education (Ed D), leadership in nursing education (Ed D), P-12 (Ed D). *Program availability:* Part-time, evening/weekend. *Faculty:* 15 full-time (11 women), 9 part-time/adjunct (5 women). *Students:* 55 full-time (40 women), 79 part-time (60 women); includes 50 minority (29 Black or African American, non-Hispanic/Latino; 1 Asian, non-Hispanic/Latino; 18 Hispanic/Latino; 2 Two or more races, non-Hispanic/Latino), 3 international. Average age 38. 20 applicants, 95% accepted, 19 enrolled. In 2016, 23 master's, 19 doctorates awarded. *Degree requirements:* For master's, comprehensive exam; for doctorate, thesis/dissertation. *Entrance requirements:* For master's, minimum GPA of 3.0, interview; for doctorate, minimum GPA of 3.5, interview, essay, resume, employment verification, 3 letters of recommendation. Additional exam requirements/recommendations for international students: Required—TOEFL (minimum score 60 iBT), IELTS (minimum score 4.5). *Application deadline:* For fall admission, 6/1 for domestic students, 4/30 priority date for international students; for spring admission, 11/1 for domestic students, 9/30 priority date for international students. Applications are processed on a rolling basis. Application fee: $35 ($135 for international students). Electronic applications accepted. *Expenses:* $885 per credit hour. *Financial support:* In 2016–17, 99 students received support. Federal Work-Study and scholarships for some active duty military personnel available. Support available to part-time students. Financial award application deadline: 6/1; financial award applicants required to submit FAFSA. *Faculty research:* Motivational orientation of preservice teachers. *Unit head:* Dr. Craig Hammonds, Director, Graduate Programs in Education, 254-295-4189, E-mail: rhammonds@umhb.edu. *Application contact:* Sharon Aguilera, Assistant Director, Graduate Admissions, 254-295-4835, Fax: 254-295-5038, E-mail: saguilera@umhb.edu.
Website: http://graduate.umhb.edu/education/

University of Maryland, Baltimore County, The Graduate School, College of Arts, Humanities and Social Sciences, Department of Education, Baltimore, MD 21250. Offers education (MAE, MAE), including K-8 mathematics instructional leadership (MAE), K-8 science education (MAE), K-8 STEM education (MAE), secondary science education (MAE), secondary STEM education (MAE); instructional systems development (MA, Graduate Certificate), including distance education (Graduate Certificate), instructional systems development, instructional technology (Graduate Certificate); teaching (MAT), including early childhood education, elementary education, teaching; teaching English to speakers of other languages (MA, Postbaccalaureate Certificate). *Accreditation:* NCATE. *Program availability:* Part-time, evening/weekend, online learning. *Faculty:* 21 full-time (15 women), 25 part-time/adjunct (19 women). *Students:* 71 full-time (52 women), 339 part-time (251 women); includes 99 minority (62 Black or African American, non-Hispanic/Latino; 1 American Indian or Alaska Native, non-Hispanic/Latino; 17 Asian, non-Hispanic/Latino; 15 Hispanic/Latino; 1 Native Hawaiian or other Pacific Islander, non-Hispanic/Latino; 3 Two or more races, non-Hispanic/Latino), 9 international. Average age 34. 90 applicants, 94% accepted, 80 enrolled. In 2016, 60 master's awarded. *Degree requirements:* For master's, comprehensive exam (for some programs), thesis (for some programs). *Entrance requirements:* For master's, GRE General Test, GRE Subject Test (for MA in TESOL); PRAXIS Core Examination or GRE with minimum score of 1000 (for MAT); PRAXIS II (for MAE), minimum GPA of 3.0. Additional exam requirements/recommendations for international students: Required—TOEFL. *Application deadline:* For fall admission, 6/1 for domestic and international students; for spring admission, 11/1 for domestic students, 6/1 for international students. Applications are processed on a rolling basis. Application fee: $50. Electronic applications accepted. *Expenses:* Tuition, state resident: full-time $13,294. Tuition, nonresident: full-time $20,286. *Financial support:* In 2016–17, 12 students received support, including teaching assistantships with full tuition reimbursements available (averaging $12,000 per year); fellowships, career-related internships or fieldwork, Federal Work-Study, scholarships/grants, tuition waivers (partial), and unspecified assistantships also available. Financial award application deadline: 3/1. *Faculty research:* Teacher leadership; STEM education; ESOL/bilingual education; early childhood education; language, literacy and culture. *Total annual research expenditures:* $100,000. *Unit head:* Dr. Jon Singer, Department Chair, 410-455-2466, Fax: 410-455-3986, E-mail: jsinger@umbc.edu. *Application contact:* Dr. Susan M. Blunck, Graduate Program Director, 410-455-2869, Fax: 410-455-3986, E-mail: blunck@umbc.edu. Website: http://www.umbc.edu/education/

University of Maryland, College Park, Academic Affairs, College of Education, College Park, MD 20742. Offers M Ed, MA, Ed D, PhD, AGSC, CAGS. *Accreditation:* NCATE. *Program availability:* Part-time, evening/weekend, online learning. *Degree requirements:* For doctorate, thesis/dissertation. *Entrance requirements:* For master's, GRE General Test or MAT, minimum GPA of 3.0. Electronic applications accepted.

University of Maryland Eastern Shore, Graduate Programs, Department of Education, Program in Teaching, Princess Anne, MD 21853-1299. Offers MAT. Program offered jointly with Salisbury University. *Accreditation:* NCATE. *Degree requirements:* For master's, comprehensive exam, internship, seminar paper, PRAXIS II. *Entrance requirements:* For master's, PRAXIS I, interview, minimum GPA of 3.0, writing sample. Additional exam requirements/recommendations for international students: Required—TOEFL (minimum score 80 iBT). Electronic applications accepted.

University of Maryland University College, The Graduate School, Master of Arts in Teaching Program, Adelphi, MD 20783. Offers MAT. *Program availability:* Part-time, evening/weekend. *Students:* 6 full-time (4 women), 100 part-time (66 women); includes 13 minority (9 Black or African American, non-Hispanic/Latino; 1 Asian, non-Hispanic/Latino; 1 Hispanic/Latino; 2 Two or more races, non-Hispanic/Latino). Average age 34. 68 applicants, 100% accepted, 25 enrolled. In 2016, 57 master's awarded. *Degree requirements:* For master's, comprehensive exam, thesis or alternative. *Application deadline:* Applications are processed on a rolling basis. Application fee: $50. Electronic applications accepted. *Expenses:* Tuition, state resident: part-time $458 per credit. Tuition, nonresident: part-time $659 per credit. *Financial support:* Application deadline: 6/1; applicants required to submit FAFSA. *Unit head:* Dr. Virginia Pilato, Chair, Education Department, 240-684-2400, Fax: 240-684-2401, E-mail: virginia.pilato@umuc.edu. *Application contact:* Coordinator, Graduate Admissions, 800-888-8682, Fax: 240-684-2151, E-mail: newgrad@umuc.edu.
Website: http://www.umuc.edu/academic-programs/masters-degrees/teaching.cfm

University of Mary Washington, College of Education, Fredericksburg, VA 22401. Offers education (M Ed); elementary education (MS). *Program availability:* Part-time, evening/weekend. *Faculty:* 12 full-time (9 women), 18 part-time/adjunct (12 women). *Students:* 102 full-time (90 women), 106 part-time (89 women); includes 34 minority (11 Black or African American, non-Hispanic/Latino; 2 Asian, non-Hispanic/Latino; 12 Hispanic/Latino; 9 Two or more races, non-Hispanic/Latino). Average age 29. 231 applicants, 59% accepted, 79 enrolled. In 2016, 107 master's awarded. *Degree requirements:* For master's, one foreign language, comprehensive exam (for some programs). *Entrance requirements:* For master's, PRAXIS Core Academic Skills for Educators (Reading; Writing; Math or Virginia Department of Education accepted equivalent). Additional exam requirements/recommendations for international students: Required—TOEFL (minimum score 570 paper-based; 88 iBT), IELTS (minimum score 6.5). *Application deadline:* For fall admission, 4/15 for domestic and international students; for spring admission, 9/15 for domestic and international students. Applications are processed on a rolling basis. Application fee: $50. Electronic applications accepted. Application fee is waived when completed online. *Expenses:* Contact institution. *Financial support:* In 2016–17, 29 students received support, including 3 fellowships with partial tuition reimbursements available (averaging $9,000 per year); research assistantships, teaching assistantships, and scholarships/grants also available. Financial award application deadline: 4/25; financial award applicants required to submit FAFSA. *Unit head:* Dr. Marie Sheckels, Dean, 540-654-1334. *Application contact:* Deanna C. Pack, Director of Graduate Admissions, 540-286-8030, Fax: 540-286-8085, E-mail: dpack@umw.edu.
Website: http://www.umw.edu/education/

University of Massachusetts Amherst, Graduate School, College of Education, Amherst, MA 01003. Offers M Ed, Ed D, PhD, Ed S. *Accreditation:* NCATE. *Program availability:* Part-time, online learning. Terminal master's awarded for partial completion of doctoral program. *Degree requirements:* For doctorate, comprehensive exam, thesis/dissertation. *Entrance requirements:* Additional exam requirements/recommendations for international students: Required—TOEFL (minimum score 550 paper-based; 80 iBT), IELTS (minimum score 6.5). Electronic applications accepted.

University of Massachusetts Boston, College of Education and Human Development, Boston, MA 02125-3393. Offers M Ed, MS, Ed D, PhD. *Program availability:* Part-time, evening/weekend. *Students:* 341 full-time (275 women), 494 part-time (364 women). *Degree requirements:* For master's, comprehensive exam; for doctorate, comprehensive exam, thesis/dissertation. *Entrance requirements:* For master's, GRE General Test or MAT; for doctorate, GRE General Test or MAT, minimum GPA of 2.75. *Application deadline:* For fall admission, 3/1 for domestic students. *Expenses:* Tuition, state resident: full-time $16,863. Tuition, nonresident: full-time $32,913. *Required fees:* $177. *Financial support:* Research assistantships with full tuition reimbursements, teaching assistantships with full tuition reimbursements, career-related internships or fieldwork, Federal Work-Study, and unspecified assistantships available. Support available to part-time students. Financial award application deadline: 3/1; financial award applicants required to submit FAFSA. *Faculty research:* Effects of ethnicity on applied psychology and education, enhancing equity and excellence in public schools, diversity and change in higher education, improving the functioning of individuals with disabilities. *Unit head:* Dr. Peter Langer, Interim Dean, 617-287-7600. *Application*

contact: Peggy Roldan Patel, Graduate Admissions Coordinator, 617-287-6400, Fax: 617-287-6236, E-mail: bos.gadm@dpc.umassp.edu.
Website: http://www.umb.edu/academics/cehd

University of Massachusetts Dartmouth, Graduate School, College of Arts and Sciences, School of Education, North Dartmouth, MA 02747-2300. Offers educational leadership (Ed D, PhD), including educational leadership and policy studies; STEM education and teacher development (MAT, PhD, Postbaccalaureate Certificate), including education ESL preK-12 (Postbaccalaureate Certificate), mathematics education (PhD), middle school education (MAT), secondary school education (Postbaccalaureate Certificate), teaching secondary school education (MAT). *Program availability:* Part-time. *Faculty:* 13 full-time (6 women), 9 part-time/adjunct (5 women). *Students:* 42 full-time (20 women), 119 part-time (76 women); includes 31 minority (9 Black or African American, non-Hispanic/Latino; 1 American Indian or Alaska Native, non-Hispanic/Latino; 3 Asian, non-Hispanic/Latino; 12 Hispanic/Latino; 6 Two or more races, non-Hispanic/Latino), 5 international. Average age 34. 75 applicants, 89% accepted, 51 enrolled. In 2016, 77 master's, 12 doctorates awarded. Terminal master's awarded for partial completion of doctoral program. *Degree requirements:* For doctorate, thesis/dissertation. *Entrance requirements:* For master's, Massachusetts Tests for Educator Licensure (MTEL) Communication and Literacy Test and Subject Matter Test, statement of purpose (minimum of 300 words), resume, 2 letters of recommendation, official transcripts; copy of Massachusetts Initial License (for professional licensure program only); for doctorate, GRE or GMAT, statement of purpose (minimum of 300 words), resume, 3 letters of recommendation, official transcripts; 10-page scholarly writing sample (for educational leadership only); for Postbaccalaureate Certificate, statement of purpose (minimum of 300 words), resume, 2 letters of recommendation, official transcripts. Additional exam requirements/recommendations for international students: Required—TOEFL (minimum score 533 paper-based; 72 iBT). *Application deadline:* For fall admission, 2/15 priority date for domestic students, 1/15 priority date for international students; for spring admission, 12/15 priority date for domestic students, 11/15 priority date for international students. Application fee: $60. Electronic applications accepted. *Expenses:* Tuition, state resident: full-time $14,994; part-time $624.75 per credit. Tuition, nonresident: full-time $27,068; part-time $1127.83 per credit. *Required fees:* $405; $25.88 per credit. Tuition and fees vary according to course load and reciprocity agreements. *Financial support:* In 2016–17, 4 fellowships (averaging $18,500 per year), 3 research assistantships (averaging $5,027 per year), 2 teaching assistantships (averaging $16,000 per year) were awarded; institutionally sponsored loans, scholarships/grants, unspecified assistantships, and doctoral support, instructional assistantships also available. Support available to part-time students. Financial award application deadline: 3/1; financial award applicants required to submit FAFSA. *Faculty research:* Role of metacognition in advanced mathematical thinking, education reform, curricular theory, higher education policy, qualitative methods, reading/special education, English education, development of specialized knowledge for science teaching. *Total annual research expenditures:* $1.9 million. *Unit head:* Amy Shapiro, Associate Dean, College of Arts and Sciences, 508-910-9101-, Fax: 508-999-9125, E-mail: ashapiro@umassd.edu. *Application contact:* Steven Briggs, Director of Marketing and Recruitment for Graduate Studies, 508-999-8604, Fax: 508-999-8183, E-mail: graduate@umassd.edu.
Website: http://www.umassd.edu/cas/schoolofeducation

University of Massachusetts Lowell, Graduate School of Education, Lowell, MA 01854. Offers curriculum and instruction (M Ed). *Accreditation:* NCATE. *Program availability:* Part-time, evening/weekend, online learning. Terminal master's awarded for partial completion of doctoral program. *Entrance requirements:* For master's, GRE General Test. Additional exam requirements/recommendations for international students: Required—TOEFL. Electronic applications accepted.

University of Memphis, Graduate School, College of Education, Memphis, TN 38152. Offers M Ed, MAT, MS, Ed D, PhD, Graduate Certificate. *Accreditation:* NCATE. *Program availability:* Part-time, evening/weekend, 100% online, blended/hybrid learning. *Faculty:* 58 full-time (36 women), 32 part-time/adjunct (21 women). *Students:* 212 full-time (164 women), 575 part-time (423 women); includes 324 minority (266 Black or African American, non-Hispanic/Latino; 1 American Indian or Alaska Native, non-Hispanic/Latino; 11 Asian, non-Hispanic/Latino; 23 Hispanic/Latino; 1 Native Hawaiian or other Pacific Islander, non-Hispanic/Latino; 22 Two or more races, non-Hispanic/Latino), 13 international. Average age 38. 377 applicants, 79% accepted, 223 enrolled. In 2016, 187 master's, 43 doctorates, 55 other advanced degrees awarded. Terminal master's awarded for partial completion of doctoral program. *Degree requirements:* For master's, comprehensive exam, thesis or alternative, practicum; for doctorate, comprehensive exam, thesis/dissertation, residency project, internship (for some). *Entrance requirements:* For master's, GRE General Test or MAT; for doctorate, GRE General Test, writing sample, interview, letters of reference; for Graduate Certificate, letters of reference. Additional exam requirements/recommendations for international students: Required—TOEFL (minimum score 550 paper-based; 79 iBT). *Application deadline:* Applications are processed on a rolling basis. Application fee: $35 ($60 for international students). Electronic applications accepted. *Expenses:* $5,231.50 per semester full-time in-state, $9,623.50 full-time out-of-state. *Financial support:* In 2016–17, 921 students received support, including 18 research assistantships with full tuition reimbursements available, 14 teaching assistantships with full tuition reimbursements available; career-related internships or fieldwork, Federal Work-Study, scholarships/grants, tuition waivers (partial), and unspecified assistantships also available. Financial award application deadline: 2/1; financial award applicants required to submit FAFSA. *Faculty research:* Urban school effectiveness, literacy development, teacher effectiveness, exercise physiology, crisis counseling. *Total annual research expenditures:* $3.3 million. *Unit head:* Dr. Kandi Hill-Clarke, Dean, 901-678-5495, Fax: 901-678-4778, E-mail: k.hill-clarke@memphis.edu. *Application contact:* Dr. Suzanne Lease, Interim Assistant Dean of Education for Graduate Programs, 901-678-2352, Fax: 901-678-4476, E-mail: slease@memphis.edu.
Website: http://www.memphis.edu/coe

University of Miami, Graduate School, School of Education and Human Development, Coral Gables, FL 33124. Offers MS Ed, Ed D, PhD, Certificate, Ed S. *Program availability:* 100% online. *Faculty:* 72 full-time (37 women), 51 part-time/adjunct (31 women). *Students:* 404 full-time (209 women), 86 part-time (61 women); includes 241 minority (81 Black or African American, non-Hispanic/Latino; 2 American Indian or Alaska Native, non-Hispanic/Latino; 11 Asian, non-Hispanic/Latino; 129 Hispanic/Latino; 2 Native Hawaiian or other Pacific Islander, non-Hispanic/Latino; 16 Two or more races, non-Hispanic/Latino), 34 international. Average age 30. 613 applicants, 44% accepted, 152 enrolled. In 2016, 100 master's, 19 doctorates, 3 other advanced degrees awarded. Terminal master's awarded for partial completion of doctoral program. *Degree requirements:* For master's, comprehensive exam (for some programs), thesis optional, electronic portfolio, special project, personal growth experience; for doctorate, thesis/dissertation, qualifying exam, portfolio. *Entrance requirements:* For master's and doctorate, GRE General Test. Additional exam requirements/recommendations for international students: Required—TOEFL (minimum score 550 paper-based; 80 iBT); Recommended—IELTS (minimum score 6.5). *Application deadline:* For fall admission, 10/1 for international students. Application fee: $65. Electronic applications accepted. *Financial support:* Fellowships, research assistantships, teaching assistantships, career-related internships or fieldwork, institutionally sponsored loans, scholarships/grants, health care benefits, tuition waivers (full and partial), and unspecified assistantships available. Support available to part-time students. Financial award application deadline: 3/1; financial award applicants required to submit FAFSA. *Faculty research:* Social skills and learning disabilities, planning for mainstreamed pupils, alcohol and drug abuse, restructuring education for all learners. *Unit head:* Dr. Walter Secada, Senior Associate Dean, 305-284-2102, Fax: 305-284-9395, E-mail: wsecada@miami.edu. *Application contact:* Lois Heffernan, Graduate Admissions Coordinator, 305-284-2167, Fax: 305-284-9395, E-mail: lheffernan@miami.edu.
Website: http://www.education.miami.edu

University of Michigan, Rackham Graduate School, Combined Program in Education and Psychology, Ann Arbor, MI 48109. Offers PhD. *Accreditation:* TEAC. *Faculty:* 20 part-time/adjunct (11 women). *Students:* 34 full-time (25 women); includes 20 minority (13 Black or African American, non-Hispanic/Latino; 3 Asian, non-Hispanic/Latino; 4 Hispanic/Latino). Average age 27. 110 applicants, 8% accepted, 6 enrolled. In 2016, 9 doctorates awarded. *Degree requirements:* For doctorate, thesis/dissertation, independent research project, preliminary exam, oral defense of dissertation. *Entrance requirements:* For doctorate, GRE General Test with Analytical Writing Test. Additional exam requirements/recommendations for international students: Required—TOEFL (minimum score 600 paper-based; 100 iBT). *Application deadline:* For fall admission, 12/1 for domestic and international students. Application fee: $75. Electronic applications accepted. *Expenses:* Contact institution. *Financial support:* In 2016–17, 34 students received support, including 16 fellowships with full tuition reimbursements available (averaging $29,605 per year), 3 research assistantships with full tuition reimbursements available (averaging $27,737 per year), 15 teaching assistantships with full tuition reimbursements available (averaging $27,737 per year); institutionally sponsored loans, scholarships/grants, health care benefits, and unspecified assistantships also available. Financial award application deadline: 4/15. *Faculty research:* Human development in context of schools, families, communities; cognitive and learning sciences; motivation and self-regulated learning; culture, ethnicity, social and class influences on learning and motivation. *Unit head:* Dr. Stephanie J. Rowley, Chair, 734-647-0626, Fax: 734-615-2164, E-mail: srowley@umich.edu. *Application contact:* Katie Schmitt, Program Coordinator, 734-763-0680, Fax: 734-615-2164, E-mail: cpep@umich.edu.
Website: http://www.soe.umich.edu/academics/doctoral_programs/ep/

University of Michigan, School of Education, Ann Arbor, MI 48109-1259. Offers MA, MS, PhD, MA/Certification, MBA/MA, MPP/MA, PhD/MA. *Accreditation:* TEAC. Terminal master's awarded for partial completion of doctoral program. *Degree requirements:* For master's, thesis optional; for doctorate, comprehensive exam, thesis/dissertation. *Entrance requirements:* For master's and doctorate, GRE General Test. Additional exam requirements/recommendations for international students: Required—TOEFL (minimum score 560 paper-based). Electronic applications accepted. *Expenses:* Tuition, state resident: full-time $21,466; part-time $1152 per credit hour. Tuition, nonresident: full-time $43,346; part-time $2367 per credit hour. Part-time tuition and fees vary according to course load, degree level and program. *Faculty research:* Teaching, learning, policy, leadership, technology.

University of Michigan–Dearborn, College of Education, Health, and Human Services, Master of Arts in Teaching Program, Dearborn, MI 48126-2638. Offers MAT. *Accreditation:* TEAC. *Program availability:* Part-time, evening/weekend. *Faculty:* 7 full-time (5 women), 8 part-time/adjunct (6 women). *Students:* 9 full-time (5 women), 8 part-time (4 women); includes 5 minority (3 Black or African American, non-Hispanic/Latino; 1 Hispanic/Latino; 1 Two or more races, non-Hispanic/Latino). Average age 38. 5 applicants, 20% accepted, 1 enrolled. In 2016, 9 master's awarded. *Entrance requirements:* For master's, Michigan Test for Teacher Certification Professional Readiness Exam, minimum cumulative GPA of 3.0, interview, 3 letters of recommendation, statement of purpose. Additional exam requirements/recommendations for international students: Required—TOEFL (minimum score 560 paper-based; 84 iBT), IELTS (minimum score 6.5). *Application deadline:* For fall admission, 8/1 priority date for domestic students, 5/1 priority date for international students; for winter admission, 12/1 priority date for domestic students, 9/1 priority date for international students; for spring admission, 4/1 priority date for domestic students, 1/1 priority date for international students. Applications are processed on a rolling basis. Application fee: $60. Electronic applications accepted. *Expenses:* Contact institution. *Financial support:* In 2016–17, 3 students received support. Career-related internships or fieldwork and scholarships/grants available. Financial award application deadline: 3/1; financial award applicants required to submit FAFSA. *Faculty research:* Educational technology, educational foundations, assessment. *Unit head:* Dr. Stein Brunvand, Director, Master's Programs, 313-583-6415, E-mail: sbrunvan@umich.edu. *Application contact:* Elizabeth Morden, Graduate Programs Assistant, 313-593-5090, E-mail: emorden@umich.edu.
Website: http://umdearborn.edu/cehhs/cehhs_mat/

University of Michigan–Dearborn, College of Education, Health, and Human Services, Master of Arts Program in Education, Dearborn, MI 48126-2638. Offers MA. *Accreditation:* TEAC. *Program availability:* Part-time, evening/weekend, 100% online. *Faculty:* 9 full-time (6 women), 4 part-time/adjunct (3 women). *Students:* 3 full-time (all women), 46 part-time (41 women); includes 3 minority (1 Black or African American, non-Hispanic/Latino; 2 Hispanic/Latino). Average age 31. 21 applicants, 95% accepted, 11 enrolled. In 2016, 33 master's awarded. *Entrance requirements:* For master's, minimum GPA of 3.0, teaching certificate, 3 letters of recommendation, statement of purpose. Additional exam requirements/recommendations for international students: Required—TOEFL (minimum score 560 paper-based; 84 iBT), IELTS (minimum score 6.5). *Application deadline:* For fall admission, 8/1 for domestic students, 5/1 for international students; for winter admission, 12/1 for domestic students, 9/1 for international students; for spring admission, 4/1 for domestic students, 1/1 for international students. Applications are processed on a rolling basis. Application fee: $60. Electronic applications accepted. *Expenses:* Contact institution. *Financial support:* In 2016–17, 4 students received support. Career-related internships or fieldwork and scholarships/grants available. Financial award application deadline: 3/1; financial award applicants required to submit FAFSA. *Faculty research:* STEM education, organizational leadership, inquiry based curriculum development, developing effective inclusive practices. *Unit head:* Dr. Stein Brunvand, Director, Master's Programs, 313-583-6415, E-mail: sbrunvan@umich.edu. *Application contact:* Elizabeth Morden, Graduate Programs Assistant, 313-593-5090, E-mail: emorden@umich.edu.
Website: http://umdearborn.edu/cehhs/cehhs_maed/

University of Michigan–Flint, School of Education and Human Services, Flint, MI 48502. Offers MA, Ed D, Ed S. *Program availability:* Part-time, 100% online, mixed mode programs. *Faculty:* 14 full-time (9 women), 30 part-time/adjunct (17 women). *Students:* 31 full-time (18 women), 200 part-time (145 women); includes 61 minority (48 Black or African American, non-Hispanic/Latino; 1 Asian, non-Hispanic/Latino; 6 Hispanic/Latino; 1 Native Hawaiian or other Pacific Islander, non-Hispanic/Latino; 5 Two or more races, non-Hispanic/Latino), 2 international. Average age 39. 124 applicants, 86% accepted, 75 enrolled. In 2016, 77 master's, 1 doctorate awarded. *Degree requirements:* For master's, thesis optional; for doctorate, thesis/dissertation. *Entrance requirements:* For master's, bachelor's degree from regionally-accredited institution,

minimum overall undergraduate GPA of 3.0; for doctorate, Ed S; minimum overall graduate GPA of 3.3 (6.0 on a 9.0 scale) or equivalent; at least 3 years of work experience in a P-16 educational institution or in an education-related position; for Ed S, MA or MS in an education-related field from accredited institution; minimum overall graduate GPA of 3.0 (6.0 on a 9.0 scale) or equivalent; at least 3 years of work experience in educational setting. Additional exam requirements/recommendations for international students: Required—TOEFL (minimum score 84 iBT), IELTS (minimum score 6.5). *Application deadline:* For fall admission, 7/1 for domestic students, 4/1 for international students; for winter admission, 11/15 for domestic students, 9/1 for international students; for spring admission, 3/15 for domestic students, 1/1 for international students. Applications are processed on a rolling basis. Application fee: $55. Electronic applications accepted. *Expenses:* Contact institution. *Financial support:* Federal Work-Study, scholarships/grants, and unspecified assistantships available. Support available to part-time students. Financial award application deadline: 3/1; financial award applicants required to submit FAFSA. *Unit head:* Dr. Bob Barnett, Dean, 810-766-6878, Fax: 810-766-6891, E-mail: rbarnett@umflint.edu. *Application contact:* Bradley T. Maki, Director of Graduate Admissions, 810-762-3171, Fax: 810-766-6789, E-mail: bmaki@umflint.edu.
Website: http://www.umflint.edu/sehs

University of Minnesota, Duluth, Graduate School, College of Education and Human Service Professions, Department of Education, Duluth, MN 55812-2496. Offers M Ed, Ed D. *Program availability:* Part-time, evening/weekend. *Degree requirements:* For doctorate, comprehensive exam. *Entrance requirements:* For doctorate, GRE, MA (preferred) minimum GPA of 3.0, 3 letters of recommendation, 3 work samples. Additional exam requirements/recommendations for international students: Required—TOEFL (minimum score 550 paper-based).

University of Minnesota, Twin Cities Campus, Graduate School, College of Education and Human Development, Minneapolis, MN 55455-0213. Offers M Ed, MA, MS, MSW, Ed D, PhD, Certificate, Ed S. *Accreditation:* NCATE. *Program availability:* Part-time. *Faculty:* 178 full-time (95 women). *Students:* 1,469 full-time (1,059 women), 768 part-time (527 women); includes 482 minority (137 Black or African American, non-Hispanic/Latino; 17 American Indian or Alaska Native, non-Hispanic/Latino; 119 Asian, non-Hispanic/Latino; 131 Hispanic/Latino; 1 Native Hawaiian or other Pacific Islander, non-Hispanic/Latino; 77 Two or more races, non-Hispanic/Latino), 179 international. Average age 32. 2,091 applicants, 53% accepted, 1005 enrolled. In 2016, 1,159 master's, 155 doctorates, 74 other advanced degrees awarded. Application fee: $75 ($95 for international students). *Financial support:* In 2016–17, 157 fellowships, 300 research assistantships with full tuition reimbursements (averaging $11,689 per year), 214 teaching assistantships with full tuition reimbursements (averaging $11,785 per year) were awarded; scholarships/grants and tuition waivers (partial) also available. Financial award applicants required to submit FAFSA. *Faculty research:* Educational equity and achievement gap; living longer, living better - healthy aging across the lifespan; children's mental health, child welfare; autism spectrum disorders, neurodevelopment, developmental disability. *Total annual research expenditures:* $51.5 million. *Unit head:* Dr. Jean K. Quam, Dean, 612-626-9252, Fax: 612-626-7496, E-mail: jquam@umn.edu. *Application contact:* Dr. Brianne Keeney, Director of Graduate Education Initiatives, 612-626-9145, E-mail: keen0113@umn.edu.
Website: http://www.cehd.umn.edu

University of Mississippi, Graduate School, School of Education, University, MS 38677. Offers M Ed, MA, Ed D, PhD, Ed S, Specialist. *Accreditation:* NCATE. *Faculty:* 58 full-time (22 women), 35 part-time/adjunct (27 women). *Students:* 203 full-time (158 women), 404 part-time (299 women); includes 219 minority (185 Black or African American, non-Hispanic/Latino; 6 Asian, non-Hispanic/Latino; 21 Hispanic/Latino; 7 Two or more races, non-Hispanic/Latino), 9 international. Average age 31. In 2016, 176 master's, 20 doctorates, 37 other advanced degrees awarded. *Degree requirements:* For doctorate, thesis/dissertation. *Entrance requirements:* For master's, GRE General Test, minimum GPA of 3.0; for doctorate, GRE General Test. Additional exam requirements/recommendations for international students: Required—TOEFL. *Application deadline:* For fall admission, 4/1 for domestic students; for spring admission, 10/1 for domestic students. Applications are processed on a rolling basis. Application fee: $40. Electronic applications accepted. *Financial support:* Scholarships/grants available. Financial award application deadline: 3/1; financial award applicants required to submit FAFSA. *Unit head:* Dr. David Rock, Dean, 662-915-7063, Fax: 662-915-7249, E-mail: soe@olemiss.edu. *Application contact:* Dr. Christy M. Wyandt, Associate Dean, 662-915-7474, Fax: 662-915-7577, E-mail: cwyandt@olemiss.edu.
Website: https://www.olemiss.edu

University of Missouri, Office of Research and Graduate Studies, College of Education, Columbia, MO 65211. Offers M Ed, MA, Ed D, PhD, Certificate, Ed S. *Accreditation:* TEAC. *Program availability:* Part-time, evening/weekend. *Faculty:* 100 full-time (62 women), 4 part-time/adjunct (1 woman). *Students:* 640 full-time (430 women), 727 part-time (471 women); includes 157 minority (70 Black or African American, non-Hispanic/Latino; 2 American Indian or Alaska Native, non-Hispanic/Latino; 14 Asian, non-Hispanic/Latino; 44 Hispanic/Latino; 1 Native Hawaiian or other Pacific Islander, non-Hispanic/Latino; 26 Two or more races, non-Hispanic/Latino), 72 international. Average age 34. Terminal master's awarded for partial completion of doctoral program. *Degree requirements:* For master's, variable foreign language requirement, thesis (for some programs); for doctorate, variable foreign language requirement, comprehensive exam (for some programs), thesis/dissertation. *Entrance requirements:* For master's, minimum GPA of 3.0; for doctorate, GRE General Test. Additional exam requirements/recommendations for international students: Required—TOEFL (minimum score 550 paper-based; 80 iBT), IELTS (minimum score 6.5). *Application deadline:* Applications are processed on a rolling basis. Application fee: $75 ($90 for international students). *Expenses:* Tuition, state resident: full-time $6347; part-time $352.60 per credit hour. Tuition, nonresident: full-time $17,379; part-time $965.50 per credit hour. *Required fees:* $1035. Tuition and fees vary according to course load, campus/location and program. *Financial support:* Fellowships, research assistantships, teaching assistantships, institutionally sponsored loans, scholarships/grants, traineeships, health care benefits, and unspecified assistantships available. Support available to part-time students.
Website: http://education.missouri.edu/

University of Missouri–Kansas City, School of Education, Kansas City, MO 64110-2499. Offers administration (Ed D); counseling and guidance (MA, Ed S), including mental health counseling (Ed S), school counseling (Ed S); counseling psychology (PhD); curriculum and instruction (MA, Ed S), including language and literacy (Ed S); education (PhD), including higher education administration, PK-12 education administration; educational administration (MA, Ed S), including advanced principal (Ed S), beginning principal (Ed S), district-level administration (Ed S); reading education (MA); special education (MA). PhD in education offered through the School of Graduate Studies. *Accreditation:* NCATE. *Program availability:* Part-time, evening/weekend. *Faculty:* 33 full-time (26 women), 51 part-time/adjunct (39 women). *Students:* 136 full-time (103 women), 275 part-time (194 women); includes 110 minority (71 Black or African American, non-Hispanic/Latino; 3 American Indian or Alaska Native, non-Hispanic/Latino; 8 Asian, non-Hispanic/Latino; 22 Hispanic/Latino; 6 Two or more races, non-Hispanic/Latino), 20 international. Average age 32. 324 applicants, 45% accepted, 108 enrolled. In 2016, 152 master's, 13 doctorates, 50 other advanced degrees awarded. *Degree requirements:* For doctorate, thesis/dissertation, internship, practicum. *Entrance requirements:* For master's, GRE, minimum GPA of 2.75, 2 letters of reference, written statement of purpose; for doctorate, GRE, minimum GPA of 3.0; for Ed S, minimum GPA of 3.0. Additional exam requirements/recommendations for international students: Required—TOEFL (minimum score 550 paper-based; 80 iBT). *Application deadline:* For fall admission, 4/1 priority date for domestic and international students; for spring admission, 11/1 priority date for domestic and international students. Applications are processed on a rolling basis. Application fee: $45 ($50 for international students). *Financial support:* In 2016–17, 12 research assistantships with partial tuition reimbursements (averaging $12,476 per year) were awarded; career-related internships or fieldwork, Federal Work-Study, institutionally sponsored loans, and tuition waivers (full and partial) also available. Support available to part-time students. Financial award application deadline: 3/1; financial award applicants required to submit FAFSA. *Faculty research:* Urban education, inquiry-based field study, theories of counseling and psychotherapy, school literacy, educational technology. *Unit head:* Justin Perry, Dean, 816-235-5663, Fax: 816-235-5270, E-mail: education@umkc.edu.
Website: http://education.umkc.edu

University of Missouri–St. Louis, College of Education, St. Louis, MO 63121. Offers M Ed, Ed D, PhD, Certificate, Ed S. *Accreditation:* NCATE. *Program availability:* Part-time, evening/weekend. *Faculty:* 62 full-time (39 women), 76 part-time/adjunct (55 women). *Students:* 198 full-time (161 women), 981 part-time (744 women); includes 331 minority (253 Black or African American, non-Hispanic/Latino; 3 American Indian or Alaska Native, non-Hispanic/Latino; 21 Asian, non-Hispanic/Latino; 41 Hispanic/Latino; 1 Native Hawaiian or other Pacific Islander, non-Hispanic/Latino; 12 Two or more races, non-Hispanic/Latino), 13 international. 469 applicants, 86% accepted, 281 enrolled. *Degree requirements:* For master's, comprehensive exam, thesis optional; for doctorate, thesis/dissertation. *Entrance requirements:* For doctorate, GRE General Test, 3 letters of recommendation. Additional exam requirements/recommendations for international students: Recommended—TOEFL (minimum score 550 paper-based; 79 iBT), IELTS (minimum score 6.5). *Application deadline:* For fall admission, 7/1 priority date for domestic and international students; for spring admission, 12/1 priority date for domestic and international students. Applications are processed on a rolling basis. Application fee: $50 ($40 for international students). Electronic applications accepted. *Financial support:* Research assistantships with tuition reimbursements and teaching assistantships with tuition reimbursements available. Financial award application deadline: 4/1; financial award applicants required to submit FAFSA. *Faculty research:* Remedial reading, literacy, educational policy and research, science education. *Unit head:* Ann Taylor, Interim Dean, 314-516-5106, Fax: 314-516-5227, E-mail: taylorann@umsl.edu. *Application contact:* 314-516-5458, Fax: 314-516-6996, E-mail: gradadm@umsl.edu.
Website: http://coe.umsl.edu/

University of Mobile, Graduate Studies, Program in Education, Mobile, AL 36613. Offers MA. *Program availability:* Part-time, 100% online. *Degree requirements:* For master's, comprehensive exam, thesis optional. *Entrance requirements:* For master's, GRE, Alabama teaching certificate. Additional exam requirements/recommendations for international students: Required—TOEFL (minimum score 550 paper-based; 80 iBT). Electronic applications accepted. *Faculty research:* Retention, writing across the curriculum.

University of Montana, Graduate School, Phyllis J. Washington College of Education and Human Sciences, Missoula, MT 59812-0002. Offers M Ed, MA, MS, Ed D, Ed S. *Accreditation:* NCATE. *Program availability:* Part-time. *Degree requirements:* For Ed S, thesis. *Entrance requirements:* For master's, GRE General Test, minimum GPA of 3.0; for Ed S, GRE General Test. Additional exam requirements/recommendations for international students: Required—TOEFL. *Faculty research:* Cooperative learning, administrative styles.

University of Montevallo, College of Education, Montevallo, AL 35115. Offers M Ed, Ed S. *Accreditation:* NCATE. *Program availability:* Part-time, evening/weekend. *Students:* 86 full-time (65 women), 186 part-time (135 women); includes 55 minority (45 Black or African American, non-Hispanic/Latino; 1 Asian, non-Hispanic/Latino; 6 Hispanic/Latino; 3 Two or more races, non-Hispanic/Latino). In 2016, 120 master's, 17 Ed Ss awarded. *Degree requirements:* For master's, comprehensive exam. *Entrance requirements:* For master's, GRE General Test, MAT, minimum undergraduate GPA of 2.5. Additional exam requirements/recommendations for international students: Required—TOEFL (minimum score 550 paper-based). *Application deadline:* For fall admission, 7/15 for domestic students; for spring admission, 11/15 for domestic students. Application fee: $25. *Expenses:* Tuition, state resident: full-time $9936. Tuition, nonresident: full-time $20,592. *Required fees:* $640. *Financial support:* Federal Work-Study, scholarships/grants, and unspecified assistantships available. *Unit head:* Dr. Anna E. McEwan, Dean, 205-665-6360, E-mail: mcewanae@montevallo.edu. *Application contact:* Kevin Thornthwaite, Director, Graduate Admissions and Records, 205-665-6350, E-mail: graduate@montevallo.edu.
Website: http://www.montevallo.edu/education/college-of-education/

University of Nebraska at Kearney, College of Education, Kearney, NE 68849-0001. Offers MA Ed, MS Ed, Ed S. *Accreditation:* NCATE. *Program availability:* Part-time, evening/weekend, 100% online. *Faculty:* 50 full-time (26 women). *Students:* 129 full-time (106 women), 569 part-time (397 women); includes 52 minority (7 Black or African American, non-Hispanic/Latino; 3 Asian, non-Hispanic/Latino; 33 Hispanic/Latino; 1 Native Hawaiian or other Pacific Islander, non-Hispanic/Latino; 8 Two or more races, non-Hispanic/Latino), 5 international. Average age 31. 223 applicants, 91% accepted, 138 enrolled. In 2016, 236 master's, 20 Ed Ss awarded. *Degree requirements:* For master's, comprehensive exam, thesis optional. *Entrance requirements:* Additional exam requirements/recommendations for international students: Recommended—TOEFL (minimum score 550 paper-based; 79 iBT), IELTS (minimum score 6.5). *Application deadline:* For fall admission, 6/15 for domestic and international students; for spring admission, 10/15 for domestic and international students; for summer admission, 3/15 for domestic and international students. Application fee: $45. Electronic applications accepted. *Expenses:* Tuition, state resident: full-time $4064; part-time $225.75 per credit hour. Tuition, nonresident: full-time $8915; part-time $495.25 per credit hour. *Required fees:* $772; $23 per credit hour. Part-time tuition and fees vary according to course load, campus/location, program and reciprocity agreements. *Financial support:* Research assistantships with full tuition reimbursements, teaching assistantships with full tuition reimbursements, career-related internships or fieldwork, scholarships/grants, health care benefits, and unspecified assistantships available. Support available to part-time students. Financial award application deadline: 2/28; financial award applicants required to submit FAFSA. *Unit head:* Dr. Sheryl Feinstein, Dean, 308-865-8502. *Application contact:* Linda Johnson, Director, Graduate Admissions and Programs, 800-717-7881, Fax: 308-865-8837, E-mail: johnsonli@unk.edu.
Website: http://www.unk.edu/coe/

University of Nebraska at Omaha, Graduate Studies, College of Education, Omaha, NE 68182. Offers MA, MS, Ed D, PhD, Certificate, Ed S. *Accreditation:* NCATE.

Program availability: Part-time, evening/weekend. *Faculty:* 33 full-time (25 women). *Students:* 201 full-time (127 women), 600 part-time (497 women); includes 89 minority (27 Black or African American, non-Hispanic/Latino; 16 Asian, non-Hispanic/Latino; 28 Hispanic/Latino; 18 Two or more races, non-Hispanic/Latino), 26 international. Average age 32. 343 applicants, 59% accepted, 162 enrolled. In 2016, 245 master's, 14 doctorates, 1 other advanced degree awarded. *Degree requirements:* For master's, comprehensive exam (for some programs), thesis (for some programs); for doctorate, comprehensive exam, thesis/dissertation. *Entrance requirements:* Additional exam requirements/recommendations for international students: Required—TOEFL, IELTS, PTE. *Application deadline:* Applications are processed on a rolling basis. Application fee: $45. Electronic applications accepted. *Financial support:* In 2016–17, 68 students received support. Fellowships, research assistantships with tuition reimbursements available, teaching assistantships with tuition reimbursements available, career-related internships or fieldwork, Federal Work-Study, institutionally sponsored loans, scholarships/grants, health care benefits, tuition waivers (full), and unspecified assistantships available. Support available to part-time students. Financial award application deadline: 3/1; financial award applicants required to submit FAFSA. *Unit head:* Dr. Nancy Edick, Dean, 402-554-2341, E-mail: graduate@unomaha.edu.

University of Nevada, Las Vegas, Graduate College, College of Education, Las Vegas, NV 89154-3001. Offers M Ed, MS, Ed D, PhD, Advanced Certificate, Certificate, Ed S, PhD/JD. *Program availability:* Part-time, evening/weekend. *Faculty:* 63 full-time (34 women), 43 part-time/adjunct (31 women). *Students:* 623 full-time (476 women), 480 part-time (338 women); includes 429 minority (119 Black or African American, non-Hispanic/Latino; 6 American Indian or Alaska Native, non-Hispanic/Latino; 49 Asian, non-Hispanic/Latino; 179 Hispanic/Latino; 7 Native Hawaiian or other Pacific Islander, non-Hispanic/Latino; 69 Two or more races, non-Hispanic/Latino), 46 international. Average age 35. 555 applicants, 74% accepted, 333 enrolled. In 2016, 356 master's, 31 doctorates, 9 other advanced degrees awarded. *Degree requirements:* For master's, comprehensive exam (for some programs), thesis (for some programs); for doctorate, comprehensive exam, thesis/dissertation; for other advanced degree, comprehensive exam (for some programs). *Entrance requirements:* For master's and doctorate, GRE General Test. Additional exam requirements/recommendations for international students: Required—TOEFL (minimum score 550 paper-based; 80 iBT), IELTS (minimum score 7). Application fee: $60 ($95 for international students). Electronic applications accepted. *Expenses:* $269.25 per credit, $792 per 3-credit course; $9,634 per year resident; $23,274 per year non-resident; $7,094 fees non-resident (7 credits or more); $1,307 annual health insurance fee. *Financial support:* In 2016–17, 44 research assistantships with partial tuition reimbursements (averaging $14,535 per year), 76 teaching assistantships with partial tuition reimbursements (averaging $15,479 per year) were awarded; institutionally sponsored loans, scholarships/grants, health care benefits, and unspecified assistantships also available. Financial award application deadline: 3/15. *Faculty research:* Technology integration in general and special education, assessment of behavioral and emotional disorders, teacher quality and student achievement, evidence-based practices in special education (autism and emotional and behavioral disorders), math and science education. *Total annual research expenditures:* $1.6 million. *Unit head:* Dr. Kim Metcalf, Dean, 702-895-3375, Fax: 702-895-4068, E-mail: kim.metcalf@unlv.edu.
Website: http://education.unlv.edu/

University of Nevada, Reno, Graduate School, College of Education, Reno, NV 89557. Offers M Ed, MA, MS, Ed D, PhD, Ed S. *Accreditation:* NCATE. Terminal master's awarded for partial completion of doctoral program. *Degree requirements:* For master's, thesis optional; for doctorate, thesis/dissertation. *Entrance requirements:* For master's, GRE, minimum GPA of 2.75; for doctorate, GRE, minimum GPA of 3.0. Additional exam requirements/recommendations for international students: Required—TOEFL (minimum score 500 paper-based; 61 iBT), IELTS (minimum score 6). Electronic applications accepted.

University of New Brunswick Fredericton, School of Graduate Studies, Faculty of Education, Fredericton, NB E3B 5A3, Canada. Offers M Ed, PhD. *Program availability:* Part-time, online learning. *Degree requirements:* For master's, variable foreign language requirement, thesis optional; for doctorate, variable foreign language requirement, comprehensive exam, thesis/dissertation. *Entrance requirements:* For master's, minimum GPA of 3.0. Additional exam requirements/recommendations for international students: Required—TOEFL (minimum score 650 paper-based); Recommended—TWE (minimum score 5.5). Electronic applications accepted. *Faculty research:* Adult education, educational administration and leadership, counseling, exceptional learners, critical studies.

University of New England, College of Graduate and Professional Studies, Portland, ME 04103. Offers applied nutrition (MS); career and technical education (MS Ed); curriculum and instruction (MS Ed); education (CAGS, Post-Master's Certificate); education leadership (Ed D); educational leadership (MS Ed); generalist (MS Ed); health informatics (MS, Graduate Certificate); inclusion education (MS Ed); literacy K-12 (MS Ed); medical education leadership (MMEL); public health (Graduate Certificate); reading specialist (MS Ed); social work (MSW). *Program availability:* Part-time, evening/weekend, online only, 100% online. *Faculty:* 67 part-time/adjunct (46 women). *Students:* 891 full-time (667 women), 359 part-time (261 women); includes 309 minority (215 Black or African American, non-Hispanic/Latino; 2 American Indian or Alaska Native, non-Hispanic/Latino; 63 Asian, non-Hispanic/Latino; 18 Hispanic/Latino; 2 Native Hawaiian or other Pacific Islander, non-Hispanic/Latino; 9 Two or more races, non-Hispanic/Latino). Average age 36. 777 applicants, 50% accepted, 316 enrolled. In 2016, 292 master's, 34 doctorates, 130 other advanced degrees awarded. *Application deadline:* Applications are processed on a rolling basis. Electronic applications accepted. Tuition and fees vary according to degree level, program and student level. *Financial support:* Application deadline: 5/1; applicants required to submit FAFSA. *Unit head:* Dr. Martha Wilson, Associate Provost for Online Worldwide Learning/Dean of the College of Graduate and Professional Studies, 207-221-4985, E-mail: mwilson13@une.edu.
Website: http://online.une.edu

University of New Hampshire, Graduate School, College of Liberal Arts, Department of Education, Durham, NH 03824. Offers early childhood education (M Ed); education (PhD); educational administration and supervision (Ed S); elementary education (M Ed); secondary education (MAT); special education (M Ed). *Accreditation:* TEAC. *Program availability:* Part-time. *Degree requirements:* For doctorate, thesis/dissertation. *Entrance requirements:* For master's, doctorate, and Ed S, GRE General Test. Additional exam requirements/recommendations for international students: Required—TOEFL (minimum score 550 paper-based; 80 iBT). Electronic applications accepted.

University of New Hampshire, Graduate School Manchester Campus, Manchester, NH 03101. Offers business administration (MBA); educational administration and supervision (Ed S); educational studies (M Ed); elementary teacher education (M Ed); information technology (MS); public administration (MPA); public health (MPH, Certificate); secondary teacher education (M Ed, MAT); social work (MSW); substance use disorders (Certificate). *Program availability:* Part-time, evening/weekend. *Degree requirements:* For master's, thesis or alternative. *Entrance requirements:* Additional exam requirements/recommendations for international students: Required—TOEFL (minimum score 550 paper-based; 80 iBT). Electronic applications accepted.

University of New Mexico, Graduate Studies, College of Education, Albuquerque, NM 87131-2039. Offers MA, MS, Ed D, PhD, Ed S, Graduate Certificate. *Accreditation:* NCATE. *Program availability:* Part-time, evening/weekend. *Faculty:* 110 full-time (70 women), 16 part-time/adjunct (12 women). *Students:* 389 full-time (253 women), 603 part-time (457 women); includes 463 minority (34 Black or African American, non-Hispanic/Latino; 68 American Indian or Alaska Native, non-Hispanic/Latino; 21 Asian, non-Hispanic/Latino; 316 Hispanic/Latino; 24 Two or more races, non-Hispanic/Latino), 81 international. Average age 37. 427 applicants, 64% accepted, 224 enrolled. In 2016, 288 master's, 33 doctorates, 39 other advanced degrees awarded. *Degree requirements:* For master's, comprehensive exam (for some programs), thesis (for some programs); for doctorate, variable foreign language requirement, comprehensive exam, thesis/dissertation. *Entrance requirements:* Additional exam requirements/recommendations for international students: Required—TOEFL (minimum score 550 paper-based), IELTS (minimum score 7). *Application deadline:* For fall admission, 3/1 for international students; for spring admission, 8/1 for international students. Application fee: $50. Electronic applications accepted. *Financial support:* Career-related internships or fieldwork, Federal Work-Study, scholarships/grants, health care benefits, and unspecified assistantships available. Support available to part-time students. Financial award application deadline: 3/1; financial award applicants required to submit FAFSA. *Faculty research:* Best practices in pedagogy, quantitative analysis and assessment, socio-cultural issues, educational leadership, health and wellness across the lifespan. *Total annual research expenditures:* $578,105. *Unit head:* Dr. Richard Howell, Dean, 505-277-2231, Fax: 505-277-8427, E-mail: rhowell@unm.edu. *Application contact:* Academic Graduate Coordinator, 505-277-3190, E-mail: coeac@unm.edu.
Website: http://coe.unm.edu/

University of New Orleans, Graduate School, College of Education and Human Development, New Orleans, LA 70148. Offers M Ed, MAT, PhD. *Accreditation:* NCATE. *Program availability:* Part-time, online learning. *Degree requirements:* For master's, comprehensive exam, thesis optional; for doctorate, comprehensive exam, thesis/dissertation. *Entrance requirements:* For master's and doctorate, GRE General Test. Additional exam requirements/recommendations for international students: Required—TOEFL (minimum score 550 paper-based; 79 iBT). Electronic applications accepted. *Faculty research:* Special education and habilitation, educational administration, exercise physiology, wellness, effective school instruction.

University of North Alabama, College of Education, Florence, AL 35632-0001. Offers MA, MA Ed, MS, Ed S. *Accreditation:* NCATE. *Program availability:* Part-time, 100% online, blended/hybrid learning. *Faculty:* 40 full-time (21 women), 4 part-time/adjunct (0 women). *Students:* 85 full-time (54 women), 215 part-time (167 women); includes 37 minority (20 Black or African American, non-Hispanic/Latino; 6 American Indian or Alaska Native, non-Hispanic/Latino; 6 Hispanic/Latino; 5 Two or more races, non-Hispanic/Latino), 3 international. Average age 33. 118 applicants, 72% accepted, 69 enrolled. In 2016, 109 master's, 25 other advanced degrees awarded. *Degree requirements:* For master's, comprehensive exam. *Entrance requirements:* For master's, GRE, MAT, PRAXIS II, or NTE, minimum GPA of 2.5, Alabama Class B Certificate or equivalent, teaching experience. Additional exam requirements/recommendations for international students: Required—TOEFL (minimum score 79 iBT), IELTS (minimum score 6), PTE (minimum score 54). *Application deadline:* Applications are processed on a rolling basis. Application fee: $50 ($100 for international students). Electronic applications accepted. *Expenses:* Tuition, state resident: full-time $2799; part-time $1866 per semester. Tuition, nonresident: full-time $5598; part-time $3732 per semester. *Required fees:* $915; $642 per semester. Tuition and fees vary according to course load. *Financial support:* In 2016–17, 33 students received support. Scholarships/grants and unspecified assistantships available. Financial award application deadline: 2/1; financial award applicants required to submit FAFSA. *Unit head:* Dr. Donna Lefort, Dean, 256-765-4252, Fax: 256-765-4664, E-mail: dpjacobs@una.edu. *Application contact:* Hillary N. Coats, Graduate Admissions Coordinator, 256-765-4447, E-mail: graduate@una.edu.
Website: http://www.una.edu/education/

The University of North Carolina at Chapel Hill, Graduate School, School of Education, Chapel Hill, NC 27514-3500. Offers M Ed, MA, MAT, MSA, Ed D, PhD. *Accreditation:* NCATE. *Program availability:* Part-time. *Degree requirements:* For master's, comprehensive exam, thesis (for some programs); for doctorate, comprehensive exam, thesis/dissertation. *Entrance requirements:* For master's and doctorate, GRE General Test, minimum GPA of 3.0 during last 2 years of undergraduate course work. Additional exam requirements/recommendations for international students: Required—TOEFL (minimum score 550 paper-based). Electronic applications accepted. *Faculty research:* Curriculum development; school success and intervention; professional development, recruitment and retention; service-learning; evaluation.

The University of North Carolina at Charlotte, Cato College of Education, Charlotte, NC 28223-0001. Offers M Ed, MA, MAT, MSA, Ed D, PhD, Graduate Certificate, Post-Master's Certificate, Postbaccalaureate Certificate. *Accreditation:* ACA (one or more programs are accredited); NCATE. *Program availability:* Part-time, evening/weekend, 100% online, blended/hybrid learning. *Faculty:* 109 full-time (66 women), 28 part-time/adjunct (20 women). *Students:* 286 full-time (228 women), 1,174 part-time (923 women); includes 422 minority (313 Black or African American, non-Hispanic/Latino; 1 American Indian or Alaska Native, non-Hispanic/Latino; 25 Asian, non-Hispanic/Latino; 62 Hispanic/Latino; 21 Two or more races, non-Hispanic/Latino), 23 international. Average age 33. 886 applicants, 85% accepted, 593 enrolled. In 2016, 212 master's, 26 doctorates, 266 other advanced degrees awarded. *Entrance requirements:* For master's, bachelor's degree, or its U.S. equivalent, from regionally-accredited college or university; minimum overall GPA of 3.0 on all previous work beyond high school; statement of purpose (essay); at least three recommendation forms; for doctorate, bachelor's degree (or its U.S. equivalent) from regionally-accredited college or university; minimum overall GPA of 3.5 in master's degree program; for other advanced degree, bachelor's degree from regionally-accredited university; minimum GPA of 2.75 on all post-secondary work attempted; transcripts; personal statement outlining why the applicant seeks admission to the program. Additional exam requirements/recommendations for international students: Required—TOEFL (minimum score 523 paper-based, 70 iBT) or IELTS (6.5). *Application deadline:* Applications are processed on a rolling basis. Application fee: $75. Electronic applications accepted. *Expenses:* Tuition, state resident: full-time $4252. Tuition, nonresident: full-time $17,423. *Required fees:* $3026. Tuition and fees vary according to course load and program. *Financial support:* In 2016–17, 51 students received support, including 1 fellowship (averaging $32,786 per year), 38 research assistantships (averaging $13,450 per year), 10 teaching assistantships (averaging $8,448 per year); career-related internships or fieldwork, institutionally sponsored loans, scholarships/grants, unspecified assistantships, and administrative assistantships also available. Support available to part-time students. Financial award application deadline: 3/1; financial award applicants required to submit FAFSA. *Faculty research:* Quality classroom instruction, culturally responsive instruction, teacher education policy and practice, early intervention, counseling practices. *Total annual research expenditures:* $8.5 million. *Unit head:* Dr. Ellen McIntyre, Dean, 704-687-8722, E-mail: ellen.mcintyre@uncc.edu. *Application*

contact: Kathy B. Giddings, Director of Graduate Admissions, 704-687-5503, Fax: 704-687-1668, E-mail: gradadm@uncc.edu.
Website: https://education.uncc.edu/

The University of North Carolina at Greensboro, Graduate School, School of Education, Greensboro, NC 27412-5001. Offers M Ed, MLIS, MS, MSA, Ed D, PhD, Certificate, Ed S, PMC, MS/Ed S, MS/PhD. *Accreditation:* NCATE. *Program availability:* Part-time, evening/weekend. *Degree requirements:* For doctorate, thesis/dissertation. *Entrance requirements:* For master's, doctorate, and other advanced degree, GRE General Test. Additional exam requirements/recommendations for international students: Required—TOEFL. Electronic applications accepted. *Faculty research:* Effects of homogeneous grouping, women in higher education, assessment of student achievement.

The University of North Carolina at Pembroke, The Graduate School, School of Education, Pembroke, NC 28372-1510. Offers counseling (MA Ed), including clinical mental health counseling, professional school counseling; elementary education (MA Ed); health and human performance (MA), including physical education; reading education (MA Ed); school administration (MSA). *Accreditation:* NCATE. *Program availability:* Part-time, evening/weekend. *Degree requirements:* For master's, comprehensive exam (for some programs), thesis optional. *Entrance requirements:* For master's, GRE General Test or MAT, minimum GPA of 3.0 in major, 2.5 overall. Additional exam requirements/recommendations for international students: Required—TOEFL.

The University of North Carolina Wilmington, Watson College of Education, Wilmington, NC 28403-3297. Offers M Ed, MAT, MS, MSA, Ed D. *Accreditation:* NCATE. *Program availability:* Part-time. *Faculty:* 68 full-time (44 women), 5 part-time/adjunct (3 women). *Students:* 180 full-time (135 women), 364 part-time (299 women); includes 144 minority (104 Black or African American, non-Hispanic/Latino; 7 American Indian or Alaska Native, non-Hispanic/Latino; 3 Asian, non-Hispanic/Latino; 18 Hispanic/Latino; 1 Native Hawaiian or other Pacific Islander, non-Hispanic/Latino; 11 Two or more races, non-Hispanic/Latino), 6 international. Average age 34. 311 applicants, 78% accepted, 181 enrolled. In 2016, 151 master's, 19 doctorates awarded. *Degree requirements:* For master's, comprehensive exam (for some programs), thesis (for some programs), e-portfolio defense, research project, capstone experience (depending on degree); for doctorate, comprehensive exam, thesis/dissertation. *Entrance requirements:* For master's, GRE General Test, MAT, minimum B average in undergraduate work, 3 letters of recommendation, statement of interest; NC Class A teacher license in related field and minimum of 3 years' teaching experience (for some programs); for doctorate, GRE, statement of interest, master's degree in education field, 3 years of leadership experience, minimum GPA of 3.0 in undergraduate and graduate work. Additional exam requirements/recommendations for international students: Required—TOEFL (minimum score 79 iBT), IELTS (minimum score 6.5). *Application deadline:* For fall admission, 5/15 for domestic students; for spring admission, 10/15 for domestic students. Applications are processed on a rolling basis. Application fee: $60. Electronic applications accepted. *Expenses:* Contact institution. *Financial support:* Scholarships/grants and unspecified assistantships available. Support available to part-time students. Financial award application deadline: 3/15; financial award applicants required to submit FAFSA. *Unit head:* Dr. Van Dempsey, Dean, 910-962-3354, Fax: 910-962-4081, E-mail: dempseyv@uncw.edu. *Application contact:* Dr. Ron Vetter, Dean, Graduate School, 910-962-3224, Fax: 910-962-3787, E-mail: vetterr@uncw.edu.
Website: http://www.uncw.edu/ed/degree_grad.html

University of North Dakota, Graduate School, College of Education and Human Development, Grand Forks, ND 58202. Offers M Ed, MA, MS, MSW, Ed D, PhD, Ed S. *Accreditation:* NCATE. *Program availability:* Part-time, evening/weekend, online learning. *Degree requirements:* For master's, comprehensive exam, thesis or alternative; for doctorate, comprehensive exam, thesis/dissertation; for Ed S, comprehensive exam (for some programs), thesis (for some programs). *Entrance requirements:* For master's, GRE General Test, MAT, GRE Subject Test, minimum GPA of 3.0; for doctorate, GRE Subject Test, minimum GPA of 3.5. Additional exam requirements/recommendations for international students: Required—TOEFL (minimum score 550 paper-based; 79 iBT), IELTS (minimum score 6.5). *Application deadline:* Applications are processed on a rolling basis. Application fee: $35. Electronic applications accepted. *Financial support:* Fellowships with full and partial tuition reimbursements, research assistantships with full and partial tuition reimbursements, teaching assistantships with full and partial tuition reimbursements, career-related internships or fieldwork, Federal Work-Study, institutionally sponsored loans, scholarships/grants, tuition waivers (full and partial), and unspecified assistantships available. Support available to part-time students. Financial award application deadline: 3/15; financial award applicants required to submit FAFSA. *Unit head:* Dr. Dan R. Rice, Dean, 701-777-4255, Fax: 701-777-4393, E-mail: dan.rice@mail.und.nodak.edu. *Application contact:* Evan Nelson, Director of Admissions and Recruitment, 701-777-2945, Fax: 701-777-3619, E-mail: evan.nelson@gradschool.und.edu.
Website: http://education.und.edu/

University of Northern British Columbia, Office of Graduate Studies, Prince George, BC V2N 4Z9, Canada. Offers business administration (Diploma); community health science (M Sc); disability management (MA); education (M Ed); first nations studies (MA); gender studies (MA); history (MA); interdisciplinary studies (MA); international studies (MA); mathematical, computer and physical sciences (M Sc); natural resources and environmental studies (M Sc, MA, MNRES, PhD); political science (MA); psychology (M Sc, PhD); social work (MSW). *Program availability:* Part-time, evening/weekend, online learning. *Degree requirements:* For master's, thesis; for doctorate, thesis/dissertation. *Entrance requirements:* For master's, GRE, minimum B average in undergraduate course work; for doctorate, candidacy exam, minimum A average in graduate course work.

University of Northern Colorado, Graduate School, College of Education and Behavioral Sciences, Greeley, CO 80639. Offers MA, MAT, MS, Ed D, PhD, Ed S. *Accreditation:* NCATE. *Program availability:* Part-time, online learning. *Degree requirements:* For master's, comprehensive exam, thesis optional; for doctorate, comprehensive exam, thesis/dissertation; for Ed S, comprehensive exam, thesis. *Entrance requirements:* For doctorate, GRE General Test. *Application deadline:* Applications are processed on a rolling basis. Application fee: $50 ($60 for international students). *Financial support:* Fellowships, research assistantships, teaching assistantships, and unspecified assistantships available. Financial award application deadline: 3/1; financial award applicants required to submit FAFSA. *Unit head:* Dr. Eugene P. Sheehan, Dean, 970-351-2817, Fax: 970-351-2312, E-mail: coeinfo@unco.edu. *Application contact:* Linda Sisson, Graduate Student Admission Coordinator, 970-351-1807, Fax: 970-351-2371, E-mail: linda.sisson@unco.edu.
Website: http://www.unco.edu/cebs/index.asp

University of Northern Iowa, Graduate College, College of Education, Cedar Falls, IA 50614. Offers MA, MAE, MS, Ed D, Ed S. *Program availability:* Part-time, evening/weekend. *Degree requirements:* For Ed S, thesis or alternative. *Entrance requirements:* For master's, minimum GPA of 3.0; for doctorate, GRE, master's degree, minimum GPA of 3.5; for Ed S, GRE General Test, GRE Subject Test. Additional exam requirements/recommendations for international students: Required—TOEFL (minimum score 500 paper-based; 61 iBT). Electronic applications accepted.

University of North Florida, College of Education and Human Services, Jacksonville, FL 32224. Offers M Ed, MS, Ed D. *Accreditation:* NCATE. *Program availability:* Part-time, evening/weekend. *Faculty:* 53 full-time (33 women), 11 part-time/adjunct (9 women). *Students:* 115 full-time (97 women), 340 part-time (248 women); includes 136 minority (84 Black or African American, non-Hispanic/Latino; 1 American Indian or Alaska Native, non-Hispanic/Latino; 10 Asian, non-Hispanic/Latino; 24 Hispanic/Latino; 1 Native Hawaiian or other Pacific Islander, non-Hispanic/Latino; 16 Two or more races, non-Hispanic/Latino), 20 international. Average age 34. 197 applicants, 53% accepted, 74 enrolled. In 2016, 174 master's, 7 doctorates awarded. Terminal master's awarded for partial completion of doctoral program. *Degree requirements:* For doctorate, thesis/dissertation. *Entrance requirements:* For master's, GRE General Test, minimum GPA of 3.0 in last 60 hours, interview, 3 letters of recommendation; for doctorate, GRE General Test, master's degree, interview, writing sample, 3 letters of recommendation. Additional exam requirements/recommendations for international students: Required—TOEFL (minimum score 500 paper-based). *Application deadline:* For fall admission, 7/1 priority date for domestic students, 5/1 for international students; for spring admission, 11/1 priority date for domestic students, 10/1 for international students. Application fee: $30. Electronic applications accepted. Tuition and fees vary according to course load, campus/location and program. *Financial support:* In 2016–17, 58 students received support, including 1 research assistantship (averaging $3,241 per year), 1 teaching assistantship (averaging $5,378 per year); career-related internships or fieldwork, Federal Work-Study, scholarships/grants, and tuition waivers (partial) also available. Support available to part-time students. Financial award application deadline: 4/1; financial award applicants required to submit FAFSA. *Faculty research:* Effective instruction, technology education, exceptional student education, multiculturalism. *Total annual research expenditures:* $854,059. *Unit head:* Dr. Diane Yendol-Hoppey, Dean, 904-620-2520, E-mail: diane.yendol-hoppey@unf.edu. *Application contact:* Dr. John Kemppainen, Director, Office of Student Services, 904-620-2530, Fax: 904-620-1135, E-mail: jkemppai@unf.edu.
Website: http://www.unf.edu/coehs/

University of North Georgia, College of Education, Dahlonega, GA 30597. Offers early childhood education (M Ed); middle grades education (M Ed, MAT); physical education (MS); school leadership (Ed S); secondary education (M Ed), including English education, history education, mathematics education, physical education. *Accreditation:* NCATE. *Program availability:* Part-time, evening/weekend, online learning. *Faculty:* 16 full-time (12 women), 3 part-time/adjunct (all women). *Students:* 11 full-time (8 women), 146 part-time (107 women); includes 19 minority (10 Black or African American, non-Hispanic/Latino; 2 Asian, non-Hispanic/Latino; 6 Hispanic/Latino; 1 Two or more races, non-Hispanic/Latino). Average age 28. 77 applicants, 83% accepted, 47 enrolled. In 2016, 79 master's awarded. *Degree requirements:* For master's, comprehensive exam, thesis optional. *Entrance requirements:* For master's, GRE or MAT, GACE, minimum GPA of 2.75; for Ed S, GRE General Test or MAT, 3 years of teaching experience, master's degree, minimum graduate GPA of 3.25, leadership position in the school. Additional exam requirements/recommendations for international students: Required—TOEFL (minimum score 550 paper-based; 79 iBT), IELTS (minimum score 6.5). *Application deadline:* For fall admission, 8/1 priority date for domestic students, 7/1 priority date for international students; for spring admission, 12/1 priority date for domestic students, 11/1 priority date for international students. Applications are processed on a rolling basis. Application fee: $40. Electronic applications accepted. *Expenses:* Contact institution. *Financial support:* Teaching assistantships, career-related internships or fieldwork, scholarships/grants, and unspecified assistantships available. Financial award application deadline: 5/1; financial award applicants required to submit CSS PROFILE or FAFSA. *Unit head:* Dr. Susan Ayers, Dean, College of Education, 706-864-1998, E-mail: susan.ayres@ung.edu. *Application contact:* Regina Boling, Teacher Education Graduate Admissions, 706-864-1533, E-mail: regina.boling@ung.edu.
Website: http://ung.edu/college-of-education/

University of North Texas, Robert B. Toulouse School of Graduate Studies, Denton, TX 76203-5459. Offers accounting (MS); applied anthropology (MA, MS); applied behavior analysis (Certificate); applied geography (MA); applied technology and performance improvement (M Ed, MS); art education (MA); art history (MA); art museum education (Certificate); arts leadership (Certificate); audiology (Au D); behavior analysis (MS); behavioral science (PhD); biochemistry and molecular biology (MS); biology (MA, MS); biomedical engineering (MS); business analysis (MS); chemistry (MS); clinical health psychology (PhD); communication studies (MA, MS); computer engineering (MS); computer science (MS); counseling (M Ed, MS), including clinical mental health counseling (MS), college and university counseling, elementary school counseling, secondary school counseling; creative writing (MA); criminal justice (MS); curriculum and instruction (M Ed); decision sciences (MBA); design (MA, MFA), including fashion design (MFA), innovation studies, interior design (MFA); early childhood studies (MS); economics (MS); educational leadership (M Ed, Ed D); educational psychology (MS, PhD), including family studies (MS), gifted and talented (MS), human development (MS), learning and cognition (MS), research, measurement and evaluation (MS); electrical engineering (MS); emergency management (MPA); engineering technology (MS); English (MA); English as a second language (MA); environmental science (MS); finance (MBA, MS); financial management (MPA); French (MA); health services management (MBA); higher education (M Ed, Ed D); history (MA, MS); hospitality management (MS); human resources management (MPA); information science (MS); information systems (PhD); information technologies (MBA); interdisciplinary studies (MA, MS); international studies (MA); international sustainable tourism (MS); jazz studies (MM); journalism (MA, MJ, Graduate Certificate), including interactive and virtual digital communication (Graduate Certificate), narrative journalism (Graduate Certificate), public relations (Graduate Certificate); kinesiology (MS); linguistics (MA); local government management (MPA); logistics (PhD); logistics and supply chain management (MBA); long-term care, senior housing, and aging services (MA); management (PhD); marketing (MBA); mathematics (MA, MS); mechanical and energy engineering (MS, PhD); music (MA), including ethnomusicology, music theory, musicology, performance; music composition (PhD); music education (MM Ed, PhD); nonprofit management (MPA); operations and supply chain management (MBA); performance (MM, DMA); philosophy (MA); political science (MA); professional and technical communication (MA); radio, television and film (MA, MFA); rehabilitation counseling (Certificate); sociology (MA); Spanish (MA); special education (M Ed); speech-language pathology (MA); strategic management (MBA); studio art (MFA); teaching (M Ed); MBA/MS. *Program availability:* Part-time, evening/weekend, online learning. Terminal master's awarded for partial completion of doctoral program. *Degree requirements:* For master's, variable foreign language requirement, comprehensive exam (for some programs), thesis (for some programs); for doctorate, variable foreign language requirement, comprehensive exam (for some programs), thesis/dissertation; for other advanced degree, variable foreign language requirement, comprehensive exam (for some programs). *Entrance requirements:* For master's and doctorate, GRE, GMAT. Additional exam requirements/recommendations for international students: Required—TOEFL (minimum score 550 paper-based; 79 iBT). Electronic applications accepted.

University of Northwestern–St. Paul, Master of Arts in Education Program, St. Paul, MN 55113-1598. Offers MA Ed. *Program availability:* Part-time, evening/weekend, online learning. *Application deadline:* Applications are processed on a rolling basis. Electronic applications accepted. *Expenses:* Contact institution. *Application contact:* College of Adult and Graduate Studies Admissions, 651-631-5200, E-mail: gradstudies@unwsp.edu.
Website: https://www.unwsp.edu/web/graduate-studies/master-of-arts-in-education

University of Notre Dame, Graduate School, College of Arts and Letters, Division of Social Science, Institute for Educational Initiatives, Notre Dame, IN 46556. Offers M Ed, MA. Enrollment restricted to participants in the Alliance for Catholic Education (ACE) program. *Entrance requirements:* For master's, GRE General Test, acceptance into the Alliance for Catholic Education program. Electronic applications accepted. *Faculty research:* Effective teaching, motivation, social and ethical development, literacy.

University of Oklahoma, Jeannine Rainbolt College of Education, Norman, OK 73019. Offers M Ed, Ed D, PhD, Graduate Certificate. *Accreditation:* NCATE. *Program availability:* Part-time, evening/weekend. *Faculty:* 77 full-time (46 women), 7 part-time/adjunct (4 women). *Students:* 293 full-time (201 women), 478 part-time (351 women); includes 230 minority (75 Black or African American, non-Hispanic/Latino; 42 American Indian or Alaska Native, non-Hispanic/Latino; 10 Asian, non-Hispanic/Latino; 47 Hispanic/Latino; 2 Native Hawaiian or other Pacific Islander, non-Hispanic/Latino; 54 Two or more races, non-Hispanic/Latino), 39 international. Average age 34. 348 applicants, 61% accepted, 158 enrolled. In 2016, 202 master's, 37 doctorates, 12 other advanced degrees awarded. Terminal master's awarded for partial completion of doctoral program. *Degree requirements:* For master's, comprehensive exam (for some programs), thesis (for some programs); for doctorate, comprehensive exam, thesis/dissertation (for some programs). *Entrance requirements:* Additional exam requirements/recommendations for international students: Required—TOEFL (minimum score 79 iBT) or IELTS (minimum score 6.5). *Application deadline:* For fall admission, 6/1 for domestic students, 3/1 for international students; for spring admission, 11/1 for domestic students, 9/1 for international students. Application fee: $50 ($100 for international students). Electronic applications accepted. *Expenses:* Tuition, state resident: full-time $4886; part-time $203.60 per credit hour. Tuition, nonresident: full-time $18,989; part-time $791.20 per credit hour. *Required fees:* $3283; $126.25 per credit hour. $126.50 per semester. *Financial support:* In 2016–17, 481 students received support, including 51 research assistantships with partial tuition reimbursements available (averaging $13,519 per year), 15 teaching assistantships with partial tuition reimbursements available (averaging $12,960 per year); fellowships with full tuition reimbursements available, career-related internships or fieldwork, Federal Work-Study, scholarships/grants, health care benefits, and unspecified assistantships also available. Support available to part-time students. Financial award application deadline: 6/1; financial award applicants required to submit FAFSA. *Total annual research expenditures:* $4.7 million. *Unit head:* Dr. Gregg Garn, Dean, 405-325-1082, Fax: 405-325-7390, E-mail: garn@ou.edu. *Application contact:* Dr. Sherry Cox, Assistant Dean, 405-325-2238, Fax: 405-325-7620, E-mail: scox@ou.edu.
Website: http://www.ou.edu/education/

University of Oregon, Graduate School, College of Education, Eugene, OR 97403. Offers M Ed, MA, MS, D Ed, PhD. *Program availability:* Part-time. Terminal master's awarded for partial completion of doctoral program. *Degree requirements:* For master's, exam, paper, or project; for doctorate, comprehensive exam, thesis/dissertation. *Entrance requirements:* Additional exam requirements/recommendations for international students: Required—TOEFL. *Faculty research:* Basic and applied research in teaching, learning and habilitation in all settings, schooling effectiveness.

University of Ottawa, Faculty of Graduate and Postdoctoral Studies, Faculty of Education, Ottawa, ON K1N 6N5, Canada. Offers M Ed, MA Ed, PhD, Certificate. *Program availability:* Online learning. *Degree requirements:* For master's, thesis or alternative; for doctorate, comprehensive exam, thesis/dissertation, seminar. *Entrance requirements:* For master's, honors degree or equivalent, minimum B average; for doctorate, master's degree, minimum B+ average. Electronic applications accepted. *Faculty research:* Teaching, learning and evaluation; second language education; organizational studies in education; society, culture and literacies; educational counseling.

University of Pennsylvania, Graduate School of Education, Philadelphia, PA 19104. Offers M Phil, MS, MS Ed, Ed D, PhD, Certificate. *Program availability:* Part-time, evening/weekend, online learning. *Faculty:* 70 full-time (28 women), 44 part-time/adjunct (23 women). *Students:* 1,039 full-time (739 women), 365 part-time (266 women); includes 468 minority (199 Black or African American, non-Hispanic/Latino; 110 Asian, non-Hispanic/Latino; 109 Hispanic/Latino; 1 Native Hawaiian or other Pacific Islander, non-Hispanic/Latino; 49 Two or more races, non-Hispanic/Latino), 324 international. Average age 31. 3,103 applicants, 50% accepted, 850 enrolled. In 2016, 559 master's, 77 doctorates awarded. Terminal master's awarded for partial completion of doctoral program. Application fee: $75. Electronic applications accepted. *Expenses: Tuition:* Full-time $31,068; part-time $5762 per course. *Required fees:* $3200; $336 per course. Full-time tuition and fees vary according to degree level, program and student level. Part-time tuition and fees vary according to course load, degree level and program.
Website: http://www.gse.upenn.edu/

University of Pennsylvania, Graduate School of Education, Division of Teaching, Learning, and Leadership, Program in Teaching, Learning, and Teacher Education, Philadelphia, PA 19104. Offers Ed D, PhD. *Expenses: Tuition:* Full-time $31,068; part-time $5762 per course. *Required fees:* $3200; $336 per course. Full-time tuition and fees vary according to degree level, program and student level. Part-time tuition and fees vary according to course load, degree level and program.

University of Phoenix–Bay Area Campus, College of Education, San Jose, CA 95134-1805. Offers administration and supervision (MA Ed); adult education and training (MA Ed); early childhood education (MA Ed); education (Ed S); educational leadership (Ed D); elementary teacher education (MA Ed); higher education administration (PhD); secondary teacher education (MA Ed); special education (MA Ed); teacher leadership (MA Ed). *Program availability:* Evening/weekend, online learning. *Degree requirements:* For master's, thesis (for some programs). *Entrance requirements:* For master's, minimum undergraduate GPA of 2.5, 3 years of work experience. Additional exam requirements/recommendations for international students: Required—TOEFL (minimum score 550 paper-based; 79 iBT). Electronic applications accepted.

University of Phoenix–Central Valley Campus, College of Education, Fresno, CA 93720-1552. Offers curriculum and instruction (MA Ed); curriculum and instruction-computer education (MA Ed); elementary teacher education (MA Ed); secondary teacher education (MA Ed).

University of Phoenix–Colorado Campus, College of Education, Lone Tree, CO 80124-5453. Offers administration and supervision (MAEd); curriculum instruction (MAEd); elementary teacher education (MAEd); school counseling (MSC); secondary teacher education (MAEd). *Program availability:* Evening/weekend. *Degree requirements:* For master's, thesis (for some programs). *Entrance requirements:* For master's, minimum undergraduate GPA of 2.5, 3 years work experience. Additional exam requirements/recommendations for international students: Required—TOEFL (minimum score 550 paper-based; 79 iBT). Electronic applications accepted.

University of Phoenix–Colorado Springs Downtown Campus, College of Education, Colorado Springs, CO 80903. Offers administration and supervision (MA Ed); curriculum and instruction (MA Ed); elementary teacher education (MA Ed); principal licensure certification (Certificate); school counseling (MSC); secondary teacher education (MA Ed). *Program availability:* Evening/weekend. *Degree requirements:* For master's, thesis (for some programs). *Entrance requirements:* For master's, minimum undergraduate GPA of 2.5, 3 years of work experience. Additional exam requirements/recommendations for international students: Required—TOEFL (minimum score 550 paper-based; 79 iBT). Electronic applications accepted.

University of Phoenix–Dallas Campus, College of Education, Dallas, TX 75251. Offers curriculum and instruction (MA Ed).

University of Phoenix–Hawaii Campus, College of Education, Honolulu, HI 96813-3800. Offers administration and supervision (MA Ed); curriculum and instruction (MA Ed); elementary education (MA Ed); secondary education (MA Ed); special education (MA Ed); teacher education for elementary licensure (MA Ed). *Program availability:* Evening/weekend. *Degree requirements:* For master's, thesis (for some programs). *Entrance requirements:* For master's, minimum undergraduate GPA of 2.5, 3 years of work experience. Additional exam requirements/recommendations for international students: Required—TOEFL (minimum score 550 paper-based; 79 iBT). Electronic applications accepted.

University of Phoenix–Houston Campus, College of Education, Houston, TX 77079-2004. Offers curriculum and instruction (MA Ed).

University of Phoenix–Las Vegas Campus, College of Education, Las Vegas, NV 89135. Offers administration and supervision (MA Ed); curriculum and instruction (MA Ed); school counseling (MSC); teacher education-elementary licensure (MA Ed). *Program availability:* Evening/weekend. *Degree requirements:* For master's, thesis (for some programs). *Entrance requirements:* For master's, minimum undergraduate GPA of 2.5, 3 years of work experience. Additional exam requirements/recommendations for international students: Required—TOEFL (minimum score 550 paper-based; 79 iBT). Electronic applications accepted.

University of Phoenix–New Mexico Campus, College of Education, Albuquerque, NM 87113-1570. Offers administration and supervision (MAEd); curriculum and instruction (MAEd); elementary teacher education (MAEd); school counseling (MSC); secondary teacher education (MAEd). *Program availability:* Evening/weekend. *Degree requirements:* For master's, thesis (for some programs). *Entrance requirements:* For master's, minimum undergraduate GPA of 2.5, 3 years of work experience. Additional exam requirements/recommendations for international students: Required—TOEFL (minimum score 550 paper-based; 79 iBT). Electronic applications accepted.

University of Phoenix–North Florida Campus, College of Education, Jacksonville, FL 32216-0959. Offers administration and supervision (MA Ed); curriculum and instruction (MA Ed), including computer education, mathematics education; early childhood education (MA Ed); elementary teacher education (MA Ed); secondary teacher education (MA Ed). *Program availability:* Evening/weekend. *Degree requirements:* For master's, thesis (for some programs). *Entrance requirements:* For master's, 3 years of work experience, minimum undergraduate GPA of 2.5. Additional exam requirements/recommendations for international students: Required—TOEFL (minimum score 550 paper-based; 49 iBT). Electronic applications accepted.

University of Phoenix–Online Campus, College of Education, Phoenix, AZ 85034-7209. Offers administration and supervision (MAEd, Certificate); adult education and training (MAEd); curriculum and instruction (MAEd), including computer education, curriculum and instruction, English as a second language, language arts, mathematics, reading; early childhood education (MAEd); educational studies (MAEd); elementary teacher education (MAEd), including early childhood, elementary teacher education, high school middle level, middle level; principal licensure (Certificate); secondary teacher education (MAEd); special education (MAEd, Certificate); teacher education (MAEd), including middle level generalist; teacher education middle level mathematics (MAEd), including middle level mathematics; teacher education middle level science (MAEd), including middle level science; teacher education secondary mathematics (MAEd); teacher education secondary science (MAEd); teacher leadership (MAEd); teachers of English learners (Certificate); transition to teaching (Certificate), including elementary education, secondary education. *Program availability:* Evening/weekend, online learning. *Entrance requirements:* Additional exam requirements/recommendations for international students: Required—TOEFL, TOEIC (Test of English as an International Communication), Berlitz Online English Proficiency Exam, PTE, or IELTS. Electronic applications accepted. *Expenses:* Contact institution.

University of Phoenix–Phoenix Campus, College of Education, Tempe, AZ 85282-2371. Offers administration and supervision (MA Ed); adult education and training (MA Ed); curriculum and instruction reading (MA Ed); early childhood education (MA Ed); education studies (MA Ed); elementary teacher education (MA Ed); secondary teacher education (MA Ed); special education (MA Ed); teacher leadership (MA Ed). *Program availability:* Evening/weekend, online learning. *Entrance requirements:* Additional exam requirements/recommendations for international students: Required—TOEFL, TOEIC (Test of English as an International Communication), Berlitz Online English Proficiency Exam, PTE, or IELTS. Electronic applications accepted. *Expenses:* Contact institution.

University of Phoenix–Sacramento Valley Campus, College of Education, Sacramento, CA 95833-4334. Offers adult education (MA Ed); curriculum instruction (MA Ed); elementary teacher education (MA Ed); secondary teacher education (MA Ed); teacher education (Certificate). *Program availability:* Evening/weekend. *Degree requirements:* For master's, thesis (for some programs). *Entrance requirements:* For master's, 3 years of work experience, minimum undergraduate GPA of 2.5. Additional exam requirements/recommendations for international students: Required—TOEFL (minimum score 550 paper-based; 79 iBT). Electronic applications accepted.

University of Phoenix–San Diego Campus, College of Education, San Diego, CA 92123. Offers curriculum and instruction (MA Ed), including computer education, curriculum and instruction, English as a second language; elementary teacher education (MA Ed); secondary teacher education (MA Ed). *Program availability:* Evening/weekend. *Degree requirements:* For master's, thesis (for some programs). *Entrance requirements:* For master's, 3 years of work experience, minimum undergraduate GPA of 3.0. Additional exam requirements/recommendations for international students: Required—TOEFL (minimum score 550 paper-based; 79 iBT). Electronic applications accepted.

University of Phoenix–Southern Arizona Campus, College of Education, Tucson, AZ 85711. Offers administration and supervision (MA Ed); adult education and training (MA Ed); curriculum instruction (MA Ed); educational counseling (MA Ed); elementary teacher education (MA Ed); school counseling (MSC); secondary teacher education (MA Ed); special education (MA Ed, Certificate). *Program availability:* Evening/weekend. *Degree requirements:* For master's, thesis (for some programs). *Entrance requirements:* For master's, minimum undergraduate GPA of 2.5, 3 years of work experience.

Additional exam requirements/recommendations for international students: Required—TOEFL (minimum score 550 paper-based; 79 iBT). Electronic applications accepted.

University of Phoenix–Southern California Campus, College of Education, Costa Mesa, CA 92626. Offers administration and supervision (MA Ed, Certificate); adult education and training (MA Ed); educational studies (MA Ed); elementary teacher education (MA Ed); secondary teacher education (MA Ed); teacher leadership (MA Ed); teachers of English learners (Certificate). *Program availability:* Evening/weekend, online learning. *Entrance requirements:* Additional exam requirements/recommendations for international students: Required—TOEFL, TOEIC (Test of English as an International Communication), Berlitz Online English Proficiency Exam, PTE, or IELTS. Electronic applications accepted. *Expenses:* Contact institution.

University of Phoenix–South Florida Campus, College of Education, Miramar, FL 33027-4145. Offers administration and supervision (MA Ed); curriculum and instruction (MA Ed), including computer education, curriculum and instruction, mathematics education; early childhood education (MA Ed); elementary teacher education (MA Ed); secondary teacher education (MA Ed). *Program availability:* Evening/weekend. *Degree requirements:* For master's, thesis (for some programs). *Entrance requirements:* For master's, 3 years of work experience, minimum undergraduate GPA of 2.5. Additional exam requirements/recommendations for international students: Required—TOEFL (minimum score 550 paper-based; 79 iBT). Electronic applications accepted.

University of Phoenix–Utah Campus, College of Education, Salt Lake City, UT 84123-4642. Offers administration and supervision (MA Ed); curriculum and instruction (MA Ed); elementary teacher education (MA Ed); school counseling (MSC); secondary teacher education (MA Ed); special education (MA Ed). *Program availability:* Evening/weekend. *Degree requirements:* For master's, thesis (for some programs). *Entrance requirements:* For master's, minimum undergraduate GPA of 2.5, 3 years work experience. Additional exam requirements/recommendations for international students: Required—TOEFL (minimum score 550 paper-based; 79 iBT). Electronic applications accepted.

University of Phoenix–Washington D.C. Campus, College of Education, Washington, DC 20001. Offers administration and supervision (MA Ed); adult education and training (MA Ed); computer education (MA Ed); curriculum and instruction (MA Ed, Ed D); early childhood education (MA Ed); education (Ed S); educational leadership (Ed D); educational technology (Ed D); elementary teacher education (MA Ed); English and language arts education (MA Ed); English as a second language (MA Ed); higher education administration (PhD); mathematics education (MA Ed); secondary teacher education (MA Ed); special education (MA Ed); teacher leadership (MA Ed).

University of Pikeville, Patton College of Education, Pikeville, KY 41501. Offers teacher leader (MA). *Program availability:* Part-time, evening/weekend. *Faculty:* 12 part-time/adjunct (9 women). *Students:* 71 full-time (61 women); includes 1 minority (Black or African American, non-Hispanic/Latino). Average age 35. *Degree requirements:* For master's, comprehensive exam. *Application deadline:* For fall admission, 8/15 for domestic students. Applications are processed on a rolling basis. Application fee: $50. *Expenses:* Contact institution. *Financial support:* Application deadline: 2/1; applicants required to submit FAFSA. *Unit head:* Coletta Parsley, Interim Dean, 606-218-5318, E-mail: colettaparsley@upike.edu. *Application contact:* Fairy Coleman, Administrative Assistant, 606-218-5314, E-mail: fairycoleman@upike.edu.
Website: http://www.upike.edu/COE/

University of Pittsburgh, School of Education, Pittsburgh, PA 15260. Offers M Ed, MA, MAT, MS, Ed D, PhD. *Program availability:* Part-time, evening/weekend, online learning. Terminal master's awarded for partial completion of doctoral program. *Degree requirements:* For master's, comprehensive exam, thesis (for some programs); for doctorate, comprehensive exam, thesis/dissertation. *Entrance requirements:* For doctorate, GRE. Additional exam requirements/recommendations for international students: Required—TOEFL (minimum score 550 paper-based; 80 iBT). Electronic applications accepted. Tuition and fees vary according to program.

See Display below and Close-Up on page 733.

University of Portland, School of Education, Portland, OR 97203-5798. Offers education (MA, MAT); educational leadership (M Ed); English for speakers of other languages (M Ed); initial administrator licensure (M Ed); neuroeducation (M Ed, Ed D); organizational leadership and development (Ed D); reading (M Ed); school leadership and development (Ed D); special education (M Ed). M Ed also available through the Graduate Outreach Program for teachers residing in the Oregon and Washington state areas. *Accreditation:* NCATE. *Program availability:* Part-time, evening/weekend. *Entrance requirements:* For master's, minimum GPA of 3.0, teaching certificate, letters of recommendation, resume, statement of goals, official transcripts. Additional exam requirements/recommendations for international students: Required—TOEFL (minimum score 550 paper-based; 80 iBT), IELTS (minimum score 7). *Faculty research:* Multicultural education, supervision/leadership.

University of Prince Edward Island, Faculty of Education, Charlottetown, PE C1A 4P3, Canada. Offers leadership and learning (M Ed). *Program availability:* Part-time. *Degree requirements:* For master's, thesis. *Entrance requirements:* For master's, 2 years of professional experience, bachelor of education, professional certificate. Additional exam requirements/recommendations for international students: Required—TOEFL (minimum score 550 paper-based; 80 iBT), Canadian Academic English Language Assessment, Michigan English Language Assessment Battery, Canadian Test of English for Scholars and Trainees. *Faculty research:* Distance learning, aboriginal communities and education leadership development, international development, immersion language learning.

University of Puerto Rico, Río Piedras Campus, College of Education, San Juan, PR 00931-3300. Offers M Ed, MS, Ed D. *Accreditation:* NCATE. *Program availability:* Part-time. *Degree requirements:* For master's, thesis; for doctorate, thesis/dissertation, internship. *Entrance requirements:* For master's, GRE or PAEG, minimum GPA of 3.0, letter of recommendation; for doctorate, GRE or PAEG, master's degree, minimum GPA of 3.0, letter of recommendation (2), interview. *Faculty research:* Curriculum, math teaching.

University of Puget Sound, School of Education, Tacoma, WA 98416. Offers M Ed, MAT. *Program availability:* Part-time. *Faculty:* 8 full-time (5 women), 2 part-time/adjunct (both women). *Students:* 26 full-time (20 women), 29 part-time (27 women); includes 11 minority (1 American Indian or Alaska Native, non-Hispanic/Latino; 3 Asian, non-Hispanic/Latino; 2 Hispanic/Latino; 5 Two or more races, non-Hispanic/Latino). Average age 29. 93 applicants, 66% accepted, 44 enrolled. In 2016, 42 master's awarded. *Degree requirements:* For master's, capstone course (for M Ed); project (for MAT). *Entrance requirements:* For master's, GRE General Test, WEST-E or NES, WEST-B or ACT/SAT, two education foundation prerequisite courses (for MAT); interview (for M Ed). Additional exam requirements/recommendations for international students: Required—TOEFL (minimum score 550 paper-based; 90 iBT). *Application deadline:* For fall admission, 3/1 priority date for domestic and international students. Applications are processed on a rolling basis. Application fee: $60. Electronic applications accepted. *Expenses:* $3,575 per unit tuition (for MAT); $3,925 per unit tuition (for M Ed). *Financial support:* In 2016–17, 24 students received support. Scholarships/grants available. Financial award application deadline: 3/31; financial award applicants required to submit FAFSA. *Faculty research:* Pre-service teacher learning and public school partnerships,

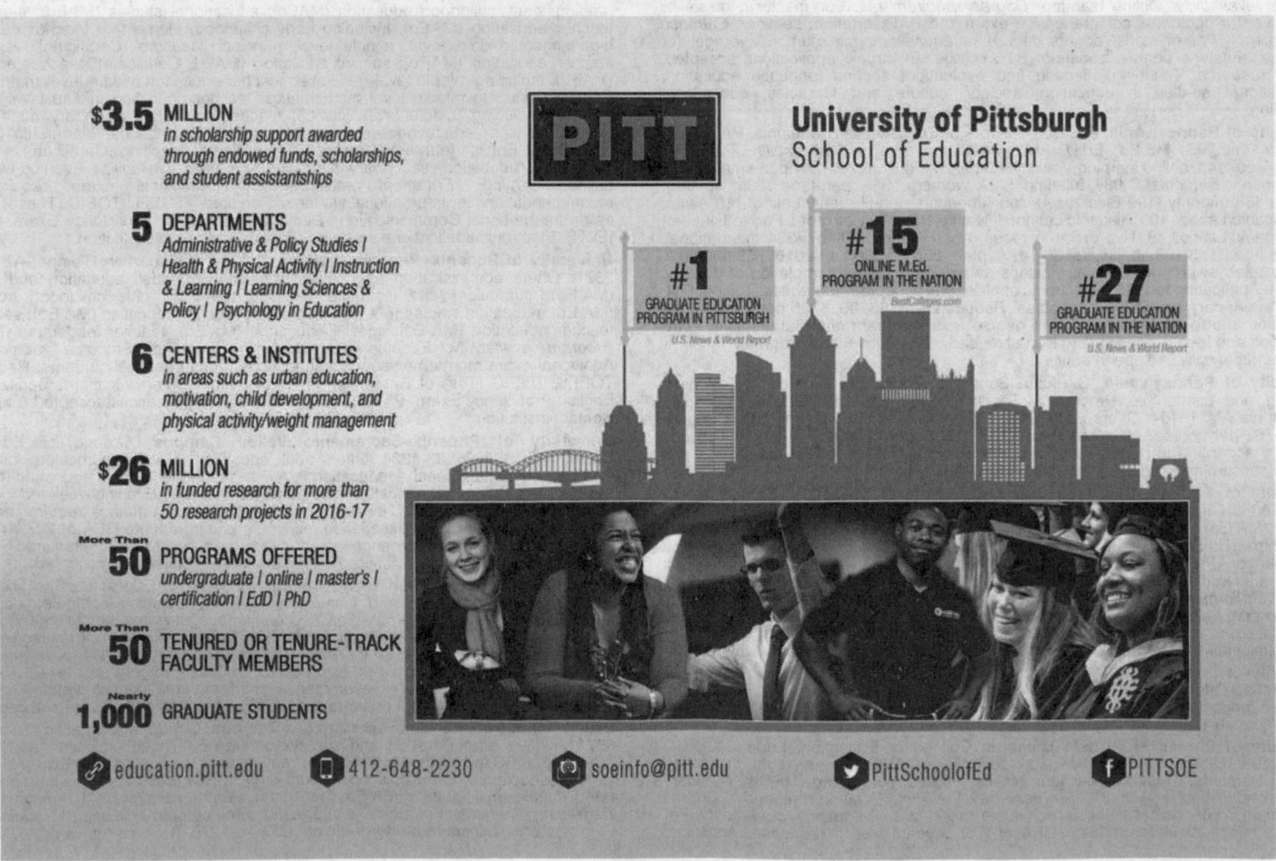
$3.5 MILLION
in scholarship support awarded through endowed funds, scholarships, and student assistantships
5 DEPARTMENTS
Administrative & Policy Studies | Health & Physical Activity | Instruction & Learning | Learning Sciences & Policy | Psychology in Education
6 CENTERS & INSTITUTES
in areas such as urban education, motivation, child development, and physical activity/weight management
$26 MILLION
in funded research for more than 50 research projects in 2016-17
More Than 50 PROGRAMS OFFERED
undergraduate | online | master's | certification | EdD | PhD
More Than 50 TENURED OR TENURE-TRACK FACULTY MEMBERS
Nearly 1,000 GRADUATE STUDENTS
PITT
University of Pittsburgh
School of Education
#1 GRADUATE EDUCATION PROGRAM IN PITTSBURGH
U.S. News & World Report
#15 ONLINE M.Ed. PROGRAM IN THE NATION
BestColleges.com
#27 GRADUATE EDUCATION PROGRAM IN THE NATION
U.S. News & World Report
education.pitt.edu
412-648-2230
soeinfo@pitt.edu
PittSchoolofEd
PITTSOE

creating equitable classrooms, literacy development, teaching social studies, suicide prevention. *Unit head:* Amy Ryken, Dean, 253-879-2810, Fax: 253-879-3926, E-mail: aryken@pugetsound.edu. *Application contact:* Karen Stump, Certification Officer/ Admission Coordinator, 253-879-3382, Fax: 253-879-3926, E-mail: kstump@ pugetsound.edu.
Website: http://www.pugetsound.edu/academics/departments-and-programs/graduate/ school-of-education/

University of Redlands, School of Education, Redlands, CA 92373-0999. Offers MA, Ed D, Certificate. *Program availability:* Part-time, evening/weekend. *Entrance requirements:* For master's, minimum undergraduate GPA of 3.0, 2 letters of recommendation. Additional exam requirements/recommendations for international students: Required—TOEFL (minimum score 550 paper-based). *Expenses:* Contact institution.

University of Regina, Faculty of Graduate Studies and Research, Faculty of Education, Regina, SK S4S 0A2, Canada. Offers M Ed, MA Ed, MHRD, PhD, Master's Certificate. *Program availability:* Part-time. *Faculty:* 50 full-time (32 women), 26 part-time/adjunct (4 women). *Students:* 96 full-time (72 women), 204 part-time (147 women). 110 applicants, 30% accepted. In 2016, 84 master's, 2 doctorates, 1 other advanced degree awarded. *Degree requirements:* For master's, thesis (for some programs), practicum, project, or thesis; for doctorate, thesis/dissertation. *Entrance requirements:* For master's, 4-year B Ed or equivalent, two years of teaching or other relevant professional experience. Additional exam requirements/recommendations for international students: Required—TOEFL (minimum score 580 paper-based; 80 iBT), IELTS (minimum score 6.5), PTE (minimum score 59). *Application deadline:* For fall admission, 2/15 for domestic and international students; for winter admission, 10/15 for domestic and international students; for spring admission, 2/15 for domestic and international students. Application fee: $100. Electronic applications accepted. *Financial support:* In 2016–17, 24 fellowships (averaging $5,042 per year), 18 teaching assistantships (averaging $2,562 per year) were awarded; career-related internships or fieldwork and scholarships/grants also available. Financial award application deadline: 6/15. *Faculty research:* Curriculum and instruction, educational administration, educational psychology, human resource development, adult education. *Unit head:* Dr. Ken Montgomery, Associate Dean, Research and Graduate Programs in Education, 306-585-5031, Fax: 306-585-5387, E-mail: ken.montgomery@uregina.ca. *Application contact:* Tania Gates, Graduate Program Coordinator, 306-585-4506, Fax: 306-585-5387, E-mail: edgrad@uregina.ca.
Website: http://www.uregina.ca/education

University of Rhode Island, Graduate School, Alan Shawn Feinstein College of Education and Professional Studies, School of Education, Kingston, RI 02881. Offers education (PhD); reading (MA); special education (MA). *Accreditation:* NCATE. *Program availability:* Part-time, evening/weekend. *Faculty:* 18 full-time (13 women). *Students:* 65 full-time (51 women), 147 part-time (108 women); includes 27 minority (7 Black or African American, non-Hispanic/Latino; 6 American Indian or Alaska Native, non-Hispanic/Latino; 7 Asian, non-Hispanic/Latino; 6 Hispanic/Latino; 1 Two or more races, non-Hispanic/Latino), 10 international. In 2016, 26 master's, 7 doctorates awarded. *Degree requirements:* For master's, comprehensive exam (for some programs), thesis optional; for doctorate, comprehensive exam, thesis/dissertation. *Entrance requirements:* For master's, 2 letters of recommendation; interview (for special education applicants); for doctorate, GRE, 3 letters of recommendation, resume. Additional exam requirements/recommendations for international students: Required—TOEFL. *Application deadline:* For fall admission, 1/15 for domestic students, 1/31 for international students; for spring admission, 11/15 for domestic students; for summer admission, 4/15 for domestic students. Application fee: $65. Electronic applications accepted. *Expenses:* Tuition, state resident: full-time $11,796; part-time $655 per credit. Tuition, nonresident: full-time $24,206; part-time $1345 per credit. *Required fees:* $1546; $44 per credit. One-time fee: $155 full-time; $35 part-time. *Financial support:* In 2016–17, 1 research assistantship with tuition reimbursement (averaging $8,592 per year), 4 teaching assistantships with tuition reimbursements (averaging $15,036 per year) were awarded. Financial award application deadline: 1/31; financial award applicants required to submit FAFSA. *Unit head:* Dr. David Byrd, Director, School of Education, 401-874-5484, Fax: 401-874-5471, E-mail: dbyrd@uri.edu. *Application contact:* Graduate Admissions, 401-874-2872, E-mail: gradadm@etal.uri.edu.
Website: http://www.uri.edu/hss/education/

University of Rio Grande, Graduate School, Rio Grande, OH 45674. Offers athletic coaching leadership (M Ed); educational leadership (M Ed); integrated arts (M Ed); intervention specialist in early childhood (M Ed); intervention specialist in mild/moderate (M Ed). *Accreditation:* NCATE. *Program availability:* Part-time. *Degree requirements:* For master's, final research project, portfolio. *Entrance requirements:* For master's, minimum GPA of 2.7 in major, 2.5 overall. Additional exam requirements/ recommendations for international students: Required—TOEFL. *Application deadline:* Applications are processed on a rolling basis. Application fee: $20. *Financial support:* Career-related internships or fieldwork available. Support available to part-time students. Financial award application deadline: 7/1; financial award applicants required to submit FAFSA. *Faculty research:* Interagency collaboration, reading and mathematics, learning styles, college access, literacy. *Unit head:* Dr. Greg Miller, Director, 740-245-7030, E-mail: gmiller@rio.edu. *Application contact:* Nancy Downs, Secretary, 740-245-7328, Fax: 740-245-7175, E-mail: ndowns@rio.edu.

University of Rochester, Margaret Warner Graduate School of Education and Human Development, Rochester, NY 14627. Offers MS, Ed D, PhD. *Accreditation:* ACA (one or more programs are accredited); NCATE. *Program availability:* Part-time, evening/ weekend. Terminal master's awarded for partial completion of doctoral program. *Degree requirements:* For master's, thesis (for some programs); for doctorate, thesis/ dissertation, qualifying exam. *Expenses: Tuition:* Full-time $47,450; part-time $1482 per credit hour. *Required fees:* $528. Tuition and fees vary according to program.

University of St. Francis, College of Education, Joliet, IL 60435-6169. Offers educational leadership (MS, Ed D); elementary education (M Ed); reading (MS); secondary education (M Ed), including English education, math education, science education, social studies education, visual arts education; special education (M Ed); teaching and learning (MS); TESOL (Certificate). *Accreditation:* NCATE. *Program availability:* Part-time, evening/weekend, 100% online, blended/hybrid learning. *Faculty:* 11 full-time (8 women), 60 part-time/adjunct (42 women). *Students:* 34 full-time (26 women), 420 part-time (318 women); includes 92 minority (51 Black or African American, non-Hispanic/Latino; 5 Asian, non-Hispanic/Latino; 31 Hispanic/Latino; 5 Two or more races, non-Hispanic/Latino), 4 international. Average age 36. 242 applicants, 48% accepted, 96 enrolled. In 2016, 229 master's, 44 doctorates, 10 other advanced degrees awarded. *Degree requirements:* For master's, comprehensive exam; for doctorate, thesis/dissertation. *Entrance requirements:* Additional exam requirements/ recommendations for international students: Required—TOEFL (minimum score 550 paper-based; 79 iBT), IELTS (minimum score 6). *Application deadline:* Applications are processed on a rolling basis. Application fee: $30. Electronic applications accepted. Application fee is waived when completed online. *Expenses:* Contact institution. *Financial support:* In 2016–17, 48 students received support. Career-related internships or fieldwork and unspecified assistantships available. Support available to part-time students. Financial award applicants required to submit FAFSA. *Unit head:* Dr. John Gambro, Dean, 815-740-3829, Fax: 815-740-2264, E-mail: jgambro@stfrancis.edu. *Application contact:* Sandra Sloka, Director of Admissions for Graduate and Degree Completion Programs, 800-735-7500, Fax: 815-740-3431, E-mail: ssloka@ stfrancis.edu.
Website: http://www.stfrancis.edu/academics/college-of-education/

University of Saint Francis, Graduate School, Department of Education, Fort Wayne, IN 46808-3994. Offers education (MAT); secondary education (MAT); special education (MS Ed), including intense intervention, mild intervention. *Accreditation:* NCATE. *Program availability:* Part-time, evening/weekend, online only, 100% online. *Faculty:* 1 (woman) full-time, 4 part-time/adjunct (2 women). *Students:* 4 full-time (3 women), 16 part-time (8 women); includes 2 minority (both Black or African American, non-Hispanic/ Latino). Average age 29. 5 applicants, 100% accepted, 4 enrolled. In 2016, 2 master's awarded. *Degree requirements:* For master's, comprehensive exam. *Entrance requirements:* For master's, GRE (minimum composite score of 280 verbal and quantitative subtests) or MAT (minimum score of 389) if undergraduate GPA is below a 2.8 or prior graduate level GPA is below 3.0; GRE, ACT, SAT, or CASA exam if no license, minimum undergraduate GPA of 2.8; resume (if GPA is below 3.0); standard teaching license and/or bachelor's degree from regionally-accredited institution; background check; two professional recommendations. Additional exam requirements/ recommendations for international students: Required—TOEFL (minimum score 550 paper-based) or IELTS (minimum score 6.5). *Application deadline:* Applications are processed on a rolling basis. Application fee: $0. Electronic applications accepted. *Expenses:* $475 per credit hour. *Financial support:* Federal Work-Study, scholarships/ grants, and unspecified assistantships available. Financial award application deadline: 3/10; financial award applicants required to submit FAFSA. *Unit head:* Mary Riepenhoff, Assistant Professor/Department Chair, 260-399-7700 Ext. 8409, Fax: 260-399-8170, E-mail: mriepenhoff@sf.edu. *Application contact:* Kyle Richardson, Enrollment Specialist, 260-399-7700 Ext. 6310, Fax: 260-399-8152, E-mail: krichardson@sf.edu.
Website: http://education.sf.edu/

University of Saint Joseph, Department of Education, West Hartford, CT 06117-2700. Offers curriculum and instruction (MA); educational technology (MA); literacy internship (MA); multiple intelligences (MA); reading/language (MA); TESOL (MA). *Program availability:* Part-time, evening/weekend. *Degree requirements:* For master's, comprehensive exam, thesis or alternative. *Entrance requirements:* For master's, 2 letters of recommendation. Electronic applications accepted. Application fee is waived when completed online. *Expenses: Tuition:* Full-time $14,580; part-time $729 per credit hour. *Required fees:* $920; $46 per credit hour. Tuition and fees vary according to course load, degree level and program.

University of Saint Mary, Graduate Programs, Program in Education, Leavenworth, KS 66048-5082. Offers MA. *Accreditation:* NCATE. *Program availability:* Part-time, evening/ weekend, online learning. *Students:* 28 full-time (19 women), 3 part-time (1 woman); includes 6 minority (2 Black or African American, non-Hispanic/Latino; 1 Asian, non-Hispanic/Latino; 1 Hispanic/Latino; 2 Two or more races, non-Hispanic/Latino), 1 international. Average age 30. In 2016, 4 master's awarded. *Degree requirements:* For master's, thesis, oral presentation. *Entrance requirements:* For master's, minimum undergraduate GPA of 2.75, bachelor's degree from accredited college, interview, official transcripts, two letters of recommendation, essay. *Application deadline:* Applications are processed on a rolling basis. Application fee: $25. Electronic applications accepted. *Expenses:* $395 per hour. *Faculty research:* Curriculum and instruction. *Unit head:* Dr. Gwen Landever, Chair, 913-758-6159, E-mail: gwen.landever@stmary.edu.
Website: http://www.stmary.edu/success/Grad-Program/Master-of-Arts-Education.aspx

University of Saint Mary, Graduate Programs, Program in Teaching, Leavenworth, KS 66048-5082. Offers MAT. *Program availability:* Part-time, online only, 100% online. *Students:* 9 full-time (7 women), 2 part-time (both women); includes 2 minority (1 Black or African American, non-Hispanic/Latino; 1 Hispanic/Latino). Average age 33. In 2016, 14 master's awarded. *Degree requirements:* For master's, thesis. *Entrance requirements:* For master's, minimum undergraduate GPA of 2.75. Application fee: $25. Electronic applications accepted. *Expenses:* Contact institution. *Unit head:* Dr. Gwen Landever, Chair, 913-758-6159.
Website: http://online.stmary.edu/MAT

University of St. Thomas, Graduate Studies, College of Education, Leadership and Counseling, St. Paul, MN 55105-1096. Offers MA, Ed D, Psy D, Certificate, Ed S. *Program availability:* Part-time, evening/weekend, 100% online, blended/hybrid learning. *Degree requirements:* For doctorate, thesis/dissertation. *Entrance requirements:* For master's, minimum GPA of 3.0 or MAT. Additional exam requirements/ recommendations for international students: Required—TOEFL (minimum score 550 paper-based; 80 iBT). *Application deadline:* For fall admission, 7/15 priority date for domestic students, 7/15 for international students; for spring admission, 12/9 priority date for domestic students, 12/9 for international students; for summer admission, 4/3 for domestic and international students. Applications are processed on a rolling basis. Electronic applications accepted. *Expenses:* Contact institution. *Financial support:* Research assistantships, career-related internships or fieldwork, institutionally sponsored loans, scholarships/grants, and unspecified assistantships available. Support available to part-time students. Financial award application deadline: 8/1; financial award applicants required to submit FAFSA. *Unit head:* Dr. Joseph L. Kreitzer, Dean, 651-962-6032, Fax: 651-962-4169, E-mail: jlkreitzer@stthomas.edu.
Website: http://www.stthomas.edu/education/

University of St. Thomas, School of Education and Human Services, Houston, TX 77006-4696. Offers all level education (M Ed); bilingual/dual language (M Ed); Catholic school teaching (M Ed); Catholic/private school leadership (M Ed); counselor education (M Ed); curriculum and instruction (M Ed); education (Ed D); educational leadership (M Ed); elementary teaching (M Ed); English as a second language (M Ed); exceptionality/educational diagnostician (M Ed); exceptionality/special education (M Ed); generalist (M Ed); reading (M Ed); secondary teaching (M Ed); teaching (MAT). *Accreditation:* TEAC. *Program availability:* Part-time, evening/weekend, online learning. *Faculty:* 44 full-time (29 women), 31 part-time/adjunct (17 women). *Students:* 65 full-time (61 women), 719 part-time (645 women); includes 515 minority (169 Black or African American, non-Hispanic/Latino; 25 Asian, non-Hispanic/Latino; 315 Hispanic/Latino; 2 Native Hawaiian or other Pacific Islander, non-Hispanic/Latino; 4 Two or more races, non-Hispanic/Latino), 24 international. Average age 36. 297 applicants, 92% accepted, 211 enrolled. In 2016, 403 master's awarded. *Degree requirements:* For master's, thesis, field experience. *Entrance requirements:* For master's, GRE or MAT if GPA is below 3.0, bachelor's degree; minimum GPA of 2.75 in bachelor's degree or last 60 credit hours; official transcripts from all institutions; goal statement of 250-300 words; 1 reference. Additional exam requirements/recommendations for international students: Required—TOEFL (minimum score 94 IBT), IELTS (minimum score 7), PTE (minimum score 53). *Application deadline:* Applications are processed on a rolling basis. Application fee: $35. Electronic applications accepted. *Expenses:* Contact institution. *Financial support:* In 2016–17, 52 students received support. Federal Work-Study, scholarships/grants, and state work-study, institutional employment available. Support available to part-time students. Financial award application deadline: 4/15; financial award applicants required to submit FAFSA. *Faculty research:* Leadership, diversity,

personality traits, second language acquisition. *Unit head:* Dr. Robert LeBlanc, Dean, 713-525-3540, Fax: 713-525-3871, E-mail: education@stthom.edu. *Application contact:* Rita Paredes, Administrative Assistant, 713-525-3442, Fax: 713-525-3871, E-mail: rparede@stthom.edu.
Website: http://www.stthom.edu/Academics/School_of_Education_and_Human_Services/Index.aqf

University of San Diego, School of Leadership and Education Sciences, San Diego, CA 92110-2492. Offers M Ed, MA, MAT, PhD, Certificate. *Accreditation:* NCATE. *Program availability:* Part-time, evening/weekend. *Faculty:* 31 full-time (17 women), 74 part-time/adjunct (46 women). *Students:* 345 full-time (281 women), 448 part-time (340 women); includes 327 minority (42 Black or African American, non-Hispanic/Latino; 1 American Indian or Alaska Native, non-Hispanic/Latino; 51 Asian, non-Hispanic/Latino; 198 Hispanic/Latino; 3 Native Hawaiian or other Pacific Islander, non-Hispanic/Latino; 32 Two or more races, non-Hispanic/Latino), 43 international. Average age 31. In 2016, 243 master's, 21 doctorates awarded. *Degree requirements:* For master's, international experience; for doctorate, comprehensive exam (for some programs), thesis/dissertation (for some programs), international experience. *Entrance requirements:* For doctorate, GRE General Test, master's degree. Additional exam requirements/recommendations for international students: Required—TOEFL (minimum score 580 paper-based; 83 iBT), TWE. Application fee: $45. *Financial support:* In 2016–17, 383 students received support. Career-related internships or fieldwork, Federal Work-Study, institutionally sponsored loans, unspecified assistantships, and stipends available. Support available to part-time students. Financial award application deadline: 4/1; financial award applicants required to submit FAFSA. *Unit head:* Dr. Nicholas Ladany, Dean, 619-260-4540, Fax: 619-260-6835, E-mail: nladany@sandiego.edu. *Application contact:* Monica Mahon, Associate Director of Graduate Admissions, 619-260-4524, Fax: 619-260-4158, E-mail: grads@sandiego.edu.
Website: http://www.sandiego.edu/soles/

University of San Francisco, School of Education, San Francisco, CA 94117-1080. Offers MA, Ed D. *Program availability:* Part-time, evening/weekend. *Faculty:* 39 full-time (26 women), 114 part-time/adjunct (70 women). *Students:* 794 full-time (616 women), 253 part-time (191 women); includes 522 minority (91 Black or African American, non-Hispanic/Latino; 140 Asian, non-Hispanic/Latino; 230 Hispanic/Latino; 9 Native Hawaiian or other Pacific Islander, non-Hispanic/Latino; 52 Two or more races, non-Hispanic/Latino), 75 international. Average age 32. 929 applicants, 83% accepted, 387 enrolled. In 2016, 364 master's, 36 doctorates awarded. *Degree requirements:* For doctorate, thesis/dissertation. *Entrance requirements:* For master's, CBEST, CSET, and/or CSET Writing Skills (depending on program); for doctorate, GRE or MAT. Additional exam requirements/recommendations for international students: Required—TOEFL (minimum score 580 paper-based; 92 iBT), IELTS (minimum score 7), PTE (minimum score 62). *Application deadline:* For fall admission, 5/1 priority date for domestic and international students; for spring admission, 10/1 priority date for domestic and international students. Applications are processed on a rolling basis. Application fee: $55 ($65 for international students). Electronic applications accepted. *Expenses: Tuition:* Full-time $23,310; part-time $1295 per credit. Tuition and fees vary according to course load, degree level, campus/location and program. *Financial support:* In 2016–17, 155 students received support. Fellowships, research assistantships, and teaching assistantships available. Financial award application deadline: 3/2; financial award applicants required to submit FAFSA. *Unit head:* Dr. Shabnam Koirala-Azad, Acting Dean, 415-422-6525. *Application contact:* Peter Cole, Admission Coordinator, 415-422-5467, E-mail: schoolofeducation@usfca.edu.

University of Saskatchewan, College of Graduate Studies and Research, College of Education, Saskatoon, SK S7N 5A2, Canada. Offers M Ed, MC Ed, PhD, Diploma. *Program availability:* Part-time. *Degree requirements:* For master's, thesis (for some programs); for doctorate, comprehensive exam (for some programs), thesis/dissertation. *Entrance requirements:* Additional exam requirements/recommendations for international students: Required—TOEFL (minimum score 80 iBT); Recommended—IELTS (minimum score 6.5). Electronic applications accepted.

The University of Scranton, Panuska College of Professional Studies, Department of Education, Scranton, PA 18510. Offers curriculum and instruction (MS); educational administration (MS); reading education (MS); secondary education (MS). *Accreditation:* NCATE; TEAC. *Program availability:* Part-time, evening/weekend, online learning. *Faculty research:* Meta-analysis as a research tool, family involvement in school activities, effect of curriculum integration on student learning and attitude, the effects of inclusion on students, development of emotional intelligence of young children.

University of Sioux Falls, Fredrikson School of Education, Sioux Falls, SD 57105-1699. Offers educational administration (Ed S), including principal leadership, superintendent and district leadership; leadership in reading (M Ed); leadership in schools (M Ed); leadership in technology (M Ed); teaching (M Ed). Admission in summer only. *Accreditation:* NCATE. *Program availability:* Part-time, evening/weekend. *Degree requirements:* For master's, comprehensive exam (for some programs), research application project; for Ed S, comprehensive exam, portfolio. *Entrance requirements:* For master's, minimum GPA of 3.0, 1 year of teaching experience; for Ed S, minimum 3 years of teaching experience, minimum cumulative GPA of 3.5, 1 year of administrative experience. Additional exam requirements/recommendations for international students: Required—TOEFL. *Faculty research:* Reading, literacy, leadership.

University of South Africa, College of Human Sciences, Pretoria, South Africa. Offers adult education (M Ed); African languages (MA, PhD); African politics (MA, PhD); Afrikaans (MA, PhD); ancient history (MA, PhD); ancient Near Eastern studies (MA, PhD); anthropology (MA, PhD); applied linguistics (MA); Arabic (MA, PhD); archaeology (MA); art history (MA); Biblical archaeology (MA); Biblical studies (M Th, D Th, PhD); Christian spirituality (M Th, D Th); church history (M Th, D Th); classical studies (MA, PhD); clinical psychology (MA); communication (MA, PhD); comparative education (M Ed, Ed D); consulting psychology (D Admin, D Com, PhD); curriculum studies (M Ed, Ed D); development studies (M Admin, MA, D Admin, PhD); didactics (M Ed, Ed D); education (M Tech); education management (M Ed, Ed D); educational psychology (M Ed); English (MA); environmental education (M Ed); French (MA, PhD); German (MA, PhD); Greek (MA); guidance and counseling (M Ed); health studies (MA, PhD), including health sciences education (MA), health services management (MA), medical and surgical nursing science (critical care general) (MA), midwifery and neonatal nursing science (MA), trauma and emergency care (MA); history (MA, PhD); history of education (Ed D); inclusive education (M Ed, Ed D); information and communications technology policy and regulation (MA); information science (MA, MIS, PhD); international politics (MA, PhD); Islamic studies (MA, PhD); Italian (MA, PhD); Judaica (MA, PhD); linguistics (MA, PhD); mathematical education (M Ed); mathematics education (MA); missiology (M Th, D Th); modern Hebrew (MA, PhD); musicology (MA, MMus, D Mus, PhD); natural science education (M Ed); New Testament (M Th, D Th); Old Testament (D Th); pastoral therapy (M Th, D Th); philosophy (MA); philosophy of education (M Ed, Ed D); politics (MA, PhD); Portuguese (MA, PhD); practical theology (M Th, D Th); psychology (MA, MS, PhD); psychology of education (M Ed, Ed D); public health (MA); religious studies (MA, D Th, PhD); Romance languages (MA); Russian (MA, PhD); Semitic languages (MA, PhD); social behavior studies in HIV/AIDS (MA); social science (mental health) (MA); social science in development studies (MA); social science in psychology (MA); social science in social work (MA); social science in sociology (MA); social work (MSW, DSW, PhD); socio-education (M Ed, Ed D); sociolinguistics (MA); sociology (MA, PhD); Spanish (MA, PhD); systematic theology (M Th, D Th); TESOL (teaching English to speakers of other languages) (MA); theological ethics (M Th, D Th); theory of literature (MA, PhD); urban ministries (D Th); urban ministry (M Th).

University of South Alabama, College of Education and Professional Studies, Mobile, AL 36688. Offers M Ed, MS, Ed D, PhD. *Accreditation:* NCATE. *Program availability:* Part-time, online learning. *Faculty:* 35 full-time (22 women), 12 part-time/adjunct (8 women). *Students:* 359 full-time (254 women), 153 part-time (120 women); includes 147 minority (113 Black or African American, non-Hispanic/Latino; 4 American Indian or Alaska Native, non-Hispanic/Latino; 5 Asian, non-Hispanic/Latino; 16 Hispanic/Latino; 2 Native Hawaiian or other Pacific Islander, non-Hispanic/Latino; 7 Two or more races, non-Hispanic/Latino), 7 international. Average age 34. 277 applicants, 54% accepted, 130 enrolled. In 2016, 124 master's, 9 doctorates awarded. *Degree requirements:* For master's, comprehensive exam; for doctorate, comprehensive exam, thesis/dissertation. *Entrance requirements:* For master's, GRE General Test or MAT; for doctorate, GRE, minimum graduate GPA of 3.25, 3 years of experience in field, 3 letters of recommendation, interview, official transcripts, statement of purpose. Additional exam requirements/recommendations for international students: Required—TOEFL (minimum score 525 paper-based; 71 iBT). *Application deadline:* For fall admission, 7/15 priority date for domestic students, 6/15 priority date for international students; for spring admission, 11/1 priority date for domestic and international students; for summer admission, 4/15 priority date for domestic students. Applications are processed on a rolling basis. Application fee: $35. Electronic applications accepted. *Expenses:* Tuition, state resident: full-time $9768; part-time $407 per credit hour. Tuition, nonresident: full-time $19,536; part-time $814 per credit hour. *Financial support:* Fellowships, research assistantships, teaching assistantships, career-related internships or fieldwork, Federal Work-Study, institutionally sponsored loans, scholarships/grants, and unspecified assistantships available. Support available to part-time students. Financial award application deadline: 5/31; financial award applicants required to submit FAFSA. *Faculty research:* Mixed methods research and program evaluation. *Unit head:* Dr. Andrea M. Kent, Dean, College of Education, 251-380-2738, Fax: 251-380-2748, E-mail: akent@southalabama.edu. *Application contact:* Dr. Susan Santoli, Director of Graduate Studies, 251-380-2738, Fax: 251-380-2758, E-mail: ssantoli@southalabama.edu.
Website: http://www.southalabama.edu/colleges/ceps/

University of South Carolina, The Graduate School, College of Education, Columbia, SC 29208. Offers IMA, M Ed, MAT, MS, MT, Ed D, PhD, Certificate, Ed S. *Accreditation:* NCATE. *Program availability:* Part-time, evening/weekend, online learning. *Degree requirements:* For master's, comprehensive exam, thesis (for some programs), foreign language (MA); for doctorate, one foreign language, comprehensive exam, thesis/dissertation. *Entrance requirements:* For master's, GRE General Test or MAT, official transcripts, letters of recommendation, letter of intent; for doctorate, GRE General Test or MAT/qualifying exams, letters of recommendation, letters of intent, interview. Electronic applications accepted. *Faculty research:* Inquiry learning, assessment of student learning, equity issues in education, multicultural education, cultural diversity.

University of South Carolina Upstate, Graduate Programs, Spartanburg, SC 29303-4999. Offers early childhood education (M Ed); elementary education (M Ed); informatics (MS); special education: visual impairment (M Ed). *Accreditation:* NCATE. *Program availability:* Part-time, evening/weekend. *Degree requirements:* For master's, professional portfolio. *Entrance requirements:* For master's, GRE General Test or MAT, interview, minimum undergraduate GPA of 2.5, teaching certificate, 2 letters of recommendation. *Faculty research:* Promoting university diversity awareness, rough and tumble play, social justice education, American Indian literatures and cultures, diversity and multicultural education, science teaching strategy.

The University of South Dakota, Graduate School, School of Education, Vermillion, SD 57069. Offers MA, MS, Ed D, PhD, Ed S. *Accreditation:* NCATE. *Program availability:* Part-time, evening/weekend, online learning. *Degree requirements:* For master's and Ed S, comprehensive exam, thesis or alternative; for doctorate, comprehensive exam, thesis/dissertation. *Entrance requirements:* For master's and doctorate, GRE General Test or MAT, minimum GPA of 2.7. Additional exam requirements/recommendations for international students: Required—TOEFL (minimum score 550 paper-based; 79 iBT). Electronic applications accepted.

University of Southern California, Graduate School, Rossier School of Education, Los Angeles, CA 90089. Offers MAT, ME, MMFT, Ed D, PhD. *Degree requirements:* For master's, thesis optional; for doctorate, thesis/dissertation. *Entrance requirements:* For master's and doctorate, GRE. Additional exam requirements/recommendations for international students: Required—TOEFL (minimum score 100 iBT). Electronic applications accepted. *Faculty research:* Data-driven decision-making in K-12 schools and districts; examination of college and university leadership and management in U. S. and Asia; studies in facilitating student learning; organizational change and the role of leaders; leadership, diversity, learning and accountability.

University of Southern Indiana, Graduate Studies, Pott College of Science, Engineering, and Education, Department of Teacher Education, Evansville, IN 47712-3590. Offers elementary education (MSE); mathematics teaching (MSE); school administration and leadership (MSE); secondary education (MSE). *Accreditation:* NCATE. *Program availability:* Part-time, evening/weekend. *Faculty:* 5 full-time (4 women), 2 part-time/adjunct (1 woman). *Students:* 9 full-time (5 women), 14 part-time (12 women), 2 international. Average age 32. In 2016, 17 master's awarded. *Entrance requirements:* For master's, PRAXIS II, bachelor's degree with minimum cumulative GPA of 2.75 from college or university accredited by NCATE or comparable association; minimum GPA of 3.0 in all courses taken at graduate level at all schools attended; teaching license. Additional exam requirements/recommendations for international students: Required—TOEFL (minimum score 550 paper-based; 79 iBT), IELTS (minimum score 6). *Application deadline:* For fall admission, 7/1 priority date for domestic students, 1/1 priority date for international students. Applications are processed on a rolling basis. Application fee: $40. Electronic applications accepted. *Expenses:* Tuition, state resident: full-time $8497. Tuition, nonresident: full-time $16,691. *Required fees:* $500. *Financial support:* Federal Work-Study, scholarships/grants, tuition waivers (full and partial), and unspecified assistantships available. Financial award application deadline: 3/1; financial award applicants required to submit FAFSA. *Unit head:* Dr. Bonnie Beach, Associate Dean, 812-465-1620, E-mail: blbeach@usi.edu. *Application contact:* Dr. Mayola Rowser, Director, Graduate Studies, 812-465-7015, Fax: 812-464-1956, E-mail: mrowser@usi.edu.
Website: http://www.usi.edu/science/teacher-education/programs/mse

University of Southern Maine, College of Management and Human Service, School of Education and Human Development, Gorham, ME 04038. Offers MS, MS Ed, Psy D, CAS, CGS. *Accreditation:* TEAC. *Program availability:* Part-time, evening/weekend, online learning. Terminal master's awarded for partial completion of doctoral program. *Degree requirements:* For master's, comprehensive exam (for some programs), thesis or alternative; for doctorate, thesis/dissertation; for other advanced degree, thesis or alternative. *Entrance requirements:* For master's, GRE General Test or MAT, proof of teacher certification; for doctorate, GRE General Test; for other advanced degree, master's degree. Additional exam requirements/recommendations for international students: Required—TOEFL (minimum score 550 paper-based; 79 iBT). Electronic applications accepted. *Faculty research:* Teacher development, library technology outreach, literacy through literature, college-bound, multicultural education, school psychology, education policy and evaluation.

University of Southern Mississippi, Graduate School, College of Education and Psychology, Hattiesburg, MS 39406. Offers M Ed, MA, MAT, MLIS, MS, Ed D, PhD, Ed S, Graduate Certificate. *Accreditation:* NCATE. *Program availability:* Part-time. Terminal master's awarded for partial completion of doctoral program. *Degree requirements:* For master's, comprehensive exam, thesis (for some programs); for doctorate, comprehensive exam, thesis/dissertation; for other advanced degree, comprehensive exam, thesis. *Entrance requirements:* For master's, GRE General Test, MAT, minimum GPA of 2.75 on last 60 hours; for doctorate, GRE General Test, minimum GPA of 3.5; for other advanced degree, GRE General Test. Additional exam requirements/recommendations for international students: Required—TOEFL, IELTS. *Application deadline:* For fall admission, 3/1 priority date for domestic students, 3/1 for international students; for spring admission, 11/1 priority date for domestic students, 11/1 for international students. Applications are processed on a rolling basis. Application fee: $60. Electronic applications accepted. *Expenses: Tuition, area resident:* Full-time $15,708; part-time $437 per credit hour. *Financial support:* Research assistantships with full tuition reimbursements, teaching assistantships with full tuition reimbursements, career-related internships or fieldwork, Federal Work-Study, institutionally sponsored loans, scholarships/grants, health care benefits, and unspecified assistantships available. Financial award application deadline: 3/15; financial award applicants required to submit FAFSA. *Faculty research:* Reading, sleep, animal cognition. *Unit head:* Dr. Trent Gould, Dean, 601-266-4224, Fax: 601-266-4175, E-mail: trent.gould@usm.edu. *Application contact:* Shonna Breland, Manager of Graduate Admissions, 601-266-6563, Fax: 601-266-5138.
Website: https://www.usm.edu/education-psychology

University of South Florida, College of Education, Tampa, FL 33620-9951. Offers M Ed, MA, MAT, Ed D, PhD, Ed S. *Accreditation:* NCATE. *Program availability:* Part-time, evening/weekend, online learning. *Faculty:* 88 full-time (54 women). *Students:* 449 full-time (309 women), 710 part-time (525 women); includes 335 minority (144 Black or African American, non-Hispanic/Latino; 2 American Indian or Alaska Native, non-Hispanic/Latino; 30 Asian, non-Hispanic/Latino; 140 Hispanic/Latino; 2 Native Hawaiian or other Pacific Islander, non-Hispanic/Latino; 17 Two or more races, non-Hispanic/Latino), 110 international. Average age 35. 716 applicants, 50% accepted, 265 enrolled. In 2016, 348 master's, 62 doctorates, 10 other advanced degrees awarded. *Degree requirements:* For master's, comprehensive exam, thesis (for some programs), project (for some programs); for doctorate, comprehensive exam, thesis/dissertation, philosophies of inquiry; multiple research methods. *Entrance requirements:* For master's, GRE General Test, minimum GPA of 3.5 in last 60 hours of course work; for doctorate, GRE General Test, minimum GPA of 3.5; for Ed S, GRE General Test. Additional exam requirements/recommendations for international students: Required—TOEFL (minimum score 550 paper-based). *Application deadline:* For fall admission, 2/15 for domestic students, 1/2 for international students; for spring admission, 10/15 for domestic students, 6/1 for international students. Application fee: $30. Electronic applications accepted. *Expenses:* Tuition, state resident: full-time $7766; part-time $431.43 per credit hour. Tuition, nonresident: full-time $15,789; part-time $877.17 per credit hour. *Required fees:* $37 per term. *Financial support:* In 2016–17, 188 students received support, including 9 fellowships with full tuition reimbursements available (averaging $15,000 per year), 2 research assistantships with full tuition reimbursements available (averaging $15,000 per year); career-related internships or fieldwork, Federal Work-Study, institutionally sponsored loans, scholarships/grants, health care benefits, and unspecified assistantships also available. Support available to part-time students. Financial award applicants required to submit FAFSA. *Faculty research:* Scholarship of teaching and learning, educator preparation, diversity issues as they relate to PK-20 education, urban education. *Total annual research expenditures:* $14.9 million. *Unit head:* Dr. Colleen S. Kennedy, Dean, 813-974-3400, Fax: 813-974-3826. *Application contact:* Dr. Diane Briscoe, Coordinator of Graduate Studies, 813-974-1804, Fax: 813-974-3391, E-mail: briscoe@usf.edu.
Website: http://www.coedu.usf.edu/

University of South Florida, St. Petersburg, College of Education, St. Petersburg, FL 33701. Offers educational leadership development (M Ed); elementary education (MA), including math/science; English education (MA); middle grades STEM education (MS); reading education (MA). *Program availability:* Part-time. *Degree requirements:* For master's, comprehensive exam, practicum, internship, comprehensive portfolio. *Entrance requirements:* For master's, State of Florida General Knowledge Test (GKT), Florida Teaching Certificate (for non-initial certification programs), letters of recommendation. Additional exam requirements/recommendations for international students: Required—TOEFL (minimum score 550 paper-based; 79 iBT); Recommended—IELTS. Electronic applications accepted.

The University of Tampa, Programs in Education, Tampa, FL 33606-1490. Offers curriculum and instruction (M Ed); instructional design and technology (MS). *Program availability:* Part-time, evening/weekend. *Faculty:* 2 full-time (1 woman), 3 part-time/adjunct (all women). *Students:* 44 full-time (38 women), 18 part-time (14 women); includes 2 minority (both Black or African American, non-Hispanic/Latino), 7 international. Average age 31. 126 applicants, 40% accepted, 29 enrolled. In 2016, 23 master's awarded. *Degree requirements:* For master's, capstone. *Entrance requirements:* For master's, GMAT or GRE, current Florida Professional Teaching Certificate, statement of eligibility for Florida Professional Teaching Certificate, or professional teaching certificate from another state; bachelor's degree in an area of education. Additional exam requirements/recommendations for international students: Required—TOEFL (minimum score 577 paper-based; 90 iBT), IELTS (minimum score 7.5). *Application deadline:* Applications are processed on a rolling basis. Application fee: $40. Electronic applications accepted. *Expenses:* $588 per credit tuition, $40 per term fees. *Financial support:* In 2016–17, 20 students received support. Career-related internships or fieldwork, scholarships/grants, and unspecified assistantships available. Financial award applicants required to submit FAFSA. *Faculty research:* Diversity in the classroom, technology integration, assessment methodologies, complex and ill-structured problem solving, communities of practice. *Unit head:* Dr. Antony Erben, Chair, 813-257-3414, E-mail: terben@ut.edu. *Application contact:* Chanelle Cox, Staff Assistant, Admissions for Graduate and Continuing Studies, 813-253-6249, E-mail: ccox@ut.edu.
Website: http://www.ut.edu/graduate/education/

The University of Tennessee, Graduate School, College of Education, Health and Human Sciences, Knoxville, TN 37996. Offers MPH, MS, Ed D, PhD, Ed S, MS/MPH. *Accreditation:* NCATE. *Program availability:* Part-time, evening/weekend, online learning. Terminal master's awarded for partial completion of doctoral program. *Degree requirements:* For master's and Ed S, thesis optional; for doctorate, thesis/dissertation. *Entrance requirements:* For master's, minimum GPA of 2.7; for doctorate and Ed S, GRE General Test, minimum GPA of 2.7. Additional exam requirements/recommendations for international students: Required—TOEFL. Electronic applications accepted.

The University of Tennessee at Chattanooga, School of Education, Chattanooga, TN 37403. Offers counseling (M Ed), including community counseling, school counseling; education (M Ed, Post-Master's Certificate), including elementary education (M Ed), school leadership, secondary education (M Ed), special education (M Ed); educational specialist (Ed S), including educational technology, school psychology; learning and leadership (Ed D), including educational leadership. *Accreditation:* ACA; NCATE. *Program availability:* Part-time. *Faculty:* 13 full-time (8 women), 2 part-time/adjunct (both women). *Students:* 50 full-time (32 women), 157 part-time (107 women); includes 42 minority (28 Black or African American, non-Hispanic/Latino; 4 Asian, non-Hispanic/Latino; 2 Hispanic/Latino; 8 Two or more races, non-Hispanic/Latino), 1 international. Average age 36. 169 applicants, 76% accepted, 49 enrolled. In 2016, 77 master's, 5 other advanced degrees awarded. *Degree requirements:* For master's, comprehensive exam, thesis optional, culminating experience; for doctorate, comprehensive exam, thesis/dissertation; for other advanced degree, internship. *Entrance requirements:* For master's, GRE General Test, PPST 1, teaching certificate; for doctorate, GRE General Test, master's degree, two years of practical work experience in organizational environment; for other advanced degree, GRE General Test, letters of reference. Additional exam requirements/recommendations for international students: Required—TOEFL (minimum score 550 paper-based; 79 iBT), IELTS (minimum score 6). *Application deadline:* For fall admission, 6/15 for domestic students, 7/1 for international students; for spring admission, 11/1 for domestic and international students. Applications are processed on a rolling basis. Application fee: $35 ($40 for international students). Electronic applications accepted. *Expenses:* $9,876 full-time in-state; $25,994 full-time out-of-state; $450 per credit part-time in-state; $1,345 per credit part-time out-of-state. *Financial support:* In 2016–17, 18 research assistantships, 5 teaching assistantships were awarded; career-related internships or fieldwork, institutionally sponsored loans, scholarships/grants, and unspecified assistantships also available. Support available to part-time students. Financial award application deadline: 7/1; financial award applicants required to submit FAFSA. *Faculty research:* School counseling, community counseling, elementary and secondary education, school leadership and administration. *Total annual research expenditures:* $247,231. *Unit head:* Dr. Renee Murley, Director, 423-425-4684, Fax: 423-425-5380, E-mail: renee-murley@utc.edu. *Application contact:* Dr. Joanne Romagni, Dean of the Graduate School, 423-425-4478, Fax: 423-425-5223, E-mail: joanne-romagni@utc.edu.
Website: http://www.utc.edu/school-education/abouttheschool/gradprograms.php

The University of Tennessee at Martin, Graduate Programs, College of Education, Health and Behavioral Sciences, Martin, TN 38238. Offers MS Ed. *Accreditation:* NCATE. *Program availability:* Part-time, online only, 100% online. *Faculty:* 45. *Students:* 35 full-time (26 women), 210 part-time (160 women); includes 34 minority (24 Black or African American, non-Hispanic/Latino; 1 Asian, non-Hispanic/Latino; 7 Hispanic/Latino; 2 Two or more races, non-Hispanic/Latino). Average age 33. 168 applicants, 70% accepted, 73 enrolled. In 2016, 51 master's awarded. *Degree requirements:* For master's, comprehensive exam. *Entrance requirements:* For master's, GRE General Test, minimum GPA of 2.5. Additional exam requirements/recommendations for international students: Required—TOEFL (minimum score 525 paper-based; 71 iBT). *Application deadline:* For fall admission, 7/27 priority date for domestic and international students; for spring admission, 12/17 priority date for domestic and international students; for summer admission, 5/10 priority date for domestic and international students. Applications are processed on a rolling basis. Application fee: $30 ($130 for international students). Electronic applications accepted. *Expenses:* Tuition, state resident: full-time $8254; part-time $459 per credit hour. Tuition, nonresident: full-time $22,198; part-time $1234 per credit hour. *Required fees:* $79 per credit hour. Part-time tuition and fees vary according to course load and campus/location. *Financial support:* In 2016–17, 13 students received support, including 2 research assistantships with full tuition reimbursements available (averaging $6,912 per year), 10 teaching assistantships with full tuition reimbursements available (averaging $6,909 per year); scholarships/grants and unspecified assistantships also available. Financial award application deadline: 2/1; financial award applicants required to submit FAFSA. *Faculty research:* Environmental education, self-concept, science education, attention deficit disorder, special education. *Unit head:* Cynthia West, Dean, 731-881-7127, Fax: 731-881-7975, E-mail: cwest@utm.edu. *Application contact:* Jolene L. Cunningham, Student Services Specialist, 731-881-7012, Fax: 731-881-7499, E-mail: jcunningham@utm.edu.
Website: http://www.utm.edu/departments/cehbs/

The University of Texas at Arlington, Graduate School, College of Education, Arlington, TX 76019. Offers M Ed, M Ed T, PhD. *Unit head:* Dr. Phil Cohen, Dean of Graduate Studies, 817-272-3186, Fax: 817-272-2625, E-mail: graduate.school@uta.edu. *Application contact:* Dr. Phil Cohen, Dean of Graduate Studies, 817-272-3186, Fax: 817-272-2625, E-mail: graduate.school@uta.edu.
Website: http://www.uta.edu/coed/index.php

The University of Texas at Austin, Graduate School, College of Education, Austin, TX 78712-1111. Offers M Ed, MA, MS, Ed D, PhD. *Program availability:* Part-time. *Entrance requirements:* For master's and doctorate, GRE General Test. Electronic applications accepted.

The University of Texas at El Paso, Graduate School, College of Education, El Paso, TX 79968-0001. Offers M Ed, MA, Ed D, PhD. *Program availability:* Part-time, evening/weekend, online learning. *Degree requirements:* For master's, thesis optional; for doctorate, thesis/dissertation. *Entrance requirements:* For master's, minimum GPA of 3.0, letter of intent, resume, letters of recommendation, copy of teaching certificate, district service record; for doctorate, GRE, resume, letters of recommendation, scholarly paper. Additional exam requirements/recommendations for international students: Required—TOEFL; Recommended—IELTS. Electronic applications accepted.

The University of Texas of the Permian Basin, Office of Graduate Studies, School of Education, Odessa, TX 79762-0001. Offers MA. *Accreditation:* NCATE. *Entrance requirements:* For master's, GRE General Test. Additional exam requirements/recommendations for international students: Required—TOEFL (minimum score 550 paper-based).

The University of Texas Rio Grande Valley, College of Education and P-16 Integration, Edinburg, TX 78539. Offers M Ed, MA, MS, Ed D, PhD. Ed D offered jointly with The University of Texas at Austin. *Program availability:* Part-time, evening/weekend. *Degree requirements:* For master's, thesis optional. *Entrance requirements:* For master's, GRE General Test. Tuition and fees vary according to course load and program. *Faculty research:* Literacy development, bilingual education, brain mapping.

University of the Cumberlands, Graduate Programs in Education, Williamsburg, KY 40769-1372. Offers all grades (P-12) (M Ed); business and marketing (MA Ed, MAT); counselor education and supervision (Ed D); director of pupil personnel (Certificate); director of special education (Certificate); educational administration and supervision (Ed S); educational leadership (Ed D); elementary education (MA Ed, MAT); instructional leadership - principalship (MA Ed); instructional leadership - school principal (Certificate); middle school education (MA Ed, MAT); reading and writing (MA Ed); school counseling (MA Ed); school superintendent (Certificate); secondary education (MA Ed, MAT); special education (MAT); supervisor of instruction

(Certificate); teacher leader (MA Ed). *Program availability:* Part-time, evening/weekend, online learning. *Degree requirements:* For master's, comprehensive exam. Electronic applications accepted.

University of the Pacific, Gladys L. Benerd School of Education, Stockton, CA 95211-0197. Offers M Ed, MA, Ed D, Ed S. *Accreditation:* NCATE. *Faculty:* 18 full-time (11 women), 37 part-time/adjunct (30 women). *Students:* 210 full-time (166 women), 234 part-time (178 women); includes 223 minority (49 Black or African American, non-Hispanic/Latino; 40 Asian, non-Hispanic/Latino; 107 Hispanic/Latino; 4 Native Hawaiian or other Pacific Islander, non-Hispanic/Latino; 23 Two or more races, non-Hispanic/Latino), 8 international. Average age 33. 182 applicants, 75% accepted, 106 enrolled. In 2016, 215 master's, 23 doctorates awarded. *Degree requirements:* For doctorate, thesis/dissertation. *Entrance requirements:* For master's, GRE General Test; for doctorate, GRE General Test, GRE Subject Test. Additional exam requirements/recommendations for international students: Required—TOEFL. *Application deadline:* For fall admission, 3/1 priority date for domestic students; for spring admission, 10/15 for domestic students. Applications are processed on a rolling basis. Application fee: $75. *Financial support:* Teaching assistantships and institutionally sponsored loans available. Support available to part-time students. Financial award application deadline: 3/1; financial award applicants required to submit FAFSA. *Unit head:* Dr. Vanessa Sheared, Dean, 209-946-2683, E-mail: lwebster@pacific.edu. *Application contact:* Office of Graduate Admissions, 209-946-2344.

University of the Sacred Heart, Graduate Programs, Department of Education, San Juan, PR 00914-0383. Offers early childhood education (M Ed); information technology and multimedia (Certificate); instruction systems and education technology (M Ed), including English, information technology and multimedia, instructional design, mathematics, Spanish. *Program availability:* Part-time, evening/weekend. *Degree requirements:* For master's, thesis. *Entrance requirements:* For master's, EXADEP, minimum undergraduate GPA of 2.75, interview.

University of the Southwest, Graduate Programs, Hobbs, NM 88240-9129. Offers business administration (MBA); curriculum and instruction (MSE); curriculum and instruction: bilingual (MSE); curriculum and instruction: TESOL (MSE); early childhood education (MSE); educational administration (MSE); mental health counseling (MSE); school counseling (MSE); special education (MSE); sports management (MBA). *Program availability:* Part-time, evening/weekend, online learning. *Degree requirements:* For master's, comprehensive exam, thesis (for some programs). *Entrance requirements:* Additional exam requirements/recommendations for international students: Recommended—TOEFL. Electronic applications accepted.

University of the Virgin Islands, School of Education, St. Thomas, VI 00802. Offers creative leadership for innovation and change (PhD); educational leadership (MA); school counseling (MA); school psychology (Ed S). *Program availability:* Part-time, evening/weekend. *Faculty:* 8 full-time (2 women), 9 part-time/adjunct (4 women). *Students:* 9 full-time (8 women), 107 part-time (89 women); includes 69 minority (67 Black or African American, non-Hispanic/Latino; 2 Hispanic/Latino), 17 international. Average age 43. 101 applicants, 80% accepted, 69 enrolled. In 2016, 9 master's awarded. *Degree requirements:* For master's, comprehensive exam, thesis or alternative; for doctorate, comprehensive exam, thesis/dissertation, qualifying examination; for Ed S, comprehensive exam. *Entrance requirements:* For master's, GRE, minimum GPA of 2.5, BA degree from accredited institution. Additional exam requirements/recommendations for international students: Required—TOEFL (minimum score 550 paper-based). *Application deadline:* For fall admission, 4/30 for domestic and international students; for spring admission, 10/30 for domestic and international students. Application fee: $25. Electronic applications accepted. *Expenses:* Contact institution. *Financial support:* Scholarships/grants available. Financial award application deadline: 4/15; financial award applicants required to submit FAFSA. *Unit head:* Dr. Linda Thomas, Dean, 340-693-1321, Fax: 340-693-1335, E-mail: lthomas2@uvi.edu. *Application contact:* Dr. Xuri M. Allen, Director of Admissions, 340-693-1224, Fax: 340-693-1167, E-mail: xallen@uvi.edu.

The University of Toledo, College of Graduate Studies, Judith Herb College of Education, Toledo, OH 43606-3390. Offers MAE, ME, MES, MME, DE, PhD, Certificate, Ed S. *Accreditation:* NCATE. *Program availability:* Part-time, evening/weekend. Terminal master's awarded for partial completion of doctoral program. *Degree requirements:* For master's, thesis; for doctorate, comprehensive exam (for some programs), thesis/dissertation (for some programs); for other advanced degree, thesis optional. *Entrance requirements:* For master's and other advanced degree, minimum cumulative GPA of 2.7 for all previous academic work, letters of recommendation, statement of purpose, transcripts from all prior institutions attended; for doctorate, GRE, minimum cumulative GPA of 2.7 for all previous academic work, 3.0 for occupational therapy and physical therapy; letters of recommendation; statement of purpose; transcripts from all prior institutions attended. Additional exam requirements/recommendations for international students: Required—TOEFL (minimum score 550 paper-based; 80 iBT). Electronic applications accepted.

University of Toronto, School of Graduate Studies, Ontario Institute for Studies in Education, Toronto, ON M5S 1A1, Canada. Offers M Ed, MA, MT, Ed D, PhD. *Program availability:* Part-time, evening/weekend. *Degree requirements:* For master's, thesis (for some programs); for doctorate, thesis/dissertation. *Entrance requirements:* For master's, minimum B average in final year, 1 year of professional experience in field (MA, M Ed); for doctorate, minimum B+ average, professional experience in education or a relevant field (Ed D). Additional exam requirements/recommendations for international students: Required—TOEFL (minimum score 580 paper-based; 93 iBT), TWE (minimum score 5). *Expenses:* Contact institution.

The University of Tulsa, Graduate School, Kendall College of Arts and Sciences, Program in Educational Studies, Tulsa, OK 74104-3189. Offers MA. *Program availability:* Part-time. *Faculty:* 5 full-time (2 women). *Students:* 5 full-time (1 woman), 6 part-time (3 women); includes 2 minority (1 American Indian or Alaska Native, non-Hispanic/Latino; 1 Two or more races, non-Hispanic/Latino), 1 international. Average age 29. 11 applicants, 36% accepted, 3 enrolled. In 2016, 7 master's awarded. *Degree requirements:* For master's, thesis optional. *Entrance requirements:* For master's, GRE. Additional exam requirements/recommendations for international students: Required—TOEFL (minimum score 90 iBT). *Application deadline:* Applications are processed on a rolling basis. Application fee: $55. Electronic applications accepted. *Expenses: Tuition:* Full-time $22,230; part-time $1235 per credit hour. *Required fees:* $990 per semester. Tuition and fees vary according to course load. *Financial support:* In 2016–17, 2 students received support, including 1 fellowship with full tuition reimbursement available (averaging $17,083 per year), 1 teaching assistantship with full tuition reimbursement available (averaging $13,410 per year); career-related internships or fieldwork, institutionally sponsored loans, scholarships/grants, health care benefits, tuition waivers (full and partial), and unspecified assistantships also available. Support available to part-time students. Financial award application deadline: 2/1. *Faculty research:* Language, discourse, and development; educational foundations. *Unit head:* Dr. Diane Beals, Chair, 918-631-2045, Fax: 918-631-3033, E-mail: diane-beals@utulsa.edu. *Application contact:* Dr. Avi Mintz, Advisor, 918-631-2919, Fax: 918-631-3033, E-mail: avi-mintz@utulsa.edu.
Website: http://artsandsciences.utulsa.edu/academics/departments-schools/educational-studies/

The University of Tulsa, Graduate School, Kendall College of Arts and Sciences, School of Urban Education, Tulsa, OK 74104-3189. Offers education (M Ed), including elementary education, secondary education; mathematics and science education (MSMSE); teaching arts (MTA), including art, biology, English, history, mathematics. *Accreditation:* TEAC. *Program availability:* Part-time. *Faculty:* 4 full-time (3 women). *Students:* 10 full-time (4 women), 2 part-time (0 women); includes 4 minority (2 Black or African American, non-Hispanic/Latino; 1 Asian, non-Hispanic/Latino; 1 Hispanic/Latino), 1 international. Average age 26. 28 applicants, 46% accepted, 9 enrolled. In 2016, 7 master's awarded. *Degree requirements:* For master's, thesis optional. *Entrance requirements:* For master's, GRE General Test. Additional exam requirements/recommendations for international students: Required—TOEFL (minimum score 577 paper-based; 91 iBT), IELTS (minimum score 6.5). *Application deadline:* For fall admission, 2/1 priority date for domestic students. Applications are processed on a rolling basis. Application fee: $55. Electronic applications accepted. *Expenses: Tuition:* Full-time $22,230; part-time $1235 per credit hour. *Required fees:* $990 per semester. Tuition and fees vary according to course load. *Financial support:* In 2016–17, 3 students received support, including 3 teaching assistantships with full tuition reimbursements available (averaging $13,410 per year); fellowships with tuition reimbursements available, research assistantships with tuition reimbursements available, career-related internships or fieldwork, Federal Work-Study, scholarships/grants, health care benefits, tuition waivers (full and partial), and unspecified assistantships also available. Support available to part-time students. Financial award application deadline: 2/1; financial award applicants required to submit FAFSA. *Faculty research:* Elementary/secondary certification, math/science education, teaching arts. *Total annual research expenditures:* $233,240. *Unit head:* Dr. Sharon Baker, Chair, 918-631-2238, Fax: 918-631-3721, E-mail: sharon-baker@utulsa.edu. *Application contact:* Dr. David Brown, Advisor, 918-631-2719, Fax: 918-631-2133, E-mail: david-brown@utulsa.edu.
Website: http://artsandsciences.utulsa.edu/academics/departments-schools/urban-education/

University of Utah, Graduate School, College of Education, Salt Lake City, UT 84112. Offers M Ed, M Stat, MA, MS, Ed D, PhD, Ed S, MPA/PhD. *Accreditation:* TEAC. *Faculty:* 52 full-time (32 women), 29 part-time/adjunct (24 women). *Students:* 298 full-time (214 women), 309 part-time (213 women); includes 158 minority (16 Black or African American, non-Hispanic/Latino; 4 American Indian or Alaska Native, non-Hispanic/Latino; 17 Asian, non-Hispanic/Latino; 95 Hispanic/Latino; 1 Native Hawaiian or other Pacific Islander, non-Hispanic/Latino; 25 Two or more races, non-Hispanic/Latino), 10 international. Average age 33. 521 applicants, 46% accepted, 207 enrolled. In 2016, 125 master's, 25 doctorates awarded. *Degree requirements:* For master's, variable foreign language requirement, comprehensive exam (for some programs), thesis (for some programs); for doctorate, variable foreign language requirement, comprehensive exam (for some programs), thesis/dissertation. *Entrance requirements:* For master's and doctorate, minimum GPA of 3.0. Additional exam requirements/recommendations for international students: Required—TOEFL. *Application deadline:* For fall admission, 2/15 for domestic and international students; for spring admission, 11/1 for domestic and international students. Application fee: $55 ($65 for international students). Electronic applications accepted. *Expenses:* Contact institution. *Financial support:* Fellowships with tuition reimbursements, research assistantships with tuition reimbursements, teaching assistantships with tuition reimbursements, career-related internships or fieldwork, Federal Work-Study, institutionally sponsored loans, scholarships/grants, health care benefits, tuition waivers (full), and unspecified assistantships available. Support available to part-time students. Financial award application deadline: 2/1; financial award applicants required to submit FAFSA. *Faculty research:* Leadership, autism, reading instruction, mental retardation, diagnosis. *Total annual research expenditures:* $767,089. *Unit head:* Maria E. Franquiz, Dean, 801-581-8221, E-mail: maria.franquiz@utah.edu.
Website: http://education.utah.edu/

University of Vermont, Graduate College, College of Education and Social Services, Burlington, VT 05405. Offers M Ed, MAT, MS, MSW, Ed D, PhD. *Accreditation:* NCATE. *Program availability:* Part-time. *Degree requirements:* For doctorate, thesis/dissertation. *Entrance requirements:* Additional exam requirements/recommendations for international students: Required—TOEFL (minimum score 550 paper-based; 80 iBT). Electronic applications accepted. *Expenses:* Tuition, state resident: full-time $5814. Tuition, nonresident: full-time $14,670.

University of Victoria, Faculty of Graduate Studies, Faculty of Education, Victoria, BC V8W 2Y2, Canada. Offers M Ed, M Sc, MA, PhD.

University of Virginia, Curry School of Education, Charlottesville, VA 22903. Offers M Ed, MT, Ed D, PhD, Ed S, MBA/M Ed, MPP/PhD. *Accreditation:* TEAC. *Faculty:* 119 full-time (70 women), 8 part-time/adjunct (6 women). *Students:* 766 full-time (601 women), 99 part-time (60 women); includes 176 minority (52 Black or African American, non-Hispanic/Latino; 49 Asian, non-Hispanic/Latino; 45 Hispanic/Latino; 30 Two or more races, non-Hispanic/Latino), 30 international. Average age 26. 1,140 applicants, 44% accepted, 301 enrolled. In 2016, 379 master's, 40 doctorates, 43 other advanced degrees awarded. *Degree requirements:* For master's, comprehensive exam (for some programs), thesis (for some programs); for doctorate, comprehensive exam (for some programs), thesis/dissertation. *Entrance requirements:* For master's, doctorate, and Ed S, GRE General Test, letters of recommendation. Additional exam requirements/recommendations for international students: Required—TOEFL (minimum score 600 paper-based; 90 iBT), IELTS (minimum score 7). *Application deadline:* Applications are processed on a rolling basis. Application fee: $60. Electronic applications accepted. *Expenses:* $15,450 tuition, $2,654 fees in-state; $25,578 tuition, $3,336 fees out-of-state. *Financial support:* Fellowships, research assistantships, teaching assistantships, and Federal Work-Study available. Financial award application deadline: 1/5; financial award applicants required to submit FAFSA. *Unit head:* Robert C. Pianta, Dean, 434-924-3334, E-mail: pianta@virginia.edu. *Application contact:* Eric Molnar, Assistant Director, Admissions and Enrollment Reporting, 434-243-2085, E-mail: eric.molnar@virginia.edu.
Website: http://curry.edschool.virginia.edu/

University of Washington, Graduate School, College of Education, Seattle, WA 98195. Offers curriculum and instruction (M Ed, Ed D, PhD), including educational technology, general curriculum (Ed D, PhD), language, literacy, and culture, mathematics education, multicultural education, reading and language arts education (Ed D), science education, social studies education, teaching and curriculum (M Ed); educational leadership and policy studies (M Ed, Ed D, PhD), including administration (Ed D), educational policy, organization, and leadership (M Ed, PhD), higher education, leadership for learning (Ed D), social and cultural foundations of education (M Ed, PhD); educational psychology (M Ed, PhD), including educational psychology (PhD), human development and cognition (M Ed), learning sciences, measurement, statistics and research design (M Ed), school psychology (M Ed); instructional leadership (M Ed); intercollegiate athletic leadership (M Ed); special education (M Ed, Ed D, PhD), including early childhood special education (M Ed), emotional and behavioral disabilities (M Ed), learning disabilities (M Ed), low-incidence disabilities (M Ed), severe disabilities (M Ed), special education (Ed D, PhD); teacher education (MIT). *Accreditation:* APA. *Program availability:* Part-time, evening/weekend. *Degree requirements:* For master's, thesis optional; for doctorate, thesis/dissertation. *Entrance requirements:* For master's and doctorate, GRE General Test, minimum GPA of 3.0. Additional exam requirements/recommendations for international students: Required—TOEFL. Electronic applications accepted. *Faculty research:* School restructuring/effective schools, special education interventions, literacy and writing, technology, school partnerships, teacher preparation.

University of Washington, Bothell, Program in Education, Bothell, WA 98011. Offers education (M Ed); leadership development for educators (M Ed); secondary/middle level endorsement (M Ed). *Program availability:* Part-time, evening/weekend. *Degree requirements:* For master's, thesis. *Entrance requirements:* Additional exam requirements/recommendations for international students: Required—TOEFL. Electronic applications accepted. *Faculty research:* Multicultural education in citizenship education, intercultural education, knowledge and practice in the principalship, educational public policy, national board certification for teachers, teacher learning in literacy, technology and its impact on teaching and learning of mathematics, reading assessments, professional development in literacy education and mobility, digital media, education and class.

University of Washington, Tacoma, Graduate Programs, Program in Education, Tacoma, WA 98402-3100. Offers education (M Ed); educational administration (principal or program administrator certification) (M Ed); elementary education teacher certification (M Ed); elementary education/special education teacher certification (M Ed); secondary science or math teacher certification (M Ed). *Program availability:* Part-time, evening/weekend. *Degree requirements:* For master's, culminating project. *Entrance requirements:* For master's, WEST-B, WEST-E (teacher certification programs only), official sealed transcript from every college/university attended, personal goal statement, letters of recommendation, copy of valid teaching certificate. Additional exam requirements/recommendations for international students: Required—TOEFL (minimum score 580 paper-based; 92 iBT). Electronic applications accepted. *Faculty research:* Global learning communities for English/Chinese languages, evaluation of mathematics and reading intervention programs, response to intervention, school-wide behavioral and emotional support, mathematics education and culturally responsive mathematics education.

The University of West Alabama, School of Graduate Studies, College of Education, Livingston, AL 35470. Offers M Ed, MAT, MSCE, Ed S. *Accreditation:* NCATE. *Program availability:* Part-time, evening/weekend, 100% online. *Faculty:* 48 full-time (28 women), 80 part-time/adjunct (50 women). *Students:* 1,945 (1,593 women); includes 723 minority (667 Black or African American, non-Hispanic/Latino; 13 American Indian or Alaska Native, non-Hispanic/Latino; 6 Asian, non-Hispanic/Latino; 13 Hispanic/Latino; 1 Native Hawaiian or other Pacific Islander, non-Hispanic/Latino; 23 Two or more races, non-Hispanic/Latino). Average age 34. 670 applicants, 87% accepted, 450 enrolled. In 2016, 523 master's, 124 other advanced degrees awarded. *Degree requirements:* For master's, comprehensive exam, thesis optional; for Ed S, comprehensive exam. *Entrance requirements:* For master's, GRE or MAT, minimum GPA of 2.75. Additional exam requirements/recommendations for international students: Required—TOEFL (minimum score 500 paper-based; 61 iBT). *Application deadline:* Applications are processed on a rolling basis. Application fee: $40. Electronic applications accepted. *Expenses:* Tuition, state resident: part-time $355 per credit hour. Tuition, nonresident: part-time $710 per credit hour. *Required fees:* $130 per semester. *Financial support:* In 2016–17, 22 teaching assistantships (averaging $7,344 per year) were awarded; Federal Work-Study, scholarships/grants, and unspecified assistantships also available. Support available to part-time students. Financial award application deadline: 3/1; financial award applicants required to submit FAFSA. *Unit head:* Dr. B. J. Kimbrough, Dean of Graduate Studies, 205-652-3647, Fax: 205-652-3706, E-mail: bkimbrough@uwa.edu.
Website: http://www.uwa.edu/coe/

The University of Western Ontario, Faculty of Graduate Studies, Social Sciences Division, Faculty of Education, London, ON N6A 5B8, Canada. Offers M Ed. *Program availability:* Part-time. *Entrance requirements:* For master's, minimum B average.

University of West Georgia, College of Education, Carrollton, GA 30118. Offers business education (M Ed); early childhood education (M Ed, Ed S); educational leadership (M Ed, Ed S); media (M Ed, Ed S); professional counseling (M Ed, Ed S); professional counseling and supervision (Ed D); reading instruction (M Ed); school improvement (Ed D); secondary education (M Ed); special education (M Ed, Ed S), including teaching (M Ed); speech language pathology (M Ed); teaching (MAT). *Accreditation:* NCATE. *Program availability:* Part-time, evening/weekend, 100% online, blended/hybrid learning. *Faculty:* 46 full-time (31 women). *Students:* 321 full-time (266 women), 1,007 part-time (813 women); includes 456 minority (389 Black or African American, non-Hispanic/Latino; 1 American Indian or Alaska Native, non-Hispanic/Latino; 13 Asian, non-Hispanic/Latino; 43 Hispanic/Latino; 10 Two or more races, non-Hispanic/Latino), 12 international. Average age 33. 541 applicants, 79% accepted, 305 enrolled. In 2016, 286 master's, 20 doctorates, 156 other advanced degrees awarded. *Entrance requirements:* Additional exam requirements/recommendations for international students: Required—TOEFL (minimum score 523 paper-based; 69 iBT); Recommended—IELTS (minimum score 6.5). *Application deadline:* For fall admission, 7/21 for domestic students, 6/1 for international students; for spring admission, 11/30 for domestic students, 10/15 for international students; for summer admission, 4/15 for domestic students, 3/30 for international students. Applications are processed on a rolling basis. Application fee: $40. Electronic applications accepted. *Expenses:* Tuition, state resident: full-time $5316; part-time $222 per semester hour. Tuition, nonresident: full-time $20,658; part-time $861 per semester hour. *Required fees:* $1962. Tuition and fees vary according to course load, degree level and program. *Financial support:* Fellowships, research assistantships, teaching assistantships, career-related internships or fieldwork, Federal Work-Study, institutionally sponsored loans, scholarships/grants, and unspecified assistantships available. Support available to part-time students. Financial award application deadline: 4/1; financial award applicants required to submit FAFSA. *Unit head:* Dr. Diane Hoff, Dean, College of Education, 678-839-6570, Fax: 678-839-6098, E-mail: dhoff@westga.edu. *Application contact:* Dr. Toby Ziglar, Assistant Dean of the Graduate School, 678-839-1394, Fax: 678-839-1395, E-mail: graduate@westga.edu.
Website: http://www.westga.edu/education/

University of Windsor, Faculty of Graduate Studies, Faculty of Education, Windsor, ON N9B 3P4, Canada. Offers education (M Ed); educational studies (PhD). *Program availability:* Part-time, evening/weekend. *Degree requirements:* For master's, thesis or alternative; for doctorate, comprehensive exam, thesis/dissertation. *Entrance requirements:* For master's, minimum B average, teaching certificate; for doctorate, M Ed or MA in education, minimum A average, evidence of research competencies. Additional exam requirements/recommendations for international students: Required—TOEFL (minimum score 600 paper-based). Electronic applications accepted. *Faculty research:* School structures, teacher morale, cognitive deficits, new technologies in art education, internal and external factors that affect learning and teaching.

University of Wisconsin–Eau Claire, College of Education and Human Sciences, Eau Claire, WI 54702-4004. Offers ME-PD, MS, MSE, MST. *Degree requirements:* For master's, comprehensive exam. *Entrance requirements:* For master's, GRE (MAT, MST, MSE, MS); pre-professional skills test (MAT), minimum undergraduate GPA of 2.75 or 3.0 in the last half of undergraduate work. Additional exam requirements/recommendations for international students: Required—TOEFL (minimum score 79 iBT). Electronic applications accepted.

University of Wisconsin–Green Bay, Graduate Studies, Program in Applied Leadership for Teaching and Learning, Green Bay, WI 54311-7001. Offers MS Ed. *Program availability:* Part-time, evening/weekend. *Faculty:* 2 full-time (1 woman), 3 part-time/adjunct (all women). *Students:* 5 full-time (4 women), 17 part-time (13 women); includes 3 minority (1 American Indian or Alaska Native, non-Hispanic/Latino; 1 Hispanic/Latino; 1 Two or more races, non-Hispanic/Latino). Average age 37. 7 applicants, 100% accepted, 7 enrolled. In 2016, 29 master's awarded. *Degree requirements:* For master's, thesis or alternative. *Entrance requirements:* For master's, minimum GPA of 3.0. *Application deadline:* For fall admission, 8/1 for domestic students; for spring admission, 11/1 for domestic students. Applications are processed on a rolling basis. Application fee: $56. Electronic applications accepted. *Expenses:* Tuition, state resident: full-time $7640; part-time $424 per credit hour. Tuition, nonresident: full-time $16,771; part-time $932 per credit hour. *Required fees:* $1580; $88 per credit hour. Tuition and fees vary according to program and reciprocity agreements. *Financial support:* In 2016–17, 3 students received support. Scholarships/grants and tuition waivers (partial) available. Financial award application deadline: 7/15. *Faculty research:* Curriculum design, assessment. *Unit head:* Dr. Tim Kaufman, Director, 920-465-2964, E-mail: kaufmant@uwgb.edu. *Application contact:* Mary Valitchka, Graduate Studies Coordinator, 920-465-2123, Fax: 920-465-2043, E-mail: valitchm@uwgb.edu.
Website: http://www.uwgb.edu/graduate/

University of Wisconsin–La Crosse, School of Education, La Crosse, WI 54601-3742. Offers English language arts elementary (Graduate Certificate); professional development (ME-PD); reading (MS Ed); special education (MS Ed). *Program availability:* Part-time, evening/weekend. *Faculty:* 5 full-time (3 women), 25 part-time/adjunct (17 women). *Students:* 85 part-time (74 women); includes 2 minority (1 Asian, non-Hispanic/Latino; 1 Hispanic/Latino). Average age 27. 32 applicants, 100% accepted, 23 enrolled. In 2016, 25 master's, 5 other advanced degrees awarded. *Entrance requirements:* For master's, GRE. Additional exam requirements/recommendations for international students: Required—TOEFL (minimum score 550 paper-based; 79 iBT). *Application deadline:* Applications are processed on a rolling basis. Electronic applications accepted. *Financial support:* Research assistantships, Federal Work-Study, scholarships/grants, health care benefits, and tuition waivers (partial) available. Support available to part-time students. Financial award application deadline: 3/15; financial award applicants required to submit FAFSA. *Unit head:* Marcie Wycoff-Horn, Dean, School of Education, 608-785-6786, E-mail: mwycoff-horn@uwlax.edu. *Application contact:* Brandon Schaller, Senior Graduate Student Status Examiner, 608-785-8941, E-mail: admissions@uwlax.edu.
Website: https://www.uwlax.edu/soe/

University of Wisconsin–Madison, Graduate School, School of Education, Madison, WI 53706-1380. Offers MA, MFA, MS, PhD, Certificate. *Degree requirements:* For doctorate, thesis/dissertation. *Entrance requirements:* Additional exam requirements/recommendations for international students: Required—TOEFL (minimum score 580 paper-based; 92 iBT), IELTS (minimum score 7).

University of Wisconsin–Milwaukee, Graduate School, School of Education, Milwaukee, WI 53201-0413. Offers MS, PhD, CAS, Ed S, Graduate Certificate. *Program availability:* Part-time. *Students:* 260 full-time (196 women), 348 part-time (255 women); includes 166 minority (67 Black or African American, non-Hispanic/Latino; 1 American Indian or Alaska Native, non-Hispanic/Latino; 18 Asian, non-Hispanic/Latino; 15 Hispanic/Latino; 1 Native Hawaiian or other Pacific Islander, non-Hispanic/Latino; 64 Two or more races, non-Hispanic/Latino), 14 international. Average age 34. 493 applicants, 55% accepted, 172 enrolled. In 2016, 218 master's, 19 doctorates, 36 other advanced degrees awarded. *Degree requirements:* For doctorate, thesis/dissertation. *Entrance requirements:* For doctorate, GRE General Test. *Application deadline:* For fall admission, 1/1 priority date for domestic students; for spring admission, 9/1 for domestic students. Applications are processed on a rolling basis. Application fee: $56 ($96 for international students). Electronic applications accepted. *Financial support:* Fellowships, teaching assistantships, career-related internships or fieldwork, Federal Work-Study, health care benefits, unspecified assistantships, and project assistantships available. Support available to part-time students. Financial award application deadline: 4/15; financial award applicants required to submit FAFSA. *Total annual research expenditures:* $1.8 million. *Unit head:* Alan Shoho, Dean, 414-229-4181, E-mail: shoho@uwm.edu. *Application contact:* Education Office of Student Services, 414-229-4721, E-mail: soeoss@uwm.edu.
Website: http://uwm.edu/education

University of Wisconsin–Oshkosh, Graduate Studies, College of Education and Human Services, Oshkosh, WI 54901. Offers MS, MSE. *Program availability:* Part-time, evening/weekend. *Degree requirements:* For master's, comprehensive exam (for some programs), thesis or alternative, field report, PPST, PRAXIS II. *Entrance requirements:* For master's, PPST, PRAXIS II, teaching license, letters of recommendation, interview. Additional exam requirements/recommendations for international students: Required—TOEFL (minimum score 550 paper-based; 79 iBT). Electronic applications accepted.

University of Wisconsin–Platteville, School of Graduate Studies, College of Liberal Arts and Education, School of Education, Platteville, WI 53818-3099. Offers adult education (MSE). *Accreditation:* NCATE. *Program availability:* Part-time, evening/weekend. *Students:* 42 full-time (30 women), 72 part-time (54 women); includes 20 minority (18 Black or African American, non-Hispanic/Latino; 1 American Indian or Alaska Native, non-Hispanic/Latino; 1 Hispanic/Latino). 37 applicants, 86% accepted, 25 enrolled. In 2016, 59 master's awarded. *Degree requirements:* For master's, comprehensive exam, thesis or alternative. *Entrance requirements:* Additional exam requirements/recommendations for international students: Required—TOEFL (minimum score 550 paper-based; 79 iBT), IELTS (minimum score 6.5). *Application deadline:* For fall admission, 9/1 for domestic students, 7/1 for international students; for spring admission, 1/1 for domestic students, 11/15 for international students. Applications are processed on a rolling basis. Application fee: $56. Electronic applications accepted. *Financial support:* Research assistantships with partial tuition reimbursements, career-related internships or fieldwork, Federal Work-Study, institutionally sponsored loans, scholarships/grants, and unspecified assistantships available. Support available to part-time students. Financial award applicants required to submit FAFSA. *Unit head:* Dr. Dominic Barraclough, Interim Director, 608-342-1131, Fax: 608-342-1133, E-mail: education@uwplatt.edu. *Application contact:* Dee Dunbar, School of Graduate Studies, 608-342-1322, Fax: 608-342-1389, E-mail: gradstudies@uwplatt.edu.
Website: http://www.uwplatt.edu/

University of Wisconsin–River Falls, Outreach and Graduate Studies, College of Education and Professional Studies, Department of Teacher Education, River Falls, WI 54022. Offers elementary education (MSE); professional development shared inquiry communities (MSE); reading (MSE). *Program availability:* Part-time. *Degree* *requirements:* For master's, comprehensive exam, thesis or alternative. *Entrance requirements:* For master's, minimum GPA of 2.75. Additional exam requirements/recommendations for international students: Required—TOEFL (minimum score 500 paper-based; 65 iBT), IELTS (minimum score 5.5). Electronic applications accepted.

University of Wisconsin–Stevens Point, College of Professional Studies, School of Education, Stevens Point, WI 54481-3897. Offers education—general/reading (MSE); education—general/special (MSE); educational administration (MSE); elementary education (MSE); guidance and counseling (MSE). *Program availability:* Part-time. *Degree requirements:* For master's, comprehensive exam, thesis or alternative. *Entrance requirements:* For master's, teacher certification, minimum undergraduate GPA of 3.0, 2 years of teaching experience, letters of recommendation. Additional exam requirements/recommendations for international students: Required—TOEFL (minimum score 523 paper-based). *Faculty research:* Gifted education, early childhood special education, curriculum and instruction, standards-based education.

University of Wisconsin–Stout, Graduate School, College of Education, Health and Human Sciences, School of Education, Menomonie, WI 54751. Offers MS, MS Ed, Ed D, Ed S. *Accreditation:* NCATE. *Program availability:* Part-time, online learning. *Degree requirements:* For master's and Ed S, thesis. *Entrance requirements:* For degree, minimum GPA of 3.25. Additional exam requirements/recommendations for international students: Required—TOEFL (minimum score 500 paper-based; 61 iBT). Electronic applications accepted.

University of Wisconsin–Superior, Graduate Division, Department of Teacher Education, Superior, WI 54880-4500. Offers instruction (MSE); special education (MSE), including emotional/behavior disabilities, learning disabilities; teaching reading (MSE). *Program availability:* Part-time, evening/weekend, online learning. *Degree requirements:* For master's, research project. *Entrance requirements:* For master's, minimum GPA of 2.75, teaching certificate. Electronic applications accepted. *Faculty research:* Science teaching.

University of Wisconsin–Whitewater, School of Graduate Studies, College of Education and Professional Studies, Whitewater, WI 53190-1790. Offers MS, MSE, Postbaccalaureate Certificate. *Accreditation:* NCATE. *Program availability:* Part-time, evening/weekend, online learning. *Entrance requirements:* Additional exam requirements/recommendations for international students: Required—TOEFL (minimum score 550 paper-based). Electronic applications accepted.

Upper Iowa University, Master of Education Program, Fayette, IA 52142-1857. Offers early childhood (M Ed); English as a second language (M Ed); higher education (M Ed); instructional strategist (M Ed); reading (M Ed); teacher leadership (M Ed).

Urbana University, College of Education and Sports Studies, Urbana, OH 43078-2091. Offers classroom education (M Ed). *Program availability:* Part-time, evening/weekend. *Degree requirements:* For master's, comprehensive oral exam, capstone research project. *Entrance requirements:* For master's, minimum GPA of 2.7, teaching license. Additional exam requirements/recommendations for international students: Required—TOEFL (minimum score 550 paper-based). *Faculty research:* Best professional practices, reading/special education, classroom management, teaching models, school finance.

Utah State University, School of Graduate Studies, Emma Eccles Jones College of Education and Human Services, Logan, UT 84322. Offers M Ed, MA, MFHD, MRC, MS, Au D, Ed D, PhD, Ed S. *Accreditation:* TEAC. *Program availability:* Part-time, evening/weekend, online learning. *Degree requirements:* For doctorate, comprehensive exam, thesis/dissertation. *Entrance requirements:* For master's, GRE General Test, minimum GPA of 3.0; for doctorate, GRE General Test, master's degree; for Ed S, GRE General Test, GRE Subject Test. Additional exam requirements/recommendations for international students: Required—TOEFL (minimum score 550 paper-based). *Faculty research:* Literacy instruction, design and delivery of instruction, children at-risk and their families, hearing assessment and management, language and literacy development.

Utah Valley University, Program in Education, Orem, UT 84058-5999. Offers educational technology (M Ed); elementary mathematics (M Ed); elementary STEM (M Ed); English as a second language (M Ed); reading (M Ed); teachers as leaders (M Ed). *Accreditation:* TEAC. *Program availability:* Part-time. *Degree requirements:* For master's, project. *Entrance requirements:* For master's, GRE, 3 letters of recommendation, interview, essay. Additional exam requirements/recommendations for international students: Required—TOEFL (minimum score 83 iBT). Electronic applications accepted. *Expenses:* Contact institution.

Utica College, Teacher Education Programs, Utica, NY 13502-4892. Offers MS, MS Ed, CAS. *Accreditation:* TEAC. *Faculty:* 10 full-time (7 women). *Students:* 17 full-time (12 women), 30 part-time (21 women); includes 3 minority (1 Black or African American, non-Hispanic/Latino; 1 Hispanic/Latino; 1 Two or more races, non-Hispanic/Latino). Average age 27. 21 applicants, 76% accepted, 14 enrolled. In 2016, 20 master's awarded. *Degree requirements:* For master's, comprehensive exam or thesis. *Entrance requirements:* For master's, CST, LAST, minimum GPA of 3.0. Additional exam requirements/recommendations for international students: Required—TOEFL (minimum score 525 paper-based). *Application deadline:* Applications are processed on a rolling basis. Application fee: $50. Electronic applications accepted. *Expenses:* Contact institution. *Financial support:* Career-related internships or fieldwork, scholarships/grants, tuition waivers (partial), and unspecified assistantships available. Support available to part-time students. Financial award application deadline: 3/15; financial award applicants required to submit FAFSA. *Unit head:* Dr. Patrice Hallock, Director, Institute for Excellence in Education, 315-792-3162, E-mail: phallock@utica.edu. *Application contact:* John D. Rowe, Director of Graduate Admissions, 315-792-3824, Fax: 315-792-3003, E-mail: jrowe@utica.edu.

Valley City State University, Online Master of Education Program, Valley City, ND 58072. Offers elementary education (M Ed); English education (M Ed); library and information technologies (M Ed); teaching (MAT); teaching and technology (M Ed); teaching English language learners (M Ed); technology education (M Ed). *Accreditation:* NCATE. *Program availability:* Part-time, evening/weekend, online only, 100% online. *Faculty:* 21 full-time (12 women), 15 part-time/adjunct (11 women). *Students:* 4 full-time (3 women), 133 part-time (92 women); includes 9 minority (1 American Indian or Alaska Native, non-Hispanic/Latino; 4 Hispanic/Latino; 4 Two or more races, non-Hispanic/Latino), 1 international. Average age 34. 35 applicants, 91% accepted, 28 enrolled. In 2016, 45 master's awarded. *Degree requirements:* For master's, action research report, comprehensive portfolio. *Entrance requirements:* For master's, GRE, MAT, PRAXIS II or National Teaching Board for Professional Standards (if GPA is less than 3.0). Additional exam requirements/recommendations for international students: Required—TOEFL (minimum score 525 paper-based; 71 iBT); Recommended—IELTS (minimum score 5.5). *Application deadline:* For fall admission, 7/21 priority date for domestic and international students; for spring admission, 12/8 priority date for domestic and international students; for summer admission, 5/5 priority date for domestic and international students. Applications are processed on a rolling basis. Application fee: $35. Electronic applications accepted. *Expenses:* $373 per credit. *Financial support:* In 2016–17, 23 students received support. Scholarships/grants, tuition waivers (full and partial), and unspecified assistantships available. Financial award application deadline: 6/14; financial award applicants required to submit FAFSA. *Faculty research:* Universal accessibility, instructional design and technology, gender communication, STEM education in K-12. *Unit head:* Dr. Gary Thompson, Dean, 701-845-7197, E-mail: gary.thompson@vcsu.edu. *Application contact:* Misty Lindgren, Graduate Studies, 701-845-7303, Fax: 701-845-7190, E-mail: misty.lindgren@vcsu.edu.
Website: http://www.vcsu.edu/graduate

Valparaiso University, Graduate School and Continuing Education, Department of Education, Valparaiso, IN 46383. Offers initial licensure (M Ed, Ed S), including humane education (M Ed), instructional leadership (M Ed), primary education (M Ed), school psychology, secondary education (M Ed); instructional leadership (M Ed); M Ed/Ed S. *Accreditation:* NCATE. *Program availability:* Part-time, evening/weekend, online learning. *Entrance requirements:* For master's, GRE General Test, minimum GPA of 3.0. Additional exam requirements/recommendations for international students: Required—TOEFL (minimum score 550 paper-based; 80 iBT), IELTS (minimum score 6). Electronic applications accepted. *Expenses: Tuition:* Full-time $11,070; part-time $615 per credit hour. *Required fees:* $116 per semester. Tuition and fees vary according to course load, degree level and program.

★ **Vanderbilt University,** Peabody College, Nashville, TN 37240-1001. Offers M Ed, MPP, Ed D. *Accreditation:* APA (one or more programs are accredited); NCATE. *Program availability:* Part-time. *Faculty:* 165 full-time (107 women), 106 part-time/adjunct (68 women). *Students:* 544 full-time (458 women), 156 part-time (100 women); includes 115 minority (47 Black or African American, non-Hispanic/Latino; 19 Asian, non-Hispanic/Latino; 29 Hispanic/Latino; 1 Native Hawaiian or other Pacific Islander, non-Hispanic/Latino; 19 Two or more races, non-Hispanic/Latino), 94 international. Average age 26. 1,394 applicants, 59% accepted, 346 enrolled. In 2016, 349 master's, 22 doctorates awarded. *Degree requirements:* For master's, comprehensive exam, thesis optional; for doctorate, thesis/dissertation, qualifying examinations, residency. *Entrance requirements:* For master's and doctorate, GRE General Test. Additional exam requirements/recommendations for international students: Required—TOEFL (minimum score 550 paper-based; 80 iBT). *Application deadline:* For fall admission, 12/31 priority date for domestic and international students; for spring admission, 11/1 priority date for domestic and international students. Applications are processed on a rolling basis. Application fee: $0. Electronic applications accepted. *Expenses:* $1,596 per credit hour tuition; $438 activity/recreation fee; $3,064 health insurance. *Financial support:* In 2016–17, 418 students received support, including 4 fellowships with partial tuition reimbursements available, 138 research assistantships with partial tuition reimbursements available, 77 teaching assistantships with partial tuition reimbursements available; career-related internships or fieldwork, Federal Work-Study, institutionally sponsored loans, scholarships/grants, traineeships, tuition waivers (partial), and unspecified assistantships also available. Support available to part-time students. Financial award application deadline: 1/15; financial award applicants required to submit FAFSA. *Total annual research expenditures:* $35.6 million. *Unit head:* Dr. Camilla P. Benbow, Dean, 615-322-8407, Fax: 615-322-8501, E-mail: camilla.benbow@vanderbilt.edu. *Application contact:* Kimberly Brazil, Director of Graduate and Professional Admissions, 615-332-8410, Fax: 615-343-3474, E-mail: kim.brazil@vanderbilt.edu.

Website: http://peabody.vanderbilt.edu/

See Display on next page and Close-Up on page 735.

Vanderbilt University, Program in Learning, Teaching and Diversity, Nashville, TN 37240-1001. Offers PhD. *Faculty:* 24 full-time (15 women). *Students:* 44 full-time (33 women), 1 part-time (0 women); includes 11 minority (2 Black or African American, non-Hispanic/Latino; 4 Asian, non-Hispanic/Latino; 1 Hispanic/Latino; 4 Two or more races, non-Hispanic/Latino), 2 international. Average age 32. 144 applicants, 6% accepted, 9 enrolled. In 2016, 4 degrees awarded. *Degree requirements:* For doctorate, comprehensive exam, thesis/dissertation, qualifying examinations. *Entrance requirements:* For doctorate, GRE General Test. Additional exam requirements/recommendations for international students: Required—TOEFL (minimum score 570 paper-based; 88 iBT). *Application deadline:* For fall admission, 12/1 for domestic and international students. Application fee: $0. Electronic applications accepted. *Expenses:* Contact institution. *Financial support:* Fellowships with partial tuition reimbursements, research assistantships with full tuition reimbursements, teaching assistantships with full tuition reimbursements, Federal Work-Study, institutionally sponsored loans, scholarships/grants, traineeships, and health care benefits available. Financial award application deadline: 1/15; financial award applicants required to submit CSS PROFILE or FAFSA. *Faculty research:* New pedagogies for math, science, and language; the support of English language learners; the uses of new technology and media in the classroom; middle school mathematics and the institutional setting of teaching. *Unit head:* Dr. Melissa Gresalfi, Director of Graduate Studies, 615-322-8227, Fax: 615-322-8014, E-mail: melissa.gresalfi@vanderbilt.edu. *Application contact:* Angela Saylor, Educational Coordinator, 615-322-8092, Fax: 615-322-8014, E-mail: angela.saylor@vanderbilt.edu.
Website: http://peabody.vanderbilt.edu/departments/tl/index.php

Vanguard University of Southern California, Graduate Programs in Education, Costa Mesa, CA 92626-9601. Offers MA. *Program availability:* Evening/weekend. *Degree requirements:* For master's, thesis or alternative. *Entrance requirements:* For master's, California Basic Educational Skills Test, California Subject Examinations for Teachers, minimum GPA of 3.0. Additional exam requirements/recommendations for international students: Required—TOEFL (minimum score 550 paper-based; 79 iBT). Electronic applications accepted. *Expenses:* Contact institution. *Faculty research:* Reading, educational administration.

Villanova University, Graduate School of Liberal Arts and Sciences, Department of Education and Counseling, Villanova, PA 19085-1699. Offers clinical mental health counseling (MS), including counseling and human relations; education (MA); education plus teacher certification (MA); elementary school counseling (MS), including counseling and human relations; secondary school counseling (MS), including counseling and human relations; teacher leadership (MA). *Program availability:* Part-time, evening/weekend. *Faculty:* 20. *Students:* 81 full-time (67 women), 35 part-time (24 women); includes 18 minority (5 Black or African American, non-Hispanic/Latino; 7 Asian, non-Hispanic/Latino; 6 Hispanic/Latino), 2 international. Average age 30. 71 applicants, 72% accepted, 38 enrolled. In 2016, 47 master's awarded. *Degree requirements:* For master's, comprehensive exam. *Entrance requirements:* For master's, GRE or MAT, minimum GPA of 3.0, statement of goals. Additional exam requirements/recommendations for international students: Required—TOEFL or IELTS. *Application deadline:* For fall admission, 3/1 priority date for domestic students, 5/1 for international students; for spring admission, 11/15 priority date for domestic students, 10/15 for international students; for summer admission, 5/1 for domestic students. Applications are processed on a rolling basis. Application fee: $50. Electronic applications accepted. *Financial support:* Research assistantships, teaching assistantships, scholarships/grants, and unspecified assistantships available. Financial award applicants required to submit FAFSA. *Unit head:* Dr. Edward Fierros, Chairperson, 610-519-4625. *Application contact:* Dean, Graduate School of Liberal Arts and Sciences.
Website: http://www.education.villanova.edu/

Virginia Commonwealth University, Graduate School, School of Education, Richmond, VA 23284-9005. Offers M Ed, MT, Ed D, PhD, Certificate. *Accreditation:* NCATE. *Program availability:* Part-time. *Degree requirements:* For doctorate, thesis/dissertation. *Entrance requirements:* For master's, GRE General Test or MAT; for doctorate, GRE (PhD only), MAT (Ed D only), interview, master's degree. Additional exam requirements/recommendations for international students: Required—TOEFL (minimum score 600 paper-based; 100 iBT); Recommended—IELTS (minimum score 6.5). Application fee: $50. Electronic applications accepted. *Financial support:* Fellowships, research assistantships, teaching assistantships, career-related internships or fieldwork, Federal Work-Study, institutionally sponsored loans, and tuition waivers (full and partial) available. Support available to part-time students. Financial award application deadline: 3/1; financial award applicants required to submit FAFSA. *Unit head:* Dr. Christine S. Walther-Thomas, Dean, 804-828-3382, E-mail: cswalthertho@vcu.edu. *Application contact:* Dr. Diane Simon, Associate Dean for Student Affairs, 804-828-3382, Fax: 804-828-1323, E-mail: dsimon@vcu.edu.
Website: http://www.soe.vcu.edu/

Virginia International University, School of Education, Fairfax, VA 22030. Offers applied linguistics (MS); education (M Ed); teaching English to speakers of other languages (MA). *Program availability:* Part-time, online learning. *Entrance requirements:* For master's, bachelor's degree. Additional exam requirements/recommendations for international students: Required—TOEFL (minimum score 550 paper-based; 80 iBT), IELTS (minimum score 6). Electronic applications accepted.

Virginia Polytechnic Institute and State University, VT Online, Blacksburg, VA 24061. Offers advanced transportation systems (Certificate); aerospace engineering (MS); agricultural and life sciences (MSLFS); business information systems (Graduate Certificate); career and technical education (MS); civil engineering (MS); computer engineering (M Eng, MS); decision support systems (Graduate Certificate); eLearning leadership (MA); electrical engineering (M Eng, MS); engineering administration (MEA); environmental engineering (Certificate); environmental politics and policy (Graduate Certificate); environmental sciences and engineering (MS); foundations of political analysis (Graduate Certificate); health product risk management (Graduate Certificate); industrial and systems engineering (MS); information policy and society (Graduate Certificate); information security (Graduate Certificate); information technology (MIT); instructional technology (MA); integrative STEM education (MA Ed); liberal arts (Graduate Certificate); life sciences: health product risk management (MS); natural resources (MNR, Graduate Certificate); networking (Graduate Certificate); nonprofit and nongovernmental organization management (Graduate Certificate); ocean engineering (MS); political science (MA); security studies (Graduate Certificate); software development (Graduate Certificate). *Expenses:* Tuition, state resident: full-time $12,467; part-time $692.50 per credit hour. Tuition, nonresident: full-time $25,095; part-time $1394.25 per credit hour. *Required fees:* $2669; $491.50 per semester. Tuition and fees vary according to course load, campus/location and program.

Virginia State University, College of Graduate Studies, College of Education, Petersburg, VA 23806-0001. Offers M Ed, MS, Ed D.

Virginia State University, College of Graduate Studies, College of Humanities and Social Sciences, Petersburg, VA 23806-0001. Offers M Ed, MA, MS. *Accreditation:* NCATE. *Program availability:* Part-time, evening/weekend.

Virginia Union University, Evelyn R. Syphax School of Education, Psychology and Interdisciplinary Studies, Richmond, VA 23220-1170. Offers curriculum and instruction (MA).

Viterbo University, Graduate Programs in Education, La Crosse, WI 54601-4797. Offers cross-categorical special education (Certificate); director of instruction (Certificate); director of special education and pupil services (Certificate); early childhood (Certificate); education (MAE); literacy coaching (Certificate); PreK-12 principal/supervisor of special education (Certificate); principal (Certificate); reading specialist endorsement (Certificate); reading teacher (Certificate); reading teacher 5-12 endorsement (Certificate); reading teacher K-8 endorsement (Certificate); superintendent (Certificate); talented and gifted endorsement (Certificate); Wisconsin school business administrator (Certificate). Weekend courses available in summer. *Accreditation:* NCATE. *Program availability:* Part-time, evening/weekend. *Degree requirements:* For master's, comprehensive exam, thesis, 30 credits of course work. *Entrance requirements:* For master's, BS, transcripts, teaching license, written narrative. Electronic applications accepted. *Expenses:* Contact institution.

Wagner College, Division of Graduate Studies, Education Department, Staten Island, NY 10301-4495. Offers childhood education/students with disabilities (MS Ed); early childhood education/students with disabilities (birth-grade 2) (MS Ed); educational leadership (MS Ed, Certificate), including school district leadership; literacy (B-6) (MS Ed); secondary education/students with disabilities (MS Ed), including secondary education 7-12. *Accreditation:* NCATE. *Program availability:* Part-time, evening/weekend. *Degree requirements:* For master's, thesis (for some programs). *Entrance requirements:* For master's, minimum GPA of 3.0. Electronic applications accepted. Tuition and fees vary according to degree level. *Faculty research:* School-community partnerships, civic engagement, educational accountability, micro-aggression and bullying, cross-cultural pedagogy with students and families.

Wake Forest University, Graduate School of Arts and Sciences, Department of Education, Winston-Salem, NC 27106. Offers secondary education (MA Ed). *Accreditation:* ACA; NCATE. *Faculty:* 8 full-time (4 women). *Students:* 12 full-time (5 women); includes 2 minority (1 Black or African American, non-Hispanic/Latino; 1 Native Hawaiian or other Pacific Islander, non-Hispanic/Latino). Average age 24. 24 applicants, 71% accepted, 12 enrolled. In 2016, 11 master's awarded. *Degree requirements:* For master's, thesis optional. *Entrance requirements:* For master's, GRE General Test. Additional exam requirements/recommendations for international students: Required—TOEFL (minimum score 550 paper-based). *Application deadline:* For fall admission, 1/15 for domestic students, 1/15 priority date for international students. Application fee: $75. Electronic applications accepted. *Expenses:* Contact institution. *Financial support:* In 2016–17, 12 students received support, including 8 fellowships with full tuition reimbursements available (averaging $49,000 per year), 3 teaching assistantships with full tuition reimbursements available (averaging $49,000 per year); scholarships/grants and tuition waivers (full and partial) also available. Financial award application deadline: 2/15. *Faculty research:* Teaching and learning. *Unit head:* Dr. Adam Friedman, Chair, 336-758-5507, Fax: 336-758-4591, E-mail: amfriedman@wfu.edu. *Application contact:* Dr. Leah McCoy, Program Director, 336-758-5498, Fax: 336-758-4591, E-mail: mccoy@wfu.edu.
Website: http://college.wfu.edu/education/graduate-program/overview-of-graduate-programs/

Walden University, Graduate Programs, Richard W. Riley College of Education and Leadership, Minneapolis, MN 55401. Offers adult education (Post-Master's Certificate); adult learning (Graduate Certificate); college teaching and learning (Graduate Certificate); community college leadership (Ed D); curriculum, instruction and assessment (Ed D, Ed S, Graduate Certificate); developmental education (Graduate Certificate); early childhood administration, management, and leadership (Graduate Certificate); early childhood education (Ed D, Ed S); early childhood public policy and advocacy (Graduate Certificate); early childhood studies (MS), including administration, management and leadership, early childhood public policy and advocacy, teaching adults in the early childhood field, teaching and diversity in early childhood education; education (MS, PhD), including adolescent literacy and learning (MS), curriculum, instruction, and assessment (grades K-12) (MS), curriculum, instruction, assessment, and evaluation (PhD), early childhood leadership and advocacy (PhD), early childhood special education (PhD), educational leadership (MS), educational leadership and administration (principal preparation) (MS), educational technology and design (PhD), elementary reading and literacy (PreK-6) (MS), elementary reading and mathematics (grades K-6) (MS), global and comparative education (PhD), higher education leadership management and policy (PhD), integrating technology in the classroom (grades K-12) (MS), learning, instruction and innovation (PhD), mathematics (grades 5-8) (MS), mathematics (grades K-6) (MS), mathematics and science (grades K-8) (MS), organizational research, assessment, and evaluation (PhD), reading and literacy with a reading K-12 endorsement (MS), reading literacy assessment and evaluation (PhD), science (grades K-8) (MS), special education (non-licensure) (grades K-12) (MS), teacher leadership (grades K-12) (MS), teaching English language learners (grades K-12) (MS); educational administration and leadership (Ed D); educational leadership and administration (principal preparation) (Ed S); educational technology (Ed D, Ed S, Post Master's Certificate); elementary reading and literacy (Graduate Certificate); engaging culturally diverse learners (Graduate Certificate); enrollment management and institutional marketing (Graduate Certificate); higher education (MS), including adult learning, college teaching and learning, enrollment management and institutional marketing, global higher education, leadership for student success, online and distance learning; higher education and adult learning (Ed D); higher education leadership and management (Ed D); higher education leadership for student success (Graduate Certificate); instructional design and technology (MS, Postbaccalaureate Certificate), including general program (MS), online learning (MS), training and performance improvement (MS); integrating technology in the classroom (Graduate Certificate); mathematics 5-8 (Graduate Certificate); mathematics K-6 (Graduate Certificate); online teaching for adult educators (Graduate Certificate); reading, literacy, and assessment (Ed D, Ed S); science K-8 (Graduate Certificate); special education (Ed D, Ed S, Graduate Certificate); special education (K-age 21) (MAT); teacher leadership (Graduate Certificate); teaching adults English as a second language (Graduate Certificate); teaching adults in the early childhood field (Graduate Certificate); teaching and diversity in early childhood education (Graduate Certificate); teaching English language learners (grades K-12) (Graduate Certificate); teaching K-12 students online (Graduate Certificate). *Accreditation:* NCATE. *Program availability:* Part-time, evening/weekend, online only, 100% online. *Degree requirements:* For doctorate, thesis/dissertation (for some programs), residency; for other advanced degree, residency (for some programs). *Entrance requirements:* For master's, bachelor's degree or higher; minimum GPA of 2.5; official transcripts; goal statement (for some programs); access to computer and Internet; for doctorate, master's degree or higher; three years of related professional or academic experience (preferred); minimum GPA of 3.0; goal statement and current resume (for select programs); official transcripts; access to computer and Internet; for other advanced degree, relevant work experience; access to computer and Internet. Additional exam requirements/recommendations for international students: Required—TOEFL (minimum score 550 paper-based, 79 iBT), IELTS (minimum score 6.5), Michigan English Language Assessment Battery (minimum score 82), or PTE (minimum score 53). Electronic applications accepted.

Walla Walla University, Graduate Studies, School of Education and Psychology, College Place, WA 99324. Offers curriculum and instruction (M Ed, MA, MAT); educational leadership (M Ed, MA, MAT); literacy instruction (M Ed, MA, MAT); students at risk (M Ed, MA, MAT); teaching (MAT). *Program availability:* Part-time. *Entrance requirements:* For master's, GRE General Test, minimum GPA of 2.75. Additional exam requirements/recommendations for international students: Required—TOEFL (minimum score 550 paper-based; 79 iBT). *Application deadline:* For fall admission, 4/1 priority date for domestic students. Applications are processed on a rolling basis. Application fee: $50. Electronic applications accepted. *Expenses: Tuition:* Part-time $592 per quarter hour. *Financial support:* Research assistantships, teaching assistantships, Federal Work-Study, and tuition waivers (partial) available. Support available to part-time students. Financial award application deadline: 4/30; financial award applicants required to submit FAFSA. *Faculty research:* Admissions/retention, instructional psychology, moral development, teaching of reading. *Unit head:* Denise Dunzweiler, Dean, 509-527-2212, Fax: 509-527-2248, E-mail: denise.dunzweiler@wallawalla.edu. *Application contact:* Dr. Joe G. Galusha, Dean of Graduate Studies, 509-527-2421, Fax: 509-527-2237, E-mail: joe.galusha@wallawalla.edu.
Website: https://wallawalla.edu/academics/areas-of-study/undergraduate-programs/education-and-psychology/

Walsh University, Graduate Programs, Program in Education, North Canton, OH 44720-3396. Offers leadership with principal license (MA Ed); reading literacy (MA Ed). *Accreditation:* NCATE. *Program availability:* Part-time, evening/weekend. *Faculty:* 5 full-time (3 women), 5 part-time/adjunct (4 women). *Students:* 27 full-time (15 women), 53 part-time (45 women); includes 2 minority (both Black or African American, non-Hispanic/Latino), 1 international. Average age 34. 27 applicants, 70% accepted, 19 enrolled. In 2016, 26 master's awarded. *Degree requirements:* For master's, comprehensive exam (for some programs), thesis optional, action research project or comprehensive exam. *Entrance requirements:* For master's, MAT (minimum score 396), GRE (minimum scores: verbal 145, quantitative 146, combined 291, writing 3.0), or minimum GPA of 3.0 on the baccalaureate transcript, interview, minimum GPA of 3.0, writing sample, 3 recommendation forms, notarized affidavit of good moral character. Additional exam requirements/recommendations for international students: Required—TOEFL (minimum score 500 paper-based; 61 iBT). *Application deadline:* For fall admission, 7/15 priority date for domestic students. Applications are processed on a rolling basis. Application fee: $25. Electronic applications accepted. Application fee is waived when completed online. *Expenses:* $664 per credit hour. *Financial support:* In 2016–17, 5 students received support, including 5 research assistantships (averaging $10,917 per year). Financial award application deadline: 12/31; financial award applicants required to submit FAFSA. *Faculty research:* Learning and the brain, primary STEM, effective assessment practices, literacy. *Unit head:* Dr. Alan Digianantonio, Director, 330-490-7336, Fax: 330-244-4777, E-mail: adigianantonio@walsh.edu. *Application contact:* Audra Dice, Graduate and Transfer Admissions Counselor, 330-490-7181, Fax: 330-244-4680, E-mail: adice@walsh.edu.

Warner Pacific College, Graduate Programs, Portland, OR 97215-4099. Offers human services (MA); not-for-profit leadership (MS); organizational leadership (MS); teaching (MAT). *Program availability:* Part-time, evening/weekend. *Degree requirements:* For master's, thesis or alternative, presentation of defense. *Entrance requirements:* For master's, interview, minimum GPA of 2.5, letters of recommendation. *Faculty research:* New Testament studies, nineteenth-century Wesleyan theology, preaching and church growth, Christian ethics.

Warner University, School of Education, Lake Wales, FL 33859. Offers curriculum and instruction (MAEd); elementary education (MAEd); science, technology, engineering, and mathematics (STEM) (MAEd). *Program availability:* Part-time, evening/weekend, online learning. *Degree requirements:* For master's, thesis, accomplished practices portfolio. *Entrance requirements:* For master's, minimum GPA of 3.0 in last 60 hours of undergraduate coursework; 2 letters of recommendation. Additional exam requirements/recommendations for international students: Required—TOEFL (minimum score 550 paper-based). *Application deadline:* Applications are processed on a rolling basis. Application fee: $50. Electronic applications accepted. *Financial support:* Scholarships/grants available. Financial award applicants required to submit FAFSA. *Unit head:* Dr. Bill Rigel, Dean, 863-638-7207, Fax: 863-638-4907, E-mail: bill.rigel@warner.edu. *Application contact:* Torshanda Howard, Admissions Advisor, 863-638-7501, Fax: 863-638-4907, E-mail: admissons@warner.edu.
Website: http://warner.edu/graduate/degrees-offered/arts-in-education/

Washburn University, College of Arts and Sciences, Department of Education, Topeka, KS 66621. Offers curriculum and instruction (M Ed); educational leadership (M Ed); reading (M Ed); special education (M Ed). *Accreditation:* NCATE. *Program availability:* Part-time. *Degree requirements:* For master's, comprehensive exam, thesis or alternative, portfolio, comprehensive paper, or action research project. *Entrance requirements:* For master's, department exam, GRE General Test, or MAT, minimum GPA of 3.0 in graduate coursework or last 60 hours of undergraduate coursework. Additional exam requirements/recommendations for international students: Required—TOEFL (minimum score 80 iBT). *Faculty research:* Reading/literature/literacy, foundations, special education, diversity, teaching and technology.

Washington State University, College of Education, Pullman, WA 99164-2114. Offers Ed M, MA, MIT, Ed D, PhD. *Degree requirements:* For master's, comprehensive exam (for some programs), thesis (for some programs), oral and written exams; for doctorate, comprehensive exam, thesis/dissertation, oral and written exams, internship. *Entrance requirements:* For master's, GRE General Test, minimum GPA of 3.0, 3 letters of recommendation, transcripts showing all college or university course work, statement of professional objectives, current curriculum vitae/resume; for doctorate, GRE General Test or MAT, minimum GPA of 3.0, 3 letters of recommendation, transcripts showing all college or university course work, statement of professional objectives, current curriculum vitae/resume. Additional exam requirements/recommendations for international students: Required—TOEFL (minimum score 550 paper-based; 80 iBT). Electronic applications accepted.

Washington University in St. Louis, The Graduate School, Department of Education, St. Louis, MO 63130-4899. Offers educational research (PhD); elementary education (MA Ed); secondary education (MAT). *Degree requirements:* For master's, thesis or alternative; for doctorate, thesis/dissertation. *Entrance requirements:* For master's and doctorate, GRE General Test. Additional exam requirements/recommendations for international students: Required—TOEFL. Electronic applications accepted. *Faculty research:* Teacher education, educational studies, urban education, policy studies, science and math education, second language research.

Wayland Baptist University, Graduate Programs, Program in Education, Plainview, TX 79072-6998. Offers education administration (M Ed); education diagnostics (M Ed); education literacy (M Ed); elementary certification (M Ed); English (M Ed); English as a second language (M Ed); higher education administration (M Ed); human resources (M Ed); instructional leadership (M Ed); instructional technology (M Ed); leadership training and development (M Ed); science education (M Ed); secondary certification (M Ed); social studies (M Ed); special education (M Ed); sports administration and management (M Ed). *Program availability:* Part-time, evening/weekend, online learning. *Degree requirements:* For master's, comprehensive exam, capstone course. *Entrance requirements:* For master's, GRE, GMAT or MAT. Additional exam requirements/recommendations for international students: Required—TOEFL (minimum score 500 paper-based; 61 iBT). Electronic applications accepted.

Wayne State College, School of Education and Counseling, Wayne, NE 68787. Offers MSE, Ed S. *Accreditation:* NCATE. *Program availability:* Part-time, evening/weekend. *Degree requirements:* For master's, comprehensive exam, thesis (for some programs). *Entrance requirements:* For master's, GRE General Test, minimum cumulative GPA of 3.0; for Ed S, GRE General Test, minimum GPA of 3.2 in all program coursework. Additional exam requirements/recommendations for international students: Required—TOEFL (minimum score 550 paper-based).

Wayne State University, College of Education, Detroit, MI 48202. Offers M Ed, MA, MAT, Ed D, PhD, Certificate, Ed S, M Ed/MA. *Accreditation:* TEAC. *Program availability:* Part-time, evening/weekend, 100% online, blended/hybrid learning. *Faculty:* 62. *Students:* 457 full-time (340 women), 942 part-time (688 women); includes 505 minority (384 Black or African American, non-Hispanic/Latino; 5 American Indian or Alaska Native, non-Hispanic/Latino; 25 Asian, non-Hispanic/Latino; 48 Hispanic/Latino; 1 Native Hawaiian or other Pacific Islander, non-Hispanic/Latino; 42 Two or more races, non-Hispanic/Latino), 60 international. Average age 35. 831 applicants, 42% accepted, 254 enrolled. In 2016, 384 master's, 40 doctorates, 65 other advanced degrees awarded. Terminal master's awarded for partial completion of doctoral program. *Degree requirements:* For master's, thesis (for some programs); for doctorate, thesis/dissertation, written exam. *Entrance requirements:* For master's, eligibility for state provisional teaching certificate (for most M Ed programs); baccalaureate degree with minimum upper-division GPA of 2.75; for doctorate, written exam of writing ability, minimum undergraduate GPA of 3.0, graduate 3.5; 3 years of teaching experience (for some programs); master's degree (for most programs); for other advanced degree, minimum upper-division GPA of 2.75 or 3.4 in master's program; master's degree; 3 years of teaching experience (for some areas). Additional exam requirements/recommendations for international students: Required—TOEFL (minimum score 550 paper-based; 79 iBT), TWE (minimum score 5.5), Michigan English Language Assessment Battery (minimum score 85); Recommended—IELTS (minimum score 6.5). *Application deadline:* For fall admission, 6/1 priority date for domestic students, 5/1 for international students; for winter admission, 10/1 priority date for domestic students, 9/1 priority date for international students; for spring admission, 2/1 priority date for domestic students, 1/1 priority date for international students. Application fee: $0. Electronic applications accepted. *Expenses:* $16,503 per year resident tuition and fees, $33,697 per year non-resident tuition and fees. *Financial support:* In 2016–17, 342 students received support, including 4 fellowships with tuition reimbursements available (averaging $11,307 per year), 12 research assistantships with tuition reimbursements available (averaging $17,994 per year), 5 teaching assistantships with tuition reimbursements available (averaging $17,994 per year); Federal Work-Study, scholarships/grants, traineeships, health care benefits, and unspecified assistantships also available. Support available to part-time students. Financial award applicants required to submit FAFSA. *Unit head:* Dr. R. Douglas Whitman, Dean, 313-577-1620, E-mail: dwhitman@wayne.edu. *Application contact:* Janice Green, Assistant Dean, 313-577-1620, E-mail: jwgreen@wayne.edu.
Website: http://coe.wayne.edu/

Weber State University, Jerry and Vickie Moyes College of Education, Ogden, UT 84408-1001. Offers M Ed, MSAT. *Accreditation:* NCATE; TEAC. *Program availability:* Part-time, evening/weekend. *Faculty:* 18 full-time (12 women). *Students:* 48 full-time (24 women), 111 part-time (86 women); includes 10 minority (4 Asian, non-Hispanic/Latino; 4 Hispanic/Latino; 2 Two or more races, non-Hispanic/Latino), 5 international. Average age 35. In 2016, 45 master's awarded. *Degree requirements:* For master's, project presentation, exam. *Entrance requirements:* For master's, GRE. Additional exam requirements/recommendations for international students: Required—TOEFL (minimum score 525 paper-based). *Application deadline:* For fall admission, 5/15 for domestic students; for spring admission, 9/15 for domestic students; for summer admission, 1/15 for domestic students. Applications are processed on a rolling basis. Application fee: $60 ($90 for international students). *Expenses:* Contact institution. *Financial support:* In

2016–17, 38 students received support. Institutionally sponsored loans, scholarships/grants, tuition waivers (full and partial), and unspecified assistantships available. Support available to part-time students. Financial award application deadline: 4/1; financial award applicants required to submit FAFSA. *Unit head:* Dr. Jack Rasmussen, Dean, 801-626-6273, Fax: 801-626-7427, E-mail: jrasmussen@weber.edu. *Application contact:* Nathan Alexander, College of Education Recruiter, 801-626-8124, Fax: 801-626-7427, E-mail: nathanalexander@weber.edu.
Website: http://www.weber.edu/education/

Webster University, School of Education, St. Louis, MO 63119-3194. Offers MA, MAT, MET, Ed S. *Accreditation:* NCATE. *Program availability:* Part-time, online learning. *Degree requirements:* For master's, thesis (for some programs). *Entrance requirements:* For master's, minimum GPA of 2.5. Additional exam requirements/recommendations for international students: Required—TOEFL. *Application deadline:* Applications are processed on a rolling basis. Application fee: $35 ($50 for international students). *Expenses: Tuition:* Full-time $21,900; part-time $730 per credit hour. Tuition and fees vary according to campus/location and program. *Financial support:* Career-related internships or fieldwork and Federal Work-Study available. Support available to part-time students. Financial award application deadline: 4/1; financial award applicants required to submit FAFSA. *Unit head:* Brenda Fyfe, Dean, 314-968-6913, Fax: 314-968-7118, E-mail: fyfebv@webster.edu. *Application contact:* Sarah Nandor, Director, Graduate and Transfer Admissions, 314-968-7109, E-mail: gadmit@webster.edu.

Wesleyan College, Department of Education, Macon, GA 31210-4462. Offers early childhood education (MA). *Program availability:* Part-time. *Degree requirements:* For master's, thesis or alternative, practicum, professional portfolio. *Entrance requirements:* For master's, GRE or MAT, interview, teaching certificate, 3 letters of recommendation. Additional exam requirements/recommendations for international students: Required—TOEFL. *Faculty research:* Neuroscience, gender bias in science and mathematics.

Wesley College, Education Program, Dover, DE 19901-3875. Offers M Ed, MA Ed, MAT. *Accreditation:* NCATE. *Program availability:* Part-time, evening/weekend. *Degree requirements:* For master's, thesis optional. *Entrance requirements:* For master's, GRE. *Faculty research:* Learning styles, community-higher education partnerships, curriculum models, science learning and teaching, literacy development in early elementary.

West Chester University of Pennsylvania, College of Education and Social Work, West Chester, PA 19383. Offers M Ed, MS, MSW, Ed D, Certificate, Post Master's Certificate, Teaching Certificate. *Accreditation:* NCATE. *Program availability:* Part-time, evening/weekend, 100% online, blended/hybrid learning. *Faculty:* 56 full-time (40 women), 21 part-time/adjunct (17 women). *Students:* 355 full-time (293 women), 606 part-time (524 women); includes 219 minority (154 Black or African American, non-Hispanic/Latino; 7 Asian, non-Hispanic/Latino; 37 Hispanic/Latino; 21 Two or more races, non-Hispanic/Latino), 3 international. Average age 30. 674 applicants, 72% accepted, 316 enrolled. In 2016, 255 master's, 53 other advanced degrees awarded. *Degree requirements:* For master's, comprehensive exam (for some programs), thesis (for some programs). *Entrance requirements:* Additional exam requirements/recommendations for international students: Required—TOEFL or IELTS. *Application deadline:* For fall admission, 5/15 for international students; for spring admission, 10/15 for international students. Applications are processed on a rolling basis. Application fee: $50. Electronic applications accepted. *Expenses:* Tuition, state resident: full-time $8694; part-time $483 per credit. Tuition, nonresident: full-time $13,050; part-time $725 per credit. *Required fees:* $2399; $119.05 per credit. Tuition and fees vary according to campus/location and program. *Financial support:* Scholarships/grants and unspecified assistantships available. Financial award application deadline: 2/15; financial award applicants required to submit FAFSA. *Unit head:* Dr. Kenneth D. Witmer, Jr., Dean, 610-436-2321, Fax: 610-436-3102, E-mail: kwitmer@wcupa.edu. *Application contact:* Office of Graduate Studies and Extended Education, 610-436-2943, Fax: 610-436-2763, E-mail: gradstudy@wcupa.edu.
Website: http://www.wcupa.edu/education-socialWork/staff.aspx

Western Carolina University, Graduate School, College of Education and Allied Professions, Cullowhee, NC 28723. Offers MA. *Accreditation:* NCATE. *Program availability:* Part-time, evening/weekend, online learning. *Degree requirements:* For master's, comprehensive exam, thesis. *Entrance requirements:* For master's, GRE, appropriate undergraduate degree with minimum GPA of 3.0, 3 recommendations, writing sample, resume, interview. Additional exam requirements/recommendations for international students: Required—TOEFL (minimum score 550 paper-based; 79 iBT). *Expenses:* Tuition, state resident: full-time $2174. Tuition, nonresident: full-time $7377. *Required fees:* $1442. Part-time tuition and fees vary according to course load. *Faculty research:* Evolutionary psychology, marital and family development, program evaluation, rural education, special education, educational leadership, employee recruitment/retention.

Western Connecticut State University, Division of Graduate Studies, School of Professional Studies, Department of Education and Educational Psychology, Danbury, CT 06810-6885. Offers clinical mental health counseling (MS); curriculum (MS); instructional leadership (Ed D); instructional technology (MS); reading (MS); school counseling (MS); special education (MS). *Accreditation:* NCATE. *Program availability:* Part-time. *Degree requirements:* For master's, thesis or alternative, completion of program in 6 years. *Entrance requirements:* For master's, MAT (if GPA is below 2.8), valid teaching certificate, letters of reference; for doctorate, GRE or MAT, resume, three recommendations (one in a supervisory capacity in an educational setting), satisfactory interview with WCSU representatives from the Ed D Admissions Committee. Additional exam requirements/recommendations for international students: Recommended—TOEFL (minimum score 550 paper-based; 79 iBT), IELTS (minimum score 6). *Expenses:* Contact institution. *Faculty research:* Cultural diversity in teacher and counselor education programs, African-American educational leaders, urban education and equity.

Western Governors University, Teachers College, Salt Lake City, UT 84107. Offers curriculum and instruction (MS); educational leadership (MS); educational studies (MA); educational studies (5-12) (MA), including mathematics; elementary education (K-8) (MAT, Postbaccalaureate Certificate); elementary education (PreK-8) (MAT); English language learning (K-12) (MA); instructional design (MAT); learning and technology (M Ed, MA); management and innovation (M Ed); mathematics (5-12) (MAT, Postbaccalaureate Certificate); mathematics (5-9) (MAT, Postbaccalaureate Certificate); mathematics education (5-12) (MA); mathematics education (5-9) (MA); mathematics education (K-6) (MA); measurement and evaluation (M Ed); science (5-12) (Postbaccalaureate Certificate); science (5-9) (MAT, Postbaccalaureate Certificate); science education (5-12) (MA), including biology, chemistry, geology, physics; science education (5-9) (MA); social science (5-12) (MAT, Postbaccalaureate Certificate); special education (MAT, MS). *Accreditation:* NCATE. *Program availability:* Evening/weekend, online learning. *Degree requirements:* For master's, capstone project. *Entrance requirements:* For master's and Postbaccalaureate Certificate, Readiness Assessment, transcripts. Additional exam requirements/recommendations for international students: Required—TOEFL (minimum score 450 paper-based; 80 iBT). Electronic applications accepted. *Expenses:* Contact institution.

Western Illinois University, School of Graduate Studies, College of Education and Human Services, Macomb, IL 61455-1390. Offers MA, MS, MS Ed, Ed D, Certificate, Ed S. *Accreditation:* NCATE. *Program availability:* Part-time, evening/weekend, online learning. *Students:* 281 full-time (155 women), 490 part-time (329 women); includes 108 minority (48 Black or African American, non-Hispanic/Latino; 1 American Indian or Alaska Native, non-Hispanic/Latino; 7 Asian, non-Hispanic/Latino; 39 Hispanic/Latino; 13 Two or more races, non-Hispanic/Latino), 26 international. Average age 30. 436 applicants, 84% accepted, 199 enrolled. *Degree requirements:* For master's, comprehensive exam (for some programs), thesis or alternative; for doctorate, comprehensive exam, thesis/dissertation, electronic portfolio. *Entrance requirements:* For master's, GRE and MAT (for selected programs); for doctorate, GRE. Additional exam requirements/recommendations for international students: Required—TOEFL. *Application deadline:* Applications are processed on a rolling basis. Application fee: $30. Electronic applications accepted. *Financial support:* Research assistantships with full tuition reimbursements, teaching assistantships with full tuition reimbursements, and unspecified assistantships available. Financial award applicants required to submit FAFSA. *Unit head:* Dr. Erskine Smith, Dean, 309-298-1690. *Application contact:* Dr. Nancy Parsons, Associate Provost and Director of Graduate Studies, 309-298-1806, Fax: 309-298-2345, E-mail: grad-office@wiu.edu.
Website: http://wiu.edu/coehs

Western Michigan University, Graduate College, College of Education and Human Development, Kalamazoo, MI 49008. Offers MA, MS, Ed D, PhD, Ed S, Graduate Certificate. *Accreditation:* NCATE. *Program availability:* Part-time. *Degree requirements:* For doctorate, thesis/dissertation; for other advanced degree, thesis.

Western New Mexico University, Graduate Division, School of Education, Silver City, NM 88062-0680. Offers bilingual education (MAT); educational leadership (MA); elementary education (MAT); reading (MAT); secondary education (MAT); special education (MAT); TESOL (teaching English to speakers of other languages) (MAT). *Accreditation:* NCATE. *Program availability:* Part-time, online learning. *Degree requirements:* For master's, comprehensive exam. *Entrance requirements:* For master's, minimum GPA of 3.0 in last 64 hours of undergraduate study. Additional exam requirements/recommendations for international students: Required—TOEFL (minimum score 550 paper-based; 79 iBT). Electronic applications accepted. *Faculty research:* International education, electronic reading assessment, developing STEM teachers.

Western Oregon University, Graduate Programs, College of Education, Monmouth, OR 97361. Offers MAT, MS, MS Ed. *Accreditation:* NCATE. *Program availability:* Part-time, evening/weekend, online learning. *Degree requirements:* For master's, comprehensive exam (for some programs), thesis optional, written exam. *Entrance requirements:* For master's, minimum GPA of 3.0. Additional exam requirements/recommendations for international students: Required—TOEFL (minimum score 550 paper-based; 79 iBT), IELTS (minimum score 6.5). *Faculty research:* Effectiveness of work, sample methodology, documentation of learning gains, appropriateness of advanced proficiency.

Western State Colorado University, Graduate Programs in Education, Gunnison, CO 81231. Offers education administrator leadership (MA); reading leadership (MA); teacher leadership (MA). *Program availability:* Online learning. *Degree requirements:* For master's, capstone.

Western Washington University, Graduate School, Woodring College of Education, Bellingham, WA 98225-5996. Offers M Ed, MA, MIT. *Accreditation:* NCATE. *Program availability:* Part-time, online learning. *Degree requirements:* For master's, comprehensive exam, thesis optional. *Entrance requirements:* For master's, GRE General Test or MAT, minimum GPA of 3.0 in last 60 semester hours or last 90 quarter hours. Additional exam requirements/recommendations for international students: Required—TOEFL (minimum score 567 paper-based). Electronic applications accepted.

Westfield State University, College of Graduate and Continuing Education, Department of Education, Westfield, MA 01086. Offers early childhood education (M Ed); elementary education (M Ed); reading specialist (M Ed); secondary education (M Ed), including biology teacher education, chemistry teacher education, general science teacher education, history teacher education, mathematics teacher education, physical education teacher education; special education (M Ed), including moderate disabilities, 5-12, moderate disabilities, preK-8; vocational technical education (M Ed). *Accreditation:* NCATE. *Program availability:* Part-time, evening/weekend. *Faculty:* 16 full-time (7 women), 33 part-time/adjunct (24 women). *Students:* 21 full-time (10 women), 168 part-time (126 women); includes 6 minority (2 Black or African American, non-Hispanic/Latino; 2 Hispanic/Latino; 2 Two or more races, non-Hispanic/Latino), 1 international. Average age 32. 47 applicants, 85% accepted, 30 enrolled. In 2016, 51 master's awarded. *Degree requirements:* For master's, comprehensive exam, practicum. *Entrance requirements:* For master's, GRE General Test or MAT, minimum undergraduate GPA of 2.8. Additional exam requirements/recommendations for international students: Recommended—TOEFL (minimum score 550 paper-based; 79 iBT). *Application deadline:* For fall admission, 6/30 for domestic students; for spring admission, 10/31 for domestic students; for summer admission, 3/31 for domestic students. Applications are processed on a rolling basis. Application fee: $50. Electronic applications accepted. *Expenses:* Tuition, state resident: part-time $318 per semester hour. Tuition, nonresident: part-time $318 per semester hour. *Required fees:* $75 per semester. Tuition and fees vary according to course load and program. *Financial support:* Unspecified assistantships and SOS scholarships for education majors only available. Financial award application deadline: 3/1; financial award applicants required to submit FAFSA. *Faculty research:* Collaborative teacher education, developmental early childhood education. *Unit head:* Dr. Sandra Berkowitz, Department Chair, 413-572-5323, E-mail: sberkowitz@westfield.ma.edu. *Application contact:* Shelly Henrichon, Coordinator of DGCE Admissions, 413-572-8022, Fax: 413-572-5227, E-mail: mhenrichon@westfield.ma.edu.
Website: http://www.westfield.ma.edu/academics/degrees/education-graduate-programs

West Liberty University, College of Education, West Liberty, WV 26074. Offers MA Ed. *Accreditation:* NCATE. *Degree requirements:* For master's, capstone experience. *Entrance requirements:* For master's, GRE or MAT, minimum GPA of 2.5, teaching license, interview. Electronic applications accepted. *Expenses:* Tuition, state resident: full-time $7074; part-time $393 per credit. Tuition, nonresident: full-time $11,124; part-time $618 per credit. *Unit head:* Dr. Keely Camden, Dean, 304-336-8247, E-mail: kcamden@westliberty.edu.
Website: http://westliberty.edu/education/

Westminster College, School of Education, Salt Lake City, UT 84105-3697. Offers community leadership (MACL); education (M Ed); teaching (MAT). *Accreditation:* TEAC. *Program availability:* Part-time, evening/weekend. *Faculty:* 13 full-time (10 women), 16 part-time/adjunct (10 women). *Students:* 56 full-time (46 women), 66 part-time (54 women); includes 26 minority (5 Black or African American, non-Hispanic/Latino; 5 Asian, non-Hispanic/Latino; 13 Hispanic/Latino; 2 Native Hawaiian or other Pacific Islander, non-Hispanic/Latino; 1 Two or more races, non-Hispanic/Latino), 5 international. Average age 34. 46 applicants, 89% accepted, 26 enrolled. In 2016, 71 master's awarded. *Degree requirements:* For master's, project or thesis. *Entrance*

requirements: For master's, GRE, PRAXIS II, personal statement (2-pages), 2 letters of recommendation, personal resume, official transcript, minimum GPA of 3.0. Additional exam requirements/recommendations for international students: Required—TOEFL (minimum score 600 paper-based; 100 iBT), IELTS (minimum score 7.5). *Application deadline:* For fall admission, 6/3 priority date for domestic and international students; for spring admission, 10/16 priority date for domestic and international students; for summer admission, 1/22 priority date for domestic and international students. Applications are processed on a rolling basis. Application fee: $50. Electronic applications accepted. *Expenses:* Contact institution. *Financial support:* In 2016–17, 39 students received support. Career-related internships or fieldwork, scholarships/grants, unspecified assistantships, and tuition reimbursements, tuition remission available. Support available to part-time students. Financial award applicants required to submit FAFSA. *Faculty research:* Identity development, space among marginalized populations, adult education, Latin American studies and economic developments, educational travel, learning in social movements. *Unit head:* Melanie Agnew, Dean, School of Education, 801-832-2470, Fax: 801-832-3105. *Application contact:* Ashley Williams, Director of Graduate Admissions, 801-832-2213, Fax: 801-832-3101, E-mail: awilliams@westminstercollege.edu.
Website: http://www.westminstercollege.edu/med

West Texas A&M University, College of Education and Social Sciences, Department of Education, Canyon, TX 79016-0001. Offers counseling (MA); curriculum and instruction (M Ed); educational diagnostician (M Ed); educational leadership (M Ed); instructional design and technology (M Ed); reading education (M Ed); school counseling (M Ed); teaching (MAT). *Program availability:* Part-time, evening/weekend, online learning. *Degree requirements:* For master's, comprehensive exam, thesis optional. *Entrance requirements:* For master's, GRE General Test. Additional exam requirements/recommendations for international students: Required—TOEFL. *Application deadline:* For fall admission, 8/1 for domestic students, 6/1 for international students; for spring admission, 12/1 for domestic students, 11/1 for international students; for summer admission, 5/1 for domestic students. Applications are processed on a rolling basis. Application fee: $40 ($75 for international students). Electronic applications accepted. *Financial support:* Application deadline: 2/1; applicants required to submit FAFSA. *Application contact:* Dr. Leigh Green, Interim Department Head, 806-651-2616.

West Virginia University, College of Education and Human Services, Morgantown, WV 26506-6122. Offers MA, MS, Au D, Ed D, PhD. *Accreditation:* NCATE. *Program availability:* Part-time, evening/weekend, online learning. *Degree requirements:* For master's, content exams; for doctorate, comprehensive exam, thesis/dissertation. *Entrance requirements:* Additional exam requirements/recommendations for international students: Required—TOEFL (minimum score 500 paper-based; 61 iBT). Electronic applications accepted. *Faculty research:* Internet training and integration for teachers, rural education, teacher preparation, organization of schools, evaluation of personnel.

West Virginia Wesleyan College, Department of Education, Buckhannon, WV 26201. Offers M Ed. *Accreditation:* NCATE.

Wheaton College, Graduate School, Department of Education, Wheaton, IL 60187-5593. Offers elementary education (MAT); secondary education (MAT). *Accreditation:* NCATE. *Faculty:* 1 full-time (0 women). *Students:* 14 full-time (10 women); includes 2 minority (both Asian, non-Hispanic/Latino). Average age 25. 11 applicants, 100% accepted, 8 enrolled. In 2016, 10 master's awarded. *Degree requirements:* For master's, thesis or alternative. *Entrance requirements:* For master's, GRE General Test or MAT. Additional exam requirements/recommendations for international students: Required—TOEFL (minimum score 550 paper-based; 80 iBT), IELTS (minimum score 6.5). *Application deadline:* For fall admission, 5/1 for domestic students, 1/1 for international students; for spring admission, 11/1 for domestic students. Applications are processed on a rolling basis. Application fee: $30. Electronic applications accepted. *Expenses: Tuition:* Full-time $19,080; part-time $795 per credit hour. Tuition and fees vary according to degree level and program. *Financial support:* Career-related internships or fieldwork and Federal Work-Study available. Financial award application deadline: 3/1; financial award applicants required to submit FAFSA. *Unit head:* Dr. Paul Egeland, Chair, 630-752-5041. *Application contact:* Dusty Di Santo, Director of Graduate Admissions, 630-752-5195, Fax: 630-752-7047, E-mail: graduate.admissions@wheaton.edu.
Website: http://www.wheaton.edu/academics/departments/education

Wheelock College, Graduate Programs, Boston, MA 02215. Offers MS, MSW. *Accreditation:* NCATE (one or more programs are accredited). *Program availability:* Part-time, evening/weekend, online learning. *Entrance requirements:* For master's, interview. Additional exam requirements/recommendations for international students: Required—TOEFL (minimum score 550 paper-based). *Faculty research:* Teacher development and leadership, national standards science education, high academic achievement for students of color, cultural influences on development, media literacy.

Whittier College, Graduate Programs, Department of Education and Child Development, Whittier, CA 90608-0634. Offers educational administration (MA Ed); elementary education (MA Ed); secondary education (MA Ed). *Program availability:* Part-time, evening/weekend. *Degree requirements:* For master's, thesis. *Entrance requirements:* For master's, GRE General Test, MAT, minimum GPA of 3.5, academic writing sample.

Whitworth University, School of Education, Graduate Studies in Education, Spokane, WA 99251-0001. Offers administration (M Ed); counseling (M Ed), including school counselors, social agency/church setting; elementary education (M Ed); gifted and talented (MAT); secondary education (M Ed); special education (MAT); teaching (MIT). *Accreditation:* NCATE. *Program availability:* Part-time, evening/weekend. *Degree requirements:* For master's, comprehensive exam, thesis (for some programs). *Entrance requirements:* For master's, GRE General Test, MAT. Additional exam requirements/recommendations for international students: Required—TOEFL. *Faculty research:* Rural program development, mainstreaming, special needs learners.

Wichita State University, Graduate School, College of Education, Wichita, KS 67260. Offers M Ed, MAT, Ed D, Ed S. *Accreditation:* NCATE. *Program availability:* Part-time, evening/weekend, 100% online, blended/hybrid learning. *Unit head:* Dr. Shirley Lefever, Dean, 316-978-3301, Fax: 316-978-3302, E-mail: shirley.lefever@wichita.edu. *Application contact:* Jordan Oleson, Admissions Coordinator, 316-978-3095, Fax: 316-978-3253, E-mail: jordan.oleson@wichita.edu.
Website: http://www.wichita.edu/education

Widener University, School of Education, Hospitality, and Continuing Studies, Chester, PA 19013-5792. Offers adult education (M Ed); counseling in higher education (M Ed); counselor education (M Ed); early childhood education (M Ed); educational foundations (M Ed); educational leadership (M Ed); educational psychology (M Ed); elementary education (M Ed); English and language arts (M Ed); health education (M Ed); higher education leadership (Ed D); home and school visitor (M Ed); human sexuality (M Ed, PhD); mathematics education (M Ed); middle school education (M Ed); principalship (M Ed); reading and language arts (Ed D); reading education (M Ed); school administration (Ed D); science education (M Ed); social studies education (M Ed); special education (M Ed); technology education (M Ed). *Accreditation:* NCATE. *Program availability:* Part-time, evening/weekend. *Faculty:* 34 full-time (22 women), 37 part-time/adjunct (14 women). *Students:* 97 full-time (64 women), 201 part-time (143 women); includes 56 minority (44 Black or African American, non-Hispanic/Latino; 1 American Indian or Alaska Native, non-Hispanic/Latino; 2 Asian, non-Hispanic/Latino; 8 Hispanic/Latino; 1 Two or more races, non-Hispanic/Latino), 32 international. Average age 39. 139 applicants, 88% accepted. In 2016, 45 master's, 21 doctorates awarded. Terminal master's awarded for partial completion of doctoral program. *Degree requirements:* For doctorate, thesis/dissertation. *Entrance requirements:* For master's, minimum GPA of 2.5; for doctorate, GRE or MAT, minimum GPA of 2.0 (undergraduate), 3.5 (graduate). *Application deadline:* Applications are processed on a rolling basis. Application fee: $25 ($300 for international students). Electronic applications accepted. *Expenses:* Contact institution. *Financial support:* Career-related internships or fieldwork, tuition waivers (full and partial), and unspecified assistantships available. Support available to part-time students. Financial award application deadline: 5/1. *Faculty research:* Reading and cognition, adult education, technology education, educational leadership, special education. *Unit head:* Dr. Shawn Fitzgerald, Dean, 610-499-4294, Fax: 610-499-4623, E-mail: smfitzgerald@widener.edu. *Application contact:* Dr. Roberta Nolan, Director of Graduate Admissions, 610-499-4125, E-mail: rdnolan@widener.edu.
Website: http://www.widener.edu/academics/schools/eics

Wilkes University, College of Graduate and Professional Studies, School of Education, Wilkes-Barre, PA 18766-0002. Offers 21st century teaching and learning (MS Ed); art and science of teaching (MS Ed); classroom technology (MS Ed); early childhood literacy (MS Ed); educational development and strategies (MS Ed); educational leadership (MS Ed, Ed D); effective teaching (MS Ed); instructional media (MS Ed); instructional technology (MS Ed); international school leadership (MS Ed); international teaching and learning (MS Ed); middle level education (MS Ed); online teaching (MS Ed); reading (MS Ed); school business leadership (MS Ed); special education (MS Ed); teaching English to speakers of other languages (MS Ed). *Program availability:* Part-time, evening/weekend, 100% online, blended/hybrid learning. *Students:* 87 full-time (70 women), 1,496 part-time (1,111 women); includes 77 minority (11 Black or African American, non-Hispanic/Latino; 2 American Indian or Alaska Native, non-Hispanic/Latino; 12 Asian, non-Hispanic/Latino; 28 Hispanic/Latino; 3 Native Hawaiian or other Pacific Islander, non-Hispanic/Latino; 21 Two or more races, non-Hispanic/Latino). Average age 33. In 2016, 524 master's, 21 doctorates awarded. *Entrance requirements:* Additional exam requirements/recommendations for international students: Required—TOEFL (minimum score 550 paper-based; 79 iBT). *Application deadline:* Applications are processed on a rolling basis. Application fee: $45. Electronic applications accepted. *Expenses:* Contact institution. *Financial support:* Unspecified assistantships available. Financial award application deadline: 3/1; financial award applicants required to submit FAFSA. *Unit head:* Dr. Rhonda Rabbitt, Dean, 570-408-4680, Fax: 570-408-7872, E-mail: rhonda.rabbitt@wilkes.edu. *Application contact:* Director of Graduate Education, 570-408-4234, Fax: 570-408-7846.
Website: http://www.wilkes.edu/academics/graduate-programs/masters-programs/graduate-education/index.aspx

William Carey University, School of Education, Hattiesburg, MS 39401-5499. Offers art education (M Ed); art of teaching (M Ed); elementary education (M Ed, Ed S); English education (M Ed); gifted education (M Ed); history and social science (M Ed); mild/moderate disabilities (M Ed); secondary education (M Ed). *Accreditation:* NCATE. *Program availability:* Part-time. *Degree requirements:* For master's, comprehensive exam. *Entrance requirements:* For master's, GRE, MAT, minimum GPA of 2.5, Class A teacher's license. Additional exam requirements/recommendations for international students: Required—TOEFL (minimum score 550 paper-based).

William Jessup University, Program in Teaching, Rocklin, CA 95765. Offers single subject English (MAT); single subject math (MAT). *Program availability:* Evening/weekend.

William Jewell College, Department of Education, Liberty, MO 64068-1843. Offers differentiated instruction (MS Ed).

William Paterson University of New Jersey, College of Education, Wayne, NJ 07470-8420. Offers curriculum and learning (M Ed); educational leadership (M Ed); elementary education (MAT); literacy (M Ed); professional counseling (M Ed); secondary education (MAT); special education (M Ed). *Accreditation:* NCATE. *Program availability:* Part-time, evening/weekend. *Faculty:* 36 full-time (25 women), 32 part-time/adjunct (27 women). *Students:* 74 full-time (51 women), 607 part-time (515 women); includes 194 minority (42 Black or African American, non-Hispanic/Latino; 21 Asian, non-Hispanic/Latino; 116 Hispanic/Latino; 15 Two or more races, non-Hispanic/Latino), 1 international. Average age 35. 390 applicants, 83% accepted, 263 enrolled. In 2016, 170 master's awarded. *Degree requirements:* For master's, comprehensive exam, thesis (for some programs), exit interview (for some programs); practicum/internship; minimum GPA of 3.0 (for some programs); exit portfolio (for some programs). *Entrance requirements:* For master's, GRE/MAT, minimum GPA of 2.75; teaching certificate; essay; interview; 2 letters of recommendation; personal statement. Additional exam requirements/recommendations for international students: Required—TOEFL (minimum score 550 paper-based; 79 iBT), IELTS (minimum score 6). *Application deadline:* For fall admission, 8/1 for domestic students, 4/1 for international students; for spring admission, 12/1 for domestic students, 11/1 for international students; for summer admission, 5/1 for domestic students, 2/1 for international students. Applications are processed on a rolling basis. Application fee: $50. Electronic applications accepted. *Expenses:* Tuition, state resident: full-time $12,480; part-time $611 per credit. Tuition, nonresident: full-time $20,263; part-time $992 per credit. *Required fees:* $1573; $77 per credit. Tuition and fees vary according to course load, degree level and program. *Financial support:* Career-related internships or fieldwork, Federal Work-Study, scholarships/grants, and unspecified assistantships available. Support available to part-time students. Financial award application deadline: 4/1; financial award applicants required to submit FAFSA. *Faculty research:* History of education, social media in classrooms and education, integrating environmental lessons into urban classrooms, minority student self-advocacy in higher education, factors affecting high school teacher retention. *Total annual research expenditures:* $289,197. *Unit head:* Dr. Candace Burns, Dean, 973-720-2137, Fax: 973-720-3467, E-mail: burnsc@wpunj.edu. *Application contact:* Liana Fornarotto, Director of Education Enrollment and Certification, 973-720-2206, Fax: 973-720-2989, E-mail: fornarottol@wpunj.edu.
Website: http://www.wpunj.edu/coe

Wilmington College, Department of Education, Wilmington, OH 45177. Offers reading (M Ed); special education (M Ed). *Accreditation:* TEAC. *Program availability:* Part-time. *Degree requirements:* For master's, comprehensive exam. *Entrance requirements:* For master's, GRE or MAT, minimum GPA of 3.0, 2 letters of recommendation. Additional exam requirements/recommendations for international students: Required—TOEFL. *Faculty research:* Reading instruction, special education practices, conflict resolution in the schools, models of higher education for teachers.

Wilmington University, College of Education, New Castle, DE 19720-6491. Offers applied technology in education (M Ed); career and technical education (M Ed); educational leadership (Ed D); elementary and secondary school counseling (M Ed); elementary studies (M Ed); ESOL literacy (M Ed); higher education leadership (Ed D); instruction: gifted and talented (M Ed); instruction: teacher of reading (M Ed); instruction:

teaching and learning (M Ed); organizational leadership (Ed D); school leadership (M Ed); secondary education (MAT); special education (M Ed). *Accreditation:* NCATE. *Program availability:* Part-time, evening/weekend. *Faculty:* 19 full-time (11 women), 178 part-time/adjunct (99 women). *Students:* 248 full-time (176 women), 999 part-time (738 women); includes 244 minority (193 Black or African American, non-Hispanic/Latino; 17 American Indian or Alaska Native, non-Hispanic/Latino; 9 Asian, non-Hispanic/Latino; 19 Hispanic/Latino; 2 Native Hawaiian or other Pacific Islander, non-Hispanic/Latino; 4 Two or more races, non-Hispanic/Latino), 7 international. Average age 34. 672 applicants, 96% accepted, 348 enrolled. In 2016, 529 master's, 87 doctorates awarded. *Entrance requirements:* For master's, 2 letters of recommendation, interview. Additional exam requirements/recommendations for international students: Required—TOEFL (minimum score 500 paper-based). *Application deadline:* For fall admission, 4/30 for domestic students. Applications are processed on a rolling basis. Application fee: $35. Electronic applications accepted. *Expenses: Tuition:* Full-time $8388; part-time $466 per credit. *Required fees:* $25 per semester. Tuition and fees vary according to degree level. *Financial support:* Applicants required to submit FAFSA. *Unit head:* Dr. John C. Gray, Dean. *Application contact:* Laura Morris, Director of Admissions, 877-967-5464, E-mail: infocenter@wilmu.edu.
Website: http://www.wilmu.edu/education/

Wilson College, Graduate Programs, Chambersburg, PA 17201-1285. Offers accounting (M Acc); choreography and visual art (MFA); education (M Ed); healthcare management for sustainability (MHM); humanities (MA), including art and culture, critical/cultural theory, English language and literature, women's studies; management (MSM); nursing (MSN), including nursing education, nursing leadership and management. *Program availability:* Evening/weekend. *Degree requirements:* For master's, project. *Entrance requirements:* For master's, PRAXIS, minimum undergraduate cumulative GPA of 3.0, 2 letters of recommendation, current certification for eligibility to teach in grades K-12, resume, personal interview. Electronic applications accepted.

Wingate University, Thayer School of Education, Wingate, NC 28174. Offers community college executive leadership (Ed D); educational leadership (MA Ed, Ed S); elementary education (MA Ed, MAT). *Accreditation:* NCATE. *Program availability:* Part-time, evening/weekend. *Degree requirements:* For master's, portfolio. *Entrance requirements:* For master's, GRE General Test or MAT, teaching certificate (MA Ed). *Application deadline:* For fall admission, 8/15 priority date for domestic students; for spring admission, 12/15 for domestic students. Applications are processed on a rolling basis. Application fee: $0. *Financial support:* Scholarships/grants available. Support available to part-time students. Financial award applicants required to submit FAFSA. *Unit head:* Dr. Annette D. Digby, Interim Dean, 704-233-8473, E-mail: a.digby@wingate.edu. *Application contact:* Theresa Gibson, Director of the Graduate Education Program, 980-359-1023, E-mail: t.gibson@wingate.edu.

Winona State University, College of Education, Department of Education, Winona, MN 55987. Offers MS. *Accreditation:* NCATE. *Program availability:* Part-time, evening/weekend. *Degree requirements:* For master's, comprehensive exam, thesis (for some programs). *Entrance requirements:* For master's, minimum GPA of 2.75/teaching license.

Winston-Salem State University, MAT Program, Winston-Salem, NC 27110-0003. Offers middle grades education (MAT); special education (MAT). *Accreditation:* NCATE. *Program availability:* Part-time, evening/weekend, online learning. *Entrance requirements:* For master's, GRE, MAT, NC teacher licensure. Electronic applications accepted. *Faculty research:* Action research on issues in elementary classroom.

Winthrop University, College of Education, Rock Hill, SC 29733. Offers M Ed, MAT. *Accreditation:* NCATE. *Program availability:* Part-time. *Degree requirements:* For master's, comprehensive exam (for some programs). *Entrance requirements:* Additional exam requirements/recommendations for international students: Required—TOEFL (minimum paper-based score of 520, iBT 68) or IELTS (minimum score of 6). Electronic applications accepted. *Expenses:* Tuition, state resident: full-time $14,312; part-time $599 per credit hour. Tuition, nonresident: full-time $27,570; part-time $1153 per credit hour.

Wittenberg University, Graduate Program, Springfield, OH 45501-0720. Offers education (MA). *Accreditation:* NCATE.

Worcester State University, Graduate Studies, Department of Education, Worcester, MA 01602-2597. Offers early childhood education (M Ed); education (M Ed); elementary education (M Ed); English as a second language (M Ed, Postbaccalaureate Certificate); health education (M Ed); leadership and administration (M Ed, CAGS, Ed S); middle school education (M Ed, Postbaccalaureate Certificate); moderate disabilities (M Ed, Postbaccalaureate Certificate); reading (M Ed, CAGS, Ed S, Postbaccalaureate Certificate); school psychology (CAGS, Ed S); secondary education (M Ed, CAGS, Ed S). *Program availability:* Part-time, evening/weekend. *Faculty:* 13 full-time (12 women), 16 part-time/adjunct (7 women). *Students:* 43 full-time (36 women), 275 part-time (205 women); includes 29 minority (6 Black or African American, non-Hispanic/Latino; 2 American Indian or Alaska Native, non-Hispanic/Latino; 1 Asian, non-Hispanic/Latino; 15 Hispanic/Latino; 5 Two or more races, non-Hispanic/Latino), 1 international. Average age 34. 320 applicants, 88% accepted, 150 enrolled. In 2016, 57 master's, 128 CAGSs awarded. *Degree requirements:* For master's, comprehensive exam (for some programs), thesis (for some programs). *Entrance requirements:* For master's, GRE General Test, MAT or GMAT, teaching certificate. Additional exam requirements/recommendations for international students: Required—TOEFL (minimum score 550 paper-based; 79 iBT). *Application deadline:* For fall admission, 6/15 for domestic and international students; for spring admission, 11/1 for domestic and international students; for summer admission, 4/1 for domestic and international students. Applications are processed on a rolling basis. Application fee: $50. Electronic applications accepted. *Expenses:* Tuition, state resident: part-time $150 per credit. Tuition, nonresident: part-time $150 per credit. *Financial support:* Career-related internships or fieldwork, scholarships/grants, and unspecified assistantships available. Financial award application deadline: 3/1; financial award applicants required to submit FAFSA. *Unit head:* Dr. Carol Donnelly, Coordinator, 508-929-8667, Fax: 508-929-8164, E-mail: cdonnelly@worcester.edu. *Application contact:* Sara Grady, Associate Dean of Graduate Studies and Professional Development, 508-929-8787, Fax: 508-929-8100, E-mail: sara.grady@worcester.edu.

Wright State University, Graduate School, College of Education and Human Services, Dayton, OH 45435. Offers M Ed, MA, MRC, MS, Ed S. *Accreditation:* NCATE. *Program availability:* Part-time, evening/weekend. *Degree requirements:* For Ed S, thesis. *Entrance requirements:* For master's, GRE General Test, MAT, PRAXIS II; for Ed S, GRE General Test, MAT. Additional exam requirements/recommendations for international students: Required—TOEFL. Application fee: $25. *Expenses:* Tuition, state resident: full-time $9952; part-time $622 per credit hour. Tuition, nonresident: full-time $16,960; part-time $1060 per credit hour. *Financial support:* Fellowships with full tuition reimbursements, research assistantships, teaching assistantships, career-related internships or fieldwork, Federal Work-Study, institutionally sponsored loans, tuition waivers (full and partial), and unspecified assistantships available. Support available to part-time students. Financial award applicants required to submit FAFSA. *Unit head:* Dr. Gregory R. Bernhardt, Dean, 937-775-2822, Fax: 937-775-4855, E-mail: gregory.bernhardt@wright.edu. *Application contact:* John Kimble, Associate Director of Graduate Admissions and Records, 937-775-2957, Fax: 937-775-2453, E-mail: john.kimble@wright.edu.
Website: http://www.ed.wright.edu/

Xavier University, College of Social Sciences, Health and Education, School of Education, Cincinnati, OH 45207. Offers M Ed, MA, MS, Ed D. *Accreditation:* TEAC. *Entrance requirements:* Additional exam requirements/recommendations for international students: Required—TOEFL (minimum score 550 paper-based; 79 iBT). Electronic applications accepted. Application fee is waived when completed online. *Expenses:* Contact institution. *Faculty research:* Early childhood literacy, service-learning, family resiliency/special needs families, technology integration, leadership theory, Montessori methodology.

Xavier University of Louisiana, Graduate School, Programs in Education, New Orleans, LA 70125. Offers counseling (MA); curriculum and instruction (MA); educational leadership (MA). *Accreditation:* NCATE. *Program availability:* Part-time, evening/weekend. *Degree requirements:* For master's, comprehensive exam, thesis or alternative. *Entrance requirements:* For master's, GRE General Test, MAT, minimum GPA of 2.5. Additional exam requirements/recommendations for international students: Required—TOEFL.

York College of Pennsylvania, Master of Education Program, York, PA 17403. Offers educational leadership (M Ed); educational technology (M Ed); reading specialist (M Ed). *Program availability:* Part-time, evening/weekend. *Faculty:* 3 full-time (2 women), 5 part-time/adjunct (2 women). *Students:* 54 part-time (39 women), 1 international. Average age 33. 51 applicants, 67% accepted, 30 enrolled. In 2016, 4 master's awarded. *Degree requirements:* For master's, comprehensive exam (for some programs), thesis (for some programs). *Entrance requirements:* For master's, PRAXIS, GRE, or MAT (within past 10 years), statement of applicant's professional and academic goals, 2 letters of recommendation, letter from current supervisor, official undergraduate and graduate transcript(s), copy of teaching certificate(s), current professional resume, interview. Additional exam requirements/recommendations for international students: Required—TOEFL. *Application deadline:* For fall admission, 7/15 priority date for domestic students; for spring admission, 11/15 priority date for domestic students; for summer admission, 4/15 priority date for domestic students. Applications are processed on a rolling basis. Application fee: $0. Electronic applications accepted. *Expenses:* $620 per credit. *Financial support:* Scholarships/grants available. Financial award applicants required to submit FAFSA. *Faculty research:* Classroom technology, assessment, educational leadership, professional development. *Unit head:* Dr. Joshua D. DeSantis, Director, Master of Education Program, 717-815-1936, E-mail: jdesant1@ycp.edu.
Website: https://www.ycp.edu/med

York University, Faculty of Graduate Studies, Faculty of Education, Toronto, ON M3J 1P3, Canada. Offers M Ed, PhD. *Program availability:* Part-time. *Degree requirements:* For master's, thesis or alternative; for doctorate, comprehensive exam, thesis/dissertation. Electronic applications accepted.

Youngstown State University, Graduate School, Beeghly College of Education, Youngstown, OH 44555-0001. Offers MS Ed, Ed D. *Accreditation:* NCATE. *Program availability:* Part-time, evening/weekend. *Degree requirements:* For master's, comprehensive exam; for doctorate, comprehensive exam, thesis/dissertation. *Entrance requirements:* For master's, minimum GPA of 2.7; for doctorate, GRE General Test, GRE Subject Test, interview, minimum GPA of 3.5. Additional exam requirements/recommendations for international students: Required—TOEFL. *Faculty research:* Euthanasia, psychometrics, ethical issues, community relations, educational law.

THE COLLEGE OF WILLIAM AND MARY

School of Education

 For more information, visit http://petersons.to/williammaryeducation

Programs of Study

Curriculum and Instruction—Teacher Education: The School of Education prepares tomorrow's educational leaders, because it attracts highly qualified students to its teacher education programs and then provides them with exemplary professional educational experiences. The School of Education offers one-year master's programs in elementary, secondary, and special education. The School also offers master's degrees to prepare for careers as a reading specialist or in gifted education. (http://education.wm.edu/academics/ci/index.php)

Counseling and School Psychology: The school psychology and counseling programs at William and Mary prepare highly qualified professionals to practice in the public schools or in related educational and mental health settings. The School offers two-year master's programs in community, family, addictions, and school counseling. For students who want to study beyond the master's level, the School offers a Ph.D. in counselor education, which can be completed in three to four years of full-time enrollment. For students interested in school psychology, the School offers a three-year Ed.S. program that culminates in a year-long internship experience. (http://education.wm.edu/academics/space/index.php)

Educational Policy, Planning and Leadership: The Educational Policy, Planning and Leadership department prepares students with the knowledge and skills necessary to guide, influence, and shape institutions at all levels of education, and to enhance the effectiveness of complex educational organizations through leadership, scholarship, and service. The School of Education offers master's degrees in K–12 administration and higher education administration. In addition, the School offers doctoral programs in general K–12 administration, gifted administration, special education administration, curriculum leadership, curriculum and educational technology, and higher education administration. Full-time students can expect to finish the doctorate in three to four years. (http://education.wm.edu/academics/eppl/index.php)

Research Facilities

The School of Education building was completed in May 2010. The facility houses W&M's nationally-ranked School of Education and brings all of its academic programs, outreach centers and research projects together in a highly professional setting designed to stimulate collaboration and innovation.

One such project, the Center for Gifted Education, provides services to educators, policy makers, graduate students, researchers, parents, and students in support of the needs of gifted and talented individuals. The center has established an international reputation for excellence in research, curriculum development, and service.

Another outreach center, the New Horizons Family Counseling Center, provides free services to families of children attending public schools in the local area. Families may be referred to the clinic by teachers, principals, counselors, school psychologists, or school social workers. Students in counseling programs complete clinical internships in the center. Under licensed faculty supervision, students serve as administrators, supervisors, and family counselors for the center.

Financial Aid

Financial assistance is available in the form of assistantships, fellowships, scholarships, and awards earmarked for School of Education students. Both full-time and part-time assistantships are available to full-time students. Awards and scholarships are merit based. Other forms of aid are available through the university's financial aid office. For more information about assistantships, prospective students should visit http://education.wm.edu/admissions/financialaid/assistantships/index.php. For more information about scholarships and awards, visit http://education.wm.edu/admissions/financialaid/soeawards/index.php.

Cost of Study

In 2017–18, the tuition and general fee for students is approximately $15,002 per year for residents of Virginia and $31,864 per year for nonresidents. Details about tuition can be found at http://education.wm.edu/admissions/graduate/tuition/index.php.

Living and Housing Costs

The College offers a limited number of graduate student housing spaces on campus, with costs averaging approximately $4,000 per semester. Application is made by submission of the housing request form after a student is admitted. In addition, the College maintains a website for off-campus student housing available in the Williamsburg community.

Student Group

The School of Education enrolls approximately 500 students each semester. Of those, 77 percent are degree-seeking students; 34 percent are pursuing doctorate degrees; 41 percent are enrolled full time; 18 percent are students of color; 19 percent are male; and 4 percent are international students. The average age is 28.

Admission is competitive. The average undergraduate GPA of admitted students is 3.4; the average GRE verbal score is the 69th percentile; the average GRE quantitative score is the 46th percentile.

Student Outcomes

Graduates of the School of Education find work in public and private K–12 schools, nonprofit organizations, clinical practices, and institutions of higher education, just to name a few.

Location

Williamsburg is on a Chesapeake Bay peninsula between the York and James rivers, 50 miles from Richmond and 150 miles from Washington, D.C. The College is located in a beautiful and historic city, constituting an integral part of Colonial Williamsburg. Williamsburg is serviced by Newport News, Norfolk, and Richmond airports; bus and railway services are also available.

The College

Although it retains the historic name under which it was chartered in 1693, the College of William and Mary in Virginia is a residential, full-time, coeducational, state-supported university. It is the second oldest college in the nation, but also a cutting-edge research university. It is selective, but also public, offering a world-class education without the sticker shock. It is a "Public Ivy"—one of only eight in the nation, which means it offers a superior education that's accessible to everyone.

Applying

Applications are available online at http://education.wm.edu/admissions/graduate/applying/index.php. The deadline for all application materials to be received, including transcripts, test scores, and letters of recommendation, is January 15 each year. The counseling and school psychology programs require the GRE (general test only); the advanced teacher education, and educational leadership and administrative programs require either the GRE or the MAT. The initial teacher preparation programs require the Praxis Core Academic Skills for Educators exam. The school psychology program and doctorate in counselor education require admission interviews. Students are notified of admission decisions no later than mid-March.

Correspondence and Information

Dorothy Smith Osborne, Assistant Dean
School of Education—Office of Academic Programs
The College of William and Mary
P.O. Box 8795
Williamsburg, Virginia 23187-8795
United States
Phone: 757-221-2317
Fax: 757-221-2293
E-mail: graded@wm.edu
Website: https://education.wm.edu/
Request Information: http://education.wm.edu/admissions/graduate/requestinfo/index.php

The College of William and Mary

THE FACULTY AND THEIR RESEARCH

The School of Education has 39 tenure-line faculty members, of which 8 hold endowed professorships, combined with other personnel for a total of 90 faculty and staff members. The School's education professors have garnered more than $64 million in research grants over the past ten years with $19 million in the past three years.

Spencer Niles, Dean and Professor—Ph.D., The Pennsylvania State University.
Virginia Ambler, Executive Assistant Professor, Ph.D., The College of William and Mary.
James Barber, Associate Professor, Ph.D., University of Michigan.
Katherine Barko-Alva, Instructor, Ph.D., University of Florida.
Stephanie Blackmon, Assistant Professor, Ph.D., University of Alabama, Tuscaloosa.
Brian Blouet, Professor, Ph.D., University of Hull.
Bruce Bracken, Professor, Ph.D., University of Georgia.
Johnston Brendel, Clinical Associate Professor, Ed.D., The College of William and Mary.
Kim Chandler, Clinical Assistant Professor, Ph.D., The College of William and Mary.
Jason Chen, Assistant Professor, Ph.D., Emory University.
Margaret A. Constatino, Ph.D., University of Southern Mississippi.
Kristen Conradi, Assistant Professor, Ph.D., University of Virginia.
Tracy Cross, Professor, Ph.D., University of Tennessee, Knoxville.
Michael DiPaola, Professor, Ed.D., Rutgers, The State University of New Jersey.
Jamel Donnor, Associate Professor, Ph.D., University of Wisconsin–Madison.
Pamela Eddy, Associate Professor, Ph.D., Michigan State University.
Thomas Farmer, Associate Dean, Ph.D., University of North Carolina–Chapel Hill.
Victoria Foster, Professor, Ed.D., North Carolina State University.
Christopher Gareis, Professor, Ed.D., The College of William and Mary.
W. Fanchon Glover, Executive Assistant Professor, Ed.D., The College of William and Mary.
Leslie Grant, Associate Professor, Ph.D., The College of William and Mary.
Charles Gressard, Professor, Ph.D., University of Iowa.
Gail Hardinge, Clinical Associate Professor, Ed.D., The College of William and Mary.
Natoya Haskins, Assistant Professor, Ph.D., The College of William and Mary.
Judith Harris, Professor, Ph.D., University of Virginia.
Mark Hofer, Professor, Ph.D., University of Virginia.
Heartley Huber, Ph.D., Vanderbilt University.
C. Denise Johnson, Professor, Ph.D., University of Memphis.
Meredith Kier, Assistant Professor, Ph.D., North Carolina State University.
Kyung Kim, Associate Professor, Ph.D., Korea University; Ph.D., University of Georgia.
Lori Korinek, Professor, Ph.D., University of Florida.
Marguerite Mason, Professor, Ph.D., University of Iowa.
Charles McAdams, Professor, Ed.D., North Carolina State University.
Gail McEachron, Professor, Ph.D., University of Texas at Austin.
Ryan J. McGill, Assistant Professor, Ph.D., Chapman University.
Patrick R. Mullin, Assistant Professor, Ph.D., University of Central Florida.
Patricia Popp, Clinical Associate Professor, Ph.D., The College of William and Mary.
Deborah Ramer, Instructor, Ed.S., University of Virginia.
Gene Roche, Executive Professor, Ed.D., Syracuse University.
Drew Stelljis, Executive Assistant Professor, Ph.D., The College of William and Mary.
Jeremy Stoddard, Associate Professor, Ph.D., University of Wisconsin–Madison.
James Stronge, Professor, Ph.D., University of Alabama at Tuscaloosa.
Carol Tieso, Professor, Ph.D., University of Connecticut.
Megan Tschannen-Moran, Professor, Ph.D., The Ohio State University.
Sandra Ward, Professor, Ph.D., The Pennsylvania State University.
Thomas Ward, Professor, The Pennsylvania State University.

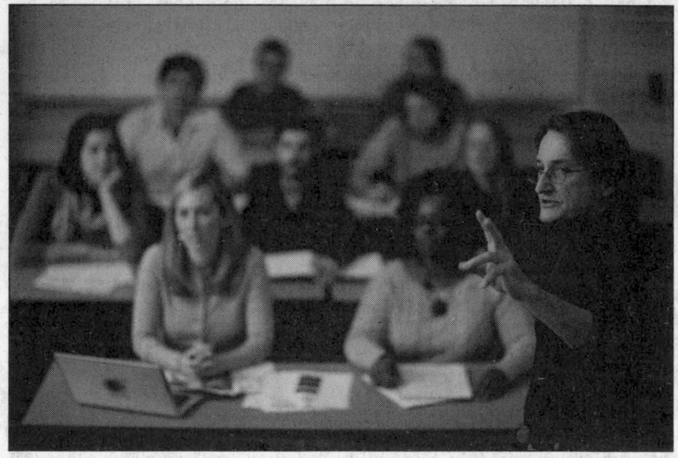

DREXEL UNIVERSITY

School of Education

 For more information, visit http://petersons.to/drexelu_education

Programs of Study

Drexel University's School of Education strives to meet the professional needs and career objectives of those who are currently working in the education field, or who wish to pursue careers as teachers, faculty members, education administrators, and staff members at all levels of education. Through challenging course work taught by experienced faculty, students are exposed to current research and trends on teaching and administration including the latest developments in pedagogy and instructional technology. The School of Education goes well beyond teacher training: it produces education leaders.

The School of Education offers undergraduate, graduate and doctoral degree programs and a wide variety of certificate, certification, and professional development programs to meet the needs of educators and educational administrators. Drexel University is a premier technology university, and the School of Education provides cutting-edge technology-based curricula with an orientation in science, technology, and math.

Graduates of the School of Education are known for their creativity, technological savvy, preparedness, and leadership skills. The School of Education's faculty members are carefully chosen for their expertise in developing these traits and skills in students. The School of Education continues to explore new opportunities for graduate programs and for collaboration and partnership with the education community. These initiatives provide additional opportunities to students who wish to make a difference in the rapidly expanding and diverse field of education.

M.S. in Applied Behavioral Analysis: Drexel's Master of Science in Applied Behavioral Analysis enables students to effectively analyze, understand, and guide change in human behavior from a systematic, data-driven approach. The M.S. in Applied Behavioral Analysis degree program with the Autism Spectrum concentration is approved by the Behavior Analyst Certification Board and is ideal for students who plan to work with children and adults who are affected by this disorder. The program offers a practicum at the A. J. Drexel Autism Institute or with EI programs, residential and community behavior health providers, or educational agencies.

M.S. in Creativity and Innovation: Drexel's online Master of Science in Creativity and Innovation degree program enables students to develop and apply their own creativity to find innovative solutions in the full gamut of work environments, from education to marketing and public relations to engineering to healthcare. Students have access to the prestigious Drexel-Torrance Center for Creativity and Innovation, a valuable resource that helps students develop leadership and problem-solving skills.

M.S. in Educational Administration (principal certification available): Drexel's online Master of Science in Educational Administration degree program offers innovative training based on a framework of state and national leadership standards for elementary and secondary instructors and counselors to become school administrators. The M.S. in Educational Administration degree program is ideal for those with an initial teaching certification who are interested in furthering their career by obtaining principal certification with a master's degree. For those interested in a singular leadership credential without principal certification, it offers leadership training that can be applied in any educational setting in the United States and around the world.

M.S. in Educational Improvement and Transformation: Drexel's flexible online Master of Science in Educational Improvement and Transformation degree program allows students to approach a master's degree in several unique ways. Students select from 10 Professional Development Concentration Sets to customize their degree, including: Collaborative Special Education Law and Process, Creativity and Innovation, Educational Policy, e-Learning Leadership, Evaluation and Assessment, Instructional Design, Leadership in Educational Settings, Learning Technologies, Special Education Leadership, and Urban Education.

Knowledge gained in this program prepares the student for leadership positions in several educational settings, including public and private schools, colleges and universities, national associations, government organizations, nonprofit organizations, learning science organizations, and more.

M.S. in Global and International Education: Drexel's online Master of Science in Global and International Education degree program prepares students to work within the complex economic, political, cultural, and social structures that shape learning in different parts of the world. Graduates of the Global and International Education program will acquire the leadership skills necessary to develop, analyze, implement, and evaluate educational policies at a variety of institutions and organizations, through interpersonal advocacy skills and cross-cultural communication, using emerging information technologies. It is ideal for those who have already completed a study-abroad program, for those who want to transition back to the international realm, for those working abroad, and individuals interested in a second career opportunity.

M.S. in Higher Education: Drexel's online Master of Science in Higher Education degree program prepares students to lead complex administrative and management positions at universities and colleges, national and international associations and organizations, government agencies, foundations, and corporations in the United States and around the world. The Higher Education program offers an interdisciplinary, experiential curriculum of coursework drawn from Drexel's School of Education. Foundation study provides a thorough overview of education from the colonial era to present-day virtual models, and examines the organizational and administrative structure of institutional hierarchy.

Students take a primary concentration in administration and organizational management and can select a secondary concentration from one of the following areas: Community College Administration and Leadership, Enrollment Management, Global and International Education, Educational Policy, Institutional Research and Planning, e-Learning Technologies and Instructional Design, Neuroscience, Learning and Online Instruction, and Student Development and Affairs.

M.S. in Learning Technologies: Drexel's online Master of Science in Learning Technologies degree program is a unique online program that prepares students as leaders who can create learning solutions for an increasingly fluid, interconnected, and complex world. The curriculum is framed by national technology standards in twenty-first century learning, digital media literacy, design thinking, learning sciences, and diverse field experiences. The Learning Technologies course work builds on Drexel's leadership in the latest educational research and technologies and provides students with a complete framework for understanding the learning sciences and media literacy—from initial concepts and development of instructional design to how individuals use learning software—from the obstacles they encounter to the solutions that help them succeed.

M.S. in Mathematics Learning and Teaching: Drexel's online Master of Science in Mathematics Learning and Teaching program trains graduates to improve mathematics in middle and high schools through shared, solution-oriented teaching methods. The Mathematics Learning and Teaching curriculum builds on leading-edge aspects of education and math in areas such as evaluation and diagnostic teaching, and offers electives that explore higher education and learning technologies. Students work independently on rigorous math assignments and collaborate on the outcome within a community of fellow students and faculty members to produce student-centered, technology-enhanced strategies for middle and high school math learners of all abilities.

M.S. in Special Education: Drexel's online Master of Science in Special Education degree program is designed to produce highly qualified professionals to expand educational horizons for all children in need. The Special Education program is a flexible online program with course work that builds on the essentials of special education. Students can hone their skills by pursuing on of four concentration areas: Autism Spectrum Disorders, Technologies for Special Education, Multisensory Reading Instruction Level 1 (includes Wilson® Language Level 1 certification), Collaborative Special Education Law and Process, and Customized Study (for individuals who already possess special education certification).

M.S. in Sport Coaching Leadership: Drexel's online Master of Science in Sport Coaching Leadership engages students in the areas of coaching theory, developing a sports program, coaching philosophy, goal–setting, understanding the needs of athletes, recruiting, developing training programs, budgeting, program planning, forecasting, NCAA compliance, and fundraising. Students will also select a concentration to specialize in a particular sport or create a custom-designed specialization to meet their career goals. Coaches at the youth, scholastic, club, collegiate, Olympic, and professional levels can customize their course to their level and sport(s) of interest. Offered fully online, this program is well-suited to coaches with a busy schedule, at any level of their career.

M.S. in Teaching, Learning and Curriculum: Drexel's online Master of Science in Teaching, Learning and Curriculum program is customized to each student's goals and is rooted in Drexel's philosophy of experiential learning through field experiences and a focus on integrated technology in research. Students have two degree options to pursue:

- Master of Science in Teaching, Learning and Curriculum: Teaching Certification
- Master of Science in Teaching, Learning and Curriculum: Advanced Studies

The degree program trains students using current learning trends, from advanced techniques of instruction and assessment to the impact of multimedia and new learning technologies. Students focus on diversities in the classroom, such as students with special needs and intercultural learners, and develop solution-oriented strategies for instructional leadership.

Ed.D. in Education Leadership and Management: Drexel's Ed.D. in Educational Leadership and Management degree program stands alone as a rigorous, accelerated doctoral program that produces leaders with the skills and knowledge to create educational reform. The Ed.D. program offers an elite professional practitioner's degree as a completely online program or in a blended delivery format that combines on-campus classes and online education.

For achievement-oriented students interested in educational management, the Ed.D. program provides a path to the Superintendent Letter of Eligibility in Pennsylvania. The program also provides a competitive creative career track into leadership roles within public school districts and private institutions, universities and colleges, national and global foundations, organizations, corporations, and government agencies.

The Ed.D. program is an expansive, leading-edge program that prepares students for a full range of educational opportunities connected to human and societal development, with a real understanding of the operations and responsibilities faced by rapidly changing, global learning environments.

Ph.D. in Education: Drexel's Ph.D. in Education program is a rigorous, highly competitive program designed for those who aspire to be leaders in the field of education as researchers, scholars, and instructors in higher education and in other educational settings. Small by design, the Ph.D. degree program admits 6–10 students per cohort and provides students with benefits such as research and teaching assistantships that offer generous stipends, tuition remission, and health insurance subsidies. The major emphasis of the program is on engaging individual students in collaborative inquiry and research with faculty experts. Specific areas of concentration for doctoral students include Science, Technology, Engineering and Mathematics (STEM) Education and Educational Leadership.

Faculty

Drexel University's School of Education has diverse faculty expertise in many areas, including teacher education, higher education, global and international education, educational administration and leadership, learning technologies, and adult education and organization development. Collaborative research associated with these areas and more is expansive, interdisciplinary, and focused, with a particular emphasis on technology-enhanced education and the learning sciences.

Research productivity, measured both by peer-reviewed publications and funded research expenditures continues to be high priority, encouraging scholarly inquiry to improve education practices locally and globally.

The School of Education's faculty directory is available online at drexel.edu/soe/faculty-research/faculty.

Financial Aid

Prospective students should visit http://drexel.edu/drexelcentral/finaid/prospective-students/grad/ for details on the financial aid application. Information for international students is also available at this site.

Costs

The most up-to-date information on tuition and fees can be found at http://drexel.edu/drexelcentral/finaid/costs/grad.

Admissions

For details on requirements for Drexel's School of Education's graduate programs, prospective students should visit http://drexel.edu/soe/admissions/graduate.

Applying

Specific information for applying to the School of Education's on-campus or blended graduate programs, as well as the online graduate programs, is available at drexel.edu/soe/admissions/apply.

Correspondence and Information

School of Education
Drexel University
3141 Chestnut Street
Philadelphia, Pennsylvania 19104
United States
Phone: 215-895-6770
E-mail: education@drexel.edu
Website: Drexel.edu/soe

Drexel University was founded as the Drexel Institute in 1891 (pictured above). It has since grown to include 3 Philadelphia campuses, regional sites, international partnerships in China and Israel, and Drexel Online.

Drexel offers robust educational offerings, both online and in-person, at its modern campus located in Philadelphia, Pennsylvania, including the Papadakis Integrated Sciences Building (left) and the James Marks Intercultural Center (right).

MANHATTANVILLE COLLEGE

School of Education

Programs of Study

The School of Education at Manhattanville College offers undergraduate and graduate programs for careers in education at all levels. All programs are registered with and approved by the New York State Education Department. The School of Education is accredited by the National Council for Accreditation of Teacher Education (NCATE).

Manhattanville offers a graduate-level accelerated teacher certification program, Jump Start, which is especially popular with adults who are changing careers. Cohorts begin twice a year, in fall and spring. Jump Start students are eligible to be in their own classrooms by September of the following year as well-prepared, fully paid teachers with full benefits while they finish the additional requirements for the master's degree. The program is usually available for dual certification with special education in the areas of childhood education, mathematics, biology, chemistry, social studies, and English, and for single certifications in physics, Spanish, visual arts, TESOL, and physical education.

Manhattanville offers three master's programs, the Master of Arts in Teaching (M.A.T.), the Master of Professional Studies (M.P.S.), and the Master in Educational Studies (M.Ed.), as well as a Doctor of Education (Ed.D.) degree in educational leadership. In addition, Manhattanville offers programs in more than sixty areas that lead to New York State certification. Manhattanville also offers post-master's certifications, certificates of advanced study, and a professional diploma.

The Master of Arts in Teaching degree program is intended for graduate students with few or no prior courses in education. On completion of the program, the candidate is eligible for New York State certification as a teacher of childhood (grades 1–6), early childhood (birth–grade 2), early childhood and childhood (birth–grade 6), biology (grades 5–12), chemistry (grades 5–12), English (grades 5–12), French (grades 7–12), Italian (grades 7–12), Latin (grades 7–12), mathematics (grades 5–12), music (all grades), physical education and sports pedagogy (all grades), physics (grades 7–12), social studies (grades 5–12), Spanish (grades 7–12), or visual arts (all grades). Most M.A.T. programs range from 36 to 39 credits. The program in childhood/early childhood is 49 credits. All M.A.T. programs include one semester of full-time student teaching or supervised fieldwork.

The Master of Professional Studies degree includes programs in educational leadership, literacy, special education, or teaching English to speakers of another language (all grades or adult and international settings). There are also dual-certification programs in childhood, early childhood, middle child/adolescence literacy and special education. M.P.S. programs require from 36 to 47 credits, depending on the program and the area in which certification is sought.

The Doctor of Education (Ed.D.) degree program in Educational Leadership is designed to meet the needs of midcareer professionals who have leadership experience in public or private schools, community programs, governmental agencies, or nongovernmental organizations with major education initiatives. This program builds on Manhattanville's educational leadership master's and professional diploma certification programs for building-level and/or district-level leadership. Also offered is the Executive Ed.D., designed for advanced doctoral students in education leadership (or related field) who have completed all course work requirements, except for the dissertation. In addition, a concentration within the thriving Ed.D., is designed for practicing and aspiring leaders in higher education seeking to help shape educational institutions in the future.

The certification programs offer students who already hold a functionally related master's degree an opportunity to complete a program of 27 to 30 credits that makes them eligible for certification in a specific field and level of education. Manhattanville also offers a 15-credit Teacher Leader program for those interested in serving as leaders in their schools.

In addition there are several advanced certificate programs in the areas of bilingual education (childhood/Spanish), health and wellness, administration of physical education, education for sustainability, and science of reading: multisensory instruction.

Research Facilities

Manhattanville's teaching library ranks among the foremost undergraduate teaching libraries in the country. The Manhattanville library provides a wide range of subscription databases, electronic journals, and electronic books to support teaching and learning at every level. The Educational Resource Center in the library building has curriculum materials to assist preservice and new teachers. Reference service is available both in person during the day and evening hours, and online at any time from anywhere in the world. Students and faculty members may also text questions to a librarian. A library mobile app delivers services to users on the go.

Manhattanville College supports instruction in French, Spanish, Russian, Italian, German, Chinese, Japanese, Hindi, Marathi, modern Hebrew, and English as a second language. The College provides tutoring in every academic subject, customized services for students with special needs, audiovisual facilities, and a leading Information Literacy instruction program. The library building is open 24 hours, 7 days a week through most of the fall and spring semesters, and it has computer labs, quiet study areas, group-study rooms, and a café where students and faculty members can meet informally. The Manhattanville College Library has a dedicated Education Librarian who works with the faculty members and undergraduate, graduate, and doctoral students to assist in any way with their research needs.

Manhattanville, which was named one of the top 100 wired colleges in the U.S., has state-of-the-art computers, computer labs, and campus networking for student use and instruction.

Financial Aid

Family Educational Loans are available to graduate students. A deferred payment plan is also available. There are a limited number of graduate assistantships, for which matriculated students work 200 hours to earn the cost of 6 credit hours. A maximum of three assistantships per student are possible, and courses must be taken concurrently with the assistantship. For further information, prospective students should contact the Office of Financial Aid, Reid Hall, Purchase, New York 10577 (telephone: 914-323-5357).

Cost of Study

Tuition was $915 per credit for 2016–17. There is a semester registration fee of $60 and there are some course fees.

Living and Housing Costs

Most School of Education graduate students live and work in their own homes and communities throughout Westchester and the surrounding counties. For campus housing information, students should call Residence Life at 914-323-5217.

Student Group

There are approximately 900 students in the School of Education at Manhattanville College. Fifty-five percent are career changers. Their average age is 30.

Location

Manhattanville's campus, 100 acres of suburban countryside, is located in New York's Westchester County, just minutes from White Plains to the west and Greenwich, Connecticut, to the east. It is 30 miles from Manhattan. The campus is accessible via public transportation.

Manhattanville College

The College

Manhattanville College is a coeducational, independent liberal arts college whose mission is to educate ethically and socially responsible leaders for the global community. Founded in 1841, the College has 1,600 undergraduate students and almost 1,200 graduate students. Of the graduate students, 820 are enrolled in the School of Education. Manhattanville offers bachelor's, master's, and doctoral degrees in more than fifty academic concentrations in the arts and sciences. Its curriculum nurtures intellectual curiosity and independent thinking.

Applying

Applications are reviewed on a continuing basis. Applicants are encouraged to apply at least sixty days in advance of the semester for which matriculation is sought (fall, spring, summer I, or summer II). Application requirements are the submission of a completed application form, a fee of $75, two recommendations, a two- to three-page typewritten essay on the applicant's background and philosophy of education, official test score report from either the Graduate Record Examination (GRE) or the Miller Analogies Test (MAT), and official transcripts of all previous college work (both undergraduate and graduate). Limited study as a nonmatriculated student is permitted.

Correspondence and Information

Jeanine Pardey-Levine
Director of Graduate Enrollment Management
School of Education
Manhattanville College
2900 Purchase Street
Purchase, New York 10577
Phone: 914-323-5142 (Admissions)
Fax: 914-694-1732
E-mail: edschool@mville.edu
Website: http://www.mville.edu/SOE

THE FACULTY

School of Education Administration

Shelley B. Wepner, Professor and Dean; Ed.D., Pennsylvania.
Katheryn T. Hathaway, Associate Dean of Accreditation and Technology; Ed.D., Columbia Teachers College.
Heidi Sakanaka, Assistant Dean for Outreach.
Jody Green, Assistant Dean for Graduate Advising; M.S.Ed., Fordham.
Danielle Wachter, Assistant to the Dean; B.S., LIU, Southampton.
Robert Cooper, Director of Jump Start; M.A., CUNY, City College.
Jeanine Pardey-Levine, Director of Graduate Enrollment Management; M.M., Hartford.
Kevin Roberts, Director of Field Placement, Certification, and Community Outreach; M.S., Adelphi.
Renee Gargano, Coordinator of Applied Research and Fieldwork, Doctoral Program; Ed.M., Boston University.

Curriculum and Instruction

Barbara Allen-Lyall, Assistant Professor, Ph.D., Lesley.
Victoria Fantozzi, Assistant Professor and Department Chair; Ph.D., Virginia
JoAnne Ferrara, Associate Professor and Associate Dean for Undergraduate Admissions and Advising; Ed.D., Nova Southeastern.
Frederick Heckendorn III, Assistant Professor of Secondary/ Social Studies Education; Ed.D., Hofstra.
Sherie McClam, Assistant Professor; Ph.D., Colorado at Boulder.

Early Childhood

Victoria Fantozzi, Assistant Professor for Early Childhood and Childhood, Ph.D., Virginia.
Patricia Vardin, Associate Professor and Department Chair; Ed.D., Columbia Teachers College.

Educational Leadership and Special Subjects

Yiping Wan, Professor; and Coordinator of the Doctoral Program Ph.D., Texas at Austin.
Lenora Boehlert, Assistant Professor, Educational Leadership; Ed.D., Vanderbilt.
Stephen Caldas, Professor for the Doctoral Program; Ph.D., LSU.
Kenneth Mitchell, Associate Professor for the Doctoral Program; Ed.D., Fordham.
Robert Monson, Visiting Associate Professor for the Doctoral Program; Ph.D., St. Louis.
Rhonda Clements, Professor and Program Director of Physical Education and Sports Pedagogy; Ed.D., Columbia Teachers College.
Diane Gomez, Associate Professor of ESL/Foreign Language and Department Chair; Ph.D., Fordham.
Laurence Krute, Associate Professor of ESL/Foreign Language and Associate Dean of Graduate Advising; Ph.D., Columbia.
Ryan Fisk, Half-time Instructor of Educational Leadership and Special Subjects; M.S., Hofstra.
Kristie Lynch, Assistant Professor of Physical Education and Sports Pedagogy; Ed.D., Columbia Teachers College.

Literacy

Katherine Cunningham, Assistant Professor; Ed.D., Columbia Teachers College.
Courtney Ryan Kelly, Associate Professor; Ph.D., Ohio State.

Special Education

Vance Austin, Associate Professor and Department Chair; Ph.D., Fordham.
Ellis I. Barowsky, Professor; Ph.D., CUNY Graduate Center.
Noor Syed, Assistant Professor of Applied Behavior Analysis; M.Phil., SUNY Binghamton; Ed.D. candidate (December 2017), Columbia Teachers College.
Nikki Josephs, Ph.D., Georgia State.
Micheline S. Malow, Associate Professor and Associate Department Chair; Ph.D., CUNY Graduate Center.

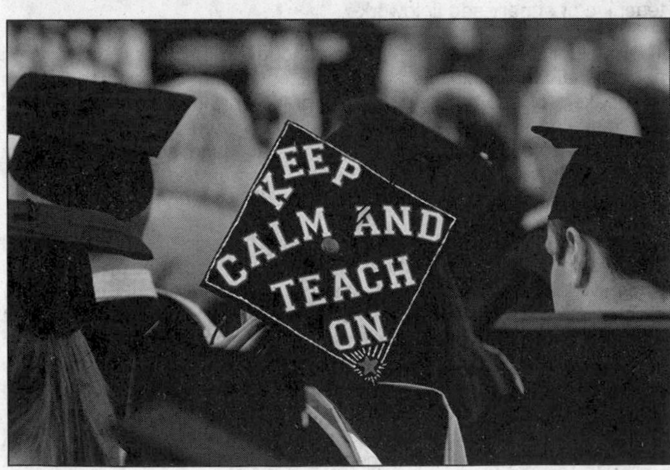

NORTHWESTERN UNIVERSITY

School of Education and Social Policy

Northwestern

SCHOOL OF **EDUCATION AND SOCIAL POLICY**

 For more information, visit http://petersons.to/northwesterneducationsocialpolicy

Programs of Study

Northwestern University's School of Education and Social Policy offers programs leading to the M.S., M.A., and Ph.D. degrees. There are four program areas: Education (M.S.), Higher Education (M.S.), Learning and Organizational Change (M.S.), Learning Sciences (M.A. and Ph.D.), and Human Development and Social Policy (Ph.D.).

The Learning Sciences M.A. and Ph.D. programs are dedicated to the preparation of researchers, developers, and practitioners qualified to advance the scientific understanding and practice of teaching and learning. Both programs in the learning sciences are interdisciplinary, offering a synthesis of computational, educational, and social science research; linguistics; computer science; anthropology; and cognitive science.

The Human Development and Social Policy Ph.D. program prepares students to bridge human development, social science, and social policy. Graduates of this program assume positions as professors, researchers, and policy makers who can bring multidisciplinary knowledge about human development to affect policy.

Concentrations in the M.S. in Education program include public and private school teaching and advanced teaching. Students enrolled full-time typically complete the program in twelve months, provided they matriculate with no course deficiencies; opportunities for part-time study toward a master's degree are also available.

Research Facilities

Northwestern's research libraries contain more than 6.9 million volumes, 4.65 million microfilm units, and 351,787 current periodical and serial publications. Research and teaching activities are supported by a state-of-the-art multimedia computing network with full Internet access. The School is actively involved with the Institute for Policy Research, a University-wide research center that promotes interdisciplinary urban policy research and training. Specialized research and service resources within the School include the Center for Talent Development, a nationally prominent center that identifies and provides programming for academically talented youth, their parents, and the professionals who work with them. The Tarry Center for Collaborative Teaching and Learning provides state-of-the-art facilities for innovative teaching with technology.

Financial Aid

Several forms of aid are available, including fellowships and scholarships. In addition, there are teaching assistantships awarded to doctoral students who work with the School's undergraduate programs. Special opportunities for research assistantships and other employment also exist within the School's and the University's many research centers. Arrangements for loans are also possible.

Cost of Study

For up-to-date tuition information, prospective students should visit the website at http://www.northwestern.edu/sfs/tuition/.

Living and Housing Costs

The University operates a residence in Evanston for the use of graduate students. For those Northwestern students interested in securing off-campus housing near the University, information and assistance are also available.

Student Group

Graduate study occurs within the context of individualized instruction, and enrollments are selective. Currently, 237 students are enrolled in master's programs, and 47 are enrolled in Ph.D. programs. Since an interdisciplinary perspective is valued, students with preparation in a wide range of disciplinary areas are encouraged to apply.

Student Outcomes

Graduates teach and conduct research in academic and nonacademic settings; occupy strategic policy positions in government, corporations, and institutions; and assume positions of responsibility in a wide range of service organizations. Potential professional settings for learning sciences graduates include University research and teaching as well as business, industry, or school system-based careers studying, designing, and/or implementing learning environments. Graduates of the Ph.D. in Human Development and Social Policy program assume positions as teachers, researchers, or policy makers who can bring multidisciplinary knowledge about human development directly to bear upon policy. Graduates of the Learning Sciences M.A. program are practitioners in the vanguard of teaching and learning systems development and instructional resource development. Most students in the M.S. in Education and Higher Education programs gain on-site experience through supervised internships for future careers as professional educators and administrators.

Location

The campus is located on Lake Michigan, 12 miles north of Chicago. The beautiful lakefront campus offers a rich cultural environment through a wealth of theatrical, musical, and athletic events. The extensive cultural resources of Chicago are readily accessible via public transportation.

The University and The School

Established in 1851, Northwestern has grown to become one of the most distinguished private universities in the country. The School of Education and Social Policy has developed from its origins as a department of pedagogy by continually broadening its scope to encompass those educative, learning, and socializing experiences that take place throughout the life span in families, schools, communities, and the workplace.

Applying

Applications for admission are reviewed and acted upon as they are received. Students should consult program brochures for specific application deadlines. Applicants planning to seek financial aid must meet early submission deadlines.

Correspondence and Information

School of Education and Social Policy
Northwestern University
2120 Campus Drive
Evanston, Illinois 60208-2610
Phone: 847-491-3790 (Office of Student Affairs)
847-467-1458 (M.S. in Education)
847-491-4620 (M.S. in Higher Education)
847-491-4329 (Human Development and Social Policy Ph.D.)
847-491-7376 (Learning and Organizational Change M.S.)
847-491-7494 (Learning Sciences M.A.)
847-491-7494 (Learning Sciences Ph.D.)
Website: http://www.sesp.northwestern.edu

THE FACULTY AND THEIR RESEARCH

Emma Adam, Ph.D., Minnesota. Parent, child, and adolescent stress and emotion; attachment; health policy.

Corey Brady, Ph.D., Massachusetts Dartmouth. Mathematics, modeling.

Lindsay Chase-Lansdale, Ph.D., Michigan. Child and adolescent development, family functioning, public policy, multidisciplinary research, poverty and welfare reform, family structure, risk and resilience.

Cynthia Coburn, Ph.D., Stanford. Relationship between instruction policy and teachers' classroom practices in urban schools.

Daniel Cohen, Ph.D., Northwestern. Holocaust education.

Jeannette Colyvas, Ph.D., Stanford. Organizations and entrepreneurship; comparing public, private, and nonprofit forms of organizing; the study of networks.

Mesmin Destin, Ph.D., Michigan. Academic motivation and achievement, small classroom-based interventions to improve school outcomes for low-income and minority youth.

Timothy Dohrer, Ph.D., Penn State. Curriculum and instruction.

Matthew Easterday, Ph.D., Carnegie Mellon. Human-computer interaction, constructionism, computer-based modeling.

David Figlio, Ph.D., Wisconsin–Madison. Accountability policy, economics of education, teacher quality, teacher labor markets, anti-poverty policy, intergenerational transmission of human capital, evaluation design.

Kenneth D. Forbus, Ph.D., MIT. Qualitative physics, cognitive simulation of analogy, intelligence tutoring systems and learning environments for science and engineering.

Wendi Gardner, Ph.D., Ohio State. Centrality of social inclusion to the self.

Dedre Gentner, Ph.D., Berkeley. Learning, reasoning, and conceptual change in adults and children; mental models; acquisition of meaning.

Elizabeth Gerber, Ph.D., Stanford. Design and innovation work practices.

Jonathan Guryan, Ph.D., MIT. Racial inequality, economics of education.

Claudia Haase, Ph.D., Jena (Germany). Emotion, motivation, life span development, aging, well-being, physical health, career success, relationship satisfaction, statistical methods.

Northwestern University

Romana Hasnain-Wynia, Ph.D., Brandeis. Equity in health care, reducing disparities in health care, quality of care for diverse populations, health policy.

Larry Hedges, Ph.D., Stanford. Statistical methods for research in education, social sciences, and policy studies; social distribution of test scores.

Susan Hespos, Ph.D., Emory. Object representation, number and spatial relationships.

Barton J. Hirsch, Ph.D., Oregon. Community psychology, social networks, ecology of adolescent development, after-school programs.

Paula Hooper, Ph.D., M.I.T. Design of learning environments.

Michael Horn, Ph.D., Tufts. Design of educational technology, learning in museums, computer programming, tangible interaction.

Simone Ispa-Landa, Ph.D., Harvard. Qualitative methods, race and ethnic relations, social identity, American family, intersectionality theory, micro-macro links.

Kirabo Jackson, Ph.D., Harvard. Economics of education, labor economics, public finance, applied econometrics, development.

Eva Lam, Ph.D., Berkeley. Second language and literacy development, digital literacy and learning, language and identity, language socialization, globalization and English learning, multilingualism and cultural diversity in education.

Carol D. Lee, Ph.D., Chicago. Cultural contexts affecting learning broadly and literacy specifically, teacher preparation and development, classroom discourse, urban education.

Dan A. Lewis, Ph.D., California, Santa Cruz. Policy analysis, urban social problems, community organization, urban school reform.

Gregory Light, Ph.D., London. Student learning in higher and professional education, faculty development, faculty concepts and approaches to teaching, variation theory.

Regina Logan, Ph.D., Northwestern. Teaching and learning processes, adulthood and aging, gender studies.

Ofer Malamud, Ph.D., Harvard. Economics and education policy, educational investment over the life course, technology in the formation of human capital, effect of general education in labor market outcomes.Jolie Matthews, Ph.D., Stanford. Learning and behavior norms in online communities, social media production and consumption practices, digital history and historical consciousness.

Dan P. McAdams, Ph.D., Harvard. Personality development, identity and life stories, intimacy, adult development, narrative psychology, modernity and the self, autobiographical memory, psychological biography.

Thomas McDade, Ph.D., Emory. Human biology, biocultural perspectives on health and human development, medical anthropology and global health, ecological immunology, stress, health disparities.

Douglas L. Medin, Ph.D., South Dakota. Learning, reasoning, and conceptual change in adults and children; mental models; acquisition of meaning; culture and education.

Quinn Mulroy, Ph.D., Columbia. Policymaking, policy implementation, law and courts, regulatory agencies, Congress, civil rights, environmental policy, American political development.

Eleanor O'Rourke, Ph.D., Washington. Technology-enabled learning experience, educational games and playful learning, growth mindset interventions, connected classroom ecosystems.

Paula M. Olszewski-Kubilius, Ph.D., Northwestern. Gifted education, child development, minority gifted child development, accelerated educational programs, needs of special populations of gifted children.

Penelope L. Peterson, Ph.D., Stanford. Learning and teaching in schools and classrooms, particularly in mathematics and literacy; teacher learning in reform contexts; relations among educational research, policy, and practice.

David Rapp, Ph.D., SUNY at Stony Brook. Experimental psychology, comprehension of texts, psychology of learning, multimedia learning, visualization and learning tools.

Brian J. Reiser, Ph.D., Yale. Intelligent tutoring systems, interactive learning environments for science and technology, scientific inquiry skills.

Christopher K. Riesbeck, Ph.D., Stanford. Natural language and analyzers, case-based reasoners, intelligent computational media.

James E. Rosenbaum, Ph.D., Harvard. Adolescent and adult development, poverty and housing, welfare reform, high school to work transition.

Terri Sabol, Ph.D., Virginia. Individual and environmental factors that lead to healthy child development.

Diane Schanzenbach, Ph.D., Princeton. Early childhood education, accountability policy, economics of education, obesity, anti-poverty policy, education and health.

Heather Schoenfeld, Ph.D., Northwestern. Law and society, race and inequality, crime and punishment, historical and comparative methods.

Kimberly Scott, Ph.D., Ohio State. Organizational effectiveness and change, organizational learning, job satisfaction.

Lilah Shapiro, Ph.D., Chicago. Sociology, social psychology, identity, life story and narrative, ethnicity, religion, assimilation and immigration, diaspora experiences, family dynamics.

Bruce Sherin, Ph.D., Berkeley. Science education, instructional technology, external representations in science and mathematical learning.

Miriam Sherin, Ph.D., Berkeley. Mathematics teaching and learning, teacher cognition, teacher education.

Ryan Smerek, Ph.D., Michigan. Organizational learning, leadership, job satisfaction, organizational culture, open-book finance.

Bruce D. Spencer, Ph.D., Yale. Social and educational measurement, statistics for policy analysis, demography, decision theory.

James P. Spillane, Ph.D., Michigan State. Educational policy, intergovernmental relations, school reform, relations between policy and local practice.

Saiying Steenbergen-Hu, Ph.D., Purdue. Academic achievement, gifted education, psychological and social-emotional development, educational measurement and assessment, meta-analysis, and research synthesis.

Reed Stevens, Ph.D., Berkeley. Curriculum design, learning in atypical settings, design of learning tools.

Linda Teplin, Ph.D., Northwestern. Epidemiologic studies of psychiatric disorders, juvenile justice, drug abuse, public health policy, HIV/AIDS risk behaviors, correlates of violence.

Lois Trautvetter, Ph.D., Michigan. Higher education, gender issues and females in science.

David H. Uttal, Ph.D., Michigan. Mental representation, cognitive development, spatial cognition, early symbolization.

Shirin Vossoughi, Ph.D., Stanford. Ethnographic study of teaching, learning, and educational equity; social, cultural, historical, and political dimensions of human development.

Laurie Wakschlag, Ph.D., Chicago. Behavioral sciences.

Ellen Wartella, Ph.D., Minnesota. Effects of media on children and adolescents, impact of food marketing on childhood obesity.

Sandra R. Waxman, Ph.D., Pennsylvania. Language and conceptual development, early cognitive development, language and thought.

Uri Wilensky, Ph.D., MIT. Science and mathematics learning and technology, connected learning, constructionism, computer-based modeling, agent-based modeling, complex systems and education.

Marcelo Worsley, Ph.D., Stanford. Learning sciences, technology design, computer science.

Michael Wolf, Ph.D., Illinois. Adult literacy, patient education, medication and safety adherence.

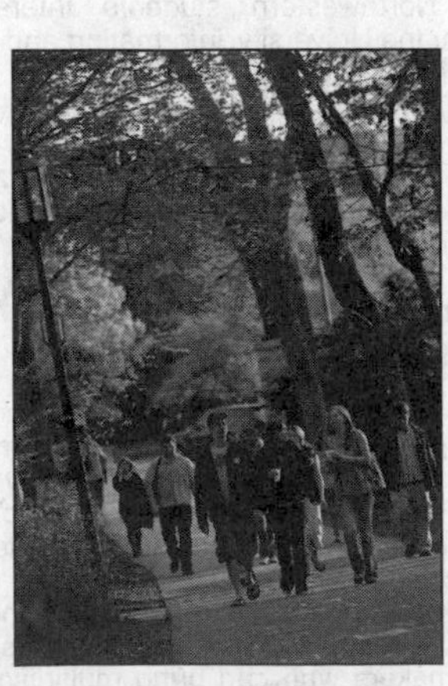

UNIVERSITY OF PITTSBURGH

Graduate Programs in Education

 For more information, visit http://petersons.to/upitt_education

Programs of Study

The University of Pittsburgh School of Education (SOE) offers numerous opportunities to pursue graduate studies in education, including over 50 graduate degree programs. As the school begins its second century, it is focused on advancing education through the following:

- Improving the educational experience for students in urban schools
- Exploring the synergy between public policy and classroom practice
- Understanding the factors and strategies that lead to success in the classroom
- Developing obesity prevention and intervention programs

The School of Education's **Department of Administrative and Policy Studies (ADMPS)** helps to develop school leaders and policymakers who can effectively advocate advancements while managing K–12 and higher education systems. Master's, Ph.D., and Ed.D. degrees are offered in higher education management, school leadership, and social and comparative analysis in education. Administrative and supervisory certificates are also offered in school leadership. More information is available online at http://www.education.pitt.edu/AcademicDepartments/AdministrativePolicyStudies.aspx.

The **Department of Health and Physical Activity (HPA)** promotes the importance of physically active lifestyles and other health-related behaviors that lead to better quality of life. Master's degrees are offered in the areas of health and fitness, as well as health, physical activity, and chronic disease. HPA also offers a Ph.D. program in exercise physiology, and an Ed.D. in health and physical activity. Additional details can be found at http://www.education.pitt.edu/AcademicDepartments/HealthPhysicalActivity.aspx.

The **Department of Instruction and Learning (DIL)** program prepares expert and leader teachers in specific subject areas by shaping an understanding of educating and learning from various perspectives. The department awards a variety of master's degrees, initial and add-on teaching certificate options, supervisory certificates, as well as Ph.D. and Ed.D. options. Areas of focus include but are not limited to: early childhood and elementary education; secondary education: English and communications, foreign language, mathematics, science, and social studies; teaching English to speakers of other languages (TESOL); language, literacy, and culture; special education; reading education; early intervention; applied behavioral analysis; and vision studies. More information is available online at http://www.education.pitt.edu/AcademicDepartments/InstructionLearning.aspx.

The **Psychology in Education (PIE) Department** prepares graduates for professional careers in and out of the classroom (applied developmental psychology) and in the lab (research methodology). Master's and Ph.D. degrees, as well as teaching certificates, are awarded in applied developmental psychology. The school also offers master's and Ph.D. degrees in research methodology. Additional details can be found at http://www.education.pitt.edu/AcademicDepartments/PsychologyinEducation.aspx.

The **Learning Sciences and Policy (LSAP) Department** at the School of Education offers a Ph.D. in LSAP, which incorporates the inclusion of learning sciences into education and teaching, and emphasizes organizational and policy change with the goal of improving instruction. The department also offers an E.D. program in Out-of-School Learning, which is intended for experienced informal learning professionals seeking advanced training for leadership positions in museums, after-school learning, media, digital design, university outreach/extension, and other areas where learning environments exist outside of schools. More information is available online at http://www.education.pitt.edu AcademicDepartments/LearningSciencesPolicy.aspx.

Research, and Outreach

The SOE has many partnerships with centers, institutes, and initiatives both on campus and regionally, and has developed some of its own centers, such as the Center for Urban Education (CUE), Healthy Lifestyle Institute (HLI), and the Center for Motivation (MC), to enhance the education of its students and students in the local communities. These include outreach programs such as the Western PA Writing Project and the Educational Leadership Initiative.

The tuition-based Falk Laboratory School, affiliated with the SOE, is a K–8 laboratory school that provides faculty members, student interns, practicum students, and researchers with opportunities to develop and support new and innovative practices in education.

Financial Aid

The School of Education offers some departmental aid options to students pursuing advanced degrees. Financial assistance is available to a limited number of graduate students through graduate student assistantships (GSA), teaching assistantships (TA), teaching fellowships (TF), graduate student researchers (GSR), and tuition remission. In addition to departmental aid, the SOE has numerous endowed scholarships and fellowships available that were established through gifts or grants.

Many of the students in the School of Education fund their schooling through the use of Federal Stafford Loans and Graduate PLUS loans, as well as private alternative educational loans. University policy holds that international students must provide evidence of their ability to fully fund their studies in the United States prior to acceptance. International students are not eligible for Federal Stafford Loan funds or private alternative loan funds.

Cost of Study

For the 2017-18 academic year, tuition for Pennsylvania students in graduate programs in the School of Education is $11,145 per term plus $425 in fees for full-time students and $898 per credit and $270 in fees for part-time students. For out-of-state residents, full-time tuition is $18,490 per term with $425 in fees and for part-time students, $1,512 per credit with $270 in fees.

Living and Housing

The University owns several hundred apartments that are available to graduate students. University-owned apartments are unfurnished and range from efficiencies to three-bedroom units. These units are not considered on-campus housing and are administered via a lease, security deposit, and monthly payments.

Applications for University-owned apartments are accepted by Off-Campus Living (http://www.ocl.pitt.edu) beginning the second Monday in January on a first-come, first-served basis. Students also may apply online.

Student Group

In the fall of 2017, there were 842 graduate students in the SOE's programs; 13.9 percent of those were international students. There were 86 graduate student appointments, 9 fellowships, 56 teaching assistants, and 21 research assistants. For the 2016-17 academic year, the SOE conferred 614 master's degrees and 174 doctoral degrees.

The Council of Graduate Students in Education (CGSE) is run by graduate students in the School of Education; students within the school are automatically members of the organization. CGSE is supported primarily through the student activity fee fund with additional support from the Dean's office.

With more than 33,000 SOE alumni across the globe, graduates are connected to a strong and involved fellowship that is changing the field of education through life-changing work.

Location

The main campus of the University of Pittsburgh is situated on 132 urban acres in Pittsburgh's historic Oakland section. Much of the campus, including its centerpiece 42-story Cathedral of Learning, falls within the Oakland Civic Center and Schenley Farms National Historic District, a park populated with buildings that replicate the city's architectural history.

The main campus borders or is within a short walking distance of many recreational, cultural, and educational institutions that also populate the Oakland neighborhood. The campus is directly adjacent to Schenley Plaza, the main branch of the Carnegie Public Library, the Carnegie Museums of Natural History and Art, and the Carnegie Music Hall.

The campus is widely recognized for its commitment to environmental sustainability and has won multiple Green Star Awards from the Professional Grounds Management Society.

The University and The School

The University of Pittsburgh (Pitt), in western Pennsylvania, was founded in 1787 and is one of the oldest public institutions of higher education in the nation. *U.S. News & World Report* ranks the University of Pittsburgh School of Education graduate program among its top 30 graduate education programs in the nation.

For more than 100 years, the University of Pittsburgh's School of Education has been dedicated to preparing students for life-changing careers, whether they desire to be teachers, researchers, public policy experts, administrators or health educators. The SOE consists of five academic departments: Administrative and Policy Studies; Health and Physical Activity; Instruction and Learning; Learning Sciences and Policy; and Psychology in Education. Through these departments, the school awards over 50 graduate degrees and offers 12 certificate programs.

Faculty

The School of Education at University of Pittsburgh has 80 full-time faculty members on staff with a 4:1 ratio of doctoral students to full-time faculty members. Faculty members and graduate students are involved in a variety of collaborative research experiences ranging from more basic research to research that is applied to school settings. Additional information and a complete listing about SOE faculty members is available at http://www.education.pitt.edu/AboutUs/Faculty.aspx.

Applying

Deadlines vary by program. Specific information regarding dates can be found on the School of Education website, specifically, on the admission requirements page for the program for which the applicant is applying. Supplemental materials that must be submitted with the online application also vary by program, and details can also be found on the admission requirement page for the program. Applicants are also welcome to direct questions to soeinfo@pitt.edu or call 412-648-2230. To begin the online application process, applicants should visit http://www.education.pitt.edu/FutureStudents/AdmissionsProcedures.aspx.

For the fall of 2016, nearly 600 students applied for admission to the various master's degree programs in the SOE; 86 percent were accepted. Approximately 230 students sought admission to the Ph.D. and Ed.D. programs; 50 percent were accepted.

Correspondence and Information

Dr. Valerie Kinloch, Dean
School of Education
University of Pittsburgh
Wesley W. Posvar Hall
230 S. Bouquet St.
Pittsburgh, Pennsylvania 15260
United States
Phone: 412-648-6944
Fax: 412-648-1825

Kaitlin Yacob
Director of Admissions
School of Education
Phone: 412-648-7362
Fax: 412-648-1899
E-mail: soeinfo@pitt.edu

The Cathedral of Learning, a Pittsburgh landmark listed in the National Register of Historic Places, is the centerpiece of the University of Pittsburgh's main campus in the Oakland neighborhood of Pittsburgh. The 42-story Late Gothic Revival Cathedral is the second-tallest university building in the world. The Cathedral of Learning contains more than 2,000 rooms and windows, and functions as one of the primary classroom and administrative centers of the university.

A point of convergence for Pitt students, faculty, and staff since it was erected in fall 2001, this panther statue greets those who enter the south side of the University's William Pitt Union. The bronze statue was cast in Parma, Italy, and serves as both a tribute to Pitt and a reminder of the University's fierce Panther Pride. A time capsule, to be opened in 2051, lies buried beneath the statue.

VANDERBILT UNIVERSITY

Peabody College

 For more information, visit http://petersons.to/vanderbilteducation

Programs of Study

Vanderbilt University's Peabody College of Education and Human Development offers programs leading to the Master of Education (M.Ed.), Master of Public Policy (M.P.P.), and Doctor of Education (Ed.D.) degrees. The Vanderbilt Graduate School, through Peabody departments, offers the Doctor of Philosophy (Ph.D.) degree. Peabody is committed to preparing students to become research scholars or innovative practitioners in the field of education and human development. Students may attend full- or part-time. Weekend courses are offered in several programs for working professionals who want to earn an advanced degree.

Students may pursue the Master of Education (M.Ed.) in child studies; clinical psychological assessment; community development and action; elementary education; English language learners; higher education administration (including specializations in administration, student life, and service learning); human development counseling (with specializations in school and community counseling); independent school leadership; international education policy and management; leadership and organizational performance; learning, diversity, and urban studies; learning and instruction (including specializations in teaching and learning; digital literacies; language, culture, and international studies; science and mathematics; or an individualized program); quantitative methods; reading education; secondary education; and special education (including specializations in applied behavior analysis, early childhood, high-incidence disabilities, and low-incidence disabilities). A Master of Public Policy is available in education policy. Peabody also offers a joint M.P.P./J.D. program and a dual degree with the Vanderbilt Divinity School.

Students interested in doctoral study may enroll in educational leadership and policy (Ed.D.); educational neuroscience (Ph.D); higher education leadership and policy (Ed.D.); community research and action (Ph.D.); leadership and learning in organizations (online Ed.D.); leadership and policy studies (Ph.D., with specializations in educational leadership and policy, higher education leadership and policy, and international education policy and management); learning, teaching, and diversity (Ph.D., with specializations in development, learning, and diversity; language, literacy, and culture; mathematics and science; and science and learning environment design); psychological sciences (Ph.D., with specializations in clinical science, cognitive science, developmental science, and quantitative methods and evaluation); and special education (Ph.D., with specializations in early childhood, high-incidence disabilities, and severe disabilities).

Peabody's teacher education and advanced certification programs are approved by the National Council for Accreditation of Teacher Education (NCATE). Programs in psychology and counseling are accredited by the American Psychological Association and the Council on Accreditation of Counseling and Related Educational Programs (CACREP), respectively.

Research Opportunities

In addition to the Vanderbilt University Library System, which has more than 2.6 million volumes, excellent research facilities and opportunities to conduct research are available through the Vanderbilt Kennedy Center for Research on Human Development, the Peabody Research Institute, the Susan Gray School, the National Center on School Choice, the National Center on Performance Initiatives, and the Center for Community Studies. The many local field sites available for research include hospitals, Metropolitan Nashville Public Schools, private schools, rehabilitation centers, schools for people with disabilities, government agencies, corporations, and nonprofit organizations.

Financial Aid

More than 70 percent of new students at Peabody receive financial aid. The College sponsors several substantial scholarship programs with offerings that range from partial to full tuition. In addition, assistantships, traineeships, loans, and part-time employment are available. Awards are made annually, and every attempt is made to meet a student's financial need. Application for financial aid does not affect the admission decision.

Cost of Study

Tuition for study at Peabody College for the 2017–18 academic year is $1,708 per semester credit hour for the M.Ed., M.P.P., and Ed.D. programs, and $1,910 per semester credit hour for programs offered through the Graduate School.

Living and Housing Costs

Vanderbilt's location in Nashville offers students the advantage of a wide range of living choices. Costs for housing, food, and other living expenses are moderate when compared with other metropolitan areas nationwide.

Student Group

Vanderbilt has a diverse student body of about 12,000. Peabody has an enrollment of approximately 1,800 students, of whom about 700 are graduate students. Women make up about 65 percent of Peabody's graduate students, while students from underrepresented groups make up about 20 percent. Students have a broad range of academic backgrounds and include recent graduates of baccalaureate programs as well as men and women who have many years of professional experience. The median age of current students is 27.

Student Outcomes

Graduates who earn a master's or doctoral degree from Peabody are prepared to work for educational, corporate, government, and service organizations in a variety of roles. More than 10,000 alumni are practicing teachers, more than 175 are school superintendents, and more than 50 are current or former college or university presidents.

Location

Nashville, the capital of Tennessee, is a cosmopolitan city with a metropolitan area population of 1.7 million. Vanderbilt University is one of more than a dozen institutions of higher learning located in Nashville and the surrounding area, leading Nashville to be called the "Athens of the South."

Nashville offers residents and visitors much in the way of music, art, and recreation. More than 100 local venues provide a wide variety of music, while classical and contemporary music is performed by the Nashville Symphony Orchestra and the Nashville Chamber Orchestra. The Tennessee Performing Arts Center (TPAC) is home to two theater companies, a ballet company, and an opera company. Vanderbilt's own Great Performances series frequently brings the best in chamber music, new music, theater, and all forms of dance to the Vanderbilt campus. Outstanding exhibitions of fine art can be seen at the Frist Center for the Visual Arts and at Cheekwood Botanical Garden and Museum of Art. There are more than 6,000 acres of public parks in the city, and the surrounding region of rolling hills and lakes is dotted with state parks and recreation areas.

Nashville has been named one of the 15 best U.S. cities for work and family by *Fortune* magazine, was ranked as the most popular U.S. city for corporate relocations by *Expansion Management* magazine, and was named by *Forbes* magazine as one of the 25 cities most likely to have the country's highest job growth over the coming five years. More information on Nashville can be found online at http://www.vanderbilt.edu/nashville.

The University and The College

Vanderbilt University, founded in 1873, is a private nondenominational institution with a strong tradition of graduate and professional education. Peabody, recognized for more than a century as one of the nation's foremost independent colleges of education, merged with Vanderbilt University in 1979. The College is currently ranked the number two graduate school of education in the nation by *U.S. News & World Report.* Peabody seeks to create knowledge through research, to prepare leaders, to support practitioners, and to strengthen communities at all levels.

Applying

Admission to professional degree programs is based on an evaluation of the applicant's potential for academic success and professional service, with consideration given to transcripts of previous course work, GRE General Test or MAT scores, letters of reference, and a letter outlining personal goals. Additional supporting credentials, such as a sample of the applicant's scholarly writing or a personal interview, may also be required.

Applicants who apply after the deadline should know that admission and financial assistance depend upon the availability of space and funds in the department in which they seek to study. Deadlines are December 1 for the Ph.D. and Ed.D. programs and December 31 for the M.Ed. and M.P.P. programs.

Correspondence and Information

Graduate Admissions
Peabody College of Vanderbilt University
Peabody Station, Box 227
Nashville, Tennessee 37203
United States
Phone: 615-322-8410
Fax: 615-322-4029
E-mail: peabody.admissions@vanderbilt.edu
Website: http://peabody.vanderbilt.edu

THE FACULTY

Department of Human and Organizational Development

Sandra Barnes, Professor; Ph.D., Georgia State.
Kimberly D. Bess, Assistant Professor; Ph.D., Vanderbilt.
Mark D. Cannon, Associate Professor; Ph.D., Harvard.
Ashley Carse, Assistant Professor; Ph.D., North Carolina at Chapel Hill.
Brian Christens, Associate Professor; Ph.D., Vanderbilt.
Nicole Cobb, Senior Lecturer; Ed.D., Tennessee.
David K. Diehl, Assistant Professor; Ph.D., Stanford.
Bradley Erford, Professor; Ph.D., Virginia.
Andrew J. Finch, Associate Professor of the Practice; Ph.D., Vanderbilt.
Anjali Forber-Pratt, Assistant Professor; Ph.D., Illinois at Urbana-Champaign.
James C. Fraser, Associate Professor; Ph.D., Georgia State.
Gina Frieden, Assistant Professor of the Practice; Ph.D., Memphis State.
Susan K. Friedman, Lecturer; M.B.A., Arizona State.
Leigh Gilchrist, Assistant Professor of the Practice; Ed.D., Vanderbilt.
Brian Griffith, Associate Clinical Professor; Ph.D., South Carolina.
Leslie Kirby, Principal Senior Lecturer; Ph.D., Vanderbilt.
Heather Lefkowitz, Lecturer; M.Div., Vanderbilt.
Mark Lipsey, Research Professor; Ph.D., Johns Hopkins.
Velma McBride Murry, Professor; Ph.D., Missouri–Columbia.

Maury Nation, Associate Professor; Ph.D., South Carolina.
Carol Nixon, Research Assistant Professor; Ph.D., Vanderbilt.
Nancy Nolan, Lecturer; M.Ed., Vanderbilt.
Douglas Perkins, Professor; Ph.D., NYU.
Jessica Perkins, Assistant Professor; Ph.D., Harvard.
Sara Safransky, Assistant Professor; Ph.D., North Carolina at Chapel Hill.
Sharon Shields, Professor of the Practice; Ph.D., George Peabody.
Marybeth Shinn, Professor; Ph.D., Michigan.
Heather Smith, Assistant Professor of the Practice; Ph.D., Central Florida.
Paul Speer, Professor; Ph.D., Missouri–Kansas City.
Sarah V. Suiter, Assistant Professor of the Practice; Ph.D., Vanderbilt.
Emily Tanner-Smith, Research Associate Professor; Ph.D., Vanderbilt.
Kristen C. Tompkins, Lecturer; M.Ed., Vanderbilt.
Andrew Van Schaack, Principal Senior Lecturer; Ph.D., Utah State.

Department of Leadership, Policy, and Organizations
Robert Dale Ballou, Associate Professor; Ph.D., Yale.
Angela Boatman, Assistant Professor; Ed.D., Harvard.
John Braxton, Professor; D.Ed., Penn State.
Christopher Candelaria; Assistant Professor; Ph.D., Stanford.
Marisa A. Cannata, Research Assistant Professor; Ph.D., Michigan.
Jose Cossa, Senior Lecturer; Ph.D., Chicago.
Xiu Cravens, Associate Professor of the Practice; Ph.D., Vanderbilt.
Susan Douglas, Assistant Professor of the Practice; Ph.D., Vanderbilt.
Corbette Doyle, Senior Lecturer; M.B.A., Vanderbilt.
William R. Doyle, Associate Professor; Ph.D., Stanford.
Mimi Engel, Assistant Professor; Ph.D., Northwestern.
Brent Evans, Assistant Professor; Ph.D., Stanford.
Seth Gershenson, Associate Professor; Ph.D., Michigan.
Joanne Golann, Assistant Professor; Ph.D., Princeton.
Ellen Goldring, Professor; Ph.D., Chicago.
Jason Grissom, Associate Professor; Ph.D., Stanford.
Carolyn J. Heinrich, Professor; Ph.D., Chicago.
Gary T. Henry, Professor; Ph.D., Wisconsin.
Brian L. Heuser, Assistant Professor; Ed.D., Vanderbilt.
Susan M. Kochanowski, Senior Lecturer; Ph.D., SUNY at Albany.
David Laird, Assistant Professor of the Practice; Ed.D., Vanderbilt.
Catherine Gavin Loss, Assistant Professor of the Practice; Ph.D., Virginia.
Christopher P. Loss, Associate Professor; Ph.D., Virginia.
Brenda McKenzie, Senior Lecturer; Ph.D., Kent.
Joseph Murphy, Professor; Ph.D., Ohio State.
Christine Quinn Trank, Associate Professor of the Practice; Ph.D., Iowa.
Patrick J. Schuermann, Assistant Professor; Ed.D., Vanderbilt.
Matthew Shaw, Assistant Professor; Ed.D., Harvard.
Claire Smrekar, Associate Professor; Ph.D., Stanford.
Adela Soliz, Assistant Professor; Ed.D., Harvard.
Matthew Springer, Associate Professor; Ph.D., Vanderbilt.
Deborah Tobey, Senior Lecturer; Ed.D., Vanderbilt.

Department of Psychology and Human Development
Camilla P. Benbow, Professor; Ed.D., Johns Hopkins.
Amy Booth, Professor; Ph.D., Pittsburgh.
James Booth, Professor; Ph.D., Maryland.
Sarah Brown-Schmidt, Associate Professor; Ph.D., Rochester.
Sun-Joo Cho, Associate Professor; Ph.D., Georgia.
David A. Cole, Professor; Ph.D., Houston.
Bruce E. Compas, Professor; Ph.D., UCLA.
Elizabeth May Dykens, Professor; Ph.D., Kansas.
Lisa K. Fazio, Assistant Professor; Ph.D., Duke.
Judy Garber, Professor; Ph.D., Minnesota, Twin Cities.
Vicki S. Harris, Assistant Clinical Professor; Ph.D., Pennsylvania.
Kathryn Humphreys, Assistant Professor; Ph.D., California.
Shane Hutton, Lecturer; Ph.D., North Carolina–Chapel Hill.
Autumn Kujawa, Assistant Professor; Ph.D., SUNY.
Jonathan Lane, Assistant Professor; Ph.D., Michigan.
Daniel T. Levin, Professor; Ph.D., Cornell.
David Lubinski, Professor; Ph.D., Minnesota.
Nina Martin, Associate Clinical Professor; Ed.D., Harvard.
Yolanda McDonald, Associate Clinical Professor; Ph.D., Texas.
Amy Needham, Professor; Ph.D., Illinois.
Julia Noland, Senior Lecturer; Ph.D., Cornell.
Laura R. Novick, Associate Professor; Ph.D., Stanford.
Georgine Pion, Research Associate Professor; Ph.D., Claremont.
Kristopher J. Preacher, Professor; Ph.D., Ohio.
Gavin Price, Assistant Professor; Ph.D., Jyväskylä (Finland).
John R. Rieser, Professor; Ph.D., Minnesota, Twin Cities.
Bethany Rittle-Johnson, Professor; Ph.D., Carnegie Mellon.
Joseph Lee Rodgers III, Professor; Ph.D., North Carolina.
Megan M. Saylor, Associate Professor; Ph.D., Oregon.
Craig A. Smith, Associate Professor; Ph.D., Stanford.
Sonya Sterba, Associate Professor; Ph.D., North Carolina–Chapel Hill.
Georgene Troseth, Associate Professor; Ph.D., Illinois at Urbana-Champaign.
Leigh Wadsworth, Senior Lecturer; Ph.D., Arizona State.
Tedra Ann Walden, Professor; Ph.D., Florida.
Duane Watson, Associate Professor; Ph.D., Rochester.
Bahr Weiss, Associate Professor; Ph.D., North Carolina–Chapel Hill.

Department of Special Education
Marcia Barnes, Professor; Ph.D., McMaster.
Erin Barton, Associate Professor; Ph.D., Vanderbilt.
Karen E. Blankenship, Assistant Professor; Ph.D., Vanderbilt.
Andrea Capizzi, Assistant Professor of the Practice; Ph.D., Vanderbilt.
Erik W. Carter, Professor; Ph.D., Vanderbilt.
Laurie Cutting, Professor; Ph.D., Northwestern.
Alex da Fonte, Assistant Professor of the Practice; M.S., Purdue.
Donna Y. Ford, Professor; Ph.D., Cleveland State.
Douglas Fuchs, Professor; Ph.D., Minnesota.
Lynn Fuchs, Professor; Ph.D., Minnesota.
Ted S. Hasselbring, Research Professor; Ed.D., Indiana.
Deborah D. Hatton, Associate Professor; Ph.D., North Carolina.
Mary Louise Hemmeter, Professor; Ph.D., Vanderbilt.
Robert Hodapp, Professor; Ph.D., Boston University.
Nealetta J. Houchins-Juarez, Instructor of the Practice; M.A., Nevada.
Ann Kaiser, Professor; Ph.D., Kansas.
Victoria Knight, Assistant Professor; Ph.D., North Carolina.
Joseph Lambert, Assistant Professor of the Practice; Ph.D., Utah State.
Jennifer Ledford, Assistant Professor; Ph.D., Vanderbilt.
Christopher Lemons, Associate Professor; Ph.D., Vanderbilt.
Blair Lloyd, Assistant Professor; Ph.D., Vanderbilt. Kim Paulsen, Professor of the Practice; Ed.D., Nevada, Las Vegas.
Naomi Tyler, Associate Professor of the Practice; Ph.D., New Mexico State.
Jeanne Wanzek, Associate Professor; Ph.D., University of Texas.
Joseph H. Wehby, Associate Professor; Ph.D., Vanderbilt.
Sandra Wilson, Research Assistant Professor; Ph.D., Vanderbilt.
Paul J. Yoder, Professor; Ph.D., North Carolina.

Department of Teaching and Learning
Corey Brady, Assistant Professor; Ph.D., Dartmouth.
Douglas Clark, Professor; Ph.D., Berkeley.
Paul A. Cobb, Research Professor; Ph.D., Georgia.
Molly F. Collins, Lecturer; Ed.D., Boston University.
Shannon M. Daniel, Lecturer; Ph.D., Maryland.
Ana Christine DaSilva, Professor of the Practice; Ph.D., Nevada.
David Dickinson, Professor; Ed.D., Harvard.
Teresa Dunleavy, Assistant Professor of the Practice; Ph.D., Washington (Seattle).
Dale C. Farran, Research Professor; Ph.D., Bryn Mawr.
Emily Galloway, Assistant Professor; D.Ed., Harvard.
Kathy A. Ganske, Professor of the Practice; Ph.D., Virginia.
Amanda P. Goodwin, Associate Professor; Ph.D., Miami.
Melissa Sommerfield Gresalfi, Associate Professor; Ph.D., Stanford.
Rogers Hall, Professor; Ph.D., California, Irvine.
Andrea W. Henrie, Lecturer; Ph.D., Tennessee.
Ilana Horn, Associate Professor; Ph.D., Berkeley.
Andrew L. Hostetler, Assistant Professor of the Practice; Ph.D., Kent State.
Melanie K. Hundley, Associate Professor of the Practice; Ph.D., Georgia.
Robert T. Jimenez, Professor; Ph.D., Illinois at Urbana-Champaign.
Heather J. Johnson, Assistant Professor of the Practice; Ph.D., Northwestern.
Nicole Joseph, Assistant Professor; Ph.D., Washington.
Ocheze Joseph, Lecturer; Ed.D., Maryland.
Kara Krinks, Lecturer; Ph.D., Vanderbilt.
Kevin Leander, Associate Professor; Ph.D., Illinois.
Deborah L. Lehrer, Lecturer; M.Ed., Edinboro.
Richard Lehrer, Professor; Ph.D., Chicago.
Luis Leyva, Assistant Professor; Ed.M., Rutgers.
Jeannette Mancilla-Martinez, Associate Professor; Ed.D., Harvard.
Ebony O. McGee, Assistant Professor; Ph.D., Illinois.
Catherine McTamaney, Senior Lecturer; Ed.D., Vanderbilt.
Kristen W. Neal, Lecturer; Ph.D., Vanderbilt.
Ann M. Neely, Associate Professor of the Practice; Ed.D., Georgia.
Amy Palmeri, Assistant Professor of the Practice; Ph.D., Indiana Bloomington.
Emily Pendergrass, Senior Lecturer; Ph.D., Georgia.
Jeanne H. Peter, Lecturer; Ed.D., Vanderbilt.
Rebecca Peterson, Lecturer; M.Ed., Vanderbilt.
Lisa Pray, Professor of the Practice; Ph.D., Arizona State.
Deborah W. Rowe, Professor; Ph.D., Indiana.
Leona Schauble, Professor; Ph.D., Columbia.
Elizabeth Self, Lecturer; Ph.D., Vanderbilt.
Virginia L. Shepherd, Research Professor; Ph.D., Iowa.
Marcy Singer-Gabella, Professor; Ph.D., Stanford.
Barbara Stengel, Professor of the Practice; Ph.D., Pittsburgh.
Anita Wager, Professor of the Practice; Ph.D., Wisconsin.

The Faye and Joe Wyatt Center for Education.

Section 23
Administration, Instruction, and Theory

This section contains a directory of institutions offering graduate work in administration, instruction, and theory. Additional information about programs listed in the directory but not augmented by an in-depth entry may be obtained by writing directly to the dean of a graduate school or chair of a department at the address given in the directory.

For programs offering related work, see also in this book *Education, Instructional Levels, Leisure Studies and Recreation, Physical Education and Kinesiology, Special Focus,* and *Subject Areas.* In other guides in this series:

Graduate Programs in the Humanities, Arts & Social Sciences
See *Psychology and Counseling (School Psychology)*
Graduate Programs in the Biological/Biomedical Sciences and Health-Related Medical Professions
See *Health-Related Professions*

CONTENTS

Program Directories

Featured Schools: Displays and Close-Ups

See also:

Curriculum and Instruction

Acadia University, Faculty of Professional Studies, School of Education, Program in Curriculum Studies, Wolfville, NS B4P 2R6, Canada. Offers cultural and media studies (M Ed); learning and technology (M Ed); science, math and technology (M Ed). *Program availability:* Part-time. *Degree requirements:* For master's, thesis optional. *Entrance requirements:* For master's, B Ed or the equivalent, minimum B average in undergraduate course work, 2 years of teaching experience. Additional exam requirements/recommendations for international students: Required—TOEFL (minimum score 580 paper-based; 93 iBT), IELTS (minimum score 6.5). *Faculty research:* Literacy development, postmodern philosophy and curriculum theory, historiography, philosophy of education, learning and technology.

American College of Education, Graduate Programs, Indianapolis, IN 46204. Offers curriculum and instruction (M Ed), including bilingual, ESL; educational leadership (M Ed); educational technology (M Ed).

American InterContinental University Online, Program in Education, Schaumburg, IL 60173. Offers curriculum and instruction (M Ed); educational assessment and evaluation (M Ed); instructional technology (M Ed); leadership of educational organizations (M Ed). *Accreditation:* TEAC. *Program availability:* Evening/weekend, online learning. *Entrance requirements:* Additional exam requirements/recommendations for international students: Required—TOEFL (minimum score 550 paper-based). Electronic applications accepted.

American Public University System, AMU/APU Graduate Programs, Charles Town, WV 25414. Offers accounting (MBA, MS); applied business analytics (MBA, MS); criminal justice (MA), including business administration, emergency and disaster management, general (MA, MS); educational leadership (M Ed); emergency and disaster management (MA); entrepreneurship (MBA); environmental policy and management (MS), including environmental planning, environmental sustainability, fish and wildlife management, general (MA, MS), global environmental management; finance (MBA); general (MBA); government contracting and acquisition (MBA); health care administration (MBA); health information management (MS); history (MA), including American history, ancient and classical history, European history, global history, public history; homeland security (MA), including business administration, counterterrorism studies, criminal justice, cyber, emergency management and public health, intelligence studies, transportation security; homeland security resource allocation (MBA); humanities (MA); information technology (MS), including digital forensics, enterprise software development, information assurance and security, IT project management; information technology management (MBA); intelligence studies (MA), including criminal intelligence, cyber, general (MA, MS), homeland security, intelligence analysis, intelligence collection, intelligence management, intelligence operations, terrorism studies; international relations and conflict resolution (MA), including comparative and security issues, conflict resolution, international and transnational security issues, peacekeeping; legal studies (MA); management (MA), including strategic consulting; marketing (MBA); military history (MA), including American military history, American Revolution, civil war, war since 1945, World War II; military studies (MA), including joint warfare, strategic leadership; national security studies (MA), including cyber, general (MA, MS), homeland security, regional security studies, security and intelligence analysis, terrorism studies; nonprofit management (MBA); political science (MA), including American politics and government, comparative government and development, general (MA, MS), international relations, public policy; psychology (MA); public administration (MPA), including disaster management, environmental policy, health policy, human resources, national security, organizational management, security management; public health (MPH); reverse logistics management (MA); security management (MA); space studies (MS), including aerospace science, general (MA, MS), planetary science; sports and health sciences (MS); sports management (MBA); teaching (M Ed), including autism spectrum disorder, curriculum and instruction for elementary teachers, elementary reading, English language learners, instructional leadership, online learning, special education, STEAM (STEM plus the arts); transportation and logistics management (MA). *Program availability:* Part-time, evening/weekend, online only, 100% online. *Faculty:* 401 full-time (228 women), 1,678 part-time/adjunct (781 women). *Students:* 378 full-time (184 women), 8,455 part-time (3,484 women); includes 2,972 minority (1,552 Black or African American, non-Hispanic/Latino; 52 American Indian or Alaska Native, non-Hispanic/Latino; 211 Asian, non-Hispanic/Latino; 791 Hispanic/Latino; 70 Native Hawaiian or other Pacific Islander, non-Hispanic/Latino; 296 Two or more races, non-Hispanic/Latino), 109 international. Average age 37. In 2016, 3,185 master's awarded. *Degree requirements:* For master's, comprehensive exam or practicum. *Entrance requirements:* For master's, official transcript showing earned bachelor's degree from institution accredited by recognized accrediting body. Additional exam requirements/recommendations for international students: Required—TOEFL (minimum score 550 paper-based), IELTS (minimum score 6.5). *Application deadline:* Applications are processed on a rolling basis. Application fee: $0. Electronic applications accepted. *Expenses: Tuition:* Part-time $350 per credit hour. *Required fees:* $50 per course. *Financial support:* Scholarships/grants available. Financial award applicants required to submit FAFSA. *Unit head:* Dr. Karan Powell, President, 877-468-6268, Fax: 304-724-3780. *Application contact:* Terry Grant, Vice President of Enrollment Management, 877-468-6268, Fax: 304-724-3780, E-mail: info@apus.edu.
Website: http://www.apus.edu

Andrews University, School of Graduate Studies, School of Education, Department of Teaching, Learning, and Curriculum, Program in Curriculum and Instruction, Berrien Springs, MI 49104. Offers MA, Ed D, PhD, Ed S. *Students:* 13 full-time (9 women), 9 part-time (all women); includes 8 minority (6 Black or African American, non-Hispanic/Latino; 2 Hispanic/Latino), 7 international. Average age 41. In 2016, 8 doctorates awarded. *Degree requirements:* For master's, thesis optional; for doctorate, thesis/dissertation. *Entrance requirements:* For master's, GRE Subject Test. Additional exam requirements/recommendations for international students: Required—TOEFL (minimum score 550 paper-based). *Application deadline:* Applications are processed on a rolling basis. Application fee: $40. *Financial support:* Fellowships, research assistantships, teaching assistantships, career-related internships or fieldwork, Federal Work-Study, institutionally sponsored loans, and tuition waivers (partial) available. Support available to part-time students. *Unit head:* Dr. Larry D. Burton, Coordinator, 269-971-6674. *Application contact:* Justina Clayburn, Supervisor of Graduate Admission, 800-253-2874, Fax: 269-471-6321, E-mail: graduate@andrews.edu.

Angelo State University, College of Graduate Studies and Research, College of Education, Department of Curriculum and Instruction, San Angelo, TX 76909. Offers curriculum and instruction (MA); educational administration (M Ed); guidance and counseling (M Ed); student development and leadership in higher education (M Ed). *Program availability:* Part-time, evening/weekend, online learning. *Students:* 400 full-time (328 women), 396 part-time (325 women); includes 242 minority (80 Black or African American, non-Hispanic/Latino; 2 American Indian or Alaska Native, non-Hispanic/Latino; 6 Asian, non-Hispanic/Latino; 148 Hispanic/Latino; 6 Two or more races, non-Hispanic/Latino), 1 international. Average age 35. *Application deadline:* For fall admission, 7/15 priority date for domestic students, 6/10 for international students; for spring admission, 12/1 priority date for domestic students, 11/1 for international students. Application fee: $40 ($50 for international students). *Expenses:* Tuition, state resident: full-time $3726; part-time $2484 per year. Tuition, nonresident: full-time $10,746; part-time $7164 per year. *Required fees:* $2538; $1702 per unit. *Unit head:* Dr. Jim Summerlin, Chair, 325-942-2647, Fax: 325-942-2039, E-mail: james.summerlin@angelo.edu. *Application contact:* Lesley Casarez, Graduate Advisor, 325-486-6775, E-mail: lesley.casarez@angelo.edu.
Website: http://www.angelo.edu/dept/ci/

Appalachian State University, Cratis D. Williams Graduate School, Department of Curriculum and Instruction, Boone, NC 28608. Offers curriculum specialist (MA); educational media (MA); elementary education (MA); middle grades education (MA), including language arts, mathematics, science, social studies. *Accreditation:* NCATE. *Program availability:* Part-time, evening/weekend, online learning. *Degree requirements:* For master's, comprehensive exam, thesis or alternative. *Entrance requirements:* For master's, GRE General Test or MAT, 3 letters of recommendation. Additional exam requirements/recommendations for international students: Required—TOEFL (minimum score 570 paper-based; 79 iBT), IELTS (minimum score 6.5). *Application deadline:* For fall admission, 3/14 for domestic students, 2/1 for international students; for spring admission, 11/1 for domestic students, 7/1 for international students. Applications are processed on a rolling basis. Application fee: $55. Electronic applications accepted. *Expenses:* Tuition, state resident: full-time $4744. Tuition, nonresident: full-time $17,913. Full-time tuition and fees vary according to program. *Financial support:* Fellowships, research assistantships, teaching assistantships, career-related internships or fieldwork, Federal Work-Study, scholarships/grants, and unspecified assistantships available. Financial award application deadline: 4/1; financial award applicants required to submit FAFSA. *Faculty research:* Media literacy, elementary teaching, curriculum development, online learning environments. *Unit head:* Dr. Michael Jacobson, Chairperson, 828-262-2224. *Application contact:* Dr. Chrystal Dean, Program Director, 828-262-8009, E-mail: deanco@appstate.edu.
Website: http://www.ced.appstate.edu/departments/ci

Arcadia University, School of Education, Glenside, PA 19038-3295. Offers art education (M Ed); computer education (CAS); curriculum (CAS); curriculum studies (M Ed); early childhood education (M Ed), including individualized, master teacher, research in child development; educational leadership (M Ed, Ed D, CAS); elementary education (M Ed); English education (MA Ed); environmental education (MA Ed); instructional technology (M Ed); language arts (M Ed); library science (M Ed); mathematics education (M Ed, MA Ed); music education (MA Ed); psychology (MA Ed); reading (M Ed, CAS); science education (M Ed, CAS); secondary education (M Ed, CAS); special education (M Ed, Ed D, CAS); theater arts (MA Ed); written communication (MA Ed). *Accreditation:* NASAD. *Program availability:* Part-time, evening/weekend, online learning. *Faculty:* 19 full-time (13 women), 3 part-time/adjunct (all women). *Students:* 22 full-time (16 women), 356 part-time (284 women); includes 84 minority (55 Black or African American, non-Hispanic/Latino; 2 American Indian or Alaska Native, non-Hispanic/Latino; 13 Asian, non-Hispanic/Latino; 11 Hispanic/Latino; 3 Two or more races, non-Hispanic/Latino), 4 international. Average age 34. 145 applicants, 73% accepted, 80 enrolled. In 2016, 95 master's, 11 doctorates awarded. *Application deadline:* Applications are processed on a rolling basis. Application fee: $50. Electronic applications accepted. *Expenses:* Contact institution. *Financial support:* Career-related internships or fieldwork, tuition waivers (partial), and unspecified assistantships available. *Unit head:* John T Groves, Interim Dean of the School of Education, 215-572-2940. *Application contact:* 215-572-2925, Fax: 215-572-2126, E-mail: grad@arcadia.edu.

Arizona State University at the Tempe campus, Mary Lou Fulton Teachers College, Program in Curriculum and Instruction, Phoenix, AZ 85069. Offers curriculum and instruction (M Ed, MA); elementary education (M Ed); physical education (MPE); secondary education (M Ed). *Program availability:* Part-time, evening/weekend, online learning. Terminal master's awarded for partial completion of doctoral program. *Degree requirements:* For master's, thesis or alternative, applied project, interactive Program of Study (iPOS) submitted before completing 50 percent of required credit hours. *Entrance requirements:* For master's, GRE or GMAT (for some programs), minimum GPA of 3.0 or equivalent in last 2 years of work leading to bachelor's degree, 3 letters of recommendation, personal statement describing research and career goals, curriculum vitae or resume, IVP fingerprint clearance card (for those seeking Arizona certification). Additional exam requirements/recommendations for international students: Required—TOEFL, IELTS, or PTE. Electronic applications accepted. *Expenses:* Contact institution. *Faculty research:* Early childhood, media and computers, elementary education, secondary education, English education, bilingual education, language and literacy, science education, engineering education, exercise and wellness education.

Arkansas Tech University, College of Education, Russellville, AR 72801. Offers college student personnel (MS); educational leadership (M Ed, Ed S); elementary education (M Ed); instructional improvement (M Ed); instructional technology (M Ed); school counseling and leadership (M Ed); school leadership (Ed D); strength and conditioning studies (MS); teaching (MAT); teaching, learning, and leadership (M Ed). *Accreditation:* NCATE. *Program availability:* Part-time, evening/weekend, online learning. *Students:* 72 full-time (43 women), 371 part-time (283 women); includes 108 minority (80 Black or African American, non-Hispanic/Latino; 1 American Indian or Alaska Native, non-Hispanic/Latino; 4 Asian, non-Hispanic/Latino; 13 Hispanic/Latino; 10 Two or more races, non-Hispanic/Latino), 6 international. Average age 33. In 2016, 181 master's, 1 other advanced degree awarded. *Degree requirements:* For master's, comprehensive exam, thesis optional, action research project. *Entrance requirements:* Additional exam requirements/recommendations for international students: Required—TOEFL (minimum score 550 paper-based; 79 iBT), IELTS (minimum score 6.5). *Application deadline:* For fall admission, 3/1 priority date for domestic students, 5/1 priority date for international students; for spring admission, 10/1 priority date for domestic and international students. Applications are processed on a rolling basis. Application fee: $25 ($75 for international students). Electronic applications accepted. *Expenses:* Tuition, state resident: full-time $4932; part-time $274 per credit hour. Tuition, nonresident: full-time $9864; part-time $548 per credit hour. *Required fees:* $513 per semester. Tuition and fees vary according to course load. *Financial support:* In 2016–17, research assistantships with full tuition reimbursements (averaging $4,800 per year), teaching assistantships with full tuition reimbursements (averaging $4,800 per year) were awarded; career-related internships or fieldwork, Federal Work-Study, scholarships/grants, health care benefits, and unspecified assistantships also available. Support available to part-time students. Financial award application deadline: 4/15;

financial award applicants required to submit FAFSA. *Unit head:* Dr. Mary Gunter, Dean, 479-964-3217, E-mail: mgunter@atu.edu.
Website: http://www.atu.edu/education/

Arlington Baptist College, Program in Education, Arlington, TX 76012-3425. Offers curriculum and instruction (M Ed); educational leadership (M Ed). *Degree requirements:* For master's, professional portfolio; internship (for educational leadership). *Entrance requirements:* For master's, bachelor's degree from accredited college or university with minimum GPA of 3.0, minimum of 12 hours in Bible; minimum of three years' classroom teaching experience in an accredited K-12 public or private school (for educational leadership only).

Armstrong State University, School of Graduate Studies, Department of Secondary, Adult, and Physical Education, Savannah, GA 31419-1997. Offers adolescent and adult education (Certificate); adult education and community leadership (M Ed); curriculum and instruction (M Ed); secondary education (MAT). *Program availability:* Part-time, evening/weekend, online learning. *Faculty:* 9 full-time (all women), 3 part-time/adjunct (all women). *Students:* 23 full-time (16 women), 103 part-time (68 women); includes 47 minority (40 Black or African American, non-Hispanic/Latino; 1 Asian, non-Hispanic/Latino; 2 Hispanic/Latino; 4 Two or more races, non-Hispanic/Latino), 1 international. Average age 32. 77 applicants, 52% accepted, 28 enrolled. In 2016, 36 master's, 1 other advanced degree awarded. *Degree requirements:* For master's, comprehensive exam (for some programs), thesis (for some programs), capstone project (for M Ed). *Entrance requirements:* For master's, edTPA (for MAT). Additional exam requirements/recommendations for international students: Required—TOEFL (minimum score 523 paper-based). *Application deadline:* For fall admission, 6/30 priority date for domestic students, 5/1 priority date for international students; for spring admission, 11/15 priority date for domestic students, 9/15 priority date for international students; for summer admission, 4/15 priority date for domestic students, 9/15 for international students. Applications are processed on a rolling basis. Application fee: $30. Electronic applications accepted. *Expenses:* Tuition, state resident: full-time $1781; part-time $161.93 per credit hour. Tuition, nonresident: full-time $6482; part-time $589.27 per credit hour. *Required fees:* $1224 per unit. $612 per semester. Tuition and fees vary according to course load, campus/location and program. *Financial support:* In 2016–17, research assistantships with full tuition reimbursements (averaging $5,000 per year) were awarded; career-related internships or fieldwork, Federal Work-Study, scholarships/grants, and unspecified assistantships also available. Support available to part-time students. Financial award application deadline: 3/15; financial award applicants required to submit FAFSA. *Faculty research:* Quality of teacher leadership, classroom management and first year teachers; edTPA preparation and success of candidates; social justice issues related to educational preparation; recruitment of STEM teachers. *Unit head:* Dr. Regina Rahimi, Interim Department Head, 912-344-2562, E-mail: regina.rahimi@armstrong.edu. *Application contact:* McKenzie Peterman, Assistant Director of Graduate Admissions, 912-344-2503, Fax: 912-344-3417, E-mail: graduate@armstrong.edu.
Website: http://www.armstrong.edu/Education/adolescent_adult_education2/aaed_welcome

Auburn University, Graduate School, College of Education, Department of Educational Foundations, Leadership, and Technology, Auburn University, AL 36849. Offers adult education (PhD, Ed S); curriculum supervision (M Ed, PhD); higher education administration (PhD); library media (Ed S); school administration (M Ed, PhD). *Accreditation:* NCATE. *Program availability:* Part-time. *Faculty:* 29 full-time (15 women), 4 part-time/adjunct (3 women). *Students:* 119 full-time (72 women), 273 part-time (170 women); includes 132 minority (114 Black or African American, non-Hispanic/Latino; 2 American Indian or Alaska Native, non-Hispanic/Latino; 4 Asian, non-Hispanic/Latino; 6 Hispanic/Latino; 1 Native Hawaiian or other Pacific Islander, non-Hispanic/Latino; 5 Two or more races, non-Hispanic/Latino), 14 international. Average age 37. 220 applicants, 71% accepted, 78 enrolled. In 2016, 67 master's, 44 doctorates, 41 other advanced degrees awarded. *Degree requirements:* For master's, thesis (for some programs); for doctorate, thesis/dissertation; for Ed S, field project. *Entrance requirements:* For master's, doctorate, and Ed S, GRE General Test. *Application deadline:* Applications are processed on a rolling basis. Application fee: $50 ($60 for international students). Electronic applications accepted. *Expenses:* Tuition, state resident: full-time $9072; part-time $504 per credit hour. Tuition, nonresident: full-time $27,216; part-time $1512 per credit hour. *Required fees:* $812 per semester. Tuition and fees vary according to degree level and program. *Financial support:* Teaching assistantships and Federal Work-Study available. Support available to part-time students. Financial award application deadline: 3/15; financial award applicants required to submit FAFSA. *Unit head:* Dr. Sherida Downer, Head, 334-844-4460. *Application contact:* Dr. George Flowers, Dean of the Graduate School, 334-844-4700.
Website: http://www.education.auburn.edu/academic_departments/eflt/

Augusta University, The Graduate School, College of Education, Program in Curriculum and Instruction, Augusta, GA 30912. Offers curriculum and instruction (Ed S); elementary education (MAT); foreign language education (MAT); instruction (M Ed); middle grades education (MAT); music education (MAT); secondary education (MAT); special education (MAT). *Degree requirements:* For master's, thesis, portfolio. *Entrance requirements:* For master's, GRE, MAT, minimum GPA of 2.5. Application fee: $20. *Financial support:* Career-related internships or fieldwork, Federal Work-Study, institutionally sponsored loans, and unspecified assistantships available. Support available to part-time students. Financial award application deadline: 4/15; financial award applicants required to submit FAFSA. *Unit head:* Dr. Gordon Eisenman, Director, 706-737-1496, Fax: 706-667-4706, E-mail: geisenman@augusta.edu. *Application contact:* Dr. Gordon Eisenman, Director, 706-737-1496, Fax: 706-667-4706, E-mail: geisenman@augusta.edu.

Aurora University, School of Education and Human Performance, Aurora, IL 60506-4892. Offers bilingual-ESL education (MA); educational leadership (MA); educational technology (MA); leadership in administration (Ed D); leadership in adult learning and higher education (Ed D); leadership in curriculum and instruction (Ed D); reading instruction (MA); special education (MA). *Accreditation:* NCATE. *Program availability:* Part-time, evening/weekend. *Faculty:* 22 full-time (12 women), 46 part-time/adjunct (27 women). *Students:* 36 full-time (30 women), 559 part-time (372 women); includes 68 minority (27 Black or African American, non-Hispanic/Latino; 1 American Indian or Alaska Native, non-Hispanic/Latino; 6 Asian, non-Hispanic/Latino; 29 Hispanic/Latino; 2 Native Hawaiian or other Pacific Islander, non-Hispanic/Latino; 3 Two or more races, non-Hispanic/Latino). Average age 37. 126 applicants, 98% accepted, 72 enrolled. In 2016, 178 master's, 27 doctorates awarded. *Degree requirements:* For master's, student teaching; for doctorate, comprehensive exam, thesis/dissertation. *Entrance requirements:* For master's, 2 years of teaching experience, valid teaching certificate; for doctorate, appropriate master's degree, two references, curriculum vitae, personal statement, professional project, reflective essay. Additional exam requirements/recommendations for international students: Required—TOEFL (minimum score 550 paper-based; 79 iBT). *Application deadline:* For fall admission, 6/1 for international students; for spring admission, 10/1 for international students. Applications are processed on a rolling basis. Application fee: $0. Electronic applications accepted. *Expenses:* Contact institution. *Financial support:* In 2016–17, 10 students received support. Federal Work-Study, scholarships/grants, and unspecified assistantships available. Support available to part-time students. Financial award applicants required to submit FAFSA. *Unit head:* Dr. Jen Buckley, Executive Director of the School of Education and Human Performance, 630-844-1542, Fax: 630-844-6155, E-mail: jbuckley@aurora.edu. *Application contact:* Elizabeth Botica, Graduate Education Recruiter, 630-947-8918, E-mail: ebotica@aurora.edu.
Website: http://aurora.edu/education

Austin Peay State University, College of Graduate Studies, College of Education, Department of Educational Specialties, Clarksville, TN 37044. Offers administration and supervision (Ed S); counseling and guidance (Ed S); curriculum and instruction (MA Ed); education leadership (MA Ed); elementary education (Ed S); reading (MA Ed); secondary education (Ed S). *Program availability:* Part-time, evening/weekend, online learning. *Faculty:* 7 full-time (4 women), 4 part-time/adjunct (3 women). *Students:* 4 full-time (3 women), 77 part-time (60 women); includes 13 minority (8 Black or African American, non-Hispanic/Latino; 1 Asian, non-Hispanic/Latino; 3 Hispanic/Latino; 1 Two or more races, non-Hispanic/Latino). Average age 37. 18 applicants, 89% accepted, 14 enrolled. In 2016, 34 master's, 9 Ed Ss awarded. *Degree requirements:* For master's, comprehensive exam, thesis optional. *Entrance requirements:* For master's, GRE General Test, MAT, minimum undergraduate GPA of 2.75. Additional exam requirements/recommendations for international students: Required—TOEFL (minimum score 500 paper-based). *Application deadline:* For fall admission, 8/9 priority date for domestic students. Applications are processed on a rolling basis. Application fee: $45 ($50 for international students). Electronic applications accepted. *Expenses:* Tuition, state resident: full-time $8300; part-time $415 per credit hour. Tuition, nonresident: full-time $22,280; part-time $1114 per credit hour. *Required fees:* $1473; $73.65 per credit hour. *Financial support:* Research assistantships with full tuition reimbursements, career-related internships or fieldwork, Federal Work-Study, institutionally sponsored loans, scholarships/grants, and unspecified assistantships available. Support available to part-time students. Financial award application deadline: 4/1; financial award applicants required to submit FAFSA. *Unit head:* Dr. Moniqueka Gold, Chair, 931-221-7696, Fax: 931-221-1292, E-mail: goldm@apsu.edu. *Application contact:* Brad Averitt, Coordinator of Graduate Admissions, 800-859-4723, Fax: 931-221-7641, E-mail: gradadmissions@apsu.edu.

Austin Peay State University, College of Graduate Studies, College of Education, Department of Teaching and Learning, Clarksville, TN 37044. Offers elementary education K-6 (MAT); reading (MA Ed); secondary education 7-12 (MAT); special education K-12 (MAT). *Program availability:* Part-time, evening/weekend, online learning. *Faculty:* 12 full-time (8 women), 1 (woman) part-time/adjunct. *Students:* 62 full-time (39 women), 79 part-time (72 women); includes 31 minority (16 Black or African American, non-Hispanic/Latino; 1 Asian, non-Hispanic/Latino; 8 Hispanic/Latino; 6 Two or more races, non-Hispanic/Latino), 2 international. Average age 33. 60 applicants, 80% accepted, 33 enrolled. In 2016, 53 master's awarded. *Degree requirements:* For master's, comprehensive exam, thesis optional. *Entrance requirements:* For master's, GRE General Test, minimum undergraduate GPA of 2.75. Additional exam requirements/recommendations for international students: Required—TOEFL (minimum score 500 paper-based). *Application deadline:* For fall admission, 8/9 priority date for domestic students. Applications are processed on a rolling basis. Application fee: $45 ($50 for international students). Electronic applications accepted. *Expenses:* Tuition, state resident: full-time $8300; part-time $415 per credit hour. Tuition, nonresident: full-time $22,280; part-time $1114 per credit hour. *Required fees:* $1473; $73.65 per credit hour. *Financial support:* Research assistantships, career-related internships or fieldwork, Federal Work-Study, institutionally sponsored loans, scholarships/grants, and unspecified assistantships available. Support available to part-time students. Financial award application deadline: 4/1; financial award applicants required to submit FAFSA. *Unit head:* Dr. Benita Bruster, Interim Chair, 931-221-6491, Fax: 931-221-1292, E-mail: brusterb@apsu.edu. *Application contact:* Brad Averitt, Coordinator of Graduate Admissions, 800-859-4723, Fax: 931-221-7641, E-mail: gradadmissions@apsu.edu.

Averett University, Master in Education Program, Danville, VA 24541-3692. Offers administration and supervision (M Ed); curriculum and instruction (M Ed); special education with endorsement (M Ed); special education with licensure (M Ed). Program offered on Danville Campus only. *Program availability:* Part-time, online only, 100% online. *Faculty:* 1 full-time (0 women), 15 part-time/adjunct (12 women). *Students:* 26 full-time (22 women), 98 part-time (73 women); includes 39 minority (34 Black or African American, non-Hispanic/Latino; 3 American Indian or Alaska Native, non-Hispanic/Latino; 2 Hispanic/Latino). Average age 36. 109 applicants, 54% accepted, 56 enrolled. In 2016, 19 master's awarded. *Degree requirements:* For master's, 30-credit core curriculum, minimum GPA of 3.0 throughout program, completion of degree requirements within six years from start of program. *Entrance requirements:* For master's, PRAXIS I, GRE, or MAT; writing proficiency test, minimum cumulative GPA of 3.0 over the last 60 hours of undergraduate study toward a baccalaureate degree, three letters of recommendation, Virginia teaching license (or eligibility). Additional exam requirements/recommendations for international students: Required—TOEFL (minimum score 600 paper-based; 100 iBT). *Application deadline:* Applications are processed on a rolling basis. Electronic applications accepted. *Expenses:* $9,600. *Financial support:* Application deadline: 3/1; applicants required to submit FAFSA. *Faculty research:* Digital story telling for instruction and assessment; online collaborative tools; digital field trips with Google Earth; teacher preparation in special education in Kenya, Malawi, Zambia, and Zimbabwe; self-efficacy of regular education teachers regarding inclusion of special education students in their classrooms. *Total annual research expenditures:* $5,000. *Unit head:* Dr. Sue Davis, Education Chair, 434-791-5741, Fax: 434-791-5020, E-mail: suedavis@averett.edu.
Website: http://gps.averett.edu/online/education/

Azusa Pacific University, School of Education, Department of Foundations and Transdisciplinary Studies, Program in Curriculum and Instruction in Multicultural Contexts, Azusa, CA 91702-7000. Offers MA Ed. *Accreditation:* NCATE. *Program availability:* Part-time, evening/weekend. *Degree requirements:* For master's, core exams, oral presentation. *Entrance requirements:* For master's, 12 units of course work in education, minimum GPA of 3.0. *Faculty research:* Diversity in teacher education programs, teacher morale, student perception of school, case study instruction.

Azusa Pacific University, School of Education, Department of Foundations and Transdisciplinary Studies, Program in Teaching, Azusa, CA 91702-7000. Offers MA Ed.

Ball State University, Graduate School, Teachers College, Department of Educational Studies, Program in Curriculum and Educational Technology, Muncie, IN 47306. Offers MA. *Accreditation:* NCATE. *Program availability:* Part-time, online only, 100% online. *Entrance requirements:* For master's, minimum baccalaureate GPA of 2.75 or 3.0 in latter half of baccalauareate. Additional exam requirements/recommendations for international students: Required—TOEFL (minimum score 550 paper-based; 79 iBT), IELTS (minimum score 6.5). Electronic applications accepted.

Ball State University, Graduate School, Teachers College, Department of Educational Studies, Program in Educational Studies, Muncie, IN 47306. Offers educational studies (PhD), including cultural and educational policy studies, curriculum, educational technology. *Program availability:* Part-time, blended/hybrid learning. *Degree requirements:* For doctorate, thesis/dissertation. *Entrance requirements:* For doctorate,

Curriculum and Instruction

GRE General Test, minimum graduate GPA of 3.2, curriculum vitae, writing sample, three letters of reference. Additional exam requirements/recommendations for international students: Required—TOEFL (minimum score 550 paper-based; 79 iBT), IELTS (minimum score 6.5). Electronic applications accepted. *Faculty research:* Emerging curriculum trends, secondary teacher preparation, issues of equity and social justice in education, teacher technology integration, teaching for transformative understanding, teacher leadership, history of educational policy and practices, ethics and education.

Barry University, School of Education, Program in Curriculum and Instruction, Miami Shores, FL 33161-6695. Offers accomplished teacher (Ed S); culture, language and literacy (TESOL) (PhD); curriculum evaluation and research (PhD); early childhood (Ed S); early childhood education (PhD); elementary (Ed S); elementary education (PhD); ESOL (Ed S); gifted (Ed S); Montessori (Ed S); PKP/elementary (Ed S); reading (Ed S); reading, language and cognition (PhD). *Entrance requirements:* For doctorate, GRE, minimum GPA of 3.25.

Baylor University, Graduate School, School of Education, Department of Curriculum and Instruction, Waco, TX 76798. Offers MA, MS Ed, Ed D, PhD. *Accreditation:* NCATE. *Program availability:* Part-time. *Faculty:* 13 full-time (9 women). *Students:* 26 full-time (19 women), 13 part-time (8 women); includes 4 minority (2 Black or African American, non-Hispanic/Latino; 2 Hispanic/Latino), 2 international. Average age 30. 26 applicants, 65% accepted, 14 enrolled. In 2016, 13 master's, 6 doctorates awarded. *Degree requirements:* For master's, 2 foreign languages, comprehensive exam, thesis optional; for doctorate, comprehensive exam, thesis/dissertation. *Entrance requirements:* For master's, GRE General Test (including Analytic Writing), 3 letters of recommendation, personal statement, interview; for doctorate, GRE General Test (including Analytic Writing), 3 letters of recommendation, personal statement, interview, writing sample. Additional exam requirements/recommendations for international students: Required—TOEFL (minimum score 550 paper-based, 80 iBT) or IELTS (minimum score 6.5). *Application deadline:* For fall admission, 3/15 priority date for domestic and international students; for spring admission, 10/15 priority date for domestic and international students. Applications are processed on a rolling basis. Application fee: $25. Electronic applications accepted. *Expenses: Tuition:* Full-time $28,494; part-time $1583 per credit hour. *Required fees:* $167 per credit hour. Tuition and fees vary according to course load and program. *Financial support:* In 2016–17, 35 students received support, including 15 research assistantships with partial tuition reimbursements available (averaging $10,000 per year), 1 teaching assistantship with full tuition reimbursement available (averaging $19,000 per year); Federal Work-Study, institutionally sponsored loans, scholarships/grants, health care benefits, and unspecified assistantships also available. Support available to part-time students. Financial award application deadline: 3/15. *Faculty research:* Curriculum and pedagogy, elementary education, English language arts education, literacy and reading education, mathematics education, qualitative research, science education, social foundations and cultural studies, social studies education, secondary education, teacher education, technology education, media literacy, civics education, historically black colleges. *Total annual research expenditures:* $75,000. *Unit head:* Dr. Trena Wilkerson, Graduate Program Director, 254-710-6162, Fax: 254-710-3160, E-mail: trena_wilkerson@baylor.edu. *Application contact:* Carol Stukenbroeker, Administrative Assistant, 254-710-2410, Fax: 254-710-3160, E-mail: carol_stukenbroeker@baylor.edu.
Website: http://www.baylor.edu/soe/ci/

Bay Path University, Program in Curriculum and Instruction, Longmeadow, MA 01106-2292. Offers MS Ed. *Program availability:* Part-time, 100% online. *Students:* 16 full-time (all women), 30 part-time (28 women); includes 8 minority (3 Black or African American, non-Hispanic/Latino; 2 Hispanic/Latino; 3 Two or more races, non-Hispanic/Latino). Average age 31. 27 applicants, 67% accepted, 15 enrolled. In 2016, 4 master's awarded. *Application deadline:* Applications are processed on a rolling basis. Application fee: $45. Electronic applications accepted. Application fee is waived when completed online. *Expenses:* $13,365. *Financial support:* Unspecified assistantships available. Financial award applicants required to submit FAFSA. *Unit head:* Andrea Hickson, Program Director, E-mail: ahickson@baypath.edu. *Application contact:* Diane Ranaldi, Dean of Graduate Admissions, 413-565-1332, Fax: 413-565-1250, E-mail: dranaldi@baypath.edu.

Benedictine University, Graduate Programs, Program in Education, Lisle, IL 60532. Offers curriculum and instruction and collaborative teaching (M Ed); elementary education (MA Ed); leadership and administration (M Ed); reading and literacy (M Ed); secondary education (MA Ed); special education (MA Ed). *Program availability:* Part-time, evening/weekend. *Students:* 17 full-time (16 women), 30 part-time (26 women); includes 2 minority (both Black or African American, non-Hispanic/Latino). 21 applicants, 62% accepted, 8 enrolled. In 2016, 68 master's awarded. *Degree requirements:* For master's, comprehensive exam, thesis (for some programs). *Entrance requirements:* For master's, GRE or MAT. Additional exam requirements/recommendations for international students: Required—TOEFL (minimum score 550 paper-based). *Application deadline:* For fall admission, 9/1 for domestic students; for winter admission, 12/1 for domestic students; for spring admission, 2/15 for domestic students. Applications are processed on a rolling basis. Application fee: $40. Electronic applications accepted. *Expenses:* Contact institution. *Financial support:* Career-related internships or fieldwork and health care benefits available. Support available to part-time students. *Unit head:* MeShelda Jackson, Director, 630-829-6282, E-mail: mjackson@ben.edu. *Application contact:* Kari Gibbons, Associate Vice President, Enrollment Center, 630-829-6200, Fax: 630-829-6584, E-mail: kgibbons@ben.edu.

Berry College, Graduate Programs, Graduate Programs in Education, Program in Curriculum and Instruction, Mount Berry, GA 30149-0159. Offers M Ed, Ed S. *Accreditation:* NCATE. *Faculty:* 5 part-time/adjunct (all women). *Students:* 5 part-time (all women). Average age 27. In 2016, 12 Ed Ss awarded. *Degree requirements:* For master's and Ed S, thesis, portfolio, oral exams. *Entrance requirements:* For master's, GRE or MAT, minimum GPA of 2.5; for Ed S, M Ed from NCATE-accredited school, minimum GPA of 3.25. Additional exam requirements/recommendations for international students: Required—TOEFL (minimum score 550 paper-based). *Application deadline:* For fall admission, 7/21 for domestic students, 5/1 for international students; for spring admission, 12/1 for domestic students, 10/1 for international students. Applications are processed on a rolling basis. Application fee: $25 ($30 for international students). Electronic applications accepted. *Expenses:* Contact institution. *Financial support:* Research assistantships and scholarships/grants available. Support available to part-time students. Financial award application deadline: 3/1; financial award applicants required to submit FAFSA. *Unit head:* Dr. Jacqueline McDowell, Dean, 706-236-1717, Fax: 706-238-5827, E-mail: jmcdowell@berry.edu. *Application contact:* Brett Kennedy, Assistant Vice President of Enrollment Management, 706-236-2215, Fax: 706-290-2178, E-mail: admissions@berry.edu.
Website: http://www.berry.edu/academics/education/graduate/

Biola University, School of Education, La Mirada, CA 90639-0001. Offers curriculum and instruction (Certificate); early childhood (MA Ed, MAT); multiple subject (MAT); single subject (MAT); special education (MA Ed, MAT, Certificate). *Program availability:* Part-time, evening/weekend, online learning. *Entrance requirements:* For master's, CBEST, CSET, GRE (waived if cumulative GPA is 3.5 or above or if CBEST and all CSET subtests are passed). Additional exam requirements/recommendations for international students: Required—TOEFL (minimum score 100 iBT). Electronic applications accepted. *Faculty research:* Early childhood education, elementary education, special education, curriculum development, teacher preparation.

Black Hills State University, Graduate Studies, Program in Curriculum and Instruction, Spearfish, SD 57799. Offers MS. *Program availability:* Part-time. *Entrance requirements:* Additional exam requirements/recommendations for international students: Required—TOEFL (minimum score 500 paper-based; 60 iBT).

Bloomsburg University of Pennsylvania, School of Graduate Studies, College of Education, Department of Teaching and Learning, Program in Curriculum and Instruction, Bloomsburg, PA 17815-1301. Offers M Ed, Certificate. *Accreditation:* NCATE. *Faculty:* 6 full-time (1 woman). *Students:* 15 full-time (3 women), 27 part-time (15 women); includes 2 minority (both Hispanic/Latino). Average age 29. 31 applicants, 68% accepted, 17 enrolled. In 2016, 18 master's awarded. *Degree requirements:* For master's, thesis. *Entrance requirements:* For master's, MAT, GRE, or PRAXIS, minimum QPA of 3.0, interview. Additional exam requirements/recommendations for international students: Required—TOEFL (minimum score 550 paper-based; 79 iBT), IELTS. *Application deadline:* Applications are processed on a rolling basis. Application fee: $35 ($60 for international students). Electronic applications accepted. *Expenses:* Tuition, state resident: full-time $9660; part-time $483 per credit. Tuition, nonresident: full-time $14,500; part-time $725 per credit. *Required fees:* $2410; $107 per credit. $75 per term. Tuition and fees vary according to course load, degree level and program. *Financial support:* Federal Work-Study and unspecified assistantships available. Financial award applicants required to submit FAFSA. *Unit head:* Dr. Ingrid Everett, Program Coordinator, 570-389-5120, Fax: 570-389-3030, E-mail: ieverett@bloomu.edu. *Application contact:* Jennifer Kessler, Administrative Assistant, 570-389-4015, Fax: 570-389-3054, E-mail: jkessler@bloomu.edu.
Website: http://www.bloomu.edu/gradschool/curriculum-instruction

Bloomsburg University of Pennsylvania, School of Graduate Studies, College of Education, Department of Teaching and Learning, Program in Educational Leadership, Bloomsburg, PA 17815-1301. Offers college student affairs (M Ed); PreK-12 curriculum and instruction (M Ed); PreK-12 school counseling (M Ed); PreK-12 school principal (M Ed). *Faculty:* 6 full-time (2 women), 1 (woman) part-time/adjunct. *Students:* 64 full-time (42 women), 39 part-time (26 women); includes 18 minority (8 Black or African American, non-Hispanic/Latino; 4 Asian, non-Hispanic/Latino; 3 Hispanic/Latino; 1 Native Hawaiian or other Pacific Islander, non-Hispanic/Latino; 2 Two or more races, non-Hispanic/Latino), 1 international. Average age 27. 87 applicants, 60% accepted, 43 enrolled. In 2016, 39 master's awarded. *Degree requirements:* For master's, practicum. *Entrance requirements:* For master's, 3 letters of recommendation, resume, minimum QPA of 3.0, personal statement, interview. Additional exam requirements/recommendations for international students: Required—TOEFL, IELTS. Application fee: $35 ($60 for international students). Electronic applications accepted. *Expenses:* Tuition, state resident: full-time $9660; part-time $483 per credit. Tuition, nonresident: full-time $14,500; part-time $725 per credit. *Required fees:* $2410; $107 per credit. $75 per term. Tuition and fees vary according to course load, degree level and program. *Financial support:* Federal Work-Study and unspecified assistantships available. Financial award applicants required to submit FAFSA. *Unit head:* Dr. Ingrid Everett, Program Coordinator, 570-389-5120, Fax: 570-389-3030, E-mail: ieverett@bloomu.edu. *Application contact:* Jennifer Kessler, Administrative Assistant, 570-389-4015, Fax: 570-389-3054, E-mail: jkessler@bloomu.edu.

Bluffton University, Programs in Education, Bluffton, OH 45817. Offers faith-based education (MA Ed); intervention specialist (MA Ed); leadership (MA Ed); reading (MA Ed). *Accreditation:* NCATE. *Program availability:* Part-time. *Faculty:* 6 full-time (3 women), 1 part-time/adjunct (0 women). *Students:* 9 full-time (all women), 10 part-time (9 women); includes 1 minority (Black or African American, non-Hispanic/Latino). Average age 34. 14 applicants, 50% accepted, 6 enrolled. In 2016, 1 master's awarded. *Degree requirements:* For master's, action research project, public presentation. *Entrance requirements:* For master's, PRAXIS I, bachelor's degree, minimum GPA of 3.0. Additional exam requirements/recommendations for international students: Required—TOEFL. *Application deadline:* For fall admission, 8/15 priority date for domestic students, 6/15 priority date for international students; for spring admission, 12/15 priority date for domestic students, 9/15 priority date for international students. Applications are processed on a rolling basis. Application fee: $25. Electronic applications accepted. Application fee is waived when completed online. *Expenses:* $453 per credit. *Financial support:* Health care benefits available. Support available to part-time students. Financial award application deadline: 9/15; financial award applicants required to submit FAFSA. *Faculty research:* Mentoring. *Unit head:* Dr. Gayle M. Trollinger, Director of Graduate Programs in Education, 419-358-3341, E-mail: trollingerg@bluffton.edu. *Application contact:* Nancey Schortgen, Program Representative, 419-358-3202, Fax: 419-358-3399, E-mail: schortgenn@bluffton.edu.
Website: http://www.bluffton.edu/grad/

Bob Jones University, Graduate Programs, Greenville, SC 29614. Offers accountancy (MS); Bible (MA); Bible translation (MA); Biblical studies (Certificate); broadcast management (MS); business administration (MBA); church history (MA, PhD); church ministries (MA); church music (MM); cinema and video production (MA); counseling (MS); curriculum and instruction (Ed D); divinity (M Div); dramatic production (MA); educational leadership (MS, Ed D, Ed S); elementary education (M Ed, MAT); English (M Ed, MA, MAT); fine arts (MA); graphic design (MA); history (M Ed, MA); illustration (MA); interpretative speech (MA); mathematics (M Ed, MAT); medical missions (Certificate); ministry (MM, D Min); multi-categorical special education (M Ed, MAT); music (M Ed); New Testament interpretation (PhD); Old Testament interpretation (PhD); orchestral instrument performance (MM); organ performance (MM); pastoral studies (MA); personnel services (MS, Ed S); piano pedagogy (MM); piano performance (MM); platform arts (MA); radio and television broadcasting (MS); rhetoric and public address (MA); secondary education (M Ed); studio art (MA); teaching Bible (MA); theology (MA, PhD); voice performance (MM); youth ministries (MA); M Div/MM.

Boise State University, College of Education, Department of Curriculum, Instruction and Foundational Studies, Boise, ID 83725-1747. Offers curriculum and instruction (MA Ed, Ed D); educational leadership (M Ed); executive educational leadership (Ed S). *Accreditation:* NCATE. *Program availability:* Part-time. *Faculty:* 36. *Students:* 24 full-time (18 women), 180 part-time (113 women); includes 19 minority (1 Black or African American, non-Hispanic/Latino; 3 American Indian or Alaska Native, non-Hispanic/Latino; 3 Asian, non-Hispanic/Latino; 12 Hispanic/Latino), 6 international. Average age 36. 79 applicants, 67% accepted, 35 enrolled. In 2016, 36 master's, 6 other advanced degrees awarded. *Degree requirements:* For master's, thesis optional. *Entrance requirements:* For master's, minimum GPA of 3.0. Additional exam requirements/recommendations for international students: Required—TOEFL (minimum score 550 paper-based; 80 iBT), IELTS (minimum score 6). *Application deadline:* For fall admission, 3/1 for domestic and international students; for spring admission, 10/15 for domestic students, 10/1 for international students. Application fee: $65 ($95 for international students). Electronic applications accepted. *Expenses:* Tuition, state resident: full-time $6058; part-time $358 per credit hour. Tuition, nonresident: full-time $20,108; part-time $608 per credit hour. *Required fees:* $2108. Tuition and fees vary

according to program. *Financial support:* In 2016–17, 41 students received support. Scholarships/grants and unspecified assistantships available. Financial award application deadline: 3/1; financial award applicants required to submit FAFSA. *Unit head:* Dr. Philip P. Kelly, Department Chair, 208-426-4977, Fax: 208-426-4365. *Application contact:* Dr. Kelly Cross, Associate Chair, 208-426-2806, E-mail: kellycross@boisestate.edu.
Website: http://education.boisestate.edu/cifs/

Boston College, Lynch School of Education, Program in Curriculum and Instruction, Chestnut Hill, MA 02467-3800. Offers M Ed, PhD, CAES, JD/M Ed. *Program availability:* Part-time, evening/weekend. *Faculty:* 19 full-time (11 women). *Students:* 59 full-time (51 women), 100 part-time (74 women); includes 23 minority (7 Black or African American, non-Hispanic/Latino; 6 Asian, non-Hispanic/Latino; 8 Hispanic/Latino; 2 Two or more races, non-Hispanic/Latino), 28 international. Average age 28. 115 applicants, 55% accepted, 28 enrolled. In 2016, 61 master's, 11 doctorates, 1 other advanced degree awarded. Terminal master's awarded for partial completion of doctoral program. *Degree requirements:* For master's and CAES, comprehensive exam; for doctorate, comprehensive exam, thesis/dissertation. *Entrance requirements:* For master's and CAES, GRE General Test or MAT; for doctorate, GRE General Test. Additional exam requirements/recommendations for international students: Required—TOEFL (minimum score 550 paper-based; 100 iBT). *Application deadline:* For fall admission, 12/1 priority date for domestic and international students; for spring admission, 11/1 priority date for domestic and international students. Application fee: $65. Electronic applications accepted. Tuition and fees vary according to program. *Financial support:* Federal Work-Study, scholarships/grants, and tuition waivers (partial) available. Support available to part-time students. Financial award applicants required to submit FAFSA. *Unit head:* Dr. Susan Bruce, Chairperson, 617-552-4214, Fax: 617-552-0398. *Application contact:* Kimberly Rose, Graduate Admission Assistant, 617-552-4214, Fax: 617-552-0398, E-mail: roseki@bc.edu.
Website: http://www.bc.edu/schools/lsoe/academics/departments/teseci/graduate/curriculum.html

Bowling Green State University, Graduate College, College of Education and Human Development, School of Teaching and Learning, Program in Curriculum and Teaching, Bowling Green, OH 43403. Offers M Ed. *Program availability:* Part-time, evening/weekend. *Degree requirements:* For master's, thesis or alternative. *Entrance requirements:* For master's, GRE General Test or PRAXIS. Additional exam requirements/recommendations for international students: Required—TOEFL. *Application deadline:* For fall admission, 3/15 priority date for domestic students. Applications are processed on a rolling basis. Application fee: $30. Electronic applications accepted. *Financial support:* Research assistantships with full tuition reimbursements, teaching assistantships with full tuition reimbursements, career-related internships or fieldwork, Federal Work-Study, and unspecified assistantships available. Financial award applicants required to submit FAFSA. *Faculty research:* Cognitive development in cultural context, sociocultural and activity theory, philosophy in education, performance assessment. *Unit head:* Dr. Mark Seals, Director. *Application contact:* Dr. Mark Seals, Director.

Bradley University, The Graduate School, College of Education and Health Sciences, Department of Teacher Education, Peoria, IL 61625-0002. Offers curriculum and instruction (MA). *Accreditation:* NCATE. *Program availability:* Part-time, evening/weekend. *Degree requirements:* For master's, comprehensive exam, thesis optional. *Entrance requirements:* For master's, GRE General Test or MAT, 2 letters of recommendation. Additional exam requirements/recommendations for international students: Required—TOEFL (minimum score 550 paper-based; 79 iBT), IELTS (minimum score 6.5). *Application deadline:* For fall admission, 5/15 priority date for domestic and international students; for spring admission, 10/15 priority date for domestic and international students. Applications are processed on a rolling basis. Application fee: $40 ($50 for international students). Electronic applications accepted. *Expenses: Tuition:* Full-time $7650; part-time $850 per credit. *Required fees:* $50 per credit. One-time fee: $100 full-time. *Financial support:* Career-related internships or fieldwork, scholarships/grants, tuition waivers (partial), and unspecified assistantships available. Financial award application deadline: 4/1. *Unit head:* Dr. Dean Cantu, Chairperson, 309-677-3190, E-mail: dcantu@bradley.edu. *Application contact:* Kayla Carroll, Director of International Admissions and Student Services, 309-677-2375, E-mail: klcarroll@fsmail.bradley.edu.
Website: http://www.bradley.edu/academic/departments/te/

Brandon University, Faculty of Education, Brandon, MB R7A 6A9, Canada. Offers curriculum and instruction (M Ed, Diploma); educational administration (M Ed, Diploma); guidance and counseling (M Ed, Diploma); special education (M Ed, Diploma). *Degree requirements:* For master's, thesis. *Entrance requirements:* For master's, minimum GPA of 3.0, teaching certificate or equivalent. Additional exam requirements/recommendations for international students: Required—TOEFL. *Faculty research:* Comparative education, environmental studies, parent/school council.

Brescia University, Program in Teacher Leadership, Owensboro, KY 42301-3023. Offers MSTL. *Program availability:* Part-time, evening/weekend. *Degree requirements:* For master's, action research project. *Entrance requirements:* For master's, PRAXIS II, NTE, or GRE, interview, minimum GPA of 2.75, BA or BS, two letters of reference, professional resume. Electronic applications accepted.

Buena Vista University, School of Education, Storm Lake, IA 50588. Offers curriculum and instruction (M Ed), including effective teaching, TESL; school guidance and counseling (MS Ed). Program offered in summer only. *Program availability:* Part-time, evening/weekend, online learning. *Degree requirements:* For master's, thesis, fieldwork/practicum, capstone portfolio. *Entrance requirements:* For master's, Analytical Writing Assessment (in-house), minimum undergraduate GPA of 2.75. Electronic applications accepted. *Faculty research:* Reading, curriculum, educational psychology, special education.

Caldwell University, Graduate Studies, Division of Education, Caldwell, NJ 07006-6195. Offers curriculum and instruction (MA); education (Ed D, Postbaccalaureate Certificate); educational administration (MA); learning disabilities teacher-consultant (Post-Master's Certificate); literacy instruction (MA); principal (Post-Master's Certificate); reading specialist (Post-Master's Certificate); special education (MA), including special education, teaching of students with disabilities, teaching of students with disabilities and learning disabilities teacher-consultant; superintendent (Post-Master's Certificate); supervisor (Post-Master's Certificate). *Program availability:* Part-time, evening/weekend. *Degree requirements:* For master's, comprehensive exam (for some programs). *Entrance requirements:* For master's, PRAXIS, 3 years of work experience, prior teaching certification. Additional exam requirements/recommendations for international students: Required—TOEFL (minimum score 580 paper-based). Electronic applications accepted. *Faculty research:* Curriculum and instruction, secondary education, special education, education and technology.

California Baptist University, Program in Education, Riverside, CA 92504-3206. Offers educational leadership (MS); educational leadership for faith-based institutions (MS); educational leadership for public institutions (MS); educational technology (MS); instructional computer applications (MS); international education (MS); leadership and adult learning (MS); leadership and organizational studies (MS); online teaching and learning (MS); reading (MS); science education (MA); special education in mild/moderate disabilities (MS); special education in moderate/severe disabilities (MS); teacher leadership (MS); teaching (MS); teaching and learning (MS). *Program availability:* Part-time, evening/weekend, 100% online, blended/hybrid learning. *Faculty:* 20 full-time (8 women), 11 part-time/adjunct (7 women). *Students:* 191 full-time (148 women), 234 part-time (178 women); includes 194 minority (23 Black or African American, non-Hispanic/Latino; 5 American Indian or Alaska Native, non-Hispanic/Latino; 15 Asian, non-Hispanic/Latino; 131 Hispanic/Latino; 4 Native Hawaiian or other Pacific Islander, non-Hispanic/Latino; 16 Two or more races, non-Hispanic/Latino), 2 international. Average age 31. 277 applicants, 61% accepted, 150 enrolled. In 2016, 280 master's awarded. *Degree requirements:* For master's, comprehensive exam, project, or thesis. *Entrance requirements:* For master's, minimum undergraduate GPA of 2.75; 500-word essay; three letters of recommendation; two prerequisite courses completed with minimum C grade. Additional exam requirements/recommendations for international students: Required—TOEFL (minimum score 80 iBT). *Application deadline:* For fall admission, 8/1 priority date for domestic students, 7/1 for international students; for spring admission, 12/1 priority date for domestic students, 11/1 for international students. Applications are processed on a rolling basis. Application fee: $45. Electronic applications accepted. *Expenses:* Contact institution. *Financial support:* In 2016–17, 162 students received support. Federal Work-Study and scholarships/grants available. Financial award applicants required to submit CSS PROFILE or FAFSA. *Faculty research:* Leadership development, complexity theory, faith and learning, special education, social and philosophical contexts of education. *Unit head:* Dr. John Shoup, Dean, School of Education, 951-343-4516, E-mail: jshoup@calbaptist.edu.
Website: http://www.calbaptist.edu/mastersined/

California Coast University, School of Education, Santa Ana, CA 92701. Offers administration (M Ed); curriculum and instruction (M Ed); educational administration (Ed D); educational psychology (Ed D); organizational leadership (Ed D). *Program availability:* Online learning.

California State Polytechnic University, Pomona, Master's Programs in Education, Pomona, CA 91768-2557. Offers curriculum and instruction (MA), including literacy studies. *Program availability:* Part-time, evening/weekend. *Students:* 21 full-time (14 women), 95 part-time (67 women); includes 69 minority (8 Black or African American, non-Hispanic/Latino; 1 American Indian or Alaska Native, non-Hispanic/Latino; 10 Asian, non-Hispanic/Latino; 48 Hispanic/Latino; 2 Two or more races, non-Hispanic/Latino), 4 international. Average age 34. 27 applicants, 93% accepted, 14 enrolled. In 2016, 50 master's awarded. *Entrance requirements:* Additional exam requirements/recommendations for international students: Required—TOEFL. *Application deadline:* Applications are processed on a rolling basis. Application fee: $55. Electronic applications accepted. *Expenses:* Contact institution. *Financial support:* Application deadline: 3/2; applicants required to submit FAFSA. *Unit head:* Kelly Mitchell, Graduate Studies Coordinator, 909-869-2358, Fax: 909-869-2722, E-mail: klmitchell@cpp.edu. *Application contact:* Andrew M Wright, Director of Admissions, 909-869-3130, Fax: 909-869-4529, E-mail: awright@cpp.edu.
Website: http://www.cpp.edu/~ceis/education/masters-programs/index.shtml

California State University, Chico, Office of Graduate Studies, College of Communication and Education, School of Education, Chico, CA 95929-0722. Offers curriculum and instruction (MA); teaching English learners and special education advising patterns (MA), including special education, teaching English learners. *Program availability:* Part-time. *Faculty:* 26 full-time (20 women), 48 part-time/adjunct (35 women). *Students:* 45 full-time (33 women), 30 part-time (23 women); includes 26 minority (1 Black or African American, non-Hispanic/Latino; 4 Asian, non-Hispanic/Latino; 16 Hispanic/Latino; 1 Native Hawaiian or other Pacific Islander, non-Hispanic/Latino; 4 Two or more races, non-Hispanic/Latino). 29 applicants, 69% accepted, 16 enrolled. In 2016, 69 master's awarded. *Degree requirements:* For master's, thesis or project and comprehensive exam. *Entrance requirements:* For master's, writing assessment, two letters of recommendation, statement of purpose. Additional exam requirements/recommendations for international students: Required—TOEFL (minimum score 550 paper-based; 80 iBT), IELTS (minimum score 6.5), PTE (minimum score 59). *Application deadline:* For fall admission, 3/1 priority date for domestic students, 3/1 for international students; for spring admission, 9/15 priority date for domestic students, 9/15 for international students. Application fee: $55. Electronic applications accepted. *Financial support:* Fellowships, career-related internships or fieldwork, scholarships/grants, and stipends available. Financial award application deadline: 3/1; financial award applicants required to submit FAFSA. *Unit head:* Dr. Deborah Summers, Director, 530-898-6421, Fax: 530-898-6177, E-mail: educ@csuchico.edu. *Application contact:* Judy L. Morris, Graduate Admission Coordinator, 530-898-5416, Fax: 530-898-3342, E-mail: jlmorris@csuchico.edu.
Website: http://www.csuchico.edu/soe/

California State University, Dominguez Hills, College of Education, Division of Graduate Education, Program in Curriculum and Instruction, Carson, CA 90747-0001. Offers MA. *Program availability:* Part-time, evening/weekend. *Degree requirements:* For master's, comprehensive exam. *Entrance requirements:* For master's, minimum GPA of 2.75. Additional exam requirements/recommendations for international students: Required—TOEFL. *Faculty research:* Cooperative learning, student engagement.

California State University, Fresno, Division of Research and Graduate Studies, Kremen School of Education and Human Development, Department of Curriculum and Instruction, Fresno, CA 93740-8027. Offers education (MA), including curriculum and instruction. *Accreditation:* NCATE. *Program availability:* Part-time, evening/weekend. *Degree requirements:* For master's, thesis or alternative. *Entrance requirements:* For master's, GRE General Test, MAT, minimum GPA of 2.75. Additional exam requirements/recommendations for international students: Required—TOEFL. *Application deadline:* For fall admission, 5/1 for domestic and international students; for spring admission, 10/1 for domestic and international students. Applications are processed on a rolling basis. Application fee: $55. Electronic applications accepted. *Financial support:* Career-related internships or fieldwork, Federal Work-Study, scholarships/grants, and research awards available. Support available to part-time students. Financial award application deadline: 3/1; financial award applicants required to submit FAFSA. *Faculty research:* Teacher excellence, teacher quality improvement, online assessment. *Unit head:* Dr. Jacques Benninga, Chair, 559-278-0240, Fax: 559-278-0107, E-mail: jackb@csufresno.edu. *Application contact:* Dr. Roy Bohlin, Graduate Program Coordinator, 559-278-0245, Fax: 559-278-0107, E-mail: royb@csufresno.edu.
Website: http://www.fresnostate.edu/kremen/departments/ci.html

California State University, Los Angeles, Graduate Studies, Charter College of Education, Division of Curriculum and Instruction, Los Angeles, CA 90032-8530. Offers elementary teaching (MA). *Program availability:* Part-time, evening/weekend. *Entrance requirements:* For master's, minimum GPA of 2.75 in last 90 units of course work, teaching certificate. Additional exam requirements/recommendations for international students: Required—TOEFL (minimum score 500 paper-based). Electronic applications accepted. *Faculty research:* Media, language arts, mathematics, computers, drug-free schools.

Curriculum and Instruction

California State University, Northridge, Graduate Studies, Michael D. Eisner College of Education, Department of Elementary Education, Northridge, CA 91330. Offers curriculum and instruction (MA); language and literacy (MA); multilingual/multicultural education (MA). *Accreditation:* NCATE. *Program availability:* Part-time, evening/weekend. *Faculty:* 12 full-time (4 women), 17 part-time/adjunct (7 women). *Students:* 37 part-time (33 women); includes 21 minority (1 Asian, non-Hispanic/Latino; 17 Hispanic/Latino; 3 Two or more races, non-Hispanic/Latino). Average age 29. 44 applicants, 55% accepted, 20 enrolled. *Degree requirements:* For master's, comprehensive exam. *Entrance requirements:* For master's, GRE General Test or minimum GPA of 3.0. Additional exam requirements/recommendations for international students: Required—TOEFL. *Application deadline:* For fall admission, 11/30 for domestic students. Application fee: $55. *Expenses:* Tuition, state resident: full-time $4152. *Financial support:* Federal Work-Study available. Financial award application deadline: 3/1. *Unit head:* Dr. Joyce Burstein, Chair, 818-677-2621.
Website: http://www.csun.edu/eisner-education/elementary-education

California State University, Sacramento, Office of Graduate Studies, College of Education, Graduate and Professional Studies in Education, Sacramento, CA 95819. Offers child development (MA); counseling (MS); curriculum and instruction (MA); education (Ed D); education leadership and policy studies (MA), including higher education, PreK-12; educational technology (MA); gender equity (MA); language and literacy (MA); multicultural education (MA); school psychology (MA); special education (MA); workforce development advocacy (MA). *Program availability:* Part-time. *Students:* 446 full-time (335 women), 125 part-time (97 women); includes 298 minority (39 Black or African American, non-Hispanic/Latino; 3 American Indian or Alaska Native, non-Hispanic/Latino; 97 Asian, non-Hispanic/Latino; 153 Hispanic/Latino; 6 Native Hawaiian or other Pacific Islander, non-Hispanic/Latino). Average age 32. 540 applicants, 76% accepted, 250 enrolled. In 2016, 107 master's, 7 doctorates awarded. *Degree requirements:* For master's, thesis or project; writing proficiency exam. *Entrance requirements:* For master's, minimum GPA of 2.5, 3.0 in last 60 units. Additional exam requirements/recommendations for international students: Required—TOEFL (minimum score 550 paper-based; 80 iBT). *Application deadline:* For fall admission, 2/15 for domestic students, 1/15 for international students. Applications are processed on a rolling basis. Application fee: $55. Electronic applications accepted. *Expenses:* $4,302 full-time tuition and fees per semester, $2,796 part-time. *Financial support:* Career-related internships or fieldwork and Federal Work-Study available. Support available to part-time students. Financial award application deadline: 3/1; financial award applicants required to submit FAFSA. *Unit head:* Dr. Susan Heredia, Chair, 916-278-5942, E-mail: coe@csus.edu. *Application contact:* Jose Martinez, Graduate Admissions Supervisor, 916-278-7871, E-mail: martinj@skymail.csus.edu.
Website: http://www.csus.edu/coe/academics/graduate/index.html

California State University, Stanislaus, College of Education, Program in Education (MA), Turlock, CA 95382. Offers curriculum and instruction (MA), including education technology, elementary education, multilingual education, physical education, reading, secondary education, special education; school administration (MA); school counseling (MA). *Program availability:* Part-time, evening/weekend. *Degree requirements:* For master's, comprehensive exam (for some programs), thesis (for some programs). *Entrance requirements:* For master's, MAT, GRE, or CBEST (varies by concentration), 3 letters of recommendation, personal statement. Additional exam requirements/recommendations for international students: Required—TOEFL (minimum score 550 paper-based). Electronic applications accepted. *Faculty research:* Children's perspectives on historical events, method elementary schools dual language education, K-12 reading programs.

Calvary University, Graduate School and Seminary, Kansas City, MO 64147. Offers Bible and theology (MS); Biblical counseling (MA); education (MS), including administration and leadership, Christian education, curriculum and instruction, elementary education; organization development (MS); pastoral studies (M Div). *Program availability:* Part-time, evening/weekend. *Faculty:* 6 full-time (2 women), 2 part-time/adjunct (1 woman). *Students:* 11 full-time (3 women), 29 part-time (15 women); includes 12 minority (4 Black or African American, non-Hispanic/Latino; 1 American Indian or Alaska Native, non-Hispanic/Latino; 6 Asian, non-Hispanic/Latino; 1 Native Hawaiian or other Pacific Islander, non-Hispanic/Latino). Average age 39. In 2016, 19 master's awarded. *Degree requirements:* For master's, variable foreign language requirement, comprehensive exam, thesis or alternative. *Entrance requirements:* For master's, minimum GPA of 2.5, BA or BS, doctrine agreement. Additional exam requirements/recommendations for international students: Required—TOEFL (minimum score 550 paper-based). *Application deadline:* Applications are processed on a rolling basis. Application fee: $0. Electronic applications accepted. *Expenses: Tuition:* Full-time $7200; part-time $4800 per credit. *Required fees:* $640; $520 per credit. $140 per semester. One-time fee: $100. Tuition and fees vary according to program. *Financial support:* In 2016–17, 8 students received support. Scholarships/grants available. Financial award application deadline: 11/5; financial award applicants required to submit FAFSA. *Unit head:* Dr. Thomas Baurain, Director of Seminary, 816-322-0110 Ext. 1502, Fax: 816-331-4474, E-mail: thomas.baurain@calvary.edu. *Application contact:* Ann Rogers, Admissions Office Assistant, 800-326-3960 Ext. 1321, Fax: 816-331-4474, E-mail: admissions@calvary.edu.
Website: http://www.calvary.edu

Calvin College, Graduate Programs in Education, Grand Rapids, MI 49546-4388. Offers curriculum and instruction (M Ed). *Accreditation:* TEAC. *Program availability:* Part-time. *Faculty:* 12 full-time (5 women). *Students:* 4 full-time (3 women), 120 part-time (80 women); includes 13 minority (3 Black or African American, non-Hispanic/Latino; 4 Asian, non-Hispanic/Latino; 1 Hispanic/Latino; 5 Two or more races, non-Hispanic/Latino), 15 international. Average age 29. 24 applicants, 100% accepted, 24 enrolled. In 2016, 23 master's awarded. *Degree requirements:* For master's, thesis or seminar. *Entrance requirements:* For master's, teaching certificate. Additional exam requirements/recommendations for international students: Required—TOEFL (minimum score 550 paper-based; 80 iBT). *Application deadline:* For fall admission, 8/1 priority date for domestic students, 5/1 priority date for international students; for spring admission, 1/1 priority date for domestic students, 12/1 priority date for international students; for summer admission, 5/18 for domestic students. Applications are processed on a rolling basis. Application fee: $0. Electronic applications accepted. *Expenses:* Contact institution. *Financial support:* Federal Work-Study, scholarships/grants, and tuition waivers (full and partial) available. Financial award application deadline: 4/3; financial award applicants required to submit FAFSA. *Faculty research:* Literacy, racialized gender and gendered identity, teacher learning, learning disabilities identification, leadership. *Unit head:* Dr. David Smith, Graduate Program Director, 616-526-6158, Fax: 616-526-6505, E-mail: dsmith@calvin.edu. *Application contact:* Cindi Hoekstra, Program Manager, 616-526-6158, Fax: 616-526-6505, E-mail: choekstr@calvin.edu.
Website: http://www.calvin.edu/academic/graduate_studies

Cambridge College, School of Education, Cambridge, MA 02138-5304. Offers autism specialist (M Ed); autism/behavior analyst (M Ed); behavior analyst (Post-Master's Certificate); behavioral management (M Ed); early childhood teacher (M Ed); education specialist in curriculum and instruction (CAGS); educational leadership (Ed D); elementary teacher (M Ed); English as a second language (M Ed, Certificate); general science (M Ed); health education (Post-Master's Certificate); health/family and consumer sciences (M Ed); history (M Ed); individualized (M Ed); information technology literacy (M Ed); instructional technology (M Ed); interdisciplinary studies (M Ed); library teacher (M Ed); literacy education (M Ed); mathematics (M Ed); mathematics specialist (Certificate); middle school mathematics and science (M Ed); school administration (M Ed, CAGS); school guidance counselor (M Ed); school nurse education (M Ed); school social worker/school adjustment counselor (M Ed); special education administrator (CAGS); special education/moderate disabilities (M Ed); teaching skills and methodologies (M Ed). *Program availability:* Part-time, evening/weekend, online learning. *Degree requirements:* For master's, thesis, internship/practicum (licensure program only); for doctorate, thesis/dissertation; for other advanced degree, thesis. *Entrance requirements:* For master's, interview, resume, documentation of licensure, 2 professional references; for doctorate, official transcripts, interview, resume, documentation of licensure (if any), written personal statement/essay, portfolio of scholarly and professional work, qualifying assessment, 2 professional references, health insurance, immunizations form; for other advanced degree, official transcripts, interview, resume, documentation of licensure (if any), written personal statement/essay, 2 professional references, health insurance, immunizations form. Additional exam requirements/recommendations for international students: Required—TOEFL (minimum score 550 paper-based; 79 iBT), Michigan English Language Assessment Battery (minimum score 85); Recommended—IELTS (minimum score 6). Electronic applications accepted. *Expenses:* Contact institution. *Faculty research:* Adult education, accelerated learning, mathematics education, brain compatible learning, special education and law.

Capella University, School of Education, Doctoral Programs in Education, Minneapolis, MN 55402. Offers curriculum and instruction (PhD); educational leadership and management (Ed D); instructional design for online learning (PhD); K-12 studies in education (PhD); leadership for higher education (PhD); leadership in educational administration (PhD); postsecondary and adult education (PhD); professional studies in education (PhD); reading and literacy (Ed D); special education leadership (PhD); training and performance improvement (PhD).

Capella University, School of Education, Master's Programs in Education, Minneapolis, MN 55402. Offers adult education (MS); curriculum and instruction (MS); early childhood education (MS); enrollment management (MS); higher education leadership and management (MS); instructional design for online learning (MS); integrative studies (MS); K-12 studies in education (MS); leadership in educational administration (MS); reading and literacy (MS); special education teaching (MS).

Caribbean University, Graduate School, Bayamón, PR 00960-0493. Offers administration and supervision (MA Ed); criminal justice (MA); curriculum and instruction (MA Ed, PhD), including elementary education (MA Ed), English education (MA Ed), history education (MA Ed), mathematics education (MA Ed), primary education (MA Ed), science education (MA Ed), Spanish education (MA Ed); educational technology in instructional systems (MA Ed); gerontology (MSN); human resources (MBA); museology, archiving and art history (MA Ed); neonatal pediatrics (MSN); physical education (MA Ed); special education (MA Ed). *Entrance requirements:* For master's, interview, minimum GPA of 2.5.

Carson-Newman University, Graduate Program in Education, Jefferson City, TN 37760. Offers curriculum and instruction (M Ed); educational leadership (M Ed); elementary education (MAT); school counseling (MS); secondary education (MAT); teaching English as a second language (MATESL). *Accreditation:* NCATE. *Program availability:* Part-time, evening/weekend, 100% online, blended/hybrid learning. *Degree requirements:* For master's, thesis or alternative. *Entrance requirements:* For master's, PRAXIS II or GRE with minimum score of 290 on the verbal and quantitative components (for MAT), minimum GPA of 3.0 in major, 2.5 overall. Additional exam requirements/recommendations for international students: Recommended—TOEFL (minimum score 79 iBT), IELTS (minimum score 6.5), TSE (minimum score 53). *Expenses: Tuition:* Full-time $10,142; part-time $461 per credit hour. *Required fees:* $300; $150 per semester. One-time fee: $150.

Castleton University, Division of Graduate Studies, Department of Education, Program in Curriculum and Instruction, Castleton, VT 05735. Offers MA Ed. *Program availability:* Part-time, evening/weekend. *Degree requirements:* For master's, thesis or alternative. *Entrance requirements:* For master's, GRE General Test, MAT, interview, minimum undergraduate GPA of 3.0.

Cedarville University, Graduate Programs, Cedarville, OH 45314. Offers business administration (MBA); curriculum (M Ed); educational administration (M Ed); family nurse practitioner (MSN); global health ministries (MSN); instruction (M Ed); ministry (M Min); pharmacy (Pharm D). *Program availability:* Part-time, evening/weekend, online learning. *Degree requirements:* For master's, thesis. *Entrance requirements:* For master's, GRE, 2 professional recommendations; for doctorate, PCAT, professional recommendation from a practicing pharmacist or current employer/supervisor, resume, essay, interview. Additional exam requirements/recommendations for international students: Required—TOEFL (minimum score 550 paper-based; 80 iBT). Electronic applications accepted. *Expenses:* Contact institution.

Central Michigan University, Central Michigan University Global Campus, Program in Education, Mount Pleasant, MI 48859. Offers college teaching (Graduate Certificate); community college (MA); curriculum and instruction (MA); educational technology (MA, DET); reading and literacy K-12 (MA); school principalship (MA), including charter school leadership; training and development (MA). *Accreditation:* TEAC. *Program availability:* Part-time, evening/weekend. *Faculty:* 24 full-time (14 women), 24 part-time/adjunct (8 women). *Students:* 888 (620 women); includes 225 minority (142 Black or African American, non-Hispanic/Latino; 8 American Indian or Alaska Native, non-Hispanic/Latino; 16 Asian, non-Hispanic/Latino; 13 Hispanic/Latino; 46 Two or more races, non-Hispanic/Latino). Average age 37. In 2016, 76 master's awarded. *Entrance requirements:* For master's, minimum GPA of 2.7 in major. Additional exam requirements/recommendations for international students: Required—TOEFL. *Application deadline:* Applications are processed on a rolling basis. Application fee: $50. Electronic applications accepted. *Financial support:* Scholarships/grants available. Support available to part-time students. *Unit head:* Kaleb Patrick, Director, 989-774-3144, E-mail: patri1kg@cmich.edu. *Application contact:* 877-268-4636, E-mail: cmuglobal@cmich.edu.

Central Michigan University, College of Graduate Studies, College of Education and Human Services, Department of Educational Leadership, Mount Pleasant, MI 48859. Offers educational leadership (Ed D), including educational technology (Ed D, Ed S), higher education leadership, K-12 curriculum, K-12 leadership; general educational administration (Ed S), including administrative leadership K-12, educational technology (Ed D, Ed S), higher education administration, instructional leadership K-12; school principalship (MA), including charter school leadership, site-based leadership; student affairs administration (MA); teacher leadership (MA). *Program availability:* Part-time, evening/weekend. *Degree requirements:* For master's and Ed S, thesis or alternative; for doctorate, thesis/dissertation. *Entrance requirements:* For doctorate, GRE or MAT, master's degree, minimum GPA of 3.5, 3 years of professional education experience.

Electronic applications accepted. *Faculty research:* Elementary administration, secondary administration, student achievement, in-service training, internships in administration.

Central Washington University, Graduate Studies and Research, College of Education and Professional Studies, Department of Educational Foundations and Curriculum, Program in Master Teacher, Ellensburg, WA 98926. Offers M Ed. *Program availability:* Part-time. *Degree requirements:* For master's, comprehensive exam (for some programs), thesis or alternative. *Entrance requirements:* For master's, minimum GPA of 3.0, 1 year of contracted teaching experience. Additional exam requirements/recommendations for international students: Required—TOEFL (minimum score 550 paper-based; 79 iBT), IELTS (minimum score 6.5). Electronic applications accepted.

Chapman University, College of Educational Studies, Orange, CA 92866. Offers counseling (MA), including school counseling (MA, Credential); education (PhD), including cultural and curricular studies, disability studies, leadership studies, school psychology (PhD, Credential); educational psychology (MA); leadership development (MA); multiple subjects (Credential), including Spanish/English bilingual; pupil personnel services (Credential), including school counseling (MA, Credential), school psychology (PhD, Credential); school psychology (Ed S); single subject (Credential); special education (MA, Credential), including mild/moderate (Credential), moderate/severe (Credential); teaching (MA), including elementary education, secondary education, secondary music education. *Accreditation:* TEAC. *Program availability:* Part-time, evening/weekend. *Faculty:* 29 full-time (14 women), 36 part-time/adjunct (28 women). *Students:* 186 full-time (148 women), 186 part-time (134 women); includes 144 minority (9 Black or African American, non-Hispanic/Latino; 39 Asian, non-Hispanic/Latino; 78 Hispanic/Latino; 2 Native Hawaiian or other Pacific Islander, non-Hispanic/Latino; 16 Two or more races, non-Hispanic/Latino), 8 international. Average age 29. 143 applicants, 63% accepted, 64 enrolled. In 2016, 111 master's, 24 doctorates awarded. *Degree requirements:* For doctorate, thesis/dissertation. *Entrance requirements:* Additional exam requirements/recommendations for international students: Required—TOEFL (minimum score 550 paper-based, 80 iBT), IELTS (6.5), PTE Academic (53), or CAE. *Application deadline:* Applications are processed on a rolling basis. Application fee: $60. Electronic applications accepted. *Expenses:* Contact institution. *Financial support:* Fellowships and scholarships/grants available. Financial award application deadline: 3/2; financial award applicants required to submit FAFSA. *Unit head:* Dr. Margaret Grogan, Dean, 714-516-5968, E-mail: grogan@chapman.edu. *Application contact:* Sara Simon, Graduate Admission Counselor, 714-997-6770, E-mail: simon@chapman.edu.
Website: http://www.chapman.edu/CES/

City University of Seattle, Graduate Division, Albright School of Education, Seattle, WA 98121. Offers administrator certification (Certificate); curriculum and instruction (M Ed); elementary education (MIT); guidance and counseling (M Ed); leadership (M Ed); reading and literacy (M Ed); school counseling (M Ed); special education (MIT); superintendent certification (Certificate). *Program availability:* Part-time, evening/weekend, online learning. *Degree requirements:* For master's, comprehensive exam (for some programs), thesis (for some programs). *Entrance requirements:* For master's, baccalaureate degree or equivalent from an accredited or otherwise recognized institution. Additional exam requirements/recommendations for international students: Required—TOEFL (minimum score 567 paper-based; 87 iBT); Recommended—IELTS. Electronic applications accepted. *Expenses:* Contact institution.

Clarion University of Pennsylvania, Office of Transfer, Adult and Graduate Admissions, Master of Education Program, Clarion, PA 16214. Offers curriculum and instruction (M Ed); early childhood (M Ed); math education (M Ed); reading (M Ed); science education (M Ed); special education (M Ed); technology (M Ed). *Accreditation:* NCATE. *Program availability:* Part-time, evening/weekend, 100% online, blended/hybrid learning. *Faculty:* 12 full-time (8 women), 5 part-time/adjunct (all women). *Students:* 17 full-time (15 women), 97 part-time (78 women); includes 1 minority (Two or more races, non-Hispanic/Latino). Average age 29. 76 applicants, 99% accepted, 48 enrolled. In 2016, 34 master's awarded. *Degree requirements:* For master's, comprehensive exam, thesis, or portfolio. *Entrance requirements:* For master's, minimum QPA of 3.0. Additional exam requirements/recommendations for international students: Required—TOEFL (minimum score 550 paper-based; 80 iBT), IELTS (minimum score 7). *Application deadline:* For fall admission, 8/1 for domestic students, 4/15 for international students; for spring admission, 8/1 for domestic students, 9/15 for international students. Applications are processed on a rolling basis. Application fee: $40. Electronic applications accepted. *Expenses:* $632.35 per credit. *Financial support:* Career-related internships or fieldwork, Federal Work-Study, scholarships/grants, and unspecified assistantships available. Support available to part-time students. Financial award application deadline: 3/1; financial award applicants required to submit FAFSA. *Unit head:* Dr. John McCullough, Chair, Department of Education, 814-393-2104, Fax: 814-393-2446, E-mail: gradstudies@clarion.edu. *Application contact:* Dana Bearer, Associate Director for Transfer, Adult, and Graduate Programs, 814-393-2337, Fax: 814-393-2722, E-mail: gradstudies@clarion.edu.

Clark Atlanta University, School of Education, Department of Curriculum, Atlanta, GA 30314. Offers special education general curriculum (MA); teaching math and science (MAT). *Program availability:* Part-time. *Faculty:* 2 full-time (both women), 1 part-time/adjunct (0 women). *Students:* 6 full-time (1 woman), 2 part-time (1 woman); includes 6 minority (all Black or African American, non-Hispanic/Latino), 1 international. Average age 34. 17 applicants, 76% accepted, 2 enrolled. In 2016, 2 master's awarded. *Degree requirements:* For master's, one foreign language, comprehensive exam. *Entrance requirements:* For master's, GRE General Test, minimum undergraduate GPA of 2.6. Additional exam requirements/recommendations for international students: Required—TOEFL (minimum score 500 paper-based; 61 iBT). *Application deadline:* For fall admission, 4/1 for domestic and international students; for spring admission, 11/1 for domestic and international students. Applications are processed on a rolling basis. Application fee: $40 ($55 for international students). *Expenses: Tuition:* Full-time $15,498; part-time $861 per credit hour. *Required fees:* $1326; $1326 per credit hour. Tuition and fees vary according to course load. *Financial support:* Career-related internships or fieldwork, Federal Work-Study, scholarships/grants, and unspecified assistantships available. Support available to part-time students. Financial award application deadline: 4/30; financial award applicants required to submit FAFSA. *Unit head:* Dr. James Young, Chairperson, 404-880-6079, E-mail: jyoung@cau.edu. *Application contact:* Graduate Program Admissions, 404-880-8483, E-mail: graduateadmissions@cau.edu.
Website: http://www.cau.edu/school-of-education/Dept-of-Curriculum-and-Instruction/index.html

Clarks Summit University, Graduate Studies, South Abington Township, PA 18411. Offers Bible (MA); counseling (MA, MS); curriculum and instruction (M Ed); educational administration (M Ed); intercultural studies (MA); literature (MA); missions (MA); organizational leadership (MA); reading specialist (M Ed); secondary English/communications (M Ed); social entrepreneurship (MA); worldview studies (MA). MA in missions program available only for Association of Baptists for World Evangelism missionary personnel. *Program availability:* Part-time, evening/weekend, online learning.

Entrance requirements: Additional exam requirements/recommendations for international students: Required—TOEFL (minimum score 500 paper-based).

Clemson University, Graduate School, College of Education, Department of Teaching and Learning, Program in Curriculum and Instruction, Clemson, SC 29634. Offers PhD. *Accreditation:* NCATE. *Program availability:* Part-time, evening/weekend. *Faculty:* 15 full-time (12 women). *Students:* 10 full-time (8 women), 14 part-time (10 women); includes 4 minority (1 Black or African American, non-Hispanic/Latino; 3 Hispanic/Latino), 4 international. Average age 35. 19 applicants, 37% accepted, 4 enrolled. In 2016, 8 doctorates awarded. *Degree requirements:* For doctorate, comprehensive exam, thesis/dissertation. *Entrance requirements:* For doctorate, GRE General Test, unofficial transcripts, resume, letter of intent, letters of recommendation. Additional exam requirements/recommendations for international students: Required—TOEFL (minimum score 540 paper-based; 80 iBT). *Application deadline:* For fall admission, 4/1 for domestic and international students. Applications are processed on a rolling basis. Application fee: $80 ($90 for international students). Electronic applications accepted. *Expenses:* $4,264 per semester full-time resident, $8,485 per semester full-time non-resident, $471 per credit hour part-time resident, $942 per credit hour part-time non-resident. *Financial support:* In 2016–17, 9 students received support, including 1 research assistantship with partial tuition reimbursement available (averaging $20,571 per year), 8 teaching assistantships with partial tuition reimbursements available (averaging $14,125 per year); career-related internships or fieldwork also available. Financial award application deadline: 4/1. *Faculty research:* Elementary and early childhood education, secondary education (English, math, social studies, and science), special education, reading and literacy. *Unit head:* Dr. Jeff Marshall, Department Chair, 864-656-2059, E-mail: marsha9@clemson.edu. *Application contact:* Alison Search, Student Services Coordinator, 864-250-8880, E-mail: alisonp@clemson.edu.
Website: http://www.clemson.edu/education/academics/doctoral-programs/phd-doctorate-curriculum-instruction/index.html

The College at Brockport, State University of New York, School of Education, Health, and Human Services, Department of Education and Human Development, Program in Childhood Curriculum Specialist, Brockport, NY 14420-2997. Offers MS Ed. *Accreditation:* NCATE. *Program availability:* Part-time. *Students:* 1 part-time (0 women). In 2016, 1 master's awarded. *Degree requirements:* For master's, thesis or alternative. *Entrance requirements:* For master's, minimum GPA of 3.0, letters of recommendation, statement of objectives, current resume. Additional exam requirements/recommendations for international students: Required—TOEFL (minimum score 550 paper-based; 79 iBT), IELTS (minimum score 6.5). *Application deadline:* For fall admission, 3/15 priority date for domestic and international students; for spring admission, 10/15 priority date for domestic and international students. Application fee: $80. Electronic applications accepted. *Expenses:* Contact institution. *Financial support:* Federal Work-Study, scholarships/grants, and unspecified assistantships available. Support available to part-time students. Financial award application deadline: 3/15; financial award applicants required to submit FAFSA. *Unit head:* Dr. Sue Robb, Chairperson, 585-395-5935, Fax: 585-395-2172, E-mail: awalton@brockport.edu. *Application contact:* Anne Walton, Coordinator of Certification and Graduate Advisement, 585-395-2326, Fax: 585-395-2172, E-mail: awalton@brockport.edu.
Website: http://www.brockport.edu/ehd

The College of Idaho, Department of Education, Caldwell, ID 83605. Offers curriculum and instruction (M Ed); teaching (MAT). *Degree requirements:* For master's, thesis. *Entrance requirements:* For master's, GRE, portfolio, minimum undergraduate GPA of 3.0, interview. *Faculty research:* Discourse analysis, at-risk youth, children's literature, research design, program evaluation.

The College of Saint Rose, Graduate Studies, Thelma P. Lally School of Education, Teacher Education Programs, Albany, NY 12203-1419. Offers adolescence education (MS Ed, Advanced Certificate); adolescence education/special education (Advanced Certificate); childhood education (MS Ed); curriculum and instruction (MS Ed); early childhood education (MS Ed). *Students:* 72 full-time (59 women), 32 part-time (26 women); includes 6 minority (4 Black or African American, non-Hispanic/Latino; 2 Hispanic/Latino), 2 international. Average age 28. 60 applicants, 78% accepted, 25 enrolled. In 2016, 37 master's awarded. *Entrance requirements:* For master's, minimum undergraduate GPA of 3.0. Additional exam requirements/recommendations for international students: Required—TOEFL (minimum score 550 paper-based; 80 iBT), IELTS (minimum score 6), PTE (minimum score 56). *Application deadline:* For fall admission, 4/1 priority date for domestic and international students; for spring admission, 10/15 priority date for domestic and international students; for summer admission, 3/15 priority date for domestic and international students. Applications are processed on a rolling basis. Application fee: $40. Electronic applications accepted. *Expenses: Tuition:* Full-time $14,382; part-time $799 per credit. *Required fees:* $814; $32 per credit. $88 per semester. Tuition and fees vary according to course load. *Financial support:* Career-related internships or fieldwork, scholarships/grants, tuition waivers (partial), and unspecified assistantships available. Support available to part-time students. Financial award application deadline: 4/15. *Unit head:* Dr. Drey Martone, Chair, 518-454-5262, E-mail: martoned@strose.edu. *Application contact:* Cris Murray, Assistant Vice President for Graduate Recruitment and Enrollment, 518-485-3390, Fax: 518-458-5479, E-mail: grad@strose.edu.
Website: https://www.strose.edu/academics/schools/school-of-education/

The College of William and Mary, School of Education, Program in Curriculum and Instruction, Williamsburg, VA 23187-8795. Offers elementary education (MA Ed); gifted education (MA Ed); literacy leadership (MA Ed); math specialist (MA Ed); secondary education (MA Ed), including English, foreign language, math, science, social studies; special education (MA Ed). *Accreditation:* NCATE. *Program availability:* Part-time. *Faculty:* 30 full-time (21 women), 48 part-time/adjunct (38 women). *Students:* 60 full-time (47 women), 14 part-time (all women); includes 13 minority (1 Black or African American, non-Hispanic/Latino; 1 American Indian or Alaska Native, non-Hispanic/Latino; 2 Asian, non-Hispanic/Latino; 7 Hispanic/Latino; 2 Two or more races, non-Hispanic/Latino). Average age 26. 134 applicants, 79% accepted, 66 enrolled. In 2016, 77 master's awarded. *Degree requirements:* For master's, project. *Entrance requirements:* For master's, GRE, MAT, PRAXIS Core Academic Skills for Educators, minimum GPA of 2.5. Additional exam requirements/recommendations for international students: Required—TOEFL (minimum score 100 iBT), IELTS (minimum score 7). *Application deadline:* For fall admission, 1/15 for domestic and international students; for spring admission, 10/1 for domestic and international students. Application fee: $50. Electronic applications accepted. *Expenses:* $14,258 per year in-state full-time, $275 per credit in-state part-time; $30,500 per year out-of-state full-time, $1,200 per credit out-of-state part-time. *Financial support:* In 2016–17, 30 students received support, including 3 research assistantships (averaging $14,259 per year); scholarships/grants and unspecified assistantships also available. Financial award application deadline: 1/15; financial award applicants required to submit FAFSA. *Faculty research:* Educational technology, professional development and evaluation, inclusive education, rural education, education policy. *Unit head:* Dr. Jeremy D. Stoddard, Department Chair, 757-221-2348, E-mail: jdstod@wm.edu. *Application contact:* Dorothy Smith Osborne,

Curriculum and Instruction

Assistant Dean for Academic Programs and Student Services, 757-221-2317, E-mail: dsosbo@wm.edu.
Website: http://education.wm.edu

The College of William and Mary, School of Education, Program in Education Policy, Planning, and Leadership, Williamsburg, VA 23187-8795. Offers curriculum and educational technology (PhD); curriculum leadership (Ed D, PhD); educational leadership (M Ed), including higher education administration (M Ed, Ed D, PhD), K-12 administration and supervision; educational policy, planning, and leadership (Ed D, PhD), including general education administration, gifted education administration, higher education administration (M Ed, Ed D, PhD). *Accreditation:* NCATE. *Program availability:* Part-time, evening/weekend. *Faculty:* 20 full-time (10 women), 21 part-time/adjunct (13 women). *Students:* 63 full-time (45 women), 143 part-time (95 women); includes 53 minority (39 Black or African American, non-Hispanic/Latino; 4 Asian, non-Hispanic/Latino; 6 Hispanic/Latino; 4 Two or more races, non-Hispanic/Latino), 4 international. Average age 38. 122 applicants, 77% accepted, 65 enrolled. In 2016, 26 master's, 24 doctorates awarded. *Degree requirements:* For doctorate, comprehensive exam, thesis/dissertation. *Entrance requirements:* For master's, GRE or MAT, minimum GPA of 2.5; for doctorate, GRE or MAT, minimum GPA of 3.0. Additional exam requirements/recommendations for international students: Required—TOEFL (minimum score 100 iBT), IELTS (minimum score 7). *Application deadline:* For fall admission, 1/15 for domestic and international students. Application fee: $50. Electronic applications accepted. *Expenses:* $14,258 per year in-state full-time, $275 per credit in-state part-time; $30,500 per year out-of-state full-time, $1,200 per credit out-of-state part-time. *Financial support:* In 2016–17, 64 students received support, including 1 fellowship (averaging $20,000 per year), 54 research assistantships (averaging $19,668 per year); institutionally sponsored loans, scholarships/grants, and unspecified assistantships also available. Support available to part-time students. Financial award application deadline: 1/15; financial award applicants required to submit FAFSA. *Faculty research:* Higher education policy, evaluation of teachers, program evaluation, civil rights and higher education, program evaluation. *Unit head:* Dr. Michael F. Dipaola, Department Chair, 757-221-2344, E-mail: mfdipa@wm.edu. *Application contact:* Dorothy Smith Osborne, Assistant Dean for Academic Programs and Student Services, 757-221-2317, E-mail: dsosbo@wm.edu.
Website: http://education.wm.edu

Colorado Christian University, Program in Curriculum and Instruction, Lakewood, CO 80226. Offers corporate education (MACI); early childhood educator (MACI); elementary educator (MACI); instructional technology (MACI); master educator (MACI); online course developer (MACI); online teaching and learning (MACI); special education generalist (MACI). *Program availability:* Part-time, evening/weekend. *Degree requirements:* For master's, thesis optional, practicum. *Entrance requirements:* For master's, interviews, letters of recommendation. Additional exam requirements/recommendations for international students: Required—TOEFL. Electronic applications accepted. *Expenses:* Contact institution.

Columbia International University, Columbia Graduate School, Columbia, SC 29230-3122. Offers Bible teaching (MABT); counseling (MACN); early childhood and elementary education (MAT); educational administration (M Ed); educational leadership (PhD); instruction and learning (M Ed); teaching English as a foreign language (Certificate); teaching English as a foreign language and intercultural studies (MATF). *Program availability:* Part-time, evening/weekend, online learning. *Degree requirements:* For master's, internships, professional project. *Entrance requirements:* For master's, MAT; GRE (for some programs), minimum GPA of 2.7. Additional exam requirements/recommendations for international students: Required—TOEFL. Electronic applications accepted.

Columbus State University, Graduate Studies, College of Education and Health Professions, Department of Counseling, Foundations, and Leadership, Columbus, GA 31907-5645. Offers clinical mental health counseling (MS); curriculum and leadership (Ed D), including curriculum, educational leadership, higher education (M Ed, Ed D); educational leadership (M Ed, Ed S), including higher education (M Ed, Ed D); school counseling (M Ed, Ed S). *Accreditation:* ACA; NCATE. *Program availability:* Part-time, evening/weekend, 100% online, blended/hybrid learning. *Faculty:* 14 full-time (4 women), 25 part-time/adjunct (14 women). *Students:* 226 full-time (159 women), 294 part-time (219 women); includes 298 minority (270 Black or African American, non-Hispanic/Latino; 1 American Indian or Alaska Native, non-Hispanic/Latino; 5 Asian, non-Hispanic/Latino; 13 Hispanic/Latino; 9 Two or more races, non-Hispanic/Latino), 1 international. Average age 39. 367 applicants, 57% accepted, 162 enrolled. In 2016, 20 master's, 7 doctorates, 121 other advanced degrees awarded. *Degree requirements:* For master's, thesis, exit exam; for doctorate, comprehensive exam, thesis/dissertation; for Ed S, thesis or alternative. *Entrance requirements:* For master's, GRE General Test, minimum undergraduate GPA of 2.75; for doctorate, GRE General Test, minimum graduate GPA of 3.5, four years of professional service; for Ed S, GRE General Test, minimum undergraduate GPA of 2.75, graduate 3.0. Additional exam requirements/recommendations for international students: Required—TOEFL (minimum score 550 paper-based; 79 iBT). *Application deadline:* For fall admission, 6/30 for domestic and international students; for spring admission, 11/1 for domestic and international students; for summer admission, 3/1 for domestic and international students. Applications are processed on a rolling basis. Application fee: $50. Electronic applications accepted. *Expenses:* Tuition, state resident: full-time $4804; part-time $2412 per semester hour. Tuition, nonresident: full-time $19,218; part-time $9612 per semester hour. *Required fees:* $1850; $1850 per semester hour. Tuition and fees vary according to program. *Financial support:* In 2016–17, 43 students received support, including 9 research assistantships with partial tuition reimbursements available (averaging $3,000 per year); career-related internships or fieldwork, Federal Work-Study, institutionally sponsored loans, scholarships/grants, tuition waivers (partial), and unspecified assistantships also available. Support available to part-time students. Financial award application deadline: 5/1; financial award applicants required to submit FAFSA. *Unit head:* Dr. Tom Hackett, Department Chair, 706-507-8968, Fax: 706-569-3134, E-mail: hackett_paul@columbusstate.edu. *Application contact:* Kristin Williams, Director of International and Graduate Recruitment, 706-507-8848, Fax: 706-568-5091, E-mail: williams_kristin@columbusstate.edu.
Website: http://cfl.columbusstate.edu/

Columbus State University, Graduate Studies, College of Education and Health Professions, Department of Teacher Education, Columbus, GA 31907-5645. Offers curriculum and instruction in accomplished teaching (M Ed); early childhood education (M Ed, MAT, Ed S); middle grades education (M Ed, MAT, Ed S); secondary education (M Ed, MAT, Ed S), including biology (MAT), chemistry (MAT), earth and space science (MAT), English/language arts, general science (M Ed), history (MAT), mathematics, science (Ed S), social science (M Ed, Ed S); special education (M Ed, MAT, Ed S), including general curriculum (M Ed, MAT); teacher leadership (M Ed). *Accreditation:* NCATE. *Program availability:* Part-time, evening/weekend, 100% online, blended/hybrid learning. *Faculty:* 20 full-time (13 women), 19 part-time/adjunct (16 women). *Students:* 92 full-time (66 women), 212 part-time (179 women); includes 113 minority (104 Black or African American, non-Hispanic/Latino; 1 American Indian or Alaska Native, non-Hispanic/Latino; 2 Asian, non-Hispanic/Latino; 4 Hispanic/Latino; 2 Two or more races, non-Hispanic/Latino), 5 international. Average age 34. 209 applicants, 56% accepted, 79 enrolled. In 2016, 111 master's, 18 other advanced degrees awarded. *Degree requirements:* For Ed S, thesis or alternative. *Entrance requirements:* For master's, GRE General Test, minimum undergraduate GPA of 2.75; for Ed S, GRE General Test, minimum undergraduate GPA of 2.75, graduate 3.0. Additional exam requirements/recommendations for international students: Required—TOEFL (minimum score 550 paper-based; 79 iBT). *Application deadline:* For fall admission, 6/30 for domestic students, 5/1 for international students; for spring admission, 11/1 for domestic and international students; for summer admission, 3/1 for domestic and international students. Applications are processed on a rolling basis. Application fee: $50. Electronic applications accepted. *Expenses:* Tuition, state resident: full-time $4804; part-time $2412 per semester hour. Tuition, nonresident: full-time $19,218; part-time $9612 per semester hour. *Required fees:* $1850; $1850 per semester hour. Tuition and fees vary according to program. *Financial support:* In 2016–17, 60 students received support, including 12 research assistantships with partial tuition reimbursements available (averaging $3,000 per year); career-related internships or fieldwork, Federal Work-Study, institutionally sponsored loans, scholarships/grants, tuition waivers (partial), and unspecified assistantships also available. Support available to part-time students. Financial award application deadline: 5/1; financial award applicants required to submit FAFSA. *Unit head:* Dr. Jan Burcham, Department Chair, 706-507-8519, Fax: 706-568-3134, E-mail: burcham_jan@columbusstate.edu. *Application contact:* Kristin Williams, Director of International and Graduate Recruitment, 706-507-8848, Fax: 706-568-5091, E-mail: williams_kristin@columbusstate.edu.
Website: http://te.columbusstate.edu/

Concordia University, College of Education, Portland, OR 97211-6099. Offers career and technical education (M Ed); curriculum and instruction (M Ed), including adolescent literacy, career and technical education, e-learning/technology education, early childhood education, English for speakers of other languages, English language development, environmental education, mathematics, methods and curriculum, reading, science, teacher leadership, the inclusive classroom; early childhood (MAT); education leadership (Ed D); educational administration (M Ed); elementary education (MAT); secondary education (MAT); special education (M Ed); teacher leadership (Ed D). *Program availability:* Part-time, online learning. *Degree requirements:* For master's, comprehensive exam, work samples/portfolio. *Entrance requirements:* For master's, California Basic Educational Skills Test or PRAXIS I, minimum undergraduate GPA of 2.8, graduate 3.0; 2 letters of recommendation. Additional exam requirements/recommendations for international students: Required—TOEFL (minimum score 525 paper-based). Electronic applications accepted. *Faculty research:* Learner-centered classroom, brain-based learning, future of online learning.

Concordia University Ann Arbor, Graduate Programs, Ann Arbor, MI 48105-2797. Offers curriculum and instruction (MS); educational leadership (MS); organizational leadership and administration (MS). *Program availability:* Part-time, evening/weekend. *Degree requirements:* For master's, thesis. *Entrance requirements:* Additional exam requirements/recommendations for international students: Required—TOEFL (minimum score 80 iBT); Recommended—IELTS (minimum score 6.5). Electronic applications accepted.

Concordia University Chicago, College of Education, Program in Curriculum and Instruction, River Forest, IL 60305-1499. Offers MA. MA offered jointly with the Chicago Consortium of Colleges and Universities. *Accreditation:* NCATE. *Program availability:* Part-time, evening/weekend. *Degree requirements:* For master's, comprehensive exam, thesis. *Entrance requirements:* For master's, minimum GPA of 2.9. Additional exam requirements/recommendations for international students: Required—TOEFL (minimum score 550 paper-based). Electronic applications accepted. *Faculty research:* School discipline, school improvement, leadership.

Concordia University Irvine, School of Education, Irvine, CA 92612-3299. Offers curriculum and instruction (MA); education and preliminary teaching credential (M Ed); educational administration and preliminary administrative services credential (MA); educational technology (MA); school counseling with pupil personnel services credential (MA). *Program availability:* Part-time, evening/weekend, online learning. *Degree requirements:* For master's, action research project. *Entrance requirements:* For master's, California Basic Educational Skills Test, California Subject Examinations for Teachers (M Ed and MA in educational administration and preliminary administrative services credential), official college transcript(s), signed statement of intent, two references, copy of credential. Additional exam requirements/recommendations for international students: Required—TOEFL. Electronic applications accepted. *Expenses:* Contact institution.

Concordia University, St. Paul, College of Education, St. Paul, MN 55104-5494. Offers classroom instruction (MA Ed), including K-12 reading; differentiated instruction (MA Ed); education (Ed D); educational leadership (MA Ed); educational technology (MA Ed); K-12 principal licensure (Ed S); special education (MA Ed, Certificate), including autism spectrum disorder (MA Ed), emotional and behavioral disorders (MA Ed), learning disabilities (MA Ed); superintendent (Ed S); teaching (MAT). *Accreditation:* NCATE. *Program availability:* Part-time, evening/weekend, 100% online, blended/hybrid learning. *Faculty:* 9 full-time (5 women), 88 part-time/adjunct (52 women). *Students:* 994 full-time (745 women), 40 part-time (34 women); includes 118 minority (40 Black or African American, non-Hispanic/Latino; 7 American Indian or Alaska Native, non-Hispanic/Latino; 33 Asian, non-Hispanic/Latino; 20 Hispanic/Latino; 18 Two or more races, non-Hispanic/Latino), 15 international. Average age 34. 549 applicants, 82% accepted, 372 enrolled. In 2016, 399 master's, 108 other advanced degrees awarded. *Degree requirements:* For master's, thesis (for some programs); for doctorate, thesis/dissertation, capstone projects; for other advanced degree, e-folio review of competencies. *Entrance requirements:* For master's, official transcripts from regionally-accredited institution stating the conferral of a bachelor's degree with minimum cumulative GPA of 3.0; personal statement; professional resume; practitioner in field through work or volunteerism; resume; for doctorate, minimum master's or specialist degree GPA of 3.25; transcript; writing sample; three letters of recommendation; current resume; on-campus interview; for other advanced degree, at least three years of teaching experience; master's degree; valid MN teaching license; writing sample; two letters of recommendation; resume. Additional exam requirements/recommendations for international students: Recommended—TOEFL (minimum score 547 paper-based; 78 iBT), IELTS (minimum score 6). *Application deadline:* For fall admission, 8/1 for domestic and international students; for spring admission, 12/1 for domestic and international students; for summer admission, 5/1 for domestic and international students. Applications are processed on a rolling basis. Application fee: $50. Electronic applications accepted. *Expenses:* Contact institution. *Financial support:* In 2016–17, 112 students received support. Scholarships/grants and unspecified assistantships available. Financial award applicants required to submit FAFSA. *Faculty research:* Differentiated instruction in K-12 educational settings; educational leadership; effective online pedagogy in higher education; equine-assisted learning; faculty development in higher education. *Unit head:* Lonn Maly, Dean, 651-641-8203, E-mail: maly@csp.edu. *Application contact:* Kimberly Craig, Associate Vice President, Cohort Enrollment Management, 651-603-6223, Fax: 651-603-6320, E-mail: craig@csp.edu.

Coppin State University, Division of Graduate Studies, Division of Education, Department of Curriculum and Instruction, Program in Curriculum and Instruction, Baltimore, MD 21216-3698. Offers M Ed. *Program availability:* Part-time, evening/weekend, online learning. *Degree requirements:* For master's, thesis. *Entrance requirements:* For master's, GRE or MAT, minimum GPA of 3.0, teacher certification.

Cornell University, Graduate School, Graduate Fields of Agriculture and Life Sciences, Field of Education, Ithaca, NY 14853. Offers adult and extension education (MPS, MS, PhD); learning, teaching, and social policy (MPS, MS, PhD); mathematics 7-12 (MS). Terminal master's awarded for partial completion of doctoral program. *Degree requirements:* For master's, thesis (MS); for doctorate, comprehensive exam, thesis/dissertation. *Entrance requirements:* For master's and doctorate, GRE General Test, sample of written work (recommended), 2 letters of recommendation. Additional exam requirements/recommendations for international students: Required—TOEFL (minimum score 550 paper-based; 77 iBT). Electronic applications accepted. *Faculty research:* Moral development and professional ethics, public issues education and community development, socio/political issues in public education, teacher education and curriculum in agricultural science and mathematics, extension research.

Dakota Wesleyan University, Program in Education, Mitchell, SD 57301-4398. Offers curriculum and instruction (MA Ed); educational policy and administration (MA Ed); preK-12 principal certification (MA Ed); secondary certification (MA Ed). *Program availability:* Part-time, evening/weekend. *Degree requirements:* For master's, comprehensive exam, thesis optional, electronic portfolio. *Entrance requirements:* For master's, minimum GPA of 2.7, elementary statistics course, statement of purpose, official transcripts, resume, three letters of recommendation. Additional exam requirements/recommendations for international students: Required—TOEFL (minimum score 500 paper-based), IELTS (minimum score 6.5). Electronic applications accepted. *Faculty research:* Math, political policy, technology in the classroom.

Dallas Baptist University, Dorothy M. Bush College of Education, Program in Curriculum and Instruction, Dallas, TX 75211-9299. Offers Christian school administration (M Ed); distance learning (M Ed); English as a second language (M Ed); instructional technology (M Ed); professional life coaching (M Ed); special education (M Ed); supervision (M Ed). *Program availability:* Part-time, evening/weekend, 100% online, blended/hybrid learning. *Application deadline:* Applications are processed on a rolling basis. Application fee: $25. Electronic applications accepted. Application fee is waived when completed online. *Expenses: Tuition:* Full-time $15,408; part-time $856 per credit hour. *Required fees:* $400 per semester. Tuition and fees vary according to course load and degree level. *Unit head:* Dr. Deborah H. Tribble, Director, 214-333-5201, E-mail: debbiet@dbu.edu. *Application contact:* Bobby Soto, Director of Admissions, 214-333-5242, E-mail: graduate@dbu.edu.
Website: http://www3.dbu.edu/graduate/curriculum_instruction.asp

Delaware State University, Graduate Programs, College of Education, Health and Public Policy, Program in Curriculum and Instruction, Dover, DE 19901-2277. Offers MA. *Program availability:* Part-time, evening/weekend. *Degree requirements:* For master's, comprehensive exam, thesis optional. *Entrance requirements:* For master's, GRE General Test, minimum GPA of 3.0 in major, 2.75 overall. Additional exam requirements/recommendations for international students: Required—TOEFL (minimum score 550 paper-based). Electronic applications accepted.

Delaware Valley University, Program in Educational Leadership, Doylestown, PA 18901-2697. Offers instruction, curriculum and technology (MS); school administration and leadership (MS). *Program availability:* Part-time, evening/weekend. *Entrance requirements:* For master's, minimum undergraduate GPA of 3.0.

DePaul University, College of Education, Chicago, IL 60614. Offers bilingual bicultural education (M Ed, MA); counseling (M Ed, MA), including clinical mental health counseling, college student development, school counseling; curriculum studies (M Ed, MA, Ed D); early childhood education (M Ed, MA, Ed D); educating adults (MA); educational leadership (M Ed, MA, Ed D), including administration and supervision (M Ed, MA), principal preparation (M Ed, MA); elementary education (MA); mathematics education (MA); mathematics for teaching (MS); middle school mathematics education (MS); reading specialist (M Ed, MA); secondary education (M Ed); social and cultural foundations in education (MA); special education (M Ed, MA); world languages education (M Ed, MA). *Program availability:* Part-time, evening/weekend, online learning. *Degree requirements:* For doctorate, thesis/dissertation. Electronic applications accepted.

DeVry University–Folsom Campus, Graduate Programs, Folsom, CA 95630. Offers accounting (M Acc); accounting and financial management (MAFM); business administration (MBA); curriculum leadership (M Ed); educational leadership (M Ed); educational technology (M Ed); higher education leadership (M Ed); human resource management (MHRM); information systems management (MISM); network and communications management (MNCM); project management (MPM); public administration (MPA).

Doane University, Program in Education, Crete, NE 68333-2430. Offers curriculum and instruction (M Ed); educational leadership (M Ed). *Accreditation:* NCATE. *Program availability:* Part-time, evening/weekend. *Faculty:* 10 full-time (7 women), 66 part-time/adjunct (50 women). *Students:* 224 full-time (167 women), 488 part-time (388 women); includes 22 minority (9 Black or African American, non-Hispanic/Latino; 2 American Indian or Alaska Native, non-Hispanic/Latino; 1 Asian, non-Hispanic/Latino; 7 Hispanic/Latino; 1 Native Hawaiian or other Pacific Islander, non-Hispanic/Latino; 2 Two or more races, non-Hispanic/Latino), 1 international. Average age 34. In 2016, 257 master's awarded. *Degree requirements:* For master's, thesis. *Entrance requirements:* For master's, minimum GPA of 2.5. Additional exam requirements/recommendations for international students: Required—TOEFL. *Application deadline:* Applications are processed on a rolling basis. Electronic applications accepted. *Expenses:* Contact institution. *Financial support:* Applicants required to submit FAFSA. *Unit head:* Dr. Lyn C. Forester, Dean, 402-826-8604, Fax: 402-826-8278. *Application contact:* Wilma Daddario, Assistant Dean, 402-464-1223, Fax: 402-466-4228, E-mail: wdaddario@doane.edu.
Website: http://www.doane.edu/masters-degrees

Drexel University, Goodwin College of Professional Studies, School of Education, Philadelphia, PA 19104-2875. Offers applied behavior analysis (MS); creativity and innovation (MS); education improvement and transformation (MS); educational administration (MS); educational leadership and management (Ed D); educational leadership development and learning technologies (PhD); global and international education (MS); higher education (MS); human resources development (MS); learning technologies (MS); mathematics, learning and teaching (MS); special education (MS); teaching, learning and curriculum (MS). *Program availability:* Part-time, evening/weekend, online learning. *Degree requirements:* For doctorate, thesis/dissertation. *Entrance requirements:* For doctorate, GRE or GMAT. Additional exam requirements/recommendations for international students: Required—TOEFL, IELTS. Electronic applications accepted. Application fee is waived when completed online. *Expenses:* Contact institution. *Faculty research:* Leadership development, mathematics education, literacy, autism, educational technology.

See Display on page 660 and Close-Up on page 727.

Drury University, Master in Education Program, Springfield, MO 5802. Offers curriculum and instruction (M Ed), including elementary, middle school, secondary; gifted education (M Ed); instructional leadership (M Ed); instructional technology (M Ed); integrated learning (M Ed); online teaching (M Ed); special education (M Ed); special reading (M Ed). *Accreditation:* NCATE. *Program availability:* Part-time, evening/weekend, 100% online, blended/hybrid learning. *Students:* 146 full-time (111 women); includes 6 minority (1 Asian, non-Hispanic/Latino; 3 Hispanic/Latino; 2 Two or more races, non-Hispanic/Latino), 1 international. Average age 34. 42 applicants, 74% accepted. In 2016, 74 master's awarded. *Entrance requirements:* For master's, GRE, bachelor's degree with minimum GPA of 2.75. Additional exam requirements/recommendations for international students: Recommended—TOEFL (minimum score 80 iBT), IELTS (minimum score 6.5). *Application deadline:* For fall admission, 8/4 priority date for domestic and international students; for spring admission, 1/5 priority date for domestic and international students; for summer admission, 5/26 priority date for domestic and international students. Applications are processed on a rolling basis. Application fee: $25 ($50 for international students). Electronic applications accepted. *Expenses:* $352 tuition per credit hour; $7 per credit hour technology fee; $100 graduation fee; $59 portfolio fee (one-time). *Financial support:* In 2016–17, 20 students received support. Career-related internships or fieldwork, scholarships/grants, tuition waivers (partial), and unspecified assistantships available. Financial award application deadline: 6/30; financial award applicants required to submit FAFSA. *Faculty research:* Gifted students, instructional technology, autism, diversity and social justice. *Unit head:* Dr. Asikaa Cosgrove, Director, Master in Education, 417-873-7806, E-mail: acosgrov@drury.edu.
Website: http://www.drury.edu/education-masters

Duquesne University, School of Education, Department of Educational Foundations and Leadership, Program in School Administration and Supervision, Pittsburgh, PA 15282-0001. Offers curriculum and instruction (Post-Master's Certificate); school administration K-12 (MS Ed, Post-Master's Certificate); school supervision (MS Ed). *Program availability:* Part-time, evening/weekend. *Faculty:* 1 (woman) full-time. *Students:* 18 full-time (13 women), 4 part-time (all women); includes 1 minority (Black or African American, non-Hispanic/Latino), 1 international. Average age 36. 17 applicants, 88% accepted, 9 enrolled. In 2016, 22 master's awarded. *Degree requirements:* For master's, thesis optional. *Entrance requirements:* For master's and Post-Master's Certificate, bachelor's degree. Additional exam requirements/recommendations for international students: Required—TOEFL (minimum score 550 paper-based), IELTS (minimum score 7). *Application deadline:* For fall admission, 9/1 for domestic students; for spring admission, 1/1 for domestic students. Applications are processed on a rolling basis. Application fee: $0. Electronic applications accepted. *Expenses: Tuition:* Full-time $22,212; part-time $1234 per credit. Tuition and fees vary according to program. *Financial support:* Research assistantships available. Support available to part-time students. *Unit head:* Dr. Fran Serenka, Associate Professor and Director, 412-396-5274, Fax: 412-396-1274, E-mail: serenkaf@duq.edu. *Application contact:* Michael Dolinger, Director of Student and Academic Services, 412-396-6647, Fax: 412-396-5585, E-mail: dolingerm@duq.edu.
Website: http://www.duq.edu/academics/schools/education/graduate-programs-education/school-admin-and-supervision

East Carolina University, Graduate School, College of Education, Department of Special Education, Foundations, and Research, Greenville, NC 27858-4353. Offers assistive technology (Certificate); autism (Certificate); behavior specialist (Certificate); deaf-blindness (Certificate); special education (MA Ed). *Program availability:* Part-time, online learning. *Degree requirements:* For master's, comprehensive exam, thesis optional. *Entrance requirements:* For master's, GRE General Test or MAT, interview, bachelor's degree in related field, minimum GPA of 2.5, teaching license. Additional exam requirements/recommendations for international students: Required—TOEFL. *Application deadline:* For fall admission, 6/1 priority date for domestic students. Applications are processed on a rolling basis. Application fee: $50. *Financial support:* Research assistantships, teaching assistantships, and Federal Work-Study available. Support available to part-time students. Financial award application deadline: 6/1; financial award applicants required to submit FAFSA. *Unit head:* Dr. Guili Zhang, Interim Chair, 252-328-4989, E-mail: zhangg@ecu.edu. *Application contact:* Dean of Graduate School, 252-328-6012, Fax: 252-328-6071, E-mail: gradschool@ecu.edu.
Website: http://www.ecu.edu/cs-educ/sefr/index.cfm

Eastern Kentucky University, The Graduate School, College of Education, Department of Curriculum and Instruction, Richmond, KY 40475-3102. Offers elementary education (MA Ed), including early elementary education, reading; library science (MA Ed); music education (MA Ed); secondary and higher education (MA Ed), including secondary education; teaching (MAT). *Accreditation:* NCATE. *Program availability:* Part-time. *Degree requirements:* For master's, portfolio is part of exam. *Entrance requirements:* For master's, GRE General Test, PRAXIS II (KY), minimum GPA of 2.5. *Faculty research:* Technology in education, reading instruction, e-portfolios, induction to teacher education, dispositions of teachers.

Eastern Michigan University, Graduate School, College of Education, Department of Teacher Education, Programs in Curriculum and Instruction, Ypsilanti, MI 48197. Offers advanced teaching and learning (MA); early literacy instruction (Graduate Certificate); instructional leadership (MA); learning, motivation and creativity (Graduate Certificate); literacy coaching (Graduate Certificate); online teaching (Certificate); secondary literacy instruction (Graduate Certificate); urban and diversity education (MA). *Students:* 1 (woman) full-time, 31 part-time (29 women); includes 6 minority (2 Black or African American, non-Hispanic/Latino; 2 Asian, non-Hispanic/Latino; 2 Two or more races, non-Hispanic/Latino), 1 international. Average age 33. 11 applicants, 73% accepted, 4 enrolled. In 2016, 8 master's, 1 other advanced degree awarded. Application fee: $45. *Application contact:* Dr. Virginia Harder, Graduate Coordinator/Advisor, 734-487-2729, Fax: 734-487-2101, E-mail: vharder1@emich.edu.

Eastern New Mexico University, Graduate School, College of Education and Technology, Department of Curriculum and Instruction, Portales, NM 88130. Offers bilingual education (M Ed); educational technology (M Ed); elementary education (M Ed); English as a second language (M Ed); pedagogy and learning (M Ed); professional technical education (M Ed); reading/literacy (M Ed). *Program availability:* Part-time, online learning. *Degree requirements:* For master's, comprehensive exam, thesis optional. *Entrance requirements:* For master's, minimum GPA of 3.0, photocopy of teaching license, writing assessment, letter of recommendation. Additional exam requirements/recommendations for international students: Required—TOEFL (minimum score 550 paper-based; 79 iBT), IELTS (minimum score 6). Electronic applications accepted.

Eastern Washington University, Graduate Studies, College of Arts, Letters and Education, Department of Education, Program in Curriculum Development, Cheney, WA 99004-2431. Offers M Ed. *Students:* 3 full-time (2 women), 2 part-time (both women). Average age 37. 3 applicants, 33% accepted, 1 enrolled. In 2016, 8 master's awarded. *Degree requirements:* For master's, comprehensive exam. *Entrance requirements:* For master's, minimum GPA of 3.0. Additional exam requirements/recommendations for international students: Required—TOEFL (minimum score 580 paper-based; 92 iBT), IELTS (minimum score 7), PTE (minimum score 63). *Application deadline:* For fall admission, 4/1 priority date for domestic students; for spring admission, 1/15 for domestic students. Applications are processed on a rolling basis. Application fee: $75. Electronic applications accepted. *Expenses:* Tuition, state resident: full-time $11,000; part-time $5500 per credit. Tuition, nonresident: full-time $24,000; part-time $12,000 per credit. *Required fees:* $1300. One-time fee: $50 full-time. Part-time tuition and fees vary according to course load, campus/location and program. *Financial support:* In 2016–17, teaching assistantships with partial tuition reimbursements (averaging $10,000 per year) were awarded; career-related internships or fieldwork, Federal Work-Study, institutionally sponsored loans, scholarships/grants, health care benefits, tuition waivers (partial), and unspecified assistantships also available. Support available to part-time students. Financial award application deadline: 2/1. *Unit head:* Robin Showalter, Program Coordinator, 509-359-6492, E-mail: rshowalter@mail.ewu.edu.

East Tennessee State University, School of Graduate Studies, College of Education, Department of Curriculum and Instruction, Johnson City, TN 37614. Offers educational technology (M Ed), including educational communications and technology, school library media; elementary education (M Ed); reading (MA), including reading education; school library professional (Post-Master's Certificate); secondary education (M Ed), including classroom technology; teacher education with multiple levels (MAT), including elementary education, middle grades education, secondary education. *Accreditation:* NCATE. *Program availability:* Part-time, evening/weekend, online learning. *Degree requirements:* For master's, comprehensive exam, thesis optional, student teaching, practicum; for Post-Master's Certificate, field work (school library); culminating experience (storytelling). *Entrance requirements:* For master's, GRE, SAT, ACT, PRAXIS, minimum GPA of 3.0; for Post-Master's Certificate, master's degree, TN teaching license. Additional exam requirements/recommendations for international students: Required—TOEFL (minimum score 550 paper-based; 79 iBT). Electronic applications accepted. *Faculty research:* Critical thinking; curriculum development in reading, math, and science education; cultural diversity; cognitive processes; effective teaching strategies.

East Texas Baptist University, Master of Education Program, Marshall, TX 75670-1498. Offers college and university leadership (M Ed); curriculum and instruction (M Ed); principal certification (M Ed); sports and exercise leadership (M Ed); teacher certification (M Ed). *Program availability:* Part-time, evening/weekend. *Faculty:* 3 full-time (1 woman), 3 part-time/adjunct (all women). *Students:* 33 part-time (19 women); includes 14 minority (10 Black or African American, non-Hispanic/Latino; 4 Hispanic/Latino), 1 international. Average age 29. 53 applicants, 51% accepted, 25 enrolled. In 2016, 20 master's awarded. *Entrance requirements:* Additional exam requirements/recommendations for international students: Recommended—TOEFL (minimum score 550 paper-based; 79 iBT). *Application deadline:* For fall admission, 8/17 for domestic students; for spring admission, 1/10 for domestic students; for summer admission, 5/2 for domestic students. Applications are processed on a rolling basis. Application fee: $50. Electronic applications accepted. *Expenses:* $700 per credit hour tuition; $150 per semester fees (6 or more hours enrolled); $75 per semester fees (1-5 hours enrolled). *Financial support:* In 2016–17, 14 students received support. Federal Work-Study, unspecified assistantships, and staff grants available. Financial award applicants required to submit FAFSA. *Unit head:* Dr. PJ Winters, Director, 903-923-2276, Fax: 903-935-4318, E-mail: med@etbu.edu. *Application contact:* Den Murley, Director of Graduate Admissions, 903-923-2079, Fax: 903-934-8115, E-mail: dmurley@etbu.edu.
Website: https://www.etbu.edu/education/master-education/

Emporia State University, Program in Curriculum and Instruction, Emporia, KS 66801-5415. Offers curriculum leadership (MS); effective practitioner (MS); national board certification (MS). *Accreditation:* NCATE. *Program availability:* Part-time, online only, 100% online. *Faculty:* 10 full-time (3 women). *Students:* 7 full-time (all women), 134 part-time (123 women); includes 6 minority (1 Black or African American, non-Hispanic/Latino; 1 American Indian or Alaska Native, non-Hispanic/Latino; 3 Hispanic/Latino; 1 Two or more races, non-Hispanic/Latino). 35 applicants, 100% accepted, 32 enrolled. In 2016, 57 master's awarded. *Degree requirements:* For master's, comprehensive exam or thesis, practicum. *Entrance requirements:* For master's, GRE or MAT, appropriate bachelor's degree, teacher certification, 1 year of teaching experience, letters of recommendation. *Application deadline:* For fall admission, 8/15 priority date for domestic students. Applications are processed on a rolling basis. Application fee: $30 ($75 for international students). Electronic applications accepted. *Expenses:* Tuition, state resident: full-time $5922; part-time $246.75 per credit hour. Tuition, nonresident: full-time $18,414; part-time $767.25 per credit hour. *Required fees:* $1884; $78.50 per credit hour. *Financial support:* Career-related internships or fieldwork, Federal Work-Study, institutionally sponsored loans, health care benefits, and unspecified assistantships available. Financial award application deadline: 3/15; financial award applicants required to submit FAFSA. *Unit head:* Dr. Daniel Stiffler, Chair, 620-341-5776, E-mail: dstiffle@emporia.edu. *Application contact:* Mary Sewell, Admissions Coordinator, 800-950-GRAD, Fax: 620-341-5909, E-mail: msewell@emporia.edu.
Website: http://www.emporia.edu/sleme/graduate-programs/ci.html

Emporia State University, Program in Instructional Specialist, Emporia, KS 66801-5415. Offers elementary subject matter (MS); reading (MS). *Accreditation:* NCATE. *Program availability:* Part-time. *Faculty:* 29 full-time (21 women), 3 part-time/adjunct (2 women). *Students:* 7 full-time (all women), 65 part-time (58 women). 23 applicants, 100% accepted, 16 enrolled. In 2016, 27 master's awarded. *Degree requirements:* For master's, comprehensive exam or thesis, practicum. *Entrance requirements:* For master's, GRE General Test or MAT, essay exam, appropriate bachelor's degree, letters of recommendation. Additional exam requirements/recommendations for international students: Required—TOEFL (minimum score 520 paper-based; 68 iBT). *Application deadline:* For fall admission, 8/15 priority date for domestic students. Applications are processed on a rolling basis. Application fee: $30 ($75 for international students). Electronic applications accepted. *Expenses:* Tuition, state resident: full-time $5922; part-time $246.75 per credit hour. Tuition, nonresident: full-time $18,414; part-time $767.25 per credit hour. *Required fees:* $1884; $78.50 per credit hour. *Financial support:* Federal Work-Study, institutionally sponsored loans, health care benefits, and unspecified assistantships available. Financial award application deadline: 3/15; financial award applicants required to submit FAFSA. *Unit head:* Dr. Matt Siemears, Chair, 620-341-6057, E-mail: msiemear@emporia.edu. *Application contact:* Mary Sewell, Admissions Coordinator, 800-950-GRAD, Fax: 620-341-5909, E-mail: msewell@emporia.edu.

Evangel University, Department of Education, Springfield, MO 65802. Offers curriculum and instruction (M Ed); educational leadership (M Ed); literacy (M Ed); secondary teaching (M Ed). *Accreditation:* NCATE. *Program availability:* Part-time, evening/weekend, 100% online, blended/hybrid learning. *Faculty:* 3 full-time (2 women), 4 part-time/adjunct (2 women). *Students:* 2 full-time (1 woman), 33 part-time (29 women); includes 1 minority (Asian, non-Hispanic/Latino). Average age 30. 10 applicants, 90% accepted, 9 enrolled. In 2016, 28 master's awarded. *Degree requirements:* For master's, comprehensive exam, thesis optional. *Entrance requirements:* For master's, PRAXIS II (preferred) or GRE, minimum undergraduate GPA of 3.0. Additional exam requirements/recommendations for international students: Required—TOEFL (minimum score 550 paper-based). *Application deadline:* For fall admission, 7/15 priority date for domestic students, 8/1 for international students; for spring admission, 11/15 priority date for domestic students, 12/1 for international students. Applications are processed on a rolling basis. Application fee: $25. Electronic applications accepted. Application fee is waived when completed online. *Expenses: Tuition:* Part-time $400 per credit hour. *Required fees:* $148 per trimester. One-time fee: $25. Tuition and fees vary according to course load, degree level and program. *Financial support:* In 2016–17, 11 students received support. Scholarships/grants and unspecified assistantships available. Financial award application deadline: 4/1; financial award applicants required to submit FAFSA. *Unit head:* Dr. Susan Langston, Program Coordinator, 417-865-2815 Ext. 8552, E-mail: langstons@evangel.edu. *Application contact:* Karen Benitez, Admissions Representative, Graduate Studies, 417-865-2815 Ext. 7416, Fax: 417-575-5484, E-mail: benitezk@evangel.edu.
Website: http://www.evangel.edu/academics/graduate-studies/graduate-programs

Evangel University, Doctor of Educational Leadership in Curriculum and Instruction Program, Springfield, MO 65802. Offers Ed D. *Program availability:* Part-time, evening/weekend. *Faculty:* 4 full-time (1 woman), 2 part-time/adjunct (1 woman). *Students:* 26 full-time (21 women), 6 part-time (2 women); includes 2 minority (1 American Indian or Alaska Native, non-Hispanic/Latino; 1 Two or more races, non-Hispanic/Latino). Average age 41. 3 applicants, 100% accepted, 3 enrolled. *Degree requirements:* For doctorate, thesis/dissertation. *Entrance requirements:* For doctorate, MA in education (preferred). Additional exam requirements/recommendations for international students: Required—TOEFL (minimum score 550 paper-based). *Application deadline:* For fall admission, 7/15 priority date for domestic students, 8/1 for international students; for spring admission, 11/15 priority date for domestic students, 12/1 for international students. Applications are processed on a rolling basis. Application fee: $25. Electronic applications accepted. *Expenses: Tuition:* Part-time $400 per credit hour. *Required fees:* $148 per trimester. One-time fee: $25. Tuition and fees vary according to course load, degree level and program. *Financial support:* In 2016–17, 8 students received support. Scholarships/grants available. Support available to part-time students. Financial award application deadline: 4/1; financial award applicants required to submit FAFSA. *Unit head:* Dr. Susan Langston, Program Coordinator, 417-865-2815 Ext. 8552, E-mail: langstons@evangel.edu. *Application contact:* Karen Benitez, Admissions Representative, Graduate Studies, 417-865-2811 Ext. 7416, Fax: 417-575-5484, E-mail: benitezk@evangel.edu.
Website: https://www.evangel.edu/programs/doctor-education-educational-leadership-curriculum-instruction/

Fairleigh Dickinson University, Metropolitan Campus, University College: Arts, Sciences, and Professional Studies, Peter Sammartino School of Education, Teaneck, NJ 07666-1914. Offers dyslexia specialist (Certificate); education for certified teachers (MA); educational leadership (MA); instructional technology (Certificate); learning disabilities (MA); literacy/reading (Certificate); multilingual education (MA); teacher of the handicapped (Certificate); teaching (MAT). *Accreditation:* TEAC. *Program availability:* Part-time. *Degree requirements:* For master's, research project (MAT).

Ferris State University, College of Education and Human Services, School of Education, Big Rapids, MI 49307. Offers curriculum and instruction (M Ed), including special education, subject area; educational leadership (MS); instructor (MSCTE); post-secondary administration (MSCTE); training and development (MSCTE). *Program availability:* Part-time, evening/weekend, blended/hybrid learning. *Faculty:* 7 full-time (4 women), 9 part-time/adjunct (6 women). *Students:* 3 full-time (1 woman), 62 part-time (34 women); includes 8 minority (3 Black or African American, non-Hispanic/Latino; 1 Hispanic/Latino; 4 Two or more races, non-Hispanic/Latino), 9 international. Average age 37. 24 applicants, 71% accepted, 10 enrolled. In 2016, 36 master's awarded. *Degree requirements:* For master's, thesis, research paper or project. *Entrance requirements:* For master's, minimum undergraduate GPA of 3.0. Additional exam requirements/recommendations for international students: Required—TOEFL (minimum score 500 paper-based, 79 iBT) or IELTS. *Application deadline:* For fall admission, 7/1 priority date for domestic and international students; for spring admission, 11/1 priority date for domestic and international students; for summer admission, 3/1 priority date for domestic and international students. Applications are processed on a rolling basis. Application fee: $30. Electronic applications accepted. Application fee is waived when completed online. Tuition and fees vary according to degree level and program. *Financial support:* Career-related internships or fieldwork and scholarships/grants available. Support available to part-time students. Financial award applicants required to submit FAFSA. *Faculty research:* Suicide prevention, reading, women in education, special needs, administration. *Unit head:* Arrick L. Jackson, Dean, 231-591-2702, Fax: 231-591-2043, E-mail: arrickJackson@ferris.edu. *Application contact:* Liza Ing, Graduate Program Coordinator, 231-591-5362, Fax: 231-591-2043, E-mail: lizaIng@ferris.edu.
Website: http://www.ferris.edu/education/education/

Fitchburg State University, Division of Graduate and Continuing Education, Program in Curriculum and Teaching, Fitchburg, MA 01420-2697. Offers M Ed. *Program availability:* Part-time, evening/weekend. *Entrance requirements:* Additional exam requirements/recommendations for international students: Required—TOEFL (minimum score 550 paper-based; 79 iBT). Electronic applications accepted. *Expenses:* Tuition, state resident: full-time $2871; part-time $1914 per year. Tuition, nonresident: full-time $2871; part-time $1914 per year. *Required fees:* $3828. Tuition and fees vary according to program.

Florida Atlantic University, College of Education, Department of Curriculum, Culture, and Educational Inquiry, Boca Raton, FL 33431-0991. Offers curriculum and instruction (M Ed, PhD, Ed S); early childhood education (M Ed); multicultural education (M Ed); TESOL and bilingual education (MA). *Program availability:* Part-time, evening/weekend. *Faculty:* 12 full-time (9 women), 1 (woman) part-time/adjunct. *Students:* 31 full-time (27 women), 93 part-time (68 women); includes 37 minority (17 Black or African American, non-Hispanic/Latino; 4 Asian, non-Hispanic/Latino; 15 Hispanic/Latino; 1 Two or more races, non-Hispanic/Latino), 2 international. Average age 35. 65 applicants, 60% accepted, 25 enrolled. In 2016, 17 master's, 18 doctorates, 3 other advanced degrees awarded. *Entrance requirements:* Additional exam requirements/recommendations for international students: Required—TOEFL (minimum score 500 paper-based; 61 iBT), IELTS (minimum score 6). *Application deadline:* For fall admission, 7/1 for domestic students, 2/15 for international students; for spring admission, 11/1 for domestic students, 7/15 for international students. Application fee: $30. *Expenses:* Tuition, state resident: full-time $7392; part-time $369.82 per credit hour. Tuition, nonresident: full-time $19,432; part-time $1024.81 per credit hour. *Faculty research:* Multicultural education, early intervention strategies, family literacy, religious diversity in schools, early childhood curriculum. *Unit head:* Dr. Dilys Schoorman, Chair, 561-297-3965, E-mail: dschoorm@fau.edu. *Application contact:* Dr. Eliah Watlington, Associate Dean, 561-296-8520, Fax: 261-297-2991, E-mail: ewatling@fau.edu.
Website: http://www.coe.fau.edu/academicdepartments/ccei/

Florida Atlantic University, College of Education, Department of Teaching and Learning, Boca Raton, FL 33431-0991. Offers curriculum and instruction (M Ed), including art, biology, chemistry, English, French, German, mathematics, music, physics, Pre-K and primary education, reading, social sciences, Spanish; elementary education (M Ed); environmental education (M Ed); reading education (M Ed); social foundations of education (M Ed), including educational psychology, educational

technology, multilingual education. *Accreditation:* NCATE. *Program availability:* Part-time, evening/weekend. *Faculty:* 15 full-time (12 women), 2 part-time/adjunct (1 woman). *Students:* 25 full-time (20 women), 41 part-time (37 women); includes 18 minority (9 Black or African American, non-Hispanic/Latino; 2 Asian, non-Hispanic/Latino; 7 Hispanic/Latino), 7 international. Average age 32. 54 applicants, 59% accepted, 18 enrolled. In 2016, 36 master's awarded. *Entrance requirements:* For master's, GRE General Test, minimum GPA of 3.0 in last 2 years of undergraduate course work. Additional exam requirements/recommendations for international students: Required—TOEFL (minimum score 500 paper-based; 61 iBT), IELTS (minimum score 6). *Application deadline:* For fall admission, 7/1 for domestic students, 2/15 for international students; for spring admission, 11/1 for domestic students, 7/15 for international students. Applications are processed on a rolling basis. Application fee: $30. *Expenses:* Tuition, state resident: full-time $7392; part-time $369.82 per credit hour. Tuition, nonresident: full-time $19,432; part-time $1024.81 per credit hour. *Financial support:* Fellowships with partial tuition reimbursements, research assistantships with partial tuition reimbursements, teaching assistantships with partial tuition reimbursements, career-related internships or fieldwork, scholarships/grants, and unspecified assistantships available. *Faculty research:* Technology, teaching English to speakers of other languages, math teaching, electronic portfolio assessment, global perspectives through social studies. *Unit head:* Dr. Barbara Ridener, Chairperson, 561-297-3588, E-mail: bridener@fau.edu. *Application contact:* Dr. Eliah Watlington, Associate Dean, 561-296-8520, Fax: 261-297-2991, E-mail: ewatling@fau.edu.
Website: http://www.coe.fau.edu/academicdepartments/tl/

Florida Gulf Coast University, College of Education, Program in Curriculum and Instruction, Fort Myers, FL 33965-6565. Offers elementary education (M Ed); English education (M Ed); gifted education (M Ed); mathematics education (M Ed); middle school education (M Ed); science education (M Ed); social science education (M Ed). *Program availability:* Part-time, evening/weekend, online learning. *Faculty:* 26 full-time (18 women), 44 part-time/adjunct (32 women). *Students:* 1 (woman) full-time, 22 part-time (20 women); includes 49 minority (19 Black or African American, non-Hispanic/Latino; 4 Asian, non-Hispanic/Latino; 24 Hispanic/Latino; 2 Two or more races, non-Hispanic/Latino), 2 international. Average age 28. 9 applicants, 78% accepted, 2 enrolled. In 2016, 9 master's awarded. *Degree requirements:* For master's, final project or portfolio. *Entrance requirements:* For master's, GRE General Test, MAT, minimum undergraduate GPA of 3.0 in last 2 years. Additional exam requirements/recommendations for international students: Required—TOEFL (minimum score 550 paper-based). *Application deadline:* For fall admission, 7/1 priority date for domestic students; for spring admission, 10/15 for domestic students. Applications are processed on a rolling basis. Application fee: $30. Electronic applications accepted. *Expenses:* Tuition, state resident: full-time $6721. Tuition, nonresident: full-time $28,170. *Required fees:* $1987. Tuition and fees vary according to course load and degree level. *Financial support:* In 2016–17, 1 student received support. Application deadline: 3/1; applicants required to submit FAFSA. *Faculty research:* Internet in schools, technology in pre-service and in-service teacher training. *Unit head:* Dr. Diane Schmidt, Department Chair, 239-590-7741, Fax: 239-590-7801, E-mail: dschmidt@fgcu.edu. *Application contact:* Keiana Desmore, Adviser/Counselor, 239-590-7759, Fax: 239-590-7801, E-mail: kdesmore@fgcu.edu.
Website: http://coe.fgcu.edu/c-imed/

Florida International University, College of Arts, Sciences, and Education, Department of Teaching and Learning, Miami, FL 33199. Offers art education (MA, MS); curriculum and instruction (MS, Ed D, PhD, Ed S), including curriculum development (MS), elementary education (MS), English education (MS), learning technologies (MS), mathematics education (MS), modern language education (MS), physical education (MS), science education (MS), social studies education (MS), special education (MS); early childhood education (MS); exceptional student education (Ed D); foreign language education (MS), including foreign language education, teaching English to speakers of other languages (TESOL); international/intercultural education (MS); language, literacy and culture (PhD); mathematics, science, and learning technologies (PhD); physical education (MS), including sport and fitness; reading education (MS). *Program availability:* Part-time, evening/weekend. *Faculty:* 34 full-time (23 women), 64 part-time/adjunct (48 women). *Students:* 182 full-time (154 women), 231 part-time (190 women); includes 323 minority (69 Black or African American, non-Hispanic/Latino; 10 Asian, non-Hispanic/Latino; 237 Hispanic/Latino; 7 Two or more races, non-Hispanic/Latino), 19 international. Average age 34. 282 applicants, 58% accepted, 113 enrolled. In 2016, 184 master's, 12 doctorates awarded. *Degree requirements:* For doctorate, comprehensive exam, thesis/dissertation. *Entrance requirements:* For master's, GRE General Test, Florida General Knowledge Test or Florida College Level Academic Skills Test; for doctorate and Ed S, GRE General Test. Additional exam requirements/recommendations for international students: Required—TOEFL (minimum score 550 paper-based; 80 iBT), IELTS (minimum score 6.3). *Application deadline:* For fall admission, 6/1 priority date for domestic students, 4/1 for international students; for winter admission, 10/1 priority date for domestic students, 9/1 for international students; for spring admission, 3/1 priority date for domestic students, 2/1 for international students. Applications are processed on a rolling basis. Application fee: $30. Electronic applications accepted. *Expenses:* Tuition, state resident: full-time $8912; part-time $446 per credit hour. Tuition, nonresident: full-time $21,393; part-time $992 per credit hour. *Required fees:* $2185; $195 per semester. Tuition and fees vary according to program. *Financial support:* Research assistantships with tuition reimbursements and teaching assistantships with tuition reimbursements available. *Unit head:* Dr. Lynn Miller, Chair, 305-348-2005, Fax: 305-348-2086, E-mail: lynne.miller@fiu.edu. *Application contact:* Nanett Rojas, Assistant Director, Graduate Admissions, 305-348-7464, Fax: 305-348-7441, E-mail: gradadm@fiu.edu.
Website: http://education.fiu.edu

Florida State University, The Graduate School, College of Education, Program in Curriculum and Instruction, Tallahassee, FL 32306. Offers curriculum and instruction (MS, PhD, Ed S), including early childhood education, elementary education, English education, English teaching (MS), exceptional student education (MS), foreign and second language education, foreign and second language teaching (MS), mathematics education, mathematics teaching (MS), reading education and language arts, science education, social science education, social science teaching (MS), special education, special education studies (MS), visual disabilities (MS, Ed S). *Program availability:* Part-time, evening/weekend. Terminal master's awarded for partial completion of doctoral program. *Degree requirements:* For master's and Ed S, comprehensive exam, thesis optional; for doctorate, comprehensive exam, thesis/dissertation, diagnostic exam, preliminary exam, prospectus defense, dissertation defense. *Entrance requirements:* For master's, doctorate, and Ed S, GRE General Test, minimum upper-division GPA of 3.0. Additional exam requirements/recommendations for international students: Required—TOEFL (minimum score 550 paper-based, 80 iBT), IELTS (minimum score 6.5), Michigan English Language Assessment Battery (minimum score 77), or PTE (minimum score 55). Application fee: $30. Electronic applications accepted. *Expenses:* Tuition, state resident: full-time $7263; part-time $403.51 per credit hour. Tuition, nonresident: full-time $18,087; part-time $1004.85 per credit hour. *Required fees:* $1365; $75.81 per credit hour. $20 per semester. Tuition and fees vary according to campus/location. *Financial support:* Fellowships, research assistantships, teaching assistantships, scholarships/grants, tuition waivers (full and partial), and unspecified assistantships available. Financial award application deadline: 1/15; financial award applicants required to submit FAFSA. *Faculty research:* Identifying effective intervention strategies to improve reading skills; improving literacy teaching and learning through technology; understanding of student sense making, problem solving, the history and structure of STEM disciplines, and teacher education to support the development of ambitious instruction that supports the STEM learning of all students; examining practices of international education; identifying ways to support the professional development of teachers. *Unit head:* Dr. Sherry Southerland, Professor/Department Chair, 850-644-4880, Fax: 850-644-7736, E-mail: ssoutherland@admin.fsu.edu. *Application contact:* Libbie Crowley, Academic Support Specialist, 850-644-2122, Fax: 850-644-7736, E-mail: ecrowley@fsu.edu.
Website: http://education.fsu.edu/degrees-and-programs/graduate-programs

Fontbonne University, Graduate Programs, St. Louis, MO 63105-3098. Offers accounting (MBA, MS); art (MA); art (K-12) (MAT); business (MBA); computer science (MS); deaf education (MA); early intervention in deaf education (MA); education (MA), including autism spectrum disorders, curriculum and instruction, diverse learners, early childhood education, reading, special education; elementary education (MAT); family and consumer sciences (MA), including multidisciplinary health communication studies; fine arts (MFA); instructional design and technology (MS); management and leadership (MM); middle school education (MAT); secondary education (MAT); special education (MAT); speech-language pathology (MS); supply chain management (MS); theatre (MA). *Program availability:* Part-time, evening/weekend, online learning. *Faculty:* 32 full-time (24 women), 43 part-time/adjunct (26 women). *Students:* 456 full-time (313 women), 102 part-time (77 women); includes 138 minority (118 Black or African American, non-Hispanic/Latino; 1 American Indian or Alaska Native, non-Hispanic/Latino; 7 Asian, non-Hispanic/Latino; 9 Hispanic/Latino; 3 Two or more races, non-Hispanic/Latino), 37 international. *Degree requirements:* For master's, comprehensive exam (for some programs), thesis (for some programs). *Entrance requirements:* Additional exam requirements/recommendations for international students: Required—TOEFL (minimum score 500 paper-based; 65 iBT). *Application deadline:* For fall admission, 8/1 for international students; for spring admission, 12/1 for international students. Applications are processed on a rolling basis. Application fee: $25 ($30 for international students). Electronic applications accepted. *Expenses: Tuition:* Full-time $8436; part-time $703 per credit hour. *Required fees:* $18 per credit hour. Tuition and fees vary according to course load. *Financial support:* Teaching assistantships with partial tuition reimbursements and scholarships/grants available. Support available to part-time students. Financial award application deadline: 4/1; financial award applicants required to submit FAFSA. *Unit head:* Dr. Carey Adams, Vice President for Academic Affairs, 314-719-3609, E-mail: cadams@fontbonne.edu. *Application contact:* Lauryn Filip, Coordinator, Graduate Admission and Professional Studies, 314-889-4650, E-mail: admissions@fontbonne.edu.
Website: https://www.fontbonne.edu/academics/graduate-programs/

Fordham University, Graduate School of Education, Division of Curriculum and Teaching, New York, NY 10023. Offers curriculum and teaching (MSE); early childhood education (MSE); elementary education (MST); special education (MSE, Adv C); teaching English as a second language (MSE). *Accreditation:* NCATE. *Program availability:* Part-time, evening/weekend. *Degree requirements:* For Adv C, thesis. *Entrance requirements:* Additional exam requirements/recommendations for international students: Required—TOEFL (minimum score 577 paper-based; 90 iBT), IELTS (minimum score 7). Electronic applications accepted.

Framingham State University, Continuing Education, Program in Curriculum and Instructional Technology, Framingham, MA 01701-9101. Offers M Ed. *Program availability:* Online learning.

Franciscan University of Steubenville, Graduate Programs, Department of Education, Steubenville, OH 43952-1763. Offers administration (MS Ed); teaching (MS Ed). *Accreditation:* NCATE. *Program availability:* Part-time, evening/weekend, online learning. *Degree requirements:* For master's, project. *Entrance requirements:* For master's, minimum undergraduate GPA of 2.5 or written exam. Additional exam requirements/recommendations for international students: Required—TOEFL. Electronic applications accepted. Application fee is waived when completed online. *Expenses:* Contact institution.

Franklin Pierce University, Graduate and Professional Studies, Rindge, NH 03461-0060. Offers curriculum and instruction (M Ed); elementary education (MS Ed); emerging network technologies (Graduate Certificate); energy and sustainability studies (MBA, Graduate Certificate); health administration (MBA, Graduate Certificate); human resource management (MBA, Graduate Certificate); information technology (MBA); leadership (MBA); nursing education (MS); nursing leadership (MS); physical therapy (DPT); physician assistant studies (MPAS); special education (M Ed); sports management (MBA). *Accreditation:* APTA. *Program availability:* Part-time, 100% online, blended/hybrid learning. *Faculty:* 47 full-time (36 women), 165 part-time/adjunct (108 women). *Students:* 380 full-time (226 women), 245 part-time (158 women); includes 52 minority (13 Black or African American, non-Hispanic/Latino; 2 American Indian or Alaska Native, non-Hispanic/Latino; 14 Asian, non-Hispanic/Latino; 22 Hispanic/Latino; 1 Native Hawaiian or other Pacific Islander, non-Hispanic/Latino), 13 international. Average age 29. 1,995 applicants, 28% accepted, 267 enrolled. In 2016, 120 master's, 86 doctorates awarded. *Degree requirements:* For master's, concentrated original research projects; student teaching; fieldwork and/or internship; leadership project; PRAXIS I and II (for M Ed); for doctorate, concentrated original research projects, clinical fieldwork and/or internship, leadership project. *Entrance requirements:* For master's, minimum GPA of 2.5, 3 letters of recommendation; competencies in accounting, economics, statistics, and computer skills through life experience or undergraduate coursework (for MBA); certification/e-portfolio, minimum C grade in all education courses (for M Ed); license to practice as RN (for MS); for doctorate, GRE, 80 hours of observation/work in PT settings; completion of anatomy, chemistry, physics, and statistics; minimum GPA of 3.0. Additional exam requirements/recommendations for international students: Required—TOEFL (minimum score 550 paper-based; 61 iBT). *Application deadline:* Applications are processed on a rolling basis. Application fee: $0. Electronic applications accepted. *Expenses: Tuition:* Full-time $15,960; part-time $665 per credit hour. Tuition and fees vary according to program. *Financial support:* Teaching assistantships with tuition reimbursements, career-related internships or fieldwork, and unspecified assistantships available. Support available to part-time students. Financial award applicants required to submit FAFSA. *Faculty research:* Evidence-based practice in sports physical therapy, human resource management in economic crisis, leadership in nursing, innovation in sports facility management, differentiated learning and understanding by design. *Unit head:* Dr. Maria Altobello, Dean, 603-647-3509, Fax: 603-229-4580, E-mail: altobellom@franklinpierce.edu. *Application contact:* Graduate Studies, 800-325-1090, Fax: 603-626-4815, E-mail: cgps@franklinpierce.edu.
Website: http://www.franklinpierce.edu/academics/gradstudies/index.htm

Freed-Hardeman University, Program in Education, Henderson, TN 38340-2399. Offers curriculum and instruction (M Ed); school counseling (M Ed), including administration and supervision, special education; school leadership (Ed S). *Accreditation:* NCATE. *Program availability:* Part-time, evening/weekend. *Degree* *requirements:* For master's, comprehensive exam, thesis optional; for Ed S, thesis. *Entrance requirements:* For master's, GRE General Test or NTE; for Ed S, 3 years of teaching experience. Additional exam requirements/recommendations for international students: Required—TOEFL (minimum score 500 paper-based).

Fresno Pacific University, Graduate Programs, School of Education, Program in Curriculum and Teaching, Fresno, CA 93702-4709. Offers MA. *Program availability:* Part-time, evening/weekend, online learning. *Degree requirements:* For master's, thesis or alternative. *Entrance requirements:* For master's, interview, statement of intent, three letters of recommendation, official transcript, BA/BS, minimum GPA of 2.75. Additional exam requirements/recommendations for international students: Required—TOEFL (minimum score 550 paper-based). Electronic applications accepted. *Expenses:* Contact institution.

Frostburg State University, Graduate School, College of Education, Department of Educational Professions, Program in Curriculum and Instruction, Frostburg, MD 21532-1099. Offers educational technology (M Ed); elementary education (M Ed); secondary education (M Ed). *Program availability:* Part-time, evening/weekend. *Degree requirements:* For master's, thesis or alternative. *Entrance requirements:* For master's, teaching certificate. Additional exam requirements/recommendations for international students: Required—TOEFL. Electronic applications accepted.

Furman University, Graduate Division, Department of Education, Greenville, SC 29613. Offers curriculum and instruction (MA); early childhood education (MA); educational leadership (Ed S); English as a second language (MA); literacy (MA); school leadership (MA); special education (MA). *Accreditation:* NCATE. *Program availability:* Part-time, online learning. *Degree requirements:* For master's, comprehensive exam (for some programs), thesis or alternative. *Entrance requirements:* For master's, PRAXIS II. *Faculty research:* Literacy, pedagogy and practice, social justice, advanced leadership, achievement in high poverty schools.

Gannon University, School of Graduate Studies, College of Humanities, Education, and Social Sciences, School of Education, Program in Curriculum and Instruction, Erie, PA 16541-0001. Offers M Ed. *Program availability:* Part-time, evening/weekend, 100% online. *Students:* 6 full-time (all women), 85 part-time (64 women); includes 5 minority (1 Black or African American, non-Hispanic/Latino; 1 American Indian or Alaska Native, non-Hispanic/Latino; 1 Asian, non-Hispanic/Latino; 2 Hispanic/Latino). Average age 32. 38 applicants, 89% accepted, 30 enrolled. In 2016, 61 master's awarded. *Degree requirements:* For master's, thesis or alternative, portfolio project. *Entrance requirements:* For master's, bachelor's degree from regionally-accredited college or university with minimum GPA of 3.0, official transcripts, 3 letters of recommendation. Additional exam requirements/recommendations for international students: Required—TOEFL (minimum score 79 iBT). *Application deadline:* Applications are processed on a rolling basis. Application fee: $25. Electronic applications accepted. Application fee is waived when completed online. *Expenses:* Contact institution. *Financial support:* Federal Work-Study available. Financial award application deadline: 7/1; financial award applicants required to submit FAFSA. *Unit head:* Dr. Bill Hallock, Program Coordinator, 814-871-7136, E-mail: hallock002@gannon.edu. *Application contact:* Bridget Philip, Director of Graduate Admissions, 814-871-5831, E-mail: graduate@gannon.edu.

Gannon University, School of Graduate Studies, College of Humanities, Education, and Social Sciences, School of Education, Program in Curriculum Supervisor, Erie, PA 16541-0001. Offers Certificate. *Program availability:* Part-time, evening/weekend, online learning. *Students:* 1 (woman) part-time. Average age 34. 4 applicants, 50% accepted, 1 enrolled. In 2016, 2 Certificates awarded. *Degree requirements:* For Certificate, internship. *Entrance requirements:* Additional exam requirements/recommendations for international students: Required—TOEFL (minimum score 79 iBT). *Application deadline:* Applications are processed on a rolling basis. Application fee: $25. Electronic applications accepted. Application fee is waived when completed online. *Expenses:* Contact institution. *Financial support:* Federal Work-Study available. Financial award application deadline: 7/1; financial award applicants required to submit FAFSA. *Unit head:* Dr. Bill Hallock, Program Coordinator, 814-871-7136, E-mail: hallock002@gannon.edu. *Application contact:* Bridget Philip, Director of Graduate Admissions, 814-871-7412, E-mail: graduate@gannon.edu.

Gardner-Webb University, Graduate School, School of Education, Program in Curriculum and Instruction, Boiling Springs, NC 28017. Offers Ed D. *Faculty:* 16 full-time (6 women), 35 part-time/adjunct (20 women). *Students:* 2 full-time (1 woman), 234 part-time (214 women); includes 77 minority (69 Black or African American, non-Hispanic/Latino; 1 American Indian or Alaska Native, non-Hispanic/Latino; 2 Asian, non-Hispanic/Latino; 5 Hispanic/Latino), 1 international. Average age 37. 143 applicants, 41% accepted, 46 enrolled. In 2016, 32 doctorates awarded. *Expenses:* Contact institution. *Unit head:* Dr. Alan D. Eury, Chair, 704-406-4402, Fax: 704-406-3921, E-mail: dsimmons@gardner-webb.edu. *Application contact:* Office of Graduate Admissions, 877-498-4723, Fax: 704-406-3895, E-mail: gradinfo@gardner-webb.edu.

George Mason University, College of Education and Human Development, Programs in Curriculum and Instruction, Fairfax, VA 22030. Offers advanced international baccalaureate (M Ed); assistive technology (M Ed); designing digital learning in schools (M Ed); early childhood education (M Ed); early childhood education for diverse learners (M Ed); elementary education (M Ed); English as a second language (M Ed); gifted child education (M Ed); history (M Ed); literacy (M Ed), including PK-12 classroom teachers, reading specialist; literacy leadership for diverse schools (M Ed), including K-12 reading; physical education (M Ed); science K-12 (M Ed); secondary education (M Ed), including biology, chemistry, earth science, English, history/social science, math, physics; special education (M Ed); teacher leadership (M Ed); teaching culturally, linguistically diverse and exceptional learners (M Ed); transformative teaching (M Ed). *Faculty:* 41 full-time (35 women), 53 part-time/adjunct (46 women). *Students:* 155 full-time (127 women), 821 part-time (697 women); includes 267 minority (82 Black or African American, non-Hispanic/Latino; 5 American Indian or Alaska Native, non-Hispanic/Latino; 75 Asian, non-Hispanic/Latino; 88 Hispanic/Latino; 1 Native Hawaiian or other Pacific Islander, non-Hispanic/Latino; 16 Two or more races, non-Hispanic/Latino), 19 international. Average age 33. 513 applicants, 90% accepted, 352 enrolled. In 2016, 347 master's awarded. *Degree requirements:* For master's, comprehensive exam, thesis (for some programs). *Entrance requirements:* For master's, PRAXIS Core (for some programs), minimum GPA of 3.0 in last 60 hours, licensed as teacher or educational administrator, official transcripts, goals statement, 3 recommendation letters, interview or writing sample (depending on program), up to 3 years' teaching experience (depending on program). Additional exam requirements/recommendations for international students: Required—TOEFL (minimum score 575 paper-based; 88 iBT), IELTS (minimum score 6.5), PTE (minimum score 59). *Application deadline:* For spring admission, 11/1 priority date for domestic and international students. Application fee: $75 ($80 for international students). Electronic applications accepted. *Expenses:* Tuition, state resident: full-time $10,628; part-time $443 per credit. Tuition, nonresident: full-time $29,306; part-time $1221 per credit. *Required fees:* $3096; $129 per credit. Tuition and fees vary according to program. *Financial support:* In 2016–17, 1 student received support, including 1 teaching assistantship (averaging $4,060 per year); career-related internships or fieldwork, Federal Work-Study, scholarships/grants, unspecified assistantships, and health care benefits (for full-time research or teaching assistantship recipients) also available. Support available to part-time students. Financial award application deadline: 3/1; financial award applicants required to submit FAFSA. *Faculty research:* Achievement gaps and superintendent decisions, constructivist view of classroom teaching, cost of cheating, creating a critical literacy milieu in kindergarten. *Unit head:* Rebecca Fox, Professor and Academic Program Coordinator, 703-993-4123, E-mail: rfox@gmu.edu.
Website: http://gse.gmu.edu/programs/gsemasters

The George Washington University, Graduate School of Education and Human Development, Department of Curriculum and Pedagogy, Program in Curriculum and Instruction, Washington, DC 20052. Offers MA Ed, Ed D, Ed S, Graduate Certificate. *Accreditation:* NCATE. *Program availability:* Evening/weekend. *Students:* 28 full-time (24 women), 48 part-time (38 women); includes 20 minority (13 Black or African American, non-Hispanic/Latino; 4 Asian, non-Hispanic/Latino; 1 Hispanic/Latino; 2 Two or more races, non-Hispanic/Latino), 15 international. Average age 33. 59 applicants, 75% accepted, 25 enrolled. In 2016, 6 master's, 3 doctorates, 1 other advanced degree awarded. *Degree requirements:* For master's and other advanced degree, comprehensive exam; for doctorate, comprehensive exam, thesis/dissertation. *Entrance requirements:* For master's, GRE General Test or MAT, minimum GPA of 2.75, resume; for doctorate and other advanced degree, GRE General Test or MAT, interview, minimum GPA of 3.3. *Application deadline:* For fall admission, 1/15 priority date for domestic students; for spring admission, 10/1 for domestic students. Applications are processed on a rolling basis. Application fee: $75. *Financial support:* In 2016–17, 25 students received support. Fellowships, research assistantships, career-related internships or fieldwork, Federal Work-Study, and tuition waivers (partial) available. Financial award application deadline: 1/15; financial award applicants required to submit FAFSA. *Faculty research:* Cognitive skills-teaching, metacognitive strategies, adult basic literacy. *Unit head:* Dr. Sharon Lynch, Faculty Coordinator, 202-994-6174, E-mail: slynch@gwu.edu. *Application contact:* Sarah Lang, Director of Graduate Admissions, 202-994-1447, Fax: 202-994-7207, E-mail: slang@gwu.edu.

Georgia Southern University, Jack N. Averitt College of Graduate Studies, College of Education, Department of Curriculum, Foundations, and Reading, Program in Curriculum Studies, Statesboro, GA 30460. Offers curriculum studies (Ed D), including cultural curriculum, instructional improvement, multicultural studies, teaching and learning. *Program availability:* Part-time. *Students:* 21 full-time (19 women), 131 part-time (99 women); includes 43 minority (35 Black or African American, non-Hispanic/Latino; 5 Hispanic/Latino; 3 Two or more races, non-Hispanic/Latino), 3 international. Average age 41. In 2016, 16 doctorates awarded. *Degree requirements:* For doctorate, comprehensive exam, thesis/dissertation, exams. *Entrance requirements:* For doctorate, GRE or MAT, letters of reference, minimum GPA of 3.5, writing sample. Additional exam requirements/recommendations for international students: Required—TOEFL (minimum score 550 paper-based; 80 iBT), IELTS (minimum score 6). *Application deadline:* For summer admission, 1/30 for domestic students. Application fee: $50. Electronic applications accepted. *Expenses:* Tuition, state resident: full-time $7236; part-time $277 per semester hour. Tuition, nonresident: full-time $27,118; part-time $1105 per semester hour. *Required fees:* $2092. *Financial support:* In 2016–17, 8 students received support. Research assistantships with partial tuition reimbursements available, career-related internships or fieldwork, Federal Work-Study, scholarships/grants, and unspecified assistantships available. Financial award application deadline: 4/15; financial award applicants required to submit FAFSA. *Faculty research:* Curriculum theory, cultural studies, narrative research, postmodern theory, critical race theory, international education, feminism, media literacy, documentary studies, post human condition, social and cultural foundations of education, democracy and education. *Unit head:* Dr. Daniel Chapman, Program Coordinator, 912-478-5715, E-mail: dechapman@georgiasouthern.edu. *Application contact:* Lydia Cross, Coordinator for Graduate Student Recruitment, 912-478-8664, E-mail: lcross@georgiasouthern.edu.
Website: http://coe.georgiasouthern.edu/cs/

Georgia Southern University, Jack N. Averitt College of Graduate Studies, College of Education, Department of Teaching and Learning, Program in Curriculum and Instruction - Accomplished Teaching, Statesboro, GA 30458. Offers M Ed. *Program availability:* Part-time, evening/weekend, blended/hybrid learning. *Students:* 40 full-time (36 women), 175 part-time (141 women); includes 74 minority (64 Black or African American, non-Hispanic/Latino; 5 Hispanic/Latino; 5 Two or more races, non-Hispanic/Latino). Average age 30. 68 applicants, 100% accepted, 48 enrolled. In 2016, 69 master's awarded. *Entrance requirements:* For master's, current Georgia teaching certificate. Additional exam requirements/recommendations for international students: Required—TOEFL (minimum score 550 paper-based; 80 iBT), IELTS (minimum score 6). *Application deadline:* For fall admission, 8/16 for domestic students; for spring admission, 1/11 for domestic students; for summer admission, 5/14 for domestic students. Applications are processed on a rolling basis. Application fee: $50. Electronic applications accepted. *Expenses:* Tuition, state resident: full-time $7236; part-time $277 per semester hour. Tuition, nonresident: full-time $27,118; part-time $1105 per semester hour. *Required fees:* $2092. *Financial support:* In 2016–17, 2 students received support, including 4 fellowships with full tuition reimbursements available (averaging $7,750 per year). Financial award application deadline: 4/20; financial award applicants required to submit FAFSA. *Faculty research:* Teacher preparation, curriculum design, assessment for improved student outcomes, reflective practices of infield teachers, diversity responsive methods in instruction. *Unit head:* Dr. Kymberly Harris, Chair, 912-478-5041, E-mail: kharris@georgiasouthern.edu. *Application contact:* Lydia Cross, Coordinator for Graduate Student Recruitment, 912-478-8664, E-mail: lcross@georgiasouthern.edu.

Georgia State University, College of Education and Human Development, Department of Middle and Secondary Education, Atlanta, GA 30302-3083. Offers curriculum and instruction (Ed D); English education (MAT); mathematics education (M Ed, MAT); middle level education (MAT); reading, language and literacy education (M Ed, MAT), including reading instruction (M Ed); science education (M Ed, MAT), including biology (MAT), broad field science (MAT), chemistry (MAT), earth science (MAT), physics (MAT); social studies education (M Ed, MAT), including economics (MAT), geography (MAT), history (MAT), political science (MAT); teaching and learning (PhD), including language and literacy, mathematics education, music education, science education, social studies education, teaching and teacher education. *Accreditation:* NCATE. *Program availability:* Part-time, evening/weekend, online learning. *Faculty:* 24 full-time (18 women). *Students:* 145 full-time (91 women), 151 part-time (102 women); includes 141 minority (104 Black or African American, non-Hispanic/Latino; 1 American Indian or Alaska Native, non-Hispanic/Latino; 16 Asian, non-Hispanic/Latino; 12 Hispanic/Latino; 8 Two or more races, non-Hispanic/Latino), 10 international. Average age 36. 115 applicants, 50% accepted, 41 enrolled. In 2016, 94 master's, 22 doctorates awarded. *Degree requirements:* For master's, comprehensive exam (for some programs), thesis or alternative, exit portfolio; for doctorate, comprehensive exam, thesis/dissertation. *Entrance requirements:* For master's, GRE; GACE I (for initial teacher preparation programs), baccalaureate degree or equivalent, resume, goals statement, two letters of recommendation, minimum undergraduate GPA of 2.5; proof of initial teacher certification in the content area (for M Ed); for doctorate, GRE, resume, goals statement, writing sample, two letters of recommendation, minimum graduate GPA of 3.3, interview. Additional exam requirements/recommendations for international students: Required—TOEFL (minimum score 550 paper-based; 79 iBT) or IELTS (minimum score 6.5).

Application deadline: For fall admission, 1/15 priority date for domestic and international students; for spring admission, 10/1 for domestic and international students. Application fee: $50. Electronic applications accepted. *Expenses:* Tuition, state resident: full-time $6876; part-time $382 per credit hour. Tuition, nonresident: full-time $22,374; part-time $1243 per credit hour. *Required fees:* $2128; $1064 per term. Part-time tuition and fees vary according to course load and program. *Financial support:* In 2016–17, fellowships with full tuition reimbursements (averaging $19,667 per year), research assistantships with full tuition reimbursements (averaging $5,436 per year), teaching assistantships with full tuition reimbursements (averaging $2,779 per year) were awarded; career-related internships or fieldwork, Federal Work-Study, scholarships/grants, health care benefits, tuition waivers (full and partial), and unspecified assistantships also available. Financial award application deadline: 3/15. *Faculty research:* Teacher education in language and literacy, mathematics, science, and social studies in urban middle and secondary school settings; learning technologies in school, community, and corporate settings; multicultural education and education for social justice; urban education; international education. *Unit head:* Dr. Dana L. Fox, Chair, 404-413-8060, Fax: 404-413-8063, E-mail: dfox@gsu.edu. *Application contact:* Bobbie Turner, Administrative Coordinator I, 404-413-8405, Fax: 404-413-8063, E-mail: bnturner@gsu.edu.
Website: http://mse.education.gsu.edu/

Graceland University, Gleazer School of Education, Independence, MO 64050. Offers curriculum and instruction (M Ed); differentiated instruction (M Ed); instructional leadership (M Ed); literacy and instruction (M Ed); management in the inclusive classroom (M Ed); special education (M Ed); technology integration (M Ed). *Accreditation:* NCATE. *Program availability:* Part-time, evening/weekend, online learning. *Faculty:* 2 full-time (both women), 9 part-time/adjunct (5 women). *Students:* 115 full-time (96 women), 20 part-time (17 women); includes 10 minority (5 Black or African American, non-Hispanic/Latino; 1 Asian, non-Hispanic/Latino; 1 Hispanic/Latino; 1 Native Hawaiian or other Pacific Islander, non-Hispanic/Latino; 2 Two or more races, non-Hispanic/Latino), 2 international. 155 applicants, 61% accepted, 85 enrolled. In 2016, 61 master's awarded. *Degree requirements:* For master's, action research project. *Entrance requirements:* For master's, minimum GPA of 3.0, teaching certificate, current teaching contract. Additional exam requirements/recommendations for international students: Required—TOEFL. *Application deadline:* For fall admission, 10/1 for domestic students; for winter admission, 11/15 for domestic students; for spring admission, 2/15 priority date for domestic students; for summer admission, 6/1 for domestic students. Applications are processed on a rolling basis. Application fee: $50. Electronic applications accepted. *Expenses:* Contact institution. *Financial support:* Institutionally sponsored loans and scholarships/grants available. Financial award application deadline: 12/15; financial award applicants required to submit FAFSA. *Faculty research:* Literacy, technology, faculty mentoring, adult literacy, e-learning, online teaching. *Unit head:* Dr. Lee Bash, Interim Dean, 641-784-5072, E-mail: bash@graceland.edu. *Application contact:* Jeanette Calipetro, Admissions Representative, 816-423-4716, Fax: 816-833-2990, E-mail: jcali1@graceland.edu.
Website: http://www.graceland.edu/education

Grambling State University, School of Graduate Studies and Research, College of Education, Department of Curriculum and Instruction, Grambling, LA 71245. Offers curriculum and instruction (MS); special education (M Ed). *Program availability:* Part-time. *Degree requirements:* For master's, comprehensive exam, thesis (for some programs). *Entrance requirements:* Additional exam requirements/recommendations for international students: Required—TOEFL (minimum score 500 paper-based; 62 iBT).

Grambling State University, School of Graduate Studies and Research, College of Education, Department of Educational Leadership, Grambling, LA 71245. Offers developmental education (MS, Ed D, PMC), including curriculum and instructional design (Ed D), English (MS), guidance and counseling (MS), higher education administration and management (Ed D), mathematics (MS), reading (MS), science (MS), student development and personnel services (Ed D); educational leadership (M Ed). *Program availability:* Part-time, evening/weekend. *Degree requirements:* For master's, comprehensive exam, thesis (for some programs); for doctorate, comprehensive exam, thesis/dissertation. *Entrance requirements:* For master's, GRE, minimum GPA of 2.5 on last degree; for doctorate, GRE (minimum score 1000, 500 on Verbal), master's degree, minimum GPA of 3.0 on last degree. Additional exam requirements/recommendations for international students: Required—TOEFL (minimum score 500 paper-based; 62 iBT). Electronic applications accepted.

Grand Canyon University, College of Education, Phoenix, AZ 85017-1097. Offers autism spectrum disorders (MA); curriculum and instruction (MA); early childhood education (M Ed); educational administration (M Ed); educational leadership (M Ed); elementary education (M Ed); gifted education (MA); instructional technology (MS); K-12 leadership (Ed S); reading (MA); secondary education (M Ed); secondary humanities education (M Ed); secondary STEM education (M Ed); special education (M Ed); teaching and learning (Ed D); teaching English to speakers of other languages (MA). *Program availability:* Part-time, evening/weekend, online learning. *Degree requirements:* For master's, publishable research paper (M Ed), e-portfolio. *Entrance requirements:* For master's, undergraduate degree from accredited, GCU-approved college, university, or program with minimum GPA 2.8. Additional exam requirements/recommendations for international students: Required—TOEFL (minimum score 550 paper-based; 79 iBT), IELTS (minimum score 6). *Application deadline:* For fall admission, 8/21 for domestic students, 7/2 for international students; for spring admission, 12/24 for domestic students, 11/1 for international students. Applications are processed on a rolling basis. Application fee: $100. Electronic applications accepted. *Financial support:* Federal Work-Study available. Support available to part-time students. Financial award applicants required to submit FAFSA. *Unit head:* Dr. Kimberly L. LaPrade, Dean, 602-639-6360, E-mail: kimberly.laprade@gcu.edu. *Application contact:* Dr. Kimberly L. LaPrade, Dean, 602-639-6360, E-mail: kimberly.laprade@gcu.edu.
Website: https://www.gcu.edu/college-of-education.php

Grand Valley State University, College of Education, Program in Instruction and Curriculum, Allendale, MI 49401-9403. Offers M Ed. *Program availability:* Part-time, evening/weekend. *Students:* 33 full-time (17 women), 155 part-time (133 women); includes 17 minority (4 Black or African American, non-Hispanic/Latino; 1 American Indian or Alaska Native, non-Hispanic/Latino; 3 Asian, non-Hispanic/Latino; 5 Hispanic/Latino; 4 Two or more races, non-Hispanic/Latino), 2 international. Average age 32. 35 applicants, 97% accepted, 14 enrolled. In 2016, 85 master's awarded. *Degree requirements:* For master's, project or thesis. *Entrance requirements:* For master's, minimum GPA of 3.0 or GRE General Test, last 60 credits from a regionally-accredited college/university, 3 letters of recommendation. Additional exam requirements/recommendations for international students: Required—TOEFL (minimum score 550 paper-based, 80 iBT), IELTS (6.5), or Michigan English Language Assessment Battery. *Application deadline:* Applications are processed on a rolling basis. Application fee: $30. Electronic applications accepted. *Expenses:* $628 per credit hour. *Financial support:* In 2016–17, 24 students received support. Unspecified assistantships available. *Unit head:* Dr. Linda Pickett, Graduate Program Director, 616-331-6663, Fax: 616-331-6515, E-mail: pickettl@gvsu.edu. *Application contact:* Thomas Owens, Student Information and Services Center, 616-331-6282, Fax: 616-331-6217, E-mail: owenst@gvsu.edu.
Website: http://www.gvsu.edu/grad/instruction/

Harvard University, Harvard Graduate School of Education, Master's Programs in Education, Cambridge, MA 02138. Offers arts in education (Ed M); education policy and management (Ed M); higher education (Ed M); human development and psychology (Ed M); international education policy (Ed M); language and literacy (Ed M); learning and teaching (Ed M); mind, brain, and education (Ed M); prevention science and practice (Ed M); school leadership (Ed M); special studies (Ed M); teacher education (Ed M); technology, innovation, and education (Ed M). *Program availability:* Part-time. *Entrance requirements:* For master's, GRE General Test, statement of purpose, 3 letters of recommendation, resume, official transcripts. Additional exam requirements/recommendations for international students: Required—TOEFL (minimum score 613 paper-based; 104 iBT), TWE (minimum score 5). Electronic applications accepted. *Faculty research:* Learning and development, educational leadership and organizations, education policy analysis.

Henderson State University, Graduate Studies, Teachers College, Department of Advanced Instructional Studies, Arkadelphia, AR 71999-0001. Offers developmental therapy (MSE); dyslexia therapy (Graduate Certificate); education (MAT); educational technology leadership (Graduate Certificate); English as a second language (MSE, Graduate Certificate); instructional facilitator (MSE, Graduate Certificate); middle level education (MAT); special education (K-12) (MAT, MSE); special education/early childhood (MAT). *Accreditation:* NCATE. *Program availability:* Part-time. *Faculty:* 12 full-time (9 women), 5 part-time/adjunct (4 women). *Students:* 13 full-time (8 women), 79 part-time (66 women); includes 14 minority (8 Black or African American, non-Hispanic/Latino; 2 American Indian or Alaska Native, non-Hispanic/Latino; 2 Hispanic/Latino; 2 Two or more races, non-Hispanic/Latino). Average age 33. 21 applicants, 100% accepted, 21 enrolled. In 2016, 29 master's awarded. *Entrance requirements:* For master's, GRE General Test or MAT, minimum GPA of 2.7, teacher certification. Additional exam requirements/recommendations for international students: Required—TOEFL (minimum score 600 paper-based); Recommended—IELTS (minimum score 6.5). *Application deadline:* For fall admission, 8/1 priority date for domestic students, 6/30 priority date for international students; for spring admission, 1/1 priority date for domestic students, 11/30 priority date for international students. Applications are processed on a rolling basis. Application fee: $25 ($75 for international students). *Expenses:* Tuition, state resident: full-time $6288; part-time $3144 per credit hour. Tuition, nonresident: full-time $12,888; part-time $6444 per credit hour. *Required fees:* $1429; $1024 per credit hour. Tuition and fees vary according to course load and student level. *Financial support:* In 2016–17, 1 teaching assistantship with partial tuition reimbursement (averaging $4,000 per year) was awarded; scholarships/grants and unspecified assistantships also available. Financial award application deadline: 4/15; financial award applicants required to submit FAFSA. *Unit head:* Dr. Gary Smithey, Coordinator, 870-230-5361, Fax: 870-230-5455, E-mail: smitheg@hsu.edu. *Application contact:* Dr. Ken Taylor, Graduate Dean, 870-230-5126, Fax: 870-230-5479, E-mail: taylorke@hsu.edu.
Website: http://www.hsu.edu/Academics/TeachersCollege/AIS/index.html

Hood College, Graduate School, Department of Education, Frederick, MD 21701-8575. Offers curriculum and instruction (MS), including elementary education, elementary science and mathematics education, secondary education, special education; educational leadership (MS); reading specialization (MS); STEM education (Certificate). *Accreditation:* NCATE. *Program availability:* Part-time-only, evening/weekend. *Faculty:* 3 full-time, 37 part-time/adjunct. *Students:* 1 (woman) full-time, 357 part-time (283 women); includes 71 minority (41 Black or African American, non-Hispanic/Latino; 6 Asian, non-Hispanic/Latino; 15 Hispanic/Latino; 9 Two or more races, non-Hispanic/Latino). Average age 33. 96 applicants, 95% accepted, 83 enrolled. In 2016, 47 master's awarded. *Degree requirements:* For master's, action research project, portfolio (for reading specialization); for Certificate, STEM capstone activity. *Entrance requirements:* For master's, minimum GPA of 2.75, teaching certification, writing sample during interview, letter of recommendation from principal (for educational leadership program only). Additional exam requirements/recommendations for international students: Required—TOEFL (minimum score 575 paper-based; 89 iBT), IELTS (minimum score 6.5). *Application deadline:* For fall admission, 8/15 priority date for domestic students, 8/5 for international students; for spring admission, 12/1 priority date for domestic students, 12/1 for international students; for summer admission, 5/1 priority date for domestic students, 4/15 for international students. Applications are processed on a rolling basis. Application fee: $35. Electronic applications accepted. *Expenses:* $450 per credit; $105 comprehensive fee per semester. *Financial support:* Tuition waivers (partial) and unspecified assistantships available. Financial award applicants required to submit FAFSA. *Faculty research:* Leadership, action research, brain research, learning styles. *Unit head:* April Boulton, Interim Dean of the Graduate School, E-mail: gofurther@hood.edu. *Application contact:* Jan Marcus, Assistant Director of Graduate Admissions, 301-696-3600, E-mail: gofurther@hood.edu.
Website: http://www.hood.edu/academics/education/index.html

Houston Baptist University, College of Education and Behavioral Sciences, Programs in Education, Houston, TX 77074-3298. Offers bilingual education (M Ed); counselor education (M Ed); curriculum and instruction (M Ed); educational administration (M Ed); educational diagnostician (M Ed); executive educational leadership (Ed D); reading education (M Ed). *Program availability:* Part-time, evening/weekend, 100% online, blended/hybrid learning. *Students:* 45 full-time (35 women), 158 part-time (136 women); includes 141 minority (87 Black or African American, non-Hispanic/Latino; 1 American Indian or Alaska Native, non-Hispanic/Latino; 5 Asian, non-Hispanic/Latino; 47 Hispanic/Latino; 1 Two or more races, non-Hispanic/Latino), 3 international. Average age 34. 320 applicants, 30% accepted, 61 enrolled. In 2016, 121 degrees awarded. *Degree requirements:* For master's, comprehensive exam; for doctorate, thesis/dissertation. *Entrance requirements:* For master's, minimum GPA of 2.75, two recommendations, resume, bachelor's degree conferred transcript; interview (for non-certified teachers); for doctorate, GRE, 3 letters of recommendation. Additional exam requirements/recommendations for international students: Required—TOEFL (minimum score 80 iBT), IELTS (minimum score 6.5). *Application deadline:* For fall admission, 8/1 for domestic students, 6/1 for international students; for spring admission, 1/1 for domestic students, 11/1 for international students; for summer admission, 5/1 for domestic students, 3/1 for international students. Applications are processed on a rolling basis. Application fee: $0 ($100 for international students). Electronic applications accepted. Application fee is waived when completed online. *Expenses:* $1,650 per 3-hour course; $1,275 annual general fee; $1,060 annual technology fee. *Financial support:* In 2016–17, 2 students received support. Research assistantships, teaching assistantships, Federal Work-Study, and scholarships/grants available. Support available to part-time students. Financial award application deadline: 4/1; financial award applicants required to submit FAFSA. *Faculty research:* Autism and inclusion, integrating technology into instruction, school change and leadership trust. *Unit head:* Dr. Charlotte Fontenot, Director, Graduate Programs, 281-649-3078, Fax: 281-649-3361, E-mail: cfontenot@hbu.edu. *Application contact:* Kristy Wright, Administrative Assistant for Graduate Programs, 281-649-3094, Fax: 281-649-3361, E-mail: kwright@hbu.edu.
Website: http://www.hbu.edu/MED

Idaho State University, Office of Graduate Studies, College of Education, Department of Educational Foundations, Pocatello, ID 83209-8059. Offers child and family studies (M Ed); curriculum leadership (M Ed); education (M Ed); educational administration

(M Ed); educational foundations (5th Year Certificate); elementary education (M Ed), including K-12 education, literacy, secondary education. *Program availability:* Part-time. *Degree requirements:* For master's, comprehensive exam, thesis optional, oral exam, written exam; for 5th Year Certificate, comprehensive exam, thesis (for some programs), oral exam, written exam. *Entrance requirements:* For master's, GRE General Test or MAT, minimum undergraduate GPA of 3.0; for 5th Year Certificate, GRE General Test, minimum undergraduate GPA of 3.0, master's degree. Additional exam requirements/ recommendations for international students: Required—TOEFL (minimum score 550 paper-based; 80 iBT). Electronic applications accepted. *Faculty research:* Child and families studies; business education; special education; math, science, and technology education.

Illinois State University, Graduate School, College of Education, Department of Curriculum and Instruction, Normal, IL 61790-2200. Offers curriculum and instruction (MS, MS Ed, Ed D); educational policies (Ed D); postsecondary education (Ed D); reading (MS Ed); supervision (Ed D). *Accreditation:* NCATE. *Degree requirements:* For master's, variable foreign language requirement, thesis or alternative; for doctorate, variable foreign language requirement, thesis/dissertation, 2 terms of residency, internship. *Entrance requirements:* For master's, GRE General Test, minimum GPA of 3.0 in last 60 hours of course work; for doctorate, GRE General Test. *Faculty research:* In-service and pre-service teacher education for teachers of English language learners; teachers for all children: developing a model for alternative, bilingual elementary certification for paraprofessionals in Illinois; Illinois Geographic Alliance, Connections Project.

Indiana State University, College of Graduate and Professional Studies, Bayh College of Education, Department of Teaching and Learning, Terre Haute, IN 47809. Offers curriculum and instruction (M Ed, PhD); educational technology (MS). *Accreditation:* NCATE. *Degree requirements:* For doctorate, thesis/dissertation. *Entrance requirements:* For doctorate, GRE General Test. Electronic applications accepted. *Faculty research:* Discipline FERPA reading, teacher strengths and needs.

Indiana University Bloomington, School of Education, Department of Curriculum and Instruction, Bloomington, IN 47405-7000. Offers art education (MS, Ed D, PhD); curriculum studies (Ed D, PhD); elementary education (MS, Ed D, PhD, Ed S); mathematics education (MS, Ed D, PhD); science education (MS, Ed D, PhD); secondary education (MS, Ed D, PhD); social studies education (MS, PhD); special education (PhD, Ed S). *Accreditation:* NCATE. *Program availability:* Part-time, evening/ weekend. Terminal master's awarded for partial completion of doctoral program. *Degree requirements:* For doctorate, thesis/dissertation; for Ed S, comprehensive exam or project. *Entrance requirements:* For master's, doctorate, and Ed S, GRE General Test. Electronic applications accepted.

Indiana University of Pennsylvania, School of Graduate Studies and Research, College of Education and Educational Technology, Department of Professional Studies in Education, Program in Curriculum and Instruction, Indiana, PA 15705. Offers D Ed. *Accreditation:* NCATE. *Program availability:* Part-time, evening/weekend. *Faculty:* 15 full-time (11 women), 3 part-time/adjunct (2 women). *Students:* 9 full-time (4 women), 85 part-time (64 women); includes 5 minority (2 Black or African American, non-Hispanic/ Latino; 1 Asian, non-Hispanic/Latino; 1 Hispanic/Latino; 1 Two or more races, non-Hispanic/Latino), 11 international. Average age 40. 56 applicants, 41% accepted, 15 enrolled. In 2016, 7 doctorates awarded. *Degree requirements:* For doctorate, one foreign language, comprehensive exam, thesis/dissertation. *Entrance requirements:* For doctorate, 2 letters of recommendation; recorded five-minute, research-based presentation; 1.5 hour online writing task. Additional exam requirements/ recommendations for international students: Required—TOEFL (minimum score 540 paper-based). *Application deadline:* Applications are processed on a rolling basis. Application fee: $50. Electronic applications accepted. *Expenses:* Contact institution. *Financial support:* In 2016–17, 3 fellowships with full tuition reimbursements (averaging $2,137 per year), 14 research assistantships with tuition reimbursements (averaging $4,690 per year), 2 teaching assistantships with partial tuition reimbursements (averaging $21,363 per year) were awarded; career-related internships or fieldwork, Federal Work-Study, scholarships/grants, and unspecified assistantships also available. Support available to part-time students. Financial award application deadline: 4/15; financial award applicants required to submit FAFSA. *Unit head:* Dr. Kelli Jo Kerry-Moran, Graduate Coordinator, 724-357-7931, E-mail: kjkmoran@iup.edu.
Website: http://www.iup.edu/grad/CandI/default.aspx

Indiana University–Purdue University Indianapolis, School of Education, Indianapolis, IN 46202-5155. Offers curriculum and instruction (MS); early childhood (MS); educational leadership (MS, Certificate); English as a second language (Certificate); kindergarten (Certificate); language education (MS); reading (Certificate); school counseling (MS); special education (MS, Certificate). *Program availability:* Part-time, evening/weekend. *Faculty:* 35 full-time (27 women), 56 part-time/adjunct (42 women). *Students:* 125 full-time (86 women), 181 part-time (139 women); includes 106 minority (78 Black or African American, non-Hispanic/Latino; 9 Asian, non-Hispanic/ Latino; 12 Hispanic/Latino; 7 Two or more races, non-Hispanic/Latino), 3 international. Average age 32. 73 applicants, 93% accepted, 68 enrolled. In 2016, 73 master's awarded. Terminal master's awarded for partial completion of doctoral program. *Degree requirements:* For master's, thesis optional. *Entrance requirements:* For master's, GRE General Test, minimum GPA of 2.5; for Certificate, official transcripts. Additional exam requirements/recommendations for international students: Required—TOEFL (minimum score 60 iBT), IELTS (minimum score 5.5). *Application deadline:* For fall admission, 5/1 for domestic students; for spring admission, 11/1 for domestic students. Application fee: $60 ($65 for international students). Electronic applications accepted. *Expenses:* $1,262 tuition, $213 general fee. *Financial support:* Applicants required to submit FAFSA. *Faculty research:* Educational policies and school leaders' responses to these; issues of intersectionality in the experiences of African American lesbian, gay, and bisexual students attending historically black colleges and universities and those who belong to black Greek-letter organizations; students' experiential knowledge and their evolving disciplinary-specific literacy and understanding; innovative program development; urban ESL teacher preparation; target-based instructional coaching. *Total annual research expenditures:* $2.1 million. *Unit head:* Dr. Robin Hughes, Executive Associate Dean, 317-274-6817, E-mail: roblhugh@iupui.edu. *Application contact:* Ky Shaw, Graduate Admissions Coordinator, 317-278-6778, E-mail: kycshaw@iupui.edu.
Website: http://education.iupui.edu/

Inter American University of Puerto Rico, Arecibo Campus, Programs in Education, Arecibo, PR 00614-4050. Offers administration and educational supervision (MA Ed); counseling and guidance (MA Ed); curriculum and teaching (MA Ed), including biology education, English as a second language, history education, math education, Spanish; elementary education (MA Ed). *Accreditation:* TEAC. *Degree requirements:* For master's, comprehensive exam, thesis optional. *Entrance requirements:* For master's, GRE, EXADEP, bachelor's degree in education or teaching license (administration and supervision) or courses in education and psychology (counseling and guidance), minimum GPA of 2.5 in last 60 credits.

Inter American University of Puerto Rico, Barranquitas Campus, Program in Education, Barranquitas, PR 00794. Offers curriculum and teaching (M Ed), including biology education, English as a second language, history education, mathematics education, Spanish; educational leadership and management (MA); elementary education (M Ed); information and library service technology (M Ed); special education (MA). *Accreditation:* TEAC. *Degree requirements:* For master's, comprehensive exam, thesis optional. *Entrance requirements:* For master's, EXADEP, letter of recommendation. Electronic applications accepted.

Inter American University of Puerto Rico, Metropolitan Campus, Graduate Programs, Program in Education, San Juan, PR 00919-1293. Offers curriculum and instruction (Ed D); educational administration (Ed D); guidance and counseling (MA, Ed D); special education administration (Ed D). *Accreditation:* TEAC. *Degree requirements:* For doctorate, comprehensive exam, thesis/dissertation. *Entrance requirements:* For doctorate, GRE, MAT, or EXADEP. Electronic applications accepted.

Inter American University of Puerto Rico, San Germán Campus, Graduate Studies Center, Program in Curriculum and Instruction, San Germán, PR 00683-5008. Offers Ed D. *Program availability:* Part-time, evening/weekend.

Iowa State University of Science and Technology, Department of Education, Ames, IA 50011. Offers curriculum and instructional technology (M Ed, MS, PhD); elementary education (M Ed, MS); historical, philosophical, and comparative studies in education (M Ed, MS); special education (M Ed, MS, PhD). *Degree requirements:* For master's, thesis or alternative; for doctorate, thesis/dissertation. *Entrance requirements:* For master's and doctorate, GRE General Test. Additional exam requirements/ recommendations for international students: Required—TOEFL (minimum score 560 paper-based; 83 iBT), IELTS (minimum score 6.5). *Application deadline:* For fall admission, 1/1 priority date for domestic and international students; for spring admission, 9/1 for domestic and international students. Application fee: $60 ($90 for international students). Electronic applications accepted. *Application contact:* Robyn Goldy, Application Contact, 515-294-1241, Fax: 515-294-4942, E-mail: rgoldy@iastate.edu.
Website: http://www.ci.hs.iastate.edu

John Brown University, Graduate Education Programs, Siloam Springs, AR 72761-2121. Offers curriculum and instruction (M Ed); secondary education (MAT). *Program availability:* Part-time, evening/weekend. *Faculty:* 1 (woman) full-time, 5 part-time/ adjunct (3 women). *Students:* 17 part-time (8 women). Average age 32. 11 applicants, 64% accepted, 5 enrolled. In 2016, 7 master's awarded. *Entrance requirements:* For master's, GRE (minimum score of 300). Additional exam requirements/ recommendations for international students: Required—TOEFL (minimum score 550 paper-based; 79 iBT). *Application deadline:* Applications are processed on a rolling basis. Application fee: $35 ($100 for international students). Electronic applications accepted. *Expenses: Tuition:* Full-time $13,000; part-time $6500 per credit hour. Part-time tuition and fees vary according to course load and program. *Financial support:* Scholarships/grants and unspecified assistantships available. *Unit head:* Dr. Connie Matchell, Graduate Program Director, 479-524-9500, E-mail: cmatchell@jbu.edu. *Application contact:* Mark Bjornsen, Graduate Education Representative, 479-631-4665, E-mail: mbjornsen@jbu.edu.
Website: http://www.jbu.edu/grad/education/

Johnson State College, Program in Education, Johnson, VT 05656. Offers applied behavior analysis (MA Ed); curriculum and instruction (MA Ed); foundations of education (MA Ed); special education (MA Ed). *Program availability:* Part-time. *Degree requirements:* For master's, thesis or alternative, exit interview. *Entrance requirements:* For master's, interview. Additional exam requirements/recommendations for international students: Required—TOEFL. *Application deadline:* For fall admission, 5/1 for domestic students, 2/1 for international students. Applications are processed on a rolling basis. Electronic applications accepted. *Expenses:* Tuition, state resident: part-time $555 per credit. Tuition, nonresident: part-time $800 per credit. *Financial support:* Scholarships/grants and unspecified assistantships available. Financial award application deadline: 3/1; financial award applicants required to submit FAFSA. *Unit head:* Dr. Kathleen Brinegar, Chair, Department of Education, 802-635-1472, Fax: 802-635-1465, E-mail: kathleen.brinegar@jsc.edu. *Application contact:* Catherine H. Higley, Administrative Assistant, 800-635-2356 Ext. 1244, Fax: 802-635-1248, E-mail: catherine.higley@jsc.edu.
Website: http://www.jsc.edu/academics/education/majors-and-minors/master-of-arts-in-education/

Kansas State University, Graduate School, College of Education, Department of Curriculum and Instruction, Manhattan, KS 66506. Offers curriculum and instruction (Ed D, PhD); digital teaching and learning (MS); educational computing, design and online learning (MS); elementary/middle level curriculum and instruction (MS); online learning (Certificate); reading specialist endorsement (MS); reading/language arts (MS); teacher leader/school improvement (MS); teaching and learning (Certificate). *Accreditation:* NCATE. *Program availability:* Part-time, online learning. *Faculty:* 36 full-time (22 women), 18 part-time/adjunct (9 women). *Students:* 59 full-time (40 women), 94 part-time (72 women); includes 21 minority (5 Black or African American, non-Hispanic/ Latino; 3 Asian, non-Hispanic/Latino; 11 Hispanic/Latino; 2 Two or more races, non-Hispanic/Latino), 20 international. Average age 35. 70 applicants, 71% accepted, 36 enrolled. In 2016, 61 master's, 12 doctorates, 9 other advanced degrees awarded. *Degree requirements:* For master's, comprehensive exam, portfolio, project, report or thesis; for doctorate, comprehensive exam, thesis/dissertation, preliminary exam; for Certificate, comprehensive exam, portfolio. *Entrance requirements:* For master's, minimum GPA of 3.0, 3 letters of recommendation; for doctorate, GRE, minimum GPA of 3.0, 3 letters of recommendation, evidence of scholarly writing; for Certificate, minimum GPA of 3.0, letters of recommendation. Additional exam requirements/recommendations for international students: Required—TOEFL (minimum score 550 paper-based; 80 iBT) or IELTS. *Application deadline:* For fall admission, 3/1 priority date for domestic students, 2/1 priority date for international students; for spring admission, 10/1 priority date for domestic students, 8/1 priority date for international students. Applications are processed on a rolling basis. Application fee: $50 ($75 for international students). Electronic applications accepted. *Expenses:* Tuition, state resident: full-time $9670. Tuition, nonresident: full-time $21,828. *Required fees:* $862. *Financial support:* In 2016–17, 1 research assistantship (averaging $19,980 per year), 8 teaching assistantships (averaging $12,620 per year) were awarded; career-related internships or fieldwork, institutionally sponsored loans, scholarships/grants, and unspecified assistantships also available. Support available to part-time students. Financial award application deadline: 3/1; financial award applicants required to submit FAFSA. *Faculty research:* Literacy and technology, critical race theory and diversity, achievement gaps, school improvement, teacher education. *Total annual research expenditures:* $647,057. *Unit head:* Dr. F. Todd Goodson, Department Chair, 785-532-5904, Fax: 785-532-7304, E-mail: tgoodson@ksu.edu. *Application contact:* Dr. Kay Ann Taylor, Director, Curriculum and Instruction Graduate Programs, 785-532-6974, Fax: 785-532-7304, E-mail: ktaylor@ksu.edu.
Website: http://www.coe.ksu.edu/edci/index.html

Kean University, College of Education, Program in Instruction and Curriculum, Union, NJ 07083. Offers bilingual/bicultural education (MA); teaching English as a second language (MA). *Accreditation:* NCATE. *Program availability:* Part-time. *Faculty:* 15 full-time (9 women). *Students:* 3 full-time (all women), 25 part-time (19 women); includes 21 minority (1 Black or African American, non-Hispanic/Latino; 20 Hispanic/Latino), 2

international. Average age 37. 21 applicants, 52% accepted, 10 enrolled. In 2016, 25 master's awarded. *Degree requirements:* For master's, comprehensive exam (for some programs), thesis optional, two-semester advanced seminar. *Entrance requirements:* For master's, GRE General Test or MAT; PRAXIS (for some programs), minimum GPA of 3.0, personal statement, professional resume/curriculum vitae, commitment to working with children, certification (for some programs), two letters of recommendation. Additional exam requirements/recommendations for international students: Required—TOEFL (minimum score 550 paper-based; 79 iBT), IELTS (minimum score 6.5). *Application deadline:* For fall admission, 6/1 for domestic and international students; for spring admission, 12/1 for domestic and international students. Applications are processed on a rolling basis. Application fee: $75. Electronic applications accepted. *Expenses:* Tuition, state resident: full-time $13,156; part-time $640 per credit. Tuition, nonresident: full-time $17,831; part-time $785 per credit. *Required fees:* $3316; $151 per credit. Tuition and fees vary according to course level, course load, degree level and program. *Financial support:* Scholarships/grants and unspecified assistantships available. Financial award applicants required to submit FAFSA. *Unit head:* Dr. Gail Verdi, Program Coordinator, 908-737-3908, E-mail: gverdi@kean.edu. *Application contact:* Brittany Gerstenhaber, Admissions Counselor, 908-737-7100, E-mail: grad-adm@kean.edu.
Website: http://grad.kean.edu/masters-programs/bilingualbicultural-education-instruction-and-curriculum

Keene State College, School of Professional and Graduate Studies, Keene, NH 03435. Offers curriculum and instruction (M Ed); education leadership (PMC); educational leadership (M Ed); safety and occupational health applied science (MS); school counselor (M Ed, PMC); special education (M Ed). *Accreditation:* NCATE. *Program availability:* Part-time, evening/weekend. *Faculty:* 9 full-time (4 women), 8 part-time/adjunct (3 women). *Students:* 24 full-time (17 women), 66 part-time (38 women); includes 3 minority (1 Black or African American, non-Hispanic/Latino; 1 Hispanic/Latino; 1 Two or more races, non-Hispanic/Latino), 1 international. Average age 33. 24 applicants, 100% accepted, 24 enrolled. In 2016, 26 master's, 1 other advanced degree awarded. *Degree requirements:* For master's, thesis (for some programs). *Entrance requirements:* For master's, PRAXIS I, 3 references; official transcripts; minimum GPA of 2.5; interview; essay; teacher/educator certificate; work/internship experience. Additional exam requirements/recommendations for international students: Required—TOEFL (minimum score 550 paper-based; 61 iBT). *Application deadline:* For fall admission, 4/1 for domestic and international students; for spring admission, 11/1 for domestic and international students; for summer admission, 3/1 for domestic and international students. Applications are processed on a rolling basis. Application fee: $50. Electronic applications accepted. *Expenses:* Tuition, state resident: full-time $9180; part-time $510 per credit. Tuition, nonresident: full-time $10,080; part-time $560 per credit. *Required fees:* $1908; $106 per credit. Tuition and fees vary according to course load. *Financial support:* In 2016–17, 27 students received support. Career-related internships or fieldwork, Federal Work-Study, institutionally sponsored loans, scholarships/grants, and unspecified assistantships available. Support available to part-time students. Financial award application deadline: 3/1; financial award applicants required to submit FAFSA. *Unit head:* Dr. Karrie Kalich, Dean of Professional and Graduate Studies, 603-358-2885, E-mail: kkalich@keene.edu. *Application contact:* Peter Tandy, Assistant Director for Graduate Studies, 603-358-2332, E-mail: kscgraduatestudies@keene.edu.
Website: http://www.keene.edu/academics/graduate/

Kent State University, College of Education, Health and Human Services, School of Teaching, Learning and Curriculum Studies, Program in Curriculum and Instruction, Kent, OH 44242-0001. Offers M Ed, PhD, Ed S. *Accreditation:* NCATE. *Program availability:* Part-time, evening/weekend. *Degree requirements:* For doctorate, comprehensive exam, thesis/dissertation. *Entrance requirements:* For master's, 2 letters of reference, goals statement; for doctorate, GRE General Test, 2 letters of reference, goals statement, writing sample, resume; for Ed S, GRE General Test, 2 letters of reference, goals statement. Additional exam requirements/recommendations for international students: Required—TOEFL (minimum score 550 paper-based; 80 iBT). Electronic applications accepted. *Expenses:* Tuition, state resident: full-time $10,864; part-time $495 per credit hour. Tuition, nonresident: full-time $18,380; part-time $837 per credit hour. *Faculty research:* Gender equity issues in teaching, learning math and science, teaching as inquiry artistry, curriculum studies for democratic humanism.

Kent State University at Stark, Graduate School of Education, Health and Human Services, Canton, OH 44720-7599. Offers curriculum and instruction studies (M Ed, MA).

Kutztown University of Pennsylvania, College of Education, Program in Secondary Education, Kutztown, PA 19530-0730. Offers biology (M Ed); curriculum and instruction (M Ed); English (M Ed); mathematics (M Ed); middle level (M Ed); social studies (M Ed); teaching (M Ed). *Accreditation:* NCATE. *Program availability:* Part-time, evening/weekend. *Faculty:* 4 full-time (2 women), 2 part-time/adjunct (0 women). *Students:* 35 full-time (23 women), 58 part-time (37 women); includes 4 minority (2 Black or African American, non-Hispanic/Latino; 2 Hispanic/Latino). Average age 31. 96 applicants, 86% accepted, 43 enrolled. In 2016, 35 master's awarded. *Degree requirements:* For master's, comprehensive exam, thesis optional. *Entrance requirements:* For master's, GRE General Test, minimum undergraduate major GPA of 3.0, 3 letters of recommendation, copy of PRAXIS II or valid instructional I or II teaching certificate. Additional exam requirements/recommendations for international students: Required—TOEFL (minimum score 550 paper-based, 79 iBT) or IELTS (minimum score 6.5). *Application deadline:* For fall admission, 8/1 for domestic and international students; for spring admission, 12/1 for domestic and international students. Application fee: $35. Electronic applications accepted. *Expenses:* Tuition, state resident: full-time $4347; part-time $483 per credit. Tuition, nonresident: full-time $6525; part-time $725 per credit. *Required fees:* $88 per credit. One-time fee: $50 full-time. *Financial support:* Career-related internships or fieldwork, Federal Work-Study, scholarships/grants, and unspecified assistantships available. Financial award application deadline: 3/1; financial award applicants required to submit FAFSA. *Unit head:* Dr. Theresa Stahler, Chairperson, 610-683-4259, Fax: 610-683-1338, E-mail: stahler@kutztown.edu. *Application contact:* Dr. Patricia Walsh Coates, Graduate Coordinator, 610-638-4289, Fax: 610-683-1338, E-mail: coates@kutztown.edu.
Website: https://www.kutztown.edu/academcs/graduate-programs/secondary-education.htm

LaGrange College, Graduate Programs, Department of Education, LaGrange, GA 30240-2999. Offers curriculum and instruction (M Ed, Ed S); middle grades (MAT); secondary education (MAT). *Program availability:* Part-time, evening/weekend. *Degree requirements:* For master's, comprehensive exam. *Entrance requirements:* For master's, GRE, MAT, minimum GPA of 2.5. Additional exam requirements/recommendations for international students: Required—TOEFL (minimum score 550 paper-based).

La Sierra University, School of Education, Department of Curriculum and Instruction, Riverside, CA 92515. Offers curriculum and instruction (MA, Ed D, Ed S); teaching (MAT). *Program availability:* Part-time, evening/weekend. *Degree requirements:* For doctorate, thesis/dissertation; for Ed S, thesis optional. *Entrance requirements:* For master's, minimum GPA of 3.0; for doctorate, GRE General Test, GRE Subject Test, minimum GPA of 3.3; for Ed S, minimum GPA of 3.3. *Faculty research:* New teacher success, politics of knowledge, computer-assisted instruction, diversity issues.

Lee University, Program in Education, Cleveland, TN 37320-3450. Offers art (MAT); curriculum and instruction (M Ed, Ed S); early childhood (MAT); educational leadership (M Ed, Ed S); elementary education (MAT); English and math (MAT); English and science (MAT); English and social studies (MAT); higher education administration (MS); history (MAT); history and economics (MAT); math and science (MAT); math and social studies (MAT); middle grades (MAT); science and social studies (MASW); secondary education (MAT); Spanish (MAT); special education (M Ed, MAT); TESOL (MAT). *Accreditation:* NCATE. *Program availability:* Part-time. *Faculty:* 13 full-time (6 women), 9 part-time/adjunct (4 women). *Students:* 35 full-time (27 women), 50 part-time (32 women); includes 12 minority (5 Black or African American, non-Hispanic/Latino; 5 Hispanic/Latino; 2 Two or more races, non-Hispanic/Latino), 4 international. Average age 30. 43 applicants, 79% accepted, 28 enrolled. In 2016, 42 master's, 6 other advanced degrees awarded. *Degree requirements:* For master's, variable foreign language requirement, thesis optional, internship. *Entrance requirements:* For master's, MAT or GRE General Test, minimum undergraduate GPA of 2.75, 3 letters of recommendation, interview, writing sample, official transcripts, background check; for Ed S, minimum undergraduate and master's GPA of 2.75, official transcripts for undergraduate and master's degrees. Additional exam requirements/recommendations for international students: Required—TOEFL (minimum score 61 iBT). *Application deadline:* For fall admission, 6/1 priority date for domestic and international students; for spring admission, 11/1 priority date for domestic and international students; for summer admission, 4/1 priority date for domestic and international students. Applications are processed on a rolling basis. Application fee: $25. Electronic applications accepted. *Expenses: Tuition:* Full-time $11,367; part-time $632 per credit hour. *Required fees:* $35 per term. One-time fee: $25. Tuition and fees vary according to program. *Financial support:* In 2016–17, 42 students received support. Career-related internships or fieldwork, Federal Work-Study, institutionally sponsored loans, scholarships/grants, and unspecified assistantships available. Financial award application deadline: 3/1; financial award applicants required to submit FAFSA. *Unit head:* Dr. William Kamm, Director, 423-614-8544, E-mail: wkamm@leeuniversity.edu. *Application contact:* Crystal Keeter, Graduate Education Secretary, 423-614-8544, E-mail: ckeeter@leeuniversity.edu.
Website: http://www.leeuniversity.edu/academics/graduate/education

Lesley University, Graduate School of Education, Cambridge, MA 02138-2790. Offers arts, community, and education (M Ed); autism studies (Certificate); curriculum and instruction (M Ed, CAGS); early childhood education (M Ed); ecological teaching and learning (MS); educational studies (PhD), including adult learning, educational leadership, individually designed; elementary education (M Ed); emergent technologies for educators (Certificate); ESLArts: language learning through the arts (M Ed); high school education (M Ed); individually designed (M Ed); integrated teaching through the arts (M Ed); literacy for K-8 classroom teachers (M Ed); mathematics education (M Ed); middle school education (M Ed); moderate disabilities (M Ed); online learning (Certificate); reading (CAGS); science in education (M Ed); severe disabilities (M Ed); special needs (CAGS); specialist teacher of reading (M Ed); teacher of visual art (M Ed); technology in education (M Ed, CAGS). *Accreditation:* TEAC. *Program availability:* Part-time, evening/weekend, online learning. *Degree requirements:* For master's, practicum; for doctorate, thesis/dissertation. *Entrance requirements:* For master's, Massachusetts Tests for Educator Licensure (MTEL), transcripts, statement of purpose, recommendations; interview (for special education); for doctorate, GRE General Test, transcripts, statement of purpose, recommendations, interview, master's degree, resume; for other advanced degree, interview, master's degree. Additional exam requirements/recommendations for international students: Required—TOEFL (minimum score 550 paper-based; 80 iBT). Electronic applications accepted. *Faculty research:* Assessment in literacy, mathematics and science; autism spectrum disorders; instructional technology and online learning; multicultural education and English language learners.

LeTourneau University, Graduate Programs, Longview, TX 75607-7001. Offers business (MBA); counseling (MA), including licensed professional counselor, marriage and family therapy, school counseling; curriculum and instruction (M Ed); educational administration (M Ed); engineering (ME, MS); engineering management (MEM); health care administration (MS); marriage and family therapy (MA); psychology (MA); strategic leadership (MSL); teacher leadership (M Ed); teaching and learning (M Ed). *Program availability:* Part-time, 100% online, blended/hybrid learning. *Faculty:* 24 full-time (7 women), 40 part-time/adjunct (15 women). *Students:* 82 full-time (48 women), 428 part-time (331 women); includes 234 minority (138 Black or African American, non-Hispanic/Latino; 5 American Indian or Alaska Native, non-Hispanic/Latino; 5 Asian, non-Hispanic/Latino; 50 Hispanic/Latino; 36 Two or more races, non-Hispanic/Latino), 15 international. Average age 37. 257 applicants, 60% accepted, 141 enrolled. In 2016, 136 master's awarded. *Degree requirements:* For master's, thesis (for some programs). *Entrance requirements:* Additional exam requirements/recommendations for international students: Required—TOEFL. *Application deadline:* For fall admission, 8/22 for domestic students, 8/29 for international students; for winter admission, 10/10 for domestic students; for spring admission, 1/2 for domestic students, 1/10 for international students; for summer admission, 5/1 for domestic and international students. Applications are processed on a rolling basis. Electronic applications accepted. *Expenses:* $10,890-$18,450 tuition per year (depending on program). *Financial support:* Research assistantships, institutionally sponsored loans, and unspecified assistantships available. Financial award applicants required to submit FAFSA. *Application contact:* Chris Fontaine, Assistant Vice President for Enrollment Services and Global Admissions, 903-233-4312, E-mail: chrisfontaine@letu.edu.
Website: http://www.letu.edu

Lewis & Clark College, Graduate School of Education and Counseling, Department of Teacher Education, Program in Curriculum and Instruction, Portland, OR 97219-7899. Offers M Ed. *Program availability:* Part-time, evening/weekend. *Entrance requirements:* For master's, minimum GPA of 2.75. Additional exam requirements/recommendations for international students: Required—TOEFL (minimum score 575 paper-based). *Application deadline:* Applications are processed on a rolling basis. Application fee: $50. Electronic applications accepted. *Financial support:* Career-related internships or fieldwork, Federal Work-Study, institutionally sponsored loans, scholarships/grants, health care benefits, and tuition waivers (partial) available. Support available to part-time students. Financial award application deadline: 3/1; financial award applicants required to submit FAFSA. *Unit head:* Kimberly Campbell, Director, 503-768-6100, Fax: 503-768-6115, E-mail: lcteach@lclark.edu. *Application contact:* Becky Haas, Director of Admissions, 503-768-6200, Fax: 503-768-6205, E-mail: gseadmit@lclark.edu.
Website: http://www.lclark.edu/graduate/departments/teacher_education/current_teachers/master_of_education/

Lincoln Memorial University, Carter and Moyers School of Education, Harrogate, TN 37752-1901. Offers administration and supervision (M Ed, Ed S); counseling and guidance (M Ed); curriculum and instruction (M Ed, Ed D, Ed S); English (M Ed); executive leadership (Ed D); higher education administration (Ed D); human resource development (Ed D); leadership and administration (Ed D). *Program availability:* Part-time, evening/weekend, online learning. *Degree requirements:* For master's, comprehensive exam, thesis optional; for Ed S, comprehensive exam. *Entrance requirements:* For master's, PRAXIS, NTE, GRE, MAT, letters of recommendation; for Ed S, graduate transcripts. Additional exam requirements/recommendations for international students: Recommended—TOEFL. *Faculty research:* Brain compatible teaching and learning; poverty in Appalachia; leadership for change; ethics, moral responsibility and social justice; human and organizational learning.

Louisiana State University in Shreveport, College of Business, Education, and Human Development, Program in Education, Shreveport, LA 71115-2399. Offers curriculum and instruction (M Ed); leadership (M Ed); leadership studies (Ed D). *Accreditation:* NCATE. *Program availability:* Part-time. *Students:* 5 full-time (all women), 236 part-time (198 women); includes 110 minority (92 Black or African American, non-Hispanic/Latino; 6 Asian, non-Hispanic/Latino; 6 Hispanic/Latino; 6 Two or more races, non-Hispanic/Latino). Average age 36. 148 applicants, 95% accepted, 39 enrolled. In 2016, 61 master's awarded. *Degree requirements:* For master's, orally-presented project, 200-hour internship (educational leadership). *Entrance requirements:* For master's, GRE, minimum GPA of 2.5; teacher certification; recommendations and interview (for educational leadership). Additional exam requirements/recommendations for international students: Required—TOEFL (minimum score 550 paper-based; 61 iBT). *Application deadline:* For fall admission, 6/30 for domestic and international students; for spring admission, 11/30 for domestic and international students; for summer admission, 4/30 for domestic and international students. Applications are processed on a rolling basis. Application fee: $20 ($30 for international students). Electronic applications accepted. *Expenses:* Tuition, state resident: full-time $5163; part-time $350 per credit hour. Tuition, nonresident: full-time $15,578; part-time $1038 per credit hour. *Required fees:* $63 per credit hour. Tuition and fees vary according to course load and program. *Financial support:* In 2016–17, 5 research assistantships (averaging $2,150 per year) were awarded. *Unit head:* Dr. Pat Doerr, Coordinator, 318-797-5033, Fax: 318-798-4144, E-mail: pat.doerr@lsus.edu. *Application contact:* Mary Catherine Harvison, Director of Admissions, 318-797-2400, Fax: 318-797-5286, E-mail: mary.harvison@lsus.edu.

Louisiana Tech University, Graduate School, College of Education, Department of Curriculum, Instruction and Leadership, Ruston, LA 71272. Offers curriculum and instruction (M Ed), including research, theory, and design, visually impaired; educational leadership (M Ed, Ed D), including higher education administration (Ed D), P-12 educational leadership (Ed D). *Accreditation:* NCATE. *Program availability:* Part-time. *Degree requirements:* For doctorate, thesis/dissertation. *Entrance requirements:* For master's and doctorate, GRE General Test. *Application deadline:* For fall admission, 7/29 for domestic students; for spring admission, 2/3 for domestic students. Application fee: $20 ($30 for international students). *Financial support:* Fellowships, research assistantships, and teaching assistantships available. Financial award application deadline: 2/1. *Unit head:* Dr. Bryan McCoy, Chair, 318-257-4609, Fax: 318-257-2379, E-mail: bmccoy@latech.edu. *Application contact:* Dr. John Harrison, Associate Dean of Graduate Studies, 318-257-3229, Fax: 318-257-2379, E-mail: johnharrison@latech.edu. Website: http://education.latech.edu/departments/cil/

Lourdes University, Graduate School, Sylvania, OH 43560-2898. Offers business (MBA); leadership (M Ed); nurse anesthesia (MSN); nurse educator (MSN); nurse leader (MSN); organizational leadership (MOL); reading (M Ed); teaching and curriculum (M Ed); theology (MA). *Program availability:* Evening/weekend. *Entrance requirements:* Additional exam requirements/recommendations for international students: Required—TOEFL.

Loyola University Chicago, School of Education, Program in Curriculum and Instruction, Chicago, IL 60660. Offers M Ed, Ed D. *Program availability:* Part-time, evening/weekend. *Faculty:* 22 full-time (16 women), 39 part-time/adjunct (31 women). *Students:* 18 full-time (15 women), 23 part-time (15 women); includes 13 minority (4 Black or African American, non-Hispanic/Latino; 1 American Indian or Alaska Native, non-Hispanic/Latino; 5 Asian, non-Hispanic/Latino; 3 Hispanic/Latino). Average age 35. 15 applicants, 67% accepted, 8 enrolled. In 2016, 5 master's, 8 doctorates awarded. Terminal master's awarded for partial completion of doctoral program. *Degree requirements:* For master's, comprehensive exam; for doctorate, comprehensive exam, thesis/dissertation. *Entrance requirements:* For master's, 3 references, minimum GPA of 3.0, resume; for doctorate, GRE, 3 references, interview, minimum GPA of 3.0, resume. Additional exam requirements/recommendations for international students: Required—TOEFL (minimum score 550 paper-based; 79 iBT). *Application deadline:* For fall admission, 1/1 for domestic and international students; for spring admission, 11/1 for domestic and international students. Applications are processed on a rolling basis. Application fee: $50. Electronic applications accepted. Application fee is waived when completed online. *Expenses: Tuition:* Full-time $18,594. *Required fees:* $848. Part-time tuition and fees vary according to course load, degree level and program. *Financial support:* In 2016–17, 6 fellowships with partial tuition reimbursements, 12 research assistantships with full tuition reimbursements (averaging $14,000 per year) were awarded; institutionally sponsored loans, scholarships/grants, and unspecified assistantships also available. Support available to part-time students. Financial award application deadline: 2/1; financial award applicants required to submit FAFSA. *Faculty research:* School improvement, technology, change, reading. *Unit head:* Dr. David Ensminger, Director, 312-915-7257, E-mail: densmin@luc.edu. *Application contact:* Marie Hatland, Information Contact, 312-915-6800, E-mail: schleduc@luc.edu.

Loyola University Maryland, Graduate Programs, School of Education, Program in Curriculum and Instruction, Baltimore, MD 21210-2699. Offers MA. *Program availability:* Part-time. *Faculty:* 34 full-time (22 women), 30 part-time/adjunct (24 women). *Students:* 17 full-time (16 women); includes 4 minority (1 Black or African American, non-Hispanic/Latino; 1 American Indian or Alaska Native, non-Hispanic/Latino; 1 Hispanic/Latino; 1 Two or more races, non-Hispanic/Latino). Average age 31. 68 applicants, 87% accepted, 56 enrolled. In 2016, 17 master's awarded. *Degree requirements:* For master's, thesis. *Entrance requirements:* For master's, essay, transcripts, resume. Additional exam requirements/recommendations for international students: Required—TOEFL (minimum score 550 paper-based), IELTS (minimum score 7). *Application deadline:* For fall admission, 6/15 for domestic students; for winter admission, 11/1 for domestic students. Applications are processed on a rolling basis. Application fee: $60. Electronic applications accepted. *Expenses:* Contact institution. *Financial support:* In 2016–17, 4 students received support. Scholarships/grants available. Financial award application deadline: 4/15; financial award applicants required to submit FAFSA. *Application contact:* Mechelle Palmer, Senior Associate Director of Graduate Admission, 410-617-7741, E-mail: mjpalmer@loyola.edu.

Lynchburg College, Graduate Studies, M Ed Program in Curriculum and Instruction, Lynchburg, VA 24501-3199. Offers instructional leadership (M Ed); teacher licensure (M Ed). *Program availability:* Part-time, evening/weekend. *Students:* 3 full-time (all women), 13 part-time (8 women); includes 2 minority (both Black or African American, non-Hispanic/Latino). In 2016, 6 master's awarded. *Degree requirements:* For master's, comprehensive exam (for some programs), National Board Certification portfolio or comprehensive exam. *Entrance requirements:* For master's, GRE, minimum GPA of 3.0 (preferred), official transcripts (bachelor's, others as relevant), three letters of recommendation, career goals statement. Additional exam requirements/recommendations for international students: Required—TOEFL (minimum score 550 paper-based; 79 iBT), IELTS (minimum score 6.5). *Application deadline:* For fall admission, 7/31 for domestic students, 6/1 for international students; for spring admission, 11/30 for domestic students, 10/15 for international students. Applications are processed on a rolling basis. Application fee: $30. Electronic applications accepted. Application fee is waived when completed online. *Expenses:* Contact institution. *Financial support:* Federal Work-Study, scholarships/grants, health care benefits, and unspecified assistantships available. Support available to part-time students. Financial award application deadline: 7/31; financial award applicants required to submit FAFSA. *Unit head:* Dr. Mary Ann Mayhew, Assistant Professor/Program Director, Curriculum and Instruction, 434-544-8515, E-mail: mayhew.m@lynchburg.edu.
Website: http://www.lynchburg.edu/graduate/master-of-education-in-curriculum-and-instruction/

Lyndon State College, Graduate Programs in Education, Department of Education, Lyndonville, VT 05851-0919. Offers curriculum and instruction (M Ed); reading specialist (M Ed); special education (M Ed); teaching and counseling (M Ed). *Program availability:* Part-time, evening/weekend. *Degree requirements:* For master's, exam or major field project. *Entrance requirements:* Additional exam requirements/recommendations for international students: Recommended—TOEFL (minimum score 500 paper-based).

Malone University, Graduate Program in Education, Canton, OH 44709. Offers curriculum and instruction (MA); curriculum, instruction, and professional development (MA); educational leadership (principal license) (MA); intervention specialist (MA). *Accreditation:* NCATE. *Program availability:* Part-time, evening/weekend. *Degree requirements:* For master's, research project. *Entrance requirements:* For master's, minimum GPA of 3.0, teaching license. Additional exam requirements/recommendations for international students: Required—TOEFL (minimum score 550 paper-based; 79 iBT). *Faculty research:* Educational leadership styles: Jesus as master teacher, assessment accommodations for English language learners, preparing culturally proficient teachers, using naturally occurring text in the classroom to meet the syntactic needs of students with learning disabilities, using tablet instructional technology to meet the needs of students with disabilities.

Marian University, School of Education, Fond du Lac, WI 54935-4699. Offers curriculum and instruction leadership (PhD); educational administration (PhD); educational leadership (MAE); educational technology (MAE); leadership studies (PhD); special education (MAE); teacher education (MAE). *Accreditation:* NCATE. *Program availability:* Part-time, evening/weekend, online learning. *Faculty:* 11 full-time (7 women), 14 part-time/adjunct (8 women). *Students:* 13 full-time (9 women), 179 part-time (113 women); includes 16 minority (6 Black or African American, non-Hispanic/Latino; 3 American Indian or Alaska Native, non-Hispanic/Latino; 2 Asian, non-Hispanic/Latino; 3 Hispanic/Latino; 2 Two or more races, non-Hispanic/Latino). Average age 39. In 2016, 72 master's, 8 doctorates awarded. *Degree requirements:* For master's, exam, field-based experience project, portfolio; for doctorate, comprehensive exam, thesis/dissertation, field-based experience. *Entrance requirements:* For master's, minimum GPA of 3.0, BA in education or related field, teaching license; for doctorate, GRE, MAT, resume, 2 writing samples, interview. Additional exam requirements/recommendations for international students: Required—TOEFL (minimum score 525 paper-based; 70 iBT). *Application deadline:* Applications are processed on a rolling basis. Application fee: $50. *Expenses: Tuition:* Full-time $5130; part-time $570 per credit hour. *Financial support:* In 2016–17, 3 students received support. Federal Work-Study available. Support available to part-time students. Financial award application deadline: 3/1; financial award applicants required to submit FAFSA. *Faculty research:* At-risk youth, multicultural issues, values in education, teaching/learning strategies. *Unit head:* Dr. Kelly Chaney, Dean, 920-923-8610, Fax: 920-923-7663, E-mail: kachaney01@marianuniversity.edu.
Website: https://www.marianuniversity.edu/academic-programs/graduate-studies/

Marquette University, Graduate School, College of Education, Department of Educational Policy and Leadership, Milwaukee, WI 53201-1881. Offers college student personnel administration (M Ed); curriculum and instruction (MA); education (MA); educational administration (M Ed); educational policy and foundations (MA); elementary education (Certificate); literacy (MA); principal (Certificate); reading specialist (Certificate); reading teacher (Certificate); secondary education (Certificate); superintendent (Certificate). *Program availability:* Part-time, evening/weekend. *Faculty:* 17 full-time (14 women), 28 part-time/adjunct (23 women). *Students:* 31 full-time (23 women), 103 part-time (66 women); includes 22 minority (7 Black or African American, non-Hispanic/Latino; 1 American Indian or Alaska Native, non-Hispanic/Latino; 6 Asian, non-Hispanic/Latino; 6 Hispanic/Latino; 2 Two or more races, non-Hispanic/Latino). Average age 31. 96 applicants, 92% accepted, 67 enrolled. In 2016, 47 master's, 3 other advanced degrees awarded. Terminal master's awarded for partial completion of doctoral program. *Degree requirements:* For master's, comprehensive exam, thesis (for some programs); for doctorate, thesis/dissertation, qualifying exam. *Entrance requirements:* For master's, GRE General Test or MAT, official transcripts from all current and previous colleges/universities except Marquette, three letters of recommendation, statement of purpose; for doctorate, GRE General Test, MAT, sample of written work, official transcripts from all current and previous colleges/universities except Marquette, three letters of recommendation, statement of purpose, resume/curriculum vitae; for Certificate, GRE General Test or MAT, master's degree. Additional exam requirements/recommendations for international students: Required—TOEFL (minimum score 530 paper-based). *Application deadline:* For fall admission, 1/15 for domestic and international students. Application fee: $50. *Expenses:* Contact institution. *Financial support:* Fellowships, research assistantships, health care benefits, tuition waivers (partial), and unspecified assistantships available. Support available to part-time students. Financial award application deadline: 2/15. *Faculty research:* Leadership; social justice in education; development of lifelong learners; race, class, and schooling in historical perspective; urban teacher education. *Unit head:* Dr. Ellen Eckman, Chair, 414-288-1561. *Application contact:* Dr. Cynthia Ellwood.

Martin Luther College, Graduate Studies, New Ulm, MN 56073. Offers early childhood director (MS Ed Admin); educational technology (MS Ed); instruction (MS Ed); leadership (MS Ed); principal (MS Ed Admin); special education (MS Ed). *Program availability:* Part-time, evening/weekend. *Faculty:* 9 full-time (1 woman), 21 part-time/adjunct (10 women). *Students:* 1 (woman) full-time, 77 part-time (30 women); includes 2 minority (1 Asian, non-Hispanic/Latino; 1 Two or more races, non-Hispanic/Latino), 4 international. Average age 37. 6 applicants, 100% accepted, 6 enrolled. In 2016, 15 master's awarded. *Degree requirements:* For master's, capstone project or comprehensive exam. *Entrance requirements:* For master's, undergraduate degree in education from an accredited college or university, minimum undergraduate GPA of 3.0. Additional exam requirements/recommendations for international students: Required—TOEFL (minimum score 550 paper-based; 80 iBT); Recommended—IELTS (minimum score 6.5). *Application deadline:* Applications are processed on a rolling basis. Application fee: $35. Electronic applications accepted. *Expenses:* $11,220 tuition, $140 graduation fee. *Financial support:* In 2016–17, 2 students received support. Scholarships/grants available. Financial award application deadline: 9/1. *Faculty research:* Principal effectiveness, principal support, cognitive load in math instruction, reading strategies in multigrade classrooms, mentor provided professional development

for new teachers. *Unit head:* John E. Meyer, Director of Graduate Studies, 507-354-8221 Ext. 398, E-mail: meyerjd@mlc-wels.edu.
Website: https://mlc-wels.edu/graduate-studies/

Massachusetts College of Liberal Arts, Graduate Programs, North Adams, MA 01247-4100. Offers business (MBA); educational administration (M Ed); educational leadership (CAGS); instruction and curriculum (M Ed); instructional technology (M Ed); physical education and health (M Ed); reading (M Ed); special education (M Ed). *Program availability:* Part-time, evening/weekend. *Degree requirements:* For master's, thesis. *Entrance requirements:* For master's, writing sample.

McDaniel College, Graduate and Professional Studies, Program in Curriculum and Instruction, Westminster, MD 21157-4390. Offers MS. *Program availability:* Part-time, evening/weekend, 100% online, blended/hybrid learning. *Faculty:* 4 full-time (all women), 18 part-time/adjunct (13 women). *Students:* 7 full-time (6 women), 326 part-time (254 women); includes 49 minority (28 Black or African American, non-Hispanic/Latino; 1 American Indian or Alaska Native, non-Hispanic/Latino; 3 Asian, non-Hispanic/Latino; 14 Hispanic/Latino; 1 Native Hawaiian or other Pacific Islander, non-Hispanic/Latino; 2 Two or more races, non-Hispanic/Latino), 1 international. Average age 31. 58 applicants, 100% accepted. In 2016, 105 master's awarded. *Degree requirements:* For master's, comprehensive exam (for some programs), thesis optional. *Entrance requirements:* For master's, one reference. Additional exam requirements/recommendations for international students: Required—TOEFL (minimum score 79 iBT), IELTS (minimum score 6). *Application deadline:* For fall admission, 6/1 priority date for domestic students; for spring admission, 11/1 priority date for domestic students; for summer admission, 3/1 priority date for domestic students. Applications are processed on a rolling basis. Application fee: $75. Electronic applications accepted. *Expenses: Tuition:* Full-time $8370; part-time $465 per credit. *Required fees:* $75 per semester. Tuition and fees vary according to course load, program and reciprocity agreements. *Financial support:* Application deadline: 3/1; applicants required to submit FAFSA. *Unit head:* Fax: 410-857-2515, E-mail: gradadms@mcdaniel.edu. *Application contact:* Penny Pfeiffer, Senior Graduate Enrollment Management Specialist, 410-857-2513, Fax: 410-857-2515, E-mail: ppfeiffer@mcdaniel.edu.

McGill University, Faculty of Graduate and Postdoctoral Studies, Faculty of Education, Department of Integrated Studies in Education, Montréal, QC H3A 2T5, Canada. Offers culture and values in education (MA, PhD); curriculum studies (MA); educational leadership (MA, Certificate); educational studies (PhD); integrated studies in education (M Ed); second language education (MA, PhD).

McKendree University, Graduate Programs, Programs in Education, Lebanon, IL 62254-1299. Offers curriculum design and instruction (Ed D, Ed S); educational administration and leadership (MA Ed); educational studies (MA Ed); higher education administrative services (MA Ed); music education (MA Ed); reading (MA Ed); special education (MA Ed); teacher leadership (MA Ed); teaching certification (MA Ed). *Accreditation:* NCATE. *Program availability:* Part-time, evening/weekend, online learning. *Entrance requirements:* For master's, official transcripts from all institutions previously attended, minimum GPA of 3.0, resume, references; for doctorate, GRE (within the past 5 years), master's degree in education and Ed S, or the equivalent, from regionally-accredited institution; official transcripts from all institutions previously attended; curriculum vitae/resume; essay/personal statement; two years of teaching/professional experience; for Ed S, GRE (within the past 5 years), master's degree in education from regionally-accredited institution of higher education; official transcripts from all institutions previously attended; curriculum vitae/resume; essay/personal statement; two years of teaching/professional experience. Additional exam requirements/recommendations for international students: Required—TOEFL. Electronic applications accepted.

McNeese State University, Doré School of Graduate Studies, Burton College of Education, Office of Graduate Education Programs, Program in Curriculum and Instruction, Lake Charles, LA 70609. Offers early childhood education (M Ed); elementary education (M Ed); reading (M Ed); secondary education (M Ed). *Program availability:* Evening/weekend. *Entrance requirements:* For master's, GRE, teaching certificate.

Medaille College, Program in Education, Buffalo, NY 14214-2695. Offers adolescent education (MS Ed); curriculum and instruction (MS Ed); education preparation (MS Ed); literacy (MS Ed); special education (MS). *Accreditation:* TEAC. *Program availability:* Part-time, evening/weekend. *Degree requirements:* For master's, comprehensive exam (for some programs), thesis or alternative. *Entrance requirements:* For master's, minimum undergraduate GPA of 2.7. Additional exam requirements/recommendations for international students: Required—TOEFL (minimum score 550 paper-based). Electronic applications accepted. *Faculty research:* Curriculum planning, truancy, tracking minority students, curriculum design, mentoring students.

Memorial University of Newfoundland, School of Graduate Studies, Faculty of Education, St. John's, NL A1C 5S7, Canada. Offers counseling psychology (M Ed); curriculum, teaching, and learning studies (M Ed); education (PhD); educational leadership studies (M Ed, Graduate Diploma); information technology (M Ed); post-secondary studies (M Ed, Diploma), including health professional education (Diploma). *Program availability:* Part-time. *Degree requirements:* For master's, thesis optional, internship, paper folio, project; for doctorate, comprehensive exam, thesis/dissertation, thesis seminar, oral defense of thesis. *Entrance requirements:* For master's, undergraduate degree with at least 2nd class standing, 1-2 years of work experience; for doctorate, minimum A average in graduate course work, MA in education, 2 years of professional experience; for other advanced degree, 2nd class degree, 2 years of work experience with adult learners, appropriate academic qualifications and work experience in a health-related field. Electronic applications accepted. *Faculty research:* Critical thinking, literacy, cognitive studies and counseling, educational change, technology in instruction.

Mercer University, Graduate Studies, Cecil B. Day Campus, Tift College of Education (Atlanta), Macon, GA 31207. Offers curriculum and instruction (PhD); early childhood education (M Ed, MAT, Ed S); educational leadership (PhD), including higher education leadership, P-12 school leadership; educational leadership P-12 (M Ed, Ed S); higher education leadership (M Ed); independent and charter school leadership (M Ed); middle grades education (M Ed, MAT); reading specialist (M Ed); secondary education (M Ed, MAT); teacher leadership (Ed S). *Accreditation:* NCATE. *Program availability:* Part-time, evening/weekend. *Faculty:* 28 full-time (15 women), 30 part-time/adjunct (27 women). *Students:* 177 full-time (150 women), 324 part-time (264 women); includes 288 minority (256 Black or African American, non-Hispanic/Latino; 1 American Indian or Alaska Native, non-Hispanic/Latino; 7 Asian, non-Hispanic/Latino; 17 Hispanic/Latino; 1 Native Hawaiian or other Pacific Islander, non-Hispanic/Latino; 6 Two or more races, non-Hispanic/Latino), 1 international. Average age 35. In 2016, 173 master's, 34 doctorates, 54 other advanced degrees awarded. *Degree requirements:* For master's and Ed S, research project; for doctorate, comprehensive exam, thesis/dissertation. *Entrance requirements:* For master's, GRE or MAT, minimum undergraduate GPA of 2.75; for doctorate, GRE; for Ed S, GRE or MAT, minimum GPA of 3.25; 3 years of certified teaching experience (for educational leadership and teacher leadership). Additional exam requirements/recommendations for international students: Required—TOEFL (minimum score 80 iBT). *Application deadline:* For fall admission, 8/1 for domestic and international students; for spring admission, 12/1 for domestic and international students; for summer admission, 5/1 for domestic and international students. Applications are processed on a rolling basis. Application fee: $25 ($50 for international students). Electronic applications accepted. *Expenses:* $590 per credit, $1,770 per course (for M Ed); $595 per credit, $1,785 per course (for MAT); $615 per credit, $1,845 per course (for Ed S); $717 per credit, $2,151 per course (for PhD); $150 per semester technology fee. *Financial support:* Federal Work-Study and unspecified assistantships available. Support available to part-time students. Financial award application deadline: 5/1; financial award applicants required to submit FAFSA. *Faculty research:* Educational technology, multicultural and minority issues in education, educational leadership (P-12 and higher education), school discipline and school bullying, standards-based mathematics education. *Unit head:* Dr. James Barta, Dean, 478-301-5355, Fax: 478-301-2280, E-mail: barta_jj@mercer.edu. *Application contact:* Renee Slaton, Associate Director of Graduate Admissions, 678-547-6084, Fax: 678-547-6055, E-mail: mercereducation@mercer.edu.
Website: http://education.mercer.edu/

Meredith College, School of Education, Health and Human Sciences, Raleigh, NC 27607-5298. Offers academically and intellectually gifted (M Ed); curriculum instruction specialist (M Ed); elementary education (M Ed, MAT); English as a second language (M Ed, MAT); health and physical education (MAT); nutrition, health and human performance (MS, Postbaccalaureate Certificate), including dietetic internship (Postbaccalaureate Certificate), nutrition (MS); reading (M Ed); special education (MAT). *Accreditation:* NCATE. *Program availability:* Part-time, evening/weekend. *Degree requirements:* For master's, thesis optional. *Entrance requirements:* For master's, GRE General Test or MAT, minimum GPA of 2.5, teaching license, recommendations. Additional exam requirements/recommendations for international students: Required—TOEFL. Electronic applications accepted. *Expenses:* Contact institution.

Merrimack College, School of Education and Social Policy, North Andover, MA 01845-5800. Offers community engagement (M Ed), including community organizations, higher education, K-12 education; criminology and criminal justice (MS); curriculum and instruction (M Ed); early childhood education (M Ed); educational leadership (CAGS), including instructional leadership; elementary education (M Ed); English as a second language (PreK-6) (M Ed); high school education (M Ed); higher education (M Ed), including leadership and organizational development, student affairs; middle school education (M Ed); moderate disabilities (PreK-8) (M Ed); school counseling (M Ed). *Program availability:* Part-time, evening/weekend, 100% online courses with immersion events and in-classroom practicum close to home. *Faculty:* 17 full-time, 34 part-time/adjunct. *Students:* 204 full-time (172 women), 83 part-time (67 women); includes 32 minority (4 Black or African American, non-Hispanic/Latino; 2 Asian, non-Hispanic/Latino; 23 Hispanic/Latino; 3 Two or more races, non-Hispanic/Latino), 1 international. Average age 27. 261 applicants, 89% accepted, 200 enrolled. In 2016, 153 master's, 2 other advanced degrees awarded. *Degree requirements:* For master's, practicum, portfolio, and state test (for licensure track); capstone (for higher education, curriculum and instruction, and community engagement tracks). *Entrance requirements:* For master's, Massachusetts Teacher Education Licensure (MTEL), official transcripts from other colleges, resume, personal statement, 2 letters of recommendation. Additional exam requirements/recommendations for international students: Required—TOEFL (minimum score 84 iBT), IELTS (minimum score 6.5), PTE (minimum score 56). *Application deadline:* For fall admission, 8/14 for domestic students, 7/14 for international students; for spring admission, 1/10 for domestic students, 12/10 for international students; for summer admission, 5/10 for domestic students, 4/10 for international students. Applications are processed on a rolling basis. Application fee: $0. Electronic applications accepted. *Expenses:* Contact institution. *Financial support:* Fellowships with full tuition reimbursements, career-related internships or fieldwork, scholarships/grants, and health care benefits available. Support available to part-time students. Financial award application deadline: 5/1; financial award applicants required to submit FAFSA. *Faculty research:* Feminist praxis in higher education, transgender student agency and belonging, campus sexual violence prevention, the scholarship of engagement; community engagement; service learning; diversity education; community-university partnerships, college going behaviors and indicators of success for inner city youth, strategies to increase students pursuit and success in STEM higher education, effective workforce development for displaced or under employed individuals, police reform, e.g. surveillance. *Application contact:* Alyssa Frey, Graduate Admissions Counselor, 978-837-3563, E-mail: freya@merrimack.edu.
Website: http://www.merrimack.edu/academics/graduate/education/

Messiah College, Program in Education, Mechanicsburg, PA 17055. Offers curriculum and instruction (M Ed); special education (M Ed); teaching English to speakers of other languages (M Ed). *Program availability:* Part-time, online learning. Electronic applications accepted. *Faculty research:* Socio-cultural perspectives on education, TESOL, autism, special education.

Michigan State University, The Graduate School, College of Education, Department of Teacher Education, East Lansing, MI 48824. Offers curriculum, instruction and teacher education (PhD, Ed S); teaching and curriculum (MA). *Entrance requirements:* Additional exam requirements/recommendations for international students: Required—TOEFL. Electronic applications accepted.

Middle Tennessee State University, College of Graduate Studies, College of Education, Department of Educational Leadership, Program in Curriculum and Instruction, Murfreesboro, TN 37132. Offers curriculum and instruction (M Ed, Ed S); English as a second language (M Ed, Ed S); secondary education (M Ed); technology and curriculum design (Ed S). *Accreditation:* NCATE. *Program availability:* Part-time, evening/weekend, online learning. *Degree requirements:* For master's, comprehensive exam; for Ed S, comprehensive exam, thesis or alternative. *Entrance requirements:* For master's and Ed S, GRE, MAT or PRAXIS. Additional exam requirements/recommendations for international students: Required—TOEFL (minimum score 525 paper-based; 71 iBT) or IELTS (minimum score 6). Electronic applications accepted.

Midwestern State University, Billie Doris McAda Graduate School, West College of Education, Program in Curriculum and Instruction, Wichita Falls, TX 76308. Offers M Ed. *Program availability:* Part-time, evening/weekend. *Degree requirements:* For master's, comprehensive exam. *Entrance requirements:* For master's, GRE General Test, MAT, or GMAT. Additional exam requirements/recommendations for international students: Required—TOEFL (minimum score 550 paper-based). Electronic applications accepted. *Faculty research:* Role of the twenty-first century principal, instructional effectiveness, motivation, curriculum theory, educational research methodology.

Minnesota State University Moorhead, Graduate Studies, College of Education and Human Services, Moorhead, MN 56563. Offers counseling and student affairs (MS); curriculum and instruction (MS); educational leadership (MS, Ed S); special education (MS); speech-language pathology (MS). *Accreditation:* NCATE. *Program availability:* Part-time, 100% online, blended/hybrid learning. *Students:* 133 full-time (116 women), 363 part-time (274 women). Average age 32. 273 applicants, 49% accepted. In 2016, 114 master's awarded. *Degree requirements:* For master's, comprehensive exam (for some programs), thesis. *Entrance requirements:* For master's, GRE, essay, letter of

intent, letters of reference, teaching license, teaching verification. Additional exam requirements/recommendations for international students: Required—TOEFL (minimum score 550 paper-based). *Application deadline:* For fall admission, 4/15 priority date for domestic students; for spring admission, 11/1 priority date for domestic students. Applications are processed on a rolling basis. Application fee: $20. Electronic applications accepted. *Expenses:* Tuition, state resident: full-time $9000; part-time $4500 per credit. Tuition, nonresident: full-time $18,000; part-time $9000 per credit. *Required fees:* $942; $39.25 per credit. One-time fee: $90 full-time. Full-time tuition and fees vary according to course load, degree level, program and reciprocity agreements. *Financial support:* Federal Work-Study and unspecified assistantships available. Financial award application deadline: 10/1; financial award applicants required to submit FAFSA. *Unit head:* Dr. Ok-Hee Lee, Dean, 218-477-2095, E-mail: okheelee@mnstate.edu. *Application contact:* Karla Wenger, Office Manager, 218-477-2344, Fax: 218-477-2482, E-mail: wengerk@mnstate.edu.
Website: http://www.mnstate.edu/cehs/

Misericordia University, College of Health Sciences and Education, Program in Education, Dallas, PA 18612-1098. Offers instructional technology (MS); reading specialist (MS); special education (MS). *Program availability:* Part-time, evening/weekend. *Entrance requirements:* For master's, minimum undergraduate GPA of 3.0. Additional exam requirements/recommendations for international students: Required—TOEFL. Electronic applications accepted.

Mississippi College, Graduate School, School of Education, Department of Teacher Education and Leadership, Clinton, MS 39058. Offers art (M Ed); biological science (M Ed); business education (M Ed); computer science (M Ed); dyslexia therapy (M Ed); educational leadership (M Ed, Ed D, Ed S); elementary education (M Ed, Ed S); English (M Ed); higher education administration (MS); mathematics (M Ed); secondary education (M Ed); social studies (history) (M Ed); teaching arts (M Ed). *Program availability:* Part-time, online learning. *Degree requirements:* For master's, comprehensive exam, thesis optional. *Entrance requirements:* For master's, NTE. Additional exam requirements/recommendations for international students: Recommended—TOEFL, IELTS. Electronic applications accepted.

Mississippi State University, College of Education, Department of Curriculum, Instruction and Special Education, Mississippi State, MS 39762. Offers early childhood education (PhD); elementary education (MS, PhD, Ed S), including early childhood education (MS), general elementary education (MS), middle level education (MS); general curriculum and instruction (PhD); middle level (MAT); reading education (PhD); secondary education (MAT, MS, PhD, Ed S); special education (MAT, MS, PhD, Ed S). *Accreditation:* NCATE. *Program availability:* Part-time, evening/weekend. *Faculty:* 21 full-time (16 women), 1 (woman) part-time/adjunct. *Students:* 39 full-time (26 women), 168 part-time (128 women); includes 49 minority (43 Black or African American, non-Hispanic/Latino; 2 American Indian or Alaska Native, non-Hispanic/Latino; 1 Hispanic/Latino; 1 Native Hawaiian or other Pacific Islander, non-Hispanic/Latino; 2 Two or more races, non-Hispanic/Latino), 4 international. Average age 33. 98 applicants, 56% accepted, 47 enrolled. In 2016, 69 master's, 6 doctorates, 10 other advanced degrees awarded. *Degree requirements:* For master's, comprehensive exam; for doctorate, thesis/dissertation; for Ed S, comprehensive exam, thesis or alternative. *Entrance requirements:* For master's, GRE, minimum GPA of 2.75 in junior and senior year, eligibility for initial teacher certification; for doctorate, GRE, minimum GPA of 3.4 on previous graduate work; for Ed S, GRE, minimum GPA of 3.2 on master's degree. Additional exam requirements/recommendations for international students: Required—TOEFL (minimum score 550 paper-based; 79 iBT); Recommended—IELTS (minimum score 6.5). *Application deadline:* For fall admission, 3/1 priority date for domestic students, 5/1 for international students; for spring admission, 9/1 priority date for domestic students, 9/1 for international students. Applications are processed on a rolling basis. Application fee: $60. Electronic applications accepted. *Expenses:* Tuition, state resident: full-time $7670; part-time $852.50 per credit hour. Tuition, nonresident: full-time $20,790; part-time $2310.50 per credit hour. Part-time tuition and fees vary according to course load. *Financial support:* In 2016–17, 8 research assistantships with partial tuition reimbursements (averaging $11,381 per year) were awarded; Federal Work-Study, institutionally sponsored loans, scholarships/grants, and unspecified assistantships also available. Financial award application deadline: 4/1; financial award applicants required to submit FAFSA. *Faculty research:* Early childhood education, reading, rural schools, multicultural education, use of technology in instruction. *Unit head:* Dr. Janice Nicholson, Interim Department Head, 662-325-3704, Fax: 662-325-7857, E-mail: jin4@msstate.edu. *Application contact:* Linda Bonner, Senior Admissions Assistant, 662-325-3363, E-mail: lbonner@grad.msstate.edu.
Website: http://www.cise.msstate.edu/

Mississippi University for Women, Graduate School, College of Education and Human Sciences, Columbus, MS 39701-9998. Offers differentiated instruction (M Ed); educational leadership (M Ed); gifted studies (M Ed); reading/literacy (M Ed); teaching (MAT). *Accreditation:* ASHA; NCATE. *Program availability:* Part-time. *Degree requirements:* For master's, comprehensive exam, thesis optional. *Entrance requirements:* For master's, GRE General Test or NTE (M Ed in gifted education or MS in speech/language pathology), MAT (M Ed in instructional management), minimum QPA of 3.0.

Montana State University, The Graduate School, College of Education, Health, and Human Development, Department of Education, Bozeman, MT 59717. Offers adult and higher education (Ed D); curriculum and instruction (M Ed, Ed D), including professional educator (M Ed), technology education (M Ed); education (M Ed), including adult and higher education, educational leadership, school counseling; educational leadership (Ed D, Ed S). *Accreditation:* TEAC. *Program availability:* Part-time, online learning. *Degree requirements:* For master's, comprehensive exam; for doctorate, comprehensive exam, thesis/dissertation. *Entrance requirements:* For master's, GRE, 3 letters of reference, essays, BA transcripts; for doctorate, GRE, MAT, 3 letters of reference, essay, BA and M Ed transcripts; for Ed S, PRAXIS. Additional exam requirements/recommendations for international students: Required—TOEFL (minimum score 550 paper-based). Electronic applications accepted. *Faculty research:* Critical literacy; standards-based education; school Improvement, organizational change, leadership in rural education, leadership in Indian education; student Learning; multicultural/culturally responsive education for social justice Native American indigenous education, community-centered education teacher preparation.

Montana State University Billings, College of Education, Department of Educational Theory and Practice, Option in General Curriculum, Billings, MT 59101. Offers K-8 (M Ed); secondary (M Ed). *Accreditation:* NCATE. *Program availability:* Part-time. *Faculty:* 15 full-time (10 women), 1 (woman) part-time/adjunct. *Students:* 62. *Degree requirements:* For master's, thesis or professional paper and/or field experience. *Entrance requirements:* For master's, GRE General Test or MAT, minimum GPA of 3.0. Additional exam requirements/recommendations for international students: Required—TOEFL (minimum score 79 iBT), IELTS (minimum score 6.5). *Application deadline:* Applications are processed on a rolling basis. Application fee: $40. Electronic applications accepted. *Expenses:* Tuition, state resident: full-time $5265; part-time $3436 per year. Tuition, nonresident: full-time $14,030; part-time $9280 per year. *International tuition:* $19,295 full-time. Tuition and fees vary according to degree level, campus/location and program. *Financial support:* Teaching assistantships with partial tuition reimbursements, career-related internships or fieldwork, Federal Work-Study, institutionally sponsored loans, scholarships/grants, tuition waivers (partial), and unspecified assistantships available. Support available to part-time students. Financial award application deadline: 5/1; financial award applicants required to submit FAFSA. *Faculty research:* Social studies education, science education. *Unit head:* Dr. Ken Miller, Chair, 406-657-2034, Fax: 406-657-2807, E-mail: kmiller@msubillings.edu. *Application contact:* David M. Sullivan, Graduate Studies Counselor, 406-657-2053, Fax: 406-657-2299, E-mail: dsullivan@msubillings.edu.

Montclair State University, The Graduate School, College of Education and Human Services, MAT Program in Teaching, Montclair, NJ 07043-1624. Offers art (MAT); biology (MAT); chemistry (MAT); earth science (MAT); English (MAT); French (MAT); health and physical education (MAT); health education (MAT); mathematics (MAT); music (MAT); physical education (MAT); physical science (MAT); social studies (MAT); Spanish (MAT); teacher of English as a second language (MAT). *Degree requirements:* For master's, comprehensive exam, thesis or alternative. *Entrance requirements:* For master's, interview, 2 letters of recommendation. Additional exam requirements/recommendations for international students: Required—TOEFL (minimum score 83 iBT), IELTS (minimum score 6.5). Electronic applications accepted. *Expenses:* Tuition, state resident: part-time $553 per credit. Tuition, nonresident: part-time $854 per credit. *Required fees:* $91 per credit. Tuition and fees vary according to program.

Moravian College, Graduate and Continuing Studies, Education Programs, Bethlehem, PA 18018-6650. Offers curriculum and instruction (M Ed); education (MAT). *Program availability:* Part-time, evening/weekend. *Faculty:* 7 full-time (4 women), 17 part-time/adjunct (12 women). *Students:* 1 (woman) full-time, 91 part-time (71 women); includes 7 minority (1 Asian, non-Hispanic/Latino; 5 Hispanic/Latino; 1 Two or more races, non-Hispanic/Latino). Average age 35. 15 applicants, 80% accepted, 11 enrolled. In 2016, 17 master's awarded. *Degree requirements:* For master's, thesis. *Entrance requirements:* For master's, state teacher certification. *Application deadline:* For fall admission, 8/1 priority date for domestic and international students; for spring admission, 1/1 priority date for domestic and international students; for summer admission, 5/1 priority date for domestic and international students. Applications are processed on a rolling basis. Electronic applications accepted. *Expenses:* Contact institution. *Financial support:* Applicants required to submit FAFSA. *Faculty research:* Teacher action research, youth participatory research, practitioner inquiry, science education, deaf and hard of hearing education. *Unit head:* Dr. Joseph Shosh, Director, 610-861-1400, Fax: 610-861-1466, E-mail: shoshj@moravian.edu. *Application contact:* 610-861-1400, Fax: 610-861-1466, E-mail: graduate@moravian.edu.

Morehead State University, Graduate Programs, College of Education, Department of Curriculum and Instruction, Morehead, KY 40351. Offers curriculum and instruction (Ed S); elementary education (MA Ed), including elementary education, international education, middle school education, reading; secondary education (MA Ed); special education (MA Ed); teaching (MAT). *Program availability:* Part-time, evening/weekend. *Degree requirements:* For master's, comprehensive exam, thesis optional; for Ed S, thesis, oral exam. *Entrance requirements:* For master's, GRE General Test, minimum GPA of 2.75, teaching certificate; for Ed S, GRE General Test, interview, master's degree, minimum GPA of 3.5, work experience. Additional exam requirements/recommendations for international students: Required—TOEFL (minimum score 500 paper-based). Electronic applications accepted. *Faculty research:* Communicative competence of learning-disabled students, teaching social studies in elementary schools, ungraded primary school organization, study skills.

Morehead State University, Graduate Programs, College of Education, Department of Foundational and Graduate Studies in Education, Morehead, KY 40351. Offers adult and higher education (MA, Ed S); certified professional counselor (Ed S); counseling P-12 (MA); curriculum and instruction (Ed S); educational technology (MA Ed); instructional leadership (Ed S); school administration (MA); school counseling (Ed S); teacher leader business and marketing content (MA Ed); teacher leader business and marketing technology (MA Ed); teacher leader educational technology (MA Ed); teacher leader English (MA Ed); teacher leader gifted education (MA Ed); teacher leader IECE certification (MA Ed); teacher leader interdisciplinary education P-5 (MA Ed); teacher leader middle grades (MA Ed); teacher leader non IECE certification (MA Ed); teacher leader reading/writing - non-certification (MA Ed); teacher leader reading/writing certification (MA Ed); teacher leader school communication - certification (MA Ed); teacher leader school communication - non-certification (MA Ed); teacher leader social studies (MA Ed); teacher leader special education (MA Ed). *Accreditation:* NCATE. *Program availability:* Part-time, evening/weekend. *Degree requirements:* For master's, thesis optional, oral and/or written comprehensive exams; for Ed S, thesis, oral exam. *Entrance requirements:* For master's, GRE General Test, minimum overall undergraduate GPA of 2.5; for Ed S, GRE General Test, interview, master's degree, minimum GPA of 3.5, work experience. Additional exam requirements/recommendations for international students: Required—TOEFL (minimum score 500 paper-based). Electronic applications accepted. *Faculty research:* Character education, school accountability, computer applications for school administrators.

Mount Saint Vincent University, Graduate Programs, Faculty of Education, Program in Curriculum Studies, Halifax, NS B3M 2J6, Canada. Offers education of young adolescents (M Ed, MA Ed, MA-R); general studies (M Ed, MA Ed, MA-R); teaching English as a second language (M Ed, MA Ed, MA-R). *Program availability:* Part-time, evening/weekend, online learning. *Degree requirements:* For master's, thesis (for some programs). *Entrance requirements:* For master's, bachelor's degree in related field, minimum B average, 1 year of teaching experience. Electronic applications accepted. *Faculty research:* Science education, cultural studies, international education, curriculum development.

National Louis University, National College of Education, Chicago, IL 60603. Offers administration and supervision (M Ed, Ed D, CAS, Ed S); curriculum and instruction (M Ed, MS Ed, CAS); early childhood administration (M Ed, CAS); early childhood education (M Ed, MAT, MS Ed, CAS); education (Ed D); educational psychology/human learning and development (M Ed, MS Ed, CAS, Ed S); elementary education (MAT); interdisciplinary curriculum and instruction (M Ed); mathematics education (M Ed, MS Ed, CAS); middle grades education (MAT); reading and language (M Ed, MS Ed, CAS); school psychology (M Ed, Ed S); science education (M Ed, MS Ed, CAS); secondary education (MAT); special education (M Ed, MAT, CAS); technology in education (M Ed, CAS). *Accreditation:* NCATE. *Program availability:* Part-time, evening/weekend. *Degree requirements:* For doctorate, comprehensive exam, thesis/dissertation. *Entrance requirements:* For master's, MAT or GRE, minimum GPA of 3.0; for doctorate, GRE General Test, minimum GPA of 3.25, interview, resume, writing sample, 4 recommendations. Additional exam requirements/recommendations for international students: Required—TOEFL (minimum score 550 paper-based; 79 iBT).

Newman University, Master of Science in Education Program, Wichita, KS 67213-2097. Offers building leadership (MS Ed); curriculum and instruction (MS Ed), including English as a second language, reading specialist; organizational leadership (MS Ed). *Accreditation:* NCATE. *Program availability:* Part-time, evening/weekend, online learning. *Degree requirements:* For master's, thesis optional. *Entrance requirements:* For master's, 3 years' full-time teaching experience, minimum GPA of 3.0, writing sample, 2 letters of recommendation, evidence of teaching certification. Additional exam requirements/recommendations for international students: Required—TOEFL (minimum score 600 paper-based; 100 iBT). Electronic applications accepted. *Expenses:* Contact institution. *Faculty research:* Online course design and deliver, staff engagement, classroom action.

New Mexico Highlands University, Graduate Studies, School of Education, Las Vegas, NM 87701. Offers curriculum and instruction (MA); educational leadership (MA); professional counseling (MA); special education (MA). *Accreditation:* NCATE. *Program availability:* Part-time. *Degree requirements:* For master's, comprehensive exam, thesis or alternative. *Entrance requirements:* For master's, minimum undergraduate GPA of 3.0. Additional exam requirements/recommendations for international students: Required—TOEFL (minimum score 540 paper-based). *Faculty research:* Middle school curriculum, integrated computer applications for pre-service classroom teachers, adolescent literacy, narrative cognitive modes in New Mexico multicultural setting, math and math education.

New Mexico State University, College of Education, Department of Curriculum and Instruction, Las Cruces, NM 88003. Offers bilingual education (MA); curriculum and instruction (Ed D); early childhood education (MA); educational diagnostics (Ed S); language, literacy and culture (MA); learning design and technologies (MA); teaching (MAT), including Spanish; teaching English to speakers of other languages (MA). *Accreditation:* NCATE. *Program availability:* Part-time, evening/weekend, 100% online. *Faculty:* 23 full-time (17 women), 7 part-time/adjunct (5 women). *Students:* 114 full-time (81 women), 219 part-time (159 women); includes 190 minority (16 Black or African American, non-Hispanic/Latino; 2 American Indian or Alaska Native, non-Hispanic/Latino; 5 Asian, non-Hispanic/Latino; 160 Hispanic/Latino; 7 Two or more races, non-Hispanic/Latino), 33 international. Average age 37. 126 applicants, 75% accepted, 65 enrolled. In 2016, 92 master's, 19 doctorates awarded. *Degree requirements:* For master's, comprehensive exam, thesis optional; for doctorate, comprehensive exam, thesis/dissertation. *Entrance requirements:* For master's, minimum cumulative GPA of 3.0; for doctorate, portfolio, minimum cumulative GPA of 3.0. Additional exam requirements/recommendations for international students: Required—TOEFL (minimum score 550 paper-based; 79 iBT), IELTS (minimum score 6.5). *Application deadline:* For fall admission, 12/15 priority date for domestic and international students; for spring admission, 11/1 for domestic students. Applications are processed on a rolling basis. Application fee: $40 ($50 for international students). Electronic applications accepted. *Expenses:* Tuition, state resident: full-time $4086. Tuition, nonresident: full-time $14,254. *Required fees:* $853. Tuition and fees vary according to course load. *Financial support:* In 2016–17, 102 students received support, including 2 fellowships (averaging $4,076 per year), 2 research assistantships (averaging $18,070 per year), 16 teaching assistantships (averaging $16,454 per year); career-related internships or fieldwork, Federal Work-Study, scholarships/grants, traineeships, health care benefits, and unspecified assistantships also available. Support available to part-time students. Financial award application deadline: 3/1. *Faculty research:* STEM education, bilingual and English as a second language education, critical pedagogy/multicultural education, learning design and technology, early childhood education. *Total annual research expenditures:* $29,926. *Unit head:* Dr. David Rutledge, Department Head, 575-646-5411, Fax: 575-646-5436, E-mail: rutledge@nmsu.edu. *Application contact:* Dr. David Rutledge, Associate Department Head for Graduate Programs, 575-646-5411, Fax: 575-646-5436, E-mail: rutledge@nmsu.edu.
Website: http://ci.education.nmsu.edu

New Mexico State University, College of Education, Department of Special Education and Communication Disorders, Las Cruces, NM 88003. Offers communication disorders (MA); curriculum and instruction (Ed S), including special education (MA, Ed S), special education/deaf-hard of hearing (MA, Ed S); education (MA), including autism spectrum disorders, special education (MA, Ed S), special education/deaf-hard of hearing (MA, Ed S), speech-language pathology; special education (Ed D, PhD), including bilingual/multicultural special education. *Accreditation:* ASHA (one or more programs are accredited); NCATE. *Program availability:* Part-time, evening/weekend, online learning. *Faculty:* 15 full-time (12 women), 4 part-time/adjunct (3 women). *Students:* 59 full-time (49 women), 64 part-time (52 women); includes 68 minority (3 Black or African American, non-Hispanic/Latino; 2 American Indian or Alaska Native, non-Hispanic/Latino; 2 Asian, non-Hispanic/Latino; 59 Hispanic/Latino; 2 Two or more races, non-Hispanic/Latino), 7 international. Average age 33. 175 applicants, 19% accepted, 29 enrolled. In 2016, 43 master's, 1 doctorate, 1 other advanced degree awarded. *Degree requirements:* For master's, comprehensive exam, thesis optional; for doctorate, comprehensive exam, thesis/dissertation. *Entrance requirements:* For master's, GRE General Test or MAT. Additional exam requirements/recommendations for international students: Required—TOEFL (minimum score 550 paper-based; 79 iBT), IELTS (minimum score 6.5). *Application deadline:* For fall admission, 2/1 priority date for domestic students. Applications are processed on a rolling basis. Application fee: $40 ($50 for international students). Electronic applications accepted. *Expenses:* Tuition, state resident: full-time $4086. Tuition, nonresident: full-time $14,254. *Required fees:* $853. Tuition and fees vary according to course load. *Financial support:* In 2016–17, 47 students received support, including 2 research assistantships (averaging $12,723 per year), 15 teaching assistantships (averaging $9,700 per year); career-related internships or fieldwork, Federal Work-Study, scholarships/grants, traineeships, health care benefits, and unspecified assistantships also available. Support available to part-time students. Financial award application deadline: 3/1. *Faculty research:* Multicultural special education, multicultural communication disorders, mild disability, multicultural assessment, deaf education, early childhood, bilingual special education. *Total annual research expenditures:* $156,279. *Unit head:* Dr. Bob Wood, Interim Department Head, 575-646-5972, Fax: 575-646-7712, E-mail: bobwood@nmsu.edu. *Application contact:* Dr. Karen Potter, Director, Special Education Program, 575-646-2402, Fax: 575-646-7712, E-mail: potterk@nmsu.edu.
Website: http://spedcd.education.nmsu.edu

Nicholls State University, Graduate Studies, College of Education, Department of Teacher Education, Thibodaux, LA 70310. Offers curriculum and instruction (M Ed); educational leadership (M Ed); elementary education (MAT); human performance education (MAT); middle school education (MAT); secondary education (MAT). *Accreditation:* NCATE. *Program availability:* Part-time, evening/weekend, online learning. *Degree requirements:* For master's, comprehensive exam, portfolio. *Entrance requirements:* For master's, GRE General Test, teaching license. Electronic applications accepted.

North Carolina State University, Graduate School, College of Education, Department of Curriculum and Instruction, Program in Curriculum and Instruction, Raleigh, NC 27695. Offers M Ed, MS, PhD. *Accreditation:* NCATE. *Degree requirements:* For master's, thesis (for some programs); for doctorate, thesis/dissertation. *Entrance requirements:* For master's, GRE General Test or MAT, minimum GPA of 3.0 in major; for doctorate, GRE General Test, minimum GPA of 3.0 in major. Electronic applications accepted. *Faculty research:* Curriculum development, teacher development, intervention for exceptional children, literacy development.

North Dakota State University, College of Graduate and Interdisciplinary Studies, College of Human Development and Education, School of Education, Program in Curriculum and Instruction, Fargo, ND 58102. Offers M Ed, MS. *Degree requirements:* For master's, comprehensive exam, thesis (for some programs). *Entrance requirements:* For master's, Cooperative English Test, GRE General Test, MAT. Additional exam requirements/recommendations for international students: Required—TOEFL.

Northern Arizona University, Graduate College, College of Education, Department of Teaching and Learning, Flagstaff, AZ 86011. Offers curriculum and instruction (Ed D); early childhood education (M Ed); elementary education (M Ed); secondary education (M Ed). *Program availability:* Part-time. *Degree requirements:* For master's, comprehensive exam (for some programs), thesis (for some programs). *Entrance requirements:* For master's, minimum GPA of 3.0. Additional exam requirements/recommendations for international students: Required—TOEFL (minimum score 550 paper-based; 80 iBT), IELTS (minimum score 7). Electronic applications accepted. *Expenses:* Tuition, state resident: full-time $8971; part-time $444 per credit hour. Tuition, nonresident: full-time $20,958; part-time $1164 per credit hour. *Required fees:* $1018; $644 per credit hour. Tuition and fees vary according to course load, campus/location and program.

Northern Illinois University, Graduate School, College of Education, Department of Special and Early Education, De Kalb, IL 60115-2854. Offers curriculum and instruction (MS Ed, Ed D), including curriculum leadership (Ed D), elementary education (Ed D), secondary education (Ed D); early childhood education (MS Ed); elementary education (MS Ed); special education (MS Ed). *Program availability:* Part-time, evening/weekend. *Faculty:* 22 full-time (14 women), 2 part-time/adjunct (both women). *Students:* 42 full-time (34 women), 85 part-time (68 women); includes 16 minority (4 Black or African American, non-Hispanic/Latino; 3 Asian, non-Hispanic/Latino; 6 Hispanic/Latino; 3 Two or more races, non-Hispanic/Latino), 6 international. Average age 33. 70 applicants, 73% accepted, 30 enrolled. In 2016, 19 master's, 1 doctorate awarded. *Degree requirements:* For master's, comprehensive exam, thesis optional; for doctorate, thesis/dissertation, candidacy exam, dissertation defense. *Entrance requirements:* For master's, GRE General Test or MAT, minimum undergraduate GPA of 2.75; for doctorate, GRE General Test or MAT, minimum undergraduate GPA of 2.75, graduate 3.2. Additional exam requirements/recommendations for international students: Required—TOEFL (minimum score 550 paper-based). *Application deadline:* For fall admission, 6/1 for domestic students, 5/1 for international students; for spring admission, 11/1 for domestic students, 10/1 for international students. Applications are processed on a rolling basis. Application fee: $40. Electronic applications accepted. *Financial support:* In 2016–17, 14 research assistantships with full tuition reimbursements were awarded; fellowships with full tuition reimbursements, teaching assistantships with full tuition reimbursements, career-related internships or fieldwork, Federal Work-Study, scholarships/grants, tuition waivers (full), and unspecified assistantships also available. Support available to part-time students. Financial award applicants required to submit FAFSA. *Faculty research:* Teacher certification, stress reduction during student teaching, teaching history, portfolios in student teaching. *Unit head:* Gregory Conderman, Chair, 815-753-1619, E-mail: seed@niu.edu. *Application contact:* Gail Myers, Clerk, Graduate Advising, 815-753-0381, E-mail: gmyers@niu.edu.
Website: http://www.cedu.niu.edu/seed/

Northern Michigan University, Office of Graduate Education and Research, College of Health Sciences and Professional Studies, School of Education, Leadership and Public Service, Marquette, MI 49855-5301. Offers administration and supervision (MAE); elementary education (MAE); higher education in student affairs (MA); instruction (MAE); learning disabilities (MAE); public administration (MPA), including criminal justice administration, human resource administration, public administration, public management, state and local government; reading education (MAE), including reading, reading specialist; science education (MS); secondary education (MAE). *Accreditation:* TEAC. *Program availability:* Part-time, online learning. *Degree requirements:* For master's, thesis (for some programs). *Entrance requirements:* For master's, minimum GPA of 3.0. Additional exam requirements/recommendations for international students: Required—TOEFL (minimum score 550 paper-based; 79 iBT), IELTS (minimum score 6.5). Electronic applications accepted.

Northern State University, MS Ed Program in Teaching and Learning, Aberdeen, SD 57401-7198. Offers MS Ed. *Accreditation:* NCATE. *Program availability:* Part-time, evening/weekend, online learning. *Degree requirements:* For master's, comprehensive exam, thesis optional. *Entrance requirements:* For master's, minimum GPA of 2.75. Additional exam requirements/recommendations for international students: Required—TOEFL (minimum score 550 paper-based; 78 iBT), IELTS (minimum score 6). Electronic applications accepted.

Northwestern Oklahoma State University, School of Professional Studies, Program in Curriculum and Instruction, Alva, OK 73717-2799. Offers M Ed. *Program availability:* Part-time. *Degree requirements:* For master's, thesis optional, portfolio. *Entrance requirements:* For master's, GRE General Test or MAT, minimum GPA of 2.75.

Northwestern State University of Louisiana, Graduate Studies and Research, College of Education and Human Development, Program in Curriculum and Instruction, Natchitoches, LA 71497. Offers M Ed. *Entrance requirements:* Additional exam requirements/recommendations for international students: Required—TOEFL. Electronic applications accepted.

Northwest Nazarene University, Graduate Education Program, Nampa, ID 83686-5897. Offers curriculum and instruction (M Ed); educational leadership (M Ed, Ed D, PhD, Ed S), including building administrator (M Ed, Ed S), director of special education (Ed S), leadership and organizational development (Ed S), superintendent (Ed S). *Accreditation:* ACA (one or more programs are accredited); NCATE. *Program availability:* Part-time, online only, 100% online, 2-week face-to-face residency (for doctoral programs). *Faculty:* 4 full-time (3 women), 17 part-time/adjunct (6 women). *Students:* 112 full-time (72 women), 73 part-time (36 women); includes 19 minority (3 Black or African American, non-Hispanic/Latino; 2 Asian, non-Hispanic/Latino; 6 Hispanic/Latino; 1 Native Hawaiian or other Pacific Islander, non-Hispanic/Latino; 7 Two or more races, non-Hispanic/Latino), 5 international. Average age 39. 96 applicants, 72% accepted, 67 enrolled. In 2016, 59 master's, 13 doctorates, 33 other advanced degrees awarded. *Degree requirements:* For master's, comprehensive exam (for some programs), action research project; for doctorate, thesis/dissertation; for Ed S, comprehensive exam, research project. *Entrance requirements:* For master's, minimum undergraduate GPA of 3.0 overall or during final 30 semester credits, undergraduate degree, valid teaching certificate; for doctorate, Ed S or equivalent, minimum GPA of 3.5; for Ed S, undergraduate degree, valid teaching certificate. Additional exam requirements/recommendations for international students: Recommended—TOEFL. *Application deadline:* Applications are processed on a rolling basis. Application fee: $50. Electronic applications accepted. *Expenses:* Contact institution. *Financial support:* In 2016–17, research assistantships (averaging $5,000 per year) were awarded. Financial award application deadline: 1/15; financial award applicants required to submit FAFSA. *Faculty research:* Action research, cooperative learning, accountability, institutional accreditation. *Unit head:* Dr. Heidi Curtis, Chair, 208-467-8250, E-mail: hlcurtis@nnu.edu. *Application contact:* Charlene Brown, Admissions Counselor, 208-467-8492, Fax: 208-467-8384, E-mail: gradeducationinfo@nnu.edu.
Website: http://www.nnu.edu/graded/

Curriculum and Instruction

Notre Dame de Namur University, Division of Academic Affairs, School of Education and Leadership, Program in Education, Belmont, CA 94002-1908. Offers curriculum and instruction (MA). *Program availability:* Part-time, evening/weekend. *Degree requirements:* For master's, thesis (for some programs). *Entrance requirements:* For master's, CBEST, CSET, valid teaching credential or substantial teaching experience. Additional exam requirements/recommendations for international students: Required—TOEFL (minimum score 550 paper-based; 79 iBT). Electronic applications accepted.

Ohio Dominican University, Division of Education, Program in Curriculum and Instruction, Columbus, OH 43219-2099. Offers M Ed. *Program availability:* Part-time, evening/weekend, 100% online, blended/hybrid learning. *Faculty:* 6 full-time (4 women), 6 part-time/adjunct (5 women). *Students:* 5 full-time (all women), 25 part-time (24 women); includes 3 minority (1 Black or African American, non-Hispanic/Latino; 1 Hispanic/Latino; 1 Two or more races, non-Hispanic/Latino). Average age 32. 14 applicants, 64% accepted, 8 enrolled. In 2016, 10 master's awarded. *Entrance requirements:* For master's, bachelor's degree from regionally-accredited institution; teaching certificate/license; currently teaching or have access to an academic classroom. Additional exam requirements/recommendations for international students: Required—TOEFL (minimum score 550 paper-based), IELTS (minimum score 6.5). *Application deadline:* For fall admission, 8/15 for domestic students, 6/10 for international students; for spring admission, 1/4 for domestic students, 11/2 for international students; for summer admission, 5/30 for domestic students. Applications are processed on a rolling basis. Application fee: $25. Electronic applications accepted. *Expenses:* $529 per credit hour, $225 per semester fees. *Financial support:* Applicants required to submit FAFSA. *Unit head:* Dr. JoAnn Hohenbrink, Associate Professor/Chair of Education Division, 614-251-4759, E-mail: hohenbrj@ohiodominican.edu. *Application contact:* John W. Naughton, Director for Graduate Admissions, 614-251-4721, Fax: 614-251-6654, E-mail: grad@ohiodominican.edu.
Website: http://www.ohiodominican.edu/academics/graduate/master-of-education/curriculum-instruction

Ohio University, Graduate College, Gladys W. and David H. Patton College of Education and Human Services, Department of Teacher Education, Athens, OH 45701-2979. Offers adolescent to young adult education (M Ed); curriculum and instruction (M Ed, PhD); early childhood/special education (M Ed); intervention specialist/mild-moderate needs (M Ed); intervention specialist/moderate-intensive needs (M Ed); middle childhood education (M Ed); reading education (M Ed). *Program availability:* Part-time, evening/weekend. *Degree requirements:* For master's, thesis or alternative; for doctorate, comprehensive exam, thesis/dissertation. *Entrance requirements:* For master's, GRE General Test or MAT (if GPA is below 2.9); for doctorate, GRE General Test, minimum GPA of 3.4, work experience. Additional exam requirements/recommendations for international students: Required—TOEFL (minimum score 550 paper-based; 80 iBT) or IELTS (minimum score 6.5). *Application deadline:* For fall admission, 5/1 priority date for domestic students, 4/1 priority date for international students; for winter admission, 11/1 priority date for domestic students, 10/1 priority date for international students; for spring admission, 2/15 priority date for domestic students, 1/1 priority date for international students. Applications are processed on a rolling basis. Application fee: $50 ($55 for international students). Electronic applications accepted. *Financial support:* Research assistantships with full tuition reimbursements, teaching assistantships with full tuition reimbursements, Federal Work-Study, institutionally sponsored loans, tuition waivers (partial), and unspecified assistantships available. Financial award application deadline: 3/1. *Faculty research:* Cognition literacy, character education, teacher's education reform, disabilities. *Unit head:* Dr. John Henning, Chair, 740-597-1830, Fax: 740-593-0477, E-mail: henningj@ohio.edu. *Application contact:* Floyd J. Doney, Director of Student Affairs, 740-593-4400, Fax: 740-593-9310, E-mail: doney@ohio.edu.
Website: http://www.cehs.ohio.edu/academics/te/index.htm

Ohio Valley University, School of Graduate Education, Vienna, WV 26105-8000. Offers curriculum and instruction (M Ed). *Program availability:* Online learning. *Entrance requirements:* For master's, 2 letters of recommendation, official transcripts from all previous institutions, essay, bachelor's degree.

Oklahoma State University, College of Education, School of Teaching and Curriculum Leadership, Stillwater, OK 74078. Offers MS, PhD. *Program availability:* Part-time. *Faculty:* 31 full-time (30 women), 28 part-time/adjunct (24 women). *Students:* 23 full-time (all women), 129 part-time (107 women); includes 40 minority (10 Black or African American, non-Hispanic/Latino; 4 American Indian or Alaska Native, non-Hispanic/Latino; 1 Asian, non-Hispanic/Latino; 7 Hispanic/Latino; 18 Two or more races, non-Hispanic/Latino), 5 international. Average age 37. 35 applicants, 89% accepted, 27 enrolled. In 2016, 58 master's, 10 doctorates awarded. *Degree requirements:* For master's, thesis or alternative; for doctorate, comprehensive exam, thesis/dissertation. *Entrance requirements:* For master's and doctorate, GRE or GMAT. Additional exam requirements/recommendations for international students: Required—TOEFL (minimum score 550 paper-based; 79 iBT). *Application deadline:* For fall admission, 3/1 priority date for international students; for spring admission, 8/1 priority date for international students. Applications are processed on a rolling basis. Application fee: $40 ($75 for international students). Electronic applications accepted. *Expenses:* Tuition, state resident: full-time $3775; part-time $209.70 per credit hour. Tuition, nonresident: full-time $14,851; part-time $825.05 per credit hour. *Required fees:* $2027; $112.60 per credit hour. Tuition and fees vary according to campus/location. *Financial support:* In 2016–17, 5 research assistantships (averaging $8,240 per year), 7 teaching assistantships (averaging $11,691 per year) were awarded; career-related internships or fieldwork, Federal Work-Study, scholarships/grants, health care benefits, tuition waivers (partial), and unspecified assistantships also available. Support available to part-time students. Financial award application deadline: 3/1; financial award applicants required to submit FAFSA. *Unit head:* Dr. Jennifer Sanders, Interim Department Head, 405-744-9214, Fax: 405-744-6290, E-mail: jenn.sanders10@okstate.edu.
Website: http://education.okstate.edu/stcl

Old Dominion University, Darden College of Education, Doctoral Program in Curriculum and Instruction, Norfolk, VA 23529. Offers PhD. *Program availability:* Part-time, evening/weekend. *Faculty:* 8 full-time (6 women). *Students:* 9 full-time (7 women), 8 part-time (all women); includes 2 minority (both Black or African American, non-Hispanic/Latino). Average age 44. 19 applicants, 53% accepted, 8 enrolled. In 2016, 5 doctorates awarded. *Degree requirements:* For doctorate, comprehensive exam, thesis/dissertation. *Entrance requirements:* For doctorate, GRE, letters of recommendation; minimum undergraduate GPA of 2.8, graduate 3.2. Additional exam requirements/recommendations for international students: Required—TOEFL (minimum score 600 paper-based). *Application deadline:* For fall admission, 3/15 priority date for domestic and international students; for spring admission, 11/15 for domestic and international students. Applications are processed on a rolling basis. Application fee: $50. Electronic applications accepted. *Expenses:* Tuition, state resident: full-time $8604; part-time $478 per credit hour. Tuition, nonresident: full-time $21,510; part-time $1195 per credit hour. *Required fees:* $66 per semester. Tuition and fees vary according to campus/location, program and reciprocity agreements. *Financial support:* In 2016–17, 7 students received support, including fellowships with full tuition reimbursements available (averaging $20,000 per year), 4 teaching assistantships with full tuition reimbursements available (averaging $20,000 per year); research assistantships also available. Financial award application deadline: 4/15. *Faculty research:* Curriculum change, language arts, library science, multicultural education, foundations in education. *Unit head:* Dr. Richard Overbaugh, Graduate Program Director, 757-683-3284, Fax: 757-683-5862, E-mail: roverbau@odu.edu. *Application contact:* William Heffelfinger, Director of Graduate Admissions, 757-683-5554, Fax: 757-683-3255, E-mail: gradadmit@odu.edu.
Website: http://education.odu.edu/eci/ciphd/

Old Dominion University, Darden College of Education, Program in Physical Education, Curriculum and Instruction Emphasis, Norfolk, VA 23529. Offers human movement sciences (PhD), including health and sport pedagogy; physical education (MS Ed), including adapted physical education, coaching education, curriculum and instruction. *Program availability:* Part-time, evening/weekend. *Faculty:* 2 full-time (0 women), 1 (woman) part-time/adjunct. *Students:* 5 full-time (2 women), 2 part-time (1 woman); includes 1 minority (Hispanic/Latino). Average age 29. 8 applicants, 75% accepted, 4 enrolled. In 2016, 4 master's awarded. *Degree requirements:* For master's, comprehensive exam (for some programs), thesis or alternative, internship, research project. *Entrance requirements:* For master's, GRE, PRAXIS Core (for licensure only), minimum GPA of 2.8 overall, 3.0 in major. Additional exam requirements/recommendations for international students: Required—TOEFL (minimum score 500 paper-based; 97 iBT). *Application deadline:* For fall admission, 3/1 priority date for domestic students; for spring admission, 11/1 for domestic students. Applications are processed on a rolling basis. Application fee: $50. Electronic applications accepted. *Expenses:* Tuition, state resident: full-time $8604; part-time $478 per credit hour. Tuition, nonresident: full-time $21,510; part-time $1195 per credit hour. *Required fees:* $66 per semester. Tuition and fees vary according to campus/location, program and reciprocity agreements. *Financial support:* In 2016–17, 2 students received support, including 1 teaching assistantship (averaging $10,000 per year); unspecified assistantships also available. Financial award application deadline: 4/15. *Faculty research:* Motor development, physical activity and fitness, motivation and learning in physical education, curriculum and instruction. *Unit head:* Dr. Lynn Ridinger, Chair, 757-683-4995, E-mail: lridinge@odu.edu. *Application contact:* William Heffelfinger, Director of Graduate Admissions, 757-683-5554, Fax: 757-683-3255, E-mail: gradadmit@odu.edu.
Website: http://education.odu.edu/eci/ciphd/

Olivet Nazarene University, Graduate School, Division of Education, Program in Curriculum and Instruction, Bourbonnais, IL 60914. Offers MAE. *Program availability:* Evening/weekend. *Degree requirements:* For master's, thesis or alternative.

Oral Roberts University, School of Education, Tulsa, OK 74171. Offers Christian school administration (K-12) (MA Ed, Ed D); Christian school curriculum development (MA Ed); college and higher education administration (Ed D); public school administration (K-12) (MA Ed, Ed D); public school teaching (MA Ed). *Accreditation:* NCATE. *Program availability:* Part-time, online learning. *Degree requirements:* For master's, comprehensive exam, thesis optional; for doctorate, comprehensive exam, thesis/dissertation. *Entrance requirements:* For master's, GRE General Test or MAT, minimum GPA of 3.0; for doctorate, minimum GPA of 3.0. Additional exam requirements/recommendations for international students: Required—TOEFL (minimum score 500 paper-based). *Expenses:* Contact institution. *Faculty research:* Teacher effectiveness, college success in high achieving African-Americans, professional development practices.

Ottawa University, Graduate Studies-Arizona, Program in Education, Ottawa, KS 66067-3399. Offers community college counseling (MA); curriculum and instruction (MA); early childhood (MA); education intervention (MA); education leadership (MA); education technology (MA); Montessori early childhood education (MA); Montessori elementary education (MA); professional development (MA); school guidance counseling (MA); special education - cross categorical (MA). Programs offered in Mesa, Phoenix, Tempe and West Valley, AZ. *Accreditation:* NCATE. *Program availability:* Part-time. *Degree requirements:* For master's, thesis or alternative. *Entrance requirements:* For master's, minimum undergraduate GPA of 3.0, copy of current state certification or teaching license. Additional exam requirements/recommendations for international students: Required—TOEFL (minimum score 550 paper-based). Electronic applications accepted. *Expenses:* Contact institution.

Our Lady of the Lake University, School of Professional Studies, Program in Curriculum and Instruction, San Antonio, TX 78207-4689. Offers integrated science teaching (M Ed). *Program availability:* Part-time, evening/weekend. *Faculty:* 4 full-time (all women), 3 part-time/adjunct (2 women). *Students:* 22 part-time (19 women); includes 16 minority (all Hispanic/Latino). Average age 38. 1 applicant. In 2016, 4 master's awarded. *Degree requirements:* For master's, comprehensive exam. *Entrance requirements:* For master's, GRE General Test or MAT, official transcripts demonstrating bachelor's degree with minimum cumulative GPA of 2.75, personal statement, 2 references, completed FERPA Consent to Release Education Records and Information form, interview. Additional exam requirements/recommendations for international students: Required—TOEFL. *Application deadline:* For fall admission, 6/15 for domestic and international students; for spring admission, 11/15 for domestic and international students; for summer admission, 4/15 for domestic and international students. Applications are processed on a rolling basis. Application fee: $40 ($50 for international students). Electronic applications accepted. Application fee is waived when completed online. *Expenses: Tuition:* Full-time $14,796. Tuition and fees vary according to course load, degree level, campus/location and program. *Financial support:* Federal Work-Study, scholarships/grants, unspecified assistantships, and tuition discounts available. Support available to part-time students. Financial award application deadline: 5/1; financial award applicants required to submit FAFSA. *Faculty research:* Multicultural Issues, technology integration, mentoring teachers, teacher retention. *Unit head:* Dr. Alycia Maurer, Chair, Education Department, 210-434-6711 Ext. 7152, E-mail: admaurer@ollusa.edu. *Application contact:* Office of Graduate Admissions, 210-431-3995, Fax: 210-431-3945, E-mail: gradadm@lake.ollusa.edu.
Website: http://www.ollusa.edu/s/1190/hybrid/default-hybrid-ollu.aspx?sid-1190&gid-1&pgid-7883

Pacific Lutheran University, School of Education and Kinesiology, Program in Initial Teaching Certification, Tacoma, WA 98447. Offers MAE. *Accreditation:* NCATE. *Program availability:* Part-time, evening/weekend. *Degree requirements:* For master's, comprehensive exam, thesis optional. *Entrance requirements:* For master's, WEST-B or WEST-B Exemption (or CBEST and/or PRAXIS for out-of-state applicants), interview. Additional exam requirements/recommendations for international students: Required—TOEFL (minimum score 550 paper-based; 88 iBT), ACTFL (American Council on the Teaching of Foreign Languages) oral proficiency exam. Electronic applications accepted. *Expenses:* Contact institution.

Park University, School of Graduate and Professional Studies, Kansas City, MO 54105. Offers adult education (M Ed); business and government leadership (Graduate Certificate); business, government, and global society (MPA); communication and leadership (MA); creative and life writing (Graduate Certificate); disaster and emergency management (MPA, Graduate Certificate); educational leadership (M Ed); finance (MBA, Graduate Certificate); general business (MBA); global business (Graduate Certificate); healthcare administration (MHA); healthcare services management and leadership (Graduate Certificate); international business (MBA); language and literacy (M Ed), including English for speakers of other languages, special reading teacher/ literacy coach; leadership of international healthcare organizations (Graduate Certificate); management information systems (MBA, Graduate Certificate); music performance (ADP, Graduate Certificate), including cello (MM, ADP), piano (MM, ADP), viola (MM, ADP), violin (MM, ADP); nonprofit and community services management (MPA); nonprofit leadership (Graduate Certificate); performance (MM), including cello (MM, ADP), piano (MM, ADP), viola (MM, ADP), violin (MM, ADP); public management (MPA); social work (MSW); teacher leadership (M Ed), including curriculum and assessment, instructional leader. *Program availability:* Part-time, evening/weekend, online learning. *Degree requirements:* For master's, comprehensive exam (for some programs), thesis (for some programs), internship (for some programs); exam (for some programs). *Entrance requirements:* For master's, GRE or GMAT (for some programs), teacher certification (for some M Ed programs), letters of recommendation, essay, resume (for some programs). Additional exam requirements/recommendations for international students: Required—TOEFL (minimum score 550 paper-based; 79 iBT), IELTS (minimum score 6). Electronic applications accepted.

Penn State Harrisburg, Graduate School, School of Behavioral Sciences and Education, Middletown, PA 17057. Offers adult education in the health and medical professions (Certificate); applied behavior analysis (MA); applied clinical psychology (MA); applied psychological research (MA); community psychology and social change (MA); English as a second language (ESL) program specialist and leadership (Certificate); folklore and ethnography (Certificate); health education (M Ed); lifelong learning and adult education (M Ed, D Ed); literacy education (M Ed); literacy leadership (Certificate); psychology: applications in clinical psychology (Certificate); psychology: health psychology (Certificate); teaching and curriculum (M Ed); training and development (M Ed, Certificate). *Program availability:* Part-time, evening/weekend. *Unit head:* Dr. Mukund S. Kulkarni, Chancellor, 717-948-6105, Fax: 717-948-6452. *Application contact:* Robert W. Coffman, Jr., Director of Enrollment Management, Recruitment and Admissions, 717-948-6250, Fax: 717-948-6325, E-mail: hbgadmit@psu.edu.
Website: https://harrisburg.psu.edu/behavioral-sciences-and-education/

Penn State University Park, Graduate School, College of Education, Department of Curriculum and Instruction, University Park, PA 16802. Offers M Ed, MS, PhD, Certificate. *Accreditation:* NCATE. *Unit head:* Dr. David H. Monk, Dean, 814-865-2523, Fax: 814-865-0555. *Application contact:* Lori Hawn, Director, Graduate Student Services, 814-865-1795, Fax: 814-863-4627, E-mail: l-gswww@lists.psu.edu.
Website: http://ed.psu.edu/c-and-i

Penn State York, Graduate School, York, PA 17403. Offers ESL specialist (Certificate); teaching and curriculum (M Ed). *Students:* 6 part-time (all women). Average age 33. 3 applicants, 33% accepted, 1 enrolled. *Unit head:* Dr. Regina Vasilatos-Younken, Vice Provost for Graduate Education/Dean, Graduate School, 814-865-2516, Fax: 814-863-4627. *Application contact:* Lori Hawn, Director, Graduate Student Services, 814-865-1795, Fax: 814-863-4627, E-mail: l-gswww@lists.psu.edu.
Website: http://www.gradschool.psu.edu/

Pensacola Christian College, Graduate Studies, Pensacola, FL 32503-2267. Offers business administration (MBA); curriculum and instruction (MS, Ed D, Ed S); dramatics (MFA); educational leadership (MS, Ed D, Ed S); graphic design (MA, MFA); music (MA); nursing (MSN); performance studies (MA); studio art (MA, MFA).

Peru State College, Graduate Programs, Program in Education, Peru, NE 68421. Offers curriculum and instruction (MS Ed). *Accreditation:* NCATE. *Program availability:* Part-time. *Degree requirements:* For master's, comprehensive exam (for some programs), thesis optional.

Piedmont College, School of Education, Demorest, GA 30535. Offers art education (MAT); curriculum and instruction (Ed S); early childhood education (MA, MAT); instructional technology (MAT); middle grades education (MA, MAT); music education (MAT); secondary education (MA, MAT); special education (MA, MAT). *Program availability:* Part-time, evening/weekend. *Students:* 290 full-time (217 women), 614 part-time (508 women); includes 131 minority (97 Black or African American, non-Hispanic/ Latino; 4 American Indian or Alaska Native, non-Hispanic/Latino; 5 Asian, non-Hispanic/ Latino; 11 Hispanic/Latino; 6 Native Hawaiian or other Pacific Islander, non-Hispanic/ Latino; 8 Two or more races, non-Hispanic/Latino), 6 international. Average age 37. 257 applicants, 64% accepted, 160 enrolled. In 2016, 288 master's, 243 other advanced degrees awarded. *Degree requirements:* For master's, thesis, field experience in the classroom teaching. *Entrance requirements:* For master's, GRE General Test, MAT, minimum undergraduate GPA of 2.5; for Ed S, minimum graduate GPA of 3.5, valid teaching certificate. Additional exam requirements/recommendations for international students: Required—TOEFL (minimum score 550 paper-based). *Application deadline:* For fall admission, 7/15 for domestic students; for spring admission, 12/1 for domestic students. Applications are processed on a rolling basis. Electronic applications accepted. *Expenses: Tuition:* Full-time $8910. *Financial support:* Career-related internships or fieldwork, Federal Work-Study, and unspecified assistantships available. Support available to part-time students. Financial award applicants required to submit FAFSA. *Unit head:* Dr. Don Gnecco, Dean, 706-778-3000 Ext. 1201, Fax: 706-776-9608, E-mail: dgnecco@piedmont.edu. *Application contact:* Kathleen Anderson, Director of Graduate Enrollment Management, 706-778-8500 Ext. 1181, Fax: 706-778-0150, E-mail: kanderson@piedmont.edu.

Piedmont International University, Graduate School, Winston-Salem, NC 27101-5197. Offers Biblical studies (PhD); curriculum and instruction (M Ed); divinity (M Div); educational leadership (M Ed); leadership (MA, PhD); ministry (MA Min, D Min); non-language track (MABS); PhD preparation track (MABS). *Program availability:* Part-time, online learning. Terminal master's awarded for partial completion of doctoral program. *Degree requirements:* For master's, 2 foreign languages, comprehensive exam, thesis or alternative; for doctorate, 2 foreign languages, comprehensive exam. *Entrance requirements:* For master's, GRE General Test; for doctorate, Hebrew and Greek proficiency, MA. Additional exam requirements/recommendations for international students: Required—TOEFL (minimum score 500 paper-based; 60 iBT). Electronic applications accepted. *Faculty research:* Theological and biblical studies.

Plymouth State University, College of Graduate Studies, Graduate Studies in Education, Program in Secondary Education, Plymouth, NH 03264-1595. Offers curriculum and instruction (M Ed); language education (M Ed); library media (M Ed); physical education (M Ed); social studies education (M Ed); special education (M Ed). *Program availability:* Part-time, evening/weekend. *Entrance requirements:* For master's, MAT.

Point Park University, School of Arts and Sciences, Department of Education, Pittsburgh, PA 15222-1984. Offers curriculum and instruction (MA); educational administration (MA); special education (M Ed); teaching and leadership (M Ed). *Program availability:* Part-time, evening/weekend. *Degree requirements:* For master's, comprehensive exam (for some programs), thesis or alternative. *Entrance requirements:* For master's, minimum GPA of 3.0, resume, 2 letters of recommendation. Additional exam requirements/recommendations for international students: Required—TOEFL. Electronic applications accepted.

Pontifical Catholic University of Puerto Rico, College of Education, Doctoral Program in Curriculum and Instruction, Ponce, PR 00717-0777. Offers PhD. *Degree requirements:* For doctorate, thesis/dissertation. *Entrance requirements:* For doctorate, EXADEP, GRE General Test or MAT, 3 letters of recommendation.

Pontifical Catholic University of Puerto Rico, College of Education, Master's Program in Curriculum and Instruction, Ponce, PR 00717-0777. Offers M Ed. *Degree requirements:* For master's, comprehensive exam, thesis (for some programs). *Entrance requirements:* For master's, GRE, 2 letters of recommendation, interview, minimum GPA of 2.75.

Prairie View A&M University, College of Education, Department of Curriculum and Instruction, Prairie View, TX 77446. Offers M Ed, MA Ed, MS Ed. *Accreditation:* NCATE. *Program availability:* Part-time, evening/weekend. *Faculty:* 4 full-time (3 women), 1 (woman) part-time/adjunct. *Students:* 14 full-time (11 women), 22 part-time (19 women); includes 23 minority (22 Black or African American, non-Hispanic/Latino; 1 Two or more races, non-Hispanic/Latino), 3 international. Average age 31. 35 applicants, 94% accepted, 21 enrolled. In 2016, 18 master's awarded. *Degree requirements:* For master's, comprehensive exam, thesis optional. *Entrance requirements:* For master's, GRE, minimum GPA of 2.5, 3 references. Additional exam requirements/ recommendations for international students: Required—TOEFL (minimum score 550 paper-based; 79 iBT). *Application deadline:* For fall admission, 5/1 priority date for domestic and international students; for spring admission, 10/1 priority date for domestic students, 9/1 priority date for international students; for summer admission, 3/1 priority date for domestic students, 2/1 priority date for international students. Applications are processed on a rolling basis. Application fee: $50. Electronic applications accepted. *Expenses:* Tuition, state resident: full-time $4362; part-time $273.48 per credit hour. Tuition, nonresident: full-time $12,390; part-time $534.10 per credit hour. *Required fees:* $2782; $178.26 per credit hour. *Financial support:* Career-related internships or fieldwork, institutionally sponsored loans, scholarships/grants, health care benefits, tuition waivers (full and partial), and unspecified assistantships available. Support available to part-time students. Financial award application deadline: 4/1; financial award applicants required to submit FAFSA. *Faculty research:* Metacognitive strategies, emotionally disturbed, language arts, teachers recruit, diversity, recruitment, retention, school collaboration. *Unit head:* Dr. Douglas Butler, Interim Department Head, 936-261-3410, Fax: 936-261-3419, E-mail: dmbutler@pvamu.edu. *Application contact:* Pauline Walker, Administrative Assistant II, Research and Graduate Studies, 936-261-3521, Fax: 936-261-3529, E-mail: gradadmissions@pvamu.edu.

Purdue University, Graduate School, College of Education, Department of Curriculum and Instruction, West Lafayette, IN 47907. Offers agricultural and extension education (MS, MS Ed, PhD, Ed S); art education (PhD); career and technical education (MS Ed, PhD, Ed S); curriculum studies (MS Ed, PhD, Ed S); educational technology (MS Ed, PhD, Ed S); elementary education (MS Ed); family and consumer sciences education (MS Ed, PhD, Ed S); foreign language education (MS Ed, PhD, Ed S); industrial technology (PhD, Ed S); language arts (MS Ed, PhD, Ed S); literacy (MS Ed, PhD, Ed S); mathematics education (MS, MS Ed, PhD, Ed S); science education (MS, MS Ed, PhD, Ed S); social studies education (MS Ed, PhD, Ed S). *Accreditation:* NCATE. *Program availability:* Part-time, evening/weekend. *Faculty:* 37 full-time (27 women), 1 (woman) part-time/adjunct. *Students:* 78 full-time (50 women), 286 part-time (195 women); includes 68 minority (25 Black or African American, non-Hispanic/Latino; 3 American Indian or Alaska Native, non-Hispanic/Latino; 10 Asian, non-Hispanic/Latino; 22 Hispanic/Latino; 1 Native Hawaiian or other Pacific Islander, non-Hispanic/Latino; 7 Two or more races, non-Hispanic/Latino), 44 international. Average age 36. 150 applicants, 79% accepted, 73 enrolled. In 2016, 107 master's, 20 doctorates, 2 other advanced degrees awarded. *Degree requirements:* For master's, thesis optional; for doctorate, thesis/dissertation, oral and written exams; for Ed S, oral presentation, project. *Entrance requirements:* For master's, GRE General Test (if undergraduate GPA is below 3.0), minimum undergraduate GPA of 3.0 or equivalent; for doctorate, GRE General Test (minimum combined verbal and quantitative score of 1000, 300 for new scoring), minimum undergraduate GPA of 3.0 or equivalent; master's degree with minimum GPA of 3.0 or equivalent; for Ed S, GRE General Test (minimum combined verbal and quantitative score of 1000, 300 for new scoring), minimum undergraduate GPA of 3.0 or equivalent; master's degree. Additional exam requirements/ recommendations for international students: Required—TOEFL (minimum score 550 paper-based; 77 iBT). *Application deadline:* For fall admission, 12/15 for domestic students, 3/1 for international students; for spring admission, 9/15 for domestic students, 8/1 for international students. Application fee: $60 ($75 for international students). Electronic applications accepted. *Financial support:* Fellowships with full tuition reimbursements, research assistantships with full tuition reimbursements, teaching assistantships with full tuition reimbursements, career-related internships or fieldwork, and tuition waivers (full) available. Support available to part-time students. Financial award application deadline: 3/1; financial award applicants required to submit FAFSA. *Faculty research:* Literacy acquisition and development, teacher beliefs and knowledge, recruitment and retention of underrepresented students, economic education, literacy discourse. *Unit head:* Janet M. Alsup, Head, 765-494-9667, E-mail: alsupj@purdue.edu. *Application contact:* Heather Brinkman, Graduate Contact, 765-494-2345, E-mail: hbrinkma@purdue.edu.
Website: http://www.edci.purdue.edu/

Quincy University, Master of Science in Education Programs, Quincy, IL 62301-2699. Offers curriculum and instruction (MS Ed), including bilingual/English as a second language; leadership (MS Ed); reading education (MS Ed); special education (MS Ed); teacher leader (MS Ed). *Program availability:* Part-time, evening/weekend, online learning. *Degree requirements:* For master's, comprehensive exam (for some programs), thesis optional. *Entrance requirements:* For master's, MAT or GRE. Additional exam requirements/recommendations for international students: Required—TOEFL (minimum score 550 paper-based; 79 iBT). Electronic applications accepted. Application fee is waived when completed online.

Randolph College, Programs in Education, Lynchburg, VA 24503. Offers curriculum and instruction (MAT); special education-learning disabilities (M Ed, MAT). *Accreditation:* TEAC. *Entrance requirements:* For master's, minimum GPA of 3.0 in prerequisite education coursework, 2.7 in major or field of interest (MAT); teaching license (M Ed); 2 recommendations; interview.

Regent University, Graduate School, School of Education, Virginia Beach, VA 23464-9800. Offers adult education (Ed D, PhD, Ed S); advanced educational leadership (Ed D, PhD, Ed S); career switcher (M Ed); character education (Ed D, PhD, Ed S); Christian education leadership (Ed D, PhD, Ed S); Christian school administration (M Ed); curriculum and instruction (M Ed), including adult education, Christian school, gifted and talented education, STEM education, teacher leader; educational leadership (M Ed); educational psychology (Ed D, PhD, Ed S); educational technology and online learning (Ed D, PhD, Ed S); elementary education (M Ed); exceptional education executive leadership (Ed D, PhD, Ed S); higher education (Ed D, PhD, Ed S); higher education leadership and management (Ed D, PhD, Ed S); individualized degree plan (M Ed); K-12 school leadership (Ed D, PhD, Ed S); K-12 special education (M Ed); K-8 leadership in mathematics education (M Ed); leadership in mathematics education (Ed S); reading specialist (M Ed); special education (Ed D, PhD, Ed S); student affairs

(M Ed); TESOL (M Ed), including adult education - collegiate, K-12. *Accreditation:* TEAC. *Program availability:* Part-time, evening/weekend, 100% online, blended/hybrid learning. *Faculty:* 22 full-time (10 women), 42 part-time/adjunct (31 women). *Students:* 89 full-time (62 women), 1,035 part-time (823 women); includes 466 minority (381 Black or African American, non-Hispanic/Latino; 3 American Indian or Alaska Native, non-Hispanic/Latino; 19 Asian, non-Hispanic/Latino; 50 Hispanic/Latino; 13 Two or more races, non-Hispanic/Latino), 11 international. Average age 39. 976 applicants, 59% accepted, 449 enrolled. In 2016, 241 master's, 22 doctorates, 4 other advanced degrees awarded. *Degree requirements:* For master's, thesis or alternative; for doctorate, comprehensive exam, thesis/dissertation. *Entrance requirements:* For master's, Virginia Communication and Literacy Assessment (VCLA), PRAXIS, college transcripts, writing sample, interview; for doctorate, GRE, writing sample, resume, transcripts, interview. Additional exam requirements/recommendations for international students: Required—TOEFL (minimum score 577 paper-based). *Application deadline:* For fall admission, 4/1 priority date for domestic students; for spring admission, 10/15 priority date for domestic students. Applications are processed on a rolling basis. Application fee: $50. Electronic applications accepted. *Expenses:* Contact institution. *Financial support:* In 2016–17, 622 students received support, including 1 fellowship (averaging $5,000 per year); career-related internships or fieldwork, scholarships/grants, and unspecified assistantships also available. Support available to part-time students. *Faculty research:* Christian school administration, curriculum and instruction, educational technology and online learning, higher education, special education. *Unit head:* Dr. Donald Finn, Dean, 757-352-4278, Fax: 757-352-4318, E-mail: dfinn@regent.edu. *Application contact:* Heidi Cece, Assistant Vice President of Enrollment Management, 800-373-5504, Fax: 757-352-4381, E-mail: admissions@regent.edu.
Website: http://www.regent.edu/soe/

Regis University, College of Contemporary Liberal Studies, Denver, CO 80221-1099. Offers creative writing (MFA); criminology (M Sc); curriculum, instruction and assessment (M Ed); education - teacher leadership (M Ed); educational leadership (M Ed); elementary education (M Ed); literacy (Certificate); reading (M Ed); secondary education (M Ed); special education (M Ed); teacher academic leadership (Certificate); teacher leadership (MA); teacher/educational leadership (M Ed); teaching the linguistically diverse (M Ed). *Program availability:* Part-time, evening/weekend, 100% online, blended/hybrid learning. *Faculty:* 18 full-time (12 women), 42 part-time/adjunct (26 women). *Students:* 302 full-time (234 women), 270 part-time (218 women); includes 148 minority (33 Black or African American, non-Hispanic/Latino; 3 American Indian or Alaska Native, non-Hispanic/Latino; 13 Asian, non-Hispanic/Latino; 83 Hispanic/Latino; 16 Two or more races, non-Hispanic/Latino), 3 international. Average age 36. 431 applicants, 90% accepted, 110 enrolled. In 2016, 308 master's awarded. *Degree requirements:* For master's, thesis (for some programs). *Entrance requirements:* For master's, official transcript reflecting baccalaureate degree awarded from regionally-accredited college or university, work experience, resume, letters of recommendation. Additional exam requirements/recommendations for international students: Required—TOEFL (minimum score 550 paper-based; 82 iBT). *Application deadline:* For fall admission, 8/15 priority date for domestic students, 7/13 for international students; for winter admission, 10/10 priority date for domestic students, 9/8 for international students; for spring admission, 1/10 priority date for domestic students, 11/17 for international students; for summer admission, 5/1 priority date for domestic students. Applications are processed on a rolling basis. Application fee: $75. Electronic applications accepted. *Expenses:* $485 per credit hour. *Financial support:* Scholarships/grants available. Financial award application deadline: 4/15; financial award applicants required to submit FAFSA. *Unit head:* Dr. Elisa Robyn, Academic Dean. *Application contact:* Cate Clark, Director of Admissions, 303-458-4900, Fax: 303-964-5534, E-mail: ruadmissions@regis.edu.
Website: http://www.regis.edu/CCLS.aspx

Rider University, Department of Graduate Education, Leadership and Counseling, Program in Curriculum, Instruction and Supervision, Lawrenceville, NJ 08648-3001. Offers curriculum, instruction and supervision (MA); supervisor (Certificate). *Accreditation:* NCATE. *Program availability:* Part-time, evening/weekend. *Degree requirements:* For master's, comprehensive exam, practicum project. *Entrance requirements:* For master's, interview, 2 letters of recommendation from current supervisors, resume. Additional exam requirements/recommendations for international students: Required—TOEFL (minimum score 550 paper-based). Electronic applications accepted. *Faculty research:* Curriculum change, curriculum development, teacher evaluation.

Rivier University, School of Graduate Studies, Department of Education, Nashua, NH 03060. Offers curriculum and instruction (M Ed); early childhood education (M Ed); educational administration (M Ed); educational studies (M Ed); elementary education (M Ed); elementary education and general special education (M Ed); emotional and behavioral disorders (M Ed); general social education (M Ed); leadership and learning (Ed D, CAGS); learning disabilities (M Ed); learning disabilities and reading (M Ed); mental health counseling (MA); reading (M Ed); school counseling (M Ed). *Program availability:* Part-time, evening/weekend. *Degree requirements:* For master's, comprehensive exam (for some programs), internships. *Entrance requirements:* For master's, GRE General Test or MAT.

St. Catherine University, Graduate Programs, Program in Education–Curriculum and Instruction, St. Paul, MN 55105. Offers MA. *Program availability:* Part-time, evening/weekend, online learning. *Degree requirements:* For master's, thesis. *Entrance requirements:* For master's, current teaching license, classroom experience, minimum GPA of 3.0. Additional exam requirements/recommendations for international students: Required—Michigan English Language Assessment Battery or TOEFL (minimum score 600 paper-based; 100 iBT). *Expenses:* Contact institution.

St. Cloud State University, School of Graduate Studies, School of Education, Department of Teacher Development, St. Cloud, MN 56301-4498. Offers curriculum and instruction (MS). *Degree requirements:* For master's, thesis or alternative. *Entrance requirements:* For master's, GRE General Test, minimum GPA of 2.75. Additional exam requirements/recommendations for international students: Required—Michigan English Language Assessment Battery; Recommended—TOEFL (minimum score 550 paper-based), IELTS (minimum score 6.5). Electronic applications accepted.

St. Francis Xavier University, Graduate Studies, Graduate Studies in Education, Antigonish, NS B2G 2W5, Canada. Offers curriculum and instruction (M Ed); educational administration and leadership (M Ed). *Program availability:* Part-time, online learning. *Degree requirements:* For master's, thesis. *Entrance requirements:* For master's, minimum undergraduate B average, 2 years of teaching experience. *Application deadline:* For fall admission, 2/15 for domestic and international students. Application fee: $40. *Expenses: Tuition:* Full-time $9060 Canadian dollars; part-time $725 Canadian dollars per credit. *Required fees:* $789 Canadian dollars; $78.84 Canadian dollars per credit. Tuition and fees vary according to course load, degree level and program. *Financial support:* Teaching assistantships available. *Faculty research:* Inclusive education, qualitative research. *Unit head:* Dr. Robert E. White, Chair, 902-867-3420, Fax: 902-867-3887, E-mail: rwhite@stfx.ca. *Application contact:* Colleen Jones, Assistant, 902-867-3906, Fax: 902-867-5154, E-mail: med@stfx.ca.

Saint Joseph's University, College of Arts and Sciences, Graduate Programs in Education, Philadelphia, PA 19131-1395. Offers curriculum supervisor (Certificate); educational leadership (MS, Ed D); elementary education (MS, Certificate); elementary/middle school education (Certificate); instructional technology (MS, Certificate); organizational development and leadership (MS); principal (Certificate); professional education (MS); reading specialist (MS, Certificate); reading supervisor (Certificate); secondary education (MS, Certificate); special education (MS); special education 7-12 (Certificate); special education PK-8 (Certificate); superintendent's letter of eligibility (Certificate); supervisor of special education (Certificate); teacher of the deaf and hard of hearing (Certificate). *Program availability:* Part-time, evening/weekend, blended/hybrid learning. *Faculty:* 26 full-time (21 women), 74 part-time/adjunct (45 women). *Students:* 107 full-time (88 women), 826 part-time (622 women); includes 170 minority (115 Black or African American, non-Hispanic/Latino; 2 American Indian or Alaska Native, non-Hispanic/Latino; 11 Asian, non-Hispanic/Latino; 31 Hispanic/Latino; 1 Native Hawaiian or other Pacific Islander, non-Hispanic/Latino; 10 Two or more races, non-Hispanic/Latino), 18 international. Average age 33. 338 applicants, 76% accepted, 173 enrolled. In 2016, 419 master's, 16 doctorates, 24 other advanced degrees awarded. *Degree requirements:* For master's, thesis or alternative; for doctorate, comprehensive exam, thesis/dissertation. *Entrance requirements:* For master's, 2 letters of recommendation, minimum GPA of 3.0, official transcripts, personal statement; for doctorate, GRE, master's degree from accredited institution, minimum graduate GPA of 3.5, computer competence, interview with program director. Additional exam requirements/recommendations for international students: Required—TOEFL (minimum score 550 paper-based; 80 iBT), IELTS (minimum score 6.5), PTE (minimum score 60). *Application deadline:* For fall admission, 7/15 for international students; for spring admission, 11/1 for international students. Applications are processed on a rolling basis. Application fee: $35. Electronic applications accepted. *Expenses:* $750 per credit, $100 education fee, $360 online organization development and leadership residency fee. *Financial support:* In 2016–17, 25 students received support. Unspecified assistantships available. Financial award application deadline: 5/1; financial award applicants required to submit FAFSA. *Faculty research:* Factors predicting early mathematics skills for low income children, early child care and development, preschool quality, parent communication and home-school collaboration issues, education of terminally ill children, preparing literacy teachers for urban schools. *Total annual research expenditures:* $18,118. *Unit head:* Dr. John Vacca, Associate Dean, Education, 610-660-3131, E-mail: gradcas@sju.edu. *Application contact:* Graduate Admissions, College of Arts and Sciences, 610-660-3131, E-mail: gradcas@sju.edu.
Website: http://sju.edu/int/academics/cas/grad/education/index.html

Saint Louis University, Graduate Education, College of Education and Public Service, Department of Educational Studies, St. Louis, MO 63103. Offers curriculum and instruction (MA, Ed D, PhD); educational foundations (MA, Ed D, PhD); special education (MA); teaching (MAT). *Accreditation:* NCATE. *Program availability:* Part-time. *Degree requirements:* For master's, comprehensive exam; for doctorate, comprehensive exam, thesis/dissertation, preliminary oral and written exams. *Entrance requirements:* For master's, GRE General Test or MAT, letters of recommendation, resume; for doctorate, GRE General Test, letters of recommendation, resumé, goal statement, transcripts. Additional exam requirements/recommendations for international students: Required—TOEFL (minimum score 525 paper-based). Electronic applications accepted. *Faculty research:* Teacher preparation, multicultural issues, children with special needs, qualitative research in education, inclusion.

Saint Vincent College, Program in Education, Latrobe, PA 15650-2690. Offers curriculum and instruction (MS); instructional design and technology (MS); school administration and supervision (MS); special education (MS). *Program availability:* Part-time, evening/weekend. *Degree requirements:* For master's, comprehensive exam. *Entrance requirements:* For master's, GRE (if undergraduate GPA less than 3.0). Additional exam requirements/recommendations for international students: Required—TOEFL (minimum score 550 paper-based). *Faculty research:* Assessment and instructional technology.

Saint Xavier University, Graduate Studies, School of Education, Chicago, IL 60655-3105. Offers counseling (MA); curriculum and instruction (MA); early childhood education (MA); educational administration (MA); elementary education (MA); individualized studies (MA), including educational technology, English as a second language (ESL), ISTEM (integrative science, technology, engineering, and math), science education; music education (MA); reading (MA); secondary education (MA); Spanish education (MA); special education (MA); teaching and leadership (MA). *Accreditation:* NCATE. *Program availability:* Part-time, evening/weekend. *Degree requirements:* For master's, thesis or project. *Entrance requirements:* For master's, minimum GPA of 3.0. *Expenses:* Contact institution.

Salem International University, School of Education, Salem, WV 26426-0500. Offers curriculum and instruction (M Ed); educational leadership (M Ed). *Program availability:* Part-time, evening/weekend, online learning. *Degree requirements:* For master's, comprehensive exam (for some programs), thesis (for some programs). *Entrance requirements:* For master's, GRE, MAT, NTE, 3 letters of recommendation. Additional exam requirements/recommendations for international students: Required—TOEFL (minimum score 550 paper-based). Electronic applications accepted. *Expenses:* Contact institution. *Faculty research:* Improved classroom effectiveness.

Salisbury University, Program in Curriculum and Instruction, Salisbury, MD 21801-6837. Offers M Ed. *Program availability:* Part-time, evening/weekend. *Faculty:* 11 full-time (6 women), 3 part-time/adjunct (2 women). *Students:* 10 full-time (6 women), 87 part-time (73 women); includes 11 minority (9 Black or African American, non-Hispanic/Latino; 2 Two or more races, non-Hispanic/Latino). Average age 30. 29 applicants, 41% accepted, 10 enrolled. In 2016, 28 master's awarded. *Entrance requirements:* Additional exam requirements/recommendations for international students: Required—TOEFL (minimum score 550 paper-based, 79 iBT) or IELTS (6.5). *Application deadline:* For fall admission, 3/1 priority date for domestic and international students; for spring admission, 10/1 priority date for domestic and international students; for summer admission, 3/1 priority date for domestic and international students. Applications are processed on a rolling basis. Application fee: $65. Electronic applications accepted. *Expenses:* $381 per credit hour resident tuition, $670 per credit hour non-resident tuition; $84 per credit hour fees. *Financial support:* In 2016–17, 1 student received support, including 5 teaching assistantships with full tuition reimbursements available (averaging $8,250 per year); career-related internships or fieldwork and scholarships/grants also available. Support available to part-time students. Financial award application deadline: 3/1; financial award applicants required to submit FAFSA. *Faculty research:* Technology; literacy; social justice; STEM; mathematics. *Unit head:* Dr. Diana Wagner, Graduate Program Director, Curriculum and Instruction, 410-677-5490, E-mail: dmwagner@salisbury.edu.
Website: http://www.salisbury.edu/gsr/gradstudies/MEDpage

Sam Houston State University, College of Education, Department of Curriculum and Instruction, Huntsville, TX 77341. Offers curriculum and instruction (M Ed). *Accreditation:* NCATE. *Program availability:* Part-time, evening/weekend. *Degree requirements:* For master's, comprehensive exam, thesis optional; for doctorate, comprehensive exam, thesis/dissertation. *Entrance requirements:* For master's, GRE

General Test; for doctorate, GRE General Test, three letters of recommendation, sample of professional work, three years of working experience. Additional exam requirements/recommendations for international students: Required—TOEFL (minimum score 550 paper-based; 79 iBT), IELTS (minimum score 6.5). Electronic applications accepted.

San Diego State University, Graduate and Research Affairs, College of Education, School of Teacher Education, Program in Elementary Curriculum and Instruction, San Diego, CA 92182. Offers MA. *Accreditation:* NCATE. *Program availability:* Evening/weekend. *Entrance requirements:* For master's, GRE General Test, letters of reference. Additional exam requirements/recommendations for international students: Required—TOEFL. Electronic applications accepted.

San Diego State University, Graduate and Research Affairs, College of Education, School of Teacher Education, Program in Secondary Curriculum and Instruction, San Diego, CA 92182. Offers MA. *Accreditation:* NCATE. *Entrance requirements:* For master's, GRE General Test, letters of reference. Additional exam requirements/recommendations for international students: Required—TOEFL. Electronic applications accepted.

San Jose State University, Graduate Studies and Research, Connie L. Lurie College of Education, San Jose, CA 95192-0001. Offers child and adolescent development (MA); common core mathematics (K-8) (Certificate, Credential); education (MA, Credential), including counseling and student personnel (MA), speech pathology (MA); educational leadership (MA, Ed D, Credential), including administration and supervision (MA), higher education (MA), preliminary administrative services (Credential), professional administrative services (Credential); elementary education (MA), including curriculum and instruction; K-12 school counseling (Credential); K-12 school counseling internship (Credential); school child welfare attendance (Credential); single subject (Credential). *Accreditation:* NCATE. *Program availability:* Evening/weekend. Electronic applications accepted.

Shawnee State University, Program in Curriculum and Instruction, Portsmouth, OH 45662. Offers M Ed. *Accreditation:* NCATE.

Shaw University, Department of Education, Raleigh, NC 27601-2399. Offers curriculum and instruction (MS), including early childhood education. *Program availability:* Part-time, evening/weekend. *Degree requirements:* For master's, comprehensive exam, thesis, practicum/internship, PRAXIS II. *Entrance requirements:* For master's, GRE General Test, letters of recommendation. Additional exam requirements/recommendations for international students: Required—TOEFL (minimum score 500 paper-based). Electronic applications accepted. *Faculty research:* Multicultural education, instructional technology.

Shepherd University, Program in Curriculum and Instruction, Shepherdstown, WV 25443. Offers MA. *Accreditation:* NCATE.

Shippensburg University of Pennsylvania, School of Graduate Studies, College of Education and Human Services, Department of Teacher Education, Shippensburg, PA 17257-2299. Offers curriculum and instruction (M Ed), including biology, early childhood education, elementary and middle level education, elementary education, geography/earth science, history, mathematics, middle school education, modern languages; literacy studies (Certificate); online instruction, learning, and technology (Certificate); reading (M Ed); teaching English as a second language (Certificate). *Accreditation:* NCATE. *Program availability:* Part-time, evening/weekend, 100% online, blended/hybrid learning. *Faculty:* 14 full-time (9 women), 5 part-time/adjunct (all women). *Students:* 11 full-time (10 women), 88 part-time (81 women); includes 8 minority (3 Black or African American, non-Hispanic/Latino; 2 Asian, non-Hispanic/Latino; 3 Hispanic/Latino), 4 international. Average age 32. 57 applicants, 60% accepted, 28 enrolled. In 2016, 18 master's awarded. *Degree requirements:* For master's, comprehensive exam (for some programs), thesis optional, practicum or internship; capstone seminar (for some programs). *Entrance requirements:* For master's, MAT or GRE (if GPA less than 2.75), interview, 3 letters of reference, questionnaire of teaching background and future goals, resume. Additional exam requirements/recommendations for international students: Required—TOEFL (minimum score 550 paper-based, 68 iBT) or IELTS (minimum score 6). *Application deadline:* For fall admission, 4/1 priority date for domestic students, 4/30 for international students; for spring admission, 9/1 priority date for domestic students, 9/30 for international students; for summer admission, 2/1 priority date for domestic students. Applications are processed on a rolling basis. Application fee: $45. Electronic applications accepted. *Expenses:* Tuition, state resident: part-time $483 per credit. Tuition, nonresident: part-time $725 per credit. *Required fees:* $141 per credit. *Financial support:* In 2016–17, 3 students received support. Career-related internships or fieldwork, scholarships/grants, unspecified assistantships, and resident hall director and student payroll positions available. Support available to part-time students. Financial award application deadline: 3/1; financial award applicants required to submit FAFSA. *Unit head:* Dr. Christine A. Royce, Chairperson, 717-477-1688, Fax: 717-477-4046, E-mail: caroyc@ship.edu. *Application contact:* Megan N. Luft, Assistant Dean of Graduate Admissions, 717-477-1231, Fax: 717-477-4016, E-mail: mnluft@ship.edu.
Website: http://www.ship.edu/teacher/

Simon Fraser University, Office of Graduate Studies and Postdoctoral Fellows, Faculty of Education, Programs in Curriculum and Instruction, Burnaby, BC V5A 1S6, Canada. Offers curriculum and instruction (M Ed); curriculum and instruction foundations (M Ed, MA); curriculum theory and implementation (PhD); educational practice (M Ed); philosophy of education (PhD). *Faculty:* 15 full-time (3 women). *Degree requirements:* For master's, comprehensive exam (for some programs), thesis (for some programs); for doctorate, comprehensive exam, thesis/dissertation. *Entrance requirements:* For master's, minimum GPA of 3.0 (on scale of 4.33) or 3.33 based on last 60 credits of undergraduate courses; for doctorate, minimum GPA of 3.5 (on scale of 4.33). Additional exam requirements/recommendations for international students: Recommended—TOEFL (minimum score 580 paper-based; 93 iBT), IELTS (minimum score 7), TWE (minimum score 5). Application fee: $90 ($125 for international students). Electronic applications accepted. *Financial support:* Scholarships/grants available. *Faculty research:* Philosophy of education, applied and comparative epistemology, ethics and moral education, critical multicultural practices. *Unit head:* Dr. Shawn Bullock, Graduate Chair, 778-782-4102, E-mail: educadgs@sfu.ca. *Application contact:* Graduate Secretary, 778-782-4787, E-mail: educmast@sfu.ca.

Simpson University, School of Education, Redding, CA 96003-8606. Offers education (MA), including curriculum, education leadership; education and preliminary administrative services credential (MA); education and preliminary teaching credential (MA); teaching (MA). *Program availability:* Part-time, evening/weekend. *Faculty:* 4 full-time (1 woman), 9 part-time/adjunct (3 women). *Students:* 8 full-time (7 women), 10 part-time (7 women); includes 1 minority (Two or more races, non-Hispanic/Latino), 1 international. Average age 37. In 2016, 16 master's awarded. *Degree requirements:* For master's, thesis optional. *Entrance requirements:* For master's, statement of purpose, 2 professional references, professional essay, interview. Additional exam requirements/recommendations for international students: Required—TOEFL (minimum score 550 paper-based). *Application deadline:* Applications are processed on a rolling basis. Application fee: $35. Electronic applications accepted. *Expenses:* $420 per credit. *Financial support:* Scholarships/grants available. Financial award application deadline: 7/15; financial award applicants required to submit FAFSA. *Unit head:* Dr. Craig Cook, Dean of Education, 530-226-4188, Fax: 530-226-4872, E-mail: ccook@simpsonu.edu. *Application contact:* Stacy Burgess, Director of Admissions for Adult and Graduate Studies, 530-226-4961, E-mail: sburgess@simpsonu.edu.

Sonoma State University, School of Education, Rohnert Park, CA 94928-3609. Offers administrative services (Credential); curriculum, teaching, and learning (MA); early childhood education (MA); education specialist (Credential); educational leadership (MA); multiple subject (Credential); reading and literacy (MA, Credential); single subject (Credential); special education (MA). *Accreditation:* NCATE. *Program availability:* Part-time, evening/weekend. *Degree requirements:* For master's, thesis or alternative. *Entrance requirements:* For master's, minimum GPA of 2.5. Additional exam requirements/recommendations for international students: Required—TOEFL (minimum score 500 paper-based). Application fee: $55. *Expenses:* Tuition, state resident: full-time $6738; part-time $3906 per unit. *Required fees:* $1916; $1916 per year. Tuition and fees vary according to course load, degree level and program. *Financial support:* Fellowships, research assistantships, career-related internships or fieldwork, and Federal Work-Study available. Support available to part-time students. Financial award application deadline: 3/2; financial award applicants required to submit FAFSA. *Unit head:* Dr. Carlos Ayala, Dean, 707-664-4412, E-mail: carlos.ayala@sonoma.edu. *Application contact:* Dr. Jennifer Mahdavi, Coordinator of Graduate Studies, 707-664-3311, E-mail: jennifer.mahdavi@sonoma.edu.
Website: http://www.sonoma.edu/education/

South Dakota State University, Graduate School, College of Education and Human Sciences, Department of Teaching, Learning and Leadership, Brookings, SD 57007. Offers agricultural education (MS); curriculum and instruction (M Ed); educational administration (M Ed). *Program availability:* Part-time, evening/weekend, online learning. *Degree requirements:* For master's, portfolio, oral exam. *Entrance requirements:* For master's, minimum GPA of 2.75. Additional exam requirements/recommendations for international students: Required—TOEFL (minimum score 550 paper-based; 80 iBT). *Faculty research:* Inclusion school climate, K-12 reform and restructuring, rural development, ESL, leadership.

Southeastern Louisiana University, College of Education, Department of Teaching and Learning, Hammond, LA 70402. Offers curriculum and instruction (M Ed); elementary education (MAT); special education (M Ed); special education: early interventionist (MAT). *Accreditation:* NCATE. *Program availability:* Part-time, evening/weekend. *Faculty:* 14 full-time (all women), 2 part-time/adjunct (1 woman). *Students:* 8 full-time (all women), 48 part-time (46 women); includes 7 minority (6 Black or African American, non-Hispanic/Latino; 1 Hispanic/Latino). Average age 32. 79 applicants, 49% accepted, 21 enrolled. In 2016, 34 master's awarded. *Degree requirements:* For master's, comprehensive exam (for some programs), thesis (for some programs), action research project, oral defense of research project, portfolio, teaching certificate, minimum cumulative GPA of 3.0. *Entrance requirements:* For master's, GRE (verbal and quantitative), PRAXIS (for MAT). Additional exam requirements/recommendations for international students: Required—TOEFL (minimum score 500 paper-based; 61 iBT). *Application deadline:* For fall admission, 7/15 priority date for domestic students, 6/1 priority date for international students; for spring admission, 12/1 priority date for domestic students, 10/1 priority date for international students. Applications are processed on a rolling basis. Application fee: $20 ($30 for international students). Electronic applications accepted. *Expenses:* Tuition, state resident: full-time $6540; part-time $465 per credit hour. Tuition, nonresident: full-time $19,017; part-time $1158 per credit hour. *Required fees:* $1829. *Financial support:* In 2016–17, 13 students received support. Research assistantships, career-related internships or fieldwork, Federal Work-Study, institutionally sponsored loans, scholarships/grants, and unspecified assistantships available. Support available to part-time students. Financial award application deadline: 5/1; financial award applicants required to submit FAFSA. *Faculty research:* Teacher in services, STEM, educational technology, pre-service teacher education. *Unit head:* Dr. Colleen Klein-Ezell, Department Head, 985-549-2221, Fax: 985-549-5009, E-mail: colleen.klein-ezell@southeastern.edu. *Application contact:* Amanda Harper, Graduate Admissions Analyst, 985-549-5620, Fax: 985-549-5632, E-mail: admissions@southeastern.edu.
Website: http://www.southeastern.edu/acad_research/depts/teach_lrn/index.html

Southeastern University, College of Education, Lakeland, FL 33801-6099. Offers curriculum and instruction (Ed D); educational leadership (M Ed); elementary education (M Ed); exceptional student education (M Ed); exceptional student education/educational therapy (M Ed); organizational leadership (Ed D); reading education (M Ed); teaching English to speakers of other languages (M Ed). *Expenses: Tuition:* Full-time $9450; part-time $6300 per credit. *Required fees:* $500; $250 per semester. One-time fee: $150. Tuition and fees vary according to degree level, campus/location and program. *Unit head:* Amy N. Bratten, Dean, 863-667-5238, E-mail: anbratten@seu.edu.
Website: http://www.seu.edu/education/

Southern Arkansas University–Magnolia, School of Graduate Studies, Magnolia, AR 71753. Offers agriculture (MS); business administration (MBA), including agri-business, social entrepreneurship, supply chain management; clinical and mental health counseling (MS); computer and information sciences (MS), including cyber security and privacy, data science, information technology; gifted and talented (M Ed), including curriculum and instruction, educational administration and supervision, gifted and talented P-8/7-12, instructional specialist P-4; higher, adult and lifelong education (M Ed); kinesiology (M Ed), including coaching; library media and information specialist (M Ed); public administration (MPA); school counseling K-12 (M Ed); student affairs and college counseling (M Ed); teaching (MAT). *Accreditation:* NCATE. *Program availability:* Part-time, 100% online, blended/hybrid learning. *Faculty:* 36 full-time (19 women), 33 part-time/adjunct (14 women). *Students:* 605 full-time (143 women), 879 part-time (352 women); includes 130 minority (113 Black or African American, non-Hispanic/Latino; 7 American Indian or Alaska Native, non-Hispanic/Latino; 2 Asian, non-Hispanic/Latino; 2 Hispanic/Latino; 6 Two or more races, non-Hispanic/Latino), 1,048 international. Average age 28. 904 applicants, 81% accepted, 262 enrolled. In 2016, 278 master's awarded. *Degree requirements:* For master's, comprehensive exam (for some programs), thesis optional. *Entrance requirements:* For master's, GRE, MAT or GMAT, minimum GPA of 2.5. Additional exam requirements/recommendations for international students: Required—TOEFL (minimum score 550 paper-based), IELTS (minimum score 6). *Application deadline:* For fall admission, 7/20 for domestic students, 7/10 for international students; for spring admission, 12/1 for domestic students, 11/15 for international students; for summer admission, 4/1 for domestic students, 5/1 for international students. Applications are processed on a rolling basis. Application fee: $25 ($50 for international students). Electronic applications accepted. *Expenses:* Tuition, state resident: full-time $2511; part-time $279 per credit hour. Tuition, nonresident: full-time $3726; part-time $414 per credit hour. *Required fees:* $307 per semester. Tuition and fees vary according to course load and program. *Financial support:* Career-related internships or fieldwork, Federal Work-Study, scholarships/grants, tuition waivers (full), and unspecified assistantships available. Financial award applicants required to submit FAFSA. *Faculty research:* Alternative certification for teachers, supervision of instruction, instructional leadership, counseling. *Unit head:* Dr. Kim Bloss, Dean, School of Graduate Studies, 870-235-4150, Fax: 870-235-5227,

E-mail: kkbloss@saumag.edu. *Application contact:* Shrijana Malakar, Admissions Specialist, 870-235-4150, Fax: 870-235-5227, E-mail: smalakar@saumag.edu.
Website: http://www.saumag.edu/graduate

Southern Illinois University Carbondale, Graduate School, College of Education and Human Services, Department of Curriculum and Instruction, Carbondale, IL 62901-4701. Offers MS Ed, PhD. *Accreditation:* NCATE. *Program availability:* Part-time. *Degree requirements:* For doctorate, variable foreign language requirement, thesis/dissertation. *Entrance requirements:* For master's, minimum GPA of 2.7; for doctorate, GRE, minimum GPA of 3.25. Additional exam requirements/recommendations for international students: Required—TOEFL. *Faculty research:* Early childhood, science/environmental education, teacher education, instructional development/technology, reading.

Southern Illinois University Edwardsville, Graduate School, School of Education, Health, and Human Behavior, Department of Curriculum and Instruction, Program in Curriculum and Instruction, Edwardsville, IL 62026. Offers MS Ed. *Accreditation:* NCATE. *Program availability:* Part-time, evening/weekend. *Degree requirements:* For master's, thesis (for some programs), final exam/paper. *Entrance requirements:* For master's, teaching certificate. Additional exam requirements/recommendations for international students: Required—TOEFL (minimum score 550 paper-based; 79 iBT), IELTS (minimum score 6.5). Electronic applications accepted.

Southern New Hampshire University, School of Education, Manchester, NH 03106-1045. Offers business education (M Ed); child development (M Ed); curriculum and instruction (M Ed), including education leadership, reading, special education, technology integration; education (M Ed); educational leadership (M Ed, Ed D); educational studies (M Ed); elementary education (M Ed); English (MAT); English for speakers of other languages (M Ed); reading and writing specialist (M Ed); school business administration (Certificate); secondary education (M Ed); special education (M Ed); technology integration specialist (M Ed). *Program availability:* Part-time, evening/weekend, online learning. *Degree requirements:* For master's, comprehensive exam (for some programs), thesis or alternative. *Entrance requirements:* For master's, PRAXIS I, minimum GPA of 2.75. Additional exam requirements/recommendations for international students: Required—TOEFL (minimum score 550 paper-based). Electronic applications accepted. *Expenses:* Contact institution.

Southwestern Adventist University, Education Department, Keene, TX 76059. Offers curriculum and instruction with reading emphasis (M Ed); educational leadership (M Ed). *Program availability:* Part-time, evening/weekend. *Degree requirements:* For master's, thesis or alternative, professional paper. *Entrance requirements:* For master's, GRE General Test.

Southwestern Assemblies of God University, Thomas F. Harrison School of Graduate Studies, Program in Education, Waxahachie, TX 75165-5735. Offers Christian school administration (MS); curriculum development (MS); early education administration (M Ed); middle and secondary education (M Ed). *Degree requirements:* For master's, comprehensive written and oral exams. *Entrance requirements:* For master's, GRE General Test, minimum GPA of 2.5. Electronic applications accepted.

Southwestern College, Education Programs, Winfield, KS 67156-2499. Offers curriculum and instruction (M Ed); early childhood education (M Ed); educational leadership (Ed D); special education (M Ed), including adaptive, functional; teaching (MA). *Accreditation:* NCATE. *Program availability:* Part-time, evening/weekend, 100% online, blended/hybrid learning. *Faculty:* 7 full-time (5 women), 15 part-time/adjunct (12 women). *Students:* 27 full-time (18 women), 102 part-time (77 women); includes 17 minority (8 Black or African American, non-Hispanic/Latino; 1 American Indian or Alaska Native, non-Hispanic/Latino; 1 Asian, non-Hispanic/Latino; 6 Hispanic/Latino; 1 Native Hawaiian or other Pacific Islander, non-Hispanic/Latino), 32 international. Average age 38. 36 applicants, 64% accepted, 16 enrolled. In 2016, 71 master's, 10 doctorates awarded. *Degree requirements:* For master's, practicum, portfolio; for doctorate, thesis/dissertation, professional portfolio. *Entrance requirements:* For master's, baccalaureate degree, minimum GPA of 3.0, valid teaching certificate (for special education); for doctorate, GRE if no master's degree, baccalaureate degree with minimum GPA of 3.25 and current teaching experience, or master's degree with minimum GPA of 3.5. Additional exam requirements/recommendations for international students: Required—TOEFL (minimum score 550 paper-based; 80 iBT). *Application deadline:* Applications are processed on a rolling basis. Application fee: $40. Electronic applications accepted. *Expenses:* $550 per credit; $485 per credit (online); $580 per credit (doctorate program). *Financial support:* In 2016–17, 8 students received support. Scholarships/grants available. Financial award applicants required to submit FAFSA. *Unit head:* Dana Thomson, Director of Education Operations, 800-846-1543 Ext. 6253, Fax: 620-229-6253, E-mail: dana.thomson@sckans.edu. *Application contact:* Dennis Russell, Director of Admissions and Student Services, 888-684-5335 Ext. 3372, Fax: 888-684-5218, E-mail: dennis.russell@sckans.edu.
Website: http://www.sckans.edu/graduate/education-med/

Stanford University, Graduate School of Education, Program in Curriculum and Teacher Education, Stanford, CA 94305-2004. Offers MA. *Degree requirements:* For master's, thesis (for some programs). *Entrance requirements:* For master's, GRE General Test. Electronic applications accepted. *Expenses: Tuition:* Full-time $47,331. *Required fees:* $609.

State University of New York at Fredonia, College of Education, Fredonia, NY 14063. Offers curriculum and instruction (MS Ed); literacy education (MS Ed), including birth-grade 12, grades 5-12; TESOL (MS Ed). *Accreditation:* NCATE. *Program availability:* Part-time. *Faculty:* 21 full-time (17 women), 11 part-time/adjunct (9 women). *Students:* 39 full-time (32 women), 54 part-time (33 women); includes 8 minority (1 Black or African American, non-Hispanic/Latino; 4 Asian, non-Hispanic/Latino; 2 Hispanic/Latino; 1 Two or more races, non-Hispanic/Latino). Average age 29. 60 applicants, 97% accepted, 39 enrolled. In 2016, 56 master's awarded. *Degree requirements:* For master's, thesis. *Entrance requirements:* For master's, GRE, minimum undergraduate GPA of 3.0. Additional exam requirements/recommendations for international students: Required—TOEFL (minimum score 79 iBT), IELTS (minimum score 6.5). *Application deadline:* For fall admission, 4/1 priority date for domestic and international students; for spring admission, 11/1 priority date for domestic students, 11/1 for international students. Applications are processed on a rolling basis. Application fee: $75. Electronic applications accepted. *Expenses:* Tuition, state resident: full-time $10,370; part-time $453 per credit. Tuition, nonresident: full-time $20,190; part-time $925 per credit. *Required fees:* $1619; $67.30 per credit hour. $403.80 per semester. *Financial support:* In 2016–17, 4 teaching assistantships with full and partial tuition reimbursements (averaging $7,075 per year) were awarded. Financial award application deadline: 3/15; financial award applicants required to submit FAFSA. *Faculty research:* Positive behavioral intervention and support (PBIS), place-based science education, peer support for education, primary source material for social studies education, policies and practices in learning English language. *Unit head:* Dr. Christine Givner, Dean, 716-673-3311, E-mail: christine.givner@fredonia.edu. *Application contact:* Wendy S. Dunst, Interim Graduate Recruitment and Admissions Associate, 716-673-3808, Fax: 716-673-3712, E-mail: wendy.dunst@fredonia.edu.
Website: http://www.fredonia.edu/coe/

State University of New York at Oswego, Graduate Studies, School of Education, Department of Curriculum and Instruction, Oswego, NY 13126. Offers adolescence education (MST); art education (MAT); childhood education (MST); curriculum and instruction (MS Ed); literacy education (MS Ed); special education (MS Ed). *Program availability:* Part-time, evening/weekend. *Degree requirements:* For master's, comprehensive exam (for some programs), thesis optional. *Entrance requirements:* For master's, GRE General Test, minimum GPA of 2.7, provisional teaching certificate. Additional exam requirements/recommendations for international students: Required—TOEFL (minimum score 560 paper-based). *Faculty research:* Classroom applications for microcomputers; classroom questioning, wait-time, and achievement; values clarification and academic achievement.

State University of New York at Plattsburgh, School of Education, Health, and Human Services, Program in Teacher Education: Teaching and Learning, Plattsburgh, NY 12901-2681. Offers MS Ed. *Program availability:* Part-time, evening/weekend. *Entrance requirements:* For master's, minimum GPA of 2.5. Additional exam requirements/recommendations for international students: Required—TOEFL.

State University of New York College at Potsdam, School of Education and Professional Studies, Program in Curriculum and Instruction, Potsdam, NY 13676. Offers childhood education (MST); curriculum and instruction (MS Ed). *Accreditation:* NCATE. *Program availability:* Online learning. *Degree requirements:* For master's, thesis (for some programs). *Entrance requirements:* For master's, minimum GPA of 2.75 in last 60 credit hours of undergraduate study. Additional exam requirements/recommendations for international students: Required—TOEFL (minimum score 550 paper-based; 80 iBT), IELTS (minimum score 6). Electronic applications accepted.

Syracuse University, School of Education, Programs in Instructional Design, Development, and Evaluation, Syracuse, NY 13244. Offers MS, PhD, CAS. *Program availability:* Part-time. *Students:* Average age 34. *Degree requirements:* For master's, thesis or alternative; for doctorate, comprehensive exam, thesis/dissertation. *Entrance requirements:* For master's, GRE or MAT, baccalaureate degree from regionally-accredited college/university, statement of goals, three letters of recommendation, transcripts; for doctorate, GRE, master's degree in instructional design or equivalent, statement of goals, three letters of recommendation, transcripts; for CAS, GRE (recommended), master's degree in instructional design or equivalent, statement of goals, three letters of recommendation, transcripts. Additional exam requirements/recommendations for international students: Required—TOEFL (minimum score 100 iBT). *Application deadline:* For fall admission, 1/15 priority date for domestic and international students; for spring admission, 10/15 priority date for domestic and international students. Applications are processed on a rolling basis. Application fee: $75. Electronic applications accepted. *Expenses: Tuition:* Full-time $25,974; part-time $1443 per credit hour. *Required fees:* $802; $50 per course. Tuition and fees vary according to course load and program. *Financial support:* Fellowships with full tuition reimbursements, research assistantships with tuition reimbursements, teaching assistantships with tuition reimbursements, career-related internships or fieldwork, and scholarships/grants available. Financial award application deadline: 1/15. *Faculty research:* Digital media production, technologies for instructional settings, strategies in educational project management, educational technology in international settings. *Unit head:* Dr. Tiffany A. Koszalka, Chair, 315-443-3703, E-mail: takoszal@syr.edu. *Application contact:* Speranza Migliore, Graduate Admissions Recruiter, 315-443-2505, E-mail: gradrcrt@syr.edu.
Website: http://soeweb.syr.edu/idde/instrucdesign.html

Syracuse University, School of Education, Programs in Teaching and Curriculum, Syracuse, NY 13244. Offers MS, PhD. *Program availability:* Part-time. *Students:* Average age 37. *Degree requirements:* For master's, thesis or alternative; for doctorate, comprehensive exam, thesis/dissertation. *Entrance requirements:* For master's, baccalaureate degree from regionally-accredited college/university, relevant work experience, three letters of recommendation, personal statement, transcripts; for doctorate, GRE, master's degree, writing sample, three years of professional experience, resume, interview. Additional exam requirements/recommendations for international students: Required—TOEFL (minimum score 100 iBT). *Application deadline:* For fall admission, 1/15 priority date for domestic students, 5/15 priority date for international students; for spring admission, 10/15 priority date for domestic and international students; for summer admission, 1/15 priority date for domestic and international students. Applications are processed on a rolling basis. Application fee: $75. Electronic applications accepted. *Expenses: Tuition:* Full-time $25,974; part-time $1443 per credit hour. *Required fees:* $802; $50 per course. Tuition and fees vary according to course load and program. *Financial support:* Fellowships with full tuition reimbursements, research assistantships, teaching assistantships with tuition reimbursements, scholarships/grants, and tuition waivers available. Financial award application deadline: 1/15. *Faculty research:* Theory and practice of curriculum, the lives and careers of teachers, policies and practices of teacher education, research design, implementation and analysis, forms of scholarly expression. *Unit head:* Dr. George Theoharis, Chair of Teaching and Leadership/Professor, 315-443-2685, E-mail: gtheohar@syr.edu. *Application contact:* Speranza Migliore, Graduate Admissions Recruiter, 315-443-2505, E-mail: gradrcrt@syr.edu.
Website: http://soeweb.syr.edu/

Tarleton State University, College of Graduate Studies, College of Education, Department of Curriculum and Instruction, Stephenville, TX 76402. Offers educational diagnostician (M Ed); elementary education (M Ed); instructional design and technology (M Ed); instructional leadership (M Ed); professional reading specialist (M Ed); secondary education (M Ed); special education (M Ed); technology applications (M Ed); technology director (M Ed). *Program availability:* Part-time, evening/weekend. *Faculty:* 9 full-time (7 women), 6 part-time/adjunct (4 women). *Students:* 17 full-time (0 women), 104 part-time (101 women); includes 28 minority (5 Black or African American, non-Hispanic/Latino; 1 American Indian or Alaska Native, non-Hispanic/Latino; 19 Hispanic/Latino; 3 Two or more races, non-Hispanic/Latino). 62 applicants, 94% accepted, 35 enrolled. In 2016, 34 master's awarded. *Degree requirements:* For master's, comprehensive exam. *Entrance requirements:* For master's, GRE General Test, minimum GPA of 3.0. Additional exam requirements/recommendations for international students: Required—TOEFL (minimum score 550 paper-based; 80 iBT). *Application deadline:* For fall admission, 8/15 priority date for domestic students; for spring admission, 1/7 for domestic students. Applications are processed on a rolling basis. Application fee: $45 ($145 for international students). Electronic applications accepted. *Expenses:* $3,672 tuition; $2,437 fees. *Financial support:* Research assistantships, teaching assistantships, career-related internships or fieldwork, Federal Work-Study, and institutionally sponsored loans available. Support available to part-time students. Financial award application deadline: 5/1; financial award applicants required to submit FAFSA. *Unit head:* Dr. Jordan Barkley, Department Head, 254-968-9089, E-mail: jbarkley@tarleton.edu. *Application contact:* Information Contact, 254-968-9104, Fax: 254-968-9670, E-mail: gradoffice@tarleton.edu.
Website: http://www.tarleton.edu/cimasters/

Teachers College, Columbia University, Department of Curriculum and Teaching, New York, NY 10027-6696. Offers curriculum and teaching (Ed M, MA, Ed D); curriculum and teaching: elementary education (MA); curriculum and teaching:

secondary education (MA); early childhood education (MA, Ed D); early childhood education: special education (MA); elementary education-gifted extension (MA); elementary inclusive education (MA); gifted education (MA); literacy specialist (MA); secondary inclusive education (MA); special inclusive elementary education (MA). *Program availability:* Part-time, evening/weekend. *Students:* 236 full-time (219 women), 198 part-time (176 women); includes 160 minority (53 Black or African American, non-Hispanic/Latino; 1 American Indian or Alaska Native, non-Hispanic/Latino; 43 Asian, non-Hispanic/Latino; 41 Hispanic/Latino; 22 Two or more races, non-Hispanic/Latino), 38 international. 399 applicants, 66% accepted, 104 enrolled. Terminal master's awarded for partial completion of doctoral program. *Degree requirements:* For doctorate, thesis/dissertation. *Expenses: Tuition:* Full-time $36,288; part-time $1512 per credit. *Required fees:* $438 per semester. One-time fee: $510 full-time. Full-time tuition and fees vary according to course load. *Unit head:* Prof. Nancy Lesko, Chair, 212-678-3264, E-mail: lesko@tc.columbia.edu. *Application contact:* David Estrella, Director of Admission, 212-678-3305, Fax: 212-678-4171, E-mail: estrella@tc.columbia.edu.

Tennessee State University, The School of Graduate Studies and Research, College of Education, Department of Teaching and Learning, Program in Curriculum and Instruction, Nashville, TN 37209-1561. Offers M Ed, Ed D. *Accreditation:* NCATE. *Degree requirements:* For master's, thesis optional; for doctorate, thesis/dissertation. *Entrance requirements:* For master's, GRE General Test or MAT, minimum GPA of 2.5; for doctorate, GRE General Test or MAT, minimum GPA of 3.25. Additional exam requirements/recommendations for international students: Required—TOEFL.

Tennessee Technological University, College of Graduate Studies, College of Education, Department of Curriculum and Instruction, Program in Curriculum, Cookeville, TN 38505. Offers MA, Ed S. *Accreditation:* NCATE. *Program availability:* Part-time, evening/weekend. *Faculty:* 2 full-time (1 woman). *Students:* 10 full-time (7 women), 26 part-time (22 women); includes 2 minority (1 American Indian or Alaska Native, non-Hispanic/Latino; 1 Two or more races, non-Hispanic/Latino), 2 international. Average age 27. 31 applicants, 45% accepted, 6 enrolled. In 2016, 19 master's, 4 other advanced degrees awarded. *Degree requirements:* For master's and Ed S, comprehensive exam, thesis or alternative. *Entrance requirements:* For master's and Ed S, MAT or GRE. Additional exam requirements/recommendations for international students: Required—TOEFL (minimum score 527 paper-based; 71 iBT), IELTS (minimum score 5.5), PTE (minimum score 48), or TOEIC (Test of English as an International Communication). *Application deadline:* For fall admission, 8/1 for domestic students, 5/1 for international students; for spring admission, 12/1 for domestic students, 10/1 for international students; for summer admission, 5/1 for domestic students, 2/1 for international students. Applications are processed on a rolling basis. Application fee: $35 ($40 for international students). Electronic applications accepted. *Expenses:* Tuition, state resident: full-time $9375; part-time $534 per credit hour. Tuition, nonresident: full-time $22,443; part-time $1260 per credit hour. *Financial support:* In 2016–17, 2 fellowships (averaging $8,000 per year) were awarded; research assistantships and teaching assistantships also available. Financial award application deadline: 4/1. *Unit head:* Dr. Jeremy Wendt, Interim Chairperson, 931-372-3181, Fax: 931-372-6270, E-mail: jwendt@tntech.edu. *Application contact:* Shelia K. Kendrick, Coordinator of Graduate Studies, 931-372-3808, Fax: 931-372-3497, E-mail: skendrick@tntech.edu.

Texas A&M International University, Office of Graduate Studies and Research, College of Education, Department of Curriculum and Pedagogy, Laredo, TX 78041-1900. Offers MS. *Degree requirements:* For master's, comprehensive exam. *Entrance requirements:* Additional exam requirements/recommendations for international students: Required—TOEFL (minimum score 550 paper-based; 79 iBT).

Texas A&M University, College of Education and Human Development, Department of Teaching, Learning, and Culture, College Station, TX 77843. Offers curriculum and instruction (M Ed, MS, Ed D, PhD). *Program availability:* Part-time. *Faculty:* 45. *Students:* 175 full-time (142 women), 285 part-time (232 women); includes 132 minority (56 Black or African American, non-Hispanic/Latino; 12 Asian, non-Hispanic/Latino; 61 Hispanic/Latino; 3 Two or more races, non-Hispanic/Latino), 61 international. Average age 34. 130 applicants, 92% accepted, 81 enrolled. In 2016, 127 master's, 26 doctorates awarded. *Degree requirements:* For master's, comprehensive exam, thesis (for some programs); for doctorate, comprehensive exam, thesis/dissertation. *Entrance requirements:* For master's, GRE General Test, minimum GPA of 3.0; for doctorate, GRE General Test, 3 years of teaching experience. Additional exam requirements/recommendations for international students: Required—TOEFL (minimum score 550 paper-based; 80 iBT), IELTS (minimum score 6), PTE (minimum score 53). *Application deadline:* For fall admission, 3/1 for domestic students, 1/1 for international students; for spring admission, 10/1 for domestic students, 8/1 for international students. Application fee: $50 ($90 for international students). Electronic applications accepted. *Expenses:* Contact institution. *Financial support:* In 2016–17, 190 students received support, including 2 fellowships with tuition reimbursements available (averaging $18,000 per year), 45 research assistantships with tuition reimbursements available (averaging $6,445 per year), 32 teaching assistantships with tuition reimbursements available (averaging $11,235 per year); career-related internships or fieldwork, institutionally sponsored loans, scholarships/grants, traineeships, health care benefits, tuition waivers (full and partial), and unspecified assistantships also available. Support available to part-time students. Financial award application deadline: 3/15; financial award applicants required to submit FAFSA. *Unit head:* Dr. Lynn Burlbaw, Professor and Interim Department Co-Head, 979-845-8384, Fax: 979-845-9663, E-mail: burlbaw@neo.tamu.edu. *Application contact:* Sarah Oakley, Academic Advisor II, 979-845-5063, Fax: 979-845-9663, E-mail: sarahoakley@tamu.edu.
Website: http://tlac.tamu.edu

Texas A&M University–Central Texas, Graduate Studies and Research, Killeen, TX 76549. Offers accounting (MS); business administration (MBA); clinical mental health counseling (MS); criminal justice (MCJ); curriculum and instruction (M Ed); educational administration (M Ed); educational psychology - experimental psychology (MS); history (MA); human resource management (MS); information systems (MS); liberal studies (MS); management and leadership (MS); marriage and family therapy (MS); mathematics (MS); political science (MA); school counseling (M Ed); school psychology (Ed S).

Texas A&M University–Commerce, College of Education and Human Services, Commerce, TX 75429-3011. Offers counseling (MS); curriculum and instruction (M Ed, MS); early childhood education (M Ed, MS); educational administration (M Ed, Ed D); educational psychology (PhD); educational technology leadership (MS); educational technology library science (MS); health, kinesiology and sports studies (MS); higher education (MS, Ed D); organization, learning, and technology (MS); psychology (MS); reading (M Ed, MS); school psychology (SSP); secondary education (M Ed, MS); social work (MSW); special education (M Ed); supervision, curriculum and instruction-elementary education (Ed D). *Program availability:* Part-time, 100% online, blended/hybrid learning. *Faculty:* 88 full-time (52 women), 31 part-time/adjunct (24 women). *Students:* 341 full-time (276 women), 1,495 part-time (1,156 women); includes 762 minority (429 Black or African American, non-Hispanic/Latino; 4 American Indian or Alaska Native, non-Hispanic/Latino; 27 Asian, non-Hispanic/Latino; 247 Hispanic/Latino; 1 Native Hawaiian or other Pacific Islander, non-Hispanic/Latino; 54 Two or more races, non-Hispanic/Latino), 18 international. Average age 37. 1,070 applicants, 54% accepted, 452 enrolled. In 2016, 579 master's, 31 doctorates awarded. *Degree requirements:* For master's, one foreign language, comprehensive exam, thesis optional, departmental qualifying exams (for some programs); for doctorate, comprehensive exam, thesis/dissertation, departmental qualifying exam; for SSP, comprehensive exam, thesis optional. *Entrance requirements:* For master's and doctorate, GRE General Test. Additional exam requirements/recommendations for international students: Required—TOEFL (minimum score 550 paper-based; 79 iBT), IELTS (minimum score 6). *Application deadline:* For fall admission, 6/1 priority date for international students; for spring admission, 10/15 priority date for international students; for summer admission, 3/15 priority date for international students. Applications are processed on a rolling basis. Application fee: $50. Electronic applications accepted. *Expenses:* $2,254 resident; $4,744 non-resident. *Financial support:* In 2016–17, 301 students received support, including 39 research assistantships with partial tuition reimbursements available (averaging $9,000 per year), 17 teaching assistantships with partial tuition reimbursements available (averaging $9,000 per year); career-related internships or fieldwork, Federal Work-Study, institutionally sponsored loans, scholarships/grants, health care benefits, and unspecified assistantships also available. Financial award application deadline: 5/1; financial award applicants required to submit FAFSA. *Faculty research:* Cognitive and bilingual education, positive behavioral intervention, literacy, math readiness. *Total annual research expenditures:* $470,963. *Unit head:* Dr. Timothy Letzring, Dean, 903-886-5181, Fax: 903-886-5905, E-mail: tim.letzring@tamuc.edu. *Application contact:* Jennifer Faunce, Graduate Recruiter, 903-886-5030, Fax: 903-886-5905, E-mail: jennifer.faunce@tamuc.edu.
Website: http://www.tamuc.edu/academics/graduateSchool/programs/education/default.aspx

Texas A&M University–Corpus Christi, College of Graduate Studies, College of Education, Program in Curriculum and Instruction, Corpus Christi, TX 78412-5503. Offers MS, PhD. *Program availability:* Part-time, evening/weekend. *Students:* 11 full-time (7 women), 54 part-time (48 women); includes 31 minority (1 Black or African American, non-Hispanic/Latino; 1 Asian, non-Hispanic/Latino; 29 Hispanic/Latino), 4 international. Average age 37. 20 applicants, 70% accepted, 8 enrolled. In 2016, 12 master's, 8 doctorates awarded. *Degree requirements:* For doctorate, comprehensive exam, thesis/dissertation. *Entrance requirements:* For master's, minimum GPA of 3.0 in last 60 hours; essay (approximately 300-400 words in length); for doctorate, GMAT/GRE (taken within 5 years), master's degree, minimum GPA of 3.0 in last 60 hours, 4 reference forms, 3 years' teaching experience, interview. Additional exam requirements/recommendations for international students: Required—TOEFL (minimum score 550 paper-based), IELTS (minimum score 6.5). *Application deadline:* For fall admission, 7/15 priority date for domestic students, 5/1 priority date for international students; for spring admission, 11/15 priority date for domestic students, 9/1 priority date for international students. Applications are processed on a rolling basis. Application fee: $50 ($70 for international students). Electronic applications accepted. *Financial support:* Research assistantships, teaching assistantships, career-related internships or fieldwork, Federal Work-Study, institutionally sponsored loans, scholarships/grants, health care benefits, and unspecified assistantships available. Support available to part-time students. Financial award application deadline: 3/15; financial award applicants required to submit FAFSA. *Unit head:* Dr. Faye Bruun, Chair, 361-825-2417, E-mail: faye.bruun@tamucc.edu. *Application contact:* Graduate Admissions Coordinator, 361-825-2177, Fax: 361-825-2755, E-mail: gradweb@tamucc.edu.
Website: http://education.tamucc.edu/

Texas A&M University–Texarkana, Graduate Studies and Research, College of Education and Liberal Arts, Texarkana, TX 75505-5518. Offers adult education (MS); curriculum and instruction (M Ed); education (MS); educational administration (M Ed); English (MA); instructional technology (MS); interdisciplinary studies (MA, MS); special education (MS). *Program availability:* Part-time, evening/weekend. *Degree requirements:* For master's, comprehensive exam (for some programs), thesis optional. *Entrance requirements:* For master's, minimum GPA of 2.5 on last 60 hours of bachelor's degree. Additional exam requirements/recommendations for international students: Required—TOEFL. Electronic applications accepted.

Texas Christian University, College of Education, Doctoral Programs in Education, Fort Worth, TX 76129. Offers counseling and counselor education (PhD); curriculum studies (PhD); educational leadership (Ed D); higher educational leadership (Ed D); science education (PhD); MBA/Ed D. *Program availability:* Part-time, evening/weekend. *Faculty:* 29 full-time (21 women), 8 part-time/adjunct (5 women). *Students:* 77 full-time (56 women), 19 part-time (7 women); includes 33 minority (12 Black or African American, non-Hispanic/Latino; 5 Asian, non-Hispanic/Latino; 15 Hispanic/Latino; 1 Two or more races, non-Hispanic/Latino), 6 international. Average age 37. 34 applicants, 56% accepted, 13 enrolled. In 2016, 5 doctorates awarded. *Degree requirements:* For doctorate, comprehensive exam, thesis/dissertation. *Entrance requirements:* For doctorate, GRE General Test. Additional exam requirements/recommendations for international students: Required—TOEFL (minimum score 550 paper-based; 80 iBT). *Application deadline:* For fall admission, 2/1 for domestic and international students; for winter admission, 2/1 for domestic and international students; for spring admission, 11/16 for domestic and international students. Application fee: $60. Electronic applications accepted. *Expenses: Tuition:* Full-time $26,640; part-time $1480 per credit hour. *Required fees:* $48. Tuition and fees vary according to program. *Financial support:* In 2016–17, 57 students received support, including 1 fellowship with full tuition reimbursement available, 10 research assistantships with full tuition reimbursements available (averaging $18,500 per year), 7 teaching assistantships with full tuition reimbursements available (averaging $18,500 per year); career-related internships or fieldwork, scholarships/grants, health care benefits, and unspecified assistantships also available. Support available to part-time students. Financial award application deadline: 2/1; financial award applicants required to submit FAFSA. *Unit head:* Dr. Jan Lacina, Associate Dean, 817-257-6786, Fax: 817-257-7466, E-mail: j.lacina@tcu.edu. *Application contact:* Lori Kimball, Administrative Program Specialist, 817-257-7661, Fax: 817-257-7466, E-mail: l.kimball@tcu.edu.
Website: http://coe.tcu.edu/graduate-overview/

Texas Christian University, College of Education, Master's Programs in Education, Fort Worth, TX 76129. Offers counseling (M Ed); curriculum and instruction (M Ed), including curriculum studies, language and literacy, math education, science education; educational leadership (M Ed); special education (M Ed). *Program availability:* Part-time, evening/weekend. *Faculty:* 29 full-time (21 women), 8 part-time/adjunct (5 women). *Students:* 112 full-time (95 women), 12 part-time (11 women); includes 39 minority (6 Black or African American, non-Hispanic/Latino; 2 Asian, non-Hispanic/Latino; 27 Hispanic/Latino; 1 Native Hawaiian or other Pacific Islander, non-Hispanic/Latino; 3 Two or more races, non-Hispanic/Latino), 2 international. Average age 29. 107 applicants, 78% accepted, 66 enrolled. In 2016, 54 master's awarded. *Degree requirements:* For master's, comprehensive exam (for some programs), thesis (for some programs). *Entrance requirements:* For master's, GRE General Test. Additional exam requirements/recommendations for international students: Required—TOEFL (minimum score 550 paper-based; 80 iBT). *Application deadline:* For fall admission, 3/1 for domestic and international students; for spring admission, 11/16 for domestic and international students; for summer admission, 3/1 for domestic and international students. Application

fee: $60. Electronic applications accepted. *Expenses: Tuition:* Full-time $26,640; part-time $1480 per credit hour. *Required fees:* $48. Tuition and fees vary according to program. *Financial support:* In 2016–17, 104 students received support, including 4 research assistantships with full tuition reimbursements available (averaging $15,000 per year), 31 teaching assistantships with full tuition reimbursements available (averaging $15,000 per year); career-related internships or fieldwork, scholarships/grants, and unspecified assistantships also available. Support available to part-time students. Financial award application deadline: 3/1; financial award applicants required to submit FAFSA. *Unit head:* Dr. Jan Lacina, Associate Dean, 817-257-6786, Fax: 817-257-7466, E-mail: j.lacina@tcu.edu. *Application contact:* Lori Kimball, Administrative Program Specialist, 817-257-7661, Fax: 817-257-7466, E-mail: l.kimball@tcu.edu.
Website: http://coe.tcu.edu/graduate-overview/

Texas Southern University, College of Education, Area of Curriculum and Instruction, Houston, TX 77004-4584. Offers bilingual education (M Ed); curriculum and instruction (Ed D); secondary education (M Ed). *Program availability:* Part-time, evening/weekend. *Degree requirements:* For master's, comprehensive exam; for doctorate, comprehensive exam, thesis/dissertation. *Entrance requirements:* For master's, GRE General Test, minimum GPA of 2.5; for doctorate, GRE General Test or MAT, master's degree, minimum B+ average. Additional exam requirements/recommendations for international students: Required—TOEFL. Electronic applications accepted.

Texas Tech University, Graduate School, College of Education, Department of Curriculum and Instruction, Lubbock, TX 79409-1071. Offers bilingual education (M Ed); curriculum and instruction (M Ed); elementary education (M Ed); language/literacy education (M Ed); multidisciplinary science (MS); secondary education (M Ed). *Accreditation:* NCATE. *Program availability:* Part-time, evening/weekend, online learning. *Faculty:* 24 full-time (17 women), 1 part-time/adjunct (0 women). *Students:* 65 full-time (52 women), 237 part-time (191 women); includes 97 minority (30 Black or African American, non-Hispanic/Latino; 1 American Indian or Alaska Native, non-Hispanic/Latino; 10 Asian, non-Hispanic/Latino; 47 Hispanic/Latino; 9 Two or more races, non-Hispanic/Latino), 41 international. Average age 39. 181 applicants, 54% accepted, 78 enrolled. In 2016, 20 master's, 28 doctorates awarded. Terminal master's awarded for partial completion of doctoral program. *Degree requirements:* For master's, comprehensive exam (for some programs), thesis optional; for doctorate, comprehensive exam, thesis/dissertation. *Entrance requirements:* For master's, bachelor's degree; resume; letter of intent; academic writing sample; 2 letters of recommendation; for doctorate, GRE, master's degree; resume; letter of intent; academic writing sample; 3 letters of recommendation. Additional exam requirements/recommendations for international students: Required—TOEFL (minimum score 550 paper-based; 79 iBT). *Application deadline:* For fall admission, 6/1 priority date for domestic students, 1/15 priority date for international students; for spring admission, 9/1 priority date for domestic students, 6/15 priority date for international students. Applications are processed on a rolling basis. Application fee: $75. Electronic applications accepted. *Expenses:* $285 per credit hour full-time resident tuition, $693 per credit hour full-time non-resident tuition; $50.50 per credit hour fee plus $608 per term fee. *Financial support:* In 2016–17, 110 students received support, including 110 fellowships (averaging $3,132 per year); research assistantships, Federal Work-Study, institutionally sponsored loans, scholarships/grants, health care benefits, and unspecified assistantships also available. Support available to part-time students. Financial award application deadline: 2/1; financial award applicants required to submit FAFSA. *Faculty research:* Teacher education, curriculum studies, bilingual education, science and math education, language and literacy education. *Total annual research expenditures:* $120,552. *Unit head:* Dr. Jian Wang, Department Chair, Curriculum and Instruction, 806-834-5165, Fax: 806-742-2179, E-mail: jian.wang@ttu.edu. *Application contact:* Brianna Sanchez, Coordinator, 806-834-2353, Fax: 806-742-2179, E-mail: brianna.sanchez@ttu.edu.
Website: http://www.educ.ttu.edu

Texas Woman's University, Graduate School, College of Professional Education, Department of Teacher Education, Denton, TX 76204-5769. Offers educational administration (M Ed, MA); special education (M Ed, MA, PhD), including educational diagnostician (M Ed, MA), intervention specialist (M Ed); teaching, learning, and curriculum (M Ed, MA). *Program availability:* Part-time. *Students:* 15 full-time (13 women), 98 part-time (85 women); includes 36 minority (13 Black or African American, non-Hispanic/Latino; 3 American Indian or Alaska Native, non-Hispanic/Latino; 3 Asian, non-Hispanic/Latino; 16 Hispanic/Latino; 1 Two or more races, non-Hispanic/Latino). Average age 38. In 2016, 111 master's, 1 doctorate awarded. Terminal master's awarded for partial completion of doctoral program. *Degree requirements:* For master's, comprehensive exam, thesis, professional paper (M Ed); for doctorate, comprehensive exam, thesis/dissertation. *Entrance requirements:* For master's, minimum GPA of 3.0 on last 60 undergraduate hours, 2 letters of reference, resume, copy of certifications, teacher service record, statement of intent; for doctorate, GRE General Test, minimum GPA of 3.0, 3 letters of reference, resume, copy of certifications, teacher service record, statement of intent. Additional exam requirements/recommendations for international students: Required—TOEFL (minimum score 550 paper-based; 79 iBT). *Application deadline:* For fall admission, 7/1 priority date for domestic students, 3/1 for international students; for spring admission, 11/1 priority date for domestic students, 7/1 for international students. Applications are processed on a rolling basis. Application fee: $50 ($75 for international students). Electronic applications accepted. *Expenses:* Tuition, state resident: full-time $9046; part-time $251 per credit hour. Tuition, nonresident: full-time $22,922; part-time $614 per credit hour. *International tuition:* $23,046 full-time. *Required fees:* $2690; $1285 per credit hour. One-time fee: $50. Tuition and fees vary according to course level, course load, program and reciprocity agreements. *Financial support:* Research assistantships, career-related internships or fieldwork, Federal Work-Study, institutionally sponsored loans, scholarships/grants, traineeships, health care benefits, and unspecified assistantships available. Support available to part-time students. Financial award application deadline: 3/1; financial award applicants required to submit FAFSA. *Faculty research:* Language and literacy, classroom management, learning disabilities, staff and professional development, leadership preparation practice. *Unit head:* Dr. Jane Pemberton, Chair, 940-898-2273, Fax: 940-898-2270, E-mail: teachereducation@twu.edu. *Application contact:* Dr. Samuel Wheeler, Assistant Director of Admissions, 940-898-3188, Fax: 940-898-3081, E-mail: wheelersr@twu.edu.
Website: http://www.twu.edu/teacher-education/

Trevecca Nazarene University, Graduate Education Program, Nashville, TN 37210-2877. Offers accountability and instructional leadership (Ed S); curriculum and instruction for Christian school educators (M Ed); curriculum and instruction K-12 (M Ed); educational leadership (M Ed); English second language (M Ed); library and information science (MLI Sc); special education: visual impairments (M Ed); teaching (MAT), including teaching 6-12, teaching K-5. *Accreditation:* NCATE. *Program availability:* Part-time, evening/weekend, online learning. *Faculty:* 5 full-time (3 women), 18 part-time/adjunct (12 women). *Students:* 80 full-time (64 women), 16 part-time (13 women); includes 19 minority (17 Black or African American, non-Hispanic/Latino; 2 Hispanic/Latino). Average age 35. In 2016, 68 master's, 7 other advanced degrees awarded. *Degree requirements:* For master's, comprehensive exam, exit assessment/e-portfolio. *Entrance requirements:* For master's, GRE (minimum score of 290) or MAT (minimum score of 378); PRAXIS (for MAT), minimum GPA of 3.0, official transcript from regionally-accredited institution, at least 3 years' successful teaching experience (for M Ed in educational leadership major). Additional exam requirements/recommendations for international students: Required—TOEFL (minimum score 550 paper-based). *Application deadline:* Applications are processed on a rolling basis. Electronic applications accepted. *Expenses:* Contact institution. *Financial support:* Applicants required to submit FAFSA. *Unit head:* Dr. Suzie Harris, Dean, School of Education/Director of Graduate Education Programs, 615-248-1201, Fax: 615-248-1597, E-mail: admissions_ged@trevecca.edu. *Application contact:* 844-TNU-GRAD, E-mail: sgcsadmissions@trevecca.edu.
Website: http://www.trevecca.edu/soe

Trinity Washington University, School of Education, Washington, DC 20017-1094. Offers clinical mental health counseling (MA); early childhood education (MAT); educating for change (M Ed); educational administration (MSA); elementary education (MAT); reading (M Ed); school counseling (MA); secondary education (MAT), including English, social studies; special education (MAT). *Accreditation:* NCATE. *Program availability:* Part-time, evening/weekend. *Degree requirements:* For master's, thesis (for some programs), capstone project(s). *Entrance requirements:* For master's, PRAXIS I, minimum GPA of 2.8. Additional exam requirements/recommendations for international students: Required—TOEFL (minimum score 550 paper-based). *Faculty research:* Technology, literacy, special education, organizations, inclusion models.

Tusculum College, Graduate and Professional Studies, Program in Curriculum and Instruction, Greeneville, TN 37743-9997. Offers mathematics education (MA Ed); special education (MA Ed). *Program availability:* Evening/weekend. *Degree requirements:* For master's, thesis or alternative. *Entrance requirements:* For master's, NTE, PRAXIS II, GRE, MAT, 3 years of work experience, minimum GPA of 3.0, bachelor's degree. Additional exam requirements/recommendations for international students: Required—TOEFL (minimum score 540 paper-based; 73 iBT). *Application deadline:* Applications are processed on a rolling basis. Application fee: $0. *Expenses: Tuition:* Full-time $7497; part-time $357 per credit hour. *Unit head:* Dr. Tricia Hunsader, Dean, School of Education, 423-636-7300 Ext. 5693, E-mail: thunsader@tusculum.edu. *Application contact:* Lindsey Seal, Director of Enrollment, 423-636-7300 Ext. 5006, E-mail: lseal@tusculum.edu.
Website: http://home.tusculum.edu/gps/graduate-degrees/master-arts-education-curriculum-instruction/

Universidad Adventista de las Antillas, EGECED Department, Mayagüez, PR 00681-0118. Offers curriculum and instruction (M Ed); medical surgical nursing (MN); school administration and supervision (M Ed). *Degree requirements:* For master's, comprehensive exam (for some programs), thesis (for some programs). *Entrance requirements:* For master's, EXADEP or GRE General Test, recommendations. Electronic applications accepted.

Universidad del Turabo, Graduate Programs, Programs in Education, Program in Curriculum and Instruction and Appropriate Environment, Gurabo, PR 00778-3030. Offers D Ed. *Program availability:* Part-time, evening/weekend. *Students:* 10 full-time (9 women), 112 part-time (84 women); all minorities (all Hispanic/Latino). Average age 45. 55 applicants, 55% accepted, 27 enrolled. In 2016, 12 doctorates awarded. *Entrance requirements:* For doctorate, EXADEP, GRE or GMAT, official transcript, recommendation letters, essay, curriculum vitae, interview. *Application deadline:* Applications are processed on a rolling basis. Application fee: $25. Electronic applications accepted. *Financial support:* Institutionally sponsored loans available. Financial award applicants required to submit FAFSA. *Unit head:* Israel Rodríguez, Dean, 787-743-7979 Ext. 4627. *Application contact:* Diriee Rodríguez, Admission's Director, 787-743-7979 Ext. 4453, E-mail: admisiones-ut@suagm.edu.
Website: http://ut.suagm.edu/es/educacion

Universidad del Turabo, Graduate Programs, Programs in Education, Program in Curriculum and Teaching, Gurabo, PR 00778-3030. Offers M Ed. *Program availability:* Part-time, evening/weekend. *Students:* 21 full-time (18 women), 16 part-time (14 women); all minorities (all Hispanic/Latino). Average age 37. 37 applicants, 57% accepted, 15 enrolled. In 2016, 16 master's awarded. *Entrance requirements:* For master's, EXADEP, GRE or GMAT, interview, official transcript, essay, recommendation letter. *Application deadline:* Applications are processed on a rolling basis. Application fee: $25. Electronic applications accepted. *Financial support:* Institutionally sponsored loans available. Financial award applicants required to submit FAFSA. *Unit head:* Israel Rodríguez, Dean, 787-743-7979 Ext. 4627. *Application contact:* Diriee Rodríguez, Admissions Director, 787-743-7979 Ext. 4453, E-mail: admisiones-ut@suagm.edu.
Website: http://ut.suagm.edu/es/educacion

Universidad Metropolitana, School of Education, Program in Curriculum and Teaching, San Juan, PR 00928-1150. Offers M Ed. *Program availability:* Part-time, evening/weekend. *Degree requirements:* For master's, thesis or alternative. *Entrance requirements:* For master's, EXADEP, interview.

Université de Montréal, Faculty of Education, Department of Didactics, Montréal, QC H3C 3J7, Canada. Offers M Ed, MA, PhD, DESS. Terminal master's awarded for partial completion of doctoral program. *Degree requirements:* For master's, thesis (for some programs); for doctorate, thesis/dissertation, general exam. Electronic applications accepted. *Faculty research:* Teaching of French as a first or second language, teaching of science and technology, teaching of mathematics, teaching of arts.

Université Laval, Faculty of Education, Department of Teaching and Learning Studies, Programs in Didactics, Québec, QC G1K 7P4, Canada. Offers MA, PhD. Terminal master's awarded for partial completion of doctoral program. *Degree requirements:* For master's, thesis (for some programs); for doctorate, comprehensive exam, thesis/dissertation. *Entrance requirements:* For master's and doctorate, English exam (comprehension of written English), knowledge of French. Electronic applications accepted.

University at Albany, State University of New York, School of Education, Department of Educational Theory and Practice, Albany, NY 12222-0001. Offers curriculum and instruction (PhD, CAS); curriculum development and instructional technology (MS); general education studies (MS). *Program availability:* Part-time, evening/weekend, 100% online, blended/hybrid learning. *Faculty:* 6 full-time (4 women), 12 part-time/adjunct (8 women). *Students:* 84 full-time (56 women), 223 part-time (155 women); includes 39 minority (12 Black or African American, non-Hispanic/Latino; 6 Asian, non-Hispanic/Latino; 14 Hispanic/Latino; 7 Two or more races, non-Hispanic/Latino), 26 international. Average age 30. 147 applicants, 78% accepted, 106 enrolled. In 2016, 99 master's, 5 doctorates, 11 other advanced degrees awarded. *Degree requirements:* For doctorate, one foreign language, thesis/dissertation. *Entrance requirements:* For doctorate, GRE General Test. Additional exam requirements/recommendations for international students: Required—TOEFL (minimum score 550 paper-based). *Application deadline:* For fall admission, 2/1 for domestic students, 1/31 for international students. Application fee: $75. Electronic applications accepted. *Expenses:* Tuition, state resident: full-time $10,870; part-time $453 per credit hour. Tuition, nonresident: full-time $22,210; part-time $925 per credit hour. *International tuition:* $21,550 full-time. *Required fees:* $1864; $96 per credit hour. *Financial support:* Fellowships available.

Total annual research expenditures: $1.2 million. *Unit head:* Arthur Appleby, Chair, 518-442-5006, E-mail: aapplebee@albany.edu.

University at Buffalo, the State University of New York, Graduate School, Graduate School of Education, Department of Learning and Instruction, Buffalo, NY 14260. Offers biology education (Ed M, Certificate); chemistry education (Ed M, Certificate); childhood education (Ed M); childhood education with bilingual extension (Ed M); college teaching (Advanced Certificate); curriculum, instruction and the science of learning (PhD); early childhood education (Ed M); early childhood education with bilingual extension (Ed M); earth science education (Ed M, Certificate); education and technology (Ed M); education studies (Ed M); educational technology and new literacies (Certificate); educational technology and new literacies (Advanced Certificate); elementary education (Ed D); English education (Ed M, Certificate); English education studies (Ed M); English for speakers of other languages (Ed M); foreign and second language education (PhD); French education (Ed M, Certificate); German education (Ed M, Certificate); gifted education (Certificate); Latin education (Ed M, Certificate); literacy education studies (Ed M); literacy specialist (Ed M); literacy teaching and learning (Certificate); mathematics education (Ed M, Certificate); music education (Ed M, Certificate); music education studies (Ed M); music learning theory (Advanced Certificate); online education (Advanced Certificate); physics education (Ed M, Certificate); science and the public (Ed M); social studies education (Ed M, Certificate); Spanish education (Ed M, Certificate); special education (PhD); teaching English to speakers of other languages (Ed M). *Program availability:* Part-time, evening/weekend, 100% online. *Faculty:* 28 full-time (21 women), 67 part-time/adjunct (49 women). *Students:* 198 full-time (153 women), 312 part-time (220 women); includes 48 minority (28 Black or African American, non-Hispanic/Latino; 4 American Indian or Alaska Native, non-Hispanic/Latino; 15 Asian, non-Hispanic/Latino; 1 Hispanic/Latino), 66 international. Average age 33. 336 applicants, 86% accepted, 178 enrolled. In 2016, 137 master's, 24 doctorates, 25 other advanced degrees awarded. *Degree requirements:* For master's, comprehensive exam; for doctorate, thesis/dissertation, research analysis exam, research experience. *Entrance requirements:* For master's, letters of reference; for doctorate, GRE General Test or MAT, interview, writing sample, letters of recommendation. Additional exam requirements/recommendations for international students: Required—TOEFL (minimum score 600 paper-based; 96 iBT). *Application deadline:* For fall admission, 2/1 priority date for domestic and international students; for spring admission, 11/15 priority date for domestic students, 10/1 for international students. Applications are processed on a rolling basis. Application fee: $50. Electronic applications accepted. *Financial support:* In 2016–17, 44 fellowships (averaging $4,010 per year), 39 research assistantships with tuition reimbursements (averaging $9,897 per year) were awarded; teaching assistantships, career-related internships or fieldwork, Federal Work-Study, institutionally sponsored loans, scholarships/grants, tuition waivers (full and partial), and unspecified assistantships also available. Financial award application deadline: 2/28; financial award applicants required to submit FAFSA. *Faculty research:* Science assessment, foreign language teaching and learning, early learning, new literacies, gender and education. *Total annual research expenditures:* $534,880. *Unit head:* Dr. Deborah Moore-Russo, Chair, 716-645-4069, Fax: 716-645-3161, E-mail: dam29@buffalo.edu. *Application contact:* Luann Zak, Admissions Assistant, 716-645-2110, Fax: 716-645-7937, E-mail: luannzak@buffalo.edu.
Website: http://gse.buffalo.edu/lai

The University of Akron, Graduate School, College of Education, Department of Curricular and Instructional Studies, Program in Curriculum and Instruction with Licensure Options, Akron, OH 44325. Offers MS. *Students:* 3. *Entrance requirements:* For master's, minimum GPA of 3.0. Additional exam requirements/recommendations for international students: Required—TOEFL (minimum score 550 paper-based; 79 iBT), IELTS (minimum score 6.5). *Application deadline:* Applications are processed on a rolling basis. Application fee: $45 ($70 for international students). *Expenses:* Tuition, state resident: full-time $8618; part-time $359 per credit hour. Tuition, nonresident: full-time $17,149; part-time $715 per credit hour. *Required fees:* $1652. *Unit head:* Dr. Susan Clark, Interim Chair, 330-972-7780, E-mail: sclark1@uakron.edu. *Application contact:* Kelly Chaff, College Program Specialist, 330-972-7028, E-mail: klchaff@uakron.edu.
Website: http://www.uakron.edu/education/academic-programs/graduate-programs.dot

The University of Alabama at Birmingham, School of Education, Program in Curriculum Education, Birmingham, AL 35294. Offers Ed S. *Program availability:* Part-time, online learning. *Degree requirements:* For Ed S, comprehensive exam, thesis optional. *Entrance requirements:* For degree, GRE General Test, MAT, minimum GPA of 3.0, master's degree. Electronic applications accepted. Full-time tuition and fees vary according to course load and program.

University of Arkansas, Graduate School, College of Education and Health Professions, Department of Curriculum and Instruction, Program in Curriculum and Instruction, Fayetteville, AR 72701. Offers M Ed, PhD, Ed S. *Program availability:* Part-time. In 2016, 5 master's, 10 doctorates awarded. *Degree requirements:* For doctorate, thesis/dissertation. *Entrance requirements:* For doctorate, GRE General Test. *Application deadline:* For fall admission, 4/1 for international students; for spring admission, 10/1 for international students. Applications are processed on a rolling basis. Application fee: $40 ($50 for international students). Electronic applications accepted. *Financial support:* In 2016–17, 12 research assistantships, 2 teaching assistantships were awarded; fellowships with tuition reimbursements also available. Financial award application deadline: 4/1. *Unit head:* Dr. Michael Daugherty, Unit Head, 479-575-4209, E-mail: mkd03@uark.edu. *Application contact:* Dr. Derrick Mears, Graduate Coordinator, 479-575-6195, Fax: 479-575-6676, E-mail: dmears@uark.edu.
Website: http://cied.uark.edu/

University of Arkansas at Little Rock, Graduate School, College of Education and Health Professions, Department of Teacher Education, Program in Curriculum and Instruction, Little Rock, AR 72204-1099. Offers M Ed. *Entrance requirements:* For master's, teaching license.

The University of British Columbia, Faculty of Education, Department of Curriculum and Pedagogy, Vancouver, BC V6T 1Z4, Canada. Offers art education (M Ed, MA); curriculum studies (M Ed, MA, PhD); home economics education (M Ed, MA); mathematics education (M Ed, MA); media and technology studies education (M Ed, MA); music education (M Ed, MA); physical education (M Ed, MA); science education (M Ed, MA); social studies education (M Ed, MA). *Program availability:* Part-time, online learning. *Degree requirements:* For master's, thesis (MA); for doctorate, comprehensive exam, thesis/dissertation. *Entrance requirements:* Additional exam requirements/recommendations for international students: Required—TOEFL, IELTS. Application fee: $100 Canadian dollars ($162 Canadian dollars for international students). Electronic applications accepted. *Expenses:* $6,865 per year tuition and fees domestic, $10,938 per year international (for MA and M Ed); $4,802 per year tuition and fees, $8,436 per year international (for PhD). *Financial support:* Fellowships with partial tuition reimbursements, research assistantships with partial tuition reimbursements, teaching assistantships with partial tuition reimbursements, and tuition waivers (partial) available. *Faculty research:* School subjects, teaching and learning. *Application contact:* Alan Jay, Graduate Programs Assistant, 604-822-5367, Fax: 604-822-4714, E-mail: edcp.grad@ubc.ca.
Website: http://www.edcp.educ.ubc.ca/

University of Calgary, Faculty of Graduate Studies, Werklund School of Education, Graduate Division of Educational Research, Calgary, AB T2N 1N4, Canada. Offers adult learning (M Ed, MA, Ed D, PhD); curriculum and learning (M Ed, MA, Ed D, PhD); educational leadership (M Ed, MA, Ed D, PhD); languages and diversity (M Ed, MA, Ed D, PhD); learning sciences (M Ed, MA, Ed D, PhD). Ed D in educational leadership offered via distance delivery. *Program availability:* Part-time, evening/weekend, online learning. *Degree requirements:* For master's, thesis (for some programs); for doctorate, thesis/dissertation, candidacy exam. *Entrance requirements:* For master's, minimum GPA of 3.0, 3 letters of reference; for doctorate, minimum GPA of 3.5, 3 letters of reference. Additional exam requirements/recommendations for international students: Required—TOEFL, IELTS. Electronic applications accepted. *Faculty research:* Curriculum, leadership, technology, contexts, gifted, second language teaching, work place and adult learning.

University of California, Davis, Graduate Studies, Graduate Group in Education, Davis, CA 95616. Offers education (MA, Ed D); instructional studies (PhD); psychological studies (PhD); sociocultural studies (PhD). Ed D offered jointly with California State University, Fresno. Terminal master's awarded for partial completion of doctoral program. *Degree requirements:* For master's, comprehensive exam (for some programs), thesis (for some programs); for doctorate, thesis/dissertation. *Entrance requirements:* For master's and doctorate, GRE. Additional exam requirements/recommendations for international students: Required—TOEFL (minimum score 550 paper-based). Electronic applications accepted. *Faculty research:* Language and literacy, mathematics education, science education, teacher development, school psychology.

University of California, San Diego, Graduate Division, Program in Education Studies, La Jolla, CA 92093. Offers education (M Ed, PhD); educational leadership (Ed D); teaching and learning (MA, Ed D), including bilingual education (MA), curriculum design (MA). Ed D offered jointly with California State University, San Marcos. *Students:* 89 full-time (59 women), 52 part-time (38 women). 228 applicants, 52% accepted, 74 enrolled. In 2016, 68 master's, 6 doctorates awarded. *Degree requirements:* For master's, thesis (for some programs), student teaching; for doctorate, comprehensive exam, thesis/dissertation. *Entrance requirements:* For master's, GRE General Test; CBEST and appropriate CSET exam (for select tracks), current teaching or educational assignment (for select tracks); for doctorate, GRE General Test, current teaching or educational assignment (for select tracks). Additional exam requirements/recommendations for international students: Required—TOEFL (minimum score 550 paper-based; 80 iBT), IELTS (minimum score 7). *Application deadline:* For fall admission, 12/1 for domestic students. Application fee: $105 ($125 for international students). Electronic applications accepted. *Expenses:* Tuition, state resident: full-time $11,220. Tuition, nonresident: full-time $26,322. *Required fees:* $1864. *Financial support:* Fellowships, career-related internships or fieldwork, and scholarships/grants available. Financial award applicants required to submit FAFSA. *Faculty research:* Language, culture and literacy development of deaf/hard of hearing children; equity issues in education; educational reform; evaluation, assessment, and research methodologies; distributed learning. *Unit head:* Alan J. Daly, Chair, 858-822-6472, E-mail: ajdaly@ucsd.edu. *Application contact:* Giselle Van Luit, Graduate Coordinator, 858-534-2958, E-mail: edsinfo@ucsd.edu.

University of Central Arkansas, Graduate School, College of Education, Department of Leadership Studies, Conway, AR 72035-0001. Offers college student personnel (MS); district-level administration (PMC); educational leadership - district level (Ed S); instructional technology (MS); library media and information technology (MS); school counseling (MS); school leadership (MS); school-based leadership adult education program administration (PMC); school-based leadership building administration (PMC); school-based leadership curriculum administration (PMC); school-based leadership gifted and talented program administration (PMC); school-based leadership special education program administration (PMC). *Accreditation:* NCATE. *Program availability:* Part-time, evening/weekend, online learning. *Degree requirements:* For master's and other advanced degree, comprehensive exam. *Entrance requirements:* For master's, GRE. Additional exam requirements/recommendations for international students: Required—TOEFL (minimum score 80 iBT). Electronic applications accepted. *Expenses:* Contact institution.

University of Central Florida, College of Education and Human Performance, Education Doctoral Programs, Orlando, FL 32816. Offers communication sciences and disorders (PhD); curriculum and instruction (Ed D); early childhood education (PhD); educational leadership (Ed D); elementary education (PhD); exceptional education (PhD); exercise physiology (PhD); higher education (PhD); instructional technology (PhD); mathematics education (PhD); methodology, measurement and analysis (PhD); reading education (PhD); science education (PhD); social science education (PhD); TESOL (PhD). *Students:* 127 full-time (91 women), 43 part-time (29 women); includes 33 minority (17 Black or African American, non-Hispanic/Latino; 5 Asian, non-Hispanic/Latino; 7 Hispanic/Latino; 4 Two or more races, non-Hispanic/Latino), 26 international. Average age 37. 163 applicants, 40% accepted, 52 enrolled. In 2016, 57 doctorates awarded. Application fee: $30. Electronic applications accepted. *Expenses:* Tuition, state resident: part-time $288.16 per credit hour. Tuition, nonresident: part-time $1071.31 per credit hour. *Financial support:* In 2016–17, 78 students received support, including 41 fellowships with partial tuition reimbursements available (averaging $5,916 per year), 44 research assistantships with partial tuition reimbursements available (averaging $7,637 per year), 48 teaching assistantships with partial tuition reimbursements available (averaging $9,633 per year). Financial award application deadline: 3/1; financial award applicants required to submit FAFSA. *Unit head:* Dr. Edward Robinson, Director of Doctoral Programs, 407-823-6106, E-mail: edward.robinson@ucf.edu. *Application contact:* Assistant Director, Graduate Admissions, 407-823-2766, Fax: 407-823-6442, E-mail: gradadmissions@ucf.edu.
Website: http://education.ucf.edu/programs.cfm?pid=g&cat=2

University of Cincinnati, Graduate School, College of Education, Criminal Justice, and Human Services, Division of Teacher Education, Program in Curriculum and Instruction, Cincinnati, OH 45221. Offers M Ed, Ed D. *Accreditation:* NCATE. *Program availability:* Part-time. *Degree requirements:* For master's, thesis; for doctorate, thesis/dissertation. *Entrance requirements:* For master's, GRE General Test; for doctorate, GRE General Test, GRE Subject Test. Additional exam requirements/recommendations for international students: Required—TOEFL (minimum score 550 paper-based), TWE (minimum score 4.5), OEPT. Electronic applications accepted. *Expenses: Tuition, area resident:* Full-time $12,790; part-time $389 per credit hour. Tuition, state resident: full-time $13,290; part-time $419 per credit hour. Tuition, nonresident: full-time $24,532, part-time $976 per credit hour. *International tuition:* $24,832 full-time. *Required fees:* $3958; $140 per credit hour. Tuition and fees vary according to course load, degree level, program and reciprocity agreements.

University of Colorado Boulder, Graduate School, School of Education, Division of Curriculum and Instruction, Boulder, CO 80309. Offers MA, PhD. *Accreditation:* NCATE. *Students:* 67 full-time (43 women), 36 part-time (30 women); includes 16 minority (2 Black or African American, non-Hispanic/Latino; 2 Asian, non-Hispanic/Latino; 10

Hispanic/Latino; 2 Two or more races, non-Hispanic/Latino), 1 international. Average age 31. 107 applicants, 60% accepted, 27 enrolled. In 2016, 27 master's, 8 doctorates awarded. Terminal master's awarded for partial completion of doctoral program. *Degree requirements:* For master's, comprehensive exam, thesis or alternative; for doctorate, one foreign language, comprehensive exam, thesis/dissertation. *Entrance requirements:* For master's, GRE General Test or MAT, minimum undergraduate GPA of 2.75; for doctorate, GRE General Test. *Application deadline:* For fall admission, 2/1 for domestic students, 12/1 for international students; for spring admission, 9/1 for domestic and international students. Application fee: $60 ($80 for international students). Electronic applications accepted. Application fee is waived when completed online. *Financial support:* In 2016–17, 147 students received support, including 52 fellowships (averaging $3,246 per year), 29 research assistantships with full and partial tuition reimbursements available (averaging $30,416 per year), 13 teaching assistantships with full and partial tuition reimbursements available (averaging $20,048 per year); institutionally sponsored loans, scholarships/grants, health care benefits, and unspecified assistantships also available. Financial award applicants required to submit FAFSA. *Application contact:* E-mail: edadvise@colorado.edu.
Website: http://www.colorado.edu/education/

University of Colorado Colorado Springs, College of Education, Colorado Springs, CO 80918. Offers counseling and human services (MA); curriculum and instruction (MA); educational leadership (MA); educational leadership, research and policy (PhD); special education (MA); teaching English to speakers of other languages (MA). *Accreditation:* ACA; NCATE. *Program availability:* Part-time, evening/weekend, 100% online, blended/hybrid learning. *Faculty:* 26 full-time (18 women), 33 part-time/adjunct (21 women). *Students:* 136 full-time (94 women), 264 part-time (177 women); includes 99 minority (17 Black or African American, non-Hispanic/Latino; 1 American Indian or Alaska Native, non-Hispanic/Latino; 8 Asian, non-Hispanic/Latino; 55 Hispanic/Latino; 18 Two or more races, non-Hispanic/Latino), 9 international. Average age 35. 152 applicants, 89% accepted, 88 enrolled. In 2016, 161 master's, 11 doctorates awarded. *Degree requirements:* For master's, comprehensive exam, thesis or alternative, microcomputer proficiency; for doctorate, comprehensive exam, thesis/dissertation, research lab. *Entrance requirements:* For master's and doctorate, GRE General Test. Additional exam requirements/recommendations for international students: Recommended—TOEFL (minimum score 550 paper-based; 80 iBT), IELTS (minimum score 6). *Application deadline:* For fall admission, 2/1 priority date for domestic students, 2/1 for international students; for spring admission, 10/15 for domestic students, 10/1 for international students. Applications are processed on a rolling basis. Application fee: $60 ($100 for international students). Electronic applications accepted. *Expenses:* Contact institution. *Financial support:* In 2016–17, 108 students received support. Career-related internships or fieldwork, Federal Work-Study, scholarships/grants, and unspecified assistantships available. Support available to part-time students. Financial award application deadline: 3/1; financial award applicants required to submit FAFSA. *Faculty research:* Linguistically diverse education (LDE), educational policy, evidence-based reading and writing instruction, relational and social aggression, positive behavior supports, inclusive schooling, K-12 education policy. *Total annual research expenditures:* $272,136. *Unit head:* Dr. Valerie Martin Conley, Dean, 719-255-4133, E-mail: vmconley@uccs.edu. *Application contact:* The College of Education Student Resource Office, 719-255-4996, E-mail: education@uccs.edu.
Website: http://www.uccs.edu/coe

University of Connecticut, Graduate School, Neag School of Education, Department of Educational Psychology, Cognition, Instruction, and Learning Technology Program, Storrs, CT 06269. Offers MA, PhD. *Degree requirements:* For master's, comprehensive exam; for doctorate, thesis/dissertation. *Entrance requirements:* For doctorate, GRE General Test. Additional exam requirements/recommendations for international students: Required—TOEFL (minimum score 550 paper-based). Electronic applications accepted.

University of Delaware, College of Education and Human Development, School of Education, Newark, DE 19716. Offers education (PhD); educational leadership (Ed D); higher education (M Ed); instruction (MI); reading (M Ed); school leadership (M Ed); school psychology (MA, Ed S); teaching English as a second language (TESL) (MA). *Accreditation:* NCATE. *Program availability:* Part-time, evening/weekend. Terminal master's awarded for partial completion of doctoral program. *Degree requirements:* For master's, comprehensive exam (for some programs), thesis (for some programs); for doctorate, comprehensive exam (for some programs), thesis/dissertation. *Entrance requirements:* For master's and doctorate, GRE, 3 letters of recommendation. Additional exam requirements/recommendations for international students: Required—TOEFL (minimum score 600 paper-based). Electronic applications accepted. *Faculty research:* Teacher education; curriculum theory and development; community based education models, educational leadership.

University of Denver, Morgridge College of Education, Denver, CO 80208. Offers child, family and school psychology (MA, PhD, Ed S); counseling psychology (MA, PhD); curriculum and instruction (MA, Ed D, PhD); curriculum instruction and teaching (Certificate); early childhood special education (MA, Certificate); educational leadership and policy studies (MA, Ed D, PhD, Certificate); higher education (Ed D, PhD); library and information science (MLIS); research methods and statistics (MA, PhD). *Accreditation:* ALA; APA (one or more programs are accredited). *Program availability:* Part-time, evening/weekend, online learning. *Faculty:* 39 full-time (29 women), 60 part-time/adjunct (42 women). *Students:* 498 full-time (392 women), 362 part-time (282 women); includes 223 minority (63 Black or African American, non-Hispanic/Latino; 6 American Indian or Alaska Native, non-Hispanic/Latino; 20 Asian, non-Hispanic/Latino; 102 Hispanic/Latino; 1 Native Hawaiian or other Pacific Islander, non-Hispanic/Latino; 31 Two or more races, non-Hispanic/Latino), 40 international. Average age 32. 1,027 applicants, 69% accepted, 386 enrolled. In 2016, 252 master's, 36 doctorates, 141 other advanced degrees awarded. Terminal master's awarded for partial completion of doctoral program. *Degree requirements:* For master's, comprehensive exam; for doctorate, 2 foreign languages, comprehensive exam, thesis/dissertation. *Entrance requirements:* For master's and doctorate, GRE General Test or GMAT. Additional exam requirements/recommendations for international students: Required—TOEFL (minimum score 550 paper-based; 80 iBT). *Application deadline:* Applications are processed on a rolling basis. Application fee: $65. Electronic applications accepted. *Expenses:* $29,022 per year full-time. *Financial support:* In 2016–17, 697 students received support, including 37 research assistantships with tuition reimbursements available (averaging $11,209 per year), 66 teaching assistantships with tuition reimbursements available (averaging $3,742 per year); career-related internships or fieldwork, Federal Work-Study, institutionally sponsored loans, scholarships/grants, and unspecified assistantships also available. Support available to part-time students. Financial award application deadline: 2/15; financial award applicants required to submit FAFSA. *Faculty research:* Early childhood education, access and equity, educational leadership, family and school partnerships, neurodevelopmental disorders. *Total annual research expenditures:* $3.3 million. *Unit head:* Dr. Karen Riley, Dean, 303-871-3665, Fax: 303-871-4456, E-mail: karen.riley@du.edu. *Application contact:* Jodi Dye, Director of Admissions, 303-871-2510, Fax: 303-871-4456, E-mail: jodi.dye@du.edu.
Website: http://morgridge.du.edu

University of Detroit Mercy, College of Liberal Arts and Education, Detroit, MI 48221. Offers addiction counseling (MA); addiction studies (Certificate); clinical mental health counseling (MA); clinical psychology (MA, PhD); computer and information systems (MS); criminal justice (MA); curriculum and instruction (MA); economics (MA); educational administration (MA); financial economics (MA); industrial/organizational psychology (MA); information assurance (MS); intelligence analysis (MA); liberal studies (MALS); religious studies (MA); school counseling (MA, Certificate); school psychology (Spec); security administration (MS); special education: emotionally impaired/behaviorally disordered (MA); special education: learning disabilities (MA). *Program availability:* Part-time, evening/weekend. *Degree requirements:* For doctorate, departmental qualifying exam. *Faculty research:* Psychology of aging, history of technology, Renaissance humanism, U.S. and Japanese economic relations.

University of Florida, Graduate School, College of Education, School of Teaching and Learning, Gainesville, FL 32611. Offers curriculum and instruction (M Ed, MAE, Ed D, PhD, Ed S); elementary education (M Ed, MAE); English education (M Ed, MAE); mathematics education (M Ed, MAE); reading education (M Ed, MAE); science education (M Ed, MAE); social studies education (M Ed, MAE). *Accreditation:* NCATE. *Program availability:* Part-time, evening/weekend, online learning. Terminal master's awarded for partial completion of doctoral program. *Degree requirements:* For master's, comprehensive exam (for some programs), thesis (for some programs); for doctorate, comprehensive exam (for some programs), thesis/dissertation (for some programs). *Entrance requirements:* For master's and doctorate, GRE General Test, minimum GPA of 3.0; for Ed S, GRE General Test. Additional exam requirements/recommendations for international students: Required—TOEFL (minimum score 550 paper-based; 80 iBT), IELTS (minimum score 6). Electronic applications accepted. *Faculty research:* STEM education; curriculum; teaching and teacher education; languages and literacy; schools, culture, and society; theories and processes of learning.

University of Hawaii at Manoa, Graduate Division, College of Education, Department of Curriculum Studies, Honolulu, HI 96822. Offers curriculum studies (M Ed); early childhood education (M Ed). *Program availability:* Part-time. *Degree requirements:* For master's, thesis optional. *Entrance requirements:* Additional exam requirements/recommendations for international students: Required—TOEFL (minimum score 500 paper-based; 61 iBT), IELTS (minimum score 5).

University of Hawaii at Manoa, Graduate Division, College of Education, PhD in Education Program, Honolulu, HI 96822. Offers curriculum and instruction (PhD); educational administration (PhD); educational foundations (PhD); educational policy studies (PhD); educational psychology (PhD); exceptionalities (PhD); kinesiology (PhD); learning design and technology (PhD). *Program availability:* Part-time, evening/weekend. *Degree requirements:* For doctorate, thesis/dissertation. *Entrance requirements:* For doctorate, GRE General Test, sample of written work. Additional exam requirements/recommendations for international students: Required—TOEFL (minimum score 600 paper-based; 100 iBT), IELTS (minimum score 7).

University of Holy Cross, Program in Education and Counseling, New Orleans, LA 70131-7399. Offers administration and supervision (M Ed); curriculum and instruction (M Ed); marriage and family counseling (MA); school counseling (M Ed, MA). *Accreditation:* ACA; NCATE. *Program availability:* Part-time, evening/weekend. *Degree requirements:* For master's, thesis. *Entrance requirements:* For master's, GRE General Test, minimum GPA of 2.7.

University of Houston, College of Education, Department of Curriculum and Instruction, Houston, TX 77204. Offers administration and supervision (M Ed); curriculum and instruction (M Ed, Ed D); professional leadership (Ed D). *Accreditation:* NCATE. *Program availability:* Part-time, evening/weekend. *Degree requirements:* For master's, comprehensive exam, thesis optional; for doctorate, comprehensive exam, thesis/dissertation. *Entrance requirements:* For master's and doctorate, GRE, minimum cumulative undergraduate GPA of 2.6, 3 letters of recommendation, resume/vita, goal statement. Additional exam requirements/recommendations for international students: Required—TOEFL (minimum score 550 paper-based; 79 iBT). Electronic applications accepted. *Faculty research:* Teaching-learning process, instructional technology in schools, teacher education, classroom management, at-risk students.

University of Houston–Clear Lake, School of Education, Program in Curriculum and Instruction, Houston, TX 77058-1002. Offers curriculum and instruction (MS); early childhood education (MS); reading (MS); school library and information science (MS). *Program availability:* Part-time, evening/weekend. *Degree requirements:* For master's, thesis (for some programs). *Entrance requirements:* For master's, GRE or minimum GPA of 3.0 in last 60 hours. Additional exam requirements/recommendations for international students: Required—TOEFL (minimum score 550 paper-based). Electronic applications accepted.

University of Houston–Downtown, College of Public Service, Department of Urban Education, Houston, TX 77002. Offers curriculum and instruction (MAT); elementary and secondary education (MAT). *Program availability:* Part-time, evening/weekend, 100% online. *Faculty:* 6 full-time (2 women), 2 part-time/adjunct (both women). *Students:* 7 full-time (3 women), 47 part-time (42 women); includes 45 minority (18 Black or African American, non-Hispanic/Latino; 6 Asian, non-Hispanic/Latino; 21 Hispanic/Latino). Average age 34. 36 applicants, 89% accepted, 28 enrolled. In 2016, 11 master's awarded. *Degree requirements:* For master's, capstone course with completed project, position paper, grant proposal, empirical study, curriculum development/revision, or advanced technology project presented at annual Graduate Project Exhibition. *Entrance requirements:* For master's, GRE, personal statement, 3 recommendation forms. Additional exam requirements/recommendations for international students: Required—TOEFL (minimum score 550 paper-based; 80 iBT). *Application deadline:* For fall admission, 7/15 for domestic and international students; for spring admission, 11/15 for domestic and international students. Application fee: $35 ($60 for international students). Electronic applications accepted. *Expenses:* $305.50 in-state, per credit; $663.50 out-of-state, per credit. *Financial support:* Federal Work-Study and scholarships/grants available. Financial award application deadline: 4/1; financial award applicants required to submit FAFSA. *Unit head:* Dr. Ron Beebe, Department Chair, 713-221-8689, Fax: 713-226-5294, E-mail: beeber@uhd.edu. *Application contact:* Ceshia Love, Director of Graduate and International Admissions, 713-221-8093, Fax: 713-223-7408, E-mail: gradadmissions@uhd.edu.
Website: https://www.uhd.edu/academics/public-service/urban-education/Pages/default.aspx

University of Houston–Victoria, School of Education, Health Professions and Human Development, Victoria, TX 77901-4450. Offers administration and supervision (M Ed); adult and higher education (M Ed); counselor education (M Ed); curriculum and instruction (M Ed); educational technology (M Ed); special education (M Ed). *Program availability:* Part-time, evening/weekend, online learning. *Degree requirements:* For master's, comprehensive exam, project or thesis. *Entrance requirements:* For master's, GRE General Test. Additional exam requirements/recommendations for international students: Required—TOEFL. Electronic applications accepted. *Faculty research:* Reading and language arts education, evaluation and diagnosis of special children's abilities.

University of Idaho, College of Graduate Studies, College of Education, Department of Curriculum and Instruction, Moscow, ID 83844. Offers career and technology education (M Ed); curriculum and instruction (M Ed, Ed S); special education (M Ed). *Faculty:* 25 full-time, 2 part-time/adjunct. *Students:* 21 full-time (16 women), 35 part-time (29 women). Average age 37. In 2016, 17 master's awarded. *Entrance requirements:* For master's, minimum GPA of 3.0. Additional exam requirements/recommendations for international students: Required—TOEFL. *Application deadline:* For fall admission, 8/1 for domestic students; for spring admission, 12/15 for domestic students. Applications are processed on a rolling basis. Application fee: $60. Electronic applications accepted. *Expenses:* Tuition, state resident: full-time $6460; part-time $414 per credit hour. Tuition, nonresident: full-time $21,268; part-time $1237 per credit hour. *Required fees:* $2070; $60 per credit hour. Full-time tuition and fees vary according to course load and reciprocity agreements. *Financial support:* Research assistantships and teaching assistantships available. Financial award applicants required to submit FAFSA. *Unit head:* Dr. Allen Kitchel, Interim Chair, 208-885-6587, E-mail: teached@uidaho.edu. *Application contact:* Sean Scoggin, Graduate Recruitment Coordinator, 208-885-4001, Fax: 208-885-4406, E-mail: graduateadmissions@uidaho.edu.
Website: http://www.uidaho.edu/ed/ci

University of Illinois at Chicago, College of Education, Department of Curriculum and Instruction, Chicago, IL 60607-7128. Offers curriculum studies (PhD); elementary education (M Ed); secondary education (M Ed). *Program availability:* Part-time, evening/weekend. *Degree requirements:* For doctorate, thesis/dissertation. *Entrance requirements:* For master's, minimum GPA of 2.75; for doctorate, GRE General Test, minimum GPA of 2.75. Additional exam requirements/recommendations for international students: Required—TOEFL. Electronic applications accepted. *Faculty research:* Curriculum theory, curriculum development, research on teaching, curriculum and context, reading/literacy.

University of Illinois at Urbana–Champaign, Graduate College, College of Education, Department of Curriculum and Instruction, Champaign, IL 61820. Offers curriculum and instruction (Ed M, MA, MS, Ed D, PhD, CAS); early childhood education (Ed M); elementary education (Ed M); secondary education (Ed M). *Program availability:* Part-time, online learning.

University of Indianapolis, Graduate Programs, School of Education, Indianapolis, IN 46227-3697. Offers art education (MAT); biology (MAT); chemistry (MAT); curriculum and instruction (MA); earth sciences (MAT); education (MA, MAT); educational leadership (MA); elementary education (MA); English (MAT); French (MAT); math (MAT); physical education (MAT); physics (MAT); secondary education (MA), including art education, education, English education, social studies education; social studies (MAT); Spanish (MAT). *Accreditation:* NCATE. *Program availability:* Part-time, evening/weekend. *Entrance requirements:* For master's, GRE Subject Test, PRAXIS I, minimum GPA of 2.5, 3 letters of recommendation, interview. Additional exam requirements/recommendations for international students: Required—TOEFL (minimum score 550 paper-based). *Faculty research:* Assessment of teacher education, perceptions of prospective teachers by parents.

University of Jamestown, Program in Education, Jamestown, ND 58405. Offers curriculum and instruction (M Ed). *Degree requirements:* For master's, thesis or project.

The University of Kansas, Graduate Studies, School of Education, Department of Curriculum and Teaching, Lawrence, KS 66045. Offers curriculum and instruction (MA, MS Ed, PhD). *Program availability:* Part-time, evening/weekend, online learning. *Students:* 90 full-time (57 women), 328 part-time (286 women); includes 55 minority (18 Black or African American, non-Hispanic/Latino; 3 American Indian or Alaska Native, non-Hispanic/Latino; 9 Asian, non-Hispanic/Latino; 6 Hispanic/Latino; 19 Two or more races, non-Hispanic/Latino), 20 international. Average age 34. 225 applicants, 85% accepted, 149 enrolled. In 2016, 70 master's, 17 doctorates awarded. *Entrance requirements:* For master's, minimum GPA of 3.0, official transcript(s), resume, statement of goals/purpose, three letters of recommendation; for doctorate, GRE General Test, minimum graduate GPA of 3.5, official transcript(s), resume, statement of goals/purpose, three letters of recommendation, writing sample. Additional exam requirements/recommendations for international students: Required—TOEFL, IELTS. *Application deadline:* For fall admission, 3/15 priority date for domestic and international students; for spring admission, 10/15 priority date for domestic and international students. Application fee: $65 ($85 for international students). Electronic applications accepted. *Financial support:* Fellowships, research assistantships, teaching assistantships, Federal Work-Study, scholarships/grants, and unspecified assistantships available. Financial award application deadline: 3/15; financial award applicants required to submit FAFSA. *Faculty research:* Community-based field experiences in teacher education, vocabulary and narrative development of primary students, narrative inquiry, engaging students in critical thinking by using technology in the classroom, argumentation and evaluation intervention in science education. *Unit head:* Dr. Steven Hugh White, Chair of Curriculum and Teaching, 785-864-9662, E-mail: s-white@ku.edu. *Application contact:* Susan M. McGee, Graduate Admissions Coordinator, 785-864-4437, E-mail: ctdepartment@ku.edu.
Website: http://ct.soe.ku.edu/

University of Kentucky, Graduate School, College of Education, Program in Curriculum and Instruction, Lexington, KY 40506-0032. Offers curriculum and instruction (Ed D, PhD); elementary education (MA Ed); instructional system design (MS Ed); literacy (MA Ed); middle school education (MA Ed, MS Ed); secondary education (MA Ed, MS Ed). *Accreditation:* NCATE. *Degree requirements:* For master's, comprehensive exam, thesis optional; for doctorate, comprehensive exam, thesis/dissertation. *Entrance requirements:* For master's, GRE General Test, minimum undergraduate GPA of 2.75; for doctorate, GRE General Test, minimum graduate GPA of 3.0. Additional exam requirements/recommendations for international students: Required—TOEFL (minimum score 550 paper-based). Electronic applications accepted. *Faculty research:* Educational reform, multicultural education, classroom instructional practices, performance based assessment, primary school programs.

University of Louisiana at Lafayette, College of Education, Graduate Studies and Research in Education, Program in Curriculum and Instruction, Lafayette, LA 70504. Offers M Ed. *Accreditation:* NCATE. *Degree requirements:* For master's, thesis or alternative. *Entrance requirements:* For master's, GRE General Test, teaching certificate. Additional exam requirements/recommendations for international students: Required—TOEFL (minimum score 550 paper-based). Electronic applications accepted.

University of Louisiana at Monroe, Graduate School, College of Arts, Education, and Sciences, School of Education, Program in Curriculum and Instruction, Monroe, LA 71209-0001. Offers art education (M Ed); biology education (M Ed); chemistry education (M Ed); curriculum and instruction (Ed D); early childhood education (M Ed); earth science education (M Ed); educational leadership (M Ed); elementary education (1-5) (M Ed); English as a second language (M Ed); English education (M Ed); family and consumer education (M Ed); French education (M Ed); history education (M Ed); math education (M Ed); middle school education (M Ed); music education (M Ed); reading education (K-12) (M Ed); Spanish education (M Ed); special education - academically gifted (M Ed); special education - early intervention (M Ed); special education - educational diagnostician (M Ed); special education - mild/moderate disabilities (M Ed); speech education (M Ed). *Accreditation:* NCATE. *Faculty:* 8 full-time (4 women), 4 part-time/adjunct (3 women). *Students:* 13 full-time (11 women), 80 part-time (65 women); includes 25 minority (19 Black or African American, non-Hispanic/Latino; 1 Asian, non-Hispanic/Latino; 3 Hispanic/Latino; 2 Two or more races, non-Hispanic/Latino). Average age 37. 118 applicants, 30% accepted, 16 enrolled. In 2016, 23 master's, 4 doctorates awarded. *Degree requirements:* For master's, comprehensive exam (for some programs), thesis; for doctorate, thesis/dissertation, internships. *Entrance requirements:* For master's, GRE General Test; for doctorate, GRE General Test, minimum undergraduate GPA of 2.75, graduate 3.25. Additional exam requirements/recommendations for international students: Required—TOEFL (minimum score 500 paper-based; 61 iBT). *Application deadline:* For fall admission, 8/24 priority date for domestic students, 7/1 for international students; for winter admission, 12/14 priority date for domestic students; for spring admission, 1/19 for domestic students, 11/1 for international students. Applications are processed on a rolling basis. Application fee: $20 ($30 for international students). Electronic applications accepted. *Expenses:* Tuition, state resident: full-time $6489. Tuition, nonresident: full-time $18,589. *Required fees:* $8984. Tuition and fees vary according to course level, course load, degree level and program. *Financial support:* Research assistantships, career-related internships or fieldwork, Federal Work-Study, and unspecified assistantships available. Financial award application deadline: 4/1; financial award applicants required to submit FAFSA. *Unit head:* Dr. Dorothy Schween, Director, 318-342-1268, Fax: 318-342-3131, E-mail: schween@ulm.edu.

University of Louisville, Graduate School, College of Education and Human Development, Department of Teaching and Learning, Louisville, KY 40292-0001. Offers art education (MAT); autism and applied behavior analysis (Certificate); curriculum and instruction (PhD); early elementary education (MAT); exercise physiology (MS); health and physical education (MAT); health professions education (Certificate); higher education (MA); human resources and organization development (MS); instructional technology (M Ed); interdisciplinary early childhood education (MAT); middle school education (MAT); music education (MAT); secondary education (MAT); special education (MAT); sport administration (MS); teacher leadership (M Ed). *Program availability:* Part-time, evening/weekend. *Students:* 116 full-time (68 women), 158 part-time (112 women); includes 46 minority (24 Black or African American, non-Hispanic/Latino; 8 Asian, non-Hispanic/Latino; 5 Hispanic/Latino; 9 Two or more races, non-Hispanic/Latino), 6 international. Average age 30. 114 applicants, 71% accepted, 57 enrolled. In 2016, 59 master's, 3 doctorates awarded. *Application deadline:* For spring admission, 1/1 priority date for international students. Application fee: $60. *Expenses:* Tuition, state resident: full-time $12,246; part-time $681 per credit hour. Tuition, nonresident: full-time $25,486; part-time $1417 per credit hour. *Required fees:* $196. Tuition and fees vary according to program and reciprocity agreements. *Financial support:* Application deadline: 6/1; applicants required to submit FAFSA. *Faculty research:* STEM teaching and learning; content literacy for English language learners; social justice in teacher education; adolescent literacy; mathematics teacher development. *Total annual research expenditures:* $1.7 million. *Unit head:* Dr. Ann E. Larson, Dean, College of Education and Human Development, 502-852-6411, Fax: 502-852-1464, E-mail: ann@louisville.edu. *Application contact:* Betty Hampton, Director of Graduate Student Services, 502-852-5597, Fax: 502-852-1465, E-mail: edadvise@louisville.edu.
Website: http://louisville.edu/delphi

University of Manitoba, Faculty of Graduate Studies, Faculty of Education, Department of Curriculum, Teaching and Learning, Winnipeg, MB R3T 2N2, Canada. Offers language and literacy (M Ed); second language education (M Ed); studies in curriculum, teaching and learning (M Ed). *Degree requirements:* For master's, thesis or alternative.

University of Mary, Liffrig Family School of Education and Behavioral Sciences, Department of Education, Bismarck, ND 58504-9652. Offers curriculum, instruction and assessment (M Ed); education (Ed D); elementary administration (M Ed); reading (M Ed); secondary administration (M Ed); special education strategist (M Ed). *Program availability:* Part-time. *Degree requirements:* For master's, portfolio or thesis. *Entrance requirements:* For master's, interview, letters of reference, minimum GPA of 2.5. Additional exam requirements/recommendations for international students: Required—TOEFL (minimum score 500 paper-based; 71 iBT). Electronic applications accepted.

University of Mary Hardin-Baylor, Graduate Studies in Education, Belton, TX 76513. Offers curriculum and instruction (M Ed); educational administration (M Ed, Ed D), including higher education (Ed D), leadership in nursing education (Ed D), P-12 (Ed D). *Program availability:* Part-time, evening/weekend. *Faculty:* 15 full-time (11 women), 9 part-time/adjunct (5 women). *Students:* 55 full-time (40 women), 79 part-time (60 women); includes 50 minority (29 Black or African American, non-Hispanic/Latino; 1 Asian, non-Hispanic/Latino; 18 Hispanic/Latino; 2 Two or more races, non-Hispanic/Latino), 3 international. Average age 38. 20 applicants, 95% accepted, 19 enrolled. In 2016, 23 master's, 19 doctorates awarded. *Degree requirements:* For master's, comprehensive exam; for doctorate, thesis/dissertation. *Entrance requirements:* For master's, minimum GPA of 3.0, interview; for doctorate, minimum GPA of 3.5, interview, essay, resume, employment verification, 3 letters of recommendation. Additional exam requirements/recommendations for international students: Required—TOEFL (minimum score 60 iBT), IELTS (minimum score 4.5). *Application deadline:* For fall admission, 6/1 for domestic students, 4/30 priority date for international students; for spring admission, 11/1 for domestic students, 9/30 priority date for international students. Applications are processed on a rolling basis. Application fee: $35 ($135 for international students). Electronic applications accepted. *Expenses:* $885 per credit hour. *Financial support:* In 2016–17, 99 students received support. Federal Work-Study and scholarships for some active duty military personnel available. Support available to part-time students. Financial award application deadline: 6/1; financial award applicants required to submit FAFSA. *Faculty research:* Motivational orientation of preservice teachers. *Unit head:* Dr. Craig Hammonds, Director, Graduate Programs in Education, 254-295-4189, E-mail: chammonds@umhb.edu. *Application contact:* Sharon Aguilera, Assistant Director, Graduate Admissions, 254-295-4835, Fax: 254-295-5038, E-mail: saguilera@umhb.edu.
Website: http://graduate.umhb.edu/education/

University of Maryland, College Park, Academic Affairs, College of Education, Department of Teaching, Learning, Policy and Leadership, College Park, MD 20742. Offers reading (M Ed, MA, PhD, CAGS); secondary education (M Ed, MA, Ed D, PhD, CAGS); teaching English to speakers of other languages (M Ed). *Accreditation:* NCATE. *Program availability:* Part-time, evening/weekend, online learning. *Degree requirements:* For master's, comprehensive exam, seminar paper; for doctorate, comprehensive exam, thesis/dissertation, published paper, oral exam. *Entrance requirements:* For master's, GRE General Test or MAT, minimum GPA of 3.0, 3 letters of recommendation; for doctorate, GRE General Test or MAT, minimum undergraduate GPA of 3.0, graduate 3.5; 3 letters of recommendation. Electronic applications accepted. *Faculty research:* Teacher preparation, curriculum study, in-service education.

University of Massachusetts Lowell, Graduate School of Education, Lowell, MA 01854. Offers curriculum and instruction (M Ed). *Accreditation:* NCATE. *Program availability:* Part-time, evening/weekend, online learning. Terminal master's awarded for partial completion of doctoral program. *Entrance requirements:* For master's, GRE

General Test. Additional exam requirements/recommendations for international students: Required—TOEFL. Electronic applications accepted.

University of Memphis, Graduate School, College of Education, Department of Instruction and Curriculum Leadership, Memphis, TN 38152. Offers advanced studies in teaching and learning (M Ed); applied behavior analysis (Graduate Certificate); autism studies (Graduate Certificate); early childhood education (MAT, MS, Ed D); elementary education (MAT); instruction and curriculum (MS, Ed D); instruction design and technology (MS, Ed D); instructional design and technology (Graduate Certificate); literacy, leadership, and coaching (Graduate Certificate); reading (MS, Ed D); school library information specialist (Graduate Certificate); secondary education (MAT); special education (MAT, MS, Ed D); STEM teacher leadership (Graduate Certificate); urban education (Graduate Certificate). *Accreditation:* NCATE (one or more programs are accredited). *Program availability:* Part-time. *Faculty:* 24 full-time (14 women), 17 part-time/adjunct (12 women). *Students:* 66 full-time (52 women), 315 part-time (243 women); includes 163 minority (132 Black or African American, non-Hispanic/Latino; 1 American Indian or Alaska Native, non-Hispanic/Latino; 6 Asian, non-Hispanic/Latino; 13 Hispanic/Latino; 1 Native Hawaiian or other Pacific Islander, non-Hispanic/Latino; 10 Two or more races, non-Hispanic/Latino), 4 international. Average age 35. 215 applicants, 78% accepted, 120 enrolled. In 2016, 111 master's, 21 doctorates, 8 other advanced degrees awarded. Terminal master's awarded for partial completion of doctoral program. *Degree requirements:* For master's, comprehensive exam, thesis or alternative; for doctorate, comprehensive exam, thesis/dissertation. *Entrance requirements:* For master's, GRE General Test, PRAXIS, minimum GPA of 2.5, letters of reference; for doctorate, GRE General Test, GRE Subject Test, 2 years of teaching experience, letters of reference, statement of purpose, interview. Additional exam requirements/recommendations for international students: Required—TOEFL (minimum score 550 paper-based; 79 iBT). *Application deadline:* For fall admission, 4/1 priority date for domestic students; for spring admission, 10/1 priority date for domestic students; for summer admission, 2/1 priority date for domestic students. Applications are processed on a rolling basis. Application fee: $35 ($60 for international students). Electronic applications accepted. *Expenses:* $5,231.50 per semester full-time in-state, $9,623.50 full-time out-of-state. *Financial support:* In 2016–17, 2 research assistantships with full tuition reimbursements (averaging $10,000 per year), 3 teaching assistantships with full tuition reimbursements (averaging $10,666 per year) were awarded; career-related internships or fieldwork, Federal Work-Study, institutionally sponsored loans, scholarships/grants, traineeships, and unspecified assistantships also available. Support available to part-time students. Financial award application deadline: 2/1; financial award applicants required to submit FAFSA. *Faculty research:* Effective urban teachers, preparation and retention of urban teachers, technology utilization in schools, field-based teacher preparation programs, effective use of online instruction. *Unit head:* Dr. Angiline Powell, Interim Chair, 901-678-3310, E-mail: apowell3@memphis.edu. *Application contact:* Dr. James Meindl, Coordinator of Graduate Studies, 901-678-3310, E-mail: jnmeindl@memphis.edu.
Website: http://www.memphis.edu/icl/

University of Michigan–Dearborn, College of Education, Health, and Human Services, Doctoral Program in Education, Dearborn, MI 48126. Offers curriculum and practice (Ed D); educational leadership (Ed D); metropolitan education (Ed D). *Program availability:* Part-time, evening/weekend. *Faculty:* 27 full-time (19 women), 5 part-time/adjunct (0 women). *Students:* 2 full-time (both women), 21 part-time (15 women); includes 9 minority (7 Black or African American, non-Hispanic/Latino; 1 Asian, non-Hispanic/Latino; 1 Hispanic/Latino). Average age 43. 14 applicants, 64% accepted, 7 enrolled. In 2016, 3 doctorates awarded. *Degree requirements:* For doctorate, comprehensive exam, thesis/dissertation. *Entrance requirements:* For doctorate, GRE (taken within the last 5 years), master's degree with minimum GPA of 3.3, 3 letters of recommendation (1 from faculty), 3 years' professional and/or teaching experience. Additional exam requirements/recommendations for international students: Required—TOEFL (minimum score 560 paper-based; 84 iBT), IELTS (minimum score 6.5). *Application deadline:* For fall admission, 3/1 for domestic and international students. Application fee: $60. Electronic applications accepted. *Expenses:* Contact institution. *Financial support:* In 2016–17, 5 students received support. Scholarships/grants available. Financial award application deadline: 3/1; financial award applicants required to submit FAFSA. *Faculty research:* Educational leadership, English language learning, community-based education, urban education, educational technology. *Unit head:* Dr. Chris Burke, Director, 313-593-5319, E-mail: cjfburke@umich.edu. *Application contact:* Joann Otlewski, Program Assistant, 313-593-5090, E-mail: joanno@umich.edu.
Website: http://umdearborn.edu/cehhs/cehhs_edd/

University of Michigan–Dearborn, College of Education, Health, and Human Services, Education Specialist Program, Dearborn, MI 48126. Offers curriculum and practice (Ed S); educational leadership (Ed S); metropolitan education (Ed S). *Program availability:* Part-time, evening/weekend. *Faculty:* 9 full-time (4 women), 4 part-time/adjunct (0 women). *Students:* 6 part-time (5 women); includes 1 minority (Black or African American, non-Hispanic/Latino). Average age 38. 3 applicants, 100% accepted, 2 enrolled. In 2016, 2 Ed Ss awarded. *Entrance requirements:* For degree, GRE, master's degree with minimum GPA of 3.3; at least 3 years' teaching experience or the equivalent experience working in a professional setting. Additional exam requirements/recommendations for international students: Required—TOEFL (minimum score 560 paper-based; 84 iBT), IELTS (minimum score 6.5). *Application deadline:* For fall admission, 8/1 for domestic students, 5/1 for international students; for winter admission, 12/1 for domestic students, 9/1 for international students; for spring admission, 4/1 for domestic students, 1/1 for international students. Applications are processed on a rolling basis. Application fee: $60. Electronic applications accepted. *Expenses:* Contact institution. *Financial support:* Scholarships/grants available. Financial award application deadline: 3/1; financial award applicants required to submit FAFSA. *Faculty research:* Educational leadership, metropolitan education, curriculum and practice, special education, assessment. *Unit head:* Dr. Bonnie Beyer, Director, 313-593-5583, E-mail: beyer@umich.edu. *Application contact:* Joann Otlewski, Graduate Programs Assistant, 313-593-5090, E-mail: joanno@umich.edu.
Website: http://umdearborn.edu/cehhs/cehhs_eds/

University of Michigan–Flint, School of Education and Human Services, Department of Education, Flint, MI 48502. Offers curriculum and instruction (Ed S); early childhood education (MA); education (Ed D); educational leadership (Ed S); educational technology (MA), including curriculum and instruction, developer; literacy education (MA); secondary education with certification (MA). *Program availability:* Part-time, evening/weekend, 100% online, mixed mode format (for some programs). *Faculty:* 14 full-time (9 women), 30 part-time/adjunct (17 women). *Students:* 31 full-time (18 women), 199 part-time (144 women); includes 61 minority (48 Black or African American, non-Hispanic/Latino; 1 Asian, non-Hispanic/Latino; 6 Hispanic/Latino; 1 Native Hawaiian or other Pacific Islander, non-Hispanic/Latino; 5 Two or more races, non-Hispanic/Latino), 2 international. Average age 39. 124 applicants, 86% accepted, 75 enrolled. In 2016, 77 master's, 1 doctorate awarded. *Degree requirements:* For master's, thesis optional; for doctorate, thesis/dissertation. *Entrance requirements:* For master's, bachelor's degree from regionally-accredited institution, minimum overall undergraduate GPA of 3.0; for doctorate, Ed S; minimum overall graduate GPA of 3.3 (6.0 on a 9.0 scale) or equivalent; at least 3 years of work experience in a P-16 educational institution or in an education-related position; for Ed S, MA or MS in education-related field from accredited institution; minimum overall graduate GPA of 3.0 (6.0 on a 9.0 scale) or equivalent; at least 3 years of work experience in an educational setting. Additional exam requirements/recommendations for international students: Required—TOEFL (minimum score 84 iBT), IELTS (minimum score 6.5). *Application deadline:* For fall admission, 8/1 for domestic students, 5/1 for international students; for winter admission, 11/15 for domestic students, 9/15 for international students; for spring admission, 3/15 for domestic students, 1/15 for international students; for summer admission, 5/15 for domestic students. Applications are processed on a rolling basis. Application fee: $55. Electronic applications accepted. *Expenses:* Contact institution. *Financial support:* Federal Work-Study, scholarships/grants, and unspecified assistantships available. Support available to part-time students. Financial award application deadline: 3/1; financial award applicants required to submit FAFSA. *Unit head:* Dr. Mary Jo Finney, Department Chair/Associate Professor, 810-766-6617, E-mail: mjfinney@umflint.edu. *Application contact:* Bradley T. Maki, Director of Graduate Admissions, 810-762-3171, Fax: 810-766-6789, E-mail: bmaki@umflint.edu.
Website: https://www.umflint.edu/education/graduate-programs

University of Minnesota, Twin Cities Campus, Graduate School, College of Education and Human Development, Department of Curriculum and Instruction, Minneapolis, MN 55455-0213. Offers art education (M Ed, MA, PhD); curriculum and instruction (M Ed, MA, PhD); elementary education (MA, PhD); English education (PhD); language and immersion education (Certificate); learning technologies (MA, PhD); literacy education (MA, PhD); second language education (MA, PhD); social studies education (MA, PhD); STEM education (MA, PhD); teaching (M Ed), including mathematics, science, social studies, teaching; teaching English to speakers of other languages (MA); technology enhanced learning (Certificate). *Faculty:* 37 full-time (20 women). *Students:* 411 full-time (288 women), 317 part-time (223 women); includes 153 minority (37 Black or African American, non-Hispanic/Latino; 7 American Indian or Alaska Native, non-Hispanic/Latino; 31 Asian, non-Hispanic/Latino; 48 Hispanic/Latino; 1 Native Hawaiian or other Pacific Islander, non-Hispanic/Latino; 29 Two or more races, non-Hispanic/Latino), 53 international. Average age 32. 672 applicants, 66% accepted, 400 enrolled. In 2016, 645 master's, 33 doctorates, 27 other advanced degrees awarded. Application fee: $75 ($95 for international students). *Financial support:* In 2016–17, 13 fellowships, 36 research assistantships with full tuition reimbursements (averaging $8,454 per year), 61 teaching assistantships with full tuition reimbursements (averaging $11,406 per year) were awarded. *Faculty research:* Teaching and learning; influence of cultural, linguistic, social, political, and technological factors on teaching, learning and educational research; relationship between educational practice and a democratic and just society; urban education; immigrant education, racial justice and education. *Total annual research expenditures:* $684,005. *Unit head:* Dr. Cynthia Lewis, Chair, 612-625-6313, E-mail: lewis@umn.edu. *Application contact:* Dr. Gillian Roehrig, Director of Graduate Studies, 612-625-0561, E-mail: roehr013@umn.edu.
Website: http://www.cehd.umn.edu/ci

University of Missouri, Office of Research and Graduate Studies, College of Education, Department of Educational, School, and Counseling Psychology, Columbia, MO 65211. Offers counseling psychology (M Ed, MA, PhD, Ed S); educational psychology (M Ed, MA, PhD, Ed S); learning and instruction (M Ed); school psychology (M Ed, MA, PhD, Ed S). *Accreditation:* APA (one or more programs are accredited). *Program availability:* Part-time. *Faculty:* 29 full-time (12 women), 1 part-time/adjunct (0 women). *Students:* 177 full-time (106 women), 204 part-time (102 women). *Degree requirements:* For doctorate, thesis/dissertation. *Entrance requirements:* For master's, doctorate, and Ed S, GRE General Test, minimum GPA of 3.0. Additional exam requirements/recommendations for international students: Required—TOEFL (minimum score 580 paper-based; 92 iBT). *Application deadline:* For fall admission, 12/1 priority date for domestic and international students. Applications are processed on a rolling basis. Application fee: $75 ($90 for international students). Electronic applications accepted. *Expenses:* Tuition, state resident: full-time $6347; part-time $352.60 per credit hour. Tuition, nonresident: full-time $17,379; part-time $965.50 per credit hour. *Required fees:* $1035. Tuition and fees vary according to course load, campus/location and program. *Financial support:* Fellowships, research assistantships, teaching assistantships, institutionally sponsored loans, traineeships, health care benefits, and unspecified assistantships available. Support available to part-time students.
Website: http://education.missouri.edu/ESCP/

University of Missouri, Office of Research and Graduate Studies, College of Education, Department of Learning, Teaching and Curriculum, Columbia, MO 65211. Offers agricultural education (M Ed, PhD, Ed S); art education (M Ed, PhD, Ed S); business and office education (M Ed, PhD, Ed S); early childhood education (M Ed, PhD, Ed S); elementary education (M Ed, PhD, Ed S); English education (M Ed, PhD, Ed S); foreign language education (M Ed, PhD, Ed S); health education and promotion (M Ed, PhD); learning and instruction (M Ed); marketing education (M Ed, PhD, Ed S); mathematics education (M Ed, PhD, Ed S); music education (M Ed, PhD, Ed S); reading education (M Ed, PhD, Ed S); science education (M Ed, PhD, Ed S); social studies education (M Ed, PhD, Ed S); vocational education (M Ed, PhD, Ed S). *Program availability:* Part-time. *Faculty:* 30 full-time (18 women), 1 (woman) part-time/adjunct. *Students:* 157 full-time (124 women), 157 part-time (125 women). Terminal master's awarded for partial completion of doctoral program. *Degree requirements:* For doctorate, thesis/dissertation. *Entrance requirements:* For master's and Ed S, GRE General Test or MAT, minimum GPA of 3.0; for doctorate, GRE General Test, minimum GPA of 3.0. Additional exam requirements/recommendations for international students: Required—TOEFL (minimum score 600 paper-based; 100 iBT). *Application deadline:* For fall admission, 12/1 priority date for domestic and international students. Applications are processed on a rolling basis. Application fee: $75 ($90 for international students). Electronic applications accepted. *Expenses:* Tuition, state resident: full-time $6347; part-time $352.60 per credit hour. Tuition, nonresident: full-time $17,379; part-time $965.50 per credit hour. *Required fees:* $1035. Tuition and fees vary according to course load, campus/location and program. *Financial support:* Fellowships, research assistantships, teaching assistantships, institutionally sponsored loans, traineeships, health care benefits, and unspecified assistantships available. Support available to part-time students.
Website: http://education.missouri.edu/LTC/index.php

University of Missouri, Office of Research and Graduate Studies, College of Education, Department of Special Education, Columbia, MO 65211. Offers administration and supervision of special education (PhD); behavior disorders (M Ed, PhD); curriculum development of exceptional students (M Ed, PhD); early childhood special education (M Ed, PhD); general special education (M Ed, MA, PhD); learning and instruction (M Ed); learning disabilities (M Ed, PhD); mental retardation (M Ed, PhD). *Accreditation:* TEAC. *Program availability:* Part-time, evening/weekend, online learning. *Faculty:* 13 full-time (11 women). *Students:* 22 full-time (20 women), 36 part-time (32 women). *Degree requirements:* For master's, comprehensive exam, thesis or alternative; for doctorate, comprehensive exam, thesis/dissertation. *Entrance requirements:* For master's and doctorate, GRE General Test, letters of recommendation. Additional exam requirements/recommendations for international students: Required—TOEFL (minimum score 500 paper-based; 61 iBT). *Application deadline:* For fall admission, 1/15 priority date for domestic and international students;

for winter admission, 11/1 priority date for domestic and international students; for spring admission, 4/1 priority date for domestic and international students. Application fee: $75 ($90 for international students). Electronic applications accepted. *Expenses:* Tuition, state resident: full-time $6347; part-time $352.60 per credit hour. Tuition, nonresident: full-time $17,379; part-time $965.50 per credit hour. *Required fees:* $1035. Tuition and fees vary according to course load, campus/location and program. *Financial support:* Fellowships with tuition reimbursements, research assistantships with tuition reimbursements, teaching assistantships with tuition reimbursements, career-related internships or fieldwork, scholarships/grants, health care benefits, and unspecified assistantships available.
Website: http://education.missouri.edu/SPED/

University of Missouri–Kansas City, School of Education, Kansas City, MO 64110-2499. Offers administration (Ed D); counseling and guidance (MA, Ed S), including mental health counseling (Ed S), school counseling (Ed S); counseling psychology (PhD); curriculum and instruction (MA, Ed S), including language and literacy (Ed S); education (PhD), including higher education administration, PK-12 education administration; educational administration (MA, Ed S), including advanced principal (Ed S), beginning principal (Ed S), district-level administration (Ed S); reading education (MA); special education (MA). PhD in education offered through the School of Graduate Studies. *Accreditation:* NCATE. *Program availability:* Part-time, evening/weekend. *Faculty:* 33 full-time (26 women), 51 part-time/adjunct (39 women). *Students:* 136 full-time (103 women), 275 part-time (194 women); includes 110 minority (71 Black or African American, non-Hispanic/Latino; 3 American Indian or Alaska Native, non-Hispanic/Latino; 8 Asian, non-Hispanic/Latino; 22 Hispanic/Latino; 6 Two or more races, non-Hispanic/Latino), 20 international. Average age 32. 324 applicants, 45% accepted, 108 enrolled. In 2016, 152 master's, 13 doctorates, 50 other advanced degrees awarded. *Degree requirements:* For doctorate, thesis/dissertation, internship, practicum. *Entrance requirements:* For master's, GRE, minimum GPA of 2.75, 2 letters of reference, written statement of purpose; for doctorate, GRE, minimum GPA of 3.0; for Ed S, minimum GPA of 3.0. Additional exam requirements/recommendations for international students: Required—TOEFL (minimum score 550 paper-based; 80 iBT). *Application deadline:* For fall admission, 4/1 priority date for domestic and international students; for spring admission, 11/1 priority date for domestic and international students. Applications are processed on a rolling basis. Application fee: $45 ($50 for international students). *Financial support:* In 2016–17, 12 research assistantships with partial tuition reimbursements (averaging $12,476 per year) were awarded; career-related internships or fieldwork, Federal Work-Study, institutionally sponsored loans, and tuition waivers (full and partial) also available. Support available to part-time students. Financial award application deadline: 3/1; financial award applicants required to submit FAFSA. *Faculty research:* Urban education, inquiry-based field study, theories of counseling and psychotherapy, school literacy, educational technology. *Unit head:* Justin Perry, Dean, 816-235-5663, Fax: 816-235-5270, E-mail: education@umkc.edu.
Website: http://education.umkc.edu

University of Missouri–St. Louis, College of Education, Department of Educator Preparation, Innovation and Research, St. Louis, MO 63121. Offers elementary education (M Ed), including early childhood, general, reading; secondary education (M Ed), including curriculum and instruction, general, middle level education, reading, teaching English to speakers of other languages (TESOL); special education (M Ed), including autism and developmental disabilities, early childhood special education. *Program availability:* Part-time, evening/weekend. *Faculty:* 26 full-time (14 women), 22 part-time/adjunct (14 women). *Students:* 151 full-time (127 women), 728 part-time (564 women); includes 222 minority (165 Black or African American, non-Hispanic/Latino; 1 American Indian or Alaska Native, non-Hispanic/Latino; 16 Asian, non-Hispanic/Latino; 31 Hispanic/Latino; 1 Native Hawaiian or other Pacific Islander, non-Hispanic/Latino; 8 Two or more races, non-Hispanic/Latino), 6 international. Average age 29. 363 applicants, 84% accepted, 211 enrolled. *Degree requirements:* For master's, comprehensive exam. *Entrance requirements:* Additional exam requirements/recommendations for international students: Recommended—TOEFL (minimum score 550 paper-based; 79 iBT), IELTS (minimum score 6.5). *Application deadline:* For fall admission, 7/1 priority date for domestic and international students; for spring admission, 12/1 priority date for domestic and international students. Application fee: $50 ($40 for international students). Electronic applications accepted. *Financial support:* Application deadline: 4/1; applicants required to submit FAFSA. *Unit head:* Dr. Gayle Wilkinson, Chair, 314-516-5791. *Application contact:* 314-516-5458, Fax: 314-516-6996, E-mail: gadadm@umsl.edu.
Website: https://coe.umsl.edu/dept/epir.html

University of Montana, Graduate School, Phyllis J. Washington College of Education and Human Sciences, Department of Teaching and Learning, Missoula, MT 59812-0002. Offers curriculum and instruction (M Ed, Ed D); early childhood education (M Ed); education (MA); teaching and learning (PhD). *Program availability:* Part-time. *Degree requirements:* For doctorate, thesis/dissertation. *Entrance requirements:* For master's, GRE General Test. Additional exam requirements/recommendations for international students: Required—TOEFL.

University of Nebraska at Kearney, College of Education, Department of Teacher Education, Kearney, NE 68849-0001. Offers curriculum and instruction (MA Ed), including early childhood education, elementary education, English as a second language, instructional effectiveness, reading/special education, secondary education; instructional technology (MS Ed), including information technology, instructional technology, school librarian; reading PK-12 (MA Ed); special education (MA Ed), including advanced practitioner: assistive technology specialist, advanced practitioner: behavioral interventionist, advanced practitioner: inclusive collaboration specialist, gifted, teacher education. *Program availability:* Part-time, evening/weekend, online only, 100% online. *Faculty:* 18 full-time (13 women). *Students:* 21 full-time (15 women), 296 part-time (240 women); includes 21 minority (3 Black or African American, non-Hispanic/Latino; 1 Asian, non-Hispanic/Latino; 14 Hispanic/Latino; 1 Native Hawaiian or other Pacific Islander, non-Hispanic/Latino; 2 Two or more races, non-Hispanic/Latino), 1 international. Average age 32. 81 applicants, 100% accepted, 61 enrolled. In 2016, 129 master's awarded. *Degree requirements:* For master's, comprehensive exam, thesis optional. *Entrance requirements:* For master's, portfolio or GRE. Additional exam requirements/recommendations for international students: Recommended—TOEFL (minimum score 550 paper-based; 79 iBT), IELTS (minimum score 6.5). *Application deadline:* For fall admission, 6/15 for domestic students, 5/15 for international students; for spring admission, 10/15 for domestic and international students; for summer admission, 3/15 for domestic and international students. Application fee: $45. Electronic applications accepted. *Expenses:* $285 per credit hour resident tuition, $415 per credit hour non-resident tuition (online). *Financial support:* In 2016–17, 6 students received support, including 6 research assistantships with full tuition reimbursements available (averaging $10,500 per year); career-related internships or fieldwork, scholarships/grants, health care benefits, and unspecified assistantships also available. Support available to part-time students. Financial award application deadline: 2/28; financial award applicants required to submit FAFSA. *Unit head:* Sarah Bartling, Administrative Assistant, 308-865-8513, E-mail: bartlingseg@unk.edu. *Application contact:* Linda Johnson, Director, Graduate Admissions and Programs, 308-865-8841, Fax: 308-865-8837, E-mail: johnsonli@unk.edu.
Website: http://www.unk.edu/academics/ted/index.php

University of Nebraska–Lincoln, Graduate College, College of Education and Human Sciences, Department of Teaching, Learning and Teacher Education, Lincoln, NE 68588. Offers adult and continuing education (MA); educational studies (Ed D, PhD), including special education (Ed D); teaching, learning and teacher education (M Ed, MA, MST, Ed D, PhD); vocational and adult education (M Ed, MA). *Accreditation:* NCATE. *Degree requirements:* For master's, thesis optional. *Entrance requirements:* Additional exam requirements/recommendations for international students: Required—TOEFL (minimum score 550 paper-based). Electronic applications accepted. *Faculty research:* Teacher education, instructional leadership, literacy education, technology, improvement of school curriculum.

University of Nebraska–Lincoln, Graduate College, College of Education and Human Sciences, Interdepartmental Area of Administration, Curriculum and Instruction, Lincoln, NE 68588. Offers Ed D, PhD, JD/PhD. *Accreditation:* NCATE. *Program availability:* Online learning. *Degree requirements:* For doctorate, comprehensive exam, thesis/dissertation. *Entrance requirements:* For doctorate, GRE, curriculum vitae. Additional exam requirements/recommendations for international students: Required—TOEFL (minimum score 550 paper-based). Electronic applications accepted.

University of Nevada, Las Vegas, Graduate College, College of Education, Department of Teaching and Learning, Las Vegas, NV 89154-3005. Offers curriculum and instruction (M Ed, MS, Ed D, PhD, Ed S), including teacher education (PhD); elementary teaching (Certificate); online teaching and training (Certificate); secondary teaching (Certificate); social justice studies (Certificate); teaching and learning (PhD). *Program availability:* Part-time, evening/weekend. *Faculty:* 26 full-time (12 women), 10 part-time/adjunct (8 women). *Students:* 280 full-time (202 women), 206 part-time (131 women); includes 188 minority (51 Black or African American, non-Hispanic/Latino; 4 American Indian or Alaska Native, non-Hispanic/Latino; 23 Asian, non-Hispanic/Latino; 72 Hispanic/Latino; 4 Native Hawaiian or other Pacific Islander, non-Hispanic/Latino; 34 Two or more races, non-Hispanic/Latino), 18 international. Average age 35. 178 applicants, 89% accepted, 142 enrolled. In 2016, 156 master's, 14 doctorates, 1 other advanced degree awarded. *Degree requirements:* For master's, comprehensive exam (for some programs), thesis (for some programs); for doctorate, comprehensive exam, thesis/dissertation, defense of dissertation; for other advanced degree, comprehensive exam (for some programs), oral presentation of special project or professional paper. *Entrance requirements:* For master's, bachelor's degree with minimum GPA 2.75; for doctorate, GRE General Test, master's degree with minimum GPA of 3.0; statement of purpose; demonstration of oral communication skills; 3 letters of recommendation; for other advanced degree, PRAXIS Core (for some programs); PRAXIS II (for some programs), bachelor's degree (for some programs). Additional exam requirements/recommendations for international students: Required—TOEFL (minimum score 550 paper-based; 80 iBT), IELTS (minimum score 7). *Application deadline:* For fall admission, 6/1 for domestic students, 5/1 for international students; for spring admission, 11/1 for domestic students, 10/1 for international students; for summer admission, 3/15 for domestic students. Application fee: $60 ($95 for international students). Electronic applications accepted. *Expenses:* $269.25 per credit, $792 per 3-credit course; $9,634 per year resident; $23,274 per year non-resident; $7,094 fees non-resident (7 credits or more); $1,307 annual health insurance fee. *Financial support:* In 2016–17, 8 research assistantships with partial tuition reimbursements (averaging $16,719 per year), 28 teaching assistantships with partial tuition reimbursements (averaging $17,023 per year) were awarded; institutionally sponsored loans, scholarships/grants, health care benefits, and unspecified assistantships also available. Financial award application deadline: 3/15. *Faculty research:* Content area and critical literacy, education in content areas, teacher education, STEM education, technology education. *Total annual research expenditures:* $652,413. *Unit head:* Dr. Emily Lin, Chair/Professor, 702-895-6407, Fax: 702-895-4898, E-mail: emily.lin@unlv.edu. *Application contact:* Dr. Travis Olson, Graduate Coordinator, 702-895-0471, Fax: 702-895-4898, E-mail: travis.olson@unlv.edu.
Website: http://tl.unlv.edu/

University of Nevada, Reno, Graduate School, College of Education, Department of Curriculum, Teaching and Learning, Program in Curriculum and Instruction, Reno, NV 89557. Offers PhD. *Degree requirements:* For doctorate, thesis/dissertation. *Entrance requirements:* For doctorate, GRE General Test, minimum GPA of 3.0. Additional exam requirements/recommendations for international students: Required—TOEFL (minimum score 500 paper-based; 61 iBT), IELTS (minimum score 6). Electronic applications accepted. *Faculty research:* Education, development, pedagogy.

University of Nevada, Reno, Graduate School, College of Education, Department of Curriculum, Teaching and Learning, Program in Curriculum, Teaching and Learning, Reno, NV 89557. Offers Ed D, PhD. *Degree requirements:* For doctorate, comprehensive exam, thesis/dissertation. *Entrance requirements:* For doctorate, GRE General Test, minimum GPA of 3.0. Additional exam requirements/recommendations for international students: Required—TOEFL (minimum score 500 paper-based; 61 iBT), IELTS (minimum score 6). Electronic applications accepted. *Faculty research:* Education, trends, pedagogy.

University of New England, College of Graduate and Professional Studies, Portland, ME 04103. Offers applied nutrition (MS); career and technical education (MS Ed); curriculum and instruction (MS Ed); education (CAGS, Post-Master's Certificate); education leadership (Ed D); educational leadership (MS Ed); generalist (MS Ed); health informatics (MS, Graduate Certificate); inclusion education (MS Ed); literacy K-12 (MS Ed); medical education leadership (MMEL); public health (Graduate Certificate); reading specialist (MS Ed); social work (MSW). *Program availability:* Part-time, evening/weekend, online only, 100% online. *Faculty:* 67 part-time/adjunct (46 women). *Students:* 891 full-time (667 women), 359 part-time (261 women); includes 309 minority (215 Black or African American, non-Hispanic/Latino; 2 American Indian or Alaska Native, non-Hispanic/Latino; 63 Asian, non-Hispanic/Latino; 18 Hispanic/Latino; 2 Native Hawaiian or other Pacific Islander, non-Hispanic/Latino; 9 Two or more races, non-Hispanic/Latino). Average age 36. 777 applicants, 50% accepted, 316 enrolled. In 2016, 292 master's, 34 doctorates, 130 other advanced degrees awarded. *Application deadline:* Applications are processed on a rolling basis. Electronic applications accepted. Tuition and fees vary according to degree level, program and student level. *Financial support:* Application deadline: 5/1; applicants required to submit FAFSA. *Unit head:* Dr. Martha Wilson, Associate Provost for Online Worldwide Learning/Dean of the College of Graduate and Professional Studies, 207-221-4985, E-mail: mwilson13@une.edu.
Website: http://online.une.edu

University of New Hampshire, Graduate School, College of Liberal Arts, Department of Education, Program in Education, Durham, NH 03824. Offers children and youth in communities (PhD); curriculum and instruction leadership (Postbaccalaureate Certificate); education (PhD). *Degree requirements:* For doctorate, thesis/dissertation. *Entrance requirements:* For doctorate, GRE General Test. Additional exam requirements/recommendations for international students: Required—TOEFL (minimum score 550 paper-based; 80 iBT). *Application deadline:* For fall admission, 2/15 priority date for domestic students, 2/15 for international students; for spring admission, 12/1 for

domestic students. Applications are processed on a rolling basis. Application fee: $65. Electronic applications accepted. *Financial support:* Fellowships, research assistantships, teaching assistantships, Federal Work-Study, scholarships/grants, and tuition waivers (full and partial) available. Support available to part-time students. Financial award application deadline: 2/15. *Faculty research:* Educational administration, curriculum and instruction, teacher development. *Unit head:* Dr. Leslie Couse, Chair, 603-862-0638. *Application contact:* Lisa Wilder, Administrative Assistant, 603-862-2381, E-mail: education.department@unh.edu.
Website: http://cola.unh.edu/education

University of New Orleans, Graduate School, College of Education and Human Development, Department of Curriculum and Instruction, New Orleans, LA 70148. Offers M Ed, PhD. *Accreditation:* NCATE. *Program availability:* Evening/weekend. *Degree requirements:* For doctorate, variable foreign language requirement, thesis/dissertation. *Entrance requirements:* For master's, GRE General Test; for doctorate, GRE General Test, GRE Subject Test. Additional exam requirements/recommendations for international students: Required—TOEFL (minimum score 550 paper-based; 79 iBT). Electronic applications accepted.

The University of North Carolina at Chapel Hill, Graduate School, School of Education, Program in Education, Chapel Hill, NC 27599. Offers culture, curriculum and change (MA, PhD); early childhood, intervention and literacy (MA, PhD); educational psychology, measurement and evaluation (MA, PhD). *Accreditation:* NCATE. *Degree requirements:* For master's, thesis; for doctorate, comprehensive exam, thesis/dissertation. *Entrance requirements:* For master's, GRE General Test, minimum GPA of 3.0 during last 2 years of undergraduates course work; for doctorate, GRE General Test, minimum GPA of 3.0 during last 2 years of undergraduate course work. Additional exam requirements/recommendations for international students: Required—TOEFL (minimum score 550 paper-based). Electronic applications accepted.

The University of North Carolina at Charlotte, Cato College of Education, Interdisciplinary Education Programs, Charlotte, NC 28223-0001. Offers art education (Graduate Certificate); child and family development: early childhood education (MAT); curriculum and instruction (PhD); elementary education (MAT); foreign language education (MAT); middle grades education (MAT); secondary education (MAT); special education (MAT); teaching (Graduate Certificate); teaching English as a second language (MAT); theatre education (Graduate Certificate). *Program availability:* Part-time, 100% online, blended/hybrid learning. *Students:* 78 full-time (59 women), 619 part-time (484 women); includes 255 minority (186 Black or African American, non-Hispanic/Latino; 1 American Indian or Alaska Native, non-Hispanic/Latino; 16 Asian, non-Hispanic/Latino; 37 Hispanic/Latino; 15 Two or more races, non-Hispanic/Latino), 10 international. Average age 33. 380 applicants, 92% accepted, 264 enrolled. In 2016, 93 master's, 8 doctorates, 176 other advanced degrees awarded. *Degree requirements:* For master's, thesis or alternative, research project/portfolio. *Entrance requirements:* For master's, GRE or MAT, bachelor's degree, or its U.S. equivalent, from regionally-accredited college or university; minimum overall GPA of 3.0 on all previous work beyond high school; statement of purpose (essay); at least three recommendation forms; for doctorate, GRE or MAT, bachelor's degree (or its U.S. equivalent) from regionally-accredited college or university; minimum overall GPA of 3.5 in master's degree program; for Graduate Certificate, bachelor's degree from regionally-accredited university; minimum GPA of 2.75 on all post-secondary work attempted; transcripts; personal statement outlining why the applicant seeks admission to the program. Additional exam requirements/recommendations for international students: Required—TOEFL (minimum score 523 paper-based, 70 iBT) or IELTS (6.5). *Application deadline:* For fall admission, 3/1 priority date for domestic and international students; for spring admission, 10/1 priority date for domestic and international students; for summer admission, 4/1 priority date for domestic and international students. Applications are processed on a rolling basis. Application fee: $75. Electronic applications accepted. *Expenses:* Tuition, state resident: full-time $4252. Tuition, nonresident: full-time $17,423. *Required fees:* $3026. Tuition and fees vary according to course load and program. *Financial support:* Career-related internships or fieldwork, institutionally sponsored loans, scholarships/grants, and unspecified assistantships available. Support available to part-time students. Financial award application deadline: 3/1; financial award applicants required to submit FAFSA. *Unit head:* Dr. Ellen McIntyre, Dean, 704-687-8722, E-mail: ellen.mcintyre@uncc.edu. *Application contact:* Kathy B. Giddings, Director of Graduate Admissions, 704-687-5503, Fax: 704-687-1668, E-mail: gradadm@uncc.edu.
Website: http://education.uncc.edu/academic-programs

The University of North Carolina at Greensboro, Graduate School, School of Education, Department of Educational Leadership and Cultural Foundations, Greensboro, NC 27412-5001. Offers curriculum and teaching (PhD), including cultural studies; educational leadership (Ed D, Ed S); school administration (MSA). *Accreditation:* NCATE. *Degree requirements:* For doctorate, thesis/dissertation. *Entrance requirements:* For master's, doctorate, and Ed S, GRE General Test. Additional exam requirements/recommendations for international students: Required—TOEFL. Electronic applications accepted.

The University of North Carolina at Greensboro, Graduate School, School of Education, Department of Teacher Education and Higher Education, Greensboro, NC 27412-5001. Offers college teaching and adult learning (Certificate); curriculum and instruction (M Ed), including chemistry education, elementary education, English as a second language, French education, instructional technology, mathematics education, middle grades education, reading education, science education, social studies education, Spanish education; curriculum and teaching (PhD), including higher education, teacher education and development; English as a second language (Certificate); higher education (M Ed); supervision (M Ed). *Accreditation:* NCATE. *Program availability:* Part-time. *Degree requirements:* For doctorate, thesis/dissertation. *Entrance requirements:* For master's and doctorate, GRE General Test. Additional exam requirements/recommendations for international students: Required—TOEFL. Electronic applications accepted. *Faculty research:* Community college literacy program, middle school mathematics/computer mathematics.

The University of North Carolina Wilmington, Watson College of Education, Department of Educational Leadership, Wilmington, NC 28403-3297. Offers curriculum, instruction and supervision (M Ed); educational leadership and administration (Ed D), including curriculum and instruction; higher education (M Ed); school administration (MSA), including school administration. *Program availability:* Part-time. *Faculty:* 25 full-time (14 women), 5 part-time/adjunct (3 women). *Students:* 49 full-time (31 women), 151 part-time (106 women); includes 55 minority (42 Black or African American, non-Hispanic/Latino; 7 American Indian or Alaska Native, non-Hispanic/Latino; 3 Asian, non-Hispanic/Latino; 1 Hispanic/Latino; 1 Native Hawaiian or other Pacific Islander, non-Hispanic/Latino; 1 Two or more races, non-Hispanic/Latino), 1 international. Average age 36. 113 applicants, 70% accepted, 57 enrolled. In 2016, 32 master's, 19 doctorates awarded. *Degree requirements:* For master's, comprehensive exam, thesis or alternative, e-portfolio defense; for doctorate, comprehensive exam, thesis/dissertation. *Entrance requirements:* For master's, GRE General Test, MAT, minimum B average in undergraduate work, 3 letters of recommendation, statement of interest, NC Class A teacher licensure in related field, minimum of 3 years' teaching experience; for doctorate, GRE, statement of interest, master's degree in education field, 3 years of leadership experience, minimum GPA of 3.0 in undergraduate and graduate work. Additional exam requirements/recommendations for international students: Required—TOEFL (minimum score 79 iBT), IELTS (minimum score 6.5). *Application deadline:* For fall admission, 5/15 for domestic students; for spring admission, 10/15 for domestic students; for summer admission, 3/15 for domestic students. Applications are processed on a rolling basis. Application fee: $60. Electronic applications accepted. *Expenses:* Contact institution. *Financial support:* Scholarships/grants and unspecified assistantships available. Support available to part-time students. Financial award application deadline: 3/15; financial award applicants required to submit FAFSA. *Unit head:* Dr. Tamara Walser, Interim Chair, 910-962-2290, Fax: 910-962-3609, E-mail: walsert@uncw.edu. *Application contact:* Dr. William Sterrett, Graduate Program Coordinator, 910-962-7995, E-mail: stewettw@uncw.edu.
Website: http://uncw.edu/ed/el/

University of Northern Colorado, Graduate School, College of Education and Behavioral Sciences, School of Teacher Education, Greeley, CO 80639. Offers curriculum studies (MAT); educational studies (Ed D); elementary education (MAT); English education (MAT); literacy (MA); multilingual education (MA), including TESOL, world languages; teaching diverse learners (MA). *Accreditation:* NCATE. *Program availability:* Part-time, evening/weekend. *Degree requirements:* For master's, comprehensive exam, thesis or alternative; for doctorate, comprehensive exam, thesis/dissertation. *Entrance requirements:* For master's and doctorate, GRE General Test, 3 letters of recommendation. *Application deadline:* Applications are processed on a rolling basis. Application fee: $50 ($60 for international students). Electronic applications accepted. *Financial support:* Fellowships, research assistantships, teaching assistantships, and unspecified assistantships available. Financial award application deadline: 3/1; financial award applicants required to submit FAFSA. *Unit head:* Dr. Alexander Sidorkin, Director, 970-351-2908, Fax: 970-351-1877. *Application contact:* Linda Sisson, Graduate Student Admission Coordinator, 970-351-1807, Fax: 970-351-2371, E-mail: linda.sisson@unco.edu.
Website: http://www.unco.edu/cebs/teachered/

University of Northern Iowa, Graduate College, College of Education, Ed D Program in Education, Cedar Falls, IA 50614. Offers allied health, recreation, and community services (Ed D); curriculum and instruction (Ed D); educational leadership (Ed D). *Program availability:* Part-time, evening/weekend. *Degree requirements:* For doctorate, thesis/dissertation. *Entrance requirements:* For doctorate, GRE, minimum GPA of 3.0, master's degree. Additional exam requirements/recommendations for international students: Required—TOEFL (minimum score 500 paper-based; 61 iBT).

University of North Texas, Robert B. Toulouse School of Graduate Studies, Denton, TX 76203-5459. Offers accounting (MS); applied anthropology (MA, MS); applied behavior analysis (Certificate); applied geography (MA); applied technology and performance improvement (M Ed, MS); art education (MA); art history (MA); art museum education (Certificate); arts leadership (Certificate); audiology (Au D); behavior analysis (MS); behavioral science (PhD); biochemistry and molecular biology (MS); biology (MA, MS); biomedical engineering (MS); business analysis (MS); chemistry (MS); clinical health psychology (PhD); communication studies (MA, MS); computer engineering (MS); computer science (MS); counseling (M Ed, MS), including clinical mental health counseling (MS), college and university counseling, elementary school counseling, secondary school counseling; creative writing (MA); criminal justice (MS); curriculum and instruction (M Ed); decision sciences (MBA); design (MA, MFA), including fashion design (MFA), innovation studies, interior design (MFA); early childhood studies (MS); economics (MS); educational leadership (M Ed, Ed D); educational psychology (MS, PhD), including family studies (MS), gifted and talented (MS), human development (MS), learning and cognition (MS), research, measurement and evaluation (MS); electrical engineering (MS); emergency management (MPA); engineering technology (MS); English (MA); English as a second language (MA); environmental science (MS); finance (MBA, MS); financial management (MPA); French (MA); health services management (MBA); higher education (M Ed, Ed D); history (MA, MS); hospitality management (MS); human resources management (MPA); information science (MS); information systems (PhD); information technologies (MBA); interdisciplinary studies (MA, MS); international studies (MA); international sustainable tourism (MS); jazz studies (MM); journalism (MA, MJ, Graduate Certificate), including interactive and virtual digital communication (Graduate Certificate), narrative journalism (Graduate Certificate), public relations (Graduate Certificate); kinesiology (MS); linguistics (MA); local government management (MPA); logistics (PhD); logistics and supply chain management (MBA); long-term care, senior housing, and aging services (MA); management (PhD); marketing (MBA); mathematics (MA, MS); mechanical and energy engineering (MS, PhD); music (MA), including ethnomusicology, music theory, musicology, performance; music composition (PhD); music education (MM Ed, PhD); nonprofit management (MPA); operations and supply chain management (MBA); performance (MM, DMA); philosophy (MA); political science (MA); professional and technical communication (MA); radio, television and film (MA, MFA); rehabilitation counseling (Certificate); sociology (MA); Spanish (MA); special education (M Ed); speech-language pathology (MA); strategic management (MBA); studio art (MFA); teaching (M Ed); MBA/MS. *Program availability:* Part-time, evening/weekend, online learning. Terminal master's awarded for partial completion of doctoral program. *Degree requirements:* For master's, variable foreign language requirement, comprehensive exam (for some programs), thesis (for some programs); for doctorate, variable foreign language requirement, comprehensive exam (for some programs), thesis/dissertation; for other advanced degree, variable foreign language requirement, comprehensive exam (for some programs). *Entrance requirements:* For master's and doctorate, GRE, GMAT. Additional exam requirements/recommendations for international students: Required—TOEFL (minimum score 550 paper-based; 79 iBT). Electronic applications accepted.

University of North Texas at Dallas, Graduate School, Dallas, TX 75241. Offers accounting (MBA); counseling (M Ed, MS); criminal justice (MS); curriculum and instruction (M Ed); educational administration (M Ed); human resources and organizational behavior (MBA); public leadership (MS); strategic management (MBA).

University of Oklahoma, Jeannine Rainbolt College of Education, Department of Educational Leadership and Policy Studies, Program in Educational Administration, Curriculum and Supervision, Norman, OK 73019. Offers M Ed, Ed D, PhD. *Accreditation:* NCATE. *Program availability:* Part-time, evening/weekend, blended/hybrid learning. *Students:* 28 full-time (22 women), 152 part-time (108 women); includes 55 minority (17 Black or African American, non-Hispanic/Latino; 13 American Indian or Alaska Native, non-Hispanic/Latino; 14 Hispanic/Latino; 11 Two or more races, non-Hispanic/Latino), 1 international. Average age 36. 42 applicants, 86% accepted, 30 enrolled. In 2016, 48 master's, 9 doctorates awarded. *Degree requirements:* For master's, comprehensive exam, thesis (for some programs); for doctorate, comprehensive exam, thesis/dissertation. *Entrance requirements:* For doctorate, GRE. Additional exam requirements/recommendations for international students: Required—TOEFL (minimum score 79 iBT) or IELTS (minimum score 6.5). *Application deadline:* Applications are processed on a rolling basis. Application fee: $50 ($100 for international students). Electronic applications accepted. *Expenses:* Tuition, state resident: full-time $4886; part-time $203.60 per credit hour. Tuition, nonresident: full-time $18,989; part-

time $791.20 per credit hour. *Required fees:* $3283; $126.25 per credit hour. $126.50 per semester. *Financial support:* In 2016–17, 74 students received support. Fellowships, research assistantships, teaching assistantships, career-related internships or fieldwork, Federal Work-Study, institutionally sponsored loans, scholarships/grants, health care benefits, tuition waivers, and unspecified assistantships available. Support available to part-time students. Financial award application deadline: 6/1; financial award applicants required to submit FAFSA. *Faculty research:* Improvement science; leadership and ethics; education and social policy; gender and equity; organizational reform and change. *Unit head:* John Jones, Associate Professor, 405-325-4165, E-mail: jjones@ou.edu.
Website: http://www.ou.edu/education/elps

University of Oklahoma, Jeannine Rainbolt College of Education, Department of Instructional Leadership and Academic Curriculum, Norman, OK 73019. Offers instructional leadership and academic curriculum (M Ed, PhD), including biomedical education (PhD), early childhood education, elementary education (M Ed), English education, instructional leadership, mathematics education, reading education, science education, social studies education, world languages education (M Ed). *Accreditation:* NCATE. *Program availability:* Part-time. *Faculty:* 19 full-time (15 women), 1 (woman) part-time/adjunct. *Students:* 66 full-time (49 women), 116 part-time (88 women); includes 49 minority (12 Black or African American, non-Hispanic/Latino; 6 American Indian or Alaska Native, non-Hispanic/Latino; 6 Asian, non-Hispanic/Latino; 11 Hispanic/Latino; 1 Native Hawaiian or other Pacific Islander, non-Hispanic/Latino; 13 Two or more races, non-Hispanic/Latino), 13 international. Average age 35. 38 applicants, 97% accepted, 28 enrolled. In 2016, 33 master's, 10 doctorates awarded. Terminal master's awarded for partial completion of doctoral program. *Degree requirements:* For master's, comprehensive exam (for some programs), thesis (for some programs); for doctorate, comprehensive exam (for some programs), thesis/dissertation. *Entrance requirements:* For doctorate, GRE. Additional exam requirements/recommendations for international students: Required—TOEFL (minimum score 79 iBT) or IELTS (minimum score 6.5). Application fee: $50 ($100 for international students). Electronic applications accepted. *Expenses:* Tuition, state resident: full-time $4886; part-time $203.60 per credit hour. Tuition, nonresident: full-time $18,989; part-time $791.20 per credit hour. *Required fees:* $3283; $126.25 per credit hour. $126.50 per semester. *Financial support:* In 2016–17, 112 students received support, including 7 research assistantships with partial tuition reimbursements available (averaging $10,373 per year), 6 teaching assistantships with partial tuition reimbursements available (averaging $11,446 per year); fellowships, scholarships/grants, and unspecified assistantships also available. Financial award application deadline: 6/1; financial award applicants required to submit FAFSA. *Faculty research:* Teacher preparation; instruction; curriculum; learning; constructivist theory. *Total annual research expenditures:* $165,297. *Unit head:* Dr. Stacy Reeder, Chair, 405-325-1498, Fax: 405-325-4061, E-mail: reeder@ou.edu. *Application contact:* Anna Steele, Graduate Programs Officer, 405-325-4525, E-mail: anna.steele@ou.edu.
Website: http://www.ou.edu/education/ilac

University of Phoenix–Central Valley Campus, College of Education, Fresno, CA 93720-1552. Offers curriculum and instruction (MA Ed); curriculum and instruction-computer education (MA Ed); elementary teacher education (MA Ed); secondary teacher education (MA Ed).

University of Phoenix–Colorado Campus, College of Education, Lone Tree, CO 80124-5453. Offers administration and supervision (MAEd); curriculum instruction (MAEd); elementary teacher education (MAEd); school counseling (MSC); secondary teacher education (MAEd). *Program availability:* Evening/weekend. *Degree requirements:* For master's, thesis (for some programs). *Entrance requirements:* For master's, minimum undergraduate GPA of 2.5, 3 years work experience. Additional exam requirements/recommendations for international students: Required—TOEFL (minimum score 550 paper-based; 79 iBT). Electronic applications accepted.

University of Phoenix–Colorado Springs Downtown Campus, College of Education, Colorado Springs, CO 80903. Offers administration and supervision (MA Ed); curriculum and instruction (MA Ed); elementary teacher education (MA Ed); principal licensure certification (Certificate); school counseling (MSC); secondary teacher education (MA Ed). *Program availability:* Evening/weekend. *Degree requirements:* For master's, thesis (for some programs). *Entrance requirements:* For master's, minimum undergraduate GPA of 2.5, 3 years of work experience. Additional exam requirements/recommendations for international students: Required—TOEFL (minimum score 550 paper-based; 79 iBT). Electronic applications accepted.

University of Phoenix–Dallas Campus, College of Education, Dallas, TX 75251. Offers curriculum and instruction (MA Ed).

University of Phoenix–Hawaii Campus, College of Education, Honolulu, HI 96813-3800. Offers administration and supervision (MA Ed); curriculum and instruction (MA Ed); elementary education (MA Ed); secondary education (MA Ed); special education (MA Ed); teacher education for elementary licensure (MA Ed). *Program availability:* Evening/weekend. *Degree requirements:* For master's, thesis (for some programs). *Entrance requirements:* For master's, minimum undergraduate GPA of 2.5, 3 years of work experience. Additional exam requirements/recommendations for international students: Required—TOEFL (minimum score 550 paper-based; 79 iBT). Electronic applications accepted.

University of Phoenix–Houston Campus, College of Education, Houston, TX 77079-2004. Offers curriculum and instruction (MA Ed).

University of Phoenix–Las Vegas Campus, College of Education, Las Vegas, NV 89135. Offers administration and supervision (MA Ed); curriculum and instruction (MA Ed); school counseling (MSC); teacher education-elementary licensure (MA Ed). *Program availability:* Evening/weekend. *Degree requirements:* For master's, thesis (for some programs). *Entrance requirements:* For master's, minimum undergraduate GPA of 2.5, 3 years of work experience. Additional exam requirements/recommendations for international students: Required—TOEFL (minimum score 550 paper-based; 79 iBT). Electronic applications accepted.

University of Phoenix–New Mexico Campus, College of Education, Albuquerque, NM 87113-1570. Offers administration and supervision (MAEd); curriculum and instruction (MAEd); elementary teacher education (MAEd); school counseling (MSC); secondary teacher education (MAEd). *Program availability:* Evening/weekend. *Degree requirements:* For master's, thesis (for some programs). *Entrance requirements:* For master's, minimum undergraduate GPA of 2.5, 3 years of work experience. Additional exam requirements/recommendations for international students: Required—TOEFL (minimum score 550 paper-based; 79 iBT). Electronic applications accepted.

University of Phoenix–North Florida Campus, College of Education, Jacksonville, FL 32216-0959. Offers administration and supervision (MA Ed); curriculum and instruction (MA Ed), including computer education, mathematics education; early childhood education (MA Ed); elementary teacher education (MA Ed); secondary teacher education (MA Ed). *Program availability:* Evening/weekend. *Degree requirements:* For master's, thesis (for some programs). *Entrance requirements:* For master's, 3 years of work experience, minimum undergraduate GPA of 2.5. Additional exam requirements/recommendations for international students: Required—TOEFL (minimum score 550 paper-based; 49 iBT). Electronic applications accepted.

University of Phoenix–Online Campus, College of Education, Phoenix, AZ 85034-7209. Offers administration and supervision (MAEd, Certificate); adult education and training (MAEd); curriculum and instruction (MAEd), including computer education, curriculum and instruction, English as a second language, language arts, mathematics, reading; early childhood education (MAEd); educational studies (MAEd); elementary teacher education (MAEd), including early childhood, elementary teacher education, high school middle level, middle level; principal licensure (Certificate); secondary teacher education (MAEd); special education (MAEd, Certificate); teacher education (MAEd), including middle level generalist; teacher education middle level mathematics (MAEd), including middle level mathematics; teacher education middle level science (MAEd), including middle level science; teacher education secondary mathematics (MAEd); teacher education secondary science (MAEd); teacher leadership (MAEd); teachers of English learners (Certificate); transition to teaching (Certificate), including elementary education, secondary education. *Program availability:* Evening/weekend, online learning. *Entrance requirements:* Additional exam requirements/recommendations for international students: Required—TOEFL, TOEIC (Test of English as an International Communication), Berlitz Online English Proficiency Exam, PTE, or IELTS. Electronic applications accepted. *Expenses:* Contact institution.

University of Phoenix–Online Campus, School of Advanced Studies, Phoenix, AZ 85034-7209. Offers business administration (DBA); education (Ed S); educational leadership (Ed D), including curriculum and instruction, education technology, educational leadership; health administration (DHA); higher education administration (PhD); industrial/organizational psychology (PhD); nursing (PhD); organizational leadership (DM), including information systems and technology, organizational leadership. *Program availability:* Evening/weekend, online learning. *Degree requirements:* For doctorate, thesis/dissertation. *Entrance requirements:* Additional exam requirements/recommendations for international students: Required—TOEFL, TOEIC (Test of English as an International Communication), Berlitz Online English Proficiency Exam, PTE, or IELTS. Electronic applications accepted. *Expenses:* Contact institution.

University of Phoenix–Phoenix Campus, College of Education, Tempe, AZ 85282-2371. Offers administration and supervision (MA Ed); adult education and training (MA Ed); curriculum and instruction reading (MA Ed); early childhood education (MA Ed); education studies (MA Ed); elementary teacher education (MA Ed); secondary teacher education (MA Ed); special education (MA Ed); teacher leadership (MA Ed). *Program availability:* Evening/weekend, online learning. *Entrance requirements:* Additional exam requirements/recommendations for international students: Required—TOEFL, TOEIC (Test of English as an International Communication), Berlitz Online English Proficiency Exam, PTE, or IELTS. Electronic applications accepted. *Expenses:* Contact institution.

University of Phoenix–Sacramento Valley Campus, College of Education, Sacramento, CA 95833-4334. Offers adult education (MA Ed); curriculum instruction (MA Ed); elementary teacher education (MA Ed); secondary teacher education (MA Ed); teacher education (Certificate). *Program availability:* Evening/weekend. *Degree requirements:* For master's, thesis (for some programs). *Entrance requirements:* For master's, 3 years of work experience, minimum undergraduate GPA of 2.5. Additional exam requirements/recommendations for international students: Required—TOEFL (minimum score 550 paper-based; 79 iBT). Electronic applications accepted.

University of Phoenix–San Antonio Campus, College of Education, San Antonio, TX 78230. Offers curriculum and instruction (MA Ed).

University of Phoenix–San Diego Campus, College of Education, San Diego, CA 92123. Offers curriculum and instruction (MA Ed), including computer education, curriculum and instruction, English as a second language; elementary teacher education (MA Ed); secondary teacher education (MA Ed). *Program availability:* Evening/weekend. *Degree requirements:* For master's, thesis (for some programs). *Entrance requirements:* For master's, 3 years of work experience, minimum undergraduate GPA of 3.0. Additional exam requirements/recommendations for international students: Required—TOEFL (minimum score 550 paper-based; 79 iBT). Electronic applications accepted.

University of Phoenix–Southern Arizona Campus, College of Education, Tucson, AZ 85711. Offers administration and supervision (MA Ed); adult education and training (MA Ed); curriculum instruction (MA Ed); educational counseling (MA Ed); elementary teacher education (MA Ed); school counseling (MSC); secondary teacher education (MA Ed); special education (MA Ed, Certificate). *Program availability:* Evening/weekend. *Degree requirements:* For master's, thesis (for some programs). *Entrance requirements:* For master's, minimum undergraduate GPA of 2.5, 3 years of work experience. Additional exam requirements/recommendations for international students: Required—TOEFL (minimum score 550 paper-based; 79 iBT). Electronic applications accepted.

University of Phoenix–South Florida Campus, College of Education, Miramar, FL 33027-4145. Offers administration and supervision (MA Ed); curriculum and instruction (MA Ed), including computer education, curriculum and instruction, mathematics education; early childhood education (MA Ed); elementary teacher education (MA Ed); secondary teacher education (MA Ed). *Program availability:* Evening/weekend. *Degree requirements:* For master's, thesis (for some programs). *Entrance requirements:* For master's, 3 years of work experience, minimum undergraduate GPA of 2.5. Additional exam requirements/recommendations for international students: Required—TOEFL (minimum score 550 paper-based; 79 iBT). Electronic applications accepted.

University of Phoenix–Utah Campus, College of Education, Salt Lake City, UT 84123-4642. Offers administration and supervision (MA Ed); curriculum and instruction (MA Ed); elementary teacher education (MA Ed); school counseling (MSC); secondary teacher education (MA Ed); special education (MA Ed). *Program availability:* Evening/weekend. *Degree requirements:* For master's, thesis (for some programs). *Entrance requirements:* For master's, minimum undergraduate GPA of 2.5, 3 years work experience. Additional exam requirements/recommendations for international students: Required—TOEFL (minimum score 550 paper-based; 79 iBT). Electronic applications accepted.

University of Phoenix–Washington D.C. Campus, College of Education, Washington, DC 20001. Offers administration and supervision (MA Ed); adult education and training (MA Ed); computer education (MA Ed); curriculum and instruction (MA Ed, Ed D); early childhood education (MA Ed); education (Ed S); educational leadership (Ed D); educational technology (Ed D); elementary teacher education (MA Ed); English and language arts education (MA Ed); English as a second language (MA Ed); higher education administration (PhD); mathematics education (MA Ed); secondary teacher education (MA Ed); special education (MA Ed); teacher leadership (MA Ed).

University of Puerto Rico, Río Piedras Campus, College of Education, Program in Curriculum and Teaching, San Juan, PR 00931-3300. Offers biology education (M Ed); chemistry education (M Ed); curriculum and teaching (Ed D); history education (M Ed); mathematics education (M Ed); physics education (M Ed); Spanish education (M Ed). *Program availability:* Part-time. *Degree requirements:* For master's, thesis; for doctorate, thesis/dissertation, internship. *Entrance requirements:* For master's, PAEG or GRE, minimum GPA of 3.0, letter of recommendation; for doctorate, GRE or PAEG, master's degree, minimum GPA of 3.0, letter of recommendation (2), interview. *Faculty research:* Curriculum, math teaching.

Curriculum and Instruction

University of Regina, Faculty of Graduate Studies and Research, Faculty of Education, Department of Curriculum and Instruction, Regina, SK S4S 0A2, Canada. Offers M Ed. *Program availability:* Part-time. *Faculty:* 38 full-time (26 women), 2 part-time/adjunct (both women). *Students:* 26 full-time (20 women), 110 part-time (85 women). 18 applicants, 67% accepted. In 2016, 37 master's awarded. *Degree requirements:* For master's, thesis (for some programs), practicum, project, or thesis. *Entrance requirements:* For master's, bachelor's degree in education, 2 years of teaching or other relevant professional experience. Additional exam requirements/recommendations for international students: Required—TOEFL (minimum score 580 paper-based; 80 iBT), IELTS (minimum score 6.5), PTE (minimum score 59). *Application deadline:* For fall admission, 2/15 for domestic and international students; for winter admission, 10/15 for domestic and international students; for spring admission, 2/15 for domestic students. Application fee: $100. Electronic applications accepted. *Financial support:* In 2016–17, 3 fellowships (averaging $6,000 per year), 5 teaching assistantships (averaging $2,501 per year) were awarded; scholarships/grants also available. Financial award application deadline: 6/15. *Faculty research:* Writing process and pedagogy: the Saskatchewan Writing Project; second language reading, writing, and spoken acquisition; assessing experiential learning; multicultural and anti-racist relations issues in curriculum; social media and open education. *Unit head:* Dr. Ken Montgomery, Associate Dean, Research and Graduate Programs in Education, 306-585-5031, Fax: 306-585-5387, E-mail: ken.montgomery@uregina.ca. *Application contact:* Tania Gates, Graduate Program Coordinator, 306-585-4506, Fax: 306-585-5387, E-mail: edgrad@uregina.ca.
Website: http://www.uregina.ca/education/

University of Rochester, Eastman School of Music, Program in Music Theory Pedagogy, Rochester, NY 14627. Offers MA. *Accreditation:* NASM. *Expenses: Tuition:* Full-time $47,450; part-time $1482 per credit hour. *Required fees:* $528. Tuition and fees vary according to program.

University of Rochester, Margaret Warner Graduate School of Education and Human Development, Doctoral Programs in Education, Rochester, NY 14627. Offers counseling (Ed D); educational administration (Ed D); educational policy and theory (PhD); higher education (PhD); human development in educational context (PhD); teaching, curriculum, and change (PhD). *Expenses: Tuition:* Full-time $47,450; part-time $1482 per credit hour. *Required fees:* $528. Tuition and fees vary according to program.

University of Rochester, Margaret Warner Graduate School of Education and Human Development, Master's Program in Teaching and Curriculum, Rochester, NY 14627. Offers MS. *Expenses: Tuition:* Full-time $47,450; part-time $1482 per credit hour. *Required fees:* $528. Tuition and fees vary according to program.

University of St. Francis, College of Education, Joliet, IL 60435-6169. Offers educational leadership (MS, Ed D); elementary education (M Ed); reading (MS); secondary education (M Ed), including English education, math education, science education, social studies education, visual arts education; special education (M Ed); teaching and learning (MS); TESOL (Certificate). *Accreditation:* NCATE. *Program availability:* Part-time, evening/weekend, 100% online, blended/hybrid learning. *Faculty:* 11 full-time (8 women), 60 part-time/adjunct (42 women). *Students:* 34 full-time (26 women), 420 part-time (318 women); includes 92 minority (51 Black or African American, non-Hispanic/Latino; 5 Asian, non-Hispanic/Latino; 31 Hispanic/Latino; 5 Two or more races, non-Hispanic/Latino), 4 international. Average age 36. 242 applicants, 48% accepted, 96 enrolled. In 2016, 229 master's, 44 doctorates, 10 other advanced degrees awarded. *Degree requirements:* For master's, comprehensive exam; for doctorate, thesis/dissertation. *Entrance requirements:* Additional exam requirements/recommendations for international students: Required—TOEFL (minimum score 550 paper-based; 79 iBT), IELTS (minimum score 6). *Application deadline:* Applications are processed on a rolling basis. Application fee: $30. Electronic applications accepted. Application fee is waived when completed online. *Expenses:* Contact institution. *Financial support:* In 2016–17, 48 students received support. Career-related internships or fieldwork and unspecified assistantships available. Support available to part-time students. Financial award applicants required to submit FAFSA. *Unit head:* Dr. John Gambro, Dean, 815-740-3829, Fax: 815-740-2264, E-mail: jgambro@stfrancis.edu. *Application contact:* Sandra Sloka, Director of Admissions for Graduate and Degree Completion Programs, 800-735-7500, Fax: 815-740-3431, E-mail: ssloka@stfrancis.edu.
Website: http://www.stfrancis.edu/academics/college-of-education/

University of Saint Joseph, Department of Education, West Hartford, CT 06117-2700. Offers curriculum and instruction (MA); educational technology (MA); literacy internship (MA); multiple intelligences (MA); reading/language (MA); TESOL (MA). *Program availability:* Part-time, evening/weekend. *Degree requirements:* For master's, comprehensive exam, thesis or alternative. *Entrance requirements:* For master's, 2 letters of recommendation. Electronic applications accepted. Application fee is waived when completed online. *Expenses: Tuition:* Full-time $14,580; part-time $729 per credit hour. *Required fees:* $920; $46 per credit hour. Tuition and fees vary according to course load, degree level and program.

University of St. Thomas, School of Education and Human Services, Houston, TX 77006-4696. Offers all level education (M Ed); bilingual/dual language (M Ed); Catholic school teaching (M Ed); Catholic/private school leadership (M Ed); counselor education (M Ed); curriculum and instruction (M Ed); education (Ed D); educational leadership (M Ed); elementary teaching (M Ed); English as a second language (M Ed); exceptionality/educational diagnostician (M Ed); exceptionality/special education (M Ed); generalist (M Ed); reading (M Ed); secondary teaching (M Ed); teaching (MAT). *Accreditation:* TEAC. *Program availability:* Part-time, evening/weekend, online learning. *Faculty:* 44 full-time (29 women), 31 part-time/adjunct (17 women). *Students:* 65 full-time (61 women), 719 part-time (645 women); includes 515 minority (169 Black or African American, non-Hispanic/Latino; 25 Asian, non-Hispanic/Latino; 315 Hispanic/Latino; 2 Native Hawaiian or other Pacific Islander, non-Hispanic/Latino; 4 Two or more races, non-Hispanic/Latino), 24 international. Average age 36. 297 applicants, 92% accepted, 211 enrolled. In 2016, 403 master's awarded. *Degree requirements:* For master's, thesis, field experience. *Entrance requirements:* For master's, GRE or MAT if GPA is below 3.0, bachelor's degree; minimum GPA of 2.75 in bachelor's degree or last 60 credit hours; official transcripts from all institutions; goal statement of 250-300 words; 1 reference. Additional exam requirements/recommendations for international students: Required—TOEFL (minimum score 94 iBT), IELTS (minimum score 7), PTE (minimum score 53). *Application deadline:* Applications are processed on a rolling basis. Application fee: $35. Electronic applications accepted. *Expenses:* Contact institution. *Financial support:* In 2016–17, 52 students received support. Federal Work-Study, scholarships/grants, and state work-study, institutional employment available. Support available to part-time students. Financial award application deadline: 4/15; financial award applicants required to submit FAFSA. *Faculty research:* Leadership, diversity, personality traits, second language acquisition. *Unit head:* Dr. Robert LeBlanc, Dean, 713-525-3540, Fax: 713-525-3871, E-mail: education@stthom.edu. *Application contact:* Rita Paredes, Administrative Assistant, 713-525-3442, Fax: 713-525-3871, E-mail: rparede@stthom.edu.
Website: http://www.stthom.edu/Academics/School_of_Education_and_Human_Services/Index.aqf

University of San Diego, School of Leadership and Education Sciences, Department of Learning and Teaching, San Diego, CA 92110-2492. Offers inclusive learning (M Ed); literacy and digital learning (M Ed); school leadership (M Ed); special education with deaf and hard of hearing (M Ed); STEAM (science, technology, engineering, arts, and mathematics) (M Ed); teaching (MAT); TESOL, literacy and culture (M Ed). *Program availability:* Part-time, evening/weekend. *Faculty:* 9 full-time (7 women), 29 part-time/adjunct (19 women). *Students:* 161 full-time (126 women), 188 part-time (153 women); includes 127 minority (4 Black or African American, non-Hispanic/Latino; 24 Asian, non-Hispanic/Latino; 86 Hispanic/Latino; 1 Native Hawaiian or other Pacific Islander, non-Hispanic/Latino; 12 Two or more races, non-Hispanic/Latino), 20 international. Average age 33. 383 applicants, 83% accepted, 194 enrolled. In 2016, 114 master's awarded. *Degree requirements:* For master's, thesis (for some programs), international experience. *Entrance requirements:* For master's, California Basic Educational Skills Test, California Subject Examination for Teachers, minimum GPA of 2.75. Additional exam requirements/recommendations for international students: Required—TOEFL (minimum score 580 paper-based; 83 iBT), TWE. *Application deadline:* Applications are processed on a rolling basis. Application fee: $45. Electronic applications accepted. *Financial support:* In 2016–17, 46 students received support. Career-related internships or fieldwork, Federal Work-Study, institutionally sponsored loans, and stipends available. Financial award application deadline: 4/1; financial award applicants required to submit FAFSA. *Faculty research:* Action research methodology, cultural studies, instructional theories and practices, second language acquisition, school reform. *Unit head:* Dr. Maya Kalyanpur, Chair, 619-260-7655, E-mail: mkalyanpur@sandiego.edu. *Application contact:* Monica Mahon, Associate Director of Graduate Admissions, 619-260-4524, Fax: 619-260-4158, E-mail: grads@sandiego.edu.
Website: http://www.sandiego.edu/soles/departments/learning-and-teaching/

University of San Francisco, School of Education, Department of Learning and Instruction, San Francisco, CA 94117-1080. Offers digital technologies for teaching and learning (MA); learning and instruction (MA, Ed D); special education (MA, Ed D); teaching reading (MA). *Program availability:* Part-time, evening/weekend. *Faculty:* 9 full-time (5 women), 2 part-time/adjunct (both women). *Students:* 79 full-time (61 women), 30 part-time (23 women); includes 41 minority (12 Black or African American, non-Hispanic/Latino; 12 Asian, non-Hispanic/Latino; 14 Hispanic/Latino; 3 Two or more races, non-Hispanic/Latino), 7 international. Average age 37. 64 applicants, 94% accepted, 41 enrolled. In 2016, 20 master's, 8 doctorates awarded. *Degree requirements:* For doctorate, thesis/dissertation. *Entrance requirements:* Additional exam requirements/recommendations for international students: Required—TOEFL, IELTS, PTE. *Application deadline:* For fall admission, 3/1 priority date for domestic and international students; for spring admission, 11/1 priority date for domestic and international students. Applications are processed on a rolling basis. Application fee: $55 ($65 for international students). Electronic applications accepted. *Expenses: Tuition:* Full-time $23,310; part-time $1295 per credit. Tuition and fees vary according to course load, degree level, campus/location and program. *Financial support:* In 2016–17, 13 students received support. Fellowships, research assistantships, and teaching assistantships available. Financial award application deadline: 3/2; financial award applicants required to submit FAFSA. *Unit head:* Dr. Kevin Oh, Chair, 415-422-2099. *Application contact:* Amy Fogliani, Admission Coordinator, 415-422-5467, E-mail: schoolofeducation@usfca.edu.

University of Saskatchewan, College of Graduate Studies and Research, College of Education, Department of Curriculum Studies, Saskatoon, SK S7N 5A2, Canada. Offers M Ed, PhD, Diploma. *Program availability:* Part-time. *Degree requirements:* For master's, thesis (for some programs); for doctorate, comprehensive exam (for some programs), thesis/dissertation. *Entrance requirements:* For master's, MAT. Additional exam requirements/recommendations for international students: Required—TOEFL (minimum score 80 iBT); Recommended—IELTS (minimum score 6.5). Electronic applications accepted.

The University of Scranton, Panuska College of Professional Studies, Department of Education, Program in Curriculum and Instruction, Scranton, PA 18510. Offers MS. *Program availability:* Part-time, evening/weekend, online only, 100% online.

University of South Africa, College of Human Sciences, Pretoria, South Africa. Offers adult education (M Ed); African languages (MA, PhD); African politics (MA, PhD); Afrikaans (MA, PhD); ancient history (MA, PhD); ancient Near Eastern studies (MA, PhD); anthropology (MA, PhD); applied linguistics (MA); Arabic (MA, PhD); archaeology (MA); art history (MA); Biblical archaeology (MA); Biblical studies (M Th, D Th, PhD); Christian spirituality (M Th, D Th); church history (M Th, D Th); classical studies (MA, PhD); clinical psychology (MA); communication (MA, PhD); comparative education (M Ed, Ed D); consulting psychology (D Admin, D Com, PhD); curriculum studies (M Ed, Ed D); development studies (M Admin, MA, D Admin, PhD); didactics (M Ed, Ed D); education (M Tech); education management (M Ed, Ed D); educational psychology (M Ed); English (MA); environmental education (M Ed); French (MA, PhD); German (MA, PhD); Greek (MA); guidance and counseling (M Ed); health studies (MA, PhD), including health sciences education (MA), health services management (MA), medical and surgical nursing science (critical care general) (MA), midwifery and neonatal nursing science (MA), trauma and emergency care (MA); history (MA, PhD); history of education (Ed D); inclusive education (M Ed, Ed D); information and communications technology policy and regulation (MA); information science (MA, MIS, PhD); international politics (MA, PhD); Islamic studies (MA, PhD); Italian (MA, PhD); Judaica (MA, PhD); linguistics (MA, PhD); mathematical education (M Ed); mathematics education (MA); missiology (M Th, D Th); modern Hebrew (MA, PhD); musicology (MA, MMus, D Mus, PhD); natural science education (M Ed); New Testament (M Th, D Th); Old Testament (D Th); pastoral therapy (M Th, D Th); philosophy (MA); philosophy of education (M Ed, Ed D); politics (MA, PhD); Portuguese (MA, PhD); practical theology (M Th, D Th); psychology (MA, MS, PhD); psychology of education (M Ed, Ed D); public health (MA); religious studies (MA, D Th, PhD); Romance languages (MA); Russian (MA, PhD); Semitic languages (MA, PhD); social behavior studies in HIV/AIDS (MA); social science (mental health) (MA); social science in development studies (MA); social science in psychology (MA); social science in social work (MA); social science in sociology (MA); social work (MSW, DSW, PhD); socio-education (M Ed, Ed D); sociolinguistics (MA); sociology (MA, PhD); Spanish (MA, PhD); systematic theology (M Th, D Th); TESOL (teaching English to speakers of other languages) (MA); theological ethics (M Th, D Th); theory of literature (MA, PhD); urban ministries (D Th); urban ministry (M Th).

University of South Carolina, The Graduate School, College of Education, Department of Instruction and Teacher Education, Program in Curriculum and Instruction, Columbia, SC 29208. Offers Ed D. This degree cuts across two departments and represents 6 different concentrations. *Accreditation:* NCATE. *Program availability:* Part-time, evening/weekend. *Degree requirements:* For doctorate, comprehensive exam, thesis/dissertation. *Entrance requirements:* For doctorate, GRE General Test or MAT, interview, resume, letter of intent, letters of reference. Electronic applications accepted. *Faculty research:* Teacher education, historian recording project, curriculum development in international areas, human sexuality.

The University of South Dakota, Graduate School, School of Education, Division of Curriculum and Instruction, Vermillion, SD 57069. Offers curriculum and instruction (Ed D, Ed S); elementary education (MA), including elementary education; secondary education (MA), including secondary education; secondary education plus certification (MA); special education (MA), including special education; technology for education and training (MS), including technology for education and training. *Accreditation:* NCATE. *Program availability:* Part-time, online learning. *Degree requirements:* For master's and Ed S, comprehensive exam, thesis or alternative; for doctorate, comprehensive exam, thesis/dissertation. *Entrance requirements:* For master's, doctorate, and Ed S, GRE General Test, MAT, minimum GPA of 2.7. Additional exam requirements/recommendations for international students: Required—TOEFL (minimum score 550 paper-based; 79 iBT). Electronic applications accepted.

University of Southern Mississippi, Graduate School, College of Education and Psychology, Department of Curriculum, Instruction and Special Education, Hattiesburg, MS 39406. Offers elementary education (M Ed, PhD); instructional technology (MS); instructional technology and design (PhD); secondary education (MAT); special education (M Ed, PhD). *Program availability:* Part-time, online learning. *Degree requirements:* For master's, comprehensive exam, thesis (for some programs); for doctorate, comprehensive exam, thesis/dissertation. *Entrance requirements:* For master's, GRE General Test, MAT, minimum GPA of 3.0; for doctorate, GRE General Test, minimum GPA of 3.5. Additional exam requirements/recommendations for international students: Required—TOEFL, IELTS. *Application deadline:* For fall admission, 3/1 priority date for domestic students, 3/1 for international students; for spring admission, 1/10 priority date for domestic and international students. Applications are processed on a rolling basis. Application fee: $60. *Expenses: Tuition, area resident:* Full-time $15,708; part-time $437 per credit hour. *Financial support:* Research assistantships with tuition reimbursements, teaching assistantships with full tuition reimbursements, Federal Work-Study, institutionally sponsored loans, scholarships/grants, health care benefits, tuition waivers (partial), and unspecified assistantships available. Financial award application deadline: 3/15; financial award applicants required to submit FAFSA. *Faculty research:* Mathematical problem solving, integrative curriculum, writing process, teacher education models. *Unit head:* Dr. Mary Ariail, Chair, 601-266-5247, Fax: 601-266-4548.
Website: https://www.usm.edu/elementary-special-technology-education

University of South Florida Sarasota-Manatee, College of Liberal Arts and Social Sciences, Sarasota, FL 34243. Offers criminal justice (MA); education (MA); educational leadership (M Ed), including curriculum leadership, K-12 public school leadership, non-public/charter school leadership; elementary education (MAT); English education (MA); social work (MSW). *Program availability:* Part-time, 100% online, blended/hybrid learning. *Faculty:* 11 full-time (9 women), 7 part-time/adjunct (5 women). *Students:* 11 full-time (all women), 55 part-time (41 women); includes 18 minority (5 Black or African American, non-Hispanic/Latino; 1 American Indian or Alaska Native, non-Hispanic/Latino; 2 Asian, non-Hispanic/Latino; 10 Hispanic/Latino). Average age 36. 40 applicants, 43% accepted, 17 enrolled. In 2016, 28 master's awarded. *Degree requirements:* For master's, comprehensive exam (for some programs). *Entrance requirements:* Additional exam requirements/recommendations for international students: Required—TOEFL (minimum score 550 paper-based; 79 iBT), IELTS (minimum score 6.5). *Application deadline:* For fall admission, 3/1 priority date for domestic students, 3/1 for international students; for spring admission, 10/1 priority date for domestic students, 10/1 for international students. Applications are processed on a rolling basis. Application fee: $30. Electronic applications accepted. *Expenses:* Contact institution. *Financial support:* In 2016–17, 9 students received support. Career-related internships or fieldwork, institutionally sponsored loans, scholarships/grants, health care benefits, and unspecified assistantships available. Support available to part-time students. Financial award application deadline: 3/1; financial award applicants required to submit FAFSA. *Faculty research:* Educational leadership, secondary education, elementary education, criminal justice, social work. *Unit head:* Dr. Jane Rose, Dean, 941-359-4469, Fax: 941-359-4778, E-mail: jane.rose@sar.usf.edu. *Application contact:* Brandon Avery, Assistant Director, Admissions, 941-359-4331, E-mail: bavery@sar.usf.edu.
Website: http://usfsm.edu/college-of-liberal-arts-sciences/

The University of Tampa, Programs in Education, Tampa, FL 33606-1490. Offers curriculum and instruction (M Ed); instructional design and technology (MS). *Program availability:* Part-time, evening/weekend. *Faculty:* 2 full-time (1 woman), 3 part-time/adjunct (all women). *Students:* 44 full-time (38 women), 18 part-time (14 women); includes 2 minority (both Black or African American, non-Hispanic/Latino), 7 international. Average age 31. 126 applicants, 40% accepted, 29 enrolled. In 2016, 23 master's awarded. *Degree requirements:* For master's, capstone. *Entrance requirements:* For master's, GMAT or GRE, current Florida Professional Teaching Certificate, statement of eligibility for Florida Professional Teaching Certificate, or professional teaching certificate from another state; bachelor's degree in an area of education. Additional exam requirements/recommendations for international students: Required—TOEFL (minimum score 577 paper-based; 90 iBT), IELTS (minimum score 7.5). *Application deadline:* Applications are processed on a rolling basis. Application fee: $40. Electronic applications accepted. *Expenses:* $588 per credit tuition, $40 per term fees. *Financial support:* In 2016–17, 20 students received support. Career-related internships or fieldwork, scholarships/grants, and unspecified assistantships available. Financial award applicants required to submit FAFSA. *Faculty research:* Diversity in the classroom, technology integration, assessment methodologies, complex and ill-structured problem solving, communities of practice. *Unit head:* Dr. Antony Erben, Chair, 813-257-3414, E-mail: terben@ut.edu. *Application contact:* Chanelle Cox, Staff Assistant, Admissions for Graduate and Continuing Studies, 813-253-6249, E-mail: ccox@ut.edu.
Website: http://www.ut.edu/graduate/education/

The University of Tennessee, Graduate School, College of Education, Health and Human Sciences, Program in Education, Knoxville, TN 37996. Offers art education (MS); counseling education (PhD); cultural studies in education (PhD); curriculum (MS, Ed S); curriculum, educational research and evaluation (Ed D, PhD); early childhood education (PhD); early childhood special education (MS); education of deaf and hard of hearing (MS); educational administration and policy studies (Ed D, PhD); educational administration and supervision (Ed S); educational psychology (Ed D, PhD); elementary education (MS, Ed S); elementary teaching (MS); English education (MS, Ed S); exercise science (PhD); foreign language/ESL education (MS, Ed S); instructional technology (MS, Ed D, PhD, Ed S); literacy, language and ESL education (PhD); literacy, language education, and ESL education (Ed D); mathematics education (MS, Ed S); modified and comprehensive special education (MS); reading education (MS, Ed S); school counseling (Ed S); school psychology (PhD, Ed S); science education (MS, Ed S); secondary teaching (MS); social foundations (MS); social science education (MS, Ed S); socio-cultural foundations of sports and education (PhD); special education (Ed S); teacher education (Ed D, PhD). *Accreditation:* NCATE. *Program availability:* Part-time, evening/weekend. *Degree requirements:* For master's and Ed S, thesis optional; for doctorate, variable foreign language requirement, thesis/dissertation. *Entrance requirements:* For master's, minimum GPA of 2.7; for doctorate and Ed S, GRE General Test, minimum GPA of 2.7. Additional exam requirements/recommendations for international students: Required—TOEFL. Electronic applications accepted.

The University of Tennessee at Martin, Graduate Programs, College of Education, Health and Behavioral Sciences, Program in Teaching, Martin, TN 38238. Offers curriculum and instruction (MS Ed), including 7-12, K-6; initial licensure (MS Ed), including elementary education, secondary education; initial licensure K-12 (MS Ed), including physical education, special education; interdisciplinary (MS Ed). *Students:* 21 full-time (14 women), 125 part-time (87 women); includes 22 minority (18 Black or African American, non-Hispanic/Latino; 3 Hispanic/Latino; 1 Two or more races, non-Hispanic/Latino). 115 applicants, 81% accepted, 51 enrolled. In 2016, 26 master's awarded. *Expenses:* Tuition, state resident: full-time $8254; part-time $459 per credit hour. Tuition, nonresident: full-time $22,198; part-time $1234 per credit hour. *Required fees:* $79 per credit hour. Part-time tuition and fees vary according to course load and campus/location. *Faculty research:* Special education, science/math/technology, school reform, reading. *Unit head:* Cynthia West, Dean, 731-881-7125, Fax: 731-881-7975, E-mail: cwest@utm.edu. *Application contact:* Jolene L. Cunningham, Student Services Specialist, 731-881-7012, Fax: 731-881-7499, E-mail: jcunningham@utm.edu.

The University of Texas at Arlington, Graduate School, College of Education, Department of Curriculum and Instruction, Arlington, TX 76019. Offers curriculum and instruction (M Ed), including literacy studies, mathematics education, mind, brain, and education, science education; teaching (with certification) (M Ed T). *Accreditation:* NCATE. *Program availability:* Part-time, evening/weekend, online learning. *Degree requirements:* For master's, comprehensive exam (for some programs), comprehensive activity, research project. *Entrance requirements:* For master's, GRE General Test, minimum undergraduate GPA of 3.0 in last 60 hours of course work, writing sample, 3 letters of recommendation. Additional exam requirements/recommendations for international students: Required—TOEFL (minimum score 550 paper-based). *Application deadline:* For fall admission, 6/1 priority date for domestic students, 4/1 priority date for international students; for spring admission, 10/15 priority date for domestic students, 9/15 priority date for international students. Applications are processed on a rolling basis. Application fee: $50. Electronic applications accepted. *Financial support:* Research assistantships, teaching assistantships, career-related internships or fieldwork, Federal Work-Study, scholarships/grants, and unspecified assistantships available. Financial award application deadline: 6/1; financial award applicants required to submit FAFSA. *Unit head:* Daniel H. Robinson, Chair, 817-272-0116, Fax: 817-272-2618, E-mail: daniel.robinson@uta.edu. *Application contact:* Caitlin Guerrero, Graduate Academic Advisor, 817-272-2956, Fax: 817-272-7624, E-mail: caitling@uta.edu.
Website: http://www.uta.edu/coed/curricandinstruct/index.php

The University of Texas at Austin, Graduate School, College of Education, Department of Curriculum and Instruction, Austin, TX 78712-1111. Offers bilingual/bicultural education (M Ed, MA, PhD); cultural studies in education (M Ed, MA, PhD); early childhood education (M Ed, MA, PhD); language and literacy studies (M Ed, PhD); learning technologies (M Ed, MA, PhD); physical education (M Ed, MA, PhD). Terminal master's awarded for partial completion of doctoral program. *Degree requirements:* For doctorate, thesis/dissertation. *Entrance requirements:* For master's and doctorate, GRE General Test. Electronic applications accepted.

The University of Texas at El Paso, Graduate School, College of Education, Department of Teacher Education, El Paso, TX 79968-0001. Offers education (MA); instruction (M Ed); reading education (M Ed); teaching, learning, and culture (PhD). *Program availability:* Part-time, evening/weekend. *Degree requirements:* For master's, thesis optional. *Entrance requirements:* For master's, GRE General Test, minimum GPA of 3.0. Additional exam requirements/recommendations for international students: Required—TOEFL. Electronic applications accepted.

The University of Texas at San Antonio, College of Education and Human Development, Department of Interdisciplinary Learning and Teaching, San Antonio, TX 78249-0617. Offers education (MA), including curriculum and instruction, early childhood and elementary education, instructional technology, reading and literacy, special education; interdisciplinary learning and teaching (PhD). *Program availability:* Part-time, evening/weekend. *Faculty:* 25 full-time (18 women), 4 part-time/adjunct (2 women). *Students:* 70 full-time (53 women), 256 part-time (222 women); includes 185 minority (22 Black or African American, non-Hispanic/Latino; 10 Asian, non-Hispanic/Latino; 148 Hispanic/Latino; 1 Native Hawaiian or other Pacific Islander, non-Hispanic/Latino; 4 Two or more races, non-Hispanic/Latino), 4 international. Average age 34. 145 applicants, 88% accepted, 100 enrolled. In 2016, 90 master's, 4 doctorates awarded. *Degree requirements:* For master's, comprehensive exam, thesis optional, 36 hours of course work without thesis (33 with thesis); for doctorate, comprehensive exam, thesis/dissertation, minimum of 60 semester credit hours. *Entrance requirements:* For master's, bachelor's degree with minimum GPA of 3.0 in last 60 hours of coursework; 18 hours of undergraduate coursework in education or related field; for doctorate, GRE, transcripts from all colleges and universities attended, professional vitae demonstrating experience in work environment where education was primary professional emphasis, 3 letters of recommendation, statement of purpose, minimum GPA of 3.5. Additional exam requirements/recommendations for international students: Required—TOEFL (minimum score 550 paper-based; 79 iBT), IELTS (minimum score 6.5). *Application deadline:* For fall admission, 7/1 for domestic students, 4/1 for international students; for spring admission, 11/1 for domestic students, 9/1 for international students. Applications are processed on a rolling basis. Application fee: $45 ($80 for international students). Electronic applications accepted. *Financial support:* Career-related internships or fieldwork, Federal Work-Study, and scholarships/grants available. Support available to part-time students. *Faculty research:* Explorations of science, learning and teaching, family involvement in early childhood, culturally-responsive literacy instruction in diverse settings, STEM education, autism spectrum disorder. *Total annual research expenditures:* $766,662. *Unit head:* Dr. Maria R. Cortez, Department Chair, 210-458-4413, Fax: 210-458-7281, E-mail: mari.cortez@utsa.edu. *Application contact:* Elizabeth Narvaes, Student Development Specialist, 210-458-7443, Fax: 210-458-7281, E-mail: elizabeth.narvaez@utsa.edu.
Website: http://education.utsa.edu/interdisciplinary_learning_and_teaching/

The University of Texas Rio Grande Valley, College of Education and P-16 Integration, Department of Teaching and Learning, Edinburg, TX 78539. Offers curriculum and instruction (M Ed, Ed D); educational technology (M Ed). *Program availability:* Part-time. *Degree requirements:* For master's, comprehensive exam, thesis optional. *Entrance requirements:* For master's, GRE. Additional exam requirements/recommendations for international students: Required—TOEFL, IELTS. Tuition and fees vary according to course load and program. *Faculty research:* Dual language instruction, literacy and technology, teacher education in diverse populations, mathematics and science education.

University of the Pacific, Gladys L. Benerd School of Education, Department of Curriculum and Instruction, Stockton, CA 95211-0197. Offers curriculum and instruction (MA); special education (MA). *Accreditation:* NCATE. *Faculty:* 9 full-time (6 women), 32 part-time/adjunct (25 women). *Students:* 6 full-time (all women), 18 part-time (12 women); includes 11 minority (1 Asian, non-Hispanic/Latino; 9 Hispanic/Latino; 1 Two or more races, non-Hispanic/Latino), 1 international. Average age 33. *Degree requirements:* For master's, thesis (for some programs). *Entrance requirements:* For master's, GRE General Test. Additional exam requirements/recommendations for international students: Required—TOEFL. *Application deadline:* For fall admission, 3/1 priority date for domestic students; for spring admission, 10/1 priority date for domestic students. Applications are processed on a rolling basis. Application fee: $75. *Financial support:* Teaching assistantships available. Financial award application deadline: 3/1; financial award applicants required to submit FAFSA. *Unit head:* Dr. Marilyn Draheim, Chairperson, 209-946-2558, E-mail: mdraheim@pacific.edu. *Application contact:* Office of Graduate Admissions, 209-946-2344.

University of the Southwest, Graduate Programs, Hobbs, NM 88240-9129. Offers business administration (MBA); curriculum and instruction (MSE); curriculum and instruction: bilingual (MSE); curriculum and instruction: TESOL (MSE); early childhood education (MSE); educational administration (MSE); mental health counseling (MSE); school counseling (MSE); special education (MSE); sports management (MBA). *Program availability:* Part-time, evening/weekend, online learning. *Degree requirements:* For master's, comprehensive exam, thesis (for some programs). *Entrance requirements:* Additional exam requirements/recommendations for international students: Recommended—TOEFL. Electronic applications accepted.

The University of Toledo, College of Graduate Studies, Judith Herb College of Education, Department of Curriculum and Instruction, Toledo, OH 43606-3390. Offers art education (ME); career and technical education (ME, Ed S); curriculum and instruction (ME, PhD, Ed S); early childhood education (Ed S); education and anthropology (MAE); education and biology (MES); education and chemistry (MES); education and classics (MAE); education and economics (MAE); education and English (MAE); education and French (MAE); education and geology (MES); education and German (MAE); education and history (MAE); education and mathematics (MAE, MES); education and physics (MES); education and political science (MAE); education and sociology (MAE); education and Spanish (MAE); educational media (PhD); educational technology (ME); educational technology: virtual educator (Certificate); elementary education (PhD); English as a second language (MAE); gifted and talented education (PhD); middle childhood education (ME); secondary education (ME, PhD); special education (PhD). *Accreditation:* NCATE. *Program availability:* Part-time, evening/weekend. *Degree requirements:* For master's, comprehensive exam, thesis or alternative; for doctorate, comprehensive exam, thesis/dissertation; for other advanced degree, thesis optional. *Entrance requirements:* For master's, doctorate, and other advanced degree, minimum cumulative GPA of 2.7 for all previous academic work, letters of recommendation. Additional exam requirements/recommendations for international students: Required—TOEFL (minimum score 550 paper-based; 80 iBT). Electronic applications accepted.

University of Vermont, Graduate College, College of Education and Social Services, Program in Curriculum and Instruction, Burlington, VT 05405. Offers MAT. *Accreditation:* NCATE. *Entrance requirements:* For master's, GRE (for M Ed), resume (for M Ed and MAT). Additional exam requirements/recommendations for international students: Required—TOEFL (minimum score 550 paper-based; 80 iBT). Electronic applications accepted. *Expenses:* Tuition, state resident: full-time $5814. Tuition, nonresident: full-time $14,670.

University of Victoria, Faculty of Graduate Studies, Faculty of Education, Department of Curriculum and Instruction, Victoria, BC V8W 2Y2, Canada. Offers art education (M Ed, PhD); curriculum studies (M Ed, MA, PhD); early childhood education (M Ed, PhD); educational studies (PhD); language and literacy (M Ed, MA, PhD); mathematics (M Ed, MA, PhD); music education (M Ed, MA, PhD); science (M Ed, MA, PhD); social studies (M Ed, MA); social, cultural and foundational studies (MA, PhD); technology and environmental education (PhD). *Program availability:* Part-time. *Degree requirements:* For master's, thesis, project (M Ed); for doctorate, comprehensive exam, thesis/dissertation. *Entrance requirements:* For master's, minimum B average. Additional exam requirements/recommendations for international students: Required—TOEFL (minimum score 575 paper-based), IELTS (minimum score 7). Electronic applications accepted. *Faculty research:* Elementary and secondary English, language arts, curriculum theory and practice, educational media and technology, educational administration and leadership, history and philosophy of education.

University of Virginia, Curry School of Education, Department of Curriculum, Instruction, and Special Education, Program in Curriculum and Instruction, Charlottesville, VA 22903. Offers curriculum and instruction (M Ed, Ed S); elementary education (M Ed, Ed D); English education (M Ed, Ed D); foreign language education (M Ed); mathematics education (M Ed, Ed D); science education (Ed D); social studies education (M Ed); MBA/M Ed. *Students:* 43 full-time (35 women), 24 part-time (16 women); includes 7 minority (1 Black or African American, non-Hispanic/Latino; 1 Asian, non-Hispanic/Latino; 2 Hispanic/Latino; 3 Two or more races, non-Hispanic/Latino), 4 international. Average age 33. 93 applicants, 78% accepted, 54 enrolled. In 2016, 52 master's, 14 other advanced degrees awarded. *Degree requirements:* For master's, comprehensive exam (for some programs); for doctorate, comprehensive exam, thesis/dissertation; for Ed S, comprehensive exam. *Entrance requirements:* For master's, doctorate, and Ed S, GRE General Test, 2 letters of recommendation. Additional exam requirements/recommendations for international students: Required—TOEFL (minimum score 600 paper-based; 90 iBT), IELTS (minimum score 7). *Application deadline:* Applications are processed on a rolling basis. Application fee: $60. Electronic applications accepted. *Expenses:* Tuition, state resident: full-time $15,026; part-time $834 per credit hour. Tuition, nonresident: full-time $25,168; part-time $1378 per credit hour. *Required fees:* $2654. *Financial support:* Fellowships with tuition reimbursements, research assistantships with tuition reimbursements, and teaching assistantships with tuition reimbursements available. Financial award application deadline: 1/5; financial award applicants required to submit FAFSA. *Unit head:* Susan Mintz, Program Area Director, 434-924-3128, E-mail: slm4r@virginia.edu. *Application contact:* Eric Molnar, Assistant Director, Admissions and Enrollment Reporting, 434-243-2085, E-mail: eric.molnar@virginia.edu.
Website: http://curry.virginia.edu/academics/areas-of-study/curriculum-teaching-learning

University of Virginia, Curry School of Education, Program in Education, Charlottesville, VA 22903. Offers administration and supervision (PhD); applied developmental science (PhD); counselor education (PhD); curriculum and instruction (PhD); early childhood special education (MT); education evaluation (PhD); educational psychology (PhD); educational research (PhD); elementary education (MT); English education (MT, PhD); foreign language education (MT); higher education (PhD); instructional technology (PhD); kinesiology (MT, PhD); math education (PhD); reading education (PhD); research, statistics and evaluation (PhD); school psychology (PhD); science education (PhD); social studies education (MT, PhD); special education (PhD); world languages education (MT). *Students:* 452 full-time (357 women), 18 part-time (13 women); includes 100 minority (28 Black or African American, non-Hispanic/Latino; 39 Asian, non-Hispanic/Latino; 18 Hispanic/Latino; 15 Two or more races, non-Hispanic/Latino), 14 international. Average age 25. 309 applicants, 51% accepted, 87 enrolled. In 2016, 144 master's, 31 doctorates awarded. *Degree requirements:* For master's, comprehensive exam (for some programs), field project; for doctorate, comprehensive exam, thesis/dissertation. *Entrance requirements:* For doctorate, GRE General Test. Additional exam requirements/recommendations for international students: Required—TOEFL (minimum score 600 paper-based; 90 iBT), IELTS (minimum score 7). *Application deadline:* Applications are processed on a rolling basis. Application fee: $60. Electronic applications accepted. *Expenses:* Tuition, state resident: full-time $15,026; part-time $834 per credit hour. Tuition, nonresident: full-time $25,168; part-time $1378 per credit hour. *Required fees:* $2654. *Financial support:* Fellowships, research assistantships, and teaching assistantships available. Financial award application deadline: 1/5; financial award applicants required to submit FAFSA. *Unit head:* Robert C. Pianta, Dean, 434-924-3334, E-mail: pianta@virginia.edu. *Application contact:* Eric Molnar, Assistant Director, Admissions and Enrollment Reporting, 434-243-2085, E-mail: eric.molnar@virginia.edu.
Website: http://curry.virginia.edu/teacher-education

University of Washington, Graduate School, College of Education, Seattle, WA 98195. Offers curriculum and instruction (M Ed, Ed D, PhD), including educational technology, general curriculum (Ed D, PhD), language, literacy, and culture, mathematics education, multicultural education, reading and language arts education (Ed D), science education, social studies education, teaching and curriculum (M Ed); educational leadership and policy studies (M Ed, Ed D, PhD), including administration (Ed D), educational policy, organization, and leadership (M Ed, PhD), higher education, leadership for learning (Ed D), social and cultural foundations of education (M Ed, PhD); educational psychology (M Ed, PhD), including educational psychology (PhD), human development and cognition (M Ed), learning sciences, measurement, statistics and research design (M Ed), school psychology (M Ed); instructional leadership (M Ed); intercollegiate athletic leadership (M Ed); special education (M Ed, Ed D, PhD), including early childhood special education (M Ed), emotional and behavioral disabilities (M Ed), learning disabilities (M Ed), low-incidence disabilities (M Ed), severe disabilities (M Ed), special education (Ed D, PhD); teacher education (MIT). *Accreditation:* APA. *Program availability:* Part-time, evening/weekend. *Degree requirements:* For master's, thesis optional; for doctorate, thesis/dissertation. *Entrance requirements:* For master's and doctorate, GRE General Test, minimum GPA of 3.0. Additional exam requirements/recommendations for international students: Required—TOEFL. Electronic applications accepted. *Faculty research:* School restructuring/effective schools, special education interventions, literacy and writing, technology, school partnerships, teacher preparation.

The University of West Alabama, School of Graduate Studies, College of Education, Departments of Instructional Leadership and Support/Curriculum and Instruction, Livingston, AL 35470. Offers continuing education (MSCE), including counseling and psychology, family counseling, general, guidance and counseling, library media, student affairs in higher education; early childhood education (M Ed, Ed S), including early childhood development (M Ed), early childhood education (Ed S), early childhood education P-3 (M Ed); elementary education (M Ed, Ed S), including elementary education (Ed S), elementary education K-6 (M Ed); instructional leadership (M Ed, Ed S), including instructional leadership, teacher leader (Ed S); library media (M Ed, Ed S); school counseling (M Ed, Ed S), including guidance counseling (Ed S), school counseling; secondary education (M Ed, MAT), including biology (MAT), English language arts (MAT), high school 6-12 (M Ed), history (MAT), mathematics (MAT), science (MAT), social science (MAT); special education (M Ed, Ed S), including collaborative special education 6-12 (Ed S), collaborative special education K-6 (Ed S), special education collaborative teacher 6-12 (M Ed), special education collaborative teacher K-6 (M Ed). *Accreditation:* NCATE. *Program availability:* Part-time, evening/weekend, 100% online. *Faculty:* 43 full-time (27 women), 79 part-time/adjunct (50 women). *Students:* 1,868 (1,571 women); includes 689 minority (635 Black or African American, non-Hispanic/Latino; 12 American Indian or Alaska Native, non-Hispanic/Latino; 6 Asian, non-Hispanic/Latino; 12 Hispanic/Latino; 1 Native Hawaiian or other Pacific Islander, non-Hispanic/Latino; 23 Two or more races, non-Hispanic/Latino). Average age 35. 637 applicants, 87% accepted, 426 enrolled. In 2016, 498 master's, 124 other advanced degrees awarded. *Degree requirements:* For master's, comprehensive exam, thesis optional; for Ed S, comprehensive exam. *Entrance requirements:* For master's, GRE or MAT, minimum GPA of 2.75. Additional exam requirements/recommendations for international students: Required—TOEFL (minimum score 500 paper-based; 61 iBT). *Application deadline:* Applications are processed on a rolling basis. Application fee: $40. Electronic applications accepted. *Expenses:* Tuition, state resident: part-time $355 per credit hour. Tuition, nonresident: part-time $710 per credit hour. *Required fees:* $130 per semester. *Financial support:* Teaching assistantships, Federal Work-Study, scholarships/grants, and unspecified assistantships available. Support available to part-time students. Financial award application deadline: 3/1; financial award applicants required to submit FAFSA. *Unit head:* Dr. Reenay Rogers, Chair of Instructional Leadership and Support, 205-652-5423, Fax: 205-652-3706, E-mail: rrogers@uwa.edu. *Application contact:* Dr. B. J. Kimbrough, Dean of Graduate Studies, 205-652-3647, Fax: 205-652-3670, E-mail: bkimbrough@uwa.edu.

The University of Western Ontario, Faculty of Graduate Studies, Social Sciences Division, Faculty of Education, Program in Educational Studies, London, ON N6A 5B8, Canada. Offers curriculum studies (M Ed); educational policy studies (M Ed); educational psychology/special education (M Ed). *Program availability:* Part-time. *Faculty research:* Reflective practice, gender and schooling, feminist pedagogy, narrative inquiry, second language, multiculturalism in Canada, education and law.

University of West Florida, College of Education and Professional Studies, Department of Research and Advanced Studies, Ed S Program in Curriculum and Instruction, Pensacola, FL 32514-5750. Offers Ed S. *Accreditation:* NCATE. *Program availability:* Evening/weekend. *Entrance requirements:* Additional exam requirements/recommendations for international students: Required—TOEFL (minimum score 550 paper-based). *Application deadline:* For fall admission, 6/1 for domestic and international students; for spring admission, 10/1 for domestic and international students. Applications are processed on a rolling basis. Application fee: $30. *Expenses:* Tuition, state resident: full-time $5316.12. Tuition, nonresident: full-time $11,308. *Required fees:* $583.92. Tuition and fees vary according to course load and program. *Financial support:* Fellowships, Federal Work-Study, institutionally sponsored loans, scholarships/grants, and tuition waivers (partial) available. Support available to part-time students. Financial award application deadline: 4/15; financial award applicants required to submit FAFSA. *Unit head:* Dr. Karen Rasmussen, Interim Chairperson, 850-474-2300, Fax: 850-857-6288, E-mail: krasmuss@uwf.edu. *Application contact:* Terry McCray, Assistant Director of Graduate Admissions, 850-473-7718, Fax: 850-473-7714, E-mail: gradadmissions@uwf.edu.

University of West Florida, College of Education and Professional Studies, Department of Teacher Education and Educational Leadership, Program in Curriculum and Instruction, Pensacola, FL 32514-5750. Offers elementary education (M Ed); middle level education (M Ed); secondary education (M Ed). *Program availability:* Part-time, evening/weekend. *Entrance requirements:* For master's, GRE (minimum score 450 verbal) or MAT (minimum score 396) if bachelor's GPA less than 3.0, state teaching certification; letter of intent; two professional references. Additional exam requirements/recommendations for international students: Required—TOEFL (minimum score 550 paper-based). *Application deadline:* For fall admission, 6/1 for domestic and international students; for spring admission, 10/1 for domestic and international students. Applications are processed on a rolling basis. Application fee: $30. *Expenses:* Tuition, state resident: full-time $5316.12. Tuition, nonresident: full-time $11,308.

Required fees: $583.92. Tuition and fees vary according to course load and program. *Financial support:* Career-related internships or fieldwork, Federal Work-Study, scholarships/grants, and tuition waivers (partial) available. Support available to part-time students. Financial award application deadline: 4/15; financial award applicants required to submit FAFSA. *Unit head:* Dr. William H. Evans, Acting Director, 850-474-2892, Fax: 850-474-2844, E-mail: wevans@uwf.edu. *Application contact:* Terry McCray, Assistant Director of Graduate Admissions, 850-473-7718, Fax: 850-473-7714, E-mail: gradadmissions@uwf.edu.

University of Wisconsin–Madison, Graduate School, School of Education, Department of Curriculum and Instruction, Madison, WI 53706-1380. Offers art education (MA); curriculum and instruction (MS, PhD); education and mathematics (MA); French education (MA); German education (MA); music education (MS); science education (MS); Spanish education (MA). *Accreditation:* NASM (one or more programs are accredited). *Degree requirements:* For doctorate, thesis/dissertation.

University of Wisconsin–Milwaukee, Graduate School, School of Education, Department of Curriculum and Instruction, Milwaukee, WI 53201-0413. Offers curriculum and instruction (MS), including cross-curricular focus, early childhood education, English education, mathematics education, middle childhood/early adolescence education, reading education, science education, urban social studies education. *Program availability:* Part-time. *Students:* 21 full-time (13 women), 44 part-time (42 women); includes 10 minority (1 Black or African American, non-Hispanic/Latino; 1 Asian, non-Hispanic/Latino; 2 Hispanic/Latino; 6 Two or more races, non-Hispanic/Latino), 2 international. Average age 33. 42 applicants, 71% accepted, 20 enrolled. In 2016, 45 master's awarded. *Degree requirements:* For master's, thesis or alternative. *Entrance requirements:* Additional exam requirements/recommendations for international students: Required—TOEFL (minimum score 550 paper-based; 79 iBT), IELTS (minimum score 6.5). *Application deadline:* For fall admission, 1/1 priority date for domestic students; for spring admission, 9/1 for domestic students. Applications are processed on a rolling basis. Application fee: $56 ($96 for international students). Electronic applications accepted. *Financial support:* In 2016–17, 1 fellowship was awarded; research assistantships, teaching assistantships, career-related internships or fieldwork, health care benefits, unspecified assistantships, and project assistantships also available. Support available to part-time students. Financial award application deadline: 4/15; financial award applicants required to submit FAFSA. *Application contact:* General Information Contact, 414-229-4721, E-mail: soeinfo@uwm.edu. Website: http://uwm.edu/education/academics/curriculum-instruction-department/

University of Wisconsin–Milwaukee, Graduate School, School of Education, Department of Exceptional Education, Milwaukee, WI 53201-0413. Offers autism spectrum disorders (Graduate Certificate); exceptional education (MS); transition for students with disabilities (Graduate Certificate); urban education (PhD), including adult, continuing and higher education leadership, art education, curriculum and instruction, exceptional education, mathematics education, multicultural studies, social foundations of education. *Program availability:* Part-time. *Students:* 50 full-time (41 women), 66 part-time (51 women); includes 42 minority (24 Black or African American, non-Hispanic/Latino; 6 Asian, non-Hispanic/Latino; 1 Hispanic/Latino; 11 Two or more races, non-Hispanic/Latino), 4 international. Average age 39. 55 applicants, 51% accepted, 22 enrolled. In 2016, 14 master's, 10 doctorates, 3 other advanced degrees awarded. *Degree requirements:* For master's, thesis. *Entrance requirements:* Additional exam requirements/recommendations for international students: Required—TOEFL (minimum score 550 paper-based; 79 iBT), IELTS (minimum score 6.5). *Application deadline:* For fall admission, 1/1 priority date for domestic students; for spring admission, 9/1 for domestic students. Applications are processed on a rolling basis. Application fee: $56 ($96 for international students). Electronic applications accepted. *Financial support:* Fellowships, research assistantships, teaching assistantships, career-related internships or fieldwork, health care benefits, and unspecified assistantships available. Support available to part-time students. Financial award application deadline: 4/15; financial award applicants required to submit FAFSA. *Faculty research:* Emotional disturbance, hearing impairment, learning disabilities, mental retardation. *Application contact:* General Information Contact, 414-229-4721, E-mail: soeinfo@uwm.edu. Website: http://uwm.edu/education/academics/exceptional-edu-department/

University of Wisconsin–Oshkosh, Graduate Studies, College of Education and Human Services, Department of Curriculum and Instruction, Oshkosh, WI 54901. Offers MSE. *Program availability:* Part-time, evening/weekend. *Degree requirements:* For master's, thesis or alternative, seminar paper. *Entrance requirements:* For master's, teaching license, letters of recommendation. Additional exam requirements/recommendations for international students: Required—TOEFL (minimum score 550 paper-based; 79 iBT). Electronic applications accepted. *Faculty research:* Early childhood, middle school teaching, literacy, elementary teaching, bilingual education.

University of Wisconsin–Superior, Graduate Division, Department of Teacher Education, Program in Instruction, Superior, WI 54880-4500. Offers MSE. *Program availability:* Part-time, evening/weekend. *Degree requirements:* For master's, comprehensive exam, thesis or alternative, research project. *Entrance requirements:* For master's, minimum GPA of 2.75, teaching certificate. Electronic applications accepted.

University of Wyoming, College of Education, Programs in Curriculum and Instruction, Laramie, WY 82071. Offers MA, Ed D, PhD. *Program availability:* Part-time, online learning. Terminal master's awarded for partial completion of doctoral program. *Degree requirements:* For master's, comprehensive exam, thesis; for doctorate, comprehensive exam, thesis/dissertation. *Entrance requirements:* For master's, minimum GPA of 3.0, 3 letters of reference, writing samples; for doctorate, accredited master's degree, 3 letters of reference, 3 years of teaching experience, writing sample. Additional exam requirements/recommendations for international students: Required—TOEFL (minimum score 525 paper-based). *Faculty research:* Teaching and learning teacher education, multi-cultural education, early childhood, discipline-specific pedagogy.

Utah State University, School of Graduate Studies, Emma Eccles Jones College of Education and Human Services, Doctoral Program in Education, Logan, UT 84322. Offers business information systems (Ed D, PhD); curriculum and instruction (Ed D, PhD); research and evaluation (PhD). *Degree requirements:* For doctorate, comprehensive exam, thesis/dissertation. *Entrance requirements:* For doctorate, GRE General Test, minimum GPA of 3.0, master's degree. Additional exam requirements/recommendations for international students: Required—TOEFL. Electronic applications accepted. *Faculty research:* Language and literacy development, math and science education, instructional technology, hearing problems/deafness, domestic violence and animal abuse.

Virginia Commonwealth University, Graduate School, School of Education, Doctoral Program in Education, Richmond, VA 23284-9005. Offers art education (PhD); counselor education and supervision (PhD); curriculum, culture and change (PhD); educational leadership (PhD); educational psychology (PhD); leadership (Ed D); research and evaluation (PhD); special education and disability leadership (PhD); sport leadership (PhD); urban services leadership (PhD). *Accreditation:* NCATE. *Program availability:* Part-time. *Degree requirements:* For doctorate, thesis/dissertation. *Entrance requirements:* For doctorate, GRE (for PhD), MAT (for Ed D), interview, master's degree, writing sample. Additional exam requirements/recommendations for international students: Required—TOEFL (minimum score 600 paper-based; 100 iBT). *Application deadline:* For fall admission, 2/15 for domestic students. Application fee: $50. Electronic applications accepted. *Financial support:* Fellowships, research assistantships, career-related internships or fieldwork, Federal Work-Study, and institutionally sponsored loans available. Financial award application deadline: 3/1; financial award applicants required to submit FAFSA. *Unit head:* Dr. Kathleen Cauley, Interim Director, 804-827-2657, E-mail: kmcauley@vcu.edu. *Application contact:* Dr. Colleen A. Thoma, Administrative Assistant, 804-827-2651, E-mail: cathoma@vcu.edu. Website: http://www.soe.vcu.edu/programs/doctoral-programs/

Virginia Polytechnic Institute and State University, Graduate School, College of Liberal Arts and Human Sciences, Blacksburg, VA 24061. Offers career and technical education (MS Ed, Ed D, PhD, Ed S); communication (MA); counselor education (MA Ed, Ed D, PhD, Ed S); creative writing (MFA); curriculum and instruction (MA Ed, Ed D, PhD, Ed S); educational leadership and policy studies (MA Ed, Ed D, PhD, Ed S); educational research and evaluation (PhD); English (MA); foreign languages, cultures, and literatures (MA); higher education (PhD); higher education and student affairs (MA Ed); history (MA); human development (MS, PhD); material culture and public humanities (MA); philosophy (MA); political science (MA); rhetoric and writing (PhD); science and technology studies (MS, PhD); social, political, ethical, and cultural thought (PhD); sociology (MS, PhD); theater arts (MFA). *Faculty:* 408 full-time (204 women), 3 part-time/adjunct (2 women). *Students:* 657 full-time (446 women), 457 part-time (292 women); includes 213 minority (114 Black or African American, non-Hispanic/Latino; 3 American Indian or Alaska Native, non-Hispanic/Latino; 29 Asian, non-Hispanic/Latino; 44 Hispanic/Latino; 23 Two or more races, non-Hispanic/Latino), 93 international. Average age 33. 805 applicants, 55% accepted, 328 enrolled. In 2016, 270 master's, 91 doctorates awarded. *Degree requirements:* For master's, comprehensive exam (for some programs), thesis (for some programs); for doctorate, comprehensive exam (for some programs), thesis/dissertation (for some programs). *Entrance requirements:* For master's and doctorate, GRE/GMAT. Additional exam requirements/recommendations for international students: Required—TOEFL (minimum score 80 iBT). *Application deadline:* For fall admission, 8/1 for domestic students, 4/1 for international students; for spring admission, 1/1 for domestic students, 9/1 for international students. Applications are processed on a rolling basis. Application fee: $75. Electronic applications accepted. *Expenses:* Tuition, state resident: full-time $12,467; part-time $692.50 per credit hour. Tuition, nonresident: full-time $25,095; part-time $1394.25 per credit hour. *Required fees:* $2669; $491.50 per semester. Tuition and fees vary according to course load, campus/location and program. *Financial support:* In 2016–17, 21 research assistantships with full tuition reimbursements (averaging $19,817 per year), 237 teaching assistantships with full tuition reimbursements (averaging $15,497 per year) were awarded. Financial award application deadline: 3/1; financial award applicants required to submit FAFSA. *Total annual research expenditures:* $6.6 million. *Unit head:* Rosemary Blieszner, Interim Dean, 540-231-6779, Fax: 540-231-7157, E-mail: liberalartsdean@vt.edu. *Application contact:* Chelsea Blanchet, Executive Assistant, 540-231-6779, Fax: 540-231-7157, E-mail: bchels1@vt.edu. Website: http://www.liberalarts.vt.edu/

Virginia Union University, Evelyn R. Syphax School of Education, Psychology and Interdisciplinary Studies, Richmond, VA 23220-1170. Offers curriculum and instruction (MA).

Walden University, Graduate Programs, Richard W. Riley College of Education and Leadership, Minneapolis, MN 55401. Offers adult education (Post-Master's Certificate); adult learning (Graduate Certificate); college teaching and learning (Graduate Certificate); community college leadership (Ed D); curriculum, instruction and assessment (Ed D, Ed S, Graduate Certificate); developmental education (Graduate Certificate); early childhood administration, management, and leadership (Graduate Certificate); early childhood education (Ed D, Ed S); early childhood public policy and advocacy (Graduate Certificate); early childhood studies (MS), including administration, management and leadership, early childhood public policy and advocacy, teaching adults in the early childhood field, teaching and diversity in early childhood education; education (MS, PhD), including adolescent literacy and learning (MS), curriculum, instruction, and assessment (grades K-12) (MS), curriculum, instruction, assessment, and evaluation (PhD), early childhood leadership and advocacy (PhD), early childhood special education (PhD), educational leadership (MS), educational leadership and administration (principal preparation) (MS), educational technology and design (PhD), elementary reading and literacy (PreK-6) (MS), elementary reading and mathematics (grades K-6) (MS), global and comparative education (PhD), higher education leadership management and policy (PhD), integrating technology in the classroom (grades K-12) (MS), learning, instruction and innovation (PhD), mathematics (grades 5-8) (MS), mathematics (grades K-6) (MS), mathematics and science (grades K-8) (MS), organizational research, assessment, and evaluation (PhD), reading and literacy with a reading K-12 endorsement (MS), reading literacy assessment and evaluation (PhD), science (grades K-8) (MS), special education (non-licensure) (grades K-12) (MS), teacher leadership (grades K-12) (MS), teaching English language learners (grades K-12) (MS); educational administration and leadership (Ed D); educational leadership and administration (principal preparation) (Ed S); educational technology (Ed D, Ed S, Post Master's Certificate); elementary reading and literacy (Graduate Certificate); engaging culturally diverse learners (Graduate Certificate); enrollment management and institutional marketing (Graduate Certificate); higher education (MS), including adult learning, college teaching and learning, enrollment management and institutional marketing, global higher education, leadership for student success, online and distance learning; higher education and adult learning (Ed D); higher education leadership and management (Ed D); higher education leadership for student success (Graduate Certificate); instructional design and technology (MS, Postbaccalaureate Certificate), including general program (MS), online learning (MS), training and performance improvement (MS); integrating technology in the classroom (Graduate Certificate); mathematics 5-8 (Graduate Certificate); mathematics K-6 (Graduate Certificate); online teaching for adult educators (Graduate Certificate); reading, literacy, and assessment (Ed D, Ed S); science K-8 (Graduate Certificate); special education (Ed D, Ed S, Graduate Certificate); special education (K-age 21) (MAT); teacher leadership (Graduate Certificate); teaching adults English as a second language (Graduate Certificate); teaching adults in the early childhood field (Graduate Certificate); teaching and diversity in early childhood education (Graduate Certificate); teaching English language learners (grades K-12) (Graduate Certificate); teaching K-12 students online (Graduate Certificate). *Accreditation:* NCATE. *Program availability:* Part-time, evening/weekend, online only, 100% online. *Degree requirements:* For doctorate, thesis/dissertation (for some programs), residency; for other advanced degree, residency (for some programs). *Entrance requirements:* For master's, bachelor's degree or higher; minimum GPA of 2.5; official transcripts; goal statement (for some programs); access to computer and Internet; for doctorate, master's degree or higher; three years of related professional or academic experience (preferred); minimum GPA of 3.0; goal statement and current resume (for select programs); official transcripts; access to computer and Internet; for other advanced degree, relevant work experience; access to computer and Internet. Additional exam requirements/recommendations for international students: Required—TOEFL (minimum score 550 paper-based, 79 iBT), IELTS (minimum score

6.5), Michigan English Language Assessment Battery (minimum score 82), or PTE (minimum score 53). Electronic applications accepted.

Walla Walla University, Graduate Studies, School of Education and Psychology, College Place, WA 99324. Offers curriculum and instruction (M Ed, MA, MAT); educational leadership (M Ed, MA, MAT); literacy instruction (M Ed, MA, MAT); students at risk (M Ed, MA, MAT); teaching (MAT). *Program availability:* Part-time. *Entrance requirements:* For master's, GRE General Test, minimum GPA of 2.75. Additional exam requirements/recommendations for international students: Required—TOEFL (minimum score 550 paper-based; 79 iBT). *Application deadline:* For fall admission, 4/1 priority date for domestic students. Applications are processed on a rolling basis. Application fee: $50. Electronic applications accepted. *Expenses: Tuition:* Part-time $592 per quarter hour. *Financial support:* Research assistantships, teaching assistantships, Federal Work-Study, and tuition waivers (partial) available. Support available to part-time students. Financial award application deadline: 4/30; financial award applicants required to submit FAFSA. *Faculty research:* Admissions/retention, instructional psychology, moral development, teaching of reading. *Unit head:* Denise Dunzweiler, Dean, 509-527-2212, Fax: 509-527-2248, E-mail: denise.dunzweiler@wallawalla.edu. *Application contact:* Dr. Joe G. Galusha, Dean of Graduate Studies, 509-527-2421, Fax: 509-527-2237, E-mail: joe.galusha@wallawalla.edu.
Website: https://wallawalla.edu/academics/areas-of-study/undergraduate-programs/education-and-psychology/

Warner University, School of Education, Lake Wales, FL 33859. Offers curriculum and instruction (MAEd); elementary education (MAEd); science, technology, engineering, and mathematics (STEM) (MAEd). *Program availability:* Part-time, evening/weekend, online learning. *Degree requirements:* For master's, thesis, accomplished practices portfolio. *Entrance requirements:* For master's, minimum GPA of 3.0 in last 60 hours of undergraduate coursework; 2 letters of recommendation. Additional exam requirements/recommendations for international students: Required—TOEFL (minimum score 550 paper-based). *Application deadline:* Applications are processed on a rolling basis. Application fee: $50. Electronic applications accepted. *Financial support:* Scholarships/grants available. Financial award applicants required to submit FAFSA. *Unit head:* Dr. Bill Rigel, Dean, 863-638-7207, Fax: 863-638-4907, E-mail: bill.rigel@warner.edu. *Application contact:* Torshanda Howard, Admissions Advisor, 863-638-7501, Fax: 863-638-4907, E-mail: admissons@warner.edu.
Website: http://warner.edu/graduate/degrees-offered/arts-in-education/

Washburn University, College of Arts and Sciences, Department of Education, Topeka, KS 66621. Offers curriculum and instruction (M Ed); educational leadership (M Ed); reading (M Ed); special education (M Ed). *Accreditation:* NCATE. *Program availability:* Part-time. *Degree requirements:* For master's, comprehensive exam, thesis or alternative, portfolio, comprehensive paper, or action research project. *Entrance requirements:* For master's, department exam, GRE General Test, or MAT, minimum GPA of 3.0 in graduate coursework or last 60 hours of undergraduate coursework. Additional exam requirements/recommendations for international students: Required—TOEFL (minimum score 80 iBT). *Faculty research:* Reading/literature/literacy, foundations, special education, diversity, teaching and technology.

Washington State University, College of Education, Department of Teaching and Learning, Pullman, WA 99164-2132. Offers cultural studies and social thought in education (PhD); curriculum and instruction (Ed M, MA); English language learners (Ed M, MA); language, literacy and technology (PhD); literacy education (Ed M, MA); mathematics education (PhD); special education (Ed M, MA, PhD); teacher leadership (Ed D); teaching (MIT), including elementary education, secondary education. Programs offered at the Pullman, Spokane, Tri-cities, Vancouver and Global (online) campuses. *Program availability:* Part-time, online learning. *Degree requirements:* For master's, comprehensive exam, thesis, oral or written exam; for doctorate, comprehensive exam, thesis/dissertation, oral and written exam. *Entrance requirements:* For master's, GRE General Test, minimum GPA of 3.0, 3 letters of recommendation, letter of intent, transcripts, resume/curriculum vitae; for doctorate, GRE General Test, minimum GPA of 3.0, 3 letters of recommendation, letter of intent, transcripts, writing sample, resume/curriculum vitae. Additional exam requirements/recommendations for international students: Required—TOEFL (minimum score 550 paper-based; 80 iBT). Electronic applications accepted. *Faculty research:* Intersection of gender, youth cultures and schooling; examination of ideology of power in children's literature; early childhood special education; analyzing pre-service and in-service teacher development; second language acquisition.

Waynesburg University, Graduate and Professional Studies, Canonsburg, PA 15370. Offers business (MBA), including energy management, finance, health systems, human resources, leadership, market development; counseling (MA), including addictions counseling, clinical mental health; counselor education and supervision (PhD); criminal investigation (MA); education (M Ed), including autism, curriculum and instruction, educational leadership, online teaching; nursing (MSN), including administration, education, informatics; nursing practice (DNP); special education (M Ed); technology (M Ed); MSN/MBA. *Accreditation:* AACN. *Program availability:* Part-time, evening/weekend. *Degree requirements:* For doctorate, thesis/dissertation. *Entrance requirements:* Additional exam requirements/recommendations for international students: Required—TOEFL. Electronic applications accepted.

Wayne State College, School of Education and Counseling, Department of Educational Foundations and Leadership, Program in Curriculum and Instruction, Wayne, NE 68787. Offers alternative education (MSE); business and information technology education (MSE); communication arts education (MSE); early childhood education (MSE); elementary education (MSE); English as a second language (MSE); English education (MSE); family and consumer sciences education (MSE); industrial technology and vocational education (MSE); learning communities (MSE); mathematics education (MSE); music education (MSE); science education (MSE); social science education (MSE). *Accreditation:* NCATE. *Program availability:* Part-time, evening/weekend. *Degree requirements:* For master's, comprehensive exam, thesis optional. *Entrance requirements:* For master's, GRE General Test. Additional exam requirements/recommendations for international students: Required—TOEFL (minimum score 550 paper-based).

Wayne State University, College of Education, Division of Teacher Education, Detroit, MI 48202. Offers art education (M Ed); bilingual/bicultural education (M Ed, Certificate); career and technical education (M Ed); curriculum and instruction (Ed D, PhD, Ed S), including art education (Ed D, PhD), bilingual education (Ed D, Ed S), career and technical education (MAT, Ed D, PhD, Ed S), early childhood education (MAT, Ed D, PhD, Ed S), elementary education, English as a second language (MAT, Ed D, Ed S), English education (MAT, Ed D, PhD, Ed S), foreign language education (MAT, Ed D, PhD), K-12 curriculum, mathematics education (MAT, Ed D, PhD, Ed S), science education (MAT, Ed D, PhD, Ed S), secondary education, social studies education (MAT, Ed D, PhD, Ed S); early childhood education (M Ed); elementary education (M Ed, MAT), including bilingual/bicultural education (MAT), early childhood education (MAT, Ed D, PhD, Ed S), English as a second language (MAT, Ed D, Ed S), general elementary education (MAT), mathematics education (MAT, Ed D, PhD, Ed S), science education (MAT, Ed D, PhD, Ed S), social studies education (MAT, Ed D, PhD, Ed S); English as a second language (Certificate); English education (M Ed); foreign language education (M Ed); mathematics education (M Ed); reading (M Ed, Ed S); reading, language and literature (Ed D); science education (M Ed); secondary education (MAT), including art education (K-12), bilingual/bicultural education, career and technical education (MAT, Ed D, PhD, Ed S), English as a second language (MAT, Ed D, Ed S), English education (MAT, Ed D, PhD, Ed S), foreign language education (MAT, Ed D, PhD), kinesiology, mathematics education (MAT, Ed D, PhD, Ed S); social studies education (M Ed); special education (M Ed, MAT, Ed D, PhD, Ed S), including autism spectrum disorders (MAT), cognitive development (MAT), emotional impairment (MAT), learning disabilities (MAT). *Program availability:* Part-time, blended/hybrid learning. *Faculty:* 29. *Students:* 106 full-time (73 women), 351 part-time (276 women); includes 115 minority (76 Black or African American, non-Hispanic/Latino; 10 Asian, non-Hispanic/Latino; 20 Hispanic/Latino; 1 Native Hawaiian or other Pacific Islander, non-Hispanic/Latino; 8 Two or more races, non-Hispanic/Latino), 12 international. Average age 37. 242 applicants, 37% accepted, 72 enrolled. In 2016, 178 master's, 19 doctorates, 17 other advanced degrees awarded. *Degree requirements:* For master's, essay or project (for some M Ed programs), professional field experience (for MAT programs); for doctorate, thesis/dissertation. *Entrance requirements:* For master's, Michigan Test for Teacher Certification, verification of participation in group work with children, Michigan State Police criminal background check; for doctorate, minimum undergraduate GPA of 3.0, graduate 3.5; interview; curriculum vitae; references. Additional exam requirements/recommendations for international students: Required—TOEFL (minimum score 550 paper-based; 79 iBT), TWE (minimum score 5.5), Michigan English Language Assessment Battery (minimum score 85); Recommended—IELTS (minimum score 6.5). *Application deadline:* For fall admission, 6/1 priority date for domestic students, 5/1 priority date for international students; for winter admission, 10/1 priority date for domestic students, 9/1 priority date for international students; for spring admission, 2/1 priority date for domestic students, 1/1 priority date for international students. Applications are processed on a rolling basis. Application fee: $50. Electronic applications accepted. *Expenses:* $16,503 per year resident tuition and fees, $33,697 per year non-resident tuition and fees. *Financial support:* In 2016–17, 101 students received support, including 3 fellowships (averaging $11,409 per year); research assistantships with tuition reimbursements available, Federal Work-Study, scholarships/grants, and unspecified assistantships also available. Support available to part-time students. Financial award applicants required to submit FAFSA. *Faculty research:* Improving students' skill achievement in mathematics, improving elementary children's understanding of informational text, teachers' use of their pedagogical and mathematical knowledge in the interactive work of teaching, the intersection of identity construction in teaching and learning, identifying effective methods of literacy instruction and assessments for bilingual students in elementary language arts classrooms. *Unit head:* Dr. Kathleen Crawford-McKinney, Assistant Dean, 313-577-0122. *Application contact:* Janice Green, Assistant Dean, 313-577-1605, E-mail: jwgreen@wayne.edu.
Website: http://coe.wayne.edu/ted/index.php

Weber State University, Jerry and Vickie Moyes College of Education, Program in Curriculum and Instruction, Ogden, UT 84408-1001. Offers M Ed. *Accreditation:* NCATE. *Program availability:* Part-time, evening/weekend. *Faculty:* 18 full-time (12 women). *Students:* 14 full-time (7 women), 109 part-time (84 women); includes 7 minority (4 Asian, non-Hispanic/Latino; 3 Hispanic/Latino), 1 international. Average age 37. In 2016, 30 master's awarded. *Degree requirements:* For master's, thesis or alternative, project presentation, exam. *Entrance requirements:* For master's, MAT or GRE, minimum GPA of 3.0. Additional exam requirements/recommendations for international students: Required—TOEFL (minimum score 85 iBT). *Application deadline:* For fall admission, 5/15 for domestic students; for spring admission, 9/15 for domestic students; for summer admission, 1/15 for domestic students. Applications are processed on a rolling basis. Application fee: $60 ($90 for international students). Electronic applications accepted. *Expenses:* Contact institution. *Financial support:* In 2016–17, 12 students received support. Scholarships/grants available. Financial award application deadline: 4/1; financial award applicants required to submit FAFSA. *Unit head:* Dr. Peggy Saunders, Director, 801-626-7673, Fax: 801-626-7427, E-mail: psaunders@weber.edu. *Application contact:* Nathan Alexander, College of Education Recruiter, 801-626-8124, Fax: 801-626-7427, E-mail: nathanalexander@weber.edu.
Website: http://www.weber.edu/COE/med.html

Western Connecticut State University, Division of Graduate Studies, School of Professional Studies, Department of Education and Educational Psychology, Curriculum Option, Danbury, CT 06810-6885. Offers MS. *Program availability:* Part-time. *Degree requirements:* For master's, thesis or alternative, thesis research project or 3 extra classes and comprehensive exam, completion of program in 6 years. *Entrance requirements:* For master's, minimum GPA of 2.8 or MAT, teaching certificate in elementary or secondary education. Additional exam requirements/recommendations for international students: Recommended—TOEFL (minimum score 550 paper-based; 79 iBT), IELTS (minimum score 6). *Faculty research:* Teaching various methods of instruction that include class discussions, lectures, independent projects, cooperative learning, experiential learning and field studies, recitals, demonstrations, shows, group projects, and technology-enhanced instruction.

Western Illinois University, School of Graduate Studies, College of Education and Human Services, Department of Curriculum and Instruction, Program in Curriculum and Instruction, Macomb, IL 61455-1390. Offers MS Ed. *Accreditation:* NCATE. *Program availability:* Part-time. *Students:* 1 (woman) full-time, 89 part-time (83 women); includes 5 minority (1 Black or African American, non-Hispanic/Latino; 3 Hispanic/Latino; 1 Two or more races, non-Hispanic/Latino). Average age 31. 18 applicants, 89% accepted, 11 enrolled. In 2016, 16 master's awarded. *Degree requirements:* For master's, thesis or alternative. *Entrance requirements:* Additional exam requirements/recommendations for international students: Required—TOEFL (minimum score 550 paper-based; 80 iBT). *Application deadline:* Applications are processed on a rolling basis. Application fee: $30. Electronic applications accepted. *Financial support:* Applicants required to submit FAFSA. *Unit head:* Dr. Barry Witten, Interim Chairperson, 309-298-1961. *Application contact:* Dr. Nancy Parsons, Assistant Director of Graduate Studies, 309-298-1806, Fax: 309-298-2345, E-mail: grad-office@wiu.edu.
Website: http://wiu.edu/curriculum

Western New England University, College of Arts and Sciences, Program in Curriculum and Instruction, Springfield, MA 01119. Offers M Ed. *Program availability:* Part-time, evening/weekend, online learning. *Faculty:* 3 full-time (2 women). *Students:* 14 part-time (13 women); includes 2 minority (1 Black or African American, non-Hispanic/Latino; 1 Hispanic/Latino). Average age 33. 5 applicants, 80% accepted, 3 enrolled. In 2016, 22 master's awarded. *Entrance requirements:* For master's, initial license for elementary teaching, two letters of recommendation, official transcript, resume, personal statement. Additional exam requirements/recommendations for international students: Required—TOEFL (minimum score 79 iBT). *Application deadline:* Applications are processed on a rolling basis. Application fee: $30. Electronic applications accepted. *Expenses:* Contact institution. *Financial support:* Application deadline: 4/15; applicants required to submit FAFSA. *Unit head:* Dr. Saeed Ghahramani, Dean, 413-782-1218, Fax: 413-796-2118, E-mail: sghahram@wne.edu. *Application contact:* Matthew Fox, Director of Admissions for Graduate Students and Adult

Learners, 413-782-1410, Fax: 413-782-1777, E-mail: study@wne.edu.
Website: http://www1.wne.edu/academics/graduate/education-curriculum-and-instruction.cfm

West Texas A&M University, College of Education and Social Sciences, Department of Education, Program in Curriculum and Instruction, Canyon, TX 79016-0001. Offers M Ed. *Program availability:* Part-time, evening/weekend, online learning. *Degree requirements:* For master's, comprehensive exam, thesis optional. *Entrance requirements:* For master's, GRE General Test, 18 semester hours of education course work. Additional exam requirements/recommendations for international students: Required—TOEFL (minimum score 550 paper-based). *Application deadline:* For fall admission, 8/1 for domestic students, 5/1 for international students; for spring admission, 12/1 for domestic students, 10/30 for international students; for summer admission, 5/1 for domestic students. Applications are processed on a rolling basis. Application fee: $40 ($75 for international students). Electronic applications accepted. *Financial support:* Research assistantships, teaching assistantships with partial tuition reimbursements, Federal Work-Study, institutionally sponsored loans, and tuition waivers (partial) available. Support available to part-time students. Financial award applicants required to submit CSS PROFILE or FAFSA. *Unit head:* Dr. Mark Riney, Associate Professor, 806-651-2618, E-mail: mriney@wtamu.edu. *Application contact:* Dr. Mark Riney, Associate Professor, 806-651-2618, E-mail: mriney@wtamu.edu.
Website: http://www.wtamu.edu/academics/education-curriculum-and-instruction-graduate-program-2.aspx

West Virginia University, College of Education and Human Services, Department of Curriculum and Instruction/Literacy Studies, Morgantown, WV 26506. Offers curriculum and instruction (Ed D); elementary education (MA); reading (MA); secondary education (MA), including higher education curriculum and teaching, secondary education; special education (Ed D), including special education. *Accreditation:* NCATE. *Program availability:* Part-time, evening/weekend. *Degree requirements:* For doctorate, comprehensive exam, thesis/dissertation. *Entrance requirements:* For master's, minimum GPA of 2.75; for doctorate, GRE General Test or MAT, 3 letters of recommendation, curriculum vitae. Additional exam requirements/recommendations for international students: Required—TOEFL. *Faculty research:* Teacher education, curriculum development, educational technology, curriculum assessment.

Wichita State University, Graduate School, College of Education, Department of Curriculum and Instruction, Wichita, KS 67260. Offers learning and instructional design (M Ed); special education (M Ed), including early childhood (M Ed, MAT), gifted, high incidence, low incidence; teaching (MAT), including early childhood (M Ed, MAT), middle level/secondary, transition to teaching. *Accreditation:* NCATE. *Program availability:* Part-time, evening/weekend, 100% online, blended/hybrid learning. *Entrance requirements:* For master's, MAT, minimum GPA of 2.75. *Unit head:* Dr. Kimberly McDowell, Department Head, 316-978-3322, E-mail: kim.mcdowell@wichita.edu. *Application contact:* Jordan Oleson, Admission Coordinator, 316-978-3095, Fax: 316-978-3253, E-mail: jordan.oleson@wichita.edu.

Wilkes University, College of Graduate and Professional Studies, School of Education, Wilkes-Barre, PA 18766-0002. Offers 21st century teaching and learning (MS Ed); art and science of teaching (MS Ed); classroom technology (MS Ed); early childhood literacy (MS Ed); educational development and strategies (MS Ed); educational leadership (MS Ed, Ed D); effective teaching (MS Ed); instructional media (MS Ed); instructional technology (MS Ed); international school leadership (MS Ed); international teaching and learning (MS Ed); middle level education (MS Ed); online teaching (MS Ed); reading (MS Ed); school business leadership (MS Ed); special education (MS Ed); teaching English to speakers of other languages (MS Ed). *Program availability:* Part-time, evening/weekend, 100% online, blended/hybrid learning. *Students:* 87 full-time (70 women), 1,496 part-time (1,111 women); includes 77 minority (11 Black or African American, non-Hispanic/Latino; 2 American Indian or Alaska Native, non-Hispanic/Latino; 12 Asian, non-Hispanic/Latino; 28 Hispanic/Latino; 3 Native Hawaiian or other Pacific Islander, non-Hispanic/Latino; 21 Two or more races, non-Hispanic/Latino). Average age 33. In 2016, 524 master's, 21 doctorates awarded. *Entrance requirements:* Additional exam requirements/recommendations for international students: Required—TOEFL (minimum score 550 paper-based; 79 iBT). *Application deadline:* Applications are processed on a rolling basis. Application fee: $45. Electronic applications accepted. *Expenses:* Contact institution. *Financial support:* Unspecified assistantships available. Financial award application deadline: 3/1; financial award applicants required to submit FAFSA. *Unit head:* Dr. Rhonda Rabbitt, Dean, 570-408-4680, Fax: 570-408-7872, E-mail: rhonda.rabbitt@wilkes.edu. *Application contact:* Director of Graduate Education, 570-408-4234, Fax: 570-408-7846.
Website: http://www.wilkes.edu/academics/graduate-programs/masters-programs/graduate-education/index.aspx

William Woods University, Graduate and Adult Studies, Fulton, MO 65251-1098. Offers administration (M Ed, Ed S); athletic/activities administration (M Ed); curriculum and instruction (M Ed, Ed S); educational leadership (Ed D); equestrian education (M Ed); health management (MBA); human resources (MBA); leadership (MBA); marketing, advertising, and public relations (MBA); teaching and technology (M Ed). *Program availability:* Part-time, evening/weekend. *Degree requirements:* For master's, capstone course (MBA), action research (M Ed); for Ed S, field experience. *Entrance requirements:* Additional exam requirements/recommendations for international students: Required—TOEFL (minimum score 550 paper-based). Electronic applications accepted. *Expenses:* Contact institution.

Wisconsin Lutheran College, College of Adult and Graduate Studies, Milwaukee, WI 53226-9942. Offers high performance instruction (MA Ed); instructional technology (MA Ed); leadership and innovation (MA Ed); science instruction (MA Ed).

Wright State University, Graduate School, College of Education and Human Services, Department of Educational Leadership, Program in Advanced Educational Leadership, Dayton, OH 45435. Offers advanced curriculum and instruction (Ed S). *Accreditation:* NCATE. *Degree requirements:* For Ed S, thesis. *Entrance requirements:* For degree, GRE General Test, MAT. Additional exam requirements/recommendations for international students: Required—TOEFL. Application fee: $25. *Expenses:* Tuition, state resident: full-time $9952; part-time $622 per credit hour. Tuition, nonresident: full-time $16,960; part-time $1060 per credit hour. *Financial support:* Available to part-time students. Applicants required to submit FAFSA. *Unit head:* Dr. Thomas Diamantes, Director, 937-775-3008, Fax: 937-775-2405, E-mail: thomas.diamantes@wright.edu. *Application contact:* John Kimble, Associate Director of Graduate Admissions and Records, 937-775-2957, Fax: 937-775-2453, E-mail: john.kimble@wright.edu.

Xavier University of Louisiana, Graduate School, Programs in Education, New Orleans, LA 70125. Offers counseling (MA); curriculum and instruction (MA); educational leadership (MA). *Accreditation:* NCATE. *Program availability:* Part-time, evening/weekend. *Degree requirements:* For master's, comprehensive exam, thesis or alternative. *Entrance requirements:* For master's, GRE General Test, MAT, minimum GPA of 2.5. Additional exam requirements/recommendations for international students: Required—TOEFL.

Youngstown State University, Graduate School, Beeghly College of Education, Department of Teacher Education, Youngstown, OH 44555-0001. Offers adolescent/young adult education (MS Ed); content area concentration (MS Ed); early childhood education (MS Ed); educational technology (MS Ed); literacy (MS Ed); middle childhood education (MS Ed); special education (MS Ed), including gifted and talented education, special education. *Accreditation:* NCATE. *Program availability:* Part-time, evening/weekend. *Degree requirements:* For master's, comprehensive exam. *Entrance requirements:* For master's, GRE, MAT, or teaching certificate; minimum GPA of 2.7. Additional exam requirements/recommendations for international students: Required—TOEFL. *Faculty research:* Multicultural literacy, hands-on mathematics teaching, integrated instruction, reading comprehension, emergent curriculum.

Distance Education Development

American Public University System, AMU/APU Graduate Programs, Charles Town, WV 25414. Offers accounting (MBA, MS); applied business analytics (MBA, MS); criminal justice (MA), including business administration, emergency and disaster management, general (MA, MS); educational leadership (M Ed); emergency and disaster management (MA); entrepreneurship (MBA); environmental policy and management (MS), including environmental planning, environmental sustainability, fish and wildlife management, general (MA, MS), global environmental management; finance (MBA); general (MBA); government contracting and acquisition (MBA); health care administration (MBA); health information management (MS); history (MA), including American history, ancient and classical history, European history, global history, public history; homeland security (MA), including business administration, counterterrorism studies, criminal justice, cyber, emergency management and public health, intelligence studies, transportation security; homeland security resource allocation (MBA); humanities (MA); information technology (MS), including digital forensics, enterprise software development, information assurance and security, IT project management; information technology management (MBA); intelligence studies (MA), including criminal intelligence, cyber, general (MA, MS), homeland security, intelligence analysis, intelligence collection, intelligence management, intelligence operations, terrorism studies; international relations and conflict resolution (MA), including comparative and security issues, conflict resolution, international and transnational security issues, peacekeeping; legal studies (MA); management (MA), including strategic consulting; marketing (MBA); military history (MA), including American military history, American Revolution, civil war, war since 1945, World War II; military studies (MA), including joint warfare, strategic leadership; national security studies (MA), including cyber, general (MA, MS), homeland security, regional security studies, security and intelligence analysis, terrorism studies; nonprofit management (MBA); political science (MA), including American politics and government, comparative government and development, general (MA, MS), international relations, public policy; psychology (MA); public administration (MPA), including disaster management, environmental policy, health policy, human resources, national security, organizational management, security management; public health (MPH); reverse logistics management (MA); security management (MA); space studies (MS), including aerospace science, general (MA, MS), planetary science; sports and health sciences (MS); sports management (MBA); teaching (M Ed), including autism spectrum disorder, curriculum and instruction for elementary teachers, elementary reading, English language learners, instructional leadership, online learning, special education, STEAM (STEM plus the arts); transportation and logistics management (MA). *Program availability:* Part-time, evening/weekend, online only, 100% online. *Faculty:* 401 full-time (228 women), 1,678 part-time/adjunct (781 women). *Students:* 378 full-time (184 women), 8,455 part-time (3,484 women); includes 2,972 minority (1,552 Black or African American, non-Hispanic/Latino; 52 American Indian or Alaska Native, non-Hispanic/Latino; 211 Asian, non-Hispanic/Latino; 791 Hispanic/Latino; 70 Native Hawaiian or other Pacific Islander, non-Hispanic/Latino; 296 Two or more races, non-Hispanic/Latino), 109 international. Average age 37. In 2016, 3,185 master's awarded. *Degree requirements:* For master's, comprehensive exam or practicum. *Entrance requirements:* For master's, official transcript showing earned bachelor's degree from institution accredited by recognized accrediting body. Additional exam requirements/recommendations for international students: Required—TOEFL (minimum score 550 paper-based), IELTS (minimum score 6.5). *Application deadline:* Applications are processed on a rolling basis. Application fee: $0. Electronic applications accepted. *Expenses: Tuition:* Part-time $350 per credit hour. *Required fees:* $50 per course. *Financial support:* Scholarships/grants available. Financial award applicants required to submit FAFSA. *Unit head:* Dr. Karan Powell, President, 877-468-6268, Fax: 304-724-3780. *Application contact:* Terry Grant, Vice President of Enrollment Management, 877-468-6268, Fax: 304-724-3780, E-mail: info@apus.edu.
Website: http://www.apus.edu

Athabasca University, Centre for Distance Education, Athabasca, AB T9S 3A3, Canada. Offers distance education (MDE, Ed D); distance education technology (Advanced Diploma). *Program availability:* Part-time, online learning. *Degree requirements:* For master's, thesis optional. *Entrance requirements:* For master's, 3- or 4-year baccalaureate degree. Electronic applications accepted. *Expenses:* Contact institution. *Faculty research:* Role development, interaction, educational technology, and communities of practice in distance education; instructional design.

Barry University, School of Education, Graduate Certificate Programs, Miami Shores, FL 33161-6695. Offers advanced teaching and learning with technology (Certificate); distance education (Certificate); higher education technology integration (Certificate); human resources: not for profit and religious organizations (Certificate); K-12 technology integration (Certificate).

Boise State University, College of Education, Department of Educational Technology, Boise, ID 83725. Offers educational technology (MET, MS, Ed D); online teaching (Graduate Certificate); school technology coordination (Graduate Certificate); technology integration (Graduate Certificate). *Accreditation:* NCATE. *Program availability:* Part-time, 100% online, blended/hybrid learning. *Faculty:* 27. *Students:* 13 full-time (7 women), 422 part-time (242 women); includes 41 minority (11 Black or

African American, non-Hispanic/Latino; 1 American Indian or Alaska Native, non-Hispanic/Latino; 9 Asian, non-Hispanic/Latino; 17 Hispanic/Latino; 1 Native Hawaiian or other Pacific Islander, non-Hispanic/Latino; 2 Two or more races, non-Hispanic/Latino), 17 international. Average age 38. 192 applicants, 68% accepted, 72 enrolled. In 2016, 151 master's awarded. Terminal master's awarded for partial completion of doctoral program. *Degree requirements:* For master's, thesis optional; for doctorate, thesis/dissertation. *Entrance requirements:* For master's, minimum GPA of 3.0; for doctorate, GRE General Test. Additional exam requirements/recommendations for international students: Required—TOEFL (minimum score 550 paper-based; 80 iBT), IELTS (minimum score 6). *Application deadline:* For fall admission, 2/15 for domestic and international students; for spring admission, 9/15 for domestic and international students. Applications are processed on a rolling basis. Application fee: $65 ($95 for international students). Electronic applications accepted. *Expenses:* Tuition, state resident: full-time $6058; part-time $358 per credit hour. Tuition, nonresident: full-time $20,108; part-time $608 per credit hour. *Required fees:* $2108. Tuition and fees vary according to program. *Financial support:* In 2016–17, 12 students received support, including 1 teaching assistantship (averaging $2,148 per year); scholarships/grants and unspecified assistantships also available. Financial award application deadline: 3/1; financial award applicants required to submit FAFSA. *Unit head:* Dr. Brett Shelton, Department Chair, 208-426-3391, E-mail: brettshelton@boisestate.edu. *Application contact:* Dr. Ross Perkins, Admissions Coordinator, 208-426-4875, E-mail: edtechdoc@boisestate.edu. Website: http://edtech.boisestate.edu/

Brandeis University, Rabb School of Continuing Studies, Division of Graduate Professional Studies, Master of Science in Instructional Design and Technology Program, Waltham, MA 02454-9110. Offers MS. *Program availability:* Part-time-only. *Faculty:* 45 part-time/adjunct (16 women). *Students:* 10 part-time (7 women); includes 1 minority (Two or more races, non-Hispanic/Latino). Average age 37. 1 applicant, 100% accepted, 1 enrolled. In 2016, 1 master's awarded. *Entrance requirements:* For master's, four-year bachelor's degree from regionally-accredited U.S. institution or equivalent; official transcript(s) from every college or university attended; resume or curriculum vitae; statement of goals; letter of recommendation. Additional exam requirements/recommendations for international students: Required—TWE (minimum score 4.5), TOEFL (minimum scores: 600 paper-based, 100 iBT), IELTS (7), or PTE (68). *Application deadline:* For fall admission, 6/21 priority date for domestic and international students; for winter admission, 9/13 priority date for domestic and international students; for spring admission, 12/20 priority date for domestic and international students; for summer admission, 3/14 priority date for domestic and international students. Applications are processed on a rolling basis. Application fee: $50. Electronic applications accepted. *Expenses:* $3,400 per course, $100 graduation fee. *Financial support:* Applicants required to submit FAFSA. *Unit head:* Brian Salerno, Chair, 781-736-3443, E-mail: bsalerno@brandeis.edu. *Application contact:* Frances Stearns, Director of Admissions and Recruitment, 781-736-8785, E-mail: fstearns@brandeis.edu.
Website: http://www.brandeis.edu/gps/future-students/learn-about-our-programs/instructional-design.html

California Baptist University, Program in Education, Riverside, CA 92504-3206. Offers educational leadership (MS); educational leadership for faith-based institutions (MS); educational leadership for public institutions (MS); educational technology (MS); instructional computer applications (MS); international education (MS); leadership and adult learning (MS); leadership and organizational studies (MS); online teaching and learning (MS); reading (MS); science education (MA); special education in mild/moderate disabilities (MS); special education in moderate/severe disabilities (MS); teacher leadership (MS); teaching (MS); teaching and learning (MS). *Program availability:* Part-time, evening/weekend, 100% online, blended/hybrid learning. *Faculty:* 20 full-time (8 women), 11 part-time/adjunct (7 women). *Students:* 191 full-time (148 women), 234 part-time (178 women); includes 194 minority (23 Black or African American, non-Hispanic/Latino; 5 American Indian or Alaska Native, non-Hispanic/Latino; 15 Asian, non-Hispanic/Latino; 131 Hispanic/Latino; 4 Native Hawaiian or other Pacific Islander, non-Hispanic/Latino; 16 Two or more races, non-Hispanic/Latino), 2 international. Average age 31. 277 applicants, 61% accepted, 150 enrolled. In 2016, 280 master's awarded. *Degree requirements:* For master's, comprehensive exam, project, or thesis. *Entrance requirements:* For master's, minimum undergraduate GPA of 2.75; 500-word essay; three letters of recommendation; two prerequisite courses completed with minimum C grade. Additional exam requirements/recommendations for international students: Required—TOEFL (minimum score 80 iBT). *Application deadline:* For fall admission, 8/1 priority date for domestic students, 7/1 for international students; for spring admission, 12/1 priority date for domestic students, 11/1 for international students. Applications are processed on a rolling basis. Application fee: $45. Electronic applications accepted. *Expenses:* Contact institution. *Financial support:* In 2016–17, 162 students received support. Federal Work-Study and scholarships/grants available. Financial award applicants required to submit CSS PROFILE or FAFSA. *Faculty research:* Leadership development, complexity theory, faith and learning, special education, social and philosophical contexts of education. *Unit head:* Dr. John Shoup, Dean, School of Education, 951-343-4516, E-mail: jshoup@calbaptist.edu.
Website: http://www.calbaptist.edu/mastersined/

Capella University, School of Education, Doctoral Programs in Education, Minneapolis, MN 55402. Offers curriculum and instruction (PhD); educational leadership and management (Ed D); instructional design for online learning (PhD); K-12 studies in education (PhD); leadership for higher education (PhD); leadership in educational administration (PhD); postsecondary and adult education (PhD); professional studies in education (PhD); reading and literacy (Ed D); special education leadership (PhD); training and performance improvement (PhD).

Capella University, School of Education, Master's Programs in Education, Minneapolis, MN 55402. Offers adult education (MS); curriculum and instruction (MS); early childhood education (MS); enrollment management (MS); higher education leadership and management (MS); instructional design for online learning (MS); integrative studies (MS); K-12 studies in education (MS); leadership in educational administration (MS); reading and literacy (MS); special education teaching (MS).

Clemson University, Graduate School, College of Behavioral, Social and Health Sciences, Department of Parks, Recreation, and Tourism Management, Clemson, SC 29634. Offers international parks and tourism (Certificate); parks, recreation and tourism management (MS, PhD), including recreational therapy (PhD); public administration (MPA); recreational therapy (MS); youth development leadership (MS); youth leadership development (Certificate). *Program availability:* Part-time, evening/weekend, 100% online. *Faculty:* 36 full-time (14 women), 2 part-time/adjunct (0 women). *Students:* 79 full-time (52 women), 159 part-time (100 women); includes 50 minority (36 Black or African American, non-Hispanic/Latino; 2 Asian, non-Hispanic/Latino; 6 Hispanic/Latino; 6 Two or more races, non-Hispanic/Latino), 14 international. Average age 32. 143 applicants, 62% accepted, 71 enrolled. In 2016, 37 master's, 4 doctorates, 38 other advanced degrees awarded. *Degree requirements:* For master's, comprehensive exam (for some programs), thesis (for some programs); for doctorate, comprehensive exam, thesis/dissertation; for Certificate, portfolio. *Entrance requirements:* For master's and doctorate, GRE General Test, unofficial transcripts, letter of intent, letters of reference; for Certificate, letter of recommendation, unofficial transcripts, personal statement, resume. Additional exam requirements/recommendations for international students: Required—TOEFL (minimum score 610 paper-based; 80 iBT), IELTS (minimum score 6.5). *Application deadline:* For fall admission, 1/15 priority date for domestic and international students; for spring admission, 11/15 priority date for domestic and international students. Applications are processed on a rolling basis. Application fee: $80 ($90 for international students). Electronic applications accepted. *Expenses:* $4,264 per semester full-time resident, $8,485 per semester full-time non-resident, $471 per credit hour part-time resident, $942 per credit hour part-time non-resident. *Financial support:* In 2016–17, 83 students received support, including 2 fellowships with partial tuition reimbursements available (averaging $1,750 per year), 4 research assistantships with partial tuition reimbursements available (averaging $9,219 per year), 69 teaching assistantships with partial tuition reimbursements available (averaging $10,425 per year); unspecified assistantships also available. Financial award application deadline: 1/15. *Faculty research:* Human behavior, land use, recreational therapy, sustainability, tourism. *Total annual research expenditures:* $97,805. *Unit head:* Dr. Fran McGuire, Chair, 864-656-3036, Fax: 864-656-2226, E-mail: lefty@clemson.edu. *Application contact:* Dr. Bill Norman, Graduate Coordinator, 864-656-2060, Fax: 864-656-2226, E-mail: wnorman@clemson.edu.
Website: http://www.clemson.edu/hehd/departments/prtm/

Coastal Carolina University, Spadoni College of Education, Conway, SC 29528-6054. Offers education (MAT); educational leadership (M Ed, Ed S); English for speakers of other languages (Certificate); instructional technology (M Ed, Ed S); learning and teaching (M Ed); online teaching and training (Certificate); special education (M Ed). *Accreditation:* NCATE. *Program availability:* Part-time, evening/weekend. *Faculty:* 16 full-time (8 women), 12 part-time/adjunct (7 women). *Students:* 74 full-time (48 women), 340 part-time (271 women); includes 78 minority (70 Black or African American, non-Hispanic/Latino; 1 American Indian or Alaska Native, non-Hispanic/Latino; 2 Asian, non-Hispanic/Latino; 4 Hispanic/Latino; 1 Two or more races, non-Hispanic/Latino), 2 international. Average age 33. 298 applicants, 93% accepted, 213 enrolled. In 2016, 167 master's, 8 other advanced degrees awarded. *Degree requirements:* For master's and other advanced degree, comprehensive exam. *Entrance requirements:* For master's, GRE, GMAT, 2 letters of recommendation, evidence of teacher certification, official transcripts; for other advanced degree, official transcripts, minimum of 3 years' teaching experience, statement of interest in the program, 3 letters of reference, master's degree in educational leadership or related field with minimum overall GPA of 3.0. Additional exam requirements/recommendations for international students: Required—TOEFL (minimum score 550 paper-based; 79 iBT), IELTS (minimum score 6.5). *Application deadline:* For fall admission, 7/1 priority date for domestic and international students; for spring admission, 11/1 priority date for domestic and international students; for summer admission, 3/1 priority date for domestic and international students. Applications are processed on a rolling basis. Application fee: $45. Electronic applications accepted. *Expenses:* Tuition, state resident: full-time $9990; part-time $555 per credit hour. Tuition, nonresident: full-time $18,108; part-time $1006 per credit hour. *Required fees:* $90; $5 per credit hour. *Financial support:* Fellowships, research assistantships, and unspecified assistantships available. Support available to part-time students. Financial award application deadline: 3/1; financial award applicants required to submit FAFSA. *Unit head:* Dr. Edward Jadallah, Dean, 843-349-2773, Fax: 843-349-2106, E-mail: ejadalla@coastal.edu. *Application contact:* Dr. James O. Luken, Associate Provost/Vice-Dean of the Coastal Environment, 843-349-2235, Fax: 843-349-6444, E-mail: joluken@coastal.edu.
Website: http://www.coastal.edu/education/

Colorado Christian University, Program in Curriculum and Instruction, Lakewood, CO 80226. Offers corporate education (MACI); early childhood educator (MACI); elementary educator (MACI); instructional technology (MACI); master educator (MACI); online course developer (MACI); online teaching and learning (MACI); special education generalist (MACI). *Program availability:* Part-time, evening/weekend. *Degree requirements:* For master's, thesis optional, practicum. *Entrance requirements:* For master's, interviews, letters of recommendation. Additional exam requirements/recommendations for international students: Required—TOEFL. Electronic applications accepted. *Expenses:* Contact institution.

Dallas Baptist University, Dorothy M. Bush College of Education, Program in Curriculum and Instruction, Dallas, TX 75211-9299. Offers Christian school administration (M Ed); distance learning (M Ed); English as a second language (M Ed); instructional technology (M Ed); professional life coaching (M Ed); special education (M Ed); supervision (M Ed). *Program availability:* Part-time, evening/weekend, 100% online, blended/hybrid learning. *Application deadline:* Applications are processed on a rolling basis. Application fee: $25. Electronic applications accepted. Application fee is waived when completed online. *Expenses: Tuition:* Full-time $15,408; part-time $856 per credit hour. *Required fees:* $400 per semester. Tuition and fees vary according to course load and degree level. *Unit head:* Dr. Deborah H. Tribble, Director, 214-333-5201, E-mail: debbiet@dbu.edu. *Application contact:* Bobby Soto, Director of Admissions, 214-333-5242, E-mail: graduate@dbu.edu.
Website: http://www3.dbu.edu/graduate/curriculum_instruction.asp

Dallas Baptist University, Dorothy M. Bush College of Education, Teaching Program, Dallas, TX 75211-9299. Offers distance learning (MAT); early childhood through grade 6 certification (MAT); early childhood-12 (MAT); elementary (MAT); English as a second language (MAT); Montessori (MAT); multisensory (MAT); secondary (MAT). *Program availability:* Part-time, evening/weekend, 100% online, blended/hybrid learning. *Application deadline:* Applications are processed on a rolling basis. Application fee: $25. Electronic applications accepted. Application fee is waived when completed online. *Expenses: Tuition:* Full-time $15,408; part-time $856 per credit hour. *Required fees:* $400 per semester. Tuition and fees vary according to course load and degree level. *Unit head:* Dr. Carolyn Spain, Director, 214-333-5217, E-mail: carolyns@dbu.edu. *Application contact:* Bobby Soto, Director of Admissions, 214-333-5242, E-mail: graduate@dbu.edu.
Website: http://www3.dbu.edu/graduate/mat.asp

Dallas Baptist University, Gary Cook School of Leadership, Program in Higher Education, Dallas, TX 75211-9299. Offers administration (M Ed), including community college leadership, distance learning, interdisciplinary studies, student affairs leadership; instructional (M Ed). *Program availability:* Part-time, evening/weekend, 100% online, blended/hybrid learning. *Application deadline:* Applications are processed on a rolling basis. Application fee: $25. Electronic applications accepted. Application fee is waived when completed online. *Expenses: Tuition:* Full-time $15,408; part-time $856 per credit hour. *Required fees:* $400 per semester. Tuition and fees vary according to course load and degree level. *Faculty research:* Enrollment management, portfolio assessment, servant leadership. *Unit head:* Mamo Ishida, Director, 214-333-5812, E-mail: mamo@dbu.edu. *Application contact:* Bobby Soto, Director of Admissions, 214-333-5242, E-mail: graduate@dbu.edu.
Website: http://www3.dbu.edu/leadership/hied/

Drury University, Master in Education Program, Springfield, MO 5802. Offers curriculum and instruction (M Ed), including elementary, middle school, secondary; gifted education (M Ed); instructional leadership (M Ed); instructional technology (M Ed);

integrated learning (M Ed); online teaching (M Ed); special education (M Ed); special reading (M Ed). *Accreditation:* NCATE. *Program availability:* Part-time, evening/weekend, 100% online, blended/hybrid learning. *Students:* 146 full-time (111 women); includes 6 minority (1 Asian, non-Hispanic/Latino; 3 Hispanic/Latino; 2 Two or more races, non-Hispanic/Latino), 1 international. Average age 34. 42 applicants, 74% accepted. In 2016, 74 master's awarded. *Entrance requirements:* For master's, GRE, bachelor's degree with minimum GPA of 2.75. Additional exam requirements/recommendations for international students: Recommended—TOEFL (minimum score 80 iBT), IELTS (minimum score 6.5). *Application deadline:* For fall admission, 8/4 priority date for domestic and international students; for spring admission, 1/5 priority date for domestic and international students; for summer admission, 5/26 priority date for domestic and international students. Applications are processed on a rolling basis. Application fee: $25 ($50 for international students). Electronic applications accepted. *Expenses:* $352 tuition per credit hour; $7 per credit hour technology fee; $100 graduation fee; $59 portfolio fee (one-time). *Financial support:* In 2016–17, 20 students received support. Career-related internships or fieldwork, scholarships/grants, tuition waivers (partial), and unspecified assistantships available. Financial award application deadline: 6/30; financial award applicants required to submit FAFSA. *Faculty research:* Gifted students, instructional technology, autism, diversity and social justice. *Unit head:* Dr. Asikaa Cosgrove, Director, Master in Education, 417-873-7806, E-mail: acosgrov@drury.edu.
Website: http://www.drury.edu/education-masters

Eastern Michigan University, Graduate School, College of Education, Department of Teacher Education, Programs in Curriculum and Instruction, Ypsilanti, MI 48197. Offers advanced teaching and learning (MA); early literacy instruction (Graduate Certificate); instructional leadership (MA); learning, motivation and creativity (Graduate Certificate); literacy coaching (Graduate Certificate); online teaching (Certificate); secondary literacy instruction (Graduate Certificate); urban and diversity education (MA). *Students:* 1 (woman) full-time, 31 part-time (29 women); includes 6 minority (2 Black or African American, non-Hispanic/Latino; 2 Asian, non-Hispanic/Latino; 2 Two or more races, non-Hispanic/Latino), 1 international. Average age 33. 11 applicants, 73% accepted, 4 enrolled. In 2016, 8 master's, 1 other advanced degree awarded. Application fee: $45. *Application contact:* Dr. Virginia Harder, Graduate Coordinator/Advisor, 734-487-2729, Fax: 734-487-2101, E-mail: vharder1@emich.edu.

Endicott College, Van Loan School of Graduate and Professional Studies, Program in Integrative Education, Beverly, MA 01915-2096. Offers M Ed. Program offered in conjunction with The Institute for Educational Studies (TIES). *Program availability:* Part-time, online only, 100% online. *Faculty:* 1 full-time (0 women). *Students:* 29 full-time (27 women). Average age 37. 13 applicants, 100% accepted, 12 enrolled. In 2016, 15 master's awarded. *Degree requirements:* For master's, thesis. *Entrance requirements:* For master's, undergraduate transcript. Additional exam requirements/recommendations for international students: Required—TOEFL. *Application deadline:* Applications are processed on a rolling basis. Application fee: $50. Electronic applications accepted. *Expenses:* Contact institution. *Financial support:* Tuition waivers (partial) available. Financial award applicants required to submit FAFSA. *Faculty research:* Neurophenomenology, autopoiesis, systems view. *Unit head:* Dr. Phil Snow Gang, Academic Dean, 888-722-4547, Fax: 978-232-3000, E-mail: ties@endicott.edu. *Application contact:* Ian Menchini, Director, Graduate Enrollment and Advising, 978-232-5292, E-mail: imenchin@endicott.edu.
Website: http://www.endicott.edu/VanLoan/Graduate-Studies/Master-Education/Integrative-Education.aspx

The George Washington University, Graduate School of Education and Human Development, Department of Educational Leadership, Program in E-Learning, Washington, DC 20052. Offers Graduate Certificate. *Students:* 4 part-time (all women); includes 3 minority (1 Black or African American, non-Hispanic/Latino; 1 Asian, non-Hispanic/Latino; 1 Hispanic/Latino). Average age 48. 2 applicants, 100% accepted, 2 enrolled. In 2016, 1 Graduate Certificate awarded. *Unit head:* Dr. Virginia Roach, Chair, 202-994-3094, E-mail: vroach@gwu.edu. *Application contact:* Sarah Lang, Director of Graduate Admissions, 202-994-1447, Fax: 202-994-7207, E-mail: slang@gwu.edu.
Website: http://gsehd.gwu.edu/e-learning-certificate

Kansas State University, Graduate School, College of Education, Department of Curriculum and Instruction, Manhattan, KS 66506. Offers curriculum and instruction (Ed D, PhD); digital teaching and learning (MS); educational computing, design and online learning (MS); elementary/middle level curriculum and instruction (MS); online learning (Certificate); reading specialist endorsement (MS); reading/language arts (MS); teacher leader/school improvement (MS); teaching and learning (Certificate). *Accreditation:* NCATE. *Program availability:* Part-time, online learning. *Faculty:* 36 full-time (22 women), 18 part-time/adjunct (9 women). *Students:* 59 full-time (40 women), 94 part-time (72 women); includes 21 minority (5 Black or African American, non-Hispanic/Latino; 3 Asian, non-Hispanic/Latino; 11 Hispanic/Latino; 2 Two or more races, non-Hispanic/Latino), 20 international. Average age 35. 70 applicants, 71% accepted, 36 enrolled. In 2016, 61 master's, 12 doctorates, 9 other advanced degrees awarded. *Degree requirements:* For master's, comprehensive exam, portfolio, project, report or thesis; for doctorate, comprehensive exam, thesis/dissertation, preliminary exam; for Certificate, comprehensive exam, portfolio. *Entrance requirements:* For master's, minimum GPA of 3.0, 3 letters of recommendation; for doctorate, GRE, minimum GPA of 3.0, 3 letters of recommendation, evidence of scholarly writing; for Certificate, minimum GPA of 3.0, letters of recommendation. Additional exam requirements/recommendations for international students: Required—TOEFL (minimum score 550 paper-based; 80 iBT) or IELTS. *Application deadline:* For fall admission, 3/1 priority date for domestic students, 2/1 priority date for international students; for spring admission, 10/1 priority date for domestic students, 8/1 priority date for international students. Applications are processed on a rolling basis. Application fee: $50 ($75 for international students). Electronic applications accepted. *Expenses:* Tuition, state resident: full-time $9670. Tuition, nonresident: full-time $21,828. *Required fees:* $862. *Financial support:* In 2016–17, 1 research assistantship (averaging $19,980 per year), 8 teaching assistantships (averaging $12,620 per year) were awarded; career-related internships or fieldwork, institutionally sponsored loans, scholarships/grants, and unspecified assistantships also available. Support available to part-time students. Financial award application deadline: 3/1; financial award applicants required to submit FAFSA. *Faculty research:* Literacy and technology, critical race theory and diversity, achievement gaps, school improvement, teacher education. *Total annual research expenditures:* $647,057. *Unit head:* Dr. F. Todd Goodson, Department Chair, 785-532-5904, Fax: 785-532-7304, E-mail: tgoodson@ksu.edu. *Application contact:* Dr. Kay Ann Taylor, Director, Curriculum and Instruction Graduate Programs, 785-532-6974, Fax: 785-532-7304, E-mail: ktaylor@ksu.edu.
Website: http://www.coe.ksu.edu/edci/index.html

Keiser University, Master of Science in Education Program, Ft. Lauderdale, FL 33309. Offers allied health teaching and leadership (MS Ed); career college administration (MS Ed); leadership (MS Ed); online teaching and learning (MS Ed); teaching and learning (MS Ed). *Program availability:* Part-time, online learning.

Lenoir-Rhyne University, Graduate Programs, School of Education, Program in Online Teaching and Instructional Design, Hickory, NC 28601. Offers MS. *Program availability:* Online learning. *Entrance requirements:* For master's, GRE or MAT, essay; minimum GPA of 2.7 undergraduate, 3.0 graduate. Additional exam requirements/recommendations for international students: Required—TOEFL (minimum score 600 paper-based). Electronic applications accepted. *Expenses:* Contact institution.

Lesley University, Graduate School of Education, Cambridge, MA 02138-2790. Offers arts, community, and education (M Ed); autism studies (Certificate); curriculum and instruction (M Ed, CAGS); early childhood education (M Ed); ecological teaching and learning (MS); educational studies (PhD), including adult learning, educational leadership, individually designed; elementary education (M Ed); emergent technologies for educators (Certificate); ESLArts: language learning through the arts (M Ed); high school education (M Ed); individually designed (M Ed); integrated teaching through the arts (M Ed); literacy for K-8 classroom teachers (M Ed); mathematics education (M Ed); middle school education (M Ed); moderate disabilities (M Ed); online learning (Certificate); reading (CAGS); science in education (M Ed); severe disabilities (M Ed); special needs (CAGS); specialist teacher of reading (M Ed); teacher of visual art (M Ed); technology in education (M Ed, CAGS). *Accreditation:* TEAC. *Program availability:* Part-time, evening/weekend, online learning. *Degree requirements:* For master's, practicum; for doctorate, thesis/dissertation. *Entrance requirements:* For master's, Massachusetts Tests for Educator Licensure (MTEL), transcripts, statement of purpose, recommendations; interview (for special education); for doctorate, GRE General Test, transcripts, statement of purpose, recommendations, interview, master's degree, resume; for other advanced degree, interview, master's degree. Additional exam requirements/recommendations for international students: Required—TOEFL (minimum score 550 paper-based; 80 iBT). Electronic applications accepted. *Faculty research:* Assessment in literacy, mathematics and science; autism spectrum disorders; instructional technology and online learning; multicultural education and English language learners.

Millersville University of Pennsylvania, College of Graduate Studies and Adult Learning, College of Education and Human Services, Department of Educational Foundations, Program in Assessment, Curriculum and Teaching - Online Teaching Option, Millersville, PA 17551-0302. Offers M Ed. *Program availability:* Part-time, online only, 100% online. *Faculty:* 20 full-time (13 women), 2 part-time/adjunct (both women). *Students:* 5 part-time (3 women). Average age 31. 5 applicants, 100% accepted, 1 enrolled. *Degree requirements:* For master's, thesis/capstone project. *Entrance requirements:* For master's, GRE or MAT (if undergraduate cumulative GPA is lower than 2.8), teaching certificate. Additional exam requirements/recommendations for international students: Required—TOEFL (minimum score 600 paper-based), IELTS (minimum score 6). *Application deadline:* Applications are processed on a rolling basis. Application fee: $40. Electronic applications accepted. *Expenses:* $483 per credit resident tuition; $566 per credit non-resident tuition. *Financial support:* Unspecified assistantships available. Financial award application deadline: 3/15; financial award applicants required to submit FAFSA. *Faculty research:* On-line instruction STEM instruction, innovative pedagogy, instructional technology. *Unit head:* Dr. Tim E. Mahoney, Chair, 717-871-7202, E-mail: tim.mahoney@millersville.edu. *Application contact:* Dr. Victor S. DeSantis, Dean of College of Graduate Studies and Adult Learning/Associate Provost for Civic and Community Engagement, 717-871-7619, Fax: 717-871-7954, E-mail: victor.desantis@millersville.edu.

Mississippi State University, College of Education, Department of Instructional Systems and Workforce Development, Mississippi State, MS 39762. Offers distance education (MSIT); instructional design (MSIT); instructional systems and workforce development (MST, PhD); multimedia (MSIT); technology (Ed S). *Faculty:* 12 full-time (8 women). *Students:* 14 full-time (10 women), 53 part-time (44 women); includes 41 minority (39 Black or African American, non-Hispanic/Latino; 1 American Indian or Alaska Native, non-Hispanic/Latino; 1 Two or more races, non-Hispanic/Latino). Average age 38. 17 applicants, 47% accepted, 8 enrolled. In 2016, 6 master's, 3 doctorates, 5 other advanced degrees awarded. *Degree requirements:* For master's, thesis optional, comprehensive oral or written exam; for doctorate, thesis/dissertation, comprehensive oral and written exam; for Ed S, thesis, comprehensive written exam. *Entrance requirements:* For master's, GRE, minimum GPA of 2.75 on undergraduate work, 3.0 graduate; for doctorate, GRE, minimum GPA of 3.4 on graduate work; for Ed S, GRE, minimum GPA of 3.2, master's degree. Additional exam requirements/recommendations for international students: Required—TOEFL (minimum score 550 paper-based; 79 iBT); Recommended—IELTS (minimum score 6.5). *Application deadline:* For fall admission, 7/1 for domestic students, 5/1 for international students; for spring admission, 11/1 for domestic students, 9/1 for international students. Applications are processed on a rolling basis. Application fee: $60. Electronic applications accepted. *Expenses:* Tuition, state resident: full-time $7670; part-time $852.50 per credit hour. Tuition, nonresident: full-time $20,790; part-time $2310.50 per credit hour. Part-time tuition and fees vary according to course load. *Financial support:* In 2016–17, 2 research assistantships with full tuition reimbursements (averaging $13,755 per year), 2 teaching assistantships with full tuition reimbursements (averaging $10,800 per year) were awarded; Federal Work-Study, institutionally sponsored loans, scholarships/grants, and unspecified assistantships also available. Financial award application deadline: 4/1; financial award applicants required to submit FAFSA. *Faculty research:* Computer technology, nontraditional students, interactive video, instructional technology, educational leadership. *Unit head:* Dr. Connie Forde, Professor and Department Head, 662-325-2281, Fax: 662-325-7599, E-mail: cforde@colled.msstate.edu. *Application contact:* Linda Bonner, Senior Admissions Assistant, 662-325-3363, E-mail: lbonner@grad.msstate.edu.
Website: http://www.iswd.msstate.edu

National University, Academic Affairs, School of Education, La Jolla, CA 92037-1011. Offers e-teaching and learning (Certificate); educational administration (MS). *Program availability:* Part-time, evening/weekend, 100% online, blended/hybrid learning. *Faculty:* 74 full-time (48 women), 422 part-time/adjunct (260 women). *Students:* 3,376 full-time (2,418 women), 2,410 part-time (1,641 women); includes 2,652 minority (357 Black or African American, non-Hispanic/Latino; 29 American Indian or Alaska Native, non-Hispanic/Latino; 337 Asian, non-Hispanic/Latino; 1,680 Hispanic/Latino; 45 Native Hawaiian or other Pacific Islander, non-Hispanic/Latino; 204 Two or more races, non-Hispanic/Latino). Average age 33. In 2016, 1,456 master's awarded. *Degree requirements:* For master's, thesis (for some programs). *Entrance requirements:* For master's, interview, minimum GPA of 2.5. Additional exam requirements/recommendations for international students: Required—TOEFL (minimum score 550 paper-based; 79 iBT), IELTS (minimum score 6). *Application deadline:* Applications are processed on a rolling basis. Application fee: $60 ($65 for international students). Electronic applications accepted. *Financial support:* Career-related internships or fieldwork, institutionally sponsored loans, scholarships/grants, and tuition waivers (partial) available. Support available to part-time students. Financial award application deadline: 6/30. *Faculty research:* Teacher education, special education, educational effectiveness, teaching abroad, school counseling. *Unit head:* School of Education, 800-628-8648, E-mail: soe@nu.edu. *Application contact:* Brandon Jouganatos, Vice President for Enrollment Services, 800-628-8648, E-mail: advisor@nu.edu.
Website: http://www.nu.edu/OurPrograms/SchoolOfEducation.html

Distance Education Development

New Mexico State University, College of Education, Online Teaching and Learning Program, Las Cruces, NM 88003. Offers Graduate Certificate. *Program availability:* Part-time, 100% online. *Students:* 4 full-time (3 women), 6 part-time (4 women); includes 6 minority (all Hispanic/Latino), 2 international. Average age 39. 7 applicants, 14% accepted. In 2016, 8 Graduate Certificates awarded. *Degree requirements:* For Graduate Certificate, minimum grade of B in all 5 courses; practicum. *Entrance requirements:* Additional exam requirements/recommendations for international students: Required—TOEFL (minimum score 550 paper-based; 79 iBT), IELTS (minimum score 6.5). *Application deadline:* Applications are processed on a rolling basis. Application fee: $40 ($50 for international students). Electronic applications accepted. *Expenses:* Tuition, state resident: full-time $4086. Tuition, nonresident: full-time $14,254. *Required fees:* $853. Tuition and fees vary according to course load. *Financial support:* Career-related internships or fieldwork, Federal Work-Study, scholarships/grants, traineeships, health care benefits, and unspecified assistantships available. Support available to part-time students. Financial award application deadline: 3/1. *Unit head:* Susie Bussmann, Director of Instructional Innovation and Quality, 575-646-1650, Fax: 575-646-2044, E-mail: suceppib@nmsu.edu. *Application contact:* 575-646-1650, Fax: 575-646-2044.
Website: http://otl.nmsu.edu/

New York Institute of Technology, School of Interdisciplinary Studies and Education, Department of Instructional Technology, Old Westbury, NY 11568-8000. Offers emerging technologies for trainers (Advanced Certificate); instructional design for global e-learning (Advanced Certificate); instructional technology (MS); school leadership and technology (Advanced Diploma); STEM education (Advanced Certificate). *Program availability:* Part-time, evening/weekend, 100% online, blended/hybrid learning. *Faculty:* 6 full-time (3 women), 6 part-time/adjunct (4 women). *Students:* 15 full-time (10 women), 192 part-time (132 women); includes 44 minority (15 Black or African American, non-Hispanic/Latino; 8 Asian, non-Hispanic/Latino; 17 Hispanic/Latino; 4 Two or more races, non-Hispanic/Latino), 1 international. Average age 33. 127 applicants, 82% accepted, 79 enrolled. In 2016, 47 master's, 13 other advanced degrees awarded. *Entrance requirements:* For master's, GRE (minimum combined score of 300) or MAT (minimum score of 400) within the last five years, bachelor's degree; minimum undergraduate GPA of 3.0; demonstrated proficiency in basic uses of instructional technologies; for other advanced degree, GRE or MAT within last 5 years, minimum undergraduate GPA of 3.0; demonstrated proficiency in basic uses of instructional technologies; master's degree, minimum 3 years' successful teaching experience, and permanent or provisional NY State teaching certification (for Advanced Diploma). Additional exam requirements/recommendations for international students: Required—TOEFL (minimum score 79 iBT), IELTS (minimum score 6). *Application deadline:* Applications are processed on a rolling basis. Application fee: $50. Electronic applications accepted. *Expenses:* $1,215 per credit. *Financial support:* Research assistantships with partial tuition reimbursements, career-related internships or fieldwork, scholarships/grants, health care benefits, tuition waivers (full and partial), and unspecified assistantships available. Support available to part-time students. Financial award application deadline: 3/1; financial award applicants required to submit FAFSA. *Faculty research:* Integration of information and communication technologies (ICTs) and media literacy education into learning environments; urban K-12 teachers' effective use of technology to enhance student achievement; instructional design and transdisciplinary curriculum studies for online instruction; STEM + computing partnerships for K-12 teachers; experiential, collaborative, and performance-based approaches to pedagogy and technology integration in the K-12 classroom. *Unit head:* Dr. Melda Yildiz, Department Chair, 516-686-1053, Fax: 516-686-7655, E-mail: myildiz@nyit.edu. *Application contact:* Alice Dolitsky, Director, Graduate Admissions, 516-686-7520, Fax: 516-686-1116, E-mail: nyitgrad@nyit.edu.
Website: http://www.nyit.edu/interdisciplinary/department_instructional_technology

Nova Southeastern University, Abraham S. Fischler College of Education, Fort Lauderdale, FL 33314. Offers education (MS, Ed D, PhD, Ed S); instructional technology and distance education (MS); teaching and learning (MA). *Accreditation:* NCATE. *Program availability:* Part-time, evening/weekend, 100% online, blended/hybrid learning. *Faculty:* 94 full-time (58 women), 204 part-time/adjunct (145 women). *Students:* 1,841 full-time (1,435 women), 1,705 part-time (1,336 women); includes 2,584 minority (1,389 Black or African American, non-Hispanic/Latino; 8 American Indian or Alaska Native, non-Hispanic/Latino; 44 Asian, non-Hispanic/Latino; 1,078 Hispanic/Latino; 2 Native Hawaiian or other Pacific Islander, non-Hispanic/Latino; 63 Two or more races, non-Hispanic/Latino), 26 international. Average age 41. 1,753 applicants, 47% accepted, 581 enrolled. In 2016, 654 master's, 387 doctorates, 119 other advanced degrees awarded. *Degree requirements:* For master's, practicum, internship; for doctorate, thesis/dissertation; for Ed S, thesis, practicum, internship. *Entrance requirements:* For master's, MAT or GRE (for some programs), CLAST, PRAXIS I, CBEST, General Knowledge Test, teaching certification, minimum GPA of 2.5, verification of teaching, BS; for doctorate, MAT or GRE, master's degree, minimum cumulative GPA of 3.0; for Ed S, MAT or GRE, master's degree, teaching certificate, minimum GPA of 3.0. Additional exam requirements/recommendations for international students: Recommended—TOEFL (minimum score 550 paper-based; 79 iBT), IELTS (minimum score 6). *Application deadline:* Applications are processed on a rolling basis. Application fee: $50. Electronic applications accepted. *Expenses:* Contact institution. *Financial support:* In 2016–17, 67 students received support. Career-related internships or fieldwork and Federal Work-Study available. Support available to part-time students. Financial award application deadline: 4/15; financial award applicants required to submit FAFSA. *Faculty research:* STEM education, educational technology, principal training, quality of life. *Total annual research expenditures:* $50,000. *Unit head:* Dr. Kim Durham, Interim Dean, 954-262-8731, Fax: 954-262-3894, E-mail: durham@nova.edu. *Application contact:* Adriana Garay, Executive Director for Marketing, Recruitment and Admissions, 800-986-3223 Ext. 8500, E-mail: fserecruit@nova.edu.
Website: http://www.fischlerschool.nova.edu/

Post University, Program in Education, Waterbury, CT 06723-2540. Offers education (M Ed); higher education administration (M Ed); instructional design and technology (M Ed); online teaching (M Ed); teaching and learning (M Ed); TESOL (teaching English to speakers of other languages) (M Ed). *Program availability:* Online learning.

Regent University, Graduate School, School of Education, Virginia Beach, VA 23464-9800. Offers adult education (Ed D, PhD, Ed S); advanced educational leadership (Ed D, PhD, Ed S); career switcher (M Ed); character education (Ed D, PhD, Ed S); Christian education leadership (Ed D, PhD, Ed S); Christian school administration (M Ed); curriculum and instruction (M Ed), including adult education, Christian school, gifted and talented education, STEM education, teacher leader; educational leadership (M Ed); educational psychology (Ed D, PhD, Ed S); educational technology and online learning (Ed D, PhD, Ed S); elementary education (M Ed); exceptional education executive leadership (Ed D, PhD, Ed S); higher education (Ed D, PhD, Ed S); higher education leadership and management (Ed D, PhD, Ed S); individualized degree plan (M Ed); K-12 school leadership (Ed D, PhD, Ed S); K-12 special education (M Ed); K-8 leadership in mathematics education (M Ed); leadership in mathematics education (Ed S); reading specialist (M Ed); special education (Ed D, PhD, Ed S); student affairs (M Ed); TESOL (M Ed), including adult education - collegiate, K-12. *Accreditation:* TEAC. *Program availability:* Part-time, evening/weekend, 100% online, blended/hybrid learning. *Faculty:* 22 full-time (10 women), 42 part-time/adjunct (31 women). *Students:* 89 full-time (62 women), 1,035 part-time (823 women); includes 466 minority (381 Black or African American, non-Hispanic/Latino; 3 American Indian or Alaska Native, non-Hispanic/Latino; 19 Asian, non-Hispanic/Latino; 50 Hispanic/Latino; 13 Two or more races, non-Hispanic/Latino), 11 international. Average age 39. 976 applicants, 59% accepted, 449 enrolled. In 2016, 241 master's, 22 doctorates, 4 other advanced degrees awarded. *Degree requirements:* For master's, thesis or alternative; for doctorate, comprehensive exam, thesis/dissertation. *Entrance requirements:* For master's, Virginia Communication and Literacy Assessment (VCLA), PRAXIS, college transcripts, writing sample, interview; for doctorate, GRE, writing sample, resume, transcripts, interview. Additional exam requirements/recommendations for international students: Required—TOEFL (minimum score 577 paper-based). *Application deadline:* For fall admission, 4/1 priority date for domestic students; for spring admission, 10/15 priority date for domestic students. Applications are processed on a rolling basis. Application fee: $50. Electronic applications accepted. *Expenses:* Contact institution. *Financial support:* In 2016–17, 622 students received support, including 1 fellowship (averaging $5,000 per year); career-related internships or fieldwork, scholarships/grants, and unspecified assistantships also available. Support available to part-time students. *Faculty research:* Christian school administration, curriculum and instruction, educational technology and online learning, higher education, special education. *Unit head:* Dr. Donald Finn, Dean, 757-352-4278, Fax: 757-352-4318, E-mail: dfinn@regent.edu. *Application contact:* Heidi Cece, Assistant Vice President of Enrollment Management, 800-373-5504, Fax: 757-352-4381, E-mail: admissions@regent.edu.
Website: http://www.regent.edu/soe/

Saginaw Valley State University, College of Education, Program in E-Learning, University Center, MI 48710. Offers MA. *Program availability:* Part-time, evening/weekend. *Degree requirements:* For master's, capstone course or thesis. *Entrance requirements:* For master's, minimum GPA of 3.0. Additional exam requirements/recommendations for international students: Required—TOEFL (minimum score 550 paper-based; 79 iBT). *Application deadline:* For fall admission, 7/15 for international students; for winter admission, 11/15 for international students; for spring admission, 4/15 for international students. Application fee: $30 ($90 for international students). *Expenses:* Tuition, state resident: full-time $9652; part-time $536 per credit hour. Tuition, nonresident: full-time $12,259; part-time $1022 per credit hour. *Required fees:* $263; $14.60 per credit hour. Tuition and fees vary according to degree level. *Financial support:* Federal Work-Study and scholarships/grants available. Support available to part-time students. *Unit head:* Dr. Carolyn Gilbreath, Associate Professor of Teaching Education, 989-749-4772, Fax: 989-964-4563, E-mail: cagilbre@svsu.edu. *Application contact:* Jenna Briggs, Director, Graduate and International Admissions, 989-964-6096, Fax: 989-964-2788, E-mail: gradadm@svsu.edu.

Shippensburg University of Pennsylvania, School of Graduate Studies, College of Education and Human Services, Department of Teacher Education, Shippensburg, PA 17257-2299. Offers curriculum and instruction (M Ed), including biology, early childhood education, elementary and middle level education, elementary education, geography/earth science, history, mathematics, middle school education, modern languages; literacy studies (Certificate); online instruction, learning, and technology (Certificate); reading (M Ed); teaching English as a second language (Certificate). *Accreditation:* NCATE. *Program availability:* Part-time, evening/weekend, 100% online, blended/hybrid learning. *Faculty:* 14 full-time (9 women), 5 part-time/adjunct (all women). *Students:* 11 full-time (10 women), 88 part-time (81 women); includes 8 minority (3 Black or African American, non-Hispanic/Latino; 2 Asian, non-Hispanic/Latino; 3 Hispanic/Latino), 4 international. Average age 32. 57 applicants, 60% accepted, 28 enrolled. In 2016, 18 master's awarded. *Degree requirements:* For master's, comprehensive exam (for some programs), thesis optional, practicum or internship; capstone seminar (for some programs). *Entrance requirements:* For master's, MAT or GRE (if GPA less than 2.75), interview, 3 letters of reference, questionnaire of teaching background and future goals, resume. Additional exam requirements/recommendations for international students: Required—TOEFL (minimum score 550 paper-based, 68 iBT) or IELTS (minimum score 6). *Application deadline:* For fall admission, 4/1 priority date for domestic students, 4/30 for international students; for spring admission, 9/1 priority date for domestic students, 9/30 for international students; for summer admission, 2/1 priority date for domestic students. Applications are processed on a rolling basis. Application fee: $45. Electronic applications accepted. *Expenses:* Tuition, state resident: part-time $483 per credit. Tuition, nonresident: part-time $725 per credit. *Required fees:* $141 per credit. *Financial support:* In 2016–17, 3 students received support. Career-related internships or fieldwork, scholarships/grants, unspecified assistantships, and resident hall director and student payroll positions available. Support available to part-time students. Financial award application deadline: 3/1; financial award applicants required to submit FAFSA. *Unit head:* Dr. Christine A. Royce, Chairperson, 717-477-1688, Fax: 717-477-4046, E-mail: caroyc@ship.edu. *Application contact:* Megan N. Luft, Assistant Dean of Graduate Admissions, 717-477-1231, Fax: 717-477-4016, E-mail: mnluft@ship.edu.
Website: http://www.ship.edu/teacher/

Télé-université, Graduate Programs, Québec, QC G1K 9H5, Canada. Offers computer science (PhD); corporate finance (MS); distance learning (MS). *Program availability:* Part-time.

Texas Tech University, Graduate School, College of Education, Department of Educational Psychology and Leadership, Lubbock, TX 79409-1071. Offers counselor education (M Ed, PhD); distance education (M Ed); educational leadership (M Ed, Ed D, PhD); educational psychology (M Ed, PhD); higher education (M Ed, Ed D); higher education research (PhD); instructional technology (M Ed, Ed D); special education (M Ed, Ed D, PhD). *Accreditation:* ACA; NCATE. *Program availability:* Part-time, evening/weekend. *Faculty:* 59 full-time (29 women), 3 part-time/adjunct (all women). *Students:* 300 full-time (218 women), 656 part-time (482 women); includes 320 minority (87 Black or African American, non-Hispanic/Latino; 5 American Indian or Alaska Native, non-Hispanic/Latino; 5 Asian, non-Hispanic/Latino; 200 Hispanic/Latino; 23 Two or more races, non-Hispanic/Latino), 51 international. Average age 36. 668 applicants, 56% accepted, 285 enrolled. In 2016, 171 master's, 47 doctorates awarded. Terminal master's awarded for partial completion of doctoral program. *Degree requirements:* For master's, comprehensive exam, thesis optional; for doctorate, comprehensive exam, thesis/dissertation. *Entrance requirements:* For master's, GRE (for some programs); for doctorate, GRE. Additional exam requirements/recommendations for international students: Required—TOEFL (minimum score 550 paper-based; 79 iBT). *Application deadline:* For fall admission, 6/1 priority date for domestic students, 1/15 priority date for international students; for spring admission, 9/1 priority date for domestic students, 6/15 priority date for international students. Applications are processed on a rolling basis. Application fee: $75. Electronic applications accepted. *Expenses:* $285 per credit hour full-time resident tuition, $693 per credit hour full-time non-resident tuition; $50.50 per credit hour fee plus $608 per term fee. *Financial support:* In 2016–17, 384 students received support, including 384 fellowships (averaging $3,632 per year); scholarships/grants and unspecified assistantships also available. Support available to part-time students. Financial award application deadline: 1/3; financial award applicants required to submit FAFSA. *Faculty research:* Cognitive, motivational, and developmental processes in learning; counseling education; instructional technology; generic special education and sensory impairment; community college administration; K-12 school

administration. *Total annual research expenditures:* $1,371. *Unit head:* Dr. Hansel Burley, Chair, 806-834-5135, Fax: 806-742-2179, E-mail: hansel.burley@ttu.edu. *Application contact:* Pam Smith, Admissions Advisor, 806-834-2969, Fax: 806-742-2179, E-mail: pam.smith@ttu.edu.
Website: http://www.educ.ttu.edu/

Thomas Edison State University, Heavin School of Arts and Sciences, Program in Online Learning and Teaching, Trenton, NJ 08608. Offers Graduate Certificate. *Program availability:* Part-time, online learning. *Entrance requirements:* Additional exam requirements/recommendations for international students: Required—TOEFL (minimum score 550 paper-based; 79 iBT). Electronic applications accepted.

University at Buffalo, the State University of New York, Graduate School, Graduate School of Education, Department of Learning and Instruction, Buffalo, NY 14260. Offers biology education (Ed M, Certificate); chemistry education (Ed M, Certificate); childhood education (Ed M); childhood education with bilingual extension (Ed M); college teaching (Advanced Certificate); curriculum, instruction and the science of learning (PhD); early childhood education (Ed M); early childhood education with bilingual extension (Ed M); earth science education (Ed M, Certificate); education and technology (Ed M); education studies (Ed M); educational technology and new literacies (Certificate); educational technology and new literacies (Advanced Certificate); elementary education (Ed D); English education (Ed M, Certificate); English education studies (Ed M); English for speakers of other languages (Ed M); foreign and second language education (PhD); French education (Ed M, Certificate); German education (Ed M, Certificate); gifted education (Certificate); Latin education (Ed M, Certificate); literacy education studies (Ed M); literacy specialist (Ed M); literacy teaching and learning (Certificate); mathematics education (Ed M, Certificate); music education (Ed M, Certificate); music education studies (Ed M); music learning theory (Advanced Certificate); online education (Advanced Certificate); physics education (Ed M, Certificate); science and the public (Ed M); social studies education (Ed M, Certificate); Spanish education (Ed M, Certificate); special education (PhD); teaching English to speakers of other languages (Ed M). *Program availability:* Part-time, evening/weekend, 100% online. *Faculty:* 28 full-time (21 women), 67 part-time/adjunct (49 women). *Students:* 198 full-time (153 women), 312 part-time (220 women); includes 48 minority (28 Black or African American, non-Hispanic/Latino; 4 American Indian or Alaska Native, non-Hispanic/Latino; 15 Asian, non-Hispanic/Latino; 1 Hispanic/Latino), 66 international. Average age 33. 336 applicants, 86% accepted, 178 enrolled. In 2016, 137 master's, 24 doctorates, 25 other advanced degrees awarded. *Degree requirements:* For master's, comprehensive exam; for doctorate, thesis/dissertation, research analysis exam, research experience. *Entrance requirements:* For master's, letters of reference; for doctorate, GRE General Test or MAT, interview, writing sample, letters of recommendation. Additional exam requirements/recommendations for international students: Required—TOEFL (minimum score 600 paper-based; 96 iBT). *Application deadline:* For fall admission, 2/1 priority date for domestic and international students; for spring admission, 11/15 priority date for domestic students, 10/1 for international students. Applications are processed on a rolling basis. Application fee: $50. Electronic applications accepted. *Financial support:* In 2016–17, 44 fellowships (averaging $4,010 per year), 39 research assistantships with tuition reimbursements (averaging $9,897 per year) were awarded; teaching assistantships, career-related internships or fieldwork, Federal Work-Study, institutionally sponsored loans, scholarships/grants, tuition waivers (full and partial), and unspecified assistantships also available. Financial award application deadline: 2/28; financial award applicants required to submit FAFSA. *Faculty research:* Science assessment, foreign language teaching and learning, early learning, new literacies, gender and education. *Total annual research expenditures:* $534,880. *Unit head:* Dr. Deborah Moore-Russo, Chair, 716-645-4069, Fax: 716-645-3161, E-mail: dam29@buffalo.edu. *Application contact:* Luann Zak, Admissions Assistant, 716-645-2110, Fax: 716-645-7937, E-mail: luannzak@buffalo.edu.
Website: http://gse.buffalo.edu/lai

University of Colorado Denver, School of Education and Human Development, Information and Learning Technologies Program, Denver, CO 80217. Offers e-learning design and implementation (MA); instructional design and adult learning (MA); K-12 teaching (MA). *Program availability:* Part-time, evening/weekend, online learning. *Students:* 68 full-time (56 women), 50 part-time (37 women); includes 16 minority (4 Black or African American, non-Hispanic/Latino; 5 Asian, non-Hispanic/Latino; 5 Hispanic/Latino; 1 Native Hawaiian or other Pacific Islander, non-Hispanic/Latino; 1 Two or more races, non-Hispanic/Latino), 2 international. Average age 38. 24 applicants, 88% accepted, 13 enrolled. In 2016, 45 master's awarded. *Degree requirements:* For master's, comprehensive exam (for some programs), comprehensive exam or online portfolio; 30 credit hours. *Entrance requirements:* For master's, GRE or MAT (if GPA is below 2.75), resume, statement of intent, three letters of recommendation, transcripts from all colleges/universities previously attended. Additional exam requirements/recommendations for international students: Required—TOEFL (minimum score 537 paper-based; 75 iBT); Recommended—IELTS (minimum score 6.5). *Application deadline:* For fall admission, 5/15 for domestic students, 5/1 for international students; for spring admission, 11/15 for domestic students, 11/1 for international students; for summer admission, 3/15 for domestic students, 3/1 for international students. Application fee: $50 ($75 for international students). Electronic applications accepted. *Expenses:* Contact institution. *Financial support:* In 2016–17, 7 students received support. Fellowships, research assistantships, teaching assistantships, Federal Work-Study, institutionally sponsored loans, scholarships/grants, and traineeships available. Financial award application deadline: 4/1; financial award applicants required to submit FAFSA. *Faculty research:* Technology for educational management, instructional design foundations, e-learning, educational design. *Unit head:* Brent Wilson, Professor, 303-720-7765, E-mail: brent.wilson@ucdenver.edu. *Application contact:* 303-315-6300, E-mail: education@ucdenver.edu.
Website: http://www.ucdenver.edu/academics/colleges/SchoolOfEducation/Academics/MASTERS/ILT/Pages/default.aspx

University of Illinois at Springfield, Graduate Programs, College of Education and Human Services, Department of Educational Leadership, Springfield, IL 62703-5407. Offers chief school business official (CAS); educational leadership (MA); educational technology (Graduate Certificate); English as a second language (Graduate Certificate); higher education online pedagogy (Graduate Certificate); leadership and learning (Graduate Certificate); legal aspects of education (Graduate Certificate); superintendent (CAS); teacher leadership (MA). *Program availability:* Part-time, evening/weekend, 100% online, blended/hybrid learning. *Faculty:* 5 full-time (2 women), 8 part-time/adjunct (7 women). *Students:* 4 full-time (2 women), 113 part-time (68 women); includes 20 minority (15 Black or African American, non-Hispanic/Latino; 1 American Indian or Alaska Native, non-Hispanic/Latino; 4 Hispanic/Latino), 1 international. Average age 36. 45 applicants, 62% accepted, 19 enrolled. In 2016, 22 master's, 2 other advanced degrees awarded. *Degree requirements:* For master's, capstone course. *Entrance requirements:* For master's, minimum undergraduate GPA of 3.0, valid Illinois Teaching License, minimum of two years of successful teaching experience, portfolio, interview. Additional exam requirements/recommendations for international students: Required—TOEFL (minimum score 500 paper-based; 61 iBT). *Application deadline:* Applications are processed on a rolling basis. Application fee: $60 ($75 for international students). Electronic applications accepted. *Expenses:* Tuition, state resident: part-time $329 per credit hour. Tuition, nonresident: part-time $675 per credit hour. *Financial support:* In 2016–17, fellowships with full tuition reimbursements (averaging $9,900 per year), research assistantships with full tuition reimbursements (averaging $9,991 per year), teaching assistantships with full tuition reimbursements (averaging $10,059 per year) were awarded; career-related internships or fieldwork, Federal Work-Study, scholarships/grants, health care benefits, and unspecified assistantships also available. Support available to part-time students. Financial award application deadline: 11/15; financial award applicants required to submit FAFSA. *Unit head:* Dr. Scott Day, Program Administrator, 217-206-7520, Fax: 217-206-6775, E-mail: day.scott@uis.edu. *Application contact:* Dr. Cecelia Cornell, Associate Vice Chancellor for Graduate Education, 217-206-7230, E-mail: ccorn1@uis.edu.
Website: http://www.uis.edu/edl/

The University of Kansas, Graduate Studies, School of Pharmacy, Department of Pharmaceutical Chemistry, Lawrence, KS 66045. Offers distance learning (MS, PhD); pharmaceutical chemistry (MS, PhD). *Program availability:* Part-time, evening/weekend, online learning. *Students:* 39 full-time (16 women), 13 part-time (5 women); includes 6 minority (1 Black or African American, non-Hispanic/Latino; 4 Asian, non-Hispanic/Latino; 1 Two or more races, non-Hispanic/Latino), 21 international. Average age 28. 51 applicants, 33% accepted, 11 enrolled. In 2016, 12 master's, 4 doctorates awarded. Terminal master's awarded for partial completion of doctoral program. *Entrance requirements:* For master's, GRE General Test, bachelor's degree in biological sciences, chemical engineering, chemistry, or pharmacy; official transcripts from all universities/institutions in which the applicant has studied; personal statement; resume; three letters of recommendation; for doctorate, GRE General Test, official transcripts from all universities/institutions in which the applicant has studied, personal statement, resume, three letters of recommendation. Additional exam requirements/recommendations for international students: Required—TOEFL. *Application deadline:* For fall admission, 1/15 priority date for domestic and international students; for spring admission, 12/15 for domestic and international students; for summer admission, 5/15 for domestic and international students. Application fee: $65 ($85 for international students). Electronic applications accepted. *Financial support:* Fellowships, research assistantships, career-related internships or fieldwork, scholarships/grants, traineeships, and unspecified assistantships available. Financial award application deadline: 1/15. *Faculty research:* Physical pharmacy, biotechnology, bioanalytical chemistry, biopharmaceutics and pharmacokinetics, nanotechnology. *Unit head:* Dr. Christian Schoneich, Chair, 785-864-4880, E-mail: schoneic@ku.edu. *Application contact:* Nancy Helm, Administrative Associate, 785-864-4822, E-mail: nhelm@ku.edu.
Website: http://www.pharmchem.ku.edu/

The University of Kansas, Graduate Studies, School of Pharmacy, Department of Pharmacology and Toxicology, Program in Pharmacology and Toxicology, Lawrence, KS 66045. Offers pharmacology and toxicology (MS), including distance learning. *Students:* 21 full-time (18 women), 1 (woman) part-time; includes 1 minority (Hispanic/Latino), 15 international. Average age 25. 59 applicants, 14% accepted, 6 enrolled. In 2016, 1 master's awarded. Terminal master's awarded for partial completion of doctoral program. *Entrance requirements:* For master's, GRE, bachelor's degree in related field, 3 letters of recommendation, resume or curriculum vitae, official transcripts, 1-2 page personal statement. Additional exam requirements/recommendations for international students: Required—TOEFL (minimum score 600 paper-based; 100 iBT). *Application deadline:* For fall admission, 1/15 priority date for domestic and international students. Application fee: $65 ($85 for international students). Electronic applications accepted. *Financial support:* Fellowships, research assistantships, teaching assistantships, and scholarships/grants available. Financial award application deadline: 2/1. *Faculty research:* Neurodegeneration, diabetes, neurological disorders, neuropharmacology, drug metabolism. *Unit head:* Nancy Muma, Chair, 785-864-4002, Fax: 785-864-5219, E-mail: nmuma@ku.edu. *Application contact:* Sarah Hoadley, Graduate Admissions Contact, 785-864-4002, E-mail: sarahhoadley@ku.edu.
Website: http://www.pharmtox.pharm.ku.edu

University of Maryland, Baltimore County, The Graduate School, College of Arts, Humanities and Social Sciences, Department of Education, Program in Instructional Systems Development, Halethorpe, MD 21227. Offers distance education (Graduate Certificate); instructional systems development (MA, Graduate Certificate), including distance education (Graduate Certificate); instructional technology (Graduate Certificate). *Program availability:* Part-time, evening/weekend, 100% online, blended/hybrid learning. *Faculty:* 2 full-time (0 women), 9 part-time/adjunct (3 women). *Students:* 4 full-time (1 woman), 103 part-time (72 women); includes 36 minority (24 Black or African American, non-Hispanic/Latino; 5 Asian, non-Hispanic/Latino; 4 Hispanic/Latino; 3 Two or more races, non-Hispanic/Latino). Average age 37. 49 applicants, 94% accepted, 40 enrolled. In 2016, 32 master's, 55 other advanced degrees awarded. *Degree requirements:* For master's, comprehensive exam (for some programs), portfolio (for some programs). *Entrance requirements:* Additional exam requirements/recommendations for international students: Required—TOEFL (minimum score 550 paper-based; 80 iBT), GRE. *Application deadline:* For fall admission, 6/1 priority date for domestic students, 1/1 priority date for international students; for spring admission, 11/1 priority date for domestic students; for summer admission, 3/1 priority date for domestic students. Applications are processed on a rolling basis. Application fee: $50. Electronic applications accepted. *Expenses:* Tuition, state resident: full-time $13,294. Tuition, nonresident: full-time $20,286. *Financial support:* Application deadline: 2/14; applicants required to submit FAFSA. *Faculty research:* E-learning, distance education, instructional design. *Unit head:* Dr. Greg Williams, Graduate Program Director, 443-543-5447, Fax: 443-543-5096, E-mail: gregw@umbc.edu. *Application contact:* Renee Eisenhuth, Graduate Program Coordinator, 443-543-5446, Fax: 443-543-5096, E-mail: reisen@umbc.edu.
Website: http://www.umbc.edu/isd

University of Maryland University College, The Graduate School, Program in Distance Education and E-learning, Adelphi, MD 20783. Offers MDE. *Program availability:* Part-time, evening/weekend, online learning. *Students:* 130 part-time (99 women); includes 57 minority (45 Black or African American, non-Hispanic/Latino; 9 Hispanic/Latino; 3 Two or more races, non-Hispanic/Latino), 9 international. Average age 41. 36 applicants, 100% accepted, 27 enrolled. In 2016, 27 master's awarded. *Degree requirements:* For master's, thesis or alternative. *Application deadline:* Applications are processed on a rolling basis. Application fee: $50. Electronic applications accepted. *Expenses:* Tuition, state resident: part-time $458 per credit. Tuition, nonresident: part-time $659 per credit. *Financial support:* Federal Work-Study and scholarships/grants available. Support available to part-time students. Financial award application deadline: 6/1; financial award applicants required to submit FAFSA. *Unit head:* Dr. Randall Hansen, Director, 240-684-2400, Fax: 240-684-2401, E-mail: randall.hansen@umuc.edu. *Application contact:* Coordinator, Graduate Admissions, 800-888-8682, Fax: 240-684-2151, E-mail: newgrad@umuc.edu.
Website: http://www.umuc.edu/academic-programs/masters-degrees/distance-education.cfm

University of Nevada, Las Vegas, Graduate College, College of Education, Department of Teaching and Learning, Las Vegas, NV 89154-3005. Offers curriculum and instruction (M Ed, MS, Ed D, PhD, Ed S), including teacher education (PhD);

elementary teaching (Certificate); online teaching and training (Certificate); secondary teaching (Certificate); social justice studies (Certificate); teaching and learning (PhD). *Program availability:* Part-time, evening/weekend. *Faculty:* 26 full-time (12 women), 10 part-time/adjunct (8 women). *Students:* 280 full-time (202 women), 206 part-time (131 women); includes 188 minority (51 Black or African American, non-Hispanic/Latino; 4 American Indian or Alaska Native, non-Hispanic/Latino; 23 Asian, non-Hispanic/Latino; 72 Hispanic/Latino; 4 Native Hawaiian or other Pacific Islander, non-Hispanic/Latino; 34 Two or more races, non-Hispanic/Latino), 18 international. Average age 35. 178 applicants, 89% accepted, 142 enrolled. In 2016, 156 master's, 14 doctorates, 1 other advanced degree awarded. *Degree requirements:* For master's, comprehensive exam (for some programs), thesis (for some programs); for doctorate, comprehensive exam, thesis/dissertation, defense of dissertation; for other advanced degree, comprehensive exam (for some programs), oral presentation of special project or professional paper. *Entrance requirements:* For master's, bachelor's degree with minimum GPA 2.75; for doctorate, GRE General Test, master's degree with minimum GPA of 3.0; statement of purpose; demonstration of oral communication skills; 3 letters of recommendation; for other advanced degree, PRAXIS Core (for some programs); PRAXIS II (for some programs), bachelor's degree (for some programs). Additional exam requirements/ recommendations for international students: Required—TOEFL (minimum score 550 paper-based; 80 iBT), IELTS (minimum score 7). *Application deadline:* For fall admission, 6/1 for domestic students, 5/1 for international students; for spring admission, 11/1 for domestic students, 10/1 for international students; for summer admission, 3/15 for domestic students. Application fee: $60 ($95 for international students). Electronic applications accepted. *Expenses:* $269.25 per credit, $792 per 3-credit course; $9,634 per year resident; $23,274 per year non-resident; $7,094 fees non-resident (7 credits or more); $1,307 annual health insurance fee. *Financial support:* In 2016–17, 8 research assistantships with partial tuition reimbursements (averaging $16,719 per year), 28 teaching assistantships with partial tuition reimbursements (averaging $17,023 per year) were awarded; institutionally sponsored loans, scholarships/grants, health care benefits, and unspecified assistantships also available. Financial award application deadline: 3/15. *Faculty research:* Content area and critical literacy, education in content areas, teacher education, STEM education, technology education. *Total annual research expenditures:* $652,413. *Unit head:* Dr. Emily Lin, Chair/Professor, 702-895-6407, Fax: 702-895-4898, E-mail: emily.lin@unlv.edu. *Application contact:* Dr. Travis Olson, Graduate Coordinator, 702-895-0471, Fax: 702-895-4898, E-mail: travis.olson@unlv.edu.
Website: http://tl.unlv.edu/

University of South Florida, Innovative Education, Tampa, FL 33620-9951. Offers adult, career and higher education (Graduate Certificate), including college teaching, leadership in developing human resources, leadership in higher education; Africana studies (Graduate Certificate), including diasporas and health disparities, genocide and human rights; aging studies (Graduate Certificate), including gerontology; art research (Graduate Certificate), including museum studies; business foundations (Graduate Certificate); chemical and biomedical engineering (Graduate Certificate), including materials science and engineering, water, health and sustainability; child and family studies (Graduate Certificate), including positive behavior support; civil and industrial engineering (Graduate Certificate), including transportation systems analysis; community and family health (Graduate Certificate), including maternal and child health, social marketing and public health, violence and injury: prevention and intervention, women's health; criminology (Graduate Certificate), including criminal justice administration; educational measurement and research (Graduate Certificate), including evaluation; English (Graduate Certificate), including comparative literary studies, creative writing, professional and technical communication; entrepreneurship (Graduate Certificate); environmental health (Graduate Certificate), including safety management; epidemiology and biostatistics (Graduate Certificate), including applied biostatistics, biostatistics, concepts and tools of epidemiology, epidemiology, epidemiology of infectious diseases; geography, environment and planning (Graduate Certificate), including community development, environmental policy and management, geographical information systems; geology (Graduate Certificate), including hydrogeology; global health (Graduate Certificate), including disaster management, global health and Latin American and Caribbean studies, global health practice, humanitarian assistance, infection control; government and international affairs (Graduate Certificate), including Cuban studies, globalization studies; health policy and management (Graduate Certificate), including health management and leadership, public health policy and programs; hearing specialist: early intervention (Graduate Certificate); industrial and management systems engineering (Graduate Certificate), including systems engineering, technology management; information studies (Graduate Certificate), including school library media specialist; information systems/decision sciences (Graduate Certificate), including analytics and business intelligence; instructional technology (Graduate Certificate), including distance education, Florida digital/virtual educator, instructional design, multimedia design, Web design; internal medicine, bioethics and medical humanities (Graduate Certificate), including biomedical ethics; Latin American and Caribbean studies (Graduate Certificate); mass communications (Graduate Certificate), including multimedia journalism; mathematics and statistics (Graduate Certificate), including mathematics; medicine (Graduate Certificate), including aging and neuroscience, bioinformatics, biotechnology, brain fitness and memory management, clinical investigation, health informatics, health sciences, integrative weight management, intellectual property, medicine and gender, metabolic and nutritional medicine, metabolic cardiology, pharmacy sciences; national and competitive intelligence (Graduate Certificate); psychological and social foundations (Graduate Certificate), including career counseling, college teaching, diversity in education, mental health counseling, school counseling; public affairs (Graduate Certificate), including nonprofit management, public management, research administration; public health (Graduate Certificate), including environmental health, health equity, public health generalist, translational research in adolescent behavioral health; public health practices (Graduate Certificate), including planning for healthy communities; rehabilitation and mental health counseling (Graduate Certificate), including integrative mental health care, marriage and family therapy, rehabilitation technology; secondary education (Graduate Certificate), including ESOL, foreign language education: culture and content, foreign language education: professional; social work (Graduate Certificate), including geriatric social work/clinical gerontology; special education (Graduate Certificate), including autism spectrum disorder, disabilities education: severe/profound; world languages (Graduate Certificate), including teaching English as a second language (TESL) or foreign language. *Expenses:* Tuition, state resident: full-time $7766; part-time $431.43 per credit hour. Tuition, nonresident: full-time $15,789; part-time $877.17 per credit hour. *Required fees:* $37 per term. *Unit head:* Kathy Barnes, Interdisciplinary Programs Coordinator, 813-974-8031, Fax: 813-974-7061, E-mail: barnesk@usf.edu. *Application contact:* Karen Tylinski, Metro Initiatives, 813-974-9943, Fax: 813-974-7061, E-mail: ktylinsk@usf.edu.
Website: http://www.usf.edu/innovative-education/

Virginia Polytechnic Institute and State University, VT Online, Blacksburg, VA 24061. Offers advanced transportation systems (Certificate); aerospace engineering (MS); agricultural and life sciences (MSLFS); business information systems (Graduate Certificate); career and technical education (MS); civil engineering (MS); computer engineering (M Eng, MS); decision support systems (Graduate Certificate); eLearning leadership (MA); electrical engineering (M Eng, MS); engineering administration (MEA); environmental engineering (Certificate); environmental politics and policy (Graduate Certificate); environmental sciences and engineering (MS); foundations of political analysis (Graduate Certificate); health product risk management (Graduate Certificate); industrial and systems engineering (MS); information policy and society (Graduate Certificate); information security (Graduate Certificate); information technology (MIT); instructional technology (MA); integrative STEM education (MA Ed); liberal arts (Graduate Certificate); life sciences: health product risk management (MS); natural resources (MNR, Graduate Certificate); networking (Graduate Certificate); nonprofit and nongovernmental organization management (Graduate Certificate); ocean engineering (MS); political science (MA); security studies (Graduate Certificate); software development (Graduate Certificate). *Expenses:* Tuition, state resident: full-time $12,467; part-time $692.50 per credit hour. Tuition, nonresident: full-time $25,095; part-time $1394.25 per credit hour. *Required fees:* $2669; $491.50 per semester. Tuition and fees vary according to course load, campus/location and program.

Walden University, Graduate Programs, Richard W. Riley College of Education and Leadership, Minneapolis, MN 55401. Offers adult education (Post-Master's Certificate); adult learning (Graduate Certificate); college teaching and learning (Graduate Certificate); community college leadership (Ed D); curriculum, instruction and assessment (Ed D, Ed S, Graduate Certificate); developmental education (Graduate Certificate); early childhood administration, management, and leadership (Graduate Certificate); early childhood education (Ed D, Ed S); early childhood public policy and advocacy (Graduate Certificate); early childhood studies (MS), including administration, management and leadership, early childhood public policy and advocacy, teaching adults in the early childhood field, teaching and diversity in early childhood education; education (MS, PhD), including adolescent literacy and learning (MS), curriculum, instruction, and assessment (grades K-12) (MS), curriculum, instruction, assessment, and evaluation (PhD), early childhood leadership and advocacy (PhD), early childhood special education (PhD), educational leadership (MS), educational leadership and administration (principal preparation) (MS), educational technology and design (PhD), elementary reading and literacy (PreK-6) (MS), elementary reading and mathematics (grades K-6) (MS), global and comparative education (PhD), higher education leadership management and policy (PhD), integrating technology in the classroom (grades K-12) (MS), learning, instruction and innovation (PhD), mathematics (grades 5-8) (MS), mathematics (grades K-6) (MS), mathematics and science (grades K-8) (MS), organizational research, assessment, and evaluation (PhD), reading and literacy with a reading K-12 endorsement (MS), reading literacy assessment and evaluation (PhD), science (grades K-8) (MS), special education (non-licensure) (grades K-12) (MS), teacher leadership (grades K-12) (MS), teaching English language learners (grades K-12) (MS); educational administration and leadership (Ed D); educational leadership and administration (principal preparation) (Ed S); educational technology (Ed D, Ed S, Post Master's Certificate); elementary reading and literacy (Graduate Certificate); engaging culturally diverse learners (Graduate Certificate); enrollment management and institutional marketing (Graduate Certificate); higher education (MS), including adult learning, college teaching and learning, enrollment management and institutional marketing, global higher education, leadership for student success, online and distance learning; higher education and adult learning (Ed D); higher education leadership and management (Ed D); higher education leadership for student success (Graduate Certificate); instructional design and technology (MS, Postbaccalaureate Certificate), including general program (MS), online learning (MS), training and performance improvement (MS); integrating technology in the classroom (Graduate Certificate); mathematics 5-8 (Graduate Certificate); mathematics K-6 (Graduate Certificate); online teaching for adult educators (Graduate Certificate); reading, literacy, and assessment (Ed D, Ed S); science K-8 (Graduate Certificate); special education (Ed D, Ed S, Graduate Certificate); special education (K-age 21) (MAT); teacher leadership (Graduate Certificate); teaching adults English as a second language (Graduate Certificate); teaching adults in the early childhood field (Graduate Certificate); teaching and diversity in early childhood education (Graduate Certificate); teaching English language learners (grades K-12) (Graduate Certificate); teaching K-12 students online (Graduate Certificate). *Accreditation:* NCATE. *Program availability:* Part-time, evening/ weekend, online only, 100% online. *Degree requirements:* For doctorate, thesis/ dissertation (for some programs), residency; for other advanced degree, residency (for some programs). *Entrance requirements:* For master's, bachelor's degree or higher; minimum GPA of 2.5; official transcripts; goal statement (for some programs); access to computer and Internet; for doctorate, master's degree or higher; three years of related professional or academic experience (preferred); minimum GPA of 3.0; goal statement and current resume (for select programs); official transcripts; access to computer and Internet; for other advanced degree, relevant work experience; access to computer and Internet. Additional exam requirements/recommendations for international students: Required—TOEFL (minimum score 550 paper-based, 79 iBT), IELTS (minimum score 6.5), Michigan English Language Assessment Battery (minimum score 82), or PTE (minimum score 53). Electronic applications accepted.

Waynesburg University, Graduate and Professional Studies, Canonsburg, PA 15370. Offers business (MBA), including energy management, finance, health systems, human resources, leadership, market development; counseling (MA), including addictions counseling, clinical mental health; counselor education and supervision (PhD); criminal investigation (MA); education (M Ed), including autism, curriculum and instruction, educational leadership, online teaching; nursing (MSN), including administration, education, informatics; nursing practice (DNP); special education (M Ed); technology (M Ed); MSN/MBA. *Accreditation:* AACN. *Program availability:* Part-time, evening/ weekend. *Degree requirements:* For doctorate, thesis/dissertation. *Entrance requirements:* Additional exam requirements/recommendations for international students: Required—TOEFL. Electronic applications accepted.

Wayne State University, College of Education, Division of Administrative and Organizational Studies, Detroit, MI 48202. Offers college and university teaching (Certificate); educational administration and supervision (Ed S); educational leadership (M Ed); educational leadership and policy studies (Ed D, PhD); educational technology (Certificate); learning design and technology (M Ed, Ed D, PhD, Ed S); online teaching (Certificate). *Program availability:* Part-time, 100% online, blended/hybrid learning. *Faculty:* 11. *Students:* 83 full-time (58 women), 223 part-time (148 women); includes 151 minority (126 Black or African American, non-Hispanic/Latino; 3 American Indian or Alaska Native, non-Hispanic/Latino; 4 Asian, non-Hispanic/Latino; 8 Hispanic/Latino; 10 Two or more races, non-Hispanic/Latino), 14 international. Average age 39. 143 applicants, 43% accepted, 38 enrolled. In 2016, 53 master's, 9 doctorates, 34 other advanced degrees awarded. *Degree requirements:* For doctorate, thesis/dissertation. *Entrance requirements:* For master's, baccalaureate degree from accredited U.S. institution or equivalent from college or university of government-recognized standing; minimum undergraduate GPA of 2.75 in upper-division coursework; personal statement; for doctorate, GRE (instructional design and technology), interview; curriculum vitae; three references (two professional and one academic); master's degree; minimum graduate GPA of 3.5; autobiographical statement; research experience. Additional exam requirements/recommendations for international students: Required—TOEFL (minimum score 550 paper-based; 79 iBT), Michigan English Language Assessment Battery

(minimum score 85); Recommended—IELTS (minimum score 6.5), TWE (minimum score 5.5). *Application deadline:* For fall admission, 6/1 priority date for domestic students, 5/1 priority date for international students; for winter admission, 10/1 priority date for domestic students, 9/1 priority date for international students; for spring admission, 2/1 priority date for domestic students, 1/1 priority date for international students. Applications are processed on a rolling basis. Application fee: $50. Electronic applications accepted. *Expenses:* $16,503 per year resident tuition and fees, $33,697 per year non-resident tuition and fees. *Financial support:* In 2016–17, 96 students received support, including 1 fellowship with tuition reimbursement available (averaging $11,000 per year), 4 research assistantships with tuition reimbursements available (averaging $17,949 per year); scholarships/grants and unspecified assistantships also available. Support available to part-time students. Financial award applicants required to submit FAFSA. *Faculty research:* Total quality management, participatory management, administering educational technology, school improvement, principalship. *Unit head:* Dr. William Hill, Assistant Dean, 313-577-9316, E-mail: ad2107@wayne.edu. *Application contact:* Janice Green, Assistant Dean, 313-577-1605, E-mail: jwgreen@wayne.edu.
Website: http://coe.wayne.edu/aos/index.php

Western Illinois University, School of Graduate Studies, College of Business and Technology, Program in Instructional Design and Technology, Macomb, IL 61455-1390. Offers educational technology specialist (Certificate); instructional design and technology (MS); instructional media development (Certificate); online and distance learning development (Certificate); technology integration in education (Certificate); workplace learning and performance (Certificate). *Program availability:* Part-time, online learning. *Students:* 8 full-time (5 women), 54 part-time (32 women); includes 9 minority (4 Black or African American, non-Hispanic/Latino; 1 American Indian or Alaska Native, non-Hispanic/Latino; 3 Asian, non-Hispanic/Latino; 1 Hispanic/Latino), 2 international. Average age 36. 22 applicants, 91% accepted, 15 enrolled. In 2016, 30 master's, 6 other advanced degrees awarded. *Degree requirements:* For master's, thesis or alternative. *Entrance requirements:* Additional exam requirements/recommendations for international students: Required—TOEFL (minimum score 550 paper-based; 80 iBT). *Application deadline:* Applications are processed on a rolling basis. Application fee: $30. Electronic applications accepted. *Financial support:* In 2016–17, 3 students received support. Teaching assistantships and unspecified assistantships available. Financial award applicants required to submit FAFSA. *Unit head:* Dr. Hoyet Hemphill, Chairperson, 309-298-1952. *Application contact:* Dr. Nancy Parsons, Associate Provost and Director of Graduate Studies, 309-298-1806, Fax: 309-298-2345, E-mail: grad-office@wiu.edu.
Website: http://wiu.edu/idt

Wilkes University, College of Graduate and Professional Studies, School of Education, Wilkes-Barre, PA 18766-0002. Offers 21st century teaching and learning (MS Ed); art and science of teaching (MS Ed); classroom technology (MS Ed); early childhood literacy (MS Ed); educational development and strategies (MS Ed); educational leadership (MS Ed, Ed D); effective teaching (MS Ed); instructional media (MS Ed); instructional technology (MS Ed); international school leadership (MS Ed); international teaching and learning (MS Ed); middle level education (MS Ed); online teaching (MS Ed); reading (MS Ed); school business leadership (MS Ed); special education (MS Ed); teaching English to speakers of other languages (MS Ed). *Program availability:* Part-time, evening/weekend, 100% online, blended/hybrid learning. *Students:* 87 full-time (70 women), 1,496 part-time (1,111 women); includes 77 minority (11 Black or African American, non-Hispanic/Latino; 2 American Indian or Alaska Native, non-Hispanic/Latino; 12 Asian, non-Hispanic/Latino; 28 Hispanic/Latino; 3 Native Hawaiian or other Pacific Islander, non-Hispanic/Latino; 21 Two or more races, non-Hispanic/Latino). Average age 33. In 2016, 524 master's, 21 doctorates awarded. *Entrance requirements:* Additional exam requirements/recommendations for international students: Required—TOEFL (minimum score 550 paper-based; 79 iBT). *Application deadline:* Applications are processed on a rolling basis. Application fee: $45. Electronic applications accepted. *Expenses:* Contact institution. *Financial support:* Unspecified assistantships available. Financial award application deadline: 3/1; financial award applicants required to submit FAFSA. *Unit head:* Dr. Rhonda Rabbitt, Dean, 570-408-4680, Fax: 570-408-7872, E-mail: rhonda.rabbitt@wilkes.edu. *Application contact:* Director of Graduate Education, 570-408-4234, Fax: 570-408-7846.
Website: http://www.wilkes.edu/academics/graduate-programs/masters-programs/graduate-education/index.aspx

Educational Leadership and Administration

Abilene Christian University, College of Graduate and Professional Studies, Instructional Leadership Program, Abilene, TX 79699. Offers instructional leadership (M Ed), including conflict resolution, learning with emerging technologies, principalship; learning with emerging technologies (Certificate), including leadership of learning. *Program availability:* Part-time, online learning. *Faculty:* 1 (woman) full-time, 1 part-time/adjunct (0 women). *Students:* 9 full-time (7 women); includes 4 minority (2 Black or African American, non-Hispanic/Latino; 2 Hispanic/Latino). 11 applicants, 100% accepted, 9 enrolled. In 2016, 16 master's awarded. *Degree requirements:* For master's, comprehensive exam, practicum. *Entrance requirements:* Additional exam requirements/recommendations for international students: Required—TOEFL (minimum score 80 iBT), IELTS (minimum score 6), PTE. *Application deadline:* For fall admission, 8/15 priority date for domestic students; for winter admission, 10/1 priority date for domestic students; for spring admission, 12/15 priority date for domestic students; for summer admission, 4/15 for domestic students. Applications are processed on a rolling basis. Application fee: $50. Electronic applications accepted. *Expenses:* $600 per credit hour. *Financial support:* Application deadline: 4/1; applicants required to submit FAFSA. *Unit head:* Dr. Peter Williams, Program Director, 877-698-2793, E-mail: peter.williams@acu.edu. *Application contact:* Graduate Admissions, 855-219-7000, E-mail: gradonline@acu.edu.
Website: http://www.acu.edu/online/academics/master-of-education-in-instructional-leadership.html

Abilene Christian University, College of Graduate and Professional Studies, Program in Organizational Leadership, Abilene, TX 79699. Offers Ed D. *Program availability:* Part-time, online only, 100% online. *Students:* 176 full-time (112 women), 91 part-time (62 women); includes 139 minority (92 Black or African American, non-Hispanic/Latino; 1 American Indian or Alaska Native, non-Hispanic/Latino; 43 Hispanic/Latino; 3 Two or more races, non-Hispanic/Latino), 5 international. 175 applicants, 92% accepted, 152 enrolled. *Degree requirements:* For doctorate, thesis/dissertation. *Entrance requirements:* Additional exam requirements/recommendations for international students: Required—TOEFL (minimum score 80 iBT), IELTS (minimum score 6). *Application deadline:* For fall admission, 8/15 priority date for domestic students; for winter admission, 10/1 priority date for domestic students; for spring admission, 12/15 priority date for domestic students; for summer admission, 4/15 priority date for domestic students. Applications are processed on a rolling basis. Application fee: $50. Electronic applications accepted. *Expenses:* $700 per credit hour. *Financial support:* In 2016–17, 1 student received support. Scholarships/grants available. Financial award application deadline: 4/1; financial award applicants required to submit FAFSA. *Unit head:* Dr. Peter Williams, Program Director, 877-698-2793, E-mail: pew15a@acu.edu. *Application contact:* Graduate Admissions, 855-219-7000, E-mail: gradonline@acu.edu.
Website: http://www.acu.edu/online/academics/organizational-leadership.html

Abilene Christian University, College of Graduate and Professional Studies, Superintendent Certification Program, Abilene, TX 79699. Offers Post-Master's Certificate. *Program availability:* Part-time, online learning. In 2016, 4 Post-Master's Certificates awarded. *Entrance requirements:* Additional exam requirements/recommendations for international students: Required—TOEFL (minimum score 80 iBT), IELTS (minimum score 6), PTE. *Application deadline:* For fall admission, 8/15 priority date for domestic students; for winter admission, 10/1 for domestic students; for spring admission, 11/15 priority date for domestic students; for summer admission, 4/15 for domestic students. Applications are processed on a rolling basis. Application fee: $50. Electronic applications accepted. *Expenses: Tuition:* Full-time $19,890; part-time $1105 per credit hour. Tuition and fees vary according to course load and program. *Financial support:* Application deadline: 4/1; applicants required to submit FAFSA. *Unit head:* Dr. Peter Williams, Program Director, 877-698-2793, E-mail: peter.williams@acu.edu. *Application contact:* Graduate Admissions, 855-219-7000, E-mail: gradonline@acu.edu.

Acacia University, American Graduate School of Education, Tempe, AZ 85284. Offers educational administration (M Ed); elementary education (MA); English as a second language (M Ed); secondary education (MA); special education (M Ed).

Acadia University, Faculty of Professional Studies, School of Education, Program in Leadership, Wolfville, NS B4P 2R6, Canada. Offers M Ed. *Program availability:* Part-time. *Degree requirements:* For master's, thesis optional. *Entrance requirements:* For master's, B Ed or the equivalent, 2 years teaching or related experience. Additional exam requirements/recommendations for international students: Required—TOEFL (minimum score 580 paper-based; 93 iBT), IELTS (minimum score 6.5). *Faculty research:* Organizational theory and structural change, professionalism, sexuality education.

Adelphi University, Ruth S. Ammon School of Education, Program in Educational Leadership, Garden City, NY 11530-0701. Offers MA, Certificate. *Students:* 10 part-time (7 women); includes 2 minority (both Black or African American, non-Hispanic/Latino). Average age 38. 12 applicants, 92% accepted, 7 enrolled. In 2016, 12 master's, 4 other advanced degrees awarded. *Entrance requirements:* For master's, 2 letters of recommendation, resume, letter attesting to teaching experience (3 years full-time K-12). Additional exam requirements/recommendations for international students: Required—TOEFL (minimum score 550 paper-based; 80 iBT), IELTS (minimum score 6.5). *Application deadline:* For fall admission, 8/15 priority date for domestic students, 4/1 for international students; for spring admission, 1/15 priority date for domestic students, 11/1 for international students. Applications are processed on a rolling basis. Application fee: $50. Electronic applications accepted. *Expenses:* Contact institution. *Financial support:* Research assistantships, teaching assistantships, career-related internships or fieldwork, institutionally sponsored loans, scholarships/grants, traineeships, and unspecified assistantships available. Support available to part-time students. Financial award application deadline: 2/15; financial award applicants required to submit FAFSA. *Faculty research:* Technology methodology focusing on in-service and pre-service curriculum. *Unit head:* Dr. Devin Thornburg, Director, 516-877-4026, E-mail: thornburg@adelphi.edu. *Application contact:* Christine Murphy, Director of Admissions, 516-877-3050, Fax: 516-877-3039, E-mail: graduateadmissions@adelphi.edu.

Alabama State University, College of Education, Department of Instructional Support Programs, Montgomery, AL 36101-0271. Offers counselor education (M Ed, MS, Ed S), including general counseling (MS, Ed S), school counseling (M Ed, Ed S); educational administration (M Ed, Ed D, Ed S), including educational administration (Ed S), educational leadership, policy and law (Ed D), instructional leadership (M Ed); library education media (M Ed, Ed S). *Program availability:* Part-time. *Faculty:* 11 full-time (6 women), 7 part-time/adjunct (5 women). *Students:* 50 full-time (32 women), 128 part-time (95 women); includes 167 minority (166 Black or African American, non-Hispanic/Latino; 1 Two or more races, non-Hispanic/Latino), 3 international. Average age 37. 84 applicants, 50% accepted, 16 enrolled. In 2016, 39 master's, 19 doctorates, 5 other advanced degrees awarded. *Degree requirements:* For master's, comprehensive exam; for Ed S, comprehensive exam, thesis. *Entrance requirements:* For master's, GRE General Test, MAT, writing competency test, bachelor's degree or its equivalent from accredited college or university with minimum GPA of 2.5; for Ed S, GRE General Test, MAT, writing competency test, minimum GPA of 3.25. Additional exam requirements/recommendations for international students: Required—TOEFL (minimum score 500 paper-based). *Application deadline:* For fall admission, 4/15 for domestic and international students; for spring admission, 11/15 for domestic and international students; for summer admission, 3/15 for domestic and international students. Applications are processed on a rolling basis. Application fee: $25. Electronic applications accepted. *Expenses:* Tuition, state resident: full-time $3087; part-time $2744 per credit. Tuition, nonresident: full-time $6174; part-time $5488 per credit. *Required fees:* $2284; $1142 per credit. $571 per semester. Tuition and fees vary according to class time, course level, course load, degree level, program and student level. *Financial support:* In 2016–17, 3 students received support. Research assistantships and unspecified assistantships available. Financial award application deadline: 6/30; financial award applicants required to submit FAFSA. *Unit head:* Dr. Necoal Driver, Chair, 334-229-4456, Fax: 334-229-6831, E-mail: ndriver@alasu.edu. *Application contact:* Dr. William Person, Dean of Graduate Studies, 334-229-4275, Fax: 334-229-4928, E-mail: wperson@alasu.edu.
Website: http://www.alasu.edu/academics/colleges—departments/college-of-education/instructional-support-programs/index.aspx

Albany State University, College of Education, Albany, GA 31705-2717. Offers early childhood education (M Ed); educational leadership (Ed S); health and physical education (M Ed); middle grades education (M Ed); school counseling (M Ed); special

education (M Ed). *Accreditation:* NCATE. *Program availability:* Part-time, evening/weekend, online learning. *Degree requirements:* For master's, comprehensive exam, internship, GACE Content Exam. *Entrance requirements:* For master's, GRE or MAT. *Application deadline:* For fall admission, 6/1 for domestic students, 5/1 for international students; for spring admission, 11/1 for domestic students, 10/1 for international students. Applications are processed on a rolling basis. Application fee: $20. Electronic applications accepted. *Financial support:* Scholarships/grants available. Financial award application deadline: 4/15; financial award applicants required to submit FAFSA. *Faculty research:* GACE preparation, STEM (science, technology, engineering, and mathematics), technology education, special education, professional teacher development, health implications liberation philosophy, NET-Q, learning community, disabled or at-risk students. *Unit head:* Dr. Rhonda C. Porter, Interim Dean, 229-430-1718, Fax: 229-430-4993. *Application contact:* Jeffrey Pierce, II, Graduate Admissions Counselor, 229-430-4646, Fax: 229-430-4105, E-mail: jeffrey.pierce@asurams.edu.
Website: https://www.asurams.edu/Academics/collegeofeducation/

Alliant International University–San Diego, Shirley M. Hufstedler School of Education, Educational Leadership Programs, San Diego, CA 92131. Offers educational administration (MA); educational leadership and management (K-12) (Ed D); higher education (Ed D, Certificate); preliminary administrative services (Credential). *Program availability:* Part-time. *Degree requirements:* For doctorate, comprehensive exam, thesis/dissertation. *Entrance requirements:* For master's, minimum GPA of 2.5, letters of recommendation; for doctorate, minimum GPA of 3.0, letters of recommendation. Additional exam requirements/recommendations for international students: Required—TOEFL (minimum score 550 paper-based; 80 iBT), TWE (minimum score 5). Electronic applications accepted. *Faculty research:* Global education, women and international educational opportunities.

Alliant International University–San Francisco, Shirley M. Hufstedler School of Education, Educational Leadership Programs, San Francisco, CA 94133. Offers community college administration (Ed D); educational administration (MA); educational leadership and management (K-12) (Ed D); higher education (Ed D); preliminary administrative services (Credential). *Program availability:* Part-time. *Degree requirements:* For doctorate, comprehensive exam, thesis/dissertation. *Entrance requirements:* For master's and doctorate, minimum GPA of 3.0, letters of recommendation. Additional exam requirements/recommendations for international students: Required—TOEFL (minimum score 550 paper-based; 80 iBT), TWE (minimum score 5). Electronic applications accepted. *Faculty research:* Leadership in higher education, community colleges.

Alverno College, School of Education, Milwaukee, WI 53234-3922. Offers adaptive education (MA); administrative leadership (MA); adult education and organizational development (MA); adult educational and instructional design (MA); adult educational and instructional technology (MA); global connections in the humanities (MA); instructional leadership (MA); instructional technology for K-12 settings (MA); professional development (MA); reading education (MA); reading education with adaptive education (MA); science education (MA); special education (MA); teaching in alternative schools (MA). *Accreditation:* NCATE. *Program availability:* Part-time, evening/weekend. *Faculty:* 4 full-time (3 women), 23 part-time/adjunct (17 women). *Students:* 58 full-time (57 women), 62 part-time (54 women); includes 32 minority (22 Black or African American, non-Hispanic/Latino; 2 Asian, non-Hispanic/Latino; 8 Hispanic/Latino), 1 international. Average age 39. 77 applicants, 99% accepted, 61 enrolled. In 2016, 85 master's awarded. *Degree requirements:* For master's, presentation/defense of proposal, conference presentation of inquiry projects. *Entrance requirements:* For master's, bachelor's degree in related field, communication samples from work setting, 3 letters of recommendation. Additional exam requirements/recommendations for international students: Required—TOEFL. *Application deadline:* For fall admission, 7/15 priority date for domestic and international students; for spring admission, 12/15 priority date for domestic and international students. Applications are processed on a rolling basis. Application fee: $0. Electronic applications accepted. *Expenses:* Contact institution. *Financial support:* In 2016–17, 17 students received support. Federal Work-Study and scholarships/grants available. Support available to part-time students. Financial award applicants required to submit FAFSA. *Faculty research:* Student self-assessment, self-reflection, integration of curriculum, identifying needs of students in strategic situations and designing appropriate classroom strategies. *Unit head:* Dr. Desiree Pointer Mace, Associate Dean, Graduate Program, 414-382-6345, Fax: 414-382-6332, E-mail: desiree.pointer-mace@alverno.edu. *Application contact:* Katie Kipp, Graduate Admissions Counselor, 414-382-6045, Fax: 414-382-6354, E-mail: katie.kipp@alverno.edu.

American College of Education, Graduate Programs, Indianapolis, IN 46204. Offers curriculum and instruction (M Ed), including bilingual, ESL; educational leadership (M Ed); educational technology (M Ed).

American InterContinental University Online, Program in Education, Schaumburg, IL 60173. Offers curriculum and instruction (M Ed); educational assessment and evaluation (M Ed); instructional technology (M Ed); leadership of educational organizations (M Ed). *Accreditation:* TEAC. *Program availability:* Evening/weekend, online learning. *Entrance requirements:* Additional exam requirements/recommendations for international students: Required—TOEFL (minimum score 550 paper-based). Electronic applications accepted.

American International College, Low Residency Programs, Springfield, MA 01109-3189. Offers counseling psychology (MA); educational leadership and supervision (Ed D); individual and institutional development (Ed D); professional counseling and supervision (Ed D); psychology (Ed D); teaching and learning (Ed D). *Expenses: Tuition:* Full-time $7902; part-time $750 per semester hour. *Required fees:* $60; $60 per semester hour. $30 per semester. One-time fee: $100. Tuition and fees vary according to course load, degree level, campus/location and program. *Application contact:* Kerry Barnes, Director of Graduate Admissions, 413-205-3703, Fax: 413-205-3051, E-mail: kerry.barnes@aic.edu.

American International College, School of Education, Springfield, MA 01109-3189. Offers early childhood education (M Ed, CAGS); elementary education (M Ed, CAGS); middle education/secondary education (M Ed, CAGS); moderate disabilities (M Ed, CAGS); reading specialist (M Ed, CAGS); school adjustment counseling (MAEP, CAGS); school guidance counseling (MAEP, CAGS); school leadership (M Ed, CAGS). *Program availability:* Evening/weekend. *Faculty:* 1 (woman) full-time, 90 part-time/adjunct (63 women). *Students:* 1,194 full-time (970 women), 118 part-time (83 women); includes 108 minority (15 Black or African American, non-Hispanic/Latino; 4 American Indian or Alaska Native, non-Hispanic/Latino; 12 Asian, non-Hispanic/Latino; 55 Hispanic/Latino; 2 Native Hawaiian or other Pacific Islander, non-Hispanic/Latino; 20 Two or more races, non-Hispanic/Latino). Average age 34. 517 applicants, 417 enrolled. In 2016, 879 master's, 194 CAGSs awarded. Terminal master's awarded for partial completion of doctoral program. *Degree requirements:* For master's, comprehensive exam (for some programs), thesis (for some programs), practicum/culminating experience; for CAGS, practicum/culminating experience. *Entrance requirements:* For master's, Communication and Literacy portion of the Massachusetts Tests for Education Licensure, graduate of accredited four-year college with minimum B- average in undergraduate course work; for CAGS, M Ed or master's degree in field related to licensure from accredited institution. *Application deadline:* Applications are processed on a rolling basis. Application fee: $50. Electronic applications accepted. *Expenses:* $439 per credit. *Financial support:* Applicants required to submit FAFSA. *Unit head:* Sylvia Mason, Dean, 413-205-1743, Fax: 413-205-3943, E-mail: sylvia.mason@aic.edu. *Application contact:* Kerry Barnes, Dean of Graduate Admissions, 413-205-3703, Fax: 413-205-3051, E-mail: kerry.barnes@aic.edu.
Website: http://www.aic.edu/school-of-education/

American Public University System, AMU/APU Graduate Programs, Charles Town, WV 25414. Offers accounting (MBA, MS); applied business analytics (MBA, MS); criminal justice (MA), including business administration, emergency and disaster management, general (MA, MS); educational leadership (M Ed); emergency and disaster management (MA); entrepreneurship (MBA); environmental policy and management (MS), including environmental planning, environmental sustainability, fish and wildlife management, general (MA, MS), global environmental management; finance (MBA); general (MBA); government contracting and acquisition (MBA); health care administration (MBA); health information management (MS); history (MA), including American history, ancient and classical history, European history, global history, public history; homeland security (MA), including business administration, counterterrorism studies, criminal justice, cyber, emergency management and public health, intelligence studies, transportation security; homeland security resource allocation (MBA); humanities (MA); information technology (MS), including digital forensics, enterprise software development, information assurance and security, IT project management; information technology management (MBA); intelligence studies (MA), including criminal intelligence, cyber, general (MA, MS), homeland security, intelligence analysis, intelligence collection, intelligence management, intelligence operations, terrorism studies; international relations and conflict resolution (MA), including comparative and security issues, conflict resolution, international and transnational security issues, peacekeeping; legal studies (MA); management (MA), including strategic consulting; marketing (MBA); military history (MA), including American military history, American Revolution, civil war, war since 1945, World War II; military studies (MA), including joint warfare, strategic leadership; national security studies (MA), including cyber, general (MA, MS), homeland security, regional security studies, security and intelligence analysis, terrorism studies; nonprofit management (MBA); political science (MA), including American politics and government, comparative government and development, general (MA, MS), international relations, public policy; psychology (MA); public administration (MPA), including disaster management, environmental policy, health policy, human resources, national security, organizational management, security management; public health (MPH); reverse logistics management (MA); security management (MA); space studies (MS), including aerospace science, general (MA, MS), planetary science; sports and health sciences (MS); sports management (MBA); teaching (M Ed), including autism spectrum disorder, curriculum and instruction for elementary teachers, elementary reading, English language learners, instructional leadership, online learning, special education, STEAM (STEM plus the arts); transportation and logistics management (MA). *Program availability:* Part-time, evening/weekend, online only, 100% online. *Faculty:* 401 full-time (228 women), 1,678 part-time/adjunct (781 women). *Students:* 378 full-time (184 women), 8,455 part-time (3,484 women); includes 2,972 minority (1,552 Black or African American, non-Hispanic/Latino; 52 American Indian or Alaska Native, non-Hispanic/Latino; 211 Asian, non-Hispanic/Latino; 791 Hispanic/Latino; 70 Native Hawaiian or other Pacific Islander, non-Hispanic/Latino; 296 Two or more races, non-Hispanic/Latino), 109 international. Average age 37. In 2016, 3,185 master's awarded. *Degree requirements:* For master's, comprehensive exam or practicum. *Entrance requirements:* For master's, official transcript showing earned bachelor's degree from institution accredited by recognized accrediting body. Additional exam requirements/recommendations for international students: Required—TOEFL (minimum score 550 paper-based), IELTS (minimum score 6.5). *Application deadline:* Applications are processed on a rolling basis. Application fee: $0. Electronic applications accepted. *Expenses: Tuition:* Part-time $350 per credit hour. *Required fees:* $50 per course. *Financial support:* Scholarships/grants available. Financial award applicants required to submit FAFSA. *Unit head:* Dr. Karan Powell, President, 877-468-6268, Fax: 304-724-3780. *Application contact:* Terry Grant, Vice President of Enrollment Management, 877-468-6268, Fax: 304-724-3780, E-mail: info@apus.edu.
Website: http://www.apus.edu

The American University in Cairo, Graduate School of Education, Cairo, Egypt. Offers educational leadership (MA); international and comparative education (MA). *Program availability:* Part-time, evening/weekend. *Faculty:* 8 full-time (7 women). *Students:* 6 full-time (5 women), 75 part-time (64 women). Average age 33. 60 applicants, 68% accepted, 27 enrolled. In 2016, 14 master's awarded. *Degree requirements:* For master's, thesis. *Entrance requirements:* Additional exam requirements/recommendations for international students: Required—TOEFL (minimum score 450 paper-based; 45 iBT), IELTS (minimum score 5). *Application deadline:* For fall admission, 2/1 priority date for domestic and international students; for spring admission, 10/15 priority date for domestic and international students. Applications are processed on a rolling basis. Application fee: $80. Electronic applications accepted. *Expenses:* Contact institution. *Financial support:* Fellowships with partial tuition reimbursements, teaching assistantships, career-related internships or fieldwork, scholarships/grants, tuition waivers (partial), and unspecified assistantships available. Financial award application deadline: 3/10. *Faculty research:* Educational reform. *Unit head:* Dr. Ted Purinton, Dean, 20-2-2615-1490, E-mail: tedpurinton@aucegypt.edu. *Application contact:* Maha Hegazi, Director for Graduate Admissions, 20-2-2615-1462, E-mail: mahahegazi@aucegypt.edu.
Website: http://www.aucegypt.edu/GSE/Pages/default.aspx

Anderson University, College of Education, Anderson, SC 29621-4035. Offers administration and supervision (M Ed); education (M Ed); elementary education (MAT). *Accreditation:* NCATE. *Program availability:* 100% online. *Expenses:* Contact institution. *Financial support:* Tuition waivers available. Financial award application deadline: 3/1; financial award applicants required to submit FAFSA. *Unit head:* Dr. Mark Butler, Dean, 864-231-2042. *Application contact:* Mallory Knight, Graduate Admission Counselor, 864-231-2182, Fax: 864-231-2115, E-mail: malloryknight@andersonuniversity.edu.
Website: https://www.andersonuniversity.edu/education

Andrews University, School of Graduate Studies, School of Education, Department of Leadership and Educational Administration, Program in Educational Administration and Leadership, Berrien Springs, MI 49104. Offers MA, Ed D, PhD, Ed S. *Students:* 15 full-time (10 women), 26 part-time (17 women); includes 22 minority (14 Black or African American, non-Hispanic/Latino; 1 Asian, non-Hispanic/Latino; 5 Hispanic/Latino; 2 Two or more races, non-Hispanic/Latino), 6 international. Average age 44. *Degree requirements:* For master's, thesis or alternative; for doctorate, thesis/dissertation. *Entrance requirements:* For master's and doctorate, GRE Subject Test. Additional exam requirements/recommendations for international students: Required—TOEFL (minimum score 550 paper-based). *Application deadline:* Applications are processed on a rolling basis. Application fee: $40. *Financial support:* Research assistantships available. *Unit head:* Dr. Robson Marinho, Coordinator, 269-471-3487. *Application contact:* Justina Clayburn, Supervisor of Graduate Admission, 800-253-2874, Fax: 269-471-6321, E-mail: graduate@andrews.edu.

Andrews University, School of Graduate Studies, School of Education, Department of Leadership and Educational Administration, Program in Leadership, Berrien Springs, MI 49104. Offers MA, Ed D, PhD, Ed S. *Students:* 28 full-time (11 women), 25 part-time (10 women); includes 14 minority (3 Black or African American, non-Hispanic/Latino; 2 Asian, non-Hispanic/Latino; 9 Hispanic/Latino), 12 international. Average age 50. In 2016, 4 master's, 6 doctorates awarded. *Entrance requirements:* For master's, GRE. Additional exam requirements/recommendations for international students: Required—TOEFL (minimum score 550 paper-based). Application fee: $40. *Unit head:* Dr. Robson Marinho, Chair, 269-471-6580. *Application contact:* Justina Clayburn, Supervisor of Graduate Admission, 800-253-2874, Fax: 269-471-6321, E-mail: graduate@andrews.edu.

Angelo State University, College of Graduate Studies and Research, College of Education, Department of Curriculum and Instruction, San Angelo, TX 76909. Offers curriculum and instruction (MA); educational administration (M Ed); guidance and counseling (M Ed); student development and leadership in higher education (M Ed). *Program availability:* Part-time, evening/weekend, online learning. *Students:* 400 full-time (328 women), 396 part-time (325 women); includes 242 minority (80 Black or African American, non-Hispanic/Latino; 2 American Indian or Alaska Native, non-Hispanic/Latino; 6 Asian, non-Hispanic/Latino; 148 Hispanic/Latino; 6 Two or more races, non-Hispanic/Latino), 1 international. Average age 35. *Application deadline:* For fall admission, 7/15 priority date for domestic students, 6/10 for international students; for spring admission, 12/1 priority date for domestic students, 11/1 for international students. Application fee: $40 ($50 for international students). *Expenses:* Tuition, state resident: full-time $3726; part-time $2484 per year. Tuition, nonresident: full-time $10,746; part-time $7164 per year. *Required fees:* $2538; $1702 per unit. *Unit head:* Dr. Jim Summerlin, Chair, 325-942-2647, Fax: 325-942-2039, E-mail: james.summerlin@angelo.edu. *Application contact:* Lesley Casarez, Graduate Advisor, 325-486-6775, E-mail: lesley.casarez@angelo.edu.
Website: http://www.angelo.edu/dept/ci/

Antioch University Midwest, Graduate Programs, School of Education, Yellow Springs, OH 45387-1609. Offers conflict management (M Ed); dyslexia (M Ed); early childhood education (M Ed); educational leadership (M Ed); intervention specialist, mild to moderate (M Ed); middle childhood education (M Ed); trauma informed education (M Ed). *Accreditation:* NCATE. *Program availability:* Part-time, evening/weekend. *Degree requirements:* For master's, thesis or alternative. *Entrance requirements:* For master's, resume, goal statement, interview. *Application deadline:* For fall admission, 9/7 for domestic students; for winter admission, 12/10 for domestic students; for spring admission, 3/10 for domestic students. Applications are processed on a rolling basis. Application fee: $50. Electronic applications accepted. *Expenses:* $675 per credit hour. *Financial support:* Federal Work-Study available. Financial award applicants required to submit FAFSA. *Unit head:* Dr. Marian Glancy, Director, 937-769-1880, Fax: 937-769-1805, E-mail: mglancy@antioch.edu. *Application contact:* Deena Kent-Hummel, Director of Admissions, 937-769-1823, Fax: 937-769-1804, E-mail: dkent@antioch.edu.
Website: https://www.antioch.edu/midwest/degrees-programs/education-degree/

Antioch University New England, Graduate School, Department of Education, Experienced Educators Program, Keene, NH 03431-3552. Offers foundations of education (M Ed), including applied behavioral analysis, autism spectrum disorders, educating for sustainability, next-generation learning using technology, problem-based learning using critical skills, teacher leadership; principal certification (PMC). *Degree requirements:* For master's, thesis, practicum. *Entrance requirements:* For master's, previous course work and work experience in education. Additional exam requirements/recommendations for international students: Required—TOEFL (minimum score 550 paper-based). Electronic applications accepted. *Expenses:* Contact institution. *Faculty research:* Classroom action research, school restructuring, problem-based learning, brain-based learning.

Appalachian State University, Cratis D. Williams Graduate School, Department of Leadership and Educational Studies, Boone, NC 28608. Offers educational administration (Ed S); educational media (MA); higher education (MA, Ed S); library science (MLS); school administration (MSA). *Program availability:* Part-time, evening/weekend, online learning. *Degree requirements:* For master's and Ed S, comprehensive exam, thesis optional. *Entrance requirements:* For master's and Ed S, GRE or MAT, 3 letters of recommendation. Additional exam requirements/recommendations for international students: Required—TOEFL (minimum score 570 paper-based; 79 iBT), IELTS (minimum score 6.5). *Application deadline:* For fall admission, 3/14 priority date for domestic students, 2/1 for international students; for spring admission, 11/1 for domestic students, 7/1 for international students. Applications are processed on a rolling basis. Application fee: $55. Electronic applications accepted. *Expenses:* Tuition, state resident: full-time $4744. Tuition, nonresident: full-time $17,913. Full-time tuition and fees vary according to program. *Financial support:* Research assistantships, career-related internships or fieldwork, scholarships/grants, and unspecified assistantships available. Financial award application deadline: 4/1; financial award applicants required to submit FAFSA. *Faculty research:* Brain, learning and meditation; leadership of teaching and learning. *Unit head:* Dr. Robert Sanders, Interim Director, 828-262-3112, E-mail: sandersrl@appstate.edu. *Application contact:* Dr. Vachel Miller, Program Director, 828-262-2287, E-mail: millervw@appstate.edu.
Website: http://www.les.appstate.edu

Arcadia University, School of Education, Glenside, PA 19038-3295. Offers art education (M Ed); computer education (CAS); curriculum (CAS); curriculum studies (M Ed); early childhood education (M Ed), including individualized, master teacher, research in child development; educational leadership (M Ed, Ed D, CAS); elementary education (M Ed); English education (MA Ed); environmental education (MA Ed); instructional technology (M Ed); language arts (M Ed); library science (M Ed); mathematics education (M Ed, MA Ed); music education (MA Ed); psychology (MA Ed); reading (M Ed, CAS); science education (M Ed, CAS); secondary education (M Ed, CAS); special education (M Ed, Ed D, CAS); theater arts (MA Ed); written communication (MA Ed). *Accreditation:* NASAD. *Program availability:* Part-time, evening/weekend, online learning. *Faculty:* 19 full-time (13 women), 3 part-time/adjunct (all women). *Students:* 22 full-time (16 women), 356 part-time (284 women); includes 84 minority (55 Black or African American, non-Hispanic/Latino; 2 American Indian or Alaska Native, non-Hispanic/Latino; 13 Asian, non-Hispanic/Latino; 11 Hispanic/Latino; 3 Two or more races, non-Hispanic/Latino), 4 international. Average age 34. 145 applicants, 73% accepted, 80 enrolled. In 2016, 95 master's, 11 doctorates awarded. *Application deadline:* Applications are processed on a rolling basis. Application fee: $50. Electronic applications accepted. *Expenses:* Contact institution. *Financial support:* Career-related internships or fieldwork, tuition waivers (partial), and unspecified assistantships available. *Unit head:* John T Groves, Interim Dean of the School of Education, 215-572-2940. *Application contact:* 215-572-2925, Fax: 215-572-2126, E-mail: grad@arcadia.edu.

Argosy University, Atlanta, College of Education, Atlanta, GA 30328. Offers educational leadership (MAEd, Ed D, Ed S), including higher education administration (Ed D), K-12 education (Ed D); teaching and learning (MAEd, Ed D, Ed S), including education technology (Ed D), higher education (Ed D), K-12 education (Ed D).

Argosy University, Chicago, College of Education, Chicago, IL 60601. Offers adult education and training (MA Ed); community college executive leadership (Ed D); educational leadership (MA Ed, Ed D, Ed S), including district leadership (Ed D), higher education administration (Ed D), K-12 education (Ed D); instructional leadership (Ed D, Ed S), including higher education (Ed D), K-12 education (Ed D). *Program availability:* Online learning.

Argosy University, Dallas, College of Education, Farmers Branch, TX 75244. Offers educational administration (MA Ed); educational leadership (Ed D); higher and postsecondary education (MA Ed); instructional leadership (MA Ed); school psychology (MA).

Argosy University, Denver, College of Education, Denver, CO 80231. Offers community college executive leadership (Ed D); educational leadership (MA Ed, Ed D), including higher education (Ed D), K-12 education (Ed D); instructional leadership (MA Ed, Ed D), including higher education administration (Ed D), K-12 education (Ed D).

Argosy University, Hawai`i, College of Education, Honolulu, HI 96813. Offers adult education and training (MAEd); educational leadership (Ed D), including higher education administration, K-12 education; instructional leadership (Ed D), including higher education, K-12 education; school psychology (MA).

Argosy University, Inland Empire, College of Education, Ontario, CA 91761. Offers community college executive leadership (Ed D); educational leadership (MA Ed, Ed D), including higher education administration (Ed D), K-12 education (Ed D); instructional leadership (MA Ed, Ed D), including higher education (Ed D), K-12 education (Ed D), multiple subject teacher preparation (MA Ed), single subject teacher preparation (MA Ed).

Argosy University, Los Angeles, College of Education, Santa Monica, CA 90045. Offers community college executive leadership (Ed D); educational leadership (MA Ed, Ed D), including higher education administration (Ed D), K-12 education (Ed D); instructional leadership (MA Ed, Ed D), including higher education (Ed D), K-12 education (Ed D), multiple subject teacher preparation (MA Ed), single subject teacher preparation (MA Ed).

Argosy University, Nashville, College of Education, Program in Educational Leadership, Nashville, TN 37214. Offers educational leadership (MA Ed, Ed S); higher education administration (Ed D); K-12 education (Ed D).

Argosy University, Nashville, College of Education, Program in Instructional Leadership, Nashville, TN 37214. Offers education technology (Ed D); higher education administration (Ed D); instructional leadership (MA Ed, Ed S); K-12 education (Ed D).

Argosy University, Northern Virginia, College of Education, Arlington, VA 22209. Offers community college executive leadership (Ed D); educational leadership (MA Ed, Ed D, Ed S), including higher education administration (Ed D), K-12 education (Ed D); instructional leadership (MA Ed, Ed D, Ed S), including higher education (Ed D), K-12 education (Ed D).

Argosy University, Orange County, College of Education, Orange, CA 92868. Offers community college executive leadership (Ed D); educational leadership (MA Ed, Ed D), including higher education administration (Ed D), K-12 education (Ed D); instructional leadership (MA Ed, Ed D), including education technology (Ed D), higher education (Ed D), K-12 education (Ed D), multiple subject teacher preparation (MA Ed), single subject teacher preparation (MA Ed).

Argosy University, Phoenix, College of Education, Phoenix, AZ 85021. Offers adult education and training (MA Ed); advanced educational administration (Ed D, Ed S); community college executive leadership (Ed D); educational administration (MA Ed); educational leadership (MA Ed, Ed D, Ed S), including education technology (Ed D), higher education administration (Ed D), K-12 education (Ed D); higher and postsecondary education (MA Ed); initial educational administration (Ed D, Ed S); school psychology (MA); teaching and learning (MA Ed, Ed D, Ed S), including education technology (Ed D), higher education (Ed D), K-12 education (Ed D).

Argosy University, Salt Lake City, College of Education, Draper, UT 84020. Offers educational leadership (MA Ed, Ed D).

Argosy University, San Diego, College of Education, San Diego, CA 92108. Offers community college executive leadership (Ed D); educational leadership (MA Ed, Ed D), including higher education administration (Ed D), K-12 education (Ed D); instructional leadership (MA Ed, Ed D), including higher education (Ed D), K-12 education (Ed D).

Argosy University, San Francisco Bay Area, College of Education, Alameda, CA 94501. Offers community college executive leadership (Ed D); educational leadership (MA Ed, Ed D), including education technology (Ed D), higher education administration (Ed D), K-12 education (Ed D); instructional leadership (MA Ed, Ed D), including education technology (Ed D), higher education (Ed D), K-12 education (Ed D), multiple subject teacher preparation (MA Ed), single subject teacher preparation (MA Ed).

Argosy University, Sarasota, College of Education, Sarasota, FL 34235. Offers community college executive leadership (Ed D); educational leadership (MA Ed, Ed D, Ed S), including higher education administration (Ed D), K-12 education (Ed D); school counseling (MA, Ed S); school psychology (MA); teaching and learning (MA Ed, Ed D, Ed S), including education technology (Ed D), higher education (Ed D), K-12 education (Ed D).

Argosy University, Seattle, College of Education, Seattle, WA 98121. Offers adult education and training (MA Ed); community college executive leadership (Ed D); educational leadership (MA Ed, Ed D), including higher education administration (Ed D), K-12 education (Ed D); higher and postsecondary education (MA Ed); instructional leadership (MA Ed, Ed D), including education technology (Ed D), higher education (Ed D), K-12 education (Ed D).

Argosy University, Tampa, College of Education, Tampa, FL 33607. Offers community college executive leadership (Ed D); educational leadership (MA Ed, Ed D, Ed S), including higher education administration (Ed D), K-12 education (Ed D); school counseling (MA); teaching and learning (MA Ed, Ed D, Ed S), including higher education (Ed D), K-12 education (Ed D).

Argosy University, Twin Cities, College of Education, Eagan, MN 55121. Offers advanced educational administration (Ed D, Ed S); educational leadership (MA Ed, Ed D, Ed S), including higher education administration (Ed D), K-12 education (Ed D); higher and postsecondary education (MA Ed); initial educational administration (Ed D, Ed S); instructional leadership (MA Ed, Ed D, Ed S), including education technology (Ed D), higher education (Ed D), K-12 education (Ed D).

Arizona State University at the Tempe campus, Mary Lou Fulton Teachers College, Program in Educational Leadership, Phoenix, AZ 85069. Offers educational leadership (M Ed); leadership and innovation (Ed D). *Program availability:* Part-time, evening/weekend, online learning. Terminal master's awarded for partial completion of doctoral program. *Degree requirements:* For master's, thesis or alternative, written portfolio, internship, interactive Program of Study (iPOS) submitted before completing 50 percent of required credit hours; for doctorate, thesis/dissertation, interactive Program of Study (iPOS) submitted before completing 50 percent of required credit hours. *Entrance requirements:* For master's, minimum GPA of 3.0 or equivalent in last 2 years of work leading to bachelor's degree, 1 year of teaching experience, 3 letters of recommendation, personal statement, writing sample, curriculum vitae or resume; for doctorate, master's degree in education or related field, resume, personal statement, writing samples based on short writing prompts, 3 letters of recommendation. Additional exam requirements/recommendations for international students: Required—TOEFL, IELTS, or PTE. Electronic applications accepted.

Arkansas State University, Graduate School, College of Education and Behavioral Science, School of Teacher Education and Leadership, State University, AR 72467. Offers community college administration (SCCT); curriculum and instruction (MSE); early childhood education (MSE); early childhood services (MS); educational leadership (MSE, Ed D, Ed S); educational theory and practice (MSE); middle level education (MAT, MSE); reading (MSE, Ed S); special education - gifted, talented, and creative (MSE); special education - instructional specialist grades 4-12 (MSE); special education - instructional specialist grades P-4 (MSE); special education, K-12 (MSE). *Accreditation:* NCATE. *Program availability:* Part-time, online learning. *Degree requirements:* For master's, comprehensive exam, thesis or alternative; for doctorate, comprehensive exam, thesis/dissertation; for other advanced degree, comprehensive exam. *Entrance requirements:* For master's, GRE General Test or MAT, appropriate bachelor's degree, official transcripts, immunization records, letters of reference, interview; for doctorate, GRE General Test or MAT, interview, master's degree, letters of reference, official transcript, personal statement, writing sample, immunization records; for other advanced degree, GRE General Test or MAT, interview, master's degree, official transcript, immunization records, letters of reference, 3 years of teaching experience, teaching license. Additional exam requirements/recommendations for international students: Required—TOEFL (minimum score 550 paper-based; 79 iBT), IELTS (minimum score 6), PTE (minimum score 56). Electronic applications accepted.

Arkansas Tech University, College of Education, Russellville, AR 72801. Offers college student personnel (MS); educational leadership (M Ed, Ed S); elementary education (M Ed); instructional improvement (M Ed); instructional technology (M Ed); school counseling and leadership (M Ed); school leadership (Ed D); strength and conditioning studies (MS); teaching (MAT); teaching, learning, and leadership (M Ed). *Accreditation:* NCATE. *Program availability:* Part-time, evening/weekend, online learning. *Students:* 72 full-time (43 women), 371 part-time (283 women); includes 108 minority (80 Black or African American, non-Hispanic/Latino; 1 American Indian or Alaska Native, non-Hispanic/Latino; 4 Asian, non-Hispanic/Latino; 13 Hispanic/Latino; 10 Two or more races, non-Hispanic/Latino), 6 international. Average age 33. In 2016, 181 master's, 1 other advanced degree awarded. *Degree requirements:* For master's, comprehensive exam, thesis optional, action research project. *Entrance requirements:* Additional exam requirements/recommendations for international students: Required—TOEFL (minimum score 550 paper-based; 79 iBT), IELTS (minimum score 6.5). *Application deadline:* For fall admission, 3/1 priority date for domestic students, 5/1 priority date for international students; for spring admission, 10/1 priority date for domestic and international students. Applications are processed on a rolling basis. Application fee: $25 ($75 for international students). Electronic applications accepted. *Expenses:* Tuition, state resident: full-time $4932; part-time $274 per credit hour. Tuition, nonresident: full-time $9864; part-time $548 per credit hour. *Required fees:* $513 per semester. Tuition and fees vary according to course load. *Financial support:* In 2016–17, research assistantships with full tuition reimbursements (averaging $4,800 per year), teaching assistantships with full tuition reimbursements (averaging $4,800 per year) were awarded; career-related internships or fieldwork, Federal Work-Study, scholarships/grants, health care benefits, and unspecified assistantships also available. Support available to part-time students. Financial award application deadline: 4/15; financial award applicants required to submit FAFSA. *Unit head:* Dr. Mary Gunter, Dean, 479-964-3217, E-mail: mgunter@atu.edu.
Website: http://www.atu.edu/education/

Arlington Baptist College, Program in Education, Arlington, TX 76012-3425. Offers curriculum and instruction (M Ed); educational leadership (M Ed). *Degree requirements:* For master's, professional portfolio; internship (for educational leadership). *Entrance requirements:* For master's, bachelor's degree from accredited college or university with minimum GPA of 3.0, minimum of 12 hours in Bible; minimum of three years' classroom teaching experience in an accredited K-12 public or private school (for educational leadership only).

Asbury University, School of Graduate and Professional Studies, Wilmore, KY 40390-1198. Offers biology: alternative certificate (MA Ed); chemistry: alternative certificate (MA Ed); English (MA Ed); English as a second language (MA Ed); ESL (MA Ed); French (MA Ed); Latin: alternative certificate (MA Ed); mathematics: alternative certificate (MA Ed); reading/writing endorsement (MA Ed); social studies (MA Ed); social work (MSW), including child and family services; Spanish (MA Ed); special education (MA Ed); special education: alternative certificate (MA Ed); teacher as leader endorsement (MA Ed). *Accreditation:* NCATE. *Program availability:* Part-time. *Degree requirements:* For master's, action research project, portfolio. *Entrance requirements:* For master's, PRAXIS/NTE, minimum GPA of 2.75, letters of recommendation. Additional exam requirements/recommendations for international students: Required—TOEFL (minimum score 550 paper-based). Electronic applications accepted.

Ashland University, Dwight Schar College of Education, Doctoral Program in Educational Leadership Studies, Ashland, OH 44805-3702. Offers Ed D. *Program availability:* Part-time, evening/weekend. *Degree requirements:* For doctorate, comprehensive exam, thesis/dissertation. *Entrance requirements:* For doctorate, GRE, master's degree, minimum GPA of 3.3, writing sample, letters of recommendation. Additional exam requirements/recommendations for international students: Required—TOEFL. *Application deadline:* For spring admission, 3/1 for domestic students. Applications are processed on a rolling basis. Application fee: $30. Electronic applications accepted. *Expenses:* Contact institution. *Financial support:* Teaching assistantships available. Financial award application deadline: 4/15. *Faculty research:* School funding, charter schools, administrative jobs, continuous improvement, marginalized groups, school finance, minority superintendent trends, teacher salaries, minority recruiting, women's issues. *Unit head:* Dr. Amy Clinger, Director, 419-289-5889, E-mail: aklinger@ashland.edu. *Application contact:* Dr. Amy Clinger, Director, 419-289-5889, E-mail: aklinger@ashland.edu.
Website: http://www.ashland.edu/edd/

Ashland University, Dwight Schar College of Education, Program in Educational Administration, Ashland, OH 44805-3702. Offers building principal (M Ed). *Program availability:* Part-time. *Degree requirements:* For master's, thesis or alternative, internship. *Entrance requirements:* For master's, teaching certificate or license, bachelor's degree, minimum cumulative GPA of 2.75. Additional exam requirements/recommendations for international students: Required—TOEFL. *Application deadline:* Applications are processed on a rolling basis. Application fee: $30. Electronic applications accepted. *Financial support:* Institutionally sponsored loans and scholarships/grants available. Financial award application deadline: 4/15. *Faculty research:* Gender and religious considerations in employment, Interstate School Leaders Licensure Consortium (ISLLC) standards, adjunct faculty training, politics of school finance, ethnicity and employment. *Unit head:* Dr. Robert Thiede, Chair, 419-289-5258, Fax: 419-207-6702, E-mail: rthiede@ashland.edu. *Application contact:* Dr. Linda Billman, Director and Chair, Graduate Studies in Education/Associate Dean, 419-289-5369, Fax: 419-289-5331, E-mail: lbillman@ashland.edu.

Auburn University, Graduate School, College of Education, Department of Educational Foundations, Leadership, and Technology, Auburn University, AL 36849. Offers adult education (PhD, Ed S); curriculum supervision (M Ed, PhD); higher education administration (PhD); library media (Ed S); school administration (M Ed, PhD). *Accreditation:* NCATE. *Program availability:* Part-time. *Faculty:* 29 full-time (15 women), 4 part-time/adjunct (3 women). *Students:* 119 full-time (72 women), 273 part-time (170 women); includes 132 minority (114 Black or African American, non-Hispanic/Latino; 2 American Indian or Alaska Native, non-Hispanic/Latino; 4 Asian, non-Hispanic/Latino; 6 Hispanic/Latino; 1 Native Hawaiian or other Pacific Islander, non-Hispanic/Latino; 5 Two or more races, non-Hispanic/Latino), 14 international. Average age 37. 220 applicants, 71% accepted, 78 enrolled. In 2016, 67 master's, 44 doctorates, 41 other advanced degrees awarded. *Degree requirements:* For master's, thesis (for some programs); for doctorate, thesis/dissertation; for Ed S, field project. *Entrance requirements:* For master's, doctorate, and Ed S, GRE General Test. *Application deadline:* Applications are processed on a rolling basis. Application fee: $50 ($60 for international students). Electronic applications accepted. *Expenses:* Tuition, state resident: full-time $9072; part-time $504 per credit hour. Tuition, nonresident: full-time $27,216; part-time $1512 per credit hour. *Required fees:* $812 per semester. Tuition and fees vary according to degree level and program. *Financial support:* Teaching assistantships and Federal Work-Study available. Support available to part-time students. Financial award application deadline: 3/15; financial award applicants required to submit FAFSA. *Unit head:* Dr. Sherida Downer, Head, 334-844-4460. *Application contact:* Dr. George Flowers, Dean of the Graduate School, 334-844-4700.
Website: http://www.education.auburn.edu/academic_departments/eflt/

Auburn University at Montgomery, College of Education, Department of Counselor, Leadership, and Special Education, Montgomery, AL 36124-4023. Offers counselor education (M Ed, Ed S), including clinical mental health counseling, school counseling; early childhood special education (M Ed); instructional leadership (M Ed, Ed S); special education/collaborative teacher (M Ed, Ed S). *Accreditation:* ACA; NCATE. *Program availability:* Part-time, evening/weekend. *Faculty:* 9 full-time (7 women), 3 part-time/adjunct (all women). *Students:* 7 full-time (5 women), 28 part-time (all women); includes 11 minority (10 Black or African American, non-Hispanic/Latino; 1 Asian, non-Hispanic/Latino). Average age 35. In 2016, 35 master's, 9 Ed Ss awarded. *Degree requirements:* For master's and Ed S, comprehensive exam. *Entrance requirements:* For master's, GRE General Test or MAT, certification, BS in teaching; for Ed S, GRE General Test or MAT, certification. Additional exam requirements/recommendations for international students: Recommended—TOEFL (minimum score 500 paper-based; 61 iBT), IELTS (minimum score 5.5), TSE (minimum score 44). *Application deadline:* Applications are processed on a rolling basis. Electronic applications accepted. *Expenses:* Tuition, state resident: full-time $6462; part-time $359 per credit hour. Tuition, nonresident: full-time $14,526; part-time $807 per credit hour. *Required fees:* $554. *Financial support:* Career-related internships or fieldwork and scholarships/grants available. Support available to part-time students. Financial award application deadline: 3/1; financial award applicants required to submit FAFSA. *Unit head:* Dr. Samuel Flynt, Head, 334-244-3835, Fax: 334-244-3101, E-mail: sflynt@aum.edu. *Application contact:* Dr. Rhonda Morton, Associate Dean/Graduate Coordinator, 334-244-3287, Fax: 334-244-3978, E-mail: rmorton@aum.edu.
Website: http://education.aum.edu/academic-departments/counselor-leadership-and-special-education

Augusta University, The Graduate School, College of Education, Department of Counselor Education, Leadership, and Research, Augusta, GA 30912. Offers counselor education (M Ed, Ed S), including clinical mental health counseling (M Ed), school counselor (M Ed). *Accreditation:* ACA; NCATE. *Program availability:* Part-time, evening/weekend. *Degree requirements:* For master's, comprehensive exam; for Ed S, comprehensive exam, thesis. *Entrance requirements:* For master's, GRE, MAT, minimum GPA of 2.5; for Ed S, GRE, MAT. *Application deadline:* For fall admission, 8/1 priority date for domestic students. Applications are processed on a rolling basis. Application fee: $20. *Financial support:* Career-related internships or fieldwork, Federal Work-Study, institutionally sponsored loans, and unspecified assistantships available. Support available to part-time students. Financial award application deadline: 4/15; financial award applicants required to submit FAFSA. *Faculty research:* Restructuring schools, financing education, student transition. *Unit head:* Dr. Richard Deaner, Director, 706-729-2443, E-mail: rdeaner@augusta.edu. *Application contact:* Dr. Richard Deaner, Director, 706-729-2443, E-mail: rdeaner@augusta.edu.

Augusta University, The Graduate School, College of Education, Program in Leadership, Augusta, GA 30912. Offers leadership (Ed S); school administration (M Ed); teacher leadership (M Ed). *Entrance requirements:* For master's, GRE or MAT, minimum baccalaureate GPA of 2.5. *Application deadline:* For spring admission, 12/2 for domestic students. *Unit head:* Dr. Olajide Agunoye, Director, 706-737-1496, E-mail: oagunoy@augusta.edu. *Application contact:* Bonnie Collins, Administrative Assistant II, 706-729-2465, E-mail: bcollin9@augusta.edu.

Aurora University, School of Education and Human Performance, Aurora, IL 60506-4892. Offers bilingual-ESL education (MA); educational leadership (MA); educational technology (MA); leadership in administration (Ed D); leadership in adult learning and higher education (Ed D); leadership in curriculum and instruction (Ed D); reading instruction (MA); special education (MA). *Accreditation:* NCATE. *Program availability:* Part-time, evening/weekend. *Faculty:* 22 full-time (12 women), 46 part-time/adjunct (27 women). *Students:* 36 full-time (30 women), 559 part-time (372 women); includes 68 minority (27 Black or African American, non-Hispanic/Latino; 1 American Indian or Alaska Native, non-Hispanic/Latino; 6 Asian, non-Hispanic/Latino; 29 Hispanic/Latino; 2 Native Hawaiian or other Pacific Islander, non-Hispanic/Latino; 3 Two or more races, non-Hispanic/Latino). Average age 37. 126 applicants, 98% accepted, 72 enrolled. In 2016, 178 master's, 27 doctorates awarded. *Degree requirements:* For master's, student teaching; for doctorate, comprehensive exam, thesis/dissertation. *Entrance requirements:* For master's, 2 years of teaching experience, valid teaching certificate; for doctorate, appropriate master's degree, two references, curriculum vitae, personal statement, professional project, reflective essay. Additional exam requirements/recommendations for international students: Required—TOEFL (minimum score 550 paper-based; 79 iBT). *Application deadline:* For fall admission, 6/1 for international students; for spring admission, 10/1 for international students. Applications are processed on a rolling basis. Application fee: $0. Electronic applications accepted. *Expenses:* Contact institution. *Financial support:* In 2016–17, 10 students received support. Federal Work-Study, scholarships/grants, and unspecified assistantships available. Support available to part-time students. Financial award applicants required to submit FAFSA. *Unit head:* Dr. Jen Buckley, Executive Director of the School of Education and Human Performance, 630-844-1542, Fax: 630-844-6155, E-mail: jbuckley@aurora.edu. *Application contact:* Elizabeth Botica, Graduate Education Recruiter, 630-947-8918, E-mail: ebotica@aurora.edu.
Website: http://aurora.edu/education

Austin Peay State University, College of Graduate Studies, College of Education, Department of Educational Specialties, Clarksville, TN 37044. Offers administration and supervision (Ed S); counseling and guidance (Ed S); curriculum and instruction (MA Ed); education leadership (MA Ed); elementary education (Ed S); reading (MA Ed); secondary education (Ed S). *Program availability:* Part-time, evening/weekend, online learning. *Faculty:* 7 full-time (4 women), 4 part-time/adjunct (3 women). *Students:* 4 full-time (3 women), 77 part-time (60 women); includes 13 minority (8 Black or African American, non-Hispanic/Latino; 1 Asian, non-Hispanic/Latino; 3 Hispanic/Latino; 1 Two or more races, non-Hispanic/Latino). Average age 37. 18 applicants, 89% accepted, 14 enrolled. In 2016, 34 master's, 9 Ed Ss awarded. *Degree requirements:* For master's, comprehensive exam, thesis optional. *Entrance requirements:* For master's, GRE General Test, MAT, minimum undergraduate GPA of 2.75. Additional exam requirements/recommendations for international students: Required—TOEFL (minimum score 500 paper-based). *Application deadline:* For fall admission, 8/9 priority date for domestic students. Applications are processed on a rolling basis. Application fee: $45 ($50 for international students). Electronic applications accepted. *Expenses:* Tuition, state resident: full-time $8300; part-time $415 per credit hour. Tuition, nonresident: full-time $22,280; part-time $1114 per credit hour. *Required fees:* $1473; $73.65 per credit hour. *Financial support:* Research assistantships with full tuition reimbursements, career-related internships or fieldwork, Federal Work-Study, institutionally sponsored loans, scholarships/grants, and unspecified assistantships available. Support available to part-time students. Financial award application deadline: 4/1; financial award applicants required to submit FAFSA. *Unit head:* Dr. Moniqueka Gold, Chair, 931-221-7696, Fax: 931-221-1292, E-mail: goldm@apsu.edu. *Application contact:* Brad Averitt, Coordinator of Graduate Admissions, 800-859-4723, Fax: 931-221-7641, E-mail: gradadmissions@apsu.edu.

Averett University, Master in Education Program, Danville, VA 24541-3692. Offers administration and supervision (M Ed); curriculum and instruction (M Ed); special education with endorsement (M Ed); special education with licensure (M Ed). Program offered on Danville Campus only. *Program availability:* Part-time, online only, 100% online. *Faculty:* 1 full-time (0 women), 15 part-time/adjunct (12 women). *Students:* 26 full-time (22 women), 98 part-time (73 women); includes 39 minority (34 Black or African American, non-Hispanic/Latino; 3 American Indian or Alaska Native, non-Hispanic/Latino; 2 Hispanic/Latino). Average age 36. 109 applicants, 54% accepted, 56 enrolled. In 2016, 19 master's awarded. *Degree requirements:* For master's, 30-credit core curriculum, minimum GPA of 3.0 throughout program, completion of degree requirements within six years from start of program. *Entrance requirements:* For master's, PRAXIS I, GRE, or MAT; writing proficiency test, minimum cumulative GPA of 3.0 over the last 60 hours of undergraduate study toward a baccalaureate degree, three letters of recommendation, Virginia teaching license (or eligibility). Additional exam requirements/recommendations for international students: Required—TOEFL (minimum score 600 paper-based; 100 iBT). *Application deadline:* Applications are processed on a rolling basis. Electronic applications accepted. *Expenses:* $9,600. *Financial support:* Application deadline: 3/1; applicants required to submit FAFSA. *Faculty research:* Digital story telling for instruction and assessment; online collaborative tools; digital field trips with Google Earth; teacher preparation in special education in Kenya, Malawi, Zambia, and Zimbabwe; self-efficacy of regular education teachers regarding inclusion of special education students in their classrooms. *Total annual research expenditures:* $5,000. *Unit head:* Dr. Sue Davis, Education Chair, 434-791-5741, Fax: 434-791-5020, E-mail: suedavis@averett.edu.
Website: http://gps.averett.edu/online/education/

Azusa Pacific University, School of Behavioral and Applied Sciences, Department of Higher Education, Program in Higher Education Leadership, Azusa, CA 91702-7000. Offers Ed D.

Azusa Pacific University, School of Education, Program in School Administration, Azusa, CA 91702-7000. Offers MA. *Program availability:* Part-time, evening/weekend. *Degree requirements:* For master's, comprehensive exam or thesis, core exams, oral presentation. *Entrance requirements:* For master's, 12 units of course work in education, minimum GPA of 3.0. *Faculty research:* Instructional supervision, outcome-based education, technology and online searching, teacher preparation.

Baldwin Wallace University, Graduate Programs, School of Education, Leadership in Higher Education Program, Berea, OH 44017-2088. Offers MA Ed. *Program availability:* Part-time, evening/weekend. *Students:* 31 full-time (21 women), 1 (woman) part-time; includes 3 minority (all Black or African American, non-Hispanic/Latino). Average age 29. 58 applicants, 43% accepted, 21 enrolled. In 2016, 14 master's awarded. *Degree requirements:* For master's, comprehensive exam (for some programs), capstone project, portfolio. *Entrance requirements:* For master's, bachelor's degree, MAT or minimum GPA of 3.0. Additional exam requirements/recommendations for international students: Required—TOEFL (minimum score 550 paper-based; 79 iBT). *Application deadline:* For fall admission, 8/15 for domestic students; for spring admission, 12/15 for domestic students. Applications are processed on a rolling basis. Application fee: $25. Electronic applications accepted. Application fee is waived when completed online. *Expenses:* $721 per credit hour. *Financial support:* Paid internships (for full-time students) available. Financial award applicants required to submit FAFSA. *Faculty research:* Program development in higher education, leadership styles, the psychology of leadership and learning in higher education. *Unit head:* Dr. Ken Schneck, Director, 440-826-8062, Fax: 440-826-3779, E-mail: kschneck@bw.edu. *Application contact:* Lydia Avery, Associate Director of Transfer, Adult and Graduate Admission, 440-826-2222, Fax: 440-826-3830, E-mail: admission@bw.edu.
Website: https://www.bw.edu/academics/master-of-arts-in-education/maed-school-leadership/

Baldwin Wallace University, Graduate Programs, School of Education, Specialization in School Leadership, Berea, OH 44017-2088. Offers MA Ed. *Program availability:* Part-time, evening/weekend, 100% online. *Students:* 25 full-time (18 women), 24 part-time (15 women); includes 4 minority (2 Black or African American, non-Hispanic/Latino; 1 Asian, non-Hispanic/Latino; 1 Two or more races, non-Hispanic/Latino). Average age 32. 23 applicants, 91% accepted, 16 enrolled. In 2016, 11 master's awarded. *Degree requirements:* For master's, comprehensive exam, 2-semester internship. *Entrance requirements:* For master's, bachelor's degree in field, MAT or minimum GPA of 3.0. Additional exam requirements/recommendations for international students: Required—TOEFL (minimum score 550 paper-based; 79 iBT). *Application deadline:* For fall admission, 8/15 priority date for domestic students; for spring admission, 12/15 priority date for domestic students. Applications are processed on a rolling basis. Application fee: $25. Electronic applications accepted. Application fee is waived when completed online. *Expenses:* $721 per credit hour. *Financial support:* Career-related internships or fieldwork available. Financial award applicants required to submit FAFSA. *Faculty research:* Leadership styles, instructional strategies, formative assessment. *Unit head:* Dr. Joseph Hruby, Coordinator, 440-826-8539, Fax: 440-826-3779, E-mail: jhruby@bw.edu. *Application contact:* Winifred W. Gerhardt, Director of Transfer, Adult and Graduate Admission, 440-826-2222, Fax: 440-826-3830, E-mail: admission@bw.edu.
Website: http://www.bw.edu/academics/master-of-arts-in-education/maed-school-leadership/

Ball State University, Graduate School, Teachers College, Department of Educational Leadership, Program in Educational Administration and Supervision, Muncie, IN 47306. Offers MA, Ed D. *Accreditation:* NCATE. *Program availability:* Part-time, 100% online, blended/hybrid learning. *Degree requirements:* For doctorate, thesis/dissertation. *Entrance requirements:* For master's, minimum baccalaureate GPA of 2.75 or 3.0 in latter half of baccalaureate; for doctorate, GRE General Test, interview, minimum graduate GPA of 3.2. Additional exam requirements/recommendations for international students: Required—TOEFL (minimum score 550 paper-based; 79 iBT), IELTS (minimum score 6.5). Electronic applications accepted.

Ball State University, Graduate School, Teachers College, Department of Educational Leadership, Program in School Superintendency, Muncie, IN 47306. Offers Ed S. *Accreditation:* NCATE. *Program availability:* Part-time, online only, 100% online. *Degree requirements:* For Ed S, thesis. *Entrance requirements:* For degree, GRE General Test, minimum graduate GPA of 3.2, professional portfolio including platform statement, writing sample, curriculum vitae, five references. Additional exam requirements/recommendations for international students: Required—TOEFL (minimum score 550 paper-based; 79 iBT), IELTS (minimum score 6.5). Electronic applications accepted.

Ball State University, Graduate School, Teachers College, Department of Educational Studies, Program in Executive Development for Public Service, Muncie, IN 47306. Offers MA. *Program availability:* Part-time, online only, 100% online, blended/hybrid learning. *Entrance requirements:* For master's, minimum baccalaureate GPA of 2.75 or 3.0 in latter half of baccalaureate. Additional exam requirements/recommendations for international students: Required—TOEFL (minimum score 550 paper-based; 79 iBT), IELTS (minimum score 6.5). Electronic applications accepted.

Ball State University, Graduate School, Teachers College, Department of Educational Studies, Program in Student Affairs Administration in Higher Education, Muncie, IN 47306. Offers MA. *Accreditation:* NCATE. *Entrance requirements:* For master's, GRE General Test, minimum baccalaureate GPA of 2.75 or 3.0 in latter half of baccalaureate, resume, three professional references. Additional exam requirements/recommendations for international students: Required—TOEFL (minimum score 550 paper-based; 79 iBT), IELTS (minimum score 6.5). Electronic applications accepted.

Bank Street College of Education, Graduate School, Programs in Educational Leadership, New York, NY 10025. Offers early childhood leadership (MS Ed); educational leadership (MS Ed); leadership for educational change (Ed M, MS Ed); leadership in community-based learning (MS Ed); leadership in mathematics education (MS Ed); leadership in museum education (MS Ed); leadership in the arts: creative writing (MS Ed); leadership in the arts: visual arts (MS Ed). *Degree requirements:* For master's, thesis. *Entrance requirements:* For master's, interview, essays, minimum of 2 years experience as a classroom teacher. Additional exam requirements/recommendations for international students: Required—TOEFL (minimum score 600 paper-based; 100 iBT), IELTS (minimum score 7). Electronic applications accepted. *Faculty research:* Leadership in urban schools, leadership in small schools, mathematics in elementary schools, professional development in early childhood, leadership in arts education, leadership in special education, museum leadership, community-based leadership.

Barry University, School of Education, Program in Educational Leadership, Miami Shores, FL 33161-6695. Offers MS, Ed D, Certificate, Ed S. *Program availability:* Part-time, evening/weekend. *Degree requirements:* For master's and other advanced degree, comprehensive exam. *Entrance requirements:* For master's, GRE General Test or MAT, minimum GPA of 3.0; for other advanced degree, GRE General Test, minimum GPA of 3.0. Electronic applications accepted.

Barry University, School of Education, Program in Higher Education Administration, Miami Shores, FL 33161-6695. Offers MS. *Program availability:* Part-time, evening/weekend. *Degree requirements:* For master's, comprehensive exam. *Entrance requirements:* For master's, GRE General Test or MAT, minimum GPA of 3.0. Electronic applications accepted.

Barry University, School of Education, Program in Leadership and Education, Miami Shores, FL 33161-6695. Offers educational technology (PhD); exceptional student education (PhD); higher education administration (PhD); human resource development (PhD); leadership (PhD). *Program availability:* Part-time, evening/weekend. *Degree requirements:* For doctorate, thesis/dissertation. *Entrance requirements:* For doctorate, GRE General Test, minimum GPA of 3.25. Electronic applications accepted.

Baruch College of the City University of New York, Austin W. Marxe School of Public and International Affairs, Program in Educational Leadership, New York, NY 10010-5585. Offers educational leadership (MS Ed); school building leadership (Advanced Certificate); school district leadership (Advanced Certificate). *Program availability:* Part-time, evening/weekend. *Degree requirements:* For master's, internship. *Entrance requirements:* For master's, GRE or master's degree. Additional exam requirements/recommendations for international students: Required—TOEFL. Electronic applications accepted. *Faculty research:* School administration, program development, school leadership, violence in schools, school leadership development, school reform, school discipline policy, program development.

Baruch College of the City University of New York, Austin W. Marxe School of Public and International Affairs, Program in Higher Education Administration, New York, NY 10010-5585. Offers MS Ed. *Program availability:* Part-time, evening/weekend. *Entrance requirements:* For master's, GRE General Test. Additional exam requirements/recommendations for international students: Required—TOEFL. Electronic applications accepted. *Expenses:* Contact institution.

Bayamón Central University, Graduate Programs, Program in Education, Bayamón, PR 00960-1725. Offers administration and supervision (MA Ed); commercial education (MA Ed); elementary education (K–3) (MA Ed); family counseling (Graduate Certificate); guidance and counseling (MA Ed); pre-elementary teacher (MA Ed); rehabilitation counseling (MA Ed); special education (MA Ed), including attention deficit disorder, education of the autistic, learning disabilities. *Program availability:* Part-time, evening/weekend. *Degree requirements:* For master's, comprehensive exam. *Entrance requirements:* For master's, EXADEP, bachelor's degree in education or related field.

Baylor University, Graduate School, School of Education, Department of Educational Leadership, Waco, TX 76798. Offers MS Ed, Ed S. *Accreditation:* NCATE. *Students:* 59 full-time (29 women), 11 part-time (5 women); includes 19 minority (9 Black or African American, non-Hispanic/Latino; 1 Asian, non-Hispanic/Latino; 2 Hispanic/Latino; 1 Native Hawaiian or other Pacific Islander, non-Hispanic/Latino; 6 Two or more races, non-Hispanic/Latino), 1 international. 90 applicants, 44% accepted. In 2016, 35 master's awarded. *Entrance requirements:* For master's, GRE General Test. *Application deadline:* Applications are processed on a rolling basis. Application fee: $25. *Expenses:* *Tuition:* Full-time $28,494; part-time $1583 per credit hour. *Required fees:* $167 per credit hour. Tuition and fees vary according to course load and program. *Financial support:* In 2016–17, 20 students received support, including 2 research assistantships; teaching assistantships, Federal Work-Study, institutionally sponsored loans, and scholarships/grants also available. *Unit head:* Dr. Robert Cloud, Graduate Program Director, 254-710-6110, Fax: 254-710-3265, E-mail: robert_cloud@baylor.edu. *Application contact:* Julie Baker, Administrative Assistant, 254-710-3050, Fax: 254-710-3870, E-mail: julie_l_baker@baylor.edu.
Website: http://www.baylor.edu/soe/edl/

Educational Leadership and Administration

Bay Path University, Program in Higher Education Administration, Longmeadow, MA 01106-2292. Offers enrollment management (MS); general administration (MS); institutional advancement (MS); online teaching and program administration (MS). *Program availability:* Part-time, online only, 100% online. *Students:* 9 full-time (8 women), 50 part-time (39 women); includes 18 minority (8 Black or African American, non-Hispanic/Latino; 1 American Indian or Alaska Native, non-Hispanic/Latino; 7 Hispanic/Latino; 2 Two or more races, non-Hispanic/Latino). Average age 36. 27 applicants, 67% accepted, 14 enrolled. In 2016, 15 master's awarded. *Degree requirements:* For master's, 8 core courses (24 credits) and 4 elective courses (12 credits) for a total of 36 credits. *Application deadline:* Applications are processed on a rolling basis. Application fee: $45. Electronic applications accepted. Application fee is waived when completed online. *Expenses:* $20,385. *Financial support:* Unspecified assistantships available. Financial award applicants required to submit FAFSA. *Unit head:* Dr. Lauren Way, Program Director, 413-565-1193, E-mail: lway@baypath.edu. *Application contact:* Diane Ranaldi, Dean of Graduate Admissions, 413-565-1332, Fax: 413-565-1250, E-mail: dranaldi@baypath.edu.
Website: http://graduate.baypath.edu/Graduate-Programs/Programs-Online/MS-Programs/Higher-Education-Administration

Bellarmine University, Annsley Frazier Thornton School of Education, Louisville, KY 40205. Offers education and district leadership (Ed D); education and social change (PhD); elementary education (MA Ed, MAT); leadership in higher education (PhD); learning and behavior disorders (MA Ed, MAT); middle grades education (MA Ed, MAT); principalship (Ed S); reading and writing (MA Ed); secondary education (MAT); teacher leadership (MA Ed). *Accreditation:* NCATE. *Program availability:* Part-time, evening/weekend. *Faculty:* 15 full-time (7 women), 44 part-time/adjunct (36 women). *Students:* 39 full-time (28 women), 211 part-time (164 women); includes 46 minority (35 Black or African American, non-Hispanic/Latino; 3 Asian, non-Hispanic/Latino; 5 Hispanic/Latino; 3 Two or more races, non-Hispanic/Latino). Average age 34. In 2016, 66 master's, 3 doctorates, 43 other advanced degrees awarded. *Degree requirements:* For master's, thesis (for some programs); for doctorate, thesis/dissertation. *Entrance requirements:* For master's, GRE, baccalaureate degree from accredited institution; minimum cumulative GPA of 2.75; recommendations from employers, supervisors, or professors attesting to applicant's potential as graduate student; statement of intent to pursue graduate degree; for doctorate, GRE, minimum GPA of 3.5 in all graduate coursework; baccalaureate and master's degrees in education or fields directly relevant to education; three letters of recommendation; two essays (no more than 1,000 words each); interview. Additional exam requirements/recommendations for international students: Required—TOEFL (minimum score 550 paper-based, 68 iBT), IELTS (minimum score 6), or Michigan English Language Assessment Battery. *Application deadline:* For fall admission, 8/1 priority date for domestic and international students; for spring admission, 12/1 priority date for domestic and international students; for summer admission, 4/10 priority date for domestic and international students. Applications are processed on a rolling basis. Application fee: $40. Electronic applications accepted. Tuition and fees vary according to program. *Financial support:* Scholarships/grants available. Financial award applicants required to submit FAFSA. *Faculty research:* Literacy, service-learning, dispositions, educational technology, special education. *Unit head:* Dr. Robert Cooter, Dean, 502-272-8191, Fax: 502-272-8189, E-mail: rcooter@bellarmine.edu. *Application contact:* Sarah Shumway Schuble, Senior Graduate Recruiter, 502-272-8271, Fax: 502-272-8002, E-mail: sshumway@bellarmine.edu.
Website: http://www.bellarmine.edu/education/graduate

Benedictine College, Master of Arts in School Leadership Program, Atchison, KS 66002-1499. Offers MA. *Accreditation:* NCATE. *Program availability:* Part-time, evening/weekend. *Faculty:* 3 part-time/adjunct (1 woman). *Students:* 12 full-time (7 women), 16 part-time (8 women), 1 international. Average age 33. 12 applicants, 83% accepted, 10 enrolled. In 2016, 8 master's awarded. *Degree requirements:* For master's, comprehensive exam, practicum. *Entrance requirements:* For master's, minimum GPA of 3.0. Additional exam requirements/recommendations for international students: Recommended—TOEFL, IELTS. *Application deadline:* Applications are processed on a rolling basis. Application fee: $50. Electronic applications accepted. Application fee is waived when completed online. *Expenses:* Contact institution. *Financial support:* Scholarships/grants and unspecified assistantships available. Financial award applicants required to submit FAFSA. *Faculty research:* Teacher leadership, special education issues, diversity in schools, Catholic school leadership, professional development. *Application contact:* Dr. Cheryl Reding, Director, Graduate Programs in Education, 913-360-7384, E-mail: creding@benedictine.edu.
Website: http://www.benedictine.edu/academics/graduate-programs/masl

Benedictine University, Graduate Programs, Program in Education, Lisle, IL 60532. Offers curriculum and instruction and collaborative teaching (M Ed); elementary education (MA Ed); leadership and administration (M Ed); reading and literacy (M Ed); secondary education (MA Ed); special education (MA Ed). *Program availability:* Part-time, evening/weekend. *Students:* 17 full-time (16 women), 30 part-time (26 women); includes 2 minority (both Black or African American, non-Hispanic/Latino). 21 applicants, 62% accepted, 8 enrolled. In 2016, 68 master's awarded. *Degree requirements:* For master's, comprehensive exam, thesis (for some programs). *Entrance requirements:* For master's, GRE or MAT. Additional exam requirements/recommendations for international students: Required—TOEFL (minimum score 550 paper-based). *Application deadline:* For fall admission, 9/1 for domestic students; for winter admission, 12/1 for domestic students; for spring admission, 2/15 for domestic students. Applications are processed on a rolling basis. Application fee: $40. Electronic applications accepted. *Expenses:* Contact institution. *Financial support:* Career-related internships or fieldwork and health care benefits available. Support available to part-time students. *Unit head:* MeShelda Jackson, Director, 630-829-6282, E-mail: mjackson@ben.edu. *Application contact:* Kari Gibbons, Associate Vice President, Enrollment Center, 630-829-6200, Fax: 630-829-6584, E-mail: kgibbons@ben.edu.

Benedictine University, Graduate Programs, Program in Higher Education and Organizational Change, Lisle, IL 60532. Offers Ed D. *Students:* 15 full-time (10 women), 34 part-time (21 women); includes 16 minority (12 Black or African American, non-Hispanic/Latino; 4 Hispanic/Latino). 32 applicants, 94% accepted, 26 enrolled. In 2016, 21 doctorates awarded. Application fee: $40. *Expenses: Tuition:* Full-time $15,600; part-time $650 per hour. *Required fees:* $300. One-time fee: $125 part-time. Tuition and fees vary according to class time, course load, campus/location and program. *Unit head:* Dr. Sunil Chand, Director, 630-829-1930, E-mail: schand@ben.edu. *Application contact:* Kari Gibbons, Associate Vice President, Enrollment Center, 630-829-6200, Fax: 630-829-6584, E-mail: kgibbons@ben.edu.

Berry College, Graduate Programs, Graduate Programs in Education, Program in Educational Leadership, Mount Berry, GA 30149-0159. Offers Ed S. *Faculty:* 2 full-time (0 women), 5 part-time/adjunct (4 women). *Students:* 34 full-time (27 women), 34 part-time (25 women); includes 21 minority (17 Black or African American, non-Hispanic/Latino; 4 Hispanic/Latino). Average age 42. In 2016, 64 Ed Ss awarded. *Degree requirements:* For Ed S, thesis, portfolio, oral exams. *Entrance requirements:* For degree, M Ed from NCATE-accredited school, minimum GPA of 3.25. Additional exam requirements/recommendations for international students: Required—TOEFL (minimum score 550 paper-based). *Application deadline:* For fall admission, 7/21 for domestic students, 5/1 for international students; for spring admission, 12/1 for domestic students, 10/1 for international students. Applications are processed on a rolling basis. Application fee: $25 ($30 for international students). Electronic applications accepted. *Expenses:* Contact institution. *Financial support:* In 2016–17, 2 students received support. Available to part-time students. Application deadline: 3/1; applicants required to submit FAFSA. *Unit head:* Dr. Jacqueline McDowell, Dean, Charter School of Education and Human Sciences, 706-236-1717, Fax: 706-238-5827, E-mail: jmcdowell@berry.edu. *Application contact:* Brett Kennedy, Assistant Vice President of Enrollment Management, 706-236-2215, Fax: 706-290-2178, E-mail: admissions@berry.edu.
Website: http://www.berry.edu/academics/education/graduate/

Bethel University, Graduate Programs, McKenzie, TN 38201. Offers administration and supervision (MA Ed); business administration (MBA); conflict resolution (MA); physician assistant studies (MS). *Program availability:* Part-time, evening/weekend. *Degree requirements:* For master's, thesis (for some programs). *Entrance requirements:* For master's, GRE General Test or MAT, minimum undergraduate GPA of 2.5.

Bethel University, Graduate School, St. Paul, MN 55112-6999. Offers business administration (MBA); classroom management (Certificate); counseling (MA); international baccalaureate teaching and learning (Certificate); K-12 education (MA); leadership (Ed D); leadership foundations (Certificate); nurse educator (MS, Certificate); nurse-midwifery (MS); physician assistant (MS); special education (MA); strategic leadership (MA); teaching (MA). *Program availability:* Part-time, evening/weekend, 100% online, blended/hybrid learning. *Faculty:* 19 full-time (15 women), 57 part-time/adjunct (37 women). *Students:* 674 full-time (466 women), 378 part-time (256 women); includes 188 minority (94 Black or African American, non-Hispanic/Latino; 3 American Indian or Alaska Native, non-Hispanic/Latino; 43 Asian, non-Hispanic/Latino; 31 Hispanic/Latino; 1 Native Hawaiian or other Pacific Islander, non-Hispanic/Latino; 16 Two or more races, non-Hispanic/Latino), 33 international. *Degree requirements:* For master's, comprehensive exam (for some programs), thesis (for some programs); for doctorate, comprehensive exam, thesis/dissertation. *Entrance requirements:* Additional exam requirements/recommendations for international students: Required—TOEFL (minimum score 550 paper-based, 80 iBT) or IELTS. *Application deadline:* Applications are processed on a rolling basis. Application fee: $0. Electronic applications accepted. *Expenses:* Contact institution. *Financial support:* Teaching assistantships, career-related internships or fieldwork, and scholarships/grants available. Support available to part-time students. Financial award applicants required to submit FAFSA. *Unit head:* Dick Crombie, Vice-President/Dean, 651-635-8000, Fax: 651-635-8004, E-mail: gs@bethel.edu. *Application contact:* Director of Admissions, 651-635-8000, Fax: 651-635-8004, E-mail: gs@bethel.edu.
Website: https://www.bethel.edu/graduate/

Binghamton University, State University of New York, Graduate School, College of Community and Public Affairs, Department of Student Affairs Administration, Binghamton, NY 13902-6000. Offers MS. *Program availability:* Part-time. *Faculty:* 3 full-time (all women), 2 part-time/adjunct (both women). *Students:* 34 full-time (19 women), 11 part-time (10 women); includes 12 minority (3 Black or African American, non-Hispanic/Latino; 3 Asian, non-Hispanic/Latino; 3 Hispanic/Latino; 3 Two or more races, non-Hispanic/Latino), 1 international. Average age 27. 53 applicants, 98% accepted, 28 enrolled. In 2016, 25 master's awarded. *Degree requirements:* For master's, comprehensive exam. *Entrance requirements:* For master's, GRE General Test. Additional exam requirements/recommendations for international students: Required—TOEFL (minimum score 80 iBT). *Application deadline:* For fall admission, 4/15 priority date for domestic and international students; for spring admission, 11/15 priority date for domestic and international students. Application fee: $75. Electronic applications accepted. *Financial support:* In 2016–17, 38 students received support. Fellowships, career-related internships or fieldwork, Federal Work-Study, institutionally sponsored loans, scholarships/grants, health care benefits, and unspecified assistantships available. Financial award applicants required to submit FAFSA. *Unit head:* Brianna King, Director of Student Admissions, 607-777-2719, E-mail: bking@binghamton.edu. *Application contact:* Ben Balkaya, Assistant Dean and Director, 607-777-2151, Fax: 607-777-2501, E-mail: balkaya@binghamton.edu.
Website: http://www2.binghamton.edu/ccpa/student-affairs-administration/

Binghamton University, State University of New York, Graduate School, Graduate School of Education, Program in Educational Theory and Practice, Binghamton, NY 13902-6000. Offers educational leadership (Certificate); educational studies (MS); educational theory and practice (Ed D). MS program also offered for working teachers in Greater New Orleans. *Program availability:* Part-time. *Students:* 5 full-time (3 women), 66 part-time (55 women); includes 7 minority (4 Black or African American, non-Hispanic/Latino; 1 American Indian or Alaska Native, non-Hispanic/Latino; 1 Asian, non-Hispanic/Latino; 1 Hispanic/Latino), 5 international. Average age 43. 30 applicants, 97% accepted, 18 enrolled. In 2016, 9 master's, 4 doctorates, 9 other advanced degrees awarded. *Degree requirements:* For master's, thesis; for doctorate, thesis/dissertation. *Entrance requirements:* For doctorate, GRE General Test; for Certificate, teaching certification. Additional exam requirements/recommendations for international students: Required—TOEFL (minimum score 550 paper-based; 80 iBT). *Application deadline:* For fall admission, 2/1 priority date for domestic and international students. Application fee: $75. Electronic applications accepted. *Financial support:* In 2016–17, 11 students received support, including 1 fellowship with full tuition reimbursement available (averaging $15,500 per year), 3 teaching assistantships with full tuition reimbursements available (averaging $15,500 per year); career-related internships or fieldwork, Federal Work-Study, institutionally sponsored loans, scholarships/grants, health care benefits, tuition waivers (full and partial), and unspecified assistantships also available. Financial award applicants required to submit FAFSA. *Unit head:* Dr. Susan Strehle, Dean, 607-777-7329, E-mail: sstrehle@binghamton.edu. *Application contact:* Ben Balkaya, Assistant Dean and Director, 607-777-2151, Fax: 607-777-2501, E-mail: balkaya@binghamton.edu.
Website: http://www2.binghamton.edu/gse/doctoral-program/index.html

Bloomsburg University of Pennsylvania, School of Graduate Studies, College of Education, Department of Teaching and Learning, Program in Educational Leadership, Bloomsburg, PA 17815-1301. Offers college student affairs (M Ed); PreK-12 curriculum and instruction (M Ed); PreK-12 school counseling (M Ed); PreK-12 school principal (M Ed). *Faculty:* 6 full-time (2 women), 1 (woman) part-time/adjunct. *Students:* 64 full-time (42 women), 39 part-time (26 women); includes 18 minority (8 Black or African American, non-Hispanic/Latino; 4 Asian, non-Hispanic/Latino; 3 Hispanic/Latino; 1 Native Hawaiian or other Pacific Islander, non-Hispanic/Latino; 2 Two or more races, non-Hispanic/Latino), 1 international. Average age 27. 87 applicants, 60% accepted, 43 enrolled. In 2016, 39 master's awarded. *Degree requirements:* For master's, practicum. *Entrance requirements:* For master's, 3 letters of recommendation, resume, minimum QPA of 3.0, personal statement, interview. Additional exam requirements/recommendations for international students: Required—TOEFL, IELTS. Application fee: $35 ($60 for international students). Electronic applications accepted. *Expenses:* Tuition, state resident: full-time $9660; part-time $483 per credit. Tuition, nonresident: full-time $14,500; part-time $725 per credit. *Required fees:* $2410; $107 per credit. $75 per term. Tuition and fees vary according to course load, degree level and program. *Financial support:* Federal Work-Study and unspecified assistantships available.

Financial award applicants required to submit FAFSA. *Unit head:* Dr. Ingrid Everett, Program Coordinator, 570-389-5120, Fax: 570-389-3030, E-mail: ieverett@bloomu.edu. *Application contact:* Jennifer Kessler, Administrative Assistant, 570-389-4015, Fax: 570-389-3054, E-mail: jkessler@bloomu.edu.

Bob Jones University, Graduate Programs, Greenville, SC 29614. Offers accountancy (MS); Bible (MA); Bible translation (MA); Biblical studies (Certificate); broadcast management (MS); business administration (MBA); church history (MA, PhD); church ministries (MA); church music (MM); cinema and video production (MA); counseling (MS); curriculum and instruction (Ed D); divinity (M Div); dramatic production (MA); educational leadership (MS, Ed D, Ed S); elementary education (M Ed, MAT); English (M Ed, MA, MAT); fine arts (MA); graphic design (MA); history (M Ed, MA); illustration (MA); interpretative speech (MA); mathematics (M Ed, MAT); medical missions (Certificate); ministry (MM, D Min); multi-categorical special education (M Ed, MAT); music (M Ed); New Testament interpretation (PhD); Old Testament interpretation (PhD); orchestral instrument performance (MM); organ performance (MM); pastoral studies (MA); personnel services (MS, Ed S); piano pedagogy (MM); piano performance (MM); platform arts (MA); radio and television broadcasting (MS); rhetoric and public address (MA); secondary education (M Ed); studio art (MA); teaching Bible (MA); theology (MA, PhD); voice performance (MM); youth ministries (MA); M Div/MM.

Boise State University, College of Education, Department of Curriculum, Instruction and Foundational Studies, Boise, ID 83725-1747. Offers curriculum and instruction (MA Ed, Ed D); educational leadership (M Ed); executive educational leadership (Ed S). *Accreditation:* NCATE. *Program availability:* Part-time. *Faculty:* 36. *Students:* 24 full-time (18 women), 180 part-time (113 women); includes 19 minority (1 Black or African American, non-Hispanic/Latino; 3 American Indian or Alaska Native, non-Hispanic/Latino; 3 Asian, non-Hispanic/Latino; 12 Hispanic/Latino), 6 international. Average age 36. 79 applicants, 67% accepted, 35 enrolled. In 2016, 36 master's, 6 other advanced degrees awarded. *Degree requirements:* For master's, thesis optional. *Entrance requirements:* For master's, minimum GPA of 3.0. Additional exam requirements/recommendations for international students: Required—TOEFL (minimum score 550 paper-based; 80 iBT), IELTS (minimum score 6). *Application deadline:* For fall admission, 3/1 for domestic and international students; for spring admission, 10/15 for domestic students, 10/1 for international students. Application fee: $65 ($95 for international students). Electronic applications accepted. *Expenses:* Tuition, state resident: full-time $6058; part-time $358 per credit hour. Tuition, nonresident: full-time $20,108; part-time $608 per credit hour. *Required fees:* $2108. Tuition and fees vary according to program. *Financial support:* In 2016–17, 41 students received support. Scholarships/grants and unspecified assistantships available. Financial award application deadline: 3/1; financial award applicants required to submit FAFSA. *Unit head:* Dr. Philip P. Kelly, Department Chair, 208-426-4977, Fax: 208-426-4365. *Application contact:* Dr. Kelly Cross, Associate Chair, 208-426-2806, E-mail: kellycross@boisestate.edu.
Website: http://education.boisestate.edu/cifs/

Boston College, Lynch School of Education, Program in Educational Leadership, Chestnut Hill, MA 02467-3800. Offers M Ed, Ed D, CAES, JD/M Ed. *Program availability:* Part-time, evening/weekend. *Faculty:* 6 full-time (3 women). *Students:* 9 full-time (3 women), 39 part-time (25 women); includes 8 minority (6 Black or African American, non-Hispanic/Latino; 1 Asian, non-Hispanic/Latino; 1 Hispanic/Latino), 6 international. Average age 38. 20 applicants, 65% accepted, 7 enrolled. In 2016, 12 master's, 1 doctorate, 1 CAES awarded. Terminal master's awarded for partial completion of doctoral program. *Degree requirements:* For master's and CAES, comprehensive exam. *Entrance requirements:* For master's and CAES, GRE General Test or MAT; for doctorate, GRE General Test. Additional exam requirements/recommendations for international students: Required—TOEFL (minimum score 100 iBT). *Application deadline:* For fall admission, 12/1 priority date for domestic and international students; for spring admission, 11/1 priority date for domestic and international students. Application fee: $65. Electronic applications accepted. Tuition and fees vary according to program. *Financial support:* Research assistantships with tuition reimbursements, Federal Work-Study, scholarships/grants, and tuition waivers (partial) available. Support available to part-time students. Financial award applicants required to submit FAFSA. *Unit head:* Lauri Johnson, Department Chair, 617-552-1039, E-mail: lauri.johnson.1@bc.edu. *Application contact:* Kimberly Rose, Graduate Admission Assistant, 617-552-4214, Fax: 617-552-0398, E-mail: roseki@bc.edu.

Bowie State University, Graduate Programs, Program in Educational Leadership/Executive Fellows, Bowie, MD 20715-9465. Offers Ed D. *Program availability:* Part-time, evening/weekend. *Degree requirements:* For doctorate, comprehensive exam, thesis/dissertation. Electronic applications accepted.

Bowie State University, Graduate Programs, Program in Elementary and Secondary School Administration, Bowie, MD 20715-9465. Offers M Ed. *Program availability:* Part-time, evening/weekend. *Degree requirements:* For master's, comprehensive exam. *Entrance requirements:* For master's, copy of teaching certificate, 3 years of teaching experience, letter of recommendation from current supervisor. Electronic applications accepted.

Bowie State University, Graduate Programs, Program in School Administration and Supervision, Bowie, MD 20715-9465. Offers M Ed. *Program availability:* Part-time, evening/weekend. *Degree requirements:* For master's, comprehensive exam, thesis optional, research paper. *Entrance requirements:* For master's, minimum undergraduate GPA of 3.0, 3 years of teaching experience, teaching certificate.

Bowling Green State University, Graduate College, College of Education and Human Development, Department of Higher Education and Student Affairs, Program in Higher Education Administration, Bowling Green, OH 43403. Offers PhD. *Accreditation:* NCATE. *Program availability:* Part-time. *Degree requirements:* For doctorate, comprehensive exam, thesis/dissertation. *Entrance requirements:* For doctorate, GRE General Test. Additional exam requirements/recommendations for international students: Required—TOEFL. *Application deadline:* For fall admission, 1/15 for domestic students. Application fee: $30. Electronic applications accepted. *Financial support:* Research assistantships with full tuition reimbursements, teaching assistantships, career-related internships or fieldwork, Federal Work-Study, institutionally sponsored loans, and unspecified assistantships available. Support available to part-time students. Financial award applicants required to submit FAFSA. *Faculty research:* Adult learners, legal issues, intellectual development. *Unit head:* Dr. Craig Mertler, Director, 419-372-9357. *Application contact:* Dr. Michael Coomes, Graduate Coordinator, 419-372-7157.

Bowling Green State University, Graduate College, College of Education and Human Development, School of Educational Foundations, Leadership and Policy, Program in Educational Administration and Supervision, Bowling Green, OH 43403. Offers educational leadership (M Ed, Ed S); leadership studies (Ed D). *Accreditation:* NCATE. *Program availability:* Part-time, evening/weekend. *Degree requirements:* For master's, thesis or alternative; for doctorate, comprehensive exam, thesis/dissertation; for Ed S, thesis or alternative, field experience or internship. *Entrance requirements:* For master's, doctorate, and Ed S, GRE General Test. Additional exam requirements/recommendations for international students: Required—TOEFL. *Application deadline:* Applications are processed on a rolling basis. Application fee: $30. Electronic applications accepted. *Financial support:* Research assistantships with full tuition reimbursements, teaching assistantships with full tuition reimbursements, career-related internships or fieldwork, Federal Work-Study, institutionally sponsored loans, tuition waivers (partial), and unspecified assistantships available. Support available to part-time students. Financial award applicants required to submit FAFSA. *Faculty research:* Professional development for school leaders, organizational development, school finance, legal challenges to school decision making, administering urban schools. *Unit head:* Dr. Craig Mertler, Director, 419-372-9357. *Application contact:* Dr. Daniel Fasko, Jr., Graduate Coordinator, 419-372-7322.

Bradley University, The Graduate School, College of Education and Health Sciences, Department of Leadership in Education, Nonprofits and Counseling, Peoria, IL 61625-0002. Offers counseling (MA), including clinical mental health counseling, professional school counseling; leadership in educational administration (MA); nonprofit leadership (MA). *Accreditation:* ACA; NCATE. *Program availability:* Part-time, evening/weekend. *Degree requirements:* For master's, comprehensive exam, thesis optional. *Entrance requirements:* For master's, GRE General Test or MAT, interview, 3 letters of recommendation. Additional exam requirements/recommendations for international students: Required—TOEFL (minimum score 550 paper-based; 79 iBT), IELTS (minimum score 6.5). *Application deadline:* For fall admission, 5/15 priority date for domestic and international students; for spring admission, 10/15 priority date for domestic and international students. Applications are processed on a rolling basis. Application fee: $40 ($50 for international students). Electronic applications accepted. *Expenses: Tuition:* Full-time $7650; part-time $850 per credit. *Required fees:* $50 per credit. One-time fee: $100 full-time. *Financial support:* Research assistantships with full and partial tuition reimbursements, career-related internships or fieldwork, scholarships/grants, tuition waivers (partial), and unspecified assistantships available. Support available to part-time students. Financial award application deadline: 4/1. *Unit head:* Jenny Tripses, Interim Chair, 309-677-3593, E-mail: jtripses@bradley.edu. *Application contact:* Kayla Carroll, Director of International Admissions and Student Services, 309-677-2375, E-mail: klcarroll@fsmail.bradley.edu.
Website: http://www.bradley.edu/academic/departments/lenc/

Brandeis University, Graduate School of Arts and Sciences, Teaching Program, Waltham, MA 02454-9110. Offers Jewish day school (MAT); public elementary education (MAT); secondary education (MAT), including Bible, biology, chemistry, Chinese, English, history, math, physics; teacher leadership (Ed M, CAGS). *Faculty:* 4 full-time (2 women), 11 part-time/adjunct (10 women). *Students:* 26 full-time (19 women), 32 part-time (26 women); includes 3 minority (all Hispanic/Latino), 10 international. 106 applicants, 70% accepted, 53 enrolled. In 2016, 39 master's awarded. *Degree requirements:* For master's, internship; research project. *Entrance requirements:* For master's, GRE General Test or MAT, official transcript(s), 2 letters of recommendation, resume, statement of purpose. Additional exam requirements/recommendations for international students: Required—TOEFL (minimum score 600 paper-based; 100 iBT); Recommended—IELTS (minimum score 7), TSE (minimum score 68). *Application deadline:* Applications are processed on a rolling basis. Application fee: $75. Electronic applications accepted. *Expenses:* Contact institution. *Financial support:* Scholarships/grants and tuition waivers (partial) available. Financial award application deadline: 4/15; financial award applicants required to submit FAFSA. *Faculty research:* Teacher education, education, teaching, elementary education, secondary education, Jewish education, English, history, biology, chemistry, physics, math, Chinese, Bible/Tanakh. *Unit head:* Prof. Marya Levenson, Director, 781-736-2002, Fax: 781-736-5020, E-mail: mlevenso@brandeis.edu. *Application contact:* Manuel Tuan, Department Coordinator, 781-736-2002, Fax: 781-736-5020, E-mail: tuan@brandeis.edu.
Website: http://www.brandeis.edu/programs/mat

Brandman University, School of Education, Irvine, CA 92618. Offers education (MA); elementary education (MAT); organizational leadership (Ed D); school counseling (MA); secondary education (MAT); special education (MA). *Expenses: Tuition:* Full-time $14,880; part-time $620 per credit hour. Tuition and fees vary according to degree level and program. *Unit head:* Dr. Christine G. Zeppos, Dean, 949-341-9948, E-mail: zeppos@brandman.edu.
Website: http://www.brandman.edu/education/

Brandon University, Faculty of Education, Brandon, MB R7A 6A9, Canada. Offers curriculum and instruction (M Ed, Diploma); educational administration (M Ed, Diploma); guidance and counseling (M Ed, Diploma); special education (M Ed, Diploma). *Degree requirements:* For master's, thesis. *Entrance requirements:* For master's, minimum GPA of 3.0, teaching certificate or equivalent. Additional exam requirements/recommendations for international students: Required—TOEFL. *Faculty research:* Comparative education, environmental studies, parent/school council.

Bridgewater State University, College of Graduate Studies, College of Education and Allied Studies, Department of Secondary Education and Professional Programs, Program in Educational Leadership, Bridgewater, MA 02325. Offers M Ed, CAGS. *Accreditation:* NCATE. *Program availability:* Part-time, evening/weekend. *Degree requirements:* For master's and CAGS, comprehensive exam. *Entrance requirements:* For master's, GRE General Test or Massachusetts Test for Educator Licensure, work experience; for CAGS, master's degree.

Brigham Young University, Graduate Studies, David O. McKay School of Education, Department of Educational Leadership and Foundations, Provo, UT 84602. Offers educational leadership and foundations (Ed D); educational leadership: education policy and social foundations (M Ed); educational leadership: school leadership (M Ed). *Program availability:* Part-time, evening/weekend. *Faculty:* 11 full-time (2 women), 1 part-time/adjunct (0 women). *Students:* 44 full-time (16 women), 26 part-time (14 women); includes 10 minority (4 Asian, non-Hispanic/Latino; 2 Hispanic/Latino; 2 Native Hawaiian or other Pacific Islander, non-Hispanic/Latino; 2 Two or more races, non-Hispanic/Latino), 3 international. Average age 42. 82 applicants, 46% accepted, 38 enrolled. In 2016, 24 master's, 6 doctorates awarded. Terminal master's awarded for partial completion of doctoral program. *Degree requirements:* For master's, comprehensive exam; for doctorate, comprehensive exam, thesis/dissertation, prospectus. *Entrance requirements:* For master's and doctorate, GRE, LSAT, or GMAT. Additional exam requirements/recommendations for international students: Required—TOEFL (minimum score 580 paper-based; 85 iBT). *Application deadline:* For fall admission, 5/1 for domestic students, 2/15 for international students; for spring admission, 1/15 for domestic students, 2/15 for international students; for summer admission, 3/1 for domestic and international students. Application fee: $50. Electronic applications accepted. *Expenses:* $393 per credit. *Financial support:* In 2016–17, 15 students received support. Research assistantships available. Financial award application deadline: 8/15. *Unit head:* Pamela Hallam, Chair, 801-422-3600, Fax: 801-422-0196, E-mail: pam_hallam@byu.edu. *Application contact:* Michele Price, Department Secretary, 801-422-3813, Fax: 801-422-0196, E-mail: michele_price@byu.edu.
Website: http://education.byu.edu/edlf/

Brooklyn College of the City University of New York, School of Education, Program in Educational Leadership, Brooklyn, NY 11210-2889. Offers school building leader (MS Ed); school district leader (MS Ed). *Program availability:* Part-time, evening/

weekend. *Entrance requirements:* For master's, 2 supervisory letters of recommendation, essay, resume, teaching certificate, interview. Additional exam requirements/recommendations for international students: Required—TOEFL (minimum score 500 paper-based; 61 iBT). Electronic applications accepted.

Buffalo State College, State University of New York, The Graduate School, Faculty of Applied Science and Education, Department of Elementary Education and Reading, Program in Educational Leadership, Buffalo, NY 14222-1095. Offers CAS. *Accreditation:* NCATE. *Program availability:* Part-time, evening/weekend. *Degree requirements:* For CAS, internship. *Entrance requirements:* For degree, master's degree, New York teaching certificate, 3 years of teaching experience. Additional exam requirements/ recommendations for international students: Required—TOEFL (minimum score 550 paper-based).

Butler University, College of Education, Indianapolis, IN 46208-3485. Offers alternative special education licensure (Certificate); educational administration (MS); effective teaching and leadership (MS); international baccalaureate teaching and learning (Certificate); licensed mental health counselor (Certificate); school counseling (MS); teachers of the visually impaired (Certificate). *Accreditation:* ACA; NCATE. *Program availability:* Part-time. *Faculty:* 13 full-time (10 women), 5 part-time/adjunct (4 women). *Students:* 9 full-time (7 women), 119 part-time (85 women); includes 14 minority (10 Black or African American, non-Hispanic/Latino; 1 Asian, non-Hispanic/Latino; 2 Hispanic/Latino; 1 Two or more races, non-Hispanic/Latino). Average age 32. 79 applicants, 76% accepted, 63 enrolled. In 2016, 42 master's, 30 other advanced degrees awarded. *Entrance requirements:* For master's, GRE (minimum score 291) or MAT (minimum score 396) unless undergraduate GPA is a 3.0 or higher, two letters of recommendation, transcripts, interview, professional resume. Additional exam requirements/recommendations for international students: Required—TOEFL (minimum score 550 paper-based; 79 iBT), IELTS (minimum score 6). *Application deadline:* For fall admission, 2/1 for domestic and international students; for spring admission, 11/1 for domestic and international students; for summer admission, 4/1 for domestic and international students. Applications are processed on a rolling basis. Application fee: $0. Electronic applications accepted. *Expenses:* Contact institution. *Financial support:* In 2016–17, 60 students received support. Scholarships/grants and unspecified assistantships available. Financial award application deadline: 7/15; financial award applicants required to submit FAFSA. *Faculty research:* Principals role in school improvement, leadership and school climate, retention of teachers in special education, the neuro-diversity brain, school counseling intervention. *Unit head:* Dr. Ena Shelley, Dean, 317-940-9752, Fax: 317-940-6481. *Application contact:* Diane Dubord, Graduate Student Services Specialist, 317-940-8100, Fax: 317-940-8250, E-mail: ddubord@butler.edu.
Website: https://www.butler.edu/coe/graduate-programs

Cairn University, School of Education, Langhorne, PA 19047-2990. Offers applied behavior analysis (MS Sp Ed, Certificate); educational leadership and administration (MS El); instruction (MS Sp Ed); teacher education (MS Ed). *Program availability:* Part-time, evening/weekend, 100% online, blended/hybrid learning. *Faculty:* 2 full-time (both women), 4 part-time/adjunct (3 women). *Students:* 3 full-time (2 women), 89 part-time (62 women); includes 18 minority (10 Black or African American, non-Hispanic/Latino; 6 Asian, non-Hispanic/Latino; 2 Hispanic/Latino), 21 international. Average age 38. 35 applicants, 100% accepted, 25 enrolled. In 2016, 17 master's awarded. *Entrance requirements:* Additional exam requirements/recommendations for international students: Required—TOEFL (minimum score 550 paper-based). *Application deadline:* Applications are processed on a rolling basis. Application fee: $25. Electronic applications accepted. Application fee is waived when completed online. *Expenses:* $655 per semester credit. *Financial support:* Scholarships/grants available. Support available to part-time students. Financial award applicants required to submit FAFSA. *Unit head:* Joseph Beeson, Interim Dean, 215-702-4498, E-mail: teacher.ed@cairn.edu. *Application contact:* Abigail Simon, Enrollment Counselor, Graduate Education, 800-572-2472, Fax: 215-702-4248, E-mail: asimon@cairn.edu.
Website: http://www.cairn.edu/academics/education

Caldwell University, Graduate Studies, Division of Education, Caldwell, NJ 07006-6195. Offers curriculum and instruction (MA); education (Ed D, Postbaccalaureate Certificate); educational administration (MA); learning disabilities teacher-consultant (Post-Master's Certificate); literacy instruction (MA); principal (Post-Master's Certificate); reading specialist (Post-Master's Certificate); special education (MA), including special education, teaching of students with disabilities, teaching of students with disabilities and learning disabilities teacher-consultant; superintendent (Post-Master's Certificate); supervisor (Post-Master's Certificate). *Program availability:* Part-time, evening/weekend. *Degree requirements:* For master's, comprehensive exam (for some programs). *Entrance requirements:* For master's, PRAXIS, 3 years of work experience, prior teaching certification. Additional exam requirements/recommendations for international students: Required—TOEFL (minimum score 580 paper-based). Electronic applications accepted. *Faculty research:* Curriculum and instruction, secondary education, special education, education and technology.

California Baptist University, Program in Education, Riverside, CA 92504-3206. Offers educational leadership (MS); educational leadership for faith-based institutions (MS); educational leadership for public institutions (MS); educational technology (MS); instructional computer applications (MS); international education (MS); leadership and adult learning (MS); leadership and organizational studies (MS); online teaching and learning (MS); reading (MS); science education (MA); special education in mild/ moderate disabilities (MS); special education in moderate/severe disabilities (MS); teacher leadership (MS); teaching (MS); teaching and learning (MS). *Program availability:* Part-time, evening/weekend, 100% online, blended/hybrid learning. *Faculty:* 20 full-time (8 women), 11 part-time/adjunct (7 women). *Students:* 191 full-time (148 women), 234 part-time (178 women); includes 194 minority (23 Black or African American, non-Hispanic/Latino; 5 American Indian or Alaska Native, non-Hispanic/ Latino; 15 Asian, non-Hispanic/Latino; 131 Hispanic/Latino; 4 Native Hawaiian or other Pacific Islander, non-Hispanic/Latino; 16 Two or more races, non-Hispanic/Latino), 2 international. Average age 31. 277 applicants, 61% accepted, 150 enrolled. In 2016, 280 master's awarded. *Degree requirements:* For master's, comprehensive exam, project, or thesis. *Entrance requirements:* For master's, minimum undergraduate GPA of 2.75; 500-word essay; three letters of recommendation; two prerequisite courses completed with minimum C grade. Additional exam requirements/recommendations for international students: Required—TOEFL (minimum score 80 iBT). *Application deadline:* For fall admission, 8/1 priority date for domestic students, 7/1 for international students; for spring admission, 12/1 priority date for domestic students, 11/1 for international students. Applications are processed on a rolling basis. Application fee: $45. Electronic applications accepted. *Expenses:* Contact institution. *Financial support:* In 2016–17, 162 students received support. Federal Work-Study and scholarships/grants available. Financial award applicants required to submit CSS PROFILE or FAFSA. *Faculty research:* Leadership development, complexity theory, faith and learning, special education, social and philosophical contexts of education. *Unit head:* Dr. John Shoup, Dean, School of Education, 951-343-4516, E-mail: jshoup@calbaptist.edu.
Website: http://www.calbaptist.edu/mastersined/

California Baptist University, Program in Leadership and Adult Learning, Riverside, CA 92504-3206. Offers MA. *Program availability:* Part-time, evening/weekend. *Degree requirements:* For master's, CCCAOE professional training or leadership tactics. *Entrance requirements:* For master's, minimum undergraduate GPA of 2.75, bachelor's degree transcripts, three letters of recommendation, essay, resume. Additional exam requirements/recommendations for international students: Required—TOEFL (minimum score 80 iBT). *Application deadline:* For fall admission, 8/1 priority date for domestic students, 7/1 priority date for international students; for spring admission, 12/1 priority date for domestic students, 11/1 priority date for international students. Applications are processed on a rolling basis. Application fee: $45. Electronic applications accepted. *Expenses:* Contact institution. *Financial support:* Applicants required to submit CSS PROFILE or FAFSA. *Unit head:* Dr. John Shoup, Dean, School of Education, 951-343-4205, E-mail: jshoup@calbaptist.edu.

California Coast University, School of Education, Santa Ana, CA 92701. Offers administration (M Ed); curriculum and instruction (M Ed); educational administration (Ed D); educational psychology (Ed D); organizational leadership (Ed D). *Program availability:* Online learning.

California Lutheran University, Graduate Studies, Graduate School of Education, Thousand Oaks, CA 91360-2787. Offers counseling and guidance (MS), including college student personnel, counseling and guidance; educational leadership (MA, Ed D), including educational leadership (K-12) (Ed D), higher education leadership (Ed D); special education (MS); teacher leadership (M Ed); teaching (M Ed). *Accreditation:* NCATE. *Program availability:* Part-time, evening/weekend. *Faculty:* 23 full-time (17 women), 39 part-time/adjunct (26 women). *Students:* 518 full-time (411 women), 79 part-time (67 women); includes 252 minority (12 Black or African American, non-Hispanic/ Latino; 3 American Indian or Alaska Native, non-Hispanic/Latino; 17 Asian, non-Hispanic/Latino; 108 Hispanic/Latino; 1 Native Hawaiian or other Pacific Islander, non-Hispanic/Latino; 111 Two or more races, non-Hispanic/Latino), 14 international. Average age 35. 319 applicants, 74% accepted, 192 enrolled. In 2016, 93 master's, 13 doctorates awarded. *Degree requirements:* For master's, comprehensive exam or thesis; for doctorate, thesis/dissertation. *Entrance requirements:* For master's, GRE General Test, interview, minimum GPA of 3.0. *Application deadline:* For fall admission, 7/1 priority date for domestic students; for spring admission, 11/1 priority date for domestic students; for summer admission, 4/1 priority date for domestic students. Applications are processed on a rolling basis. Application fee: $50. Electronic applications accepted. *Unit head:* Dr. Michael Hillis, Dean, 805-493-3421. *Application contact:* 805-493-3325, Fax: 805-493-3861, E-mail: clugrad@callutheran.edu.

California State Polytechnic University, Pomona, Ed D Program in Educational Leadership, Pomona, CA 91768-2557. Offers Ed D. *Program availability:* Part-time, evening/weekend. *Students:* 51 part-time (37 women); includes 36 minority (8 Black or African American, non-Hispanic/Latino; 5 Asian, non-Hispanic/Latino; 21 Hispanic/ Latino; 2 Two or more races, non-Hispanic/Latino), 1 international. Average age 43. 21 applicants, 100% accepted, 15 enrolled. In 2016, 14 doctorates awarded. *Entrance requirements:* Additional exam requirements/recommendations for international students: Required—TOEFL. *Application deadline:* Applications are processed on a rolling basis. Application fee: $55. Electronic applications accepted. *Expenses:* Contact institution. *Financial support:* Applicants required to submit FAFSA. *Unit head:* Michael M. Bandoni, Doctoral Studies Coordinator, 909-869-3060, Fax: 909-869-5416, E-mail: mmbandoni@cpp.edu. *Application contact:* Andrew M. Wright, Director of Admissions.
Website: http://www.cpp.edu/~doctoralstudies/

California State University, Bakersfield, Division of Graduate Studies, School of Social Sciences and Education, Program in Educational Administration, Bakersfield, CA 93311. Offers MA. *Degree requirements:* For master's, thesis or alternative, project or culminating exam. *Application deadline:* Applications are processed on a rolling basis. Application fee: $55. *Expenses:* Tuition, state resident: full-time $2246; part-time $1302 per semester. *Unit head:* D. Danny Whetton, Graduate Coordinator, 661-664-3055, Fax: 661-664-2479, E-mail: dwhetton@csub.edu. *Application contact:* Debbie Blowers, Assistant Director of Admissions and Evaluations, 661-664-3381, E-mail: dblowers@csub.edu.
Website: https://www.csub.edu/sse/departments/advancededucationalstudies/educational_administration/index.html

California State University, Bakersfield, Division of Graduate Studies, School of Social Sciences and Education, Program in Educational Leadership, Bakersfield, CA 93311. Offers Ed D. *Students:* 18 part-time (13 women); includes 9 minority (1 Black or African American, non-Hispanic/Latino; 1 American Indian or Alaska Native, non-Hispanic/Latino; 2 Asian, non-Hispanic/Latino; 4 Hispanic/Latino; 1 Two or more races, non-Hispanic/Latino). Average age 40. 23 applicants, 96% accepted, 19 enrolled. *Degree requirements:* For doctorate, thesis/dissertation. *Expenses:* Tuition, state resident: full-time $2246; part-time $1302 per semester. *Financial support:* In 2016–17, fellowships (averaging $1,850 per year) were awarded; Federal Work-Study, scholarships/grants, and tuition waivers (full and partial) also available. Financial award application deadline: 3/2; financial award applicants required to submit FAFSA. *Unit head:* D. Danny Whetton, Director, 661-654-3055, E-mail: edd@csub.edu. *Application contact:* Debbie Blowers, Assistant Director of Admissions, 661-664-3381, E-mail: dblowers@csub.edu.

California State University, Dominguez Hills, College of Education, Division of Graduate Education, Program in School Leadership, Carson, CA 90747-0001. Offers MA. *Program availability:* Part-time, evening/weekend. *Degree requirements:* For master's, comprehensive exam. *Entrance requirements:* For master's, minimum GPA of 2.75. *Faculty research:* Educational leadership, teacher retention, accountability, decision-making.

California State University, East Bay, Office of Graduate Studies, College of Education and Allied Studies, Department of Educational Leadership, Hayward, CA 94542-3000. Offers MS, Ed D. *Accreditation:* NCATE. *Program availability:* Part-time, evening/weekend, online learning. *Students:* 67 full-time (45 women), 79 part-time (60 women); includes 76 minority (25 Black or African American, non-Hispanic/Latino; 1 American Indian or Alaska Native, non-Hispanic/Latino; 16 Asian, non-Hispanic/Latino; 29 Hispanic/Latino; 2 Native Hawaiian or other Pacific Islander, non-Hispanic/Latino; 3 Two or more races, non-Hispanic/Latino). Average age 42. 66 applicants, 83% accepted, 42 enrolled. In 2016, 60 master's, 16 doctorates awarded. *Degree requirements:* For master's, comprehensive exam, project or thesis; for doctorate, thesis/dissertation. *Entrance requirements:* For master's, CBEST, teaching or services credential and experience; minimum GPA of 3.0; for doctorate, GRE, MA with minimum GPA of 3.0; PK-12 leadership position; portfolio of work samples; employer/district support agreement. Additional exam requirements/recommendations for international students: Required—TOEFL (minimum score 550 paper-based). *Application deadline:* For fall admission, 6/30 for domestic and international students. Application fee: $55. Electronic applications accepted. *Financial support:* Career-related internships or fieldwork, Federal Work-Study, and institutionally sponsored loans available. Support available to part-time students. Financial award application deadline: 3/2; financial award applicants required to submit FAFSA. *Unit head:* Prof. Peg Winkelman, Chair, 510-885-4145, E-mail: peg.winkelman@csueastbay.edu. *Application contact:* Prof. Gilberto Arriaza, Graduate Advisor, 510-885-2905, E-mail: gilberto.arriaza@

csueastbay.edu.
Website: http://www20.csueastbay.edu/ceas/departments/el/

California State University, East Bay, Office of Graduate Studies, College of Education and Allied Studies, Department of Teacher Education, Hayward, CA 94542-3000. Offers education (MS), including curriculum, early childhood education, educational technology and leadership, reading instruction. *Program availability:* Online learning. *Students:* 55 full-time (43 women), 21 part-time (15 women); includes 34 minority (5 Black or African American, non-Hispanic/Latino; 1 American Indian or Alaska Native, non-Hispanic/Latino; 14 Asian, non-Hispanic/Latino; 10 Hispanic/Latino; 1 Native Hawaiian or other Pacific Islander, non-Hispanic/Latino; 3 Two or more races, non-Hispanic/Latino), 6 international. Average age 33. 65 applicants, 91% accepted, 11 enrolled. In 2016, 67 master's awarded. *Degree requirements:* For master's, project or thesis. *Entrance requirements:* For master's, minimum GPA of 3.0 in field, 2.5 overall; teaching experience; baccalaureate degree; 3 letters of recommendation. Additional exam requirements/recommendations for international students: Required—TOEFL (minimum score 550 paper-based), IELTS. *Application deadline:* For fall admission, 6/30 for domestic and international students. Application fee: $55. Electronic applications accepted. *Financial support:* Career-related internships or fieldwork, Federal Work-Study, and institutionally sponsored loans available. Support available to part-time students. Financial award application deadline: 3/2; financial award applicants required to submit FAFSA. *Faculty research:* Online, pedagogy, writing, learning, teaching. *Unit head:* Dr. Eric Engdahl, Chair, 510-885-4599, E-mail: eric.engdahl@csueastbay.edu. *Application contact:* Prof. Valerie Helgren-Lempesis, Education Graduate Advisor, 510-885-3006, Fax: 510-885-4632, E-mail: valerie.helgren-lempesis@csueastbay.edu.
Website: http://www20.csueastbay.edu/ceas/departments/ted/index.html

California State University, Fresno, Division of Research and Graduate Studies, Kremen School of Education and Human Development, Department of Educational Leadership, Fresno, CA 93740-8027. Offers education (MA), including educational leadership and administration. *Accreditation:* NCATE. *Program availability:* Part-time, evening/weekend. *Degree requirements:* For master's, thesis or alternative. *Entrance requirements:* For master's, GRE General Test, MAT, minimum GPA of 2.75. Additional exam requirements/recommendations for international students: Required—TOEFL. *Application deadline:* For fall admission, 5/1 for domestic and international students; for spring admission, 10/1 for domestic and international students. Applications are processed on a rolling basis. Application fee: $55. Electronic applications accepted. *Financial support:* Career-related internships or fieldwork, Federal Work-Study, scholarships/grants, and research awards available. Support available to part-time students. Financial award application deadline: 3/1; financial award applicants required to submit FAFSA. *Faculty research:* Substance abuse on youth education. *Unit head:* Dr. Linda Hauser, Chair, 559-278-0350, Fax: 559-278-0370, E-mail: lhauser@csufresno.edu. *Application contact:* Dr. Jennifer Moradian Watson, Coordinator, 559-278-0354, Fax: 559-278-0370, E-mail: jmoradianwatson@csufresno.edu.
Website: http://www.fresnostate.edu/kremen/departments/era.html

California State University, Fresno, Division of Research and Graduate Studies, Kremen School of Education and Human Development, Doctoral Program in Educational Leadership, Fresno, CA 93740-8027. Offers Ed D. *Program availability:* Part-time. *Degree requirements:* For doctorate, thesis/dissertation. *Entrance requirements:* For doctorate, GRE, minimum GPA of 3.0, master's degree, personal interview, written statement of purpose. Additional exam requirements/recommendations for international students: Required—TOEFL. *Application deadline:* For fall admission, 5/31 for domestic students. Application fee: $55. Electronic applications accepted. *Expenses:* $5,961 per term. *Financial support:* Career-related internships or fieldwork and scholarships/grants available. Support available to part-time students. Financial award application deadline: 3/1; financial award applicants required to submit FAFSA. *Faculty research:* Minority special education leadership, literacy, ethics of leadership, organizational planning, language development. *Unit head:* Kenneth Magdaleno, Director, 559-278-0294, Fax: 559-278-0457, E-mail: kmagdaleno@csufresno.edu. *Application contact:* Tiffany Jennings, Administrative Support Coordinator II, 559-278-2448, Fax: 559-278-4658, E-mail: tijennings@csufresno.edu.
Website: http://www.fresnostate.edu/kremen/dpelfs/

California State University, Fullerton, Graduate Studies, College of Education, Department of Educational Leadership, Fullerton, CA 92834-9480. Offers educational administration (MS); educational leadership (Ed D). *Accreditation:* NCATE. *Program availability:* Part-time. *Degree requirements:* For master's, thesis or alternative, project. *Entrance requirements:* For master's, minimum GPA of 2.5. Application fee: $55. *Expenses:* Tuition, state resident: full-time $3369; part-time $1953 per unit. Tuition, nonresident: full-time $3915; part-time $2499 per unit. Tuition and fees vary according to course load, degree level and program. *Financial support:* Career-related internships or fieldwork, Federal Work-Study, institutionally sponsored loans, and scholarships/grants available. Support available to part-time students. Financial award application deadline: 3/1; financial award applicants required to submit FAFSA. *Faculty research:* Creation of a substance abuse prevention training and demonstration program. *Unit head:* Jennifer Goldstein, Head, 657-278-3963. *Application contact:* Admissions/Applications, 657-278-2371.

California State University, Long Beach, Graduate Studies, College of Education, Department of Advanced Studies in Education and Counseling, Long Beach, CA 90840. Offers counseling (MS), including marriage and family therapy, school counseling, student development in higher education; education (MA, Ed D); educational administration (MA, Ed D); educational psychology (MA); special education (MS). *Program availability:* Part-time, evening/weekend. *Entrance requirements:* For master's, GRE General Test, minimum GPA of 2.75. *Application deadline:* For fall admission, 3/1 for domestic students. Applications are processed on a rolling basis. Application fee: $55. Electronic applications accepted. *Financial support:* Federal Work-Study, institutionally sponsored loans, and scholarships/grants available. Financial award application deadline: 3/2. *Unit head:* Dr. Hiromi Masunaga, Chair, 562-985-4517, E-mail: asec@csulb.edu.

California State University, Northridge, Graduate Studies, Michael D. Eisner College of Education, Department of Educational Leadership and Policy Studies, Northridge, CA 91330. Offers education (MA); educational administration (MA); educational leadership (Ed D). *Accreditation:* NCATE. *Program availability:* Part-time, evening/weekend. *Faculty:* 8 full-time (3 women), 24 part-time/adjunct (12 women). *Students:* 44 full-time (25 women), 185 part-time (145 women); includes 143 minority (12 Black or African American, non-Hispanic/Latino; 1 American Indian or Alaska Native, non-Hispanic/Latino; 11 Asian, non-Hispanic/Latino; 113 Hispanic/Latino; 6 Two or more races, non-Hispanic/Latino), 2 international. Average age 38. 129 applicants, 87% accepted, 93 enrolled. *Entrance requirements:* For master's, 2 letters of recommendation. Additional exam requirements/recommendations for international students: Required—TOEFL. *Application deadline:* For fall admission, 11/30 for domestic students. Application fee: $55. *Expenses:* Tuition, state resident: full-time $4152. *Financial support:* Fellowships available. Financial award application deadline: 3/1. *Faculty research:* Bilingual educational training. *Unit head:* Jody Dunlap, Chair, 818-677-2591, E-mail: jody.dunlap@csun.edu.
Website: http://www.csun.edu/eisner-education/educational-leadership-policy-studies

California State University, Sacramento, Office of Graduate Studies, College of Education, Graduate and Professional Studies in Education, Sacramento, CA 95819. Offers child development (MA); counseling (MS); curriculum and instruction (MA); education (Ed D); education leadership and policy studies (MA), including higher education, PreK-12; educational technology (MA); gender equity (MA); language and literacy (MA); multicultural education (MA); school psychology (MA); special education (MA); workforce development advocacy (MA). *Program availability:* Part-time. *Students:* 446 full-time (335 women), 125 part-time (97 women); includes 298 minority (39 Black or African American, non-Hispanic/Latino; 3 American Indian or Alaska Native, non-Hispanic/Latino; 97 Asian, non-Hispanic/Latino; 153 Hispanic/Latino; 6 Native Hawaiian or other Pacific Islander, non-Hispanic/Latino). Average age 32. 540 applicants, 76% accepted, 250 enrolled. In 2016, 107 master's, 7 doctorates awarded. *Degree requirements:* For master's, thesis or project; writing proficiency exam. *Entrance requirements:* For master's, minimum GPA of 2.5, 3.0 in last 60 units. Additional exam requirements/recommendations for international students: Required—TOEFL (minimum score 550 paper-based; 80 iBT). *Application deadline:* For fall admission, 2/15 for domestic students, 1/15 for international students. Applications are processed on a rolling basis. Application fee: $55. Electronic applications accepted. *Expenses:* $4,302 full-time tuition and fees per semester, $2,796 part-time. *Financial support:* Career-related internships or fieldwork and Federal Work-Study available. Support available to part-time students. Financial award application deadline: 3/1; financial award applicants required to submit FAFSA. *Unit head:* Dr. Susan Heredia, Chair, 916-278-5942, E-mail: coe@csus.edu. *Application contact:* Jose Martinez, Graduate Admissions Supervisor, 916-278-7871, E-mail: martinj@skymail.csus.edu.
Website: http://www.csus.edu/coe/academics/graduate/index.html

California State University, San Bernardino, Graduate Studies, College of Education, Program in Educational Administration, San Bernardino, CA 92407. Offers MA. *Program availability:* Part-time, evening/weekend. *Faculty:* 25 full-time (15 women), 42 part-time/adjunct (28 women). *Students:* 41 full-time (25 women), 40 part-time (25 women); includes 42 minority (7 Black or African American, non-Hispanic/Latino; 1 American Indian or Alaska Native, non-Hispanic/Latino; 3 Asian, non-Hispanic/Latino; 28 Hispanic/Latino; 3 Two or more races, non-Hispanic/Latino), 1 international. 44 applicants, 86% accepted, 31 enrolled. In 2016, 32 master's awarded. *Degree requirements:* For master's, thesis or alternative. *Entrance requirements:* Additional exam requirements/recommendations for international students: Required—TOEFL. *Application deadline:* For fall admission, 7/16 for domestic students; for winter admission, 10/16 for domestic students; for spring admission, 2/5 for domestic students. Application fee: $55. *Expenses:* Tuition, state resident: full-time $7843; part-time $5011.20 per year. Tuition and fees vary according to course load, degree level, program and reciprocity agreements. *Unit head:* Dr. Jay Fiene, Dean, 909-537-5600, E-mail: jfiene@csusb.edu. *Application contact:* Dr. Francisca Beer, Dean of Graduate Studies, 909-537-5058, E-mail: fbeer@csusb.edu.

California State University, San Bernardino, Graduate Studies, College of Education, Program in Educational Leadership: Community College Specialization, San Bernardino, CA 92407. Offers MA. *Program availability:* Part-time, evening/weekend. *Students:* 2 full-time (both women), 16 part-time (6 women); includes 10 minority (1 Asian, non-Hispanic/Latino; 8 Hispanic/Latino; 1 Two or more races, non-Hispanic/Latino), 1 international. 24 applicants, 67% accepted, 15 enrolled. *Degree requirements:* For master's, thesis optional. *Entrance requirements:* Additional exam requirements/recommendations for international students: Required—TOEFL. *Application deadline:* For fall admission, 7/17 for domestic students. Application fee: $55. *Expenses:* Tuition, state resident: full-time $7843; part-time $5011.20 per year. Tuition and fees vary according to course load, degree level, program and reciprocity agreements. *Unit head:* Dr. Jay Fiene, Dean, 909-537-7621, E-mail: jfiene@csusb.edu. *Application contact:* Dr. Francisca Beer, Dean of Graduate Studies, 909-537-5058, E-mail: fbeer@csusb.edu.

California State University, San Bernardino, Graduate Studies, College of Education, Program in Educational Leadership: P-12 Specialization, San Bernardino, CA 92407. Offers Ed D. *Students:* 9 full-time (5 women), 52 part-time (34 women); includes 39 minority (14 Black or African American, non-Hispanic/Latino; 2 Asian, non-Hispanic/Latino; 22 Hispanic/Latino; 1 Two or more races, non-Hispanic/Latino). 22 applicants, 55% accepted, 12 enrolled. In 2016, 3 doctorates awarded. *Entrance requirements:* Additional exam requirements/recommendations for international students: Required—TOEFL. *Application deadline:* For fall admission, 7/16 for domestic students. Application fee: $55. *Expenses:* Tuition, state resident: full-time $7843; part-time $5011.20 per year. Tuition and fees vary according to course load, degree level, program and reciprocity agreements. *Unit head:* Dr. Jay Fiene, Dean, 909-537-7621, E-mail: jfiene@csusb.edu. *Application contact:* Dr. Francisca Beer, Dean of Graduate Studies, 909-537-5058, E-mail: fbeer@csusb.edu.

California State University, San Marcos, College of Education, Health and Human Services, School of Education, San Marcos, CA 92096-0001. Offers educational administration (MA); educational leadership (Ed D); general education (MA); literacy education (MA); special education (MA). *Accreditation:* NCATE (one or more programs are accredited). *Program availability:* Part-time, evening/weekend. *Degree requirements:* For master's, thesis. *Entrance requirements:* For master's, minimum GPA of 3.0, teaching credentials, 1 year of teaching experience. *Expenses:* Tuition, state resident: full-time $6738. Tuition, nonresident: full-time $13,434. *Required fees:* $1906. Tuition and fees vary according to campus/location and program. *Faculty research:* Multicultural literature, art as knowledge, poetry and second language acquisition, restructuring K–12 education and improving the training of K–8 science teachers.

California State University, Stanislaus, College of Education, Program in Education (MA), Turlock, CA 95382. Offers curriculum and instruction (MA), including education technology, elementary education, multilingual education, physical education, reading, secondary education, special education; school administration (MA); school counseling (MA). *Program availability:* Part-time, evening/weekend. *Degree requirements:* For master's, comprehensive exam (for some programs), thesis (for some programs). *Entrance requirements:* For master's, MAT, GRE, or CBEST (varies by concentration), 3 letters of recommendation, personal statement. Additional exam requirements/recommendations for international students: Required—TOEFL (minimum score 550 paper-based). Electronic applications accepted. *Faculty research:* Children's perspectives on historical events, method elementary schools dual language education, K-12 reading programs.

California State University, Stanislaus, College of Education, Programs in Educational Leadership (Ed D), Turlock, CA 95382. Offers community college leadership (Ed D); P-12 leadership (Ed D). *Program availability:* Part-time, evening/weekend. *Degree requirements:* For doctorate, thesis/dissertation. *Entrance requirements:* For doctorate, GRE, minimum GPA of 3.0, 3 letters of reference, interview, personal statement. Additional exam requirements/recommendations for international students: Required—TOEFL (minimum score 550 paper-based). Electronic applications accepted.

Educational Leadership and Administration

California University of Pennsylvania, School of Graduate Studies and Research, College of Education and Human Services, Program in School Administration, California, PA 15419-1394. Offers M Ed. *Accreditation:* NCATE. *Program availability:* Part-time, evening/weekend, online learning. *Degree requirements:* For master's, comprehensive exam, thesis optional. *Entrance requirements:* For master's, MAT, interview, minimum GPA of 3.0, teaching certificate, 2 years of teaching experience. Additional exam requirements/recommendations for international students: Required—TOEFL (minimum score 550 paper-based; 80 iBT). Electronic applications accepted. *Expenses:* Tuition, state resident: full-time $11,592; part-time $483 per credit. Tuition, nonresident: full-time $17,400; part-time $725 per credit. *Required fees:* $3916. Tuition and fees vary according to course load, degree level, campus/location and reciprocity agreements. *Faculty research:* Educational leadership, peer coaching, online education-effective teaching strategies, instruction strategies, school law.

Calumet College of Saint Joseph, Program in Leadership in Teaching, Whiting, IN 46394-2195. Offers MS Ed.

Calvary University, Graduate School and Seminary, Kansas City, MO 64147. Offers Bible and theology (MS); Biblical counseling (MA); education (MS), including administration and leadership, Christian education, curriculum and instruction, elementary education; organization development (MS); pastoral studies (M Div). *Program availability:* Part-time, evening/weekend. *Faculty:* 6 full-time (2 women), 2 part-time/adjunct (1 woman). *Students:* 11 full-time (3 women), 29 part-time (15 women); includes 12 minority (4 Black or African American, non-Hispanic/Latino; 1 American Indian or Alaska Native, non-Hispanic/Latino; 6 Asian, non-Hispanic/Latino; 1 Native Hawaiian or other Pacific Islander, non-Hispanic/Latino). Average age 39. In 2016, 19 master's awarded. *Degree requirements:* For master's, variable foreign language requirement, comprehensive exam, thesis or alternative. *Entrance requirements:* For master's, minimum GPA of 2.5, BA or BS, doctrine agreement. Additional exam requirements/recommendations for international students: Required—TOEFL (minimum score 550 paper-based). *Application deadline:* Applications are processed on a rolling basis. Application fee: $0. Electronic applications accepted. *Expenses: Tuition:* Full-time $7200; part-time $4800 per credit. *Required fees:* $640; $520 per credit. $140 per semester. One-time fee: $100. Tuition and fees vary according to program. *Financial support:* In 2016–17, 8 students received support. Scholarships/grants available. Financial award application deadline: 11/5; financial award applicants required to submit FAFSA. *Unit head:* Dr. Thomas Baurain, Director of Seminary, 816-322-0110 Ext. 1502, Fax: 816-331-4474, E-mail: thomas.baurain@calvary.edu. *Application contact:* Ann Rogers, Admissions Office Assistant, 800-326-3960 Ext. 1321, Fax: 816-331-4474, E-mail: admissions@calvary.edu.
Website: http://www.calvary.edu

Cambridge College, School of Education, Cambridge, MA 02138-5304. Offers autism specialist (M Ed); autism/behavior analyst (M Ed); behavior analyst (Post-Master's Certificate); behavioral management (M Ed); early childhood teacher (M Ed); education specialist in curriculum and instruction (CAGS); educational leadership (Ed D); elementary teacher (M Ed); English as a second language (M Ed, Certificate); general science (M Ed); health education (Post-Master's Certificate); health/family and consumer sciences (M Ed); history (M Ed); individualized (M Ed); information technology literacy (M Ed); instructional technology (M Ed); interdisciplinary studies (M Ed); library teacher (M Ed); literacy education (M Ed); mathematics (M Ed); mathematics specialist (Certificate); middle school mathematics and science (M Ed); school administration (M Ed, CAGS); school guidance counselor (M Ed); school nurse education (M Ed); school social worker/school adjustment counselor (M Ed); special education administrator (CAGS); special education/moderate disabilities (M Ed); teaching skills and methodologies (M Ed). *Program availability:* Part-time, evening/weekend, online learning. *Degree requirements:* For master's, thesis, internship/practicum (licensure program only); for doctorate, thesis/dissertation; for other advanced degree, thesis. *Entrance requirements:* For master's, interview, resume, documentation of licensure, 2 professional references; for doctorate, official transcripts, interview, resume, documentation of licensure (if any), written personal statement/essay, portfolio of scholarly and professional work, qualifying assessment, 2 professional references, health insurance, immunizations form; for other advanced degree, official transcripts, interview, resume, documentation of licensure (if any), written personal statement/essay, 2 professional references, health insurance, immunizations form. Additional exam requirements/recommendations for international students: Required—TOEFL (minimum score 550 paper-based; 79 iBT), Michigan English Language Assessment Battery (minimum score 85); Recommended—IELTS (minimum score 6). Electronic applications accepted. *Expenses:* Contact institution. *Faculty research:* Adult education, accelerated learning, mathematics education, brain compatible learning, special education and law.

Cameron University, Office of Graduate Studies, Program in Educational Leadership, Lawton, OK 73505-6377. Offers MS. *Program availability:* Part-time, evening/weekend. *Degree requirements:* For master's, portfolio.

Campbell University, Graduate and Professional Programs, School of Education, Buies Creek, NC 27506. Offers elementary education (M Ed); interdisciplinary studies (M Ed); middle grades education (M Ed); physical education (M Ed); school administration (MSA); school counseling (M Ed); secondary education (M Ed). *Accreditation:* NCATE. *Program availability:* Part-time, evening/weekend. *Degree requirements:* For master's, comprehensive exam. *Entrance requirements:* For master's, GRE General Test, minimum GPA of 2.7. *Faculty research:* Spiritual values and wellness issues in counseling, stress and professional burnout among counselors, thinking strategies, leadership, adaptive technology.

Canisius College, Graduate Division, School of Education and Human Services, Department of Graduate Education and Leadership, Buffalo, NY 14208-1098. Offers business and marketing education (MS Ed); college student personnel (MS Ed); deaf education (MS Ed); deaf/adolescent education, grades 7-12 (MS Ed); deaf/childhood education, grades 1-6 (MS Ed); differentiated instruction (MS Ed); education administration (MS); educational administration (MS Ed); educational technologies (Certificate); gifted education extension (Certificate); literacy (MS Ed); reading (Certificate); school building leadership (MS Ed, Certificate); school district leadership (Certificate); teacher leader (Certificate); TESOL (MS Ed). *Accreditation:* NCATE. *Program availability:* Part-time, evening/weekend, 100% online, blended/hybrid learning. *Faculty:* 5 full-time (all women), 23 part-time/adjunct (16 women). *Students:* 95 full-time (78 women), 223 part-time (177 women); includes 31 minority (15 Black or African American, non-Hispanic/Latino; 2 American Indian or Alaska Native, non-Hispanic/Latino; 4 Asian, non-Hispanic/Latino; 9 Hispanic/Latino; 1 Two or more races, non-Hispanic/Latino), 1 international. Average age 30. 162 applicants, 89% accepted, 135 enrolled. In 2016, 135 master's, 39 other advanced degrees awarded. *Entrance requirements:* For master's, GRE (if cumulative GPA less than 2.7), transcripts, two letters of recommendation. Additional exam requirements/recommendations for international students: Required—TOEFL (minimum score 550 paper-based, 79 iBT), IELTS (minimum score 6.5), or CAEL (minimum score 70). *Application deadline:* Applications are processed on a rolling basis. Application fee: $25. Electronic applications accepted. Application fee is waived when completed online. *Expenses: Tuition:* Full-time $14,742. *Required fees:* $724. *Financial support:* Career-related internships or fieldwork, Federal Work-Study, scholarships/grants, tuition waivers (partial), and unspecified assistantships available. Support available to part-time students. Financial award application deadline: 4/30; financial award applicants required to submit FAFSA. *Faculty research:* Asperger's disease, autism, private higher education, reading strategies. *Unit head:* Dr. Rosemary K. Murray, Chair/Associate Professor of Graduate Education and Leadership, 716-888-3723, E-mail: murray1@canisius.edu. *Application contact:* Kathleen B. Davis, Vice President of Enrollment Management, 716-888-2500, Fax: 716-888-3195, E-mail: daviskb@canisius.edu.
Website: http://www.canisius.edu/graduate/

Capella University, School of Education, Doctoral Programs in Education, Minneapolis, MN 55402. Offers curriculum and instruction (PhD); educational leadership and management (Ed D); instructional design for online learning (PhD); K-12 studies in education (PhD); leadership for higher education (PhD); leadership in educational administration (PhD); postsecondary and adult education (PhD); professional studies in education (PhD); reading and literacy (Ed D); special education leadership (PhD); training and performance improvement (PhD).

Capella University, School of Education, Master's Programs in Education, Minneapolis, MN 55402. Offers adult education (MS); curriculum and instruction (MS); early childhood education (MS); enrollment management (MS); higher education leadership and management (MS); instructional design for online learning (MS); integrative studies (MS); K-12 studies in education (MS); leadership in educational administration (MS); reading and literacy (MS); special education teaching (MS).

Cardinal Stritch University, College of Education and Leadership, Department of Education, Milwaukee, WI 53217-3985. Offers educational leadership (MS); higher education student affairs leadership (MS); leadership for the advancement of learning and service (Ed D, PhD); leadership for the advancement of learning and service in higher education (Ed D, PhD); teaching (MAT); urban education (MA). *Accreditation:* NCATE. *Program availability:* Evening/weekend. *Degree requirements:* For master's, comprehensive exam, thesis (for some programs), research project, faculty recommendation; for doctorate, thesis/dissertation, practica, field experience. *Entrance requirements:* For master's, 3 letters of recommendation, minimum GPA of 3.0; for doctorate, minimum GPA of 3.5 in master's coursework, 3 letters of recommendation. *Application deadline:* For fall admission, 7/15 priority date for domestic students; for spring admission, 12/15 priority date for domestic students. Applications are processed on a rolling basis. Application fee: $25. *Expenses: Tuition:* Full-time $11,890; part-time $765 per credit hour. Tuition and fees vary according to class time, course load, degree level, program and student's religious affiliation. *Financial support:* Fellowships, research assistantships with partial tuition reimbursements, career-related internships or fieldwork, Federal Work-Study, and scholarships/grants available. Financial award applicants required to submit FAFSA. *Unit head:* Dr. Nancy Blair, Chair, 414-410-4367. *Application contact:* 800-347-8822 Ext. 4042, E-mail: gradadm@stritch.edu.

Caribbean University, Graduate School, Bayamón, PR 00960-0493. Offers administration and supervision (MA Ed); criminal justice (MA); curriculum and instruction (MA Ed, PhD), including elementary education (MA Ed), English education (MA Ed), history education (MA Ed), mathematics education (MA Ed), primary education (MA Ed), science education (MA Ed), Spanish education (MA Ed); educational technology in instructional systems (MA Ed); gerontology (MSN); human resources (MBA); museology, archiving and art history (MA Ed); neonatal pediatrics (MSN); physical education (MA Ed); special education (MA Ed). *Entrance requirements:* For master's, interview, minimum GPA of 2.5.

Carlow University, College of Learning and Innovation, Program in Educational Leadership for High Performance Learning, Pittsburgh, PA 15213-3165. Offers educational leadership for high performance learning (MS); educational leadership for high performance learning with principal certification (MS). *Program availability:* Online only, 100% online. *Students:* 23 full-time (21 women); includes 1 minority (Black or African American, non-Hispanic/Latino). Average age 37. 5 applicants, 100% accepted. *Degree requirements:* For master's, internship. *Entrance requirements:* For master's, personal essay; resume or curriculum vitae; two recommendations; official transcripts; interview; minimum undergraduate GPA of 3.0; instructional I or II teaching certificate (for principal certification program). Additional exam requirements/recommendations for international students: Required—TOEFL (minimum score 550 paper-based). *Application deadline:* Applications are processed on a rolling basis. Electronic applications accepted. *Expenses: Tuition:* Full-time $11,855; part-time $801 per credit. *Required fees:* $182; $13 per credit. Tuition and fees vary according to course load, degree level and program. *Financial support:* Application deadline: 4/1; applicants required to submit FAFSA. *Unit head:* Dr. Pat McMahon, Program Director, 412-578-6013, Fax: 412-578-8816, E-mail: plmcmahon@carlow.edu.
Website: http://www.carlow.edu/educational_leadership.aspx

Carroll University, Graduate Programs in Education, Waukesha, WI 53186-5593. Offers adult and continuing education (M Ed); educational leadership (MS); pk-12 (M Ed). *Program availability:* Part-time, evening/weekend. *Faculty:* 7 full-time (5 women), 14 part-time/adjunct (all women). *Students:* 11 full-time (10 women), 163 part-time (125 women); includes 11 minority (3 Black or African American, non-Hispanic/Latino; 3 American Indian or Alaska Native, non-Hispanic/Latino; 2 Asian, non-Hispanic/Latino; 3 Hispanic/Latino), 1 international. Average age 34. 96 applicants, 38% accepted, 18 enrolled. In 2016, 43 master's awarded. *Degree requirements:* For master's, thesis. *Entrance requirements:* For master's, minimum undergraduate GPA of 2.5 in related field. Additional exam requirements/recommendations for international students: Required—TOEFL. *Application deadline:* For fall admission, 8/15 priority date for domestic students. Applications are processed on a rolling basis. Application fee: $0. Electronic applications accepted. *Expenses: Tuition:* Full-time $10,548; part-time $586 per credit. *Required fees:* $520 per semester. Tuition and fees vary according to course load, degree level and program. *Financial support:* Available to part-time students. Application deadline: 3/15; applicants required to submit FAFSA. *Faculty research:* Qualitative research methods, whole language approaches to teaching, the writing process, multicultural education, gifted/talented learners. *Unit head:* Dr. Kathrine Kramer, Director of Graduate Studies, 262-650-4917, E-mail: kkramer@carrollu.edu. *Application contact:* Lori Aliota, Graduate Admission Counselor, 262-524-7226, E-mail: laliota@carrollu.edu.
Website: http://www.carrollu.edu/gradprograms/education/default.asp

Carson-Newman University, Graduate Program in Education, Jefferson City, TN 37760. Offers curriculum and instruction (M Ed); educational leadership (M Ed); elementary education (MAT); school counseling (MS); secondary education (MAT); teaching English as a second language (MATESL). *Accreditation:* NCATE. *Program availability:* Part-time, evening/weekend, 100% online, blended/hybrid learning. *Degree requirements:* For master's, thesis or alternative. *Entrance requirements:* For master's, PRAXIS II or GRE with minimum score of 290 on the verbal and quantitative components (for MAT), minimum GPA of 3.0 in major, 2.5 overall. Additional exam requirements/recommendations for international students: Recommended—TOEFL (minimum score 79 iBT), IELTS (minimum score 6.5), TSE (minimum score 53). *Expenses: Tuition:* Full-time $10,142; part-time $461 per credit hour. *Required fees:* $300; $150 per semester. One-time fee: $150.

Carthage College, Division of Teacher Education, Kenosha, WI 53140. Offers classroom guidance and counseling (M Ed); creative arts (M Ed); gifted and talented children (M Ed); language arts (M Ed); modern language (M Ed); natural sciences (M Ed); reading (M Ed, Certificate); social sciences (M Ed); teacher leadership (M Ed). *Program availability:* Part-time, evening/weekend. *Degree requirements:* For master's, thesis optional. *Entrance requirements:* For master's, MAT, minimum B average, letters of reference.

Castleton University, Division of Graduate Studies, Department of Education, Program in Educational Leadership, Castleton, VT 05735. Offers MA Ed, CAGS. *Program availability:* Part-time, evening/weekend. *Degree requirements:* For master's, thesis or alternative; for CAGS, publishable paper. *Entrance requirements:* For master's, GRE General Test, MAT, interview, minimum undergraduate GPA of 3.0; for CAGS, educational research, master's degree, minimum undergraduate GPA of 3.0.

The Catholic University of America, School of Arts and Sciences, Department of Education, Washington, DC 20064. Offers Catholic school leadership (MA); education (Certificate); secondary education (MA); special education (MA), including early childhood, non-categorical. *Accreditation:* NCATE. *Program availability:* Part-time. *Faculty:* 8 full-time (7 women), 2 part-time/adjunct (both women). *Students:* 7 full-time (6 women), 21 part-time (13 women); includes 5 minority (2 Black or African American, non-Hispanic/Latino; 3 Hispanic/Latino), 3 international. Average age 38. 22 applicants, 45% accepted, 3 enrolled. In 2016, 14 master's awarded. *Degree requirements:* For master's, comprehensive exam, thesis or alternative; for Certificate, action research project. *Entrance requirements:* For master's, GRE General Test or MAT, statement of purpose, official copies of academic transcripts, three letters of recommendation, interview; for Certificate, PRAXIS I, statement of purpose, official copies of academic transcripts, three letters of recommendation, interview. Additional exam requirements/recommendations for international students: Required—TOEFL (minimum score 550 paper-based; 80 iBT). *Application deadline:* For fall admission, 7/15 priority date for domestic students, 7/1 for international students; for spring admission, 11/15 priority date for domestic students, 11/1 for international students. Applications are processed on a rolling basis. Application fee: $55. Electronic applications accepted. *Expenses:* $42,850 per year; $1,170 per credit; $200 per semester part-time fees. *Financial support:* Fellowships, research assistantships, teaching assistantships, Federal Work-Study, scholarships/grants, tuition waivers (full and partial), and unspecified assistantships available. Financial award application deadline: 2/1; financial award applicants required to submit FAFSA. *Faculty research:* Special education, early childhood education, educational psychology, Catholic school administration, leadership and policy studies, counseling, curriculum and instruction. *Total annual research expenditures:* $54,518. *Unit head:* Dr. John Convey, Chair, 202-319-5810, Fax: 202-319-5815, E-mail: convey@cua.edu. *Application contact:* Director of Graduate Admissions, 202-319-5057, Fax: 202-319-6533, E-mail: cua-admissions@cua.edu.
Website: http://education.cua.edu/

Cedarville University, Graduate Programs, Cedarville, OH 45314. Offers business administration (MBA); curriculum (M Ed); educational administration (M Ed); family nurse practitioner (MSN); global health ministries (MSN); instruction (M Ed); ministry (M Min); pharmacy (Pharm D). *Program availability:* Part-time, evening/weekend, online learning. *Degree requirements:* For master's, thesis. *Entrance requirements:* For master's, GRE, 2 professional recommendations; for doctorate, PCAT, professional recommendation from a practicing pharmacist or current employer/supervisor, resume, essay, interview. Additional exam requirements/recommendations for international students: Required—TOEFL (minimum score 550 paper-based; 80 iBT). Electronic applications accepted. *Expenses:* Contact institution.

Centenary University, Program in Education, Hackettstown, NJ 07840-2100. Offers education practice (M Ed); educational leadership (MA, Ed D); instructional leadership (MA); reading (M Ed); special education (MA). *Accreditation:* TEAC. *Program availability:* Part-time, evening/weekend, online learning. *Degree requirements:* For master's, thesis. *Entrance requirements:* For master's, interview, minimum undergraduate GPA of 2.8.

Central Connecticut State University, School of Graduate Studies, School of Education and Professional Studies, Department of Educational Leadership, Policy and Instructional Technology, New Britain, CT 06050-4010. Offers MS, Ed D, AC, Sixth Year Certificate. *Program availability:* Part-time, evening/weekend. *Faculty:* 17 full-time (7 women), 15 part-time/adjunct (7 women). *Students:* 9 full-time (6 women), 322 part-time (231 women); includes 51 minority (25 Black or African American, non-Hispanic/Latino; 7 Asian, non-Hispanic/Latino; 13 Hispanic/Latino; 1 Native Hawaiian or other Pacific Islander, non-Hispanic/Latino; 5 Two or more races, non-Hispanic/Latino). Average age 37. 53 applicants, 85% accepted, 34 enrolled. In 2016, 75 master's, 5 doctorates, 90 other advanced degrees awarded. *Degree requirements:* For master's, thesis or alternative; for doctorate, thesis/dissertation or alternative; for other advanced degree, thesis or alternative, qualifying exam. *Entrance requirements:* For master's, minimum undergraduate GPA of 2.7; for doctorate, GRE, master's degree, minimum GPA of 3.0 on all graduate coursework, essay, interview, resume, letters of recommendation; for other advanced degree, master's degree with minimum GPA of 3.0, essay, portfolio, letters of recommendation. Additional exam requirements/recommendations for international students: Required—TOEFL (minimum score 550 paper-based; 79 iBT). *Application deadline:* For fall admission, 6/1 for domestic and international students; for spring admission, 11/1 for domestic and international students. Applications are processed on a rolling basis. Application fee: $50. Electronic applications accepted. *Expenses: Tuition, area resident:* Full-time $6497; part-time $606 per credit. Tuition, state resident: full-time $9748; part-time $622 per credit. Tuition, nonresident: full-time $18,102; part-time $622 per credit. *Required fees:* $4459; $246 per credit. *Financial support:* In 2016–17, 6 students received support. Career-related internships or fieldwork, Federal Work-Study, and scholarships/grants available. Support available to part-time students. Financial award application deadline: 3/1; financial award applicants required to submit FAFSA. *Faculty research:* Curriculum development, organizational leadership in educational settings, educational planning and development. *Unit head:* Dr. Anthony Rigazio-Digilio, Chair, 860-832-2130, E-mail: digilio@ccsu.edu. *Application contact:* Patricia Gardner, Associate Director of Graduate Studies, 860-832-2350, Fax: 860-832-2362.
Website: http://web.ccsu.edu/seps/departments/eduLeadership/default.asp

Central Connecticut State University, School of Graduate Studies, School of Engineering, Science and Technology, Department of Mathematical Sciences, New Britain, CT 06050-4010. Offers data mining (MS, Certificate); mathematics (MA, MS), including actuarial science (MA), computer science (MA), statistics (MA); mathematics education leadership (Sixth Year Certificate); mathematics for secondary education (Certificate). *Program availability:* Part-time, evening/weekend, 100% online. *Faculty:* 14 full-time (4 women). *Students:* 8 full-time (5 women), 73 part-time (37 women); includes 17 minority (4 Black or African American, non-Hispanic/Latino; 7 Asian, non-Hispanic/Latino; 4 Hispanic/Latino; 2 Two or more races, non-Hispanic/Latino), 4 international. Average age 37. 44 applicants, 68% accepted, 21 enrolled. In 2016, 23 master's, 1 other advanced degree awarded. *Degree requirements:* For master's, comprehensive exam, thesis or alternative, special project; for other advanced degree, qualifying exam. *Entrance requirements:* For master's, minimum undergraduate GPA of 2.7; for other advanced degree, minimum undergraduate GPA of 3.0, essay, letters of recommendation. Additional exam requirements/recommendations for international students: Required—TOEFL (minimum score 550 paper-based; 79 iBT). *Application deadline:* For fall admission, 5/1 for domestic and international students; for spring admission, 11/1 for domestic and international students. Applications are processed on a rolling basis. Application fee: $50. Electronic applications accepted. *Expenses: Tuition, area resident:* Full-time $6497; part-time $606 per credit. Tuition, state resident: full-time $9748; part-time $622 per credit. Tuition, nonresident: full-time $18,102; part-time $622 per credit. *Required fees:* $4459; $246 per credit. *Financial support:* In 2016–17, 18 students received support. Career-related internships or fieldwork, Federal Work-Study, and scholarships/grants available. Support available to part-time students. Financial award application deadline: 3/1; financial award applicants required to submit FAFSA. *Faculty research:* Statistics, actuarial mathematics, computer systems and engineering, computer programming techniques, operations research. *Unit head:* Dr. Philip Halloran, Chair, 860-832-2835, E-mail: halloranp@ccsu.edu. *Application contact:* Patricia Gardner, Associate Director of Graduate Studies, 860-832-2350, Fax: 860-832-2362.
Website: http://www.ccsu.edu/mathematics/

Central Michigan University, Central Michigan University Global Campus, Program in Education, Mount Pleasant, MI 48859. Offers college teaching (Graduate Certificate); community college (MA); curriculum and instruction (MA); educational technology (MA, DET); reading and literacy K-12 (MA); school principalship (MA), including charter school leadership; training and development (MA). *Accreditation:* TEAC. *Program availability:* Part-time, evening/weekend. *Faculty:* 24 full-time (14 women), 24 part-time/adjunct (8 women). *Students:* 888 (620 women); includes 225 minority (142 Black or African American, non-Hispanic/Latino; 8 American Indian or Alaska Native, non-Hispanic/Latino; 16 Asian, non-Hispanic/Latino; 13 Hispanic/Latino; 46 Two or more races, non-Hispanic/Latino). Average age 37. In 2016, 76 master's awarded. *Entrance requirements:* For master's, minimum GPA of 2.7 in major. Additional exam requirements/recommendations for international students: Required—TOEFL. *Application deadline:* Applications are processed on a rolling basis. Application fee: $50. Electronic applications accepted. *Financial support:* Scholarships/grants available. Support available to part-time students. *Unit head:* Kaleb Patrick, Director, 989-774-3144, E-mail: patri1kg@cmich.edu. *Application contact:* 877-268-4636, E-mail: cmuglobal@cmich.edu.

Central Michigan University, Central Michigan University Global Campus, Program in Educational Leadership, Mount Pleasant, MI 48859. Offers K-12 leadership (Ed D). *Program availability:* Part-time, evening/weekend. *Faculty:* 14 full-time (5 women), 17 part-time/adjunct (7 women). *Students:* 43 (27 women); includes 13 minority (11 Black or African American, non-Hispanic/Latino; 2 Two or more races, non-Hispanic/Latino). Average age 43. In 2016, 3 doctorates awarded. *Entrance requirements:* Additional exam requirements/recommendations for international students: Required—TOEFL. *Application deadline:* Applications are processed on a rolling basis. Application fee: $50. Electronic applications accepted. *Financial support:* Scholarships/grants available. Support available to part-time students. *Unit head:* Patrick Graham, Coordinator, New Program and Cohort Enrollment Support, 989-774-1661, E-mail: graha1pm@cmich.edu. *Application contact:* 877-268-4636, E-mail: cmuglobal@cmich.edu.

Central Michigan University, College of Graduate Studies, College of Education and Human Services, Department of Educational Leadership, Mount Pleasant, MI 48859. Offers educational leadership (Ed D), including educational technology (Ed D, Ed S), higher education leadership, K-12 curriculum, K-12 leadership; general educational administration (Ed S), including administrative leadership K-12, educational technology (Ed D, Ed S), higher education administration, instructional leadership K-12; school principalship (MA), including charter school leadership, site-based leadership; student affairs administration (MA); teacher leadership (MA). *Program availability:* Part-time, evening/weekend. *Degree requirements:* For master's and Ed S, thesis or alternative; for doctorate, thesis/dissertation. *Entrance requirements:* For doctorate, GRE or MAT, master's degree, minimum GPA of 3.5, 3 years of professional education experience. Electronic applications accepted. *Faculty research:* Elementary administration, secondary administration, student achievement, in-service training, internships in administration.

Central Washington University, Graduate Studies and Research, College of Education and Professional Studies, Department of Advanced Programs, Ellensburg, WA 98926. Offers higher education (M Ed); school administration (M Ed); school instructional leadership (M Ed). *Program availability:* Part-time. *Degree requirements:* For master's, comprehensive exam, thesis or alternative. *Entrance requirements:* Additional exam requirements/recommendations for international students: Required—TOEFL (minimum score 550 paper-based), IELTS (minimum score 6.5). Electronic applications accepted.

Chadron State College, School of Professional and Graduate Studies, Department of Education, Chadron, NE 69337. Offers business (MA Ed); community counseling (MA Ed); educational administration (MS Ed, Sp Ed); elementary education (MS Ed); history (MA Ed); language and literature (MA Ed); secondary administration (MS Ed); secondary education (MS Ed). *Accreditation:* NCATE. *Program availability:* Part-time, evening/weekend, online learning. *Degree requirements:* For master's, thesis optional. *Entrance requirements:* For master's, GRE General Test, GRE Writing Test, minimum GPA of 2.75 or 12 graduate hours at CSC with minimum GPA of 3.25. Additional exam requirements/recommendations for international students: Required—TOEFL. Electronic applications accepted. *Faculty research:* Rural education, technology, mental health.

Chaminade University of Honolulu, Office of Professional and Continuing Education, Program in Education, Honolulu, HI 96816-1578. Offers child development (M Ed); early childhood education (MAT); educational leadership (M Ed); elementary education (MAT); instructional leadership (M Ed); Montessori (M Ed); secondary education (MAT); special education (MAT). *Program availability:* Part-time, evening/weekend, 100% online, blended/hybrid learning. *Faculty:* 7 full-time (4 women), 8 part-time/adjunct (6 women). *Students:* 98 full-time (80 women), 82 part-time (62 women); includes 110 minority (6 Black or African American, non-Hispanic/Latino; 2 American Indian or Alaska Native, non-Hispanic/Latino; 51 Asian, non-Hispanic/Latino; 9 Hispanic/Latino; 41 Native Hawaiian or other Pacific Islander, non-Hispanic/Latino; 1 Two or more races, non-Hispanic/Latino), 1 international. Average age 35. 38 applicants, 100% accepted, 29 enrolled. In 2016, 79 master's awarded. *Degree requirements:* For master's, thesis or alternative. *Entrance requirements:* For master's, PRAXIS (for MAT), minimum GPA of 2.75 (for M Ed), 3.0 (for MAT); 2 letters of recommendation, resume, writing sample (for MAT). Additional exam requirements/recommendations for international students: Required—TOEFL (minimum score 550 paper-based; 79 iBT). *Application deadline:* Applications are processed on a rolling basis. Application fee: $40. Electronic applications accepted. *Expenses:* $740 per credit hour plus $93 fee per online course. *Financial support:* Applicants required to submit FAFSA. *Unit head:* Dr. Dale Fryxell, Interim Dean, 808-739-4684, Fax: 808-739-4607, E-mail: edu-advising@chaminade.edu. *Application contact:* 808-735-4755, E-mail: gradserv@chaminade.edu.
Website: http://www.chaminade.edu/education

Educational Leadership and Administration

Chapman University, College of Educational Studies, Orange, CA 92866. Offers counseling (MA), including school counseling (MA, Credential); education (PhD), including cultural and curricular studies, disability studies, leadership studies, school psychology (PhD, Credential); educational psychology (MA); leadership development (MA); multiple subjects (Credential), including Spanish/English bilingual; pupil personnel services (Credential), including school counseling (MA, Credential), school psychology (PhD, Credential); school psychology (Ed S); single subject (Credential); special education (MA, Credential), including mild/moderate (Credential), moderate/severe (Credential); teaching (MA), including elementary education, secondary education, secondary music education. *Accreditation:* TEAC. *Program availability:* Part-time, evening/weekend. *Faculty:* 29 full-time (14 women), 36 part-time/adjunct (28 women). *Students:* 186 full-time (148 women), 186 part-time (134 women); includes 144 minority (9 Black or African American, non-Hispanic/Latino; 39 Asian, non-Hispanic/Latino; 78 Hispanic/Latino; 2 Native Hawaiian or other Pacific Islander, non-Hispanic/Latino; 16 Two or more races, non-Hispanic/Latino), 8 international. Average age 29. 143 applicants, 63% accepted, 64 enrolled. In 2016, 111 master's, 24 doctorates awarded. *Degree requirements:* For doctorate, thesis/dissertation. *Entrance requirements:* Additional exam requirements/recommendations for international students: Required—TOEFL (minimum score 550 paper-based, 80 iBT), IELTS (6.5), PTE Academic (53), or CAE. *Application deadline:* Applications are processed on a rolling basis. Application fee: $60. Electronic applications accepted. *Expenses:* Contact institution. *Financial support:* Fellowships and scholarships/grants available. Financial award application deadline: 3/2; financial award applicants required to submit FAFSA. *Unit head:* Dr. Margaret Grogan, Dean, 714-516-5968, E-mail: grogan@chapman.edu. *Application contact:* Sara Simon, Graduate Admission Counselor, 714-997-6770, E-mail: simon@chapman.edu.
Website: http://www.chapman.edu/CES/

Charleston Southern University, School of Education, Charleston, SC 29423-8087. Offers elementary administration and supervision (M Ed); elementary education (M Ed); secondary administration and supervision (M Ed). *Accreditation:* NCATE. *Program availability:* Part-time, evening/weekend. *Degree requirements:* For master's, thesis optional. *Entrance requirements:* For master's, GRE or MAT. Additional exam requirements/recommendations for international students: Required—TOEFL (minimum score 550 paper-based; 79 iBT). *Application deadline:* Applications are processed on a rolling basis. Application fee: $40. *Expenses:* Contact institution. *Financial support:* Research assistantships with full tuition reimbursements, career-related internships or fieldwork, and Federal Work-Study available. Financial award application deadline: 4/15; financial award applicants required to submit FAFSA. *Unit head:* Dr. Melanie G. Reynolds-Murphy, Interim Dean, 843-863-7765, Fax: 843-863-7784, E-mail: mmurphy@csuniv.edu. *Application contact:* Dr. Melanie G. Reynolds-Murphy, Interim Dean, 843-863-7765, Fax: 843-863-7784, E-mail: mmurphy@csuniv.edu.
Website: http://www.csuniv.edu/education/

Chestnut Hill College, School of Graduate Studies, Department of Education, Program in Educational Leadership, Philadelphia, PA 19118-2693. Offers M Ed. *Program availability:* Part-time, evening/weekend. *Degree requirements:* For master's, thesis optional. *Entrance requirements:* For master's, PRAXIS I or proof of teaching certification, letters of recommendation, writing sample, 6 graduate credits with minimum B grade if undergraduate GPA less than 3.0. Additional exam requirements/recommendations for international students: Required—TOEFL (minimum score 500 paper-based), IELTS (minimum score 6.0), or TWE (minimum score 22). Electronic applications accepted. *Expenses:* Contact institution. *Faculty research:* Mentoring and induction program.

Cheyney University of Pennsylvania, Graduate Programs, Principal Certification Program (K-12), Cheyney, PA 19319. Offers Certificate. Program also offered on campus of West Chester University of Pennsylvania. *Entrance requirements:* For degree, five years of professional school experience.

Cheyney University of Pennsylvania, Graduate Programs, Program in Educational Leadership, Cheyney, PA 19319. Offers M Ed, Certificate. *Program availability:* Part-time, evening/weekend. *Degree requirements:* For master's, thesis or alternative; for Certificate, internship. *Entrance requirements:* For master's, minimum GPA of 3.0, writing sample. Electronic applications accepted. *Faculty research:* Teacher motivation, critical thinking.

Chicago State University, School of Graduate and Professional Studies, College of Education, Department of Educational Leadership, Curriculum and Foundations, Program in Educational Leadership, Chicago, IL 60628. Offers educational leadership (Ed D); general administration (MA); higher education administration (MA). *Accreditation:* NCATE. *Degree requirements:* For master's, comprehensive exam, thesis optional. *Entrance requirements:* For master's, minimum GPA of 2.75.

Christian Brothers University, School of Arts, Memphis, TN 38104-5581. Offers Catholic studies (MACS); educational leadership (MSEL); teacher-leadership (M Ed); teaching (MAT). *Program availability:* Part-time, evening/weekend. *Entrance requirements:* For master's, GRE, GMAT, PRAXIS II. *Expenses:* Contact institution.

The Citadel, The Military College of South Carolina, Citadel Graduate College, Zucker Family School of Education, Charleston, SC 29409. Offers elementary/secondary school administration and supervision (M Ed); elementary/secondary school counseling (M Ed); interdisciplinary STEM education (M Ed); literacy education (M Ed, Graduate Certificate); middle grades (MAT), including English, mathematics, science, social studies; physical education (grades K-12) (MAT); school superintendency (Ed S); secondary education (MAT), including biology, English, mathematics, social studies; student affairs (Graduate Certificate); student affairs and college counseling (M Ed). *Accreditation:* NCATE. *Program availability:* Part-time, evening/weekend, 100% online, blended/hybrid learning. *Faculty:* 9 full-time (4 women), 9 part-time/adjunct (5 women). *Students:* 70 full-time (58 women), 249 part-time (200 women); includes 87 minority (70 Black or African American, non-Hispanic/Latino; 1 Asian, non-Hispanic/Latino; 9 Hispanic/Latino; 7 Two or more races, non-Hispanic/Latino), 2 international. 146 applicants, 98% accepted, 105 enrolled. In 2016, 85 master's, 7 other advanced degrees awarded. *Degree requirements:* For master's, comprehensive exam (for some programs). *Entrance requirements:* For master's, GRE (minimum combined verbal and quantitative score of 290) or MAT (minimum score 396). Additional exam requirements/recommendations for international students: Required—TOEFL (minimum score 550 paper-based; 79 iBT). *Application deadline:* Applications are processed on a rolling basis. Application fee: $40. Electronic applications accepted. *Expenses:* Tuition, state resident: full-time $5121; part-time $569 per credit hour. Tuition, nonresident: full-time $8613; part-time $957 per credit hour. *Required fees:* $90 per term. *Financial support:* Fellowships and unspecified assistantships available. Support available to part-time students. Financial award application deadline: 7/1; financial award applicants required to submit FAFSA. *Unit head:* Dr. Larry G. Daniel, Dean, 843-953-5097, E-mail: ldaniel@citadel.edu. *Application contact:* Dr. Tammy J. Graham, Associate Professor, 843-953-6854, E-mail: tammy.graham@citadel.edu.
Website: http://www.citadel.edu/root/education-graduate-programs

City College of the City University of New York, Graduate School, School of Education, Department of Leadership and Special Education, New York, NY 10031-9198. Offers educational leadership (MS, AC); teacher of students with disabilities in adolescent education (MS Ed); teacher of students with disabilities in childhood education (MS Ed). *Degree requirements:* For master's, thesis, research paper. *Entrance requirements:* For master's, Liberal Arts and Sciences Test (LAST), Content Specialty Test (CST), interview; minimum GPA of 3.0 in major, 2.5 overall. Additional exam requirements/recommendations for international students: Required—TOEFL. Tuition and fees vary according to course load, degree level and program. *Faculty research:* Dynamics of organizational change, impact of laws on educational policy, leadership development in schools.

City University of Seattle, Graduate Division, Albright School of Education, Seattle, WA 98121. Offers administrator certification (Certificate); curriculum and instruction (M Ed); elementary education (MIT); guidance and counseling (M Ed); leadership (M Ed); reading and literacy (M Ed); school counseling (M Ed); special education (MIT); superintendent certification (Certificate). *Program availability:* Part-time, evening/weekend, online learning. *Degree requirements:* For master's, comprehensive exam (for some programs), thesis (for some programs). *Entrance requirements:* For master's, baccalaureate degree or equivalent from an accredited or otherwise recognized institution. Additional exam requirements/recommendations for international students: Required—TOEFL (minimum score 567 paper-based; 87 iBT); Recommended—IELTS. Electronic applications accepted. *Expenses:* Contact institution.

City University of Seattle, Graduate Division, Division of Doctoral Studies, Seattle, WA 98121. Offers leadership (Ed D). *Program availability:* Online learning. *Entrance requirements:* For doctorate, master's degree from an accredited or otherwise recognized institution; resume/curriculum vitae that demonstrates two or more years in a leadership capacity; interview with a member of the program faculty.

Claremont Graduate University, Graduate Programs, School of Educational Studies, Claremont, CA 91711-6160. Offers Africana education (Certificate); education and policy (MA, PhD); higher education/student affairs (MA, PhD); human development (MA, PhD); public school administration (MA, PhD); quantitative evaluation (MA, PhD); special education (MA, PhD); teacher education (MA); teaching and learning (MA, PhD); urban leadership (PhD); MBA/PhD. PhD program offered jointly with San Diego State University. *Program availability:* Part-time. *Faculty:* 14 full-time (9 women), 1 part-time/adjunct (0 women). *Students:* 195 full-time (143 women), 196 part-time (137 women); includes 217 minority (43 Black or African American, non-Hispanic/Latino; 4 American Indian or Alaska Native, non-Hispanic/Latino; 32 Asian, non-Hispanic/Latino; 117 Hispanic/Latino; 2 Native Hawaiian or other Pacific Islander, non-Hispanic/Latino; 19 Two or more races, non-Hispanic/Latino), 14 international. Average age 38. In 2016, 48 master's, 39 doctorates, 7 other advanced degrees awarded. Terminal master's awarded for partial completion of doctoral program. *Entrance requirements:* For master's and doctorate, GRE General Test. Additional exam requirements/recommendations for international students: Required—TOEFL (minimum score 75 iBT). *Application deadline:* For fall admission, 3/1 priority date for domestic and international students. Applications are processed on a rolling basis. Application fee: $80. Electronic applications accepted. *Expenses: Tuition:* Full-time $44,328; part-time $1847 per unit. *Required fees:* $600; $300 per semester. Tuition and fees vary according to course load and program. *Financial support:* Fellowships, research assistantships, Federal Work-Study, institutionally sponsored loans, and scholarships/grants available. Support available to part-time students. Financial award application deadline: 2/15; financial award applicants required to submit FAFSA. *Faculty research:* Education administration, K-12 and higher education, multicultural education, education policy, diversity in higher education, faculty issues. *Unit head:* Allen Omoto, Dean, 909-607-3786, E-mail: allen.omoto@cgu.edu. *Application contact:* Rachel Camacho, Senior Assistant Director of Admission, 909-607-9418, E-mail: camacho@cgu.edu.
Website: https://www.cgu.edu/school/school-of-educational-studies/

Clark Atlanta University, School of Education, Department of Educational Leadership, Atlanta, GA 30314. Offers MA, Ed D, Ed S. *Program availability:* Part-time, evening/weekend. *Faculty:* 4 full-time (2 women), 8 part-time/adjunct (6 women). *Students:* 50 full-time (27 women), 39 part-time (24 women); includes 65 minority (63 Black or African American, non-Hispanic/Latino; 1 Asian, non-Hispanic/Latino; 1 Hispanic/Latino), 14 international. Average age 36. 26 applicants, 81% accepted, 12 enrolled. In 2016, 8 master's, 12 doctorates, 2 other advanced degrees awarded. *Degree requirements:* For master's and Ed S, comprehensive exam; for doctorate, comprehensive exam, thesis/dissertation. *Entrance requirements:* For master's, GRE General Test, minimum undergraduate GPA of 2.6; for doctorate and Ed S, GRE General Test, minimum graduate GPA of 3.0. Additional exam requirements/recommendations for international students: Required—TOEFL (minimum score 500 paper-based; 61 iBT). *Application deadline:* For fall admission, 4/1 for domestic and international students; for spring admission, 11/1 for domestic and international students. Applications are processed on a rolling basis. Application fee: $40 ($55 for international students). Electronic applications accepted. *Expenses: Tuition:* Full-time $15,498; part-time $861 per credit hour. *Required fees:* $1326; $1326 per credit hour. Tuition and fees vary according to course load. *Financial support:* Career-related internships or fieldwork, Federal Work-Study, scholarships/grants, and unspecified assistantships available. Support available to part-time students. Financial award application deadline: 4/30; financial award applicants required to submit FAFSA. *Unit head:* Dr. Barbara Hill, Chairperson, 404-880-6126, E-mail: bhill@cau.edu. *Application contact:* Graduate Program Admissions, 404-880-8483, E-mail: graduateadmissions@cau.edu.

Clarke University, Program in Education, Dubuque, IA 52001-3198. Offers instructional leadership (MAE). *Program availability:* Part-time, 100% online, blended/hybrid learning. *Faculty:* 6 full-time (all women), 1 (woman) part-time/adjunct. *Students:* 6 full-time (all women), 13 part-time (all women); includes 2 minority (1 Hispanic/Latino; 1 Two or more races, non-Hispanic/Latino). Average age 26. 17 applicants, 82% accepted, 10 enrolled. In 2016, 16 master's awarded. *Degree requirements:* For master's, thesis optional. *Entrance requirements:* For master's, official transcripts documenting completion of undergraduate degree from accredited college or university, copy of teaching certificates and licenses, two recommendation forms, statement of goals and career plans, minimum GPA of 2.75. Additional exam requirements/recommendations for international students: Required—TOEFL (minimum score 550 paper-based, 80 iBT) or IELTS (6.5). *Application deadline:* Applications are processed on a rolling basis. Application fee: $35. Electronic applications accepted. *Expenses:* $500 per credit. *Financial support:* Applicants required to submit FAFSA. *Unit head:* Dr. Paula Schmidt, Director of Graduate Education, 563-588-6573, E-mail: paula.schmidt@clarke.edu. *Application contact:* Kimberly Roush, Director of Admission, Graduate and Adult Programs, 563-588-6539, Fax: 563-552-7994, E-mail: graduate@clarke.edu.

Clarks Summit University, Graduate Studies, South Abington Township, PA 18411. Offers Bible (MA); counseling (MA, MS); curriculum and instruction (M Ed); educational administration (M Ed); intercultural studies (MA); literature (MA); missions (MA); organizational leadership (MA); reading specialist (M Ed); secondary English/communications (M Ed); social entrepreneurship (MA); worldview studies (MA). MA in missions program available only for Association of Baptists for World Evangelism missionary personnel. *Program availability:* Part-time, evening/weekend, online learning. *Entrance requirements:* Additional exam requirements/recommendations for international students: Required—TOEFL (minimum score 500 paper-based).

Clemson University, Graduate School, College of Education, Clemson, SC 29634-0702. Offers administration and supervision (K-12) (M Ed, Ed S); education and organizational leadership (MS), including athletic leadership; educational leadership (PhD), including P-12; human resource development (MHRD); middle-level education (MAT). *Program availability:* Part-time, evening/weekend, 100% online. *Faculty:* 75 full-time (54 women), 1 part-time/adjunct (0 women). *Students:* 120 full-time (84 women), 309 part-time (206 women); includes 96 minority (68 Black or African American, non-Hispanic/Latino; 1 American Indian or Alaska Native, non-Hispanic/Latino; 3 Asian, non-Hispanic/Latino; 19 Hispanic/Latino; 5 Two or more races, non-Hispanic/Latino), 11 international. Average age 34. 417 applicants, 50% accepted, 133 enrolled. In 2016, 239 master's, 21 doctorates, 59 other advanced degrees awarded. *Degree requirements:* For master's, comprehensive exam (for some programs), thesis (for some programs); for doctorate, comprehensive exam, thesis/dissertation. *Entrance requirements:* For master's, doctorate, and other advanced degree, GRE General Test, unofficial transcripts, letters of recommendation. Additional exam requirements/recommendations for international students: Required—TOEFL (minimum score 80 iBT), IELTS (minimum score 7). *Application deadline:* Applications are processed on a rolling basis. Application fee: $80 ($90 for international students). Electronic applications accepted. *Expenses:* Contact institution. *Financial support:* In 2016–17, 75 students received support, including 22 fellowships with partial tuition reimbursements available (averaging $6,316 per year), 28 research assistantships with partial tuition reimbursements available (averaging $15,399 per year), 5 teaching assistantships with partial tuition reimbursements available (averaging $30,000 per year); unspecified assistantships also available. *Faculty research:* Early literacy and motivation, STEAM education, legal/policy issues in education, leadership, special education interventions/assessment/policy. *Total annual research expenditures:* $2.8 million. *Unit head:* Dr. George Petersen, Dean, 864-656-4444, Fax: 864-656-0311, E-mail: soedean@clemson.edu. *Application contact:* Dr. David Fleming, Graduate Programs Coordinator, 864-656-1881, Fax: 864-656-0311, E-mail: dflemin@clemson.edu.
Website: http://www.clemson.edu/education/

Clemson University, Graduate School, College of Education, Department of Educational and Organizational Leadership Development, Program in Administration and Supervision, Clemson, SC 29634. Offers M Ed, Ed S. *Program availability:* Part-time, evening/weekend. *Faculty:* 20 full-time (13 women), 1 part-time/adjunct (0 women). *Students:* 1 (woman) full-time, 76 part-time (61 women); includes 15 minority (10 Black or African American, non-Hispanic/Latino; 4 Hispanic/Latino; 1 Two or more races, non-Hispanic/Latino). Average age 33. 40 applicants, 85% accepted, 31 enrolled. In 2016, 25 master's, 21 Ed Ss awarded. *Degree requirements:* For master's, comprehensive exam, PRAXIS; for Ed S, comprehensive exam. *Entrance requirements:* For master's, GRE General Test, unofficial transcripts, statement of interest, letters of recommendation; for Ed S, GRE General Test, 1 year of teaching experience. Additional exam requirements/recommendations for international students: Required—TOEFL (minimum score 80 iBT), IELTS (minimum score 7). *Application deadline:* For fall admission, 6/10 for domestic students; for summer admission, 4/10 for domestic students. Applications are processed on a rolling basis. Application fee: $80 ($90 for international students). Electronic applications accepted. *Expenses:* $4,027 per semester full-time resident, $8,013 per semester full-time non-resident, $437 per credit hour part-time resident, $874 per credit hour part-time non-resident. *Faculty research:* School finance, educational assessment and accountability policies, politics of education, school improvement, complex organizations, school law. *Unit head:* Dr. George Petersen, Dean, School of Education, 864-656-4444, Fax: 864-656-0311, E-mail: soedean@clemson.edu. *Application contact:* Dr. Frederick Buskey, Graduate Program Coordinator, 864-656-4777, E-mail: bbuskey@clemson.edu.
Website: http://www.clemson.edu/education/academics/masters-specialist-programs/masters-administration-supervision/index.html

Clemson University, Graduate School, College of Education, Department of Educational and Organizational Leadership Development, Program in Educational Leadership, Clemson, SC 29634. Offers educational leadership (PhD), including higher education, P-12. *Accreditation:* NCATE. *Program availability:* Part-time, evening/weekend. *Faculty:* 12 full-time (5 women). *Students:* 29 full-time (20 women), 76 part-time (44 women); includes 24 minority (22 Black or African American, non-Hispanic/Latino; 2 Hispanic/Latino), 3 international. Average age 39. 31 applicants, 32% accepted, 6 enrolled. In 2016, 13 doctorates awarded. *Degree requirements:* For doctorate, comprehensive exam, thesis/dissertation, preliminary exam. *Entrance requirements:* For doctorate, GRE General Test, unofficial transcripts, letters of recommendation. Additional exam requirements/recommendations for international students: Required—TOEFL (minimum score 80 iBT), IELTS (minimum score 7). *Application deadline:* For fall admission, 3/1 priority date for domestic and international students; for spring admission, 10/1 priority date for domestic and international students. Application fee: $80 ($90 for international students). Electronic applications accepted. *Expenses:* $4,264 per semester full-time resident, $8,485 per semester full-time non-resident, $471 per credit hour part-time resident, $942 per credit hour part-time non-resident. *Financial support:* In 2016–17, 29 students received support, including 5 fellowships with partial tuition reimbursements available (averaging $5,000 per year), 7 research assistantships with partial tuition reimbursements available (averaging $14,596 per year), 1 teaching assistantship with partial tuition reimbursement available (averaging $18,000 per year); unspecified assistantships also available. Financial award application deadline: 3/1. *Faculty research:* Higher education leadership, P-12 educational leadership. *Unit head:* Dr. George Petersen, Dean, 864-656-4444, Fax: 864-656-0311, E-mail: soedean@clemson.edu. *Application contact:* Dr. Frederick Buskey, Program Coordinator, 864-656-4777, E-mail: bbuskey@clemson.edu.
Website: http://www.clemson.edu/education/departments/educational-organizational-leadership-development/academics/index.html

Cleveland State University, College of Graduate Studies, College of Education and Human Services, Department of Counseling, Administration, Supervision and Adult Learning (CASAL), Cleveland, OH 44115. Offers adult learning and development (M Ed), counselor education (PhD); early childhood mental health counseling (Certificate); educational administration and supervision (M Ed). *Accreditation:* ACA (one or more programs are accredited). *Program availability:* Part-time, evening/weekend. *Faculty:* 15 full-time (8 women), 19 part-time/adjunct (10 women). *Students:* 104 full-time (85 women), 259 part-time (197 women); includes 138 minority (115 Black or African American, non-Hispanic/Latino; 1 American Indian or Alaska Native, non-Hispanic/Latino; 3 Asian, non-Hispanic/Latino; 16 Hispanic/Latino; 3 Two or more races, non-Hispanic/Latino), 8 international. Average age 34. 57 applicants, 93% accepted, 51 enrolled. In 2016, 102 master's awarded. *Degree requirements:* For master's, comprehensive exam (for some programs), thesis optional, internship. *Entrance requirements:* For master's, GRE General Test or MAT, letter of recommendation and minimum GPA of 2.75 (for counseling); 2 letters of recommendation and interviews (for organizational leadership). Additional exam requirements/recommendations for international students: Required—TOEFL (minimum score 550 paper-based; 78 iBT), IELTS (minimum score 6). *Application deadline:* For fall admission, 6/21 for domestic students, 5/15 for international students; for spring admission, 8/31 for domestic students, 11/1 for international students. Application fee: $40. Electronic applications accepted. *Expenses:* Tuition, state resident: full-time $9565. Tuition, nonresident: full-time $17,980. Tuition and fees vary according to program. *Financial support:* In 2016–17, 19 students received support, including 10 research assistantships with tuition reimbursements available (averaging $11,882 per year), 5 teaching assistantships with tuition reimbursements available (averaging $11,882 per year); scholarships/grants and unspecified assistantships also available. Support available to part-time students. *Faculty research:* Education law, career development, bullying, psychopharmacology, counseling and spirituality. *Total annual research expenditures:* $225,821. *Unit head:* Dr. Ann L. Bauer, Chairperson, 216-687-4582, Fax: 216-687-5378, E-mail: a.l.bauer@csuohio.edu. *Application contact:* Deborah L. Brown, Interim Assistant Director, Graduate Admissions, 216-523-7572, Fax: 216-687-5400, E-mail: d.l.brown@csuohio.edu.
Website: http://www.csuohio.edu/cehs/departments/CASAL/casal_dept.html

Cleveland State University, College of Graduate Studies, College of Education and Human Services, Program in Urban Education, Specialization in School Administration, Cleveland, OH 44115. Offers PhD. *Program availability:* Part-time. *Faculty:* 4 full-time (0 women). *Students:* 8 part-time (3 women); includes 4 minority (3 Black or African American, non-Hispanic/Latino; 1 Hispanic/Latino). Average age 38. 10 applicants, 40% accepted. In 2016, 3 doctorates awarded. *Degree requirements:* For doctorate, one foreign language, comprehensive exam, thesis/dissertation. *Entrance requirements:* For doctorate, GRE General Test (minimum score of 297 for combined Verbal and Quantitative exams, 4.0 preferred for Analytical Writing), minimum graduate GPA of 3.25, curriculum vitae or resume, personal statement, 2 letters of recommendation. Additional exam requirements/recommendations for international students: Required—TOEFL (minimum score 550 paper-based; 78 iBT), IELTS (minimum score 6). *Application deadline:* For fall admission, 1/15 for domestic and international students. Application fee: $40. Electronic applications accepted. *Expenses:* Tuition, state resident: full-time $9565. Tuition, nonresident: full-time $17,980. Tuition and fees vary according to program. *Financial support:* In 2016–17, 1 student received support, including 1 teaching assistantship with full tuition reimbursement available (averaging $5,900 per year); tuition waivers also available. Support available to part-time students. Financial award application deadline: 4/1; financial award applicants required to submit FAFSA. *Faculty research:* Theory and practice of management and leadership in educational, government, human resource development, and social service settings. *Unit head:* Dr. Graham Stead, Director, Doctoral Studies, 216-687-3828, E-mail: g.b.stead@csuohio.edu. *Application contact:* Rita M. Grabowski, Administrative Coordinator, 216-687-4697, Fax: 216-875-9697, E-mail: r.grabowski@csuohio.edu.
Website: http://www.csuohio.edu/cehs/casal/programs-1

Coastal Carolina University, Spadoni College of Education, Conway, SC 29528-6054. Offers education (MAT); educational leadership (M Ed, Ed S); English for speakers of other languages (Certificate); instructional technology (M Ed, Ed S); learning and teaching (M Ed); online teaching and training (Certificate); special education (M Ed). *Accreditation:* NCATE. *Program availability:* Part-time, evening/weekend. *Faculty:* 16 full-time (8 women), 12 part-time/adjunct (7 women). *Students:* 74 full-time (48 women), 340 part-time (271 women); includes 78 minority (70 Black or African American, non-Hispanic/Latino; 1 American Indian or Alaska Native, non-Hispanic/Latino; 2 Asian, non-Hispanic/Latino; 4 Hispanic/Latino; 1 Two or more races, non-Hispanic/Latino), 2 international. Average age 33. 298 applicants, 93% accepted, 213 enrolled. In 2016, 167 master's, 8 other advanced degrees awarded. *Degree requirements:* For master's and other advanced degree, comprehensive exam. *Entrance requirements:* For master's, GRE, GMAT, 2 letters of recommendation, evidence of teacher certification, official transcripts; for other advanced degree, official transcripts, minimum of 3 years' teaching experience, statement of interest in the program, 3 letters of reference, master's degree in educational leadership or related field with minimum overall GPA of 3.0. Additional exam requirements/recommendations for international students: Required—TOEFL (minimum score 550 paper-based; 79 iBT), IELTS (minimum score 6.5). *Application deadline:* For fall admission, 7/1 priority date for domestic and international students; for spring admission, 11/1 priority date for domestic and international students; for summer admission, 3/1 priority date for domestic and international students. Applications are processed on a rolling basis. Application fee: $45. Electronic applications accepted. *Expenses:* Tuition, state resident: full-time $9990; part-time $555 per credit hour. Tuition, nonresident: full-time $18,108; part-time $1006 per credit hour. *Required fees:* $90; $5 per credit hour. *Financial support:* Fellowships, research assistantships, and unspecified assistantships available. Support available to part-time students. Financial award application deadline: 3/1; financial award applicants required to submit FAFSA. *Unit head:* Dr. Edward Jadallah, Dean, 843-349-2773, Fax: 843-349-2106, E-mail: ejadalla@coastal.edu. *Application contact:* Dr. James O. Luken, Associate Provost/Vice-Dean of the Coastal Environment, 843-349-2235, Fax: 843-349-6444, E-mail: joluken@coastal.edu.
Website: http://www.coastal.edu/education/

The College at Brockport, State University of New York, School of Education, Health, and Human Services, Department of Counselor Education, Brockport, NY 14420-2997. Offers college counseling (MS Ed, CAS); mental health counseling (MS, CAS); school counseling (MS Ed, CAS); school counselor supervision (CAS). *Accreditation:* ACA (one or more programs are accredited). *Program availability:* Part-time. *Faculty:* 5 full-time (3 women), 6 part-time/adjunct (4 women). *Students:* 26 full-time (20 women), 75 part-time (60 women); includes 22 minority (12 Black or African American, non-Hispanic/Latino; 1 American Indian or Alaska Native, non-Hispanic/Latino; 1 Asian, non-Hispanic/Latino; 3 Hispanic/Latino; 5 Two or more races, non-Hispanic/Latino). 102 applicants, 34% accepted, 26 enrolled. In 2016, 20 master's, 4 other advanced degrees awarded. *Degree requirements:* For master's, thesis, internship. *Entrance requirements:* For master's, group interview, letters of recommendation, written objectives, audio response; for CAS, master's degree, New York state school counselor certificate. Additional exam requirements/recommendations for international students: Required—TOEFL (minimum score 550 paper-based; 79 iBT), IELTS (minimum score 6.5). *Application deadline:* For fall admission, 2/1 priority date for domestic and international students; for spring admission, 9/1 priority date for domestic and international students; for summer admission, 2/1 priority date for domestic and international students. Application fee: $80. Electronic applications accepted. *Expenses:* Contact institution. *Financial support:* In 2016–17, 1 fellowship with full tuition reimbursement (averaging $7,500 per year), 1 teaching assistantship with full tuition reimbursement (averaging $6,000 per year) were awarded; Federal Work-Study, scholarships/grants, and unspecified assistantships also available. Support available to part-time students. Financial award application deadline: 3/15; financial award applicants required to submit FAFSA. *Faculty research:* Gender and diversity issues; counseling outcomes; spirituality; school, college and mental health counseling; obesity. *Unit head:* Dr. Susan Seem, Chair, 585-395-5492, Fax: 585-395-2366, E-mail: sseem@brockport.edu. *Application contact:* Danielle A. Welch, Graduate Admissions Counselor, 585-395-5465, Fax: 585-395-2515.
Website: http://www.brockport.edu/edc/

The College at Brockport, State University of New York, School of Education, Health, and Human Services, Department of Educational Administration, Brockport, NY 14420-2997. Offers school building leader (CAS); school building leader/school district leader (CAS); school district business leader (CAS); school district leader (CAS); teacher leadership (Graduate Certificate). *Program availability:* Part-time. *Faculty:* 3 full-

time (1 woman), 6 part-time/adjunct (3 women). *Students:* 7 full-time (4 women), 91 part-time (59 women); includes 5 minority (2 Black or African American, non-Hispanic/Latino; 1 American Indian or Alaska Native, non-Hispanic/Latino; 1 Hispanic/Latino; 1 Two or more races, non-Hispanic/Latino). 31 applicants, 90% accepted, 25 enrolled. In 2016, 50 CASs awarded. *Degree requirements:* For other advanced degree, thesis or alternative, internship. *Entrance requirements:* For degree, minimum GPA of 3.0, letter of recommendation. Additional exam requirements/recommendations for international students: Required—TOEFL (minimum score 550 paper-based; 79 iBT), IELTS (minimum score 6.5). *Application deadline:* For fall admission, 7/15 priority date for domestic and international students; for spring admission, 11/15 priority date for domestic and international students. Application fee: $80. Electronic applications accepted. *Expenses:* Contact institution. *Financial support:* Federal Work-Study, scholarships/grants, and unspecified assistantships available. Support available to part-time students. Financial award application deadline: 3/15; financial award applicants required to submit FAFSA. *Faculty research:* Superintendency, budgeting, school business administration, leadership, special education administration. *Unit head:* Jeffrey Linn, Graduate Director, 585-395-2661, Fax: 585-395-2172, E-mail: jlinn@brockport.edu. *Application contact:* Danielle A. Welch, Graduate Admissions Counselor, 585-395-2525, Fax: 585-395-2515.
Website: http://www.brockport.edu/edadmin/

The College of New Jersey, Office of Graduate and Advancing Education, School of Education, Department of Educational Administration and Secondary Education, Program in Educational Leadership, Ewing, NJ 08628. Offers M Ed, Certificate. *Program availability:* Part-time, evening/weekend. *Degree requirements:* For master's, comprehensive exam. *Entrance requirements:* For master's, GRE, minimum GPA of 3.0 in field or 2.75 overall; for Certificate, previous master's degree or higher. Additional exam requirements/recommendations for international students: Required—TOEFL. Electronic applications accepted.

The College of New Rochelle, Graduate School, Division of Education, Program in Educational Leadership, New Rochelle, NY 10805-2308. Offers school building leader (MS, Advanced Certificate); school district leader (MS, Advanced Diploma). *Degree requirements:* For master's, internship. *Entrance requirements:* For master's, interview, minimum GPA of 3.0 in field, 2.7 overall, minimum 3 years teaching or education administration experience.

College of Saint Elizabeth, Department of Educational Leadership, Morristown, NJ 07960-6989. Offers assistive technology (Certificate); education (MA); educational leadership (MA, Ed D). *Program availability:* Part-time. *Degree requirements:* For master's, thesis or alternative; for doctorate, thesis/dissertation. *Entrance requirements:* For master's, GRE, GMAT, baccalaureate degree with minimum GPA of 2.75, standard teaching certificate, three years of exemplary certified teaching experience, writing sample, two letters of recommendation from school(s) of employment, personal interiew (for educational leadership); for doctorate, GRE, MA in educational leadership or related field; leadership experience including certification as principal and/or supervisor; letter of recommendation from college/university professor attesting to candidate's ability to perform a high level of academic work in the program; for Certificate, MA in education; certification; baccalaureate degree with minimum GPA of 2.75; personal written statement; two letters of recommendation; official transcripts from all colleges attended. Additional exam requirements/recommendations for international students: Required—TOEFL (minimum score 550 paper-based; 79 iBT), IELTS (minimum score 6.5). Electronic applications accepted. Application fee is waived when completed online. *Expenses:* Contact institution.

College of Saint Mary, Program in Education, Omaha, NE 68106. Offers assessment leadership (MSE); English as a second language (MSE). *Program availability:* Part-time. *Entrance requirements:* For master's, technology competency test or equivalent, minimum cumulative GPA of 3.0, teaching certificate, 2 letters of reference, resume.

The College of Saint Rose, Graduate Studies, Thelma P. Lally School of Education, Programs in Educational Leadership and Administration, Albany, NY 12203-1419. Offers educational leadership (MS Ed); school building leader (Certificate); school district business leader (Certificate); school district leader (Certificate). *Program availability:* Part-time, evening/weekend. *Students:* 78 full-time (57 women), 738 part-time (582 women); includes 329 minority (164 Black or African American, non-Hispanic/Latino; 3 American Indian or Alaska Native, non-Hispanic/Latino; 32 Asian, non-Hispanic/Latino; 120 Hispanic/Latino; 1 Native Hawaiian or other Pacific Islander, non-Hispanic/Latino; 9 Two or more races, non-Hispanic/Latino), 1 international. Average age 37. 493 applicants, 77% accepted, 349 enrolled. In 2016, 89 master's, 579 Certificates awarded. *Degree requirements:* For master's, comprehensive exam or thesis. *Entrance requirements:* For master's, minimum undergraduate GPA of 3.0, timed writing sample, interview, permanent certification or 3 years of teaching experience. Additional exam requirements/recommendations for international students: Required—TOEFL (minimum score 550 paper-based; 80 iBT), IELTS (minimum score 6), PTE (minimum score 56). *Application deadline:* For fall admission, 4/1 priority date for domestic and international students; for spring admission, 10/15 priority date for domestic and international students; for summer admission, 3/15 priority date for domestic students, 3/14 priority date for international students. Applications are processed on a rolling basis. Application fee: $40. Electronic applications accepted. *Expenses: Tuition:* Full-time $14,382; part-time $799 per credit. *Required fees:* $814; $32 per credit. $88 per semester. Tuition and fees vary according to course load. *Financial support:* Career-related internships or fieldwork, scholarships/grants, tuition waivers (partial), and unspecified assistantships available. Support available to part-time students. Financial award application deadline: 4/15. *Unit head:* Dr. Kevin S. Baughman, Program Director, 518-454-5259, E-mail: baughmak@strose.edu. *Application contact:* Cris Murray, Assistant Vice President for Graduate Recruitment and Enrollment, 518-485-3390, Fax: 518-458-5479, E-mail: grad@strose.edu.
Website: https://www.strose.edu/educational-leadership-and-administration/

The College of Saint Rose, Graduate Studies, Thelma P. Lally School of Education, Programs in Higher Education Leadership and Administration, Albany, NY 12203-1419. Offers MS Ed, Advanced Certificate. *Program availability:* Part-time, evening/weekend. *Students:* 17 part-time (7 women); includes 3 minority (2 Black or African American, non-Hispanic/Latino; 1 Hispanic/Latino), 1 international. Average age 31. 13 applicants, 85% accepted, 5 enrolled. In 2016, 11 master's, 1 Advanced Certificate awarded. *Degree requirements:* For master's, capstone seminar. *Entrance requirements:* For master's, resume, letter of recommendation. Additional exam requirements/recommendations for international students: Required—TOEFL (minimum score 550 paper-based; 80 iBT), IELTS (minimum score 6), PTE (minimum score 56). *Application deadline:* For fall admission, 4/1 priority date for domestic and international students; for spring admission, 10/15 priority date for domestic and international students; for summer admission, 3/15 priority date for domestic and international students. Applications are processed on a rolling basis. Application fee: $40. Electronic applications accepted. *Expenses: Tuition:* Full-time $14,382; part-time $799 per credit. *Required fees:* $814; $32 per credit. $88 per semester. Tuition and fees vary according to course load. *Financial support:* Scholarships/grants, tuition waivers (partial), and unspecified assistantships available. Support available to part-time students. Financial award application deadline: 4/15. *Unit head:* Dr. R. Mark Sullivan, Director, 518-454-5122, E-mail: sullivam@strose.edu. *Application contact:* Cris Murray, Assistant Vice President for Graduate Recruitment and Enrollment, 518-454-5136, Fax: 518-458-5479, E-mail: grad@strose.edu.
Website: https://www.strose.edu/higher-education-leadership-and-administration/

College of Staten Island of the City University of New York, Graduate Programs, School of Education, Program in Leadership in Education, Staten Island, NY 10314-6600. Offers school administrator and supervisor (Post-Master's Certificate); school building leader (Post-Master's Certificate); school district leader (Post-Master's Certificate). *Program availability:* Part-time, evening/weekend. *Faculty:* 2 full-time, 3 part-time/adjunct. *Students:* 36 part-time. Average age 36. 29 applicants, 86% accepted, 23 enrolled. In 2016, 26 Post-Master's Certificates awarded. *Degree requirements:* For Post-Master's Certificate, 30 credits within a cohort model: 24 credits in supervision, administration, curriculum, policy analysis, human relations; theory, research, and practice in educational leadership; 6 credits in a field experience seminar (SBL/SDL); 9 credits with courses including a fieldwork component and project over district level issues (SDL). *Entrance requirements:* For degree, master's degree with minimum GPA of 3.0, 3 professional recommendations, letter of intent, interview with faculty. Additional exam requirements/recommendations for international students: Required—TOEFL (minimum score 550 paper-based; 79 iBT), IELTS (minimum score 6.5). *Application deadline:* For fall admission, 6/20 priority date for domestic and international students; for spring admission, 12/2 priority date for domestic and international students. Applications are processed on a rolling basis. Application fee: $125. Electronic applications accepted. *Expenses:* Tuition, state resident: full-time $10,130; part-time $425 per credit. Tuition, nonresident: full-time $18,720; part-time $780 per credit. *Required fees:* $181.10 per semester. Tuition and fees vary according to program. *Faculty research:* Supervision of instruction, school-community partnerships, education reform, history of education, organizational theory. *Unit head:* Dr. Ruth Powers-Silverberg, Graduate Faculty Advisor, 718-982-3726, E-mail: ruth.silverberg@csi.cuny.edu. *Application contact:* Sasha Spence, Associate Director for Graduate Admissions, 718-982-2019, Fax: 718-982-2500, E-mail: sasha.spence@csi.cuny.edu.
Website: http://www.csi.cuny.edu/catalog/graduate/graduate-programs-in-education.htm#o2614

The College of William and Mary, School of Education, Program in Education Policy, Planning, and Leadership, Williamsburg, VA 23187-8795. Offers curriculum and educational technology (PhD); curriculum leadership (Ed D, PhD); educational leadership (M Ed), including higher education administration (M Ed, Ed D, PhD), K-12 administration and supervision; educational policy, planning, and leadership (Ed D, PhD), including general education administration, gifted education administration, higher education administration (M Ed, Ed D, PhD). *Accreditation:* NCATE. *Program availability:* Part-time, evening/weekend. *Faculty:* 20 full-time (10 women), 21 part-time/adjunct (13 women). *Students:* 63 full-time (45 women), 143 part-time (95 women); includes 53 minority (39 Black or African American, non-Hispanic/Latino; 4 Asian, non-Hispanic/Latino; 6 Hispanic/Latino; 4 Two or more races, non-Hispanic/Latino), 4 international. Average age 38. 122 applicants, 77% accepted, 65 enrolled. In 2016, 26 master's, 24 doctorates awarded. *Degree requirements:* For doctorate, comprehensive exam, thesis/dissertation. *Entrance requirements:* For master's, GRE or MAT, minimum GPA of 2.5; for doctorate, GRE or MAT, minimum GPA of 3.0. Additional exam requirements/recommendations for international students: Required—TOEFL (minimum score 100 iBT), IELTS (minimum score 7). *Application deadline:* For fall admission, 1/15 for domestic and international students. Application fee: $50. Electronic applications accepted. *Expenses:* $14,258 per year in-state full-time, $275 per credit in-state part-time; $30,500 per year out-of-state full-time, $1,200 per credit out-of-state part-time. *Financial support:* In 2016–17, 64 students received support, including 1 fellowship (averaging $20,000 per year), 54 research assistantships (averaging $19,668 per year); institutionally sponsored loans, scholarships/grants, and unspecified assistantships also available. Support available to part-time students. Financial award application deadline: 1/15; financial award applicants required to submit FAFSA. *Faculty research:* Higher education policy, evaluation of teachers, program evaluation, civil rights and higher education, program evaluation. *Unit head:* Dr. Michael F. Dipaola, Department Chair, 757-221-2344, E-mail: mfdipa@wm.edu. *Application contact:* Dorothy Smith Osborne, Assistant Dean for Academic Programs and Student Services, 757-221-2317, E-mail: dsosbo@wm.edu.
Website: http://education.wm.edu

Colorado Mesa University, Center for Teacher Education, Grand Junction, CO 81501-3122. Offers educational leadership (MAEd); English for speakers of other languages (MAEd); exceptional learner/special education (MAEd); teacher education (Graduate Certificate); teacher leader (MAEd). *Accreditation:* NCATE. *Program availability:* Part-time. *Faculty:* 6 full-time (5 women), 12 part-time/adjunct (6 women). *Students:* 18 full-time (13 women), 35 part-time (28 women); includes 4 minority (1 American Indian or Alaska Native, non-Hispanic/Latino; 3 Hispanic/Latino), 1 international. Average age 34. 28 applicants, 25% accepted, 6 enrolled. In 2016, 26 master's, 36 other advanced degrees awarded. *Degree requirements:* For master's, comprehensive exam (for some programs), capstone presentation. *Entrance requirements:* For master's, 3 professional letters of recommendation, Colorado teaching license, minimum baccalaureate GPA of 3.0; for Graduate Certificate, minimum baccalaureate GPA of 3.0. Additional exam requirements/recommendations for international students: Required—TOEFL (minimum score 550 paper-based). *Application deadline:* For fall admission, 6/1 priority date for domestic and international students; for spring admission, 11/1 priority date for domestic and international students; for summer admission, 3/1 priority date for domestic and international students. Applications are processed on a rolling basis. Application fee: $50. Electronic applications accepted. *Expenses:* $406.43 per credit hour resident tuition and fees, $1,092.43 per credit hour non-resident tuition and fees. *Financial support:* In 2016–17, 2 students received support. Scholarships/grants available. Financial award applicants required to submit FAFSA. *Faculty research:* K-8 STEM instruction, special education inclusion, elementary math literacy, secondary literacy, elementary/early childhood education literacy. *Unit head:* Dr. Blake Bickham, Department Head, 970-248-1729, E-mail: bbickham@coloradomesa.edu. *Application contact:* Mary Kienietz, Administrative Assistant, 970-248-1786, E-mail: mkieniet@coloradomesa.edu.
Website: http://coloradomesa.edu/teachered/index.html

Colorado State University, College of Health and Human Sciences, School of Education, Fort Collins, CO 80523-1588. Offers adult education and training (M Ed); counseling and career development (M Ed); education sciences (PhD); higher education leadership (PhD); organization learning, performance, and change (PhD); organizational learning, performance, and change (M Ed); student affairs in higher education (MS); teaching and learning (M Ed), including principal licensure, teacher licensure. *Accreditation:* ACA; TEAC. *Program availability:* Part-time, online only, 100% online, blended/hybrid learning, face-to-face off-campus courses. *Faculty:* 29 full-time (21 women), 23 part-time/adjunct (11 women). *Students:* 80 full-time (56 women), 541 part-time (353 women); includes 142 minority (26 Black or African American, non-Hispanic/Latino; 2 American Indian or Alaska Native, non-Hispanic/Latino; 22 Asian, non-Hispanic/Latino; 71 Hispanic/Latino; 21 Two or more races, non-Hispanic/Latino), 18 international. Average age 37. 483 applicants, 31% accepted, 137 enrolled. In 2016, 183 master's, 33 doctorates awarded. *Degree requirements:* For master's, thesis optional,

professional portfolio; for doctorate, comprehensive exam, thesis/dissertation. *Entrance requirements:* For master's, bachelor's degree; minimum GPA of 3.0 in last degree earned; for doctorate, GRE or GMAT (depending upon specialization), master's degree; minimum GPA of 3.0 in last degree earned. Additional exam requirements/ recommendations for international students: Required—TOEFL (minimum score 550 paper-based; 80 iBT), IELTS (minimum score 6.5), PTE (minimum score 58). *Application deadline:* Applications are processed on a rolling basis. Application fee: $60 ($70 for international students). Electronic applications accepted. *Expenses:* Contact institution. *Financial support:* In 2016–17, 3 students received support, including 7 research assistantships with full tuition reimbursements available (averaging $11,749 per year), 5 teaching assistantships with full tuition reimbursements available (averaging $15,886 per year); fellowships with full tuition reimbursements available, scholarships/ grants, and unspecified assistantships also available. Financial award application deadline: 3/1; financial award applicants required to submit FAFSA. *Faculty research:* Higher education leadership; research methods; human resource development; K-16 education; diversity, equity, and inclusion. *Total annual research expenditures:* $499,898. *Unit head:* Dr. Louise Jennings, Co-Director, 970-491-6317, Fax: 970-491-1317, E-mail: louise.jennings@colostate.edu. *Application contact:* Kelli Clark, Graduate Programs Coordinator, 970-491-2093, Fax: 970-491-1317, E-mail: kelli.clark@ colostate.edu.
Website: http://www.soe.chhs.colostate.edu/

Colorado State University–Global Campus, Graduate Programs, Greenwood Village, CO 80111. Offers criminal justice and law enforcement administration (MS); education leadership (MS); finance (MS); healthcare administration and management (MS); human resource management (MHRM); information technology management (MITM); international management (MS); management (MS); organizational leadership (MS); professional accounting (MPA); project management (MS); teaching and learning (MS). *Accreditation:* ACBSP. *Program availability:* Online learning.

Columbia College, Graduate Programs, Education Division, Columbia, SC 29203-5998. Offers divergent learning (M Ed); higher education administration (M Ed). *Accreditation:* NCATE. *Program availability:* Part-time, evening/weekend, online learning. *Degree requirements:* For master's, thesis. *Entrance requirements:* For master's, GRE General Test, MAT, 2 recommendations, current South Carolina teaching certificate, minimum GPA of 3.2. Electronic applications accepted. *Expenses:* Contact institution.

Columbia College, Master of Education in Educational Leadership Program, Columbia, MO 65216-0002. Offers M Ed. *Program availability:* Part-time, evening/weekend, 100% online, blended/hybrid learning. *Faculty:* 1 (woman) full-time, 4 part-time/adjunct (all women). *Students:* 4 full-time (3 women), 39 part-time (12 women); includes 3 minority (2 Black or African American, non-Hispanic/Latino; 1 Asian, non-Hispanic/Latino). Average age 33. 8 applicants, 100% accepted, 6 enrolled. In 2016, 4 master's awarded. *Entrance requirements:* Additional exam requirements/recommendations for international students: Required—TOEFL (minimum score 550 paper-based; 61 iBT). *Application deadline:* For fall admission, 8/9 priority date for domestic and international students; for spring admission, 12/27 priority date for domestic and international students. Applications are processed on a rolling basis. Application fee: $55. Electronic applications accepted. *Expenses:* Contact institution. *Financial support:* Federal Work-Study and scholarships/grants available. Financial award application deadline: 3/1; financial award applicants required to submit FAFSA. *Unit head:* Teresa VanDover, M Ed Coordinator, 573-875-7794, E-mail: tmvandover@ccis.edu. *Application contact:* Stephanie Johnson, Director of Admissions, 573-875-7352, Fax: 573-875-7506, E-mail: sjohnson@ccis.edu.

Columbia International University, Columbia Graduate School, Columbia, SC 29230-3122. Offers Bible teaching (MABT); counseling (MACN); early childhood and elementary education (MAT); educational administration (M Ed); educational leadership (PhD); instruction and learning (M Ed); teaching English as a foreign language (Certificate); teaching English as a foreign language and intercultural studies (MATF). *Program availability:* Part-time, evening/weekend, online learning. *Degree requirements:* For master's, internships, professional project. *Entrance requirements:* For master's, MAT; GRE (for some programs), minimum GPA of 2.7. Additional exam requirements/ recommendations for international students: Required—TOEFL. Electronic applications accepted.

Columbus State University, Graduate Studies, College of Education and Health Professions, Department of Counseling, Foundations, and Leadership, Columbus, GA 31907-5645. Offers clinical mental health counseling (MS); curriculum and leadership (Ed D), including curriculum, educational leadership, higher education (M Ed, Ed D); educational leadership (M Ed, Ed S), including higher education (M Ed, Ed D); school counseling (M Ed, Ed S). *Accreditation:* ACA; NCATE. *Program availability:* Part-time, evening/weekend, 100% online, blended/hybrid learning. *Faculty:* 14 full-time (4 women), 25 part-time/adjunct (14 women). *Students:* 226 full-time (159 women), 294 part-time (219 women); includes 298 minority (270 Black or African American, non-Hispanic/Latino; 1 American Indian or Alaska Native, non-Hispanic/Latino; 5 Asian, non-Hispanic/Latino; 13 Hispanic/Latino; 9 Two or more races, non-Hispanic/Latino), 1 international. Average age 39. 367 applicants, 57% accepted, 162 enrolled. In 2016, 20 master's, 7 doctorates, 121 other advanced degrees awarded. *Degree requirements:* For master's, thesis, exit exam; for doctorate, comprehensive exam, thesis/dissertation; for Ed S, thesis or alternative. *Entrance requirements:* For master's, GRE General Test, minimum undergraduate GPA of 2.75; for doctorate, GRE General Test, minimum graduate GPA of 3.5, four years of professional service; for Ed S, GRE General Test, minimum undergraduate GPA of 2.75, graduate 3.0. Additional exam requirements/ recommendations for international students: Required—TOEFL (minimum score 550 paper-based; 79 iBT). *Application deadline:* For fall admission, 6/30 for domestic and international students; for spring admission, 11/1 for domestic and international students; for summer admission, 3/1 for domestic and international students. Applications are processed on a rolling basis. Application fee: $50. Electronic applications accepted. *Expenses:* Tuition, state resident: full-time $4804; part-time $2412 per semester hour. Tuition, nonresident: full-time $19,218; part-time $9612 per semester hour. *Required fees:* $1850; $1850 per semester hour. Tuition and fees vary according to program. *Financial support:* In 2016–17, 43 students received support, including 9 research assistantships with partial tuition reimbursements available (averaging $3,000 per year); career-related internships or fieldwork, Federal Work-Study, institutionally sponsored loans, scholarships/grants, tuition waivers (partial), and unspecified assistantships also available. Support available to part-time students. Financial award application deadline: 5/1; financial award applicants required to submit FAFSA. *Unit head:* Dr. Tom Hackett, Department Chair, 706-507-8968, Fax: 706-569-3134, E-mail: hackett_paul@columbusstate.edu. *Application contact:* Kristin Williams, Director of International and Graduate Recruitment, 706-507-8848, Fax: 706-568-5091, E-mail: williams_kristin@columbusstate.edu.
Website: http://cfl.columbusstate.edu/

Columbus State University, Graduate Studies, College of Education and Health Professions, Department of Teacher Education, Columbus, GA 31907-5645. Offers curriculum and instruction in accomplished teaching (M Ed); early childhood education (M Ed, MAT, Ed S); middle grades education (M Ed, MAT, Ed S); secondary education (M Ed, MAT, Ed S), including biology (MAT), chemistry (MAT), earth and space science (MAT), English/language arts, general science (M Ed), history (MAT), mathematics, science (Ed S), social science (M Ed, Ed S); special education (M Ed, MAT, Ed S), including general curriculum (M Ed, MAT); teacher leadership (M Ed). *Accreditation:* NCATE. *Program availability:* Part-time, evening/weekend, 100% online, blended/hybrid learning. *Faculty:* 20 full-time (13 women), 19 part-time/adjunct (16 women). *Students:* 92 full-time (66 women), 212 part-time (179 women); includes 113 minority (104 Black or African American, non-Hispanic/Latino; 1 American Indian or Alaska Native, non-Hispanic/Latino; 2 Asian, non-Hispanic/Latino; 4 Hispanic/Latino; 2 Two or more races, non-Hispanic/Latino), 5 international. Average age 34. 209 applicants, 56% accepted, 79 enrolled. In 2016, 111 master's, 18 other advanced degrees awarded. *Degree requirements:* For Ed S, thesis or alternative. *Entrance requirements:* For master's, GRE General Test, minimum undergraduate GPA of 2.75; for Ed S, GRE General Test, minimum undergraduate GPA of 2.75, graduate 3.0. Additional exam requirements/ recommendations for international students: Required—TOEFL (minimum score 550 paper-based; 79 iBT). *Application deadline:* For fall admission, 6/30 for domestic students, 5/1 for international students; for spring admission, 11/1 for domestic and international students; for summer admission, 3/1 for domestic and international students. Applications are processed on a rolling basis. Application fee: $50. Electronic applications accepted. *Expenses:* Tuition, state resident: full-time $4804; part-time $2412 per semester hour. Tuition, nonresident: full-time $19,218; part-time $9612 per semester hour. *Required fees:* $1850; $1850 per semester hour. Tuition and fees vary according to program. *Financial support:* In 2016–17, 60 students received support, including 12 research assistantships with partial tuition reimbursements available (averaging $3,000 per year); career-related internships or fieldwork, Federal Work-Study, institutionally sponsored loans, scholarships/grants, tuition waivers (partial), and unspecified assistantships also available. Support available to part-time students. Financial award application deadline: 5/1; financial award applicants required to submit FAFSA. *Unit head:* Dr. Jan Burcham, Department Chair, 706-507-8519, Fax: 706-568-3134, E-mail: burcham_jan@columbusstate.edu. *Application contact:* Kristin Williams, Director of International and Graduate Recruitment, 706-507-8848, Fax: 706-568-5091, E-mail: williams_kristin@columbusstate.edu.
Website: http://te.columbusstate.edu/

Concordia University, College of Education, Portland, OR 97211-6099. Offers career and technical education (M Ed); curriculum and instruction (M Ed), including adolescent literacy, career and technical education, e-learning/technology education, early childhood education, English for speakers of other languages, English language development, environmental education, mathematics, methods and curriculum, reading, science, teacher leadership, the inclusive classroom; early childhood (MAT); education leadership (Ed D); educational administration (M Ed); elementary education (MAT); secondary education (MAT); special education (M Ed); teacher leadership (Ed D). *Program availability:* Part-time, online learning. *Degree requirements:* For master's, comprehensive exam, work samples/portfolio. *Entrance requirements:* For master's, California Basic Educational Skills Test or PRAXIS I, minimum undergraduate GPA of 2.8, graduate 3.0; 2 letters of recommendation. Additional exam requirements/ recommendations for international students: Required—TOEFL (minimum score 525 paper-based). Electronic applications accepted. *Faculty research:* Learner-centered classroom, brain-based learning, future of online learning.

Concordia University Ann Arbor, Graduate Programs, Ann Arbor, MI 48105-2797. Offers curriculum and instruction (MS); educational leadership (MS); organizational leadership and administration (MS). *Program availability:* Part-time, evening/weekend. *Degree requirements:* For master's, thesis. *Entrance requirements:* Additional exam requirements/recommendations for international students: Required—TOEFL (minimum score 80 iBT); Recommended—IELTS (minimum score 6.5). Electronic applications accepted.

Concordia University Chicago, College of Education, Program in School Leadership, River Forest, IL 60305-1499. Offers MA, Ed D, CAS. MA offered jointly with the Chicago Consortium of Colleges and Universities. *Accreditation:* NCATE. *Program availability:* Part-time, evening/weekend. *Degree requirements:* For master's, comprehensive exam, thesis optional; for CAS, thesis, final project. *Entrance requirements:* For master's, minimum GPA of 2.9; for CAS, master's degree. Additional exam requirements/ recommendations for international students: Required—TOEFL (minimum score 550 paper-based). Electronic applications accepted. *Faculty research:* Effectiveness of urban Lutheran schools in impacting children's faith development, effectiveness of centers for urban ministries in supporting urban ministry and teaching science.

Concordia University Irvine, School of Education, Irvine, CA 92612-3299. Offers curriculum and instruction (MA); education and preliminary teaching credential (M Ed); educational administration and preliminary administrative services credential (MA); educational technology (MA); school counseling with pupil personnel services credential (MA). *Program availability:* Part-time, evening/weekend, online learning. *Degree requirements:* For master's, action research project. *Entrance requirements:* For master's, California Basic Educational Skills Test, California Subject Examinations for Teachers (M Ed and MA in educational administration and preliminary administrative services credential), official college transcript(s), signed statement of intent, two references, copy of credential. Additional exam requirements/recommendations for international students: Required—TOEFL. Electronic applications accepted. *Expenses:* Contact institution.

Concordia University, Nebraska, Graduate Programs in Education, Program in Educational Administration, Seward, NE 68434-1556. Offers elementary and secondary education (M Ed); elementary education (M Ed); secondary education (M Ed). *Accreditation:* NCATE. *Program availability:* Part-time. *Degree requirements:* For master's, thesis or alternative. *Entrance requirements:* For master's, GRE, MAT, or NTE, BS in education or equivalent, minimum GPA of 3.0.

Concordia University, St. Paul, College of Education, St. Paul, MN 55104-5494. Offers classroom instruction (MA Ed), including K-12 reading; differentiated instruction (MA Ed); education (Ed D); educational leadership (MA Ed); educational technology (MA Ed); K-12 principal licensure (Ed S); special education (MA Ed, Certificate), including autism spectrum disorder (MA Ed), emotional and behavioral disorders (MA Ed), learning disabilities (MA Ed); superintendent (Ed S); teaching (MAT). *Accreditation:* NCATE. *Program availability:* Part-time, evening/weekend, 100% online, blended/hybrid learning. *Faculty:* 9 full-time (5 women), 88 part-time/adjunct (52 women). *Students:* 994 full-time (745 women), 40 part-time (34 women); includes 118 minority (40 Black or African American, non-Hispanic/Latino; 7 American Indian or Alaska Native, non-Hispanic/Latino; 33 Asian, non-Hispanic/Latino; 20 Hispanic/Latino; 18 Two or more races, non-Hispanic/Latino), 15 international. Average age 34. 549 applicants, 82% accepted, 372 enrolled. In 2016, 399 master's, 108 other advanced degrees awarded. *Degree requirements:* For master's, thesis (for some programs); for doctorate, thesis/dissertation, capstone projects; for other advanced degree, e-folio review of competencies. *Entrance requirements:* For master's, official transcripts from regionally-accredited institution stating the conferral of a bachelor's degree with minimum cumulative GPA of 3.0; personal statement; professional resume; practitioner in field through work or volunteerism; resume; for doctorate, minimum master's or specialist degree GPA of 3.25; transcript; writing sample; three letters of recommendation; current resume; on-campus interview; for other advanced degree, at least three years of teaching experience; master's degree; valid MN teaching license; writing sample; two letters of recommendation; resume. Additional exam requirements/recommendations for international students: Recommended—TOEFL (minimum score 547 paper-based; 78 iBT), IELTS (minimum score 6). *Application deadline:* For fall admission, 8/1 for domestic and international students; for spring admission, 12/1 for domestic and international students; for summer admission, 5/1 for domestic and international students. Applications are processed on a rolling basis. Application fee: $50. Electronic applications accepted. *Expenses:* Contact institution. *Financial support:* In 2016–17, 112 students received support. Scholarships/grants and unspecified assistantships available. Financial award applicants required to submit FAFSA. *Faculty research:* Differentiated instruction in K-12 educational settings; educational leadership; effective online pedagogy in higher education; equine-assisted learning; faculty development in higher education. *Unit head:* Lonn Maly, Dean, 651-641-8203, E-mail: maly@csp.edu. *Application contact:* Kimberly Craig, Associate Vice President, Cohort Enrollment Management, 651-603-6223, Fax: 651-603-6320, E-mail: craig@csp.edu.

Concordia University Wisconsin, Graduate Programs, Department of Education, Program in Educational Administration, Mequon, WI 53097-2402. Offers MS Ed. *Program availability:* Part-time, evening/weekend, online learning. *Degree requirements:* For master's, comprehensive exam, thesis or alternative. *Entrance requirements:* For master's, minimum GPA of 3.0. Additional exam requirements/recommendations for international students: Required—TOEFL. Application fee: $35. *Financial support:* Application deadline: 8/1. *Unit head:* Dr. Ross Stueber, Head, 262-243-4285, Fax: 262-243-4428, E-mail: ross.stueber@cuw.edu. *Application contact:* Graduate Admissions, 262-243-4248, Fax: 262-243-4428.

Concord University, Graduate Studies, Athens, WV 24712-1000. Offers educational leadership and supervision (M Ed); health promotion (MA); reading specialist (M Ed); social work (MSW); special education (M Ed); teaching (MAT). *Program availability:* Part-time, evening/weekend, online learning. *Faculty:* 16 full-time (10 women), 7 part-time/adjunct (4 women). *Students:* 129 full-time (105 women), 220 part-time (169 women); includes 28 minority (26 Black or African American, non-Hispanic/Latino; 1 American Indian or Alaska Native, non-Hispanic/Latino; 1 Hispanic/Latino), 2 international. *Degree requirements:* For master's, thesis (for some programs). *Entrance requirements:* For master's, GRE or MAT, baccalaureate degree with minimum GPA of 2.5 from regionally-accredited institution; teaching license; 2 letters of recommendation; completed disposition assessment form. *Application deadline:* Applications are processed on a rolling basis. Application fee: $30. Electronic applications accepted. *Expenses:* Tuition, state resident: full-time $3800; part-time $2539 per semester. Tuition, nonresident: full-time $6627; part-time $4416 per semester. Tuition and fees vary according to course load. *Financial support:* Tuition waivers and unspecified assistantships available. Financial award applicants required to submit FAFSA. *Unit head:* Dr. Cheryl Barnes, Director, 304-384-6306, E-mail: cbarnes@concord.edu. *Application contact:* Debra Moore, Special Events Assistant, 304-384-5113, E-mail: dlm@concord.edu.
Website: http://www.concord.edu/graduate

Converse College, School of Education and Graduate Studies, Education Specialist Program, Spartanburg, SC 29302. Offers administration and leadership (Ed S); administration and supervision (Ed S); literacy (Ed S). *Accreditation:* AAMFT/COAMFTE. *Program availability:* Part-time. *Entrance requirements:* For degree, GRE or MAT (marriage and family therapy), minimum GPA of 3.0. *Application deadline:* For fall admission, 8/1 for domestic and international students; for winter admission, 11/15 for domestic and international students; for spring admission, 1/15 for domestic and international students. Applications are processed on a rolling basis. Application fee: $40. Electronic applications accepted. *Expenses: Tuition:* Full-time $3600; part-time $400 per credit hour. *Required fees:* $70 per term. *Unit head:* Dr. Kathy Good, Dean of the School of Education and Graduate Studies, 864-596-9082, E-mail: kathy.good@converse.edu. *Application contact:* Jill Feist, Administrative Assistant to the Dean of the School of Education and Graduate Studies, 864-596-9220, Fax: 864-596-9221, E-mail: jill.feist@converse.edu.

Converse College, School of Education and Graduate Studies, Program in Leadership, Spartanburg, SC 29302. Offers administration and supervision (M Ed). *Degree requirements:* For master's, capstone paper. *Entrance requirements:* For master's, NTE, minimum GPA of 2.75, nomination by school district, 3 recommendations. *Application deadline:* For fall admission, 8/1 for domestic and international students; for winter admission, 11/15 for domestic and international students; for spring admission, 1/15 for domestic and international students. Application fee: $40. Electronic applications accepted. *Expenses: Tuition:* Full-time $3600; part-time $400 per credit hour. *Required fees:* $70 per term. *Unit head:* Dr. Kathy Good, Dean of the School of Education and Graduate Studies, 864-596-9082, E-mail: kathy.good@converse.edu. *Application contact:* 864-596-9404, E-mail: graduate@converse.edu.

Creighton University, Graduate School, College of Arts and Sciences, Department of Education, Program in Educational Leadership, Omaha, NE 68178-0001. Offers MS. *Program availability:* Part-time, online only, 100% online, blended/hybrid learning. *Faculty:* 10 full-time (5 women). *Students:* 97 part-time (66 women); includes 4 minority (2 Black or African American, non-Hispanic/Latino; 2 Hispanic/Latino). Average age 34. 20 applicants, 85% accepted, 17 enrolled. In 2016, 12 master's awarded. *Degree requirements:* For master's, portfolio. *Entrance requirements:* For master's, 2 writing samples, 3 letters of recommendation. Additional exam requirements/recommendations for international students: Required—TOEFL (minimum score 90 iBT). *Application deadline:* For fall admission, 7/1 for domestic students, 3/1 for international students; for winter admission, 10/1 for domestic students, 5/1 for international students; for spring admission, 3/1 for domestic students, 10/1 for international students. Applications are processed on a rolling basis. Application fee: $50. Electronic applications accepted. *Expenses: Tuition:* Full-time $14,400; part-time $800 per credit hour. *Required fees:* $158 per semester. Tuition and fees vary according to course load, campus/location, program, reciprocity agreements and student's religious affiliation. *Financial support:* Scholarships/grants and tuition waivers (partial) available. Support available to part-time students. Financial award application deadline: 5/1; financial award applicants required to submit FAFSA. *Faculty research:* Catholic school leadership, early childhood education. *Unit head:* Dr. Timothy J. Cook, Professor of Education, 402-280-2561, E-mail: timcook@creighton.edu. *Application contact:* Lindsay Johnson, Director of Graduate and Adult Recruitment, 402-280-2703, Fax: 402-280-2423, E-mail: gradschool@creighton.edu.

Creighton University, Graduate School, Department of Interdisciplinary Studies, Interdisciplinary Ed D Program in Leadership, Omaha, NE 68178-0001. Offers Ed D. *Program availability:* Part-time, online only, blended/hybrid learning. *Faculty:* 7 full-time (5 women), 23 part-time/adjunct (12 women). *Students:* 26 full-time (21 women), 151 part-time (109 women); includes 11 minority (4 Black or African American, non-Hispanic/Latino; 1 American Indian or Alaska Native, non-Hispanic/Latino; 1 Asian, non-Hispanic/Latino; 4 Hispanic/Latino; 1 Two or more races, non-Hispanic/Latino). Average age 42. 69 applicants, 80% accepted, 41 enrolled. In 2016, 57 doctorates awarded. *Degree requirements:* For doctorate, thesis/dissertation. *Entrance requirements:* For doctorate, master's or equivalent professional degree, current resume, official transcripts, three recommendations. Additional exam requirements/recommendations for international students: Required—TOEFL (minimum score 90 iBT). *Application deadline:* For fall admission, 6/15 priority date for domestic students, 6/15 for international students; for winter admission, 10/15 for domestic and international students; for spring admission, 3/15 priority date for domestic students, 3/15 for international students; for summer admission, 3/1 for domestic and international students. Applications are processed on a rolling basis. Application fee: $50. Electronic applications accepted. *Expenses:* $989 per credit hour. *Financial support:* In 2016–17, 8 students received support. Scholarships/grants available. Financial award application deadline: 5/1; financial award applicants required to submit FAFSA. *Unit head:* Dr. Jennifer Moss Breen, Director, 402-280-3952, E-mail: jennifermossbreen@creighton.edu. *Application contact:* Tara Waln-Lewellyn, Program Manager, 402-280-2392, Fax: 402-280-2423, E-mail: tarawaln-lewellyn@creighton.edu.
Website: https://www.creighton.edu/gradschool/edd/home/

Dakota Wesleyan University, Program in Education, Mitchell, SD 57301-4398. Offers curriculum and instruction (MA Ed); educational policy and administration (MA Ed); preK-12 principal certification (MA Ed); secondary certification (MA Ed). *Program availability:* Part-time, evening/weekend. *Degree requirements:* For master's, comprehensive exam, thesis optional, electronic portfolio. *Entrance requirements:* For master's, minimum GPA of 2.7, elementary statistics course, statement of purpose, official transcripts, resume, three letters of recommendation. Additional exam requirements/recommendations for international students: Required—TOEFL (minimum score 500 paper-based), IELTS (minimum score 6.5). Electronic applications accepted. *Faculty research:* Math, political policy, technology in the classroom.

Dallas Baptist University, Dorothy M. Bush College of Education, Program in Curriculum and Instruction, Dallas, TX 75211-9299. Offers Christian school administration (M Ed); distance learning (M Ed); English as a second language (M Ed); instructional technology (M Ed); professional life coaching (M Ed); special education (M Ed); supervision (M Ed). *Program availability:* Part-time, evening/weekend, 100% online, blended/hybrid learning. *Application deadline:* Applications are processed on a rolling basis. Application fee: $25. Electronic applications accepted. Application fee is waived when completed online. *Expenses: Tuition:* Full-time $15,408; part-time $856 per credit hour. *Required fees:* $400 per semester. Tuition and fees vary according to course load and degree level. *Unit head:* Dr. Deborah H. Tribble, Director, 214-333-5201, E-mail: debbiet@dbu.edu. *Application contact:* Bobby Soto, Director of Admissions, 214-333-5242, E-mail: graduate@dbu.edu.
Website: http://www3.dbu.edu/graduate/curriculum_instruction.asp

Dallas Baptist University, Dorothy M. Bush College of Education, Program in Educational Leadership, Dallas, TX 75211-9299. Offers charter school administration (M Ed); educational leadership K-12 (Ed D); principal certification (M Ed). *Program availability:* Part-time, evening/weekend, 100% online, blended/hybrid learning. *Application deadline:* Applications are processed on a rolling basis. Application fee: $25. Electronic applications accepted. Application fee is waived when completed online. *Expenses: Tuition:* Full-time $15,408; part-time $856 per credit hour. *Required fees:* $400 per semester. Tuition and fees vary according to course load and degree level. *Unit head:* Dr. Tam Jones, Program Administrator, 214-333-6841, E-mail: tamj@dbu.edu. *Application contact:* Bobby Soto, Director of Admissions, 214-333-5242, E-mail: graduate@dbu.edu.
Website: http://www3.dbu.edu/graduate/education.asp

Dallas Baptist University, Gary Cook School of Leadership, Program in Higher Education, Dallas, TX 75211-9299. Offers administration (M Ed), including community college leadership, distance learning, interdisciplinary studies, student affairs leadership; instructional (M Ed). *Program availability:* Part-time, evening/weekend, 100% online, blended/hybrid learning. *Application deadline:* Applications are processed on a rolling basis. Application fee: $25. Electronic applications accepted. Application fee is waived when completed online. *Expenses: Tuition:* Full-time $15,408; part-time $856 per credit hour. *Required fees:* $400 per semester. Tuition and fees vary according to course load and degree level. *Faculty research:* Enrollment management, portfolio assessment, servant leadership. *Unit head:* Mamo Ishida, Director, 214-333-5812, E-mail: mamo@dbu.edu. *Application contact:* Bobby Soto, Director of Admissions, 214-333-5242, E-mail: graduate@dbu.edu.
Website: http://www3.dbu.edu/leadership/hied/

Dallas Theological Seminary, Graduate Programs, Dallas, TX 75204-6499. Offers adult education (Th M); apologetics (Th M); Bible backgrounds (Th M); Bible translation (Th M); Biblical and theological studies (Certificate); biblical counseling (MA); biblical exegesis and linguistics (MA); biblical exposition (PhD); biblical studies (MA); Biblical theology (Th M); children's education (Th M); Christian education (MA, D Min); Christian leadership (MA); cross-cultural ministries (MA); educational administration (Th M); educational leadership (Th M); evangelism and discipleship (Th M); exposition of Biblical books (Th M); family life education (Th M); general studies (Th M); Hebrew and cognate studies (Th M); hermeneutics (Th M); historical theology (Th M); homiletics (Th M); intercultural ministries (Th M); Jesus studies (Th M); leadership studies (Th M); media and communication (MA); media arts (Th M); ministry (D Min); ministry with women (Th M); New Testament studies (Th M, PhD); Old Testament studies (Th M, PhD); parachurch ministries (Th M); pastoral care and counseling (Th M); pastoral theology and practice (Th M); philosophy (Th M); sacred theology (STM); spiritual formation (Th M); systematic theology (Th M); teaching in Christian institutions (Th M); theological studies (PhD); urban ministries (Th M); worship studies (Th M); youth education (Th M). *Program availability:* Part-time, online learning. *Degree requirements:* For master's, variable foreign language requirement, thesis (for some programs); for doctorate, 2 foreign languages, thesis/dissertation. *Entrance requirements:* For master's, GRE or MAT (if minimum undergraduate cumulative GPA is below 2.5 or undergraduate degree is unaccredited). Additional exam requirements/recommendations for international students: Required—TOEFL (minimum score 575 paper-based; 85 iBT), TWE. Electronic applications accepted.

Delaware State University, Graduate Programs, College of Education, Health and Public Policy, Program in Educational Leadership, Dover, DE 19901-2277. Offers MA, Ed D. *Entrance requirements:* Additional exam requirements/recommendations for international students: Required—TOEFL (minimum score 550 paper-based).

Delaware Valley University, Program in Educational Leadership, Doylestown, PA 18901-2697. Offers instruction, curriculum and technology (MS); school administration and leadership (MS). *Program availability:* Part-time, evening/weekend. *Entrance requirements:* For master's, minimum undergraduate GPA of 3.0.

Delta State University, Graduate Programs, College of Education, Division of Teacher Education, Leadership, and Research, Program in Professional Studies, Cleveland, MS 38733-0001. Offers counselor education (Ed D); elementary education (Ed D); higher education (Ed D). *Program availability:* Part-time, evening/weekend. *Degree requirements:* For doctorate, thesis/dissertation. *Entrance requirements:* For doctorate, GRE General Test.

Delta State University, Graduate Programs, College of Education, Division of Teacher Education, Leadership, and Research, Programs in Educational Administration and Supervision, Cleveland, MS 38733-0001. Offers M Ed, Ed S. *Accreditation:* NCATE.

Program availability: Part-time, evening/weekend. *Degree requirements:* For master's, thesis optional. *Entrance requirements:* For master's, GRE General Test or MAT; for Ed S, master's degree, teaching certificate.

DePaul University, College of Education, Chicago, IL 60614. Offers bilingual bicultural education (M Ed, MA); counseling (M Ed, MA), including clinical mental health counseling, college student development, school counseling; curriculum studies (M Ed, MA, Ed D); early childhood education (M Ed, MA, Ed D); educating adults (MA); educational leadership (M Ed, MA, Ed D), including administration and supervision (M Ed, MA), principal preparation (M Ed, MA); elementary education (MA); mathematics education (MA); mathematics for teaching (MS); middle school mathematics education (MS); reading specialist (M Ed, MA); secondary education (M Ed); social and cultural foundations in education (MA); special education (M Ed, MA); world languages education (M Ed, MA). *Program availability:* Part-time, evening/weekend, online learning. *Degree requirements:* For doctorate, thesis/dissertation. Electronic applications accepted.

DeVry University–Folsom Campus, Graduate Programs, Folsom, CA 95630. Offers accounting (M Acc); accounting and financial management (MAFM); business administration (MBA); curriculum leadership (M Ed); educational leadership (M Ed); educational technology (M Ed); higher education leadership (M Ed); human resource management (MHRM); information systems management (MISM); network and communications management (MNCM); project management (MPM); public administration (MPA).

Doane University, Program in Education, Crete, NE 68333-2430. Offers curriculum and instruction (M Ed); educational leadership (M Ed). *Accreditation:* NCATE. *Program availability:* Part-time, evening/weekend. *Faculty:* 10 full-time (7 women), 66 part-time/adjunct (50 women). *Students:* 224 full-time (167 women), 488 part-time (388 women); includes 22 minority (9 Black or African American, non-Hispanic/Latino; 2 American Indian or Alaska Native, non-Hispanic/Latino; 1 Asian, non-Hispanic/Latino; 7 Hispanic/Latino; 1 Native Hawaiian or other Pacific Islander, non-Hispanic/Latino; 2 Two or more races, non-Hispanic/Latino), 1 international. Average age 34. In 2016, 257 master's awarded. *Degree requirements:* For master's, thesis. *Entrance requirements:* For master's, minimum GPA of 2.5. Additional exam requirements/recommendations for international students: Required—TOEFL. *Application deadline:* Applications are processed on a rolling basis. Electronic applications accepted. *Expenses:* Contact institution. *Financial support:* Applicants required to submit FAFSA. *Unit head:* Dr. Lyn C. Forester, Dean, 402-826-8604, Fax: 402-826-8278. *Application contact:* Wilma Daddario, Assistant Dean, 402-464-1223, Fax: 402-466-4228, E-mail: wdaddario@doane.edu.
Website: http://www.doane.edu/masters-degrees

Drexel University, Goodwin College of Professional Studies, School of Education, Philadelphia, PA 19104-2875. Offers applied behavior analysis (MS); creativity and innovation (MS); education improvement and transformation (MS); educational administration (MS); educational leadership and management (Ed D); educational leadership development and learning technologies (PhD); global and international education (MS); higher education (MS); human resources development (MS); learning technologies (MS); mathematics, learning and teaching (MS); special education (MS); teaching, learning and curriculum (MS). *Program availability:* Part-time, evening/weekend, online learning. *Degree requirements:* For doctorate, thesis/dissertation. *Entrance requirements:* For doctorate, GRE or GMAT. Additional exam requirements/recommendations for international students: Required—TOEFL, IELTS. Electronic applications accepted. Application fee is waived when completed online. *Expenses:* Contact institution. *Faculty research:* Leadership development, mathematics education, literacy, autism, educational technology.

See Display on page 660 and Close-Up on page 727.

Drury University, Master in Education Program, Springfield, MO 5802. Offers curriculum and instruction (M Ed), including elementary, middle school, secondary; gifted education (M Ed); instructional leadership (M Ed); instructional technology (M Ed); integrated learning (M Ed); online teaching (M Ed); special education (M Ed); special reading (M Ed). *Accreditation:* NCATE. *Program availability:* Part-time, evening/weekend, 100% online, blended/hybrid learning. *Students:* 146 full-time (111 women); includes 6 minority (1 Asian, non-Hispanic/Latino; 3 Hispanic/Latino; 2 Two or more races, non-Hispanic/Latino), 1 international. Average age 34. 42 applicants, 74% accepted. In 2016, 74 master's awarded. *Entrance requirements:* For master's, GRE, bachelor's degree with minimum GPA of 2.75. Additional exam requirements/recommendations for international students: Recommended—TOEFL (minimum score 80 iBT), IELTS (minimum score 6.5). *Application deadline:* For fall admission, 8/4 priority date for domestic and international students; for spring admission, 1/5 priority date for domestic and international students; for summer admission, 5/26 priority date for domestic and international students. Applications are processed on a rolling basis. Application fee: $25 ($50 for international students). Electronic applications accepted. *Expenses:* $352 tuition per credit hour; $7 per credit hour technology fee; $100 graduation fee; $59 portfolio fee (one-time). *Financial support:* In 2016–17, 20 students received support. Career-related internships or fieldwork, scholarships/grants, tuition waivers (partial), and unspecified assistantships available. Financial award application deadline: 6/30; financial award applicants required to submit FAFSA. *Faculty research:* Gifted students, instructional technology, autism, diversity and social justice. *Unit head:* Dr. Asikaa Cosgrove, Director, Master in Education, 417-873-7806, E-mail: acosgrov@drury.edu.
Website: http://www.drury.edu/education-masters

Duquesne University, School of Education, Department of Educational Foundations and Leadership, Ed D in Educational Leadership Program, Pittsburgh, PA 15282-0001. Offers Ed D. *Program availability:* Part-time, evening/weekend. *Faculty:* 7 full-time (3 women). *Students:* 35 full-time (24 women), 2 part-time (1 woman); includes 11 minority (all Black or African American, non-Hispanic/Latino), 2 international. Average age 45. 25 applicants, 60% accepted, 14 enrolled. In 2016, 12 doctorates awarded. *Degree requirements:* For doctorate, thesis/dissertation. *Entrance requirements:* For doctorate, GRE, letters of recommendation, essay, interview, master's degree. Additional exam requirements/recommendations for international students: Required—TOEFL (minimum score 550 paper-based), IELTS (minimum score 7). *Application deadline:* For fall admission, 3/1 for domestic students. Application fee: $0. Electronic applications accepted. *Expenses: Tuition:* Full-time $22,212; part-time $1234 per credit. Tuition and fees vary according to program. *Unit head:* Dr. Connie Moss, Associate Professor, 412-396-4433, Fax: 412-396-6017, E-mail: moss@duq.edu. *Application contact:* Michael Dolinger, Director of Student and Academic Services, 412-396-6647, Fax: 412-396-5585, E-mail: dolingerm@duq.edu.
Website: http://wwwtest.duq.edu/academics/schools/education/graduate-programs-education/educational-leadership

Duquesne University, School of Education, Department of Educational Foundations and Leadership, Program in School Administration and Supervision, Pittsburgh, PA 15282-0001. Offers curriculum and instruction (Post-Master's Certificate); school administration K-12 (MS Ed, Post-Master's Certificate); school supervision (MS Ed). *Program availability:* Part-time, evening/weekend. *Faculty:* 1 (woman) full-time. *Students:* 18 full-time (13 women), 4 part-time (all women); includes 1 minority (Black or African American, non-Hispanic/Latino), 1 international. Average age 36. 17 applicants, 88% accepted, 9 enrolled. In 2016, 22 master's awarded. *Degree requirements:* For master's, thesis optional. *Entrance requirements:* For master's and Post-Master's Certificate, bachelor's degree. Additional exam requirements/recommendations for international students: Required—TOEFL (minimum score 550 paper-based), IELTS (minimum score 7). *Application deadline:* For fall admission, 9/1 for domestic students; for spring admission, 1/1 for domestic students. Applications are processed on a rolling basis. Application fee: $0. Electronic applications accepted. *Expenses: Tuition:* Full-time $22,212; part-time $1234 per credit. Tuition and fees vary according to program. *Financial support:* Research assistantships available. Support available to part-time students. *Unit head:* Dr. Fran Serenka, Associate Professor and Director, 412-396-5274, Fax: 412-396-1274, E-mail: serenkaf@duq.edu. *Application contact:* Michael Dolinger, Director of Student and Academic Services, 412-396-6647, Fax: 412-396-5585, E-mail: dolingerm@duq.edu.
Website: http://www.duq.edu/academics/schools/education/graduate-programs-education/school-admin-and-supervision

D'Youville College, Department of Education, Buffalo, NY 14201-1084. Offers educational leadership (Ed D); elementary education (MS Ed); secondary education (MS Ed); special education (MS Ed). *Program availability:* Part-time, evening/weekend. *Degree requirements:* For master's, one foreign language, comprehensive exam, project or thesis. *Entrance requirements:* For master's, GRE (if GPA less than 2.75), minimum GPA of 3.0. Additional exam requirements/recommendations for international students: Required—TOEFL (minimum score 500 paper-based). Electronic applications accepted. *Faculty research:* Developmental disabilities, multiculturalism, early childhood education.

East Carolina University, Graduate School, College of Education, Department of Educational Leadership, Greenville, NC 27858-4353. Offers educational administration and supervision (Ed S); educational leadership (Ed D); school administration (MSA). *Accreditation:* NCATE. *Program availability:* Part-time, evening/weekend, online learning. *Students:* 12 full-time (all women), 270 part-time (174 women); includes 74 minority (58 Black or African American, non-Hispanic/Latino; 2 American Indian or Alaska Native, non-Hispanic/Latino; 2 Asian, non-Hispanic/Latino; 8 Hispanic/Latino; 4 Two or more races, non-Hispanic/Latino), 7 international. Average age 40. 156 applicants, 96% accepted, 131 enrolled. In 2016, 50 master's, 13 doctorates, 4 other advanced degrees awarded. *Degree requirements:* For master's, comprehensive exam, thesis optional; for doctorate, thesis/dissertation. *Entrance requirements:* For master's, GRE General Test or MAT, interview, minimum GPA of 2.5, bachelor's degree in related field, teaching license (MA Ed); for doctorate, GRE or MAT, interview, minimum GPA of 3.5. Additional exam requirements/recommendations for international students: Required—TOEFL. *Application deadline:* For fall admission, 6/1 priority date for domestic students. Applications are processed on a rolling basis. Application fee: $50. *Financial support:* Research assistantships with partial tuition reimbursements, teaching assistantships with partial tuition reimbursements, and Federal Work-Study available. Support available to part-time students. Financial award application deadline: 6/1. *Unit head:* Wiliam A. Rouse, Interim Chair, 252-328-6135, E-mail: rousew@ecu.edu. *Application contact:* Dean of Graduate School, 252-328-6012, Fax: 252-328-6071, E-mail: gradschool@ecu.edu.
Website: http://www.ecu.edu/cs-educ/leed/index.cfm

Eastern Illinois University, Graduate School, College of Education and Professional Studies, Department of Educational Leadership, Charleston, IL 61920. Offers MS Ed, Ed S. *Accreditation:* NCATE. *Program availability:* Part-time, evening/weekend. *Degree requirements:* For master's, comprehensive exam; for Ed S, comprehensive exam, thesis. *Entrance requirements:* For master's and Ed S, GMAT or GRE. Additional exam requirements/recommendations for international students: Required—TOEFL (minimum score 500 paper-based; 61 iBT), IELTS (minimum score 6). Electronic applications accepted.

Eastern Kentucky University, The Graduate School, College of Education, Department of Counseling and Educational Leadership, Richmond, KY 40475-3102. Offers human services (MA); instructional leadership (MA Ed); mental health counseling (MA); school counseling (MA Ed). *Accreditation:* ACA (one or more programs are accredited); NCATE. *Program availability:* Part-time, online learning. *Entrance requirements:* For master's, GRE General Test, minimum GPA of 2.5.

Eastern Michigan University, Graduate School, College of Education, Department of Leadership and Counseling, Programs in Educational Leadership, Ypsilanti, MI 48197. Offers community college leadership (Graduate Certificate); educational leadership (MA, Ed D, SPA); higher education/general administration (MA); higher education/student affairs (MA); K-12 administration (MA); K-12 basic administration (Post Master's Certificate). *Program availability:* Part-time, evening/weekend, online learning. *Students:* 52 full-time (39 women), 298 part-time (198 women); includes 103 minority (81 Black or African American, non-Hispanic/Latino; 3 American Indian or Alaska Native, non-Hispanic/Latino; 4 Asian, non-Hispanic/Latino; 10 Hispanic/Latino; 5 Two or more races, non-Hispanic/Latino), 2 international. Average age 35. 185 applicants, 70% accepted, 67 enrolled. In 2016, 85 master's, 28 doctorates, 23 other advanced degrees awarded. *Degree requirements:* For master's, portfolio. *Entrance requirements:* For doctorate, GRE. Additional exam requirements/recommendations for international students: Required—TOEFL. *Application deadline:* For winter admission, 2/1 for domestic and international students. Applications are processed on a rolling basis. Application fee: $45. *Financial support:* Fellowships, research assistantships with full tuition reimbursements, teaching assistantships with full tuition reimbursements, career-related internships or fieldwork, Federal Work-Study, institutionally sponsored loans, scholarships/grants, tuition waivers (partial), and unspecified assistantships available. Support available to part-time students. *Application contact:* Dr. Jaclynn Tracy, Coordinator of Advising, Programs in Educational Leadership, 734-487-0255, Fax: 734-487-4608, E-mail: jtracy@emich.edu.

Eastern Michigan University, Graduate School, College of Education, Department of Special Education, Programs in Special Education, Ypsilanti, MI 48197. Offers administration and supervision (SPA); curriculum development (SPA); special education (MA). *Accreditation:* NCATE. *Program availability:* Part-time, evening/weekend, online learning. *Students:* 4 full-time (3 women), 23 part-time (20 women); includes 4 minority (2 Black or African American, non-Hispanic/Latino; 1 Asian, non-Hispanic/Latino; 1 Hispanic/Latino), 3 international. Average age 40. 13 applicants, 85% accepted, 7 enrolled. In 2016, 1 master's, 5 other advanced degrees awarded. *Entrance requirements:* For master's, GRE General Test. Additional exam requirements/recommendations for international students: Required—TOEFL. *Application deadline:* Applications are processed on a rolling basis. Application fee: $45. *Financial support:* Fellowships, research assistantships with full tuition reimbursements, teaching assistantships with full tuition reimbursements, career-related internships or fieldwork, Federal Work-Study, institutionally sponsored loans, scholarships/grants, tuition waivers (partial), and unspecified assistantships available. Support available to part-time students. Financial award applicants required to submit FAFSA. *Application contact:* Dr. Derrick Fries, Advisor, 734-487-3300, Fax: 734-487-2473, E-mail: dfries@emich.edu.

Educational Leadership and Administration

Eastern Michigan University, Graduate School, College of Education, Department of Teacher Education, Programs in Curriculum and Instruction, Ypsilanti, MI 48197. Offers advanced teaching and learning (MA); early literacy instruction (Graduate Certificate); instructional leadership (MA); learning, motivation and creativity (Graduate Certificate); literacy coaching (Graduate Certificate); online teaching (Certificate); secondary literacy instruction (Graduate Certificate); urban and diversity education (MA). *Students:* 1 (woman) full-time, 31 part-time (29 women); includes 6 minority (2 Black or African American, non-Hispanic/Latino; 2 Asian, non-Hispanic/Latino; 2 Two or more races, non-Hispanic/Latino), 1 international. Average age 33. 11 applicants, 73% accepted, 4 enrolled. In 2016, 8 master's, 1 other advanced degree awarded. Application fee: $45. *Application contact:* Dr. Virginia Harder, Graduate Coordinator/Advisor, 734-487-2729, Fax: 734-487-2101, E-mail: vharder1@emich.edu.

Eastern Nazarene College, Adult and Graduate Studies, Division of Teacher Education, Quincy, MA 02170. Offers administration (M Ed); early childhood education (M Ed, Certificate); elementary education (M Ed, Certificate); English as a second language (Certificate); instructional enrichment and development (Certificate); middle school education (M Ed, Certificate); moderate special needs education (Certificate); principal (Certificate); program development and supervision (Certificate); secondary education (M Ed, Certificate); special education administrator (Certificate); special needs (M Ed); supervisor (Certificate); teacher of reading (M Ed, Certificate). M Ed also available through weekend program for administration, special needs, and teacher of reading only. *Program availability:* Part-time, evening/weekend. *Entrance requirements:* Additional exam requirements/recommendations for international students: Required—TOEFL (minimum score 550 paper-based).

Eastern New Mexico University, Graduate School, College of Education and Technology, Department of Educational Studies, Portales, NM 88130. Offers counseling (MA); education (M Ed), including educational administration, secondary education; school counseling (M Ed); special education (M Sp Ed), including early childhood special education, general. *Accreditation:* NCATE. *Program availability:* Part-time, evening/weekend, online learning. *Degree requirements:* For master's, comprehensive exam, thesis optional. *Entrance requirements:* For master's, minimum GPA of 3.0, letter of recommendation, photocopy of teaching license, writing assessment, Level II teaching license (for M Ed in educational administration). Additional exam requirements/recommendations for international students: Required—TOEFL (minimum score 550 paper-based; 79 iBT), IELTS (minimum score 6). Electronic applications accepted.

Eastern University, Loeb School of Education, St. Davids, PA 19087-3696. Offers ESL program specialist (K-12) (Certificate); general supervisor (PreK-12) (Certificate); health and physical education (K-12) (Certificate); middle level (4-8) (Certificate); multicultural education (M Ed); organizational leadership with education (PhD); Pre K-4 (Certificate); Pre K-4 with special education (Certificate); reading (M Ed); reading specialist (K-12) (Certificate); reading supervisor (K-12) (Certificate); school health supervisor (Certificate); school nurse (K-12) (Certificate); secondary biology education (7-12) (Certificate); secondary chemistry education (7-12) (Certificate); secondary communication education (7-12) (Certificate); secondary education (7-12) (Certificate); secondary English education (7-12) (Certificate); secondary math education (7-12) (Certificate); secondary social studies education (7-12) (Certificate); special education (M Ed); special education (7-12) (Certificate); special education (Pre K-8) (Certificate); special education supervisor (N-12) (Certificate); TESOL (M Ed); world language (Certificate), including French, Spanish. *Program availability:* Part-time, evening/weekend, online learning. *Students:* 41 full-time (32 women), 89 part-time (68 women); includes 54 minority (38 Black or African American, non-Hispanic/Latino; 3 Asian, non-Hispanic/Latino; 11 Hispanic/Latino; 2 Two or more races, non-Hispanic/Latino), 2 international. Average age 37. In 2016, 64 master's awarded. *Entrance requirements:* Additional exam requirements/recommendations for international students: Required—TOEFL. *Application deadline:* Applications are processed on a rolling basis. Application fee: $35. Electronic applications accepted. Application fee is waived when completed online. *Expenses:* $690 per credit. *Unit head:* Michael Dziedziak, Executive Director of Enrollment, 800-452-0996, E-mail: gpsadmissions@eastern.edu.
Website: http://www.eastern.edu/academics/programs/loeb-school-education-0

East Tennessee State University, School of Graduate Studies, College of Education, Department of Educational Leadership and Policy Analysis, Johnson City, TN 37614. Offers M Ed, Ed D, Ed S. *Accreditation:* NCATE. *Program availability:* Part-time, online learning. *Degree requirements:* For master's, comprehensive exam, portfolio development and presentation, performance assessment; for doctorate, comprehensive exam, thesis/dissertation, residency, internship; for Ed S, comprehensive exam, field experience; internship (for some programs). *Entrance requirements:* For master's, writing assessment, minimum GPA of 2.75, professional resume, teaching certificate, teaching experience, interview, four letters of recommendation; for doctorate, GRE General Test, writing assessment, professional resume, teaching certificate (for some programs), interview, four letters of recommendation; for Ed S, writing assessment, professional resume, teaching certificate (for some programs), four letters of recommendation. Additional exam requirements/recommendations for international students: Required—TOEFL (minimum score 550 paper-based; 79 iBT). Electronic applications accepted. *Faculty research:* Assessment and evaluation; examining school leadership, management, and accountability systems that limit learning; college and university enrollment and retention issues.

East Texas Baptist University, Master of Education Program, Marshall, TX 75670-1498. Offers college and university leadership (M Ed); curriculum and instruction (M Ed); principal certification (M Ed); sports and exercise leadership (M Ed); teacher certification (M Ed). *Program availability:* Part-time, evening/weekend. *Faculty:* 3 full-time (1 woman), 3 part-time/adjunct (all women). *Students:* 33 part-time (19 women); includes 14 minority (10 Black or African American, non-Hispanic/Latino; 4 Hispanic/Latino), 1 international. Average age 29. 53 applicants, 51% accepted, 25 enrolled. In 2016, 20 master's awarded. *Entrance requirements:* Additional exam requirements/recommendations for international students: Recommended—TOEFL (minimum score 550 paper-based; 79 iBT). *Application deadline:* For fall admission, 8/17 for domestic students; for spring admission, 1/10 for domestic students; for summer admission, 5/2 for domestic students. Applications are processed on a rolling basis. Application fee: $50. Electronic applications accepted. *Expenses:* $700 per credit hour tuition; $150 per semester fees (6 or more hours enrolled); $75 per semester fees (1-5 hours enrolled). *Financial support:* In 2016–17, 14 students received support. Federal Work-Study, unspecified assistantships, and staff grants available. Financial award applicants required to submit FAFSA. *Unit head:* Dr. PJ Winters, Director, 903-923-2276, Fax: 903-935-4318, E-mail: med@etbu.edu. *Application contact:* Den Murley, Director of Graduate Admissions, 903-923-2079, Fax: 903-934-8115, E-mail: dmurley@etbu.edu.
Website: https://www.etbu.edu/education/master-education/

Edgewood College, Program in Education, Madison, WI 53711-1997. Offers adult learning (MA Ed); director of special education and pupil services (Certificate); education (MA Ed); teaching and learning (MA Ed). *Accreditation:* NCATE (one or more programs are accredited). *Program availability:* Part-time, evening/weekend. *Faculty:* 13 full-time (9 women), 15 part-time/adjunct (10 women). *Students:* 137 full-time (91 women), 215 part-time (150 women); includes 51 minority (23 Black or African American, non-Hispanic/Latino; 3 American Indian or Alaska Native, non-Hispanic/Latino; 5 Asian, non-Hispanic/Latino; 17 Hispanic/Latino; 3 Two or more races, non-Hispanic/Latino), 18 international. Average age 37. In 2016, 74 master's, 18 doctorates awarded. *Degree requirements:* For master's, practicum, research project; for doctorate, comprehensive exam, thesis/dissertation. *Entrance requirements:* For master's, minimum GPA of 2.75, 2 letters of recommendation, personal statement; for doctorate, resume, letter of intent, 2 letters of recommendation, interview, writing sample. Additional exam requirements/recommendations for international students: Required—TOEFL (minimum score 525 paper-based; 72 iBT). *Application deadline:* For fall admission, 8/15 for domestic students, 5/1 for international students; for spring admission, 1/8 for domestic students, 11/1 for international students. Applications are processed on a rolling basis. Application fee: $30. Electronic applications accepted. *Expenses: Tuition:* Part-time $898 per credit. Tuition and fees vary according to course load. *Financial support:* Applicants required to submit FAFSA. *Faculty research:* Urban high schools, transgender students, literacy pedagogy, funds of knowledge, English language learners. *Unit head:* Dr. Timothy D. Slekar, Dean, E-mail: tslekar@edgewood.edu. *Application contact:* Joann Eastman, Admissions Counselor, 608-663-3250, Fax: 608-663-2214, E-mail: gps@edgewood.edu.
Website: https://www.edgewood.edu/academics/schools/school-of-education

Edinboro University of Pennsylvania, Department of Middle and Secondary Education and Educational Leadership, Edinboro, PA 16444. Offers educational leadership (M Ed); middle and secondary instruction (M Ed). *Program availability:* Part-time, evening/weekend. *Degree requirements:* For master's, comprehensive exam, thesis or alternative, project. *Entrance requirements:* For master's, GRE or MAT, minimum QPA of 2.5. Electronic applications accepted.

Elizabeth City State University, School of Education and Psychology, Master of School Administration Program, Elizabeth City, NC 27909-7806. Offers MSA. *Program availability:* Part-time, evening/weekend. *Degree requirements:* For master's, thesis or alternative, electronic portfolio. *Entrance requirements:* For master's, MAT, GRE, minimum GPA of 3.0, 3 years of teaching experience, 3 letters of recommendation, two official transcripts from all undergraduate/graduate schools attended, teacher license, 3-4 page statement of purpose. Additional exam requirements/recommendations for international students: Required—TOEFL (minimum score 550 paper-based, 80 iBT) or IELTS (minimum score 6.5). Electronic applications accepted. *Faculty research:* Mentoring, assessment, professional learning communities, common core standards, Interstate School Leaders Licensure Consortium (ISLLC), differentiating instruction.

Elmhurst College, Graduate Programs, Program in Teacher Leadership, Elmhurst, IL 60126-3296. Offers M Ed. *Program availability:* Part-time, evening/weekend. *Faculty:* 4 full-time (all women), 1 (woman) part-time/adjunct. *Students:* 2 full-time (both women), 41 part-time (34 women); includes 3 minority (1 American Indian or Alaska Native, non-Hispanic/Latino; 2 Hispanic/Latino). Average age 31. 28 applicants, 82% accepted, 23 enrolled. In 2016, 3 master's awarded. *Entrance requirements:* For master's, 3 recommendations, resume, statement of purpose. Additional exam requirements/recommendations for international students: Required—TOEFL (minimum score 550 paper-based; 79 iBT). *Application deadline:* Applications are processed on a rolling basis. Application fee: $0. Electronic applications accepted. *Expenses:* $450 per semester hour. *Financial support:* In 2016–17, 17 students received support. Scholarships/grants available. Support available to part-time students. Financial award application deadline: 3/1; financial award applicants required to submit FAFSA. *Application contact:* Timothy J. Panfil, Director of Enrollment Management, School for Professional Studies, 630-617-3300 Ext. 3256, Fax: 630-617-6471, E-mail: panfilt@elmhurst.edu.
Website: http://www.elmhurst.edu/tl

Emporia State University, Program in Curriculum and Instruction, Emporia, KS 66801-5415. Offers curriculum leadership (MS); effective practitioner (MS); national board certification (MS). *Accreditation:* NCATE. *Program availability:* Part-time, online only, 100% online. *Faculty:* 10 full-time (3 women). *Students:* 7 full-time (all women), 134 part-time (123 women); includes 6 minority (1 Black or African American, non-Hispanic/Latino; 1 American Indian or Alaska Native, non-Hispanic/Latino; 3 Hispanic/Latino; 1 Two or more races, non-Hispanic/Latino). 35 applicants, 100% accepted, 32 enrolled. In 2016, 57 master's awarded. *Degree requirements:* For master's, comprehensive exam or thesis, practicum. *Entrance requirements:* For master's, GRE or MAT, appropriate bachelor's degree, teacher certification, 1 year of teaching experience, letters of recommendation. *Application deadline:* For fall admission, 8/15 priority date for domestic students. Applications are processed on a rolling basis. Application fee: $30 ($75 for international students). Electronic applications accepted. *Expenses:* Tuition, state resident: full-time $5922; part-time $246.75 per credit hour. Tuition, nonresident: full-time $18,414; part-time $767.25 per credit hour. *Required fees:* $1884; $78.50 per credit hour. *Financial support:* Career-related internships or fieldwork, Federal Work-Study, institutionally sponsored loans, health care benefits, and unspecified assistantships available. Financial award application deadline: 3/15; financial award applicants required to submit FAFSA. *Unit head:* Dr. Daniel Stiffler, Chair, 620-341-5776, E-mail: dstiffle@emporia.edu. *Application contact:* Mary Sewell, Admissions Coordinator, 800-950-GRAD, Fax: 620-341-5909, E-mail: msewell@emporia.edu.
Website: http://www.emporia.edu/sleme/graduate-programs/ci.html

Emporia State University, Program in Educational Administration, Emporia, KS 66801-5415. Offers elementary administration (MS); elementary/secondary administration (MS); secondary administration (MS). *Accreditation:* NCATE. *Program availability:* Part-time. *Faculty:* 10 full-time (3 women). *Students:* 5 full-time (4 women), 1 part-time (45 women); includes 7 minority (4 Black or African American, non-Hispanic/Latino; 1 Asian, non-Hispanic/Latino; 1 Hispanic/Latino; 1 Two or more races, non-Hispanic/Latino). 28 applicants, 100% accepted, 11 enrolled. In 2016, 61 master's awarded. *Degree requirements:* For master's, comprehensive exam or thesis, practicum. *Entrance requirements:* For master's, GRE or MAT, appropriate bachelor's degree, letters of recommendation, teacher certification, 1 year of teaching experience. *Application deadline:* For fall admission, 8/15 priority date for domestic students. Applications are processed on a rolling basis. Application fee: $30 ($75 for international students). Electronic applications accepted. *Expenses:* Tuition, state resident: full-time $5922; part-time $246.75 per credit hour. Tuition, nonresident: full-time $18,414; part-time $767.25 per credit hour. *Required fees:* $1884; $78.50 per credit hour. *Financial support:* Career-related internships or fieldwork, Federal Work-Study, institutionally sponsored loans, health care benefits, and unspecified assistantships available. Financial award application deadline: 3/15; financial award applicants required to submit FAFSA. *Unit head:* Dr. Daniel Stiffler, Chair, 620-341-5776, E-mail: dstiffle@emporia.edu. *Application contact:* Mary Sewell, Admissions Coordinator, 800-950-GRAD, Fax: 620-341-5909, E-mail: msewell@emporia.edu.

Endicott College, Van Loan School of Graduate and Professional Studies, Program in Administrative Leadership, Beverly, MA 01915-2096. Offers M Ed. *Program availability:* Part-time, evening/weekend. *Faculty:* 6 part-time/adjunct (3 women). *Students:* 40 full-time (23 women), 6 part-time (1 woman); includes 1 minority (Asian, non-Hispanic/Latino). Average age 37. In 2016, 27 master's awarded. *Entrance requirements:* For master's, Massachusetts Tests for Educator Licensure (MTEL) Communication and Literacy Test; MAT or GRE, baccalaureate degree, at least three years of school-based employment. Additional exam requirements/recommendations for international students:

Required—TOEFL. *Application deadline:* Applications are processed on a rolling basis. Application fee: $50. Electronic applications accepted. *Expenses:* Contact institution. *Financial support:* Scholarships/grants available. Financial award applicants required to submit FAFSA. *Unit head:* Dr. Aubry Threlkeld, Director of Graduate Licensure Programs, 978-232-2408, E-mail: athrelke@endicott.edu. *Application contact:* Ian Menchini, Director, Graduate Enrollment and Advising, 978-232-5292.

Endicott College, Van Loan School of Graduate and Professional Studies, Program in Educational Leadership, Beverly, MA 01915-2096. Offers Ed D. *Program availability:* Part-time, evening/weekend. *Faculty:* 2 full-time (both women), 7 part-time/adjunct (4 women). *Students:* 4 full-time (all women), 15 part-time (9 women); includes 1 minority (Black or African American, non-Hispanic/Latino). Average age 42. 7 applicants, 100% accepted, 6 enrolled. In 2016, 2 doctorates awarded. *Degree requirements:* For doctorate, comprehensive exam, thesis/dissertation, apprenticeship. *Entrance requirements:* For doctorate, GRE or MAT, official undergraduate and graduate transcripts, three letters of recommendation, personal statement, resume or curriculum vitae, writing sample, interview. Additional exam requirements/recommendations for international students: Required—TOEFL. *Application deadline:* For fall admission, 6/1 for domestic students. Application fee: $50. *Expenses:* Contact institution. *Faculty research:* Learning styles in post-secondary education, leadership in the professoriate, collapsing boundaries PreK-PhD. *Unit head:* Dr. Lynne Celli, Associate Dean of Graduate Education, 978-816-7651, Fax: 978-232-3000, E-mail: lcelli@endicott.edu. *Application contact:* Ian Menchini, Director, Graduate Enrollment and Advising, 978-232-5292, Fax: 978-232-3000, E-mail: imenchin@endicott.edu.
Website: http://www.endicott.edu/VanLoan/Graduate-Studies/Doctoral-Studies.aspx

Evangel University, Department of Education, Springfield, MO 65802. Offers curriculum and instruction (M Ed); educational leadership (M Ed); literacy (M Ed); secondary teaching (M Ed). *Accreditation:* NCATE. *Program availability:* Part-time, evening/weekend, 100% online, blended/hybrid learning. *Faculty:* 3 full-time (2 women), 4 part-time/adjunct (2 women). *Students:* 2 full-time (1 woman), 33 part-time (29 women); includes 1 minority (Asian, non-Hispanic/Latino). Average age 30. 10 applicants, 90% accepted, 9 enrolled. In 2016, 28 master's awarded. *Degree requirements:* For master's, comprehensive exam, thesis optional. *Entrance requirements:* For master's, PRAXIS II (preferred) or GRE, minimum undergraduate GPA of 3.0. Additional exam requirements/recommendations for international students: Required—TOEFL (minimum score 550 paper-based). *Application deadline:* For fall admission, 7/15 priority date for domestic students, 8/1 for international students; for spring admission, 11/15 priority date for domestic students, 12/1 for international students. Applications are processed on a rolling basis. Application fee: $25. Electronic applications accepted. Application fee is waived when completed online. *Expenses: Tuition:* Part-time $400 per credit hour. *Required fees:* $148 per trimester. One-time fee: $25. Tuition and fees vary according to course load, degree level and program. *Financial support:* In 2016–17, 11 students received support. Scholarships/grants and unspecified assistantships available. Financial award application deadline: 4/1; financial award applicants required to submit FAFSA. *Unit head:* Dr. Susan Langston, Program Coordinator, 417-865-2815 Ext. 8552, E-mail: langstons@evangel.edu. *Application contact:* Karen Benitez, Admissions Representative, Graduate Studies, 417-865-2815 Ext. 7416, Fax: 417-575-5484, E-mail: benitezk@evangel.edu.
Website: http://www.evangel.edu/academics/graduate-studies/graduate-programs

Evangel University, Doctor of Educational Leadership in Curriculum and Instruction Program, Springfield, MO 65802. Offers Ed D. *Program availability:* Part-time, evening/weekend. *Faculty:* 4 full-time (1 woman), 2 part-time/adjunct (1 woman). *Students:* 26 full-time (21 women), 6 part-time (2 women); includes 2 minority (1 American Indian or Alaska Native, non-Hispanic/Latino; 1 Two or more races, non-Hispanic/Latino). Average age 41. 3 applicants, 100% accepted, 3 enrolled. *Degree requirements:* For doctorate, thesis/dissertation. *Entrance requirements:* For doctorate, MA in education (preferred). Additional exam requirements/recommendations for international students: Required—TOEFL (minimum score 550 paper-based). *Application deadline:* For fall admission, 7/15 priority date for domestic students, 8/1 for international students; for spring admission, 11/15 priority date for domestic students, 12/1 for international students. Applications are processed on a rolling basis. Application fee: $25. Electronic applications accepted. *Expenses: Tuition:* Part-time $400 per credit hour. *Required fees:* $148 per trimester. One-time fee: $25. Tuition and fees vary according to course load, degree level and program. *Financial support:* In 2016–17, 8 students received support. Scholarships/grants available. Support available to part-time students. Financial award application deadline: 4/1; financial award applicants required to submit FAFSA. *Unit head:* Dr. Susan Langston, Program Coordinator, 417-865-2815 Ext. 8552, E-mail: langstons@evangel.edu. *Application contact:* Karen Benitez, Admissions Representative, Graduate Studies, 417-865-2811 Ext. 7416, Fax: 417-575-5484, E-mail: benitezk@evangel.edu.
Website: https://www.evangel.edu/programs/doctor-education-educational-leadership-curriculum-instruction/

Fairleigh Dickinson University, College at Florham, University College: Arts, Sciences, and Professional Studies, Peter Sammartino School of Education, Program in Educational Leadership, Madison, NJ 07940-1099. Offers MA.

Fairleigh Dickinson University, Metropolitan Campus, University College: Arts, Sciences, and Professional Studies, Peter Sammartino School of Education, Program in Educational Leadership, Teaneck, NJ 07666-1914. Offers MA.

Fayetteville State University, Graduate School, Programs in Educational Leadership and School Administration, Fayetteville, NC 28301-4298. Offers school administration (MSA). *Accreditation:* NCATE (one or more programs are accredited). *Program availability:* Part-time, evening/weekend. *Faculty:* 7 full-time (4 women), 2 part-time/adjunct (1 woman). *Students:* 63 full-time (46 women), 37 part-time (25 women); includes 70 minority (62 Black or African American, non-Hispanic/Latino; 1 American Indian or Alaska Native, non-Hispanic/Latino; 1 Asian, non-Hispanic/Latino; 3 Hispanic/Latino; 3 Two or more races, non-Hispanic/Latino), 1 international. Average age 42. 32 applicants, 100% accepted, 32 enrolled. In 2016, 22 master's, 6 doctorates awarded. *Degree requirements:* For master's, internship, written and oral exams. *Entrance requirements:* For master's, GRE or MAT, minimum GPA of 2.5. Additional exam requirements/recommendations for international students: Required—TOEFL. *Application deadline:* For fall admission, 4/1 for domestic students. Applications are processed on a rolling basis. Application fee: $40. Electronic applications accepted. *Financial support:* Application deadline: 3/1; applicants required to submit FAFSA. *Faculty research:* First-generation college students and academic successes, educational law and higher education, educational policy and K-12/higher education. *Total annual research expenditures:* $20,000. *Unit head:* Dr. Linda Wilson-Jones, Chair and Professor, Department of Educational Leadership, 910-672-1731, Fax: 910-672-2075, E-mail: lwilson-jones@uncfsu.edu. *Application contact:* Mable Hawkins, Administrative Support Associate, 910-672-1731, Fax: 910-672-2075, E-mail: mhawkins@uncfsu.edu.

Felician University, Program in Education, Lodi, NJ 07644-2117. Offers education (MA); educational leadership (principal/supervision) (MA); educational supervision (PMC); principal (PMC). *Accreditation:* TEAC. *Program availability:* Part-time, evening/weekend. *Faculty:* 2 full-time (1 woman), 7 part-time/adjunct (2 women). *Students:* 4 full-time (3 women), 65 part-time (60 women); includes 19 minority (9 Black or African American, non-Hispanic/Latino; 2 Asian, non-Hispanic/Latino; 8 Hispanic/Latino), 1 international. Average age 36. 36 applicants, 78% accepted, 16 enrolled. In 2016, 18 master's, 11 other advanced degrees awarded. *Degree requirements:* For master's and PMC, presentation. *Entrance requirements:* For master's, PRAXIS Core (Reading/Writing/Math), minimum GPA of 3.0, two professional letters of recommendation, personal statement, personal interview. Additional exam requirements/recommendations for international students: Required—TOEFL (minimum score 650 paper-based; 79 iBT), IELTS (minimum score 6.5). *Application deadline:* Applications are processed on a rolling basis. Application fee: $40. Electronic applications accepted. Application fee is waived when completed online. *Expenses:* $790 per credit, $290 comprehensive fees, $165 mandatory fees. *Financial support:* Federal Work-Study and scholarships/grants available. Financial award applicants required to submit FAFSA. *Faculty research:* Educational leadership, administration, supervision, curriculum. *Unit head:* Dr. Rose Rudnitski, Dean and Professor, School of Education, 201-559-3551, E-mail: rudnitskir@felician.edu. *Application contact:* Michael Szarek, Assistant Vice-President, Graduate Admissions, 201-559-1450, E-mail: szarekm@felician.edu.

Ferris State University, College of Education and Human Services, School of Education, Big Rapids, MI 49307. Offers curriculum and instruction (M Ed), including special education, subject area; educational leadership (MS); instructor (MSCTE); post-secondary administration (MSCTE); training and development (MSCTE). *Program availability:* Part-time, evening/weekend, blended/hybrid learning. *Faculty:* 7 full-time (4 women), 9 part-time/adjunct (6 women). *Students:* 3 full-time (1 woman), 62 part-time (34 women); includes 8 minority (3 Black or African American, non-Hispanic/Latino; 1 Hispanic/Latino; 4 Two or more races, non-Hispanic/Latino), 9 international. Average age 37. 24 applicants, 71% accepted, 10 enrolled. In 2016, 36 master's awarded. *Degree requirements:* For master's, thesis, research paper or project. *Entrance requirements:* For master's, minimum undergraduate GPA of 3.0. Additional exam requirements/recommendations for international students: Required—TOEFL (minimum score 500 paper-based, 79 iBT) or IELTS. *Application deadline:* For fall admission, 7/1 priority date for domestic and international students; for spring admission, 11/1 priority date for domestic and international students; for summer admission, 3/1 priority date for domestic and international students. Applications are processed on a rolling basis. Application fee: $30. Electronic applications accepted. Application fee is waived when completed online. Tuition and fees vary according to degree level and program. *Financial support:* Career-related internships or fieldwork and scholarships/grants available. Support available to part-time students. Financial award applicants required to submit FAFSA. *Faculty research:* Suicide prevention, reading, women in education, special needs, administration. *Unit head:* Arrick L. Jackson, Dean, 231-591-2702, Fax: 231-591-2043, E-mail: arrickJackson@ferris.edu. *Application contact:* Liza Ing, Graduate Program Coordinator, 231-591-5362, Fax: 231-591-2043, E-mail: lizaIng@ferris.edu.
Website: http://www.ferris.edu/education/education/

Ferris State University, Extended and International Operations, Big Rapids, MI 49307. Offers community college leadership (Ed D). *Program availability:* Evening/weekend, blended/hybrid learning. *Faculty:* 23 part-time/adjunct (14 women). *Students:* 94 full-time (70 women), 4 part-time (1 woman); includes 21 minority (16 Black or African American, non-Hispanic/Latino; 5 Hispanic/Latino). Average age 46. 28 applicants, 75% accepted, 19 enrolled. In 2016, 11 doctorates awarded. *Degree requirements:* For doctorate, thesis/dissertation, e-portfolio demonstrating completion of program outcomes. *Entrance requirements:* For doctorate, master's degree with minimum GPA of 3.25, fierce commitment to the mission of community colleges, essay, writing samples. *Application deadline:* For fall admission, 12/15 for domestic and international students; for winter admission, 1/27 for domestic and international students; for spring admission, 4/15 for domestic students, 4/18 for international students. Applications are processed on a rolling basis. Application fee: $0. Electronic applications accepted. *Expenses:* Contact institution. *Financial support:* In 2016–17, 4 teaching assistantships (averaging $1,000 per year) were awarded. Financial award application deadline: 5/1; financial award applicants required to submit FAFSA. *Unit head:* Dr. Roberta Teahen, Director, 231-591-3805, E-mail: robertateahen@ferris.edu. *Application contact:* Megan Biller, Coordinator, 231-591-2710, Fax: 231-591-3539, E-mail: meganbiller@ferris.edu.

Fielding Graduate University, Graduate Programs, School of Leadership Studies, Programs in Education, Santa Barbara, CA 93105-3814. Offers digital teaching and learning (MA); educational administration (Certificate); leadership for change (Ed D). *Program availability:* 100% online, blended/hybrid learning. *Faculty:* 7 full-time (5 women), 15 part-time/adjunct (11 women). *Students:* 93 full-time (65 women), 5 part-time (3 women); includes 56 minority (30 Black or African American, non-Hispanic/Latino; 4 American Indian or Alaska Native, non-Hispanic/Latino; 2 Asian, non-Hispanic/Latino; 12 Hispanic/Latino; 8 Two or more races, non-Hispanic/Latino), 1 international. Average age 50. 19 applicants, 95% accepted, 12 enrolled. In 2016, 5 master's, 27 doctorates awarded. *Degree requirements:* For doctorate, thesis/dissertation. *Entrance requirements:* For master's, bachelor's degree from regionally-accredited U.S. institution or equivalent, resume, statement of purpose, official transcript; for doctorate, bachelor's or master's degree from regionally-accredited U.S. institution or equivalent, resume, statement of purpose, reflexive essay, official transcript; for Certificate, bachelor's degree from regionally-accredited U.S. institution or equivalent, resume, statement of purpose, 3 letters of recommendation, official transcript, copy of professional license. *Application deadline:* For fall admission, 7/15 for domestic and international students; for spring admission, 11/1 for domestic and international students; for summer admission, 3/1 for domestic and international students. Application fee: $75. Electronic applications accepted. *Expenses:* $8,275 per term (for Ed D); $3,500 per term (for MA). *Financial support:* In 2016–17, 9 students received support. Scholarships/grants available. Financial award applicants required to submit FAFSA. *Unit head:* Dr. Barbara Mink, Program Director, E-mail: bmink@fielding.edu. *Application contact:* Enrollment Coordinator, 800-340-1099 Ext. 4098, Fax: 805-687-9793, E-mail: admissions@fielding.edu.
Website: http://www.fielding.edu/our-programs/school-of-leadership-studies/

Fitchburg State University, Division of Graduate and Continuing Education, Program in Educational Leadership and Management, Fitchburg, MA 01420-2697. Offers educational leadership and management (M Ed, CAGS); educational technology (Certificate); school principal (M Ed, CAGS); supervisor/director (M Ed, CAGS); technology leader (M Ed, CAGS). *Accreditation:* NCATE. *Program availability:* Part-time, evening/weekend. *Entrance requirements:* Additional exam requirements/recommendations for international students: Required—TOEFL (minimum score 550 paper-based; 79 iBT). Electronic applications accepted. *Expenses:* Tuition, state resident: full-time $2871; part-time $1914 per year. Tuition, nonresident: full-time $2871; part-time $1914 per year. *Required fees:* $3828. Tuition and fees vary according to program.

Florida Agricultural and Mechanical University, Division of Graduate Studies, Research, and Continuing Education, College of Education, Department of Educational Leadership and Human Services, Tallahassee, FL 32307-3200. Offers administration and supervision (M Ed, MS, PhD); adult education (M Ed, MS); educational leadership (PhD); guidance and counseling (M Ed, MS). *Accreditation:* NCATE. *Degree* *requirements:* For master's, thesis (for some programs); for doctorate, thesis/dissertation. *Entrance requirements:* For master's, GRE General Test, minimum GPA of 3.0. Additional exam requirements/recommendations for international students: Required—TOEFL.

Florida Atlantic University, College of Education, Department of Educational Leadership and Research Methodology, Boca Raton, FL 33431-0991. Offers adult and community education (M Ed, PhD, Ed S); educational leadership (M Ed, PhD, Ed S); higher education (M Ed, PhD); K-12 school leadership (M Ed, PhD, Ed S). *Accreditation:* NCATE. *Program availability:* Part-time, evening/weekend, online learning. *Faculty:* 24 full-time (12 women), 20 part-time/adjunct (9 women). *Students:* 110 full-time (71 women), 221 part-time (155 women); includes 166 minority (100 Black or African American, non-Hispanic/Latino; 6 Asian, non-Hispanic/Latino; 49 Hispanic/Latino; 1 Native Hawaiian or other Pacific Islander, non-Hispanic/Latino; 10 Two or more races, non-Hispanic/Latino), 6 international. Average age 36. 186 applicants, 65% accepted, 97 enrolled. In 2016, 66 master's, 19 doctorates, 8 other advanced degrees awarded. *Degree requirements:* For doctorate, comprehensive exam, thesis/dissertation, departmental qualifying exam; for Ed S, departmental qualifying exam. *Entrance requirements:* For master's, GRE General Test, minimum GPA of 3.0 during previous 2 years; for doctorate, GRE General Test, minimum GPA of 3.5; for Ed S, GRE General Test. Additional exam requirements/recommendations for international students: Required—TOEFL (minimum score 500 paper-based; 61 iBT), IELTS (minimum score 6). *Application deadline:* For fall admission, 7/1 for domestic students, 2/15 for international students; for spring admission, 9/15 for domestic students, 7/15 for international students. Applications are processed on a rolling basis. Application fee: $30. Electronic applications accepted. *Expenses:* Tuition, state resident: full-time $7392; part-time $369.82 per credit hour. Tuition, nonresident: full-time $19,432; part-time $1024.81 per credit hour. *Financial support:* Fellowships, research assistantships, teaching assistantships, career-related internships or fieldwork, and tuition waivers (partial) available. *Faculty research:* Self-directed learning, school reform issues, legal issues, mentoring, school leadership. *Unit head:* Dr. Robert E. Shockley, Chair, 561-297-3550, Fax: 561-297-3618, E-mail: shockley@fau.edu. *Application contact:* Kathy DuBois, Senior Secretary, 561-297-3550, Fax: 561-297-3618, E-mail: edleadership@fau.edu.
Website: http://www.coe.fau.edu/academicdepartments/el/

Florida Gulf Coast University, College of Education, Program in Educational Leadership, Fort Myers, FL 33965-6565. Offers M Ed, MA. *Program availability:* Part-time, evening/weekend. *Faculty:* 26 full-time (18 women), 44 part-time/adjunct (32 women). *Students:* 3 full-time (all women), 57 part-time (43 women); includes 15 minority (6 Black or African American, non-Hispanic/Latino; 2 Asian, non-Hispanic/Latino; 7 Hispanic/Latino), 1 international. Average age 32. 25 applicants, 76% accepted, 15 enrolled. In 2016, 14 master's awarded. *Degree requirements:* For master's, thesis or alternative, learning and professional portfolios. *Entrance requirements:* For master's, GRE General Test, MAT, minimum GPA of 3.0. Additional exam requirements/recommendations for international students: Required—TOEFL (minimum score 550 paper-based). *Application deadline:* For fall admission, 7/1 priority date for domestic students; for spring admission, 10/15 for domestic students. Applications are processed on a rolling basis. Application fee: $30. Electronic applications accepted. *Expenses:* Tuition, state resident: full-time $6721. Tuition, nonresident: full-time $28,170. *Required fees:* $1987. Tuition and fees vary according to course load and degree level. *Financial support:* In 2016–17, 1 student received support. Application deadline: 3/1; applicants required to submit FAFSA. *Faculty research:* Inclusion, technology in teaching, curriculum development in educational leadership, education policy and law. *Unit head:* Dr. Cecil Carter, Department Chair, 239-590-7794, Fax: 239-590-7801, E-mail: ccarter@fgcu.edu. *Application contact:* Keiana Desmore, Adviser/Counselor, 239-590-7759, Fax: 239-590-7801, E-mail: kdesmore@fgcu.edu.

Florida International University, College of Arts, Sciences, and Education, Department of Leadership and Professional Studies, Miami, FL 33199. Offers adult education and human resource development (MS, Ed D); counseling (MS), including rehabilitation counseling, school counseling; counselor education (MS), including clinical mental health counseling; educational administration and supervision (Ed D); educational leadership (MS, Certificate, Ed S); higher education (Ed D); higher education administration (MS); international and comparative education (MS); recreation and sport management (MS), including recreation and sport management, recreational therapy; school psychology (Ed S); urban education (MS), including instruction in urban settings, learning technologies, multicultural/bilingual, multicultural/TESOL, urban education. *Program availability:* Part-time, evening/weekend. *Faculty:* 27 full-time (19 women), 38 part-time/adjunct (25 women). *Students:* 253 full-time (191 women), 306 part-time (241 women); includes 444 minority (129 Black or African American, non-Hispanic/Latino; 3 Asian, non-Hispanic/Latino; 304 Hispanic/Latino; 8 Two or more races, non-Hispanic/Latino), 18 international. Average age 31. 366 applicants, 60% accepted, 115 enrolled. In 2016, 193 master's, 8 doctorates awarded. *Degree requirements:* For doctorate, thesis/dissertation. *Entrance requirements:* For master's, minimum GPA of 3.0; for doctorate and other advanced degree, GRE General Test. Additional exam requirements/recommendations for international students: Required—TOEFL (minimum score 550 paper-based; 80 iBT), IELTS (minimum score 6.3). *Application deadline:* For fall admission, 6/1 priority date for domestic students, 4/1 for international students; for winter admission, 10/1 priority date for domestic students, 9/1 for international students; for spring admission, 3/1 priority date for domestic students, 2/1 for international students. Applications are processed on a rolling basis. Application fee: $30. Electronic applications accepted. *Expenses:* Tuition, state resident: full-time $8912; part-time $446 per credit hour. Tuition, nonresident: full-time $21,393; part-time $992 per credit hour. *Required fees:* $2185; $195 per semester. Tuition and fees vary according to program. *Financial support:* Fellowships, research assistantships with tuition reimbursements, teaching assistantships with tuition reimbursements, Federal Work-Study, and tuition waivers (full and partial) available. Support available to part-time students. Financial award applicants required to submit FAFSA. *Unit head:* Dr. Benjamin Baez, Chair, 305-348-3214, Fax: 305-348-1515, E-mail: benjamin.baez@fiu.edu. *Application contact:* Nanett Rojas, Assistant Director, Graduate Admissions, 305-348-7464, Fax: 305-348-7441, E-mail: gradadm@fiu.edu.
Website: http://education.fiu.edu

Florida Southern College, Programs in Teaching, Lakeland, FL 33801-5698. Offers collaborative teaching and learning (M Ed); educational leadership (M Ed, Ed D); teaching (MAT). *Program availability:* Part-time, evening/weekend. *Faculty:* 7 full-time (3 women), 8 part-time/adjunct (5 women). *Students:* 49 full-time (40 women), 31 part-time (19 women); includes 19 minority (9 Black or African American, non-Hispanic/Latino; 1 American Indian or Alaska Native, non-Hispanic/Latino; 7 Hispanic/Latino; 1 Native Hawaiian or other Pacific Islander, non-Hispanic/Latino; 1 Two or more races, non-Hispanic/Latino), 2 international. Average age 40. 133 applicants, 54% accepted, 50 enrolled. In 2016, 1 master's awarded. *Degree requirements:* For master's, comprehensive exam (for some programs), thesis (for some programs), FICE General Knowledge test and professional education exam (for MAT), eligibility for the Florida Professional Teacher Certificate (for M Ed); for doctorate, thesis/dissertation. *Entrance requirements:* For master's, Florida Teacher Certification exam (for MAT), letter of reference, resume, personal statement. Additional exam requirements/recommendations for international students: Required—TOEFL (minimum score 550 paper-based; 79 iBT), IELTS (minimum score 6.5). *Application deadline:* For fall admission, 8/1 for domestic and international students; for winter admission, 4/1 for domestic and international students; for spring admission, 12/1 for domestic and international students. Applications are processed on a rolling basis. Application fee: $30. Electronic applications accepted. *Expenses:* $410 per credit hour tuition, $100 per term fees. *Financial support:* In 2016–17, 3 students received support. Scholarships/grants available. Support available to part-time students. Financial award applicants required to submit FAFSA. *Unit head:* Dr. Tracey Tedder, Dean, 863-680-4177, Fax: 863-680-4102, E-mail: ttedder@flsouthern.edu. *Application contact:* Kathy Connelly, Evening Program Assistant Director, 863-680-4205, Fax: 863-680-3872, E-mail: kconnelly@flsouthern.edu.

Florida State University, The Graduate School, College of Education, Program in Educational Leadership and Policy, Tallahassee, FL 32306. Offers education policy and evaluation (MS, Ed D, PhD); educational leadership/administration (MS, Ed D, PhD, Certificate, Ed S); program evaluation (Certificate). *Program availability:* Part-time, evening/weekend, blended/hybrid learning. Terminal master's awarded for partial completion of doctoral program. *Degree requirements:* For master's and other advanced degree, comprehensive exam, thesis optional; for doctorate, comprehensive exam, thesis/dissertation, diagnostic exam, preliminary exam, prospectus defense, dissertation defense. *Entrance requirements:* For master's, doctorate, and other advanced degree, GRE General Test, minimum upper-division GPA of 3.0. Additional exam requirements/recommendations for international students: Required—TOEFL (minimum score 550 paper-based, 80 iBT), IELTS (minimum score 6.5), Michigan English Language Assessment Battery (minimum score 77), or PTE (minimum score 55). Application fee: $30. Electronic applications accepted. *Expenses:* Tuition, state resident: full-time $7263; part-time $403.51 per credit hour. Tuition, nonresident: full-time $18,087; part-time $1004.85 per credit hour. *Required fees:* $1365; $75.81 per credit hour. $20 per semester. Tuition and fees vary according to campus/location. *Financial support:* Fellowships, research assistantships, teaching assistantships, scholarships/grants, tuition waivers (full and partial), and unspecified assistantships available. Financial award application deadline: 1/15; financial award applicants required to submit FAFSA. *Faculty research:* Educational leadership in traditional public and charter institutions, educational evaluation and policy, policy and politics of K-12 education, pre-service teacher and teacher policy and professional education, economics and finance of education. *Unit head:* Dr. Motoko Akiba, Professor/Program Coordinator, 850-644-5553, Fax: 850-644-1258, E-mail: makiba@fsu.edu. *Application contact:* Linda J. Lyons, Academic Support Assistant, 850-644-7077, Fax: 850-644-1258, E-mail: ljlyons@fsu.edu.
Website: http://education.fsu.edu/degrees-and-programs/graduate-programs

Fordham University, Graduate School of Education, Division of Educational Leadership, Administration and Policy, New York, NY 10023. Offers administration and supervision (MSE, Adv C); administration and supervision for church leaders (PhD); educational administration and supervision (Ed D, PhD). *Accreditation:* NCATE. *Program availability:* Part-time, evening/weekend. *Degree requirements:* For master's, comprehensive exam (for some programs); for doctorate, comprehensive exam (for some programs), thesis/dissertation. *Entrance requirements:* For doctorate, MAT, GRE General Test. Electronic applications accepted.

Fort Hays State University, Graduate School, College of Education, Department of Educational Administration and Counseling, Program in Educational Administration, Hays, KS 67601-4099. Offers MS, Ed S. *Accreditation:* NCATE. *Degree requirements:* For master's and Ed S, comprehensive exam, thesis or alternative. *Entrance requirements:* For master's, GRE General Test or MAT. Additional exam requirements/recommendations for international students: Required—TOEFL (minimum score 550 paper-based). Electronic applications accepted. *Faculty research:* Guide to negotiations, nutrition program for disadvantaged, accountability, student insurance practices, student liability.

Fort Lewis College, Program in Teacher Leadership, Durango, CO 81301-3999. Offers MA, Certificate. *Degree requirements:* For master's, culminating research project. *Entrance requirements:* For master's and Certificate, baccalaureate degree from regionally-accredited college or university; minimum cumulative undergraduate and graduate GPA of 3.0; one year of full-time teaching experience in P-12 schools.

Framingham State University, Continuing Education, Program in Educational Leadership, Framingham, MA 01701-9101. Offers MA. *Program availability:* Part-time, evening/weekend. *Entrance requirements:* For master's, MAT.

Franciscan University of Steubenville, Graduate Programs, Department of Education, Steubenville, OH 43952-1763. Offers administration (MS Ed); teaching (MS Ed). *Accreditation:* NCATE. *Program availability:* Part-time, evening/weekend, online learning. *Degree requirements:* For master's, project. *Entrance requirements:* For master's, minimum undergraduate GPA of 2.5 or written exam. Additional exam requirements/recommendations for international students: Required—TOEFL. Electronic applications accepted. Application fee is waived when completed online. *Expenses:* Contact institution.

Freed-Hardeman University, Program in Education, Henderson, TN 38340-2399. Offers curriculum and instruction (M Ed); school counseling (M Ed), including administration and supervision, special education; school leadership (Ed S). *Accreditation:* NCATE. *Program availability:* Part-time, evening/weekend. *Degree requirements:* For master's, comprehensive exam, thesis optional; for Ed S, thesis. *Entrance requirements:* For master's, GRE General Test or NTE; for Ed S, 3 years of teaching experience. Additional exam requirements/recommendations for international students: Required—TOEFL (minimum score 500 paper-based).

Fresno Pacific University, Graduate Programs, School of Education, Division of Administrative Services, Fresno, CA 93702-4709. Offers MA. *Program availability:* Part-time, evening/weekend. *Degree requirements:* For master's, thesis or alternative, 4 practica. *Entrance requirements:* Additional exam requirements/recommendations for international students: Required—TOEFL (minimum score 550 paper-based). Electronic applications accepted. *Expenses:* Contact institution.

Frostburg State University, Graduate School, College of Education, Department of Educational Professions, Program in Educational Administration and Supervision, Frostburg, MD 21532-1099. Offers elementary (M Ed); secondary (M Ed). *Program availability:* Part-time, evening/weekend. *Degree requirements:* For master's, thesis or alternative. *Entrance requirements:* For master's, teaching certificate. Additional exam requirements/recommendations for international students: Required—TOEFL. Electronic applications accepted. *Faculty research:* Practicum experience in schools.

Furman University, Graduate Division, Department of Education, Greenville, SC 29613. Offers curriculum and instruction (MA); early childhood education (MA); educational leadership (Ed S); English as a second language (MA); literacy (MA); school leadership (MA); special education (MA). *Accreditation:* NCATE. *Program availability:* Part-time, online learning. *Degree requirements:* For master's, comprehensive exam (for some programs), thesis or alternative. *Entrance requirements:* For master's, PRAXIS II.

Faculty research: Literacy, pedagogy and practice, social justice, advanced leadership, achievement in high poverty schools.

Gannon University, School of Graduate Studies, College of Humanities, Education, and Social Sciences, School of Education, Program in Principal Certification, Erie, PA 16541-0001. Offers Certificate. *Program availability:* Part-time, evening/weekend. *Students:* 9 part-time (7 women). Average age 38. 22 applicants, 68% accepted, 9 enrolled. In 2016, 6 Certificates awarded. *Degree requirements:* For Certificate, internship, portfolio. *Entrance requirements:* For degree, transcripts, master's degree in education or related field from regionally-accredited college or university with minimum GPA of 3.0, 3 letters of recommendation, documentation of 3 years of educational experience working under a certificate. Additional exam requirements/recommendations for international students: Required—TOEFL (minimum score 79 iBT). *Application deadline:* Applications are processed on a rolling basis. Application fee: $25. Electronic applications accepted. Application fee is waived when completed online. *Expenses:* Contact institution. *Financial support:* Federal Work-Study available. Financial award application deadline: 7/1; financial award applicants required to submit FAFSA. *Unit head:* Dr. Bill Hallock, Program Coordinator, 814-871-7136, E-mail: hallock002@gannon.edu. *Application contact:* Bridget Philip, Director of Graduate Admissions, 814-871-7412, E-mail: graduate@gannon.edu.

Gannon University, School of Graduate Studies, College of Humanities, Education, and Social Sciences, School of Education, Program in Superintendent Letter of Eligibility Certification, Erie, PA 16541-0001. Offers Certificate. *Program availability:* Part-time, evening/weekend. *Students:* 4 part-time (2 women). Average age 35. 6 applicants, 100% accepted, 5 enrolled. In 2016, 3 Certificates awarded. *Degree requirements:* For Certificate, thesis or alternative, superintendent internship, portfolio. *Entrance requirements:* For degree, transcripts, master's degree in education or related field from regionally-accredited college or university with minimum GPA of 3.0, 3 letters of recommendation, documentation of 6 years of educational experience working under a certificate. Additional exam requirements/recommendations for international students: Required—TOEFL (minimum score 79 iBT). *Application deadline:* Applications are processed on a rolling basis. Application fee: $25. Electronic applications accepted. Application fee is waived when completed online. *Expenses:* Contact institution. *Financial support:* Federal Work-Study available. Financial award application deadline: 7/1; financial award applicants required to submit FAFSA. *Unit head:* Dr. Bill Hallock, Program Coordinator, 814-871-7136, E-mail: hallock002@gannon.edu. *Application contact:* Bridget Philip, Director of Graduate Admission, 814-871-7412, E-mail: graduate@gannon.edu.

Gannon University, School of Graduate Studies, College of Humanities, Education, and Social Sciences, School of Humanities, Program in Organizational Learning and Leadership, Erie, PA 16541-0001. Offers PhD. *Program availability:* Part-time, evening/weekend. *Students:* 1 (woman) full-time, 65 part-time (37 women); includes 2 minority (1 Asian, non-Hispanic/Latino; 1 Hispanic/Latino), 2 international. Average age 41. 27 applicants, 59% accepted, 10 enrolled. In 2016, 2 doctorates awarded. *Degree requirements:* For doctorate, thesis/dissertation. *Entrance requirements:* For doctorate, GRE, master's or other post-baccalaureate professional graduate-level degree from regionally-accredited institution of higher education with minimum GPA of 3.5; 2 years of post-baccalaureate work experience; 3 letters of recommendation; transcripts; resume; statement of purpose. Additional exam requirements/recommendations for international students: Required—TOEFL (minimum score 79 iBT). *Application deadline:* For spring admission, 2/1 for domestic students. Applications are processed on a rolling basis. Application fee: $25. Electronic applications accepted. Application fee is waived when completed online. *Expenses: Tuition:* Full-time $17,370. *Required fees:* $550. Tuition and fees vary according to course load and program. *Financial support:* Federal Work-Study and unspecified assistantships available. Financial award application deadline: 7/1; financial award applicants required to submit FAFSA. *Unit head:* Dr. Bill Hallock, Director, 814-871-7136, E-mail: hallock002@gannon.edu. *Application contact:* Bridget Philip, Director of Graduate Admissions, 814-871-7412, E-mail: graduate@gannon.edu.

Gardner-Webb University, Graduate School, School of Education, Program in Educational Leadership, Boiling Springs, NC 28017. Offers Ed D. *Faculty:* 16 full-time (6 women), 35 part-time/adjunct (20 women). *Students:* 8 full-time (6 women), 135 part-time (92 women); includes 63 minority (61 Black or African American, non-Hispanic/Latino; 1 American Indian or Alaska Native, non-Hispanic/Latino; 1 Asian, non-Hispanic/Latino). Average age 41. 45 applicants, 29% accepted, 13 enrolled. In 2016, 18 doctorates awarded. *Expenses:* Contact institution. *Unit head:* Dr. Alan D. Eury, Chair, 704-406-4402, Fax: 704-406-3921, E-mail: dsimmons@gardner-webb.edu. *Application contact:* Office of Graduate Admissions, 877-498-4723, Fax: 704-406-3895, E-mail: gradinfo@gardner-webb.edu.

Gardner-Webb University, Graduate School, School of Education, Program in Executive Leadership Studies, Boiling Springs, NC 28017. Offers MA, Ed S. *Faculty:* 16 full-time (6 women), 35 part-time/adjunct (20 women). *Students:* 186 part-time (126 women); includes 71 minority (62 Black or African American, non-Hispanic/Latino; 2 American Indian or Alaska Native, non-Hispanic/Latino; 2 Asian, non-Hispanic/Latino; 4 Hispanic/Latino; 1 Two or more races, non-Hispanic/Latino). Average age 35. 118 applicants, 64% accepted, 62 enrolled. *Expenses:* Contact institution. *Unit head:* Dr. Alan D. Eury, Dean, 704-406-4402, Fax: 704-406-3921, E-mail: dsimmons@gardner-webb.edu. *Application contact:* Office of Graduate Admissions, 877-498-4723, Fax: 704-406-3895, E-mail: gradinfo@gardner-webb.edu.

Gardner-Webb University, Graduate School, School of Education, Program in School Administration, Boiling Springs, NC 28017. Offers MA. *Accreditation:* NCATE. *Program availability:* Part-time, evening/weekend. *Faculty:* 16 full-time (6 women), 35 part-time/adjunct (20 women). *Students:* 87 part-time (69 women); includes 50 minority (47 Black or African American, non-Hispanic/Latino; 1 American Indian or Alaska Native, non-Hispanic/Latino; 2 Hispanic/Latino). Average age 37. 102 applicants, 62% accepted, 49 enrolled. *Degree requirements:* For master's, comprehensive exam. *Entrance requirements:* For master's, GRE General Test or NTE, PRAXIS, minimum GPA of 2.5. *Application deadline:* For fall admission, 8/1 priority date for domestic students. Applications are processed on a rolling basis. Electronic applications accepted. *Expenses:* Contact institution. *Financial support:* Unspecified assistantships available. *Unit head:* Dr. Alan D. Eury, Dean of the School of Education, 704-406-4402. *Application contact:* Office of Graduate Admissions, 877-498-4723, Fax: 704-406-3895, E-mail: gradinfo@gardner-webb.edu.

Gateway Seminary, Graduate and Professional Programs, Ontario, CA 91761-8642. Offers divinity (M Div); early childhood education (Certificate); education leadership (MAEL, Diploma); ministry (D Min); theological studies (MTS); theology (Th M); youth ministry (Certificate). *Accreditation:* ACIPE. *Program availability:* Part-time, evening/weekend. *Degree requirements:* For master's, thesis (for some programs); for doctorate, 2 foreign languages, thesis/dissertation. *Entrance requirements:* For doctorate, MAT. Additional exam requirements/recommendations for international students: Required—TOEFL (minimum score 550 paper-based). Electronic applications accepted.

Geneva College, Master of Arts in Higher Education Program, Beaver Falls, PA 15010-3599. Offers campus ministry (MA); college teaching (MA); educational leadership (MA); student affairs administration (MA). *Program availability:* Part-time, evening/weekend, blended/hybrid learning. *Faculty:* 2 full-time (0 women), 11 part-time/adjunct (4 women). *Students:* 49 full-time (30 women), 7 part-time (2 women); includes 6 minority (3 Black or African American, non-Hispanic/Latino; 1 Hispanic/Latino; 2 Two or more races, non-Hispanic/Latino), 1 international. Average age 26. 47 applicants, 74% accepted, 23 enrolled. In 2016, 23 master's awarded. *Degree requirements:* For master's, 36 hours (27 in core courses) including a capstone research project. *Entrance requirements:* For master's, minimum GPA of 3.0, writing sample, 3 letters of recommendation, essay on motivation for participation in the program. Additional exam requirements/recommendations for international students: Required—TOEFL. *Application deadline:* For fall admission, 9/1 priority date for domestic students; for winter admission, 1/2 priority date for domestic students; for spring admission, 3/11 priority date for domestic students. Applications are processed on a rolling basis. Electronic applications accepted. *Expenses:* $655 per credit. *Financial support:* In 2016–17, 37 students received support. Unspecified assistantships available. Financial award application deadline: 8/1; financial award applicants required to submit FAFSA. *Faculty research:* Learning theories, church-related higher education, organizational culture, sexual assault and transgender students at Christian colleges, emerging technology in higher education. *Unit head:* Dr. Keith Martel, Program Director, 724-847-6884, Fax: 724-847-6107, E-mail: hed@geneva.edu. *Application contact:* Jerryn S. Carson, Program Coordinator, 724-847-6510, Fax: 724-847-6696, E-mail: hed@geneva.edu.
Website: http://www.geneva.edu/page/higher_ed

George Fox University, College of Education, Doctor of Education in Educational Leadership Program, Newberg, OR 97132-2697. Offers Ed D. *Program availability:* Online learning.

George Fox University, College of Education, Graduate Teaching and Leading Program, Newberg, OR 97132-2697. Offers administrative leadership (Ed S); continuing administrator license (Certificate); educational leadership (M Ed); educational technology (M Ed); English for speakers of other languages (M Ed); ESOL (Certificate); initial administrator license (Certificate); reading (M Ed, Certificate); special education (M Ed); teaching (MAT). *Accreditation:* NCATE. *Program availability:* Part-time, evening/weekend, online learning. *Degree requirements:* For master's, thesis (for some programs). *Entrance requirements:* For master's, minimum undergraduate GPA of 3.0 during previous 2 years of course work, resume, 3 professional recommendations on university forms, official transcripts. Additional exam requirements/recommendations for international students: Required—TOEFL (minimum score 577 paper-based; 90 iBT). Electronic applications accepted. *Expenses:* Contact institution.

George Mason University, College of Education and Human Development, Program in Education Leadership, Fairfax, VA 22030. Offers M Ed, Certificate. *Accreditation:* NCATE. *Faculty:* 5 full-time (2 women), 8 part-time/adjunct (4 women). *Students:* 4 full-time (3 women), 347 part-time (276 women); includes 87 minority (47 Black or African American, non-Hispanic/Latino; 10 Asian, non-Hispanic/Latino; 25 Hispanic/Latino; 5 Two or more races, non-Hispanic/Latino). Average age 36. 156 applicants, 88% accepted, 103 enrolled. In 2016, 83 master's, 4 Certificates awarded. *Entrance requirements:* For master's, bachelor's degree from regionally-accredited institution with minimum GPA of 3.0 overall or in last 60 credit hours; 2 official transcripts; expanded goals statement; 3 letters of recommendation; 3 years of documented teaching experience. Additional exam requirements/recommendations for international students: Required—TOEFL (minimum score 575 paper-based; 88 iBT), IELTS (minimum score 6.5), PTE (minimum score 59). *Application deadline:* For spring admission, 11/1 priority date for domestic and international students. Application fee: $75 ($80 for international students). Electronic applications accepted. *Expenses:* Tuition, state resident: full-time $10,628; part-time $443 per credit. Tuition, nonresident: full-time $29,306; part-time $1221 per credit. *Required fees:* $3096; $129 per credit. Tuition and fees vary according to program. *Financial support:* In 2016–17, 1 student received support, including 1 teaching assistantship (averaging $6,900 per year); career-related internships or fieldwork, Federal Work-Study, scholarships/grants, unspecified assistantships, and health care benefits (for full-time research or teaching assistantship recipients) also available. Financial award application deadline: 3/1; financial award applicants required to submit FAFSA. *Faculty research:* Understanding of the complexities of change in schools, communities, and organizations; education law; foundations of education leadership, history and leadership. *Unit head:* Farnoosh Shahrokhi, Academic Program Coordinator, 703-993-2009, E-mail: fshahrok@gmu.edu.
Website: http://gse.gmu.edu/programs/edleadership/

George Mason University, College of Education and Human Development, Programs in Curriculum and Instruction, Fairfax, VA 22030. Offers advanced international baccalaureate (M Ed); assistive technology (M Ed); designing digital learning in schools (M Ed); early childhood education (M Ed); early childhood education for diverse learners (M Ed); elementary education (M Ed); English as a second language (M Ed); gifted child education (M Ed); history (M Ed); literacy (M Ed), including PK-12 classroom teachers, reading specialist; literacy leadership for diverse schools (M Ed), including K-12 reading; physical education (M Ed); science K-12 (M Ed); secondary education (M Ed), including biology, chemistry, earth science, English, history/social science, math, physics; special education (M Ed); teacher leadership (M Ed); teaching culturally, linguistically diverse and exceptional learners (M Ed); transformative teaching (M Ed). *Faculty:* 41 full-time (35 women), 53 part-time/adjunct (46 women). *Students:* 155 full-time (127 women), 821 part-time (697 women); includes 267 minority (82 Black or African American, non-Hispanic/Latino; 5 American Indian or Alaska Native, non-Hispanic/Latino; 75 Asian, non-Hispanic/Latino; 88 Hispanic/Latino; 1 Native Hawaiian or other Pacific Islander, non-Hispanic/Latino; 16 Two or more races, non-Hispanic/Latino), 19 international. Average age 33. 513 applicants, 90% accepted, 352 enrolled. In 2016, 347 master's awarded. *Degree requirements:* For master's, comprehensive exam, thesis (for some programs). *Entrance requirements:* For master's, PRAXIS Core (for some programs), minimum GPA of 3.0 in last 60 hours, licensed as teacher or educational administrator, official transcripts, goals statement, 3 recommendation letters, interview or writing sample (depending on program), up to 3 years' teaching experience (depending on program). Additional exam requirements/recommendations for international students: Required—TOEFL (minimum score 575 paper-based; 88 iBT), IELTS (minimum score 6.5), PTE (minimum score 59). *Application deadline:* For spring admission, 11/1 priority date for domestic and international students. Application fee: $75 ($80 for international students). Electronic applications accepted. *Expenses:* Tuition, state resident: full-time $10,628; part-time $443 per credit. Tuition, nonresident: full-time $29,306; part-time $1221 per credit. *Required fees:* $3096; $129 per credit. Tuition and fees vary according to program. *Financial support:* In 2016–17, 1 student received support, including 1 teaching assistantship (averaging $4,060 per year); career-related internships or fieldwork, Federal Work-Study, scholarships/grants, unspecified assistantships, and health care benefits (for full-time research or teaching assistantship recipients) also available. Support available to part-time students. Financial award application deadline: 3/1; financial award applicants required to submit FAFSA. *Faculty research:* Achievement gaps and superintendent decisions, constructivist view of classroom teaching, cost of cheating, creating a critical literacy milieu in kindergarten. *Unit head:* Rebecca Fox, Professor and Academic Program Coordinator, 703-993-4123, E-mail: rfox@gmu.edu.
Website: http://gse.gmu.edu/programs/gsemasters

Educational Leadership and Administration

The George Washington University, Graduate School of Education and Human Development, Department of Educational Leadership, Program in Educational Administration and Policy Studies, Washington, DC 20052. Offers education policy (Ed D); educational administration (Ed D). Ed D in educational administration offered at Newport News and Alexandria, VA. *Accreditation:* NCATE. *Students:* 10 full-time (8 women), 126 part-time (86 women); includes 60 minority (45 Black or African American, non-Hispanic/Latino; 7 Asian, non-Hispanic/Latino; 5 Hispanic/Latino; 1 Native Hawaiian or other Pacific Islander, non-Hispanic/Latino; 2 Two or more races, non-Hispanic/Latino), 2 international. Average age 40. 50 applicants, 58% accepted, 18 enrolled. In 2016, 27 doctorates awarded. *Degree requirements:* For doctorate, comprehensive exam, thesis/dissertation. *Entrance requirements:* For doctorate, GRE General Test or MAT, interview, minimum GPA of 3.3. *Application deadline:* For fall admission, 1/15 priority date for domestic students; for spring admission, 10/1 for domestic students. Applications are processed on a rolling basis. Application fee: $75. *Financial support:* In 2016–17, 9 students received support. Fellowships, research assistantships, teaching assistantships, career-related internships or fieldwork, Federal Work-Study, and tuition waivers (partial) available. Financial award application deadline: 1/15; financial award applicants required to submit FAFSA. *Unit head:* Michael Feuer, Dean, 202-994-6161, E-mail: mjfeuer@gwu.edu. *Application contact:* Sarah Lang, Director, Admissions and Marketing, 202-994-1447, Fax: 202-994-7207, E-mail: slang@gwu.edu.

The George Washington University, Graduate School of Education and Human Development, Department of Educational Leadership, Program in Educational Leadership and Administration, Washington, DC 20052. Offers MA Ed, Certificate, Ed S. Programs offered at Newport News and Alexandria, VA. *Accreditation:* NCATE. *Program availability:* Evening/weekend. *Students:* 23 full-time (17 women), 175 part-time (138 women); includes 84 minority (63 Black or African American, non-Hispanic/Latino; 1 American Indian or Alaska Native, non-Hispanic/Latino; 1 Asian, non-Hispanic/Latino; 10 Hispanic/Latino; 9 Two or more races, non-Hispanic/Latino), 7 international. Average age 36. 248 applicants, 75% accepted, 147 enrolled. In 2016, 20 master's, 23 Certificates awarded. *Degree requirements:* For master's, comprehensive exam. *Entrance requirements:* For master's, GRE General Test or MAT, interview, minimum GPA of 2.75. *Application deadline:* For fall admission, 1/15 priority date for domestic students; for spring admission, 10/1 for domestic students. Applications are processed on a rolling basis. Application fee: $75. *Financial support:* Fellowships, teaching assistantships, career-related internships or fieldwork, and Federal Work-Study available. Financial award application deadline: 1/15; financial award applicants required to submit FAFSA. *Faculty research:* Organizational learning. *Unit head:* Michael Feuer, Dean, 202-994-6161, E-mail: mjfeuer@gwu.edu. *Application contact:* Sarah Lang, Director of Graduate Admissions, 202-994-1447, Fax: 202-994-7207, E-mail: slang@gwu.edu.

The George Washington University, Graduate School of Education and Human Development, Department of Educational Leadership, Program in Higher Education Administration, Washington, DC 20052. Offers college teaching and academic leadership (MA Ed/HD, Ed S); general administration (MA Ed/HD, Ed S); higher education administration (Ed D); higher education finance (MA Ed/HD, Ed S); international education (MA Ed/HD, Ed S); policy (MA Ed/HD, Ed S); student affairs administration (MA Ed/HD, Ed S). *Accreditation:* NCATE. *Students:* 23 full-time (18 women), 70 part-time (51 women); includes 35 minority (20 Black or African American, non-Hispanic/Latino; 8 Asian, non-Hispanic/Latino; 6 Hispanic/Latino; 1 Two or more races, non-Hispanic/Latino), 3 international. Average age 31. 148 applicants, 74% accepted, 37 enrolled. In 2016, 30 master's, 9 doctorates, 1 other advanced degree awarded. *Degree requirements:* For master's and Ed S, comprehensive exam; for doctorate, comprehensive exam, thesis/dissertation. *Entrance requirements:* For master's, GRE General Test or MAT, minimum GPA of 2.75; for doctorate, GRE General Test or MAT, interview, minimum GPA of 3.3; for Ed S, GRE General Test or MAT, minimum GPA of 3.3. *Application deadline:* For fall admission, 1/15 priority date for domestic students; for spring admission, 10/1 for domestic students. Applications are processed on a rolling basis. Application fee: $75. *Financial support:* In 2016–17, 17 students received support. Fellowships, research assistantships, career-related internships or fieldwork, Federal Work-Study, and tuition waivers (partial) available. Financial award application deadline: 1/15; financial award applicants required to submit FAFSA. *Faculty research:* Technology in higher education administration. *Unit head:* Michael Feuer, Dean, 202-994-6161, E-mail: mjfeuer@gwu.edu. *Application contact:* Sarah Lang, Director of Graduate Admissions, 202-994-1447, Fax: 202-994-7207, E-mail: slang@gwu.edu.

The George Washington University, Graduate School of Education and Human Development, Department of Educational Leadership, Program in Leadership in Educational Technology, Washington, DC 20052. Offers Graduate Certificate. *Students:* 1 part-time (0 women). Average age 37. 1 applicant. In 2016, 1 Graduate Certificate awarded. *Unit head:* Dr. Natalie Milman, Coordinator, 202-994-1884, E-mail: nmilman@gwu.edu. *Application contact:* Sarah Lang, Director of Graduate Admissions, 202-994-1447, Fax: 202-994-7207, E-mail: slang@gwu.edu.
Website: http://gsehd.gwu.edu/

Georgia College & State University, Graduate School, The John H. Lounsbury College of Education, Program in Educational Leadership, Milledgeville, GA 31061. Offers Ed S. *Accreditation:* NCATE. *Program availability:* Part-time, evening/weekend. *Students:* 73 full-time (49 women), 1 part-time (0 women); includes 36 minority (33 Black or African American, non-Hispanic/Latino; 1 Asian, non-Hispanic/Latino; 1 Hispanic/Latino; 1 Two or more races, non-Hispanic/Latino). Average age 38. 58 applicants, 100% accepted, 44 enrolled. In 2016, 48 Ed Ss awarded. *Degree requirements:* For Ed S, comprehensive exam, minimum GPA of 3.0, complete program within 4 years. *Entrance requirements:* For degree, GACE, master's degree, 2 years of teaching experience, 2 professional recommendations, level 5 GA teacher certificate, minimum GPA of 3.25, transcripts, verification of immunization, transcript. *Application deadline:* For fall admission, 7/1 priority date for domestic students; for spring admission, 11/1 priority date for domestic students; for summer admission, 4/1 priority date for domestic students. Applications are processed on a rolling basis. Application fee: $40. Electronic applications accepted. *Expenses:* $288 per credit hour in-state tuition; $1,027 per credit hour out-of-state; fees vary by hours enrolled. *Financial support:* Application deadline: 3/1; applicants required to submit FAFSA. *Unit head:* Dr. Joseph Peters, Dean, College of Education, 478-445-2518, Fax: 478-445-6582, E-mail: joseph.peters@gcsu.edu. *Application contact:* Shanda Brand, Graduate Admission Advisor, 478-445-1383.

Georgian Court University, School of Education, Lakewood, NJ 08701-2697. Offers administration and leadership (MA); autism spectrum disorders (Certificate); education (MA); instructional technology (Certificate). *Accreditation:* TEAC. *Program availability:* Part-time, evening/weekend. *Faculty:* 14 full-time (8 women), 31 part-time/adjunct (18 women). *Students:* 66 full-time (55 women), 376 part-time (312 women); includes 92 minority (44 Black or African American, non-Hispanic/Latino; 1 American Indian or Alaska Native, non-Hispanic/Latino; 8 Asian, non-Hispanic/Latino; 34 Hispanic/Latino; 5 Two or more races, non-Hispanic/Latino). Average age 34. 409 applicants, 62% accepted, 174 enrolled. In 2016, 95 master's, 1 other advanced degree awarded. *Degree requirements:* For master's, comprehensive exam (for some programs), thesis (for some programs). *Entrance requirements:* For master's, GRE, GMAT or NTE/PRAXIS, 3 letters of recommendation. Additional exam requirements/recommendations for international students: Required—TOEFL (minimum score 550 paper-based). *Application deadline:* For fall admission, 8/15 priority date for domestic students, 5/1 for international students; for spring admission, 1/15 priority date for domestic students, 10/1 for international students. Applications are processed on a rolling basis. Application fee: $40. Electronic applications accepted. *Expenses: Tuition:* Full-time $15,079; part-time $839 per credit. *Required fees:* $968; $496 per credit. Tuition and fees vary according to campus/location and program. *Financial support:* Scholarships/grants, health care benefits, and unspecified assistantships available. Financial award application deadline: 4/15; financial award applicants required to submit FAFSA. *Unit head:* Dr. Lynn DeCapua, Dean, 732-987-2729, E-mail: ldecapua@georgian.edu. *Application contact:* Patrick Givens, Director of Graduate and Professional Studies Admissions, 732-987-2736, Fax: 732-987-2000, E-mail: gps@georgian.edu.
Website: http://georgian.edu/academics/school-of-education/

Georgia Southern University, Jack N. Averitt College of Graduate Studies, College of Education, Department of Leadership, Technology, and Human Development, Program in Educational Leadership, Statesboro, GA 30460. Offers higher education leadership (Ed D); P-12 leadership (Ed D). *Program availability:* Part-time, evening/weekend. *Students:* 37 part-time (28 women); includes 20 minority (17 Black or African American, non-Hispanic/Latino; 2 Hispanic/Latino; 1 Two or more races, non-Hispanic/Latino). Average age 43. In 2016, 14 doctorates awarded. *Degree requirements:* For doctorate, comprehensive exam, thesis/dissertation, exams. *Entrance requirements:* For doctorate, GRE General Test or MAT, minimum GPA of 3.5, letters of reference, resume. Additional exam requirements/recommendations for international students: Required—TOEFL (minimum score 550 paper-based; 80 iBT), IELTS (minimum score 6). *Application deadline:* For fall admission, 4/1 for domestic students, 3/1 for international students; for spring admission, 11/1 for domestic students, 10/1 for international students. Application fee: $50. Electronic applications accepted. *Expenses:* Tuition, state resident: full-time $7236; part-time $277 per semester hour. Tuition, nonresident: full-time $27,118; part-time $1105 per semester hour. *Required fees:* $2092. *Financial support:* In 2016–17, 2 fellowships with full tuition reimbursements (averaging $7,750 per year) were awarded; research assistantships with partial tuition reimbursements, teaching assistantships with partial tuition reimbursements, Federal Work-Study, scholarships/grants, tuition waivers (full), and unspecified assistantships also available. Support available to part-time students. Financial award application deadline: 4/15; financial award applicants required to submit FAFSA. *Faculty research:* National and local policies regarding school renewal, student achievement, and university leadership; roles and responsibilities of the assistant principal/deputy head teacher in the U.S., U.K. and China; development of an instrument to measure student dispositions; the impact of cultural context on leadership practices and behaviors; technology leadership preparation. *Unit head:* Dr. Teri Melton, Program Coordinator, 912-478-7267, Fax: 912-478-7140, E-mail: tamelton@georgiasouthern.edu. *Application contact:* Lydia Cross, Graduate Academic Service Center, 912-478-8664, E-mail: lcross@georgiasouthern.edu.
Website: http://coe.georgiasouthern.edu/edld/

Georgia Southern University, Jack N. Averitt College of Graduate Studies, College of Education, Department of Leadership, Technology, and Human Development, Program in Higher Education Administration, Statesboro, GA 30458. Offers M Ed. *Program availability:* Part-time, evening/weekend. *Students:* 45 full-time (30 women), 108 part-time (78 women); includes 69 minority (57 Black or African American, non-Hispanic/Latino; 2 Asian, non-Hispanic/Latino; 9 Hispanic/Latino; 1 Two or more races, non-Hispanic/Latino). Average age 30. 61 applicants, 98% accepted, 46 enrolled. In 2016, 35 master's awarded. *Entrance requirements:* For master's, GRE, minimum GPA of 2.5. Additional exam requirements/recommendations for international students: Required—TOEFL (minimum score 550 paper-based; 80 iBT), IELTS (minimum score 6). *Application deadline:* For fall admission, 4/1 for domestic students; for spring admission, 11/1 for domestic students. Application fee: $50. Electronic applications accepted. *Expenses:* Tuition, state resident: full-time $7236; part-time $277 per semester hour. Tuition, nonresident: full-time $27,118; part-time $1105 per semester hour. *Required fees:* $2092. *Financial support:* In 2016–17, 4 students received support, including 3 fellowships with full tuition reimbursements available (averaging $7,750 per year). Financial award application deadline: 4/20; financial award applicants required to submit FAFSA. *Faculty research:* Higher education administration, student affairs. *Unit head:* Dr. Daniel Calhoun, Program Director, 912-478-1428, Fax: 912-478-7104, E-mail: dwcalhoun@georgiasouthern.edu.

Georgia Southern University, Jack N. Averitt College of Graduate Studies, College of Education, Department of Leadership, Technology, and Human Development, Program in P-12 Leadership, Statesboro, GA 30460. Offers M Ed, Ed D, Ed S. *Accreditation:* NCATE. *Program availability:* Part-time, evening/weekend. *Students:* 15 full-time (8 women), 83 part-time (56 women); includes 37 minority (32 Black or African American, non-Hispanic/Latino; 4 Hispanic/Latino; 1 Two or more races, non-Hispanic/Latino), 1 international. Average age 38. 61 applicants, 64% accepted, 22 enrolled. In 2016, 7 master's, 6 other advanced degrees awarded. *Degree requirements:* For master's, comprehensive exam, transition point assessments; for doctorate, comprehensive exam, thesis/dissertation; for Ed S, transition point assessments. *Entrance requirements:* For master's, GRE General Test or MAT, minimum GPA of 2.5, 3 years of teaching experience; for Ed S, GRE General Test or MAT, minimum graduate GPA of 3.25. Additional exam requirements/recommendations for international students: Required—TOEFL (minimum score 550 paper-based; 80 iBT), IELTS (minimum score 6). *Application deadline:* For fall admission, 4/1 for domestic students, 3/1 for international students; for spring admission, 10/1 for domestic and international students. Application fee: $50. Electronic applications accepted. *Expenses:* Tuition, state resident: full-time $7236; part-time $277 per semester hour. Tuition, nonresident: full-time $27,118; part-time $1105 per semester hour. *Required fees:* $2092. *Financial support:* In 2016–17, 3 students received support, including 1 fellowship with full tuition reimbursement available (averaging $7,750 per year); research assistantships with partial tuition reimbursements available, teaching assistantships with partial tuition reimbursements available, career-related internships or fieldwork, Federal Work-Study, scholarships/grants, tuition waivers (full), and unspecified assistantships also available. Support available to part-time students. Financial award application deadline: 4/15; financial award applicants required to submit FAFSA. *Faculty research:* Principalship, performance-based leadership preparation, instructional technology for school leaders, dispositions of educational leaders, school/system-wide support services, student-oriented support services, universal vs. cultural contextuality of international educational leadership characteristics and behaviors. *Unit head:* Dr. Teri Melton, Program Coordinator, 912-478-0510, Fax: 912-478-7104, E-mail: tamelton@georgiasouthern.edu. *Application contact:* Lydia Cross, Coordinator for Graduate Academic Services Center, 912-478-8664, E-mail: lcross@georgiasouthern.edu.
Website: http://cogs.georgiasouthern.edu/admission/GraduatePrograms/coe_mededleader.php

Georgia State University, College of Education and Human Development, Department of Educational Policy Studies, Program in Educational Leadership, Atlanta, GA 30302-3083. Offers educational leadership (M Ed, Ed D, Ed S); urban teacher leadership (M Ed). *Accreditation:* NCATE. *Program availability:* Part-time. *Degree requirements:*

For master's, comprehensive exam, thesis or alternative, 36 semester hours; for doctorate, comprehensive exam, thesis/dissertation, 54 semester hours (for Ed D); 69 semester hours (for PhD); for Ed S, thesis, 30 semester hours of coursework. *Entrance requirements:* For master's, GRE; for doctorate and Ed S, GRE, MAT. Additional exam requirements/recommendations for international students: Required—TOEFL (minimum score 550 paper-based; 79 iBT) or IELTS (minimum score 6.5). *Application deadline:* For fall admission, 5/1 for domestic and international students; for winter admission, 2/1 for domestic students; for spring admission, 10/1 for domestic and international students. Applications are processed on a rolling basis. Application fee: $50. Electronic applications accepted. *Expenses:* Tuition, state resident: full-time $6876; part-time $382 per credit hour. Tuition, nonresident: full-time $22,374; part-time $1243 per credit hour. *Required fees:* $2128; $1064 per term. Part-time tuition and fees vary according to course load and program. *Financial support:* In 2016–17, research assistantships with full tuition reimbursements (averaging $6,000 per year) were awarded; fellowships, teaching assistantships with full tuition reimbursements, career-related internships or fieldwork, scholarships/grants, health care benefits, tuition waivers, and unspecified assistantships also available. Support available to part-time students. Financial award application deadline: 3/15. *Faculty research:* Practices with diverse populations, leadership and success, the cohort model of instruction, technology in the schools, instructional supervision and academic coaching. *Unit head:* Dr. Jami Berry, Clinical Assistant Professor, 404-413-8030, Fax: 404-413-8003, E-mail: jberry2@gsu.edu. *Application contact:* Aishah Cowan, Administrative Academic Specialist, 404-413-8273, Fax: 404-413-8033, E-mail: acowan@gsu.edu.
Website: http://eps.education.gsu.edu/programs-courses/educational-leadership/

Gordon College, Graduate Education Program, Wenham, MA 01984-1899. Offers early childhood (M Ed); educational leadership (M Ed, Ed S); elementary education (M Ed); English as a second language (M Ed, Ed S); math specialist (M Ed); mathematics specialist (Ed S); middle school education (M Ed); moderate disabilities (M Ed); Montessori education (M Ed); reading (M Ed, Ed S); secondary education (M Ed). *Program availability:* Part-time, evening/weekend. *Faculty:* 17 full-time (9 women), 41 part-time/adjunct (34 women). *Students:* 81 full-time (61 women), 109 part-time (87 women); includes 28 minority (2 Black or African American, non-Hispanic/Latino; 11 Asian, non-Hispanic/Latino; 13 Hispanic/Latino; 2 Two or more races, non-Hispanic/Latino), 12 international. Average age 34. 190 applicants, 100% accepted, 141 enrolled. In 2016, 110 master's, 16 Ed Ss awarded. *Degree requirements:* For master's, action research or clinical experience (for most programs); for Ed S, action research or clinical experience (for some programs). *Entrance requirements:* For master's, minimum undergraduate GPA of 3.0; 2 official undergraduate transcripts; professional resume; 3 recommendation letters (one professional reference, one academic reference, one personal reference); 500-700 word statement of purpose; for Ed S, minimum master's GPA of 3.3; 2 official transcripts from undergraduate and graduate schools; professional resume; 3 recommendation letters (one professional reference, one academic reference, one personal reference); 500-700 word statement of purpose. Additional exam requirements/recommendations for international students: Required—TOEFL (minimum score 550 paper-based, 80 iBT) or IELTS (minimum score 6.5). *Application deadline:* Applications are processed on a rolling basis. Application fee: $75. *Expenses:* $325 per credit tuition, $75 per term fee. *Financial support:* Applicants required to submit FAFSA. *Faculty research:* Reading, early childhood development, English language learners, universal design for learning. *Unit head:* Dr. Janet Arndt, Director of Graduate Studies, 978-867-4355, Fax: 978-867-4663. *Application contact:* Julie Lenocker, Program Administrator, 978-867-4322, Fax: 978-867-4663, E-mail: graduate-education@gordon.edu.
Website: http://www.gordon.edu/graduate

Gordon College, Graduate Leadership Program, Wenham, MA 01984-1899. Offers leadership (MA, Ed S). *Faculty:* 5 part-time/adjunct (2 women). *Students:* 9 full-time (6 women), 10 part-time (all women); includes 2 minority (1 Asian, non-Hispanic/Latino; 1 Hispanic/Latino), 1 international. Average age 39. 13 applicants, 100% accepted, 10 enrolled. *Degree requirements:* For master's, capstone research. *Entrance requirements:* For master's, official transcripts of all degrees from undergraduate schools; professional resume; 3 references (one academic, one personal, one professional); 500-700 words statement of purpose. *Application deadline:* For summer admission, 4/7 for domestic students. Application fee: $75. *Expenses:* $700 per credit tuition, $75 per term fee. *Unit head:* Dr. Janet Arndt, Director of Graduate Studies, 978-867-4663. *Application contact:* Julie Lenocker, Program Administrator, 978-867-4322, Fax: 978-867-4663, E-mail: graduate-education@gordon.edu.
Website: http://www.gordon.edu/graduate/leadership

Goucher College, Graduate Programs in Education, Baltimore, MD 21204-2794. Offers at-risk and diverse learners (M Ed, Certificate); athletic program leadership and administration (M Ed, Certificate); elementary and special education (MAT); elementary education (MAT); literacy strategies for content learning (M Ed, Certificate); middle school (M Ed, Certificate); Montessori studies (M Ed); reading instruction (M Ed, Certificate); school improvement leadership (M Ed, Certificate); school mediation (M Ed, Certificate); secondary and special education (MAT); secondary education (MAT); special education (MAT), including elementary education, secondary education; special education for certified teachers (M Ed, Certificate); teacher as leader in technology (M Ed, Certificate). *Program availability:* Part-time, evening/weekend. *Faculty:* 3 full-time (all women), 52 part-time/adjunct (40 women). *Students:* 29 full-time (20 women), 285 part-time (217 women); includes 54 minority (41 Black or African American, non-Hispanic/Latino; 3 Asian, non-Hispanic/Latino; 7 Hispanic/Latino; 3 Two or more races, non-Hispanic/Latino), 1 international. Average age 34. 85 applicants, 100% accepted, 61 enrolled. In 2016, 207 master's awarded. *Degree requirements:* For master's, thesis (M Ed), final presentation (MAT). *Entrance requirements:* For master's, minimum GPA of 3.0. Additional exam requirements/recommendations for international students: Required—TOEFL (minimum score 560 paper-based). *Application deadline:* For fall admission, 9/1 for domestic students; for spring admission, 1/15 for domestic students. Applications are processed on a rolling basis. Application fee: $75. Electronic applications accepted. *Expenses:* Contact institution. *Financial support:* Career-related internships or fieldwork and unspecified assistantships available. Support available to part-time students. Financial award application deadline: 4/15; financial award applicants required to submit FAFSA. *Faculty research:* Urban education, middle school, school improvement, teacher education, at-risk student achievement. *Unit head:* Dr. Phyllis Sunshine, Assistant Provost, 410-337-6047, Fax: 410-337-6394, E-mail: psunshin@goucher.edu. *Application contact:* Shelby Hillers, Admissions Coordinator, 410-337-6200, Fax: 410-337-6085, E-mail: shelby.hillers@goucher.edu.
Website: http://www.goucher.edu/graduate-programs/graduate-programs-in-education

Governors State University, College of Education, Program in Educational Administration and Supervision, University Park, IL 60484. Offers MA. *Program availability:* Part-time. *Faculty:* 47 full-time (31 women), 49 part-time/adjunct (39 women). *Students:* 3 full-time (2 women), 70 part-time (40 women); includes 28 minority (20 Black or African American, non-Hispanic/Latino; 1 Asian, non-Hispanic/Latino; 6 Hispanic/Latino; 1 Two or more races, non-Hispanic/Latino). Average age 36. 54 applicants, 69% accepted, 34 enrolled. In 2016, 26 master's awarded. *Entrance requirements:* Additional exam requirements/recommendations for international students: Required—TOEFL (minimum score 550 paper-based; 80 iBT), IELTS. *Application deadline:* For fall admission, 4/1 for domestic students. Application fee: $50. Electronic applications accepted. *Expenses:* $307 per credit hour; $38 per term or $76 per credit hour fees. *Financial support:* Application deadline: 5/1; applicants required to submit FAFSA. *Unit head:* Timothy Harrington, Chair, Division of Education, 708-534-4361, E-mail: tharrington2@govst.edu. *Application contact:* Yakeea Daniels, Assistant Vice President for Enrollment Services/Director of Admission, 708-534-4510, E-mail: ydaniels@govst.edu.

Governors State University, College of Education, Program in Interdisciplinary Leadership, University Park, IL 60484. Offers higher education administration (Ed D); not-for-profit/social entrepreneurship (Ed D); superintendent (P-12) (Ed D). *Program availability:* Part-time. *Faculty:* 47 full-time (31 women), 49 part-time/adjunct (39 women). *Students:* 25 full-time (16 women), 18 part-time (8 women); includes 22 minority (19 Black or African American, non-Hispanic/Latino; 2 Hispanic/Latino; 1 Two or more races, non-Hispanic/Latino). Average age 42. 56 applicants, 32% accepted, 15 enrolled. In 2016, 17 doctorates awarded. *Entrance requirements:* Additional exam requirements/recommendations for international students: Required—TOEFL (minimum score 577 paper-based; 91 iBT), IELTS. *Application deadline:* For fall admission, 4/1 for domestic students. Application fee: $75. Electronic applications accepted. *Expenses:* $415 per credit hour tuition; $38 per term or $76 per credit hour fees. *Financial support:* Application deadline: 5/1; applicants required to submit FAFSA. *Unit head:* Timothy Harrington, Chair, Division of Education, 708-534-4361, E-mail: tharrington2@govst.edu. *Application contact:* Yakeea Daniels, Assistant Vice President for Enrollment Services/Director of Admission, 708-534-4510, E-mail: ydaniels@govst.edu.

Graceland University, Gleazer School of Education, Independence, MO 64050. Offers curriculum and instruction (M Ed); differentiated instruction (M Ed); instructional leadership (M Ed); literacy and instruction (M Ed); management in the inclusive classroom (M Ed); special education (M Ed); technology integration (M Ed). *Accreditation:* NCATE. *Program availability:* Part-time, evening/weekend, online learning. *Faculty:* 2 full-time (both women), 9 part-time/adjunct (5 women). *Students:* 115 full-time (96 women), 20 part-time (17 women); includes 10 minority (5 Black or African American, non-Hispanic/Latino; 1 Asian, non-Hispanic/Latino; 1 Hispanic/Latino; 1 Native Hawaiian or other Pacific Islander, non-Hispanic/Latino; 2 Two or more races, non-Hispanic/Latino), 2 international. 155 applicants, 61% accepted, 85 enrolled. In 2016, 61 master's awarded. *Degree requirements:* For master's, action research project. *Entrance requirements:* For master's, minimum GPA of 3.0, teaching certificate, current teaching contract. Additional exam requirements/recommendations for international students: Required—TOEFL. *Application deadline:* For fall admission, 10/1 for domestic students; for winter admission, 11/15 for domestic students; for spring admission, 2/15 priority date for domestic students; for summer admission, 6/1 for domestic students. Applications are processed on a rolling basis. Application fee: $50. Electronic applications accepted. *Expenses:* Contact institution. *Financial support:* Institutionally sponsored loans and scholarships/grants available. Financial award application deadline: 12/15; financial award applicants required to submit FAFSA. *Faculty research:* Literacy, technology, faculty mentoring, adult literacy, e-learning, online teaching. *Unit head:* Dr. Lee Bash, Interim Dean, 641-784-5072, E-mail: bash@graceland.edu. *Application contact:* Jeanette Calipetro, Admissions Representative, 816-423-4716, Fax: 816-833-2990, E-mail: jcali1@graceland.edu.
Website: http://www.graceland.edu/education

Grambling State University, School of Graduate Studies and Research, College of Education, Department of Educational Leadership, Grambling, LA 71245. Offers developmental education (MS, Ed D, PMC), including curriculum and instructional design (Ed D), English (MS), guidance and counseling (MS), higher education administration and management (Ed D), mathematics (MS), reading (MS), science (MS), student development and personnel services (Ed D); educational leadership (M Ed). *Program availability:* Part-time, evening/weekend. *Degree requirements:* For master's, comprehensive exam, thesis (for some programs); for doctorate, comprehensive exam, thesis/dissertation. *Entrance requirements:* For master's, GRE, minimum GPA of 2.5 on last degree; for doctorate, GRE (minimum score 1000, 500 on Verbal), master's degree, minimum GPA of 3.0 on last degree. Additional exam requirements/recommendations for international students: Required—TOEFL (minimum score 500 paper-based; 62 iBT). Electronic applications accepted.

Grand Canyon University, College of Education, Phoenix, AZ 85017-1097. Offers autism spectrum disorders (MA); curriculum and instruction (MA); early childhood education (M Ed); educational administration (M Ed); educational leadership (M Ed); elementary education (M Ed); gifted education (MA); instructional technology (MS); K-12 leadership (Ed S); reading (MA); secondary education (M Ed); secondary humanities education (M Ed); secondary STEM education (M Ed); special education (M Ed); teaching and learning (Ed D); teaching English to speakers of other languages (MA). *Program availability:* Part-time, evening/weekend, online learning. *Degree requirements:* For master's, publishable research paper (M Ed), e-portfolio. *Entrance requirements:* For master's, undergraduate degree from accredited, GCU-approved college, university, or program with minimum GPA 2.8. Additional exam requirements/recommendations for international students: Required—TOEFL (minimum score 550 paper-based; 79 iBT), IELTS (minimum score 6). *Application deadline:* For fall admission, 8/21 for domestic students, 7/2 for international students; for spring admission, 12/24 for domestic students, 11/1 for international students. Applications are processed on a rolling basis. Application fee: $100. Electronic applications accepted. *Financial support:* Federal Work-Study available. Support available to part-time students. Financial award applicants required to submit FAFSA. *Unit head:* Dr. Kimberly L. LaPrade, Dean, 602-639-6360, E-mail: kimberly.laprade@gcu.edu. *Application contact:* Dr. Kimberly L. LaPrade, Dean, 602-639-6360, E-mail: kimberly.laprade@gcu.edu.
Website: https://www.gcu.edu/college-of-education.php

Grand Valley State University, College of Education, Program in Educational Leadership, Allendale, MI 49401-9403. Offers M Ed. *Program availability:* Part-time. *Students:* 16 full-time (11 women), 200 part-time (173 women); includes 43 minority (26 Black or African American, non-Hispanic/Latino; 4 Asian, non-Hispanic/Latino; 8 Hispanic/Latino; 5 Two or more races, non-Hispanic/Latino). Average age 34. 47 applicants, 98% accepted, 25 enrolled. In 2016, 66 master's awarded. *Degree requirements:* For master's, thesis or project. *Entrance requirements:* For master's, undergraduate minimum GPA of 3.0 or GRE General Test, last 60 credits from regionally-accredited college/university, 3 letters of recommendation. Additional exam requirements/recommendations for international students: Required—TOEFL (minimum score 550 paper-based, 80 iBT), IELTS (6.5), or Michigan English Language Assessment Battery. *Application deadline:* Applications are processed on a rolling basis. Electronic applications accepted. *Expenses:* $628 per credit hour. *Financial support:* In 2016–17, 57 students received support. Unspecified assistantships available. *Unit head:* Michael Stearns, 616-331-6821, Fax: 616-331-6241, E-mail: stearnsm@gvsu.edu. *Application contact:* Thomas Owens, Director, Student Information and Services Center, 616-331-6282, Fax: 616-331-2000, E-mail: owenst@gvsu.edu.
Website: http://www.gvsu.edu/grad/eduleadership/

Grand Valley State University, College of Education, Program in Leadership, Allendale, MI 49401-9403. Offers Ed S. *Program availability:* Part-time, evening/weekend. *Students:* 32 part-time (17 women); includes 12 minority (10 Black or African

American, non-Hispanic/Latino; 2 Hispanic/Latino). Average age 38. 8 applicants, 100% accepted, 4 enrolled. In 2016, 12 Ed Ss awarded. *Entrance requirements:* For degree, GRE, master's degree with minimum GPA of 3.0, resume, 3 recommendations. Additional exam requirements/recommendations for international students: Required—TOEFL (minimum score 550 paper-based, 80 iBT), IELTS (6.5), or Michigan English Language Assessment Battery. *Application deadline:* Applications are processed on a rolling basis. Application fee: $30. Electronic applications accepted. *Expenses:* $628 per credit hour. *Financial support:* In 2016–17, 5 students received support. Unspecified assistantships available. *Unit head:* Cathy Meyer-Looze, Program Coordinator, 616-331-6280, E-mail: meyerlca@gvsu.edu. *Application contact:* Thomas Owens, Director, Student Information and Services Center, 616-331-6282, Fax: 616-331-6217, E-mail: owenst@gvsu.edu.

Grand Valley State University, College of Education, Programs in General Education, Allendale, MI 49401-9403. Offers adult and higher education (M Ed); early childhood education (M Ed); educational differentiation (M Ed); educational leadership (M Ed); educational technology integration (M Ed); elementary education (M Ed); middle level education (M Ed); school library media services (M Ed); secondary level education (M Ed); teaching English to speakers of other languages (M Ed). *Program availability:* Part-time, evening/weekend, 100% online, blended/hybrid learning. *Students:* 28 part-time (20 women); includes 6 minority (4 Black or African American, non-Hispanic/Latino; 1 American Indian or Alaska Native, non-Hispanic/Latino; 1 Hispanic/Latino). Average age 42. In 2016, 17 master's awarded. *Degree requirements:* For master's, project or thesis. *Entrance requirements:* For master's, GRE General Test or minimum GPA of 3.0, last 60 credits from regionally-accredited college/university, 3 letters of recommendation. Additional exam requirements/recommendations for international students: Required—TOEFL (minimum score 550 paper-based, 80 iBT), IELTS (6.5), or Michigan English Language Assessment Battery. *Application deadline:* Applications are processed on a rolling basis. Application fee: $30. Electronic applications accepted. *Expenses:* $628 per credit hour. *Financial support:* In 2016–17, 2 students received support. Career-related internships or fieldwork, Federal Work-Study, scholarships/grants, and unspecified assistantships available. *Faculty research:* Effectiveness of technology in education, parental involvement, effective teaching, effective schools research. *Unit head:* Dr. Doug Busman, Graduate Program Director, 616-331-6250, E-mail: busmando@gvsu.edu. *Application contact:* Thomas Owens, Director, Student Information and Services Center, 616-331-6282, Fax: 616-331-6217, E-mail: owenst@gvsu.edu.
Website: http://www.gvsu.edu/coe/

Grand View University, Graduate Studies, Des Moines, IA 50316-1599. Offers athletic training (MS); clinical nurse leader (MSN, Post Master's Certificate); nursing education (MSN, Post Master's Certificate); organizational leadership (MS); sport management (MS); teacher leadership (M Ed); urban education (M Ed). *Program availability:* Part-time, evening/weekend. *Degree requirements:* For master's, completion of all required coursework in common core and selected track with minimum cumulative GPA of 3.0 and no more than two grades of C. *Entrance requirements:* For master's, GRE, GMAT, or essay, minimum undergraduate GPA of 3.0, professional resume, 3 letters of recommendation, interview. Additional exam requirements/recommendations for international students: Required—TOEFL (minimum score 550 paper-based). Electronic applications accepted.

Gratz College, Graduate Programs, Program in Jewish Education, Melrose Park, PA 19027. Offers education leadership (Ed D); Jewish instructional education (MA); MA/MA. *Program availability:* Part-time, evening/weekend, online learning. *Degree requirements:* For master's, one foreign language, internship. *Entrance requirements:* For master's, interview. *Application deadline:* Applications are processed on a rolling basis. Application fee: $50. *Financial support:* Fellowships, career-related internships or fieldwork, Federal Work-Study, and unspecified assistantships available. Support available to part-time students. Financial award application deadline: 4/15; financial award applicants required to submit FAFSA. *Unit head:* Coordinator, 215-635-7300, Fax: 215-635-7320. *Application contact:* Joanna Boeing Bratton, Director of Admissions, 215-635-7300 Ext. 140, Fax: 215-635-7399, E-mail: admissions@gratz.edu.
Website: https://www.gratz.edu/academics/jewish-education-graduate

Gwynedd Mercy University, School of Education, Gwynedd Valley, PA 19437-0901. Offers educational administration (MS); master teacher (MS); school counseling (MS); special education (MS). *Program availability:* Part-time, evening/weekend, 100% online. *Faculty:* 8 full-time (5 women), 38 part-time/adjunct (24 women). *Students:* 466 full-time (355 women); includes 93 minority (66 Black or African American, non-Hispanic/Latino; 12 Asian, non-Hispanic/Latino; 15 Hispanic/Latino). Average age 36. 127 applicants, 18% accepted, 9 enrolled. In 2016, 86 master's awarded. *Degree requirements:* For master's, thesis, internship, practicum. *Entrance requirements:* For master's, GRE or MAT; PRAXIS I, minimum GPA of 3.0. *Application deadline:* Applications are processed on a rolling basis. *Expenses: Tuition:* Full-time $14,400; part-time $800 per credit hour. One-time fee: $165. Tuition and fees vary according to degree level and program. *Financial support:* In 2016–17, 2 research assistantships were awarded; career-related internships or fieldwork, Federal Work-Study, institutionally sponsored loans, tuition waivers (full and partial), and unspecified assistantships also available. Financial award applicants required to submit FAFSA. *Faculty research:* Learning and the brain, reading literacy, ethics and moral judgment, leadership, teaching and multicultural education. *Unit head:* Dr. Heather Pfleger, Dean, 215-646-7300 Ext. 21581, E-mail: pfleger.h@gmercyu.edu. *Application contact:* Graduate Program Coordinator, 877-499-6333, E-mail: graduate@gmercyu.edu.
Website: https://www.gmercyu.edu/academics/graduate-education-programs

Hampton University, School of Education and Human Development, Program in Educational Leadership, Virginia Beach, VA 23668. Offers MA. *Faculty:* 1 (woman) full-time, 1 (woman) part-time/adjunct. *Entrance requirements:* For master's, GRE. Additional exam requirements/recommendations for international students: Required—TOEFL (minimum score 525 paper-based) or IELTS (6.5). *Application deadline:* For fall admission, 6/1 priority date for domestic students, 4/1 priority date for international students; for spring admission, 11/1 priority date for domestic students, 9/1 priority date for international students; for summer admission, 4/1 priority date for domestic students, 2/1 priority date for international students. Applications are processed on a rolling basis. Application fee: $35. Electronic applications accepted. *Expenses: Tuition:* Full-time $10,776; part-time $548 per credit hour. *Required fees:* $35; $35 per credit hour. Tuition and fees vary according to course load and program. *Unit head:* Dr. Martha Jallim-Hall, Graduate Program Coordinator, 757-727-5793, E-mail: martha-jallim-hall@hamptonu.edu.

Hampton University, School of Education and Human Development, Program in Educational Management, Hampton, VA 23668. Offers PhD. *Faculty:* 7 full-time (5 women), 2 part-time/adjunct (both women). *Students:* 11 full-time (9 women), 40 part-time (27 women); includes 47 minority (all Black or African American, non-Hispanic/Latino). Average age 42. 3 applicants, 100% accepted, 3 enrolled. In 2016, 12 doctorates awarded. *Degree requirements:* For doctorate, comprehensive exam, thesis/dissertation. *Entrance requirements:* Additional exam requirements/recommendations for international students: Required—TOEFL (minimum score 525 paper-based), IELTS (minimum score 6.5). *Application deadline:* For summer admission, 1/15 for domestic students. Applications are processed on a rolling basis. Application fee: $50. Electronic applications accepted. *Expenses: Tuition:* Full-time $10,776; part-time $548 per credit hour. *Required fees:* $35; $35 per credit hour. Tuition and fees vary according to course load and program. *Financial support:* Application deadline: 6/30; applicants required to submit FAFSA. *Unit head:* Dr. Barbara Holmes, Program Coordinator, 757-727-2072. *Application contact:* Keisha Thompson, 757-727-4829.

Harding University, Cannon-Clary College of Education, Searcy, AR 72149-0001. Offers advanced studies in teaching and learning (M Ed); art (MSE); behavioral science (MSE); counseling (MS, Ed S); early childhood special education (M Ed, MSE); education (MSE); educational leadership (M Ed, Ed S); elementary education (M Ed); English (MSE); French (MSE); history/social science (MSE); kinesiology (MSE); math (MSE); reading (M Ed); secondary education (M Ed); Spanish (MSE); teaching (MAT); teaching English as a second language (MSE). *Accreditation:* NCATE. *Program availability:* Part-time, evening/weekend. *Faculty:* 22 full-time (9 women), 51 part-time/adjunct (37 women). *Students:* 130 full-time (94 women), 321 part-time (234 women); includes 83 minority (50 Black or African American, non-Hispanic/Latino; 4 American Indian or Alaska Native, non-Hispanic/Latino; 6 Asian, non-Hispanic/Latino; 13 Hispanic/Latino; 10 Two or more races, non-Hispanic/Latino), 11 international. Average age 35. 125 applicants, 88% accepted, 110 enrolled. In 2016, 124 master's, 27 other advanced degrees awarded. *Degree requirements:* For master's, comprehensive exam (for some programs), thesis optional, portfolio(s); for Ed S, comprehensive exam, portfolio, project. *Entrance requirements:* For master's, GRE, MAT, PRAXIS; for Ed S, MAT or GRE. Additional exam requirements/recommendations for international students: Required—TOEFL (minimum score 550 paper-based; 79 iBT). *Application deadline:* For fall admission, 8/1 for domestic and international students; for spring admission, 1/1 for domestic and international students. Applications are processed on a rolling basis. Application fee: $35. Tuition and fees vary according to degree level and program. *Financial support:* In 2016–17, 31 students received support. Unspecified assistantships available. *Faculty research:* Reading, comprehension, school violence, educational technology, behavior, college choice, differentiated instruction, brain-based teaching. *Unit head:* Dr. Clara Carroll, Chair, 501-279-4501, Fax: 501-279-4083, E-mail: ccarroll@harding.edu. *Application contact:* Information Contact, 501-279-4315, E-mail: gradstudiesedu@harding.edu.
Website: http://www.harding.edu/education

Hardin-Simmons University, Graduate School, Irvin School of Education, Program in Education Leadership, Abilene, TX 79698-0001. Offers Ed D. *Program availability:* Part-time. *Faculty:* 5 full-time (2 women), 3 part-time/adjunct (0 women). *Students:* 27 part-time (22 women); includes 3 minority (all Hispanic/Latino), 1 international. Average age 40. In 2016, 3 doctorates awarded. *Application deadline:* For fall admission, 7/15 priority date for domestic students, 4/1 for international students; for spring admission, 1/5 priority date for domestic students, 8/1 for international students. Applications are processed on a rolling basis. Application fee: $50. Electronic applications accepted. *Expenses: Tuition:* Full-time $12,510; part-time $695 per credit hour. *Required fees:* $325; $110 per semester. *Financial support:* In 2016–17, 23 students received support, including 1 fellowship (averaging $6,000 per year); scholarships/grants also available. Support available to part-time students. Financial award application deadline: 6/30; financial award applicants required to submit FAFSA. *Unit head:* Dr. Mary Christopher, Program Director, 325-670-1510, Fax: 325-670-5859, E-mail: leadership@hsutx.edu. *Application contact:* Dr. Nancy Kucinski, Dean of Graduate Studies, 325-670-1298, Fax: 325-670-1564, E-mail: gradoff@hsutx.edu.
Website: http://www.hsutx.edu/doctorateinleadership

Harvard University, Harvard Graduate School of Education, Doctor of Education Leadership (Ed.L.D.) Program, Cambridge, MA 02138. Offers Ed L D. *Degree requirements:* For doctorate, thesis/dissertation, capstone project. *Entrance requirements:* For doctorate, GRE or GMAT, statement of purpose, 3 letters of recommendation, resume, official transcripts, 2 short essay questions. Additional exam requirements/recommendations for international students: Required—TOEFL (minimum score 613 paper-based; 104 iBT), TWE (minimum score 5). Electronic applications accepted. *Expenses:* Contact institution. *Faculty research:* System level leadership in education.

Harvard University, Harvard Graduate School of Education, Master's Programs in Education, Cambridge, MA 02138. Offers arts in education (Ed M); education policy and management (Ed M); higher education (Ed M); human development and psychology (Ed M); international education policy (Ed M); language and literacy (Ed M); learning and teaching (Ed M); mind, brain, and education (Ed M); prevention science and practice (Ed M); school leadership (Ed M); special studies (Ed M); teacher education (Ed M); technology, innovation, and education (Ed M). *Program availability:* Part-time. *Entrance requirements:* For master's, GRE General Test, statement of purpose, 3 letters of recommendation, resume, official transcripts. Additional exam requirements/recommendations for international students: Required—TOEFL (minimum score 613 paper-based; 104 iBT), TWE (minimum score 5). Electronic applications accepted. *Faculty research:* Learning and development, educational leadership and organizations, education policy analysis.

Henderson State University, Graduate Studies, Teachers College, Department of Advanced Instructional Studies, Arkadelphia, AR 71999-0001. Offers developmental therapy (MSE); dyslexia therapy (Graduate Certificate); education (MAT); educational technology leadership (Graduate Certificate); English as a second language (MSE, Graduate Certificate); instructional facilitator (MSE, Graduate Certificate); middle level education (MAT); special education (K-12) (MAT, MSE); special education/early childhood (MAT). *Accreditation:* NCATE. *Program availability:* Part-time. *Faculty:* 12 full-time (9 women), 5 part-time/adjunct (4 women). *Students:* 13 full-time (8 women), 79 part-time (66 women); includes 14 minority (8 Black or African American, non-Hispanic/Latino; 2 American Indian or Alaska Native, non-Hispanic/Latino; 2 Hispanic/Latino; 2 Two or more races, non-Hispanic/Latino). Average age 33. 21 applicants, 100% accepted, 21 enrolled. In 2016, 29 master's awarded. *Entrance requirements:* For master's, GRE General Test or MAT, minimum GPA of 2.7, teacher certification. Additional exam requirements/recommendations for international students: Required—TOEFL (minimum score 600 paper-based); Recommended—IELTS (minimum score 6.5). *Application deadline:* For fall admission, 8/1 priority date for domestic students, 6/30 priority date for international students; for spring admission, 1/1 priority date for domestic students, 11/30 priority date for international students. Applications are processed on a rolling basis. Application fee: $25 ($75 for international students). *Expenses:* Tuition, state resident: full-time $6288; part-time $3144 per credit hour. Tuition, nonresident: full-time $12,888; part-time $6444 per credit hour. *Required fees:* $1429; $1024 per credit hour. Tuition and fees vary according to course load and student level. *Financial support:* In 2016–17, 1 teaching assistantship with partial tuition reimbursement (averaging $4,000 per year) was awarded; scholarships/grants and unspecified assistantships also available. Financial award application deadline: 4/15; financial award applicants required to submit FAFSA. *Unit head:* Dr. Gary Smithey, Coordinator, 870-230-5361, Fax: 870-230-5455, E-mail: smitheg@hsu.edu. *Application contact:* Dr. Ken Taylor, Graduate Dean, 870-230-5126, Fax: 870-230-5479, E-mail: taylorke@hsu.edu.
Website: http://www.hsu.edu/Academics/TeachersCollege/AIS/index.html

Henderson State University, Graduate Studies, Teachers College, Department of Educational Leadership, Arkadelphia, AR 71999-0001. Offers curriculum leadership (Ed S); educational leadership (MSE, Ed S, Graduate Certificate). *Program availability:* Part-time, 100% online. *Faculty:* 5 full-time (4 women). *Students:* 5 full-time (4 women), 77 part-time (50 women); includes 20 minority (15 Black or African American, non-Hispanic/Latino; 1 Asian, non-Hispanic/Latino; 1 Hispanic/Latino; 3 Two or more races, non-Hispanic/Latino). Average age 38. 14 applicants, 100% accepted, 14 enrolled. In 2016, 3 master's, 9 other advanced degrees awarded. *Entrance requirements:* For master's, GRE or MAT, minimum GPA of 2.7, teacher licensure. Additional exam requirements/recommendations for international students: Required—TOEFL (minimum score 600 paper-based); Recommended—IELTS (minimum score 6.5). *Application deadline:* For fall admission, 8/1 priority date for domestic students, 6/30 priority date for international students; for spring admission, 1/1 priority date for domestic students, 11/30 priority date for international students. Applications are processed on a rolling basis. Application fee: $25 ($75 for international students). *Expenses:* Tuition, state resident: full-time $6288; part-time $3144 per credit hour. Tuition, nonresident: full-time $12,888; part-time $6444 per credit hour. *Required fees:* $1429; $1024 per credit hour. Tuition and fees vary according to course load and student level. *Financial support:* In 2016–17, 1 teaching assistantship with partial tuition reimbursement (averaging $4,000 per year) was awarded; scholarships/grants and unspecified assistantships also available. Financial award application deadline: 4/15; financial award applicants required to submit FAFSA. *Unit head:* Dr. Pat Weaver, Coordinator, 870-230-5351, E-mail: weaverp@hsu.edu. *Application contact:* Dr. Ken Taylor, Graduate Dean, 870-230-5126, Fax: 870-230-5479, E-mail: taylorke@hsu.edu.

Heritage University, Graduate Programs in Education, Program in Educational Administration, Toppenish, WA 98948-9599. Offers M Ed. *Program availability:* Part-time, evening/weekend. *Degree requirements:* For master's, comprehensive exam, thesis optional, special project. *Entrance requirements:* For master's, valid teaching certificate, 3 years of teaching experience, interview, letters of recommendation.

High Point University, Norcross Graduate School, High Point, NC 27268. Offers business administration (MBA); educational leadership (M Ed); elementary education (M Ed); history (MA); nonprofit management (MA); secondary math (M Ed); special education (M Ed); strategic communication (MA); teaching elementary education k-6 (MAT); teaching secondary mathematics 9-12 (MAT). *Accreditation:* NCATE. *Program availability:* Part-time, evening/weekend. *Degree requirements:* For master's, comprehensive exam (for some programs), thesis (for some programs). *Entrance requirements:* For master's, GMAT (MBA), GRE, MAT, minimum GPA of 3.0. Additional exam requirements/recommendations for international students: Required—TOEFL (minimum score 550 paper-based). Electronic applications accepted.

Hofstra University, School of Education, Specialized Programs in Education, Hempstead, NY 11549. Offers applied behavior analysis (Advanced Certificate); early childhood special education (MS Ed, Advanced Certificate); educational and policy leadership (Ed D); educational leadership (Advanced Certificate), including school building leader/school district business leader; educational leadership and policy studies (MS Ed), including K-12; gifted education (Advanced Certificate), including school building leader/school district business leader; health education PK-12 teaching certification (MS); inclusive early childhood special education (MS Ed); inclusive elementary special education (MS Ed); inclusive secondary special education (MS Ed); literacy studies (MS Ed, Ed D, PhD, Advanced Certificate), including birth-grade 6 (MS Ed, Advanced Certificate), birth-grade 6 and special education (birth-grade2) (MS Ed), grades 5-12 (MS Ed, Advanced Certificate); physical education (MS); secondary education generalist (MS Ed), including students with disabilities 7-12; special education (MS Ed, Advanced Certificate); special education assessment and diagnosis (Advanced Certificate); special education generalist (MS Ed), including extension in secondary education; sport science (MS), including strength and conditioning; teaching students with severe or multiple disabilities (Advanced Certificate). *Program availability:* Part-time, evening/weekend, 100% online, blended/hybrid learning. *Students:* 149 full-time (115 women), 258 part-time (187 women); includes 97 minority (50 Black or African American, non-Hispanic/Latino; 1 American Indian or Alaska Native, non-Hispanic/Latino; 11 Asian, non-Hispanic/Latino; 34 Hispanic/Latino; 1 Native Hawaiian or other Pacific Islander, non-Hispanic/Latino), 5 international. Average age 32. 250 applicants, 88% accepted, 146 enrolled. In 2016, 85 master's, 13 doctorates, 35 other advanced degrees awarded. *Degree requirements:* For master's, one foreign language, comprehensive exam (for some programs), thesis (for some programs), electronic portfolio, capstone course, internship, practicum, student teaching, seminars, minimum GPA of 3.0; for doctorate, one foreign language, comprehensive exam, thesis/dissertation, qualifying hearing. *Entrance requirements:* For master's, GRE, interview, letters of recommendation, portfolio, essay, certification; for doctorate, GRE or MAT, interview, resume, essay, master's degree, 3 letters of recommendation, writing sample; for Advanced Certificate, GRE, interview, letters of recommendation, essay, professional experience, resume, master's degree. Additional exam requirements/recommendations for international students: Required—TOEFL (minimum score 550 paper-based; 80 iBT). *Application deadline:* Applications are processed on a rolling basis. Application fee: $75. Electronic applications accepted. *Expenses: Tuition:* Full-time $1240. *Required fees:* $970. Tuition and fees vary according to program. *Financial support:* In 2016–17, 244 students received support, including 117 fellowships with full and partial tuition reimbursements available (averaging $3,705 per year), 12 research assistantships with full and partial tuition reimbursements available (averaging $6,490 per year); career-related internships or fieldwork, Federal Work-Study, institutionally sponsored loans, scholarships/grants, traineeships, tuition waivers (full and partial), and unspecified assistantships also available. Support available to part-time students. Financial award applicants required to submit FAFSA. *Faculty research:* Collaborative teaching and learning; language and culture; new media literacies; applied behavior analysis; K-12 leadership development. *Unit head:* Dr. Elfreda Blue, Chairperson, 516-463-5762, Fax: 516-463-6184, E-mail: elfreda.blue@hofstra.edu. *Application contact:* Sunil Samuel, Assistant Vice President of Admissions, 516-463-4723, Fax: 516-463-4664, E-mail: graduateadmission@hofstra.edu.
Website: http://www.hofstra.edu/education/

Holy Family University, Division of Academic Affairs, Philadelphia, PA 19114. Offers accountancy (MS); business administration (MBA); counseling psychology (MS); criminal justice (MA); education (M Ed); educational leadership (Ed D); nursing (MS). *Accreditation:* ACBSP. *Program availability:* Part-time, evening/weekend. *Faculty:* 28 full-time (19 women), 66 part-time/adjunct (36 women). *Students:* 329 full-time (281 women), 458 part-time (327 women); includes 153 minority (83 Black or African American, non-Hispanic/Latino; 1 American Indian or Alaska Native, non-Hispanic/Latino; 27 Asian, non-Hispanic/Latino; 41 Hispanic/Latino; 1 Native Hawaiian or other Pacific Islander, non-Hispanic/Latino), 4 international. Average age 34. 467 applicants, 69% accepted, 262 enrolled. In 2016, 6 master's, 2 doctorates awarded. *Degree requirements:* For master's, comprehensive exam, thesis or alternative; for doctorate, comprehensive exam, thesis/dissertation. *Entrance requirements:* For master's, minimum GPA of 3.0, interview, essay/professional statement, 2 recommendations, current resume, official transcripts of college or university work. Additional exam requirements/recommendations for international students: Required—TOEFL (minimum score 550 paper-based; 79 iBT), IELTS (minimum score 6). *Application deadline:* For fall admission, 7/1 priority date for domestic and international students; for spring admission, 11/1 priority date for domestic and international students; for summer admission, 4/1 priority date for domestic and international students. Applications are processed on a rolling basis. Application fee: $25. Electronic applications accepted. *Expenses:* $9,292 per year. *Financial support:* Available to part-time students. Applicants required to submit FAFSA. *Unit head:* Dr. Michael Markowitz, Vice President of Academic Affairs, 267-341-3286, E-mail: mmarkowitz@holyfamily.edu. *Application contact:* Don Reinmold, Director of Graduate Admissions, 267-341-5001 Ext. 3230, Fax: 215-633-0558, E-mail: dreinmold@holyfamily.edu.

Holy Family University, Graduate and Professional Programs, School of Education, Doctor of Education Programs, Philadelphia, PA 19114. Offers educational leadership and professional studies (Ed D). *Students:* 5 full-time, 21 part-time. 3 applicants, 67% accepted, 1 enrolled. In 2016, 5 doctorates awarded. *Degree requirements:* For doctorate, thesis/dissertation. *Application deadline:* Applications are processed on a rolling basis. Application fee: $25. Electronic applications accepted. *Expenses: Tuition:* Part-time $751 per hour. *Required fees:* $140 per semester. One-time fee: $165 part-time. Part-time tuition and fees vary according to degree level and program. *Unit head:* Dr. Kevin Zook, Dean, 267-341-3565, E-mail: kzook@holyfamily.edu. *Application contact:* Donald Reimold, Director of Graduate Admissions, 267-341-5001, Fax: 215-637-1478, E-mail: dreimold@holyfamily.edu.

Holy Family University, Graduate and Professional Programs, School of Education, Master of Education Programs, Philadelphia, PA 19114. Offers early elementary education (PreK-Grade 4) (M Ed); education leadership (M Ed); general education (M Ed); reading specialist (M Ed); special education (M Ed); TESOL and literacy (M Ed). *Program availability:* Part-time. *Students:* 202 full-time, 58 part-time. 209 applicants, 77% accepted, 140 enrolled. In 2016, 123 master's awarded. *Degree requirements:* For master's, thesis optional. *Application deadline:* Applications are processed on a rolling basis. Application fee: $25. Electronic applications accepted. *Expenses: Tuition:* Part-time $751 per hour. *Required fees:* $140 per semester. One-time fee: $165 part-time. Part-time tuition and fees vary according to degree level and program. *Unit head:* Dr. Kevin Zook, Dean, 267-341-3246, Fax: 215-824-2438, E-mail: kzook@holyfamily.edu. *Application contact:* Donald Reimold, Director of Graduate Admissions, 267-341-5001, Fax: 215-637-1478, E-mail: dreimold@holyfamily.edu.

Hood College, Graduate School, Department of Education, Frederick, MD 21701-8575. Offers curriculum and instruction (MS), including elementary education, elementary science and mathematics education, secondary education, special education; educational leadership (MS); reading specialization (MS); STEM education (Certificate). *Accreditation:* NCATE. *Program availability:* Part-time-only, evening/weekend. *Faculty:* 3 full-time, 37 part-time/adjunct. *Students:* 1 (woman) full-time, 357 part-time (283 women); includes 71 minority (41 Black or African American, non-Hispanic/Latino; 6 Asian, non-Hispanic/Latino; 15 Hispanic/Latino; 9 Two or more races, non-Hispanic/Latino). Average age 33. 96 applicants, 95% accepted, 83 enrolled. In 2016, 47 master's awarded. *Degree requirements:* For master's, action research project, portfolio (for reading specialization); for Certificate, STEM capstone activity. *Entrance requirements:* For master's, minimum GPA of 2.75, teaching certification, writing sample during interview, letter of recommendation from principal (for educational leadership program only). Additional exam requirements/recommendations for international students: Required—TOEFL (minimum score 575 paper-based; 89 iBT), IELTS (minimum score 6.5). *Application deadline:* For fall admission, 8/15 priority date for domestic students, 8/5 for international students; for spring admission, 12/1 priority date for domestic students, 12/1 for international students; for summer admission, 5/1 priority date for domestic students, 4/15 for international students. Applications are processed on a rolling basis. Application fee: $35. Electronic applications accepted. *Expenses:* $450 per credit; $105 comprehensive fee per semester. *Financial support:* Tuition waivers (partial) and unspecified assistantships available. Financial award applicants required to submit FAFSA. *Faculty research:* Leadership, action research, brain research, learning styles. *Unit head:* April Boulton, Interim Dean of the Graduate School, E-mail: gofurther@hood.edu. *Application contact:* Jan Marcus, Assistant Director of Graduate Admissions, 301-696-3600, E-mail: gofurther@hood.edu.
Website: http://www.hood.edu/academics/education/index.html

Hope International University, School of Graduate and Professional Studies, Program in Education, Fullerton, CA 92831-3138. Offers education administration (MA); elementary education (ME); secondary education (ME). *Program availability:* Part-time, evening/weekend. *Degree requirements:* For master's, comprehensive exam (for some programs), thesis. *Entrance requirements:* For master's, minimum GPA of 3.0, 2 references. Additional exam requirements/recommendations for international students: Required—TOEFL (minimum score 550 paper-based; 86 iBT); Recommended—IELTS (minimum score 6.5). Electronic applications accepted. *Expenses:* Contact institution. *Faculty research:* Distance education.

Houston Baptist University, College of Education and Behavioral Sciences, Programs in Education, Houston, TX 77074-3298. Offers bilingual education (M Ed); counselor education (M Ed); curriculum and instruction (M Ed); educational administration (M Ed); educational diagnostician (M Ed); executive educational leadership (Ed D); reading education (M Ed). *Program availability:* Part-time, evening/weekend, 100% online, blended/hybrid learning. *Students:* 45 full-time (35 women), 158 part-time (136 women); includes 141 minority (87 Black or African American, non-Hispanic/Latino; 1 American Indian or Alaska Native, non-Hispanic/Latino; 5 Asian, non-Hispanic/Latino; 47 Hispanic/Latino; 1 Two or more races, non-Hispanic/Latino), 3 international. Average age 34. 320 applicants, 30% accepted, 61 enrolled. In 2016, 121 degrees awarded. *Degree requirements:* For master's, comprehensive exam; for doctorate, thesis/dissertation. *Entrance requirements:* For master's, minimum GPA of 2.75, two recommendations, resume, bachelor's degree conferred transcript; interview (for non-certified teachers); for doctorate, GRE, 3 letters of recommendation. Additional exam requirements/recommendations for international students: Required—TOEFL (minimum score 80 iBT), IELTS (minimum score 6.5). *Application deadline:* For fall admission, 8/1 for domestic students, 6/1 for international students; for spring admission, 1/1 for domestic students, 11/1 for international students; for summer admission, 5/1 for domestic students, 3/1 for international students. Applications are processed on a rolling basis. Application fee: $0 ($100 for international students). Electronic applications accepted. Application fee is waived when completed online. *Expenses:* $1,650 per 3-hour course; $1,275 annual general fee; $1,060 annual technology fee. *Financial support:* In 2016–17, 2 students received support. Research assistantships, teaching assistantships, Federal Work-Study, and scholarships/grants available. Support available to part-time students. Financial award application deadline: 4/1; financial award applicants required to submit FAFSA. *Faculty research:* Autism and inclusion, integrating technology into instruction, school change and leadership trust. *Unit head:* Dr. Charlotte Fontenot, Director, Graduate Programs, 281-649-3078, Fax: 281-649-3361, E-mail: cfontenot@hbu.edu. *Application contact:* Kristy Wright, Administrative Assistant for Graduate Programs, 281-649-3094, Fax: 281-649-3361, E-mail: kwright@hbu.edu.
Website: http://www.hbu.edu/MED

Howard Payne University, Program in Instructional Leadership, Brownwood, TX 76801-2715. Offers M Ed. *Program availability:* Part-time, evening/weekend, online

only. *Faculty:* 1 full-time (0 women), 2 part-time/adjunct (1 woman). *Students:* 9 full-time (8 women), 5 part-time (3 women); includes 3 minority (1 Black or African American, non-Hispanic/Latino; 2 Hispanic/Latino). Average age 34. 10 applicants, 80% accepted, 8 enrolled. In 2016, 4 master's awarded. *Degree requirements:* For master's, comprehensive exam (for some programs), thesis or alternative. *Entrance requirements:* For master's, undergraduate degree, valid teaching certificate. Additional exam requirements/recommendations for international students: Required—TOEFL (minimum score 79 iBT). *Application deadline:* For fall admission, 7/1 for domestic students; for spring admission, 12/1 for domestic students. Applications are processed on a rolling basis. Application fee: $0. Electronic applications accepted. *Expenses:* Contact institution. *Financial support:* Application deadline: 3/15; applicants required to submit FAFSA. *Unit head:* Dr. Joe Robinson, Director of Instructional Leadership Graduate Program/Professor of Education, 325-649-8205, E-mail: jrobinson@hputx.edu. *Application contact:* Susan Sharp, Administrative Assistant, School of Education/ Certification Officer, 325-649-8144, E-mail: ssharp@hputx.edu.
Website: http://www.hputx.edu/academics/schools/school-of-education/school-of-education-graduate-program/

Howard University, School of Education, Department of Educational Leadership and Policy Studies, Washington, DC 20059. Offers educational administration (Ed D); educational administration and supervision (M Ed, CAGS). *Program availability:* Part-time. *Degree requirements:* For master's, comprehensive exam, School Leaders Licensure Assessment, practicum; for doctorate, comprehensive exam, thesis/ dissertation, internship; for CAGS, thesis. *Entrance requirements:* For master's, minimum GPA of 2.7; for doctorate, minimum GPA of 3.0. Additional exam requirements/recommendations for international students: Required—TOEFL (minimum score 550 paper-based; 79 iBT). Electronic applications accepted.

Hunter College of the City University of New York, Graduate School, School of Education, Department of Curriculum and Teaching, Program in Educational Supervision and Administration, New York, NY 10065-5085. Offers administration and supervision (AC); instructional leadership (Ed D). *Degree requirements:* For AC, portfolio review. *Entrance requirements:* For degree, minimum B average in graduate course work, teaching certificate, minimum 3 years of full-time teaching experience, interview, 2 letters of support. Additional exam requirements/recommendations for international students: Required—TOEFL. *Application deadline:* For fall admission, 4/1 for domestic students, 2/1 for international students; for spring admission, 11/1 for domestic students, 9/1 for international students. Applications are processed on a rolling basis. *Financial support:* Federal Work-Study and tuition waivers (partial) available. Support available to part-time students. *Faculty research:* Supervision of instruction, theory in action, human relations and leadership. *Unit head:* Dr. Marcia Knoll, Coordinator, 212-772-4761, E-mail: mknoll@hunter.cuny.edu. *Application contact:* Milena Solo, Director for Graduate Admissions, 212-772-4482, E-mail: admissions@hunter.cuny.edu.

Huston-Tillotson University, Graduate Programs, Austin, TX 78702-2795. Offers educational leadership (M Ed).

Idaho State University, Office of Graduate Studies, College of Education, Department of Educational Foundations, Pocatello, ID 83209-8059. Offers child and family studies (M Ed); curriculum leadership (M Ed); education (M Ed); educational administration (M Ed); educational foundations (5th Year Certificate); elementary education (M Ed), including K-12 education, literacy, secondary education. *Program availability:* Part-time. *Degree requirements:* For master's, comprehensive exam, thesis optional, oral exam, written exam; for 5th Year Certificate, comprehensive exam, thesis (for some programs), oral exam, written exam. *Entrance requirements:* For master's, GRE General Test or MAT, minimum undergraduate GPA of 3.0; for 5th Year Certificate, GRE General Test, minimum undergraduate GPA of 3.0, master's degree. Additional exam requirements/ recommendations for international students: Required—TOEFL (minimum score 550 paper-based; 80 iBT). Electronic applications accepted. *Faculty research:* Child and families studies; business education; special education; math, science, and technology education.

Idaho State University, Office of Graduate Studies, College of Education, Department of Educational Leadership and Instructional Design, Pocatello, ID 83209-8059. Offers educational administration (M Ed, 6th Year Certificate, Ed S); educational leadership (Ed D), including education training and development, educational administration, educational technology, higher education administration; educational leadership and instructional design (PhD); instructional technology (M Ed). *Program availability:* Part-time. *Degree requirements:* For master's, comprehensive exam, thesis optional, internship, oral exam or deferred thesis; for doctorate, comprehensive exam, thesis/ dissertation, written exam; for other advanced degree, comprehensive exam, thesis (for some programs), written and oral exam. *Entrance requirements:* For master's, MAT, bachelor's degree, minimum GPA of 3.0, 1 year of training experience; for doctorate, GRE General Test or MAT, minimum GPA of 3.0 (undergraduate), 3.5 (graduate); departmental interview; for other advanced degree, GRE General Test, minimum GPA of 3.0, master's degree. Additional exam requirements/recommendations for international students: Required—TOEFL (minimum score 550 paper-based; 80 iBT). Electronic applications accepted. *Faculty research:* Educational leadership, gender issues in education and sport, staff development.

Illinois State University, Graduate School, College of Education, Department of Educational Administration and Foundations, Normal, IL 61790-2200. Offers college student personnel administration (MS); educational administration (MS, MS Ed, Ed D, PhD). *Accreditation:* NCATE. *Degree requirements:* For doctorate, variable foreign language requirement, thesis/dissertation, 2 terms of residency. *Entrance requirements:* For master's, GRE General Test, minimum GPA of 2.6 in last 60 hours of course work; for doctorate, GRE General Test, master's degree or equivalent, minimum GPA of 3.5. *Faculty research:* Illinois Principals Association, special populations professional development and technical assistance project, Illinois state action for education leadership project.

Immaculata University, College of Graduate Studies, Program in Educational Leadership, Immaculata, PA 19345. Offers educational leadership (MA, Ed D); principal (Certificate); secondary education (Certificate); supervisor of special education (Certificate). *Program availability:* Part-time, evening/weekend. *Degree requirements:* For master's, comprehensive exam, thesis optional; for doctorate, comprehensive exam, thesis/dissertation. *Entrance requirements:* For master's, GRE or MAT, minimum GPA of 3.0; for doctorate, GRE General Test or MAT, minimum GPA of 3.5. Additional exam requirements/recommendations for international students: Required—TOEFL. Electronic applications accepted. *Faculty research:* Cooperative learning, school-based management, whole language, performance assessment.

Indiana State University, College of Graduate and Professional Studies, Bayh College of Education, Department of Educational Leadership, Terre Haute, IN 47809. Offers educational administration (PhD); higher education leadership (PhD); K-12 district leadership (PhD); school administration (Ed S); school administration and supervision (M Ed); student affairs and higher education (MS). *Accreditation:* NCATE. *Program availability:* Part-time, evening/weekend. Terminal master's awarded for partial completion of doctoral program. *Degree requirements:* For master's, thesis; for doctorate, thesis/dissertation. *Entrance requirements:* For master's, GRE General Test, minimum undergraduate GPA of 2.5; for doctorate, GRE General Test, minimum undergraduate GPA of 3.5; for Ed S, GRE General Test, minimum graduate GPA of 3.25. Electronic applications accepted.

Indiana University Bloomington, School of Education, Department of Educational Leadership and Policy Studies, Bloomington, IN 47405. Offers educational leadership (MS, Ed D, Ed S); higher education (Ed D, PhD); higher education and student affairs (MS); history and philosophy of education (MS); history, philosophy, and policy in education (PhD), including education policy studies, history of education, philosophy of education; international and comparative education (MS). *Accreditation:* NCATE. *Faculty:* 32 full-time (18 women). *Students:* 223 full-time (140 women), 94 part-time (50 women); includes 80 minority (44 Black or African American, non-Hispanic/Latino; 13 Asian, non-Hispanic/Latino; 18 Hispanic/Latino; 1 Native Hawaiian or other Pacific Islander, non-Hispanic/Latino; 4 Two or more races, non-Hispanic/Latino), 29 international. Average age 34. 309 applicants, 40% accepted, 57 enrolled. In 2016, 60 master's, 18 doctorates, 5 other advanced degrees awarded. *Degree requirements:* For master's, thesis optional; for doctorate, comprehensive exam, thesis/dissertation; for Ed S, comprehensive exam or project. *Entrance requirements:* For master's, doctorate, and Ed S, GRE General Test. Additional exam requirements/recommendations for international students: Required—TOEFL (minimum score 79 iBT). *Application deadline:* For fall admission, 1/15 priority date for domestic students, 12/1 priority date for international students; for spring admission, 9/1 priority date for domestic and international students. Applications are processed on a rolling basis. Application fee: $55 ($65 for international students). Electronic applications accepted. *Financial support:* Fellowships with full and partial tuition reimbursements, research assistantships with full and partial tuition reimbursements, teaching assistantships with full and partial tuition reimbursements, career-related internships or fieldwork, scholarships/grants, health care benefits, and unspecified assistantships available. *Faculty research:* Culturally engaging campus environments, school choice policy analysis, democracy and education in the national and international context, and principal leadership. *Unit head:* Dr. Dionne Danns, Interim Chair, 812-856-8398. *Application contact:* Maria Jensen, Department Administrator, 812-856-8370, Fax: 812-856-8394, E-mail: jensen5@indiana.edu.
Website: http://education.indiana.edu/about/departments/leadership/index.html

Indiana University Northwest, School of Education, Gary, IN 46408. Offers educational leadership (MS Ed); elementary education (MS Ed); K-12 online teaching (Graduate Certificate); secondary education (MS Ed). *Accreditation:* NCATE. *Program availability:* Part-time, evening/weekend. *Faculty:* 10 full-time (5 women), 2 part-time/ adjunct (both women). *Students:* 11 full-time (8 women), 67 part-time (47 women); includes 32 minority (25 Black or African American, non-Hispanic/Latino; 7 Hispanic/ Latino). Average age 38. 24 applicants, 96% accepted, 14 enrolled. In 2016, 22 master's awarded. *Entrance requirements:* For master's, GRE General Test or MAT, minimum GPA of 3.0. *Application deadline:* For fall admission, 7/15 priority date for domestic students; for spring admission, 11/15 for domestic students. Application fee: $40 ($60 for international students). Electronic applications accepted. *Expenses:* $276.98 per credit hour in-state; $652.54 per credit hour out-of-state. *Financial support:* Applicants required to submit FAFSA. *Unit head:* Dr. Charles Hobsen, Interim Dean, 219-980-6903, Fax: 219-680-4208, E-mail: chobson@iun.edu. *Application contact:* Kelly Zieba, Director of Enrollment Management, Finance, and Operations, 219-980-6879, Fax: 219-980-4208, E-mail: kmzieba@iun.edu.
Website: http://www.iun.edu/education/degrees/masters.htm

Indiana University of Pennsylvania, School of Graduate Studies and Research, College of Education and Educational Technology, Department of Professional Studies in Education, Doctoral Program in Administration and Leadership Studies, Indiana, PA 15705. Offers D Ed. Program also offered jointly with East Stroudsburg University of Pennsylvania. *Program availability:* Part-time, evening/weekend. *Faculty:* 15 full-time (11 women), 3 part-time/adjunct (2 women). *Students:* 2 full-time (1 woman), 104 part-time (55 women); includes 25 minority (14 Black or African American, non-Hispanic/ Latino; 4 Hispanic/Latino; 1 Native Hawaiian or other Pacific Islander, non-Hispanic/ Latino; 6 Two or more races, non-Hispanic/Latino), 2 international. Average age 40. 71 applicants, 79% accepted, 39 enrolled. In 2016, 22 doctorates awarded. *Degree requirements:* For doctorate, one foreign language, comprehensive exam, thesis/ dissertation, written exam. *Entrance requirements:* For doctorate, 2 letters of recommendation, interview. *Application deadline:* Applications are processed on a rolling basis. Application fee: $50. Electronic applications accepted. *Expenses:* Tuition, state resident: full-time $8694; part-time $483 per credit. Tuition, nonresident: full-time $13,050; part-time $725 per credit. *Required fees:* $157 per credit. $50 per term. Tuition and fees vary according to course load and program. *Financial support:* In 2016–17, 10 fellowships with full tuition reimbursements (averaging $496 per year), 7 research assistantships with tuition reimbursements (averaging $4,719 per year) were awarded; teaching assistantships, career-related internships or fieldwork, Federal Work-Study, scholarships/grants, and unspecified assistantships also available. Support available to part-time students. Financial award application deadline: 4/15; financial award applicants required to submit FAFSA. *Unit head:* Dr. Robert Millward, Graduate Coordinator, 724-357-5593, E-mail: robert.millward@iup.edu.
Website: http://www.iup.edu/pse/grad/administration-leadership-studies-ded/default.aspx

Indiana University of Pennsylvania, School of Graduate Studies and Research, College of Education and Educational Technology, Department of Professional Studies in Education, Principal Certification Program, Indiana, PA 15705. Offers Certificate. *Program availability:* Part-time, evening/weekend. *Faculty:* 15 full-time (11 women), 3 part-time/adjunct (2 women). *Students:* 15 part-time (9 women). Average age 37. 29 applicants, 83% accepted, 14 enrolled. *Entrance requirements:* For degree, 2 letters of recommendation. Additional exam requirements/recommendations for international students: Required—TOEFL (minimum score 540 paper-based). *Application deadline:* For fall admission, 7/1 priority date for domestic students; for spring admission, 11/1 for domestic students. Applications are processed on a rolling basis. Application fee: $50. Electronic applications accepted. *Expenses:* Tuition, state resident: full-time $8694; part-time $483 per credit. Tuition, nonresident: full-time $13,050; part-time $725 per credit. *Required fees:* $157 per credit. $50 per term. Tuition and fees vary according to course load and program. *Financial support:* Career-related internships or fieldwork, Federal Work-Study, and scholarships/grants available. Support available to part-time students. Financial award application deadline: 4/15; financial award applicants required to submit FAFSA. *Unit head:* Dr. Valeri Helterbran, Graduate Coordinator, 724-357-2400, E-mail: vhelter@iup.edu.
Website: http://www.iup.edu/pse/programs/principalcert/default.aspx

Indiana University–Purdue University Fort Wayne, College of Education and Public Policy, Department of Professional Studies, Fort Wayne, IN 46805-1499. Offers couple and family counseling (MS Ed); educational leadership (MS Ed); school counseling (MS Ed); special education (MS Ed, Certificate). *Program availability:* Part-time. *Degree requirements:* For master's, comprehensive exam, practicum, internship, portfolio. *Entrance requirements:* For master's, minimum GPA of 2.5, three professional letters of recommendation. Additional exam requirements/recommendations for international students: Required—TOEFL (minimum score 550 paper-based; 79 iBT). *Faculty research:* Learning opportunities with deafness and the hearing impaired, adolescent emotion, student evaluation of teaching.

Indiana University–Purdue University Indianapolis, School of Education, Indianapolis, IN 46202-5155. Offers curriculum and instruction (MS); early childhood (MS); educational leadership (MS, Certificate); English as a second language (Certificate); kindergarten (Certificate); language education (MS); reading (Certificate); school counseling (MS); special education (MS, Certificate). *Program availability:* Part-time, evening/weekend. *Faculty:* 35 full-time (27 women), 56 part-time/adjunct (42 women). *Students:* 125 full-time (86 women), 181 part-time (139 women); includes 106 minority (78 Black or African American, non-Hispanic/Latino; 9 Asian, non-Hispanic/Latino; 12 Hispanic/Latino; 7 Two or more races, non-Hispanic/Latino), 3 international. Average age 32. 73 applicants, 93% accepted, 68 enrolled. In 2016, 73 master's awarded. Terminal master's awarded for partial completion of doctoral program. *Degree requirements:* For master's, thesis optional. *Entrance requirements:* For master's, GRE General Test, minimum GPA of 2.5; for Certificate, official transcripts. Additional exam requirements/recommendations for international students: Required—TOEFL (minimum score 60 iBT), IELTS (minimum score 5.5). *Application deadline:* For fall admission, 5/1 for domestic students; for spring admission, 11/1 for domestic students. Application fee: $60 ($65 for international students). Electronic applications accepted. *Expenses:* $1,262 tuition, $213 general fee. *Financial support:* Applicants required to submit FAFSA. *Faculty research:* Educational policies and school leaders' responses to these; issues of intersectionality in the experiences of African American lesbian, gay, and bisexual students attending historically black colleges and universities and those who belong to black Greek-letter organizations; students' experiential knowledge and their evolving disciplinary-specific literacy and understanding; innovative program development; urban ESL teacher preparation; target-based instructional coaching. *Total annual research expenditures:* $2.1 million. *Unit head:* Dr. Robin Hughes, Executive Associate Dean, 317-274-6817, E-mail: roblhugh@iupui.edu. *Application contact:* Ky Shaw, Graduate Admissions Coordinator, 317-278-6778, E-mail: kycshaw@iupui.edu.
Website: http://education.iupui.edu/

Indiana University South Bend, School of Education, South Bend, IN 46634-7111. Offers addiction counseling (MS Ed); alcohol and drug counseling (Graduate Certificate); clinical mental health counseling (MS Ed); educational leadership (MS Ed); elementary education (MS Ed); marriage, couple, and family counseling (MS Ed); school counseling (MS Ed); secondary education (MS Ed); special education (MAT, MS Ed), including intense intervention (MS Ed), mild intervention (MS Ed). *Accreditation:* NCATE. *Program availability:* Part-time, evening/weekend. *Faculty:* 21 full-time (11 women), 9 part-time/adjunct (3 women). *Students:* 26 full-time (19 women), 104 part-time (80 women); includes 22 minority (13 Black or African American, non-Hispanic/Latino; 5 Hispanic/Latino; 4 Two or more races, non-Hispanic/Latino). Average age 35. 51 applicants, 69% accepted, 22 enrolled. In 2016, 31 master's, 2 other advanced degrees awarded. *Degree requirements:* For master's, thesis or alternative, exit project. *Entrance requirements:* For master's, letters of recommendation, GRE or minimum GPA of 3.0. Additional exam requirements/recommendations for international students: Required—TOEFL. *Application deadline:* For fall admission, 7/1 for domestic students; for spring admission, 11/1 for domestic students. Applications are processed on a rolling basis. Application fee: $40 ($60 for international students). Electronic applications accepted. *Expenses:* $276.98 per credit hour in-state; $652.54 per credit hour out-of-state. *Financial support:* Career-related internships or fieldwork available. Support available to part-time students. Financial award application deadline: 3/1; financial award applicants required to submit FAFSA. *Faculty research:* Professional dispositions, early childhood literacy, online learning, program assessments, problem-based learning. *Unit head:* Dr. Marvin Lynn, Dean, 574-520-4339, E-mail: lynnm@iusb.edu. *Application contact:* Yvonne Walker, Student Services Representative, 574-520-4185, E-mail: ydwalker@iusb.edu.
Website: https://www.iusb.edu/education/index.php

Indiana Wesleyan University, College of Adult and Professional Studies, School of Educational Leadership, Marion, IN 46953. Offers M Ed, Ed S. *Accreditation:* NCATE. *Program availability:* Part-time, evening/weekend, online learning. *Degree requirements:* For master's, portfolio. *Entrance requirements:* For master's, minimum GPA of 2.75, teaching experience, teaching license. Additional exam requirements/recommendations for international students: Required—TOEFL (minimum score 550 paper-based). Electronic applications accepted. *Faculty research:* Mentoring, performance-based assessments, faith integration, integration of technology, program assessment.

Instituto Tecnologico de Santo Domingo, Graduate School, Area of Humanities and Social Sciences, Santo Domingo, Dominican Republic. Offers accounting (Certificate); adult education (Certificate); applied linguistics (MA); economics (MA); education (M Ed); educational psychology (MA, Certificate); gender and development (MA, Certificate); humanistic studies (MA); international marketing management (Certificate); international relations in the Caribbean basin (Certificate); intervention systems in family therapy (MA); linguistic and literary communication (Certificate); pedagogical support (MA); social science education (M Ed); sustainable human development (MA); terminal illness and death psychology (Certificate); youth and adult education (M Ed).

Instituto Tecnológico y de Estudios Superiores de Monterrey, Campus Central de Veracruz, Graduate Programs, Córdoba, Mexico. Offers administration (MA); administration of information technologies (MTI); computer sciences (MCC); education (MEE); educational institution administration (MAD); educational technology (MTE); electronic commerce (MCE); finance (MAF); humanistic studies (MEH); international business for Latin America (MNL); marketing (MMT); science (MCP). *Program availability:* Part-time, evening/weekend, online learning. *Degree requirements:* For master's, thesis (for some programs). *Entrance requirements:* For master's, PAEP College Board. Electronic applications accepted.

Instituto Tecnológico y de Estudios Superiores de Monterrey, Campus Ciudad Juárez, Program in Educational Administration, Ciudad Juárez, Mexico. Offers MEA.

Instituto Tecnológico y de Estudios Superiores de Monterrey, Campus Estado de México, Professional and Graduate Division, Estado de Mexico, Mexico. Offers administration of information technologies (MITA); architecture (M Arch); business administration (GMBA, MBA); computer sciences (MCS, PhD); education (M Ed); educational institution administration (MAD); educational technology and innovation (PhD); electronic commerce (MEC); environmental systems (MS); finance (MAF); humanistic studies (MHS); information sciences and knowledge management (MISKM); information systems (MS); manufacturing systems (MS); marketing (MEM); quality systems and productivity (MS); science and materials engineering (PhD); telecommunications management (MTM). *Program availability:* Part-time, online learning. *Degree requirements:* For master's, one foreign language, thesis (for some programs); for doctorate, one foreign language, thesis/dissertation. *Entrance requirements:* For master's, E-PAEP 500, interview; for doctorate, E-PAEP 500, research proposal. Additional exam requirements/recommendations for international students: Required—TOEFL (minimum score 550 paper-based). *Faculty research:* Surface treatments by plasmas, mechanical properties, robotics, graphical computing, mechatronics security protocols.

Instituto Tecnológico y de Estudios Superiores de Monterrey, Campus Irapuato, Graduate Programs, Irapuato, Mexico. Offers administration (MBA); administration of information technology (MAIT); administration of telecommunications (MAT); architecture (M Arch); computer science (MCS); education (M Ed); educational administration (MEA); educational innovation and technology (DEIT); educational technology (MET); electronic commerce (MBA); environmental administration and planning (MEAP); environmental systems (MES); finances (MBA); humanistic studies (MHS); international management for Latin American executives (MIMLAE); library and information science (MLIS); manufacturing quality management (MMQM); marketing research (MBA).

Inter American University of Puerto Rico, Aguadilla Campus, Graduate School, Aguadilla, PR 00605. Offers accounting (MBA); counseling psychology specializing in family (MS); criminal justice (MA); educative management and leadership (MA); elementary education (M Ed); finance (MBA); human resources (MBA); industrial management (MBA); management information systems (MBA); marketing (MBA). *Program availability:* Part-time, evening/weekend. *Degree requirements:* For master's, comprehensive exam. *Entrance requirements:* For master's, EXADEP, 2 letters of recommendation, minimum GPA of 2.5. Electronic applications accepted.

Inter American University of Puerto Rico, Arecibo Campus, Programs in Education, Arecibo, PR 00614-4050. Offers administration and educational supervision (MA Ed); counseling and guidance (MA Ed); curriculum and teaching (MA Ed), including biology education, English as a second language, history education, math education, Spanish; elementary education (MA Ed). *Accreditation:* TEAC. *Degree requirements:* For master's, comprehensive exam, thesis optional. *Entrance requirements:* For master's, GRE, EXADEP, bachelor's degree in education or teaching license (administration and supervision) or courses in education and psychology (counseling and guidance), minimum GPA of 2.5 in last 60 credits.

Inter American University of Puerto Rico, Barranquitas Campus, Program in Education, Barranquitas, PR 00794. Offers curriculum and teaching (M Ed), including biology education, English as a second language, history education, mathematics education, Spanish; educational leadership and management (MA); elementary education (M Ed); information and library service technology (M Ed); special education (MA). *Accreditation:* TEAC. *Degree requirements:* For master's, comprehensive exam, thesis optional. *Entrance requirements:* For master's, EXADEP, letter of recommendation. Electronic applications accepted.

Inter American University of Puerto Rico, Fajardo Campus, Graduate Programs, Fajardo, PR 00738-7003. Offers computer science (MS); educational management and leadership (MA Ed); elementary education (MA Ed); general business (MBA); management information systems (MBA); marketing (MBA); special education (MA Ed).

Inter American University of Puerto Rico, Metropolitan Campus, Graduate Programs, Program in Education, San Juan, PR 00919-1293. Offers curriculum and instruction (Ed D); educational administration (Ed D); guidance and counseling (MA, Ed D); special education administration (Ed D). *Accreditation:* TEAC. *Degree requirements:* For doctorate, comprehensive exam, thesis/dissertation. *Entrance requirements:* For doctorate, GRE, MAT, or EXADEP. Electronic applications accepted.

Iona College, School of Arts and Science, Department of Education, New Rochelle, NY 10801-1890. Offers adolescence education: biology (MS Ed, MST); adolescence education: English (MS Ed); adolescence education: mathematics (MST); adolescence education: social studies (MS Ed, MST); adolescence education: Spanish (MS Ed); adolescence special education 5-12 (MST); childhood and special education (MST); early childhood and childhood (MST); educational leadership (MS Ed). *Accreditation:* NCATE. *Program availability:* Part-time, evening/weekend. *Faculty:* 7 full-time (6 women), 4 part-time/adjunct (2 women). *Students:* 27 full-time (19 women), 27 part-time (18 women); includes 18 minority (4 Black or African American, non-Hispanic/Latino; 1 Asian, non-Hispanic/Latino; 12 Hispanic/Latino; 1 Two or more races, non-Hispanic/Latino). Average age 26. 6 applicants, 67% accepted, 3 enrolled. In 2016, 25 master's awarded. *Degree requirements:* For master's, thesis or alternative. *Entrance requirements:* For master's, minimum GPA of 3.0, NY State teaching certificate and bachelor's degree (for MS Ed). Additional exam requirements/recommendations for international students: Required—TOEFL (minimum score 550 paper-based; 80 iBT), IELTS (minimum score 6.5). *Application deadline:* For fall admission, 8/1 priority date for domestic students, 5/1 priority date for international students; for spring admission, 1/1 priority date for domestic students, 9/1 priority date for international students. Applications are processed on a rolling basis. Application fee: $50. Electronic applications accepted. *Expenses: Tuition:* Full-time $19,692; part-time $1094 per credit. *Required fees:* $245 per term. Tuition and fees vary according to program. *Financial support:* In 2016–17, 3 students received support. Unspecified assistantships available. Support available to part-time students. Financial award application deadline: 4/15; financial award applicants required to submit FAFSA. *Faculty research:* Engaging teacher educators in scientific process, cross-national comparisons of mathematics teaching, questioning strategies in the classroom, research methods, literacy development. *Unit head:* Margaret Smith, PhD, Chair, 914-633-2210, Fax: 914-633-2608, E-mail: msmith@iona.edu. *Application contact:* Richard McMahon, Coordinator, Graduate School of Education, 914-633-2552, E-mail: rmcmahon@iona.edu.
Website: http://www.iona.edu/Academics/School-of-Arts-Science/Departments/Education/Graduate-Programs.aspx

Iowa State University of Science and Technology, Department of Educational Leadership and Policy Studies, Ames, IA 50011. Offers counselor education (M Ed, MS); educational administration (M Ed, MS); educational leadership (PhD); higher education (M Ed, MS); organizational learning and human resource development (M Ed, MS); research and evaluation (MS); student affairs (MS). *Degree requirements:* For master's, thesis or alternative; for doctorate, thesis/dissertation. *Entrance requirements:* For master's and doctorate, GRE General Test. Additional exam requirements/recommendations for international students: Required—TOEFL (minimum score 560 paper-based; 83 iBT), IELTS (minimum score 6.5). *Application deadline:* For fall admission, 1/1 priority date for domestic and international students. Application fee: $60 ($90 for international students). Electronic applications accepted. *Application contact:* Robyn Goldy, Application Contact, 515-294-1241, Fax: 515-294-4942, E-mail: rgoldy@iastate.edu.
Website: http://www.elps.hs.iastate.edu/

Jackson State University, Graduate School, College of Education and Human Development, Department of Educational Leadership, Jackson, MS 39217. Offers education administration and supervision (Ed S); educational administration and supervision (MS Ed, PhD); higher education (Ed S). *Accreditation:* NCATE. *Program availability:* Part-time, evening/weekend, online only, 100% online, blended/hybrid learning. *Faculty:* 12 full-time (9 women), 3 part-time/adjunct (0 women). *Students:* 44 full-time (8 women), 238 part-time (181 women); includes 255 minority (all Black or African American, non-Hispanic/Latino). Average age 38. 158 applicants, 60% accepted, 64 enrolled. In 2016, 8 master's, 18 doctorates, 13 other advanced degrees awarded. *Degree requirements:* For master's and Ed S, comprehensive exam, thesis; for doctorate, comprehensive exam, thesis/dissertation. *Entrance requirements:* For master's, GRE General Test; for doctorate, MAT, GRE, teaching experience. Additional

exam requirements/recommendations for international students: Required—TOEFL (minimum score 520 paper-based; 67 iBT). *Application deadline:* For fall admission, 3/1 priority date for domestic students, 3/1 for international students; for spring admission, 10/1 for domestic and international students. Applications are processed on a rolling basis. Application fee: $25. Electronic applications accepted. *Expenses:* Contact institution. *Financial support:* Career-related internships or fieldwork, Federal Work-Study, scholarships/grants, and unspecified assistantships available. Support available to part-time students. Financial award application deadline: 3/1; financial award applicants required to submit FAFSA. *Unit head:* Dr. Benjamin Ngwudike, Chair, 601-979-2351, Fax: 601-979-7048, E-mail: benjamin.c.ngwudike@jsums.edu. *Application contact:* Dr. Benjamin Ngwudike, Chair, 601-979-2351, Fax: 601-979-7048, E-mail: benjamin.c.ngwudike@jsums.edu.
Website: http://www.jsums.edu/eduleadership/

Jacksonville State University, College of Graduate Studies and Continuing Education, College of Education and Professional Studies, Program in Instructional Leadership, Jacksonville, AL 36265-1602. Offers MS Ed, Ed S. *Accreditation:* NCATE. *Program availability:* Part-time, evening/weekend. *Faculty:* 11 full-time (9 women), 1 (woman) part-time/adjunct. *Students:* 3 full-time (all women), 77 part-time (47 women); includes 11 minority (10 Black or African American, non-Hispanic/Latino; 1 American Indian or Alaska Native, non-Hispanic/Latino). Average age 36. 50 applicants, 64% accepted, 27 enrolled. In 2016, 47 master's, 5 Ed Ss awarded. *Degree requirements:* For master's, comprehensive exam, thesis (for some programs). *Entrance requirements:* For master's, GRE General Test or MAT. Additional exam requirements/recommendations for international students: Required—TOEFL (minimum score 500 paper-based; 61 iBT). *Application deadline:* Applications are processed on a rolling basis. Application fee: $35. Electronic applications accepted. *Financial support:* Available to part-time students. Application deadline: 4/1; applicants required to submit FAFSA. *Unit head:* Dr. Tommy Turner, Head, 256-782-5180, E-mail: tturner@jsu.edu. *Application contact:* Dr. Jean Pugliese, Associate Dean, 256-782-8278, Fax: 256-782-5321, E-mail: pugliese@jsu.edu.

Jacksonville University, College of Arts and Sciences, MS in Education Leadership Program, Jacksonville, FL 32211. Offers MS. *Program availability:* Part-time, evening/weekend. *Degree requirements:* For master's, comprehensive exam, practicum. *Entrance requirements:* For master's, GRE General Test, minimum GPA of 3.0. Additional exam requirements/recommendations for international students: Required—TOEFL. *Expenses: Tuition:* Full-time $13,320. One-time fee: $50 part-time. Tuition and fees vary according to course load, degree level, campus/location and program.

James Madison University, The Graduate School, College of Education, Program in Education, Harrisonburg, VA 22807. Offers early childhood education (preK-3) (MAT); educational leadership (M Ed); educational technology (M Ed); elementary education (MAT); equity and cultural diversity (M Ed); inclusive early childhood education (MAT); K-8 mathematics specialist (M Ed); middle education (MAT); reading education (M Ed); secondary education (MAT); Spanish language and culture for educators (M Ed); TESOL (MAT). *Accreditation:* NCATE. *Program availability:* Part-time, evening/weekend. *Faculty:* 21 full-time (12 women), 5 part-time/adjunct (2 women). *Students:* 249 full-time (220 women), 123 part-time (86 women); includes 43 minority (7 Black or African American, non-Hispanic/Latino; 7 Asian, non-Hispanic/Latino; 17 Hispanic/Latino; 12 Two or more races, non-Hispanic/Latino), 2 international. Average age 30. 355 applicants, 98% accepted, 312 enrolled. In 2016, 247 master's awarded. Application fee: $55. Electronic applications accepted. *Financial support:* In 2016–17, 16 students received support. Career-related internships or fieldwork, Federal Work-Study, and 22 assistantships (averaging $7911) available. Financial award application deadline: 3/1; financial award applicants required to submit FAFSA. *Unit head:* Dr. Phillip M. Wishon, Dean, 540-568-6572, E-mail: wishonpm@jmu.edu. *Application contact:* Lynette D. Michael, Director of Graduate Admissions, 540-568-6131 Ext. 6395, Fax: 540-568-7860, E-mail: michaeld@jmu.edu.
Website: http://www.jmu.edu/coe/index.shtml

Johns Hopkins University, School of Education, Certificate Programs in Education, Baltimore, MD 21218. Offers advanced methods for differentiated instruction and inclusive education (Graduate Certificate); applied behavior analysis (Post-Master's Certificate); clinical mental health counseling (Post-Master's Certificate); counseling (Advanced Certificate); data-based decision making and organizational improvement (Graduate Certificate); early intervention/preschool special education specialist (Graduate Certificate); education of students with autism and other pervasive developmental disorders (Graduate Certificate); educational leadership for independent schools (Graduate Certificate); evidence-based teaching in the health professions (Post-Master's Certificate); gifted education (Graduate Certificate); leadership in technology integration (Graduate Certificate); mind, brain and teaching (Graduate Certificate); school administration and supervision (Graduate Certificate); urban education (Graduate Certificate). *Program availability:* Part-time-only, evening/weekend, 100% online, blended/hybrid learning. *Students:* 5 full-time (all women), 194 part-time (164 women); includes 46 minority (29 Black or African American, non-Hispanic/Latino; 2 American Indian or Alaska Native, non-Hispanic/Latino; 3 Asian, non-Hispanic/Latino; 8 Hispanic/Latino; 4 Two or more races, non-Hispanic/Latino), 7 international. Average age 37. 240 applicants, 75% accepted, 143 enrolled. In 2016, 167 Advanced Certificates awarded. *Entrance requirements:* For degree, minimum of bachelor's degree from regionally- or nationally-accredited institution (master's degree for some programs); minimum GPA of 3.0 in all previous programs of study; official transcripts from all post-secondary institutions attended; essay; curriculum vitae/resume; two letters of recommendation; dispositions survey. *Application deadline:* For fall admission, 4/1 priority date for domestic students; for spring admission, 10/1 priority date for domestic students; for summer admission, 2/1 priority date for domestic students. Applications are processed on a rolling basis. Application fee: $80. Electronic applications accepted. *Expenses:* Contact institution. *Financial support:* Application deadline: 4/1; applicants required to submit FAFSA. *Unit head:* Dr. Christopher C. Morphew, Dean. *Application contact:* Elisabeth Woodward, Director of Admissions, 410-516-9796, Fax: 410-516-9817, E-mail: soe.info@jhu.edu.
Website: http://education.jhu.edu

Johns Hopkins University, School of Education, Doctoral Programs in Education, Baltimore, MD 21218. Offers Ed D, PhD. *Program availability:* Part-time, evening/weekend, 100% online. *Students:* 22 full-time (14 women), 215 part-time (149 women); includes 82 minority (35 Black or African American, non-Hispanic/Latino; 14 Asian, non-Hispanic/Latino; 25 Hispanic/Latino; 8 Two or more races, non-Hispanic/Latino), 20 international. Average age 37. 416 applicants, 27% accepted, 82 enrolled. In 2016, 11 doctorates awarded. *Degree requirements:* For doctorate, comprehensive exam, thesis/dissertation. *Entrance requirements:* For doctorate, GRE (for PhD only), master's degree from regionally- or nationally-accredited institution; minimum GPA of 3.0 in previous undergraduate and graduate studies (for Ed D only); official transcripts from all post-secondary institutions attended; three letters of recommendation; curriculum vitae/resume; personal statement; dispositions survey. Additional exam requirements/recommendations for international students: Required—TOEFL (minimum score 600 paper-based; 100 iBT), IELTS (minimum score 7). *Application deadline:* For fall admission, 12/1 for domestic and international students. Application fee: $80. Electronic applications accepted. *Expenses:* Contact institution. *Financial support:* Fellowships, research assistantships, and teaching assistantships available. Financial award application deadline: 4/1; financial award applicants required to submit FAFSA. *Unit head:* Dr. Christopher C. Morphew, Dean. *Application contact:* Elisabeth Woodward, Director of Admissions, 410-516-9796, Fax: 410-516-9817, E-mail: soe.info@jhu.edu.
Website: http://education.jhu.edu

Johns Hopkins University, School of Education, Master's Programs in Education, Baltimore, MD 21218. Offers counseling (MS), including clinical mental health counseling, school counseling; education (MS), including educational studies, gifted education, reading, school administration and supervision, technology for educators; elementary education (MAT); health professions (M Ed); intelligence analysis (MS); organizational leadership (MS); secondary education (MAT), including biology, chemistry, earth/space science, English, physics, social studies; special education (MS), including early childhood special education, general special education studies, mild to moderate disabilities, severe disabilities. *Program availability:* Part-time, evening/weekend, 100% online, blended/hybrid learning. *Students:* 345 full-time (265 women), 1,601 part-time (1,245 women); includes 837 minority (392 Black or African American, non-Hispanic/Latino; 7 American Indian or Alaska Native, non-Hispanic/Latino; 141 Asian, non-Hispanic/Latino; 207 Hispanic/Latino; 7 Native Hawaiian or other Pacific Islander, non-Hispanic/Latino; 83 Two or more races, non-Hispanic/Latino), 55 international. Average age 27. 1,352 applicants, 76% accepted, 819 enrolled. In 2016, 642 master's awarded. *Degree requirements:* For master's, comprehensive exam (for some programs), portfolio, capstone project and/or internship; PRAXIS II (subject area assessments) for initial teacher preparation programs that lead to licensure. *Entrance requirements:* For master's, GRE (for full-time programs only); PRAXIS I/core or state-approved alternative (for initial teacher preparation programs that lead to licensure), minimum of bachelor's degree from regionally- or nationally-accredited institution; minimum GPA of 3.0 in all previous programs of study; official transcripts from all post-secondary institutions attended; essay; curriculum vitae/resume; letters of recommendation (3 for full-time programs, 2 for part-time programs); dispositions survey. Additional exam requirements/recommendations for international students: Required—TOEFL (minimum score 600 paper-based; 100 iBT), IELTS (minimum score 7). *Application deadline:* For fall admission, 4/1 priority date for domestic students, 4/1 for international students; for spring admission, 10/1 priority date for domestic students, 10/1 for international students; for summer admission, 2/1 priority date for domestic students, 2/1 for international students. Applications are processed on a rolling basis. Application fee: $80. Electronic applications accepted. *Expenses:* Contact institution. *Financial support:* Application deadline: 4/1; applicants required to submit FAFSA. *Unit head:* Dr. Christopher C. Morphew, Dean. *Application contact:* Elisabeth Woodward, Director of Admissions, 410-516-9796, Fax: 410-516-9817, E-mail: soe.info@jhu.edu.
Website: http://education.jhu.edu

Johnson & Wales University, Graduate Studies, Ed D Program in Educational Leadership, Providence, RI 02903-3703. Offers Ed D. *Program availability:* Part-time. *Degree requirements:* For doctorate, thesis/dissertation. *Entrance requirements:* For doctorate, MAT, minimum GPA of 3.25; master's degree in appropriate field from accredited institution. Additional exam requirements/recommendations for international students: Required—TOEFL (minimum score 550 paper-based); Recommended—IELTS, TWE. *Faculty research:* Site-based management, collaborative learning, technology and education, K-16 education.

Kansas State University, Graduate School, College of Education, Department of Curriculum and Instruction, Manhattan, KS 66506. Offers curriculum and instruction (Ed D, PhD); digital teaching and learning (MS); educational computing, design and online learning (MS); elementary/middle level curriculum and instruction (MS); online learning (Certificate); reading specialist endorsement (MS); reading/language arts (MS); teacher leader/school improvement (MS); teaching and learning (Certificate). *Accreditation:* NCATE. *Program availability:* Part-time, online learning. *Faculty:* 36 full-time (22 women), 18 part-time/adjunct (9 women). *Students:* 59 full-time (40 women), 94 part-time (72 women); includes 21 minority (5 Black or African American, non-Hispanic/Latino; 3 Asian, non-Hispanic/Latino; 11 Hispanic/Latino; 2 Two or more races, non-Hispanic/Latino), 20 international. Average age 35. 70 applicants, 71% accepted, 36 enrolled. In 2016, 61 master's, 12 doctorates, 9 other advanced degrees awarded. *Degree requirements:* For master's, comprehensive exam, portfolio, project, report or thesis; for doctorate, comprehensive exam, thesis/dissertation, preliminary exam; for Certificate, comprehensive exam, portfolio. *Entrance requirements:* For master's, minimum GPA of 3.0, 3 letters of recommendation; for doctorate, GRE, minimum GPA of 3.0, 3 letters of recommendation, evidence of scholarly writing; for Certificate, minimum GPA of 3.0, letters of recommendation. Additional exam requirements/recommendations for international students: Required—TOEFL (minimum score 550 paper-based; 80 iBT) or IELTS. *Application deadline:* For fall admission, 3/1 priority date for domestic students, 2/1 priority date for international students; for spring admission, 10/1 priority date for domestic students, 8/1 priority date for international students. Applications are processed on a rolling basis. Application fee: $50 ($75 for international students). Electronic applications accepted. *Expenses:* Tuition, state resident: full-time $9670. Tuition, nonresident: full-time $21,828. *Required fees:* $862. *Financial support:* In 2016–17, 1 research assistantship (averaging $19,980 per year), 8 teaching assistantships (averaging $12,620 per year) were awarded; career-related internships or fieldwork, institutionally sponsored loans, scholarships/grants, and unspecified assistantships also available. Support available to part-time students. Financial award application deadline: 3/1; financial award applicants required to submit FAFSA. *Faculty research:* Literacy and technology, critical race theory and diversity, achievement gaps, school improvement, teacher education. *Total annual research expenditures:* $647,057. *Unit head:* Dr. F. Todd Goodson, Department Chair, 785-532-5904, Fax: 785-532-7304, E-mail: tgoodson@ksu.edu. *Application contact:* Dr. Kay Ann Taylor, Director, Curriculum and Instruction Graduate Programs, 785-532-6974, Fax: 785-532-7304, E-mail: ktaylor@ksu.edu.
Website: http://www.coe.ksu.edu/edci/index.html

Kansas State University, Graduate School, College of Education, Department of Educational Leadership, Manhattan, KS 66506. Offers adult learning (Certificate); educational leadership (MS, Ed D, PhD); leadership dynamics for adult learners (Certificate); qualitative research (Certificate); social justice education (Certificate); teaching English as a second language for adult learners (Certificate). *Accreditation:* NCATE. *Program availability:* Online learning. *Faculty:* 14 full-time (9 women), 3 part-time/adjunct (2 women). *Students:* 42 full-time (20 women), 300 part-time (187 women); includes 65 minority (24 Black or African American, non-Hispanic/Latino; 6 American Indian or Alaska Native, non-Hispanic/Latino; 3 Asian, non-Hispanic/Latino; 21 Hispanic/Latino; 1 Native Hawaiian or other Pacific Islander, non-Hispanic/Latino; 10 Two or more races, non-Hispanic/Latino), 1 international. Average age 38. 180 applicants, 84% accepted, 126 enrolled. In 2016, 110 master's, 2 doctorates, 2 other advanced degrees awarded. *Degree requirements:* For master's, comprehensive exam; for doctorate, comprehensive exam, thesis/dissertation. *Entrance requirements:* For master's, minimum undergraduate GPA of 3.0; for doctorate, MAT (for educational administration); GRE General Test (for adult education), minimum GPA of 3.0 in last 60 hours. Additional exam requirements/recommendations for international students: Required—TOEFL. *Application deadline:* For fall admission, 2/1 priority date for

domestic and international students; for spring admission, 8/1 priority date for domestic and international students. Applications are processed on a rolling basis. Application fee: $50 ($75 for international students). Electronic applications accepted. *Expenses:* Tuition, state resident: full-time $9670. Tuition, nonresident: full-time $21,828. *Required fees:* $862. *Financial support:* Research assistantships, institutionally sponsored loans, and scholarships/grants available. Financial award application deadline: 3/1; financial award applicants required to submit FAFSA. *Faculty research:* Educational law, school finance, school facilities, organizational leadership, adult learning, distance learning/ education. *Total annual research expenditures:* $21,235. *Unit head:* Dr. David C. Thompson, Head, 785-532-5535, Fax: 785-532-7304, E-mail: thomsond@ksu.edu. *Application contact:* Jody Ellis, Applications Contact, 785-532-5535, E-mail: foxksu@ ksu.edu.
Website: http://www.coe.k-state.edu/departments/edlea/index.html

Kaplan University, Davenport Campus, School of Higher Education Studies, Davenport, IA 52807. Offers college administration and leadership (MS); college teaching and learning (MS); student services (MS). *Program availability:* Part-time, evening/weekend, online learning. *Entrance requirements:* Additional exam requirements/recommendations for international students: Required—TOEFL (minimum score 550 paper-based; 80 iBT).

Kean University, College of Natural, Applied and Health Sciences, Program in Nursing Educational Leadership, Union, NJ 07083. Offers educational leadership (PhD). *Accreditation:* ACEN. *Faculty:* 9 full-time (all women). *Students:* 30 part-time (28 women); includes 9 minority (8 Black or African American, non-Hispanic/Latino; 1 Asian, non-Hispanic/Latino). Average age 50. 3 applicants. *Degree requirements:* For doctorate, comprehensive exam, thesis/dissertation. *Entrance requirements:* For doctorate, GRE, MSN, minimum cumulative GPA of 3.2 in last degree obtained, official transcripts from all institutions attended, valid RN license, three letters of recommendation, professional resume/curriculum vitae, personal statement. Additional exam requirements/recommendations for international students: Required—TOEFL (minimum score 550 paper-based; 79 iBT), IELTS (minimum score 6.5). *Application deadline:* For fall admission, 5/1 for domestic students; for spring admission, 12/1 for domestic and international students. Application fee: $75. Electronic applications accepted. *Expenses:* Contact institution. *Financial support:* Scholarships/grants and unspecified assistantships available. *Unit head:* Dr. Virginia Fitzsimons, Coordinator, 609-361-4798, E-mail: vfitzsim@kean.edu. *Application contact:* Pedro Lopes, Admissions Counselor, 908-737-7100, E-mail: grad-adm@kean.edu.
Website: http://grad.kean.edu/doctoral-programs/doctor-nursing-educational-leadership

Kean University, Nathan Weiss Graduate College, Program in Educational Administration, Union, NJ 07083. Offers school business administrator (MA); supervisor and principal (MA); supervisors, principals, and school business administrators (MA). *Accreditation:* NCATE. *Program availability:* Part-time, 100% online. *Faculty:* 3 full-time (2 women). *Students:* 12 full-time (8 women), 80 part-time (46 women); includes 32 minority (13 Black or African American, non-Hispanic/Latino; 2 Asian, non-Hispanic/ Latino; 17 Hispanic/Latino), 1 international. Average age 33. 184 applicants, 49% accepted, 80 enrolled. In 2016, 31 master's awarded. *Degree requirements:* For master's, comprehensive exam (for some programs), portfolio, field experience, research component, internship, teaching experience. *Entrance requirements:* For master's, GRE General Test or MAT, minimum GPA of 3.0; New Jersey or out-of-state Standard Instructional or Educational Services Certificate; one year of experience under the appropriate certificate; official transcripts from all institutions attended; two letters of recommendation; personal statement; professional resume/curriculum vitae. Additional exam requirements/recommendations for international students: Required—TOEFL (minimum score 550 paper-based; 79 iBT), IELTS (minimum score 6.5). *Application deadline:* For fall admission, 6/1 for domestic and international students; for spring admission, 12/1 for domestic and international students. Applications are processed on a rolling basis. Application fee: $75. Electronic applications accepted. *Expenses:* Tuition, state resident: full-time $13,156; part-time $640 per credit. Tuition, nonresident: full-time $17,831; part-time $785 per credit. *Required fees:* $3316; $151 per credit. Tuition and fees vary according to course level, course load, degree level and program. *Financial support:* Scholarships/grants and unspecified assistantships available. Financial award applicants required to submit FAFSA. *Unit head:* Dr. Steven Locasio, Program Coordinator, 908-737-5977, E-mail: locascst@kean.edu. *Application contact:* Brittany Gerstenhaber, Admissions Counselor, 908-737-7100, E-mail: grad-adm@ kean.edu.
Website: http://grad.kean.edu/edleadership/ma-combined

Kean University, Nathan Weiss Graduate College, Program in Educational Leadership, Union, NJ 07083. Offers Ed D. *Program availability:* Part-time. *Faculty:* 3 full-time (2 women). *Students:* 3 full-time (1 woman), 43 part-time (30 women); includes 29 minority (22 Black or African American, non-Hispanic/Latino; 1 American Indian or Alaska Native, non-Hispanic/Latino; 1 Asian, non-Hispanic/Latino; 5 Hispanic/Latino). Average age 44. 21 applicants, 48% accepted, 9 enrolled. In 2016, 12 doctorates awarded. *Degree requirements:* For doctorate, comprehensive exam, thesis/dissertation. *Entrance requirements:* For doctorate, GRE or MAT, master's degree from accredited college or university, minimum GPA of 3.0 in last degree attained, substantial experience working in education or family support agencies, 2 letters of recommendation, personal interview, transcripts, leadership portfolio, resume, letter of endorsement from superintendent or agency director. Additional exam requirements/recommendations for international students: Required—TOEFL (minimum score 550 paper-based; 79 iBT), IELTS (minimum score 6.5). *Application deadline:* For fall admission, 5/1 for domestic and international students; for spring admission, 12/1 for domestic and international students. Applications are processed on a rolling basis. Application fee: $75. Electronic applications accepted. *Expenses:* Contact institution. *Financial support:* Scholarships/ grants and unspecified assistantships available. Financial award applicants required to submit FAFSA. *Unit head:* Dr. Soundaram Ramaswami, Program Coordinator, 908-737-5979, E-mail: sramaswa@kean.edu. *Application contact:* Brittany Gerstenhaber, Admissions Counselor, 908-737-7100, E-mail: grad-adm@kean.edu.
Website: http://grad.kean.edu/edleadership/edd

Keene State College, School of Professional and Graduate Studies, Keene, NH 03435. Offers curriculum and instruction (M Ed); education leadership (PMC); educational leadership (M Ed); safety and occupational health applied science (MS); school counselor (M Ed, PMC); special education (M Ed). *Accreditation:* NCATE. *Program availability:* Part-time, evening/weekend. *Faculty:* 9 full-time (4 women), 8 part-time/ adjunct (3 women). *Students:* 24 full-time (17 women), 66 part-time (38 women); includes 3 minority (1 Black or African American, non-Hispanic/Latino; 1 Hispanic/ Latino; 1 Two or more races, non-Hispanic/Latino), 1 international. Average age 33. 24 applicants, 100% accepted, 24 enrolled. In 2016, 26 master's, 1 other advanced degree awarded. *Degree requirements:* For master's, thesis (for some programs). *Entrance requirements:* For master's, PRAXIS I, 3 references; official transcripts; minimum GPA of 2.5; interview; essay; teacher/educator certificate; work/internship experience. Additional exam requirements/recommendations for international students: Required—TOEFL (minimum score 550 paper-based; 61 iBT). *Application deadline:* For fall admission, 4/1 for domestic and international students; for spring admission, 11/1 for domestic and international students; for summer admission, 3/1 for domestic and international students. Applications are processed on a rolling basis. Application fee: $50. Electronic applications accepted. *Expenses:* Tuition, state resident: full-time $9180; part-time $510 per credit. Tuition, nonresident: full-time $10,080; part-time $560 per credit. *Required fees:* $1908; $106 per credit. Tuition and fees vary according to course load. *Financial support:* In 2016–17, 27 students received support. Career-related internships or fieldwork, Federal Work-Study, institutionally sponsored loans, scholarships/grants, and unspecified assistantships available. Support available to part-time students. Financial award application deadline: 3/1; financial award applicants required to submit FAFSA. *Unit head:* Dr. Karrie Kalich, Dean of Professional and Graduate Studies, 603-358-2885, E-mail: kkalich@keene.edu. *Application contact:* Peter Tandy, Assistant Director for Graduate Studies, 603-358-2332, E-mail: kscgraduatestudies@keene.edu.
Website: http://www.keene.edu/academics/graduate/

Keiser University, EdS in Educational Leadership Program, Ft. Lauderdale, FL 33309. Offers Ed S.

Keiser University, Joint MS Ed/MBA Program, Ft. Lauderdale, FL 33309. Offers MS Ed/MBA.

Keiser University, Master of Science in Education Program, Ft. Lauderdale, FL 33309. Offers allied health teaching and leadership (MS Ed); career college administration (MS Ed); leadership (MS Ed); online teaching and learning (MS Ed); teaching and learning (MS Ed). *Program availability:* Part-time, online learning.

Keiser University, PhD in Educational Leadership Program, Ft. Lauderdale, FL 33309. Offers PhD.

Kennesaw State University, Leland and Clarice C. Bagwell College of Education, Program in Graduate Education, Kennesaw, GA 30144. Offers educational leadership (M Ed); educational leadership technology (M Ed); elementary and early childhood education (M Ed); instructional technology (M Ed); middle grades education (M Ed); reading (M Ed); secondary education (M Ed); special education (M Ed); teaching English to speakers of other languages (M Ed). *Accreditation:* NCATE. *Program availability:* Part-time. *Degree requirements:* For master's, thesis or alternative. *Entrance requirements:* For master's, GRE General Test, T-4 state certification, minimum GPA of 2.75. Additional exam requirements/recommendations for international students: Required—TOEFL (minimum score 550 paper-based; 80 iBT), IELTS (minimum score 6.5). Electronic applications accepted.

Kennesaw State University, Leland and Clarice C. Bagwell College of Education, Program in Leadership for Learning, Kennesaw, GA 30144. Offers Ed D, Ed S. *Program availability:* Part-time, evening/weekend. *Degree requirements:* For doctorate, thesis/ dissertation. *Entrance requirements:* For doctorate, GRE General Test, minimum graduate GPA of 3.0, resume. Additional exam requirements/recommendations for international students: Required—TOEFL (minimum score 550 paper-based; 80 iBT), IELTS (minimum score 6.5). Electronic applications accepted.

Kent State University, College of Education, Health and Human Services, School of Foundations, Leadership and Administration, Program in K-12 Leadership, Kent, OH 44242-0001. Offers M Ed, PhD, Ed S. *Degree requirements:* For master's, thesis optional; for doctorate, comprehensive exam, thesis/dissertation. *Entrance requirements:* For master's, GRE if GPA is below 3.0, 2 letters of reference, goals statement; for doctorate, GRE, minimum master's-level GPA of 3.5, interview, resume, 2 letters of reference, goals statement; for Ed S, GRE. Additional exam requirements/ recommendations for international students: Required—TOEFL (minimum score 550 paper-based; 80 iBT). Electronic applications accepted. *Expenses:* Tuition, state resident: full-time $10,864; part-time $495 per credit hour. Tuition, nonresident: full-time $18,380; part-time $837 per credit hour.

Keystone College, Program in Early Childhood Education Leadership, La Plume, PA 18440. Offers M Ed. *Program availability:* Part-time, blended/hybrid learning. *Faculty:* 3 full-time (all women), 2 part-time/adjunct (both women). *Students:* 44 part-time (37 women). 35 applicants, 77% accepted, 23 enrolled. *Degree requirements:* For master's, internship, professional contribution, or addressing a grant initiative. *Entrance requirements:* For master's, GRE, college transcripts, resume or curriculum vitae, current clearances. Additional exam requirements/recommendations for international students: Required—TOEFL (minimum score 80 iBT) or IELTS (minimum score 6.5). *Application deadline:* For fall admission, 8/1 for domestic students; for spring admission, 12/1 for domestic students; for summer admission, 5/1 for domestic students. Applications are processed on a rolling basis. Application fee: $50. Electronic applications accepted. *Expenses:* Contact institution. *Financial support:* Unspecified assistantships available. Financial award application deadline: 5/1; financial award applicants required to submit FAFSA. *Unit head:* Fran Langan, PhD, Dean, School of Professional Studies, 570-945-8472, E-mail: fran.langan@keystone.edu. *Application contact:* Jennifer Sekol, Director of Admissions, 570-945-8117, Fax: 570-945-7916, E-mail: jennifer.sekol@keystone.edu.

Kutztown University of Pennsylvania, College of Education, Program in Student Affairs in Higher Education, Kutztown, PA 19530-0730. Offers M Ed. *Accreditation:* NCATE. *Program availability:* Part-time, evening/weekend. *Faculty:* 1 (woman) full-time. *Students:* 27 full-time (22 women), 19 part-time (13 women); includes 14 minority (7 Black or African American, non-Hispanic/Latino; 1 Asian, non-Hispanic/Latino; 6 Hispanic/Latino). Average age 26. 26 applicants, 65% accepted, 9 enrolled. In 2016, 12 master's awarded. *Degree requirements:* For master's, comprehensive exam. *Entrance requirements:* For master's, GRE General Test, 3 letters of recommendation, minimum undergraduate GPA of 3.0, department interview, statement of knowledge and experience in student affairs. Additional exam requirements/recommendations for international students: Required—TOEFL (minimum score 550 paper-based, 79 iBT) or IELTS (minimum score 6.5). *Application deadline:* For fall admission, 3/1 for domestic and international students; for spring admission, 10/1 for domestic and international students. Application fee: $35. Electronic applications accepted. *Expenses:* Tuition, state resident: full-time $4347; part-time $483 per credit. Tuition, nonresident: full-time $6525; part-time $725 per credit. *Required fees:* $88 per credit. One-time fee: $50 full-time. *Financial support:* Career-related internships or fieldwork, Federal Work-Study, scholarships/grants, and unspecified assistantships available. Financial award application deadline: 3/1; financial award applicants required to submit FAFSA. *Unit head:* Dr. Helen S. Hamlet, Department Chair, 610-683-4204, Fax: 610-683-1585, E-mail: hamlet@kutztown.edu.
Website: https://www.kutztown.edu/academics/graduate-programs/counseling.htm

Lamar University, College of Graduate Studies, College of Education and Human Development, Department of Educational Leadership, Beaumont, TX 77710. Offers digital learning and leading (M Ed); education administration (M Ed); educational leadership (Ed D), educational technology (M Ed). *Program availability:* Part-time, evening/weekend. *Faculty:* 29 full-time (17 women), 15 part-time/adjunct (6 women). *Students:* 8 full-time (all women), 2,215 part-time (1,490 women); includes 848 minority (387 Black or African American, non-Hispanic/Latino; 6 American Indian or Alaska Native, non-Hispanic/Latino; 30 Asian, non-Hispanic/Latino; 375 Hispanic/Latino; 50 Two or more races, non-Hispanic/Latino), 3 international. Average age 38. 869 applicants, 89% accepted, 542 enrolled. In 2016, 977 master's, 82 doctorates awarded. Terminal master's awarded for partial completion of doctoral program. *Degree*

requirements: For master's, comprehensive exam, thesis optional; for doctorate, thesis/dissertation. *Entrance requirements:* For master's, GRE General Test, minimum GPA of 2.5; for doctorate, GRE. Additional exam requirements/recommendations for international students: Required—TOEFL (minimum score 550 paper-based; 79 iBT), IELTS (minimum score 6.5). *Application deadline:* For fall admission, 8/10 priority date for domestic students, 7/1 for international students; for spring admission, 1/5 priority date for domestic students, 12/1 for international students. Applications are processed on a rolling basis. Application fee: $25 ($50 for international students). Electronic applications accepted. *Expenses:* $8,134 in-state full-time, $5,574 in-state part-time; $15,604 out-of-state full-time, $10,554 out-of-state part-time per year. *Financial support:* Fellowships, research assistantships with tuition reimbursements, teaching assistantships with tuition reimbursements, career-related internships or fieldwork, and scholarships/grants available. Support available to part-time students. Financial award application deadline: 4/1; financial award applicants required to submit FAFSA. *Faculty research:* School dropouts, suicide prevention in public school students, school climate and gifted performance, teacher evaluation. *Unit head:* Dr. Kaye Shelton, Director, 409-880-8689, Fax: 409-880-8685. *Application contact:* Deidre Mayer, Interim Director, Admissions and Academic Services, 409-880-8888, Fax: 409-880-7419, E-mail: gradmissions@lamar.edu.
Website: http://education.lamar.edu/educational-leadership

Lamar University, College of Graduate Studies, College of Education and Human Development, Department of Teacher Education, Beaumont, TX 77710. Offers teacher leadership (M Ed). *Faculty:* 7 full-time (6 women). *Students:* 213 part-time (191 women); includes 74 minority (33 Black or African American, non-Hispanic/Latino; 2 American Indian or Alaska Native, non-Hispanic/Latino; 4 Asian, non-Hispanic/Latino; 34 Hispanic/Latino; 1 Two or more races, non-Hispanic/Latino). Average age 37. 136 applicants, 99% accepted, 69 enrolled. In 2016, 146 master's awarded. *Entrance requirements:* Additional exam requirements/recommendations for international students: Required—TOEFL (minimum score 550 paper-based; 79 iBT), IELTS (minimum score 6.5). *Application deadline:* For fall admission, 8/10 for domestic students, 7/1 for international students; for spring admission, 1/5 for domestic and international students. *Expenses:* $8,134 in-state full-time, $5,574 in-state part-time; $15,604 out-of-state full-time, $10,554 out-of-state part-time per year. *Financial support:* Application deadline: 4/1; applicants required to submit FAFSA. *Unit head:* Dr. Lulu Henry, 409-880-8217, Fax: 409-880-7788. *Application contact:* Deidre Mayer, Interim Director, Admissions and Academic Services, 409-880-8888, Fax: 409-880-7419, E-mail: gradmissions@lamar.edu.
Website: http://education.lamar.edu/teacher-education

La Salle University, School of Arts and Sciences, Program in Education, Philadelphia, PA 19141-1199. Offers autism spectrum disorders (MA, Certificate); bilingual/bicultural studies (MA); classroom management (MA); dual early childhood and special education (MA); dual middle-level science and math and special education (MA); education (MA); English (MA); English as a second language (Certificate); history (MA); instructional coach (Certificate); instructional leadership (MA); reading specialist (MA, Certificate); secondary education (MA); special education (MA, Certificate). *Program availability:* Part-time, evening/weekend. *Faculty:* 5 full-time (4 women), 12 part-time/adjunct (8 women). *Students:* 10 full-time (all women), 98 part-time (74 women); includes 28 minority (13 Black or African American, non-Hispanic/Latino; 1 American Indian or Alaska Native, non-Hispanic/Latino; 1 Asian, non-Hispanic/Latino; 10 Hispanic/Latino; 3 Two or more races, non-Hispanic/Latino). Average age 34. 128 applicants, 84% accepted, 69 enrolled. In 2016, 53 master's awarded. *Degree requirements:* For master's, comprehensive exam. *Entrance requirements:* For master's, MAT or GRE, 2 letters of recommendation; for Certificate, GMAT or GRE, 2 letters of recommendation. Additional exam requirements/recommendations for international students: Required—TOEFL. *Application deadline:* For fall admission, 8/15 priority date for domestic students, 7/15 for international students; for spring admission, 12/15 priority date for domestic students, 11/15 for international students; for summer admission, 4/15 priority date for domestic students, 3/15 for international students. Applications are processed on a rolling basis. Application fee: $35. Electronic applications accepted. Application fee is waived when completed online. *Expenses:* Contact institution. *Financial support:* In 2016–17, 27 students received support. Scholarships/grants available. Support available to part-time students. Financial award application deadline: 8/31; financial award applicants required to submit FAFSA. *Unit head:* Dr. Greer Richardson, Director, 215-951-1806, Fax: 215-951-1843, E-mail: graded@lasalle.edu. *Application contact:* Elizabeth Heenan, Director, Graduate and Adult Enrollment, 215-951-1100, Fax: 215-951-1462, E-mail: heenan@lasalle.edu.
Website: http://www.lasalle.edu/grad-education-programs/

La Sierra University, School of Education, Department of Administration and Leadership, Riverside, CA 92515. Offers MA, Ed D, Ed S. *Program availability:* Part-time, evening/weekend. Terminal master's awarded for partial completion of doctoral program. *Degree requirements:* For master's, thesis optional; for doctorate, thesis/dissertation, fieldwork, qualifying exam; for Ed S, thesis optional, fieldwork. *Entrance requirements:* For master's, minimum GPA of 3.0; for doctorate, GRE General Test, GRE Subject Test, minimum GPA of 3.3, Ed S; for Ed S, master's degree, minimum GPA of 3.3.

Lee University, Program in Education, Cleveland, TN 37320-3450. Offers art (MAT); curriculum and instruction (M Ed, Ed S); early childhood (MAT); educational leadership (M Ed, Ed S); elementary education (MAT); English and math (MAT); English and science (MAT); English and social studies (MAT); higher education administration (MS); history (MAT); history and economics (MAT); math and science (MAT); math and social studies (MAT); middle grades (MAT); science and social studies (MASW); secondary education (MAT); Spanish (MAT); special education (M Ed, MAT); TESOL (MAT). *Accreditation:* NCATE. *Program availability:* Part-time. *Faculty:* 13 full-time (6 women), 9 part-time/adjunct (4 women). *Students:* 35 full-time (27 women), 50 part-time (32 women); includes 12 minority (5 Black or African American, non-Hispanic/Latino; 5 Hispanic/Latino; 2 Two or more races, non-Hispanic/Latino), 4 international. Average age 30. 43 applicants, 79% accepted, 28 enrolled. In 2016, 42 master's, 6 other advanced degrees awarded. *Degree requirements:* For master's, variable foreign language requirement, thesis optional, internship. *Entrance requirements:* For master's, MAT or GRE General Test, minimum undergraduate GPA of 2.75, 3 letters of recommendation, interview, writing sample, official transcripts, background check; for Ed S, minimum undergraduate and master's GPA of 2.75, official transcripts for undergraduate and master's degrees. Additional exam requirements/recommendations for international students: Required—TOEFL (minimum score 61 iBT). *Application deadline:* For fall admission, 6/1 priority date for domestic and international students; for spring admission, 11/1 priority date for domestic and international students; for summer admission, 4/1 priority date for domestic and international students. Applications are processed on a rolling basis. Application fee: $25. Electronic applications accepted. *Expenses: Tuition:* Full-time $11,367; part-time $632 per credit hour. *Required fees:* $35 per term. One-time fee: $25. Tuition and fees vary according to program. *Financial support:* In 2016–17, 42 students received support. Career-related internships or fieldwork, Federal Work-Study, institutionally sponsored loans, scholarships/grants, and unspecified assistantships available. Financial award application deadline: 3/1; financial award applicants required to submit FAFSA. *Unit head:* Dr. William Kamm, Director, 423-614-8544, E-mail: wkamm@leeuniversity.edu. *Application contact:* Crystal Keeter, Graduate Education Secretary, 423-614-8544, E-mail: ckeeter@leeuniversity.edu.
Website: http://www.leeuniversity.edu/academics/graduate/education

Lehigh University, College of Education, Program in Educational Leadership, Bethlehem, PA 18015. Offers M Ed, Ed D, Certificate, MBA/M Ed. *Program availability:* Part-time, evening/weekend, blended/hybrid learning. *Faculty:* 6 full-time (2 women), 5 part-time/adjunct (3 women). *Students:* 6 full-time (5 women), 117 part-time (70 women); includes 10 minority (2 Black or African American, non-Hispanic/Latino; 3 Asian, non-Hispanic/Latino; 5 Hispanic/Latino), 6 international. Average age 35. 89 applicants, 76% accepted, 13 enrolled. In 2016, 42 master's, 5 doctorates awarded. *Degree requirements:* For doctorate, comprehensive exam, thesis/dissertation. *Entrance requirements:* For master's and Certificate, minimum undergraduate GPA of 3.0; for doctorate, GRE General Test or MAT, minimum graduate GPA of 3.6, 2 letters of recommendation, essay, transcript. Additional exam requirements/recommendations for international students: Required—TOEFL (minimum score 600 paper-based; 93 iBT). *Application deadline:* For fall admission, 1/15 for domestic and international students; for spring admission, 12/1 for domestic and international students; for summer admission, 5/1 for domestic and international students. Applications are processed on a rolling basis. Application fee: $65. Electronic applications accepted. *Expenses:* $565 per credit. *Financial support:* In 2016–17, 7 students received support. Scholarships/grants, tuition waivers, and unspecified assistantships available. Financial award application deadline: 1/31; financial award applicants required to submit FAFSA. *Faculty research:* Supervision of instruction, middle-level education, organizational change, leadership preparation and development, international school leadership, urban school leadership, comparative education, social justice. *Unit head:* Dr. Floyd D. Beachum, Director, 610-758-5955, Fax: 610-758-3227, E-mail: fdb209@lehigh.edu. *Application contact:* Lauryn Woodman, Coordinator, 610-758-3250, Fax: 610-758-6223, E-mail: laa314@lehigh.edu.
Website: http://ed.lehigh.edu/academics/disciplines/edl

Le Moyne College, Department of Education, Syracuse, NY 13214. Offers adolescent education (MS Ed, MST); adolescent education/special education (MS Ed, MST); adolescent English (MST), including grades 7-12; adolescent English/special education (MST), including grades 7-12; adolescent foreign language (MST), including grades 7-12; adolescent history (MST), including grades 7-12; childhood education (MS Ed); childhood education/special education (MS Ed); elementary education (MS Ed); general education (MS Ed); inclusive childhood education (MST); literacy education (MS Ed), including birth to grade 6, grades 5-12; school building leader (MS Ed); school building leadership (CAS); school district business leader (MS Ed, CAS); school district leader (MS Ed); school district leadership (CAS); secondary education (MS Ed); special education (MS Ed); teaching English to speakers of other languages (MS Ed); urban studies (MS Ed). *Accreditation:* TEAC. *Program availability:* Part-time, evening/weekend. *Faculty:* 8 full-time (5 women), 20 part-time/adjunct (12 women). *Students:* 66 full-time (40 women), 155 part-time (117 women); includes 13 minority (4 Black or African American, non-Hispanic/Latino; 2 American Indian or Alaska Native, non-Hispanic/Latino; 2 Asian, non-Hispanic/Latino; 5 Hispanic/Latino), 3 international. Average age 30. 74 applicants, 99% accepted, 66 enrolled. In 2016, 81 master's, 53 CASs awarded. *Degree requirements:* For master's, thesis. *Entrance requirements:* For master's, bachelor's degree with minimum undergraduate GPA of 3.0, 2 letters of recommendation, transcripts. Additional exam requirements/recommendations for international students: Required—TOEFL (minimum score 550 paper-based; 79 iBT); Recommended—IELTS (minimum score 6.5). *Application deadline:* For fall admission, 4/1 priority date for domestic and international students; for spring admission, 10/1 priority date for domestic and international students; for summer admission, 3/1 priority date for domestic and international students. Applications are processed on a rolling basis. Application fee: $50. Electronic applications accepted. *Expenses:* $700 per credit hour. *Financial support:* In 2016–17, 21 students received support. Career-related internships or fieldwork, scholarships/grants, and health care benefits available. Support available to part-time students. Financial award applicants required to submit FAFSA. *Faculty research:* Minority teachers, special education, multiculturalism, literacy, technology, media literacy learning, autism, school district organization, service-learning, higher level problem solving, teacher leadership. *Unit head:* Dr. Stephen C. Fleury, Chair, Department of Education, 315-445-4376, Fax: 315-445-4744, E-mail: fleurysc@lemoyne.edu. *Application contact:* Kristen P. Richards, Senior Director of Enrollment Management, 315-445-5444, Fax: 315-445-6092, E-mail: trapaskp@lemoyne.edu.
Website: http://www.lemoyne.edu/education

Lenoir-Rhyne University, Graduate Programs, School of Education, Program in Leadership, Hickory, NC 28601. Offers community and nonprofit leadership (MA); general management (MA); higher education leadership (MA); second language community services (MA). *Program availability:* Online learning. *Entrance requirements:* Additional exam requirements/recommendations for international students: Required—TOEFL (minimum score 600 paper-based). Electronic applications accepted. *Expenses:* Contact institution.

Lesley University, Graduate School of Education, Cambridge, MA 02138-2790. Offers arts, community, and education (M Ed); autism studies (Certificate); curriculum and instruction (M Ed, CAGS); early childhood education (M Ed); ecological teaching and learning (MS); educational studies (PhD), including adult learning, educational leadership, individually designed; elementary education (M Ed); emergent technologies for educators (Certificate); ESLArts: language learning through the arts (M Ed); high school education (M Ed); individually designed (M Ed); integrated teaching through the arts (M Ed); literacy for K-8 classroom teachers (M Ed); mathematics education (M Ed); middle school education (M Ed); moderate disabilities (M Ed); online learning (Certificate); reading (CAGS); science in education (M Ed); severe disabilities (M Ed); special needs (CAGS); specialist teacher of reading (M Ed); teacher of visual art (M Ed); technology in education (M Ed, CAGS). *Accreditation:* TEAC. *Program availability:* Part-time, evening/weekend, online learning. *Degree requirements:* For master's, practicum; for doctorate, thesis/dissertation. *Entrance requirements:* For master's, Massachusetts Tests for Educator Licensure (MTEL), transcripts, statement of purpose, recommendations; interview (for special education); for doctorate, GRE General Test, transcripts, statement of purpose, recommendations, interview, master's degree, resume; for other advanced degree, interview, master's degree. Additional exam requirements/recommendations for international students: Required—TOEFL (minimum score 550 paper-based; 80 iBT). Electronic applications accepted. *Faculty research:* Assessment in literacy, mathematics and science; autism spectrum disorders; instructional technology and online learning; multicultural education and English language learners.

LeTourneau University, Graduate Programs, Longview, TX 75607-7001. Offers business (MBA); counseling (MA), including licensed professional counselor, marriage and family therapy, school counseling; curriculum and instruction (M Ed); educational administration (M Ed); engineering (ME, MS); engineering management (MEM); health care administration (MS); marriage and family therapy (MA); psychology (MA); strategic leadership (MSL); teacher leadership (M Ed); teaching and learning (M Ed). *Program availability:* Part-time, 100% online, blended/hybrid learning. *Faculty:* 24 full-time (7 women), 40 part-time/adjunct (15 women). *Students:* 82 full-time (48 women), 428 part-

time (331 women); includes 234 minority (138 Black or African American, non-Hispanic/Latino; 5 American Indian or Alaska Native, non-Hispanic/Latino; 5 Asian, non-Hispanic/Latino; 50 Hispanic/Latino; 36 Two or more races, non-Hispanic/Latino), 15 international. Average age 37. 257 applicants, 60% accepted, 141 enrolled. In 2016, 136 master's awarded. *Degree requirements:* For master's, thesis (for some programs). *Entrance requirements:* Additional exam requirements/recommendations for international students: Required—TOEFL. *Application deadline:* For fall admission, 8/22 for domestic students, 8/29 for international students; for winter admission, 10/10 for domestic students; for spring admission, 1/2 for domestic students, 1/10 for international students; for summer admission, 5/1 for domestic and international students. Applications are processed on a rolling basis. Electronic applications accepted. *Expenses:* $10,890-$18,450 tuition per year (depending on program). *Financial support:* Research assistantships, institutionally sponsored loans, and unspecified assistantships available. Financial award applicants required to submit FAFSA. *Application contact:* Chris Fontaine, Assistant Vice President for Enrollment Services and Global Admissions, 903-233-4312, E-mail: chrisfontaine@letu.edu.
Website: http://www.letu.edu

Lewis & Clark College, Graduate School of Education and Counseling, Department of Educational Leadership, Program in Educational Leadership, Portland, OR 97219-7899. Offers educational administration (M Ed, Ed S); educational leadership (Ed D); student affairs administration (MA). *Program availability:* Part-time, evening/weekend. *Degree requirements:* For doctorate, thesis/dissertation. *Entrance requirements:* For master's, minimum undergraduate GPA of 2.75, Oregon teaching or personnel service license, three years of successful teaching and/or personnel service experience in the public schools or regionally-accredited private schools; for doctorate, master's degree plus minimum of 14 degree-applicable, post-master's semester credits; minimum undergraduate GPA of 2.75. Additional exam requirements/recommendations for international students: Required—TOEFL (minimum score 575 paper-based). *Application deadline:* For fall admission, 5/1 for domestic and international students. Applications are processed on a rolling basis. Application fee: $50. Electronic applications accepted. *Financial support:* Career-related internships or fieldwork, Federal Work-Study, institutionally sponsored loans, health care benefits, and tuition waivers (partial) available. Support available to part-time students. Financial award application deadline: 3/1; financial award applicants required to submit FAFSA. *Unit head:* Mollie Galloway, Department Chair, 503-768-6080, Fax: 503-768-6085, E-mail: eda@lclark.edu. *Application contact:* Becky Haas, Director of Admissions, 503-768-6200, Fax: 503-768-6205, E-mail: gseadmit@lclark.edu.
Website: http://www.lclark.edu/dept/eda/

Lewis University, College of Education, Program in Educational Leadership, Romeoville, IL 60446. Offers M Ed, MA. *Program availability:* Part-time, evening/weekend. *Students:* 10 part-time (3 women); includes 2 minority (both Black or African American, non-Hispanic/Latino). Average age 34. *Degree requirements:* For master's, departmental qualifying exams. *Entrance requirements:* For master's, writing exam, minimum GPA of 2.75, 2 letters of recommendation, interview. Additional exam requirements/recommendations for international students: Required—TOEFL (minimum score 550 paper-based; 80 iBT). *Application deadline:* For fall admission, 5/1 priority date for international students; for spring admission, 11/15 priority date for international students. Applications are processed on a rolling basis. Application fee: $40. Electronic applications accepted. *Expenses: Tuition:* Full-time $13,860; part-time $770 per credit hour. *Required fees:* $75 per semester. Tuition and fees vary according to degree level and program. *Financial support:* Career-related internships or fieldwork, Federal Work-Study, scholarships/grants, and unspecified assistantships available. Financial award application deadline: 5/1; financial award applicants required to submit FAFSA. *Unit head:* Dr. Lauren Hoffman, Director, 815-838-0500 Ext. 5501, Fax: 815-836-5879, E-mail: hoffmanla@lewisu.edu. *Application contact:* Nina Nowaczyk, Assistant Director, Graduate Admission, 815-836-5811, E-mail: nowaczni@lewisu.edu.

Lewis University, College of Education, Program in Educational Leadership for Teaching and Learning, Romeoville, IL 60446. Offers Ed D. *Program availability:* Part-time-only, evening/weekend. *Students:* 59 part-time (33 women); includes 27 minority (18 Black or African American, non-Hispanic/Latino; 1 Asian, non-Hispanic/Latino; 8 Hispanic/Latino), 2 international. Average age 41. *Degree requirements:* For doctorate, thesis/dissertation. *Entrance requirements:* For doctorate, letters of recommendation, personal statement, academic and scholarly work. Additional exam requirements/recommendations for international students: Required—TOEFL (minimum score 550 paper-based; 80 iBT). Application fee: $40. Electronic applications accepted. *Expenses: Tuition:* Full-time $13,860; part-time $770 per credit hour. *Required fees:* $75 per semester. Tuition and fees vary according to degree level and program. *Financial support:* Application deadline: 5/1; applicants required to submit FAFSA. *Unit head:* Dr. Lauren Hoffman, Program Director, 815-838-0500 Ext. 5501, E-mail: hoffmala@lewisu.edu. *Application contact:* Nina Nowaczyk, Office of Graduate Admission, 815-836-5610, E-mail: grad@lewisu.edu.

Liberty University, School of Education, Lynchburg, VA 24515. Offers educational leadership (Ed D); gifted education (Certificate); math specialist (M Ed); middle grades (MAT, Certificate); reading specialist (M Ed); school leadership (Certificate); secondary education (MAT); sport management (MS), including administration, outdoor recreation, sport management, tourism. *Accreditation:* NCATE. *Program availability:* Part-time, online learning. *Students:* 1,910 full-time (1,427 women), 4,420 part-time (3,311 women); includes 1,451 minority (1,182 Black or African American, non-Hispanic/Latino; 33 American Indian or Alaska Native, non-Hispanic/Latino; 44 Asian, non-Hispanic/Latino; 46 Hispanic/Latino; 11 Native Hawaiian or other Pacific Islander, non-Hispanic/Latino; 135 Two or more races, non-Hispanic/Latino), 87 international. Average age 37. 5,120 applicants, 44% accepted, 1193 enrolled. In 2016, 1,378 master's, 151 doctorates, 497 other advanced degrees awarded. *Degree requirements:* For doctorate, comprehensive exam, thesis/dissertation. *Entrance requirements:* For master's, GRE General Test or MAT (if taken in or before 1999), 2 letters of recommendation, minimum undergraduate GPA of 3.0, curriculum vitae; for doctorate and Certificate, GRE General Test or MAT (if taken before 1999), minimum master's GPA of 3.0, 3 years of teaching experience. Additional exam requirements/recommendations for international students: Required—TOEFL (minimum score 600 paper-based; 100 iBT). *Application deadline:* For fall admission, 6/1 for domestic students; for spring admission, 11/1 for domestic students. Applications are processed on a rolling basis. Application fee: $50. Electronic applications accepted. *Expenses:* Contact institution. *Financial support:* Federal Work-Study and tuition waivers (partial) available. *Faculty research:* Self-determination, character education, bibliotherapy, learning styles, distance education. *Unit head:* Dr. Heather Schoffstall, Dean, 434-582-2445, Fax: 434-582-2468, E-mail: awgunter@liberty.edu. *Application contact:* Jay Bridge, Director of Graduate Admissions, 800-424-9595, Fax: 800-628-7977, E-mail: gradadmissions@liberty.edu.
Website: http://www.liberty.edu/academics/education/graduate/

Lincoln Memorial University, Carter and Moyers School of Education, Harrogate, TN 37752-1901. Offers administration and supervision (M Ed, Ed S); counseling and guidance (M Ed); curriculum and instruction (M Ed, Ed D, Ed S); English (M Ed); executive leadership (Ed D); higher education administration (Ed D); human resource development (Ed D); leadership and administration (Ed D). *Program availability:* Part-time, evening/weekend, online learning. *Degree requirements:* For master's, comprehensive exam, thesis optional; for Ed S, comprehensive exam. *Entrance requirements:* For master's, PRAXIS, NTE, GRE, MAT, letters of recommendation; for Ed S, graduate transcripts. Additional exam requirements/recommendations for international students: Recommended—TOEFL. *Faculty research:* Brain compatible teaching and learning; poverty in Appalachia; leadership for change; ethics, moral responsibility and social justice; human and organizational learning.

Lincoln University, Graduate Programs, Philadelphia, PA 19104. Offers counseling (MSC); early childhood education (M Ed), including PreK-4; early childhood education and special education (M Ed); educational leadership (M Ed), including principal certification; finance (MSB); human resources management (MSB); human services (MAHS). *Program availability:* Part-time, evening/weekend. *Faculty:* 11 full-time (5 women), 45 part-time/adjunct (24 women). *Students:* 191 full-time (131 women), 77 part-time (60 women); includes 245 minority (236 Black or African American, non-Hispanic/Latino; 1 American Indian or Alaska Native, non-Hispanic/Latino; 7 Hispanic/Latino; 1 Two or more races, non-Hispanic/Latino), 4 international. Average age 34. 221 applicants, 58% accepted, 55 enrolled. In 2016, 97 master's awarded. *Degree requirements:* For master's, thesis or alternative. *Entrance requirements:* For master's, official academic transcript from accredited institution presenting conferred bachelor's degree. *Application deadline:* For fall admission, 6/1 priority date for domestic and international students. Applications are processed on a rolling basis. Application fee: $50. Electronic applications accepted. *Expenses:* Tuition, state resident: full-time $12,264; part-time $511 per credit hour. Tuition, nonresident: full-time $21,264; part-time $886 per credit hour. *Required fees:* $1344; $56 per credit hour. Tuition and fees vary according to course load. *Financial support:* In 2016–17, 9 students received support. Scholarships/grants available. Financial award application deadline: 8/1; financial award applicants required to submit FAFSA. *Unit head:* Dr. Patricia Joseph, Dean, College of Professional, Graduate and Extended Studies, 484-365-7659, E-mail: joseph@lincoln.edu. *Application contact:* Jernice Lea, Director of Graduate Admissions, 215-590-8231, Fax: 215-387-3859, E-mail: jlea@lincoln.edu.
Website: http://www.lincoln.edu/academics/graduate-programs

Lindenwood University, Graduate Programs, School of Education, St. Charles, MO 63301-1695. Offers education (MA), including autism spectrum disorders, character education, early intervention in autism and sensory impairment, gifted, technology; educational administration (MA, Ed D, Ed S); English to speakers of other languages (MA); instructional leadership (Ed D, Ed S); library media (MA); professional counseling (MA); school administration (MA, Ed S); school counseling (MA); teaching (MA). *Program availability:* Part-time, evening/weekend, 100% online, blended/hybrid learning. *Faculty:* 39 full-time (27 women), 210 part-time/adjunct (136 women). *Students:* 292 full-time (227 women), 1,580 part-time (1,203 women); includes 404 minority (333 Black or African American, non-Hispanic/Latino; 4 American Indian or Alaska Native, non-Hispanic/Latino; 10 Asian, non-Hispanic/Latino; 36 Hispanic/Latino; 1 Native Hawaiian or other Pacific Islander, non-Hispanic/Latino; 20 Two or more races, non-Hispanic/Latino), 20 international. Average age 36. 558 applicants, 72% accepted, 353 enrolled. In 2016, 491 master's, 72 doctorates, 111 other advanced degrees awarded. *Degree requirements:* For master's, thesis (for some programs), minimum GPA of 3.0; for doctorate, thesis/dissertation, minimum GPA of 3.0; for Ed S, comprehensive exam, project, minimum GPA of 3.0. *Entrance requirements:* For master's, interview, minimum undergraduate cumulative GPA of 3.0, writing sample, letter of recommendation; for doctorate, GRE, minimum graduate GPA of 3.4, resume, interview, writing sample, 4 letters of recommendation; for Ed S, master's degree in education, relevant work experience. Additional exam requirements/recommendations for international students: Required—TOEFL (minimum score 550 paper-based; 80 iBT); Recommended—IELTS (minimum score 6.5). *Application deadline:* For fall admission, 8/28 priority date for domestic and international students; for spring admission, 1/8 priority date for domestic and international students; for summer admission, 6/5 priority date for domestic and international students. Applications are processed on a rolling basis. Application fee: $30 ($100 for international students). Electronic applications accepted. *Expenses: Tuition:* Full-time $15,672; part-time $453 per credit hour. *Required fees:* $205 per semester. Tuition and fees vary according to course level, course load and degree level. *Financial support:* In 2016–17, 334 students received support. Career-related internships or fieldwork, Federal Work-Study, institutionally sponsored loans, scholarships/grants, tuition waivers (partial), and unspecified assistantships available. Financial award application deadline: 6/30; financial award applicants required to submit FAFSA. *Unit head:* Dr. Cynthia Bice, Dean, School of Education, 636-949-4618, Fax: 636-949-4197, E-mail: cbice@lindenwood.edu. *Application contact:* Tyler Kostich, Director, Evening and Graduate Admissions, 636-949-4138, Fax: 636-949-4109, E-mail: adultadmissions@lindenwood.edu.
Website: http://www.lindenwood.edu/academics/academic-schools/school-of-education/

Lindenwood University–Belleville, Graduate Programs, Belleville, IL 62226. Offers business administration (MBA); communications (MA), including digital and multimedia, media management, promotions, training and development; counseling (MA); criminal justice administration (MS); education (MA); healthcare administration (MS); human resource management (MS); school administration (MA); teaching (MAT).

Lindsey Wilson College, Division of Education, Columbia, KY 42728. Offers teacher as leader (M Ed). *Program availability:* Online learning. *Entrance requirements:* For master's, bachelor's degree from accredited institution, minimum undergraduate GPA of 3.0, letters of recommendation.

Lipscomb University, College of Education, Nashville, TN 37204-3951. Offers applied behavior analysis (MS, Certificate); educational leadership (M Ed, Ed S); English language learning (M Ed, Ed S); instructional coaching (M Ed, Certificate, Ed S); instructional practice (M Ed); learning organizations and strategic change (Ed D); literacy coaching (Certificate); reading specialty (M Ed, Ed S); special education (M Ed); teaching, learning, and leading (M Ed); technology integration (M Ed, Ed S); technology integration specialist (Certificate). *Accreditation:* NCATE. *Program availability:* Part-time, evening/weekend, 100% online. *Faculty:* 21 full-time (15 women), 38 part-time/adjunct (26 women). *Students:* 111 full-time (80 women), 345 part-time (292 women); includes 104 minority (70 Black or African American, non-Hispanic/Latino; 1 American Indian or Alaska Native, non-Hispanic/Latino; 3 Asian, non-Hispanic/Latino; 20 Hispanic/Latino; 10 Two or more races, non-Hispanic/Latino), 1 international. Average age 33. In 2016, 201 master's, 36 doctorates, 86 other advanced degrees awarded. *Degree requirements:* For master's, comprehensive exam, portfolio, research project and presentation; for doctorate, practical capstone project in experiential setting. *Entrance requirements:* For master's, MAT (minimum score 31) or GRE General Test (minimum score 294), 2 reference letters, goals statement, writing sample, interview; for doctorate, MAT or GRE General Test, 3 reference letters, artifact of demonstrated academic excellence, written personal statements, interview. Additional exam requirements/recommendations for international students: Required—TOEFL (minimum score 570 paper-based; 80 iBT). *Application deadline:* For fall admission, 8/29 priority date for domestic students; for spring admission, 1/15 priority date for domestic students. Applications are processed on a rolling basis. Application fee: $50 ($75 for international students). Electronic applications accepted. *Expenses:* $934 per hour; $570 per hour (Teach for America). *Financial support:* Scholarships/grants, unspecified

assistantships, and partnerships with local school districts available. Financial award applicants required to submit FAFSA. *Faculty research:* Facilitative learning styles, leadership, student assessment, interactive multimedia inclusion, learning organizations and strategic change. *Unit head:* Dr. Deborah Boyd, Director of Graduate Studies, 615-966-6263, E-mail: deborah.boyd@lipscomb.edu. *Application contact:* Amanda Logsdon, Director of Enrollment and Outreach, 615-966-7199, E-mail: amanda.logsdon@lipscomb.edu.
Website: http://www.lipscomb.edu/education/graduate-programs

Lock Haven University of Pennsylvania, College of Liberal Arts and Education, Lock Haven, PA 17745-2390. Offers alternative education (M Ed); educational leadership (M Ed); teaching and learning (M Ed). *Accreditation:* NCATE. *Program availability:* Part-time, evening/weekend, online learning. *Degree requirements:* For master's, thesis. *Entrance requirements:* For master's, minimum undergraduate GPA of 3.0. Additional exam requirements/recommendations for international students: Required—TOEFL. Electronic applications accepted.

Long Island University–Hudson, Graduate School, Purchase, NY 10577. Offers autism (Advanced Certificate); childhood education (MS Ed); early childhood education (MS Ed); educational leadership (MS Ed); finance (MBA); health administration (MPA); healthcare sector management (MBA); literacy (MS Ed); management (MBA); marriage and family therapy (MS); mental health counseling (MS), including credentialed alcoholism and substance abuse counselor; middle childhood and adolescence education (MS Ed); pharmaceutics (MS), including cosmetic science, industrial pharmacy; public administration (MPA); school counseling (MS Ed, Advanced Certificate); school psychology (MS Ed); special education (MS Ed); TESOL (all grades) (Advanced Certificate); TESOL and bilingual education (MS Ed); the business of pharmaceutics and biotechnology (MBA). *Program availability:* Part-time, evening/weekend, online learning. *Faculty:* 7 full-time (5 women), 42 part-time/adjunct (25 women). *Students:* 55 full-time (41 women), 158 part-time (123 women); includes 40 minority (8 Black or African American, non-Hispanic/Latino; 1 Asian, non-Hispanic/Latino; 31 Hispanic/Latino). Average age 35. *Entrance requirements:* Additional exam requirements/recommendations for international students: Required—TOEFL (minimum score 550 paper-based; 79 iBT). *Application deadline:* Applications are processed on a rolling basis. Application fee: $50. Electronic applications accepted. *Expenses:* Contact institution. *Unit head:* Dr. Sylvia Blake, Dean and Chief Operating Officer, 914-831-2700, E-mail: westchester@liu.edu. *Application contact:* Cindy Pagnotta, Director of Marketing and Enrollment, 914-831-2701, Fax: 914-251-5959, E-mail: cindy.pagnotta@liu.edu.

Long Island University–LIU Brooklyn, School of Education, Brooklyn, NY 11201-8423. Offers adolescence urban education (MS Ed); applied behavior analysis (Advanced Certificate); bilingual education (Advanced Certificate); bilingual school counselor (MS Ed, Advanced Certificate); childhood urban education (MS Ed); childhood/early childhood urban education (MS Ed); early childhood urban education (MS Ed, Advanced Certificate); educational leadership (Advanced Certificate); marriage and family therapy (MS, Advanced Certificate); mental health counseling (MS, Advanced Certificate); school building district leader (Advanced Certificate); school counselor (MS Ed, Advanced Certificate); school psychologist (MS Ed); teaching urban children/adolescents with disabilities (MS Ed); TESOL (MS Ed). *Accreditation:* TEAC. *Program availability:* Part-time, evening/weekend. *Faculty:* 23 full-time (17 women), 44 part-time/adjunct (32 women). *Students:* 161 full-time (144 women), 594 part-time (461 women); includes 493 minority (229 Black or African American, non-Hispanic/Latino; 1 American Indian or Alaska Native, non-Hispanic/Latino; 30 Asian, non-Hispanic/Latino; 218 Hispanic/Latino; 2 Native Hawaiian or other Pacific Islander, non-Hispanic/Latino; 13 Two or more races, non-Hispanic/Latino), 9 international. 513 applicants, 73% accepted, 272 enrolled. In 2016, 262 master's, 18 other advanced degrees awarded. *Degree requirements:* For master's, thesis optional, electronic portfolio. *Entrance requirements:* For master's, GRE (for MS Ed). Additional exam requirements/recommendations for international students: Required—TOEFL (minimum score 527 paper-based; 75 iBT). *Application deadline:* Applications are processed on a rolling basis. Application fee: $50. Electronic applications accepted. *Expenses: Tuition:* Full-time $28,272; part-time $1178 per credit. *Required fees:* $451 per term. Tuition and fees vary according to degree level, program and student level. *Financial support:* In 2016–17, 81 students received support. Career-related internships or fieldwork, Federal Work-Study, institutionally sponsored loans, scholarships/grants, and unspecified assistantships available. Support available to part-time students. Financial award application deadline: 2/15; financial award applicants required to submit FAFSA. *Faculty research:* Technology in education, teaching civics and sustainability, biliteracy and dual language instruction, diversity in organizations and leadership, counseling diverse couples and families. *Unit head:* Dr. Amy Ginsberg, Dean, 718-246-6308, E-mail: amy.ginsberg@liu.edu. *Application contact:* Gabrielle Gannon, Director of Graduate Admissions, 718-488-1011, Fax: 718-780-6110, E-mail: bkln-admissions@liu.edu.
Website: http://www.liu.edu/Brooklyn/Academics/School-of-Education

Long Island University–LIU Post, College of Education, Information and Technology, Brookville, NY 11548-1300. Offers adolescence education (MS); adolescence education 7-12 (MS); archives and records management (AC); art education (MS); childhood education (MS); childhood teaching literacy B-6 (MS); childhood/special education (MS); clinical mental health counseling (MS, AC); early childhood education (MS); early childhood education/childhood education (MS); educational leadership (AC); educational technology (MS); information studies (PhD); interdisciplinary educational studies (Ed D); middle childhood education (MS); music education (MS); school counselor (MS); special education (MS Ed); speech-language pathology (MA); students with disabilities, 7-12 generalist (AC); TESOL (MA). *Accreditation:* TEAC. *Program availability:* Part-time, 100% online, blended/hybrid learning. *Faculty:* 55 full-time (35 women), 104 part-time/adjunct (57 women). *Students:* 464 full-time (390 women), 740 part-time (580 women); includes 265 minority (99 Black or African American, non-Hispanic/Latino; 45 Asian, non-Hispanic/Latino; 113 Hispanic/Latino; 1 Native Hawaiian or other Pacific Islander, non-Hispanic/Latino; 7 Two or more races, non-Hispanic/Latino), 33 international. 928 applicants, 76% accepted, 406 enrolled. In 2016, 334 master's, 10 doctorates, 137 other advanced degrees awarded. Terminal master's awarded for partial completion of doctoral program. *Degree requirements:* For master's, variable foreign language requirement, comprehensive exam (for some programs), thesis optional; for doctorate, comprehensive exam, thesis/dissertation. *Entrance requirements:* For master's and AC, GRE. Additional exam requirements/recommendations for international students: Required—PTE, TOEFL (minimum score 550 paper-based, 75 iBT) or IELTS. *Application deadline:* Applications are processed on a rolling basis. Application fee: $50. Electronic applications accepted. *Expenses: Tuition:* Full-time $28,272; part-time $1178 per credit. *Required fees:* $451 per term. Tuition and fees vary according to degree level and program. *Financial support:* Career-related internships or fieldwork, Federal Work-Study, institutionally sponsored loans, scholarships/grants, tuition waivers (partial), and unspecified assistantships available. Support available to part-time students. Financial award application deadline: 2/15; financial award applicants required to submit FAFSA. *Faculty research:* English language learners, early childhood literacy development through play, sleep, social justice through education, using a structured protocol for discussing bad news. *Total annual research expenditures:* $575,000. *Unit head:* Dr. Albert Inserra, Dean, 516-299-2210, E-mail: albert.inserra@liu.edu. *Application contact:* Carol Zerah, Director of Graduate Admissions, 516-299-2900, Fax: 516-299-2137, E-mail: post-enroll@liu.edu.
Website: http://liu.edu/CWPost/Academics/College-of-Education-Information-and-Technology

Loras College, Graduate Division, Program in Educational Leadership, Dubuque, IA 52004-0178. Offers MA. *Program availability:* Part-time, evening/weekend. *Degree requirements:* For master's, comprehensive exam, thesis optional. *Entrance requirements:* For master's, minimum cumulative undergraduate GPA of 3.0.

Louisiana State University and Agricultural & Mechanical College, Graduate School, College of Human Sciences and Education, Department of Educational Theory, Policy and Practice, Baton Rouge, LA 70803. Offers counseling (M Ed, MA, Ed S); educational administration (M Ed, MA, PhD, Ed S); educational technology (MA); elementary education (M Ed, MAT); higher education (PhD); research methodology (PhD); secondary education (M Ed, MAT). *Accreditation:* ACA (one or more programs are accredited); NCATE.

Louisiana State University in Shreveport, College of Business, Education, and Human Development, Program in Education, Shreveport, LA 71115-2399. Offers curriculum and instruction (M Ed); leadership (M Ed); leadership studies (Ed D). *Accreditation:* NCATE. *Program availability:* Part-time. *Students:* 5 full-time (all women), 236 part-time (198 women); includes 110 minority (92 Black or African American, non-Hispanic/Latino; 6 Asian, non-Hispanic/Latino; 6 Hispanic/Latino; 6 Two or more races, non-Hispanic/Latino). Average age 36. 148 applicants, 95% accepted, 39 enrolled. In 2016, 61 master's awarded. *Degree requirements:* For master's, orally-presented project, 200-hour internship (educational leadership). *Entrance requirements:* For master's, GRE, minimum GPA of 2.5; teacher certification; recommendations and interview (for educational leadership). Additional exam requirements/recommendations for international students: Required—TOEFL (minimum score 550 paper-based; 61 iBT). *Application deadline:* For fall admission, 6/30 for domestic and international students; for spring admission, 11/30 for domestic and international students; for summer admission, 4/30 for domestic and international students. Applications are processed on a rolling basis. Application fee: $20 ($30 for international students). Electronic applications accepted. *Expenses:* Tuition, state resident: full-time $5163; part-time $350 per credit hour. Tuition, nonresident: full-time $15,578; part-time $1038 per credit hour. *Required fees:* $63 per credit hour. Tuition and fees vary according to course load and program. *Financial support:* In 2016–17, 5 research assistantships (averaging $2,150 per year) were awarded. *Unit head:* Dr. Pat Doerr, Coordinator, 318-797-5033, Fax: 318-798-4144, E-mail: pat.doerr@lsus.edu. *Application contact:* Mary Catherine Harvison, Director of Admissions, 318-797-2400, Fax: 318-797-5286, E-mail: mary.harvison@lsus.edu.

Louisiana Tech University, Graduate School, College of Education, Department of Curriculum, Instruction and Leadership, Ruston, LA 71272. Offers curriculum and instruction (M Ed), including research, theory, and design, visually impaired; educational leadership (M Ed, Ed D), including higher education administration (Ed D), P-12 educational leadership (Ed D). *Accreditation:* NCATE. *Program availability:* Part-time. *Degree requirements:* For doctorate, thesis/dissertation. *Entrance requirements:* For master's and doctorate, GRE General Test. *Application deadline:* For fall admission, 7/29 for domestic students; for spring admission, 2/3 for domestic students. Application fee: $20 ($30 for international students). *Financial support:* Fellowships, research assistantships, and teaching assistantships available. Financial award application deadline: 2/1. *Unit head:* Dr. Bryan McCoy, Chair, 318-257-4609, Fax: 318-257-2379, E-mail: bmccoy@latech.edu. *Application contact:* Dr. John Harrison, Associate Dean of Graduate Studies, 318-257-3229, Fax: 318-257-2379, E-mail: johnharrison@latech.edu.
Website: http://education.latech.edu/departments/cil/

Lourdes University, Graduate School, Sylvania, OH 43560-2898. Offers business (MBA); leadership (M Ed); nurse anesthesia (MSN); nurse educator (MSN); nurse leader (MSN); organizational leadership (MOL); reading (M Ed); teaching and curriculum (M Ed); theology (MA). *Program availability:* Evening/weekend. *Entrance requirements:* Additional exam requirements/recommendations for international students: Required—TOEFL.

Loyola Marymount University, School of Education, Department of Educational Leadership, Doctorate in Educational Leadership for Social Justice Program, Los Angeles, CA 90045-2659. Offers Ed D. *Program availability:* Part-time. *Students:* 17 full-time (11 women), 45 part-time (25 women); includes 40 minority (14 Black or African American, non-Hispanic/Latino; 3 Asian, non-Hispanic/Latino; 21 Hispanic/Latino; 2 Two or more races, non-Hispanic/Latino), 1 international. Average age 39. 68 applicants, 31% accepted, 16 enrolled. In 2016, 26 doctorates awarded. *Degree requirements:* For doctorate, thesis/dissertation. *Entrance requirements:* For doctorate, GRE, interview, resume, 3 letters of recommendation. Additional exam requirements/recommendations for international students: Required—TOEFL (minimum score 600 paper-based; 100 iBT). *Application deadline:* For fall admission, 1/25 for domestic students. Application fee: $50. Electronic applications accepted. Application fee is waived when completed online. *Financial support:* In 2016–17, 48 students received support, including 4 research assistantships, 4 teaching assistantships; institutionally sponsored loans, scholarships/grants, and unspecified assistantships also available. Support available to part-time students. Financial award application deadline: 6/30; financial award applicants required to submit FAFSA. *Unit head:* Dr. Jill Bickett, Director, 310-338-3777, E-mail: jbickett@lmu.edu. *Application contact:* Chake H. Kouyoumjian, Associate Dean of Graduate Studies, 310-338-2721, E-mail: ckouyoum@lmu.edu.
Website: http://soe.lmu.edu/admissions/programs/edd/

Loyola Marymount University, School of Education, Department of Educational Leadership, Program in Catholic School Administration, Los Angeles, CA 90045-2659. Offers MA. *Program availability:* Part-time. *Students:* 9 full-time (5 women), 10 part-time (5 women); includes 10 minority (5 Asian, non-Hispanic/Latino; 5 Hispanic/Latino), 2 international. Average age 36. 8 applicants, 100% accepted, 10 enrolled. In 2016, 23 master's awarded. *Entrance requirements:* For master's, CBEST, CSET, 2 letters of recommendation, full-time employment in the Archdiocese of Los Angeles. Additional exam requirements/recommendations for international students: Required—TOEFL (minimum score 600 paper-based; 100 iBT). *Application deadline:* For fall admission, 6/15 for domestic students; for spring admission, 11/15 for domestic students. Application fee: $50. Electronic applications accepted. *Financial support:* In 2016–17, 19 students received support. Institutionally sponsored loans, scholarships/grants, and unspecified assistantships available. Financial award application deadline: 6/30; financial award applicants required to submit FAFSA. *Unit head:* Dr. Anthony Sabatino, Director, 310-338-7862, E-mail: asabati3@lmu.edu. *Application contact:* Chake H. Kouyoumjian, Associate Dean of Graduate Studies, 310-338-2721, E-mail: ckouyoum@lmu.edu.
Website: http://soe.lmu.edu/academics/catholicschooladministrationma/

Loyola Marymount University, School of Education, Department of Educational Leadership, Program in School Administration, Los Angeles, CA 90045-2659. Offers MA. *Program availability:* Part-time, evening/weekend. *Students:* 8 full-time (6 women), 2 part-time (both women); includes 6 minority (4 Black or African American, non-Hispanic/Latino; 1 Asian, non-Hispanic/Latino; 1 Hispanic/Latino). Average age 33. 11 applicants, 100% accepted, 8 enrolled. In 2016, 5 master's awarded. *Entrance requirements:* For master's, CBEST, 2 letters of recommendation. Additional exam

requirements/recommendations for international students: Required—TOEFL (minimum score 600 paper-based; 100 iBT). *Application deadline:* For summer admission, 4/1 for domestic students. Application fee: $50. Electronic applications accepted. *Financial support:* In 2016–17, 8 students received support. Scholarships/grants and unspecified assistantships available. Support available to part-time students. Financial award application deadline: 6/30; financial award applicants required to submit FAFSA. *Unit head:* Dr. Manuel Ponce, Program Director, 310-258-5438, E-mail: mponce8@lmu.edu. *Application contact:* Chake H. Kouyoumjian, Associate Dean of Graduate Studies, 310-338-2721, E-mail: ckouyoum@lmu.edu.
Website: http://soe.lmu.edu/academics/isla/academics/mainschooladministration/

Loyola University Chicago, School of Education, Program in Administration and Supervision, Chicago, IL 60660. Offers M Ed, Ed D, Certificate. *Program availability:* Part-time, evening/weekend. *Faculty:* 6 full-time (5 women), 8 part-time/adjunct (4 women). *Students:* 44 full-time (34 women), 68 part-time (50 women); includes 51 minority (33 Black or African American, non-Hispanic/Latino; 6 Asian, non-Hispanic/Latino; 12 Hispanic/Latino). Average age 35. 35 applicants, 97% accepted, 28 enrolled. In 2016, 12 doctorates awarded. *Degree requirements:* For master's, comprehensive exam; for doctorate, comprehensive exam, thesis/dissertation. *Entrance requirements:* For master's, minimum GPA of 3.0, letters of recommendation, resume, transcripts; for doctorate, GRE General Test, interview, minimum GPA of 3.0, letters of recommendation, resume. Additional exam requirements/recommendations for international students: Required—TOEFL (minimum score 550 paper-based; 79 iBT). *Application deadline:* For fall admission, 2/15 for domestic and international students. Applications are processed on a rolling basis. Application fee: $50. Electronic applications accepted. Application fee is waived when completed online. *Expenses: Tuition:* Full-time $18,594. *Required fees:* $848. Part-time tuition and fees vary according to course load, degree level and program. *Financial support:* In 2016–17, 41 fellowships, 3 research assistantships (averaging $14,000 per year) were awarded; career-related internships or fieldwork, institutionally sponsored loans, scholarships/grants, and unspecified assistantships also available. Support available to part-time students. Financial award application deadline: 2/1; financial award applicants required to submit FAFSA. *Faculty research:* Leadership, school law, school administration, supervision, ethics. *Unit head:* Dr. Celia Arresola, Director, 312-915-7022, Fax: 312-915-6980, E-mail: carreso@luc.edu. *Application contact:* Marie Hatland, Information Contact, 312-915-6800, E-mail: schleduc@luc.edu.

Loyola University Maryland, Graduate Programs, School of Education, Program in Educational Leadership, Baltimore, MD 21210-2699. Offers M Ed, CAS. *Program availability:* Part-time. *Faculty:* 34 full-time (22 women), 30 part-time/adjunct (24 women). *Students:* 7 full-time (5 women), 139 part-time (98 women); includes 78 minority (61 Black or African American, non-Hispanic/Latino; 3 Asian, non-Hispanic/Latino; 8 Hispanic/Latino; 6 Two or more races, non-Hispanic/Latino), 1 international. Average age 34. 155 applicants, 52% accepted, 74 enrolled. In 2016, 16 master's awarded. *Entrance requirements:* For master's, transcripts, essay, resume. Additional exam requirements/recommendations for international students: Required—TOEFL (minimum score 550 paper-based), IELTS (minimum score 7). *Application deadline:* For fall admission, 6/15 priority date for domestic students; for winter admission, 11/1 for domestic students; for spring admission, 3/15 priority date for domestic students. Applications are processed on a rolling basis. Application fee: $60. Electronic applications accepted. *Expenses:* Contact institution. *Financial support:* Application deadline: 4/15; applicants required to submit FAFSA. *Application contact:* Mechelle Palmer, Senior Associate Director of Graduate Admission, 410-617-7741, E-mail: mjpalmer@loyola.edu.

Lynchburg College, Graduate Studies, Ed D in Leadership Studies Program, Lynchburg, VA 24501-3199. Offers Ed D. *Program availability:* Part-time, evening/weekend. *Students:* 4 full-time (all women), 20 part-time (11 women); includes 7 minority (6 Black or African American, non-Hispanic/Latino; 1 Two or more races, non-Hispanic/Latino), 3 international. In 2016, 14 doctorates awarded. *Degree requirements:* For doctorate, comprehensive exam, thesis/dissertation. *Entrance requirements:* For doctorate, GRE or GMAT, current resume or curriculum vitae, career goals statement, master's degree, official transcripts (bachelor's, master's, others of relevance), master's-level research course, three letters of recommendation, evidence of strong writing skills. Additional exam requirements/recommendations for international students: Required—TOEFL (minimum score 550 paper-based; 79 iBT), IELTS (minimum score 6.5). *Application deadline:* For fall admission, 7/31 for domestic students, 6/1 for international students; for spring admission, 11/30 for domestic students, 10/15 for international students. Applications are processed on a rolling basis. Application fee: $30. Electronic applications accepted. Application fee is waived when completed online. *Expenses:* Contact institution. *Financial support:* Unspecified assistantships available. Financial award application deadline: 7/31; financial award applicants required to submit FAFSA. *Unit head:* Dr. John Walker, Program Director, 434-544-8032, E-mail: walker.jc@lynchburg.edu.
Website: http://www.lynchburg.edu/graduate/doctor-of-education-edd-in-leadership-studies/

Lynchburg College, Graduate Studies, M Ed Program in Educational Leadership, Lynchburg, VA 24501-3199. Offers higher education (M Ed); PK-12 administrative and supervisory (M Ed). *Program availability:* Part-time, evening/weekend. *Students:* 16 full-time (10 women), 49 part-time (37 women); includes 5 minority (4 Black or African American, non-Hispanic/Latino; 1 Hispanic/Latino). In 2016, 34 master's awarded. *Degree requirements:* For master's, comprehensive exam (for some programs), internship; ISLLC exam or comprehensive exam. *Entrance requirements:* For master's, GRE, minimum GPA of 3.0 (preferred), official transcripts (bachelor's, others as relevant), three letters of recommendation, career goals statement. Additional exam requirements/recommendations for international students: Required—TOEFL (minimum score 550 paper-based; 79 iBT), IELTS (minimum score 6.5). *Application deadline:* For fall admission, 7/31 for domestic students, 6/1 for international students; for spring admission, 11/30 for domestic students, 10/5 for international students. Applications are processed on a rolling basis. Application fee: $30. Electronic applications accepted. Application fee is waived when completed online. *Expenses:* Contact institution. *Financial support:* Career-related internships or fieldwork, Federal Work-Study, scholarships/grants, health care benefits, and unspecified assistantships available. Support available to part-time students. Financial award application deadline: 7/31; financial award applicants required to submit FAFSA. *Unit head:* Dr. John Walker, Professor/Director, Leadership Studies, 434-544-8032, E-mail: walker.jc@lynchburg.edu.
Website: http://www.lynchburg.edu/graduate/master-of-education-in-educational-leadership/

Lynn University, Donald E. and Helen L. Ross College of Education, Boca Raton, FL 33431-5598. Offers educational leadership (M Ed, Ed D), including K-12 (Ed D); exceptional student education (M Ed), including school administration K-12. *Program availability:* Part-time, evening/weekend, online learning. *Faculty:* 5 full-time (4 women), 8 part-time/adjunct (all women). *Students:* 85 full-time (63 women), 10 part-time (6 women); includes 27 minority (19 Black or African American, non-Hispanic/Latino; 7 Hispanic/Latino; 1 Two or more races, non-Hispanic/Latino), 4 international. Average age 36. 17 applicants, 94% accepted, 11 enrolled. In 2016, 24 master's, 22 doctorates awarded. *Degree requirements:* For master's, comprehensive exam, thesis (for some programs); for doctorate, thesis/dissertation, mid-program review. *Entrance requirements:* For master's, bachelor's degree from accredited institution, letter of recommendation, statement of professional goals, official transcripts; for doctorate, master's degree from accredited institution, resume, 2 letters of recommendation, professional practice statement, official transcripts. Additional exam requirements/recommendations for international students: Required—TOEFL (minimum score 550 paper-based; 80 iBT), IELTS (minimum score 6.5). *Application deadline:* For fall admission, 8/18 for domestic students, 8/4 for international students; for spring admission, 12/15 for domestic students, 12/1 for international students; for summer admission, 4/17 for domestic students, 4/3 for international students. Applications are processed on a rolling basis. Application fee: $45. Electronic applications accepted. *Expenses:* $850 per credit hour, $44,200 per year tuition and fees (for Ed D); $725 per credit hour, $29,000 per year tuition and fees (for master's). *Financial support:* In 2016–17, 74 students received support. Career-related internships or fieldwork, Federal Work-Study, scholarships/grants, tuition waivers (partial), and unspecified assistantships available. Support available to part-time students. Financial award application deadline: 3/1; financial award applicants required to submit FAFSA. *Unit head:* Dr. Kathleen Weigel, Dean, College of Education, 561-237-7441, E-mail: kweigel@lynn.edu. *Application contact:* Steven Pruitt, Director of Graduate and Undergraduate Evening Admission, 561-237-7834, Fax: 561-237-7100, E-mail: spruitt@lynn.edu.
Website: http://www.lynn.edu/academics/colleges/education

Madonna University, Programs in Education, Livonia, MI 48150-1173. Offers Catholic school leadership (MSA); educational leadership (MSA); learning disabilities (MAT); literacy education (MAT); teaching and learning (MAT). *Accreditation:* NCATE. *Program availability:* Part-time, evening/weekend. *Degree requirements:* For master's, thesis or alternative. Electronic applications accepted.

Malone University, Graduate Program in Education, Canton, OH 44709. Offers curriculum and instruction (MA); curriculum, instruction, and professional development (MA); educational leadership (principal license) (MA); intervention specialist (MA). *Accreditation:* NCATE. *Program availability:* Part-time, evening/weekend. *Degree requirements:* For master's, research project. *Entrance requirements:* For master's, minimum GPA of 3.0, teaching license. Additional exam requirements/recommendations for international students: Required—TOEFL (minimum score 550 paper-based; 79 iBT). *Faculty research:* Educational leadership styles: Jesus as master teacher, assessment accommodations for English language learners, preparing culturally proficient teachers, using naturally occurring text in the classroom to meet the syntactic needs of students with learning disabilities, using tablet instructional technology to meet the needs of students with disabilities.

Manhattan College, Graduate Programs, School of Education and Health, Program in Educational Leadership, Riverdale, NY 10471. Offers advanced leadership studies (MS Ed, Advanced Certificate), including school district leadership; school building leadership (MS Ed, Advanced Certificate). *Program availability:* Part-time, evening/weekend. *Faculty:* 1 (woman) full-time, 6 part-time/adjunct (3 women). *Students:* 39 part-time (34 women); includes 20 minority (12 Black or African American, non-Hispanic/Latino; 2 Asian, non-Hispanic/Latino; 6 Hispanic/Latino). Average age 34. 53 applicants, 64% accepted, 29 enrolled. In 2016, 3 master's, 23 Advanced Certificates awarded. *Degree requirements:* For master's, thesis, internship; for Advanced Certificate, internship. *Entrance requirements:* For master's, baccalaureate degree, minimum GPA of 3.0, 3 years of pupil personnel service, professional recommendation; for Advanced Certificate, master's degree; 3 years of personnel service; minimum GPA of 3.0; professional recommendations. Additional exam requirements/recommendations for international students: Required—TOEFL. *Application deadline:* For fall admission, 8/1 priority date for domestic students, 4/1 priority date for international students; for spring admission, 1/1 priority date for domestic students, 9/1 priority date for international students. Applications are processed on a rolling basis. Application fee: $60. Electronic applications accepted. *Expenses:* Contact institution. *Financial support:* In 2016–17, 5 students received support. Scholarships/grants and unspecified assistantships available. Financial award application deadline: 4/1; financial award applicants required to submit FAFSA. *Faculty research:* Distance learning and teacher efficacy, leadership and student achievement, professional development and student achievement, leadership development, professional development for teachers. *Unit head:* Dr. Remigia Kushner, Program Director, 718-862-7473, Fax: 718-862-7816, E-mail: sr.remigia.kushner@manhattan.edu.
Website: http://manhattan.edu/academics/education/school-building-leadership

Manhattanville College, School of Education, Program in Educational Leadership, Purchase, NY 10577-2132. Offers education leadership (Ed D); higher education leadership (Ed D); school building leader (MPS); school district leader (PD). *Program availability:* Part-time, evening/weekend. *Students:* 22 applicants, 68% accepted, 11 enrolled. In 2016, 1 master's, 8 doctorates, 10 other advanced degrees awarded. *Degree requirements:* For master's, comprehensive exam (for some programs), thesis (for some programs), student teaching, research seminars, portfolios, internships, writing assessment; for doctorate, thesis/dissertation, professional portfolio; for PD, comprehensive exam (for some programs). *Entrance requirements:* For master's, GRE or MAT, minimum undergraduate GPA of 3.0, 2 letters of recommendation, interview, writing sample, resume; for doctorate, GRE or MAT, minimum GPA of 3.0, 2 letters of recommendation, interview, writing sample, resume. Additional exam requirements/recommendations for international students: Required—TOEFL (minimum score 85 iBT); Recommended—IELTS. *Application deadline:* For fall admission, 7/1 priority date for domestic and international students; for spring admission, 11/1 priority date for domestic and international students; for summer admission, 4/1 priority date for domestic and international students. Applications are processed on a rolling basis. Application fee: $75. Electronic applications accepted. *Expenses: Tuition:* Full-time $16,470; part-time $915 per credit. *Required fees:* $60 per semester. Part-time tuition and fees vary according to course load and program. *Financial support:* Teaching assistantships, career-related internships or fieldwork, Federal Work-Study, institutionally sponsored loans, scholarships/grants, and unspecified assistantships available. Financial award applicants required to submit FAFSA. *Faculty research:* School leadership in relation to national and statewide policy development; professional development schools, full service community schools, and higher education partnerships. *Unit head:* Robert Monson, Program Coordinator, 914-323-5370, E-mail: robert.monson@mville.edu. *Application contact:* Jeanine Pardey-Levine, Director of Graduate Enrollment Management, 914-323-3208, Fax: 914-694-1732, E-mail: edschool@mville.edu.
Website: http://www.mville.edu/programs/educational-leadership

Marconi International University, Graduate Programs, Pembroke Pines, FL 33028. Offers business administration (DBA); education leadership (Ed D); education leadership, management and emerging technologies (M Ed); international business administration (IMBA).

Marian University, School of Education, Fond du Lac, WI 54935-4699. Offers curriculum and instruction leadership (PhD); educational administration (PhD); educational leadership (MAE); educational technology (MAE); leadership studies (PhD);

special education (MAE); teacher education (MAE). *Accreditation:* NCATE. *Program availability:* Part-time, evening/weekend, online learning. *Faculty:* 11 full-time (7 women), 14 part-time/adjunct (8 women). *Students:* 13 full-time (9 women), 179 part-time (113 women); includes 16 minority (6 Black or African American, non-Hispanic/Latino; 3 American Indian or Alaska Native, non-Hispanic/Latino; 2 Asian, non-Hispanic/Latino; 3 Hispanic/Latino; 2 Two or more races, non-Hispanic/Latino). Average age 39. In 2016, 72 master's, 8 doctorates awarded. *Degree requirements:* For master's, exam, field-based experience project, portfolio; for doctorate, comprehensive exam, thesis/dissertation, field-based experience. *Entrance requirements:* For master's, minimum GPA of 3.0, BA in education or related field, teaching license; for doctorate, GRE, MAT, resume, 2 writing samples, interview. Additional exam requirements/recommendations for international students: Required—TOEFL (minimum score 525 paper-based; 70 iBT). *Application deadline:* Applications are processed on a rolling basis. Application fee: $50. *Expenses: Tuition:* Full-time $5130; part-time $570 per credit hour. *Financial support:* In 2016–17, 3 students received support. Federal Work-Study available. Support available to part-time students. Financial award application deadline: 3/1; financial award applicants required to submit FAFSA. *Faculty research:* At-risk youth, multicultural issues, values in education, teaching/learning strategies. *Unit head:* Dr. Kelly Chaney, Dean, 920-923-8610, Fax: 920-923-7663, E-mail: kachaney01@marianuniversity.edu.
Website: https://www.marianuniversity.edu/academic-programs/graduate-studies/

Marquette University, Graduate School, College of Education, Department of Educational Policy and Leadership, Milwaukee, WI 53201-1881. Offers college student personnel administration (M Ed); curriculum and instruction (MA); education (MA); educational administration (M Ed); educational policy and foundations (MA); elementary education (Certificate); literacy (MA); principal (Certificate); reading specialist (Certificate); reading teacher (Certificate); secondary education (Certificate); superintendent (Certificate). *Program availability:* Part-time, evening/weekend. *Faculty:* 17 full-time (14 women), 28 part-time/adjunct (23 women). *Students:* 31 full-time (23 women), 103 part-time (66 women); includes 22 minority (7 Black or African American, non-Hispanic/Latino; 1 American Indian or Alaska Native, non-Hispanic/Latino; 6 Asian, non-Hispanic/Latino; 6 Hispanic/Latino; 2 Two or more races, non-Hispanic/Latino). Average age 31. 96 applicants, 92% accepted, 67 enrolled. In 2016, 47 master's, 3 other advanced degrees awarded. Terminal master's awarded for partial completion of doctoral program. *Degree requirements:* For master's, comprehensive exam, thesis (for some programs); for doctorate, thesis/dissertation, qualifying exam. *Entrance requirements:* For master's, GRE General Test or MAT, official transcripts from all current and previous colleges/universities except Marquette, three letters of recommendation, statement of purpose; for doctorate, GRE General Test, MAT, sample of written work, official transcripts from all current and previous colleges/universities except Marquette, three letters of recommendation, statement of purpose, resume/curriculum vitae; for Certificate, GRE General Test or MAT, master's degree. Additional exam requirements/recommendations for international students: Required—TOEFL (minimum score 530 paper-based). *Application deadline:* For fall admission, 1/15 for domestic and international students. Application fee: $50. *Expenses:* Contact institution. *Financial support:* Fellowships, research assistantships, health care benefits, tuition waivers (partial), and unspecified assistantships available. Support available to part-time students. Financial award application deadline: 2/15. *Faculty research:* Leadership; social justice in education; development of lifelong learners; race, class, and schooling in historical perspective; urban teacher education. *Unit head:* Dr. Ellen Eckman, Chair, 414-288-1561. *Application contact:* Dr. Cynthia Ellwood.

Marshall University, Academic Affairs Division, College of Education and Professional Development, Program in Leadership Studies, Huntington, WV 25755. Offers MA, MS, Ed D, Certificate, Ed S. *Program availability:* Part-time, evening/weekend. *Degree requirements:* For master's, thesis optional, comprehensive or oral assessment. *Entrance requirements:* For master's, GRE General Test or MAT.

Martin Luther College, Graduate Studies, New Ulm, MN 56073. Offers early childhood director (MS Ed Admin); educational technology (MS Ed); instruction (MS Ed); leadership (MS Ed); principal (MS Ed Admin); special education (MS Ed). *Program availability:* Part-time, evening/weekend. *Faculty:* 9 full-time (1 woman), 21 part-time/adjunct (10 women). *Students:* 1 (woman) full-time, 77 part-time (30 women); includes 2 minority (1 Asian, non-Hispanic/Latino; 1 Two or more races, non-Hispanic/Latino), 4 international. Average age 37. 6 applicants, 100% accepted, 6 enrolled. In 2016, 15 master's awarded. *Degree requirements:* For master's, capstone project or comprehensive exam. *Entrance requirements:* For master's, undergraduate degree in education from an accredited college or university, minimum undergraduate GPA of 3.0. Additional exam requirements/recommendations for international students: Required—TOEFL (minimum score 550 paper-based; 80 iBT); Recommended—IELTS (minimum score 6.5). *Application deadline:* Applications are processed on a rolling basis. Application fee: $35. Electronic applications accepted. *Expenses:* $11,220 tuition, $140 graduation fee. *Financial support:* In 2016–17, 2 students received support. Scholarships/grants available. Financial award application deadline: 9/1. *Faculty research:* Principal effectiveness, principal support, cognitive load in math instruction, reading strategies in multigrade classrooms, mentor provided professional development for new teachers. *Unit head:* John E. Meyer, Director of Graduate Studies, 507-354-8221 Ext. 398, E-mail: meyerjd@mlc-wels.edu.
Website: https://mlc-wels.edu/graduate-studies/

Marygrove College, Graduate Division, Program in Educational Leadership, Detroit, MI 48221-2599. Offers MA. *Program availability:* Part-time, evening/weekend. *Degree requirements:* For master's, research project. *Entrance requirements:* For master's, MAT, interview, minimum undergraduate GPA of 3.0.

Maryville University of Saint Louis, School of Education, St. Louis, MO 63141-7299. Offers early childhood education (MA Ed); educational leadership (Ed D); educational leadership: principal certification (MA Ed); elementary education (MA Ed); gifted education (MA Ed); higher education leadership (Ed D); literacy specialist (MA Ed); middle grades education (MA Ed); secondary teaching and inquiry (MA Ed); teacher as leader (MA Ed); teacher leadership (Ed D). *Accreditation:* NCATE. *Program availability:* Part-time, evening/weekend. *Faculty:* 17 full-time (11 women), 21 part-time/adjunct (17 women). *Students:* 12 full-time (11 women), 297 part-time (208 women); includes 92 minority (79 Black or African American, non-Hispanic/Latino; 4 Asian, non-Hispanic/Latino; 4 Hispanic/Latino; 5 Two or more races, non-Hispanic/Latino), 4 international. Average age 38. In 2016, 32 master's, 61 doctorates awarded. *Degree requirements:* For master's, thesis, project. *Entrance requirements:* For master's, minimum cumulative GPA of 3.0, 3 professional recommendations, essays, interview with program faculty; for doctorate, minimum GPA of 3.0, 3 professional recommendations, essay, interview, on-site writing sample. Additional exam requirements/recommendations for international students: Required—TOEFL (minimum score 550 paper-based). *Application deadline:* Applications are processed on a rolling basis. Electronic applications accepted. *Expenses:* $879 per credit (for Ed D); $781 per credit (for master's). *Financial support:* Career-related internships or fieldwork, Federal Work-Study, tuition waivers (partial), and professional educator discounts available. Financial award application deadline: 3/1; financial award applicants required to submit FAFSA. *Faculty research:* Collaboration with public schools, pre-service program development, mathematics, diversity, literacy. *Unit head:* Dr. Cathy Bear, Dean, 314-529-9692, Fax: 314-529-9921, E-mail: cbear@maryville.edu. *Application contact:* Stacey Ruffin, Coordinator of Clinical Experiences and Graduate Programs, 314-529-9542, Fax: 314-529-9921, E-mail: teachered@maryville.edu.
Website: http://www.maryville.edu/ed/graduate-programs/

Marywood University, Academic Affairs, Center for Interdisciplinary Studies, Scranton, PA 18509-1598. Offers human development (PhD), including educational administration, health promotion, higher education administration, instructional leadership, social work. *Program availability:* Part-time. Electronic applications accepted. *Expenses:* Contact institution.

Marywood University, Academic Affairs, Reap College of Education and Human Development, Department of Education, Program in Higher Education Administration, Scranton, PA 18509-1598. Offers MS. *Program availability:* Part-time, evening/weekend. Electronic applications accepted. *Faculty research:* Integrated thematic instruction.

Marywood University, Academic Affairs, Reap College of Education and Human Development, Department of Education, Program in Instructional Leadership, Scranton, PA 18509-1598. Offers M Ed. *Program availability:* Part-time. Electronic applications accepted.

Marywood University, Academic Affairs, Reap College of Education and Human Development, Department of Education, Program in School Leadership, Scranton, PA 18509-1598. Offers MS. *Accreditation:* NCATE. *Program availability:* Part-time. Electronic applications accepted.

Marywood University, Academic Affairs, Reap College of Education and Human Development, Department of Education, Program in Special Education Administration and Supervision, Scranton, PA 18509-1598. Offers MS. *Accreditation:* NCATE. *Program availability:* Part-time. Electronic applications accepted.

Massachusetts College of Liberal Arts, Graduate Programs, North Adams, MA 01247-4100. Offers business (MBA); educational administration (M Ed); educational leadership (CAGS); instruction and curriculum (M Ed); instructional technology (M Ed); physical education and health (M Ed); reading (M Ed); special education (M Ed). *Program availability:* Part-time, evening/weekend. *Degree requirements:* For master's, thesis. *Entrance requirements:* For master's, writing sample.

McDaniel College, Graduate and Professional Studies, Program in Educational Leadership, Westminster, MD 21157-4390. Offers MS. *Program availability:* Part-time-only, evening/weekend. *Faculty:* 2 full-time (1 woman), 16 part-time/adjunct (6 women). *Students:* 1 (woman) full-time, 322 part-time (251 women); includes 66 minority (51 Black or African American, non-Hispanic/Latino; 7 Asian, non-Hispanic/Latino; 5 Hispanic/Latino; 2 Native Hawaiian or other Pacific Islander, non-Hispanic/Latino; 1 Two or more races, non-Hispanic/Latino). Average age 38. 145 applicants, 100% accepted. In 2016, 10 master's awarded. *Degree requirements:* For master's, comprehensive exam (for some programs), thesis optional, portfolio. *Entrance requirements:* For master's, 3 recommendations, Principal Mentor Form. Additional exam requirements/recommendations for international students: Required—TOEFL (minimum score 79 iBT), IELTS (minimum score 6). *Application deadline:* For fall admission, 6/1 priority date for domestic students; for spring admission, 11/1 priority date for domestic students; for summer admission, 3/1 priority date for domestic students. Applications are processed on a rolling basis. Application fee: $75. Electronic applications accepted. *Expenses: Tuition:* Full-time $8370; part-time $465 per credit. *Required fees:* $75 per semester. Tuition and fees vary according to course load, program and reciprocity agreements. *Financial support:* Career-related internships or fieldwork available. Financial award application deadline: 3/1; financial award applicants required to submit FAFSA. *Unit head:* Fax: 410-857-2515, E-mail: gradadms@mcdaniel.edu. *Application contact:* Penny Pfeiffer, Senior Graduate Enrollment Management Specialist, 410-857-2513, Fax: 410-857-2515, E-mail: ppfeiffer@mcdaniel.edu.

McGill University, Faculty of Graduate and Postdoctoral Studies, Faculty of Education, Department of Integrated Studies in Education, Montréal, QC H3A 2T5, Canada. Offers culture and values in education (MA, PhD); curriculum studies (MA); educational leadership (MA, Certificate); educational studies (PhD); integrated studies in education (M Ed); second language education (MA, PhD).

McKendree University, Graduate Programs, Programs in Education, Lebanon, IL 62254-1299. Offers curriculum design and instruction (Ed D, Ed S); educational administration and leadership (MA Ed); educational studies (MA Ed); higher education administrative services (MA Ed); music education (MA Ed); reading (MA Ed); special education (MA Ed); teacher leadership (MA Ed); teaching certification (MA Ed). *Accreditation:* NCATE. *Program availability:* Part-time, evening/weekend, online learning. *Entrance requirements:* For master's, official transcripts from all institutions previously attended, minimum GPA of 3.0, resume, references; for doctorate, GRE (within the past 5 years), master's degree in education and Ed S, or the equivalent, from regionally-accredited institution; official transcripts from all institutions previously attended; curriculum vitae/resume; essay/personal statement; two years of teaching/professional experience; for Ed S, GRE (within the past 5 years), master's degree in education from regionally-accredited institution of higher education; official transcripts from all institutions previously attended; curriculum vitae/resume; essay/personal statement; two years of teaching/professional experience. Additional exam requirements/recommendations for international students: Required—TOEFL. Electronic applications accepted.

McNeese State University, Doré School of Graduate Studies, Burton College of Education, Office of Graduate Education Programs, Program in Educational Leadership, Lake Charles, LA 70609. Offers educational leadership (M Ed, Ed S); educational technology (Ed S). *Program availability:* Evening/weekend. *Degree requirements:* For Ed S, comprehensive exam. *Entrance requirements:* For master's, GRE, teaching certificate, 3 years of full-time teaching experience; for Ed S, teaching certificate, 3 years of teaching experience, 1 year of administration or supervision experience, master's degree with 12 semester hours in education.

Memorial University of Newfoundland, School of Graduate Studies, Faculty of Education, St. John's, NL A1C 5S7, Canada. Offers counseling psychology (M Ed); curriculum, teaching, and learning studies (M Ed); education (PhD); educational leadership studies (M Ed, Graduate Diploma); information technology (M Ed); post-secondary studies (M Ed, Diploma), including health professional education (Diploma). *Program availability:* Part-time. *Degree requirements:* For master's, thesis optional, internship, paper folio, project; for doctorate, comprehensive exam, thesis/dissertation, thesis seminar, oral defense of thesis. *Entrance requirements:* For master's, undergraduate degree with at least 2nd class standing, 1-2 years of work experience; for doctorate, minimum A average in graduate course work, MA in education, 2 years of professional experience; for other advanced degree, 2nd class degree, 2 years of work experience with adult learners, appropriate academic qualifications and work experience in a health-related field. Electronic applications accepted. *Faculty research:* Critical thinking, literacy, cognitive studies and counseling, educational change, technology in instruction.

Mercer University, Graduate Studies, Cecil B. Day Campus, Tift College of Education (Atlanta), Macon, GA 31207. Offers curriculum and instruction (PhD); early childhood

education (M Ed, MAT, Ed S); educational leadership (PhD), including higher education leadership, P-12 school leadership; educational leadership P-12 (M Ed, Ed S); higher education leadership (M Ed); independent and charter school leadership (M Ed); middle grades education (M Ed, MAT); reading specialist (M Ed); secondary education (M Ed, MAT); teacher leadership (Ed S). *Accreditation:* NCATE. *Program availability:* Part-time, evening/weekend. *Faculty:* 28 full-time (15 women), 30 part-time/adjunct (27 women). *Students:* 177 full-time (150 women), 324 part-time (264 women); includes 288 minority (256 Black or African American, non-Hispanic/Latino; 1 American Indian or Alaska Native, non-Hispanic/Latino; 7 Asian, non-Hispanic/Latino; 17 Hispanic/Latino; 1 Native Hawaiian or other Pacific Islander, non-Hispanic/Latino; 6 Two or more races, non-Hispanic/Latino), 1 international. Average age 35. In 2016, 173 master's, 34 doctorates, 54 other advanced degrees awarded. *Degree requirements:* For master's and Ed S, research project; for doctorate, comprehensive exam, thesis/dissertation. *Entrance requirements:* For master's, GRE or MAT, minimum undergraduate GPA of 2.75; for doctorate, GRE; for Ed S, GRE or MAT, minimum GPA of 3.25; 3 years of certified teaching experience (for educational leadership and teacher leadership). Additional exam requirements/recommendations for international students: Required—TOEFL (minimum score 80 iBT). *Application deadline:* For fall admission, 8/1 for domestic and international students; for spring admission, 12/1 for domestic and international students; for summer admission, 5/1 for domestic and international students. Applications are processed on a rolling basis. Application fee: $25 ($50 for international students). Electronic applications accepted. *Expenses:* $590 per credit, $1,770 per course (for M Ed); $595 per credit, $1,785 per course (for MAT); $615 per credit, $1,845 per course (for Ed S); $717 per credit, $2,151 per course (for PhD); $150 per semester technology fee. *Financial support:* Federal Work-Study and unspecified assistantships available. Support available to part-time students. Financial award application deadline: 5/1; financial award applicants required to submit FAFSA. *Faculty research:* Educational technology, multicultural and minority issues in education, educational leadership (P-12 and higher education), school discipline and school bullying, standards-based mathematics education. *Unit head:* Dr. James Barta, Dean, 478-301-5355, Fax: 478-301-2280, E-mail: barta_jj@mercer.edu. *Application contact:* Renee Slaton, Associate Director of Graduate Admissions, 678-547-6084, Fax: 678-547-6055, E-mail: mercereducation@mercer.edu.
Website: http://education.mercer.edu/

Mercer University, Graduate Studies, Macon Campus, Tift College of Education (Macon), Macon, GA 31207. Offers early childhood education (M Ed, Ed S); educational leadership (M Ed, PhD, Ed S), including higher education (PhD), P-12; higher education leadership (M Ed); teacher leadership (Ed S). *Accreditation:* NCATE. *Program availability:* Part-time, evening/weekend, 100% online, blended/hybrid learning. *Faculty:* 14 full-time (11 women), 1 part-time/adjunct (0 women). *Students:* 61 full-time (39 women), 39 part-time (30 women); includes 39 minority (34 Black or African American, non-Hispanic/Latino; 1 Asian, non-Hispanic/Latino; 2 Hispanic/Latino; 1 Native Hawaiian or other Pacific Islander, non-Hispanic/Latino; 1 Two or more races, non-Hispanic/Latino), 3 international. Average age 33. In 2016, 23 master's, 13 doctorates awarded. *Degree requirements:* For master's, research project report; for doctorate, comprehensive exam, thesis/dissertation. *Entrance requirements:* For master's, GRE or MAT, minimum GPA of 2.75; for doctorate, GRE, minimum GPA of 3.5; interview; writing sample; 3 recommendations; for Ed S, GRE or MAT, minimum GPA of 3.5 (for teacher leadership), 3.0 (for educational leadership). Additional exam requirements/recommendations for international students: Required—TOEFL (minimum score 80 iBT). *Application deadline:* For fall admission, 8/1 for domestic and international students; for spring admission, 12/1 for domestic and international students. Applications are processed on a rolling basis. Application fee: $35. Electronic applications accepted. *Expenses:* Contact institution. *Financial support:* Federal Work-Study, institutionally sponsored loans, and unspecified assistantships available. Support available to part-time students. Financial award application deadline: 5/1; financial award applicants required to submit FAFSA. *Faculty research:* Teacher effectiveness, specific learning disabilities, inclusion. *Unit head:* Dr. James Barta, Dean, 478-301-5397, Fax: 478-301-2280, E-mail: barta_jj@mercer.edu. *Application contact:* Tracey M. Wofford, Associate Director of Admissions, 678-547-6422, Fax: 678-547-6367, E-mail: wofford_tm@mercer.edu.
Website: http://education.mercer.edu/

Mercy College, School of Education, Advanced Certificate Program in Educational Leadership, Dobbs Ferry, NY 10522-1189. Offers educational leadership (Advanced Certificate). *Program availability:* Part-time, evening/weekend. *Students:* 9 part-time (7 women); includes 5 minority (all Black or African American, non-Hispanic/Latino). Average age 37. 1 applicant, 100% accepted, 1 enrolled. *Degree requirements:* For Advanced Certificate, thesis or alternative, capstone. *Entrance requirements:* For degree, initial or professional teaching certification; interview with program director or faculty advisor; two years of teaching or specialty area experience; resume; master's degree from accredited institution. Additional exam requirements/recommendations for international students: Required—TOEFL (minimum score 600 paper-based; 100 iBT), IELTS (minimum score 8). *Application deadline:* For fall admission, 8/1 for international students. Applications are processed on a rolling basis. Application fee: $40. Electronic applications accepted. *Expenses: Tuition:* Full-time $15,156; part-time $842 per credit hour. *Required fees:* $620; $155 per term. Tuition and fees vary according to course load and program. *Financial support:* Career-related internships or fieldwork, Federal Work-Study, scholarships/grants, and unspecified assistantships available. Support available to part-time students. Financial award applicants required to submit FAFSA. *Faculty research:* School law, leadership, supervision. *Unit head:* Dr. Rose Rudnitski, 914-674-7447, Fax: 914-674-7352, E-mail: rrudnitski@mercy.edu. *Application contact:* Mary Ellen Hoffman, Director, Graduate Education Programs, 914-674-7334, E-mail: mhoffman@mercy.edu.
Website: https://www.mercy.edu/education/educational-leadership

Mercy College, School of Education, Program in Educational Leadership, Dobbs Ferry, NY 10522-1189. Offers MS. *Program availability:* Part-time, evening/weekend, blended/hybrid learning. *Students:* 7 full-time (6 women), 129 part-time (93 women); includes 79 minority (41 Black or African American, non-Hispanic/Latino; 1 American Indian or Alaska Native, non-Hispanic/Latino; 1 Asian, non-Hispanic/Latino; 35 Hispanic/Latino; 1 Two or more races, non-Hispanic/Latino). Average age 32. 25 applicants, 60% accepted, 10 enrolled. In 2016, 50 master's awarded. *Degree requirements:* For master's, comprehensive exam (for some programs), thesis (for some programs). *Entrance requirements:* For master's, GRE, resume, interview, undergraduate transcript. Additional exam requirements/recommendations for international students: Required—TOEFL (minimum score 600 paper-based; 100 iBT), IELTS (minimum score 8). *Application deadline:* For fall admission, 8/1 for international students. Applications are processed on a rolling basis. Application fee: $40. Electronic applications accepted. *Expenses: Tuition:* Full-time $15,156; part-time $842 per credit hour. *Required fees:* $620; $155 per term. Tuition and fees vary according to course load and program. *Financial support:* Career-related internships or fieldwork, Federal Work-Study, scholarships/grants, and unspecified assistantships available. Support available to part-time students. Financial award applicants required to submit FAFSA. *Unit head:* Dr. Rose Rudnitski, Dean for the School of Education, 914-674-7447, Fax: 914-674-7352, E-mail: rrudnitski@mercy.edu. *Application contact:* Allison Gurdineer, Senior Director of Admissions, 877-637-2946, Fax: 914-674-7382, E-mail: admissions@mercy.edu.
Website: https://www.mercy.edu/education/educational-leadership

Mercyhurst University, Graduate Studies, Program in Organizational Leadership, Erie, PA 16546. Offers accounting (MS); higher education administration (MS); human resources (MS); organizational leadership (MS, Certificate); sports leadership (MS); strategy and innovation (MS). *Program availability:* Part-time, evening/weekend. *Degree requirements:* For master's, thesis. *Entrance requirements:* For master's, GRE General Test or MAT, interview, resume, essay, three professional references, transcripts. Additional exam requirements/recommendations for international students: Required—TOEFL (minimum score 80 iBT), IELTS (minimum score 6.5). Electronic applications accepted. *Faculty research:* Leadership training, organizational communication, leadership pedagogy.

Merrimack College, School of Education and Social Policy, North Andover, MA 01845-5800. Offers community engagement (M Ed), including community organizations, higher education, K-12 education; criminology and criminal justice (MS); curriculum and instruction (M Ed); early childhood education (M Ed); educational leadership (CAGS), including instructional leadership; elementary education (M Ed); English as a second language (PreK-6) (M Ed); high school education (M Ed); higher education (M Ed), including leadership and organizational development, student affairs; middle school education (M Ed); moderate disabilities (PreK-8) (M Ed); school counseling (M Ed). *Program availability:* Part-time, evening/weekend, 100% online courses with immersion events and in-classroom practicum close to home. *Faculty:* 17 full-time, 34 part-time/adjunct. *Students:* 204 full-time (172 women), 83 part-time (67 women); includes 32 minority (4 Black or African American, non-Hispanic/Latino; 2 Asian, non-Hispanic/Latino; 23 Hispanic/Latino; 3 Two or more races, non-Hispanic/Latino), 1 international. Average age 27. 261 applicants, 89% accepted, 200 enrolled. In 2016, 153 master's, 2 other advanced degrees awarded. *Degree requirements:* For master's, practicum, portfolio, and state test (for licensure track); capstone (for higher education, curriculum and instruction, and community engagement tracks). *Entrance requirements:* For master's, Massachusetts Teacher Education Licensure (MTEL), official transcripts from other colleges, resume, personal statement, 2 letters of recommendation. Additional exam requirements/recommendations for international students: Required—TOEFL (minimum score 84 iBT), IELTS (minimum score 6.5), PTE (minimum score 56). *Application deadline:* For fall admission, 8/14 for domestic students, 7/14 for international students; for spring admission, 1/10 for domestic students, 12/10 for international students; for summer admission, 5/10 for domestic students, 4/10 for international students. Applications are processed on a rolling basis. Application fee: $0. Electronic applications accepted. *Expenses:* Contact institution. *Financial support:* Fellowships with full tuition reimbursements, career-related internships or fieldwork, scholarships/grants, and health care benefits available. Support available to part-time students. Financial award application deadline: 5/1; financial award applicants required to submit FAFSA. *Faculty research:* Feminist praxis in higher education, transgender student agency and belonging, campus sexual violence prevention, the scholarship of engagement; community engagement; service learning; diversity education; community-university partnerships, college going behaviors and indicators of success for inner city youth, strategies to increase students pursuit and success in STEM higher education, effective workforce development for displaced or under employed individuals, police reform, e.g. surveillance. *Application contact:* Alyssa Frey, Graduate Admissions Counselor, 978-837-3563, E-mail: freya@merrimack.edu.
Website: http://www.merrimack.edu/academics/graduate/education/

Michigan State University, The Graduate School, College of Education, Department of Educational Administration, East Lansing, MI 48824. Offers higher, adult and lifelong education (MA, PhD); K–12 educational administration (MA, PhD, Ed S); student affairs administration (MA). *Program availability:* Part-time. *Entrance requirements:* Additional exam requirements/recommendations for international students: Required—TOEFL. Electronic applications accepted.

Middle Tennessee State University, College of Graduate Studies, College of Education, Department of Educational Leadership, Program in Administration and Supervision, Murfreesboro, TN 37132. Offers M Ed, Ed S. *Program availability:* Part-time, evening/weekend, online learning. *Degree requirements:* For master's, comprehensive exam; for Ed S, comprehensive exam, thesis or alternative. *Entrance requirements:* For master's and Ed S, GRE, MAT or current teaching license. Additional exam requirements/recommendations for international students: Required—TOEFL (minimum score 525 paper-based; 71 iBT) or IELTS (minimum score 6). Electronic applications accepted.

Midwestern State University, Billie Doris McAda Graduate School, West College of Education, Programs in Educational Leadership and Technology, Wichita Falls, TX 76308. Offers educational leadership (M Ed); educational technology (M Ed). *Program availability:* Part-time, evening/weekend. *Degree requirements:* For master's, comprehensive exam. *Entrance requirements:* For master's, GRE General Test or MAT. Additional exam requirements/recommendations for international students: Required—TOEFL (minimum score 550 paper-based). Electronic applications accepted. *Faculty research:* Role of the principal in the twenty-first century, culturally proficient leadership, human diversity, immigration, teacher collaboration.

Millersville University of Pennsylvania, College of Graduate Studies and Adult Learning, College of Education and Human Services, Department of Educational Foundations, Program in Educational Leadership, Millersville, PA 17551-0302. Offers Ed D. Program offered in partnership with Shippensburg University of Pennsylvania. *Program availability:* Part-time, evening/weekend, online only, blended/hybrid learning. *Faculty:* 20 full-time (13 women), 2 part-time/adjunct (both women). *Students:* 12 part-time (5 women); includes 1 minority (Black or African American, non-Hispanic/Latino). Average age 39. 6 applicants, 83% accepted, 3 enrolled. *Degree requirements:* For doctorate, comprehensive exam, thesis/dissertation, candidacy exam. *Entrance requirements:* For doctorate, teaching certificate; interview; 3-5 years of professional experience; 500- to 1000-word goal statement addressing goals and objectives for doctoral study in educational leadership and how program will assist in achieving those outcomes. Additional exam requirements/recommendations for international students: Required—TOEFL (minimum score 600 paper-based), IELTS (minimum score 6). *Application deadline:* Applications are processed on a rolling basis. Application fee: $40. Electronic applications accepted. *Expenses:* Contact institution. *Financial support:* Unspecified assistantships available. Financial award application deadline: 3/15; financial award applicants required to submit FAFSA. *Faculty research:* Supervision and poverty, student centered instruction, Follett management methods. *Unit head:* Dr. Tim E. Mahoney, Coordinator, 717-871-7202, E-mail: tim.mahoney@millersville.edu. *Application contact:* Dr. Victor S. DeSantis, Dean of College of Graduate Studies and Adult Learning/Associate Provost for Civic and Community Engagement, 717-871-7619, Fax: 717-871-7954, E-mail: victor.desantis@millersville.edu.
Website: http://www.millersville.edu/graduate/programs/doctorate/doctorate-of-education-in-educational-leadership.php

Millersville University of Pennsylvania, College of Graduate Studies and Adult Learning, College of Education and Human Services, Department of Educational Foundations, Program in Leadership for Teaching and Learning, Millersville, PA 17551-0302. Offers M Ed. *Program availability:* Part-time, evening/weekend. *Faculty:* 20 full-

time (13 women), 2 part-time/adjunct (both women). *Students:* 1 full-time (0 women), 19 part-time (9 women); includes 2 minority (1 Black or African American, non-Hispanic/Latino; 1 Hispanic/Latino). Average age 30. 4 applicants, 100% accepted, 2 enrolled. In 2016, 6 master's awarded. *Degree requirements:* For master's, applied practicum experience, portfolio review. *Entrance requirements:* For master's, GRE or MAT, teaching certificate; interview. Additional exam requirements/recommendations for international students: Required—TOEFL (minimum score 600 paper-based), IELTS (minimum score 6). *Application deadline:* Applications are processed on a rolling basis. Application fee: $40. Electronic applications accepted. *Expenses:* $483 per credit resident tuition; $725 per credit non-resident tuition. *Financial support:* In 2016–17, 1 student received support. Unspecified assistantships available. Financial award application deadline: 3/15; financial award applicants required to submit FAFSA. *Faculty research:* Mary Parker Follett management, poverty and supervision. *Unit head:* Dr. Tim E. Mahoney, Chair, 717-871-7202, E-mail: tim.mahoney@millersville.edu. *Application contact:* Dr. Victor S. DeSantis, Dean of College of Graduate Studies and Adult Learning/Associate Provost for Civic and Community Engagement, 717-871-7619, Fax: 717-871-7954, E-mail: victor.desantis@millersville.edu.
Website: https://www.millersville.edu/edfoundations/m_ed_leadership.php

Milligan College, Area of Education, Milligan College, TN 37682. Offers combined preK-3/K-5 education (M Ed); educational leadership (Ed D, Ed S); K-5 education (M Ed); middle grades education (M Ed); preK-3 education (M Ed); preK-3 special education (M Ed); secondary education (M Ed). *Accreditation:* NCATE. *Program availability:* Part-time. *Faculty:* 5 full-time (3 women), 3 part-time/adjunct (1 woman). *Students:* 26 full-time (19 women), 20 part-time (10 women); includes 2 minority (1 Black or African American, non-Hispanic/Latino; 1 Hispanic/Latino), 2 international. Average age 28. 16 applicants, 81% accepted, 11 enrolled. In 2016, 19 master's awarded. *Degree requirements:* For master's, thesis, portfolio, research project; for doctorate, thesis/dissertation, portfolio, research project. *Entrance requirements:* For master's, MAT, GRE General Test, ACT, SAT, or PRAXIS, undergraduate degree and supporting transcripts, professional recommendations, interview; for doctorate, MAT or GRE, master's degree and supporting transcripts, demonstrated scholastic ability, recognized leadership role within education, professional recommendations, essay/personal statement, portfolio (professional development plan, evidence of ability, knowledge and qualities), interview. Additional exam requirements/recommendations for international students: Required—TOEFL (minimum score 550 paper-based, 79 iBT) or IELTS (6.5). *Application deadline:* For fall admission, 8/1 priority date for domestic students, 6/1 for international students; for spring admission, 11/15 priority date for domestic students, 12/1 for international students; for summer admission, 4/1 for domestic students. Applications are processed on a rolling basis. Application fee: $30. Electronic applications accepted. *Expenses:* $360 per hour tuition (for M Ed); $475 per hour tuition (for Ed D and Ed S); $325 per semester tech/activity fees. *Financial support:* Scholarships/grants available. Financial award application deadline: 12/1; financial award applicants required to submit FAFSA. *Faculty research:* Assessment; school mental health; literacy; technology; educator preparation. *Unit head:* Dr. Angela Hilton-Prillhart, Area Chair of Education, 423-461-8769, Fax: 423-461-3103, E-mail: anhilton-prillhart@milligan.edu. *Application contact:* Melissa Dillow, Graduate Admissions Recruiter, Education, 423-461-8306, Fax: 423-461-8982, E-mail: msdillow@milligan.edu.
Website: http://www.Milligan.edu/GPS

Mills College, Graduate Studies, MBA/MA Program in Educational Leadership, Oakland, CA 94613-1000. Offers MBA/MA. Program offered jointly between School of Education and Lorry I. Lokey Graduate School of Business. *Faculty:* 12 full-time (10 women), 12 part-time/adjunct (8 women). *Students:* 8 full-time (all women), 3 part-time (2 women); includes 10 minority (6 Black or African American, non-Hispanic/Latino; 1 Asian, non-Hispanic/Latino; 2 Hispanic/Latino; 1 Two or more races, non-Hispanic/Latino). Average age 39. 8 applicants, 88% accepted, 1 enrolled. *Entrance requirements:* Additional exam requirements/recommendations for international students: Required—TOEFL (minimum score 550 paper-based; 80 iBT) or IELTS (minimum score 6). *Application deadline:* For fall admission, 2/1 priority date for domestic students, 12/15 priority date for international students. Applications are processed on a rolling basis. Application fee: $50. Electronic applications accepted. *Expenses: Tuition:* Full-time $31,620. *Required fees:* $1118. Tuition and fees vary according to course load, degree level and program. *Financial support:* In 2016–17, 15 students received support, including 14 fellowships with tuition reimbursements available (averaging $9,678 per year), 1 teaching assistantship with tuition reimbursement available (averaging $1,986 per year). Financial award application deadline: 2/1; financial award applicants required to submit FAFSA. *Unit head:* Alice McDonald, Program Head, E-mail: amcdonald@mills.edu. *Application contact:* Robynne Lofton, Director of Admissions, 510-430-3295, Fax: 510-430-2159, E-mail: grad-admission@mills.edu.
Website: http://www.mills.edu/MBAMAEdLdrshp

Minnesota State University Mankato, College of Graduate Studies and Research, College of Education, Department of Educational Leadership, Program in Experiential Education, Mankato, MN 56001. Offers MS. *Accreditation:* NCATE. *Program availability:* Part-time, evening/weekend. *Students:* 8 full-time (3 women), 20 part-time (10 women). *Degree requirements:* For master's, thesis or alternative. *Entrance requirements:* For master's, minimum GPA of 3.0 during previous 2 years. Additional exam requirements/recommendations for international students: Required—TOEFL. *Application deadline:* For fall admission, 7/1 priority date for domestic students; for spring admission, 11/1 for domestic students. Applications are processed on a rolling basis. Application fee: $40. Electronic applications accepted. *Financial support:* Research assistantships with full tuition reimbursements, teaching assistantships with full tuition reimbursements, career-related internships or fieldwork, Federal Work-Study, and unspecified assistantships available. Support available to part-time students. Financial award application deadline: 3/15; financial award applicants required to submit FAFSA.
Website: http://ed.mnsu.edu/edleadership/msexperientialed/

Minnesota State University Moorhead, Graduate Studies, College of Education and Human Services, Moorhead, MN 56563. Offers counseling and student affairs (MS); curriculum and instruction (MS); educational leadership (MS, Ed S); special education (MS); speech-language pathology (MS). *Accreditation:* NCATE. *Program availability:* Part-time, 100% online, blended/hybrid learning. *Students:* 133 full-time (116 women), 363 part-time (274 women). Average age 32. 273 applicants, 49% accepted. In 2016, 114 master's awarded. *Degree requirements:* For master's, comprehensive exam (for some programs), thesis. *Entrance requirements:* For master's, GRE, essay, letter of intent, letters of reference, teaching license, teaching verification. Additional exam requirements/recommendations for international students: Required—TOEFL (minimum score 550 paper-based). *Application deadline:* For fall admission, 4/15 priority date for domestic students; for spring admission, 11/1 priority date for domestic students. Applications are processed on a rolling basis. Application fee: $20. Electronic applications accepted. *Expenses:* Tuition, state resident: full-time $9000; part-time $4500 per credit. Tuition, nonresident: full-time $18,000; part-time $9000 per credit. *Required fees:* $942; $39.25 per credit. One-time fee: $90 full-time. Full-time tuition and fees vary according to course load, degree level, program and reciprocity agreements. *Financial support:* Federal Work-Study and unspecified assistantships available. Financial award application deadline: 10/1; financial award applicants required to submit FAFSA. *Unit head:* Dr. Ok-Hee Lee, Dean, 218-477-2095, E-mail: okheelee@mnstate.edu. *Application contact:* Karla Wenger, Office Manager, 218-477-2344, Fax: 218-477-2482, E-mail: wengerk@mnstate.edu.
Website: http://www.mnstate.edu/cehs/

Mississippi College, Graduate School, School of Education, Department of Teacher Education and Leadership, Clinton, MS 39058. Offers art (M Ed); biological science (M Ed); business education (M Ed); computer science (M Ed); dyslexia therapy (M Ed); educational leadership (M Ed, Ed D, Ed S); elementary education (M Ed, Ed S); English (M Ed); higher education administration (MS); mathematics (M Ed); secondary education (M Ed); social studies (history) (M Ed); teaching arts (M Ed). *Program availability:* Part-time, online learning. *Degree requirements:* For master's, comprehensive exam, thesis optional. *Entrance requirements:* For master's, NTE. Additional exam requirements/recommendations for international students: Recommended—TOEFL, IELTS. Electronic applications accepted.

Mississippi College, Graduate School, School of Education, Program in Higher Education Administration, Clinton, MS 39058. Offers MS. *Program availability:* Part-time, online learning. *Degree requirements:* For master's, comprehensive exam, thesis optional. *Entrance requirements:* For master's, GRE or GMAT, minimum GPA of 3.0. Additional exam requirements/recommendations for international students: Recommended—TOEFL, IELTS.

Mississippi State University, College of Agriculture and Life Sciences, School of Human Sciences, Mississippi State, MS 39762. Offers agriculture and extension education (MS, PhD), including agriculture and extension education (PhD), leadership (MS), teaching (MS); human development and family studies (MS, PhD). *Accreditation:* NCATE (one or more programs are accredited). *Program availability:* Part-time. *Faculty:* 23 full-time (13 women), 1 part-time/adjunct (0 women). *Students:* 35 full-time (25 women), 61 part-time (45 women); includes 19 minority (15 Black or African American, non-Hispanic/Latino; 2 Hispanic/Latino; 2 Two or more races, non-Hispanic/Latino), 5 international. Average age 35. 22 applicants, 73% accepted, 12 enrolled. In 2016, 8 master's, 4 doctorates awarded. *Degree requirements:* For master's, thesis optional, comprehensive oral or written exam. *Entrance requirements:* For master's, GRE, minimum GPA of 2.75 in last 4 semesters of course work; for doctorate, minimum GPA of 3.0 on prior graduate work. Additional exam requirements/recommendations for international students: Required—TOEFL (minimum score 477 paper-based; 53 iBT); Recommended—IELTS (minimum score 4.5). *Application deadline:* For fall admission, 7/1 for domestic students, 5/1 for international students; for spring admission, 11/1 for domestic students, 9/1 for international students. Applications are processed on a rolling basis. Application fee: $60. Electronic applications accepted. *Expenses:* Tuition, state resident: full-time $7670; part-time $852.50 per credit hour. Tuition, nonresident: full-time $20,790; part-time $2310.50 per credit hour. Part-time tuition and fees vary according to course load. *Financial support:* Federal Work-Study, institutionally sponsored loans, and unspecified assistantships available. Financial award application deadline: 4/1; financial award applicants required to submit FAFSA. *Faculty research:* Animal welfare, agro science, information technology, learning styles, problem solving. *Unit head:* Dr. Michael Newman, Director and Professor, 662-325-2950, E-mail: mnewman@humansci.msstate.edu. *Application contact:* Marina Hunt, Admissions and Enrollment Assistant, 662-325-5188, E-mail: mhunt@grad.msstate.edu.
Website: http://www.humansci.msstate.edu

Mississippi State University, College of Education, Educational Leadership Program, Mississippi State, MS 39762. Offers community college education (MAT, PhD); elementary, middle and secondary education administration (PhD); school administration (MS, Ed S); workforce education leadership (MS). MS in workforce education leadership held jointly with Alcorn State University. *Faculty:* 16 full-time (10 women). *Students:* 32 full-time (16 women), 158 part-time (101 women); includes 82 minority (80 Black or African American, non-Hispanic/Latino; 1 Hispanic/Latino; 1 Two or more races, non-Hispanic/Latino). Average age 38. 60 applicants, 58% accepted, 34 enrolled. In 2016, 24 master's, 15 doctorates, 5 other advanced degrees awarded. *Degree requirements:* For master's and Ed S, comprehensive exam, thesis; for doctorate, comprehensive exam, thesis/dissertation. *Entrance requirements:* For master's, GRE, minimum GPA of 2.75 in junior and senior courses; for doctorate, GRE, minimum GPA of 3.4 on previous graduate work; for Ed S, GRE, minimum GPA of 3.2, master's degree. Additional exam requirements/recommendations for international students: Required—TOEFL (minimum score 550 paper-based; 79 iBT); Recommended—IELTS (minimum score 6.5). *Application deadline:* For fall admission, 7/1 for domestic students, 5/1 for international students; for spring admission, 11/1 for domestic students, 9/1 for international students. Application fee: $60. Electronic applications accepted. *Expenses:* Tuition, state resident: full-time $7670; part-time $852.50 per credit hour. Tuition, nonresident: full-time $20,790; part-time $2310.50 per credit hour. Part-time tuition and fees vary according to course load. *Financial support:* In 2016–17, 2 research assistantships with full tuition reimbursements (averaging $12,940 per year) were awarded; Federal Work-Study, institutionally sponsored loans, and unspecified assistantships also available. Financial award application deadline: 4/1; financial award applicants required to submit FAFSA. *Unit head:* Dr. Ed Davis, Interim Department Head/Professor, 662-325-0969, Fax: 662-325-0975, E-mail: jed11@colled.msstate.edu. *Application contact:* Linda Bonner, Senior Admissions Assistant, 662-325-3363, E-mail: lbonner@grad.msstate.edu.
Website: http://www.educationalleadership.msstate.edu/

Mississippi University for Women, Graduate School, College of Education and Human Sciences, Columbus, MS 39701-9998. Offers differentiated instruction (M Ed); educational leadership (M Ed); gifted studies (M Ed); reading/literacy (M Ed); teaching (MAT). *Accreditation:* ASHA; NCATE. *Program availability:* Part-time. *Degree requirements:* For master's, comprehensive exam, thesis optional. *Entrance requirements:* For master's, GRE General Test or NTE (M Ed in gifted education or MS in speech/language pathology), MAT (M Ed in instructional management), minimum QPA of 3.0.

Missouri Baptist University, Graduate Programs, St. Louis, MO 63141-8660. Offers business administration (MBA); Christian ministries (MACM); counseling (MAC); education (MSE); education administration (MEA); educational leadership (MSE, Ed S); teaching (MAT).

Missouri State University, Graduate College, College of Education, Department of Counseling, Leadership, and Special Education, Program in Educational Administration, Springfield, MO 65897. Offers elementary principal (MS Ed, Ed S); secondary principal (MS Ed, Ed S); superintendent (Ed S). *Program availability:* Part-time, evening/weekend. *Students:* 2 full-time (0 women), 60 part-time (40 women); includes 6 minority (2 Black or African American, non-Hispanic/Latino; 1 American Indian or Alaska Native, non-Hispanic/Latino; 2 Hispanic/Latino; 1 Two or more races, non-Hispanic/Latino). Average age 34. 6 applicants, 67% accepted, 3 enrolled. In 2016, 34 master's, 15 Ed Ss awarded. *Degree requirements:* For master's and Ed S, comprehensive exam, thesis or alternative. *Entrance requirements:* For master's, minimum GPA of 2.75; for Ed S, GRE General Test, MAT, minimum GPA of 2.75. Additional exam requirements/recommendations for international students: Required—TOEFL (minimum score 550 paper-based; 79 iBT), IELTS (minimum score 6). *Application deadline:* For fall

admission, 7/20 priority date for domestic students, 5/1 for international students; for spring admission, 12/20 priority date for domestic students, 9/1 for international students; for summer admission, 5/20 priority date for domestic students. Applications are processed on a rolling basis. Application fee: $35 ($50 for international students). Electronic applications accepted. *Expenses:* Tuition, state resident: full-time $5830. Tuition, nonresident: full-time $10,708. *Required fees:* $1130. Tuition and fees vary according to class time, course level, course load and program. *Financial support:* Career-related internships or fieldwork, Federal Work-Study, institutionally sponsored loans, scholarships/grants, and unspecified assistantships available. Financial award application deadline: 3/31; financial award applicants required to submit FAFSA. *Unit head:* Dr. James Satterfield, Department Head, 417-836-5392, Fax: 417-836-4918, E-mail: clse@missouristate.edu. *Application contact:* Michael Edwards, Coordinator of Graduate Admissions, 417-836-5330, Fax: 417-836-6200, E-mail: michaeledwards@missouristate.edu.
Website: http://education.missouristate.edu/edadmin/

Missouri State University, Graduate College, College of Education, Department of Reading, Foundations, and Technology, Springfield, MO 65897. Offers educational technology (MS Ed); literacy (MS Ed, Certificate); teacher leadership (Certificate, Ed S); teaching (MAT); teaching and learning (MA, Certificate). *Program availability:* Part-time, evening/weekend, 100% online, blended/hybrid learning. *Faculty:* 13 full-time (6 women), 8 part-time/adjunct (7 women). *Students:* 29 full-time (24 women), 180 part-time (152 women); includes 14 minority (12 Hispanic/Latino; 2 Two or more races, non-Hispanic/Latino), 6 international. Average age 32. 65 applicants, 72% accepted, 33 enrolled. In 2016, 50 master's awarded. *Degree requirements:* For master's, comprehensive exam, thesis or alternative. *Entrance requirements:* Additional exam requirements/recommendations for international students: Required—TOEFL (minimum score 550 paper-based; 79 iBT), IELTS (minimum score 6). *Application deadline:* For fall admission, 7/20 priority date for domestic students, 5/1 for international students; for spring admission, 12/20 priority date for domestic students, 9/1 for international students; for summer admission, 5/20 priority date for domestic students. Applications are processed on a rolling basis. Application fee: $35 ($50 for international students). Electronic applications accepted. *Expenses:* Tuition, state resident: full-time $5830. Tuition, nonresident: full-time $10,708. *Required fees:* $1130. Tuition and fees vary according to class time, course level, course load and program. *Financial support:* Federal Work-Study, institutionally sponsored loans, scholarships/grants, and unspecified assistantships available. Financial award application deadline: 3/31; financial award applicants required to submit FAFSA. *Faculty research:* Literacy and technology, struggling readers, community service learning. *Unit head:* Dr. Cathy Pearman, Department Head, 417-836-6769, Fax: 417-836-6252, E-mail: rft@missouristate.edu. *Application contact:* Michael Edwards, Coordinator of Graduate Admissions, 417-836-5330, Fax: 417-836-6200, E-mail: michaeledwards@missouristate.edu.
Website: http://education.missouristate.edu/rft/

Monmouth University, Graduate Studies, School of Education, West Long Branch, NJ 07764-1898. Offers applied behavior analysis (Certificate); autism (Certificate); director of school counseling services (Post-Master's Certificate); early childhood (M Ed); educational leadership (Ed D); elementary education (MAT), including elementary level, secondary level; English as a second language (M Ed); learning disabilities teacher-consultant (Post-Master's Certificate); literacy (MS Ed); school counseling (MS Ed); special education (MS Ed), including autism, learning disabilities teacher-consultant, teacher of students with disabilities, teaching in inclusive settings; speech-language pathology (MS Ed); student affairs and college counseling (MS Ed); supervisor (Post-Master's Certificate); teaching English to speakers of other languages (Certificate). *Accreditation:* NCATE. *Program availability:* Part-time, evening/weekend, 100% online, blended/hybrid learning. *Faculty:* 23 full-time (19 women), 33 part-time/adjunct (25 women). *Students:* 191 full-time (172 women), 141 part-time (122 women); includes 56 minority (10 Black or African American, non-Hispanic/Latino; 9 Asian, non-Hispanic/Latino; 31 Hispanic/Latino; 6 Two or more races, non-Hispanic/Latino). Average age 26. 423 applicants, 53% accepted, 139 enrolled. In 2016, 148 master's, 4 other advanced degrees awarded. *Entrance requirements:* For master's, GRE taken within last 5 years (for MS Ed in speech-language pathology); SAT (minimum combined score of 1660 in 3 sections), ACT (23), GRE (minimum score of 4.0 on analytical writing section and minimum combined score of 310 on quantitative and verbal sections), or passing scores on 3 parts of Core Academic Skills Educators, minimum GPA of 3.0 in major; 2 letters of recommendation (for some programs); resume, personal statement or essay (depending on program). Additional exam requirements/recommendations for international students: Required—TOEFL (minimum score 550 paper-based; 79 iBT), IELTS (minimum score 6), Michigan English Language Assessment Battery (minimum score 77) or Certificate of Advanced English (minimum score B2). *Application deadline:* For fall admission, 7/15 priority date for domestic students, 7/1 for international students; for spring admission, 12/1 priority date for domestic students, 11/1 for international students; for summer admission, 5/1 for domestic students. Applications are processed on a rolling basis. Application fee: $50. Electronic applications accepted. *Expenses: Tuition, area resident:* Full-time $19,764; part-time $1098 per credit hour. *Required fees:* $175 per semester. Tuition and fees vary according to program. *Financial support:* In 2016–17, 349 students received support, including 305 fellowships (averaging $3,558 per year), 48 teaching assistantships (averaging $9,619 per year); research assistantships, institutionally sponsored loans, scholarships/grants, and unspecified assistantships also available. Support available to part-time students. Financial award application deadline: 2/1; financial award applicants required to submit FAFSA. *Faculty research:* Multicultural literacy, science and mathematics teaching strategies, teacher as reflective practitioner, children with disabilities. *Unit head:* Dr. John E. Henning, Dean, 732-263-5513, Fax: 732-263-5277. *Application contact:* Laurie Kuhn, Associate Director of Graduate Admission, 732-571-3452, Fax: 732-263-5123, E-mail: gradadm@monmouth.edu.
Website: http://www.monmouth.edu/academics/schools/education/default.asp

Montana State University, The Graduate School, College of Education, Health, and Human Development, Department of Education, Bozeman, MT 59717. Offers adult and higher education (Ed D); curriculum and instruction (M Ed, Ed D), including professional educator (M Ed), technology education (M Ed); education (M Ed), including adult and higher education, educational leadership, school counseling; educational leadership (Ed D, Ed S). *Accreditation:* TEAC. *Program availability:* Part-time, online learning. *Degree requirements:* For master's, comprehensive exam; for doctorate, comprehensive exam, thesis/dissertation. *Entrance requirements:* For master's, GRE, 3 letters of reference, essays, BA transcripts; for doctorate, GRE, MAT, 3 letters of reference, essay, BA and M Ed transcripts; for Ed S, PRAXIS. Additional exam requirements/recommendations for international students: Required—TOEFL (minimum score 550 paper-based). Electronic applications accepted. *Faculty research:* Critical literacy; standards-based education; school Improvement, organizational change, leadership in rural education, leadership in Indian education; student Learning; multicultural/culturally responsive education for social justice Native American indigenous education, community-centered education teacher preparation.

Montclair State University, The Graduate School, College of Education and Human Services, Doctoral Program in Teacher Education and Teacher Development, Montclair, NJ 07043-1624. Offers PhD. *Program availability:* Part-time, evening/weekend. *Degree requirements:* For doctorate, comprehensive exam (for some programs), thesis/dissertation. *Entrance requirements:* For doctorate, GRE General Test, interview, 3 letters of recommendation, essay. Additional exam requirements/recommendations for international students: Required—TOEFL (minimum score 83 iBT), IELTS (minimum score 6.5). Electronic applications accepted. *Expenses:* Tuition, state resident: part-time $553 per credit. Tuition, nonresident: part-time $854 per credit. *Required fees:* $91 per credit. Tuition and fees vary according to program.

Montclair State University, The Graduate School, College of Education and Human Services, Program in Educational Leadership, Montclair, NJ 07043-1624. Offers MA. *Program availability:* Part-time, evening/weekend. *Degree requirements:* For master's, comprehensive exam, thesis or alternative. *Entrance requirements:* For master's, GRE General Test, interview, 2 letters of recommendation. Additional exam requirements/recommendations for international students: Required—TOEFL (minimum score 83 iBT), IELTS (minimum score 6.5). Electronic applications accepted. *Expenses:* Tuition, state resident: part-time $553 per credit. Tuition, nonresident: part-time $854 per credit. *Required fees:* $91 per credit. Tuition and fees vary according to program.

Morehead State University, Graduate Programs, College of Education, Department of Foundational and Graduate Studies in Education, Morehead, KY 40351. Offers adult and higher education (MA, Ed S); certified professional counselor (Ed S); counseling P-12 (MA); curriculum and instruction (Ed S); educational technology (MA Ed); instructional leadership (Ed S); school administration (MA); school counseling (Ed S); teacher leader business and marketing content (MA Ed); teacher leader business and marketing technology (MA Ed); teacher leader educational technology (MA Ed); teacher leader English (MA Ed); teacher leader gifted education (MA Ed); teacher leader IECE certification (MA Ed); teacher leader interdisciplinary education P-5 (MA Ed); teacher leader middle grades (MA Ed); teacher leader non IECE certification (MA Ed); teacher leader reading/writing - non-certification (MA Ed); teacher leader reading/writing certification (MA Ed); teacher leader school communication - certification (MA Ed); teacher leader school communication - non-certification (MA Ed); teacher leader social studies (MA Ed); teacher leader special education (MA Ed). *Accreditation:* NCATE. *Program availability:* Part-time, evening/weekend. *Degree requirements:* For master's, thesis optional, oral and/or written comprehensive exams; for Ed S, thesis, oral exam. *Entrance requirements:* For master's, GRE General Test, minimum overall undergraduate GPA of 2.5; for Ed S, GRE General Test, interview, master's degree, minimum GPA of 3.5, work experience. Additional exam requirements/recommendations for international students: Required—TOEFL (minimum score 500 paper-based). Electronic applications accepted. *Faculty research:* Character education, school accountability, computer applications for school administrators.

Morgan State University, School of Graduate Studies, School of Education and Urban Studies, Department of Advanced Studies, Leadership and Policy, Program in Community College Leadership, Baltimore, MD 21251. Offers Ed D. *Accreditation:* NCATE. *Program availability:* Part-time, evening/weekend. *Degree requirements:* For doctorate, comprehensive exam, thesis/dissertation. *Entrance requirements:* For doctorate, GRE General Test or MAT. Additional exam requirements/recommendations for international students: Required—TOEFL (minimum score 550 paper-based). *Faculty research:* Multicultural education, cooperative learning, psychology of cognition.

Morgan State University, School of Graduate Studies, School of Education and Urban Studies, Department of Advanced Studies, Leadership and Policy, Program in Educational Administration and Supervision, Baltimore, MD 21251. Offers urban educational leadership (Ed D). *Accreditation:* NCATE. *Program availability:* Part-time, evening/weekend. *Faculty research:* Multicultural education, cooperative learning, psychology of cognition.

Morgan State University, School of Graduate Studies, School of Education and Urban Studies, Department of Advanced Studies, Leadership and Policy, Program in Higher Education Administration, Baltimore, MD 21251. Offers higher education (PhD); higher education administration (MA). *Degree requirements:* For doctorate, comprehensive exam, thesis/dissertation. *Entrance requirements:* For doctorate, GRE General Test or MAT, minimum GPA of 3.0.

Mount Holyoke College, Professional and Graduate Education (PaGE), South Hadley, MA 01075. Offers mathematics teaching (MAMT); teacher leadership (MATL); teaching (MAT). *Program availability:* Part-time, 100% online, blended/hybrid learning. *Faculty:* 4 full-time (3 women), 12 part-time/adjunct (10 women). *Students:* 23 full-time (21 women), 84 part-time (76 women); includes 11 minority (4 Black or African American, non-Hispanic/Latino; 2 Asian, non-Hispanic/Latino; 4 Hispanic/Latino; 1 Two or more races, non-Hispanic/Latino), 7 international. Average age 37. In 2016, 30 master's awarded. *Degree requirements:* For master's, practicum (for MAT); capstone course (for MATL); capstone portfolio (for MAMT). *Entrance requirements:* For master's, Massachusetts Tests for Education Licensure (MTEL), bachelor's degree; subject area knowledge in desired teaching discipline; personal statement; essay; official transcripts; two letters of recommendation; history of effective classroom teaching (for MATL). *Application deadline:* Applications are processed on a rolling basis. Application fee: $0. Electronic applications accepted. *Expenses: Tuition:* Full-time $24,500; part-time $770 per credit hour. *Required fees:* $117. Tuition and fees vary according to course load and program. *Financial support:* Scholarships/grants available. Financial award applicants required to submit FAFSA. *Faculty research:* Teacher leadership, state education policy, novice teacher development, global immersion experiences, mathematics education. *Unit head:* Dr. Tiffany Espinosa, Executive Director of Professional and Graduate Education, 413-538-3478, Fax: 413-538-3098.
Website: https://www.mtholyoke.edu/professional-graduate

Mount Mercy University, Program in Education, Cedar Rapids, IA 52402-4797. Offers reading (MA Ed); special education (MA Ed); teacher leadership (MA Ed). *Entrance requirements:* For master's, minimum cumulative GPA of 3.0, 2 letters of recommendation, resume, valid teaching license. Additional exam requirements/recommendations for international students: Required—TOEFL (minimum score 570 paper-based; 88 iBT). Electronic applications accepted.

Murray State University, College of Education, Department of Educational Studies, Leadership and Counseling, Program in School Administration, Murray, KY 42071. Offers MA Ed, Ed S. *Accreditation:* NCATE. *Program availability:* Part-time. *Degree requirements:* For master's and Ed S, comprehensive exam. *Entrance requirements:* For degree, GRE General Test. Additional exam requirements/recommendations for international students: Required—TOEFL.

National Louis University, National College of Education, Chicago, IL 60603. Offers administration and supervision (M Ed, Ed D, CAS, Ed S); curriculum and instruction (M Ed, MS Ed, CAS); early childhood administration (M Ed, CAS); early childhood education (M Ed, MAT, MS Ed, CAS); education (Ed D); educational psychology/human learning and development (M Ed, MS Ed, CAS, Ed S); elementary education (MAT); interdisciplinary curriculum and instruction (M Ed); mathematics education (M Ed, MS Ed, CAS); middle grades education (MAT); reading and language (M Ed, MS Ed, CAS); school psychology (M Ed, Ed S); science education (M Ed, MS Ed, CAS); secondary education (MAT); special education (M Ed, MAT, CAS); technology in education (M Ed, CAS). *Accreditation:* NCATE. *Program availability:* Part-time, evening/weekend. *Degree requirements:* For doctorate, comprehensive exam, thesis/

dissertation. *Entrance requirements:* For master's, MAT or GRE, minimum GPA of 3.0; for doctorate, GRE General Test, minimum GPA of 3.25, interview, resume, writing sample, 4 recommendations. Additional exam requirements/recommendations for international students: Required—TOEFL (minimum score 550 paper-based; 79 iBT).

National University, Academic Affairs, School of Education, La Jolla, CA 92037-1011. Offers e-teaching and learning (Certificate); educational administration (MS). *Program availability:* Part-time, evening/weekend, 100% online, blended/hybrid learning. *Faculty:* 74 full-time (48 women), 422 part-time/adjunct (260 women). *Students:* 3,376 full-time (2,418 women), 2,410 part-time (1,641 women); includes 2,652 minority (357 Black or African American, non-Hispanic/Latino; 29 American Indian or Alaska Native, non-Hispanic/Latino; 337 Asian, non-Hispanic/Latino; 1,680 Hispanic/Latino; 45 Native Hawaiian or other Pacific Islander, non-Hispanic/Latino; 204 Two or more races, non-Hispanic/Latino). Average age 33. In 2016, 1,456 master's awarded. *Degree requirements:* For master's, thesis (for some programs). *Entrance requirements:* For master's, interview, minimum GPA of 2.5. Additional exam requirements/recommendations for international students: Required—TOEFL (minimum score 550 paper-based; 79 iBT), IELTS (minimum score 6). *Application deadline:* Applications are processed on a rolling basis. Application fee: $60 ($65 for international students). Electronic applications accepted. *Financial support:* Career-related internships or fieldwork, institutionally sponsored loans, scholarships/grants, and tuition waivers (partial) available. Support available to part-time students. Financial award application deadline: 6/30. *Faculty research:* Teacher education, special education, educational effectiveness, teaching abroad, school counseling. *Unit head:* School of Education, 800-628-8648, E-mail: soe@nu.edu. *Application contact:* Brandon Jouganatos, Vice President for Enrollment Services, 800-628-8648, E-mail: advisor@nu.edu.
Website: http://www.nu.edu/OurPrograms/SchoolOfEducation.html

Neumann University, Graduate Program in Education, Aston, PA 19014-1298. Offers education (MS), including administrative (principal K-12), autism, early elementary education, secondary education, special education. *Program availability:* Part-time, evening/weekend, 100% online, blended/hybrid learning. *Faculty:* 6 full-time (5 women), 18 part-time/adjunct (7 women). *Students:* 80 full-time (64 women), 108 part-time (91 women); includes 40 minority (30 Black or African American, non-Hispanic/Latino; 6 Hispanic/Latino; 4 Two or more races, non-Hispanic/Latino), 1 international. Average age 34. 152 applicants, 67% accepted, 82 enrolled. In 2016, 42 master's awarded. *Entrance requirements:* For master's, official transcripts from all institutions attended, letter of intent, three professional references, copy of any teaching certifications. Additional exam requirements/recommendations for international students: Required—TOEFL (minimum score 70 iBT). *Application deadline:* Applications are processed on a rolling basis. Application fee: $0. Electronic applications accepted. *Expenses:* $700 per credit on-campus tuition; $480 per credit online or off-campus tuition; additional $320 for student teaching course. *Financial support:* Scholarships/grants and health care benefits available. Support available to part-time students. Financial award application deadline: 3/15; financial award applicants required to submit FAFSA. *Unit head:* Dr. Stephanie Smith-Budhai, Director of Graduate Education, 610-358-4249, E-mail: budhais@neumann.edu. *Application contact:* Dr. Erika Davis, Director of Adult and Graduate Admissions, 800-9-NEUMANN Ext. 5208, Fax: 610-361-2548, E-mail: GradAdultAdmiss@neumann.edu.
Website: https://www.neumann.edu/academics/grad/education/index.asp

Neumann University, Program in Educational Leadership, Aston, PA 19014-1298. Offers educational leadership (Ed D), including PreK-12, superintendent's letter of eligibility. *Program availability:* Part-time, evening/weekend. *Faculty:* 3 full-time (1 woman), 2 part-time/adjunct (1 woman). *Students:* 43 part-time (25 women); includes 12 minority (11 Black or African American, non-Hispanic/Latino; 1 Asian, non-Hispanic/Latino). Average age 41. 27 applicants, 44% accepted, 8 enrolled. In 2016, 6 doctorates awarded. *Degree requirements:* For doctorate, comprehensive exam, thesis/dissertation. *Entrance requirements:* For doctorate, master's degree, official transcripts from all institutions attended, resume or curriculum vitae, three official letters of recommendation, two essays. Additional exam requirements/recommendations for international students: Required—TOEFL (minimum score 70 iBT). *Application deadline:* For fall admission, 7/1 for domestic and international students. Applications are processed on a rolling basis. Application fee: $0. Electronic applications accepted. *Expenses:* $830 per credit. *Financial support:* Scholarships/grants and health care benefits available. Support available to part-time students. Financial award application deadline: 3/15; financial award applicants required to submit FAFSA. *Unit head:* Dr. Cynthia Speace, Director of Ed D Program, 610-358-4243, E-mail: speacec@neumann.edu. *Application contact:* Dr. Erika Davis, Director of Adult and Graduate Admissions, 800-9-NEUMANN Ext. 5208, Fax: 610-361-2548, E-mail: GradAdultAdmiss@neumann.edu.

New England College, Program in Education, Henniker, NH 03242-3293. Offers higher education administration (MS, Ed D); K-12 leadership (Ed D); literacy and language arts (M Ed); meeting the needs of all learners/special education (M Ed); teacher leadership/school reform (M Ed). *Program availability:* Part-time, evening/weekend.

New Jersey City University, Debra Cannon Partridge Wolfe College of Education, Department of Educational Leadership and Counseling, Jersey City, NJ 07305-1597. Offers counselor education (MA); educational administration and supervision (MA); urban education (MA). *Accreditation:* TEAC. *Program availability:* Part-time, evening/weekend. *Entrance requirements:* Additional exam requirements/recommendations for international students: Required—TOEFL (minimum score 79 iBT).

Newman University, Master of Science in Education Program, Wichita, KS 67213-2097. Offers building leadership (MS Ed); curriculum and instruction (MS Ed), including English as a second language, reading specialist; organizational leadership (MS Ed). *Accreditation:* NCATE. *Program availability:* Part-time, evening/weekend, online learning. *Degree requirements:* For master's, thesis optional. *Entrance requirements:* For master's, 3 years' full-time teaching experience, minimum GPA of 3.0, writing sample, 2 letters of recommendation, evidence of teaching certification. Additional exam requirements/recommendations for international students: Required—TOEFL (minimum score 600 paper-based; 100 iBT). Electronic applications accepted. *Expenses:* Contact institution. *Faculty research:* Online course design and deliver, staff engagement, classroom action.

New Mexico Highlands University, Graduate Studies, School of Education, Las Vegas, NM 87701. Offers curriculum and instruction (MA); educational leadership (MA); professional counseling (MA); special education (MA). *Accreditation:* NCATE. *Program availability:* Part-time. *Degree requirements:* For master's, comprehensive exam, thesis or alternative. *Entrance requirements:* For master's, minimum undergraduate GPA of 3.0. Additional exam requirements/recommendations for international students: Required—TOEFL (minimum score 540 paper-based). *Faculty research:* Middle school curriculum, integrated computer applications for pre-service classroom teachers, adolescent literacy, narrative cognitive modes in New Mexico multicultural setting, math and math education.

New Mexico State University, College of Education, Department of Educational Leadership and Administration, Las Cruces, NM 88003. Offers educational administration (MA), including community college and university administration, PK-12 public school administration; educational leadership (Ed D, PhD). *Accreditation:* NCATE. *Program availability:* Part-time-only, evening/weekend, blended/hybrid learning. *Faculty:* 7 full-time (5 women), 1 part-time/adjunct (0 women). *Students:* 18 full-time (15 women), 110 part-time (82 women); includes 83 minority (2 Black or African American, non-Hispanic/Latino; 7 American Indian or Alaska Native, non-Hispanic/Latino; 4 Asian, non-Hispanic/Latino; 68 Hispanic/Latino; 1 Native Hawaiian or other Pacific Islander, non-Hispanic/Latino; 1 Two or more races, non-Hispanic/Latino), 3 international. Average age 41. 22 applicants, 27% accepted, 6 enrolled. In 2016, 24 master's, 6 doctorates awarded. *Degree requirements:* For master's, comprehensive exam, thesis optional, internship; for doctorate, comprehensive exam, thesis/dissertation, internship. *Entrance requirements:* For master's, minimum GPA of 3.0, current U.S. teaching license, and minimum 3 years of teaching in PK-12 sector (for PK-12 public school administration); minimum bachelor's degree GPA of 3.0 (for community college and university administration); for doctorate, minimum GPA of 3.0, master's degree. Additional exam requirements/recommendations for international students: Required—TOEFL (minimum score 550 paper-based; 79 iBT), IELTS (minimum score 6.5). *Application deadline:* For spring admission, 11/15 for domestic and international students. Application fee: $40 ($50 for international students). Electronic applications accepted. *Expenses:* Tuition, state resident: full-time $4086. Tuition, nonresident: full-time $14,254. *Required fees:* $853. Tuition and fees vary according to course load. *Financial support:* In 2016–17, 14 students received support, including 1 research assistantship (averaging $17,368 per year), 2 teaching assistantships (averaging $17,166 per year); career-related internships or fieldwork, Federal Work-Study, scholarships/grants, traineeships, health care benefits, and unspecified assistantships also available. Support available to part-time students. Financial award application deadline: 3/1. *Faculty research:* Leadership in PK-12 and postsecondary education, community college administration, distance education administration, leadership for social justice, educational change. *Total annual research expenditures:* $2,656. *Unit head:* Dr. Azadeh Osanloo, Department Head, 575-646-5976, Fax: 575-646-4767, E-mail: azadeh@nmsu.edu. *Application contact:* Denise Rodgiguez-Strawn, 575-646-3825, Fax: 575-646-4767, E-mail: edmandev@nmsu.edu.
Website: http://ela.nmsu.edu/

New York University, Steinhardt School of Culture, Education, and Human Development, Department of Administration, Leadership, and Technology, Program in Educational Leadership, New York, NY 10012. Offers educational leadership (Ed D, PhD); educational leadership, politics and advocacy (MA); school building leader (MA); school district leader (Advanced Certificate). *Program availability:* Part-time, evening/weekend. *Degree requirements:* For master's, thesis (for some programs); for doctorate, thesis/dissertation. *Entrance requirements:* For doctorate, GRE General Test, interview; for Advanced Certificate, master's degree. Additional exam requirements/recommendations for international students: Required—TOEFL (minimum score 100 iBT). Electronic applications accepted. *Faculty research:* Schools and communities; critical theories of race, class and gender; school restructuring; educational reform; social organization of schools, educational advocacy.

New York University, Steinhardt School of Culture, Education, and Human Development, Department of Administration, Leadership, and Technology, Program in Higher Education, New York, NY 10012. Offers higher and postsecondary education (PhD); higher education administration (Ed D); higher education and student affairs (MA). *Accreditation:* TEAC. *Program availability:* Part-time. *Degree requirements:* For master's, thesis (for some programs); for doctorate, thesis/dissertation. *Entrance requirements:* For master's, interview, 2 letters of recommendation; for doctorate, GRE General Test, interview. Additional exam requirements/recommendations for international students: Required—TOEFL (minimum score 100 iBT). Electronic applications accepted. *Faculty research:* Organizational theory and culture, systemic change, leadership development, access, equity and diversity.

Niagara University, Graduate Division of Education, Concentration in Educational Leadership, Niagara University, NY 14109. Offers school building leader (MS Ed); school district business leader (Certificate); school district leader (MS Ed, Certificate). *Program availability:* Part-time, evening/weekend, 100% online. *Students:* 40 full-time (24 women), 109 part-time (69 women); includes 21 minority (10 Black or African American, non-Hispanic/Latino; 2 Asian, non-Hispanic/Latino; 5 Hispanic/Latino; 4 Two or more races, non-Hispanic/Latino), 32 international. Average age 39. In 2016, 22 master's, 14 Certificates awarded. *Entrance requirements:* For master's, GRE General Test or MAT; for Certificate, GRE General Test and GRE Subject Test or MAT. Additional exam requirements/recommendations for international students: Required—TOEFL (minimum score 550 paper-based; 79 iBT), IELTS (minimum score 6). *Application deadline:* For fall admission, 8/1 for domestic students. Applications are processed on a rolling basis. Application fee: $30. *Expenses:* Contact institution. *Financial support:* In 2016–17, 1 research assistantship with tuition reimbursement was awarded; teaching assistantships with tuition reimbursements, career-related internships or fieldwork, Federal Work-Study, scholarships/grants, and unspecified assistantships also available. Support available to part-time students. Financial award application deadline: 4/15; financial award applicants required to submit FAFSA. *Unit head:* Dr. Kristine Augustyniak, Chair, 716-286-8548, E-mail: kma@niagara.edu. *Application contact:* Evan Pierce, Associate Director, Graduate Studies, 716-286-8327, E-mail: epierce@niagara.edu.
Website: http://www.niagara.edu/educational-leadership-online

Nicholls State University, Graduate Studies, College of Education, Department of Teacher Education, Thibodaux, LA 70310. Offers curriculum and instruction (M Ed); educational leadership (M Ed); elementary education (MAT); human performance education (MAT); middle school education (MAT); secondary education (MAT). *Accreditation:* NCATE. *Program availability:* Part-time, evening/weekend, online learning. *Degree requirements:* For master's, comprehensive exam, portfolio. *Entrance requirements:* For master's, GRE General Test, teaching license. Electronic applications accepted.

Norfolk State University, School of Graduate Studies, School of Education, Department of Secondary Education and School Leadership, Norfolk, VA 23504. Offers principal preparation (MA); secondary education (MAT); urban education/administration (MA), including teaching. *Accreditation:* NCATE. *Program availability:* Part-time. *Entrance requirements:* For master's, GRE General Test, PRAXIS I, minimum GPA of 3.0 in major, 2.5 overall. Additional exam requirements/recommendations for international students: Required—TOEFL (minimum score 500 paper-based).

North American University, Program in Educational Leadership, Stafford, TX 77477. Offers M Ed.

North Carolina Agricultural and Technical State University, School of Graduate Studies, School of Education, Department of Human Development and Services, Greensboro, NC 27411. Offers adult education (MS); counseling (MS); school administration (MS). *Accreditation:* ACA. *Program availability:* Part-time, evening/weekend. *Degree requirements:* For master's, comprehensive exam, thesis, qualifying exam. *Entrance requirements:* For master's, GRE General Test, minimum GPA of 3.0.

North Carolina Central University, School of Education, Program in School Administration, Durham, NC 27707-3129. Offers MSA.

North Carolina State University, Graduate School, College of Education, Department of Adult and Higher Education, Program in Higher Education Administration, Raleigh, NC 27695. Offers M Ed, MS, Ed D. *Degree requirements:* For master's, thesis (for some programs); for doctorate, thesis/dissertation. *Entrance requirements:* For master's and doctorate, GRE General Test or MAT, minimum GPA of 3.0 in major. Electronic applications accepted.

North Carolina State University, Graduate School, College of Education, Department of Educational Leadership and Policy Studies, Program in Educational Administration and Supervision, Raleigh, NC 27695. Offers Ed D. *Degree requirements:* For doctorate, thesis/dissertation. *Entrance requirements:* For doctorate, GRE General Test or MAT, minimum GPA of 3.0, interview, sample of work. Electronic applications accepted.

North Carolina State University, Graduate School, College of Education, Department of Educational Leadership and Policy Studies, Program in School Administration, Raleigh, NC 27695. Offers MSA. *Degree requirements:* For master's, comprehensive exam, thesis optional. *Entrance requirements:* For master's, GRE General Test or MAT, minimum GPA of 3.0 in major, 3 years of teaching experience. Electronic applications accepted. *Faculty research:* State and national policy, educational evaluation, cohort preparation programs.

North Central College, School of Graduate and Professional Studies, Program in Leadership Studies, Naperville, IL 60566-7063. Offers MLD. *Program availability:* Part-time, evening/weekend. *Faculty:* 8 full-time (5 women), 8 part-time/adjunct (4 women). *Students:* 38 full-time (22 women), 19 part-time (12 women); includes 12 minority (6 Black or African American, non-Hispanic/Latino; 4 Hispanic/Latino; 2 Two or more races, non-Hispanic/Latino), 2 international. Average age 26. 111 applicants, 46% accepted, 25 enrolled. In 2016, 33 master's awarded. *Degree requirements:* For master's, thesis optional, project. *Entrance requirements:* For master's, interview. Additional exam requirements/recommendations for international students: Required—TOEFL (minimum score 550 paper-based; 80 iBT), IELTS (minimum score 6.5). *Application deadline:* For fall admission, 8/15 for domestic students, 7/15 for international students; for winter admission, 12/1 for domestic students, 11/1 for international students; for spring admission, 2/1 for domestic students, 12/1 for international students. Applications are processed on a rolling basis. Application fee: $25. Electronic applications accepted. Application fee is waived when completed online. *Expenses:* Contact institution. *Financial support:* Scholarships/grants available. Support available to part-time students. Financial award applicants required to submit FAFSA. *Unit head:* Dr. Pamela Monaco, Dean of Graduate and Professional Studies, 630-637-5384, E-mail: pjmonaco@noctrl.edu. *Application contact:* Wendy Kulpinski, Director of Graduate and Professional Studies Admission, 630-637-5808, Fax: 630-637-5844, E-mail: wekulpinski@noctrl.edu.

North Dakota State University, College of Graduate and Interdisciplinary Studies, College of Human Development and Education, School of Education, Program in Educational Leadership, Fargo, ND 58102. Offers M Ed, MS, Ed S. MS and Ed S offered jointly with Minnesota State University Moorhead. *Accreditation:* NCATE. *Program availability:* Part-time, evening/weekend, online learning. *Entrance requirements:* For degree, GRE General Test, master's degree, minimum GPA of 3.25. Additional exam requirements/recommendations for international students: Required—TOEFL. *Faculty research:* Organizational change and development, goal setting and systematic planning, beginning teacher assistance.

Northeastern Illinois University, College of Graduate Studies and Research, College of Education, Program in Human Resource Development, Chicago, IL 60625-4699. Offers educational leadership (MA); human resource development (MA). *Program availability:* Part-time, evening/weekend. *Degree requirements:* For master's, comprehensive papers. *Entrance requirements:* For master's, minimum GPA of 2.75, BA in human resource development. Additional exam requirements/recommendations for international students: Required—TOEFL (minimum score 550 paper-based; 79 iBT). Electronic applications accepted. *Faculty research:* Analogics, development of expertise, case-based instruction, action science organizational development, theoretical model building.

Northeastern Illinois University, College of Graduate Studies and Research, College of Education, Program in School Leadership, Chicago, IL 60625-4699. Offers educational administration and supervision (MA), including chief school business official, community college administration. *Program availability:* Part-time, evening/weekend. *Degree requirements:* For master's, comprehensive exam, practicum. *Entrance requirements:* For master's, 2 years of teaching experience, minimum GPA of 2.75. Additional exam requirements/recommendations for international students: Required—TOEFL (minimum score 550 paper-based; 79 iBT). Electronic applications accepted. *Faculty research:* Student motivation, leadership, teacher expectation, educational partnerships, community/school relations.

Northeastern State University, College of Education, Department of Educational Leadership, Program in Higher Education Leadership, Tahlequah, OK 74464-2399. Offers MS. *Faculty:* 8 full-time (6 women), 1 (woman) part-time/adjunct. *Students:* 7 full-time (all women), 25 part-time (20 women); includes 18 minority (3 Black or African American, non-Hispanic/Latino; 11 American Indian or Alaska Native, non-Hispanic/Latino; 1 Asian, non-Hispanic/Latino; 3 Two or more races, non-Hispanic/Latino), 1 international. Average age 34. In 2016, 26 master's awarded. *Degree requirements:* For master's, thesis. *Entrance requirements:* For master's, MAT or GRE. Additional exam requirements/recommendations for international students: Required—TOEFL. *Application deadline:* For fall admission, 6/1 priority date for domestic students. Applications are processed on a rolling basis. Application fee: $25. Electronic applications accepted. *Expenses:* Tuition, state resident: full-time $2816; part-time $216.60 per credit hour. Tuition, nonresident: full-time $6365; part-time $489.60 per credit hour. *Required fees:* $37.40 per credit hour. *Financial support:* Application deadline: 3/1. *Unit head:* Dr. Jim Ferrell, Department Chair, 918-444-3722, E-mail: ferrellj@nsuok.edu. *Application contact:* Josh McCollum, Graduate Coordinator, 918-444-2093, E-mail: mccolluj@nsuok.edu.
Website: http://academics.nsuok.edu/education/DegreePrograms/GraduatePrograms/HigherEducationLeadership.aspx

Northeastern State University, College of Education, Department of Educational Leadership, Program in Instructional Leadership, Tahlequah, OK 74464-2399. Offers M Ed. *Program availability:* Part-time, evening/weekend. *Faculty:* 11 full-time (8 women), 1 (woman) part-time/adjunct. *Students:* 6 full-time (4 women), 16 part-time (12 women); includes 11 minority (1 Black or African American, non-Hispanic/Latino; 5 American Indian or Alaska Native, non-Hispanic/Latino; 1 Asian, non-Hispanic/Latino; 4 Two or more races, non-Hispanic/Latino). Average age 35. In 2016, 9 master's awarded. *Degree requirements:* For master's, thesis. *Entrance requirements:* For master's, MAT or GRE. Additional exam requirements/recommendations for international students: Required—TOEFL. *Application deadline:* For fall admission, 7/1 priority date for domestic and international students; for spring admission, 10/1 priority date for domestic and international students. Applications are processed on a rolling basis. Application fee: $25. Electronic applications accepted. *Expenses:* Tuition, state resident: full-time $2816; part-time $216.60 per credit hour. Tuition, nonresident: full-time $6365; part-time $489.60 per credit hour. *Required fees:* $37.40 per credit hour. *Financial support:* Federal Work-Study available. Financial award application deadline: 3/1. *Unit head:* Dr. Jim Ferrell, Department Chair, 918-444-3722, E-mail: ferrellj@nsuok.edu. *Application contact:* Josh McCollum, Graduate Coordinator, 918-444-2093, E-mail: mccolluj@nsuok.edu.

Northeastern State University, College of Education, Department of Educational Leadership, Program in School Administration, Tahlequah, OK 74464-2399. Offers M Ed. *Program availability:* Part-time, evening/weekend. *Faculty:* 8 full-time (6 women), 1 (woman) part-time/adjunct. *Students:* 16 full-time (13 women), 65 part-time (48 women); includes 28 minority (1 Black or African American, non-Hispanic/Latino; 17 American Indian or Alaska Native, non-Hispanic/Latino; 1 Asian, non-Hispanic/Latino; 1 Hispanic/Latino; 8 Two or more races, non-Hispanic/Latino). Average age 36. In 2016, 20 master's awarded. *Degree requirements:* For master's, thesis. *Entrance requirements:* For master's, MAT or GRE, minimum GPA of 3.0. Additional exam requirements/recommendations for international students: Required—TOEFL. *Application deadline:* For fall admission, 6/1 priority date for domestic students. Applications are processed on a rolling basis. Application fee: $25. Electronic applications accepted. *Expenses:* Tuition, state resident: full-time $2816; part-time $216.60 per credit hour. Tuition, nonresident: full-time $6365; part-time $489.60 per credit hour. *Required fees:* $37.40 per credit hour. *Financial support:* Teaching assistantships and Federal Work-Study available. Financial award application deadline: 3/1. *Unit head:* Dr. Jim Ferrell, Department Chair, 918-444-3722, E-mail: ferrellj@nsuok.edu. *Application contact:* Josh McCollum, Graduate Coordinator, 918-444-2093, E-mail: mccolluj@nsuok.edu.
Website: http://academics.nsuok.edu/education/DegreePrograms/GraduatePrograms/SchoolAdministration.aspx

Northeastern University, College of Professional Studies, Boston, MA 02115-5096. Offers applied nutrition (MS); college athletics administration (MSL); commerce and economic development (MS); corporate and organizational communication (MS); criminal justice (MS); digital media (MPS); elearning and instructional design (M Ed); elementary education (MAT); geographic information technology (MPS); global studies and international relations (MS); higher education administration (M Ed); homeland security (MA); human services (MS); informatics (MPS); leadership (MS); learning analytics (M Ed); learning and instruction (M Ed); nonprofit management (MS); professional sports administration (MSL); project management (MS); regulatory affairs for drugs, biologics, and medical devices (MS); respiratory care leadership (MS); special education (M Ed); technical communication (MS). *Program availability:* Part-time, evening/weekend, 100% online, blended/hybrid learning. *Faculty:* 82 full-time (51 women), 853 part-time/adjunct (366 women). *Students:* 4,947 part-time (3,076 women). In 2016, 1,456 master's awarded. *Application deadline:* Applications are processed on a rolling basis. Application fee: $0. Electronic applications accepted. *Expenses:* Contact institution. *Financial support:* Applicants required to submit FAFSA. *Unit head:* Dr. Mary Loeffelholz, Interim Dean of the College of Professional Studies.
Website: http://www.cps.neu.edu/

Northern Arizona University, Graduate College, College of Education, Department of Educational Leadership, Flagstaff, AZ 86011. Offers community college teaching and learning (Certificate); community college/higher education (M Ed); educational foundations (M Ed); educational leadership (M Ed, Ed D); principal (Certificate); principal K-12 (M Ed); school leadership K-12 (M Ed); superintendent (Certificate). *Program availability:* Part-time. *Degree requirements:* For master's, comprehensive exam, thesis (for some programs); for doctorate, comprehensive exam, thesis/dissertation. *Entrance requirements:* For master's, minimum GPA of 3.0; for doctorate, GRE or MAT, minimum GPA of 3.5. Additional exam requirements/recommendations for international students: Required—TOEFL (minimum score 550 paper-based; 80 iBT), IELTS (minimum score 7). Electronic applications accepted. *Expenses:* Tuition, state resident: full-time $8971; part-time $444 per credit hour. Tuition, nonresident: full-time $20,958; part-time $1164 per credit hour. *Required fees:* $1018; $644 per credit hour. Tuition and fees vary according to course load, campus/location and program.

Northern Illinois University, Graduate School, College of Education, Department of Leadership, Educational Psychology and Foundations, De Kalb, IL 60115-2854. Offers educational administration (MS Ed, Ed D, Ed S); educational psychology (MS Ed, Ed D); foundations of education (MS Ed); school business management (MS Ed). *Program availability:* Part-time, evening/weekend, online learning. *Faculty:* 23 full-time (12 women). *Students:* 13 full-time (8 women), 230 part-time (133 women); includes 33 minority (13 Black or African American, non-Hispanic/Latino; 3 Asian, non-Hispanic/Latino; 9 Hispanic/Latino; 8 Two or more races, non-Hispanic/Latino), 4 international. Average age 39. 132 applicants, 43% accepted, 31 enrolled. In 2016, 36 master's, 30 doctorates, 17 other advanced degrees awarded. *Degree requirements:* For master's, comprehensive exam, thesis optional; for doctorate, thesis/dissertation, candidacy exam, dissertation defense. *Entrance requirements:* For master's, minimum undergraduate GPA of 2.75; for doctorate, GRE General Test, minimum undergraduate GPA of 2.75, 3.2 graduate; for Ed S, GRE General Test, minimum GPA of 2.75 (undergraduate), 3.2 (graduate). Additional exam requirements/recommendations for international students: Required—TOEFL (minimum score 550 paper-based). *Application deadline:* For fall admission, 6/1 for domestic students, 5/1 for international students; for spring admission, 11/1 for domestic students, 10/1 for international students. Applications are processed on a rolling basis. Application fee: $40. Electronic applications accepted. *Financial support:* In 2016–17, 4 research assistantships with full tuition reimbursements, 2 teaching assistantships with full tuition reimbursements were awarded; fellowships with full tuition reimbursements, career-related internships or fieldwork, Federal Work-Study, scholarships/grants, tuition waivers (full), and staff assistantships also available. Support available to part-time students. Financial award applicants required to submit FAFSA. *Faculty research:* Interpersonal forgiveness, learner-centered education, psychedelic studies, senior theory, professional growth. *Unit head:* Carolyn V. Schee, Chair, 815-753-4404, E-mail: lepf@niu.edu. *Application contact:* Graduate School Office, 815-753-0395, E-mail: gradsch@niu.edu.
Website: http://cedu.niu.edu/LEPF/

Northern Illinois University, Graduate School, College of Education, Department of Special and Early Education, De Kalb, IL 60115-2854. Offers curriculum and instruction (MS Ed, Ed D), including curriculum leadership (Ed D), elementary education (Ed D), secondary education (Ed D); early childhood education (MS Ed); elementary education (MS Ed); special education (MS Ed). *Program availability:* Part-time, evening/weekend. *Faculty:* 22 full-time (14 women), 2 part-time/adjunct (both women). *Students:* 42 full-time (34 women), 85 part-time (68 women); includes 16 minority (4 Black or African American, non-Hispanic/Latino; 3 Asian, non-Hispanic/Latino; 6 Hispanic/Latino; 3 Two or more races, non-Hispanic/Latino), 6 international. Average age 33. 70 applicants, 73% accepted, 30 enrolled. In 2016, 19 master's, 1 doctorate awarded. *Degree requirements:* For master's, comprehensive exam, thesis optional; for doctorate, thesis/dissertation, candidacy exam, dissertation defense. *Entrance requirements:* For master's, GRE General Test or MAT, minimum undergraduate GPA of 2.75; for doctorate, GRE General Test or MAT, minimum undergraduate GPA of 2.75, graduate 3.2. Additional exam requirements/recommendations for international students: Required—TOEFL (minimum score 550 paper-based). *Application deadline:* For fall admission, 6/1 for domestic students, 5/1 for international students; for spring admission, 11/1 for domestic students, 10/1 for international students. Applications are processed on a rolling basis. Application fee: $40. Electronic applications accepted. *Financial support:* In 2016–17, 14 research assistantships with full tuition reimbursements were awarded; fellowships with full tuition reimbursements, teaching assistantships with full tuition reimbursements, career-related internships or fieldwork, Federal Work-Study, scholarships/grants, tuition waivers (full), and unspecified assistantships also available. Support available to part-time students. Financial award applicants required to submit FAFSA. *Faculty research:* Teacher certification, stress reduction during student teaching, teaching history, portfolios in student teaching. *Unit head:* Gregory Conderman, Chair, 815-753-1619, E-mail: seed@niu.edu. *Application contact:* Gail Myers, Clerk, Graduate Advising, 815-753-0381, E-mail: gmyers@niu.edu. Website: http://www.cedu.niu.edu/seed/

Northern Kentucky University, Office of Graduate Programs, College of Education and Human Services, Doctor of Education in Educational Leadership Program, Highland Heights, KY 41099. Offers Ed D. *Program availability:* Part-time, evening/weekend. *Entrance requirements:* For doctorate, master's (or specialist) degree in education or a related field; minimum GPA of 3.25; five or more years of educational leadership experience; letter describing educational and leadership background, goals, style, and philosophy; professional vitae; leadership situation account; 3 letters of recommendation; interview. Additional exam requirements/recommendations for international students: Required—TOEFL (minimum score 79 iBT); Recommended—IELTS (minimum score 6.5). Electronic applications accepted. *Faculty research:* Educator dispositions, civic engagement and service-learning in education, school leadership, technology in education, professional development.

Northern Kentucky University, Office of Graduate Programs, College of Education and Human Services, Education Program: Teacher as a Leader, Highland Heights, KY 41099. Offers MA, Certificate. *Program availability:* Part-time, evening/weekend, online learning. *Degree requirements:* For master's, thesis optional, portfolio. *Entrance requirements:* For master's, GRE, teacher certification, bachelor's degree in appropriate subject area, minimum GPA of 2.5, 3 letters of recommendation, 1 year of teaching experience, statement of personal goals. Additional exam requirements/recommendations for international students: Required—TOEFL (minimum score 79 iBT); Recommended—IELTS (minimum score 6.5). Electronic applications accepted. *Faculty research:* Teaching with technology, middle school education, children with disabilities, teaching in the content areas, diversifying faculty.

Northern Kentucky University, Office of Graduate Programs, College of Education and Human Services, Education Specialist in Educational Leadership Program, Highland Heights, KY 41099. Offers Ed S. *Degree requirements:* For Ed S, capstone and two presentations. *Entrance requirements:* For degree, copy of valid teaching certificate showing successful completion of 3 years' full-time documented classroom teaching experience, official transcripts, 3 letters of recommendation, minimum GPA of 3.5, 3 essays, professional folio, interview. Additional exam requirements/recommendations for international students: Required—TOEFL (minimum score 79 iBT); Recommended—IELTS (minimum score 6.5). Electronic applications accepted.

Northern Michigan University, Office of Graduate Education and Research, College of Health Sciences and Professional Studies, School of Education, Leadership and Public Service, Marquette, MI 49855-5301. Offers administration and supervision (MAE); elementary education (MAE); higher education in student affairs (MA); instruction (MAE); learning disabilities (MAE); public administration (MPA), including criminal justice administration, human resource administration, public administration, public management, state and local government; reading education (MAE), including reading, reading specialist; science education (MS); secondary education (MAE). *Accreditation:* TEAC. *Program availability:* Part-time, online learning. *Degree requirements:* For master's, thesis (for some programs). *Entrance requirements:* For master's, minimum GPA of 3.0. Additional exam requirements/recommendations for international students: Required—TOEFL (minimum score 550 paper-based; 79 iBT), IELTS (minimum score 6.5). Electronic applications accepted.

Northern State University, MS Ed Program in Leadership and Administration, Aberdeen, SD 57401-7198. Offers MS Ed. *Accreditation:* NCATE. *Program availability:* Part-time, evening/weekend, online learning. *Degree requirements:* For master's, comprehensive exam, thesis optional. *Entrance requirements:* For master's, minimum GPA of 2.75. Additional exam requirements/recommendations for international students: Required—TOEFL (minimum score 550 paper-based; 78 iBT), IELTS (minimum score 6). Electronic applications accepted.

Northwestern College, Program in Education, Orange City, IA 51041-1996. Offers early childhood (M Ed); master teacher (M Ed); teacher leadership (M Ed, Graduate Certificate). *Program availability:* Online learning.

Northwestern Oklahoma State University, School of Professional Studies, Program in Educational Leadership, Alva, OK 73717-2799. Offers M Ed. *Program availability:* Part-time. *Degree requirements:* For master's, thesis optional, portfolio. *Entrance requirements:* For master's, GRE General Test or MAT, minimum GPA of 2.75.

Northwestern State University of Louisiana, Graduate Studies and Research, College of Education and Human Development, Programs in Educational Leadership and Instruction, Natchitoches, LA 71497. Offers counseling (Ed S); educational leadership (M Ed, Ed S); educational technology (Ed S); elementary teaching (Ed S); reading (Ed S); secondary teaching (Ed S); special education (Ed S). *Accreditation:* NASAD. *Degree requirements:* For master's, comprehensive exam, thesis (for some programs). *Entrance requirements:* For master's and Ed S, GRE General Test. Additional exam requirements/recommendations for international students: Required—TOEFL. Electronic applications accepted.

Northwestern University, The Graduate School, School of Education and Social Policy, Education and Social Policy Program, Evanston, IL 60035. Offers elementary teaching (MS); secondary teaching (MS); teacher leadership (MS). *Program availability:* Part-time, evening/weekend. *Degree requirements:* For master's, research project. *Entrance requirements:* For master's, GRE General Test, Illinois State Board of Education Basic Skills Exam (secondary and elementary), bachelor's degree. Additional exam requirements/recommendations for international students: Recommended—TOEFL. Electronic applications accepted. *Faculty research:* Cultural context and literacy, philosophy of education and interpretive discussion, productivity, enhancing research and teaching, motivation, new and junior faculty issues, professional development for K-12 teachers to improve math and science teaching, female/underrepresented students/faculty in STEM disciplines.

Northwest Missouri State University, Graduate School, School of Education, Maryville, MO 64468-6001. Offers early childhood education (MS Ed); education leadership (MS Ed), including elementary, K-12, secondary; educational leadership (Ed S), including elementary school principalship, secondary school principalship, superintendency; educational leadership and policy analysis (Ed D); elementary education (MS Ed); elementary mathematics (MS Ed); higher education leadership (MS); middle school education (MS Ed); reading (MS Ed); special education (MS Ed); teacher leadership (MS Ed); teaching English language learners (MS Ed). *Accreditation:* NCATE. *Program availability:* Part-time. *Students:* 15 full-time (11 women), 150 part-time (103 women). In 2016, 46 master's awarded. *Degree requirements:* For master's, comprehensive exam; for Ed S, comprehensive exam, thesis. *Entrance requirements:* For master's, GRE General Test, writing sample; for Ed S, minimum graduate GPA of 3.25. Additional exam requirements/recommendations for international students: Required—TOEFL (minimum score 550 paper-based). *Application deadline:* For fall admission, 7/1 for domestic and international students; for spring admission, 11/15 for domestic and international students. Applications are processed on a rolling basis. Application fee: $0 ($50 for international students). Electronic applications accepted. *Expenses:* Tuition, state resident: full-time $3447; part-time $383 per credit hour. Tuition, nonresident: full-time $5724; part-time $636 per credit hour. *Required fees:* $130 per credit hour. *Financial support:* Research assistantships with full tuition reimbursements, teaching assistantships with full tuition reimbursements, and unspecified assistantships available. Financial award application deadline: 4/1; financial award applicants required to submit FAFSA. *Faculty research:* Great books of educational administration. *Unit head:* Dr. Tim Wall, Dean, 660-562-1179, E-mail: timwall@nwmissouri.edu.
Website: http://www.nwmissouri.edu/academics/ed/

Northwest Nazarene University, Graduate Education Program, Nampa, ID 83686-5897. Offers curriculum and instruction (M Ed); educational leadership (M Ed, Ed D, PhD, Ed S), including building administrator (M Ed, Ed S), director of special education (Ed S), leadership and organizational development (Ed S), superintendent (Ed S). *Accreditation:* ACA (one or more programs are accredited); NCATE. *Program availability:* Part-time, online only, 100% online, 2-week face-to-face residency (for doctoral programs). *Faculty:* 4 full-time (3 women), 17 part-time/adjunct (6 women). *Students:* 112 full-time (72 women), 73 part-time (36 women); includes 19 minority (3 Black or African American, non-Hispanic/Latino; 2 Asian, non-Hispanic/Latino; 6 Hispanic/Latino; 1 Native Hawaiian or other Pacific Islander, non-Hispanic/Latino; 7 Two or more races, non-Hispanic/Latino), 5 international. Average age 39. 96 applicants, 72% accepted, 67 enrolled. In 2016, 59 master's, 13 doctorates, 33 other advanced degrees awarded. *Degree requirements:* For master's, comprehensive exam (for some programs), action research project; for doctorate, thesis/dissertation; for Ed S, comprehensive exam, research project. *Entrance requirements:* For master's, minimum undergraduate GPA of 3.0 overall or during final 30 semester credits, undergraduate degree, valid teaching certificate; for doctorate, Ed S or equivalent, minimum GPA of 3.5; for Ed S, undergraduate degree, valid teaching certificate. Additional exam requirements/recommendations for international students: Recommended—TOEFL. *Application deadline:* Applications are processed on a rolling basis. Application fee: $50. Electronic applications accepted. *Expenses:* Contact institution. *Financial support:* In 2016–17, research assistantships (averaging $5,000 per year) were awarded. Financial award application deadline: 1/15; financial award applicants required to submit FAFSA. *Faculty research:* Action research, cooperative learning, accountability, institutional accreditation. *Unit head:* Dr. Heidi Curtis, Chair, 208-467-8250, E-mail: hlcurtis@nnu.edu. *Application contact:* Charlene Brown, Admissions Counselor, 208-467-8492, Fax: 208-467-8384, E-mail: gradeducationinfo@nnu.edu.
Website: http://www.nnu.edu/graded/

Notre Dame de Namur University, Division of Academic Affairs, School of Education and Leadership, Program in School Administration, Belmont, CA 94002-1908. Offers MA. *Program availability:* Part-time, evening/weekend. *Degree requirements:* For master's, thesis optional, capstone course. *Entrance requirements:* For master's, interview, valid teaching credential, minimum 1 year of classroom teaching experience. Additional exam requirements/recommendations for international students: Required—TOEFL (minimum score 550 paper-based; 79 iBT). Electronic applications accepted.

Notre Dame of Maryland University, Graduate Studies, Leadership in Teaching Program, Baltimore, MD 21210-2476. Offers MA. *Entrance requirements:* For master's, interview, 1 year of teaching experience, minimum GPA of 3.0. Additional exam requirements/recommendations for international students: Required—TOEFL (minimum score 500 paper-based; 61 iBT). Electronic applications accepted.

Notre Dame of Maryland University, Graduate Studies, Program in Instructional Leadership for Changing Populations, Baltimore, MD 21210-2476. Offers PhD. *Entrance requirements:* Additional exam requirements/recommendations for international students: Required—TOEFL (minimum score 500 paper-based; 61 iBT).

Oakland City University, School of Education, Oakland City, IN 47660-1099. Offers educational leadership (Ed D); teaching (MA). *Accreditation:* NCATE. Terminal master's awarded for partial completion of doctoral program. *Degree requirements:* For master's, thesis; for doctorate, comprehensive exam, thesis/dissertation. *Entrance requirements:* For master's, MAT, minimum GPA of 3.0, interview, resume, letters of recommendation; for doctorate, MAT, GRE, minimum GPA of 3.2, interview, resume, letters of recommendation. *Expenses:* Contact institution. *Faculty research:* Assessment, cultural diversity, teacher education, education leadership.

Oakland University, Graduate Study and Lifelong Learning, School of Education and Human Services, Department of Organizational Leadership, Rochester, MI 48309-4401. Offers educational leadership (M Ed, PhD); higher education (Certificate); school administration (Ed S). *Entrance requirements:* Additional exam requirements/recommendations for international students: Required—TOEFL (minimum score 550 paper-based).

Oakland University, Graduate Study and Lifelong Learning, School of Education and Human Services, Department of Teacher Development and Educational Studies, Rochester, MI 48309-4401. Offers educational studies (M Ed); elementary education (MAT); secondary education (MAT); teaching and learning (Graduate Certificate). *Entrance requirements:* For master's, minimum GPA of 3.0. Electronic applications accepted.

Oglala Lakota College, Graduate Studies, Program in Educational Administration, Kyle, SD 57752-0490. Offers MA. *Program availability:* Part-time, evening/weekend. *Entrance requirements:* For master's, minimum GPA of 2.5.

Ohio Dominican University, Division of Education, Program in Educational Leadership, Columbus, OH 43219-2099. Offers M Ed. *Program availability:* Part-time, evening/weekend, 100% online, blended/hybrid learning. *Faculty:* 6 full-time (4 women), 6 part-time/adjunct (5 women). *Students:* 2 full-time (both women), 61 part-time (47 women); includes 6 minority (4 Black or African American, non-Hispanic/Latino; 1 Hispanic/Latino; 1 Two or more races, non-Hispanic/Latino), 2 international. Average age 32. 21 applicants, 67% accepted, 13 enrolled. In 2016, 15 master's awarded. *Entrance requirements:* For master's, bachelor's degree from regionally-accredited institution; teaching certificate/license; currently teaching or have access to an academic classroom. Additional exam requirements/recommendations for international students: Required—TOEFL (minimum score 550 paper-based), IELTS (minimum score 6.5). *Application deadline:* For fall admission, 8/15 for domestic students, 6/10 for international students; for spring admission, 1/4 for domestic students, 11/2 for international students; for summer admission, 5/30 for domestic students. Applications are processed on a rolling basis. Application fee: $25. Electronic applications accepted. *Expenses:* $529 per credit hour, $225 per semester fees. *Financial support:* Applicants required to submit FAFSA. *Unit head:* Dr. JoAnn Hohenbrink, Associate Professor/Chair of Education Division, 614-251-4759, E-mail: hohenbrj@ohiodominican.edu. *Application contact:* John W. Naughton, Director for Graduate Admissions, 614-251-4721, Fax: 614-

251-6654, E-mail: grad@ohiodominican.edu.
Website: http://www.ohiodominican.edu/academics/graduate/master-of-education/educational-leadership

The Ohio State University, Graduate School, College of Education and Human Ecology, Department of Educational Studies, Columbus, OH 43210. Offers M Ed, MA, PhD, Ed S. *Accreditation:* NCATE. *Program availability:* Part-time. *Faculty:* 52. *Students:* 322 full-time (222 women), 147 part-time (102 women); includes 98 minority (54 Black or African American, non-Hispanic/Latino; 15 Asian, non-Hispanic/Latino; 19 Hispanic/Latino; 10 Two or more races, non-Hispanic/Latino), 52 international. Average age 31. In 2016, 111 master's, 13 doctorates, 7 other advanced degrees awarded. *Degree requirements:* For master's, thesis optional; for doctorate, thesis/dissertation. *Entrance requirements:* For master's and doctorate, GRE General Test. Additional exam requirements/recommendations for international students: Required—TOEFL (minimum score 550 paper-based; 79 iBT), Michigan English Language Assessment Battery (minimum score 82); Recommended—IELTS (minimum score 7). *Application deadline:* For fall admission, 12/1 priority date for domestic and international students; for spring admission, 11/1 for domestic and international students; for summer admission, 3/1 for domestic and international students. Applications are processed on a rolling basis. Application fee: $60 ($70 for international students). Electronic applications accepted. *Financial support:* Fellowships with tuition reimbursements, research assistantships with tuition reimbursements, teaching assistantships with tuition reimbursements, Federal Work-Study, institutionally sponsored loans, and unspecified assistantships available. Support available to part-time students. *Unit head:* Dr. Eric Anderman, Chair and Professor, 614-688-5721, E-mail: anderman.1@osu.edu. *Application contact:* Deb Zabloudil, Director of Graduate Student Services, 614-688-4007, E-mail: zabloudil.1@osu.edu.
Website: http://ehe.osu.edu/educational-studies/

Ohio University, Graduate College, Gladys W. and David H. Patton College of Education and Human Services, Department of Educational Studies, Athens, OH 45701-2979. Offers computer education and technology (M Ed); educational administration (M Ed, Ed D); educational research and evaluation (M Ed, PhD); instructional technology (PhD). *Program availability:* Part-time, evening/weekend, online learning. *Degree requirements:* For master's, thesis or alternative; for doctorate, comprehensive exam, thesis/dissertation. *Entrance requirements:* For master's, GRE General Test (if GPA less than 2.9); for doctorate, GRE General Test, GRE Subject Test, minimum GPA of 2.9, work experience, 3 letters of reference, autobiography. Additional exam requirements/recommendations for international students: Required—TOEFL (minimum score 550 paper-based; 80 iBT) or IELTS (minimum score 6.5). *Application deadline:* For fall admission, 3/1 priority date for domestic and international students; for winter admission, 10/1 priority date for domestic and international students; for spring admission, 1/30 priority date for domestic students, 1/1 priority date for international students. Applications are processed on a rolling basis. Application fee: $50 ($55 for international students). Electronic applications accepted. *Financial support:* Research assistantships with full tuition reimbursements, teaching assistantships with full tuition reimbursements, Federal Work-Study, institutionally sponsored loans, tuition waivers (partial), and unspecified assistantships available. Financial award application deadline: 3/1. *Faculty research:* Race, class and gender; computer programs; development and organization theory; evaluation/development of instruments, leadership. *Unit head:* Dr. David Richard Moore, Chair, 740-597-1322, Fax: 740-593-0477, E-mail: moored3@ohio.edu. *Application contact:* Floyd J. Doney, Director of Student Affairs, 740-593-4400, Fax: 740-593-9310, E-mail: doney@ohio.edu.
Website: http://www.cehs.ohio.edu/academics/es/

Oklahoma State University, College of Education, School of Teaching and Curriculum Leadership, Stillwater, OK 74078. Offers MS, PhD. *Program availability:* Part-time. *Faculty:* 31 full-time (30 women), 28 part-time/adjunct (24 women). *Students:* 23 full-time (all women), 129 part-time (107 women); includes 40 minority (10 Black or African American, non-Hispanic/Latino; 4 American Indian or Alaska Native, non-Hispanic/Latino; 1 Asian, non-Hispanic/Latino; 7 Hispanic/Latino; 18 Two or more races, non-Hispanic/Latino), 5 international. Average age 37. 35 applicants, 89% accepted, 27 enrolled. In 2016, 58 master's, 10 doctorates awarded. *Degree requirements:* For master's, thesis or alternative; for doctorate, comprehensive exam, thesis/dissertation. *Entrance requirements:* For master's and doctorate, GRE or GMAT. Additional exam requirements/recommendations for international students: Required—TOEFL (minimum score 550 paper-based; 79 iBT). *Application deadline:* For fall admission, 3/1 priority date for international students; for spring admission, 8/1 priority date for international students. Applications are processed on a rolling basis. Application fee: $40 ($75 for international students). Electronic applications accepted. *Expenses:* Tuition, state resident: full-time $3775; part-time $209.70 per credit hour. Tuition, nonresident: full-time $14,851; part-time $825.05 per credit hour. *Required fees:* $2027; $112.60 per credit hour. Tuition and fees vary according to campus/location. *Financial support:* In 2016–17, 5 research assistantships (averaging $8,240 per year), 7 teaching assistantships (averaging $11,691 per year) were awarded; career-related internships or fieldwork, Federal Work-Study, scholarships/grants, health care benefits, tuition waivers (partial), and unspecified assistantships also available. Support available to part-time students. Financial award application deadline: 3/1; financial award applicants required to submit FAFSA. *Unit head:* Dr. Jennifer Sanders, Interim Department Head, 405-744-9214, Fax: 405-744-6290, E-mail: jenn.sanders10@okstate.edu.
Website: http://education.okstate.edu/stcl

Old Dominion University, Darden College of Education, Educational Leadership Services Programs, Norfolk, VA 23529. Offers educational leadership (MS Ed, PhD, Ed S). *Accreditation:* NCATE. *Program availability:* Part-time, evening/weekend, 100% online, blended/hybrid learning. *Faculty:* 5 full-time (1 woman), 14 part-time/adjunct (6 women). *Students:* 7 full-time (6 women), 195 part-time (141 women); includes 70 minority (55 Black or African American, non-Hispanic/Latino; 2 Asian, non-Hispanic/Latino; 6 Hispanic/Latino; 7 Two or more races, non-Hispanic/Latino). Average age 35. 42 applicants, 98% accepted, 34 enrolled. In 2016, 80 master's, 8 doctorates, 49 other advanced degrees awarded. *Degree requirements:* For master's and Ed S, comprehensive exam, thesis optional, internship, portfolio, school leadership licensure assessment; for doctorate, comprehensive exam, thesis/dissertation. *Entrance requirements:* For master's, minimum GPA of 3.0 in major, letters of recommendation, resume, 2 essays; for doctorate, GRE, minimum graduate GPA of 3.5, 3 letters of recommendation, essays, resume; for Ed S, minimum GPA of 3.0 in major, 2 letters of recommendation, essays, resume. Additional exam requirements/recommendations for international students: Required—TOEFL (minimum score 550 paper-based). *Application deadline:* For fall admission, 8/15 priority date for domestic students, 2/15 priority date for international students; for winter admission, 10/1 priority date for international students; for spring admission, 1/1 priority date for domestic students, 2/1 priority date for international students; for summer admission, 5/1 for domestic students. Applications are processed on a rolling basis. Application fee: $50. Electronic applications accepted. *Expenses:* Tuition, state resident: full-time $8604; part-time $478 per credit hour. Tuition, nonresident: full-time $21,510; part-time $1195 per credit hour. *Required fees:* $66 per semester. Tuition and fees vary according to campus/location, program and reciprocity agreements. *Financial support:* In 2016–17, 2 students received support, including 2 fellowships (averaging $7,500 per year); teaching assistantships, career-related internships or fieldwork, scholarships/grants, and tuition waivers also available. Support available to part-time students. Financial award application deadline: 2/15; financial award applicants required to submit FAFSA. *Faculty research:* Leadership preparation, supervision, policy studies, finance, learning sciences. *Total annual research expenditures:* $500,000. *Unit head:* Dr. Karen L. Sanzo, Graduate Program Director, 757-683-6698, Fax: 757-683-4413, E-mail: ksanzo@odu.edu. *Application contact:* William Heffelfinger, Director of Graduate Admissions, 757-683-5554, Fax: 757-683-3255, E-mail: gradadmit@odu.edu.
Website: https://www.odu.edu/efl/academics/els#.WO1RPbznsow

Olivet Nazarene University, Graduate School, Division of Education, Program in School Leadership, Bourbonnais, IL 60914. Offers MAE.

Oral Roberts University, School of Education, Tulsa, OK 74171. Offers Christian school administration (K-12) (MA Ed, Ed D); Christian school curriculum development (MA Ed); college and higher education administration (Ed D); public school administration (K-12) (MA Ed, Ed D); public school teaching (MA Ed). *Accreditation:* NCATE. *Program availability:* Part-time, online learning. *Degree requirements:* For master's, comprehensive exam, thesis optional; for doctorate, comprehensive exam, thesis/dissertation. *Entrance requirements:* For master's, GRE General Test or MAT, minimum GPA of 3.0; for doctorate, minimum GPA of 3.0. Additional exam requirements/recommendations for international students: Required—TOEFL (minimum score 500 paper-based). *Expenses:* Contact institution. *Faculty research:* Teacher effectiveness, college success in high achieving African-Americans, professional development practices.

Oregon State University, College of Education, Program in Adult and Higher Education, Corvallis, OR 97331. Offers Ed M, Ed D, PhD. *Accreditation:* NCATE. *Program availability:* Part-time, blended/hybrid learning. *Faculty:* 5 full-time (all women), 4 part-time/adjunct (2 women). *Students:* 2 full-time (both women), 34 part-time (25 women); includes 8 minority (2 Black or African American, non-Hispanic/Latino; 2 Asian, non-Hispanic/Latino; 2 Hispanic/Latino; 2 Two or more races, non-Hispanic/Latino). Average age 43. 36 applicants, 72% accepted, 22 enrolled. *Degree requirements:* For master's, thesis or alternative. *Entrance requirements:* For master's, minimum GPA of 3.0 in last 90 hours. Additional exam requirements/recommendations for international students: Required—TOEFL (minimum score 575 paper-based). *Application deadline:* For fall admission, 3/15 for domestic students. Applications are processed on a rolling basis. Application fee: $75 ($85 for international students). *Expenses:* Tuition, state resident: full-time $12,150; part-time $450 per credit. Tuition, nonresident: full-time $21,789; part-time $807 per credit. *Required fees:* $1651; $1507 per credit. One-time fee: $350. Tuition and fees vary according to course load, campus/location and program. *Financial support:* Research assistantships, teaching assistantships, career-related internships or fieldwork, Federal Work-Study, and institutionally sponsored loans available. Support available to part-time students. *Unit head:* Dr. Shelley Dubkin-Lee, Adult and Higher Education Graduate Programs Coordinator and Instructor, E-mail: shelley.dubkin-lee@oregonstate.edu.
Website: http://education.oregonstate.edu/adult-education-masters-degree-program

Ottawa University, Graduate Studies-Arizona, Program in Education, Ottawa, KS 66067-3399. Offers community college counseling (MA); curriculum and instruction (MA); early childhood (MA); education intervention (MA); education leadership (MA); education technology (MA); Montessori early childhood education (MA); Montessori elementary education (MA); professional development (MA); school guidance counseling (MA); special education - cross categorical (MA). Programs offered in Mesa, Phoenix, Tempe and West Valley, AZ. *Accreditation:* NCATE. *Program availability:* Part-time. *Degree requirements:* For master's, thesis or alternative. *Entrance requirements:* For master's, minimum undergraduate GPA of 3.0, copy of current state certification or teaching license. Additional exam requirements/recommendations for international students: Required—TOEFL (minimum score 550 paper-based). Electronic applications accepted. *Expenses:* Contact institution.

Park University, School of Graduate and Professional Studies, Kansas City, MO 54105. Offers adult education (M Ed); business and government leadership (Graduate Certificate); business, government, and global society (MPA); communication and leadership (MA); creative and life writing (Graduate Certificate); disaster and emergency management (MPA, Graduate Certificate); educational leadership (M Ed); finance (MBA, Graduate Certificate); general business (MBA); global business (Graduate Certificate); healthcare administration (MHA); healthcare services management and leadership (Graduate Certificate); international business (MBA); language and literacy (M Ed), including English for speakers of other languages, special reading teacher/literacy coach; leadership of international healthcare organizations (Graduate Certificate); management information systems (MBA, Graduate Certificate); music performance (ADP, Graduate Certificate), including cello (MM, ADP), piano (MM, ADP), viola (MM, ADP), violin (MM, ADP); nonprofit and community services management (MPA); nonprofit leadership (Graduate Certificate); performance (MM), including cello (MM, ADP), piano (MM, ADP), viola (MM, ADP), violin (MM, ADP); public management (MPA); social work (MSW); teacher leadership (M Ed), including curriculum and assessment, instructional leader. *Program availability:* Part-time, evening/weekend, online learning. *Degree requirements:* For master's, comprehensive exam (for some programs), thesis (for some programs), internship (for some programs); exam (for some programs). *Entrance requirements:* For master's, GRE or GMAT (for some programs), teacher certification (for some M Ed programs), letters of recommendation, essay, resume (for some programs). Additional exam requirements/recommendations for international students: Required—TOEFL (minimum score 550 paper-based; 79 iBT), IELTS (minimum score 6). Electronic applications accepted.

Penn State University Park, Graduate School, College of Education, Department of Education Policy Studies, University Park, PA 16802. Offers educational leadership (M Ed, D Ed, PhD, Certificate); educational theory and policy (MA, PhD); higher education (M Ed, MS, D Ed, PhD). *Accreditation:* NCATE. *Program availability:* Online learning. *Unit head:* Dr. David H. Monk, Dean, 814-865-2523, Fax: 814-865-0555. *Application contact:* Lori Hawn, Director, Graduate Student Services, 814-865-1795, Fax: 814-863-4627, E-mail: l-gswww@lists.psu.edu.
Website: http://ed.psu.edu/eps

Pensacola Christian College, Graduate Studies, Pensacola, FL 32503-2267. Offers business administration (MBA); curriculum and instruction (MS, Ed D, Ed S); dramatics (MFA); educational leadership (MS, Ed D, Ed S); graphic design (MA, MFA); music (MA); nursing (MSN); performance studies (MA); studio art (MA, MFA).

Pepperdine University, Graduate School of Education and Psychology, Division of Education, Los Angeles, CA 90045. Offers administration and preliminary administrative services (MS); education (MA); educational leadership, administration, and policy (Ed D); global leadership and change (PhD); learning technologies (MA, Ed D); organizational leadership (Ed D); social entrepreneurship and change (MA); teaching (MA); teaching: TESOL (MA). *Program availability:* Part-time, evening/weekend, online learning. *Students:* 262 full-time (169 women), 385 part-time (264 women); includes 286 minority (123 Black or African American, non-Hispanic/Latino; 4 American Indian or Alaska Native, non-Hispanic/Latino; 59 Asian, non-Hispanic/Latino; 77 Hispanic/Latino; 6 Native Hawaiian or other Pacific Islander, non-Hispanic/Latino; 17 Two or more races,

non-Hispanic/Latino), 46 international. Average age 38. 372 applicants, 95% accepted, 200 enrolled. In 2016, 142 master's, 66 doctorates awarded. *Degree requirements:* For doctorate, thesis/dissertation. *Entrance requirements:* For master's, GRE General Test; for doctorate, GRE General Test, MAT. Additional exam requirements/recommendations for international students: Required—TOEFL. *Application deadline:* Applications are processed on a rolling basis. Application fee: $55. *Expenses:* $1,165 per unit (for master's); $1,460 per unit (for doctorate). *Financial support:* Research assistantships, teaching assistantships, career-related internships or fieldwork, institutionally sponsored loans, and scholarships/grants available. Support available to part-time students. Financial award application deadline: 7/1; financial award applicants required to submit FAFSA. *Unit head:* Dr. Martine Jago, Associate Dean, Education Division, 310-568-2828, E-mail: martine.jago@pepperdine.edu. *Application contact:* Chris Costa, Director of Enrollment, 310-568-2850, E-mail: chris.costa@pepperdine.edu.
Website: http://gsep.pepperdine.edu/masters-education/

Piedmont International University, Graduate School, Winston-Salem, NC 27101-5197. Offers Biblical studies (PhD); curriculum and instruction (M Ed); divinity (M Div); educational leadership (M Ed); leadership (MA, PhD); ministry (MA Min, D Min); non-language track (MABS); PhD preparation track (MABS). *Program availability:* Part-time, online learning. Terminal master's awarded for partial completion of doctoral program. *Degree requirements:* For master's, 2 foreign languages, comprehensive exam, thesis or alternative; for doctorate, 2 foreign languages, comprehensive exam. *Entrance requirements:* For master's, GRE General Test; for doctorate, Hebrew and Greek proficiency, MA. Additional exam requirements/recommendations for international students: Required—TOEFL (minimum score 500 paper-based; 60 iBT). Electronic applications accepted. *Faculty research:* Theological and biblical studies.

Pittsburg State University, Graduate School, College of Education, Department of Teaching and Leadership, Advanced Studies in Leadership Program, Pittsburg, KS 66762. Offers advanced studies in leadership (Ed S), including general school administration, special education. *Program availability:* Part-time, online only, 100% online. *Students:* 16. In 2016, 11 Ed Ss awarded. *Degree requirements:* For Ed S, thesis optional. *Entrance requirements:* Additional exam requirements/recommendations for international students: Required—TOEFL (minimum score 520 paper-based; 68 iBT), IELTS (minimum score 6), PTE (minimum score 47). *Application deadline:* For fall admission, 6/1 for international students; for spring admission, 10/15 for international students; for summer admission, 4/1 for international students. Applications are processed on a rolling basis. Application fee: $35 ($65 for international students). Electronic applications accepted. *Expenses:* Contact institution. *Financial support:* Application deadline: 2/1; applicants required to submit FAFSA. *Unit head:* Dr. Brenda Roberts, Program Coordinator, 620-235-4498, Fax: 620-235-4520, E-mail: broberts@pittstate.edu. *Application contact:* Lisa Allen, Assistant Director of Graduate and Continuing Studies, 620-235-4218, Fax: 620-235-4219, E-mail: lallen@pittstate.edu.

Pittsburg State University, Graduate School, College of Education, Department of Teaching and Leadership, Program in Educational Leadership, Pittsburg, KS 66762. Offers MS. *Program availability:* Part-time-only, online only, 100% online. *Students:* 105. In 2016, 42 master's awarded. Terminal master's awarded for partial completion of doctoral program. *Degree requirements:* For master's, thesis optional. *Entrance requirements:* Additional exam requirements/recommendations for international students: Required—TOEFL (minimum score 520 paper-based; 68 iBT), IELTS (minimum score 6), PTE (minimum score 47). *Application deadline:* For fall admission, 7/15 for domestic students, 6/1 for international students; for spring admission, 12/15 for domestic students, 10/15 for international students; for summer admission, 5/15 for domestic students, 4/1 for international students. Applications are processed on a rolling basis. Electronic applications accepted. *Expenses:* Contact institution. *Financial support:* Application deadline: 2/1; applicants required to submit FAFSA. *Unit head:* Dr. Brenda Roberts, Program Coordinator, 620-235-4498, Fax: 620-235-4520, E-mail: broberts@pittstate.edu. *Application contact:* Lisa Allen, Assistant Director of Graduate and Continuing Studies, 620-235-4223, Fax: 620-235-4219, E-mail: lallen@pittstate.edu.

Plymouth State University, College of Graduate Studies, Graduate Studies in Education, Certificate of Advanced Graduate Studies Programs, Plymouth, NH 03264-1595. Offers clinical mental health counseling (CAGS); educational leadership (CAGS); higher education (CAGS); school psychology (CAGS). *Program availability:* Part-time, evening/weekend.

Plymouth State University, College of Graduate Studies, Graduate Studies in Education, Program in Educational Leadership, Plymouth, NH 03264-1595. Offers M Ed. *Accreditation:* NCATE. *Program availability:* Part-time, evening/weekend. *Degree requirements:* For master's, thesis optional, PRAXIS. *Entrance requirements:* For master's, MAT, minimum GPA of 3.0.

Point Loma Nazarene University, School of Education, Program in Education, San Diego, CA 92106-2899. Offers counseling and guidance (MA); educational administration (MA); leadership in learning (MA). *Program availability:* Part-time, evening/weekend. *Students:* 68 full-time (50 women), 146 part-time (116 women); includes 124 minority (8 Black or African American, non-Hispanic/Latino; 12 Asian, non-Hispanic/Latino; 96 Hispanic/Latino; 1 Native Hawaiian or other Pacific Islander, non-Hispanic/Latino; 7 Two or more races, non-Hispanic/Latino), 4 international. Average age 34. 91 applicants, 86% accepted, 67 enrolled. In 2016, 85 master's awarded. *Entrance requirements:* For master's, interview, letters of recommendation, essay. Additional exam requirements/recommendations for international students: Required—TOEFL. *Application deadline:* For fall admission, 8/4 priority date for domestic students; for spring admission, 12/8 priority date for domestic students; for summer admission, 4/12 priority date for domestic students. Applications are processed on a rolling basis. Application fee: $50. Electronic applications accepted. *Expenses:* $610 per credit (for San Diego campus), $595 per credit (for Bakersfield campus). *Financial support:* Federal Work-Study and scholarships/grants available. Support available to part-time students. Financial award applicants required to submit FAFSA. *Unit head:* Conni Campbell, Associate Dean of the School of Education, 619-849-2532, Fax: 619-849-2532, E-mail: connicampbell@pointloma.edu. *Application contact:* Claire Buckley, Director of Graduate Admission, 866-692-4723, E-mail: gradinfo@pointloma.edu.
Website: http://gps.pointloma.edu/education

Point Park University, Center for Innovative Learning, Pittsburgh, PA 15222-1984. Offers community engagement (PhD); leadership and administration (Ed D).

Point Park University, School of Arts and Sciences, Department of Education, Pittsburgh, PA 15222-1984. Offers curriculum and instruction (MA); educational administration (MA); special education (M Ed); teaching and leadership (M Ed). *Program availability:* Part-time, evening/weekend. *Degree requirements:* For master's, comprehensive exam (for some programs), thesis or alternative. *Entrance requirements:* For master's, minimum GPA of 3.0, resume, 2 letters of recommendation. Additional exam requirements/recommendations for international students: Required—TOEFL. Electronic applications accepted.

Pontifical Catholic University of Puerto Rico, College of Education, Program in Educational Leadership and Administration, Ponce, PR 00717-0777. Offers PhD.

Post University, Program in Education, Waterbury, CT 06723-2540. Offers education (M Ed); higher education administration (M Ed); instructional design and technology (M Ed); online teaching (M Ed); teaching and learning (M Ed); TESOL (teaching English to speakers of other languages) (M Ed). *Program availability:* Online learning.

Prairie View A&M University, College of Education, Department of Educational Leadership and Counseling, Prairie View, TX 77446. Offers M Ed, MA, MS Ed, PhD. *Accreditation:* NCATE. *Program availability:* Part-time, evening/weekend. *Faculty:* 16 full-time (6 women), 10 part-time/adjunct (8 women). *Students:* 113 full-time (94 women), 318 part-time (250 women); includes 406 minority (383 Black or African American, non-Hispanic/Latino; 2 American Indian or Alaska Native, non-Hispanic/Latino; 1 Asian, non-Hispanic/Latino; 17 Hispanic/Latino; 3 Two or more races, non-Hispanic/Latino), 5 international. Average age 35. 270 applicants, 83% accepted, 176 enrolled. In 2016, 121 master's, 6 doctorates awarded. *Degree requirements:* For master's, thesis optional; for doctorate, comprehensive exam, thesis/dissertation. *Entrance requirements:* For master's, GRE General Test, 3 letters of reference, minimum undergraduate GPA of 2.5; for doctorate, GRE General Test, 3 letters of reference. Additional exam requirements/recommendations for international students: Required—TOEFL (minimum score 550 paper-based; 79 iBT). *Application deadline:* For fall admission, 5/1 priority date for domestic students, 5/1 for international students; for spring admission, 10/1 priority date for domestic students, 9/1 for international students; for summer admission, 3/1 for domestic students, 2/1 for international students. Applications are processed on a rolling basis. Application fee: $50. Electronic applications accepted. *Expenses:* Tuition, state resident: full-time $4362; part-time $273.48 per credit hour. Tuition, nonresident: full-time $12,390; part-time $534.10 per credit hour. *Required fees:* $2782; $178.26 per credit hour. *Financial support:* Career-related internships or fieldwork available. Support available to part-time students. Financial award application deadline: 4/1; financial award applicants required to submit FAFSA. *Faculty research:* Mentoring, personality assessment, holistic/humanistic education. *Unit head:* Dr. Abul Pitre, Department Head, 936-261-3530, Fax: 936-261-3617, E-mail: abpitre@pvamu.edu. *Application contact:* Pauline Walker, Administrative Assistant II, Research and Graduate Studies, 936-261-3521, Fax: 936-261-3529, E-mail: gradadmissions@pvamu.edu.

Prescott College, Graduate Programs, Program in Education, Prescott, AZ 86301. Offers early childhood education (MA); early childhood special education (MA); education (MA); elementary education (MA); environmental education leadership and administration (MA); equine-assisted learning (MA); school guidance counseling (MA); secondary education (MA); special education: learning disabilities (MA); special education: mental retardation (MA); special education: serious emotional disabilities (MA); student-directed independent study (MA); sustainability education (PhD). *Program availability:* Part-time, online learning. *Faculty:* 3 full-time (all women). *Students:* 9 full-time (8 women), 30 part-time (20 women); includes 11 minority (3 Black or African American, non-Hispanic/Latino; 2 American Indian or Alaska Native, non-Hispanic/Latino; 6 Hispanic/Latino). Average age 36. 66 applicants, 82% accepted, 32 enrolled. In 2016, 12 master's, 8 doctorates awarded. *Degree requirements:* For master's, thesis, fieldwork or internship, practicum; for doctorate, thesis/dissertation. *Entrance requirements:* For master's, 2 letters of recommendation, resume; for doctorate, 3 letters of recommendation, resume, official transcripts, personal statement, program proposal. Additional exam requirements/recommendations for international students: Required—TOEFL (minimum score 500 paper-based). *Application deadline:* For fall admission, 4/15 priority date for domestic and international students; for spring admission, 9/15 priority date for domestic and international students. Applications are processed on a rolling basis. Application fee: $40. Electronic applications accepted. *Expenses: Tuition:* Full-time $19,680. One-time fee: $260 part-time. *Financial support:* Fellowships, research assistantships, teaching assistantships, career-related internships or fieldwork, Federal Work-Study, institutionally sponsored loans, scholarships/grants, traineeships, health care benefits, tuition waivers, and unspecified assistantships available. Support available to part-time students. Financial award applicants required to submit FAFSA. *Unit head:* Bob Ellis, 928-350-2217, E-mail: bellis@prescott.edu. *Application contact:* Melanie Lefever, Assistant Director, Limited-residency Programs, 928-350-2106, Fax: 928-776-5242, E-mail: mlefever@prescott.edu.

Providence College, Programs in Administration, Providence, RI 02918. Offers elementary administration (M Ed); secondary administration (M Ed). *Program availability:* Part-time, evening/weekend. *Faculty:* 6 full-time (4 women), 33 part-time/adjunct (21 women). *Students:* 2 full-time (both women), 47 part-time (30 women); includes 3 minority (1 Asian, non-Hispanic/Latino; 2 Hispanic/Latino). Average age 37. 23 applicants, 100% accepted, 13 enrolled. In 2016, 16 master's awarded. *Degree requirements:* For master's, comprehensive exam, portfolio. *Entrance requirements:* Additional exam requirements/recommendations for international students: Required—TOEFL (minimum score 577 paper-based; 90 iBT). *Application deadline:* For fall admission, 7/15 priority date for domestic and international students; for spring admission, 11/15 priority date for domestic and international students; for summer admission, 3/15 priority date for domestic students, 3/15 for international students. Application fee: $55. *Expenses: Tuition:* Part-time $1260 per course. One-time fee: $265. Tuition and fees vary according to course load and program. *Financial support:* Career-related internships or fieldwork, institutionally sponsored loans, and unspecified assistantships available. Support available to part-time students. Financial award application deadline: 8/1; financial award applicants required to submit FAFSA. *Application contact:* Rev. Mark D. Nowel, Dean of Undergraduate and Graduate Studies, 401-865-2649, Fax: 401-865-1496, E-mail: mnowel@providence.edu.
Website: http://www.providence.edu/professional-studies/graduate-degrees/Pages/master-education-administration.aspx

Purdue University, Graduate School, College of Education, Department of Educational Studies, West Lafayette, IN 47907. Offers administration (MS Ed, PhD, Ed S); counseling and development (MS Ed, PhD); education of the gifted (MS Ed); educational psychology (MS Ed, PhD); foundations of education (MS Ed, PhD); higher education administration (MS Ed, PhD); special education (MS Ed, PhD). *Accreditation:* ACA (one or more programs are accredited); NCATE (one or more programs are accredited). *Program availability:* Part-time, evening/weekend. *Faculty:* 29 full-time (22 women), 1 part-time/adjunct (0 women). *Students:* 78 full-time (60 women), 226 part-time (162 women); includes 45 minority (16 Black or African American, non-Hispanic/Latino; 8 Asian, non-Hispanic/Latino; 15 Hispanic/Latino; 6 Two or more races, non-Hispanic/Latino), 45 international. Average age 32. 214 applicants, 53% accepted, 70 enrolled. In 2016, 38 master's, 20 doctorates, 4 other advanced degrees awarded. *Degree requirements:* For master's, thesis optional; for doctorate, thesis/dissertation, oral and written exams; for Ed S, oral presentation, project. *Entrance requirements:* For master's, GRE General Test (except for special education if undergraduate GPA is higher than a 3.0), minimum undergraduate GPA of 3.0; for doctorate and Ed S, GRE General Test (minimum combined score of 1000, 300 for new scoring), minimum undergraduate GPA of 3.0. Additional exam requirements/recommendations for international students: Required—TOEFL (minimum score 550 paper-based; 77 iBT), TWE (minimum score 5). *Application deadline:* Applications are processed on a rolling basis. Application fee: $60 ($75 for international students). Electronic applications accepted. *Financial support:* Fellowships with full tuition reimbursements, research assistantships with full tuition reimbursements, teaching assistantships with full tuition

reimbursements, career-related internships or fieldwork, and tuition waivers (full) available. Support available to part-time students. Financial award application deadline: 3/1; financial award applicants required to submit FAFSA. *Faculty research:* Motivation, learning disabilities, school learning, group processes, cognitive development. *Unit head:* F. Richard Olenchak, Head, 765-494-9170, E-mail: olenchak@purdue.edu. *Application contact:* Heather Brinkman, Graduate Contact, 765-494-2345, Fax: 765-494-5832, E-mail: hbrinkma@purdue.edu.
Website: http://www.edst.purdue.edu/

Purdue University Northwest, Graduate Studies Office, School of Education, Program in Educational Administration, Hammond, IN 46323-2094. Offers MS Ed. *Entrance requirements:* Additional exam requirements/recommendations for international students: Required—TOEFL.

Queens College of the City University of New York, Division of Education, Department of Educational and Community Programs, Queens, NY 11367-1597. Offers bilingual pupil personnel (AC); counselor education (MS Ed); mental health counseling (MS); school building leader (AC); school district leader (AC); school psychologist (MS Ed); special education-childhood education (AC); special education-early childhood (MS Ed); teacher of special education 1-6 (MS Ed); teacher of special education birth-2 (MS Ed); teaching students with disabilities, grades 7-12 (MS Ed, AC). *Program availability:* Part-time. *Faculty:* 20 full-time (14 women), 50 part-time/adjunct (26 women). *Students:* 101 full-time (85 women), 459 part-time (383 women); includes 230 minority (44 Black or African American, non-Hispanic/Latino; 3 American Indian or Alaska Native, non-Hispanic/Latino; 46 Asian, non-Hispanic/Latino; 128 Hispanic/Latino; 1 Native Hawaiian or other Pacific Islander, non-Hispanic/Latino; 8 Two or more races, non-Hispanic/Latino), 3 international. Average age 28. 515 applicants, 57% accepted, 230 enrolled. In 2016, 158 master's, 68 other advanced degrees awarded. *Degree requirements:* For master's, research project; for AC, internship. *Entrance requirements:* For master's, minimum GPA of 3.0. Additional exam requirements/recommendations for international students: Required—TOEFL, IELTS. *Application deadline:* For fall admission, 3/1 for domestic students. Applications are processed on a rolling basis. Application fee: $125. Electronic applications accepted. *Expenses:* Tuition, state resident: full-time $5065; part-time $425 per credit. Tuition, nonresident: part-time $780 per credit. *Required fees:* $522; $397 per credit. Part-time tuition and fees vary according to course load and program. *Financial support:* Career-related internships or fieldwork available. Financial award application deadline: 4/1; financial award applicants required to submit FAFSA. *Unit head:* Dr. Lynn Howell, Chairperson, 718-997-5250, E-mail: lynn.howell@qc.cuny.edu.

Queens University of Charlotte, Wayland H. Cato, Jr. School of Education, Charlotte, NC 28274-0002. Offers educational leadership (MA); K-6 (MAT); literacy K-12 (M Ed). *Accreditation:* NCATE. *Program availability:* Part-time, evening/weekend, online learning. *Degree requirements:* For master's, comprehensive exam. *Entrance requirements:* For master's, GRE General Test. *Expenses:* Contact institution.

Quincy University, Master of Science in Education Programs, Quincy, IL 62301-2699. Offers curriculum and instruction (MS Ed), including bilingual/English as a second language; leadership (MS Ed); reading education (MS Ed); special education (MS Ed); teacher leader (MS Ed). *Program availability:* Part-time, evening/weekend, online learning. *Degree requirements:* For master's, comprehensive exam (for some programs), thesis optional. *Entrance requirements:* For master's, MAT or GRE. Additional exam requirements/recommendations for international students: Required—TOEFL (minimum score 550 paper-based; 79 iBT). Electronic applications accepted. Application fee is waived when completed online.

Quinnipiac University, School of Education, Program in Educational Leadership, Hamden, CT 06518-1940. Offers Diploma. *Program availability:* Part-time-only, evening/weekend. *Faculty:* 1 (woman) full-time, 5 part-time/adjunct (2 women). *Students:* 2 full-time (both women), 58 part-time (42 women); includes 4 minority (2 Black or African American, non-Hispanic/Latino; 1 Hispanic/Latino; 1 Two or more races, non-Hispanic/Latino). 26 applicants, 96% accepted, 24 enrolled. In 2016, 23 Diplomas awarded. *Entrance requirements:* For degree, 3 years of experience in pre K-12 setting, interview, 3 credits in special education course. *Application deadline:* For fall admission, 7/30 priority date for domestic students; for spring admission, 12/15 priority date for domestic students; for summer admission, 5/30 priority date for domestic students. Applications are processed on a rolling basis. Application fee: $45. Electronic applications accepted. *Expenses:* Contact institution. *Financial support:* Federal Work-Study and unspecified assistantships available. Financial award application deadline: 6/1; financial award applicants required to submit FAFSA. *Faculty research:* Leadership and teacher quality, leadership and student achievement. *Unit head:* Gail Gilmore, Program Director, 203-582-3289, E-mail: gail.gilmore@qu.edu. *Application contact:* Office of Graduate Admissions, 800-462-1944, Fax: 203-582-3443, E-mail: graduate@qu.edu.
Website: http://www.qu.edu/edleadership

Quinnipiac University, School of Education, Program in Teacher Leadership, Hamden, CT 06518-1940. Offers MS. *Program availability:* Part-time-only, evening/weekend, online only, 100% online. *Faculty:* 2 full-time (both women), 4 part-time/adjunct (3 women). *Students:* 40 part-time (33 women). 17 applicants, 82% accepted, 14 enrolled. In 2016, 14 master's awarded. *Degree requirements:* For master's, capstone experience. *Application deadline:* For fall admission, 8/15 for domestic students; for spring admission, 1/15 for domestic students. Applications are processed on a rolling basis. Application fee: $45. Electronic applications accepted. *Expenses:* Contact institution. *Financial support:* Federal Work-Study and unspecified assistantships available. Financial award application deadline: 6/1; financial award applicants required to submit FAFSA. *Faculty research:* Leadership and school climate, distributed leadership, teacher retention. *Unit head:* Gail Gilmore, Program Director, 203-582-3289, E-mail: gail.gilmore@qu.edu. *Application contact:* Quinnipiac University Online Admissions Office, 800-462-1944, E-mail: quonlineadmissions@qu.edu.
Website: https://quonline.quinnipiac.edu/online-programs/online-graduate-programs/ms-in-teacher-leadership/

Radford University, College of Graduate Studies and Research, Program in Educational Leadership, Radford, VA 24142. Offers MS. *Accreditation:* NCATE. *Program availability:* Part-time, evening/weekend, 100% online, blended/hybrid learning. *Faculty:* 2 full-time (1 woman), 2 part-time/adjunct (0 women). *Students:* 45 part-time (26 women); includes 4 minority (all Black or African American, non-Hispanic/Latino). Average age 36. 21 applicants, 100% accepted, 19 enrolled. In 2016, 23 master's awarded. *Degree requirements:* For master's, comprehensive exam. *Entrance requirements:* For master's, GRE or MAT (waived for any applicant with advanced degree), minimum GPA of 2.75, 3 years of K-12 classroom experience, writing sample, 3 letters of reference, resume, official transcripts. Additional exam requirements/recommendations for international students: Required—TOEFL (minimum score 550 paper-based; 79 iBT), IELTS (minimum score 6.5). *Application deadline:* For fall admission, 2/15 priority date for domestic students, 12/1 for international students; for spring admission, 7/1 for international students. Applications are processed on a rolling basis. Application fee: $50. Electronic applications accepted. *Expenses:* Tuition, state resident: full-time $7868; part-time $328 per credit hour. Tuition, nonresident: full-time $16,394; part-time $683 per credit hour. *Required fees:* $3090; $130 per credit hour. Tuition and fees vary according to course load and program. *Financial support:* In 2016–17, 1 student received support. Career-related internships or fieldwork, scholarships/grants, and unspecified assistantships available. Support available to part-time students. Financial award application deadline: 3/1; financial award applicants required to submit FAFSA. *Unit head:* Dr. Brad Bizzell, Coordinator, 540-831-5302, E-mail: stel@radford.edu.
Website: http://www.radford.edu/content/cehd/home/teacher-ed/programs/education-leadership.html

Ramapo College of New Jersey, Master of Arts in Educational Leadership Program, Mahwah, NJ 07430-1680. Offers MA. *Program availability:* Part-time. *Faculty:* 2 full-time (0 women), 10 part-time/adjunct (2 women). *Students:* 39 full-time (22 women), 30 part-time (21 women); includes 9 minority (3 Black or African American, non-Hispanic/Latino; 1 Asian, non-Hispanic/Latino; 4 Hispanic/Latino; 1 Two or more races, non-Hispanic/Latino). Average age 36. 57 applicants, 91% accepted, 35 enrolled. In 2016, 23 master's awarded. *Degree requirements:* For master's, thesis. *Entrance requirements:* For master's, PRAXIS, official transcript of baccalaureate degree from accredited institution with minimum recommended GPA of 3.0; personal statement; 2 letters of recommendation; resume; state-issued teaching certificate. Additional exam requirements/recommendations for international students: Required—TOEFL (minimum score 550 paper-based; 79 iBT); Recommended—IELTS (minimum score 6). *Application deadline:* For fall admission, 5/1 for domestic and international students; for spring admission, 12/1 for domestic and international students. Applications are processed on a rolling basis. Application fee: $60. Electronic applications accepted. *Expenses:* $606.05 per credit tuition, $130.45 per credit fees. *Financial support:* Career-related internships or fieldwork available. Financial award application deadline: 3/1; financial award applicants required to submit FAFSA. *Unit head:* Dr. Brian P. Chinni, Associate Professor, Educational Leadership, 201-684-7613, E-mail: bchinni@ramapo.edu. *Application contact:* M. Joyce Wilson, Secretarial Assistant, 201-684-7721, Fax: 201-684-6699, E-mail: jwilson@ramapo.edu.
Website: http://www.ramapo.edu/mael/

Regent University, Graduate School, School of Education, Virginia Beach, VA 23464-9800. Offers adult education (Ed D, PhD, Ed S); advanced educational leadership (Ed D, PhD, Ed S); career switcher (M Ed); character education (Ed D, PhD, Ed S); Christian education leadership (Ed D, PhD, Ed S); Christian school administration (M Ed); curriculum and instruction (M Ed), including adult education, Christian school, gifted and talented education, STEM education, teacher leader; educational leadership (M Ed); educational psychology (Ed D, PhD, Ed S); educational technology and online learning (Ed D, PhD, Ed S); elementary education (M Ed); exceptional education executive leadership (Ed D, PhD, Ed S); higher education (Ed D, PhD, Ed S); higher education leadership and management (Ed D, PhD, Ed S); individualized degree plan (M Ed); K-12 school leadership (Ed D, PhD, Ed S); K-12 special education (M Ed); K-8 leadership in mathematics education (M Ed); leadership in mathematics education (Ed S); reading specialist (M Ed); special education (Ed D, PhD, Ed S); student affairs (M Ed); TESOL (M Ed), including adult education - collegiate, K-12. *Accreditation:* TEAC. *Program availability:* Part-time, evening/weekend, 100% online, blended/hybrid learning. *Faculty:* 22 full-time (10 women), 42 part-time/adjunct (31 women). *Students:* 89 full-time (62 women), 1,035 part-time (823 women); includes 466 minority (381 Black or African American, non-Hispanic/Latino; 3 American Indian or Alaska Native, non-Hispanic/Latino; 19 Asian, non-Hispanic/Latino; 50 Hispanic/Latino; 13 Two or more races, non-Hispanic/Latino), 11 international. Average age 39. 976 applicants, 59% accepted, 449 enrolled. In 2016, 241 master's, 22 doctorates, 4 other advanced degrees awarded. *Degree requirements:* For master's, thesis or alternative; for doctorate, comprehensive exam, thesis/dissertation. *Entrance requirements:* For master's, Virginia Communication and Literacy Assessment (VCLA), PRAXIS, college transcripts, writing sample, interview; for doctorate, GRE, writing sample, resume, transcripts, interview. Additional exam requirements/recommendations for international students: Required—TOEFL (minimum score 577 paper-based). *Application deadline:* For fall admission, 4/1 priority date for domestic students; for spring admission, 10/15 priority date for domestic students. Applications are processed on a rolling basis. Application fee: $50. Electronic applications accepted. *Expenses:* Contact institution. *Financial support:* In 2016–17, 622 students received support, including 1 fellowship (averaging $5,000 per year); career-related internships or fieldwork, scholarships/grants, and unspecified assistantships also available. Support available to part-time students. *Faculty research:* Christian school administration, curriculum and instruction, educational technology and online learning, higher education, special education. *Unit head:* Dr. Donald Finn, Dean, 757-352-4278, Fax: 757-352-4318, E-mail: dfinn@regent.edu. *Application contact:* Heidi Cece, Assistant Vice President of Enrollment Management, 800-373-5504, Fax: 757-352-4381, E-mail: admissions@regent.edu.
Website: http://www.regent.edu/soe/

Regis College, Department of Education, Weston, MA 02493. Offers elementary teacher (MAT); higher education leadership (Ed D); reading (MAT); special education (MAT). *Program availability:* Part-time, evening/weekend, blended/hybrid learning. *Degree requirements:* For master's, thesis. *Entrance requirements:* For master's, GRE or MAT. Additional exam requirements/recommendations for international students: Required—TOEFL; Recommended—IELTS. *Application deadline:* Applications are processed on a rolling basis. Application fee: $50. Electronic applications accepted. *Financial support:* Federal Work-Study, scholarships/grants, and unspecified assistantships available. Financial award applicants required to submit FAFSA. *Unit head:* Dr. Priscilla Boerger, Department Chair/Graduate Program Director, 781-768-7422, E-mail: priscilla.boerger@regiscollege.edu.

Regis University, College of Contemporary Liberal Studies, Denver, CO 80221-1099. Offers creative writing (MFA); criminology (M Sc); curriculum, instruction and assessment (M Ed); education - teacher leadership (M Ed); educational leadership (M Ed); elementary education (M Ed); literacy (Certificate); reading (M Ed); secondary education (M Ed); special education (M Ed); teacher academic leadership (Certificate); teacher leadership (MA); teacher/educational leadership (M Ed); teaching the linguistically diverse (M Ed). *Program availability:* Part-time, evening/weekend, 100% online, blended/hybrid learning. *Faculty:* 18 full-time (12 women), 42 part-time/adjunct (26 women). *Students:* 302 full-time (234 women), 270 part-time (218 women); includes 148 minority (33 Black or African American, non-Hispanic/Latino; 3 American Indian or Alaska Native, non-Hispanic/Latino; 13 Asian, non-Hispanic/Latino; 83 Hispanic/Latino; 16 Two or more races, non-Hispanic/Latino), 3 international. Average age 36. 431 applicants, 90% accepted, 110 enrolled. In 2016, 308 master's awarded. *Degree requirements:* For master's, thesis (for some programs). *Entrance requirements:* For master's, official transcript reflecting baccalaureate degree awarded from regionally-accredited college or university, work experience, resume, letters of recommendation. Additional exam requirements/recommendations for international students: Required—TOEFL (minimum score 550 paper-based; 82 iBT). *Application deadline:* For fall admission, 8/15 priority date for domestic students, 7/13 for international students; for winter admission, 10/10 priority date for domestic students, 9/8 for international students; for spring admission, 1/10 priority date for domestic students, 11/17 for international students; for summer admission, 5/1 priority date for domestic students. Applications are processed on a rolling basis. Application fee: $75. Electronic applications accepted. *Expenses:* $485 per credit hour. *Financial support:* Scholarships/grants available. Financial award application deadline: 4/15; financial award applicants

required to submit FAFSA. *Unit head:* Dr. Elisa Robyn, Academic Dean. *Application contact:* Cate Clark, Director of Admissions, 303-458-4900, Fax: 303-964-5534, E-mail: ruadmissions@regis.edu.
Website: http://www.regis.edu/CCLS.aspx

Rhode Island College, School of Graduate Studies, Feinstein School of Education and Human Development, Department of Counseling, Educational Leadership, and School Psychology, Providence, RI 02908-1991. Offers advanced counseling (CGS); agency counseling (MA); clinical mental health counseling (MS); co-occurring disorders (MA, CGS); educational leadership (M Ed); mental health counseling (CAGS); school counseling (MA); school psychology (CAGS); teacher leadership (CGS). *Accreditation:* ACA; NCATE. *Program availability:* Part-time, evening/weekend. *Faculty:* 9 full-time (5 women), 10 part-time/adjunct (all women). *Students:* 34 full-time (28 women), 83 part-time (72 women); includes 16 minority (5 Black or African American, non-Hispanic/Latino; 1 Asian, non-Hispanic/Latino; 10 Hispanic/Latino). Average age 33. In 2016, 50 master's, 34 other advanced degrees awarded. *Degree requirements:* For master's and other advanced degree, comprehensive exam (for some programs), thesis (for some programs). *Entrance requirements:* For master's, GRE General Test or MAT, undergraduate transcripts; minimum undergraduate GPA of 3.0; for other advanced degree, GRE or MAT (for most programs), undergraduate transcripts; minimum undergraduate GPA of 3.0; 3 letters of recommendation; current resume. Additional exam requirements/recommendations for international students: Recommended—TOEFL (minimum score 550 paper-based; 79 iBT). *Application deadline:* For fall admission, 3/1 for domestic students; for spring admission, 11/1 for domestic students. Applications are processed on a rolling basis. Application fee: $50. Electronic applications accepted. *Expenses:* Tuition, state resident: full-time $8928; part-time $372 per credit. Tuition, nonresident: full-time $17,376; part-time $724 per credit. *Required fees:* $604; $22 per credit. One-time fee: $74. *Financial support:* In 2016–17, 3 teaching assistantships with full tuition reimbursements (averaging $2,500 per year) were awarded; career-related internships or fieldwork, Federal Work-Study, scholarships/grants, health care benefits, and unspecified assistantships also available. Support available to part-time students. Financial award application deadline: 5/15; financial award applicants required to submit FAFSA. *Unit head:* Dr. Andrew Snyder, Chair, 401-456-9633. *Application contact:* Graduate Studies, 401-456-8700.
Website: http://www.ric.edu/counselingEducationalLeadershipSchoolPsychology/index.php

Rider University, Department of Graduate Education, Leadership and Counseling, Program in Curriculum, Instruction and Supervision, Lawrenceville, NJ 08648-3001. Offers curriculum, instruction and supervision (MA); supervisor (Certificate). *Accreditation:* NCATE. *Program availability:* Part-time, evening/weekend. *Degree requirements:* For master's, comprehensive exam, practicum project. *Entrance requirements:* For master's, interview, 2 letters of recommendation from current supervisors, resume. Additional exam requirements/recommendations for international students: Required—TOEFL (minimum score 550 paper-based). Electronic applications accepted. *Faculty research:* Curriculum change, curriculum development, teacher evaluation.

Rider University, Department of Graduate Education, Leadership and Counseling, Program in Educational Administration, Lawrenceville, NJ 08648-3001. Offers educational administration (MA); principal (Certificate); school administrator (Certificate). *Accreditation:* NCATE. *Program availability:* Part-time, evening/weekend. *Degree requirements:* For master's, comprehensive exam, research project. *Entrance requirements:* For master's, interview, resume, 2 letters of recommendation. Additional exam requirements/recommendations for international students: Required—TOEFL (minimum score 550 paper-based). Electronic applications accepted. *Faculty research:* National/state standards, urban education, administrative leadership, financing public education, community school linkages.

Rivier University, School of Graduate Studies, Department of Education, Nashua, NH 03060. Offers curriculum and instruction (M Ed); early childhood education (M Ed); educational administration (M Ed); educational studies (M Ed); elementary education (M Ed); elementary education and general special education (M Ed); emotional and behavioral disorders (M Ed); general social education (M Ed); leadership and learning (Ed D, CAGS); learning disabilities (M Ed); learning disabilities and reading (M Ed); mental health counseling (MA); reading (M Ed); school counseling (M Ed). *Program availability:* Part-time, evening/weekend. *Degree requirements:* For master's, comprehensive exam (for some programs), internships. *Entrance requirements:* For master's, GRE General Test or MAT.

Robert Morris University, School of Education and Social Sciences, Moon Township, PA 15108-1189. Offers business education (MS); counseling psychology (MS); education (Postbaccalaureate Certificate); higher education (MS); instructional leadership (MS), including education; instructional management and leadership (PhD); literacy (MS); special education (MS). *Accreditation:* TEAC. *Program availability:* Part-time, evening/weekend, online learning. *Faculty:* 17 full-time (9 women), 4 part-time/adjunct (3 women). *Students:* 154 part-time (104 women); includes 18 minority (11 Black or African American, non-Hispanic/Latino; 2 Hispanic/Latino; 5 Two or more races, non-Hispanic/Latino), 1 international. Average age 26. 69 applicants, 26% accepted, 18 enrolled. In 2016, 40 master's, 15 doctorates awarded. *Degree requirements:* For doctorate, thesis/dissertation. *Entrance requirements:* Additional exam requirements/recommendations for international students: Required—TOEFL (minimum score 550 paper-based; 79 iBT). *Application deadline:* For fall admission, 7/1 priority date for domestic and international students; for spring admission, 11/1 priority date for domestic and international students. Applications are processed on a rolling basis. Application fee: $35. Electronic applications accepted. *Expenses:* $840 per credit (for master's degree). *Unit head:* Dr. Mary Ann Rafoth, Dean, 412-397-6020, Fax: 412-397-6044, E-mail: rafoth@rmu.edu.
Website: http://www.rmu.edu/web/cms/schools/sess/

Robert Morris University Illinois, Morris Graduate School of Management, Chicago, IL 60605. Offers accounting (MBA); accounting/finance (MBA); business analytics (MIS); design and media (MM); design management (MM); educational technology (MM); health care administration (MM); higher education administration (MM); human resource management (MBA); information security (MIS); information systems (MBA, MIS); law enforcement administration (MM); management (MBA); management/finance (MBA); management/human resource management (MBA); mobile computing (MIS); sports administration (MM). *Program availability:* Part-time, evening/weekend. *Faculty:* 4 full-time (1 woman), 25 part-time/adjunct (5 women). *Students:* 196 full-time (98 women), 151 part-time (85 women); includes 200 minority (114 Black or African American, non-Hispanic/Latino; 17 Asian, non-Hispanic/Latino; 67 Hispanic/Latino; 2 Two or more races, non-Hispanic/Latino), 23 international. Average age 33. 174 applicants, 61% accepted, 97 enrolled. In 2016, 190 master's awarded. *Entrance requirements:* For master's, official transcripts and letters of recommendation (for some programs); written personal statement. Additional exam requirements/recommendations for international students: Required—TOEFL (minimum score 550 paper-based). *Application deadline:* Applications are processed on a rolling basis. Application fee: $20 ($100 for international students). Electronic applications accepted. *Expenses: Tuition:* Full-time $16,500; part-time $2750 per course. *Financial support:* In 2016–17, 444 students received support. Federal Work-Study, scholarships/grants, and unspecified assistantships available. Support available to part-time students. Financial award applicants required to submit FAFSA. *Unit head:* Kayed Akkawi, Dean, 312-935-6050, Fax: 312-935-6020, E-mail: kakkawi@robertmorris.edu. *Application contact:* Danielle Naffziger, Vice President of Marketing and Enrollment, 312-935-4812, Fax: 312-935-6020, E-mail: dnaffziger@robertmorris.edu.

Rocky Mountain College, Program in Educational Leadership, Billings, MT 59102-1796. Offers M Ed. *Faculty:* 2 full-time (both women), 3 part-time/adjunct (1 woman). *Students:* 18 full-time (10 women); includes 1 minority (Hispanic/Latino). Average age 36. In 2016, 22 master's awarded. *Entrance requirements:* Additional exam requirements/recommendations for international students: Required—TOEFL (minimum score 570 paper-based; 88 iBT), IELTS (minimum score 6.5). *Application deadline:* Applications are processed on a rolling basis. Application fee: $35 ($40 for international students). Electronic applications accepted. Application fee is waived when completed online. *Expenses:* Contact institution. *Financial support:* In 2016–17, 18 students received support. Scholarships/grants available. Financial award applicants required to submit FAFSA. *Unit head:* Dr. Stevie Schmitz, Director of Educational Leadership and Distance Education, 406-657-1134, E-mail: schmitzs@rocky.edu.
Website: http://rocky.edu/academics/academic-programs/graduate-programs/mel/index.php

Rowan University, Graduate School, College of Education, Department of Educational Services and Leadership, Program in Educational Leadership, Glassboro, NJ 08028-1701. Offers Ed D, CAGS. *Accreditation:* NCATE. *Program availability:* Part-time, evening/weekend. *Degree requirements:* For doctorate, thesis/dissertation. *Entrance requirements:* For doctorate, GMAT or GRE General Test, master's degree. Additional exam requirements/recommendations for international students: Required—TOEFL.

Rowan University, Graduate School, College of Education, Department of Educational Services and Leadership, Program in Higher Education Administration, Glassboro, NJ 08028-1701. Offers MA. *Accreditation:* NCATE. *Program availability:* Part-time, evening/weekend. *Degree requirements:* For master's, comprehensive exam, thesis. *Entrance requirements:* For master's, GRE General Test, minimum GPA of 2.8, 2 years of teaching experience. Additional exam requirements/recommendations for international students: Required—TOEFL. Electronic applications accepted.

Rowan University, Graduate School, College of Education, Department of Educational Services and Leadership, Program in Principal Preparation, Glassboro, NJ 08028-1701. Offers CAGS. *Program availability:* Part-time, evening/weekend. *Degree requirements:* For CAGS, comprehensive exam, thesis, internship. *Entrance requirements:* For degree, GRE General Test, minimum GPA of 2.81, 1 year of teaching experience. Additional exam requirements/recommendations for international students: Required—TOEFL. Electronic applications accepted.

Rowan University, Graduate School, College of Education, Department of Educational Services and Leadership, Program in School Administration, Glassboro, NJ 08028-1701. Offers MA. Electronic applications accepted.

Rowan University, Graduate School, College of Education, Department of Educational Services and Leadership, Program in Supervisor Certification, Glassboro, NJ 08028-1701. Offers CAGS. Electronic applications accepted.

Rowan University, Graduate School, College of Education, Department of Interdisciplinary and Inclusive Education, Program in Teacher Leadership, Glassboro, NJ 08028-1701. Offers M Ed. *Program availability:* Part-time, evening/weekend. *Degree requirements:* For master's, thesis. *Entrance requirements:* For master's, GRE General Test, minimum GPA of 2.8, 1 year of teaching experience. Additional exam requirements/recommendations for international students: Required—TOEFL. Electronic applications accepted.

Rutgers University–Camden, Graduate School of Arts and Sciences, Department of Public Policy and Administration, Camden, NJ 08102. Offers education policy and leadership (MPA); international public service and development (MPA); public management (MPA); JD/MPA; MPA/MA. *Accreditation:* NASPAA. *Program availability:* Part-time, evening/weekend. *Degree requirements:* For master's, directed study, research workshop, 42 credits. *Entrance requirements:* For master's, GRE General Test, GMAT or LSAT, 3 letters of recommendation; resume. Additional exam requirements/recommendations for international students: Required—TOEFL (minimum score 550 paper-based), IELTS. Electronic applications accepted. *Faculty research:* Nonprofit management, county and municipal administration, health and human services, government communication, administrative law, educational finance.

Rutgers University–New Brunswick, Graduate School of Education, Department of Educational Theory, Policy and Administration, Programs in Educational Administration and Supervision, Piscataway, NJ 08854-8097. Offers Ed M, Ed D. *Program availability:* Part-time, evening/weekend. *Degree requirements:* For doctorate, thesis/dissertation, qualifying exam. *Entrance requirements:* For master's, GRE General Test, minimum GPA of 3.0; for doctorate, GRE General Test, minimum GPA of 3.0, master's degree in educational administration. Additional exam requirements/recommendations for international students: Required—TOEFL. Electronic applications accepted. *Faculty research:* Leadership of education, finance, law, schools as organizations.

Sacred Heart University, Graduate Programs, Isabelle Farrington College of Education, Department of Leadership/Literacy, Fairfield, CT 06825. Offers advanced studies in administration (Professional Certificate); advanced studies in literacy (Professional Certificate). *Program availability:* Part-time, evening/weekend. *Faculty:* 8 full-time (2 women), 18 part-time/adjunct (9 women). *Students:* 52 part-time (49 women). Average age 41. 16 applicants, 100% accepted, 8 enrolled. In 2016, 25 Professional Certificates awarded. *Degree requirements:* For Professional Certificate, thesis or alternative. *Entrance requirements:* For degree, proof of teacher certification. Additional exam requirements/recommendations for international students: Required—TOEFL (minimum score 570 paper-based, 80 iBT), TWE, or IELTS (6.5); Recommended—TSE. *Application deadline:* Applications are processed on a rolling basis. Application fee: $75. Electronic applications accepted. *Expenses:* $705 per credit. *Financial support:* Unspecified assistantships available. Financial award applicants required to submit FAFSA. *Unit head:* Ann Clark, Chair/Associate Clinical Professor, 203-365-4876, E-mail: clarka@sacredheart.edu. *Application contact:* William Sweeney, Director of Graduate Admissions Operations, 203-365-4827, E-mail: sweeneyw@sacredheart.edu.

Sage Graduate School, Esteves School of Education, Program in Educational Leadership, Troy, NY 12180-4115. Offers Ed D. *Program availability:* Part-time. *Faculty:* 7 full-time (4 women), 6 part-time/adjunct (2 women). *Students:* 105 part-time (74 women); includes 61 minority (40 Black or African American, non-Hispanic/Latino; 4 Asian, non-Hispanic/Latino; 15 Hispanic/Latino; 2 Two or more races, non-Hispanic/Latino). Average age 47. 111 applicants, 52% accepted, 41 enrolled. In 2016, 26 doctorates awarded. *Degree requirements:* For doctorate, comprehensive exam. *Entrance requirements:* For doctorate, three letters of professional reference that address candidate's potential in relationship to New York State Education Department's nine essential characteristics of effective school leader; on-demand writing sample to determine readiness and capability for scholarly writing; current resume; statement of career goals. Additional exam requirements/recommendations for international students:

Required—TOEFL (minimum score 550 paper-based). *Application deadline:* Applications are processed on a rolling basis. Application fee: $40. Electronic applications accepted. *Expenses:* Contact institution. *Financial support:* Fellowships, research assistantships, Federal Work-Study, scholarships/grants, and unspecified assistantships available. Support available to part-time students. Financial award applicants required to submit FAFSA. *Unit head:* Dr. John Pelizza, Interim Dean, Esteves School of Education, 518-244-2051, Fax: 518-244-2334, E-mail: pelizj@sage.edu. *Application contact:* Janice White, Chair, Doctor of Education Program in Educational Leadership, 518-244-4588, Fax: 518-266-1391, E-mail: whitej5@sage.edu.

Saginaw Valley State University, College of Education, Program in Educational Leadership, University Center, MI 48710. Offers M Ed, Ed S. *Accreditation:* NCATE. *Program availability:* Part-time, evening/weekend, online learning. *Students:* 61 part-time (34 women); includes 3 minority (2 Black or African American, non-Hispanic/Latino; 1 Two or more races, non-Hispanic/Latino). Average age 35. 28 applicants, 96% accepted, 15 enrolled. In 2016, 33 master's, 24 Ed Ss awarded. *Degree requirements:* For master's, capstone course. *Entrance requirements:* For master's, minimum GPA of 3.0, teaching certificate; for Ed S, master's degree with minimum GPA of 3.3. Additional exam requirements/recommendations for international students: Required—TOEFL (minimum score 550 paper-based; 79 iBT). *Application deadline:* For fall admission, 7/15 for international students; for winter admission, 11/15 for international students; for spring admission, 4/15 for international students. Applications are processed on a rolling basis. Application fee: $30 ($90 for international students). Electronic applications accepted. *Expenses:* Tuition, state resident: full-time $9652; part-time $536 per credit hour. Tuition, nonresident: full-time $12,259; part-time $1022 per credit hour. *Required fees:* $263; $14.60 per credit hour. Tuition and fees vary according to degree level. *Financial support:* Federal Work-Study and scholarships/grants available. Support available to part-time students. Financial award applicants required to submit FAFSA. *Unit head:* Dr. Jonathan Gould, Associate Professor of Teacher Education, 989-964-4978, Fax: 989-964-4981, E-mail: jagould@svsu.edu. *Application contact:* Jenna Briggs, Director, Graduate and International Admissions, 989-964-6096, Fax: 989-964-2788, E-mail: gradadm@svsu.edu.

St. Ambrose University, College of Education and Health Sciences, Program in Educational Administration, Davenport, IA 52803-2898. Offers MEA. *Program availability:* Part-time, evening/weekend. *Entrance requirements:* Additional exam requirements/recommendations for international students: Required—TOEFL. Electronic applications accepted.

St. Bonaventure University, School of Graduate Studies, School of Education, Program in Educational Leadership, St. Bonaventure, NY 14778-2284. Offers educational leadership (MS Ed); school building leader (Adv C); school district leader (Adv C). Hybrid format offered in Olean and Buffalo Center (Hamburg, NY). *Program availability:* Part-time, evening/weekend, online learning. *Faculty:* 1 (woman) full-time, 2 part-time/adjunct (both women). *Students:* 23 part-time (22 women); includes 3 minority (2 Black or African American, non-Hispanic/Latino; 1 Hispanic/Latino). Average age 37. 11 applicants, 100% accepted, 1 enrolled. In 2016, 7 master's, 13 Adv Cs awarded. *Degree requirements:* For master's, comprehensive exam, thesis optional, minimum cumulative GPA of 3.0, practicum, internship, electronic portfolio; for Adv C, comprehensive exam, minimum cumulative GPA of 3.0, practicum, internship, electronic portfolio. *Entrance requirements:* For master's, teaching, counseling or other school certification; three years of K-12 school experience; transcripts from all colleges previously attended; two references (one from supervising principal or superintendent); interview; writing sample (academic or professional); for Adv C, master's degree in education or certification-related area; three years of K-12 school experience; teaching or counseling certification; transcripts from all colleges previously attended; two references (one from supervising principal or superintendent); interview; writing sample. Additional exam requirements/recommendations for international students: Required—TOEFL (minimum score 550 paper-based; 79 iBT). *Application deadline:* For fall admission, 6/15 priority date for domestic students, 2/1 priority date for international students; for spring admission, 11/1 for domestic students. Applications are processed on a rolling basis. Application fee: $0. Electronic applications accepted. *Expenses:* Contact institution. *Financial support:* Federal Work-Study, scholarships/grants, health care benefits, and unspecified assistantships available. Support available to part-time students. Financial award application deadline: 4/15; financial award applicants required to submit FAFSA. *Unit head:* Dr. Nancy Casey, Director, 716-375-2394, Fax: 716-375-2360, E-mail: ncasey@sbu.edu. *Application contact:* Bruce Campbell, Director of Graduate Admissions, 716-375-2429, Fax: 716-375-4015, E-mail: gradsch@sbu.edu.
Website: http://www.sbu.edu/academics/schools/education/graduate-degrees-certificates/msed-in-educational-leadership

St. Cloud State University, School of Graduate Studies, School of Education, Department of Educational Leadership and Higher Education, Program in Higher Education Administration, St. Cloud, MN 56301-4498. Offers MS, Ed D.

St. Cloud State University, School of Graduate Studies, School of Health and Human Services, Department of Counseling and Community Psychology, Program in Educational Administration and Leadership, St. Cloud, MN 56301-4498. Offers MS. *Program availability:* Part-time. *Degree requirements:* For master's, comprehensive exam (for some programs), thesis or alternative. *Entrance requirements:* For master's, GRE General Test, minimum GPA of 2.75. Additional exam requirements/recommendations for international students: Required—Michigan English Language Assessment Battery; Recommended—TOEFL (minimum score 550 paper-based), IELTS (minimum score 6.5). Electronic applications accepted.

Saint Francis University, Graduate Education Program, Loretto, PA 15940-0600. Offers education (M Ed); leadership (M Ed); reading (M Ed). *Program availability:* Part-time, 100% online, blended/hybrid learning. *Degree requirements:* For master's, comprehensive exam, thesis optional. *Entrance requirements:* For master's, GRE or MAT (if undergraduate GPA less than 3.0). Additional exam requirements/recommendations for international students: Required—TOEFL (minimum score 550 paper-based; 75 iBT), IELTS (minimum score 6.5), International Test of English Proficiency (minimum score 4). *Expenses:* Contact institution.

St. Francis Xavier University, Graduate Studies, Graduate Studies in Education, Antigonish, NS B2G 2W5, Canada. Offers curriculum and instruction (M Ed); educational administration and leadership (M Ed). *Program availability:* Part-time, online learning. *Degree requirements:* For master's, thesis. *Entrance requirements:* For master's, minimum undergraduate B average, 2 years of teaching experience. *Application deadline:* For fall admission, 2/15 for domestic and international students. Application fee: $40. *Expenses: Tuition:* Full-time $9060 Canadian dollars; part-time $725 Canadian dollars per credit. *Required fees:* $789 Canadian dollars; $78.84 Canadian dollars per credit. Tuition and fees vary according to course load, degree level and program. *Financial support:* Teaching assistantships available. *Faculty research:* Inclusive education, qualitative research. *Unit head:* Dr. Robert E. White, Chair, 902-867-3420, Fax: 902-867-3887, E-mail: rwhite@stfx.ca. *Application contact:* Colleen Jones, Assistant, 902-867-3906, Fax: 902-867-5154, E-mail: med@stfx.ca.

St. John Fisher College, Ralph C. Wilson Jr. School of Education, Educational Leadership Program, Rochester, NY 14618-3597. Offers MS Ed. *Program availability:* Part-time, evening/weekend. *Faculty:* 1 (woman) full-time, 4 part-time/adjunct (3 women). *Students:* 19 part-time (14 women); includes 3 minority (2 Black or African American, non-Hispanic/Latino; 1 Asian, non-Hispanic/Latino). Average age 37. 16 applicants, 69% accepted, 10 enrolled. In 2016, 11 master's awarded. *Degree requirements:* For master's, capstone project, internship. *Entrance requirements:* For master's, teacher certification, minimum 2 years of teaching experience, 2 letters of recommendation, current resume. Additional exam requirements/recommendations for international students: Required—TOEFL (minimum score 575 paper-based; 80 iBT). *Application deadline:* Applications are processed on a rolling basis. Application fee: $30. Electronic applications accepted. *Expenses:* $885 per credit hour. *Financial support:* Scholarships/grants available. Financial award applicants required to submit FAFSA. *Faculty research:* Urban school leadership, assessment, effective school leadership. *Unit head:* Dr. Diane Reed, Director, 585-385-7257, E-mail: dreed@sjfc.edu. *Application contact:* Michelle Gosier, Associate Director of Transfer and Graduate Admissions, 585-385-8064, E-mail: mgosier@sjfc.edu.
Website: https://www.sjfc.edu/graduate-programs/ms-in-educational-leadership/

St. John Fisher College, Ralph C. Wilson Jr. School of Education, Executive Leadership Program, Rochester, NY 14618-3597. Offers Ed D. *Program availability:* Evening/weekend. *Faculty:* 12 full-time (8 women), 6 part-time/adjunct (3 women). *Students:* 123 full-time (88 women), 18 part-time (11 women); includes 77 minority (56 Black or African American, non-Hispanic/Latino; 3 American Indian or Alaska Native, non-Hispanic/Latino; 1 Asian, non-Hispanic/Latino; 14 Hispanic/Latino; 3 Two or more races, non-Hispanic/Latino). Average age 45. 92 applicants, 74% accepted, 55 enrolled. In 2016, 41 doctorates awarded. *Degree requirements:* For doctorate, comprehensive exam, thesis/dissertation, field experiences. *Entrance requirements:* For doctorate, 3 professional writing samples, 2 letters of reference, interview, minimum of 3 years' management experience, master's degree. Additional exam requirements/recommendations for international students: Required—TOEFL (minimum score 575 paper-based; 80 iBT). *Application deadline:* For fall admission, 3/1 for domestic and international students. Applications are processed on a rolling basis. Electronic applications accepted. *Expenses:* $1,350 per credit hour. *Financial support:* Scholarships/grants available. Financial award applicants required to submit FAFSA. *Faculty research:* Leadership, organizational development. *Unit head:* Dr. Jeannine Dingus-Eason, Program Director, 585-385-8002, E-mail: jdingus@sjfc.edu. *Application contact:* Michelle Gosier, Associate Director of Transfer and Graduate Admissions, 585-385-8064, E-mail: mgosier@sjfc.edu.
Website: https://www.sjfc.edu/graduate-programs/executive-leadership-edd/

St. John's University, The School of Education, Division of Administrative and Instructional Leadership, Instructional Leadership Program, Queens, NY 11439. Offers Ed D, Adv C. *Program availability:* Part-time, evening/weekend. *Degree requirements:* For doctorate, comprehensive exam, thesis/dissertation. *Entrance requirements:* For doctorate, GRE General Test, interview, minimum GPA of 3.2, 2 letters of recommendation, resume, writing samples, master's degree in education or related field; for Adv C, official transcript, minimum GPA of 3.0, 2 letters of recommendation, master's degree in education or related field. Additional exam requirements/recommendations for international students: Required—TOEFL (minimum score 600 paper-based; 100 iBT), IELTS (minimum score 7). Electronic applications accepted. *Faculty research:* Mathematics learning disabilities and difficulties with students identified as learning disabled or students who are English Language Learners, identification of mathematical giftedness in students who are English Language Learners, effects of parental participation and parenting behaviors on the science and mathematics academic achievement of school-age students, analysis of major theoretical perspectives in curriculum design and implementation.

St. John's University, The School of Education, Division of Administrative and Instructional Leadership, Program in Educational Administration and Supervision, Queens, NY 11439. Offers administration and supervision (Ed D). *Program availability:* Part-time, evening/weekend, online learning. *Degree requirements:* For doctorate, thesis/dissertation, clinical residency. *Entrance requirements:* For doctorate, GRE General Test, interview, minimum GPA of 3.0, 2 letters of recommendation, resume, writing samples, minimum 3 years of professional experience. Additional exam requirements/recommendations for international students: Required—TOEFL (minimum score 600 paper-based; 100 iBT), IELTS (minimum score 5.5). Electronic applications accepted. *Faculty research:* School administrators' accountability in response to New York State and federal regulations and reforms, including merit pay, decision-making in technology within the framework of instructional design; budgetary and expenditure decision-making among school district administrators in response to fiscal restraints, compliance, and changing demographics; twenty-first century technological tools in today's schools; teacher decision-making models based on decision theory.

St. John's University, The School of Education, Division of Administrative and Instructional Leadership, Program in School Building Leadership, Queens, NY 11439. Offers MS Ed, Adv C. *Program availability:* Part-time, evening/weekend, online learning. *Degree requirements:* For master's and Adv C, comprehensive exam, internship. *Entrance requirements:* For master's, official transcript with minimum GPA of 3.0, minimum 3 years of successful teaching experience, New York State Permanent Teaching Certification, bachelor's degree; for Adv C, minimum GPA of 3.5, minimum 3 years of successful teaching experience, New York State Permanent Teaching Certification, essay, 2 letters of reference, transcripts. Additional exam requirements/recommendations for international students: Required—TOEFL (minimum score 600 paper-based; 100 iBT), IELTS (minimum score 7). Electronic applications accepted. *Faculty research:* Analysis of non-public school graduate student outcomes in programs and certification, Catholic school parents' perceptions of school and after school programs, issues in school business leadership from a financial management perspective.

St. John's University, The School of Education, Division of Administrative and Instructional Leadership, Program in School District Leadership, Queens, NY 11439. Offers Adv C. *Program availability:* Part-time, evening/weekend, online learning. *Degree requirements:* For Adv C, comprehensive exam. *Entrance requirements:* For degree, minimum GPA of 3.0, minimum 3 years of successful teaching experience, New York State Permanent Teaching Certification, bachelor's degree. Additional exam requirements/recommendations for international students: Required—TOEFL (minimum score 600 paper-based; 100 iBT), IELTS (minimum score 7). Electronic applications accepted. *Faculty research:* Analysis of school district finances related to resource allocation and decision-making, responsiveness of districts to New York State proposition 13 (property tax caps), implementation of technology planning for the twenty-first century at the school district level.

St. Joseph's College, Long Island Campus, Programs in Education, Field in Educational Leadership, Patchogue, NY 11772-2399. Offers MA. *Program availability:* Part-time, evening/weekend. *Faculty:* 2 part-time/adjunct (1 woman). *Students:* 8 part-time (7 women); includes 2 minority (1 Black or African American, non-Hispanic/Latino; 1 Hispanic/Latino). Average age 30. 16 applicants, 81% accepted, 9 enrolled. *Entrance requirements:* Additional exam requirements/recommendations for international students: Recommended—TOEFL (minimum score 550 paper-based). *Application deadline:* Applications are processed on a rolling basis. Application fee: $25. Electronic

applications accepted. *Expenses:* Contact institution. *Financial support:* In 2016–17, 1 student received support. *Unit head:* Dr. S. Nancy Gilchriest, Associate Professor/ Department Chair, 631-687-1472, E-mail: ngilchriest@sjcny.edu. *Application contact:* Jodi A. Duffy, Senior Associate Director of Graduate Admissions, 631-687-4525, E-mail: jduffy@sjcny.edu.
Website: http://www.sjcny.edu/long-island

St. Joseph's College, New York, Programs in Education, Field in Educational Leadership, Brooklyn, NY 11205-3688. Offers MA. *Program availability:* Part-time, evening/weekend. *Faculty:* 2 part-time/adjunct (both women). *Students:* 2 applicants, 50% accepted. *Entrance requirements:* For master's, GRE, PRAXIS, or MAT, official transcripts, teaching certificate, 2 letters of recommendation, personal statement, resume. Additional exam requirements/recommendations for international students: Required—TOEFL (minimum score 80 iBT). *Application deadline:* Applications are processed on a rolling basis. Application fee: $25. Electronic applications accepted. *Expenses:* Contact institution. *Financial support:* Alumni grants and/or Alumni Excellence Awards available. Financial award applicants required to submit FAFSA. *Unit head:* Sr. Nancy Gilchriest, Associate Professor/Department Chair, 631-687-1472, E-mail: ngilchriest@sjcny.edu.
Website: https://www.sjcny.edu

Saint Joseph's College of Maine, Master of Science in Education Program, Standish, ME 04084. Offers adult education and training (MS Ed); Catholic school leadership (MS Ed); health care educator (MS Ed); school educator (MS Ed). Program available by correspondence. *Program availability:* Part-time, online learning. Electronic applications accepted.

Saint Joseph's University, College of Arts and Sciences, Graduate Programs in Education, Philadelphia, PA 19131-1395. Offers curriculum supervisor (Certificate); educational leadership (MS, Ed D); elementary education (MS, Certificate); elementary/ middle school education (Certificate); instructional technology (MS, Certificate); organizational development and leadership (MS); principal (Certificate); professional education (MS); reading specialist (MS, Certificate); reading supervisor (Certificate); secondary education (MS, Certificate); special education (MS); special education 7-12 (Certificate); special education PK-8 (Certificate); superintendent's letter of eligibility (Certificate); supervisor of special education (Certificate); teacher of the deaf and hard of hearing (Certificate). *Program availability:* Part-time, evening/weekend, blended/hybrid learning. *Faculty:* 26 full-time (21 women), 74 part-time/adjunct (45 women). *Students:* 107 full-time (88 women), 826 part-time (622 women); includes 170 minority (115 Black or African American, non-Hispanic/Latino; 2 American Indian or Alaska Native, non-Hispanic/Latino; 11 Asian, non-Hispanic/Latino; 31 Hispanic/Latino; 1 Native Hawaiian or other Pacific Islander, non-Hispanic/Latino; 10 Two or more races, non-Hispanic/ Latino), 18 international. Average age 33. 338 applicants, 76% accepted, 173 enrolled. In 2016, 419 master's, 16 doctorates, 24 other advanced degrees awarded. *Degree requirements:* For master's, thesis or alternative; for doctorate, comprehensive exam, thesis/dissertation. *Entrance requirements:* For master's, 2 letters of recommendation, minimum GPA of 3.0, official transcripts, personal statement; for doctorate, GRE, master's degree from accredited institution, minimum graduate GPA of 3.5, computer competence, interview with program director. Additional exam requirements/ recommendations for international students: Required—TOEFL (minimum score 550 paper-based; 80 iBT), IELTS (minimum score 6.5), PTE (minimum score 60). *Application deadline:* For fall admission, 7/15 for international students; for spring admission, 11/1 for international students. Applications are processed on a rolling basis. Application fee: $35. Electronic applications accepted. *Expenses:* $750 per credit, $100 education fee, $360 online organization development and leadership residency fee. *Financial support:* In 2016–17, 25 students received support. Unspecified assistantships available. Financial award application deadline: 5/1; financial award applicants required to submit FAFSA. *Faculty research:* Factors predicting early mathematics skills for low income children, early child care and development, preschool quality, parent communication and home-school collaboration issues, education of terminally ill children, preparing literacy teachers for urban schools. *Total annual research expenditures:* $18,118. *Unit head:* Dr. John Vacca, Associate Dean, Education, 610-660-3131, E-mail: gradcas@sju.edu. *Application contact:* Graduate Admissions, College of Arts and Sciences, 610-660-3131, E-mail: gradcas@sju.edu.
Website: http://sju.edu/int/academics/cas/grad/education/index.html

St. Lawrence University, Department of Education, Program in Educational Leadership, Canton, NY 13617. Offers combined school building leadership/school district leadership (CAS); educational leadership (M Ed); school building leadership (M Ed); school district leadership (CAS). *Program availability:* Part-time, evening/ weekend. *Entrance requirements:* For master's, GRE General Test. *Faculty research:* Leadership.

Saint Leo University, Graduate Studies in Education, Saint Leo, FL 33574-6665. Offers educational leadership (M Ed), including Catholic school administration; exceptional student education (M Ed); instructional design (MS, Certificate); instructional leadership (M Ed); reading (M Ed, Certificate); school leadership (Ed S). *Program availability:* Part-time, evening/weekend, online learning. *Faculty:* 11 full-time (10 women), 22 part-time/ adjunct (15 women). *Students:* 424 part-time (335 women); includes 94 minority (54 Black or African American, non-Hispanic/Latino; 2 Asian, non-Hispanic/Latino; 32 Hispanic/Latino; 6 Two or more races, non-Hispanic/Latino), 1 international. Average age 37. 260 applicants, 76% accepted, 107 enrolled. In 2016, 166 master's, 6 other advanced degrees awarded. *Degree requirements:* For master's, appropriate State of Florida certification tests. *Entrance requirements:* For master's, GRE (minimum score of 1000), MAT (minimum score of 410), or minimum undergraduate GPA of 3.0 in final 2 years, official transcripts, current resumé, 2 professional recommendations, personal statement, bachelor's degree from regionally-accredited university, valid professional teaching certificate; for other advanced degree, valid professional teaching certificate (for Ed S). Additional exam requirements/recommendations for international students: Required—TOEFL (minimum score 550 paper-based; 80 iBT). *Application deadline:* For fall admission, 7/1 priority date for domestic students, 7/1 for international students; for winter admission, 7/1 for international students; for spring admission, 11/1 priority date for domestic students. Applications are processed on a rolling basis. Application fee: $80. Electronic applications accepted. *Expenses:* $465 per semester hour (for MS); $480 per semester hour (for M Ed); $670 per semester hour (for Ed S). *Financial support:* In 2016–17, 17 students received support. Career-related internships or fieldwork, scholarships/grants, and health care benefits available. Financial award application deadline: 3/1; financial award applicants required to submit FAFSA. *Faculty research:* Student achievement in literacy, leadership, instructional technology. *Unit head:* Dr. Fern Aefsky, Director of Graduate Studies in Education, 352-588-8309, Fax: 352-588-8861, E-mail: kara.winkler@saintleo.edu. *Application contact:* Jennifer Shelley, Senior Associate Director of Graduate Admissions, 800-707-8846, Fax: 352-588-7873, E-mail: grad.admissions@saintleo.edu.
Website: http://www.saintleo.edu/academics/graduate.aspx

Saint Louis University, Graduate Education, College of Education and Public Service and Graduate Education, Department of Educational Leadership and Higher Education, St. Louis, MO 63103. Offers Catholic school leadership (MA); educational administration (MA, Ed D, PhD, Ed S); higher education (MA, Ed D, PhD); student personnel administration (MA). *Accreditation:* NCATE. *Program availability:* Part-time. *Degree requirements:* For master's, comprehensive written and oral exam; for doctorate, comprehensive exam, thesis/dissertation, preliminary oral and written exams. *Entrance requirements:* For master's, GRE General Test, MAT, LSAT, GMAT or MCAT, letters of recommendation, resume; for doctorate and Ed S, GRE General Test, LSAT, GMAT or MCAT, letters of recommendation, resumé, goal statement, transcripts. Additional exam requirements/recommendations for international students: Required—TOEFL (minimum score 525 paper-based). Electronic applications accepted. *Faculty research:* Superintendent of schools, school finance, school facilities, student personal administration, building leadership.

Saint Mary's College of California, Kalmanovitz School of Education, Program in Early Childhood Education, Moraga, CA 94575. Offers supervision and leadership (MA). *Program availability:* Part-time, evening/weekend. *Degree requirements:* For master's, thesis or alternative. *Entrance requirements:* For master's, interview, minimum GPA of 3.0.

Saint Mary's College of California, Kalmanovitz School of Education, Program in Educational Leadership, Moraga, CA 94575. Offers educational administration (MA); educational leadership (Ed D); preliminary administrative services (Credential). *Program availability:* Part-time, evening/weekend. *Degree requirements:* For master's, thesis or alternative; for doctorate, thesis/dissertation. *Entrance requirements:* For master's, interview, minimum GPA of 3.0, teaching credential; for doctorate, GRE or MAT, interview, MA, minimum GPA of 3.0. *Faculty research:* Building communities, programs in educational leadership, alignment of curriculum to standards.

Saint Mary's College of California, Kalmanovitz School of Education, Teaching Leadership Program, Moraga, CA 94575. Offers MA.

St. Mary's University, Graduate Studies, Program in Catholic School Leadership, San Antonio, TX 78228-8507. Offers MA. *Program availability:* Part-time, evening/weekend, online learning. *Students:* 5 part-time (all women); includes 4 minority (2 Asian, non-Hispanic/Latino; 2 Hispanic/Latino). Average age 35. 6 applicants, 50% accepted, 3 enrolled. In 2016, 8 master's awarded. *Degree requirements:* For master's, comprehensive exam. *Entrance requirements:* For master's, GRE, minimum undergraduate GPA of 2.7. Additional exam requirements/recommendations for international students: Required—TOEFL (minimum score 550 paper-based; 80 iBT), IELTS (minimum score 6). *Application deadline:* For fall admission, 7/1 for domestic students; for spring admission, 11/15 for domestic students; for summer admission, 4/1 for domestic students. Applications are processed on a rolling basis. Application fee: $0. Electronic applications accepted. *Expenses: Tuition:* Full-time $15,600; part-time $865 per credit hour. *Required fees:* $148 per semester. *Financial support:* Career-related internships or fieldwork, Federal Work-Study, institutionally sponsored loans, scholarships/grants, health care benefits, and unspecified assistantships available. Financial award application deadline: 3/31; financial award applicants required to submit FAFSA. *Faculty research:* Classical American philosophy, philosophy of education. *Unit head:* Dr. Dan Higgins, Program Director, 210-436-3121, E-mail: dhiggins@ stmarytx.edu. *Application contact:* Kim Thornton, Director, Graduate and Adult Enrollment Services, 210-436-3101, E-mail: kthornton@stmarytx.edu.
Website: https://www.stmarytx.edu/academics/graduate/masters/catholicschool/

St. Mary's University, Graduate Studies, Program in Educational Leadership, San Antonio, TX 78228-8507. Offers MA. *Program availability:* Part-time, evening/weekend. *Students:* 5 full-time (4 women), 11 part-time (9 women); includes 6 minority (all Hispanic/Latino), 3 international. Average age 26. 18 applicants, 39% accepted, 6 enrolled. In 2016, 6 master's awarded. *Entrance requirements:* For master's, GRE, minimum undergraduate GPA of 2.7. Additional exam requirements/recommendations for international students: Required—TOEFL (minimum score 550 paper-based; 80 iBT), IELTS (minimum score 6). *Application deadline:* For fall admission, 7/1 for domestic students; for spring admission, 11/15 for domestic students; for summer admission, 4/1 for domestic students. Applications are processed on a rolling basis. Application fee: $0. Electronic applications accepted. *Expenses: Tuition:* Full-time $15,600; part-time $865 per credit hour. *Required fees:* $148 per semester. *Financial support:* Fellowships, career-related internships or fieldwork, Federal Work-Study, institutionally sponsored loans, scholarships/grants, health care benefits, and unspecified assistantships available. Financial award application deadline: 3/31; financial award applicants required to submit FAFSA. *Faculty research:* Philosophy of education. *Unit head:* Dr. Dan Higgins, Program Director, 210-436-3121, E-mail: dhiggins@stmarytx.edu. *Application contact:* Kim Thornton, Director, Graduate and Adult Enrollment Services, 210-436-3101, E-mail: kthornton@stmarytx.edu.
Website: https://www.stmarytx.edu/academics/graduate/masters/educational-leadership/

Saint Mary's University of Minnesota, Schools of Graduate and Professional Programs, Graduate School of Education, Educational Administration Program, Winona, MN 55987-1399. Offers educational administration (Certificate, Ed S), including director of special education, K-12 principal, superintendent. Tuition and fees vary according to degree level and program. *Unit head:* Dr. William Bjorum, Director, 612-728-5126, Fax: 612-728-5121, E-mail: wbjorum@smumn.edu. *Application contact:* James Callinan, Director of Admissions for Graduate and Professional Programs, 612-728-5185, Fax: 612-728-5121, E-mail: jcallina@smumn.edu.

Saint Mary's University of Minnesota, Schools of Graduate and Professional Programs, Graduate School of Education, Educational Leadership Program, Winona, MN 55987-1399. Offers MA, Ed D. *Program availability:* Online learning. Tuition and fees vary according to degree level and program. *Unit head:* Dr. John McClure, Director, 612-728-5216, Fax: 612-728-5121, E-mail: jmcclure@smumn.edu. *Application contact:* James Callinan, Director of Admissions for Graduate and Professional Programs, 612-728-5185, Fax: 612-728-5121, E-mail: jcallina@smumn.edu.
Website: http://www.smumn.edu/graduate-home/areas-of-study/graduate-school-of-education/edd-in-leadership

Saint Mary's University of Minnesota, Schools of Graduate and Professional Programs, Graduate School of Education, Institute for LaSallian Studies, Winona, MN 55987-1399. Offers LaSallian leadership (MA); LaSallian studies (MA). Tuition and fees vary according to degree level and program. *Unit head:* Dr. Roxanne Eubank, Director, 612-728-5217, E-mail: reubank@smumn.edu. *Application contact:* James Callinan, Director of Admissions for Graduate and Professional Programs, 612-728-5185, Fax: 612-728-5121, E-mail: jcallina@smumn.edu.
Website: http://www.smumn.edu/graduate-home/areas-of-study/graduate-school-of-education/ma-in-lasallian-studies

Saint Michael's College, Graduate Programs, Program in Education, Colchester, VT 05439. Offers arts in education (CAGS); literacy (M Ed); school leadership (CAGS); special education (M Ed). *Program availability:* Part-time, evening/weekend. *Students:* 5 full-time (4 women), 239 part-time (199 women); includes 9 minority (2 Black or African American, non-Hispanic/Latino; 1 American Indian or Alaska Native, non-Hispanic/ Latino; 1 Asian, non-Hispanic/Latino; 4 Hispanic/Latino; 1 Two or more races, non-Hispanic/Latino), 1 international. Average age 36. In 2016, 31 master's awarded. *Degree requirements:* For master's, thesis. *Entrance requirements:* For master's, minimum GPA of 3.0, official transcripts, essay, interview. *Application deadline:*

Applications are processed on a rolling basis. Application fee: $50. Electronic applications accepted. *Expenses: Tuition:* Full-time $10,620; part-time $590 per credit. Part-time tuition and fees vary according to course load and program. *Financial support:* Fellowships with partial tuition reimbursements and scholarships/grants available. Support available to part-time students. Financial award applicants required to submit FAFSA. *Faculty research:* Integrative curriculum, moral and spiritual dimensions of education, learning styles, multiple intelligences, integrating technology into the curriculum. *Unit head:* Jonathan Silverman, Department Chair, 802-654-2306, Fax: 802-654-2664, E-mail: jsilverman@smcvt.edu. *Application contact:* Lindsay A. Damici, Marketing Communications Manager, 802-654-2556, Fax: 802-654-2732.
Website: http://www.smcvt.edu/graduate-programs/academic-programs/education.aspx

Saint Peter's University, Graduate Programs in Education, Program in Educational Leadership, Jersey City, NJ 07306-5997. Offers MA Ed, Ed D. *Program availability:* Part-time, evening/weekend. *Degree requirements:* For master's, comprehensive exam; for doctorate, comprehensive exam, thesis/dissertation. *Entrance requirements:* For master's and doctorate, GRE or MAT. Additional exam requirements/recommendations for international students: Required—TOEFL. Electronic applications accepted.

St. Thomas Aquinas College, Division of Teacher Education, Sparkill, NY 10976. Offers adolescence education (MST); childhood and special education (MST); childhood education (MST); educational leadership (MS Ed); reading (MS Ed, PMC); special education (MS Ed, PMC); teaching (MS Ed), including elementary education, middle school education, secondary education. *Accreditation:* NCATE. *Program availability:* Part-time, evening/weekend. *Degree requirements:* For master's, comprehensive exam, comprehensive professional portfolio; for PMC, action research project. *Entrance requirements:* For master's, New York State Qualifying Exam, GRE General Test or minimum GPA of 3.0, teaching certificate; for PMC, GRE General Test or minimum GPA of 3.0. Electronic applications accepted. *Faculty research:* Computer applications in education, adolescent special education students, literacy development, inclusive practices for special education students.

St. Thomas University, School of Leadership Studies, Institute for Education, Miami Gardens, FL 33054-6459. Offers earth/space science (Certificate); educational administration (MS, Certificate); educational leadership (Ed D); elementary education (MS); ESOL (Certificate); gifted education (Certificate); instructional technology (MS, Certificate); professional/studies (Certificate); reading (MS, Certificate); special education (MS). *Program availability:* Part-time, evening/weekend. *Degree requirements:* For master's, comprehensive exam; for doctorate, comprehensive exam, thesis/dissertation. *Entrance requirements:* For master's, interview, minimum GPA of 3.0 or GRE; for doctorate, GRE or MAT. Additional exam requirements/recommendations for international students: Required—TOEFL (minimum score 550 paper-based; 79 iBT). Electronic applications accepted.

Saint Vincent College, Program in Education, Latrobe, PA 15650-2690. Offers curriculum and instruction (MS); instructional design and technology (MS); school administration and supervision (MS); special education (MS). *Program availability:* Part-time, evening/weekend. *Degree requirements:* For master's, comprehensive exam. *Entrance requirements:* For master's, GRE (if undergraduate GPA less than 3.0). Additional exam requirements/recommendations for international students: Required—TOEFL (minimum score 550 paper-based). *Faculty research:* Assessment and instructional technology.

Saint Xavier University, Graduate Studies, School of Education, Chicago, IL 60655-3105. Offers counseling (MA); curriculum and instruction (MA); early childhood education (MA); educational administration (MA); elementary education (MA); individualized studies (MA), including educational technology, English as a second language (ESL), ISTEM (integrative science, technology, engineering, and math), science education; music education (MA); reading (MA); secondary education (MA); Spanish education (MA); special education (MA); teaching and leadership (MA). *Accreditation:* NCATE. *Program availability:* Part-time, evening/weekend. *Degree requirements:* For master's, thesis or project. *Entrance requirements:* For master's, minimum GPA of 3.0. *Expenses:* Contact institution.

Salem International University, School of Education, Salem, WV 26426-0500. Offers curriculum and instruction (M Ed); educational leadership (M Ed). *Program availability:* Part-time, evening/weekend, online learning. *Degree requirements:* For master's, comprehensive exam (for some programs), thesis (for some programs). *Entrance requirements:* For master's, GRE, MAT, NTE, 3 letters of recommendation. Additional exam requirements/recommendations for international students: Required—TOEFL (minimum score 550 paper-based). Electronic applications accepted. *Expenses:* Contact institution. *Faculty research:* Improved classroom effectiveness.

Salem State University, School of Graduate Studies, Program in Higher Education in Student Affairs, Salem, MA 01970-5353. Offers M Ed. *Program availability:* Part-time, evening/weekend. *Entrance requirements:* For master's, GRE or MAT. Additional exam requirements/recommendations for international students: Required—TOEFL (minimum score 550 paper-based; 80 iBT) or IELTS (minimum score 5.5).

Salisbury University, Program in Educational Leadership, Salisbury, MD 21801-6837. Offers M Ed. *Program availability:* Part-time, evening/weekend. *Faculty:* 2 full-time (0 women), 2 part-time/adjunct (1 woman). *Students:* 1 (woman) full-time, 31 part-time (17 women); includes 3 minority (1 Black or African American, non-Hispanic/Latino; 1 Hispanic/Latino; 1 Two or more races, non-Hispanic/Latino). Average age 32. 5 applicants, 40% accepted, 2 enrolled. In 2016, 10 master's awarded. *Degree requirements:* For master's, comprehensive exam. *Entrance requirements:* Additional exam requirements/recommendations for international students: Required—TOEFL (minimum score 550 paper-based, 79 iBT) or IELTS (6.5). *Application deadline:* For fall admission, 3/1 priority date for domestic and international students; for spring admission, 10/1 priority date for domestic and international students; for summer admission, 3/1 priority date for domestic and international students. Applications are processed on a rolling basis. Application fee: $65. Electronic applications accepted. *Expenses:* $381 per credit hour resident tuition, $670 per credit hour non-resident tuition; $84 per credit hour fees. *Financial support:* In 2016–17, 1 student received support. Career-related internships or fieldwork and scholarships/grants available. Support available to part-time students. Financial award application deadline: 3/1; financial award applicants required to submit FAFSA. *Faculty research:* Leadership; organizational change; school administration. *Unit head:* Dr. Douglas DeWitt, Graduate Program Director, Educational Leadership, 410-543-6286, Fax: 410-677-0249, E-mail: dmdewitt@salisbury.edu. *Application contact:* Claire Williams, Program Management Specialist, 410-677-0001, E-mail: clwilliams@salisbury.edu.
Website: http://www.salisbury.edu/gsr/gradstudies/MEDpage.html

Samford University, Orlean Beeson School of Education, Birmingham, AL 35229. Offers education (Ed D, Certificate); educational leadership: policy, organizations, leadership (MSE); elementary education (MS Ed); gifted certification (MSE); instructional design and technology (MSE); instructional leadership (MSE, Ed S); K-12 collaborative special education (MSE); teacher leader (Ed S). *Accreditation:* NCATE. *Program availability:* Part-time, evening/weekend, 100% online, blended/hybrid learning. *Faculty:* 15 full-time (9 women), 17 part-time/adjunct (12 women). *Students:* 219 full-time (161 women), 86 part-time (55 women); includes 97 minority (86 Black or African American, non-Hispanic/Latino; 5 American Indian or Alaska Native, non-Hispanic/Latino; 1 Asian, non-Hispanic/Latino; 1 Hispanic/Latino; 4 Two or more races, non-Hispanic/Latino), 2 international. Average age 38. 244 applicants, 52% accepted, 112 enrolled. In 2016, 84 master's, 22 doctorates, 12 Certificates awarded. *Degree requirements:* For master's, comprehensive exam (for some programs); for doctorate, comprehensive exam, thesis/dissertation; for other advanced degree, comprehensive exam. *Entrance requirements:* For master's, GRE or MAT; Alabama Educator Certification Testing Program (AECTP), transcripts, essays, recommendations; for doctorate, professional resume, recommendations, transcripts, interview, essays; for other advanced degree, recommendations, transcripts. Additional exam requirements/recommendations for international students: Required—TOEFL (minimum score 90 iBT), IELTS (minimum score 6.5). *Application deadline:* For fall admission, 7/15 for domestic students, 7/1 for international students; for spring admission, 11/15 for domestic and international students; for summer admission, 4/15 for domestic and international students. Application fee: $35. Electronic applications accepted. *Expenses: Tuition:* Full-time $18,530; part-time $789 per credit hour. *Required fees:* $610. Tuition and fees vary according to course load, degree level, program and student level. *Financial support:* In 2016–17, 246 students received support. Scholarships/grants available. Financial award application deadline: 3/1; financial award applicants required to submit FAFSA. *Faculty research:* Standards-based grading in K-12 schools, effective school principal leadership, effective educational leadership preparation programs, teacher/administrator shortages and job retention, instructional strategies to maximize student learning. *Total annual research expenditures:* $254,360. *Unit head:* Dr. Jean Box, Dean, 205-726-2565, Fax: 205-726-4233, E-mail: jabox@samford.edu. *Application contact:* Brooke Karr, Graduate Admissions Coordinator, 205-729-2783, Fax: 205-726-4233, E-mail: kbgilrea@samford.edu.
Website: http://www.samford.edu/education/

Sam Houston State University, College of Education, Department of Educational Leadership, Huntsville, TX 77341. Offers administration (M Ed); developmental education administration (Ed D); educational leadership (Ed D); higher education administration (MA); instructional leadership (M Ed, MA). *Program availability:* Part-time, evening/weekend, online learning. *Degree requirements:* For master's, comprehensive exam (for some programs), thesis (for some programs); for doctorate, comprehensive exam, thesis/dissertation. *Entrance requirements:* For master's, GRE General Test, references, personal essay, resume, professional statement; for doctorate, GRE General Test, master's degree, references, personal essay, resume. Additional exam requirements/recommendations for international students: Required—TOEFL (minimum score 550 paper-based; 79 iBT), IELTS (minimum score 6.5). Electronic applications accepted.

San Diego State University, Graduate and Research Affairs, College of Education, Department of Administration, Rehabilitation and Post-Secondary Education, San Diego, CA 92182. Offers educational leadership in post-secondary education (MA); rehabilitation counseling (MS), including deafness. *Program availability:* Evening/weekend, online learning. *Degree requirements:* For master's, comprehensive exam (for some programs), thesis (for some programs). *Entrance requirements:* For master's, GRE General Test, letters of reference. Additional exam requirements/recommendations for international students: Required—TOEFL. Electronic applications accepted. *Faculty research:* Rehabilitation in cultural diversity, distance learning technology.

San Diego State University, Graduate and Research Affairs, College of Education, Department of Educational Leadership, San Diego, CA 92182. Offers MA. *Accreditation:* NCATE. *Program availability:* Evening/weekend. *Entrance requirements:* For master's, GRE General Test, letters of reference. Additional exam requirements/recommendations for international students: Required—TOEFL. Electronic applications accepted.

San Francisco State University, Division of Graduate Studies, College of Education, Department of Equity, Leadership Studies, and Instructional Technologies, Program in Educational Administration, San Francisco, CA 94132-1722. Offers MA, Credential. *Accreditation:* NCATE. *Application deadline:* Applications are processed on a rolling basis. *Expenses:* Tuition, state resident: full-time $6738. Tuition, nonresident: full-time $15,666. *Required fees:* $1012. Tuition and fees vary according to degree level and program. *Unit head:* Dr. Doris Flowers, Chair, 415-338-2614, Fax: 415-338-0568, E-mail: dflowers@sfsu.edu. *Application contact:* Dr. Davide Celoria, Graduate Coordinator, 415-405-3659, Fax: 415-338-0568, E-mail: deceloria@sfsu.edu.
Website: http://gcoe.sfsu.edu/

San Francisco State University, Division of Graduate Studies, College of Education, Program in Educational Leadership, San Francisco, CA 94132-1722. Offers Ed D. *Expenses:* Tuition, state resident: full-time $6738. Tuition, nonresident: full-time $15,666. *Required fees:* $1012. Tuition and fees vary according to degree level and program. *Unit head:* Dr. Barbara Henderson, Interim Director, 415-405-4103, Fax: 415-338-7019, E-mail: barbarah@sfsu.edu. *Application contact:* Dr. Andrea Goldfien, Graduate Coordinator, 415 338-7873, Fax: 415-338-7019, E-mail: goldfien@sfsu.edu.
Website: http://edd.sfsu.edu/

San Jose State University, Graduate Studies and Research, Connie L. Lurie College of Education, San Jose, CA 95192-0001. Offers child and adolescent development (MA); common core mathematics (K-8) (Certificate, Credential); education (MA, Credential), including counseling and student personnel (MA), speech pathology (MA); educational leadership (MA, Ed D, Credential), including administration and supervision (MA), higher education (MA), preliminary administrative services (Credential), professional administrative services (Credential); elementary education (MA), including curriculum and instruction; K-12 school counseling (Credential); K-12 school counseling internship (Credential); school child welfare attendance (Credential); single subject (Credential). *Accreditation:* NCATE. *Program availability:* Evening/weekend. Electronic applications accepted.

Santa Clara University, School of Education and Counseling Psychology, Santa Clara, CA 95053. Offers Catholic school teaching (MA); counseling (MA); counseling psychology (MA); educational leadership (MA); interdisciplinary education (MA); teaching multiple subjects (MA); teaching single subjects (MA). *Program availability:* Part-time, evening/weekend. *Faculty:* 32 full-time (22 women), 40 part-time/adjunct (25 women). *Students:* 265 full-time (213 women), 333 part-time (270 women); includes 282 minority (16 Black or African American, non-Hispanic/Latino; 1 American Indian or Alaska Native, non-Hispanic/Latino; 78 Asian, non-Hispanic/Latino; 156 Hispanic/Latino; 31 Two or more races, non-Hispanic/Latino), 46 international. Average age 30. 266 applicants, 74% accepted, 126 enrolled. In 2016, 253 master's awarded. *Entrance requirements:* For master's, transcript, letters of recommendation, statement of purpose, resume. Additional exam requirements/recommendations for international students: Required—TOEFL (minimum score 90 iBT) or IELTS (6.5). *Application deadline:* Applications are processed on a rolling basis. Application fee: $50. Electronic applications accepted. *Expenses:* $581 per unit. *Financial support:* Fellowships, research assistantships, teaching assistantships, career-related internships or fieldwork, Federal Work-Study, scholarships/grants, traineeships, health care benefits, and tuition waivers available. Support available to part-time students. Financial award applicants required to submit FAFSA. *Unit head:* Dr. Sabrina Zirkel, Dean, 408-551-3074, Fax:

408-554-4367, E-mail: szirkel@scu.edu. *Application contact:* Victoria Rodriguez, Graduate Admissions Advisor, 408-554-4723, E-mail: v1rodriguez@scu.edu.
Website: http://www.scu.edu/ecp/

Schreiner University, Department of Education, Kerrville, TX 78028-5697. Offers education (M Ed); principal (Certificate). *Program availability:* Part-time, evening/weekend, online learning. *Entrance requirements:* For master's, GRE (waived if undergraduate cumulative GPA is 3.0 or above), 3 references; transcripts; interview. Additional exam requirements/recommendations for international students: Required—TOEFL. Electronic applications accepted.

Seattle Pacific University, Educational Leadership Programs, Seattle, WA 98119-1997. Offers educational leadership (M Ed, Ed D); principal (Certificate); program administrator (Certificate); superintendent (Certificate). *Accreditation:* NCATE. *Program availability:* Part-time, evening/weekend. *Degree requirements:* For master's, comprehensive exam; for doctorate, comprehensive exam, thesis/dissertation. *Entrance requirements:* For master's, GRE (minimum combined verbal and quantitative score of 950) or MAT (minimum 385 scaled score), or minimum undergraduate GPA of 3.0 cumulative or in last 45 credits of completed undergraduate coursework, copy of teaching certificate, official transcript(s) from each college/university attended, resume, personal statement (1-2 pages); for doctorate, GRE General Test or MAT, minimum GPA of 3.0, formal interview. Electronic applications accepted.

Seattle Pacific University, Master of Education in Teacher Leadership Program, Seattle, WA 98119-1997. Offers M Ed. *Accreditation:* NCATE. *Program availability:* Part-time, evening/weekend. *Degree requirements:* For master's, comprehensive exam. *Entrance requirements:* For master's, GRE General Test or MAT, copy of teaching certificate, official transcript(s), resume, personal statement, two letters of recommendation. Additional exam requirements/recommendations for international students: Required—TOEFL (minimum score 550 paper-based). Electronic applications accepted. *Expenses:* Contact institution. *Faculty research:* Educational technology, classroom environments, character education.

Seattle University, College of Education, Program in Educational Administration, Seattle, WA 98122-1090. Offers M Ed, MA, Certificate, Ed S. *Accreditation:* NCATE. *Program availability:* Part-time, evening/weekend. *Faculty:* 4 full-time (1 woman), 3 part-time/adjunct (all women). *Students:* 15 part-time (7 women); includes 3 minority (1 Black or African American, non-Hispanic/Latino; 2 Hispanic/Latino). Average age 38. 1 applicant, 100% accepted, 1 enrolled. In 2016, 13 master's, 1 other advanced degree awarded. *Degree requirements:* For master's and other advanced degree, comprehensive exam. *Entrance requirements:* For master's, GRE, MAT, or minimum GPA of 3.0; interview; 1 year of related experience. Additional exam requirements/recommendations for international students: Required—TOEFL. *Application deadline:* For fall admission, 8/20 priority date for domestic students; for winter admission, 11/20 for domestic students; for spring admission, 2/20 for domestic students. Applications are processed on a rolling basis. Application fee: $55. *Financial support:* In 2016–17, 6 students received support. Career-related internships or fieldwork and Federal Work-Study available. Support available to part-time students. Financial award applicants required to submit FAFSA. *Unit head:* Dr. Michael Silver, Director, 206-296-5798, E-mail: silverm@seattleu.edu. *Application contact:* Janet Shandley, Associate Dean of Graduate Admissions, 206-296-5900, Fax: 206-298-5656, E-mail: grad_admissions@seattleu.edu.
Website: https://www.seattleu.edu/education/edadmin/

Seattle University, College of Education, Program in Educational Leadership, Seattle, WA 98122-1090. Offers Ed D. *Accreditation:* NCATE. *Program availability:* Part-time, evening/weekend. *Faculty:* 6 full-time (3 women), 2 part-time/adjunct (both women). *Students:* 7 full-time (4 women), 52 part-time (30 women); includes 22 minority (7 Black or African American, non-Hispanic/Latino; 2 American Indian or Alaska Native, non-Hispanic/Latino; 6 Asian, non-Hispanic/Latino; 3 Hispanic/Latino; 4 Two or more races, non-Hispanic/Latino), 4 international. Average age 45. In 2016, 10 doctorates awarded. *Degree requirements:* For doctorate, comprehensive exam, thesis/dissertation. *Entrance requirements:* For doctorate, GRE General Test, MAT, interview, MA, minimum GPA of 3.5, 3 years of related experience. Additional exam requirements/recommendations for international students: Required—TOEFL. *Application deadline:* For fall admission, 4/1 for domestic students. Application fee: $55. *Expenses:* Contact institution. *Financial support:* In 2016–17, 7 students received support. Career-related internships or fieldwork and Federal Work-Study available. Support available to part-time students. Financial award applicants required to submit FAFSA. *Unit head:* Dr. Laurie Stevahn, Chair, 206-296-5750, E-mail: stevahnl@seattleu.edu. *Application contact:* Janet Shandley, Associate Dean of Graduate Admissions, 206-296-5900, Fax: 206-298-5656, E-mail: grad_admissions@seattleu.edu.
Website: https://www.seattleu.edu/education/edlr/

Seattle University, College of Education, Program in Student Development Administration, Seattle, WA 98122-1090. Offers M Ed, MA. *Program availability:* Part-time, evening/weekend. *Faculty:* 4 full-time (3 women). *Students:* 29 full-time (19 women), 32 part-time (25 women); includes 37 minority (3 Black or African American, non-Hispanic/Latino; 1 American Indian or Alaska Native, non-Hispanic/Latino; 11 Asian, non-Hispanic/Latino; 16 Hispanic/Latino; 1 Native Hawaiian or other Pacific Islander, non-Hispanic/Latino; 5 Two or more races, non-Hispanic/Latino). Average age 26. 123 applicants, 53% accepted, 30 enrolled. In 2016, 29 master's awarded. *Degree requirements:* For master's, comprehensive exam. *Entrance requirements:* For master's, GRE, MAT, or minimum GPA of 3.0; two recommendations; resume; self-assessment form; autobiography. Additional exam requirements/recommendations for international students: Required—TOEFL. *Application deadline:* For fall admission, 1/15 priority date for domestic students; for winter admission, 11/20 for domestic students; for spring admission, 2/20 for domestic students. Applications are processed on a rolling basis. Application fee: $55. *Financial support:* In 2016–17, 13 students received support. Career-related internships or fieldwork, Federal Work-Study, and unspecified assistantships available. Support available to part-time students. Financial award applicants required to submit FAFSA. *Unit head:* Dr. Jeremy Stringer, Coordinator, 206-296-6170, E-mail: stringer@seattleu.edu. *Application contact:* Janet Shandley, Associate Dean of Graduate Admissions, 206-296-5900, Fax: 206-298-5656, E-mail: grad_admissions@seattleu.edu.
Website: https://www.seattleu.edu/coe/sda/

Seton Hall University, College of Education and Human Services, Department of Education Leadership, Management and Policy, Program in Higher Education Administration, South Orange, NJ 07079-2697. Offers Ed D, PhD. *Accreditation:* NCATE. *Program availability:* Part-time, evening/weekend. *Faculty:* 12 full-time (4 women), 1 part-time/adjunct (0 women). *Students:* 20 full-time (12 women), 78 part-time (50 women); includes 39 minority (26 Black or African American, non-Hispanic/Latino; 5 Asian, non-Hispanic/Latino; 8 Hispanic/Latino), 2 international. Average age 41. 37 applicants, 84% accepted, 15 enrolled. In 2016, 8 doctorates awarded. *Degree requirements:* For doctorate, comprehensive exam, thesis/dissertation, internship. *Entrance requirements:* For doctorate, GRE or MAT, interview, minimum GPA of 3.5. Additional exam requirements/recommendations for international students: Required—TOEFL. *Application deadline:* For fall admission, 2/1 priority date for domestic students; for spring admission, 10/1 for domestic students. Applications are processed on a rolling basis. Application fee: $75. *Financial support:* In 2016–17, 7 research assistantships with tuition reimbursements (averaging $4,500 per year) were awarded. Financial award application deadline: 2/1. *Unit head:* Dr. Elaine Walker, Chair, 973-275-2307, E-mail: elaine.walker@shu.edu. *Application contact:* Diana Minakakis, Associate Dean, 973-275-2824, Fax: 973-275-2187, E-mail: diana.minakakis@shu.edu.
Website: http://www.shu.edu/academics/education/edd-higher-ed/index.cfm

Seton Hall University, College of Education and Human Services, Department of Education Leadership, Management and Policy, Program in K–12 Leadership, Management and Policy, South Orange, NJ 07079-2697. Offers Ed D, Exec Ed D, Ed S. *Program availability:* Part-time, evening/weekend. *Faculty:* 12 full-time (4 women), 1 part-time/adjunct (0 women). *Students:* 36 full-time (21 women), 232 part-time (145 women); includes 60 minority (41 Black or African American, non-Hispanic/Latino; 4 Asian, non-Hispanic/Latino; 15 Hispanic/Latino), 2 international. Average age 43. 39 applicants, 77% accepted, 25 enrolled. In 2016, 21 doctorates, 10 other advanced degrees awarded. *Degree requirements:* For doctorate, comprehensive exam, thesis/dissertation. *Entrance requirements:* For doctorate, MAT or GRE, interview. Additional exam requirements/recommendations for international students: Required—TOEFL. *Application deadline:* For fall admission, 2/1 for domestic students; for spring admission, 12/1 for domestic students. Applications are processed on a rolling basis. Application fee: $75. *Financial support:* In 2016–17, 2 research assistantships with full tuition reimbursements (averaging $4,500 per year) were awarded; unspecified assistantships also available. Financial award application deadline: 2/1. *Unit head:* Dr. Elaine Walker, Chair, 973-275-2307, E-mail: elaine.walker@shu.edu. *Application contact:* Diana Minakakis, Director of Graduate Admissions, 973-275-2824.
Website: http://www.shu.edu/academics/education/edd-k-12-administration/index.cfm

Shasta Bible College, Program in School and Church Administration, Redding, CA 96002. Offers MS. *Program availability:* Part-time, evening/weekend. *Degree requirements:* For master's, comprehensive exam (for some programs), thesis or alternative. *Entrance requirements:* For master's, cumulative GPA of 3.0, 9 semester hours of education or psychology courses. Additional exam requirements/recommendations for international students: Required—TOEFL (minimum score 550 paper-based).

Shenandoah University, School of Education and Human Development, Winchester, VA 22601-5195. Offers administrative leadership (D Ed); educational administration (MSE); emphasis in teaching (MSE); health and physical education (Certificate); individual focus (MSE); literacy education (MS); middle school teacher education (Certificate); organizational leadership (MS, D Prof); secondary school teacher education (Certificate); special education (MSE). *Accreditation:* TEAC. *Program availability:* Part-time, evening/weekend. *Faculty:* 9 full-time (7 women), 43 part-time/adjunct (33 women). *Students:* 31 full-time (25 women), 236 part-time (160 women); includes 39 minority (19 Black or African American, non-Hispanic/Latino; 1 American Indian or Alaska Native, non-Hispanic/Latino; 10 Asian, non-Hispanic/Latino; 7 Hispanic/Latino; 1 Native Hawaiian or other Pacific Islander, non-Hispanic/Latino; 1 Two or more races, non-Hispanic/Latino), 4 international. Average age 37. 90 applicants, 97% accepted, 56 enrolled. In 2016, 113 master's, 13 doctorates, 38 other advanced degrees awarded. *Degree requirements:* For master's, comprehensive exam (for some programs), thesis (for some programs); for doctorate, comprehensive exam, thesis/dissertation. *Entrance requirements:* For degree, PRAXIS Academic Core, SAT/ACT, PRAXIS Academic Core Math, or VCLA, three letters of recommendation, writing sample, undergraduate degree. Additional exam requirements/recommendations for international students: Required—TOEFL (minimum score 550 paper-based; 79 iBT), IELTS (minimum score 6.5). *Application deadline:* For fall admission, 5/1 priority date for domestic students, 5/1 for international students; for spring admission, 10/15 priority date for domestic students, 10/15 for international students; for summer admission, 3/15 priority date for domestic students, 3/15 for international students. Application fee: $30. Electronic applications accepted. *Expenses:* Contact institution. *Financial support:* In 2016–17, 18 students received support. Scholarships/grants and unspecified assistantships available. Financial award applicants required to submit FAFSA. *Faculty research:* Exploring helplessness and anxiety in learning statistics, facilitating effective classroom group work, expert-novice dynamics in teaching, K-12 policy implementation and change, adult education, family-school-community relations, mentoring of first-year school principals. *Total annual research expenditures:* $2,000. *Unit head:* Dennis William Kellison, PhD, Director, 540-535-7324, Fax: 540-665-4726, E-mail: dkelliso@su.edu. *Application contact:* Andrew Woodall, Executive Director of Recruitment and Admissions, 540-665-4581, Fax: 540-665-4627, E-mail: admit@su.edu.
Website: http://www.su.edu/education/

Shippensburg University of Pennsylvania, School of Graduate Studies, College of Education and Human Services, Department of Educational Leadership and Special Education, Shippensburg, PA 17257-2299. Offers educational leadership (M Ed, Ed D); special education (M Ed), including behavior disorders, comprehensive, learning disabilities, mental retardation/developmental disabilities. *Accreditation:* NCATE. *Program availability:* Part-time, evening/weekend, blended/hybrid learning. *Faculty:* 7 full-time (1 woman), 6 part-time/adjunct (all women). *Students:* 14 full-time (9 women), 89 part-time (47 women); includes 5 minority (3 Black or African American, non-Hispanic/Latino; 2 Two or more races, non-Hispanic/Latino), 11 international. Average age 34. 118 applicants, 69% accepted, 68 enrolled. In 2016, 40 master's awarded. *Degree requirements:* For master's, candidacy, thesis, or practicum; for doctorate, comprehensive exam, thesis/dissertation, candidacy exam; 24 credits (six 4-credit residencies) of field-based courses leading to the superintendent's letter of eligibility. *Entrance requirements:* For master's, GRE or MAT (if GPA is less than 2.75), 2 years of successful teaching experience; for doctorate, resume; three letters of recommendation; 500-1000 word goals statement; teaching certifications and endorsements currently held; experience as public school administrator or supervisor that requires an administrative/supervisory certificate. Additional exam requirements/recommendations for international students: Required—TOEFL (minimum score 550 paper-based, 68 iBT) or IELTS (minimum score 6). *Application deadline:* For fall admission, 2/1 for domestic students, 4/30 for international students; for spring admission, 7/1 for domestic students, 9/30 for international students. Applications are processed on a rolling basis. Application fee: $45. Electronic applications accepted. *Expenses:* Tuition, state resident: part-time $483 per credit. Tuition, nonresident: part-time $725 per credit. *Required fees:* $141 per credit. *Financial support:* In 2016–17, 4 students received support. Career-related internships or fieldwork, scholarships/grants, unspecified assistantships, and resident hall director and student payroll positions available. Support available to part-time students. Financial award application deadline: 3/1; financial award applicants required to submit FAFSA. *Unit head:* Dr. Thomas C. Gibbon, Interim Departmental Chair, 717-477-1498, Fax: 717-477-4036, E-mail: tcgibb@ship.edu. *Application contact:* Megan N. Luft, Assistant Dean of Graduate Admissions, 717-477-1231, Fax: 717-477-4016, E-mail: mnluft@ship.edu.
Website: http://www.ship.edu/else/

Siena Heights University, Graduate College, Adrian, MI 49221-1796. Offers clinical mental health counseling (MA); educational leadership (Specialist); leadership (MA), including health care leadership, organizational leadership; teacher education (MA), including early childhood education, early childhood education: Montessori, education leadership: principal, elementary education: reading K-12, leadership: higher education, secondary education: reading K-12, special education: cognitive impairment, special education: learning disabilities. *Program availability:* Part-time, evening/weekend. *Degree requirements:* For master's, thesis, presentation. *Entrance requirements:* For master's, minimum GPA of 3.0, current resume, essay, all post-secondary transcripts, 3 letters of reference, conviction disclosure form; copy of teaching certificate (for some education programs); for Specialist, master's degree, minimum GPA of 3.0, current resume, essay, all post-secondary transcripts, 3 letters of reference, conviction disclosure form; copy of teaching certificate (for some education programs). Electronic applications accepted.

Sierra Nevada College, Teacher Education Program, Incline Village, NV 89451. Offers advanced teaching and leadership (M Ed); elementary education (MAT); secondary education (MAT). *Program availability:* Part-time, evening/weekend, online learning. *Degree requirements:* For master's, comprehensive exam, thesis, PRAXIS I and II. *Entrance requirements:* For master's, 2 letters of recommendation, minimum GPA of 3.0. Electronic applications accepted.

Silver Lake College of the Holy Family, Graduate School, Graduate Education Program, Manitowoc, WI 54220-9319. Offers administrative leadership (MA Ed); teacher leadership (MA Ed). *Program availability:* Part-time, evening/weekend, blended/hybrid learning. *Faculty:* 2 full-time (both women), 4 part-time/adjunct (2 women). *Students:* 16 full-time (8 women), 10 part-time (8 women); includes 2 minority (both Black or African American, non-Hispanic/Latino). Average age 38. In 2016, 18 master's awarded. *Degree requirements:* For master's, comprehensive exam, thesis or alternative, capstone culminating project, comprehensive portfolio, or public presentation of project. *Entrance requirements:* For master's, ACT (preferred) or SAT, minimum undergraduate GPA of 3.0. Additional exam requirements/recommendations for international students: Required—TOEFL (minimum score 550 paper-based; 89 iBT). *Application deadline:* For fall admission, 8/1 for domestic and international students; for spring admission, 12/1 for domestic and international students. Applications are processed on a rolling basis. Application fee: $50. Electronic applications accepted. *Expenses:* $540 per credit; $220 comprehensive fee. *Financial support:* Federal Work-Study, scholarships/grants, and unspecified assistantships available. Support available to part-time students. Financial award application deadline: 6/1; financial award applicants required to submit FAFSA. *Faculty research:* Student development; school administration. *Unit head:* Nancy Sim, Director of Graduate Education Programs, 920-686-6117, Fax: 920-686-6322, E-mail: nancy.sim@sl.edu. *Application contact:* Jamie A. Grant, Executive Director of Enrollment Management, 920-686-6175, Fax: 920-686-6322, E-mail: jamie.grant@sl.edu.
Website: http://www.sl.edu/future-students/graduate-programs/degrees-offered/master-of-arts-in-education

Simon Fraser University, Office of Graduate Studies and Postdoctoral Fellows, Faculty of Education, Program in Educational Leadership, Burnaby, BC V5A 1S6, Canada. Offers M Ed, MA, Ed D. *Program availability:* Part-time, evening/weekend. *Faculty:* 8 full-time (5 women). *Degree requirements:* For master's, comprehensive exam (for some programs), thesis (for some programs); for doctorate, comprehensive exam, thesis/dissertation. *Entrance requirements:* For master's, minimum GPA of 3.0 (on scale of 4.33) or 3.33 based on last 60 credits of undergraduate courses; for doctorate, minimum GPA of 3.5 (on scale of 4.33). Additional exam requirements/recommendations for international students: Recommended—TOEFL (minimum score 580 paper-based; 93 iBT), IELTS (minimum score 7), TWE (minimum score 5). *Application deadline:* For fall admission, 1/28 for domestic and international students. Application fee: $90 ($125 for international students). Electronic applications accepted. *Financial support:* In 2016–17, fellowships (averaging $6,250 per year) were awarded; research assistantships, teaching assistantships, career-related internships or fieldwork, and scholarships/grants also available. *Faculty research:* Language learning, assessment and accountability policy, intersections between student affairs and services, recruitment and retention, indigenous peoples, student success in post-secondary education. *Unit head:* Dr. Shawn Bullock, Graduate Chair, 778-782-4102. *Application contact:* Graduate Secretary, 778-782-5891, E-mail: cpmed@sfu.ca.

Simpson University, School of Education, Redding, CA 96003-8606. Offers education (MA), including curriculum, education leadership; education and preliminary administrative services credential (MA); education and preliminary teaching credential (MA); teaching (MA). *Program availability:* Part-time, evening/weekend. *Faculty:* 4 full-time (1 woman), 9 part-time/adjunct (3 women). *Students:* 8 full-time (7 women), 10 part-time (7 women); includes 1 minority (Two or more races, non-Hispanic/Latino), 1 international. Average age 37. In 2016, 16 master's awarded. *Degree requirements:* For master's, thesis optional. *Entrance requirements:* For master's, statement of purpose, 2 professional references, professional essay, interview. Additional exam requirements/recommendations for international students: Required—TOEFL (minimum score 550 paper-based). *Application deadline:* Applications are processed on a rolling basis. Application fee: $35. Electronic applications accepted. *Expenses:* $420 per credit. *Financial support:* Scholarships/grants available. Financial award application deadline: 7/15; financial award applicants required to submit FAFSA. *Unit head:* Dr. Craig Cook, Dean of Education, 530-226-4188, Fax: 530-226-4872, E-mail: ccook@simpsonu.edu. *Application contact:* Stacy Burgess, Director of Admissions for Adult and Graduate Studies, 530-226-4961, E-mail: sburgess@simpsonu.edu.

Slippery Rock University of Pennsylvania, Graduate Studies (Recruitment), College of Education, Department of Special Education, Slippery Rock, PA 16057-1383. Offers autism (M Ed); master teacher (M Ed), including birth to grade 8, grades 7 to 12; special education (Ed D); supervision (M Ed); technology for online instruction (M Ed). *Accreditation:* NCATE. *Program availability:* Part-time, evening/weekend, 100% online. *Faculty:* 13 full-time (7 women). *Students:* 42 full-time (36 women), 278 part-time (230 women); includes 7 minority (3 Black or African American, non-Hispanic/Latino; 1 Asian, non-Hispanic/Latino; 2 Hispanic/Latino; 1 Two or more races, non-Hispanic/Latino). Average age 32. 231 applicants, 77% accepted, 100 enrolled. In 2016, 134 master's awarded. *Degree requirements:* For master's, thesis optional. *Entrance requirements:* For master's, minimum GPA of 3.0, official transcripts, teaching certification. Additional exam requirements/recommendations for international students: Required—TOEFL (minimum score 550 paper-based; 80 iBT). *Application deadline:* For fall admission, 3/1 priority date for domestic students, 5/1 priority date for international students; for spring admission, 10/1 priority date for domestic students, 9/1 priority date for international students. Applications are processed on a rolling basis. Application fee: $25 ($30 for international students). Electronic applications accepted. *Expenses:* $646.50 per credit in-state, $936.80 per credit out-of-state; $581.45 per online credit in-state, $648.65 per online credit out-of-state. *Financial support:* In 2016–17, 14 students received support. Career-related internships or fieldwork, Federal Work-Study, institutionally sponsored loans, scholarships/grants, tuition waivers (partial), and unspecified assistantships available. Support available to part-time students. Financial award application deadline: 5/1; financial award applicants required to submit FAFSA. *Unit head:* Dr. Rachel Barger-Anderson, Graduate Coordinator, 724-738-2873, Fax: 724-738-4395, E-mail: rachel.barger-ander@sru.edu. *Application contact:* Brandi Weber-Mortimer, Director of Graduate Admissions, 724-738-2051, Fax: 724-738-2146, E-mail: graduate.admissions@sru.edu.
Website: http://www.sru.edu/academics/colleges-and-departments/coe/departments/special-education/graduate-programs

Soka University of America, Graduate School of Education, Aliso Viejo, CA 92656. Offers MA. *Program availability:* Evening/weekend. *Entrance requirements:* For master's, GRE. Additional exam requirements/recommendations for international students: Required—TOEFL (minimum score 600 paper-based; 100 iBT).

See Display on next page and Close-Up on page 945.

Sonoma State University, School of Education, Rohnert Park, CA 94928-3609. Offers administrative services (Credential); curriculum, teaching, and learning (MA); early childhood education (MA); education specialist (Credential); educational leadership (MA); multiple subject (Credential); reading and literacy (MA, Credential); single subject (Credential); special education (MA). *Accreditation:* NCATE. *Program availability:* Part-time, evening/weekend. *Degree requirements:* For master's, thesis or alternative. *Entrance requirements:* For master's, minimum GPA of 2.5. Additional exam requirements/recommendations for international students: Required—TOEFL (minimum score 500 paper-based). Application fee: $55. *Expenses:* Tuition, state resident: full-time $6738; part-time $3906 per unit. *Required fees:* $1916; $1916 per year. Tuition and fees vary according to course load, degree level and program. *Financial support:* Fellowships, research assistantships, career-related internships or fieldwork, and Federal Work-Study available. Support available to part-time students. Financial award application deadline: 3/2; financial award applicants required to submit FAFSA. *Unit head:* Dr. Carlos Ayala, Dean, 707-664-4412, E-mail: carlos.ayala@sonoma.edu. *Application contact:* Dr. Jennifer Mahdavi, Coordinator of Graduate Studies, 707-664-3311, E-mail: jennifer.mahdavi@sonoma.edu.
Website: http://www.sonoma.edu/education/

South Carolina State University, College of Graduate and Professional Studies, Department of Educational Leadership, Orangeburg, SC 29117-0001. Offers educational leadership and administration (Ed D, Ed S). *Accreditation:* ACA; NCATE. *Program availability:* Part-time, evening/weekend. *Faculty:* 5 full-time (1 woman), 2 part-time/adjunct (0 women). *Students:* 17 full-time (10 women), 73 part-time (52 women); includes 84 minority (82 Black or African American, non-Hispanic/Latino; 1 American Indian or Alaska Native, non-Hispanic/Latino; 1 Asian, non-Hispanic/Latino). Average age 42. 35 applicants, 100% accepted, 35 enrolled. In 2016, 16 doctorates, 10 other advanced degrees awarded. *Degree requirements:* For doctorate, comprehensive exam, thesis/dissertation, preliminary exams, internship, practicum; for Ed S, thesis. *Entrance requirements:* For doctorate, GRE General Test or MAT, teaching certificate, teaching experience; for Ed S, GRE General Test or MAT, interview, teaching certificate, teaching experience. *Application deadline:* For fall admission, 6/15 priority date for domestic students, 6/15 for international students; for spring admission, 11/1 for domestic and international students. Application fee: $25. Electronic applications accepted. *Expenses:* Tuition, state resident: full-time $8938; part-time $579 per credit hour. Tuition, nonresident: full-time $19,018; part-time $1139 per credit hour. *Required fees:* $1482; $82 per credit hour. *Financial support:* Career-related internships or fieldwork available. Financial award application deadline: 6/1. *Unit head:* Dr. Frederick Evans, Interim Chair, Department of Educational Leadership, 803-536-4734, Fax: 803-536-8812, E-mail: fevans6@scsu.edu. *Application contact:* Curtis Foskey, Coordinator of Graduate Enrollment, 803-536-8809, Fax: 803-536-8812, E-mail: cfoskey@scsu.edu.
Website: http://www.scsu.edu/schoolofgraduatestudies/doctorofeducation.aspx

South Dakota State University, Graduate School, College of Education and Human Sciences, Department of Teaching, Learning and Leadership, Brookings, SD 57007. Offers agricultural education (MS); curriculum and instruction (M Ed); educational administration (M Ed). *Program availability:* Part-time, evening/weekend, online learning. *Degree requirements:* For master's, portfolio, oral exam. *Entrance requirements:* For master's, minimum GPA of 2.75. Additional exam requirements/recommendations for international students: Required—TOEFL (minimum score 550 paper-based; 80 iBT). *Faculty research:* Inclusion school climate, K-12 reform and restructuring, rural development, ESL, leadership.

Southeastern Louisiana University, College of Education, Department of Educational Leadership and Technology, Hammond, LA 70402. Offers educational leadership (M Ed, Ed D). *Program availability:* Part-time. *Faculty:* 22 full-time (19 women), 4 part-time/adjunct (1 woman). *Students:* 10 full-time (all women), 162 part-time (136 women); includes 58 minority (51 Black or African American, non-Hispanic/Latino; 5 Hispanic/Latino; 2 Two or more races, non-Hispanic/Latino), 1 international. Average age 37. 27 applicants, 89% accepted, 9 enrolled. In 2016, 69 master's, 2 doctorates awarded. *Degree requirements:* For master's, comprehensive exam; for doctorate, comprehensive exam, thesis/dissertation. *Entrance requirements:* For master's, GRE (minimum score of 500); for doctorate, GRE (minimum scores: Verbal 145; Quantitative 145 taken August 2011 or after). Additional exam requirements/recommendations for international students: Required—TOEFL (minimum score 500 paper-based; 61 iBT). *Application deadline:* For fall admission, 7/15 priority date for domestic students, 6/1 priority date for international students; for spring admission, 12/1 priority date for domestic students, 10/1 priority date for international students. Applications are processed on a rolling basis. Application fee: $20 ($30 for international students). Electronic applications accepted. *Expenses:* Tuition, state resident: full-time $6540; part-time $465 per credit hour. Tuition, nonresident: full-time $19,017; part-time $1158 per credit hour. *Required fees:* $1829. *Financial support:* In 2016–17, 7 students received support. Research assistantships, career-related internships or fieldwork, Federal Work-Study, institutionally sponsored loans, scholarships/grants, and unspecified assistantships available. Support available to part-time students. Financial award application deadline: 5/1; financial award applicants required to submit FAFSA. *Faculty research:* School effectiveness, online instruction, federal constitutional rights of students and teachers, using data to drive instruction, change leadership. *Unit head:* Dr. Thomas Devaney, Department Head, 985-549-5713, Fax: 985-549-5712, E-mail: tdevaney@southeastern.edu. *Application contact:* Amanda Harper, Graduate Admissions Analyst, 985-549-2066, Fax: 985-549-5632, E-mail: admissions@southeastern.edu.
Website: http://www.southeastern.edu/acad_research/depts/edlt

Southeastern Oklahoma State University, School of Education, Durant, OK 74701-0609. Offers math specialist (M Ed); reading specialist (M Ed); school administration (M Ed); school counseling (M Ed). *Accreditation:* NCATE. *Program availability:* Part-time, evening/weekend. *Degree requirements:* For master's, comprehensive exam, thesis optional, portfolio (M Ed). *Entrance requirements:* For master's, GRE General Test (for school counseling), minimum GPA of 3.0 in last 60 hours or 2.75 overall. Additional exam requirements/recommendations for international students: Required—TOEFL (minimum score 550 paper-based; 79 iBT). Electronic applications accepted.

Southeastern University, College of Education, Lakeland, FL 33801-6099. Offers curriculum and instruction (Ed D); educational leadership (M Ed); elementary education (M Ed); exceptional student education (M Ed); exceptional student education/educational therapy (M Ed); organizational leadership (Ed D); reading education (M Ed); teaching English to speakers of other languages (M Ed). *Expenses: Tuition:* Full-time $9450; part-time $6300 per credit. *Required fees:* $500; $250 per semester. One-time fee: $150. Tuition and fees vary according to degree level, campus/location and program. *Unit head:* Amy N. Bratten, Dean, 863-667-5238, E-mail: anbratten@seu.edu. Website: http://www.seu.edu/education/

Southeast Missouri State University, School of Graduate Studies, Department of Educational Leadership and Counseling, Program in Educational Administration, Cape Girardeau, MO 63701-4799. Offers educational leadership (Ed D); higher education administration (MA); secondary administration (MA); teacher leadership (MA, Ed S). *Accreditation:* NCATE. *Program availability:* Part-time, evening/weekend, online only, 100% online. *Faculty:* 7 full-time (4 women), 4 part-time/adjunct (1 woman). *Students:* 48 full-time (31 women), 166 part-time (107 women); includes 23 minority (19 Black or African American, non-Hispanic/Latino; 2 Asian, non-Hispanic/Latino; 2 Hispanic/Latino), 14 international. Average age 33. 79 applicants, 100% accepted, 79 enrolled. In 2016, 27 master's, 36 other advanced degrees awarded. *Degree requirements:* For master's and Ed S, comprehensive exam, thesis or alternative, paper; for doctorate, comprehensive exam, thesis/dissertation. *Entrance requirements:* For master's, minimum GPA of 3.5; for doctorate, GRE, interview; for Ed S, minimum GPA of 3.7. Additional exam requirements/recommendations for international students: Required—TOEFL (minimum score 550 paper-based; 79 iBT), IELTS (minimum score 6), PTE (minimum score 53). *Application deadline:* For fall admission, 8/1 for domestic students, 6/1 for international students; for spring admission, 11/21 for domestic students, 10/1 for international students; for summer admission, 5/15 for domestic students. Applications are processed on a rolling basis. Application fee: $30 ($40 for international students). Electronic applications accepted. *Expenses:* Tuition, state resident: full-time $3130; part-time $260.80 per credit hour. Tuition, nonresident: full-time $5842; part-time $486.80 per credit hour. *Required fees:* $33.70 per credit hour. *Financial support:* In 2016–17, 31 students received support. Career-related internships or fieldwork, Federal Work-Study, scholarships/grants, traineeships, tuition waivers (full), and unspecified assistantships available. Financial award application deadline: 6/30; financial award applicants required to submit FAFSA. *Faculty research:* Learning and technology; leadership, equity and social justice in P-12 schools and higher education; school culture; leadership and academic achievement; school leadership and student success. *Unit head:* Dr. C. P. Gause, Professor/Chair, 573-651-2137, Fax: 573-986-6512, E-mail: cgause@semo.edu. *Application contact:* Dr. Lisa Bertrand, Professor/Coordinator, 573-651-5080, Fax: 573-986-6512, E-mail: lbertrand@semo.edu.
Website: http://www.semo.edu/eduleadcounsel/

Southern Adventist University, School of Education and Psychology, Collegedale, TN 37315-0370. Offers clinical mental health counseling (MS); inclusive education (MS Ed); instructional leadership (MS Ed); literacy education (MS Ed); outdoor teacher education (MS Ed); school counseling (MS). *Accreditation:* NCATE. *Program availability:* Part-time, evening/weekend. *Degree requirements:* For master's, comprehensive exam (for some programs), thesis optional, position paper (MS), portfolio (MS Ed in outdoor teacher education). *Entrance requirements:* For master's, interview (MS); 9 semester hours of upper-division course work in psychology or related field, including 1 course in psychology research or statistics; 9 semester hours of education (MS Ed). Additional exam requirements/recommendations for international students: Required—TOEFL (minimum score 600 paper-based; 100 iBT). Electronic applications accepted.

Southern Arkansas University–Magnolia, School of Graduate Studies, Magnolia, AR 71753. Offers agriculture (MS); business administration (MBA), including agri-business, social entrepreneurship, supply chain management; clinical and mental health counseling (MS); computer and information sciences (MS), including cyber security and privacy, data science, information technology; gifted and talented (M Ed), including curriculum and instruction, educational administration and supervision, gifted and talented P-8/7-12, instructional specialist P-4; higher, adult and lifelong education (M Ed); kinesiology (M Ed), including coaching; library media and information specialist (M Ed); public administration (MPA); school counseling K-12 (M Ed); student affairs and college counseling (M Ed); teaching (MAT). *Accreditation:* NCATE. *Program availability:* Part-time, 100% online, blended/hybrid learning. *Faculty:* 36 full-time (19 women), 33 part-time/adjunct (14 women). *Students:* 605 full-time (143 women), 879 part-time (352 women); includes 130 minority (113 Black or African American, non-Hispanic/Latino; 7 American Indian or Alaska Native, non-Hispanic/Latino; 2 Asian, non-Hispanic/Latino; 2 Hispanic/Latino; 6 Two or more races, non-Hispanic/Latino), 1,048 international. Average age 28. 904 applicants, 81% accepted, 262 enrolled. In 2016, 278 master's awarded. *Degree requirements:* For master's, comprehensive exam (for some programs), thesis optional. *Entrance requirements:* For master's, GRE, MAT or GMAT, minimum GPA of 2.5. Additional exam requirements/recommendations for international students: Required—TOEFL (minimum score 550 paper-based), IELTS (minimum score 6). *Application deadline:* For fall admission, 7/20 for domestic students, 7/10 for international students; for spring admission, 12/1 for domestic students, 11/15 for international students; for summer admission, 4/1 for domestic students, 5/1 for international students. Applications are processed on a rolling basis. Application fee: $25 ($50 for international students). Electronic applications accepted. *Expenses:* Tuition, state resident: full-time $2511; part-time $279 per credit hour. Tuition, nonresident: full-time $3726; part-time $414 per credit hour. *Required fees:* $307 per semester. Tuition and fees vary according to course load and program. *Financial support:* Career-related internships or fieldwork, Federal Work-Study, scholarships/grants, tuition waivers (full), and unspecified assistantships available. Financial award applicants required to submit FAFSA. *Faculty research:* Alternative certification for teachers, supervision of instruction, instructional leadership, counseling. *Unit head:* Dr. Kim Bloss, Dean, School of Graduate Studies, 870-235-4150, Fax: 870-235-5227, E-mail: kkbloss@saumag.edu. *Application contact:* Shrijana Malakar, Admissions Specialist, 870-235-4150, Fax: 870-235-5227, E-mail: smalakar@saumag.edu.
Website: http://www.saumag.edu/graduate

Southern Connecticut State University, School of Graduate Studies, School of Education, Department of Educational Leadership, New Haven, CT 06515-1355. Offers educational leadership (Ed D, Diploma); research, statistics, and measurement (MS). *Program availability:* Part-time, evening/weekend. *Faculty:* 8 full-time (4 women), 6 part-time/adjunct (3 women). *Students:* 5 full-time (4 women), 155 part-time (106 women); includes 24 minority (16 Black or African American, non-Hispanic/Latino; 1 American Indian or Alaska Native, non-Hispanic/Latino; 5 Hispanic/Latino; 2 Two or more races, non-Hispanic/Latino). Average age 38. 141 applicants, 47% accepted, 50 enrolled. In 2016, 15 doctorates, 164 other advanced degrees awarded. *Entrance requirements:* For degree, master's degree, minimum GPA of 3.0, writing sample. *Application deadline:* For fall admission, 7/15 priority date for domestic students. Applications are processed on a rolling basis. Application fee: $50. Electronic applications accepted. *Expenses:* Tuition, state resident: full-time $6497; part-time $519 per credit hour. Tuition, nonresident: full-time $18,102; part-time $535 per credit hour. *Required fees:* $4722; $55 per semester. Tuition and fees vary according to program. *Financial support:* Career-related internships or fieldwork, scholarships/grants, and unspecified assistantships available. Financial award application deadline: 4/15; financial award applicants required to submit FAFSA. *Unit head:* Dr. Gladys Labas, Chairperson, 203-392-9927, Fax: 203-392-5341, E-mail: labasg1@southernct.edu. *Application contact:* Lisa Galvin, Director of Graduate Admissions, 203-392-5240, Fax: 203-392-5235, E-mail: galvinl1@southernct.edu.

Southern Illinois University Carbondale, Graduate School, College of Education and Human Services, Department of Educational Administration and Higher Education, Program in Educational Administration, Carbondale, IL 62901-4701. Offers MS Ed, PhD. PhD offered jointly with Southeast Missouri State University. *Accreditation:* NCATE. *Program availability:* Part-time. *Degree requirements:* For master's, thesis or alternative; for doctorate, thesis/dissertation. *Entrance requirements:* For master's, minimum GPA of 2.7; for doctorate, GRE General Test, MAT, minimum GPA of 3.5. Additional exam requirements/recommendations for international students: Required—TOEFL. *Faculty research:* School principalship, history and philosophy of education, supervision.

Southern Illinois University Edwardsville, Graduate School, School of Education, Health, and Human Behavior, Department of Educational Leadership, Program in Educational Administration, Edwardsville, IL 62026. Offers MS Ed, Ed S. *Accreditation:* NCATE. *Program availability:* Part-time, evening/weekend. *Degree requirements:* For master's, thesis or alternative, portfolio. *Entrance requirements:* Additional exam requirements/recommendations for international students: Required—TOEFL (minimum score 550 paper-based; 79 iBT), IELTS (minimum score 6.5). Electronic applications accepted.

Southern Illinois University Edwardsville, Graduate School, School of Education, Health, and Human Behavior, Department of Educational Leadership, Program in Educational Leadership, Edwardsville, IL 62026. Offers Ed D. *Program availability:* Part-time, evening/weekend. *Degree requirements:* For doctorate, thesis/dissertation or alternative, project. *Entrance requirements:* For doctorate, GRE. Additional exam requirements/recommendations for international students: Required—TOEFL (minimum score 550 paper-based; 79 iBT), IELTS (minimum score 6.5). Electronic applications accepted.

Southern New Hampshire University, School of Education, Manchester, NH 03106-1045. Offers business education (M Ed); child development (M Ed); curriculum and instruction (M Ed), including education leadership, reading, special education, technology integration; education (M Ed); educational leadership (M Ed, Ed D); educational studies (M Ed); elementary education (M Ed); English (MAT); English for speakers of other languages (M Ed); reading and writing specialist (M Ed); school business administration (Certificate); secondary education (M Ed); special education (M Ed); technology integration specialist (M Ed). *Program availability:* Part-time, evening/weekend, online learning. *Degree requirements:* For master's, comprehensive exam (for some programs), thesis or alternative. *Entrance requirements:* For master's, PRAXIS I, minimum GPA of 2.75. Additional exam requirements/recommendations for international students: Required—TOEFL (minimum score 550 paper-based). Electronic applications accepted. *Expenses:* Contact institution.

Southern Oregon University, Graduate Studies, School of Education, Ashland, OR 97520. Offers elementary education (MA Ed, MS Ed), including classroom teacher, early childhood, handicapped learner, reading, supervision; secondary education (MA Ed, MS Ed), including classroom teacher, handicapped learner, reading, supervision; teaching (MAT). *Program availability:* Online learning. *Faculty:* 15 full-time (10 women), 27 part-time/adjunct (21 women). *Students:* 116 full-time (82 women), 86 part-time (68 women); includes 22 minority (1 American Indian or Alaska Native, non-Hispanic/Latino; 4 Asian, non-Hispanic/Latino; 8 Hispanic/Latino; 9 Two or more races, non-Hispanic/Latino). Average age 34. 81 applicants, 80% accepted, 49 enrolled. In 2016, 107 master's awarded. *Degree requirements:* For master's, thesis optional. *Entrance requirements:* For master's, GRE General Test, minimum cumulative GPA of 3.0 in the last 90 quarter credits (60 semester credits) of undergraduate coursework. Additional exam requirements/recommendations for international students: Required—TOEFL (minimum score 540 paper-based; 76 iBT), IELTS (minimum score 6), ELPT (minimum score 964) or ELS (minimum score 112). *Application deadline:* For fall admission, 7/31 priority date for domestic and international students; for winter admission, 11/15 priority date for domestic and international students; for spring admission, 1/7 priority date for domestic and international students. Applications are processed on a rolling basis. Application fee: $60. Electronic applications accepted. *Expenses:* Tuition, state resident: full-time $10,719; part-time $397 per credit. Tuition, nonresident: full-time $13,419; part-time $497 per credit. *Required fees:* $548. *Financial support:* In 2016–17, 2 students received support. Career-related internships or fieldwork, institutionally sponsored loans, scholarships/grants, and unspecified assistantships available. *Unit head:* Dr. Gerry McCain, Graduate Program Coordinator, 541-552-6934, E-mail: mccaing@sou.edu. *Application contact:* Kelly Moutsatson, Director of Admissions, 541-552-6411, Fax: 541-552-8403, E-mail: admissions@sou.edu.
Website: http://www.sou.edu/education/

Southern University and Agricultural and Mechanical College, Graduate School, College of Education, Department of Behavioral Studies and Educational Leadership, Program in Administration and Supervision, Baton Rouge, LA 70813. Offers M Ed.

Southern University and Agricultural and Mechanical College, Graduate School, College of Education, Department of Behavioral Studies and Educational Leadership, Program in Educational Leadership, Baton Rouge, LA 70813. Offers M Ed. *Entrance requirements:* For master's, GRE General Test.

Southwest Baptist University, Program in Education, Bolivar, MO 65613-2597. Offers education (MS); educational administration (MS, Ed S). *Program availability:* Part-time. *Degree requirements:* For master's, comprehensive exam, thesis optional, 6-hour residency; for Ed S, comprehensive exam, 5-hour residency. *Entrance requirements:* For master's, GRE or PRAXIS II, interviews, minimum GPA of 2.75; for Ed S, master's degree. Additional exam requirements/recommendations for international students: Required—TOEFL (minimum score 550 paper-based). *Faculty research:* At-risk programs, principal retention, mentoring beginning principals.

Southwestern Adventist University, Education Department, Keene, TX 76059. Offers curriculum and instruction with reading emphasis (M Ed); educational leadership (M Ed). *Program availability:* Part-time, evening/weekend. *Degree requirements:* For master's, thesis or alternative, professional paper. *Entrance requirements:* For master's, GRE General Test.

Southwestern Assemblies of God University, Thomas F. Harrison School of Graduate Studies, Program in Education, Waxahachie, TX 75165-5735. Offers Christian school administration (MS); curriculum development (MS); early education administration (M Ed); middle and secondary education (M Ed). *Degree requirements:* For master's, comprehensive written and oral exams. *Entrance requirements:* For master's, GRE General Test, minimum GPA of 2.5. Electronic applications accepted.

Southwestern College, Education Programs, Winfield, KS 67156-2499. Offers curriculum and instruction (M Ed); early childhood education (M Ed); educational leadership (Ed D); special education (M Ed), including adaptive, functional; teaching (MA). *Accreditation:* NCATE. *Program availability:* Part-time, evening/weekend, 100% online, blended/hybrid learning. *Faculty:* 7 full-time (5 women), 15 part-time/adjunct (12 women). *Students:* 27 full-time (18 women), 102 part-time (77 women); includes 17 minority (8 Black or African American, non-Hispanic/Latino; 1 American Indian or Alaska Native, non-Hispanic/Latino; 1 Asian, non-Hispanic/Latino; 6 Hispanic/Latino; 1 Native Hawaiian or other Pacific Islander, non-Hispanic/Latino), 32 international. Average age 38. 36 applicants, 64% accepted, 16 enrolled. In 2016, 71 master's, 10 doctorates awarded. *Degree requirements:* For master's, practicum, portfolio; for doctorate, thesis/dissertation, professional portfolio. *Entrance requirements:* For master's, baccalaureate degree, minimum GPA of 3.0, valid teaching certificate (for special education); for doctorate, GRE if no master's degree, baccalaureate degree with minimum GPA of 3.25 and current teaching experience, or master's degree with minimum GPA of 3.5. Additional exam requirements/recommendations for international students: Required—TOEFL (minimum score 550 paper-based; 80 iBT). *Application deadline:* Applications are processed on a rolling basis. Application fee: $40. Electronic applications accepted. *Expenses:* $550 per credit; $485 per credit (online); $580 per credit (doctorate program). *Financial support:* In 2016–17, 8 students received support. Scholarships/grants available. Financial award applicants required to submit FAFSA. *Unit head:* Dana Thomson, Director of Education Operations, 800-846-1543 Ext. 6253, Fax: 620-229-6253, E-mail: dana.thomson@sckans.edu. *Application contact:* Dennis Russell, Director of Admissions and Student Services, 888-684-5335 Ext. 3372, Fax: 888-684-5218, E-mail: dennis.russell@sckans.edu.
Website: http://www.sckans.edu/graduate/education-med/

Southwestern Oklahoma State University, College of Professional and Graduate Studies, School of Behavioral Sciences and Education, Specialization in Educational Administration, Weatherford, OK 73096-3098. Offers M Ed. M Ed distance learning degree program offered to Oklahoma residents only. *Accreditation:* NCATE. *Program availability:* Part-time, evening/weekend, online learning. *Degree requirements:* For master's, exam. *Entrance requirements:* For master's, GRE General Test or minimum undergraduate GPA of 3.0, portfolio. Additional exam requirements/recommendations for international students: Required—TOEFL.

Southwest Minnesota State University, Department of Education, Marshall, MN 56258. Offers ESL (MS); math (MS); reading (MS); special education (MS), including developmental disabilities, early childhood education, emotional behavioral disorders, learning disabilities; teaching, learning and leadership (MS). *Program availability:* Part-time, evening/weekend, online learning. *Entrance requirements:* Additional exam requirements/recommendations for international students: Required—TOEFL or IELTS; Recommended—TOEFL (minimum score 550 paper-based; 80 iBT), IELTS.

Spalding University, Graduate Studies, College of Education, Program in Leadership Education, Louisville, KY 40203-2188. Offers executive (Ed D); scholar-practitioner (Ed D). *Accreditation:* NCATE. *Program availability:* Part-time, evening/weekend. *Faculty:* 7 full-time (3 women), 13 part-time/adjunct (9 women). *Students:* 26 full-time (16 women), 26 part-time (19 women); includes 28 minority (25 Black or African American, non-Hispanic/Latino; 2 Hispanic/Latino; 1 Two or more races, non-Hispanic/Latino). Average age 46. 22 applicants, 73% accepted, 16 enrolled. In 2016, 8 doctorates awarded. *Degree requirements:* For doctorate, comprehensive exam, thesis/dissertation. *Entrance requirements:* For doctorate, GRE General Test or MAT, interview, letters of recommendation, resume, transcripts. Additional exam requirements/recommendations for international students: Required—TOEFL (minimum score 535 paper-based). *Application deadline:* Applications are processed on a rolling basis. Application fee: $30. Electronic applications accepted. *Expenses: Tuition:* Full-time $15,300. *Financial support:* Research assistantships, scholarships/grants, and unspecified assistantships available. Financial award applicants required to submit FAFSA. *Faculty research:* Leadership of schools, achievement gap, women in leadership. *Unit head:* Dr. Chris Walsh, Associate Dean, 502-873-4272, E-mail: cwalsh@spalding.edu. *Application contact:* Dr. Linda Beattie, Director, 502-873-4190, E-mail: lbeattie@spalding.edu.

Spalding University, Graduate Studies, College of Education, Programs in Education, Louisville, KY 40203-2188. Offers art teacher education (MAT); business teacher education (MAT); elementary school education (MAT); foreign language (MAT); high school education (MAT); middle school education (MAT); secondary education (MAT); special education (learning and behavioral disorders) (MAT); student guidance counselor (MA); teacher leader (M Ed). *Accreditation:* NCATE. *Program availability:* Part-time, evening/weekend. *Faculty:* 39 full-time (26 women), 13 part-time/adjunct (4 women). *Students:* 97 full-time (76 women), 31 part-time (23 women); includes 39 minority (33 Black or African American, non-Hispanic/Latino; 1 Asian, non-Hispanic/Latino; 3 Hispanic/Latino; 2 Two or more races, non-Hispanic/Latino). Average age 35. 62 applicants, 55% accepted, 33 enrolled. In 2016, 49 master's awarded. *Entrance requirements:* For master's, GRE General Test or MAT, interview, letters of recommendation, resume. Additional exam requirements/recommendations for international students: Required—TOEFL (minimum score 535 paper-based). *Application deadline:* Applications are processed on a rolling basis. Application fee: $30. Electronic applications accepted. *Expenses: Tuition:* Full-time $15,300. *Financial support:* Scholarships/grants, traineeships, and unspecified assistantships available. Financial award applicants required to submit FAFSA. *Faculty research:* Instructional technology, achievement gap, classroom management, assessment. *Unit head:* Dr. Chris Walsh, Associate Dean, 502-873-4272, Fax: 502-585-7123, E-mail: cwalsh@spalding.edu. *Application contact:* Valerie Anderson, Administrative Assistant, 502-873-4260, E-mail: vanderson@spalding.edu.

Stanford University, Graduate School of Education, Program in Policy, Organization, and Leadership Studies, Stanford, CA 94305-2004. Offers MA, MA/MBA. *Degree requirements:* For master's, thesis (for some programs). *Entrance requirements:* For master's, GRE General Test. Electronic applications accepted. *Expenses: Tuition:* Full-time $47,331. *Required fees:* $609.

State University of New York at New Paltz, Graduate School, School of Education, Department of Educational Administration, New Paltz, NY 12561. Offers educational leadership (MS Ed); school building leader (CAS); school district business leader (CAS); school district leader (CAS). *Program availability:* Part-time, evening/weekend. *Students:* 6 full-time (3 women), 45 part-time (28 women); includes 6 minority (3 Black or African American, non-Hispanic/Latino; 3 Hispanic/Latino). 13 applicants, 85% accepted, 9 enrolled. In 2016, 2 master's, 29 CASs awarded. *Entrance requirements:* For master's, GRE General Test or MAT, minimum GPA of 3.0, New York state teaching certificate; for CAS, minimum GPA of 3.0, proof of 3 years' teaching experience, New York state teaching certificate. Additional exam requirements/recommendations for international students: Required—TOEFL (minimum score 550 paper-based; 80 iBT), IELTS (minimum score 6.5). *Application deadline:* Applications are processed on a rolling basis. Application fee: $50. Electronic applications accepted. *Financial support:* Application deadline: 8/1. *Faculty research:* Time management of administrators, social justice, women in educational leadership, diversity in educational leadership, superintendency. *Unit head:* Prof. Devon Duhaney, Program Director, 845-257-2853, E-mail: duhaneyd@newpaltz.edu. *Application contact:* Vika Shock, Director of Graduate Admissions, 845-257-3286, Fax: 845-257-3284, E-mail: gradschool@newpaltz.edu.
Website: http://www.newpaltz.edu/edadmin/

State University of New York at Oswego, Graduate Studies, School of Education, Department of Educational Administration, Oswego, NY 13126. Offers educational administration (CAS); school building leadership (CAS). *Program availability:* Part-time. *Degree requirements:* For CAS, comprehensive exam, internship. *Entrance requirements:* For degree, interview, MA or MS, minimum GPA of 3.0, teaching certificate. Additional exam requirements/recommendations for international students: Required—TOEFL (minimum score 560 paper-based). *Faculty research:* Professional growth and development, leadership, governance, strategic planning, shared decision-making.

State University of New York at Plattsburgh, School of Education, Health, and Human Services, Program in Educational Leadership, Plattsburgh, NY 12901-2681. Offers CAS. *Program availability:* Part-time, evening/weekend. *Entrance requirements:* Additional exam requirements/recommendations for international students: Required—TOEFL.

Educational Leadership and Administration

State University of New York College at Cortland, Graduate Studies, School of Education, Program in Educational Leadership, Cortland, NY 13045. Offers school building leader (CAS); school building leader and school district leader (CAS); school district business leader (CAS); school district leader (CAS). *Program availability:* Part-time, evening/weekend. *Degree requirements:* For CAS, one foreign language. *Entrance requirements:* For degree, MS in education, permanent New York teaching certificate. Additional exam requirements/recommendations for international students: Required—TOEFL.

Stephen F. Austin State University, Graduate School, College of Education, Department of Secondary Education and Educational Leadership, Nacogdoches, TX 75962. Offers educational leadership (Ed D); secondary education (M Ed). *Accreditation:* NCATE. *Degree requirements:* For master's, comprehensive exam; for doctorate, thesis/dissertation. *Entrance requirements:* For master's, GRE General Test; for doctorate, GRE General Test, interview, writing sample. Additional exam requirements/recommendations for international students: Required—TOEFL. Electronic applications accepted.

Stetson University, College of Arts and Sciences, Division of Education, DeLand, FL 32723. Offers counselor education (MS), including marriage, couple and family counseling, mental health counseling, school counseling; teacher education (M Ed), including educating for social justice, educational leadership. *Accreditation:* NCATE (one or more programs are accredited). *Program availability:* Part-time, evening/weekend. *Faculty:* 12 full-time (8 women), 8 part-time/adjunct (7 women). *Students:* 190 full-time (160 women), 17 part-time (13 women); includes 56 minority (20 Black or African American, non-Hispanic/Latino; 1 Asian, non-Hispanic/Latino; 30 Hispanic/Latino; 5 Two or more races, non-Hispanic/Latino), 3 international. Average age 32. 145 applicants, 81% accepted, 98 enrolled. In 2016, 47 master's awarded. *Entrance requirements:* For master's, GRE or MAT. *Application deadline:* For fall admission, 8/1 priority date for domestic students; for spring admission, 1/1 priority date for domestic students; for summer admission, 5/1 priority date for domestic students. Applications are processed on a rolling basis. Application fee: $50. Electronic applications accepted. *Expenses:* $886 per credit hour. *Financial support:* In 2016–17, 119 students received support. Career-related internships or fieldwork, Federal Work-Study, institutionally sponsored loans, scholarships/grants, unspecified assistantships, and tuition waivers for staff and dependents available. Support available to part-time students. *Faculty research:* School leadership succession planning; restorative practices in schools; literacy and art teacher evaluation and support in place of personnel appraisal; mission-driven leadership. *Unit head:* Dr. Karen Ryan, Dean, 386-822-7515. *Application contact:* Jamie Vanderlip, Senior Associate Director of Graduate Admissions, 386-822-7100, Fax: 386-822-7112, E-mail: jlvander@stetson.edu.

Stetson University, College of Arts and Sciences, Division of Education, Department of Teacher Education, Program in Educational Leadership, DeLand, FL 32723. Offers M Ed. *Accreditation:* NCATE. *Program availability:* Evening/weekend. *Faculty:* 5 full-time (3 women), 1 part-time/adjunct (0 women). *Students:* 76 full-time (58 women), 4 part-time (all women); includes 20 minority (11 Black or African American, non-Hispanic/Latino; 9 Hispanic/Latino). Average age 36. 84 applicants, 88% accepted, 61 enrolled. In 2016, 26 master's awarded. *Degree requirements:* For master's, comprehensive exam. *Entrance requirements:* For master's, GRE or MAT, transcripts, three letters of recommendation, copy of professional teaching certificate. Additional exam requirements/recommendations for international students: Required—TOEFL (minimum score 90 iBT), IELTS (minimum score 7). *Application deadline:* For fall admission, 8/1 priority date for domestic students; for spring admission, 1/1 priority date for domestic students; for summer admission, 5/1 priority date for domestic students. Applications are processed on a rolling basis. Application fee: $50. Electronic applications accepted. *Expenses:* $886 per credit hour. *Financial support:* In 2016–17, 74 students received support. Career-related internships or fieldwork, Federal Work-Study, scholarships/grants, tuition waivers, unspecified assistantships, and tuition waivers are available for staff and dependents available. Support available to part-time students. *Faculty research:* School leadership succession planning; restorative practices in schools; literacy and art teacher evaluation and support in place of personnel appraisal; mission-driven leadership. *Unit head:* Dr. Debra Touchton, Coordinator, 386-822-7075. *Application contact:* Jamie Vanderlip, Senior Associate Director of Graduate Admissions, 386-822-7100, Fax: 386-822-7112, E-mail: jlvander@stetson.edu.

Stony Brook University, State University of New York, School of Professional Development, Stony Brook, NY 11794-443. Offers biology (MAT); chemistry (MAT); coaching (Graduate Certificate); earth science (MAT); educational computing (Graduate Certificate); educational leadership (Advanced Certificate); English (MAT); environmental management (MPS, Graduate Certificate); French (MAT); German (MAT); higher education administration (MA, Certificate); human resource management (MS, Graduate Certificate); industrial management (Graduate Certificate); information systems management (Graduate Certificate); Italian (MAT); liberal studies (MA); mathematics (MAT); operations research (Graduate Certificate); physics (MAT); school district business leadership (Advanced Certificate); social studies (MAT); Spanish (MAT). *Program availability:* Part-time, evening/weekend, online learning. *Faculty:* 4 full-time (3 women), 77 part-time/adjunct (34 women). *Students:* 197 full-time (125 women), 965 part-time (674 women); includes 222 minority (79 Black or African American, non-Hispanic/Latino; 2 American Indian or Alaska Native, non-Hispanic/Latino; 35 Asian, non-Hispanic/Latino; 87 Hispanic/Latino; 1 Native Hawaiian or other Pacific Islander, non-Hispanic/Latino; 18 Two or more races, non-Hispanic/Latino), 5 international. Average age 33. 462 applicants, 87% accepted, 317 enrolled. In 2016, 348 master's, 159 other advanced degrees awarded. *Degree requirements:* For master's, one foreign language, thesis or alternative. *Entrance requirements:* Additional exam requirements/recommendations for international students: Required—TOEFL (minimum score 85 iBT). *Application deadline:* For fall admission, 1/15 for domestic students, 6/1 for international students; for spring admission, 10/1 for domestic and international students. Applications are processed on a rolling basis. Application fee: $100. *Expenses:* Contact institution. *Financial support:* Fellowships, research assistantships, teaching assistantships, and career-related internships or fieldwork available. Support available to part-time students. *Unit head:* Dr. Ken Lindblom, Dean, 631-632-7049, Fax: 631-632-9046, E-mail: kenneth.lindblom@stonybrook.edu. *Application contact:* Melissa Jordan, Assistant Dean, 631-632-7751, E-mail: melissa.jordan@stonybrook.edu.
Website: http://www.stonybrook.edu/spd/

Suffolk University, College of Arts and Sciences, Department of Philosophy, Boston, MA 02108-2770. Offers administration of higher education (M Ed, CAGS); ethics and public policy (MS). *Program availability:* Part-time, evening/weekend. *Faculty:* 4 full-time (0 women), 2 part-time/adjunct (0 women). *Students:* 22 full-time (16 women), 29 part-time (24 women); includes 10 minority (1 Black or African American, non-Hispanic/Latino; 6 Hispanic/Latino; 3 Two or more races, non-Hispanic/Latino), 1 international. Average age 28. 56 applicants, 75% accepted, 19 enrolled. In 2016, 34 master's awarded. *Degree requirements:* For master's, internship or thesis; practicum (for M Ed). *Entrance requirements:* For master's, GRE General Test, MAT, GMAT, statement of professional goals, official transcripts, 2 letters of recommendation, resume. Additional exam requirements/recommendations for international students: Required—TOEFL (minimum score 550 paper-based; 80 iBT). *Application deadline:* For fall admission, 3/15 priority date for domestic and international students; for spring admission, 10/15 priority date for domestic and international students. Applications are processed on a rolling basis. Application fee: $50. Electronic applications accepted. *Expenses:* Contact institution. *Financial support:* In 2016–17, 38 students received support, including 30 fellowships (averaging $6,556 per year); career-related internships or fieldwork, Federal Work-Study, institutionally sponsored loans, and unspecified assistantships also available. Support available to part-time students. Financial award application deadline: 4/1; financial award applicants required to submit FAFSA. *Faculty research:* Predicting competent Head Start preschoolers, cultural differences, school counseling technology, sibling attachment in divorce cases, consequences of ethical breaches by human resource professionals. *Unit head:* Dr. Greg Fried, Chair of Philosophy Department, 617-573-8109, E-mail: gfried@suffolk.edu. *Application contact:* Mara Marzocchi, Associate Director of Graduate Admissions, 617-573-8302, Fax: 617-305-1733, E-mail: grad.admission@suffolk.edu.
Website: http://www.suffolk.edu/college/graduate/69296.php

Sul Ross State University, College of Professional Studies, Department of Education, Program in School Administration, Alpine, TX 79832. Offers M Ed. *Program availability:* Part-time, evening/weekend. *Degree requirements:* For master's, thesis optional. *Entrance requirements:* For master's, GMAT or GRE General Test, minimum GPA of 2.5 in last 60 hours of undergraduate work.

Sul Ross State University, Rio Grande College of Sul Ross State University, Alpine, TX 79832. Offers business administration (MBA); teacher education (M Ed), including bilingual education, counseling, educational diagnostics, elementary education, general education, reading, school administration, secondary education. *Program availability:* Part-time, evening/weekend, online learning. *Degree requirements:* For master's, comprehensive exam, thesis optional, minimum GPA of 3.0. *Entrance requirements:* For master's, GMAT or GRE General Test, minimum GPA of 2.5 in last 60 hours of undergraduate work. Additional exam requirements/recommendations for international students: Required—TOEFL.

Syracuse University, School of Education, CAS Program in School District Business Leadership, Syracuse, NY 13244. Offers CAS. *Program availability:* Part-time. *Degree requirements:* For CAS, thesis or alternative, internship. *Entrance requirements:* For degree, master's degree, transcripts, resume. Additional exam requirements/recommendations for international students: Required—TOEFL (minimum score 100 iBT). *Application deadline:* For fall admission, 1/15 priority date for domestic and international students; for spring admission, 10/15 priority date for domestic and international students; for summer admission, 4/15 priority date for domestic and international students. Applications are processed on a rolling basis. Electronic applications accepted. *Expenses: Tuition:* Full-time $25,974; part-time $1443 per credit hour. *Required fees:* $802; $50 per course. Tuition and fees vary according to course load and program. *Financial support:* Fellowships, research assistantships, teaching assistantships, career-related internships or fieldwork, and scholarships/grants available. Financial award application deadline: 1/15. *Faculty research:* Education management, procurement, human resource management, educational leadership and administration, long-term strategic planning. *Unit head:* Dr. George Theoharis, Chair of Teaching and Leadership/Professor, 315-443-2685, E-mail: gtheohar@syr.edu. *Application contact:* Speranza Migliore, Graduate Admissions Recruiter, 315-443-2505, E-mail: gradrcrt@syr.edu.
Website: http://soeweb.syr.edu/academic/teaching_and_leadership/graduate/CAS/school_district_business_leadership/default.aspx

Syracuse University, School of Education, Programs in Educational Leadership, Syracuse, NY 13244. Offers MS, Ed D, CAS. *Program availability:* Part-time. In 2016, 1 master's, 1 doctorate, 22 other advanced degrees awarded. *Degree requirements:* For master's, thesis or alternative; for doctorate, comprehensive exam, thesis/dissertation; for CAS, thesis. *Entrance requirements:* For master's, personal statement, transcripts, three letters of recommendation, resume; for doctorate, GRE, master's degree, writing sample, resume, three letters of recommendation, transcripts; for CAS, master's degree, minimum three years of teaching experience, resume, personal statement, three letters of reference. Additional exam requirements/recommendations for international students: Required—TOEFL (minimum score 100 iBT). *Application deadline:* For fall admission, 6/15 for domestic and international students; for spring admission, 12/1 for domestic students, 10/15 for international students; for summer admission, 3/1 for domestic and international students. Applications are processed on a rolling basis. Application fee: $75. Electronic applications accepted. *Expenses: Tuition:* Full-time $25,974; part-time $1443 per credit hour. *Required fees:* $802; $50 per course. Tuition and fees vary according to course load and program. *Financial support:* Fellowships with full tuition reimbursements, research assistantships with tuition reimbursements, teaching assistantships with tuition reimbursements, career-related internships or fieldwork, and scholarships/grants available. Financial award application deadline: 1/15; financial award applicants required to submit FAFSA. *Faculty research:* Curriculum and instruction leadership for equity and excellence, information management in school, supervision of instruction, leadership for literacy development, assessment of teaching. *Unit head:* Dr. George Theoharis, Chair of Teaching and Leadership/Professor, 315-443-2685, E-mail: gtheohar@syr.edu. *Application contact:* Speranza Migliore, Graduate Admissions Recruiter, 315-443-2505, E-mail: gradrcrt@syr.edu.
Website: http://soe.syr.edu/academic/teaching_and_leadership/graduate/CAS/educational_leadership/default.aspx

Tarleton State University, College of Graduate Studies, College of Education, Department of Curriculum and Instruction, Stephenville, TX 76402. Offers educational diagnostician (M Ed); elementary education (M Ed); instructional design and technology (M Ed); instructional leadership (M Ed); professional reading specialist (M Ed); secondary education (M Ed); special education (M Ed); technology applications (M Ed); technology director (M Ed). *Program availability:* Part-time, evening/weekend. *Faculty:* 9 full-time (7 women), 6 part-time/adjunct (4 women). *Students:* 17 full-time (0 women), 104 part-time (101 women); includes 28 minority (5 Black or African American, non-Hispanic/Latino; 1 American Indian or Alaska Native, non-Hispanic/Latino; 19 Hispanic/Latino; 3 Two or more races, non-Hispanic/Latino). 62 applicants, 94% accepted, 35 enrolled. In 2016, 34 master's awarded. *Degree requirements:* For master's, comprehensive exam. *Entrance requirements:* For master's, GRE General Test, minimum GPA of 3.0. Additional exam requirements/recommendations for international students: Required—TOEFL (minimum score 550 paper-based; 80 iBT). *Application deadline:* For fall admission, 8/15 priority date for domestic students; for spring admission, 1/7 for domestic students. Applications are processed on a rolling basis. Application fee: $45 ($145 for international students). Electronic applications accepted. *Expenses:* $3,672 tuition; $2,437 fees. *Financial support:* Research assistantships, teaching assistantships, career-related internships or fieldwork, Federal Work-Study, and institutionally sponsored loans available. Support available to part-time students. Financial award application deadline: 5/1; financial award applicants required to submit FAFSA. *Unit head:* Dr. Jordan Barkley, Department Head, 254-968-9089, E-mail: jbarkley@tarleton.edu. *Application contact:* Information Contact, 254-968-9104, Fax: 254-968-9670, E-mail: gradoffice@tarleton.edu.
Website: http://www.tarleton.edu/cimasters/

Tarleton State University, College of Graduate Studies, College of Education, Department of Educational Leadership and Policy Studies, Stephenville, TX 76402. Offers educational administration (M Ed); educational leadership (Ed D, Certificate). *Program availability:* Part-time, evening/weekend, 100% online, blended/hybrid learning. *Faculty:* 8 full-time (4 women), 9 part-time/adjunct (6 women). *Students:* 19 full-time (12 women), 203 part-time (140 women); includes 66 minority (39 Black or African American, non-Hispanic/Latino; 4 American Indian or Alaska Native, non-Hispanic/Latino; 2 Asian, non-Hispanic/Latino; 18 Hispanic/Latino; 3 Two or more races, non-Hispanic/Latino), 1 international. 20 applicants, 95% accepted, 7 enrolled. In 2016, 29 master's, 13 doctorates awarded. *Degree requirements:* For master's, comprehensive exam, thesis optional; for doctorate, thesis/dissertation. *Entrance requirements:* For doctorate, GRE, 4 letters of reference, leadership portfolio. Additional exam requirements/recommendations for international students: Required—TOEFL (minimum score 550 paper-based; 80 iBT). *Application deadline:* For fall admission, 8/15 priority date for domestic students; for spring admission, 1/7 for domestic students. Applications are processed on a rolling basis. Application fee: $45 ($145 for international students). Electronic applications accepted. *Expenses:* $3,672 tuition; $2,437 fees. *Financial support:* Teaching assistantships, career-related internships or fieldwork, Federal Work-Study, and institutionally sponsored loans available. Support available to part-time students. Financial award application deadline: 5/1; financial award applicants required to submit FAFSA. *Unit head:* Dr. Tod Allen Farmer, Department Head, 254-968-1936, E-mail: farmer@tarleton.edu. *Application contact:* Information Contact, 254-968-9104, Fax: 254-968-9670, E-mail: gradoffice@tarleton.edu.
Website: http://www.tarleton.edu/edlps/

Teachers College, Columbia University, Department of Organization and Leadership, New York, NY 10027-6696. Offers adult education guided intensive study (Ed D); adult learning and leadership (Ed M, MA, Ed D); educational leadership (Ed D); higher and postsecondary education (MA, Ed D); leadership, policy and politics (Ed D); nurse executive (MA, Ed D), including administration studies (MA), professorial studies (MA); private school leadership (Ed M, MA); public school building leadership (Ed M, MA); social and organizational psychology (MA); urban education leaders (Ed D); MA/MBA. *Program availability:* Part-time, evening/weekend. *Students:* 310 full-time (214 women), 390 part-time (250 women); includes 276 minority (116 Black or African American, non-Hispanic/Latino; 3 American Indian or Alaska Native, non-Hispanic/Latino; 61 Asian, non-Hispanic/Latino; 79 Hispanic/Latino; 17 Two or more races, non-Hispanic/Latino), 93 international. 624 applicants, 57% accepted, 172 enrolled. *Degree requirements:* For doctorate, thesis/dissertation. *Expenses: Tuition:* Full-time $36,288; part-time $1512 per credit. *Required fees:* $438 per semester. One-time fee: $510 full-time. Full-time tuition and fees vary according to course load. *Unit head:* Prof. Anna Neumann, Chair, 212-678-3272, Fax: 212-678-3036, E-mail: neumann@tc.columbia.edu. *Application contact:* David Estrella, Director of Admission, 212-678-3305, E-mail: estrella@tc.columbia.edu.

Tennessee Technological University, College of Graduate Studies, College of Education, Department of Curriculum and Instruction, Program in Instructional Leadership, Cookeville, TN 38505. Offers MA, Ed S. *Accreditation:* NCATE. *Program availability:* Part-time, evening/weekend. *Faculty:* 9 full-time (3 women). *Students:* 4 full-time (3 women), 33 part-time (19 women); includes 6 minority (4 Black or African American, non-Hispanic/Latino; 2 Two or more races, non-Hispanic/Latino). Average age 27. 30 applicants, 63% accepted, 14 enrolled. In 2016, 4 master's, 9 other advanced degrees awarded. *Degree requirements:* For master's and Ed S, comprehensive exam, thesis or alternative. *Entrance requirements:* For master's and Ed S, MAT or GRE. Additional exam requirements/recommendations for international students: Required—TOEFL (minimum score 527 paper-based; 71 iBT), IELTS (minimum score 5.5), PTE (minimum score 48), or TOEIC (Test of English as an International Communication). *Application deadline:* For fall admission, 8/1 for domestic students, 5/1 for international students; for spring admission, 12/1 for domestic students, 10/1 for international students; for summer admission, 5/1 for domestic students, 2/1 for international students. Applications are processed on a rolling basis. Application fee: $35 ($40 for international students). Electronic applications accepted. *Expenses:* Tuition, state resident: full-time $9375; part-time $534 per credit hour. Tuition, nonresident: full-time $22,443; part-time $1260 per credit hour. *Financial support:* Fellowships, research assistantships, teaching assistantships, and career-related internships or fieldwork available. Financial award application deadline: 4/1. *Faculty research:* School board member training, community school education. *Unit head:* Dr. Jeremy Wendt, Interim Chairperson, 931-372-3181, Fax: 931-372-6270, E-mail: jwendt@tntech.edu. *Application contact:* Shelia K. Kendrick, Coordinator of Graduate Studies, 931-372-3808, Fax: 931-372-3497, E-mail: skendrick@tntech.edu.

Texas A&M International University, Office of Graduate Studies and Research, College of Education, Department of Professional Programs, Laredo, TX 78041-1900. Offers educational administration (MS Ed); generic special education (MS Ed); school counseling (MS). *Entrance requirements:* Additional exam requirements/recommendations for international students: Required—TOEFL (minimum score 550 paper-based; 79 iBT).

Texas A&M University, College of Education and Human Development, Department of Educational Administration and Human Resource Development, College Station, TX 77843. Offers educational administration (M Ed, MS, Ed D, PhD); educational human resource development (MS, PhD). *Program availability:* Part-time. *Students:* 117 full-time (86 women), 273 part-time (171 women); includes 153 minority (49 Black or African American, non-Hispanic/Latino; 13 Asian, non-Hispanic/Latino; 80 Hispanic/Latino; 2 Native Hawaiian or other Pacific Islander, non-Hispanic/Latino; 9 Two or more races, non-Hispanic/Latino), 33 international. Average age 36. 153 applicants, 64% accepted, 84 enrolled. In 2016, 83 master's, 27 doctorates awarded. *Degree requirements:* For master's, thesis optional; for doctorate, thesis/dissertation. *Entrance requirements:* For master's, GRE General Test, writing exam, interview, professional experience; for doctorate, GRE General Test, writing exam, interview/presentation, professional experience. Additional exam requirements/recommendations for international students: Required—TOEFL (minimum score 550 paper-based; 80 iBT), IELTS (minimum score 6), PTE (minimum score 53). *Application deadline:* For fall admission, 12/1 for domestic and international students; for spring admission, 8/15 for domestic and international students. Application fee: $50 ($90 for international students). Electronic applications accepted. *Expenses:* Contact institution. *Financial support:* In 2016–17, 192 students received support, including 5 fellowships with tuition reimbursements available (averaging $8,239 per year), 45 research assistantships with tuition reimbursements available (averaging $5,380 per year), 16 teaching assistantships with tuition reimbursements available (averaging $9,494 per year); career-related internships or fieldwork, institutionally sponsored loans, scholarships/grants, traineeships, health care benefits, tuition waivers (full and partial), and unspecified assistantships also available. Support available to part-time students. Financial award application deadline: 3/15; financial award applicants required to submit FAFSA. *Faculty research:* Higher education administration, public school administration, student affairs. *Unit head:* Dr. Fred M. Nafukho, Head, 979-862-3395, Fax: 979-862-4347, E-mail: fnafukho@tamu.edu. *Application contact:* Joyce Nelson, Director of Academic Advising, 979-845-3017, Fax: 979-862-4347, E-mail: eahradvisor@tamu.edu.
Website: http://eahr.tamu.edu

Texas A&M University–Central Texas, Graduate Studies and Research, Killeen, TX 76549. Offers accounting (MS); business administration (MBA); clinical mental health counseling (MS); criminal justice (MCJ); curriculum and instruction (M Ed); educational administration (M Ed); educational psychology - experimental psychology (MS); history (MA); human resource management (MS); information systems (MS); liberal studies (MS); management and leadership (MS); marriage and family therapy (MS); mathematics (MS); political science (MA); school counseling (M Ed); school psychology (Ed S).

Texas A&M University–Commerce, College of Education and Human Services, Commerce, TX 75429-3011. Offers counseling (MS); curriculum and instruction (M Ed, MS); early childhood education (M Ed, MS); educational administration (M Ed, Ed D); educational psychology (PhD); educational technology leadership (MS); educational technology library science (MS); health, kinesiology and sports studies (MS); higher education (MS, Ed D); organization, learning, and technology (MS); psychology (MS); reading (M Ed, MS); school psychology (SSP); secondary education (M Ed, MS); social work (MSW); special education (M Ed); supervision, curriculum and instruction-elementary education (Ed D). *Program availability:* Part-time, 100% online, blended/hybrid learning. *Faculty:* 88 full-time (52 women), 31 part-time/adjunct (24 women). *Students:* 341 full-time (276 women), 1,495 part-time (1,156 women); includes 762 minority (429 Black or African American, non-Hispanic/Latino; 4 American Indian or Alaska Native, non-Hispanic/Latino; 27 Asian, non-Hispanic/Latino; 247 Hispanic/Latino; 1 Native Hawaiian or other Pacific Islander, non-Hispanic/Latino; 54 Two or more races, non-Hispanic/Latino), 18 international. Average age 37. 1,070 applicants, 54% accepted, 452 enrolled. In 2016, 579 master's, 31 doctorates awarded. *Degree requirements:* For master's, one foreign language, comprehensive exam, thesis optional, departmental qualifying exams (for some programs); for doctorate, comprehensive exam, thesis/dissertation, departmental qualifying exam; for SSP, comprehensive exam, thesis optional. *Entrance requirements:* For master's and doctorate, GRE General Test. Additional exam requirements/recommendations for international students: Required—TOEFL (minimum score 550 paper-based; 79 iBT), IELTS (minimum score 6). *Application deadline:* For fall admission, 6/1 priority date for international students; for spring admission, 10/15 priority date for international students; for summer admission, 3/15 priority date for international students. Applications are processed on a rolling basis. Application fee: $50. Electronic applications accepted. *Expenses:* $2,254 resident; $4,744 non-resident. *Financial support:* In 2016–17, 301 students received support, including 39 research assistantships with partial tuition reimbursements available (averaging $9,000 per year), 17 teaching assistantships with partial tuition reimbursements available (averaging $9,000 per year); career-related internships or fieldwork, Federal Work-Study, institutionally sponsored loans, scholarships/grants, health care benefits, and unspecified assistantships also available. Financial award application deadline: 5/1; financial award applicants required to submit FAFSA. *Faculty research:* Cognitive and bilingual education, positive behavioral intervention, literacy, math readiness. *Total annual research expenditures:* $470,963. *Unit head:* Dr. Timothy Letzring, Dean, 903-886-5181, Fax: 903-886-5905, E-mail: tim.letzring@tamuc.edu. *Application contact:* Jennifer Faunce, Graduate Recruiter, 903-886-5030, Fax: 903-886-5905, E-mail: jennifer.faunce@tamuc.edu.
Website: http://www.tamuc.edu/academics/graduateSchool/programs/education/default.aspx

Texas A&M University–Corpus Christi, College of Graduate Studies, College of Education, Program in Educational Administration, Corpus Christi, TX 78412-5503. Offers MS. *Program availability:* Part-time, evening/weekend. *Students:* 6 full-time (5 women), 35 part-time (22 women); includes 33 minority (3 Black or African American, non-Hispanic/Latino; 1 Asian, non-Hispanic/Latino; 29 Hispanic/Latino). Average age 33. 21 applicants, 71% accepted, 14 enrolled. In 2016, 15 master's awarded. *Degree requirements:* For master's, comprehensive exam. *Entrance requirements:* For master's, minimum GPA of 3.0 in last 60 hours; essay (approximately 300-400 words in length). Additional exam requirements/recommendations for international students: Required—TOEFL (minimum score 550 paper-based; 79 iBT), IELTS (minimum score 6.5). *Application deadline:* For fall admission, 6/1 priority date for domestic students, 5/1 priority date for international students; for spring admission, 10/15 priority date for domestic students, 9/1 priority date for international students; for summer admission, 4/15 priority date for domestic students, 2/1 priority date for international students. Applications are processed on a rolling basis. Application fee: $50 ($70 for international students). Electronic applications accepted. *Financial support:* In 2016–17, 8 students received support. Research assistantships, teaching assistantships, career-related internships or fieldwork, Federal Work-Study, institutionally sponsored loans, scholarships/grants, health care benefits, and unspecified assistantships available. Support available to part-time students. Financial award application deadline: 3/15; financial award applicants required to submit FAFSA. *Unit head:* Dr. Lynn Hemmer, Chair, 361-825-3702, E-mail: lynn.hemmer@tamucc.edu. *Application contact:* Graduate Admissions Coordinator, 361-825-2177, Fax: 361-825-2755, E-mail: gradweb@tamucc.edu.
Website: http://education.tamucc.edu/

Texas A&M University–Corpus Christi, College of Graduate Studies, College of Education, Program in Educational Leadership, Corpus Christi, TX 78412-5503. Offers Ed D. Program offered jointly with Texas A&M University-Kingsville. *Program availability:* Part-time, evening/weekend. *Students:* 5 full-time (4 women), 53 part-time (41 women); includes 36 minority (1 Black or African American, non-Hispanic/Latino; 1 American Indian or Alaska Native, non-Hispanic/Latino; 1 Asian, non-Hispanic/Latino; 33 Hispanic/Latino), 3 international. Average age 44. 7 applicants, 57% accepted, 5 enrolled. In 2016, 8 doctorates awarded. *Degree requirements:* For doctorate, comprehensive exam, thesis/dissertation. *Entrance requirements:* For doctorate, GMAT/GRE (taken within 5 years), master's degree, minimum graduate GPA of 3.0 in last 60 hours, essay (300-400 words in length), 4 reference forms, interview. Additional exam requirements/recommendations for international students: Required—TOEFL (minimum score 550 paper-based; 79 iBT), IELTS (minimum score 6.5). *Application deadline:* For fall admission, 6/1 priority date for domestic and international students; for spring admission, 10/1 priority date for domestic and international students; for summer admission, 2/1 priority date for domestic and international students. Applications are processed on a rolling basis. Application fee: $50 ($70 for international students). Electronic applications accepted. *Financial support:* Research assistantships, career-related internships or fieldwork, Federal Work-Study, institutionally sponsored loans, scholarships/grants, health care benefits, and unspecified assistantships available. Support available to part-time students. Financial award application deadline: 3/15; financial award applicants required to submit FAFSA. *Unit head:* Dr. Randall Bowden, Associate Professor, 361-825-6034, E-mail: randall.bowden@tamucc.edu. *Application contact:* Graduate Admissions Coordinator, 361-825-2177, Fax: 361-825-2755, E-mail: gradweb@tamucc.edu.
Website: http://elci.tamucc.edu/

Texas A&M University–Kingsville, College of Graduate Studies, College of Education and Human Performance, Department of Educational Leadership and Counseling, Program in Educational Administration, Kingsville, TX 78363. Offers MA, MS. *Program availability:* Part-time, evening/weekend, online only, 100% online, blended/hybrid learning. *Entrance requirements:* Additional exam requirements/recommendations for international students: Required—TOEFL (minimum score 550 paper-based; 79 iBT); Recommended—IELTS. Electronic applications accepted.

Texas A&M University–Kingsville, College of Graduate Studies, College of Education and Human Performance, Department of Educational Leadership and Counseling, Program in Educational Leadership, Kingsville, TX 78363. Offers PhD. Program offered jointly with Texas A&M University. *Program availability:* Part-time, evening/weekend. *Degree requirements:* For doctorate, variable foreign language requirement, comprehensive exam, thesis/dissertation (for some programs). *Entrance requirements:* For doctorate, GRE, MAT, GMAT, two-page statement of desire to pursue doctoral degree in educational leadership; 3 letters of recommendation; curriculum vitae listing accomplishments or any other evidence of scholarship, leadership, and/or professionalism. Additional exam requirements/recommendations for international students: Required—TOEFL (minimum score 550 paper-based; 79 iBT). Electronic applications accepted.

Texas A&M University–San Antonio, Department of Leadership and Counseling, San Antonio, TX 78224. Offers counseling and guidance (MA); educational leadership (MA). *Program availability:* Part-time, evening/weekend. *Degree requirements:* For master's, comprehensive exam, thesis or alternative. *Entrance requirements:* For master's, MAT. Additional exam requirements/recommendations for international students: Required—TOEFL (minimum score 550 paper-based; 80 iBT), IELTS (minimum score 6). Electronic applications accepted.

Texas A&M University–Texarkana, Graduate Studies and Research, College of Education and Liberal Arts, Texarkana, TX 75505-5518. Offers adult education (MS); curriculum and instruction (M Ed); education (MS); educational administration (M Ed); English (MA); instructional technology (MS); interdisciplinary studies (MA, MS); special education (MS). *Program availability:* Part-time, evening/weekend. *Degree requirements:* For master's, comprehensive exam (for some programs), thesis optional. *Entrance requirements:* For master's, minimum GPA of 2.5 on last 60 hours of bachelor's degree. Additional exam requirements/recommendations for international students: Required—TOEFL. Electronic applications accepted.

Texas Christian University, College of Education, Doctoral Programs in Education, Fort Worth, TX 76129. Offers counseling and counselor education (PhD); curriculum studies (PhD); educational leadership (Ed D); higher educational leadership (Ed D); science education (PhD); MBA/Ed D. *Program availability:* Part-time, evening/weekend. *Faculty:* 29 full-time (21 women), 8 part-time/adjunct (5 women). *Students:* 77 full-time (56 women), 19 part-time (7 women); includes 33 minority (12 Black or African American, non-Hispanic/Latino; 5 Asian, non-Hispanic/Latino; 15 Hispanic/Latino; 1 Two or more races, non-Hispanic/Latino), 6 international. Average age 37. 34 applicants, 56% accepted, 13 enrolled. In 2016, 5 doctorates awarded. *Degree requirements:* For doctorate, comprehensive exam, thesis/dissertation. *Entrance requirements:* For doctorate, GRE General Test. Additional exam requirements/recommendations for international students: Required—TOEFL (minimum score 550 paper-based; 80 iBT). *Application deadline:* For fall admission, 2/1 for domestic and international students; for winter admission, 2/1 for domestic and international students; for spring admission, 11/16 for domestic and international students. Application fee: $60. Electronic applications accepted. *Expenses: Tuition:* Full-time $26,640; part-time $1480 per credit hour. *Required fees:* $48. Tuition and fees vary according to program. *Financial support:* In 2016–17, 57 students received support, including 1 fellowship with full tuition reimbursement available, 10 research assistantships with full tuition reimbursements available (averaging $18,500 per year), 7 teaching assistantships with full tuition reimbursements available (averaging $18,500 per year); career-related internships or fieldwork, scholarships/grants, health care benefits, and unspecified assistantships also available. Support available to part-time students. Financial award application deadline: 2/1; financial award applicants required to submit FAFSA. *Unit head:* Dr. Jan Lacina, Associate Dean, 817-257-6786, Fax: 817-257-7466, E-mail: j.lacina@tcu.edu. *Application contact:* Lori Kimball, Administrative Program Specialist, 817-257-7661, Fax: 817-257-7466, E-mail: l.kimball@tcu.edu.
Website: http://coe.tcu.edu/graduate-overview/

Texas Christian University, College of Education, Master's Programs in Education, Fort Worth, TX 76129. Offers counseling (M Ed); curriculum and instruction (M Ed), including curriculum studies, language and literacy, math education, science education; educational leadership (M Ed); special education (M Ed). *Program availability:* Part-time, evening/weekend. *Faculty:* 29 full-time (21 women), 8 part-time/adjunct (5 women). *Students:* 112 full-time (95 women), 12 part-time (11 women); includes 39 minority (6 Black or African American, non-Hispanic/Latino; 2 Asian, non-Hispanic/Latino; 27 Hispanic/Latino; 1 Native Hawaiian or other Pacific Islander, non-Hispanic/Latino; 3 Two or more races, non-Hispanic/Latino), 2 international. Average age 29. 107 applicants, 78% accepted, 66 enrolled. In 2016, 54 master's awarded. *Degree requirements:* For master's, comprehensive exam (for some programs), thesis (for some programs). *Entrance requirements:* For master's, GRE General Test. Additional exam requirements/recommendations for international students: Required—TOEFL (minimum score 550 paper-based; 80 iBT). *Application deadline:* For fall admission, 3/1 for domestic and international students; for spring admission, 11/16 for domestic and international students; for summer admission, 3/1 for domestic and international students. Application fee: $60. Electronic applications accepted. *Expenses: Tuition:* Full-time $26,640; part-time $1480 per credit hour. *Required fees:* $48. Tuition and fees vary according to program. *Financial support:* In 2016–17, 104 students received support, including 4 research assistantships with full tuition reimbursements available (averaging $15,000 per year), 31 teaching assistantships with full tuition reimbursements available (averaging $15,000 per year); career-related internships or fieldwork, scholarships/grants, and unspecified assistantships also available. Support available to part-time students. Financial award application deadline: 3/1; financial award applicants required to submit FAFSA. *Unit head:* Dr. Jan Lacina, Associate Dean, 817-257-6786, Fax: 817-257-7466, E-mail: j.lacina@tcu.edu. *Application contact:* Lori Kimball, Administrative Program Specialist, 817-257-7661, Fax: 817-257-7466, E-mail: l.kimball@tcu.edu.
Website: http://coe.tcu.edu/graduate-overview/

Texas Southern University, College of Education, Department of Educational Administration and Foundation, Houston, TX 77004-4584. Offers educational administration (M Ed, Ed D). *Program availability:* Part-time, evening/weekend. *Degree requirements:* For master's, comprehensive exam; for doctorate, comprehensive exam, thesis/dissertation. *Entrance requirements:* For master's, GRE General Test, minimum GPA of 2.5; for doctorate, GRE General Test or MAT, master's degree, minimum B+ average. Additional exam requirements/recommendations for international students: Required—TOEFL. Electronic applications accepted.

Texas State University, The Graduate College, College of Education, Program in Educational Leadership, San Marcos, TX 78666. Offers educational leadership (M Ed); instructional leadership (MA). *Program availability:* Part-time, evening/weekend. *Faculty:* 1 (woman) full-time, 11 part-time/adjunct (8 women). *Students:* 6 full-time (5 women), 99 part-time (69 women); includes 45 minority (10 Black or African American, non-Hispanic/Latino; 2 Asian, non-Hispanic/Latino; 31 Hispanic/Latino; 2 Two or more races, non-Hispanic/Latino), 2 international. Average age 36. 48 applicants, 63% accepted, 16 enrolled. In 2016, 58 degrees awarded. *Degree requirements:* For master's, comprehensive exam, thesis (for some programs). *Entrance requirements:* For master's, GRE General Test (preferred), baccalaureate degree from regionally-accredited institution with minimum GPA of 2.75 in last 60 hours of undergraduate course work. Additional exam requirements/recommendations for international students: Required—TOEFL (minimum score 550 paper-based; 78 iBT), IELTS (minimum score 6.5). *Application deadline:* For fall admission, 3/1 priority date for domestic and international students; for summer admission, 5/1 for domestic students, 3/15 for international students. Applications are processed on a rolling basis. Application fee: $40 ($90 for international students). Electronic applications accepted. *Expenses:* $4,851 per semester. *Financial support:* In 2016–17, 26 students received support, including 1 research assistantship (averaging $13,502 per year); teaching assistantships, career-related internships or fieldwork, Federal Work-Study, institutionally sponsored loans, and scholarships/grants also available. Support available to part-time students. Financial award application deadline: 3/1; financial award applicants required to submit FAFSA. *Faculty research:* Superintendence, middle management, supervision, junior college. *Unit head:* Dr. Bergeron Harris, Graduate Advisor, 512-245-9909, E-mail: bh26@txstate.edu. *Application contact:* Dr. Andrea Golato, Dean of Graduate School, 512-245-2581, Fax: 512-245-8365, E-mail: gradcollege@txstate.edu.
Website: http://www.txstate.edu/clas/Educational-Leadership.html

Texas State University, The Graduate College, College of Education, Program in School Improvement, San Marcos, TX 78666. Offers PhD. *Program availability:* Part-time. *Faculty:* 14 full-time (5 women), 4 part-time/adjunct (2 women). *Students:* 17 full-time (10 women), 62 part-time (33 women); includes 38 minority (7 Black or African American, non-Hispanic/Latino; 31 Hispanic/Latino). Average age 41. 40 applicants, 45% accepted, 16 enrolled. In 2016, 9 doctorates awarded. *Degree requirements:* For doctorate, comprehensive exam, thesis/dissertation. *Entrance requirements:* For doctorate, baccalaureate and master's degree from regionally-accredited university (master's degree in an area related to proposed studies with minimum graduate GPA of 3.5); statement of purpose (500 words); 3 letters of reference addressing professional and academic background; resume. Additional exam requirements/recommendations for international students: Required—TOEFL (minimum score 78 iBT), IELTS (minimum score 6.5). *Application deadline:* For fall admission, 2/1 for domestic and international students. Applications are processed on a rolling basis. Application fee: $40 ($90 for international students). Electronic applications accepted. *Expenses:* $4,851 per semester. *Financial support:* In 2016–17, 43 students received support, including 8 research assistantships (averaging $28,310 per year); teaching assistantships and scholarships/grants also available. Financial award application deadline: 3/1; financial award applicants required to submit FAFSA. *Faculty research:* Increasing college readiness and creating a college-going culture, building an educational research and improvement partnership with Chile. *Total annual research expenditures:* $59,331. *Unit head:* Dr. Melissa Martinez, PhD Program Director, 512-245-4587, E-mail: mm224@txstate.edu. *Application contact:* Dr. Andrea Golato, Dean of Graduate School, 512-245-2581, Fax: 512-245-8365, E-mail: gradcollege@txstate.edu.
Website: http://si.education.txstate.edu

Texas Tech University, Graduate School, College of Education, Department of Educational Psychology and Leadership, Lubbock, TX 79409-1071. Offers counselor education (M Ed, PhD); distance education (M Ed); educational leadership (M Ed, Ed D, PhD); educational psychology (M Ed, PhD); higher education (M Ed, Ed D); higher education research (PhD); instructional technology (M Ed, Ed D); special education (M Ed, Ed D, PhD). *Accreditation:* ACA; NCATE. *Program availability:* Part-time, evening/weekend. *Faculty:* 59 full-time (29 women), 3 part-time/adjunct (all women). *Students:* 300 full-time (218 women), 656 part-time (482 women); includes 320 minority (87 Black or African American, non-Hispanic/Latino; 5 American Indian or Alaska Native, non-Hispanic/Latino; 5 Asian, non-Hispanic/Latino; 200 Hispanic/Latino; 23 Two or more races, non-Hispanic/Latino), 51 international. Average age 36. 668 applicants, 56% accepted, 285 enrolled. In 2016, 171 master's, 47 doctorates awarded. Terminal master's awarded for partial completion of doctoral program. *Degree requirements:* For master's, comprehensive exam, thesis optional; for doctorate, comprehensive exam, thesis/dissertation. *Entrance requirements:* For master's, GRE (for some programs); for doctorate, GRE. Additional exam requirements/recommendations for international students: Required—TOEFL (minimum score 550 paper-based; 79 iBT). *Application deadline:* For fall admission, 6/1 priority date for domestic students, 1/15 priority date for international students; for spring admission, 9/1 priority date for domestic students, 6/15 priority date for international students. Applications are processed on a rolling basis. Application fee: $75. Electronic applications accepted. *Expenses:* $285 per credit hour full-time resident tuition, $693 per credit hour full-time non-resident tuition; $50.50 per credit hour fee plus $608 per term fee. *Financial support:* In 2016–17, 384 students received support, including 384 fellowships (averaging $3,632 per year); scholarships/grants and unspecified assistantships also available. Support available to part-time students. Financial award application deadline: 1/3; financial award applicants required to submit FAFSA. *Faculty research:* Cognitive, motivational, and developmental processes in learning; counseling education; instructional technology; generic special education and sensory impairment; community college administration; K-12 school administration. *Total annual research expenditures:* $1,371. *Unit head:* Dr. Hansel Burley, Chair, 806-834-5135, Fax: 806-742-2179, E-mail: hansel.burley@ttu.edu. *Application contact:* Pam Smith, Admissions Advisor, 806-834-2969, Fax: 806-742-2179, E-mail: pam.smith@ttu.edu.
Website: http://www.educ.ttu.edu/

Texas Woman's University, Graduate School, College of Professional Education, Department of Teacher Education, Denton, TX 76204-5769. Offers educational administration (M Ed, MA); special education (M Ed, MA, PhD), including educational diagnostician (M Ed, MA), intervention specialist (M Ed); teaching, learning, and curriculum (M Ed, MA). *Program availability:* Part-time. *Students:* 15 full-time (13 women), 98 part-time (85 women); includes 36 minority (13 Black or African American, non-Hispanic/Latino; 3 American Indian or Alaska Native, non-Hispanic/Latino; 3 Asian, non-Hispanic/Latino; 16 Hispanic/Latino; 1 Two or more races, non-Hispanic/Latino). Average age 38. In 2016, 111 master's, 1 doctorate awarded. Terminal master's awarded for partial completion of doctoral program. *Degree requirements:* For master's, comprehensive exam, thesis, professional paper (M Ed); for doctorate, comprehensive exam, thesis/dissertation. *Entrance requirements:* For master's, minimum GPA of 3.0 on last 60 undergraduate hours, 2 letters of reference, resume, copy of certifications, teacher service record, statement of intent; for doctorate, GRE General Test, minimum GPA of 3.0, 3 letters of reference, resume, copy of certifications, teacher service record, statement of intent. Additional exam requirements/recommendations for international students: Required—TOEFL (minimum score 550 paper-based; 79 iBT). *Application deadline:* For fall admission, 7/1 priority date for domestic students, 3/1 for international students; for spring admission, 11/1 priority date for domestic students, 7/1 for international students. Applications are processed on a rolling basis. Application fee: $50 ($75 for international students). Electronic applications accepted. *Expenses:* Tuition, state resident: full-time $9046; part-time $251 per credit hour. Tuition, nonresident: full-time $22,922; part-time $614 per credit hour. *International tuition:* $23,046 full-time. *Required fees:* $2690; $1285 per credit hour. One-time fee: $50. Tuition and fees vary according to course level, course load, program and reciprocity agreements. *Financial support:* Research assistantships, career-related internships or fieldwork, Federal Work-Study, institutionally sponsored loans, scholarships/grants,

traineeships, health care benefits, and unspecified assistantships available. Support available to part-time students. Financial award application deadline: 3/1; financial award applicants required to submit FAFSA. *Faculty research:* Language and literacy, classroom management, learning disabilities, staff and professional development, leadership preparation practice. *Unit head:* Dr. Jane Pemberton, Chair, 940-898-2273, Fax: 940-898-2270, E-mail: teachereducation@twu.edu. *Application contact:* Dr. Samuel Wheeler, Assistant Director of Admissions, 940-898-3188, Fax: 940-898-3081, E-mail: wheelersr@twu.edu.
Website: http://www.twu.edu/teacher-education/

Thomas Edison State University, Heavin School of Arts and Sciences, Program in Educational Leadership, Trenton, NJ 08608. Offers MAEL. *Program availability:* Part-time, online learning. *Degree requirements:* For master's, field-based practicum, professional portfolio development. *Entrance requirements:* For master's, at least 3 years of teaching experience; valid teacher's certification; letter of recommendation from a building-level administrator; school setting and on-site mentor available to conduct site-based fieldwork and inquiry projects successfully for each course; statement of goals and objectives. Additional exam requirements/recommendations for international students: Required—TOEFL (minimum score 550 paper-based; 79 iBT). Electronic applications accepted.

Thomas More College, Program in Teacher Leader, Crestview Hills, KY 41017-3495. Offers M Ed. *Program availability:* Part-time, evening/weekend. *Degree requirements:* For master's, comprehensive exam. *Entrance requirements:* For master's, GRE, minimum undergraduate cumulative GPA of 2.7. Additional exam requirements/recommendations for international students: Required—TOEFL (minimum score 100 iBT). Electronic applications accepted.

Tiffin University, Program in Education, Tiffin, OH 44883-2161. Offers educational technology management (M Ed); higher education administration (M Ed). *Program availability:* Part-time, evening/weekend, online only, 100% online, blended/hybrid learning. *Students:* 99 part-time (75 women); includes 26 minority (20 Black or African American, non-Hispanic/Latino; 1 Asian, non-Hispanic/Latino; 4 Hispanic/Latino; 1 Two or more races, non-Hispanic/Latino). Average age 32. 31 applicants, 90% accepted, 24 enrolled. In 2016, 45 master's awarded. *Entrance requirements:* Additional exam requirements/recommendations for international students: Required—TOEFL. *Application deadline:* Applications are processed on a rolling basis. Electronic applications accepted. *Expenses:* Contact institution. *Financial support:* Unspecified assistantships available. *Application contact:* Nikki Hintze, Director of Graduate Admissions and Student Services, 800-968-6446 Ext. 3445, Fax: 419-443-5002, E-mail: hintzenm@tiffin.edu.

Touro College, Graduate School of Education, New York, NY 10010. Offers education and special education (MS); education biology (MS); instructional technology (MS); mathematics education (MS); school leadership (MS); teaching English to speakers of other languages (MS); teaching literacy (MS). *Accreditation:* TEAC. *Program availability:* Part-time, evening/weekend, online learning. *Faculty:* 52 full-time (34 women), 199 part-time/adjunct (136 women). *Students:* 578 full-time (483 women), 1,932 part-time (1,626 women); includes 749 minority (318 Black or African American, non-Hispanic/Latino; 5 American Indian or Alaska Native, non-Hispanic/Latino; 108 Asian, non-Hispanic/Latino; 288 Hispanic/Latino; 2 Native Hawaiian or other Pacific Islander, non-Hispanic/Latino; 28 Two or more races, non-Hispanic/Latino), 17 international. Average age 32. 1,422 applicants, 50% accepted, 675 enrolled. In 2016, 6 master's awarded. *Entrance requirements:* Additional exam requirements/recommendations for international students: Required—TOEFL (minimum score 83 iBT), IELTS (minimum score 6.5). *Application deadline:* For fall admission, 8/26 for domestic students, 7/15 for international students; for spring admission, 12/31 for domestic students, 12/15 for international students. Applications are processed on a rolling basis. Application fee: $50. *Financial support:* Federal Work-Study available. Financial award applicants required to submit FAFSA. *Faculty research:* Equity assistance, language development, scholarly communications, Latin American studies and cultural sensitivity, behavior management techniques and strategies in special education. *Unit head:* Dr. Arnold Spinner, Dean, 212-463-0400 Ext. 5561, Fax: 212-462-4889, E-mail: aspinner@touro.edu. *Application contact:* Luna Feliciano, Admissions, 212-463-0400.

Towson University, Program in Action Research for School Improvement, Towson, MD 21252-0001. Offers Postbaccalaureate Certificate. *Degree requirements:* For Postbaccalaureate Certificate, research project. *Entrance requirements:* For degree, minimum undergraduate or graduate GPA of 3.0, prior transcripts. Additional exam requirements/recommendations for international students: Required—TOEFL. *Application deadline:* Applications are processed on a rolling basis. Application fee: $45. Electronic applications accepted. *Expenses:* Tuition, state resident: full-time $7580; part-time $379 per unit. Tuition, nonresident: full-time $15,700; part-time $785 per unit. *Required fees:* $2480. *Unit head:* Carla Finkelstein, Director, 410-704-2974, E-mail: cfinkelstein@towson.edu. *Application contact:* Coverley Beidleman, Assistant Director of Graduate Admissions, 410-704-2113, Fax: 410-704-3030, E-mail: grads@towson.edu.
Website: http://www.towson.edu/coe/departments/leadership/grad/schoolimprovement

Towson University, Program in Human Resource Development, Towson, MD 21252-0001. Offers education leadership (MS); general (MS). *Program availability:* Part-time, evening/weekend. *Students:* 13 full-time (all women), 248 part-time (192 women); includes 59 minority (36 Black or African American, non-Hispanic/Latino; 1 American Indian or Alaska Native, non-Hispanic/Latino; 7 Asian, non-Hispanic/Latino; 7 Hispanic/Latino; 8 Two or more races, non-Hispanic/Latino). *Degree requirements:* For master's, comprehensive exam. *Entrance requirements:* For master's, bachelor's degree, 2 letters of recommendation, minimum GPA of 3.0, essay, resume. Additional exam requirements/recommendations for international students: Required—TOEFL. *Application deadline:* Applications are processed on a rolling basis. Application fee: $45. Electronic applications accepted. *Expenses:* Tuition, state resident: full-time $7580; part-time $379 per unit. Tuition, nonresident: full-time $15,700; part-time $785 per unit. *Required fees:* $2480. *Financial support:* Application deadline: 4/1. *Unit head:* Dr. Abby Mello, Graduate Program Director, 410-704-3364, E-mail: amello@towson.edu. *Application contact:* Coverley Beidleman, Assistant Director of Graduate Admissions, 410-704-2113, Fax: 410-704-3030, E-mail: grads@towson.edu.
Website: http://www.towson.edu/cla/departments/interdisciplinary/grad/hr/

Towson University, Program in Integrated STEM Instructional Leadership, Towson, MD 21252-0001. Offers Postbaccalaureate Certificate. *Students:* 14 part-time (12 women); includes 1 minority (Two or more races, non-Hispanic/Latino). *Entrance requirements:* For degree, bachelor's degree, two years of teaching experience, minimum GPA of 3.0, two letters of recommendation, one-page personal statement, resume. Electronic applications accepted. *Expenses:* Tuition, state resident: full-time $7580; part-time $379 per unit. Tuition, nonresident: full-time $15,700; part-time $785 per unit. *Required fees:* $2480. *Unit head:* Dr. Pam Lottero-Perdue, Director, 410-704-4598, E-mail: plotteroperdue@towson.edu. *Application contact:* Coverley Beidleman, Assistant Director of Graduate Admissions, 410-704-2113, Fax: 410-704-3030, E-mail: grads@towson.edu.
Website: http://www.towson.edu/fcsm/departments/physics/grad/stempbc/

Trevecca Nazarene University, Graduate Education Program, Nashville, TN 37210-2877. Offers accountability and instructional leadership (Ed S); curriculum and instruction for Christian school educators (M Ed); curriculum and instruction K-12 (M Ed); educational leadership (M Ed); English second language (M Ed); library and information science (MLI Sc); special education: visual impairments (M Ed); teaching (MAT), including teaching 6-12, teaching K-5. *Accreditation:* NCATE. *Program availability:* Part-time, evening/weekend, online learning. *Faculty:* 5 full-time (3 women), 18 part-time/adjunct (12 women). *Students:* 80 full-time (64 women), 16 part-time (13 women); includes 19 minority (17 Black or African American, non-Hispanic/Latino; 2 Hispanic/Latino). Average age 35. In 2016, 68 master's, 7 other advanced degrees awarded. *Degree requirements:* For master's, comprehensive exam, exit assessment/e-portfolio. *Entrance requirements:* For master's, GRE (minimum score of 290) or MAT (minimum score of 378); PRAXIS (for MAT), minimum GPA of 3.0, official transcript from regionally-accredited institution, at least 3 years' successful teaching experience (for M Ed in educational leadership major). Additional exam requirements/recommendations for international students: Required—TOEFL (minimum score 550 paper-based). *Application deadline:* Applications are processed on a rolling basis. Electronic applications accepted. *Expenses:* Contact institution. *Financial support:* Applicants required to submit FAFSA. *Unit head:* Dr. Suzie Harris, Dean, School of Education/Director of Graduate Education Programs, 615-248-1201, Fax: 615-248-1597, E-mail: admissions_ged@trevecca.edu. *Application contact:* 844-TNU-GRAD, E-mail: sgcsadmissions@trevecca.edu.
Website: http://www.trevecca.edu/soe

Trevecca Nazarene University, Graduate Leadership Programs, Nashville, TN 37210-2877. Offers leadership and professional practice (Ed D); organizational leadership (MOL). *Program availability:* Online learning. *Faculty:* 10 full-time (4 women), 19 part-time/adjunct (6 women). *Students:* 209 full-time (150 women), 220 part-time (159 women); includes 240 minority (209 Black or African American, non-Hispanic/Latino; 1 American Indian or Alaska Native, non-Hispanic/Latino; 2 Asian, non-Hispanic/Latino; 16 Hispanic/Latino; 12 Two or more races, non-Hispanic/Latino), 1 international. Average age 39. In 2016, 32 master's, 43 doctorates awarded. *Degree requirements:* For master's, capstone course; for doctorate, thesis/dissertation, proposal study, symposium presentation. *Entrance requirements:* For master's, minimum GPA of 2.5, official transcript from regionally accredited institution; for doctorate, minimum GPA of 3.4, official transcript from regionally-accredited institution, resume, writing sample, interview, reference forms. Additional exam requirements/recommendations for international students: Required—TOEFL (minimum score 550 paper-based; 80 iBT). *Application deadline:* Applications are processed on a rolling basis. Application fee: $0. Electronic applications accepted. *Expenses:* $395 per credit hour (MOL); $699 per credit hour (Ed D). *Financial support:* Applicants required to submit FAFSA. *Unit head:* Dr. Tom Middendorf, Associate Vice President for Academic Services/Director of Master of Organizational Leadership, 615-248-1529, E-mail: sgcsadmissions@trevecca.edu. *Application contact:* 844-TNU-GRAD, E-mail: sgcsadmissions@trevecca.edu.

Trident University International, College of Education, Program in Educational Leadership, Cypress, CA 90630. Offers e-learning leadership (MA Ed, PhD); educational leadership (MA Ed); higher education leadership (PhD); K-12 leadership (PhD). *Program availability:* Part-time, evening/weekend, online learning. *Degree requirements:* For doctorate, comprehensive exam, thesis/dissertation, defense of dissertation. *Entrance requirements:* For master's, minimum GPA of 2.5 (students with GPA 3.0 or greater may transfer up to 30% of graduate level credits); for doctorate, minimum GPA of 3.4, course work in research methods or statistics. Additional exam requirements/recommendations for international students: Required—TOEFL. Electronic applications accepted.

Trinity Baptist College, Graduate Programs, Jacksonville, FL 32221. Offers educational leadership (M Ed); special education (M Ed). *Program availability:* Online learning. *Entrance requirements:* For master's, GRE (for M Ed), 2 letters of recommendation; minimum GPA of 2.5 (for M Min), 3.0 (for M Ed); computer proficiency.

Trinity University, Department of Education, Master of Education in School Leadership Program, San Antonio, TX 78212-7200. Offers M Ed. *Accreditation:* NCATE. *Program availability:* Part-time, evening/weekend. *Entrance requirements:* For master's, GRE or MAT, nomination from home school district, phone interview, interactive daylong leadership simulation process. *Expenses: Tuition:* Full-time $38,974. *Required fees:* $586.

Trinity Washington University, School of Education, Washington, DC 20017-1094. Offers clinical mental health counseling (MA); early childhood education (MAT); educating for change (M Ed); educational administration (MSA); elementary education (MAT); reading (M Ed); school counseling (MA); secondary education (MAT), including English, social studies; special education (MAT). *Accreditation:* NCATE. *Program availability:* Part-time, evening/weekend. *Degree requirements:* For master's, thesis (for some programs), capstone project(s). *Entrance requirements:* For master's, PRAXIS I, minimum GPA of 2.8. Additional exam requirements/recommendations for international students: Required—TOEFL (minimum score 550 paper-based). *Faculty research:* Technology, literacy, special education, organizations, inclusion models.

Trinity Western University, School of Graduate Studies, Program in Leadership, Langley, BC V2Y 1Y1, Canada. Offers business (MA, Certificate); Christian ministry (MA); education (MA, Certificate); healthcare (MA, Certificate); non-profit (MA, Certificate). *Program availability:* Online learning. *Degree requirements:* For master's, major project. *Entrance requirements:* For master's, minimum GPA of 2.7. Additional exam requirements/recommendations for international students: Required—TOEFL (minimum score 620 paper-based; 105 iBT). Electronic applications accepted. *Expenses:* Contact institution. *Faculty research:* Servant leadership.

Troy University, Graduate School, College of Education, Program in Educational Administration/Leadership, Troy, AL 36082. Offers MS, Ed S. *Accreditation:* NCATE. *Program availability:* Part-time, evening/weekend. *Faculty:* 7 full-time (2 women). *Students:* 9 full-time (5 women), 28 part-time (21 women); includes 9 minority (8 Black or African American, non-Hispanic/Latino; 1 Hispanic/Latino). Average age 37. 28 applicants, 96% accepted, 12 enrolled. In 2016, 2 master's, 7 other advanced degrees awarded. *Degree requirements:* For master's, comprehensive exam, thesis, internship. *Entrance requirements:* For master's, GRE (minimum score of 850 on old exam or 290 on new exam), GMAT (minimum score of 380), or MAT (minimum score of 385), bachelor's degree; minimum undergraduate GPA of 2.5 or 3.0 on last 30 semester hours, letter of recommendation; 3 years of teaching experience; for Ed S, GRE (minimum score of 850 on old exam or 290 on new exam), GMAT (minimum score of 380), or MAT (minimum score of 380), master's degree. Additional exam requirements/recommendations for international students: Required—TOEFL (minimum score 523 paper-based; 70 iBT), IELTS (minimum score 6). *Application deadline:* Applications are processed on a rolling basis. Application fee: $50. Electronic applications accepted. *Expenses:* Tuition, state resident: full-time $7146; part-time $397 per credit hour. Tuition, nonresident: full-time $14,292; part-time $794 per credit hour. *Required fees:* $802; $50 per semester. Tuition and fees vary according to campus/location and program. *Financial support:* Available to part-time students. Applicants required to submit FAFSA. *Unit head:* Dr. Jan Oliver, Associate Professor, 334-670-3444, Fax: 334-

670-3474, E-mail: oliverj@troy.edu. *Application contact:* Jessica A. Kimbro, Graduate Admissions, 334-670-3178, E-mail: jacord@troy.edu.

Union College, Graduate Programs, Department of Education, Barbourville, KY 40906-1499. Offers elementary education (MA); health and physical education (MA); middle grades (MA); music education (MA); principalship (MA); reading specialist (MA); secondary education (MA); special education (MA). *Degree requirements:* For master's, thesis optional. *Entrance requirements:* For master's, GRE General Test, NTE.

Union College, Graduate Programs, Educational Leadership Program, Barbourville, KY 40906-1499. Offers principalship (MA).

Union University, School of Education, Jackson, TN 38305-3697. Offers education (M Ed, MA Ed); education administration generalist (Ed S); educational leadership (Ed D); educational supervision (Ed S); higher education (Ed D). M Ed also available at Germantown campus. *Accreditation:* NCATE. *Program availability:* Part-time, evening/weekend, online learning. *Degree requirements:* For master's, thesis (for some programs), capstone research course (for MA Ed); performance exhibition (for M Ed); for doctorate, comprehensive exam, thesis/dissertation; for Ed S, thesis or alternative. *Entrance requirements:* For master's, MAT, PRAXIS II or GRE, minimum GPA of 3.0, teaching license (for M Ed only), writing sample; for doctorate, GRE, minimum graduate GPA of 3.2, writing sample; for Ed S, PRAXIS II, minimum graduate GPA of 3.2, writing sample. Additional exam requirements/recommendations for international students: Required—TOEFL (minimum score 560 paper-based; 80 iBT). Electronic applications accepted. *Expenses:* Contact institution. *Faculty research:* Mathematics education, brain compatible learning, transformational teaching, cognitive strategy development, instructional technology.

Universidad Adventista de las Antillas, EGECED Department, Mayagüez, PR 00681-0118. Offers curriculum and instruction (M Ed); medical surgical nursing (MN); school administration and supervision (M Ed). *Degree requirements:* For master's, comprehensive exam (for some programs), thesis (for some programs). *Entrance requirements:* For master's, EXADEP or GRE General Test, recommendations. Electronic applications accepted.

Universidad del Turabo, Graduate Programs, Programs in Education, Program in Educational Administration, Gurabo, PR 00778-3030. Offers M Ed. *Program availability:* Part-time, evening/weekend. *Students:* 43 full-time (30 women), 21 part-time (19 women); all minorities (all Hispanic/Latino). Average age 37. 54 applicants, 76% accepted, 34 enrolled. In 2016, 11 master's awarded. *Entrance requirements:* For master's, GRE, EXADEP, GMAT, interview, official transcript, essay, recommendation letters. *Application deadline:* Applications are processed on a rolling basis. Application fee: $25. Electronic applications accepted. *Financial support:* Institutionally sponsored loans available. Financial award applicants required to submit FAFSA. *Unit head:* Israel Rodríguez, Dean, 787-743-7979 Ext. 4627. *Application contact:* Diriee Rodríguez, Admissions Director, 787-743-7979 Ext. 4453, E-mail: admisiones-ut@suagm.edu.
Website: http://ut.suagm.edu/es/educacion

Universidad del Turabo, Graduate Programs, Programs in Education, Program in Educational Leadership, Gurabo, PR 00778-3030. Offers D Ed. *Program availability:* Part-time, evening/weekend. *Students:* 1 (woman) full-time, 69 part-time (41 women); all minorities (all Hispanic/Latino). Average age 42. 41 applicants, 46% accepted, 15 enrolled. In 2016, 5 doctorates awarded. *Entrance requirements:* For doctorate, GRE, EXADEP, GMAT, official transcript, recommendation letters, essay, curriculum vitae, interview. *Application deadline:* Applications are processed on a rolling basis. Application fee: $25. Electronic applications accepted. *Financial support:* Institutionally sponsored loans available. Financial award applicants required to submit FAFSA. *Unit head:* Israel Rodríguez, Dean, 787-743-7979 Ext. 4627. *Application contact:* Diriee Rodríguez, Admissions Director, 787-743-7979 Ext. 4453, E-mail: admisiones-ut@suagm.edu.
Website: http://ut.suagm.edu/es/educacion

Universidad Iberoamericana, Graduate School, Santo Domingo D.N., Dominican Republic. Offers business administration (MBA, PMBA); constitutional law (LL M); dentistry (DMD); educational management (MA); integrated marketing communication (MA); psychopedagogical intervention (M Ed); real estate law (LL M); strategic management of human talent (MM).

Universidad Metropolitana, School of Education, Program in Educational Administration and Supervision, San Juan, PR 00928-1150. Offers M Ed. *Program availability:* Part-time. *Degree requirements:* For master's, thesis or alternative. *Entrance requirements:* For master's, EXADEP, interview. Electronic applications accepted.

Universidad Metropolitana, School of Education, Program in Pre-School Centers Administration, San Juan, PR 00928-1150. Offers M Ed. *Program availability:* Part-time. *Degree requirements:* For master's, thesis or alternative. *Entrance requirements:* For master's, EXADEP, interview. Electronic applications accepted.

Université de Moncton, Faculty of Education, Graduate Studies in Education, Moncton, NB E1A 3E9, Canada. Offers educational psychology (M Ed, MA Ed); guidance (M Ed, MA Ed); school administration (M Ed, MA Ed); teaching (M Ed, MA Ed). *Program availability:* Part-time. *Degree requirements:* For master's, proficiency in English and French. *Entrance requirements:* For master's, minimum GPA of 3.0. *Faculty research:* Guidance, ethnolinguistic vitality, children's rights, ecological education, entrepreneurship.

Université de Montréal, Faculty of Education, Department of Administration and Foundations of Education, Montréal, QC H3C 3J7, Canada. Offers M Ed, MA, PhD, DESS. *Program availability:* Part-time. *Degree requirements:* For master's, thesis; for doctorate, thesis/dissertation, general exam. *Entrance requirements:* For master's and DESS, bachelor's degree in related field with minimum B average; for doctorate, master's degree in related field with minimum B average. Electronic applications accepted. *Faculty research:* Pluriethnicity, formative education, comparative education, diagnostic evaluation.

Université de Sherbrooke, Faculty of Education, Program in School Administration, Sherbrooke, QC J1K 2R1, Canada. Offers M Ed. *Program availability:* Part-time, evening/weekend. *Degree requirements:* For master's, thesis.

Université du Québec à Trois-Rivières, Graduate Programs, Program in Educational Administration, Trois-Rivières, QC G9A 5H7, Canada. Offers DESS.

Université Laval, Faculty of Education, Department of Foundations and Interventions in Education, Programs in Educational Administration and Evaluation, Québec, QC G1K 7P4, Canada. Offers MA, PhD. Terminal master's awarded for partial completion of doctoral program. *Degree requirements:* For master's, thesis (for some programs); for doctorate, comprehensive exam, thesis/dissertation. *Entrance requirements:* For master's and doctorate, English exam (comprehension of written English), knowledge of French and English. Electronic applications accepted.

Université Laval, Faculty of Education, Department of Foundations and Interventions in Education, Programs in Educational Practice, Québec, QC G1K 7P4, Canada. Offers educational pedagogy (Diploma); pedagogy management and development (Diploma); school adaptation (Diploma). *Program availability:* Part-time. *Entrance requirements:* For degree, English exam (comprehension of written English), knowledge of French and English. Electronic applications accepted.

University at Albany, State University of New York, School of Education, Department of Educational Policy and Leadership, Albany, NY 12222-0001. Offers educational policy and leadership (MS, PhD); higher education (MS); international education management (CAS). *Program availability:* Evening/weekend. *Faculty:* 10 full-time (4 women), 7 part-time/adjunct (6 women). *Students:* 27 full-time (11 women), 103 part-time (53 women); includes 24 minority (14 Black or African American, non-Hispanic/Latino; 1 Asian, non-Hispanic/Latino; 9 Hispanic/Latino), 15 international. Average age 31. 48 applicants, 75% accepted, 33 enrolled. In 2016, 16 master's, 9 doctorates, 11 other advanced degrees awarded. *Degree requirements:* For doctorate, one foreign language, thesis/dissertation. *Entrance requirements:* For doctorate, GRE General Test, GRE Subject Test. Additional exam requirements/recommendations for international students: Required—TOEFL (minimum score 550 paper-based). *Application deadline:* For fall admission, 2/1 for domestic students, 5/1 for international students; for spring admission, 9/1 for domestic students, 11/1 for international students. Applications are processed on a rolling basis. Application fee: $75. Electronic applications accepted. *Expenses:* Tuition, state resident: full-time $10,870; part-time $453 per credit hour. Tuition, nonresident: full-time $22,210; part-time $925 per credit hour. *International tuition:* $21,550 full-time. *Required fees:* $1864; $96 per credit hour. *Financial support:* Fellowships and career-related internships or fieldwork available. Financial award application deadline: 3/15. *Total annual research expenditures:* $273,985. *Unit head:* Kevin Kinser, Chair, 518-442-5092, E-mail: kkinser@albany.edu.
Website: http://www.albany.edu/epl/

University at Buffalo, the State University of New York, Graduate School, Graduate School of Education, Department of Educational Leadership and Policy, Buffalo, NY 14260. Offers economics and education policy analysis (MA); education studies (Ed M); educational administration (Ed M, Ed D, PhD); educational culture, policy and society (PhD); higher education administration (Ed M, PhD); school building leadership (Certificate); school business and human resource administration (Certificate); school district business leadership (Certificate); school district leadership (Certificate). *Program availability:* Part-time, evening/weekend. *Faculty:* 15 full-time (9 women), 8 part-time/adjunct (6 women). *Students:* 77 full-time (51 women), 122 part-time (76 women); includes 30 minority (23 Black or African American, non-Hispanic/Latino; 4 Asian, non-Hispanic/Latino; 3 Hispanic/Latino), 22 international. Average age 34. 144 applicants, 75% accepted, 63 enrolled. In 2016, 59 master's, 11 doctorates, 29 other advanced degrees awarded. *Degree requirements:* For master's, comprehensive exam (for some programs), thesis optional; for doctorate, comprehensive exam, thesis/dissertation. *Entrance requirements:* For master's, interview, letters of reference; for doctorate, GRE General Test or MAT, writing sample, letters of reference. Additional exam requirements/recommendations for international students: Required—TOEFL (minimum score 550 paper-based; 79 iBT). *Application deadline:* For fall admission, 2/1 priority date for domestic students, 2/1 for international students; for spring admission, 11/15 priority date for domestic students, 10/1 for international students. Applications are processed on a rolling basis. Application fee: $50. Electronic applications accepted. *Financial support:* In 2016–17, 13 fellowships (averaging $6,862 per year), 32 research assistantships with tuition reimbursements (averaging $10,496 per year) were awarded; career-related internships or fieldwork, Federal Work-Study, institutionally sponsored loans, scholarships/grants, health care benefits, tuition waivers (full and partial), and unspecified assistantships also available. Financial award application deadline: 3/15; financial award applicants required to submit FAFSA. *Faculty research:* College access and choice, school leadership preparation and practice, public policy, curriculum and pedagogy, comparative and international education. *Total annual research expenditures:* $435,404. *Unit head:* Dr. Janina C. Brutt-Griffler, Chair, 716-645-2471, Fax: 716-645-2481, E-mail: bruttg@buffalo.edu. *Application contact:* Veronica Kase, Admission Assistant, 716-645-2110, Fax: 716-645-7937, E-mail: vakase@buffalo.edu.
Website: http://gse.buffalo.edu/elp

The University of Akron, Graduate School, College of Education, Department of Educational Foundations and Leadership, Program in Higher Education Administration, Akron, OH 44325. Offers MA, MS. *Accreditation:* NCATE. *Students:* 16 full-time (10 women), 21 part-time (15 women); includes 8 minority (4 Black or African American, non-Hispanic/Latino; 1 Hispanic/Latino; 3 Two or more races, non-Hispanic/Latino), 1 international. Average age 32. 26 applicants, 50% accepted, 9 enrolled. In 2016, 21 master's awarded. *Degree requirements:* For master's, comprehensive exam. *Entrance requirements:* For master's, GRE, minimum GPA of 2.75, declaration of intent that includes statement of professional goals and reasons for choosing the field of higher education administration and The University of Akron. Additional exam requirements/recommendations for international students: Required—TOEFL (minimum score 550 paper-based; 79 iBT), IELTS (minimum score 6.5). *Application deadline:* Applications are processed on a rolling basis. Application fee: $45 ($70 for international students). Electronic applications accepted. *Expenses:* Tuition, state resident: full-time $8618; part-time $359 per credit hour. Tuition, nonresident: full-time $17,149; part-time $715 per credit hour. *Required fees:* $1652. *Financial support:* Research assistantships and teaching assistantships available. *Unit head:* Dr. Susan Clark, Interim Chair, 330-972-7780, E-mail: sclark1@uakron.edu. *Application contact:* Kelly Chaff, College Program Specialist, 330-972-7028, E-mail: klchaff@uakron.edu.

The University of Akron, Graduate School, College of Education, Department of Educational Foundations and Leadership, Program in Principalship, Akron, OH 44325. Offers MA, MS. *Students:* 1 full-time (0 women), 8 part-time (3 women); includes 1 minority (Black or African American, non-Hispanic/Latino). Average age 34. 5 applicants, 80% accepted, 2 enrolled. In 2016, 21 master's awarded. *Degree requirements:* For master's, internship. *Entrance requirements:* For master's, minimum GPA of 2.75, valid Ohio teacher license. Additional exam requirements/recommendations for international students: Required—TOEFL (minimum score 550 paper-based; 79 iBT), IELTS (minimum score 6.5). *Application deadline:* Applications are processed on a rolling basis. Application fee: $45 ($70 for international students). Electronic applications accepted. *Expenses:* Tuition, state resident: full-time $8618; part-time $359 per credit hour. Tuition, nonresident: full-time $17,149; part-time $715 per credit hour. *Required fees:* $1652. *Unit head:* Dr. Susan Clark, Interim Chair, 330-972-7780, E-mail: sclark1@uakron.edu. *Application contact:* Kelly Chaff, College Program Specialist, 330-972-7028, E-mail: klchaff@uakron.edu.

The University of Alabama, Graduate School, College of Education, Department of Educational Leadership, Policy, and Technology Studies, Educational Administration Program, Tuscaloosa, AL 35487. Offers Ed D, PhD. *Program availability:* Part-time, evening/weekend. *Students:* 1 (woman) full-time, 26 part-time (14 women); includes 8 minority (6 Black or African American, non-Hispanic/Latino; 1 American Indian or Alaska Native, non-Hispanic/Latino; 1 Hispanic/Latino), 1 international. Average age 41. 2 applicants. In 2016, 8 doctorates awarded. *Degree requirements:* For doctorate, comprehensive exam, thesis/dissertation. *Entrance requirements:* For doctorate, GRE or MAT, master's degree in field, minimum GPA of 3.0. Additional exam requirements/recommendations for international students: Recommended—TOEFL. *Application deadline:* For fall admission, 4/30 priority date for domestic and international students; for winter admission, 11/1 priority date for domestic students, 11/1 for international

students; for spring admission, 11/1 priority date for domestic and international students. Applications are processed on a rolling basis. Application fee: $50 ($60 for international students). Electronic applications accepted. *Expenses:* Tuition, state resident: full-time $10,470. Tuition, nonresident: full-time $26,950. *Financial support:* In 2016–17, 2 research assistantships with tuition reimbursements (averaging $11,900 per year) were awarded; health care benefits and unspecified assistantships also available. Financial award application deadline: 4/1. *Faculty research:* Organizational theory, instructional supervision, data-based decision-making. *Unit head:* Dr. David R. Dagley, Professor of Educational Leadership, 205-348-5159, Fax: 205-348-2161, E-mail: ddagley@bamaed.ua.edu. *Application contact:* Dr. Kathy S. Wetzel, Assistant Dean for Student Services, 205-348-1154, Fax: 205-348-0080, E-mail: kwetzel@bamaed.ua.edu.
Website: http://www.elpts.ua.edu

The University of Alabama, Graduate School, College of Education, Department of Educational Leadership, Policy, and Technology Studies, Educational Leadership Program, Tuscaloosa, AL 35487. Offers MA, Ed S. *Program availability:* Part-time, evening/weekend. *Students:* 3 full-time (1 woman), 42 part-time (29 women); includes 11 minority (10 Black or African American, non-Hispanic/Latino; 1 Asian, non-Hispanic/Latino). Average age 36. 22 applicants, 73% accepted, 15 enrolled. In 2016, 23 master's, 23 other advanced degrees awarded. *Degree requirements:* For master's, comprehensive exam, internship. *Entrance requirements:* For master's, MAT or GRE, 3 years of teaching experience, teaching certification, interview, portfolio, minimum GPA of 3.0; for Ed S, MAT or GRE, master's degree, minimum GPA of 3.0. Additional exam requirements/recommendations for international students: Required—TOEFL. *Application deadline:* For fall admission, 4/30 priority date for domestic and international students; for winter admission, 11/1 priority date for domestic and international students; for spring admission, 11/1 priority date for domestic and international students. Application fee: $50 ($60 for international students). Electronic applications accepted. *Expenses:* Tuition, state resident: full-time $10,470. Tuition, nonresident: full-time $26,950. *Financial support:* In 2016–17, 2 research assistantships with full tuition reimbursements (averaging $11,900 per year) were awarded; health care benefits also available. *Faculty research:* Instructional supervision, school effectiveness, organizational theory, politics of education, educational law. *Unit head:* Dr. David R. Dagley, Professor, 205-348-5159, Fax: 205-348-2161, E-mail: ddagley@bamaed.ua.edu. *Application contact:* Dr. Kathy S. Wetzel, Assistant Dean for Student Services, 205-348-1154, Fax: 205-348-0080, E-mail: kwetzel@bamaed.ua.edu.
Website: http://education.ua.edu/academics/elpts/edle/

The University of Alabama, Graduate School, College of Education, Department of Educational Leadership, Policy, and Technology Studies, Higher Education Administration Program, Tuscaloosa, AL 35487. Offers MA, Ed D, PhD. *Program availability:* Evening/weekend, 100% online. *Students:* 60 full-time (38 women), 86 part-time (36 women); includes 54 minority (42 Black or African American, non-Hispanic/Latino; 2 Asian, non-Hispanic/Latino; 5 Hispanic/Latino; 5 Two or more races, non-Hispanic/Latino). Average age 38. 77 applicants, 49% accepted, 27 enrolled. In 2016, 14 master's, 15 doctorates awarded. Terminal master's awarded for partial completion of doctoral program. *Degree requirements:* For master's, capstone seminar; for doctorate, comprehensive exam, thesis/dissertation. *Entrance requirements:* For master's, GRE or MAT, minimum GPA of 3.0; for doctorate, GRE (for PhD), GRE or MAT (for Ed D), master's degree, minimum GPA of 3.0. Additional exam requirements/recommendations for international students: Required—TOEFL. *Application deadline:* For fall admission, 1/15 priority date for domestic and international students. Application fee: $60 ($75 for international students). Electronic applications accepted. *Expenses:* Tuition, state resident: full-time $10,470. Tuition, nonresident: full-time $26,950. *Financial support:* In 2016–17, 5 students received support, including 2 research assistantships with full tuition reimbursements available (averaging $11,900 per year); career-related internships or fieldwork, scholarships/grants, health care benefits, and unspecified assistantships also available. *Faculty research:* College teaching and learning, faculty-administration relations, community colleges, organizational change, student affairs. *Unit head:* Dr. Karri Holley, Coordinator and Associate Professor, 205-348-7825, Fax: 205-348-2161, E-mail: kaholley@ua.edu. *Application contact:* Donna Smith, Administrative Assistant, 205-348-6871, Fax: 205-348-2161, E-mail: dbsmith@ua.edu.
Website: http://education.ua.edu/academics/elpts/hea/

The University of Alabama, Graduate School, College of Education, Department of Educational Leadership, Policy, and Technology Studies, Instructional Leadership Program, Tuscaloosa, AL 35487. Offers Ed D, PhD. *Program availability:* Part-time, evening/weekend. *Students:* 48 full-time (38 women), 127 part-time (104 women); includes 51 minority (41 Black or African American, non-Hispanic/Latino; 2 American Indian or Alaska Native, non-Hispanic/Latino; 1 Asian, non-Hispanic/Latino; 3 Hispanic/Latino; 1 Native Hawaiian or other Pacific Islander, non-Hispanic/Latino; 3 Two or more races, non-Hispanic/Latino), 2 international. Average age 43. 31 applicants, 74% accepted, 18 enrolled. In 2016, 27 doctorates awarded. *Degree requirements:* For doctorate, comprehensive exam, thesis/dissertation. *Entrance requirements:* Additional exam requirements/recommendations for international students: Recommended—TOEFL. *Application deadline:* Applications are processed on a rolling basis. Application fee: $50 ($60 for international students). Electronic applications accepted. *Expenses:* Tuition, state resident: full-time $10,470. Tuition, nonresident: full-time $26,950. *Financial support:* In 2016–17, 2 research assistantships with tuition reimbursements (averaging $11,900 per year), 2 teaching assistantships with tuition reimbursements (averaging $11,900 per year) were awarded; health care benefits and unspecified assistantships also available. Financial award application deadline: 5/15. *Unit head:* Dr. John Petrovic, Professor in Social and Cultural Studies in Education, 205-348-0465, Fax: 205-348-2161, E-mail: petrovic@ua.edu. *Application contact:* Dr. John Petrovic, Professor in Social and Cultural Studies in Education, 205-348-0465, Fax: 205-348-2161, E-mail: petrovic@ua.edu.
Website: http://www.elpts.ua.edu

The University of Alabama at Birmingham, School of Education, Program in Educational Leadership, Birmingham, AL 35294. Offers MA Ed, Ed D, Ed S. Ed D, PhD offered jointly with The University of Alabama (Tuscaloosa). *Accreditation:* NCATE. *Program availability:* Part-time. *Degree requirements:* For master's, thesis optional; for doctorate, thesis/dissertation; for Ed S, comprehensive exam, thesis optional. *Entrance requirements:* For master's, MAT, minimum GPA of 3.0, 3 years' teaching, interview; for doctorate, MAT (at or above 50th percentile), minimum GPA of 3.0, Ed S in educational leadership, school leadership experience, references, writing sample; for Ed S, MAT (minimum score of 388), minimum GPA of 3.0, master's degree or Class A certification, references. Electronic applications accepted. Full-time tuition and fees vary according to course load and program. *Faculty research:* Roles of assistant principals; mission, vision, and values of K-12; bullying.

University of Alaska Anchorage, College of Education, Program in Educational Leadership, Anchorage, AK 99508. Offers educational leadership (M Ed); principal licensure (Certificate); superintendent (Certificate). *Program availability:* Part-time. *Entrance requirements:* For master's, GRE or MAT, interview, minimum GPA of 3.0. Additional exam requirements/recommendations for international students: Required—TOEFL (minimum score 550 paper-based).

University of Alaska Southeast, Graduate Programs, Program in Education, Juneau, AK 99801. Offers educational leadership (M Ed); elementary education (MAT); learning design and technology (M Ed); mathematics education (M Ed); reading specialist (M Ed); secondary education (MAT); special education (M Ed, MAT). *Accreditation:* NCATE. *Program availability:* Part-time, evening/weekend, online learning. *Degree requirements:* For master's, comprehensive exam or project, portfolio. *Entrance requirements:* For master's, PRAXIS, minimum GPA of 3.0, writing sample, letters of recommendation. *Application deadline:* For fall admission, 3/8 for domestic students. Applications are processed on a rolling basis. Application fee: $60. Electronic applications accepted. *Expenses:* Tuition, state resident: part-time $466 per credit. Tuition, nonresident: part-time $979 per credit. *Required fees:* $19 per credit. Part-time tuition and fees vary according to course level, campus/location and reciprocity agreements. *Financial support:* Federal Work-Study, scholarships/grants, and tuition waivers (full and partial) available. Support available to part-time students. Financial award applicants required to submit FAFSA. *Faculty research:* Applied classroom research, culturally responsive practices, action research, teaching effectiveness. *Unit head:* Dr. Larry Harris, Dean, 907-796-6551, Fax: 907-796-6550, E-mail: larry.harris@uas.alaska.edu. *Application contact:* Susan A. Stuck, Administrative Assistant, 866-465-6424, Fax: 866-465-5159, E-mail: jnsas@uas.alaska.edu.

University of Alberta, Faculty of Graduate Studies and Research, Department of Educational Policy Studies, Edmonton, AB T6G 2E1, Canada. Offers adult education (M Ed, Ed D, PhD); educational administration and leadership (M Ed, Ed D, PhD, Postgraduate Diploma); First Nations education (M Ed, Ed D, PhD); theoretical, cultural and international studies in education (M Ed, Ed D, PhD). *Degree requirements:* For master's, thesis (for some programs); for doctorate, thesis/dissertation. *Entrance requirements:* For master's, minimum GPA of 6.5 on a 9.0 scale; for doctorate, minimum GPA of 7.5 on a 9.0 scale. Additional exam requirements/recommendations for international students: Required—TOEFL (minimum score 580 paper-based). Electronic applications accepted.

The University of Arizona, College of Education, Department of Educational Policy Studies and Practice, Program of Educational Leadership, Tucson, AZ 85721. Offers M Ed, Ed D, Ed S. *Program availability:* Part-time. *Degree requirements:* For master's and Ed S, capstone experience; for doctorate, comprehensive exam, thesis/dissertation. *Entrance requirements:* For master's, leadership experience; for doctorate, GRE General Test, minimum GPA of 3.5, 3 letters of recommendation, curriculum vitae, writing sample. Additional exam requirements/recommendations for international students: Required—TOEFL (minimum score 550 paper-based; 79 iBT). Electronic applications accepted. *Faculty research:* School governance, higher order thinking, restructuring schools, bilingual education policy, authority in education.

University of Arkansas, Graduate School, College of Education and Health Professions, Department of Curriculum and Instruction, Program in Educational Leadership, Fayetteville, AR 72701. Offers M Ed, Ed D, Ed S. *Accreditation:* NCATE. *Program availability:* Part-time, evening/weekend. In 2016, 8 master's, 2 doctorates awarded. *Degree requirements:* For doctorate, thesis/dissertation. *Entrance requirements:* For master's, GRE General Test, MAT or minimum GPA of 3.0; for doctorate, GRE General Test or MAT. *Application deadline:* For fall admission, 4/1 for international students; for spring admission, 10/1 for international students. Applications are processed on a rolling basis. Application fee: $40 ($50 for international students). Electronic applications accepted. *Financial support:* Fellowships with tuition reimbursements, research assistantships, teaching assistantships, career-related internships or fieldwork, and Federal Work-Study available. Support available to part-time students. Financial award application deadline: 4/1; financial award applicants required to submit FAFSA. *Unit head:* Dr. Michael Daugherty, Departmental Chairperson, 479-575-4209, Fax: 479-575-5119, E-mail: mkd03@uark.edu. *Application contact:* Dr. Ed Bengtson, Graduate Coordinator, 479-575-5092, Fax: 479-575-6676, E-mail: egbents@uark.edu.
Website: http://cied.uark.edu

University of Arkansas at Little Rock, Graduate School, College of Education and Health Professions, Department of Educational Leadership, Program in Educational Administration and Supervision, Little Rock, AR 72204-1099. Offers M Ed, Ed D, Ed S. *Program availability:* Part-time, evening/weekend. *Degree requirements:* For master's, comprehensive exam; for doctorate, comprehensive exam, oral defense of dissertation, residency; for Ed S, comprehensive exam, professional project. *Entrance requirements:* For master's, GRE General Test or MAT, 4 years of work experience (minimum 3 in teaching), interview, minimum GPA of 2.75, teaching certificate; for doctorate, GRE General Test or MAT, 4 years of work experience, minimum graduate GPA of 3.0, teaching certificate; for Ed S, GRE General Test or MAT, 4 years of work experience, minimum GPA of 2.75, teaching certificate.

University of Arkansas at Little Rock, Graduate School, College of Education and Health Professions, Department of Educational Leadership, Program in Higher Education, Little Rock, AR 72204-1099. Offers administration (MA); college student affairs (MA); health professions teaching and learning (MA); higher education (Ed D); two-year college teaching (MA). *Degree requirements:* For doctorate, comprehensive exam, oral defense of dissertation, residency. *Entrance requirements:* For master's, GRE General Test or MAT, interview, minimum graduate GPA of 3.0; for doctorate, GRE General Test, interview, minimum graduate GPA of 3.5, teaching certificate, three years of work experience.

University of Arkansas at Monticello, School of Education, Monticello, AR 71656. Offers education (M Ed, MAT); educational leadership (M Ed). *Accreditation:* NCATE. *Program availability:* Part-time, evening/weekend, online learning. *Degree requirements:* For master's, comprehensive exam. *Entrance requirements:* For master's, minimum GPA of 3.0. Additional exam requirements/recommendations for international students: Required—TOEFL (minimum score 550 paper-based). Electronic applications accepted.

University of Bridgeport, School of Education, Department of Education, Bridgeport, CT 06604. Offers education (MS); educational management (Ed D, Diploma), including intermediate administrator or supervisor (Diploma), leadership (Ed D); elementary education (MS, Diploma), including early childhood education, elementary education; middle school education (MS); music education (MS); remedial reading and language arts (Diploma); secondary education (MS, Diploma), including computer specialist (Diploma), international education (Diploma), reading specialist, secondary education. *Program availability:* Part-time, evening/weekend. *Degree requirements:* For master's, final exam, final project, or thesis; for doctorate, comprehensive exam, thesis/dissertation; for Diploma, thesis or alternative, final project. *Entrance requirements:* For master's, minimum undergraduate QPA of 2.67; for doctorate, GRE, MAT; for Diploma, GRE General Test or MAT, minimum graduate QPA of 3.0. Additional exam requirements/recommendations for international students: Recommended—TOEFL (minimum score 550 paper-based; 80 iBT), IELTS (minimum score 6.5). Electronic applications accepted. *Expenses:* Contact institution.

University of Bridgeport, School of Education, Department of Educational Leadership, Bridgeport, CT 06604. Offers intermediate administrator or supervisor (Diploma); leadership (Ed D). *Degree requirements:* For doctorate, comprehensive exam, thesis/dissertation; for Diploma, thesis or alternative, final project. *Entrance requirements:* For doctorate, GRE, MAT; for Diploma, GRE General Test or MAT, minimum graduate QPA of 3.0. Additional exam requirements/recommendations for international students: Recommended—TOEFL (minimum score 550 paper-based; 80 iBT), IELTS (minimum score 6.5). Electronic applications accepted. *Expenses:* Contact institution.

The University of British Columbia, Faculty of Education, Department of Educational Studies, Vancouver, BC V6T 1Z1, Canada. Offers adult learning and education (M Ed); adult learning and global change (M Ed); curriculum and leadership (M Ed); educational administration and leadership (M Ed); educational leadership and policy (Ed D); educational studies (M Ed, MA, PhD); higher education (M Ed); society, culture and politics in education (M Ed). *Program availability:* Part-time, evening/weekend. *Faculty:* 25 full-time (14 women), 3 part-time/adjunct (2 women). *Students:* 222 full-time (157 women), 62 part-time (44 women). Average age 35. 166 applicants, 66% accepted, 74 enrolled. In 2016, 103 master's, 13 doctorates awarded. Terminal master's awarded for partial completion of doctoral program. *Degree requirements:* For master's, thesis; for doctorate, comprehensive exam, thesis/dissertation. *Entrance requirements:* For master's, minimum B+ average, 4-year undergraduate degree, field-related experience; for doctorate, minimum B+ average, 4-year undergraduate degree, master's degree, field-related experience. Additional exam requirements/recommendations for international students: Required—TOEFL (minimum score 600 paper-based; 100 iBT) or IELTS (minimum score 6.5). Application fee: $90 ($150 for international students). Electronic applications accepted. *Expenses:* Contact institution. *Financial support:* In 2016–17, 7 fellowships with tuition reimbursements (averaging $17,000 per year), 12 research assistantships (averaging $4,000 per year), 8 teaching assistantships (averaging $5,000 per year) were awarded. *Faculty research:* Educational leadership educational administration adult education politics in education, global change and adult learning. *Total annual research expenditures:* $632,000. *Unit head:* Dr. Tara Fenwick, Head, 604-822-5359, Fax: 604-822-4244. *Application contact:* Christine Adams, Graduate Secretary, 604-822-6647, Fax: 604-822-4244, E-mail: grad.edst@ubc.ca.
Website: http://www.edst.educ.ubc.ca/

University of Calgary, Faculty of Graduate Studies, Werklund School of Education, Graduate Division of Educational Research, Calgary, AB T2N 1N4, Canada. Offers adult learning (M Ed, MA, Ed D, PhD); curriculum and learning (M Ed, MA, Ed D, PhD); educational leadership (M Ed, MA, Ed D, PhD); languages and diversity (M Ed, MA, Ed D, PhD); learning sciences (M Ed, MA, Ed D, PhD). Ed D in educational leadership offered via distance delivery. *Program availability:* Part-time, evening/weekend, online learning. *Degree requirements:* For master's, thesis (for some programs); for doctorate, thesis/dissertation, candidacy exam. *Entrance requirements:* For master's, minimum GPA of 3.0, 3 letters of reference; for doctorate, minimum GPA of 3.5, 3 letters of reference. Additional exam requirements/recommendations for international students: Required—TOEFL, IELTS. Electronic applications accepted. *Faculty research:* Curriculum, leadership, technology, contexts, gifted, second language teaching, work place and adult learning.

University of California, Berkeley, Graduate Division, School of Education, Programs in Education, Berkeley, CA 94720-1500. Offers development in mathematics and science (MA); education in mathematics, science, and technology (MA, PhD); human development and education (MA, PhD); leadership education (MA); special education (PhD); teacher education (MA); MA/Credential; PhD/Credential; PhD/MA. *Students:* 286 full-time (207 women); includes 133 minority (31 Black or African American, non-Hispanic/Latino; 2 American Indian or Alaska Native, non-Hispanic/Latino; 44 Asian, non-Hispanic/Latino; 56 Hispanic/Latino), 29 international. Average age 33. 643 applicants, 84 enrolled. In 2016, 105 master's, 31 doctorates awarded. Terminal master's awarded for partial completion of doctoral program. *Degree requirements:* For master's, exam or thesis; for doctorate, thesis/dissertation, oral qualifying exam. *Entrance requirements:* For master's and doctorate, GRE General Test, minimum GPA of 3.0 during last 2 years of undergraduate course work. *Application deadline:* For fall admission, 12/16 for domestic students. Application fee: $105 ($125 for international students). Electronic applications accepted. *Financial support:* Fellowships, research assistantships, teaching assistantships, institutionally sponsored loans, health care benefits, and unspecified assistantships available. *Faculty research:* Human development, social and moral educational psychology, developmental teacher preparation. *Unit head:* Prof. Prudence L. Carter, Dean, 510-642-3726, E-mail: gsedeansoffice@lists.berkeley.edu.
Website: https://gse.berkeley.edu

University of California, Irvine, School of Education, Irvine, CA 92697. Offers educational administration (Ed D); educational administration and leadership (Ed D); elementary and secondary education (MAT). *Program availability:* Part-time, evening/weekend. *Students:* 189 full-time (139 women), 1 part-time (0 women); includes 101 minority (44 Asian, non-Hispanic/Latino; 40 Hispanic/Latino; 1 Native Hawaiian or other Pacific Islander, non-Hispanic/Latino; 16 Two or more races, non-Hispanic/Latino), 16 international. Average age 27. 456 applicants, 54% accepted, 131 enrolled. In 2016, 139 master's, 16 doctorates awarded. *Degree requirements:* For doctorate, thesis/dissertation. *Entrance requirements:* For master's, GRE, minimum GPA of 3.0; for doctorate, GRE General Test, minimum GPA of 3.0. Additional exam requirements/recommendations for international students: Required—TOEFL (minimum score 550 paper-based). *Application deadline:* For fall admission, 1/2 priority date for domestic students, 1/2 for international students. Application fee: $105 ($125 for international students). Electronic applications accepted. *Financial support:* Fellowships, research assistantships with full tuition reimbursements, institutionally sponsored loans, traineeships, health care benefits, and unspecified assistantships available. Financial award application deadline: 3/1; financial award applicants required to submit FAFSA. *Faculty research:* Education technology, learning theory, social theory, cultural diversity, postmodernism. *Unit head:* Richard Arum, Dean, 949-824-2534, E-mail: richard.arum@uci.edu. *Application contact:* Denise Earley, Assistant Director of Student Affairs, 949-824-4022, E-mail: denise.earley@uci.edu.
Website: http://education.uci.edu/

University of California, Los Angeles, Graduate Division, Graduate School of Education and Information Studies, Program in Educational Leadership, Los Angeles, CA 90095. Offers Ed D. *Program availability:* Evening/weekend. *Degree requirements:* For doctorate, thesis/dissertation, oral and written qualifying exams. *Entrance requirements:* For doctorate, GRE General Test, minimum undergraduate GPA of 3.0, resume. Electronic applications accepted.

University of California, Riverside, Graduate Division, Graduate School of Education, Riverside, CA 92521-0102. Offers autism (M Ed); diversity and equity (M Ed); education specialist (Credential); education, society, and culture (MA, PhD); educational psychology (MA, PhD); general education (M Ed); higher education administration and policy (M Ed, PhD); multiple subject (Credential); reading (M Ed); school psychology (PhD); single subject (Credential); special education (M Ed, MA, PhD); TESOL (M Ed). Terminal master's awarded for partial completion of doctoral program. *Degree requirements:* For master's, thesis optional, comprehensive exams or thesis (MA), case study or analytical report (M Ed); for doctorate, thesis/dissertation, written and oral qualifying exams, college teaching practicum. *Entrance requirements:* For master's, GRE General Test (for MA); CBEST and CSET (for M Ed in general education only), UCR Extension TESOL certificate (for M Ed with TESOL emphasis only); for doctorate, GRE General Test, writing sample; for Credential, CBEST, CSET. Additional exam requirements/recommendations for international students: Required—TOEFL (minimum score 550 paper-based; 80 iBT), IELTS (minimum score 7). Electronic applications accepted. *Expenses:* Tuition, state resident: full-time $16,666. Tuition, nonresident: full-time $31,768. *Required fees:* $11,055.54 per quarter. $3685.18 per quarter. Tuition and fees vary according to campus/location and program. *Faculty research:* Responsiveness to intervention, faculty core, response to intervention of English language learners, advanced modeling techniques, study on social capital, trust, and motivation.

University of California, San Diego, Graduate Division, Program in Education Studies, La Jolla, CA 92093. Offers education (M Ed, PhD); educational leadership (Ed D); teaching and learning (MA, Ed D), including bilingual education (MA), curriculum design (MA). Ed D offered jointly with California State University, San Marcos. *Students:* 89 full-time (59 women), 52 part-time (38 women). 228 applicants, 52% accepted, 74 enrolled. In 2016, 68 master's, 6 doctorates awarded. *Degree requirements:* For master's, thesis (for some programs), student teaching; for doctorate, comprehensive exam, thesis/dissertation. *Entrance requirements:* For master's, GRE General Test; CBEST and appropriate CSET exam (for select tracks), current teaching or educational assignment (for select tracks); for doctorate, GRE General Test, current teaching or educational assignment (for select tracks). Additional exam requirements/recommendations for international students: Required—TOEFL (minimum score 550 paper-based; 80 iBT), IELTS (minimum score 7). *Application deadline:* For fall admission, 12/1 for domestic students. Application fee: $105 ($125 for international students). Electronic applications accepted. *Expenses:* Tuition, state resident: full-time $11,220. Tuition, nonresident: full-time $26,322. *Required fees:* $1864. *Financial support:* Fellowships, career-related internships or fieldwork, and scholarships/grants available. Financial award applicants required to submit FAFSA. *Faculty research:* Language, culture and literacy development of deaf/hard of hearing children; equity issues in education; educational reform; evaluation, assessment, and research methodologies; distributed learning. *Unit head:* Alan J. Daly, Chair, 858-822-6472, E-mail: ajdaly@ucsd.edu. *Application contact:* Giselle Van Luit, Graduate Coordinator, 858-534-2958, E-mail: edsinfo@ucsd.edu.

University of Central Arkansas, Graduate School, College of Education, Department of Leadership Studies, Conway, AR 72035-0001. Offers college student personnel (MS); district-level administration (PMC); educational leadership - district level (Ed S); instructional technology (MS); library media and information technology (MS); school counseling (MS); school leadership (MS); school-based leadership adult education program administration (PMC); school-based leadership building administration (PMC); school-based leadership curriculum administration (PMC); school-based leadership gifted and talented program administration (PMC); school-based leadership special education program administration (PMC). *Accreditation:* NCATE. *Program availability:* Part-time, evening/weekend, online learning. *Degree requirements:* For master's and other advanced degree, comprehensive exam. *Entrance requirements:* For master's, GRE. Additional exam requirements/recommendations for international students: Required—TOEFL (minimum score 80 iBT). Electronic applications accepted. *Expenses:* Contact institution.

University of Central Florida, College of Education and Human Performance, Department of Educational and Human Sciences, Program in Educational Leadership, Orlando, FL 32816. Offers educational leadership (MA, Ed D, Ed S), including community college education (MA), higher education (Ed D), student personnel (MA). *Program availability:* Part-time, evening/weekend. *Students:* 121 full-time (78 women), 274 part-time (203 women); includes 147 minority (69 Black or African American, non-Hispanic/Latino; 7 Asian, non-Hispanic/Latino; 65 Hispanic/Latino; 6 Two or more races, non-Hispanic/Latino), 1 international. Average age 31. 258 applicants, 69% accepted, 101 enrolled. In 2016, 84 master's, 24 doctorates awarded. *Degree requirements:* For master's, thesis or alternative; for doctorate, thesis/dissertation, candidacy exam; for Ed S, thesis or alternative, final exam. *Entrance requirements:* For master's, GRE General Test; for doctorate, GRE General Test, GRE Subject Test, minimum GPA of 3.0, resume; for Ed S, GRE General Test, minimum GPA of 3.0, resume. Additional exam requirements/recommendations for international students: Required—TOEFL. *Application deadline:* For fall admission, 2/20 for domestic students; for spring admission, 9/20 for domestic students. Application fee: $30. Electronic applications accepted. *Expenses:* Tuition, state resident: part-time $288.16 per credit hour. Tuition, nonresident: part-time $1071.31 per credit hour. *Financial support:* In 2016–17, 22 students received support, including 1 fellowship with partial tuition reimbursement available (averaging $2,500 per year), 21 research assistantships with partial tuition reimbursements available (averaging $8,064 per year), 2 teaching assistantships with partial tuition reimbursements available (averaging $11,154 per year); career-related internships or fieldwork, Federal Work-Study, institutionally sponsored loans, tuition waivers (partial), and unspecified assistantships also available. Financial award application deadline: 3/1; financial award applicants required to submit FAFSA. *Unit head:* Dr. Kenneth Murray, Program Coordinator, 407-832-1468, E-mail: kenneth.murray@ucf.edu. *Application contact:* Assistant Director, Graduate Admissions, 407-823-2766, Fax: 407-823-6442, E-mail: gradadmissions@ucf.edu.
Website: http://education.ucf.edu/highered/index.cfm

University of Central Florida, College of Education and Human Performance, Education Doctoral Programs, Orlando, FL 32816. Offers communication sciences and disorders (PhD); curriculum and instruction (Ed D); early childhood education (PhD); educational leadership (Ed D); elementary education (PhD); exceptional education (PhD); exercise physiology (PhD); higher education (PhD); instructional technology (PhD); mathematics education (PhD); methodology, measurement and analysis (PhD); reading education (PhD); science education (PhD); social science education (PhD); TESOL (PhD). *Students:* 127 full-time (91 women), 43 part-time (29 women); includes 33 minority (17 Black or African American, non-Hispanic/Latino; 5 Asian, non-Hispanic/Latino; 7 Hispanic/Latino; 4 Two or more races, non-Hispanic/Latino), 26 international. Average age 37. 163 applicants, 40% accepted, 52 enrolled. In 2016, 57 doctorates awarded. Application fee: $30. Electronic applications accepted. *Expenses:* Tuition, state resident: part-time $288.16 per credit hour. Tuition, nonresident: part-time $1071.31 per credit hour. *Financial support:* In 2016–17, 78 students received support, including 41 fellowships with partial tuition reimbursements available (averaging $5,916 per year), 44 research assistantships with partial tuition reimbursements available (averaging $7,637 per year), 48 teaching assistantships with partial tuition reimbursements available (averaging $9,633 per year). Financial award application deadline: 3/1; financial award applicants required to submit FAFSA. *Unit head:* Dr. Edward Robinson, Director of Doctoral Programs, 407-823-6106, E-mail: edward.robinson@ucf.edu. *Application contact:* Assistant Director, Graduate Admissions, 407-823-2766, Fax: 407-823-6442, E-mail: gradadmissions@ucf.edu.
Website: http://education.ucf.edu/programs.cfm?pid=g&cat=2

University of Central Florida, College of Education and Human Performance, School of Teaching, Learning, and Leadership, Orlando, FL 32816. Offers applied learning and instruction (MA); art education (M Ed), including teacher leadership; educational and instructional technology (MA), including instructional design and technology; educational leadership (Ed S); elementary education (M Ed, MA); English language arts education (M Ed), including teacher leadership; K-8 mathematics and science education (M Ed, Certificate); reading education (M Ed); science education (M Ed), including teacher

leadership; social science education (M Ed), including teacher leadership; teacher education (MAT), including art education, English language, mathematics education, middle school mathematics, middle school science, science education, social science education; teacher leadership (M Ed); teaching excellence (Certificate). *Program availability:* Part-time, evening/weekend. *Faculty:* 72 full-time (53 women), 55 part-time/adjunct (42 women). *Students:* 75 full-time (64 women), 304 part-time (257 women); includes 125 minority (46 Black or African American, non-Hispanic/Latino; 2 American Indian or Alaska Native, non-Hispanic/Latino; 11 Asian, non-Hispanic/Latino; 59 Hispanic/Latino; 7 Two or more races, non-Hispanic/Latino), 4 international. Average age 32. 229 applicants, 76% accepted, 102 enrolled. In 2016, 151 master's, 34 other advanced degrees awarded. *Degree requirements:* For other advanced degree, thesis or alternative. *Entrance requirements:* For degree, GRE General Test, minimum GPA of 3.0. Additional exam requirements/recommendations for international students: Required—TOEFL. *Application deadline:* For fall admission, 7/15 for domestic students; for spring admission, 12/15 for domestic students. Application fee: $30. Electronic applications accepted. *Expenses:* Tuition, state resident: part-time $288.16 per credit hour. Tuition, nonresident: part-time $1071.31 per credit hour. *Financial support:* In 2016–17, 2 students received support, including 2 research assistantships with partial tuition reimbursements available (averaging $9,463 per year); teaching assistantships, career-related internships or fieldwork, Federal Work-Study, institutionally sponsored loans, tuition waivers (partial), and unspecified assistantships also available. Financial award application deadline: 3/1; financial award applicants required to submit FAFSA. *Unit head:* Dr. Michael Hynes, Co-Director, 407-823-6076, E-mail: michael.hynes@ucf.edu. *Application contact:* Assistant Director, Graduate Admissions, 407-823-2766, Fax: 407-823-6442, E-mail: gradadmissions@ucf.edu.
Website: http://education.ucf.edu/stll/

University of Central Missouri, The Graduate School, Warrensburg, MO 64093. Offers accountancy (MA); accounting (MBA); applied mathematics (MS); aviation safety (MA); biology (MS); business administration (MBA); career and technical education leadership (MS); college student personnel administration (MS); communication (MA); computer science (MS); counseling (MS); criminal justice (MS); educational leadership (Ed D); educational technology (MS); elementary and early childhood education (MSE); English (MA); environmental studies (MA); finance (MBA); history (MA); human services/educational technology (Ed S); human services/learning resources (Ed S); human services/professional counseling (Ed S); industrial hygiene (MS); industrial management (MS); information systems (MBA); information technology (MS); kinesiology (MS); library science and information services (MS); literacy education (MSE); marketing (MBA); mathematics (MS); music (MA); occupational safety management (MS); psychology (MS); rural family nursing (MS); school administration (MSE); social gerontology (MS); sociology (MA); special education (MSE); speech language pathology (MS); superintendency (Ed S); teaching (MAT); teaching English as a second language (MA); technology (MS); technology management (PhD); theatre (MA). *Program availability:* Part-time, 100% online, blended/hybrid learning. *Degree requirements:* For master's and Ed S, comprehensive exam (for some programs), thesis (for some programs). *Entrance requirements:* Additional exam requirements/recommendations for international students: Required—TOEFL (minimum score 550 paper-based; 79 iBT). Electronic applications accepted.

University of Central Oklahoma, The Jackson College of Graduate Studies, College of Education and Professional Studies, Department of Advanced Professional and Special Services, Edmond, OK 73034-5209. Offers educational leadership (M Ed); library media education (M Ed); reading (M Ed); school counseling (M Ed); special education (M Ed), including mild/moderate disabilities, severe-profound/multiple disabilities, special education; speech-language pathology (MS). *Accreditation:* ASHA. *Program availability:* Part-time. *Degree requirements:* For master's, comprehensive exam (for some programs), thesis (for some programs). *Entrance requirements:* For master's, GRE. Additional exam requirements/recommendations for international students: Required—TOEFL (minimum score 550 paper-based; 79 iBT), IELTS (minimum score 6.5). Electronic applications accepted. *Faculty research:* Intellectual freedom, fair use copyright, technology integration, young adult literature, distance learning.

University of Cincinnati, Graduate School, College of Education, Criminal Justice, and Human Services, School of Education, Program in Educational Leadership, Cincinnati, OH 45221. Offers M Ed, Ed S. *Accreditation:* NCATE. *Program availability:* Part-time, online learning. *Degree requirements:* For master's, thesis or alternative. *Entrance requirements:* For master's, GRE General Test, 3 letters of reference, resume, minimum GPA of 2.8; for Ed S, references, interview. Additional exam requirements/recommendations for international students: Required—TOEFL (minimum score 550 paper-based). Electronic applications accepted. *Expenses: Tuition, area resident:* Full-time $12,790; part-time $389 per credit hour. Tuition, state resident: full-time $13,290; part-time $419 per credit hour. Tuition, nonresident: full-time $24,532; part-time $976 per credit hour. *International tuition:* $24,832 full-time. *Required fees:* $3958; $140 per credit hour. Tuition and fees vary according to course load, degree level, program and reciprocity agreements.

University of Cincinnati, Graduate School, College of Education, Criminal Justice, and Human Services, School of Education, Program in Urban Educational Leadership, Cincinnati, OH 45221. Offers Ed D. *Degree requirements:* For doctorate, thesis/dissertation. *Entrance requirements:* For doctorate, GRE General Test, GRE Subject Test. Additional exam requirements/recommendations for international students: Required—TOEFL (minimum score 550 paper-based), OEPT. *Expenses: Tuition, area resident:* Full-time $12,790; part-time $389 per credit hour. Tuition, state resident: full-time $13,290; part-time $419 per credit hour. Tuition, nonresident: full-time $24,532; part-time $976 per credit hour. *International tuition:* $24,832 full-time. *Required fees:* $3958; $140 per credit hour. Tuition and fees vary according to course load, degree level, program and reciprocity agreements.

University of Colorado Colorado Springs, College of Education, Colorado Springs, CO 80918. Offers counseling and human services (MA); curriculum and instruction (MA); educational leadership (MA); educational leadership, research and policy (PhD); special education (MA); teaching English to speakers of other languages (MA). *Accreditation:* ACA; NCATE. *Program availability:* Part-time, evening/weekend, 100% online, blended/hybrid learning. *Faculty:* 26 full-time (18 women), 33 part-time/adjunct (21 women). *Students:* 136 full-time (94 women), 264 part-time (177 women); includes 99 minority (17 Black or African American, non-Hispanic/Latino; 1 American Indian or Alaska Native, non-Hispanic/Latino; 8 Asian, non-Hispanic/Latino; 55 Hispanic/Latino; 18 Two or more races, non-Hispanic/Latino), 9 international. Average age 35. 152 applicants, 89% accepted, 88 enrolled. In 2016, 161 master's, 11 doctorates awarded. *Degree requirements:* For master's, comprehensive exam, thesis or alternative, microcomputer proficiency; for doctorate, comprehensive exam, thesis/dissertation, research lab. *Entrance requirements:* For master's and doctorate, GRE General Test. Additional exam requirements/recommendations for international students: Recommended—TOEFL (minimum score 550 paper-based; 80 iBT), IELTS (minimum score 6). *Application deadline:* For fall admission, 2/1 priority date for domestic students, 2/1 for international students; for spring admission, 10/15 for domestic students, 10/1 for international students. Applications are processed on a rolling basis. Application fee: $60 ($100 for international students). Electronic applications accepted. *Expenses:* Contact institution. *Financial support:* In 2016–17, 108 students received support. Career-related internships or fieldwork, Federal Work-Study, scholarships/grants, and unspecified assistantships available. Support available to part-time students. Financial award application deadline: 3/1; financial award applicants required to submit FAFSA. *Faculty research:* Linguistically diverse education (LDE), educational policy, evidence-based reading and writing instruction, relational and social aggression, positive behavior supports, inclusive schooling, K-12 education policy. *Total annual research expenditures:* $272,136. *Unit head:* Dr. Valerie Martin Conley, Dean, 719-255-4133, E-mail: vmconley@uccs.edu. *Application contact:* The College of Education Student Resource Office, 719-255-4996, E-mail: education@uccs.edu.
Website: http://www.uccs.edu/coe

University of Colorado Denver, School of Education and Human Development, Administrative Leadership and Policy Studies Program, Denver, CO 80217. Offers MA, Ed S. *Accreditation:* NCATE. *Program availability:* Part-time, evening/weekend. *Students:* 84 full-time (60 women), 16 part-time (11 women); includes 11 minority (3 Black or African American, non-Hispanic/Latino; 1 Asian, non-Hispanic/Latino; 7 Hispanic/Latino). Average age 38. 19 applicants, 95% accepted, 17 enrolled. In 2016, 29 master's, 20 other advanced degrees awarded. *Degree requirements:* For master's, comprehensive exam, 9 credit hours beyond the 32 required for principal-administrator licensure; for Ed S, comprehensive exam, 9 credit hours beyond the 32 required for principal-administrator licensure (for those already holding MA). *Entrance requirements:* For master's and Ed S, GRE or MAT (if GPA is below 2.75), minimum GPA of 2.75, interview, 3 letters of recommendation, resume. Additional exam requirements/recommendations for international students: Required—TOEFL (minimum score 525 paper-based; 71 iBT); Recommended—IELTS (minimum score 6.3). *Application deadline:* For fall admission, 5/15 for domestic and international students; for spring admission, 10/15 for domestic students, 9/15 for international students; for summer admission, 3/15 for domestic students, 2/15 for international students. Application fee: $50 ($75 for international students). Electronic applications accepted. *Expenses:* Contact institution. *Financial support:* In 2016–17, 6 students received support. Fellowships, research assistantships, teaching assistantships, Federal Work-Study, institutionally sponsored loans, scholarships/grants, and traineeships available. Financial award application deadline: 4/1; financial award applicants required to submit FAFSA. *Faculty research:* Learning cultures, teaching and learning in educational administration. *Unit head:* Connie Fulmer, Professor, 303-315-4962, E-mail: connie.fulmer@ucdenver.edu. *Application contact:* Rebecca Schell, Academic Advisor, 303-315-4978, E-mail: rebecca.schell@ucdenver.edu.
Website: http://www.ucdenver.edu/academics/colleges/SchoolOfEducation/Academics/MASTERS/PrincipalandSchoolLeadership/Pages/AdministrativeLeadership.aspx

University of Colorado Denver, School of Education and Human Development, Program in Educational Leadership and Innovation, Denver, CO 80217. Offers educational studies and research (PhD), including administrative leadership and policy, early childhood special education, math education, research, assessment and evaluation, science education, urban ecologies. *Program availability:* Part-time, evening/weekend. *Students:* 30 full-time (25 women), 14 part-time (11 women); includes 16 minority (7 Black or African American, non-Hispanic/Latino; 1 American Indian or Alaska Native, non-Hispanic/Latino; 1 Asian, non-Hispanic/Latino; 6 Hispanic/Latino; 1 Two or more races, non-Hispanic/Latino), 5 international. Average age 40. 21 applicants, 67% accepted, 8 enrolled. In 2016, 3 doctorates awarded. *Degree requirements:* For doctorate, comprehensive exam, thesis/dissertation, 75 credit hours (for PhD). *Entrance requirements:* For doctorate, GRE or equivalent, resume or curriculum vitae, letters of recommendation, master's degree or equivalent, completion of basic or advanced statistics course with minimum B grade. Additional exam requirements/recommendations for international students: Required—TOEFL (minimum score 537 paper-based; 75 iBT); Recommended—IELTS (minimum score 6.5). *Application deadline:* For fall admission, 12/1 priority date for domestic students, 11/1 priority date for international students. Applications are processed on a rolling basis. Application fee: $50 ($75 for international students). Electronic applications accepted. *Expenses:* Contact institution. *Financial support:* In 2016–17, 45 students received support. Fellowships, research assistantships, teaching assistantships, Federal Work-Study, institutionally sponsored loans, scholarships/grants, and traineeships available. Financial award application deadline: 4/1; financial award applicants required to submit FAFSA. *Faculty research:* Administrative leadership and policy studies, early childhood education, research in diversity, paraprofessionals in education, urban schools lab. *Unit head:* 303-315-6300, E-mail: education@ucdenver.edu. *Application contact:* 303-315-6300, E-mail: education@ucdenver.edu.
Website: http://www.ucdenver.edu/academics/colleges/SchoolOfEducation/Academics/Doctorate/Pages/PhD%20in%20Education%20and%20Human%20Development.aspx

University of Colorado Denver, School of Education and Human Development, Program in Leadership for Educational Equity, Denver, CO 80217. Offers executive leadership (Ed D); instructional leadership (Ed D). *Students:* 92 full-time (64 women), 21 part-time (15 women); includes 40 minority (7 Black or African American, non-Hispanic/Latino; 3 Asian, non-Hispanic/Latino; 28 Hispanic/Latino; 2 Two or more races, non-Hispanic/Latino), 1 international. Average age 41. 1 applicant, 100% accepted, 1 enrolled. In 2016, 13 doctorates awarded. *Degree requirements:* For doctorate, thesis/dissertation, 69 credit hours, including 24 in dissertation and independent study. *Entrance requirements:* For doctorate, GRE General Test, resume with minimum of 5 years experience in an educational background, 2-3 professional artifacts illuminating leadership experiences, three professional letters of recommendation, master's degree with recommended minimum GPA of 3.2. Additional exam requirements/recommendations for international students: Required—TOEFL (minimum score 550 paper-based; 80 iBT); Recommended—IELTS (minimum score 6.8). *Application deadline:* For fall admission, 5/1 for domestic students, 4/15 for international students; for spring admission, 10/1 for international students; for summer admission, 12/1 for domestic and international students. Applications are processed on a rolling basis. Application fee: $50 ($75 for international students). Electronic applications accepted. *Expenses:* Tuition, state resident: full-time $11,006; part-time $474 per credit. Tuition, nonresident: full-time $28,212; part-time $1264 per credit hour. *Required fees:* $256 per semester. One-time fee: $94.32. Tuition and fees vary according to campus/location and program. *Financial support:* In 2016–17, 38 students received support. Fellowships, research assistantships, teaching assistantships, Federal Work-Study, institutionally sponsored loans, scholarships/grants, and traineeships available. Financial award application deadline: 4/1; financial award applicants required to submit FAFSA. *Unit head:* Shelley Zion, Executive Director of the Center for Continuing Professional Education, 303-315-4985, E-mail: shelley.zion@ucdenver.edu. *Application contact:* 303-315-6300, E-mail: education@ucdenver.edu.
Website: http://www.ucdenver.edu/academics/colleges/SchoolOfEducation/Academics/Doctorate/Pages/EdD.aspx

University of Connecticut, Graduate School, Neag School of Education, Department of Educational Leadership, Field of Educational Administration, Storrs, CT 06269. Offers MA. *Accreditation:* NCATE. *Entrance requirements:* Additional exam requirements/recommendations for international students: Required—TOEFL (minimum score 550 paper-based). Electronic applications accepted.

Educational Leadership and Administration

University of Dayton, Department of Counselor Education and Human Services, Dayton, OH 45469. Offers clinical mental health counseling (MS Ed); college student personnel (MS Ed); higher education administration (MS Ed); human services (MS Ed); school counseling (MS Ed); school psychology (MS Ed, Ed S). *Accreditation:* ACA; NCATE. *Program availability:* Part-time, evening/weekend. *Faculty:* 10 full-time (6 women), 24 part-time/adjunct (15 women). *Students:* 198 full-time (155 women), 95 part-time (75 women); includes 15 minority (8 Black or African American, non-Hispanic/Latino; 2 Asian, non-Hispanic/Latino; 2 Hispanic/Latino; 3 Two or more races, non-Hispanic/Latino), 3 international. Average age 36. 426 applicants, 28% accepted. In 2016, 115 master's, 9 Ed Ss awarded. *Degree requirements:* For Ed S, thesis. *Entrance requirements:* For master's, MAT or GRE (if GPA less than 2.75), essays (for some programs). Additional exam requirements/recommendations for international students: Required—TOEFL (minimum score 550 paper-based; 80 iBT); Recommended—IELTS. *Application deadline:* For fall admission, 3/10 priority date for domestic and international students; for spring admission, 9/10 priority date for domestic and international students; for summer admission, 12/1 priority date for domestic and international students. Application fee: $0 ($50 for international students). Electronic applications accepted. *Expenses:* $620 per credit hour (for master's degree programs); $740 per credit hour (for Ed S). *Financial support:* In 2016–17, 7 research assistantships with partial tuition reimbursements (averaging $8,038 per year), 4 teaching assistantships with partial tuition reimbursements (averaging $9,390 per year) were awarded; career-related internships or fieldwork, institutionally sponsored loans, health care benefits, and unspecified assistantships also available. Financial award application deadline: 1/9; financial award applicants required to submit FAFSA. *Faculty research:* School bonding, traumatic brain injuries, second-year student experience, impact of physical space on learning, integrative health and mental health care. *Total annual research expenditures:* $1,500. *Unit head:* Dr. Alan Demmitt, Chair, 937-229-3644, Fax: 937-229-1055, E-mail: ademmitt1@udayton.edu. *Application contact:* Kathleen Brown, Administrative Assistant, 937-229-3644, Fax: 937-229-1055, E-mail: kbrown1@udayton.edu.
Website: https://www.udayton.edu/education/departments_and_programs/edc/

University of Dayton, Department of Educational Administration, Dayton, OH 45469. Offers Catholic school leadership (MS Ed); educational administration (Ed S); educational leadership (MS Ed); leadership for educational systems (MS Ed). *Program availability:* Part-time, blended/hybrid learning. *Faculty:* 6 full-time (3 women), 21 part-time/adjunct (9 women). *Students:* 49 full-time (30 women), 66 part-time (45 women); includes 7 minority (4 Black or African American, non-Hispanic/Latino; 1 Hispanic/Latino; 2 Two or more races, non-Hispanic/Latino), 13 international. Average age 34. 121 applicants, 47% accepted. In 2016, 87 master's, 3 Ed Ss awarded. *Degree requirements:* For master's, thesis (for some programs). *Entrance requirements:* For master's, MAT or GRE if undergraduate GPA is below 2.75. Additional exam requirements/recommendations for international students: Required—TOEFL (minimum score 550 paper-based; 80 iBT). *Application deadline:* For fall admission, 5/1 priority date for domestic and international students; for spring admission, 11/1 priority date for domestic and international students. Application fee: $0 ($50 for international students). Electronic applications accepted. *Expenses:* $620 per credit hour, $25 registration fee per term. *Financial support:* In 2016–17, 5 research assistantships with partial tuition reimbursements (averaging $8,038 per year) were awarded; career-related internships or fieldwork and institutionally sponsored loans also available. Financial award application deadline: 3/15; financial award applicants required to submit FAFSA. *Faculty research:* Ohio teacher evaluation system. *Unit head:* Dr. David D. Dolph, Chair, 937-229-3105, Fax: 937-229-1055, E-mail: ddolph1@udayton.edu. *Application contact:* Janice Keivel, Administrative Associate, 937-229-3738, Fax: 937-229-1055, E-mail: jkeivel1@udayton.edu.
Website: https://www.udayton.edu/education/departments_and_programs/eda/index.php

University of Dayton, Department of Teacher Education, Dayton, OH 45469. Offers early childhood leadership and advocacy (MS Ed); interdisciplinary education studies (MS Ed); leadership in educational systems (MS Ed); literacy (MS Ed); mathematics education (MS Ed); music education (MS Ed); teacher as leader (MS Ed); teacher education (MS Ed); technology-enhanced learning (MS Ed); trans-disciplinary early childhood education (MS Ed). *Program availability:* Part-time, evening/weekend, blended/hybrid learning. *Faculty:* 23 full-time (18 women), 49 part-time/adjunct (42 women). *Students:* 52 full-time (47 women), 89 part-time (76 women); includes 6 minority (2 Black or African American, non-Hispanic/Latino; 2 Hispanic/Latino; 2 Two or more races, non-Hispanic/Latino), 24 international. Average age 31. 106 applicants, 28% accepted. In 2016, 69 master's awarded. *Degree requirements:* For master's, variable foreign language requirement, thesis optional. *Entrance requirements:* For master's, GRE (minimum score of 149 verbal, 4 on writing) or MAT (minimum score of 396) if undergraduate GPA was under 2.75, minimum GPA of 2.75, 3 letters of recommendation, personal statement or resume, official transcripts. Additional exam requirements/recommendations for international students: Required—TOEFL (minimum score 550 paper-based; 80 iBT); Recommended—IELTS (minimum score 6.5). *Application deadline:* Applications are processed on a rolling basis. Application fee: $0 ($50 for international students). Electronic applications accepted. *Expenses:* $620 per credit hour, $25 registration fee per term. *Financial support:* Institutionally sponsored loans available. Financial award application deadline: 3/1; financial award applicants required to submit FAFSA. *Faculty research:* Educational technology; facilitating teacher reflection; teacher preparation in dyslexia. *Unit head:* Dr. Connie L. Bowman, Chair, 937-229-3305, E-mail: cbowman1@udayton.edu. *Application contact:* Gina Seiter, Graduate Program Advisor, 937-229-3103, E-mail: gseiter1@udayton.edu.
Website: https://www.udayton.edu/education/departments_and_programs/edt

University of Dayton, PhD Program in Educational Leadership, Dayton, OH 45469-2963. Offers educational leadership (PhD); higher education administration (PhD); PreK-12 school administration (PhD). *Program availability:* Part-time, blended/hybrid learning. *Faculty:* 5 full-time (3 women), 1 part-time/adjunct (0 women). *Students:* 50 full-time (26 women); includes 6 minority (4 Black or African American, non-Hispanic/Latino; 1 Hispanic/Latino; 1 Two or more races, non-Hispanic/Latino), 2 international. Average age 41. 59 applicants, 17% accepted. In 2016, 6 doctorates awarded. *Degree requirements:* For doctorate, comprehensive exam, thesis/dissertation. *Entrance requirements:* For doctorate, GRE (minimum score of 149 in verbal and 4.0 in analytical writing), official transcripts, 3 letters of recommendation, 500-700 word essay, current resume, interview. Additional exam requirements/recommendations for international students: Required—TOEFL (minimum score 550 paper-based; 80 iBT), GRE. *Application deadline:* Applications are processed on a rolling basis. Application fee: $0 ($50 for international students). Electronic applications accepted. *Expenses:* $808 per credit hour, $25 registration fee per term. *Financial support:* In 2016–17, 1 fellowship (averaging $2,400 per year) was awarded; institutionally sponsored loans also available. Financial award application deadline: 3/1; financial award applicants required to submit FAFSA. *Faculty research:* School law; principalship; school finance; leadership. *Unit head:* Dr. Charles J. Russo, Director, 937-229-3722, Fax: 937-229-4824, E-mail: crusso1@udayton.edu. *Application contact:* Elizabeth Pearn, Administrative Assistant, 937-229-4003, Fax: 937-229-4729, E-mail: epearn1@udayton.edu.
Website: https://www.udayton.edu/education/departments_and_programs/phd/index.php

University of Delaware, College of Education and Human Development, School of Education, Newark, DE 19716. Offers education (PhD); educational leadership (Ed D); higher education (M Ed); instruction (MI); reading (M Ed); school leadership (M Ed); school psychology (MA, Ed S); teaching English as a second language (TESL) (MA). *Accreditation:* NCATE. *Program availability:* Part-time, evening/weekend. Terminal master's awarded for partial completion of doctoral program. *Degree requirements:* For master's, comprehensive exam (for some programs), thesis (for some programs); for doctorate, comprehensive exam (for some programs), thesis/dissertation. *Entrance requirements:* For master's and doctorate, GRE, 3 letters of recommendation. Additional exam requirements/recommendations for international students: Required—TOEFL (minimum score 600 paper-based). Electronic applications accepted. *Faculty research:* Teacher education; curriculum theory and development; community based education models, educational leadership.

University of Denver, Morgridge College of Education, Denver, CO 80208. Offers child, family and school psychology (MA, PhD, Ed S); counseling psychology (MA, PhD); curriculum and instruction (MA, Ed D, PhD); curriculum instruction and teaching (Certificate); early childhood special education (MA, Certificate); educational leadership and policy studies (MA, Ed D, PhD, Certificate); higher education (Ed D, PhD); library and information science (MLIS); research methods and statistics (MA, PhD). *Accreditation:* ALA; APA (one or more programs are accredited). *Program availability:* Part-time, evening/weekend, online learning. *Faculty:* 39 full-time (29 women), 60 part-time/adjunct (42 women). *Students:* 498 full-time (392 women), 362 part-time (282 women); includes 223 minority (63 Black or African American, non-Hispanic/Latino; 6 American Indian or Alaska Native, non-Hispanic/Latino; 20 Asian, non-Hispanic/Latino; 102 Hispanic/Latino; 1 Native Hawaiian or other Pacific Islander, non-Hispanic/Latino; 31 Two or more races, non-Hispanic/Latino), 40 international. Average age 32. 1,027 applicants, 69% accepted, 386 enrolled. In 2016, 252 master's, 36 doctorates, 141 other advanced degrees awarded. Terminal master's awarded for partial completion of doctoral program. *Degree requirements:* For master's, comprehensive exam; for doctorate, 2 foreign languages, comprehensive exam, thesis/dissertation. *Entrance requirements:* For master's and doctorate, GRE General Test or GMAT. Additional exam requirements/recommendations for international students: Required—TOEFL (minimum score 550 paper-based; 80 iBT). *Application deadline:* Applications are processed on a rolling basis. Application fee: $65. Electronic applications accepted. *Expenses:* $29,022 per year full-time. *Financial support:* In 2016–17, 697 students received support, including 37 research assistantships with tuition reimbursements available (averaging $11,209 per year), 66 teaching assistantships with tuition reimbursements available (averaging $3,742 per year); career-related internships or fieldwork, Federal Work-Study, institutionally sponsored loans, scholarships/grants, and unspecified assistantships also available. Support available to part-time students. Financial award application deadline: 2/15; financial award applicants required to submit FAFSA. *Faculty research:* Early childhood education, access and equity, educational leadership, family and school partnerships, neurodevelopmental disorders. *Total annual research expenditures:* $3.3 million. *Unit head:* Dr. Karen Riley, Dean, 303-871-3665, Fax: 303-871-4456, E-mail: karen.riley@du.edu. *Application contact:* Jodi Dye, Director of Admissions, 303-871-2510, Fax: 303-871-4456, E-mail: jodi.dye@du.edu.
Website: http://morgridge.du.edu

University of Detroit Mercy, College of Liberal Arts and Education, Detroit, MI 48221. Offers addiction counseling (MA); addiction studies (Certificate); clinical mental health counseling (MA); clinical psychology (MA, PhD); computer and information systems (MS); criminal justice (MA); curriculum and instruction (MA); economics (MA); educational administration (MA); financial economics (MA); industrial/organizational psychology (MA); information assurance (MS); intelligence analysis (MA); liberal studies (MALS); religious studies (MA); school counseling (MA, Certificate); school psychology (Spec); security administration (MS); special education: emotionally impaired/behaviorally disordered (MA); special education: learning disabilities (MA). *Program availability:* Part-time, evening/weekend. *Degree requirements:* For doctorate, departmental qualifying exam. *Faculty research:* Psychology of aging, history of technology, Renaissance humanism, U.S. and Japanese economic relations.

The University of Findlay, Office of Graduate Admissions, Findlay, OH 45840-3653. Offers applied security and analytics (MSAS); athletic training (MAT); business (MBA), including certified management accountant, certified public accountant, health care management, hospitality management; education (MA Ed, Ed D), including children's literature (MA Ed), curriculum and teaching (MA Ed), education (MA Ed), educational administration (MA Ed), human resource development (MA Ed), reading (MA Ed), science education (MA Ed), superintendent (Ed D), teaching (Ed D), technology (MA Ed); environmental, safety and health management (MSEM); health informatics (MS); occupational therapy (MOT); pharmacy (Pharm D); physical therapy (DPT); physician assistant (MPA); rhetoric and writing (MA); teaching English to speakers of other languages (TESOL) and bilingual education (MA). *Program availability:* Part-time, evening/weekend, 100% online, blended/hybrid learning. *Faculty:* 114 full-time (63 women), 44 part-time/adjunct (18 women). *Students:* 751 full-time (452 women), 573 part-time (323 women); includes 164 minority (82 Black or African American, non-Hispanic/Latino; 1 American Indian or Alaska Native, non-Hispanic/Latino; 27 Asian, non-Hispanic/Latino; 37 Hispanic/Latino; 17 Two or more races, non-Hispanic/Latino), 280 international. Average age 28. 661 applicants, 52% accepted, 288 enrolled. In 2016, 366 master's, 137 doctorates awarded. *Degree requirements:* For master's, comprehensive exam (for some programs), thesis, cumulative project, capstone project; for doctorate, thesis/dissertation. *Entrance requirements:* For master's, GRE (for some programs), bachelor's degree from accredited institution, minimum undergraduate GPA of 3.0 in last 64 hours of course work; for doctorate, MAT, minimum cumulative GPA of 3.0, master's degree. Additional exam requirements/recommendations for international students: Recommended—TOEFL (minimum score 79 iBT), IELTS (minimum score 7). *Application deadline:* For fall admission, 6/15 for international students; for spring admission, 12/1 for international students; for summer admission, 4/1 for international students. Applications are processed on a rolling basis. Electronic applications accepted. *Expenses:* Contact institution. *Financial support:* In 2016–17, 139 students received support, including 15 research assistantships with partial tuition reimbursements available (averaging $7,200 per year), 25 teaching assistantships with partial tuition reimbursements available (averaging $7,200 per year); Federal Work-Study, institutionally sponsored loans, and unspecified assistantships also available. Financial award application deadline: 4/1; financial award applicants required to submit FAFSA. *Unit head:* Christopher M. Harris, Director of Admissions, 419-434-4347, E-mail: harrisc1@findlay.edu. *Application contact:* Madeline Fauser Brennan, Graduate Admissions Counselor, 419-434-4636, Fax: 419-434-4898, E-mail: fauserbrennan@findlay.edu.
Website: http://www.findlay.edu/admissions/graduate/Pages/default.aspx

University of Florida, Graduate School, College of Education, School of Human Development and Organizational Studies in Education, Gainesville, FL 32611. Offers counseling and counselor education (Ed D, PhD), including counseling and counselor education, marriage and family counseling, mental health counseling, school counseling and guidance; educational leadership (M Ed, MAE, Ed D, PhD, Ed S), including educational leadership (Ed D, PhD), educational policy (Ed D, PhD); higher education administration (Ed D, PhD), including education policy (Ed D), educational policy, higher education administration; marriage and family counseling (M Ed, MAE, Ed D, PhD, Ed S); mental health counseling (M Ed, MAE, Ed D, PhD, Ed S); research and evaluation methodology (M Ed, MAE, Ed D, PhD); school counseling and guidance (M Ed, MAE, Ed D, PhD, Ed S); student personnel in higher education (M Ed, MAE). *Accreditation:* ACA (one or more programs are accredited); NCATE. *Program availability:* Part-time, online learning. Terminal master's awarded for partial completion of doctoral program. *Degree requirements:* For master's, thesis optional; for doctorate, comprehensive exam, thesis/dissertation. *Entrance requirements:* For master's and doctorate, GRE General Test, minimum GPA of 3.0 (undergraduate), 3.5 (graduate); for Ed S, GRE General Test. Additional exam requirements/recommendations for international students: Required—TOEFL (minimum score 550 paper-based; 80 iBT), IELTS (minimum score 6). Electronic applications accepted.

University of Georgia, College of Education, Department of Lifelong Education, Administration and Policy, Athens, GA 30602. Offers adult education (Ed D, Ed S); lifelong education, administration and policy (PhD). *Accreditation:* NCATE. *Faculty:* 25 full-time (18 women), 1 part-time/adjunct (0 women). *Students:* 74 full-time (56 women), 216 part-time (136 women); includes 73 minority (62 Black or African American, non-Hispanic/Latino; 4 Asian, non-Hispanic/Latino; 3 Hispanic/Latino; 4 Two or more races, non-Hispanic/Latino), 23 international. Average age 37. 123 applicants, 64% accepted, 45 enrolled. In 2016, 19 doctorates, 14 other advanced degrees awarded. *Entrance requirements:* For doctorate, GRE General Test; for Ed S, GRE General Test or MAT. *Application deadline:* For fall admission, 7/1 priority date for domestic students; for spring admission, 11/15 for domestic students. Application fee: $50. Electronic applications accepted. *Unit head:* Dr. Janette Hill, Head, 706-542-4035, Fax: 706-542-5873, E-mail: janette@.uga.edu. *Application contact:* Dr. Robert B. Hill, Graduate Coordinator, 706-542-4016, Fax: 706-542-5873, E-mail: bobhill@uga.edu.
Website: http://www.coe.uga.edu/leap/

University of Guam, Office of Graduate Studies, School of Education, Program in Administration and Supervision, Mangilao, GU 96923. Offers M Ed. *Degree requirements:* For master's, comprehensive oral and written exams, special project or thesis. *Entrance requirements:* For master's, GRE General Test. Additional exam requirements/recommendations for international students: Required—TOEFL.

University of Hartford, College of Education, Nursing, and Health Professions, Doctoral Program in Educational Leadership, West Hartford, CT 06117-1599. Offers Ed D. *Accreditation:* NCATE. *Program availability:* Part-time, evening/weekend. *Degree requirements:* For doctorate, thesis/dissertation. *Entrance requirements:* For doctorate, MAT, 3 letters of recommendation, writing samples, interview, resume, letter of support from employer. *Expenses:* Contact institution.

University of Hartford, College of Education, Nursing, and Health Professions, Program in Educational Leadership, West Hartford, CT 06117-1599. Offers administration and supervision (CAGS). *Accreditation:* NCATE. *Program availability:* Part-time, evening/weekend. *Degree requirements:* For CAGS, comprehensive exam or research project. *Entrance requirements:* For degree, GRE General Test or MAT, interview. Additional exam requirements/recommendations for international students: Required—TOEFL (minimum score 550 paper-based). Electronic applications accepted.

University of Hawaii at Manoa, Graduate Division, College of Education, Department of Educational Administration, Honolulu, HI 96822. Offers M Ed. *Program availability:* Part-time. *Degree requirements:* For master's, thesis optional. *Entrance requirements:* Additional exam requirements/recommendations for international students: Required—TOEFL (minimum score 600 paper-based; 100 iBT), IELTS (minimum score 7). *Faculty research:* Leadership, educational policy, organizational processes, finance.

University of Hawaii at Manoa, Graduate Division, College of Education, Ed D in Professional Practice Program, Honolulu, HI 96822. Offers Ed D. *Entrance requirements:* Additional exam requirements/recommendations for international students: Required—TOEFL (minimum score 600 paper-based; 100 iBT).

University of Hawaii at Manoa, Graduate Division, College of Education, PhD in Education Program, Honolulu, HI 96822. Offers curriculum and instruction (PhD); educational administration (PhD); educational foundations (PhD); educational policy studies (PhD); educational psychology (PhD); exceptionalities (PhD); kinesiology (PhD); learning design and technology (PhD). *Program availability:* Part-time, evening/weekend. *Degree requirements:* For doctorate, thesis/dissertation. *Entrance requirements:* For doctorate, GRE General Test, sample of written work. Additional exam requirements/recommendations for international students: Required—TOEFL (minimum score 600 paper-based; 100 iBT), IELTS (minimum score 7).

University of Holy Cross, Program in Education and Counseling, New Orleans, LA 70131-7399. Offers administration and supervision (M Ed); curriculum and instruction (M Ed); marriage and family counseling (MA); school counseling (M Ed, MA). *Accreditation:* ACA; NCATE. *Program availability:* Part-time, evening/weekend. *Degree requirements:* For master's, thesis. *Entrance requirements:* For master's, GRE General Test, minimum GPA of 2.7.

University of Houston, College of Education, Department of Curriculum and Instruction, Houston, TX 77204. Offers administration and supervision (M Ed); curriculum and instruction (M Ed, Ed D); professional leadership (Ed D). *Accreditation:* NCATE. *Program availability:* Part-time, evening/weekend. *Degree requirements:* For master's, comprehensive exam, thesis optional; for doctorate, comprehensive exam, thesis/dissertation. *Entrance requirements:* For master's and doctorate, GRE, minimum cumulative undergraduate GPA of 2.6, 3 letters of recommendation, resume/vita, goal statement. Additional exam requirements/recommendations for international students: Required—TOEFL (minimum score 550 paper-based; 79 iBT). Electronic applications accepted. *Faculty research:* Teaching-learning process, instructional technology in schools, teacher education, classroom management, at-risk students.

University of Houston, College of Education, Department of Educational Leadership and Cultural Studies, Houston, TX 77204. Offers administration and supervision (M Ed, Ed D); higher education (M Ed); historical, social, and cultural foundations of education (M Ed). *Accreditation:* NCATE. *Program availability:* Part-time, evening/weekend. *Degree requirements:* For master's, comprehensive exam or thesis; for doctorate, comprehensive exam, thesis/dissertation. *Entrance requirements:* For master's, GRE General Test, minimum cumulative GPA of 2.6, 3 letters of recommendation, resume/vitae, goal statement; for doctorate, GRE General Test, minimum cumulative GPA of 2.6, 3 letters of recommendation, resume/vitae, goal statement, writing sample, interview. Additional exam requirements/recommendations for international students: Required—TOEFL (minimum score 550 paper-based; 79 iBT). Electronic applications accepted. *Faculty research:* Change, supervision, multiculturalism, evaluation, policy.

University of Houston, College of Education, Department of Educational Psychology, Houston, TX 77204. Offers administration and supervision higher education (M Ed); counseling (M Ed); counseling psychology (PhD); educational psychology (M Ed); school psychology (PhD); school psychology and individual differences (PhD); special education (M Ed). *Accreditation:* NCATE. *Program availability:* Part-time, evening/weekend, online learning. *Degree requirements:* For master's, comprehensive exam or thesis; for doctorate, comprehensive exam, thesis/dissertation. *Entrance requirements:* For master's, GRE, transcripts, 3 letters of recommendation, curriculum vita, goal statement; for doctorate, GRE, transcripts, 3 letters of recommendation, curriculum vita, goal statement, writing sample, interview. Additional exam requirements/recommendations for international students: Required—TOEFL (minimum score 550 paper-based; 79 iBT), IELTS (minimum score 6.5). Electronic applications accepted. *Faculty research:* Evidence-based assessment and intervention, multicultural issues in psychology, social and cultural context of learning, systemic barriers to college, motivational aspects of self-regulated learning.

University of Houston–Clear Lake, School of Education, Program in Educational Leadership, Houston, TX 77058-1002. Offers educational leadership (Ed D); educational management (MS). *Degree requirements:* For master's, thesis optional; for doctorate, comprehensive exam, thesis/dissertation.

University of Houston–Victoria, School of Education, Health Professions and Human Development, Victoria, TX 77901-4450. Offers administration and supervision (M Ed); adult and higher education (M Ed); counselor education (M Ed); curriculum and instruction (M Ed); educational technology (M Ed); special education (M Ed). *Program availability:* Part-time, evening/weekend, online learning. *Degree requirements:* For master's, comprehensive exam, project or thesis. *Entrance requirements:* For master's, GRE General Test. Additional exam requirements/recommendations for international students: Required—TOEFL. Electronic applications accepted. *Faculty research:* Reading and language arts education, evaluation and diagnosis of special children's abilities.

University of Idaho, College of Graduate Studies, College of Education, Department of Leadership and Counseling, Boise, ID 83702. Offers adult/organizational learning and leadership (MS, Ed S); educational leadership (M Ed, Ed S); rehabilitation counseling and human services (M Ed, MS); school counseling (M Ed, MS); special education (M Ed). *Faculty:* 14 full-time, 7 part-time/adjunct. *Students:* 37 full-time (26 women), 154 part-time (84 women). Average age 39. In 2016, 75 master's, 21 other advanced degrees awarded. *Entrance requirements:* For master's, minimum GPA of 3.0. Additional exam requirements/recommendations for international students: Required—TOEFL. *Application deadline:* Applications are processed on a rolling basis. Application fee: $60. Electronic applications accepted. *Expenses:* Tuition, state resident: full-time $6460; part-time $414 per credit hour. Tuition, nonresident: full-time $21,268; part-time $1237 per credit hour. *Required fees:* $2070; $60 per credit hour. Full-time tuition and fees vary according to course load and reciprocity agreements. *Financial support:* Applicants required to submit FAFSA. *Unit head:* Dr. Kathy Canfield-Davis, Chair, 208-364-4047, E-mail: lead@uidaho.edu. *Application contact:* Sean Scoggin, Graduate Recruitment Coordinator, 208-885-4723, Fax: 208-885-4406, E-mail: graduateadmissions@uidaho.edu.
Website: https://www.uidaho.edu/ed/lc

University of Illinois at Chicago, College of Education, Department of Educational Policy Studies, Chicago, IL 60607-7128. Offers policy studies (M Ed); policy studies in urban education (PhD); urban education leadership (Ed D). *Faculty research:* Social foundations of education, educational organizations and leadership, education policy analysis, understanding and addressing educational problems in urban contexts.

University of Illinois at Springfield, Graduate Programs, College of Education and Human Services, Department of Educational Leadership, Springfield, IL 62703-5407. Offers chief school business official (CAS); educational leadership (MA); educational technology (Graduate Certificate); English as a second language (Graduate Certificate); higher education online pedagogy (Graduate Certificate); leadership and learning (Graduate Certificate); legal aspects of education (Graduate Certificate); superintendent (CAS); teacher leadership (MA). *Program availability:* Part-time, evening/weekend, 100% online, blended/hybrid learning. *Faculty:* 5 full-time (2 women), 8 part-time/adjunct (7 women). *Students:* 4 full-time (2 women), 113 part-time (68 women); includes 20 minority (15 Black or African American, non-Hispanic/Latino; 1 American Indian or Alaska Native, non-Hispanic/Latino; 4 Hispanic/Latino), 1 international. Average age 36. 45 applicants, 62% accepted, 19 enrolled. In 2016, 22 master's, 2 other advanced degrees awarded. *Degree requirements:* For master's, capstone course. *Entrance requirements:* For master's, minimum undergraduate GPA of 3.0, valid Illinois Teaching License, minimum of two years of successful teaching experience, portfolio, interview. Additional exam requirements/recommendations for international students: Required—TOEFL (minimum score 500 paper-based; 61 iBT). *Application deadline:* Applications are processed on a rolling basis. Application fee: $60 ($75 for international students). Electronic applications accepted. *Expenses:* Tuition, state resident: part-time $329 per credit hour. Tuition, nonresident: part-time $675 per credit hour. *Financial support:* In 2016–17, fellowships with full tuition reimbursements (averaging $9,900 per year), research assistantships with full tuition reimbursements (averaging $9,991 per year), teaching assistantships with full tuition reimbursements (averaging $10,059 per year) were awarded; career-related internships or fieldwork, Federal Work-Study, scholarships/grants, health care benefits, and unspecified assistantships also available. Support available to part-time students. Financial award application deadline: 11/15; financial award applicants required to submit FAFSA. *Unit head:* Dr. Scott Day, Program Administrator, 217-206-7520, Fax: 217-206-6775, E-mail: day.scott@uis.edu. *Application contact:* Dr. Cecelia Cornell, Associate Vice Chancellor for Graduate Education, 217-206-7230, E-mail: ccorn1@uis.edu.
Website: http://www.uis.edu/edl/

University of Illinois at Urbana–Champaign, Graduate College, College of Education, Department of Education Policy, Organization, and Leadership, Champaign, IL 61820. Offers educational organization and leadership (Ed M, MS, Ed D, PhD, CAS); educational policy studies (Ed M, MA, PhD); human resource education (Ed M, MS, Ed D, PhD, CAS). *Program availability:* Part-time, online learning.

University of Indianapolis, Graduate Programs, School of Education, Indianapolis, IN 46227-3697. Offers art education (MAT); biology (MAT); chemistry (MAT); curriculum and instruction (MA); earth sciences (MAT); education (MA, MAT); educational leadership (MA); elementary education (MA); English (MAT); French (MAT); math (MAT); physical education (MAT); physics (MAT); secondary education (MA), including art education, education, English education, social studies education; social studies (MAT); Spanish (MAT). *Accreditation:* NCATE. *Program availability:* Part-time, evening/weekend. *Entrance requirements:* For master's, GRE Subject Test, PRAXIS I, minimum GPA of 2.5, 3 letters of recommendation, interview. Additional exam requirements/recommendations for international students: Required—TOEFL (minimum score 550 paper-based). *Faculty research:* Assessment of teacher education, perceptions of prospective teachers by parents.

The University of Iowa, Graduate College, College of Education, Department of Educational Policy and Leadership Studies, Program in Educational Leadership, Iowa City, IA 52242-1316. Offers MA, PhD, Ed S. *Degree requirements:* For master's and Ed S, exam; for doctorate, comprehensive exam, thesis/dissertation. *Entrance requirements:* For master's, doctorate, and Ed S, GRE General Test, minimum GPA of 3.0. Additional exam requirements/recommendations for international students: Required—TOEFL (minimum score 550 paper-based; 81 iBT). Electronic applications accepted.

The University of Kansas, Graduate Studies, School of Education, Department of Educational Leadership and Policy Studies, Education Leadership and Policy Program,

Lawrence, KS 66045-3101. Offers policy studies (PhD); social and cultural studies in education (MSE, PhD). *Program availability:* Part-time, evening/weekend. *Students:* 123 full-time (66 women), 35 part-time (17 women); includes 31 minority (12 Black or African American, non-Hispanic/Latino; 2 American Indian or Alaska Native, non-Hispanic/Latino; 3 Asian, non-Hispanic/Latino; 7 Hispanic/Latino; 7 Two or more races, non-Hispanic/Latino), 24 international. Average age 38. 36 applicants, 72% accepted, 16 enrolled. In 2016, 26 doctorates awarded. *Entrance requirements:* For master's, minimum GPA of 3.0, resume or curriculum vitae, statement of purpose, official academic transcripts, three letters of recommendation; for doctorate, GRE General Test, minimum graduate GPA of 3.5, resume or curriculum vitae, statement of purpose, official academic transcripts, three letters of recommendation, writing sample. Additional exam requirements/recommendations for international students: Required—TOEFL or IELTS. *Application deadline:* For fall admission, 7/1 for domestic and international students; for spring admission, 11/1 for domestic and international students; for summer admission, 4/1 for domestic and international students. Application fee: $65 ($85 for international students). Electronic applications accepted. *Financial support:* Fellowships, research assistantships, teaching assistantships, scholarships/grants, and unspecified assistantships available. Financial award application deadline: 3/15. *Faculty research:* Historical and philosophical issues in education, education policy and leadership, higher education faculty, research on college students, education technology. *Unit head:* Dr. Susan B. Twombly, Chair, 785-864-9721, E-mail: stwombly@ku.edu. *Application contact:* Denise Brubaker, Admissions Coordinator, 785-864-7973, E-mail: brubaker@ku.edu.
Website: http://elps.soe.ku.edu/

The University of Kansas, Graduate Studies, School of Education, Department of Educational Leadership and Policy Studies, Program in Educational Administration, Lawrence, KS 66045-3101. Offers MSE, Ed D, PhD. Program begins in Summer semester only. *Program availability:* Part-time, evening/weekend, online learning. *Students:* 4 full-time (0 women), 115 part-time (71 women); includes 25 minority (15 Black or African American, non-Hispanic/Latino; 3 American Indian or Alaska Native, non-Hispanic/Latino; 1 Asian, non-Hispanic/Latino; 4 Hispanic/Latino; 2 Two or more races, non-Hispanic/Latino), 1 international. Average age 33. 88 applicants, 90% accepted, 62 enrolled. In 2016, 11 degrees awarded. *Entrance requirements:* For master's, minimum GPA of 3.0, resume, statement of purpose, official transcript, three letters of recommendation; for doctorate, GRE General Test, minimum graduate GPA of 3.5, resume, statement of purpose, academic transcripts, three letters of recommendation, writing sample. Additional exam requirements/recommendations for international students: Required—TOEFL or IELTS. *Application deadline:* For summer admission, 4/1 for domestic and international students. Application fee: $65 ($85 for international students). Electronic applications accepted. *Financial support:* Research assistantships, teaching assistantships, Federal Work-Study, scholarships/grants, and unspecified assistantships available. Financial award application deadline: 3/1. *Unit head:* Dr. Susan B. Twombly, Chair, 785-864-9721, Fax: 785-864-4697, E-mail: stwombly@ku.edu. *Application contact:* Denise Brubaker, Admissions Coordinator, 785-864-7973, Fax: 785-864-4697, E-mail: brubaker@ku.edu.
Website: http://elps.soe.ku.edu/academics/edadmin/mse

The University of Kansas, Graduate Studies, School of Education, Department of Special Education, Lawrence, KS 66045. Offers autism spectrum disorder (MS Ed, Certificate); early childhood unified (MS Ed); high incidence disabilities (MS Ed); leadership in special and inclusive education (Certificate); low incidence disabilities (MS Ed); secondary special education and transition (MS Ed); special education (PhD). *Accreditation:* NCATE. *Program availability:* Part-time, online learning. *Students:* 91 full-time (82 women), 293 part-time (255 women); includes 50 minority (19 Black or African American, non-Hispanic/Latino; 4 American Indian or Alaska Native, non-Hispanic/Latino; 6 Asian, non-Hispanic/Latino; 7 Hispanic/Latino; 14 Two or more races, non-Hispanic/Latino), 28 international. Average age 33. 759 applicants, 27% accepted, 166 enrolled. In 2016, 51 master's, 3 doctorates awarded. *Median time to degree:* Of those who began their doctoral program in fall 2008, 90% received their degree in 8 years or less. *Entrance requirements:* For master's, minimum GPA of 3.0, official transcripts, 3 letters of reference, professional resume; for doctorate, GRE General Test, official transcripts, 3 letters of reference, professional resume, professional writing sample. Additional exam requirements/recommendations for international students: Required—TOEFL or IELTS. Application fee: $65 ($85 for international students). Electronic applications accepted. *Financial support:* Fellowships, research assistantships, teaching assistantships, Federal Work-Study, scholarships/grants, and unspecified assistantships available. Support available to part-time students. Financial award application deadline: 2/21; financial award applicants required to submit FAFSA. *Faculty research:* Autism spectrum disorders, learning disabilities research, leadership development, qualitative research and evaluation. *Unit head:* Elizabeth B. Kozleski, Chair, 785-864-0556, E-mail: elizabeth.kozleski@ku.edu. *Application contact:* Graduate Admission Contact, 785-864-4342, E-mail: specialeduadm@ku.edu.
Website: http://specialedu.ku.edu/

University of Kentucky, Graduate School, College of Education, Program in Educational Leadership Studies, Lexington, KY 40506-0032. Offers educational leadership (M Ed, Ed D, PhD, Ed S); educational sciences (PhD); family resource and youth services (M Ed, Ed S); principalship (Ed D, Ed S); school technology leadership (M Ed, PhD, Ed S); teacher leadership (M Ed, Ed S). *Degree requirements:* For master's and Ed S, comprehensive exam; for doctorate, comprehensive exam, thesis/dissertation. *Entrance requirements:* For master's, GRE General Test, minimum undergraduate GPA of 2.75; for doctorate, GRE General Test, minimum graduate GPA of 3.0. Additional exam requirements/recommendations for international students: Required—TOEFL (minimum score 550 paper-based). Electronic applications accepted. *Faculty research:* School governance, teacher empowerment, planned change, systemic reform, issues of equity and fairness.

University of La Verne, LaFetra College of Education, Doctoral Program in Organizational Leadership, La Verne, CA 91750-4443. Offers Ed D. *Program availability:* Part-time. *Students:* 111 full-time (82 women), 56 part-time (29 women); includes 73 minority (15 Black or African American, non-Hispanic/Latino; 6 Asian, non-Hispanic/Latino; 50 Hispanic/Latino; 2 Two or more races, non-Hispanic/Latino), 1 international. Average age 44. *Degree requirements:* For doctorate, thesis/dissertation. *Entrance requirements:* For doctorate, GRE or MAT, minimum graduate GPA of 3.0, resume or curriculum vitae, 2 endorsement forms. Additional exam requirements/recommendations for international students: Required—TOEFL (minimum score 550 paper-based). *Application deadline:* Applications are processed on a rolling basis. Application fee: $75. *Expenses:* Contact institution. *Financial support:* Institutionally sponsored loans and scholarships/grants available. Financial award application deadline: 3/2; financial award applicants required to submit FAFSA. *Unit head:* Dr. Barbara Poling, Professor of Organizational Leadership, 909-448-4380, E-mail: bpoling@laverne.edu. *Application contact:* Christy Ranells, Program and Admission Specialist, 909-448-4644, Fax: 909-971-2295, E-mail: cranells@laverne.edu.
Website: https://sites.laverne.edu/organizational-leadership/

University of La Verne, LaFetra College of Education, Master's Program in Education, La Verne, CA 91750-4443. Offers advanced teaching skills (M Ed); education (M Ed); educational leadership (M Ed); special emphasis (M Ed). *Accreditation:* NCATE. *Program availability:* Part-time. *Students:* 37 full-time (31 women), 107 part-time (83 women); includes 74 minority (6 Black or African American, non-Hispanic/Latino; 1 American Indian or Alaska Native, non-Hispanic/Latino; 3 Asian, non-Hispanic/Latino; 62 Hispanic/Latino; 2 Two or more races, non-Hispanic/Latino). Average age 31. *Degree requirements:* For master's, thesis optional. *Entrance requirements:* For master's, California Basic Educational Skills Test, interview, writing sample, minimum GPA of 3.0, 3 letters of recommendation. Additional exam requirements/recommendations for international students: Required—TOEFL (minimum score 550 paper-based). *Application deadline:* Applications are processed on a rolling basis. Application fee: $50. *Expenses:* Contact institution. *Financial support:* Institutionally sponsored loans and scholarships/grants available. Financial award application deadline: 3/2; financial award applicants required to submit FAFSA. *Unit head:* Dr. Jessica Decker, Chair, 909-448-4582, E-mail: jdecker@laverne.edu. *Application contact:* Christy Ranells, Program and Admission Specialist, 909-448-4644, Fax: 909-392-2744, E-mail: cranells@laverne.edu.
Website: http://www.laverne.edu/education/

University of La Verne, Regional and Online Campuses, Graduate Credential Program in Education, California Statewide Campus, La Verne, CA 91750-4443. Offers administration services (preliminary) (Credential); education specialist: mild/moderate (Credential); English (Certificate); multiple subject teaching (Credential); pupil personnel services: school counseling (Credential); single subject teaching (Credential); special education (MS); special emphasis (M Ed). *Accreditation:* NCATE. *Program availability:* Part-time. *Entrance requirements:* For degree, California Basic Educational Skills Test, minimum undergraduate GPA of 2.75, 3 letters of recommendation, interview. *Expenses:* Contact institution.

University of La Verne, Regional and Online Campuses, Graduate Programs, Central Coast/Vandenberg Air Force Base Campuses, La Verne, CA 91750-4443. Offers business administration for experienced professionals (MBA), including health services management, information technology; education (special emphasis) (M Ed); educational counseling (MS); educational leadership (M Ed); multiple subject (elementary) (Credential); preliminary administrative services (Credential); pupil personnel services (Credential); single subject (secondary) (Credential). *Program availability:* Part-time. *Expenses:* Contact institution.

University of La Verne, Regional and Online Campuses, Graduate Programs, High Desert Campus, Victorville, CA 92392. Offers business administration for experienced professionals (MBA); educational counseling (MS); educational leadership (M Ed); multiple subject (elementary) (Credential); preliminary administrative services (Credential); pupil personnel services (Credential); single subject (secondary) (Credential). *Expenses:* Contact institution.

University of La Verne, Regional and Online Campuses, Graduate Programs, Kern County Campus, Bakersfield, CA 93301. Offers business administration for experienced professionals (MBA-EP); education (special emphasis) (M Ed); educational counseling (MS); educational leadership (M Ed); health administration (MHA); leadership and management (MS); mild/moderate education specialist (Credential); multiple subject (elementary) (Credential); organizational leadership (Ed D); preliminary administrative services (Credential); single subject (secondary) (Credential); special education studies (MS). *Program availability:* Part-time, evening/weekend. *Expenses:* Contact institution.

University of La Verne, Regional and Online Campuses, Graduate Programs, Orange County Campus, Irvine, CA 92840. Offers business administration for experienced professionals (MBA); educational counseling (MS); educational leadership (M Ed); health administration (MHA); leadership and management (MS); preliminary administrative services (Credential); pupil personnel services (Credential). *Program availability:* Part-time. *Expenses:* Contact institution.

University of La Verne, Regional and Online Campuses, Graduate Programs, San Fernando Valley Campus, Burbank, CA 91505. Offers business administration for experienced professionals (MBA-EP); educational counseling (MS); educational leadership (M Ed); leadership and management (MS); preliminary administrative services (Credential); pupil personnel services (Credential). *Program availability:* Part-time, evening/weekend. *Expenses:* Contact institution.

University of La Verne, Regional and Online Campuses, Graduate Programs, Ventura County/Point Mugu Naval Air Station Campuses, Oxnard, CA 93036. Offers business administration for experienced professionals (MS); educational counseling (MS); educational leadership (M Ed); leadership and management (MS); multiple subject (elementary) (Credential); pupil personnel services (Credential); single subject (secondary) (Credential). *Program availability:* Part-time, evening/weekend. *Expenses:* Contact institution.

University of La Verne, Regional and Online Campuses, Master's Programs in Education, California Statewide Campus, La Verne, CA 91750-4443. Offers administration services (preliminary) (Credential); education specialist: mild/moderate (Credential); educational counseling (MS); educational leadership (M Ed); multiple subject teaching (Credential); pupil personnel services: school counseling (Credential); single subject teaching (Credential); special education studies (MS); special emphasis (M Ed). *Accreditation:* NCATE. *Entrance requirements:* For master's, California Basic Educational Skills Test, 3 letters of recommendation, teaching credential. *Expenses:* Contact institution.

University of Lethbridge, School of Graduate Studies, Lethbridge, AB T1K 3M4, Canada. Offers addictions counseling (M Sc); agricultural biotechnology (M Sc); agricultural studies (M Sc, MA); anthropology (MA); archaeology (M Sc, MA); art (MA, MFA); biochemistry (M Sc); biological sciences (M Sc); biomolecular science (PhD); biosystems and biodiversity (PhD); Canadian studies (MA); chemistry (M Sc); computer science (M Sc); computer science and geographical information science (M Sc); counseling (MC); counseling psychology (M Ed); dramatic arts (MA); earth, space, and physical science (PhD); economics (MA); education (MA, PhD); educational leadership (M Ed); English (MA); environmental science (M Sc); evolution and behavior (PhD); exercise science (M Sc); French (MA); French/German (MA); French/Spanish (MA); general education (M Ed); geography (M Sc, MA); German (MA); health sciences (M Sc); individualized multidisciplinary (M Sc, MA); kinesiology (M Sc, MA); management (M Sc), including accounting, finance, human resource management and labor relations, information systems, international management, marketing, policy and strategy; mathematics (M Sc); music (M Mus, MA); Native American studies (MA); neuroscience (M Sc, PhD); new media (MA, MFA); nursing (M Sc, MN); philosophy (MA); physics (M Sc); political science (MA); psychology (M Sc, MA); religious studies (MA); sociology (MA); theatre and dramatic arts (MFA); theoretical and computational science (PhD); urban and regional studies (MA); women and gender studies (MA). *Program availability:* Part-time, evening/weekend. *Degree requirements:* For master's, thesis (for some programs); for doctorate, comprehensive exam, thesis/dissertation. *Entrance requirements:* For master's, GMAT (for M Sc in management), bachelor's degree in related field, minimum GPA of 3.0 during previous 20 graded semester courses, 2 years' teaching or related experience (M Ed); for doctorate, master's degree, minimum graduate GPA of 3.5. Additional exam requirements/recommendations for international students: Required—TOEFL (minimum score 580 paper-based; 93 iBT).

Electronic applications accepted. *Faculty research:* Movement and brain plasticity, gibberellin physiology, photosynthesis, carbon cycling, molecular properties of main-group ring components.

University of Louisiana at Lafayette, College of Education, Graduate Studies and Research in Education, Program in Administration and Supervision, Lafayette, LA 70504. Offers M Ed. *Degree requirements:* For master's, thesis or alternative. *Entrance requirements:* For master's, GRE General Test, teaching certificate. Additional exam requirements/recommendations for international students: Required—TOEFL (minimum score 550 paper-based). Electronic applications accepted.

University of Louisiana at Lafayette, College of Education, Graduate Studies and Research in Education, Program in Educational Leadership, Lafayette, LA 70504. Offers M Ed, Ed D. *Entrance requirements:* Additional exam requirements/recommendations for international students: Required—TOEFL (minimum score 550 paper-based).

University of Louisiana at Monroe, Graduate School, College of Arts, Education, and Sciences, School of Education, Program in Curriculum and Instruction, Monroe, LA 71209-0001. Offers art education (M Ed); biology education (M Ed); chemistry education (M Ed); curriculum and instruction (Ed D); early childhood education (M Ed); earth science education (M Ed); educational leadership (M Ed); elementary education (1-5) (M Ed); English as a second language (M Ed); English education (M Ed); family and consumer education (M Ed); French education (M Ed); history education (M Ed); math education (M Ed); middle school education (M Ed); music education (M Ed); reading education (K-12) (M Ed); Spanish education (M Ed); special education - academically gifted (M Ed); special education - early intervention (M Ed); special education - educational diagnostician (M Ed); special education - mild/moderate disabilities (M Ed); speech education (M Ed). *Accreditation:* NCATE. *Faculty:* 8 full-time (4 women), 4 part-time/adjunct (3 women). *Students:* 13 full-time (11 women), 80 part-time (65 women); includes 25 minority (19 Black or African American, non-Hispanic/Latino; 1 Asian, non-Hispanic/Latino; 3 Hispanic/Latino; 2 Two or more races, non-Hispanic/Latino). Average age 37. 118 applicants, 30% accepted, 16 enrolled. In 2016, 23 master's, 4 doctorates awarded. *Degree requirements:* For master's, comprehensive exam (for some programs), thesis; for doctorate, thesis/dissertation, internships. *Entrance requirements:* For master's, GRE General Test; for doctorate, GRE General Test, minimum undergraduate GPA of 2.75, graduate 3.25. Additional exam requirements/recommendations for international students: Required—TOEFL (minimum score 500 paper-based; 61 iBT). *Application deadline:* For fall admission, 8/24 priority date for domestic students, 7/1 for international students; for winter admission, 12/14 priority date for domestic students; for spring admission, 1/19 for domestic students, 11/1 for international students. Applications are processed on a rolling basis. Application fee: $20 ($30 for international students). Electronic applications accepted. *Expenses:* Tuition, state resident: full-time $6489. Tuition, nonresident: full-time $18,589. *Required fees:* $8984. Tuition and fees vary according to course level, course load, degree level and program. *Financial support:* Research assistantships, career-related internships or fieldwork, Federal Work-Study, and unspecified assistantships available. Financial award application deadline: 4/1; financial award applicants required to submit FAFSA. *Unit head:* Dr. Dorothy Schween, Director, 318-342-1268, Fax: 318-342-3131, E-mail: schween@ulm.edu.

University of Louisville, Graduate School, College of Education and Human Development, Department of Educational Leadership, Evaluation and Organizational Development, Louisville, KY 40292-0001. Offers educational leadership and organizational development (Ed D, PhD), including evaluation (PhD), human resource development (PhD), P-12 administration (PhD), post-secondary administration (PhD), sport administration (PhD); health professions education (Certificate); higher education administration (MA); human resources and organization development (MS), including health professions education, human resource leadership, workplace learning and performance; P-12 educational administration (Ed S), including principalship, supervisor of instruction. *Accreditation:* NCATE. *Program availability:* Part-time, evening/weekend, online learning. *Students:* 278 full-time (65 women), 409 part-time (260 women); includes 202 minority (121 Black or African American, non-Hispanic/Latino; 1 American Indian or Alaska Native, non-Hispanic/Latino; 13 Asian, non-Hispanic/Latino; 44 Hispanic/Latino; 3 Native Hawaiian or other Pacific Islander, non-Hispanic/Latino; 20 Two or more races, non-Hispanic/Latino), 5 international. Average age 36. 233 applicants, 78% accepted, 129 enrolled. In 2016, 58 master's, 4 doctorates, 17 other advanced degrees awarded. Application fee: $60. *Expenses:* Tuition, state resident: full-time $12,246; part-time $681 per credit hour. Tuition, nonresident: full-time $25,486; part-time $1417 per credit hour. *Required fees:* $196. Tuition and fees vary according to program and reciprocity agreements. *Financial support:* Application deadline: 6/1; applicants required to submit FAFSA. *Faculty research:* Urban educational leadership and policy, human resources, organizational development, program evaluation, military education, community partnerships, higher education administration. *Total annual research expenditures:* $256,111. *Unit head:* Dr. Jeffrey Sun, Chair and Professor, 502-852-0618, E-mail: jeffrey.sun@louisville.edu. *Application contact:* Betty Hampton, Director of Graduate Student Services, 502-852-5597, Fax: 502-852-1465, E-mail: edadvise@louisville.edu.
Website: http://louisville.edu/education/departments/eleod

University of Louisville, Graduate School, College of Education and Human Development, Department of Teaching and Learning, Louisville, KY 40292-0001. Offers art education (MAT); autism and applied behavior analysis (Certificate); curriculum and instruction (PhD); early elementary education (MAT); exercise physiology (MS); health and physical education (MAT); health professions education (Certificate); higher education (MA); human resources and organization development (MS); instructional technology (M Ed); interdisciplinary early childhood education (MAT); middle school education (MAT); music education (MAT); secondary education (MAT); special education (MAT); sport administration (MS); teacher leadership (M Ed). *Program availability:* Part-time, evening/weekend. *Students:* 116 full-time (68 women), 158 part-time (112 women); includes 46 minority (24 Black or African American, non-Hispanic/Latino; 8 Asian, non-Hispanic/Latino; 5 Hispanic/Latino; 9 Two or more races, non-Hispanic/Latino), 6 international. Average age 30. 114 applicants, 71% accepted, 57 enrolled. In 2016, 59 master's, 3 doctorates awarded. *Application deadline:* For spring admission, 1/1 priority date for international students. Application fee: $60. *Expenses:* Tuition, state resident: full-time $12,246; part-time $681 per credit hour. Tuition, nonresident: full-time $25,486; part-time $1417 per credit hour. *Required fees:* $196. Tuition and fees vary according to program and reciprocity agreements. *Financial support:* Application deadline: 6/1; applicants required to submit FAFSA. *Faculty research:* STEM teaching and learning; content literacy for English language learners; social justice in teacher education; adolescent literacy; mathematics teacher development. *Total annual research expenditures:* $1.7 million. *Unit head:* Dr. Ann E. Larson, Dean, College of Education and Human Development, 502-852-6411, Fax: 502-852-1464, E-mail: ann@louisville.edu. *Application contact:* Betty Hampton, Director of Graduate Student Services, 502-852-5597, Fax: 502-852-1465, E-mail: edadvise@louisville.edu.
Website: http://louisville.edu/delphi

University of Maine, Graduate School, College of Education and Human Development, School of Educational Leadership, Higher Education, and Human Development, Orono, ME 04469. Offers educational leadership (M Ed, CAS); higher education (CAS); human development (MS). *Program availability:* Part-time. *Students:* 48 full-time (32 women), 84 part-time (62 women); includes 10 minority (3 Black or African American, non-Hispanic/Latino; 2 American Indian or Alaska Native, non-Hispanic/Latino; 3 Hispanic/Latino; 2 Two or more races, non-Hispanic/Latino), 2 international. Average age 38. 85 applicants, 93% accepted, 61 enrolled. In 2016, 28 master's, 2 doctorates, 10 other advanced degrees awarded. *Degree requirements:* For master's, thesis (for some programs); for doctorate, comprehensive exam, thesis/dissertation. *Entrance requirements:* For master's, GRE General Test, MAT; for doctorate, GRE. Additional exam requirements/recommendations for international students: Required—TOEFL. *Application deadline:* For fall admission, 2/1 priority date for domestic students. Applications are processed on a rolling basis. Application fee: $65. Electronic applications accepted. *Expenses:* Tuition, state resident: full-time $7524; part-time $2508 per credit. Tuition, nonresident: full-time $24,498; part-time $8166 per credit. *Required fees:* $1148; $571 per credit. *Financial support:* In 2016–17, 22 students received support, including 4 teaching assistantships (averaging $14,600 per year); career-related internships or fieldwork, Federal Work-Study, institutionally sponsored loans, tuition waivers (full and partial), and unspecified assistantships also available. Financial award application deadline: 3/1. *Faculty research:* Leadership formation, school organization, collective efficacy and collaborative climate of high schools, change process in high schools, principalship; equity policy; gender and education; doctoral student development, retention, and attrition; faculty development and socialization; sexuality education and curriculum development; family/domestic violence; friendship/kin relationships; early childhood education; support for families with members with disabilities. *Unit head:* Dr. Jim Artesani, Associate Dean of Accreditation and Graduate Affairs, 207-581-4061, Fax: 207-581-3120. *Application contact:* Scott G. Delcourt, Senior Associate Dean of the Graduate School, 207-581-3291, Fax: 207-581-3232, E-mail: graduate@maine.edu.
Website: http://www.umaine.edu/edhd/

University of Maine at Farmington, Graduate Programs in Education, Farmington, ME 04938. Offers early childhood education (MS Ed); educational leadership (MS Ed); instructional technology (M Ed). M Ed offered in collaboration with University of Maine and University of Southern Maine. *Accreditation:* NCATE. *Program availability:* Part-time-only, evening/weekend, 100% online, blended/hybrid learning. *Faculty:* 7 full-time (6 women), 6 part-time/adjunct (3 women). *Students:* 90 part-time (76 women). Average age 36. 30 applicants, 100% accepted, 29 enrolled. In 2016, 14 master's awarded. *Degree requirements:* For master's, thesis, capstone project (for educational leadership). *Entrance requirements:* For master's, baccalaureate degree from accredited institution, valid teaching certificate or professional experience in education. Additional exam requirements/recommendations for international students: Required—TOEFL. *Application deadline:* For fall admission, 8/10 for domestic students; for spring admission, 1/5 for domestic students; for summer admission, 4/10 for domestic students. Applications are processed on a rolling basis. Application fee: $60. Electronic applications accepted. *Expenses:* Contact institution. *Financial support:* Applicants required to submit FAFSA. *Faculty research:* Teacher leadership, school improvement strategies, technology integration. *Unit head:* Dr. Johanna Prince, Director of Graduate Programs in Education, 207-778-7066, E-mail: gradstudies@maine.edu. *Application contact:* Valerie Soucie, Administrative Specialist, 207-778-7502, Fax: 207-778-8134, E-mail: gradstudies@maine.edu.
Website: http://www2.umf.maine.edu/gradstudies/

University of Manitoba, Faculty of Graduate Studies, Faculty of Education, Department of Educational Administration, Foundations and Psychology, Winnipeg, MB R3T 2N2, Canada. Offers adult and post-secondary education (M Ed); educational administration (M Ed); guidance and counseling (M Ed); inclusive special education (M Ed); social foundations of education (M Ed). *Degree requirements:* For master's, thesis or alternative.

University of Mary, Liffrig Family School of Education and Behavioral Sciences, Department of Education, Bismarck, ND 58504-9652. Offers curriculum, instruction and assessment (M Ed); education (Ed D); elementary administration (M Ed); reading (M Ed); secondary administration (M Ed); special education strategist (M Ed). *Program availability:* Part-time. *Degree requirements:* For master's, portfolio or thesis. *Entrance requirements:* For master's, interview, letters of reference, minimum GPA of 2.5. Additional exam requirements/recommendations for international students: Required—TOEFL (minimum score 500 paper-based; 71 iBT). Electronic applications accepted.

University of Mary Hardin-Baylor, Graduate Studies in Education, Belton, TX 76513. Offers curriculum and instruction (M Ed); educational administration (M Ed, Ed D), including higher education (Ed D), leadership in nursing education (Ed D), P-12 (Ed D). *Program availability:* Part-time, evening/weekend. *Faculty:* 15 full-time (11 women), 9 part-time/adjunct (5 women). *Students:* 55 full-time (40 women), 79 part-time (60 women); includes 50 minority (29 Black or African American, non-Hispanic/Latino; 1 Asian, non-Hispanic/Latino; 18 Hispanic/Latino; 2 Two or more races, non-Hispanic/Latino), 3 international. Average age 38. 20 applicants, 95% accepted, 19 enrolled. In 2016, 23 master's, 19 doctorates awarded. *Degree requirements:* For master's, comprehensive exam; for doctorate, thesis/dissertation. *Entrance requirements:* For master's, minimum GPA of 3.0, interview; for doctorate, minimum GPA of 3.5, interview, essay, resume, employment verification, 3 letters of recommendation. Additional exam requirements/recommendations for international students: Required—TOEFL (minimum score 60 iBT), IELTS (minimum score 4.5). *Application deadline:* For fall admission, 6/1 for domestic students, 4/30 priority date for international students; for spring admission, 11/1 for domestic students, 9/30 priority date for international students. Applications are processed on a rolling basis. Application fee: $35 ($135 for international students). Electronic applications accepted. *Expenses:* $885 per credit hour. *Financial support:* In 2016–17, 99 students received support. Federal Work-Study and scholarships for some active duty military personnel available. Support available to part-time students. Financial award application deadline: 6/1; financial award applicants required to submit FAFSA. *Faculty research:* Motivational orientation of preservice teachers. *Unit head:* Dr. Craig Hammonds, Director, Graduate Programs in Education, 254-295-4189, E-mail: rhammonds@umhb.edu. *Application contact:* Sharon Aguilera, Assistant Director, Graduate Admissions, 254-295-4835, Fax: 254-295-5038, E-mail: saguilera@umhb.edu.
Website: http://graduate.umhb.edu/education/

University of Maryland, College Park, Academic Affairs, College of Education, Department of Counseling, Higher Education and Special Education, College Park, MD 20742. Offers college student personnel (M Ed, MA); college student personnel administration (PhD); community counseling (CAGS); community/career counseling (M Ed, MA); counseling and personnel services (M Ed, MA, PhD), including art therapy (M Ed), college student personnel (M Ed), counseling and personnel services (PhD), counseling psychology (M Ed), mental health counseling (M Ed), school counseling (M Ed); counseling psychology (PhD); counselor education (PhD); rehabilitation counseling (M Ed, MA, AGSC); school counseling (M Ed, MA); school psychology (M Ed, MA, PhD). *Accreditation:* ACA (one or more programs are accredited); APA (one or more programs are accredited); NCATE. *Program availability:* Part-time, evening/weekend, online learning. *Degree requirements:* For master's, thesis (for some programs); for doctorate, thesis/dissertation. *Entrance requirements:* For master's, GRE General Test or MAT, minimum GPA of 3.0, 3 letters of recommendation; for doctorate, GRE General Test or MAT, minimum GPA of 3.5, 3 letters of recommendation. Additional exam requirements/recommendations for international students: Required—TOEFL. Electronic applications accepted. *Faculty research:* Educational psychology, counseling, health.

University of Maryland, College Park, Academic Affairs, College of Education, Department of Education Policy and Leadership, College Park, MD 20742. Offers curriculum and educational communications (M Ed, MA, Ed D, PhD); social foundations of education (M Ed, MA, Ed D, PhD, CAGS). *Accreditation:* NCATE. *Program availability:* Part-time, evening/weekend, online learning. *Degree requirements:* For master's, thesis or alternative, internship and/or field experience; for doctorate, comprehensive exam, thesis/dissertation, practicum or internship. *Entrance requirements:* For master's, GRE General Test or MAT, minimum GPA of 3.0, scholarly writing sample, 3 letters of recommendation; for doctorate, GRE General Test or MAT, scholarly writing sample; minimum undergraduate GPA of 3.0, graduate 3.5. *Faculty research:* Educational technology, adult and higher education.

University of Maryland Eastern Shore, Graduate Programs, Department of Education, Program in Education Leadership, Princess Anne, MD 21853-1299. Offers Ed D. *Program availability:* Evening/weekend. *Degree requirements:* For doctorate, comprehensive exam, thesis/dissertation, internship. *Entrance requirements:* For doctorate, interview, writing sample, state certification in a standard area, 3 years of recent teaching or successful professional experience in K-12 school setting. Additional exam requirements/recommendations for international students: Required—TOEFL (minimum score 80 iBT). Electronic applications accepted.

University of Massachusetts Amherst, Graduate School, College of Education, Program in Education, Amherst, MA 01003. Offers bilingual, English as a second language, and multicultural education (M Ed, Ed S); child study and early education (M Ed); children, families and schools (Ed D, Ed S); early childhood and elementary teacher education (M Ed); educational leadership (M Ed); educational policy and leadership (Ed D); higher education (M Ed); international education (M Ed); language, literacy and culture (Ed D); learning, media and technology (M Ed, Ed S); mathematics, science, and learning technologies (Ed D); reading and writing (M Ed); research, educational measurement and psychometrics (Ed D); school counselor education (M Ed, Ed S); school psychology (Ed S); science education (Ed S); secondary teacher education (M Ed); social justice education (M Ed, Ed D, Ed S); special education (M Ed, Ed D, Ed S); teacher education and school improvement (Ed D, Ed S). *Accreditation:* NCATE. *Program availability:* Part-time, online learning. Terminal master's awarded for partial completion of doctoral program. *Degree requirements:* For doctorate, comprehensive exam, thesis/dissertation. *Entrance requirements:* Additional exam requirements/recommendations for international students: Required—TOEFL (minimum score 550 paper-based; 80 iBT), IELTS (minimum score 6.5). Electronic applications accepted.

University of Massachusetts Boston, College of Education and Human Development, Program in Educational Administration, Boston, MA 02125-3393. Offers M Ed, CAGS. *Program availability:* Part-time, evening/weekend. *Expenses:* Tuition, state resident: full-time $16,863. Tuition, nonresident: full-time $32,913. *Required fees:* $177. *Faculty research:* Power in the classroom, teacher leadership, professional development schools.

University of Massachusetts Boston, College of Education and Human Development, Program in Urban Education, Leadership, and Policy Studies, Boston, MA 02125-3393. Offers Ed D, PhD. *Program availability:* Part-time, evening/weekend. *Degree requirements:* For doctorate, comprehensive exam, thesis/dissertation. *Entrance requirements:* For doctorate, GRE General Test or MAT, minimum GPA of 2.75. *Expenses:* Tuition, state resident: full-time $16,863. Tuition, nonresident: full-time $32,913. *Required fees:* $177. *Faculty research:* School reform, race and culture in schools, race and higher education, language, literacy and writing.

University of Massachusetts Dartmouth, Graduate School, College of Arts and Sciences, School of Education, Department of Educational Leadership, North Dartmouth, MA 02747-2300. Offers educational leadership and policy studies (Ed D, PhD). *Program availability:* Part-time. *Faculty:* 4 full-time (0 women), 3 part-time/adjunct (2 women). *Students:* 17 full-time (8 women), 32 part-time (21 women); includes 16 minority (6 Black or African American, non-Hispanic/Latino; 1 American Indian or Alaska Native, non-Hispanic/Latino; 1 Asian, non-Hispanic/Latino; 5 Hispanic/Latino; 3 Two or more races, non-Hispanic/Latino), 2 international. Average age 41. 22 applicants, 86% accepted, 13 enrolled. In 2016, 12 doctorates awarded. *Degree requirements:* For doctorate, thesis/dissertation. *Entrance requirements:* For doctorate, GRE or GMAT, statement of purpose (minimum of 300 words), resume, 3 letters of recommendation, official transcripts, scholarly writing sample (minimum of 10 pages). Additional exam requirements/recommendations for international students: Required—TOEFL (minimum score 600 paper-based). *Application deadline:* For fall admission, 4/30 priority date for domestic students, 3/30 priority date for international students. Application fee: $60. Electronic applications accepted. *Expenses:* Tuition, state resident: full-time $14,994; part-time $624.75 per credit. Tuition, nonresident: full-time $27,068; part-time $1127.83 per credit. *Required fees:* $405; $25.88 per credit. Tuition and fees vary according to course load and reciprocity agreements. *Financial support:* In 2016–17, 1 fellowship (averaging $6,000 per year) was awarded; institutionally sponsored loans, scholarships/grants, and doctoral support also available. Support available to part-time students. Financial award application deadline: 3/1; financial award applicants required to submit FAFSA. *Faculty research:* Curricular theory, higher education policy, qualitative methods, critical theory. *Total annual research expenditures:* $528,000. *Unit head:* Ricardo Rosa, Graduate Program Director, 508-910-9035, E-mail: rrosa2@umassd.edu. *Application contact:* Steven Briggs, Director of Marketing and Recruitment for Graduate Studies, 508-999-8604, Fax: 508-999-8183, E-mail: graduate@umassd.edu.
Website: http://www.umassd.edu/educationalleadership/

University of Memphis, Graduate School, College of Education, Department of Instruction and Curriculum Leadership, Memphis, TN 38152. Offers advanced studies in teaching and learning (M Ed); applied behavior analysis (Graduate Certificate); autism studies (Graduate Certificate); early childhood education (MAT, MS, Ed D); elementary education (MAT); instruction and curriculum (MS, Ed D); instruction design and technology (MS, Ed D); instructional design and technology (Graduate Certificate); literacy, leadership, and coaching (Graduate Certificate); reading (MS, Ed D); school library information specialist (Graduate Certificate); secondary education (MAT); special education (MAT, MS, Ed D); STEM teacher leadership (Graduate Certificate); urban education (Graduate Certificate). *Accreditation:* NCATE (one or more programs are accredited). *Program availability:* Part-time. *Faculty:* 24 full-time (14 women), 17 part-time/adjunct (12 women). *Students:* 66 full-time (52 women), 315 part-time (243 women); includes 163 minority (132 Black or African American, non-Hispanic/Latino; 1 American Indian or Alaska Native, non-Hispanic/Latino; 6 Asian, non-Hispanic/Latino; 13 Hispanic/Latino; 1 Native Hawaiian or other Pacific Islander, non-Hispanic/Latino; 10 Two or more races, non-Hispanic/Latino), 4 international. Average age 35. 215 applicants, 78% accepted, 120 enrolled. In 2016, 111 master's, 21 doctorates, 8 other advanced degrees awarded. Terminal master's awarded for partial completion of doctoral program. *Degree requirements:* For master's, comprehensive exam, thesis or alternative; for doctorate, comprehensive exam, thesis/dissertation. *Entrance requirements:* For master's, GRE General Test, PRAXIS, minimum GPA of 2.5, letters of reference; for doctorate, GRE General Test, GRE Subject Test, 2 years of teaching experience, letters of reference, statement of purpose, interview. Additional exam requirements/recommendations for international students: Required—TOEFL (minimum score 550 paper-based; 79 iBT). *Application deadline:* For fall admission, 4/1 priority date for domestic students; for spring admission, 10/1 priority date for domestic students; for summer admission, 2/1 priority date for domestic students. Applications are processed on a rolling basis. Application fee: $35 ($60 for international students). Electronic applications accepted. *Expenses:* $5,231.50 per semester full-time in-state, $9,623.50 full-time out-of-state. *Financial support:* In 2016–17, 2 research assistantships with full tuition reimbursements (averaging $10,000 per year), 3 teaching assistantships with full tuition reimbursements (averaging $10,666 per year) were awarded; career-related internships or fieldwork, Federal Work-Study, institutionally sponsored loans, scholarships/grants, traineeships, and unspecified assistantships also available. Support available to part-time students. Financial award application deadline: 2/1; financial award applicants required to submit FAFSA. *Faculty research:* Effective urban teachers, preparation and retention of urban teachers, technology utilization in schools, field-based teacher preparation programs, effective use of online instruction. *Unit head:* Dr. Angiline Powell, Interim Chair, 901-678-3310, E-mail: apowell3@memphis.edu. *Application contact:* Dr. James Meindl, Coordinator of Graduate Studies, 901-678-3310, E-mail: jnmeindl@memphis.edu.
Website: http://www.memphis.edu/icl/

University of Memphis, Graduate School, College of Education, Department of Leadership, Memphis, TN 38152. Offers adult education (Ed D); community college teaching and leadership (Graduate Certificate); community education (Ed D); educational leadership (Ed D); higher education (Ed D); leadership (MS); policy studies (Ed D); school administration and supervision (MS); student personnel (MS). *Accreditation:* NCATE. *Program availability:* Part-time, evening/weekend, online learning. *Faculty:* 8 full-time (4 women), 5 part-time/adjunct (2 women). *Students:* 20 full-time (12 women), 155 part-time (99 women); includes 84 minority (75 Black or African American, non-Hispanic/Latino; 1 Asian, non-Hispanic/Latino; 4 Hispanic/Latino; 4 Two or more races, non-Hispanic/Latino), 2 international. Average age 40. 59 applicants, 92% accepted, 49 enrolled. In 2016, 11 master's, 14 doctorates, 3 other advanced degrees awarded. *Degree requirements:* For master's, comprehensive exam, thesis optional; for doctorate, comprehensive exam, thesis/dissertation. *Entrance requirements:* For master's, GRE, resume, letters of reference, statement of professional goals, current teacher certification, sample work, interview; for doctorate, GRE, resume, letters of reference, statement of professional goals, interview. Additional exam requirements/recommendations for international students: Required—TOEFL (minimum score 550 paper-based; 79 iBT). *Application deadline:* For fall admission, 6/15 for domestic students; for spring admission, 9/15 for domestic students; for summer admission, 2/15 for domestic students. Application fee: $35 ($60 for international students). Electronic applications accepted. *Expenses:* $5,231.50 per semester full-time in-state, $9,623.50 full-time out-of-state. *Financial support:* In 2016–17, 70 students received support, including 3 research assistantships with full tuition reimbursements available (averaging $16,800 per year); teaching assistantships, Federal Work-Study, scholarships/grants, and unspecified assistantships also available. Financial award application deadline: 2/1; financial award applicants required to submit FAFSA. *Faculty research:* School improvement, social justice, online learning, adult learning, diversity. *Unit head:* Dr. Reginald Green, Interim Chair, 901-678-3445, E-mail: rlgreen1@memphis.edu.
Website: http://www.memphis.edu/lead

University of Michigan–Dearborn, College of Education, Health, and Human Services, Doctoral Program in Education, Dearborn, MI 48126. Offers curriculum and practice (Ed D); educational leadership (Ed D); metropolitan education (Ed D). *Program availability:* Part-time, evening/weekend. *Faculty:* 27 full-time (19 women), 5 part-time/adjunct (0 women). *Students:* 2 full-time (both women), 21 part-time (15 women); includes 9 minority (7 Black or African American, non-Hispanic/Latino; 1 Asian, non-Hispanic/Latino; 1 Hispanic/Latino). Average age 43. 14 applicants, 64% accepted, 7 enrolled. In 2016, 3 doctorates awarded. *Degree requirements:* For doctorate, comprehensive exam, thesis/dissertation. *Entrance requirements:* For doctorate, GRE (taken within the last 5 years), master's degree with minimum GPA of 3.3, 3 letters of recommendation (1 from faculty), 3 years' professional and/or teaching experience. Additional exam requirements/recommendations for international students: Required—TOEFL (minimum score 560 paper-based; 84 iBT), IELTS (minimum score 6.5). *Application deadline:* For fall admission, 3/1 for domestic and international students. Application fee: $60. Electronic applications accepted. *Expenses:* Contact institution. *Financial support:* In 2016–17, 5 students received support. Scholarships/grants available. Financial award application deadline: 3/1; financial award applicants required to submit FAFSA. *Faculty research:* Educational leadership, English language learning, community-based education, urban education, educational technology. *Unit head:* Dr. Chris Burke, Director, 313-593-5319, E-mail: cjfburke@umich.edu. *Application contact:* Joann Otlewski, Program Assistant, 313-593-5090, E-mail: joanno@umich.edu.
Website: http://umdearborn.edu/cehhs/cehhs_edd/

University of Michigan–Dearborn, College of Education, Health, and Human Services, Education Specialist Program, Dearborn, MI 48126. Offers curriculum and practice (Ed S); educational leadership (Ed S); metropolitan education (Ed S). *Program availability:* Part-time, evening/weekend. *Faculty:* 9 full-time (4 women), 4 part-time/adjunct (0 women). *Students:* 6 part-time (5 women); includes 1 minority (Black or African American, non-Hispanic/Latino). Average age 38. 3 applicants, 100% accepted, 2 enrolled. In 2016, 2 Ed Ss awarded. *Entrance requirements:* For degree, GRE, master's degree with minimum GPA of 3.3; at least 3 years' teaching experience or the equivalent experience working in a professional setting. Additional exam requirements/recommendations for international students: Required—TOEFL (minimum score 560 paper-based; 84 iBT), IELTS (minimum score 6.5). *Application deadline:* For fall admission, 8/1 for domestic students, 5/1 for international students; for winter admission, 12/1 for domestic students, 9/1 for international students; for spring admission, 4/1 for domestic students, 1/1 for international students. Applications are processed on a rolling basis. Application fee: $60. Electronic applications accepted. *Expenses:* Contact institution. *Financial support:* Scholarships/grants available. Financial award application deadline: 3/1; financial award applicants required to submit FAFSA. *Faculty research:* Educational leadership, metropolitan education, curriculum and practice, special education, assessment. *Unit head:* Dr. Bonnie Beyer, Director, 313-593-5583, E-mail: beyer@umich.edu. *Application contact:* Joann Otlewski, Graduate Programs Assistant, 313-593-5090, E-mail: joanno@umich.edu.
Website: http://umdearborn.edu/cehhs/cehhs_eds/

University of Michigan–Dearborn, College of Education, Health, and Human Services, Master of Arts Program in Educational Leadership, Dearborn, MI 48126. Offers MA. *Program availability:* Part-time, evening/weekend. *Faculty:* 2 full-time (1 woman), 2 part-time/adjunct (0 women). *Students:* 1 (woman) full-time, 28 part-time (22 women); includes 6 minority (4 Black or African American, non-Hispanic/Latino; 2 Two or more races, non-Hispanic/Latino). Average age 34. 4 applicants, 50% accepted, 2 enrolled. In

2016, 8 master's awarded. *Entrance requirements:* Additional exam requirements/recommendations for international students: Required—TOEFL (minimum score 560 paper-based; 84 iBT), IELTS (minimum score 6.5). *Application deadline:* For fall admission, 8/1 priority date for domestic students, 5/1 for international students; for winter admission, 12/1 priority date for domestic students, 9/1 for international students; for spring admission, 4/1 priority date for domestic students, 1/1 for international students. Applications are processed on a rolling basis. Application fee: $60. Electronic applications accepted. *Expenses:* Contact institution. *Financial support:* In 2016–17, 2 students received support. Scholarships/grants available. Financial award application deadline: 3/1; financial award applicants required to submit FAFSA. *Faculty research:* STEM education, organizational leadership, inquiry based curriculum development, health inequalities, developing effective inclusive practices. *Unit head:* Dr. Stein Brunvand, Director, Master's Programs, 313-583-6415, E-mail: sbrunvan@umich.edu. *Application contact:* Elizabeth Morden, Graduate Programs Assistant, 313-593-5090, E-mail: emorden@umich.edu.
Website: http://umdearborn.edu/cehhs/cehhs_mael/

University of Michigan–Flint, Graduate Programs, Program in Public Administration, Flint, MI 48502. Offers administration of non-profit agencies (MPA); criminal justice administration (MPA); educational administration (MPA); general public administration (MPA); healthcare administration (MPA). *Program availability:* Part-time. *Faculty:* 1 full-time (0 women), 3 part-time/adjunct (all women). *Students:* 13 full-time (10 women), 97 part-time (59 women); includes 45 minority (35 Black or African American, non-Hispanic/Latino; 1 Asian, non-Hispanic/Latino; 3 Hispanic/Latino; 1 Native Hawaiian or other Pacific Islander, non-Hispanic/Latino; 5 Two or more races, non-Hispanic/Latino), 5 international. Average age 35. 60 applicants, 78% accepted, 38 enrolled. In 2016, 52 master's awarded. *Degree requirements:* For master's, thesis or alternative, internship. *Entrance requirements:* For master's, bachelor's degree from regionally-accredited institution, minimum overall undergraduate GPA of 3.0. Additional exam requirements/recommendations for international students: Required—TOEFL (minimum score 84 iBT), IELTS (minimum score 6.5). *Application deadline:* For fall admission, 8/1 for domestic students, 5/1 for international students; for winter admission, 11/15 for domestic students, 9/1 for international students; for spring admission, 3/15 for domestic students, 1/1 for international students; for summer admission, 5/15 for domestic students. Applications are processed on a rolling basis. Application fee: $55. Electronic applications accepted. *Expenses:* Contact institution. *Financial support:* Career-related internships or fieldwork, Federal Work-Study, and scholarships/grants available. Support available to part-time students. Financial award application deadline: 3/1; financial award applicants required to submit FAFSA. *Unit head:* Dr. Kathryn Schellenberg, Director, 810-762-3340, E-mail: kathsch@umflint.edu. *Application contact:* Bradley T. Maki, Director of Graduate Admissions, 810-762-3171, Fax: 810-766-6789, E-mail: bmaki@umflint.edu.
Website: http://www.umflint.edu/graduateprograms/public-administration-mpa

University of Michigan–Flint, School of Education and Human Services, Department of Education, Flint, MI 48502. Offers curriculum and instruction (Ed S); early childhood education (MA); education (Ed D); educational leadership (Ed S); educational technology (MA), including curriculum and instruction, developer; literacy education (MA); secondary education with certification (MA). *Program availability:* Part-time, evening/weekend, 100% online, mixed mode format (for some programs). *Faculty:* 14 full-time (9 women), 30 part-time/adjunct (17 women). *Students:* 31 full-time (18 women), 199 part-time (144 women); includes 61 minority (48 Black or African American, non-Hispanic/Latino; 1 Asian, non-Hispanic/Latino; 6 Hispanic/Latino; 1 Native Hawaiian or other Pacific Islander, non-Hispanic/Latino; 5 Two or more races, non-Hispanic/Latino), 2 international. Average age 39. 124 applicants, 86% accepted, 75 enrolled. In 2016, 77 master's, 1 doctorate awarded. *Degree requirements:* For master's, thesis optional; for doctorate, thesis/dissertation. *Entrance requirements:* For master's, bachelor's degree from regionally-accredited institution, minimum overall undergraduate GPA of 3.0; for doctorate, Ed S; minimum overall graduate GPA of 3.3 (6.0 on a 9.0 scale) or equivalent; at least 3 years of work experience in a P-16 educational institution or in an education-related position; for Ed S, MA or MS in education-related field from accredited institution; minimum overall graduate GPA of 3.0 (6.0 on a 9.0 scale) or equivalent; at least 3 years of work experience in an educational setting. Additional exam requirements/recommendations for international students: Required—TOEFL (minimum score 84 iBT), IELTS (minimum score 6.5). *Application deadline:* For fall admission, 8/1 for domestic students, 5/1 for international students; for winter admission, 11/15 for domestic students, 9/15 for international students; for spring admission, 3/15 for domestic students, 1/15 for international students; for summer admission, 5/15 for domestic students. Applications are processed on a rolling basis. Application fee: $55. Electronic applications accepted. *Expenses:* Contact institution. *Financial support:* Federal Work-Study, scholarships/grants, and unspecified assistantships available. Support available to part-time students. Financial award application deadline: 3/1; financial award applicants required to submit FAFSA. *Unit head:* Dr. Mary Jo Finney, Department Chair/Associate Professor, 810-766-6617, E-mail: mjfinney@umflint.edu. *Application contact:* Bradley T. Maki, Director of Graduate Admissions, 810-762-3171, Fax: 810-766-6789, E-mail: bmaki@umflint.edu.
Website: https://www.umflint.edu/education/graduate-programs

University of Minnesota, Twin Cities Campus, Graduate School, College of Education and Human Development, Department of Organizational Leadership, Policy and Development, Program in Education Policy and Leadership, Minneapolis, MN 55455-0213. Offers educational policy and leadership (MA, Ed D, PhD); leadership in education (M Ed). *Students:* 87 full-time (48 women), 70 part-time (43 women); includes 33 minority (13 Black or African American, non-Hispanic/Latino; 5 Asian, non-Hispanic/Latino; 13 Hispanic/Latino; 2 Two or more races, non-Hispanic/Latino), 7 international. Average age 48. 152 applicants, 66% accepted, 90 enrolled. In 2016, 4 master's, 10 doctorates awarded. Application fee: $75 ($95 for international students). *Unit head:* Dr. Heidi Barajas, Chair, 612-625-4823, E-mail: hbarajas@umn.edu. *Application contact:* Dr. Jeremy J Hernandez, Director of Graduate Studies, 612-626-9377, E-mail: herna220@umn.edu.
Website: http://www.cehd.umn.edu/OLPD/grad-programs/EPL/

University of Missouri, Office of Research and Graduate Studies, College of Education, Department of Educational Leadership and Policy Analysis, Columbia, MO 65211. Offers education administration (M Ed, MA, Ed D, PhD, Ed S); higher and adult education (M Ed, MA, Ed D, PhD, Ed S). *Program availability:* Part-time. *Faculty:* 14 full-time (9 women), 1 part-time/adjunct (0 women). *Students:* 185 full-time (105 women), 143 part-time (86 women). *Degree requirements:* For doctorate, variable foreign language requirement, comprehensive exam (for some programs), thesis/dissertation. *Entrance requirements:* For master's, doctorate, and Ed S, minimum GPA of 3.0. Additional exam requirements/recommendations for international students: Required—TOEFL (minimum score 500 paper-based; 61 iBT), IELTS (minimum score 5.5). *Application deadline:* For fall admission, 1/15 priority date for domestic and international students; for winter admission, 9/15 priority date for domestic and international students; for spring admission, 10/15 for domestic students. Applications are processed on a rolling basis. Application fee: $75 ($90 for international students). Electronic applications accepted. *Expenses:* Tuition, state resident: full-time $6347; part-time $352.60 per credit hour. Tuition, nonresident: full-time $17,379; part-time $965.50 per credit hour. *Required fees:* $1035. Tuition and fees vary according to course load, campus/location and program. *Financial support:* Fellowships with full tuition reimbursements, research assistantships with full tuition reimbursements, teaching assistantships with full tuition reimbursements, institutionally sponsored loans, scholarships/grants, health care benefits, and unspecified assistantships available.
Website: http://elpa.missouri.edu/

University of Missouri–Kansas City, School of Education, Kansas City, MO 64110-2499. Offers administration (Ed D); counseling and guidance (MA, Ed S), including mental health counseling (Ed S), school counseling (Ed S); counseling psychology (PhD); curriculum and instruction (MA, Ed S), including language and literacy (Ed S); education (PhD), including higher education administration, PK-12 education administration; educational administration (MA, Ed S), including advanced principal (Ed S), beginning principal (Ed S), district-level administration (Ed S); reading education (MA); special education (MA). PhD in education offered through the School of Graduate Studies. *Accreditation:* NCATE. *Program availability:* Part-time, evening/weekend. *Faculty:* 33 full-time (26 women), 51 part-time/adjunct (39 women). *Students:* 136 full-time (103 women), 275 part-time (194 women); includes 110 minority (71 Black or African American, non-Hispanic/Latino; 3 American Indian or Alaska Native, non-Hispanic/Latino; 8 Asian, non-Hispanic/Latino; 22 Hispanic/Latino; 6 Two or more races, non-Hispanic/Latino), 20 international. Average age 32. 324 applicants, 45% accepted, 108 enrolled. In 2016, 152 master's, 13 doctorates, 50 other advanced degrees awarded. *Degree requirements:* For doctorate, thesis/dissertation, internship, practicum. *Entrance requirements:* For master's, GRE, minimum GPA of 2.75, 2 letters of reference, written statement of purpose; for doctorate, GRE, minimum GPA of 3.0; for Ed S, minimum GPA of 3.0. Additional exam requirements/recommendations for international students: Required—TOEFL (minimum score 550 paper-based; 80 iBT). *Application deadline:* For fall admission, 4/1 priority date for domestic and international students; for spring admission, 11/1 priority date for domestic and international students. Applications are processed on a rolling basis. Application fee: $45 ($50 for international students). *Financial support:* In 2016–17, 12 research assistantships with partial tuition reimbursements (averaging $12,476 per year) were awarded; career-related internships or fieldwork, Federal Work-Study, institutionally sponsored loans, and tuition waivers (full and partial) also available. Support available to part-time students. Financial award application deadline: 3/1; financial award applicants required to submit FAFSA. *Faculty research:* Urban education, inquiry-based field study, theories of counseling and psychotherapy, school literacy, educational technology. *Unit head:* Justin Perry, Dean, 816-235-5663, Fax: 816-235-5270, E-mail: education@umkc.edu.
Website: http://education.umkc.edu

University of Missouri–St. Louis, College of Education, Department of Education Sciences and Professional Programs, St. Louis, MO 63121. Offers adult and higher education (M Ed); educational leadership and policy studies (PhD); educational psychology (M Ed), including character and citizenship education, research and program evaluation; program evaluation (Certificate); school psychology (Ed S). *Faculty:* 36 full-time (25 women), 53 part-time/adjunct (40 women). *Students:* 47 full-time (34 women), 247 part-time (175 women); includes 107 minority (86 Black or African American, non-Hispanic/Latino; 2 American Indian or Alaska Native, non-Hispanic/Latino; 5 Asian, non-Hispanic/Latino; 10 Hispanic/Latino; 4 Two or more races, non-Hispanic/Latino), 7 international. 106 applicants, 92% accepted, 70 enrolled. *Degree requirements:* For other advanced degree, comprehensive exam, thesis or alternative, internship. *Entrance requirements:* For degree, GRE General Test, 2-4 letters of recommendation, personal interview. Additional exam requirements/recommendations for international students: Required—IELTS (minimum score 6.5); Recommended—TOEFL (minimum score 550 paper-based; 79 iBT). *Application deadline:* For fall admission, 2/15 priority date for domestic students, 2/15 for international students. Application fee: $50 ($40 for international students). Electronic applications accepted. *Financial support:* Application deadline: 4/1; applicants required to submit FAFSA. *Faculty research:* Child/adolescent psychology, quantitative and qualitative methodology, evaluation processes, measurement and assessment. *Unit head:* Dr. Donald Gouwens, Chairperson, 314-516-4773, Fax: 314-516-5784, E-mail: gouwensd@umsl.edu. *Application contact:* 314-516-5458, Fax: 314-516-6996, E-mail: gradadm@umsl.edu. Website: https://coe.umsl.edu/dept/espp.html

University of Missouri–St. Louis, College of Education, Interdisciplinary Doctoral Programs, St. Louis, MO 63121. Offers counseling (PhD); educational leadership and policy studies (PhD); educational psychology (PhD); leadership in educational practice (Ed D); teaching-learning processes (PhD). *Degree requirements:* For doctorate, thesis/dissertation. *Entrance requirements:* For doctorate, GRE General Test, 3 letters of recommendation; personal interview. Additional exam requirements/recommendations for international students: Recommended—TOEFL (minimum score 550 paper-based; 79 iBT), IELTS (minimum score 6.5). *Application deadline:* For fall admission, 3/1 for domestic and international students; for spring admission, 10/1 for domestic and international students. Application fee: $50 ($40 for international students). Electronic applications accepted. *Financial support:* Research assistantships and teaching assistantships available. Financial award application deadline: 4/1; financial award applicants required to submit FAFSA. *Faculty research:* Higher education law and policy, gender and higher education, student retention, lifelong learning orientation, school counselor's role in violence prevention. *Unit head:* Dr. Kathleen Haywood, Director of Graduate Studies, 314-516-5483, Fax: 314-516-5227, E-mail: kathleen_haywood@umsl.edu. *Application contact:* 314-516-5458, Fax: 314-516-6996, E-mail: gradadm@umsl.edu.

University of Montana, Graduate School, Phyllis J. Washington College of Education and Human Sciences, Department of Educational Leadership, Missoula, MT 59812-0002. Offers M Ed, Ed D, Ed S. *Degree requirements:* For doctorate, thesis/dissertation; for Ed S, thesis. *Entrance requirements:* For master's and Ed S, GRE General Test. Additional exam requirements/recommendations for international students: Required—TOEFL.

University of Montevallo, College of Education, Program in Educational Administration, Montevallo, AL 35115. Offers M Ed, Ed S. *Accreditation:* NCATE. *Program availability:* Part-time, evening/weekend. *Students:* 49 part-time (35 women); includes 8 minority (7 Black or African American, non-Hispanic/Latino; 1 Two or more races, non-Hispanic/Latino). In 2016, 14 master's, 17 Ed Ss awarded. *Degree requirements:* For master's and Ed S, comprehensive exam. *Entrance requirements:* For master's, GRE General Test or MAT. Additional exam requirements/recommendations for international students: Required—TOEFL (minimum score 550 paper-based). *Application deadline:* For fall admission, 7/15 for domestic students; for spring admission, 11/15 for domestic students. Application fee: $25. *Expenses:* Tuition, state resident: full-time $9936. Tuition, nonresident: full-time $20,592. *Required fees:* $640. *Financial support:* Federal Work-Study, scholarships/grants, and unspecified assistantships available. *Unit head:* Dr. Anna E. McEwan, Dean of Education, 205-665-6360, E-mail: mcewanae@montevallo.edu. *Application contact:* Kevin Thornthwaite, Director, Graduate Admissions and Records, 205-665-6350, E-mail: graduate@montevallo.edu.
Website: http://www.montevallo.edu/education/college-of-education/traditional-masters-degrees/leadership/

Educational Leadership and Administration

University of Mount Union, Program in Educational Leadership, Alliance, OH 44601-3993. Offers MA. *Program availability:* Part-time, online only, blended/hybrid learning. *Faculty:* 1 (woman) full-time. *Students:* 37 full-time (23 women), 2 part-time (1 woman); includes 1 minority (Hispanic/Latino). 61 applicants, 39% accepted, 18 enrolled. In 2016, 13 master's awarded. *Entrance requirements:* For master's, MAT and/or GRE General Test, two recommendations, official transcript from each college or university previously attended, curriculum vitae or resume, personal statement. Additional exam requirements/recommendations for international students: Required—TOEFL (minimum score 100 iBT). *Application deadline:* For fall admission, 8/15 for domestic and international students. Applications are processed on a rolling basis. Application fee: $30. Electronic applications accepted. *Expenses:* Contact institution. *Financial support:* Applicants required to submit FAFSA. *Unit head:* Dr. Mandy Capel, Director, 800-992-6682, E-mail: capelml@mountunion.edu. *Application contact:* Jess Canavan, Director of Admissions, 330-823-2579, E-mail: canavajl@mountunion.edu.
Website: http://www.mountunion.edu/mael

University of Nebraska at Kearney, College of Education, Department of Educational Administration, Kearney, NE 68849-0001. Offers curriculum supervisor of academic area (MA Ed); school principalship 7-12 (MA Ed); school principalship PK-8 (MA Ed); school superintendent (Ed S); supervisor of special education (MA Ed). *Accreditation:* NCATE. *Program availability:* Part-time, evening/weekend, online only, 100% online. *Faculty:* 4 full-time (1 woman). *Students:* 4 full-time (2 women), 131 part-time (59 women); includes 5 minority (all Hispanic/Latino). Average age 35. 18 applicants, 94% accepted, 9 enrolled. In 2016, 40 master's, 7 Ed Ss awarded. *Degree requirements:* For master's and Ed S, comprehensive exam, thesis optional. *Entrance requirements:* For master's, letters of recommendation, resume, letter of interest; for Ed S, letters of recommendation, resume, essay. Additional exam requirements/recommendations for international students: Recommended—TOEFL (minimum score 550 paper-based; 79 iBT), IELTS (minimum score 6.5). *Application deadline:* For fall admission, 6/15 for domestic and international students; for spring admission, 10/15 for domestic and international students; for summer admission, 3/15 for domestic and international students. Application fee: $45. Electronic applications accepted. *Expenses:* Tuition, state resident: full-time $4064; part-time $225.75 per credit hour. Tuition, nonresident: full-time $8915; part-time $495.25 per credit hour. *Required fees:* $772; $23 per credit hour. Part-time tuition and fees vary according to course load, campus/location, program and reciprocity agreements. *Financial support:* In 2016–17, 2 students received support, including 2 research assistantships with full tuition reimbursements available (averaging $10,500 per year); career-related internships or fieldwork, scholarships/grants, health care benefits, and unspecified assistantships also available. Support available to part-time students. Financial award application deadline: 2/28; financial award applicants required to submit FAFSA. *Faculty research:* Leadership and organizational behavior. *Unit head:* Dr. Richard Meyer, Chair, Educational Administration, 308-865-8512, E-mail: meyerdc@unk.edu. *Application contact:* Linda Johnson, Director, Graduate Admissions and Programs, 308-865-8841, Fax: 308-865-8837, E-mail: johnsonli@unk.edu.
Website: http://www.unk.edu/academics/edad/

University of Nebraska at Omaha, Graduate Studies, College of Education, Department of Educational Leadership, Omaha, NE 68182. Offers educational administration and supervision (Ed D); educational leadership (MS, Ed S). *Accreditation:* NCATE. *Program availability:* Part-time, evening/weekend. *Faculty:* 5 full-time (4 women). *Students:* 6 full-time (5 women), 102 part-time (70 women); includes 15 minority (6 Black or African American, non-Hispanic/Latino; 1 Asian, non-Hispanic/Latino; 3 Hispanic/Latino; 5 Two or more races, non-Hispanic/Latino), 4 international. Average age 38. 19 applicants, 79% accepted, 10 enrolled. In 2016, 26 master's, 13 doctorates, 1 other advanced degree awarded. *Degree requirements:* For master's, comprehensive exam, thesis (for some programs); for doctorate, comprehensive exam, thesis/dissertation; for Ed S, comprehensive exam, thesis. *Entrance requirements:* For master's, minimum GPA of 3.0, transcripts, resume, copy of teaching certificate, 3 letters of recommendation, statement of purpose; for doctorate, GRE General Test, resume, 3 samples of research/written work, 3 letters of recommendation, statement of purpose, transcripts. Additional exam requirements/recommendations for international students: Required—TOEFL, IELTS, PTE. *Application deadline:* For fall admission, 6/1 priority date for domestic and international students; for spring admission, 10/1 priority date for domestic and international students; for summer admission, 2/1 for domestic and international students. Applications are processed on a rolling basis. Application fee: $45. Electronic applications accepted. *Financial support:* In 2016–17, 4 students received support, including 3 research assistantships with tuition reimbursements available, 1 teaching assistantship with tuition reimbursement available; Federal Work-Study, institutionally sponsored loans, scholarships/grants, health care benefits, tuition waivers (partial), and unspecified assistantships also available. Support available to part-time students. Financial award application deadline: 3/1. *Unit head:* Dr. Kay Keiser, Director and Graduate Program Chair, 402-554-2341, E-mail: graduate@unomaha.edu.

University of Nebraska–Lincoln, Graduate College, College of Education and Human Sciences, Department of Educational Administration, Lincoln, NE 68588. Offers M Ed, MA, Ed D, Certificate. Ed D offered jointly with University of Nebraska at Omaha. *Accreditation:* NCATE. *Degree requirements:* For master's, thesis optional; for doctorate, comprehensive exam, thesis/dissertation. *Entrance requirements:* For master's, GRE or MAT; for doctorate, GRE General Test, administrative certification. Additional exam requirements/recommendations for international students: Required—TOEFL (minimum score 550 paper-based). Electronic applications accepted. *Faculty research:* Educational policy, school finance, school law, school restructuring, leadership behavior.

University of Nebraska–Lincoln, Graduate College, College of Education and Human Sciences, Interdepartmental Area of Administration, Curriculum and Instruction, Lincoln, NE 68588. Offers Ed D, PhD, JD/PhD. *Accreditation:* NCATE. *Program availability:* Online learning. *Degree requirements:* For doctorate, comprehensive exam, thesis/dissertation. *Entrance requirements:* For doctorate, GRE, curriculum vitae. Additional exam requirements/recommendations for international students: Required—TOEFL (minimum score 550 paper-based). Electronic applications accepted.

University of Nevada, Las Vegas, Graduate College, College of Education, Department of Educational Psychology and Higher Education, Las Vegas, NV 89154-3002. Offers chief diversity officer in higher education (Certificate); college sport leadership (Certificate); educational psychology (M Ed, MS, PhD, Ed S); higher education (M Ed, PhD, Certificate); psychology/learning and technology (PhD), including learning and technology; workforce development/educational leadership (PhD); PhD/JD. *Program availability:* Part-time, evening/weekend, 100% online, blended/hybrid learning. *Faculty:* 20 full-time (14 women), 5 part-time/adjunct (3 women). *Students:* 74 full-time (55 women), 100 part-time (69 women); includes 60 minority (17 Black or African American, non-Hispanic/Latino; 11 Asian, non-Hispanic/Latino; 26 Hispanic/Latino; 6 Two or more races, non-Hispanic/Latino), 5 international. Average age 36. 121 applicants, 58% accepted, 46 enrolled. In 2016, 22 master's, 14 doctorates, 8 other advanced degrees awarded. *Degree requirements:* For master's, comprehensive exam (for some programs), thesis (for some programs); for doctorate, comprehensive exam, thesis/dissertation. *Entrance requirements:* For master's, GRE General Test or GMAT (for some programs), letters of recommendation; writing sample; bachelor's degree; for doctorate, GMAT or GRE General Test, writing exam; for other advanced degree, GRE General Test (for some programs). Additional exam requirements/recommendations for international students: Required—TOEFL (minimum score 550 paper-based; 80 iBT), IELTS (minimum score 7). *Application deadline:* For fall admission, 3/15 for domestic students, 5/1 for international students. Application fee: $60 ($95 for international students). Electronic applications accepted. *Expenses:* $269.25 per credit, $792 per 3-credit course; $9,634 per year resident; $23,274 per year non-resident; $7,094 fees non-resident (7 credits or more); $1,307 annual health insurance fee. *Financial support:* In 2016–17, 24 research assistantships with partial tuition reimbursements (averaging $14,790 per year), 21 teaching assistantships with partial tuition reimbursements (averaging $15,631 per year) were awarded; institutionally sponsored loans, scholarships/grants, health care benefits, and unspecified assistantships also available. Financial award application deadline: 3/15. *Faculty research:* Innovation and change in educational settings; educational policy, finance, and marketing; psycho-educational assessment; student retention, persistence, development, language, and culture; statistical modeling, program evaluation, qualitative and quantitative research methods. *Total annual research expenditures:* $158,780. *Unit head:* Dr. LeAnn Putney, Chair/Professor, 702-895-4879, Fax: 702-895-1658, E-mail: leann.putney@unlv.edu. *Application contact:* Dr. Steve McCafferty, Graduate Coordinator, 702-895-3245, Fax: 702-895-1658, E-mail: mccaffes@unlv.nevada.edu.
Website: http://education.unlv.edu/ephe/

University of Nevada, Reno, Graduate School, College of Education, Department of Educational Leadership, Reno, NV 89557. Offers M Ed, MA, MS, Ed D, PhD, Ed S. *Accreditation:* NCATE. Terminal master's awarded for partial completion of doctoral program. *Degree requirements:* For master's, comprehensive exam, thesis optional; for doctorate, comprehensive exam, thesis/dissertation. *Entrance requirements:* For master's, minimum GPA of 2.75; for doctorate, GRE General Test, minimum GPA of 3.0. Additional exam requirements/recommendations for international students: Required—TOEFL (minimum score 500 paper-based; 61 iBT), IELTS (minimum score 6). Electronic applications accepted. *Faculty research:* Law, finance, supervision, organizational theory, principalship.

University of New England, College of Graduate and Professional Studies, Portland, ME 04103. Offers applied nutrition (MS); career and technical education (MS Ed); curriculum and instruction (MS Ed); education (CAGS, Post-Master's Certificate); education leadership (Ed D); educational leadership (MS Ed); generalist (MS Ed); health informatics (MS, Graduate Certificate); inclusion education (MS Ed); literacy K-12 (MS Ed); medical education leadership (MMEL); public health (Graduate Certificate); reading specialist (MS Ed); social work (MSW). *Program availability:* Part-time, evening/weekend, online only, 100% online. *Faculty:* 67 part-time/adjunct (46 women). *Students:* 891 full-time (667 women), 359 part-time (261 women); includes 309 minority (215 Black or African American, non-Hispanic/Latino; 2 American Indian or Alaska Native, non-Hispanic/Latino; 63 Asian, non-Hispanic/Latino; 18 Hispanic/Latino; 2 Native Hawaiian or other Pacific Islander, non-Hispanic/Latino; 9 Two or more races, non-Hispanic/Latino). Average age 36. 777 applicants, 50% accepted, 316 enrolled. In 2016, 292 master's, 34 doctorates, 130 other advanced degrees awarded. *Application deadline:* Applications are processed on a rolling basis. Electronic applications accepted. Tuition and fees vary according to degree level, program and student level. *Financial support:* Application deadline: 5/1; applicants required to submit FAFSA. *Unit head:* Dr. Martha Wilson, Associate Provost for Online Worldwide Learning/Dean of the College of Graduate and Professional Studies, 207-221-4985, E-mail: mwilson13@une.edu.
Website: http://online.une.edu

University of New Hampshire, Graduate School, College of Liberal Arts, Department of Education, Program in Educational Administration and Supervision, Durham, NH 03824. Offers Ed S. *Program availability:* Part-time. *Students:* 6 part-time. *Entrance requirements:* For degree, GRE General Test. Additional exam requirements/recommendations for international students: Required—TOEFL (minimum score 550 paper-based; 80 iBT). *Application deadline:* For fall admission, 2/1 priority date for domestic students, 2/1 for international students; for spring admission, 12/1 for domestic students. Applications are processed on a rolling basis. Application fee: $65. *Financial support:* Fellowships, research assistantships, teaching assistantships, career-related internships or fieldwork, Federal Work-Study, scholarships/grants, and tuition waivers (full and partial) available. Support available to part-time students. Financial award application deadline: 2/15. *Faculty research:* School principalship, supervision, superintendency. *Unit head:* Leslie Couse, Chair, 603-862-0638, E-mail: education.department@unh.edu. *Application contact:* Lisa Wilder, Administrative Assistant, 603-862-2381, E-mail: education.department@unh.edu.
Website: http://cola.unh.edu/education

University of New Hampshire, Graduate School, College of Liberal Arts, Department of Education, Program in Special Education, Durham, NH 03824. Offers special education (M Ed); special education administration (Postbaccalaureate Certificate). *Program availability:* Part-time. *Degree requirements:* For master's, thesis or alternative. *Entrance requirements:* For master's, GRE General Test. Additional exam requirements/recommendations for international students: Required—TOEFL (minimum score 550 paper-based; 80 iBT). *Application deadline:* For fall admission, 6/1 priority date for domestic students, 4/1 for international students; for spring admission, 12/1 for domestic students. Applications are processed on a rolling basis. Application fee: $65. Electronic applications accepted. *Financial support:* Fellowships, research assistantships, teaching assistantships, career-related internships or fieldwork, Federal Work-Study, scholarships/grants, and tuition waivers (full and partial) available. Support available to part-time students. Financial award application deadline: 2/15. *Unit head:* Leslie Couse, Chair, 603-862-0638, E-mail: education.department@unh.edu. *Application contact:* Lisa Wilder, Administrative Assistant, 603-862-2381, E-mail: education.department@unh.edu.
Website: http://cola.unh.edu/education

University of New Hampshire, Graduate School Manchester Campus, Manchester, NH 03101. Offers business administration (MBA); educational administration and supervision (Ed S); educational studies (M Ed); elementary teacher education (M Ed); information technology (MS); public administration (MPA); public health (MPH, Certificate); secondary teacher education (M Ed, MAT); social work (MSW); substance use disorders (Certificate). *Program availability:* Part-time, evening/weekend. *Degree requirements:* For master's, thesis or alternative. *Entrance requirements:* Additional exam requirements/recommendations for international students: Required—TOEFL (minimum score 550 paper-based; 80 iBT). Electronic applications accepted.

University of New Mexico, Graduate Studies, College of Education, Program in Educational Leadership, Albuquerque, NM 87131-2039. Offers MA, Ed D, Ed S. *Accreditation:* NCATE. *Program availability:* Part-time, evening/weekend, online learning. *Faculty:* 9 full-time (5 women). *Students:* 24 full-time (15 women), 111 part-time (81 women); includes 71 minority (4 Black or African American, non-Hispanic/Latino; 22 American Indian or Alaska Native, non-Hispanic/Latino; 1 Asian, non-Hispanic/Latino; 41 Hispanic/Latino; 3 Two or more races, non-Hispanic/Latino), 2 international. Average age 42. 50 applicants, 78% accepted, 34 enrolled. In 2016, 13 master's, 5 doctorates, 17 other advanced degrees awarded. *Degree requirements:* For

master's, comprehensive exam; for doctorate, comprehensive exam, thesis/dissertation. *Entrance requirements:* For master's, bachelor's degree; for doctorate, GRE, master's degree. *Application deadline:* For fall admission, 6/1 for domestic students; for spring admission, 10/1 for domestic students. Applications are processed on a rolling basis. Application fee: $50. Electronic applications accepted. *Financial support:* Research assistantships, career-related internships or fieldwork, and scholarships/grants available. Financial award application deadline: 3/1; financial award applicants required to submit FAFSA. *Faculty research:* K-20 educational and organizational leadership, individual and organizational learning, policy, legal and political contexts. *Unit head:* Dr. Patricia Boverie, Head, 505-277-2408, Fax: 505-277-5553, E-mail: pboverie@unm.edu. *Application contact:* Linda Wood, Information Contact, 505-277-0441, Fax: 505-277-5553, E-mail: woodl@unm.edu.
Website: http://coe.unm.edu/departments-programs/teelp/education-leadership-program/index.html

University of New Orleans, Graduate School, College of Education and Human Development, Department of Educational Leadership, Counseling, and Foundations, Program in Educational Leadership, New Orleans, LA 70148. Offers M Ed, PhD. *Accreditation:* NCATE. *Program availability:* Evening/weekend. Terminal master's awarded for partial completion of doctoral program. *Degree requirements:* For doctorate, variable foreign language requirement, thesis/dissertation. *Entrance requirements:* For master's and doctorate, GRE General Test. Additional exam requirements/recommendations for international students: Required—TOEFL (minimum score 550 paper-based; 79 iBT). Electronic applications accepted.

University of North Alabama, College of Education, Department of Secondary Education, Program in Education Leadership, Florence, AL 35632-0001. Offers instructional leadership (MA Ed); secondary education (MA Ed); teacher education multiple levels (MA Ed). *Accreditation:* NCATE. *Program availability:* Part-time, 100% online, blended/hybrid learning. *Faculty:* 24 full-time (10 women), 2 part-time/adjunct (0 women). *Students:* 18 full-time (12 women), 62 part-time (43 women); includes 11 minority (8 Black or African American, non-Hispanic/Latino; 1 American Indian or Alaska Native, non-Hispanic/Latino; 1 Hispanic/Latino; 1 Two or more races, non-Hispanic/Latino). Average age 38. 32 applicants, 69% accepted, 20 enrolled. In 2016, 44 master's awarded. *Entrance requirements:* Additional exam requirements/recommendations for international students: Required—TOEFL (minimum score 79 iBT), IELTS (minimum score 6), PTE (minimum score 54). *Application deadline:* Applications are processed on a rolling basis. Application fee: $50 ($100 for international students). Electronic applications accepted. *Expenses:* Tuition, state resident: full-time $2799; part-time $1866 per semester. Tuition, nonresident: full-time $5598; part-time $3732 per semester. *Required fees:* $915; $642 per semester. Tuition and fees vary according to course load. *Financial support:* In 2016–17, 10 students received support. Application deadline: 2/1; applicants required to submit FAFSA. *Unit head:* Dr. Leah Whitten, Interim Chair, 256-765-4575, E-mail: lswhitten@una.edu. *Application contact:* Hillary N. Coats, Graduate Admissions Counselor, 256-765-4447, E-mail: graduate@una.edu.
Website: https://www.una.edu/education/departments/secondary-education.html

The University of North Carolina at Chapel Hill, Graduate School, School of Education, Programs in Educational Leadership and School Administration, Chapel Hill, NC 27599. Offers educational leadership (Ed D); school administration (MSA). *Accreditation:* NCATE. *Program availability:* Part-time. *Degree requirements:* For master's, comprehensive exam; for doctorate, comprehensive exam, thesis/dissertation. *Entrance requirements:* For master's, GRE General Test or MAT, minimum GPA of 3.2 during last 2 years of undergraduate course work, 3 years of school-based professional experience; for doctorate, GRE General Test, minimum GPA of 3.2 during last 2 years of undergraduate course work, 3 years of school-based professional experience. Additional exam requirements/recommendations for international students: Required—TOEFL (minimum score 550 paper-based). *Faculty research:* Gender, race, and class issues; school leadership; school finance and reform.

The University of North Carolina at Charlotte, Cato College of Education, Department of Educational Leadership, Charlotte, NC 28223-0001. Offers education research, measurement, and evaluation (PhD); educational leadership (Ed D); instructional systems technology (M Ed, Graduate Certificate); quantitative analysis (Graduate Certificate); school administration (MSA, Post-Master's Certificate); university and college teaching (Graduate Certificate). *Program availability:* Part-time, evening/weekend, 100% online, blended/hybrid learning. *Faculty:* 19 full-time (12 women), 6 part-time/adjunct (4 women). *Students:* 32 full-time (25 women), 221 part-time (137 women); includes 65 minority (54 Black or African American, non-Hispanic/Latino; 6 Asian, non-Hispanic/Latino; 4 Hispanic/Latino; 1 Two or more races, non-Hispanic/Latino), 4 international. Average age 37. 115 applicants, 86% accepted, 83 enrolled. In 2016, 32 master's, 8 doctorates, 26 other advanced degrees awarded. *Degree requirements:* For master's, thesis or alternative, internship, capstone project; for doctorate, comprehensive exam (for some programs), thesis/dissertation, portfolio. *Entrance requirements:* For master's, GRE or MAT, bachelor's degree, or its U.S. equivalent, from regionally-accredited college or university; minimum overall GPA of 3.5 on all previous work beyond high school; statement of purpose (essay); at least three recommendation forms; for doctorate, GRE or MAT, bachelor's degree (or its U.S. equivalent) from regionally-accredited college or university; minimum overall GPA of 3.5 in master's degree program; for other advanced degree, bachelor's degree from regionally-accredited university; minimum GPA of 2.75 on all post-secondary work attempted; transcripts; personal statement outlining why the applicant seeks admission to the program. Additional exam requirements/recommendations for international students: Required—TOEFL (minimum score 523 paper-based, 70 iBT) or IELTS (6.5). *Application deadline:* For fall admission, 3/1 priority date for domestic and international students; for spring admission, 10/1 priority date for domestic and international students; for summer admission, 4/1 priority date for domestic and international students. Applications are processed on a rolling basis. Application fee: $75. Electronic applications accepted. *Expenses:* Tuition, state resident: full-time $4252. Tuition, nonresident: full-time $17,423. *Required fees:* $3026. Tuition and fees vary according to course load and program. *Financial support:* In 2016–17, 8 students received support, including 7 research assistantships (averaging $11,650 per year), 1 teaching assistantship (averaging $11,136 per year); career-related internships or fieldwork, institutionally sponsored loans, scholarships/grants, and unspecified assistantships also available. Support available to part-time students. Financial award application deadline: 3/1; financial award applicants required to submit FAFSA. *Total annual research expenditures:* $4 million. *Unit head:* Dr. Claudia Flowers, Chair, 704-687-8862, E-mail: cpflower@uncc.edu. *Application contact:* Kathy B. Giddings, Director of Graduate Admissions, 704-687-5503, Fax: 704-687-1668, E-mail: gradadm@uncc.edu.
Website: http://edld.uncc.edu/

The University of North Carolina at Charlotte, Cato College of Education, Interdisciplinary Education Programs, Charlotte, NC 28223-0001. Offers art education (Graduate Certificate); child and family development: early childhood education (MAT); curriculum and instruction (PhD); elementary education (MAT); foreign language education (MAT); middle grades education (MAT); secondary education (MAT); special education (MAT); teaching (Graduate Certificate); teaching English as a second language (MAT); theatre education (Graduate Certificate). *Program availability:* Part-time, 100% online, blended/hybrid learning. *Students:* 78 full-time (59 women), 619 part-time (484 women); includes 255 minority (186 Black or African American, non-Hispanic/Latino; 1 American Indian or Alaska Native, non-Hispanic/Latino; 16 Asian, non-Hispanic/Latino; 37 Hispanic/Latino; 15 Two or more races, non-Hispanic/Latino), 10 international. Average age 33. 380 applicants, 92% accepted, 264 enrolled. In 2016, 93 master's, 8 doctorates, 176 other advanced degrees awarded. *Degree requirements:* For master's, thesis or alternative, research project/portfolio. *Entrance requirements:* For master's, GRE or MAT, bachelor's degree, or its U.S. equivalent, from regionally-accredited college or university; minimum overall GPA of 3.0 on all previous work beyond high school; statement of purpose (essay); at least three recommendation forms; for doctorate, GRE or MAT, bachelor's degree (or its U.S. equivalent) from regionally-accredited college or university; minimum overall GPA of 3.5 in master's degree program; for Graduate Certificate, bachelor's degree from regionally-accredited university; minimum GPA of 2.75 on all post-secondary work attempted; transcripts; personal statement outlining why the applicant seeks admission to the program. Additional exam requirements/recommendations for international students: Required—TOEFL (minimum score 523 paper-based, 70 iBT) or IELTS (6.5). *Application deadline:* For fall admission, 3/1 priority date for domestic and international students; for spring admission, 10/1 priority date for domestic and international students; for summer admission, 4/1 priority date for domestic and international students. Applications are processed on a rolling basis. Application fee: $75. Electronic applications accepted. *Expenses:* Tuition, state resident: full-time $4252. Tuition, nonresident: full-time $17,423. *Required fees:* $3026. Tuition and fees vary according to course load and program. *Financial support:* Career-related internships or fieldwork, institutionally sponsored loans, scholarships/grants, and unspecified assistantships available. Support available to part-time students. Financial award application deadline: 3/1; financial award applicants required to submit FAFSA. *Unit head:* Dr. Ellen McIntyre, Dean, 704-687-8722, E-mail: ellen.mcintyre@uncc.edu. *Application contact:* Kathy B. Giddings, Director of Graduate Admissions, 704-687-5503, Fax: 704-687-1668, E-mail: gradadm@uncc.edu.
Website: http://education.uncc.edu/academic-programs

The University of North Carolina at Greensboro, Graduate School, School of Education, Department of Educational Leadership and Cultural Foundations, Greensboro, NC 27412-5001. Offers curriculum and teaching (PhD), including cultural studies; educational leadership (Ed D, Ed S); school administration (MSA). *Accreditation:* NCATE. *Degree requirements:* For doctorate, thesis/dissertation. *Entrance requirements:* For master's, doctorate, and Ed S, GRE General Test. Additional exam requirements/recommendations for international students: Required—TOEFL. Electronic applications accepted.

The University of North Carolina at Greensboro, Graduate School, School of Education, Department of Teacher Education and Higher Education, Greensboro, NC 27412-5001. Offers college teaching and adult learning (Certificate); curriculum and instruction (M Ed), including chemistry education, elementary education, English as a second language, French education, instructional technology, mathematics education, middle grades education, reading education, science education, social studies education, Spanish education; curriculum and teaching (PhD), including higher education, teacher education and development; English as a second language (Certificate); higher education (M Ed); supervision (M Ed). *Accreditation:* NCATE. *Program availability:* Part-time. *Degree requirements:* For doctorate, thesis/dissertation. *Entrance requirements:* For master's and doctorate, GRE General Test. Additional exam requirements/recommendations for international students: Required—TOEFL. Electronic applications accepted. *Faculty research:* Community college literacy program, middle school mathematics/computer mathematics.

The University of North Carolina at Pembroke, The Graduate School, School of Education, Program in School Administration, Pembroke, NC 28372-1510. Offers MSA. *Program availability:* Part-time, evening/weekend. *Degree requirements:* For master's, internship. *Entrance requirements:* For master's, GRE General Test or MAT, minimum GPA of 3.0 in major, 2.5 overall; 3 years of teaching experience; two recommendations. Additional exam requirements/recommendations for international students: Required—TOEFL.

The University of North Carolina Wilmington, Watson College of Education, Department of Early Childhood, Elementary, Middle, Literacy and Special Education, Wilmington, NC 28403-3297. Offers educational leadership, policy, and advocacy (M Ed); elementary education (M Ed, MAT); language and literacy (M Ed); middle grades education (M Ed, MAT). *Accreditation:* NCATE. *Program availability:* Part-time. *Faculty:* 26 full-time (19 women). *Students:* 121 full-time (89 women), 139 part-time (135 women); includes 70 minority (47 Black or African American, non-Hispanic/Latino; 1 Asian, non-Hispanic/Latino; 14 Hispanic/Latino; 8 Two or more races, non-Hispanic/Latino). Average age 34. 109 applicants, 78% accepted, 65 enrolled. In 2016, 83 master's awarded. *Degree requirements:* For master's, comprehensive exam, capstone experience. *Entrance requirements:* For master's, GRE General Test, MAT, minimum GPA of 3.0 in undergraduate work, 3 letters of recommendations, NC Class A teacher license in related field, statement of interest. *Application deadline:* For fall admission, 5/15 for domestic students; for spring admission, 10/15 for domestic students; for summer admission, 3/15 for domestic students. Applications are processed on a rolling basis. Application fee: $60. Electronic applications accepted. *Expenses:* Contact institution. *Financial support:* Scholarships/grants and unspecified assistantships available. Support available to part-time students. Financial award application deadline: 3/15; financial award applicants required to submit FAFSA. *Unit head:* Dr. Kathy Fox, Chair, 910-962-3240, Fax: 910-962-3988, E-mail: foxk@uncw.edu. *Application contact:* Dr. Elizabeth Crawford, Graduate Program Coordinator, 910-962-2916, Fax: 910-962-3988, E-mail: crawforde@uncw.edu.
Website: http://www.uncw.edu/ed/eemls/index.html

The University of North Carolina Wilmington, Watson College of Education, Department of Educational Leadership, Wilmington, NC 28403-3297. Offers curriculum, instruction and supervision (M Ed); educational leadership and administration (Ed D), including curriculum and instruction; higher education (M Ed); school administration (MSA), including school administration. *Program availability:* Part-time. *Faculty:* 25 full-time (14 women), 5 part-time/adjunct (3 women). *Students:* 49 full-time (31 women), 151 part-time (106 women); includes 55 minority (42 Black or African American, non-Hispanic/Latino; 7 American Indian or Alaska Native, non-Hispanic/Latino; 3 Asian, non-Hispanic/Latino; 1 Hispanic/Latino; 1 Native Hawaiian or other Pacific Islander, non-Hispanic/Latino; 1 Two or more races, non-Hispanic/Latino), 1 international. Average age 36. 113 applicants, 70% accepted, 57 enrolled. In 2016, 32 master's, 19 doctorates awarded. *Degree requirements:* For master's, comprehensive exam, thesis or alternative, e-portfolio defense; for doctorate, comprehensive exam, thesis/dissertation. *Entrance requirements:* For master's, GRE General Test, MAT, minimum B average in undergraduate work, 3 letters of recommendation, statement of interest, NC Class A teacher licensure in related field, minimum of 3 years' teaching experience; for doctorate, GRE, statement of interest, master's degree in education field, 3 years of leadership experience, minimum GPA of 3.0 in undergraduate and graduate work. Additional exam requirements/recommendations for international students: Required—TOEFL (minimum score 79 iBT), IELTS (minimum score 6.5). *Application deadline:* For

fall admission, 5/15 for domestic students; for spring admission, 10/15 for domestic students; for summer admission, 3/15 for domestic students. Applications are processed on a rolling basis. Application fee: $60. Electronic applications accepted. *Expenses:* Contact institution. *Financial support:* Scholarships/grants and unspecified assistantships available. Support available to part-time students. Financial award application deadline: 3/15; financial award applicants required to submit FAFSA. *Unit head:* Dr. Tamara Walser, Interim Chair, 910-962-2290, Fax: 910-962-3609, E-mail: walsert@uncw.edu. *Application contact:* Dr. William Sterrett, Graduate Program Coordinator, 910-962-7995, E-mail: stewettw@uncw.edu.
Website: http://uncw.edu/ed/el/

University of North Dakota, Graduate School, College of Education and Human Development, Department of Educational Leadership, Grand Forks, ND 58202. Offers M Ed, Ed D, PhD, Ed S. *Accreditation:* NCATE. *Program availability:* Part-time, evening/weekend, online learning. *Degree requirements:* For master's and Ed S, comprehensive exam, thesis or alternative; for doctorate, comprehensive exam, thesis/dissertation, final exam. *Entrance requirements:* For master's, minimum GPA of 3.0; for doctorate, minimum GPA of 3.5. Additional exam requirements/recommendations for international students: Required—TOEFL (minimum score 550 paper-based; 79 iBT), IELTS (minimum score 6.5). *Application deadline:* For fall admission, 8/1 priority date for domestic students, 5/1 priority date for international students; for spring admission, 12/1 priority date for domestic students, 9/1 priority date for international students. Applications are processed on a rolling basis. Application fee: $35. Electronic applications accepted. *Financial support:* Fellowships with full and partial tuition reimbursements, research assistantships with full and partial tuition reimbursements, teaching assistantships with full tuition reimbursements, career-related internships or fieldwork, Federal Work-Study, institutionally sponsored loans, scholarships/grants, health care benefits, tuition waivers (full and partial), and unspecified assistantships available. Support available to part-time students. Financial award application deadline: 3/15; financial award applicants required to submit FAFSA. *Unit head:* Dr. David Nguyen, JD, Graduate Director, 701-777-2394, Fax: 701-777-4365, E-mail: david.hk.nguyen@und.edu. *Application contact:* Staci Wells, Admissions Associate, 701-777-2945, Fax: 701-777-3619, E-mail: staci.wells@gradschool.und.edu.
Website: http://education.und.edu/educational-leadership/index.cfm

University of Northern Colorado, Graduate School, College of Education and Behavioral Sciences, Department of Leadership, Policy and Development: Higher Education and P-12 Education, Educational Leadership and Policy Studies Program, Greeley, CO 80639. Offers educational leadership (MA, Ed S); educational leadership and policy studies (Ed D). *Accreditation:* NCATE. *Program availability:* Part-time, evening/weekend, online learning. *Faculty:* 5 full-time (3 women). *Students:* 17 full-time (9 women), 53 part-time (36 women); includes 21 minority (3 Black or African American, non-Hispanic/Latino; 3 American Indian or Alaska Native, non-Hispanic/Latino; 1 Asian, non-Hispanic/Latino; 14 Hispanic/Latino). Average age 37. 25 applicants, 80% accepted, 15 enrolled. In 2016, 31 master's, 5 doctorates, 23 other advanced degrees awarded. *Degree requirements:* For master's, comprehensive exam, thesis or alternative; for doctorate, comprehensive exam, thesis/dissertation; for Ed S, comprehensive exam, thesis. *Entrance requirements:* For master's, resume, interview; for doctorate, GRE General Test, resume, interview; for Ed S, resume. *Application deadline:* For fall admission, 5/1 for domestic and international students. Applications are processed on a rolling basis. Application fee: $50 ($60 for international students). Electronic applications accepted. *Financial support:* In 2016–17, 38 students received support, including 6 research assistantships (averaging $10,306 per year); fellowships, teaching assistantships, and unspecified assistantships also available. Financial award application deadline: 3/1; financial award applicants required to submit FAFSA. *Unit head:* Dr. Linda Vogel, Program Coordinator, 970-351-2861, E-mail: elps@unco.edu. *Application contact:* Linda Sisson, Graduate Student Admission Coordinator, 970-351-1807, Fax: 970-351-2371, E-mail: linda.sisson@unco.edu.
Website: http://www.unco.edu/cebs/elps/

University of Northern Colorado, Graduate School, College of Education and Behavioral Sciences, School of Teacher Education, Program in Educational Studies, Greeley, CO 80639. Offers Ed D. *Program availability:* Part-time, evening/weekend. *Application deadline:* Applications are processed on a rolling basis. Application fee: $50 ($60 for international students). Electronic applications accepted. *Financial support:* Research assistantships and teaching assistantships available. Financial award application deadline: 3/1; financial award applicants required to submit FAFSA. *Unit head:* Dr. Alexander Sidorkin, Director, 970-351-2908, Fax: 970-351-1877. *Application contact:* Linda Sisson, Graduate Student Admission Coordinator, 970-351-1807, Fax: 970-351-2371, E-mail: linda.sisson@unco.edu.
Website: http://www.unco.edu/cebs/teachered/

University of Northern Iowa, Graduate College, College of Education, Department of Educational Leadership and Postsecondary Education, MAE Program in Principalship, Cedar Falls, IA 50614. Offers MAE. *Program availability:* Part-time, evening/weekend. *Degree requirements:* For master's, comprehensive exam (for some programs), thesis or alternative, minimum of 1 year of successful teaching appropriate to the major. *Entrance requirements:* For master's, minimum GPA of 3.0. Additional exam requirements/recommendations for international students: Required—TOEFL (minimum score 500 paper-based; 61 iBT). Electronic applications accepted.

University of Northern Iowa, Graduate College, College of Education, Ed D Program in Education, Cedar Falls, IA 50614. Offers allied health, recreation, and community services (Ed D); curriculum and instruction (Ed D); educational leadership (Ed D). *Program availability:* Part-time, evening/weekend. *Degree requirements:* For doctorate, thesis/dissertation. *Entrance requirements:* For doctorate, GRE, minimum GPA of 3.0, master's degree. Additional exam requirements/recommendations for international students: Required—TOEFL (minimum score 500 paper-based; 61 iBT).

University of North Florida, College of Education and Human Services, Department of Leadership, School Counseling and Sport Management, Jacksonville, FL 32224. Offers counselor education (M Ed), including school counseling; educational leadership (M Ed, Ed D), including athletic administration (M Ed), educational leadership, educational technology (M Ed), instructional leadership (M Ed). *Program availability:* Part-time, evening/weekend. *Faculty:* 18 full-time (10 women), 1 (woman) part-time/adjunct. *Students:* 74 full-time (61 women), 219 part-time (149 women); includes 93 minority (65 Black or African American, non-Hispanic/Latino; 1 American Indian or Alaska Native, non-Hispanic/Latino; 3 Asian, non-Hispanic/Latino; 15 Hispanic/Latino; 1 Native Hawaiian or other Pacific Islander, non-Hispanic/Latino; 8 Two or more races, non-Hispanic/Latino), 14 international. Average age 34. 128 applicants, 57% accepted, 55 enrolled. In 2016, 94 master's, 7 doctorates awarded. *Degree requirements:* For doctorate, thesis/dissertation. *Entrance requirements:* For master's, GRE General Test, minimum GPA of 3.0 in last 60 hours, interview, 3 letters of recommendation; for doctorate, GRE General Test, master's degree, interview, 3 letters of recommendation, writing sample. Additional exam requirements/recommendations for international students: Required—TOEFL (minimum score 500 paper-based). *Application deadline:* For fall admission, 5/1 priority date for domestic students, 5/1 for international students. Application fee: $30. Electronic applications accepted. Tuition and fees vary according to course load, campus/location and program. *Financial support:* In 2016–17, 48 students received support, including 1 research assistantship (averaging $4,445 per year), 1 teaching assistantship (averaging $5,378 per year); career-related internships or fieldwork, Federal Work-Study, scholarships/grants, tuition waivers (partial), and unspecified assistantships also available. Support available to part-time students. Financial award application deadline: 4/1; financial award applicants required to submit FAFSA. *Faculty research:* Counseling: ethics; lesbian, bisexual and transgender issues; educational leadership: school culture and climate; educational assessment and accountability; school safety and student discipline. *Total annual research expenditures:* $45,589. *Unit head:* Dr. Liz Gregg, Chair, 904-620-5199, E-mail: liz.gregg@unf.edu. *Application contact:* Dr. Amanda Pascale, Director, The Graduate School, 904-620-1360, Fax: 904-620-1362, E-mail: graduateschool@unf.edu.
Website: http://www.unf.edu/coehs/lscsm/

University of North Georgia, College of Education, Dahlonega, GA 30597. Offers early childhood education (M Ed); middle grades education (M Ed, MAT); physical education (MS); school leadership (Ed S); secondary education (M Ed), including English education, history education, mathematics education, physical education. *Accreditation:* NCATE. *Program availability:* Part-time, evening/weekend, online learning. *Faculty:* 16 full-time (12 women), 3 part-time/adjunct (all women). *Students:* 11 full-time (8 women), 146 part-time (107 women); includes 19 minority (10 Black or African American, non-Hispanic/Latino; 2 Asian, non-Hispanic/Latino; 6 Hispanic/Latino; 1 Two or more races, non-Hispanic/Latino). Average age 28. 77 applicants, 83% accepted, 47 enrolled. In 2016, 79 master's awarded. *Degree requirements:* For master's, comprehensive exam, thesis optional. *Entrance requirements:* For master's, GRE or MAT, GACE, minimum GPA of 2.75; for Ed S, GRE General Test or MAT, 3 years of teaching experience, master's degree, minimum graduate GPA of 3.25, leadership position in the school. Additional exam requirements/recommendations for international students: Required—TOEFL (minimum score 550 paper-based; 79 iBT), IELTS (minimum score 6.5). *Application deadline:* For fall admission, 8/1 priority date for domestic students, 7/1 priority date for international students; for spring admission, 12/1 priority date for domestic students, 11/1 priority date for international students. Applications are processed on a rolling basis. Application fee: $40. Electronic applications accepted. *Expenses:* Contact institution. *Financial support:* Teaching assistantships, career-related internships or fieldwork, scholarships/grants, and unspecified assistantships available. Financial award application deadline: 5/1; financial award applicants required to submit CSS PROFILE or FAFSA. *Unit head:* Dr. Susan Ayers, Dean, College of Education, 706-864-1998, E-mail: susan.ayres@ung.edu. *Application contact:* Regina Boling, Teacher Education Graduate Admissions, 706-864-1533, E-mail: regina.boling@ung.edu.
Website: http://ung.edu/college-of-education/

University of North Texas, Robert B. Toulouse School of Graduate Studies, Denton, TX 76203-5459. Offers accounting (MS); applied anthropology (MA, MS); applied behavior analysis (Certificate); applied geography (MA); applied technology and performance improvement (M Ed, MS); art education (MA); art history (MA); art museum education (Certificate); arts leadership (Certificate); audiology (Au D); behavior analysis (MS); behavioral science (PhD); biochemistry and molecular biology (MS); biology (MA, MS); biomedical engineering (MS); business analysis (MS); chemistry (MS); clinical health psychology (PhD); communication studies (MA, MS); computer engineering (MS); computer science (MS); counseling (M Ed, MS), including clinical mental health counseling (MS), college and university counseling, elementary school counseling, secondary school counseling; creative writing (MA); criminal justice (MS); curriculum and instruction (M Ed); decision sciences (MBA); design (MA, MFA), including fashion design (MFA), innovation studies, interior design (MFA); early childhood studies (MS); economics (MS); educational leadership (M Ed, Ed D); educational psychology (MS, PhD), including family studies (MS), gifted and talented (MS), human development (MS), learning and cognition (MS), research, measurement and evaluation (MS); electrical engineering (MS); emergency management (MPA); engineering technology (MS); English (MA); English as a second language (MA); environmental science (MS); finance (MBA, MS); financial management (MPA); French (MA); health services management (MBA); higher education (M Ed, Ed D); history (MA, MS); hospitality management (MS); human resources management (MPA); information science (MS); information systems (PhD); information technologies (MBA); interdisciplinary studies (MA, MS); international studies (MA); international sustainable tourism (MS); jazz studies (MM); journalism (MA, MJ, Graduate Certificate), including interactive and virtual digital communication (Graduate Certificate), narrative journalism (Graduate Certificate), public relations (Graduate Certificate); kinesiology (MS); linguistics (MA); local government management (MPA); logistics (PhD); logistics and supply chain management (MBA); long-term care, senior housing, and aging services (MA); management (PhD); marketing (MBA); mathematics (MA, MS); mechanical and energy engineering (MS, PhD); music (MA), including ethnomusicology, music theory, musicology, performance; music composition (PhD); music education (MM Ed, PhD); nonprofit management (MPA); operations and supply chain management (MBA); performance (MM, DMA); philosophy (MA); political science (MA); professional and technical communication (MA); radio, television and film (MA, MFA); rehabilitation counseling (Certificate); sociology (MA); Spanish (MA); special education (M Ed); speech-language pathology (MA); strategic management (MBA); studio art (MFA); teaching (M Ed); MBA/MS. *Program availability:* Part-time, evening/weekend, online learning. Terminal master's awarded for partial completion of doctoral program. *Degree requirements:* For master's, variable foreign language requirement, comprehensive exam (for some programs), thesis (for some programs); for doctorate, variable foreign language requirement, comprehensive exam (for some programs), thesis/dissertation; for other advanced degree, variable foreign language requirement, comprehensive exam (for some programs). *Entrance requirements:* For master's and doctorate, GRE, GMAT. Additional exam requirements/recommendations for international students: Required—TOEFL (minimum score 550 paper-based; 79 iBT). Electronic applications accepted.

University of North Texas at Dallas, Graduate School, Dallas, TX 75241. Offers accounting (MBA); counseling (M Ed, MS); criminal justice (MS); curriculum and instruction (M Ed); educational administration (M Ed); human resources and organizational behavior (MBA); public leadership (MS); strategic management (MBA).

University of Oklahoma, Jeannine Rainbolt College of Education, Department of Educational Leadership and Policy Studies, Program in Educational Administration, Curriculum and Supervision, Norman, OK 73019. Offers M Ed, Ed D, PhD. *Accreditation:* NCATE. *Program availability:* Part-time, evening/weekend, blended/hybrid learning. *Students:* 28 full-time (22 women), 152 part-time (108 women); includes 55 minority (17 Black or African American, non-Hispanic/Latino; 13 American Indian or Alaska Native, non-Hispanic/Latino; 14 Hispanic/Latino; 11 Two or more races, non-Hispanic/Latino), 1 international. Average age 36. 42 applicants, 86% accepted, 30 enrolled. In 2016, 48 master's, 9 doctorates awarded. *Degree requirements:* For master's, comprehensive exam, thesis (for some programs); for doctorate, comprehensive exam, thesis/dissertation. *Entrance requirements:* For doctorate, GRE. Additional exam requirements/recommendations for international students: Required—TOEFL (minimum score 79 iBT) or IELTS (minimum score 6.5). *Application deadline:* Applications are processed on a rolling basis. Application fee: $50 ($100 for international students). Electronic applications accepted. *Expenses:* Tuition, state resident: full-time $4886; part-time $203.60 per credit hour. Tuition, nonresident: full-time $18,989; part-

time $791.20 per credit hour. *Required fees:* $3283; $126.25 per credit hour. $126.50 per semester. *Financial support:* In 2016–17, 74 students received support. Fellowships, research assistantships, teaching assistantships, career-related internships or fieldwork, Federal Work-Study, institutionally sponsored loans, scholarships/grants, health care benefits, tuition waivers, and unspecified assistantships available. Support available to part-time students. Financial award application deadline: 6/1; financial award applicants required to submit FAFSA. *Faculty research:* Improvement science; leadership and ethics; education and social policy; gender and equity; organizational reform and change. *Unit head:* John Jones, Associate Professor, 405-325-4165, E-mail: jjones@ou.edu.
Website: http://www.ou.edu/education/elps

University of Oklahoma, Jeannine Rainbolt College of Education, Department of Instructional Leadership and Academic Curriculum, Norman, OK 73019. Offers instructional leadership and academic curriculum (M Ed, PhD), including biomedical education (PhD), early childhood education, elementary education (M Ed), English education, instructional leadership, mathematics education, reading education, science education, social studies education, world languages education (M Ed). *Accreditation:* NCATE. *Program availability:* Part-time. *Faculty:* 19 full-time (15 women), 1 (woman) part-time/adjunct. *Students:* 66 full-time (49 women), 116 part-time (88 women); includes 49 minority (12 Black or African American, non-Hispanic/Latino; 6 American Indian or Alaska Native, non-Hispanic/Latino; 6 Asian, non-Hispanic/Latino; 11 Hispanic/Latino; 1 Native Hawaiian or other Pacific Islander, non-Hispanic/Latino; 13 Two or more races, non-Hispanic/Latino), 13 international. Average age 35. 38 applicants, 97% accepted, 28 enrolled. In 2016, 33 master's, 10 doctorates awarded. Terminal master's awarded for partial completion of doctoral program. *Degree requirements:* For master's, comprehensive exam (for some programs), thesis (for some programs); for doctorate, comprehensive exam (for some programs), thesis/dissertation. *Entrance requirements:* For doctorate, GRE. Additional exam requirements/recommendations for international students: Required—TOEFL (minimum score 79 iBT) or IELTS (minimum score 6.5). Application fee: $50 ($100 for international students). Electronic applications accepted. *Expenses:* Tuition, state resident: full-time $4886; part-time $203.60 per credit hour. Tuition, nonresident: full-time $18,989; part-time $791.20 per credit hour. *Required fees:* $3283; $126.25 per credit hour. $126.50 per semester. *Financial support:* In 2016–17, 112 students received support, including 7 research assistantships with partial tuition reimbursements available (averaging $10,373 per year), 6 teaching assistantships with partial tuition reimbursements available (averaging $11,446 per year); fellowships, scholarships/grants, and unspecified assistantships also available. Financial award application deadline: 6/1; financial award applicants required to submit FAFSA. *Faculty research:* Teacher preparation; instruction; curriculum; learning; constructivist theory. *Total annual research expenditures:* $165,297. *Unit head:* Dr. Stacy Reeder, Chair, 405-325-1498, Fax: 405-325-4061, E-mail: reeder@ou.edu. *Application contact:* Anna Steele, Graduate Programs Officer, 405-325-4525, E-mail: anna.steele@ou.edu.
Website: http://www.ou.edu/education/ilac

University of Pennsylvania, Graduate School of Education, Division of Teaching, Learning, and Leadership, Program in Educational Leadership, Philadelphia, PA 19104. Offers MS Ed, Ed D, PhD. *Program availability:* Part-time. *Students:* 19 full-time (10 women), 1 part-time (0 women); includes 7 minority (3 Asian, non-Hispanic/Latino; 4 Two or more races, non-Hispanic/Latino). Average age 36. 36 applicants, 6% accepted, 1 enrolled. In 2016, 1 doctorate awarded. *Entrance requirements:* For master's, GRE or MAT; for doctorate, GRE. *Expenses: Tuition:* Full-time $31,068; part-time $5762 per course. *Required fees:* $3200; $336 per course. Full-time tuition and fees vary according to degree level, program and student level. Part-time tuition and fees vary according to course load, degree level and program.

University of Pennsylvania, Graduate School of Education, Division of Teaching, Learning, and Leadership, Program in School Leadership, Philadelphia, PA 19104. Offers MS Ed. *Program availability:* Part-time, evening/weekend. *Students:* 36 full-time (21 women), 10 part-time (8 women); includes 14 minority (5 Black or African American, non-Hispanic/Latino; 4 Asian, non-Hispanic/Latino; 5 Hispanic/Latino). Average age 35. 87 applicants, 64% accepted, 47 enrolled. In 2016, 24 master's awarded. *Degree requirements:* For master's, thesis. *Entrance requirements:* For master's, bachelor's degree. Additional exam requirements/recommendations for international students: Required—TOEFL, IELTS. *Application deadline:* Applications are processed on a rolling basis. Application fee: $75. Electronic applications accepted. *Expenses: Tuition:* Full-time $31,068; part-time $5762 per course. *Required fees:* $3200; $336 per course. Full-time tuition and fees vary according to degree level, program and student level. Part-time tuition and fees vary according to course load, degree level and program. *Financial support:* In 2016–17, 27 students received support. Scholarships/grants available. *Faculty research:* Governance issues in schools, teacher professional development, independent schools, leadership identification and development, curriculum innovation and design. *Unit head:* Dr. Earl Ball, Director. *Application contact:* Amara Rockar, Administrative Coordinator, 215-746-2718, E-mail: arockar@upenn.edu.
Website: http://www.gse.upenn.edu/tll/slp

University of Pennsylvania, Graduate School of Education, Division of Teaching, Learning, and Leadership, Program in Teaching, Learning, and Leadership, Philadelphia, PA 19104. Offers educational leadership (MS Ed); teaching and learning (MS Ed). *Program availability:* Part-time. *Students:* 75 full-time (45 women), 31 part-time (26 women); includes 39 minority (16 Black or African American, non-Hispanic/Latino; 10 Asian, non-Hispanic/Latino; 9 Hispanic/Latino; 4 Two or more races, non-Hispanic/Latino), 12 international. Average age 34. 240 applicants, 44% accepted, 71 enrolled. In 2016, 24 master's awarded. *Expenses: Tuition:* Full-time $31,068; part-time $5762 per course. *Required fees:* $3200; $336 per course. Full-time tuition and fees vary according to degree level, program and student level. Part-time tuition and fees vary according to course load, degree level and program.

University of Pennsylvania, Graduate School of Education, Mid-Career Doctoral Program in Educational Leadership, Philadelphia, PA 19104. Offers Ed D. *Program availability:* Evening/weekend. *Students:* 91 full-time (54 women), 2 part-time (0 women); includes 47 minority (28 Black or African American, non-Hispanic/Latino; 3 Asian, non-Hispanic/Latino; 11 Hispanic/Latino; 5 Two or more races, non-Hispanic/Latino), 1 international. Average age 43. 81 applicants, 49% accepted, 24 enrolled. In 2016, 19 doctorates awarded. *Degree requirements:* For doctorate, comprehensive exam, thesis/dissertation. *Entrance requirements:* For doctorate, master's degree. *Application deadline:* For summer admission, 2/1 priority date for domestic and international students. Application fee: $75. Electronic applications accepted. *Expenses: Tuition:* Full-time $31,068; part-time $5762 per course. *Required fees:* $3200; $336 per course. Full-time tuition and fees vary according to degree level, program and student level. Part-time tuition and fees vary according to course load, degree level and program. *Faculty research:* Educational leadership, district reform, team effectiveness, identity development and social identification, racial/ethnic socialization and negotiation. *Unit head:* Martha Williams, Program Coordinator, 215-746-6573, E-mail: marthaw@upenn.edu.
Website: http://www2.gse.upenn.edu/midcareer/

University of Pennsylvania, Graduate School of Education, Penn Chief Learning Officer (CLO) Executive Doctoral Program, Philadelphia, PA 19104. Offers Ed D. *Program availability:* Evening/weekend. *Students:* 60 full-time (23 women); includes 21 minority (13 Black or African American, non-Hispanic/Latino; 5 Asian, non-Hispanic/Latino; 2 Hispanic/Latino; 1 Two or more races, non-Hispanic/Latino), 9 international. Average age 47. 43 applicants, 58% accepted, 24 enrolled. In 2016, 6 doctorates awarded. Terminal master's awarded for partial completion of doctoral program. *Degree requirements:* For doctorate, comprehensive exam, thesis/dissertation. *Entrance requirements:* For doctorate, bachelor's degree. *Application deadline:* For fall admission, 7/1 priority date for domestic and international students; for spring admission, 10/1 priority date for domestic and international students; for summer admission, 3/2 priority date for domestic and international students. Applications are processed on a rolling basis. Application fee: $75. Electronic applications accepted. *Expenses: Tuition:* Full-time $31,068; part-time $5762 per course. *Required fees:* $3200; $336 per course. Full-time tuition and fees vary according to degree level, program and student level. Part-time tuition and fees vary according to course load, degree level and program. *Faculty research:* Strategic leadership, workplace learning, business acumen, evidenced-best decision making, technology in the work place. *Unit head:* Elizabeth Ulivella, Associate Director, 215-573-0591, E-mail: ulivella@upenn.edu.
Website: http://www.pennclo.com/

University of Phoenix–Bay Area Campus, College of Education, San Jose, CA 95134-1805. Offers administration and supervision (MA Ed); adult education and training (MA Ed); early childhood education (MA Ed); education (Ed S); educational leadership (Ed D); elementary teacher education (MA Ed); higher education administration (PhD); secondary teacher education (MA Ed); special education (MA Ed); teacher leadership (MA Ed). *Program availability:* Evening/weekend, online learning. *Degree requirements:* For master's, thesis (for some programs). *Entrance requirements:* For master's, minimum undergraduate GPA of 2.5, 3 years of work experience. Additional exam requirements/recommendations for international students: Required—TOEFL (minimum score 550 paper-based; 79 iBT). Electronic applications accepted.

University of Phoenix–Colorado Campus, College of Education, Lone Tree, CO 80124-5453. Offers administration and supervision (MAEd); curriculum instruction (MAEd); elementary teacher education (MAEd); school counseling (MSC); secondary teacher education (MAEd). *Program availability:* Evening/weekend. *Degree requirements:* For master's, thesis (for some programs). *Entrance requirements:* For master's, minimum undergraduate GPA of 2.5, 3 years work experience. Additional exam requirements/recommendations for international students: Required—TOEFL (minimum score 550 paper-based; 79 iBT). Electronic applications accepted.

University of Phoenix–Colorado Springs Downtown Campus, College of Education, Colorado Springs, CO 80903. Offers administration and supervision (MA Ed); curriculum and instruction (MA Ed); elementary teacher education (MA Ed); principal licensure certification (Certificate); school counseling (MSC); secondary teacher education (MA Ed). *Program availability:* Evening/weekend. *Degree requirements:* For master's, thesis (for some programs). *Entrance requirements:* For master's, minimum undergraduate GPA of 2.5, 3 years of work experience. Additional exam requirements/recommendations for international students: Required—TOEFL (minimum score 550 paper-based; 79 iBT). Electronic applications accepted.

University of Phoenix–Hawaii Campus, College of Education, Honolulu, HI 96813-3800. Offers administration and supervision (MA Ed); curriculum and instruction (MA Ed); elementary education (MA Ed); secondary education (MA Ed); special education (MA Ed); teacher education for elementary licensure (MA Ed). *Program availability:* Evening/weekend. *Degree requirements:* For master's, thesis (for some programs). *Entrance requirements:* For master's, minimum undergraduate GPA of 2.5, 3 years of work experience. Additional exam requirements/recommendations for international students: Required—TOEFL (minimum score 550 paper-based; 79 iBT). Electronic applications accepted.

University of Phoenix–Las Vegas Campus, College of Education, Las Vegas, NV 89135. Offers administration and supervision (MA Ed); curriculum and instruction (MA Ed); school counseling (MSC); teacher education-elementary licensure (MA Ed). *Program availability:* Evening/weekend. *Degree requirements:* For master's, thesis (for some programs). *Entrance requirements:* For master's, minimum undergraduate GPA of 2.5, 3 years of work experience. Additional exam requirements/recommendations for international students: Required—TOEFL (minimum score 550 paper-based; 79 iBT). Electronic applications accepted.

University of Phoenix–New Mexico Campus, College of Education, Albuquerque, NM 87113-1570. Offers administration and supervision (MAEd); curriculum and instruction (MAEd); elementary teacher education (MAEd); school counseling (MSC); secondary teacher education (MAEd). *Program availability:* Evening/weekend. *Degree requirements:* For master's, thesis (for some programs). *Entrance requirements:* For master's, minimum undergraduate GPA of 2.5, 3 years of work experience. Additional exam requirements/recommendations for international students: Required—TOEFL (minimum score 550 paper-based; 79 iBT). Electronic applications accepted.

University of Phoenix–North Florida Campus, College of Education, Jacksonville, FL 32216-0959. Offers administration and supervision (MA Ed); curriculum and instruction (MA Ed), including computer education, mathematics education; early childhood education (MA Ed); elementary teacher education (MA Ed); secondary teacher education (MA Ed). *Program availability:* Evening/weekend. *Degree requirements:* For master's, thesis (for some programs). *Entrance requirements:* For master's, 3 years of work experience, minimum undergraduate GPA of 2.5. Additional exam requirements/recommendations for international students: Required—TOEFL (minimum score 550 paper-based; 49 iBT). Electronic applications accepted.

University of Phoenix–Online Campus, College of Education, Phoenix, AZ 85034-7209. Offers administration and supervision (MAEd, Certificate); adult education and training (MAEd); curriculum and instruction (MAEd), including computer education, curriculum and instruction, English as a second language, language arts, mathematics, reading; early childhood education (MAEd); educational studies (MAEd); elementary teacher education (MAEd), including early childhood, elementary teacher education, high school middle level, middle level; principal licensure (Certificate); secondary teacher education (MAEd); special education (MAEd, Certificate); teacher education (MAEd), including middle level generalist; teacher education middle level mathematics (MAEd), including middle level mathematics; teacher education middle level science (MAEd), including middle level science; teacher education secondary mathematics (MAEd); teacher education secondary science (MAEd); teacher leadership (MAEd); teachers of English learners (Certificate); transition to teaching (Certificate), including elementary education, secondary education. *Program availability:* Evening/weekend, online learning. *Entrance requirements:* Additional exam requirements/recommendations for international students: Required—TOEFL, TOEIC (Test of English as an International Communication), Berlitz Online English Proficiency Exam, PTE, or IELTS. Electronic applications accepted. *Expenses:* Contact institution.

University of Phoenix–Online Campus, School of Advanced Studies, Phoenix, AZ 85034-7209. Offers business administration (DBA); education (Ed S); educational leadership (Ed D), including curriculum and instruction, education technology, educational leadership; health administration (DHA); higher education administration (PhD); industrial/organizational psychology (PhD); nursing (PhD); organizational leadership (DM), including information systems and technology, organizational leadership. *Program availability:* Evening/weekend, online learning. *Degree requirements:* For doctorate, thesis/dissertation. *Entrance requirements:* Additional exam requirements/recommendations for international students: Required—TOEFL, TOEIC (Test of English as an International Communication), Berlitz Online English Proficiency Exam, PTE, or IELTS. Electronic applications accepted. *Expenses:* Contact institution.

University of Phoenix–Phoenix Campus, College of Education, Tempe, AZ 85282-2371. Offers administration and supervision (MA Ed); adult education and training (MA Ed); curriculum and instruction reading (MA Ed); early childhood education (MA Ed); education studies (MA Ed); elementary teacher education (MA Ed); secondary teacher education (MA Ed); special education (MA Ed); teacher leadership (MA Ed). *Program availability:* Evening/weekend, online learning. *Entrance requirements:* Additional exam requirements/recommendations for international students: Required—TOEFL, TOEIC (Test of English as an International Communication), Berlitz Online English Proficiency Exam, PTE, or IELTS. Electronic applications accepted. *Expenses:* Contact institution.

University of Phoenix–Southern Arizona Campus, College of Education, Tucson, AZ 85711. Offers administration and supervision (MA Ed); adult education and training (MA Ed); curriculum instruction (MA Ed); educational counseling (MA Ed); elementary teacher education (MA Ed); school counseling (MSC); secondary teacher education (MA Ed); special education (MA Ed, Certificate). *Program availability:* Evening/weekend. *Degree requirements:* For master's, thesis (for some programs). *Entrance requirements:* For master's, minimum undergraduate GPA of 2.5, 3 years of work experience. Additional exam requirements/recommendations for international students: Required—TOEFL (minimum score 550 paper-based; 79 iBT). Electronic applications accepted.

University of Phoenix–Southern California Campus, College of Education, Costa Mesa, CA 92626. Offers administration and supervision (MA Ed, Certificate); adult education and training (MA Ed); educational studies (MA Ed); elementary teacher education (MA Ed); secondary teacher education (MA Ed); teacher leadership (MA Ed); teachers of English learners (Certificate). *Program availability:* Evening/weekend, online learning. *Entrance requirements:* Additional exam requirements/recommendations for international students: Required—TOEFL, TOEIC (Test of English as an International Communication), Berlitz Online English Proficiency Exam, PTE, or IELTS. Electronic applications accepted. *Expenses:* Contact institution.

University of Phoenix–South Florida Campus, College of Education, Miramar, FL 33027-4145. Offers administration and supervision (MA Ed); curriculum and instruction (MA Ed), including computer education, curriculum and instruction, mathematics education; early childhood education (MA Ed); elementary teacher education (MA Ed); secondary teacher education (MA Ed). *Program availability:* Evening/weekend. *Degree requirements:* For master's, thesis (for some programs). *Entrance requirements:* For master's, 3 years of work experience, minimum undergraduate GPA of 2.5. Additional exam requirements/recommendations for international students: Required—TOEFL (minimum score 550 paper-based; 79 iBT). Electronic applications accepted.

University of Phoenix–Utah Campus, College of Education, Salt Lake City, UT 84123-4642. Offers administration and supervision (MA Ed); curriculum and instruction (MA Ed); elementary teacher education (MA Ed); school counseling (MSC); secondary teacher education (MA Ed); special education (MA Ed). *Program availability:* Evening/weekend. *Degree requirements:* For master's, thesis (for some programs). *Entrance requirements:* For master's, minimum undergraduate GPA of 2.5, 3 years work experience. Additional exam requirements/recommendations for international students: Required—TOEFL (minimum score 550 paper-based; 79 iBT). Electronic applications accepted.

University of Phoenix–Washington D.C. Campus, College of Education, Washington, DC 20001. Offers administration and supervision (MA Ed); adult education and training (MA Ed); computer education (MA Ed); curriculum and instruction (MA Ed, Ed D); early childhood education (MA Ed); education (Ed S); educational leadership (Ed D); educational technology (Ed D); elementary teacher education (MA Ed); English and language arts education (MA Ed); English as a second language (MA Ed); higher education administration (PhD); mathematics education (MA Ed); secondary teacher education (MA Ed); special education (MA Ed); teacher leadership (MA Ed).

University of Pikeville, Patton College of Education, Pikeville, KY 41501. Offers teacher leader (MA). *Program availability:* Part-time, evening/weekend. *Faculty:* 12 part-time/adjunct (9 women). *Students:* 71 full-time (61 women); includes 1 minority (Black or African American, non-Hispanic/Latino). Average age 35. *Degree requirements:* For master's, comprehensive exam. *Application deadline:* For fall admission, 8/15 for domestic students. Applications are processed on a rolling basis. Application fee: $50. *Expenses:* Contact institution. *Financial support:* Application deadline: 2/1; applicants required to submit FAFSA. *Unit head:* Coletta Parsley, Interim Dean, 606-218-5318, E-mail: colettaparsley@upike.edu. *Application contact:* Fairy Coleman, Administrative Assistant, 606-218-5314, E-mail: fairycoleman@upike.edu.
Website: http://www.upike.edu/COE/

University of Pittsburgh, School of Education, Department of Administrative and Policy Studies, Program in School Leadership, Pittsburgh, PA 15260. Offers M Ed, Ed D, PhD. *Program availability:* Part-time, evening/weekend. *Degree requirements:* For master's, thesis; for doctorate, thesis/dissertation. *Entrance requirements:* For doctorate, GRE General Test. Additional exam requirements/recommendations for international students: Required—TOEFL (minimum score 80 iBT). Electronic applications accepted. Tuition and fees vary according to program.

University of Portland, School of Education, Portland, OR 97203-5798. Offers education (MA, MAT); educational leadership (M Ed); English for speakers of other languages (M Ed); initial administrator licensure (M Ed); neuroeducation (M Ed, Ed D); organizational leadership and development (Ed D); reading (M Ed); school leadership and development (Ed D); special education (M Ed). M Ed also available through the Graduate Outreach Program for teachers residing in the Oregon and Washington state areas. *Accreditation:* NCATE. *Program availability:* Part-time, evening/weekend. *Entrance requirements:* For master's, minimum GPA of 3.0, teaching certificate, letters of recommendation, resume, statement of goals, official transcripts. Additional exam requirements/recommendations for international students: Required—TOEFL (minimum score 550 paper-based; 80 iBT), IELTS (minimum score 7). *Faculty research:* Multicultural education, supervision/leadership.

University of Prince Edward Island, Faculty of Education, Charlottetown, PE C1A 4P3, Canada. Offers leadership and learning (M Ed). *Program availability:* Part-time. *Degree requirements:* For master's, thesis. *Entrance requirements:* For master's, 2 years of professional experience, bachelor of education, professional certificate. Additional exam requirements/recommendations for international students: Required—TOEFL (minimum score 550 paper-based; 80 iBT), Canadian Academic English Language Assessment, Michigan English Language Assessment Battery, Canadian Test of English for Scholars and Trainees. *Faculty research:* Distance learning, aboriginal communities and education leadership development, international development, immersion language learning.

University of Puerto Rico, Río Piedras Campus, College of Education, Program in School Administration and Supervision, San Juan, PR 00931-3300. Offers M Ed, Ed D. *Program availability:* Part-time. *Degree requirements:* For master's, thesis; for doctorate, thesis/dissertation, internship. *Entrance requirements:* For master's, PAEG or GRE, minimum GPA of 3.0, letter of recommendation; for doctorate, GRE or PAEG, interview, master's degree, minimum GPA of 3.0, letter of recommendation.

University of Regina, Faculty of Graduate Studies and Research, Faculty of Education, Department of Educational Administration, Regina, SK S4S 0A2, Canada. Offers M Ed. *Program availability:* Part-time. *Faculty:* 4 full-time (2 women), 20 part-time/adjunct (11 women). *Students:* 5 full-time (2 women), 55 part-time (35 women). 20 applicants, 30% accepted. In 2016, 19 master's awarded. *Degree requirements:* For master's, thesis (for some programs), practicum, project, or thesis. *Entrance requirements:* For master's, bachelor's degree in education, 2 years of teaching or other relevant professional experience. Additional exam requirements/recommendations for international students: Required—TOEFL (minimum score 580 paper-based; 80 iBT), IELTS (minimum score 6.5), PTE (minimum score 59). *Application deadline:* For fall admission, 2/15 for domestic and international students; for winter admission, 10/15 for domestic and international students; for spring admission, 2/15 for domestic and international students. Application fee: $100. Electronic applications accepted. *Financial support:* In 2016–17, 2 fellowships (averaging $6,000 per year) were awarded; teaching assistantships also available. Financial award application deadline: 6/15. *Faculty research:* Legal aspects of school administration, economics of education, education planning, politics of education, administrative behavior in education. *Unit head:* Dr. Ken Montgomery, Associate Dean, Research and Graduate Programs in Education, 306-585-5031, Fax: 306-585-5387, E-mail: ken.montgomery@uregina.ca. *Application contact:* Tania Gates, Graduate Program Coordinator, 306-585-4506, Fax: 306-585-5387, E-mail: edgrad@uregina.ca.
Website: http://www.uregina.ca/education/

University of Rio Grande, Graduate School, Rio Grande, OH 45674. Offers athletic coaching leadership (M Ed); educational leadership (M Ed); integrated arts (M Ed); intervention specialist in early childhood (M Ed); intervention specialist in mild/moderate (M Ed). *Accreditation:* NCATE. *Program availability:* Part-time. *Degree requirements:* For master's, final research project, portfolio. *Entrance requirements:* For master's, minimum GPA of 2.7 in major, 2.5 overall. Additional exam requirements/recommendations for international students: Required—TOEFL. *Application deadline:* Applications are processed on a rolling basis. Application fee: $20. *Financial support:* Career-related internships or fieldwork available. Support available to part-time students. Financial award application deadline: 7/1; financial award applicants required to submit FAFSA. *Faculty research:* Interagency collaboration, reading and mathematics, learning styles, college access, literacy. *Unit head:* Dr. Greg Miller, Director, 740-245-7030, E-mail: gmiller@rio.edu. *Application contact:* Nancy Downs, Secretary, 740-245-7328, Fax: 740-245-7175, E-mail: ndowns@rio.edu.

University of Rochester, Margaret Warner Graduate School of Education and Human Development, Doctoral Programs in Education, Rochester, NY 14627. Offers counseling (Ed D); educational administration (Ed D); educational policy and theory (PhD); higher education (PhD); human development in educational context (PhD); teaching, curriculum, and change (PhD). *Expenses: Tuition:* Full-time $47,450; part-time $1482 per credit hour. *Required fees:* $528. Tuition and fees vary according to program.

University of Rochester, Margaret Warner Graduate School of Education and Human Development, Master's Program in School Leadership, Rochester, NY 14627. Offers MS. *Expenses: Tuition:* Full-time $47,450; part-time $1482 per credit hour. *Required fees:* $528. Tuition and fees vary according to program.

University of St. Francis, College of Education, Joliet, IL 60435-6169. Offers educational leadership (MS, Ed D); elementary education (M Ed); reading (MS); secondary education (M Ed), including English education, math education, science education, social studies education, visual arts education; special education (M Ed); teaching and learning (MS); TESOL (Certificate). *Accreditation:* NCATE. *Program availability:* Part-time, evening/weekend, 100% online, blended/hybrid learning. *Faculty:* 11 full-time (8 women), 60 part-time/adjunct (42 women). *Students:* 34 full-time (26 women), 420 part-time (318 women); includes 92 minority (51 Black or African American, non-Hispanic/Latino; 5 Asian, non-Hispanic/Latino; 31 Hispanic/Latino; 5 Two or more races, non-Hispanic/Latino), 4 international. Average age 36. 242 applicants, 48% accepted, 96 enrolled. In 2016, 229 master's, 44 doctorates, 10 other advanced degrees awarded. *Degree requirements:* For master's, comprehensive exam; for doctorate, thesis/dissertation. *Entrance requirements:* Additional exam requirements/recommendations for international students: Required—TOEFL (minimum score 550 paper-based; 79 iBT), IELTS (minimum score 6). *Application deadline:* Applications are processed on a rolling basis. Application fee: $30. Electronic applications accepted. Application fee is waived when completed online. *Expenses:* Contact institution. *Financial support:* In 2016–17, 48 students received support. Career-related internships or fieldwork and unspecified assistantships available. Support available to part-time students. Financial award applicants required to submit FAFSA. *Unit head:* Dr. John Gambro, Dean, 815-740-3829, Fax: 815-740-2264, E-mail: jgambro@stfrancis.edu. *Application contact:* Sandra Sloka, Director of Admissions for Graduate and Degree Completion Programs, 800-735-7500, Fax: 815-740-3431, E-mail: ssloka@stfrancis.edu.
Website: http://www.stfrancis.edu/academics/college-of-education/

University of St. Thomas, Graduate Studies, College of Education, Leadership and Counseling, Department of Leadership, Policy and Administration, St. Paul, MN 55105-1096. Offers education leadership and administration (MA); educational leadership and learning (Ed D); executive coaching (Certificate); K-12 administration (Ed S); leadership in student affairs (MA). *Program availability:* Part-time, evening/weekend. Terminal master's awarded for partial completion of doctoral program. *Degree requirements:* For master's, thesis (for some programs); for doctorate, thesis/dissertation; for other advanced degree, thesis or alternative. *Entrance requirements:* For master's, minimum GPA of 3.0 or MAT; for doctorate, MAT, minimum graduate GPA of 3.5; for other advanced degree, minimum graduate GPA of 3.25 or MAT. Additional exam requirements/recommendations for international students: Required—TOEFL (minimum score 550 paper-based). *Application deadline:* For fall admission, 7/15 priority date for domestic and international students; for spring admission, 12/9 priority date for domestic and international students; for summer admission, 4/3 priority date for domestic and international students. Applications are processed on a rolling basis. Electronic applications accepted. *Expenses:* Contact institution. *Financial support:* Fellowships, research assistantships, institutionally sponsored loans, and scholarships/grants available. Support available to part-time students. Financial award application deadline: 8/1; financial award applicants required to submit FAFSA. *Application contact:* Jackie Grossklaus, Department Assistant, 651-962-4885, Fax: 651-962-4169, E-mail: jmgrossklaus@stthomas.edu.

University of St. Thomas, School of Education and Human Services, Houston, TX 77006-4696. Offers all level education (M Ed); bilingual/dual language (M Ed); Catholic school teaching (M Ed); Catholic/private school leadership (M Ed); counselor education (M Ed); curriculum and instruction (M Ed); education (Ed D); educational leadership (M Ed); elementary teaching (M Ed); English as a second language (M Ed);

exceptionality/educational diagnostician (M Ed); exceptionality/special education (M Ed); generalist (M Ed); reading (M Ed); secondary teaching (M Ed); teaching (MAT). *Accreditation:* TEAC. *Program availability:* Part-time, evening/weekend, online learning. *Faculty:* 44 full-time (29 women), 31 part-time/adjunct (17 women). *Students:* 65 full-time (61 women), 719 part-time (645 women); includes 515 minority (169 Black or African American, non-Hispanic/Latino; 25 Asian, non-Hispanic/Latino; 315 Hispanic/Latino; 2 Native Hawaiian or other Pacific Islander, non-Hispanic/Latino; 4 Two or more races, non-Hispanic/Latino), 24 international. Average age 36. 297 applicants, 92% accepted, 211 enrolled. In 2016, 403 master's awarded. *Degree requirements:* For master's, thesis, field experience. *Entrance requirements:* For master's, GRE or MAT if GPA is below 3.0, bachelor's degree; minimum GPA of 2.75 in bachelor's degree or last 60 credit hours; official transcripts from all institutions; goal statement of 250-300 words; 1 reference. Additional exam requirements/recommendations for international students: Required—TOEFL (minimum score 94 iBT), IELTS (minimum score 7), PTE (minimum score 53). *Application deadline:* Applications are processed on a rolling basis. Application fee: $35. Electronic applications accepted. *Expenses:* Contact institution. *Financial support:* In 2016–17, 52 students received support. Federal Work-Study, scholarships/grants, and state work-study, institutional employment available. Support available to part-time students. Financial award application deadline: 4/15; financial award applicants required to submit FAFSA. *Faculty research:* Leadership, diversity, personality traits, second language acquisition. *Unit head:* Dr. Robert LeBlanc, Dean, 713-525-3540, Fax: 713-525-3871, E-mail: education@stthom.edu. *Application contact:* Rita Paredes, Administrative Assistant, 713-525-3442, Fax: 713-525-3871, E-mail: rparede@stthom.edu.
Website: http://www.stthom.edu/Academics/School_of_Education_and_Human_Services/Index.aqf

University of San Diego, School of Leadership and Education Sciences, Department of Leadership Studies, San Diego, CA 92110-2492. Offers higher education leadership (MA); leadership studies (MA, PhD, Certificate); nonprofit leadership and management (MA). *Program availability:* Part-time, evening/weekend. *Faculty:* 11 full-time (5 women), 17 part-time/adjunct (9 women). *Students:* 40 full-time (26 women), 219 part-time (149 women); includes 120 minority (28 Black or African American, non-Hispanic/Latino; 15 Asian, non-Hispanic/Latino; 62 Hispanic/Latino; 2 Native Hawaiian or other Pacific Islander, non-Hispanic/Latino; 13 Two or more races, non-Hispanic/Latino), 21 international. Average age 33. 312 applicants, 75% accepted, 110 enrolled. In 2016, 57 master's, 21 doctorates awarded. *Degree requirements:* For master's, thesis (for some programs), international experience; for doctorate, comprehensive exam, thesis/dissertation, international experience. *Entrance requirements:* For master's, GRE (recommended with GPA less than 3.25), minimum GPA of 3.0, interview; for doctorate, GRE (less than 5 years old), master's degree, minimum GPA of 3.5 (recommended), resume. Additional exam requirements/recommendations for international students: Required—TOEFL (minimum score 580 paper-based; 83 iBT), TWE. Application fee: $45. Electronic applications accepted. *Financial support:* In 2016–17, 186 students received support. Career-related internships or fieldwork, Federal Work-Study, institutionally sponsored loans, unspecified assistantships, and stipends available. Support available to part-time students. Financial award application deadline: 4/1; financial award applicants required to submit FAFSA. *Faculty research:* Higher education administration policy and relations, organizational leadership, nonprofits and philanthropy, student affairs leadership. *Unit head:* Dr. Lea Hubbard, Graduate Program Director, 619-260-7818, E-mail: lhubbard@sandiego.edu. *Application contact:* Monica Mahon, Associate Director of Graduate Admissions, 619-260-4524, Fax: 619-260-4158, E-mail: grads@sandiego.edu.
Website: https://www.sandiego.edu/soles/departments/leadership-studies/

University of San Diego, School of Leadership and Education Sciences, Department of Learning and Teaching, San Diego, CA 92110-2492. Offers inclusive learning (M Ed); literacy and digital learning (M Ed); school leadership (M Ed); special education with deaf and hard of hearing (M Ed); STEAM (science, technology, engineering, arts, and mathematics) (M Ed); teaching (MAT); TESOL, literacy and culture (M Ed). *Program availability:* Part-time, evening/weekend. *Faculty:* 9 full-time (7 women), 29 part-time/adjunct (19 women). *Students:* 161 full-time (126 women), 188 part-time (153 women); includes 127 minority (4 Black or African American, non-Hispanic/Latino; 24 Asian, non-Hispanic/Latino; 86 Hispanic/Latino; 1 Native Hawaiian or other Pacific Islander, non-Hispanic/Latino; 12 Two or more races, non-Hispanic/Latino), 20 international. Average age 33. 383 applicants, 83% accepted, 194 enrolled. In 2016, 114 master's awarded. *Degree requirements:* For master's, thesis (for some programs), international experience. *Entrance requirements:* For master's, California Basic Educational Skills Test, California Subject Examination for Teachers, minimum GPA of 2.75. Additional exam requirements/recommendations for international students: Required—TOEFL (minimum score 580 paper-based; 83 iBT), TWE. *Application deadline:* Applications are processed on a rolling basis. Application fee: $45. Electronic applications accepted. *Financial support:* In 2016–17, 46 students received support. Career-related internships or fieldwork, Federal Work-Study, institutionally sponsored loans, and stipends available. Financial award application deadline: 4/1; financial award applicants required to submit FAFSA. *Faculty research:* Action research methodology, cultural studies, instructional theories and practices, second language acquisition, school reform. *Unit head:* Dr. Maya Kalyanpur, Chair, 619-260-7655, E-mail: mkalyanpur@sandiego.edu. *Application contact:* Monica Mahon, Associate Director of Graduate Admissions, 619-260-4524, Fax: 619-260-4158, E-mail: grads@sandiego.edu.
Website: http://www.sandiego.edu/soles/departments/learning-and-teaching/

University of San Francisco, School of Education, Catholic Educational Leadership Program, San Francisco, CA 94117-1080. Offers Catholic school leadership (Ed D). *Program availability:* Part-time, evening/weekend. *Faculty:* 1 (woman) part-time/adjunct. *Students:* 14 full-time (6 women), 15 part-time (6 women); includes 6 minority (1 Black or African American, non-Hispanic/Latino; 2 Asian, non-Hispanic/Latino; 2 Hispanic/Latino; 1 Two or more races, non-Hispanic/Latino), 7 international. Average age 38. 7 applicants, 100% accepted, 4 enrolled. In 2016, 16 master's, 5 doctorates awarded. *Degree requirements:* For doctorate, thesis/dissertation. *Entrance requirements:* Additional exam requirements/recommendations for international students: Required—TOEFL, IELTS, PTE. Application fee: $55 ($65 for international students). Electronic applications accepted. *Expenses: Tuition:* Full-time $23,310; part-time $1295 per credit. Tuition and fees vary according to course load, degree level, campus/location and program. *Financial support:* In 2016–17, 9 students received support. Fellowships, research assistantships, and teaching assistantships available. Financial award application deadline: 3/2; financial award applicants required to submit FAFSA. *Unit head:* Dr. Patricia Mitchell, Chair, 415-422-6226. *Application contact:* Peter Cole, Admission Coordinator, 415-422-5467, E-mail: schoolofeducation@usfca.edu.
Website: https://www.usfca.edu/catalog/graduate/school-of-education/programs-catholic-educational-leadership

University of San Francisco, School of Education, Leadership Studies Program, San Francisco, CA 94117-1080. Offers MA, Ed D. *Program availability:* Part-time, evening/weekend. *Faculty:* 9 full-time (7 women), 5 part-time/adjunct (3 women). *Students:* 121 full-time (79 women), 38 part-time (27 women); includes 102 minority (30 Black or African American, non-Hispanic/Latino; 29 Asian, non-Hispanic/Latino; 31 Hispanic/Latino; 3 Native Hawaiian or other Pacific Islander, non-Hispanic/Latino; 9 Two or more races, non-Hispanic/Latino), 14 international. Average age 33. 171 applicants, 73% accepted, 51 enrolled. In 2016, 50 master's, 11 doctorates awarded. *Degree requirements:* For doctorate, thesis/dissertation. *Entrance requirements:* Additional exam requirements/recommendations for international students: Required—TOEFL, IELTS, PTE. *Application deadline:* For fall admission, 3/1 priority date for domestic and international students; for spring admission, 10/15 priority date for domestic and international students. Applications are processed on a rolling basis. Application fee: $55 ($65 for international students). Electronic applications accepted. *Expenses: Tuition:* Full-time $23,310; part-time $1295 per credit. Tuition and fees vary according to course load, degree level, campus/location and program. *Financial support:* In 2016–17, 33 students received support. Fellowships, research assistantships, and teaching assistantships available. Financial award application deadline: 3/2; financial award applicants required to submit FAFSA. *Unit head:* Dr. Patricia Mitchell, Chair, 415-422-6551. *Application contact:* Peter Cole, Admission Coordinator, 415-422-5467, E-mail: schoolofeducation@usfca.edu.
Website: https://www.usfca.edu/catalog/graduate/school-of-education/programs-organization-and-leadership

University of Saskatchewan, College of Graduate Studies and Research, College of Education, Department of Educational Administration, Saskatoon, SK S7N 5A2, Canada. Offers M Ed, PhD, Diploma. *Program availability:* Part-time. *Degree requirements:* For master's, thesis (for some programs); for doctorate, comprehensive exam (for some programs), thesis/dissertation. *Entrance requirements:* Additional exam requirements/recommendations for international students: Required—TOEFL (minimum score 80 iBT); Recommended—IELTS (minimum score 6.5). Electronic applications accepted.

The University of Scranton, Panuska College of Professional Studies, Department of Education, Program in Educational Administration, Scranton, PA 18510. Offers MS. *Accreditation:* NCATE. *Program availability:* Part-time, evening/weekend, online only, 100% online.

University of Sioux Falls, Fredrikson School of Education, Sioux Falls, SD 57105-1699. Offers educational administration (Ed S), including principal leadership, superintendent and district leadership; leadership in reading (M Ed); leadership in schools (M Ed); leadership in technology (M Ed); teaching (M Ed). Admission in summer only. *Accreditation:* NCATE. *Program availability:* Part-time, evening/weekend. *Degree requirements:* For master's, comprehensive exam (for some programs), research application project; for Ed S, comprehensive exam, portfolio. *Entrance requirements:* For master's, minimum GPA of 3.0, 1 year of teaching experience; for Ed S, minimum 3 years of teaching experience, minimum cumulative GPA of 3.5, 1 year of administrative experience. Additional exam requirements/recommendations for international students: Required—TOEFL. *Faculty research:* Reading, literacy, leadership.

University of South Africa, College of Human Sciences, Pretoria, South Africa. Offers adult education (M Ed); African languages (MA, PhD); African politics (MA, PhD); Afrikaans (MA, PhD); ancient history (MA, PhD); ancient Near Eastern studies (MA, PhD); anthropology (MA, PhD); applied linguistics (MA); Arabic (MA, PhD); archaeology (MA); art history (MA); Biblical archaeology (MA); Biblical studies (M Th, D Th, PhD); Christian spirituality (M Th, D Th); church history (M Th, D Th); classical studies (MA, PhD); clinical psychology (MA); communication (MA, PhD); comparative education (M Ed, Ed D); consulting psychology (D Admin, D Com, PhD); curriculum studies (M Ed, Ed D); development studies (M Admin, MA, D Admin, PhD); didactics (M Ed, Ed D); education (M Tech); education management (M Ed, Ed D); educational psychology (M Ed); English (MA); environmental education (M Ed); French (MA, PhD); German (MA, PhD); Greek (MA); guidance and counseling (M Ed); health studies (MA, PhD), including health sciences education (MA), health services management (MA), medical and surgical nursing science (critical care general) (MA), midwifery and neonatal nursing science (MA), trauma and emergency care (MA); history (MA, PhD); history of education (Ed D); inclusive education (M Ed, Ed D); information and communications technology policy and regulation (MA); information science (MA, MIS, PhD); international politics (MA, PhD); Islamic studies (MA, PhD); Italian (MA, PhD); Judaica (MA, PhD); linguistics (MA, PhD); mathematical education (M Ed); mathematics education (MA); missiology (M Th, D Th); modern Hebrew (MA, PhD); musicology (MA, MMus, D Mus, PhD); natural science education (M Ed); New Testament (M Th, D Th); Old Testament (D Th); pastoral therapy (M Th, D Th); philosophy (MA); philosophy of education (M Ed, Ed D); politics (MA, PhD); Portuguese (MA, PhD); practical theology (M Th, D Th); psychology (MA, MS, PhD); psychology of education (M Ed, Ed D); public health (MA); religious studies (MA, D Th, PhD); Romance languages (MA); Russian (MA, PhD); Semitic languages (MA, PhD); social behavior studies in HIV/AIDS (MA); social science (mental health) (MA); social science in development studies (MA); social science in psychology (MA); social science in social work (MA); social science in sociology (MA); social work (MSW, DSW, PhD); socio-education (M Ed, Ed D); sociolinguistics (MA); sociology (MA, PhD); Spanish (MA, PhD); systematic theology (M Th, D Th); TESOL (teaching English to speakers of other languages) (MA); theological ethics (M Th, D Th); theory of literature (MA, PhD); urban ministries (D Th); urban ministry (M Th).

University of South Alabama, College of Education and Professional Studies, Department of Leadership and Teacher Education, Mobile, AL 36688. Offers art education (M Ed); early childhood education (M Ed); educational leadership (M Ed, Ed D); elementary education (M Ed); reading education (M Ed); science education (M Ed); secondary education (M Ed); special education (M Ed). *Accreditation:* NCATE. *Program availability:* Part-time, 100% online, blended/hybrid learning. *Faculty:* 16 full-time (12 women), 6 part-time/adjunct (3 women). *Students:* 198 full-time (150 women), 77 part-time (58 women); includes 77 minority (61 Black or African American, non-Hispanic/Latino; 2 American Indian or Alaska Native, non-Hispanic/Latino; 2 Asian, non-Hispanic/Latino; 7 Hispanic/Latino; 1 Native Hawaiian or other Pacific Islander, non-Hispanic/Latino; 4 Two or more races, non-Hispanic/Latino). Average age 34. 153 applicants, 53% accepted, 69 enrolled. In 2016, 80 master's, 1 doctorate awarded. *Degree requirements:* For master's, comprehensive exam, thesis (for some programs); for doctorate, comprehensive exam, thesis/dissertation. *Entrance requirements:* For master's, GRE General Test or MAT, minimum GPA of 3.0; for doctorate, GRE, minimum graduate GPA of 3.25, 3 years of experience in field, 3 letters of recommendation, interview, official transcripts. Additional exam requirements/recommendations for international students: Required—TOEFL. *Application deadline:* For fall admission, 7/15 for domestic students; for spring admission, 11/15 for domestic students; for summer admission, 4/15 for domestic students. Applications are processed on a rolling basis. Application fee: $35. Electronic applications accepted. *Expenses:* Tuition, state resident: full-time $9768; part-time $407 per credit hour. Tuition, nonresident: full-time $19,536; part-time $814 per credit hour. *Financial support:* Fellowships, research assistantships, teaching assistantships, career-related internships or fieldwork, Federal Work-Study, institutionally sponsored loans, scholarships/grants, and unspecified assistantships available. Support available to part-time students. Financial award application deadline: 5/31; financial award applicants required to submit FAFSA. *Unit head:* Dr. Susan Santoli, Department Chair, 251-380-2836, Fax: 251-380-2758, E-mail: ssantoli@southalabama.edu. *Application contact:* Dr.

Educational Leadership and Administration

Susan Santoli, Director of Graduate Studies, 251-380-2836, Fax: 251-380-2758, E-mail: ssantoli@southalabama.edu.
Website: http://www.southalabama.edu/colleges/coe/lte/index.html

University of South Carolina, The Graduate School, College of Education, Department of Educational Leadership and Policies, Program in Educational Administration, Columbia, SC 29208. Offers M Ed, PhD, Ed S. *Accreditation:* NCATE. *Program availability:* Part-time, evening/weekend, online learning. *Degree requirements:* For master's, comprehensive exam, thesis (for some programs), foreign language (MA); for doctorate, comprehensive exam, thesis/dissertation. *Entrance requirements:* For master's, GRE General Test or MAT, letter of reference, resume; for doctorate and Ed S, GRE General Test or MAT, interview, letter of intent, letter of reference, transcripts, resum&e. Electronic applications accepted.

The University of South Dakota, Graduate School, School of Education, Division of Educational Administration, Vermillion, SD 57069. Offers educational administration (MA, Ed D, Ed S), including adult and higher education (MA, Ed D), curriculum director, director of special education (Ed D, Ed S), preK-12 principal, school district superintendent. *Accreditation:* NCATE. *Program availability:* Part-time, evening/weekend, 100% online, blended/hybrid learning. *Degree requirements:* For master's and Ed S, comprehensive exam, thesis or alternative; for doctorate, comprehensive exam, thesis/dissertation. *Entrance requirements:* For master's and doctorate, GRE General Test, MAT, minimum GPA of 2.7. Additional exam requirements/recommendations for international students: Required—TOEFL (minimum score 550 paper-based; 79 iBT). Electronic applications accepted.

University of Southern California, Graduate School, Rossier School of Education, Doctor of Education Programs, Los Angeles, CA 90089. Offers educational psychology (Ed D); higher education administration (Ed D); K-12 leadership in urban school settings (Ed D); teacher education in multicultural societies (Ed D). *Program availability:* Part-time, evening/weekend. *Degree requirements:* For doctorate, thesis/dissertation. *Entrance requirements:* For doctorate, GRE. Additional exam requirements/recommendations for international students: Required—TOEFL (minimum score 100 iBT). Electronic applications accepted. *Faculty research:* Data-driven decision-making in K-12 schools and districts; examination of college and university leadership and management in U. S. and Asia; studies in facilitating student learning; organizational change and the role of leaders; leadership, diversity, learning and accountability.

University of Southern California, Graduate School, Rossier School of Education, Doctor of Philosophy in Education Programs, Los Angeles, CA 90089. Offers educational psychology (PhD); higher education administration and policy (PhD); K-12 policy and practice (PhD). *Degree requirements:* For doctorate, thesis/dissertation, 63 units; qualifying exam; dissertation proposal and defense. *Entrance requirements:* For doctorate, GRE. Additional exam requirements/recommendations for international students: Required—TOEFL (minimum score 100 iBT). Electronic applications accepted. *Faculty research:* Diversity in higher education, organizational change, educational psychology, policy and politics of educational reform, economics of education and education policy.

University of Southern Indiana, Graduate Studies, Pott College of Science, Engineering, and Education, Department of Teacher Education, Program in School Administration and Leadership, Evansville, IN 47712-3590. Offers MSE. *Program availability:* Part-time, evening/weekend. *Faculty:* 5 full-time (4 women), 2 part-time/adjunct (1 woman). *Students:* 6 full-time (3 women), 1 international. Average age 32. *Entrance requirements:* For master's, PRAXIS II, bachelor's degree with minimum cumulative GPA of 2.75 from college or university accredited by NCATE or comparable association; minimum GPA of 3.0 in all courses taken at graduate level at all schools attended; teaching license. Additional exam requirements/recommendations for international students: Required—TOEFL (minimum score 550 paper-based; 79 iBT), IELTS (minimum score 6). *Application deadline:* Applications are processed on a rolling basis. Application fee: $40. Electronic applications accepted. *Expenses:* Tuition, state resident: full-time $8497. Tuition, nonresident: full-time $16,691. *Required fees:* $500. *Financial support:* Federal Work-Study, scholarships/grants, tuition waivers (full and partial), and unspecified assistantships available. Financial award application deadline: 3/1; financial award applicants required to submit FAFSA. *Unit head:* Dr. Bonnie Beach, Associate Dean, 812-465-1620, E-mail: blbeach@usi.edu. *Application contact:* Dr. Mayola Rowser, Director, Graduate Studies, 812-465-7015, Fax: 812-464-1956, E-mail: mrowser@usi.edu.
Website: http://www.usi.edu/science/teacher-education/programs/mse

University of Southern Maine, College of Management and Human Service, School of Education and Human Development, Educational Leadership Program, Portland, ME 04103. Offers assistant principal (CGS); educational leadership (MS Ed, CAS). *Program availability:* Part-time, evening/weekend, online learning. *Degree requirements:* For master's, thesis or alternative, practicum, internship; for other advanced degree, thesis or alternative. *Entrance requirements:* For master's, three years of documented teaching; for other advanced degree, master's degree. Additional exam requirements/recommendations for international students: Required—TOEFL (minimum score 550 paper-based; 79 iBT). Electronic applications accepted. *Faculty research:* Teaching strategies, technology-enhanced leadership, school-community partnerships, workforce development, higher education.

University of Southern Mississippi, Graduate School, College of Education and Psychology, Department of Educational Research and Administration, Hattiesburg, MS 39406. Offers educational administration (M Ed, Ed D, PhD, Ed S); educational administration and supervision (M Ed); educational studies and research (MS); higher education (Ed D); higher education administration (PhD); higher education: student affairs (M Ed); research, evaluation, statistics, assessment (PhD). *Degree requirements:* For master's and Ed S, comprehensive exam, thesis (for some programs); for doctorate, comprehensive exam, thesis/dissertation. *Entrance requirements:* For master's and doctorate, GRE General Test, minimum GPA of 2.75. Additional exam requirements/recommendations for international students: Required—TOEFL. *Application deadline:* For fall admission, 2/1 for domestic students, 3/1 for international students. Applications are processed on a rolling basis. Application fee: $60. *Expenses: Tuition, area resident:* Full-time $15,708; part-time $437 per credit hour. *Financial support:* Career-related internships or fieldwork, Federal Work-Study, and institutionally sponsored loans available. Financial award application deadline: 3/15; financial award applicants required to submit FAFSA. *Unit head:* Dr. Lilian Hill, Co-Chair, 601-266-4622. *Application contact:* Shonna Breland, Manager of Graduate Admissions, 601-266-6563, Fax: 601-266-5138.
Website: https://www.usm.edu/educational-research-administration

University of South Florida, College of Education, Department of Leadership, Counseling, Adult, Career and Higher Education, Tampa, FL 33620-9951. Offers adult education (MA, Ed D, PhD, Ed S); career and technical education (MA); career and workforce education (PhD); higher education/community college teaching (MA, Ed D, PhD); vocational education (Ed S). *Faculty:* 17 full-time (10 women). *Students:* 137 full-time (96 women), 331 part-time (237 women); includes 170 minority (75 Black or African American, non-Hispanic/Latino; 2 American Indian or Alaska Native, non-Hispanic/Latino; 12 Asian, non-Hispanic/Latino; 71 Hispanic/Latino; 2 Native Hawaiian or other Pacific Islander, non-Hispanic/Latino; 8 Two or more races, non-Hispanic/Latino), 18 international. Average age 35. 175 applicants, 66% accepted, 93 enrolled. In 2016, 111 master's, 22 doctorates, 1 other advanced degree awarded. Application fee: $30. *Expenses:* Tuition, state resident: full-time $7766; part-time $431.43 per credit hour. Tuition, nonresident: full-time $15,789; part-time $877.17 per credit hour. *Required fees:* $37 per term. *Total annual research expenditures:* $545,936. *Unit head:* Dr. Judith Ponticell, Chair, 813-974-4897, Fax: 813-974-5423, E-mail: jponticell@usf.edu.
Website: http://www.coedu.usf.edu/main/departments/ache/ache.html

University of South Florida, Innovative Education, Tampa, FL 33620-9951. Offers adult, career and higher education (Graduate Certificate), including college teaching, leadership in developing human resources, leadership in higher education; Africana studies (Graduate Certificate), including diasporas and health disparities, genocide and human rights; aging studies (Graduate Certificate), including gerontology; art research (Graduate Certificate), including museum studies; business foundations (Graduate Certificate); chemical and biomedical engineering (Graduate Certificate), including materials science and engineering, water, health and sustainability; child and family studies (Graduate Certificate), including positive behavior support; civil and industrial engineering (Graduate Certificate), including transportation systems analysis; community and family health (Graduate Certificate), including maternal and child health, social marketing and public health, violence and injury: prevention and intervention, women's health; criminology (Graduate Certificate), including criminal justice administration; educational measurement and research (Graduate Certificate), including evaluation; English (Graduate Certificate), including comparative literary studies, creative writing, professional and technical communication; entrepreneurship (Graduate Certificate); environmental health (Graduate Certificate), including safety management; epidemiology and biostatistics (Graduate Certificate), including applied biostatistics, biostatistics, concepts and tools of epidemiology, epidemiology, epidemiology of infectious diseases; geography, environment and planning (Graduate Certificate), including community development, environmental policy and management, geographical information systems; geology (Graduate Certificate), including hydrogeology; global health (Graduate Certificate), including disaster management, global health and Latin American and Caribbean studies, global health practice, humanitarian assistance, infection control; government and international affairs (Graduate Certificate), including Cuban studies, globalization studies; health policy and management (Graduate Certificate), including health management and leadership, public health policy and programs; hearing specialist: early intervention (Graduate Certificate); industrial and management systems engineering (Graduate Certificate), including systems engineering, technology management; information studies (Graduate Certificate), including school library media specialist; information systems/decision sciences (Graduate Certificate), including analytics and business intelligence; instructional technology (Graduate Certificate), including distance education, Florida digital/virtual educator, instructional design, multimedia design, Web design; internal medicine, bioethics and medical humanities (Graduate Certificate), including biomedical ethics; Latin American and Caribbean studies (Graduate Certificate); mass communications (Graduate Certificate), including multimedia journalism; mathematics and statistics (Graduate Certificate), including mathematics; medicine (Graduate Certificate), including aging and neuroscience, bioinformatics, biotechnology, brain fitness and memory management, clinical investigation, health informatics, health sciences, integrative weight management, intellectual property, medicine and gender, metabolic and nutritional medicine, metabolic cardiology, pharmacy sciences; national and competitive intelligence (Graduate Certificate); psychological and social foundations (Graduate Certificate), including career counseling, college teaching, diversity in education, mental health counseling, school counseling; public affairs (Graduate Certificate), including nonprofit management, public management, research administration; public health (Graduate Certificate), including environmental health, health equity, public health generalist, translational research in adolescent behavioral health; public health practices (Graduate Certificate), including planning for healthy communities; rehabilitation and mental health counseling (Graduate Certificate), including integrative mental health care, marriage and family therapy, rehabilitation technology; secondary education (Graduate Certificate), including ESOL, foreign language education: culture and content, foreign language education: professional; social work (Graduate Certificate), including geriatric social work/clinical gerontology; special education (Graduate Certificate), including autism spectrum disorder, disabilities education: severe/profound; world languages (Graduate Certificate), including teaching English as a second language (TESL) or foreign language. *Expenses:* Tuition, state resident: full-time $7766; part-time $431.43 per credit hour. Tuition, nonresident: full-time $15,789; part-time $877.17 per credit hour. *Required fees:* $37 per term. *Unit head:* Kathy Barnes, Interdisciplinary Programs Coordinator, 813-974-8031, Fax: 813-974-7061, E-mail: barnesk@usf.edu. *Application contact:* Karen Tylinski, Metro Initiatives, 813-974-9943, Fax: 813-974-7061, E-mail: ktylinsk@usf.edu.
Website: http://www.usf.edu/innovative-education/

University of South Florida, St. Petersburg, College of Education, St. Petersburg, FL 33701. Offers educational leadership development (M Ed); elementary education (MA), including math/science; English education (MA); middle grades STEM education (MS); reading education (MA). *Program availability:* Part-time. *Degree requirements:* For master's, comprehensive exam, practicum, internship, comprehensive portfolio. *Entrance requirements:* For master's, State of Florida General Knowledge Test (GKT), Florida Teaching Certificate (for non-initial certification programs), letters of recommendation. Additional exam requirements/recommendations for international students: Required—TOEFL (minimum score 550 paper-based; 79 iBT); Recommended—IELTS. Electronic applications accepted.

University of South Florida Sarasota-Manatee, College of Liberal Arts and Social Sciences, Sarasota, FL 34243. Offers criminal justice (MA); education (MA); educational leadership (M Ed), including curriculum leadership, K-12 public school leadership, non-public/charter school leadership; elementary education (MAT); English education (MA); social work (MSW). *Program availability:* Part-time, 100% online, blended/hybrid learning. *Faculty:* 11 full-time (9 women), 7 part-time/adjunct (5 women). *Students:* 11 full-time (all women), 55 part-time (41 women); includes 18 minority (5 Black or African American, non-Hispanic/Latino; 1 American Indian or Alaska Native, non-Hispanic/Latino; 2 Asian, non-Hispanic/Latino; 10 Hispanic/Latino). Average age 36. 40 applicants, 43% accepted, 17 enrolled. In 2016, 28 master's awarded. *Degree requirements:* For master's, comprehensive exam (for some programs). *Entrance requirements:* Additional exam requirements/recommendations for international students: Required—TOEFL (minimum score 550 paper-based; 79 iBT), IELTS (minimum score 6.5). *Application deadline:* For fall admission, 3/1 priority date for domestic students, 3/1 for international students; for spring admission, 10/1 priority date for domestic students, 10/1 for international students. Applications are processed on a rolling basis. Application fee: $30. Electronic applications accepted. *Expenses:* Contact institution. *Financial support:* In 2016–17, 9 students received support. Career-related internships or fieldwork, institutionally sponsored loans, scholarships/grants, health care benefits, and unspecified assistantships available. Support available to part-time students. Financial award application deadline: 3/1; financial award applicants required to submit FAFSA. *Faculty research:* Educational leadership, secondary education, elementary education, criminal justice, social work. *Unit head:* Dr. Jane Rose, Dean, 941-359-4469, Fax: 941-359-4778, E-mail: jane.rose@sar.usf.edu. *Application contact:*

Brandon Avery, Assistant Director, Admissions, 941-359-4331, E-mail: bavery@sar.usf.edu.
Website: http://usfsm.edu/college-of-liberal-arts-sciences/

The University of Tennessee, Graduate School, College of Education, Health and Human Sciences, Program in Education, Knoxville, TN 37996. Offers art education (MS); counseling education (PhD); cultural studies in education (PhD); curriculum (MS, Ed S); curriculum, educational research and evaluation (Ed D, PhD); early childhood education (PhD); early childhood special education (MS); education of deaf and hard of hearing (MS); educational administration and policy studies (Ed D, PhD); educational administration and supervision (Ed S); educational psychology (Ed D, PhD); elementary education (MS, Ed S); elementary teaching (MS); English education (MS, Ed S); exercise science (PhD); foreign language/ESL education (MS, Ed S); instructional technology (MS, Ed D, PhD, Ed S); literacy, language and ESL education (PhD); literacy, language education, and ESL education (Ed D); mathematics education (MS, Ed S); modified and comprehensive special education (MS); reading education (MS, Ed S); school counseling (Ed S); school psychology (PhD, Ed S); science education (MS, Ed S); secondary teaching (MS); social foundations (MS); social science education (MS, Ed S); socio-cultural foundations of sports and education (PhD); special education (Ed S); teacher education (Ed D, PhD). *Accreditation:* NCATE. *Program availability:* Part-time, evening/weekend. *Degree requirements:* For master's and Ed S, thesis optional; for doctorate, variable foreign language requirement, thesis/dissertation. *Entrance requirements:* For master's, minimum GPA of 2.7; for doctorate and Ed S, GRE General Test, minimum GPA of 2.7. Additional exam requirements/recommendations for international students: Required—TOEFL. Electronic applications accepted.

The University of Tennessee, Graduate School, College of Education, Health and Human Sciences, Program in Educational Administration and Policy Studies, Knoxville, TN 37996. Offers educational administration and policy studies (Ed D); educational administration and supervision (MS). *Accreditation:* NCATE. *Program availability:* Part-time, evening/weekend, online learning. *Degree requirements:* For master's, thesis optional. *Entrance requirements:* For master's, minimum GPA of 2.7. Additional exam requirements/recommendations for international students: Required—TOEFL. Electronic applications accepted.

The University of Tennessee at Chattanooga, School of Education, Chattanooga, TN 37403. Offers counseling (M Ed), including community counseling, school counseling; education (M Ed, Post-Master's Certificate), including elementary education (M Ed), school leadership, secondary education (M Ed), special education (M Ed); educational specialist (Ed S), including educational technology, school psychology; learning and leadership (Ed D), including educational leadership. *Accreditation:* ACA; NCATE. *Program availability:* Part-time. *Faculty:* 13 full-time (8 women), 2 part-time/adjunct (both women). *Students:* 50 full-time (32 women), 157 part-time (107 women); includes 42 minority (28 Black or African American, non-Hispanic/Latino; 4 Asian, non-Hispanic/Latino; 2 Hispanic/Latino; 8 Two or more races, non-Hispanic/Latino), 1 international. Average age 36. 169 applicants, 76% accepted, 49 enrolled. In 2016, 77 master's, 5 other advanced degrees awarded. *Degree requirements:* For master's, comprehensive exam, thesis optional, culminating experience; for doctorate, comprehensive exam, thesis/dissertation; for other advanced degree, internship. *Entrance requirements:* For master's, GRE General Test, PPST 1, teaching certificate; for doctorate, GRE General Test, master's degree, two years of practical work experience in organizational environment; for other advanced degree, GRE General Test, letters of reference. Additional exam requirements/recommendations for international students: Required—TOEFL (minimum score 550 paper-based; 79 iBT), IELTS (minimum score 6). *Application deadline:* For fall admission, 6/15 for domestic students, 7/1 for international students; for spring admission, 11/1 for domestic and international students. Applications are processed on a rolling basis. Application fee: $35 ($40 for international students). Electronic applications accepted. *Expenses:* $9,876 full-time in-state; $25,994 full-time out-of-state; $450 per credit part-time in-state; $1,345 per credit part-time out-of-state. *Financial support:* In 2016–17, 18 research assistantships, 5 teaching assistantships were awarded; career-related internships or fieldwork, institutionally sponsored loans, scholarships/grants, and unspecified assistantships also available. Support available to part-time students. Financial award application deadline: 7/1; financial award applicants required to submit FAFSA. *Faculty research:* School counseling, community counseling, elementary and secondary education, school leadership and administration. *Total annual research expenditures:* $247,231. *Unit head:* Dr. Renee Murley, Director, 423-425-4684, Fax: 423-425-5380, E-mail: renee-murley@utc.edu. *Application contact:* Dr. Joanne Romagni, Dean of the Graduate School, 423-425-4478, Fax: 423-425-5223, E-mail: joanne-romagni@utc.edu.
Website: http://www.utc.edu/school-education/abouttheschool/gradprograms.php

The University of Tennessee at Martin, Graduate Programs, College of Education, Health and Behavioral Sciences, Program in Educational Leadership, Martin, TN 38238. Offers MS Ed. *Program availability:* Part-time, online only, 100% online. *Students:* 23 part-time (14 women); includes 1 minority (Hispanic/Latino). Average age 36. 13 applicants, 46% accepted, 4 enrolled. In 2016, 8 master's awarded. *Degree requirements:* For master's, comprehensive exam. *Entrance requirements:* For master's, GRE General Test, minimum GPA of 2.5, letters of reference, teaching license, resume, teaching experience. Additional exam requirements/recommendations for international students: Required—TOEFL (minimum score 525 paper-based; 71 iBT). *Application deadline:* For fall admission, 7/27 priority date for domestic and international students; for spring admission, 12/17 priority date for domestic and international students; for summer admission, 5/10 priority date for domestic and international students. Applications are processed on a rolling basis. Application fee: $30 ($130 for international students). Electronic applications accepted. *Expenses:* Tuition, state resident: full-time $8254; part-time $459 per credit hour. Tuition, nonresident: full-time $22,198; part-time $1234 per credit hour. *Required fees:* $79 per credit hour. Part-time tuition and fees vary according to course load and campus/location. *Financial support:* Research assistantships with full tuition reimbursements, teaching assistantships with full tuition reimbursements, scholarships/grants, and unspecified assistantships available. Financial award application deadline: 2/1; financial award applicants required to submit FAFSA. *Unit head:* Cynthia West, Dean, 731-881-7125, Fax: 731-881-7975, E-mail: cwest@utm.edu. *Application contact:* Jolene L. Cunningham, Student Services Specialist, 731-881-7012, Fax: 731-881-7499, E-mail: jcunningham@utm.edu.

The University of Texas at Arlington, Graduate School, College of Education, Department of Educational Leadership and Policy Studies, Arlington, TX 76019. Offers educational leadership (PhD); higher education (M Ed); principal certification (M Ed). *Program availability:* Part-time, evening/weekend, online learning. *Degree requirements:* For master's, 2 field-based practica; for doctorate, comprehensive exam, thesis/dissertation, 2 research-based practica. *Entrance requirements:* For master's, GRE, 3 references forms, minimum undergraduate GPA of 3.0 in the last 60 hours of course work; for doctorate, GRE, resume, statement of intent, 3 reference forms, applicable master's degree. Application fee: $50. *Financial support:* Fellowships and research assistantships available. Financial award applicants required to submit FAFSA. *Faculty research:* Lived realities of students of color in K-16 contexts, K-16 faculty, K-16 policy and law, K-16 student access, K-16 student success. *Unit head:* Dr. Adrienne E. Hyle, Chair, 817-272-2841, Fax: 817-272-2127, E-mail: ahyle@uta.edu. *Application contact:* Paige Cordor, Graduate Advisor, 817-272-5051, Fax: 817-272-2127, E-mail: paigec@uta.edu.
Website: http://www.uta.edu/coehp/educleadership/

The University of Texas at Austin, Graduate School, College of Education, Department of Educational Administration, Austin, TX 78712-1111. Offers M Ed, Ed D, PhD. *Degree requirements:* For doctorate, thesis/dissertation. *Entrance requirements:* For master's and doctorate, GRE General Test. Electronic applications accepted.

The University of Texas at Austin, Graduate School, College of Education, Department of Special Education, Austin, TX 78712-1111. Offers autism and developmental disabilities (Ed D, PhD); autism and developmental disability (M Ed, MA); early childhood special education (M Ed, MA, Ed D, PhD); learning disabilities (Ed D, PhD); learning disabilities/behavior disorders (M Ed, MA); multicultural special education (M Ed, MA, Ed D, PhD); rehabilitation counselor (M Ed); rehabilitation counselor education (Ed D, PhD); special education administration (Ed D, PhD). *Accreditation:* CORE. *Program availability:* Part-time, evening/weekend, online learning. *Degree requirements:* For master's, thesis or alternative; for doctorate, thesis/dissertation. *Entrance requirements:* For master's and doctorate, GRE General Test. *Faculty research:* Anchored instruction, reading disabilities, multicultural/bilingual.

The University of Texas at El Paso, Graduate School, College of Education, Department of Educational Leadership and Foundations, El Paso, TX 79968-0001. Offers educational administration (M Ed); educational leadership and administration (Ed D). *Program availability:* Part-time, evening/weekend. *Degree requirements:* For master's, thesis optional; for doctorate, thesis/dissertation. *Entrance requirements:* For doctorate, GRE General Test, minimum graduate GPA of 3.0. Additional exam requirements/recommendations for international students: Required—TOEFL. Electronic applications accepted.

The University of Texas at San Antonio, College of Education and Human Development, Department of Educational Leadership and Policy Studies, San Antonio, TX 78249-0617. Offers educational leadership (Ed D); educational leadership and policy studies (M Ed), including educational leadership, higher education administration. *Program availability:* Part-time. *Faculty:* 19 full-time (6 women), 15 part-time/adjunct (7 women). *Students:* 64 full-time (46 women), 274 part-time (189 women); includes 220 minority (36 Black or African American, non-Hispanic/Latino; 2 Asian, non-Hispanic/Latino; 176 Hispanic/Latino; 6 Two or more races, non-Hispanic/Latino), 3 international. Average age 36. 103 applicants, 79% accepted, 54 enrolled. In 2016, 95 master's, 21 doctorates awarded. *Degree requirements:* For master's, comprehensive exam, thesis or alternative; for doctorate, comprehensive exam, thesis/dissertation. *Entrance requirements:* For master's, transcripts, statement of purpose, resume or curriculum vitae; for doctorate, GRE General Test, minimum GPA of 3.5 in a master's program, resume, three letters of recommendation, statement of purpose. Additional exam requirements/recommendations for international students: Required—TOEFL (minimum score 550 paper-based; 79 iBT), IELTS (minimum score 6.5). *Application deadline:* For fall admission, 7/1 for domestic students, 4/1 for international students; for spring admission, 11/1 for domestic students, 9/1 for international students. Application fee: $45 ($80 for international students). *Financial support:* In 2016–17, 6 students received support, including 6 fellowships (averaging $41,666 per year). Financial award application deadline: 2/1. *Faculty research:* Urban and international school leadership, student success, college access, higher education policy, multiculturalism, minority student achievement. *Total annual research expenditures:* $9,119. *Unit head:* Dr. Enrique Aleman, Department Chair, 210-458-5411, E-mail: enrique.aleman@utsa.edu. *Application contact:* Elisha Reynolds, Student Development Specialist, 210-458-6620, Fax: 210-458-5848, E-mail: elisha.reynolds@utsa.edu.
Website: http://education.utsa.edu/educational_leadership_and_policy_studies/

The University of Texas at Tyler, College of Education and Psychology, Department of Educational Leadership, Tyler, TX 75799-0001. Offers M Ed. *Program availability:* Part-time, evening/weekend, online learning. *Degree requirements:* For master's, comprehensive exam, 2 years of teaching experience. *Entrance requirements:* For master's, GRE General Test. Additional exam requirements/recommendations for international students: Required—TOEFL. *Faculty research:* Effective schools, restructuring of schools, leadership.

The University of Texas of the Permian Basin, Office of Graduate Studies, School of Education, Program in Educational Leadership, Odessa, TX 79762-0001. Offers MA. *Degree requirements:* For master's, comprehensive exam (for some programs), thesis (for some programs). *Entrance requirements:* For master's, GRE General Test. Additional exam requirements/recommendations for international students: Required—TOEFL (minimum score 550 paper-based).

The University of Texas Rio Grande Valley, College of Education and P-16 Integration, Department of Organization and School Leadership, Edinburg, TX 78539. Offers educational leadership (M Ed, Ed D). *Program availability:* Part-time, evening/weekend. *Degree requirements:* For master's, comprehensive exam, thesis optional; for doctorate, comprehensive exam, thesis/dissertation. *Entrance requirements:* For master's, GRE; for doctorate, master's degree. Additional exam requirements/recommendations for international students: Required—TOEFL. Electronic applications accepted. Tuition and fees vary according to course load and program. *Faculty research:* Community perceptions of education, leadership and gender studies, continuous improvement processes, leadership.

University of the Cumberlands, Graduate Programs in Education, Williamsburg, KY 40769-1372. Offers all grades (P-12) (M Ed); business and marketing (MA Ed, MAT); counselor education and supervision (Ed D); director of pupil personnel (Certificate); director of special education (Certificate); educational administration and supervision (Ed S); educational leadership (Ed D); elementary education (MA Ed, MAT); instructional leadership - principalship (MA Ed); instructional leadership - school principal (Certificate); middle school education (MA Ed, MAT); reading and writing (MA Ed); school counseling (MA Ed); school superintendent (Certificate); secondary education (MA Ed, MAT); special education (MAT); supervisor of instruction (Certificate); teacher leader (MA Ed). *Program availability:* Part-time, evening/weekend, online learning. *Degree requirements:* For master's, comprehensive exam. Electronic applications accepted.

University of the Pacific, Gladys L. Benerd School of Education, Department of Educational Administration and Leadership, Stockton, CA 95211-0197. Offers educational administration (MA, Ed D). *Accreditation:* NCATE. *Students:* 204 full-time (160 women), 212 part-time (162 women). *Degree requirements:* For master's, thesis (for some programs); for doctorate, thesis/dissertation. *Entrance requirements:* For master's and doctorate, GRE General Test, GRE Subject Test. Additional exam requirements/recommendations for international students: Required—TOEFL. *Application deadline:* For fall admission, 3/1 priority date for domestic students; for spring admission, 10/1 priority date for domestic students. Applications are processed on a rolling basis. Application fee: $75. *Financial support:* Teaching assistantships available. Financial award application deadline: 3/1; financial award applicants required to submit FAFSA. *Unit head:* Dr. Linda Skrla, Chairperson, 209-946-2580, E-mail: lskrla@pacific.edu. *Application contact:* Office of Graduate Admissions, 209-946-2344.

Educational Leadership and Administration

University of the Southwest, Graduate Programs, Hobbs, NM 88240-9129. Offers business administration (MBA); curriculum and instruction (MSE); curriculum and instruction: bilingual (MSE); curriculum and instruction: TESOL (MSE); early childhood education (MSE); educational administration (MSE); mental health counseling (MSE); school counseling (MSE); special education (MSE); sports management (MBA). *Program availability:* Part-time, evening/weekend, online learning. *Degree requirements:* For master's, comprehensive exam, thesis (for some programs). *Entrance requirements:* Additional exam requirements/recommendations for international students: Recommended—TOEFL. Electronic applications accepted.

University of the Virgin Islands, School of Education, St. Thomas, VI 00802. Offers creative leadership for innovation and change (PhD); educational leadership (MA); school counseling (MA); school psychology (Ed S). *Program availability:* Part-time, evening/weekend. *Faculty:* 8 full-time (2 women), 9 part-time/adjunct (4 women). *Students:* 9 full-time (8 women), 107 part-time (89 women); includes 69 minority (67 Black or African American, non-Hispanic/Latino; 2 Hispanic/Latino), 17 international. Average age 43. 101 applicants, 80% accepted, 69 enrolled. In 2016, 9 master's awarded. *Degree requirements:* For master's, comprehensive exam, thesis or alternative; for doctorate, comprehensive exam, thesis/dissertation, qualifying examination; for Ed S, comprehensive exam. *Entrance requirements:* For master's, GRE, minimum GPA of 2.5, BA degree from accredited institution. Additional exam requirements/recommendations for international students: Required—TOEFL (minimum score 550 paper-based). *Application deadline:* For fall admission, 4/30 for domestic and international students; for spring admission, 10/30 for domestic and international students. Application fee: $25. Electronic applications accepted. *Expenses:* Contact institution. *Financial support:* Scholarships/grants available. Financial award application deadline: 4/15; financial award applicants required to submit FAFSA. *Unit head:* Dr. Linda Thomas, Dean, 340-693-1321, Fax: 340-693-1335, E-mail: lthomas2@uvi.edu. *Application contact:* Dr. Xuri M. Allen, Director of Admissions, 340-693-1224, Fax: 340-693-1167, E-mail: xallen@uvi.edu.

The University of Toledo, College of Graduate Studies, Judith Herb College of Education, Department of Educational Foundations and Leadership, Toledo, OH 43606-3390. Offers educational administration and supervision (ME, DE, Ed S); educational psychology (ME, PhD); educational research and measurement (ME, PhD); educational sociology (PhD); educational theory and social foundations (ME); foundations of education (DE, PhD); history of education (PhD); philosophy of education (PhD). *Accreditation:* NCATE. *Program availability:* Part-time, evening/weekend. *Degree requirements:* For master's, comprehensive exam, thesis or alternative; for doctorate, comprehensive exam, thesis/dissertation; for Ed S, thesis optional. *Entrance requirements:* For master's, doctorate, and Ed S, minimum cumulative GPA of 2.7 for all previous academic work, letters of recommendation. Additional exam requirements/recommendations for international students: Required—TOEFL (minimum score 550 paper-based; 80 iBT). Electronic applications accepted.

University of Utah, Graduate School, College of Education, Department of Educational Leadership and Policy, Salt Lake City, UT 84084. Offers educational leadership and policy (Ed D, PhD), including higher education administration (Ed D), K-12 (Ed D); K-12 school administration (M Ed); K-12 teacher instructional leadership (M Ed); student affairs (M Ed); MPA/PhD. *Program availability:* Part-time, evening/weekend. *Faculty:* 11 full-time (7 women), 3 part-time/adjunct (all women). *Students:* 79 full-time (47 women), 134 part-time (95 women); includes 63 minority (7 Black or African American, non-Hispanic/Latino; 2 American Indian or Alaska Native, non-Hispanic/Latino; 7 Asian, non-Hispanic/Latino; 38 Hispanic/Latino; 9 Two or more races, non-Hispanic/Latino), 1 international. Average age 35. 154 applicants, 67% accepted, 86 enrolled. In 2016, 42 master's, 8 doctorates awarded. *Degree requirements:* For master's, comprehensive exam (for some programs), internship, capstone; for doctorate, thesis/dissertation, qualifying exam. *Entrance requirements:* For master's, minimum undergraduate GPA of 3.0, valid bachelor's degree, 3 years' teaching or leadership experience, Level 1 or 2 UT educator's license (for K-12 programs only); for doctorate, GRE General Test (taken with five years of applying), minimum undergraduate GPA of 3.0, valid master's degree. Additional exam requirements/recommendations for international students: Required—TOEFL (minimum score 500 paper-based). *Application deadline:* For fall admission, 1/15 priority date for domestic and international students; for winter admission, 2/1 for domestic and international students; for spring admission, 11/1 priority date for domestic and international students; for summer admission, 3/1 priority date for domestic and international students. Applications are processed on a rolling basis. Application fee: $55 ($65 for international students). Electronic applications accepted. *Expenses:* Contact institution. *Financial support:* In 2016–17, 47 students received support, including 1 fellowship with full tuition reimbursement available (averaging $14,500 per year), 2 research assistantships with full tuition reimbursements available (averaging $15,000 per year), 6 teaching assistantships with full tuition reimbursements available (averaging $15,000 per year); career-related internships or fieldwork, scholarships/grants, health care benefits, and unspecified assistantships also available. Support available to part-time students. Financial award application deadline: 3/1; financial award applicants required to submit FAFSA. *Faculty research:* Education accountability, college student diversity, K-12 educational administration and school leadership, student affairs, higher education. *Unit head:* Dr. Gerardo Lopez, Chair, 801-581-6627, Fax: 801-585-6756, E-mail: gerardo.lopez@utah.edu. *Application contact:* Marilynn S. Howard, Academic Coordinator, 801-581-6714, Fax: 801-585-6756, E-mail: marilynn.howard@utah.edu.
Website: http://elp.utah.edu/

University of Vermont, Graduate College, College of Education and Social Services, Department of Leadership and Developmental Sciences, Program in Educational Leadership, Burlington, VT 05405. Offers M Ed. *Accreditation:* NCATE. *Degree requirements:* For master's, thesis or alternative. *Entrance requirements:* Additional exam requirements/recommendations for international students: Required—TOEFL (minimum score 550 paper-based; 80 iBT). Electronic applications accepted. *Expenses:* Tuition, state resident: full-time $5814. Tuition, nonresident: full-time $14,670.

University of Vermont, Graduate College, College of Education and Social Services, Department of Leadership and Developmental Sciences, Program in Educational Leadership and Policy Studies, Burlington, VT 05405. Offers Ed D, PhD. *Accreditation:* NCATE. *Degree requirements:* For doctorate, thesis/dissertation. *Entrance requirements:* For doctorate, GRE, resume (for Ed D), writing sample. Additional exam requirements/recommendations for international students: Required—TOEFL (minimum score 550 paper-based; 80 iBT). Electronic applications accepted. *Expenses:* Tuition, state resident: full-time $5814. Tuition, nonresident: full-time $14,670.

University of Vermont, Graduate College, College of Education and Social Services, Department of Leadership and Developmental Sciences, Program in Higher Education and Student Affairs Administration, Burlington, VT 05405. Offers M Ed. *Accreditation:* NCATE. *Degree requirements:* For master's, thesis or alternative. *Entrance requirements:* For master's, resume. Additional exam requirements/recommendations for international students: Required—TOEFL (minimum score 550 paper-based; 80 iBT). Electronic applications accepted. *Expenses:* Tuition, state resident: full-time $5814. Tuition, nonresident: full-time $14,670.

University of Victoria, Faculty of Graduate Studies, Faculty of Education, Department of Educational Psychology and Leadership Studies, Victoria, BC V8W 2Y2, Canada. Offers aboriginal communities counseling (M Ed); counseling (M Ed, MA); educational psychology (M Ed, MA, PhD), including counseling psychology (M Ed, MA), leadership studies (PhD), learning and development (MA, PhD), measurement and evaluation, special education (M Ed, MA); leadership studies (M Ed, MA). *Program availability:* Part-time. *Degree requirements:* For master's, thesis (for some programs), comprehensive exam (M Ed); for doctorate, comprehensive exam, thesis/dissertation, candidacy exam. *Entrance requirements:* For master's, 2 years of work experience in a relevant field; for doctorate, GRE, 2 years of work experience in a relevant field, minimum B average. Additional exam requirements/recommendations for international students: Required—TOEFL (minimum score 575 paper-based), IELTS (minimum score 7). *Faculty research:* Learning and development (child, adolescent and adult), special education and exceptional children.

University of Virginia, Curry School of Education, Department of Leadership, Foundations and Policy, Program in Administration and Supervision, Charlottesville, VA 22903. Offers M Ed, Ed D, Ed S. *Students:* 12 part-time (4 women); includes 1 minority (Hispanic/Latino). Average age 34. 22 applicants, 68% accepted, 14 enrolled. In 2016, 8 master's, 3 doctorates, 23 other advanced degrees awarded. *Entrance requirements:* For master's, doctorate, and Ed S, GRE General Test, letters of recommendation. *Application deadline:* Applications are processed on a rolling basis. Application fee: $60. Electronic applications accepted. *Expenses:* Tuition, state resident: full-time $15,026; part-time $834 per credit hour. Tuition, nonresident: full-time $25,168; part-time $1378 per credit hour. *Required fees:* $2654. *Financial support:* Fellowships, research assistantships, and teaching assistantships available. Financial award applicants required to submit FAFSA. *Unit head:* Pam Tucker, Program Coordinator, 434-924-7846, E-mail: pdtucker@virginia.edu. *Application contact:* Eric Molnar, Assistant Director, Admissions and Enrollment Reporting, 434-243-2085, E-mail: eric.molnar@virginia.edu.
Website: http://curry.virginia.edu/academics/areas-of-study/administration-supervision

University of Virginia, Curry School of Education, Program in Education, Charlottesville, VA 22903. Offers administration and supervision (PhD); applied developmental science (PhD); counselor education (PhD); curriculum and instruction (PhD); early childhood special education (MT); education evaluation (PhD); educational psychology (PhD); educational research (PhD); elementary education (MT); English education (MT, PhD); foreign language education (MT); higher education (PhD); instructional technology (PhD); kinesiology (MT, PhD); math education (PhD); reading education (PhD); research, statistics and evaluation (PhD); school psychology (PhD); science education (PhD); social studies education (MT, PhD); special education (PhD); world languages education (MT). *Students:* 452 full-time (357 women), 18 part-time (13 women); includes 100 minority (28 Black or African American, non-Hispanic/Latino; 39 Asian, non-Hispanic/Latino; 18 Hispanic/Latino; 15 Two or more races, non-Hispanic/Latino), 14 international. Average age 25. 309 applicants, 51% accepted, 87 enrolled. In 2016, 144 master's, 31 doctorates awarded. *Degree requirements:* For master's, comprehensive exam (for some programs), field project; for doctorate, comprehensive exam, thesis/dissertation. *Entrance requirements:* For doctorate, GRE General Test. Additional exam requirements/recommendations for international students: Required—TOEFL (minimum score 600 paper-based; 90 iBT), IELTS (minimum score 7). *Application deadline:* Applications are processed on a rolling basis. Application fee: $60. Electronic applications accepted. *Expenses:* Tuition, state resident: full-time $15,026; part-time $834 per credit hour. Tuition, nonresident: full-time $25,168; part-time $1378 per credit hour. *Required fees:* $2654. *Financial support:* Fellowships, research assistantships, and teaching assistantships available. Financial award application deadline: 1/5; financial award applicants required to submit FAFSA. *Unit head:* Robert C. Pianta, Dean, 434-924-3334, E-mail: pianta@virginia.edu. *Application contact:* Eric Molnar, Assistant Director, Admissions and Enrollment Reporting, 434-243-2085, E-mail: eric.molnar@virginia.edu.
Website: http://curry.virginia.edu/teacher-education

University of Washington, Graduate School, College of Education, Seattle, WA 98195. Offers curriculum and instruction (M Ed, Ed D, PhD), including educational technology, general curriculum (Ed D, PhD), language, literacy, and culture, mathematics education, multicultural education, reading and language arts education (Ed D), science education, social studies education, teaching and curriculum (M Ed); educational leadership and policy studies (M Ed, Ed D, PhD), including administration (Ed D), educational policy, organization, and leadership (M Ed, PhD), higher education, leadership for learning (Ed D), social and cultural foundations of education (M Ed, PhD); educational psychology (M Ed, PhD), including educational psychology (PhD), human development and cognition (M Ed), learning sciences, measurement, statistics and research design (M Ed), school psychology (M Ed); instructional leadership (M Ed); intercollegiate athletic leadership (M Ed); special education (M Ed, Ed D, PhD), including early childhood special education (M Ed), emotional and behavioral disabilities (M Ed), learning disabilities (M Ed), low-incidence disabilities (M Ed), severe disabilities (M Ed), special education (Ed D, PhD); teacher education (MIT). *Accreditation:* APA. *Program availability:* Part-time, evening/weekend. *Degree requirements:* For master's, thesis optional; for doctorate, thesis/dissertation. *Entrance requirements:* For master's and doctorate, GRE General Test, minimum GPA of 3.0. Additional exam requirements/recommendations for international students: Required—TOEFL. Electronic applications accepted. *Faculty research:* School restructuring/effective schools, special education interventions, literacy and writing, technology, school partnerships, teacher preparation.

University of Washington, Bothell, Program in Education, Bothell, WA 98011. Offers education (M Ed); leadership development for educators (M Ed); secondary/middle level endorsement (M Ed). *Program availability:* Part-time, evening/weekend. *Degree requirements:* For master's, thesis. *Entrance requirements:* Additional exam requirements/recommendations for international students: Required—TOEFL. Electronic applications accepted. *Faculty research:* Multicultural education in citizenship education, intercultural education, knowledge and practice in the principalship, educational public policy, national board certification for teachers, teacher learning in literacy, technology and its impact on teaching and learning of mathematics, reading assessments, professional development in literacy education and mobility, digital media, education and class.

University of Washington, Tacoma, Graduate Programs, Program in Education, Tacoma, WA 98402-3100. Offers education (M Ed); educational administration (principal or program administrator certification) (M Ed); elementary education teacher certification (M Ed); elementary education/special education teacher certification (M Ed); secondary science or math teacher certification (M Ed). *Program availability:* Part-time, evening/weekend. *Degree requirements:* For master's, culminating project. *Entrance requirements:* For master's, WEST-B, WEST-E (teacher certification programs only), official sealed transcript from every college/university attended, personal goal statement, letters of recommendation, copy of valid teaching certificate. Additional exam requirements/recommendations for international students: Required—TOEFL (minimum score 580 paper-based; 92 iBT). Electronic applications accepted. *Faculty research:* Global learning communities for English/Chinese languages, evaluation of mathematics and reading intervention programs, response to intervention, school-wide behavioral and emotional support, mathematics education and culturally responsive mathematics education.

The University of West Alabama, School of Graduate Studies, College of Education, Departments of Instructional Leadership and Support/Curriculum and Instruction, Program in Instructional Leadership, Livingston, AL 35470. Offers instructional leadership (M Ed, Ed S); teacher leader (Ed S). *Accreditation:* NCATE. *Program availability:* Part-time, evening/weekend, 100% online. *Faculty:* 3 full-time (2 women), 14 part-time/adjunct (7 women). *Students:* 224 (151 women); includes 75 minority (69 Black or African American, non-Hispanic/Latino; 1 Asian, non-Hispanic/Latino; 1 Hispanic/Latino; 4 Two or more races, non-Hispanic/Latino). Average age 37. 105 applicants, 86% accepted, 54 enrolled. In 2016, 20 master's, 32 Ed Ss awarded. *Degree requirements:* For master's, comprehensive exam, thesis optional; for Ed S, comprehensive exam. *Entrance requirements:* For master's, GRE General Test, MAT, minimum GPA of 2.75. Additional exam requirements/recommendations for international students: Required—TOEFL (minimum score 500 paper-based; 61 iBT). *Application deadline:* Applications are processed on a rolling basis. Application fee: $40. Electronic applications accepted. *Expenses:* Tuition, state resident: part-time $355 per credit hour. Tuition, nonresident: part-time $710 per credit hour. *Required fees:* $130 per semester. *Financial support:* Teaching assistantships, Federal Work-Study, scholarships/grants, and unspecified assistantships available. Support available to part-time students. Financial award application deadline: 3/1; financial award applicants required to submit FAFSA. *Unit head:* Dr. Reenay Rogers, Chair of Instructional Leadership and Support, 205-652-5423, Fax: 205-652-3706, E-mail: rrogers@uwa.edu. *Application contact:* Dr. B. J. Kimbrough, Dean of Graduate Studies, 205-652-3647, Fax: 205-652-3706, E-mail: bkimbrough@uwa.edu.
Website: http://www.uwa.edu/medinstructionalleadership.aspx

University of West Florida, College of Education and Professional Studies, Department of Teacher Education and Educational Leadership, Program in Educational Leadership, Pensacola, FL 32514-5750. Offers M Ed. *Accreditation:* NCATE. *Program availability:* Part-time, evening/weekend, online learning. *Degree requirements:* For master's, thesis optional. *Entrance requirements:* For master's, GRE General Test or minimum GPA of 3.0. Additional exam requirements/recommendations for international students: Required—TOEFL (minimum score 550 paper-based). *Application deadline:* For fall admission, 6/1 for domestic students, 5/15 for international students; for spring admission, 10/1 for domestic and international students. Applications are processed on a rolling basis. Application fee: $30. *Expenses:* Tuition, state resident: full-time $5316.12. Tuition, nonresident: full-time $11,308. *Required fees:* $583.92. Tuition and fees vary according to course load and program. *Financial support:* Career-related internships or fieldwork, Federal Work-Study, scholarships/grants, and tuition waivers (partial) available. Support available to part-time students. Financial award application deadline: 4/15; financial award applicants required to submit FAFSA. *Unit head:* Dr. Karen Rasmussen, Interim Chairperson, 850-474-2300, Fax: 850-857-6288, E-mail: krasmuss@uwf.edu. *Application contact:* Terry McCray, Assistant Director of Graduate Admissions, 850-473-7718, Fax: 850-473-7714, E-mail: gradadmissions@uwf.edu.
Website: http://uwf.edu/education/educationalleadership_med.cfm

University of West Florida, College of Education and Professional Studies, Ed D Programs, Specialization in Administrative and Leadership Studies, Pensacola, FL 32514-5750. Offers Ed D. *Degree requirements:* For doctorate, comprehensive exam, thesis/dissertation. *Entrance requirements:* For doctorate, GRE, MAT, or GMAT, letter of intent; writing sample; three letters of recommendation; two completed disposition assessment forms; written statement of goals; interview with admissions committee. Additional exam requirements/recommendations for international students: Required—TOEFL (minimum score 550 paper-based). *Application deadline:* For fall admission, 6/1 for domestic and international students; for spring admission, 10/1 for domestic students. *Expenses:* Tuition, state resident: full-time $5316.12. Tuition, nonresident: full-time $11,308. *Required fees:* $583.92. Tuition and fees vary according to course load and program. *Unit head:* Dr. Carla Thompson, Director, 850-473-7327, E-mail: cthompson1@uwf.edu. *Application contact:* Terry McCray, Assistant Director of Graduate Admissions, 850-473-7718, Fax: 850-473-7714, E-mail: gradadmissions@uwf.edu.
Website: http://uwf.edu/edd/administration.cfm

University of West Georgia, College of Education, Carrollton, GA 30118. Offers business education (M Ed); early childhood education (M Ed, Ed S); educational leadership (M Ed, Ed S); media (M Ed, Ed S); professional counseling (M Ed, Ed S); professional counseling and supervision (Ed D); reading instruction (M Ed); school improvement (Ed D); secondary education (M Ed); special education (M Ed, Ed S), including teaching (M Ed); speech language pathology (M Ed); teaching (MAT). *Accreditation:* NCATE. *Program availability:* Part-time, evening/weekend, 100% online, blended/hybrid learning. *Faculty:* 46 full-time (31 women). *Students:* 321 full-time (266 women), 1,007 part-time (813 women); includes 456 minority (389 Black or African American, non-Hispanic/Latino; 1 American Indian or Alaska Native, non-Hispanic/Latino; 13 Asian, non-Hispanic/Latino; 43 Hispanic/Latino; 10 Two or more races, non-Hispanic/Latino), 12 international. Average age 33. 541 applicants, 79% accepted, 305 enrolled. In 2016, 286 master's, 20 doctorates, 156 other advanced degrees awarded. *Entrance requirements:* Additional exam requirements/recommendations for international students: Required—TOEFL (minimum score 523 paper-based; 69 iBT); Recommended—IELTS (minimum score 6.5). *Application deadline:* For fall admission, 7/21 for domestic students, 6/1 for international students; for spring admission, 11/30 for domestic students, 10/15 for international students; for summer admission, 4/15 for domestic students, 3/30 for international students. Applications are processed on a rolling basis. Application fee: $40. Electronic applications accepted. *Expenses:* Tuition, state resident: full-time $5316; part-time $222 per semester hour. Tuition, nonresident: full-time $20,658; part-time $861 per semester hour. *Required fees:* $1962. Tuition and fees vary according to course load, degree level and program. *Financial support:* Fellowships, research assistantships, teaching assistantships, career-related internships or fieldwork, Federal Work-Study, institutionally sponsored loans, scholarships/grants, and unspecified assistantships available. Support available to part-time students. Financial award application deadline: 4/1; financial award applicants required to submit FAFSA. *Unit head:* Dr. Diane Hoff, Dean, College of Education, 678-839-6570, Fax: 678-839-6098, E-mail: dhoff@westga.edu. *Application contact:* Dr. Toby Ziglar, Assistant Dean of the Graduate School, 678-839-1394, Fax: 678-839-1395, E-mail: graduate@westga.edu.
Website: http://www.westga.edu/education/

University of Wisconsin–Madison, Graduate School, School of Education, Department of Educational Leadership and Policy Analysis, Madison, WI 53706-1380. Offers administration (Certificate); educational policy (MS, PhD); global higher education (MS). *Degree requirements:* For doctorate, thesis/dissertation. *Entrance requirements:* For master's and doctorate, GRE General Test. Electronic applications accepted.

University of Wisconsin–Milwaukee, Graduate School, School of Education, Department of Administrative Leadership, Milwaukee, WI 53201-0413. Offers administrative leadership (MS, Graduate Certificate), including adult and continuing education leadership (MS), educational administration and supervision (MS), higher education administration (MS); support services for online students in higher education (Graduate Certificate); teaching and learning in higher education (Graduate Certificate). *Program availability:* Part-time. *Students:* 22 full-time (16 women), 157 part-time (102 women); includes 52 minority (21 Black or African American, non-Hispanic/Latino; 4 Asian, non-Hispanic/Latino; 2 Hispanic/Latino; 25 Two or more races, non-Hispanic/Latino), 2 international. Average age 34. 108 applicants, 72% accepted, 48 enrolled. In 2016, 72 master's, 19 other advanced degrees awarded. *Degree requirements:* For master's, comprehensive exam, thesis or alternative. *Entrance requirements:* For master's, GRE General Test. Additional exam requirements/recommendations for international students: Required—TOEFL (minimum score 550 paper-based; 79 iBT), IELTS (minimum score 6.5). *Application deadline:* For fall admission, 1/1 priority date for domestic students; for spring admission, 9/1 for domestic students. Applications are processed on a rolling basis. Application fee: $56 ($96 for international students). Electronic applications accepted. *Financial support:* In 2016–17, 2 fellowships were awarded; research assistantships, teaching assistantships, career-related internships or fieldwork, health care benefits, unspecified assistantships, and project assistantships also available. Support available to part-time students. Financial award application deadline: 4/15; financial award applicants required to submit FAFSA. *Unit head:* Alan Shoho, Dean, 414-229-4181, E-mail: shoho@uwm.edu. *Application contact:* General Contact, 414-229-4721, E-mail: soeinfo@uwm.edu.
Website: http://uwm.edu/education/academics/administrative-leadership-department/

University of Wisconsin–Milwaukee, Graduate School, School of Education, Department of Exceptional Education, Milwaukee, WI 53201-0413. Offers autism spectrum disorders (Graduate Certificate); exceptional education (MS); transition for students with disabilities (Graduate Certificate); urban education (PhD), including adult, continuing and higher education leadership, art education, curriculum and instruction, exceptional education, mathematics education, multicultural studies, social foundations of education. *Program availability:* Part-time. *Students:* 50 full-time (41 women), 66 part-time (51 women); includes 42 minority (24 Black or African American, non-Hispanic/Latino; 6 Asian, non-Hispanic/Latino; 1 Hispanic/Latino; 11 Two or more races, non-Hispanic/Latino), 4 international. Average age 39. 55 applicants, 51% accepted, 22 enrolled. In 2016, 14 master's, 10 doctorates, 3 other advanced degrees awarded. *Degree requirements:* For master's, thesis. *Entrance requirements:* Additional exam requirements/recommendations for international students: Required—TOEFL (minimum score 550 paper-based; 79 iBT), IELTS (minimum score 6.5). *Application deadline:* For fall admission, 1/1 priority date for domestic students; for spring admission, 9/1 for domestic students. Applications are processed on a rolling basis. Application fee: $56 ($96 for international students). Electronic applications accepted. *Financial support:* Fellowships, research assistantships, teaching assistantships, career-related internships or fieldwork, health care benefits, and unspecified assistantships available. Support available to part-time students. Financial award application deadline: 4/15; financial award applicants required to submit FAFSA. *Faculty research:* Emotional disturbance, hearing impairment, learning disabilities, mental retardation. *Application contact:* General Information Contact, 414-229-4721, E-mail: soeinfo@uwm.edu.
Website: http://uwm.edu/education/academics/exceptional-edu-department/

University of Wisconsin–Oshkosh, Graduate Studies, College of Education and Human Services, Department of Educational Leadership and Human Services, Oshkosh, WI 54901. Offers educational leadership (MS). *Program availability:* Part-time, evening/weekend. *Degree requirements:* For master's, comprehensive exam, thesis optional. *Entrance requirements:* For master's, bachelor's degree in education or related field. Additional exam requirements/recommendations for international students: Required—TOEFL (minimum score 550 paper-based; 79 iBT). Electronic applications accepted. *Faculty research:* Supervision models, learning styles, total quality management, cooperative learning, school choice.

University of Wisconsin–Stevens Point, College of Professional Studies, School of Education, Program in Educational Administration, Stevens Point, WI 54481-3897. Offers MSE. Program offered jointly with University of Wisconsin–Superior. *Degree requirements:* For master's, comprehensive exam, thesis or alternative.

University of Wisconsin–Superior, Graduate Division, Department of Educational Administration, Superior, WI 54880-4500. Offers MSE, Ed S. Programs offered jointly with University of Wisconsin - Eau Claire, University of Wisconsin - Stevens Point. *Program availability:* Part-time, evening/weekend, online learning. *Degree requirements:* For master's, thesis or alternative, research project or position paper, written exam; for Ed S, thesis, internship, oral and written exams. *Entrance requirements:* For master's, GRE General Test or MAT, minimum GPA of 2.75, teaching license, 3 years of teaching experience; for Ed S, MAT, GRE, master's degree, 3 years of teaching experience, teaching license. *Faculty research:* Postsecondary disabilities, educational partnerships, K-12.

University of Wisconsin–Whitewater, School of Graduate Studies, College of Business and Economics, Program in School Business Management, Whitewater, WI 53190-1790. Offers MSE. *Program availability:* Part-time, evening/weekend, online learning. *Entrance requirements:* For master's, minimum GPA of 2.75. Additional exam requirements/recommendations for international students: Required—TOEFL (minimum score 550 paper-based; 80 iBT), IELTS (minimum score 6). Electronic applications accepted.

University of Wyoming, College of Education, Programs in Educational Leadership, Laramie, WY 82071. Offers MA, Ed D, Certificate. *Program availability:* Part-time, online learning. *Degree requirements:* For master's, thesis; for doctorate, comprehensive exam, thesis/dissertation; for Certificate, comprehensive exam, thesis, residency. *Entrance requirements:* For master's and Certificate, GRE; for doctorate, MA, 3 years' teaching experience. Additional exam requirements/recommendations for international students: Required—TOEFL (minimum score 520 paper-based). *Faculty research:* School leadership, leadership preparation, leadership skills.

Upper Iowa University, Master of Education Program, Fayette, IA 52142-1857. Offers early childhood (M Ed); English as a second language (M Ed); higher education (M Ed); instructional strategist (M Ed); reading (M Ed), teacher leadership (M Ed).

Ursuline College, School of Graduate Studies, Program in Educational Administration, Pepper Pike, OH 44124-4398. Offers MA. *Program availability:* Part-time. *Faculty:* 6 part-time/adjunct (3 women). *Students:* 24 full-time (16 women), 19 part-time (12 women); includes 13 minority (all Black or African American, non-Hispanic/Latino). Average age 34. 18 applicants, 100% accepted, 14 enrolled. In 2016, 25 master's awarded. *Degree requirements:* For master's, thesis or alternative. *Entrance requirements:* For master's, minimum undergraduate GPA of 3.0, teaching certificate, professional experience. Additional exam requirements/recommendations for international students: Required—TOEFL (minimum score 500 paper-based; 80 iBT). *Application deadline:* For fall admission, 8/1 priority date for domestic students. Applications are processed on a rolling basis. Application fee: $25. Electronic applications accepted. *Expenses:* $632 per credit hour. *Financial support:* In 2016–17, 8 students received support. Scholarships/grants available. Support available to part-time students. Financial award application deadline: 3/1; financial award applicants required to submit FAFSA. *Unit head:* Dr. James Connell, Director, 440-449-3413, Fax: 440-646-8328, E-mail: jconnell@ursuline.edu. *Application contact:* Melanie Steele,

Educational Leadership and Administration

Director, Graduate Admission, 440-646-8146, Fax: 440-684-6138, E-mail: graduateadmissions@ursuline.edu.

Utah Valley University, Program in Education, Orem, UT 84058-5999. Offers educational technology (M Ed); elementary mathematics (M Ed); elementary STEM (M Ed); English as a second language (M Ed); reading (M Ed); teachers as leaders (M Ed). *Accreditation:* TEAC. *Program availability:* Part-time. *Degree requirements:* For master's, project. *Entrance requirements:* For master's, GRE, 3 letters of recommendation, interview, essay. Additional exam requirements/recommendations for international students: Required—TOEFL (minimum score 83 iBT). Electronic applications accepted. *Expenses:* Contact institution.

Valdosta State University, Program in Educational Leadership, Valdosta, GA 31698. Offers M Ed. *Accreditation:* NCATE. *Program availability:* 100% online, blended/hybrid learning. *Degree requirements:* For master's, thesis (for some programs), comprehensive written and/or oral exams. *Entrance requirements:* For master's, GRE General Test or MAT. Additional exam requirements/recommendations for international students: Required—TOEFL (minimum score 523 paper-based); Recommended—IELTS. Electronic applications accepted. *Expenses:* Contact institution. *Faculty research:* Mentoring in higher education, contemporary issues in higher education.

Valparaiso University, Graduate School and Continuing Education, Department of Education, Valparaiso, IN 46383. Offers initial licensure (M Ed, Ed S), including humane education (M Ed), instructional leadership (M Ed), primary education (M Ed), school psychology, secondary education (M Ed); instructional leadership (M Ed); M Ed/Ed S. *Accreditation:* NCATE. *Program availability:* Part-time, evening/weekend, online learning. *Entrance requirements:* For master's, GRE General Test, minimum GPA of 3.0. Additional exam requirements/recommendations for international students: Required—TOEFL (minimum score 550 paper-based; 80 iBT), IELTS (minimum score 6). Electronic applications accepted. *Expenses: Tuition:* Full-time $11,070; part-time $615 per credit hour. *Required fees:* $116 per semester. Tuition and fees vary according to course load, degree level and program.

Vanderbilt University, Peabody College, Department of Leadership, Policy, and Organizations, Nashville, TN 37240-1001. Offers education policy (MPP); educational leadership and policy (Ed D); higher education (M Ed); higher education leadership and policy (Ed D); independent school leadership (M Ed); international education policy and management (M Ed); leadership and organizational performance (M Ed). *Program availability:* Part-time. *Faculty:* 29 full-time (14 women), 21 part-time/adjunct (5 women). *Students:* 166 full-time (124 women), 107 part-time (63 women); includes 50 minority (25 Black or African American, non-Hispanic/Latino; 7 Asian, non-Hispanic/Latino; 9 Hispanic/Latino; 1 Native Hawaiian or other Pacific Islander, non-Hispanic/Latino; 8 Two or more races, non-Hispanic/Latino), 32 international. Average age 29. 543 applicants, 63% accepted, 133 enrolled. In 2016, 109 master's, 22 doctorates awarded. *Degree requirements:* For master's, comprehensive exam, thesis optional; for doctorate, thesis/dissertation, qualifying exams, residency. *Entrance requirements:* For master's and doctorate, GRE General Test. Additional exam requirements/recommendations for international students: Required—TOEFL (minimum score 550 paper-based; 80 iBT). *Application deadline:* For fall admission, 12/31 priority date for domestic and international students; for spring admission, 11/1 priority date for domestic and international students. Applications are processed on a rolling basis. Application fee: $0. Electronic applications accepted. *Expenses: Tuition:* Part-time $1854 per credit hour. *Financial support:* Fellowships with partial tuition reimbursements, research assistantships with partial tuition reimbursements, teaching assistantships with partial tuition reimbursements, Federal Work-Study, institutionally sponsored loans, scholarships/grants, tuition waivers (partial), and unspecified assistantships available. Support available to part-time students. Financial award application deadline: 1/15; financial award applicants required to submit FAFSA. *Faculty research:* Higher education, educational leadership, education policy, international education, educator effectiveness. *Unit head:* Dr. Ellen B. Goldring, Chair, 615-322-8000, Fax: 615-343-7094, E-mail: ellen.b.goldring@vanderbilt.edu. *Application contact:* Rosie Moody, Educational Coordinator, 615-322-8019, Fax: 615-343-7094, E-mail: rosie.moody@vanderbilt.edu.
Website: http://peabody.vanderbilt.edu/departments/lpo/index.php

Vanderbilt University, Program in Leadership and Policy Studies, Nashville, TN 37240-1001. Offers higher education leadership and policy (PhD); K-12 educational leadership and policy (PhD). *Faculty:* 23 full-time (9 women). *Students:* 38 full-time (16 women); includes 13 minority (3 Black or African American, non-Hispanic/Latino; 6 Asian, non-Hispanic/Latino; 3 Hispanic/Latino; 1 Two or more races, non-Hispanic/Latino), 2 international. Average age 31. 114 applicants, 11% accepted, 8 enrolled. In 2016, 4 degrees awarded. *Degree requirements:* For doctorate, comprehensive exam, thesis/dissertation, qualifying examinations. *Entrance requirements:* For doctorate, GRE General Test. Additional exam requirements/recommendations for international students: Required—TOEFL (minimum score 570 paper-based; 88 iBT). *Application deadline:* For fall admission, 12/1 for domestic and international students. Application fee: $0. Electronic applications accepted. *Expenses:* Contact institution. *Financial support:* Fellowships with full tuition reimbursements, research assistantships with full tuition reimbursements, teaching assistantships with full tuition reimbursements, Federal Work-Study, institutionally sponsored loans, scholarships/grants, traineeships, and health care benefits available. Financial award application deadline: 1/15; financial award applicants required to submit CSS PROFILE or FAFSA. *Faculty research:* Charter schooling, pay for performance, access and equity for immigrant and at-risk students, higher-education policy, race and ethnic relations, college student departure, college student success, and international comparisons. *Unit head:* Dr. Ron Zimmer, Director of Graduate Studies, 615-322-0722, Fax: 615-343-7094, E-mail: ronald.w.zimmer@vanderbilt.edu. *Application contact:* Rosie Moody, Admissions and Education Coordinator, 615-322-8019, Fax: 615-343-7094, E-mail: rosie.moody@vanderbilt.edu.
Website: http://peabody.vanderbilt.edu/departments/lpo/graduate_and_professional_programs/phd/index.php

Villanova University, Graduate School of Liberal Arts and Sciences, Department of Education and Counseling, Villanova, PA 19085-1699. Offers clinical mental health counseling (MS), including counseling and human relations; education (MA); education plus teacher certification (MA); elementary school counseling (MS), including counseling and human relations; secondary school counseling (MS), including counseling and human relations; teacher leadership (MA). *Program availability:* Part-time, evening/weekend. *Faculty:* 20. *Students:* 81 full-time (67 women), 35 part-time (24 women); includes 18 minority (5 Black or African American, non-Hispanic/Latino; 7 Asian, non-Hispanic/Latino; 6 Hispanic/Latino), 2 international. Average age 30. 71 applicants, 72% accepted, 38 enrolled. In 2016, 47 master's awarded. *Degree requirements:* For master's, comprehensive exam. *Entrance requirements:* For master's, GRE or MAT, minimum GPA of 3.0, statement of goals. Additional exam requirements/recommendations for international students: Required—TOEFL or IELTS. *Application deadline:* For fall admission, 3/1 priority date for domestic students, 5/1 for international students; for spring admission, 11/15 priority date for domestic students, 10/15 for international students; for summer admission, 5/1 for domestic students. Applications are processed on a rolling basis. Application fee: $50. Electronic applications accepted. *Financial support:* Research assistantships, teaching assistantships, scholarships/grants, and unspecified assistantships available. Financial award applicants required to submit FAFSA. *Unit head:* Dr. Edward Fierros, Chairperson, 610-519-4625. *Application contact:* Dean, Graduate School of Liberal Arts and Sciences.
Website: http://www.education.villanova.edu/

Virginia Commonwealth University, Graduate School, School of Education, Doctoral Program in Education, Richmond, VA 23284-9005. Offers art education (PhD); counselor education and supervision (PhD); curriculum, culture and change (PhD); educational leadership (PhD); educational psychology (PhD); leadership (Ed D); research and evaluation (PhD); special education and disability leadership (PhD); sport leadership (PhD); urban services leadership (PhD). *Accreditation:* NCATE. *Program availability:* Part-time. *Degree requirements:* For doctorate, thesis/dissertation. *Entrance requirements:* For doctorate, GRE (for PhD), MAT (for Ed D), interview, master's degree, writing sample. Additional exam requirements/recommendations for international students: Required—TOEFL (minimum score 600 paper-based; 100 iBT). *Application deadline:* For fall admission, 2/15 for domestic students. Application fee: $50. Electronic applications accepted. *Financial support:* Fellowships, research assistantships, career-related internships or fieldwork, Federal Work-Study, and institutionally sponsored loans available. Financial award application deadline: 3/1; financial award applicants required to submit FAFSA. *Unit head:* Dr. Kathleen Cauley, Interim Director, 804-827-2657, E-mail: kmcauley@vcu.edu. *Application contact:* Dr. Colleen A. Thoma, Administrative Assistant, 804-827-2651, E-mail: cathoma@vcu.edu.
Website: http://www.soe.vcu.edu/programs/doctoral-programs/

Virginia Commonwealth University, Graduate School, School of Education, Program in Educational Leadership, Richmond, VA 23284-9005. Offers M Ed. *Entrance requirements:* Additional exam requirements/recommendations for international students: Required—TOEFL (minimum score 600 paper-based; 100 iBT); Recommended—IELTS. *Application deadline:* For fall admission, 2/15 for domestic students. Application fee: $50. Electronic applications accepted. *Financial support:* Applicants required to submit FAFSA. *Unit head:* Dr. Colleen A. Thoma, Director, Doctoral Studies in Education, 804-827-2657, E-mail: kmcauley@vcu.edu. *Application contact:* Dr. Brenda Cowlbeck, Coordinator, 804-827-2615, E-mail: bfcowlbeck@vcu.edu.
Website: http://www.soe.vcu.edu/academics/el/EDd_leadership.html

Virginia Polytechnic Institute and State University, Graduate School, College of Liberal Arts and Human Sciences, Blacksburg, VA 24061. Offers career and technical education (MS Ed, Ed D, PhD, Ed S); communication (MA); counselor education (MA Ed, Ed D, PhD, Ed S); creative writing (MFA); curriculum and instruction (MA Ed, Ed D, PhD, Ed S); educational leadership and policy studies (MA Ed, Ed D, PhD, Ed S); educational research and evaluation (PhD); English (MA); foreign languages, cultures, and literatures (MA); higher education (PhD); higher education and student affairs (MA Ed); history (MA); human development (MS, PhD); material culture and public humanities (MA); philosophy (MA); political science (MA); rhetoric and writing (PhD); science and technology studies (MS, PhD); social, political, ethical, and cultural thought (PhD); sociology (MS, PhD); theater arts (MFA). *Faculty:* 408 full-time (204 women), 3 part-time/adjunct (2 women). *Students:* 657 full-time (446 women), 457 part-time (292 women); includes 213 minority (114 Black or African American, non-Hispanic/Latino; 3 American Indian or Alaska Native, non-Hispanic/Latino; 29 Asian, non-Hispanic/Latino; 44 Hispanic/Latino; 23 Two or more races, non-Hispanic/Latino), 93 international. Average age 33. 805 applicants, 55% accepted, 328 enrolled. In 2016, 270 master's, 91 doctorates awarded. *Degree requirements:* For master's, comprehensive exam (for some programs), thesis (for some programs); for doctorate, comprehensive exam (for some programs), thesis/dissertation (for some programs). *Entrance requirements:* For master's and doctorate, GRE/GMAT. Additional exam requirements/recommendations for international students: Required—TOEFL (minimum score 80 iBT). *Application deadline:* For fall admission, 8/1 for domestic students, 4/1 for international students; for spring admission, 1/1 for domestic students, 9/1 for international students. Applications are processed on a rolling basis. Application fee: $75. Electronic applications accepted. *Expenses:* Tuition, state resident: full-time $12,467; part-time $692.50 per credit hour. Tuition, nonresident: full-time $25,095; part-time $1394.25 per credit hour. *Required fees:* $2669; $491.50 per semester. Tuition and fees vary according to course load, campus/location and program. *Financial support:* In 2016–17, 21 research assistantships with full tuition reimbursements (averaging $19,817 per year), 237 teaching assistantships with full tuition reimbursements (averaging $15,497 per year) were awarded. Financial award application deadline: 3/1; financial award applicants required to submit FAFSA. *Total annual research expenditures:* $6.6 million. *Unit head:* Rosemary Blieszner, Interim Dean, 540-231-6779, Fax: 540-231-7157, E-mail: liberalartsdean@vt.edu. *Application contact:* Chelsea Blanchet, Executive Assistant, 540-231-6779, Fax: 540-231-7157, E-mail: bchels1@vt.edu.
Website: http://www.liberalarts.vt.edu/

Virginia State University, College of Graduate Studies, College of Education, Department of Administrative and Organizational Leadership, Petersburg, VA 23806-0001. Offers administration and supervision (M Ed). *Accreditation:* NCATE. *Degree requirements:* For master's, thesis optional.

Virginia State University, College of Graduate Studies, College of Education, Department of Doctoral Studies, Petersburg, VA 23806-0001. Offers educational administration and supervision (Ed D).

Virginia Theological Seminary, Graduate and Professional Programs, Alexandria, VA 22304. Offers Christian spirituality (D Min); educational leadership (D Ed Min, D Min); ministry development (D Min); theology (M Div, MA). *Accreditation:* ATS. *Program availability:* Part-time. *Faculty:* 26 full-time (11 women), 29 part-time/adjunct (11 women). *Students:* 220. *Degree requirements:* For master's, 2 foreign languages, thesis; for doctorate, thesis/dissertation. *Entrance requirements:* For master's and doctorate, GRE General Test. *Application deadline:* For fall admission, 5/1 for domestic students. Application fee: $0. *Expenses: Tuition:* Full-time $13,800; part-time $636 per credit hour. *Required fees:* $140. *Financial support:* Career-related internships or fieldwork, Federal Work-Study, and institutionally sponsored loans available. *Application contact:* Rachel Holm, Associate Director for Admissions, Financial Aid and Housing, 703-370-6600.

Viterbo University, Graduate Programs in Education, La Crosse, WI 54601-4797. Offers cross-categorical special education (Certificate); director of instruction (Certificate); director of special education and pupil services (Certificate); early childhood (Certificate); education (MAE); literacy coaching (Certificate); PreK-12 principal/supervisor of special education (Certificate); principal (Certificate); reading specialist endorsement (Certificate); reading teacher (Certificate); reading teacher 5-12 endorsement (Certificate); reading teacher K-8 endorsement (Certificate); superintendent (Certificate); talented and gifted endorsement (Certificate); Wisconsin school business administrator (Certificate). Weekend courses available in summer. *Accreditation:* NCATE. *Program availability:* Part-time, evening/weekend. *Degree requirements:* For master's, comprehensive exam, thesis, 30 credits of course work. *Entrance requirements:* For master's, BS, transcripts, teaching license, written narrative. Electronic applications accepted. *Expenses:* Contact institution.

Wagner College, Division of Graduate Studies, Education Department, Program in Educational Leadership, Staten Island, NY 10301-4495. Offers school district leadership (MS Ed, Certificate). *Program availability:* Part-time, evening/weekend. *Entrance requirements:* For master's, minimum GPA of 3.0, valid initial NY State Certificate or equivalent, interview, recommendations. Electronic applications accepted. Tuition and fees vary according to degree level.

Walden University, Graduate Programs, Richard W. Riley College of Education and Leadership, Minneapolis, MN 55401. Offers adult education (Post-Master's Certificate); adult learning (Graduate Certificate); college teaching and learning (Graduate Certificate); community college leadership (Ed D); curriculum, instruction and assessment (Ed D, Ed S, Graduate Certificate); developmental education (Graduate Certificate); early childhood administration, management, and leadership (Graduate Certificate); early childhood education (Ed D, Ed S); early childhood public policy and advocacy (Graduate Certificate); early childhood studies (MS), including administration, management and leadership, early childhood public policy and advocacy, teaching adults in the early childhood field, teaching and diversity in early childhood education; education (MS, PhD), including adolescent literacy and learning (MS), curriculum, instruction, and assessment (grades K-12) (MS), curriculum, instruction, assessment, and evaluation (PhD), early childhood leadership and advocacy (PhD), early childhood special education (PhD), educational leadership (MS), educational leadership and administration (principal preparation) (MS), educational technology and design (PhD), elementary reading and literacy (PreK-6) (MS), elementary reading and mathematics (grades K-6) (MS), global and comparative education (PhD), higher education leadership management and policy (PhD), integrating technology in the classroom (grades K-12) (MS), learning, instruction and innovation (PhD), mathematics (grades 5-8) (MS), mathematics (grades K-6) (MS), mathematics and science (grades K-8) (MS), organizational research, assessment, and evaluation (PhD), reading and literacy with a reading K-12 endorsement (MS), reading literacy assessment and evaluation (PhD), science (grades K-8) (MS), special education (non-licensure) (grades K-12) (MS), teacher leadership (grades K-12) (MS), teaching English language learners (grades K-12) (MS); educational administration and leadership (Ed D); educational leadership and administration (principal preparation) (Ed S); educational technology (Ed D, Ed S, Post Master's Certificate); elementary reading and literacy (Graduate Certificate); engaging culturally diverse learners (Graduate Certificate); enrollment management and institutional marketing (Graduate Certificate); higher education (MS), including adult learning, college teaching and learning, enrollment management and institutional marketing, global higher education, leadership for student success, online and distance learning; higher education and adult learning (Ed D); higher education leadership and management (Ed D); higher education leadership for student success (Graduate Certificate); instructional design and technology (MS, Postbaccalaureate Certificate), including general program (MS), online learning (MS), training and performance improvement (MS); integrating technology in the classroom (Graduate Certificate); mathematics 5-8 (Graduate Certificate); mathematics K-6 (Graduate Certificate); online teaching for adult educators (Graduate Certificate); reading, literacy, and assessment (Ed D, Ed S); science K-8 (Graduate Certificate); special education (Ed D, Ed S, Graduate Certificate); special education (K-age 21) (MAT); teacher leadership (Graduate Certificate); teaching adults English as a second language (Graduate Certificate); teaching adults in the early childhood field (Graduate Certificate); teaching and diversity in early childhood education (Graduate Certificate); teaching English language learners (grades K-12) (Graduate Certificate); teaching K-12 students online (Graduate Certificate). *Accreditation:* NCATE. *Program availability:* Part-time, evening/weekend, online only, 100% online. *Degree requirements:* For doctorate, thesis/dissertation (for some programs), residency; for other advanced degree, residency (for some programs). *Entrance requirements:* For master's, bachelor's degree or higher; minimum GPA of 2.5; official transcripts; goal statement (for some programs); access to computer and Internet; for doctorate, master's degree or higher; three years of related professional or academic experience (preferred); minimum GPA of 3.0; goal statement and current resume (for select programs); official transcripts; access to computer and Internet; for other advanced degree, relevant work experience; access to computer and Internet. Additional exam requirements/recommendations for international students: Required—TOEFL (minimum score 550 paper-based, 79 iBT), IELTS (minimum score 6.5), Michigan English Language Assessment Battery (minimum score 82), or PTE (minimum score 53). Electronic applications accepted.

Waldorf University, Program in Organizational Leadership, Forest City, IA 50436. Offers criminal justice leadership (MA); emergency management leadership (MA); fire/rescue executive leadership (MA); human resource development (MA); public administration (MA); sport management (MA); teacher leader (MA).

Walla Walla University, Graduate Studies, School of Education and Psychology, College Place, WA 99324. Offers curriculum and instruction (M Ed, MA, MAT); educational leadership (M Ed, MA, MAT); literacy instruction (M Ed, MA, MAT); students at risk (M Ed, MA, MAT); teaching (MAT). *Program availability:* Part-time. *Entrance requirements:* For master's, GRE General Test, minimum GPA of 2.75. Additional exam requirements/recommendations for international students: Required—TOEFL (minimum score 550 paper-based; 79 iBT). *Application deadline:* For fall admission, 4/1 priority date for domestic students. Applications are processed on a rolling basis. Application fee: $50. Electronic applications accepted. *Expenses: Tuition:* Part-time $592 per quarter hour. *Financial support:* Research assistantships, teaching assistantships, Federal Work-Study, and tuition waivers (partial) available. Support available to part-time students. Financial award application deadline: 4/30; financial award applicants required to submit FAFSA. *Faculty research:* Admissions/retention, instructional psychology, moral development, teaching of reading. *Unit head:* Denise Dunzweiler, Dean, 509-527-2212, Fax: 509-527-2248, E-mail: denise.dunzweiler@wallawalla.edu. *Application contact:* Dr. Joe G. Galusha, Dean of Graduate Studies, 509-527-2421, Fax: 509-527-2237, E-mail: joe.galusha@wallawalla.edu.
Website: https://wallawalla.edu/academics/areas-of-study/undergraduate-programs/education-and-psychology/

Washburn University, College of Arts and Sciences, Department of Education, Topeka, KS 66621. Offers curriculum and instruction (M Ed); educational leadership (M Ed); reading (M Ed); special education (M Ed). *Accreditation:* NCATE. *Program availability:* Part-time. *Degree requirements:* For master's, comprehensive exam, thesis or alternative, portfolio, comprehensive paper, or action research project. *Entrance requirements:* For master's, department exam, GRE General Test, or MAT, minimum GPA of 3.0 in graduate coursework or last 60 hours of undergraduate coursework. Additional exam requirements/recommendations for international students: Required—TOEFL (minimum score 80 iBT). *Faculty research:* Reading/literature/literacy, foundations, special education, diversity, teaching and technology.

Washington State University, College of Education, Department of Educational Leadership, Sports Studies, and Educational/Counseling Psychology, Pullman, WA 99164-2136. Offers counseling psychology (PhD); educational leadership (Ed M, MA, Ed D, PhD); educational psychology (MA, PhD); sport management (MA). Programs also offered at the Spokane, Tri-Cities, Vancouver and Global (online) campuses. *Program availability:* Part-time, online learning. *Degree requirements:* For master's, comprehensive exam (for some programs), thesis (for some programs), oral or written exam; for doctorate, comprehensive exam, thesis/dissertation, oral and written exam, internship. *Entrance requirements:* For master's and doctorate, GRE General Test, minimum GPA of 3.0, 3 letters of recommendation, transcripts showing all college or university course work, statement of professional objectives, current curriculum vitae/resume. Additional exam requirements/recommendations for international students: Required—TOEFL (minimum score 550 paper-based; 80 iBT). Electronic applications accepted. *Faculty research:* Multicultural counseling and career development, educational and psychological measurement issues, business decision-making process and power relationships, leadership practices and processes as suffused with and constituted by emotion work.

Washington State University, College of Education, Department of Teaching and Learning, Pullman, WA 99164-2132. Offers cultural studies and social thought in education (PhD); curriculum and instruction (Ed M, MA); English language learners (Ed M, MA); language, literacy and technology (PhD); literacy education (Ed M, MA); mathematics education (PhD); special education (Ed M, MA, PhD); teacher leadership (Ed D); teaching (MIT), including elementary education, secondary education. Programs offered at the Pullman, Spokane, Tri-cities, Vancouver and Global (online) campuses. *Program availability:* Part-time, online learning. *Degree requirements:* For master's, comprehensive exam, thesis, oral or written exam; for doctorate, comprehensive exam, thesis/dissertation, oral and written exam. *Entrance requirements:* For master's, GRE General Test, minimum GPA of 3.0, 3 letters of recommendation, letter of intent, transcripts, resume/curriculum vitae; for doctorate, GRE General Test, minimum GPA of 3.0, 3 letters of recommendation, letter of intent, transcripts, writing sample, resume/curriculum vitae. Additional exam requirements/recommendations for international students: Required—TOEFL (minimum score 550 paper-based; 80 iBT). Electronic applications accepted. *Faculty research:* Intersection of gender, youth cultures and schooling; examination of ideology of power in children's literature; early childhood special education; analyzing pre-service and in-service teacher development; second language acquisition.

Wayland Baptist University, Graduate Programs, Program in Education, Plainview, TX 79072-6998. Offers education administration (M Ed); education diagnostics (M Ed); education literacy (M Ed); elementary certification (M Ed); English (M Ed); English as a second language (M Ed); higher education administration (M Ed); human resources (M Ed); instructional leadership (M Ed); instructional technology (M Ed); leadership training and development (M Ed); science education (M Ed); secondary certification (M Ed); social studies (M Ed); special education (M Ed); sports administration and management (M Ed). *Program availability:* Part-time, evening/weekend, online learning. *Degree requirements:* For master's, comprehensive exam, capstone course. *Entrance requirements:* For master's, GRE, GMAT or MAT. Additional exam requirements/recommendations for international students: Required—TOEFL (minimum score 500 paper-based; 61 iBT). Electronic applications accepted.

Waynesburg University, Graduate and Professional Studies, Canonsburg, PA 15370. Offers business (MBA), including energy management, finance, health systems, human resources, leadership, market development; counseling (MA), including addictions counseling, clinical mental health; counselor education and supervision (PhD); criminal investigation (MA); education (M Ed), including autism, curriculum and instruction, educational leadership, online teaching; nursing (MSN), including administration, education, informatics; nursing practice (DNP); special education (M Ed); technology (M Ed); MSN/MBA. *Accreditation:* AACN. *Program availability:* Part-time, evening/weekend. *Degree requirements:* For doctorate, thesis/dissertation. *Entrance requirements:* Additional exam requirements/recommendations for international students: Required—TOEFL. Electronic applications accepted.

Wayne State College, School of Education and Counseling, Department of Educational Foundations and Leadership, Program in Educational Administration, Wayne, NE 68787. Offers educational administration (Ed S); elementary administration (MSE); elementary and secondary administration (MSE); secondary administration (MSE). *Accreditation:* NCATE. *Program availability:* Part-time, evening/weekend. *Degree requirements:* For master's, comprehensive exam, thesis optional, research paper. *Entrance requirements:* For master's, GRE General Test, minimum GPA of 2.5; for Ed S, GRE General Test, minimum GPA of 3.2. Additional exam requirements/recommendations for international students: Required—TOEFL (minimum score 550 paper-based). Electronic applications accepted.

Wayne State University, College of Education, Division of Administrative and Organizational Studies, Detroit, MI 48202. Offers college and university teaching (Certificate); educational administration and supervision (Ed S); educational leadership (M Ed); educational leadership and policy studies (Ed D, PhD); educational technology (Certificate); learning design and technology (M Ed, Ed D, PhD, Ed S); online teaching (Certificate). *Program availability:* Part-time, 100% online, blended/hybrid learning. *Faculty:* 11. *Students:* 83 full-time (58 women), 223 part-time (148 women); includes 151 minority (126 Black or African American, non-Hispanic/Latino; 3 American Indian or Alaska Native, non-Hispanic/Latino; 4 Asian, non-Hispanic/Latino; 8 Hispanic/Latino; 10 Two or more races, non-Hispanic/Latino), 14 international. Average age 39. 143 applicants, 43% accepted, 38 enrolled. In 2016, 53 master's, 9 doctorates, 34 other advanced degrees awarded. *Degree requirements:* For doctorate, thesis/dissertation. *Entrance requirements:* For master's, baccalaureate degree from accredited U.S. institution or equivalent from college or university of government-recognized standing; minimum undergraduate GPA of 2.75 in upper-division coursework; personal statement; for doctorate, GRE (instructional design and technology), interview; curriculum vitae; three references (two professional and one academic); master's degree; minimum graduate GPA of 3.5; autobiographical statement; research experience. Additional exam requirements/recommendations for international students: Required—TOEFL (minimum score 550 paper-based; 79 iBT), Michigan English Language Assessment Battery (minimum score 85); Recommended—IELTS (minimum score 6.5), TWE (minimum score 5.5). *Application deadline:* For fall admission, 6/1 priority date for domestic students, 5/1 priority date for international students; for winter admission, 10/1 priority date for domestic students, 9/1 priority date for international students; for spring admission, 2/1 priority date for domestic students, 1/1 priority date for international students. Applications are processed on a rolling basis. Application fee: $50. Electronic applications accepted. *Expenses:* $16,503 per year resident tuition and fees, $33,697 per year non-resident tuition and fees. *Financial support:* In 2016–17, 96 students received support, including 1 fellowship with tuition reimbursement available (averaging $11,000 per year), 4 research assistantships with tuition reimbursements available (averaging $17,949 per year); scholarships/grants and unspecified assistantships also available. Support available to part-time students. Financial award applicants required to submit FAFSA. *Faculty research:* Total quality management, participatory management, administering educational technology, school improvement, principalship. *Unit head:* Dr. William Hill, Assistant Dean, 313-577-9316, E-mail: ad2107@wayne.edu. *Application contact:* Janice Green, Assistant Dean, 313-577-1605, E-mail: jwgreen@wayne.edu.
Website: http://coe.wayne.edu/aos/index.php

West Chester University of Pennsylvania, College of Education and Social Work, Department of Early and Middle Grades Education, West Chester, PA 19383. Offers applied studies in teaching and learning (M Ed); early childhood education (M Ed), including accomplished teacher, program administrators; grades 4-8 (Teaching

Certificate); grades preK-4 (Teaching Certificate). *Accreditation:* NCATE. *Program availability:* Part-time, 100% online. *Faculty:* 7 full-time (6 women), 1 (woman) part-time/adjunct. *Students:* 14 full-time (13 women), 97 part-time (83 women); includes 21 minority (14 Black or African American, non-Hispanic/Latino; 2 Asian, non-Hispanic/Latino; 4 Hispanic/Latino; 1 Two or more races, non-Hispanic/Latino), 1 international. Average age 30. 31 applicants, 87% accepted, 17 enrolled. In 2016, 24 master's, 21 other advanced degrees awarded. *Degree requirements:* For master's, teacher research project, portfolio. *Entrance requirements:* For master's, one year of full time teaching, minimum GPA of 3.0; for Teaching Certificate, math, social studies, or science concentration exams (for middle grades preparation), minimum GPA of 3.0. Additional exam requirements/recommendations for international students: Required—TOEFL or IELTS. *Application deadline:* For fall admission, 5/15 for international students; for spring admission, 10/15 for international students. Applications are processed on a rolling basis. Application fee: $50. Electronic applications accepted. *Expenses:* Tuition, state resident: full-time $8694; part-time $483 per credit. Tuition, nonresident: full-time $13,050; part-time $725 per credit. *Required fees:* $2399; $119.05 per credit. Tuition and fees vary according to campus/location and program. *Financial support:* Scholarships/grants and unspecified assistantships available. Financial award application deadline: 2/15; financial award applicants required to submit FAFSA. *Faculty research:* Cooperative learning, creative expression and critical thinking, teacher research, learning styles, middle school education. *Unit head:* Dr. Heather Leaman, Chair, 610-436-2944, Fax: 610-436-3102, E-mail: hleaman@wcupa.edu. *Application contact:* Office of Graduate Studies and Extended Education, 610-436-2943, Fax: 610-436-2763, E-mail: gradstudy@wcupa.edu.
Website: http://www.wcupa.edu/education-socialWork/earlyMiddleGrades/

West Chester University of Pennsylvania, College of Education and Social Work, Program in Policy, Planning, and Administration, West Chester, PA 19383. Offers Ed D. *Program availability:* Part-time, evening/weekend. *Students:* 15 part-time (8 women); includes 1 minority (Hispanic/Latino). Average age 36. 27 applicants, 78% accepted, 15 enrolled. *Degree requirements:* For doctorate, comprehensive exam. *Entrance requirements:* For doctorate, GRE if master's GPA lower than 3.85, master's degree from regionally-accredited college or university, three letters of recommendation from education professionals, professional writing demonstration at time of application (waived for applicants who present GRE analytical writing score of 4.5 or higher), resume or curriculum vitae, interview (upon Committee request). Additional exam requirements/recommendations for international students: Required—TOEFL or IELTS. *Application deadline:* For fall admission, 5/15 for international students; for spring admission, 10/15 for international students. Applications are processed on a rolling basis. Application fee: $50. Electronic applications accepted. *Expenses:* Tuition, state resident: full-time $8694; part-time $483 per credit. Tuition, nonresident: full-time $13,050; part-time $725 per credit. *Required fees:* $2399; $119.05 per credit. Tuition and fees vary according to campus/location and program. *Financial support:* Application deadline: 2/15; applicants required to submit FAFSA. *Faculty research:* Literacy, special education, critical pedagogy, social and cultural foundations of education, educational technology. *Unit head:* Dr. Kenneth D. Witmer, Jr., Dean, 610-436-2321, Fax: 610-436-3102, E-mail: kwitmer@wcupa.edu. *Application contact:* Robert Haworth, Graduate Coordinator, 610-436-2246, E-mail: rhaworth@wcupa.edu.
Website: http://www.wcupa.edu/education-socialWork/doctorate/

Western Connecticut State University, Division of Graduate Studies, School of Professional Studies, Department of Education and Educational Psychology, Program in Instructional Leadership, Danbury, CT 06810-6885. Offers Ed D. *Program availability:* Part-time. *Degree requirements:* For doctorate, comprehensive exam, thesis/dissertation, completion of program in 6 years. *Entrance requirements:* For doctorate, GRE or MAT, resume, three recommendations (one in a supervisory capacity in an educational setting), satisfactory interview with WCSU representatives from the Ed D Admissions Committee. Additional exam requirements/recommendations for international students: Recommended—TOEFL (minimum score 550 paper-based; 79 iBT), IELTS (minimum score 6). *Expenses:* Contact institution. *Faculty research:* Differentiated instruction, the transition of teacher learning, teacher retention, relationship building through the evaluation process, leadership development.

Western Governors University, Teachers College, Salt Lake City, UT 84107. Offers curriculum and instruction (MS); educational leadership (MS); educational studies (MA); educational studies (5-12) (MA), including mathematics; elementary education (K-8) (MAT, Postbaccalaureate Certificate); elementary education (PreK-8) (MAT); English language learning (K-12) (MA); instructional design (MAT); learning and technology (M Ed, MA); management and innovation (M Ed); mathematics (5-12) (MAT, Postbaccalaureate Certificate); mathematics (5-9) (MAT, Postbaccalaureate Certificate); mathematics education (5-12) (MA); mathematics education (5-9) (MA); mathematics education (K-6) (MA); measurement and evaluation (M Ed); science (5-12) (Postbaccalaureate Certificate); science (5-9) (MAT, Postbaccalaureate Certificate); science education (5-12) (MA), including biology, chemistry, geology, physics; science education (5-9) (MA); social science (5-12) (MAT, Postbaccalaureate Certificate); special education (MAT, MS). *Accreditation:* NCATE. *Program availability:* Evening/weekend, online learning. *Degree requirements:* For master's, capstone project. *Entrance requirements:* For master's and Postbaccalaureate Certificate, Readiness Assessment, transcripts. Additional exam requirements/recommendations for international students: Required—TOEFL (minimum score 450 paper-based; 80 iBT). Electronic applications accepted. *Expenses:* Contact institution.

Western Illinois University, School of Graduate Studies, College of Education and Human Services, Department of Educational Studies, Program in College Student Personnel, Macomb, IL 61455-1390. Offers college student personnel (MS), including higher education leadership, student affairs. *Accreditation:* NCATE. *Program availability:* Part-time. *Students:* 56 full-time (37 women), 19 part-time (15 women); includes 19 minority (7 Black or African American, non-Hispanic/Latino; 1 Asian, non-Hispanic/Latino; 8 Hispanic/Latino; 3 Two or more races, non-Hispanic/Latino), 2 international. Average age 27. 110 applicants, 79% accepted, 28 enrolled. In 2016, 27 master's awarded. *Degree requirements:* For master's, thesis or alternative. *Entrance requirements:* For master's, interview. Additional exam requirements/recommendations for international students: Required—TOEFL (minimum score 550 paper-based; 80 iBT). *Application deadline:* For fall admission, 1/5 priority date for domestic students. Application fee: $30. Electronic applications accepted. *Financial support:* In 2016–17, 55 students received support. Unspecified assistantships available. Financial award applicants required to submit FAFSA. *Unit head:* Dr. Tracy Davis, Coordinator, 309-298-1183. *Application contact:* Dr. Nancy Parsons, Associate Provost and Director of Graduate Studies, 309-298-1806, Fax: 309-298-2345, E-mail: grad-office@wiu.edu.
Website: http://wiu.edu/csp/

Western Illinois University, School of Graduate Studies, College of Education and Human Services, Department of Educational Studies, Program in Educational Leadership, Macomb, IL 61455-1390. Offers MS Ed, Ed D, Ed S. *Accreditation:* NCATE. *Program availability:* Part-time, evening/weekend. *Students:* 19 full-time (9 women), 156 part-time (64 women); includes 13 minority (7 Black or African American, non-Hispanic/Latino; 5 Hispanic/Latino; 1 Two or more races, non-Hispanic/Latino), 1 international. Average age 39. 35 applicants, 94% accepted, 26 enrolled. In 2016, 14 master's, 12 doctorates, 18 other advanced degrees awarded. *Degree requirements:* For master's, thesis or alternative; for doctorate, comprehensive exam, thesis/dissertation, electronic portfolio. *Entrance requirements:* For master's and Ed S, interview; for doctorate, GRE General Test. Additional exam requirements/recommendations for international students: Required—TOEFL (minimum score 575 paper-based; 88 iBT). *Application deadline:* Applications are processed on a rolling basis. Application fee: $30. Electronic applications accepted. *Financial support:* In 2016–17, 3 students received support. Unspecified assistantships available. Financial award applicants required to submit FAFSA. *Unit head:* Dr. Greg Montalvo, Interim Chairperson, 309-298-1070. *Application contact:* Dr. Nancy Parsons, Associate Provost and Director of Graduate Studies, 309-298-1806, Fax: 309-298-2345, E-mail: grad-office@wiu.edu.

Western Kentucky University, Graduate Studies, College of Education and Behavioral Sciences, Department of Educational Administration, Leadership, and Research, Bowling Green, KY 42101. Offers adult education (MAE); educational leadership (Ed D); school administration (Ed S); school principal (MAE). *Accreditation:* NCATE. *Program availability:* Part-time, evening/weekend. *Degree requirements:* For master's, comprehensive exam, thesis or applied project and oral defense; for Ed S, thesis. *Entrance requirements:* For master's, GRE General Test, minimum GPA of 2.75. Additional exam requirements/recommendations for international students: Required—TOEFL (minimum score 555 paper-based; 79 iBT). *Faculty research:* Principal internship, superintendent assessment, administrative leadership, group training for residential workers.

Western Michigan University, Graduate College, College of Education and Human Development, Department of Educational Leadership, Research and Technology, Kalamazoo, MI 49008. Offers educational leadership (MA, PhD, Ed S), including educational leadership (MA); educational technology (MA, Graduate Certificate); evaluation, measurement and research (MA, PhD); organizational learning and performance (MA).

Western New Mexico University, Graduate Division, School of Education, Silver City, NM 88062-0680. Offers bilingual education (MAT); educational leadership (MA); elementary education (MAT); reading (MAT); secondary education (MAT); special education (MAT); TESOL (teaching English to speakers of other languages) (MAT). *Accreditation:* NCATE. *Program availability:* Part-time, online learning. *Degree requirements:* For master's, comprehensive exam. *Entrance requirements:* For master's, minimum GPA of 3.0 in last 64 hours of undergraduate study. Additional exam requirements/recommendations for international students: Required—TOEFL (minimum score 550 paper-based; 79 iBT). Electronic applications accepted. *Faculty research:* International education, electronic reading assessment, developing STEM teachers.

Western State Colorado University, Graduate Programs in Education, Gunnison, CO 81231. Offers education administrator leadership (MA); reading leadership (MA); teacher leadership (MA). *Program availability:* Online learning. *Degree requirements:* For master's, capstone.

Western Washington University, Graduate School, Woodring College of Education, Department of Educational Leadership, Educational Administration Program, Bellingham, WA 98225-5996. Offers M Ed. *Accreditation:* NCATE. *Program availability:* Part-time. *Degree requirements:* For master's, comprehensive exam, thesis optional. *Entrance requirements:* For master's, GRE General Test or MAT, minimum GPA of 3.0 in last 60 semester hours or last 90 quarter hours, certification. Additional exam requirements/recommendations for international students: Required—TOEFL (minimum score 567 paper-based). Electronic applications accepted. *Faculty research:* Principal efficacy, collaborative school leadership, school/university partnerships, case study methodology, ethical leadership.

Western Washington University, Graduate School, Woodring College of Education, Department of Educational Leadership, Program in Student Affairs Administration, Bellingham, WA 98225-5996. Offers M Ed. *Accreditation:* NCATE. *Program availability:* Part-time. *Degree requirements:* For master's, comprehensive exam, thesis optional, research project. *Entrance requirements:* For master's, GRE General Test or MAT, minimum GPA of 3.0 in last 60 semester hours or last 90 quarter hours. Additional exam requirements/recommendations for international students: Required—TOEFL (minimum score 567 paper-based). Electronic applications accepted. *Faculty research:* Outcomes assessment, adult learning, best practices/student affairs, college health promotion, cultural pluralism.

Westminster College, Graduate School, Program in Educational Administration, New Wilmington, PA 16172-0001. Offers school principal K-12 (M Ed); school superintendent (Certificate). *Expenses: Tuition:* Full-time $1362; part-time $454 per semester hour. One-time fee: $235.50 full-time. *Unit head:* Dr. Robert L. Zorn, Graduate School Director, 724-946-7031, Fax: 724-946-6158. *Application contact:* Dr. Darwin W. Huey, Graduate Education Director, 724-946-7186, Fax: 724-946-6158, E-mail: hueydw@westminster.edu.

West Texas A&M University, College of Education and Social Sciences, Department of Education, Program in Educational Leadership, Canyon, TX 79016-0001. Offers M Ed. *Program availability:* Part-time, evening/weekend, online learning. *Degree requirements:* For master's, comprehensive exam, thesis optional. *Entrance requirements:* For master's, GRE General Test. Additional exam requirements/recommendations for international students: Required—TOEFL (minimum score 550 paper-based). *Application deadline:* For fall admission, 8/1 for domestic students, 5/1 for international students; for spring admission, 12/1 for domestic students, 10/30 for international students; for summer admission, 5/1 for domestic students. Applications are processed on a rolling basis. Application fee: $40 ($75 for international students). Electronic applications accepted. *Financial support:* Research assistantships with partial tuition reimbursements, teaching assistantships with partial tuition reimbursements, career-related internships or fieldwork, Federal Work-Study, institutionally sponsored loans, and tuition waivers (partial) available. Support available to part-time students. Financial award applicants required to submit CSS PROFILE or FAFSA. *Faculty research:* Teacher quality, leadership, recruitment, retention. *Unit head:* Dr. Gary Bigham, Chair, 806-651-3622. *Application contact:* Dr. Gary Bigham, Chair, 806-651-3622.
Website: http://www.wtamu.edu/academics/educational-leadership.aspx

West Virginia University, College of Education and Human Services, Department of Educational Leadership Studies, Morgantown, WV 26506. Offers educational leadership (Ed D); higher education administration (MA); public school administration (MA). *Accreditation:* NCATE. *Program availability:* Part-time. *Degree requirements:* For master's, content exams; for doctorate, comprehensive exam, thesis/dissertation. *Entrance requirements:* For master's, minimum GPA of 2.75 or MA Degree or MAT of 4107; for doctorate, GRE General Test or MAT, minimum GPA of 3.25. Additional exam requirements/recommendations for international students: Required—TOEFL. Electronic applications accepted. *Faculty research:* Evaluation, collective bargaining, educational law, international higher education, superintendency.

Wheeling Jesuit University, Department of Education, Wheeling, WV 26003-6295. Offers MEL. *Program availability:* Part-time, evening/weekend, online learning. *Degree requirements:* For master's, thesis. *Entrance requirements:* For master's, GRE or MAT, minimum GPA of 2.5, professional teaching certificate. Additional exam requirements/recommendations for international students: Required—TOEFL (minimum score 600 paper-based; 100 iBT). Electronic applications accepted. Application fee is waived when completed online. *Faculty research:* Education leadership, school improvement, student achievement, leadership in special education.

Wheelock College, Graduate Programs, Division of Education, Boston, MA 02215. Offers early childhood education (MS); education leadership (MS); elementary education (MS); language, literacy, and reading (MS); teaching students with moderate disabilities (MS). *Accreditation:* NCATE. *Program availability:* Online learning. *Degree requirements:* For master's, comprehensive exam. *Entrance requirements:* Additional exam requirements/recommendations for international students: Required—TOEFL. Electronic applications accepted. *Faculty research:* Symbolic learning, emergent literacy, diversity inclusion, beginning reading language and culture, math education.

Whittier College, Graduate Programs, Department of Education and Child Development, Program in Educational Administration, Whittier, CA 90608-0634. Offers MA Ed. *Program availability:* Part-time, evening/weekend. *Degree requirements:* For master's, thesis. *Entrance requirements:* For master's, GRE General Test, MAT. *Faculty research:* Candidate leadership development.

Whitworth University, School of Education, Graduate Studies in Education, Program in Administration, Spokane, WA 99251-0001. Offers M Ed. *Accreditation:* NCATE. *Program availability:* Part-time, evening/weekend. *Degree requirements:* For master's, comprehensive exam, internship, practicum, research project, or thesis. *Entrance requirements:* For master's, GRE General Test, MAT. *Faculty research:* Rural staff development.

Wichita State University, Graduate School, College of Education, Department of Counseling, Educational Leadership, Educational and School Psychology, Wichita, KS 67260. Offers counseling (M Ed); educational leadership (M Ed, Ed D); educational psychology (M Ed); school psychology (Ed S). *Accreditation:* NCATE. *Program availability:* Part-time, evening/weekend. Application fee: $50 ($65 for international students). *Unit head:* Dr. Jody Fiorini, Department Head, 316-978-3325, Fax: 316-978-3102, E-mail: jody.fiorini@wichita.edu. *Application contact:* Jordan Oleson, Admissions Coordinator, 316-978-3095, Fax: 316-978-3253, E-mail: jordan.oleson@wichita.edu.
Website: http://www.wichita.edu/cles

Widener University, School of Education, Hospitality, and Continuing Studies, Chester, PA 19013-5792. Offers adult education (M Ed); counseling in higher education (M Ed); counselor education (M Ed); early childhood education (M Ed); educational foundations (M Ed); educational leadership (M Ed); educational psychology (M Ed); elementary education (M Ed); English and language arts (M Ed); health education (M Ed); higher education leadership (Ed D); home and school visitor (M Ed); human sexuality (M Ed, PhD); mathematics education (M Ed); middle school education (M Ed); principalship (M Ed); reading and language arts (Ed D); reading education (M Ed); school administration (Ed D); science education (M Ed); social studies education (M Ed); special education (M Ed); technology education (M Ed). *Accreditation:* NCATE. *Program availability:* Part-time, evening/weekend. *Faculty:* 34 full-time (22 women), 37 part-time/adjunct (14 women). *Students:* 97 full-time (64 women), 201 part-time (143 women); includes 56 minority (44 Black or African American, non-Hispanic/Latino; 1 American Indian or Alaska Native, non-Hispanic/Latino; 2 Asian, non-Hispanic/Latino; 8 Hispanic/Latino; 1 Two or more races, non-Hispanic/Latino), 32 international. Average age 39. 139 applicants, 88% accepted. In 2016, 45 master's, 21 doctorates awarded. Terminal master's awarded for partial completion of doctoral program. *Degree requirements:* For doctorate, thesis/dissertation. *Entrance requirements:* For master's, minimum GPA of 2.5; for doctorate, GRE or MAT, minimum GPA of 2.0 (undergraduate), 3.5 (graduate). *Application deadline:* Applications are processed on a rolling basis. Application fee: $25 ($300 for international students). Electronic applications accepted. *Expenses:* Contact institution. *Financial support:* Career-related internships or fieldwork, tuition waivers (full and partial), and unspecified assistantships available. Support available to part-time students. Financial award application deadline: 5/1. *Faculty research:* Reading and cognition, adult education, technology education, educational leadership, special education. *Unit head:* Dr. Shawn Fitzgerald, Dean, 610-499-4294, Fax: 610-499-4623, E-mail: smfitzgerald@widener.edu. *Application contact:* Dr. Roberta Nolan, Director of Graduate Admissions, 610-499-4125, E-mail: rdnolan@widener.edu.
Website: http://www.widener.edu/academics/schools/eics

Wilkes University, College of Graduate and Professional Studies, School of Education, Wilkes-Barre, PA 18766-0002. Offers 21st century teaching and learning (MS Ed); art and science of teaching (MS Ed); classroom technology (MS Ed); early childhood literacy (MS Ed); educational development and strategies (MS Ed); educational leadership (MS Ed, Ed D); effective teaching (MS Ed); instructional media (MS Ed); instructional technology (MS Ed); international school leadership (MS Ed); international teaching and learning (MS Ed); middle level education (MS Ed); online teaching (MS Ed); reading (MS Ed); school business leadership (MS Ed); special education (MS Ed); teaching English to speakers of other languages (MS Ed). *Program availability:* Part-time, evening/weekend, 100% online, blended/hybrid learning. *Students:* 87 full-time (70 women), 1,496 part-time (1,111 women); includes 77 minority (11 Black or African American, non-Hispanic/Latino; 2 American Indian or Alaska Native, non-Hispanic/Latino; 12 Asian, non-Hispanic/Latino; 28 Hispanic/Latino; 3 Native Hawaiian or other Pacific Islander, non-Hispanic/Latino; 21 Two or more races, non-Hispanic/Latino). Average age 33. In 2016, 524 master's, 21 doctorates awarded. *Entrance requirements:* Additional exam requirements/recommendations for international students: Required—TOEFL (minimum score 550 paper-based; 79 iBT). *Application deadline:* Applications are processed on a rolling basis. Application fee: $45. Electronic applications accepted. *Expenses:* Contact institution. *Financial support:* Unspecified assistantships available. Financial award application deadline: 3/1; financial award applicants required to submit FAFSA. *Unit head:* Dr. Rhonda Rabbitt, Dean, 570-408-4680, Fax: 570-408-7872, E-mail: rhonda.rabbitt@wilkes.edu. *Application contact:* Director of Graduate Education, 570-408-4234, Fax: 570-408-7846.
Website: http://www.wilkes.edu/academics/graduate-programs/masters-programs/graduate-education/index.aspx

William Paterson University of New Jersey, College of Education, Wayne, NJ 07470-8420. Offers curriculum and learning (M Ed); educational leadership (M Ed); elementary education (MAT); literacy (M Ed); professional counseling (M Ed); secondary education (MAT); special education (M Ed). *Accreditation:* NCATE. *Program availability:* Part-time, evening/weekend. *Faculty:* 36 full-time (25 women), 32 part-time/adjunct (27 women). *Students:* 74 full-time (51 women), 607 part-time (515 women); includes 194 minority (42 Black or African American, non-Hispanic/Latino; 21 Asian, non-Hispanic/Latino; 116 Hispanic/Latino; 15 Two or more races, non-Hispanic/Latino), 1 international. Average age 35. 390 applicants, 83% accepted, 263 enrolled. In 2016, 170 master's awarded. *Degree requirements:* For master's, comprehensive exam, thesis (for some programs), exit interview (for some programs); practicum/internship; minimum GPA of 3.0 (for some programs); exit portfolio (for some programs). *Entrance requirements:* For master's, GRE/MAT, minimum GPA of 2.75; teaching certificate; essay; interview; 2 letters of recommendation; personal statement. Additional exam requirements/recommendations for international students: Required—TOEFL (minimum score 550 paper-based; 79 iBT), IELTS (minimum score 6). *Application deadline:* For fall admission, 8/1 for domestic students, 4/1 for international students; for spring admission, 12/1 for domestic students, 11/1 for international students; for summer admission, 5/1 for domestic students, 2/1 for international students. Applications are processed on a rolling basis. Application fee: $50. Electronic applications accepted. *Expenses:* Tuition, state resident: full-time $12,480; part-time $611 per credit. Tuition, nonresident: full-time $20,263; part-time $992 per credit. *Required fees:* $1573; $77 per credit. Tuition and fees vary according to course load, degree level and program. *Financial support:* Career-related internships or fieldwork, Federal Work-Study, scholarships/grants, and unspecified assistantships available. Support available to part-time students. Financial award application deadline: 4/1; financial award applicants required to submit FAFSA. *Faculty research:* History of education, social media in classrooms and education, integrating environmental lessons into urban classrooms, minority student self-advocacy in higher education, factors affecting high school teacher retention. *Total annual research expenditures:* $289,197. *Unit head:* Dr. Candace Burns, Dean, 973-720-2137, Fax: 973-720-3467, E-mail: burnsc@wpunj.edu. *Application contact:* Liana Fornarotto, Director of Education Enrollment and Certification, 973-720-2206, Fax: 973-720-2989, E-mail: fornarottol@wpunj.edu.
Website: http://www.wpunj.edu/coe

William Woods University, Graduate and Adult Studies, Fulton, MO 65251-1098. Offers administration (M Ed, Ed S); athletic/activities administration (M Ed); curriculum and instruction (M Ed, Ed S); educational leadership (Ed D); equestrian education (M Ed); health management (MBA); human resources (MBA); leadership (MBA); marketing, advertising, and public relations (MBA); teaching and technology (M Ed). *Program availability:* Part-time, evening/weekend. *Degree requirements:* For master's, capstone course (MBA), action research (M Ed); for Ed S, field experience. *Entrance requirements:* Additional exam requirements/recommendations for international students: Required—TOEFL (minimum score 550 paper-based). Electronic applications accepted. *Expenses:* Contact institution.

Wilmington University, College of Education, New Castle, DE 19720-6491. Offers applied technology in education (M Ed); career and technical education (M Ed); educational leadership (Ed D); elementary and secondary school counseling (M Ed); elementary studies (M Ed); ESOL literacy (M Ed); higher education leadership (Ed D); instruction: gifted and talented (M Ed); instruction: teacher of reading (M Ed); instruction: teaching and learning (M Ed); organizational leadership (Ed D); school leadership (M Ed); secondary education (MAT); special education (M Ed). *Accreditation:* NCATE. *Program availability:* Part-time, evening/weekend. *Faculty:* 19 full-time (11 women), 178 part-time/adjunct (99 women). *Students:* 248 full-time (176 women), 999 part-time (738 women); includes 244 minority (193 Black or African American, non-Hispanic/Latino; 17 American Indian or Alaska Native, non-Hispanic/Latino; 9 Asian, non-Hispanic/Latino; 19 Hispanic/Latino; 2 Native Hawaiian or other Pacific Islander, non-Hispanic/Latino; 4 Two or more races, non-Hispanic/Latino), 7 international. Average age 34. 672 applicants, 96% accepted, 348 enrolled. In 2016, 529 master's, 87 doctorates awarded. *Entrance requirements:* For master's, 2 letters of recommendation, interview. Additional exam requirements/recommendations for international students: Required—TOEFL (minimum score 500 paper-based). *Application deadline:* For fall admission, 4/30 for domestic students. Applications are processed on a rolling basis. Application fee: $35. Electronic applications accepted. *Expenses: Tuition:* Full-time $8388; part-time $466 per credit. *Required fees:* $25 per semester. Tuition and fees vary according to degree level. *Financial support:* Applicants required to submit FAFSA. *Unit head:* Dr. John C. Gray, Dean. *Application contact:* Laura Morris, Director of Admissions, 877-967-5464, E-mail: infocenter@wilmu.edu.
Website: http://www.wilmu.edu/education/

Wingate University, Thayer School of Education, Wingate, NC 28174. Offers community college executive leadership (Ed D); educational leadership (MA Ed, Ed S); elementary education (MA Ed, MAT). *Accreditation:* NCATE. *Program availability:* Part-time, evening/weekend. *Degree requirements:* For master's, portfolio. *Entrance requirements:* For master's, GRE General Test or MAT, teaching certificate (MA Ed). *Application deadline:* For fall admission, 8/15 priority date for domestic students; for spring admission, 12/15 for domestic students. Applications are processed on a rolling basis. Application fee: $0. *Financial support:* Scholarships/grants available. Support available to part-time students. Financial award applicants required to submit FAFSA. *Unit head:* Dr. Annette D. Digby, Interim Dean, 704-233-8473, E-mail: a.digby@wingate.edu. *Application contact:* Theresa Gibson, Director of the Graduate Education Program, 980-359-1023, E-mail: t.gibson@wingate.edu.

Winona State University, College of Education, Department of Education Leadership, Winona, MN 55987. Offers educational leadership (Ed S), including general superintendency, K-12 principalship; general school leadership (MS); K-12 principalship (MS); outdoor education/adventure-based leadership (MS); sports management (MS); teacher leadership (MS). *Accreditation:* NCATE. *Program availability:* Part-time, evening/weekend. *Degree requirements:* For master's, comprehensive exam, thesis optional; for Ed S, thesis optional.

Winthrop University, College of Education, Program in Educational Leadership, Rock Hill, SC 29733. Offers M Ed. *Entrance requirements:* For master's, GRE General Test or MAT, 3 years of experience, South Carolina Class III Teaching Certificate, recommendations from current principal and district-level administrator. Additional exam requirements/recommendations for international students: Required—TOEFL (minimum score 550 paper-based; 79 iBT), IELTS (minimum score 6). Electronic applications accepted. *Expenses:* Tuition, state resident: full-time $14,312; part-time $599 per credit hour. Tuition, nonresident: full-time $27,570; part-time $1153 per credit hour.

Wisconsin Lutheran College, College of Adult and Graduate Studies, Milwaukee, WI 53226-9942. Offers high performance instruction (MA Ed); instructional technology (MA Ed); leadership and innovation (MA Ed); science instruction (MA Ed).

Worcester State University, Graduate Studies, Department of Education, Program in Leadership and Administration, Worcester, MA 01602-2597. Offers M Ed, CAGS, Ed S. *Program availability:* Part-time. *Faculty:* 13 full-time (12 women), 16 part-time/adjunct (7 women). *Students:* 1 (woman) full-time, 80 part-time (64 women); includes 8 minority (3 Black or African American, non-Hispanic/Latino; 1 American Indian or Alaska Native, non-Hispanic/Latino; 2 Hispanic/Latino; 2 Two or more races, non-Hispanic/Latino). Average age 40. 61 applicants, 95% accepted, 43 enrolled. In 2016, 5 master's awarded. *Degree requirements:* For master's, comprehensive exam (for some programs), thesis optional. *Entrance requirements:* For master's, GRE or MAT, MTEL Communication and Literacy exam, teaching license; essay explaining interest in becoming school administrator; 3 reference letters; at least 2 years of teaching experience; for other advanced degree, M Ed or master's degree in related field with minimum GPA of 3.0; completion of 1-year induction program with mentor; initial license in school administration. Additional exam requirements/recommendations for international students: Required—TOEFL (minimum score 550 paper-based; 79 iBT). *Application deadline:* For fall admission, 6/15 for domestic and international students; for spring admission, 11/1 for domestic and international students; for summer admission, 4/1 for domestic and international students. Applications are processed on a rolling basis. Application fee: $50. Electronic applications accepted. *Expenses:* Tuition, state resident: part-time $150 per credit. Tuition, nonresident: part-time $150 per credit. *Financial support:* Career-related internships or fieldwork, scholarships/grants, and unspecified assistantships available. Financial award application deadline: 3/1; financial award applicants required to submit FAFSA. *Unit head:* Dr. Audrey Wright, Coordinator,

508-929-8594, Fax: 508-929-8164, E-mail: awright1@worcester.edu. *Application contact:* Sara Grady, Associate Dean for Graduate Studies and Professional Development, 508-929-8787, Fax: 508-929-8100, E-mail: sara.grady@worcester.edu.

Wright State University, Graduate School, College of Education and Human Services, Department of Educational Leadership, Program in Advanced Educational Leadership, Dayton, OH 45435. Offers advanced curriculum and instruction (Ed S). *Accreditation:* NCATE. *Degree requirements:* For Ed S, thesis. *Entrance requirements:* For degree, GRE General Test, MAT. Additional exam requirements/recommendations for international students: Required—TOEFL. Application fee: $25. *Expenses:* Tuition, state resident: full-time $9952; part-time $622 per credit hour. Tuition, nonresident: full-time $16,960; part-time $1060 per credit hour. *Financial support:* Available to part-time students. Applicants required to submit FAFSA. *Unit head:* Dr. Thomas Diamantes, Director, 937-775-3008, Fax: 937-775-2405, E-mail: thomas.diamantes@wright.edu. *Application contact:* John Kimble, Associate Director of Graduate Admissions and Records, 937-775-2957, Fax: 937-775-2453, E-mail: john.kimble@wright.edu.

Xavier University, College of Social Sciences, Health and Education, School of Education, Department of Educational Leadership and Human Resource Development, Cincinnati, OH 45207. Offers educational administration (M Ed); human resource development (MS). *Program availability:* Part-time, evening/weekend. *Degree requirements:* For master's, internship; for doctorate, comprehensive exam, thesis/dissertation. *Entrance requirements:* For master's, GRE or MAT, resume; 2 letters of recommendation; goal statement; official transcript; for doctorate, GRE, GMAT, LSAT or MAT, official transcript; 1,000-word goal statement; resume; 3 letters of recommendation. Additional exam requirements/recommendations for international students: Required—TOEFL (minimum score 550 paper-based; 79 iBT). Electronic applications accepted. Application fee is waived when completed online. *Expenses:* Contact institution.

Xavier University of Louisiana, Graduate School, Programs in Education, New Orleans, LA 70125. Offers counseling (MA); curriculum and instruction (MA); educational leadership (MA). *Accreditation:* NCATE. *Program availability:* Part-time, evening/weekend. *Degree requirements:* For master's, comprehensive exam, thesis or alternative. *Entrance requirements:* For master's, GRE General Test, MAT, minimum GPA of 2.5. Additional exam requirements/recommendations for international students: Required—TOEFL.

Yeshiva University, Azrieli Graduate School of Jewish Education and Administration, New York, NY 10033-4391. Offers MS, Ed D, Specialist. *Accreditation:* TEAC. *Program availability:* Part-time, evening/weekend. Terminal master's awarded for partial completion of doctoral program. *Degree requirements:* For master's, one foreign language, student teaching experience, comprehensive exam or thesis; for doctorate, one foreign language, comprehensive exam, thesis/dissertation, certifying exams, internship; for Specialist, one foreign language, comprehensive exam, certifying exams, internship. *Entrance requirements:* For master's, GRE General Test, BA in Jewish studies or equivalent; for doctorate and Specialist, GRE General Test, master's degree in Jewish education, 2 years of teaching experience. *Expenses:* Contact institution. *Faculty research:* Social patterns of American and Israeli Jewish population, special education, adult education, technology in education, return to religious values.

York College of Pennsylvania, Master of Education Program, York, PA 17403. Offers educational leadership (M Ed); educational technology (M Ed); reading specialist (M Ed). *Program availability:* Part-time, evening/weekend. *Faculty:* 3 full-time (2 women), 5 part-time/adjunct (2 women). *Students:* 54 part-time (39 women), 1 international. Average age 33. 51 applicants, 67% accepted, 30 enrolled. In 2016, 4 master's awarded. *Degree requirements:* For master's, comprehensive exam (for some programs), thesis (for some programs). *Entrance requirements:* For master's, PRAXIS, GRE, or MAT (within past 10 years), statement of applicant's professional and academic goals, 2 letters of recommendation, letter from current supervisor, official undergraduate and graduate transcript(s), copy of teaching certificate(s), current professional resume, interview. Additional exam requirements/recommendations for international students: Required—TOEFL. *Application deadline:* For fall admission, 7/15 priority date for domestic students; for spring admission, 11/15 priority date for domestic students; for summer admission, 4/15 priority date for domestic students. Applications are processed on a rolling basis. Application fee: $0. Electronic applications accepted. *Expenses:* $620 per credit. *Financial support:* Scholarships/grants available. Financial award applicants required to submit FAFSA. *Faculty research:* Classroom technology, assessment, educational leadership, professional development. *Unit head:* Dr. Joshua D. DeSantis, Director, Master of Education Program, 717-815-1936, E-mail: jdesant1@ycp.edu. Website: https://www.ycp.edu/med

Youngstown State University, Graduate School, Beeghly College of Education, Department of Educational Foundations, Research, Technology, and Leadership, Youngstown, OH 44555-0001. Offers educational administration (MS Ed); educational leadership (Ed D). *Accreditation:* NCATE. *Program availability:* Part-time, evening/weekend. *Degree requirements:* For master's, comprehensive exam; for doctorate, comprehensive exam, thesis/dissertation. *Entrance requirements:* For master's, GRE, MAT, or teaching certificate; minimum GPA of 2.7; for doctorate, GRE General Test, GRE Subject Test, interview, minimum GPA of 3.5. Additional exam requirements/recommendations for international students: Required—TOEFL. *Faculty research:* Administrative theory, computer applications, education law, school and community relations, finance principalship.

Educational Measurement and Evaluation

American InterContinental University Online, Program in Education, Schaumburg, IL 60173. Offers curriculum and instruction (M Ed); educational assessment and evaluation (M Ed); instructional technology (M Ed); leadership of educational organizations (M Ed). *Accreditation:* TEAC. *Program availability:* Evening/weekend, online learning. *Entrance requirements:* Additional exam requirements/recommendations for international students: Required—TOEFL (minimum score 550 paper-based). Electronic applications accepted.

American University, School of Professional and Extended Studies, Washington, DC 20016. Offers healthcare management (MS, Graduate Certificate); human resource analytics and management (Graduate Certificate); measurement and evaluation (MS); project monitoring and evaluation (Graduate Certificate); sports analytics and management (MS, Graduate Certificate). *Program availability:* 100% online. *Faculty:* 28 full-time (12 women), 8 part-time/adjunct (4 women). *Students:* 26 part-time (22 women); includes 1 minority (American Indian or Alaska Native, non-Hispanic/Latino), 2 international. Average age 38. 37 applicants, 100% accepted, 22 enrolled. *Entrance requirements:* For master's, statement of purpose, current resume/curriculum vitae, official transcripts from all academic institutions, letters of recommendation. Additional exam requirements/recommendations for international students: Required—TOEFL or IELTS. *Application deadline:* Applications are processed on a rolling basis. Application fee: $55. Electronic applications accepted. *Expenses:* $1,579 per credit; $690 mandatory fees; some programs charge different fee for spring enrollment. *Financial support:* Applicants required to submit FAFSA. *Unit head:* Carola Weil, Dean, 202-885-5990, Fax: 202-895-4960, E-mail: weil@american.edu. *Application contact:* Heather Broberg, Assistant Director for Recruitment and Admission, 202-895-4953, E-mail: broberg@american.edu.
Website: http://www.american.edu/spexs/

Arizona State University at the Tempe campus, Mary Lou Fulton Teachers College, Program in Educational Policy and Evaluation, Phoenix, AZ 85069. Offers PhD. Fall admission only. *Degree requirements:* For doctorate, comprehensive exam, thesis/dissertation, interactive Program of Study (iPOS) submitted before completing 50 percent of required credit hours. *Entrance requirements:* For doctorate, GRE, minimum GPA of 3.0 or equivalent in last 2 years of work leading to bachelor's degree, 3 letters of recommendation, personal statement, writing sample, curriculum vitae or resume. Additional exam requirements/recommendations for international students: Required—TOEFL, IELTS, or PTE. Electronic applications accepted. *Expenses:* Contact institution. *Faculty research:* Education policy analysis, school finance and quantitative methods, school improvement in ethnically, linguistically and economically diverse communities, parent/teacher engagement, school choice, accountability polices, school finance litigation, school segregation.

Ball State University, Graduate School, Teachers College, Department of Educational Psychology, Muncie, IN 47306. Offers educational psychology (MA, MS), including educational psychology (MA, MS, PhD); educational psychology (PhD), including educational psychology (MA, MS, PhD); gifted and talented education (Certificate); human development and learning (Certificate); instructional design and assessment (Certificate); neuropsychology (Certificate); quantitative psychology (MS); response to intervention (Certificate); school psychology (MA, PhD), including school psychology (MA, PhD, Ed S); school psychology (Ed S), including school psychology (MA, PhD, Ed S). *Program availability:* 100% online. *Degree requirements:* For doctorate, thesis/dissertation; for other advanced degree, thesis. *Entrance requirements:* For master's, GRE General Test, minimum baccalaureate GPA of 2.75 or 3.0 in latter half of baccalauareate, professional goals and self-assessment; for doctorate, GRE General Test, minimum graduate GPA of 3.2; for other advanced degree, GRE General Test. Additional exam requirements/recommendations for international students: Required—TOEFL (minimum score 550 paper-based; 79 iBT), IELTS (minimum score 6.5). Electronic applications accepted.

Baylor University, Graduate School, School of Education, Department of Educational Psychology, Waco, TX 76798. Offers applied behavior analysis (MS Ed); educational psychology (MA, MS Ed, PhD); exceptionalities (PhD); gifted and talented studies (MS Ed); learning and development (PhD); measurement (PhD); quantitative methods (MA); school psychology (Ed S). *Accreditation:* NCATE. *Faculty:* 11 full-time (6 women). *Students:* 48 full-time (42 women), 17 part-time (15 women); includes 15 minority (4 Black or African American, non-Hispanic/Latino; 2 Asian, non-Hispanic/Latino; 8 Hispanic/Latino; 1 Two or more races, non-Hispanic/Latino), 2 international. Average age 29. 90 applicants, 33% accepted, 30 enrolled. In 2016, 13 master's, 4 doctorates, 7 other advanced degrees awarded. Terminal master's awarded for partial completion of doctoral program. *Degree requirements:* For master's, thesis optional; for doctorate, comprehensive exam, thesis/dissertation; for Ed S, comprehensive exam, thesis or alternative. *Entrance requirements:* For master's, GRE, minimum GPA of 3.0; for doctorate, GRE General Test, master's degree; for Ed S, GRE General Test. Additional exam requirements/recommendations for international students: Required—TOEFL (minimum score 550 paper-based; 80 iBT), IELTS (minimum score 6.5). *Application deadline:* For fall admission, 2/1 priority date for domestic and international students. Application fee: $80. Electronic applications accepted. *Expenses: Tuition:* Full-time $28,494; part-time $1583 per credit hour. *Required fees:* $167 per credit hour. Tuition and fees vary according to course load and program. *Financial support:* In 2016–17, 42 students received support, including 20 fellowships with full and partial tuition reimbursements available, 22 research assistantships with full and partial tuition reimbursements available; career-related internships or fieldwork, Federal Work-Study, institutionally sponsored loans, scholarships/grants, health care benefits, tuition waivers (full and partial), unspecified assistantships, and stipends also available. Financial award application deadline: 2/1; financial award applicants required to submit FAFSA. *Faculty research:* Individual differences, quantitative methods, gifted and talented, special education, school psychology, autism, applied behavior analysis, learning, human development. *Total annual research expenditures:* $300,000. *Unit head:* Dr. Terrill F. Saxon, Professor and Chairman, 254-710-6101, E-mail: terrill_saxon@baylor.edu. *Application contact:* Heather Tindle, Office Manager, 254-710-3112, E-mail: heather_tindle@baylor.edu.
Website: http://www.baylor.edu/soe/EDP/

Boston College, Lynch School of Education, Program in Educational Research, Measurement, and Evaluation, Chestnut Hill, MA 02467-3800. Offers M Ed, MS, PhD. *Program availability:* Part-time, evening/weekend. *Faculty:* 8 full-time (4 women). *Students:* 31 full-time (21 women), 33 part-time (25 women); includes 11 minority (3 Black or African American, non-Hispanic/Latino; 4 Asian, non-Hispanic/Latino; 1 Hispanic/Latino; 3 Two or more races, non-Hispanic/Latino), 24 international. Average age 31. 65 applicants, 69% accepted, 19 enrolled. In 2016, 8 master's, 4 doctorates awarded. Terminal master's awarded for partial completion of doctoral program. *Degree requirements:* For master's, comprehensive exam; for doctorate, comprehensive exam, thesis/dissertation. *Entrance requirements:* For master's, GRE General Test or MAT; for doctorate, GRE General Test. Additional exam requirements/recommendations for international students: Required—TOEFL (minimum score 100 iBT). *Application deadline:* For fall admission, 12/1 priority date for domestic and international students; for spring admission, 11/1 priority date for domestic and international students. Application fee: $65. Electronic applications accepted. Tuition and fees vary according to program. *Financial support:* Research assistantships with full tuition reimbursements, teaching assistantships with partial tuition reimbursements, Federal Work-Study, scholarships/grants, and tuition waivers (full and partial) available. Support available to part-time students. Financial award applicants required to submit FAFSA. *Unit head:* Dr.

Larry Ludlow, Department Chair, 617-552-4221, E-mail: ludlow@bc.edu. *Application contact:* Kimberly Rose, Graduate Admission Assistant, 617-552-4214, Fax: 617-552-0398, E-mail: roseki@bc.edu.

Brandeis University, Rabb School of Continuing Studies, Division of Graduate Professional Studies, Graduate Certificate in Learning Analytics Program, Waltham, MA 02454-9110. Offers Graduate Certificate. *Program availability:* Part-time-only, online only, 100% online. *Faculty:* 45 part-time/adjunct (16 women). *Students:* 1 (woman) part-time. Average age 37. *Entrance requirements:* For degree, three years of work experience; master's or doctoral degree in analytics, instructional design or a related field; master's degree from regionally-accredited U.S. institution or equivalent; official transcript(s) from every college or university attended; resume or curriculum vitae; statement of goals; letter of recommendation. Additional exam requirements/recommendations for international students: Required—TWE (minimum score 4.5), TOEFL (minimum scores: 600 paper-based, 100 iBT), IELTS (7), or PTE (68). *Application deadline:* For fall admission, 6/21 priority date for domestic and international students; for winter admission, 9/13 priority date for domestic and international students; for spring admission, 12/20 priority date for domestic and international students; for summer admission, 3/14 priority date for domestic and international students. Applications are processed on a rolling basis. Application fee: $50. Electronic applications accepted. *Expenses:* $3,400 per course, $100 graduation fee. *Financial support:* Applicants required to submit FAFSA. *Unit head:* Brian Salerno, Chair, 781-736-3443, E-mail: bsalerno@brandeis.edu. *Application contact:* Frances Stearns, Director of Admissions and Recruitment, 781-736-8785, E-mail: fstearns@brandeis.edu.

Brigham Young University, Graduate Studies, David O. McKay School of Education, Program in Educational Inquiry, Measurement, and Evaluation, Provo, UT 84602. Offers PhD. *Faculty:* 10 full-time (4 women), 1 part-time/adjunct (0 women). *Students:* 20 full-time (9 women); includes 2 minority (1 Asian, non-Hispanic/Latino; 1 Hispanic/Latino). Average age 36. 13 applicants, 38% accepted, 4 enrolled. In 2016, 4 doctorates awarded. *Degree requirements:* For doctorate, comprehensive exam, thesis/dissertation, internship. *Entrance requirements:* For doctorate, GRE, master's degree. Additional exam requirements/recommendations for international students: Required—TOEFL. *Application deadline:* For fall admission, 2/1 for domestic students. Application fee: $50. Electronic applications accepted. *Expenses:* Contact institution. *Financial support:* Research assistantships, health care benefits, and tuition waivers available. *Faculty research:* Educational research methods, structural equation modeling, quantitative methods, qualitative methods. *Unit head:* Dr. Richard R. Sudweeks, Program Coordinator, 801-422-7078, Fax: 801-422-0200, E-mail: richard_sudweeks@byu.edu. *Application contact:* Ashley C. Gordon, Program Manager, 801-422-4717, Fax: 801-422-0195, E-mail: eime@byu.edu.
Website: http://education.byu.edu/eime

Cambridge College, School of Education, Cambridge, MA 02138-5304. Offers autism specialist (M Ed); autism/behavior analyst (M Ed); behavior analyst (Post-Master's Certificate); behavioral management (M Ed); early childhood teacher (M Ed); education specialist in curriculum and instruction (CAGS); educational leadership (Ed D); elementary teacher (M Ed); English as a second language (M Ed, Certificate); general science (M Ed); health education (Post-Master's Certificate); health/family and consumer sciences (M Ed); history (M Ed); individualized (M Ed); information technology literacy (M Ed); instructional technology (M Ed); interdisciplinary studies (M Ed); library teacher (M Ed); literacy education (M Ed); mathematics (M Ed); mathematics specialist (Certificate); middle school mathematics and science (M Ed); school administration (M Ed, CAGS); school guidance counselor (M Ed); school nurse education (M Ed); school social worker/school adjustment counselor (M Ed); special education administrator (CAGS); special education/moderate disabilities (M Ed); teaching skills and methodologies (M Ed). *Program availability:* Part-time, evening/weekend, online learning. *Degree requirements:* For master's, thesis, internship/practicum (licensure program only); for doctorate, thesis/dissertation; for other advanced degree, thesis. *Entrance requirements:* For master's, interview, resume, documentation of licensure, 2 professional references; for doctorate, official transcripts, interview, resume, documentation of licensure (if any), written personal statement/essay, portfolio of scholarly and professional work, qualifying assessment, 2 professional references, health insurance, immunizations form; for other advanced degree, official transcripts, interview, resume, documentation of licensure (if any), written personal statement/essay, 2 professional references, health insurance, immunizations form. Additional exam requirements/recommendations for international students: Required—TOEFL (minimum score 550 paper-based; 79 iBT), Michigan English Language Assessment Battery (minimum score 85); Recommended—IELTS (minimum score 6). Electronic applications accepted. *Expenses:* Contact institution. *Faculty research:* Adult education, accelerated learning, mathematics education, brain compatible learning, special education and law.

Claremont Graduate University, Graduate Programs, School of Educational Studies, Claremont, CA 91711-6160. Offers Africana education (Certificate); education and policy (MA, PhD); higher education/student affairs (MA, PhD); human development (MA, PhD); public school administration (MA, PhD); quantitative evaluation (MA, PhD); special education (MA, PhD); teacher education (MA); teaching and learning (MA, PhD); urban leadership (PhD); MBA/PhD. PhD program offered jointly with San Diego State University. *Program availability:* Part-time. *Faculty:* 14 full-time (9 women), 1 part-time/adjunct (0 women). *Students:* 195 full-time (143 women), 196 part-time (137 women); includes 217 minority (43 Black or African American, non-Hispanic/Latino; 4 American Indian or Alaska Native, non-Hispanic/Latino; 32 Asian, non-Hispanic/Latino; 117 Hispanic/Latino; 2 Native Hawaiian or other Pacific Islander, non-Hispanic/Latino; 19 Two or more races, non-Hispanic/Latino), 14 international. Average age 38. In 2016, 48 master's, 39 doctorates, 7 other advanced degrees awarded. Terminal master's awarded for partial completion of doctoral program. *Entrance requirements:* For master's and doctorate, GRE General Test. Additional exam requirements/recommendations for international students: Required—TOEFL (minimum score 75 iBT). *Application deadline:* For fall admission, 3/1 priority date for domestic and international students. Applications are processed on a rolling basis. Application fee: $80. Electronic applications accepted. *Expenses: Tuition:* Full-time $44,328; part-time $1847 per unit. *Required fees:* $600; $300 per semester. Tuition and fees vary according to course load and program. *Financial support:* Fellowships, research assistantships, Federal Work-Study, institutionally sponsored loans, and scholarships/grants available. Support available to part-time students. Financial award application deadline: 2/15; financial award applicants required to submit FAFSA. *Faculty research:* Education administration, K-12 and higher education, multicultural education, education policy, diversity in higher education, faculty issues. *Unit head:* Allen Omoto, Dean, 909-607-3786, E-mail: allen.omoto@cgu.edu. *Application contact:* Rachel Camacho, Senior Assistant Director of Admission, 909-607-9418, E-mail: camacho@cgu.edu.
Website: https://www.cgu.edu/school/school-of-educational-studies/

Clemson University, Graduate School, College of Education, Department of Education and Human Development, Program in Learning Sciences, Clemson, SC 29634. Offers PhD. *Program availability:* Part-time. *Faculty:* 9 full-time (6 women). *Students:* 8 full-time (6 women), 5 part-time (2 women); includes 5 minority (3 Black or African American, non-Hispanic/Latino; 1 Asian, non-Hispanic/Latino; 1 Hispanic/Latino), 1 international. Average age 33. 9 applicants, 44% accepted, 3 enrolled. *Degree requirements:* For doctorate, comprehensive exam, thesis/dissertation. *Entrance requirements:* For doctorate, GRE General Test, unofficial transcripts, 2 letters of recommendation, resume/curriculum vitae, letter of intent. Additional exam requirements/recommendations for international students: Required—TOEFL (minimum score 80 iBT), IELTS (minimum score 7). *Application deadline:* For fall admission, 4/1 for domestic and international students. Application fee: $80 ($90 for international students). Electronic applications accepted. *Expenses:* $4,264 per semester full-time resident, $8,485 per semester full-time non-resident, $471 per credit hour part-time resident, $942 per credit hour part-time non-resident. *Financial support:* In 2016–17, 7 students received support, including 5 teaching assistantships with partial tuition reimbursements available (averaging $15,000 per year); unspecified assistantships also available. Financial award application deadline: 1/1. *Faculty research:* Digital media and games for learning, discipline literacies, psychometrics, classroom practice influence on child development, quantitative research methodology. *Unit head:* Dr. Debi Switzer, Department Chair, 864-656-5098, E-mail: debi@clemson.edu. *Application contact:* Julie Jones, Student Services Program Coordinator, 864-656-5096, E-mail: jgambre@clemson.edu.
Website: http://www.clemson.edu/education/academics/doctoral-programs/phd-doctorate-learning-sciences/index.html

College of Saint Mary, Program in Education, Omaha, NE 68106. Offers assessment leadership (MSE); English as a second language (MSE). *Program availability:* Part-time. *Entrance requirements:* For master's, technology competency test or equivalent, minimum cumulative GPA of 3.0, teaching certificate, 2 letters of reference, resume.

Duquesne University, School of Education, Department of Educational Foundations and Leadership, Program in Educational Studies, Pittsburgh, PA 15282-0001. Offers educational studies (MS Ed); program evaluation (MS Ed). *Program availability:* Part-time, evening/weekend, 100% online. *Faculty:* 1 full-time (0 women). *Students:* 10 full-time (8 women), 11 part-time (8 women); includes 6 minority (5 Black or African American, non-Hispanic/Latino; 1 Hispanic/Latino), 11 international. Average age 34. 17 applicants, 94% accepted, 4 enrolled. In 2016, 10 master's awarded. *Degree requirements:* For master's, thesis optional. *Entrance requirements:* For master's, bachelor's degree. Additional exam requirements/recommendations for international students: Required—TOEFL (minimum score 550 paper-based), IELTS (minimum score 7). *Application deadline:* For fall admission, 9/1 for domestic students; for spring admission, 1/1 for domestic students. Applications are processed on a rolling basis. Application fee: $0. Electronic applications accepted. *Expenses: Tuition:* Full-time $22,212; part-time $1234 per credit. Tuition and fees vary according to program. *Financial support:* Research assistantships available. Support available to part-time students. *Unit head:* Dr. Gibbs Kanyongo, Associate Professor, 412-396-5190, Fax: 412-396-5454, E-mail: kanyongog@duq.edu. *Application contact:* Michael Dolinger, Director of Student and Academic Services, 412-396-6647, Fax: 412-396-5585, E-mail: dolingerm@duq.edu.

Eastern Michigan University, Graduate School, College of Education, Department of Teacher Education, Programs in Educational Psychology and Assessment, Ypsilanti, MI 48197. Offers educational assessment (Graduate Certificate); educational psychology (MA). *Accreditation:* NCATE. *Program availability:* Part-time, evening/weekend, online learning. *Students:* 31 part-time (29 women); includes 9 minority (4 Black or African American, non-Hispanic/Latino; 1 American Indian or Alaska Native, non-Hispanic/Latino; 1 Hispanic/Latino; 3 Two or more races, non-Hispanic/Latino). Average age 34. 21 applicants, 67% accepted, 5 enrolled. In 2016, 19 master's, 3 other advanced degrees awarded. *Degree requirements:* For master's, thesis or alternative. *Entrance requirements:* For master's, GRE. Additional exam requirements/recommendations for international students: Required—TOEFL. *Application deadline:* Applications are processed on a rolling basis. Application fee: $45. *Financial support:* Fellowships, research assistantships with full tuition reimbursements, teaching assistantships with full tuition reimbursements, career-related internships or fieldwork, Federal Work-Study, institutionally sponsored loans, scholarships/grants, tuition waivers (partial), and unspecified assistantships available. Support available to part-time students. Financial award applicants required to submit FAFSA. *Application contact:* Dr. Alane Starko, Coordinator, 734-487-3260, Fax: 734-487-2101, E-mail: astarko@emich.edu.

Florida State University, The Graduate School, College of Education, Program in Educational Leadership and Policy, Tallahassee, FL 32306. Offers education policy and evaluation (MS, Ed D, PhD); educational leadership/administration (MS, Ed D, PhD, Certificate, Ed S); program evaluation (Certificate). *Program availability:* Part-time, evening/weekend, blended/hybrid learning. Terminal master's awarded for partial completion of doctoral program. *Degree requirements:* For master's and other advanced degree, comprehensive exam, thesis optional; for doctorate, comprehensive exam, thesis/dissertation, diagnostic exam, preliminary exam, prospectus defense, dissertation defense. *Entrance requirements:* For master's, doctorate, and other advanced degree, GRE General Test, minimum upper-division GPA of 3.0. Additional exam requirements/recommendations for international students: Required—TOEFL (minimum score 550 paper-based, 80 iBT), IELTS (minimum score 6.5), Michigan English Language Assessment Battery (minimum score 77), or PTE (minimum score 55). Application fee: $30. Electronic applications accepted. *Expenses:* Tuition, state resident: full-time $7263; part-time $403.51 per credit hour. Tuition, nonresident: full-time $18,087; part-time $1004.85 per credit hour. *Required fees:* $1365; $75.81 per credit hour. $20 per semester. Tuition and fees vary according to campus/location. *Financial support:* Fellowships, research assistantships, teaching assistantships, scholarships/grants, tuition waivers (full and partial), and unspecified assistantships available. Financial award application deadline: 1/15; financial award applicants required to submit FAFSA. *Faculty research:* Educational leadership in traditional public and charter institutions, educational evaluation and policy, policy and politics of K-12 education, pre-service teacher and teacher policy and professional education, economics and finance of education. *Unit head:* Dr. Motoko Akiba, Professor/Program Coordinator, 850-644-5553, Fax: 850-644-1258, E-mail: makiba@fsu.edu. *Application contact:* Linda J. Lyons, Academic Support Assistant, 850-644-7077, Fax: 850-644-1258, E-mail: ljlyons@fsu.edu.
Website: http://education.fsu.edu/degrees-and-programs/graduate-programs

Florida State University, The Graduate School, College of Education, Program in Measurement and Statistics, Tallahassee, FL 32306. Offers measurement and statistics (MS, PhD, Certificate). *Degree requirements:* For master's, comprehensive exam, thesis optional; for doctorate, comprehensive exam, thesis/dissertation, diagnostic exam, preliminary exam, prospectus defense, dissertation defense. *Entrance requirements:* For master's, doctorate, and Certificate, GRE General Test, minimum upper-division GPA of 3.0. Additional exam requirements/recommendations for international students: Required—TOEFL (minimum score 550 paper-based, 80 iBT), IELTS (minimum score 6.5), Michigan English Language Assessment Battery (minimum score 77), or PTE (minimum score 55). Application fee: $30. Electronic applications accepted. *Expenses:* Tuition, state resident: full-time $7263; part-time $403.51 per credit hour. Tuition, nonresident: full-time $18,087; part-time $1004.85 per credit hour. *Required fees:* $1365; $75.81 per credit hour. $20 per semester. Tuition and fees vary according to campus/location. *Financial support:* Fellowships, research assistantships, teaching

assistantships, Federal Work-Study, scholarships/grants, health care benefits, and unspecified assistantships available. Financial award application deadline: 1/15; financial award applicants required to submit FAFSA. *Faculty research:* Evidence-centered assessment design; meta-analysis methods, Bayesian analysis; psychometric methods, item response modeling, large-scale assessment, teacher qualifications; factor analysis, structural equation modeling; longitudinal data analysis, multilevel modeling, missing data problems. *Unit head:* Dr. Betsy Becker, Professor/Department Chair, 850-645-2371, Fax: 850-644-8776, E-mail: bbecker@fsu.edu. *Application contact:* Mary Kate McKee, Academic Program Specialist, 850-644-8792, Fax: 850-644-8776, E-mail: mmckee@fsu.edu.
Website: http://education.fsu.edu/degrees-and-programs/graduate-programs

Georgia Southern University, Jack N. Averitt College of Graduate Studies, College of Education, Department of Curriculum, Foundations, and Reading, Statesboro, GA 30460. Offers curriculum studies (Ed D), including curriculum studies; evaluation, assessment, research, and learning (M Ed); reading education (M Ed, Ed S). *Accreditation:* NCATE. *Program availability:* Part-time, evening/weekend. *Students:* 25 full-time (22 women), 153 part-time (121 women); includes 49 minority (40 Black or African American, non-Hispanic/Latino; 5 Hispanic/Latino; 4 Two or more races, non-Hispanic/Latino), 3 international. Average age 40. 11 applicants, 91% accepted, 7 enrolled. In 2016, 9 master's, 16 doctorates, 1 other advanced degree awarded. *Degree requirements:* For master's, comprehensive exam; for doctorate, comprehensive exam, thesis/dissertation, exams. *Entrance requirements:* For master's, GRE General Test or MAT, minimum GPA of 2.5; for doctorate, GRE General Test or MAT, minimum GPA of 3.5, letters of reference, writing sample. Additional exam requirements/recommendations for international students: Required—TOEFL (minimum score 550 paper-based; 80 iBT), IELTS (minimum score 6). *Application deadline:* For fall admission, 3/1 priority date for domestic and international students; for spring admission, 10/1 priority date for domestic students, 10/1 for international students. Applications are processed on a rolling basis. Application fee: $50. Electronic applications accepted. *Expenses:* Tuition, state resident: full-time $7236; part-time $277 per semester hour. Tuition, nonresident: full-time $27,118; part-time $1105 per semester hour. *Required fees:* $2092. *Financial support:* In 2016–17, 10 students received support, including 1 research assistantship with full tuition reimbursement available (averaging $7,750 per year); fellowships, scholarships/grants, and unspecified assistantships also available. Financial award application deadline: 4/15; financial award applicants required to submit FAFSA. *Faculty research:* Curriculum theories, at-risk students, gifted female adolescents, cognitive mapping, faculty evaluation, learning environments, research methodology, social and cultural conditions of learning, preservice teacher education. *Unit head:* Dr. Kent Rittschoff, Chair, 912-478-0698, Fax: 912-478-5382, E-mail: kent_r@georgiasouthern.edu. *Application contact:* Lydia Cross, Graduate Academic Services Center, 912-478-8664, E-mail: lcross@georgiasouthern.edu.
Website: http://coe.georgiasouthern.edu/cfr/

Georgia State University, College of Education and Human Development, Department of Educational Policy Studies, Program in Educational Research, Atlanta, GA 30302-3083. Offers MS, PhD. MS offered jointly with Department of Counseling and Psychological Services. *Accreditation:* NCATE. *Program availability:* Part-time. *Degree requirements:* For master's, 36 semester hours, thesis or project; for doctorate, comprehensive exam, thesis/dissertation, 69 semester hours. *Entrance requirements:* For master's and doctorate, GRE. Additional exam requirements/recommendations for international students: Required—TOEFL (minimum score 550 paper-based; 79 iBT) or IELTS (minimum score 6.5). *Application deadline:* For fall admission, 1/15 for domestic and international students; for winter admission, 2/1 for domestic students; for spring admission, 10/1 for domestic and international students. Applications are processed on a rolling basis. Application fee: $50. Electronic applications accepted. *Expenses:* Tuition, state resident: full-time $6876; part-time $382 per credit hour. Tuition, nonresident: full-time $22,374; part-time $1243 per credit hour. *Required fees:* $2128; $1064 per term. Part-time tuition and fees vary according to course load and program. *Financial support:* In 2016–17, research assistantships with full tuition reimbursements (averaging $10,886 per year) were awarded; fellowships, teaching assistantships with full tuition reimbursements, career-related internships or fieldwork, scholarships/grants, health care benefits, tuition waivers (full), and unspecified assistantships also available. Support available to part-time students. Financial award application deadline: 3/15. *Faculty research:* Program evaluation, item response theory, quantitative research methodology, qualitative research methodology, gender and identity studies. *Unit head:* Dr. Janice Fournillier, Associate Professor, 404-413-8030, Fax: 404-413-8003, E-mail: jfournillier@gsu.edu. *Application contact:* Aishah Cowan, Administrative Academic Specialist, 404-413-8273, Fax: 404-413-8003, E-mail: acowan@gsu.edu.
Website: http://eps.education.gsu.edu/programs-courses/rms/educational-research-m-s/

Houston Baptist University, College of Education and Behavioral Sciences, Programs in Education, Houston, TX 77074-3298. Offers bilingual education (M Ed); counselor education (M Ed); curriculum and instruction (M Ed); educational administration (M Ed); educational diagnostician (M Ed); executive educational leadership (Ed D); reading education (M Ed). *Program availability:* Part-time, evening/weekend, 100% online, blended/hybrid learning. *Students:* 45 full-time (35 women), 158 part-time (136 women); includes 141 minority (87 Black or African American, non-Hispanic/Latino; 1 American Indian or Alaska Native, non-Hispanic/Latino; 5 Asian, non-Hispanic/Latino; 47 Hispanic/Latino; 1 Two or more races, non-Hispanic/Latino), 3 international. Average age 34. 320 applicants, 30% accepted, 61 enrolled. In 2016, 121 degrees awarded. *Degree requirements:* For master's, comprehensive exam; for doctorate, thesis/dissertation. *Entrance requirements:* For master's, minimum GPA of 2.75, two recommendations, resume, bachelor's degree conferred transcript; interview (for non-certified teachers); for doctorate, GRE, 3 letters of recommendation. Additional exam requirements/recommendations for international students: Required—TOEFL (minimum score 80 iBT), IELTS (minimum score 6.5). *Application deadline:* For fall admission, 8/1 for domestic students, 6/1 for international students; for spring admission, 1/1 for domestic students, 11/1 for international students; for summer admission, 5/1 for domestic students, 3/1 for international students. Applications are processed on a rolling basis. Application fee: $0 ($100 for international students). Electronic applications accepted. Application fee is waived when completed online. *Expenses:* $1,650 per 3-hour course; $1,275 annual general fee; $1,060 annual technology fee. *Financial support:* In 2016–17, 2 students received support. Research assistantships, teaching assistantships, Federal Work-Study, and scholarships/grants available. Support available to part-time students. Financial award application deadline: 4/1; financial award applicants required to submit FAFSA. *Faculty research:* Autism and inclusion, integrating technology into instruction, school change and leadership trust. *Unit head:* Dr. Charlotte Fontenot, Director, Graduate Programs, 281-649-3078, Fax: 281-649-3361, E-mail: cfontenot@hbu.edu. *Application contact:* Kristy Wright, Administrative Assistant for Graduate Programs, 281-649-3094, Fax: 281-649-3361, E-mail: kwright@hbu.edu.
Website: http://www.hbu.edu/MED

Indiana University Bloomington, School of Education, Department of Counseling and Educational Psychology, Bloomington, IN 47405-1006. Offers counseling (MS, PhD, Ed S); counselor education (MS, Ed S); educational psychology (MS, PhD); inquiry methodology (PhD); learning and developmental sciences (MS, PhD); school psychology (PhD, Ed S). *Accreditation:* ACA (one or more programs are accredited); APA (one or more programs are accredited); NCATE. Terminal master's awarded for partial completion of doctoral program. *Degree requirements:* For master's, thesis optional; for doctorate, thesis/dissertation; for Ed S, comprehensive exam or project. *Entrance requirements:* For master's, doctorate, and Ed S, GRE General Test. Additional exam requirements/recommendations for international students: Required—TOEFL. Electronic applications accepted. *Faculty research:* Counseling psychology, inquiry methodology, school psychology, learning sciences, human development, educational psychology.

Indiana University Bloomington, School of Education, Program in Inquiry Methodology, Bloomington, IN 47405-7000. Offers PhD.

Iowa State University of Science and Technology, Department of Educational Leadership and Policy Studies, Ames, IA 50011. Offers counselor education (M Ed, MS); educational administration (M Ed, MS); educational leadership (PhD); higher education (M Ed, MS); organizational learning and human resource development (M Ed, MS); research and evaluation (MS); student affairs (MS). *Degree requirements:* For master's, thesis or alternative; for doctorate, thesis/dissertation. *Entrance requirements:* For master's and doctorate, GRE General Test. Additional exam requirements/recommendations for international students: Required—TOEFL (minimum score 560 paper-based; 83 iBT), IELTS (minimum score 6.5). *Application deadline:* For fall admission, 1/1 priority date for domestic and international students. Application fee: $60 ($90 for international students). Electronic applications accepted. *Application contact:* Robyn Goldy, Application Contact, 515-294-1241, Fax: 515-294-4942, E-mail: rgoldy@iastate.edu.
Website: http://www.elps.hs.iastate.edu/

James Madison University, The Graduate School, College of Education, Program in Adult Education and Human Resource Development, Harrisonburg, VA 22802. Offers higher education (MS Ed); human resource management (MS Ed); individualized (MS Ed); instructional design (MS Ed); leadership and facilitation (MS Ed); program evaluation and measurement (MS Ed). *Accreditation:* NCATE. *Program availability:* Part-time, evening/weekend. *Students:* 10 full-time (8 women), 11 part-time (10 women); includes 7 minority (4 Black or African American, non-Hispanic/Latino; 1 Hispanic/Latino; 2 Two or more races, non-Hispanic/Latino), 1 international. Average age 30. 23 applicants, 91% accepted, 18 enrolled. In 2016, 17 master's awarded. Application fee: $55. Electronic applications accepted. *Financial support:* In 2016–17, 15 students received support. Teaching assistantships, Federal Work-Study, and 8 assistantships (averaging $7911), 1 athletic assistantship (averaging $9284) available. Financial award application deadline: 3/1; financial award applicants required to submit FAFSA. *Unit head:* Dr. Jane B. Thall, Department Head, 540-568-5531, E-mail: thalljb@jmu.edu. *Application contact:* Lynette D. Michael, Director of Graduate Admissions, 540-568-6131 Ext. 6395, Fax: 540-568-7860, E-mail: michaeld@jmu.edu.

James Madison University, The Graduate School, College of Health and Behavioral Sciences, Program in Assessment and Measurement, Harrisonburg, VA 22807. Offers PhD. *Program availability:* Part-time. *Students:* 13 full-time (9 women), 2 part-time (both women); includes 3 minority (2 Black or African American, non-Hispanic/Latino; 1 Asian, non-Hispanic/Latino). Average age 30. 5 applicants, 20% accepted. Application fee: $55. Electronic applications accepted. *Financial support:* In 2016–17, 10 students received support, including 1 fellowship; Federal Work-Study, unspecified assistantships, and 13 doctoral assistantships (stipend varies) also available. Financial award application deadline: 3/1; financial award applicants required to submit FAFSA. *Unit head:* Dr. Deborah L. Bandalos, Graduate Program Director, 540-568-7132, E-mail: bandaldl@jmu.edu. *Application contact:* Lynette D. Michael, Director of Graduate Admissions and Student Records, 540-568-6131 Ext. 6395, Fax: 540-568-7860, E-mail: michaeld@jmu.edu.
Website: http://www.psyc.jmu.edu/assessment/

Kent State University, College of Education, Health and Human Services, School of Foundations, Leadership and Administration, Program in Evaluation and Measurement, Kent, OH 44242-0001. Offers M Ed, PhD. *Degree requirements:* For doctorate, comprehensive exam, thesis/dissertation. *Entrance requirements:* For master's, minimum GPA of 2.75, 2 letters of reference, goals statement; for doctorate, GRE, minimum GPA of 3.5 from master's degree, resume, 2 letters of reference, goal statement. Additional exam requirements/recommendations for international students: Required—TOEFL (minimum score 550 paper-based; 80 iBT). *Expenses:* Tuition, state resident: full-time $10,864; part-time $495 per credit hour. Tuition, nonresident: full-time $18,380; part-time $837 per credit hour.

Louisiana State University and Agricultural & Mechanical College, Graduate School, College of Human Sciences and Education, Department of Educational Theory, Policy and Practice, Baton Rouge, LA 70803. Offers counseling (M Ed, MA, Ed S); educational administration (M Ed, MA, PhD, Ed S); educational technology (MA); elementary education (M Ed, MAT); higher education (PhD); research methodology (PhD); secondary education (M Ed, MAT). *Accreditation:* ACA (one or more programs are accredited); NCATE.

Loyola University Chicago, School of Education, Program in Research Methods, Chicago, IL 60660. Offers MA, PhD. *Program availability:* Part-time, evening/weekend. *Faculty:* 4 full-time (3 women), 1 (woman) part-time/adjunct. *Students:* 16 full-time (11 women), 4 part-time (0 women); includes 3 minority (1 Black or African American, non-Hispanic/Latino; 2 Hispanic/Latino), 1 international. Average age 38. 11 applicants, 55% accepted, 4 enrolled. In 2016, 1 master's, 1 doctorate awarded. *Degree requirements:* For master's, comprehensive exam (M Ed), thesis (MA); for doctorate, comprehensive exam, thesis/dissertation. *Entrance requirements:* For master's, GRE General Test, letters of recommendation, resume, minimum GPA of 3.0; for doctorate, GRE General Test, interview. Additional exam requirements/recommendations for international students: Required—TOEFL (minimum score 550 paper-based; 79 iBT). *Application deadline:* For fall admission, 12/1 for domestic and international students. Applications are processed on a rolling basis. Application fee: $50. Electronic applications accepted. Application fee is waived when completed online. *Expenses:* $949 per hour; $2,847 per course; $8,541-$11,388 per semester plus fees $432 per semester and $225 the first semester. *Financial support:* In 2016–17, 22 students received support, including 3 research assistantships with full tuition reimbursements available (averaging $14,000 per year), 19 teaching assistantships (averaging $4,000 per year); institutionally sponsored loans, scholarships/grants, health care benefits, and unspecified assistantships also available. Support available to part-time students. Financial award application deadline: 2/1; financial award applicants required to submit FAFSA. *Faculty research:* Circular statistics, program evaluation, psychological measurement, infant attachment, adolescent development. *Unit head:* Dr. Leanne Kallemeyn, Program Chair, 312-915-6909, E-mail: lkallemeyn@luc.edu. *Application contact:* Thomas Ott, Information Contact, 312-915-8907, E-mail: tott@luc.edu.

McNeese State University, Doré School of Graduate Studies, Burton College of Education, Office of Graduate Education Programs, Program in Special Education, Lake Charles, LA 70609. Offers advanced professional (M Ed); autism (M Ed); educational diagnostician (M Ed). *Entrance requirements:* For master's, GRE, teaching certificate.

McNeese State University, Doré School of Graduate Studies, Burton College of Education, Office of Student Teaching and Professional Education Services, Program in Educational Diagnostician, Lake Charles, LA 70609. Offers Graduate Certificate. *Entrance requirements:* For degree, bachelor's degree, teaching certificate.

Michigan State University, The Graduate School, College of Education, Department of Counseling, Educational Psychology and Special Education, East Lansing, MI 48824. Offers counseling (MA); educational psychology and educational technology (PhD); educational technology (MA); measurement and quantitative methods (PhD); rehabilitation counseling (MA); rehabilitation counselor education (PhD); school psychology (MA, PhD, Ed S); special education (MA, PhD). *Accreditation:* APA (one or more programs are accredited); CORE (one or more programs are accredited). *Program availability:* Part-time. *Entrance requirements:* Additional exam requirements/recommendations for international students: Required—TOEFL. Electronic applications accepted.

Missouri State University, Graduate College, College of Education, Department of Counseling, Leadership, and Special Education, Program in Counseling and Assessment, Springfield, MO 65897. Offers Ed S. *Program availability:* Part-time. *Students:* 1 (woman) full-time, 4 part-time (all women). Average age 35. 3 applicants, 33% accepted, 1 enrolled. In 2016, 1 Ed S awarded. *Degree requirements:* For Ed S, comprehensive exam. *Entrance requirements:* For degree, GRE. Additional exam requirements/recommendations for international students: Required—TOEFL (minimum score 550 paper-based; 79 iBT), IELTS (minimum score 6). *Application deadline:* For fall admission, 2/1 for domestic and international students. Application fee: $35 ($50 for international students). Electronic applications accepted. *Expenses:* Tuition, state resident: full-time $5830. Tuition, nonresident: full-time $10,708. *Required fees:* $1130. Tuition and fees vary according to class time, course level, course load and program. *Financial support:* Federal Work-Study, institutionally sponsored loans, scholarships/grants, and unspecified assistantships available. Financial award application deadline: 3/31; financial award applicants required to submit FAFSA. *Unit head:* Dr. James Satterfield, Department Head, 417-836-5392, Fax: 417-836-4918, E-mail: clse@missouristate.edu. *Application contact:* Michael Edwards, Coordinator of Graduate Admissions, 417-836-5330, Fax: 417-836-6200, E-mail: michaeledwards@missouristate.edu.
Website: http://education.missouristate.edu/assessment/

Missouri Western State University, Program in Assessment, St. Joseph, MO 64507-2294. Offers autism spectrum disorders (MAS, Graduate Certificate); TESOL (MAS, Graduate Certificate); writing (MAS). *Program availability:* Part-time. *Students:* 1 (woman) full-time, 33 part-time (25 women). Average age 37. 9 applicants, 100% accepted, 5 enrolled. In 2016, 6 master's, 1 other advanced degree awarded. *Entrance requirements:* For master's, minimum GPA of 2.75. Additional exam requirements/recommendations for international students: Recommended—TOEFL (minimum score 79 iBT), IELTS (minimum score 6). *Application deadline:* For fall admission, 7/15 for domestic and international students; for spring admission, 10/1 for domestic and international students; for summer admission, 3/15 for domestic students. Applications are processed on a rolling basis. Application fee: $50. Electronic applications accepted. *Expenses:* Tuition, state resident: full-time $6548; part-time $327.39 per credit hour. Tuition, nonresident: full-time $11,848; part-time $592.39 per credit hour. *Required fees:* $542; $99 per credit hour. $176 per semester. One-time fee: $50. Tuition and fees vary according to course load and program. *Financial support:* Scholarships/grants and unspecified assistantships available. Support available to part-time students. *Unit head:* Dr. Susan Bashinski, Director of Graduate Programs in Education, 816-271-5629, E-mail: sbashinski@missouriwestern.edu. *Application contact:* Dr. Benjamin D. Caldwell, Dean of the Graduate School, 816-271-4394, Fax: 816-271-4525, E-mail: graduate@missouriwestern.edu.
Website: https://www.missouriwestern.edu/masa/

Montclair State University, The Graduate School, College of Education and Human Services, Program Evaluation Certificate Program, Montclair, NJ 07043-1624. Offers Certificate. *Expenses:* Tuition, state resident: part-time $553 per credit. Tuition, nonresident: part-time $854 per credit. *Required fees:* $91 per credit. Tuition and fees vary according to program.

New Mexico State University, College of Education, Department of Counseling and Educational Psychology, Las Cruces, NM 88003. Offers counseling psychology (PhD); educational diagnostics (MA), including counseling and guidance, educational diagnostics; school psychology (Ed S). *Accreditation:* ACA; APA (one or more programs are accredited); NCATE. *Program availability:* Part-time. *Faculty:* 11 full-time (9 women), 4 part-time/adjunct (2 women). *Students:* 74 full-time (56 women), 12 part-time (9 women); includes 58 minority (2 Black or African American, non-Hispanic/Latino; 1 American Indian or Alaska Native, non-Hispanic/Latino; 6 Asian, non-Hispanic/Latino; 48 Hispanic/Latino; 1 Two or more races, non-Hispanic/Latino), 1 international. Average age 29. 115 applicants, 36% accepted, 26 enrolled. In 2016, 12 master's, 6 doctorates, 9 other advanced degrees awarded. *Degree requirements:* For master's, comprehensive exam, thesis optional, internship; for doctorate, comprehensive exam, thesis/dissertation, internship; for Ed S, comprehensive exam, thesis or alternative, internship. *Entrance requirements:* For master's, doctorate, and Ed S, GRE General Test, minimum GPA of 3.0. Additional exam requirements/recommendations for international students: Required—TOEFL (minimum score 550 paper-based; 79 iBT), IELTS (minimum score 6.5). *Application deadline:* For fall admission, 12/15 for domestic and international students; for spring admission, 2/1 priority date for domestic students, 2/1 for international students. Application fee: $40 ($50 for international students). Electronic applications accepted. *Expenses:* Tuition, state resident: full-time $4086. Tuition, nonresident: full-time $14,254. *Required fees:* $853. Tuition and fees vary according to course load. *Financial support:* In 2016–17, 69 students received support, including 6 fellowships (averaging $4,088 per year), 5 research assistantships (averaging $12,036 per year), 23 teaching assistantships (averaging $12,358 per year); career-related internships or fieldwork, Federal Work-Study, scholarships/grants, traineeships, health care benefits, and unspecified assistantships also available. Support available to part-time students. Financial award application deadline: 3/1. *Faculty research:* Multicultural counseling and training, school and counseling psychology, social justice, integrated primary care behavioral health training, mental health disparities. *Total annual research expenditures:* $122,042. *Unit head:* Dr. Gladys DeNecochea, Interim Department Head, 575-646-2121, Fax: 575-646-8035, E-mail: gdenecoc@nmsu.edu. *Application contact:* Norma Arrieta, Student Program Coordinator, 575-646-2121, Fax: 575-646-8035, E-mail: cep@nmsu.edu.
Website: http://cep.education.nmsu.edu

New Mexico State University, College of Education, Department of Curriculum and Instruction, Las Cruces, NM 88003. Offers bilingual education (MA); curriculum and instruction (Ed D); early childhood education (MA); educational diagnostics (Ed S); language, literacy and culture (MA); learning design and technologies (MA); teaching (MAT), including Spanish; teaching English to speakers of other languages (MA). *Accreditation:* NCATE. *Program availability:* Part-time, evening/weekend, 100% online. *Faculty:* 23 full-time (17 women), 7 part-time/adjunct (5 women). *Students:* 114 full-time (81 women), 219 part-time (159 women); includes 190 minority (16 Black or African American, non-Hispanic/Latino; 2 American Indian or Alaska Native, non-Hispanic/Latino; 5 Asian, non-Hispanic/Latino; 160 Hispanic/Latino; 7 Two or more races, non-Hispanic/Latino), 33 international. Average age 37. 126 applicants, 75% accepted, 65 enrolled. In 2016, 92 master's, 19 doctorates awarded. *Degree requirements:* For master's, comprehensive exam, thesis optional; for doctorate, comprehensive exam, thesis/dissertation. *Entrance requirements:* For master's, minimum cumulative GPA of 3.0; for doctorate, portfolio, minimum cumulative GPA of 3.0. Additional exam requirements/recommendations for international students: Required—TOEFL (minimum score 550 paper-based; 79 iBT), IELTS (minimum score 6.5). *Application deadline:* For fall admission, 12/15 priority date for domestic and international students; for spring admission, 11/1 for domestic students. Applications are processed on a rolling basis. Application fee: $40 ($50 for international students). Electronic applications accepted. *Expenses:* Tuition, state resident: full-time $4086. Tuition, nonresident: full-time $14,254. *Required fees:* $853. Tuition and fees vary according to course load. *Financial support:* In 2016–17, 102 students received support, including 2 fellowships (averaging $4,076 per year), 2 research assistantships (averaging $18,070 per year), 16 teaching assistantships (averaging $16,454 per year); career-related internships or fieldwork, Federal Work-Study, scholarships/grants, traineeships, health care benefits, and unspecified assistantships also available. Support available to part-time students. Financial award application deadline: 3/1. *Faculty research:* STEM education, bilingual and English as a second language education, critical pedagogy/multicultural education, learning design and technology, early childhood education. *Total annual research expenditures:* $29,926. *Unit head:* Dr. David Rutledge, Department Head, 575-646-5411, Fax: 575-646-5436, E-mail: rutledge@nmsu.edu. *Application contact:* Dr. David Rutledge, Associate Department Head for Graduate Programs, 575-646-5411, Fax: 575-646-5436, E-mail: rutledge@nmsu.edu.
Website: http://ci.education.nmsu.edu

North Carolina State University, Graduate School, College of Education, Department of Educational Leadership and Policy Studies, Program in Educational Research and Policy Analysis, Raleigh, NC 27695. Offers PhD. *Degree requirements:* For doctorate, thesis/dissertation. *Entrance requirements:* For doctorate, GRE General Test, minimum GPA of 3.0, interview, sample of work. Electronic applications accepted.

Ohio University, Graduate College, Gladys W. and David H. Patton College of Education and Human Services, Department of Educational Studies, Athens, OH 45701-2979. Offers computer education and technology (M Ed); educational administration (M Ed, Ed D); educational research and evaluation (M Ed, PhD); instructional technology (PhD). *Program availability:* Part-time, evening/weekend, online learning. *Degree requirements:* For master's, thesis or alternative; for doctorate, comprehensive exam, thesis/dissertation. *Entrance requirements:* For master's, GRE General Test (if GPA less than 2.9); for doctorate, GRE General Test, GRE Subject Test, minimum GPA of 2.9, work experience, 3 letters of reference, autobiography. Additional exam requirements/recommendations for international students: Required—TOEFL (minimum score 550 paper-based; 80 iBT) or IELTS (minimum score 6.5). *Application deadline:* For fall admission, 3/1 priority date for domestic and international students; for winter admission, 10/1 priority date for domestic and international students; for spring admission, 1/30 priority date for domestic students, 1/1 priority date for international students. Applications are processed on a rolling basis. Application fee: $50 ($55 for international students). Electronic applications accepted. *Financial support:* Research assistantships with full tuition reimbursements, teaching assistantships with full tuition reimbursements, Federal Work-Study, institutionally sponsored loans, tuition waivers (partial), and unspecified assistantships available. Financial award application deadline: 3/1. *Faculty research:* Race, class and gender; computer programs; development and organization theory; evaluation/development of instruments, leadership. *Unit head:* Dr. David Richard Moore, Chair, 740-597-1322, Fax: 740-593-0477, E-mail: moored3@ohio.edu. *Application contact:* Floyd J. Doney, Director of Student Affairs, 740-593-4400, Fax: 740-593-9310, E-mail: doney@ohio.edu.
Website: http://www.cehs.ohio.edu/academics/es/

Old Dominion University, Darden College of Education, Program in Educational Psychology and Program Evaluation, Norfolk, VA 23529. Offers education (PhD), including educational psychology, program evaluation. *Program availability:* Part-time, evening/weekend. *Faculty:* 5 full-time (2 women). *Students:* 4 full-time (all women), 2 part-time (both women); includes 1 minority (Black or African American, non-Hispanic/Latino), 2 international. Average age 40. 3 applicants, 100% accepted, 1 enrolled. *Degree requirements:* For doctorate, comprehensive exam, thesis/dissertation. *Entrance requirements:* Additional exam requirements/recommendations for international students: Required—TOEFL. *Application deadline:* Applications are processed on a rolling basis. Application fee: $50. Electronic applications accepted. *Expenses:* $30,000. *Financial support:* In 2016–17, 4 students received support, including 4 fellowships with full tuition reimbursements available (averaging $15,000 per year), 10 research assistantships with full tuition reimbursements available (averaging $15,000 per year), 2 teaching assistantships with full tuition reimbursements available (averaging $15,000 per year); unspecified assistantships also available. Financial award application deadline: 2/1. *Faculty research:* Motivation self-regulated learning distance learning calibration assessment. *Unit head:* Shana Pribesh, Coordinator, 757-683-6684, E-mail: spribesh@odu.edu. *Application contact:* Nechell Bonds, Director of Admissions, 757-683-3685, Fax: 757-683-3255, E-mail: gradadmit@odu.edu.
Website: http://www.odu.edu/efl/academics/eppe

Rutgers University–New Brunswick, Graduate School of Education, Department of Educational Psychology, Program in Educational Statistics, Measurement and Evaluation, Piscataway, NJ 08854-8097. Offers Ed M. *Program availability:* Part-time, evening/weekend. *Entrance requirements:* For master's, GRE General Test, 3 letters of recommendation. Additional exam requirements/recommendations for international students: Required—TOEFL (minimum score 550 paper-based; 83 iBT). Electronic applications accepted. *Faculty research:* Program evaluation of student assessment, Type I error and power comparisons, test performance factors, theory building in participatory program evaluation, test validity in higher education admissions.

Seton Hall University, College of Education and Human Services, Department of Education Leadership, Management and Policy, South Orange, NJ 07079-2697. Offers college student personnel administration (MA); education research, assessment and program evaluation (PhD); higher education administration (Ed D, PhD); human resource training and development (MA); K–12 administration and supervision (Ed D, Exec Ed D, Ed S); K–12 leadership, management and policy (Ed D, Exec Ed D, Ed S). *Program availability:* Part-time, evening/weekend, blended/hybrid learning. *Faculty:* 18 full-time (7 women), 25 part-time/adjunct (8 women). *Students:* 50 full-time (35 women), 839 part-time (500 women); includes 270 minority (157 Black or African American, non-Hispanic/Latino; 5 American Indian or Alaska Native, non-Hispanic/Latino; 19 Asian, non-Hispanic/Latino; 87 Hispanic/Latino; 2 Native Hawaiian or other Pacific Islander, non-Hispanic/Latino), 6 international. Average age 37. 199 applicants, 74% accepted, 127 enrolled. In 2016, 83 master's, 26 doctorates, 52 other advanced degrees awarded. *Degree requirements:* For master's, comprehensive exam, thesis or alternative; for doctorate, thesis/dissertation, oral exam, written exam; for Ed S, internship, research project. *Entrance requirements:* For master's, GRE or MAT, minimum GPA of 3.0; for doctorate, GRE or MAT, interview, minimum GPA of 3.5; for Ed S, GRE or MAT, minimum GPA of 3.5. Additional exam requirements/recommendations for international students: Required—TOEFL. *Application deadline:* Applications are processed on a rolling basis. Application fee: $75. *Expenses:* $1,212 per credit. *Financial support:* In 2016–17, 2 research assistantships with full tuition reimbursements (averaging $4,500 per year) were awarded; unspecified assistantships also available. Financial award application deadline: 2/1; financial award applicants required to submit FAFSA. *Unit head:* Dr. Elaine Walker, Chair, 973-275-2307, E-mail: elaine.walker@shu.edu. *Application contact:* Diana Minakakis, Director of Graduate Admissions, 973-275-2824, Fax: 973-275-2187, E-mail: diana.minakakis@shu.edu.

Southern Connecticut State University, School of Graduate Studies, School of Education, Department of Educational Leadership, New Haven, CT 06515-1355. Offers educational leadership (Ed D, Diploma); research, statistics, and measurement (MS). *Program availability:* Part-time, evening/weekend. *Faculty:* 8 full-time (4 women), 6 part-time/adjunct (3 women). *Students:* 5 full-time (4 women), 155 part-time (106 women); includes 24 minority (16 Black or African American, non-Hispanic/Latino; 1 American Indian or Alaska Native, non-Hispanic/Latino; 5 Hispanic/Latino; 2 Two or more races, non-Hispanic/Latino). Average age 38. 141 applicants, 47% accepted, 50 enrolled. In 2016, 15 doctorates, 164 other advanced degrees awarded. *Entrance requirements:* For degree, master's degree, minimum GPA of 3.0, writing sample. *Application deadline:* For fall admission, 7/15 priority date for domestic students. Applications are processed on a rolling basis. Application fee: $50. Electronic applications accepted. *Expenses:* Tuition, state resident: full-time $6497; part-time $519 per credit hour. Tuition, nonresident: full-time $18,102; part-time $535 per credit hour. *Required fees:* $4722; $55 per semester. Tuition and fees vary according to program. *Financial support:* Career-related internships or fieldwork, scholarships/grants, and unspecified assistantships available. Financial award application deadline: 4/15; financial award applicants required to submit FAFSA. *Unit head:* Dr. Gladys Labas, Chairperson, 203-392-9927, Fax: 203-392-5341, E-mail: labasg1@southernct.edu. *Application contact:* Lisa Galvin, Director of Graduate Admissions, 203-392-5240, Fax: 203-392-5235, E-mail: galvinl1@southernct.edu.

Southwestern Oklahoma State University, College of Professional and Graduate Studies, School of Behavioral Sciences and Education, Specialization in School Psychometry, Weatherford, OK 73096-3098. Offers M Ed. M Ed distance learning degree program offered to Oklahoma residents only. *Accreditation:* NCATE. *Program availability:* Part-time, evening/weekend. *Degree requirements:* For master's, exam. *Entrance requirements:* For master's, GRE General Test or minimum undergraduate GPA of 3.0, portfolio. Additional exam requirements/recommendations for international students: Required—TOEFL.

Sul Ross State University, College of Professional Studies, Department of Education, Program in Educational Diagnostics, Alpine, TX 79832. Offers M Ed, Certificate. *Program availability:* Part-time, evening/weekend. *Degree requirements:* For master's, thesis optional. *Entrance requirements:* For master's, GMAT or GRE General Test, minimum GPA of 2.5 in last 60 hours of undergraduate work.

Sul Ross State University, Rio Grande College of Sul Ross State University, Alpine, TX 79832. Offers business administration (MBA); teacher education (M Ed), including bilingual education, counseling, educational diagnostics, elementary education, general education, reading, school administration, secondary education. *Program availability:* Part-time, evening/weekend, online learning. *Degree requirements:* For master's, comprehensive exam, thesis optional, minimum GPA of 3.0. *Entrance requirements:* For master's, GMAT or GRE General Test, minimum GPA of 2.5 in last 60 hours of undergraduate work. Additional exam requirements/recommendations for international students: Required—TOEFL.

Syracuse University, School of Education, Programs in Instructional Design, Development, and Evaluation, Syracuse, NY 13244. Offers MS, PhD, CAS. *Program availability:* Part-time. *Students:* Average age 34. *Degree requirements:* For master's, thesis or alternative; for doctorate, comprehensive exam, thesis/dissertation. *Entrance requirements:* For master's, GRE or MAT, baccalaureate degree from regionally-accredited college/university, statement of goals, three letters of recommendation, transcripts; for doctorate, GRE, master's degree in instructional design or equivalent, statement of goals, three letters of recommendation, transcripts; for CAS, GRE (recommended), master's degree in instructional design or equivalent, statement of goals, three letters of recommendation, transcripts. Additional exam requirements/recommendations for international students: Required—TOEFL (minimum score 100 iBT). *Application deadline:* For fall admission, 1/15 priority date for domestic and international students; for spring admission, 10/15 priority date for domestic and international students. Applications are processed on a rolling basis. Application fee: $75. Electronic applications accepted. *Expenses: Tuition:* Full-time $25,974; part-time $1443 per credit hour. *Required fees:* $802; $50 per course. Tuition and fees vary according to course load and program. *Financial support:* Fellowships with full tuition reimbursements, research assistantships with tuition reimbursements, teaching assistantships with tuition reimbursements, career-related internships or fieldwork, and scholarships/grants available. Financial award application deadline: 1/15. *Faculty research:* Digital media production, technologies for instructional settings, strategies in educational project management, educational technology in international settings. *Unit head:* Dr. Tiffany A. Koszalka, Chair, 315-443-3703, E-mail: takoszal@syr.edu. *Application contact:* Speranza Migliore, Graduate Admissions Recruiter, 315-443-2505, E-mail: gradrcrt@syr.edu.
Website: http://soeweb.syr.edu/idde/instrucdesign.html

Teachers College, Columbia University, Department of Human Development, New York, NY 10027-6696. Offers applied statistics (MS); cognitive studies in education (MA, Ed D, PhD); developmental psychology (MA, Ed D, PhD); educational psychology-human cognition and learning (Ed M, MA, Ed D, PhD); learning analytics (MS); measurement and evaluation (ME, Ed D, PhD); measurement, evaluation, and statistics (MA, MS, Ed D, PhD). *Program availability:* Part-time. *Students:* 217 full-time (168 women), 131 part-time (93 women); includes 83 minority (30 Black or African American, non-Hispanic/Latino; 31 Asian, non-Hispanic/Latino; 18 Hispanic/Latino; 4 Two or more races, non-Hispanic/Latino), 182 international. 450 applicants, 69% accepted, 132 enrolled. *Expenses: Tuition:* Full-time $36,288; part-time $1512 per credit. *Required fees:* $438 per semester. One-time fee: $510 full-time. Full-time tuition and fees vary according to course load. *Unit head:* Prof. Matthew S. Johnson, Chair, 212-678-3882, Fax: 212-678-3837, E-mail: johnson@tc.columbia.edu. *Application contact:* David Estrella, Director of Admission, 212-678-3305, E-mail: estrella@tc.columbia.edu.
Website: http://www.tc.columbia.edu/human-development/

Tennessee Technological University, College of Graduate Studies, College of Education, Department of Curriculum and Instruction, Program in Exceptional Learning, Cookeville, TN 38505. Offers applied behavior analysis (PhD); literacy (PhD); program planning and evaluation (PhD); STEM education (PhD). *Program availability:* Part-time, evening/weekend. *Students:* 10 full-time (6 women), 28 part-time (21 women); includes 2 minority (1 Black or African American, non-Hispanic/Latino; 1 Two or more races, non-Hispanic/Latino), 2 international. 15 applicants, 67% accepted, 7 enrolled. In 2016, 5 doctorates awarded. *Degree requirements:* For doctorate, comprehensive exam, thesis/dissertation. *Entrance requirements:* For doctorate, GRE, minimum GPA of 3.0. Additional exam requirements/recommendations for international students: Required—TOEFL (minimum score 550 paper-based; 79 iBT), IELTS (minimum score 5.5), PTE (minimum score 53), or TOEIC (Test of English as an International Communication). *Application deadline:* For fall admission, 8/1 for domestic students, 5/1 for international students; for spring admission, 12/1 for domestic students, 10/1 for international students; for summer admission, 5/1 for domestic students, 2/1 for international students. Applications are processed on a rolling basis. Application fee: $35 ($40 for international students). Electronic applications accepted. *Expenses:* Tuition, state resident: full-time $9375; part-time $534 per credit hour. Tuition, nonresident: full-time $22,443; part-time $1260 per credit hour. *Financial support:* In 2016–17, 4 fellowships (averaging $8,000 per year), 9 research assistantships (averaging $12,000 per year), 2 teaching assistantships (averaging $12,000 per year) were awarded. Financial award application deadline: 4/1. *Unit head:* Dr. Lisa Zagumny, Director, 931-372-3078, Fax: 931-372-3517, E-mail: lzagumny@tntech.edu. *Application contact:* Shelia K. Kendrick, Coordinator of Graduate Studies, 931-372-3808, Fax: 931-372-3497, E-mail: skendrick@tntech.edu.
Website: https://www.tntech.edu/education/elphd/

Texas A&M University–San Antonio, Department of Curriculum and Kinesiology, San Antonio, TX 78224. Offers bilingual education (MA); early childhood education (M Ed); kinesiology (MS); reading (MS); special education (M Ed), including educational diagnostician, instructional specialist. *Program availability:* Part-time, evening/weekend. *Degree requirements:* For master's, comprehensive exam, thesis or alternative. *Entrance requirements:* For master's, MAT. Additional exam requirements/recommendations for international students: Required—TOEFL (minimum score 550 paper-based; 80 iBT), IELTS (minimum score 6). Electronic applications accepted.

Université Laval, Faculty of Education, Department of Foundations and Interventions in Education, Québec, QC G1K 7P4, Canada. Offers educational administration and evaluation (MA, PhD); educational practice (Diploma), including educational pedagogy, pedagogy management and development, school adaptation; orientation sciences (MA, PhD). *Degree requirements:* For doctorate, comprehensive exam, thesis/dissertation. Electronic applications accepted.

University at Albany, State University of New York, School of Education, Division of Educational Psychology and Methodology, Albany, NY 12222-0001. Offers educational psychology (PhD); educational psychology and methodology (MS); educational research (CAS). *Accreditation:* APA (one or more programs are accredited). *Program availability:* Evening/weekend. *Faculty:* 19 full-time (9 women), 18 part-time/adjunct (14 women). *Students:* 194 full-time (158 women), 101 part-time (87 women); includes 55 minority (16 Black or African American, non-Hispanic/Latino; 1 American Indian or Alaska Native, non-Hispanic/Latino; 15 Asian, non-Hispanic/Latino; 18 Hispanic/Latino; 5 Two or more races, non-Hispanic/Latino), 24 international. Average age 31. 185 applicants, 43% accepted, 102 enrolled. In 2016, 89 master's, 18 doctorates, 10 other advanced degrees awarded. *Degree requirements:* For doctorate, thesis/dissertation. *Entrance requirements:* For doctorate, GRE General Test. Additional exam requirements/recommendations for international students: Required—TOEFL (minimum score 550 paper-based). Application fee: $75. Electronic applications accepted. *Expenses:* Tuition, state resident: full-time $10,870; part-time $453 per credit hour. Tuition, nonresident: full-time $22,210; part-time $925 per credit hour. *International tuition:* $21,550 full-time. *Required fees:* $1864; $96 per credit hour. *Financial support:* Fellowships and career-related internships or fieldwork available. *Total annual research expenditures:* $1.3 million. *Unit head:* Kevin Quinn, Chair, 518-442-5074, E-mail: kquinn@albany.edu.
Website: http://www.albany.edu/educational_psychology/

The University of Akron, Graduate School, College of Education, Department of Educational Foundations and Leadership, Program in Assessment and Evaluation, Akron, OH 44325. Offers MA, Certificate. *Program availability:* Online learning. *Students:* 4 full-time (all women), 24 part-time (22 women); includes 10 minority (7 Black or African American, non-Hispanic/Latino; 1 Asian, non-Hispanic/Latino; 2 Two or more races, non-Hispanic/Latino). Average age 38. 23 applicants, 91% accepted, 13 enrolled. In 2016, 8 master's awarded. *Degree requirements:* For master's, project, culminating portfolio. *Entrance requirements:* Additional exam requirements/recommendations for international students: Required—TOEFL (minimum score 550 paper-based; 79 iBT), IELTS (minimum score 6.5). *Application deadline:* Applications are processed on a rolling basis. Application fee: $45 ($70 for international students). *Expenses:* Tuition, state resident: full-time $8618; part-time $359 per credit hour. Tuition, nonresident: full-time $17,149; part-time $715 per credit hour. *Required fees:* $1652. *Unit head:* Dr. Susan Clark, Interim Chair, 330-972-7780, E-mail: sclark1@uakron.edu. *Application contact:* Kelly Chaff, College Program Specialist, 330-972-7028, E-mail: klchaff@uakron.edu.

University of Arkansas, Graduate School, College of Education and Health Professions, Department of Curriculum and Instruction, Program in Educational Statistics and Research Methods, Fayetteville, AR 72701. Offers MS, PhD. In 2016, 2 doctorates awarded. *Application deadline:* For fall admission, 4/1 for international students; for spring admission, 10/1 for international students. Applications are processed on a rolling basis. Application fee: $40 ($50 for international students). Electronic applications accepted. *Financial support:* In 2016–17, 14 research assistantships were awarded; fellowships and teaching assistantships also available. *Unit head:* Dr. Michael Daugherty, Departmental Chairperson, 479-575-4209, Fax: 479-575-5119, E-mail: mkd03@uark.edu. *Application contact:* Dr. Wen-Juo Lo, Graduate Coordinator, 479-575-6321, Fax: 479-575-6676, E-mail: wlo@uark.edu.
Website: http://cied.uark.edu/

The University of British Columbia, Faculty of Education, Department of Educational and Counseling Psychology, and Special Education, Vancouver, BC V6T 1Z4, Canada. Offers counseling psychology (M Ed, MA, PhD); guidance studies (Diploma); human development, learning and culture (M Ed, MA, PhD); measurement, evaluation, and research methodology (M Ed, MA, PhD); school psychology (M Ed, MA, PhD); special education (M Ed, MA, PhD, Diploma). *Program availability:* Part-time. *Degree requirements:* For master's, thesis (for some programs); for doctorate, comprehensive exam, thesis/dissertation. *Entrance requirements:* For master's, GRE General Test (counseling psychology MA); for doctorate, GRE General Test. Additional exam requirements/recommendations for international students: Required—TOEFL. Application fee: $102 Canadian dollars ($165 Canadian dollars for international students). Electronic applications accepted. *Expenses:* $6,865 per year tuition, $10,938 per year international (for MA, M Ed); $4,802 per year tuition, $8,436 per year international (for PhD). *Financial support:* Fellowships, research assistantships, teaching assistantships, career-related internships or fieldwork, Federal Work-Study, institutionally sponsored loans, scholarships/grants, health care benefits, tuition waivers (full and partial), and unspecified assistantships available. *Faculty research:* Women, family, social problems, career transition, stress and coping problems. *Application contact:* Karen Yan, Graduate Program Assistant, 604-822-6371, Fax: 604-822-3302, E-mail: karen.yan@ubc.ca.
Website: http://ecps.educ.ubc.ca/

University of Calgary, Faculty of Graduate Studies, Werklund School of Education, Graduate Division of Educational Research, Calgary, AB T2N 1N4, Canada. Offers adult learning (M Ed, MA, Ed D, PhD); curriculum and learning (M Ed, MA, Ed D, PhD); educational leadership (M Ed, MA, Ed D, PhD); languages and diversity (M Ed, MA, Ed D, PhD); learning sciences (M Ed, MA, Ed D, PhD). Ed D in educational leadership offered via distance delivery. *Program availability:* Part-time, evening/weekend, online learning. *Degree requirements:* For master's, thesis (for some programs); for doctorate, thesis/dissertation, candidacy exam. *Entrance requirements:* For master's, minimum GPA of 3.0, 3 letters of reference; for doctorate, minimum GPA of 3.5, 3 letters of reference. Additional exam requirements/recommendations for international students: Required—TOEFL, IELTS. Electronic applications accepted. *Faculty research:* Curriculum, leadership, technology, contexts, gifted, second language teaching, work place and adult learning.

University of Colorado Boulder, Graduate School, School of Education, Division of Research and Evaluation Methodology, Boulder, CO 80309. Offers PhD. *Accreditation:* NCATE. *Students:* 8 full-time (4 women); includes 1 minority (Native Hawaiian or other Pacific Islander, non-Hispanic/Latino), 1 international. Average age 35. 16 applicants, 31% accepted, 2 enrolled. In 2016, 1 doctorate awarded. *Degree requirements:* For doctorate, one foreign language, comprehensive exam, thesis/dissertation. *Entrance requirements:* For doctorate, GRE General Test, minimum undergraduate GPA of 2.75. *Application deadline:* For fall admission, 2/1 for domestic students, 12/1 for international students; for spring admission, 9/1 for domestic and international students. Application fee: $60 ($80 for international students). Electronic applications accepted. Application fee is waived when completed online. *Financial support:* In 2016–17, 30 students received support, including 7 fellowships (averaging $4,534 per year), 8 research assistantships with full and partial tuition reimbursements available (averaging $35,008 per year), 2 teaching assistantships with full and partial tuition reimbursements available (averaging $14,305 per year); institutionally sponsored loans, scholarships/grants, health care benefits, and unspecified assistantships also available. Financial award applicants required to submit FAFSA. *Application contact:* E-mail: edadvise@colorado.edu.
Website: http://www.colorado.edu/education/

University of Colorado Denver, School of Education and Human Development, Program in Educational Leadership and Innovation, Denver, CO 80217. Offers educational studies and research (PhD), including administrative leadership and policy, early childhood special education, math education, research, assessment and evaluation, science education, urban ecologies. *Program availability:* Part-time, evening/weekend. *Students:* 30 full-time (25 women), 14 part-time (11 women); includes 16 minority (7 Black or African American, non-Hispanic/Latino; 1 American Indian or Alaska Native, non-Hispanic/Latino; 1 Asian, non-Hispanic/Latino; 6 Hispanic/Latino; 1 Two or more races, non-Hispanic/Latino), 5 international. Average age 40. 21 applicants, 67% accepted, 8 enrolled. In 2016, 3 doctorates awarded. *Degree requirements:* For doctorate, comprehensive exam, thesis/dissertation, 75 credit hours (for PhD). *Entrance requirements:* For doctorate, GRE or equivalent, resume or curriculum vitae, letters of recommendation, master's degree or equivalent, completion of basic or advanced statistics course with minimum B grade. Additional exam requirements/recommendations for international students: Required—TOEFL (minimum score 537 paper-based; 75 iBT); Recommended—IELTS (minimum score 6.5). *Application deadline:* For fall admission, 12/1 priority date for domestic students, 11/1 priority date for international students. Applications are processed on a rolling basis. Application fee: $50 ($75 for international students). Electronic applications accepted. *Expenses:* Contact institution. *Financial support:* In 2016–17, 45 students received support. Fellowships, research assistantships, teaching assistantships, Federal Work-Study, institutionally sponsored loans, scholarships/grants, and traineeships available. Financial award application deadline: 4/1; financial award applicants required to submit FAFSA. *Faculty research:* Administrative leadership and policy studies, early childhood education, research in diversity, paraprofessionals in education, urban schools lab. *Unit head:* 303-315-6300, E-mail: education@ucdenver.edu. *Application contact:* 303-315-6300, E-mail: education@ucdenver.edu.
Website: http://www.ucdenver.edu/academics/colleges/SchoolOfEducation/Academics/Doctorate/Pages/PhD%20in%20Education%20and%20Human%20Development.aspx

University of Colorado Denver, School of Education and Human Development, Programs in Educational and School Psychology, Denver, CO 80217. Offers educational psychology (MA), including educational assessment, educational psychology, human development, human learning, research and evaluation; school psychology (Psy D, Ed S). MA program also offered in partnership with Boulder Journey School, Friends School and Stanley British Primary School. *Program availability:* Part-time, evening/weekend. *Students:* 210 full-time (171 women), 79 part-time (71 women); includes 47 minority (5 Black or African American, non-Hispanic/Latino; 2 American Indian or Alaska Native, non-Hispanic/Latino; 5 Asian, non-Hispanic/Latino; 28 Hispanic/Latino; 7 Two or more races, non-Hispanic/Latino), 6 international. Average age 30. 179 applicants, 94% accepted, 126 enrolled. In 2016, 166 master's, 7 doctorates, 11 other advanced degrees awarded. *Degree requirements:* For master's, comprehensive exam, 9 hours of core courses, embedded within a minimum of 36 to 38 hours of relevant coursework, including an educational psychology practicum, independent study project or thesis (recommended); for Ed S, comprehensive exam, minimum of 75 semester hours (61 hours of coursework, 6 of 500-hour practicum in field, and 8 of 1200-hour internship); PRAXIS II. *Entrance requirements:* For master's, GRE if undergraduate GPA below 2.75, resume, three letters of recommendation, transcripts; for Ed S, GRE, resume, letters of recommendation, transcripts. Additional exam requirements/recommendations for international students: Required—TOEFL (minimum score 537 paper-based; 75 iBT); Recommended—IELTS (minimum score 6.5). *Application deadline:* For fall admission, 4/15 for domestic students, 4/1 for international students; for spring admission, 9/15 for domestic students, 9/1 for international students. Application fee: $50 ($75 for international students). Electronic applications accepted. *Expenses:* Contact institution. *Financial support:* In 2016–17, 90 students received support. Research assistantships, Federal Work-Study, institutionally sponsored loans, scholarships/grants, and traineeships available. Financial award application deadline: 4/1; financial award applicants required to submit FAFSA. *Faculty research:* Crisis response and intervention, school violence prevention, immigrant experience, educational environments for English language learners, culturally competent assessment and intervention, child and youth suicide. *Unit head:* Francie Crepeau-Hobson, Associate Professor and Program Director, 303-315-6315, E-mail: franci.creapeau-hobson@ucdenver.edu. *Application contact:* 303-315-6300, E-mail: education@ucdenver.edu.
Website: http://www.ucdenver.edu/academics/colleges/SchoolOfEducation/Academics/MASTERS/EPSY/Pages/default.aspx

University of Denver, Morgridge College of Education, Denver, CO 80208. Offers child, family and school psychology (MA, PhD, Ed S); counseling psychology (MA, PhD); curriculum and instruction (MA, Ed D, PhD); curriculum instruction and teaching (Certificate); early childhood special education (MA, Certificate); educational leadership and policy studies (MA, Ed D, PhD, Certificate); higher education (Ed D, PhD); library and information science (MLIS); research methods and statistics (MA, PhD). *Accreditation:* ALA; APA (one or more programs are accredited). *Program availability:* Part-time, evening/weekend, online learning. *Faculty:* 39 full-time (29 women), 60 part-time/adjunct (42 women). *Students:* 498 full-time (392 women), 362 part-time (282 women); includes 223 minority (63 Black or African American, non-Hispanic/Latino; 6 American Indian or Alaska Native, non-Hispanic/Latino; 20 Asian, non-Hispanic/Latino; 102 Hispanic/Latino; 1 Native Hawaiian or other Pacific Islander, non-Hispanic/Latino; 31 Two or more races, non-Hispanic/Latino), 40 international. Average age 32. 1,027 applicants, 69% accepted, 386 enrolled. In 2016, 252 master's, 36 doctorates, 141 other advanced degrees awarded. Terminal master's awarded for partial completion of doctoral program. *Degree requirements:* For master's, comprehensive exam; for doctorate, 2 foreign languages, comprehensive exam, thesis/dissertation. *Entrance requirements:* For master's and doctorate, GRE General Test or GMAT. Additional exam requirements/recommendations for international students: Required—TOEFL (minimum score 550 paper-based; 80 iBT). *Application deadline:* Applications are processed on a rolling basis. Application fee: $65. Electronic applications accepted. *Expenses:* $29,022 per year full-time. *Financial support:* In 2016–17, 697 students received support, including 37 research assistantships with tuition reimbursements available (averaging $11,209 per year), 66 teaching assistantships with tuition reimbursements available (averaging $3,742 per year); career-related internships or fieldwork, Federal Work-Study, institutionally sponsored loans, scholarships/grants, and unspecified assistantships also available. Support available to part-time students. Financial award application deadline: 2/15; financial award applicants required to submit FAFSA. *Faculty research:* Early childhood education, access and equity, educational leadership, family and school partnerships, neurodevelopmental disorders. *Total annual research expenditures:* $3.3 million. *Unit head:* Dr. Karen Riley, Dean, 303-871-3665, Fax: 303-871-4456, E-mail: karen.riley@du.edu. *Application contact:* Jodi Dye, Director of Admissions, 303-871-2510, Fax: 303-871-4456, E-mail: jodi.dye@du.edu.
Website: http://morgridge.du.edu

University of Florida, Graduate School, College of Education, School of Human Development and Organizational Studies in Education, Gainesville, FL 32611. Offers counseling and counselor education (Ed D, PhD), including counseling and counselor education, marriage and family counseling, mental health counseling, school counseling and guidance; educational leadership (M Ed, MAE, Ed D, PhD, Ed S), including educational leadership (Ed D, PhD), educational policy (Ed D, PhD); higher education administration (Ed D, PhD), including education policy (Ed D), educational policy, higher education administration; marriage and family counseling (M Ed, MAE, Ed D, PhD, Ed S); mental health counseling (M Ed, MAE, Ed D, PhD, Ed S); research and evaluation methodology (M Ed, MAE, Ed D, PhD); school counseling and guidance (M Ed, MAE, Ed D, PhD, Ed S); student personnel in higher education (M Ed, MAE). *Accreditation:* ACA (one or more programs are accredited); NCATE. *Program availability:* Part-time, online learning. Terminal master's awarded for partial completion of doctoral program. *Degree requirements:* For master's, thesis optional; for doctorate, comprehensive exam, thesis/dissertation. *Entrance requirements:* For master's and doctorate, GRE General Test, minimum GPA of 3.0 (undergraduate), 3.5 (graduate); for Ed S, GRE General Test. Additional exam requirements/recommendations for international students: Required—TOEFL (minimum score 550 paper-based; 80 iBT), IELTS (minimum score 6). Electronic applications accepted.

University of Illinois at Chicago, College of Education, Department of Educational Psychology, Chicago, IL 60607-7128. Offers early childhood education (M Ed); educational psychology (PhD); measurement, evaluation, statistics, and assessment (M Ed); youth development (M Ed). *Program availability:* Part-time, online learning. *Faculty research:* Children's construction of morality, development of resilience in the face of enduring economical difficulties, cognition and cognitive development, test fairness.

The University of Iowa, Graduate College, College of Education, Department of Psychological and Quantitative Foundations, Iowa City, IA 52242-1316. Offers counseling psychology (PhD); educational measurement and statistics (MA, PhD); educational psychology (MA, PhD); school psychology (PhD, Ed S). *Accreditation:* APA. *Degree requirements:* For master's, thesis optional, exam; for doctorate, comprehensive exam, thesis/dissertation; for Ed S, exam. *Entrance requirements:* For master's, doctorate, and Ed S, GRE General Test, minimum GPA of 3.0. Additional exam requirements/recommendations for international students: Required—TOEFL (minimum score 550 paper-based; 81 iBT). Electronic applications accepted.

The University of Kansas, Graduate Studies, School of Education, Department of Educational Psychology, Program in Educational Psychology and Research, Lawrence, KS 66045. Offers MS Ed, PhD. *Program availability:* Part-time. *Students:* 36 full-time (22 women), 5 part-time (3 women); includes 6 minority (2 Black or African American, non-Hispanic/Latino; 3 Asian, non-Hispanic/Latino; 1 Hispanic/Latino), 18 international. Average age 31. 17 applicants, 71% accepted, 6 enrolled. In 2016, 2 master's, 6 doctorates awarded. *Entrance requirements:* For master's, GRE General Test, minimum GPA of 3.0, resume, statement of purpose, official transcripts, three recommendation letters; for doctorate, GRE General Test, resume, statement of purpose, official transcripts, three recommendation letters. Additional exam requirements/recommendations for international students: Required—TOEFL or IELTS. *Application deadline:* For fall admission, 12/15 for domestic and international students. Application fee: $65 ($85 for international students). Electronic applications accepted. *Financial support:* Fellowships, research assistantships, teaching assistantships, career-related internships or fieldwork, institutionally sponsored loans, scholarships/grants, traineeships, health care benefits, tuition waivers (full and partial), and unspecified assistantships available. Support available to part-time students. Financial award application deadline: 12/15. *Faculty research:* Educational measurement, applied statistics, research design, program evaluation, learning and development. *Unit head:* Steven Wayne Lee, Chair, 785-864-9701, E-mail: swlee@ku.edu. *Application contact:* Penny Fritts, Admissions Coordinator, 785-864-9645, E-mail: fritts@ku.edu.
Website: http://www.soe.ku.edu/PRE/

University of Kentucky, Graduate School, College of Education, Program in Educational Policy Studies and Evaluation, Lexington, KY 40506-0032. Offers educational policy studies and evaluation (Ed D); higher education (MS Ed, PhD); social and philosophical studies (MS Ed). *Accreditation:* NCATE. Terminal master's awarded for partial completion of doctoral program. *Degree requirements:* For master's, comprehensive exam, thesis optional; for doctorate, comprehensive exam, thesis/dissertation. *Entrance requirements:* For master's, GRE General Test, minimum undergraduate GPA of 2.75; for doctorate, GRE General Test, minimum graduate GPA of 3.0. Additional exam requirements/recommendations for international students: Required—TOEFL (minimum score 550 paper-based). Electronic applications accepted. *Faculty research:* Studies in higher education; comparative and international education; evaluation of educational programs, policies, and reform; student, teacher, and faculty cultures; gender and education.

University of Louisiana at Monroe, Graduate School, College of Arts, Education, and Sciences, School of Education, Program in Curriculum and Instruction, Monroe, LA 71209-0001. Offers art education (M Ed); biology education (M Ed); chemistry education (M Ed); curriculum and instruction (Ed D); early childhood education (M Ed); earth science education (M Ed); educational leadership (M Ed); elementary education (1-5) (M Ed); English as a second language (M Ed); English education (M Ed); family and consumer education (M Ed); French education (M Ed); history education (M Ed); math education (M Ed); middle school education (M Ed); music education (M Ed); reading education (K-12) (M Ed); Spanish education (M Ed); special education - academically gifted (M Ed); special education - early intervention (M Ed); special education - educational diagnostician (M Ed); special education - mild/moderate disabilities (M Ed);

speech education (M Ed). *Accreditation:* NCATE. *Faculty:* 8 full-time (4 women), 4 part-time/adjunct (3 women). *Students:* 13 full-time (11 women), 80 part-time (65 women); includes 25 minority (19 Black or African American, non-Hispanic/Latino; 1 Asian, non-Hispanic/Latino; 3 Hispanic/Latino; 2 Two or more races, non-Hispanic/Latino). Average age 37. 118 applicants, 30% accepted, 16 enrolled. In 2016, 23 master's, 4 doctorates awarded. *Degree requirements:* For master's, comprehensive exam (for some programs), thesis; for doctorate, thesis/dissertation, internships. *Entrance requirements:* For master's, GRE General Test; for doctorate, GRE General Test, minimum undergraduate GPA of 2.75, graduate 3.25. Additional exam requirements/recommendations for international students: Required—TOEFL (minimum score 500 paper-based; 61 iBT). *Application deadline:* For fall admission, 8/24 priority date for domestic students, 7/1 for international students; for winter admission, 12/14 priority date for domestic students; for spring admission, 1/19 for domestic students, 11/1 for international students. Applications are processed on a rolling basis. Application fee: $20 ($30 for international students). Electronic applications accepted. *Expenses:* Tuition, state resident: full-time $6489. Tuition, nonresident: full-time $18,589. *Required fees:* $8984. Tuition and fees vary according to course level, course load, degree level and program. *Financial support:* Research assistantships, career-related internships or fieldwork, Federal Work-Study, and unspecified assistantships available. Financial award application deadline: 4/1; financial award applicants required to submit FAFSA. *Unit head:* Dr. Dorothy Schween, Director, 318-342-1268, Fax: 318-342-3131, E-mail: schween@ulm.edu.

University of Louisville, Graduate School, College of Education and Human Development, Department of Counseling and Human Development, Louisville, KY 40292-0001. Offers counseling and personnel services (M Ed, PhD), including art therapy (M Ed), clinical mental health counseling (M Ed), college student personnel, counseling psychology, counselor education and supervision (PhD), educational psychology, measurement, and evaluation (PhD), school counseling (M Ed). *Accreditation:* APA; NCATE. *Program availability:* Part-time, evening/weekend. *Students:* 148 full-time (115 women), 58 part-time (42 women); includes 52 minority (36 Black or African American, non-Hispanic/Latino; 1 American Indian or Alaska Native, non-Hispanic/Latino; 4 Asian, non-Hispanic/Latino; 7 Hispanic/Latino; 4 Two or more races, non-Hispanic/Latino), 2 international. Average age 28. 206 applicants, 56% accepted, 73 enrolled. In 2016, 38 master's, 1 doctorate awarded. *Degree requirements:* For doctorate, comprehensive exam, thesis/dissertation. *Entrance requirements:* For master's and doctorate, GRE General Test. Application fee: $60. *Expenses:* Tuition, state resident: full-time $12,246; part-time $681 per credit hour. Tuition, nonresident: full-time $25,486; part-time $1417 per credit hour. *Required fees:* $196. Tuition and fees vary according to program and reciprocity agreements. *Financial support:* Fellowships, research assistantships, teaching assistantships, career-related internships or fieldwork, Federal Work-Study, scholarships/grants, health care benefits, and unspecified assistantships available. Financial award application deadline: 6/1; financial award applicants required to submit FAFSA. *Faculty research:* Mental health services and under-served populations; health disparities and outcomes; well-being identity development; measurement and evaluation. *Total annual research expenditures:* $295,684. *Unit head:* Dr. Mark M. Leach, Interim Chair/Professor, 502-852-0588, Fax: 502-852-0629, E-mail: m.leach@louisville.edu. *Application contact:* Betty Hampton, Director of Graduate Student Services, 502-852-5597, Fax: 502-852-1465, E-mail: edadvise@louisville.edu.
Website: http://www.louisville.edu/education/departments/ecpy

University of Maryland, College Park, Academic Affairs, College of Education, Department of Human Development and Quantitative Methodology, College Park, MD 20742. Offers MA, Ed D, PhD. *Entrance requirements:* Additional exam requirements/recommendations for international students: Required—TOEFL.

University of Massachusetts Amherst, Graduate School, College of Education, Program in Education, Amherst, MA 01003. Offers bilingual, English as a second language, and multicultural education (M Ed, Ed S); child study and early education (M Ed); children, families and schools (Ed D, Ed S); early childhood and elementary teacher education (M Ed); educational leadership (M Ed); educational policy and leadership (Ed D); higher education (M Ed); international education (M Ed); language, literacy and culture (Ed D); learning, media and technology (M Ed, Ed S); mathematics, science, and learning technologies (Ed D); reading and writing (M Ed); research, educational measurement and psychometrics (Ed D); school counselor education (M Ed, Ed S); school psychology (Ed S); science education (Ed S); secondary teacher education (M Ed); social justice education (M Ed, Ed D, Ed S); special education (M Ed, Ed D, Ed S); teacher education and school improvement (Ed D, Ed S). *Accreditation:* NCATE. *Program availability:* Part-time, online learning. Terminal master's awarded for partial completion of doctoral program. *Degree requirements:* For doctorate, comprehensive exam, thesis/dissertation. *Entrance requirements:* Additional exam requirements/recommendations for international students: Required—TOEFL (minimum score 550 paper-based; 80 iBT), IELTS (minimum score 6.5). Electronic applications accepted.

University of Memphis, Graduate School, College of Education, Department of Counseling, Educational Psychology and Research, Memphis, TN 38152. Offers counseling (MS, Ed D), including clinical mental health counseling (MS), clinical rehabilitation counseling (MS), rehabilitation counseling (MS), school counseling (MS); counseling psychology (PhD); educational psychology and research (MS, PhD), including educational psychology, educational research. *Accreditation:* ACA (one or more programs are accredited); APA (one or more programs are accredited); CORE (one or more programs are accredited); NCATE. *Program availability:* Blended/hybrid learning. *Faculty:* 26 full-time (18 women), 10 part-time/adjunct (7 women). *Students:* 124 full-time (99 women), 79 part-time (60 women); includes 64 minority (48 Black or African American, non-Hispanic/Latino; 3 Asian, non-Hispanic/Latino; 6 Hispanic/Latino; 7 Two or more races, non-Hispanic/Latino), 7 international. Average age 32. 82 applicants, 68% accepted, 39 enrolled. In 2016, 65 master's, 8 doctorates awarded. *Degree requirements:* For master's, comprehensive exam, thesis or alternative, internship; for doctorate, comprehensive exam, thesis/dissertation, practicum, internship, residency, scholarly work. *Entrance requirements:* For master's, GRE General Test or MAT, minimum GPA of 2.5, letters of reference, interview; for doctorate, GRE General Test, master's degree or equivalent, letters of reference, interview, curriculum vitae, personal statement. Additional exam requirements/recommendations for international students: Required—TOEFL (minimum score 550 paper-based; 79 iBT). *Application deadline:* For fall admission, 10/1 priority date for domestic students; for spring admission, 4/1 priority date for domestic students. Applications are processed on a rolling basis. Application fee: $35 ($60 for international students). Electronic applications accepted. *Expenses:* $5,231.50 per semester full-time in-state, $9,623.50 full-time out-of-state. *Financial support:* In 2016–17, 130 students received support, including 13 research assistantships with full tuition reimbursements available (averaging $14,820 per year), 11 teaching assistantships with full tuition reimbursements available (averaging $15,600 per year); fellowships with full tuition reimbursements available, career-related internships or fieldwork, Federal Work-Study, scholarships/grants, and unspecified assistantships also available. Financial award application deadline: 2/1; financial award applicants required to submit FAFSA. *Faculty research:* Anger management, aging and disability, supervision, multicultural counseling. *Unit head:* Dr. Steve West, Chair, 901-678-2841, Fax: 901-678-5114, E-mail: slwest@memphis.edu. *Application contact:* Dr. Suzanne Lease, Interim Assistant Dean of Education and Graduate Programs, 901-678-4476, Fax: 901-678-4778, E-mail: slease@memphis.edu.
Website: http://www.memphis.edu/cepr/

University of Miami, Graduate School, School of Education and Human Development, Department of Educational and Psychological Studies, Program in Research, Measurement, and Evaluation, Coral Gables, FL 33124. Offers MS Ed, PhD. *Program availability:* Part-time, evening/weekend. *Faculty:* 2 full-time (1 woman). *Students:* 5 full-time (3 women), 7 part-time (3 women); includes 4 minority (1 Black or African American, non-Hispanic/Latino; 3 Hispanic/Latino), 5 international. Average age 32. 12 applicants, 50% accepted, 5 enrolled. In 2016, 4 master's awarded. Terminal master's awarded for partial completion of doctoral program. *Degree requirements:* For master's, comprehensive exam, thesis optional; for doctorate, thesis/dissertation, qualifying exam. *Entrance requirements:* For master's and doctorate, GRE General Test. Additional exam requirements/recommendations for international students: Required—TOEFL (minimum score 550 paper-based; 80 iBT); Recommended—IELTS (minimum score 6.5). *Application deadline:* For fall admission, 10/1 for international students. Applications are processed on a rolling basis. Application fee: $65. Electronic applications accepted. *Financial support:* In 2016–17, 3 students received support. Fellowships, research assistantships, teaching assistantships, institutionally sponsored loans, scholarships/grants, health care benefits, tuition waivers (full and partial), and unspecified assistantships available. Support available to part-time students. Financial award application deadline: 3/1; financial award applicants required to submit FAFSA. *Faculty research:* Psychometric theory, computer-based testing, quantitative research methods. *Unit head:* Dr. Soyeon Ahn, Associate Professor and Program Director, 305-284-5389, E-mail: s.ahn@miami.edu. *Application contact:* Lois Heffernan, Graduate Admissions Coordinator, 305-284-2167, Fax: 305-284-9395, E-mail: lheffernan@miami.edu.
Website: http://www.education.miami.edu

University of Michigan–Dearborn, College of Education, Health, and Human Services, Master of Arts Program in Program Evaluation and Assessment, Dearborn, MI 48126. Offers MA. *Program availability:* Part-time, evening/weekend. *Faculty:* 6 full-time (all women). *Degree requirements:* For master's, essay. *Entrance requirements:* Additional exam requirements/recommendations for international students: Required—TOEFL (minimum score 560 paper-based; 84 iBT), IELTS (minimum score 6.5). *Application deadline:* For fall admission, 8/1 for domestic students, 5/1 for international students; for winter admission, 12/1 for domestic students, 9/1 for international students; for spring admission, 4/1 for domestic students, 1/1 for international students. Applications are processed on a rolling basis. Application fee: $60. Electronic applications accepted. *Expenses:* Contact institution. *Financial support:* Application deadline: 3/1; applicants required to submit FAFSA. *Faculty research:* Urban education, multicultural education, assessment, evaluation and research methodology, pedagogy and interventions. *Unit head:* Dr. Janine Janosky, Dean, 313-593-5435, E-mail: jjanosky@umich.edu. *Application contact:* Dr. Stein Brunvand, Director, Master's Programs, 313-583-6415, E-mail: sbrunvan@umich.edu.
Website: https://umdearborn.edu/cehhs/graduate-programs/areas-study/ma-program-evaluation-and-assessment

University of Minnesota, Twin Cities Campus, Graduate School, College of Education and Human Development, Department of Organizational Leadership, Policy and Development, Program in Evaluation Studies, Minneapolis, MN 55455-0213. Offers MA, PhD. *Students:* 15 full-time (10 women), 12 part-time (9 women); includes 8 minority (3 Black or African American, non-Hispanic/Latino; 2 Asian, non-Hispanic/Latino; 1 Hispanic/Latino; 2 Two or more races, non-Hispanic/Latino), 1 international. Average age 41. 22 applicants, 36% accepted, 8 enrolled. In 2016, 3 master's, 8 doctorates awarded. Application fee: $75 ($95 for international students). *Unit head:* Dr. Heidi Barajas, Chair, 612-625-4823, E-mail: hbarajas@umn.edu. *Application contact:* Dr. Jeremy J. Hernandez, Director of Graduate Studies, 612-626-9377, E-mail: herna220@umn.edu.
Website: http://www.cehd.umn.edu/OLPD/grad-programs/ES/

University of Missouri–St. Louis, College of Education, Department of Education Sciences and Professional Programs, St. Louis, MO 63121. Offers adult and higher education (M Ed); educational leadership and policy studies (PhD); educational psychology (M Ed), including character and citizenship education, research and program evaluation; program evaluation (Certificate); school psychology (Ed S). *Faculty:* 36 full-time (25 women), 53 part-time/adjunct (40 women). *Students:* 47 full-time (34 women), 247 part-time (175 women); includes 107 minority (86 Black or African American, non-Hispanic/Latino; 2 American Indian or Alaska Native, non-Hispanic/Latino; 5 Asian, non-Hispanic/Latino; 10 Hispanic/Latino; 4 Two or more races, non-Hispanic/Latino), 7 international. 106 applicants, 92% accepted, 70 enrolled. *Degree requirements:* For other advanced degree, comprehensive exam, thesis or alternative, internship. *Entrance requirements:* For degree, GRE General Test, 2-4 letters of recommendation, personal interview. Additional exam requirements/recommendations for international students: Required—IELTS (minimum score 6.5); Recommended—TOEFL (minimum score 550 paper-based; 79 iBT). *Application deadline:* For fall admission, 2/15 priority date for domestic students, 2/15 for international students. Application fee: $50 ($40 for international students). Electronic applications accepted. *Financial support:* Application deadline: 4/1; applicants required to submit FAFSA. *Faculty research:* Child/adolescent psychology, quantitative and qualitative methodology, evaluation processes, measurement and assessment. *Unit head:* Dr. Donald Gouwens, Chairperson, 314-516-4773, Fax: 314-516-5784, E-mail: gouwensd@umsl.edu. *Application contact:* 314-516-5458, Fax: 314-516-6996, E-mail: gradadm@umsl.edu.
Website: https://coe.umsl.edu/dept/espp.html

University of Missouri–St. Louis, Graduate School, Program in Public Policy Administration, St. Louis, MO 63121. Offers local government management (MPPA, Certificate); nonprofit management and leadership (MPPA, Certificate); policy and program evaluation (MPPA, Certificate). *Accreditation:* NASPAA. *Program availability:* Part-time, evening/weekend. *Faculty:* 2 full-time (both women), 6 part-time/adjunct (2 women). *Students:* 10 full-time (5 women), 43 part-time (26 women); includes 14 minority (12 Black or African American, non-Hispanic/Latino; 2 Asian, non-Hispanic/Latino). Average age 33. 28 applicants, 89% accepted, 17 enrolled. *Degree requirements:* For master's, exit project. *Entrance requirements:* For master's, 3 letters of recommendation, personal statement. Additional exam requirements/recommendations for international students: Recommended—TOEFL (minimum score 550 paper-based), IELTS (minimum score 6.5). *Application deadline:* For fall admission, 7/1 priority date for domestic and international students; for spring admission, 12/1 priority date for domestic and international students. Applications are processed on a rolling basis. Application fee: $50 ($40 for international students). Electronic applications accepted. *Financial support:* Research assistantships with tuition reimbursements and career-related internships or fieldwork available. Financial award application deadline: 4/1; financial award applicants required to submit FAFSA. *Faculty research:* Urban policy, public finance, evaluation. *Unit head:* Dr. Deborah Balser, Director, 314-516-5146, Fax:

314-516-5210, E-mail: balserd@umsl.edu. *Application contact:* 314-516-5458, Fax: 314-516-6996, E-mail: gradadm@umsl.edu.
Website: http://www.umsl.edu/gradschool/ppa/

University of Nebraska–Lincoln, Graduate College, College of Education and Human Sciences, Department of Educational Psychology, Lincoln, NE 68588. Offers cognition, learning and development (MA); counseling psychology (MA); educational psychology (MA, Ed S); psychological studies in education (PhD), including cognition, learning and development, counseling psychology, quantitative, qualitative, and psychometric methods, school psychology; quantitative, qualitative, and psychometric methods (MA); school psychology (MA, Ed S). *Accreditation:* APA (one or more programs are accredited); NCATE. *Degree requirements:* For master's, thesis optional. *Entrance requirements:* For master's, GRE General Test. Additional exam requirements/recommendations for international students: Required—TOEFL (minimum score 500 paper-based). Electronic applications accepted. *Faculty research:* Measurement and assessment, metacognition, academic skills, child development, multicultural education and counseling.

The University of North Carolina at Chapel Hill, Graduate School, School of Education, Program in Education, Chapel Hill, NC 27599. Offers culture, curriculum and change (MA, PhD); early childhood, intervention and literacy (MA, PhD); educational psychology, measurement and evaluation (MA, PhD). *Accreditation:* NCATE. *Degree requirements:* For master's, thesis; for doctorate, comprehensive exam, thesis/dissertation. *Entrance requirements:* For master's, GRE General Test, minimum GPA of 3.0 during last 2 years of undergraduate course work; for doctorate, GRE General Test, minimum GPA of 3.0 during last 2 years of undergraduate course work. Additional exam requirements/recommendations for international students: Required—TOEFL (minimum score 550 paper-based). Electronic applications accepted.

The University of North Carolina at Greensboro, Graduate School, School of Education, Department of Educational Research Methodology, Greensboro, NC 27412-5001. Offers educational research, measurement and evaluation (PhD); MS/PhD. *Accreditation:* NCATE. *Degree requirements:* For doctorate, thesis/dissertation. *Entrance requirements:* For doctorate, GRE General Test. Additional exam requirements/recommendations for international students: Required—TOEFL. Electronic applications accepted.

University of Northern Colorado, Graduate School, College of Education and Behavioral Sciences, Department of Applied Statistics and Research Methods, Greeley, CO 80639. Offers MS, PhD. *Program availability:* Part-time. *Degree requirements:* For master's, comprehensive exam; for doctorate, comprehensive exam, thesis/dissertation. *Entrance requirements:* For master's, 3 letters of reference; for doctorate, GRE General Test, 3 letters of reference. *Application deadline:* Applications are processed on a rolling basis. Application fee: $50 ($60 for international students). Electronic applications accepted. *Financial support:* Fellowships, research assistantships, and teaching assistantships available. Financial award application deadline: 3/1. *Unit head:* Dr. Susan Hutchinson, Program Coordinator, 970-351-2807, Fax: 970-351-1669. *Application contact:* Linda Sisson, Graduate Student Admission Coordinator, 970-351-1807, Fax: 970-351-2371, E-mail: linda.sisson@unco.edu.
Website: http://www.unco.edu/cebs/asrm

University of Northern Iowa, Graduate College, College of Education, Department of Educational Psychology and Foundations, MAE Program in Educational Psychology: Context and Techniques of Assessment, Cedar Falls, IA 50614. Offers MAE. *Entrance requirements:* For master's, GRE, official transcripts, statement of purpose, three reference letters, writing sample.

University of North Texas, Robert B. Toulouse School of Graduate Studies, Denton, TX 76203-5459. Offers accounting (MS); applied anthropology (MA, MS); applied behavior analysis (Certificate); applied geography (MA); applied technology and performance improvement (M Ed, MS); art education (MA); art history (MA); art museum education (Certificate); arts leadership (Certificate); audiology (Au D); behavior analysis (MS); behavioral science (PhD); biochemistry and molecular biology (MS); biology (MA, MS); biomedical engineering (MS); business analysis (MS); chemistry (MS); clinical health psychology (PhD); communication studies (MA, MS); computer engineering (MS); computer science (MS); counseling (M Ed, MS), including clinical mental health counseling (MS), college and university counseling, elementary school counseling, secondary school counseling; creative writing (MA); criminal justice (MS); curriculum and instruction (M Ed); decision sciences (MBA); design (MA, MFA), including fashion design (MFA), innovation studies, interior design (MFA); early childhood studies (MS); economics (MS); educational leadership (M Ed, Ed D); educational psychology (MS, PhD), including family studies (MS), gifted and talented (MS), human development (MS), learning and cognition (MS), research, measurement and evaluation (MS); electrical engineering (MS); emergency management (MPA); engineering technology (MS); English (MA); English as a second language (MA); environmental science (MS); finance (MBA, MS); financial management (MPA); French (MA); health services management (MBA); higher education (M Ed, Ed D); history (MA, MS); hospitality management (MS); human resources management (MPA); information science (MS); information systems (PhD); information technologies (MBA); interdisciplinary studies (MA, MS); international studies (MA); international sustainable tourism (MS); jazz studies (MM); journalism (MA, MJ, Graduate Certificate), including interactive and virtual digital communication (Graduate Certificate), narrative journalism (Graduate Certificate), public relations (Graduate Certificate); kinesiology (MS); linguistics (MA); local government management (MPA); logistics (PhD); logistics and supply chain management (MBA); long-term care, senior housing, and aging services (MA); management (PhD); marketing (MBA); mathematics (MA, MS); mechanical and energy engineering (MS, PhD); music (MA), including ethnomusicology, music theory, musicology, performance; music composition (PhD); music education (MM Ed, PhD); nonprofit management (MPA); operations and supply chain management (MBA); performance (MM, DMA); philosophy (MA); political science (MA); professional and technical communication (MA); radio, television and film (MA, MFA); rehabilitation counseling (Certificate); sociology (MA); Spanish (MA); special education (M Ed); speech-language pathology (MA); strategic management (MBA); studio art (MFA); teaching (M Ed); MBA/MS. *Program availability:* Part-time, evening/weekend, online learning. Terminal master's awarded for partial completion of doctoral program. *Degree requirements:* For master's, variable foreign language requirement, comprehensive exam (for some programs), thesis (for some programs); for doctorate, variable foreign language requirement, comprehensive exam (for some programs), thesis/dissertation; for other advanced degree, variable foreign language requirement, comprehensive exam (for some programs). *Entrance requirements:* For master's and doctorate, GRE, GMAT. Additional exam requirements/recommendations for international students: Required—TOEFL (minimum score 550 paper-based; 79 iBT). Electronic applications accepted.

University of Pennsylvania, Graduate School of Education, Division of Human Development and Quantitative Methods, Program in Quantitative Methods, Philadelphia, PA 19104. Offers M Phil, MS, PhD. *Program availability:* Part-time. *Students:* 9 full-time (6 women), 1 (woman) part-time; includes 5 minority (2 Asian, non-Hispanic/Latino; 3 Two or more races, non-Hispanic/Latino), 3 international. Average age 30. 6 applicants, 33% accepted, 2 enrolled. In 2016, 1 doctorate awarded. *Entrance requirements:* For master's, bachelor's degree. *Expenses: Tuition:* Full-time $31,068; part-time $5762 per course. *Required fees:* $3200; $336 per course. Full-time tuition and fees vary according to degree level, program and student level. Part-time tuition and fees vary according to course load, degree level and program. *Financial support:* In 2016–17, 20 students received support. Applicants required to submit FAFSA.

University of Pennsylvania, Graduate School of Education, Division of Human Development and Quantitative Methods, Program in Statistics, Measurement, Assessment, and Research Technology (SMART), Philadelphia, PA 19104. Offers MS. *Students:* 38 full-time (25 women), 9 part-time (8 women); includes 2 minority (1 Black or African American, non-Hispanic/Latino; 1 Asian, non-Hispanic/Latino), 40 international. Average age 25. 220 applicants, 34% accepted, 31 enrolled. In 2016, 21 master's awarded. *Expenses: Tuition:* Full-time $31,068; part-time $5762 per course. *Required fees:* $3200; $336 per course. Full-time tuition and fees vary according to degree level, program and student level. Part-time tuition and fees vary according to course load, degree level and program.

University of Pittsburgh, School of Education, Department of Psychology in Education, Program in Research Methodology, Pittsburgh, PA 15260. Offers M Ed, MA, PhD. *Program availability:* Part-time, evening/weekend. Terminal master's awarded for partial completion of doctoral program. *Degree requirements:* For master's, thesis; for doctorate, thesis/dissertation. *Entrance requirements:* For doctorate, GRE General Test. Additional exam requirements/recommendations for international students: Required—TOEFL. Electronic applications accepted. Tuition and fees vary according to program.

University of Puerto Rico, Río Piedras Campus, College of Education, Program in Educational Research and Evaluation, San Juan, PR 00931-3300. Offers M Ed. *Program availability:* Part-time. *Degree requirements:* For master's, thesis. *Entrance requirements:* For master's, PAEG or GRE, interview, minimum GPA of 3.0, letter of recommendation.

University of St. Thomas, School of Education and Human Services, Houston, TX 77006-4696. Offers all level education (M Ed); bilingual/dual language (M Ed); Catholic school teaching (M Ed); Catholic/private school leadership (M Ed); counselor education (M Ed); curriculum and instruction (M Ed); education (Ed D); educational leadership (M Ed); elementary teaching (M Ed); English as a second language (M Ed); exceptionality/educational diagnostician (M Ed); exceptionality/special education (M Ed); generalist (M Ed); reading (M Ed); secondary teaching (M Ed); teaching (MAT). *Accreditation:* TEAC. *Program availability:* Part-time, evening/weekend, online learning. *Faculty:* 44 full-time (29 women), 31 part-time/adjunct (17 women). *Students:* 65 full-time (61 women), 719 part-time (645 women); includes 515 minority (169 Black or African American, non-Hispanic/Latino; 25 Asian, non-Hispanic/Latino; 315 Hispanic/Latino; 2 Native Hawaiian or other Pacific Islander, non-Hispanic/Latino; 4 Two or more races, non-Hispanic/Latino), 24 international. Average age 36. 297 applicants, 92% accepted, 211 enrolled. In 2016, 403 master's awarded. *Degree requirements:* For master's, thesis, field experience. *Entrance requirements:* For master's, GRE or MAT if GPA is below 3.0, bachelor's degree; minimum GPA of 2.75 in bachelor's degree or last 60 credit hours; official transcripts from all institutions; goal statement of 250-300 words; 1 reference. Additional exam requirements/recommendations for international students: Required—TOEFL (minimum score 94 iBT), IELTS (minimum score 7), PTE (minimum score 53). *Application deadline:* Applications are processed on a rolling basis. Application fee: $35. Electronic applications accepted. *Expenses:* Contact institution. *Financial support:* In 2016–17, 52 students received support. Federal Work-Study, scholarships/grants, and state work-study, institutional employment available. Support available to part-time students. Financial award application deadline: 4/15; financial award applicants required to submit FAFSA. *Faculty research:* Leadership, diversity, personality traits, second language acquisition. *Unit head:* Dr. Robert LeBlanc, Dean, 713-525-3540, Fax: 713-525-3871, E-mail: education@stthom.edu. *Application contact:* Rita Paredes, Administrative Assistant, 713-525-3442, Fax: 713-525-3871, E-mail: rparede@stthom.edu.
Website: http://www.stthom.edu/Academics/School_of_Education_and_Human_Services/Index.aqf

University of South Carolina, The Graduate School, College of Education, Department of Educational Studies, Program in Educational Psychology, Research, Columbia, SC 29208. Offers M Ed, PhD. *Accreditation:* NCATE. *Program availability:* Part-time. *Degree requirements:* For master's, comprehensive exam, thesis (for some programs); for doctorate, comprehensive exam, thesis/dissertation. *Entrance requirements:* For master's, GRE General Test; for doctorate, GRE General Test, interview. Electronic applications accepted. *Faculty research:* Problem solving, higher order thinking skills, psychometric research, methodology.

University of Southern Mississippi, Graduate School, College of Education and Psychology, Department of Educational Research and Administration, Hattiesburg, MS 39406. Offers educational administration (M Ed, Ed D, PhD, Ed S); educational administration and supervision (M Ed); educational studies and research (MS); higher education (Ed D); higher education administration (PhD); higher education: student affairs (M Ed); research, evaluation, statistics, assessment (PhD). *Degree requirements:* For master's and Ed S, comprehensive exam, thesis (for some programs); for doctorate, comprehensive exam, thesis/dissertation. *Entrance requirements:* For master's and doctorate, GRE General Test, minimum GPA of 2.75. Additional exam requirements/recommendations for international students: Required—TOEFL. *Application deadline:* For fall admission, 2/1 for domestic students, 3/1 for international students. Applications are processed on a rolling basis. Application fee: $60. *Expenses: Tuition, area resident:* Full-time $15,708; part-time $437 per credit hour. *Financial support:* Career-related internships or fieldwork, Federal Work-Study, and institutionally sponsored loans available. Financial award application deadline: 3/15; financial award applicants required to submit FAFSA. *Unit head:* Dr. Lilian Hill, Co-Chair, 601-266-4622. *Application contact:* Shonna Breland, Manager of Graduate Admissions, 601-266-6563, Fax: 601-266-5138.
Website: https://www.usm.edu/educational-research-administration

University of South Florida, Innovative Education, Tampa, FL 33020-9951. Offers adult, career and higher education (Graduate Certificate), including college teaching, leadership in developing human resources, leadership in higher education; Africana studies (Graduate Certificate), including diasporas and health disparities, genocide and human rights; aging studies (Graduate Certificate), including gerontology; art research (Graduate Certificate), including museum studies; business foundations (Graduate Certificate); chemical and biomedical engineering (Graduate Certificate), including materials science and engineering, water, health and sustainability; child and family studies (Graduate Certificate), including positive behavior support; civil and industrial engineering (Graduate Certificate), including transportation systems analysis; community and family health (Graduate Certificate), including maternal and child health, social marketing and public health, violence and injury: prevention and intervention, women's health; criminology (Graduate Certificate), including criminal justice administration; educational measurement and research (Graduate Certificate), including evaluation; English (Graduate Certificate), including comparative literary studies, creative writing, professional and technical communication; entrepreneurship (Graduate Certificate); environmental health (Graduate Certificate), including safety management; epidemiology and biostatistics (Graduate Certificate), including applied biostatistics, biostatistics, concepts and tools of epidemiology, epidemiology, epidemiology of infectious diseases; geography, environment and planning (Graduate Certificate),

including community development, environmental policy and management, geographical information systems; geology (Graduate Certificate), including hydrogeology; global health (Graduate Certificate), including disaster management, global health and Latin American and Caribbean studies, global health practice, humanitarian assistance, infection control; government and international affairs (Graduate Certificate), including Cuban studies, globalization studies; health policy and management (Graduate Certificate), including health management and leadership, public health policy and programs; hearing specialist: early intervention (Graduate Certificate); industrial and management systems engineering (Graduate Certificate), including systems engineering, technology management; information studies (Graduate Certificate), including school library media specialist; information systems/decision sciences (Graduate Certificate), including analytics and business intelligence; instructional technology (Graduate Certificate), including distance education, Florida digital/virtual educator, instructional design, multimedia design, Web design; internal medicine, bioethics and medical humanities (Graduate Certificate), including biomedical ethics; Latin American and Caribbean studies (Graduate Certificate); mass communications (Graduate Certificate), including multimedia journalism; mathematics and statistics (Graduate Certificate), including mathematics; medicine (Graduate Certificate), including aging and neuroscience, bioinformatics, biotechnology, brain fitness and memory management, clinical investigation, health informatics, health sciences, integrative weight management, intellectual property, medicine and gender, metabolic and nutritional medicine, metabolic cardiology, pharmacy sciences; national and competitive intelligence (Graduate Certificate); psychological and social foundations (Graduate Certificate), including career counseling, college teaching, diversity in education, mental health counseling, school counseling; public affairs (Graduate Certificate), including nonprofit management, public management, research administration; public health (Graduate Certificate), including environmental health, health equity, public health generalist, translational research in adolescent behavioral health; public health practices (Graduate Certificate), including planning for healthy communities; rehabilitation and mental health counseling (Graduate Certificate), including integrative mental health care, marriage and family therapy, rehabilitation technology; secondary education (Graduate Certificate), including ESOL, foreign language education: culture and content, foreign language education: professional; social work (Graduate Certificate), including geriatric social work/clinical gerontology; special education (Graduate Certificate), including autism spectrum disorder, disabilities education: severe/profound; world languages (Graduate Certificate), including teaching English as a second language (TESL) or foreign language. *Expenses:* Tuition, state resident: full-time $7766; part-time $431.43 per credit hour. Tuition, nonresident: full-time $15,789; part-time $877.17 per credit hour. *Required fees:* $37 per term. *Unit head:* Kathy Barnes, Interdisciplinary Programs Coordinator, 813-974-8031, Fax: 813-974-7061, E-mail: barnesk@usf.edu. *Application contact:* Karen Tylinski, Metro Initiatives, 813-974-9943, Fax: 813-974-7061, E-mail: ktylinsk@usf.edu.
Website: http://www.usf.edu/innovative-education/

The University of Tennessee, Graduate School, College of Education, Health and Human Sciences, Program in Education, Knoxville, TN 37996. Offers art education (MS); counseling education (PhD); cultural studies in education (PhD); curriculum (MS, Ed S); curriculum, educational research and evaluation (Ed D, PhD); early childhood education (PhD); early childhood special education (MS); education of deaf and hard of hearing (MS); educational administration and policy studies (Ed D, PhD); educational administration and supervision (Ed S); educational psychology (Ed D, PhD); elementary education (MS, Ed S); elementary teaching (MS); English education (MS, Ed S); exercise science (PhD); foreign language/ESL education (MS, Ed S); instructional technology (MS, Ed D, PhD, Ed S); literacy, language and ESL education (PhD); literacy, language education, and ESL education (Ed D); mathematics education (MS, Ed S); modified and comprehensive special education (MS); reading education (MS, Ed S); school counseling (Ed S); school psychology (PhD, Ed S); science education (MS, Ed S); secondary teaching (MS); social foundations (MS); social science education (MS, Ed S); socio-cultural foundations of sports and education (PhD); special education (Ed S); teacher education (Ed D, PhD). *Accreditation:* NCATE. *Program availability:* Part-time, evening/weekend. *Degree requirements:* For master's and Ed S, thesis optional; for doctorate, variable foreign language requirement, thesis/dissertation. *Entrance requirements:* For master's, minimum GPA of 2.7; for doctorate and Ed S, GRE General Test, minimum GPA of 2.7. Additional exam requirements/recommendations for international students: Required—TOEFL. Electronic applications accepted.

The University of Texas at El Paso, Graduate School, College of Education, Department of Educational Psychology and Special Services, El Paso, TX 79968-0001. Offers educational diagnostics (M Ed); guidance and counseling (M Ed); special education (M Ed). *Program availability:* Part-time, evening/weekend. *Degree requirements:* For master's, thesis optional. *Entrance requirements:* For master's, minimum GPA of 3.0. Additional exam requirements/recommendations for international students: Required—TOEFL. Electronic applications accepted.

The University of Texas Rio Grande Valley, College of Education and P-16 Integration, Department of Human Development and School Services, Edinburg, TX 78539. Offers early childhood education (M Ed); early childhood special education (M Ed); educational diagnostician (M Ed); school psychology (MA). *Program availability:* Part-time, evening/weekend. *Degree requirements:* For master's, comprehensive exam (for some programs), thesis (for some programs). *Entrance requirements:* For master's, GRE General Test, interview. Tuition and fees vary according to course load and program. *Faculty research:* Reading instruction, assessment practice, behavior interventions consultation, mental retardation.

The University of Toledo, College of Graduate Studies, Judith Herb College of Education, Department of Educational Foundations and Leadership, Toledo, OH 43606-3390. Offers educational administration and supervision (ME, DE, Ed S); educational psychology (ME, PhD); educational research and measurement (ME, PhD); educational sociology (PhD); educational theory and social foundations (ME); foundations of education (DE, PhD); history of education (PhD); philosophy of education (PhD). *Accreditation:* NCATE. *Program availability:* Part-time, evening/weekend. *Degree requirements:* For master's, comprehensive exam, thesis or alternative; for doctorate, comprehensive exam, thesis/dissertation; for Ed S, thesis optional. *Entrance requirements:* For master's, doctorate, and Ed S, minimum cumulative GPA of 2.7 for all previous academic work, letters of recommendation. Additional exam requirements/recommendations for international students: Required—TOEFL (minimum score 550 paper-based; 80 iBT). Electronic applications accepted.

University of Victoria, Faculty of Graduate Studies, Faculty of Education, Department of Educational Psychology and Leadership Studies, Victoria, BC V8W 2Y2, Canada. Offers aboriginal communities counseling (M Ed); counseling (M Ed, MA); educational psychology (M Ed, MA, PhD), including counseling psychology (M Ed, MA), leadership studies (PhD), learning and development (MA, PhD), measurement and evaluation, special education (M Ed, MA); leadership studies (M Ed, MA). *Program availability:* Part-time. *Degree requirements:* For master's, thesis (for some programs), comprehensive exam (M Ed); for doctorate, comprehensive exam, thesis/dissertation, candidacy exam. *Entrance requirements:* For master's, 2 years of work experience in a relevant field; for doctorate, GRE, 2 years of work experience in a relevant field, minimum B average. Additional exam requirements/recommendations for international students: Required—TOEFL (minimum score 575 paper-based), IELTS (minimum score 7). *Faculty research:* Learning and development (child, adolescent and adult), special education and exceptional children.

University of Virginia, Curry School of Education, Department of Leadership, Foundations and Policy, Program in Educational Psychology, Charlottesville, VA 22903. Offers applied developmental science (M Ed); educational evaluation (M Ed); educational psychology (M Ed, Ed D, Ed S); educational research (Ed D); gifted education (M Ed); instructional technology (M Ed, Ed S); research statistics and evaluation (Ed D); school psychology (Ed D). *Students:* 28 full-time (15 women), 10 part-time (7 women); includes 8 minority (2 Black or African American, non-Hispanic/Latino; 2 Asian, non-Hispanic/Latino; 3 Hispanic/Latino; 1 Two or more races, non-Hispanic/Latino), 7 international. Average age 26. 85 applicants, 80% accepted, 33 enrolled. In 2016, 35 master's, 1 other advanced degree awarded. *Degree requirements:* For master's, comprehensive exam. *Entrance requirements:* For master's and doctorate, GRE General Test, 2 letters of recommendation. Additional exam requirements/recommendations for international students: Required—TOEFL (minimum score 600 paper-based; 90 iBT), IELTS (minimum score 7). *Application deadline:* Applications are processed on a rolling basis. Application fee: $60. Electronic applications accepted. *Expenses:* Tuition, state resident: full-time $15,026; part-time $834 per credit hour. Tuition, nonresident: full-time $25,168; part-time $1378 per credit hour. *Required fees:* $2654. *Financial support:* Fellowships, research assistantships, and teaching assistantships available. Financial award application deadline: 1/5; financial award applicants required to submit FAFSA. *Unit head:* Sara Rimm-Kaufman, Program Director, 434-982-2863, E-mail: serk@virginia.edu. *Application contact:* Eric Molnar, Assistant Director, Admissions and Enrollment Reporting, 434-243-2085, E-mail: eric.molnar@virginia.edu.
Website: http://curry.virginia.edu/academics/areas-of-study/educational-psychology

University of Virginia, Curry School of Education, Program in Education, Charlottesville, VA 22903. Offers administration and supervision (PhD); applied developmental science (PhD); counselor education (PhD); curriculum and instruction (PhD); early childhood special education (MT); education evaluation (PhD); educational psychology (PhD); educational research (PhD); elementary education (MT); English education (MT, PhD); foreign language education (MT); higher education (PhD); instructional technology (PhD); kinesiology (MT, PhD); math education (PhD); reading education (PhD); research, statistics and evaluation (PhD); school psychology (PhD); science education (PhD); social studies education (MT, PhD); special education (PhD); world languages education (MT). *Students:* 452 full-time (357 women), 18 part-time (13 women); includes 100 minority (28 Black or African American, non-Hispanic/Latino; 39 Asian, non-Hispanic/Latino; 18 Hispanic/Latino; 15 Two or more races, non-Hispanic/Latino), 14 international. Average age 25. 309 applicants, 51% accepted, 87 enrolled. In 2016, 144 master's, 31 doctorates awarded. *Degree requirements:* For master's, comprehensive exam (for some programs), field project; for doctorate, comprehensive exam, thesis/dissertation. *Entrance requirements:* For doctorate, GRE General Test. Additional exam requirements/recommendations for international students: Required—TOEFL (minimum score 600 paper-based; 90 iBT), IELTS (minimum score 7). *Application deadline:* Applications are processed on a rolling basis. Application fee: $60. Electronic applications accepted. *Expenses:* Tuition, state resident: full-time $15,026; part-time $834 per credit hour. Tuition, nonresident: full-time $25,168; part-time $1378 per credit hour. *Required fees:* $2654. *Financial support:* Fellowships, research assistantships, and teaching assistantships available. Financial award application deadline: 1/5; financial award applicants required to submit FAFSA. *Unit head:* Robert C. Pianta, Dean, 434-924-3334, E-mail: pianta@virginia.edu. *Application contact:* Eric Molnar, Assistant Director, Admissions and Enrollment Reporting, 434-243-2085, E-mail: eric.molnar@virginia.edu.
Website: http://curry.virginia.edu/teacher-education

University of Washington, Graduate School, College of Education, Program in Educational Psychology, Seattle, WA 98195. Offers educational psychology (PhD); human development and cognition (M Ed); learning sciences (M Ed, PhD); measurement, statistics and research design (M Ed); school psychology (M Ed). *Accreditation:* APA. *Degree requirements:* For master's, thesis optional; for doctorate, thesis/dissertation. *Entrance requirements:* For master's and doctorate, GRE General Test, minimum GPA of 3.0. Additional exam requirements/recommendations for international students: Required—TOEFL.

University of Wisconsin–Milwaukee, Graduate School, School of Education, Department of Educational Psychology, Milwaukee, WI 53201-0413. Offers children's mental health for school professionals (Graduate Certificate); community counseling (MS); counseling psychology (PhD); educational statistics and measurement (MS, PhD); learning and development (MS, PhD); multicultural knowledge of mental health practices (Graduate Certificate); school counseling (MS); school counseling (Graduate Certificate); school psychology (MS, PhD, Ed S). *Accreditation:* APA. *Program availability:* Part-time. *Students:* 161 full-time (121 women), 53 part-time (39 women); includes 47 minority (12 Black or African American, non-Hispanic/Latino; 1 American Indian or Alaska Native, non-Hispanic/Latino; 5 Asian, non-Hispanic/Latino; 8 Hispanic/Latino; 1 Native Hawaiian or other Pacific Islander, non-Hispanic/Latino; 20 Two or more races, non-Hispanic/Latino), 6 international. Average age 30. 266 applicants, 45% accepted, 71 enrolled. In 2016, 73 master's, 9 doctorates, 18 other advanced degrees awarded. *Degree requirements:* For master's, comprehensive exam, thesis; for doctorate, thesis/dissertation. *Entrance requirements:* For master's, minimum GPA of 3.0; for doctorate, GRE General Test, minimum GPA of 3.0. Additional exam requirements/recommendations for international students: Required—TOEFL (minimum score 550 paper-based; 79 iBT), IELTS (minimum score 6.5). *Application deadline:* For fall admission, 1/1 priority date for domestic students; for spring admission, 9/1 for domestic students. Applications are processed on a rolling basis. Application fee: $56 ($96 for international students). Electronic applications accepted. *Financial support:* In 2016–17, 14 fellowships, 1 research assistantship, 8 teaching assistantships were awarded; career-related internships or fieldwork, health care benefits, unspecified assistantships, and project assistantships also available. Support available to part-time students. Financial award application deadline: 4/15; financial award applicants required to submit FAFSA. *Application contact:* General Information Contact, 414-229-4721, E-mail: soeinfo@uwm.edu.
Website: http://uwm.edu/education/academics/educational-psychology-department/

Utah State University, School of Graduate Studies, Emma Eccles Jones College of Education and Human Services, Department of Psychology, Logan, UT 84322. Offers clinical/counseling/school psychology (PhD); research and evaluation methodology (PhD); school counseling (MS); school psychology (MS). *Accreditation:* APA (one or more programs are accredited). *Program availability:* Part-time, evening/weekend, online learning. Terminal master's awarded for partial completion of doctoral program. *Degree requirements:* For master's, thesis (for some programs); for doctorate, thesis/dissertation. *Entrance requirements:* For master's, GRE General Test (school psychology), MAT (school counseling), minimum GPA of 3.5; for doctorate, GRE General Test, minimum GPA of 3.5. Additional exam requirements/recommendations for international students: Required—TOEFL. *Faculty research:* Hearing loss detection in infancy, ADHD, eating disorders, domestic violence, neuropsychology, bilingual/Spanish speaking students/parents.

Utah State University, School of Graduate Studies, Emma Eccles Jones College of Education and Human Services, Doctoral Program in Education, Logan, UT 84322. Offers business information systems (Ed D, PhD); curriculum and instruction (Ed D, PhD); research and evaluation (PhD). *Degree requirements:* For doctorate, comprehensive exam, thesis/dissertation. *Entrance requirements:* For doctorate, GRE General Test, minimum GPA of 3.0, master's degree. Additional exam requirements/recommendations for international students: Required—TOEFL. Electronic applications accepted. *Faculty research:* Language and literacy development, math and science education, instructional technology, hearing problems/deafness, domestic violence and animal abuse.

Virginia Commonwealth University, Graduate School, School of Education, Doctoral Program in Education, Richmond, VA 23284-9005. Offers art education (PhD); counselor education and supervision (PhD); curriculum, culture and change (PhD); educational leadership (PhD); educational psychology (PhD); leadership (Ed D); research and evaluation (PhD); special education and disability leadership (PhD); sport leadership (PhD); urban services leadership (PhD). *Accreditation:* NCATE. *Program availability:* Part-time. *Degree requirements:* For doctorate, thesis/dissertation. *Entrance requirements:* For doctorate, GRE (for PhD), MAT (for Ed D), interview, master's degree, writing sample. Additional exam requirements/recommendations for international students: Required—TOEFL (minimum score 600 paper-based; 100 iBT). *Application deadline:* For fall admission, 2/15 for domestic students. Application fee: $50. Electronic applications accepted. *Financial support:* Fellowships, research assistantships, career-related internships or fieldwork, Federal Work-Study, and institutionally sponsored loans available. Financial award application deadline: 3/1; financial award applicants required to submit FAFSA. *Unit head:* Dr. Kathleen Cauley, Interim Director, 804-827-2657, E-mail: kmcauley@vcu.edu. *Application contact:* Dr. Colleen A. Thoma, Administrative Assistant, 804-827-2651, E-mail: cathoma@vcu.edu.
Website: http://www.soe.vcu.edu/programs/doctoral-programs/

Virginia Polytechnic Institute and State University, Graduate School, College of Liberal Arts and Human Sciences, Blacksburg, VA 24061. Offers career and technical education (MS Ed, Ed D, PhD, Ed S); communication (MA); counselor education (MA Ed, Ed D, PhD, Ed S); creative writing (MFA); curriculum and instruction (MA Ed, Ed D, PhD, Ed S); educational leadership and policy studies (MA Ed, Ed D, PhD, Ed S); educational research and evaluation (PhD); English (MA); foreign languages, cultures, and literatures (MA); higher education (PhD); higher education and student affairs (MA Ed); history (MA); human development (MS, PhD); material culture and public humanities (MA); philosophy (MA); political science (MA); rhetoric and writing (PhD); science and technology studies (MS, PhD); social, political, ethical, and cultural thought (PhD); sociology (MS, PhD); theater arts (MFA). *Faculty:* 408 full-time (204 women), 3 part-time/adjunct (2 women). *Students:* 657 full-time (446 women), 457 part-time (292 women); includes 213 minority (114 Black or African American, non-Hispanic/Latino; 3 American Indian or Alaska Native, non-Hispanic/Latino; 29 Asian, non-Hispanic/Latino; 44 Hispanic/Latino; 23 Two or more races, non-Hispanic/Latino), 93 international. Average age 33. 805 applicants, 55% accepted, 328 enrolled. In 2016, 270 master's, 91 doctorates awarded. *Degree requirements:* For master's, comprehensive exam (for some programs), thesis (for some programs); for doctorate, comprehensive exam (for some programs), thesis/dissertation (for some programs). *Entrance requirements:* For master's and doctorate, GRE/GMAT. Additional exam requirements/recommendations for international students: Required—TOEFL (minimum score 80 iBT). *Application deadline:* For fall admission, 8/1 for domestic students, 4/1 for international students; for spring admission, 1/1 for domestic students, 9/1 for international students. Applications are processed on a rolling basis. Application fee: $75. Electronic applications accepted. *Expenses:* Tuition, state resident: full-time $12,467; part-time $692.50 per credit hour. Tuition, nonresident: full-time $25,095; part-time $1394.25 per credit hour. *Required fees:* $2669; $491.50 per semester. Tuition and fees vary according to course load, campus/location and program. *Financial support:* In 2016–17, 21 research assistantships with full tuition reimbursements (averaging $19,817 per year), 237 teaching assistantships with full tuition reimbursements (averaging $15,497 per year) were awarded. Financial award application deadline: 3/1; financial award applicants required to submit FAFSA. *Total annual research expenditures:* $6.6 million. *Unit head:* Rosemary Blieszner, Interim Dean, 540-231-6779, Fax: 540-231-7157, E-mail: liberalartsdean@vt.edu. *Application contact:* Chelsea Blanchet, Executive Assistant, 540-231-6779, Fax: 540-231-7157, E-mail: bchels1@vt.edu.
Website: http://www.liberalarts.vt.edu/

Walden University, Graduate Programs, Richard W. Riley College of Education and Leadership, Minneapolis, MN 55401. Offers adult education (Post-Master's Certificate); adult learning (Graduate Certificate); college teaching and learning (Graduate Certificate); community college leadership (Ed D); curriculum, instruction and assessment (Ed D, Ed S, Graduate Certificate); developmental education (Graduate Certificate); early childhood administration, management, and leadership (Graduate Certificate); early childhood education (Ed D, Ed S); early childhood public policy and advocacy (Graduate Certificate); early childhood studies (MS), including administration, management and leadership, early childhood public policy and advocacy, teaching adults in the early childhood field, teaching and diversity in early childhood education; education (MS, PhD), including adolescent literacy and learning (MS), curriculum, instruction, and assessment (grades K-12) (MS), curriculum, instruction, assessment, and evaluation (PhD), early childhood leadership and advocacy (PhD), early childhood special education (PhD), educational leadership (MS), educational leadership and administration (principal preparation) (MS), educational technology and design (PhD), elementary reading and literacy (PreK-6) (MS), elementary reading and mathematics (grades K-6) (MS), global and comparative education (PhD), higher education leadership management and policy (PhD), integrating technology in the classroom (grades K-12) (MS), learning, instruction and innovation (PhD), mathematics (grades 5-8) (MS), mathematics (grades K-6) (MS), mathematics and science (grades K-8) (MS), organizational research, assessment, and evaluation (PhD), reading and literacy with a reading K-12 endorsement (MS), reading literacy assessment and evaluation (PhD), science (grades K-8) (MS), special education (non-licensure) (grades K-12) (MS), teacher leadership (grades K-12) (MS), teaching English language learners (grades K-12) (MS); educational administration and leadership (Ed D); educational leadership and administration (principal preparation) (Ed S); educational technology (Ed D, Ed S, Post Master's Certificate); elementary reading and literacy (Graduate Certificate); engaging culturally diverse learners (Graduate Certificate); enrollment management and institutional marketing (Graduate Certificate); higher education (MS), including adult learning, college teaching and learning, enrollment management and institutional marketing, global higher education, leadership for student success, online and distance learning; higher education and adult learning (Ed D); higher education leadership and management (Ed D); higher education leadership for student success (Graduate Certificate); instructional design and technology (MS, Postbaccalaureate Certificate), including general program (MS), online learning (MS), training and performance improvement (MS); integrating technology in the classroom (Graduate Certificate); mathematics 5-8 (Graduate Certificate); mathematics K-6 (Graduate Certificate); online teaching for adult educators (Graduate Certificate); reading, literacy, and assessment (Ed D, Ed S); science K-8 (Graduate Certificate); special education (Ed D, Ed S, Graduate Certificate); special education (K-age 21) (MAT); teacher leadership (Graduate Certificate); teaching adults English as a second language (Graduate Certificate); teaching adults in the early childhood field (Graduate Certificate); teaching and diversity in early childhood education (Graduate Certificate); teaching English language learners (grades K-12) (Graduate Certificate); teaching K-12 students online (Graduate Certificate). *Accreditation:* NCATE. *Program availability:* Part-time, evening/weekend, online only, 100% online. *Degree requirements:* For doctorate, thesis/dissertation (for some programs), residency; for other advanced degree, residency (for some programs). *Entrance requirements:* For master's, bachelor's degree or higher; minimum GPA of 2.5; official transcripts; goal statement (for some programs); access to computer and Internet; for doctorate, master's degree or higher; three years of related professional or academic experience (preferred); minimum GPA of 3.0; goal statement and current resume (for select programs); official transcripts; access to computer and Internet; for other advanced degree, relevant work experience; access to computer and Internet. Additional exam requirements/recommendations for international students: Required—TOEFL (minimum score 550 paper-based, 79 iBT), IELTS (minimum score 6.5), Michigan English Language Assessment Battery (minimum score 82), or PTE (minimum score 53). Electronic applications accepted.

Washington University in St. Louis, The Graduate School, Department of Education, Program in Educational Research, St. Louis, MO 63130-4899. Offers PhD. *Entrance requirements:* For doctorate, GRE General Test. Additional exam requirements/recommendations for international students: Required—TOEFL. Electronic applications accepted.

Wayland Baptist University, Graduate Programs, Program in Education, Plainview, TX 79072-6998. Offers education administration (M Ed); education diagnostics (M Ed); education literacy (M Ed); elementary certification (M Ed); English (M Ed); English as a second language (M Ed); higher education administration (M Ed); human resources (M Ed); instructional leadership (M Ed); instructional technology (M Ed); leadership training and development (M Ed); science education (M Ed); secondary certification (M Ed); social studies (M Ed); special education (M Ed); sports administration and management (M Ed). *Program availability:* Part-time, evening/weekend, online learning. *Degree requirements:* For master's, comprehensive exam, capstone course. *Entrance requirements:* For master's, GRE, GMAT or MAT. Additional exam requirements/recommendations for international students: Required—TOEFL (minimum score 500 paper-based; 61 iBT). Electronic applications accepted.

Wayne State University, College of Education, Division of Theoretical and Behavioral Foundations, Detroit, MI 48202. Offers applied behavior analysis (Certificate); counseling (M Ed, MA, Ed D, PhD, Ed S); counseling psychology (MA); education evaluation and research (M Ed, Ed D, PhD); educational psychology (M Ed, PhD), including learning and instruction sciences (PhD); rehabilitation counseling and community inclusion (MA); school and community psychology (MA); school psychology (Certificate). *Accreditation:* ACA (one or more programs are accredited); CORE (one or more programs are accredited). *Program availability:* Evening/weekend. *Faculty:* 12. *Students:* 211 full-time (179 women), 237 part-time (196 women); includes 167 minority (119 Black or African American, non-Hispanic/Latino; 1 American Indian or Alaska Native, non-Hispanic/Latino; 10 Asian, non-Hispanic/Latino; 17 Hispanic/Latino; 20 Two or more races, non-Hispanic/Latino), 24 international. Average age 32. 294 applicants, 34% accepted, 72 enrolled. In 2016, 87 master's, 12 doctorates, 14 other advanced degrees awarded. *Degree requirements:* For master's, thesis (for some programs); for doctorate, thesis/dissertation. *Entrance requirements:* For master's, GRE, interview, personal statement, portfolio (art therapy); for doctorate, GRE, department-written exam, interview, curriculum vitae, references, master's degree in closely-related field with minimum GPA of 3.5, demonstration of counseling skills (counseling); for other advanced degree, master's degree in counseling and counseling license (for Ed S); good standing in school and community psychology MA program (for Certificate). Additional exam requirements/recommendations for international students: Required—TOEFL (minimum score 550 paper-based; 79 iBT), Michigan English Language Assessment Battery (minimum score 85); Recommended—IELTS (minimum score 6.5), TWE (minimum score 5.5). *Application deadline:* For fall admission, 6/1 priority date for domestic students, 5/1 priority date for international students; for winter admission, 10/1 priority date for domestic students, 9/1 priority date for international students; for spring admission, 2/1 priority date for domestic students, 1/1 priority date for international students. Applications are processed on a rolling basis. Application fee: $50. Electronic applications accepted. *Expenses:* $16,503 per year resident tuition and fees, $33,697 per year non-resident tuition and fees. *Financial support:* In 2016–17, 92 students received support, including 2 research assistantships with tuition reimbursements available (averaging $17,994 per year); fellowships with tuition reimbursements available, teaching assistantships with tuition reimbursements available, Federal Work-Study, scholarships/grants, health care benefits, and unspecified assistantships also available. Support available to part-time students. Financial award applicants required to submit FAFSA. *Faculty research:* Adolescents at risk, supervision of counseling. *Unit head:* Dr. Cheryl Somers, Assistant Dean, 313-577-1670, E-mail: c.somers@wayne.edu. *Application contact:* Janice Green, Assistant Dean, 313-577-1605, E-mail: jwgreen@wayne.edu.
Website: http://coe.wayne.edu/tbf/index.php

Western Governors University, Teachers College, Salt Lake City, UT 84107. Offers curriculum and instruction (MS); educational leadership (MS); educational studies (MA); educational studies (5-12) (MA), including mathematics; elementary education (K-8) (MAT, Postbaccalaureate Certificate); elementary education (PreK-8) (MAT); English language learning (K-12) (MA); instructional design (MAT); learning and technology (M Ed, MA); management and innovation (M Ed); mathematics (5-12) (MAT, Postbaccalaureate Certificate); mathematics (5-9) (MAT, Postbaccalaureate Certificate); mathematics education (5-12) (MA); mathematics education (5-9) (MA); mathematics education (K-6) (MA); measurement and evaluation (M Ed); science (5-12) (Postbaccalaureate Certificate); science (5-9) (MAT, Postbaccalaureate Certificate); science education (5-12) (MA), including biology, chemistry, geology, physics; science education (5-9) (MA); social science (5-12) (MAT, Postbaccalaureate Certificate); special education (MAT, MS). *Accreditation:* NCATE. *Program availability:* Evening/weekend, online learning. *Degree requirements:* For master's, capstone project. *Entrance requirements:* For master's and Postbaccalaureate Certificate, Readiness Assessment, transcripts. Additional exam requirements/recommendations for international students: Required—TOEFL (minimum score 450 paper-based; 80 iBT). Electronic applications accepted. *Expenses:* Contact institution.

Western Michigan University, Graduate College, College of Education and Human Development, Department of Educational Leadership, Research and Technology, Kalamazoo, MI 49008. Offers educational leadership (MA, PhD, Ed S), including educational leadership (MA); educational technology (MA, Graduate Certificate); evaluation, measurement and research (MA, PhD); organizational learning and performance (MA).

Educational Measurement and Evaluation

Western Michigan University, Graduate College, College of Education and Human Development, Department of Interdisciplinary Education, Kalamazoo, MI 49008. Offers PhD.

West Texas A&M University, College of Education and Social Sciences, Department of Education, Program in Educational Diagnostician, Canyon, TX 79016-0001. Offers M Ed. *Program availability:* Part-time, online learning. *Faculty:* 3 full-time (all women). *Students:* 2 full-time (both women), 15 part-time (14 women); includes 1 minority (Hispanic/Latino). Average age 34. 23 applicants, 74% accepted, 17 enrolled. In 2016, 6 degrees awarded. *Degree requirements:* For master's, comprehensive exam, thesis optional. *Entrance requirements:* For master's, GRE General Test, 3 years' teaching experience, competency in diagnosis and prescription. Additional exam requirements/recommendations for international students: Required—TOEFL (minimum score 550 paper-based). *Application deadline:* For fall admission, 8/1 for domestic students, 5/1 for international students; for spring admission, 12/1 for domestic students, 10/30 for international students; for summer admission, 5/1 for domestic students. Applications are processed on a rolling basis. Application fee: $40 ($75 for international students). Electronic applications accepted. *Financial support:* In 2016–17, research assistantships with partial tuition reimbursements (averaging $6,500 per year), teaching assistantships with partial tuition reimbursements (averaging $6,700 per year) were awarded; Federal Work-Study, institutionally sponsored loans, and tuition waivers (partial) also available. Support available to part-time students. Financial award applicants required to submit CSS PROFILE or FAFSA. *Faculty research:* Teacher preparation through web-based instruction, developmental disabilities. *Application contact:* Dr. Frank Goode, Assistant Professor, 806-651-3621.

Wilkes University, College of Graduate and Professional Studies, School of Education, Wilkes-Barre, PA 18766-0002. Offers 21st century teaching and learning (MS Ed); art and science of teaching (MS Ed); classroom technology (MS Ed); early childhood literacy (MS Ed); educational development and strategies (MS Ed); educational leadership (MS Ed, Ed D); effective teaching (MS Ed); instructional media (MS Ed); instructional technology (MS Ed); international school leadership (MS Ed); international teaching and learning (MS Ed); middle level education (MS Ed); online teaching (MS Ed); reading (MS Ed); school business leadership (MS Ed); special education (MS Ed); teaching English to speakers of other languages (MS Ed). *Program availability:* Part-time, evening/weekend, 100% online, blended/hybrid learning. *Students:* 87 full-time (70 women), 1,496 part-time (1,111 women); includes 77 minority (11 Black or African American, non-Hispanic/Latino; 2 American Indian or Alaska Native, non-Hispanic/Latino; 12 Asian, non-Hispanic/Latino; 28 Hispanic/Latino; 3 Native Hawaiian or other Pacific Islander, non-Hispanic/Latino; 21 Two or more races, non-Hispanic/Latino). Average age 33. In 2016, 524 master's, 21 doctorates awarded. *Entrance requirements:* Additional exam requirements/recommendations for international students: Required—TOEFL (minimum score 550 paper-based; 79 iBT). *Application deadline:* Applications are processed on a rolling basis. Application fee: $45. Electronic applications accepted. *Expenses:* Contact institution. *Financial support:* Unspecified assistantships available. Financial award application deadline: 3/1; financial award applicants required to submit FAFSA. *Unit head:* Dr. Rhonda Rabbitt, Dean, 570-408-4680, Fax: 570-408-7872, E-mail: rhonda.rabbitt@wilkes.edu. *Application contact:* Director of Graduate Education, 570-408-4234, Fax: 570-408-7846.
Website: http://www.wilkes.edu/academics/graduate-programs/masters-programs/graduate-education/index.aspx

Educational Media/Instructional Technology

Abilene Christian University, College of Graduate and Professional Studies, Instructional Leadership Program, Abilene, TX 79699. Offers instructional leadership (M Ed), including conflict resolution, learning with emerging technologies, principalship; learning with emerging technologies (Certificate), including leadership of learning. *Program availability:* Part-time, online learning. *Faculty:* 1 (woman) full-time, 1 part-time/adjunct (0 women). *Students:* 9 full-time (7 women); includes 4 minority (2 Black or African American, non-Hispanic/Latino; 2 Hispanic/Latino). 11 applicants, 100% accepted, 9 enrolled. In 2016, 16 master's awarded. *Degree requirements:* For master's, comprehensive exam, practicum. *Entrance requirements:* Additional exam requirements/recommendations for international students: Required—TOEFL (minimum score 80 iBT), IELTS (minimum score 6), PTE. *Application deadline:* For fall admission, 8/15 priority date for domestic students; for winter admission, 10/1 priority date for domestic students; for spring admission, 12/15 priority date for domestic students; for summer admission, 4/15 for domestic students. Applications are processed on a rolling basis. Application fee: $50. Electronic applications accepted. *Expenses:* $600 per credit hour. *Financial support:* Application deadline: 4/1; applicants required to submit FAFSA. *Unit head:* Dr. Peter Williams, Program Director, 877-698-2793, E-mail: peter.williams@acu.edu. *Application contact:* Graduate Admissions, 855-219-7000, E-mail: gradonline@acu.edu.
Website: http://www.acu.edu/online/academics/master-of-education-in-instructional-leadership.html

Acadia University, Faculty of Professional Studies, School of Education, Program in Curriculum Studies, Wolfville, NS B4P 2R6, Canada. Offers cultural and media studies (M Ed); learning and technology (M Ed); science, math and technology (M Ed). *Program availability:* Part-time. *Degree requirements:* For master's, thesis optional. *Entrance requirements:* For master's, B Ed or the equivalent, minimum B average in undergraduate course work, 2 years of teaching experience. Additional exam requirements/recommendations for international students: Required—TOEFL (minimum score 580 paper-based; 93 iBT), IELTS (minimum score 6.5). *Faculty research:* Literacy development, postmodern philosophy and curriculum theory, historiography, philosophy of education, learning and technology.

Adelphi University, Ruth S. Ammon School of Education, Program in Educational Technology, Garden City, NY 11530-0701. Offers MA. *Program availability:* Online learning. *Students:* 5 full-time (4 women), 5 part-time (3 women); includes 4 minority (3 Black or African American, non-Hispanic/Latino; 1 Hispanic/Latino). Average age 29. 8 applicants, 88% accepted, 4 enrolled. *Entrance requirements:* For master's, personal statement, two letters of reference, current resume or curriculum vitae. Additional exam requirements/recommendations for international students: Required—TOEFL (minimum score 550 paper-based; 80 iBT), IELTS (minimum score 6.5). *Expenses: Tuition:* Full-time $37,623; part-time $1179 per credit hour. *Required fees:* $1335; $405 per semester. Tuition and fees vary according to degree level, campus/location and program. *Unit head:* Dr. Jane Ashdown, Dean, 516-877-4065, E-mail: jashdown@adelphi.edu. *Application contact:* Christine Murphy, Director of Admissions, 516-877-3050, Fax: 516-877-3039, E-mail: graduateadmissions@adelphi.edu.
Website: http://education-ci.adelphi.edu/educational-technology/

Alabama Agricultural and Mechanical University, School of Graduate Studies, College of Education, Humanities, and Behavioral Sciences, Department of Educational Leadership and Secondary Education, Huntsville, AL 35811. Offers biology (M Ed); business/marketing education (M Ed, Ed S); chemistry (M Ed); collaborative teacher secondary education (M Ed, Ed S); education (M Ed, Ed S); English language arts (M Ed); family/consumer science education (M Ed, Ed S); general science (M Ed); general social science (M Ed); mathematics (M Ed, Ed S); physics (M Ed, Ed S); technology education (M Ed). *Accreditation:* NCATE. *Program availability:* Evening/weekend. *Degree requirements:* For master's, comprehensive exam; for Ed S, thesis. *Entrance requirements:* For master's, GRE General Test. Additional exam requirements/recommendations for international students: Required—TOEFL (minimum score 500 paper-based; 61 iBT). *Application deadline:* For fall admission, 5/1 for domestic students. Applications are processed on a rolling basis. Application fee: $25. Electronic applications accepted. *Expenses:* Tuition, nonresident: part-time $826 per credit hour. Full-time tuition and fees vary according to course load and program. *Financial support:* Research assistantships, career-related internships or fieldwork, Federal Work-Study, institutionally sponsored loans, and traineeships available. Financial award application deadline: 4/1. *Faculty research:* World peace through education, computer-assisted instruction. *Unit head:* Dr. Derrick Davis, Chair, 256-372-4047, Fax: 256-372-5526.

Alabama State University, College of Education, Department of Instructional Support Programs, Montgomery, AL 36101-0271. Offers counselor education (M Ed, MS, Ed S), including general counseling (MS, Ed S), school counseling (M Ed, Ed S); educational administration (M Ed, Ed D, Ed S), including educational administration (Ed S), educational leadership, policy and law (Ed D), instructional leadership (M Ed); library education media (M Ed, Ed S). *Program availability:* Part-time. *Faculty:* 11 full-time (6 women), 7 part-time/adjunct (5 women). *Students:* 50 full-time (32 women), 128 part-time (95 women); includes 167 minority (166 Black or African American, non-Hispanic/Latino; 1 Two or more races, non-Hispanic/Latino), 3 international. Average age 37. 84 applicants, 50% accepted, 16 enrolled. In 2016, 39 master's, 19 doctorates, 5 other advanced degrees awarded. *Degree requirements:* For master's, comprehensive exam; for Ed S, comprehensive exam, thesis. *Entrance requirements:* For master's, GRE General Test, MAT, writing competency test, bachelor's degree or its equivalent from accredited college or university with minimum GPA of 2.5; for Ed S, GRE General Test, MAT, writing competency test, minimum GPA of 3.25. Additional exam requirements/recommendations for international students: Required—TOEFL (minimum score 500 paper-based). *Application deadline:* For fall admission, 4/15 for domestic and international students; for spring admission, 11/15 for domestic and international students; for summer admission, 3/15 for domestic and international students. Applications are processed on a rolling basis. Application fee: $25. Electronic applications accepted. *Expenses:* Tuition, state resident: full-time $3087; part-time $2744 per credit. Tuition, nonresident: full-time $6174; part-time $5488 per credit. *Required fees:* $2284; $1142 per credit. $571 per semester. Tuition and fees vary according to class time, course level, course load, degree level, program and student level. *Financial support:* In 2016–17, 3 students received support. Research assistantships and unspecified assistantships available. Financial award application deadline: 6/30; financial award applicants required to submit FAFSA. *Unit head:* Dr. Necoal Driver, Chair, 334-229-4456, Fax: 334-229-6831, E-mail: ndriver@alasu.edu. *Application contact:* Dr. William Person, Dean of Graduate Studies, 334-229-4275, Fax: 334-229-4928, E-mail: wperson@alasu.edu.
Website: http://www.alasu.edu/academics/colleges—departments/college-of-education/instructional-support-programs/index.aspx

Alverno College, School of Education, Milwaukee, WI 53234-3922. Offers adaptive education (MA); administrative leadership (MA); adult education and organizational development (MA); adult educational and instructional design (MA); adult educational and instructional technology (MA); global connections in the humanities (MA); instructional leadership (MA); instructional technology for K-12 settings (MA); professional development (MA); reading education (MA); reading education with adaptive education (MA); science education (MA); special education (MA); teaching in alternative schools (MA). *Accreditation:* NCATE. *Program availability:* Part-time, evening/weekend. *Faculty:* 4 full-time (3 women), 23 part-time/adjunct (17 women). *Students:* 58 full-time (57 women), 62 part-time (54 women); includes 32 minority (22 Black or African American, non-Hispanic/Latino; 2 Asian, non-Hispanic/Latino; 8 Hispanic/Latino), 1 international. Average age 39. 77 applicants, 99% accepted, 61 enrolled. In 2016, 85 master's awarded. *Degree requirements:* For master's, presentation/defense of proposal, conference presentation of inquiry projects. *Entrance requirements:* For master's, bachelor's degree in related field, communication samples from work setting, 3 letters of recommendation. Additional exam requirements/recommendations for international students: Required—TOEFL. *Application deadline:* For fall admission, 7/15 priority date for domestic and international students; for spring admission, 12/15 priority date for domestic and international students. Applications are processed on a rolling basis. Application fee: $0. Electronic applications accepted. *Expenses:* Contact institution. *Financial support:* In 2016–17, 17 students received support. Federal Work-Study and scholarships/grants available. Support available to part-time students. Financial award applicants required to submit FAFSA. *Faculty research:* Student self-assessment, self-reflection, integration of curriculum, identifying needs of students in strategic situations and designing appropriate classroom strategies. *Unit head:* Dr. Desiree Pointer Mace, Associate Dean, Graduate Program, 414-382-6345, Fax: 414-382-6332, E-mail: desiree.pointer-mace@alverno.edu. *Application contact:* Katie Kipp, Graduate Admissions Counselor, 414-382-6045, Fax: 414-382-6354, E-mail: katie.kipp@alverno.edu.

American College of Education, Graduate Programs, Indianapolis, IN 46204. Offers curriculum and instruction (M Ed), including bilingual, ESL; educational leadership (M Ed); educational technology (M Ed).

American InterContinental University Online, Program in Education, Schaumburg, IL 60173. Offers curriculum and instruction (M Ed); educational assessment and evaluation (M Ed); instructional technology (M Ed); leadership of educational organizations (M Ed). *Accreditation:* TEAC. *Program availability:* Evening/weekend, online learning. *Entrance requirements:* Additional exam requirements/recommendations for international students: Required—TOEFL (minimum score 550 paper-based). Electronic applications accepted.

Antioch University New England, Graduate School, Department of Education, Experienced Educators Program, Keene, NH 03431-3552. Offers foundations of education (M Ed), including applied behavioral analysis, autism spectrum disorders, educating for sustainability, next-generation learning using technology, problem-based learning using critical skills, teacher leadership; principal certification (PMC). *Degree requirements:* For master's, thesis, practicum. *Entrance requirements:* For master's, previous course work and work experience in education. Additional exam requirements/recommendations for international students: Required—TOEFL (minimum score 550 paper-based). Electronic applications accepted. *Expenses:* Contact institution. *Faculty research:* Classroom action research, school restructuring, problem-based learning, brain-based learning.

Appalachian State University, Cratis D. Williams Graduate School, Department of Curriculum and Instruction, Boone, NC 28608. Offers curriculum specialist (MA); educational media (MA); elementary education (MA); middle grades education (MA), including language arts, mathematics, science, social studies. *Accreditation:* NCATE. *Program availability:* Part-time, evening/weekend, online learning. *Degree requirements:* For master's, comprehensive exam, thesis or alternative. *Entrance requirements:* For master's, GRE General Test or MAT, 3 letters of recommendation. Additional exam requirements/recommendations for international students: Required—TOEFL (minimum score 570 paper-based; 79 iBT), IELTS (minimum score 6.5). *Application deadline:* For fall admission, 3/14 for domestic students, 2/1 for international students; for spring admission, 11/1 for domestic students, 7/1 for international students. Applications are processed on a rolling basis. Application fee: $55. Electronic applications accepted. *Expenses:* Tuition, state resident: full-time $4744. Tuition, nonresident: full-time $17,913. Full-time tuition and fees vary according to program. *Financial support:* Fellowships, research assistantships, teaching assistantships, career-related internships or fieldwork, Federal Work-Study, scholarships/grants, and unspecified assistantships available. Financial award application deadline: 4/1; financial award applicants required to submit FAFSA. *Faculty research:* Media literacy, elementary teaching, curriculum development, online learning environments. *Unit head:* Dr. Michael Jacobson, Chairperson, 828-262-2224. *Application contact:* Dr. Chrystal Dean, Program Director, 828-262-8009, E-mail: deanco@appstate.edu.
Website: http://www.ced.appstate.edu/departments/ci

Appalachian State University, Cratis D. Williams Graduate School, Department of Leadership and Educational Studies, Boone, NC 28608. Offers educational administration (Ed S); educational media (MA); higher education (MA, Ed S); library science (MLS); school administration (MSA). *Program availability:* Part-time, evening/weekend, online learning. *Degree requirements:* For master's and Ed S, comprehensive exam, thesis optional. *Entrance requirements:* For master's and Ed S, GRE or MAT, 3 letters of recommendation. Additional exam requirements/recommendations for international students: Required—TOEFL (minimum score 570 paper-based; 79 iBT), IELTS (minimum score 6.5). *Application deadline:* For fall admission, 3/14 priority date for domestic students, 2/1 for international students; for spring admission, 11/1 for domestic students, 7/1 for international students. Applications are processed on a rolling basis. Application fee: $55. Electronic applications accepted. *Expenses:* Tuition, state resident: full-time $4744. Tuition, nonresident: full-time $17,913. Full-time tuition and fees vary according to program. *Financial support:* Research assistantships, career-related internships or fieldwork, scholarships/grants, and unspecified assistantships available. Financial award application deadline: 4/1; financial award applicants required to submit FAFSA. *Faculty research:* Brain, learning and meditation; leadership of teaching and learning. *Unit head:* Dr. Robert Sanders, Interim Director, 828-262-3112, E-mail: sandersrl@appstate.edu. *Application contact:* Dr. Vachel Miller, Program Director, 828-262-2287, E-mail: millervw@appstate.edu.
Website: http://www.les.appstate.edu

Arcadia University, School of Education, Glenside, PA 19038-3295. Offers art education (M Ed); computer education (CAS); curriculum (CAS); curriculum studies (M Ed); early childhood education (M Ed), including individualized, master teacher, research in child development; educational leadership (M Ed, Ed D, CAS); elementary education (M Ed); English education (MA Ed); environmental education (MA Ed); instructional technology (M Ed); language arts (M Ed); library science (M Ed); mathematics education (M Ed, MA Ed); music education (MA Ed); psychology (MA Ed); reading (M Ed, CAS); science education (M Ed, CAS); secondary education (M Ed, CAS); special education (M Ed, Ed D, CAS); theater arts (MA Ed); written communication (MA Ed). *Accreditation:* NASAD. *Program availability:* Part-time, evening/weekend, online learning. *Faculty:* 19 full-time (13 women), 3 part-time/adjunct (all women). *Students:* 22 full-time (16 women), 356 part-time (284 women); includes 84 minority (55 Black or African American, non-Hispanic/Latino; 2 American Indian or Alaska Native, non-Hispanic/Latino; 13 Asian, non-Hispanic/Latino; 11 Hispanic/Latino; 3 Two or more races, non-Hispanic/Latino), 4 international. Average age 34. 145 applicants, 73% accepted, 80 enrolled. In 2016, 95 master's, 11 doctorates awarded. *Application deadline:* Applications are processed on a rolling basis. Application fee: $50. Electronic applications accepted. *Expenses:* Contact institution. *Financial support:* Career-related internships or fieldwork, tuition waivers (partial), and unspecified assistantships available. *Unit head:* John T Groves, Interim Dean of the School of Education, 215-572-2940. *Application contact:* 215-572-2925, Fax: 215-572-2126, E-mail: grad@arcadia.edu.

Argosy University, Atlanta, College of Education, Atlanta, GA 30328. Offers educational leadership (MAEd, Ed D, Ed S), including higher education administration (Ed D), K-12 education (Ed D); teaching and learning (MAEd, Ed D, Ed S), including education technology (Ed D), higher education (Ed D), K-12 education (Ed D).

Argosy University, Denver, College of Education, Denver, CO 80231. Offers community college executive leadership (Ed D); educational leadership (MA Ed, Ed D), including higher education (Ed D), K-12 education (Ed D); instructional leadership (MA Ed, Ed D), including higher education administration (Ed D), K-12 education (Ed D).

Argosy University, Nashville, College of Education, Program in Instructional Leadership, Nashville, TN 37214. Offers education technology (Ed D); higher education administration (Ed D); instructional leadership (MA Ed, Ed S); K-12 education (Ed D).

Argosy University, Orange County, College of Education, Orange, CA 92868. Offers community college executive leadership (Ed D); educational leadership (MA Ed, Ed D), including higher education administration (Ed D), K-12 education (Ed D); instructional leadership (MA Ed, Ed D), including education technology (Ed D), higher education (Ed D), K-12 education (Ed D), multiple subject teacher preparation (MA Ed), single subject teacher preparation (MA Ed).

Argosy University, Phoenix, College of Education, Phoenix, AZ 85021. Offers adult education and training (MA Ed); advanced educational administration (Ed D, Ed S); community college executive leadership (Ed D); educational administration (MA Ed); educational leadership (MA Ed, Ed D, Ed S), including education technology (Ed D), higher education administration (Ed D), K-12 education (Ed D); higher and postsecondary education (MA Ed); initial educational administration (Ed D, Ed S); school psychology (MA); teaching and learning (MA Ed, Ed D, Ed S), including education technology (Ed D), higher education (Ed D), K-12 education (Ed D).

Argosy University, San Francisco Bay Area, College of Education, Alameda, CA 94501. Offers community college executive leadership (Ed D); educational leadership (MA Ed, Ed D), including education technology (Ed D), higher education administration (Ed D), K-12 education (Ed D); instructional leadership (MA Ed, Ed D), including education technology (Ed D), higher education (Ed D), K-12 education (Ed D), multiple subject teacher preparation (MA Ed), single subject teacher preparation (MA Ed).

Argosy University, Sarasota, College of Education, Sarasota, FL 34235. Offers community college executive leadership (Ed D); educational leadership (MA Ed, Ed D, Ed S), including higher education administration (Ed D), K-12 education (Ed D); school counseling (MA, Ed S); school psychology (MA); teaching and learning (MA Ed, Ed D, Ed S), including education technology (Ed D), higher education (Ed D), K-12 education (Ed D).

Argosy University, Seattle, College of Education, Seattle, WA 98121. Offers adult education and training (MA Ed); community college executive leadership (Ed D); educational leadership (MA Ed, Ed D), including higher education administration (Ed D), K-12 education (Ed D); higher and postsecondary education (MA Ed); instructional leadership (MA Ed, Ed D), including education technology (Ed D), higher education (Ed D), K-12 education (Ed D).

Argosy University, Twin Cities, College of Education, Eagan, MN 55121. Offers advanced educational administration (Ed D, Ed S); educational leadership (MA Ed, Ed D, Ed S), including higher education administration (Ed D), K-12 education (Ed D); higher and postsecondary education (MA Ed); initial educational administration (Ed D, Ed S); instructional leadership (MA Ed, Ed D, Ed S), including education technology (Ed D), higher education (Ed D), K-12 education (Ed D).

Arizona State University at the Tempe campus, Mary Lou Fulton Teachers College, Program in Educational Technology, Phoenix, AZ 85069. Offers educational technology (M Ed); instructional design and performance improvement (Graduate Certificate); online teaching for grades K-12 (Graduate Certificate). *Program availability:* Part-time, evening/weekend, online learning. Terminal master's awarded for partial completion of doctoral program. *Degree requirements:* For master's, thesis or alternative, applied project, interactive Program of Study (iPOS) submitted before completing 50 percent of required credit hours. *Entrance requirements:* For master's, GRE (Verbal section) or MAT (for students with less than 3 years of professional experience as teacher, trainer or instructional designer), minimum GPA of 3.0 or equivalent in last 2 years of work leading to bachelor's degree, 3 letters of recommendation, personal statement, curriculum vitae or resume. Additional exam requirements/recommendations for international students: Required—TOEFL (minimum score 600 paper-based; 100 iBT). Electronic applications accepted. *Faculty research:* Virtual environments; innovative technologies; theory, design, and implementation of computer-based learning environments; impact of technology into curricula on student achievement/attitude; electronic portfolios for learning and assessment.

Arkansas Tech University, College of Education, Russellville, AR 72801. Offers college student personnel (MS); educational leadership (M Ed, Ed S); elementary education (M Ed); instructional improvement (M Ed); instructional technology (M Ed); school counseling and leadership (M Ed); school leadership (Ed D); strength and conditioning studies (MS); teaching (MAT); teaching, learning, and leadership (M Ed). *Accreditation:* NCATE. *Program availability:* Part-time, evening/weekend, online learning. *Students:* 72 full-time (43 women), 371 part-time (283 women); includes 108 minority (80 Black or African American, non-Hispanic/Latino; 1 American Indian or Alaska Native, non-Hispanic/Latino; 4 Asian, non-Hispanic/Latino; 13 Hispanic/Latino; 10 Two or more races, non-Hispanic/Latino), 6 international. Average age 33. In 2016, 181 master's, 1 other advanced degree awarded. *Degree requirements:* For master's, comprehensive exam, thesis optional, action research project. *Entrance requirements:* Additional exam requirements/recommendations for international students: Required—TOEFL (minimum score 550 paper-based; 79 iBT), IELTS (minimum score 6.5). *Application deadline:* For fall admission, 3/1 priority date for domestic students, 5/1 priority date for international students; for spring admission, 10/1 priority date for domestic and international students. Applications are processed on a rolling basis. Application fee: $25 ($75 for international students). Electronic applications accepted. *Expenses:* Tuition, state resident: full-time $4932; part-time $274 per credit hour. Tuition, nonresident: full-time $9864; part-time $548 per credit hour. *Required fees:* $513 per semester. Tuition and fees vary according to course load. *Financial support:* In 2016–17, research assistantships with full tuition reimbursements (averaging $4,800 per year), teaching assistantships with full tuition reimbursements (averaging $4,800 per year) were awarded; career-related internships or fieldwork, Federal Work-Study, scholarships/grants, health care benefits, and unspecified assistantships also available. Support available to part-time students. Financial award application deadline: 4/15; financial award applicants required to submit FAFSA. *Unit head:* Dr. Mary Gunter, Dean, 479-964-3217, E-mail: mgunter@atu.edu.
Website: http://www.atu.edu/education/

Ashland University, Dwight Schar College of Education, Department of Educational Foundations and Instruction, Ashland, OH 44805-3702. Offers educational technology (M Ed); literacy (M Ed); teaching and learning in the 21st century (M Ed). *Program availability:* Part-time, evening/weekend. *Degree requirements:* For master's, inquiry seminar, internship, or thesis. *Entrance requirements:* For master's, teaching certificate or license, bachelor's degree, minimum cumulative GPA of 2.75. Additional exam requirements/recommendations for international students: Required—TOEFL. *Application deadline:* Applications are processed on a rolling basis. Application fee: $30. Electronic applications accepted. *Financial support:* Application deadline: 4/15. *Faculty research:* Character education, teacher reflection, religion and education, professional education, environmental education. *Unit head:* Dr. Louise Fleming, Chair, 419-289-5347, E-mail: lfleming@ashland.edu. *Application contact:* Dr. Linda Billman, Associate Dean, 419-289-5369, Fax: 419-289-5331, E-mail: lbillman@ashland.edu.
Website: http://www.ashland.edu/academics/education/edfoundations/

Auburn University, Graduate School, College of Education, Department of Educational Foundations, Leadership, and Technology, Auburn University, AL 36849. Offers adult education (PhD, Ed S); curriculum supervision (M Ed, PhD); higher education administration (PhD); library media (Ed S); school administration (M Ed, PhD). *Accreditation:* NCATE. *Program availability:* Part-time. *Faculty:* 29 full-time (15 women), 4 part-time/adjunct (3 women). *Students:* 119 full-time (72 women), 273 part-time (170 women); includes 132 minority (114 Black or African American, non-Hispanic/Latino; 2 American Indian or Alaska Native, non-Hispanic/Latino; 4 Asian, non-Hispanic/Latino; 6 Hispanic/Latino; 1 Native Hawaiian or other Pacific Islander, non-Hispanic/Latino; 5 Two or more races, non-Hispanic/Latino), 14 international. Average age 37. 220 applicants, 71% accepted, 78 enrolled. In 2016, 67 master's, 44 doctorates, 41 other advanced degrees awarded. *Degree requirements:* For master's, thesis (for some programs); for doctorate, thesis/dissertation; for Ed S, field project. *Entrance requirements:* For master's, doctorate, and Ed S, GRE General Test. *Application deadline:* Applications are processed on a rolling basis. Application fee: $50 ($60 for international students). Electronic applications accepted. *Expenses:* Tuition, state resident: full-time $9072; part-time $504 per credit hour. Tuition, nonresident: full-time $27,216; part-time $1512 per credit hour. *Required fees:* $812 per semester. Tuition and fees vary according to degree level and program. *Financial support:* Teaching assistantships and Federal

Work-Study available. Support available to part-time students. Financial award application deadline: 3/15; financial award applicants required to submit FAFSA. *Unit head:* Dr. Sherida Downer, Head, 334-844-4460. *Application contact:* Dr. George Flowers, Dean of the Graduate School, 334-844-4700.
Website: http://www.education.auburn.edu/academic_departments/eflt/

Auburn University at Montgomery, College of Education, Department of Counselor, Leadership, and Special Education, Montgomery, AL 36124-4023. Offers counselor education (M Ed, Ed S), including clinical mental health counseling, school counseling; early childhood special education (M Ed); instructional leadership (M Ed, Ed S); special education/collaborative teacher (M Ed, Ed S). *Accreditation:* ACA; NCATE. *Program availability:* Part-time, evening/weekend. *Faculty:* 9 full-time (7 women), 3 part-time/adjunct (all women). *Students:* 7 full-time (5 women), 28 part-time (all women); includes 11 minority (10 Black or African American, non-Hispanic/Latino; 1 Asian, non-Hispanic/Latino). Average age 35. In 2016, 35 master's, 9 Ed Ss awarded. *Degree requirements:* For master's and Ed S, comprehensive exam. *Entrance requirements:* For master's, GRE General Test or MAT, certification, BS in teaching; for Ed S, GRE General Test or MAT, certification. Additional exam requirements/recommendations for international students: Recommended—TOEFL (minimum score 500 paper-based; 61 iBT), IELTS (minimum score 5.5), TSE (minimum score 44). *Application deadline:* Applications are processed on a rolling basis. Electronic applications accepted. *Expenses:* Tuition, state resident: full-time $6462; part-time $359 per credit hour. Tuition, nonresident: full-time $14,526; part-time $807 per credit hour. *Required fees:* $554. *Financial support:* Career-related internships or fieldwork and scholarships/grants available. Support available to part-time students. Financial award application deadline: 3/1; financial award applicants required to submit FAFSA. *Unit head:* Dr. Samuel Flynt, Head, 334-244-3835, Fax: 334-244-3101, E-mail: sflynt@aum.edu. *Application contact:* Dr. Rhonda Morton, Associate Dean/Graduate Coordinator, 334-244-3287, Fax: 334-244-3978, E-mail: rmorton@aum.edu.
Website: http://education.aum.edu/academic-departments/counselor-leadership-and-special-education

Auburn University at Montgomery, College of Education, Department of Curriculum, Instruction, and Technology, Montgomery, AL 36124-4023. Offers elementary education (M Ed, Ed S); instructional technology (Ed S); secondary education (M Ed). *Faculty:* 10 full-time (6 women), 6 part-time/adjunct (4 women). *Students:* 18 full-time (15 women), 23 part-time (22 women); includes 11 minority (10 Black or African American, non-Hispanic/Latino; 1 Asian, non-Hispanic/Latino), 1 international. *Entrance requirements:* Additional exam requirements/recommendations for international students: Recommended—TOEFL (minimum score 500 paper-based; 61 iBT), IELTS (minimum score 5.5), TSE (minimum score 44). *Expenses:* Tuition, state resident: full-time $6462; part-time $359 per credit hour. Tuition, nonresident: full-time $14,526; part-time $807 per credit hour. *Required fees:* $554. *Financial support:* Application deadline: 3/1; applicants required to submit FAFSA. *Unit head:* Dr. Kellie Shumack, Head, 334-244-3737, Fax: 334-244-3835, E-mail: kshumack@aum.edu. *Application contact:* Dr. Rhonda Morton, Associate Dean/Graduate Coordinator, 334-224-3287, Fax: 334-244-3978, E-mail: rmorton@aum.edu.
Website: http://education.aum.edu/academic-departments/curriculum-instruction-technology

Augustana University, MA in Education Program, Sioux Falls, SD 57197. Offers instructional strategies (MA); reading (MA); special populations (MA); STEM (MA); technology (MA). *Accreditation:* NCATE. *Program availability:* Part-time, evening/weekend, online only, 100% online. *Degree requirements:* For master's, thesis. *Entrance requirements:* For master's, appropriate bachelor's degree, minimum GPA of 3.0, teaching certificate. Additional exam requirements/recommendations for international students: Required—TOEFL (minimum score 550 paper-based). *Application deadline:* For fall admission, 8/1 for domestic and international students; for spring admission, 11/1 for domestic and international students; for summer admission, 4/1 for domestic and international students. Applications are processed on a rolling basis. Application fee: $50. Electronic applications accepted. *Expenses:* Contact institution. *Financial support:* Application deadline: 3/1; applicants required to submit FAFSA. *Unit head:* Dr. Laurie Daily, Chair, 605-274-5211, E-mail: laurie.daily@augie.edu. *Application contact:* Jody Nitz, Graduate Coordinator, 605-274-4043, Fax: 605-274-4450, E-mail: graduate@augie.edu.
Website: http://www.augie.edu/master-arts-education

Augusta University, The Graduate School, College of Education, Program in Educational Innovation, Augusta, GA 30912. Offers educational innovation (Ed D). *Unit head:* Dr. Wayne Lord, Director, 706-729-2455, E-mail: elord1@augusta.edu. *Application contact:* Mary Ann Cooke, Administrative Specialist II, 706-737-1497, E-mail: mcooke@augusta.edu.
Website: http://www.augusta.edu/education/advanced-studies-innovation/edd-ei.php

Aurora University, School of Education and Human Performance, Aurora, IL 60506-4892. Offers bilingual-ESL education (MA); educational leadership (MA); educational technology (MA); leadership in administration (Ed D); leadership in adult learning and higher education (Ed D); leadership in curriculum and instruction (Ed D); reading instruction (MA); special education (MA). *Accreditation:* NCATE. *Program availability:* Part-time, evening/weekend. *Faculty:* 22 full-time (12 women), 46 part-time/adjunct (27 women). *Students:* 36 full-time (30 women), 559 part-time (372 women); includes 68 minority (27 Black or African American, non-Hispanic/Latino; 1 American Indian or Alaska Native, non-Hispanic/Latino; 6 Asian, non-Hispanic/Latino; 29 Hispanic/Latino; 2 Native Hawaiian or other Pacific Islander, non-Hispanic/Latino; 3 Two or more races, non-Hispanic/Latino). Average age 37. 126 applicants, 98% accepted, 72 enrolled. In 2016, 178 master's, 27 doctorates awarded. *Degree requirements:* For master's, student teaching; for doctorate, comprehensive exam, thesis/dissertation. *Entrance requirements:* For master's, 2 years of teaching experience, valid teaching certificate; for doctorate, appropriate master's degree, two references, curriculum vitae, personal statement, professional project, reflective essay. Additional exam requirements/recommendations for international students: Required—TOEFL (minimum score 550 paper-based; 79 iBT). *Application deadline:* For fall admission, 6/1 for international students; for spring admission, 10/1 for international students. Applications are processed on a rolling basis. Application fee: $0. Electronic applications accepted. *Expenses:* Contact institution. *Financial support:* In 2016–17, 10 students received support. Federal Work-Study, scholarships/grants, and unspecified assistantships available. Support available to part-time students. Financial award applicants required to submit FAFSA. *Unit head:* Dr. Jen Buckley, Executive Director of the School of Education and Human Performance, 630-844-1542, Fax: 630-844-6155, E-mail: jbuckley@aurora.edu. *Application contact:* Elizabeth Botica, Graduate Education Recruiter, 630-947-8918, E-mail: ebotica@aurora.edu.
Website: http://aurora.edu/education

Avila University, School of Professional Studies, Kansas City, MO 64145-1698. Offers executive leadership development (MS); fundraising (MA); instructional design and technology (MA, MS); leadership coaching (MS); organizational development (MS); project management (MA); strategic human resources (MS). *Program availability:* Part-time-only, evening/weekend, 100% online, blended/hybrid learning. *Faculty:* 15 part-time/adjunct (9 women). *Students:* 90 full-time (59 women), 47 part-time (40 women); includes 50 minority (38 Black or African American, non-Hispanic/Latino; 1 American Indian or Alaska Native, non-Hispanic/Latino; 3 Asian, non-Hispanic/Latino; 7 Hispanic/Latino; 1 Two or more races, non-Hispanic/Latino), 6 international. Average age 38. 95 applicants, 58% accepted, 38 enrolled. In 2016, 37 master's awarded. *Degree requirements:* For master's, thesis optional. *Entrance requirements:* For master's, 2 letters of recommendation, minimum GPA of 3.0 during last 60 hours, resume, statement of intent. Additional exam requirements/recommendations for international students: Required—TOEFL (minimum score 550 paper-based; 79 iBT). *Application deadline:* Applications are processed on a rolling basis. Application fee: $0. Electronic applications accepted. *Expenses:* $545 per credit hour. *Financial support:* In 2016–17, 14 students received support. Unspecified assistantships available. Support available to part-time students. Financial award applicants required to submit FAFSA. *Unit head:* Dr. Steve Iliff, Associate Dean/Director, 816-501-3675, Fax: 816-941-4650, E-mail: advantage@avila.edu. *Application contact:* Jessica Burson, Graduate Admission Advisor, 816-501-2482, Fax: 816-941-4650, E-mail: advantage@avila.edu.
Website: https://www.avila.edu/mrk/advantage-3

Azusa Pacific University, School of Education, Department of Advanced Studies, Program in Digital Teaching and Learning, Azusa, CA 91702-7000. Offers MA Ed.

Azusa Pacific University, School of Education, Department of Advanced Studies, Program in Educational Technology, Azusa, CA 91702-7000. Offers M Ed. *Program availability:* Part-time, evening/weekend. *Degree requirements:* For master's, comprehensive exam, core exam, oral presentation. *Entrance requirements:* For master's, 12 units of course work in education, minimum GPA of 3.0.

Azusa Pacific University, School of Education, Department of Advanced Studies, Program in Educational Technology and Learning, Azusa, CA 91702-7000. Offers MA. *Program availability:* Online learning.

Azusa Pacific University, School of Education, Department of Special Education, Program in Special Education and Educational Technology, Azusa, CA 91702-7000. Offers M Ed.

Baldwin Wallace University, Graduate Programs, School of Education, Technology Leadership Program, Berea, OH 44017-2088. Offers MA Ed. *Program availability:* Part-time, evening/weekend, 100% online. *Students:* 8 full-time (4 women), 8 part-time (3 women); includes 1 minority (Black or African American, non-Hispanic/Latino). Average age 33. 5 applicants, 60% accepted, 3 enrolled. In 2016, 4 master's awarded. *Degree requirements:* For master's, comprehensive exam, portfolio. *Entrance requirements:* For master's, bachelor's degree in field, MAT or minimum GPA of 3.0. Additional exam requirements/recommendations for international students: Required—TOEFL (minimum score 550 paper-based; 79 iBT). *Application deadline:* For fall admission, 8/15 priority date for domestic students; for spring admission, 12/15 priority date for domestic students. Applications are processed on a rolling basis. Application fee: $25. Electronic applications accepted. Application fee is waived when completed online. *Expenses:* $721 per credit hour. *Financial support:* Career-related internships or fieldwork available. Financial award applicants required to submit FAFSA. *Faculty research:* No-cost software, online resources for building a classroom learning management system. *Unit head:* Dr. Karen Kaye, Coordinator, 440-826-8064, Fax: 440-826-3779, E-mail: sfinelli@bw.edu. *Application contact:* Winifred W. Gerhardt, Director of Transfer, Adult and Graduate Admission, 440-826-2222, Fax: 440-826-3830, E-mail: admission@bw.edu.
Website: http://www.bw.edu/academics/master-of-arts-in-education/maed-technology-leadership/

Ball State University, Graduate School, Teachers College, Department of Educational Studies, Program in Curriculum and Educational Technology, Muncie, IN 47306. Offers MA. *Accreditation:* NCATE. *Program availability:* Part-time, online only, 100% online. *Entrance requirements:* For master's, minimum baccalaureate GPA of 2.75 or 3.0 in latter half of baccalauareate. Additional exam requirements/recommendations for international students: Required—TOEFL (minimum score 550 paper-based; 79 iBT), IELTS (minimum score 6.5). Electronic applications accepted.

Ball State University, Graduate School, Teachers College, Department of Educational Studies, Program in Educational Studies, Muncie, IN 47306. Offers educational studies (PhD), including cultural and educational policy studies, curriculum, educational technology. *Program availability:* Part-time, blended/hybrid learning. *Degree requirements:* For doctorate, thesis/dissertation. *Entrance requirements:* For doctorate, GRE General Test, minimum graduate GPA of 3.2, curriculum vitae, writing sample, three letters of reference. Additional exam requirements/recommendations for international students: Required—TOEFL (minimum score 550 paper-based; 79 iBT), IELTS (minimum score 6.5). Electronic applications accepted. *Faculty research:* Emerging curriculum trends, secondary teacher preparation, issues of equity and social justice in education, teacher technology integration, teaching for transformative understanding, teacher leadership, history of educational policy and practices, ethics and education.

Barry University, School of Education, Graduate Certificate Programs, Miami Shores, FL 33161-6695. Offers advanced teaching and learning with technology (Certificate); distance education (Certificate); higher education technology integration (Certificate); human resources: not for profit and religious organizations (Certificate); K-12 technology integration (Certificate).

Barry University, School of Education, Program in Educational Technology Applications, Miami Shores, FL 33161-6695. Offers educational computing and technology (MS, Ed S). *Program availability:* Part-time, evening/weekend, online learning. *Degree requirements:* For master's and Ed S, comprehensive exam. *Entrance requirements:* For master's, GRE General Test or MAT, minimum GPA of 3.0; for Ed S, GRE General Test, minimum GPA of 3.0.

Barry University, School of Education, Program in Leadership and Education, Miami Shores, FL 33161-6695. Offers educational technology (PhD); exceptional student education (PhD); higher education administration (PhD); human resource development (PhD); leadership (PhD). *Program availability:* Part-time, evening/weekend. *Degree requirements:* For doctorate, thesis/dissertation. *Entrance requirements:* For doctorate, GRE General Test, minimum GPA of 3.25. Electronic applications accepted.

Barry University, School of Education, Program in Technology and TESOL, Miami Shores, FL 33161-6695. Offers MS, Ed S.

Bay Path University, Program in Higher Education Administration, Longmeadow, MA 01106-2292. Offers enrollment management (MS); general administration (MS); institutional advancement (MS); online teaching and program administration (MS). *Program availability:* Part-time, online only, 100% online. *Students:* 9 full-time (8 women), 50 part-time (39 women); includes 18 minority (8 Black or African American, non-Hispanic/Latino; 1 American Indian or Alaska Native, non-Hispanic/Latino; 7 Hispanic/Latino; 2 Two or more races, non-Hispanic/Latino). Average age 36. 27 applicants, 67% accepted, 14 enrolled. In 2016, 15 master's awarded. *Degree requirements:* For master's, 8 core courses (24 credits) and 4 elective courses (12 credits) for a total of 36 credits. *Application deadline:* Applications are processed on a rolling basis. Application fee: $45. Electronic applications accepted. Application fee is waived when completed online. *Expenses:* $20,385. *Financial support:* Unspecified

assistantships available. Financial award applicants required to submit FAFSA. *Unit head:* Dr. Lauren Way, Program Director, 413-565-1193, E-mail: lway@baypath.edu. *Application contact:* Diane Ranaldi, Dean of Graduate Admissions, 413-565-1332, Fax: 413-565-1250, E-mail: dranaldi@baypath.edu.
Website: http://graduate.baypath.edu/Graduate-Programs/Programs-Online/MS-Programs/Higher-Education-Administration

Belhaven University, School of Education, Jackson, MS 39202-1789. Offers educational technology (M Ed); elementary education (M Ed, MAT); reading literacy (M Ed); secondary education (M Ed, MAT). *Program availability:* Part-time, evening/weekend, 100% online, blended/hybrid learning. *Faculty:* 36 full-time (27 women), 9 part-time/adjunct (6 women). *Students:* 319 full-time (270 women), 403 part-time (318 women); includes 502 minority (486 Black or African American, non-Hispanic/Latino; 2 Asian, non-Hispanic/Latino; 3 Hispanic/Latino; 11 Two or more races, non-Hispanic/Latino). Average age 35. In 2016, 78 master's awarded. *Degree requirements:* For master's, comprehensive exam, portfolio. *Entrance requirements:* For master's, PRAXIS I and II, minimum GPA of 2.8. *Application deadline:* Applications are processed on a rolling basis. Application fee: $25. Electronic applications accepted. *Expenses:* $495 per credit hour plus $75 technology fee per course. *Financial support:* Applicants required to submit FAFSA. *Unit head:* Dr. David Hand, Dean, 601-965-7020, E-mail: dhand@belhaven.edu. *Application contact:* Sean Kirnan, Assistant Vice President for Adult and Graduate Enrollment and Student Services, 601-968-8727, Fax: 601-968-5953, E-mail: gradadmission@belhaven.edu.
Website: http://graduateed.belhaven.edu

Bellevue University, Graduate School, College of Professional Studies, Bellevue, NE 68005-3098. Offers instructional design and development (MS); justice administration and criminal management (MS); leadership (MA); organizational performance (MS); public administration (MPA); security management (MS).

Bloomsburg University of Pennsylvania, School of Graduate Studies, College of Science and Technology, Department of Instructional Technology, Bloomsburg, PA 17815-1301. Offers corporate instructional technology (MS); eLearning developer (Certificate). *Program availability:* Online learning. *Faculty:* 5 full-time (1 woman), 3 part-time/adjunct (2 women). *Students:* 21 full-time (12 women), 46 part-time (28 women); includes 13 minority (5 Black or African American, non-Hispanic/Latino; 3 Asian, non-Hispanic/Latino; 4 Hispanic/Latino; 1 Two or more races, non-Hispanic/Latino). Average age 32. 41 applicants, 66% accepted, 24 enrolled. In 2016, 47 master's, 1 other advanced degree awarded. *Degree requirements:* For master's, thesis optional. *Entrance requirements:* For master's, minimum QPA of 2.8, 3 letters of recommendation, personal statement. Additional exam requirements/recommendations for international students: Required—TOEFL (minimum score 550 paper-based), IELTS. *Application deadline:* Applications are processed on a rolling basis. Application fee: $35 ($60 for international students). Electronic applications accepted. *Expenses:* Tuition, state resident: full-time $9660; part-time $483 per credit. Tuition, nonresident: full-time $14,500; part-time $725 per credit. *Required fees:* $2410; $107 per credit. $75 per term. Tuition and fees vary according to course load, degree level and program. *Financial support:* Career-related internships or fieldwork, Federal Work-Study, and unspecified assistantships available. Financial award applicants required to submit FAFSA. *Unit head:* Dr. Helmut Doll, MS Program Coordinator, 570-389-4848, Fax: 570-389-4943, E-mail: hdoll@bloomu.edu. *Application contact:* Jennifer Kessler, Administrative Assistant, 570-389-4015, Fax: 570-389-3054, E-mail: jkessler@bloomu.edu.
Website: http://iit.bloomu.edu/

Boise State University, College of Education, Department of Educational Technology, Boise, ID 83725. Offers educational technology (MET, MS, Ed D); online teaching (Graduate Certificate); school technology coordination (Graduate Certificate); technology integration (Graduate Certificate). *Accreditation:* NCATE. *Program availability:* Part-time, 100% online, blended/hybrid learning. *Faculty:* 27. *Students:* 13 full-time (7 women), 422 part-time (242 women); includes 41 minority (11 Black or African American, non-Hispanic/Latino; 1 American Indian or Alaska Native, non-Hispanic/Latino; 9 Asian, non-Hispanic/Latino; 17 Hispanic/Latino; 1 Native Hawaiian or other Pacific Islander, non-Hispanic/Latino; 2 Two or more races, non-Hispanic/Latino), 17 international. Average age 38. 192 applicants, 68% accepted, 72 enrolled. In 2016, 151 master's awarded. Terminal master's awarded for partial completion of doctoral program. *Degree requirements:* For master's, thesis optional; for doctorate, thesis/dissertation. *Entrance requirements:* For master's, minimum GPA of 3.0; for doctorate, GRE General Test. Additional exam requirements/recommendations for international students: Required—TOEFL (minimum score 550 paper-based; 80 iBT), IELTS (minimum score 6). *Application deadline:* For fall admission, 2/15 for domestic and international students; for spring admission, 9/15 for domestic and international students. Applications are processed on a rolling basis. Application fee: $65 ($95 for international students). Electronic applications accepted. *Expenses:* Tuition, state resident: full-time $6058; part-time $358 per credit hour. Tuition, nonresident: full-time $20,108; part-time $608 per credit hour. *Required fees:* $2108. Tuition and fees vary according to program. *Financial support:* In 2016–17, 12 students received support, including 1 teaching assistantship (averaging $2,148 per year); scholarships/grants and unspecified assistantships also available. Financial award application deadline: 3/1; financial award applicants required to submit FAFSA. *Unit head:* Dr. Brett Shelton, Department Chair, 208-426-3391, E-mail: brettshelton@boisestate.edu. *Application contact:* Dr. Ross Perkins, Admissions Coordinator, 208-426-4875, E-mail: edtechdoc@boisestate.edu.
Website: http://edtech.boisestate.edu/

Bowling Green State University, Graduate College, College of Education and Human Development, School of Teaching and Learning, Program in Classroom Technology, Bowling Green, OH 43403. Offers M Ed. *Accreditation:* NCATE. *Program availability:* Part-time, evening/weekend. *Degree requirements:* For master's, thesis or alternative. *Entrance requirements:* For master's, GRE General Test. Additional exam requirements/recommendations for international students: Required—TOEFL. *Application deadline:* Applications are processed on a rolling basis. Application fee: $30. Electronic applications accepted. *Financial support:* Research assistantships with full tuition reimbursements, teaching assistantships with full tuition reimbursements, career-related internships or fieldwork, Federal Work-Study, and institutionally sponsored loans available. Financial award applicants required to submit FAFSA. *Unit head:* Dr. Cindy Hendricks, Director, 419-372-7341. *Application contact:* Dr. Gregg Brownell, Graduate Coordinator, 419-372-9546.

Bridgewater State University, College of Graduate Studies, College of Education and Allied Studies, Department of Secondary Education and Professional Programs, Program in Instructional Technology, Bridgewater, MA 02325. Offers M Ed. *Program availability:* Part-time, evening/weekend. *Entrance requirements:* For master's, GRE General Test or Massachusetts Test for Educator Licensure.

Brigham Young University, Graduate Studies, David O. McKay School of Education, Department of Instructional Psychology and Technology, Provo, UT 84602. Offers MS, PhD. *Faculty:* 10 full-time (1 woman). *Students:* 40 full-time (15 women), 32 part-time (14 women); includes 3 minority (all Native Hawaiian or other Pacific Islander, non-Hispanic/Latino), 1 international. Average age 36. 46 applicants, 52% accepted, 21 enrolled. In 2016, 18 master's, 12 doctorates awarded. *Degree requirements:* For master's, thesis; for doctorate, comprehensive exam, thesis/dissertation. *Entrance requirements:* For master's and doctorate, GRE General Test. Additional exam requirements/recommendations for international students: Required—TOEFL. *Application deadline:* For fall admission, 1/2 for domestic students, 2/1 for international students; for winter admission, 2/1 for international students; for summer admission, 2/1 for international students. Application fee: $50. Electronic applications accepted. *Expenses: Tuition:* Full-time $6680; part-time $393 per credit. Tuition and fees vary according to course load, program and student's religious affiliation. *Financial support:* In 2016–17, 21 students received support, including 22 research assistantships with tuition reimbursements available (averaging $10,000 per year), 12 teaching assistantships with tuition reimbursements available (averaging $7,000 per year); career-related internships or fieldwork, scholarships/grants, tuition waivers (full and partial), and unspecified assistantships also available. Support available to part-time students. Financial award application deadline: 4/15. *Faculty research:* Interactive learning, learning theory, instructional designed development, research and evaluation, measurement. *Unit head:* Dr. Charles R. Graham, Department Chair, 801-422-4110, Fax: 801-422-0314, E-mail: charles.graham@byu.edu. *Application contact:* Michele Bray, Department Secretary, 801-422-2746, Fax: 801-422-0314, E-mail: michele_bray@byu.edu.
Website: http://education.byu.edu/ipt/

Brigham Young University, Graduate Studies, Ira A. Fulton College of Engineering and Technology, School of Technology, Provo, UT 84602. Offers construction management (MS); information technology (MS); manufacturing engineering technology (MS); technology and engineering education (MS). *Faculty:* 25 full-time (0 women), 3 part-time/adjunct (0 women). *Students:* 36 full-time (4 women); includes 5 minority (2 American Indian or Alaska Native, non-Hispanic/Latino; 2 Asian, non-Hispanic/Latino; 1 Hispanic/Latino). Average age 29. 14 applicants, 100% accepted, 13 enrolled. In 2016, 11 master's awarded. *Degree requirements:* For master's, thesis. *Entrance requirements:* For master's, GRE General Test; GMAT or GRE (for construction management emphasis), minimum GPA of 3.0 in last 60 hours of course work. Additional exam requirements/recommendations for international students: Required—TOEFL (minimum score 580 paper-based; 85 iBT). *Application deadline:* For fall admission, 2/15 for domestic and international students; for winter admission, 9/10 for domestic students, 9/15 for international students; for spring admission, 2/15 for domestic and international students; for summer admission, 2/15 for domestic and international students. Application fee: $50. Electronic applications accepted. *Expenses: Tuition:* Full-time $6680; part-time $393 per credit. Tuition and fees vary according to course load, program and student's religious affiliation. *Financial support:* In 2016–17, 28 students received support, including 3 research assistantships (averaging $18,288 per year), 11 teaching assistantships (averaging $7,500 per year); scholarships/grants also available. *Faculty research:* Information assurance and security, HEI and databases, manufacturing materials, processes and systems, innovation in construction management scheduling and delivery methods. *Total annual research expenditures:* $844,333. *Unit head:* Dr. Barry M. Lunt, Director, 801-422-6300, Fax: 801-422-0490, E-mail: blunt@byu.edu. *Application contact:* Clifton Farnsworth, Graduate Coordinator, 801-422-6494, Fax: 801-422-0490, E-mail: clifton_farnsworth@byu.edu.
Website: http://www.et.byu.edu/sot/

Buffalo State College, State University of New York, The Graduate School, Faculty of Applied Science and Education, Department of Computer Information Systems, Program in Educational Computing, Buffalo, NY 14222-1095. Offers MS Ed. *Accreditation:* NCATE. *Program availability:* Part-time, evening/weekend. *Degree requirements:* For master's, thesis, project. *Entrance requirements:* Additional exam requirements/recommendations for international students: Required—TOEFL (minimum score 550 paper-based).

California Baptist University, Program in Education, Riverside, CA 92504-3206. Offers educational leadership (MS); educational leadership for faith-based institutions (MS); educational leadership for public institutions (MS); educational technology (MS); instructional computer applications (MS); international education (MS); leadership and adult learning (MS); leadership and organizational studies (MS); online teaching and learning (MS); reading (MS); science education (MA); special education in mild/moderate disabilities (MS); special education in moderate/severe disabilities (MS); teacher leadership (MS); teaching (MS); teaching and learning (MS). *Program availability:* Part-time, evening/weekend, 100% online, blended/hybrid learning. *Faculty:* 20 full-time (8 women), 11 part-time/adjunct (7 women). *Students:* 191 full-time (148 women), 234 part-time (178 women); includes 194 minority (23 Black or African American, non-Hispanic/Latino; 5 American Indian or Alaska Native, non-Hispanic/Latino; 15 Asian, non-Hispanic/Latino; 131 Hispanic/Latino; 4 Native Hawaiian or other Pacific Islander, non-Hispanic/Latino; 16 Two or more races, non-Hispanic/Latino), 2 international. Average age 31. 277 applicants, 61% accepted, 150 enrolled. In 2016, 280 master's awarded. *Degree requirements:* For master's, comprehensive exam, project, or thesis. *Entrance requirements:* For master's, minimum undergraduate GPA of 2.75; 500-word essay; three letters of recommendation; two prerequisite courses completed with minimum C grade. Additional exam requirements/recommendations for international students: Required—TOEFL (minimum score 80 iBT). *Application deadline:* For fall admission, 8/1 priority date for domestic students, 7/1 for international students; for spring admission, 12/1 priority date for domestic students, 11/1 for international students. Applications are processed on a rolling basis. Application fee: $45. Electronic applications accepted. *Expenses:* Contact institution. *Financial support:* In 2016–17, 162 students received support. Federal Work-Study and scholarships/grants available. Financial award applicants required to submit CSS PROFILE or FAFSA. *Faculty research:* Leadership development, complexity theory, faith and learning, special education, social and philosophical contexts of education. *Unit head:* Dr. John Shoup, Dean, School of Education, 951-343-4516, E-mail: jshoup@calbaptist.edu.
Website: http://www.calbaptist.edu/mastersined/

California State University, East Bay, Office of Graduate Studies, College of Education and Allied Studies, Department of Teacher Education, Hayward, CA 94542-3000. Offers education (MS), including curriculum, early childhood education, educational technology and leadership, reading instruction. *Program availability:* Online learning. *Students:* 55 full-time (43 women), 21 part-time (15 women); includes 34 minority (5 Black or African American, non-Hispanic/Latino; 1 American Indian or Alaska Native, non-Hispanic/Latino; 14 Asian, non-Hispanic/Latino; 10 Hispanic/Latino; 1 Native Hawaiian or other Pacific Islander, non-Hispanic/Latino; 3 Two or more races, non-Hispanic/Latino), 6 international. Average age 33. 65 applicants, 91% accepted, 11 enrolled. In 2016, 67 master's awarded. *Degree requirements:* For master's, project or thesis. *Entrance requirements:* For master's, minimum GPA of 3.0 in field, 2.5 overall; teaching experience; baccalaureate degree; 3 letters of recommendation. Additional exam requirements/recommendations for international students: Required—TOEFL (minimum score 550 paper-based), IELTS. *Application deadline:* For fall admission, 6/30 for domestic and international students. Application fee: $55. Electronic applications accepted. *Financial support:* Career-related internships or fieldwork, Federal Work-Study, and institutionally sponsored loans available. Support available to part-time students. Financial award application deadline: 3/2; financial award applicants required to submit FAFSA. *Faculty research:* Online, pedagogy, writing, learning, teaching. *Unit head:* Dr. Eric Engdahl, Chair, 510-885-4599, E-mail: eric.engdahl@csueastbay.edu.

Application contact: Prof. Valerie Helgren-Lempesis, Education Graduate Advisor, 510-885-3006, Fax: 510-885-4632, E-mail: valerie.helgren-lempesis@csueastbay.edu.
Website: http://www20.csueastbay.edu/ceas/departments/ted/index.html

California State University, Fullerton, Graduate Studies, College of Education, Department of Elementary and Bilingual Education, Fullerton, CA 92834-9480. Offers bilingual/bicultural education (MS); educational technology (MS); elementary curriculum and instruction (MS). *Accreditation:* NCATE. *Program availability:* Part-time. *Degree requirements:* For master's, comprehensive exam, project or thesis. *Entrance requirements:* For master's, minimum GPA of 2.5, teaching certificate. Application fee: $55. *Expenses:* Tuition, state resident: full-time $3369; part-time $1953 per unit. Tuition, nonresident: full-time $3915; part-time $2499 per unit. Tuition and fees vary according to course load, degree level and program. *Financial support:* Career-related internships or fieldwork, Federal Work-Study, institutionally sponsored loans, and scholarships/grants available. Support available to part-time students. Financial award application deadline: 3/1; financial award applicants required to submit FAFSA. *Faculty research:* Teacher training and tracking, model for improvement of teaching. *Unit head:* Lisa Kirtman, Chair, 657-278-4731. *Application contact:* Admissions/Applications, 657-278-2371.
Website: http://ed.fullerton.edu/EDEL/

California State University, Fullerton, Graduate Studies, College of Education, Program in Instructional Design and Technology, Fullerton, CA 92834-9480. Offers MS. *Program availability:* Part-time, online learning. Application fee: $55. *Expenses:* Tuition, state resident: full-time $3369; part-time $1953 per unit. Tuition, nonresident: full-time $3915; part-time $2499 per unit. Tuition and fees vary according to course load, degree level and program. *Financial support:* Career-related internships or fieldwork, Federal Work-Study, institutionally sponsored loans, and scholarships/grants available. Support available to part-time students. Financial award application deadline: 3/1; financial award applicants required to submit FAFSA. *Unit head:* Dr. Jo Ann Carter-Wells, Chair, 657-278-3357. *Application contact:* Admissions/Applications, 657-278-2371.
Website: http://ed.fullerton.edu/msidt/

California State University, Northridge, Graduate Studies, Michael D. Eisner College of Education, Department of Secondary Education, Northridge, CA 91330. Offers educational technology (MA); English education (MA); mathematics education (MA); secondary science education (MA); teaching and learning (MA). *Accreditation:* NCATE. *Program availability:* Part-time. *Faculty:* 10 full-time (5 women), 50 part-time/adjunct (24 women). *Students:* 17 full-time (10 women), 87 part-time (55 women); includes 41 minority (3 Black or African American, non-Hispanic/Latino; 11 Asian, non-Hispanic/Latino; 24 Hispanic/Latino; 1 Native Hawaiian or other Pacific Islander, non-Hispanic/Latino; 2 Two or more races, non-Hispanic/Latino), 4 international. Average age 37. 80 applicants, 80% accepted, 50 enrolled. *Degree requirements:* For master's, thesis optional. *Entrance requirements:* For master's, GRE General Test or minimum GPA of 3.0. Additional exam requirements/recommendations for international students: Required—TOEFL. *Application deadline:* For fall admission, 11/30 for domestic students. Application fee: $55. *Expenses:* Tuition, state resident: full-time $4152. *Financial support:* Application deadline: 3/1. *Unit head:* Dr. Julie Gainsburg, Chair, 818-677-2580. *Application contact:* Dr. Michael Rivas, Graduate Advisor, 818-677-6792, E-mail: michael.rivas@csun.edu.
Website: http://www.csun.edu/eisner-education/secondary-education

California State University, Sacramento, Office of Graduate Studies, College of Education, Graduate and Professional Studies in Education, Sacramento, CA 95819. Offers child development (MA); counseling (MS); curriculum and instruction (MA); education (Ed D); education leadership and policy studies (MA), including higher education, PreK-12; educational technology (MA); gender equity (MA); language and literacy (MA); multicultural education (MA); school psychology (MA); special education (MA); workforce development advocacy (MA). *Program availability:* Part-time. *Students:* 446 full-time (335 women), 125 part-time (97 women); includes 298 minority (39 Black or African American, non-Hispanic/Latino; 3 American Indian or Alaska Native, non-Hispanic/Latino; 97 Asian, non-Hispanic/Latino; 153 Hispanic/Latino; 6 Native Hawaiian or other Pacific Islander, non-Hispanic/Latino). Average age 32. 540 applicants, 76% accepted, 250 enrolled. In 2016, 107 master's, 7 doctorates awarded. *Degree requirements:* For master's, thesis or project; writing proficiency exam. *Entrance requirements:* For master's, minimum GPA of 2.5, 3.0 in last 60 units. Additional exam requirements/recommendations for international students: Required—TOEFL (minimum score 550 paper-based; 80 iBT). *Application deadline:* For fall admission, 2/15 for domestic students, 1/15 for international students. Applications are processed on a rolling basis. Application fee: $55. Electronic applications accepted. *Expenses:* $4,302 full-time tuition and fees per semester, $2,796 part-time. *Financial support:* Career-related internships or fieldwork and Federal Work-Study available. Support available to part-time students. Financial award application deadline: 3/1; financial award applicants required to submit FAFSA. *Unit head:* Dr. Susan Heredia, Chair, 916-278-5942, E-mail: coe@csus.edu. *Application contact:* Jose Martinez, Graduate Admissions Supervisor, 916-278-7871, E-mail: martinj@skymail.csus.edu.
Website: http://www.csus.edu/coe/academics/graduate/index.html

California State University, Stanislaus, College of Education, Program in Education (MA), Turlock, CA 95382. Offers curriculum and instruction (MA), including education technology, elementary education, multilingual education, physical education, reading, secondary education, special education; school administration (MA); school counseling (MA). *Program availability:* Part-time, evening/weekend. *Degree requirements:* For master's, comprehensive exam (for some programs), thesis (for some programs). *Entrance requirements:* For master's, MAT, GRE, or CBEST (varies by concentration), 3 letters of recommendation, personal statement. Additional exam requirements/recommendations for international students: Required—TOEFL (minimum score 550 paper-based). Electronic applications accepted. *Faculty research:* Children's perspectives on historical events, method elementary schools dual language education, K-12 reading programs.

Cambridge College, School of Education, Cambridge, MA 02138-5304. Offers autism specialist (M Ed); autism/behavior analyst (M Ed); behavior analyst (Post-Master's Certificate); behavioral management (M Ed); early childhood teacher (M Ed); education specialist in curriculum and instruction (CAGS); educational leadership (Ed D); elementary teacher (M Ed); English as a second language (M Ed, Certificate); general science (M Ed); health education (Post-Master's Certificate); health/family and consumer sciences (M Ed); history (M Ed); individualized (M Ed); information technology literacy (M Ed); instructional technology (M Ed); interdisciplinary studies (M Ed); library teacher (M Ed); literacy education (M Ed); mathematics (M Ed); mathematics specialist (Certificate); middle school mathematics and science (M Ed); school administration (M Ed, CAGS); school guidance counselor (M Ed); school nurse education (M Ed); school social worker/school adjustment counselor (M Ed); special education administrator (CAGS); special education/moderate disabilities (M Ed); teaching skills and methodologies (M Ed). *Program availability:* Part-time, evening/weekend, online learning. *Degree requirements:* For master's, thesis, internship/practicum (licensure program only); for doctorate, thesis/dissertation; for other advanced degree, thesis. *Entrance requirements:* For master's, interview, resume, documentation of licensure, 2 professional references; for doctorate, official transcripts, interview, resume, documentation of licensure (if any), written personal statement/essay, portfolio of scholarly and professional work, qualifying assessment, 2 professional references, health insurance, immunizations form; for other advanced degree, official transcripts, interview, resume, documentation of licensure (if any), written personal statement/essay, 2 professional references, health insurance, immunizations form. Additional exam requirements/recommendations for international students: Required—TOEFL (minimum score 550 paper-based; 79 iBT), Michigan English Language Assessment Battery (minimum score 85); Recommended—IELTS (minimum score 6). Electronic applications accepted. *Expenses:* Contact institution. *Faculty research:* Adult education, accelerated learning, mathematics education, brain compatible learning, special education and law.

Canisius College, Graduate Division, School of Education and Human Services, Department of Graduate Education and Leadership, Buffalo, NY 14208-1098. Offers business and marketing education (MS Ed); college student personnel (MS Ed); deaf education (MS Ed); deaf/adolescent education, grades 7-12 (MS Ed); deaf/childhood education, grades 1-6 (MS Ed); differentiated instruction (MS Ed); education administration (MS); educational administration (MS Ed); educational technologies (Certificate); gifted education extension (Certificate); literacy (MS Ed); reading (Certificate); school building leadership (MS Ed, Certificate); school district leadership (Certificate); teacher leader (Certificate); TESOL (MS Ed). *Accreditation:* NCATE. *Program availability:* Part-time, evening/weekend, 100% online, blended/hybrid learning. *Faculty:* 5 full-time (all women), 23 part-time/adjunct (16 women). *Students:* 95 full-time (78 women), 223 part-time (177 women); includes 31 minority (15 Black or African American, non-Hispanic/Latino; 2 American Indian or Alaska Native, non-Hispanic/Latino; 4 Asian, non-Hispanic/Latino; 9 Hispanic/Latino; 1 Two or more races, non-Hispanic/Latino), 1 international. Average age 30. 162 applicants, 89% accepted, 135 enrolled. In 2016, 135 master's, 39 other advanced degrees awarded. *Entrance requirements:* For master's, GRE (if cumulative GPA less than 2.7), transcripts, two letters of recommendation. Additional exam requirements/recommendations for international students: Required—TOEFL (minimum score 550 paper-based, 79 iBT), IELTS (minimum score 6.5), or CAEL (minimum score 70). *Application deadline:* Applications are processed on a rolling basis. Application fee: $25. Electronic applications accepted. Application fee is waived when completed online. *Expenses:* *Tuition:* Full-time $14,742. *Required fees:* $724. *Financial support:* Career-related internships or fieldwork, Federal Work-Study, scholarships/grants, tuition waivers (partial), and unspecified assistantships available. Support available to part-time students. Financial award application deadline: 4/30; financial award applicants required to submit FAFSA. *Faculty research:* Asperger's disease, autism, private higher education, reading strategies. *Unit head:* Dr. Rosemary K. Murray, Chair/Associate Professor of Graduate Education and Leadership, 716-888-3723, E-mail: murray1@canisius.edu. *Application contact:* Kathleen B. Davis, Vice President of Enrollment Management, 716-888-2500, Fax: 716-888-3195, E-mail: daviskb@canisius.edu.
Website: http://www.canisius.edu/graduate/

Capella University, School of Education, Doctoral Programs in Education, Minneapolis, MN 55402. Offers curriculum and instruction (PhD); educational leadership and management (Ed D); instructional design for online learning (PhD); K-12 studies in education (PhD); leadership for higher education (PhD); leadership in educational administration (PhD); postsecondary and adult education (PhD); professional studies in education (PhD); reading and literacy (Ed D); special education leadership (PhD); training and performance improvement (PhD).

Capella University, School of Education, Master's Programs in Education, Minneapolis, MN 55402. Offers adult education (MS); curriculum and instruction (MS); early childhood education (MS); enrollment management (MS); higher education leadership and management (MS); instructional design for online learning (MS); integrative studies (MS); K-12 studies in education (MS); leadership in educational administration (MS); reading and literacy (MS); special education teaching (MS).

Caribbean University, Graduate School, Bayamón, PR 00960-0493. Offers administration and supervision (MA Ed); criminal justice (MA); curriculum and instruction (MA Ed, PhD), including elementary education (MA Ed), English education (MA Ed), history education (MA Ed), mathematics education (MA Ed), primary education (MA Ed), science education (MA Ed), Spanish education (MA Ed); educational technology in instructional systems (MA Ed); gerontology (MSN); human resources (MBA); museology, archiving and art history (MA Ed); neonatal pediatrics (MSN); physical education (MA Ed); special education (MA Ed). *Entrance requirements:* For master's, interview, minimum GPA of 2.5.

Central Michigan University, Central Michigan University Global Campus, Program in Education, Mount Pleasant, MI 48859. Offers college teaching (Graduate Certificate); community college (MA); curriculum and instruction (MA); educational technology (MA, DET); reading and literacy K-12 (MA); school principalship (MA), including charter school leadership; training and development (MA). *Accreditation:* TEAC. *Program availability:* Part-time, evening/weekend. *Faculty:* 24 full-time (14 women), 24 part-time/adjunct (8 women). *Students:* 888 (620 women); includes 225 minority (142 Black or African American, non-Hispanic/Latino; 8 American Indian or Alaska Native, non-Hispanic/Latino; 16 Asian, non-Hispanic/Latino; 13 Hispanic/Latino; 46 Two or more races, non-Hispanic/Latino). Average age 37. In 2016, 76 master's awarded. *Entrance requirements:* For master's, minimum GPA of 2.7 in major. Additional exam requirements/recommendations for international students: Required—TOEFL. *Application deadline:* Applications are processed on a rolling basis. Application fee: $50. Electronic applications accepted. *Financial support:* Scholarships/grants available. Support available to part-time students. *Unit head:* Kaleb Patrick, Director, 989-774-3144, E-mail: patri1kg@cmich.edu. *Application contact:* 877-268-4636, E-mail: cmuglobal@cmich.edu.

Central Michigan University, College of Graduate Studies, College of Education and Human Services, Department of Educational Leadership, Mount Pleasant, MI 48859. Offers educational leadership (Ed D), including educational technology (Ed D, Ed S), higher education leadership, K-12 curriculum, K-12 leadership; general educational administration (Ed S), including administrative leadership K-12, educational technology (Ed D, Ed S), higher education administration, instructional leadership K-12; school principalship (MA), including charter school leadership, site-based leadership; student affairs administration (MA); teacher leadership (MA). *Program availability:* Part-time, evening/weekend. *Degree requirements:* For master's and Ed S, thesis or alternative; for doctorate, thesis/dissertation. *Entrance requirements:* For doctorate, GRE or MAT, master's degree, minimum GPA of 3.5, 3 years of professional education experience. Electronic applications accepted. *Faculty research:* Elementary administration, secondary administration, student achievement, in-service training, internships in administration.

Central Michigan University, College of Graduate Studies, College of Education and Human Services, Department of Teacher Education and Professional Development, Mount Pleasant, MI 48859. Offers educational technology (MA, Graduate Certificate); elementary education (MA), including classroom teaching, early childhood; reading and literacy K-12 (MA); secondary education (MA). *Program availability:* Part-time, evening/weekend. *Degree requirements:* For master's, thesis or alternative. Electronic applications accepted. *Faculty research:* Integrating literacy across the curriculum, science teaching and aesthetic learning in science, diversity education, educational technology, educational psychology and child development.

Chestnut Hill College, School of Graduate Studies, Program in Instructional Technology, Philadelphia, PA 19118-2693. Offers instructional technology (MS, CAS), including instructional design and e-learning, instructional design and e-learning with instructional technology specialist certification preparation. *Program availability:* Part-time, evening/weekend. *Degree requirements:* For master's, special project/internship. *Entrance requirements:* For master's, GRE General Test or MAT, letters of recommendation, writing sample. Additional exam requirements/recommendations for international students: Required—TOEFL (minimum score 500 paper-based), IELTS (minimum score 6.0), or TWE (minimum score 22). Electronic applications accepted. *Expenses:* Contact institution. *Faculty research:* Instructional design, learning management systems and related technologies, video as a teaching and learning tool, Web 2.0 technologies and virtual worlds as a learning tool, utilization of laptops and iPads in the classroom.

Chicago State University, School of Graduate and Professional Studies, College of Education, Department of Reading, Elementary Education, Library Information and Media Studies, Program in Library Information and Media Studies, Chicago, IL 60628. Offers MS Ed. *Entrance requirements:* For master's, minimum GPA of 2.75.

Chicago State University, School of Graduate and Professional Studies, College of Education, Department of Technology and Education, Chicago, IL 60628. Offers secondary education (MAT); technology and education (MS Ed). *Program availability:* Online learning. *Degree requirements:* For master's, thesis optional. *Entrance requirements:* For master's, minimum GPA of 2.75.

Cleary University, Online Program in Business Administration, Howell, MI 48843. Offers analytics, technology, and innovation (MBA, Graduate Certificate); financial planning (Graduate Certificate); global leadership (MBA, Graduate Certificate); health care leadership (MBA, Graduate Certificate). *Program availability:* Part-time, evening/weekend, online learning. *Faculty:* 13 part-time/adjunct (6 women). *Students:* 92 full-time (47 women), 25 part-time (14 women). *Degree requirements:* For master's, thesis. *Entrance requirements:* For master's, bachelor's degree; minimum GPA of 2.5; professional resume indicating minimum of 2 years of management or related experience; undergraduate degree from accredited college or university with at least 18 quarter hours (or 12 semester hours) of accounting study (for MBA in accounting). Additional exam requirements/recommendations for international students: Required—TOEFL (minimum score 550 paper-based; 79 iBT), Michigan English Language Assessment Battery (minimum score 75). *Application deadline:* For fall admission, 8/15 for domestic students, 7/15 for international students; for spring admission, 4/2 for domestic students, 1/2 for international students. Applications are processed on a rolling basis. Application fee: $50. Electronic applications accepted. *Expenses: Tuition:* Full-time $16,560; part-time $920 per credit hour. *Required fees:* $100 per semester. *Financial support:* Fellowships, Federal Work-Study, and scholarships/grants available. Support available to part-time students. Financial award application deadline: 8/15; financial award applicants required to submit FAFSA. *Unit head:* Dr. Lance B. Lewis, Provost and Chief Academic Officer, 800-686-1883, E-mail: llewis@cleary.edu. *Application contact:* Cassandra Tarnowski, Director of Admissions, 800-686-1883, Fax: 517-338-3336, E-mail: ctarnowski@cleary.edu.

Cleveland State University, College of Graduate Studies, College of Education and Human Services, Program in Urban Education, Specialization in Learning and Development, Cleveland, OH 44115. Offers PhD. *Program availability:* Part-time. *Faculty:* 17 full-time (9 women). *Students:* 1 (woman) full-time, 13 part-time (10 women); includes 6 minority (5 Black or African American, non-Hispanic/Latino; 1 Asian, non-Hispanic/Latino), 2 international. Average age 47. 18 applicants, 28% accepted. In 2016, 9 doctorates awarded. *Degree requirements:* For doctorate, one foreign language, comprehensive exam, thesis/dissertation. *Entrance requirements:* For doctorate, GRE General Test (minimum score of 297 for combined Verbal and Quantitative exams, 4.0 preferred for Analytical Writing), minimum graduate GPA of 3.25 in educational psychology, school psychology and/or special education; curriculum vitae or resume; personal statement; 2 letters of recommendation. Additional exam requirements/recommendations for international students: Required—TOEFL (minimum score 550 paper-based; 78 iBT), IELTS (minimum score 6). *Application deadline:* For fall admission, 1/15 for domestic and international students. Application fee: $40. Electronic applications accepted. *Expenses:* Tuition, state resident: full-time $9565. Tuition, nonresident: full-time $17,980. Tuition and fees vary according to program. *Financial support:* In 2016–17, 5 students received support, including 1 research assistantship with full tuition reimbursement available, 2 teaching assistantships with full tuition reimbursements available (averaging $10,325 per year); tuition waivers also available. Support available to part-time students. Financial award application deadline: 4/1; financial award applicants required to submit FAFSA. *Faculty research:* Implications of human variability to instruction service delivery in educational and social agencies. *Unit head:* Dr. Graham Stead, Director, Doctoral Studies, 216-875-9869, E-mail: g.b.stead@csuohio.edu. *Application contact:* Rita M. Grabowski, Administrative Coordinator, 216-687-4697, Fax: 216-875-9697, E-mail: r.grabowski@csuohio.edu.
Website: http://www.csuohio.edu/cehs/casal/programs-0

Coastal Carolina University, Spadoni College of Education, Conway, SC 29528-6054. Offers education (MAT); educational leadership (M Ed, Ed S); English for speakers of other languages (Certificate); instructional technology (M Ed, Ed S); learning and teaching (M Ed); online teaching and training (Certificate); special education (M Ed). *Accreditation:* NCATE. *Program availability:* Part-time, evening/weekend. *Faculty:* 16 full-time (8 women), 12 part-time/adjunct (7 women). *Students:* 74 full-time (48 women), 340 part-time (271 women); includes 78 minority (70 Black or African American, non-Hispanic/Latino; 1 American Indian or Alaska Native, non-Hispanic/Latino; 2 Asian, non-Hispanic/Latino; 4 Hispanic/Latino; 1 Two or more races, non-Hispanic/Latino), 2 international. Average age 33. 298 applicants, 93% accepted, 213 enrolled. In 2016, 167 master's, 8 other advanced degrees awarded. *Degree requirements:* For master's and other advanced degree, comprehensive exam. *Entrance requirements:* For master's, GRE, GMAT, 2 letters of recommendation, evidence of teacher certification, official transcripts; for other advanced degree, official transcripts, minimum of 3 years' teaching experience, statement of interest in the program, 3 letters of reference, master's degree in educational leadership or related field with minimum overall GPA of 3.0. Additional exam requirements/recommendations for international students: Required—TOEFL (minimum score 550 paper-based; 79 iBT), IELTS (minimum score 6.5). *Application deadline:* For fall admission, 7/1 priority date for domestic and international students; for spring admission, 11/1 priority date for domestic and international students; for summer admission, 3/1 priority date for domestic and international students. Applications are processed on a rolling basis. Application fee: $45. Electronic applications accepted. *Expenses:* Tuition, state resident: full-time $9990; part-time $555 per credit hour. Tuition, nonresident: full-time $18,108; part-time $1006 per credit hour. *Required fees:* $90; $5 per credit hour. *Financial support:* Fellowships, research assistantships, and unspecified assistantships available. Support available to part-time students. Financial award application deadline: 3/1; financial award applicants required to submit FAFSA. *Unit head:* Dr. Edward Jadallah, Dean, 843-349-2773, Fax: 843-349-2106, E-mail: ejadalla@coastal.edu. *Application contact:* Dr. James O. Luken, Associate Provost/Vice-Dean of the Coastal Environment, 843-349-2235, Fax: 843-349-6444, E-mail: joluken@coastal.edu.
Website: http://www.coastal.edu/education/

College of Mount Saint Vincent, School of Professional and Graduate Studies, Department of Teacher Education, Riverdale, NY 10471-1093. Offers instructional technology and global perspectives (Certificate); middle level education (Certificate); multicultural studies (Certificate); teaching English to speakers of other languages (MS Ed); urban and multicultural education (MS Ed). *Accreditation:* TEAC. *Program availability:* Part-time. *Degree requirements:* For master's, comprehensive exam. *Entrance requirements:* For master's, interview, New York teaching certificate. Additional exam requirements/recommendations for international students: Required—TOEFL.

College of Saint Elizabeth, Department of Educational Leadership, Morristown, NJ 07960-6989. Offers assistive technology (Certificate); education (MA); educational leadership (MA, Ed D). *Program availability:* Part-time. *Degree requirements:* For master's, thesis or alternative; for doctorate, thesis/dissertation. *Entrance requirements:* For master's, GRE, GMAT, baccalaureate degree with minimum GPA of 2.75, standard teaching certificate, three years of exemplary certified teaching experience, writing sample, two letters of recommendation from school(s) of employment, personal interview (for educational leadership); for doctorate, GRE, MA in educational leadership or related field; leadership experience including certification as principal and/or supervisor; letter of recommendation from college/university professor attesting to candidate's ability to perform a high level of academic work in the program; for Certificate, MA in education; certification; baccalaureate degree with minimum GPA of 2.75; personal written statement; two letters of recommendation; official transcripts from all colleges attended. Additional exam requirements/recommendations for international students: Required—TOEFL (minimum score 550 paper-based; 79 iBT), IELTS (minimum score 6.5). Electronic applications accepted. Application fee is waived when completed online. *Expenses:* Contact institution.

The College of William and Mary, School of Education, Program in Education Policy, Planning, and Leadership, Williamsburg, VA 23187-8795. Offers curriculum and educational technology (PhD); curriculum leadership (Ed D, PhD); educational leadership (M Ed), including higher education administration (M Ed, Ed D, PhD), K-12 administration and supervision; educational policy, planning, and leadership (Ed D, PhD), including general education administration, gifted education administration, higher education administration (M Ed, Ed D, PhD). *Accreditation:* NCATE. *Program availability:* Part-time, evening/weekend. *Faculty:* 20 full-time (10 women), 21 part-time/adjunct (13 women). *Students:* 63 full-time (45 women), 143 part-time (95 women); includes 53 minority (39 Black or African American, non-Hispanic/Latino; 4 Asian, non-Hispanic/Latino; 6 Hispanic/Latino; 4 Two or more races, non-Hispanic/Latino), 4 international. Average age 38. 122 applicants, 77% accepted, 65 enrolled. In 2016, 26 master's, 24 doctorates awarded. *Degree requirements:* For doctorate, comprehensive exam, thesis/dissertation. *Entrance requirements:* For master's, GRE or MAT, minimum GPA of 2.5; for doctorate, GRE or MAT, minimum GPA of 3.0. Additional exam requirements/recommendations for international students: Required—TOEFL (minimum score 100 iBT), IELTS (minimum score 7). *Application deadline:* For fall admission, 1/15 for domestic and international students. Application fee: $50. Electronic applications accepted. *Expenses:* $14,258 per year in-state full-time, $275 per credit in-state part-time; $30,500 per year out-of-state full-time, $1,200 per credit out-of-state part-time. *Financial support:* In 2016–17, 64 students received support, including 1 fellowship (averaging $20,000 per year), 54 research assistantships (averaging $19,668 per year); institutionally sponsored loans, scholarships/grants, and unspecified assistantships also available. Support available to part-time students. Financial award application deadline: 1/15; financial award applicants required to submit FAFSA. *Faculty research:* Higher education policy, evaluation of teachers, program evaluation, civil rights and higher education, program evaluation. *Unit head:* Dr. Michael F. Dipaola, Department Chair, 757-221-2344, E-mail: mfdipa@wm.edu. *Application contact:* Dorothy Smith Osborne, Assistant Dean for Academic Programs and Student Services, 757-221-2317, E-mail: dsosbo@wm.edu.
Website: http://education.wm.edu

Colorado Christian University, Program in Curriculum and Instruction, Lakewood, CO 80226. Offers corporate education (MACI); early childhood educator (MACI); elementary educator (MACI); instructional technology (MACI); master educator (MACI); online course developer (MACI); online teaching and learning (MACI); special education generalist (MACI). *Program availability:* Part-time, evening/weekend. *Degree requirements:* For master's, thesis optional, practicum. *Entrance requirements:* For master's, interviews, letters of recommendation. Additional exam requirements/recommendations for international students: Required—TOEFL. Electronic applications accepted. *Expenses:* Contact institution.

Colorado State University–Pueblo, College of Education, Engineering and Professional Studies, Education Program, Pueblo, CO 81001-4901. Offers art education (M Ed); foreign language education (M Ed); health and physical education (M Ed); instructional technology (M Ed); linguistically diverse education (M Ed); music education (M Ed); special education (M Ed). *Accreditation:* TEAC. *Program availability:* Part-time. *Degree requirements:* For master's, portfolio. *Entrance requirements:* For master's, 3 recommendations, teaching license. Additional exam requirements/recommendations for international students: Required—TOEFL (minimum score 500 paper-based). Electronic applications accepted. *Faculty research:* Portfolio assessment, math education, science education.

Concordia University, College of Education, Portland, OR 97211-6099. Offers career and technical education (M Ed); curriculum and instruction (M Ed), including adolescent literacy, career and technical education, e-learning/technology education, early childhood education, English for speakers of other languages, English language development, environmental education, mathematics, methods and curriculum, reading, science, teacher leadership, the inclusive classroom; early childhood (MAT); education leadership (Ed D); educational administration (M Ed); elementary education (MAT); secondary education (MAT); special education (M Ed); teacher leadership (Ed D). *Program availability:* Part-time, online learning. *Degree requirements:* For master's, comprehensive exam, work samples/portfolio. *Entrance requirements:* For master's, California Basic Educational Skills Test or PRAXIS I, minimum undergraduate GPA of 2.8, graduate 3.0; 2 letters of recommendation. Additional exam requirements/recommendations for international students: Required—TOEFL (minimum score 525 paper-based). Electronic applications accepted. *Faculty research:* Learner-centered classroom, brain-based learning, future of online learning.

Concordia University, School of Graduate Studies, Faculty of Arts and Science, Department of Education, Program in Educational Technology, Montréal, QC H3G 1M8, Canada. Offers MA. *Degree requirements:* For master's, one foreign language, thesis optional, internship. *Faculty research:* Instructional design and tele-education, educational cybernetics and systems analysis, media research and theory development, distance education.

Educational Media/Instructional Technology

Concordia University, School of Graduate Studies, Faculty of Arts and Science, Department of Education, Program in Instructional Technology, Montréal, QC H3G 1M8, Canada. Offers Diploma. *Entrance requirements:* For degree, BA in related field.

Concordia University Chicago, College of Graduate and Innovative Programs, Program in Educational Technology, River Forest, IL 60305-1499. Offers MA.

Concordia University Irvine, School of Education, Irvine, CA 92612-3299. Offers curriculum and instruction (MA); education and preliminary teaching credential (M Ed); educational administration and preliminary administrative services credential (MA); educational technology (MA); school counseling with pupil personnel services credential (MA). *Program availability:* Part-time, evening/weekend, online learning. *Degree requirements:* For master's, action research project. *Entrance requirements:* For master's, California Basic Educational Skills Test, California Subject Examinations for Teachers (M Ed and MA in educational administration and preliminary administrative services credential), official college transcript(s), signed statement of intent, two references, copy of credential. Additional exam requirements/recommendations for international students: Required—TOEFL. Electronic applications accepted. *Expenses:* Contact institution.

Concordia University, St. Paul, College of Education, St. Paul, MN 55104-5494. Offers classroom instruction (MA Ed), including K-12 reading; differentiated instruction (MA Ed); education (Ed D); educational leadership (MA Ed); educational technology (MA Ed); K-12 principal licensure (Ed S); special education (MA Ed, Certificate), including autism spectrum disorder (MA Ed), emotional and behavioral disorders (MA Ed), learning disabilities (MA Ed); superintendent (Ed S); teaching (MAT). *Accreditation:* NCATE. *Program availability:* Part-time, evening/weekend, 100% online, blended/hybrid learning. *Faculty:* 9 full-time (5 women), 88 part-time/adjunct (52 women). *Students:* 994 full-time (745 women), 40 part-time (34 women); includes 118 minority (40 Black or African American, non-Hispanic/Latino; 7 American Indian or Alaska Native, non-Hispanic/Latino; 33 Asian, non-Hispanic/Latino; 20 Hispanic/Latino; 18 Two or more races, non-Hispanic/Latino), 15 international. Average age 34. 549 applicants, 82% accepted, 372 enrolled. In 2016, 399 master's, 108 other advanced degrees awarded. *Degree requirements:* For master's, thesis (for some programs); for doctorate, thesis/dissertation, capstone projects; for other advanced degree, e-folio review of competencies. *Entrance requirements:* For master's, official transcripts from regionally-accredited institution stating the conferral of a bachelor's degree with minimum cumulative GPA of 3.0; personal statement; professional resume; practitioner in field through work or volunteerism; resume; for doctorate, minimum master's or specialist degree GPA of 3.25; transcript; writing sample; three letters of recommendation; current resume; on-campus interview; for other advanced degree, at least three years of teaching experience; master's degree; valid MN teaching license; writing sample; two letters of recommendation; resume. Additional exam requirements/recommendations for international students: Recommended—TOEFL (minimum score 547 paper-based; 78 iBT), IELTS (minimum score 6). *Application deadline:* For fall admission, 8/1 for domestic and international students; for spring admission, 12/1 for domestic and international students; for summer admission, 5/1 for domestic and international students. Applications are processed on a rolling basis. Application fee: $50. Electronic applications accepted. *Expenses:* Contact institution. *Financial support:* In 2016–17, 112 students received support. Scholarships/grants and unspecified assistantships available. Financial award applicants required to submit FAFSA. *Faculty research:* Differentiated instruction in K-12 educational settings; educational leadership; effective online pedagogy in higher education; equine-assisted learning; faculty development in higher education. *Unit head:* Lonn Maly, Dean, 651-641-8203, E-mail: maly@csp.edu. *Application contact:* Kimberly Craig, Associate Vice President, Cohort Enrollment Management, 651-603-6223, Fax: 651-603-6320, E-mail: craig@csp.edu.

Dakota State University, College of Education, Madison, SD 57042-1799. Offers educational technology (MSET). *Accreditation:* NCATE. *Program availability:* Part-time-only, evening/weekend, online only, 100% online. *Degree requirements:* For master's, thesis, portfolio. *Entrance requirements:* For master's, GRE General Test, demonstration of technology skills, minimum GPA of 2.7. *Application deadline:* For fall admission, 6/15 for domestic students; for spring admission, 11/15 for domestic students; for summer admission, 4/15 for domestic students. Applications are processed on a rolling basis. Application fee: $35. *Expenses:* Tuition, state resident: full-time $7310. Tuition, nonresident: full-time $13,824. *Required fees:* $930. Tuition and fees vary according to program and reciprocity agreements. *Financial support:* Fellowships with partial tuition reimbursements, career-related internships or fieldwork, Federal Work-Study, scholarships/grants, unspecified assistantships, and administrative assistantships available. Support available to part-time students. Financial award applicants required to submit FAFSA. *Faculty research:* Educational technology evaluation, computer-supported collaborative learning, cognitive theory and visual representation of the effects of ubiquitous wireless computing on student learning and productivity, accessible learning, pedagogies for exceptional children. *Unit head:* Dr. Crystal Pauli, Dean, 605-256-5799. *Application contact:* Mark Hawkes, Dean of Graduate Studies and Research/Academic Coordinator, 605-256-5274, Fax: 605-256-5093, E-mail: mark.hawkes@dsu.edu.
Website: http://dsu.edu/graduate-students/mset

Dallas Baptist University, Dorothy M. Bush College of Education, Program in Curriculum and Instruction, Dallas, TX 75211-9299. Offers Christian school administration (M Ed); distance learning (M Ed); English as a second language (M Ed); instructional technology (M Ed); professional life coaching (M Ed); special education (M Ed); supervision (M Ed). *Program availability:* Part-time, evening/weekend, 100% online, blended/hybrid learning. *Application deadline:* Applications are processed on a rolling basis. Application fee: $25. Electronic applications accepted. Application fee is waived when completed online. *Expenses: Tuition:* Full-time $15,408; part-time $856 per credit hour. *Required fees:* $400 per semester. Tuition and fees vary according to course load and degree level. *Unit head:* Dr. Deborah H. Tribble, Director, 214-333-5201, E-mail: debbiet@dbu.edu. *Application contact:* Bobby Soto, Director of Admissions, 214-333-5242, E-mail: graduate@dbu.edu.
Website: http://www3.dbu.edu/graduate/curriculum_instruction.asp

Delaware Valley University, Program in Educational Leadership, Doylestown, PA 18901-2697. Offers instruction, curriculum and technology (MS); school administration and leadership (MS). *Program availability:* Part-time, evening/weekend. *Entrance requirements:* For master's, minimum undergraduate GPA of 3.0.

DeSales University, Division of Liberal Arts and Social Sciences, Center Valley, PA 18034-9568. Offers criminal justice (MCJ); digital forensics (MCJ, Postbaccalaureate Certificate); education (M Ed), including instructional technology, secondary education, special education, teaching English to speakers of other languages; investigative forensics (MCJ, Postbaccalaureate Certificate). *Program availability:* Part-time, 100% online, blended/hybrid learning. *Faculty:* 5 full-time (3 women), 20 part-time/adjunct (13 women). *Students:* 55 full-time (36 women), 100 part-time (64 women); includes 25 minority (5 Black or African American, non-Hispanic/Latino; 14 Hispanic/Latino; 6 Two or more races, non-Hispanic/Latino). Average age 33. 145 applicants, 80% accepted, 103 enrolled. In 2016, 36 master's awarded. *Entrance requirements:* For master's, bachelor's degree from accredited institution, minimum undergraduate GPA of 3.0, personal statement showing potential of graduate work, three letters of recommendation, professional goal statement. Additional exam requirements/recommendations for international students: Required—TOEFL. *Application deadline:* Applications are processed on a rolling basis. Application fee: $50. Electronic applications accepted. *Expenses: Tuition:* Part-time $815 per credit hour. Tuition and fees vary according to degree level and program. *Financial support:* Applicants required to submit FAFSA. *Unit head:* Dr. Brain Kane, Division Head of Liberal Arts and Social Studies, 610-282-1100 Ext. 1274, E-mail: brian.kane@desales.edu. *Application contact:* Julia Ferraro, Director of Graduate Admissions, 610-282-1100 Ext. 1768, E-mail: gradadmissions@desales.edu.

DeVry University–Folsom Campus, Graduate Programs, Folsom, CA 95630. Offers accounting (M Acc); accounting and financial management (MAFM); business administration (MBA); curriculum leadership (M Ed); educational leadership (M Ed); educational technology (M Ed); higher education leadership (M Ed); human resource management (MHRM); information systems management (MISM); network and communications management (MNCM); project management (MPM); public administration (MPA).

Drexel University, Goodwin College of Professional Studies, School of Education, Philadelphia, PA 19104-2875. Offers applied behavior analysis (MS); creativity and innovation (MS); education improvement and transformation (MS); educational administration (MS); educational leadership and management (Ed D); educational leadership development and learning technologies (PhD); global and international education (MS); higher education (MS); human resources development (MS); learning technologies (MS); mathematics, learning and teaching (MS); special education (MS); teaching, learning and curriculum (MS). *Program availability:* Part-time, evening/weekend, online learning. *Degree requirements:* For doctorate, thesis/dissertation. *Entrance requirements:* For doctorate, GRE or GMAT. Additional exam requirements/recommendations for international students: Required—TOEFL, IELTS. Electronic applications accepted. Application fee is waived when completed online. *Expenses:* Contact institution. *Faculty research:* Leadership development, mathematics education, literacy, autism, educational technology.

See Display on page 660 and Close-Up on page 727.

Drexel University, Goodwin College of Professional Studies, School of Technology and Professional Studies, Philadelphia, PA 19104-2875. Offers construction management (MS); creativity and innovation (MS); engineering technology (MS); food science (MS); hospitality management (MS); professional studies: creativity studies (MS); professional studies: e-learning leadership (MS); professional studies: homeland security management (MS); project management (MS); property management (MS); sport management (MS). *Program availability:* Part-time, evening/weekend. *Faculty:* 37 full-time (14 women). *Students:* 13 full-time, 462 part-time; includes 133 minority (86 Black or African American, non-Hispanic/Latino; 24 Asian, non-Hispanic/Latino; 23 Hispanic/Latino). In 2016, 88 master's awarded. *Entrance requirements:* Additional exam requirements/recommendations for international students: Required—TOEFL, IELTS. *Application deadline:* For fall admission, 9/1 for domestic students; for winter admission, 12/1 for domestic students; for spring admission, 3/1 for domestic students. Applications are processed on a rolling basis. Application fee: $75. Electronic applications accepted. Application fee is waived when completed online. *Expenses: Tuition:* Full-time $32,184; part-time $1192 per credit hour. *Required fees:* $280. Tuition and fees vary according to campus/location and program. *Financial support:* Applicants required to submit FAFSA. *Unit head:* Dr. William F. Lynch, Dean, 215-895-2159, E-mail: goodwin@drexel.edu. *Application contact:* Matthew Gray, Manager, Recruitment and Enrollment, 215-895-6255, Fax: 215-895-2153, E-mail: mdg67@drexel.edu.
Website: http://drexel.edu/grad/programs/goodwin/

Drury University, Master in Education Program, Springfield, MO 5802. Offers curriculum and instruction (M Ed), including elementary, middle school, secondary; gifted education (M Ed); instructional leadership (M Ed); instructional technology (M Ed); integrated learning (M Ed); online teaching (M Ed); special education (M Ed); special reading (M Ed). *Accreditation:* NCATE. *Program availability:* Part-time, evening/weekend, 100% online, blended/hybrid learning. *Students:* 146 full-time (111 women); includes 6 minority (1 Asian, non-Hispanic/Latino; 3 Hispanic/Latino; 2 Two or more races, non-Hispanic/Latino), 1 international. Average age 34. 42 applicants, 74% accepted. In 2016, 74 master's awarded. *Entrance requirements:* For master's, GRE, bachelor's degree with minimum GPA of 2.75. Additional exam requirements/recommendations for international students: Recommended—TOEFL (minimum score 80 iBT), IELTS (minimum score 6.5). *Application deadline:* For fall admission, 8/4 priority date for domestic and international students; for spring admission, 1/5 priority date for domestic and international students; for summer admission, 5/26 priority date for domestic and international students. Applications are processed on a rolling basis. Application fee: $25 ($50 for international students). Electronic applications accepted. *Expenses:* $352 tuition per credit hour; $7 per credit hour technology fee; $100 graduation fee; $59 portfolio fee (one-time). *Financial support:* In 2016–17, 20 students received support. Career-related internships or fieldwork, scholarships/grants, tuition waivers (partial), and unspecified assistantships available. Financial award application deadline: 6/30; financial award applicants required to submit FAFSA. *Faculty research:* Gifted students, instructional technology, autism, diversity and social justice. *Unit head:* Dr. Asikaa Cosgrove, Director, Master in Education, 417-873-7806, E-mail: acosgrov@drury.edu.
Website: http://www.drury.edu/education-masters

Duquesne University, Graduate School of Liberal Arts, Department of Media, Pittsburgh, PA 15282-0001. Offers MS, Certificate. *Program availability:* Part-time, evening/weekend, blended/hybrid learning. *Faculty:* 10 full-time (2 women), 3 part-time/adjunct (0 women). *Students:* 21 full-time (14 women), 4 part-time (2 women); includes 2 minority (1 Black or African American, non-Hispanic/Latino; 1 Two or more races, non-Hispanic/Latino), 9 international. Average age 28. 17 applicants, 100% accepted, 9 enrolled. In 2016, 15 master's awarded. *Entrance requirements:* For master's, GRE General Test, portfolio, writing sample. Additional exam requirements/recommendations for international students: Required—TOEFL. *Application deadline:* For fall admission, 8/1 for domestic students, 5/1 for international students; for spring admission, 11/1 for domestic students. Applications are processed on a rolling basis. Application fee: $0. Electronic applications accepted. *Expenses: Tuition:* Full-time $22,212; part-time $1234 per credit. Tuition and fees vary according to program. *Financial support:* In 2016–17, 10 students received support, including 10 teaching assistantships with full tuition reimbursements available (averaging $8,000 per year); Federal Work-Study also available. Support available to part-time students. Financial award application deadline: 5/1. *Unit head:* Dr. Michael Dillon, Director, 412-396-6448, E-mail: dillonm@duq.edu. *Application contact:* Linda Rendulic, Assistant to the Dean, 412-396-6400, Fax: 412-396-5265, E-mail: rendulic@duq.edu.
Website: http://www.duq.edu/academics/schools/liberal-arts/graduate-school/programs/media-arts-and-technology

Duquesne University, School of Education, Department of Instruction and Leadership, Program in Instructional Technology, Pittsburgh, PA 15282-0001. Offers MS Ed, Ed D, Post-Master's Certificate. *Program availability:* Part-time, evening/weekend, minimal on-campus study. *Faculty:* 3 full-time (1 woman). *Students:* 53 full-time (35 women), 9 part-

time (8 women); includes 3 minority (2 Black or African American, non-Hispanic/Latino; 1 Hispanic/Latino), 9 international. Average age 36. 40 applicants, 95% accepted, 14 enrolled. In 2016, 10 master's, 5 doctorates awarded. *Degree requirements:* For master's, thesis optional; for doctorate, thesis/dissertation. *Entrance requirements:* For master's, bachelor's degree; for doctorate, GRE, master's degree; for Post-Master's Certificate, bachelor's/master's degree. Additional exam requirements/recommendations for international students: Required—TOEFL (minimum score 550 paper-based), IELTS (minimum score 7). *Application deadline:* For fall admission, 9/1 for domestic students; for spring admission, 1/1 for domestic students. Applications are processed on a rolling basis. Application fee: $0. Electronic applications accepted. *Expenses: Tuition:* Full-time $22,212; part-time $1234 per credit. Tuition and fees vary according to program. *Financial support:* Available to part-time students. *Unit head:* Dr. David Carbonara, Assistant Professor/Director, 412-396-4039, Fax: 412-396-1997, E-mail: carbonara@duq.edu. *Application contact:* Michael Dolinger, Director of Student and Academic Services, 412-396-6647, Fax: 412-396-5585, E-mail: dolingerm@duq.edu.
Website: http://www.duq.edu/academics/schools/education/graduate-programs/instructional-technology

East Carolina University, Graduate School, College of Education, Department of Mathematics, Science, and Instructional Technology Education, Greenville, NC 27858-4353. Offers elementary mathematics (Certificate); instructional technology (MA Ed, MS); mathematics education (MA Ed); science education (MA Ed, MAT). *Program availability:* Part-time, evening/weekend. *Students:* 15 full-time (10 women), 266 part-time (213 women); includes 52 minority (34 Black or African American, non-Hispanic/Latino; 3 American Indian or Alaska Native, non-Hispanic/Latino; 4 Asian, non-Hispanic/Latino; 9 Hispanic/Latino; 2 Two or more races, non-Hispanic/Latino), 1 international. Average age 37. 131 applicants, 100% accepted, 116 enrolled. In 2016, 30 master's awarded. *Degree requirements:* For master's, comprehensive exam, thesis optional. *Entrance requirements:* For master's, GRE General Test or MAT, interview, minimum GPA of 2.5, bachelor's degree in related field, teaching license (MA Ed). Additional exam requirements/recommendations for international students: Required—TOEFL. *Application deadline:* For fall admission, 6/1 priority date for domestic students. Applications are processed on a rolling basis. Application fee: $50. *Financial support:* Research assistantships, teaching assistantships, and Federal Work-Study available. Support available to part-time students. Financial award application deadline: 6/1. *Unit head:* Susan Ganter, Chair, 252-737-3001, E-mail: ganters@ecu.edu. *Application contact:* Dean of Graduate School, 252-328-6012, Fax: 252-328-6071, E-mail: gradschool@ecu.edu.
Website: http://www.ecu.edu/cs-educ/msite/

East Carolina University, Graduate School, College of Education, Department of Special Education, Foundations, and Research, Greenville, NC 27858-4353. Offers assistive technology (Certificate); autism (Certificate); behavior specialist (Certificate); deaf-blindness (Certificate); special education (MA Ed). *Program availability:* Part-time, online learning. *Degree requirements:* For master's, comprehensive exam, thesis optional. *Entrance requirements:* For master's, GRE General Test or MAT, interview, bachelor's degree in related field, minimum GPA of 2.5, teaching license. Additional exam requirements/recommendations for international students: Required—TOEFL. *Application deadline:* For fall admission, 6/1 priority date for domestic students. Applications are processed on a rolling basis. Application fee: $50. *Financial support:* Research assistantships, teaching assistantships, and Federal Work-Study available. Support available to part-time students. Financial award application deadline: 6/1; financial award applicants required to submit FAFSA. *Unit head:* Dr. Guili Zhang, Interim Chair, 252-328-4989, E-mail: zhangg@ecu.edu. *Application contact:* Dean of Graduate School, 252-328-6012, Fax: 252-328-6071, E-mail: gradschool@ecu.edu.
Website: http://www.ecu.edu/cs-educ/sefr/index.cfm

Eastern Connecticut State University, School of Education and Professional Studies/Graduate Division, Program in Educational Technology, Willimantic, CT 06226-2295. Offers MS. *Program availability:* Part-time, evening/weekend, 100% online, blended/hybrid learning. *Faculty:* 2 full-time (1 woman). *Students:* 2 full-time (1 woman), 9 part-time (4 women); includes 1 minority (Asian, non-Hispanic/Latino). Average age 36. 4 applicants, 50% accepted, 2 enrolled. In 2016, 9 master's awarded. *Degree requirements:* For master's, comprehensive exam, thesis optional, culminating portfolio. *Entrance requirements:* For master's, minimum GPA of 2.7, bachelor's degree from accredited institution. Additional exam requirements/recommendations for international students: Required—TOEFL (minimum score 550 paper-based; 79 iBT); Recommended—IELTS (minimum score 6). *Application deadline:* For fall admission, 7/6 priority date for domestic and international students; for spring admission, 11/3 priority date for domestic and international students. Applications are processed on a rolling basis. Application fee: $50. Electronic applications accepted. *Expenses: Tuition, area resident:* Full-time $11,781; part-time $560 per credit. Tuition, state resident: full-time $15,031; part-time $568 per credit. Tuition, nonresident: full-time $24,581; part-time $568 per credit. *Required fees:* $40 per semester. Full-time tuition and fees vary according to course level, course load and reciprocity agreements. *Financial support:* Research assistantships, teaching assistantships, career-related internships or fieldwork, institutionally sponsored loans, and unspecified assistantships available. Financial award application deadline: 3/1; financial award applicants required to submit FAFSA. *Unit head:* Dr. David Stoloff, Advisor, 860-465-5501, Fax: 860-465-5099, E-mail: stoloff@easternct.edu. *Application contact:* Paula Goyette, Graduate Division, School of Education and Professional Studies, 860-465-5292, Fax: 860-465-5710, E-mail: graduateadmissions@easternct.edu.

Eastern Michigan University, Graduate School, College of Education, Department of Teacher Education, Programs in Curriculum and Instruction, Ypsilanti, MI 48197. Offers advanced teaching and learning (MA); early literacy instruction (Graduate Certificate); instructional leadership (MA); learning, motivation and creativity (Graduate Certificate); literacy coaching (Graduate Certificate); online teaching (Certificate); secondary literacy instruction (Graduate Certificate); urban and diversity education (MA). *Students:* 1 (woman) full-time, 31 part-time (29 women); includes 6 minority (2 Black or African American, non-Hispanic/Latino; 2 Asian, non-Hispanic/Latino; 2 Two or more races, non-Hispanic/Latino), 1 international. Average age 33. 11 applicants, 73% accepted, 4 enrolled. In 2016, 8 master's, 1 other advanced degree awarded. Application fee: $45. *Application contact:* Dr. Virginia Harder, Graduate Coordinator/Advisor, 734-487-2729, Fax: 734-487-2101, E-mail: vharder1@emich.edu.

Eastern Michigan University, Graduate School, College of Education, Department of Teacher Education, Programs in Educational Media and Technology, Ypsilanti, MI 48197. Offers MA, Graduate Certificate. *Program availability:* Part-time, evening/weekend, online learning. *Students:* 24 part-time (13 women); includes 2 minority (both Hispanic/Latino). Average age 35. 9 applicants, 78% accepted, 3 enrolled. In 2016, 12 master's awarded. *Entrance requirements:* Additional exam requirements/recommendations for international students: Required—TOEFL. *Application deadline:* Applications are processed on a rolling basis. Application fee: $45. *Financial support:* Fellowships, research assistantships with full tuition reimbursements, teaching assistantships with full tuition reimbursements, career-related internships or fieldwork, Federal Work-Study, institutionally sponsored loans, scholarships/grants, tuition waivers (partial), and unspecified assistantships available. Support available to part-time students. Financial award applicants required to submit FAFSA. *Application contact:* Dr. Toni Stokes Jones, Coordinator, 734-487-3260, Fax: 734-487-2101, E-mail: tjones1@emich.edu.

Eastern New Mexico University, Graduate School, College of Education and Technology, Department of Curriculum and Instruction, Portales, NM 88130. Offers bilingual education (M Ed); educational technology (M Ed); elementary education (M Ed); English as a second language (M Ed); pedagogy and learning (M Ed); professional technical education (M Ed); reading/literacy (M Ed). *Program availability:* Part-time, online learning. *Degree requirements:* For master's, comprehensive exam, thesis optional. *Entrance requirements:* For master's, minimum GPA of 3.0, photocopy of teaching license, writing assessment, letter of recommendation. Additional exam requirements/recommendations for international students: Required—TOEFL (minimum score 550 paper-based; 79 iBT), IELTS (minimum score 6). Electronic applications accepted.

East Stroudsburg University of Pennsylvania, Graduate and Extended Studies, College of Education, Department of Digital Media Technologies, East Stroudsburg, PA 18301-2999. Offers M Ed. *Program availability:* Part-time, evening/weekend, online learning. *Degree requirements:* For master's, comprehensive exam, comprehensive portfolio, internship. *Entrance requirements:* For master's, two letters of recommendation, portfolio or interview, minimum overall undergraduate QPA of 2.5. Additional exam requirements/recommendations for international students: Recommended—TOEFL (minimum score 560 paper-based; 83 iBT), IELTS. *Application deadline:* For fall admission, 7/31 priority date for domestic students, 6/30 priority date for international students; for spring admission, 11/30 for domestic students, 10/31 for international students. Applications are processed on a rolling basis. Application fee: $50. Electronic applications accepted. *Expenses:* Tuition, state resident: full-time $8694; part-time $5796 per year. Tuition, nonresident: full-time $13,050; part-time $8700 per year. *Required fees:* $2550; $1690 per unit. $845 per semester. Tuition and fees vary according to course load, campus/location and program. *Financial support:* Research assistantships with tuition reimbursements, career-related internships or fieldwork, Federal Work-Study, and unspecified assistantships available. Support available to part-time students. Financial award application deadline: 3/1; financial award applicants required to submit FAFSA. *Unit head:* Dr. Richard Otto, Chair, 570-422-3763, Fax: 570-422-3876, E-mail: rotto@esu.edu. *Application contact:* Kevin Quintero, Associate Director, Graduate and Extended Studies, 570-422-3890, Fax: 570-422-2711, E-mail: kquintero@esu.edu.

East Tennessee State University, School of Graduate Studies, College of Education, Department of Curriculum and Instruction, Johnson City, TN 37614. Offers educational technology (M Ed), including educational communications and technology, school library media; elementary education (M Ed); reading (MA), including reading education; school library professional (Post-Master's Certificate); secondary education (M Ed), including classroom technology; teacher education with multiple levels (MAT), including elementary education, middle grades education, secondary education. *Accreditation:* NCATE. *Program availability:* Part-time, evening/weekend, online learning. *Degree requirements:* For master's, comprehensive exam, thesis optional, student teaching, practicum; for Post-Master's Certificate, field work (school library); culminating experience (storytelling). *Entrance requirements:* For master's, GRE, SAT, ACT, PRAXIS, minimum GPA of 3.0; for Post-Master's Certificate, master's degree, TN teaching license. Additional exam requirements/recommendations for international students: Required—TOEFL (minimum score 550 paper-based; 79 iBT). Electronic applications accepted. *Faculty research:* Critical thinking; curriculum development in reading, math, and science education; cultural diversity; cognitive processes; effective teaching strategies.

Emporia State University, Department of Instructional Design and Technology, Emporia, KS 66801-5415. Offers MS. *Accreditation:* NCATE. *Program availability:* Part-time, online only, 100% online. *Faculty:* 7 full-time (3 women). *Students:* 34 full-time (16 women), 53 part-time (41 women); includes 9 minority (5 Black or African American, non-Hispanic/Latino; 2 Asian, non-Hispanic/Latino; 1 Hispanic/Latino; 1 Two or more races, non-Hispanic/Latino), 29 international. 40 applicants, 98% accepted, 17 enrolled. In 2016, 42 master's awarded. *Degree requirements:* For master's, comprehensive exam (for some programs), thesis (for some programs), project. *Entrance requirements:* For master's, appropriate bachelor's degree, letters of recommendation. Additional exam requirements/recommendations for international students: Required—TOEFL (minimum score 520 paper-based; 68 iBT). *Application deadline:* For fall admission, 8/15 priority date for domestic students. Applications are processed on a rolling basis. Application fee: $30 ($75 for international students). Electronic applications accepted. *Expenses:* Tuition, state resident: full-time $5922; part-time $246.75 per credit hour. Tuition, nonresident: full-time $18,414; part-time $767.25 per credit hour. *Required fees:* $1884; $78.50 per credit hour. *Financial support:* In 2016–17, 11 teaching assistantships with full tuition reimbursements (averaging $7,344 per year) were awarded; Federal Work-Study, institutionally sponsored loans, health care benefits, and unspecified assistantships also available. Financial award application deadline: 3/15; financial award applicants required to submit FAFSA. *Unit head:* Dr. Zeni Colorado, Chair, 620-341-5477, E-mail: jcolorad@emporia.edu. *Application contact:* Mary Sewell, Admissions Coordinator, 800-950-GRAD, Fax: 620-341-5909, E-mail: msewell@emporia.edu.
Website: http://www.emporia.edu/idt/

Fairfield University, Graduate School of Education and Allied Professions, Fairfield, CT 06824. Offers applied behavior analysis (ATC); applied psychology (MA); clinical mental health counseling (MA, CAS); educational technology (MA); elementary education (MA, CAS); family studies (MA); integration of spirituality and religion in counseling (ATC); marriage and family therapy (MA); reading and language development (Sixth Year Certificate); school counseling (MA, CAS); school psychology (MA, CAS); school-based marriage and family therapy (ATC); secondary education (MA); special education (MA, CAS); substance abuse counseling (ATC); teaching (Certificate); teaching and foundations (MA, CAS); TESOL, world languages, and bilingual education (MA, CAS). *Accreditation:* NCATE. *Program availability:* Part-time, evening/weekend. *Faculty:* 19 full-time (15 women), 38 part-time/adjunct (26 women). *Students:* 153 full-time (132 women), 302 part-time (252 women); includes 97 minority (24 Black or African American, non-Hispanic/Latino; 12 Asian, non-Hispanic/Latino; 55 Hispanic/Latino; 6 Two or more races, non-Hispanic/Latino), 6 international. Average age 32. 283 applicants, 61% accepted, 97 enrolled. In 2016, 130 master's awarded. *Degree requirements:* For master's, comprehensive exam. *Entrance requirements:* For master's, minimum GPA of 3.0, 2 recommendations, resume. Additional exam requirements/recommendations for international students: Required—TOEFL (minimum score 550 paper-based; 84 iBT) or IELTS (minimum score 7.5). *Application deadline:* For fall admission, 2/15 for international students; for spring admission, 10/1 for international students. Application fee: $60. Electronic applications accepted. *Expenses:* $725 per credit hour. *Financial support:* In 2016–17, 42 students received support. Career-related internships or fieldwork and unspecified assistantships available. Support available to part-time students. Financial award applicants required to submit FAFSA. *Faculty research:* Reading and literacy, writing, social justice and inequality in

education, addictions and mental health issues, therapeutic relationships and clinical supervision. *Unit head:* Dr. Robert D. Hannafin, Dean, 203-254-4250, Fax: 203-254-4241, E-mail: rhannafin@fairfield.edu. *Application contact:* Marianne Gumpper, Director of Graduate Admission, 203-254-4184, Fax: 203-254-4073, E-mail: gradadmis@fairfield.edu.
Website: http://www.fairfield.edu/gseap

Fairleigh Dickinson University, College at Florham, University College: Arts, Sciences, and Professional Studies, Peter Sammartino School of Education, Madison, NJ 07940-1099. Offers education for certified teachers (MA, Certificate); educational leadership (MA); instructional technology (Certificate); literacy/reading (Certificate); teaching (MAT).

Fairleigh Dickinson University, Metropolitan Campus, University College: Arts, Sciences, and Professional Studies, Peter Sammartino School of Education, Teaneck, NJ 07666-1914. Offers dyslexia specialist (Certificate); education for certified teachers (MA); educational leadership (MA); instructional technology (Certificate); learning disabilities (MA); literacy/reading (Certificate); multilingual education (MA); teacher of the handicapped (Certificate); teaching (MAT). *Accreditation:* TEAC. *Program availability:* Part-time. *Degree requirements:* For master's, research project (MAT).

Fairmont State University, Programs in Education, Fairmont, WV 26554. Offers digital media, new literacies and learning (M Ed); education (MAT); exercise science, fitness and wellness (M Ed); professional studies (M Ed); reading (M Ed); special education (M Ed). *Accreditation:* NCATE. *Program availability:* Part-time, evening/weekend, 100% online. *Faculty:* 18 full-time (11 women), 5 part-time/adjunct (3 women). *Students:* 62 full-time (52 women), 102 part-time (82 women); includes 6 minority (2 Black or African American, non-Hispanic/Latino; 1 American Indian or Alaska Native, non-Hispanic/Latino; 1 Hispanic/Latino; 2 Two or more races, non-Hispanic/Latino). Average age 33. 68 applicants, 84% accepted, 47 enrolled. In 2016, 44 degrees awarded. *Entrance requirements:* For master's, GRE. Additional exam requirements/recommendations for international students: Required—TOEFL (minimum score 80 iBT), IELTS (minimum score 6.5). *Application deadline:* For fall admission, 5/1 for domestic and international students. Applications are processed on a rolling basis. Application fee: $40. Electronic applications accepted. *Expenses:* Tuition, state resident: full-time $7504; part-time $405 per credit hour. Tuition, nonresident: full-time $16,060; part-time $880 per credit hour. Part-time tuition and fees vary according to course load. *Financial support:* In 2016–17, 20 students received support. Research assistantships, teaching assistantships, scholarships/grants, and unspecified assistantships available. Financial award applicants required to submit FAFSA. *Unit head:* Dr. Carolyn Crislip-Tacy, Interim Dean, School of Education, 304-367-4143, Fax: 304-367-4599, E-mail: carolyn.crislip-tacy@fairmontstate.edu. *Application contact:* Jack Kirby, Director of Graduate Studies, 304-367-4101, E-mail: jack.kirby@fairmontstate.edu.
Website: http://www.fairmontstate.edu/graduatestudies/

Florida Atlantic University, College of Education, Department of Teaching and Learning, Boca Raton, FL 33431-0991. Offers curriculum and instruction (M Ed), including art, biology, chemistry, English, French, German, mathematics, music, physics, Pre-K and primary education, reading, social sciences, Spanish; elementary education (M Ed); environmental education (M Ed); reading education (M Ed); social foundations of education (M Ed), including educational psychology, educational technology, multilingual education. *Accreditation:* NCATE. *Program availability:* Part-time, evening/weekend. *Faculty:* 15 full-time (12 women), 2 part-time/adjunct (1 woman). *Students:* 25 full-time (20 women), 41 part-time (37 women); includes 18 minority (9 Black or African American, non-Hispanic/Latino; 2 Asian, non-Hispanic/Latino; 7 Hispanic/Latino), 7 international. Average age 32. 54 applicants, 59% accepted, 18 enrolled. In 2016, 36 master's awarded. *Entrance requirements:* For master's, GRE General Test, minimum GPA of 3.0 in last 2 years of undergraduate course work. Additional exam requirements/recommendations for international students: Required—TOEFL (minimum score 500 paper-based; 61 iBT), IELTS (minimum score 6). *Application deadline:* For fall admission, 7/1 for domestic students, 2/15 for international students; for spring admission, 11/1 for domestic students, 7/15 for international students. Applications are processed on a rolling basis. Application fee: $30. *Expenses:* Tuition, state resident: full-time $7392; part-time $369.82 per credit hour. Tuition, nonresident: full-time $19,432; part-time $1024.81 per credit hour. *Financial support:* Fellowships with partial tuition reimbursements, research assistantships with partial tuition reimbursements, teaching assistantships with partial tuition reimbursements, career-related internships or fieldwork, scholarships/grants, and unspecified assistantships available. *Faculty research:* Technology, teaching English to speakers of other languages, math teaching, electronic portfolio assessment, global perspectives through social studies. *Unit head:* Dr. Barbara Ridener, Chairperson, 561-297-3588, E-mail: bridener@fau.edu. *Application contact:* Dr. Eliah Watlington, Associate Dean, 561-296-8520, Fax: 261-297-2991, E-mail: ewatling@fau.edu.
Website: http://www.coe.fau.edu/academicdepartments/tl/

Florida Institute of Technology, College of Science, Program in Educational Technology, Melbourne, FL 32901-6975. Offers MS. *Program availability:* Part-time. *Students:* 1 (woman) full-time, 4 part-time (all women); includes 1 minority (Black or African American, non-Hispanic/Latino), 4 international. Average age 31. *Degree requirements:* For master's, comprehensive exam (for some programs), thesis or oral final exam, 30 credit hours. *Entrance requirements:* For master's, resume, statement of objectives. Additional exam requirements/recommendations for international students: Required—TOEFL (minimum score 550 paper-based; 79 iBT). *Application deadline:* Applications are processed on a rolling basis. Electronic applications accepted. *Expenses: Tuition:* Full-time $22,338; part-time $1241 per credit hour. *Required fees:* $250. Tuition and fees vary according to degree level, campus/location and program. *Financial support:* Applicants required to submit FAFSA. *Unit head:* Dr. Scott R. Tilley, Program Chair, 321-674-8126, E-mail: stilley@fit.edu. *Application contact:* Cheryl A. Brown, Associate Director of Graduate Admissions, 321-674-7581, Fax: 321-723-9468, E-mail: cbrown@fit.edu.
Website: http://www.fit.edu/programs/8115/ms-educational-technology#.VT_h8k10ypo

Florida International University, College of Arts, Sciences, and Education, Department of Leadership and Professional Studies, Miami, FL 33199. Offers adult education and human resource development (MS, Ed D); counseling (MS), including rehabilitation counseling, school counseling; counselor education (MS), including clinical mental health counseling; educational administration and supervision (Ed D); educational leadership (MS, Certificate, Ed S); higher education (Ed D); higher education administration (MS); international and comparative education (MS); recreation and sport management (MS), including recreation and sport management, recreational therapy; school psychology (Ed S); urban education (MS), including instruction in urban settings, learning technologies, multicultural/bilingual, multicultural/TESOL, urban education. *Program availability:* Part-time, evening/weekend. *Faculty:* 27 full-time (19 women), 38 part-time/adjunct (25 women). *Students:* 253 full-time (191 women), 306 part-time (241 women); includes 444 minority (129 Black or African American, non-Hispanic/Latino; 3 Asian, non-Hispanic/Latino; 304 Hispanic/Latino; 8 Two or more races, non-Hispanic/Latino), 18 international. Average age 31. 366 applicants, 60% accepted, 115 enrolled. In 2016, 193 master's, 8 doctorates awarded. *Degree requirements:* For doctorate, thesis/dissertation. *Entrance requirements:* For master's, minimum GPA of 3.0; for doctorate and other advanced degree, GRE General Test. Additional exam requirements/recommendations for international students: Required—TOEFL (minimum score 550 paper-based; 80 iBT), IELTS (minimum score 6.3). *Application deadline:* For fall admission, 6/1 priority date for domestic students, 4/1 for international students; for winter admission, 10/1 priority date for domestic students, 9/1 for international students; for spring admission, 3/1 priority date for domestic students, 2/1 for international students. Applications are processed on a rolling basis. Application fee: $30. Electronic applications accepted. *Expenses:* Tuition, state resident: full-time $8912; part-time $446 per credit hour. Tuition, nonresident: full-time $21,393; part-time $992 per credit hour. *Required fees:* $2185; $195 per semester. Tuition and fees vary according to program. *Financial support:* Fellowships, research assistantships with tuition reimbursements, teaching assistantships with tuition reimbursements, Federal Work-Study, and tuition waivers (full and partial) available. Support available to part-time students. Financial award applicants required to submit FAFSA. *Unit head:* Dr. Benjamin Baez, Chair, 305-348-3214, Fax: 305-348-1515, E-mail: benjamin.baez@fiu.edu. *Application contact:* Nanett Rojas, Assistant Director, Graduate Admissions, 305-348-7464, Fax: 305-348-7441, E-mail: gradadm@fiu.edu.
Website: http://education.fiu.edu

Florida International University, College of Arts, Sciences, and Education, Department of Teaching and Learning, Miami, FL 33199. Offers art education (MA, MS); curriculum and instruction (MS, Ed D, PhD, Ed S), including curriculum development (MS), elementary education (MS), English education (MS), learning technologies (MS), mathematics education (MS), modern language education (MS), physical education (MS), science education (MS), social studies education (MS), special education (MS); early childhood education (MS); exceptional student education (Ed D); foreign language education (MS), including foreign language education, teaching English to speakers of other languages (TESOL); international/intercultural education (MS); language, literacy and culture (PhD); mathematics, science, and learning technologies (PhD); physical education (MS), including sport and fitness; reading education (MS). *Program availability:* Part-time, evening/weekend. *Faculty:* 34 full-time (23 women), 64 part-time/adjunct (48 women). *Students:* 182 full-time (154 women), 231 part-time (190 women); includes 323 minority (69 Black or African American, non-Hispanic/Latino; 10 Asian, non-Hispanic/Latino; 237 Hispanic/Latino; 7 Two or more races, non-Hispanic/Latino), 19 international. Average age 34. 282 applicants, 58% accepted, 113 enrolled. In 2016, 184 master's, 12 doctorates awarded. *Degree requirements:* For doctorate, comprehensive exam, thesis/dissertation. *Entrance requirements:* For master's, GRE General Test, Florida General Knowledge Test or Florida College Level Academic Skills Test; for doctorate and Ed S, GRE General Test. Additional exam requirements/recommendations for international students: Required—TOEFL (minimum score 550 paper-based; 80 iBT), IELTS (minimum score 6.3). *Application deadline:* For fall admission, 6/1 priority date for domestic students, 4/1 for international students; for winter admission, 10/1 priority date for domestic students, 9/1 for international students; for spring admission, 3/1 priority date for domestic students, 2/1 for international students. Applications are processed on a rolling basis. Application fee: $30. Electronic applications accepted. *Expenses:* Tuition, state resident: full-time $8912; part-time $446 per credit hour. Tuition, nonresident: full-time $21,393; part-time $992 per credit hour. *Required fees:* $2185; $195 per semester. Tuition and fees vary according to program. *Financial support:* Research assistantships with tuition reimbursements and teaching assistantships with tuition reimbursements available. *Unit head:* Dr. Lynn Miller, Chair, 305-348-2005, Fax: 305-348-2086, E-mail: lynne.miller@fiu.edu. *Application contact:* Nanett Rojas, Assistant Director, Graduate Admissions, 305-348-7464, Fax: 305-348-7441, E-mail: gradadm@fiu.edu.
Website: http://education.fiu.edu

Florida State University, The Graduate School, College of Education, Program in Instructional Systems and Learning Technologies, Tallahassee, FL 32306. Offers human performance technology (Certificate); instructional systems and learning technologies (MS, PhD); online instructional development (Certificate). *Degree requirements:* For master's and Certificate, comprehensive exam, thesis optional; for doctorate, comprehensive exam, thesis/dissertation, diagnostic exam, preliminary exam, prospectus defense, dissertation defense. *Entrance requirements:* For master's, doctorate, and Certificate, GRE General Test, minimum upper-division GPA of 3.0. Additional exam requirements/recommendations for international students: Required—TOEFL (minimum score 550 paper-based, 80 iBT), IELTS (minimum score 6.5), Michigan English Language Assessment Battery (minimum score 77), or PTE (minimum score 55). Application fee: $30. Electronic applications accepted. *Expenses:* Tuition, state resident: full-time $7263; part-time $403.51 per credit hour. Tuition, nonresident: full-time $18,087; part-time $1004.85 per credit hour. *Required fees:* $1365; $75.81 per credit hour. $20 per semester. Tuition and fees vary according to campus/location. *Financial support:* Fellowships, research assistantships, teaching assistantships, scholarships/grants, tuition waivers (full and partial), and unspecified assistantships available. Financial award application deadline: 1/15; financial award applicants required to submit FAFSA. *Faculty research:* Instructional design and development; performance improvement and learning analytics; emerging technologies (mobile, social media); game-based learning and stealth assessment; online learning (discussion, communities). *Unit head:* Dr. Vanessa Dennen, Associate Professor/Program Coordinator, 850-644-8783, Fax: 850-644-8776, E-mail: vdennen@fsu.edu. *Application contact:* Mary Kate McKee, Academic Program Specialist, 850-644-8792, Fax: 850-644-8776, E-mail: mmckee@campus.fsu.edu.
Website: http://education.fsu.edu/degrees-and-programs/graduate-programs

Fontbonne University, Graduate Programs, St. Louis, MO 63105-3098. Offers accounting (MBA, MS); art (MA); art (K-12) (MAT); business (MBA); computer science (MS); deaf education (MA); early intervention in deaf education (MA); education (MA), including autism spectrum disorders, curriculum and instruction, diverse learners, early childhood education, reading, special education; elementary education (MAT); family and consumer sciences (MA), including multidisciplinary health communication studies; fine arts (MFA); instructional design and technology (MS); management and leadership (MM); middle school education (MAT); secondary education (MAT); special education (MAT); speech-language pathology (MS); supply chain management (MS); theatre (MA). *Program availability:* Part-time, evening/weekend, online learning. *Faculty:* 32 full-time (24 women), 43 part-time/adjunct (26 women). *Students:* 456 full-time (313 women), 102 part-time (77 women); includes 138 minority (118 Black or African American, non-Hispanic/Latino; 1 American Indian or Alaska Native, non-Hispanic/Latino; 7 Asian, non-Hispanic/Latino; 9 Hispanic/Latino; 3 Two or more races, non-Hispanic/Latino), 37 international. *Degree requirements:* For master's, comprehensive exam (for some programs), thesis (for some programs). *Entrance requirements:* Additional exam requirements/recommendations for international students: Required—TOEFL (minimum score 500 paper-based; 65 iBT). *Application deadline:* For fall admission, 8/1 for international students; for spring admission, 12/1 for international students. Applications are processed on a rolling basis. Application fee: $25 ($30 for international students). Electronic applications accepted. *Expenses: Tuition:* Full-time $8436; part-time $703 per credit hour. *Required fees:* $18 per credit hour. Tuition and fees vary according to course load. *Financial support:* Teaching assistantships with partial tuition reimbursements and scholarships/grants available. Support available to part-time students. Financial award application deadline: 4/1; financial award applicants

required to submit FAFSA. *Unit head:* Dr. Carey Adams, Vice President for Academic Affairs, 314-719-3609, E-mail: cadams@fontbonne.edu. *Application contact:* Lauryn Filip, Coordinator, Graduate Admission and Professional Studies, 314-889-4650, E-mail: admissions@fontbonne.edu.
Website: https://www.fontbonne.edu/academics/graduate-programs/

Fort Hays State University, Graduate School, College of Education, Department of Technology Studies, Hays, KS 67601-4099. Offers instructional technology (MS). *Degree requirements:* For master's, comprehensive exam, thesis or alternative. *Entrance requirements:* Additional exam requirements/recommendations for international students: Required—TOEFL (minimum score 550 paper-based). Electronic applications accepted.

Framingham State University, Continuing Education, Program in Curriculum and Instructional Technology, Framingham, MA 01701-9101. Offers M Ed. *Program availability:* Online learning.

Franklin University, Instructional Design and Performance Technology Program, Columbus, OH 43215-5399. Offers MS.

Fresno Pacific University, Graduate Programs, School of Education, Program in Educational Technology, Fresno, CA 93702-4709. Offers MA. *Program availability:* Part-time, evening/weekend, online learning. *Degree requirements:* For master's, thesis or alternative. *Entrance requirements:* For master's, three references. Additional exam requirements/recommendations for international students: Required—TOEFL (minimum score 550 paper-based). *Expenses:* Contact institution.

Fresno Pacific University, Graduate Programs, School of Education, Program in School Library and Information Technology, Fresno, CA 93702-4709. Offers MA Ed. *Program availability:* Part-time, evening/weekend, online learning. *Degree requirements:* For master's, thesis or alternative. *Entrance requirements:* For master's, CBEST. Additional exam requirements/recommendations for international students: Required—TOEFL (minimum score 550 paper-based). Electronic applications accepted. *Expenses:* Contact institution.

Frostburg State University, Graduate School, College of Education, Department of Educational Professions, Program in Curriculum and Instruction, Frostburg, MD 21532-1099. Offers educational technology (M Ed); elementary education (M Ed); secondary education (M Ed). *Program availability:* Part-time, evening/weekend. *Degree requirements:* For master's, thesis or alternative. *Entrance requirements:* For master's, teaching certificate. Additional exam requirements/recommendations for international students: Required—TOEFL. Electronic applications accepted.

Full Sail University, Education Media Design and Technology Master of Science Program - Online, Winter Park, FL 32792-7437. Offers MS. *Program availability:* Online learning. *Entrance requirements:* Additional exam requirements/recommendations for international students: Required—TOEFL (minimum score 550 paper-based; 79 iBT).

George Fox University, College of Education, Graduate Teaching and Leading Program, Newberg, OR 97132-2697. Offers administrative leadership (Ed S); continuing administrator license (Certificate); educational leadership (M Ed); educational technology (M Ed); English for speakers of other languages (M Ed); ESOL (Certificate); initial administrator license (Certificate); reading (M Ed, Certificate); special education (M Ed); teaching (MAT). *Accreditation:* NCATE. *Program availability:* Part-time, evening/weekend, online learning. *Degree requirements:* For master's, thesis (for some programs). *Entrance requirements:* For master's, minimum undergraduate GPA of 3.0 during previous 2 years of course work, resume, 3 professional recommendations on university forms, official transcripts. Additional exam requirements/recommendations for international students: Required—TOEFL (minimum score 577 paper-based; 90 iBT). Electronic applications accepted. *Expenses:* Contact institution.

George Mason University, College of Education and Human Development, Programs in Curriculum and Instruction, Fairfax, VA 22030. Offers advanced international baccalaureate (M Ed); assistive technology (M Ed); designing digital learning in schools (M Ed); early childhood education (M Ed); early childhood education for diverse learners (M Ed); elementary education (M Ed); English as a second language (M Ed); gifted child education (M Ed); history (M Ed); literacy (M Ed), including PK-12 classroom teachers, reading specialist; literacy leadership for diverse schools (M Ed), including K-12 reading; physical education (M Ed); science K-12 (M Ed); secondary education (M Ed), including biology, chemistry, earth science, English, history/social science, math, physics; special education (M Ed); teacher leadership (M Ed); teaching culturally, linguistically diverse and exceptional learners (M Ed); transformative teaching (M Ed). *Faculty:* 41 full-time (35 women), 53 part-time/adjunct (46 women). *Students:* 155 full-time (127 women), 821 part-time (697 women); includes 267 minority (82 Black or African American, non-Hispanic/Latino; 5 American Indian or Alaska Native, non-Hispanic/Latino; 75 Asian, non-Hispanic/Latino; 88 Hispanic/Latino; 1 Native Hawaiian or other Pacific Islander, non-Hispanic/Latino; 16 Two or more races, non-Hispanic/Latino), 19 international. Average age 33. 513 applicants, 90% accepted, 352 enrolled. In 2016, 347 master's awarded. *Degree requirements:* For master's, comprehensive exam, thesis (for some programs). *Entrance requirements:* For master's, PRAXIS Core (for some programs), minimum GPA of 3.0 in last 60 hours, licensed as teacher or educational administrator, official transcripts, goals statement, 3 recommendation letters, interview or writing sample (depending on program), up to 3 years' teaching experience (depending on program). Additional exam requirements/recommendations for international students: Required—TOEFL (minimum score 575 paper-based; 88 iBT), IELTS (minimum score 6.5), PTE (minimum score 59). *Application deadline:* For spring admission, 11/1 priority date for domestic and international students. Application fee: $75 ($80 for international students). Electronic applications accepted. *Expenses:* Tuition, state resident: full-time $10,628; part-time $443 per credit. Tuition, nonresident: full-time $29,306; part-time $1221 per credit. *Required fees:* $3096; $129 per credit. Tuition and fees vary according to program. *Financial support:* In 2016–17, 1 student received support, including 1 teaching assistantship (averaging $4,060 per year); career-related internships or fieldwork, Federal Work-Study, scholarships/grants, unspecified assistantships, and health care benefits (for full-time research or teaching assistantship recipients) also available. Support available to part-time students. Financial award application deadline: 3/1; financial award applicants required to submit FAFSA. *Faculty research:* Achievement gaps and superintendent decisions, constructivist view of classroom teaching, cost of cheating, creating a critical literacy milieu in kindergarten. *Unit head:* Rebecca Fox, Professor and Academic Program Coordinator, 703-993-4123, E-mail: rfox@gmu.edu.
Website: http://gse.gmu.edu/programs/gsemasters

The George Washington University, Graduate School of Education and Human Development, Department of Educational Leadership, Program in Educational Technology Leadership, Washington, DC 20052. Offers MA Ed. *Accreditation:* NCATE. *Program availability:* Part-time, evening/weekend. *Students:* 3 full-time (2 women), 75 part-time (49 women); includes 25 minority (8 Black or African American, non-Hispanic/Latino; 2 Asian, non-Hispanic/Latino; 11 Hispanic/Latino; 4 Two or more races, non-Hispanic/Latino), 1 international. Average age 35. 52 applicants, 90% accepted, 37 enrolled. In 2016, 32 master's awarded. *Degree requirements:* For master's, comprehensive exam, thesis or alternative. *Entrance requirements:* For master's, GRE General Test or MAT, minimum GPA of 2.75. *Application deadline:* For fall admission, 1/15 priority date for domestic students; for spring admission, 10/1 for domestic students. Applications are processed on a rolling basis. Application fee: $75. *Expenses:* Contact institution. *Financial support:* Fellowships, research assistantships, teaching assistantships, and career-related internships or fieldwork available. Financial award application deadline: 1/15. *Faculty research:* Interactive multimedia, distance education, federal technology policy. *Unit head:* Dr. Natalie Milman, Coordinator, 202-994-1884, E-mail: milman@gwu.edu. *Application contact:* Sarah Lang, Director of Graduate Admissions, 202-994-1447, Fax: 202-994-7207, E-mail: slang@gwu.edu.

The George Washington University, Graduate School of Education and Human Development, Department of Educational Leadership, Program in Instructional Design, Washington, DC 20052. Offers Graduate Certificate. *Students:* 13 part-time (10 women); includes 2 minority (both Asian, non-Hispanic/Latino). Average age 41. 11 applicants, 82% accepted, 5 enrolled. In 2016, 5 Graduate Certificates awarded. *Unit head:* Michael Feuer, Dean, 202-994-6161, E-mail: mjfeuer@gwu.edu. *Application contact:* Sarah Lang, Director of Graduate Admissions, 202-994-1447, Fax: 202-994-7207, E-mail: slang@gwu.edu.
Website: http://gsehd.gwu.edu/instructional-design-certificate

The George Washington University, Graduate School of Education and Human Development, Department of Educational Leadership, Program in Integrating Technology into Education, Washington, DC 20052. Offers Graduate Certificate. *Students:* 1 applicant, 100% accepted. In 2016, 1 Graduate Certificate awarded. *Unit head:* Dr. Natalie Milman, Coordinator, 202-994-1884, E-mail: nmilman@gwu.edu. *Application contact:* Sarah Lang, Director of Graduate Admissions, 202-994-1447, Fax: 202-994-7207, E-mail: slang@gwu.edu.
Website: http://gsehd.gwu.edu/integrating-technology-education-certificate

The George Washington University, Graduate School of Education and Human Development, Department of Educational Leadership, Program in Leadership in Educational Technology, Washington, DC 20052. Offers Graduate Certificate. *Students:* 1 part-time (0 women). Average age 37. 1 applicant. In 2016, 1 Graduate Certificate awarded. *Unit head:* Dr. Natalie Milman, Coordinator, 202-994-1884, E-mail: nmilman@gwu.edu. *Application contact:* Sarah Lang, Director of Graduate Admissions, 202-994-1447, Fax: 202-994-7207, E-mail: slang@gwu.edu.
Website: http://gsehd.gwu.edu/

The George Washington University, Graduate School of Education and Human Development, Department of Educational Leadership, Program in Multimedia Development, Washington, DC 20052. Offers Graduate Certificate. *Students:* 2 part-time (1 woman); both minorities (1 Black or African American, non-Hispanic/Latino; 1 Hispanic/Latino). Average age 42. 1 applicant, 100% accepted, 1 enrolled. *Unit head:* Michael Feuer, Dean, 202-994-6161, E-mail: mjfeuer@gwu.edu. *Application contact:* Sarah Lang, Director of Graduate Admissions, 202-994-1447, Fax: 202-994-7207, E-mail: slang@gwu.edu.
Website: http://gsehd.gwu.edu/multimedia-development-certificate

The George Washington University, Graduate School of Education and Human Development, Department of Educational Leadership, Program in Training and Educational Technology, Washington, DC 20052. Offers Graduate Certificate. *Students:* 2 part-time (both women); includes 1 minority (Black or African American, non-Hispanic/Latino). Average age 44. 2 applicants, 100% accepted, 1 enrolled. In 2016, 1 Graduate Certificate awarded. *Unit head:* Dr. Natalie Milman, Coordinator, 202-994-1884, E-mail: nmilman@gwu.edu. *Application contact:* Sarah Lang, Director of Graduate Admissions, 202-994-1447, Fax: 202-994-7207, E-mail: slang@gwu.edu.
Website: http://gsehd.gwu.edu/training-and-educational-technology-certificate

Georgia College & State University, Graduate School, The John H. Lounsbury College of Education, Program in Library Media, Milledgeville, GA 31061. Offers M Ed. *Program availability:* Part-time, evening/weekend, online only, 100% online. *Students:* 6 full-time (5 women), 37 part-time (30 women); includes 18 minority (16 Black or African American, non-Hispanic/Latino; 1 Hispanic/Latino; 1 Two or more races, non-Hispanic/Latino). Average age 34. 10 applicants, 100% accepted, 7 enrolled. In 2016, 16 master's awarded. *Degree requirements:* For master's, comprehensive exam, minimum GPA of 3.0, complete program within 4 years. *Entrance requirements:* For master's, on-site writing assessment, GRE General Test taken within six years (minimum scores 1,000 verbal and quantitative combined if taken before August 1, 2011, 305 if taken on or after August 1, 2011), or MAT (minimum score 400), level 4 teaching certificate, 2 professional recommendations, transcripts, proof of immunization, minimum GPA of 2.75. *Application deadline:* For fall admission, 7/1 priority date for domestic students; for spring admission, 11/1 priority date for domestic students; for summer admission, 4/1 priority date for domestic students. Applications are processed on a rolling basis. Application fee: $40. Electronic applications accepted. *Expenses:* $288 per credit hour in-state tuition; $1,027 per credit hour out-of-state; fees vary by hours enrolled. *Financial support:* In 2016–17, 3 students received support. Unspecified assistantships available. Financial award application deadline: 3/1; financial award applicants required to submit FAFSA. *Unit head:* Dr. Joseph Peters, Dean, College of Education, 478-445-2518, Fax: 478-445-6582, E-mail: joseph.peters@gcsu.edu. *Application contact:* Shanda Brand, Graduate Admissions Advisor, 478-445-1383, Fax: 478-445-6582, E-mail: shanda.brand@gcsu.edu.

Georgian Court University, School of Education, Lakewood, NJ 08701-2697. Offers administration and leadership (MA); autism spectrum disorders (Certificate); education (MA); instructional technology (Certificate). *Accreditation:* TEAC. *Program availability:* Part-time, evening/weekend. *Faculty:* 14 full-time (8 women), 31 part-time/adjunct (18 women). *Students:* 66 full-time (55 women), 376 part-time (312 women); includes 92 minority (44 Black or African American, non-Hispanic/Latino; 1 American Indian or Alaska Native, non-Hispanic/Latino; 8 Asian, non-Hispanic/Latino; 34 Hispanic/Latino; 5 Two or more races, non-Hispanic/Latino). Average age 34. 409 applicants, 62% accepted, 174 enrolled. In 2016, 95 master's, 1 other advanced degree awarded. *Degree requirements:* For master's, comprehensive exam (for some programs), thesis (for some programs). *Entrance requirements:* For master's, GRE, GMAT or NTE/PRAXIS, 3 letters of recommendation. Additional exam requirements/recommendations for international students: Required—TOEFL (minimum score 550 paper-based). *Application deadline:* For fall admission, 8/15 priority date for domestic students, 5/1 for international students; for spring admission, 1/15 priority date for domestic students, 10/1 for international students. Applications are processed on a rolling basis. Application fee: $40. Electronic applications accepted. *Expenses: Tuition:* Full-time $15,079; part-time $839 per credit. *Required fees:* $968; $496 per credit. Tuition and fees vary according to campus/location and program. *Financial support:* Scholarships/grants, health care benefits, and unspecified assistantships available. Financial award application deadline: 4/15; financial award applicants required to submit FAFSA. *Unit head:* Dr. Lynn DeCapua, Dean, 732-987-2729, E-mail: ldecapua@georgian.edu. *Application contact:* Patrick Givens, Director of Graduate and Professional Studies Admissions, 732-987-2736, Fax: 732-987-2000, E-mail: gps@georgian.edu.
Website: http://georgian.edu/academics/school-of-education/

Georgia Southern University, Jack N. Averitt College of Graduate Studies, College of Education, Department of Leadership, Technology, and Human Development, Program in Instructional Technology, Statesboro, GA 30460. Offers instructional technology

(M Ed, Ed S); school library media (M Ed, Ed S). *Program availability:* Part-time, evening/weekend, blended/hybrid learning. *Students:* 7 full-time (all women), 143 part-time (119 women); includes 38 minority (31 Black or African American, non-Hispanic/Latino; 1 American Indian or Alaska Native, non-Hispanic/Latino; 1 Asian, non-Hispanic/Latino; 3 Hispanic/Latino; 2 Two or more races, non-Hispanic/Latino). Average age 35. 58 applicants, 97% accepted, 22 enrolled. In 2016, 45 master's, 14 Ed Ss awarded. *Degree requirements:* For master's, portfolio, transition point assessments. *Entrance requirements:* For master's, GRE General Test or MAT, minimum GPA of 2.5. Additional exam requirements/recommendations for international students: Required—TOEFL (minimum score 550 paper-based; 80 iBT), IELTS (minimum score 6). *Application deadline:* For fall admission, 8/16 for domestic students, 3/1 priority date for international students; for spring admission, 1/11 for domestic students, 10/1 for international students; for summer admission, 5/10 for domestic students. Application fee: $50. Electronic applications accepted. *Expenses:* Tuition, state resident: full-time $7236; part-time $277 per semester hour. Tuition, nonresident: full-time $27,118; part-time $1105 per semester hour. *Required fees:* $2092. *Financial support:* In 2016–17, 2 students received support. Research assistantships, teaching assistantships, career-related internships or fieldwork, and scholarships/grants available. Support available to part-time students. Financial award application deadline: 4/15; financial award applicants required to submit FAFSA. *Faculty research:* Online learning in higher education and K-12, instructional technology leadership, school library media programs, twenty-first century skills, instructional technology in the content areas. *Unit head:* Dr. Lucy Green, Program Coordinator, 912-478-0275, Fax: 912-478-7104, E-mail: lgreen@georgiasouthern.edu. *Application contact:* Lydia Cross, Coordinator for Graduate Academic Services Center, 912-478-8664, E-mail: lcross@georgiasouthern.edu.
Website: http://coe.georgiasouthern.edu/itec/

Georgia State University, College of Education and Human Development, Learning Technologies Division, Atlanta, GA 30302-3083. Offers instructional design and technology (MS); instructional technology (PhD). *Program availability:* Part-time, evening/weekend. *Faculty:* 7 full-time (3 women). *Students:* 13 full-time (10 women), 34 part-time (19 women); includes 17 minority (11 Black or African American, non-Hispanic/Latino; 2 Asian, non-Hispanic/Latino; 1 Hispanic/Latino; 3 Two or more races, non-Hispanic/Latino), 1 international. Average age 39. 26 applicants, 38% accepted, 6 enrolled. In 2016, 8 master's, 2 doctorates awarded. *Degree requirements:* For master's, comprehensive exam; for doctorate, comprehensive exam, thesis/dissertation. *Entrance requirements:* For master's, GRE General Test, minimum GPA of 2.5; for doctorate, GRE General Test or MAT, minimum GPA of 3.3. Additional exam requirements/recommendations for international students: Required—TOEFL. Application fee: $50. Electronic applications accepted. *Expenses:* Tuition, state resident: full-time $6876; part-time $382 per credit hour. Tuition, nonresident: full-time $22,374; part-time $1243 per credit hour. *Required fees:* $2128; $1064 per term. Part-time tuition and fees vary according to course load and program. *Financial support:* Federal Work-Study and institutionally sponsored loans available. *Unit head:* Dr. Paul A. Alberto, Interim Dean, 404-413-8100, Fax: 404-413-8103, E-mail: palberto@gsu.edu. *Application contact:* Nancy Keita, Director, Office of Academic Assistance and Graduate Admissions, 404-413-8001, E-mail: nkeita@gsu.edu.
Website: http://ltd.education.gsu.edu/

Goucher College, Graduate Programs in Education, Baltimore, MD 21204-2794. Offers at-risk and diverse learners (M Ed, Certificate); athletic program leadership and administration (M Ed, Certificate); elementary and special education (MAT); elementary education (MAT); literacy strategies for content learning (M Ed, Certificate); middle school (M Ed, Certificate); Montessori studies (M Ed); reading instruction (M Ed, Certificate); school improvement leadership (M Ed, Certificate); school mediation (M Ed, Certificate); secondary and special education (MAT); secondary education (MAT); special education (MAT), including elementary education, secondary education; special education for certified teachers (M Ed, Certificate); teacher as leader in technology (M Ed, Certificate). *Program availability:* Part-time, evening/weekend. *Faculty:* 3 full-time (all women), 52 part-time/adjunct (40 women). *Students:* 29 full-time (20 women), 285 part-time (217 women); includes 54 minority (41 Black or African American, non-Hispanic/Latino; 3 Asian, non-Hispanic/Latino; 7 Hispanic/Latino; 3 Two or more races, non-Hispanic/Latino), 1 international. Average age 34. 85 applicants, 100% accepted, 61 enrolled. In 2016, 207 master's awarded. *Degree requirements:* For master's, thesis (M Ed), final presentation (MAT). *Entrance requirements:* For master's, minimum GPA of 3.0. Additional exam requirements/recommendations for international students: Required—TOEFL (minimum score 560 paper-based). *Application deadline:* For fall admission, 9/1 for domestic students; for spring admission, 1/15 for domestic students. Applications are processed on a rolling basis. Application fee: $75. Electronic applications accepted. *Expenses:* Contact institution. *Financial support:* Career-related internships or fieldwork and unspecified assistantships available. Support available to part-time students. Financial award application deadline: 4/15; financial award applicants required to submit FAFSA. *Faculty research:* Urban education, middle school, school improvement, teacher education, at-risk student achievement. *Unit head:* Dr. Phyllis Sunshine, Assistant Provost, 410-337-6047, Fax: 410-337-6394, E-mail: psunshin@goucher.edu. *Application contact:* Shelby Hillers, Admissions Coordinator, 410-337-6200, Fax: 410-337-6085, E-mail: shelby.hillers@goucher.edu.
Website: http://www.goucher.edu/graduate-programs/graduate-programs-in-education

Graceland University, Gleazer School of Education, Independence, MO 64050. Offers curriculum and instruction (M Ed); differentiated instruction (M Ed); instructional leadership (M Ed); literacy and instruction (M Ed); management in the inclusive classroom (M Ed); special education (M Ed); technology integration (M Ed). *Accreditation:* NCATE. *Program availability:* Part-time, evening/weekend, online learning. *Faculty:* 2 full-time (both women), 9 part-time/adjunct (5 women). *Students:* 115 full-time (96 women), 20 part-time (17 women); includes 10 minority (5 Black or African American, non-Hispanic/Latino; 1 Asian, non-Hispanic/Latino; 1 Hispanic/Latino; 1 Native Hawaiian or other Pacific Islander, non-Hispanic/Latino; 2 Two or more races, non-Hispanic/Latino), 2 international. 155 applicants, 61% accepted, 85 enrolled. In 2016, 61 master's awarded. *Degree requirements:* For master's, action research project. *Entrance requirements:* For master's, minimum GPA of 3.0, teaching certificate, current teaching contract. Additional exam requirements/recommendations for international students: Required—TOEFL. *Application deadline:* For fall admission, 10/1 for domestic students; for winter admission, 11/15 for domestic students; for spring admission, 2/15 priority date for domestic students; for summer admission, 6/1 for domestic students. Applications are processed on a rolling basis. Application fee: $50. Electronic applications accepted. *Expenses:* Contact institution. *Financial support:* Institutionally sponsored loans and scholarships/grants available. Financial award application deadline: 12/15; financial award applicants required to submit FAFSA. *Faculty research:* Literacy, technology, faculty mentoring, adult literacy, e-learning, online teaching. *Unit head:* Dr. Lee Bash, Interim Dean, 641-784-5072, E-mail: bash@graceland.edu. *Application contact:* Jeanette Calipetro, Admissions Representative, 816-423-4716, Fax: 816-833-2990, E-mail: jcali1@graceland.edu.
Website: http://www.graceland.edu/education

Grambling State University, School of Graduate Studies and Research, College of Education, Department of Educational Leadership, Grambling, LA 71245. Offers developmental education (MS, Ed D, PMC), including curriculum and instructional design (Ed D), English (MS), guidance and counseling (MS), higher education administration and management (Ed D), mathematics (MS), reading (MS), science (MS), student development and personnel services (Ed D); educational leadership (M Ed). *Program availability:* Part-time, evening/weekend. *Degree requirements:* For master's, comprehensive exam, thesis (for some programs); for doctorate, comprehensive exam, thesis/dissertation. *Entrance requirements:* For master's, GRE, minimum GPA of 2.5 on last degree; for doctorate, GRE (minimum score 1000, 500 on Verbal), master's degree, minimum GPA of 3.0 on last degree. Additional exam requirements/recommendations for international students: Required—TOEFL (minimum score 500 paper-based; 62 iBT). Electronic applications accepted.

Grand Canyon University, College of Education, Phoenix, AZ 85017-1097. Offers autism spectrum disorders (MA); curriculum and instruction (MA); early childhood education (M Ed); educational administration (M Ed); educational leadership (M Ed); elementary education (M Ed); gifted education (MA); instructional technology (MS); K-12 leadership (Ed S); reading (MA); secondary education (M Ed); secondary humanities education (M Ed); secondary STEM education (M Ed); special education (M Ed); teaching and learning (Ed D); teaching English to speakers of other languages (MA). *Program availability:* Part-time, evening/weekend, online learning. *Degree requirements:* For master's, publishable research paper (M Ed), e-portfolio. *Entrance requirements:* For master's, undergraduate degree from accredited, GCU-approved college, university, or program with minimum GPA 2.8. Additional exam requirements/recommendations for international students: Required—TOEFL (minimum score 550 paper-based; 79 iBT), IELTS (minimum score 6). *Application deadline:* For fall admission, 8/21 for domestic students, 7/2 for international students; for spring admission, 12/24 for domestic students, 11/1 for international students. Applications are processed on a rolling basis. Application fee: $100. Electronic applications accepted. *Financial support:* Federal Work-Study available. Support available to part-time students. Financial award applicants required to submit FAFSA. *Unit head:* Dr. Kimberly L. LaPrade, Dean, 602-639-6360, E-mail: kimberly.laprade@gcu.edu. *Application contact:* Dr. Kimberly L. LaPrade, Dean, 602-639-6360, E-mail: kimberly.laprade@gcu.edu.
Website: https://www.gcu.edu/college-of-education.php

Grand Valley State University, College of Education, Program in Educational Technology, Allendale, MI 49401-9403. Offers M Ed. *Accreditation:* NCATE. *Program availability:* Part-time, evening/weekend, 100% online. *Students:* 16 full-time (10 women), 52 part-time (36 women); includes 5 minority (2 Black or African American, non-Hispanic/Latino; 1 Asian, non-Hispanic/Latino; 1 Hispanic/Latino; 1 Two or more races, non-Hispanic/Latino), 1 international. Average age 30. 15 applicants, 100% accepted, 15 enrolled. In 2016, 13 master's awarded. *Degree requirements:* For master's, project or thesis. *Entrance requirements:* For master's, GRE General Test or minimum GPA of 3.0, last 60 credits from regionally-accredited college/university, 3 letters of recommendation. Additional exam requirements/recommendations for international students: Required—TOEFL (minimum score 550 paper-based, 80 iBT), IELTS (6.5), or Michigan English Language Assessment Battery. *Application deadline:* Applications are processed on a rolling basis. Application fee: $30. Electronic applications accepted. *Expenses:* $628 per credit hour. *Financial support:* In 2016–17, 2 students received support. Unspecified assistantships available. *Unit head:* Dr. Jason Siko, Department Director, 616-331-6652, Fax: 616-331-6285, E-mail: sikoj@gvsu.edu. *Application contact:* Thomas Owens, Director, Student Information and Services Center, 616-331-6282, Fax: 616-331-6217, E-mail: owenst@gvsu.edu.

Grand Valley State University, College of Education, Programs in General Education, Allendale, MI 49401-9403. Offers adult and higher education (M Ed); early childhood education (M Ed); educational differentiation (M Ed); educational leadership (M Ed); educational technology integration (M Ed); elementary education (M Ed); middle level education (M Ed); school library media services (M Ed); secondary level education (M Ed); teaching English to speakers of other languages (M Ed). *Program availability:* Part-time, evening/weekend, 100% online, blended/hybrid learning. *Students:* 28 part-time (20 women); includes 6 minority (4 Black or African American, non-Hispanic/Latino; 1 American Indian or Alaska Native, non-Hispanic/Latino; 1 Hispanic/Latino). Average age 42. In 2016, 17 master's awarded. *Degree requirements:* For master's, project or thesis. *Entrance requirements:* For master's, GRE General Test or minimum GPA of 3.0, last 60 credits from regionally-accredited college/university, 3 letters of recommendation. Additional exam requirements/recommendations for international students: Required—TOEFL (minimum score 550 paper-based, 80 iBT), IELTS (6.5), or Michigan English Language Assessment Battery. *Application deadline:* Applications are processed on a rolling basis. Application fee: $30. Electronic applications accepted. *Expenses:* $628 per credit hour. *Financial support:* In 2016–17, 2 students received support. Career-related internships or fieldwork, Federal Work-Study, scholarships/grants, and unspecified assistantships available. *Faculty research:* Effectiveness of technology in education, parental involvement, effective teaching, effective schools research. *Unit head:* Dr. Doug Busman, Graduate Program Director, 616-331-6250, E-mail: busmando@gvsu.edu. *Application contact:* Thomas Owens, Director, Student Information and Services Center, 616-331-6282, Fax: 616-331-6217, E-mail: owenst@gvsu.edu.
Website: http://www.gvsu.edu/coe/

Harrisburg University of Science and Technology, Learning Technologies and Media Systems Program, Harrisburg, PA 17101. Offers games and simulations (MS); instructional design (MS); instructional development (MS); instructional technology (MS); integration and leadership (MS). *Program availability:* Part-time, evening/weekend. *Faculty:* 1 full-time (0 women), 5 part-time/adjunct (3 women). *Students:* 23 full-time (19 women), 13 part-time (7 women), 25 international. In 2016, 4 master's awarded. *Degree requirements:* For master's, thesis optional. *Entrance requirements:* Additional exam requirements/recommendations for international students: Required—TOEFL (minimum score 520 paper-based; 80 iBT); Recommended—IELTS (minimum score 6). *Application deadline:* Applications are processed on a rolling basis. Application fee: $0. Electronic applications accepted. *Expenses: Tuition:* Full-time $4800; part-time $800 per semester hour. *Financial support:* Applicants required to submit FAFSA. *Faculty research:* User compatibility with technology, teaching and training, curriculum development, instructional design, gamification. *Unit head:* Dr. Richard Kordel, Program Lead, 717-901-5167, E-mail: rkordel@harrisburgu.edu.

Harvard University, Extension School, Cambridge, MA 02138-3722. Offers applied sciences (CAS); biotechnology (ALM); educational technologies (ALM); educational technology (CET); English for graduate and professional studies (DGP); environmental management (ALM, CEM); information technology (ALM); journalism (ALM); liberal arts (ALM); management (ALM, CM); mathematics for teaching (ALM); museum studies (ALM); premedical studies (Diploma); publication and communication (CPC). *Program availability:* Part-time, evening/weekend. *Degree requirements:* For master's, thesis. *Entrance requirements:* For master's, 3 completed graduate courses with grade of B or higher. Additional exam requirements/recommendations for international students: Required—TOEFL (minimum score 600 paper-based), TWE (minimum score 5). *Expenses:* Contact institution.

Harvard University, Harvard Graduate School of Education, Master's Programs in Education, Cambridge, MA 02138. Offers arts in education (Ed M); education policy and management (Ed M); higher education (Ed M); human development and psychology

(Ed M); international education policy (Ed M); language and literacy (Ed M); learning and teaching (Ed M); mind, brain, and education (Ed M); prevention science and practice (Ed M); school leadership (Ed M); special studies (Ed M); teacher education (Ed M); technology, innovation, and education (Ed M). *Program availability:* Part-time. *Entrance requirements:* For master's, GRE General Test, statement of purpose, 3 letters of recommendation, resume, official transcripts. Additional exam requirements/recommendations for international students: Required—TOEFL (minimum score 613 paper-based; 104 iBT), TWE (minimum score 5). Electronic applications accepted. *Faculty research:* Learning and development, educational leadership and organizations, education policy analysis.

Hofstra University, School of Education, Programs in Teacher Education, Hempstead, NY 11549. Offers bilingual education (MA, Advanced Certificate); bilingual extension (Advanced Certificate), including education/speech language pathology; business education (MS Ed); early childhood and childhood education (MS Ed); early childhood education (MA, MS Ed); education technology (Advanced Certificate); elementary education (MA, MS Ed), including science, technology, engineering, and mathematics (STEM) (MA); English education (MS Ed); family and consumer science (MS Ed); fine arts and music education (Advanced Certificate); fine arts education (MS Ed); foreign language and TESOL (MS Ed); foreign language education (MS Ed), including French, German, Russian, Spanish; learning and teaching (Ed D), including applied linguistics, art education, arts and humanities, early childhood education, English education, human development, math education, math, science, and technology, multicultural education, physical education, science education, social studies education, special education; mathematics education (MA, MS Ed); middle school extension (Advanced Certificate), including grades 5-6, grades 7-9; music education (MA, MS Ed); science education (MA, MS Ed), including biology, chemistry, earth science, geology, physics; secondary education (Advanced Certificate); social studies education (MA, MS Ed); teaching languages other than English and TESOL (MS Ed); TESOL (MS Ed, Advanced Certificate). *Program availability:* Part-time, evening/weekend, blended/hybrid learning. *Students:* 139 full-time (97 women), 145 part-time (106 women); includes 60 minority (15 Black or African American, non-Hispanic/Latino; 1 American Indian or Alaska Native, non-Hispanic/Latino; 12 Asian, non-Hispanic/Latino; 31 Hispanic/Latino; 1 Two or more races, non-Hispanic/Latino), 21 international. Average age 29. 255 applicants, 86% accepted, 122 enrolled. In 2016, 101 master's, 4 doctorates, 43 other advanced degrees awarded. *Degree requirements:* For master's, comprehensive exam, thesis (for some programs), exit project, student teaching, fieldwork, electronic portfolio, curriculum project, minimum GPA of 3.0; for doctorate, thesis/dissertation; for Advanced Certificate, 3 foreign languages, comprehensive exam (for some programs), thesis project. *Entrance requirements:* For master's, GRE, MAT, 2 letters of recommendation, portfolio, teacher certification (MA), interview, essay; for doctorate, GMAT, GRE, LSAT, or MAT; for Advanced Certificate, 2 letters of recommendation, essay, interview and/or portfolio, teaching certificate. Additional exam requirements/recommendations for international students: Required—TOEFL (minimum score 550 paper-based; 80 iBT). *Application deadline:* Applications are processed on a rolling basis. Application fee: $75. Electronic applications accepted. *Expenses: Tuition:* Full-time $1240. *Required fees:* $970. Tuition and fees vary according to program. *Financial support:* In 2016–17, 149 students received support, including 58 fellowships with full and partial tuition reimbursements available (averaging $5,309 per year), 5 research assistantships with full and partial tuition reimbursements available (averaging $7,073 per year); career-related internships or fieldwork, Federal Work-Study, institutionally sponsored loans, scholarships/grants, traineeships, tuition waivers (full and partial), and unspecified assistantships also available. Support available to part-time students. Financial award applicants required to submit FAFSA. *Faculty research:* Educational interventions that foster critical-thinking skills; teachers' attitudes about professional development; threats to teacher quality. *Unit head:* Dr. Eustace Thompson, Chairperson, 516-463-5749, Fax: 516-463-6275, E-mail: eustace.g.thompson@hofstra.edu. *Application contact:* Sunil Samuel, Assistant Vice President of Admissions, 516-463-4723, Fax: 516-463-4664, E-mail: graduateadmission@hofstra.edu.
Website: http://www.hofstra.edu/education/

Idaho State University, Office of Graduate Studies, College of Education, Department of Educational Leadership and Instructional Design, Pocatello, ID 83209-8059. Offers educational administration (M Ed, 6th Year Certificate, Ed S); educational leadership (Ed D), including education training and development, educational administration, educational technology, higher education administration; educational leadership and instructional design (PhD); instructional technology (M Ed). *Program availability:* Part-time. *Degree requirements:* For master's, comprehensive exam, thesis optional, internship, oral exam or deferred thesis; for doctorate, comprehensive exam, thesis/dissertation, written exam; for other advanced degree, comprehensive exam, thesis (for some programs), written and oral exam. *Entrance requirements:* For master's, MAT, bachelor's degree, minimum GPA of 3.0, 1 year of training experience; for doctorate, GRE General Test or MAT, minimum GPA of 3.0 (undergraduate), 3.5 (graduate); departmental interview; for other advanced degree, GRE General Test, minimum GPA of 3.0, master's degree. Additional exam requirements/recommendations for international students: Required—TOEFL (minimum score 550 paper-based; 80 iBT). Electronic applications accepted. *Faculty research:* Educational leadership, gender issues in education and sport, staff development.

Idaho State University, Office of Graduate Studies, College of Education, Program in Instructional Methods and Technology, Pocatello, ID 83209. Offers instructional design (PhD); instructional technology (M Ed). *Program availability:* Part-time. *Degree requirements:* For master's, comprehensive exam, thesis optional, minimum 36 credits; for doctorate, comprehensive exam, thesis/dissertation (for some programs). *Entrance requirements:* For master's, GRE or MAT, bachelor's degree; for doctorate, GRE or MAT, master's degree. Additional exam requirements/recommendations for international students: Required—TOEFL (minimum score 550 paper-based; 80 iBT). Electronic applications accepted.

Indiana State University, College of Graduate and Professional Studies, Bayh College of Education, Department of Teaching and Learning, Terre Haute, IN 47809. Offers curriculum and instruction (M Ed, PhD); educational technology (MS). *Accreditation:* NCATE. *Degree requirements:* For doctorate, thesis/dissertation. *Entrance requirements:* For doctorate, GRE General Test. Electronic applications accepted. *Faculty research:* Discipline FERPA reading, teacher strengths and needs.

Indiana University Bloomington, School of Education, Department of Instructional Systems Technology, Bloomington, IN 47405-1006. Offers MS, PhD. *Program availability:* Online learning. Terminal master's awarded for partial completion of doctoral program. *Degree requirements:* For master's, thesis optional, portfolio; for doctorate, comprehensive exam, thesis/dissertation, dossier review. *Entrance requirements:* For master's and doctorate, GRE General Test, minimum GPA of 2.75. Additional exam requirements/recommendations for international students: Required—TOEFL. Electronic applications accepted. *Faculty research:* Instructional design and theory development, e-learning and distance education, systemic change, serious simulations and games, human performance improvement, technology integration in education.

Indiana University of Pennsylvania, School of Graduate Studies and Research, College of Education and Educational Technology, Department of Adult and Community Education, Program in Adult and Community Education/Communications Technology, Indiana, PA 15705. Offers MA. *Program availability:* Part-time, evening/weekend. *Faculty:* 2 full-time (1 woman). *Students:* 12 full-time (4 women), 6 part-time (4 women); includes 6 minority (3 Black or African American, non-Hispanic/Latino; 2 Hispanic/Latino; 1 Two or more races, non-Hispanic/Latino), 8 international. Average age 27. 28 applicants, 71% accepted, 13 enrolled. In 2016, 21 master's awarded. *Degree requirements:* For master's, thesis optional. *Entrance requirements:* For master's, 2 letters of recommendation, resume. Additional exam requirements/recommendations for international students: Required—TOEFL (minimum score 540 paper-based; 76 iBT). *Application deadline:* Applications are processed on a rolling basis. Application fee: $50. Electronic applications accepted. *Expenses:* Tuition, state resident: full-time $8694; part-time $483 per credit. Tuition, nonresident: full-time $13,050; part-time $725 per credit. *Required fees:* $157 per credit. $50 per term. Tuition and fees vary according to course load and program. *Financial support:* In 2016–17, 11 research assistantships with tuition reimbursements (averaging $4,698 per year) were awarded; fellowships, teaching assistantships, career-related internships or fieldwork, Federal Work-Study, scholarships/grants, and unspecified assistantships also available. Support available to part-time students. Financial award application deadline: 4/15; financial award applicants required to submit FAFSA. *Unit head:* Dr. Gary Dean, Graduate Coordinator, 724-357-2470, E-mail: gjdean@iup.edu.
Website: http://www.iup.edu/aec

Indiana University of Pennsylvania, School of Graduate Studies and Research, College of Education and Educational Technology, Department of Communications Media, Program in Communications Media and Instructional Technology, Indiana, PA 15705. Offers PhD. *Faculty:* 10 full-time (4 women). *Students:* 13 full-time (3 women), 37 part-time (15 women); includes 4 minority (3 Black or African American, non-Hispanic/Latino; 1 Two or more races, non-Hispanic/Latino), 5 international. Average age 38. 65 applicants, 26% accepted, 6 enrolled. In 2016, 10 doctorates awarded. Application fee: $50. *Expenses:* Contact institution. *Financial support:* In 2016–17, 2 fellowships with full tuition reimbursements (averaging $2,296 per year), 7 research assistantships with tuition reimbursements (averaging $5,769 per year), 3 teaching assistantships with partial tuition reimbursements (averaging $23,305 per year) were awarded. *Unit head:* Dr. Zachary Stiegler, Coordinator, 724-357-3219, E-mail: zachary.stiegler@iup.edu.
Website: http://www.iup.edu/commmedia/programs/phdcmit/

Indiana University South Bend, College of Liberal Arts and Sciences, South Bend, IN 46634-7111. Offers advanced computer programming (Graduate Certificate); applied informatics (Graduate Certificate); applied mathematics and computer science (MS); behavior modification (Graduate Certificate); computer applications (Graduate Certificate); computer programming (Graduate Certificate); correctional management and supervision (Graduate Certificate); English (MA); health systems management (Graduate Certificate); international studies (Graduate Certificate); liberal studies (MLS); nonprofit management (Graduate Certificate); paralegal studies (Graduate Certificate); professional writing (Graduate Certificate); public affairs (MPA); public management (Graduate Certificate); social and cultural diversity (Graduate Certificate); strategic sustainability leadership (Graduate Certificate); technology for administration (Graduate Certificate). *Program availability:* Part-time, evening/weekend. *Faculty:* 79 full-time (33 women). *Students:* 31 full-time (11 women), 92 part-time (53 women); includes 28 minority (9 Black or African American, non-Hispanic/Latino; 8 Asian, non-Hispanic/Latino; 5 Hispanic/Latino; 6 Two or more races, non-Hispanic/Latino), 19 international. Average age 38. 51 applicants, 84% accepted, 31 enrolled. In 2016, 30 master's, 6 other advanced degrees awarded. *Degree requirements:* For master's, variable foreign language requirement, thesis (for some programs). *Entrance requirements:* For master's, minimum GPA of 3.0. Additional exam requirements/recommendations for international students: Required—TOEFL (minimum score 550 paper-based; 80 iBT). *Application deadline:* For fall admission, 7/31 priority date for domestic students, 7/1 priority date for international students; for spring admission, 3/31 priority date for domestic students, 11/1 priority date for international students. Applications are processed on a rolling basis. Application fee: $40 ($60 for international students). *Expenses:* $276.98 per credit hour in-state; $652.54 per credit hour out-of-state. *Financial support:* In 2016–17, 5 teaching assistantships were awarded; Federal Work-Study also available. Support available to part-time students. Financial award application deadline: 3/10. *Faculty research:* Artificial intelligence, bioinformatics, English language and literature, creative writing, computer networks. *Total annual research expenditures:* $127,000. *Unit head:* Dr. Elizabeth E. Dunn, Dean, 574-520-4290, E-mail: elizdunn@iusb.edu. *Application contact:* Admissions Counselor, 574-520-4839, Fax: 574-520-4834, E-mail: graduate@iusb.edu.
Website: https://www.iusb.edu/clas/

Instituto Tecnológico y de Estudios Superiores de Monterrey, Campus Central de Veracruz, Graduate Programs, Córdoba, Mexico. Offers administration (MA); administration of information technologies (MTI); computer sciences (MCC); education (MEE); educational institution administration (MAD); educational technology (MTE); electronic commerce (MCE); finance (MAF); humanistic studies (MEH); international business for Latin America (MNL); marketing (MMT); science (MCP). *Program availability:* Part-time, evening/weekend, online learning. *Degree requirements:* For master's, thesis (for some programs). *Entrance requirements:* For master's, PAEP College Board. Electronic applications accepted.

Instituto Tecnológico y de Estudios Superiores de Monterrey, Campus Ciudad de México, Virtual University Division, Ciudad de Mexico, Mexico. Offers administration of information technologies (MA); computer sciences (MA); education (MA, PhD); educational technology (MA); environmental engineering (MA); environmental systems (MA); humanistic studies (MA); industrial engineering (MA); international business for Latin America (MA); quality systems (MA); quality systems and productivity (MA). *Program availability:* Part-time, evening/weekend, online learning. *Entrance requirements:* For master's and doctorate, Instituto entrance exam. Additional exam requirements/recommendations for international students: Required—TOEFL.

Instituto Tecnológico y de Estudios Superiores de Monterrey, Campus Ciudad Juárez, Program in Educational Innovation, Ciudad Juárez, Mexico. Offers DE.

Instituto Tecnológico y de Estudios Superiores de Monterrey, Campus Ciudad Juárez, Program in Educational Technology, Ciudad Juárez, Mexico. Offers MTE.

Instituto Tecnológico y de Estudios Superiores de Monterrey, Campus Estado de México, Professional and Graduate Division, Estado de Mexico, Mexico. Offers administration of information technologies (MITA); architecture (M Arch); business administration (GMBA, MBA); computer sciences (MCS, PhD); education (M Ed); educational institution administration (MAD); educational technology and innovation (PhD); electronic commerce (MEC); environmental systems (MS); finance (MAF); humanistic studies (MHS); information sciences and knowledge management (MISKM); information systems (MS); manufacturing systems (MS); marketing (MEM); quality systems and productivity (MS); science and materials engineering (PhD); telecommunications management (MTM). *Program availability:* Part-time, online learning. *Degree requirements:* For master's, one foreign language, thesis (for some programs); for doctorate, one foreign language, thesis/dissertation. *Entrance requirements:* For master's, E-PAEP 500, interview; for doctorate, E-PAEP 500, research proposal. Additional exam requirements/recommendations for international students: Required—TOEFL (minimum score 550 paper-based). *Faculty research:* Surface treatments by plasmas, mechanical properties, robotics, graphical computing, mechatronics security protocols.

Instituto Tecnológico y de Estudios Superiores de Monterrey, Campus Irapuato, Graduate Programs, Irapuato, Mexico. Offers administration (MBA); administration of information technology (MAIT); administration of telecommunications (MAT); architecture (M Arch); computer science (MCS); education (M Ed); educational administration (MEA); educational innovation and technology (DEIT); educational technology (MET); electronic commerce (MBA); environmental administration and planning (MEAP); environmental systems (MES); finances (MBA); humanistic studies (MHS); international management for Latin American executives (MIMLAE); library and information science (MLIS); manufacturing quality management (MMQM); marketing research (MBA).

Inter American University of Puerto Rico, Metropolitan Campus, Graduate Programs, Program in Educational Computing, San Juan, PR 00919-1293. Offers MA. *Degree requirements:* For master's, comprehensive exam, portfolio. *Entrance requirements:* For master's, GRE or EXADEP, minimum GPA of 2.5. Electronic applications accepted. *Faculty research:* Effectiveness of multimedia, World Wide Web for distance learning.

Iowa State University of Science and Technology, Department of Education, Ames, IA 50011. Offers curriculum and instructional technology (M Ed, MS, PhD); elementary education (M Ed, MS); historical, philosophical, and comparative studies in education (M Ed, MS); special education (M Ed, MS, PhD). *Degree requirements:* For master's, thesis or alternative; for doctorate, thesis/dissertation. *Entrance requirements:* For master's and doctorate, GRE General Test. Additional exam requirements/ recommendations for international students: Required—TOEFL (minimum score 560 paper-based; 83 iBT), IELTS (minimum score 6.5). *Application deadline:* For fall admission, 1/1 priority date for domestic and international students; for spring admission, 9/1 for domestic and international students. Application fee: $60 ($90 for international students). Electronic applications accepted. *Application contact:* Robyn Goldy, Application Contact, 515-294-1241, Fax: 515-294-4942, E-mail: rgoldy@iastate.edu.
Website: http://www.ci.hs.iastate.edu

Jacksonville State University, College of Graduate Studies and Continuing Education, College of Education and Professional Studies, Program in Library Media, Jacksonville, AL 36265-1602. Offers MS Ed. *Program availability:* Part-time, evening/weekend. *Faculty:* 10 full-time (6 women), 12 part-time/adjunct (5 women). *Students:* 5 full-time (all women), 9 part-time (7 women); includes 1 minority (Black or African American, non-Hispanic/Latino). Average age 38. 6 applicants, 50% accepted, 2 enrolled. In 2016, 11 master's awarded. *Degree requirements:* For master's, comprehensive exam, thesis (for some programs). *Entrance requirements:* For master's, GRE General Test or MAT. Additional exam requirements/recommendations for international students: Required—TOEFL (minimum score 500 paper-based; 61 iBT). *Application deadline:* Applications are processed on a rolling basis. Application fee: $35. Electronic applications accepted. *Financial support:* In 2016–17, 3 students received support. Available to part-time students. Application deadline: 4/1; applicants required to submit FAFSA. *Unit head:* Dr. Tommy Turner, Head, 256-782-5180, E-mail: tturner@jsu.edu. *Application contact:* Dr. Jean Pugliese, Associate Dean, 256-782-8278, Fax: 256-782-5321, E-mail: pugliese@jsu.edu.

James Madison University, The Graduate School, College of Education, Program in Education, Harrisonburg, VA 22807. Offers early childhood education (preK-3) (MAT); educational leadership (M Ed); educational technology (M Ed); elementary education (MAT); equity and cultural diversity (M Ed); inclusive early childhood education (MAT); K-8 mathematics specialist (M Ed); middle education (MAT); reading education (M Ed); secondary education (MAT); Spanish language and culture for educators (M Ed); TESOL (MAT). *Accreditation:* NCATE. *Program availability:* Part-time, evening/ weekend. *Faculty:* 21 full-time (12 women), 5 part-time/adjunct (2 women). *Students:* 249 full-time (220 women), 123 part-time (86 women); includes 43 minority (7 Black or African American, non-Hispanic/Latino; 7 Asian, non-Hispanic/Latino; 17 Hispanic/ Latino; 12 Two or more races, non-Hispanic/Latino), 2 international. Average age 30. 355 applicants, 98% accepted, 312 enrolled. In 2016, 247 master's awarded. Application fee: $55. Electronic applications accepted. *Financial support:* In 2016–17, 16 students received support. Career-related internships or fieldwork, Federal Work-Study, and 22 assistantships (averaging $7911) available. Financial award application deadline: 3/1; financial award applicants required to submit FAFSA. *Unit head:* Dr. Phillip M. Wishon, Dean, 540-568-6572, E-mail: wishonpm@jmu.edu. *Application contact:* Lynette D. Michael, Director of Graduate Admissions, 540-568-6131 Ext. 6395, Fax: 540-568-7860, E-mail: michaeld@jmu.edu.
Website: http://www.jmu.edu/coe/index.shtml

Johns Hopkins University, School of Education, Master's Programs in Education, Baltimore, MD 21218. Offers counseling (MS), including clinical mental health counseling, school counseling; education (MS), including educational studies, gifted education, reading, school administration and supervision, technology for educators; elementary education (MAT); health professions (M Ed); intelligence analysis (MS); organizational leadership (MS); secondary education (MAT), including biology, chemistry, earth/space science, English, physics, social studies; special education (MS), including early childhood special education, general special education studies, mild to moderate disabilities, severe disabilities. *Program availability:* Part-time, evening/ weekend, 100% online, blended/hybrid learning. *Students:* 345 full-time (265 women), 1,601 part-time (1,245 women); includes 837 minority (392 Black or African American, non-Hispanic/Latino; 7 American Indian or Alaska Native, non-Hispanic/Latino; 141 Asian, non-Hispanic/Latino; 207 Hispanic/Latino; 7 Native Hawaiian or other Pacific Islander, non-Hispanic/Latino; 83 Two or more races, non-Hispanic/Latino), 55 international. Average age 27. 1,352 applicants, 76% accepted, 819 enrolled. In 2016, 642 master's awarded. *Degree requirements:* For master's, comprehensive exam (for some programs), portfolio, capstone project and/or internship; PRAXIS II (subject area assessments) for initial teacher preparation programs that lead to licensure. *Entrance requirements:* For master's, GRE (for full-time programs only); PRAXIS I/core or state-approved alternative (for initial teacher preparation programs that lead to licensure), minimum of bachelor's degree from regionally- or nationally-accredited institution; minimum GPA of 3.0 in all previous programs of study; official transcripts from all post-secondary institutions attended; essay; curriculum vitae/resume; letters of recommendation (3 for full-time programs, 2 for part-time programs); dispositions survey. Additional exam requirements/recommendations for international students: Required—TOEFL (minimum score 600 paper-based; 100 iBT), IELTS (minimum score 7). *Application deadline:* For fall admission, 4/1 priority date for domestic students, 4/1 for international students; for spring admission, 10/1 priority date for domestic students, 10/1 for international students; for summer admission, 2/1 priority date for domestic students, 2/1 for international students. Applications are processed on a rolling basis. Application fee: $80. Electronic applications accepted. *Expenses:* Contact institution. *Financial support:* Application deadline: 4/1; applicants required to submit FAFSA. *Unit head:* Dr. Christopher C. Morphew, Dean. *Application contact:* Elisabeth Woodward, Director of Admissions, 410-516-9796, Fax: 410-516-9817, E-mail: soe.info@jhu.edu.
Website: http://education.jhu.edu

Johnson University, Graduate and Professional Programs, Knoxville, TN 37998-1001. Offers biblical interpretation (Graduate Certificate); business administration (MBA); Christian ministries (Graduate Certificate); clinical mental health counseling (MA); educational technology (MA); intercultural studies (MA); leadership (MBA); leadership studies (PhD); New Testament (MA); nonprofit management (MBA); school counseling (MA); spiritual formation and leadership (Graduate Certificate); strategic ministry (MA); teacher education (MA). *Program availability:* Part-time, evening/weekend, 100% online, blended/hybrid learning. *Faculty:* 26 full-time (10 women), 32 part-time/adjunct (9 women). *Students:* 126 full-time (46 women), 170 part-time (65 women); includes 33 minority (13 Black or African American, non-Hispanic/Latino; 1 American Indian or Alaska Native, non-Hispanic/Latino; 4 Asian, non-Hispanic/Latino; 8 Hispanic/Latino; 7 Two or more races, non-Hispanic/Latino), 21 international. Average age 35. In 2016, 106 master's, 3 doctorates awarded. *Degree requirements:* For master's, variable foreign language requirement, comprehensive exam, thesis (for some programs), internships; for doctorate, variable foreign language requirement, comprehensive exam, thesis/dissertation, internships. *Entrance requirements:* For master's, PRAXIS (for MA in teacher education); MAT (for counseling); GRE or GMAT (for MBA), interview, 3 references, transcripts, essay, minimum GPA of 2.5 or 3.0 (depending on program); for doctorate, GRE or MAT (taken not less than 5 years prior), interview, 3 references, transcripts, essay, minimum GPA of 3.0; for Graduate Certificate, interview, 3 references, transcripts, essay, minimum GPA of 3.0. Additional exam requirements/ recommendations for international students: Required—TOEFL (minimum score 527 paper-based; 71 iBT). *Application deadline:* For fall admission, 7/1 for domestic students; for spring admission, 11/1 for domestic students; for summer admission, 4/1 for domestic students. Application fee: $50. Electronic applications accepted. *Expenses:* Contact institution. *Financial support:* Scholarships/grants available. Financial award application deadline: 4/15; financial award applicants required to submit FAFSA. *Unit head:* Richard Clark, Vice President for External Relations, 865-251-2327, E-mail: rclark@johnsonu.edu. *Application contact:* Lisa Tarwater, Director of Graduate Admissions, 865-251-3400, E-mail: ltarwater@johnsonu.edu.

Kansas State University, Graduate School, College of Education, Department of Curriculum and Instruction, Manhattan, KS 66506. Offers curriculum and instruction (Ed D, PhD); digital teaching and learning (MS); educational computing, design and online learning (MS); elementary/middle level curriculum and instruction (MS); online learning (Certificate); reading specialist endorsement (MS); reading/language arts (MS); teacher leader/school improvement (MS); teaching and learning (Certificate). *Accreditation:* NCATE. *Program availability:* Part-time, online learning. *Faculty:* 36 full-time (22 women), 18 part-time/adjunct (9 women). *Students:* 59 full-time (40 women), 94 part-time (72 women); includes 21 minority (5 Black or African American, non-Hispanic/ Latino; 3 Asian, non-Hispanic/Latino; 11 Hispanic/Latino; 2 Two or more races, non-Hispanic/Latino), 20 international. Average age 35. 70 applicants, 71% accepted, 36 enrolled. In 2016, 61 master's, 12 doctorates, 9 other advanced degrees awarded. *Degree requirements:* For master's, comprehensive exam, portfolio, project, report or thesis; for doctorate, comprehensive exam, thesis/dissertation, preliminary exam; for Certificate, comprehensive exam, portfolio. *Entrance requirements:* For master's, minimum GPA of 3.0, 3 letters of recommendation; for doctorate, GRE, minimum GPA of 3.0, 3 letters of recommendation, evidence of scholarly writing; for Certificate, minimum GPA of 3.0, letters of recommendation. Additional exam requirements/recommendations for international students: Required—TOEFL (minimum score 550 paper-based; 80 iBT) or IELTS. *Application deadline:* For fall admission, 3/1 priority date for domestic students, 2/1 priority date for international students; for spring admission, 10/1 priority date for domestic students, 8/1 priority date for international students. Applications are processed on a rolling basis. Application fee: $50 ($75 for international students). Electronic applications accepted. *Expenses:* Tuition, state resident: full-time $9670. Tuition, nonresident: full-time $21,828. *Required fees:* $862. *Financial support:* In 2016–17, 1 research assistantship (averaging $19,980 per year), 8 teaching assistantships (averaging $12,620 per year) were awarded; career-related internships or fieldwork, institutionally sponsored loans, scholarships/grants, and unspecified assistantships also available. Support available to part-time students. Financial award application deadline: 3/1; financial award applicants required to submit FAFSA. *Faculty research:* Literacy and technology, critical race theory and diversity, achievement gaps, school improvement, teacher education. *Total annual research expenditures:* $647,057. *Unit head:* Dr. F. Todd Goodson, Department Chair, 785-532-5904, Fax: 785-532-7304, E-mail: tgoodson@ksu.edu. *Application contact:* Dr. Kay Ann Taylor, Director, Curriculum and Instruction Graduate Programs, 785-532-6974, Fax: 785-532-7304, E-mail: ktaylor@ksu.edu.
Website: http://www.coe.ksu.edu/edci/index.html

Kaplan University, Davenport Campus, School of Teacher Education, Davenport, IA 52807. Offers education (M Ed); secondary education (M Ed); teaching and learning (MA); teaching literacy and language: grades 6-12 (MA); teaching literacy and language: grades K-6 (MA); teaching mathematics: grades 6-8 (MA); teaching mathematics: grades 9-12 (MA); teaching mathematics: grades K-5 (MA); teaching science: grades 6-12 (MA); teaching science: grades K-6 (MA); teaching students with special needs (MA); teaching with technology (MA). *Program availability:* Part-time, evening/weekend, online learning. *Entrance requirements:* Additional exam requirements/recommendations for international students: Required—TOEFL (minimum score 550 paper-based; 80 iBT).

Keiser University, EdS in Instructional Design and Technology Program, Ft. Lauderdale, FL 33309. Offers Ed S.

Keiser University, PhD in Instructional Design and Technology Program, Ft. Lauderdale, FL 33309. Offers PhD.

Kennesaw State University, Leland and Clarice C. Bagwell College of Education, Program in Graduate Education, Kennesaw, GA 30144. Offers educational leadership (M Ed); educational leadership technology (M Ed); elementary and early childhood education (M Ed); instructional technology (M Ed); middle grades education (M Ed); reading (M Ed); secondary education (M Ed); special education (M Ed); teaching English to speakers of other languages (M Ed). *Accreditation:* NCATE. *Program availability:* Part-time. *Degree requirements:* For master's, thesis or alternative. *Entrance requirements:* For master's, GRE General Test, T-4 state certification, minimum GPA of 2.75. Additional exam requirements/recommendations for international students: Required—TOEFL (minimum score 550 paper-based; 80 iBT), IELTS (minimum score 6.5). Electronic applications accepted.

Kent State University, College of Education, Health and Human Services, School of Lifespan Development and Educational Sciences, Program in Instructional Technology, Kent, OH 44242-0001. Offers computer technology (M Ed); educational psychology (PhD), including instructional technology; general instructional technology (M Ed). *Accreditation:* NCATE. *Degree requirements:* For master's, thesis (for some programs). *Entrance requirements:* For master's, 2 letters of reference, goals statement, minimum GPA of 2.75. Additional exam requirements/recommendations for international students: Required—TOEFL (minimum score 550 paper-based; 80 iBT). *Expenses:* Tuition, state resident: full-time $10,864; part-time $495 per credit hour. Tuition, nonresident: full-time

$18,380; part-time $837 per credit hour. *Faculty research:* Cooperative learning, aesthetics, computers in schools.

Kutztown University of Pennsylvania, College of Education, Program in Instructional Technology, Kutztown, PA 19530-0730. Offers M Ed. *Program availability:* Part-time, evening/weekend, 100% online, blended/hybrid learning. *Faculty:* 3 full-time (2 women). *Students:* 3 full-time (1 woman), 58 part-time (38 women); includes 2 minority (1 Black or African American, non-Hispanic/Latino; 1 Two or more races, non-Hispanic/Latino). Average age 31. 31 applicants, 100% accepted, 19 enrolled. In 2016, 9 master's awarded. *Degree requirements:* For master's, comprehensive exam. *Entrance requirements:* For master's, GRE or valid PA teaching certificate, 3 letters of recommendation. Additional exam requirements/recommendations for international students: Required—TOEFL (minimum score 550 paper-based, 79 iBT) or IELTS (minimum score 6.5). *Application deadline:* For fall admission, 8/1 for domestic and international students; for spring admission, 12/1 for domestic and international students. Application fee: $35. Electronic applications accepted. *Expenses:* Tuition, state resident: full-time $4347; part-time $483 per credit. Tuition, nonresident: full-time $6525; part-time $725 per credit. *Required fees:* $88 per credit. One-time fee: $50 full-time. *Financial support:* Career-related internships or fieldwork, Federal Work-Study, scholarships/grants, and unspecified assistantships available. Financial award application deadline: 3/1; financial award applicants required to submit FAFSA. *Unit head:* Dr. Andrea Harmer, Chairperson, 610-683-4301, Fax: 610-683-1326, E-mail: harmer@kutztown.edu.
Website: https://www.kutztown.edu/academics/graduate-programs/instructional-technology.htm

Lamar University, College of Graduate Studies, College of Education and Human Development, Department of Educational Leadership, Beaumont, TX 77710. Offers digital learning and leading (M Ed); education administration (M Ed); educational leadership (Ed D); educational technology (M Ed). *Program availability:* Part-time, evening/weekend. *Faculty:* 29 full-time (17 women), 15 part-time/adjunct (6 women). *Students:* 8 full-time (all women), 2,215 part-time (1,490 women); includes 848 minority (387 Black or African American, non-Hispanic/Latino; 6 American Indian or Alaska Native, non-Hispanic/Latino; 30 Asian, non-Hispanic/Latino; 375 Hispanic/Latino; 50 Two or more races, non-Hispanic/Latino), 3 international. Average age 38. 869 applicants, 89% accepted, 542 enrolled. In 2016, 977 master's, 82 doctorates awarded. Terminal master's awarded for partial completion of doctoral program. *Degree requirements:* For master's, comprehensive exam, thesis optional; for doctorate, thesis/dissertation. *Entrance requirements:* For master's, GRE General Test, minimum GPA of 2.5; for doctorate, GRE. Additional exam requirements/recommendations for international students: Required—TOEFL (minimum score 550 paper-based; 79 iBT), IELTS (minimum score 6.5). *Application deadline:* For fall admission, 8/10 priority date for domestic students, 7/1 for international students; for spring admission, 1/5 priority date for domestic students, 12/1 for international students. Applications are processed on a rolling basis. Application fee: $25 ($50 for international students). Electronic applications accepted. *Expenses:* $8,134 in-state full-time, $5,574 in-state part-time; $15,604 out-of-state full-time, $10,554 out-of-state part-time per year. *Financial support:* Fellowships, research assistantships with tuition reimbursements, teaching assistantships with tuition reimbursements, career-related internships or fieldwork, and scholarships/grants available. Support available to part-time students. Financial award application deadline: 4/1; financial award applicants required to submit FAFSA. *Faculty research:* School dropouts, suicide prevention in public school students, school climate and gifted performance, teacher evaluation. *Unit head:* Dr. Kaye Shelton, Director, 409-880-8689, Fax: 409-880-8685. *Application contact:* Deidre Mayer, Interim Director, Admissions and Academic Services, 409-880-8888, Fax: 409-880-7419, E-mail: gradmissions@lamar.edu.
Website: http://education.lamar.edu/educational-leadership

La Salle University, School of Arts and Sciences, Program in Instructional Technology Management, Philadelphia, PA 19141-1199. Offers MS, Certificate. *Program availability:* Part-time, evening/weekend, online only, 100% online. *Faculty:* 5 part-time/adjunct (3 women). *Students:* 16 part-time (13 women); includes 12 minority (9 Black or African American, non-Hispanic/Latino; 2 Hispanic/Latino; 1 Two or more races, non-Hispanic/Latino), 1 international. Average age 36. 9 applicants, 78% accepted, 4 enrolled. In 2016, 15 master's, 1 other advanced degree awarded. *Degree requirements:* For master's, capstone project. *Entrance requirements:* For master's and Certificate, baccalaureate degree; two letters of recommendation; 3 years of professional experience in corporate training, human resources, information technology or business. Additional exam requirements/recommendations for international students: Required—TOEFL. *Application deadline:* For fall admission, 8/15 priority date for domestic students; for spring admission, 12/15 priority date for domestic students; for summer admission, 4/15 priority date for domestic students. Applications are processed on a rolling basis. Application fee: $35. Electronic applications accepted. Application fee is waived when completed online. *Expenses:* Contact institution. *Financial support:* In 2016–17, 1 student received support. Scholarships/grants available. Support available to part-time students. Financial award application deadline: 8/31; financial award applicants required to submit FAFSA. *Unit head:* Margaret M. McCoey, Director, 215-951-1136, E-mail: mccoey@lasalle.edu. *Application contact:* Elizabeth Heenan, Director, Graduate and Adult Enrollment, 215-951-1100, Fax: 215-951-1462, E-mail: heenan@lasalle.edu.
Website: http://www.lasalle.edu/instructional-technology-management/

Lawrence Technological University, College of Arts and Sciences, Southfield, MI 48075-1058. Offers bioinformatics (Graduate Certificate); computer science (MS), including data science, big data, and data mining, intelligent systems; instructional design, communication, and presentation (Graduate Certificate); instructional technology (Graduate Certificate); premedical studies (Graduate Certificate); technical and professional communication (MS, Graduate Certificate); writing for the digital age (Graduate Certificate). *Program availability:* Part-time, evening/weekend. *Faculty:* 6 full-time (2 women), 10 part-time/adjunct (5 women). *Students:* 37 part-time (18 women); includes 4 minority (1 Black or African American, non-Hispanic/Latino; 1 Asian, non-Hispanic/Latino; 2 Hispanic/Latino), 8 international. Average age 33. 301 applicants, 23% accepted, 9 enrolled. In 2016, 22 master's, 2 other advanced degrees awarded. *Degree requirements:* For master's, thesis (for some programs). *Entrance requirements:* Additional exam requirements/recommendations for international students: Required—TOEFL (minimum score 550 paper-based; 79 iBT), IELTS (minimum score 6.5). *Application deadline:* For fall admission, 5/22 for international students; for spring admission, 10/11 for international students; for summer admission, 2/16 for international students. Applications are processed on a rolling basis. Application fee: $50. Electronic applications accepted. *Expenses: Tuition:* Full-time $14,868; part-time $1062 per credit. *Required fees:* $75 per semester. Tuition and fees vary according to campus/location. *Financial support:* In 2016–17, 9 students received support. Scholarships/grants and tuition reduction available. Financial award application deadline: 4/1; financial award applicants required to submit FAFSA. *Faculty research:* Computer analysis of visual art, psychology of numbers games, neural basis of moral judgement, synthesis of glycosylated warfarin analogs for potential use as antiviral drugs, observation of chemotaxis behavior in c. elegans. *Total annual research expenditures:* $530,625. *Unit head:* Dr. Hsiao-Ping Moore, Dean, 248-204-3500, Fax: 248-204-3518, E-mail: scidean@ltu.edu. *Application contact:* Jane Rohrback, Director of Admissions, 248-204-3160, Fax: 248-204-2228, E-mail: admissions@ltu.edu.

Lehigh University, College of Education, Program in Teaching, Learning and Technology, Bethlehem, PA 18015. Offers elementary education (M Ed); instructional technology (MS); teaching, learning and technology (PhD); technology use in the schools (Graduate Certificate); M Ed/MA. *Program availability:* Part-time. *Faculty:* 7 full-time (3 women), 4 part-time/adjunct (2 women). *Students:* 29 full-time (22 women), 61 part-time (48 women); includes 10 minority (1 Black or African American, non-Hispanic/Latino; 4 Asian, non-Hispanic/Latino; 3 Hispanic/Latino; 1 Native Hawaiian or other Pacific Islander, non-Hispanic/Latino; 1 Two or more races, non-Hispanic/Latino), 7 international. Average age 31. 65 applicants, 82% accepted, 12 enrolled. In 2016, 25 master's, 1 doctorate awarded. Terminal master's awarded for partial completion of doctoral program. *Degree requirements:* For doctorate, comprehensive exam, thesis/dissertation, qualifying exam. *Entrance requirements:* For master's, minimum GPA of 3.0, 2 letters of recommendation, essay, transcript; for doctorate, GRE General Test, minimum graduate GPA of 3.0, writing sample, 2 letters of recommendation, essay, transcript. Additional exam requirements/recommendations for international students: Required—TOEFL (minimum score 600 paper-based; 93 iBT). *Application deadline:* For fall admission, 4/1 for domestic and international students; for summer admission, 4/1 for domestic and international students. Applications are processed on a rolling basis. Application fee: $65. Electronic applications accepted. *Expenses:* $565 per credit. *Financial support:* In 2016–17, 2 research assistantships (averaging $21,473 per year) were awarded; fellowships also available. Financial award application deadline: 1/31. *Faculty research:* Teaching and learning, K-16 curriculum development, Web-based learning, teaching and technology, language and literacy. *Unit head:* Dr. Lynn Columba, Director, 610-758-3237, Fax: 610-758-3243, E-mail: hlc0@lehigh.edu. *Application contact:* Donna Toothman, Coordinator, 610-758-3230, Fax: 610-758-3243, E-mail: djt2@lehigh.edu.
Website: http://ed.lehigh.edu/academics/degrees

Lenoir-Rhyne University, Graduate Programs, School of Education, Program in Online Teaching and Instructional Design, Hickory, NC 28601. Offers MS. *Program availability:* Online learning. *Entrance requirements:* For master's, GRE or MAT, essay; minimum GPA of 2.7 undergraduate, 3.0 graduate. Additional exam requirements/recommendations for international students: Required—TOEFL (minimum score 600 paper-based). Electronic applications accepted. *Expenses:* Contact institution.

Lesley University, Graduate School of Education, Cambridge, MA 02138-2790. Offers arts, community, and education (M Ed); autism studies (Certificate); curriculum and instruction (M Ed, CAGS); early childhood education (M Ed); ecological teaching and learning (MS); educational studies (PhD), including adult learning, educational leadership, individually designed; elementary education (M Ed); emergent technologies for educators (Certificate); ESLArts: language learning through the arts (M Ed); high school education (M Ed); individually designed (M Ed); integrated teaching through the arts (M Ed); literacy for K-8 classroom teachers (M Ed); mathematics education (M Ed); middle school education (M Ed); moderate disabilities (M Ed); online learning (Certificate); reading (CAGS); science in education (M Ed); severe disabilities (M Ed); special needs (CAGS); specialist teacher of reading (M Ed); teacher of visual art (M Ed); technology in education (M Ed, CAGS). *Accreditation:* TEAC. *Program availability:* Part-time, evening/weekend, online learning. *Degree requirements:* For master's, practicum; for doctorate, thesis/dissertation. *Entrance requirements:* For master's, Massachusetts Tests for Educator Licensure (MTEL), transcripts, statement of purpose, recommendations; interview (for special education); for doctorate, GRE General Test, transcripts, statement of purpose, recommendations, interview, master's degree, resume; for other advanced degree, interview, master's degree. Additional exam requirements/recommendations for international students: Required—TOEFL (minimum score 550 paper-based; 80 iBT). Electronic applications accepted. *Faculty research:* Assessment in literacy, mathematics and science; autism spectrum disorders; instructional technology and online learning; multicultural education and English language learners.

Lewis University, College of Education, Program in Curriculum and Instruction: Instructional Technology, Romeoville, IL 60446. Offers M Ed. *Program availability:* Part-time, evening/weekend. *Students:* 2 full-time (1 woman), 9 part-time (4 women), 1 international. Average age 29. *Degree requirements:* For master's, departmental qualifying exam. *Entrance requirements:* For master's, writing exam, minimum GPA of 2.75, 2 letters of recommendation, interview. Additional exam requirements/recommendations for international students: Required—TOEFL (minimum score 550 paper-based; 80 iBT). *Application deadline:* For fall admission, 5/1 priority date for international students; for spring admission, 11/15 priority date for international students. Applications are processed on a rolling basis. Application fee: $40. Electronic applications accepted. *Expenses: Tuition:* Full-time $13,860; part-time $770 per credit hour. *Required fees:* $75 per semester. Tuition and fees vary according to degree level and program. *Financial support:* Career-related internships or fieldwork, institutionally sponsored loans, and unspecified assistantships available. Support available to part-time students. Financial award application deadline: 5/1; financial award applicants required to submit FAFSA. *Unit head:* Dr. Seung Kim, Program Director, 815-838-0500, E-mail: kimse@lewisu.edu. *Application contact:* Linda Campbell, Graduate Admission Counselor, 815-836-5610 Ext. 5704, Fax: 815-836-5578, E-mail: campbeli@lewisu.edu.

Lindenwood University, Graduate Programs, School of Education, St. Charles, MO 63301-1695. Offers education (MA), including autism spectrum disorders, character education, early intervention in autism and sensory impairment, gifted, technology; educational administration (MA, Ed D, Ed S); English to speakers of other languages (MA); instructional leadership (Ed D, Ed S); library media (MA); professional counseling (MA); school administration (MA, Ed S); school counseling (MA); teaching (MA). *Program availability:* Part-time, evening/weekend, 100% online, blended/hybrid learning. *Faculty:* 39 full-time (27 women), 210 part-time/adjunct (136 women). *Students:* 292 full-time (227 women), 1,580 part-time (1,200 women); includes 404 minority (333 Black or African American, non-Hispanic/Latino; 4 American Indian or Alaska Native, non-Hispanic/Latino; 10 Asian, non-Hispanic/Latino; 36 Hispanic/Latino; 1 Native Hawaiian or other Pacific Islander, non-Hispanic/Latino; 20 Two or more races, non-Hispanic/Latino), 20 international. Average age 36. 558 applicants, 72% accepted, 353 enrolled. In 2016, 491 master's, 72 doctorates, 111 other advanced degrees awarded. *Degree requirements:* For master's, thesis (for some programs), minimum GPA of 3.0; for doctorate, thesis/dissertation, minimum GPA of 3.0; for Ed S, comprehensive exam, project, minimum GPA of 3.0. *Entrance requirements:* For master's, interview, minimum undergraduate cumulative GPA of 3.0, writing sample, letter of recommendation; for doctorate, GRE, minimum graduate GPA of 3.4, resume, interview, writing sample, 4 letters of recommendation; for Ed S, master's degree in education, relevant work experience. Additional exam requirements/recommendations for international students: Required—TOEFL (minimum score 550 paper-based; 80 iBT); Recommended—IELTS (minimum score 6.5). *Application deadline:* For fall admission, 8/28 priority date for domestic and international students; for spring admission, 1/8 priority date for domestic and international students; for summer admission, 6/5 priority date for domestic and international students. Applications are processed on a rolling basis. Application fee: $30 ($100 for international students). Electronic applications accepted. *Expenses:*

Tuition: Full-time $15,672; part-time $453 per credit hour. *Required fees:* $205 per semester. Tuition and fees vary according to course level, course load and degree level. *Financial support:* In 2016–17, 334 students received support. Career-related internships or fieldwork, Federal Work-Study, institutionally sponsored loans, scholarships/grants, tuition waivers (partial), and unspecified assistantships available. Financial award application deadline: 6/30; financial award applicants required to submit FAFSA. *Unit head:* Dr. Cynthia Bice, Dean, School of Education, 636-949-4618, Fax: 636-949-4197, E-mail: cbice@lindenwood.edu. *Application contact:* Tyler Kostich, Director, Evening and Graduate Admissions, 636-949-4138, Fax: 636-949-4109, E-mail: adultadmissions@lindenwood.edu.
Website: http://www.lindenwood.edu/academics/academic-schools/school-of-education/

Lipscomb University, College of Education, Nashville, TN 37204-3951. Offers applied behavior analysis (MS, Certificate); educational leadership (M Ed, Ed S); English language learning (M Ed, Ed S); instructional coaching (M Ed, Certificate, Ed S); instructional practice (M Ed); learning organizations and strategic change (Ed D); literacy coaching (Certificate); reading specialty (M Ed, Ed S); special education (M Ed); teaching, learning, and leading (M Ed); technology integration (M Ed, Ed S); technology integration specialist (Certificate). *Accreditation:* NCATE. *Program availability:* Part-time, evening/weekend, 100% online. *Faculty:* 21 full-time (15 women), 38 part-time/adjunct (26 women). *Students:* 111 full-time (80 women), 345 part-time (292 women); includes 104 minority (70 Black or African American, non-Hispanic/Latino; 1 American Indian or Alaska Native, non-Hispanic/Latino; 3 Asian, non-Hispanic/Latino; 20 Hispanic/Latino; 10 Two or more races, non-Hispanic/Latino), 1 international. Average age 33. In 2016, 201 master's, 36 doctorates, 86 other advanced degrees awarded. *Degree requirements:* For master's, comprehensive exam, portfolio, research project and presentation; for doctorate, practical capstone project in experiential setting. *Entrance requirements:* For master's, MAT (minimum score 31) or GRE General Test (minimum score 294), 2 reference letters, goals statement, writing sample, interview; for doctorate, MAT or GRE General Test, 3 reference letters, artifact of demonstrated academic excellence, written personal statements, interview. Additional exam requirements/recommendations for international students: Required—TOEFL (minimum score 570 paper-based; 80 iBT). *Application deadline:* For fall admission, 8/29 priority date for domestic students; for spring admission, 1/15 priority date for domestic students. Applications are processed on a rolling basis. Application fee: $50 ($75 for international students). Electronic applications accepted. *Expenses:* $934 per hour; $570 per hour (Teach for America). *Financial support:* Scholarships/grants, unspecified assistantships, and partnerships with local school districts available. Financial award applicants required to submit FAFSA. *Faculty research:* Facilitative learning styles, leadership, student assessment, interactive multimedia inclusion, learning organizations and strategic change. *Unit head:* Dr. Deborah Boyd, Director of Graduate Studies, 615-966-6263, E-mail: deborah.boyd@lipscomb.edu. *Application contact:* Amanda Logsdon, Director of Enrollment and Outreach, 615-966-7199, E-mail: amanda.logsdon@lipscomb.edu.
Website: http://www.lipscomb.edu/education/graduate-programs

Long Island University–LIU Post, College of Education, Information and Technology, Brookville, NY 11548-1300. Offers adolescence education (MS); adolescence education 7-12 (MS); archives and records management (AC); art education (MS); childhood education (MS); childhood teaching literacy B-6 (MS); childhood/special education (MS); clinical mental health counseling (MS, AC); early childhood education (MS); early childhood education/childhood education (MS); educational leadership (AC); educational technology (MS); information studies (PhD); interdisciplinary educational studies (Ed D); middle childhood education (MS); music education (MS); school counselor (MS); special education (MS Ed); speech-language pathology (MA); students with disabilities, 7-12 generalist (AC); TESOL (MA). *Accreditation:* TEAC. *Program availability:* Part-time, 100% online, blended/hybrid learning. *Faculty:* 55 full-time (35 women), 104 part-time/adjunct (57 women). *Students:* 464 full-time (390 women), 740 part-time (580 women); includes 265 minority (99 Black or African American, non-Hispanic/Latino; 45 Asian, non-Hispanic/Latino; 113 Hispanic/Latino; 1 Native Hawaiian or other Pacific Islander, non-Hispanic/Latino; 7 Two or more races, non-Hispanic/Latino), 33 international. 928 applicants, 76% accepted, 406 enrolled. In 2016, 334 master's, 10 doctorates, 137 other advanced degrees awarded. Terminal master's awarded for partial completion of doctoral program. *Degree requirements:* For master's, variable foreign language requirement, comprehensive exam (for some programs), thesis optional; for doctorate, comprehensive exam, thesis/dissertation. *Entrance requirements:* For master's and AC, GRE. Additional exam requirements/recommendations for international students: Required—PTE, TOEFL (minimum score 550 paper-based, 75 iBT) or IELTS. *Application deadline:* Applications are processed on a rolling basis. Application fee: $50. Electronic applications accepted. *Expenses: Tuition:* Full-time $28,272; part-time $1178 per credit. *Required fees:* $451 per term. Tuition and fees vary according to degree level and program. *Financial support:* Career-related internships or fieldwork, Federal Work-Study, institutionally sponsored loans, scholarships/grants, tuition waivers (partial), and unspecified assistantships available. Support available to part-time students. Financial award application deadline: 2/15; financial award applicants required to submit FAFSA. *Faculty research:* English language learners, early childhood literacy development through play, sleep, social justice through education, using a structured protocol for discussing bad news. *Total annual research expenditures:* $575,000. *Unit head:* Dr. Albert Inserra, Dean, 516-299-2210, E-mail: albert.inserra@liu.edu. *Application contact:* Carol Zerah, Director of Graduate Admissions, 516-299-2900, Fax: 516-299-2137, E-mail: post-enroll@liu.edu.
Website: http://liu.edu/CWPost/Academics/College-of-Education-Information-and-Technology

Longwood University, College of Graduate and Professional Studies, College of Education and Human Services, Program in School Librarianship, Farmville, VA 23909. Offers M Ed. *Program availability:* Part-time, evening/weekend. *Degree requirements:* For master's, professional portfolio. *Entrance requirements:* For master's, PRAXIS I (for initial teaching licensure track), bachelor's degree from regionally-accredited institution, 2 recommendations, minimum 500-word personal essay, official transcripts, minimum GPA of 2.75, valid teaching license. Additional exam requirements/recommendations for international students: Required—TOEFL (minimum score 570 paper-based; 80 iBT), IELTS (minimum score 6.5). Electronic applications accepted. *Expenses:* Contact institution.

Louisiana State University and Agricultural & Mechanical College, Graduate School, College of Human Sciences and Education, Department of Educational Theory, Policy and Practice, Baton Rouge, LA 70803. Offers counseling (M Ed, MA, Ed S); educational administration (M Ed, MA, PhD, Ed S); educational technology (MA); elementary education (M Ed, MAT); higher education (PhD); research methodology (PhD); secondary education (M Ed, MAT). *Accreditation:* ACA (one or more programs are accredited); NCATE.

Loyola University Maryland, Graduate Programs, School of Education, Program in Educational Technology, Baltimore, MD 21210-2699. Offers M Ed, MA. *Program availability:* Part-time. *Faculty:* 34 full-time (22 women), 30 part-time/adjunct (24 women). *Students:* 137 full-time (113 women); includes 32 minority (19 Black or African American, non-Hispanic/Latino; 4 Asian, non-Hispanic/Latino; 6 Hispanic/Latino; 1 Native Hawaiian or other Pacific Islander, non-Hispanic/Latino; 2 Two or more races, non-Hispanic/Latino). Average age 31. In 2016, 9 master's awarded. *Degree requirements:* For master's, thesis. *Entrance requirements:* For master's, transcript, essay. Additional exam requirements/recommendations for international students: Required—TOEFL (minimum score 550 paper-based), IELTS (minimum score 7). Application fee: $60. Electronic applications accepted. *Expenses:* Contact institution. *Financial support:* Scholarships/grants available. Financial award application deadline: 4/15; financial award applicants required to submit FAFSA. *Application contact:* Mechelle Palmer, Senior Associate Director of Graduate Admission, 410-617-7741, E-mail: mjpalmer@loyola.edu.

Manhattan College, Graduate Programs, School of Education and Health, Program in Instructional Design and Delivery, Riverdale, NY 10471. Offers MS. *Program availability:* Part-time, evening/weekend. *Faculty:* 1 (woman) full-time, 6 part-time/adjunct (3 women). *Students:* 14 full-time (12 women); includes 8 minority (4 Black or African American, non-Hispanic/Latino; 4 Hispanic/Latino). Average age 32. 16 applicants, 88% accepted, 14 enrolled. *Degree requirements:* For master's, thesis. *Entrance requirements:* For master's, GRE. *Application deadline:* For fall admission, 8/1 priority date for domestic students; for spring admission, 1/1 priority date for domestic students; for summer admission, 4/15 priority date for domestic students. Applications are processed on a rolling basis. Application fee: $105. Electronic applications accepted. *Expenses:* $925 per credit. *Financial support:* In 2016–17, 2 students received support. Scholarships/grants, tuition waivers, and unspecified assistantships available. Financial award application deadline: 8/1; financial award applicants required to submit FAFSA. *Faculty research:* Simulations, gaming, adult technology integration, pre-service training, STEM integration into curriculum, web 2.0 tool development, LMS development. *Unit head:* Dr. Shawna Bushell, Director, 718-862-7147, E-mail: bushell@manhattan.edu. *Application contact:* William Bisset, Vice President for Enrollment, 718-862-7199, Fax: 718-862-8019, E-mail: william.bisset@manhattan.edu.
Website: http://manhattan.edu/academics/education/idd

Marconi International University, Graduate Programs, Pembroke Pines, FL 33028. Offers business administration (DBA); education leadership (Ed D); education leadership, management and emerging technologies (M Ed); international business administration (IMBA).

Marian University, School of Education, Fond du Lac, WI 54935-4699. Offers curriculum and instruction leadership (PhD); educational administration (PhD); educational leadership (MAE); educational technology (MAE); leadership studies (PhD); special education (MAE); teacher education (MAE). *Accreditation:* NCATE. *Program availability:* Part-time, evening/weekend, online learning. *Faculty:* 11 full-time (7 women), 14 part-time/adjunct (8 women). *Students:* 13 full-time (9 women), 179 part-time (113 women); includes 16 minority (6 Black or African American, non-Hispanic/Latino; 3 American Indian or Alaska Native, non-Hispanic/Latino; 2 Asian, non-Hispanic/Latino; 3 Hispanic/Latino; 2 Two or more races, non-Hispanic/Latino). Average age 39. In 2016, 72 master's, 8 doctorates awarded. *Degree requirements:* For master's, exam, field-based experience project, portfolio; for doctorate, comprehensive exam, thesis/dissertation, field-based experience. *Entrance requirements:* For master's, minimum GPA of 3.0, BA in education or related field, teaching license; for doctorate, GRE, MAT, resume, 2 writing samples, interview. Additional exam requirements/recommendations for international students: Required—TOEFL (minimum score 525 paper-based; 70 iBT). *Application deadline:* Applications are processed on a rolling basis. Application fee: $50. *Expenses: Tuition:* Full-time $5130; part-time $570 per credit hour. *Financial support:* In 2016–17, 3 students received support. Federal Work-Study available. Support available to part-time students. Financial award application deadline: 3/1; financial award applicants required to submit FAFSA. *Faculty research:* At-risk youth, multicultural issues, values in education, teaching/learning strategies. *Unit head:* Dr. Kelly Chaney, Dean, 920-923-8610, Fax: 920-923-7663, E-mail: kachaney01@marianuniversity.edu.
Website: https://www.marianuniversity.edu/academic-programs/graduate-studies/

Marlboro College, Graduate and Professional Studies, Program in Teaching with Technology, Marlboro, VT 05344. Offers educational technology (Certificate); teaching with technology (MAT). *Program availability:* Part-time, evening/weekend, blended/hybrid learning. *Faculty:* 1 full-time (0 women), 8 part-time/adjunct (5 women). *Students:* 6 full-time (3 women), 13 part-time (5 women); includes 3 minority (1 Black or African American, non-Hispanic/Latino; 2 Two or more races, non-Hispanic/Latino). Average age 44. 8 applicants, 88% accepted, 7 enrolled. In 2016, 5 master's awarded. *Degree requirements:* For master's, 36 credits including capstone project. *Entrance requirements:* For master's, statement of intent, 2 letters of recommendation, transcripts. *Application deadline:* For fall admission, 7/1 priority date for domestic students; for winter admission, 11/1 priority date for domestic students; for spring admission, 3/1 priority date for domestic students. Applications are processed on a rolling basis. Application fee: $0. Electronic applications accepted. *Expenses:* $765 per credit. *Financial support:* In 2016–17, 2 students received support. Scholarships/grants available. Financial award application deadline: 8/5; financial award applicants required to submit FAFSA. *Unit head:* Caleb Clark, Degree Chair, 802-258-9207, Fax: 802-258-9201, E-mail: cclark@gradschool.marlboro.edu. *Application contact:* Don Parker, Admissions Assistant, 802-451-7505, Fax: 802-258-9201, E-mail: graduateadmissions@marlboro.edu.
Website: https://www.marlboro.edu/academics/graduate/mat

Martin Luther College, Graduate Studies, New Ulm, MN 56073. Offers early childhood director (MS Ed Admin); educational technology (MS Ed); instruction (MS Ed); leadership (MS Ed); principal (MS Ed Admin); special education (MS Ed). *Program availability:* Part-time, evening/weekend. *Faculty:* 9 full-time (1 woman), 21 part-time/adjunct (10 women). *Students:* 1 (woman) full-time, 77 part-time (30 women); includes 2 minority (1 Asian, non-Hispanic/Latino; 1 Two or more races, non-Hispanic/Latino), 4 international. Average age 37. 6 applicants, 100% accepted, 6 enrolled. In 2016, 15 master's awarded. *Degree requirements:* For master's, capstone project or comprehensive exam. *Entrance requirements:* For master's, undergraduate degree in education from an accredited college or university, minimum undergraduate GPA of 3.0. Additional exam requirements/recommendations for international students: Required—TOEFL (minimum score 550 paper-based; 80 iBT); Recommended—IELTS (minimum score 6.5). *Application deadline:* Applications are processed on a rolling basis. Application fee: $35. Electronic applications accepted. *Expenses:* $11,220 tuition, $140 graduation fee. *Financial support:* In 2016–17, 2 students received support. Scholarships/grants available. Financial award application deadline: 9/1. *Faculty research:* Principal effectiveness, principal support, cognitive load in math instruction, reading strategies in multigrade classrooms, mentor provided professional development for new teachers. *Unit head:* John E. Meyer, Director of Graduate Studies, 507-354-8221 Ext. 398, E-mail: meyerjd@mlc-wels.edu.
Website: https://mlc-wels.edu/graduate-studies/

Marygrove College, Graduate Division, Program in Educational Technology, Detroit, MI 48221-2599. Offers M Ed. Program offered in partnership with Lawrence Technological University.

Massachusetts College of Liberal Arts, Graduate Programs, North Adams, MA 01247-4100. Offers business (MBA); educational administration (M Ed); educational leadership (CAGS); instruction and curriculum (M Ed); instructional technology (M Ed);

physical education and health (M Ed); reading (M Ed); special education (M Ed). *Program availability:* Part-time, evening/weekend. *Degree requirements:* For master's, thesis. *Entrance requirements:* For master's, writing sample.

McDaniel College, Graduate and Professional Studies, Program in School Librarianship, Westminster, MD 21157-4390. Offers MS. *Program availability:* Part-time, evening/weekend, online only, 100% online. *Faculty:* 1 (woman) full-time, 5 part-time/adjunct (all women). *Students:* 3 full-time (all women), 51 part-time (47 women); includes 3 minority (1 Black or African American, non-Hispanic/Latino; 2 Asian, non-Hispanic/Latino). Average age 37. 15 applicants, 80% accepted. In 2016, 6 master's awarded. *Degree requirements:* For master's, comprehensive exam, thesis optional. *Entrance requirements:* For master's, PRAXIS, 3 recommendations, essay. Additional exam requirements/recommendations for international students: Required—TOEFL (minimum score 79 iBT), IELTS (minimum score 6). *Application deadline:* For fall admission, 6/1 priority date for domestic students; for spring admission, 11/1 priority date for domestic students; for summer admission, 3/1 priority date for domestic students. Applications are processed on a rolling basis. Application fee: $75. Electronic applications accepted. *Expenses: Tuition:* Full-time $8370; part-time $465 per credit. *Required fees:* $75 per semester. Tuition and fees vary according to course load, program and reciprocity agreements. *Financial support:* Career-related internships or fieldwork available. Financial award application deadline: 3/1; financial award applicants required to submit FAFSA. *Unit head:* Fax: 410-857-2515, E-mail: gradadms@mcdaniel.edu. *Application contact:* Crystal L. Perry, Assistant Director, Graduate Enrollment Management, 410-857-2516, Fax: 410-857-2515, E-mail: cperry@mcdaniel.edu.

McNeese State University, Doré School of Graduate Studies, Burton College of Education, Office of Graduate Education Programs, Program in Educational Leadership, Lake Charles, LA 70609. Offers educational leadership (M Ed, Ed S); educational technology (Ed S). *Program availability:* Evening/weekend. *Degree requirements:* For Ed S, comprehensive exam. *Entrance requirements:* For master's, GRE, teaching certificate, 3 years of full-time teaching experience; for Ed S, teaching certificate, 3 years of teaching experience, 1 year of administration or supervision experience, master's degree with 12 semester hours in education.

McNeese State University, Doré School of Graduate Studies, Burton College of Education, Office of Graduate Education Programs, Program in Educational Technology Leadership, Lake Charles, LA 70609. Offers M Ed. *Program availability:* Evening/weekend. *Entrance requirements:* For master's, GRE, teaching certificate.

McNeese State University, Doré School of Graduate Studies, Burton College of Education, Office of Graduate Education Programs, Program in Instructional Technology, Lake Charles, LA 70609. Offers MS. *Program availability:* Evening/weekend. *Entrance requirements:* For master's, GRE.

Memorial University of Newfoundland, School of Graduate Studies, Faculty of Education, St. John's, NL A1C 5S7, Canada. Offers counseling psychology (M Ed); curriculum, teaching, and learning studies (M Ed); education (PhD); educational leadership studies (M Ed, Graduate Diploma); information technology (M Ed); post-secondary studies (M Ed, Diploma), including health professional education (Diploma). *Program availability:* Part-time. *Degree requirements:* For master's, thesis optional, internship, paper folio, project; for doctorate, comprehensive exam, thesis/dissertation, thesis seminar, oral defense of thesis. *Entrance requirements:* For master's, undergraduate degree with at least 2nd class standing, 1-2 years of work experience; for doctorate, minimum A average in graduate course work, MA in education, 2 years of professional experience; for other advanced degree, 2nd class degree, 2 years of work experience with adult learners, appropriate academic qualifications and work experience in a health-related field. Electronic applications accepted. *Faculty research:* Critical thinking, literacy, cognitive studies and counseling, educational change, technology in instruction.

Michigan State University, The Graduate School, College of Education, Department of Counseling, Educational Psychology and Special Education, East Lansing, MI 48824. Offers counseling (MA); educational psychology and educational technology (PhD); educational technology (MA); measurement and quantitative methods (PhD); rehabilitation counseling (MA); rehabilitation counselor education (PhD); school psychology (MA, PhD, Ed S); special education (MA, PhD). *Accreditation:* APA (one or more programs are accredited); CORE (one or more programs are accredited). *Program availability:* Part-time. *Entrance requirements:* Additional exam requirements/recommendations for international students: Required—TOEFL. Electronic applications accepted.

MidAmerica Nazarene University, Professional and Graduate Studies in Education, Olathe, KS 66062-1899. Offers ESOL (M Ed); reading specialist (M Ed); technology enhanced teaching (M Ed). *Accreditation:* NCATE. *Program availability:* Part-time, evening/weekend, online only, 100% online. *Faculty:* 5 full-time (3 women), 12 part-time/adjunct (7 women). *Students:* 22 full-time (16 women), 43 part-time (38 women); includes 6 minority (3 Black or African American, non-Hispanic/Latino; 1 Asian, non-Hispanic/Latino; 2 Two or more races, non-Hispanic/Latino). Average age 32. 18 applicants, 22% accepted, 2 enrolled. In 2016, 41 master's awarded. *Entrance requirements:* For master's, bachelor's degree from an accredited college or university, minimum undergraduate GPA of 3.0, valid teaching license. Additional exam requirements/recommendations for international students: Required—TOEFL (minimum score 81 iBT), IELTS (minimum score 6). *Application deadline:* For fall admission, 8/6 for domestic students; for spring admission, 12/15 for domestic students; for summer admission, 5/7 for domestic students. Applications are processed on a rolling basis. Electronic applications accepted. *Expenses:* Contact institution. *Financial support:* Scholarships/grants available. Financial award applicants required to submit FAFSA. *Unit head:* Dr. Ramona Stowe, Chair, 913-971-3524, Fax: 913-971-3407, E-mail: rsstowe@mnu.edu. *Application contact:* Glenna Murray, Administrative Assistant, 913-971-3292, Fax: 913-971-3002, E-mail: gkmurray@mnu.edu.
Website: http://www.mnu.edu/education.html

Middle Tennessee State University, College of Graduate Studies, College of Education, Department of Educational Leadership, Program in Curriculum and Instruction, Murfreesboro, TN 37132. Offers curriculum and instruction (M Ed, Ed S); English as a second language (M Ed, Ed S); secondary education (M Ed); technology and curriculum design (Ed S). *Accreditation:* NCATE. *Program availability:* Part-time, evening/weekend, online learning. *Degree requirements:* For master's, comprehensive exam; for Ed S, comprehensive exam, thesis or alternative. *Entrance requirements:* For master's and Ed S, GRE, MAT or PRAXIS. Additional exam requirements/recommendations for international students: Required—TOEFL (minimum score 525 paper-based; 71 iBT) or IELTS (minimum score 6). Electronic applications accepted.

Midwestern State University, Billie Doris McAda Graduate School, West College of Education, Programs in Educational Leadership and Technology, Wichita Falls, TX 76308. Offers educational leadership (M Ed); educational technology (M Ed). *Program availability:* Part-time, evening/weekend. *Degree requirements:* For master's, comprehensive exam. *Entrance requirements:* For master's, GRE General Test or MAT. Additional exam requirements/recommendations for international students: Required—TOEFL (minimum score 550 paper-based). Electronic applications accepted. *Faculty research:* Role of the principal in the twenty-first century, culturally proficient leadership, human diversity, immigration, teacher collaboration.

Misericordia University, College of Health Sciences and Education, Program in Education, Dallas, PA 18612-1098. Offers instructional technology (MS); reading specialist (MS); special education (MS). *Program availability:* Part-time, evening/weekend. *Entrance requirements:* For master's, minimum undergraduate GPA of 3.0. Additional exam requirements/recommendations for international students: Required—TOEFL. Electronic applications accepted.

Mississippi State University, College of Education, Department of Instructional Systems and Workforce Development, Mississippi State, MS 39762. Offers distance education (MSIT); instructional design (MSIT); instructional systems and workforce development (MST, PhD); multimedia (MSIT); technology (Ed S). *Faculty:* 12 full-time (8 women). *Students:* 14 full-time (10 women), 53 part-time (44 women); includes 41 minority (39 Black or African American, non-Hispanic/Latino; 1 American Indian or Alaska Native, non-Hispanic/Latino; 1 Two or more races, non-Hispanic/Latino). Average age 38. 17 applicants, 47% accepted, 8 enrolled. In 2016, 6 master's, 3 doctorates, 5 other advanced degrees awarded. *Degree requirements:* For master's, thesis optional, comprehensive oral or written exam; for doctorate, thesis/dissertation, comprehensive oral and written exam; for Ed S, thesis, comprehensive written exam. *Entrance requirements:* For master's, GRE, minimum GPA of 2.75 on undergraduate work, 3.0 graduate; for doctorate, GRE, minimum GPA of 3.4 on graduate work; for Ed S, GRE, minimum GPA of 3.2, master's degree. Additional exam requirements/recommendations for international students: Required—TOEFL (minimum score 550 paper-based; 79 iBT); Recommended—IELTS (minimum score 6.5). *Application deadline:* For fall admission, 7/1 for domestic students, 5/1 for international students; for spring admission, 11/1 for domestic students, 9/1 for international students. Applications are processed on a rolling basis. Application fee: $60. Electronic applications accepted. *Expenses:* Tuition, state resident: full-time $7670; part-time $852.50 per credit hour. Tuition, nonresident: full-time $20,790; part-time $2310.50 per credit hour. Part-time tuition and fees vary according to course load. *Financial support:* In 2016–17, 2 research assistantships with full tuition reimbursements (averaging $13,755 per year), 2 teaching assistantships with full tuition reimbursements (averaging $10,800 per year) were awarded; Federal Work-Study, institutionally sponsored loans, scholarships/grants, and unspecified assistantships also available. Financial award application deadline: 4/1; financial award applicants required to submit FAFSA. *Faculty research:* Computer technology, nontraditional students, interactive video, instructional technology, educational leadership. *Unit head:* Dr. Connie Forde, Professor and Department Head, 662-325-2281, Fax: 662-325-7599, E-mail: cforde@colled.msstate.edu. *Application contact:* Linda Bonner, Senior Admissions Assistant, 662-325-3363, E-mail: lbonner@grad.msstate.edu.
Website: http://www.iswd.msstate.edu

Missouri Southern State University, Program in Instructional Technology, Joplin, MO 64801-1595. Offers MS Ed. Program offered jointly with Northwest Missouri State University. *Degree requirements:* For master's, comprehensive exam, research paper. *Entrance requirements:* For master's, GRE (minimum combined score of 700), writing assessment, minimum overall undergraduate GPA of 3.0.

Missouri State University, Graduate College, College of Education, Department of Reading, Foundations, and Technology, Program in Educational Technology, Springfield, MO 65897. Offers MS Ed. *Program availability:* Part-time. *Students:* 9 full-time (7 women), 25 part-time (19 women); includes 1 minority (Hispanic/Latino), 5 international. Average age 33. 18 applicants, 67% accepted, 11 enrolled. In 2016, 18 master's awarded. *Degree requirements:* For master's, comprehensive exam, thesis or alternative. *Entrance requirements:* Additional exam requirements/recommendations for international students: Required—TOEFL (minimum score 550 paper-based; 79 iBT), IELTS (minimum score 6). *Application deadline:* For fall admission, 7/20 priority date for domestic students, 5/1 for international students; for spring admission, 12/20 priority date for domestic students, 9/1 for international students; for summer admission, 5/20 priority date for domestic students. Applications are processed on a rolling basis. Application fee: $35 ($50 for international students). Electronic applications accepted. *Expenses:* Tuition, state resident: full-time $5830. Tuition, nonresident: full-time $10,708. *Required fees:* $1130. Tuition and fees vary according to class time, course level, course load and program. *Financial support:* Federal Work-Study, institutionally sponsored loans, scholarships/grants, and unspecified assistantships available. Financial award application deadline: 3/31; financial award applicants required to submit FAFSA. *Unit head:* Dr. Cathy Pearman, Department Head, 417-836-6769, E-mail: rft@missouristate.edu. *Application contact:* Michael Edwards, Coordinator of Graduate Admissions, 417-836-5330, Fax: 417-836-6200, E-mail: michaeledwards@missouristate.edu.
Website: http://education.missouristate.edu/rft/

Molloy College, Graduate Education Program, Rockville Centre, NY 11571-5002. Offers adolescent education in biology (MS Ed); adolescent special education (Advanced Certificate); bilingual extension (Advanced Certificate); childhood education (MS Ed); childhood special education (Advanced Certificate); early childhood education (MS Ed); educational technology (MS Ed); English (MS Ed); mathematics (MS Ed); social studies (MS Ed); Spanish (MS Ed); special education on both childhood and adolescent levels (MS Ed); teaching English to speakers of other languages (TESOL) in grades Pre-K to 12 (MS Ed); TESOL (Advanced Certificate). *Accreditation:* NCATE. *Program availability:* Part-time, evening/weekend. *Faculty:* 17 full-time (16 women), 23 part-time/adjunct (19 women). *Students:* 95 full-time (75 women), 221 part-time (177 women); includes 59 minority (14 Black or African American, non-Hispanic/Latino; 6 Asian, non-Hispanic/Latino; 38 Hispanic/Latino; 1 Two or more races, non-Hispanic/Latino), 1 international. Average age 42. 214 applicants, 66% accepted, 125 enrolled. In 2016, 95 master's, 4 Advanced Certificates awarded. *Entrance requirements:* Additional exam requirements/recommendations for international students: Required—TOEFL (minimum score 550 paper-based; 79 iBT). *Application deadline:* Applications are processed on a rolling basis. Application fee: $60. Electronic applications accepted. *Expenses: Tuition:* Full-time $19,170; part-time $1065 per credit. *Required fees:* $950; $790 per credit. Tuition and fees vary according to course load. *Financial support:* Applicants required to submit FAFSA. *Faculty research:* ESL - general education teacher collaboration; special education; school desegregation; American intellectual and social history; families and schools. *Unit head:* Joanne O'Brien, Associate Dean/Director, 516-323-3116, E-mail: jobrien@molloy.edu. *Application contact:* Jaclyn Machowicz, Assistant Director for Admissions, 516-323-4010, E-mail: jmachowicz@molloy.edu.

Montana State University Billings, College of Education, Department of Educational Theory and Practice, Option in Online Instructional Technologies, Billings, MT 59101. Offers M Ed. *Accreditation:* NCATE. *Program availability:* Part-time. *Degree requirements:* For master's, professional paper or thesis. *Entrance requirements:* For master's, GRE General Test or MAT, minimum GPA of 3.0. Additional exam requirements/recommendations for international students: Required—TOEFL (minimum score 79 iBT), IELTS (minimum score 6.5). *Application deadline:* For fall admission, 7/15 for domestic students; for spring admission, 12/1 for domestic students. Applications are processed on a rolling basis. Application fee: $40. Electronic applications accepted.

Expenses: Tuition, state resident: full-time $5265; part-time $3436 per year. Tuition, nonresident: full-time $14,030; part-time $9280 per year. *International tuition:* $19,295 full-time. Tuition and fees vary according to degree level, campus/location and program. *Financial support:* Teaching assistantships with partial tuition reimbursements, career-related internships or fieldwork, Federal Work-Study, institutionally sponsored loans, scholarships/grants, tuition waivers (partial), and unspecified assistantships available. Support available to part-time students. Financial award application deadline: 5/1; financial award applicants required to submit FAFSA. *Unit head:* Dr. Ken Miller, Chair, 406-657-2034, E-mail: kmiller@msubillings.edu. *Application contact:* David M. Sullivan, Graduate Studies Counselor, 406-657-2053, Fax: 406-657-2299, E-mail: dsullivan@msubillings.edu.

Morehead State University, Graduate Programs, College of Education, Department of Foundational and Graduate Studies in Education, Morehead, KY 40351. Offers adult and higher education (MA, Ed S); certified professional counselor (Ed S); counseling P-12 (MA); curriculum and instruction (Ed S); educational technology (MA Ed); instructional leadership (Ed S); school administration (MA); school counseling (Ed S); teacher leader business and marketing content (MA Ed); teacher leader business and marketing technology (MA Ed); teacher leader educational technology (MA Ed); teacher leader English (MA Ed); teacher leader gifted education (MA Ed); teacher leader IECE certification (MA Ed); teacher leader interdisciplinary education P-5 (MA Ed); teacher leader middle grades (MA Ed); teacher leader non IECE certification (MA Ed); teacher leader reading/writing - non-certification (MA Ed); teacher leader reading/writing certification (MA Ed); teacher leader school communication - certification (MA Ed); teacher leader school communication - non-certification (MA Ed); teacher leader social studies (MA Ed); teacher leader special education (MA Ed). *Accreditation:* NCATE. *Program availability:* Part-time, evening/weekend. *Degree requirements:* For master's, thesis optional, oral and/or written comprehensive exams; for Ed S, thesis, oral exam. *Entrance requirements:* For master's, GRE General Test, minimum overall undergraduate GPA of 2.5; for Ed S, GRE General Test, interview, master's degree, minimum GPA of 3.5, work experience. Additional exam requirements/recommendations for international students: Required—TOEFL (minimum score 500 paper-based). Electronic applications accepted. *Faculty research:* Character education, school accountability, computer applications for school administrators.

National Louis University, National College of Education, Chicago, IL 60603. Offers administration and supervision (M Ed, Ed D, CAS, Ed S); curriculum and instruction (M Ed, MS Ed, CAS); early childhood administration (M Ed, CAS); early childhood education (M Ed, MAT, MS Ed, CAS); education (Ed D); educational psychology/human learning and development (M Ed, MS Ed, CAS, Ed S); elementary education (MAT); interdisciplinary curriculum and instruction (M Ed); mathematics education (M Ed, MS Ed, CAS); middle grades education (MAT); reading and language (M Ed, MS Ed, CAS); school psychology (M Ed, Ed S); science education (M Ed, MS Ed, CAS); secondary education (MAT); special education (M Ed, MAT, CAS); technology in education (M Ed, CAS). *Accreditation:* NCATE. *Program availability:* Part-time, evening/weekend. *Degree requirements:* For doctorate, comprehensive exam, thesis/dissertation. *Entrance requirements:* For master's, MAT or GRE, minimum GPA of 3.0; for doctorate, GRE General Test, minimum GPA of 3.25, interview, resume, writing sample, 4 recommendations. Additional exam requirements/recommendations for international students: Required—TOEFL (minimum score 550 paper-based; 79 iBT).

Nazareth College of Rochester, Graduate Studies, Department of Education, Program of Educational Technology, Rochester, NY 14618. Offers MS Ed. *Program availability:* Part-time, evening/weekend. *Entrance requirements:* For master's, minimum GPA of 3.0. Additional exam requirements/recommendations for international students: Required—TOEFL or IELTS. *Application deadline:* For fall admission, 4/1 priority date for domestic students; for spring admission, 10/1 priority date for domestic students. Application fee: $40. *Expenses: Tuition:* Part-time $880 per credit hour. Part-time tuition and fees vary according to course load, degree level and program. *Financial support:* Unspecified assistantships available. Financial award application deadline: 3/1; financial award applicants required to submit FAFSA. *Unit head:* Dr. James Fenwick, Director, 585-389-2630, E-mail: jfenwic3@naz.edu. *Application contact:* Judith Baker, Director, Transfer and Graduate Admissions, 585-531-1154, Fax: 585-389-2826, E-mail: gradadmissions@naz.edu.

New Jersey City University, Debra Cannon Partridge Wolfe College of Education, Department of Educational Technology, Jersey City, NJ 07305-1597. Offers educational technology (MA); educational technology leadership (Ed D). *Accreditation:* NCATE. *Program availability:* Part-time, evening/weekend, online learning. *Degree requirements:* For master's, internship. *Entrance requirements:* Additional exam requirements/recommendations for international students: Required—TOEFL (minimum score 79 iBT).

New York Institute of Technology, School of Interdisciplinary Studies and Education, Department of Instructional Technology, Old Westbury, NY 11568-8000. Offers emerging technologies for trainers (Advanced Certificate); instructional design for global e-learning (Advanced Certificate); instructional technology (MS); school leadership and technology (Advanced Diploma); STEM education (Advanced Certificate). *Program availability:* Part-time, evening/weekend, 100% online, blended/hybrid learning. *Faculty:* 6 full-time (3 women), 6 part-time/adjunct (4 women). *Students:* 15 full-time (10 women), 192 part-time (132 women); includes 44 minority (15 Black or African American, non-Hispanic/Latino; 8 Asian, non-Hispanic/Latino; 17 Hispanic/Latino; 4 Two or more races, non-Hispanic/Latino), 1 international. Average age 33. 127 applicants, 82% accepted, 79 enrolled. In 2016, 47 master's, 13 other advanced degrees awarded. *Entrance requirements:* For master's, GRE (minimum combined score of 300) or MAT (minimum score of 400) within the last five years, bachelor's degree; minimum undergraduate GPA of 3.0; demonstrated proficiency in basic uses of instructional technologies; for other advanced degree, GRE or MAT within last 5 years, minimum undergraduate GPA of 3.0; demonstrated proficiency in basic uses of instructional technologies; master's degree, minimum 3 years' successful teaching experience, and permanent or provisional NY State teaching certification (for Advanced Diploma). Additional exam requirements/recommendations for international students: Required—TOEFL (minimum score 79 iBT), IELTS (minimum score 6). *Application deadline:* Applications are processed on a rolling basis. Application fee: $50. Electronic applications accepted. *Expenses:* $1,215 per credit. *Financial support:* Research assistantships with partial tuition reimbursements, career-related internships or fieldwork, scholarships/grants, health care benefits, tuition waivers (full and partial), and unspecified assistantships available. Support available to part-time students. Financial award application deadline: 3/1; financial award applicants required to submit FAFSA. *Faculty research:* Integration of information and communication technologies (ICTs) and media literacy education into learning environments; urban K-12 teachers' effective use of technology to enhance student achievement; instructional design and transdisciplinary curriculum studies for online instruction; STEM + computing partnerships for K-12 teachers; experiential, collaborative, and performance-based approaches to pedagogy and technology integration in the K-12 classroom. *Unit head:* Dr. Melda Yildiz, Department Chair, 516-686-1053, Fax: 516-686-7655, E-mail: myildiz@nyit.edu. *Application contact:* Alice Dolitsky, Director, Graduate Admissions, 516-686-7520, Fax: 516-686-1116, E-mail: nyitgrad@nyit.edu.
Website: http://www.nyit.edu/interdisciplinary/department_instructional_technology

New York University, Steinhardt School of Culture, Education, and Human Development, Department of Administration, Leadership, and Technology, Programs in Educational Communication and Technology, Brooklyn, NY 11201. Offers digital media design for learning (MA, Advanced Certificate); educational communication and technology (PhD); games for learning (MS). *Program availability:* Part-time. *Degree requirements:* For master's, thesis (for some programs); for doctorate, thesis/dissertation. *Entrance requirements:* For doctorate, GRE General Test, interview; for Advanced Certificate, master's degree. Additional exam requirements/recommendations for international students: Required—TOEFL (minimum score 100 iBT). Electronic applications accepted. *Faculty research:* Digital design for learning, critical evaluation of games, multimedia, cognitive science, individual differences in multimedia learning, serious games.

North Carolina Agricultural and Technical State University, School of Graduate Studies, School of Education, Department of Curriculum and Instruction, Greensboro, NC 27411. Offers elementary education (MA Ed); instructional technology (MS); reading education (MA Ed); teaching (MAT). *Accreditation:* NCATE. *Program availability:* Part-time, evening/weekend. *Degree requirements:* For master's, comprehensive exam, qualifying exam. *Entrance requirements:* For master's, GRE General Test, minimum GPA of 3.0.

North Carolina Central University, School of Education, Program in Educational Technology, Durham, NC 27707-3129. Offers MA. *Accreditation:* NCATE. *Program availability:* Part-time, evening/weekend. *Degree requirements:* For master's, comprehensive exam, thesis or alternative. *Entrance requirements:* For master's, GRE, minimum GPA of 3.0 in major, 2.5 overall. Additional exam requirements/recommendations for international students: Required—TOEFL.

North Carolina Central University, School of Education, Program in Instructional Technology, Durham, NC 27707-3129. Offers M Ed.

North Carolina State University, Graduate School, College of Education, Department of Curriculum and Instruction, Program in Instructional Technology, Raleigh, NC 27695. Offers M Ed, MS. *Entrance requirements:* For master's, MAT or GRE, minimum GPA of 3.0, 3 letters of reference.

North Carolina State University, Graduate School, College of Education, Department of Mathematics, Science, and Technology Education, Program in Technology Education, Raleigh, NC 27695. Offers M Ed, MS, Ed D. *Degree requirements:* For master's, thesis (for some programs); for doctorate, thesis/dissertation. *Entrance requirements:* For master's, GRE or MAT; for doctorate, GRE General Test or MAT, minimum GPA of 3.0, interview. Electronic applications accepted.

Northeastern State University, College of Education, Department of Curriculum and Instruction, Program in Library Media and Information Technology, Tahlequah, OK 74464-2399. Offers MS. *Faculty:* 13 full-time (10 women). *Students:* 5 full-time (all women), 30 part-time (all women); includes 7 minority (1 Black or African American, non-Hispanic/Latino; 3 American Indian or Alaska Native, non-Hispanic/Latino; 3 Two or more races, non-Hispanic/Latino). Average age 38. In 2016, 11 master's awarded. *Entrance requirements:* Additional exam requirements/recommendations for international students: Required—TOEFL. *Application deadline:* For fall admission, 7/1 for domestic and international students; for spring admission, 11/1 for domestic and international students. Applications are processed on a rolling basis. Application fee: $25. Electronic applications accepted. *Expenses:* Tuition, state resident: full-time $2816; part-time $216.60 per credit hour. Tuition, nonresident: full-time $6365; part-time $489.60 per credit hour. *Required fees:* $37.40 per credit hour. *Unit head:* Dr. Kelli Carney, Program Chair, 918-449-6365, E-mail: carneyka@nsuok.edu. *Application contact:* Josh McCollum, Graduate Coordinator, 918-444-2093, E-mail: mccolluj@nsuok.edu.
Website: http://academics.nsuok.edu/education/DegreePrograms/GraduatePrograms/LibraryMediaInformationTechnology.aspx

Northern Arizona University, Graduate College, College of Education, Department of Educational Specialties, Flagstaff, AZ 86011. Offers autism spectrum disorders (Certificate); bilingual/multicultural education (M Ed), including bilingual education, ESL education; career and technical education (M Ed, Certificate); culturally and linguistically diverse special education (Certificate); early childhood special education (M Ed); educational technology (M Ed, Certificate); English as a second language (Certificate); mild/moderate disabilities (M Ed); positive behavior support (Certificate); special education (M Ed). *Degree requirements:* For master's, comprehensive exam (for some programs), thesis (for some programs). *Entrance requirements:* For master's, minimum GPA of 3.0. Additional exam requirements/recommendations for international students: Required—TOEFL (minimum score 550 paper-based; 80 iBT), IELTS (minimum score 7). Electronic applications accepted. *Expenses:* Tuition, state resident: full-time $8971; part-time $444 per credit hour. Tuition, nonresident: full-time $20,958; part-time $1164 per credit hour. *Required fees:* $1018; $644 per credit hour. Tuition and fees vary according to course load, campus/location and program.

Northern Illinois University, Graduate School, College of Education, Department of Educational Technology, Research and Assessment, De Kalb, IL 60115-2854. Offers educational research and evaluation (MS); instructional technology (MS Ed, Ed D). *Program availability:* Part-time, evening/weekend. *Faculty:* 13 full-time (7 women). *Students:* 65 full-time (37 women), 98 part-time (70 women); includes 28 minority (15 Black or African American, non-Hispanic/Latino; 5 Asian, non-Hispanic/Latino; 6 Hispanic/Latino; 2 Two or more races, non-Hispanic/Latino), 41 international. Average age 39. 33 applicants, 64% accepted, 12 enrolled. In 2016, 38 master's, 10 doctorates awarded. Terminal master's awarded for partial completion of doctoral program. *Degree requirements:* For master's, comprehensive exam, thesis optional; for doctorate, thesis/dissertation, candidacy exam, dissertation defense. *Entrance requirements:* For master's, GRE General Test or MAT, minimum GPA of 2.75; for doctorate, GRE General Test or MAT, minimum undergraduate GPA of 2.75, 3.2 graduate. Additional exam requirements/recommendations for international students: Required—TOEFL (minimum score 550 paper-based). *Application deadline:* For fall admission, 6/1 for domestic students, 5/1 for international students; for spring admission, 11/1 for domestic students, 10/1 for international students. Applications are processed on a rolling basis. Application fee: $40. Electronic applications accepted. *Financial support:* In 2016–17, 3 research assistantships with full tuition reimbursements, 27 teaching assistantships with full tuition reimbursements were awarded; fellowships with full tuition reimbursements, career-related internships or fieldwork, Federal Work-Study, scholarships/grants, tuition waivers (full), and unspecified assistantships also available. Support available to part-time students. Financial award applicants required to submit FAFSA. *Faculty research:* Distance education, Web-based training, copyright assessment during student teaching, instructional software. *Unit head:* Dr. Wei-Chen Hung, Chair, 815-753-9339, E-mail: etra@niu.edu. *Application contact:* Graduate School Office, 815-753-0395, E-mail: gradsch@niu.edu.
Website: http://www.cedu.niu.edu/etra/index.html

Northern State University, MS Ed Program in Instructional Design in E-learning, Aberdeen, SD 57401-7198. Offers MS Ed. *Program availability:* Part-time, online learning. *Degree requirements:* For master's, comprehensive exam, thesis optional. *Entrance requirements:* For master's, minimum GPA of 2.75. Additional exam requirements/recommendations for international students: Required—TOEFL (minimum score 550 paper-based; 78 iBT), IELTS (minimum score 6). Electronic applications accepted.

Northern State University, MS Program in Training and Development in E-learning, Aberdeen, SD 57401-7198. Offers MS. *Program availability:* Part-time, online learning. *Degree requirements:* For master's, comprehensive exam, thesis optional. *Entrance requirements:* For master's, minimum GPA of 2.75. Additional exam requirements/ recommendations for international students: Required—TOEFL (minimum score 550 paper-based; 78 iBT), IELTS (minimum score 6). Electronic applications accepted.

Northwestern State University of Louisiana, Graduate Studies and Research, College of Education and Human Development, Program in Educational Technology Leadership, Natchitoches, LA 71497. Offers M Ed. *Degree requirements:* For master's, comprehensive exam, thesis (for some programs). *Entrance requirements:* For master's, GRE General Test. Additional exam requirements/recommendations for international students: Required—TOEFL. Electronic applications accepted.

Northwestern State University of Louisiana, Graduate Studies and Research, College of Education and Human Development, Programs in Educational Leadership and Instruction, Natchitoches, LA 71497. Offers counseling (Ed S); educational leadership (M Ed, Ed S); educational technology (Ed S); elementary teaching (Ed S); reading (Ed S); secondary teaching (Ed S); special education (Ed S). *Accreditation:* NASAD. *Degree requirements:* For master's, comprehensive exam, thesis (for some programs). *Entrance requirements:* For master's and Ed S, GRE General Test. Additional exam requirements/recommendations for international students: Required—TOEFL. Electronic applications accepted.

Northwestern University, The Graduate School, School of Education and Social Policy, Program in Learning Sciences, Evanston, IL 60208. Offers MA, PhD. Admissions and degrees offered through The Graduate School. Terminal master's awarded for partial completion of doctoral program. *Degree requirements:* For master's, thesis or alternative, portfolio; for doctorate, thesis/dissertation, qualifying exam. *Entrance requirements:* For doctorate, GRE General Test. Additional exam requirements/ recommendations for international students: Required—TOEFL (minimum score 600 paper-based; 100 iBT). Electronic applications accepted. *Expenses:* Contact institution. *Faculty research:* Technologically supported learning environments; inquiry-based learning in mathematics, science, and literacy; learning social contexts; cognitive models of learning and problem solving; changing roles for teachers involved in innovative design and practice.

Northwest Missouri State University, Graduate School, School of Computer Science and Information Systems, Maryville, MO 64468-6001. Offers applied computer science (MS); information systems (MS); instructional technology (MS). *Program availability:* Part-time. *Degree requirements:* For master's, comprehensive exam. *Entrance requirements:* For master's, GRE General Test, minimum GPA of 3.0. Additional exam requirements/recommendations for international students: Required—TOEFL (minimum score 550 paper-based). *Expenses:* Tuition, state resident: full-time $3447; part-time $383 per credit hour. Tuition, nonresident: full-time $5724; part-time $636 per credit hour. *Required fees:* $130 per credit hour.

Nova Southeastern University, Abraham S. Fischler College of Education, Fort Lauderdale, FL 33314. Offers education (MS, Ed D, PhD, Ed S); instructional technology and distance education (MS); teaching and learning (MA). *Accreditation:* NCATE. *Program availability:* Part-time, evening/weekend, 100% online, blended/hybrid learning. *Faculty:* 94 full-time (58 women), 204 part-time/adjunct (145 women). *Students:* 1,841 full-time (1,435 women), 1,705 part-time (1,336 women); includes 2,584 minority (1,389 Black or African American, non-Hispanic/Latino; 8 American Indian or Alaska Native, non-Hispanic/Latino; 44 Asian, non-Hispanic/Latino; 1,078 Hispanic/ Latino; 2 Native Hawaiian or other Pacific Islander, non-Hispanic/Latino; 63 Two or more races, non-Hispanic/Latino), 26 international. Average age 41. 1,753 applicants, 47% accepted, 581 enrolled. In 2016, 654 master's, 387 doctorates, 119 other advanced degrees awarded. *Degree requirements:* For master's, practicum, internship; for doctorate, thesis/dissertation; for Ed S, thesis, practicum, internship. *Entrance requirements:* For master's, MAT or GRE (for some programs), CLAST, PRAXIS I, CBEST, General Knowledge Test, teaching certification, minimum GPA of 2.5, verification of teaching, BS; for doctorate, MAT or GRE, master's degree, minimum cumulative GPA of 3.0; for Ed S, MAT or GRE, master's degree, teaching certificate, minimum GPA of 3.0. Additional exam requirements/recommendations for international students: Recommended—TOEFL (minimum score 550 paper-based; 79 iBT), IELTS (minimum score 6). *Application deadline:* Applications are processed on a rolling basis. Application fee: $50. Electronic applications accepted. *Expenses:* Contact institution. *Financial support:* In 2016–17, 67 students received support. Career-related internships or fieldwork and Federal Work-Study available. Support available to part-time students. Financial award application deadline: 4/15; financial award applicants required to submit FAFSA. *Faculty research:* STEM education, educational technology, principal training, quality of life. *Total annual research expenditures:* $50,000. *Unit head:* Dr. Kim Durham, Interim Dean, 954-262-8731, Fax: 954-262-3894, E-mail: durham@nova.edu. *Application contact:* Adriana Garay, Executive Director for Marketing, Recruitment and Admissions, 800-986-3223 Ext. 8500, E-mail: fserecruit@nova.edu.
Website: http://www.fischlerschool.nova.edu/

Ohio University, Graduate College, Gladys W. and David H. Patton College of Education and Human Services, Department of Educational Studies, Athens, OH 45701-2979. Offers computer education and technology (M Ed); educational administration (M Ed, Ed D); educational research and evaluation (M Ed, PhD); instructional technology (PhD). *Program availability:* Part-time, evening/weekend, online learning. *Degree requirements:* For master's, thesis or alternative; for doctorate, comprehensive exam, thesis/dissertation. *Entrance requirements:* For master's, GRE General Test (if GPA less than 2.9); for doctorate, GRE General Test, GRE Subject Test, minimum GPA of 2.9, work experience, 3 letters of reference, autobiography. Additional exam requirements/recommendations for international students: Required—TOEFL (minimum score 550 paper-based; 80 iBT) or IELTS (minimum score 6.5). *Application deadline:* For fall admission, 3/1 priority date for domestic and international students; for winter admission, 10/1 priority date for domestic and international students; for spring admission, 1/30 priority date for domestic students, 1/1 priority date for international students. Applications are processed on a rolling basis. Application fee: $50 ($55 for international students). Electronic applications accepted. *Financial support:* Research assistantships with full tuition reimbursements, teaching assistantships with full tuition reimbursements, Federal Work-Study, institutionally sponsored loans, tuition waivers (partial), and unspecified assistantships available. Financial award application deadline: 3/1. *Faculty research:* Race, class and gender; computer programs; development and organization theory; evaluation/development of instruments, leadership. *Unit head:* Dr. David Richard Moore, Chair, 740-597-1322, Fax: 740-593-0477, E-mail: moored3@ohio.edu. *Application contact:* Floyd J. Doney, Director of Student Affairs, 740-593-4400, Fax: 740-593-9310, E-mail: doney@ohio.edu.
Website: http://www.cehs.ohio.edu/academics/es/

Old Dominion University, Darden College of Education, Program in Elementary/Middle Education, Norfolk, VA 23529. Offers elementary education (Postbaccalaureate Certificate); instructional technology (MS Ed); library science (MS Ed). *Accreditation:* NCATE. *Program availability:* Part-time, evening/weekend, 100% online, blended/hybrid learning. *Faculty:* 21 full-time (19 women), 24 part-time/adjunct (22 women). *Students:* 120 full-time (112 women), 138 part-time (125 women); includes 60 minority (36 Black or African American, non-Hispanic/Latino; 1 American Indian or Alaska Native, non-Hispanic/Latino; 5 Asian, non-Hispanic/Latino; 12 Hispanic/Latino; 6 Two or more races, non-Hispanic/Latino). Average age 33. 213 applicants, 88% accepted, 172 enrolled. In 2016, 127 master's awarded. *Degree requirements:* For master's, comprehensive exam. *Entrance requirements:* For master's, GRE General Test or MAT; PRAXIS I, SAT or ACT, minimum GPA of 2.8. Additional exam requirements/recommendations for international students: Required—TOEFL (minimum score 600 paper-based). *Application deadline:* For fall admission, 6/1 priority date for domestic students; for winter admission, 11/1 priority date for domestic students; for spring admission, 3/1 priority date for domestic students. Applications are processed on a rolling basis. Application fee: $50. Electronic applications accepted. *Expenses:* $478 per credit hour in-state; $1,195 per credit hour out-of-state. *Financial support:* In 2016–17, 180 students received support. Unspecified assistantships available. Financial award application deadline: 2/15; financial award applicants required to submit FAFSA. *Faculty research:* Education pre-K to 6, school librarianship, reading, TESOL, literacy. *Unit head:* Dr. KaaVonia Hinton, Chair, Department of Teaching and Learning, 757-683-3284, Fax: 757-683-5862, E-mail: khintonj@odu.edu. *Application contact:* William Heffelfinger, Director of Graduate Admissions, 757-683-5554, Fax: 757-683-3255, E-mail: gradadmit@odu.edu.
Website: http://education.odu.edu/eci/

Old Dominion University, Darden College of Education, Program in Instructional Design and Technology, Norfolk, VA 23529. Offers PhD. *Program availability:* Part-time, evening/weekend, 100% online, blended/hybrid learning. *Faculty:* 4 full-time (3 women), 1 (woman) part-time/adjunct. *Students:* 6 full-time (5 women), 41 part-time (28 women); includes 10 minority (8 Black or African American, non-Hispanic/Latino; 1 Hispanic/ Latino; 1 Two or more races, non-Hispanic/Latino), 2 international. Average age 43. 30 applicants, 43% accepted, 13 enrolled. In 2016, 5 doctorates awarded. *Degree requirements:* For doctorate, comprehensive exam, thesis/dissertation. *Entrance requirements:* For doctorate, GRE, references, interview, essay of 500 words. Additional exam requirements/recommendations for international students: Required—TOEFL (minimum score 550 paper-based). *Application deadline:* For fall admission, 4/1 priority date for domestic students, 3/1 priority date for international students; for winter admission, 11/1 priority date for domestic students, 10/1 priority date for international students; for spring admission, 4/1 for domestic students, 2/1 priority date for international students. Applications are processed on a rolling basis. Application fee: $50. Electronic applications accepted. *Expenses:* Tuition, state resident: full-time $8604; part-time $478 per credit hour. Tuition, nonresident: full-time $21,510; part-time $1195 per credit hour. *Required fees:* $66 per semester. Tuition and fees vary according to campus/location, program and reciprocity agreements. *Financial support:* In 2016–17, 4 students received support, including 3 research assistantships with full tuition reimbursements available (averaging $15,000 per year); career-related internships or fieldwork and unspecified assistantships also available. Financial award application deadline: 2/15; financial award applicants required to submit FAFSA. *Faculty research:* Instructional design, distance education, instructional strategies, human performance technology, simulation design. *Total annual research expenditures:* $2 million. *Unit head:* Dr. Jill E. Stefaniak, Graduate Program Director, 757-683-6696, Fax: 757-683-5227, E-mail: jstefani@odu.edu. *Application contact:* William Heffelfinger, Director of Graduate Admissions, 757-683-5554, Fax: 757-683-3255, E-mail: gradadmit@odu.edu.
Website: http://education.odu.edu/eci/idt

Ottawa University, Graduate Studies-Arizona, Program in Education, Ottawa, KS 66067-3399. Offers community college counseling (MA); curriculum and instruction (MA); early childhood (MA); education intervention (MA); education leadership (MA); education technology (MA); Montessori early childhood education (MA); Montessori elementary education (MA); professional development (MA); school guidance counseling (MA); special education - cross categorical (MA). Programs offered in Mesa, Phoenix, Tempe and West Valley, AZ. *Accreditation:* NCATE. *Program availability:* Part-time. *Degree requirements:* For master's, thesis or alternative. *Entrance requirements:* For master's, minimum undergraduate GPA of 3.0, copy of current state certification or teaching license. Additional exam requirements/recommendations for international students: Required—TOEFL (minimum score 550 paper-based). Electronic applications accepted. *Expenses:* Contact institution.

Pace University, School of Education, New York, NY 10038. Offers adolescent education (MST), including biology, business education, chemistry, earth science, English, foreign languages, mathematics, physics, social studies, visual arts; childhood education (MST); early childhood development, learning and intervention (MST); educational technology studies (MS); inclusive adolescent education (MST), including biology, business education, chemistry, earth science, English, foreign languages, mathematics, physics, social studies, visual arts; integrated instruction for educational technology (Certificate); integrated instruction for literacy and technology (Certificate); literacy (MS Ed); special education (MS Ed). *Accreditation:* NCATE. *Program availability:* Part-time, evening/weekend, blended/hybrid learning. *Faculty:* 19 full-time (13 women), 86 part-time/adjunct (49 women). *Students:* 115 full-time (97 women), 543 part-time (381 women); includes 280 minority (137 Black or African American, non-Hispanic/Latino; 1 American Indian or Alaska Native, non-Hispanic/Latino; 40 Asian, non-Hispanic/Latino; 87 Hispanic/Latino; 15 Two or more races, non-Hispanic/Latino), 13 international. Average age 30. 181 applicants, 78% accepted, 72 enrolled. In 2016, 193 master's, 9 other advanced degrees awarded. *Degree requirements:* For master's, certification exams. *Entrance requirements:* For master's, GRE, interview, teaching certificate (except for MST). Additional exam requirements/recommendations for international students: Required—TOEFL (minimum score 88 iBT), IELTS or PTE. *Application deadline:* For fall admission, 8/1 priority date for domestic students, 6/1 for international students; for spring admission, 12/1 priority date for domestic students, 10/ 1 for international students. Applications are processed on a rolling basis. Application fee: $70. Electronic applications accepted. *Expenses:* Contact institution. *Financial support:* In 2016–17, 17 students received support, including 17 research assistantships with partial tuition reimbursements available (averaging $6,020 per year); career-related internships or fieldwork and Federal Work-Study also available. Financial award application deadline: 9/1; financial award applicants required to submit FAFSA. *Faculty research:* STEM education, TESOL, teacher education, special education, language and literary development. *Total annual research expenditures:* $290,153. *Unit head:* Dr. Xiao-Lei Wang, Dean, School of Education, 914-773-3876, E-mail: xwang@pace.edu. *Application contact:* Susan Ford-Goldschein, Director of Graduate Admissions, 212-346-1531, Fax: 212-346-1585, E-mail: graduateadmission@pace.edu.
Website: http://www.pace.edu/school-of-education

Penn State University Park, Graduate School, College of Education, Department of Learning and Performance Systems, University Park, PA 16802. Offers adult education (M Ed, D Ed, PhD, Certificate); corporate training (MPS); learning, design, and technology (M Ed, MS, PhD, Certificate); lifelong learning and adult education (M Ed,

D Ed, PhD, Certificate); organization development and change (MPS); workforce education and development (M Ed, MS, PhD). *Unit head:* Dr. David H. Monk, Dean, 814-865-2523, Fax: 814-865-0555. *Application contact:* Lori Hawn, Director, Graduate Student Services, 814-865-1795, Fax: 814-863-4627, E-mail: l-gswww@lists.psu.edu.
Website: http://ed.psu.edu/lps/dept-lps

Pepperdine University, Graduate School of Education and Psychology, Division of Education, Los Angeles, CA 90045. Offers administration and preliminary administrative services (MS); education (MA); educational leadership, administration, and policy (Ed D); global leadership and change (PhD); learning technologies (MA, Ed D); organizational leadership (Ed D); social entrepreneurship and change (MA); teaching (MA); teaching: TESOL (MA). *Program availability:* Part-time, evening/weekend, online learning. *Students:* 262 full-time (169 women), 385 part-time (264 women); includes 286 minority (123 Black or African American, non-Hispanic/Latino; 4 American Indian or Alaska Native, non-Hispanic/Latino; 59 Asian, non-Hispanic/Latino; 77 Hispanic/Latino; 6 Native Hawaiian or other Pacific Islander, non-Hispanic/Latino; 17 Two or more races, non-Hispanic/Latino), 46 international. Average age 38. 372 applicants, 95% accepted, 200 enrolled. In 2016, 142 master's, 66 doctorates awarded. *Degree requirements:* For doctorate, thesis/dissertation. *Entrance requirements:* For master's, GRE General Test; for doctorate, GRE General Test, MAT. Additional exam requirements/recommendations for international students: Required—TOEFL. *Application deadline:* Applications are processed on a rolling basis. Application fee: $55. *Expenses:* $1,165 per unit (for master's); $1,460 per unit (for doctorate). *Financial support:* Research assistantships, teaching assistantships, career-related internships or fieldwork, institutionally sponsored loans, and scholarships/grants available. Support available to part-time students. Financial award application deadline: 7/1; financial award applicants required to submit FAFSA. *Unit head:* Dr. Martine Jago, Associate Dean, Education Division, 310-568-2828, E-mail: martine.jago@pepperdine.edu. *Application contact:* Chris Costa, Director of Enrollment, 310-568-2850, E-mail: chris.costa@pepperdine.edu.
Website: http://gsep.pepperdine.edu/masters-education/

Piedmont College, School of Education, Demorest, GA 30535. Offers art education (MAT); curriculum and instruction (Ed S); early childhood education (MA, MAT); instructional technology (MAT); middle grades education (MA, MAT); music education (MAT); secondary education (MA, MAT); special education (MA, MAT). *Program availability:* Part-time, evening/weekend. *Students:* 290 full-time (217 women), 614 part-time (508 women); includes 131 minority (97 Black or African American, non-Hispanic/Latino; 4 American Indian or Alaska Native, non-Hispanic/Latino; 5 Asian, non-Hispanic/Latino; 11 Hispanic/Latino; 6 Native Hawaiian or other Pacific Islander, non-Hispanic/Latino; 8 Two or more races, non-Hispanic/Latino), 6 international. Average age 37. 257 applicants, 64% accepted, 160 enrolled. In 2016, 288 master's, 243 other advanced degrees awarded. *Degree requirements:* For master's, thesis, field experience in the classroom teaching. *Entrance requirements:* For master's, GRE General Test, MAT, minimum undergraduate GPA of 2.5; for Ed S, minimum graduate GPA of 3.5, valid teaching certificate. Additional exam requirements/recommendations for international students: Required—TOEFL (minimum score 550 paper-based). *Application deadline:* For fall admission, 7/15 for domestic students; for spring admission, 12/1 for domestic students. Applications are processed on a rolling basis. Electronic applications accepted. *Expenses: Tuition:* Full-time $8910. *Financial support:* Career-related internships or fieldwork, Federal Work-Study, and unspecified assistantships available. Support available to part-time students. Financial award applicants required to submit FAFSA. *Unit head:* Dr. Don Gnecco, Dean, 706-778-3000 Ext. 1201, Fax: 706-776-9608, E-mail: dgnecco@piedmont.edu. *Application contact:* Kathleen Anderson, Director of Graduate Enrollment Management, 706-778-8500 Ext. 1181, Fax: 706-778-0150, E-mail: kanderson@piedmont.edu.

Pittsburg State University, Graduate School, College of Education, Department of Teaching and Leadership, Program in Educational Technology, Pittsburg, KS 66762. Offers MS. *Accreditation:* NCATE. *Program availability:* Part-time, online only, 100% online. *Students:* 54. In 2016, 58 master's awarded. *Degree requirements:* For master's, thesis or alternative. *Entrance requirements:* For master's, PPST. Additional exam requirements/recommendations for international students: Required—TOEFL (minimum score 520 paper-based; 68 iBT), IELTS (minimum score 6), PTE (minimum score 47). *Application deadline:* For fall admission, 7/15 for domestic students, 6/1 for international students; for spring admission, 12/15 for domestic students, 10/15 for international students; for summer admission, 5/15 for domestic students, 4/1 for international students. Applications are processed on a rolling basis. Application fee: $35 ($60 for international students). Electronic applications accepted. *Expenses:* Contact institution. *Financial support:* In 2016–17, teaching assistantships (averaging $5,000 per year) were awarded; career-related internships or fieldwork, Federal Work-Study, and unspecified assistantships also available. Financial award application deadline: 2/1; financial award applicants required to submit FAFSA. *Unit head:* Dr. Brenda Roberts, Program Coordinator, 620-235-4498, Fax: 620-235-4520, E-mail: broberts@pittstate.edu. *Application contact:* Lisa Allen, Assistant Director of Graduate and Continuing Studies, 620-235-4218, Fax: 620-235-4219, E-mail: lallen@pittstate.edu.

Plymouth State University, College of Graduate Studies, Graduate Studies in Education, Program in Secondary Education, Plymouth, NH 03264-1595. Offers curriculum and instruction (M Ed); language education (M Ed); library media (M Ed); physical education (M Ed); social studies education (M Ed); special education (M Ed). *Program availability:* Part-time, evening/weekend. *Entrance requirements:* For master's, MAT.

Post University, Program in Education, Waterbury, CT 06723-2540. Offers education (M Ed); higher education administration (M Ed); instructional design and technology (M Ed); online teaching (M Ed); teaching and learning (M Ed); TESOL (teaching English to speakers of other languages) (M Ed). *Program availability:* Online learning.

Purdue University, Graduate School, College of Education, Department of Curriculum and Instruction, West Lafayette, IN 47907. Offers agricultural and extension education (MS, MS Ed, PhD, Ed S); art education (PhD); career and technical education (MS Ed, PhD, Ed S); curriculum studies (MS Ed, PhD, Ed S); educational technology (MS Ed, PhD, Ed S); elementary education (MS Ed); family and consumer sciences education (MS Ed, PhD, Ed S); foreign language education (MS Ed, PhD, Ed S); industrial technology (PhD, Ed S); language arts (MS Ed, PhD, Ed S); literacy (MS Ed, PhD, Ed S); mathematics education (MS, MS Ed, PhD, Ed S); science education (MS, MS Ed, PhD, Ed S); social studies education (MS Ed, PhD, Ed S). *Accreditation:* NCATE. *Program availability:* Part-time, evening/weekend. *Faculty:* 37 full-time (27 women), 1 (woman) part-time/adjunct. *Students:* 78 full-time (50 women), 286 part-time (195 women); includes 68 minority (25 Black or African American, non-Hispanic/Latino; 3 American Indian or Alaska Native, non-Hispanic/Latino; 10 Asian, non-Hispanic/Latino; 22 Hispanic/Latino; 1 Native Hawaiian or other Pacific Islander, non-Hispanic/Latino; 7 Two or more races, non-Hispanic/Latino), 44 international. Average age 36. 150 applicants, 79% accepted, 73 enrolled. In 2016, 107 master's, 20 doctorates, 2 other advanced degrees awarded. *Degree requirements:* For master's, thesis optional; for doctorate, thesis/dissertation, oral and written exams; for Ed S, oral presentation, project. *Entrance requirements:* For master's, GRE General Test (if undergraduate GPA is below 3.0), minimum undergraduate GPA of 3.0 or equivalent; for doctorate, GRE General Test (minimum combined verbal and quantitative score of 1000, 300 for new scoring), minimum undergraduate GPA of 3.0 or equivalent; master's degree with minimum GPA of 3.0 or equivalent; for Ed S, GRE General Test (minimum combined verbal and quantitative score of 1000, 300 for new scoring), minimum undergraduate GPA of 3.0 or equivalent; master's degree. Additional exam requirements/recommendations for international students: Required—TOEFL (minimum score 550 paper-based; 77 iBT). *Application deadline:* For fall admission, 12/15 for domestic students, 3/1 for international students; for spring admission, 9/15 for domestic students, 8/1 for international students. Application fee: $60 ($75 for international students). Electronic applications accepted. *Financial support:* Fellowships with full tuition reimbursements, research assistantships with full tuition reimbursements, teaching assistantships with full tuition reimbursements, career-related internships or fieldwork, and tuition waivers (full) available. Support available to part-time students. Financial award application deadline: 3/1; financial award applicants required to submit FAFSA. *Faculty research:* Literacy acquisition and development, teacher beliefs and knowledge, recruitment and retention of underrepresented students, economic education, literacy discourse. *Unit head:* Janet M. Alsup, Head, 765-494-9667, E-mail: alsupj@purdue.edu. *Application contact:* Heather Brinkman, Graduate Contact, 765-494-2345, E-mail: hbrinkma@purdue.edu.
Website: http://www.edci.purdue.edu/

Purdue University Northwest, Graduate Studies Office, School of Education, Program in Instructional Technology, Hammond, IN 46323-2094. Offers MS Ed. *Entrance requirements:* Additional exam requirements/recommendations for international students: Required—TOEFL.

Quinnipiac University, School of Education, Program in Instructional Design, Hamden, CT 06518-1940. Offers MS. *Program availability:* Part-time-only, evening/weekend, online only, 100% online. *Faculty:* 2 full-time (both women), 2 part-time/adjunct (0 women). *Students:* 1 (woman) full-time, 45 part-time (37 women); includes 7 minority (1 Black or African American, non-Hispanic/Latino; 4 Hispanic/Latino; 2 Two or more races, non-Hispanic/Latino). 16 applicants, 81% accepted, 11 enrolled. In 2016, 7 master's awarded. *Application deadline:* For fall admission, 8/15 for domestic students; for spring admission, 1/15 for domestic students. Applications are processed on a rolling basis. Application fee: $45. Electronic applications accepted. *Expenses:* Contact institution. *Financial support:* Federal Work-Study and unspecified assistantships available. Financial award application deadline: 6/1; financial award applicants required to submit FAFSA. *Unit head:* Ruth Schwartz, Director, 203-582-8419, E-mail: ruth.schwartz@qu.edu. *Application contact:* Quinnipiac University Online Admissions, 800-462-1944, Fax: 203-582-3443, E-mail: quonlineadmissions@qu.edu.
Website: https://quonline.quinnipiac.edu/online-programs/online-graduate-programs/ms-in-instructional-design/

Ramapo College of New Jersey, Master of Science in Educational Technology Program, Mahwah, NJ 07430-1680. Offers MS. *Program availability:* Part-time, evening/weekend. *Faculty:* 12 part-time/adjunct (5 women). *Students:* 2 full-time (both women), 142 part-time (103 women); includes 18 minority (2 Black or African American, non-Hispanic/Latino; 3 Asian, non-Hispanic/Latino; 13 Hispanic/Latino), 3 international. Average age 34. 72 applicants, 93% accepted, 55 enrolled. In 2016, 37 master's awarded. *Degree requirements:* For master's, capstone course. *Entrance requirements:* For master's, official transcript of baccalaureate degree from accredited institution with minimum recommended GPA of 3.0; personal statement; letter of recommendation; resume. Additional exam requirements/recommendations for international students: Required—TOEFL (minimum score 550 paper-based; 79 iBT); Recommended—IELTS (minimum score 6). *Application deadline:* For fall admission, 5/1 for domestic and international students; for spring admission, 12/1 for domestic and international students. Applications are processed on a rolling basis. Application fee: $60. Electronic applications accepted. *Expenses:* $606.05 per credit tuition, $130.45 per credit fees. *Financial support:* Career-related internships or fieldwork available. Financial award application deadline: 3/1; financial award applicants required to submit FAFSA. *Faculty research:* Integrating technology in the curriculum of K-12 learning environment. *Unit head:* Dr. Richard Russo, Director of the Master in Educational Technology Program, 201-684-7899, Fax: 201-684-6699, E-mail: rrusso@ramapo.edu. *Application contact:* M. Joyce Wilson, Administrative Assistant, 201-684-7721, Fax: 201-684-6699, E-mail: jwilson@ramapo.edu.
Website: http://www.ramapo.edu/mset/

Regent University, Graduate School, School of Education, Virginia Beach, VA 23464-9800. Offers adult education (Ed D, PhD, Ed S); advanced educational leadership (Ed D, PhD, Ed S); career switcher (M Ed); character education (Ed D, PhD, Ed S); Christian education leadership (Ed D, PhD, Ed S); Christian school administration (M Ed); curriculum and instruction (M Ed), including adult education, Christian school, gifted and talented education, STEM education, teacher leader; educational leadership (M Ed); educational psychology (Ed D, PhD, Ed S); educational technology and online learning (Ed D, PhD, Ed S); elementary education (M Ed); exceptional education executive leadership (Ed D, PhD, Ed S); higher education (Ed D, PhD, Ed S); higher education leadership and management (Ed D, PhD, Ed S); individualized degree plan (M Ed); K-12 school leadership (Ed D, PhD, Ed S); K-12 special education (M Ed); K-8 leadership in mathematics education (M Ed); leadership in mathematics education (Ed S); reading specialist (M Ed); special education (Ed D, PhD, Ed S); student affairs (M Ed); TESOL (M Ed), including adult education - collegiate, K-12. *Accreditation:* TEAC. *Program availability:* Part-time, evening/weekend, 100% online, blended/hybrid learning. *Faculty:* 22 full-time (10 women), 42 part-time/adjunct (31 women). *Students:* 89 full-time (62 women), 1,035 part-time (823 women); includes 466 minority (381 Black or African American, non-Hispanic/Latino; 3 American Indian or Alaska Native, non-Hispanic/Latino; 19 Asian, non-Hispanic/Latino; 50 Hispanic/Latino; 13 Two or more races, non-Hispanic/Latino), 11 international. Average age 39. 976 applicants, 59% accepted, 449 enrolled. In 2016, 241 master's, 22 doctorates, 4 other advanced degrees awarded. *Degree requirements:* For master's, thesis or alternative; for doctorate, comprehensive exam, thesis/dissertation. *Entrance requirements:* For master's, Virginia Communication and Literacy Assessment (VCLA), PRAXIS, college transcripts, writing sample, interview; for doctorate, GRE, writing sample, resume, transcripts, interview. Additional exam requirements/recommendations for international students: Required—TOEFL (minimum score 577 paper-based). *Application deadline:* For fall admission, 4/1 priority date for domestic students; for spring admission, 10/15 priority date for domestic students. Applications are processed on a rolling basis. Application fee: $50. Electronic applications accepted. *Expenses:* Contact institution. *Financial support:* In 2016–17, 622 students received support, including 1 fellowship (averaging $5,000 per year); career-related internships or fieldwork, scholarships/grants, and unspecified assistantships also available. Support available to part-time students. *Faculty research:* Christian school administration, curriculum and instruction, educational technology and online learning, higher education, special education. *Unit head:* Dr. Donald Finn, Dean, 757-352-4278, Fax: 757-352-4318, E-mail: dfinn@regent.edu. *Application contact:* Heidi Cece, Assistant Vice President of Enrollment Management, 800-373-5504, Fax: 757-352-4381, E-mail: admissions@regent.edu.
Website: http://www.regent.edu/soe/

Robert Morris University Illinois, Morris Graduate School of Management, Chicago, IL 60605. Offers accounting (MBA); accounting/finance (MBA); business analytics (MIS); design and media (MM); design management (MM); educational technology (MM); health care administration (MM); higher education administration (MM); human resource management (MBA); information security (MIS); information systems (MBA, MIS); law enforcement administration (MM); management (MBA); management/finance (MBA); management/human resource management (MBA); mobile computing (MIS); sports administration (MM). *Program availability:* Part-time, evening/weekend. *Faculty:* 4 full-time (1 woman), 25 part-time/adjunct (5 women). *Students:* 196 full-time (98 women), 151 part-time (85 women); includes 200 minority (114 Black or African American, non-Hispanic/Latino; 17 Asian, non-Hispanic/Latino; 67 Hispanic/Latino; 2 Two or more races, non-Hispanic/Latino), 23 international. Average age 33. 174 applicants, 61% accepted, 97 enrolled. In 2016, 190 master's awarded. *Entrance requirements:* For master's, official transcripts and letters of recommendation (for some programs); written personal statement. Additional exam requirements/recommendations for international students: Required—TOEFL (minimum score 550 paper-based). *Application deadline:* Applications are processed on a rolling basis. Application fee: $20 ($100 for international students). Electronic applications accepted. *Expenses: Tuition:* Full-time $16,500; part-time $2750 per course. *Financial support:* In 2016–17, 444 students received support. Federal Work-Study, scholarships/grants, and unspecified assistantships available. Support available to part-time students. Financial award applicants required to submit FAFSA. *Unit head:* Kayed Akkawi, Dean, 312-935-6050, Fax: 312-935-6020, E-mail: kakkawi@robertmorris.edu. *Application contact:* Danielle Naffziger, Vice President of Marketing and Enrollment, 312-935-4812, Fax: 312-935-6020, E-mail: dnaffziger@robertmorris.edu.

Rockford University, Graduate Studies, Department of Education, Program in Instructional Strategies, Rockford, IL 61108-2393. Offers MAT. *Program availability:* Part-time, evening/weekend, online learning. *Degree requirements:* For master's, professional portfolio. *Entrance requirements:* For master's, GRE General Test, official transcripts, three letter of recommendation forms, essay. Additional exam requirements/recommendations for international students: Required—TOEFL (minimum score 550 paper-based; 79 iBT). *Application deadline:* Applications are processed on a rolling basis. Application fee: $50. Electronic applications accepted. *Expenses:* Contact institution. *Financial support:* Scholarships/grants and unspecified assistantships available. Support available to part-time students. Financial award application deadline: 3/1; financial award applicants required to submit FAFSA. *Application contact:* Michelle Mehren, Assistant Director, Office of Graduate Studies, 815-226-4040, Fax: 815-394-3706, E-mail: mmehren@rockford.edu.
Website: https://www.rockford.edu/admission/graduate/mat/

Rowan University, Graduate School, College of Education, Department of Interdisciplinary and Inclusive Education, Glassboro, NJ 08028-1701. Offers autism spectrum disorders (CGS); bilingual/bicultural education (CGS); educational technology (CGS); elementary education (MST); learning disabilities (MA, CGS); music education (MA); science teaching (MST); secondary education (MST); special education (MA, CGS); teacher leadership (M Ed); teacher of students with disabilities (Postbaccalaureate Certificate); teaching and learning (CGS); teaching STEM (MA). *Accreditation:* NCATE. *Program availability:* Part-time, evening/weekend. *Degree requirements:* For master's, comprehensive exam, thesis. *Entrance requirements:* For master's, GRE General Test, PRAXIS I, PRAXIS II, interview, minimum GPA of 2.8. Additional exam requirements/recommendations for international students: Required—TOEFL. Electronic applications accepted.

Saginaw Valley State University, College of Education, Program in Instructional Technology, University Center, MI 48710. Offers MA. *Program availability:* Part-time, evening/weekend. *Students:* 1 (woman) full-time, 30 part-time (22 women); includes 3 minority (1 Black or African American, non-Hispanic/Latino; 2 Hispanic/Latino). Average age 35. 11 applicants, 100% accepted, 8 enrolled. In 2016, 22 master's awarded. *Degree requirements:* For master's, capstone course or thesis. *Entrance requirements:* For master's, minimum GPA of 3.0. Additional exam requirements/recommendations for international students: Required—TOEFL (minimum score 550 paper-based; 79 iBT). *Application deadline:* For fall admission, 7/15 for international students; for winter admission, 11/15 for international students; for spring admission, 4/15 for international students. Applications are processed on a rolling basis. Application fee: $30 ($90 for international students). Electronic applications accepted. *Expenses:* Tuition, state resident: full-time $9652; part-time $536 per credit hour. Tuition, nonresident: full-time $12,259; part-time $1022 per credit hour. *Required fees:* $263; $14.60 per credit hour. Tuition and fees vary according to degree level. *Financial support:* Federal Work-Study and scholarships/grants available. Support available to part-time students. Financial award applicants required to submit FAFSA. *Unit head:* Dr. Carolyn Gilbreath, Associate Professor of Teaching Education, 989-749-4772, Fax: 989-964-4563, E-mail: cagilbre@svsu.edu. *Application contact:* Jenna Briggs, Director, Graduate and International Admissions, 989-964-6096, Fax: 989-964-2788, E-mail: gradadm@svsu.edu.

St. Cloud State University, School of Graduate Studies, School of Education, Center for Information Media, St. Cloud, MN 56301-4498. Offers MS. *Program availability:* Part-time, evening/weekend, online learning. *Degree requirements:* For master's, comprehensive exam, thesis or alternative. *Entrance requirements:* For master's, minimum overall GPA of 2.75 in previous undergraduate and graduate records or in last half of undergraduate work. Additional exam requirements/recommendations for international students: Required—Michigan English Language Assessment Battery; Recommended—TOEFL (minimum score 550 paper-based; 79 iBT), IELTS (minimum score 6.5). Electronic applications accepted.

Saint Joseph's University, College of Arts and Sciences, Graduate Programs in Education, Philadelphia, PA 19131-1395. Offers curriculum supervisor (Certificate); educational leadership (MS, Ed D); elementary education (MS, Certificate); elementary/middle school education (Certificate); instructional technology (MS, Certificate); organizational development and leadership (MS); principal (Certificate); professional education (MS); reading specialist (MS, Certificate); reading supervisor (Certificate); secondary education (MS, Certificate); special education (MS); special education 7-12 (Certificate); special education PK-8 (Certificate); superintendent's letter of eligibility (Certificate); supervisor of special education (Certificate); teacher of the deaf and hard of hearing (Certificate). *Program availability:* Part-time, evening/weekend, blended/hybrid learning. *Faculty:* 26 full-time (21 women), 74 part-time/adjunct (45 women). *Students:* 107 full-time (88 women), 826 part-time (622 women); includes 170 minority (115 Black or African American, non-Hispanic/Latino; 2 American Indian or Alaska Native, non-Hispanic/Latino; 11 Asian, non-Hispanic/Latino; 31 Hispanic/Latino; 1 Native Hawaiian or other Pacific Islander, non-Hispanic/Latino; 10 Two or more races, non-Hispanic/Latino), 18 international. Average age 33. 338 applicants, 76% accepted, 173 enrolled. In 2016, 419 master's, 16 doctorates, 24 other advanced degrees awarded. *Degree requirements:* For master's, thesis or alternative; for doctorate, comprehensive exam, thesis/dissertation. *Entrance requirements:* For master's, 2 letters of recommendation, minimum GPA of 3.0, official transcripts, personal statement; for doctorate, GRE, master's degree from accredited institution, minimum graduate GPA of 3.5, computer competence, interview with program director. Additional exam requirements/recommendations for international students: Required—TOEFL (minimum score 550 paper-based; 80 iBT), IELTS (minimum score 6.5), PTE (minimum score 60). *Application deadline:* For fall admission, 7/15 for international students; for spring admission, 11/1 for international students. Applications are processed on a rolling basis. Application fee: $35. Electronic applications accepted. *Expenses:* $750 per credit, $100 education fee, $360 online organization development and leadership residency fee. *Financial support:* In 2016–17, 25 students received support. Unspecified assistantships available. Financial award application deadline: 5/1; financial award applicants required to submit FAFSA. *Faculty research:* Factors predicting early mathematics skills for low income children, early child care and development, preschool quality, parent communication and home-school collaboration issues, education of terminally ill children, preparing literacy teachers for urban schools. *Total annual research expenditures:* $18,118. *Unit head:* Dr. John Vacca, Associate Dean, Education, 610-660-3131, E-mail: gradcas@sju.edu. *Application contact:* Graduate Admissions, College of Arts and Sciences, 610-660-3131, E-mail: gradcas@sju.edu.
Website: http://sju.edu/int/academics/cas/grad/education/index.html

Saint Leo University, Graduate Studies in Education, Saint Leo, FL 33574-6665. Offers educational leadership (M Ed), including Catholic school administration; exceptional student education (M Ed); instructional design (MS, Certificate); instructional leadership (M Ed); reading (M Ed, Certificate); school leadership (Ed S). *Program availability:* Part-time, evening/weekend, online learning. *Faculty:* 11 full-time (10 women), 22 part-time/adjunct (15 women). *Students:* 424 part-time (335 women); includes 94 minority (54 Black or African American, non-Hispanic/Latino; 2 Asian, non-Hispanic/Latino; 32 Hispanic/Latino; 6 Two or more races, non-Hispanic/Latino), 1 international. Average age 37. 260 applicants, 76% accepted, 107 enrolled. In 2016, 166 master's, 6 other advanced degrees awarded. *Degree requirements:* For master's, appropriate State of Florida certification tests. *Entrance requirements:* For master's, GRE (minimum score of 1000), MAT (minimum score of 410), or minimum undergraduate GPA of 3.0 in final 2 years, official transcripts, current resumé, 2 professional recommendations, personal statement, bachelor's degree from regionally-accredited university, valid professional teaching certificate; for other advanced degree, valid professional teaching certificate (for Ed S). Additional exam requirements/recommendations for international students: Required—TOEFL (minimum score 550 paper-based; 80 iBT). *Application deadline:* For fall admission, 7/1 priority date for domestic students, 7/1 for international students; for winter admission, 7/1 for international students; for spring admission, 11/1 priority date for domestic students. Applications are processed on a rolling basis. Application fee: $80. Electronic applications accepted. *Expenses:* $465 per semester hour (for MS); $480 per semester hour (for M Ed); $670 per semester hour (for Ed S). *Financial support:* In 2016–17, 17 students received support. Career-related internships or fieldwork, scholarships/grants, and health care benefits available. Financial award application deadline: 3/1; financial award applicants required to submit FAFSA. *Faculty research:* Student achievement in literacy, leadership, instructional technology. *Unit head:* Dr. Fern Aefsky, Director of Graduate Studies in Education, 352-588-8309, Fax: 352-588-8861, E-mail: kara.winkler@saintleo.edu. *Application contact:* Jennifer Shelley, Senior Associate Director of Graduate Admissions, 800-707-8846, Fax: 352-588-7873, E-mail: grad.admissions@saintleo.edu.
Website: http://www.saintleo.edu/academics/graduate.aspx

Saint Mary's University of Minnesota, Schools of Graduate and Professional Programs, Graduate School of Education, Learning Design and Technology Program, Winona, MN 55987-1399. Offers M Ed. *Program availability:* Online learning. Tuition and fees vary according to degree level and program. *Unit head:* Nancy Van Erp, Associate Program Director, 320-260-5116, E-mail: nvanerp@smumn.edu. *Application contact:* James Callinan, Director of Admissions for Graduate and Professional Programs, 612-728-5185, Fax: 612-728-5121, E-mail: jcallina@smumn.edu.
Website: http://www.smumn.edu/graduate-home/areas-of-study/graduate-school-of-education/med-in-learning-design-technology

St. Thomas University, School of Leadership Studies, Institute for Education, Miami Gardens, FL 33054-6459. Offers earth/space science (Certificate); educational administration (MS, Certificate); educational leadership (Ed D); elementary education (MS); ESOL (Certificate); gifted education (Certificate); instructional technology (MS, Certificate); professional/studies (Certificate); reading (MS, Certificate); special education (MS). *Program availability:* Part-time, evening/weekend. *Degree requirements:* For master's, comprehensive exam; for doctorate, comprehensive exam, thesis/dissertation. *Entrance requirements:* For master's, interview, minimum GPA of 3.0 or GRE; for doctorate, GRE or MAT. Additional exam requirements/recommendations for international students: Required—TOEFL (minimum score 550 paper-based; 79 iBT). Electronic applications accepted.

Saint Vincent College, Program in Education, Latrobe, PA 15650-2690. Offers curriculum and instruction (MS); instructional design and technology (MS); school administration and supervision (MS); special education (MS). *Program availability:* Part-time, evening/weekend. *Degree requirements:* For master's, comprehensive exam. *Entrance requirements:* For master's, GRE (if undergraduate GPA less than 3.0). Additional exam requirements/recommendations for international students: Required—TOEFL (minimum score 550 paper-based). *Faculty research:* Assessment and instructional technology.

Saint Xavier University, Graduate Studies, School of Education, Chicago, IL 60655-3105. Offers counseling (MA); curriculum and instruction (MA); early childhood education (MA); educational administration (MA); elementary education (MA); individualized studies (MA), including educational technology, English as a second language (ESL), ISTEM (integrative science, technology, engineering, and math), science education; music education (MA); reading (MA); secondary education (MA); Spanish education (MA); special education (MA); teaching and leadership (MA). *Accreditation:* NCATE. *Program availability:* Part-time, evening/weekend. *Degree requirements:* For master's, thesis or project. *Entrance requirements:* For master's, minimum GPA of 3.0. *Expenses:* Contact institution.

Salem State University, School of Graduate Studies, Program in Library Media Studies, Salem, MA 01970-5353. Offers M Ed. *Accreditation:* NCATE. *Program availability:* Part-time, evening/weekend. *Entrance requirements:* For master's, GRE or MAT. Additional exam requirements/recommendations for international students: Required—TOEFL (minimum score 550 paper-based; 80 iBT) or IELTS (minimum score 5.5).

Samford University, Orlean Beeson School of Education, Birmingham, AL 35229. Offers education (Ed D, Certificate); educational leadership: policy, organizations, leadership (MSE); elementary education (MS Ed); gifted certification (MSE); instructional design and technology (MSE); instructional leadership (MSE, Ed S); K-12 collaborative special education (MSE); teacher leader (Ed S). *Accreditation:* NCATE. *Program availability:* Part-time, evening/weekend, 100% online, blended/hybrid learning. *Faculty:* 15 full-time (9 women), 17 part-time/adjunct (12 women). *Students:* 219 full-time (161 women), 86 part-time (55 women); includes 97 minority (86 Black or African American, non-Hispanic/Latino; 5 American Indian or Alaska Native, non-Hispanic/Latino; 1 Asian, non-Hispanic/Latino; 1 Hispanic/Latino; 4 Two or more races, non-Hispanic/Latino), 2 international. Average age 38. 244 applicants, 52% accepted, 112 enrolled. In 2016, 84 master's, 22 doctorates, 12 Certificates awarded. *Degree requirements:* For master's, comprehensive exam (for some programs); for doctorate,

comprehensive exam, thesis/dissertation; for other advanced degree, comprehensive exam. *Entrance requirements:* For master's, GRE or MAT; Alabama Educator Certification Testing Program (AECTP), transcripts, essays, recommendations; for doctorate, professional resume, recommendations, transcripts, interview, essays; for other advanced degree, recommendations, transcripts. Additional exam requirements/recommendations for international students: Required—TOEFL (minimum score 90 iBT), IELTS (minimum score 6.5). *Application deadline:* For fall admission, 7/15 for domestic students, 7/1 for international students; for spring admission, 11/15 for domestic and international students; for summer admission, 4/15 for domestic and international students. Application fee: $35. Electronic applications accepted. *Expenses: Tuition:* Full-time $18,530; part-time $789 per credit hour. *Required fees:* $610. Tuition and fees vary according to course load, degree level, program and student level. *Financial support:* In 2016–17, 246 students received support. Scholarships/grants available. Financial award application deadline: 3/1; financial award applicants required to submit FAFSA. *Faculty research:* Standards-based grading in K-12 schools, effective school principal leadership, effective educational leadership preparation programs, teacher/administrator shortages and job retention, instructional strategies to maximize student learning. *Total annual research expenditures:* $254,360. *Unit head:* Dr. Jean Box, Dean, 205-726-2565, Fax: 205-726-4233, E-mail: jabox@samford.edu. *Application contact:* Brooke Karr, Graduate Admissions Coordinator, 205-729-2783, Fax: 205-726-4233, E-mail: kbgilrea@samford.edu.
Website: http://www.samford.edu/education/

San Diego State University, Graduate and Research Affairs, College of Education, Department of Educational Technology, San Diego, CA 92182. Offers educational technology (MA); educational technology and teaching and learning (Ed D). *Accreditation:* NCATE. *Program availability:* Evening/weekend. *Entrance requirements:* For master's, GRE General Test, letters of reference. Additional exam requirements/recommendations for international students: Required—TOEFL. Electronic applications accepted.

San Francisco State University, Division of Graduate Studies, College of Education, Department of Equity, Leadership Studies, and Instructional Technologies, Program in Instructional Technologies, San Francisco, CA 94132-1722. Offers MA. *Expenses:* Tuition, state resident: full-time $6738. Tuition, nonresident: full-time $15,666. *Required fees:* $1012. Tuition and fees vary according to degree level and program. *Unit head:* Dr. Doris Flowers, Chair, 415-338-2614, Fax: 415-338-0568, E-mail: dflowers@sfsu.edu. *Application contact:* Dr. Patricia Donohue, Program Coordinator, 415-338-7833, Fax: 415-338-0568, E-mail: pdonohue@sfsu.edu.
Website: http://gcoe.sfsu.edu/

Seattle Pacific University, Program in Digital Education Leadership, Seattle, WA 98119-1997. Offers M Ed.

Seton Hall University, College of Education and Human Services, Department of Educational Studies, South Orange, NJ 07079-2697. Offers instructional design and technology (MA); special education (MA). *Program availability:* Part-time, evening/weekend, blended/hybrid learning. *Faculty:* 6 full-time (3 women), 13 part-time/adjunct (8 women). *Students:* 6 full-time (4 women), 50 part-time (43 women); includes 6 minority (2 Asian, non-Hispanic/Latino; 4 Hispanic/Latino). Average age 32. 39 applicants, 90% accepted, 27 enrolled. In 2016, 13 master's awarded. *Degree requirements:* For master's, comprehensive exam, capstone project. *Entrance requirements:* For master's, GRE or MAT, PRAXIS (for certification candidates), minimum GPA of 2.75. *Application deadline:* For fall admission, 5/1 for domestic students; for spring admission, 10/1 for domestic students. Applications are processed on a rolling basis. Application fee: $75. Electronic applications accepted. *Expenses:* $1,212 per credit. *Financial support:* In 2016–17, 3 research assistantships with full tuition reimbursements (averaging $4,000 per year) were awarded; fellowships, career-related internships or fieldwork, institutionally sponsored loans, and unspecified assistantships also available. Financial award application deadline: 2/1; financial award applicants required to submit FAFSA. *Faculty research:* Special education, applied behavioral analysis, educational technology. *Unit head:* Dr. Daniel Katz, Chair, 973-275-2724, E-mail: daniel.katz@shu.edu.
Website: http://www.shu.edu/academics/education/graduate-studies.cfm

Simon Fraser University, Office of Graduate Studies and Postdoctoral Fellows, Faculty of Education, Program in Educational Technology and Learning Design, Burnaby, BC V5A 1S6, Canada. Offers M Ed, MA, PhD. *Program availability:* Part-time, evening/weekend. *Faculty:* 7 full-time (2 women). *Degree requirements:* For master's, comprehensive exam (for some programs), thesis (for some programs); for doctorate, comprehensive exam, thesis/dissertation. *Entrance requirements:* For master's, minimum GPA of 3.0 (on scale of 4.33) or 3.33 based on last 60 credits of undergraduate courses; for doctorate, minimum GPA of 3.5 (on scale of 4.33). Additional exam requirements/recommendations for international students: Recommended—TOEFL (minimum score 580 paper-based; 93 iBT), IELTS (minimum score 7), TWE (minimum score 5). *Application deadline:* For fall admission, 1/15 for domestic students. Application fee: $90 ($125 for international students). *Financial support:* In 2016–17, fellowships (averaging $6,250 per year) were awarded; career-related internships or fieldwork and scholarships/grants also available. *Faculty research:* Integration of technological applications in post-secondary education, problems in learning and teaching science, gaming and simulation for learning, adaptive software for researching and promoting self-regulated learning, design and use of online environments for learning. *Unit head:* Dr. Shawn Bullock, Graduate Chair, 778-782-4102. *Application contact:* Graduate Secretary, 778-782-4215, E-mail: educmast@sfu.ca.

Slippery Rock University of Pennsylvania, Graduate Studies (Recruitment), College of Education, Department of Special Education, Slippery Rock, PA 16057-1383. Offers autism (M Ed); master teacher (M Ed), including birth to grade 8, grades 7 to 12; special education (Ed D); supervision (M Ed); technology for online instruction (M Ed). *Accreditation:* NCATE. *Program availability:* Part-time, evening/weekend, 100% online. *Faculty:* 13 full-time (7 women). *Students:* 42 full-time (36 women), 278 part-time (230 women); includes 7 minority (3 Black or African American, non-Hispanic/Latino; 1 Asian, non-Hispanic/Latino; 2 Hispanic/Latino; 1 Two or more races, non-Hispanic/Latino). Average age 32. 231 applicants, 77% accepted, 100 enrolled. In 2016, 134 master's awarded. *Degree requirements:* For master's, thesis optional. *Entrance requirements:* For master's, minimum GPA of 3.0, official transcripts, teaching certification. Additional exam requirements/recommendations for international students: Required—TOEFL (minimum score 550 paper-based; 80 iBT). *Application deadline:* For fall admission, 3/1 priority date for domestic students, 5/1 priority date for international students; for spring admission, 10/1 priority date for domestic students, 9/1 priority date for international students. Applications are processed on a rolling basis. Application fee: $25 ($30 for international students). Electronic applications accepted. *Expenses:* $646.50 per credit in-state, $936.80 per credit out-of-state; $581.45 per online credit in-state, $648.65 per online credit out-of-state. *Financial support:* In 2016–17, 14 students received support. Career-related internships or fieldwork, Federal Work-Study, institutionally sponsored loans, scholarships/grants, tuition waivers (partial), and unspecified assistantships available. Support available to part-time students. Financial award application deadline: 5/1; financial award applicants required to submit FAFSA. *Unit head:* Dr. Rachel Barger-Anderson, Graduate Coordinator, 724-738-2873, Fax: 724-738-4395, E-mail: rachel.barger-ander@sru.edu. *Application contact:* Brandi Weber-Mortimer, Director of Graduate Admissions, 724-738-2051, Fax: 724-738-2146, E-mail: graduate.admissions@sru.edu.
Website: http://www.sru.edu/academics/colleges-and-departments/coe/departments/special-education/graduate-programs

Southern Illinois University Edwardsville, Graduate School, School of Education, Health, and Human Behavior, Department of Educational Leadership, Program in Instructional Technology, Edwardsville, IL 62026. Offers MS Ed. *Accreditation:* NCATE. *Program availability:* Part-time, evening/weekend. *Degree requirements:* For master's, thesis or alternative, portfolio. *Entrance requirements:* Additional exam requirements/recommendations for international students: Required—TOEFL (minimum score 550 paper-based; 79 iBT), IELTS (minimum score 6.5). Electronic applications accepted.

Southern Illinois University Edwardsville, Graduate School, School of Education, Health, and Human Behavior, Department of Educational Leadership, Program in Web-Based Learning, Edwardsville, IL 62026. Offers Postbaccalaureate Certificate. *Program availability:* Part-time. *Entrance requirements:* Additional exam requirements/recommendations for international students: Required—TOEFL (minimum score 550 paper-based; 79 iBT), IELTS (minimum score 6.5). Electronic applications accepted.

Southern New Hampshire University, School of Education, Manchester, NH 03106-1045. Offers business education (M Ed); child development (M Ed); curriculum and instruction (M Ed), including education leadership, reading, special education, technology integration; education (M Ed); educational leadership (M Ed, Ed D); educational studies (M Ed); elementary education (M Ed); English (MAT); English for speakers of other languages (M Ed); reading and writing specialist (M Ed); school business administration (Certificate); secondary education (M Ed); special education (M Ed); technology integration specialist (M Ed). *Program availability:* Part-time, evening/weekend, online learning. *Degree requirements:* For master's, comprehensive exam (for some programs), thesis or alternative. *Entrance requirements:* For master's, PRAXIS I, minimum GPA of 2.75. Additional exam requirements/recommendations for international students: Required—TOEFL (minimum score 550 paper-based). Electronic applications accepted. *Expenses:* Contact institution.

Southern University and Agricultural and Mechanical College, Graduate School, College of Education, Department of Curriculum and Instruction, Baton Rouge, LA 70813. Offers elementary education (M Ed); media (M Ed); secondary education (M Ed). *Degree requirements:* For master's, comprehensive exam, thesis optional. *Entrance requirements:* For master's, GMAT or GRE General Test. Additional exam requirements/recommendations for international students: Required—TOEFL (minimum score 525 paper-based).

Stanford University, Graduate School of Education, Program in Learning, Design, and Technology, Stanford, CA 94305-2004. Offers MA. Electronic applications accepted. *Expenses: Tuition:* Full-time $47,331. *Required fees:* $609.

State University of New York College at Potsdam, School of Education and Professional Studies, Program in Information and Communication Technology, Potsdam, NY 13676. Offers educational technology specialist (MS Ed); organizational performance, leadership and technology (MS Ed). *Program availability:* Part-time, evening/weekend. *Degree requirements:* For master's, culminating experience. *Entrance requirements:* For master's, minimum GPA of 3.0 in last 60 hours of course work. Additional exam requirements/recommendations for international students: Required—TOEFL (minimum score 550 paper-based; 80 iBT), IELTS (minimum score 6). Electronic applications accepted.

State University of New York Empire State College, School for Graduate Studies, Programs in Education, Saratoga Springs, NY 12866-4391. Offers adult learning (MA); learning and emerging technologies (MA); teaching (MAT); teaching and learning (M Ed). *Program availability:* Online learning.

Stockton University, Office of Graduate Studies, Program in Instructional Technology, Galloway, NJ 08205-9441. Offers MA. *Program availability:* Part-time, evening/weekend. *Faculty:* 2 full-time (both women), 1 (woman) part-time/adjunct. *Students:* 4 full-time (2 women), 32 part-time (28 women); includes 5 minority (1 Black or African American, non-Hispanic/Latino; 3 Hispanic/Latino; 1 Two or more races, non-Hispanic/Latino). Average age 35. 19 applicants, 79% accepted, 11 enrolled. In 2016, 23 master's awarded. *Degree requirements:* For master's, final project. *Entrance requirements:* For master's, GRE or MAT, minimum GPA of 3.0. Additional exam requirements/recommendations for international students: Required—TOEFL. *Application deadline:* For fall admission, 7/1 priority date for domestic students, 7/1 for international students; for spring admission, 12/1 for domestic students, 11/1 for international students. Applications are processed on a rolling basis. Application fee: $50. Electronic applications accepted. *Expenses:* $772 per credit in-state. *Financial support:* Fellowships, research assistantships, career-related internships or fieldwork, Federal Work-Study, scholarships/grants, and unspecified assistantships available. Support available to part-time students. Financial award application deadline: 3/1; financial award applicants required to submit FAFSA. *Faculty research:* Ethics, digital imaging, virtual reality in the classroom, 3D art in multimedia, technology projects for job-skills training, community computing networks. *Unit head:* Dr. Doug Harvey, Director, 609-626-3640, E-mail: mait@stockton.edu. *Application contact:* Tara Williams, Assistant Director of Graduate Enrollment, 609-626-3640, Fax: 609-626-6050, E-mail: gradschool@stockton.edu.
Website: http://www.stockton.edu/grad

Stony Brook University, State University of New York, Graduate School, College of Engineering and Applied Sciences, Department of Technology and Society, Program in Educational Technology, Stony Brook, NY 11794. Offers MS. *Accreditation:* NCATE. *Entrance requirements:* For master's, GRE, minimum GPA of 3.0, statement of purpose. Additional exam requirements/recommendations for international students: Required—TOEFL (minimum score 85 iBT), IELTS (minimum score 6.5). *Application deadline:* For fall admission, 8/2 for domestic students, 4/15 for international students; for spring admission, 12/1 for domestic students, 10/5 for international students. Electronic applications accepted. *Expenses:* Contact institution. *Financial support:* Research assistantships and teaching assistantships available. *Unit head:* Dr. David Ferguson, Chair, 631-632-8763, E-mail: david.ferguson@stonybrook.edu. *Application contact:* Marypat Taveras, Coordinator, 631-632-8762, Fax: 631-632-7809, E-mail: marypat.taveras@stonybrook.edu.
Website: http://www.stonybrook.edu/est/graduate/msedtech.shtml

Stony Brook University, State University of New York, School of Professional Development, Stony Brook, NY 11794-443. Offers biology (MAT); chemistry (MAT); coaching (Graduate Certificate); earth science (MAT); educational computing (Graduate Certificate); educational leadership (Advanced Certificate); English (MAT); environmental management (MPS, Graduate Certificate); French (MAT); German (MAT); higher education administration (MA, Certificate); human resource management (MS, Graduate Certificate); industrial management (Graduate Certificate); information systems management (Graduate Certificate); Italian (MAT); liberal studies (MA); mathematics (MAT); operations research (Graduate Certificate); physics (MAT); school district business leadership (Advanced Certificate); social studies (MAT); Spanish

(MAT). *Program availability:* Part-time, evening/weekend, online learning. *Faculty:* 4 full-time (3 women), 77 part-time/adjunct (34 women). *Students:* 197 full-time (125 women), 965 part-time (674 women); includes 222 minority (79 Black or African American, non-Hispanic/Latino; 2 American Indian or Alaska Native, non-Hispanic/Latino; 35 Asian, non-Hispanic/Latino; 87 Hispanic/Latino; 1 Native Hawaiian or other Pacific Islander, non-Hispanic/Latino; 18 Two or more races, non-Hispanic/Latino), 5 international. Average age 33. 462 applicants, 87% accepted, 317 enrolled. In 2016, 348 master's, 159 other advanced degrees awarded. *Degree requirements:* For master's, one foreign language, thesis or alternative. *Entrance requirements:* Additional exam requirements/recommendations for international students: Required—TOEFL (minimum score 85 iBT). *Application deadline:* For fall admission, 1/15 for domestic students, 6/1 for international students; for spring admission, 10/1 for domestic and international students. Applications are processed on a rolling basis. Application fee: $100. *Expenses:* Contact institution. *Financial support:* Fellowships, research assistantships, teaching assistantships, and career-related internships or fieldwork available. Support available to part-time students. *Unit head:* Dr. Ken Lindblom, Dean, 631-632-7049, Fax: 631-632-9046, E-mail: kenneth.lindblom@stonybrook.edu. *Application contact:* Melissa Jordan, Assistant Dean, 631-632-7751, E-mail: melissa.jordan@stonybrook.edu.
Website: http://www.stonybrook.edu/spd/

Strayer University, Graduate Studies, Washington, DC 20005-2603. Offers accounting (MS); acquisition (MBA); business administration (MBA); communications technology (MS); educational management (M Ed); finance (MBA); health services administration (MHSA); hospitality and tourism management (MBA); human resource management (MBA); information systems (MS), including computer security management, decision support system management, enterprise resource management, network management, software engineering management, systems development management; management (MBA); management information systems (MS); marketing (MBA); professional accounting (MS), including accounting information systems, controllership, taxation; public administration (MPA); supply chain management (MBA); technology in education (M Ed). Programs also offered at campus locations in Birmingham, AL; Chamblee, GA; Cobb County, GA; Morrow, GA; White Marsh, MD; Charleston, SC; Columbia, SC; Greensboro, NC; Greenville, SC; Lexington, KY; Louisville, KY; Nashville, TN; North Raleigh, NC; Washington, DC. *Accreditation:* ACBSP. *Program availability:* Part-time, evening/weekend, online learning. *Degree requirements:* For master's, thesis. *Entrance requirements:* For master's, GMAT, GRE General Test, bachelor's degree from an accredited college or university, minimum undergraduate GPA of 2.75. Electronic applications accepted.

Syracuse University, School of Education, CAS Program in Educational Technology, Syracuse, NY 13244. Offers CAS. *Accreditation:* ACA. *Program availability:* Part-time. *Entrance requirements:* For degree, baccalaureate degree from regionally-accredited college/university, statement of goals, three recommendation letters, transcripts. Additional exam requirements/recommendations for international students: Required—TOEFL (minimum score 100 iBT). *Application deadline:* Applications are processed on a rolling basis. Application fee: $75. Electronic applications accepted. *Expenses: Tuition:* Full-time $25,974; part-time $1443 per credit hour. *Required fees:* $802; $50 per course. Tuition and fees vary according to course load and program. *Financial support:* Fellowships, research assistantships, teaching assistantships, career-related internships or fieldwork, and scholarships/grants available. Financial award application deadline: 1/15. *Faculty research:* Instructional design, learning with digital technologies, training and professional development, designing effective and efficient instruction, designing digital instruction. *Unit head:* Dr. Tiffany A. Koszalka, Chair, 315-443-3703, E-mail: takoszal@syr.edu. *Application contact:* Speranza Migliore, Graduate Admissions Recruiter, 315-443-2505, E-mail: gradrcrt@syr.edu.
Website: http://soeweb.syr.edu/chs/

Syracuse University, School of Education, MS Program in Instructional Technology, Syracuse, NY 13244. Offers MS. *Program availability:* Part-time. *Students:* Average age 25. In 2016, 2 master's awarded. *Entrance requirements:* For master's, GRE, baccalaureate degree from regionally-accredited college/university, initial New York State teaching certification, statement of goals, three letters of recommendation, transcripts. Additional exam requirements/recommendations for international students: Required—TOEFL (minimum score 100 iBT). *Application deadline:* For fall admission, 1/15 for domestic students, 1/15 priority date for international students. Application fee: $75. Electronic applications accepted. *Expenses: Tuition:* Full-time $25,974; part-time $1443 per credit hour. *Required fees:* $802; $50 per course. Tuition and fees vary according to course load and program. *Financial support:* Fellowships with full tuition reimbursements, research assistantships with tuition reimbursements, teaching assistantships, career-related internships or fieldwork, and scholarships/grants available. Financial award application deadline: 1/15. *Unit head:* Dr. Tiffany A. Koszalka, Chair, 315-443-3703, E-mail: takoszal@syr.edu. *Application contact:* Speranza Migliore, Graduate Admissions Recruiter, 315-443-2505, E-mail: gradrcrt@syr.edu.
Website: http://soeweb.syr.edu/academic/Instructional_Design_Development_and_Evaluation/graduate/masters/instructional_technology/default.aspx

Syracuse University, School of Information Studies, CAS Program in School Media, Syracuse, NY 13244. Offers CAS. *Program availability:* Part-time, evening/weekend, online learning. *Entrance requirements:* For degree, MS in library and information science, letter of recommendation, personal statement, resume, official transcripts. Additional exam requirements/recommendations for international students: Required—TOEFL (minimum score 100 iBT). *Application deadline:* For fall admission, 1/1 priority date for domestic and international students; for spring admission, 10/15 priority date for domestic and international students; for summer admission, 2/1 priority date for domestic and international students. Applications are processed on a rolling basis. Application fee: $75. Electronic applications accepted. *Expenses: Tuition:* Full-time $25,974; part-time $1443 per credit hour. *Required fees:* $802; $50 per course. Tuition and fees vary according to course load and program. *Financial support:* Application deadline: 1/1. *Faculty research:* Managing a school library, literacy through school libraries, information technologies in educational organizations, information services to students with disabilities. *Unit head:* Prof. Jill Hurst-Wahl, Program Director, 315-443-1070, E-mail: igrad@syr.edu. *Application contact:* Susan Corieri, Director of Enrollment Management, 315-443-2575, E-mail: igrad@syr.edu.
Website: http://ischool.syr.edu/

Syracuse University, School of Information Studies, MS Program in Library and Information Science: School Media, Syracuse, NY 13244. Offers MS. *Program availability:* Part-time, evening/weekend, online learning. *Students:* Average age 34. *Entrance requirements:* For master's, GRE General Test, personal statement, two letters of recommendation, resume. Additional exam requirements/recommendations for international students: Required—TOEFL (minimum score 100 iBT). *Application deadline:* For fall admission, 1/1 priority date for domestic and international students; for spring admission, 10/15 priority date for domestic and international students. Applications are processed on a rolling basis. Application fee: $75. Electronic applications accepted. *Expenses: Tuition:* Full-time $25,974; part-time $1443 per credit hour. *Required fees:* $802; $50 per course. Tuition and fees vary according to course load and program. *Financial support:* Fellowships with full tuition reimbursements, research assistantships with partial tuition reimbursements, and teaching assistantships with partial tuition reimbursements available. Financial award application deadline: 1/1. *Faculty research:* Collection management based on a unified media concept, use of information resources from a problem-solving perspective, digital literacy, curriculum consultation and technology innovation. *Unit head:* Prof. Jill Hurst-Wahl, Program Director, 315-443-1070, E-mail: igrad@syr.edu. *Application contact:* Susan Corieri, Director of Enrollment Management, 315-443-2575, E-mail: ischool@syr.edu.
Website: https://ischool.syr.edu/academics/graduate/masters-degrees/ms-library-information-science-school-media/

Tarleton State University, College of Graduate Studies, College of Education, Department of Curriculum and Instruction, Stephenville, TX 76402. Offers educational diagnostician (M Ed); elementary education (M Ed); instructional design and technology (M Ed); instructional leadership (M Ed); professional reading specialist (M Ed); secondary education (M Ed); special education (M Ed); technology applications (M Ed); technology director (M Ed). *Program availability:* Part-time, evening/weekend. *Faculty:* 9 full-time (7 women), 6 part-time/adjunct (4 women). *Students:* 17 full-time (0 women), 104 part-time (101 women); includes 28 minority (5 Black or African American, non-Hispanic/Latino; 1 American Indian or Alaska Native, non-Hispanic/Latino; 19 Hispanic/Latino; 3 Two or more races, non-Hispanic/Latino). 62 applicants, 94% accepted, 35 enrolled. In 2016, 34 master's awarded. *Degree requirements:* For master's, comprehensive exam. *Entrance requirements:* For master's, GRE General Test, minimum GPA of 3.0. Additional exam requirements/recommendations for international students: Required—TOEFL (minimum score 550 paper-based; 80 iBT). *Application deadline:* For fall admission, 8/15 priority date for domestic students; for spring admission, 1/7 for domestic students. Applications are processed on a rolling basis. Application fee: $45 ($145 for international students). Electronic applications accepted. *Expenses:* $3,672 tuition; $2,437 fees. *Financial support:* Research assistantships, teaching assistantships, career-related internships or fieldwork, Federal Work-Study, and institutionally sponsored loans available. Support available to part-time students. Financial award application deadline: 5/1; financial award applicants required to submit FAFSA. *Unit head:* Dr. Jordan Barkley, Department Head, 254-968-9089, E-mail: jbarkley@tarleton.edu. *Application contact:* Information Contact, 254-968-9104, Fax: 254-968-9670, E-mail: gradoffice@tarleton.edu.
Website: http://www.tarleton.edu/cimasters/

Teachers College, Columbia University, Department of Mathematics, Science and Technology, New York, NY 10027-6696. Offers biology 7-12 (MA); chemistry 7-12 (MA); communication and education (MA, Ed D); computing in education (MA); earth science 7-12 (MA); instructional technology and media (Ed M, MA, Ed D); mathematics education (Ed M, MA, Ed D, Ed DCT, PhD); physics 7-12 (MA); science and dental education (MA); science education (Ed M, MS, Ed DCT, PhD); supervisor/teacher of science education (MA); technology specialist (MA). *Program availability:* Part-time, evening/weekend, online learning. *Students:* 195 full-time (133 women), 222 part-time (139 women); includes 152 minority (44 Black or African American, non-Hispanic/Latino; 66 Asian, non-Hispanic/Latino; 32 Hispanic/Latino; 10 Two or more races, non-Hispanic/Latino), 106 international. 368 applicants, 65% accepted, 123 enrolled. Terminal master's awarded for partial completion of doctoral program. *Degree requirements:* For doctorate, thesis/dissertation. *Expenses: Tuition:* Full-time $36,288; part-time $1512 per credit. *Required fees:* $438 per semester. One-time fee: $510 full-time. Full-time tuition and fees vary according to course load. *Unit head:* Dr. O. Roger Anderson, Chair, 212-678-3405, Fax: 212-678-8129, E-mail: ora@ldeo.columbia.edu. *Application contact:* David Estrella, Director of Admission, 212-678-3305, E-mail: estrella@tc.columbia.edu.
Website: http://www.tc.columbia.edu/mathematics-science-and-technology/

Tennessee Technological University, College of Graduate Studies, College of Education, Department of Curriculum and Instruction, Program in Educational Technology, Cookeville, TN 38505. Offers MA, Ed S. *Program availability:* Part-time, evening/weekend. *Students:* 4 full-time (all women), 16 part-time (12 women); includes 1 minority (Two or more races, non-Hispanic/Latino). 13 applicants, 92% accepted, 12 enrolled. In 2016, 4 master's, 3 other advanced degrees awarded. *Degree requirements:* For master's, comprehensive exam, thesis or alternative. *Entrance requirements:* For master's, MAT or GRE. Additional exam requirements/recommendations for international students: Required—TOEFL (minimum score 527 paper-based; 71 iBT), IELTS (minimum score 5.5), PTE (minimum score 48), or TOEIC (Test of English as an International Communication). *Application deadline:* For fall admission, 8/1 for domestic students, 5/1 for international students; for spring admission, 12/1 for domestic students, 10/1 for international students; for summer admission, 5/1 for domestic students, 2/1 for international students. Application fee: $35 ($40 for international students). Electronic applications accepted. *Expenses:* Tuition, state resident: full-time $9375; part-time $534 per credit hour. Tuition, nonresident: full-time $22,443; part-time $1260 per credit hour. *Unit head:* Dr. Jeremy Wendt, Interim Chairperson, 931-372-3181, Fax: 931-372-6270, E-mail: jwendt@tntech.edu. *Application contact:* Shelia K. Kendrick, Coordinator of Graduate Studies, 931-372-3808, Fax: 931-372-3497, E-mail: skendrick@tntech.edu.

Texas A&M University, College of Education and Human Development, Department of Educational Psychology, College Station, TX 77843. Offers bilingual education (M Ed, MS); counseling psychology (PhD); educational psychology (M Ed, MS, PhD); educational technology (M Ed); school psychology (PhD); special education (M Ed, MS). *Accreditation:* APA (one or more programs are accredited). *Program availability:* Part-time, evening/weekend, blended/hybrid learning. *Faculty:* 42. *Students:* 172 full-time (139 women), 281 part-time (233 women); includes 144 minority (27 Black or African American, non-Hispanic/Latino; 1 American Indian or Alaska Native, non-Hispanic/Latino; 19 Asian, non-Hispanic/Latino; 86 Hispanic/Latino; 1 Native Hawaiian or other Pacific Islander, non-Hispanic/Latino; 10 Two or more races, non-Hispanic/Latino), 48 international. Average age 33. 181 applicants, 44% accepted, 45 enrolled. In 2016, 99 master's, 27 doctorates awarded. *Degree requirements:* For master's, thesis optional; for doctorate, thesis/dissertation. *Entrance requirements:* For master's and doctorate, GRE General Test. Additional exam requirements/recommendations for international students: Required—TOEFL (minimum score 550 paper-based; 80 iBT), IELTS (minimum score 6), PTE (minimum score 53). *Application deadline:* For fall admission, 12/1 for domestic students; for spring admission, 10/15 for domestic students. Application fee: $50 ($90 for international students). Electronic applications accepted. *Expenses:* Contact institution. *Financial support:* In 2016–17, 231 students received support, including 8 fellowships with tuition reimbursements available (averaging $9,919 per year), 98 research assistantships with tuition reimbursements available (averaging $6,004 per year), 13 teaching assistantships with tuition reimbursements available (averaging $9,368 per year); career-related internships or fieldwork, institutionally sponsored loans, scholarships/grants, traineeships, health care benefits, tuition waivers (full and partial), and unspecified assistantships also available. Support available to part-time students. Financial award application deadline: 3/15; financial award applicants required to submit FAFSA. *Unit head:* Dr. Victor Willson, Department Head, 979-845-1394, E-mail: v-willson@tamu.edu. *Application contact:* Kristie Stramaski, Senior Academic Advisor, 979-845-1833, E-mail: epsyadvisor@tamu.edu.
Website: http://epsy.tamu.edu

Texas A&M University–Commerce, College of Education and Human Services, Commerce, TX 75429-3011. Offers counseling (MS); curriculum and instruction (M Ed,

MS); early childhood education (M Ed, MS); educational administration (M Ed, Ed D); educational psychology (PhD); educational technology leadership (MS); educational technology library science (MS); health, kinesiology and sports studies (MS); higher education (MS, Ed D); organization, learning, and technology (MS); psychology (MS); reading (M Ed, MS); school psychology (SSP); secondary education (M Ed, MS); social work (MSW); special education (M Ed); supervision, curriculum and instruction-elementary education (Ed D). *Program availability:* Part-time, 100% online, blended/hybrid learning. *Faculty:* 88 full-time (52 women), 31 part-time/adjunct (24 women). *Students:* 341 full-time (276 women), 1,495 part-time (1,156 women); includes 762 minority (429 Black or African American, non-Hispanic/Latino; 4 American Indian or Alaska Native, non-Hispanic/Latino; 27 Asian, non-Hispanic/Latino; 247 Hispanic/Latino; 1 Native Hawaiian or other Pacific Islander, non-Hispanic/Latino; 54 Two or more races, non-Hispanic/Latino), 18 international. Average age 37. 1,070 applicants, 54% accepted, 452 enrolled. In 2016, 579 master's, 31 doctorates awarded. *Degree requirements:* For master's, one foreign language, comprehensive exam, thesis optional, departmental qualifying exams (for some programs); for doctorate, comprehensive exam, thesis/dissertation, departmental qualifying exam; for SSP, comprehensive exam, thesis optional. *Entrance requirements:* For master's and doctorate, GRE General Test. Additional exam requirements/recommendations for international students: Required—TOEFL (minimum score 550 paper-based; 79 iBT), IELTS (minimum score 6). *Application deadline:* For fall admission, 6/1 priority date for international students; for spring admission, 10/15 priority date for international students; for summer admission, 3/15 priority date for international students. Applications are processed on a rolling basis. Application fee: $50. Electronic applications accepted. *Expenses:* $2,254 resident; $4,744 non-resident. *Financial support:* In 2016–17, 301 students received support, including 39 research assistantships with partial tuition reimbursements available (averaging $9,000 per year), 17 teaching assistantships with partial tuition reimbursements available (averaging $9,000 per year); career-related internships or fieldwork, Federal Work-Study, institutionally sponsored loans, scholarships/grants, health care benefits, and unspecified assistantships also available. Financial award application deadline: 5/1; financial award applicants required to submit FAFSA. *Faculty research:* Cognitive and bilingual education, positive behavioral intervention, literacy, math readiness. *Total annual research expenditures:* $470,963. *Unit head:* Dr. Timothy Letzring, Dean, 903-886-5181, Fax: 903-886-5905, E-mail: tim.letzring@tamuc.edu. *Application contact:* Jennifer Faunce, Graduate Recruiter, 903-886-5030, Fax: 903-886-5905, E-mail: jennifer.faunce@tamuc.edu.
Website: http://www.tamuc.edu/academics/graduateSchool/programs/education/default.aspx

Texas A&M University–Corpus Christi, College of Graduate Studies, College of Education, Corpus Christi, TX 78412-5503. Offers counseling (MS), including counseling; counselor education (PhD); curriculum and instruction (MS, PhD); early childhood education (MS); educational administration (MS); educational leadership (Ed D); elementary education (MS); instructional design and educational technology (MS); kinesiology (MS); reading (MS); secondary education (MS); special education (MS). *Program availability:* Part-time, evening/weekend, online learning. *Faculty:* 50 full-time (29 women), 29 part-time/adjunct (18 women). *Students:* 158 full-time (130 women), 344 part-time (281 women); includes 288 minority (28 Black or African American, non-Hispanic/Latino; 2 American Indian or Alaska Native, non-Hispanic/Latino; 8 Asian, non-Hispanic/Latino; 246 Hispanic/Latino; 4 Two or more races, non-Hispanic/Latino), 22 international. Average age 35. 273 applicants, 60% accepted, 142 enrolled. In 2016, 67 master's, 13 doctorates awarded. *Degree requirements:* For master's, comprehensive exam, capstone; for doctorate, thesis/dissertation. *Entrance requirements:* For master's, GRE General Test, essay (300 words); for doctorate, GRE, essay, resume, 3-4 reference forms. *Application deadline:* For fall admission, 7/15 priority date for domestic students, 5/1 priority date for international students; for spring admission, 11/15 priority date for domestic students, 9/1 priority date for international students. Applications are processed on a rolling basis. Application fee: $50 ($70 for international students). Electronic applications accepted. *Financial support:* Research assistantships, teaching assistantships, career-related internships or fieldwork, Federal Work-Study, institutionally sponsored loans, scholarships/grants, health care benefits, and unspecified assistantships available. Support available to part-time students. Financial award application deadline: 3/15; financial award applicants required to submit FAFSA. *Unit head:* Dr. Arthur Hernandez, Dean, 361-825-2660, E-mail: art.hernandez@tamucc.edu. *Application contact:* Graduate Admissions Coordinator, 361-825-2177, Fax: 361-825-2755, E-mail: gradweb@tamucc.edu.
Website: http://education.tamucc.edu/

Texas A&M University–Kingsville, College of Graduate Studies, College of Education and Human Performance, Department of Educational Leadership and Counseling, Program in Instructional Technology, Kingsville, TX 78363. Offers MS. *Program availability:* Part-time, evening/weekend. *Degree requirements:* For master's, variable foreign language requirement, comprehensive exam, thesis (for some programs). *Entrance requirements:* For master's, GRE, MAT, GMAT. Additional exam requirements/recommendations for international students: Required—TOEFL (minimum score 550 paper-based; 79 iBT). Electronic applications accepted.

Texas A&M University–Texarkana, Graduate Studies and Research, College of Education and Liberal Arts, Texarkana, TX 75505-5518. Offers adult education (MS); curriculum and instruction (M Ed); education (MS); educational administration (M Ed); English (MA); instructional technology (MS); interdisciplinary studies (MA, MS); special education (MS). *Program availability:* Part-time, evening/weekend. *Degree requirements:* For master's, comprehensive exam (for some programs), thesis optional. *Entrance requirements:* For master's, minimum GPA of 2.5 on last 60 hours of bachelor's degree. Additional exam requirements/recommendations for international students: Required—TOEFL. Electronic applications accepted.

Texas State University, The Graduate College, College of Education, Program in Educational Technology, San Marcos, TX 78666. Offers M Ed. *Program availability:* Part-time, evening/weekend. *Faculty:* 3 full-time (1 woman). *Students:* 5 full-time (4 women), 13 part-time (9 women); includes 7 minority (1 Black or African American, non-Hispanic/Latino; 5 Hispanic/Latino; 1 Two or more races, non-Hispanic/Latino). Average age 35. 12 applicants, 75% accepted, 7 enrolled. In 2016, 9 master's awarded. *Degree requirements:* For master's, comprehensive exam. *Entrance requirements:* For master's, GRE (preferred), baccalaureate degree from regionally-accredited institution with minimum GPA of 2.75 in undergraduate work, statement of purpose. Additional exam requirements/recommendations for international students: Required—TOEFL (minimum score 550 paper-based; 78 iBT), IELTS (minimum score 6.5). *Application deadline:* For fall admission, 6/15 priority date for domestic students, 6/1 for international students; for spring admission, 10/15 priority date for domestic students, 10/1 for international students; for summer admission, 4/15 for domestic students, 3/15 for international students. Applications are processed on a rolling basis. Application fee: $40 ($90 for international students). Electronic applications accepted. *Expenses:* $4,851 per semester. *Financial support:* In 2016–17, 6 students received support, including 1 research assistantship (averaging $13,172 per year); teaching assistantships and scholarships/grants also available. Financial award application deadline: 3/1; financial award applicants required to submit FAFSA. *Unit head:* Dr. David Bynum, Graduate Advisor, 512-245-2038, Fax: 512-245-7911, E-mail: db15@txstate.edu. *Application contact:* Dr. Andrea Golato, Dean of Graduate School, 512-245-2581, Fax: 512-245-8365, E-mail: gradcollege@txstate.edu.
Website: http://www.education.txstate.edu/ci/degrees-programs/graduate/edtech.html

Texas Tech University, Graduate School, College of Education, Department of Educational Psychology and Leadership, Lubbock, TX 79409-1071. Offers counselor education (M Ed, PhD); distance education (M Ed); educational leadership (M Ed, Ed D, PhD); educational psychology (M Ed, PhD); higher education (M Ed, Ed D); higher education research (PhD); instructional technology (M Ed, Ed D); special education (M Ed, Ed D, PhD). *Accreditation:* ACA; NCATE. *Program availability:* Part-time, evening/weekend. *Faculty:* 59 full-time (29 women), 3 part-time/adjunct (all women). *Students:* 300 full-time (218 women), 656 part-time (482 women); includes 320 minority (87 Black or African American, non-Hispanic/Latino; 5 American Indian or Alaska Native, non-Hispanic/Latino; 5 Asian, non-Hispanic/Latino; 200 Hispanic/Latino; 23 Two or more races, non-Hispanic/Latino), 51 international. Average age 36. 668 applicants, 56% accepted, 285 enrolled. In 2016, 171 master's, 47 doctorates awarded. Terminal master's awarded for partial completion of doctoral program. *Degree requirements:* For master's, comprehensive exam, thesis optional; for doctorate, comprehensive exam, thesis/dissertation. *Entrance requirements:* For master's, GRE (for some programs); for doctorate, GRE. Additional exam requirements/recommendations for international students: Required—TOEFL (minimum score 550 paper-based; 79 iBT). *Application deadline:* For fall admission, 6/1 priority date for domestic students, 1/15 priority date for international students; for spring admission, 9/1 priority date for domestic students, 6/15 priority date for international students. Applications are processed on a rolling basis. Application fee: $75. Electronic applications accepted. *Expenses:* $285 per credit hour full-time resident tuition, $693 per credit hour full-time non-resident tuition; $50.50 per credit hour fee plus $608 per term fee. *Financial support:* In 2016–17, 384 students received support, including 384 fellowships (averaging $3,632 per year); scholarships/grants and unspecified assistantships also available. Support available to part-time students. Financial award application deadline: 1/3; financial award applicants required to submit FAFSA. *Faculty research:* Cognitive, motivational, and developmental processes in learning; counseling education; instructional technology; generic special education and sensory impairment; community college administration; K-12 school administration. *Total annual research expenditures:* $1,371. *Unit head:* Dr. Hansel Burley, Chair, 806-834-5135, Fax: 806-742-2179, E-mail: hansel.burley@ttu.edu. *Application contact:* Pam Smith, Admissions Advisor, 806-834-2969, Fax: 806-742-2179, E-mail: pam.smith@ttu.edu.
Website: http://www.educ.ttu.edu/

Thomas Edison State University, Heavin School of Arts and Sciences, Program in Online Learning and Teaching, Trenton, NJ 08608. Offers Graduate Certificate. *Program availability:* Part-time, online learning. *Entrance requirements:* Additional exam requirements/recommendations for international students: Required—TOEFL (minimum score 550 paper-based; 79 iBT). Electronic applications accepted.

Tiffin University, Program in Education, Tiffin, OH 44883-2161. Offers educational technology management (M Ed); higher education administration (M Ed). *Program availability:* Part-time, evening/weekend, online only, 100% online, blended/hybrid learning. *Students:* 99 part-time (75 women); includes 26 minority (20 Black or African American, non-Hispanic/Latino; 1 Asian, non-Hispanic/Latino; 4 Hispanic/Latino; 1 Two or more races, non-Hispanic/Latino). Average age 32. 31 applicants, 90% accepted, 24 enrolled. In 2016, 45 master's awarded. *Entrance requirements:* Additional exam requirements/recommendations for international students: Required—TOEFL. *Application deadline:* Applications are processed on a rolling basis. Electronic applications accepted. *Expenses:* Contact institution. *Financial support:* Unspecified assistantships available. *Application contact:* Nikki Hintze, Director of Graduate Admissions and Student Services, 800-968-6446 Ext. 3445, Fax: 419-443-5002, E-mail: hintzenm@tiffin.edu.

Touro College, Graduate School of Education, New York, NY 10010. Offers education and special education (MS); education biology (MS); instructional technology (MS); mathematics education (MS); school leadership (MS); teaching English to speakers of other languages (MS); teaching literacy (MS). *Accreditation:* TEAC. *Program availability:* Part-time, evening/weekend, online learning. *Faculty:* 52 full-time (34 women), 199 part-time/adjunct (136 women). *Students:* 578 full-time (483 women), 1,932 part-time (1,626 women); includes 749 minority (318 Black or African American, non-Hispanic/Latino; 5 American Indian or Alaska Native, non-Hispanic/Latino; 108 Asian, non-Hispanic/Latino; 288 Hispanic/Latino; 2 Native Hawaiian or other Pacific Islander, non-Hispanic/Latino; 28 Two or more races, non-Hispanic/Latino), 17 international. Average age 32. 1,422 applicants, 50% accepted, 675 enrolled. In 2016, 6 master's awarded. *Entrance requirements:* Additional exam requirements/recommendations for international students: Required—TOEFL (minimum score 83 iBT), IELTS (minimum score 6.5). *Application deadline:* For fall admission, 8/26 for domestic students, 7/15 for international students; for spring admission, 12/31 for domestic students, 12/15 for international students. Applications are processed on a rolling basis. Application fee: $50. *Financial support:* Federal Work-Study available. Financial award applicants required to submit FAFSA. *Faculty research:* Equity assistance, language development, scholarly communications, Latin American studies and cultural sensitivity, behavior management techniques and strategies in special education. *Unit head:* Dr. Arnold Spinner, Dean, 212-463-0400 Ext. 5561, Fax: 212-462-4889, E-mail: aspinner@touro.edu. *Application contact:* Luna Feliciano, Admissions, 212-463-0400.

Touro College, Graduate School of Technology, New York, NY 10010. Offers information systems (MS); instructional technology (MS); Web and multimedia design (MA). *Faculty:* 18 part-time/adjunct (6 women). *Students:* 100 full-time (37 women), 122 part-time (59 women); includes 78 minority (31 Black or African American, non-Hispanic/Latino; 1 American Indian or Alaska Native, non-Hispanic/Latino; 25 Asian, non-Hispanic/Latino; 18 Hispanic/Latino; 3 Two or more races, non-Hispanic/Latino), 83 international. Average age 34. *Entrance requirements:* Additional exam requirements/recommendations for international students: Required—TOEFL (minimum score 83 iBT), IELTS (minimum score 6.5), PTE (minimum score 58). *Unit head:* Dr. Issac Herskowitz, Dean of the Graduate School of Technology, 202-463-0400 Ext. 5231, E-mail: issac.herskowitz@touro.edu. *Application contact:* Jack Romano, Program Director, 212-463-0400 Ext. 5462.
Website: http://www.touro.edu/gst/

Towson University, Program in Instructional Technology, Towson, MD 21252-0001. Offers instructional design and training (MS). *Program availability:* Part-time, evening/weekend. *Students:* 26 full-time (20 women), 214 part-time (186 women); includes 26 minority (17 Black or African American, non-Hispanic/Latino; 2 Asian, non-Hispanic/Latino; 5 Hispanic/Latino; 2 Two or more races, non-Hispanic/Latino), 3 international. *Degree requirements:* For master's, thesis optional; for doctorate, comprehensive exam, thesis/dissertation. *Entrance requirements:* For master's, minimum GPA of 3.0, technological literacy; for doctorate, GRE, master's degree in computer science, information systems, information technology, or closely-related area; minimum GPA of 3.0; 2 letters of recommendation; letter of intent; writing sample; digital learning sample. Additional exam requirements/recommendations for international students: Required—TOEFL. *Application deadline:* For fall admission, 8/1 for domestic students, 7/15 for international students. Application fee: $45. Electronic applications accepted. *Expenses:*

Tuition, state resident: full-time $7580; part-time $379 per unit. Tuition, nonresident: full-time $15,700; part-time $785 per unit. *Required fees:* $2480. *Financial support:* Application deadline: 4/1. *Unit head:* Dr. Gilda Martinez-Alba, Graduate Program Director, 410-704-2576, E-mail: gmartinez@towson.edu. *Application contact:* Coverley Beidleman, Assistant Director of Graduate Admissions, 410-704-2113, Fax: 410-704-3030, E-mail: grads@towson.edu.
Website: https://www.towson.edu/coe/departments/edtech/grad/index.html

Trevecca Nazarene University, Graduate Instructional Design and Technology Program, Nashville, TN 37210-2877. Offers MS. *Program availability:* Online only. *Faculty:* 1 (woman) full-time, 1 (woman) part-time/adjunct. *Students:* 10 full-time (9 women); includes 1 minority (Black or African American, non-Hispanic/Latino). Average age 40. *Degree requirements:* For master's, capstone. *Entrance requirements:* For master's, minimum GPA of 2.75, minimum math grade of C, minimum English composition grade of C. Additional exam requirements/recommendations for international students: Required—TOEFL (minimum score 550 paper-based; 80 iBT). *Application deadline:* Applications are processed on a rolling basis. Application fee: $0. Electronic applications accepted. *Expenses:* $395 per credit hour. *Financial support:* Applicants required to submit FAFSA. *Unit head:* 615-248-1529, E-mail: sgcsadmissions@trevecca.edu. *Application contact:* 844-TNU-GRAD, E-mail: sgcsadmissions@trevecca.edu.
Website: http://online.trevecca.edu/idt

Trident University International, College of Education, Program in Educational Leadership, Cypress, CA 90630. Offers e-learning leadership (MA Ed, PhD); educational leadership (MA Ed); higher education leadership (PhD); K-12 leadership (PhD). *Program availability:* Part-time, evening/weekend, online learning. *Degree requirements:* For doctorate, comprehensive exam, thesis/dissertation, defense of dissertation. *Entrance requirements:* For master's, minimum GPA of 2.5 (students with GPA 3.0 or greater may transfer up to 30% of graduate level credits); for doctorate, minimum GPA of 3.4, course work in research methods or statistics. Additional exam requirements/recommendations for international students: Required—TOEFL. Electronic applications accepted.

Université Laval, Faculty of Education, Department of Teaching and Learning Studies, Programs in Teaching Technology, Québec, QC G1K 7P4, Canada. Offers MA, PhD. Terminal master's awarded for partial completion of doctoral program. *Degree requirements:* For master's, thesis (for some programs); for doctorate, comprehensive exam, thesis/dissertation. *Entrance requirements:* For master's and doctorate, English exam (comprehension of written English), knowledge of French. Electronic applications accepted.

University at Albany, State University of New York, School of Education, Department of Educational Theory and Practice, Albany, NY 12222-0001. Offers curriculum and instruction (PhD, CAS); curriculum development and instructional technology (MS); general education studies (MS). *Program availability:* Part-time, evening/weekend, 100% online, blended/hybrid learning. *Faculty:* 6 full-time (4 women), 12 part-time/adjunct (8 women). *Students:* 84 full-time (56 women), 223 part-time (155 women); includes 39 minority (12 Black or African American, non-Hispanic/Latino; 6 Asian, non-Hispanic/Latino; 14 Hispanic/Latino; 7 Two or more races, non-Hispanic/Latino), 26 international. Average age 30. 147 applicants, 78% accepted, 106 enrolled. In 2016, 99 master's, 5 doctorates, 11 other advanced degrees awarded. *Degree requirements:* For doctorate, one foreign language, thesis/dissertation. *Entrance requirements:* For doctorate, GRE General Test. Additional exam requirements/recommendations for international students: Required—TOEFL (minimum score 550 paper-based). *Application deadline:* For fall admission, 2/1 for domestic students, 1/31 for international students. Application fee: $75. Electronic applications accepted. *Expenses:* Tuition, state resident: full-time $10,870; part-time $453 per credit hour. Tuition, nonresident: full-time $22,210; part-time $925 per credit hour. *International tuition:* $21,550 full-time. *Required fees:* $1864; $96 per credit hour. *Financial support:* Fellowships available. *Total annual research expenditures:* $1.2 million. *Unit head:* Arthur Appleby, Chair, 518-442-5006, E-mail: aapplebee@albany.edu.

University at Buffalo, the State University of New York, Graduate School, Graduate School of Education, Department of Learning and Instruction, Buffalo, NY 14260. Offers biology education (Ed M, Certificate); chemistry education (Ed M, Certificate); childhood education (Ed M); childhood education with bilingual extension (Ed M); college teaching (Advanced Certificate); curriculum, instruction and the science of learning (PhD); early childhood education (Ed M); early childhood education with bilingual extension (Ed M); earth science education (Ed M, Certificate); education and technology (Ed M); education studies (Ed M); educational technology and new literacies (Certificate); educational technology and new literacies (Advanced Certificate); elementary education (Ed D); English education (Ed M, Certificate); English education studies (Ed M); English for speakers of other languages (Ed M); foreign and second language education (PhD); French education (Ed M, Certificate); German education (Ed M, Certificate); gifted education (Certificate); Latin education (Ed M, Certificate); literacy education studies (Ed M); literacy specialist (Ed M); literacy teaching and learning (Certificate); mathematics education (Ed M, Certificate); music education (Ed M, Certificate); music education studies (Ed M); music learning theory (Advanced Certificate); online education (Advanced Certificate); physics education (Ed M, Certificate); science and the public (Ed M); social studies education (Ed M, Certificate); Spanish education (Ed M, Certificate); special education (PhD); teaching English to speakers of other languages (Ed M). *Program availability:* Part-time, evening/weekend, 100% online. *Faculty:* 28 full-time (21 women), 67 part-time/adjunct (49 women). *Students:* 198 full-time (153 women), 312 part-time (220 women); includes 48 minority (28 Black or African American, non-Hispanic/Latino; 4 American Indian or Alaska Native, non-Hispanic/Latino; 15 Asian, non-Hispanic/Latino; 1 Hispanic/Latino), 66 international. Average age 33. 336 applicants, 86% accepted, 178 enrolled. In 2016, 137 master's, 24 doctorates, 25 other advanced degrees awarded. *Degree requirements:* For master's, comprehensive exam; for doctorate, thesis/dissertation, research analysis exam, research experience. *Entrance requirements:* For master's, letters of reference; for doctorate, GRE General Test or MAT, interview, writing sample, letters of recommendation. Additional exam requirements/recommendations for international students: Required—TOEFL (minimum score 600 paper-based; 96 iBT). *Application deadline:* For fall admission, 2/1 priority date for domestic and international students; for spring admission, 11/15 priority date for domestic students, 10/1 for international students. Applications are processed on a rolling basis. Application fee: $50. Electronic applications accepted. *Financial support:* In 2016–17, 44 fellowships (averaging $4,010 per year), 39 research assistantships with tuition reimbursements (averaging $9,897 per year) were awarded; teaching assistantships, career-related internships or fieldwork, Federal Work Study, institutionally sponsored loans, scholarships/grants, tuition waivers (full and partial), and unspecified assistantships also available. Financial award application deadline: 2/28; financial award applicants required to submit FAFSA. *Faculty research:* Science assessment, foreign language teaching and learning, early learning, new literacies, gender and education. *Total annual research expenditures:* $534,880. *Unit head:* Dr. Deborah Moore-Russo, Chair, 716-645-4069, Fax: 716-645-3161, E-mail: dam29@buffalo.edu. *Application contact:* Luann Zak, Admissions Assistant, 716-645-2110, Fax: 716-645-7937, E-mail: luannzak@buffalo.edu.
Website: http://gse.buffalo.edu/lai

University at Buffalo, the State University of New York, Graduate School, Graduate School of Education, Department of Library and Information Studies, Buffalo, NY 14260. Offers information and library science (MS); library and information studies (Certificate); school librarianship (MS). *Accreditation:* ALA (one or more programs are accredited). *Program availability:* Part-time, 100% online. *Faculty:* 10 full-time (6 women), 9 part-time/adjunct (6 women). *Students:* 35 full-time (28 women), 144 part-time (112 women); includes 9 minority (4 Black or African American, non-Hispanic/Latino; 1 American Indian or Alaska Native, non-Hispanic/Latino; 4 Asian, non-Hispanic/Latino), 6 international. Average age 33. 93 applicants, 91% accepted, 63 enrolled. In 2016, 81 master's awarded. *Degree requirements:* For master's, thesis optional; for Certificate, thesis. *Entrance requirements:* For master's, letters of recommendation. Additional exam requirements/recommendations for international students: Required—TOEFL (minimum score 550 paper-based; 79 iBT). *Application deadline:* For fall admission, 4/1 priority date for domestic and international students; for spring admission, 10/15 priority date for domestic students, 10/15 for international students. Applications are processed on a rolling basis. Application fee: $50. Electronic applications accepted. *Financial support:* In 2016–17, 19 fellowships (averaging $2,816 per year), 6 research assistantships with tuition reimbursements (averaging $10,128 per year) were awarded; teaching assistantships, Federal Work-Study, scholarships/grants, tuition waivers (full and partial), and unspecified assistantships also available. Support available to part-time students. Financial award application deadline: 3/1; financial award applicants required to submit FAFSA. *Faculty research:* Information-seeking behavior, thesauri, impact of technology, questioning behaviors, educational informatics. *Total annual research expenditures:* $91,973. *Unit head:* Dr. Heidi Julien, Chair, 716-645-1474, Fax: 716-645-3775, E-mail: heidijul@buffalo.edu. *Application contact:* Pat Glinski, Admissions Assistant, 716-645-2110, Fax: 716-645-7937, E-mail: gse-info@buffalo.edu.
Website: http://www.gse.buffalo.edu/lis/

The University of Akron, Graduate School, College of Education, Department of Educational Foundations and Leadership, Program in Instructional Technology, Akron, OH 44325. Offers MA. *Program availability:* Online learning. *Students:* 6 full-time (3 women), 31 part-time (17 women); includes 4 minority (2 Black or African American, non-Hispanic/Latino; 1 Hispanic/Latino; 1 Two or more races, non-Hispanic/Latino), 3 international. Average age 34. 12 applicants, 100% accepted, 11 enrolled. In 2016, 27 master's awarded. *Degree requirements:* For master's, electronic portfolio. *Entrance requirements:* Additional exam requirements/recommendations for international students: Required—TOEFL (minimum score 550 paper-based; 79 iBT), IELTS (minimum score 6.5). *Application deadline:* Applications are processed on a rolling basis. Application fee: $45 ($70 for international students). Electronic applications accepted. *Expenses:* Tuition, state resident: full-time $8618; part-time $359 per credit hour. Tuition, nonresident: full-time $17,149; part-time $715 per credit hour. *Required fees:* $1652. *Unit head:* Dr. Susan Clark, Interim Chair, 330-972-7780, E-mail: sclark1@uakron.edu. *Application contact:* Kelly Chaff, College Program Specialist, 330-972-7028, E-mail: klchaff@uakron.edu.

University of Alaska Southeast, Graduate Programs, Program in Education, Juneau, AK 99801. Offers educational leadership (M Ed); elementary education (MAT); learning design and technology (M Ed); mathematics education (M Ed); reading specialist (M Ed); secondary education (MAT); special education (M Ed, MAT). *Accreditation:* NCATE. *Program availability:* Part-time, evening/weekend, online learning. *Degree requirements:* For master's, comprehensive exam or project, portfolio. *Entrance requirements:* For master's, PRAXIS, minimum GPA of 3.0, writing sample, letters of recommendation. *Application deadline:* For fall admission, 3/8 for domestic students. Applications are processed on a rolling basis. Application fee: $60. Electronic applications accepted. *Expenses:* Tuition, state resident: part-time $466 per credit. Tuition, nonresident: part-time $979 per credit. *Required fees:* $19 per credit. Part-time tuition and fees vary according to course level, campus/location and reciprocity agreements. *Financial support:* Federal Work-Study, scholarships/grants, and tuition waivers (full and partial) available. Support available to part-time students. Financial award applicants required to submit FAFSA. *Faculty research:* Applied classroom research, culturally responsive practices, action research, teaching effectiveness. *Unit head:* Dr. Larry Harris, Dean, 907-796-6551, Fax: 907-796-6550, E-mail: larry.harris@uas.alaska.edu. *Application contact:* Susan A. Stuck, Administrative Assistant, 866-465-6424, Fax: 866-465-5159, E-mail: jnsas@uas.alaska.edu.

University of Alberta, Faculty of Graduate Studies and Research, Department of Educational Psychology, Edmonton, AB T6G 2E1, Canada. Offers counseling psychology (M Ed, PhD); educational psychology (M Ed, PhD); instructional technology (M Ed); school counseling (M Ed); school psychology (M Ed, PhD); special education (M Ed, PhD); special education-deafness studies (M Ed); teaching English as a second language (M Ed). *Program availability:* Part-time. *Degree requirements:* For master's, thesis optional; for doctorate, comprehensive exam, thesis/dissertation. *Entrance requirements:* For master's and doctorate, minimum GPA of 3.0. Additional exam requirements/recommendations for international students: Required—TOEFL. *Faculty research:* Human learning, development and assessment.

University of Arkansas, Graduate School, College of Education and Health Professions, Department of Curriculum and Instruction, Program in Educational Technology, Fayetteville, AR 72701. Offers M Ed. *Accreditation:* NCATE. *Program availability:* Part-time, evening/weekend. In 2016, 12 master's awarded. *Entrance requirements:* For master's, GRE General Test, MAT or minimum GPA of 3.0. *Application deadline:* For fall admission, 4/1 for international students; for spring admission, 10/1 for international students. Applications are processed on a rolling basis. Application fee: $40 ($50 for international students). Electronic applications accepted. *Financial support:* Fellowships with tuition reimbursements, research assistantships, teaching assistantships, career-related internships or fieldwork, and Federal Work-Study available. Support available to part-time students. Financial award application deadline: 4/1; financial award applicants required to submit FAFSA. *Unit head:* Dr. Michael Daugherty, Departmental Chairperson, 479-575-4209, E-mail: mkd03@uark.edu. *Application contact:* Dr. Cheryl Murphy, Graduate Coordinator, 479-575-5111, Fax: 479-575-6676, E-mail: cmurphy@uark.edu.
Website: http://etec.uark.edu/

University of Arkansas at Little Rock, Graduate School, College of Education and Health Professions, Department of Educational Leadership, Program in Learning Systems Technology Education, Little Rock, AR 72204-1099. Offers M Ed. *Degree requirements:* For master's, comprehensive exam or defense of portfolio. *Faculty research:* Instructional program development, educational technology product development, educational technology management.

University of California, Irvine, Francisco J. Ayala School of Biological Sciences, Program in Biological Sciences and Educational Media Design, Irvine, CA 92697. Offers MS. *Degree requirements:* For master's, capstone project. *Entrance requirements:* For master's, BS in biological sciences with minimum GPA of 3.0. Application fee: $105 ($125 for international students). *Unit head:* Dr. Brad Hughes, Director, 949-824-6614, E-mail: bhughes@uci.edu. *Application contact:* Renee Frigo, Program Manager, 949-

824-8145, Fax: 949-824-1965, E-mail: rfrigo@uci.edu.
Website: http://bsemd.bio.uci.edu/

University of Central Arkansas, Graduate School, College of Education, Department of Leadership Studies, Program in Library Media and Information Technology, Conway, AR 72035-0001. Offers MS. *Program availability:* Part-time, evening/weekend, online learning. *Degree requirements:* For master's, comprehensive exam. *Entrance requirements:* For master's, GRE General Test, minimum GPA of 2.7. Additional exam requirements/recommendations for international students: Required—TOEFL (minimum score 550 paper-based). Electronic applications accepted.

University of Central Florida, College of Education and Human Performance, Department of Educational and Human Sciences, Program in Instructional Design and Technology, Orlando, FL 32816. Offers e-learning professional development (Certificate); instructional design and technology (MA); instructional design for simulations (Certificate); instructional/educational technology (Certificate). *Program availability:* Part-time. *Students:* 7 full-time (6 women), 46 part-time (36 women); includes 18 minority (6 Black or African American, non-Hispanic/Latino; 12 Hispanic/Latino), 1 international. Average age 38. 21 applicants, 76% accepted, 15 enrolled. In 2016, 9 master's, 9 other advanced degrees awarded. *Degree requirements:* For master's, thesis or alternative. *Entrance requirements:* Additional exam requirements/recommendations for international students: Required—TOEFL. *Application deadline:* For fall admission, 7/15 for domestic students; for spring admission, 12/1 for domestic students. Application fee: $30. Electronic applications accepted. *Expenses:* Tuition, state resident: part-time $288.16 per credit hour. Tuition, nonresident: part-time $1071.31 per credit hour. *Financial support:* In 2016–17, 1 student received support, including 1 teaching assistantship with partial tuition reimbursement available (averaging $9,088 per year). Financial award application deadline: 3/1; financial award applicants required to submit FAFSA. *Unit head:* Dr. Richard Hartshorne, Program Coordinator, 407-823-1861, E-mail: richard.hartshorne@ucf.edu. *Application contact:* Assistant Director, Graduate Admissions, 407-823-2766, Fax: 407-823-6442, E-mail: gradadmissions@ucf.edu.
Website: http://education.ucf.edu/insttech/

University of Central Florida, College of Education and Human Performance, Education Doctoral Programs, Orlando, FL 32816. Offers communication sciences and disorders (PhD); curriculum and instruction (Ed D); early childhood education (PhD); educational leadership (Ed D); elementary education (PhD); exceptional education (PhD); exercise physiology (PhD); higher education (PhD); instructional technology (PhD); mathematics education (PhD); methodology, measurement and analysis (PhD); reading education (PhD); science education (PhD); social science education (PhD); TESOL (PhD). *Students:* 127 full-time (91 women), 43 part-time (29 women); includes 33 minority (17 Black or African American, non-Hispanic/Latino; 5 Asian, non-Hispanic/Latino; 7 Hispanic/Latino; 4 Two or more races, non-Hispanic/Latino), 26 international. Average age 37. 163 applicants, 40% accepted, 52 enrolled. In 2016, 57 doctorates awarded. Application fee: $30. Electronic applications accepted. *Expenses:* Tuition, state resident: part-time $288.16 per credit hour. Tuition, nonresident: part-time $1071.31 per credit hour. *Financial support:* In 2016–17, 78 students received support, including 41 fellowships with partial tuition reimbursements available (averaging $5,916 per year), 44 research assistantships with partial tuition reimbursements available (averaging $7,637 per year), 48 teaching assistantships with partial tuition reimbursements available (averaging $9,633 per year). Financial award application deadline: 3/1; financial award applicants required to submit FAFSA. *Unit head:* Dr. Edward Robinson, Director of Doctoral Programs, 407-823-6106, E-mail: edward.robinson@ucf.edu. *Application contact:* Assistant Director, Graduate Admissions, 407-823-2766, Fax: 407-823-6442, E-mail: gradadmissions@ucf.edu.
Website: http://education.ucf.edu/programs.cfm?pid=g&cat=2

University of Central Florida, College of Education and Human Performance, School of Teaching, Learning, and Leadership, Orlando, FL 32816. Offers applied learning and instruction (MA); art education (M Ed), including teacher leadership; educational and instructional technology (MA), including instructional design and technology; educational leadership (Ed S); elementary education (M Ed, MA); English language arts education (M Ed), including teacher leadership; K-8 mathematics and science education (M Ed, Certificate); reading education (M Ed); science education (M Ed), including teacher leadership; social science education (M Ed), including teacher leadership; teacher education (MAT), including art education, English language, mathematics education, middle school mathematics, middle school science, science education, social science education; teacher leadership (M Ed); teaching excellence (Certificate). *Program availability:* Part-time, evening/weekend. *Faculty:* 72 full-time (53 women), 55 part-time/adjunct (42 women). *Students:* 75 full-time (64 women), 304 part-time (257 women); includes 125 minority (46 Black or African American, non-Hispanic/Latino; 2 American Indian or Alaska Native, non-Hispanic/Latino; 11 Asian, non-Hispanic/Latino; 59 Hispanic/Latino; 7 Two or more races, non-Hispanic/Latino), 4 international. Average age 32. 229 applicants, 76% accepted, 102 enrolled. In 2016, 151 master's, 34 other advanced degrees awarded. *Degree requirements:* For other advanced degree, thesis or alternative. *Entrance requirements:* For degree, GRE General Test, minimum GPA of 3.0. Additional exam requirements/recommendations for international students: Required—TOEFL. *Application deadline:* For fall admission, 7/15 for domestic students; for spring admission, 12/15 for domestic students. Application fee: $30. Electronic applications accepted. *Expenses:* Tuition, state resident: part-time $288.16 per credit hour. Tuition, nonresident: part-time $1071.31 per credit hour. *Financial support:* In 2016–17, 2 students received support, including 2 research assistantships with partial tuition reimbursements available (averaging $9,463 per year); teaching assistantships, career-related internships or fieldwork, Federal Work-Study, institutionally sponsored loans, tuition waivers (partial), and unspecified assistantships also available. Financial award application deadline: 3/1; financial award applicants required to submit FAFSA. *Unit head:* Dr. Michael Hynes, Co-Director, 407-823-6076, E-mail: michael.hynes@ucf.edu. *Application contact:* Assistant Director, Graduate Admissions, 407-823-2766, Fax: 407-823-6442, E-mail: gradadmissions@ucf.edu.
Website: http://education.ucf.edu/stll/

University of Central Missouri, The Graduate School, Warrensburg, MO 64093. Offers accountancy (MA); accounting (MBA); applied mathematics (MS); aviation safety (MA); biology (MS); business administration (MBA); career and technical education leadership (MS); college student personnel administration (MS); communication (MA); computer science (MS); counseling (MS); criminal justice (MS); educational leadership (Ed D); educational technology (MS); elementary and early childhood education (MSE); English (MA); environmental studies (MA); finance (MBA); history (MA); human services/educational technology (Ed S); human services/learning resources (Ed S); human services/professional counseling (Ed S); industrial hygiene (MS); industrial management (MS); information systems (MBA); information technology (MS); kinesiology (MS); library science and information services (MS); literacy education (MSE); marketing (MBA); mathematics (MS); music (MA); occupational safety management (MS); psychology (MS); rural family nursing (MS); school administration (MSE); social gerontology (MS); sociology (MA); special education (MSE); speech language pathology (MS); superintendency (Ed S); teaching (MAT); teaching English as a second language (MA); technology (MS); technology management (PhD); theatre (MA). *Program availability:* Part-time, 100% online, blended/hybrid learning. *Degree requirements:* For master's and Ed S, comprehensive exam (for some programs), thesis (for some programs). *Entrance requirements:* Additional exam requirements/recommendations for international students: Required—TOEFL (minimum score 550 paper-based; 79 iBT). Electronic applications accepted.

University of Central Oklahoma, The Jackson College of Graduate Studies, College of Education and Professional Studies, Department of Advanced Professional and Special Services, Edmond, OK 73034-5209. Offers educational leadership (M Ed); library media education (M Ed); reading (M Ed); school counseling (M Ed); special education (M Ed), including mild/moderate disabilities, severe-profound/multiple disabilities, special education; speech-language pathology (MS). *Accreditation:* ASHA. *Program availability:* Part-time. *Degree requirements:* For master's, comprehensive exam (for some programs), thesis (for some programs). *Entrance requirements:* For master's, GRE. Additional exam requirements/recommendations for international students: Required—TOEFL (minimum score 550 paper-based; 79 iBT), IELTS (minimum score 6.5). Electronic applications accepted. *Faculty research:* Intellectual freedom, fair use copyright, technology integration, young adult literature, distance learning.

University of Colorado Denver, School of Education and Human Development, Information and Learning Technologies Program, Denver, CO 80217. Offers e-learning design and implementation (MA); instructional design and adult learning (MA); K-12 teaching (MA). *Program availability:* Part-time, evening/weekend, online learning. *Students:* 68 full-time (56 women), 50 part-time (37 women); includes 16 minority (4 Black or African American, non-Hispanic/Latino; 5 Asian, non-Hispanic/Latino; 5 Hispanic/Latino; 1 Native Hawaiian or other Pacific Islander, non-Hispanic/Latino; 1 Two or more races, non-Hispanic/Latino), 2 international. Average age 38. 24 applicants, 88% accepted, 13 enrolled. In 2016, 45 master's awarded. *Degree requirements:* For master's, comprehensive exam (for some programs), comprehensive exam or online portfolio; 30 credit hours. *Entrance requirements:* For master's, GRE or MAT (if GPA is below 2.75), resume, statement of intent, three letters of recommendation, transcripts from all colleges/universities previously attended. Additional exam requirements/recommendations for international students: Required—TOEFL (minimum score 537 paper-based; 75 iBT); Recommended—IELTS (minimum score 6.5). *Application deadline:* For fall admission, 5/15 for domestic students, 5/1 for international students; for spring admission, 11/15 for domestic students, 11/1 for international students; for summer admission, 3/15 for domestic students, 3/1 for international students. Application fee: $50 ($75 for international students). Electronic applications accepted. *Expenses:* Contact institution. *Financial support:* In 2016–17, 7 students received support. Fellowships, research assistantships, teaching assistantships, Federal Work-Study, institutionally sponsored loans, scholarships/grants, and traineeships available. Financial award application deadline: 4/1; financial award applicants required to submit FAFSA. *Faculty research:* Technology for educational management, instructional design foundations, e-learning, educational design. *Unit head:* Brent Wilson, Professor, 303-720-7765, E-mail: brent.wilson@ucdenver.edu. *Application contact:* 303-315-6300, E-mail: education@ucdenver.edu.
Website: http://www.ucdenver.edu/academics/colleges/SchoolOfEducation/Academics/MASTERS/ILT/Pages/default.aspx

University of Connecticut, Graduate School, Neag School of Education, Department of Educational Psychology, Cognition, Instruction, and Learning Technology Program, Storrs, CT 06269. Offers MA, PhD. *Degree requirements:* For master's, comprehensive exam; for doctorate, thesis/dissertation. *Entrance requirements:* For doctorate, GRE General Test. Additional exam requirements/recommendations for international students: Required—TOEFL (minimum score 550 paper-based). Electronic applications accepted.

University of Dayton, Department of Teacher Education, Dayton, OH 45469. Offers early childhood leadership and advocacy (MS Ed); interdisciplinary education studies (MS Ed); leadership in educational systems (MS Ed); literacy (MS Ed); mathematics education (MS Ed); music education (MS Ed); teacher as leader (MS Ed); teacher education (MS Ed); technology-enhanced learning (MS Ed); trans-disciplinary early childhood education (MS Ed). *Program availability:* Part-time, evening/weekend, blended/hybrid learning. *Faculty:* 23 full-time (18 women), 49 part-time/adjunct (42 women). *Students:* 52 full-time (47 women), 89 part-time (76 women); includes 6 minority (2 Black or African American, non-Hispanic/Latino; 2 Hispanic/Latino; 2 Two or more races, non-Hispanic/Latino), 24 international. Average age 31. 106 applicants, 28% accepted. In 2016, 69 master's awarded. *Degree requirements:* For master's, variable foreign language requirement, thesis optional. *Entrance requirements:* For master's, GRE (minimum score of 149 verbal, 4 on writing) or MAT (minimum score of 396) if undergraduate GPA was under 2.75, minimum GPA of 2.75, 3 letters of recommendation, personal statement or resume, official transcripts. Additional exam requirements/recommendations for international students: Required—TOEFL (minimum score 550 paper-based; 80 iBT); Recommended—IELTS (minimum score 6.5). *Application deadline:* Applications are processed on a rolling basis. Application fee: $0 ($50 for international students). Electronic applications accepted. *Expenses:* $620 per credit hour, $25 registration fee per term. *Financial support:* Institutionally sponsored loans available. Financial award application deadline: 3/1; financial award applicants required to submit FAFSA. *Faculty research:* Educational technology; facilitating teacher reflection; teacher preparation in dyslexia. *Unit head:* Dr. Connie L. Bowman, Chair, 937-229-3305, E-mail: cbowman1@udayton.edu. *Application contact:* Gina Seiter, Graduate Program Advisor, 937-229-3103, E-mail: gseiter1@udayton.edu.
Website: https://www.udayton.edu/education/departments_and_programs/edt

The University of Findlay, Office of Graduate Admissions, Findlay, OH 45840-3653. Offers applied security and analytics (MSAS); athletic training (MAT); business (MBA), including certified management accountant, certified public accountant, health care management, hospitality management; education (MA Ed, Ed D), including children's literature (MA Ed), curriculum and teaching (MA Ed), education (MA Ed), educational administration (MA Ed), human resource development (MA Ed), reading (MA Ed), science education (MA Ed), superintendent (Ed D), teaching (Ed D), technology (MA Ed); environmental, safety and health management (MSEM); health informatics (MS); occupational therapy (MOT); pharmacy (Pharm D); physical therapy (DPT); physician assistant (MPA); rhetoric and writing (MA); teaching English to speakers of other languages (TESOL) and bilingual education (MA). *Program availability:* Part-time, evening/weekend, 100% online, blended/hybrid learning. *Faculty:* 114 full-time (63 women), 44 part-time/adjunct (18 women). *Students:* 751 full-time (452 women), 573 part-time (323 women); includes 164 minority (82 Black or African American, non-Hispanic/Latino; 1 American Indian or Alaska Native, non-Hispanic/Latino; 27 Asian, non-Hispanic/Latino; 37 Hispanic/Latino; 17 Two or more races, non-Hispanic/Latino), 280 international. Average age 28. 661 applicants, 52% accepted, 288 enrolled. In 2016, 366 master's, 137 doctorates awarded. *Degree requirements:* For master's, comprehensive exam (for some programs), thesis, cumulative project, capstone project; for doctorate, thesis/dissertation. *Entrance requirements:* For master's, GRE (for some programs), bachelor's degree from accredited institution, minimum undergraduate GPA of 3.0 in last 64 hours of course work; for doctorate, MAT, minimum cumulative GPA of 3.0, master's degree. Additional exam requirements/recommendations for international students: Recommended—TOEFL (minimum score 79 iBT), IELTS (minimum score 7).

Application deadline: For fall admission, 6/15 for international students; for spring admission, 12/1 for international students; for summer admission, 4/1 for international students. Applications are processed on a rolling basis. Electronic applications accepted. *Expenses:* Contact institution. *Financial support:* In 2016–17, 139 students received support, including 15 research assistantships with partial tuition reimbursements available (averaging $7,200 per year), 25 teaching assistantships with partial tuition reimbursements available (averaging $7,200 per year); Federal Work-Study, institutionally sponsored loans, and unspecified assistantships also available. Financial award application deadline: 4/1; financial award applicants required to submit FAFSA. *Unit head:* Christopher M. Harris, Director of Admissions, 419-434-4347, E-mail: harrisc1@findlay.edu. *Application contact:* Madeline Fauser Brennan, Graduate Admissions Counselor, 419-434-4636, Fax: 419-434-4898, E-mail: fauserbrennan@findlay.edu.
Website: http://www.findlay.edu/admissions/graduate/Pages/default.aspx

University of Georgia, College of Education, Department of Career and Information Studies, Athens, GA 30602. Offers learning, design, and technology (M Ed, PhD, Ed S), including instructional design and development (M Ed, Ed S); workforce education (MAT, Ed D), including business education (MAT). *Accreditation:* NCATE. *Faculty:* 14 full-time (7 women). *Students:* 27 full-time (15 women), 70 part-time (46 women); includes 24 minority (23 Black or African American, non-Hispanic/Latino; 1 Native Hawaiian or other Pacific Islander, non-Hispanic/Latino), 5 international. Average age 37. 40 applicants, 63% accepted, 8 enrolled. In 2016, 16 master's, 23 doctorates, 5 other advanced degrees awarded. *Entrance requirements:* For master's, GRE General Test, MAT; for doctorate, GRE General Test; for Ed S, GRE General Test or MAT. *Application deadline:* For fall admission, 7/1 priority date for domestic students; for spring admission, 11/15 for domestic students. Application fee: $50. Electronic applications accepted. *Financial support:* Fellowships, research assistantships, teaching assistantships, and unspecified assistantships available. *Unit head:* Dr. Robert C. Branch, Head, 706-542-4100, Fax: 706-542-4054. *Application contact:* Dr. Robert C. Wicklein, Graduate Coordinator, 706-542-4503, Fax: 706-542-4054, E-mail: wickone@uga.edu.
Website: http://www.coe.uga.edu/cis/

University of Hartford, College of Education, Nursing, and Health Professions, Program in Educational Technology, West Hartford, CT 06117-1599. Offers M Ed. *Accreditation:* NCATE. *Program availability:* Part-time, evening/weekend. *Degree requirements:* For master's, comprehensive exam. *Entrance requirements:* For master's, interview, 2 letters of recommendation. Additional exam requirements/recommendations for international students: Required—TOEFL (minimum score 550 paper-based). Electronic applications accepted.

University of Hawaii at Manoa, Graduate Division, College of Education, Department of Educational Technology, Honolulu, HI 96822. Offers M Ed. *Program availability:* Part-time. *Degree requirements:* For master's, thesis optional. *Entrance requirements:* Additional exam requirements/recommendations for international students: Required—TOEFL (minimum score 650 paper-based; 114 iBT), IELTS (minimum score 7). *Faculty research:* Distance education-interaction via electronic means.

University of Hawaii at Manoa, Graduate Division, College of Education, PhD in Education Program, Honolulu, HI 96822. Offers curriculum and instruction (PhD); educational administration (PhD); educational foundations (PhD); educational policy studies (PhD); educational psychology (PhD); exceptionalities (PhD); kinesiology (PhD); learning design and technology (PhD). *Program availability:* Part-time, evening/weekend. *Degree requirements:* For doctorate, thesis/dissertation. *Entrance requirements:* For doctorate, GRE General Test, sample of written work. Additional exam requirements/recommendations for international students: Required—TOEFL (minimum score 600 paper-based; 100 iBT), IELTS (minimum score 7).

University of Houston–Clear Lake, School of Education, Program in Curriculum and Instruction, Houston, TX 77058-1002. Offers curriculum and instruction (MS); early childhood education (MS); reading (MS); school library and information science (MS). *Program availability:* Part-time, evening/weekend. *Degree requirements:* For master's, thesis (for some programs). *Entrance requirements:* For master's, GRE or minimum GPA of 3.0 in last 60 hours. Additional exam requirements/recommendations for international students: Required—TOEFL (minimum score 550 paper-based). Electronic applications accepted.

University of Houston–Clear Lake, School of Education, Program in Foundations and Professional Studies, Houston, TX 77058-1002. Offers counseling (MS); instructional technology (MS); multicultural studies (MS). *Program availability:* Part-time, evening/weekend. *Degree requirements:* For master's, thesis optional. *Entrance requirements:* For master's, GRE or minimum GPA of 3.0 in last 60 hours. Additional exam requirements/recommendations for international students: Required—TOEFL (minimum score 550 paper-based). Electronic applications accepted.

University of Houston–Victoria, School of Education, Health Professions and Human Development, Victoria, TX 77901-4450. Offers administration and supervision (M Ed); adult and higher education (M Ed); counselor education (M Ed); curriculum and instruction (M Ed); educational technology (M Ed); special education (M Ed). *Program availability:* Part-time, evening/weekend, online learning. *Degree requirements:* For master's, comprehensive exam, project or thesis. *Entrance requirements:* For master's, GRE General Test. Additional exam requirements/recommendations for international students: Required—TOEFL. Electronic applications accepted. *Faculty research:* Reading and language arts education, evaluation and diagnosis of special children's abilities.

University of Illinois at Springfield, Graduate Programs, College of Education and Human Services, Department of Educational Leadership, Springfield, IL 62703-5407. Offers chief school business official (CAS); educational leadership (MA); educational technology (Graduate Certificate); English as a second language (Graduate Certificate); higher education online pedagogy (Graduate Certificate); leadership and learning (Graduate Certificate); legal aspects of education (Graduate Certificate); superintendent (CAS); teacher leadership (MA). *Program availability:* Part-time, evening/weekend, 100% online, blended/hybrid learning. *Faculty:* 5 full-time (2 women), 8 part-time/adjunct (7 women). *Students:* 4 full-time (2 women), 113 part-time (68 women); includes 20 minority (15 Black or African American, non-Hispanic/Latino; 1 American Indian or Alaska Native, non-Hispanic/Latino; 4 Hispanic/Latino), 1 international. Average age 36. 45 applicants, 62% accepted, 19 enrolled. In 2016, 22 master's, 2 other advanced degrees awarded. *Degree requirements:* For master's, capstone course. *Entrance requirements:* For master's, minimum undergraduate GPA of 3.0, valid Illinois Teaching License, minimum of two years of successful teaching experience, portfolio, interview. Additional exam requirements/recommendations for international students: Required—TOEFL (minimum score 500 paper-based; 61 iBT). *Application deadline:* Applications are processed on a rolling basis. Application fee: $60 ($75 for international students). Electronic applications accepted. *Expenses:* Tuition, state resident: part-time $329 per credit hour. Tuition, nonresident: part-time $675 per credit hour. *Financial support:* In 2016–17, fellowships with full tuition reimbursements (averaging $9,900 per year), research assistantships with full tuition reimbursements (averaging $9,991 per year), teaching assistantships with full tuition reimbursements (averaging $10,059 per year) were awarded; career-related internships or fieldwork, Federal Work-Study, scholarships/grants, health care benefits, and unspecified assistantships also available. Support available to part-time students. Financial award application deadline: 11/15; financial award applicants required to submit FAFSA. *Unit head:* Dr. Scott Day, Program Administrator, 217-206-7520, Fax: 217-206-6775, E-mail: day.scott@uis.edu. *Application contact:* Dr. Cecelia Cornell, Associate Vice Chancellor for Graduate Education, 217-206-7230, E-mail: ccorn1@uis.edu.
Website: http://www.uis.edu/edl/

The University of Kansas, Graduate Studies, School of Education, Department of Educational Leadership and Policy Studies, Program in Educational Technology, Lawrence, KS 66045. Offers MS Ed, PhD. *Program availability:* Part-time, evening/weekend. *Students:* 9 full-time (8 women), 17 part-time (10 women); includes 4 minority (1 American Indian or Alaska Native, non-Hispanic/Latino; 2 Asian, non-Hispanic/Latino; 1 Hispanic/Latino), 6 international. Average age 34. 16 applicants, 81% accepted, 10 enrolled. In 2016, 12 master's awarded. *Entrance requirements:* For master's, resume or electronic portfolio, official transcripts, statement of purpose, three letters of recommendation; for doctorate, GRE, resume or electronic portfolio, official transcripts, statement of purpose, three letters of recommendation, sample of academic writing. Additional exam requirements/recommendations for international students: Required—TOEFL, IELTS. *Application deadline:* For fall admission, 6/1 priority date for domestic and international students; for spring admission, 11/1 for domestic and international students; for summer admission, 4/1 for domestic and international students. Application fee: $65 ($85 for international students). Electronic applications accepted. *Financial support:* Research assistantships, teaching assistantships, and unspecified assistantships available. Financial award application deadline: 2/21. *Unit head:* Dr. Susan B. Twombly, Chair, 785-864-9721, E-mail: stwombly@ku.edu. *Application contact:* Denise Brubaker, Admissions Coordinator, 785-864-4458, Fax: 785-864-4697, E-mail: elps@ku.edu.
Website: http://edtech.ku.edu/

University of Kentucky, Graduate School, College of Education, Program in Curriculum and Instruction, Lexington, KY 40506-0032. Offers curriculum and instruction (Ed D, PhD); elementary education (MA Ed); instructional system design (MS Ed); literacy (MA Ed); middle school education (MA Ed, MS Ed); secondary education (MA Ed, MS Ed). *Accreditation:* NCATE. *Degree requirements:* For master's, comprehensive exam, thesis optional; for doctorate, comprehensive exam, thesis/dissertation. *Entrance requirements:* For master's, GRE General Test, minimum undergraduate GPA of 2.75; for doctorate, GRE General Test, minimum graduate GPA of 3.0. Additional exam requirements/recommendations for international students: Required—TOEFL (minimum score 550 paper-based). Electronic applications accepted. *Faculty research:* Educational reform, multicultural education, classroom instructional practices, performance based assessment, primary school programs.

University of Maine, Graduate School, College of Education and Human Development, School of Kinesiology, Physical Education and Athletic Training, Orono, ME 04469. Offers classroom technology integrationist (CGS); education data specialist (CGS); educational technology coordinator (CGS); kinesiology and physical education (M Ed, MS); science education (M Ed, MS); STEM education (PhD). *Program availability:* Part-time, evening/weekend. *Students:* 13 full-time (4 women), 1 (woman) part-time; includes 1 minority (Hispanic/Latino), 1 international. Average age 24. 15 applicants, 100% accepted, 7 enrolled. In 2016, 16 master's, 10 other advanced degrees awarded. *Degree requirements:* For master's, thesis (for some programs); for doctorate, comprehensive exam, thesis/dissertation. *Entrance requirements:* For master's, GRE General Test, MAT; for doctorate, GRE General Test. Additional exam requirements/recommendations for international students: Required—TOEFL. *Application deadline:* For fall admission, 1/15 for domestic students. Applications are processed on a rolling basis. Application fee: $65. Electronic applications accepted. *Expenses:* Tuition, state resident: full-time $7524; part-time $2508 per credit. Tuition, nonresident: full-time $24,498; part-time $8166 per credit. *Required fees:* $1148; $571 per credit. *Financial support:* In 2016–17, 9 students received support, including 1 research assistantship with full tuition reimbursement available (averaging $14,600 per year), 6 teaching assistantships (averaging $14,600 per year); Federal Work-Study, scholarships/grants, and unspecified assistantships also available. Financial award application deadline: 3/1. *Faculty research:* Integration of technology in K-12 classrooms, instructional theory and practice in science, inquiry-based teaching, professional development, exercise science, adaptive physical education, neuromuscular function/dysfunction. *Unit head:* Dr. Jim Artesani, Associate Dean of Accreditation and Graduate Affairs, 207-581-4061, Fax: 207-581-2423. *Application contact:* Scott G. Delcourt, Assistant Vice President for Graduate Studies and Senior Associate Dean, 207-581-3291, Fax: 207-581-3232, E-mail: graduate@maine.edu.
Website: http://umaine.edu/edhd/

University of Maine at Farmington, Graduate Programs in Education, Farmington, ME 04938. Offers early childhood education (MS Ed); educational leadership (MS Ed); instructional technology (M Ed). M Ed offered in collaboration with University of Maine and University of Southern Maine. *Accreditation:* NCATE. *Program availability:* Part-time-only, evening/weekend, 100% online, blended/hybrid learning. *Faculty:* 7 full-time (6 women), 6 part-time/adjunct (3 women). *Students:* 90 part-time (76 women). Average age 36. 30 applicants, 100% accepted, 29 enrolled. In 2016, 14 master's awarded. *Degree requirements:* For master's, thesis, capstone project (for educational leadership). *Entrance requirements:* For master's, baccalaureate degree from accredited institution, valid teaching certificate or professional experience in education. Additional exam requirements/recommendations for international students: Required—TOEFL. *Application deadline:* For fall admission, 8/10 for domestic students; for spring admission, 1/5 for domestic students; for summer admission, 4/10 for domestic students. Applications are processed on a rolling basis. Application fee: $60. Electronic applications accepted. *Expenses:* Contact institution. *Financial support:* Applicants required to submit FAFSA. *Faculty research:* Teacher leadership, school improvement strategies, technology integration. *Unit head:* Dr. Johanna Prince, Director of Graduate Programs in Education, 207-778-7066, E-mail: gradstudies@maine.edu. *Application contact:* Valerie Soucie, Administrative Specialist, 207-778-7502, Fax: 207-778-8134, E-mail: gradstudies@maine.edu.
Website: http://www2.umf.maine.edu/gradstudies/

University of Maryland, Baltimore County, The Graduate School, College of Arts, Humanities and Social Sciences, Department of Education, Program in Instructional Systems Development, Halethorpe, MD 21227. Offers distance education (Graduate Certificate); instructional systems development (MA, Graduate Certificate), including distance education (Graduate Certificate); instructional technology (Graduate Certificate). *Program availability:* Part-time, evening/weekend, 100% online, blended/hybrid learning. *Faculty:* 2 full-time (0 women), 9 part-time/adjunct (3 women). *Students:* 4 full-time (1 woman), 103 part-time (72 women); includes 36 minority (24 Black or African American, non-Hispanic/Latino; 5 Asian, non-Hispanic/Latino; 4 Hispanic/Latino; 3 Two or more races, non-Hispanic/Latino). Average age 37. 49 applicants, 94% accepted, 40 enrolled. In 2016, 32 master's, 55 other advanced degrees awarded. *Degree requirements:* For master's, comprehensive exam (for some programs), portfolio (for some programs). *Entrance requirements:* Additional exam requirements/

recommendations for international students: Required—TOEFL (minimum score 550 paper-based; 80 iBT), GRE. *Application deadline:* For fall admission, 6/1 priority date for domestic students, 1/1 priority date for international students; for spring admission, 11/1 priority date for domestic students; for summer admission, 3/1 priority date for domestic students. Applications are processed on a rolling basis. Application fee: $50. Electronic applications accepted. *Expenses:* Tuition, state resident: full-time $13,294. Tuition, nonresident: full-time $20,286. *Financial support:* Application deadline: 2/14; applicants required to submit FAFSA. *Faculty research:* E-learning, distance education, instructional design. *Unit head:* Dr. Greg Williams, Graduate Program Director, 443-543-5447, Fax: 443-543-5096, E-mail: gregw@umbc.edu. *Application contact:* Renee Eisenhuth, Graduate Program Coordinator, 443-543-5446, Fax: 443-543-5096, E-mail: reisen@umbc.edu.
Website: http://www.umbc.edu/isd

University of Maryland, College Park, Academic Affairs, College of Education, Department of Education Policy and Leadership, College Park, MD 20742. Offers curriculum and educational communications (M Ed, MA, Ed D, PhD); social foundations of education (M Ed, MA, Ed D, PhD, CAGS). *Accreditation:* NCATE. *Program availability:* Part-time, evening/weekend, online learning. *Degree requirements:* For master's, thesis or alternative, internship and/or field experience; for doctorate, comprehensive exam, thesis/dissertation, practicum or internship. *Entrance requirements:* For master's, GRE General Test or MAT, minimum GPA of 3.0, scholarly writing sample, 3 letters of recommendation; for doctorate, GRE General Test or MAT, scholarly writing sample; minimum undergraduate GPA of 3.0, graduate 3.5. *Faculty research:* Educational technology, adult and higher education.

University of Maryland University College, The Graduate School, Program in Learning Design and Technology, Adelphi, MD 20783. Offers MS. *Program availability:* Part-time, evening/weekend. *Students:* 20 full-time (15 women); includes 9 minority (8 Black or African American, non-Hispanic/Latino; 1 Two or more races, non-Hispanic/Latino), 1 international. Average age 37. 21 applicants, 100% accepted, 16 enrolled. *Application deadline:* Applications are processed on a rolling basis. Application fee: $50. Electronic applications accepted. *Expenses:* Tuition, state resident: part-time $458 per credit. Tuition, nonresident: part-time $659 per credit. *Financial support:* Scholarships/grants available. Financial award application deadline: 6/1; financial award applicants required to submit FAFSA. *Unit head:* E-mail: graddean@umuc.edu. *Application contact:* Coordinator, Graduate Admissions, 800-888-8682, Fax: 240-684-2151, E-mail: newgrad@umuc.edu.
Website: http://www.umuc.edu/academic-programs/masters-degrees/learning-design-technology-ms.cfm

University of Massachusetts Amherst, Graduate School, College of Education, Program in Education, Amherst, MA 01003. Offers bilingual, English as a second language, and multicultural education (M Ed, Ed S); child study and early education (M Ed); children, families and schools (Ed D, Ed S); early childhood and elementary teacher education (M Ed); educational leadership (M Ed); educational policy and leadership (Ed D); higher education (M Ed); international education (M Ed); language, literacy and culture (Ed D); learning, media and technology (M Ed, Ed S); mathematics, science, and learning technologies (Ed D); reading and writing (M Ed); research, educational measurement and psychometrics (Ed D); school counselor education (M Ed, Ed S); school psychology (Ed S); science education (Ed S); secondary teacher education (M Ed); social justice education (M Ed, Ed D, Ed S); special education (M Ed, Ed D, Ed S); teacher education and school improvement (Ed D, Ed S). *Accreditation:* NCATE. *Program availability:* Part-time, online learning. Terminal master's awarded for partial completion of doctoral program. *Degree requirements:* For doctorate, comprehensive exam, thesis/dissertation. *Entrance requirements:* Additional exam requirements/recommendations for international students: Required—TOEFL (minimum score 550 paper-based; 80 iBT), IELTS (minimum score 6.5). Electronic applications accepted.

University of Massachusetts Boston, College of Advancing and Professional Studies, Program in Instructional Design, Boston, MA 02125-3393. Offers M Ed, Certificate. *Program availability:* Part-time, evening/weekend. *Students:* 4 full-time (3 women), 62 part-time (43 women); includes 5 minority (1 Black or African American, non-Hispanic/Latino; 1 Asian, non-Hispanic/Latino; 2 Hispanic/Latino; 1 Two or more races, non-Hispanic/Latino), 3 international. Average age 40. 16 applicants, 94% accepted, 6 enrolled. In 2016, 32 master's awarded. *Degree requirements:* For master's, comprehensive exam, thesis optional, practicum. *Entrance requirements:* For master's, MAT, minimum GPA of 2.75. *Application deadline:* For fall admission, 3/1 for domestic students; for spring admission, 11/1 for domestic students. *Expenses:* Tuition, state resident: full-time $16,863. Tuition, nonresident: full-time $32,913. *Required fees:* $177. *Financial support:* Research assistantships with full tuition reimbursements, teaching assistantships with full tuition reimbursements, career-related internships or fieldwork, Federal Work-Study, and unspecified assistantships available. Support available to part-time students. Financial award application deadline: 3/1; financial award applicants required to submit FAFSA. *Faculty research:* Distance education, adult education. *Application contact:* Peggy Roldan Patel, Graduate Admissions Coordinator, 617-287-6400, Fax: 617-287-6236, E-mail: bos.gadm@dpc.umassp.edu.

University of Memphis, Graduate School, College of Education, Department of Instruction and Curriculum Leadership, Memphis, TN 38152. Offers advanced studies in teaching and learning (M Ed); applied behavior analysis (Graduate Certificate); autism studies (Graduate Certificate); early childhood education (MAT, MS, Ed D); elementary education (MAT); instruction and curriculum (MS, Ed D); instruction design and technology (MS, Ed D); instructional design and technology (Graduate Certificate); literacy, leadership, and coaching (Graduate Certificate); reading (MS, Ed D); school library information specialist (Graduate Certificate); secondary education (MAT); special education (MAT, MS, Ed D); STEM teacher leadership (Graduate Certificate); urban education (Graduate Certificate). *Accreditation:* NCATE (one or more programs are accredited). *Program availability:* Part-time. *Faculty:* 24 full-time (14 women), 17 part-time/adjunct (12 women). *Students:* 66 full-time (52 women), 315 part-time (243 women); includes 163 minority (132 Black or African American, non-Hispanic/Latino; 1 American Indian or Alaska Native, non-Hispanic/Latino; 6 Asian, non-Hispanic/Latino; 13 Hispanic/Latino; 1 Native Hawaiian or other Pacific Islander, non-Hispanic/Latino; 10 Two or more races, non-Hispanic/Latino), 4 international. Average age 35. 215 applicants, 78% accepted, 120 enrolled. In 2016, 111 master's, 21 doctorates, 8 other advanced degrees awarded. Terminal master's awarded for partial completion of doctoral program. *Degree requirements:* For master's, comprehensive exam, thesis or alternative; for doctorate, comprehensive exam, thesis/dissertation. *Entrance requirements:* For master's, GRE General Test, PRAXIS, minimum GPA of 2.5, letters of reference; for doctorate, GRE General Test, GRE Subject Test, 2 years of teaching experience, letters of reference, statement of purpose, interview. Additional exam requirements/recommendations for international students: Required—TOEFL (minimum score 550 paper-based; 79 iBT). *Application deadline:* For fall admission, 4/1 priority date for domestic students; for spring admission, 10/1 priority date for domestic students; for summer admission, 2/1 priority date for domestic students. Applications are processed on a rolling basis. Application fee: $35 ($60 for international students). Electronic applications accepted. *Expenses:* $5,231.50 per semester full-time in-state, $9,623.50 full-time out-of-state. *Financial support:* In 2016–17, 2 research assistantships with full tuition reimbursements (averaging $10,000 per year), 3 teaching assistantships with full tuition reimbursements (averaging $10,666 per year) were awarded; career-related internships or fieldwork, Federal Work-Study, institutionally sponsored loans, scholarships/grants, traineeships, and unspecified assistantships also available. Support available to part-time students. Financial award application deadline: 2/1; financial award applicants required to submit FAFSA. *Faculty research:* Effective urban teachers, preparation and retention of urban teachers, technology utilization in schools, field-based teacher preparation programs, effective use of online instruction. *Unit head:* Dr. Angiline Powell, Interim Chair, 901-678-3310, E-mail: apowell3@memphis.edu. *Application contact:* Dr. James Meindl, Coordinator of Graduate Studies, 901-678-3310, E-mail: jnmeindl@memphis.edu.
Website: http://www.memphis.edu/icl/

University of Michigan–Dearborn, College of Education, Health, and Human Services, Master of Arts Program in Educational Technology, Dearborn, MI 48126. Offers MA. *Program availability:* Part-time, evening/weekend, online only, 100% online. *Faculty:* 8 full-time (4 women), 1 part-time/adjunct (0 women). *Students:* 30 part-time (15 women); includes 5 minority (2 Black or African American, non-Hispanic/Latino; 2 Hispanic/Latino; 1 Two or more races, non-Hispanic/Latino). Average age 31. 7 applicants, 100% accepted, 6 enrolled. In 2016, 21 master's awarded. *Entrance requirements:* Additional exam requirements/recommendations for international students: Required—TOEFL (minimum score 560 paper-based; 84 iBT), IELTS (minimum score 6.5). *Application deadline:* For fall admission, 8/1 priority date for domestic students, 5/1 priority date for international students; for winter admission, 12/1 priority date for domestic students, 9/1 priority date for international students; for spring admission, 4/1 priority date for domestic students, 1/1 priority date for international students. Applications are processed on a rolling basis. Application fee: $60. Electronic applications accepted. *Expenses:* Contact institution. *Financial support:* In 2016–17, 6 students received support. Scholarships/grants available. Financial award application deadline: 3/1; financial award applicants required to submit FAFSA. *Faculty research:* Educational technology, foundations, constructivist education. *Unit head:* Dr. Stein Brunvand, Director, Master's Programs, 313-583-6415, E-mail: sbrunvan@umich.edu. *Application contact:* Elizabeth Morden, Graduate Programs Assistant, 313-593-5090, E-mail: emorden@umich.edu.
Website: http://umdearborn.edu/cehhs/cehhs_ma_ed_tech/

University of Michigan–Flint, School of Education and Human Services, Department of Education, Flint, MI 48502. Offers curriculum and instruction (Ed S); early childhood education (MA); education (Ed D); educational leadership (Ed S); educational technology (MA), including curriculum and instruction, developer; literacy education (MA); secondary education with certification (MA). *Program availability:* Part-time, evening/weekend, 100% online, mixed mode format (for some programs). *Faculty:* 14 full-time (9 women), 30 part-time/adjunct (17 women). *Students:* 31 full-time (18 women), 199 part-time (144 women); includes 61 minority (48 Black or African American, non-Hispanic/Latino; 1 Asian, non-Hispanic/Latino; 6 Hispanic/Latino; 1 Native Hawaiian or other Pacific Islander, non-Hispanic/Latino; 5 Two or more races, non-Hispanic/Latino), 2 international. Average age 39. 124 applicants, 86% accepted, 75 enrolled. In 2016, 77 master's, 1 doctorate awarded. *Degree requirements:* For master's, thesis optional; for doctorate, thesis/dissertation. *Entrance requirements:* For master's, bachelor's degree from regionally-accredited institution, minimum overall undergraduate GPA of 3.0; for doctorate, Ed S; minimum overall graduate GPA of 3.3 (6.0 on a 9.0 scale) or equivalent; at least 3 years of work experience in a P-16 educational institution or in an education-related position; for Ed S, MA or MS in education-related field from accredited institution; minimum overall graduate GPA of 3.0 (6.0 on a 9.0 scale) or equivalent; at least 3 years of work experience in an educational setting. Additional exam requirements/recommendations for international students: Required—TOEFL (minimum score 84 iBT), IELTS (minimum score 6.5). *Application deadline:* For fall admission, 8/1 for domestic students, 5/1 for international students; for winter admission, 11/15 for domestic students, 9/15 for international students; for spring admission, 3/15 for domestic students, 1/15 for international students; for summer admission, 5/15 for domestic students. Applications are processed on a rolling basis. Application fee: $55. Electronic applications accepted. *Expenses:* Contact institution. *Financial support:* Federal Work-Study, scholarships/grants, and unspecified assistantships available. Support available to part-time students. Financial award application deadline: 3/1; financial award applicants required to submit FAFSA. *Unit head:* Dr. Mary Jo Finney, Department Chair/Associate Professor, 810-766-6617, E-mail: mjfinney@umflint.edu. *Application contact:* Bradley T. Maki, Director of Graduate Admissions, 810-762-3171, Fax: 810-766-6789, E-mail: bmaki@umflint.edu.
Website: https://www.umflint.edu/education/graduate-programs

University of Minnesota, Twin Cities Campus, Graduate School, College of Education and Human Development, Department of Curriculum and Instruction, Minneapolis, MN 55455-0213. Offers art education (M Ed, MA, PhD); curriculum and instruction (M Ed, MA, PhD); elementary education (MA, PhD); English education (PhD); language and immersion education (Certificate); learning technologies (MA, PhD); literacy education (MA, PhD); second language education (MA, PhD); social studies education (MA, PhD); STEM education (MA, PhD); teaching (M Ed), including mathematics, science, social studies, teaching; teaching English to speakers of other languages (MA); technology enhanced learning (Certificate). *Faculty:* 37 full-time (20 women). *Students:* 411 full-time (288 women), 317 part-time (223 women); includes 153 minority (37 Black or African American, non-Hispanic/Latino; 7 American Indian or Alaska Native, non-Hispanic/Latino; 31 Asian, non-Hispanic/Latino; 48 Hispanic/Latino; 1 Native Hawaiian or other Pacific Islander, non-Hispanic/Latino; 29 Two or more races, non-Hispanic/Latino), 53 international. Average age 32. 672 applicants, 66% accepted, 400 enrolled. In 2016, 645 master's, 33 doctorates, 27 other advanced degrees awarded. Application fee: $75 ($95 for international students). *Financial support:* In 2016–17, 13 fellowships, 36 research assistantships with full tuition reimbursements (averaging $8,454 per year), 61 teaching assistantships with full tuition reimbursements (averaging $11,406 per year) were awarded. *Faculty research:* Teaching and learning; influence of cultural, linguistic, social, political, and technological factors on teaching, learning and educational research; relationship between educational practice and a democratic and just society; urban education; immigrant education, racial justice and education. *Total annual research expenditures:* $684,005. *Unit head:* Dr. Cynthia Lewis, Chair, 612-625-6313, E-mail: lewis@umn.edu. *Application contact:* Dr. Gillian Roehrig, Director of Graduate Studies, 612-625-0561, E-mail: roehr013@umn.edu.
Website: http://www.cehd.umn.edu/ci

University of Missouri, Office of Research and Graduate Studies, College of Education, School of Information Science and Learning Technologies, Columbia, MO 65211. Offers educational technology (M Ed, Ed S); information science and learning technology (PhD, Certificate); library science (MA). *Accreditation:* ALA (one or more programs are accredited). *Program availability:* Part-time, evening/weekend. *Faculty:* 13 full-time (11 women), 1 part-time/adjunct (0 women). *Students:* 99 full-time (75 women), 187 part-time (126 women). *Entrance requirements:* For master's, GRE General Test or MAT, minimum GPA of 3.0. Additional exam requirements/recommendations for international students: Required—TOEFL (minimum score 540 paper-based; 76 iBT). *Application deadline:* For fall admission, 2/15 priority date for domestic and international students; for winter admission, 9/15 priority date for domestic and international students;

for spring admission, 3/1 priority date for domestic students. Applications are processed on a rolling basis. Application fee: $75 ($90 for international students). Electronic applications accepted. *Expenses:* Tuition, state resident: full-time $6347; part-time $352.60 per credit hour. Tuition, nonresident: full-time $17,379; part-time $965.50 per credit hour. *Required fees:* $1035. Tuition and fees vary according to course load, campus/location and program. *Financial support:* Fellowships, teaching assistantships, scholarships/grants, health care benefits, and unspecified assistantships available. Support available to part-time students.
Website: http://education.missouri.edu/information-science-learning-technologies/

University of Nebraska at Kearney, College of Education, Department of Teacher Education, Kearney, NE 68849-0001. Offers curriculum and instruction (MA Ed), including early childhood education, elementary education, English as a second language, instructional effectiveness, reading/special education, secondary education; instructional technology (MS Ed), including information technology, instructional technology, school librarian; reading PK-12 (MA Ed); special education (MA Ed), including advanced practitioner: assistive technology specialist, advanced practitioner: behavioral interventionist, advanced practitioner: inclusive collaboration specialist, gifted, teacher education. *Program availability:* Part-time, evening/weekend, online only, 100% online. *Faculty:* 18 full-time (13 women). *Students:* 21 full-time (15 women), 296 part-time (240 women); includes 21 minority (3 Black or African American, non-Hispanic/ Latino; 1 Asian, non-Hispanic/Latino; 14 Hispanic/Latino; 1 Native Hawaiian or other Pacific Islander, non-Hispanic/Latino; 2 Two or more races, non-Hispanic/Latino), 1 international. Average age 32. 81 applicants, 100% accepted, 61 enrolled. In 2016, 129 master's awarded. *Degree requirements:* For master's, comprehensive exam, thesis optional. *Entrance requirements:* For master's, portfolio or GRE. Additional exam requirements/recommendations for international students: Recommended—TOEFL (minimum score 550 paper-based; 79 iBT), IELTS (minimum score 6.5). *Application deadline:* For fall admission, 6/15 for domestic students, 5/15 for international students; for spring admission, 10/15 for domestic and international students; for summer admission, 3/15 for domestic and international students. Application fee: $45. Electronic applications accepted. *Expenses:* $285 per credit hour resident tuition, $415 per credit hour non-resident tuition (online). *Financial support:* In 2016–17, 6 students received support, including 6 research assistantships with full tuition reimbursements available (averaging $10,500 per year); career-related internships or fieldwork, scholarships/ grants, health care benefits, and unspecified assistantships also available. Support available to part-time students. Financial award application deadline: 2/28; financial award applicants required to submit FAFSA. *Unit head:* Sarah Bartling, Administrative Assistant, 308-865-8513, E-mail: bartlingseg@unk.edu. *Application contact:* Linda Johnson, Director, Graduate Admissions and Programs, 308-865-8841, Fax: 308-865-8837, E-mail: johnsonli@unk.edu.
Website: http://www.unk.edu/academics/ted/index.php

University of Nevada, Las Vegas, Graduate College, College of Education, Department of Educational Psychology and Higher Education, Las Vegas, NV 89154-3002. Offers chief diversity officer in higher education (Certificate); college sport leadership (Certificate); educational psychology (M Ed, MS, PhD, Ed S); higher education (M Ed, PhD, Certificate); psychology/learning and technology (PhD), including learning and technology; workforce development/educational leadership (PhD); PhD/JD. *Program availability:* Part-time, evening/weekend, 100% online, blended/hybrid learning. *Faculty:* 20 full-time (14 women), 5 part-time/adjunct (3 women). *Students:* 74 full-time (55 women), 100 part-time (69 women); includes 60 minority (17 Black or African American, non-Hispanic/Latino; 11 Asian, non-Hispanic/Latino; 26 Hispanic/Latino; 6 Two or more races, non-Hispanic/Latino), 5 international. Average age 36. 121 applicants, 58% accepted, 46 enrolled. In 2016, 22 master's, 14 doctorates, 8 other advanced degrees awarded. *Degree requirements:* For master's, comprehensive exam (for some programs), thesis (for some programs); for doctorate, comprehensive exam, thesis/dissertation. *Entrance requirements:* For master's, GRE General Test or GMAT (for some programs), letters of recommendation; writing sample; bachelor's degree; for doctorate, GMAT or GRE General Test, writing exam; for other advanced degree, GRE General Test (for some programs). Additional exam requirements/recommendations for international students: Required—TOEFL (minimum score 550 paper-based; 80 iBT), IELTS (minimum score 7). *Application deadline:* For fall admission, 3/15 for domestic students, 5/1 for international students. Application fee: $60 ($95 for international students). Electronic applications accepted. *Expenses:* $269.25 per credit, $792 per 3-credit course; $9,634 per year resident; $23,274 per year non-resident; $7,094 fees non-resident (7 credits or more); $1,307 annual health insurance fee. *Financial support:* In 2016–17, 24 research assistantships with partial tuition reimbursements (averaging $14,790 per year), 21 teaching assistantships with partial tuition reimbursements (averaging $15,631 per year) were awarded; institutionally sponsored loans, scholarships/grants, health care benefits, and unspecified assistantships also available. Financial award application deadline: 3/15. *Faculty research:* Innovation and change in educational settings; educational policy, finance, and marketing; psycho-educational assessment; student retention, persistence, development, language, and culture; statistical modeling, program evaluation, qualitative and quantitative research methods. *Total annual research expenditures:* $158,780. *Unit head:* Dr. LeAnn Putney, Chair/ Professor, 702-895-4879, Fax: 702-895-1658, E-mail: leann.putney@unlv.edu. *Application contact:* Dr. Steve McCafferty, Graduate Coordinator, 702-895-3245, Fax: 702-895-1658, E-mail: mccaffes@unlv.nevada.edu.
Website: http://education.unlv.edu/ephe/

University of New Hampshire, Graduate School, College of Health and Human Services, Department of Occupational Therapy, Durham, NH 03824. Offers assistive technology (Postbaccalaureate Certificate); occupational therapy (MS). *Accreditation:* AOTA. *Program availability:* Part-time. *Degree requirements:* For master's, thesis or alternative. *Entrance requirements:* For master's, GRE General Test, current certification as an OTR from the American Occupational Therapy Board or World Federation of Occupational Therapy. Additional exam requirements/recommendations for international students: Required—TOEFL (minimum score 550 paper-based; 80 iBT). *Application deadline:* For fall admission, 4/1 for domestic and international students. Applications are processed on a rolling basis. Application fee: $65. Electronic applications accepted. *Financial support:* Fellowships, research assistantships, teaching assistantships, career-related internships or fieldwork, Federal Work-Study, and scholarships/grants available. Support available to part-time students. Financial award application deadline: 2/15. *Unit head:* Lou Ann Griswold, Chair, 603-862-3416. *Application contact:* Deb Smith, 603-862-3221, E-mail: deb.smith@unh.edu.
Website: http://www.chhs.unh.edu/ot

University of New Mexico, Graduate Studies, College of University Libraries and Learning Sciences, Albuquerque, NM 87131-2039. Offers organization, information and learning sciences (MA, PhD, Ed S). *Accreditation:* NCATE. *Program availability:* Part-time, evening/weekend, online learning. *Faculty:* 12 full-time (9 women). *Students:* 26 full-time (15 women), 76 part-time (51 women); includes 42 minority (1 Black or African American, non-Hispanic/Latino; 4 American Indian or Alaska Native, non-Hispanic/ Latino; 5 Asian, non-Hispanic/Latino; 29 Hispanic/Latino; 3 Two or more races, non-Hispanic/Latino), 6 international. Average age 45. 30 applicants, 80% accepted, 21 enrolled. In 2016, 19 master's, 4 doctorates awarded. *Degree requirements:* For master's, comprehensive exam, thesis or alternative; for doctorate, comprehensive exam, thesis/dissertation. *Entrance requirements:* For master's, minimum GPA of 3.0 in last 60 hours of course work, bachelor's degree; for doctorate, GRE General Test, MAT, master's degree, minimum GPA of 3.5. Additional exam requirements/recommendations for international students: Required—TOEFL. *Application deadline:* For fall admission, 3/ 15 for domestic and international students; for spring admission, 10/15 for domestic and international students. Application fee: $50. Electronic applications accepted. *Financial support:* Fellowships, research assistantships, teaching assistantships with tuition reimbursements, and career-related internships or fieldwork available. Financial award application deadline: 3/1; financial award applicants required to submit FAFSA. *Faculty research:* Adult learning, distance education, instructional multimedia, organizational learning and development, transformational learning, workplace and learning environment factors that enhance learning and productivity, program and organization evaluation and reform, effects of technology on learning and problem solving. *Total annual research expenditures:* $50,371. *Unit head:* Dr. Charlotte Gunawardens, Program Director, 505-277-5046, Fax: 505-277-1427, E-mail: lani@unm.edu. *Application contact:* Linda Wood, Program Coordinator, 505-277-4131, Fax: 505-277-1427, E-mail: woodl@unm.edu.
Website: http://oils.unm.edu/

The University of North Carolina at Charlotte, Cato College of Education, Department of Educational Leadership, Charlotte, NC 28223-0001. Offers education research, measurement, and evaluation (PhD); educational leadership (Ed D); instructional systems technology (M Ed, Graduate Certificate); quantitative analysis (Graduate Certificate); school administration (MSA, Post-Master's Certificate); university and college teaching (Graduate Certificate). *Program availability:* Part-time, evening/ weekend, 100% online, blended/hybrid learning. *Faculty:* 19 full-time (12 women), 6 part-time/adjunct (4 women). *Students:* 32 full-time (25 women), 221 part-time (137 women); includes 65 minority (54 Black or African American, non-Hispanic/Latino; 6 Asian, non-Hispanic/Latino; 4 Hispanic/Latino; 1 Two or more races, non-Hispanic/ Latino), 4 international. Average age 37. 115 applicants, 86% accepted, 83 enrolled. In 2016, 32 master's, 8 doctorates, 26 other advanced degrees awarded. *Degree requirements:* For master's, thesis or alternative, internship, capstone project; for doctorate, comprehensive exam (for some programs), thesis/dissertation, portfolio. *Entrance requirements:* For master's, GRE or MAT, bachelor's degree, or its U.S. equivalent, from regionally-accredited college or university; minimum overall GPA of 3.5 on all previous work beyond high school; statement of purpose (essay); at least three recommendation forms; for doctorate, GRE or MAT, bachelor's degree (or its U.S. equivalent) from regionally-accredited college or university; minimum overall GPA of 3.5 in master's degree program; for other advanced degree, bachelor's degree from regionally-accredited university; minimum GPA of 2.75 on all post-secondary work attempted; transcripts; personal statement outlining why the applicant seeks admission to the program. Additional exam requirements/recommendations for international students: Required—TOEFL (minimum score 523 paper-based, 70 iBT) or IELTS (6.5). *Application deadline:* For fall admission, 3/1 priority date for domestic and international students; for spring admission, 10/1 priority date for domestic and international students; for summer admission, 4/1 priority date for domestic and international students. Applications are processed on a rolling basis. Application fee: $75. Electronic applications accepted. *Expenses:* Tuition, state resident: full-time $4252. Tuition, nonresident: full-time $17,423. *Required fees:* $3026. Tuition and fees vary according to course load and program. *Financial support:* In 2016–17, 8 students received support, including 7 research assistantships (averaging $11,650 per year), 1 teaching assistantship (averaging $11,136 per year); career-related internships or fieldwork, institutionally sponsored loans, scholarships/grants, and unspecified assistantships also available. Support available to part-time students. Financial award application deadline: 3/1; financial award applicants required to submit FAFSA. *Total annual research expenditures:* $4 million. *Unit head:* Dr. Claudia Flowers, Chair, 704-687-8862, E-mail: cpflower@uncc.edu. *Application contact:* Kathy B. Giddings, Director of Graduate Admissions, 704-687-5503, Fax: 704-687-1668, E-mail: gradadm@uncc.edu.
Website: http://edld.uncc.edu/

The University of North Carolina at Greensboro, Graduate School, School of Education, Department of Teacher Education and Higher Education, Greensboro, NC 27412-5001. Offers college teaching and adult learning (Certificate); curriculum and instruction (M Ed), including chemistry education, elementary education, English as a second language, French education, instructional technology, mathematics education, middle grades education, reading education, science education, social studies education, Spanish education; curriculum and teaching (PhD), including higher education, teacher education and development; English as a second language (Certificate); higher education (M Ed); supervision (M Ed). *Accreditation:* NCATE. *Program availability:* Part-time. *Degree requirements:* For doctorate, thesis/dissertation. *Entrance requirements:* For master's and doctorate, GRE General Test. Additional exam requirements/recommendations for international students: Required—TOEFL. Electronic applications accepted. *Faculty research:* Community college literacy program, middle school mathematics/computer mathematics.

The University of North Carolina Wilmington, Watson College of Education, Department of Instructional Technology, Foundations and Secondary Education, Wilmington, NC 28403-3297. Offers academically or intellectually gifted (M Ed); English as a second language (M Ed, MAT); instructional technology (MS); physical education and health (M Ed, MAT); secondary education (M Ed, MAT); Spanish (MAT); Spanish education (MASS). *Program availability:* Part-time. *Faculty:* 17 full-time (11 women). *Students:* 36 full-time (22 women), 62 part-time (49 women); includes 17 minority (12 Black or African American, non-Hispanic/Latino; 3 Hispanic/Latino; 2 Two or more races, non-Hispanic/Latino), 5 international. Average age 34. 89 applicants, 89% accepted, 59 enrolled. In 2016, 36 master's awarded. *Degree requirements:* For master's, comprehensive exam (for some programs), thesis (for some programs), thesis or research project. *Entrance requirements:* For master's, GRE or MAT, statement of interest, 3 letters of recommendation, minimum GPA of 3.0 in undergraduate work. Additional exam requirements/recommendations for international students: Required—TOEFL (minimum score 79 iBT), IELTS (minimum score 6.5). *Application deadline:* For fall admission, 5/15 for domestic students; for spring admission, 10/15 for domestic students; for summer admission, 3/15 for domestic students. Applications are processed on a rolling basis. Application fee: $60. Electronic applications accepted. *Expenses:* Contact institution. *Financial support:* Scholarships/grants and unspecified assistantships available. Financial award application deadline: 3/15; financial award applicants required to submit FAFSA. *Unit head:* Dr. Donyell Roseboro, Chair, 910-962-2289, Fax: 910-962-3609, E-mail: roseborod@uncw.edu. *Application contact:* Dr. Mahnaz Moallem, Graduate Coordinator, 910-962-4183, E-mail: moallemm@uncw.edu.
Website: http://www.uncw.edu/ed/itfse/

University of North Dakota, Graduate School, College of Education and Human Development, Program in Instructional Design and Technology, Grand Forks, ND 58202. Offers M Ed, MS. *Degree requirements:* For master's, comprehensive exam, thesis or alternative. *Entrance requirements:* For master's, minimum GPA of 3.0. Additional exam requirements/recommendations for international students: Required—TOEFL (minimum score 550 paper-based; 79 iBT), IELTS (minimum score 6.5). *Application deadline:* For fall admission, 8/1 priority date for domestic students, 5/1 priority date for international students; for spring admission, 12/1 priority date for domestic students, 9/1 priority date for international students. Applications are processed on a rolling basis. Application fee: $35. Electronic applications accepted. *Financial support:* Fellowships with full and partial tuition reimbursements, research assistantships with full and partial tuition reimbursements, teaching assistantships with full tuition reimbursements, Federal Work-Study, institutionally sponsored loans, scholarships/grants, health care benefits, and unspecified assistantships available. Support available to part-time students. Financial award application deadline: 3/15; financial award applicants required to submit FAFSA. *Unit head:* Dr. Richard Van Eck, Graduate Director, 701-777-3239, Fax: 701-777-4365, E-mail: richard.vaneck@und.edu. *Application contact:* Staci Wells, Admissions Specialist, 701-777-0748, Fax: 701-777-3619, E-mail: staci.wells@gradschool.und.edu.

University of Northern Iowa, Graduate College, College of Education, Department of Curriculum and Instruction, MA Program in Instructional Technology, Cedar Falls, IA 50614. Offers instructional technology (MA); performance and training technology (MA); school library endorsement (MA). *Degree requirements:* For master's, comprehensive exam, thesis or alternative. *Entrance requirements:* For master's, minimum GPA of 3.0. Additional exam requirements/recommendations for international students: Required—TOEFL (minimum score 500 paper-based; 61 iBT). Electronic applications accepted.

University of Northern Iowa, Graduate College, College of Education, Department of Curriculum and Instruction, MA Program in School Library Studies, Cedar Falls, IA 50614. Offers MA. *Program availability:* Part-time, evening/weekend. *Degree requirements:* For master's, comprehensive exam (for some programs), thesis or alternative, comprehensive portfolio. *Entrance requirements:* For master's, minimum GPA of 3.0. Additional exam requirements/recommendations for international students: Required—TOEFL (minimum score 500 paper-based; 61 iBT). Electronic applications accepted.

University of North Florida, College of Education and Human Services, Department of Leadership, School Counseling and Sport Management, Jacksonville, FL 32224. Offers counselor education (M Ed), including school counseling; educational leadership (M Ed, Ed D), including athletic administration (M Ed), educational leadership, educational technology (M Ed), instructional leadership (M Ed). *Program availability:* Part-time, evening/weekend. *Faculty:* 18 full-time (10 women), 1 (woman) part-time/adjunct. *Students:* 74 full-time (61 women), 219 part-time (149 women); includes 93 minority (65 Black or African American, non-Hispanic/Latino; 1 American Indian or Alaska Native, non-Hispanic/Latino; 3 Asian, non-Hispanic/Latino; 15 Hispanic/Latino; 1 Native Hawaiian or other Pacific Islander, non-Hispanic/Latino; 8 Two or more races, non-Hispanic/Latino), 14 international. Average age 34. 128 applicants, 57% accepted, 55 enrolled. In 2016, 94 master's, 7 doctorates awarded. *Degree requirements:* For doctorate, thesis/dissertation. *Entrance requirements:* For master's, GRE General Test, minimum GPA of 3.0 in last 60 hours, interview, 3 letters of recommendation; for doctorate, GRE General Test, master's degree, interview, 3 letters of recommendation, writing sample. Additional exam requirements/recommendations for international students: Required—TOEFL (minimum score 500 paper-based). *Application deadline:* For fall admission, 5/1 priority date for domestic students, 5/1 for international students. Application fee: $30. Electronic applications accepted. Tuition and fees vary according to course load, campus/location and program. *Financial support:* In 2016–17, 48 students received support, including 1 research assistantship (averaging $4,445 per year), 1 teaching assistantship (averaging $5,378 per year); career-related internships or fieldwork, Federal Work-Study, scholarships/grants, tuition waivers (partial), and unspecified assistantships also available. Support available to part-time students. Financial award application deadline: 4/1; financial award applicants required to submit FAFSA. *Faculty research:* Counseling: ethics; lesbian, bisexual and transgender issues; educational leadership: school culture and climate; educational assessment and accountability; school safety and student discipline. *Total annual research expenditures:* $45,589. *Unit head:* Dr. Liz Gregg, Chair, 904-620-5199, E-mail: liz.gregg@unf.edu. *Application contact:* Dr. Amanda Pascale, Director, The Graduate School, 904-620-1360, Fax: 904-620-1362, E-mail: graduateschool@unf.edu.
Website: http://www.unf.edu/coehs/lscsm/

University of Oklahoma, Jeannine Rainbolt College of Education, Department of Educational Psychology, Program in Instructional Psychology and Technology, Norman, OK 73019. Offers 21st century teaching and learning (M Ed); educational psychology (M Ed); instructional design and technology (M Ed); instructional psychology and technology (PhD); integrating technology in teaching (M Ed). *Program availability:* Part-time. *Students:* 15 full-time (13 women), 29 part-time (21 women); includes 6 minority (1 Black or African American, non-Hispanic/Latino; 1 American Indian or Alaska Native, non-Hispanic/Latino; 1 Asian, non-Hispanic/Latino; 3 Hispanic/Latino), 13 international. Average age 33. 28 applicants, 61% accepted, 12 enrolled. In 2016, 11 master's, 2 doctorates awarded. Terminal master's awarded for partial completion of doctoral program. *Degree requirements:* For doctorate, comprehensive exam, thesis/dissertation. *Entrance requirements:* For doctorate, GRE. Additional exam requirements/recommendations for international students: Required—TOEFL (minimum score 79 iBT) or IELTS (minimum score 6.5). *Application deadline:* Applications are processed on a rolling basis. Application fee: $50 ($100 for international students). Electronic applications accepted. *Expenses:* Tuition, state resident: full-time $4886; part-time $203.60 per credit hour. Tuition, nonresident: full-time $18,989; part-time $791.20 per credit hour. *Required fees:* $3283; $126.25 per credit hour. $126.50 per semester. *Financial support:* In 2016–17, 28 students received support. Fellowships with full and partial tuition reimbursements available, research assistantships with full and partial tuition reimbursements available, teaching assistantships with full and partial tuition reimbursements available, and scholarships/grants available. Financial award application deadline: 6/1; financial award applicants required to submit FAFSA. *Faculty research:* Social and cultural implications of technologies; girls interest in stem; epistemic stance; teacher learning and development. *Unit head:* Dr. Nancy E. Marchand-Martella, Chair, Department of Educational Psychology, 405-325-0624, Fax: 405-325-6655, E-mail: nmarchand-martella@ou.edu. *Application contact:* Anna Steele, Graduate Programs Specialist, 405-325-4525, Fax: 405-325-7390, E-mail: jrcoe_gps@ou.edu.
Website: http://www.ou.edu/education/edpy

University of Pennsylvania, Graduate School of Education, Division of Teaching, Learning, and Leadership, Program in Learning Sciences and Technologies, Philadelphia, PA 19104. Offers MS Ed. *Students:* 17 full-time (13 women), 5 part-time (4 women); includes 5 minority (2 Black or African American, non-Hispanic/Latino; 2 Asian, non-Hispanic/Latino; 1 Hispanic/Latino), 13 international. Average age 27. 60 applicants, 70% accepted, 10 enrolled. In 2016, 14 master's awarded. *Expenses:* *Tuition:* Full-time $31,068; part-time $5762 per course. *Required fees:* $3200; $336 per course. Full-time tuition and fees vary according to degree level, program and student level. Part-time tuition and fees vary according to course load, degree level and program.

University of Phoenix–Online Campus, School of Advanced Studies, Phoenix, AZ 85034-7209. Offers business administration (DBA); education (Ed S); educational leadership (Ed D), including curriculum and instruction, education technology, educational leadership; health administration (DHA); higher education administration (PhD); industrial/organizational psychology (PhD); nursing (PhD); organizational leadership (DM), including information systems and technology, organizational leadership. *Program availability:* Evening/weekend, online learning. *Degree requirements:* For doctorate, thesis/dissertation. *Entrance requirements:* Additional exam requirements/recommendations for international students: Required—TOEFL, TOEIC (Test of English as an International Communication), Berlitz Online English Proficiency Exam, PTE, or IELTS. Electronic applications accepted. *Expenses:* Contact institution.

University of Phoenix–Washington D.C. Campus, College of Education, Washington, DC 20001. Offers administration and supervision (MA Ed); adult education and training (MA Ed); computer education (MA Ed); curriculum and instruction (MA Ed, Ed D); early childhood education (MA Ed); education (Ed S); educational leadership (Ed D); educational technology (Ed D); elementary teacher education (MA Ed); English and language arts education (MA Ed); English as a second language (MA Ed); higher education administration (PhD); mathematics education (MA Ed); secondary teacher education (MA Ed); special education (MA Ed); teacher leadership (MA Ed).

University of St. Francis, College of Business and Health Administration, School of Professional Studies, Joliet, IL 60435-6169. Offers e-learning (Certificate); management of training and development (Certificate); training and development (MS); training specialist (Certificate). *Accreditation:* ACBSP. *Program availability:* Part-time, evening/weekend, 100% online. *Faculty:* 1 (woman) full-time, 2 part-time/adjunct (both women). *Students:* 6 full-time (4 women), 49 part-time (37 women); includes 20 minority (13 Black or African American, non-Hispanic/Latino; 1 Asian, non-Hispanic/Latino; 5 Hispanic/Latino; 1 Native Hawaiian or other Pacific Islander, non-Hispanic/Latino). Average age 42. 36 applicants, 47% accepted, 13 enrolled. In 2016, 26 master's, 3 other advanced degrees awarded. *Entrance requirements:* Additional exam requirements/recommendations for international students: Required—TOEFL (minimum score 550 paper-based; 79 iBT), IELTS (minimum score 6). *Application deadline:* Applications are processed on a rolling basis. Application fee: $30. Electronic applications accepted. Application fee is waived when completed online. *Expenses:* *Tuition:* Part-time $739 per credit hour. *Required fees:* $125 per semester. Part-time tuition and fees vary according to degree level and program. *Financial support:* In 2016–17, 8 students received support. Tuition waivers (partial) and unspecified assistantships available. Support available to part-time students. Financial award applicants required to submit FAFSA. *Unit head:* Dr. Orlando Griego, Dean, 815-740-3395, Fax: 815-740-3537, E-mail: ogriego@stfrancis.edu. *Application contact:* Sandra Sloka, Director of Admissions for Graduate and Degree Completion Programs, 800-735-7500, Fax: 815-740-3431, E-mail: ssloka@stfrancis.edu.
Website: http://www.stfrancis.edu/academics/college-of-business-health-administration

University of Saint Joseph, Department of Education, West Hartford, CT 06117-2700. Offers curriculum and instruction (MA); educational technology (MA); literacy internship (MA); multiple intelligences (MA); reading/language (MA); TESOL (MA). *Program availability:* Part-time, evening/weekend. *Degree requirements:* For master's, comprehensive exam, thesis or alternative. *Entrance requirements:* For master's, 2 letters of recommendation. Electronic applications accepted. Application fee is waived when completed online. *Expenses:* *Tuition:* Full-time $14,580; part-time $729 per credit hour. *Required fees:* $920; $46 per credit hour. Tuition and fees vary according to course load, degree level and program.

University of San Francisco, School of Education, Department of Learning and Instruction, San Francisco, CA 94117-1080. Offers digital technologies for teaching and learning (MA); learning and instruction (MA, Ed D); special education (MA, Ed D); teaching reading (MA). *Program availability:* Part-time, evening/weekend. *Faculty:* 9 full-time (5 women), 2 part-time/adjunct (both women). *Students:* 79 full-time (61 women), 30 part-time (23 women); includes 41 minority (12 Black or African American, non-Hispanic/Latino; 12 Asian, non-Hispanic/Latino; 14 Hispanic/Latino; 3 Two or more races, non-Hispanic/Latino), 7 international. Average age 37. 64 applicants, 94% accepted, 41 enrolled. In 2016, 20 master's, 8 doctorates awarded. *Degree requirements:* For doctorate, thesis/dissertation. *Entrance requirements:* Additional exam requirements/recommendations for international students: Required—TOEFL, IELTS, PTE. *Application deadline:* For fall admission, 3/1 priority date for domestic and international students; for spring admission, 11/1 priority date for domestic and international students. Applications are processed on a rolling basis. Application fee: $55 ($65 for international students). Electronic applications accepted. *Expenses:* *Tuition:* Full-time $23,310; part-time $1295 per credit. Tuition and fees vary according to course load, degree level, campus/location and program. *Financial support:* In 2016–17, 13 students received support. Fellowships, research assistantships, and teaching assistantships available. Financial award application deadline: 3/2; financial award applicants required to submit FAFSA. *Unit head:* Dr. Kevin Oh, Chair, 415-422-2099. *Application contact:* Amy Fogliani, Admission Coordinator, 415-422-5467, E-mail: schoolofeducation@usfca.edu.

University of San Francisco, School of Education, Department of Teacher Education, San Francisco, CA 94117-1080. Offers digital media and learning (MA); teaching (MA); teaching reading (MA); teaching urban education and social justice (MA). *Program availability:* Part-time. *Faculty:* 6 full-time (2 women), 50 part-time/adjunct (33 women). *Students:* 212 full-time (154 women), 25 part-time (20 women); includes 106 minority (16 Black or African American, non-Hispanic/Latino; 30 Asian, non-Hispanic/Latino; 48 Hispanic/Latino; 2 Native Hawaiian or other Pacific Islander, non-Hispanic/Latino; 10 Two or more races, non-Hispanic/Latino), 1 international. Average age 29. 246 applicants, 95% accepted, 125 enrolled. In 2016, 127 master's awarded. *Entrance requirements:* Additional exam requirements/recommendations for international students: Required—TOEFL, IELTS, PTE. *Application deadline:* For fall admission, 3/1 priority date for domestic and international students; for spring admission, 10/15 priority date for domestic students, 10/1 for international students. Applications are processed on a rolling basis. Electronic applications accepted. *Expenses:* *Tuition:* Full-time $23,310; part-time $1295 per credit. Tuition and fees vary according to course load, degree level, campus/location and program. *Financial support:* In 2016–17, 25 students received support. Applicants required to submit FAFSA. *Unit head:* Dr. Noah Borrero, Chair, 415-422-6481. *Application contact:* Peter Cole, Admission Coordinator, 415-422-5467, E-mail: schoolofeducation@usfca.edu.
Website: https://www.usfca.edu/catalog/graduate/school-of-education/programs-teacher-education

University of Sioux Falls, Fredrikson School of Education, Sioux Falls, SD 57105-1699. Offers educational administration (Ed S), including principal leadership, superintendent and district leadership; leadership in reading (M Ed); leadership in schools (M Ed); leadership in technology (M Ed); teaching (M Ed). Admission in summer only. *Accreditation:* NCATE. *Program availability:* Part-time, evening/weekend. *Degree requirements:* For master's, comprehensive exam (for some programs), research application project; for Ed S, comprehensive exam, portfolio. *Entrance requirements:* For master's, minimum GPA of 3.0, 1 year of teaching experience; for Ed S, minimum 3 years of teaching experience, minimum cumulative GPA of 3.5, 1 year of administrative experience. Additional exam requirements/recommendations for international students: Required—TOEFL. *Faculty research:* Reading, literacy, leadership.

University of South Africa, College of Human Sciences, Pretoria, South Africa. Offers adult education (M Ed); African languages (MA, PhD); African politics (MA, PhD);

Afrikaans (MA, PhD); ancient history (MA, PhD); ancient Near Eastern studies (MA, PhD); anthropology (MA, PhD); applied linguistics (MA); Arabic (MA, PhD); archaeology (MA); art history (MA); Biblical archaeology (MA); Biblical studies (M Th, D Th, PhD); Christian spirituality (M Th, D Th); church history (M Th, D Th); classical studies (MA, PhD); clinical psychology (MA); communication (MA, PhD); comparative education (M Ed, Ed D); consulting psychology (D Admin, D Com, PhD); curriculum studies (M Ed, Ed D); development studies (M Admin, MA, D Admin, PhD); didactics (M Ed, Ed D); education (M Tech); education management (M Ed, Ed D); educational psychology (M Ed); English (MA); environmental education (M Ed); French (MA, PhD); German (MA, PhD); Greek (MA); guidance and counseling (M Ed); health studies (MA, PhD), including health sciences education (MA), health services management (MA), medical and surgical nursing science (critical care general) (MA), midwifery and neonatal nursing science (MA), trauma and emergency care (MA); history (MA, PhD); history of education (Ed D); inclusive education (M Ed, Ed D); information and communications technology policy and regulation (MA); information science (MA, MIS, PhD); international politics (MA, PhD); Islamic studies (MA, PhD); Italian (MA, PhD); Judaica (MA, PhD); linguistics (MA, PhD); mathematical education (M Ed); mathematics education (MA); missiology (M Th, D Th); modern Hebrew (MA, PhD); musicology (MA, MMus, D Mus, PhD); natural science education (M Ed); New Testament (M Th, D Th); Old Testament (D Th); pastoral therapy (M Th, D Th); philosophy (MA); philosophy of education (M Ed, Ed D); politics (MA, PhD); Portuguese (MA, PhD); practical theology (M Th, D Th); psychology (MA, MS, PhD); psychology of education (M Ed, Ed D); public health (MA); religious studies (MA, D Th, PhD); Romance languages (MA); Russian (MA, PhD); Semitic languages (MA, PhD); social behavior studies in HIV/AIDS (MA); social science (mental health) (MA); social science in development studies (MA); social science in psychology (MA); social science in social work (MA); social science in sociology (MA); social work (MSW, DSW, PhD); socio-education (M Ed, Ed D); sociolinguistics (MA); sociology (MA, PhD); Spanish (MA, PhD); systematic theology (M Th, D Th); TESOL (teaching English to speakers of other languages) (MA); theological ethics (M Th, D Th); theory of literature (MA, PhD); urban ministries (D Th); urban ministry (M Th).

University of South Alabama, College of Education and Professional Studies, Department of Counseling and Instructional Sciences, Mobile, AL 36688. Offers clinical mental health counseling (MS); educational media (M Ed, MS); instructional design and development (MS, PhD); school counseling (M Ed). *Accreditation:* NCATE. *Program availability:* Part-time. *Faculty:* 12 full-time (8 women), 6 part-time/adjunct (5 women). *Students:* 104 full-time (83 women), 67 part-time (56 women); includes 49 minority (35 Black or African American, non-Hispanic/Latino; 2 American Indian or Alaska Native, non-Hispanic/Latino; 2 Asian, non-Hispanic/Latino; 8 Hispanic/Latino; 1 Native Hawaiian or other Pacific Islander, non-Hispanic/Latino; 1 Two or more races, non-Hispanic/Latino), 4 international. Average age 35. 59 applicants, 51% accepted, 26 enrolled. In 2016, 28 master's, 8 doctorates awarded. *Degree requirements:* For master's, comprehensive exam; for doctorate, comprehensive exam, thesis/dissertation. *Entrance requirements:* For master's, GRE General Test or MAT, minimum GPA of 3.0, two letters of recommendation; for doctorate, GRE, three letters of recommendation, master's degree in field or completion of prerequisites, resume. Additional exam requirements/recommendations for international students: Required—TOEFL (minimum score 525 paper-based; 71 iBT). *Application deadline:* For fall admission, 6/15 for domestic students, 5/15 for international students; for spring admission, 12/1 for domestic students, 11/1 for international students; for summer admission, 4/1 for domestic students. Applications are processed on a rolling basis. Application fee: $35. Electronic applications accepted. *Expenses:* Tuition, state resident: full-time $9768; part-time $407 per credit hour. Tuition, nonresident: full-time $19,536; part-time $814 per credit hour. *Financial support:* Fellowships, research assistantships, teaching assistantships, career-related internships or fieldwork, Federal Work-Study, institutionally sponsored loans, scholarships/grants, and unspecified assistantships available. Support available to part-time students. Financial award application deadline: 5/31; financial award applicants required to submit FAFSA. *Faculty research:* Agency counseling, rehabilitation counseling, school psychometry. *Unit head:* Dr. Tres Stefurak, Department Chair, 251-380-2734, Fax: 251-380-2713, E-mail: jstefurak@southalabama.edu. *Application contact:* Dr. Susan Santoli, Director of Graduate Studies, 251-380-2836, Fax: 251-380-2758, E-mail: ssantoli@southalabama.edu.
Website: http://www.southalabama.edu/colleges/ceps/cins/

University of South Carolina, The Graduate School, College of Education, Department of Educational Studies, Program in Educational Technology, Columbia, SC 29208. Offers M Ed. *Accreditation:* NCATE. *Program availability:* Part-time, online learning. *Degree requirements:* For master's, comprehensive exam. *Entrance requirements:* For master's, GRE or MAT, interview, letters of intent and reference.

University of South Carolina Aiken, Program in Educational Technology, Aiken, SC 29801. Offers M Ed. Program offered with University of South Carolina in Columbia. *Program availability:* Part-time, evening/weekend, online only, 100% online. *Faculty:* 4 full-time (2 women). *Students:* 4 part-time (2 women); includes 1 minority (Black or African American, non-Hispanic/Latino). Average age 33. 3 applicants, 33% accepted, 1 enrolled. In 2016, 4 master's awarded. *Degree requirements:* For master's, culminating electronic portfolio, professional conference presentations. *Entrance requirements:* For master's, GRE or MAT. Additional exam requirements/recommendations for international students: Required—TOEFL (minimum score 550 paper-based; 80 iBT). *Application deadline:* Applications are processed on a rolling basis. Application fee: $45. Electronic applications accepted. *Expenses:* Tuition, state resident: full-time $12,798; part-time $533 per credit hour. Tuition, nonresident: full-time $27,408; part-time $1142 per credit hour. *Required fees:* $11 per credit hour. $25 per semester. Full-time tuition and fees vary according to course load. *Financial support:* In 2016–17, 1 student received support. Fellowships with partial tuition reimbursements available, career-related internships or fieldwork, Federal Work-Study, scholarships/grants, tuition waivers (partial), and unspecified assistantships available. Support available to part-time students. Financial award application deadline: 3/15; financial award applicants required to submit FAFSA. *Faculty research:* Educational technology, e-learning, online and distance education, professional learning, and mobile learning, technology-enhanced learning environments, instructional design, and curriculum development. *Total annual research expenditures:* $1.2 million. *Unit head:* Dr. Erin Besser, Educational Technology Program Coordinator, 803-641-3712, E-mail: erinbe@usca.edu. *Application contact:* Dan Robb, Associate Vice Chancellor for Enrollment Management, 803-641-3487, Fax: 803-641-3727, E-mail: danr@usca.edu.
Website: http://edtech.usca.edu/

The University of South Dakota, Graduate School, School of Education, Division of Curriculum and Instruction, Program in Technology for Education and Training, Vermillion, SD 57069. Offers MS. *Program availability:* Part-time, evening/weekend, 100% online, blended/hybrid learning. *Degree requirements:* For master's, comprehensive exam, thesis or alternative. *Entrance requirements:* For master's, GRE, minimum GPA of 2.7. Additional exam requirements/recommendations for international students: Required—TOEFL (minimum score 550 paper-based; 79 iBT). Electronic applications accepted.

University of Southern Mississippi, Graduate School, College of Education and Psychology, Department of Curriculum, Instruction and Special Education, Hattiesburg, MS 39406. Offers elementary education (M Ed, PhD); instructional technology (MS); instructional technology and design (PhD); secondary education (MAT); special education (M Ed, PhD). *Program availability:* Part-time, online learning. *Degree requirements:* For master's, comprehensive exam, thesis (for some programs); for doctorate, comprehensive exam, thesis/dissertation. *Entrance requirements:* For master's, GRE General Test, MAT, minimum GPA of 3.0; for doctorate, GRE General Test, minimum GPA of 3.5. Additional exam requirements/recommendations for international students: Required—TOEFL, IELTS. *Application deadline:* For fall admission, 3/1 priority date for domestic students, 3/1 for international students; for spring admission, 1/10 priority date for domestic and international students. Applications are processed on a rolling basis. Application fee: $60. *Expenses: Tuition, area resident:* Full-time $15,708; part-time $437 per credit hour. *Financial support:* Research assistantships with tuition reimbursements, teaching assistantships with full tuition reimbursements, Federal Work-Study, institutionally sponsored loans, scholarships/grants, health care benefits, tuition waivers (partial), and unspecified assistantships available. Financial award application deadline: 3/15; financial award applicants required to submit FAFSA. *Faculty research:* Mathematical problem solving, integrative curriculum, writing process, teacher education models. *Unit head:* Dr. Mary Ariail, Chair, 601-266-5247, Fax: 601-266-4548.
Website: https://www.usm.edu/elementary-special-technology-education

University of South Florida, Innovative Education, Tampa, FL 33620-9951. Offers adult, career and higher education (Graduate Certificate), including college teaching, leadership in developing human resources, leadership in higher education; Africana studies (Graduate Certificate), including diasporas and health disparities, genocide and human rights; aging studies (Graduate Certificate), including gerontology; art research (Graduate Certificate), including museum studies; business foundations (Graduate Certificate); chemical and biomedical engineering (Graduate Certificate), including materials science and engineering, water, health and sustainability; child and family studies (Graduate Certificate), including positive behavior support; civil and industrial engineering (Graduate Certificate), including transportation systems analysis; community and family health (Graduate Certificate), including maternal and child health, social marketing and public health, violence and injury: prevention and intervention, women's health; criminology (Graduate Certificate), including criminal justice administration; educational measurement and research (Graduate Certificate), including evaluation; English (Graduate Certificate), including comparative literary studies, creative writing, professional and technical communication; entrepreneurship (Graduate Certificate); environmental health (Graduate Certificate), including safety management; epidemiology and biostatistics (Graduate Certificate), including applied biostatistics, biostatistics, concepts and tools of epidemiology, epidemiology, epidemiology of infectious diseases; geography, environment and planning (Graduate Certificate), including community development, environmental policy and management, geographical information systems; geology (Graduate Certificate), including hydrogeology; global health (Graduate Certificate), including disaster management, global health and Latin American and Caribbean studies, global health practice, humanitarian assistance, infection control; government and international affairs (Graduate Certificate), including Cuban studies, globalization studies; health policy and management (Graduate Certificate), including health management and leadership, public health policy and programs; hearing specialist: early intervention (Graduate Certificate); industrial and management systems engineering (Graduate Certificate), including systems engineering, technology management; information studies (Graduate Certificate), including school library media specialist; information systems/decision sciences (Graduate Certificate), including analytics and business intelligence; instructional technology (Graduate Certificate), including distance education, Florida digital/virtual educator, instructional design, multimedia design, Web design; internal medicine, bioethics and medical humanities (Graduate Certificate), including biomedical ethics; Latin American and Caribbean studies (Graduate Certificate); mass communications (Graduate Certificate), including multimedia journalism; mathematics and statistics (Graduate Certificate), including mathematics; medicine (Graduate Certificate), including aging and neuroscience, bioinformatics, biotechnology, brain fitness and memory management, clinical investigation, health informatics, health sciences, integrative weight management, intellectual property, medicine and gender, metabolic and nutritional medicine, metabolic cardiology, pharmacy sciences; national and competitive intelligence (Graduate Certificate); psychological and social foundations (Graduate Certificate), including career counseling, college teaching, diversity in education, mental health counseling, school counseling; public affairs (Graduate Certificate), including nonprofit management, public management, research administration; public health (Graduate Certificate), including environmental health, health equity, public health generalist, translational research in adolescent behavioral health; public health practices (Graduate Certificate), including planning for healthy communities; rehabilitation and mental health counseling (Graduate Certificate), including integrative mental health care, marriage and family therapy, rehabilitation technology; secondary education (Graduate Certificate), including ESOL, foreign language education: culture and content, foreign language education: professional; social work (Graduate Certificate), including geriatric social work/clinical gerontology; special education (Graduate Certificate), including autism spectrum disorder, disabilities education: severe/profound; world languages (Graduate Certificate), including teaching English as a second language (TESL) or foreign language. *Expenses:* Tuition, state resident: full-time $7766; part-time $431.43 per credit hour. Tuition, nonresident: full-time $15,789; part-time $877.17 per credit hour. *Required fees:* $37 per term. *Unit head:* Kathy Barnes, Interdisciplinary Programs Coordinator, 813-974-8031, Fax: 813-974-7061, E-mail: barnesk@usf.edu. *Application contact:* Karen Tylinski, Metro Initiatives, 813-974-9943, Fax: 813-974-7061, E-mail: ktylinsk@usf.edu.
Website: http://www.usf.edu/innovative-education/

The University of Tampa, Programs in Education, Tampa, FL 33606-1490. Offers curriculum and instruction (M Ed); instructional design and technology (MS). *Program availability:* Part-time, evening/weekend. *Faculty:* 2 full-time (1 woman), 0 part-time/adjunct (all women). *Students:* 44 full-time (38 women), 18 part-time (14 women); includes 2 minority (both Black or African American, non-Hispanic/Latino), 7 international. Average age 31. 126 applicants, 40% accepted, 29 enrolled. In 2016, 23 master's awarded. *Degree requirements:* For master's, capstone. *Entrance requirements:* For master's, GMAT or GRE, current Florida Professional Teaching Certificate, statement of eligibility for Florida Professional Teaching Certificate, or professional teaching certificate from another state; bachelor's degree in an area of education. Additional exam requirements/recommendations for international students: Required—TOEFL (minimum score 577 paper-based; 90 iBT), IELTS (minimum score 7.5). *Application deadline:* Applications are processed on a rolling basis. Application fee: $40. Electronic applications accepted. *Expenses:* $588 per credit tuition, $40 per term fees. *Financial support:* In 2016–17, 20 students received support. Career-related internships or fieldwork, scholarships/grants, and unspecified assistantships available. Financial award applicants required to submit FAFSA. *Faculty research:* Diversity in the classroom, technology integration, assessment methodologies, complex and ill-structured problem solving, communities of practice. *Unit head:* Dr. Antony Erben, Chair, 813-257-3414, E-mail: terben@ut.edu. *Application contact:* Chanelle Cox, Staff Assistant, Admissions for Graduate and Continuing Studies, 813-253-6249, E-mail:

ccox@ut.edu.
Website: http://www.ut.edu/graduate/education/

The University of Tennessee, Graduate School, College of Education, Health and Human Sciences, Program in Education, Knoxville, TN 37996. Offers art education (MS); counseling education (PhD); cultural studies in education (PhD); curriculum (MS, Ed S); curriculum, educational research and evaluation (Ed D, PhD); early childhood education (PhD); early childhood special education (MS); education of deaf and hard of hearing (MS); educational administration and policy studies (Ed D, PhD); educational administration and supervision (Ed S); educational psychology (Ed D, PhD); elementary education (MS, Ed S); elementary teaching (MS); English education (MS, Ed S); exercise science (PhD); foreign language/ESL education (MS, Ed S); instructional technology (MS, Ed D, PhD, Ed S); literacy, language and ESL education (PhD); literacy, language education, and ESL education (Ed D); mathematics education (MS, Ed S); modified and comprehensive special education (MS); reading education (MS, Ed S); school counseling (Ed S); school psychology (PhD, Ed S); science education (MS, Ed S); secondary teaching (MS); social foundations (MS); social science education (MS, Ed S); socio-cultural foundations of sports and education (PhD); special education (Ed S); teacher education (Ed D, PhD). *Accreditation:* NCATE. *Program availability:* Part-time, evening/weekend. *Degree requirements:* For master's and Ed S, thesis optional; for doctorate, variable foreign language requirement, thesis/dissertation. *Entrance requirements:* For master's, minimum GPA of 2.7; for doctorate and Ed S, GRE General Test, minimum GPA of 2.7. Additional exam requirements/recommendations for international students: Required—TOEFL. Electronic applications accepted.

The University of Tennessee at Chattanooga, School of Education, Chattanooga, TN 37403. Offers counseling (M Ed), including community counseling, school counseling; education (M Ed, Post-Master's Certificate), including elementary education (M Ed), school leadership, secondary education (M Ed), special education (M Ed); educational specialist (Ed S), including educational technology, school psychology; learning and leadership (Ed D), including educational leadership. *Accreditation:* ACA; NCATE. *Program availability:* Part-time. *Faculty:* 13 full-time (8 women), 2 part-time/adjunct (both women). *Students:* 50 full-time (32 women), 157 part-time (107 women); includes 42 minority (28 Black or African American, non-Hispanic/Latino; 4 Asian, non-Hispanic/Latino; 2 Hispanic/Latino; 8 Two or more races, non-Hispanic/Latino), 1 international. Average age 36. 169 applicants, 76% accepted, 49 enrolled. In 2016, 77 master's, 5 other advanced degrees awarded. *Degree requirements:* For master's, comprehensive exam, thesis optional, culminating experience; for doctorate, comprehensive exam, thesis/dissertation; for other advanced degree, internship. *Entrance requirements:* For master's, GRE General Test, PPST 1, teaching certificate; for doctorate, GRE General Test, master's degree, two years of practical work experience in organizational environment; for other advanced degree, GRE General Test, letters of reference. Additional exam requirements/recommendations for international students: Required—TOEFL (minimum score 550 paper-based; 79 iBT), IELTS (minimum score 6). *Application deadline:* For fall admission, 6/15 for domestic students, 7/1 for international students; for spring admission, 11/1 for domestic and international students. Applications are processed on a rolling basis. Application fee: $35 ($40 for international students). Electronic applications accepted. *Expenses:* $9,876 full-time in-state; $25,994 full-time out-of-state; $450 per credit part-time in-state; $1,345 per credit part-time out-of-state. *Financial support:* In 2016–17, 18 research assistantships, 5 teaching assistantships were awarded; career-related internships or fieldwork, institutionally sponsored loans, scholarships/grants, and unspecified assistantships also available. Support available to part-time students. Financial award application deadline: 7/1; financial award applicants required to submit FAFSA. *Faculty research:* School counseling, community counseling, elementary and secondary education, school leadership and administration. *Total annual research expenditures:* $247,231. *Unit head:* Dr. Renee Murley, Director, 423-425-4684, Fax: 423-425-5380, E-mail: renee-murley@utc.edu. *Application contact:* Dr. Joanne Romagni, Dean of the Graduate School, 423-425-4478, Fax: 423-425-5223, E-mail: joanne-romagni@utc.edu.
Website: http://www.utc.edu/school-education/abouttheschool/gradprograms.php

The University of Texas at Austin, Graduate School, College of Education, Department of Curriculum and Instruction, Austin, TX 78712-1111. Offers bilingual/bicultural education (M Ed, MA, PhD); cultural studies in education (M Ed, MA, PhD); early childhood education (M Ed, MA, PhD); language and literacy studies (M Ed, PhD); learning technologies (M Ed, MA, PhD); physical education (M Ed, MA, PhD). Terminal master's awarded for partial completion of doctoral program. *Degree requirements:* For doctorate, thesis/dissertation. *Entrance requirements:* For master's and doctorate, GRE General Test. Electronic applications accepted.

The University of Texas at San Antonio, College of Education and Human Development, Department of Educational Psychology, San Antonio, TX 78207. Offers applied behavioral analysis (Certificate); digital learning design (Certificate); language acquisition and bilingual psychoeducational assessment (Certificate); school psychology (MA). *Program availability:* Part-time. *Faculty:* 11 full-time (6 women), 1 (woman) part-time/adjunct. *Students:* 38 full-time (31 women), 29 part-time (25 women); includes 43 minority (4 Black or African American, non-Hispanic/Latino; 1 Asian, non-Hispanic/Latino; 35 Hispanic/Latino; 3 Two or more races, non-Hispanic/Latino). Average age 28. 23 applicants, 78% accepted, 13 enrolled. In 2016, 16 master's, 16 other advanced degrees awarded. *Degree requirements:* For master's, comprehensive exam, thesis (for some programs). *Entrance requirements:* For master's, GRE, bachelor's degree with 18 credit hours in field of study or in another appropriate field of study, two letters of recommendation, statement of purpose; for Certificate, 18 hours in psychology, sociology, education, or anything related (for applied behavioral analysis); minimum GPA of 2.7 in last 30 hours (for language acquisition and bilingual psychoeducational assessment). Additional exam requirements/recommendations for international students: Required—TOEFL (minimum score 550 paper-based; 79 iBT), IELTS (minimum score 6.5). *Application deadline:* For fall admission, 7/1 for domestic students, 4/1 for international students; for spring admission, 11/1 for domestic students, 9/1 for international students; for summer admission, 3/1 for international students. Applications are processed on a rolling basis. Application fee: $45 ($80 for international students). Electronic applications accepted. *Financial support:* In 2016–17, 9 research assistantships (averaging $2,829 per year) were awarded. Financial award application deadline: 3/5; financial award applicants required to submit FAFSA. *Faculty research:* Teacher consultation and culturally responsive school psychology practices, youth mentoring, cross-age peer mentoring, adolescent connectedness, pair counseling. *Total annual research expenditures:* $91,630. *Unit head:* Dr. Jeremy Sullivan, Department Chair, 210-458-2378, Fax: 210-458-2019, E-mail: jeremy.sullivan@utsa.edu. *Application contact:* Dr. John Pruiett, Development Specialist, 210-458-2721, Fax: 210-458-2019, E-mail: johnny.pruiett@utsa.edu.
Website: http://education.utsa.edu/educational_psychology

The University of Texas at San Antonio, College of Education and Human Development, Department of Interdisciplinary Learning and Teaching, San Antonio, TX 78249-0617. Offers education (MA), including curriculum and instruction, early childhood and elementary education, instructional technology, reading and literacy, special education; interdisciplinary learning and teaching (PhD). *Program availability:* Part-time, evening/weekend. *Faculty:* 25 full-time (18 women), 4 part-time/adjunct (2 women). *Students:* 70 full-time (53 women), 256 part-time (222 women); includes 185 minority (22 Black or African American, non-Hispanic/Latino; 10 Asian, non-Hispanic/Latino; 148 Hispanic/Latino; 1 Native Hawaiian or other Pacific Islander, non-Hispanic/Latino; 4 Two or more races, non-Hispanic/Latino), 4 international. Average age 34. 145 applicants, 88% accepted, 100 enrolled. In 2016, 90 master's, 4 doctorates awarded. *Degree requirements:* For master's, comprehensive exam, thesis optional, 36 hours of course work without thesis (33 with thesis); for doctorate, comprehensive exam, thesis/dissertation, minimum of 60 semester credit hours. *Entrance requirements:* For master's, bachelor's degree with minimum GPA of 3.0 in last 60 hours of coursework; 18 hours of undergraduate coursework in education or related field; for doctorate, GRE, transcripts from all colleges and universities attended, professional vitae demonstrating experience in work environment where education was primary professional emphasis, 3 letters of recommendation, statement of purpose, minimum GPA of 3.5. Additional exam requirements/recommendations for international students: Required—TOEFL (minimum score 550 paper-based; 79 iBT), IELTS (minimum score 6.5). *Application deadline:* For fall admission, 7/1 for domestic students, 4/1 for international students; for spring admission, 11/1 for domestic students, 9/1 for international students. Applications are processed on a rolling basis. Application fee: $45 ($80 for international students). Electronic applications accepted. *Financial support:* Career-related internships or fieldwork, Federal Work-Study, and scholarships/grants available. Support available to part-time students. *Faculty research:* Explorations of science, learning and teaching, family involvement in early childhood, culturally-responsive literacy instruction in diverse settings, STEM education, autism spectrum disorder. *Total annual research expenditures:* $766,662. *Unit head:* Dr. Maria R. Cortez, Department Chair, 210-458-4413, Fax: 210-458-7281, E-mail: mari.cortez@utsa.edu. *Application contact:* Elizabeth Narvaes, Student Development Specialist, 210-458-7443, Fax: 210-458-7281, E-mail: elizabeth.narvaez@utsa.edu.
Website: http://education.utsa.edu/interdisciplinary_learning_and_teaching/

The University of Texas Rio Grande Valley, College of Education and P-16 Integration, Department of Teaching and Learning, Edinburg, TX 78539. Offers curriculum and instruction (M Ed, Ed D); educational technology (M Ed). *Program availability:* Part-time. *Degree requirements:* For master's, comprehensive exam, thesis optional. *Entrance requirements:* For master's, GRE. Additional exam requirements/recommendations for international students: Required—TOEFL, IELTS. Tuition and fees vary according to course load and program. *Faculty research:* Dual language instruction, literacy and technology, teacher education in diverse populations, mathematics and science education.

University of the Sacred Heart, Graduate Programs, Department of Education, Program in Instruction Systems and Education Technology, San Juan, PR 00914-0383. Offers M Ed. *Program availability:* Part-time, evening/weekend. *Degree requirements:* For master's, thesis. *Entrance requirements:* For master's, EXADEP, interview, minimum undergraduate GPA of 2.75.

The University of Toledo, College of Graduate Studies, Judith Herb College of Education, Department of Curriculum and Instruction, Toledo, OH 43606-3390. Offers art education (ME); career and technical education (ME, Ed S); curriculum and instruction (ME, PhD, Ed S); early childhood education (Ed S); education and anthropology (MAE); education and biology (MES); education and chemistry (MES); education and classics (MAE); education and economics (MAE); education and English (MAE); education and French (MAE); education and geology (MES); education and German (MAE); education and history (MAE); education and mathematics (MAE, MES); education and physics (MES); education and political science (MAE); education and sociology (MAE); education and Spanish (MAE); educational media (PhD); educational technology (ME); educational technology: virtual educator (Certificate); elementary education (PhD); English as a second language (MAE); gifted and talented education (PhD); middle childhood education (ME); secondary education (ME, PhD); special education (PhD). *Accreditation:* NCATE. *Program availability:* Part-time, evening/weekend. *Degree requirements:* For master's, comprehensive exam, thesis or alternative; for doctorate, comprehensive exam, thesis/dissertation; for other advanced degree, thesis optional. *Entrance requirements:* For master's, doctorate, and other advanced degree, minimum cumulative GPA of 2.7 for all previous academic work, letters of recommendation. Additional exam requirements/recommendations for international students: Required—TOEFL (minimum score 550 paper-based; 80 iBT). Electronic applications accepted.

University of Utah, Graduate School, College of Education, Department of Educational Psychology, Salt Lake City, UT 84112. Offers clinical mental health counseling (M Ed); counseling psychology (PhD); elementary education (M Ed); instructional design and educational technology (M Ed); instructional design and technology (MS); learning and cognition (MS, PhD); reading and literacy (M Ed, PhD); school counseling (M Ed); school psychology (M Ed, PhD, Ed S); statistics (M Stat). *Accreditation:* APA (one or more programs are accredited). *Faculty:* 23 full-time (12 women), 15 part-time/adjunct (10 women). *Students:* 119 full-time (95 women), 106 part-time (74 women); includes 37 minority (2 Black or African American, non-Hispanic/Latino; 6 Asian, non-Hispanic/Latino; 22 Hispanic/Latino; 7 Two or more races, non-Hispanic/Latino), 6 international. Average age 31. 296 applicants, 27% accepted, 73 enrolled. In 2016, 47 master's, 8 doctorates awarded. Terminal master's awarded for partial completion of doctoral program. *Degree requirements:* For master's, variable foreign language requirement, comprehensive exam (for some programs), thesis (for some programs), projects; for doctorate, variable foreign language requirement, comprehensive exam, thesis/dissertation, oral exam. *Entrance requirements:* For master's and doctorate, GRE General Test, minimum GPA of 3.0. Additional exam requirements/recommendations for international students: Required—TOEFL (minimum score 80 iBT). *Application deadline:* For fall admission, 12/15 for domestic and international students; for winter admission, 11/1 for domestic and international students; for spring admission, 3/15 for domestic and international students. Application fee: $55 ($65 for international students). Electronic applications accepted. *Expenses:* Contact institution. *Financial support:* In 2016–17, 84 students received support, including 12 fellowships with full and partial tuition reimbursements available (averaging $18,000 per year), 21 research assistantships with full and partial tuition reimbursements available (averaging $14,500 per year), 57 teaching assistantships with full and partial tuition reimbursements available (averaging $14,500 per year); career-related internships or fieldwork, Federal Work-Study, institutionally sponsored loans, scholarships/grants, traineeships, health care benefits, and unspecified assistantships also available. Financial award application deadline: 4/1; financial award applicants required to submit FAFSA. *Faculty research:* Autism, computer technology and instruction, cognitive behavior, aging, group counseling. *Total annual research expenditures:* $620,935. *Unit head:* Dr. Anne E. Cook, Chair, 801-581-7148, Fax: 801-581-5566, E-mail: anne.cook@utah.edu. *Application contact:* JoLynn N. Yates, Academic Coordinator, 801-581-7148, Fax: 801-581-5566, E-mail: jo.yates@utah.edu.
Website: http://www.ed.utah.edu/edps/

University of Virginia, Curry School of Education, Department of Leadership, Foundations and Policy, Program in Educational Psychology, Charlottesville, VA 22903. Offers applied developmental science (M Ed); educational evaluation (M Ed);

educational psychology (M Ed, Ed D, Ed S); educational research (Ed D); gifted education (M Ed); instructional technology (M Ed, Ed S); research statistics and evaluation (Ed D); school psychology (Ed D). *Students:* 28 full-time (15 women), 10 part-time (7 women); includes 8 minority (2 Black or African American, non-Hispanic/Latino; 2 Asian, non-Hispanic/Latino; 3 Hispanic/Latino; 1 Two or more races, non-Hispanic/Latino), 7 international. Average age 26. 85 applicants, 80% accepted, 33 enrolled. In 2016, 35 master's, 1 other advanced degree awarded. *Degree requirements:* For master's, comprehensive exam. *Entrance requirements:* For master's and doctorate, GRE General Test, 2 letters of recommendation. Additional exam requirements/recommendations for international students: Required—TOEFL (minimum score 600 paper-based; 90 iBT), IELTS (minimum score 7). *Application deadline:* Applications are processed on a rolling basis. Application fee: $60. Electronic applications accepted. *Expenses:* Tuition, state resident: full-time $15,026; part-time $834 per credit hour. Tuition, nonresident: full-time $25,168; part-time $1378 per credit hour. *Required fees:* $2654. *Financial support:* Fellowships, research assistantships, and teaching assistantships available. Financial award application deadline: 1/5; financial award applicants required to submit FAFSA. *Unit head:* Sara Rimm-Kaufman, Program Director, 434-982-2863, E-mail: serk@virginia.edu. *Application contact:* Eric Molnar, Assistant Director, Admissions and Enrollment Reporting, 434-243-2085, E-mail: eric.molnar@virginia.edu.
Website: http://curry.virginia.edu/academics/areas-of-study/educational-psychology

University of Virginia, Curry School of Education, Program in Education, Charlottesville, VA 22903. Offers administration and supervision (PhD); applied developmental science (PhD); counselor education (PhD); curriculum and instruction (PhD); early childhood special education (MT); education evaluation (PhD); educational psychology (PhD); educational research (PhD); elementary education (MT); English education (MT, PhD); foreign language education (MT); higher education (PhD); instructional technology (PhD); kinesiology (MT, PhD); math education (PhD); reading education (PhD); research, statistics and evaluation (PhD); school psychology (PhD); science education (PhD); social studies education (MT, PhD); special education (PhD); world languages education (MT). *Students:* 452 full-time (357 women), 18 part-time (13 women); includes 100 minority (28 Black or African American, non-Hispanic/Latino; 39 Asian, non-Hispanic/Latino; 18 Hispanic/Latino; 15 Two or more races, non-Hispanic/Latino), 14 international. Average age 25. 309 applicants, 51% accepted, 87 enrolled. In 2016, 144 master's, 31 doctorates awarded. *Degree requirements:* For master's, comprehensive exam (for some programs), field project; for doctorate, comprehensive exam, thesis/dissertation. *Entrance requirements:* For doctorate, GRE General Test. Additional exam requirements/recommendations for international students: Required—TOEFL (minimum score 600 paper-based; 90 iBT), IELTS (minimum score 7). *Application deadline:* Applications are processed on a rolling basis. Application fee: $60. Electronic applications accepted. *Expenses:* Tuition, state resident: full-time $15,026; part-time $834 per credit hour. Tuition, nonresident: full-time $25,168; part-time $1378 per credit hour. *Required fees:* $2654. *Financial support:* Fellowships, research assistantships, and teaching assistantships available. Financial award application deadline: 1/5; financial award applicants required to submit FAFSA. *Unit head:* Robert C. Pianta, Dean, 434-924-3334, E-mail: pianta@virginia.edu. *Application contact:* Eric Molnar, Assistant Director, Admissions and Enrollment Reporting, 434-243-2085, E-mail: eric.molnar@virginia.edu.
Website: http://curry.virginia.edu/teacher-education

University of Washington, Graduate School, College of Education, Seattle, WA 98195. Offers curriculum and instruction (M Ed, Ed D, PhD), including educational technology, general curriculum (Ed D, PhD), language, literacy, and culture, mathematics education, multicultural education, reading and language arts education (Ed D), science education, social studies education, teaching and curriculum (M Ed); educational leadership and policy studies (M Ed, Ed D, PhD), including administration (Ed D), educational policy, organization, and leadership (M Ed, PhD), higher education, leadership for learning (Ed D), social and cultural foundations of education (M Ed, PhD); educational psychology (M Ed, PhD), including educational psychology (PhD), human development and cognition (M Ed), learning sciences, measurement, statistics and research design (M Ed), school psychology (M Ed); instructional leadership (M Ed); intercollegiate athletic leadership (M Ed); special education (M Ed, Ed D, PhD), including early childhood special education (M Ed), emotional and behavioral disabilities (M Ed), learning disabilities (M Ed), low-incidence disabilities (M Ed), severe disabilities (M Ed), special education (Ed D, PhD); teacher education (MIT). *Accreditation:* APA. *Program availability:* Part-time, evening/weekend. *Degree requirements:* For master's, thesis optional; for doctorate, thesis/dissertation. *Entrance requirements:* For master's and doctorate, GRE General Test, minimum GPA of 3.0. Additional exam requirements/recommendations for international students: Required—TOEFL. Electronic applications accepted. *Faculty research:* School restructuring/effective schools, special education interventions, literacy and writing, technology, school partnerships, teacher preparation.

The University of West Alabama, School of Graduate Studies, College of Education, Departments of Instructional Leadership and Support/Curriculum and Instruction, Program in Continuing Education, Livingston, AL 35470. Offers counseling and psychology (MSCE); family counseling (MSCE); general (MSCE); guidance and counseling (MSCE); library media (MSCE); student affairs in higher education (MSCE). *Accreditation:* NCATE. *Program availability:* Part-time, evening/weekend, 100% online. *Faculty:* 14 full-time (11 women), 45 part-time/adjunct (31 women). *Students:* 352 (295 women); includes 247 minority (234 Black or African American, non-Hispanic/Latino; 3 American Indian or Alaska Native, non-Hispanic/Latino; 1 Asian, non-Hispanic/Latino; 3 Hispanic/Latino; 1 Native Hawaiian or other Pacific Islander, non-Hispanic/Latino; 5 Two or more races, non-Hispanic/Latino). Average age 34. 92 applicants, 90% accepted, 72 enrolled. In 2016, 117 master's awarded. *Degree requirements:* For master's, comprehensive exam, thesis optional. *Entrance requirements:* For master's, GRE General Test, MAT, minimum GPA of 2.75. Additional exam requirements/recommendations for international students: Required—TOEFL (minimum score 500 paper-based; 61 iBT). *Application deadline:* Applications are processed on a rolling basis. Application fee: $40. Electronic applications accepted. *Expenses:* Tuition, state resident: part-time $355 per credit hour. Tuition, nonresident: part-time $710 per credit hour. *Required fees:* $130 per semester. *Financial support:* Teaching assistantships, Federal Work-Study, scholarships/grants, and unspecified assistantships available. Support available to part-time students. Financial award applicants required to submit FAFSA. *Unit head:* Dr. Reenay Rogers, Chair of Instructional Leadership and Support, 205-652-5423, Fax: 205-652-3706, E-mail: rrogers@uwa.edu. *Application contact:* Dr. B. J. Kimbrough, Dean of Graduate Studies, 205-652-3647, Fax: 205-652-3670, E-mail: bkimbrough@uwa.edu.

The University of West Alabama, School of Graduate Studies, College of Education, Departments of Instructional Leadership and Support/Curriculum and Instruction, Program in Library Media, Livingston, AL 35470. Offers M Ed, Ed S. *Program availability:* Part-time, evening/weekend, 100% online. *Faculty:* 3 full-time (2 women), 14 part-time/adjunct (7 women). *Students:* 136 (132 women); includes 26 minority (23 Black or African American, non-Hispanic/Latino; 1 American Indian or Alaska Native, non-Hispanic/Latino; 2 Two or more races, non-Hispanic/Latino). Average age 35. 35 applicants, 80% accepted, 23 enrolled. In 2016, 65 master's, 9 Ed Ss awarded. *Degree requirements:* For master's, comprehensive exam, thesis optional; for Ed S, comprehensive exam. *Entrance requirements:* For master's, GRE General Test, MAT, minimum GPA of 2.75. Additional exam requirements/recommendations for international students: Required—TOEFL (minimum score 500 paper-based; 61 iBT). *Application deadline:* Applications are processed on a rolling basis. Application fee: $40. Electronic applications accepted. *Expenses:* Tuition, state resident: part-time $355 per credit hour. Tuition, nonresident: part-time $710 per credit hour. *Required fees:* $130 per semester. *Financial support:* Teaching assistantships, Federal Work-Study, scholarships/grants, and unspecified assistantships available. Support available to part-time students. Financial award application deadline: 3/1; financial award applicants required to submit FAFSA. *Unit head:* Dr. Reenay Rogers, Chair of Instructional Leadership and Support, 205-652-5423, Fax: 205-652-3706, E-mail: rrogers@uwa.edu. *Application contact:* Dr. B. J. Kimbrough, Dean of Graduate Studies, 205-652-3647, Fax: 205-652-3706, E-mail: bkimbrough@uwa.edu.
Website: http://www.uwa.edu/medlibrarymedia.aspx

University of West Florida, College of Education and Professional Studies, Department of Instructional, Workforce and Applied Technology, Pensacola, FL 32514-5750. Offers instructional design and technology (M Ed, Ed D), including instructional design and technology (M Ed), technology leadership (M Ed); network operations, performance and security (M Ed). *Entrance requirements:* For master's, GRE, GMAT, or MAT, letter of intent, names of references. Additional exam requirements/recommendations for international students: Required—TOEFL (minimum score 550 paper-based). *Application deadline:* For fall admission, 6/1 for domestic and international students; for spring admission, 10/1 for domestic and international students. Applications are processed on a rolling basis. Electronic applications accepted. *Expenses:* Tuition, state resident: full-time $5316.12. Tuition, nonresident: full-time $11,308. *Required fees:* $583.92. Tuition and fees vary according to course load and program. *Financial support:* Fellowships, research assistantships with partial tuition reimbursements, teaching assistantships with partial tuition reimbursements, and unspecified assistantships available. *Unit head:* Chair, 850-474-2300. *Application contact:* Terry McCray, Assistant Director of Graduate Admissions, 850-473-7718, Fax: 850-473-7714, E-mail: gradadmissions@uwf.edu.
Website: http://uwf.edu/ceps/departments/instructional-workforce-and-applied-technology/

University of West Florida, College of Education and Professional Studies, Ed D Programs, Specialization in Instructional Design and Technology, Pensacola, FL 32514-5750. Offers Ed D. *Degree requirements:* For doctorate, comprehensive exam, thesis/dissertation. *Entrance requirements:* For doctorate, GRE, MAT, or GMAT, letter of intent; writing sample; three letters of recommendation; two completed disposition assessment forms; written statement of goals; interview with admissions committee. Additional exam requirements/recommendations for international students: Required—TOEFL (minimum score 550 paper-based). *Application deadline:* For fall admission, 6/1 for domestic and international students; for spring admission, 10/1 for domestic students. Applications are processed on a rolling basis. Application fee: $30. *Expenses:* Tuition, state resident: full-time $5316.12. Tuition, nonresident: full-time $11,308. *Required fees:* $583.92. Tuition and fees vary according to course load and program. *Unit head:* Dr. Nancy B. Hastings, Chair, 850-474-3013, E-mail: nhastings@uwf.edu. *Application contact:* Terry McCray, Assistant Director of Graduate Admissions, 850-473-7718, Fax: 850-473-7714, E-mail: gradadmissions@uwf.edu.

University of West Georgia, College of Education, Carrollton, GA 30118. Offers business education (M Ed); early childhood education (M Ed, Ed S); educational leadership (M Ed, Ed S); media (M Ed, Ed S); professional counseling (M Ed, Ed S); professional counseling and supervision (Ed D); reading instruction (M Ed); school improvement (Ed D); secondary education (M Ed); special education (M Ed, Ed S), including teaching (M Ed); speech language pathology (M Ed); teaching (MAT). *Accreditation:* NCATE. *Program availability:* Part-time, evening/weekend, 100% online, blended/hybrid learning. *Faculty:* 46 full-time (31 women). *Students:* 321 full-time (266 women), 1,007 part-time (813 women); includes 456 minority (389 Black or African American, non-Hispanic/Latino; 1 American Indian or Alaska Native, non-Hispanic/Latino; 13 Asian, non-Hispanic/Latino; 43 Hispanic/Latino; 10 Two or more races, non-Hispanic/Latino), 12 international. Average age 33. 541 applicants, 79% accepted, 305 enrolled. In 2016, 286 master's, 20 doctorates, 156 other advanced degrees awarded. *Entrance requirements:* Additional exam requirements/recommendations for international students: Required—TOEFL (minimum score 523 paper-based; 69 iBT); Recommended—IELTS (minimum score 6.5). *Application deadline:* For fall admission, 7/21 for domestic students, 6/1 for international students; for spring admission, 11/30 for domestic students, 10/15 for international students; for summer admission, 4/15 for domestic students, 3/30 for international students. Applications are processed on a rolling basis. Application fee: $40. Electronic applications accepted. *Expenses:* Tuition, state resident: full-time $5316; part-time $222 per semester hour. Tuition, nonresident: full-time $20,658; part-time $861 per semester hour. *Required fees:* $1962. Tuition and fees vary according to course load, degree level and program. *Financial support:* Fellowships, research assistantships, teaching assistantships, career-related internships or fieldwork, Federal Work-Study, institutionally sponsored loans, scholarships/grants, and unspecified assistantships available. Support available to part-time students. Financial award application deadline: 4/1; financial award applicants required to submit FAFSA. *Unit head:* Dr. Diane Hoff, Dean, College of Education, 678-839-6570, Fax: 678-839-6098, E-mail: dhoff@westga.edu. *Application contact:* Dr. Toby Ziglar, Assistant Dean of the Graduate School, 678-839-1394, Fax: 678-839-1395, E-mail: graduate@westga.edu.
Website: http://www.westga.edu/education/

University of Wisconsin–Milwaukee, Graduate School, College of Health Sciences, Department of Occupational Science and Technology, Milwaukee, WI 53201-0413. Offers assistive technology and design (MS); ergonomics (MS). *Accreditation:* AOTA. *Students:* 92 full-time (84 women), 4 part-time (3 women); includes 7 minority (3 Asian, non-Hispanic/Latino; 1 Hispanic/Latino; 3 Two or more races, non-Hispanic/Latino). Average age 26. 90 applicants, 40% accepted, 32 enrolled. In 2016, 34 master's awarded. *Degree requirements:* For master's, thesis or alternative. *Entrance requirements:* Additional exam requirements/recommendations for international students: Required—TOEFL (minimum score 550 paper-based; 79 iBT), IELTS (minimum score 6.5). *Application deadline:* For fall admission, 1/1 priority date for domestic students; for spring admission, 9/1 for domestic students. Applications are processed on a rolling basis. Application fee: $56 ($75 for international students). *Financial support:* Fellowships, research assistantships, teaching assistantships, and unspecified assistantships available. Support available to part-time students. Financial award application deadline: 4/15. *Unit head:* Jay Kapellusch, PhD, Department Chair, 414-229-5292, Fax: 414-229-2619, E-mail: kap@uwm.edu. *Application contact:* Bhagwant S. Sindhu, PhD, Graduate Program Coordinator, 414-229-1180, Fax: 414-229-5100, E-mail: sindhu@uwm.edu.
Website: http://uwm.edu/healthsciences/academics/occupational-science-technology/

University of Wisconsin–Milwaukee, Graduate School, College of Health Sciences, Program in Assistive Technology and Accessible Design, Milwaukee, WI 53201-0413. Offers assistive technology and accessible design (Graduate Certificate). *Accreditation:* NAACLS. *Program availability:* Part-time. *Students:* 5 part-time (4 women); includes 2

minority (1 Asian, non-Hispanic/Latino; 1 Hispanic/Latino), 1 international. Average age 34. 2 applicants, 100% accepted. In 2016, 9 Graduate Certificates awarded. *Entrance requirements:* Additional exam requirements/recommendations for international students: Required—TOEFL (minimum score 550 paper-based; 79 iBT), IELTS (minimum score 6.5). *Application deadline:* For fall admission, 1/1 priority date for domestic students; for spring admission, 9/1 for domestic students. Applications are processed on a rolling basis. Application fee: $56 ($96 for international students). *Financial support:* Fellowships, research assistantships, teaching assistantships, career-related internships or fieldwork, and unspecified assistantships available. Support available to part-time students. Financial award application deadline: 4/15. *Application contact:* Michelle Silverman, Coordinator, 414-229-3556, E-mail: silverm2@uwm.edu.
Website: http://uwm.edu/healthsciences/academics/certificate-in-assistive-technology-accessible-design/

University of Wyoming, College of Education, Program in Instructional Technology, Laramie, WY 82071. Offers MS, Ed D, PhD. *Program availability:* Part-time, online learning. *Degree requirements:* For master's, thesis or alternative; for doctorate, comprehensive exam, thesis/dissertation. *Entrance requirements:* For master's, GRE, minimum GPA of 3.0; for doctorate, MS or MA, minimum GPA of 3.0. Additional exam requirements/recommendations for international students: Required—TOEFL. Electronic applications accepted. *Faculty research:* Web based instruction, instructional decision, adult education history, literacy in adults, international distance education.

Utah State University, School of Graduate Studies, Emma Eccles Jones College of Education and Human Services, Department of Instructional Technology and Learning Sciences, Logan, UT 84322. Offers M Ed, MS, PhD, Ed S. *Program availability:* Part-time, evening/weekend, online learning. Terminal master's awarded for partial completion of doctoral program. *Degree requirements:* For master's, thesis (for some programs); for doctorate, comprehensive exam, thesis/dissertation. *Entrance requirements:* For master's, GRE General Test or MAT, minimum GPA of 3.0, 3 recommendation letters; for doctorate, GRE General Test, minimum GPA of 3.0, 3 recommendation letters, transcripts, letter of intent; for Ed S, GRE General Test, GRE Subject Test, minimum GPA of 3.0. Additional exam requirements/recommendations for international students: Required—TOEFL (minimum score 550 paper-based). Electronic applications accepted. *Faculty research:* Interactive learning environments, computer-assisted instruction, learning, distance education, corporate training.

Utah Valley University, Program in Education, Orem, UT 84058-5999. Offers educational technology (M Ed); elementary mathematics (M Ed); elementary STEM (M Ed); English as a second language (M Ed); reading (M Ed); teachers as leaders (M Ed). *Accreditation:* TEAC. *Program availability:* Part-time. *Degree requirements:* For master's, project. *Entrance requirements:* For master's, GRE, 3 letters of recommendation, interview, essay. Additional exam requirements/recommendations for international students: Required—TOEFL (minimum score 83 iBT). Electronic applications accepted. *Expenses:* Contact institution.

Valley City State University, Online Master of Education Program, Valley City, ND 58072. Offers elementary education (M Ed); English education (M Ed); library and information technologies (M Ed); teaching (MAT); teaching and technology (M Ed); teaching English language learners (M Ed); technology education (M Ed). *Accreditation:* NCATE. *Program availability:* Part-time, evening/weekend, online only, 100% online. *Faculty:* 21 full-time (12 women), 15 part-time/adjunct (11 women). *Students:* 4 full-time (3 women), 133 part-time (92 women); includes 9 minority (1 American Indian or Alaska Native, non-Hispanic/Latino; 4 Hispanic/Latino; 4 Two or more races, non-Hispanic/Latino), 1 international. Average age 34. 35 applicants, 91% accepted, 28 enrolled. In 2016, 45 master's awarded. *Degree requirements:* For master's, action research report, comprehensive portfolio. *Entrance requirements:* For master's, GRE, MAT, PRAXIS II or National Teaching Board for Professional Standards (if GPA is less than 3.0). Additional exam requirements/recommendations for international students: Required—TOEFL (minimum score 525 paper-based; 71 iBT); Recommended—IELTS (minimum score 5.5). *Application deadline:* For fall admission, 7/21 priority date for domestic and international students; for spring admission, 12/8 priority date for domestic and international students; for summer admission, 5/5 priority date for domestic and international students. Applications are processed on a rolling basis. Application fee: $35. Electronic applications accepted. *Expenses:* $373 per credit. *Financial support:* In 2016–17, 23 students received support. Scholarships/grants, tuition waivers (full and partial), and unspecified assistantships available. Financial award application deadline: 6/14; financial award applicants required to submit FAFSA. *Faculty research:* Universal accessibility, instructional design and technology, gender communication, STEM education in K-12. *Unit head:* Dr. Gary Thompson, Dean, 701-845-7197, E-mail: gary.thompson@vcsu.edu. *Application contact:* Misty Lindgren, Graduate Studies, 701-845-7303, Fax: 701-845-7190, E-mail: misty.lindgren@vcsu.edu.
Website: http://www.vcsu.edu/graduate

Valparaiso University, Graduate School and Continuing Education, Department of Education, Program in Initial Licensure, Valparaiso, IN 46383. Offers humane education (M Ed); instructional leadership (M Ed); primary education (M Ed); school psychology (M Ed, Ed S); secondary education (M Ed). *Program availability:* Part-time, evening/weekend. *Entrance requirements:* For master's, GRE General Test, Pre-Professional Skills Test (PPST), minimum GPA of 3.0. Additional exam requirements/recommendations for international students: Required—TOEFL (minimum score 550 paper-based; 80 iBT), IELTS (minimum score 6). Electronic applications accepted. *Expenses: Tuition:* Full-time $11,070; part-time $615 per credit hour. *Required fees:* $116 per semester. Tuition and fees vary according to course load, degree level and program.

Virginia Commonwealth University, Graduate School, School of Education, Program in Adult Learning, Richmond, VA 23284-9005. Offers adult literacy (M Ed); human resource development (M Ed); teaching and learning with technology (M Ed). *Accreditation:* NCATE. *Program availability:* Part-time. *Entrance requirements:* For master's, GRE General Test or MAT. Additional exam requirements/recommendations for international students: Required—TOEFL (minimum score 600 paper-based; 100 iBT). *Application deadline:* For fall admission, 3/15 for domestic students; for spring admission, 11/1 for domestic students. Applications are processed on a rolling basis. Application fee: $50. Electronic applications accepted. *Financial support:* Career-related internships or fieldwork and Federal Work-Study available. Financial award application deadline: 3/1; financial award applicants required to submit FAFSA. *Faculty research:* Adult development and learning, program planning and evaluation. *Unit head:* Dr. Leila Christenbury, Interim Department Chair, 804-828-1306, Fax: 804-827-0676, E-mail: lchriste@vcu.edu. *Application contact:* Dr. Robin R. Hurst, Graduate Program Director, 804-828-8021, E-mail: rrhurst@vcu.edu.
Website: http://www.soe.vcu.edu/programs.html#graduate

Virginia Polytechnic Institute and State University, VT Online, Blacksburg, VA 24061. Offers advanced transportation systems (Certificate); aerospace engineering (MS); agricultural and life sciences (MSLFS); business information systems (Graduate Certificate); career and technical education (MS); civil engineering (MS); computer engineering (M Eng, MS); decision support systems (Graduate Certificate); eLearning leadership (MA); electrical engineering (M Eng, MS); engineering administration (MEA); environmental engineering (Certificate); environmental politics and policy (Graduate Certificate); environmental sciences and engineering (MS); foundations of political analysis (Graduate Certificate); health product risk management (Graduate Certificate); industrial and systems engineering (MS); information policy and society (Graduate Certificate); information security (Graduate Certificate); information technology (MIT); instructional technology (MA); integrative STEM education (MA Ed); liberal arts (Graduate Certificate); life sciences: health product risk management (MS); natural resources (MNR, Graduate Certificate); networking (Graduate Certificate); nonprofit and nongovernmental organization management (Graduate Certificate); ocean engineering (MS); political science (MA); security studies (Graduate Certificate); software development (Graduate Certificate). *Expenses:* Tuition, state resident: full-time $12,467; part-time $692.50 per credit hour. Tuition, nonresident: full-time $25,095; part-time $1394.25 per credit hour. *Required fees:* $2669; $491.50 per semester. Tuition and fees vary according to course load, campus/location and program.

Walden University, Graduate Programs, Richard W. Riley College of Education and Leadership, Minneapolis, MN 55401. Offers adult education (Post-Master's Certificate); adult learning (Graduate Certificate); college teaching and learning (Graduate Certificate); community college leadership (Ed D); curriculum, instruction and assessment (Ed D, Ed S, Graduate Certificate); developmental education (Graduate Certificate); early childhood administration, management, and leadership (Graduate Certificate); early childhood education (Ed D, Ed S); early childhood public policy and advocacy (Graduate Certificate); early childhood studies (MS), including administration, management and leadership, early childhood public policy and advocacy, teaching adults in the early childhood field, teaching and diversity in early childhood education; education (MS, PhD), including adolescent literacy and learning (MS), curriculum, instruction, and assessment (grades K-12) (MS), curriculum, instruction, assessment, and evaluation (PhD), early childhood leadership and advocacy (PhD), early childhood special education (PhD), educational leadership (MS), educational leadership and administration (principal preparation) (MS), educational technology and design (PhD), elementary reading and literacy (PreK-6) (MS), elementary reading and mathematics (grades K-6) (MS), global and comparative education (PhD), higher education leadership management and policy (PhD), integrating technology in the classroom (grades K-12) (MS), learning, instruction and innovation (PhD), mathematics (grades 5-8) (MS), mathematics (grades K-6) (MS), mathematics and science (grades K-8) (MS), organizational research, assessment, and evaluation (PhD), reading and literacy with a reading K-12 endorsement (MS), reading literacy assessment and evaluation (PhD), science (grades K-8) (MS), special education (non-licensure) (grades K-12) (MS), teacher leadership (grades K-12) (MS), teaching English language learners (grades K-12) (MS); educational administration and leadership (Ed D); educational leadership and administration (principal preparation) (Ed S); educational technology (Ed D, Ed S, Post Master's Certificate); elementary reading and literacy (Graduate Certificate); engaging culturally diverse learners (Graduate Certificate); enrollment management and institutional marketing (Graduate Certificate); higher education (MS), including adult learning, college teaching and learning, enrollment management and institutional marketing, global higher education, leadership for student success, online and distance learning; higher education and adult learning (Ed D); higher education leadership and management (Ed D); higher education leadership for student success (Graduate Certificate); instructional design and technology (MS, Postbaccalaureate Certificate), including general program (MS), online learning (MS), training and performance improvement (MS); integrating technology in the classroom (Graduate Certificate); mathematics 5-8 (Graduate Certificate); mathematics K-6 (Graduate Certificate); online teaching for adult educators (Graduate Certificate); reading, literacy, and assessment (Ed D, Ed S); science K-8 (Graduate Certificate); special education (Ed D, Ed S, Graduate Certificate); special education (K-age 21) (MAT); teacher leadership (Graduate Certificate); teaching adults English as a second language (Graduate Certificate); teaching adults in the early childhood field (Graduate Certificate); teaching and diversity in early childhood education (Graduate Certificate); teaching English language learners (grades K-12) (Graduate Certificate); teaching K-12 students online (Graduate Certificate). *Accreditation:* NCATE. *Program availability:* Part-time, evening/weekend, online only, 100% online. *Degree requirements:* For doctorate, thesis/dissertation (for some programs), residency; for other advanced degree, residency (for some programs). *Entrance requirements:* For master's, bachelor's degree or higher; minimum GPA of 2.5; official transcripts; goal statement (for some programs); access to computer and Internet; for doctorate, master's degree or higher; three years of related professional or academic experience (preferred); minimum GPA of 3.0; goal statement and current resume (for select programs); official transcripts; access to computer and Internet; for other advanced degree, relevant work experience; access to computer and Internet. Additional exam requirements/recommendations for international students: Required—TOEFL (minimum score 550 paper-based, 79 iBT), IELTS (minimum score 6.5), Michigan English Language Assessment Battery (minimum score 82), or PTE (minimum score 53). Electronic applications accepted.

Walden University, Graduate Programs, School of Psychology, Minneapolis, MN 55401. Offers clinical psychology (MS), including counseling, general program; forensic psychology (MS), including forensic psychology in the community, general program, mental health applications, program planning and evaluation in forensic settings, psychology and legal systems; industrial organizational (MS, PhD), including consulting psychology, forensic (MS), forensic psychology (PhD), general practice, leadership development and coaching (MS), organizational diversity and social change, research evaluation (PhD); online teaching in psychology (Post-Master's Certificate); organizational psychology and development (Postbaccalaureate Certificate); psychology (MS, PhD), including applied psychology (MS), clinical psychology (PhD), crisis management and response (MS), educational psychology, forensic psychology (PhD), general psychology (MS), general psychology research (PhD), general psychology teaching (PhD), health psychology, leadership development and coaching (MS), psychology of culture (MS), psychology, public administration, and social change (MS), social psychology, terrorism and security (MS); psychology respecialization (Post-Doctoral Certificate). *Program availability:* Part-time, evening/weekend, online only, 100% online. Terminal master's awarded for partial completion of doctoral program. *Degree requirements:* For master's, thesis optional; for doctorate, thesis/dissertation, residency. *Entrance requirements:* For master's, bachelor's degree or higher; minimum GPA of 2.5; official transcripts; goal statement (for some programs); access to computer and Internet; for doctorate, master's degree or higher; three years of related professional or academic experience (preferred); minimum GPA of 3.0; goal statement and current resume (for select programs); official transcripts; access to computer and Internet; for other advanced degree, relevant work experience; access to computer and Internet. Additional exam requirements/recommendations for international students: Required—TOEFL (minimum score 550 paper-based, 79 iBT), IELTS (minimum score 6.5), Michigan English Language Assessment Battery (minimum score 82), or PTE (minimum score 53). Electronic applications accepted.

Warner University, School of Education, Lake Wales, FL 33859. Offers curriculum and instruction (MAEd); elementary education (MAEd); science, technology, engineering, and mathematics (STEM) (MAEd). *Program availability:* Part-time, evening/weekend, online learning. *Degree requirements:* For master's, thesis, accomplished practices portfolio. *Entrance requirements:* For master's, minimum GPA of 3.0 in last 60 hours of

undergraduate coursework; 2 letters of recommendation. Additional exam requirements/recommendations for international students: Required—TOEFL (minimum score 550 paper-based). *Application deadline:* Applications are processed on a rolling basis. Application fee: $50. Electronic applications accepted. *Financial support:* Scholarships/grants available. Financial award applicants required to submit FAFSA. *Unit head:* Dr. Bill Rigel, Dean, 863-638-7207, Fax: 863-638-4907, E-mail: bill.rigel@warner.edu. *Application contact:* Torshanda Howard, Admissions Advisor, 863-638-7501, Fax: 863-638-4907, E-mail: admissons@warner.edu.
Website: http://warner.edu/graduate/degrees-offered/arts-in-education/

Wayland Baptist University, Graduate Programs, Program in Education, Plainview, TX 79072-6998. Offers education administration (M Ed); education diagnostics (M Ed); education literacy (M Ed); elementary certification (M Ed); English (M Ed); English as a second language (M Ed); higher education administration (M Ed); human resources (M Ed); instructional leadership (M Ed); instructional technology (M Ed); leadership training and development (M Ed); science education (M Ed); secondary certification (M Ed); social studies (M Ed); special education (M Ed); sports administration and management (M Ed). *Program availability:* Part-time, evening/weekend, online learning. *Degree requirements:* For master's, comprehensive exam, capstone course. *Entrance requirements:* For master's, GRE, GMAT or MAT. Additional exam requirements/recommendations for international students: Required—TOEFL (minimum score 500 paper-based; 61 iBT). Electronic applications accepted.

Waynesburg University, Graduate and Professional Studies, Canonsburg, PA 15370. Offers business (MBA), including energy management, finance, health systems, human resources, leadership, market development; counseling (MA), including addictions counseling, clinical mental health; counselor education and supervision (PhD); criminal investigation (MA); education (M Ed), including autism, curriculum and instruction, educational leadership, online teaching; nursing (MSN), including administration, education, informatics; nursing practice (DNP); special education (M Ed); technology (M Ed); MSN/MBA. *Accreditation:* AACN. *Program availability:* Part-time, evening/weekend. *Degree requirements:* For doctorate, thesis/dissertation. *Entrance requirements:* Additional exam requirements/recommendations for international students: Required—TOEFL. Electronic applications accepted.

Wayne State University, College of Education, Division of Administrative and Organizational Studies, Detroit, MI 48202. Offers college and university teaching (Certificate); educational administration and supervision (Ed S); educational leadership (M Ed); educational leadership and policy studies (Ed D, PhD); educational technology (Certificate); learning design and technology (M Ed, Ed D, PhD, Ed S); online teaching (Certificate). *Program availability:* Part-time, 100% online, blended/hybrid learning. *Faculty:* 11. *Students:* 83 full-time (58 women), 223 part-time (148 women); includes 151 minority (126 Black or African American, non-Hispanic/Latino; 3 American Indian or Alaska Native, non-Hispanic/Latino; 4 Asian, non-Hispanic/Latino; 8 Hispanic/Latino; 10 Two or more races, non-Hispanic/Latino), 14 international. Average age 39. 143 applicants, 43% accepted, 38 enrolled. In 2016, 53 master's, 9 doctorates, 34 other advanced degrees awarded. *Degree requirements:* For doctorate, thesis/dissertation. *Entrance requirements:* For master's, baccalaureate degree from accredited U.S. institution or equivalent from college or university of government-recognized standing; minimum undergraduate GPA of 2.75 in upper-division coursework; personal statement; for doctorate, GRE (instructional design and technology), interview; curriculum vitae; three references (two professional and one academic); master's degree; minimum graduate GPA of 3.5; autobiographical statement; research experience. Additional exam requirements/recommendations for international students: Required—TOEFL (minimum score 550 paper-based; 79 iBT), Michigan English Language Assessment Battery (minimum score 85); Recommended—IELTS (minimum score 6.5), TWE (minimum score 5.5). *Application deadline:* For fall admission, 6/1 priority date for domestic students, 5/1 priority date for international students; for winter admission, 10/1 priority date for domestic students, 9/1 priority date for international students; for spring admission, 2/1 priority date for domestic students, 1/1 priority date for international students. Applications are processed on a rolling basis. Application fee: $50. Electronic applications accepted. *Expenses:* $16,503 per year resident tuition and fees, $33,697 per year non-resident tuition and fees. *Financial support:* In 2016–17, 96 students received support, including 1 fellowship with tuition reimbursement available (averaging $11,000 per year), 4 research assistantships with tuition reimbursements available (averaging $17,949 per year); scholarships/grants and unspecified assistantships also available. Support available to part-time students. Financial award applicants required to submit FAFSA. *Faculty research:* Total quality management, participatory management, administering educational technology, school improvement, principalship. *Unit head:* Dr. William Hill, Assistant Dean, 313-577-9316, E-mail: ad2107@wayne.edu. *Application contact:* Janice Green, Assistant Dean, 313-577-1605, E-mail: jwgreen@wayne.edu.
Website: http://coe.wayne.edu/aos/index.php

Webster University, School of Education, Department of Multidisciplinary Studies, St. Louis, MO 63119-3194. Offers applied educational psychology (MA, Ed S); communication arts (MA); early childhood education (MA, MAT); education and innovation (MA); educational technology (MET); elementary education (MAT); mathematics for educators (MA); middle school education (MAT); multidisciplinary studies (MAT); multimodal literacy for global impact (MA); reading (MA); secondary school education (MAT); special education (MA, MAT); teaching English as a second language (MA); transformative learning in the global community (Ed S). *Program availability:* Part-time. *Entrance requirements:* For master's, minimum GPA of 2.5. Additional exam requirements/recommendations for international students: Required—TOEFL. *Application deadline:* Applications are processed on a rolling basis. Application fee: $35 ($50 for international students). *Expenses: Tuition:* Full-time $21,900; part-time $730 per credit hour. Tuition and fees vary according to campus/location and program. *Financial support:* Federal Work-Study available. Support available to part-time students. Financial award application deadline: 4/1; financial award applicants required to submit FAFSA. *Unit head:* Dr. Deborah Stiles, Chair, 314-968-7056, Fax: 314-968-7118, E-mail: stilesda@webster.edu.

West Chester University of Pennsylvania, College of Education and Social Work, Department of Professional and Secondary Education, West Chester, PA 19383. Offers education for sustainability (Certificate); educational technology (Certificate); entrepreneurial education (Certificate); transformative education and social change (MS). *Program availability:* Part-time. *Faculty:* 10 full-time (3 women). *Students:* 6 full-time (5 women), 35 part-time (22 women); includes 2 minority (1 Hispanic/Latino; 1 Two or more races, non-Hispanic/Latino). Average age 30. 24 applicants, 88% accepted, 17 enrolled. In 2016, 7 master's, 3 other advanced degrees awarded. *Degree requirements:* For master's, comprehensive exam (for some programs), thesis, 36 credits. *Entrance requirements:* For master's, teaching certification (strongly recommended); for Certificate, minimum GPA of 3.0. Additional exam requirements/recommendations for international students: Required—TOEFL or IELTS. *Application deadline:* For fall admission, 5/15 for international students; for spring admission, 10/15 for international students. Applications are processed on a rolling basis. Application fee: $50. Electronic applications accepted. *Expenses:* Tuition, state resident: full-time $8694; part-time $483 per credit. Tuition, nonresident: full-time $13,050; part-time $725 per credit. *Required fees:* $2399; $119.05 per credit. Tuition and fees vary according to campus/location and program. *Financial support:* Scholarships/grants and unspecified assistantships available. Financial award application deadline: 2/15; financial award applicants required to submit FAFSA. *Faculty research:* Technology integration: preparing our teachers for the twenty-first century, critical pedagogy. *Unit head:* Dr. John Elmore, Chair, 610-436-6934, Fax: 610-436-3102, E-mail: jelmore@wcupa.edu. *Application contact:* Dr. Matthew Kruger-Ross, Graduate Coordinator, 610-436-2106, Fax: 610-436-3102, E-mail: mkruger-ross@wcupa.edu.
Website: http://www.wcupa.edu/education-socialWork/profsecedu/

West Chester University of Pennsylvania, College of Education and Social Work, Department of Special Education, West Chester, PA 19383. Offers autism (Certificate); special education (Teaching Certificate); special education (M Ed); universal design for learning and assistive technology (Certificate). *Accreditation:* NCATE. *Program availability:* Part-time, 100% online. *Faculty:* 8 full-time (7 women), 1 (woman) part-time/adjunct. *Students:* 13 full-time (10 women), 182 part-time (165 women); includes 14 minority (8 Black or African American, non-Hispanic/Latino; 1 Asian, non-Hispanic/Latino; 3 Hispanic/Latino; 2 Two or more races, non-Hispanic/Latino), 1 international. Average age 29. 84 applicants, 89% accepted, 60 enrolled. In 2016, 38 master's, 26 Certificates awarded. *Degree requirements:* For master's, minimum GPA of 3.0, action research; for other advanced degree, minimum GPA of 3.0; modified student teaching. *Entrance requirements:* For master's, GRE if GPA is below 3.0, two letters of recommendation; for other advanced degree, GRE if GPA is below 3.0. Additional exam requirements/recommendations for international students: Required—TOEFL or IELTS. *Application deadline:* For fall admission, 5/15 for international students; for spring admission, 10/15 for international students. Applications are processed on a rolling basis. Application fee: $50. Electronic applications accepted. *Expenses:* Tuition, state resident: full-time $8694; part-time $483 per credit. Tuition, nonresident: full-time $13,050; part-time $725 per credit. *Required fees:* $2399; $119.05 per credit. Tuition and fees vary according to campus/location and program. *Financial support:* Scholarships/grants and unspecified assistantships available. Financial award application deadline: 2/15; financial award applicants required to submit FAFSA. *Faculty research:* Instructional strategies for students with moderate to severe disabilities; family involvement for families of students with disabilities; instructional strategies for students with autism; math instruction for students with learning disabilities; transitions for students with disabilities; behavior management for students with behavior disorders. *Unit head:* Dr. Corrine Murphy, Chair, 610-436-0040, Fax: 610-436-3102, E-mail: cmurphy@wcupa.edu. *Application contact:* Dr. S. Christy Hicks, Graduate Coordinator, 610-436-3067, E-mail: shicks@wcupa.edu.
Website: http://www.wcupa.edu/education-socialWork/specialEducation/

Western Connecticut State University, Division of Graduate Studies, School of Professional Studies, Department of Education and Educational Psychology, Instructional Technology Option, Danbury, CT 06810-6885. Offers MS. *Program availability:* Part-time. *Degree requirements:* For master's, thesis or research project, completion of program in 6 years. *Entrance requirements:* For master's, minimum GPA of 2.8, teaching certificate. Additional exam requirements/recommendations for international students: Recommended—TOEFL (minimum score 550 paper-based; 79 iBT), IELTS (minimum score 6). *Faculty research:* Connectivism in education.

Western Governors University, Teachers College, Salt Lake City, UT 84107. Offers curriculum and instruction (MS); educational leadership (MS); educational studies (MA); educational studies (5-12) (MA), including mathematics; elementary education (K-8) (MAT, Postbaccalaureate Certificate); elementary education (PreK-8) (MAT); English language learning (K-12) (MA); instructional design (MAT); learning and technology (M Ed, MA); management and innovation (M Ed); mathematics (5-12) (MAT, Postbaccalaureate Certificate); mathematics (5-9) (MAT, Postbaccalaureate Certificate); mathematics education (5-12) (MA); mathematics education (5-9) (MA); mathematics education (K-6) (MA); measurement and evaluation (M Ed); science (5-12) (Postbaccalaureate Certificate); science (5-9) (MAT, Postbaccalaureate Certificate); science education (5-12) (MA), including biology, chemistry, geology, physics; science education (5-9) (MA); social science (5-12) (MAT, Postbaccalaureate Certificate); special education (MAT, MS). *Accreditation:* NCATE. *Program availability:* Evening/weekend, online learning. *Degree requirements:* For master's, capstone project. *Entrance requirements:* For master's and Postbaccalaureate Certificate, Readiness Assessment, transcripts. Additional exam requirements/recommendations for international students: Required—TOEFL (minimum score 450 paper-based; 80 iBT). Electronic applications accepted. *Expenses:* Contact institution.

Western Illinois University, School of Graduate Studies, College of Business and Technology, Program in Instructional Design and Technology, Macomb, IL 61455-1390. Offers educational technology specialist (Certificate); instructional design and technology (MS); instructional media development (Certificate); online and distance learning development (Certificate); technology integration in education (Certificate); workplace learning and performance (Certificate). *Program availability:* Part-time, online learning. *Students:* 8 full-time (5 women), 54 part-time (32 women); includes 9 minority (4 Black or African American, non-Hispanic/Latino; 1 American Indian or Alaska Native, non-Hispanic/Latino; 3 Asian, non-Hispanic/Latino; 1 Hispanic/Latino), 2 international. Average age 36. 22 applicants, 91% accepted, 15 enrolled. In 2016, 30 master's, 6 other advanced degrees awarded. *Degree requirements:* For master's, thesis or alternative. *Entrance requirements:* Additional exam requirements/recommendations for international students: Required—TOEFL (minimum score 550 paper-based; 80 iBT). *Application deadline:* Applications are processed on a rolling basis. Application fee: $30. Electronic applications accepted. *Financial support:* In 2016–17, 3 students received support. Teaching assistantships and unspecified assistantships available. Financial award applicants required to submit FAFSA. *Unit head:* Dr. Hoyet Hemphill, Chairperson, 309-298-1952. *Application contact:* Dr. Nancy Parsons, Associate Provost and Director of Graduate Studies, 309-298-1806, Fax: 309-298-2345, E-mail: grad-office@wiu.edu.
Website: http://wiu.edu/idt

Western Kentucky University, Graduate Studies, College of Education and Behavioral Sciences, School of Teacher Education, Bowling Green, KY 42101. Offers elementary education (MAE, Ed S); exceptional education: learning and behavioral disorders (MAE); exceptional education: moderate and severe disabilities (MAE); instructional design (MS); interdisciplinary early childhood education (MAE); library media education (MS); literacy education (MAE); middle grades education (MAE); secondary education (MAE, Ed S). *Program availability:* Part-time, evening/weekend, online learning. *Degree requirements:* For master's, comprehensive exam. *Entrance requirements:* For master's, GRE General Test. Additional exam requirements/recommendations for international students: Required—TOEFL (minimum score 555 paper-based; 79 iBT). *Faculty research:* Teacher preparation in moderate/severe disabilities.

Western Michigan University, Graduate College, College of Education and Human Development, Department of Educational Leadership, Research and Technology, Kalamazoo, MI 49008. Offers educational leadership (MA, PhD, Ed S), including educational leadership (MA); educational technology (MA, Graduate Certificate); evaluation, measurement and research (MA, PhD); organizational learning and performance (MA).

Western Oregon University, Graduate Programs, College of Education, Division of Teacher Education, Program in Information Technology, Monmouth, OR 97361. Offers MS Ed. *Accreditation:* NCATE. *Program availability:* Part-time, evening/weekend, online learning. *Degree requirements:* For master's, written exams. *Entrance requirements:* For master's, interview, minimum GPA of 3.0, teaching license. Additional exam requirements/recommendations for international students: Required—TOEFL (minimum score 550 paper-based; 79 iBT), IELTS (minimum score 6.5). *Faculty research:* Impact of technology on teaching and learning.

West Texas A&M University, College of Education and Social Sciences, Department of Education, Program in Instructional Design and Technology, Canyon, TX 79016-0001. Offers M Ed. *Program availability:* Part-time, evening/weekend, 100% online. *Degree requirements:* For master's, comprehensive exam, thesis optional. *Entrance requirements:* For master's, GRE General Test, approval from the instructional technology admissions committee. Additional exam requirements/recommendations for international students: Required—TOEFL (minimum score 550 paper-based). *Application deadline:* For fall admission, 8/1 for domestic students, 5/1 for international students; for spring admission, 12/1 for domestic students, 10/30 for international students; for summer admission, 5/1 for domestic students. Applications are processed on a rolling basis. Application fee: $40 ($75 for international students). Electronic applications accepted. *Financial support:* Research assistantships, teaching assistantships with partial tuition reimbursements, career-related internships or fieldwork, Federal Work-Study, institutionally sponsored loans, and tuition waivers (partial) available. Support available to part-time students. Financial award applicants required to submit CSS PROFILE or FAFSA. *Faculty research:* Mathematics and science instruction, technology, developing online courses for freshmen, integrity of online courses. *Unit head:* Dr. Rich Rose, Associate Professor, 806-676-9456. *Application contact:* Dr. Rich Rose, Associate Professor, 806-676-9456.
Website: http://www.wtamu.edu/academics/instructional-design-technology-graduate-program.aspx

West Virginia University, College of Education and Human Services, Department of Technology, Learning and Culture, Program in Instructional Design and Technology, Morgantown, WV 26506. Offers MA, Ed D. *Accreditation:* NCATE. *Degree requirements:* For master's, thesis; for doctorate, thesis/dissertation. *Entrance requirements:* For master's, GRE General Test, minimum GPA of 2.75; for doctorate, GRE, minimum GPA of 2.75. Additional exam requirements/recommendations for international students: Required—TOEFL. *Faculty research:* Appropriate technology, alternative energy, computer applications for education and training, telecommunication, professional development.

Widener University, School of Education, Hospitality, and Continuing Studies, Chester, PA 19013-5792. Offers adult education (M Ed); counseling in higher education (M Ed); counselor education (M Ed); early childhood education (M Ed); educational foundations (M Ed); educational leadership (M Ed); educational psychology (M Ed); elementary education (M Ed); English and language arts (M Ed); health education (M Ed); higher education leadership (Ed D); home and school visitor (M Ed); human sexuality (M Ed, PhD); mathematics education (M Ed); middle school education (M Ed); principalship (M Ed); reading and language arts (Ed D); reading education (M Ed); school administration (Ed D); science education (M Ed); social studies education (M Ed); special education (M Ed); technology education (M Ed). *Accreditation:* NCATE. *Program availability:* Part-time, evening/weekend. *Faculty:* 34 full-time (22 women), 37 part-time/adjunct (14 women). *Students:* 97 full-time (64 women), 201 part-time (143 women); includes 56 minority (44 Black or African American, non-Hispanic/Latino; 1 American Indian or Alaska Native, non-Hispanic/Latino; 2 Asian, non-Hispanic/Latino; 8 Hispanic/Latino; 1 Two or more races, non-Hispanic/Latino), 32 international. Average age 39. 139 applicants, 88% accepted. In 2016, 45 master's, 21 doctorates awarded. Terminal master's awarded for partial completion of doctoral program. *Degree requirements:* For doctorate, thesis/dissertation. *Entrance requirements:* For master's, minimum GPA of 2.5; for doctorate, GRE or MAT, minimum GPA of 2.0 (undergraduate), 3.5 (graduate). *Application deadline:* Applications are processed on a rolling basis. Application fee: $25 ($300 for international students). Electronic applications accepted. *Expenses:* Contact institution. *Financial support:* Career-related internships or fieldwork, tuition waivers (full and partial), and unspecified assistantships available. Support available to part-time students. Financial award application deadline: 5/1. *Faculty research:* Reading and cognition, adult education, technology education, educational leadership, special education. *Unit head:* Dr. Shawn Fitzgerald, Dean, 610-499-4294, Fax: 610-499-4623, E-mail: smfitzgerald@widener.edu. *Application contact:* Dr. Roberta Nolan, Director of Graduate Admissions, 610-499-4125, E-mail: rdnolan@widener.edu.
Website: http://www.widener.edu/academics/schools/eics

Wilkes University, College of Graduate and Professional Studies, School of Education, Wilkes-Barre, PA 18766-0002. Offers 21st century teaching and learning (MS Ed); art and science of teaching (MS Ed); classroom technology (MS Ed); early childhood literacy (MS Ed); educational development and strategies (MS Ed); educational leadership (MS Ed, Ed D); effective teaching (MS Ed); instructional media (MS Ed); instructional technology (MS Ed); international school leadership (MS Ed); international teaching and learning (MS Ed); middle level education (MS Ed); online teaching (MS Ed); reading (MS Ed); school business leadership (MS Ed); special education (MS Ed); teaching English to speakers of other languages (MS Ed). *Program availability:* Part-time, evening/weekend, 100% online, blended/hybrid learning. *Students:* 87 full-time (70 women), 1,496 part-time (1,111 women); includes 77 minority (11 Black or African American, non-Hispanic/Latino; 2 American Indian or Alaska Native, non-Hispanic/Latino; 12 Asian, non-Hispanic/Latino; 28 Hispanic/Latino; 3 Native Hawaiian or other Pacific Islander, non-Hispanic/Latino; 21 Two or more races, non-Hispanic/Latino). Average age 33. In 2016, 524 master's, 21 doctorates awarded. *Entrance requirements:* Additional exam requirements/recommendations for international students: Required—TOEFL (minimum score 550 paper-based; 79 iBT). *Application deadline:* Applications are processed on a rolling basis. Application fee: $45. Electronic applications accepted. *Expenses:* Contact institution. *Financial support:* Unspecified assistantships available. Financial award application deadline: 3/1; financial award applicants required to submit FAFSA. *Unit head:* Dr. Rhonda Rabbitt, Dean, 570-408-4680, Fax: 570-408-7872, E-mail: rhonda.rabbitt@wilkes.edu. *Application contact:* Director of Graduate Education, 570-408-4234, Fax: 570-408-7846.
Website: http://www.wilkes.edu/academics/graduate-programs/masters-programs/graduate-education/index.aspx

William Woods University, Graduate and Adult Studies, Fulton, MO 65251-1098. Offers administration (M Ed, Ed S); athletic/activities administration (M Ed); curriculum and instruction (M Ed, Ed S); educational leadership (Ed D); equestrian education (M Ed); health management (MBA); human resources (MBA); leadership (MBA); marketing, advertising, and public relations (MBA); teaching and technology (M Ed). *Program availability:* Part-time, evening/weekend. *Degree requirements:* For master's, capstone course (MBA), action research (M Ed); for Ed S, field experience. *Entrance requirements:* Additional exam requirements/recommendations for international students: Required—TOEFL (minimum score 550 paper-based). Electronic applications accepted. *Expenses:* Contact institution.

Wilmington University, College of Education, New Castle, DE 19720-6491. Offers applied technology in education (M Ed); career and technical education (M Ed); educational leadership (Ed D); elementary and secondary school counseling (M Ed); elementary studies (M Ed); ESOL literacy (M Ed); higher education leadership (Ed D); instruction: gifted and talented (M Ed); instruction: teacher of reading (M Ed); instruction: teaching and learning (M Ed); organizational leadership (Ed D); school leadership (M Ed); secondary education (MAT); special education (M Ed). *Accreditation:* NCATE. *Program availability:* Part-time, evening/weekend. *Faculty:* 19 full-time (11 women), 178 part-time/adjunct (99 women). *Students:* 248 full-time (176 women), 999 part-time (738 women); includes 244 minority (193 Black or African American, non-Hispanic/Latino; 17 American Indian or Alaska Native, non-Hispanic/Latino; 9 Asian, non-Hispanic/Latino; 19 Hispanic/Latino; 2 Native Hawaiian or other Pacific Islander, non-Hispanic/Latino; 4 Two or more races, non-Hispanic/Latino), 7 international. Average age 34. 672 applicants, 96% accepted, 348 enrolled. In 2016, 529 master's, 87 doctorates awarded. *Entrance requirements:* For master's, 2 letters of recommendation, interview. Additional exam requirements/recommendations for international students: Required—TOEFL (minimum score 500 paper-based). *Application deadline:* For fall admission, 4/30 for domestic students. Applications are processed on a rolling basis. Application fee: $35. Electronic applications accepted. *Expenses: Tuition:* Full-time $8388; part-time $466 per credit. *Required fees:* $25 per semester. Tuition and fees vary according to degree level. *Financial support:* Applicants required to submit FAFSA. *Unit head:* Dr. John C. Gray, Dean. *Application contact:* Laura Morris, Director of Admissions, 877-967-5464, E-mail: infocenter@wilmu.edu.
Website: http://www.wilmu.edu/education/

Wisconsin Lutheran College, College of Adult and Graduate Studies, Milwaukee, WI 53226-9942. Offers high performance instruction (MA Ed); instructional technology (MA Ed); leadership and innovation (MA Ed); science instruction (MA Ed).

Worcester Polytechnic Institute, Graduate Studies and Research, Program in Learning Sciences and Technologies, Worcester, MA 01609-2280. Offers MS, PhD. Program offered jointly between Department of Social Science and Policy Studies and Department of Computer Science. *Program availability:* Part-time, evening/weekend. *Students:* 7 full-time (4 women), 1 part-time (0 women); includes 1 minority (Two or more races, non-Hispanic/Latino). 3 applicants, 100% accepted, 2 enrolled. In 2016, 3 master's awarded. *Entrance requirements:* For master's and doctorate, GRE (strongly recommended), statement of purpose, brief sample of scholarly writing. Additional exam requirements/recommendations for international students: Required—TOEFL (minimum score 563 paper-based; 84 iBT), IELTS (minimum score 7). *Application deadline:* For fall admission, 1/1 for domestic and international students; for spring admission, 10/1 for domestic and international students. Applications are processed on a rolling basis. Application fee: $70. Electronic applications accepted. *Financial support:* Research assistantships, teaching assistantships, career-related internships or fieldwork, health care benefits, and unspecified assistantships available. Financial award application deadline: 1/1; financial award applicants required to submit FAFSA. *Unit head:* Ivon Arroyo, Co-Director, 508-831-5296, E-mail: iarriyo@wpi.edu. *Application contact:* Tricia Desmarais, Administrative Assistant, 508-831-5296, Fax: 508-831-5896, E-mail: td@wpi.edu.
Website: http://www.wpi.edu/academics/lst

York College of Pennsylvania, Master of Education Program, York, PA 17403. Offers educational leadership (M Ed); educational technology (M Ed); reading specialist (M Ed). *Program availability:* Part-time, evening/weekend. *Faculty:* 3 full-time (2 women), 5 part-time/adjunct (2 women). *Students:* 54 part-time (39 women), 1 international. Average age 33. 51 applicants, 67% accepted, 30 enrolled. In 2016, 4 master's awarded. *Degree requirements:* For master's, comprehensive exam (for some programs), thesis (for some programs). *Entrance requirements:* For master's, PRAXIS, GRE, or MAT (within past 10 years), statement of applicant's professional and academic goals, 2 letters of recommendation, letter from current supervisor, official undergraduate and graduate transcript(s), copy of teaching certificate(s), current professional resume, interview. Additional exam requirements/recommendations for international students: Required—TOEFL. *Application deadline:* For fall admission, 7/15 priority date for domestic students; for spring admission, 11/15 priority date for domestic students; for summer admission, 4/15 priority date for domestic students. Applications are processed on a rolling basis. Application fee: $0. Electronic applications accepted. *Expenses:* $620 per credit. *Financial support:* Scholarships/grants available. Financial award applicants required to submit FAFSA. *Faculty research:* Classroom technology, assessment, educational leadership, professional development. *Unit head:* Dr. Joshua D. DeSantis, Director, Master of Education Program, 717-815-1936, E-mail: jdesant1@ycp.edu.
Website: https://www.ycp.edu/med

Youngstown State University, Graduate School, Beeghly College of Education, Department of Teacher Education, Youngstown, OH 44555-0001. Offers adolescent/young adult education (MS Ed); content area concentration (MS Ed); early childhood education (MS Ed); educational technology (MS Ed); literacy (MS Ed); middle childhood education (MS Ed); special education (MS Ed), including gifted and talented education, special education. *Accreditation:* NCATE. *Program availability:* Part-time, evening/weekend. *Degree requirements:* For master's, comprehensive exam. *Entrance requirements:* For master's, GRE, MAT, or teaching certificate; minimum GPA of 2.7. Additional exam requirements/recommendations for international students: Required—TOEFL. *Faculty research:* Multicultural literacy, hands-on mathematics teaching, integrated instruction, reading comprehension, emergent curriculum.

Educational Policy

Alabama State University, College of Education, Department of Instructional Support Programs, Montgomery, AL 36101-0271. Offers counselor education (M Ed, MS, Ed S), including general counseling (MS, Ed S), school counseling (M Ed, Ed S); educational administration (M Ed, Ed D, Ed S), including educational administration (Ed S), educational leadership, policy and law (Ed D), instructional leadership (M Ed); library education media (M Ed, Ed S). *Program availability:* Part-time. *Faculty:* 11 full-time (6

women), 7 part-time/adjunct (5 women). *Students:* 50 full-time (32 women), 128 part-time (95 women); includes 167 minority (166 Black or African American, non-Hispanic/Latino; 1 Two or more races, non-Hispanic/Latino), 3 international. Average age 37. 84 applicants, 50% accepted, 16 enrolled. In 2016, 39 master's, 19 doctorates, 5 other advanced degrees awarded. *Degree requirements:* For master's, comprehensive exam; for Ed S, comprehensive exam, thesis. *Entrance requirements:* For master's, GRE General Test, MAT, writing competency test, bachelor's degree or its equivalent from accredited college or university with minimum GPA of 2.5; for Ed S, GRE General Test, MAT, writing competency test, minimum GPA of 3.25. Additional exam requirements/recommendations for international students: Required—TOEFL (minimum score 500 paper-based). *Application deadline:* For fall admission, 4/15 for domestic and international students; for spring admission, 11/15 for domestic and international students; for summer admission, 3/15 for domestic and international students. Applications are processed on a rolling basis. Application fee: $25. Electronic applications accepted. *Expenses:* Tuition, state resident: full-time $3087; part-time $2744 per credit. Tuition, nonresident: full-time $6174; part-time $5488 per credit. *Required fees:* $2284; $1142 per credit. $571 per semester. Tuition and fees vary according to class time, course level, course load, degree level, program and student level. *Financial support:* In 2016–17, 3 students received support. Research assistantships and unspecified assistantships available. Financial award application deadline: 6/30; financial award applicants required to submit FAFSA. *Unit head:* Dr. Necoal Driver, Chair, 334-229-4456, Fax: 334-229-6831, E-mail: ndriver@alasu.edu. *Application contact:* Dr. William Person, Dean of Graduate Studies, 334-229-4275, Fax: 334-229-4928, E-mail: wperson@alasu.edu.
Website: http://www.alasu.edu/academics/colleges—departments/college-of-education/instructional-support-programs/index.aspx

American University, School of Education, Education Policy and Leadership Program, Washington, DC 20016-8001. Offers M Ed, Certificate, M Ed/MPA, M Ed/MPP. *Students:* 21 full-time (18 women), 21 part-time (16 women); includes 19 minority (9 Black or African American, non-Hispanic/Latino; 3 Asian, non-Hispanic/Latino; 6 Hispanic/Latino; 1 Two or more races, non-Hispanic/Latino). Average age 27. 37 applicants, 89% accepted, 21 enrolled. *Degree requirements:* For master's, comprehensive exam. *Entrance requirements:* For master's, GRE, statement of purpose, transcripts, 2 letters of recommendation, resume; for Certificate, statement of purpose, transcripts, 2 letters of recommendation, resume. Additional exam requirements/recommendations for international students: Required—TOEFL (minimum score 100 iBT), IELTS (minimum score 7), PTE (minimum score 68). *Application deadline:* For fall admission, 2/1 for domestic students; for spring admission, 11/1 for domestic students. Application fee: $55. *Expenses:* $1,579 per credit tuition; $690 mandatory fees. *Financial support:* Unspecified assistantships available. Financial award applicants required to submit FAFSA. *Unit head:* Fax: 202-885-6900, E-mail: edpolicy@american.edu. *Application contact:* Kathleen Clowery, Director, Graduate Admissions, 202-885-3620, Fax: 202-885-1344, E-mail: clowery@american.edu.

Arizona State University at the Tempe campus, Mary Lou Fulton Teachers College, Program in Educational Policy and Evaluation, Phoenix, AZ 85069. Offers PhD. Fall admission only. *Degree requirements:* For doctorate, comprehensive exam, thesis/dissertation, interactive Program of Study (iPOS) submitted before completing 50 percent of required credit hours. *Entrance requirements:* For doctorate, GRE, minimum GPA of 3.0 or equivalent in last 2 years of work leading to bachelor's degree, 3 letters of recommendation, personal statement, writing sample, curriculum vitae or resume. Additional exam requirements/recommendations for international students: Required—TOEFL, IELTS, or PTE. Electronic applications accepted. *Expenses:* Contact institution. *Faculty research:* Education policy analysis, school finance and quantitative methods, school improvement in ethnically, linguistically and economically diverse communities, parent/teacher engagement, school choice, accountability polices, school finance litigation, school segregation.

Ball State University, Graduate School, Teachers College, Department of Educational Studies, Program in Educational Studies, Muncie, IN 47306. Offers educational studies (PhD), including cultural and educational policy studies, curriculum, educational technology. *Program availability:* Part-time, blended/hybrid learning. *Degree requirements:* For doctorate, thesis/dissertation. *Entrance requirements:* For doctorate, GRE General Test, minimum graduate GPA of 3.2, curriculum vitae, writing sample, three letters of reference. Additional exam requirements/recommendations for international students: Required—TOEFL (minimum score 550 paper-based; 79 iBT), IELTS (minimum score 6.5). Electronic applications accepted. *Faculty research:* Emerging curriculum trends, secondary teacher preparation, issues of equity and social justice in education, teacher technology integration, teaching for transformative understanding, teacher leadership, history of educational policy and practices, ethics and education.

Brigham Young University, Graduate Studies, David O. McKay School of Education, Department of Educational Leadership and Foundations, Provo, UT 84602. Offers educational leadership and foundations (Ed D); educational leadership: education policy and social foundations (M Ed); educational leadership: school leadership (M Ed). *Program availability:* Part-time, evening/weekend. *Faculty:* 11 full-time (2 women), 1 part-time/adjunct (0 women). *Students:* 44 full-time (16 women), 26 part-time (14 women); includes 10 minority (4 Asian, non-Hispanic/Latino; 2 Hispanic/Latino; 2 Native Hawaiian or other Pacific Islander, non-Hispanic/Latino; 2 Two or more races, non-Hispanic/Latino), 3 international. Average age 42. 82 applicants, 46% accepted, 38 enrolled. In 2016, 24 master's, 6 doctorates awarded. Terminal master's awarded for partial completion of doctoral program. *Degree requirements:* For master's, comprehensive exam; for doctorate, comprehensive exam, thesis/dissertation, prospectus. *Entrance requirements:* For master's and doctorate, GRE, LSAT, or GMAT. Additional exam requirements/recommendations for international students: Required—TOEFL (minimum score 580 paper-based; 85 iBT). *Application deadline:* For fall admission, 5/1 for domestic students, 2/15 for international students; for spring admission, 1/15 for domestic students, 2/15 for international students; for summer admission, 3/1 for domestic and international students. Application fee: $50. Electronic applications accepted. *Expenses:* $393 per credit. *Financial support:* In 2016–17, 15 students received support. Research assistantships available. Financial award application deadline: 8/15. *Unit head:* Pamela Hallam, Chair, 801-422-3600, Fax: 801-422-0196, E-mail: pam_hallam@byu.edu. *Application contact:* Michele Price, Department Secretary, 801-422-3813, Fax: 801-422-0196, E-mail: michele_price@byu.edu.
Website: http://education.byu.edu/edlf/

California State University, Sacramento, Office of Graduate Studies, College of Education, Graduate and Professional Studies in Education, Sacramento, CA 95819. Offers child development (MA); counseling (MS); curriculum and instruction (MA); education (Ed D); education leadership and policy studies (MA), including higher education, PreK-12; educational technology (MA); gender equity (MA); language and literacy (MA); multicultural education (MA); school psychology (MA); special education (MA); workforce development advocacy (MA). *Program availability:* Part-time. *Students:* 446 full-time (335 women), 125 part-time (97 women); includes 298 minority (39 Black or African American, non-Hispanic/Latino; 3 American Indian or Alaska Native, non-Hispanic/Latino; 97 Asian, non-Hispanic/Latino; 153 Hispanic/Latino; 6 Native Hawaiian or other Pacific Islander, non-Hispanic/Latino). Average age 32. 540 applicants, 76% accepted, 250 enrolled. In 2016, 107 master's, 7 doctorates awarded. *Degree requirements:* For master's, thesis or project; writing proficiency exam. *Entrance requirements:* For master's, minimum GPA of 2.5, 3.0 in last 60 units. Additional exam requirements/recommendations for international students: Required—TOEFL (minimum score 550 paper-based; 80 iBT). *Application deadline:* For fall admission, 2/15 for domestic students, 1/15 for international students. Applications are processed on a rolling basis. Application fee: $55. Electronic applications accepted. *Expenses:* $4,302 full-time tuition and fees per semester, $2,796 part-time. *Financial support:* Career-related internships or fieldwork and Federal Work-Study available. Support available to part-time students. Financial award application deadline: 3/1; financial award applicants required to submit FAFSA. *Unit head:* Dr. Susan Heredia, Chair, 916-278-5942, E-mail: coe@csus.edu. *Application contact:* Jose Martinez, Graduate Admissions Supervisor, 916-278-7871, E-mail: martinj@skymail.csus.edu.
Website: http://www.csus.edu/coe/academics/graduate/index.html

Cleveland State University, College of Graduate Studies, College of Education and Human Services, Program in Urban Education, Specialization in Policy Studies, Cleveland, OH 44115. Offers PhD. *Program availability:* Part-time. *Faculty:* 6 full-time (1 woman). *Students:* 5 full-time (3 women), 17 part-time (10 women); includes 10 minority (8 Black or African American, non-Hispanic/Latino; 1 Hispanic/Latino; 1 Two or more races, non-Hispanic/Latino), 1 international. Average age 44. 6 applicants, 33% accepted, 2 enrolled. In 2016, 4 doctorates awarded. *Degree requirements:* For doctorate, one foreign language, comprehensive exam, thesis/dissertation. *Entrance requirements:* For doctorate, GRE General Test (minimum score of 297 for combined Verbal and Quantitative exams, 4.0 preferred for Analytical Writing), minimum graduate GPA of 3.25, curriculum vitae or resume, personal statement, 2 letters of recommendation. Additional exam requirements/recommendations for international students: Required—TOEFL (minimum score 550 paper-based; 78 iBT), IELTS (minimum score 6). *Application deadline:* For fall admission, 1/15 for domestic and international students. Application fee: $40. Electronic applications accepted. *Expenses:* Tuition, state resident: full-time $9565. Tuition, nonresident: full-time $17,980. Tuition and fees vary according to program. *Financial support:* In 2016–17, 5 students received support, including 2 research assistantships with full tuition reimbursements available, 1 teaching assistantship with full tuition reimbursement available (averaging $8,850 per year); tuition waivers (full and partial) also available. Support available to part-time students. Financial award application deadline: 4/1; financial award applicants required to submit FAFSA. *Faculty research:* Historical, theoretical and practical aspects of educational policy formation; relationship of educational policy within the larger context of urban affairs, public policy, and school reform. *Unit head:* Dr. Graham Stead, Director, 216-875-9869, Fax: 216-875-9697, E-mail: g.b.stead@csuohio.edu. *Application contact:* Rita M. Grabowski, Administrative Coordinator, 216-687-4697, Fax: 216-875-9697, E-mail: r.grabowski@csuohio.edu.
Website: http://www.csuohio.edu/cehs/departments/DOC/ep_doc.html

The College of William and Mary, School of Education, Program in Education Policy, Planning, and Leadership, Williamsburg, VA 23187-8795. Offers curriculum and educational technology (PhD); curriculum leadership (Ed D, PhD); educational leadership (M Ed), including higher education administration (M Ed, Ed D, PhD), K-12 administration and supervision; educational policy, planning, and leadership (Ed D, PhD), including general education administration, gifted education administration, higher education administration (M Ed, Ed D, PhD). *Accreditation:* NCATE. *Program availability:* Part-time, evening/weekend. *Faculty:* 20 full-time (10 women), 21 part-time/adjunct (13 women). *Students:* 63 full-time (45 women), 143 part-time (95 women); includes 53 minority (39 Black or African American, non-Hispanic/Latino; 4 Asian, non-Hispanic/Latino; 6 Hispanic/Latino; 4 Two or more races, non-Hispanic/Latino), 4 international. Average age 38. 122 applicants, 77% accepted, 65 enrolled. In 2016, 26 master's, 24 doctorates awarded. *Degree requirements:* For doctorate, comprehensive exam, thesis/dissertation. *Entrance requirements:* For master's, GRE or MAT, minimum GPA of 2.5; for doctorate, GRE or MAT, minimum GPA of 3.0. Additional exam requirements/recommendations for international students: Required—TOEFL (minimum score 100 iBT), IELTS (minimum score 7). *Application deadline:* For fall admission, 1/15 for domestic and international students. Application fee: $50. Electronic applications accepted. *Expenses:* $14,258 per year in-state full-time, $275 per credit in-state part-time; $30,500 per year out-of-state full-time, $1,200 per credit out-of-state part-time. *Financial support:* In 2016–17, 64 students received support, including 1 fellowship (averaging $20,000 per year), 54 research assistantships (averaging $19,668 per year); institutionally sponsored loans, scholarships/grants, and unspecified assistantships also available. Support available to part-time students. Financial award application deadline: 1/15; financial award applicants required to submit FAFSA. *Faculty research:* Higher education policy, evaluation of teachers, program evaluation, civil rights and higher education, program evaluation. *Unit head:* Dr. Michael F. Dipaola, Department Chair, 757-221-2344, E-mail: mfdipa@wm.edu. *Application contact:* Dorothy Smith Osborne, Assistant Dean for Academic Programs and Student Services, 757-221-2317, E-mail: dsosbo@wm.edu.
Website: http://education.wm.edu

Cornell University, Graduate School, Graduate Fields of Agriculture and Life Sciences, Field of Education, Ithaca, NY 14853. Offers adult and extension education (MPS, MS, PhD); learning, teaching, and social policy (MPS, MS, PhD); mathematics 7-12 (MS). Terminal master's awarded for partial completion of doctoral program. *Degree requirements:* For master's, thesis (MS); for doctorate, comprehensive exam, thesis/dissertation. *Entrance requirements:* For master's and doctorate, GRE General Test, sample of written work (recommended), 2 letters of recommendation. Additional exam requirements/recommendations for international students: Required—TOEFL (minimum score 550 paper-based; 77 iBT). Electronic applications accepted. *Faculty research:* Moral development and professional ethics, public issues education and community development, socio/political issues in public education, teacher education and curriculum in agricultural science and mathematics, extension research.

Eastern Michigan University, Graduate School, College of Arts and Sciences, Department of Sociology, Anthropology and Criminology, Program in Schools, Society and Violence, Ypsilanti, MI 48197. Offers MA. *Students:* 2 full-time (1 woman), 3 part-time (1 woman); includes 1 minority (American Indian or Alaska Native, non-Hispanic/Latino). Average age 25. 6 applicants, 67% accepted, 4 enrolled. In 2016, 1 master's awarded. Application fee: $45. *Application contact:* Dr. Solage Simoes, Coordinator, 734-487-0012, Fax: 734-487-9666, E-mail: ssimoes@emich.edu.
Website: http://www.emich.edu/sac/

Florida State University, The Graduate School, College of Education, Program in Educational Leadership and Policy, Tallahassee, FL 32306. Offers education policy and evaluation (MS, Ed D, PhD); educational leadership/administration (MS, Ed D, PhD, Certificate, Ed S); program evaluation (Certificate). *Program availability:* Part-time, evening/weekend, blended/hybrid learning. Terminal master's awarded for partial completion of doctoral program. *Degree requirements:* For master's and other advanced degree, comprehensive exam, thesis optional; for doctorate, comprehensive exam, thesis/dissertation, diagnostic exam, preliminary exam, prospectus defense, dissertation

defense. *Entrance requirements:* For master's, doctorate, and other advanced degree, GRE General Test, minimum upper-division GPA of 3.0. Additional exam requirements/recommendations for international students: Required—TOEFL (minimum score 550 paper-based, 80 iBT), IELTS (minimum score 6.5), Michigan English Language Assessment Battery (minimum score 77), or PTE (minimum score 55). Application fee: $30. Electronic applications accepted. *Expenses:* Tuition, state resident: full-time $7263; part-time $403.51 per credit hour. Tuition, nonresident: full-time $18,087; part-time $1004.85 per credit hour. *Required fees:* $1365; $75.81 per credit hour. $20 per semester. Tuition and fees vary according to campus/location. *Financial support:* Fellowships, research assistantships, teaching assistantships, scholarships/grants, tuition waivers (full and partial), and unspecified assistantships available. Financial award application deadline: 1/15; financial award applicants required to submit FAFSA. *Faculty research:* Educational leadership in traditional public and charter institutions, educational evaluation and policy, policy and politics of K-12 education, pre-service teacher and teacher policy and professional education, economics and finance of education. *Unit head:* Dr. Motoko Akiba, Professor/Program Coordinator, 850-644-5553, Fax: 850-644-1258, E-mail: makiba@fsu.edu. *Application contact:* Linda J. Lyons, Academic Support Assistant, 850-644-7077, Fax: 850-644-1258, E-mail: ljlyons@fsu.edu.
Website: http://education.fsu.edu/degrees-and-programs/graduate-programs

The George Washington University, Graduate School of Education and Human Development, Department of Educational Leadership, Program in Educational Administration and Policy Studies, Washington, DC 20052. Offers education policy (Ed D); educational administration (Ed D). Ed D in educational administration offered at Newport News and Alexandria, VA. *Accreditation:* NCATE. *Students:* 10 full-time (8 women), 126 part-time (86 women); includes 60 minority (45 Black or African American, non-Hispanic/Latino; 7 Asian, non-Hispanic/Latino; 5 Hispanic/Latino; 1 Native Hawaiian or other Pacific Islander, non-Hispanic/Latino; 2 Two or more races, non-Hispanic/Latino), 2 international. Average age 40. 50 applicants, 58% accepted, 18 enrolled. In 2016, 27 doctorates awarded. *Degree requirements:* For doctorate, comprehensive exam, thesis/dissertation. *Entrance requirements:* For doctorate, GRE General Test or MAT, interview, minimum GPA of 3.3. *Application deadline:* For fall admission, 1/15 priority date for domestic students; for spring admission, 10/1 for domestic students. Applications are processed on a rolling basis. Application fee: $75. *Financial support:* In 2016–17, 9 students received support. Fellowships, research assistantships, teaching assistantships, career-related internships or fieldwork, Federal Work-Study, and tuition waivers (partial) available. Financial award application deadline: 1/15; financial award applicants required to submit FAFSA. *Unit head:* Michael Feuer, Dean, 202-994-6161, E-mail: mjfeuer@gwu.edu. *Application contact:* Sarah Lang, Director, Admissions and Marketing, 202-994-1447, Fax: 202-994-7207, E-mail: slang@gwu.edu.

The George Washington University, Graduate School of Education and Human Development, Department of Educational Leadership, Program in Education Policy Studies, Washington, DC 20052. Offers MA Ed. *Accreditation:* NCATE. *Students:* 18 full-time (15 women), 2 part-time (both women); includes 5 minority (2 Black or African American, non-Hispanic/Latino; 3 Hispanic/Latino), 3 international. Average age 28. 55 applicants, 71% accepted, 12 enrolled. In 2016, 12 master's awarded. *Degree requirements:* For master's, comprehensive exam. *Entrance requirements:* For master's, GRE General Test or MAT, interview, minimum GPA of 2.75. *Application deadline:* For fall admission, 1/15 priority date for domestic students; for spring admission, 10/1 for domestic students. Applications are processed on a rolling basis. Application fee: $75. *Financial support:* In 2016–17, 10 students received support. Fellowships, career-related internships or fieldwork, Federal Work-Study, and tuition waivers (partial) available. Financial award application deadline: 1/15. *Unit head:* Michael Feuer, Dean, 202-994-6161, E-mail: mjfeuer@gwu.edu. *Application contact:* Sarah Lang, Director of Graduate Admissions, 202-994-1447, Fax: 202-994-7207, E-mail: slang@gwu.edu.

The George Washington University, Graduate School of Education and Human Development, Department of Educational Leadership, Program in Higher Education Administration, Washington, DC 20052. Offers college teaching and academic leadership (MA Ed/HD, Ed S); general administration (MA Ed/HD, Ed S); higher education administration (Ed D); higher education finance (MA Ed/HD, Ed S); international education (MA Ed/HD, Ed S); policy (MA Ed/HD, Ed S); student affairs administration (MA Ed/HD, Ed S). *Accreditation:* NCATE. *Students:* 23 full-time (18 women), 70 part-time (51 women); includes 35 minority (20 Black or African American, non-Hispanic/Latino; 8 Asian, non-Hispanic/Latino; 6 Hispanic/Latino; 1 Two or more races, non-Hispanic/Latino), 3 international. Average age 31. 148 applicants, 74% accepted, 37 enrolled. In 2016, 30 master's, 9 doctorates, 1 other advanced degree awarded. *Degree requirements:* For master's and Ed S, comprehensive exam; for doctorate, comprehensive exam, thesis/dissertation. *Entrance requirements:* For master's, GRE General Test or MAT, minimum GPA of 2.75; for doctorate, GRE General Test or MAT, interview, minimum GPA of 3.3; for Ed S, GRE General Test or MAT, minimum GPA of 3.3. *Application deadline:* For fall admission, 1/15 priority date for domestic students; for spring admission, 10/1 for domestic students. Applications are processed on a rolling basis. Application fee: $75. *Financial support:* In 2016–17, 17 students received support. Fellowships, research assistantships, career-related internships or fieldwork, Federal Work-Study, and tuition waivers (partial) available. Financial award application deadline: 1/15; financial award applicants required to submit FAFSA. *Faculty research:* Technology in higher education administration. *Unit head:* Michael Feuer, Dean, 202-994-6161, E-mail: mjfeuer@gwu.edu. *Application contact:* Sarah Lang, Director of Graduate Admissions, 202-994-1447, Fax: 202-994-7207, E-mail: slang@gwu.edu.

Georgia State University, College of Education and Human Development, Department of Educational Policy Studies, Atlanta, GA 30302-3083. Offers educational leadership (M Ed, Ed D, Ed S), including educational leadership, urban teacher leadership (M Ed); educational research (MS, PhD); social foundations of education (MS, PhD). *Program availability:* Part-time. *Faculty:* 20 full-time (14 women). *Students:* 48 full-time (30 women), 88 part-time (61 women); includes 73 minority (58 Black or African American, non-Hispanic/Latino; 6 Asian, non-Hispanic/Latino; 6 Hispanic/Latino; 3 Two or more races, non-Hispanic/Latino), 2 international. Average age 38. 74 applicants, 53% accepted, 25 enrolled. In 2016, 9 master's, 24 doctorates, 15 other advanced degrees awarded. *Degree requirements:* For master's, thesis optional, 36 semester hours; for doctorate, comprehensive exam, thesis/dissertation, 54 semester hours (for Ed D); 69 semester hours (for PhD); for Ed S, thesis, 30 semester hours of coursework. *Entrance requirements:* For master's, GRE; for doctorate and Ed S, GRE, MAT. Additional exam requirements/recommendations for international students: Required—TOEFL (minimum score 550 paper-based; 79 iBT) or IELTS (minimum score 6.5). *Application deadline:* For fall admission, 1/15 for domestic and international students; for winter admission, 2/1 for domestic and international students; for spring admission, 10/1 for domestic and international students. Applications are processed on a rolling basis. Application fee: $50. Electronic applications accepted. *Expenses:* Tuition, state resident: full-time $6876; part-time $382 per credit hour. Tuition, nonresident: full-time $22,374; part-time $1243 per credit hour. *Required fees:* $2128; $1064 per term. Part-time tuition and fees vary according to course load and program. *Financial support:* In 2016–17, fellowships with full tuition reimbursements (averaging $23,000 per year), research assistantships with full tuition reimbursements (averaging $27,671 per year), teaching assistantships with full tuition reimbursements (averaging $2,300 per year) were awarded; career-related internships or fieldwork, institutionally sponsored loans, scholarships/grants, health care benefits, tuition waivers (full), and unspecified assistantships also available. Support available to part-time students. Financial award application deadline: 3/15. *Faculty research:* Social and cultural influences on schools, equity and social justice, research methodology, program evaluation, leadership and instruction in schools. *Unit head:* Dr. Bill Curlette, Chair, 404-413-8030, Fax: 404-413-8003, E-mail: wcurlette@gsu.edu. *Application contact:* Aishah Cowan, Administrative Academic Specialist, 404-413-8273, Fax: 404-413-8033, E-mail: acowan@gsu.edu.
Website: http://eps.education.gsu.edu/

Harvard University, Harvard Graduate School of Education, Master's Programs in Education, Cambridge, MA 02138. Offers arts in education (Ed M); education policy and management (Ed M); higher education (Ed M); human development and psychology (Ed M); international education policy (Ed M); language and literacy (Ed M); learning and teaching (Ed M); mind, brain, and education (Ed M); prevention science and practice (Ed M); school leadership (Ed M); special studies (Ed M); teacher education (Ed M); technology, innovation, and education (Ed M). *Program availability:* Part-time. *Entrance requirements:* For master's, GRE General Test, statement of purpose, 3 letters of recommendation, resume, official transcripts. Additional exam requirements/recommendations for international students: Required—TOEFL (minimum score 613 paper-based; 104 iBT), TWE (minimum score 5). Electronic applications accepted. *Faculty research:* Learning and development, educational leadership and organizations, education policy analysis.

Howard University, School of Education, Department of Educational Leadership and Policy Studies, Washington, DC 20059. Offers educational administration (Ed D); educational administration and supervision (M Ed, CAGS). *Program availability:* Part-time. *Degree requirements:* For master's, comprehensive exam, School Leaders Licensure Assessment, practicum; for doctorate, comprehensive exam, thesis/dissertation, internship; for CAGS, thesis. *Entrance requirements:* For master's, minimum GPA of 2.7; for doctorate, minimum GPA of 3.0. Additional exam requirements/recommendations for international students: Required—TOEFL (minimum score 550 paper-based; 79 iBT). Electronic applications accepted.

Illinois State University, Graduate School, College of Education, Department of Curriculum and Instruction, Normal, IL 61790-2200. Offers curriculum and instruction (MS, MS Ed, Ed D); educational policies (Ed D); postsecondary education (Ed D); reading (MS Ed); supervision (Ed D). *Accreditation:* NCATE. *Degree requirements:* For master's, variable foreign language requirement, thesis or alternative; for doctorate, variable foreign language requirement, thesis/dissertation, 2 terms of residency, internship. *Entrance requirements:* For master's, GRE General Test, minimum GPA of 3.0 in last 60 hours of course work; for doctorate, GRE General Test. *Faculty research:* In-service and pre-service teacher education for teachers of English language learners; teachers for all children: developing a model for alternative, bilingual elementary certification for paraprofessionals in Illinois; Illinois Geographic Alliance, Connections Project.

Indiana University Bloomington, School of Education, Department of Educational Leadership and Policy Studies, Bloomington, IN 47405. Offers educational leadership (MS, Ed D, Ed S); higher education (Ed D, PhD); higher education and student affairs (MS); history and philosophy of education (MS); history, philosophy, and policy in education (PhD), including education policy studies, history of education, philosophy of education; international and comparative education (MS). *Accreditation:* NCATE. *Faculty:* 32 full-time (18 women). *Students:* 223 full-time (140 women), 94 part-time (50 women); includes 80 minority (44 Black or African American, non-Hispanic/Latino; 13 Asian, non-Hispanic/Latino; 18 Hispanic/Latino; 1 Native Hawaiian or other Pacific Islander, non-Hispanic/Latino; 4 Two or more races, non-Hispanic/Latino), 29 international. Average age 34. 309 applicants, 40% accepted, 57 enrolled. In 2016, 60 master's, 18 doctorates, 5 other advanced degrees awarded. *Degree requirements:* For master's, thesis optional; for doctorate, comprehensive exam, thesis/dissertation; for Ed S, comprehensive exam or project. *Entrance requirements:* For master's, doctorate, and Ed S, GRE General Test. Additional exam requirements/recommendations for international students: Required—TOEFL (minimum score 79 iBT). *Application deadline:* For fall admission, 1/15 priority date for domestic students, 12/1 priority date for international students; for spring admission, 9/1 priority date for domestic and international students. Applications are processed on a rolling basis. Application fee: $55 ($65 for international students). Electronic applications accepted. *Financial support:* Fellowships with full and partial tuition reimbursements, research assistantships with full and partial tuition reimbursements, teaching assistantships with full and partial tuition reimbursements, career-related internships or fieldwork, scholarships/grants, health care benefits, and unspecified assistantships available. *Faculty research:* Culturally engaging campus environments, school choice policy analysis, democracy and education in the national and international context, and principal leadership. *Unit head:* Dr. Dionne Danns, Interim Chair, 812-856-8398. *Application contact:* Maria Jensen, Department Administrator, 812-856-8370, Fax: 812-856-8394, E-mail: jensen5@indiana.edu.
Website: http://education.indiana.edu/about/departments/leadership/index.html

Johns Hopkins University, School of Education, Doctoral Programs in Education, Baltimore, MD 21218. Offers Ed D, PhD. *Program availability:* Part-time, evening/weekend, 100% online. *Students:* 22 full-time (14 women), 215 part-time (149 women); includes 82 minority (35 Black or African American, non-Hispanic/Latino; 14 Asian, non-Hispanic/Latino; 25 Hispanic/Latino; 8 Two or more races, non-Hispanic/Latino), 20 international. Average age 37. 416 applicants, 27% accepted, 82 enrolled. In 2016, 11 doctorates awarded. *Degree requirements:* For doctorate, comprehensive exam, thesis/dissertation. *Entrance requirements:* For doctorate, GRE (for PhD only), master's degree from regionally- or nationally-accredited institution; minimum GPA of 3.0 in previous undergraduate and graduate studies (for Ed D only); official transcripts from all post-secondary institutions attended; three letters of recommendation; curriculum vitae/resume; personal statement; dispositions survey. Additional exam requirements/recommendations for international students: Required—TOEFL (minimum score 600 paper-based; 100 iBT), IELTS (minimum score 7). *Application deadline:* For fall admission, 12/1 for domestic and international students. Application fee: $80. Electronic applications accepted. *Expenses:* Contact institution. *Financial support:* Fellowships, research assistantships, and teaching assistantships available. Financial award application deadline: 4/1; financial award applicants required to submit FAFSA. *Unit head:* Dr. Christopher C. Morphew, Dean. *Application contact:* Elisabeth Woodward, Director of Admissions, 410-516-9796, Fax: 410-516-9817, E-mail: soe.info@jhu.edu.
Website: http://education.jhu.edu

Loyola University Chicago, School of Education, Program in Cultural and Educational Policy Studies, Chicago, IL 60660. Offers M Ed, MA, PhD. *Program availability:* Part-time. *Faculty:* 5 full-time (3 women), 5 part-time/adjunct (2 women). *Students:* 53 full-time (41 women), 8 part-time (5 women); includes 32 minority (20 Black or African American, non-Hispanic/Latino; 1 American Indian or Alaska Native, non-Hispanic/Latino; 3 Asian, non-Hispanic/Latino; 7 Hispanic/Latino; 1 Native Hawaiian or other Pacific Islander, non-Hispanic/Latino). Average age 30. 70 applicants, 71% accepted,

32 enrolled. In 2016, 11 master's, 3 doctorates awarded. *Degree requirements:* For master's, comprehensive exam (M Ed), thesis (MA); for doctorate, comprehensive exam, thesis/dissertation, oral candidacy exam. *Entrance requirements:* For master's, letters of recommendation, minimum GPA of 3.0; for doctorate, GRE General Test, interview, letter of recommendation, resume, minimum GPA of 3.0. Additional exam requirements/recommendations for international students: Required—TOEFL (minimum score 550 paper-based; 79 iBT). *Application deadline:* For fall admission, 4/1 for domestic and international students; for spring admission, 11/1 for domestic and international students. Applications are processed on a rolling basis. Application fee: $50. Electronic applications accepted. Application fee is waived when completed online. *Expenses: Tuition:* Full-time $18,594. *Required fees:* $848. Part-time tuition and fees vary according to course load, degree level and program. *Financial support:* In 2016–17, 5 research assistantships with full tuition reimbursements (averaging $14,000 per year), 24 teaching assistantships (averaging $4,000 per year) were awarded; career-related internships or fieldwork, institutionally sponsored loans, scholarships/grants, health care benefits, and unspecified assistantships also available. Support available to part-time students. Financial award application deadline: 2/1; financial award applicants required to submit FAFSA. *Faculty research:* Politics of education, cultural foundations, policy studies, qualitative research methods, multicultural diversity. *Unit head:* Dr. Noah Sobe, Director, 312-915-6954, E-mail: nsobe@luc.edu. *Application contact:* Marie Hatland, Information Contact, 312-915-6800, E-mail: schleduc@luc.edu.

Marquette University, Graduate School, College of Education, Department of Educational Policy and Leadership, Milwaukee, WI 53201-1881. Offers college student personnel administration (M Ed); curriculum and instruction (MA); education (MA); educational administration (M Ed); educational policy and foundations (MA); elementary education (Certificate); literacy (MA); principal (Certificate); reading specialist (Certificate); reading teacher (Certificate); secondary education (Certificate); superintendent (Certificate). *Program availability:* Part-time, evening/weekend. *Faculty:* 17 full-time (14 women), 28 part-time/adjunct (23 women). *Students:* 31 full-time (23 women), 103 part-time (66 women); includes 22 minority (7 Black or African American, non-Hispanic/Latino; 1 American Indian or Alaska Native, non-Hispanic/Latino; 6 Asian, non-Hispanic/Latino; 6 Hispanic/Latino; 2 Two or more races, non-Hispanic/Latino). Average age 31. 96 applicants, 92% accepted, 67 enrolled. In 2016, 47 master's, 3 other advanced degrees awarded. Terminal master's awarded for partial completion of doctoral program. *Degree requirements:* For master's, comprehensive exam, thesis (for some programs); for doctorate, thesis/dissertation, qualifying exam. *Entrance requirements:* For master's, GRE General Test or MAT, official transcripts from all current and previous colleges/universities except Marquette, three letters of recommendation, statement of purpose; for doctorate, GRE General Test, MAT, sample of written work, official transcripts from all current and previous colleges/universities except Marquette, three letters of recommendation, statement of purpose, resume/curriculum vitae; for Certificate, GRE General Test or MAT, master's degree. Additional exam requirements/recommendations for international students: Required—TOEFL (minimum score 530 paper-based). *Application deadline:* For fall admission, 1/15 for domestic and international students. Application fee: $50. *Expenses:* Contact institution. *Financial support:* Fellowships, research assistantships, health care benefits, tuition waivers (partial), and unspecified assistantships available. Support available to part-time students. Financial award application deadline: 2/15. *Faculty research:* Leadership; social justice in education; development of lifelong learners; race, class, and schooling in historical perspective; urban teacher education. *Unit head:* Dr. Ellen Eckman, Chair, 414-288-1561. *Application contact:* Dr. Cynthia Ellwood.

Michigan State University, The Graduate School, College of Education, Program in Educational Policy, East Lansing, MI 48824. Offers PhD. *Entrance requirements:* Additional exam requirements/recommendations for international students: Required—TOEFL. Electronic applications accepted.

New York University, Steinhardt School of Culture, Education, and Human Development, Department of Humanities and Social Sciences in the Professions, Program in Sociology of Education, New York, NY 10003. Offers education policy (MA); social and cultural studies of education (MA); sociology of education (PhD). *Program availability:* Part-time. *Degree requirements:* For master's, thesis (for some programs); for doctorate, thesis/dissertation. *Entrance requirements:* For master's, letters of recommendation; for doctorate, GRE General Test, interview. Additional exam requirements/recommendations for international students: Required—TOEFL (minimum score 100 iBT). Electronic applications accepted. *Faculty research:* Legal and institutional environments of schools; social inequality; high school reform and achievement; urban schooling, economics and education, educational policy.

Northwest Missouri State University, Graduate School, School of Education, Maryville, MO 64468-6001. Offers early childhood education (MS Ed); education leadership (MS Ed), including elementary, K-12, secondary; educational leadership (Ed S), including elementary school principalship, secondary school principalship, superintendency; educational leadership and policy analysis (Ed D); elementary education (MS Ed); elementary mathematics (MS Ed); higher education leadership (MS); middle school education (MS Ed); reading (MS Ed); special education (MS Ed); teacher leadership (MS Ed); teaching English language learners (MS Ed). *Accreditation:* NCATE. *Program availability:* Part-time. *Students:* 15 full-time (11 women), 150 part-time (103 women). In 2016, 46 master's awarded. *Degree requirements:* For master's, comprehensive exam; for Ed S, comprehensive exam, thesis. *Entrance requirements:* For master's, GRE General Test, writing sample; for Ed S, minimum graduate GPA of 3.25. Additional exam requirements/recommendations for international students: Required—TOEFL (minimum score 550 paper-based). *Application deadline:* For fall admission, 7/1 for domestic and international students; for spring admission, 11/15 for domestic and international students. Applications are processed on a rolling basis. Application fee: $0 ($50 for international students). Electronic applications accepted. *Expenses:* Tuition, state resident: full-time $3447; part-time $383 per credit hour. Tuition, nonresident: full-time $5724; part-time $636 per credit hour. *Required fees:* $130 per credit hour. *Financial support:* Research assistantships with full tuition reimbursements, teaching assistantships with full tuition reimbursements, and unspecified assistantships available. Financial award application deadline: 4/1; financial award applicants required to submit FAFSA. *Faculty research:* Great books of educational administration. *Unit head:* Dr. Tim Wall, Dean, 660-562-1179, E-mail: timwall@nwmissouri.edu.
Website: http://www.nwmissouri.edu/academics/ed/

The Ohio State University, Graduate School, College of Education and Human Ecology, Department of Educational Studies, Columbus, OH 43210. Offers M Ed, MA, PhD, Ed S. *Accreditation:* NCATE. *Program availability:* Part-time. *Faculty:* 52. *Students:* 322 full-time (222 women), 147 part-time (102 women); includes 98 minority (54 Black or African American, non-Hispanic/Latino; 15 Asian, non-Hispanic/Latino; 19 Hispanic/Latino; 10 Two or more races, non-Hispanic/Latino), 52 international. Average age 31. In 2016, 111 master's, 13 doctorates, 7 other advanced degrees awarded. *Degree requirements:* For master's, thesis optional; for doctorate, thesis/dissertation. *Entrance requirements:* For master's and doctorate, GRE General Test. Additional exam requirements/recommendations for international students: Required—TOEFL (minimum score 550 paper-based; 79 iBT), Michigan English Language Assessment Battery (minimum score 82); Recommended—IELTS (minimum score 7). *Application deadline:* For fall admission, 12/1 priority date for domestic and international students; for spring admission, 11/1 for domestic and international students; for summer admission, 3/1 for domestic and international students. Applications are processed on a rolling basis. Application fee: $60 ($70 for international students). Electronic applications accepted. *Financial support:* Fellowships with tuition reimbursements, research assistantships with tuition reimbursements, teaching assistantships with tuition reimbursements, Federal Work-Study, institutionally sponsored loans, and unspecified assistantships available. Support available to part-time students. *Unit head:* Dr. Eric Anderman, Chair and Professor, 614-688-5721, E-mail: anderman.1@osu.edu. *Application contact:* Deb Zabloudil, Director of Graduate Student Services, 614-688-4007, E-mail: zabloudil.1@osu.edu.
Website: http://ehe.osu.edu/educational-studies/

Oregon State University, College of Education, Program in Education, Corvallis, OR 97331. Offers advanced science and mathematics education (Ed M); agricultural education (PhD); education (Ed D); free-choice learning (Ed M); language equity and educational policy (PhD); mathematics education (MS); pre-K-12 English to speakers of other languages (ESOL) (Ed M); science education (MS); science/mathematics education (PhD); social justice in education (Ed M). *Program availability:* Part-time, 100% online, blended/hybrid learning. *Faculty:* 9 full-time (8 women), 6 part-time/adjunct (2 women). *Students:* 14 full-time (8 women), 76 part-time (53 women); includes 25 minority (6 Black or African American, non-Hispanic/Latino; 2 American Indian or Alaska Native, non-Hispanic/Latino; 5 Asian, non-Hispanic/Latino; 10 Hispanic/Latino; 2 Two or more races, non-Hispanic/Latino), 3 international. Average age 38. 72 applicants, 69% accepted, 40 enrolled. In 2016, 14 master's, 21 doctorates awarded. Terminal master's awarded for partial completion of doctoral program. *Degree requirements:* For master's, variable foreign language requirement, thesis (for some programs); for doctorate, variable foreign language requirement, thesis/dissertation. *Entrance requirements:* Additional exam requirements/recommendations for international students: Required—TOEFL (minimum score 575 paper-based). Application fee: $75 ($85 for international students). *Expenses:* Tuition, state resident: full-time $12,150; part-time $450 per credit. Tuition, nonresident: full-time $21,789; part-time $807 per credit. *Required fees:* $1651; $1507 per credit. One-time fee: $350. Tuition and fees vary according to course load, campus/location and program. *Financial support:* Fellowships, research assistantships, teaching assistantships, career-related internships or fieldwork, Federal Work-Study, and institutionally sponsored loans available. Support available to part-time students. *Faculty research:* School administration, educational foundations, research methodology, education policy development, higher education administration. *Unit head:* Dr. Larry Flick, Dean. *Application contact:* E-mail: askcoed@oregonstate.edu.

Penn State University Park, Graduate School, College of Education, Department of Education Policy Studies, University Park, PA 16802. Offers educational leadership (M Ed, D Ed, PhD, Certificate); educational theory and policy (MA, PhD); higher education (M Ed, MS, D Ed, PhD). *Accreditation:* NCATE. *Program availability:* Online learning. *Unit head:* Dr. David H. Monk, Dean, 814-865-2523, Fax: 814-865-0555. *Application contact:* Lori Hawn, Director, Graduate Student Services, 814-865-1795, Fax: 814-863-4627, E-mail: l-gswww@lists.psu.edu.
Website: http://ed.psu.edu/eps

Rutgers University–Camden, Graduate School of Arts and Sciences, Department of Public Policy and Administration, Camden, NJ 08102. Offers education policy and leadership (MPA); international public service and development (MPA); public management (MPA); JD/MPA; MPA/MA. *Accreditation:* NASPAA. *Program availability:* Part-time, evening/weekend. *Degree requirements:* For master's, directed study, research workshop, 42 credits. *Entrance requirements:* For master's, GRE General Test, GMAT or LSAT, 3 letters of recommendation; resume. Additional exam requirements/recommendations for international students: Required—TOEFL (minimum score 550 paper-based), IELTS. Electronic applications accepted. *Faculty research:* Nonprofit management, county and municipal administration, health and human services, government communication, administrative law, educational finance.

Rutgers University–New Brunswick, Graduate School of Education, Doctoral Program in Education, New Brunswick, NJ 08901. Offers educational policy (PhD); educational psychology (PhD); literacy education (PhD); mathematics education (PhD). *Program availability:* Part-time. *Degree requirements:* For doctorate, thesis/dissertation, qualifying exam. *Entrance requirements:* For doctorate, GRE General Test, GRE Subject Test (mathematics education). Additional exam requirements/recommendations for international students: Required—TOEFL (minimum score 575 paper-based; 83 iBT). Electronic applications accepted. *Faculty research:* Literacy education, math education, educational psychology, educational policy, learning sciences.

Stanford University, Graduate School of Education, Program in Policy, Organization, and Leadership Studies, Stanford, CA 94305-2004. Offers MA, MA/MBA. *Degree requirements:* For master's, thesis (for some programs). *Entrance requirements:* For master's, GRE General Test. Electronic applications accepted. *Expenses: Tuition:* Full-time $47,331. *Required fees:* $609.

Syracuse University, School of Education, CAS Program in Instructional Design Foundations, Syracuse, NY 13244. Offers CAS. *Program availability:* Part-time. *Entrance requirements:* For degree, baccalaureate degree from regionally-accredited college/university, statement of goals, three recommendation letters, transcripts. *Application deadline:* Applications are processed on a rolling basis. Application fee: $75. Electronic applications accepted. *Expenses: Tuition:* Full-time $25,974; part-time $1443 per credit hour. *Required fees:* $802; $50 per course. Tuition and fees vary according to course load and program. *Financial support:* Fellowships, research assistantships, teaching assistantships, career-related internships or fieldwork, and scholarships/grants available. Financial award application deadline: 1/15. *Unit head:* Dr. Tiffany A. Koszalka, Chair, 315-443-3703, E-mail: takoszal@syr.edu. *Application contact:* Speranza Migliore, Graduate Admissions Recruiter, 315-443-2505, E-mail: gradrcrt@syr.edu.
Website: http://soe.syr.edu/academic/Instructional_Design_Development_and_Evaluation/graduate/certificates/default.aspx

Teachers College, Columbia University, Department of Education Policy and Social Analysis, New York, NY 10027. Offers economics and education (Ed M, MA, PhD); education policy (Ed M, MA, Ed D, PhD); politics and education (Ed M, MA, Ed D, PhD); sociology and education (Ed M, MA, Ed D, PhD). *Students:* 148 full-time (110 women), 107 part-time (85 women); includes 95 minority (40 Black or African American, non-Hispanic/Latino; 23 Asian, non-Hispanic/Latino; 26 Hispanic/Latino; 6 Two or more races, non-Hispanic/Latino), 74 international. 516 applicants, 54% accepted, 98 enrolled. *Expenses: Tuition:* Full-time $36,288; part-time $1512 per credit. *Required fees:* $438 per semester. One-time fee: $510 full-time. Full-time tuition and fees vary according to course load. *Unit head:* Dr. Jeffrey Henig, Chair, 212-678-8313, Fax: 212-678 3589, E-mail: henig@tc.columbia.edu. *Application contact:* David Estrella, Director of Admissions, 212-678-3305, E-mail: estrella@tc.columbia.edu.
Website: http://www.tc.columbia.edu/education-policy-and-social-analysis/

Teachers College, Columbia University, Department of Organization and Leadership, New York, NY 10027-6696. Offers adult education guided intensive study (Ed D); adult learning and leadership (Ed M, MA, Ed D); educational leadership (Ed D); higher and postsecondary education (MA, Ed D); leadership, policy and politics (Ed D); nurse executive (MA, Ed D), including administration studies (MA), professorial studies (MA); private school leadership (Ed M, MA); public school building leadership (Ed M, MA); social and organizational psychology (MA); urban education leaders (Ed D); MA/MBA. *Program availability:* Part-time, evening/weekend. *Students:* 310 full-time (214 women), 390 part-time (250 women); includes 276 minority (116 Black or African American, non-Hispanic/Latino; 3 American Indian or Alaska Native, non-Hispanic/Latino; 61 Asian, non-Hispanic/Latino; 79 Hispanic/Latino; 17 Two or more races, non-Hispanic/Latino), 93 international. 624 applicants, 57% accepted, 172 enrolled. *Degree requirements:* For doctorate, thesis/dissertation. *Expenses: Tuition:* Full-time $36,288; part-time $1512 per credit. *Required fees:* $438 per semester. One-time fee: $510 full-time. Full-time tuition and fees vary according to course load. *Unit head:* Prof. Anna Neumann, Chair, 212-678-3272, Fax: 212-678-3036, E-mail: neumann@tc.columbia.edu. *Application contact:* David Estrella, Director of Admission, 212-678-3305, E-mail: estrella@tc.columbia.edu.

University at Albany, State University of New York, School of Education, Department of Educational Policy and Leadership, Albany, NY 12222-0001. Offers educational policy and leadership (MS, PhD); higher education (MS); international education management (CAS). *Program availability:* Evening/weekend. *Faculty:* 10 full-time (4 women), 7 part-time/adjunct (6 women). *Students:* 27 full-time (11 women), 103 part-time (53 women); includes 24 minority (14 Black or African American, non-Hispanic/Latino; 1 Asian, non-Hispanic/Latino; 9 Hispanic/Latino), 15 international. Average age 31. 48 applicants, 75% accepted, 33 enrolled. In 2016, 16 master's, 9 doctorates, 11 other advanced degrees awarded. *Degree requirements:* For doctorate, one foreign language, thesis/dissertation. *Entrance requirements:* For doctorate, GRE General Test, GRE Subject Test. Additional exam requirements/recommendations for international students: Required—TOEFL (minimum score 550 paper-based). *Application deadline:* For fall admission, 2/1 for domestic students, 5/1 for international students; for spring admission, 9/1 for domestic students, 11/1 for international students. Applications are processed on a rolling basis. Application fee: $75. Electronic applications accepted. *Expenses:* Tuition, state resident: full-time $10,870; part-time $453 per credit hour. Tuition, nonresident: full-time $22,210; part-time $925 per credit hour. *International tuition:* $21,550 full-time. *Required fees:* $1864; $96 per credit hour. *Financial support:* Fellowships and career-related internships or fieldwork available. Financial award application deadline: 3/15. *Total annual research expenditures:* $273,985. *Unit head:* Kevin Kinser, Chair, 518-442-5092, E-mail: kkinser@albany.edu.
Website: http://www.albany.edu/epl/

University of Alberta, Faculty of Graduate Studies and Research, Department of Educational Policy Studies, Edmonton, AB T6G 2E1, Canada. Offers adult education (M Ed, Ed D, PhD); educational administration and leadership (M Ed, Ed D, PhD, Postgraduate Diploma); First Nations education (M Ed, Ed D, PhD); theoretical, cultural and international studies in education (M Ed, Ed D, PhD). *Degree requirements:* For master's, thesis (for some programs); for doctorate, thesis/dissertation. *Entrance requirements:* For master's, minimum GPA of 6.5 on a 9.0 scale; for doctorate, minimum GPA of 7.5 on a 9.0 scale. Additional exam requirements/recommendations for international students: Required—TOEFL (minimum score 580 paper-based). Electronic applications accepted.

University of Arkansas, Graduate School, College of Education and Health Professions, Department of Education Reform, Fayetteville, AR 72701. Offers education policy (PhD). In 2016, 4 doctorates awarded. *Application deadline:* For fall admission, 4/1 for international students; for spring admission, 10/1 for international students. Applications are processed on a rolling basis. Electronic applications accepted. *Financial support:* In 2016–17, 14 research assistantships were awarded; fellowships and teaching assistantships also available. *Unit head:* Dr. Jay Greene, Department Head, 479-575-3172, E-mail: jpg@uark.edu. *Application contact:* Dr. Dirk C. van Raemdonck, Graduate Admissions, 479-575-5597, Fax: 479-575-6676, E-mail: dvanraem@uark.edu.
Website: http://edre.uark.edu/

The University of British Columbia, Faculty of Education, Department of Educational Studies, Vancouver, BC V6T 1Z1, Canada. Offers adult learning and education (M Ed); adult learning and global change (M Ed); curriculum and leadership (M Ed); educational administration and leadership (M Ed); educational leadership and policy (Ed D); educational studies (M Ed, MA, PhD); higher education (M Ed); society, culture and politics in education (M Ed). *Program availability:* Part-time, evening/weekend. *Faculty:* 25 full-time (14 women), 3 part-time/adjunct (2 women). *Students:* 222 full-time (157 women), 62 part-time (44 women). Average age 35. 166 applicants, 66% accepted, 74 enrolled. In 2016, 103 master's, 13 doctorates awarded. Terminal master's awarded for partial completion of doctoral program. *Degree requirements:* For master's, thesis; for doctorate, comprehensive exam, thesis/dissertation. *Entrance requirements:* For master's, minimum B+ average, 4-year undergraduate degree, field-related experience; for doctorate, minimum B+ average, 4-year undergraduate degree, master's degree, field-related experience. Additional exam requirements/recommendations for international students: Required—TOEFL (minimum score 600 paper-based; 100 iBT) or IELTS (minimum score 6.5). Application fee: $90 ($150 for international students). Electronic applications accepted. *Expenses:* Contact institution. *Financial support:* In 2016–17, 7 fellowships with tuition reimbursements (averaging $17,000 per year), 12 research assistantships (averaging $4,000 per year), 8 teaching assistantships (averaging $5,000 per year) were awarded. *Faculty research:* Educational leadership educational administration adult education politics in education, global change and adult learning. *Total annual research expenditures:* $632,000. *Unit head:* Dr. Tara Fenwick, Head, 604-822-5359, Fax: 604-822-4244. *Application contact:* Christine Adams, Graduate Secretary, 604-822-6647, Fax: 604-822-4244, E-mail: grad.edst@ubc.ca.
Website: http://www.edst.educ.ubc.ca/

University of Colorado Boulder, Graduate School, School of Education, Division of Educational Foundations, Policy, and Practice, Boulder, CO 80309. Offers MA, PhD. *Students:* 26 full-time (18 women), 10 part-time (8 women); includes 17 minority (5 Black or African American, non-Hispanic/Latino; 2 Asian, non-Hispanic/Latino; 7 Hispanic/Latino; 3 Two or more races, non-Hispanic/Latino). Average age 31. 69 applicants, 42% accepted, 11 enrolled. In 2016, 10 master's, 3 doctorates awarded. *Entrance requirements:* For master's, minimum undergraduate GPA of 2.75. *Application deadline:* For fall admission, 2/1 for domestic students, 12/1 for international students; for spring admission, 9/1 for domestic and international students. Application fee: $60 ($80 for international students). Electronic applications accepted. Application fee is waived when completed online. *Financial support:* In 2016–17, 77 students received support, including 21 fellowships (averaging $2,781 per year), 16 research assistantships with full and partial tuition reimbursements available (averaging $33,632 per year), 8 teaching assistantships with full and partial tuition reimbursements available (averaging $19,119 per year); institutionally sponsored loans, scholarships/grants, health care benefits, and unspecified assistantships also available. Financial award applicants required to submit FAFSA. *Application contact:* E-mail: edadvise@colorado.edu.
Website: http://www.colorado.edu/education/

University of Colorado Denver, School of Education and Human Development, Program in Educational Leadership and Innovation, Denver, CO 80217. Offers educational studies and research (PhD), including administrative leadership and policy, early childhood special education, math education, research, assessment and evaluation, science education, urban ecologies. *Program availability:* Part-time, evening/weekend. *Students:* 30 full-time (25 women), 14 part-time (11 women); includes 16 minority (7 Black or African American, non-Hispanic/Latino; 1 American Indian or Alaska Native, non-Hispanic/Latino; 1 Asian, non-Hispanic/Latino; 6 Hispanic/Latino; 1 Two or more races, non-Hispanic/Latino), 5 international. Average age 40. 21 applicants, 67% accepted, 8 enrolled. In 2016, 3 doctorates awarded. *Degree requirements:* For doctorate, comprehensive exam, thesis/dissertation, 75 credit hours (for PhD). *Entrance requirements:* For doctorate, GRE or equivalent, resume or curriculum vitae, letters of recommendation, master's degree or equivalent, completion of basic or advanced statistics course with minimum B grade. Additional exam requirements/recommendations for international students: Required—TOEFL (minimum score 537 paper-based; 75 iBT); Recommended—IELTS (minimum score 6.5). *Application deadline:* For fall admission, 12/1 priority date for domestic students, 11/1 priority date for international students. Applications are processed on a rolling basis. Application fee: $50 ($75 for international students). Electronic applications accepted. *Expenses:* Contact institution. *Financial support:* In 2016–17, 45 students received support. Fellowships, research assistantships, teaching assistantships, Federal Work-Study, institutionally sponsored loans, scholarships/grants, and traineeships available. Financial award application deadline: 4/1; financial award applicants required to submit FAFSA. *Faculty research:* Administrative leadership and policy studies, early childhood education, research in diversity, paraprofessionals in education, urban schools lab. *Unit head:* 303-315-6300, E-mail: education@ucdenver.edu. *Application contact:* 303-315-6300, E-mail: education@ucdenver.edu.
Website: http://www.ucdenver.edu/academics/colleges/SchoolOfEducation/Academics/Doctorate/Pages/PhD%20in%20Education%20and%20Human%20Development.aspx

University of Denver, Morgridge College of Education, Denver, CO 80208. Offers child, family and school psychology (MA, PhD, Ed S); counseling psychology (MA, PhD); curriculum and instruction (MA, Ed D, PhD); curriculum instruction and teaching (Certificate); early childhood special education (MA, Certificate); educational leadership and policy studies (MA, Ed D, PhD, Certificate); higher education (Ed D, PhD); library and information science (MLIS); research methods and statistics (MA, PhD). *Accreditation:* ALA; APA (one or more programs are accredited). *Program availability:* Part-time, evening/weekend, online learning. *Faculty:* 39 full-time (29 women), 60 part-time/adjunct (42 women). *Students:* 498 full-time (392 women), 362 part-time (282 women); includes 223 minority (63 Black or African American, non-Hispanic/Latino; 6 American Indian or Alaska Native, non-Hispanic/Latino; 20 Asian, non-Hispanic/Latino; 102 Hispanic/Latino; 1 Native Hawaiian or other Pacific Islander, non-Hispanic/Latino; 31 Two or more races, non-Hispanic/Latino), 40 international. Average age 32. 1,027 applicants, 69% accepted, 386 enrolled. In 2016, 252 master's, 36 doctorates, 141 other advanced degrees awarded. Terminal master's awarded for partial completion of doctoral program. *Degree requirements:* For master's, comprehensive exam; for doctorate, 2 foreign languages, comprehensive exam, thesis/dissertation. *Entrance requirements:* For master's and doctorate, GRE General Test or GMAT. Additional exam requirements/recommendations for international students: Required—TOEFL (minimum score 550 paper-based; 80 iBT). *Application deadline:* Applications are processed on a rolling basis. Application fee: $65. Electronic applications accepted. *Expenses:* $29,022 per year full-time. *Financial support:* In 2016–17, 697 students received support, including 37 research assistantships with tuition reimbursements available (averaging $11,209 per year), 66 teaching assistantships with tuition reimbursements available (averaging $3,742 per year); career-related internships or fieldwork, Federal Work-Study, institutionally sponsored loans, scholarships/grants, and unspecified assistantships also available. Support available to part-time students. Financial award application deadline: 2/15; financial award applicants required to submit FAFSA. *Faculty research:* Early childhood education, access and equity, educational leadership, family and school partnerships, neurodevelopmental disorders. *Total annual research expenditures:* $3.3 million. *Unit head:* Dr. Karen Riley, Dean, 303-871-3665, Fax: 303-871-4456, E-mail: karen.riley@du.edu. *Application contact:* Jodi Dye, Director of Admissions, 303-871-2510, Fax: 303-871-4456, E-mail: jodi.dye@du.edu.
Website: http://morgridge.du.edu

University of Florida, Graduate School, College of Education, School of Human Development and Organizational Studies in Education, Gainesville, FL 32611. Offers counseling and counselor education (Ed D, PhD), including counseling and counselor education, marriage and family counseling, mental health counseling, school counseling and guidance; educational leadership (M Ed, MAE, Ed D, PhD, Ed S), including educational leadership (Ed D, PhD), educational policy (Ed D, PhD); higher education administration (Ed D, PhD), including education policy (Ed D), educational policy, higher education administration; marriage and family counseling (M Ed, MAE, Ed D, PhD, Ed S); mental health counseling (M Ed, MAE, Ed D, PhD, Ed S); research and evaluation methodology (M Ed, MAE, Ed D, PhD); school counseling and guidance (M Ed, MAE, Ed D, PhD, Ed S); student personnel in higher education (M Ed, MAE). *Accreditation:* ACA (one or more programs are accredited); NCATE. *Program availability:* Part-time, online learning. Terminal master's awarded for partial completion of doctoral program. *Degree requirements:* For master's, thesis optional; for doctorate, comprehensive exam, thesis/dissertation. *Entrance requirements:* For master's and doctorate, GRE General Test, minimum GPA of 3.0 (undergraduate), 3.5 (graduate); for Ed S, GRE General Test. Additional exam requirements/recommendations for international students: Required—TOEFL (minimum score 550 paper-based; 80 iBT), IELTS (minimum score 6). Electronic applications accepted.

University of Florida, Graduate School, College of Liberal Arts and Sciences, Department of Political Science, Gainesville, FL 32611. Offers educational policy (PhD); international development policy and administration (MA, Certificate); international relations (MA, MAT); political campaigning (MA, Certificate); political science (MA, PhD); public affairs (MA, Certificate); tropical conservation and development (MA, PhD); JD/MA. Terminal master's awarded for partial completion of doctoral program. *Degree requirements:* For master's, variable foreign language requirement, comprehensive exam (for some programs), thesis or alternative, internship (for some programs); for doctorate, variable foreign language requirement, comprehensive exam, thesis/dissertation. *Entrance requirements:* For master's and doctorate, GRE General Test (minimum score: 308 combined verbal/quantitative), minimum GPA of 3.5. Additional exam requirements/recommendations for international students: Required—TOEFL (minimum score 550 paper-based; 80 iBT), IELTS (minimum score 6). Electronic applications accepted. *Faculty research:* American electoral politics and political institutions, comparative democratization and development, theories of international relation, and political theory.

University of Georgia, College of Education, Department of Lifelong Education, Administration and Policy, Athens, GA 30602. Offers adult education (Ed D, Ed S); lifelong education, administration and policy (PhD). *Accreditation:* NCATE. *Faculty:* 25 full-time (18 women), 1 part-time/adjunct (0 women). *Students:* 74 full-time (56 women), 216 part-time (136 women); includes 73 minority (62 Black or African American, non-Hispanic/Latino; 4 Asian, non-Hispanic/Latino; 3 Hispanic/Latino; 4 Two or more races, non-Hispanic/Latino), 23 international. Average age 37. 123 applicants, 64% accepted, 45 enrolled. In 2016, 19 doctorates, 14 other advanced degrees awarded. *Entrance requirements:* For doctorate, GRE General Test; for Ed S, GRE General Test or MAT.

Application deadline: For fall admission, 7/1 priority date for domestic students; for spring admission, 11/15 for domestic students. Application fee: $50. Electronic applications accepted. *Unit head:* Dr. Janette Hill, Head, 706-542-4035, Fax: 706-542-5873, E-mail: janette@.uga.edu. *Application contact:* Dr. Robert B. Hill, Graduate Coordinator, 706-542-4016, Fax: 706-542-5873, E-mail: bobhill@uga.edu.
Website: http://www.coe.uga.edu/leap/

University of Hawaii at Manoa, Graduate Division, College of Education, PhD in Education Program, Honolulu, HI 96822. Offers curriculum and instruction (PhD); educational administration (PhD); educational foundations (PhD); educational policy studies (PhD); educational psychology (PhD); exceptionalities (PhD); kinesiology (PhD); learning design and technology (PhD). *Program availability:* Part-time, evening/weekend. *Degree requirements:* For doctorate, thesis/dissertation. *Entrance requirements:* For doctorate, GRE General Test, sample of written work. Additional exam requirements/recommendations for international students: Required—TOEFL (minimum score 600 paper-based; 100 iBT), IELTS (minimum score 7).

University of Illinois at Chicago, College of Education, Department of Educational Policy Studies, Chicago, IL 60607-7128. Offers policy studies (M Ed); policy studies in urban education (PhD); urban education leadership (Ed D). *Faculty research:* Social foundations of education, educational organizations and leadership, education policy analysis, understanding and addressing educational problems in urban contexts.

University of Illinois at Urbana–Champaign, Graduate College, College of Education, Department of Education Policy, Organization, and Leadership, Champaign, IL 61820. Offers educational organization and leadership (Ed M, MS, Ed D, PhD, CAS); educational policy studies (Ed M, MA, PhD); human resource education (Ed M, MS, Ed D, PhD, CAS). *Program availability:* Part-time, online learning.

The University of Iowa, Graduate College, College of Education, Department of Educational Policy and Leadership Studies, Iowa City, IA 52242-1316. Offers educational leadership (MA, PhD, Ed S); higher education and student affairs (MA, PhD); schools, culture, and society (MA, PhD). *Degree requirements:* For master's and Ed S, exam; for doctorate, comprehensive exam, thesis/dissertation. *Entrance requirements:* For master's, doctorate, and Ed S, GRE General Test, minimum GPA of 3.0. Additional exam requirements/recommendations for international students: Required—TOEFL (minimum score 550 paper-based; 81 iBT). Electronic applications accepted.

The University of Kansas, Graduate Studies, School of Education, Department of Educational Leadership and Policy Studies, Education Leadership and Policy Program, Lawrence, KS 66045-3101. Offers policy studies (PhD); social and cultural studies in education (MSE, PhD). *Program availability:* Part-time, evening/weekend. *Students:* 123 full-time (66 women), 35 part-time (17 women); includes 31 minority (12 Black or African American, non-Hispanic/Latino; 2 American Indian or Alaska Native, non-Hispanic/Latino; 3 Asian, non-Hispanic/Latino; 7 Hispanic/Latino; 7 Two or more races, non-Hispanic/Latino), 24 international. Average age 38. 36 applicants, 72% accepted, 16 enrolled. In 2016, 26 doctorates awarded. *Entrance requirements:* For master's, minimum GPA of 3.0, resume or curriculum vitae, statement of purpose, official academic transcripts, three letters of recommendation; for doctorate, GRE General Test, minimum graduate GPA of 3.5, resume or curriculum vitae, statement of purpose, official academic transcripts, three letters of recommendation, writing sample. Additional exam requirements/recommendations for international students: Required—TOEFL or IELTS. *Application deadline:* For fall admission, 7/1 for domestic and international students; for spring admission, 11/1 for domestic and international students; for summer admission, 4/1 for domestic and international students. Application fee: $65 ($85 for international students). Electronic applications accepted. *Financial support:* Fellowships, research assistantships, teaching assistantships, scholarships/grants, and unspecified assistantships available. Financial award application deadline: 3/15. *Faculty research:* Historical and philosophical issues in education, education policy and leadership, higher education faculty, research on college students, education technology. *Unit head:* Dr. Susan B. Twombly, Chair, 785-864-9721, E-mail: stwombly@ku.edu. *Application contact:* Denise Brubaker, Admissions Coordinator, 785-864-7973, E-mail: brubaker@ku.edu.
Website: http://elps.soe.ku.edu/

University of Kentucky, Graduate School, College of Education, Program in Educational Policy Studies and Evaluation, Lexington, KY 40506-0032. Offers educational policy studies and evaluation (Ed D); higher education (MS Ed, PhD); social and philosophical studies (MS Ed). *Accreditation:* NCATE. Terminal master's awarded for partial completion of doctoral program. *Degree requirements:* For master's, comprehensive exam, thesis optional; for doctorate, comprehensive exam, thesis/dissertation. *Entrance requirements:* For master's, GRE General Test, minimum undergraduate GPA of 2.75; for doctorate, GRE General Test, minimum graduate GPA of 3.0. Additional exam requirements/recommendations for international students: Required—TOEFL (minimum score 550 paper-based). Electronic applications accepted. *Faculty research:* Studies in higher education; comparative and international education; evaluation of educational programs, policies, and reform; student, teacher, and faculty cultures; gender and education.

University of Maryland, Baltimore County, The Graduate School, College of Arts, Humanities and Social Sciences, School of Public Policy, Baltimore, MD 21250. Offers public policy (MPP, PhD), including economics (PhD), educational policy, emergency services (PhD), environmental policy, evaluation and analytical methods, health policy, policy history (PhD), public management, urban policy. *Program availability:* Part-time, evening/weekend. *Faculty:* 10 full-time (4 women), 1 part-time/adjunct (0 women). *Students:* 48 full-time (23 women), 66 part-time (36 women); includes 23 minority (14 Black or African American, non-Hispanic/Latino; 4 Asian, non-Hispanic/Latino; 3 Hispanic/Latino; 1 Native Hawaiian or other Pacific Islander, non-Hispanic/Latino; 1 Two or more races, non-Hispanic/Latino), 6 international. Average age 37. 49 applicants, 65% accepted, 16 enrolled. In 2016, 15 master's, 6 doctorates awarded. Terminal master's awarded for partial completion of doctoral program. *Degree requirements:* For master's, thesis, policy analysis paper, internship for pre-service; for doctorate, thesis/dissertation, comprehensive and field qualifying exams. *Entrance requirements:* For master's and doctorate, GRE General Test, 3 academic letters of reference, resume, research paper, official transcripts. Additional exam requirements/recommendations for international students: Required—TOEFL (minimum score 550 paper-based; 80 iBT). *Application deadline:* For fall admission, 1/15 priority date for domestic students, 1/1 priority date for international students; for spring admission, 11/1 priority date for domestic students, 5/1 priority date for international students. Applications are processed on a rolling basis. Application fee: $50. Electronic applications accepted. *Expenses:* $733 per credit hour in-state tuition and fees, $1,127 per credit hour out-of-state; $27,321 tuition and fees in-state, $41,899 out-of-state (for MPP); $38,316 tuition and fees in-state, $58,804 out-of-state (PhD). *Financial support:* In 2016–17, 25 students received support, including 2 fellowships with full tuition reimbursements available (averaging $14,000 per year), 23 research assistantships with full tuition reimbursements available (averaging $20,000 per year); career-related internships or fieldwork, Federal Work-Study, scholarships/grants, health care benefits, and unspecified assistantships also available. Financial award application deadline: 1/15; financial award applicants required to submit FAFSA. *Faculty research:* Education policy, health policy, urban policy, public management, evaluation and analytical method. *Unit head:* Dr. Donald F. Norris, Director, 410-455-3201, Fax: 410-455-1172, E-mail: norris@umbc.edu. *Application contact:* Sally F. Helms, Administrator of Academic Affairs, 410-455-3202, Fax: 410-455-1172, E-mail: gradpubpol@umbc.edu.
Website: http://publicpolicy.umbc.edu/

University of Massachusetts Amherst, Graduate School, College of Education, Program in Education, Amherst, MA 01003. Offers bilingual, English as a second language, and multicultural education (M Ed, Ed S); child study and early education (M Ed); children, families and schools (Ed D, Ed S); early childhood and elementary teacher education (M Ed); educational leadership (M Ed); educational policy and leadership (Ed D); higher education (M Ed); international education (M Ed); language, literacy and culture (Ed D); learning, media and technology (M Ed, Ed S); mathematics, science, and learning technologies (Ed D); reading and writing (M Ed); research, educational measurement and psychometrics (Ed D); school counselor education (M Ed, Ed S); school psychology (Ed S); science education (Ed S); secondary teacher education (M Ed); social justice education (M Ed, Ed D, Ed S); special education (M Ed, Ed D, Ed S); teacher education and school improvement (Ed D, Ed S). *Accreditation:* NCATE. *Program availability:* Part-time, online learning. Terminal master's awarded for partial completion of doctoral program. *Degree requirements:* For doctorate, comprehensive exam, thesis/dissertation. *Entrance requirements:* Additional exam requirements/recommendations for international students: Required—TOEFL (minimum score 550 paper-based; 80 iBT), IELTS (minimum score 6.5). Electronic applications accepted.

University of Massachusetts Boston, College of Education and Human Development, Program in Urban Education, Leadership, and Policy Studies, Boston, MA 02125-3393. Offers Ed D, PhD. *Program availability:* Part-time, evening/weekend. *Degree requirements:* For doctorate, comprehensive exam, thesis/dissertation. *Entrance requirements:* For doctorate, GRE General Test or MAT, minimum GPA of 2.75. *Expenses:* Tuition, state resident: full-time $16,863. Tuition, nonresident: full-time $32,913. *Required fees:* $177. *Faculty research:* School reform, race and culture in schools, race and higher education, language, literacy and writing.

University of Massachusetts Dartmouth, Graduate School, College of Arts and Sciences, Department of Public Policy, North Dartmouth, MA 02747-2300. Offers educational policy (Graduate Certificate); environmental policy (Graduate Certificate); public management (Graduate Certificate); public policy (MPP). *Program availability:* Part-time, 100% online. *Faculty:* 4 full-time (0 women), 1 part-time/adjunct (0 women). *Students:* 7 full-time (5 women), 70 part-time (43 women); includes 14 minority (5 Black or African American, non-Hispanic/Latino; 1 Asian, non-Hispanic/Latino; 5 Hispanic/Latino; 3 Two or more races, non-Hispanic/Latino). Average age 36. 66 applicants, 94% accepted, 40 enrolled. In 2016, 15 master's, 17 other advanced degrees awarded. *Degree requirements:* For master's, e-portfolio. *Entrance requirements:* For master's, GRE (waived if applicant has already earned a master's degree or higher, has successfully completed the educational policy or environmental policy post baccalaureate certificates, or is submitting LSAT scores as a joint JD/MPP program applicant), statement of purpose (minimum of 300 words), resume, 2 letters of recommendation, official transcripts; for Graduate Certificate, statement of purpose (minimum of 300 words), resume, official transcripts. Additional exam requirements/recommendations for international students: Required—TOEFL (minimum score 600 paper-based). *Application deadline:* Applications are processed on a rolling basis. Application fee: $60. Electronic applications accepted. *Expenses:* Tuition, state resident: full-time $14,994; part-time $624.75 per credit. Tuition, nonresident: full-time $27,068; part-time $1127.83 per credit. *Required fees:* $405; $25.88 per credit. Tuition and fees vary according to course load and reciprocity agreements. *Financial support:* In 2016–17, 3 research assistantships (averaging $3,400 per year) were awarded; career-related internships or fieldwork, institutionally sponsored loans, scholarships/grants, and unspecified assistantships also available. Support available to part-time students. Financial award application deadline: 3/1; financial award applicants required to submit FAFSA. *Faculty research:* Demographic analysis, legal and regulatory framework, human rights policy, globalization policies, women's public policy issues, educational leadership, environmental law, effects of evaluation models, international trade and finance, corporate social responsibility. *Total annual research expenditures:* $3,000. *Unit head:* Michael Goodman, Graduate Program Director, Public Policy, 508-910-6986, Fax: 508-999-8374, E-mail: mgoodman@umassd.edu. *Application contact:* Steven Briggs, Director of Marketing and Recruitment for Graduate Studies, 508-999-8604, Fax: 508-999-8183, E-mail: graduate@umassd.edu.
Website: http://www.umassd.edu/cas/departmentsanddegreeprograms/publicpolicy/

University of Massachusetts Dartmouth, Graduate School, College of Arts and Sciences, School of Education, Department of Educational Leadership, North Dartmouth, MA 02747-2300. Offers educational leadership and policy studies (Ed D, PhD). *Program availability:* Part-time. *Faculty:* 4 full-time (0 women), 3 part-time/adjunct (2 women). *Students:* 17 full-time (8 women), 32 part-time (21 women); includes 16 minority (6 Black or African American, non-Hispanic/Latino; 1 American Indian or Alaska Native, non-Hispanic/Latino; 1 Asian, non-Hispanic/Latino; 5 Hispanic/Latino; 3 Two or more races, non-Hispanic/Latino), 2 international. Average age 41. 22 applicants, 86% accepted, 13 enrolled. In 2016, 12 doctorates awarded. *Degree requirements:* For doctorate, thesis/dissertation. *Entrance requirements:* For doctorate, GRE or GMAT, statement of purpose (minimum of 300 words), resume, 3 letters of recommendation, official transcripts, scholarly writing sample (minimum of 10 pages). Additional exam requirements/recommendations for international students: Required—TOEFL (minimum score 600 paper-based). *Application deadline:* For fall admission, 4/30 priority date for domestic students, 3/30 priority date for international students. Application fee: $60. Electronic applications accepted. *Expenses:* Tuition, state resident: full-time $14,994; part-time $624.75 per credit. Tuition, nonresident: full-time $27,068; part-time $1127.83 per credit. *Required fees:* $405; $25.88 per credit. Tuition and fees vary according to course load and reciprocity agreements. *Financial support:* In 2016–17, 1 fellowship (averaging $6,000 per year) was awarded; institutionally sponsored loans, scholarships/grants, and doctoral support also available. Support available to part-time students. Financial award application deadline: 3/1; financial award applicants required to submit FAFSA. *Faculty research:* Curricular theory, higher education policy, qualitative methods, critical theory. *Total annual research expenditures:* $528,000. *Unit head:* Ricardo Rosa, Graduate Program Director, 508-910-9035, E-mail: rrosa2@umassd.edu. *Application contact:* Steven Briggs, Director of Marketing and Recruitment for Graduate Studies, 508-999-8604, Fax: 508-999-8183, E-mail: graduate@umassd.edu.
Website: http://www.umassd.edu/educationalleadership/

University of Minnesota, Twin Cities Campus, Graduate School, College of Education and Human Development, Department of Organizational Leadership, Policy and Development, Program in Education Policy and Leadership, Minneapolis, MN 55455-0213. Offers educational policy and leadership (MA, Ed D, PhD); leadership in education (M Ed). *Students:* 87 full-time (48 women), 70 part-time (43 women); includes 33 minority (13 Black or African American, non-Hispanic/Latino; 5 Asian, non-Hispanic/Latino; 13 Hispanic/Latino; 2 Two or more races, non-Hispanic/Latino), 7 international. Average age 48. 152 applicants, 66% accepted, 90 enrolled. In 2016, 4 master's, 10 doctorates awarded. Application fee: $75 ($95 for international students). *Unit head:* Dr.

Educational Policy

Heidi Barajas, Chair, 612-625-4823, E-mail: hbarajas@umn.edu. *Application contact:* Dr. Jeremy J. Hernandez, Director of Graduate Studies, 612-626-9377, E-mail: herna220@umn.edu.
Website: http://www.cehd.umn.edu/OLPD/grad-programs/EPL/

University of Missouri–St. Louis, College of Education, Department of Education Sciences and Professional Programs, St. Louis, MO 63121. Offers adult and higher education (M Ed); educational leadership and policy studies (PhD); educational psychology (M Ed), including character and citizenship education, research and program evaluation; program evaluation (Certificate); school psychology (Ed S). *Faculty:* 36 full-time (25 women), 53 part-time/adjunct (40 women). *Students:* 47 full-time (34 women), 247 part-time (175 women); includes 107 minority (86 Black or African American, non-Hispanic/Latino; 2 American Indian or Alaska Native, non-Hispanic/Latino; 5 Asian, non-Hispanic/Latino; 10 Hispanic/Latino; 4 Two or more races, non-Hispanic/Latino), 7 international. 106 applicants, 92% accepted, 70 enrolled. *Degree requirements:* For other advanced degree, comprehensive exam, thesis or alternative, internship. *Entrance requirements:* For degree, GRE General Test, 2-4 letters of recommendation, personal interview. Additional exam requirements/recommendations for international students: Required—IELTS (minimum score 6.5); Recommended—TOEFL (minimum score 550 paper-based; 79 iBT). *Application deadline:* For fall admission, 2/15 priority date for domestic students, 2/15 for international students. Application fee: $50 ($40 for international students). Electronic applications accepted. *Financial support:* Application deadline: 4/1; applicants required to submit FAFSA. *Faculty research:* Child/adolescent psychology, quantitative and qualitative methodology, evaluation processes, measurement and assessment. *Unit head:* Dr. Donald Gouwens, Chairperson, 314-516-4773, Fax: 314-516-5784, E-mail: gouwensd@umsl.edu. *Application contact:* 314-516-5458, Fax: 314-516-6996, E-mail: gradadm@umsl.edu.
Website: https://coe.umsl.edu/dept/espp.html

University of Missouri–St. Louis, College of Education, Interdisciplinary Doctoral Programs, St. Louis, MO 63121. Offers counseling (PhD); educational leadership and policy studies (PhD); educational psychology (PhD); leadership in educational practice (Ed D); teaching-learning processes (PhD). *Degree requirements:* For doctorate, thesis/dissertation. *Entrance requirements:* For doctorate, GRE General Test, 3 letters of recommendation; personal interview. Additional exam requirements/recommendations for international students: Recommended—TOEFL (minimum score 550 paper-based; 79 iBT), IELTS (minimum score 6.5). *Application deadline:* For fall admission, 3/1 for domestic and international students; for spring admission, 10/1 for domestic and international students. Application fee: $50 ($40 for international students). Electronic applications accepted. *Financial support:* Research assistantships and teaching assistantships available. Financial award application deadline: 4/1; financial award applicants required to submit FAFSA. *Faculty research:* Higher education law and policy, gender and higher education, student retention, lifelong learning orientation, school counselor's role in violence prevention. *Unit head:* Dr. Kathleen Haywood, Director of Graduate Studies, 314-516-5483, Fax: 314-516-5227, E-mail: kathleen_haywood@umsl.edu. *Application contact:* 314-516-5458, Fax: 314-516-6996, E-mail: gradadm@umsl.edu.

The University of North Carolina Wilmington, Watson College of Education, Department of Early Childhood, Elementary, Middle, Literacy and Special Education, Wilmington, NC 28403-3297. Offers educational leadership, policy, and advocacy (M Ed); elementary education (M Ed, MAT); language and literacy (M Ed); middle grades education (M Ed, MAT). *Accreditation:* NCATE. *Program availability:* Part-time. *Faculty:* 26 full-time (19 women). *Students:* 121 full-time (89 women), 139 part-time (135 women); includes 70 minority (47 Black or African American, non-Hispanic/Latino; 1 Asian, non-Hispanic/Latino; 14 Hispanic/Latino; 8 Two or more races, non-Hispanic/Latino). Average age 34. 109 applicants, 78% accepted, 65 enrolled. In 2016, 83 master's awarded. *Degree requirements:* For master's, comprehensive exam, capstone experience. *Entrance requirements:* For master's, GRE General Test, MAT, minimum GPA of 3.0 in undergraduate work, 3 letters of recommendations, NC Class A teacher license in related field, statement of interest. *Application deadline:* For fall admission, 5/15 for domestic students; for spring admission, 10/15 for domestic students; for summer admission, 3/15 for domestic students. Applications are processed on a rolling basis. Application fee: $60. Electronic applications accepted. *Expenses:* Contact institution. *Financial support:* Scholarships/grants and unspecified assistantships available. Support available to part-time students. Financial award application deadline: 3/15; financial award applicants required to submit FAFSA. *Unit head:* Dr. Kathy Fox, Chair, 910-962-3240, Fax: 910-962-3988, E-mail: foxk@uncw.edu. *Application contact:* Dr. Elizabeth Crawford, Graduate Program Coordinator, 910-962-2916, Fax: 910-962-3988, E-mail: crawforde@uncw.edu.
Website: http://www.uncw.edu/ed/eemls/index.html

University of Northern Colorado, Graduate School, College of Education and Behavioral Sciences, Department of Leadership, Policy and Development: Higher Education and P-12 Education, Educational Leadership and Policy Studies Program, Greeley, CO 80639. Offers educational leadership (MA, Ed S); educational leadership and policy studies (Ed D). *Accreditation:* NCATE. *Program availability:* Part-time, evening/weekend, online learning. *Faculty:* 5 full-time (3 women). *Students:* 17 full-time (9 women), 53 part-time (36 women); includes 21 minority (3 Black or African American, non-Hispanic/Latino; 3 American Indian or Alaska Native, non-Hispanic/Latino; 1 Asian, non-Hispanic/Latino; 14 Hispanic/Latino). Average age 37. 25 applicants, 80% accepted, 15 enrolled. In 2016, 31 master's, 5 doctorates, 23 other advanced degrees awarded. *Degree requirements:* For master's, comprehensive exam, thesis or alternative; for doctorate, comprehensive exam, thesis/dissertation; for Ed S, comprehensive exam, thesis. *Entrance requirements:* For master's, resume, interview; for doctorate, GRE General Test, resume, interview; for Ed S, resume. *Application deadline:* For fall admission, 5/1 for domestic and international students. Applications are processed on a rolling basis. Application fee: $50 ($60 for international students). Electronic applications accepted. *Financial support:* In 2016–17, 38 students received support, including 6 research assistantships (averaging $10,306 per year); fellowships, teaching assistantships, and unspecified assistantships also available. Financial award application deadline: 3/1; financial award applicants required to submit FAFSA. *Unit head:* Dr. Linda Vogel, Program Coordinator, 970-351-2861, E-mail: elps@unco.edu. *Application contact:* Linda Sisson, Graduate Student Admission Coordinator, 970-351-1807, Fax: 970-351-2371, E-mail: linda.sisson@unco.edu.
Website: http://www.unco.edu/cebs/elps/

University of Oklahoma, Jeannine Rainbolt College of Education, Department of Educational Leadership and Policy Studies, Norman, OK 73019. Offers adult and higher education (M Ed, PhD), including adult and higher education; educational administration, curriculum and supervision (M Ed, Ed D, PhD), including educational administration (M Ed, Ed D), educational leadership and policy (PhD); educational studies (M Ed, PhD). *Accreditation:* NCATE. *Program availability:* Part-time, evening/weekend, blended/hybrid learning. *Faculty:* 34 full-time (14 women), 5 part-time/adjunct (2 women). *Students:* 147 full-time (91 women), 245 part-time (168 women); includes 122 minority (49 Black or African American, non-Hispanic/Latino; 26 American Indian or Alaska Native, non-Hispanic/Latino; 22 Hispanic/Latino; 1 Native Hawaiian or other Pacific Islander, non-Hispanic/Latino; 24 Two or more races, non-Hispanic/Latino), 8 international. Average age 33. 129 applicants, 72% accepted, 73 enrolled. In 2016, 121 master's, 15 doctorates awarded. Terminal master's awarded for partial completion of doctoral program. *Degree requirements:* For master's, comprehensive exam, thesis (for some programs); for doctorate, comprehensive exam, thesis/dissertation. *Entrance requirements:* Additional exam requirements/recommendations for international students: Required—TOEFL (minimum score 79 iBT) or IELTS (minimum score 6.5). *Application deadline:* For fall admission, 2/1 for domestic and international students; for spring admission, 10/1 for domestic and international students; for summer admission, 4/1 for domestic and international students. Applications are processed on a rolling basis. Application fee: $50 ($100 for international students). Electronic applications accepted. *Expenses:* Tuition, state resident: full-time $4886; part-time $203.60 per credit hour. Tuition, nonresident: full-time $18,989; part-time $791.20 per credit hour. *Required fees:* $3283; $126.25 per credit hour. $126.50 per semester. *Financial support:* In 2016–17, 253 students received support, including 15 research assistantships (averaging $15,906 per year), 1 teaching assistantship (averaging $11,250 per year); fellowships, career-related internships or fieldwork, Federal Work-Study, institutionally sponsored loans, scholarships/grants, traineeships, health care benefits, and unspecified assistantships also available. Support available to part-time students. Financial award application deadline: 6/1; financial award applicants required to submit FAFSA. *Faculty research:* Improvement science, leadership and ethics, education and social policy, gender and equity, collegiate athletics. *Total annual research expenditures:* $421,212. *Unit head:* Curt Adams, Associate Professor and Interim Chair, 918-660-3891, E-mail: curt_adams-1@ou.edu.
Website: http://www.ou.edu/education/elps

University of Pennsylvania, Graduate School of Education, Division of Education Policy, Philadelphia, PA 19104. Offers MS Ed, PhD. *Program availability:* Part-time. *Students:* 38 full-time (27 women), 6 part-time (4 women); includes 15 minority (7 Black or African American, non-Hispanic/Latino; 3 Asian, non-Hispanic/Latino; 4 Hispanic/Latino; 1 Two or more races, non-Hispanic/Latino), 11 international. Average age 28. 250 applicants, 50% accepted, 34 enrolled. In 2016, 16 master's, 2 doctorates awarded. *Degree requirements:* For master's, thesis or alternative, research practicum; for doctorate, comprehensive exam, thesis/dissertation. *Entrance requirements:* For master's, GRE, bachelor's degree; for doctorate, GRE, bachelor's degree; master's degree (preferred). Additional exam requirements/recommendations for international students: Required—TOEFL, IELTS. *Application deadline:* For fall admission, 12/8 priority date for domestic and international students. Applications are processed on a rolling basis. Application fee: $75. Electronic applications accepted. *Expenses: Tuition:* Full-time $31,068; part-time $5762 per course. *Required fees:* $3200; $336 per course. Full-time tuition and fees vary according to degree level, program and student level. Part-time tuition and fees vary according to course load, degree level and program. *Financial support:* In 2016–17, 13 students received support. Fellowships, research assistantships, teaching assistantships, Federal Work-Study, scholarships/grants, and health care benefits available. *Faculty research:* Teachers and teaching policy, school reform, standards, and assessment, early childhood education, program evaluation and policy analysis, career and college readiness. *Unit head:* Krista Featherstone, Program Manager, 215-573-8075, E-mail: kfeat@upenn.edu.
Website: http://www.gse.upenn.edu/ep

University of Pittsburgh, School of Education, Learning Sciences and Policy Program, Pittsburgh, PA 15260. Offers PhD. *Program availability:* Part-time, evening/weekend. *Degree requirements:* For doctorate, comprehensive exam, thesis/dissertation. *Entrance requirements:* Additional exam requirements/recommendations for international students: Required—TOEFL (minimum score 550 paper-based; 80 iBT). Tuition and fees vary according to program.

University of Rochester, Margaret Warner Graduate School of Education and Human Development, Doctoral Programs in Education, Rochester, NY 14627. Offers counseling (Ed D); educational administration (Ed D); educational policy and theory (PhD); higher education (PhD); human development in educational context (PhD); teaching, curriculum, and change (PhD). *Expenses: Tuition:* Full-time $47,450; part-time $1482 per credit hour. *Required fees:* $528. Tuition and fees vary according to program.

University of Rochester, Margaret Warner Graduate School of Education and Human Development, Master's Program in Educational Policy, Rochester, NY 14627. Offers MS. *Expenses: Tuition:* Full-time $47,450; part-time $1482 per credit hour. *Required fees:* $528. Tuition and fees vary according to program.

University of Southern California, Graduate School, Rossier School of Education, Doctor of Philosophy in Education Programs, Los Angeles, CA 90089. Offers educational psychology (PhD); higher education administration and policy (PhD); K-12 policy and practice (PhD). *Degree requirements:* For doctorate, thesis/dissertation, 63 units; qualifying exam; dissertation proposal and defense. *Entrance requirements:* For doctorate, GRE. Additional exam requirements/recommendations for international students: Required—TOEFL (minimum score 100 iBT). Electronic applications accepted. *Faculty research:* Diversity in higher education, organizational change, educational psychology, policy and politics of educational reform, economics of education and education policy.

The University of Texas at Arlington, Graduate School, College of Education, Department of Educational Leadership and Policy Studies, Arlington, TX 76019. Offers educational leadership (PhD); higher education (M Ed); principal certification (M Ed). *Program availability:* Part-time, evening/weekend, online learning. *Degree requirements:* For master's, 2 field-based practica; for doctorate, comprehensive exam, thesis/dissertation, 2 research-based practica. *Entrance requirements:* For master's, GRE, 3 references forms, minimum undergraduate GPA of 3.0 in the last 60 hours of course work; for doctorate, GRE, resume, statement of intent, 3 reference forms, applicable master's degree. Application fee: $50. *Financial support:* Fellowships and research assistantships available. Financial award applicants required to submit FAFSA. *Faculty research:* Lived realities of students of color in K-16 contexts, K-16 faculty, K-16 policy and law, K-16 student access, K-16 student success. *Unit head:* Dr. Adrienne E. Hyle, Chair, 817-272-2841, Fax: 817-272-2127, E-mail: ahyle@uta.edu. *Application contact:* Paige Cordor, Graduate Advisor, 817-272-5051, Fax: 817-272-2127, E-mail: paigec@uta.edu.
Website: http://www.uta.edu/coehp/educleadership/

University of Virginia, Curry School of Education, Department of Leadership, Foundations and Policy, Program in Educational Policy, Charlottesville, VA 22903. Offers PhD, PhD/MPP. *Entrance requirements:* For doctorate, GRE General Test, 2 letters of recommendation. Additional exam requirements/recommendations for international students: Required—TOEFL (minimum score 600 paper-based; 90 iBT), IELTS (minimum score 7). *Application deadline:* Applications are processed on a rolling basis. Application fee: $60. Electronic applications accepted. *Expenses:* Tuition, state resident: full-time $15,026; part-time $834 per credit hour. Tuition, nonresident: full-time $25,168; part-time $1378 per credit hour. *Required fees:* $2654. *Financial support:* Fellowships, research assistantships, and teaching assistantships available. Financial award application deadline: 1/5; financial award applicants required to submit FAFSA. *Unit head:* James H. Wyckoff, Director, Educational Policy PhD Program, 434-924-0842, E-mail: jhw4n@virginia.edu. *Application contact:* Eric Molnar, Assistant Director,

Admissions and Enrollment Reporting, 434-243-2085, E-mail: eric.molnar@virginia.edu.
Website: http://curry.virginia.edu/academics/areas-of-study/education-policy

University of Washington, Graduate School, College of Education, Seattle, WA 98195. Offers curriculum and instruction (M Ed, Ed D, PhD), including educational technology, general curriculum (Ed D, PhD), language, literacy, and culture, mathematics education, multicultural education, reading and language arts education (Ed D), science education, social studies education, teaching and curriculum (M Ed); educational leadership and policy studies (M Ed, Ed D, PhD), including administration (Ed D), educational policy, organization, and leadership (M Ed, PhD), higher education, leadership for learning (Ed D), social and cultural foundations of education (M Ed, PhD); educational psychology (M Ed, PhD), including educational psychology (PhD), human development and cognition (M Ed), learning sciences, measurement, statistics and research design (M Ed), school psychology (M Ed); instructional leadership (M Ed); intercollegiate athletic leadership (M Ed); special education (M Ed, Ed D, PhD), including early childhood special education (M Ed), emotional and behavioral disabilities (M Ed), learning disabilities (M Ed), low-incidence disabilities (M Ed), severe disabilities (M Ed), special education (Ed D, PhD); teacher education (MIT). *Accreditation:* APA. *Program availability:* Part-time, evening/weekend. *Degree requirements:* For master's, thesis optional; for doctorate, thesis/dissertation. *Entrance requirements:* For master's and doctorate, GRE General Test, minimum GPA of 3.0. Additional exam requirements/recommendations for international students: Required—TOEFL. Electronic applications accepted. *Faculty research:* School restructuring/effective schools, special education interventions, literacy and writing, technology, school partnerships, teacher preparation.

The University of Western Ontario, Faculty of Graduate Studies, Social Sciences Division, Faculty of Education, Program in Educational Studies, London, ON N6A 5B8, Canada. Offers curriculum studies (M Ed); educational policy studies (M Ed); educational psychology/special education (M Ed). *Program availability:* Part-time. *Faculty research:* Reflective practice, gender and schooling, feminist pedagogy, narrative inquiry, second language, multiculturalism in Canada, education and law.

University of Wisconsin–Madison, Graduate School, School of Education, Department of Educational Leadership and Policy Analysis, Madison, WI 53706-1380. Offers administration (Certificate); educational policy (MS, PhD); global higher education (MS). *Degree requirements:* For doctorate, thesis/dissertation. *Entrance requirements:* For master's and doctorate, GRE General Test. Electronic applications accepted.

University of Wisconsin–Madison, Graduate School, School of Education, Department of Educational Policy Studies, Madison, WI 53706-1380. Offers MA, PhD. *Degree requirements:* For doctorate, thesis/dissertation. *Entrance requirements:* For master's and doctorate, GRE General Test. Electronic applications accepted.

University of Wisconsin–Milwaukee, Graduate School, School of Education, Department of Educational Policy and Community Studies, Milwaukee, WI 53201-0413. Offers cultural foundations of community engagement and education (MS), including alternative education, community engagement and partnerships, educational policy, race relations, youth work; educational policy (Graduate Certificate). *Program availability:* Part-time. *Students:* 6 full-time (5 women), 28 part-time (21 women); includes 15 minority (9 Black or African American, non-Hispanic/Latino; 2 Asian, non-Hispanic/Latino; 2 Hispanic/Latino; 2 Two or more races, non-Hispanic/Latino). Average age 35. 28 applicants, 64% accepted, 11 enrolled. In 2016, 18 master's, 1 other advanced degree awarded. *Entrance requirements:* Additional exam requirements/recommendations for international students: Required—TOEFL (minimum score 550 paper-based; 79 iBT), IELTS (minimum score 6.5). *Application deadline:* For fall admission, 1/1 priority date for domestic students; for spring admission, 9/1 for domestic students. Applications are processed on a rolling basis. Application fee: $56 ($96 for international students). Electronic applications accepted. *Financial support:* In 2016–17, 3 fellowships with full tuition reimbursements were awarded; research assistantships, teaching assistantships, career-related internships or fieldwork, health care benefits, and unspecified assistantships also available. Support available to part-time students. Financial award application deadline: 4/15; financial award applicants required to submit FAFSA. *Application contact:* General Information Contact, 414-229-4721, E-mail: soeinfo@uwm.edu.
Website: http://uwm.edu/education/academics/edu-policy-community-studies-department/

Vanderbilt University, Peabody College, Department of Leadership, Policy, and Organizations, Nashville, TN 37240-1001. Offers education policy (MPP); educational leadership and policy (Ed D); higher education (M Ed); higher education leadership and policy (Ed D); independent school leadership (M Ed); international education policy and management (M Ed); leadership and organizational performance (M Ed). *Program availability:* Part-time. *Faculty:* 29 full-time (14 women), 21 part-time/adjunct (5 women). *Students:* 166 full-time (124 women), 107 part-time (63 women); includes 50 minority (25 Black or African American, non-Hispanic/Latino; 7 Asian, non-Hispanic/Latino; 9 Hispanic/Latino; 1 Native Hawaiian or other Pacific Islander, non-Hispanic/Latino; 8 Two or more races, non-Hispanic/Latino), 32 international. Average age 29. 543 applicants, 63% accepted, 133 enrolled. In 2016, 109 master's, 22 doctorates awarded. *Degree requirements:* For master's, comprehensive exam, thesis optional; for doctorate, thesis/dissertation, qualifying exams, residency. *Entrance requirements:* For master's and doctorate, GRE General Test. Additional exam requirements/recommendations for international students: Required—TOEFL (minimum score 550 paper-based; 80 iBT). *Application deadline:* For fall admission, 12/31 priority date for domestic and international students; for spring admission, 11/1 priority date for domestic and international students. Applications are processed on a rolling basis. Application fee: $0. Electronic applications accepted. *Expenses: Tuition:* Part-time $1854 per credit hour. *Financial support:* Fellowships with partial tuition reimbursements, research assistantships with partial tuition reimbursements, teaching assistantships with partial tuition reimbursements, Federal Work-Study, institutionally sponsored loans, scholarships/grants, tuition waivers (partial), and unspecified assistantships available. Support available to part-time students. Financial award application deadline: 1/15; financial award applicants required to submit FAFSA. *Faculty research:* Higher education, educational leadership, education policy, international education, educator effectiveness. *Unit head:* Dr. Ellen B. Goldring, Chair, 615-322-8000, Fax: 615-343-7094, E-mail: ellen.b.goldring@vanderbilt.edu. *Application contact:* Rosie Moody, Educational Coordinator, 615-322-8019, Fax: 615-343-7094, E-mail: rosie.moody@vanderbilt.edu.
Website: http://peabody.vanderbilt.edu/departments/lpo/index.php

Virginia Polytechnic Institute and State University, Graduate School, College of Liberal Arts and Human Sciences, Blacksburg, VA 24061. Offers career and technical education (MS Ed, Ed D, PhD, Ed S); communication (MA); counselor education (MA Ed, Ed D, PhD, Ed S); creative writing (MFA); curriculum and instruction (MA Ed, Ed D, PhD, Ed S); educational leadership and policy studies (MA Ed, Ed D, PhD, Ed S); educational research and evaluation (PhD); English (MA); foreign languages, cultures, and literatures (MA); higher education (PhD); higher education and student affairs (MA Ed); history (MA); human development (MS, PhD); material culture and public humanities (MA); philosophy (MA); political science (MA); rhetoric and writing (PhD); science and technology studies (MS, PhD); social, political, ethical, and cultural thought (PhD); sociology (MS, PhD); theater arts (MFA). *Faculty:* 408 full-time (204 women), 3 part-time/adjunct (2 women). *Students:* 657 full-time (446 women), 457 part-time (292 women); includes 213 minority (114 Black or African American, non-Hispanic/Latino; 3 American Indian or Alaska Native, non-Hispanic/Latino; 29 Asian, non-Hispanic/Latino; 44 Hispanic/Latino; 23 Two or more races, non-Hispanic/Latino), 93 international. Average age 33. 805 applicants, 55% accepted, 328 enrolled. In 2016, 270 master's, 91 doctorates awarded. *Degree requirements:* For master's, comprehensive exam (for some programs), thesis (for some programs); for doctorate, comprehensive exam (for some programs), thesis/dissertation (for some programs). *Entrance requirements:* For master's and doctorate, GRE/GMAT. Additional exam requirements/recommendations for international students: Required—TOEFL (minimum score 80 iBT). *Application deadline:* For fall admission, 8/1 for domestic students, 4/1 for international students; for spring admission, 1/1 for domestic students, 9/1 for international students. Applications are processed on a rolling basis. Application fee: $75. Electronic applications accepted. *Expenses:* Tuition, state resident: full-time $12,467; part-time $692.50 per credit hour. Tuition, nonresident: full-time $25,095; part-time $1394.25 per credit hour. *Required fees:* $2669; $491.50 per semester. Tuition and fees vary according to course load, campus/location and program. *Financial support:* In 2016–17, 21 research assistantships with full tuition reimbursements (averaging $19,817 per year), 237 teaching assistantships with full tuition reimbursements (averaging $15,497 per year) were awarded. Financial award application deadline: 3/1; financial award applicants required to submit FAFSA. *Total annual research expenditures:* $6.6 million. *Unit head:* Rosemary Blieszner, Interim Dean, 540-231-6779, Fax: 540-231-7157, E-mail: liberalartsdean@vt.edu. *Application contact:* Chelsea Blanchet, Executive Assistant, 540-231-6779, Fax: 540-231-7157, E-mail: bchels1@vt.edu.
Website: http://www.liberalarts.vt.edu/

Wayne State University, College of Education, Division of Administrative and Organizational Studies, Detroit, MI 48202. Offers college and university teaching (Certificate); educational administration and supervision (Ed S); educational leadership (M Ed); educational leadership and policy studies (Ed D, PhD); educational technology (Certificate); learning design and technology (M Ed, Ed D, PhD, Ed S); online teaching (Certificate). *Program availability:* Part-time, 100% online, blended/hybrid learning. *Faculty:* 11. *Students:* 83 full-time (58 women), 223 part-time (148 women); includes 151 minority (126 Black or African American, non-Hispanic/Latino; 3 American Indian or Alaska Native, non-Hispanic/Latino; 4 Asian, non-Hispanic/Latino; 8 Hispanic/Latino; 10 Two or more races, non-Hispanic/Latino), 14 international. Average age 39. 143 applicants, 43% accepted, 38 enrolled. In 2016, 53 master's, 9 doctorates, 34 other advanced degrees awarded. *Degree requirements:* For doctorate, thesis/dissertation. *Entrance requirements:* For master's, baccalaureate degree from accredited U.S. institution or equivalent from college or university of government-recognized standing; minimum undergraduate GPA of 2.75 in upper-division coursework; personal statement; for doctorate, GRE (instructional design and technology), interview; curriculum vitae; three references (two professional and one academic); master's degree; minimum graduate GPA of 3.5; autobiographical statement; research experience. Additional exam requirements/recommendations for international students: Required—TOEFL (minimum score 550 paper-based; 79 iBT), Michigan English Language Assessment Battery (minimum score 85); Recommended—IELTS (minimum score 6.5), TWE (minimum score 5.5). *Application deadline:* For fall admission, 6/1 priority date for domestic students, 5/1 priority date for international students; for winter admission, 10/1 priority date for domestic students, 9/1 priority date for international students; for spring admission, 2/1 priority date for domestic students, 1/1 priority date for international students. Applications are processed on a rolling basis. Application fee: $50. Electronic applications accepted. *Expenses:* $16,503 per year resident tuition and fees, $33,697 per year non-resident tuition and fees. *Financial support:* In 2016–17, 96 students received support, including 1 fellowship with tuition reimbursement available (averaging $11,000 per year), 4 research assistantships with tuition reimbursements available (averaging $17,949 per year); scholarships/grants and unspecified assistantships also available. Support available to part-time students. Financial award applicants required to submit FAFSA. *Faculty research:* Total quality management, participatory management, administering educational technology, school improvement, principalship. *Unit head:* Dr. William Hill, Assistant Dean, 313-577-9316, E-mail: ad2107@wayne.edu. *Application contact:* Janice Green, Assistant Dean, 313-577-1605, E-mail: jwgreen@wayne.edu.
Website: http://coe.wayne.edu/aos/index.php

West Chester University of Pennsylvania, College of Education and Social Work, Program in Policy, Planning, and Administration, West Chester, PA 19383. Offers Ed D. *Program availability:* Part-time, evening/weekend. *Students:* 15 part-time (8 women); includes 1 minority (Hispanic/Latino). Average age 36. 27 applicants, 78% accepted, 15 enrolled. *Degree requirements:* For doctorate, comprehensive exam. *Entrance requirements:* For doctorate, GRE if master's GPA lower than 3.85, master's degree from regionally-accredited college or university, three letters of recommendation from education professionals, professional writing demonstration at time of application (waived for applicants who present GRE analytical writing score of 4.5 or higher), resume or curriculum vitae, interview (upon Committee request). Additional exam requirements/recommendations for international students: Required—TOEFL or IELTS. *Application deadline:* For fall admission, 5/15 for international students; for spring admission, 10/15 for international students. Applications are processed on a rolling basis. Application fee: $50. Electronic applications accepted. *Expenses:* Tuition, state resident: full-time $8694; part-time $483 per credit. Tuition, nonresident: full-time $13,050; part-time $725 per credit. *Required fees:* $2399; $119.05 per credit. Tuition and fees vary according to campus/location and program. *Financial support:* Application deadline: 2/15; applicants required to submit FAFSA. *Faculty research:* Literacy, special education, critical pedagogy, social and cultural foundations of education, educational technology. *Unit head:* Dr. Kenneth D. Witmer, Jr., Dean, 610-436-2321, Fax: 610-436-3102, E-mail: kwitmer@wcupa.edu. *Application contact:* Robert Haworth, Graduate Coordinator, 610-436-2246, E-mail: rhaworth@wcupa.edu.
Website: http://www.wcupa.edu/education-socialWork/doctorate/

Educational Psychology

Alliant International University–Irvine, Shirley M. Hufstedler School of Education, Educational Psychology Programs, Irvine, CA 92606. Offers educational psychology (Psy D); pupil personnel services (Credential); school psychology (MA). *Program availability:* Part-time. *Degree requirements:* For doctorate, thesis/dissertation. *Entrance requirements:* For master's, minimum GPA of 2.5, letters of recommendation; for doctorate, interview, minimum GPA of 3.0, letters of recommendation. Additional exam requirements/recommendations for international students: Required—TOEFL (minimum score 550 paper-based; 80 iBT), TWE (minimum score 5). *Faculty research:* School-based mental health.

Alliant International University–Los Angeles, Shirley M. Hufstedler School of Education, Educational Psychology Programs, Alhambra, CA 91803. Offers educational psychology (Psy D); pupil personnel services (Credential); school psychology (MA). *Program availability:* Part-time. *Degree requirements:* For doctorate, comprehensive exam, thesis/dissertation. *Entrance requirements:* For master's, minimum GPA of 2.5, letters of recommendation; for doctorate, interview, minimum GPA of 3.0, letters of recommendation. Additional exam requirements/recommendations for international students: Required—TOEFL (minimum score 550 paper-based), TWE (minimum score 5). Electronic applications accepted. *Faculty research:* Early identification and intervention with high-risk preschoolers, pediatric neuropsychology, interpersonal violence, ADHD, learning theories.

Alliant International University–San Diego, Shirley M. Hufstedler School of Education, Educational Psychology Programs, San Diego, CA 92131. Offers educational psychology (Psy D); pupil personnel services (Credential); school neuropsychology (Certificate); school psychology (MA); school-based mental health (Certificate). *Program availability:* Part-time. *Degree requirements:* For doctorate, comprehensive exam, thesis/dissertation, internship. *Entrance requirements:* For master's, minimum GPA of 2.5, letters of recommendation; for doctorate, minimum GPA of 3.0, letters of recommendation. Additional exam requirements/recommendations for international students: Required—TOEFL (minimum score 550 paper-based; 80 iBT), TWE (minimum score 5). Electronic applications accepted. *Faculty research:* School-based mental health, pupil personnel services, childhood mood, school-based assessment.

Alliant International University–San Francisco, Shirley M. Hufstedler School of Education, Educational Psychology Programs, San Francisco, CA 94133. Offers educational psychology (Psy D); pupil personnel services (Credential); school psychology (MA). *Program availability:* Part-time. Terminal master's awarded for partial completion of doctoral program. *Degree requirements:* For doctorate, thesis/dissertation. *Entrance requirements:* For master's, minimum GPA of 3.0, letters of recommendation; for doctorate, interview, minimum GPA of 3.0, letters of recommendation. Additional exam requirements/recommendations for international students: Required—TOEFL (minimum score 550 paper-based), TWE (minimum score 5). Electronic applications accepted. *Faculty research:* Social skills, ADHD, cognitive functioning and learning, innovative teaching methods.

American International College, Low Residency Programs, Springfield, MA 01109-3189. Offers counseling psychology (MA); educational leadership and supervision (Ed D); individual and institutional development (Ed D); professional counseling and supervision (Ed D); psychology (Ed D); teaching and learning (Ed D). *Expenses: Tuition:* Full-time $7902; part-time $750 per semester hour. *Required fees:* $60; $60 per semester hour. $30 per semester. One-time fee: $100. Tuition and fees vary according to course load, degree level, campus/location and program. *Application contact:* Kerry Barnes, Director of Graduate Admissions, 413-205-3703, Fax: 413-205-3051, E-mail: kerry.barnes@aic.edu.

American International College, School of Business, Arts and Sciences, Springfield, MA 01109-3189. Offers accounting and taxation (MS); business administration (MBA); clinical psychology (MA); educational psychology (Ed D); forensic psychology (MS); general psychology (MA, CAGS); management (CAGS); resort and casino management (MBA, CAGS). *Program availability:* Part-time, evening/weekend. *Degree requirements:* For master's, comprehensive exam (for some programs), thesis (for some programs), practicum; for doctorate, comprehensive exam (for some programs), thesis/dissertation; for CAGS, comprehensive exam (for some programs), thesis (for some programs). *Entrance requirements:* For master's, BS or BA; for doctorate, interview. Additional exam requirements/recommendations for international students: Required—TOEFL (minimum score 550 paper-based; 80 iBT). *Expenses: Tuition:* Full-time $7902; part-time $750 per semester hour. *Required fees:* $60; $60 per semester hour. $30 per semester. One-time fee: $100. Tuition and fees vary according to course load, degree level, campus/location and program.

Andrews University, School of Graduate Studies, School of Education, Department of Graduate Psychology and Counseling, Program in Educational and Developmental Psychology, Berrien Springs, MI 49104. Offers educational and developmental psychology (MA); educational psychology (Ed D, PhD). *Students:* 17 full-time (12 women), 3 part-time (2 women); includes 9 minority (6 Black or African American, non-Hispanic/Latino; 3 Hispanic/Latino), 5 international. Average age 37. In 2016, 9 master's, 1 doctorate awarded. *Degree requirements:* For master's, thesis optional. *Entrance requirements:* For master's, GRE. Additional exam requirements/recommendations for international students: Required—TOEFL (minimum score 550 paper-based). *Application deadline:* Applications are processed on a rolling basis. Application fee: $40. *Unit head:* Dr. Jimmy Kijai, Coordinator, 269-471-6240. *Application contact:* Justina Clayburn, Supervisor of Graduate Admission, 800-253-2874, Fax: 269-471-6321, E-mail: graduate@andrews.edu.

Ball State University, Graduate School, Teachers College, Department of Educational Psychology, Program in Educational Psychology, Muncie, IN 47306. Offers MA, MS, PhD. *Accreditation:* NCATE. *Program availability:* Part-time, 100% online. *Degree requirements:* For doctorate, thesis/dissertation. *Entrance requirements:* For master's, GRE General Test (for MS only), minimum baccalaureate GPA of 2.75 or 3.0 in latter half of baccalauareate; for doctorate, GRE General Test, minimum graduate GPA of 3.2. Additional exam requirements/recommendations for international students: Required—TOEFL (minimum score 550 paper-based; 79 iBT), IELTS (minimum score 6.5). Electronic applications accepted.

Baylor University, Graduate School, School of Education, Department of Educational Psychology, Waco, TX 76798. Offers applied behavior analysis (MS Ed); educational psychology (MA, MS Ed, PhD); exceptionalities (PhD); gifted and talented studies (MS Ed); learning and development (PhD); measurement (PhD); quantitative methods (MA); school psychology (Ed S). *Accreditation:* NCATE. *Faculty:* 11 full-time (6 women). *Students:* 48 full-time (42 women), 17 part-time (15 women); includes 15 minority (4 Black or African American, non-Hispanic/Latino; 2 Asian, non-Hispanic/Latino; 8 Hispanic/Latino; 1 Two or more races, non-Hispanic/Latino), 2 international. Average age 29. 90 applicants, 33% accepted, 30 enrolled. In 2016, 13 master's, 4 doctorates, 7 other advanced degrees awarded. Terminal master's awarded for partial completion of doctoral program. *Degree requirements:* For master's, thesis optional; for doctorate, comprehensive exam, thesis/dissertation; for Ed S, comprehensive exam, thesis or alternative. *Entrance requirements:* For master's, GRE, minimum GPA of 3.0; for doctorate, GRE General Test, master's degree; for Ed S, GRE General Test. Additional exam requirements/recommendations for international students: Required—TOEFL (minimum score 550 paper-based; 80 iBT), IELTS (minimum score 6.5). *Application deadline:* For fall admission, 2/1 priority date for domestic and international students. Application fee: $80. Electronic applications accepted. *Expenses: Tuition:* Full-time $28,494; part-time $1583 per credit hour. *Required fees:* $167 per credit hour. Tuition and fees vary according to course load and program. *Financial support:* In 2016–17, 42 students received support, including 20 fellowships with full and partial tuition reimbursements available, 22 research assistantships with full and partial tuition reimbursements available; career-related internships or fieldwork, Federal Work-Study, institutionally sponsored loans, scholarships/grants, health care benefits, tuition waivers (full and partial), unspecified assistantships, and stipends also available. Financial award application deadline: 2/1; financial award applicants required to submit FAFSA. *Faculty research:* Individual differences, quantitative methods, gifted and talented, special education, school psychology, autism, applied behavior analysis, learning, human development. *Total annual research expenditures:* $300,000. *Unit head:* Dr. Terrill F. Saxon, Professor and Chairman, 254-710-6101, E-mail: terrill_saxon@baylor.edu. *Application contact:* Heather Tindle, Office Manager, 254-710-3112, E-mail: heather_tindle@baylor.edu.
Website: http://www.baylor.edu/soe/EDP/

Boston College, Lynch School of Education, Program in Applied Developmental and Educational Psychology, Chestnut Hill, MA 02467-3800. Offers MA, PhD. *Program availability:* Part-time, evening/weekend. *Faculty:* 11 full-time (8 women). *Students:* 19 full-time (18 women), 21 part-time (20 women); includes 8 minority (2 Black or African American, non-Hispanic/Latino; 2 Asian, non-Hispanic/Latino; 3 Hispanic/Latino; 1 Two or more races, non-Hispanic/Latino), 8 international. Average age 27. 97 applicants, 48% accepted, 14 enrolled. In 2016, 15 master's, 2 doctorates awarded. Terminal master's awarded for partial completion of doctoral program. *Degree requirements:* For master's, comprehensive exam; for doctorate, comprehensive exam, thesis/dissertation. *Entrance requirements:* For master's and doctorate, GRE General Test. Additional exam requirements/recommendations for international students: Required—TOEFL (minimum score 100 iBT). *Application deadline:* For fall admission, 12/1 priority date for domestic and international students; for spring admission, 11/1 for domestic and international students. Application fee: $65. Electronic applications accepted. Tuition and fees vary according to program. *Financial support:* Fellowships with tuition reimbursements, research assistantships with tuition reimbursements, teaching assistantships with tuition reimbursements, career-related internships or fieldwork, Federal Work-Study, scholarships/grants, traineeships, health care benefits, tuition waivers (full and partial), and unspecified assistantships available. Support available to part-time students. Financial award applicants required to submit FAFSA. *Faculty research:* Cognitive learning and culture, effects of social policy reform on children and families, psychosocial trauma, human rights and international justice, positive youth development, children and adolescents living in poverty. *Unit head:* Dr. Penny Hauser-Cram, Chairperson, 617-552-4214, Fax: 617-552-4710. *Application contact:* Kimberly Rose, Graduate Admission Assistant, 617-552-4214, Fax: 617-552-0398, E-mail: roseki@bc.edu.
Website: http://www.bc.edu/schools/lsoe/academics/departments/cdep/adep/madevelop.html

Brigham Young University, Graduate Studies, David O. McKay School of Education, Department of Instructional Psychology and Technology, Provo, UT 84602. Offers MS, PhD. *Faculty:* 10 full-time (1 woman). *Students:* 40 full-time (15 women), 32 part-time (14 women); includes 3 minority (all Native Hawaiian or other Pacific Islander, non-Hispanic/Latino), 1 international. Average age 36. 46 applicants, 52% accepted, 21 enrolled. In 2016, 18 master's, 12 doctorates awarded. *Degree requirements:* For master's, thesis; for doctorate, comprehensive exam, thesis/dissertation. *Entrance requirements:* For master's and doctorate, GRE General Test. Additional exam requirements/recommendations for international students: Required—TOEFL. *Application deadline:* For fall admission, 1/2 for domestic students, 2/1 for international students; for winter admission, 2/1 for international students; for summer admission, 2/1 for international students. Application fee: $50. Electronic applications accepted. *Expenses: Tuition:* Full-time $6680; part-time $393 per credit. Tuition and fees vary according to course load, program and student's religious affiliation. *Financial support:* In 2016–17, 21 students received support, including 22 research assistantships with tuition reimbursements available (averaging $10,000 per year), 12 teaching assistantships with tuition reimbursements available (averaging $7,000 per year); career-related internships or fieldwork, scholarships/grants, tuition waivers (full and partial), and unspecified assistantships also available. Support available to part-time students. Financial award application deadline: 4/15. *Faculty research:* Interactive learning, learning theory, instructional designed development, research and evaluation, measurement. *Unit head:* Dr. Charles R. Graham, Department Chair, 801-422-4110, Fax: 801-422-0314, E-mail: charles.graham@byu.edu. *Application contact:* Michele Bray, Department Secretary, 801-422-2746, Fax: 801-422-0314, E-mail: michele_bray@byu.edu.
Website: http://education.byu.edu/ipt/

California Coast University, School of Education, Santa Ana, CA 92701. Offers administration (M Ed); curriculum and instruction (M Ed); educational administration (Ed D); educational psychology (Ed D); organizational leadership (Ed D). *Program availability:* Online learning.

California State University, Long Beach, Graduate Studies, College of Education, Department of Advanced Studies in Education and Counseling, Long Beach, CA 90840. Offers counseling (MS), including marriage and family therapy, school counseling, student development in higher education; education (MA, Ed D); educational administration (MA, Ed D); educational psychology (MA); special education (MS). *Program availability:* Part-time, evening/weekend. *Entrance requirements:* For master's, GRE General Test, minimum GPA of 2.75. *Application deadline:* For fall admission, 3/1 for domestic students. Applications are processed on a rolling basis. Application fee: $55. Electronic applications accepted. *Financial support:* Federal Work-Study, institutionally sponsored loans, and scholarships/grants available. Financial award application deadline: 3/2. *Unit head:* Dr. Hiromi Masunaga, Chair, 562-985-4517, E-mail: asec@csulb.edu.

California State University, Northridge, Graduate Studies, Michael D. Eisner College of Education, Department of Educational Psychology and Counseling, Northridge, CA

91330. Offers counseling (MS), including career counseling, college counseling and student services, marriage and family therapy, school counseling, school psychology; educational psychology (MA Ed), including development, learning, and instruction, early childhood education. *Accreditation:* ACA (one or more programs are accredited); NCATE. *Program availability:* Part-time, evening/weekend. *Faculty:* 17 full-time (4 women), 46 part-time/adjunct (15 women). *Students:* 283 full-time (235 women), 79 part-time (72 women); includes 180 minority (8 Black or African American, non-Hispanic/Latino; 22 Asian, non-Hispanic/Latino; 132 Hispanic/Latino; 18 Two or more races, non-Hispanic/Latino), 13 international. Average age 29. 411 applicants, 36% accepted, 129 enrolled. *Entrance requirements:* For master's, GRE General Test or minimum GPA of 3.0. Additional exam requirements/recommendations for international students: Required—TOEFL. *Application deadline:* For fall admission, 11/30 for domestic students. Application fee: $55. *Expenses:* Tuition, state resident: full-time $4152. *Financial support:* Scholarships/grants available. Support available to part-time students. Financial award application deadline: 3/1. *Unit head:* Dr. Shari Tarver-Behring, Chair, 818-677-2599. *Application contact:* 818-677-3755.
Website: http://www.csun.edu/eisner-education/educational-psychology-counseling

Capella University, Harold Abel School of Social and Behavioral Science, Doctoral Programs in Psychology, Minneapolis, MN 55402. Offers addiction psychology (PhD); clinical psychology (Psy D); educational psychology (PhD); general advanced studies in human behavior (PhD); general psychology (PhD); industrial/organizational psychology (PhD); school psychology (Psy D).

Capella University, Harold Abel School of Social and Behavioral Science, Master's Programs in Psychology, Minneapolis, MN 55402. Offers applied behavior analysis (MS); clinical psychology (MS); counseling psychology (MS); educational psychology (MS); evaluation, research, and measurement (MS); general advanced studies in human behavior (MS); general psychology (MS); industrial/organizational psychology (MS); leadership coaching psychology (MS); school psychology (MS); sport psychology (MS).

Chapman University, College of Educational Studies, Orange, CA 92866. Offers counseling (MA), including school counseling (MA, Credential); education (PhD), including cultural and curricular studies, disability studies, leadership studies, school psychology (PhD, Credential); educational psychology (MA); leadership development (MA); multiple subjects (Credential), including Spanish/English bilingual; pupil personnel services (Credential), including school counseling (MA, Credential), school psychology (PhD, Credential); school psychology (Ed S); single subject (Credential); special education (MA, Credential), including mild/moderate (Credential), moderate/severe (Credential); teaching (MA), including elementary education, secondary education, secondary music education. *Accreditation:* TEAC. *Program availability:* Part-time, evening/weekend. *Faculty:* 29 full-time (14 women), 36 part-time/adjunct (28 women). *Students:* 186 full-time (148 women), 186 part-time (134 women); includes 144 minority (9 Black or African American, non-Hispanic/Latino; 39 Asian, non-Hispanic/Latino; 78 Hispanic/Latino; 2 Native Hawaiian or other Pacific Islander, non-Hispanic/Latino; 16 Two or more races, non-Hispanic/Latino), 8 international. Average age 29. 143 applicants, 63% accepted, 64 enrolled. In 2016, 111 master's, 24 doctorates awarded. *Degree requirements:* For doctorate, thesis/dissertation. *Entrance requirements:* Additional exam requirements/recommendations for international students: Required—TOEFL (minimum score 550 paper-based, 80 iBT), IELTS (6.5), PTE Academic (53), or CAE. *Application deadline:* Applications are processed on a rolling basis. Application fee: $60. Electronic applications accepted. *Expenses:* Contact institution. *Financial support:* Fellowships and scholarships/grants available. Financial award application deadline: 3/2; financial award applicants required to submit FAFSA. *Unit head:* Dr. Margaret Grogan, Dean, 714-516-5968, E-mail: grogan@chapman.edu. *Application contact:* Sara Simon, Graduate Admission Counselor, 714-997-6770, E-mail: simon@chapman.edu.
Website: http://www.chapman.edu/CES/

Clark Atlanta University, School of Education, Department of Counseling and Psychological Studies, Atlanta, GA 30314. Offers MA. *Accreditation:* ACA. *Program availability:* Part-time. *Faculty:* 4 full-time (2 women), 2 part-time/adjunct (both women). *Students:* 29 full-time (21 women), 8 part-time (4 women); includes 30 minority (all Black or African American, non-Hispanic/Latino), 1 international. Average age 28. 20 applicants, 100% accepted, 11 enrolled. In 2016, 26 master's awarded. *Degree requirements:* For master's, comprehensive exam. *Entrance requirements:* For master's, GRE General Test, minimum undergraduate GPA of 2.6. Additional exam requirements/recommendations for international students: Required—TOEFL (minimum score 500 paper-based; 61 iBT). *Application deadline:* For fall admission, 4/1 for domestic and international students; for spring admission, 11/1 for domestic and international students. Applications are processed on a rolling basis. Application fee: $40 ($55 for international students). Electronic applications accepted. *Expenses: Tuition:* Full-time $15,498; part-time $861 per credit hour. *Required fees:* $1326; $1326 per credit hour. Tuition and fees vary according to course load. *Financial support:* Career-related internships or fieldwork, Federal Work-Study, scholarships/grants, and unspecified assistantships available. Support available to part-time students. Financial award application deadline: 4/30; financial award applicants required to submit FAFSA. *Unit head:* Dr. Ken Sanders, Chairperson, 404-880-8519, E-mail: ksanders1@cau.edu. *Application contact:* Graduate Program Admissions, 404-880-8483, E-mail: graduateadmissions@cau.edu.

The College of Saint Rose, Graduate Studies, Thelma P. Lally School of Education, Educational and School Psychology Programs, Albany, NY 12203-1419. Offers educational psychology (MS Ed, Certificate); school psychology (MS Ed). *Students:* 37 full-time (32 women), 9 part-time (6 women); includes 7 minority (1 Black or African American, non-Hispanic/Latino; 1 American Indian or Alaska Native, non-Hispanic/Latino; 1 Asian, non-Hispanic/Latino; 3 Hispanic/Latino; 1 Two or more races, non-Hispanic/Latino), 4 international. Average age 33. 47 applicants, 77% accepted, 21 enrolled. In 2016, 23 master's awarded. *Entrance requirements:* For master's, minimum undergraduate GPA of 3.0. Additional exam requirements/recommendations for international students: Required—TOEFL (minimum score 550 paper-based; 80 iBT), IELTS (minimum score 6), PTE (minimum score 56). *Application deadline:* For fall admission, 2/15 priority date for domestic and international students. Applications are processed on a rolling basis. Application fee: $40. Electronic applications accepted. *Expenses: Tuition:* Full-time $14,382; part-time $799 per credit. *Required fees:* $814; $32 per credit. $88 per semester. Tuition and fees vary according to course load. *Financial support:* Career-related internships or fieldwork, scholarships/grants, tuition waivers (partial), and unspecified assistantships available. Support available to part-time students. Financial award application deadline: 4/15. *Unit head:* Dr. Andrew Shanock, Chair, 518-337-5694, E-mail: shanocka@strose.edu. *Application contact:* Cris Murray, Assistant Vice President for Graduate Recruitment and Enrollment, 518-485-3390, Fax: 518-458-5479, E-mail: grad@strose.edu.
Website: https://www.strose.edu/school-psychology/

Eastern Michigan University, Graduate School, College of Education, Department of Teacher Education, Programs in Educational Psychology and Assessment, Ypsilanti, MI 48197. Offers educational assessment (Graduate Certificate); educational psychology (MA). *Accreditation:* NCATE. *Program availability:* Part-time, evening/weekend, online learning. *Students:* 31 part-time (29 women); includes 9 minority (4 Black or African American, non-Hispanic/Latino; 1 American Indian or Alaska Native, non-Hispanic/Latino; 1 Hispanic/Latino; 3 Two or more races, non-Hispanic/Latino). Average age 34. 21 applicants, 67% accepted, 5 enrolled. In 2016, 19 master's, 3 other advanced degrees awarded. *Degree requirements:* For master's, thesis or alternative. *Entrance requirements:* For master's, GRE. Additional exam requirements/recommendations for international students: Required—TOEFL. *Application deadline:* Applications are processed on a rolling basis. Application fee: $45. *Financial support:* Fellowships, research assistantships with full tuition reimbursements, teaching assistantships with full tuition reimbursements, career-related internships or fieldwork, Federal Work-Study, institutionally sponsored loans, scholarships/grants, tuition waivers (partial), and unspecified assistantships available. Support available to part-time students. Financial award applicants required to submit FAFSA. *Application contact:* Dr. Alane Starko, Coordinator, 734-487-3260, Fax: 734-487-2101, E-mail: astarko@emich.edu.

Edinboro University of Pennsylvania, Department of Counseling, School Psychology and Special Education, Edinboro, PA 16444. Offers counseling (MA), including art therapy, clinical mental health counseling, college counseling, rehabilitation counseling, school counseling; educational psychology (M Ed); school psychology (Ed S); special education (M Ed), including autism, behavior management. *Accreditation:* ACA. *Program availability:* Part-time, evening/weekend. *Degree requirements:* For master's, thesis or alternative, competency exam; for Ed S, thesis or alternative. *Entrance requirements:* For master's and Ed S, GRE or MAT, minimum QPA of 2.5. Electronic applications accepted.

Florida Atlantic University, College of Education, Department of Teaching and Learning, Boca Raton, FL 33431-0991. Offers curriculum and instruction (M Ed), including art, biology, chemistry, English, French, German, mathematics, music, physics, Pre-K and primary education, reading, social sciences, Spanish; elementary education (M Ed); environmental education (M Ed); reading education (M Ed); social foundations of education (M Ed), including educational psychology, educational technology, multilingual education. *Accreditation:* NCATE. *Program availability:* Part-time, evening/weekend. *Faculty:* 15 full-time (12 women), 2 part-time/adjunct (1 woman). *Students:* 25 full-time (20 women), 41 part-time (37 women); includes 18 minority (9 Black or African American, non-Hispanic/Latino; 2 Asian, non-Hispanic/Latino; 7 Hispanic/Latino), 7 international. Average age 32. 54 applicants, 59% accepted, 18 enrolled. In 2016, 36 master's awarded. *Entrance requirements:* For master's, GRE General Test, minimum GPA of 3.0 in last 2 years of undergraduate course work. Additional exam requirements/recommendations for international students: Required—TOEFL (minimum score 500 paper-based; 61 iBT), IELTS (minimum score 6). *Application deadline:* For fall admission, 7/1 for domestic students, 2/15 for international students; for spring admission, 11/1 for domestic students, 7/15 for international students. Applications are processed on a rolling basis. Application fee: $30. *Expenses:* Tuition, state resident: full-time $7392; part-time $369.82 per credit hour. Tuition, nonresident: full-time $19,432; part-time $1024.81 per credit hour. *Financial support:* Fellowships with partial tuition reimbursements, research assistantships with partial tuition reimbursements, teaching assistantships with partial tuition reimbursements, career-related internships or fieldwork, scholarships/grants, and unspecified assistantships available. *Faculty research:* Technology, teaching English to speakers of other languages, math teaching, electronic portfolio assessment, global perspectives through social studies. *Unit head:* Dr. Barbara Ridener, Chairperson, 561-297-3588, E-mail: bridener@fau.edu. *Application contact:* Dr. Eliah Watlington, Associate Dean, 561-297-6520, Fax: 261-297-2991, E-mail: ewatling@fau.edu.
Website: http://www.coe.fau.edu/academicdepartments/tl/

Florida State University, The Graduate School, College of Education, Program in Educational Psychology, Tallahassee, FL 32306. Offers learning and cognition (MS, PhD); sport psychology (MS, PhD). Terminal master's awarded for partial completion of doctoral program. *Degree requirements:* For master's, comprehensive exam, thesis optional; for doctorate, comprehensive exam, thesis/dissertation, diagnostic exam, preliminary exam, prospectus defense, dissertation defense. *Entrance requirements:* For master's and doctorate, GRE General Test, minimum upper-division GPA of 3.0. Additional exam requirements/recommendations for international students: Required—TOEFL (minimum score 550 paper-based, 80 iBT), IELTS (minimum score 6.5), Michigan English Language Assessment Battery (minimum score 77), or PTE (minimum score 55). Application fee: $30. Electronic applications accepted. *Expenses:* Tuition, state resident: full-time $7263; part-time $403.51 per credit hour. Tuition, nonresident: full-time $18,087; part-time $1004.85 per credit hour. *Required fees:* $1365; $75.81 per credit hour. $20 per semester. Tuition and fees vary according to campus/location. *Financial support:* Fellowships, research assistantships, teaching assistantships, scholarships/grants, tuition waivers (full and partial), and unspecified assistantships available. Financial award application deadline: 1/15; financial award applicants required to submit FAFSA. *Faculty research:* Motivation/emotion/cognition/critical thinking; human performance, adult learning, teacher quality; language/literacy development and instruction; evaluation of evidence-based interventions; well-being of underrepresented, high-need groups. *Unit head:* Dr. Betsy Becker, Professor/Department Chair, 850-644-2371, Fax: 850-644-8776, E-mail: bbecker@fsu.edu. *Application contact:* Eileen Sirois, Academic Program Assistant, 850-644-8786, Fax: 850-644-8776, E-mail: esirois@fsu.edu.
Website: http://education.fsu.edu/degrees-and-programs/graduate-programs

Fordham University, Graduate School of Education, Division of Psychological and Educational Services, New York, NY 10023. Offers counseling and personnel services (MSE); counseling psychology (PhD); school psychology (PhD). *Accreditation:* APA (one or more programs are accredited); NCATE. *Program availability:* Part-time, evening/weekend. Terminal master's awarded for partial completion of doctoral program. *Degree requirements:* For master's, comprehensive exam (for some programs); for doctorate, comprehensive exam (for some programs), thesis/dissertation. *Entrance requirements:* For doctorate, GRE General Test. Additional exam requirements/recommendations for international students: Required—TOEFL (minimum score 577 paper-based; 90 iBT), IELTS (minimum score 7). Electronic applications accepted.

George Mason University, College of Education and Human Development, Program in Educational Psychology, Fairfax, VA 22030. Offers MS, Certificate. *Faculty:* 6 full-time (all women), 2 part-time/adjunct (1 woman). *Students:* 9 full-time (5 women), 22 part-time (20 women); includes 4 minority (2 Black or African American, non-Hispanic/Latino; 1 Asian, non-Hispanic/Latino; 1 Hispanic/Latino), 5 international. Average age 29. 22 applicants, 64% accepted, 7 enrolled. In 2016, 22 master's awarded. *Entrance requirements:* For master's, GRE, official transcripts; 3 letters of recommendation; expanded goals statement. Additional exam requirements/recommendations for international students: Required—TOEFL (minimum score 575 paper-based; 80 iBT), IELTS (minimum score 6.5), PTE (minimum score 59). *Application deadline:* For spring admission, 11/1 priority date for domestic and international students. Application fee: $75 ($80 for international students). Electronic applications accepted. *Expenses:* Tuition, state resident: full-time $10,628; part-time $443 per credit. Tuition, nonresident: full-time $29,306; part-time $1221 per credit. *Required fees:* $3096; $129 per credit. Tuition and fees vary according to program. *Financial support:* In 2016–17, 1 student

received support, including 1 research assistantship with tuition reimbursement available (averaging $12,480 per year); career-related internships or fieldwork, Federal Work-Study, scholarships/grants, unspecified assistantships, and health care benefits (for full-time research or teaching assistantship recipients) also available. Support available to part-time students. Financial award application deadline: 3/1; financial award applicants required to submit FAFSA. *Faculty research:* Learning, cognition, motivation measurement, evaluation assessment, educational policy. *Unit head:* Erin Peters-Burton, Academic Program Coordinator, 703-993-9695, Fax: 703-993-3678, E-mail: epeters1@gmu.edu. *Application contact:* Kim Howe, Office Manager, 703-993-3679, Fax: 703-993-3678, E-mail: khowe1@gmu.edu.
Website: http://gse.gmu.edu/programs/edpsych/

Georgia State University, College of Education and Human Development, Department of Educational Psychology, Special Education, and Communication Disorders, Program in Educational Psychology, Atlanta, GA 30302-3083. Offers MS, PhD. *Accreditation:* NCATE. *Program availability:* Part-time, evening/weekend, online learning. *Degree requirements:* For master's, comprehensive exam (for some programs), thesis (for some programs); for doctorate, comprehensive exam, thesis/dissertation. *Entrance requirements:* For master's and doctorate, GRE. Additional exam requirements/ recommendations for international students: Required—TOEFL (minimum score 550 paper-based; 79 iBT) or IELTS (minimum score 6.5). *Application deadline:* For fall admission, 1/15 for domestic and international students; for winter admission, 9/1 for domestic and international students. Applications are processed on a rolling basis. Application fee: $50. Electronic applications accepted. *Expenses:* Tuition, state resident: full-time $6876; part-time $382 per credit hour. Tuition, nonresident: full-time $22,374; part-time $1243 per credit hour. *Required fees:* $2128; $1064 per term. Part-time tuition and fees vary according to course load and program. *Financial support:* In 2016–17, fellowships with full tuition reimbursements (averaging $28,000 per year) were awarded; research assistantships with full tuition reimbursements, teaching assistantships with full tuition reimbursements, institutionally sponsored loans, scholarships/grants, tuition waivers, and unspecified assistantships also available. Financial award applicants required to submit FAFSA. *Faculty research:* Language and literacy, social emotional development, cognitive development, applied behavior analysis, motivation and metacognition. *Unit head:* Dr. Miles Anthony Irving, Program Coordinator, 404-413-3808, E-mail: iam@gsu.edu. *Application contact:* Sandy Vaughn, Senior Administrative Coordinator, 404-413-8318, E-mail: svaughn@gsu.edu.
Website: http://esc.education.gsu.edu/academics-and-admissions/educational-psychology/

The Graduate Center, City University of New York, Graduate Studies, Program in Educational Psychology, New York, NY 10016-4039. Offers PhD. *Accreditation:* APA. *Degree requirements:* For doctorate, 2 foreign languages, thesis/dissertation. *Entrance requirements:* For doctorate, GRE General Test, interview, minimum GPA of 3.0. Additional exam requirements/recommendations for international students: Required—TOEFL. Electronic applications accepted.

Harvard University, Harvard Graduate School of Education, Master's Programs in Education, Cambridge, MA 02138. Offers arts in education (Ed M); education policy and management (Ed M); higher education (Ed M); human development and psychology (Ed M); international education policy (Ed M); language and literacy (Ed M); learning and teaching (Ed M); mind, brain, and education (Ed M); prevention science and practice (Ed M); school leadership (Ed M); special studies (Ed M); teacher education (Ed M); technology, innovation, and education (Ed M). *Program availability:* Part-time. *Entrance requirements:* For master's, GRE General Test, statement of purpose, 3 letters of recommendation, resume, official transcripts. Additional exam requirements/ recommendations for international students: Required—TOEFL (minimum score 613 paper-based; 104 iBT), TWE (minimum score 5). Electronic applications accepted. *Faculty research:* Learning and development, educational leadership and organizations, education policy analysis.

Holy Names University, Graduate Division, Department of Education, Oakland, CA 94619-1699. Offers educational therapy (Certificate); mild/moderate disabilities (Ed S); multiple subject teaching (Credential); single subject teaching (Credential); urban education: educational therapy (M Ed); urban education: K-12 education (M Ed); urban education: special education (M Ed). *Program availability:* Part-time. *Students:* 18 full-time (11 women), 111 part-time (79 women); includes 74 minority (37 Black or African American, non-Hispanic/Latino; 1 American Indian or Alaska Native, non-Hispanic/ Latino; 10 Asian, non-Hispanic/Latino; 24 Hispanic/Latino; 1 Native Hawaiian or other Pacific Islander, non-Hispanic/Latino; 1 Two or more races, non-Hispanic/Latino), 3 international. Average age 35. 62 applicants, 81% accepted, 39 enrolled. In 2016, 11 master's, 33 Certificates awarded. *Degree requirements:* For master's, comprehensive exam, research paper, thesis or project. *Entrance requirements:* For master's, minimum undergraduate GPA of 2.6 overall, 3.0 in major; personal statement; two recommendations; interview. Additional exam requirements/recommendations for international students: Required—TOEFL (minimum score 550 paper-based; 79 iBT). *Application deadline:* For fall admission, 8/1 priority date for domestic students, 7/15 for international students; for spring admission, 12/1 priority date for domestic students, 12/ 1 for international students; for summer admission, 5/1 priority date for domestic students, 5/1 for international students. Applications are processed on a rolling basis. Application fee: $65. Electronic applications accepted. Application fee is waived when completed online. *Expenses: Tuition:* Full-time $17,532; part-time $974 per credit hour. *Required fees:* $500; $250 per credit hour. *Financial support:* Career-related internships or fieldwork, Federal Work-Study, scholarships/grants, and unspecified assistantships available. Support available to part-time students. Financial award application deadline: 3/2; financial award applicants required to submit FAFSA. *Faculty research:* Cognitive development, language development, learning handicaps. *Unit head:* Dr. Kimberly Mayfield, Chair, 510-436-1396, Fax: 510-436-1325, E-mail: mayfield@hnu.edu. *Application contact:* Graduate Admission, 800-430-1321, Fax: 510-436-1325, E-mail: graduateadmissions@hnu.edu.
Website: http://www.hnu.edu/academics/graduatePrograms/education.html

Howard University, School of Education, Department of Human Development and Psychoeducational Studies, Program in Educational Psychology, Washington, DC 20059-0002. Offers PhD. *Program availability:* Part-time. *Degree requirements:* For doctorate, one foreign language, comprehensive exam, thesis/dissertation, expository writing exam, internship. *Entrance requirements:* For doctorate, GRE General Test, minimum GPA of 3.4. Additional exam requirements/recommendations for international students: Required—TOEFL (minimum score 550 paper-based; 79 iBT). Electronic applications accepted.

Immaculata University, College of Graduate Studies, Department of Psychology, Immaculata, PA 19345. Offers clinical mental health counseling (MA); clinical psychology (Psy D); forensic psychology (Graduate Certificate); integrative psychotherapy (Graduate Certificate); neuropsychology (Graduate Certificate); psychodynamic psychotherapy (Graduate Certificate); psychological testing (Graduate Certificate); school counseling (MA, Graduate Certificate); school psychology (MA). *Accreditation:* APA. *Program availability:* Part-time, evening/weekend. Terminal master's awarded for partial completion of doctoral program. *Degree requirements:* For master's, comprehensive exam, thesis optional; for doctorate, comprehensive exam, thesis/dissertation. *Entrance requirements:* For master's, GRE General Test or MAT, minimum GPA of 3.0; for doctorate, GRE General Test or MAT, minimum GPA of 3.5. Additional exam requirements/recommendations for international students: Required—TOEFL, IELTS. Electronic applications accepted. *Faculty research:* Supervision ethics, psychology of teaching, gender.

Indiana University Bloomington, School of Education, Department of Counseling and Educational Psychology, Bloomington, IN 47405-1006. Offers counseling (MS, PhD, Ed S); counselor education (MS, Ed S); educational psychology (MS, PhD); inquiry methodology (PhD); learning and developmental sciences (MS, PhD); school psychology (PhD, Ed S). *Accreditation:* ACA (one or more programs are accredited); APA (one or more programs are accredited); NCATE. Terminal master's awarded for partial completion of doctoral program. *Degree requirements:* For master's, thesis optional; for doctorate, thesis/dissertation; for Ed S, comprehensive exam or project. *Entrance requirements:* For master's, doctorate, and Ed S, GRE General Test. Additional exam requirements/recommendations for international students: Required—TOEFL. Electronic applications accepted. *Faculty research:* Counseling psychology, inquiry methodology, school psychology, learning sciences, human development, educational psychology.

Indiana University of Pennsylvania, School of Graduate Studies and Research, College of Education and Educational Technology, Department of Educational and School Psychology, Program in Educational Psychology, Indiana, PA 15705. Offers M Ed, Certificate. *Accreditation:* NCATE. *Program availability:* Part-time. *Faculty:* 8 full-time (3 women). *Students:* 10 full-time (7 women); includes 3 minority (all Black or African American, non-Hispanic/Latino). Average age 24. 26 applicants, 58% accepted, 10 enrolled. In 2016, 12 master's awarded. *Degree requirements:* For master's, thesis optional. *Entrance requirements:* For master's, GRE General Test, 2 letters of recommendation. Additional exam requirements/recommendations for international students: Required—TOEFL (minimum score 540 paper-based; 76 iBT). *Application deadline:* For fall admission, 2/1 priority date for domestic students. Application fee: $50. Electronic applications accepted. *Expenses:* Tuition, state resident: full-time $8694; part-time $483 per credit. Tuition, nonresident: full-time $13,050; part-time $725 per credit. *Required fees:* $157 per credit. $50 per term. Tuition and fees vary according to course load and program. *Financial support:* In 2016–17, 9 research assistantships with tuition reimbursements (averaging $3,627 per year) were awarded; fellowships with full tuition reimbursements, teaching assistantships with partial tuition reimbursements, career-related internships or fieldwork, Federal Work-Study, scholarships/grants, and unspecified assistantships also available. Support available to part-time students. Financial award application deadline: 4/15; financial award applicants required to submit FAFSA. *Unit head:* Dr. Mark R. McGowan, Graduate Coordinator, 724-357-2174, E-mail: mmcgowan@iup.edu.
Website: http://www.iup.edu/schoolpsychology/grad/educational-psychology-med/default.aspx

Instituto Tecnologico de Santo Domingo, Graduate School, Area of Humanities and Social Sciences, Santo Domingo, Dominican Republic. Offers accounting (Certificate); adult education (Certificate); applied linguistics (MA); economics (MA); education (M Ed); educational psychology (MA, Certificate); gender and development (MA, Certificate); humanistic studies (MA); international marketing management (Certificate); international relations in the Caribbean basin (Certificate); intervention systems in family therapy (MA); linguistic and literary communication (Certificate); pedagogical support (MA); social science education (M Ed); sustainable human development (MA); terminal illness and death psychology (Certificate); youth and adult education (M Ed).

John Carroll University, Graduate Studies, Programs in Educational and School Psychology, University Heights, OH 44118-4581. Offers educational psychology (M Ed); school psychology (M Ed, Ed S). *Accreditation:* NCATE. *Program availability:* Part-time, evening/weekend. *Degree requirements:* For master's, comprehensive exam, research essay or thesis (MA only). *Entrance requirements:* For master's, GRE General Test or MAT, minimum GPA of 2.75, degree in education or psychology, interview. *Application deadline:* For fall admission, 2/1 for domestic students; for spring admission, 10/15 for domestic students. Applications are processed on a rolling basis. Application fee: $25 ($35 for international students). Electronic applications accepted. *Expenses: Tuition:* Full-time $10,425; part-time $695 per credit hour. One-time fee: $200 full-time. Tuition and fees vary according to course load, campus/location and program. *Financial support:* Teaching assistantships, scholarships/grants, and unspecified assistantships available. Financial award application deadline: 3/1; financial award applicants required to submit FAFSA. *Unit head:* Dr. Catherine A. Rosemary, Chair, 216-397-4632, Fax: 216-397-3045. *Application contact:* Jennifer L. Tucker, Records Management Assistant, 216-397-1925, Fax: 216-397-1835, E-mail: jtucker@jcu.edu.

Kent State University, College of Education, Health and Human Services, School of Lifespan Development and Educational Sciences, Program in Educational Psychology, Kent, OH 44242-0001. Offers M Ed, MA. *Degree requirements:* For master's, thesis optional. *Entrance requirements:* For master's, 2 letters of reference, minimum GPA of 3.5, goals statement. Additional exam requirements/recommendations for international students: Required—TOEFL (minimum score 550 paper-based; 80 iBT). Electronic applications accepted. *Expenses:* Tuition, state resident: full-time $10,864; part-time $495 per credit hour. Tuition, nonresident: full-time $18,380; part-time $837 per credit hour.

La Sierra University, School of Education, Department of School Psychology and Counseling, Riverside, CA 92515. Offers counseling (MA); educational psychology (Ed S); school psychology (Ed S). *Program availability:* Part-time, evening/weekend. *Degree requirements:* For master's, thesis optional; for Ed S, practicum (educational psychology). *Entrance requirements:* For master's, California Basic Educational Skills Test, NTE, minimum GPA of 3.0; for Ed S, minimum GPA of 3.3. *Faculty research:* Equivalent score scales, self perception.

McGill University, Faculty of Graduate and Postdoctoral Studies, Faculty of Education, Department of Educational and Counseling Psychology, Montréal, QC H3A 2T5, Canada. Offers counseling psychology (MA, PhD); educational psychology (M Ed, MA, PhD); school/applied child psychology and applied developmental psychology (M Ed, MA, PhD, Diploma), including school psychology. *Accreditation:* APA.

Memorial University of Newfoundland, School of Graduate Studies, Faculty of Education, St. John's, NL A1C 5S7, Canada. Offers counseling psychology (M Ed); curriculum, teaching, and learning studies (M Ed); education (PhD); educational leadership studies (M Ed, Graduate Diploma); information technology (M Ed); post-secondary studies (M Ed, Diploma), including health professional education (Diploma). *Program availability:* Part-time. *Degree requirements:* For master's, thesis optional, internship, paper folio, project; for doctorate, comprehensive exam, thesis/dissertation, thesis seminar, oral defense of thesis. *Entrance requirements:* For master's, undergraduate degree with at least 2nd class standing, 1-2 years of work experience; for doctorate, minimum A average in graduate course work, MA in education, 2 years of professional experience; for other advanced degree, 2nd class degree, 2 years of work experience with adult learners, appropriate academic qualifications and work experience in a health-related field. Electronic applications accepted. *Faculty research:* Critical thinking, literacy, cognitive studies and counseling, educational change, technology in instruction.

Miami University, College of Education, Health and Society, Department of Educational Psychology, Oxford, OH 45056. Offers M Ed, MA, MS, Ed S. *Accreditation:* NCATE. *Students:* 44 full-time (38 women), 86 part-time (66 women); includes 12 minority (7 Black or African American, non-Hispanic/Latino; 2 Asian, non-Hispanic/Latino; 1 Hispanic/Latino; 2 Two or more races, non-Hispanic/Latino), 12 international. Average age 31. In 2016, 49 master's awarded. *Expenses:* Tuition, state resident: full-time $12,890; part-time $564 per credit hour. Tuition, nonresident: full-time $29,604; part-time $1260 per credit hour. *Required fees:* $638. Part-time tuition and fees vary according to course load and program. *Unit head:* Dr. Raymond Witte, Chair and Professor, 513-529-6621, E-mail: edp@miamioh.edu. *Application contact:* 513-529-6621, E-mail: edp@miamioh.edu.
Website: http://www.MiamiOH.edu/EDP

Michigan School of Professional Psychology, MA and Psy D Programs in Clinical Psychology, Farmington Hills, MI 48334. Offers MA, Psy D. *Accreditation:* APA. *Program availability:* Part-time. *Faculty:* 8 full-time (4 women), 13 part-time/adjunct (11 women). *Students:* 84 full-time (66 women), 56 part-time (46 women); includes 42 minority (29 Black or African American, non-Hispanic/Latino; 2 Asian, non-Hispanic/Latino; 5 Hispanic/Latino; 6 Two or more races, non-Hispanic/Latino), 1 international. Average age 34. 155 applicants, 54% accepted, 61 enrolled. In 2016, 42 master's, 17 doctorates awarded. *Degree requirements:* For master's, practicum; for doctorate, comprehensive exam, thesis/dissertation, internship, practicum. *Entrance requirements:* For master's, undergraduate degree from accredited institution with minimum GPA of 2.5; major in psychology, social work, or counseling; for doctorate, GRE General Test, undergraduate degree from accredited institution with minimum GPA of 2.5; graduate degree in psychology, social work, or counseling from accredited institution with minimum GPA of 3.25; graduate-level practicum. Additional exam requirements/recommendations for international students: Required—TOEFL (minimum score 550 paper-based; 79 iBT). *Application deadline:* For fall admission, 8/15 for domestic students; for winter admission, 12/1 for domestic students; for spring admission, 4/3 for domestic students. Applications are processed on a rolling basis. Application fee: $75. Electronic applications accepted. *Expenses:* Contact institution. *Financial support:* In 2016–17, 6 students received support, including 1 research assistantship, 5 teaching assistantships (averaging $14,436 per year); institutionally sponsored loans, scholarships/grants, and unspecified assistantships also available. Financial award application deadline: 8/30; financial award applicants required to submit FAFSA. *Faculty research:* Health psychology, trauma. *Unit head:* Dr. Frances Brown, Program Director, 248-476-1122, Fax: 248-476-1125. *Application contact:* Carrie Hauser, Coordinator of Admissions and Student Engagement, 248-476-1122 Ext. 117, Fax: 248-476-1125, E-mail: chauser@mispp.edu.
Website: http://www.mispp.edu

Michigan State University, The Graduate School, College of Education, Department of Counseling, Educational Psychology and Special Education, East Lansing, MI 48824. Offers counseling (MA); educational psychology and educational technology (PhD); educational technology (MA); measurement and quantitative methods (PhD); rehabilitation counseling (MA); rehabilitation counselor education (PhD); school psychology (MA, PhD, Ed S); special education (MA, PhD). *Accreditation:* APA (one or more programs are accredited); CORE (one or more programs are accredited). *Program availability:* Part-time. *Entrance requirements:* Additional exam requirements/recommendations for international students: Required—TOEFL. Electronic applications accepted.

Mississippi State University, College of Education, Department of Counseling, Educational Psychology, and Foundations, Mississippi State, MS 39762. Offers clinical mental health (MS); college counseling (MS); college/post secondary student counseling and personnel services (PhD); counselor education (Ed S); counselor education/student counseling and guidance services (PhD); general educational psychology (MS); psychometry (MS); rehabilitation (MS); school counseling (MS); school psychology (PhD, Ed S); student affairs (MS). *Accreditation:* ACA (one or more programs are accredited); APA; CORE (one or more programs are accredited); NCATE. *Program availability:* Part-time, blended/hybrid learning. *Faculty:* 21 full-time (14 women), 2 part-time/adjunct (both women). *Students:* 125 full-time (94 women), 70 part-time (60 women); includes 63 minority (48 Black or African American, non-Hispanic/Latino; 1 American Indian or Alaska Native, non-Hispanic/Latino; 4 Asian, non-Hispanic/Latino; 5 Hispanic/Latino; 5 Two or more races, non-Hispanic/Latino), 6 international. Average age 30. 151 applicants, 64% accepted, 70 enrolled. In 2016, 49 master's, 3 doctorates, 4 other advanced degrees awarded. Terminal master's awarded for partial completion of doctoral program. *Degree requirements:* For master's, comprehensive exam, thesis optional; for doctorate, thesis/dissertation, comprehensive oral and written exam. *Entrance requirements:* For master's, GRE (taken within the last five years), BS with minimum GPA of 2.75 on last 60 hours; for doctorate, GRE, MS from CACREP- or CORE-accredited program in counseling; for Ed S, GRE, MS in counseling or related field, minimum GPA of 3.3 on all graduate work. Additional exam requirements/recommendations for international students: Required—TOEFL (minimum score 550 paper-based; 79 iBT); Recommended—IELTS (minimum score 6.5). *Application deadline:* For fall admission, 2/1 priority date for domestic and international students. Applications are processed on a rolling basis. Application fee: $60. Electronic applications accepted. *Expenses:* Tuition, state resident: full-time $7670; part-time $852.50 per credit hour. Tuition, nonresident: full-time $20,790; part-time $2310.50 per credit hour. Part-time tuition and fees vary according to course load. *Financial support:* In 2016–17, 9 teaching assistantships with full tuition reimbursements (averaging $8,401 per year) were awarded; career-related internships or fieldwork, Federal Work-Study, institutionally sponsored loans, and unspecified assistantships also available. Financial award application deadline: 2/1; financial award applicants required to submit FAFSA. *Faculty research:* HIV/AIDS in college population, substance abuse in youth and college students, ADHD and conduct disorders in youth, assessment and identification of early childhood disabilities, assessment and vocational transition of the disabled. *Unit head:* Dr. David Morse, Professor and Head, 662-325-3426, Fax: 662-325-3263, E-mail: dmorse@colled.msstate.edu. *Application contact:* Linda Bonner, Senior Admissions Assistant, 662-325-3363, E-mail: lbonner@grad.msstate.edu.
Website: http://www.cep.msstate.edu/

Mount Saint Vincent University, Graduate Programs, Faculty of Education, Program in Educational Psychology, Halifax, NS B3M 2J6, Canada. Offers education of the blind or visually impaired (M Ed, MA Ed); education of the deaf or hard of hearing (M Ed, MA Ed); educational psychology (MA-R); human relations (M Ed, MA Ed). *Program availability:* Part-time, evening/weekend, online learning. *Degree requirements:* For master's, thesis (for some programs). *Entrance requirements:* For master's, bachelor's degree in related field, 1 year of teaching experience. Electronic applications accepted. *Faculty research:* Personality measurement, values reasoning, aggression and sexuality, power and control, quantitative and qualitative research methodologies.

National Louis University, National College of Education, Chicago, IL 60603. Offers administration and supervision (M Ed, Ed D, CAS, Ed S); curriculum and instruction (M Ed, MS Ed, CAS); early childhood administration (M Ed, CAS); early childhood education (M Ed, MAT, MS Ed, CAS); education (Ed D); educational psychology/human learning and development (M Ed, MS Ed, CAS, Ed S); elementary education (MAT); interdisciplinary curriculum and instruction (M Ed); mathematics education (M Ed, MS Ed, CAS); middle grades education (MAT); reading and language (M Ed, MS Ed, CAS); school psychology (M Ed, Ed S); science education (M Ed, MS Ed, CAS); secondary education (MAT); special education (M Ed, MAT, CAS); technology in education (M Ed, CAS). *Accreditation:* NCATE. *Program availability:* Part-time, evening/weekend. *Degree requirements:* For doctorate, comprehensive exam, thesis/dissertation. *Entrance requirements:* For master's, MAT or GRE, minimum GPA of 3.0; for doctorate, GRE General Test, minimum GPA of 3.25, interview, resume, writing sample, 4 recommendations. Additional exam requirements/recommendations for international students: Required—TOEFL (minimum score 550 paper-based; 79 iBT).

New York University, Steinhardt School of Culture, Education, and Human Development, Department of Applied Psychology, Programs in Educational and Developmental Psychology, New York, NY 10003. Offers developmental psychology (PhD); human development and social intervention (MA); psychology and social intervention (PhD). *Accreditation:* APA (one or more programs are accredited). *Program availability:* Part-time. *Degree requirements:* For master's, thesis (for some programs); for doctorate, thesis/dissertation. *Entrance requirements:* For doctorate, GRE General Test, interview. Additional exam requirements/recommendations for international students: Required—TOEFL. Electronic applications accepted. *Faculty research:* Schools and communities, self-regulation and academic achievement, intervention and social change, trauma and resilience, cognition.

Northern Arizona University, Graduate College, College of Education, Department of Educational Psychology, Flagstaff, AZ 86011. Offers counseling (MA); educational psychology (PhD), including counseling psychology, school psychology; human relations (M Ed); school counseling (M Ed); school psychology (Ed S); student affairs (M Ed). *Program availability:* Part-time, online learning. Terminal master's awarded for partial completion of doctoral program. *Degree requirements:* For master's, internship (for some programs); for doctorate, comprehensive exam, thesis/dissertation, internship. *Entrance requirements:* Additional exam requirements/recommendations for international students: Required—TOEFL (minimum score 550 paper-based; 80 iBT), IELTS (minimum score 7). Electronic applications accepted. *Expenses:* Tuition, state resident: full-time $8971; part-time $444 per credit hour. Tuition, nonresident: full-time $20,958; part-time $1164 per credit hour. *Required fees:* $1018; $644 per credit hour. Tuition and fees vary according to course load, campus/location and program.

Northern Illinois University, Graduate School, College of Education, Department of Leadership, Educational Psychology and Foundations, De Kalb, IL 60115-2854. Offers educational administration (MS Ed, Ed D, Ed S); educational psychology (MS Ed, Ed D); foundations of education (MS Ed); school business management (MS Ed). *Program availability:* Part-time, evening/weekend, online learning. *Faculty:* 23 full-time (12 women). *Students:* 13 full-time (8 women), 230 part-time (133 women); includes 33 minority (13 Black or African American, non-Hispanic/Latino; 3 Asian, non-Hispanic/Latino; 9 Hispanic/Latino; 8 Two or more races, non-Hispanic/Latino), 4 international. Average age 39. 132 applicants, 43% accepted, 31 enrolled. In 2016, 36 master's, 30 doctorates, 17 other advanced degrees awarded. *Degree requirements:* For master's, comprehensive exam, thesis optional; for doctorate, thesis/dissertation, candidacy exam, dissertation defense. *Entrance requirements:* For master's, minimum undergraduate GPA of 2.75; for doctorate, GRE General Test, minimum undergraduate GPA of 2.75, 3.2 graduate; for Ed S, GRE General Test, minimum GPA of 2.75 (undergraduate), 3.2 (graduate). Additional exam requirements/recommendations for international students: Required—TOEFL (minimum score 550 paper-based). *Application deadline:* For fall admission, 6/1 for domestic students, 5/1 for international students; for spring admission, 11/1 for domestic students, 10/1 for international students. Applications are processed on a rolling basis. Application fee: $40. Electronic applications accepted. *Financial support:* In 2016–17, 4 research assistantships with full tuition reimbursements, 2 teaching assistantships with full tuition reimbursements were awarded; fellowships with full tuition reimbursements, career-related internships or fieldwork, Federal Work-Study, scholarships/grants, tuition waivers (full), and staff assistantships also available. Support available to part-time students. Financial award applicants required to submit FAFSA. *Faculty research:* Interpersonal forgiveness, learner-centered education, psychedelic studies, senior theory, professional growth. *Unit head:* Carolyn V. Schee, Chair, 815-753-4404, E-mail: lepf@niu.edu. *Application contact:* Graduate School Office, 815-753-0395, E-mail: gradsch@niu.edu.
Website: http://cedu.niu.edu/LEPF/

Oklahoma State University, College of Education, School of Applied Health and Educational Psychology, Stillwater, OK 74078. Offers applied behavioral studies (Ed D); applied health and educational psychology (MS, PhD, Ed S). *Accreditation:* APA (one or more programs are accredited). *Program availability:* Part-time. *Faculty:* 38 full-time (22 women), 11 part-time/adjunct (6 women). *Students:* 168 full-time (122 women), 140 part-time (80 women); includes 86 minority (21 Black or African American, non-Hispanic/Latino; 10 American Indian or Alaska Native, non-Hispanic/Latino; 3 Asian, non-Hispanic/Latino; 24 Hispanic/Latino; 28 Two or more races, non-Hispanic/Latino), 13 international. Average age 30. 157 applicants, 51% accepted, 73 enrolled. In 2016, 73 master's, 21 doctorates awarded. *Degree requirements:* For master's, thesis (for some programs); for doctorate, comprehensive exam, thesis/dissertation. *Entrance requirements:* For master's and doctorate, GRE or GMAT. Additional exam requirements/recommendations for international students: Required—TOEFL (minimum score 550 paper-based; 79 iBT). *Application deadline:* For fall admission, 3/1 priority date for international students; for spring admission, 8/1 priority date for international students. Applications are processed on a rolling basis. Application fee: $40 ($75 for international students). Electronic applications accepted. *Expenses:* Tuition, state resident: full-time $3775; part-time $209.70 per credit hour. Tuition, nonresident: full-time $14,851; part-time $825.05 per credit hour. *Required fees:* $2027; $112.60 per credit hour. Tuition and fees vary according to campus/location. *Financial support:* In 2016–17, 31 research assistantships (averaging $9,791 per year), 64 teaching assistantships (averaging $11,347 per year) were awarded; career-related internships or fieldwork, Federal Work-Study, scholarships/grants, health care benefits, tuition waivers (partial), and unspecified assistantships also available. Support available to part-time students. Financial award application deadline: 3/1; financial award applicants required to submit FAFSA. *Unit head:* Dr. Aric Warren, Head, 405-744-6040, Fax: 405-744-6779, E-mail: aric.warren@okstate.edu.
Website: http://education.okstate.edu/sahep

Old Dominion University, Darden College of Education, Program in Educational Psychology and Program Evaluation, Norfolk, VA 23529. Offers education (PhD), including educational psychology, program evaluation. *Program availability:* Part-time, evening/weekend. *Faculty:* 5 full-time (2 women). *Students:* 4 full-time (all women), 2 part-time (both women); includes 1 minority (Black or African American, non-Hispanic/Latino), 2 international. Average age 40. 3 applicants, 100% accepted, 1 enrolled. *Degree requirements:* For doctorate, comprehensive exam, thesis/dissertation. *Entrance requirements:* Additional exam requirements/recommendations for international students: Required—TOEFL. *Application deadline:* Applications are processed on a rolling basis. Application fee: $50. Electronic applications accepted.

Educational Psychology

Expenses: $30,000. *Financial support:* In 2016–17, 4 students received support, including 4 fellowships with full tuition reimbursements available (averaging $15,000 per year), 10 research assistantships with full tuition reimbursements available (averaging $15,000 per year), 2 teaching assistantships with full tuition reimbursements available (averaging $15,000 per year); unspecified assistantships also available. Financial award application deadline: 2/1. *Faculty research:* Motivation self-regulated learning distance learning calibration assessment. *Unit head:* Shana Pribesh, Coordinator, 757-683-6684, E-mail: spribesh@odu.edu. *Application contact:* Nechell Bonds, Director of Admissions, 757-683-3685, Fax: 757-683-3255, E-mail: gradadmit@odu.edu.
Website: http://www.odu.edu/efl/academics/eppe

Penn State University Park, Graduate School, College of Education, Department of Educational Psychology, Counseling, and Special Education, University Park, PA 16802. Offers counselor education (M Ed, D Ed, PhD, Certificate); educational psychology (MS, PhD, Certificate); school psychology (M Ed, MS, PhD, Certificate); special education (M Ed, MS, PhD, Certificate). *Unit head:* Dr. David H. Monk, Dean, 814-865-2523, Fax: 814-865-0555. *Application contact:* Lori Hawn, Director, Graduate Student Services, 814-865-1795, Fax: 814-863-4627, E-mail: l-gswww@lists.psu.edu.
Website: http://ed.psu.edu/epcse

Pontifical Catholic University of Puerto Rico, College of Education, Program in Educational Psychology, Ponce, PR 00717-0777. Offers M Ed. *Degree requirements:* For master's, comprehensive exam, thesis (for some programs). *Entrance requirements:* For master's, GRE, 2 letters of recommendation, interview, minimum GPA of 2.75.

Purdue University, Graduate School, College of Education, Department of Educational Studies, West Lafayette, IN 47907. Offers administration (MS Ed, PhD, Ed S); counseling and development (MS Ed, PhD); education of the gifted (MS Ed); educational psychology (MS Ed, PhD); foundations of education (MS Ed, PhD); higher education administration (MS Ed, PhD); special education (MS Ed, PhD). *Accreditation:* ACA (one or more programs are accredited); NCATE (one or more programs are accredited). *Program availability:* Part-time, evening/weekend. *Faculty:* 29 full-time (22 women), 1 part-time/adjunct (0 women). *Students:* 78 full-time (60 women), 226 part-time (162 women); includes 45 minority (16 Black or African American, non-Hispanic/Latino; 8 Asian, non-Hispanic/Latino; 15 Hispanic/Latino; 6 Two or more races, non-Hispanic/Latino), 45 international. Average age 32. 214 applicants, 53% accepted, 70 enrolled. In 2016, 38 master's, 20 doctorates, 4 other advanced degrees awarded. *Degree requirements:* For master's, thesis optional; for doctorate, thesis/dissertation, oral and written exams; for Ed S, oral presentation, project. *Entrance requirements:* For master's, GRE General Test (except for special education if undergraduate GPA is higher than a 3.0), minimum undergraduate GPA of 3.0; for doctorate and Ed S, GRE General Test (minimum combined score of 1000, 300 for new scoring), minimum undergraduate GPA of 3.0. Additional exam requirements/recommendations for international students: Required—TOEFL (minimum score 550 paper-based; 77 iBT), TWE (minimum score 5). *Application deadline:* Applications are processed on a rolling basis. Application fee: $60 ($75 for international students). Electronic applications accepted. *Financial support:* Fellowships with full tuition reimbursements, research assistantships with full tuition reimbursements, teaching assistantships with full tuition reimbursements, career-related internships or fieldwork, and tuition waivers (full) available. Support available to part-time students. Financial award application deadline: 3/1; financial award applicants required to submit FAFSA. *Faculty research:* Motivation, learning disabilities, school learning, group processes, cognitive development. *Unit head:* F. Richard Olenchak, Head, 765-494-9170, E-mail: olenchak@purdue.edu. *Application contact:* Heather Brinkman, Graduate Contact, 765-494-2345, Fax: 765-494-5832, E-mail: hbrinkma@purdue.edu.
Website: http://www.edst.purdue.edu/

Regent University, Graduate School, School of Education, Virginia Beach, VA 23464-9800. Offers adult education (Ed D, PhD, Ed S); advanced educational leadership (Ed D, PhD, Ed S); career switcher (M Ed); character education (Ed D, PhD, Ed S); Christian education leadership (Ed D, PhD, Ed S); Christian school administration (M Ed); curriculum and instruction (M Ed), including adult education, Christian school, gifted and talented education, STEM education, teacher leader; educational leadership (M Ed); educational psychology (Ed D, PhD, Ed S); educational technology and online learning (Ed D, PhD, Ed S); elementary education (M Ed); exceptional education executive leadership (Ed D, PhD, Ed S); higher education (Ed D, PhD, Ed S); higher education leadership and management (Ed D, PhD, Ed S); individualized degree plan (M Ed); K-12 school leadership (Ed D, PhD, Ed S); K-12 special education (M Ed); K-8 leadership in mathematics education (M Ed); leadership in mathematics education (Ed S); reading specialist (M Ed); special education (Ed D, PhD, Ed S); student affairs (M Ed); TESOL (M Ed), including adult education - collegiate, K-12. *Accreditation:* TEAC. *Program availability:* Part-time, evening/weekend, 100% online, blended/hybrid learning. *Faculty:* 22 full-time (10 women), 42 part-time/adjunct (31 women). *Students:* 89 full-time (62 women), 1,035 part-time (823 women); includes 466 minority (381 Black or African American, non-Hispanic/Latino; 3 American Indian or Alaska Native, non-Hispanic/Latino; 19 Asian, non-Hispanic/Latino; 50 Hispanic/Latino; 13 Two or more races, non-Hispanic/Latino), 11 international. Average age 39. 976 applicants, 59% accepted, 449 enrolled. In 2016, 241 master's, 22 doctorates, 4 other advanced degrees awarded. *Degree requirements:* For master's, thesis or alternative; for doctorate, comprehensive exam, thesis/dissertation. *Entrance requirements:* For master's, Virginia Communication and Literacy Assessment (VCLA), PRAXIS, college transcripts, writing sample, interview; for doctorate, GRE, writing sample, resume, transcripts, interview. Additional exam requirements/recommendations for international students: Required—TOEFL (minimum score 577 paper-based). *Application deadline:* For fall admission, 4/1 priority date for domestic students; for spring admission, 10/15 priority date for domestic students. Applications are processed on a rolling basis. Application fee: $50. Electronic applications accepted. *Expenses:* Contact institution. *Financial support:* In 2016–17, 622 students received support, including 1 fellowship (averaging $5,000 per year); career-related internships or fieldwork, scholarships/grants, and unspecified assistantships also available. Support available to part-time students. *Faculty research:* Christian school administration, curriculum and instruction, educational technology and online learning, higher education, special education. *Unit head:* Dr. Donald Finn, Dean, 757-352-4278, Fax: 757-352-4318, E-mail: dfinn@regent.edu. *Application contact:* Heidi Cece, Assistant Vice President of Enrollment Management, 800-373-5504, Fax: 757-352-4381, E-mail: admissions@regent.edu.
Website: http://www.regent.edu/soe/

Rutgers University–New Brunswick, Graduate School of Education, Department of Educational Psychology, Program in Learning, Cognition and Development, Piscataway, NJ 08854-8097. Offers Ed M. *Program availability:* Part-time, evening/weekend. *Entrance requirements:* For master's, GRE General Test, 3 letters of recommendation. Additional exam requirements/recommendations for international students: Required—TOEFL (minimum score 550 paper-based; 83 iBT). Electronic applications accepted. *Faculty research:* Cognitive development, gender roles, cognition and instruction, peer learning, infancy and early childhood.

Rutgers University–New Brunswick, Graduate School of Education, Doctoral Program in Education, New Brunswick, NJ 08901. Offers educational policy (PhD); educational psychology (PhD); literacy education (PhD); mathematics education (PhD). *Program availability:* Part-time. *Degree requirements:* For doctorate, thesis/dissertation, qualifying exam. *Entrance requirements:* For doctorate, GRE General Test, GRE Subject Test (mathematics education). Additional exam requirements/recommendations for international students: Required—TOEFL (minimum score 575 paper-based; 83 iBT). Electronic applications accepted. *Faculty research:* Literacy education, math education, educational psychology, educational policy, learning sciences.

Simon Fraser University, Office of Graduate Studies and Postdoctoral Fellows, Faculty of Education, Program in Educational Psychology, Burnaby, BC V5A 1S6, Canada. Offers M Ed, MA, PhD. *Program availability:* Part-time, evening/weekend. *Faculty:* 10 full-time (5 women). *Degree requirements:* For master's, comprehensive exam (for some programs), thesis (for some programs), project or thesis; for doctorate, comprehensive exam, thesis/dissertation. *Entrance requirements:* For master's, minimum GPA of 3.0 (on scale of 4.33) or 3.33 based on last 60 credits of undergraduate courses; for doctorate, GRE, minimum GPA of 3.5 (on scale of 4.33). Additional exam requirements/recommendations for international students: Recommended—TOEFL (minimum score 580 paper-based; 93 iBT), IELTS (minimum score 7), TWE (minimum score 5). *Application deadline:* For fall admission, 1/31 for domestic and international students. Application fee: $90 ($125 for international students). Electronic applications accepted. *Financial support:* In 2016–17, fellowships (averaging $6,250 per year), teaching assistantships (averaging $5,608 per year) were awarded; research assistantships, career-related internships or fieldwork, and scholarships/grants also available. *Faculty research:* Autism and social interaction; cultural and personal dimensions in psychological development; early childhood education; social and emotional development; historical emergence, practice, and ongoing development of the constructs of learning disabilities. *Unit head:* Dr. Shawn Bullock, Graduate Chair, 778-782-4858. *Application contact:* Graduate Secretary, 778-782-4215, E-mail: educmast@sfu.ca.

Southern Illinois University Carbondale, Graduate School, College of Education and Human Services, Department of Educational Psychology and Special Education, Program in Educational Psychology, Carbondale, IL 62901-4701. Offers MS Ed, PhD. *Accreditation:* NCATE. *Degree requirements:* For master's, thesis; for doctorate, thesis/dissertation. *Entrance requirements:* For master's, GRE General Test, minimum GPA of 2.7; for doctorate, minimum GPA of 3.25. Additional exam requirements/recommendations for international students: Required—TOEFL. *Faculty research:* Career development, problem-solving, learning and instruction, cognitive development, family assessment.

State University of New York College at Oneonta, Graduate Programs, Division of Education, Department of Educational Psychology, Counseling and Special Education, Oneonta, NY 13820-4015. Offers school counselor K-12 (MS Ed, CAS); special education (MS Ed). *Accreditation:* NCATE. *Program availability:* Part-time, evening/weekend. *Degree requirements:* For master's, comprehensive exam. *Entrance requirements:* For master's, GRE General Test. *Application deadline:* For fall admission, 3/1 for domestic students. Application fee: $50. *Unit head:* Dr. Dawn Hamlin, Chair, 607-436-3526, Fax: 607-436-3799, E-mail: dawn.hamlin@oneonta.edu. *Application contact:* Patrick J. Mente, Director of Graduate Studies, 607-436-2523, Fax: 607-436-3084, E-mail: gradstudies@oneonta.edu.
Website: http://www.oneonta.edu/academics/ed/edpsych/

Teachers College, Columbia University, Department of Health and Behavior Studies, New York, NY 10027-6696. Offers applied behavior analysis (MA, PhD); applied educational psychology: school psychology (Ed M, PhD); behavioral nutrition (PhD), including nutrition (Ed D, PhD); community health education (MS); community nutrition education (Ed M), including community nutrition education; education of deaf and hard of hearing (MA, PhD); health education (MA, Ed D); hearing impairment (Ed D); intellectual disability/autism (MA, Ed D, PhD); nursing education (Ed D, Advanced Certificate); nutrition and education (MS); nutrition and exercise physiology (MS); nutrition and public health (MS); nutrition education (Ed D), including nutrition (Ed D, PhD); physical disabilities (Ed D); reading specialist (MA); severe or multiple disabilities (MA); special education (Ed M, MA, Ed D); teaching of sign language (MA). *Program availability:* Part-time, evening/weekend. *Students:* 282 full-time (262 women), 262 part-time (222 women); includes 180 minority (54 Black or African American, non-Hispanic/Latino; 1 American Indian or Alaska Native, non-Hispanic/Latino; 56 Asian, non-Hispanic/Latino; 56 Hispanic/Latino; 1 Native Hawaiian or other Pacific Islander, non-Hispanic/Latino; 12 Two or more races, non-Hispanic/Latino), 55 international. 503 applicants, 57% accepted, 146 enrolled. Terminal master's awarded for partial completion of doctoral program. *Expenses: Tuition:* Full-time $36,288; part-time $1512 per credit. *Required fees:* $438 per semester. One-time fee: $510 full-time. Full-time tuition and fees vary according to course load. *Unit head:* Prof. Stephen T. Peverly, Chair, 212-678-3964, Fax: 212-678-8259, E-mail: stp4@columbia.edu. *Application contact:* David Estrella, Director of Admission, 212-678-3305, E-mail: estrella@tc.columbia.edu.
Website: http://www.tc.columbia.edu/health-and-behavior-studies/

Teachers College, Columbia University, Department of Human Development, New York, NY 10027-6696. Offers applied statistics (MS); cognitive studies in education (MA, Ed D, PhD); developmental psychology (MA, Ed D, PhD); educational psychology-human cognition and learning (Ed M, MA, Ed D, PhD); learning analytics (MS); measurement and evaluation (ME, Ed D, PhD); measurement, evaluation, and statistics (MA, MS, Ed D, PhD). *Program availability:* Part-time. *Students:* 217 full-time (168 women), 131 part-time (93 women); includes 83 minority (30 Black or African American, non-Hispanic/Latino; 31 Asian, non-Hispanic/Latino; 18 Hispanic/Latino; 4 Two or more races, non-Hispanic/Latino), 182 international. 450 applicants, 69% accepted, 132 enrolled. *Expenses: Tuition:* Full-time $36,288; part-time $1512 per credit. *Required fees:* $438 per semester. One-time fee: $510 full-time. Full-time tuition and fees vary according to course load. *Unit head:* Prof. Matthew S. Johnson, Chair, 212-678-3882, Fax: 212-678-3837, E-mail: johnson@tc.columbia.edu. *Application contact:* David Estrella, Director of Admission, 212-678-3305, E-mail: estrella@tc.columbia.edu.
Website: http://www.tc.columbia.edu/human-development/

Temple University, College of Education, Department of Psychological Studies in Education, Philadelphia, PA 19122-6096. Offers applied behavior analysis (MS Ed); counseling psychology (Ed M), including agency counseling, school counseling; educational psychology (Ed M); school psychology (PhD, Ed S). *Accreditation:* APA (one or more programs are accredited). *Program availability:* Part-time, evening/weekend. *Faculty:* 25 full-time (12 women), 23 part-time/adjunct (11 women). *Students:* 284 full-time (213 women), 170 part-time (120 women); includes 144 minority (95 Black or African American, non-Hispanic/Latino; 2 American Indian or Alaska Native, non-Hispanic/Latino; 17 Asian, non-Hispanic/Latino; 20 Hispanic/Latino; 10 Two or more races, non-Hispanic/Latino), 24 international. 517 applicants, 61% accepted, 180 enrolled. In 2016, 127 master's, 26 doctorates, 15 other advanced degrees awarded. Terminal master's awarded for partial completion of doctoral program. *Degree requirements:* For master's, thesis or alternative; for doctorate, thesis/dissertation. *Entrance requirements:* Additional exam requirements/recommendations for international students: Required—TOEFL (minimum score 550 paper-based; 79 iBT). *Application deadline:* For fall admission, 12/15 for international students; for spring admission, 8/1 for international students. Application fee: $60. *Financial support:*

Fellowships, research assistantships with full tuition reimbursements, and teaching assistantships with full tuition reimbursements available. Financial award application deadline: 1/15; financial award applicants required to submit FAFSA. *Unit head:* Dr. Catherine Fiorello, Chair, 215-204-6254, E-mail: catherine.fiorello@temple.edu. *Application contact:* Dr. Catherine Fiorello, Chair, 215-204-6254, E-mail: catherine.fiorello@temple.edu.
Website: http://education.temple.edu/pse

Tennessee Technological University, College of Graduate Studies, College of Education, Department of Counseling and Psychology, Cookeville, TN 38505. Offers MA, Ed S. *Accreditation:* NCATE (one or more programs are accredited). *Program availability:* Part-time, evening/weekend. *Faculty:* 24 full-time (6 women). *Students:* 38 full-time (34 women), 33 part-time (28 women); includes 11 minority (5 Black or African American, non-Hispanic/Latino; 1 Asian, non-Hispanic/Latino; 3 Hispanic/Latino; 2 Two or more races, non-Hispanic/Latino). Average age 27. 46 applicants, 59% accepted, 17 enrolled. In 2016, 24 master's, 7 other advanced degrees awarded. *Degree requirements:* For master's and Ed S, comprehensive exam, thesis or alternative. *Entrance requirements:* For master's and Ed S, GRE. Additional exam requirements/recommendations for international students: Required—FLS International (completion of Level 18). *Application deadline:* For fall admission, 8/1 for domestic students, 5/1 for international students; for spring admission, 12/1 for domestic students, 10/1 for international students; for summer admission, 5/1 for domestic students, 2/1 for international students. Applications are processed on a rolling basis. Application fee: $35 ($40 for international students). Electronic applications accepted. *Expenses:* Tuition, state resident: full-time $9375; part-time $534 per credit hour. Tuition, nonresident: full-time $22,443; part-time $1260 per credit hour. *Financial support:* In 2016–17, 1 fellowship (averaging $8,000 per year), 1 teaching assistantship (averaging $8,000 per year) were awarded; research assistantships and career-related internships or fieldwork also available. Financial award application deadline: 4/1. *Unit head:* Dr. Barry Stein, Chairperson, 931-372-3457, Fax: 931-372-6319, E-mail: bstein@tntech.edu. *Application contact:* Shelia K. Kendrick, Coordinator of Graduate Studies, 931-372-3808, Fax: 931-372-3497, E-mail: skendrick@tntech.edu.

Texas A&M University, College of Education and Human Development, Department of Educational Psychology, College Station, TX 77843. Offers bilingual education (M Ed, MS); counseling psychology (PhD); educational psychology (M Ed, MS, PhD); educational technology (M Ed); school psychology (PhD); special education (M Ed, MS). *Accreditation:* APA (one or more programs are accredited). *Program availability:* Part-time, evening/weekend, blended/hybrid learning. *Faculty:* 42. *Students:* 172 full-time (139 women), 281 part-time (233 women); includes 144 minority (27 Black or African American, non-Hispanic/Latino; 1 American Indian or Alaska Native, non-Hispanic/Latino; 19 Asian, non-Hispanic/Latino; 86 Hispanic/Latino; 1 Native Hawaiian or other Pacific Islander, non-Hispanic/Latino; 10 Two or more races, non-Hispanic/Latino), 48 international. Average age 33. 181 applicants, 44% accepted, 45 enrolled. In 2016, 99 master's, 27 doctorates awarded. *Degree requirements:* For master's, thesis optional; for doctorate, thesis/dissertation. *Entrance requirements:* For master's and doctorate, GRE General Test. Additional exam requirements/recommendations for international students: Required—TOEFL (minimum score 550 paper-based; 80 iBT), IELTS (minimum score 6), PTE (minimum score 53). *Application deadline:* For fall admission, 12/1 for domestic students; for spring admission, 10/15 for domestic students. Application fee: $50 ($90 for international students). Electronic applications accepted. *Expenses:* Contact institution. *Financial support:* In 2016–17, 231 students received support, including 8 fellowships with tuition reimbursements available (averaging $9,919 per year), 98 research assistantships with tuition reimbursements available (averaging $6,004 per year), 13 teaching assistantships with tuition reimbursements available (averaging $9,368 per year); career-related internships or fieldwork, institutionally sponsored loans, scholarships/grants, traineeships, health care benefits, tuition waivers (full and partial), and unspecified assistantships also available. Support available to part-time students. Financial award application deadline: 3/15; financial award applicants required to submit FAFSA. *Unit head:* Dr. Victor Willson, Department Head, 979-845-1394, E-mail: v-willson@tamu.edu. *Application contact:* Kristie Stramaski, Senior Academic Advisor, 979-845-1833, E-mail: epsyadvisor@tamu.edu.
Website: http://epsy.tamu.edu

Texas A&M University–Central Texas, Graduate Studies and Research, Killeen, TX 76549. Offers accounting (MS); business administration (MBA); clinical mental health counseling (MS); criminal justice (MCJ); curriculum and instruction (M Ed); educational administration (M Ed); educational psychology - experimental psychology (MS); history (MA); human resource management (MS); information systems (MS); liberal studies (MS); management and leadership (MS); marriage and family therapy (MS); mathematics (MS); political science (MA); school counseling (M Ed); school psychology (Ed S).

Texas A&M University–Commerce, College of Education and Human Services, Commerce, TX 75429-3011. Offers counseling (MS); curriculum and instruction (M Ed, MS); early childhood education (M Ed, MS); educational administration (M Ed, Ed D); educational psychology (PhD); educational technology leadership (MS); educational technology library science (MS); health, kinesiology and sports studies (MS); higher education (MS, Ed D); organization, learning, and technology (MS); psychology (MS); reading (M Ed, MS); school psychology (SSP); secondary education (M Ed, MS); social work (MSW); special education (M Ed); supervision, curriculum and instruction-elementary education (Ed D). *Program availability:* Part-time, 100% online, blended/hybrid learning. *Faculty:* 88 full-time (52 women), 31 part-time/adjunct (24 women). *Students:* 341 full-time (276 women), 1,495 part-time (1,156 women); includes 762 minority (429 Black or African American, non-Hispanic/Latino; 4 American Indian or Alaska Native, non-Hispanic/Latino; 27 Asian, non-Hispanic/Latino; 247 Hispanic/Latino; 1 Native Hawaiian or other Pacific Islander, non-Hispanic/Latino; 54 Two or more races, non-Hispanic/Latino), 18 international. Average age 37. 1,070 applicants, 54% accepted, 452 enrolled. In 2016, 579 master's, 31 doctorates awarded. *Degree requirements:* For master's, one foreign language, comprehensive exam, thesis optional, departmental qualifying exams (for some programs); for doctorate, comprehensive exam, thesis/dissertation, departmental qualifying exam; for SSP, comprehensive exam, thesis optional. *Entrance requirements:* For master's and doctorate, GRE General Test. Additional exam requirements/recommendations for international students: Required—TOEFL (minimum score 550 paper-based; 79 iBT), IELTS (minimum score 6). *Application deadline:* For fall admission, 6/1 priority date for international students; for spring admission, 10/15 priority date for international students; for summer admission, 3/15 priority date for international students. Applications are processed on a rolling basis. Application fee: $50. Electronic applications accepted. *Expenses:* $2,254 resident; $4,744 non-resident. *Financial support:* In 2016–17, 301 students received support, including 39 research assistantships with partial tuition reimbursements available (averaging $9,000 per year), 17 teaching assistantships with partial tuition reimbursements available (averaging $9,000 per year); career-related internships or fieldwork, Federal Work-Study, institutionally sponsored loans, scholarships/grants, health care benefits, and unspecified assistantships also available. Financial award application deadline: 5/1; financial award applicants required to submit FAFSA. *Faculty research:* Cognitive and bilingual education, positive behavioral intervention, literacy, math readiness. *Total annual research expenditures:* $470,963. *Unit head:* Dr. Timothy Letzring, Dean, 903-886-5181, Fax: 903-886-5905, E-mail: tim.letzring@tamuc.edu. *Application contact:* Jennifer Faunce, Graduate Recruiter, 903-886-5030, Fax: 903-886-5905, E-mail: jennifer.faunce@tamuc.edu.
Website: http://www.tamuc.edu/academics/graduateSchool/programs/education/default.aspx

Texas Tech University, Graduate School, College of Education, Department of Educational Psychology and Leadership, Lubbock, TX 79409-1071. Offers counselor education (M Ed, PhD); distance education (M Ed); educational leadership (M Ed, Ed D, PhD); educational psychology (M Ed, PhD); higher education (M Ed, Ed D); higher education research (PhD); instructional technology (M Ed, Ed D); special education (M Ed, Ed D, PhD). *Accreditation:* ACA; NCATE. *Program availability:* Part-time, evening/weekend. *Faculty:* 59 full-time (29 women), 3 part-time/adjunct (all women). *Students:* 300 full-time (218 women), 656 part-time (482 women); includes 320 minority (87 Black or African American, non-Hispanic/Latino; 5 American Indian or Alaska Native, non-Hispanic/Latino; 5 Asian, non-Hispanic/Latino; 200 Hispanic/Latino; 23 Two or more races, non-Hispanic/Latino), 51 international. Average age 36. 668 applicants, 56% accepted, 285 enrolled. In 2016, 171 master's, 47 doctorates awarded. Terminal master's awarded for partial completion of doctoral program. *Degree requirements:* For master's, comprehensive exam, thesis optional; for doctorate, comprehensive exam, thesis/dissertation. *Entrance requirements:* For master's, GRE (for some programs); for doctorate, GRE. Additional exam requirements/recommendations for international students: Required—TOEFL (minimum score 550 paper-based; 79 iBT). *Application deadline:* For fall admission, 6/1 priority date for domestic students, 1/15 priority date for international students; for spring admission, 9/1 priority date for domestic students, 6/15 priority date for international students. Applications are processed on a rolling basis. Application fee: $75. Electronic applications accepted. *Expenses:* $285 per credit hour full-time resident tuition, $693 per credit hour full-time non-resident tuition; $50.50 per credit hour fee plus $608 per term fee. *Financial support:* In 2016–17, 384 students received support, including 384 fellowships (averaging $3,632 per year); scholarships/grants and unspecified assistantships also available. Support available to part-time students. Financial award application deadline: 1/3; financial award applicants required to submit FAFSA. *Faculty research:* Cognitive, motivational, and developmental processes in learning; counseling education; instructional technology; generic special education and sensory impairment; community college administration; K-12 school administration. *Total annual research expenditures:* $1,371. *Unit head:* Dr. Hansel Burley, Chair, 806-834-5135, Fax: 806-742-2179, E-mail: hansel.burley@ttu.edu. *Application contact:* Pam Smith, Admissions Advisor, 806-834-2969, Fax: 806-742-2179, E-mail: pam.smith@ttu.edu.
Website: http://www.educ.ttu.edu/

Universidad de Iberoamerica, Graduate School, San Jose, Costa Rica. Offers clinical neuropsychology (PhD); clinical psychology (M Psych); educational psychology (M Psych); forensic psychology (M Psych); hospital management (MHA); intensive care nursing (MN); medicine (MD).

Université de Moncton, Faculty of Education, Graduate Studies in Education, Moncton, NB E1A 3E9, Canada. Offers educational psychology (M Ed, MA Ed); guidance (M Ed, MA Ed); school administration (M Ed, MA Ed); teaching (M Ed, MA Ed). *Program availability:* Part-time. *Degree requirements:* For master's, proficiency in English and French. *Entrance requirements:* For master's, minimum GPA of 3.0. *Faculty research:* Guidance, ethnolinguistic vitality, children's rights, ecological education, entrepreneurship.

Université de Montréal, Faculty of Education, Department of Psychopedagogy and Andragogy, Montréal, QC H3C 3J7, Canada. Offers M Ed, MA, PhD, DESS. *Program availability:* Part-time, evening/weekend. Terminal master's awarded for partial completion of doctoral program. *Degree requirements:* For master's, thesis (for some programs); for doctorate, thesis/dissertation, general exam. *Entrance requirements:* For doctorate, MA or M Ed. Electronic applications accepted.

Université du Québec à Trois-Rivières, Graduate Programs, Program in Psychoeducation, Trois-Rivières, QC G9A 5H7, Canada. Offers M Ed, PhD. M Ed offered jointly with Université du Québec en Outaouais. *Entrance requirements:* For master's, appropriate bachelor's degree, proficiency in French. *Faculty research:* Troubled youth intervention.

Université du Québec en Outaouais, Graduate Programs, Program in Psychoeducation, Gatineau, QC J8X 3X7, Canada. Offers M Ed, MA. *Program availability:* Part-time. *Degree requirements:* For master's, thesis (for some programs). *Entrance requirements:* For master's, appropriate bachelor's degree, proficiency in French.

Université Laval, Faculty of Education, Department of Teaching and Learning Studies, Programs in Educational Psychology, Québec, QC G1K 7P4, Canada. Offers MA, PhD. Terminal master's awarded for partial completion of doctoral program. *Degree requirements:* For master's, thesis (for some programs); for doctorate, comprehensive exam, thesis/dissertation. *Entrance requirements:* For master's and doctorate, English exam (comprehension of written English), knowledge of French. Electronic applications accepted. *Faculty research:* Emotional, social, and cognitive development; learning and motivation in school; language development; reading acquisition; computer and learning strategies.

University at Albany, State University of New York, School of Education, Division of Educational Psychology and Methodology, Albany, NY 12222-0001. Offers educational psychology (PhD); educational psychology and methodology (MS); educational research (CAS). *Accreditation:* APA (one or more programs are accredited). *Program availability:* Evening/weekend. *Faculty:* 19 full-time (9 women), 18 part-time/adjunct (14 women). *Students:* 194 full-time (158 women), 101 part-time (87 women); includes 55 minority (16 Black or African American, non-Hispanic/Latino; 1 American Indian or Alaska Native, non-Hispanic/Latino; 15 Asian, non-Hispanic/Latino; 18 Hispanic/Latino; 5 Two or more races, non-Hispanic/Latino), 24 international. Average age 31. 185 applicants, 43% accepted, 102 enrolled. In 2016, 89 master's, 18 doctorates, 10 other advanced degrees awarded. *Degree requirements:* For doctorate, thesis/dissertation. *Entrance requirements:* For doctorate, GRE General Test. Additional exam requirements/recommendations for international students: Required—TOEFL (minimum score 550 paper-based). Application fee: $75. Electronic applications accepted. *Expenses:* Tuition, state resident: full-time $10,870; part-time $453 per credit hour. Tuition, nonresident: full-time $22,210; part-time $925 per credit hour. *International tuition:* $21,550 full-time. *Required fees:* $1864; $96 per credit hour. *Financial support:* Fellowships and career-related internships or fieldwork available. *Total annual research expenditures:* $1.3 million. *Unit head:* Kevin Quinn, Chair, 518-442-5074, E-mail: kquinn@albany.edu.
Website: http://www.albany.edu/educational_psychology/

University at Buffalo, the State University of New York, Graduate School, Graduate School of Education, Department of Counseling, School, and Educational Psychology, Buffalo, NY 14260. Offers applied statistical analysis (Advanced Certificate); counseling/school psychology (PhD); counselor education (PhD); education studies (Ed M); educational psychology (MA, PhD); mental health counseling (MS, Certificate); mindful counseling for wellness and engagement (Advanced Certificate); rehabilitation

counseling (MS, Advanced Certificate); school counseling (Ed M, Certificate). *Accreditation:* CORE (one or more programs are accredited). *Program availability:* Part-time, 100% online. *Faculty:* 27 full-time (11 women), 52 part-time/adjunct (45 women). *Students:* 161 full-time (131 women), 140 part-time (109 women); includes 30 minority (22 Black or African American, non-Hispanic/Latino; 2 American Indian or Alaska Native, non-Hispanic/Latino; 3 Asian, non-Hispanic/Latino; 3 Hispanic/Latino), 20 international. Average age 32. 321 applicants, 56% accepted, 113 enrolled. In 2016, 62 master's, 10 doctorates, 47 other advanced degrees awarded. *Degree requirements:* For master's, comprehensive exam (for some programs), thesis (for some programs); for doctorate, comprehensive exam, thesis/dissertation. *Entrance requirements:* For master's, GRE General Test, interview, letters of reference; for doctorate, GRE General Test, interview, letters of reference, writing sample. Additional exam requirements/recommendations for international students: Required—TOEFL (minimum score 79 iBT). *Application deadline:* For fall admission, 2/1 priority date for domestic and international students. Application fee: $50. Electronic applications accepted. *Financial support:* In 2016–17, 20 fellowships (averaging $8,477 per year), 33 research assistantships with tuition reimbursements (averaging $10,419 per year) were awarded; teaching assistantships, career-related internships or fieldwork, Federal Work-Study, institutionally sponsored loans, scholarships/grants, tuition waivers (full and partial), and unspecified assistantships also available. Financial award application deadline: 2/1; financial award applicants required to submit FAFSA. *Faculty research:* Multicultural counseling, class size effects, good work in counseling, eating disorders, outcome assessment, change agents and therapeutic factors in group counseling. *Total annual research expenditures:* $1.3 million. *Unit head:* Dr. Jeremy Finn, Chair, 716-645-1126, Fax: 716-645-6616, E-mail: finn@buffalo.edu. *Application contact:* Joanne Laska, Admissions Assistant, 716-645-2110, Fax: 716-645-7937, E-mail: jlaska@buffalo.edu.
Website: http://gse.buffalo.edu/csep

University of Alberta, Faculty of Graduate Studies and Research, Department of Educational Psychology, Edmonton, AB T6G 2E1, Canada. Offers counseling psychology (M Ed, PhD); educational psychology (M Ed, PhD); instructional technology (M Ed); school counseling (M Ed); school psychology (M Ed, PhD); special education (M Ed, PhD); special education-deafness studies (M Ed); teaching English as a second language (M Ed). *Program availability:* Part-time. *Degree requirements:* For master's, thesis optional; for doctorate, comprehensive exam, thesis/dissertation. *Entrance requirements:* For master's and doctorate, minimum GPA of 3.0. Additional exam requirements/recommendations for international students: Required—TOEFL. *Faculty research:* Human learning, development and assessment.

The University of Arizona, College of Education, Department of Educational Psychology, Tucson, AZ 85721. Offers educational psychology (MA, PhD); educational research methodology (Certificate); motivating learning environments (Certificate). *Accreditation:* APA (one or more programs are accredited). *Program availability:* Part-time. Terminal master's awarded for partial completion of doctoral program. *Degree requirements:* For master's, comprehensive exam (for some programs), thesis optional; for doctorate, comprehensive exam, thesis/dissertation. *Entrance requirements:* For master's, minimum GPA of 3.0, 3 letters of recommendation, 500-word professional writing sample; for doctorate, GRE General Test, minimum GPA of 3.0, 3 letters of recommendation, statement of purpose, 500-word professional writing sample. Additional exam requirements/recommendations for international students: Required—TOEFL (minimum score 600 paper-based). Electronic applications accepted. *Faculty research:* School reform, motivational learning in classroom settings, measurement and evaluation of learning outcomes, student resilience, preadolescent and adolescent development.

University of California, Davis, Graduate Studies, Graduate Group in Education, Davis, CA 95616. Offers education (MA, Ed D); instructional studies (PhD); psychological studies (PhD); sociocultural studies (PhD). Ed D offered jointly with California State University, Fresno. Terminal master's awarded for partial completion of doctoral program. *Degree requirements:* For master's, comprehensive exam (for some programs), thesis (for some programs); for doctorate, thesis/dissertation. *Entrance requirements:* For master's and doctorate, GRE. Additional exam requirements/recommendations for international students: Required—TOEFL (minimum score 550 paper-based). Electronic applications accepted. *Faculty research:* Language and literacy, mathematics education, science education, teacher development, school psychology.

University of California, Riverside, Graduate Division, Graduate School of Education, Riverside, CA 92521-0102. Offers autism (M Ed); diversity and equity (M Ed); education specialist (Credential); education, society, and culture (MA, PhD); educational psychology (MA, PhD); general education (M Ed); higher education administration and policy (M Ed, PhD); multiple subject (Credential); reading (M Ed); school psychology (PhD); single subject (Credential); special education (M Ed, MA, PhD); TESOL (M Ed). Terminal master's awarded for partial completion of doctoral program. *Degree requirements:* For master's, thesis optional, comprehensive exams or thesis (MA), case study or analytical report (M Ed); for doctorate, thesis/dissertation, written and oral qualifying exams, college teaching practicum. *Entrance requirements:* For master's, GRE General Test (for MA); CBEST and CSET (for M Ed in general education only), UCR Extension TESOL certificate (for M Ed with TESOL emphasis only); for doctorate, GRE General Test, writing sample; for Credential, CBEST, CSET. Additional exam requirements/recommendations for international students: Required—TOEFL (minimum score 550 paper-based; 80 iBT), IELTS (minimum score 7). Electronic applications accepted. *Expenses:* Tuition, state resident: full-time $16,666. Tuition, nonresident: full-time $31,768. *Required fees:* $11,055.54 per quarter. $3685.18 per quarter. Tuition and fees vary according to campus/location and program. *Faculty research:* Responsiveness to intervention, faculty core, response to intervention of English language learners, advanced modeling techniques, study on social capital, trust, and motivation.

University of Colorado Boulder, Graduate School, School of Education, Division of Educational and Psychological Studies, Boulder, CO 80309. Offers MA, PhD. *Accreditation:* NCATE. *Students:* 19 full-time (11 women), 6 part-time (2 women); includes 11 minority (5 Black or African American, non-Hispanic/Latino; 5 Hispanic/Latino; 1 Native Hawaiian or other Pacific Islander, non-Hispanic/Latino), 1 international. Average age 33. 60 applicants, 30% accepted, 11 enrolled. In 2016, 4 doctorates awarded. Terminal master's awarded for partial completion of doctoral program. *Degree requirements:* For master's, comprehensive exam, thesis or alternative; for doctorate, one foreign language, comprehensive exam, thesis/dissertation. *Entrance requirements:* For master's, GRE General Test or MAT, minimum undergraduate GPA of 2.75; for doctorate, GRE General Test. *Application deadline:* For fall admission, 2/1 for domestic students, 12/1 for international students; for spring admission, 9/1 for domestic and international students. Application fee: $60 ($80 for international students). Electronic applications accepted. Application fee is waived when completed online. *Financial support:* In 2016–17, 61 students received support, including 19 fellowships (averaging $4,217 per year), 13 research assistantships with full and partial tuition reimbursements available (averaging $31,975 per year), 6 teaching assistantships with full and partial tuition reimbursements available (averaging $27,466 per year); institutionally sponsored loans, scholarships/grants, health care benefits, and unspecified assistantships also available. Financial award applicants required to submit FAFSA. *Application contact:* E-mail: edadvise@colorado.edu.
Website: http://www.colorado.edu/education/

University of Colorado Denver, School of Education and Human Development, Programs in Educational and School Psychology, Denver, CO 80217. Offers educational psychology (MA), including educational assessment, educational psychology, human development, human learning, research and evaluation; school psychology (Psy D, Ed S). MA program also offered in partnership with Boulder Journey School, Friends School and Stanley British Primary School. *Program availability:* Part-time, evening/weekend. *Students:* 210 full-time (171 women), 79 part-time (71 women); includes 47 minority (5 Black or African American, non-Hispanic/Latino; 2 American Indian or Alaska Native, non-Hispanic/Latino; 5 Asian, non-Hispanic/Latino; 28 Hispanic/Latino; 7 Two or more races, non-Hispanic/Latino), 6 international. Average age 30. 179 applicants, 94% accepted, 126 enrolled. In 2016, 166 master's, 7 doctorates, 11 other advanced degrees awarded. *Degree requirements:* For master's, comprehensive exam, 9 hours of core courses, embedded within a minimum of 36 to 38 hours of relevant coursework, including an educational psychology practicum, independent study project or thesis (recommended); for Ed S, comprehensive exam, minimum of 75 semester hours (61 hours of coursework, 6 of 500-hour practicum in field, and 8 of 1200-hour internship); PRAXIS II. *Entrance requirements:* For master's, GRE if undergraduate GPA below 2.75, resume, three letters of recommendation, transcripts; for Ed S, GRE, resume, letters of recommendation, transcripts. Additional exam requirements/recommendations for international students: Required—TOEFL (minimum score 537 paper-based; 75 iBT); Recommended—IELTS (minimum score 6.5). *Application deadline:* For fall admission, 4/15 for domestic students, 4/1 for international students; for spring admission, 9/15 for domestic students, 9/1 for international students. Application fee: $50 ($75 for international students). Electronic applications accepted. *Expenses:* Contact institution. *Financial support:* In 2016–17, 90 students received support. Research assistantships, Federal Work-Study, institutionally sponsored loans, scholarships/grants, and traineeships available. Financial award application deadline: 4/1; financial award applicants required to submit FAFSA. *Faculty research:* Crisis response and intervention, school violence prevention, immigrant experience, educational environments for English language learners, culturally competent assessment and intervention, child and youth suicide. *Unit head:* Francie Crepeau-Hobson, Associate Professor and Program Director, 303-315-6315, E-mail: franci.creapeau-hobson@ucdenver.edu. *Application contact:* 303-315-6300, E-mail: education@ucdenver.edu.
Website: http://www.ucdenver.edu/academics/colleges/SchoolOfEducation/Academics/MASTERS/EPSY/Pages/default.aspx

University of Connecticut, Graduate School, Neag School of Education, Department of Educational Psychology, Storrs, CT 06269. Offers cognition and instruction (MA, PhD). *Degree requirements:* For master's, comprehensive exam; for doctorate, thesis/dissertation. *Entrance requirements:* For doctorate, GRE General Test. Additional exam requirements/recommendations for international students: Required—TOEFL (minimum score 550 paper-based). Electronic applications accepted.

University of Georgia, College of Education, Department of Educational Psychology, Athens, GA 30602. Offers educational psychology (Ed S). *Accreditation:* NCATE. *Entrance requirements:* For degree, GRE General Test or MAT. *Application deadline:* For fall admission, 7/1 priority date for domestic students; for spring admission, 11/15 for domestic students. Application fee: $50. Electronic applications accepted. *Financial support:* Fellowships, research assistantships, teaching assistantships, and unspecified assistantships available. *Unit head:* Dr. Roy P. Martin, Acting Head, 706-542-4261, Fax: 706-542-4240, E-mail: rpmartin@uga.edu. *Application contact:* Michelle Lease, Graduate Coordinator, 706-542-4110, E-mail: epsygc@uga.edu.
Website: http://www.coe.uga.edu/epit

University of Hawaii at Manoa, Graduate Division, College of Education, Department of Educational Psychology, Honolulu, HI 96822. Offers M Ed, PhD. *Program availability:* Part-time. *Degree requirements:* For master's, thesis optional; for doctorate, comprehensive exam, thesis/dissertation. *Entrance requirements:* Additional exam requirements/recommendations for international students: Required—TOEFL (minimum score 600 paper-based; 100 iBT), IELTS (minimum score 7). *Faculty research:* Human learning and development, measurement, research methods, statistics.

University of Hawaii at Manoa, Graduate Division, College of Education, PhD in Education Program, Honolulu, HI 96822. Offers curriculum and instruction (PhD); educational administration (PhD); educational foundations (PhD); educational policy studies (PhD); educational psychology (PhD); exceptionalities (PhD); kinesiology (PhD); learning design and technology (PhD). *Program availability:* Part-time, evening/weekend. *Degree requirements:* For doctorate, thesis/dissertation. *Entrance requirements:* For doctorate, GRE General Test, sample of written work. Additional exam requirements/recommendations for international students: Required—TOEFL (minimum score 600 paper-based; 100 iBT), IELTS (minimum score 7).

University of Houston, College of Education, Department of Educational Psychology, Houston, TX 77204. Offers administration and supervision - higher education (M Ed); counseling (M Ed); counseling psychology (PhD); educational psychology (M Ed); school psychology (PhD); school psychology and individual differences (PhD); special education (M Ed). *Accreditation:* NCATE. *Program availability:* Part-time, evening/weekend, online learning. *Degree requirements:* For master's, comprehensive exam or thesis; for doctorate, comprehensive exam, thesis/dissertation. *Entrance requirements:* For master's, GRE, transcripts, 3 letters of recommendation, curriculum vita, goal statement; for doctorate, GRE, transcripts, 3 letters of recommendation, curriculum vita, goal statement, writing sample, interview. Additional exam requirements/recommendations for international students: Required—TOEFL (minimum score 550 paper-based; 79 iBT), IELTS (minimum score 6.5). Electronic applications accepted. *Faculty research:* Evidence-based assessment and intervention, multicultural issues in psychology, social and cultural context of learning, systemic barriers to college, motivational aspects of self-regulated learning.

University of Illinois at Chicago, College of Education, Department of Educational Psychology, Chicago, IL 60607-7128. Offers early childhood education (M Ed); educational psychology (PhD); measurement, evaluation, statistics, and assessment (M Ed); youth development (M Ed). *Program availability:* Part-time, online learning. *Faculty research:* Children's construction of morality, development of resilience in the face of enduring economical difficulties, cognition and cognitive development, test fairness.

University of Illinois at Urbana–Champaign, Graduate College, College of Education, Department of Educational Psychology, Champaign, IL 61820. Offers Ed M, MA, MS, PhD, CAS. *Accreditation:* APA (one or more programs are accredited). *Program availability:* Part-time, online learning.

The University of Iowa, Graduate College, College of Education, Department of Psychological and Quantitative Foundations, Iowa City, IA 52242-1316. Offers counseling psychology (PhD); educational measurement and statistics (MA, PhD); educational psychology (MA, PhD); school psychology (PhD, Ed S). *Accreditation:* APA. *Degree requirements:* For master's, thesis optional, exam; for doctorate, comprehensive exam, thesis/dissertation; for Ed S, exam. *Entrance requirements:* For master's, doctorate, and Ed S, GRE General Test, minimum GPA of 3.0. Additional exam requirements/recommendations for international students: Required—TOEFL (minimum score 550 paper-based; 81 iBT). Electronic applications accepted.

The University of Kansas, Graduate Studies, School of Education, Department of Educational Psychology, Program in Educational Psychology and Research, Lawrence, KS 66045. Offers MS Ed, PhD. *Program availability:* Part-time. *Students:* 36 full-time (22 women), 5 part-time (3 women); includes 6 minority (2 Black or African American, non-Hispanic/Latino; 3 Asian, non-Hispanic/Latino; 1 Hispanic/Latino), 18 international. Average age 31. 17 applicants, 71% accepted, 6 enrolled. In 2016, 2 master's, 6 doctorates awarded. *Entrance requirements:* For master's, GRE General Test, minimum GPA of 3.0, resume, statement of purpose, official transcripts, three recommendation letters; for doctorate, GRE General Test, resume, statement of purpose, official transcripts, three recommendation letters. Additional exam requirements/recommendations for international students: Required—TOEFL or IELTS. *Application deadline:* For fall admission, 12/15 for domestic and international students. Application fee: $65 ($85 for international students). Electronic applications accepted. *Financial support:* Fellowships, research assistantships, teaching assistantships, career-related internships or fieldwork, institutionally sponsored loans, scholarships/grants, traineeships, health care benefits, tuition waivers (full and partial), and unspecified assistantships available. Support available to part-time students. Financial award application deadline: 12/15. *Faculty research:* Educational measurement, applied statistics, research design, program evaluation, learning and development. *Unit head:* Steven Wayne Lee, Chair, 785-864-9701, E-mail: swlee@ku.edu. *Application contact:* Penny Fritts, Admissions Coordinator, 785-864-9645, E-mail: fritts@ku.edu.
Website: http://www.soe.ku.edu/PRE/

University of Kentucky, Graduate School, College of Education, Program in Educational and Counseling Psychology, Lexington, KY 40506-0032. Offers counseling psychology (MS, PhD, Ed S); educational psychology (MS, PhD); school psychology (PhD, Ed S). *Accreditation:* APA (one or more programs are accredited); NCATE. *Degree requirements:* For doctorate, comprehensive exam, thesis/dissertation; for Ed S, comprehensive exam. *Entrance requirements:* For doctorate, GRE General Test, minimum graduate GPA of 3.0; for Ed S, GRE General Test. Additional exam requirements/recommendations for international students: Required—TOEFL (minimum score 550 paper-based). Electronic applications accepted.

University of Louisville, Graduate School, College of Education and Human Development, Department of Counseling and Human Development, Louisville, KY 40292-0001. Offers counseling and personnel services (M Ed, PhD), including art therapy (M Ed), clinical mental health counseling (M Ed), college student personnel, counseling psychology, counselor education and supervision (PhD), educational psychology, measurement, and evaluation (PhD), school counseling (M Ed). *Accreditation:* APA; NCATE. *Program availability:* Part-time, evening/weekend. *Students:* 148 full-time (115 women), 58 part-time (42 women); includes 52 minority (36 Black or African American, non-Hispanic/Latino; 1 American Indian or Alaska Native, non-Hispanic/Latino; 4 Asian, non-Hispanic/Latino; 7 Hispanic/Latino; 4 Two or more races, non-Hispanic/Latino), 2 international. Average age 28. 206 applicants, 56% accepted, 73 enrolled. In 2016, 38 master's, 1 doctorate awarded. *Degree requirements:* For doctorate, comprehensive exam, thesis/dissertation. *Entrance requirements:* For master's and doctorate, GRE General Test. Application fee: $60. *Expenses:* Tuition, state resident: full-time $12,246; part-time $681 per credit hour. Tuition, nonresident: full-time $25,486; part-time $1417 per credit hour. *Required fees:* $196. Tuition and fees vary according to program and reciprocity agreements. *Financial support:* Fellowships, research assistantships, teaching assistantships, career-related internships or fieldwork, Federal Work-Study, scholarships/grants, health care benefits, and unspecified assistantships available. Financial award application deadline: 6/1; financial award applicants required to submit FAFSA. *Faculty research:* Mental health services and under-served populations; health disparities and outcomes; well-being identity development; measurement and evaluation. *Total annual research expenditures:* $295,684. *Unit head:* Dr. Mark M. Leach, Interim Chair/Professor, 502-852-0588, Fax: 502-852-0629, E-mail: m.leach@louisville.edu. *Application contact:* Betty Hampton, Director of Graduate Student Services, 502-852-5597, Fax: 502-852-1465, E-mail: edadvise@louisville.edu.
Website: http://www.louisville.edu/education/departments/ecpy

The University of Manchester, School of Education, Manchester, United Kingdom. Offers counseling (D Couns); counseling psychology (D Couns); education (M Phil, Ed D, PhD); educational and child psychology (Ed D); educational psychology (Ed D).

University of Manitoba, Faculty of Graduate Studies, Faculty of Education, Department of Educational Administration, Foundations and Psychology, Winnipeg, MB R3T 2N2, Canada. Offers adult and post-secondary education (M Ed); educational administration (M Ed); guidance and counseling (M Ed); inclusive special education (M Ed); social foundations of education (M Ed). *Degree requirements:* For master's, thesis or alternative.

University of Memphis, Graduate School, College of Education, Department of Counseling, Educational Psychology and Research, Memphis, TN 38152. Offers counseling (MS, Ed D), including clinical mental health counseling (MS), clinical rehabilitation counseling (MS), rehabilitation counseling (MS), school counseling (MS); counseling psychology (PhD); educational psychology and research (MS, PhD), including educational psychology, educational research. *Accreditation:* ACA (one or more programs are accredited); APA (one or more programs are accredited); CORE (one or more programs are accredited); NCATE. *Program availability:* Blended/hybrid learning. *Faculty:* 26 full-time (18 women), 10 part-time/adjunct (7 women). *Students:* 124 full-time (99 women), 79 part-time (60 women); includes 64 minority (48 Black or African American, non-Hispanic/Latino; 3 Asian, non-Hispanic/Latino; 6 Hispanic/Latino; 7 Two or more races, non-Hispanic/Latino), 7 international. Average age 32. 82 applicants, 68% accepted, 39 enrolled. In 2016, 65 master's, 8 doctorates awarded. *Degree requirements:* For master's, comprehensive exam, thesis or alternative, internship; for doctorate, comprehensive exam, thesis/dissertation, practicum, internship, residency, scholarly work. *Entrance requirements:* For master's, GRE General Test or MAT, minimum GPA of 2.5, letters of reference, interview; for doctorate, GRE General Test, master's degree or equivalent, letters of reference, interview, curriculum vitae, personal statement. Additional exam requirements/recommendations for international students: Required—TOEFL (minimum score 550 paper-based; 79 iBT). *Application deadline:* For fall admission, 10/1 priority date for domestic students; for spring admission, 4/1 priority date for domestic students. Applications are processed on a rolling basis. Application fee: $35 ($60 for international students). Electronic applications accepted. *Expenses:* $5,231.50 per semester full-time in-state, $9,623.50 full-time out-of-state. *Financial support:* In 2016–17, 130 students received support, including 13 research assistantships with full tuition reimbursements available (averaging $14,820 per year), 11 teaching assistantships with full tuition reimbursements available (averaging $15,600 per year); fellowships with full tuition reimbursements available, career-related internships or fieldwork, Federal Work-Study, scholarships/grants, and unspecified assistantships also available. Financial award application deadline: 2/1; financial award applicants required to submit FAFSA. *Faculty research:* Anger management, aging and disability, supervision, multicultural counseling. *Unit head:* Dr. Steve West, Chair, 901-678-2841, Fax: 901-678-5114, E-mail: slwest@memphis.edu. *Application contact:* Dr. Suzanne Lease, Interim Assistant Dean of Education and Graduate Programs, 901-678-4476, Fax: 901-678-4778, E-mail: slease@memphis.edu.
Website: http://www.memphis.edu/cepr/

University of Minnesota, Twin Cities Campus, Graduate School, College of Education and Human Development, Department of Educational Psychology, Minneapolis, MN 55455-0213. Offers autism spectrum disorder (Certificate); counseling and student personnel psychology (MA); early childhood special education (M Ed); psychological foundations of education (MA, PhD); quantitative methods in education (MA, PhD); school psychology (MA, PhD, Ed S); special education (M Ed, MA, PhD); talent development and gifted education (Certificate). *Accreditation:* APA (one or more programs are accredited). *Faculty:* 31 full-time (16 women). *Students:* 261 full-time (197 women), 63 part-time (47 women); includes 46 minority (6 Black or African American, non-Hispanic/Latino; 19 Asian, non-Hispanic/Latino; 12 Hispanic/Latino; 9 Two or more races, non-Hispanic/Latino), 27 international. Average age 29. 285 applicants, 42% accepted, 110 enrolled. In 2016, 153 master's, 35 doctorates, 10 other advanced degrees awarded. Application fee: $75 ($95 for international students). *Financial support:* In 2016–17, 26 fellowships, 61 research assistantships (averaging $14,168 per year), 31 teaching assistantships (averaging $12,522 per year) were awarded. *Faculty research:* Achievement gap; autism; behavioral and social-emotional development; improving skills in mathematics, reading, and comprehension; measuring and analyzing student change. *Total annual research expenditures:* $5.3 million. *Unit head:* Dr. Geoffrey Maruyama, Chair, 612-624-1003, Fax: 612-625-5861, E-mail: geoff@umn.edu. *Application contact:* Dr. Ernest Davenport, Director of Graduate Studies, 612-624-1040, E-mail: lqr6576@umn.edu.
Website: http://www.cehd.umn.edu/EdPsych

University of Missouri, Office of Research and Graduate Studies, College of Education, Department of Educational, School, and Counseling Psychology, Columbia, MO 65211. Offers counseling psychology (M Ed, MA, PhD, Ed S); educational psychology (M Ed, MA, PhD, Ed S); learning and instruction (M Ed); school psychology (M Ed, MA, PhD, Ed S). *Accreditation:* APA (one or more programs are accredited). *Program availability:* Part-time. *Faculty:* 29 full-time (12 women), 1 part-time/adjunct (0 women). *Students:* 177 full-time (106 women), 204 part-time (102 women). *Degree requirements:* For doctorate, thesis/dissertation. *Entrance requirements:* For master's, doctorate, and Ed S, GRE General Test, minimum GPA of 3.0. Additional exam requirements/recommendations for international students: Required—TOEFL (minimum score 580 paper-based; 92 iBT). *Application deadline:* For fall admission, 12/1 priority date for domestic and international students. Applications are processed on a rolling basis. Application fee: $75 ($90 for international students). Electronic applications accepted. *Expenses:* Tuition, state resident: full-time $6347; part-time $352.60 per credit hour. Tuition, nonresident: full-time $17,379; part-time $965.50 per credit hour. *Required fees:* $1035. Tuition and fees vary according to course load, campus/location and program. *Financial support:* Fellowships, research assistantships, teaching assistantships, institutionally sponsored loans, traineeships, health care benefits, and unspecified assistantships available. Support available to part-time students.
Website: http://education.missouri.edu/ESCP/

University of Missouri–St. Louis, College of Education, Interdisciplinary Doctoral Programs, St. Louis, MO 63121. Offers counseling (PhD); educational leadership and policy studies (PhD); educational psychology (PhD); leadership in educational practice (Ed D); teaching-learning processes (PhD). *Degree requirements:* For doctorate, thesis/dissertation. *Entrance requirements:* For doctorate, GRE General Test, 3 letters of recommendation; personal interview. Additional exam requirements/recommendations for international students: Recommended—TOEFL (minimum score 550 paper-based; 79 iBT), IELTS (minimum score 6.5). *Application deadline:* For fall admission, 3/1 for domestic and international students; for spring admission, 10/1 for domestic and international students. Application fee: $50 ($40 for international students). Electronic applications accepted. *Financial support:* Research assistantships and teaching assistantships available. Financial award application deadline: 4/1; financial award applicants required to submit FAFSA. *Faculty research:* Higher education law and policy, gender and higher education, student retention, lifelong learning orientation, school counselor's role in violence prevention. *Unit head:* Dr. Kathleen Haywood, Director of Graduate Studies, 314-516-5483, Fax: 314-516-5227, E-mail: kathleen_haywood@umsl.edu. *Application contact:* 314-516-5458, Fax: 314-516-6996, E-mail: gradadm@umsl.edu.

University of Nebraska–Lincoln, Graduate College, College of Education and Human Sciences, Department of Educational Psychology, Lincoln, NE 68588. Offers cognition, learning and development (MA); counseling psychology (MA); educational psychology (MA, Ed S); psychological studies in education (PhD), including cognition, learning and development, counseling psychology, quantitative, qualitative, and psychometric methods, school psychology; quantitative, qualitative, and psychometric methods (MA); school psychology (MA, Ed S). *Accreditation:* APA (one or more programs are accredited); NCATE. *Degree requirements:* For master's, thesis optional. *Entrance requirements:* For master's, GRE General Test. Additional exam requirements/recommendations for international students: Required—TOEFL (minimum score 500 paper-based). Electronic applications accepted. *Faculty research:* Measurement and assessment, metacognition, academic skills, child development, multicultural education and counseling.

University of Nevada, Reno, Graduate School, College of Education, Department of Counseling and Educational Psychology, Reno, NV 89557. Offers M Ed, MA, MS, Ed D, PhD, Ed S. *Accreditation:* ACA (one or more programs are accredited); NCATE. Terminal master's awarded for partial completion of doctoral program. *Degree requirements:* For master's, comprehensive exam, thesis optional; for doctorate, comprehensive exam, thesis/dissertation, qualifying exam. *Entrance requirements:* For master's, GRE, minimum GPA of 2.75; for doctorate, GRE, minimum GPA of 3.0. Additional exam requirements/recommendations for international students: Required—TOEFL (minimum score 500 paper-based; 61 iBT), IELTS (minimum score 6). Electronic applications accepted. *Faculty research:* Marriage and family counseling, substance abuse attitudes of teachers, current supply of counseling educators, HIV-positive services for patients, family counseling for youth at risk.

University of New Mexico, Graduate Studies, College of Education, Program in Educational Psychology, Albuquerque, NM 87131. Offers MA, PhD. *Accreditation:* NCATE. *Program availability:* Part-time, evening/weekend. *Faculty:* 6 full-time (4 women). *Students:* 14 full-time (10 women), 12 part-time (10 women); includes 10 minority (1 Black or African American, non-Hispanic/Latino; 4 American Indian or Alaska Native, non-Hispanic/Latino; 4 Hispanic/Latino; 1 Two or more races, non-Hispanic/Latino), 1 international. Average age 36. 10 applicants, 60% accepted, 6 enrolled. In 2016, 4 master's, 4 doctorates awarded. Terminal master's awarded for partial completion of doctoral program. *Degree requirements:* For master's, comprehensive exam (for some programs), thesis (for some programs); for doctorate, comprehensive exam, thesis/dissertation. *Entrance requirements:* For master's, GRE General Test or MAT, minimum GPA of 3.0 in last 2 years of undergraduate study, 3 letters of reference, interview with 3 faculty; for doctorate, GRE General Test or MAT, minimum GPA of 3.0

in last 2 years of undergraduate study, 3 letters of reference, interview with 3 faculty, writing sample. Additional exam requirements/recommendations for international students: Required—TOEFL. *Application deadline:* For fall admission, 3/1 for domestic and international students; for spring admission, 10/1 for domestic and international students. Application fee: $50. Electronic applications accepted. *Financial support:* Teaching assistantships with tuition reimbursements and unspecified assistantships available. Financial award application deadline: 3/1; financial award applicants required to submit FAFSA. *Faculty research:* Measurement and assessment, cognitive strategies, accountability, motivation, instructional technology, educational research, human lifespan development, beliefs. *Unit head:* Dr. Jay Parkes, Department Chair, 505-277-3320, Fax: 505-277-8361, E-mail: edpsy@unm.edu. *Application contact:* Cynthia Salas, Department Administrator, 505-277-4535, Fax: 505-277-8361, E-mail: divbse@unm.edu.
Website: https://coe.unm.edu/departments-programs/ifce/educational-psychology/

The University of North Carolina at Chapel Hill, Graduate School, School of Education, Program in Education, Chapel Hill, NC 27599. Offers culture, curriculum and change (MA, PhD); early childhood, intervention and literacy (MA, PhD); educational psychology, measurement and evaluation (MA, PhD). *Accreditation:* NCATE. *Degree requirements:* For master's, thesis; for doctorate, comprehensive exam, thesis/dissertation. *Entrance requirements:* For master's, GRE General Test, minimum GPA of 3.0 during last 2 years of undergraduates course work; for doctorate, GRE General Test, minimum GPA of 3.0 during last 2 years of undergraduate course work. Additional exam requirements/recommendations for international students: Required—TOEFL (minimum score 550 paper-based). Electronic applications accepted.

University of Northern Colorado, Graduate School, College of Education and Behavioral Sciences, School of Psychological Sciences, Greeley, CO 80639. Offers educational psychology (MA, PhD). *Program availability:* Part-time. *Degree requirements:* For master's, comprehensive exam, thesis or alternative; for doctorate, comprehensive exam, thesis/dissertation. *Entrance requirements:* For master's and doctorate, GRE General Test, letters of recommendation. *Application deadline:* Applications are processed on a rolling basis. Application fee: $50 ($60 for international students). Electronic applications accepted. *Financial support:* Fellowships, research assistantships, teaching assistantships, and unspecified assistantships available. Financial award application deadline: 3/1; financial award applicants required to submit FAFSA. *Unit head:* Dr. Mark Alcorn, Director, 970-351-2957, Fax: 970-351-1103. *Application contact:* Linda Sisson, Graduate Student Admission Coordinator, 970-351-1807, Fax: 970-351-2371, E-mail: linda.sisson@unco.edu.
Website: http://www.unco.edu/cebs/psychsci

University of Northern Iowa, Graduate College, College of Education, Department of Educational Psychology and Foundations, MAE Program in Educational Psychology: Professional Development for Teachers, Cedar Falls, IA 50614. Offers MAE. *Program availability:* Online learning.

University of North Texas, Robert B. Toulouse School of Graduate Studies, Denton, TX 76203-5459. Offers accounting (MS); applied anthropology (MA, MS); applied behavior analysis (Certificate); applied geography (MA); applied technology and performance improvement (M Ed, MS); art education (MA); art history (MA); art museum education (Certificate); arts leadership (Certificate); audiology (Au D); behavior analysis (MS); behavioral science (PhD); biochemistry and molecular biology (MS); biology (MA, MS); biomedical engineering (MS); business analysis (MS); chemistry (MS); clinical health psychology (PhD); communication studies (MA, MS); computer engineering (MS); computer science (MS); counseling (M Ed, MS), including clinical mental health counseling (MS), college and university counseling, elementary school counseling, secondary school counseling; creative writing (MA); criminal justice (MS); curriculum and instruction (M Ed); decision sciences (MBA); design (MA, MFA), including fashion design (MFA), innovation studies, interior design (MFA); early childhood studies (MS); economics (MS); educational leadership (M Ed, Ed D); educational psychology (MS, PhD), including family studies (MS), gifted and talented (MS), human development (MS), learning and cognition (MS), research, measurement and evaluation (MS); electrical engineering (MS); emergency management (MPA); engineering technology (MS); English (MA); English as a second language (MA); environmental science (MS); finance (MBA, MS); financial management (MPA); French (MA); health services management (MBA); higher education (M Ed, Ed D); history (MA, MS); hospitality management (MS); human resources management (MPA); information science (MS); information systems (PhD); information technologies (MBA); interdisciplinary studies (MA, MS); international studies (MA); international sustainable tourism (MS); jazz studies (MM); journalism (MA, MJ, Graduate Certificate), including interactive and virtual digital communication (Graduate Certificate), narrative journalism (Graduate Certificate), public relations (Graduate Certificate); kinesiology (MS); linguistics (MA); local government management (MPA); logistics (PhD); logistics and supply chain management (MBA); long-term care, senior housing, and aging services (MA); management (PhD); marketing (MBA); mathematics (MA, MS); mechanical and energy engineering (MS, PhD); music (MA), including ethnomusicology, music theory, musicology, performance; music composition (PhD); music education (MM Ed, PhD); nonprofit management (MPA); operations and supply chain management (MBA); performance (MM, DMA); philosophy (MA); political science (MA); professional and technical communication (MA); radio, television and film (MA, MFA); rehabilitation counseling (Certificate); sociology (MA); Spanish (MA); special education (M Ed); speech-language pathology (MA); strategic management (MBA); studio art (MFA); teaching (M Ed); MBA/MS. *Program availability:* Part-time, evening/weekend, online learning. Terminal master's awarded for partial completion of doctoral program. *Degree requirements:* For master's, variable foreign language requirement, comprehensive exam (for some programs), thesis (for some programs); for doctorate, variable foreign language requirement, comprehensive exam (for some programs), thesis/dissertation; for other advanced degree, variable foreign language requirement, comprehensive exam (for some programs). *Entrance requirements:* For master's and doctorate, GRE, GMAT. Additional exam requirements/recommendations for international students: Required—TOEFL (minimum score 550 paper-based; 79 iBT). Electronic applications accepted.

University of Oklahoma, Jeannine Rainbolt College of Education, Department of Educational Psychology, Program in Instructional Psychology and Technology, Norman, OK 73019. Offers 21st century teaching and learning (M Ed); educational psychology (M Ed); instructional design and technology (M Ed); instructional psychology and technology (PhD); integrating technology in teaching (M Ed). *Program availability:* Part-time. *Students:* 15 full-time (13 women), 29 part-time (21 women); includes 6 minority (1 Black or African American, non-Hispanic/Latino; 1 American Indian or Alaska Native, non-Hispanic/Latino; 1 Asian, non-Hispanic/Latino; 3 Hispanic/Latino), 13 international. Average age 33. 28 applicants, 61% accepted, 12 enrolled. In 2016, 11 master's, 2 doctorates awarded. Terminal master's awarded for partial completion of doctoral program. *Degree requirements:* For doctorate, comprehensive exam, thesis/dissertation. *Entrance requirements:* For doctorate, GRE. Additional exam requirements/recommendations for international students: Required—TOEFL (minimum score 79 iBT) or IELTS (minimum score 6.5). *Application deadline:* Applications are processed on a rolling basis. Application fee: $50 ($100 for international students). Electronic applications accepted. *Expenses:* Tuition, state resident: full-time $4886; part-time $203.60 per credit hour. Tuition, nonresident: full-time $18,989; part-time $791.20 per credit hour. *Required fees:* $3283; $126.25 per credit hour. $126.50 per semester. *Financial support:* In 2016–17, 28 students received support. Fellowships with full and partial tuition reimbursements available, research assistantships with full and partial tuition reimbursements available, teaching assistantships with full and partial tuition reimbursements available, and scholarships/grants available. Financial award application deadline: 6/1; financial award applicants required to submit FAFSA. *Faculty research:* Social and cultural implications of technologies; girls interest in stem; epistemic stance; teacher learning and development. *Unit head:* Dr. Nancy E. Marchand-Martella, Chair, Department of Educational Psychology, 405-325-0624, Fax: 405-325-6655, E-mail: nmarchand-martella@ou.edu. *Application contact:* Anna Steele, Graduate Programs Specialist, 405-325-4525, Fax: 405-325-7390, E-mail: jrcoe_gps@ou.edu.
Website: http://www.ou.edu/education/edpy

University of Phoenix–Southern Arizona Campus, College of Education, Tucson, AZ 85711. Offers administration and supervision (MA Ed); adult education and training (MA Ed); curriculum instruction (MA Ed); educational counseling (MA Ed); elementary teacher education (MA Ed); school counseling (MSC); secondary teacher education (MA Ed); special education (MA Ed, Certificate). *Program availability:* Evening/weekend. *Degree requirements:* For master's, thesis (for some programs). *Entrance requirements:* For master's, minimum undergraduate GPA of 2.5, 3 years of work experience. Additional exam requirements/recommendations for international students: Required—TOEFL (minimum score 550 paper-based; 79 iBT). Electronic applications accepted.

University of Regina, Faculty of Graduate Studies and Research, Faculty of Education, Department of Educational Psychology, Regina, SK S4S 0A2, Canada. Offers M Ed. *Program availability:* Part-time. *Faculty:* 5 full-time (2 women), 20 part-time/adjunct (11 women). *Students:* 31 full-time (27 women), 34 part-time (24 women). 33 applicants, 12% accepted. In 2016, 14 master's awarded. *Degree requirements:* For master's, thesis (for some programs), practicum, project, or thesis. *Entrance requirements:* For master's, bachelor's degree in education. Additional exam requirements/recommendations for international students: Required—TOEFL (minimum score 580 paper-based; 80 iBT), IELTS (minimum score 6.5), PTE (minimum score 59). *Application deadline:* For fall admission, 2/15 for domestic and international students; for winter admission, 10/15 for domestic and international students; for spring admission, 2/15 for domestic and international students. Application fee: $100. Electronic applications accepted. *Financial support:* In 2016–17, 6 fellowships (averaging $6,000 per year), 2 teaching assistantships (averaging $2,501 per year) were awarded; career-related internships or fieldwork and scholarships/grants also available. Financial award application deadline: 6/15. *Faculty research:* Theories of counseling, psychology of learning, aptitude and achievement analysis, education and vocational guidance, resilience: re-conceptualizing PRAXIS. *Unit head:* Dr. Ken Montgomery, Associate Dean, Research and Graduate Programs, 306-585-5031, Fax: 306-585-5387, E-mail: ken.montgomery@uregina.ca. *Application contact:* Tania Gates, Graduate Program Coordinator, 306-585-4506, Fax: 306-585-5387, E-mail: edgrad@uregina.ca.
Website: http://www.uregina.ca/education/

University of Saskatchewan, College of Graduate Studies and Research, College of Education, Department of Educational Psychology and Special Education, Saskatoon, SK S7N 5A2, Canada. Offers M Ed, PhD, Diploma. *Degree requirements:* For master's, thesis (for some programs); for doctorate, comprehensive exam (for some programs), thesis/dissertation. *Entrance requirements:* Additional exam requirements/recommendations for international students: Required—TOEFL (minimum score 80 iBT); Recommended—IELTS (minimum score 6.5). Electronic applications accepted.

University of South Africa, College of Human Sciences, Pretoria, South Africa. Offers adult education (M Ed); African languages (MA, PhD); African politics (MA, PhD); Afrikaans (MA, PhD); ancient history (MA, PhD); ancient Near Eastern studies (MA, PhD); anthropology (MA, PhD); applied linguistics (MA); Arabic (MA, PhD); archaeology (MA); art history (MA); Biblical archaeology (MA); Biblical studies (M Th, D Th, PhD); Christian spirituality (M Th, D Th); church history (M Th, D Th); classical studies (MA, PhD); clinical psychology (MA); communication (MA, PhD); comparative education (M Ed, Ed D); consulting psychology (D Admin, D Com, PhD); curriculum studies (M Ed, Ed D); development studies (M Admin, MA, D Admin, PhD); didactics (M Ed, Ed D); education (M Tech); education management (M Ed, Ed D); educational psychology (M Ed); English (MA); environmental education (M Ed); French (MA, PhD); German (MA, PhD); Greek (MA); guidance and counseling (M Ed); health studies (MA, PhD), including health sciences education (MA), health services management (MA), medical and surgical nursing science (critical care general) (MA), midwifery and neonatal nursing science (MA), trauma and emergency care (MA); history (MA, PhD); history of education (Ed D); inclusive education (M Ed, Ed D); information and communications technology policy and regulation (MA); information science (MA, MIS, PhD); international politics (MA, PhD); Islamic studies (MA, PhD); Italian (MA, PhD); Judaica (MA, PhD); linguistics (MA, PhD); mathematical education (M Ed); mathematics education (MA); missiology (M Th, D Th); modern Hebrew (MA, PhD); musicology (MA, MMus, D Mus, PhD); natural science education (M Ed); New Testament (M Th, D Th); Old Testament (D Th); pastoral therapy (M Th, D Th); philosophy (MA); philosophy of education (M Ed, Ed D); politics (MA, PhD); Portuguese (MA, PhD); practical theology (M Th, D Th); psychology (MA, MS, PhD); psychology of education (M Ed, Ed D); public health (MA); religious studies (MA, D Th, PhD); Romance languages (MA); Russian (MA, PhD); Semitic languages (MA, PhD); social behavior studies in HIV/AIDS (MA); social science (mental health) (MA); social science in development studies (MA); social science in psychology (MA); social science in social work (MA); social science in sociology (MA); social work (MSW, DSW, PhD); socio-education (M Ed, Ed D); sociolinguistics (MA); sociology (MA, PhD); Spanish (MA, PhD); systematic theology (M Th, D Th); TESOL (teaching English to speakers of other languages) (MA); theological ethics (M Th, D Th); theory of literature (MA, PhD); urban ministries (D Th); urban ministry (M Th).

University of South Carolina, The Graduate School, College of Education, Department of Educational Studies, Program in Educational Psychology, Research, Columbia, SC 29208. Offers M Ed, PhD. *Accreditation:* NCATE. *Program availability:* Part-time. *Degree requirements:* For master's, comprehensive exam, thesis (for some programs); for doctorate, comprehensive exam, thesis/dissertation. *Entrance requirements:* For master's, GRE General Test; for doctorate, GRE General Test, interview. Electronic applications accepted. *Faculty research:* Problem solving, higher order thinking skills, psychometric research, methodology.

The University of South Dakota, Graduate School, School of Education, Division of Counseling and Psychology in Education, Vermillion, SD 57069. Offers counseling (MA, PhD, Ed S); human development and educational psychology (MA, PhD, Ed S); school psychology (PhD, Ed S). *Accreditation:* ACA (one or more programs are accredited); NCATE. *Program availability:* Part-time. *Degree requirements:* For master's and Ed S, comprehensive exam, thesis or alternative; for doctorate, comprehensive exam, thesis/dissertation. *Entrance requirements:* For master's and doctorate, GRE General Test, minimum GPA of 3.0. Additional exam requirements/recommendations for international students: Required—TOEFL (minimum score 550 paper-based; 79 iBT). Electronic applications accepted.

University of Southern California, Graduate School, Rossier School of Education, Doctor of Education Programs, Los Angeles, CA 90089. Offers educational psychology (Ed D); higher education administration (Ed D); K-12 leadership in urban school settings (Ed D); teacher education in multicultural societies (Ed D). *Program availability:* Part-time, evening/weekend. *Degree requirements:* For doctorate, thesis/dissertation. *Entrance requirements:* For doctorate, GRE. Additional exam requirements/recommendations for international students: Required—TOEFL (minimum score 100 iBT). Electronic applications accepted. *Faculty research:* Data-driven decision-making in K-12 schools and districts; examination of college and university leadership and management in U. S. and Asia; studies in facilitating student learning; organizational change and the role of leaders; leadership, diversity, learning and accountability.

University of Southern California, Graduate School, Rossier School of Education, Doctor of Philosophy in Education Programs, Los Angeles, CA 90089. Offers educational psychology (PhD); higher education administration and policy (PhD); K-12 policy and practice (PhD). *Degree requirements:* For doctorate, thesis/dissertation, 63 units; qualifying exam; dissertation proposal and defense. *Entrance requirements:* For doctorate, GRE. Additional exam requirements/recommendations for international students: Required—TOEFL (minimum score 100 iBT). Electronic applications accepted. *Faculty research:* Diversity in higher education, organizational change, educational psychology, policy and politics of educational reform, economics of education and education policy.

University of Southern Maine, College of Management and Human Service, School of Education and Human Development, Program in Educational Psychology, Portland, ME 04103. Offers applied behavior analysis (MS, CGS). *Program availability:* Part-time, evening/weekend. *Entrance requirements:* For master's, GRE or MAT. Additional exam requirements/recommendations for international students: Required—TOEFL (minimum score 550 paper-based; 79 iBT). Electronic applications accepted. *Faculty research:* Applied behavior analysis, functional behavioral analysis, positive behavioral interventions and supports.

University of South Florida, College of Education, Department of Educational and Psychological Studies, Tampa, FL 33620-9951. Offers college student affairs (M Ed); counselor education (MA, PhD, Ed S); interdisciplinary (PhD, Ed S); school psychology (PhD, Ed S). *Faculty:* 25 full-time (12 women). *Students:* 97 full-time (66 women), 94 part-time (62 women); includes 52 minority (22 Black or African American, non-Hispanic/Latino; 8 Asian, non-Hispanic/Latino; 19 Hispanic/Latino; 3 Two or more races, non-Hispanic/Latino), 25 international. Average age 34. 132 applicants, 45% accepted, 46 enrolled. In 2016, 94 master's, 7 doctorates, 8 other advanced degrees awarded. Application fee: $30. *Expenses:* Tuition, state resident: full-time $7766; part-time $431.43 per credit hour. Tuition, nonresident: full-time $15,789; part-time $877.17 per credit hour. *Required fees:* $37 per term. *Faculty research:* College student affairs, counselor education, educational psychology, school psychology, social foundations. *Total annual research expenditures:* $11.1 million. *Unit head:* Dr. Barabara Shircliff, Chair, 813-974-4001, E-mail: shirclif@usf.edu.
Website: http://www.coedu.usf.edu/main/departments/psf/psf.html

The University of Tennessee, Graduate School, College of Education, Health and Human Sciences, Department of Educational Psychology and Counseling, Knoxville, TN 37996. Offers adult education (MS); applied educational psychology (MS); collaborative learning (Ed D); college student personnel (MS); mental health counseling (MS); rehabilitation counseling (MS); school counseling (MS). *Accreditation:* ACA (one or more programs are accredited); CORE (one or more programs are accredited); NCATE. *Program availability:* Part-time, evening/weekend. *Degree requirements:* For master's, thesis optional. *Entrance requirements:* For master's, GRE General Test, minimum GPA of 2.7. Additional exam requirements/recommendations for international students: Required—TOEFL. Electronic applications accepted.

The University of Tennessee, Graduate School, College of Education, Health and Human Sciences, Program in Education, Knoxville, TN 37996. Offers art education (MS); counseling education (PhD); cultural studies in education (PhD); curriculum (MS, Ed S); curriculum, educational research and evaluation (Ed D, PhD); early childhood education (PhD); early childhood special education (MS); education of deaf and hard of hearing (MS); educational administration and policy studies (Ed D, PhD); educational administration and supervision (Ed S); educational psychology (Ed D, PhD); elementary education (MS, Ed S); elementary teaching (MS); English education (MS, Ed S); exercise science (PhD); foreign language/ESL education (MS, Ed S); instructional technology (MS, Ed D, PhD, Ed S); literacy, language and ESL education (PhD); literacy, language education, and ESL education (Ed D); mathematics education (MS, Ed S); modified and comprehensive special education (MS); reading education (MS, Ed S); school counseling (Ed S); school psychology (PhD, Ed S); science education (MS, Ed S); secondary teaching (MS); social foundations (MS); social science education (MS, Ed S); socio-cultural foundations of sports and education (PhD); special education (Ed S); teacher education (Ed D, PhD). *Accreditation:* NCATE. *Program availability:* Part-time, evening/weekend. *Degree requirements:* For master's and Ed S, thesis optional; for doctorate, variable foreign language requirement, thesis/dissertation. *Entrance requirements:* For master's, minimum GPA of 2.7; for doctorate and Ed S, GRE General Test, minimum GPA of 2.7. Additional exam requirements/recommendations for international students: Required—TOEFL. Electronic applications accepted.

The University of Texas at Austin, Graduate School, College of Education, Department of Educational Psychology, Austin, TX 78712-1111. Offers academic educational psychology (M Ed, MA); counseling psychology (PhD); counselor education (M Ed); human development, culture and learning sciences (PhD); program evaluation (MA); quantitative methods (M Ed, MA, PhD); school psychology (MA, PhD). *Accreditation:* APA (one or more programs are accredited). *Degree requirements:* For master's, thesis optional; for doctorate, thesis/dissertation. *Entrance requirements:* For master's and doctorate, GRE General Test, 3 letters of recommendation. Additional exam requirements/recommendations for international students: Required—TOEFL.

The University of Texas at El Paso, Graduate School, College of Education, Department of Educational Psychology and Special Services, El Paso, TX 79968-0001. Offers educational diagnostics (M Ed); guidance and counseling (M Ed); special education (M Ed). *Program availability:* Part-time, evening/weekend. *Degree requirements:* For master's, thesis optional. *Entrance requirements:* For master's, minimum GPA of 3.0. Additional exam requirements/recommendations for international students: Required—TOEFL. Electronic applications accepted.

The University of Texas Rio Grande Valley, College of Education and P-16 Integration, Department of Human Development and School Services, Edinburg, TX 78539. Offers early childhood education (M Ed); early childhood special education (M Ed); educational diagnostician (M Ed); school psychology (MA). *Program availability:* Part-time, evening/weekend. *Degree requirements:* For master's, comprehensive exam (for some programs), thesis (for some programs). *Entrance requirements:* For master's, GRE General Test, interview. Tuition and fees vary according to course load and program. *Faculty research:* Reading instruction, assessment practice, behavior interventions consultation, mental retardation.

University of the Pacific, Gladys L. Benerd School of Education, Department of Educational and School Psychology, Stockton, CA 95211-0197. Offers educational psychology (MA, Ed D); school psychology (Ed S). *Accreditation:* NCATE. *Students:* 4 part-time (all women); includes 3 minority (all Hispanic/Latino). Average age 33. *Degree requirements:* For master's, thesis; for doctorate, thesis/dissertation. *Entrance requirements:* For master's and doctorate, GRE General Test, GRE Subject Test. Additional exam requirements/recommendations for international students: Required—TOEFL. *Application deadline:* For fall admission, 3/1 priority date for domestic students; for spring admission, 10/1 priority date for domestic students. Applications are processed on a rolling basis. Application fee: $75. *Financial support:* Teaching assistantships available. Financial award application deadline: 3/1; financial award applicants required to submit FAFSA. *Unit head:* Dr. Linda Webster, Chairperson, 209-946-2559, E-mail: lwebster@pacific.edu. *Application contact:* Office of Graduate Admissions, 209-946-2344.

The University of Toledo, College of Graduate Studies, Judith Herb College of Education, Department of Educational Foundations and Leadership, Toledo, OH 43606-3390. Offers educational administration and supervision (ME, DE, Ed S); educational psychology (ME, PhD); educational research and measurement (ME, PhD); educational sociology (PhD); educational theory and social foundations (ME); foundations of education (DE, PhD); history of education (PhD); philosophy of education (PhD). *Accreditation:* NCATE. *Program availability:* Part-time, evening/weekend. *Degree requirements:* For master's, comprehensive exam, thesis or alternative; for doctorate, comprehensive exam, thesis/dissertation; for Ed S, thesis optional. *Entrance requirements:* For master's, doctorate, and Ed S, minimum cumulative GPA of 2.7 for all previous academic work, letters of recommendation. Additional exam requirements/recommendations for international students: Required—TOEFL (minimum score 550 paper-based; 80 iBT). Electronic applications accepted.

University of Utah, Graduate School, College of Education, Department of Educational Psychology, Salt Lake City, UT 84112. Offers clinical mental health counseling (M Ed); counseling psychology (PhD); elementary education (M Ed); instructional design and educational technology (M Ed); instructional design and technology (MS); learning and cognition (MS, PhD); reading and literacy (M Ed, PhD); school counseling (M Ed); school psychology (M Ed, PhD, Ed S); statistics (M Stat). *Accreditation:* APA (one or more programs are accredited). *Faculty:* 23 full-time (12 women), 15 part-time/adjunct (10 women). *Students:* 119 full-time (95 women), 106 part-time (74 women); includes 37 minority (2 Black or African American, non-Hispanic/Latino; 6 Asian, non-Hispanic/Latino; 22 Hispanic/Latino; 7 Two or more races, non-Hispanic/Latino), 6 international. Average age 31. 296 applicants, 27% accepted, 73 enrolled. In 2016, 47 master's, 8 doctorates awarded. Terminal master's awarded for partial completion of doctoral program. *Degree requirements:* For master's, variable foreign language requirement, comprehensive exam (for some programs), thesis (for some programs), projects; for doctorate, variable foreign language requirement, comprehensive exam, thesis/dissertation, oral exam. *Entrance requirements:* For master's and doctorate, GRE General Test, minimum GPA of 3.0. Additional exam requirements/recommendations for international students: Required—TOEFL (minimum score 80 iBT). *Application deadline:* For fall admission, 12/15 for domestic and international students; for winter admission, 11/1 for domestic and international students; for spring admission, 3/15 for domestic and international students. Application fee: $55 ($65 for international students). Electronic applications accepted. *Expenses:* Contact institution. *Financial support:* In 2016–17, 84 students received support, including 12 fellowships with full and partial tuition reimbursements available (averaging $18,000 per year), 21 research assistantships with full and partial tuition reimbursements available (averaging $14,500 per year), 57 teaching assistantships with full and partial tuition reimbursements available (averaging $14,500 per year); career-related internships or fieldwork, Federal Work-Study, institutionally sponsored loans, scholarships/grants, traineeships, health care benefits, and unspecified assistantships also available. Financial award application deadline: 4/1; financial award applicants required to submit FAFSA. *Faculty research:* Autism, computer technology and instruction, cognitive behavior, aging, group counseling. *Total annual research expenditures:* $620,935. *Unit head:* Dr. Anne E. Cook, Chair, 801-581-7148, Fax: 801-581-5566, E-mail: anne.cook@utah.edu. *Application contact:* JoLynn N. Yates, Academic Coordinator, 801-581-7148, Fax: 801-581-5566, E-mail: jo.yates@utah.edu.
Website: http://www.ed.utah.edu/edps/

University of Utah, Graduate School, Interdepartmental Program in Statistics, Salt Lake City, UT 84112-1107. Offers biostatistics (M Stat); econometrics (M Stat); educational psychology (M Stat); mathematics (M Stat); sociology (M Stat). *Program availability:* Part-time. *Students:* 30 full-time (9 women), 29 part-time (8 women); includes 10 minority (7 Asian, non-Hispanic/Latino; 3 Hispanic/Latino), 12 international. Average age 31. 50 applicants, 70% accepted, 27 enrolled. In 2016, 20 master's awarded. *Degree requirements:* For master's, comprehensive exam (for some programs), projects. *Entrance requirements:* For master's, GRE General Test (for all but biostatistics); GRE Subject Test (for mathematics), minimum GPA of 3.0; course work in calculus, matrix theory, statistics. Additional exam requirements/recommendations for international students: Required—TOEFL (minimum score 500 paper-based; 61 iBT). *Application deadline:* For fall admission, 7/1 for domestic students, 4/1 for international students. Applications are processed on a rolling basis. Application fee: $55 ($65 for international students). Electronic applications accepted. *Expenses:* Tuition, state resident: full-time $7011; part-time $3918.24 per credit hour. Tuition, nonresident: full-time $22,154; part-time $11,665.42 per credit hour. *Financial support:* In 2016–17, 10 students received support, including 10 research assistantships with tuition reimbursements available (averaging $1,000 per year); career-related internships or fieldwork, scholarships/grants, and unspecified assistantships also available. *Faculty research:* Biostatistics, sociology, economics, educational psychology, mathematics. *Unit head:* Xiaoming Sheng, Chair, University Statistics Committee, 801-213-3729, E-mail: xiaoming.sheng@utah.edu. *Application contact:* Laura Egbert, Coordinator, 801-585-6853, E-mail: laura.egbert@utah.edu.
Website: http://www.mstat.utah.edu

University of Victoria, Faculty of Graduate Studies, Faculty of Education, Department of Educational Psychology and Leadership Studies, Victoria, BC V8W 2Y2, Canada. Offers aboriginal communities counseling (M Ed); counseling (M Ed, MA); educational psychology (M Ed, MA, PhD), including counseling psychology (M Ed, MA), leadership studies (PhD), learning and development (MA, PhD), measurement and evaluation, special education (M Ed, MA); leadership studies (M Ed, MA). *Program availability:* Part-time. *Degree requirements:* For master's, thesis (for some programs), comprehensive exam (M Ed); for doctorate, comprehensive exam, thesis/dissertation, candidacy exam. *Entrance requirements:* For master's, 2 years of work experience in a relevant field; for doctorate, GRE, 2 years of work experience in a relevant field, minimum B average. Additional exam requirements/recommendations for international students: Required—TOEFL (minimum score 575 paper-based), IELTS (minimum score 7). *Faculty research:* Learning and development (child, adolescent and adult), special education and exceptional children.

University of Virginia, Curry School of Education, Department of Leadership, Foundations and Policy, Program in Educational Psychology, Charlottesville, VA 22903.

Offers applied developmental science (M Ed); educational evaluation (M Ed); educational psychology (M Ed, Ed D, Ed S); educational research (Ed D); gifted education (M Ed); instructional technology (M Ed, Ed S); research statistics and evaluation (Ed D); school psychology (Ed D). *Students:* 28 full-time (15 women), 10 part-time (7 women); includes 8 minority (2 Black or African American, non-Hispanic/Latino; 2 Asian, non-Hispanic/Latino; 3 Hispanic/Latino; 1 Two or more races, non-Hispanic/Latino), 7 international. Average age 26. 85 applicants, 80% accepted, 33 enrolled. In 2016, 35 master's, 1 other advanced degree awarded. *Degree requirements:* For master's, comprehensive exam. *Entrance requirements:* For master's and doctorate, GRE General Test, 2 letters of recommendation. Additional exam requirements/recommendations for international students: Required—TOEFL (minimum score 600 paper-based; 90 iBT), IELTS (minimum score 7). *Application deadline:* Applications are processed on a rolling basis. Application fee: $60. Electronic applications accepted. *Expenses:* Tuition, state resident: full-time $15,026; part-time $834 per credit hour. Tuition, nonresident: full-time $25,168; part-time $1378 per credit hour. *Required fees:* $2654. *Financial support:* Fellowships, research assistantships, and teaching assistantships available. Financial award application deadline: 1/5; financial award applicants required to submit FAFSA. *Unit head:* Sara Rimm-Kaufman, Program Director, 434-982-2863, E-mail: serk@virginia.edu. *Application contact:* Eric Molnar, Assistant Director, Admissions and Enrollment Reporting, 434-243-2085, E-mail: eric.molnar@virginia.edu.
Website: http://curry.virginia.edu/academics/areas-of-study/educational-psychology

University of Virginia, Curry School of Education, Program in Education, Charlottesville, VA 22903. Offers administration and supervision (PhD); applied developmental science (PhD); counselor education (PhD); curriculum and instruction (PhD); early childhood special education (MT); education evaluation (PhD); educational psychology (PhD); educational research (PhD); elementary education (MT); English education (MT, PhD); foreign language education (MT); higher education (PhD); instructional technology (PhD); kinesiology (MT, PhD); math education (PhD); reading education (PhD); research, statistics and evaluation (PhD); school psychology (PhD); science education (PhD); social studies education (MT, PhD); special education (PhD); world languages education (MT). *Students:* 452 full-time (357 women), 18 part-time (13 women); includes 100 minority (28 Black or African American, non-Hispanic/Latino; 39 Asian, non-Hispanic/Latino; 18 Hispanic/Latino; 15 Two or more races, non-Hispanic/Latino), 14 international. Average age 25. 309 applicants, 51% accepted, 87 enrolled. In 2016, 144 master's, 31 doctorates awarded. *Degree requirements:* For master's, comprehensive exam (for some programs), field project; for doctorate, comprehensive exam, thesis/dissertation. *Entrance requirements:* For doctorate, GRE General Test. Additional exam requirements/recommendations for international students: Required—TOEFL (minimum score 600 paper-based; 90 iBT), IELTS (minimum score 7). *Application deadline:* Applications are processed on a rolling basis. Application fee: $60. Electronic applications accepted. *Expenses:* Tuition, state resident: full-time $15,026; part-time $834 per credit hour. Tuition, nonresident: full-time $25,168; part-time $1378 per credit hour. *Required fees:* $2654. *Financial support:* Fellowships, research assistantships, and teaching assistantships available. Financial award application deadline: 1/5; financial award applicants required to submit FAFSA. *Unit head:* Robert C. Pianta, Dean, 434-924-3334, E-mail: pianta@virginia.edu. *Application contact:* Eric Molnar, Assistant Director, Admissions and Enrollment Reporting, 434-243-2085, E-mail: eric.molnar@virginia.edu.
Website: http://curry.virginia.edu/teacher-education

University of Washington, Graduate School, College of Education, Program in Educational Psychology, Seattle, WA 98195. Offers educational psychology (PhD); human development and cognition (M Ed); learning sciences (M Ed, PhD); measurement, statistics and research design (M Ed); school psychology (M Ed). *Accreditation:* APA. *Degree requirements:* For master's, thesis optional; for doctorate, thesis/dissertation. *Entrance requirements:* For master's and doctorate, GRE General Test, minimum GPA of 3.0. Additional exam requirements/recommendations for international students: Required—TOEFL.

The University of Western Ontario, Faculty of Graduate Studies, Social Sciences Division, Faculty of Education, Program in Educational Studies, London, ON N6A 5B8, Canada. Offers curriculum studies (M Ed); educational policy studies (M Ed); educational psychology/special education (M Ed). *Program availability:* Part-time. *Faculty research:* Reflective practice, gender and schooling, feminist pedagogy, narrative inquiry, second language, multiculturalism in Canada, education and law.

University of Wisconsin–Madison, Graduate School, School of Education, Department of Educational Psychology, Madison, WI 53706-1380. Offers MS, PhD. *Accreditation:* APA (one or more programs are accredited). *Degree requirements:* For doctorate, thesis/dissertation. *Entrance requirements:* For master's and doctorate, GRE General Test. Electronic applications accepted.

University of Wisconsin–Milwaukee, Graduate School, School of Education, Department of Educational Psychology, Milwaukee, WI 53201-0413. Offers children's mental health for school professionals (Graduate Certificate); community counseling (MS); counseling psychology (PhD); educational statistics and measurement (MS, PhD); learning and development (MS, PhD); multicultural knowledge of mental health practices (Graduate Certificate); school counseling (MS); school counseling (Graduate Certificate); school psychology (MS, PhD, Ed S). *Accreditation:* APA. *Program availability:* Part-time. *Students:* 161 full-time (121 women), 53 part-time (39 women); includes 47 minority (12 Black or African American, non-Hispanic/Latino; 1 American Indian or Alaska Native, non-Hispanic/Latino; 5 Asian, non-Hispanic/Latino; 8 Hispanic/Latino; 1 Native Hawaiian or other Pacific Islander, non-Hispanic/Latino; 20 Two or more races, non-Hispanic/Latino), 6 international. Average age 30. 266 applicants, 45% accepted, 71 enrolled. In 2016, 73 master's, 9 doctorates, 18 other advanced degrees awarded. *Degree requirements:* For master's, comprehensive exam, thesis; for doctorate, thesis/dissertation. *Entrance requirements:* For master's, minimum GPA of 3.0; for doctorate, GRE General Test, minimum GPA of 3.0. Additional exam requirements/recommendations for international students: Required—TOEFL (minimum score 550 paper-based; 79 iBT), IELTS (minimum score 6.5). *Application deadline:* For fall admission, 1/1 priority date for domestic students; for spring admission, 9/1 for domestic students. Applications are processed on a rolling basis. Application fee: $56 ($96 for international students). Electronic applications accepted. *Financial support:* In 2016–17, 14 fellowships, 1 research assistantship, 8 teaching assistantships were awarded; career-related internships or fieldwork, health care benefits, unspecified assistantships, and project assistantships also available. Support available to part-time students. Financial award application deadline: 4/15; financial award applicants required to submit FAFSA. *Application contact:* General Information Contact, 414-229-4721, E-mail: soeinfo@uwm.edu.
Website: http://uwm.edu/education/academics/educational-psychology-department/

Virginia Commonwealth University, Graduate School, School of Education, Doctoral Program in Education, Richmond, VA 23284-9005. Offers art education (PhD); counselor education and supervision (PhD); curriculum, culture and change (PhD); educational leadership (PhD); educational psychology (PhD); leadership (Ed D); research and evaluation (PhD); special education and disability leadership (PhD); sport leadership (PhD); urban services leadership (PhD). *Accreditation:* NCATE. *Program availability:* Part-time. *Degree requirements:* For doctorate, thesis/dissertation. *Entrance requirements:* For doctorate, GRE (for PhD), MAT (for Ed D), interview, master's degree, writing sample. Additional exam requirements/recommendations for international students: Required—TOEFL (minimum score 600 paper-based; 100 iBT). *Application deadline:* For fall admission, 2/15 for domestic students. Application fee: $50. Electronic applications accepted. *Financial support:* Fellowships, research assistantships, career-related internships or fieldwork, Federal Work-Study, and institutionally sponsored loans available. Financial award application deadline: 3/1; financial award applicants required to submit FAFSA. *Unit head:* Dr. Kathleen Cauley, Interim Director, 804-827-2657, E-mail: kmcauley@vcu.edu. *Application contact:* Dr. Colleen A. Thoma, Administrative Assistant, 804-827-2651, E-mail: cathoma@vcu.edu.
Website: http://www.soe.vcu.edu/programs/doctoral-programs/

Walden University, Graduate Programs, School of Psychology, Minneapolis, MN 55401. Offers clinical psychology (MS), including counseling, general program; forensic psychology (MS), including forensic psychology in the community, general program, mental health applications, program planning and evaluation in forensic settings, psychology and legal systems; industrial organizational (MS, PhD), including consulting psychology, forensic (MS), forensic psychology (PhD), general practice, leadership development and coaching (MS), organizational diversity and social change, research evaluation (PhD); online teaching in psychology (Post-Master's Certificate); organizational psychology and development (Postbaccalaureate Certificate); psychology (MS, PhD), including applied psychology (MS), clinical psychology (PhD), crisis management and response (MS), educational psychology, forensic psychology (PhD), general psychology (MS), general psychology research (PhD), general psychology teaching (PhD), health psychology, leadership development and coaching (MS), psychology of culture (MS), psychology, public administration, and social change (MS), social psychology, terrorism and security (MS); psychology respecialization (Post-Doctoral Certificate). *Program availability:* Part-time, evening/weekend, online only, 100% online. Terminal master's awarded for partial completion of doctoral program. *Degree requirements:* For master's, thesis optional; for doctorate, thesis/dissertation, residency. *Entrance requirements:* For master's, bachelor's degree or higher; minimum GPA of 2.5; official transcripts; goal statement (for some programs); access to computer and Internet; for doctorate, master's degree or higher; three years of related professional or academic experience (preferred); minimum GPA of 3.0; goal statement and current resume (for select programs); official transcripts; access to computer and Internet; for other advanced degree, relevant work experience; access to computer and Internet. Additional exam requirements/recommendations for international students: Required—TOEFL (minimum score 550 paper-based, 79 iBT), IELTS (minimum score 6.5), Michigan English Language Assessment Battery (minimum score 82), or PTE (minimum score 53). Electronic applications accepted.

Washington State University, College of Education, Department of Educational Leadership, Sports Studies, and Educational/Counseling Psychology, Pullman, WA 99164-2136. Offers counseling psychology (PhD); educational leadership (Ed M, MA, Ed D, PhD); educational psychology (MA, PhD); sport management (MA). Programs also offered at the Spokane, Tri-Cities, Vancouver and Global (online) campuses. *Program availability:* Part-time, online learning. *Degree requirements:* For master's, comprehensive exam (for some programs), thesis (for some programs), oral or written exam; for doctorate, comprehensive exam, thesis/dissertation, oral and written exam, internship. *Entrance requirements:* For master's and doctorate, GRE General Test, minimum GPA of 3.0, 3 letters of recommendation, transcripts showing all college or university course work, statement of professional objectives, current curriculum vitae/resume. Additional exam requirements/recommendations for international students: Required—TOEFL (minimum score 550 paper-based; 80 iBT). Electronic applications accepted. *Faculty research:* Multicultural counseling and career development, educational and psychological measurement issues, business decision-making process and power relationships, leadership practices and processes as suffused with and constituted by emotion work.

Wayne State University, College of Education, Division of Theoretical and Behavioral Foundations, Detroit, MI 48202. Offers applied behavior analysis (Certificate); counseling (M Ed, MA, Ed D, PhD, Ed S); counseling psychology (MA); education evaluation and research (M Ed, Ed D, PhD); educational psychology (M Ed, PhD), including learning and instruction sciences (PhD); rehabilitation counseling and community inclusion (MA); school and community psychology (MA); school psychology (Certificate). *Accreditation:* ACA (one or more programs are accredited); CORE (one or more programs are accredited). *Program availability:* Evening/weekend. *Faculty:* 12. *Students:* 211 full-time (179 women), 237 part-time (196 women); includes 167 minority (119 Black or African American, non-Hispanic/Latino; 1 American Indian or Alaska Native, non-Hispanic/Latino; 10 Asian, non-Hispanic/Latino; 17 Hispanic/Latino; 20 Two or more races, non-Hispanic/Latino), 24 international. Average age 32. 294 applicants, 34% accepted, 72 enrolled. In 2016, 87 master's, 12 doctorates, 14 other advanced degrees awarded. *Degree requirements:* For master's, thesis (for some programs); for doctorate, thesis/dissertation. *Entrance requirements:* For master's, GRE, interview, personal statement, portfolio (art therapy); for doctorate, GRE, department-written exam, interview, curriculum vitae, references, master's degree in closely-related field with minimum GPA of 3.5, demonstration of counseling skills (counseling); for other advanced degree, master's degree in counseling and counseling license (for Ed S); good standing in school and community psychology MA program (for Certificate). Additional exam requirements/recommendations for international students: Required—TOEFL (minimum score 550 paper-based; 79 iBT), Michigan English Language Assessment Battery (minimum score 85); Recommended—IELTS (minimum score 6.5), TWE (minimum score 5.5). *Application deadline:* For fall admission, 6/1 priority date for domestic students, 5/1 priority date for international students; for winter admission, 10/1 priority date for domestic students, 9/1 priority date for international students; for spring admission, 2/1 priority date for domestic students, 1/1 priority date for international students. Applications are processed on a rolling basis. Application fee: $50. Electronic applications accepted. *Expenses:* $16,503 per year resident tuition and fees, $33,697 per year non-resident tuition and fees. *Financial support:* In 2016–17, 92 students received support, including 2 research assistantships with tuition reimbursements available (averaging $17,994 per year); fellowships with tuition reimbursements available, teaching assistantships with tuition reimbursements available, Federal Work-Study, scholarships/grants, health care benefits, and unspecified assistantships also available. Support available to part-time students. Financial award applicants required to submit FAFSA. *Faculty research:* Adolescents at risk, supervision of counseling. *Unit head:* Dr. Cheryl Somers, Assistant Dean, 313-577-1670, E-mail: c.somers@wayne.edu. *Application contact:* Janice Green, Assistant Dean, 313-577-1605, E-mail: jwgreen@wayne.edu.
Website: http://coe.wayne.edu/tbf/index.php

Webster University, School of Education, Department of Multidisciplinary Studies, St. Louis, MO 63119-3194. Offers applied educational psychology (MA, Ed S); communication arts (MA); early childhood education (MA, MAT); education and innovation (MA); educational technology (MET); elementary education (MAT); mathematics for educators (MA); middle school education (MAT); multidisciplinary studies (MAT); multimodal literacy for global impact (MA); reading (MA); secondary school education (MAT); special education (MA, MAT); teaching English as a second language (MA); transformative learning in the global community (Ed S). *Program availability:* Part-time. *Entrance requirements:* For master's, minimum GPA of 2.5. Additional exam requirements/recommendations for international students: Required—TOEFL. *Application deadline:* Applications are processed on a rolling basis. Application fee: $35 ($50 for international students). *Expenses: Tuition:* Full-time $21,900; part-time $730 per credit hour. Tuition and fees vary according to campus/location and program. *Financial support:* Federal Work-Study available. Support available to part-time students. Financial award application deadline: 4/1; financial award applicants required to submit FAFSA. *Unit head:* Dr. Deborah Stiles, Chair, 314-968-7056, Fax: 314-968-7118, E-mail: stilesda@webster.edu.

West Virginia University, College of Education and Human Services, Department of Technology, Learning and Culture, Program in Educational Psychology, Morgantown, WV 26506. Offers MA. *Accreditation:* NCATE. *Program availability:* Evening/weekend. *Degree requirements:* For master's, thesis, content exams. *Entrance requirements:* For master's, GRE General Test (minimum score 1100 verbal and quantitative) or MAT (minimum score 55), minimum GPA of 3.0, interview. Additional exam requirements/recommendations for international students: Required—TOEFL (minimum score 550 paper-based). *Faculty research:* Learning, development, instructional design, stimulus control, rehabilitation.

Wichita State University, Graduate School, College of Education, Department of Counseling, Educational Leadership, Educational and School Psychology, Wichita, KS 67260. Offers counseling (M Ed); educational leadership (M Ed, Ed D); educational psychology (M Ed); school psychology (Ed S). *Accreditation:* NCATE. *Program availability:* Part-time, evening/weekend. Application fee: $50 ($65 for international students). *Unit head:* Dr. Jody Fiorini, Department Head, 316-978-3325, Fax: 316-978-3102, E-mail: jody.fiorini@wichita.edu. *Application contact:* Jordan Oleson, Admissions Coordinator, 316-978-3095, Fax: 316-978-3253, E-mail: jordan.oleson@wichita.edu.
Website: http://www.wichita.edu/cles

Widener University, School of Education, Hospitality, and Continuing Studies, Chester, PA 19013-5792. Offers adult education (M Ed); counseling in higher education (M Ed); counselor education (M Ed); early childhood education (M Ed); educational foundations (M Ed); educational leadership (M Ed); educational psychology (M Ed); elementary education (M Ed); English and language arts (M Ed); health education (M Ed); higher education leadership (Ed D); home and school visitor (M Ed); human sexuality (M Ed, PhD); mathematics education (M Ed); middle school education (M Ed); principalship (M Ed); reading and language arts (Ed D); reading education (M Ed); school administration (Ed D); science education (M Ed); social studies education (M Ed); special education (M Ed); technology education (M Ed). *Accreditation:* NCATE. *Program availability:* Part-time, evening/weekend. *Faculty:* 34 full-time (22 women), 37 part-time/adjunct (14 women). *Students:* 97 full-time (64 women), 201 part-time (143 women); includes 56 minority (44 Black or African American, non-Hispanic/Latino; 1 American Indian or Alaska Native, non-Hispanic/Latino; 2 Asian, non-Hispanic/Latino; 8 Hispanic/Latino; 1 Two or more races, non-Hispanic/Latino), 32 international. Average age 39. 139 applicants, 88% accepted. In 2016, 45 master's, 21 doctorates awarded. Terminal master's awarded for partial completion of doctoral program. *Degree requirements:* For doctorate, thesis/dissertation. *Entrance requirements:* For master's, minimum GPA of 2.5; for doctorate, GRE or MAT, minimum GPA of 2.0 (undergraduate), 3.5 (graduate). *Application deadline:* Applications are processed on a rolling basis. Application fee: $25 ($300 for international students). Electronic applications accepted. *Expenses:* Contact institution. *Financial support:* Career-related internships or fieldwork, tuition waivers (full and partial), and unspecified assistantships available. Support available to part-time students. Financial award application deadline: 5/1. *Faculty research:* Reading and cognition, adult education, technology education, educational leadership, special education. *Unit head:* Dr. Shawn Fitzgerald, Dean, 610-499-4294, Fax: 610-499-4623, E-mail: smfitzgerald@widener.edu. *Application contact:* Dr. Roberta Nolan, Director of Graduate Admissions, 610-499-4125, E-mail: rdnolan@widener.edu.
Website: http://www.widener.edu/academics/schools/eics

Foundations and Philosophy of Education

Antioch University New England, Graduate School, Department of Education, Experienced Educators Program, Keene, NH 03431-3552. Offers foundations of education (M Ed), including applied behavioral analysis, autism spectrum disorders, educating for sustainability, next-generation learning using technology, problem-based learning using critical skills, teacher leadership; principal certification (PMC). *Degree requirements:* For master's, thesis, practicum. *Entrance requirements:* For master's, previous course work and work experience in education. Additional exam requirements/recommendations for international students: Required—TOEFL (minimum score 550 paper-based). Electronic applications accepted. *Expenses:* Contact institution. *Faculty research:* Classroom action research, school restructuring, problem-based learning, brain-based learning.

Arkansas State University, Graduate School, College of Education and Behavioral Science, School of Teacher Education and Leadership, State University, AR 72467. Offers community college administration (SCCT); curriculum and instruction (MSE); early childhood education (MSE); early childhood services (MS); educational leadership (MSE, Ed D, Ed S); educational theory and practice (MSE); middle level education (MAT, MSE); reading (MSE, Ed S); special education - gifted, talented, and creative (MSE); special education - instructional specialist grades 4-12 (MSE); special education - instructional specialist grades P-4 (MSE); special education, K-12 (MSE). *Accreditation:* NCATE. *Program availability:* Part-time, online learning. *Degree requirements:* For master's, comprehensive exam, thesis or alternative; for doctorate, comprehensive exam, thesis/dissertation; for other advanced degree, comprehensive exam. *Entrance requirements:* For master's, GRE General Test or MAT, appropriate bachelor's degree, official transcripts, immunization records, letters of reference, interview; for doctorate, GRE General Test or MAT, interview, master's degree, letters of reference, official transcript, personal statement, writing sample, immunization records; for other advanced degree, GRE General Test or MAT, interview, master's degree, official transcript, immunization records, letters of reference, 3 years of teaching experience, teaching license. Additional exam requirements/recommendations for international students: Required—TOEFL (minimum score 550 paper-based; 79 iBT), IELTS (minimum score 6), PTE (minimum score 56). Electronic applications accepted.

Ashland University, Dwight Schar College of Education, Department of Educational Foundations and Instruction, Ashland, OH 44805-3702. Offers educational technology (M Ed); literacy (M Ed); teaching and learning in the 21st century (M Ed). *Program availability:* Part-time, evening/weekend. *Degree requirements:* For master's, inquiry seminar, internship, or thesis. *Entrance requirements:* For master's, teaching certificate or license, bachelor's degree, minimum cumulative GPA of 2.75. Additional exam requirements/recommendations for international students: Required—TOEFL. *Application deadline:* Applications are processed on a rolling basis. Application fee: $30. Electronic applications accepted. *Financial support:* Application deadline: 4/15. *Faculty research:* Character education, teacher reflection, religion and education, professional education, environmental education. *Unit head:* Dr. Louise Fleming, Chair, 419-289-5347, E-mail: lfleming@ashland.edu. *Application contact:* Dr. Linda Billman, Associate Dean, 419-289-5369, Fax: 419-289-5331, E-mail: lbillman@ashland.edu.
Website: http://www.ashland.edu/academics/education/edfoundations/

Azusa Pacific University, School of Education, Department of Foundations and Transdisciplinary Studies, Azusa, CA 91702-7000. Offers curriculum and instruction in multicultural contexts (MA Ed); teaching (MA Ed).

Ball State University, Graduate School, Teachers College, Department of Educational Studies, Program in Educational Studies, Muncie, IN 47306. Offers educational studies (PhD), including cultural and educational policy studies, curriculum, educational technology. *Program availability:* Part-time, blended/hybrid learning. *Degree requirements:* For doctorate, thesis/dissertation. *Entrance requirements:* For doctorate, GRE General Test, minimum graduate GPA of 3.2, curriculum vitae, writing sample, three letters of reference. Additional exam requirements/recommendations for international students: Required—TOEFL (minimum score 550 paper-based; 79 iBT), IELTS (minimum score 6.5). Electronic applications accepted. *Faculty research:* Emerging curriculum trends, secondary teacher preparation, issues of equity and social justice in education, teacher technology integration, teaching for transformative understanding, teacher leadership, history of educational policy and practices, ethics and education.

Bank Street College of Education, Graduate School, Studies in Education Program, New York, NY 10025. Offers Ed M, MS Ed. *Degree requirements:* For master's, thesis. *Entrance requirements:* For master's, interview, essays. Additional exam requirements/recommendations for international students: Required—TOEFL (minimum score 600 paper-based; 100 iBT), IELTS (minimum score 7). Electronic applications accepted.

Binghamton University, State University of New York, Graduate School, Graduate School of Education, Program in Educational Theory and Practice, Binghamton, NY 13902-6000. Offers educational leadership (Certificate); educational studies (MS); educational theory and practice (Ed D). MS program also offered for working teachers in Greater New Orleans. *Program availability:* Part-time. *Students:* 5 full-time (3 women), 66 part-time (55 women); includes 7 minority (4 Black or African American, non-Hispanic/Latino; 1 American Indian or Alaska Native, non-Hispanic/Latino; 1 Asian, non-Hispanic/Latino; 1 Hispanic/Latino), 5 international. Average age 43. 30 applicants, 97% accepted, 18 enrolled. In 2016, 9 master's, 4 doctorates, 9 other advanced degrees awarded. *Degree requirements:* For master's, thesis; for doctorate, thesis/dissertation. *Entrance requirements:* For doctorate, GRE General Test; for Certificate, teaching certification. Additional exam requirements/recommendations for international students: Required—TOEFL (minimum score 550 paper-based; 80 iBT). *Application deadline:* For fall admission, 2/1 priority date for domestic and international students. Application fee: $75. Electronic applications accepted. *Financial support:* In 2016–17, 11 students received support, including 1 fellowship with full tuition reimbursement available (averaging $15,500 per year), 3 teaching assistantships with full tuition reimbursements available (averaging $15,500 per year); career-related internships or fieldwork, Federal Work-Study, institutionally sponsored loans, scholarships/grants, health care benefits, tuition waivers (full and partial), and unspecified assistantships also available. Financial award applicants required to submit FAFSA. *Unit head:* Dr. Susan Strehle, Dean, 607-777-7329, E-mail: sstrehle@binghamton.edu. *Application contact:* Ben Balkaya, Assistant Dean and Director, 607-777-2151, Fax: 607-777-2501, E-mail: balkaya@binghamton.edu.
Website: http://www2.binghamton.edu/gse/doctoral-program/index.html

Brigham Young University, Graduate Studies, David O. McKay School of Education, Department of Educational Leadership and Foundations, Provo, UT 84602. Offers educational leadership and foundations (Ed D); educational leadership: education policy and social foundations (M Ed); educational leadership: school leadership (M Ed). *Program availability:* Part-time, evening/weekend. *Faculty:* 11 full-time (2 women), 1 part-time/adjunct (0 women). *Students:* 44 full-time (16 women), 26 part-time (14 women); includes 10 minority (4 Asian, non-Hispanic/Latino; 2 Hispanic/Latino; 2 Native Hawaiian or other Pacific Islander, non-Hispanic/Latino; 2 Two or more races, non-Hispanic/Latino), 3 international. Average age 42. 82 applicants, 46% accepted, 38 enrolled. In 2016, 24 master's, 6 doctorates awarded. Terminal master's awarded for partial completion of doctoral program. *Degree requirements:* For master's, comprehensive exam; for doctorate, comprehensive exam, thesis/dissertation, prospectus. *Entrance requirements:* For master's and doctorate, GRE, LSAT, or GMAT. Additional exam requirements/recommendations for international students: Required—TOEFL (minimum score 580 paper-based; 85 iBT). *Application deadline:* For fall admission, 5/1 for domestic students, 2/15 for international students; for spring admission, 1/15 for domestic students, 2/15 for international students; for summer admission, 3/1 for domestic and international students. Application fee: $50. Electronic applications accepted. *Expenses:* $393 per credit. *Financial support:* In 2016–17, 15 students received support. Research assistantships available. Financial award application deadline: 8/15. *Unit head:* Pamela Hallam, Chair, 801-422-3600, Fax: 801-422-0196, E-mail: pam_hallam@byu.edu. *Application contact:* Michele Price, Department Secretary, 801-422-3813, Fax: 801-422-0196, E-mail: michele_price@byu.edu.
Website: http://education.byu.edu/edlf/

Central Washington University, Graduate Studies and Research, College of Education and Professional Studies, Department of Educational Foundations and Curriculum, Ellensburg, WA 98926. Offers master teacher (M Ed). *Program availability:* Part-time. *Degree requirements:* For master's, comprehensive exam (for some programs), thesis or alternative. *Entrance requirements:* For master's, 1 year contracted teaching experience. Additional exam requirements/recommendations for international students: Required—TOEFL (minimum score 550 paper-based; 79 iBT), IELTS (minimum score 6.5). Electronic applications accepted.

Chicago State University, School of Graduate and Professional Studies, College of Education, Department of Educational Leadership, Curriculum and Foundations, Program in Curriculum and Instruction, Chicago, IL 60628. Offers instructional foundations (MS Ed). *Degree requirements:* For master's, comprehensive exam, thesis optional. *Entrance requirements:* For master's, minimum GPA of 2.75.

College of Staten Island of the City University of New York, Graduate Programs, School of Education, Program in Childhood Education, Staten Island, NY 10314-6600. Offers learning and development (MS Ed); literacy education (MS Ed); mathematics education (MS Ed); music education (MS Ed); science education (MS Ed); social foundations of education (MS Ed); social studies education (MS Ed). *Program availability:* Part-time, evening/weekend. *Faculty:* 2 full-time, 11 part-time/adjunct. *Students:* 16 full-time, 53 part-time. Average age 30. 40 applicants, 53% accepted, 13 enrolled. In 2016, 20 master's awarded. *Degree requirements:* For master's, educational research project; ten courses and a minimum of 32-38 credits in five required areas of study or minimum of 45-49 credits in six required core courses before selecting from array of advanced courses. *Entrance requirements:* For master's, GRE General Test or an approved equivalent examination, relevant bachelor's degree, letters of recommendation, one- or two-page personal statement. Additional exam requirements/recommendations for international students: Required—TOEFL (minimum score 550 paper-based; 79 iBT), IELTS (minimum score 6.5). *Application deadline:* For fall admission, 4/25 for domestic and international students; for spring admission, 11/25 for domestic and international students. Applications are processed on a rolling basis. Application fee: $125. Electronic applications accepted. *Expenses:* Tuition, state resident: full-time $10,130; part-time $425 per credit. Tuition, nonresident: full-time $18,720; part-time $780 per credit. *Required fees:* $181.10 per semester. Tuition and fees vary according to program. *Faculty research:* Preservice teacher preparation, music integration, music education through children's songs, literacy, emergent bilingual. *Unit head:* Dr. Vivian Shulman, Graduate Faculty Advisor, 718-982-4086, E-mail: vivian.shulman@csi.cuny.edu. *Application contact:* Sasha Spence, Associate Director for Graduate Admissions, 718-982-2019, Fax: 718-982-2500, E-mail: sasha.spence@csi.cuny.edu.
Website: http://www.csi.cuny.edu/admissions/grad/pdf/Education%20Fact%20Sheet.pdf

Columbia University, Graduate School of Arts and Sciences, New York, NY 10027. Offers African-American studies (MA); American studies (MA); anthropology (MA, PhD); art history and archaeology (MA, PhD); astronomy (PhD); biological sciences (PhD); biotechnology (MA); chemical physics (PhD); chemistry (PhD); classical studies (MA, PhD); classics (MA, PhD); climate and society (MA); conservation biology (MA); earth and environmental sciences (PhD); East Asia: regional studies (MA); East Asian languages and cultures (MA, PhD); ecology, evolution and environmental biology (MA), including conservation biology; ecology, evolution, and environmental biology (PhD), including ecology and evolutionary biology, evolutionary primatology; economics (MA, PhD); English and comparative literature (MA, PhD); French and Romance philology (MA, PhD); Germanic languages (MA, PhD); global French studies (MA); global thought (MA); Hispanic cultural studies (MA); history (PhD); history and literature (MA); human rights studies (MA); Islamic studies (MA); Italian (MA, PhD); Japanese pedagogy (MA); Jewish studies (MA); Latin America and the Caribbean: regional studies (MA); Latin American and Iberian cultures (PhD); mathematics (MA, PhD), including finance (MA); medieval and Renaissance studies (MA); Middle Eastern, South Asian, and African studies (MA, PhD); modern art: critical and curatorial studies (MA); modern European studies (MA); museum anthropology (MA); music (DMA, PhD); oral history (MA); philosophical foundations of physics (MA); philosophy (MA, PhD); physics (PhD); political science (MA, PhD); psychology (PhD); quantitative methods in the social sciences (MA); religion (MA, PhD); Russia, Eurasia and East Europe: regional studies (MA); Russian translation (MA); Slavic cultures (MA); Slavic languages (MA, PhD); sociology (MA, PhD); South Asian studies (MA); statistics (MA, PhD); theatre (PhD). Dual-degree programs require admission to both Graduate School of Arts and Sciences and another Columbia school. *Program availability:* Part-time. Terminal master's awarded for partial completion of doctoral program. *Degree requirements:* For master's, variable foreign language requirement, comprehensive exam (for some programs), thesis (for some programs); for doctorate, variable foreign language requirement, comprehensive exam (for some programs), thesis/dissertation. *Entrance requirements:* For master's and doctorate, GRE General Test, GRE Subject Test (for some programs). Additional exam requirements/recommendations for international students: Required—TOEFL, IELTS. Electronic applications accepted.

Curry College, Graduate Studies, Program in Education, Milton, MA 02186-9984. Offers elementary education (M Ed); foundations (non-license) (M Ed); reading (M Ed, Certificate); special education (M Ed). *Program availability:* Part-time, evening/weekend. *Degree requirements:* For master's, project or thesis. *Entrance requirements:* For master's, interview, recommendations, resume, written statement. Additional exam requirements/recommendations for international students: Required—TOEFL (minimum score 550 paper-based; 80 iBT). *Expenses:* Contact institution. *Faculty research:* Classroom trauma, therapeutic writing, inclusionary practices.

DePaul University, College of Education, Chicago, IL 60614. Offers bilingual bicultural education (M Ed, MA); counseling (M Ed, MA), including clinical mental health counseling, college student development, school counseling; curriculum studies (M Ed, MA, Ed D); early childhood education (M Ed, MA, Ed D); educating adults (MA); educational leadership (M Ed, MA, Ed D), including administration and supervision (M Ed, MA), principal preparation (M Ed, MA); elementary education (MA); mathematics education (MA); mathematics for teaching (MS); middle school mathematics education (MS); reading specialist (M Ed, MA); secondary education (M Ed); social and cultural foundations in education (MA); special education (M Ed, MA); world languages education (M Ed, MA). *Program availability:* Part-time, evening/weekend, online learning. *Degree requirements:* For doctorate, thesis/dissertation. Electronic applications accepted.

Duquesne University, School of Education, Department of Educational Foundations and Leadership, Program in Educational Studies, Pittsburgh, PA 15282-0001. Offers educational studies (MS Ed); program evaluation (MS Ed). *Program availability:* Part-time, evening/weekend, 100% online. *Faculty:* 1 full-time (0 women). *Students:* 10 full-time (8 women), 11 part-time (8 women); includes 6 minority (5 Black or African American, non-Hispanic/Latino; 1 Hispanic/Latino), 11 international. Average age 34. 17 applicants, 94% accepted, 4 enrolled. In 2016, 10 master's awarded. *Degree requirements:* For master's, thesis optional. *Entrance requirements:* For master's, bachelor's degree. Additional exam requirements/recommendations for international students: Required—TOEFL (minimum score 550 paper-based), IELTS (minimum score 7). *Application deadline:* For fall admission, 9/1 for domestic students; for spring admission, 1/1 for domestic students. Applications are processed on a rolling basis. Application fee: $0. Electronic applications accepted. *Expenses: Tuition:* Full-time $22,212; part-time $1234 per credit. Tuition and fees vary according to program. *Financial support:* Research assistantships available. Support available to part-time students. *Unit head:* Dr. Gibbs Kanyongo, Associate Professor, 412-396-5190, Fax: 412-396-5454, E-mail: kanyongog@duq.edu. *Application contact:* Michael Dolinger, Director of Student and Academic Services, 412-396-6647, Fax: 412-396-5585, E-mail: dolingerm@duq.edu.

Eastern Michigan University, Graduate School, College of Education, Department of Teacher Education, Program in Social Foundations, Ypsilanti, MI 48197. Offers MA. *Accreditation:* NCATE. *Program availability:* Part-time, evening/weekend, online learning. *Students:* 12 part-time (9 women); includes 2 minority (both Hispanic/Latino), 1 international. Average age 31. 8 applicants, 100% accepted, 1 enrolled. In 2016, 2 master's awarded. *Entrance requirements:* For master's, GRE. Additional exam requirements/recommendations for international students: Required—TOEFL. *Application deadline:* Applications are processed on a rolling basis. Application fee: $45. *Financial support:* Fellowships, research assistantships with full tuition reimbursements, teaching assistantships with full tuition reimbursements, career-related internships or fieldwork, Federal Work-Study, institutionally sponsored loans, scholarships/grants, tuition waivers (partial), and unspecified assistantships available. Support available to part-time students. Financial award applicants required to submit FAFSA. *Application contact:* Dr. Paul Ramsey, Coordinator, 734-487-3260, Fax: 734-487-2101, E-mail: pramsey1@emich.edu.

Eastern Washington University, Graduate Studies, College of Arts, Letters and Education, Department of Education, Program in Educational Foundations, Cheney, WA 99004-2431. Offers M Ed. *Degree requirements:* For master's, comprehensive exam. *Entrance requirements:* For master's, minimum GPA of 3.0. *Expenses:* Tuition, state resident: full-time $11,000; part-time $5500 per credit. Tuition, nonresident: full-time $24,000; part-time $12,000 per credit. *Required fees:* $1300. One-time fee: $50 full-time. Part-time tuition and fees vary according to course load, campus/location and program.

Fairfield University, Graduate School of Education and Allied Professions, Fairfield, CT 06824. Offers applied behavior analysis (ATC); applied psychology (MA); clinical mental health counseling (MA, CAS); educational technology (MA); elementary education (MA, CAS); family studies (MA); integration of spirituality and religion in counseling (ATC); marriage and family therapy (MA); reading and language development (Sixth Year Certificate); school counseling (MA, CAS); school psychology (MA, CAS); school-based marriage and family therapy (ATC); secondary education (MA); special education (MA, CAS); substance abuse counseling (ATC); teaching (Certificate); teaching and foundations (MA, CAS); TESOL, world languages, and bilingual education (MA, CAS). *Accreditation:* NCATE. *Program availability:* Part-time, evening/weekend. *Faculty:* 19 full-time (15 women), 38 part-time/adjunct (26 women). *Students:* 153 full-time (132 women), 302 part-time (252 women); includes 97 minority (24 Black or African American, non-Hispanic/Latino; 12 Asian, non-Hispanic/Latino; 55 Hispanic/Latino; 6 Two or more races, non-Hispanic/Latino), 6 international. Average age 32. 283 applicants, 61% accepted, 97 enrolled. In 2016, 130 master's awarded. *Degree requirements:* For master's, comprehensive exam. *Entrance requirements:* For master's, minimum GPA of 3.0, 2 recommendations, resume. Additional exam requirements/recommendations for international students: Required—TOEFL (minimum score 550 paper-based; 84 iBT) or IELTS (minimum score 7.5). *Application deadline:* For fall admission, 2/15 for international students; for spring admission, 10/1 for international students. Application fee: $60. Electronic applications accepted. *Expenses:* $725 per credit hour. *Financial support:* In 2016–17, 42 students received support. Career-related internships or fieldwork and unspecified assistantships available. Support available to part-time students. Financial award applicants required to submit FAFSA. *Faculty research:* Reading and literacy, writing, social justice and inequality in education, addictions and mental health issues, therapeutic relationships and clinical supervision. *Unit head:* Dr. Robert D. Hannafin, Dean, 203-254-4250, Fax: 203-254-4241, E-mail: rhannafin@fairfield.edu. *Application contact:* Marianne Gumpper, Director of Graduate Admission, 203-254-4184, Fax: 203-254-4073, E-mail: gradadmis@fairfield.edu.
Website: http://www.fairfield.edu/gseap

Fairleigh Dickinson University, Metropolitan Campus, University College: Arts, Sciences, and Professional Studies, School of Computer Sciences and Engineering, Program in Mathematical Foundation, Teaneck, NJ 07666-1914. Offers MS.

Florida Atlantic University, College of Education, Department of Teaching and Learning, Boca Raton, FL 33431-0991. Offers curriculum and instruction (M Ed), including art, biology, chemistry, English, French, German, mathematics, music, physics, Pre-K and primary education, reading, social sciences, Spanish; elementary education (M Ed); environmental education (M Ed); reading education (M Ed); social foundations of education (M Ed), including educational psychology, educational technology, multilingual education. *Accreditation:* NCATE. *Program availability:* Part-time, evening/weekend. *Faculty:* 15 full-time (12 women), 2 part-time/adjunct (1 woman). *Students:* 25 full-time (20 women), 41 part-time (37 women); includes 18 minority (9 Black or African American, non-Hispanic/Latino; 2 Asian, non-Hispanic/Latino; 7 Hispanic/Latino), 7 international. Average age 32. 54 applicants, 59% accepted, 18 enrolled. In 2016, 36 master's awarded. *Entrance requirements:* For master's, GRE General Test, minimum GPA of 3.0 in last 2 years of undergraduate course work. Additional exam requirements/recommendations for international students: Required—TOEFL (minimum score 500 paper-based; 61 iBT), IELTS (minimum score 6). *Application deadline:* For fall admission, 7/1 for domestic students, 2/15 for international students; for spring admission, 11/1 for domestic students, 7/15 for international students. Applications are processed on a rolling basis. Application fee: $30. *Expenses:* Tuition, state resident: full-time $7392; part-time $369.82 per credit hour. Tuition, nonresident: full-time $19,432; part-time $1024.81 per credit hour. *Financial support:* Fellowships with partial tuition reimbursements, research assistantships with partial tuition reimbursements, teaching assistantships with partial tuition reimbursements, career-related internships or fieldwork, scholarships/grants, and unspecified assistantships available. *Faculty research:* Technology, teaching English to speakers of other languages, math teaching, electronic portfolio assessment, global perspectives through social studies. *Unit head:* Dr. Barbara Ridener, Chairperson, 561-297-3588, E-mail: bridener@fau.edu. *Application contact:* Dr. Eliah Watlington, Associate Dean, 561-296-8520, Fax: 261-297-2991, E-mail: ewatling@fau.edu.
Website: http://www.coe.fau.edu/academicdepartments/tl/

Florida State University, The Graduate School, College of Education, Program in Foundations of Education, Tallahassee, FL 32306. Offers social, historical and philosophical foundations of education (MS, PhD); sociocultural and international development education studies (MS, Ed D, PhD). *Program availability:* Part-time, evening/weekend. Terminal master's awarded for partial completion of doctoral program. *Degree requirements:* For master's, comprehensive exam, thesis optional; for doctorate, comprehensive exam, thesis/dissertation, diagnostic exam, preliminary exam, prospectus defense, dissertation defense. *Entrance requirements:* For master's and doctorate, GRE General Test, minimum upper-division GPA of 3.0. Additional exam requirements/recommendations for international students: Required—TOEFL (minimum score 550 paper-based, 80 iBT), IELTS (minimum score 6.5), Michigan English Language Assessment Battery (minimum score 77), or PTE (minimum score 55). Application fee: $30. Electronic applications accepted. *Expenses:* Tuition, state resident: full-time $7263; part-time $403.51 per credit hour. Tuition, nonresident: full-time $18,087; part-time $1004.85 per credit hour. *Required fees:* $1365; $75.81 per credit hour. $20 per semester. Tuition and fees vary according to campus/location. *Financial support:* Fellowships, research assistantships, teaching assistantships, scholarships/grants, tuition waivers (full and partial), and unspecified assistantships available. Financial award application deadline: 1/15; financial award applicants required

to submit FAFSA. *Faculty research:* Socio-cultural foundations of education, policy and politics of international and comparative education; design, management, and evaluation of international education projects; issues of educational equity and equality in domestic and international educational settings, philosophy of education. *Unit head:* Dr. Ayesha Khurshid, Assistant Professor/Program Coordinator, 850-644-7078, Fax: 850-644-1258, E-mail: akhurshid@fsu.edu. *Application contact:* Linda J. Lyons, Academic Support Assistant, 850-644-7077, Fax: 850-644-1258, E-mail: ljlyons@fsu.edu.
Website: http://education.fsu.edu/degrees-and-programs/graduate-programs

Georgia State University, College of Education and Human Development, Department of Educational Policy Studies, Program in Social Foundations of Education, Atlanta, GA 30302-3083. Offers MS, PhD. *Accreditation:* NCATE. *Program availability:* Part-time. *Degree requirements:* For master's, 36 semester hours, thesis or project; for doctorate, comprehensive exam, thesis/dissertation, 69 semester hours. *Entrance requirements:* For master's and doctorate, GRE. Additional exam requirements/recommendations for international students: Required—TOEFL (minimum score 550 paper-based; 79 iBT) or IELTS (minimum score 6.5). *Application deadline:* For fall admission, 1/15 for domestic and international students; for winter admission, 2/1 for domestic students; for spring admission, 10/1 for domestic and international students. Applications are processed on a rolling basis. Application fee: $50. Electronic applications accepted. *Expenses:* Tuition, state resident: full-time $6876; part-time $382 per credit hour. Tuition, nonresident: full-time $22,374; part-time $1243 per credit hour. *Required fees:* $2128; $1064 per term. Part-time tuition and fees vary according to course load and program. *Financial support:* In 2016–17, research assistantships with full tuition reimbursements (averaging $10,886 per year) were awarded; fellowships, teaching assistantships with full tuition reimbursements, career-related internships or fieldwork, institutionally sponsored loans, scholarships/grants, health care benefits, tuition waivers, and unspecified assistantships also available. Financial award application deadline: 3/15. *Faculty research:* Social and cultural influences on schools, globalization and the workforce, history of women teachers in the U.S., school-corporate nexus, curriculum transformation for equity and inclusion. *Unit head:* Dr. Richard Lakes, Professor, 404-413-8030, Fax: 404-413-8003, E-mail: rlakes@gsu.edu. *Application contact:* Aishah Cowan, Administrative Academic Specialist, 404-413-8273, Fax: 404-413-8033, E-mail: acowan@gsu.edu.
Website: http://eps.education.gsu.edu/programs-courses/social-foundations-education/ms-sfd/

Harvard University, Extension School, Cambridge, MA 02138-3722. Offers applied sciences (CAS); biotechnology (ALM); educational technologies (ALM); educational technology (CET); English for graduate and professional studies (DGP); environmental management (ALM, CEM); information technology (ALM); journalism (ALM); liberal arts (ALM); management (ALM, CM); mathematics for teaching (ALM); museum studies (ALM); premedical studies (Diploma); publication and communication (CPC). *Program availability:* Part-time, evening/weekend. *Degree requirements:* For master's, thesis. *Entrance requirements:* For master's, 3 completed graduate courses with grade of B or higher. Additional exam requirements/recommendations for international students: Required—TOEFL (minimum score 600 paper-based), TWE (minimum score 5). *Expenses:* Contact institution.

Indiana University Bloomington, School of Education, Department of Educational Leadership and Policy Studies, Bloomington, IN 47405. Offers educational leadership (MS, Ed D, Ed S); higher education (Ed D, PhD); higher education and student affairs (MS); history and philosophy of education (MS); history, philosophy, and policy in education (PhD), including education policy studies, history of education, philosophy of education; international and comparative education (MS). *Accreditation:* NCATE. *Faculty:* 32 full-time (18 women). *Students:* 223 full-time (140 women), 94 part-time (50 women); includes 80 minority (44 Black or African American, non-Hispanic/Latino; 13 Asian, non-Hispanic/Latino; 18 Hispanic/Latino; 1 Native Hawaiian or other Pacific Islander, non-Hispanic/Latino; 4 Two or more races, non-Hispanic/Latino), 29 international. Average age 34. 309 applicants, 40% accepted, 57 enrolled. In 2016, 60 master's, 18 doctorates, 5 other advanced degrees awarded. *Degree requirements:* For master's, thesis optional; for doctorate, comprehensive exam, thesis/dissertation; for Ed S, comprehensive exam or project. *Entrance requirements:* For master's, doctorate, and Ed S, GRE General Test. Additional exam requirements/recommendations for international students: Required—TOEFL (minimum score 79 iBT). *Application deadline:* For fall admission, 1/15 priority date for domestic students, 12/1 priority date for international students; for spring admission, 9/1 priority date for domestic and international students. Applications are processed on a rolling basis. Application fee: $55 ($65 for international students). Electronic applications accepted. *Financial support:* Fellowships with full and partial tuition reimbursements, research assistantships with full and partial tuition reimbursements, teaching assistantships with full and partial tuition reimbursements, career-related internships or fieldwork, scholarships/grants, health care benefits, and unspecified assistantships available. *Faculty research:* Culturally engaging campus environments, school choice policy analysis, democracy and education in the national and international context, and principal leadership. *Unit head:* Dr. Dionne Danns, Interim Chair, 812-856-8398. *Application contact:* Maria Jensen, Department Administrator, 812-856-8370, Fax: 812-856-8394, E-mail: jensen5@indiana.edu.
Website: http://education.indiana.edu/about/departments/leadership/index.html

Indiana University Bloomington, University Graduate School, College of Arts and Sciences, School of Global and International Studies, Department of East Asian Languages and Cultures, Bloomington, IN 47408. Offers Chinese (MA, PhD); Chinese language pedagogy (MA); East Asian studies (MA); Japanese (MA, PhD); Japanese language pedagogy (MA). *Program availability:* Part-time. *Degree requirements:* For master's, one foreign language, thesis; for doctorate, 2 foreign languages, comprehensive exam, thesis/dissertation. *Entrance requirements:* Additional exam requirements/recommendations for international students: Required—TOEFL (minimum score 93 iBT). Electronic applications accepted. *Faculty research:* Modern East Asian history; politics and society; traditional Chinese thought and society; medieval and premodern Japanese history, literature and society; modern Chinese and Japanese film and literature; Chinese, Japanese, Korean language and linguistics.

Iowa State University of Science and Technology, Department of Education, Ames, IA 50011. Offers curriculum and instructional technology (M Ed, MS, PhD); elementary education (M Ed, MS); historical, philosophical, and comparative studies in education (M Ed, MS); special education (M Ed, MS, PhD). *Degree requirements:* For master's, thesis or alternative; for doctorate, thesis/dissertation. *Entrance requirements:* For master's and doctorate, GRE General Test. Additional exam requirements/recommendations for international students: Required—TOEFL (minimum score 560 paper-based; 83 iBT), IELTS (minimum score 6.5). *Application deadline:* For fall admission, 1/1 priority date for domestic and international students; for spring admission, 9/1 for domestic and international students. Application fee: $60 ($90 for international students). Electronic applications accepted. *Application contact:* Robyn Goldy, Application Contact, 515-294-1241, Fax: 515-294-4942, E-mail: rgoldy@iastate.edu.
Website: http://www.ci.hs.iastate.edu

Johnson State College, Program in Education, Johnson, VT 05656. Offers applied behavior analysis (MA Ed); curriculum and instruction (MA Ed); foundations of education (MA Ed); special education (MA Ed). *Program availability:* Part-time. *Degree requirements:* For master's, thesis or alternative, exit interview. *Entrance requirements:* For master's, interview. Additional exam requirements/recommendations for international students: Required—TOEFL. *Application deadline:* For fall admission, 5/1 for domestic students, 2/1 for international students. Applications are processed on a rolling basis. Electronic applications accepted. *Expenses:* Tuition, state resident: part-time $555 per credit. Tuition, nonresident: part-time $800 per credit. *Financial support:* Scholarships/grants and unspecified assistantships available. Financial award application deadline: 3/1; financial award applicants required to submit FAFSA. *Unit head:* Dr. Kathleen Brinegar, Chair, Department of Education, 802-635-1472, Fax: 802-635-1465, E-mail: kathleen.brinegar@jsc.edu. *Application contact:* Catherine H. Higley, Administrative Assistant, 800-635-2356 Ext. 1244, Fax: 802-635-1248, E-mail: catherine.higley@jsc.edu.
Website: http://www.jsc.edu/academics/education/majors-and-minors/master-of-arts-in-education/

Kent State University, College of Education, Health and Human Services, School of Foundations, Leadership and Administration, Program in Cultural Foundations, Kent, OH 44242-0001. Offers M Ed, MA, PhD. *Accreditation:* NCATE. *Degree requirements:* For master's, thesis optional; for doctorate, comprehensive exam, thesis/dissertation. *Entrance requirements:* For master's, minimum GPA of 2.75, 2 letters of reference, goal statement; for doctorate, GRE General Test, minimum GPA of 3.5, master's degree, resume, interview, goal statement, 2 letters of reference. Additional exam requirements/recommendations for international students: Required—TOEFL (minimum score 550 paper-based; 80 iBT). Electronic applications accepted. *Expenses:* Tuition, state resident: full-time $10,864; part-time $495 per credit hour. Tuition, nonresident: full-time $18,380; part-time $837 per credit hour. *Faculty research:* Public politics, intercultural communication and training, research paradigms, comparative and international education.

Marquette University, Graduate School, College of Education, Department of Educational Policy and Leadership, Milwaukee, WI 53201-1881. Offers college student personnel administration (M Ed); curriculum and instruction (MA); education (MA); educational administration (M Ed); educational policy and foundations (MA); elementary education (Certificate); literacy (MA); principal (Certificate); reading specialist (Certificate); reading teacher (Certificate); secondary education (Certificate); superintendent (Certificate). *Program availability:* Part-time, evening/weekend. *Faculty:* 17 full-time (14 women), 28 part-time/adjunct (23 women). *Students:* 31 full-time (23 women), 103 part-time (66 women); includes 22 minority (7 Black or African American, non-Hispanic/Latino; 1 American Indian or Alaska Native, non-Hispanic/Latino; 6 Asian, non-Hispanic/Latino; 6 Hispanic/Latino; 2 Two or more races, non-Hispanic/Latino). Average age 31. 96 applicants, 92% accepted, 67 enrolled. In 2016, 47 master's, 3 other advanced degrees awarded. Terminal master's awarded for partial completion of doctoral program. *Degree requirements:* For master's, comprehensive exam, thesis (for some programs); for doctorate, thesis/dissertation, qualifying exam. *Entrance requirements:* For master's, GRE General Test or MAT, official transcripts from all current and previous colleges/universities except Marquette, three letters of recommendation, statement of purpose; for doctorate, GRE General Test, MAT, sample of written work, official transcripts from all current and previous colleges/universities except Marquette, three letters of recommendation, statement of purpose, resume/curriculum vitae; for Certificate, GRE General Test or MAT, master's degree. Additional exam requirements/recommendations for international students: Required—TOEFL (minimum score 530 paper-based). *Application deadline:* For fall admission, 1/15 for domestic and international students. Application fee: $50. *Expenses:* Contact institution. *Financial support:* Fellowships, research assistantships, health care benefits, tuition waivers (partial), and unspecified assistantships available. Support available to part-time students. Financial award application deadline: 2/15. *Faculty research:* Leadership; social justice in education; development of lifelong learners; race, class, and schooling in historical perspective; urban teacher education. *Unit head:* Dr. Ellen Eckman, Chair, 414-288-1561. *Application contact:* Dr. Cynthia Ellwood.

McGill University, Faculty of Graduate and Postdoctoral Studies, Faculty of Education, Department of Integrated Studies in Education, Montréal, QC H3A 2T5, Canada. Offers culture and values in education (MA, PhD); curriculum studies (MA); educational leadership (MA, Certificate); educational studies (PhD); integrated studies in education (M Ed); second language education (MA, PhD).

Mount Saint Vincent University, Graduate Programs, Faculty of Education, Program in Educational Foundations, Halifax, NS B3M 2J6, Canada. Offers M Ed, MA Ed, MA-R. *Program availability:* Part-time, evening/weekend. *Degree requirements:* For master's, thesis (for some programs). *Entrance requirements:* For master's, bachelor's degree in related field, minimum B average. Electronic applications accepted. *Faculty research:* Research paradigms, moral aspects of education and teaching, private/independent schools, theory of critical thinking, teachers as workers and as agents of social change.

New York University, Steinhardt School of Culture, Education, and Human Development, Department of Humanities and Social Sciences in the Professions, Program in History of Education, New York, NY 10003. Offers MA, PhD. *Program availability:* Part-time. *Degree requirements:* For master's, thesis (for some programs); for doctorate, thesis/dissertation. *Entrance requirements:* For doctorate, GRE General Test, interview. Additional exam requirements/recommendations for international students: Required—TOEFL (minimum score 100 iBT). Electronic applications accepted. *Faculty research:* American educational thought, democratic community and education, twentieth century history of education, Jewish history.

Northern Arizona University, Graduate College, College of Education, Department of Educational Leadership, Flagstaff, AZ 86011. Offers community college teaching and learning (Certificate); community college/higher education (M Ed); educational foundations (M Ed); educational leadership (M Ed, Ed D); principal (Certificate); principal K-12 (M Ed); school leadership K-12 (M Ed); superintendent (Certificate). *Program availability:* Part-time. *Degree requirements:* For master's, comprehensive exam, thesis (for some programs); for doctorate, comprehensive exam, thesis/dissertation. *Entrance requirements:* For master's, minimum GPA of 3.0; for doctorate, GRE or MAT, minimum GPA of 3.5. Additional exam requirements/recommendations for international students: Required—TOEFL (minimum score 550 paper-based; 80 iBT), IELTS (minimum score 7). Electronic applications accepted. *Expenses:* Tuition, state resident: full-time $8971; part-time $444 per credit hour. Tuition, nonresident: full-time $20,958; part-time $1164 per credit hour. *Required fees:* $1018; $644 per credit hour. Tuition and fees vary according to course load, campus/location and program.

Northern Illinois University, Graduate School, College of Education, Department of Leadership, Educational Psychology and Foundations, De Kalb, IL 60115-2854. Offers educational administration (MS Ed, Ed D, Ed S); educational psychology (MS Ed, Ed D); foundations of education (MS Ed); school business management (MS Ed). *Program availability:* Part-time, evening/weekend, online learning. *Faculty:* 23 full-time (12 women). *Students:* 13 full-time (8 women), 230 part-time (133 women); includes 33 minority (13 Black or African American, non-Hispanic/Latino; 3 Asian, non-Hispanic/Latino; 9 Hispanic/Latino; 8 Two or more races, non-Hispanic/Latino), 4 international.

Average age 39. 132 applicants, 43% accepted, 31 enrolled. In 2016, 36 master's, 30 doctorates, 17 other advanced degrees awarded. *Degree requirements:* For master's, comprehensive exam, thesis optional; for doctorate, thesis/dissertation, candidacy exam, dissertation defense. *Entrance requirements:* For master's, minimum undergraduate GPA of 2.75; for doctorate, GRE General Test, minimum undergraduate GPA of 2.75, 3.2 graduate; for Ed S, GRE General Test, minimum GPA of 2.75 (undergraduate), 3.2 (graduate). Additional exam requirements/recommendations for international students: Required—TOEFL (minimum score 550 paper-based). *Application deadline:* For fall admission, 6/1 for domestic students, 5/1 for international students; for spring admission, 11/1 for domestic students, 10/1 for international students. Applications are processed on a rolling basis. Application fee: $40. Electronic applications accepted. *Financial support:* In 2016–17, 4 research assistantships with full tuition reimbursements, 2 teaching assistantships with full tuition reimbursements were awarded; fellowships with full tuition reimbursements, career-related internships or fieldwork, Federal Work-Study, scholarships/grants, tuition waivers (full), and staff assistantships also available. Support available to part-time students. Financial award applicants required to submit FAFSA. *Faculty research:* Interpersonal forgiveness, learner-centered education, psychedelic studies, senior theory, professional growth. *Unit head:* Carolyn V. Schee, Chair, 815-753-4404, E-mail: lepf@niu.edu. *Application contact:* Graduate School Office, 815-753-0395, E-mail: gradsch@niu.edu.
Website: http://cedu.niu.edu/LEPF/

Penn State University Park, Graduate School, College of Education, Department of Education Policy Studies, University Park, PA 16802. Offers educational leadership (M Ed, D Ed, PhD, Certificate); educational theory and policy (MA, PhD); higher education (M Ed, MS, D Ed, PhD). *Accreditation:* NCATE. *Program availability:* Online learning. *Unit head:* Dr. David H. Monk, Dean, 814-865-2523, Fax: 814-865-0555. *Application contact:* Lori Hawn, Director, Graduate Student Services, 814-865-1795, Fax: 814-863-4627, E-mail: l-gswww@lists.psu.edu.
Website: http://ed.psu.edu/eps

Purdue University, Graduate School, College of Education, Department of Educational Studies, West Lafayette, IN 47907. Offers administration (MS Ed, PhD, Ed S); counseling and development (MS Ed, PhD); education of the gifted (MS Ed); educational psychology (MS Ed, PhD); foundations of education (MS Ed, PhD); higher education administration (MS Ed, PhD); special education (MS Ed, PhD). *Accreditation:* ACA (one or more programs are accredited); NCATE (one or more programs are accredited). *Program availability:* Part-time, evening/weekend. *Faculty:* 29 full-time (22 women), 1 part-time/adjunct (0 women). *Students:* 78 full-time (60 women), 226 part-time (162 women); includes 45 minority (16 Black or African American, non-Hispanic/Latino; 8 Asian, non-Hispanic/Latino; 15 Hispanic/Latino; 6 Two or more races, non-Hispanic/Latino), 45 international. Average age 32. 214 applicants, 53% accepted, 70 enrolled. In 2016, 38 master's, 20 doctorates, 4 other advanced degrees awarded. *Degree requirements:* For master's, thesis optional; for doctorate, thesis/dissertation, oral and written exams; for Ed S, oral presentation, project. *Entrance requirements:* For master's, GRE General Test (except for special education if undergraduate GPA is higher than a 3.0), minimum undergraduate GPA of 3.0; for doctorate and Ed S, GRE General Test (minimum combined score of 1000, 300 for new scoring), minimum undergraduate GPA of 3.0. Additional exam requirements/recommendations for international students: Required—TOEFL (minimum score 550 paper-based; 77 iBT), TWE (minimum score 5). *Application deadline:* Applications are processed on a rolling basis. Application fee: $60 ($75 for international students). Electronic applications accepted. *Financial support:* Fellowships with full tuition reimbursements, research assistantships with full tuition reimbursements, teaching assistantships with full tuition reimbursements, career-related internships or fieldwork, and tuition waivers (full) available. Support available to part-time students. Financial award application deadline: 3/1; financial award applicants required to submit FAFSA. *Faculty research:* Motivation, learning disabilities, school learning, group processes, cognitive development. *Unit head:* F. Richard Olenchak, Head, 765-494-9170, E-mail: olenchak@purdue.edu. *Application contact:* Heather Brinkman, Graduate Contact, 765-494-2345, Fax: 765-494-5832, E-mail: hbrinkma@purdue.edu.
Website: http://www.edst.purdue.edu/

Rutgers University–New Brunswick, Graduate School of Education, Department of Educational Theory, Policy and Administration, Program in Social and Philosophical Foundations of Education, Piscataway, NJ 08854-8097. Offers Ed M, Ed D. *Program availability:* Part-time, evening/weekend. *Degree requirements:* For doctorate, thesis/dissertation, qualifying exam. *Entrance requirements:* For master's, GRE General Test; for doctorate, GRE General Test, writing sample. Additional exam requirements/recommendations for international students: Required—TOEFL. Electronic applications accepted. *Faculty research:* Anthropology, history, sociology, philosophy, comparative education.

Saint Louis University, Graduate Education, College of Education and Public Service, Department of Educational Studies, St. Louis, MO 63103. Offers curriculum and instruction (MA, Ed D, PhD); educational foundations (MA, Ed D, PhD); special education (MA); teaching (MAT). *Accreditation:* NCATE. *Program availability:* Part-time. *Degree requirements:* For master's, comprehensive exam; for doctorate, comprehensive exam, thesis/dissertation, preliminary oral and written exams. *Entrance requirements:* For master's, GRE General Test or MAT, letters of recommendation, resume; for doctorate, GRE General Test, letters of recommendation, resumé, goal statement, transcripts. Additional exam requirements/recommendations for international students: Required—TOEFL (minimum score 525 paper-based). Electronic applications accepted. *Faculty research:* Teacher preparation, multicultural issues, children with special needs, qualitative research in education, inclusion.

Simon Fraser University, Office of Graduate Studies and Postdoctoral Fellows, Faculty of Education, Programs in Curriculum and Instruction, Burnaby, BC V5A 1S6, Canada. Offers curriculum and instruction (M Ed); curriculum and instruction foundations (M Ed, MA); curriculum theory and implementation (PhD); educational practice (M Ed); philosophy of education (PhD). *Faculty:* 15 full-time (3 women). *Degree requirements:* For master's, comprehensive exam (for some programs), thesis (for some programs); for doctorate, comprehensive exam, thesis/dissertation. *Entrance requirements:* For master's, minimum GPA of 3.0 (on scale of 4.33) or 3.33 based on last 60 credits of undergraduate courses; for doctorate, minimum GPA of 3.5 (on scale of 4.33). Additional exam requirements/recommendations for international students: Recommended—TOEFL (minimum score 580 paper-based; 93 iBT), IELTS (minimum score 7), TWE (minimum score 5). Application fee: $90 ($125 for international students). Electronic applications accepted. *Financial support:* Scholarships/grants available. *Faculty research:* Philosophy of education, applied and comparative epistemology, ethics and moral education, critical multicultural practices. *Unit head:* Dr. Shawn Bullock, Graduate Chair, 778-782-4102, E-mail: educadgs@sfu.ca. *Application contact:* Graduate Secretary, 778-782-4787, E-mail: educmast@sfu.ca.

Southern Illinois University Edwardsville, Graduate School, School of Education, Health, and Human Behavior, Department of Educational Leadership, Program in Learning, Culture, and Society, Edwardsville, IL 62026. Offers MS Ed. *Program availability:* Part-time, evening/weekend. *Degree requirements:* For master's, thesis or alternative, project, oral defense. *Entrance requirements:* Additional exam requirements/recommendations for international students: Required—TOEFL (minimum score 550 paper-based; 79 iBT), IELTS (minimum score 6.5). Electronic applications accepted.

Spring Hill College, Graduate Programs, Program in Education, Mobile, AL 36608-1791. Offers early childhood education (MAT, MS Ed); educational theory (MS Ed); elementary education (MAT, MS Ed); secondary education (MAT, MS Ed). *Program availability:* Part-time. *Faculty:* 3 full-time (all women). *Students:* 3 full-time (all women), 7 part-time (5 women); includes 1 minority (Black or African American, non-Hispanic/Latino). Average age 26. In 2016, 10 master's awarded. *Degree requirements:* For master's, comprehensive exam, completion of program within 6 calendar years of entrance into graduate studies at Spring Hill; documentation of course field assignments (MS) or completion of internship (MAT). *Entrance requirements:* For master's, GRE, MAT, or PRAXIS (varies by program), bachelor's degree with minimum undergraduate GPA of 3.0; class B certificate (for MS); minimum number of hours in specific fields (for MAT). Additional exam requirements/recommendations for international students: Required—TOEFL (minimum score 550 paper-based; 80 iBT), IELTS (minimum score 6.5), CPE or CAE (minimum score C), Michigan English Language Assessment Battery (minimum score 90). *Application deadline:* For fall admission, 8/1 priority date for domestic and international students; for spring admission, 12/1 priority date for domestic and international students. Applications are processed on a rolling basis. Application fee: $25 ($35 for international students). Electronic applications accepted. *Expenses:* Contact institution. *Financial support:* Applicants required to submit FAFSA. *Unit head:* Dr. Lori P. Aultman, Chair of Education, 251-380-3473, Fax: 251-460-2184, E-mail: laultman@shc.edu. *Application contact:* Robert Stewart, Vice President of Enrollment, 251-380-3030, Fax: 251-460-2186, E-mail: rstewart@shc.edu.
Website: http://ug.shc.edu/graduate-degrees/master-science-education/

Syracuse University, School of Education, Programs in Cultural Foundations of Education, Syracuse, NY 13244. Offers MS, PhD, CAS. *Program availability:* Part-time. In 2016, 4 master's, 4 doctorates awarded. *Degree requirements:* For master's, thesis or alternative; for doctorate, comprehensive exam, thesis/dissertation. *Entrance requirements:* For master's, baccalaureate degree from regionally-accredited college/university, writing sample; for doctorate, GRE, master's degree (preferred); writing sample; interview (recommended); personal statement. Additional exam requirements/recommendations for international students: Required—TOEFL (minimum score 100 iBT). *Application deadline:* For fall admission, 1/15 priority date for domestic and international students. Applications are processed on a rolling basis. Application fee: $75. Electronic applications accepted. *Expenses: Tuition:* Full-time $25,974; part-time $1443 per credit hour. *Required fees:* $802; $50 per course. Tuition and fees vary according to course load and program. *Financial support:* Fellowships with full tuition reimbursements, research assistantships with tuition reimbursements, teaching assistantships with tuition reimbursements, career-related internships or fieldwork, and scholarships/grants available. Financial award application deadline: 1/15; financial award applicants required to submit FAFSA. *Faculty research:* Gender and education, history of women's education, the role of science in liberal education, student attrition, inequality in education. *Unit head:* Dr. Barbara Applebaum, Chair, 315-443-3343, E-mail: bappleba@syr.edu. *Application contact:* Speranza Migliore, Graduate Admissions Recruiter, 315-443-2505, E-mail: gradrcrt@syr.edu.
Website: http://soeweb.syr.edu/cfe/culturalfound.html

Teachers College, Columbia University, Department of Arts and Humanities, New York, NY 10027. Offers applied linguistics (MA, Ed D); art and art education (Ed M, MA, Ed D, Ed DCT); arts administration (MA); bilingual and bicultural education (MA); global competence (Certificate); history and education (Ed D, PhD); music and music education (Ed DCT); philosophy and education (MA, Ed D, PhD); social studies education (Ed M, PhD); teaching English to speakers of other languages (Ed M); teaching of English and English education (Ed M, MA, Ed D, PhD), including English education (Ed M, Ed D, PhD), teaching of English (MA); teaching of social studies (MA); TESOL (MA, Ed D). *Program availability:* Part-time, evening/weekend. *Students:* 429 full-time (329 women), 467 part-time (332 women); includes 268 minority (62 Black or African American, non-Hispanic/Latino; 1 American Indian or Alaska Native, non-Hispanic/Latino; 108 Asian, non-Hispanic/Latino; 76 Hispanic/Latino; 21 Two or more races, non-Hispanic/Latino), 212 international. 1,068 applicants, 53% accepted, 272 enrolled. Terminal master's awarded for partial completion of doctoral program. *Expenses: Tuition:* Full-time $36,288; part-time $1512 per credit. *Required fees:* $438 per semester. One-time fee: $510 full-time. Full-time tuition and fees vary according to course load. *Financial support:* Fellowships, research assistantships, teaching assistantships, career-related internships or fieldwork, Federal Work-Study, institutionally sponsored loans, tuition waivers (full and partial), and unspecified assistantships available. Support available to part-time students. *Unit head:* Prof. William Gaudelli, Department Chair, 212-678-3150, E-mail: wg74@columbia.edu. *Application contact:* David Estrella, Director of Admissions, 212-678-3305, Fax: 212-678-4171, E-mail: estrella@tc.columbia.edu.
Website: http://www.tc.edu/a%26h/

University at Buffalo, the State University of New York, Graduate School, Graduate School of Education, Department of Educational Leadership and Policy, Buffalo, NY 14260. Offers economics and education policy analysis (MA); education studies (Ed M); educational administration (Ed M, Ed D, PhD); educational culture, policy and society (PhD); higher education administration (Ed M, PhD); school building leadership (Certificate); school business and human resource administration (Certificate); school district business leadership (Certificate); school district leadership (Certificate). *Program availability:* Part-time, evening/weekend. *Faculty:* 15 full-time (9 women), 8 part-time/adjunct (6 women). *Students:* 77 full-time (51 women), 122 part-time (76 women); includes 30 minority (23 Black or African American, non-Hispanic/Latino; 4 Asian, non-Hispanic/Latino; 3 Hispanic/Latino), 22 international. Average age 34. 144 applicants, 75% accepted, 63 enrolled. In 2016, 59 master's, 11 doctorates, 29 other advanced degrees awarded. *Degree requirements:* For master's, comprehensive exam (for some programs), thesis optional; for doctorate, comprehensive exam, thesis/dissertation. *Entrance requirements:* For master's, interview, letters of reference; for doctorate, GRE General Test or MAT, writing sample, letters of reference. Additional exam requirements/recommendations for international students: Required—TOEFL (minimum score 550 paper-based; 79 iBT). *Application deadline:* For fall admission, 2/1 priority date for domestic students, 2/1 for international students; for spring admission, 11/15 priority date for domestic students, 10/1 for international students. Applications are processed on a rolling basis. Application fee: $50. Electronic applications accepted. *Financial support:* In 2016–17, 13 fellowships (averaging $6,862 per year), 32 research assistantships with tuition reimbursements (averaging $10,496 per year) were awarded; career-related internships or fieldwork, Federal Work-Study, institutionally sponsored loans, scholarships/grants, health care benefits, tuition waivers (full and partial), and unspecified assistantships also available. Financial award application deadline: 3/15; financial award applicants required to submit FAFSA. *Faculty research:* College access and choice, school leadership preparation and practice, public policy, curriculum and pedagogy, comparative and international education. *Total annual research expenditures:* $435,404. *Unit head:* Dr. Janina C. Brutt-Griffler, Chair, 716-645-2471, Fax: 716-645-2481, E-mail: bruttg@buffalo.edu. *Application contact:* Veronica Kase,

Admission Assistant, 716-645-2110, Fax: 716-645-7937, E-mail: vakase@buffalo.edu.
Website: http://gse.buffalo.edu/elp

The University of British Columbia, Faculty of Education, Department of Educational Studies, Vancouver, BC V6T 1Z1, Canada. Offers adult learning and education (M Ed); adult learning and global change (M Ed); curriculum and leadership (M Ed); educational administration and leadership (M Ed); educational leadership and policy (Ed D); educational studies (M Ed, MA, PhD); higher education (M Ed); society, culture and politics in education (M Ed). *Program availability:* Part-time, evening/weekend. *Faculty:* 25 full-time (14 women), 3 part-time/adjunct (2 women). *Students:* 222 full-time (157 women), 62 part-time (44 women). Average age 35. 166 applicants, 66% accepted, 74 enrolled. In 2016, 103 master's, 13 doctorates awarded. Terminal master's awarded for partial completion of doctoral program. *Degree requirements:* For master's, thesis; for doctorate, comprehensive exam, thesis/dissertation. *Entrance requirements:* For master's, minimum B+ average, 4-year undergraduate degree, field-related experience; for doctorate, minimum B+ average, 4-year undergraduate degree, master's degree, field-related experience. Additional exam requirements/recommendations for international students: Required—TOEFL (minimum score 600 paper-based; 100 iBT) or IELTS (minimum score 6.5). Application fee: $90 ($150 for international students). Electronic applications accepted. *Expenses:* Contact institution. *Financial support:* In 2016–17, 7 fellowships with tuition reimbursements (averaging $17,000 per year), 12 research assistantships (averaging $4,000 per year), 8 teaching assistantships (averaging $5,000 per year) were awarded. *Faculty research:* Educational leadership educational administration adult education politics in education, global change and adult learning. *Total annual research expenditures:* $632,000. *Unit head:* Dr. Tara Fenwick, Head, 604-822-5359, Fax: 604-822-4244. *Application contact:* Christine Adams, Graduate Secretary, 604-822-6647, Fax: 604-822-4244, E-mail: grad.edst@ubc.ca.
Website: http://www.edst.educ.ubc.ca/

University of California, Riverside, Graduate Division, Graduate School of Education, Riverside, CA 92521-0102. Offers autism (M Ed); diversity and equity (M Ed); education specialist (Credential); education, society, and culture (MA, PhD); educational psychology (MA, PhD); general education (M Ed); higher education administration and policy (M Ed, PhD); multiple subject (Credential); reading (M Ed); school psychology (PhD); single subject (Credential); special education (M Ed, MA, PhD); TESOL (M Ed). Terminal master's awarded for partial completion of doctoral program. *Degree requirements:* For master's, thesis optional, comprehensive exams or thesis (MA), case study or analytical report (M Ed); for doctorate, thesis/dissertation, written and oral qualifying exams, college teaching practicum. *Entrance requirements:* For master's, GRE General Test (for MA); CBEST and CSET (for M Ed in general education only), UCR Extension TESOL certificate (for M Ed with TESOL emphasis only); for doctorate, GRE General Test, writing sample; for Credential, CBEST, CSET. Additional exam requirements/recommendations for international students: Required—TOEFL (minimum score 550 paper-based; 80 iBT), IELTS (minimum score 7). Electronic applications accepted. *Expenses:* Tuition, state resident: full-time $16,666. Tuition, nonresident: full-time $31,768. *Required fees:* $11,055.54 per quarter. $3685.18 per quarter. Tuition and fees vary according to campus/location and program. *Faculty research:* Responsiveness to intervention, faculty core, response to intervention of English language learners, advanced modeling techniques, study on social capital, trust, and motivation.

University of Cincinnati, Graduate School, College of Education, Criminal Justice, and Human Services, School of Education, Program in Educational Studies, Cincinnati, OH 45221. Offers M Ed, PhD. *Accreditation:* NCATE. *Program availability:* Part-time. *Degree requirements:* For master's, thesis optional; for doctorate, comprehensive exam, thesis/dissertation. *Entrance requirements:* For master's, GRE General Test; for doctorate, GRE General Test, GRE Subject Test. Additional exam requirements/recommendations for international students: Required—TOEFL (minimum score 520 paper-based), OEPT 3. Electronic applications accepted. *Expenses: Tuition, area resident:* Full-time $12,790; part-time $389 per credit hour. Tuition, state resident: full-time $13,290; part-time $419 per credit hour. Tuition, nonresident: full-time $24,532; part-time $976 per credit hour. *International tuition:* $24,832 full-time. *Required fees:* $3958; $140 per credit hour. Tuition and fees vary according to course load, degree level, program and reciprocity agreements.

University of Hawaii at Manoa, Graduate Division, College of Education, Department of Educational Foundations, Honolulu, HI 96822. Offers M Ed. *Program availability:* Part-time, evening/weekend. *Degree requirements:* For master's, thesis optional. *Entrance requirements:* Additional exam requirements/recommendations for international students: Required—TOEFL (minimum score 580 paper-based; 92 iBT), IELTS (minimum score 5). *Faculty research:* Multicultural-ethnic education, comparative education, educational policy, interdisciplinary inquiry, moral/political education.

University of Hawaii at Manoa, Graduate Division, College of Education, PhD in Education Program, Honolulu, HI 96822. Offers curriculum and instruction (PhD); educational administration (PhD); educational foundations (PhD); educational policy studies (PhD); educational psychology (PhD); exceptionalities (PhD); kinesiology (PhD); learning design and technology (PhD). *Program availability:* Part-time, evening/weekend. *Degree requirements:* For doctorate, thesis/dissertation. *Entrance requirements:* For doctorate, GRE General Test, sample of written work. Additional exam requirements/recommendations for international students: Required—TOEFL (minimum score 600 paper-based; 100 iBT), IELTS (minimum score 7).

University of Houston, College of Education, Department of Educational Leadership and Cultural Studies, Houston, TX 77204. Offers administration and supervision (M Ed, Ed D); higher education (M Ed); historical, social, and cultural foundations of education (M Ed). *Accreditation:* NCATE. *Program availability:* Part-time, evening/weekend. *Degree requirements:* For master's, comprehensive exam or thesis; for doctorate, comprehensive exam, thesis/dissertation. *Entrance requirements:* For master's, GRE General Test, minimum cumulative GPA of 2.6, 3 letters of recommendation, resume/vitae, goal statement; for doctorate, GRE General Test, minimum cumulative GPA of 2.6, 3 letters of recommendation, resume/vitae, goal statement, writing sample, interview. Additional exam requirements/recommendations for international students: Required—TOEFL (minimum score 550 paper-based; 79 iBT). Electronic applications accepted. *Faculty research:* Change, supervision, multiculturalism, evaluation, policy.

University of Houston–Clear Lake, School of Education, Program in Foundations and Professional Studies, Houston, TX 77058-1002. Offers counseling (MS); instructional technology (MS); multicultural studies (MS). *Program availability:* Part-time, evening/weekend. *Degree requirements:* For master's, thesis optional. *Entrance requirements:* For master's, GRE or minimum GPA of 3.0 in last 60 hours. Additional exam requirements/recommendations for international students: Required—TOEFL (minimum score 550 paper-based). Electronic applications accepted.

The University of Iowa, Graduate College, College of Education, Department of Educational Policy and Leadership Studies, Program in Schools, Culture, and Society, Iowa City, IA 52242-1316. Offers MA, PhD. *Degree requirements:* For master's, thesis optional, exam; for doctorate, comprehensive exam, thesis/dissertation. *Entrance requirements:* For master's and doctorate, GRE General Test, minimum GPA of 3.0. Additional exam requirements/recommendations for international students: Required—TOEFL (minimum score 550 paper-based; 81 iBT). Electronic applications accepted.

The University of Iowa, Graduate College, College of Education, Department of Psychological and Quantitative Foundations, Iowa City, IA 52242-1316. Offers counseling psychology (PhD); educational measurement and statistics (MA, PhD); educational psychology (MA, PhD); school psychology (PhD, Ed S). *Accreditation:* APA. *Degree requirements:* For master's, thesis optional, exam; for doctorate, comprehensive exam, thesis/dissertation; for Ed S, exam. *Entrance requirements:* For master's, doctorate, and Ed S, GRE General Test, minimum GPA of 3.0. Additional exam requirements/recommendations for international students: Required—TOEFL (minimum score 550 paper-based; 81 iBT). Electronic applications accepted.

University of Manitoba, Faculty of Graduate Studies, Faculty of Education, Department of Educational Administration, Foundations and Psychology, Winnipeg, MB R3T 2N2, Canada. Offers adult and post-secondary education (M Ed); educational administration (M Ed); guidance and counseling (M Ed); inclusive special education (M Ed); social foundations of education (M Ed). *Degree requirements:* For master's, thesis or alternative.

University of Maryland, College Park, Academic Affairs, College of Education, Department of Education Policy and Leadership, College Park, MD 20742. Offers curriculum and educational communications (M Ed, MA, Ed D, PhD); social foundations of education (M Ed, MA, Ed D, PhD, CAGS). *Accreditation:* NCATE. *Program availability:* Part-time, evening/weekend, online learning. *Degree requirements:* For master's, thesis or alternative, internship and/or field experience; for doctorate, comprehensive exam, thesis/dissertation, practicum or internship. *Entrance requirements:* For master's, GRE General Test or MAT, minimum GPA of 3.0, scholarly writing sample, 3 letters of recommendation; for doctorate, GRE General Test or MAT, scholarly writing sample; minimum undergraduate GPA of 3.0, graduate 3.5. *Faculty research:* Educational technology, adult and higher education.

University of Minnesota, Twin Cities Campus, Graduate School, College of Education and Human Development, Department of Educational Psychology, Program in Psychological Foundations of Education, Minneapolis, MN 55455-0213. Offers MA, PhD. *Students:* 37 full-time (21 women), 18 part-time (12 women); includes 11 minority (1 Black or African American, non-Hispanic/Latino; 6 Asian, non-Hispanic/Latino; 2 Hispanic/Latino; 2 Two or more races, non-Hispanic/Latino), 13 international. Average age 33. 63 applicants, 17% accepted, 8 enrolled. In 2016, 4 master's, 8 doctorates awarded. Application fee: $75 ($95 for international students). *Unit head:* Dr. Geoffrey Maruyama, Chair, 612-625-5861, Fax: 612-624-8241, E-mail: geoff@umn.edu. *Application contact:* Dr. Ernest Davenport, Director of Graduate Studies, 612-624-1040, E-mail: lqr6576@umn.edu.
Website: http://www.cehd.umn.edu/EdPsych/programs/Foundations/

University of New Mexico, Graduate Studies, College of Education, Program in Language, Literacy and Sociocultural Studies, Albuquerque, NM 87131. Offers American Indian education (MA); bilingual education (MA, PhD); educational linguistics (PhD); educational thought and sociocultural studies (MA, PhD); literacy/language arts (MA, PhD); social studies (MA); TESOL (MA, PhD). *Faculty:* 17 full-time (10 women), 4 part-time/adjunct (3 women). *Students:* 57 full-time (38 women), 129 part-time (105 women); includes 102 minority (8 Black or African American, non-Hispanic/Latino; 16 American Indian or Alaska Native, non-Hispanic/Latino; 6 Asian, non-Hispanic/Latino; 67 Hispanic/Latino; 5 Two or more races, non-Hispanic/Latino), 32 international. Average age 39. 50 applicants, 60% accepted, 23 enrolled. In 2016, 36 master's, 4 doctorates awarded. *Degree requirements:* For master's, comprehensive exam, thesis optional; for doctorate, comprehensive exam, thesis/dissertation, research skills. *Entrance requirements:* For master's, letter of intent, 3 letters of recommendation, resume, BA/BS, department demographic form, transcripts; for doctorate, writing sample, letter of intent, 3 letters of recommendation, resume, BA/BS, MA, department demographic form, transcripts. Additional exam requirements/recommendations for international students: Required—TOEFL. *Application deadline:* For fall admission, 12/1 for domestic and international students; for spring admission, 9/15 for domestic and international students. Application fee: $50. Electronic applications accepted. *Financial support:* Fellowships, research assistantships, teaching assistantships with tuition reimbursements, career-related internships or fieldwork, institutionally sponsored loans, scholarships/grants, and unspecified assistantships available. Support available to part-time students. Financial award application deadline: 3/1; financial award applicants required to submit FAFSA. *Faculty research:* School reform, professional development, history of education, Native American education, politics of education, feminism and issues of sexual identity, critical race theory, bilingualism, literacy reading, adolescent literature, second language acquisition, critical theory and schooling, indigenous languages. *Unit head:* Dr. Lois M. Meyer, Chair, 505-277-7244, Fax: 505-277-8362, E-mail: lsmeyer@unm.edu. *Application contact:* Debra Schaffer, Administrative Assistant, 505-277-0437, Fax: 505-277-8362, E-mail: schaffer@unm.edu.
Website: http://coe.unm.edu/departments-programs/llss/index.html

University of Pennsylvania, Graduate School of Education, Division of Literacy, Culture, and International Education, Program in Education, Culture and Society, Philadelphia, PA 19104. Offers MS Ed, PhD. *Students:* 39 full-time (32 women), 8 part-time (5 women); includes 19 minority (7 Black or African American, non-Hispanic/Latino; 5 Asian, non-Hispanic/Latino; 6 Hispanic/Latino; 1 Two or more races, non-Hispanic/Latino), 7 international. Average age 29. 187 applicants, 32% accepted, 30 enrolled. In 2016, 11 master's, 4 doctorates awarded. *Expenses: Tuition:* Full-time $31,068; part-time $5762 per course. *Required fees:* $3200; $336 per course. Full-time tuition and fees vary according to degree level, program and student level. Part-time tuition and fees vary according to course load, degree level and program.

University of Pittsburgh, School of Education, Department of Administrative and Policy Studies, Program in Social and Comparative Analysis in Education, Pittsburgh, PA 15260. Offers M Ed, MA, Ed D, PhD. *Program availability:* Evening/weekend. *Degree requirements:* For master's, thesis; for doctorate, thesis/dissertation. *Entrance requirements:* For doctorate, GRE General Test. Additional exam requirements/recommendations for international students: Required—TOEFL (minimum score 80 iBT). Electronic applications accepted. Tuition and fees vary according to program.

University of Rochester, Margaret Warner Graduate School of Education and Human Development, Doctoral Programs in Education, Rochester, NY 14627. Offers counseling (Ed D); educational administration (Ed D); educational policy and theory (PhD); higher education (PhD); human development in educational context (PhD); teaching, curriculum, and change (PhD). *Expenses: Tuition:* Full-time $47,450; part-time $1482 per credit hour. *Required fees:* $528. Tuition and fees vary according to program.

University of Saskatchewan, College of Graduate Studies and Research, College of Education, Department of Educational Foundations, Saskatoon, SK S7N 5A2, Canada. Offers M Ed, MC Ed, PhD, Diploma. *Program availability:* Part-time. *Degree requirements:* For master's, thesis (for some programs); for doctorate, comprehensive exam (for some programs), thesis/dissertation. *Entrance requirements:* Additional exam requirements/recommendations for international students: Required—TOEFL (minimum score 80 iBT); Recommended—IELTS (minimum score 6.5). Electronic applications accepted. *Faculty research:* Indian and northern education, adult and continuing education, international education.

Foundations and Philosophy of Education

University of South Africa, College of Human Sciences, Pretoria, South Africa. Offers adult education (M Ed); African languages (MA, PhD); African politics (MA, PhD); Afrikaans (MA, PhD); ancient history (MA, PhD); ancient Near Eastern studies (MA, PhD); anthropology (MA, PhD); applied linguistics (MA); Arabic (MA, PhD); archaeology (MA); art history (MA); Biblical archaeology (MA); Biblical studies (M Th, D Th, PhD); Christian spirituality (M Th, D Th); church history (M Th, D Th); classical studies (MA, PhD); clinical psychology (MA); communication (MA, PhD); comparative education (M Ed, Ed D); consulting psychology (D Admin, D Com, PhD); curriculum studies (M Ed, Ed D); development studies (M Admin, MA, D Admin, PhD); didactics (M Ed, Ed D); education (M Tech); education management (M Ed, Ed D); educational psychology (M Ed); English (MA); environmental education (M Ed); French (MA, PhD); German (MA, PhD); Greek (MA); guidance and counseling (M Ed); health studies (MA, PhD), including health sciences education (MA), health services management (MA), medical and surgical nursing science (critical care general) (MA), midwifery and neonatal nursing science (MA), trauma and emergency care (MA); history (MA, PhD); history of education (Ed D); inclusive education (M Ed, Ed D); information and communications technology policy and regulation (MA); information science (MA, MIS, PhD); international politics (MA, PhD); Islamic studies (MA, PhD); Italian (MA, PhD); Judaica (MA, PhD); linguistics (MA, PhD); mathematical education (M Ed); mathematics education (MA); missiology (M Th, D Th); modern Hebrew (MA, PhD); musicology (MA, MMus, D Mus, PhD); natural science education (M Ed); New Testament (M Th, D Th); Old Testament (D Th); pastoral therapy (M Th, D Th); philosophy (MA); philosophy of education (M Ed, Ed D); politics (MA, PhD); Portuguese (MA, PhD); practical theology (M Th, D Th); psychology (MA, MS, PhD); psychology of education (M Ed, Ed D); public health (MA); religious studies (MA, D Th, PhD); Romance languages (MA); Russian (MA, PhD); Semitic languages (MA, PhD); social behavior studies in HIV/AIDS (MA); social science (mental health) (MA); social science in development studies (MA); social science in psychology (MA); social science in social work (MA); social science in sociology (MA); social work (MSW, DSW, PhD); socio-education (M Ed, Ed D); sociolinguistics (MA); sociology (MA, PhD); Spanish (MA, PhD); systematic theology (M Th, D Th); TESOL (teaching English to speakers of other languages) (MA); theological ethics (M Th, D Th); theory of literature (MA, PhD); urban ministries (D Th); urban ministry (M Th).

University of South Carolina, The Graduate School, College of Education, Department of Educational Studies, Program in Foundations in Education, Columbia, SC 29208. Offers PhD. *Accreditation:* NCATE. *Program availability:* Part-time. *Degree requirements:* For doctorate, comprehensive exam, thesis/dissertation. *Entrance requirements:* For doctorate, GRE General Test or MAT, interview. Electronic applications accepted. *Faculty research:* Oral history, educational biography, home schooling, international education.

The University of Tennessee, Graduate School, College of Education, Health and Human Sciences, Program in Education, Knoxville, TN 37996. Offers art education (MS); counseling education (PhD); cultural studies in education (PhD); curriculum (MS, Ed S); curriculum, educational research and evaluation (Ed D, PhD); early childhood education (PhD); early childhood special education (MS); education of deaf and hard of hearing (MS); educational administration and policy studies (Ed D, PhD); educational administration and supervision (Ed S); educational psychology (Ed D, PhD); elementary education (MS, Ed S); elementary teaching (MS); English education (MS, Ed S); exercise science (PhD); foreign language/ESL education (MS, Ed S); instructional technology (MS, Ed D, PhD, Ed S); literacy, language and ESL education (PhD); literacy, language education, and ESL education (Ed D); mathematics education (MS, Ed S); modified and comprehensive special education (MS); reading education (MS, Ed S); school counseling (Ed S); school psychology (PhD, Ed S); science education (MS, Ed S); secondary teaching (MS); social foundations (MS); social science education (MS, Ed S); socio-cultural foundations of sports and education (PhD); special education (Ed S); teacher education (Ed D, PhD). *Accreditation:* NCATE. *Program availability:* Part-time, evening/weekend. *Degree requirements:* For master's and Ed S, thesis optional; for doctorate, variable foreign language requirement, thesis/dissertation. *Entrance requirements:* For master's, minimum GPA of 2.7; for doctorate and Ed S, GRE General Test, minimum GPA of 2.7. Additional exam requirements/recommendations for international students: Required—TOEFL. Electronic applications accepted.

The University of Texas of the Permian Basin, Office of Graduate Studies, School of Education, Program in Professional Education, Odessa, TX 79762-0001. Offers MA. *Degree requirements:* For master's, comprehensive exam (for some programs), thesis (for some programs). *Entrance requirements:* For master's, GRE General Test. Additional exam requirements/recommendations for international students: Required—TOEFL (minimum score 550 paper-based).

The University of Toledo, College of Graduate Studies, Judith Herb College of Education, Department of Educational Foundations and Leadership, Toledo, OH 43606-3390. Offers educational administration and supervision (ME, DE, Ed S); educational psychology (ME, PhD); educational research and measurement (ME, PhD); educational sociology (PhD); educational theory and social foundations (ME); foundations of education (DE, PhD); history of education (PhD); philosophy of education (PhD). *Accreditation:* NCATE. *Program availability:* Part-time, evening/weekend. *Degree requirements:* For master's, comprehensive exam, thesis or alternative; for doctorate, comprehensive exam, thesis/dissertation; for Ed S, thesis optional. *Entrance requirements:* For master's, doctorate, and Ed S, minimum cumulative GPA of 2.7 for all previous academic work, letters of recommendation. Additional exam requirements/recommendations for international students: Required—TOEFL (minimum score 550 paper-based; 80 iBT). Electronic applications accepted.

University of Utah, Graduate School, College of Education, Department of Education, Culture, and Society, Salt Lake City, UT 84112. Offers M Ed, MA, MS, PhD. *Program availability:* Evening/weekend. *Faculty:* 12 full-time (8 women). *Students:* 48 full-time (27 women), 49 part-time (29 women); includes 52 minority (7 Black or African American, non-Hispanic/Latino; 2 American Indian or Alaska Native, non-Hispanic/Latino; 2 Asian, non-Hispanic/Latino; 32 Hispanic/Latino; 1 Native Hawaiian or other Pacific Islander, non-Hispanic/Latino; 8 Two or more races, non-Hispanic/Latino), 3 international. Average age 34. 41 applicants, 61% accepted, 20 enrolled. In 2016, 19 master's, 7 doctorates awarded. Terminal master's awarded for partial completion of doctoral program. *Degree requirements:* For master's, comprehensive exam, thesis (for some programs); for doctorate, thesis/dissertation. *Entrance requirements:* For master's, minimum GPA of 3.0; for doctorate, minimum GPA of 3.5. Additional exam requirements/recommendations for international students: Required—TOEFL (minimum score 650 paper-based; 114 iBT). *Application deadline:* For fall admission, 2/1 priority date for domestic and international students. Application fee: $55 ($65 for international students). Electronic applications accepted. *Expenses:* Tuition, state resident: full-time $7011; part-time $3918.24 per credit hour. Tuition, nonresident: full-time $22,154; part-time $11,665.42 per credit hour. *Financial support:* In 2016–17, 8 students received support, including 5 fellowships with full tuition reimbursements available (averaging $13,500 per year), 3 research assistantships with full tuition reimbursements available (averaging $13,500 per year), 8 teaching assistantships with full tuition reimbursements available (averaging $15,000 per year); scholarships/grants, health care benefits, tuition waivers (full and partial), and unspecified assistantships also available. Financial award application deadline: 4/1; financial award applicants required to submit FAFSA. *Faculty research:* History, philosophy and sociology of education, language, culture and curriculum. *Total annual research expenditures:* $6,404. *Unit head:* Dr. Edward Buendía, Department Chair, 801-587-7803, E-mail: ed.buendia@utah.edu. *Application contact:* Amy Suzanne Wright, Academic Program Support Specialist, 801-587-7814, E-mail: amy.wright@utah.edu.
Website: http://ecs.utah.edu/

University of Victoria, Faculty of Graduate Studies, Faculty of Education, Department of Curriculum and Instruction, Victoria, BC V8W 2Y2, Canada. Offers art education (M Ed, PhD); curriculum studies (M Ed, MA, PhD); early childhood education (M Ed, PhD); educational studies (PhD); language and literacy (M Ed, MA, PhD); mathematics (M Ed, MA, PhD); music education (M Ed, MA, PhD); science (M Ed, MA, PhD); social studies (M Ed, MA); social, cultural and foundational studies (MA, PhD); technology and environmental education (PhD). *Program availability:* Part-time. *Degree requirements:* For master's, thesis, project (M Ed); for doctorate, comprehensive exam, thesis/dissertation. *Entrance requirements:* For master's, minimum B average. Additional exam requirements/recommendations for international students: Required—TOEFL (minimum score 575 paper-based), IELTS (minimum score 7). Electronic applications accepted. *Faculty research:* Elementary and secondary English, language arts, curriculum theory and practice, educational media and technology, educational administration and leadership, history and philosophy of education.

University of Washington, Graduate School, College of Education, Seattle, WA 98195. Offers curriculum and instruction (M Ed, Ed D, PhD), including educational technology, general curriculum (Ed D, PhD), language, literacy, and culture, mathematics education, multicultural education, reading and language arts education (Ed D), science education, social studies education, teaching and curriculum (M Ed); educational leadership and policy studies (M Ed, Ed D, PhD), including administration (Ed D), educational policy, organization, and leadership (M Ed, PhD), higher education, leadership for learning (Ed D), social and cultural foundations of education (M Ed, PhD); educational psychology (M Ed, PhD), including educational psychology (PhD), human development and cognition (M Ed), learning sciences, measurement, statistics and research design (M Ed), school psychology (M Ed); instructional leadership (M Ed); intercollegiate athletic leadership (M Ed); special education (M Ed, Ed D, PhD), including early childhood special education (M Ed), emotional and behavioral disabilities (M Ed), learning disabilities (M Ed), low-incidence disabilities (M Ed), severe disabilities (M Ed), special education (Ed D, PhD); teacher education (MIT). *Accreditation:* APA. *Program availability:* Part-time, evening/weekend. *Degree requirements:* For master's, thesis optional; for doctorate, thesis/dissertation. *Entrance requirements:* For master's and doctorate, GRE General Test, minimum GPA of 3.0. Additional exam requirements/recommendations for international students: Required—TOEFL. Electronic applications accepted. *Faculty research:* School restructuring/effective schools, special education interventions, literacy and writing, technology, school partnerships, teacher preparation.

University of Wisconsin–Milwaukee, Graduate School, School of Education, Department of Educational Policy and Community Studies, Milwaukee, WI 53201-0413. Offers cultural foundations of community engagement and education (MS), including alternative education, community engagement and partnerships, educational policy, race relations, youth work; educational policy (Graduate Certificate). *Program availability:* Part-time. *Students:* 6 full-time (5 women), 28 part-time (21 women); includes 15 minority (9 Black or African American, non-Hispanic/Latino; 2 Asian, non-Hispanic/Latino; 2 Hispanic/Latino; 2 Two or more races, non-Hispanic/Latino). Average age 35. 28 applicants, 64% accepted, 11 enrolled. In 2016, 18 master's, 1 other advanced degree awarded. *Entrance requirements:* Additional exam requirements/recommendations for international students: Required—TOEFL (minimum score 550 paper-based; 79 iBT), IELTS (minimum score 6.5). *Application deadline:* For fall admission, 1/1 priority date for domestic students; for spring admission, 9/1 for domestic students. Applications are processed on a rolling basis. Application fee: $56 ($96 for international students). Electronic applications accepted. *Financial support:* In 2016–17, 3 fellowships with full tuition reimbursements were awarded; research assistantships, teaching assistantships, career-related internships or fieldwork, health care benefits, and unspecified assistantships also available. Support available to part-time students. Financial award application deadline: 4/15; financial award applicants required to submit FAFSA. *Application contact:* General Information Contact, 414-229-4721, E-mail: soeinfo@uwm.edu.
Website: http://uwm.edu/education/academics/edu-policy-community-studies-department/

University of Wisconsin–Milwaukee, Graduate School, School of Education, Department of Exceptional Education, Milwaukee, WI 53201-0413. Offers autism spectrum disorders (Graduate Certificate); exceptional education (MS); transition for students with disabilities (Graduate Certificate); urban education (PhD), including adult, continuing and higher education leadership, art education, curriculum and instruction, exceptional education, mathematics education, multicultural studies, social foundations of education. *Program availability:* Part-time. *Students:* 50 full-time (41 women), 66 part-time (51 women); includes 42 minority (24 Black or African American, non-Hispanic/Latino; 6 Asian, non-Hispanic/Latino; 1 Hispanic/Latino; 11 Two or more races, non-Hispanic/Latino), 4 international. Average age 39. 55 applicants, 51% accepted, 22 enrolled. In 2016, 14 master's, 10 doctorates, 3 other advanced degrees awarded. *Degree requirements:* For master's, thesis. *Entrance requirements:* Additional exam requirements/recommendations for international students: Required—TOEFL (minimum score 550 paper-based; 79 iBT), IELTS (minimum score 6.5). *Application deadline:* For fall admission, 1/1 priority date for domestic students; for spring admission, 9/1 for domestic students. Applications are processed on a rolling basis. Application fee: $56 ($96 for international students). Electronic applications accepted. *Financial support:* Fellowships, research assistantships, teaching assistantships, career-related internships or fieldwork, health care benefits, and unspecified assistantships available. Support available to part-time students. Financial award application deadline: 4/15; financial award applicants required to submit FAFSA. *Faculty research:* Emotional disturbance, hearing impairment, learning disabilities, mental retardation. *Application contact:* General Information Contact, 414-229-4721, E-mail: soeinfo@uwm.edu.
Website: http://uwm.edu/education/academics/exceptional-edu-department/

Wayne State University, College of Education, Division of Theoretical and Behavioral Foundations, Detroit, MI 48202. Offers applied behavior analysis (Certificate); counseling (M Ed, MA, Ed D, PhD, Ed S); counseling psychology (MA); education evaluation and research (M Ed, Ed D, PhD); educational psychology (M Ed, PhD), including learning and instruction sciences (PhD); rehabilitation counseling and community inclusion (MA); school and community psychology (MA); school psychology (Certificate). *Accreditation:* ACA (one or more programs are accredited); CORE (one or more programs are accredited). *Program availability:* Evening/weekend. *Faculty:* 12. *Students:* 211 full-time (179 women), 237 part-time (196 women); includes 167 minority (119 Black or African American, non-Hispanic/Latino; 1 American Indian or Alaska Native, non-Hispanic/Latino; 10 Asian, non-Hispanic/Latino; 17 Hispanic/Latino; 20 Two or more races, non-Hispanic/Latino), 24 international. Average age 32. 294 applicants, 34% accepted, 72 enrolled. In 2016, 87 master's, 12 doctorates, 14 other advanced degrees awarded. *Degree requirements:* For master's, thesis (for some programs); for

doctorate, thesis/dissertation. *Entrance requirements:* For master's, GRE, interview, personal statement, portfolio (art therapy); for doctorate, GRE, department-written exam, interview, curriculum vitae, references, master's degree in closely-related field with minimum GPA of 3.5, demonstration of counseling skills (counseling); for other advanced degree, master's degree in counseling and counseling license (for Ed S); good standing in school and community psychology MA program (for Certificate). Additional exam requirements/recommendations for international students: Required—TOEFL (minimum score 550 paper-based; 79 iBT), Michigan English Language Assessment Battery (minimum score 85); Recommended—IELTS (minimum score 6.5), TWE (minimum score 5.5). *Application deadline:* For fall admission, 6/1 priority date for domestic students, 5/1 priority date for international students; for winter admission, 10/1 priority date for domestic students, 9/1 priority date for international students; for spring admission, 2/1 priority date for domestic students, 1/1 priority date for international students. Applications are processed on a rolling basis. Application fee: $50. Electronic applications accepted. *Expenses:* $16,503 per year resident tuition and fees, $33,697 per year non-resident tuition and fees. *Financial support:* In 2016–17, 92 students received support, including 2 research assistantships with tuition reimbursements available (averaging $17,994 per year); fellowships with tuition reimbursements available, teaching assistantships with tuition reimbursements available, Federal Work-Study, scholarships/grants, health care benefits, and unspecified assistantships also available. Support available to part-time students. Financial award applicants required to submit FAFSA. *Faculty research:* Adolescents at risk, supervision of counseling. *Unit head:* Dr. Cheryl Somers, Assistant Dean, 313-577-1670, E-mail: c.somers@wayne.edu. *Application contact:* Janice Green, Assistant Dean, 313-577-1605, E-mail: jwgreen@wayne.edu.
Website: http://coe.wayne.edu/tbf/index.php

Western Illinois University, School of Graduate Studies, College of Education and Human Services, Department of Educational Studies, Program in Educational and Interdisciplinary Studies, Macomb, IL 61455-1390. Offers educational and interdisciplinary studies (MS Ed); teaching English to speakers of other languages (Certificate). *Accreditation:* NCATE. *Program availability:* Part-time. *Students:* 4 full-time (all women), 23 part-time (19 women); includes 6 minority (1 Asian, non-Hispanic/Latino; 3 Hispanic/Latino; 2 Two or more races, non-Hispanic/Latino), 1 international. Average age 31. 7 applicants, 100% accepted, 3 enrolled. In 2016, 7 master's, 3 Certificates awarded. *Degree requirements:* For master's, thesis or alternative. *Entrance requirements:* For master's, minimum GPA of 2.75, interview. Additional exam requirements/recommendations for international students: Required—TOEFL (minimum score 550 paper-based; 80 iBT). *Application deadline:* Applications are processed on a rolling basis. Application fee: $30. Electronic applications accepted. *Financial support:* In 2016–17, 5 students received support, including 1 research assistantship with full tuition reimbursement available (averaging $7,544 per year); unspecified assistantships also available. Financial award applicants required to submit FAFSA. *Unit head:* Dr. Greg Montalvo, Interim Chairperson, 309-298-1183. *Application contact:* Dr. Nancy Parsons, Associate Provost and Director of Graduate Studies, 309-298-1806, Fax: 309-298-2345, E-mail: grad-office@wiu.edu.
Website: http://www.wiu.edu/coehs/es/programs/eis/eis.php

Widener University, School of Education, Hospitality, and Continuing Studies, Chester, PA 19013-5792. Offers adult education (M Ed); counseling in higher education (M Ed); counselor education (M Ed); early childhood education (M Ed); educational foundations (M Ed); educational leadership (M Ed); educational psychology (M Ed); elementary education (M Ed); English and language arts (M Ed); health education (M Ed); higher education leadership (Ed D); home and school visitor (M Ed); human sexuality (M Ed, PhD); mathematics education (M Ed); middle school education (M Ed); principalship (M Ed); reading and language arts (Ed D); reading education (M Ed); school administration (Ed D); science education (M Ed); social studies education (M Ed); special education (M Ed); technology education (M Ed). *Accreditation:* NCATE. *Program availability:* Part-time, evening/weekend. *Faculty:* 34 full-time (22 women), 37 part-time/adjunct (14 women). *Students:* 97 full-time (64 women), 201 part-time (143 women); includes 56 minority (44 Black or African American, non-Hispanic/Latino; 1 American Indian or Alaska Native, non-Hispanic/Latino; 2 Asian, non-Hispanic/Latino; 8 Hispanic/Latino; 1 Two or more races, non-Hispanic/Latino), 32 international. Average age 39. 139 applicants, 88% accepted. In 2016, 45 master's, 21 doctorates awarded. Terminal master's awarded for partial completion of doctoral program. *Degree requirements:* For doctorate, thesis/dissertation. *Entrance requirements:* For master's, minimum GPA of 2.5; for doctorate, GRE or MAT, minimum GPA of 2.0 (undergraduate), 3.5 (graduate). *Application deadline:* Applications are processed on a rolling basis. Application fee: $25 ($300 for international students). Electronic applications accepted. *Expenses:* Contact institution. *Financial support:* Career-related internships or fieldwork, tuition waivers (full and partial), and unspecified assistantships available. Support available to part-time students. Financial award application deadline: 5/1. *Faculty research:* Reading and cognition, adult education, technology education, educational leadership, special education. *Unit head:* Dr. Shawn Fitzgerald, Dean, 610-499-4294, Fax: 610-499-4623, E-mail: smfitzgerald@widener.edu. *Application contact:* Dr. Roberta Nolan, Director of Graduate Admissions, 610-499-4125, E-mail: rdnolan@widener.edu.
Website: http://www.widener.edu/academics/schools/eics

William Paterson University of New Jersey, College of Humanities and Social Sciences, Wayne, NJ 07470-8420. Offers applied sociology (MA); clinical and counseling psychology (MA); clinical psychology (Psy D); creative and professional writing (MFA); English (MA); history (MA); political science and public policy (MA); public policy and international affairs (MA). *Program availability:* Part-time, evening/weekend. *Faculty:* 35 full-time (19 women), 8 part-time/adjunct (5 women). *Students:* 58 full-time (38 women), 62 part-time (46 women); includes 40 minority (9 Black or African American, non-Hispanic/Latino; 6 Asian, non-Hispanic/Latino; 21 Hispanic/Latino; 4 Two or more races, non-Hispanic/Latino), 4 international. Average age 32. 160 applicants, 55% accepted, 50 enrolled. In 2016, 56 master's awarded. *Degree requirements:* For master's, thesis (for some programs), internship (for some programs). *Entrance requirements:* For master's, GRE/MAT, minimum GPA of 3.0; 2 letters of recommendation; writing sample/personal statement. Additional exam requirements/recommendations for international students: Required—TOEFL (minimum score 550 paper-based; 79 iBT), IELTS (minimum score 6). *Application deadline:* For fall admission, 8/1 for domestic students, 4/1 for international students; for spring admission, 12/1 for domestic students, 11/1 for international students; for summer admission, 5/1 for domestic students, 2/1 for international students. Applications are processed on a rolling basis. Application fee: $50. Electronic applications accepted. *Expenses:* Tuition, state resident: full-time $12,480; part-time $611 per credit. Tuition, nonresident: full-time $20,263; part-time $992 per credit. *Required fees:* $1573; $77 per credit. Tuition and fees vary according to course load, degree level and program. *Financial support:* Career-related internships or fieldwork, Federal Work-Study, scholarships/grants, and unspecified assistantships available. Support available to part-time students. Financial award applicants required to submit FAFSA. *Faculty research:* Relationship violence among adolescents; autism in young children; game theory; gender, governance and empowerment in India; Chinese development policies concerning Africa. *Total annual research expenditures:* $162,900. *Unit head:* Dr. Kara Rabbitt, Dean, 973-720-2180, Fax: 973-720-2955, E-mail: rabbittk@wpunj.edu. *Application contact:* Tinu Adeniran, Associate Director, Graduate Admissions, 973-720-2764, Fax: 973-720-2035, E-mail: adenirant@wpunj.edu.
Website: http://www.wpunj.edu/cohss

International and Comparative Education

American University, School of Education, Program in International Training and Education, Washington, DC 20016-8001. Offers MA. *Students:* 27 full-time (22 women), 21 part-time (20 women); includes 17 minority (4 Black or African American, non-Hispanic/Latino; 5 Asian, non-Hispanic/Latino; 5 Hispanic/Latino; 3 Two or more races, non-Hispanic/Latino), 5 international. Average age 28. 81 applicants, 94% accepted, 23 enrolled. In 2016, 23 master's awarded. *Degree requirements:* For master's, one foreign language, comprehensive exam. *Entrance requirements:* For master's, GRE General Test, minimum GPA of 3.0, six months of international/cultural experience (preferred), statement of purpose, transcript, 2 letters of recommendation, resume. Additional exam requirements/recommendations for international students: Required—TOEFL (minimum score 100 iBT), IELTS (minimum score 7), PTE (minimum score 68). *Application deadline:* For fall admission, 2/1 priority date for domestic students; for spring admission, 11/1 for domestic students. Applications are processed on a rolling basis. Application fee: $55. *Expenses:* $1,579 per credit tuition; $690 mandatory fees. *Financial support:* Application deadline: 2/1. *Unit head:* Cynthia Miller-Idriss, Director, 202-885-3740, E-mail: cynthia@american.edu. *Application contact:* Kathleen Clowery, Director, Graduate Admissions, 202-885-3620, Fax: 202-885-1344, E-mail: clowery@american.edu.
Website: http://www.american.edu/cas/seth/itep/index.cfm

The American University in Cairo, Graduate School of Education, Cairo, Egypt. Offers educational leadership (MA); international and comparative education (MA). *Program availability:* Part-time, evening/weekend. *Faculty:* 8 full-time (7 women). *Students:* 6 full-time (5 women), 75 part-time (64 women). Average age 33. 60 applicants, 68% accepted, 27 enrolled. In 2016, 14 master's awarded. *Degree requirements:* For master's, thesis. *Entrance requirements:* Additional exam requirements/recommendations for international students: Required—TOEFL (minimum score 450 paper-based; 45 iBT), IELTS (minimum score 5). *Application deadline:* For fall admission, 2/1 priority date for domestic and international students; for spring admission, 10/15 priority date for domestic and international students. Applications are processed on a rolling basis. Application fee: $80. Electronic applications accepted. *Expenses:* Contact institution. *Financial support:* Fellowships with partial tuition reimbursements, teaching assistantships, career-related internships or fieldwork, scholarships/grants, tuition waivers (partial), and unspecified assistantships available. Financial award application deadline: 3/10. *Faculty research:* Educational reform. *Unit head:* Dr. Ted Purinton, Dean, 20-2-2615-1490, E-mail: tedpurinton@aucegypt.edu. *Application contact:* Maha Hegazi, Director for Graduate Admissions, 20-2-2615-1462, E-mail: mahahegazi@aucegypt.edu.
Website: http://www.aucegypt.edu/GSE/Pages/default.aspx

Andrews University, School of Graduate Studies, College of Arts and Sciences, Department of Behavioral Science, Berrien Springs, MI 49104. Offers international development (MSCID), including community and international development. *Faculty:* 10 full-time (2 women), 1 part-time/adjunct (0 women). *Students:* 15 full-time (13 women), 6 part-time (3 women); includes 9 minority (4 Black or African American, non-Hispanic/Latino; 2 Asian, non-Hispanic/Latino; 3 Hispanic/Latino), 8 international. Average age 32. In 2016, 12 master's awarded. *Entrance requirements:* For master's, GRE. Additional exam requirements/recommendations for international students: Required—TOEFL (minimum score 550 paper-based). *Application deadline:* Applications are processed on a rolling basis. Application fee: $40. *Faculty research:* Risk behaviors. *Unit head:* Dr. Duane C. McBride, Chair, 269-471-3152. *Application contact:* Justina Clayburn, Supervisor of Graduate Admission, 800-253-2874, Fax: 269-471-6321, E-mail: graduate@andrews.edu.

Avila University, School of Education, Kansas City, MO 64145-1698. Offers English language learners (Advanced Certificate); international advocacy and leadership (MA, Certificate); literacy (MA); special reading (Advanced Certificate); teaching and learning (MA); TESL (MA). *Program availability:* Part-time, evening/weekend, online learning. *Faculty:* 6 full-time (5 women), 11 part-time/adjunct (6 women). *Students:* 65 full-time (50 women), 23 part-time (17 women); includes 12 minority (8 Black or African American, non-Hispanic/Latino; 2 Asian, non-Hispanic/Latino; 1 Hispanic/Latino; 1 Two or more races, non-Hispanic/Latino), 3 international. Average age 34. 135 applicants, 44% accepted, 33 enrolled. In 2016, 29 master's awarded. *Entrance requirements:* For master's, minimum GPA of 3.0, writing sample, recommendation, interview; for other advanced degree, foreign language. Additional exam requirements/recommendations for international students: Required—TOEFL (minimum score 580 paper-based; 92 iBT). *Application deadline:* Applications are processed on a rolling basis. Electronic applications accepted. *Expenses:* $483 per credit hour. *Financial support:* In 2016–17, 6 students received support. Unspecified assistantships available. Financial award applicants required to submit FAFSA. *Unit head:* Dr. Stacy Keith, Director of Graduate Education, 816-501-2446, Fax: 816-501-2915, E-mail: stacy.keith@avila.edu. *Application contact:* Cory Roup, Graduate Education Enrollment and Academic Advisor, 816-501-2464, E-mail: cory.roup@avila.edu.
Website: https://www.avila.edu/academics/graduate-studies/grad-education

Boston College, Lynch School of Education, Program in International Higher Education, Chestnut Hill, MA 02467-3800. Offers MA. *Students:* 4 full-time (2 women), 4 part-time (3 women); includes 2 minority (both Asian, non-Hispanic/Latino), 3 international. Average age 27. 11 applicants, 91% accepted, 9 enrolled. *Application deadline:* Applications are processed on a rolling basis. Application fee: $65. Tuition and fees vary according to program. *Unit head:* Hans de Wit, Director. *Application contact:*

International and Comparative Education

Laura E. Rumbley, Coordinator, 617-552-4185.
Website: http://www.bc.edu/schools/lsoe/academics/departments/eahe/graduate/maihe

Bowling Green State University, Graduate College, College of Education and Human Development, School of Educational Foundations, Leadership and Policy, Program in Cross-Cultural and International Education, Bowling Green, OH 43403. Offers MA. *Program availability:* Part-time. *Degree requirements:* For master's, thesis or alternative. *Entrance requirements:* For master's, GRE General Test. Additional exam requirements/ recommendations for international students: Required—TOEFL. Application fee: $30. *Financial support:* Research assistantships with full tuition reimbursements, teaching assistantships with full tuition reimbursements, and unspecified assistantships available. *Unit head:* Dr. Craig Mertler, Director, 419-372-9357. *Application contact:* Dr. Alexander Goberman, Graduate Coordinator, 419-372-9950, E-mail: boothmz@bgsu.edu.

California Baptist University, Program in Education, Riverside, CA 92504-3206. Offers educational leadership (MS); educational leadership for faith-based institutions (MS); educational leadership for public institutions (MS); educational technology (MS); instructional computer applications (MS); international education (MS); leadership and adult learning (MS); leadership and organizational studies (MS); online teaching and learning (MS); reading (MS); science education (MA); special education in mild/ moderate disabilities (MS); special education in moderate/severe disabilities (MS); teacher leadership (MS); teaching (MS); teaching and learning (MS). *Program availability:* Part-time, evening/weekend, 100% online, blended/hybrid learning. *Faculty:* 20 full-time (8 women), 11 part-time/adjunct (7 women). *Students:* 191 full-time (148 women), 234 part-time (178 women); includes 194 minority (23 Black or African American, non-Hispanic/Latino; 5 American Indian or Alaska Native, non-Hispanic/ Latino; 15 Asian, non-Hispanic/Latino; 131 Hispanic/Latino; 4 Native Hawaiian or other Pacific Islander, non-Hispanic/Latino; 16 Two or more races, non-Hispanic/Latino), 2 international. Average age 31. 277 applicants, 61% accepted, 150 enrolled. In 2016, 280 master's awarded. *Degree requirements:* For master's, comprehensive exam, project, or thesis. *Entrance requirements:* For master's, minimum undergraduate GPA of 2.75; 500-word essay; three letters of recommendation; two prerequisite courses completed with minimum C grade. Additional exam requirements/recommendations for international students: Required—TOEFL (minimum score 80 iBT). *Application deadline:* For fall admission, 8/1 priority date for domestic students, 7/1 for international students; for spring admission, 12/1 priority date for domestic students, 11/1 for international students. Applications are processed on a rolling basis. Application fee: $45. Electronic applications accepted. *Expenses:* Contact institution. *Financial support:* In 2016–17, 162 students received support. Federal Work-Study and scholarships/grants available. Financial award applicants required to submit CSS PROFILE or FAFSA. *Faculty research:* Leadership development, complexity theory, faith and learning, special education, social and philosophical contexts of education. *Unit head:* Dr. John Shoup, Dean, School of Education, 951-343-4516, E-mail: jshoup@calbaptist.edu.
Website: http://www.calbaptist.edu/mastersined/

California State University, Dominguez Hills, College of Extended and International Education, Carson, CA 90747-0001. Offers MA, MS. *Program availability:* Part-time, evening/weekend, online learning. *Degree requirements:* For master's, thesis. *Entrance requirements:* Additional exam requirements/recommendations for international students: Required—TOEFL. Electronic applications accepted. *Expenses:* Contact institution.

The College of New Jersey, Office of Graduate and Advancing Education, Office of Global Programs, Program in Overseas Education, Ewing, NJ 08628. Offers M Ed, Certificate. *Program availability:* Part-time. *Degree requirements:* For master's, comprehensive exam. *Entrance requirements:* For master's, GRE, minimum GPA of 3.0 in field or 2.75 overall; for Certificate, previous master's degree or higher. Additional exam requirements/recommendations for international students: Required—TOEFL. Electronic applications accepted.

Drexel University, Goodwin College of Professional Studies, School of Education, Philadelphia, PA 19104-2875. Offers applied behavior analysis (MS); creativity and innovation (MS); education improvement and transformation (MS); educational administration (MS); educational leadership and management (Ed D); educational leadership development and learning technologies (PhD); global and international education (MS); higher education (MS); human resources development (MS); learning technologies (MS); mathematics, learning and teaching (MS); special education (MS); teaching, learning and curriculum (MS). *Program availability:* Part-time, evening/ weekend, online learning. *Degree requirements:* For doctorate, thesis/dissertation. *Entrance requirements:* For doctorate, GRE or GMAT. Additional exam requirements/ recommendations for international students: Required—TOEFL, IELTS. Electronic applications accepted. Application fee is waived when completed online. *Expenses:* Contact institution. *Faculty research:* Leadership development, mathematics education, literacy, autism, educational technology.

See Display on page 660 and Close-Up on page 727.

Florida International University, College of Arts, Sciences, and Education, Department of Leadership and Professional Studies, Miami, FL 33199. Offers adult education and human resource development (MS, Ed D); counseling (MS), including rehabilitation counseling, school counseling; counselor education (MS), including clinical mental health counseling; educational administration and supervision (Ed D); educational leadership (MS, Certificate, Ed S); higher education (Ed D); higher education administration (MS); international and comparative education (MS); recreation and sport management (MS), including recreation and sport management, recreational therapy; school psychology (Ed S); urban education (MS), including instruction in urban settings, learning technologies, multicultural/bilingual, multicultural/TESOL, urban education. *Program availability:* Part-time, evening/weekend. *Faculty:* 27 full-time (19 women), 38 part-time/adjunct (25 women). *Students:* 253 full-time (191 women), 306 part-time (241 women); includes 444 minority (129 Black or African American, non-Hispanic/Latino; 3 Asian, non-Hispanic/Latino; 304 Hispanic/Latino; 8 Two or more races, non-Hispanic/Latino), 18 international. Average age 31. 366 applicants, 60% accepted, 115 enrolled. In 2016, 193 master's, 8 doctorates awarded. *Degree requirements:* For doctorate, thesis/dissertation. *Entrance requirements:* For master's, minimum GPA of 3.0; for doctorate and other advanced degree, GRE General Test. Additional exam requirements/recommendations for international students: Required—TOEFL (minimum score 550 paper-based; 80 iBT), IELTS (minimum score 6.3). *Application deadline:* For fall admission, 6/1 priority date for domestic students, 4/1 for international students; for winter admission, 10/1 priority date for domestic students, 9/1 for international students; for spring admission, 3/1 priority date for domestic students, 2/ 1 for international students. Applications are processed on a rolling basis. Application fee: $30. Electronic applications accepted. *Expenses:* Tuition, state resident: full-time $8912; part-time $446 per credit hour. Tuition, nonresident: full-time $21,393; part-time $992 per credit hour. *Required fees:* $2185; $195 per semester. Tuition and fees vary according to program. *Financial support:* Fellowships, research assistantships with tuition reimbursements, teaching assistantships with tuition reimbursements, Federal Work-Study, and tuition waivers (full and partial) available. Support available to part-time students. Financial award applicants required to submit FAFSA. *Unit head:* Dr. Benjamin Baez, Chair, 305-348-3214, Fax: 305-348-1515, E-mail: benjamin.baez@fiu.edu. *Application contact:* Nanett Rojas, Assistant Director, Graduate Admissions, 305-348-7464, Fax: 305-348-7441, E-mail: gradadm@fiu.edu.
Website: http://education.fiu.edu

Florida International University, College of Arts, Sciences, and Education, Department of Teaching and Learning, Miami, FL 33199. Offers art education (MA, MS); curriculum and instruction (MS, Ed D, PhD, Ed S), including curriculum development (MS), elementary education (MS), English education (MS), learning technologies (MS), mathematics education (MS), modern language education (MS), physical education (MS), science education (MS), social studies education (MS), special education (MS); early childhood education (MS); exceptional student education (Ed D); foreign language education (MS), including foreign language education, teaching English to speakers of other languages (TESOL); international/intercultural education (MS); language, literacy and culture (PhD); mathematics, science, and learning technologies (PhD); physical education (MS), including sport and fitness; reading education (MS). *Program availability:* Part-time, evening/weekend. *Faculty:* 34 full-time (23 women), 64 part-time/ adjunct (48 women). *Students:* 182 full-time (154 women), 231 part-time (190 women); includes 323 minority (69 Black or African American, non-Hispanic/Latino; 10 Asian, non-Hispanic/Latino; 237 Hispanic/Latino; 7 Two or more races, non-Hispanic/Latino), 19 international. Average age 34. 282 applicants, 58% accepted, 113 enrolled. In 2016, 184 master's, 12 doctorates awarded. *Degree requirements:* For doctorate, comprehensive exam, thesis/dissertation. *Entrance requirements:* For master's, GRE General Test, Florida General Knowledge Test or Florida College Level Academic Skills Test; for doctorate and Ed S, GRE General Test. Additional exam requirements/ recommendations for international students: Required—TOEFL (minimum score 550 paper-based; 80 iBT), IELTS (minimum score 6.3). *Application deadline:* For fall admission, 6/1 priority date for domestic students, 4/1 for international students; for winter admission, 10/1 priority date for domestic students, 9/1 for international students; for spring admission, 3/1 priority date for domestic students, 2/1 for international students. Applications are processed on a rolling basis. Application fee: $30. Electronic applications accepted. *Expenses:* Tuition, state resident: full-time $8912; part-time $446 per credit hour. Tuition, nonresident: full-time $21,393; part-time $992 per credit hour. *Required fees:* $2185; $195 per semester. Tuition and fees vary according to program. *Financial support:* Research assistantships with tuition reimbursements and teaching assistantships with tuition reimbursements available. *Unit head:* Dr. Lynn Miller, Chair, 305-348-2005, Fax: 305-348-2086, E-mail: lynne.miller@fiu.edu. *Application contact:* Nanett Rojas, Assistant Director, Graduate Admissions, 305-348-7464, Fax: 305-348-7441, E-mail: gradadm@fiu.edu.
Website: http://education.fiu.edu

Florida State University, The Graduate School, College of Education, Program in Foundations of Education, Tallahassee, FL 32306. Offers social, historical and philosophical foundations of education (MS, PhD); sociocultural and international development education studies (MS, Ed D, PhD). *Program availability:* Part-time, evening/weekend. Terminal master's awarded for partial completion of doctoral program. *Degree requirements:* For master's, comprehensive exam, thesis optional; for doctorate, comprehensive exam, thesis/dissertation, diagnostic exam, preliminary exam, prospectus defense, dissertation defense. *Entrance requirements:* For master's and doctorate, GRE General Test, minimum upper-division GPA of 3.0. Additional exam requirements/recommendations for international students: Required—TOEFL (minimum score 550 paper-based, 80 iBT), IELTS (minimum score 6.5), Michigan English Language Assessment Battery (minimum score 77), or PTE (minimum score 55). Application fee: $30. Electronic applications accepted. *Expenses:* Tuition, state resident: full-time $7263; part-time $403.51 per credit hour. Tuition, nonresident: full-time $18,087; part-time $1004.85 per credit hour. *Required fees:* $1365; $75.81 per credit hour. $20 per semester. Tuition and fees vary according to campus/location. *Financial support:* Fellowships, research assistantships, teaching assistantships, scholarships/grants, tuition waivers (full and partial), and unspecified assistantships available. Financial award application deadline: 1/15; financial award applicants required to submit FAFSA. *Faculty research:* Socio-cultural foundations of education, policy and politics of international and comparative education; design, management, and evaluation of international education projects; issues of educational equity and equality in domestic and international educational settings, philosophy of education. *Unit head:* Dr. Ayesha Khurshid, Assistant Professor/Program Coordinator, 850-644-7078, Fax: 850-644-1258, E-mail: akhurshid@fsu.edu. *Application contact:* Linda J. Lyons, Academic Support Assistant, 850-644-7077, Fax: 850-644-1258, E-mail: ljlyons@ fsu.edu.
Website: http://education.fsu.edu/degrees-and-programs/graduate-programs

Gallaudet University, The Graduate School, Washington, DC 20002-3625. Offers American Sign Language/English bilingual early childhood deaf education: birth to 5 (Certificate); audiology (Au D); clinical psychology (PhD); deaf and hard of hearing infants, toddlers, and their families (Certificate); deaf education (MA, Ed S); deaf history (Certificate); deaf studies (Certificate); educating deaf students with disabilities (Certificate); education: teacher preparation (MA), including deaf education, early childhood education and deaf education, elementary education and deaf education, secondary education and deaf education; educational neuroscience (PhD); hearing, speech and language sciences (MS, PhD); international development (MA); interpretation (MA, PhD), including combined interpreting practice and research (MA), interpreting research (MA); linguistics (MA, PhD); mental health counseling (MA); peer mentoring (Certificate); public administration (MPA); school counseling (MA); school psychology (Psy S); sign language teaching (MA); social work (MSW); speech-language pathology (MS). *Program availability:* Part-time. *Students:* 297 full-time (231 women), 129 part-time (97 women); includes 105 minority (35 Black or African American, non-Hispanic/Latino; 20 Asian, non-Hispanic/Latino; 39 Hispanic/Latino; 11 Two or more races, non-Hispanic/Latino), 22 international. Average age 30. 471 applicants, 52% accepted, 147 enrolled. In 2016, 138 master's, 25 doctorates, 14 other advanced degrees awarded. Terminal master's awarded for partial completion of doctoral program. *Degree requirements:* For master's, comprehensive exam (for some programs), thesis optional; for doctorate, comprehensive exam, thesis/dissertation. *Entrance requirements:* For master's and doctorate, GRE General Test or MAT, letters of recommendation, interviews, goals statement, American Sign Language proficiency interview, written English competency. Additional exam requirements/recommendations for international students: Required—TOEFL. *Application deadline:* For fall admission, 2/ 15 for domestic students. Applications are processed on a rolling basis. Application fee: $75. Electronic applications accepted. *Expenses: Tuition:* Full-time $17,100; part-time $950 per credit hour. *Required fees:* $3725; $276 per semester. *Financial support:* Fellowships, research assistantships, teaching assistantships, career-related internships or fieldwork, Federal Work-Study, scholarships/grants, tuition waivers (partial), and unspecified assistantships available. Support available to part-time students. Financial award application deadline: 7/1; financial award applicants required to submit FAFSA. *Faculty research:* Signing math dictionaries, telecommunications access, cancer genetics, linguistics, visual language and visual learning, integrated quantum materials, deaf legal discourse, advance recruitment and retention in geosciences. *Unit head:* Dr. Gaurav Mathur, Dean, Graduate School and Continuing Studies, 202-250-2380, Fax: 202-651-5027, E-mail: gaurav.mathur@gallaudet.edu.

Application contact: Wednesday Luria, Coordinator of Prospective Graduate Student Services, 202-651-5400, Fax: 202-651-5295, E-mail: graduate.school@gallaudet.edu.

George Mason University, College of Humanities and Social Sciences, Program in Global Affairs, Fairfax, VA 22030. Offers MA. *Faculty:* 18 full-time (8 women), 5 part-time/adjunct (3 women). *Students:* 23 full-time (13 women), 20 part-time (13 women); includes 16 minority (6 Black or African American, non-Hispanic/Latino; 1 Asian, non-Hispanic/Latino; 8 Hispanic/Latino; 1 Two or more races, non-Hispanic/Latino), 4 international. Average age 29. 42 applicants, 93% accepted, 17 enrolled. In 2016, 33 master's awarded. *Degree requirements:* For master's, capstone seminar. *Entrance requirements:* For master's, GRE, expanded goals statement, 2 letters of recommendation, evidence of professional competency in a second language tested through Language Testing International or other means approved by the department. Additional exam requirements/recommendations for international students: Required—TOEFL (minimum score 575 paper-based; 88 iBT), IELTS (minimum score 6.5), PTE (minimum score 59). *Application deadline:* For fall admission, 3/15 for domestic students. Application fee: $75 ($80 for international students). Electronic applications accepted. *Expenses:* Tuition, state resident: full-time $10,628; part-time $443 per credit. Tuition, nonresident: full-time $29,306; part-time $1221 per credit. *Required fees:* $3096; $129 per credit. Tuition and fees vary according to program. *Financial support:* Career-related internships or fieldwork, Federal Work-Study, and scholarships/grants available. Financial award application deadline: 3/1; financial award applicants required to submit FAFSA. *Faculty research:* Social movements, globalization, law and economics, comparative politics, global environmentalism and governance, international business and economic development. *Unit head:* Lisa Breglia, Director, 703-993-9184, Fax: 703-993-1244, E-mail: lbreglia@gmu.edu. *Application contact:* Stephanie Lister, Graduate Coordinator, 703-993-5056, Fax: 703-993-1244, E-mail: slister1@gmu.edu. Website: http://globalaffairs.gmu.edu

The George Washington University, Graduate School of Education and Human Development, Department of Educational Leadership, Program in Higher Education Administration, Washington, DC 20052. Offers college teaching and academic leadership (MA Ed/HD, Ed S); general administration (MA Ed/HD, Ed S); higher education administration (Ed D); higher education finance (MA Ed/HD, Ed S); international education (MA Ed/HD, Ed S); policy (MA Ed/HD, Ed S); student affairs administration (MA Ed/HD, Ed S). *Accreditation:* NCATE. *Students:* 23 full-time (18 women), 70 part-time (51 women); includes 35 minority (20 Black or African American, non-Hispanic/Latino; 8 Asian, non-Hispanic/Latino; 6 Hispanic/Latino; 1 Two or more races, non-Hispanic/Latino), 3 international. Average age 31. 148 applicants, 74% accepted, 37 enrolled. In 2016, 30 master's, 9 doctorates, 1 other advanced degree awarded. *Degree requirements:* For master's and Ed S, comprehensive exam; for doctorate, comprehensive exam, thesis/dissertation. *Entrance requirements:* For master's, GRE General Test or MAT, minimum GPA of 2.75; for doctorate, GRE General Test or MAT, interview, minimum GPA of 3.3; for Ed S, GRE General Test or MAT, minimum GPA of 3.3. *Application deadline:* For fall admission, 1/15 priority date for domestic students; for spring admission, 10/1 for domestic students. Applications are processed on a rolling basis. Application fee: $75. *Financial support:* In 2016–17, 17 students received support. Fellowships, research assistantships, career-related internships or fieldwork, Federal Work-Study, and tuition waivers (partial) available. Financial award application deadline: 1/15; financial award applicants required to submit FAFSA. *Faculty research:* Technology in higher education administration. *Unit head:* Michael Feuer, Dean, 202-994-6161, E-mail: mjfeuer@gwu.edu. *Application contact:* Sarah Lang, Director of Graduate Admissions, 202-994-1447, Fax: 202-994-7207, E-mail: slang@gwu.edu.

The George Washington University, Graduate School of Education and Human Development, Department of Educational Leadership, Program in International Education, Washington, DC 20052. Offers MA Ed. *Accreditation:* NCATE. *Students:* 35 full-time (31 women), 42 part-time (37 women); includes 23 minority (8 Black or African American, non-Hispanic/Latino; 1 American Indian or Alaska Native, non-Hispanic/Latino; 7 Asian, non-Hispanic/Latino; 4 Hispanic/Latino; 3 Two or more races, non-Hispanic/Latino), 17 international. Average age 27. 111 applicants, 90% accepted, 32 enrolled. In 2016, 34 master's awarded. *Degree requirements:* For master's, comprehensive exam. *Entrance requirements:* For master's, GRE General Test or MAT, minimum GPA of 2.75. *Application deadline:* For fall admission, 1/15 priority date for domestic students; for spring admission, 10/1 for domestic students. Applications are processed on a rolling basis. Application fee: $75. *Financial support:* In 2016–17, 13 students received support. Fellowships, research assistantships, career-related internships or fieldwork, Federal Work-Study, and tuition waivers available. Financial award application deadline: 1/15; financial award applicants required to submit FAFSA. *Faculty research:* Education and development. *Unit head:* Dr. William K. Cummings, Coordinator, 202-994-4698, E-mail: wkcum@gwu.edu. *Application contact:* Sarah Lang, Director of Graduate Admissions, 202-994-1447, Fax: 202-994-7207, E-mail: slang@gwu.edu.

Harvard University, Harvard Graduate School of Education, Master's Programs in Education, Cambridge, MA 02138. Offers arts in education (Ed M); education policy and management (Ed M); higher education (Ed M); human development and psychology (Ed M); international education policy (Ed M); language and literacy (Ed M); learning and teaching (Ed M); mind, brain, and education (Ed M); prevention science and practice (Ed M); school leadership (Ed M); special studies (Ed M); teacher education (Ed M); technology, innovation, and education (Ed M). *Program availability:* Part-time. *Entrance requirements:* For master's, GRE General Test, statement of purpose, 3 letters of recommendation, resume, official transcripts. Additional exam requirements/recommendations for international students: Required—TOEFL (minimum score 613 paper-based; 104 iBT), TWE (minimum score 5). Electronic applications accepted. *Faculty research:* Learning and development, educational leadership and organizations, education policy analysis.

Indiana University Bloomington, School of Education, Department of Educational Leadership and Policy Studies, Bloomington, IN 47405. Offers educational leadership (MS, Ed D, Ed S); higher education (Ed D, PhD); higher education and student affairs (MS); history and philosophy of education (MS); history, philosophy, and policy in education (PhD), including education policy studies, history of education, philosophy of education; international and comparative education (MS). *Accreditation:* NCATE. *Faculty:* 32 full-time (18 women). *Students:* 223 full-time (140 women), 94 part-time (50 women); includes 80 minority (44 Black or African American, non-Hispanic/Latino; 13 Asian, non-Hispanic/Latino; 18 Hispanic/Latino; 1 Native Hawaiian or other Pacific Islander, non-Hispanic/Latino; 4 Two or more races, non-Hispanic/Latino), 29 international. Average age 34. 309 applicants, 40% accepted, 57 enrolled. In 2016, 60 master's, 18 doctorates, 5 other advanced degrees awarded. *Degree requirements:* For master's, thesis optional; for doctorate, comprehensive exam, thesis/dissertation; for Ed S, comprehensive exam or project. *Entrance requirements:* For master's, doctorate, and Ed S, GRE General Test. Additional exam requirements/recommendations for international students: Required—TOEFL (minimum score 79 iBT). *Application deadline:* For fall admission, 1/15 priority date for domestic students, 12/1 priority date for international students; for spring admission, 9/1 priority date for domestic and international students. Applications are processed on a rolling basis. Application fee: $55 ($65 for international students). Electronic applications accepted. *Financial support:* Fellowships with full and partial tuition reimbursements, research assistantships with full and partial tuition reimbursements, teaching assistantships with full and partial tuition reimbursements, career-related internships or fieldwork, scholarships/grants, health care benefits, and unspecified assistantships available. *Faculty research:* Culturally engaging campus environments, school choice policy analysis, democracy and education in the national and international context, and principal leadership. *Unit head:* Dr. Dionne Danns, Interim Chair, 812-856-8398. *Application contact:* Maria Jensen, Department Administrator, 812-856-8370, Fax: 812-856-8394, E-mail: jensen5@indiana.edu.
Website: http://education.indiana.edu/about/departments/leadership/index.html

Lehigh University, College of Education, Program in Comparative and International Education, Bethlehem, PA 18015. Offers comparative and international education (MA, PhD); globalization and educational change (M Ed); international development in education (Certificate). *Program availability:* Part-time, blended/hybrid learning. *Faculty:* 4 full-time (2 women), 1 part-time/adjunct (0 women). *Students:* 25 full-time (20 women), 29 part-time (24 women); includes 4 minority (1 Black or African American, non-Hispanic/Latino; 1 Asian, non-Hispanic/Latino; 2 Hispanic/Latino), 13 international. Average age 34. 77 applicants, 66% accepted, 10 enrolled. In 2016, 14 master's awarded. *Degree requirements:* For master's, thesis (MA); for doctorate, comprehensive exam, thesis/dissertation. *Entrance requirements:* For master's, 2 letters of recommendation, transcripts, essays, resume; for doctorate, GRE, transcripts, 2 letters of recommendation, essay, curriculum vitae, 2 writing samples. Additional exam requirements/recommendations for international students: Required—TOEFL (minimum score 93 iBT). *Application deadline:* For fall and spring admission, 2/1 for domestic and international students. Application fee: $65. Electronic applications accepted. *Expenses:* $565 per credit. *Financial support:* In 2016–17, 1 research assistantship with full tuition reimbursement was awarded; fellowships, scholarships/grants, health care benefits, tuition waivers, and unspecified assistantships also available. Financial award application deadline: 1/31; financial award applicants required to submit FAFSA. *Faculty research:* Comparative education, rural education, gender equity in education, educational borrowing, comparing education systems, education policy and globalization, family-school relationships, China, international testing, social inequities, European Education Policy and school-work transition. *Total annual research expenditures:* $24,949. *Unit head:* Dr. Arpana Inman, Program Director/Professor, 610-758-4443, Fax: 610-758-6223, E-mail: agi2@lehigh.edu. *Application contact:* Sharon Y. Warden, Coordinator, 610-758-3256, Fax: 610-758-6223, E-mail: sy00@lehigh.edu.
Website: http://ed.lehigh.edu

Louisiana State University and Agricultural & Mechanical College, Graduate School, College of Human Sciences and Education, School of Human Resource Education and Workforce Development, Baton Rouge, LA 70803. Offers agriculture and extension education and youth development (MS, PhD); career and technical education (MS, PhD); comprehensive vocational education (MS, PhD); extension and international education (MS, PhD); human resource and leadership development (MS, PhD); industrial education (MS); vocational agriculture education (MS, PhD); vocational business education (MS); vocational home economics education (MS). *Accreditation:* NCATE.

Middlebury Institute of International Studies at Monterey, Graduate School of International Policy and Management, Program in International Education Management, Monterey, CA 93940-2691. Offers MA. *Degree requirements:* For master's, one foreign language, practicum. *Entrance requirements:* For master's, minimum GPA of 3.0, proficiency in a foreign language. Additional exam requirements/recommendations for international students: Required—TOEFL (minimum score 550 paper-based; 80 iBT). Electronic applications accepted. Application fee is waived when completed online. *Expenses: Tuition:* Full-time $38,250; part-time $1820 per credit. *Required fees:* $78 per semester.

Morehead State University, Graduate Programs, College of Education, Department of Curriculum and Instruction, Morehead, KY 40351. Offers curriculum and instruction (Ed S); elementary education (MA Ed), including elementary education, international education, middle school education, reading; secondary education (MA Ed); special education (MA Ed); teaching (MAT). *Program availability:* Part-time, evening/weekend. *Degree requirements:* For master's, comprehensive exam, thesis optional; for Ed S, thesis, oral exam. *Entrance requirements:* For master's, GRE General Test, minimum GPA of 2.75, teaching certificate; for Ed S, GRE General Test, interview, master's degree, minimum GPA of 3.5, work experience. Additional exam requirements/recommendations for international students: Required—TOEFL (minimum score 500 paper-based). Electronic applications accepted. *Faculty research:* Communicative competence of learning-disabled students, teaching social studies in elementary schools, ungraded primary school organization, study skills.

New York University, Steinhardt School of Culture, Education, and Human Development, Department of Humanities and Social Sciences in the Professions, Program in International Education, New York, NY 10003. Offers MA, PhD, Advanced Certificate. *Program availability:* Part-time. *Degree requirements:* For master's, thesis (for some programs); for doctorate, thesis/dissertation. *Entrance requirements:* For doctorate, GRE General Test, interview; for Advanced Certificate, master's degree. Additional exam requirements/recommendations for international students: Required—TOEFL (minimum score 100 iBT). Electronic applications accepted. *Faculty research:* Civic education, ethnic identity among students and teachers, comparative education, education during emergencies, cross-cultural exchange.

SIT Graduate Institute, Graduate Programs, Master's Programs in Intercultural Service, Leadership, and Management, Program in International Education, Brattleboro, VT 05302-0676. Offers MA.

Stanford University, Graduate School of Education, Program in International Comparative Education, Stanford, CA 94305-2004. Offers MA, PhD. *Expenses: Tuition:* Full-time $47,331. *Required fees:* $609.

Teachers College, Columbia University, Department of International and Transcultural Studies, New York, NY 10027-6696. Offers anthropology and education (MA, Ed D, PhD); applied anthropology (PhD); comparative and international education (MA, Ed D, PhD); international educational development (Ed M, MA, Ed D, PhD). *Program availability:* Part-time. *Students:* 151 full-time (128 women), 119 part-time (95 women); includes 83 minority (17 Black or African American, non-Hispanic/Latino; 32 Asian, non-Hispanic/Latino; 23 Hispanic/Latino; 11 Two or more races, non-Hispanic/Latino), 97 international. 422 applicants, 67% accepted, 138 enrolled. *Degree requirements:* For doctorate, thesis/dissertation. *Expenses: Tuition:* Full-time $36,288; part-time $1512 per credit. *Required fees:* $438 per semester. One-time fee: $510 full-time. Full-time tuition and fees vary according to course load. *Unit head:* Prof. Herve Varenne, Chair, 212-678-3190, E-mail: varenne@tc.columbia.edu. *Application contact:* David Estrella, Director of Admission, 212-678-3305, E-mail: estrella@tc.columbia.edu.

University at Albany, State University of New York, School of Education, Department of Educational Policy and Leadership, Albany, NY 12222-0001. Offers educational policy and leadership (MS, PhD); higher education (MS); international education management (CAS). *Program availability:* Evening/weekend. *Faculty:* 10 full-time (4

women), 7 part-time/adjunct (6 women). *Students:* 27 full-time (11 women), 103 part-time (53 women); includes 24 minority (14 Black or African American, non-Hispanic/Latino; 1 Asian, non-Hispanic/Latino; 9 Hispanic/Latino), 15 international. Average age 31. 48 applicants, 75% accepted, 33 enrolled. In 2016, 16 master's, 9 doctorates, 11 other advanced degrees awarded. *Degree requirements:* For doctorate, one foreign language, thesis/dissertation. *Entrance requirements:* For doctorate, GRE General Test, GRE Subject Test. Additional exam requirements/recommendations for international students: Required—TOEFL (minimum score 550 paper-based). *Application deadline:* For fall admission, 2/1 for domestic students, 5/1 for international students; for spring admission, 9/1 for domestic students, 11/1 for international students. Applications are processed on a rolling basis. Application fee: $75. Electronic applications accepted. *Expenses:* Tuition, state resident: full-time $10,870; part-time $453 per credit hour. Tuition, nonresident: full-time $22,210; part-time $925 per credit hour. *International tuition:* $21,550 full-time. *Required fees:* $1864; $96 per credit hour. *Financial support:* Fellowships and career-related internships or fieldwork available. Financial award application deadline: 3/15. *Total annual research expenditures:* $273,985. *Unit head:* Kevin Kinser, Chair, 518-442-5092, E-mail: kkinser@albany.edu.
Website: http://www.albany.edu/epl/

University of Bridgeport, School of Education, Department of Education, Bridgeport, CT 06604. Offers education (MS); educational management (Ed D, Diploma), including intermediate administrator or supervisor (Diploma), leadership (Ed D); elementary education (MS, Diploma), including early childhood education, elementary education; middle school education (MS); music education (MS); remedial reading and language arts (Diploma); secondary education (MS, Diploma), including computer specialist (Diploma), international education (Diploma), reading specialist, secondary education. *Program availability:* Part-time, evening/weekend. *Degree requirements:* For master's, final exam, final project, or thesis; for doctorate, comprehensive exam, thesis/dissertation; for Diploma, thesis or alternative, final project. *Entrance requirements:* For master's, minimum undergraduate QPA of 2.67; for doctorate, GRE, MAT; for Diploma, GRE General Test or MAT, minimum graduate QPA of 3.0. Additional exam requirements/recommendations for international students: Recommended—TOEFL (minimum score 550 paper-based; 80 iBT), IELTS (minimum score 6.5). Electronic applications accepted. *Expenses:* Contact institution.

University of Massachusetts Amherst, Graduate School, College of Education, Program in Education, Amherst, MA 01003. Offers bilingual, English as a second language, and multicultural education (M Ed, Ed S); child study and early education (M Ed); children, families and schools (Ed D, Ed S); early childhood and elementary teacher education (M Ed); educational leadership (M Ed); educational policy and leadership (Ed D); higher education (M Ed); international education (M Ed); language, literacy and culture (Ed D); learning, media and technology (M Ed, Ed S); mathematics, science, and learning technologies (Ed D); reading and writing (M Ed); research, educational measurement and psychometrics (Ed D); school counselor education (M Ed, Ed S); school psychology (Ed S); science education (Ed S); secondary teacher education (M Ed); social justice education (M Ed, Ed D, Ed S); special education (M Ed, Ed D, Ed S); teacher education and school improvement (Ed D, Ed S). *Accreditation:* NCATE. *Program availability:* Part-time, online learning. Terminal master's awarded for partial completion of doctoral program. *Degree requirements:* For doctorate, comprehensive exam, thesis/dissertation. *Entrance requirements:* Additional exam requirements/recommendations for international students: Required—TOEFL (minimum score 550 paper-based; 80 iBT), IELTS (minimum score 6.5). Electronic applications accepted.

University of Minnesota, Twin Cities Campus, Graduate School, College of Education and Human Development, Department of Organizational Leadership, Policy and Development, Program in Comparative and International Development Education, Minneapolis, MN 55455-0213. Offers MA, PhD. *Students:* 51 full-time (38 women), 39 part-time (22 women); includes 15 minority (7 Black or African American, non-Hispanic/Latino; 4 Asian, non-Hispanic/Latino; 4 Hispanic/Latino), 20 international. Average age 35. 78 applicants, 32% accepted, 24 enrolled. In 2016, 14 master's, 12 doctorates awarded. Application fee: $75 ($95 for international students). *Unit head:* Dr. Frances Vavrus, Chair, 612-624-1006, Fax: 612-624-3377, E-mail: vavru003@umn.edu. *Application contact:* Dr. Jeremy J. Hernandez, Director of Graduate Studies, 612-626-9377, E-mail: herna220@umn.edu.
Website: http://www.cehd.umn.edu/OLPD/grad-programs/CIDE/

University of Pennsylvania, Graduate School of Education, Division of Literacy, Culture, and International Education, Program in International Educational Development, Philadelphia, PA 19104. Offers MS Ed. *Students:* 37 full-time (29 women), 10 part-time (8 women); includes 18 minority (6 Black or African American, non-Hispanic/Latino; 5 Asian, non-Hispanic/Latino; 4 Hispanic/Latino; 3 Two or more races, non-Hispanic/Latino), 17 international. Average age 26. 159 applicants, 60% accepted, 33 enrolled. In 2016, 26 master's awarded. *Expenses: Tuition:* Full-time $31,068; part-time $5762 per course. *Required fees:* $3200; $336 per course. Full-time tuition and fees vary according to degree level, program and student level. Part-time tuition and fees vary according to course load, degree level and program.

University of Pittsburgh, School of Education, Department of Administrative and Policy Studies, Program in Social and Comparative Analysis in Education, Pittsburgh, PA 15260. Offers M Ed, MA, Ed D, PhD. *Program availability:* Evening/weekend. *Degree requirements:* For master's, thesis; for doctorate, thesis/dissertation. *Entrance requirements:* For doctorate, GRE General Test. Additional exam requirements/recommendations for international students: Required—TOEFL (minimum score 80 iBT). Electronic applications accepted. Tuition and fees vary according to program.

University of San Francisco, School of Education, Department of International and Multicultural Education, San Francisco, CA 94117-1080. Offers MA, Ed D. *Program availability:* Part-time, evening/weekend. *Faculty:* 11 full-time (9 women), 8 part-time/adjunct (6 women). *Students:* 128 full-time (112 women), 73 part-time (56 women); includes 86 minority (14 Black or African American, non-Hispanic/Latino; 21 Asian, non-Hispanic/Latino; 39 Hispanic/Latino; 1 Native Hawaiian or other Pacific Islander, non-Hispanic/Latino; 11 Two or more races, non-Hispanic/Latino), 40 international. Average age 34. 169 applicants, 96% accepted, 58 enrolled. In 2016, 57 master's, 12 doctorates awarded. *Degree requirements:* For doctorate, thesis/dissertation. *Entrance requirements:* Additional exam requirements/recommendations for international students: Required—TOEFL, IELTS, PTE. *Application deadline:* For fall admission, 3/1 priority date for domestic students, 3/1 for international students; for spring admission, 10/15 priority date for domestic and international students. Applications are processed on a rolling basis. Application fee: $55 ($65 for international students). Electronic applications accepted. *Expenses: Tuition:* Full-time $23,310; part-time $1295 per credit. Tuition and fees vary according to course load, degree level, campus/location and program. *Financial support:* In 2016–17, 41 students received support. Fellowships, research assistantships, and teaching assistantships available. Financial award application deadline: 3/2; financial award applicants required to submit FAFSA. *Unit head:* Dr. Emma Fuentes, Chair, 415-422-6878. *Application contact:* Peter Cole, Admission Coordinator, 415-422-5467, E-mail: schoolofeducation@usfca.edu.

University of South Africa, College of Human Sciences, Pretoria, South Africa. Offers adult education (M Ed); African languages (MA, PhD); African politics (MA, PhD); Afrikaans (MA, PhD); ancient history (MA, PhD); ancient Near Eastern studies (MA, PhD); anthropology (MA, PhD); applied linguistics (MA); Arabic (MA, PhD); archaeology (MA); art history (MA); Biblical archaeology (MA); Biblical studies (M Th, D Th, PhD); Christian spirituality (M Th, D Th); church history (M Th, D Th); classical studies (MA, PhD); clinical psychology (MA); communication (MA, PhD); comparative education (M Ed, Ed D); consulting psychology (D Admin, D Com, PhD); curriculum studies (M Ed, Ed D); development studies (M Admin, MA, D Admin, PhD); didactics (M Ed, Ed D); education (M Tech); education management (M Ed, Ed D); educational psychology (M Ed); English (MA); environmental education (M Ed); French (MA, PhD); German (MA, PhD); Greek (MA); guidance and counseling (M Ed); health studies (MA, PhD), including health sciences education (MA), health services management (MA), medical and surgical nursing science (critical care general) (MA), midwifery and neonatal nursing science (MA), trauma and emergency care (MA); history (MA, PhD); history of education (Ed D); inclusive education (M Ed, Ed D); information and communications technology policy and regulation (MA); information science (MA, MIS, PhD); international politics (MA, PhD); Islamic studies (MA, PhD); Italian (MA, PhD); Judaica (MA, PhD); linguistics (MA, PhD); mathematical education (M Ed); mathematics education (MA); missiology (M Th, D Th); modern Hebrew (MA, PhD); musicology (MA, MMus, D Mus, PhD); natural science education (M Ed); New Testament (M Th, D Th); Old Testament (D Th); pastoral therapy (M Th, D Th); philosophy (MA); philosophy of education (M Ed, Ed D); politics (MA, PhD); Portuguese (MA, PhD); practical theology (M Th, D Th); psychology (MA, MS, PhD); psychology of education (M Ed, Ed D); public health (MA); religious studies (MA, D Th, PhD); Romance languages (MA); Russian (MA, PhD); Semitic languages (MA, PhD); social behavior studies in HIV/AIDS (MA); social science (mental health) (MA); social science in development studies (MA); social science in psychology (MA); social science in social work (MA); social science in sociology (MA); social work (MSW, DSW, PhD); socio-education (M Ed, Ed D); sociolinguistics (MA); sociology (MA, PhD); Spanish (MA, PhD); systematic theology (M Th, D Th); TESOL (teaching English to speakers of other languages) (MA); theological ethics (M Th, D Th); theory of literature (MA, PhD); urban ministries (D Th); urban ministry (M Th).

University of Wisconsin–Madison, Graduate School, School of Education, Department of Educational Leadership and Policy Analysis, Madison, WI 53706-1380. Offers administration (Certificate); educational policy (MS, PhD); global higher education (MS). *Degree requirements:* For doctorate, thesis/dissertation. *Entrance requirements:* For master's and doctorate, GRE General Test. Electronic applications accepted.

Vanderbilt University, Peabody College, Department of Leadership, Policy, and Organizations, Nashville, TN 37240-1001. Offers education policy (MPP); educational leadership and policy (Ed D); higher education (M Ed); higher education leadership and policy (Ed D); independent school leadership (M Ed); international education policy and management (M Ed); leadership and organizational performance (M Ed). *Program availability:* Part-time. *Faculty:* 29 full-time (14 women), 21 part-time/adjunct (5 women). *Students:* 166 full-time (124 women), 107 part-time (63 women); includes 50 minority (25 Black or African American, non-Hispanic/Latino; 7 Asian, non-Hispanic/Latino; 9 Hispanic/Latino; 1 Native Hawaiian or other Pacific Islander, non-Hispanic/Latino; 8 Two or more races, non-Hispanic/Latino), 32 international. Average age 29. 543 applicants, 63% accepted, 133 enrolled. In 2016, 109 master's, 22 doctorates awarded. *Degree requirements:* For master's, comprehensive exam, thesis optional; for doctorate, thesis/dissertation, qualifying exams, residency. *Entrance requirements:* For master's and doctorate, GRE General Test. Additional exam requirements/recommendations for international students: Required—TOEFL (minimum score 550 paper-based; 80 iBT). *Application deadline:* For fall admission, 12/31 priority date for domestic and international students; for spring admission, 11/1 priority date for domestic and international students. Applications are processed on a rolling basis. Application fee: $0. Electronic applications accepted. *Expenses: Tuition:* Part-time $1854 per credit hour. *Financial support:* Fellowships with partial tuition reimbursements, research assistantships with partial tuition reimbursements, teaching assistantships with partial tuition reimbursements, Federal Work-Study, institutionally sponsored loans, scholarships/grants, tuition waivers (partial), and unspecified assistantships available. Support available to part-time students. Financial award application deadline: 1/15; financial award applicants required to submit FAFSA. *Faculty research:* Higher education, educational leadership, education policy, international education, educator effectiveness. *Unit head:* Dr. Ellen B. Goldring, Chair, 615-322-8000, Fax: 615-343-7094, E-mail: ellen.b.goldring@vanderbilt.edu. *Application contact:* Rosie Moody, Educational Coordinator, 615-322-8019, Fax: 615-343-7094, E-mail: rosie.moody@vanderbilt.edu.
Website: http://peabody.vanderbilt.edu/departments/lpo/index.php

Walden University, Graduate Programs, Richard W. Riley College of Education and Leadership, Minneapolis, MN 55401. Offers adult education (Post-Master's Certificate); adult learning (Graduate Certificate); college teaching and learning (Graduate Certificate); community college leadership (Ed D); curriculum, instruction and assessment (Ed D, Ed S, Graduate Certificate); developmental education (Graduate Certificate); early childhood administration, management, and leadership (Graduate Certificate); early childhood education (Ed D, Ed S); early childhood public policy and advocacy (Graduate Certificate); early childhood studies (MS), including administration, management and leadership, early childhood public policy and advocacy, teaching adults in the early childhood field, teaching and diversity in early childhood education; education (MS, PhD), including adolescent literacy and learning (MS), curriculum, instruction, and assessment (grades K-12) (MS), curriculum, instruction, assessment, and evaluation (PhD), early childhood leadership and advocacy (PhD), early childhood special education (PhD), educational leadership (MS), educational leadership and administration (principal preparation) (MS), educational technology and design (PhD), elementary reading and literacy (PreK-6) (MS), elementary reading and mathematics (grades K-6) (MS), global and comparative education (PhD), higher education leadership management and policy (PhD), integrating technology in the classroom (grades K-12) (MS), learning, instruction and innovation (PhD), mathematics (grades 5-8) (MS), mathematics (grades K-6) (MS), mathematics and science (grades K-8) (MS), organizational research, assessment, and evaluation (PhD), reading and literacy with a reading K-12 endorsement (MS), reading literacy assessment and evaluation (PhD), science (grades K-8) (MS), special education (non-licensure) (grades K-12) (MS), teacher leadership (grades K-12) (MS), teaching English language learners (grades K-12) (MS); educational administration and leadership (Ed D); educational leadership and administration (principal preparation) (Ed S); educational technology (Ed D, Ed S, Post Master's Certificate); elementary reading and literacy (Graduate Certificate); engaging culturally diverse learners (Graduate Certificate); enrollment management and institutional marketing (Graduate Certificate); higher education (MS), including adult learning, college teaching and learning, enrollment management and institutional marketing, global higher education, leadership for student success, online and distance learning; higher education and adult learning (Ed D); higher education leadership and management (Ed D); higher education leadership for student success (Graduate Certificate); instructional design and technology (MS, Postbaccalaureate Certificate), including general program (MS), online learning (MS), training and performance improvement (MS); integrating technology in the classroom (Graduate Certificate); mathematics 5-8 (Graduate Certificate); mathematics K-6 (Graduate Certificate); online teaching for adult educators (Graduate Certificate); reading, literacy, and assessment

(Ed D, Ed S); science K-8 (Graduate Certificate); special education (Ed D, Ed S, Graduate Certificate); special education (K-age 21) (MAT); teacher leadership (Graduate Certificate); teaching adults English as a second language (Graduate Certificate); teaching adults in the early childhood field (Graduate Certificate); teaching and diversity in early childhood education (Graduate Certificate); teaching English language learners (grades K-12) (Graduate Certificate); teaching K-12 students online (Graduate Certificate). *Accreditation:* NCATE. *Program availability:* Part-time, evening/weekend, online only, 100% online. *Degree requirements:* For doctorate, thesis/dissertation (for some programs), residency; for other advanced degree, residency (for some programs). *Entrance requirements:* For master's, bachelor's degree or higher; minimum GPA of 2.5; official transcripts; goal statement (for some programs); access to computer and Internet; for doctorate, master's degree or higher; three years of related professional or academic experience (preferred); minimum GPA of 3.0; goal statement and current resume (for select programs); official transcripts; access to computer and Internet; for other advanced degree, relevant work experience; access to computer and Internet. Additional exam requirements/recommendations for international students: Required—TOEFL (minimum score 550 paper-based, 79 iBT), IELTS (minimum score 6.5), Michigan English Language Assessment Battery (minimum score 82), or PTE (minimum score 53). Electronic applications accepted.

Wilkes University, College of Graduate and Professional Studies, School of Education, Wilkes-Barre, PA 18766-0002. Offers 21st century teaching and learning (MS Ed); art and science of teaching (MS Ed); classroom technology (MS Ed); early childhood literacy (MS Ed); educational development and strategies (MS Ed); educational leadership (MS Ed, Ed D); effective teaching (MS Ed); instructional media (MS Ed); instructional technology (MS Ed); international school leadership (MS Ed); international teaching and learning (MS Ed); middle level education (MS Ed); online teaching (MS Ed); reading (MS Ed); school business leadership (MS Ed); special education (MS Ed); teaching English to speakers of other languages (MS Ed). *Program availability:* Part-time, evening/weekend, 100% online, blended/hybrid learning. *Students:* 87 full-time (70 women), 1,496 part-time (1,111 women); includes 77 minority (11 Black or African American, non-Hispanic/Latino; 2 American Indian or Alaska Native, non-Hispanic/Latino; 12 Asian, non-Hispanic/Latino; 28 Hispanic/Latino; 3 Native Hawaiian or other Pacific Islander, non-Hispanic/Latino; 21 Two or more races, non-Hispanic/Latino). Average age 33. In 2016, 524 master's, 21 doctorates awarded. *Entrance requirements:* Additional exam requirements/recommendations for international students: Required—TOEFL (minimum score 550 paper-based; 79 iBT). *Application deadline:* Applications are processed on a rolling basis. Application fee: $45. Electronic applications accepted. *Expenses:* Contact institution. *Financial support:* Unspecified assistantships available. Financial award application deadline: 3/1; financial award applicants required to submit FAFSA. *Unit head:* Dr. Rhonda Rabbitt, Dean, 570-408-4680, Fax: 570-408-7872, E-mail: rhonda.rabbitt@wilkes.edu. *Application contact:* Director of Graduate Education, 570-408-4234, Fax: 570-408-7846.
Website: http://www.wilkes.edu/academics/graduate-programs/masters-programs/graduate-education/index.aspx

Student Affairs

Alfred University, Graduate School, Division of Education, Alfred, NY 14802-1205. Offers college student development (MS Ed); literacy (MS Ed). *Accreditation:* TEAC. *Program availability:* Part-time. *Faculty:* 4 full-time (3 women), 3 part-time/adjunct (2 women). *Students:* 50 full-time (38 women), 245 part-time (195 women); includes 169 minority (91 Black or African American, non-Hispanic/Latino; 2 American Indian or Alaska Native, non-Hispanic/Latino; 7 Asian, non-Hispanic/Latino; 69 Hispanic/Latino). Average age 34. In 2016, 21 master's awarded. *Entrance requirements:* For master's, Liberal Arts and Sciences Test (LAST), Assessment of Teaching Skills (written) (ATS-W), Content Specialty Test (CST). Additional exam requirements/recommendations for international students: Required—TOEFL (minimum score 590 paper-based; 90 iBT), IELTS (minimum score 6.5). *Application deadline:* For fall admission, 8/1 for domestic students, 3/15 for international students; for spring admission, 12/1 for domestic students, 10/1 for international students. Applications are processed on a rolling basis. Application fee: $60. Electronic applications accepted. *Expenses: Tuition:* Full-time $38,020; part-time $810 per credit. *Required fees:* $970; $82 per semester. *Financial support:* Research assistantships with partial tuition reimbursements, tuition waivers (partial), and unspecified assistantships available. Financial award applicants required to submit FAFSA. *Unit head:* Kevin Curtin, Program Director, 607-871-2699. *Application contact:* Sara Love, Coordinator of Graduate Admissions, 607-871-2115, Fax: 607-871-2198, E-mail: gradinquiry@alfred.edu.
Website: http://www.alfred.edu/gradschool/education/

Alliant International University–Los Angeles, Shirley M. Hufstedler School of Education, Educational Psychology Programs, Alhambra, CA 91803. Offers educational psychology (Psy D); pupil personnel services (Credential); school psychology (MA). *Program availability:* Part-time. *Degree requirements:* For doctorate, comprehensive exam, thesis/dissertation. *Entrance requirements:* For master's, minimum GPA of 2.5, letters of recommendation; for doctorate, interview, minimum GPA of 3.0, letters of recommendation. Additional exam requirements/recommendations for international students: Required—TOEFL (minimum score 550 paper-based), TWE (minimum score 5). Electronic applications accepted. *Faculty research:* Early identification and intervention with high-risk preschoolers, pediatric neuropsychology, interpersonal violence, ADHD, learning theories.

Alliant International University–San Diego, Shirley M. Hufstedler School of Education, Educational Psychology Programs, San Diego, CA 92131. Offers educational psychology (Psy D); pupil personnel services (Credential); school neuropsychology (Certificate); school psychology (MA); school-based mental health (Certificate). *Program availability:* Part-time. *Degree requirements:* For doctorate, comprehensive exam, thesis/dissertation, internship. *Entrance requirements:* For master's, minimum GPA of 2.5, letters of recommendation; for doctorate, minimum GPA of 3.0, letters of recommendation. Additional exam requirements/recommendations for international students: Required—TOEFL (minimum score 550 paper-based; 80 iBT), TWE (minimum score 5). Electronic applications accepted. *Faculty research:* School-based mental health, pupil personnel services, childhood mood, school-based assessment.

Appalachian State University, Cratis D. Williams Graduate School, Department of Human Development and Psychological Counseling, Boone, NC 28608. Offers clinical mental health counseling (MA); college student development (MA); marriage and family therapy (MA); school counseling (MA). *Accreditation:* AAMFT/COAMFTE; ACA; NCATE. *Program availability:* Part-time. *Degree requirements:* For master's, comprehensive exam (for some programs), thesis optional, internships. *Entrance requirements:* For master's, GRE General Test, 3 letters of recommendation. Additional exam requirements/recommendations for international students: Required—TOEFL (minimum score 570 paper-based; 79 iBT), IELTS (minimum score 6.5). *Application deadline:* For fall admission, 2/1 priority date for domestic students, 2/1 for international students; for spring admission, 2/1 for international students. Applications are processed on a rolling basis. Application fee: $55. Electronic applications accepted. *Expenses:* Tuition, state resident: full-time $4744. Tuition, nonresident: full-time $17,913. Full-time tuition and fees vary according to program. *Financial support:* Fellowships, research assistantships, teaching assistantships, career-related internships or fieldwork, Federal Work-Study, scholarships/grants, and unspecified assistantships available. Financial award application deadline: 4/1; financial award applicants required to submit FAFSA. *Faculty research:* Multicultural counseling, addictions counseling, play therapy, expressive arts, child and adolescent therapy, sexual abuse counseling. *Unit head:* Dr. Lee Baruth, Chairman, 828-262-2055, E-mail: baruthlg@appstate.edu. *Application contact:* Dr. Mark Schwarze, Program Director, 828-262-6046, E-mail: asucmhc@appstate.edu.
Website: http://www.ced.appstate.edu/departments/hpc

Arkansas State University, Graduate School, College of Education and Behavioral Science, Department of Psychology and Counseling, State University, AR 72467. Offers clinical mental health counseling (Graduate Certificate); college student personnel services (MS); dyslexia therapy (Graduate Certificate); psychological science (MS); psychology and counseling (Ed S); rehabilitation counseling (MRC); school counseling (MSE); student affairs (Graduate Certificate). *Accreditation:* ACA (one or more programs are accredited); CORE (one or more programs are accredited); NCATE. *Program availability:* Part-time. *Degree requirements:* For master's and other advanced degree, comprehensive exam, thesis or alternative. *Entrance requirements:* For master's, GRE General Test or MAT (for MSE), appropriate bachelor's degree, interview, letters of reference, official transcripts, immunization records, written statement, 2-3 page autobiography; for other advanced degree, GRE General Test, interview, master's degree, letters of reference, official transcript, personal statement, immunization records. Additional exam requirements/recommendations for international students: Required—TOEFL (minimum score 550 paper-based; 79 iBT), IELTS (minimum score 6), PTE (minimum score 56). Electronic applications accepted.

Arkansas Tech University, College of Education, Russellville, AR 72801. Offers college student personnel (MS); educational leadership (M Ed, Ed S); elementary education (M Ed); instructional improvement (M Ed); instructional technology (M Ed); school counseling and leadership (M Ed); school leadership (Ed D); strength and conditioning studies (MS); teaching (MAT); teaching, learning, and leadership (M Ed). *Accreditation:* NCATE. *Program availability:* Part-time, evening/weekend, online learning. *Students:* 72 full-time (43 women), 371 part-time (283 women); includes 108 minority (80 Black or African American, non-Hispanic/Latino; 1 American Indian or Alaska Native, non-Hispanic/Latino; 4 Asian, non-Hispanic/Latino; 13 Hispanic/Latino; 10 Two or more races, non-Hispanic/Latino), 6 international. Average age 33. In 2016, 181 master's, 1 other advanced degree awarded. *Degree requirements:* For master's, comprehensive exam, thesis optional, action research project. *Entrance requirements:* Additional exam requirements/recommendations for international students: Required—TOEFL (minimum score 550 paper-based; 79 iBT), IELTS (minimum score 6.5). *Application deadline:* For fall admission, 3/1 priority date for domestic students, 5/1 priority date for international students; for spring admission, 10/1 priority date for domestic and international students. Applications are processed on a rolling basis. Application fee: $25 ($75 for international students). Electronic applications accepted. *Expenses:* Tuition, state resident: full-time $4932; part-time $274 per credit hour. Tuition, nonresident: full-time $9864; part-time $548 per credit hour. *Required fees:* $513 per semester. Tuition and fees vary according to course load. *Financial support:* In 2016–17, research assistantships with full tuition reimbursements (averaging $4,800 per year), teaching assistantships with full tuition reimbursements (averaging $4,800 per year) were awarded; career-related internships or fieldwork, Federal Work-Study, scholarships/grants, health care benefits, and unspecified assistantships also available. Support available to part-time students. Financial award application deadline: 4/15; financial award applicants required to submit FAFSA. *Unit head:* Dr. Mary Gunter, Dean, 479-964-3217, E-mail: mgunter@atu.edu.
Website: http://www.atu.edu/education/

Azusa Pacific University, School of Behavioral and Applied Sciences, Department of Leadership and Organizational Psychology, Program in College Student Affairs, Azusa, CA 91702-7000. Offers M Ed. *Program availability:* Part-time, evening/weekend. *Degree requirements:* For master's, exam. *Entrance requirements:* For master's, 12 units of course work in social science, minimum GPA of 3.0.

Binghamton University, State University of New York, Graduate School, College of Community and Public Affairs, Department of Student Affairs Administration, Binghamton, NY 13902-6000. Offers MS. *Program availability:* Part-time. *Faculty:* 3 full-time (all women), 2 part-time/adjunct (both women). *Students:* 34 full-time (19 women), 11 part-time (10 women); includes 12 minority (3 Black or African American, non-Hispanic/Latino; 3 Asian, non-Hispanic/Latino; 3 Hispanic/Latino; 3 Two or more races, non-Hispanic/Latino), 1 international. Average age 27. 50 applicants, 90% accepted, 28 enrolled. In 2016, 25 master's awarded. *Degree requirements:* For master's, comprehensive exam. *Entrance requirements:* For master's, GRE General Test. Additional exam requirements/recommendations for international students: Required—TOEFL (minimum score 80 iBT). *Application deadline:* For fall admission, 4/15 priority date for domestic and international students; for spring admission, 11/15 priority date for domestic and international students. Application fee: $75. Electronic applications accepted. *Financial support:* In 2016–17, 38 students received support. Fellowships, career-related internships or fieldwork, Federal Work-Study, institutionally sponsored loans, scholarships/grants, health care benefits, and unspecified assistantships available. Financial award applicants required to submit FAFSA. *Unit head:* Brianna King, Director of Student Admissions, 607-777-2719, E-mail: bking@binghamton.edu. *Application contact:* Ben Balkaya, Assistant Dean and Director, 607-777-2151, Fax: 607-777-2501, E-mail: balkaya@binghamton.edu.
Website: http://www2.binghamton.edu/ccpa/student-affairs-administration/

Bloomsburg University of Pennsylvania, School of Graduate Studies, College of Education, Department of Teaching and Learning, Program in Educational Leadership, Bloomsburg, PA 17815-1301. Offers college student affairs (M Ed); PreK-12 curriculum and instruction (M Ed); PreK-12 school counseling (M Ed); PreK-12 school principal

(M Ed). *Faculty:* 6 full-time (2 women), 1 (woman) part-time/adjunct. *Students:* 64 full-time (42 women), 39 part-time (26 women); includes 18 minority (8 Black or African American, non-Hispanic/Latino; 4 Asian, non-Hispanic/Latino; 3 Hispanic/Latino; 1 Native Hawaiian or other Pacific Islander, non-Hispanic/Latino; 2 Two or more races, non-Hispanic/Latino), 1 international. Average age 27. 87 applicants, 60% accepted, 43 enrolled. In 2016, 39 master's awarded. *Degree requirements:* For master's, practicum. *Entrance requirements:* For master's, 3 letters of recommendation, resume, minimum QPA of 3.0, personal statement, interview. Additional exam requirements/recommendations for international students: Required—TOEFL, IELTS. Application fee: $35 ($60 for international students). Electronic applications accepted. *Expenses:* Tuition, state resident: full-time $9660; part-time $483 per credit. Tuition, nonresident: full-time $14,500; part-time $725 per credit. *Required fees:* $2410; $107 per credit. $75 per term. Tuition and fees vary according to course load, degree level and program. *Financial support:* Federal Work-Study and unspecified assistantships available. Financial award applicants required to submit FAFSA. *Unit head:* Dr. Ingrid Everett, Program Coordinator, 570-389-5120, Fax: 570-389-3030, E-mail: ieverett@bloomu.edu. *Application contact:* Jennifer Kessler, Administrative Assistant, 570-389-4015, Fax: 570-389-3054, E-mail: jkessler@bloomu.edu.

Bob Jones University, Graduate Programs, Greenville, SC 29614. Offers accountancy (MS); Bible (MA); Bible translation (MA); Biblical studies (Certificate); broadcast management (MS); business administration (MBA); church history (MA, PhD); church ministries (MA); church music (MM); cinema and video production (MA); counseling (MS); curriculum and instruction (Ed D); divinity (M Div); dramatic production (MA); educational leadership (MS, Ed D, Ed S); elementary education (M Ed, MAT); English (M Ed, MA, MAT); fine arts (MA); graphic design (MA); history (M Ed, MA); illustration (MA); interpretative speech (MA); mathematics (M Ed, MAT); medical missions (Certificate); ministry (MM, D Min); multi-categorical special education (M Ed, MAT); music (M Ed); New Testament interpretation (PhD); Old Testament interpretation (PhD); orchestral instrument performance (MM); organ performance (MM); pastoral studies (MA); personnel services (MS, Ed S); piano pedagogy (MM); piano performance (MM); platform arts (MA); radio and television broadcasting (MS); rhetoric and public address (MA); secondary education (M Ed); studio art (MA); teaching Bible (MA); theology (MA, PhD); voice performance (MM); youth ministries (MA); M Div/MM.

Bowling Green State University, Graduate College, College of Education and Human Development, Department of Higher Education and Student Affairs, Program in College Student Personnel, Bowling Green, OH 43403. Offers MA. *Program availability:* Part-time. *Degree requirements:* For master's, thesis or alternative. *Entrance requirements:* For master's, GRE General Test, interview. Additional exam requirements/recommendations for international students: Required—TOEFL. *Application deadline:* For fall admission, 1/1 priority date for domestic students. Application fee: $30. Electronic applications accepted. *Financial support:* Research assistantships with full tuition reimbursements, teaching assistantships with full tuition reimbursements, career-related internships or fieldwork, institutionally sponsored loans, and unspecified assistantships available. Financial award applicants required to submit FAFSA. *Faculty research:* Adult learning, legal issues, moral and ethical development. *Unit head:* Dr. Craig Mertler, Director, 419-372-9357. *Application contact:* Dr. Michael Coomes, Graduate Coordinator, 419-372-7157.

Bucknell University, Graduate Studies, College of Arts and Sciences, Department of Education, Lewisburg, PA 17837. Offers college student personnel (MS Ed). *Program availability:* Part-time. *Degree requirements:* For master's, comprehensive exam (for some programs), thesis or alternative. *Entrance requirements:* For master's, GRE General Test, minimum GPA of 3.0. Additional exam requirements/recommendations for international students: Required—TOEFL (minimum score 600 paper-based). *Application deadline:* For fall admission, 2/1 priority date for domestic students, 1/1 priority date for international students. Application fee: $25. *Expenses: Tuition:* Part-time $5475 per course. *Financial support:* Fellowships with full and partial tuition reimbursements, scholarships/grants, and tuition waivers (full and partial) available. Financial award application deadline: 2/1. *Unit head:* Dr. Joe Murray, Head, 717-577-1324. *Application contact:* Gretchen H. Fegley, Coordinator, 570-577-3655, Fax: 570-577-3760, E-mail: gfegley@bucknell.edu.
Website: http://www.bucknell.edu/education

Buffalo State College, State University of New York, The Graduate School, Faculty of Applied Science and Education, Department of Educational Foundations, Program in Student Personnel Administration, Buffalo, NY 14222-1095. Offers MS. *Degree requirements:* For master's, comprehensive exam. *Entrance requirements:* For master's, minimum GPA of 2.75 in last 60 hours of undergraduate course work. Additional exam requirements/recommendations for international students: Required—TOEFL (minimum score 550 paper-based).

California State University, Bakersfield, Division of Graduate Studies, School of Social Sciences and Education, Program in Counseling, Bakersfield, CA 93311. Offers school counseling (MS); student affairs (MS). *Accreditation:* NCATE. *Students:* 64 full-time (57 women), 7 part-time (6 women); includes 55 minority (1 Black or African American, non-Hispanic/Latino; 1 Asian, non-Hispanic/Latino; 49 Hispanic/Latino; 4 Two or more races, non-Hispanic/Latino), 1 international. Average age 28. 74 applicants, 59% accepted, 38 enrolled. In 2016, 35 master's awarded. *Degree requirements:* For master's, thesis or alternative, culminating projects. *Entrance requirements:* For master's, CBEST (for school counseling). *Application deadline:* Applications are processed on a rolling basis. Application fee: $55. *Expenses:* Tuition, state resident: full-time $2246; part-time $1302 per semester. *Financial support:* In 2016–17, fellowships (averaging $1,850 per year) were awarded; Federal Work-Study, scholarships/grants, and tuition waivers (full and partial) also available. Financial award application deadline: 3/2; financial award applicants required to submit FAFSA. *Unit head:* Dr. Yvonne Ortiz-Bush, Graduate Coordinator, 661-654-3087, Fax: 661-654-2479, E-mail: yortiz_bush@csub.edu. *Application contact:* Debbie Blowers, Assistant Director of Admissions and Evaluations, 661-664-3381, E-mail: dblowers@csub.edu.
Website: https://www.csub.edu/psychology/mscounselingpsych/index.html

California State University, Fresno, Division of Research and Graduate Studies, Kremen School of Education and Human Development, Department of Counselor Education and Rehabilitation, Program in Student Affairs and College Counseling, Fresno, CA 93740-8027. Offers MS. *Accreditation:* NCATE. *Program availability:* Part-time, evening/weekend. *Degree requirements:* For master's, thesis or alternative. *Entrance requirements:* For master's, GRE General Test, MAT, minimum GPA of 3.0. Additional exam requirements/recommendations for international students: Required—TOEFL. *Application deadline:* For fall admission, 5/1 for domestic and international students; for spring admission, 10/1 for domestic and international students. Applications are processed on a rolling basis. Application fee: $55. Electronic applications accepted. *Financial support:* Career-related internships or fieldwork, Federal Work-Study, scholarships/grants, and research awards available. Support available to part-time students. Financial award application deadline: 3/1; financial award applicants required to submit FAFSA. *Unit head:* Dr. Kyoung Mi Choi, Facilitator, 559-278-0070, Fax: 559-278-0045, E-mail: kchoi@csufresno.edu.

California State University, Long Beach, Graduate Studies, College of Education, Department of Advanced Studies in Education and Counseling, Long Beach, CA 90840. Offers counseling (MS), including marriage and family therapy, school counseling, student development in higher education; education (MA, Ed D); educational administration (MA, Ed D); educational psychology (MA); special education (MS). *Program availability:* Part-time, evening/weekend. *Entrance requirements:* For master's, GRE General Test, minimum GPA of 2.75. *Application deadline:* For fall admission, 3/1 for domestic students. Applications are processed on a rolling basis. Application fee: $55. Electronic applications accepted. *Financial support:* Federal Work-Study, institutionally sponsored loans, and scholarships/grants available. Financial award application deadline: 3/2. *Unit head:* Dr. Hiromi Masunaga, Chair, 562-985-4517, E-mail: asec@csulb.edu.

Canisius College, Graduate Division, School of Education and Human Services, Department of Graduate Education and Leadership, Buffalo, NY 14208-1098. Offers business and marketing education (MS Ed); college student personnel (MS Ed); deaf education (MS Ed); deaf/adolescent education, grades 7-12 (MS Ed); deaf/childhood education, grades 1-6 (MS Ed); differentiated instruction (MS Ed); education administration (MS); educational administration (MS Ed); educational technologies (Certificate); gifted education extension (Certificate); literacy (MS Ed); reading (Certificate); school building leadership (MS Ed, Certificate); school district leadership (Certificate); teacher leader (Certificate); TESOL (MS Ed). *Accreditation:* NCATE. *Program availability:* Part-time, evening/weekend, 100% online, blended/hybrid learning. *Faculty:* 5 full-time (all women), 23 part-time/adjunct (16 women). *Students:* 95 full-time (78 women), 223 part-time (177 women); includes 31 minority (15 Black or African American, non-Hispanic/Latino; 2 American Indian or Alaska Native, non-Hispanic/Latino; 4 Asian, non-Hispanic/Latino; 9 Hispanic/Latino; 1 Two or more races, non-Hispanic/Latino), 1 international. Average age 30. 162 applicants, 89% accepted, 135 enrolled. In 2016, 135 master's, 39 other advanced degrees awarded. *Entrance requirements:* For master's, GRE (if cumulative GPA less than 2.7), transcripts, two letters of recommendation. Additional exam requirements/recommendations for international students: Required—TOEFL (minimum score 550 paper-based, 79 iBT), IELTS (minimum score 6.5), or CAEL (minimum score 70). *Application deadline:* Applications are processed on a rolling basis. Application fee: $25. Electronic applications accepted. Application fee is waived when completed online. *Expenses: Tuition:* Full-time $14,742. *Required fees:* $724. *Financial support:* Career-related internships or fieldwork, Federal Work-Study, scholarships/grants, tuition waivers (partial), and unspecified assistantships available. Support available to part-time students. Financial award application deadline: 4/30; financial award applicants required to submit FAFSA. *Faculty research:* Asperger's disease, autism, private higher education, reading strategies. *Unit head:* Dr. Rosemary K. Murray, Chair/Associate Professor of Graduate Education and Leadership, 716-888-3723, E-mail: murray1@canisius.edu. *Application contact:* Kathleen B. Davis, Vice President of Enrollment Management, 716-888-2500, Fax: 716-888-3195, E-mail: daviskb@canisius.edu.
Website: http://www.canisius.edu/graduate/

Cardinal Stritch University, College of Education and Leadership, Department of Education, Milwaukee, WI 53217-3985. Offers educational leadership (MS); higher education student affairs leadership (MS); leadership for the advancement of learning and service (Ed D, PhD); leadership for the advancement of learning and service in higher education (Ed D, PhD); teaching (MAT); urban education (MA). *Accreditation:* NCATE. *Program availability:* Evening/weekend. *Degree requirements:* For master's, comprehensive exam, thesis (for some programs), research project, faculty recommendation; for doctorate, thesis/dissertation, practica, field experience. *Entrance requirements:* For master's, 3 letters of recommendation, minimum GPA of 3.0; for doctorate, minimum GPA of 3.5 in master's coursework, 3 letters of recommendation. *Application deadline:* For fall admission, 7/15 priority date for domestic students; for spring admission, 12/15 priority date for domestic students. Applications are processed on a rolling basis. Application fee: $25. *Expenses: Tuition:* Full-time $11,890; part-time $765 per credit hour. Tuition and fees vary according to class time, course load, degree level, program and student's religious affiliation. *Financial support:* Fellowships, research assistantships with partial tuition reimbursements, career-related internships or fieldwork, Federal Work-Study, and scholarships/grants available. Financial award applicants required to submit FAFSA. *Unit head:* Dr. Nancy Blair, Chair, 414-410-4367. *Application contact:* 800-347-8822 Ext. 4042, E-mail: gradadm@stritch.edu.

Central Michigan University, College of Graduate Studies, College of Education and Human Services, Department of Educational Leadership, Mount Pleasant, MI 48859. Offers educational leadership (Ed D), including educational technology (Ed D, Ed S), higher education leadership, K-12 curriculum, K-12 leadership; general educational administration (Ed S), including administrative leadership K-12, educational technology (Ed D, Ed S), higher education administration, instructional leadership K-12; school principalship (MA), including charter school leadership, site-based leadership; student affairs administration (MA); teacher leadership (MA). *Program availability:* Part-time, evening/weekend. *Degree requirements:* For master's and Ed S, thesis or alternative; for doctorate, thesis/dissertation. *Entrance requirements:* For doctorate, GRE or MAT, master's degree, minimum GPA of 3.5, 3 years of professional education experience. Electronic applications accepted. *Faculty research:* Elementary administration, secondary administration, student achievement, in-service training, internships in administration.

The Citadel, The Military College of South Carolina, Citadel Graduate College, Zucker Family School of Education, Charleston, SC 29409. Offers elementary/secondary school administration and supervision (M Ed); elementary/secondary school counseling (M Ed); interdisciplinary STEM education (M Ed); literacy education (M Ed, Graduate Certificate); middle grades (MAT), including English, mathematics, science, social studies; physical education (grades K-12) (MAT); school superintendency (Ed S); secondary education (MAT), including biology, English, mathematics, social studies; student affairs (Graduate Certificate); student affairs and college counseling (M Ed). *Accreditation:* NCATE. *Program availability:* Part-time, evening/weekend, 100% online, blended/hybrid learning. *Faculty:* 9 full-time (4 women), 9 part-time/adjunct (5 women). *Students:* 70 full-time (58 women), 249 part-time (200 women); includes 87 minority (70 Black or African American, non-Hispanic/Latino; 1 Asian, non-Hispanic/Latino; 9 Hispanic/Latino; 7 Two or more races, non-Hispanic/Latino), 2 international. 146 applicants, 98% accepted, 105 enrolled. In 2016, 85 master's, 7 other advanced degrees awarded. *Degree requirements:* For master's, comprehensive exam (for some programs). *Entrance requirements:* For master's, GRE (minimum combined verbal and quantitative score of 290) or MAT (minimum score 396). Additional exam requirements/recommendations for international students: Required—TOEFL (minimum score 550 paper-based; 79 iBT). *Application deadline:* Applications are processed on a rolling basis. Application fee: $40. Electronic applications accepted. *Expenses:* Tuition, state resident: full-time $5121; part-time $569 per credit hour. Tuition, nonresident: full-time $8613; part-time $957 per credit hour. *Required fees:* $90 per term. *Financial support:* Fellowships and unspecified assistantships available. Support available to part-time students. Financial award application deadline: 7/1; financial award applicants required to submit FAFSA. *Unit head:* Dr. Larry G. Daniel, Dean, 843-953-5097, E-mail: ldaniel@citadel.edu. *Application contact:* Dr. Tammy J. Graham, Associate Professor, 843-953-6854, E-mail: tammy.graham@citadel.edu.
Website: http://www.citadel.edu/root/education-graduate-programs

Claremont Graduate University, Graduate Programs, School of Educational Studies, Claremont, CA 91711-6160. Offers Africana education (Certificate); education and policy (MA, PhD); higher education/student affairs (MA, PhD); human development (MA, PhD); public school administration (MA, PhD); quantitative evaluation (MA, PhD); special education (MA, PhD); teacher education (MA); teaching and learning (MA, PhD); urban leadership (PhD); MBA/PhD. PhD program offered jointly with San Diego State University. *Program availability:* Part-time. *Faculty:* 14 full-time (9 women), 1 part-time/adjunct (0 women). *Students:* 195 full-time (143 women), 196 part-time (137 women); includes 217 minority (43 Black or African American, non-Hispanic/Latino; 4 American Indian or Alaska Native, non-Hispanic/Latino; 32 Asian, non-Hispanic/Latino; 117 Hispanic/Latino; 2 Native Hawaiian or other Pacific Islander, non-Hispanic/Latino; 19 Two or more races, non-Hispanic/Latino), 14 international. Average age 38. In 2016, 48 master's, 39 doctorates, 7 other advanced degrees awarded. Terminal master's awarded for partial completion of doctoral program. *Entrance requirements:* For master's and doctorate, GRE General Test. Additional exam requirements/recommendations for international students: Required—TOEFL (minimum score 75 iBT). *Application deadline:* For fall admission, 3/1 priority date for domestic and international students. Applications are processed on a rolling basis. Application fee: $80. Electronic applications accepted. *Expenses: Tuition:* Full-time $44,328; part-time $1847 per unit. *Required fees:* $600; $300 per semester. Tuition and fees vary according to course load and program. *Financial support:* Fellowships, research assistantships, Federal Work-Study, institutionally sponsored loans, and scholarships/grants available. Support available to part-time students. Financial award application deadline: 2/15; financial award applicants required to submit FAFSA. *Faculty research:* Education administration, K-12 and higher education, multicultural education, education policy, diversity in higher education, faculty issues. *Unit head:* Allen Omoto, Dean, 909-607-3786, E-mail: allen.omoto@cgu.edu. *Application contact:* Rachel Camacho, Senior Assistant Director of Admission, 909-607-9418, E-mail: camacho@cgu.edu.
Website: https://www.cgu.edu/school/school-of-educational-studies/

Clemson University, Graduate School, College of Education, Department of Educational and Organizational Leadership Development, Clemson, SC 29634. Offers administration and supervision (M Ed, Ed S); athletic leadership (MS, Certificate); educational leadership (PhD), including educational leadership; human resource development (MHRD), including human resource development; student affairs (M Ed). *Program availability:* Part-time, evening/weekend, 100% online. *Faculty:* 20 full-time (13 women), 1 part-time/adjunct (0 women). *Students:* 36 full-time (22 women), 243 part-time (150 women); includes 70 minority (53 Black or African American, non-Hispanic/Latino; 1 American Indian or Alaska Native, non-Hispanic/Latino; 2 Asian, non-Hispanic/Latino; 11 Hispanic/Latino; 3 Two or more races, non-Hispanic/Latino), 3 international. Average age 35. 136 applicants, 67% accepted, 79 enrolled. In 2016, 83 master's, 13 doctorates, 21 other advanced degrees awarded. *Degree requirements:* For master's, thesis (for some programs); for doctorate, comprehensive exam, thesis/dissertation. *Entrance requirements:* For master's and doctorate, GRE General Test, unofficial transcripts, letters of recommendation. Additional exam requirements/recommendations for international students: Required—TOEFL (minimum score 80 iBT), IELTS (minimum score 7). *Application deadline:* For fall admission, 3/1 priority date for domestic and international students; for spring admission, 10/1 priority date for domestic and international students. Applications are processed on a rolling basis. Application fee: $80 ($90 for international students). Electronic applications accepted. *Expenses:* $4,264 per semester full-time resident, $8,485 per semester full-time non-resident, $471 per credit hour part-time resident, $942 per credit hour part-time non-resident. *Financial support:* In 2016–17, 29 students received support, including 5 fellowships with partial tuition reimbursements available (averaging $5,000 per year), 7 research assistantships with partial tuition reimbursements available (averaging $14,596 per year), 1 teaching assistantship with partial tuition reimbursement available (averaging $18,000 per year); career-related internships or fieldwork and unspecified assistantships also available. Financial award application deadline: 3/1. *Total annual research expenditures:* $31,201. *Unit head:* Dr. Robert Knoeppel, Department Chair, 864-656-1882, E-mail: rck@clemson.edu. *Application contact:* Dr. David Fleming, Graduate Programs Coordinator, 864-656-1881, Fax: 864-656-0311, E-mail: dflemin@clemson.edu.
Website: http://www.clemson.edu/education/departments/educational-organizational-leadership-development/index.html

College of Saint Elizabeth, Department of Psychology, Morristown, NJ 07960-6989. Offers counseling psychology (MA); forensic psychology (MA); mental health counseling (Certificate); psychology (Psy D); student affairs in higher education (Certificate). *Program availability:* Part-time. *Degree requirements:* For master's, thesis or alternative. *Entrance requirements:* For master's, minimum GPA of 3.0, BA in psychology (preferred), 12 credits of course work in psychology; for doctorate, GRE, 3 letters of recommendation from professionals who can comment on the applicant's qualifications for doctoral study; master's degree in counseling psychology, forensic psychology and counseling, or its equivalent. Additional exam requirements/recommendations for international students: Required—TOEFL (minimum score 550 paper-based; 79 iBT), IELTS (minimum score 6.5). Electronic applications accepted. *Expenses:* Contact institution.

The College of Saint Rose, Graduate Studies, Thelma P. Lally School of Education, Program in College Student Services Administration, Albany, NY 12203-1419. Offers MS Ed. *Accreditation:* NCATE. *Program availability:* Part-time, evening/weekend. *Students:* 9 full-time (6 women), 6 part-time (all women); includes 6 minority (1 Black or African American, non-Hispanic/Latino; 1 Asian, non-Hispanic/Latino; 4 Hispanic/Latino), 1 international. Average age 25. 13 applicants, 92% accepted, 6 enrolled. In 2016, 5 master's awarded. *Degree requirements:* For master's, comprehensive exam or thesis. *Entrance requirements:* For master's, interview, minimum undergraduate GPA of 3.0, 9 hours of psychology coursework. Additional exam requirements/recommendations for international students: Required—TOEFL (minimum score 550 paper-based; 80 iBT), IELTS (minimum score 6), PTE (minimum score 56). *Application deadline:* For fall admission, 4/1 for domestic and international students; for spring admission, 10/15 priority date for domestic and international students; for summer admission, 3/15 for domestic and international students. Applications are processed on a rolling basis. Application fee: $40. Electronic applications accepted. *Expenses: Tuition:* Full-time $14,382; part-time $799 per credit. *Required fees:* $814; $32 per credit. $88 per semester. Tuition and fees vary according to course load. *Financial support:* Career-related internships or fieldwork, scholarships/grants, tuition waivers (partial), and unspecified assistantships available. Support available to part-time students. Financial award application deadline: 4/15. *Unit head:* Dr. Jelane Kennedy, Chair, 518-454-5289, E-mail: kennedyj@strose.edu. *Application contact:* Cris Murray, Assistant Vice President for Graduate Recruitment and Enrollment, 518-485-3390, Fax: 518-458-5479, E-mail: grad@strose.edu.
Website: https://www.strose.edu/academics/agraduate-programs/college-student-services-administration-ms/

Colorado State University, College of Health and Human Sciences, School of Education, Fort Collins, CO 80523-1588. Offers adult education and training (M Ed); counseling and career development (M Ed); education sciences (PhD); higher education leadership (PhD); organization learning, performance, and change (PhD); organizational learning, performance, and change (M Ed); student affairs in higher education (MS); teaching and learning (M Ed), including principal licensure, teacher licensure. *Accreditation:* ACA; TEAC. *Program availability:* Part-time, online only, 100% online, blended/hybrid learning, face-to-face off-campus courses. *Faculty:* 29 full-time (21 women), 23 part-time/adjunct (11 women). *Students:* 80 full-time (56 women), 541 part-time (353 women); includes 142 minority (26 Black or African American, non-Hispanic/Latino; 2 American Indian or Alaska Native, non-Hispanic/Latino; 22 Asian, non-Hispanic/Latino; 71 Hispanic/Latino; 21 Two or more races, non-Hispanic/Latino), 18 international. Average age 37. 483 applicants, 31% accepted, 137 enrolled. In 2016, 183 master's, 33 doctorates awarded. *Degree requirements:* For master's, thesis optional, professional portfolio; for doctorate, comprehensive exam, thesis/dissertation. *Entrance requirements:* For master's, bachelor's degree; minimum GPA of 3.0 in last degree earned; for doctorate, GRE or GMAT (depending upon specialization), master's degree; minimum GPA of 3.0 in last degree earned. Additional exam requirements/recommendations for international students: Required—TOEFL (minimum score 550 paper-based; 80 iBT), IELTS (minimum score 6.5), PTE (minimum score 58). *Application deadline:* Applications are processed on a rolling basis. Application fee: $60 ($70 for international students). Electronic applications accepted. *Expenses:* Contact institution. *Financial support:* In 2016–17, 3 students received support, including 7 research assistantships with full tuition reimbursements available (averaging $11,749 per year), 5 teaching assistantships with full tuition reimbursements available (averaging $15,886 per year); fellowships with full tuition reimbursements available, scholarships/grants, and unspecified assistantships also available. Financial award application deadline: 3/1; financial award applicants required to submit FAFSA. *Faculty research:* Higher education leadership; research methods; human resource development; K-16 education; diversity, equity, and inclusion. *Total annual research expenditures:* $499,898. *Unit head:* Dr. Louise Jennings, Co-Director, 970-491-6317, Fax: 970-491-1317, E-mail: louise.jennings@colostate.edu. *Application contact:* Kelli Clark, Graduate Programs Coordinator, 970-491-2093, Fax: 970-491-1317, E-mail: kelli.clark@colostate.edu.
Website: http://www.soe.chhs.colostate.edu/

Dallas Baptist University, Gary Cook School of Leadership, Program in Higher Education, Dallas, TX 75211-9299. Offers administration (M Ed), including community college leadership, distance learning, interdisciplinary studies, student affairs leadership; instructional (M Ed). *Program availability:* Part-time, evening/weekend, 100% online, blended/hybrid learning. *Application deadline:* Applications are processed on a rolling basis. Application fee: $25. Electronic applications accepted. Application fee is waived when completed online. *Expenses: Tuition:* Full-time $15,408; part-time $856 per credit hour. *Required fees:* $400 per semester. Tuition and fees vary according to course load and degree level. *Faculty research:* Enrollment management, portfolio assessment, servant leadership. *Unit head:* Mamo Ishida, Director, 214-333-5812, E-mail: mamo@dbu.edu. *Application contact:* Bobby Soto, Director of Admissions, 214-333-5242, E-mail: graduate@dbu.edu.
Website: http://www3.dbu.edu/leadership/hied/

DePaul University, College of Education, Chicago, IL 60614. Offers bilingual bicultural education (M Ed, MA); counseling (M Ed, MA), including clinical mental health counseling, college student development, school counseling; curriculum studies (M Ed, MA, Ed D); early childhood education (M Ed, MA, Ed D); educating adults (MA); educational leadership (M Ed, MA, Ed D), including administration and supervision (M Ed, MA), principal preparation (M Ed, MA); elementary education (MA); mathematics education (MA); mathematics for teaching (MS); middle school mathematics education (MS); reading specialist (M Ed, MA); secondary education (M Ed); social and cultural foundations in education (MA); special education (M Ed, MA); world languages education (M Ed, MA). *Program availability:* Part-time, evening/weekend, online learning. *Degree requirements:* For doctorate, thesis/dissertation. Electronic applications accepted.

Eastern Illinois University, Graduate School, College of Education and Professional Studies, Department of Counseling and Student Development, Charleston, IL 61920. Offers college student affairs (MS); counseling (MS). *Accreditation:* ACA; NCATE. *Program availability:* Part-time, evening/weekend. *Degree requirements:* For master's, comprehensive exam (for some programs), thesis (for some programs). *Entrance requirements:* For master's, GMAT or GRE. Additional exam requirements/recommendations for international students: Required—TOEFL (minimum score 500 paper-based; 61 iBT), IELTS (minimum score 6). Electronic applications accepted.

Eastern Michigan University, Graduate School, Academic and Student Affairs Division, Ypsilanti, MI 48197. Offers individualized studies (MA, MS); integrated marketing communications (MS). *Students:* 2 full-time (both women), 50 part-time (33 women); includes 8 minority (3 Black or African American, non-Hispanic/Latino; 4 Asian, non-Hispanic/Latino; 1 Two or more races, non-Hispanic/Latino), 1 international. 84 applicants, 83% accepted, 31 enrolled. *Entrance requirements:* Additional exam requirements/recommendations for international students: Required—TOEFL. Application fee: $45. *Unit head:* Dr. Wade Tornquist, Interim Dean, 734-487-0042, Fax: 734-487-0050, E-mail: wade.tornquist@emich.edu. *Application contact:* Graduate Admissions, 734-487-2400, Fax: 734-487-6559, E-mail: graduate.admissions@emich.edu.

Eastern Michigan University, Graduate School, College of Education, Department of Leadership and Counseling, Programs in Educational Leadership, Ypsilanti, MI 48197. Offers community college leadership (Graduate Certificate); educational leadership (MA, Ed D, SPA); higher education/general administration (MA); higher education/student affairs (MA); K-12 administration (MA); K-12 basic administration (Post Master's Certificate). *Program availability:* Part-time, evening/weekend, online learning. *Students:* 52 full-time (39 women), 298 part-time (198 women); includes 103 minority (81 Black or African American, non-Hispanic/Latino; 3 American Indian or Alaska Native, non-Hispanic/Latino; 4 Asian, non-Hispanic/Latino; 10 Hispanic/Latino; 5 Two or more races, non-Hispanic/Latino), 2 international. Average age 35. 185 applicants, 70% accepted, 67 enrolled. In 2016, 85 master's, 28 doctorates, 23 other advanced degrees awarded. *Degree requirements:* For master's, portfolio. *Entrance requirements:* For doctorate, GRE. Additional exam requirements/recommendations for international students: Required—TOEFL. *Application deadline:* For winter admission, 2/1 for domestic and international students. Applications are processed on a rolling basis. Application fee: $45. *Financial support:* Fellowships, research assistantships with full tuition reimbursements, teaching assistantships with full tuition reimbursements, career-related internships or fieldwork, Federal Work-Study, institutionally sponsored loans, scholarships/grants, tuition waivers (partial), and unspecified assistantships available. Support available to part-time students. *Application contact:* Dr. Jaclynn Tracy, Coordinator of Advising, Programs in Educational Leadership, 734-487-0255, Fax: 734-487-4608, E-mail: jtracy@emich.edu.

Fresno Pacific University, Graduate Programs, School of Education, Division of Pupil Personnel Services, Fresno, CA 93702-4709. Offers board certified associate behavior analyst (Certificate); school counseling (MA); school psychology (MA). *Program availability:* Part-time. *Degree requirements:* For master's, thesis or alternative. *Entrance requirements:* Additional exam requirements/recommendations for international students: Required—TOEFL (minimum score 550 paper-based).

The George Washington University, Graduate School of Education and Human Development, Department of Educational Leadership, Program in Higher Education Administration, Washington, DC 20052. Offers college teaching and academic leadership (MA Ed/HD, Ed S); general administration (MA Ed/HD, Ed S); higher education administration (Ed D); higher education finance (MA Ed/HD, Ed S); international education (MA Ed/HD, Ed S); policy (MA Ed/HD, Ed S); student affairs administration (MA Ed/HD, Ed S). *Accreditation:* NCATE. *Students:* 23 full-time (18 women), 70 part-time (51 women); includes 35 minority (20 Black or African American, non-Hispanic/Latino; 8 Asian, non-Hispanic/Latino; 6 Hispanic/Latino; 1 Two or more races, non-Hispanic/Latino), 3 international. Average age 31. 148 applicants, 74% accepted, 37 enrolled. In 2016, 30 master's, 9 doctorates, 1 other advanced degree awarded. *Degree requirements:* For master's and Ed S, comprehensive exam; for doctorate, comprehensive exam, thesis/dissertation. *Entrance requirements:* For master's, GRE General Test or MAT, minimum GPA of 2.75; for doctorate, GRE General Test or MAT, interview, minimum GPA of 3.3; for Ed S, GRE General Test or MAT, minimum GPA of 3.3. *Application deadline:* For fall admission, 1/15 priority date for domestic students; for spring admission, 10/1 for domestic students. Applications are processed on a rolling basis. Application fee: $75. *Financial support:* In 2016–17, 17 students received support. Fellowships, research assistantships, career-related internships or fieldwork, Federal Work-Study, and tuition waivers (partial) available. Financial award application deadline: 1/15; financial award applicants required to submit FAFSA. *Faculty research:* Technology in higher education administration. *Unit head:* Michael Feuer, Dean, 202-994-6161, E-mail: mjfeuer@gwu.edu. *Application contact:* Sarah Lang, Director of Graduate Admissions, 202-994-1447, Fax: 202-994-7207, E-mail: slang@gwu.edu.

Grambling State University, School of Graduate Studies and Research, College of Education, Department of Educational Leadership, Grambling, LA 71245. Offers developmental education (MS, Ed D, PMC), including curriculum and instructional design (Ed D), English (MS), guidance and counseling (MS), higher education administration and management (Ed D), mathematics (MS), reading (MS), science (MS), student development and personnel services (Ed D); educational leadership (M Ed). *Program availability:* Part-time, evening/weekend. *Degree requirements:* For master's, comprehensive exam, thesis (for some programs); for doctorate, comprehensive exam, thesis/dissertation. *Entrance requirements:* For master's, GRE, minimum GPA of 2.5 on last degree; for doctorate, GRE (minimum score 1000, 500 on Verbal), master's degree, minimum GPA of 3.0 on last degree. Additional exam requirements/recommendations for international students: Required—TOEFL (minimum score 500 paper-based; 62 iBT). Electronic applications accepted.

Hampton University, School of Education and Human Development, Program in Counseling, Hampton, VA 23668. Offers college student development (MA); community agency counseling (MA); counseling (Ed S); counselor education and supervision (PhD); pastoral counseling (MA); school counseling (MA). *Accreditation:* ACA; NCATE. *Program availability:* Part-time, evening/weekend, online learning. *Faculty:* 4 full-time (2 women). *Students:* 37 full-time (34 women), 17 part-time (16 women); includes 49 minority (all Black or African American, non-Hispanic/Latino), 1 international. Average age 32. 55 applicants, 53% accepted, 19 enrolled. In 2016, 20 master's awarded. *Degree requirements:* For master's, comprehensive exam; for doctorate, comprehensive exam, thesis/dissertation. *Entrance requirements:* For master's, GRE General Test, personal statement, two letters of recommendation; for doctorate, GRE General Test, personal statement, writing sample, three letters of recommendation; for Ed S, personal statement, two letters of recommendation. Additional exam requirements/recommendations for international students: Required—TOEFL (minimum score 525 paper-based) or IELTS (6.5). *Application deadline:* For fall admission, 6/1 priority date for domestic students, 4/1 priority date for international students; for winter admission, 9/1 priority date for international students; for spring admission, 11/1 priority date for domestic students, 9/1 for international students; for summer admission, 4/1 priority date for domestic students, 2/1 priority date for international students. Applications are processed on a rolling basis. Application fee: $35. Electronic applications accepted. *Expenses: Tuition:* Full-time $10,776; part-time $548 per credit hour. *Required fees:* $35; $35 per credit hour. Tuition and fees vary according to course load and program. *Financial support:* Fellowships, research assistantships, teaching assistantships, career-related internships or fieldwork, Federal Work-Study, institutionally sponsored loans, and scholarships/grants available. Support available to part-time students. Financial award application deadline: 6/30; financial award applicants required to submit FAFSA. *Faculty research:* Personality development, temperament, post-traumatic stress disorder, continuum of normal to abnormal personality. *Unit head:* Dr. Spencer R. Baker, Chair, 757-637-2232, E-mail: spencer.baker@hamptonu.edu.
Website: http://edhd.hamptonu.edu/counseling/

Illinois State University, Graduate School, College of Education, Department of Educational Administration and Foundations, Program in College Student Personnel Administration, Normal, IL 61790-2200. Offers MS.

Indiana State University, College of Graduate and Professional Studies, Bayh College of Education, Department of Educational Leadership, Terre Haute, IN 47809. Offers educational administration (PhD); higher education leadership (PhD); K-12 district leadership (PhD); school administration (Ed S); school administration and supervision (M Ed); student affairs and higher education (MS). *Accreditation:* NCATE. *Program availability:* Part-time, evening/weekend. Terminal master's awarded for partial completion of doctoral program. *Degree requirements:* For master's, thesis; for doctorate, thesis/dissertation. *Entrance requirements:* For master's, GRE General Test, minimum undergraduate GPA of 2.5; for doctorate, GRE General Test, minimum undergraduate GPA of 3.5; for Ed S, GRE General Test, minimum graduate GPA of 3.25. Electronic applications accepted.

Indiana University Bloomington, School of Education, Department of Educational Leadership and Policy Studies, Bloomington, IN 47405. Offers educational leadership (MS, Ed D, Ed S); higher education (Ed D, PhD); higher education and student affairs (MS); history and philosophy of education (MS); history, philosophy, and policy in education (PhD), including education policy studies, history of education, philosophy of education; international and comparative education (MS). *Accreditation:* NCATE. *Faculty:* 32 full-time (18 women). *Students:* 223 full-time (140 women), 94 part-time (50 women); includes 80 minority (44 Black or African American, non-Hispanic/Latino; 13 Asian, non-Hispanic/Latino; 18 Hispanic/Latino; 1 Native Hawaiian or other Pacific Islander, non-Hispanic/Latino; 4 Two or more races, non-Hispanic/Latino), 29 international. Average age 34. 309 applicants, 40% accepted, 57 enrolled. In 2016, 60 master's, 18 doctorates, 5 other advanced degrees awarded. *Degree requirements:* For master's, thesis optional; for doctorate, comprehensive exam, thesis/dissertation; for Ed S, comprehensive exam or project. *Entrance requirements:* For master's, doctorate, and Ed S, GRE General Test. Additional exam requirements/recommendations for international students: Required—TOEFL (minimum score 79 iBT). *Application deadline:* For fall admission, 1/15 priority date for domestic students, 12/1 priority date for international students; for spring admission, 9/1 priority date for domestic and international students. Applications are processed on a rolling basis. Application fee: $55 ($65 for international students). Electronic applications accepted. *Financial support:* Fellowships with full and partial tuition reimbursements, research assistantships with full and partial tuition reimbursements, teaching assistantships with full and partial tuition reimbursements, career-related internships or fieldwork, scholarships/grants, health care benefits, and unspecified assistantships available. *Faculty research:* Culturally engaging campus environments, school choice policy analysis, democracy and education in the national and international context, and principal leadership. *Unit head:* Dr. Dionne Danns, Interim Chair, 812-856-8398. *Application contact:* Maria Jensen, Department Administrator, 812-856-8370, Fax: 812-856-8394, E-mail: jensen5@indiana.edu.
Website: http://education.indiana.edu/about/departments/leadership/index.html

Indiana University of Pennsylvania, School of Graduate Studies and Research, College of Education and Educational Technology, Department of Student Affairs in Higher Education, Indiana, PA 15705. Offers MA. *Accreditation:* NCATE. *Program availability:* Part-time. *Faculty:* 4 full-time (2 women), 1 part-time/adjunct (0 women). *Students:* 45 full-time (37 women), 5 part-time (4 women); includes 11 minority (6 Black or African American, non-Hispanic/Latino; 3 Hispanic/Latino; 1 Native Hawaiian or other Pacific Islander, non-Hispanic/Latino; 1 Two or more races, non-Hispanic/Latino). Average age 24. 101 applicants, 61% accepted, 26 enrolled. In 2016, 21 master's awarded. *Degree requirements:* For master's, comprehensive exam, thesis optional. *Entrance requirements:* For master's, resume, interview, 2 letters of recommendation, writing sample, minimum GPA of 2.8. Additional exam requirements/recommendations for international students: Required—TOEFL (minimum score 540 paper-based). *Application deadline:* For fall admission, 1/15 priority date for domestic students. Application fee: $50. Electronic applications accepted. *Expenses:* Contact institution. *Financial support:* In 2016–17, 21 research assistantships with tuition reimbursements (averaging $5,445 per year) were awarded; fellowships, career-related internships or fieldwork, Federal Work-Study, scholarships/grants, and unspecified assistantships also available. Support available to part-time students. Financial award application deadline: 4/15; financial award applicants required to submit FAFSA. *Unit head:* Dr. John Wesley Lowery, Chairperson, 724-357-4545, E-mail: jlowery@iup.edu.
Website: http://www.iup.edu/sahe

Iowa State University of Science and Technology, Department of Educational Leadership and Policy Studies, Ames, IA 50011. Offers counselor education (M Ed, MS); educational administration (M Ed, MS); educational leadership (PhD); higher education (M Ed, MS); organizational learning and human resource development (M Ed, MS); research and evaluation (MS); student affairs (MS). *Degree requirements:* For master's, thesis or alternative; for doctorate, thesis/dissertation. *Entrance requirements:* For master's and doctorate, GRE General Test. Additional exam requirements/recommendations for international students: Required—TOEFL (minimum score 560 paper-based; 83 iBT), IELTS (minimum score 6.5). *Application deadline:* For fall admission, 1/1 priority date for domestic and international students. Application fee: $60 ($90 for international students). Electronic applications accepted. *Application contact:* Robyn Goldy, Application Contact, 515-294-1241, Fax: 515-294-4942, E-mail: rgoldy@iastate.edu.
Website: http://www.elps.hs.iastate.edu/

Kansas State University, Graduate School, College of Education, Department of Special Education, Counseling and Student Affairs, Manhattan, KS 66506. Offers academic advising (MS, Certificate); counseling and student development (MS), including college student development, school counseling; special education (MS, Ed D); special education, counseling, and student affairs (PhD). *Accreditation:* ACA; NCATE. *Program availability:* Part-time, online learning. *Faculty:* 16 full-time (11 women), 11 part-time/adjunct (5 women). *Students:* 108 full-time (63 women), 252 part-time (193 women); includes 83 minority (33 Black or African American, non-Hispanic/Latino; 4 American Indian or Alaska Native, non-Hispanic/Latino; 7 Asian, non-Hispanic/Latino; 28 Hispanic/Latino; 2 Native Hawaiian or other Pacific Islander, non-Hispanic/Latino; 9 Two or more races, non-Hispanic/Latino), 6 international. Average age 33. 189 applicants, 82% accepted, 96 enrolled. In 2016, 134 master's, 4 doctorates, 70 other advanced degrees awarded. *Degree requirements:* For master's, comprehensive exam; for doctorate, comprehensive exam, thesis/dissertation. *Entrance requirements:* For master's, minimum undergraduate GPA of 3.0; for doctorate, GRE General Test, minimum GPA of 3.0 in last 60 hours. Additional exam requirements/recommendations for international students: Required—TOEFL. *Application deadline:* For fall admission, 2/1 for domestic students, 1/1 priority date for international students; for spring admission, 8/1 for domestic students, 8/1 priority date for international students; for summer admission, 12/1 priority date for international students. Applications are processed on a rolling basis. Application fee: $50 ($75 for international students). Electronic applications accepted. *Expenses:* Tuition, state resident: full-time $9670. Tuition, nonresident: full-time $21,828. *Required fees:* $862. *Financial support:* In 2016–17, 3 teaching assistantships (averaging $14,727 per year) were awarded; career-related internships or fieldwork, institutionally sponsored loans, and scholarships/grants also available. Financial award application deadline: 3/1; financial award applicants required to submit FAFSA. *Faculty research:* Counseling supervision, academic advising, career development, student development, universal design for learning, autism, learning disabilities. *Total annual research expenditures:* $17,900. *Unit head:* Dr. Kenneth Hughey, Head, 785-532-5541, Fax: 785-532-7304, E-mail: khughey@ksu.edu. *Application contact:* Cassandra Llewelyn, Application Contact, 785-532-5541, Fax: 785-532-7304, E-mail: cjwalker@ksu.edu.
Website: http://www.coe.k-state.edu/departments/secsa/

Kaplan University, Davenport Campus, School of Higher Education Studies, Davenport, IA 52807. Offers college administration and leadership (MS); college teaching and learning (MS); student services (MS). *Program availability:* Part-time, evening/weekend, online learning. *Entrance requirements:* Additional exam requirements/recommendations for international students: Required—TOEFL (minimum score 550 paper-based; 80 iBT).

Kent State University, College of Education, Health and Human Services, School of Foundations, Leadership and Administration, Program in Higher Education and Student Personnel, Kent, OH 44242-0001. Offers M Ed. *Accreditation:* NCATE. *Program availability:* Part-time, evening/weekend. *Entrance requirements:* For master's, GRE if undergraduate GPA is below 3.0, resume, interview, 2 letters of recommendation, goals statement. Additional exam requirements/recommendations for international students: Required—TOEFL (minimum score 550 paper-based; 80 iBT). Electronic applications accepted. *Expenses:* Tuition, state resident: full-time $10,864; part-time $495 per credit hour. Tuition, nonresident: full-time $18,380; part-time $837 per credit hour. *Faculty research:* History/sociology of higher education, organization and administration in higher education.

Lewis & Clark College, Graduate School of Education and Counseling, Department of Educational Leadership, Program in Educational Leadership, Portland, OR 97219-7899. Offers educational administration (M Ed, Ed S); educational leadership (Ed D); student affairs administration (MA). *Program availability:* Part-time, evening/weekend. *Degree requirements:* For doctorate, thesis/dissertation. *Entrance requirements:* For master's, minimum undergraduate GPA of 2.75, Oregon teaching or personnel service license, three years of successful teaching and/or personnel service experience in the public schools or regionally-accredited private schools; for doctorate, master's degree plus

minimum of 14 degree-applicable, post-master's semester credits; minimum undergraduate GPA of 2.75. Additional exam requirements/recommendations for international students: Required—TOEFL (minimum score 575 paper-based). *Application deadline:* For fall admission, 5/1 for domestic and international students. Applications are processed on a rolling basis. Application fee: $50. Electronic applications accepted. *Financial support:* Career-related internships or fieldwork, Federal Work-Study, institutionally sponsored loans, health care benefits, and tuition waivers (partial) available. Support available to part-time students. Financial award application deadline: 3/1; financial award applicants required to submit FAFSA. *Unit head:* Mollie Galloway, Department Chair, 503-768-6080, Fax: 503-768-6085, E-mail: eda@lclark.edu. *Application contact:* Becky Haas, Director of Admissions, 503-768-6200, Fax: 503-768-6205, E-mail: gseadmit@lclark.edu.
Website: http://www.lclark.edu/dept/eda/

Lewis University, College of Arts and Sciences, Program in Organizational Leadership, Romeoville, IL 60446. Offers higher education/student services (MA); non-profit management (MA); organizational management (MA); professional and executive coaching (MA); training and development (MA). *Program availability:* Part-time, evening/weekend, 100% online. *Students:* 15 full-time (12 women), 176 part-time (130 women); includes 75 minority (51 Black or African American, non-Hispanic/Latino; 2 American Indian or Alaska Native, non-Hispanic/Latino; 2 Asian, non-Hispanic/Latino; 16 Hispanic/Latino; 4 Two or more races, non-Hispanic/Latino), 2 international. Average age 36. *Entrance requirements:* For master's, bachelor's degree, at least 24 years of age, minimum of 3 years of work experience, minimum GPA of 3.0, letter of recommendation. Additional exam requirements/recommendations for international students: Required—TOEFL (minimum score 550 paper-based; 80 iBT). *Application deadline:* For fall admission, 5/1 priority date for international students; for spring admission, 11/15 priority date for international students. Applications are processed on a rolling basis. Application fee: $40. Electronic applications accepted. *Expenses: Tuition:* Full-time $13,860; part-time $770 per credit hour. *Required fees:* $75 per semester. Tuition and fees vary according to degree level and program. *Financial support:* Tuition waivers and unspecified assistantships available. Financial award application deadline: 5/1; financial award applicants required to submit FAFSA. *Unit head:* Dr. Keith Lavine, Chair of Organizational Leadership, 815-838-0500, E-mail: lavineke@lewisu.edu. *Application contact:* Nancy Wiksten, Graduate Admission Counselor, 815-836-5628, Fax: 815-836-5578, E-mail: grad@lewisu.edu.

Manhattan College, Graduate Programs, School of Education and Health, Program in Counseling, Riverdale, NY 10471. Offers bilingual pupil personnel services (Professional Diploma); mental health counseling (MS, Professional Diploma); school counseling (MA, Professional Diploma). *Program availability:* Part-time, evening/weekend. *Faculty:* 2 full-time (both women), 17 part-time/adjunct (8 women). *Students:* 70 full-time (55 women), 33 part-time (24 women); includes 56 minority (22 Black or African American, non-Hispanic/Latino; 2 Asian, non-Hispanic/Latino; 32 Hispanic/Latino). Average age 32. 51 applicants, 88% accepted, 38 enrolled. In 2016, 38 master's, 10 other advanced degrees awarded. *Degree requirements:* For master's, thesis, internship. *Entrance requirements:* For master's, minimum GPA of 3.0. Additional exam requirements/recommendations for international students: Required—TOEFL. *Application deadline:* For fall admission, 7/1 priority date for domestic students; for spring admission, 12/20 priority date for domestic students. Applications are processed on a rolling basis. Application fee: $75. Electronic applications accepted. *Expenses:* $925 per credit tuition; $175 per term information fee; $375 graduation fee; $105 per term registration fee. *Financial support:* Federal Work-Study, health care benefits, and unspecified assistantships available. Financial award application deadline: 2/1; financial award applicants required to submit FAFSA. *Faculty research:* Cognitive development, college and career readiness, group counseling, cultural attitudes, bullying, family social environments. *Unit head:* Dr. Corine Fitzpatrick, Director, 718-862-7497, Fax: 718-862-7472, E-mail: corine.fitzpatrick@manhattan.edu. *Application contact:* William Bisset, Vice President for Enrollment, 718-862-7199, Fax: 718-862-8019, E-mail: william.bisset@manhattan.edu.

Marquette University, Graduate School, College of Education, Department of Educational Policy and Leadership, Milwaukee, WI 53201-1881. Offers college student personnel administration (M Ed); curriculum and instruction (MA); education (MA); educational administration (M Ed); educational policy and foundations (MA); elementary education (Certificate); literacy (MA); principal (Certificate); reading specialist (Certificate); reading teacher (Certificate); secondary education (Certificate); superintendent (Certificate). *Program availability:* Part-time, evening/weekend. *Faculty:* 17 full-time (14 women), 28 part-time/adjunct (23 women). *Students:* 31 full-time (23 women), 103 part-time (66 women); includes 22 minority (7 Black or African American, non-Hispanic/Latino; 1 American Indian or Alaska Native, non-Hispanic/Latino; 6 Asian, non-Hispanic/Latino; 6 Hispanic/Latino; 2 Two or more races, non-Hispanic/Latino). Average age 31. 96 applicants, 92% accepted, 67 enrolled. In 2016, 47 master's, 3 other advanced degrees awarded. Terminal master's awarded for partial completion of doctoral program. *Degree requirements:* For master's, comprehensive exam, thesis (for some programs); for doctorate, thesis/dissertation, qualifying exam. *Entrance requirements:* For master's, GRE General Test or MAT, official transcripts from all current and previous colleges/universities except Marquette, three letters of recommendation, statement of purpose; for doctorate, GRE General Test, MAT, sample of written work, official transcripts from all current and previous colleges/universities except Marquette, three letters of recommendation, statement of purpose, resume/curriculum vitae; for Certificate, GRE General Test or MAT, master's degree. Additional exam requirements/recommendations for international students: Required—TOEFL (minimum score 530 paper-based). *Application deadline:* For fall admission, 1/15 for domestic and international students. Application fee: $50. *Expenses:* Contact institution. *Financial support:* Fellowships, research assistantships, health care benefits, tuition waivers (partial), and unspecified assistantships available. Support available to part-time students. Financial award application deadline: 2/15. *Faculty research:* Leadership; social justice in education; development of lifelong learners; race, class, and schooling in historical perspective; urban teacher education. *Unit head:* Dr. Ellen Eckman, Chair, 414-288-1561. *Application contact:* Dr. Cynthia Ellwood.

Merrimack College, School of Education and Social Policy, North Andover, MA 01845-5800. Offers community engagement (M Ed), including community organizations, higher education, K-12 education; criminology and criminal justice (MS); curriculum and instruction (M Ed); early childhood education (M Ed); educational leadership (CAGS), including instructional leadership; elementary education (M Ed); English as a second language (PreK-6) (M Ed); high school education (M Ed); higher education (M Ed), including leadership and organizational development, student affairs; middle school education (M Ed); moderate disabilities (PreK-8) (M Ed); school counseling (M Ed). *Program availability:* Part-time, evening/weekend, 100% online courses with immersion events and in-classroom practicum close to home. *Faculty:* 17 full-time, 34 part-time/adjunct. *Students:* 204 full-time (172 women), 83 part-time (67 women); includes 32 minority (4 Black or African American, non-Hispanic/Latino; 2 Asian, non-Hispanic/Latino; 23 Hispanic/Latino; 3 Two or more races, non-Hispanic/Latino), 1 international. Average age 27. 261 applicants, 89% accepted, 200 enrolled. In 2016, 153 master's, 2 other advanced degrees awarded. *Degree requirements:* For master's, practicum, portfolio, and state test (for licensure track); capstone (for higher education, curriculum and instruction, and community engagement tracks). *Entrance requirements:* For master's, Massachusetts Teacher Education Licensure (MTEL), official transcripts from other colleges, resume, personal statement, 2 letters of recommendation. Additional exam requirements/recommendations for international students: Required—TOEFL (minimum score 84 iBT), IELTS (minimum score 6.5), PTE (minimum score 56). *Application deadline:* For fall admission, 8/14 for domestic students, 7/14 for international students; for spring admission, 1/10 for domestic students, 12/10 for international students; for summer admission, 5/10 for domestic students, 4/10 for international students. Applications are processed on a rolling basis. Application fee: $0. Electronic applications accepted. *Expenses:* Contact institution. *Financial support:* Fellowships with full tuition reimbursements, career-related internships or fieldwork, scholarships/grants, and health care benefits available. Support available to part-time students. Financial award application deadline: 5/1; financial award applicants required to submit FAFSA. *Faculty research:* Feminist praxis in higher education, transgender student agency and belonging, campus sexual violence prevention, the scholarship of engagement; community engagement; service learning; diversity education; community-university partnerships, college going behaviors and indicators of success for inner city youth, strategies to increase students pursuit and success in STEM higher education, effective workforce development for displaced or under employed individuals, police reform, e.g. surveillance. *Application contact:* Alyssa Frey, Graduate Admissions Counselor, 978-837-3563, E-mail: freya@merrimack.edu.
Website: http://www.merrimack.edu/academics/graduate/education/

Messiah College, Program in Higher Education, Mechanicsburg, PA 17055. Offers college athletics management (MA); self-designed concentration (MA); student affairs (MA). *Program availability:* Part-time. Electronic applications accepted. *Faculty research:* College athletics management, assessment and student learning outcomes, the life and legacy of Ernest L. Boyer, common learning, student affairs practice.

Minnesota State University Mankato, College of Graduate Studies and Research, College of Education, Department of Counseling and Student Personnel, Mankato, MN 56001. Offers college student affairs (MS); counselor education and supervision (Ed D); mental health counseling (MS); professional school counseling (K-12) (MS). *Accreditation:* ACA (one or more programs are accredited); NCATE. *Students:* 77 full-time (68 women), 38 part-time (26 women). *Degree requirements:* For master's, comprehensive exam, thesis or alternative. *Entrance requirements:* For master's, GRE General Test or MAT (if GPA less than 3.0 for last 2 years), minimum GPA of 3.0 during previous 2 years, 3 letters of reference. Additional exam requirements/recommendations for international students: Required—TOEFL. *Application deadline:* For fall admission, 1/15 priority date for domestic students. Applications are processed on a rolling basis. Application fee: $40. Electronic applications accepted. *Financial support:* Research assistantships with full tuition reimbursements, teaching assistantships with full tuition reimbursements, career-related internships or fieldwork, Federal Work-Study, institutionally sponsored loans, and unspecified assistantships available. Support available to part-time students. Financial award application deadline: 3/15; financial award applicants required to submit FAFSA. *Unit head:* Dr. Jackie Lewis, Chair, E-mail: jacqueline.lewis@mnsu.edu.
Website: http://ed.mnsu.edu/csp/

Mississippi State University, College of Education, Department of Counseling, Educational Psychology, and Foundations, Mississippi State, MS 39762. Offers clinical mental health (MS); college counseling (MS); college/post secondary student counseling and personnel services (PhD); counselor education (Ed S); counselor education/student counseling and guidance services (PhD); general educational psychology (MS); psychometry (MS); rehabilitation (MS); school counseling (MS); school psychology (PhD, Ed S); student affairs (MS). *Accreditation:* ACA (one or more programs are accredited); APA; CORE (one or more programs are accredited); NCATE. *Program availability:* Part-time, blended/hybrid learning. *Faculty:* 21 full-time (14 women), 2 part-time/adjunct (both women). *Students:* 125 full-time (94 women), 70 part-time (60 women); includes 63 minority (48 Black or African American, non-Hispanic/Latino; 1 American Indian or Alaska Native, non-Hispanic/Latino; 4 Asian, non-Hispanic/Latino; 5 Hispanic/Latino; 5 Two or more races, non-Hispanic/Latino), 6 international. Average age 30. 151 applicants, 64% accepted, 70 enrolled. In 2016, 49 master's, 3 doctorates, 4 other advanced degrees awarded. Terminal master's awarded for partial completion of doctoral program. *Degree requirements:* For master's, comprehensive exam, thesis optional; for doctorate, thesis/dissertation, comprehensive oral and written exam. *Entrance requirements:* For master's, GRE (taken within the last five years), BS with minimum GPA of 2.75 on last 60 hours; for doctorate, GRE, MS from CACREP- or CORE-accredited program in counseling; for Ed S, GRE, MS in counseling or related field, minimum GPA of 3.3 on all graduate work. Additional exam requirements/recommendations for international students: Required—TOEFL (minimum score 550 paper-based; 79 iBT); Recommended—IELTS (minimum score 6.5). *Application deadline:* For fall admission, 2/1 priority date for domestic and international students. Applications are processed on a rolling basis. Application fee: $60. Electronic applications accepted. *Expenses:* Tuition, state resident: full-time $7670; part-time $852.50 per credit hour. Tuition, nonresident: full-time $20,790; part-time $2310.50 per credit hour. Part-time tuition and fees vary according to course load. *Financial support:* In 2016–17, 9 teaching assistantships with full tuition reimbursements (averaging $8,401 per year) were awarded; career-related internships or fieldwork, Federal Work-Study, institutionally sponsored loans, and unspecified assistantships also available. Financial award application deadline: 2/1; financial award applicants required to submit FAFSA. *Faculty research:* HIV/AIDS in college population, substance abuse in youth and college students, ADHD and conduct disorders in youth, assessment and identification of early childhood disabilities, assessment and vocational transition of the disabled. *Unit head:* Dr. David Morse, Professor and Head, 662-325-3426, Fax: 662-325-3263, E-mail: dmorse@colled.msstate.edu. *Application contact:* Linda Bonner, Senior Admissions Assistant, 662-325-3363, E-mail: lbonner@grad.msstate.edu.
Website: http://www.cep.msstate.edu/

Missouri State University, Graduate College, College of Education, Department of Counseling, Leadership, and Special Education, Program in Student Affairs in Higher Education, Springfield, MO 65897. Offers MS. *Program availability:* Part-time. *Students:* 32 full-time (26 women), 4 part-time (3 women); includes 6 minority (3 Black or African American, non-Hispanic/Latino; 1 Hispanic/Latino; 2 Two or more races, non-Hispanic/Latino), 3 international. Average age 26. 39 applicants, 69% accepted, 13 enrolled. In 2016, 10 master's awarded. *Degree requirements:* For master's, comprehensive exam, thesis or alternative. *Entrance requirements:* For master's, GRE, statement of purpose; three references. Additional exam requirements/recommendations for international students: Required—TOEFL (minimum score 550 paper-based; 79 iBT), IELTS (minimum score 6). *Application deadline:* For fall admission, 2/1 priority date for domestic students, 2/1 for international students. Applications are processed on a rolling basis. Application fee: $35 ($50 for international students). Electronic applications accepted. *Expenses:* Tuition, state resident: full-time $5830. Tuition, nonresident: full-time $10,708. *Required fees:* $1130. Tuition and fees vary according to class time, course level, course load and program. *Financial support:* Federal Work-Study, institutionally sponsored loans, scholarships/grants, and unspecified assistantships available. Financial award application deadline: 3/31; financial award applicants required to submit FAFSA. *Unit head:* Dr. James Satterfield, Department Head, 417-836-5392,

E-mail: clse@missouristate.edu. *Application contact:* Michael Edwards, Coordinator of Graduate Admissions, 417-836-5330, Fax: 417-836-6200, E-mail: michaeledwards@missouristate.edu.
Website: http://education.missouristate.edu/edadmin/MSEDSA.htm

Monmouth University, Graduate Studies, School of Education, West Long Branch, NJ 07764-1898. Offers applied behavior analysis (Certificate); autism (Certificate); director of school counseling services (Post-Master's Certificate); early childhood (M Ed); educational leadership (Ed D); elementary education (MAT), including elementary level, secondary level; English as a second language (M Ed); learning disabilities teacher-consultant (Post-Master's Certificate); literacy (MS Ed); school counseling (MS Ed); special education (MS Ed), including autism, learning disabilities teacher-consultant, teacher of students with disabilities, teaching in inclusive settings; speech-language pathology (MS Ed); student affairs and college counseling (MS Ed); supervisor (Post-Master's Certificate); teaching English to speakers of other languages (Certificate). *Accreditation:* NCATE. *Program availability:* Part-time, evening/weekend, 100% online, blended/hybrid learning. *Faculty:* 23 full-time (19 women), 33 part-time/adjunct (25 women). *Students:* 191 full-time (172 women), 141 part-time (122 women); includes 56 minority (10 Black or African American, non-Hispanic/Latino; 9 Asian, non-Hispanic/Latino; 31 Hispanic/Latino; 6 Two or more races, non-Hispanic/Latino). Average age 26. 423 applicants, 53% accepted, 139 enrolled. In 2016, 148 master's, 4 other advanced degrees awarded. *Entrance requirements:* For master's, GRE taken within last 5 years (for MS Ed in speech-language pathology); SAT (minimum combined score of 1660 in 3 sections), ACT (23), GRE (minimum score of 4.0 on analytical writing section and minimum combined score of 310 on quantitative and verbal sections), or passing scores on 3 parts of Core Academic Skills Educators, minimum GPA of 3.0 in major; 2 letters of recommendation (for some programs); resume, personal statement or essay (depending on program). Additional exam requirements/recommendations for international students: Required—TOEFL (minimum score 550 paper-based; 79 iBT), IELTS (minimum score 6), Michigan English Language Assessment Battery (minimum score 77) or Certificate of Advanced English (minimum score B2). *Application deadline:* For fall admission, 7/15 priority date for domestic students, 7/1 for international students; for spring admission, 12/1 priority date for domestic students, 11/1 for international students; for summer admission, 5/1 for domestic students. Applications are processed on a rolling basis. Application fee: $50. Electronic applications accepted. *Expenses: Tuition, area resident:* Full-time $19,764; part-time $1098 per credit hour. *Required fees:* $175 per semester. Tuition and fees vary according to program. *Financial support:* In 2016–17, 349 students received support, including 305 fellowships (averaging $3,558 per year), 48 teaching assistantships (averaging $9,619 per year); research assistantships, institutionally sponsored loans, scholarships/grants, and unspecified assistantships also available. Support available to part-time students. Financial award application deadline: 2/1; financial award applicants required to submit FAFSA. *Faculty research:* Multicultural literacy, science and mathematics teaching strategies, teacher as reflective practitioner, children with disabilities. *Unit head:* Dr. John E. Henning, Dean, 732-263-5513, Fax: 732-263-5277. *Application contact:* Laurie Kuhn, Associate Director of Graduate Admission, 732-571-3452, Fax: 732-263-5123, E-mail: gradadm@monmouth.edu.
Website: http://www.monmouth.edu/academics/schools/education/default.asp

New York University, Steinhardt School of Culture, Education, and Human Development, Department of Administration, Leadership, and Technology, Program in Higher Education, New York, NY 10012. Offers higher and postsecondary education (PhD); higher education administration (Ed D); higher education and student affairs (MA). *Accreditation:* TEAC. *Program availability:* Part-time. *Degree requirements:* For master's, thesis (for some programs); for doctorate, thesis/dissertation. *Entrance requirements:* For master's, interview, 2 letters of recommendation; for doctorate, GRE General Test, interview. Additional exam requirements/recommendations for international students: Required—TOEFL (minimum score 100 iBT). Electronic applications accepted. *Faculty research:* Organizational theory and culture, systemic change, leadership development, access, equity and diversity.

Northern Arizona University, Graduate College, College of Education, Department of Educational Psychology, Flagstaff, AZ 86011. Offers counseling (MA); educational psychology (PhD), including counseling psychology, school psychology; human relations (M Ed); school counseling (M Ed); school psychology (Ed S); student affairs (M Ed). *Program availability:* Part-time, online learning. Terminal master's awarded for partial completion of doctoral program. *Degree requirements:* For master's, internship (for some programs); for doctorate, comprehensive exam, thesis/dissertation, internship. *Entrance requirements:* Additional exam requirements/recommendations for international students: Required—TOEFL (minimum score 550 paper-based; 80 iBT), IELTS (minimum score 7). Electronic applications accepted. *Expenses:* Tuition, state resident: full-time $8971; part-time $444 per credit hour. Tuition, nonresident: full-time $20,958; part-time $1164 per credit hour. *Required fees:* $1018; $644 per credit hour. Tuition and fees vary according to course load, campus/location and program.

Northern Michigan University, Office of Graduate Education and Research, College of Health Sciences and Professional Studies, School of Education, Leadership and Public Service, Marquette, MI 49855-5301. Offers administration and supervision (MAE); elementary education (MAE); higher education in student affairs (MA); instruction (MAE); learning disabilities (MAE); public administration (MPA), including criminal justice administration, human resource administration, public administration, public management, state and local government; reading education (MAE), including reading, reading specialist; science education (MS); secondary education (MAE). *Accreditation:* TEAC. *Program availability:* Part-time, online learning. *Degree requirements:* For master's, thesis (for some programs). *Entrance requirements:* For master's, minimum GPA of 3.0. Additional exam requirements/recommendations for international students: Required—TOEFL (minimum score 550 paper-based; 79 iBT), IELTS (minimum score 6.5). Electronic applications accepted.

Northwestern State University of Louisiana, Graduate Studies and Research, College of Education and Human Development, Program in Student Affairs in Higher Education, Natchitoches, LA 71497. Offers MA. *Accreditation:* NCATE. *Degree requirements:* For master's, comprehensive exam, thesis or alternative. *Entrance requirements:* For master's, GRE General Test, GRE Subject Test, minimum undergraduate GPA of 2.5. Additional exam requirements/recommendations for international students: Required—TOEFL. Electronic applications accepted.

Nova Southeastern University, College of Arts, Humanities, and Social Sciences, Fort Lauderdale, FL 33314-7796. Offers advanced conflict resolution practice (Graduate Certificate); college student affairs (MS); conflict analysis and resolution (MS, PhD); cross-disciplinary studies (MA); family studies (Graduate Certificate); family systems health care (Graduate Certificate); family therapy (MS, PhD); marriage and family therapy (DMFT); peace studies (Graduate Certificate); qualitative research (Graduate Certificate); solution focused coaching (Graduate Certificate). *Accreditation:* AAMFT/COAMFTE (one or more programs are accredited). *Program availability:* Part-time, evening/weekend, 100% online, blended/hybrid learning. *Faculty:* 29 full-time (18 women), 27 part-time/adjunct (21 women). *Students:* 306 full-time (242 women), 889 part-time (683 women); includes 677 minority (403 Black or African American, non-Hispanic/Latino; 2 American Indian or Alaska Native, non-Hispanic/Latino; 20 Asian, non-Hispanic/Latino; 224 Hispanic/Latino; 1 Native Hawaiian or other Pacific Islander, non-Hispanic/Latino; 27 Two or more races, non-Hispanic/Latino), 53 international. Average age 37. 624 applicants, 61% accepted, 285 enrolled. In 2016, 303 master's, 71 doctorates, 34 other advanced degrees awarded. *Degree requirements:* For master's, thesis optional, comprehensive exams, portfolios (for some programs), table-top exams (for some programs); for doctorate, comprehensive exam, thesis/dissertation, qualifying exams, portfolios (for some programs). *Entrance requirements:* For master's, interview, minimum GPA of 3.0, writing sample; for doctorate, interview, minimum GPA of 3.5, master's degree in related field, writing sample; for Graduate Certificate, minimum GPA of 3.0. Additional exam requirements/recommendations for international students: Required—TOEFL. *Application deadline:* For fall admission, 5/17 priority date for domestic and international students; for winter admission, 12/1 priority date for domestic and international students; for spring admission, 4/1 priority date for domestic and international students. Applications are processed on a rolling basis. Application fee: $50. Electronic applications accepted. *Expenses:* $1,005. *Financial support:* In 2016–17, 170 students received support. Career-related internships or fieldwork, Federal Work-Study, scholarships/grants, and unspecified assistantships available. Financial award application deadline: 4/1; financial award applicants required to submit CSS PROFILE. *Faculty research:* Conflict resolution, family therapy, peace research, international conflict, multi-disciplinary studies, college student affairs, national security affairs, health care conflict resolution, family systems health care, advanced family systems, qualitative research, solution-focused coaching. *Unit head:* Dr. Honggang Yang, Dean, 954-262-3016, Fax: 954-262-3968, E-mail: yangh@nova.edu. *Application contact:* Marcia Arango, Student Recruitment Coordinator, 954-262-3006, Fax: 954-262-3968, E-mail: marango@nsu.nova.edu.
Website: http://cahss.nova.edu/

Ohio University, Graduate College, Gladys W. and David H. Patton College of Education and Human Services, Department of Counseling and Higher Education, Athens, OH 45701-2979. Offers college student personnel (M Ed); community/agency counseling (M Ed); counselor education (PhD); higher education (PhD); rehabilitation counseling (M Ed); school counseling (M Ed). *Accreditation:* ACA; CORE. *Program availability:* Part-time, evening/weekend. *Degree requirements:* For master's, comprehensive exam (for some programs), thesis or alternative; for doctorate, comprehensive exam, thesis/dissertation. *Entrance requirements:* For master's, GRE General Test or MAT (if GPA less than 2.9), 3 letters of reference; for doctorate, GRE General Test, work experience, minimum GPA of 3.4. Additional exam requirements/recommendations for international students: Required—TOEFL (minimum score 550 paper-based; 80 iBT) or IELTS (minimum score 6.5). *Application deadline:* For fall admission, 1/15 for domestic and international students. Application fee: $50 ($55 for international students). Electronic applications accepted. *Financial support:* Research assistantships with full tuition reimbursements, teaching assistantships with full tuition reimbursements, Federal Work-Study, institutionally sponsored loans, tuition waivers (partial), and unspecified assistantships available. Financial award application deadline: 1/15. *Faculty research:* Youth violence, gender studies, student affairs, chemical dependency, disabilities issues. *Unit head:* Dr. Tracy Leinbaugh, Chair, 740-593-0846, Fax: 740-593-0477, E-mail: leinbaug@ohio.edu. *Application contact:* Floyd J. Doney, Director of Student Affairs, 740-593-4400, Fax: 740-593-9310, E-mail: doney@ohio.edu.
Website: http://www.cehs.ohio.edu/academics/che/

Oregon State University, College of Liberal Arts, Program in College Student Services Administration, Corvallis, OR 97331. Offers Ed M, MS. *Faculty:* 6 full-time (5 women), 4 part-time/adjunct (2 women). *Students:* 27 full-time (19 women), 9 part-time (5 women); includes 13 minority (1 Black or African American, non-Hispanic/Latino; 4 Asian, non-Hispanic/Latino; 5 Hispanic/Latino; 3 Two or more races, non-Hispanic/Latino), 5 international. Average age 28. 67 applicants, 43% accepted, 19 enrolled. In 2016, 16 master's awarded. *Degree requirements:* For master's, thesis or alternative. *Entrance requirements:* For master's, minimum GPA of 3.0 in last 90 hours of course work. Additional exam requirements/recommendations for international students: Required—TOEFL (minimum score 80 iBT), IELTS (minimum score 6.5). *Application deadline:* For fall admission, 12/15 for domestic students. Application fee: $75 ($85 for international students). *Expenses:* Tuition, state resident: full-time $12,150; part-time $450 per credit. Tuition, nonresident: full-time $21,789; part-time $807 per credit. *Required fees:* $1651; $1507 per credit. One-time fee: $350. Tuition and fees vary according to course load, campus/location and program. *Financial support:* Teaching assistantships, career-related internships or fieldwork, Federal Work-Study, and institutionally sponsored loans available. Support available to part-time students. *Unit head:* Dr. Larry Roper, Interim Director, School of Language, Culture and Society/Professor, E-mail: larry.roper@oregonstate.edu.

Providence University College & Theological Seminary, Theological Seminary, Otterburne, MB R0A 1G0, Canada. Offers children's ministry (Certificate); Christian studies (MA, Certificate); counseling (MA); cross-cultural discipleship (Certificate); divinity (M Div); educational studies (MA), including counseling psychology, educational ministries, student development, teaching English to speakers of other languages, training teachers of English to speakers of other languages; global studies (MA); lay counseling (Diploma); ministry (D Min); teaching English to speakers of other languages (Certificate); theological studies (MA); training teacher of English to speakers of other languages (Certificate); youth ministry (Certificate). *Accreditation:* ATS. *Program availability:* Part-time. *Degree requirements:* For master's, variable foreign language requirement, thesis (for some programs); for doctorate, thesis/dissertation. *Entrance requirements:* Additional exam requirements/recommendations for international students: Recommended—TOEFL (minimum score 550 paper-based). *Faculty research:* Studies in Isaiah, theology of sin.

Regent University, Graduate School, School of Education, Virginia Beach, VA 23464-9800. Offers adult education (Ed D, PhD, Ed S); advanced educational leadership (Ed D, PhD, Ed S); career switcher (M Ed); character education (Ed D, PhD, Ed S); Christian education leadership (Ed D, PhD, Ed S); Christian school administration (M Ed); curriculum and instruction (M Ed), including adult education, Christian school, gifted and talented education, STEM education, teacher leader; educational leadership (M Ed); educational psychology (Ed D, PhD, Ed S); educational technology and online learning (Ed D, PhD, Ed S); elementary education (M Ed); exceptional education executive leadership (Ed D, PhD, Ed S); higher education (Ed D, PhD, Ed S); higher education leadership and management (Ed D, PhD, Ed S); individualized degree plan (M Ed); K-12 school leadership (Ed D, PhD, Ed S); K-12 special education (M Ed); K-8 leadership in mathematics education (M Ed); leadership in mathematics education (Ed S); reading specialist (M Ed); special education (Ed D, PhD, Ed S); student affairs (M Ed); TESOL (M Ed), including adult education - collegiate, K-12. *Accreditation:* TEAC. *Program availability:* Part-time, evening/weekend, 100% online, blended/hybrid learning. *Faculty:* 22 full-time (10 women), 42 part-time/adjunct (31 women). *Students:* 89 full-time (62 women), 1,035 part-time (823 women); includes 466 minority (381 Black or African American, non-Hispanic/Latino; 3 American Indian or Alaska Native, non-Hispanic/Latino; 19 Asian, non-Hispanic/Latino; 50 Hispanic/Latino; 13 Two or more races, non-Hispanic/Latino), 11 international. Average age 39. 976 applicants, 59% accepted, 449 enrolled. In 2016, 241 master's, 22 doctorates, 4 other advanced degrees awarded. *Degree requirements:* For master's, thesis or alternative; for doctorate, comprehensive exam, thesis/dissertation. *Entrance requirements:* For master's, Virginia Communication and Literacy Assessment (VCLA), PRAXIS, college transcripts, writing

sample, interview; for doctorate, GRE, writing sample, resume, transcripts, interview. Additional exam requirements/recommendations for international students: Required—TOEFL (minimum score 577 paper-based). *Application deadline:* For fall admission, 4/1 priority date for domestic students; for spring admission, 10/15 priority date for domestic students. Applications are processed on a rolling basis. Application fee: $50. Electronic applications accepted. *Expenses:* Contact institution. *Financial support:* In 2016–17, 622 students received support, including 1 fellowship (averaging $5,000 per year); career-related internships or fieldwork, scholarships/grants, and unspecified assistantships also available. Support available to part-time students. *Faculty research:* Christian school administration, curriculum and instruction, educational technology and online learning, higher education, special education. *Unit head:* Dr. Donald Finn, Dean, 757-352-4278, Fax: 757-352-4318, E-mail: dfinn@regent.edu. *Application contact:* Heidi Cece, Assistant Vice President of Enrollment Management, 800-373-5504, Fax: 757-352-4381, E-mail: admissions@regent.edu.
Website: http://www.regent.edu/soe/

Rutgers University–New Brunswick, Graduate School of Education, Department of Educational Psychology, Program in College Student Affairs, Piscataway, NJ 08854-8097. Offers Ed M. *Accreditation:* ACA. *Degree requirements:* For master's, comprehensive exam. *Entrance requirements:* For master's, GRE General Test, 3 letters of recommendation, resume. Additional exam requirements/recommendations for international students: Required—TOEFL (minimum score 550 paper-based; 83 iBT). Electronic applications accepted. *Faculty research:* Higher education equality, Latino college student experience.

St. Cloud State University, School of Graduate Studies, School of Education, Department of Educational Leadership and Higher Education, Program in College Counseling and Student Development, St. Cloud, MN 56301-4498. Offers MS. *Degree requirements:* For master's, comprehensive exam, thesis or alternative. *Entrance requirements:* For master's, GRE General Test, minimum GPA of 2.75. Additional exam requirements/recommendations for international students: Required—Michigan English Language Assessment Battery; Recommended—TOEFL (minimum score 550 paper-based), IELTS (minimum score 6.5). Electronic applications accepted.

St. Edward's University, New College, Program in College Student Development, Austin, TX 78704. Offers MA. *Program availability:* Part-time-only, evening/weekend. *Students:* 21 part-time (17 women); includes 11 minority (3 Black or African American, non-Hispanic/Latino; 6 Hispanic/Latino; 2 Two or more races, non-Hispanic/Latino). Average age 33. 16 applicants, 81% accepted, 7 enrolled. In 2016, 5 master's awarded. *Degree requirements:* For master's, 36 hours of coursework with minimum cumulative GPA of 3.0. *Entrance requirements:* For master's, GRE, minimum GPA of 3.0 on the last 60 semester hours of work, 2.75 on all college-level work. Additional exam requirements/recommendations for international students: Required—TOEFL (minimum score 79 iBT), IELTS (minimum score 6). *Application deadline:* For fall admission, 6/1 priority date for domestic and international students; for spring admission, 10/1 priority date for domestic and international students; for summer admission, 3/1 priority date for domestic and international students. Applications are processed on a rolling basis. Application fee: $50. Electronic applications accepted. *Expenses: Tuition:* Full-time $25,092; part-time $1394 per credit hour. *Required fees:* $75 per trimester. Full-time tuition and fees vary according to course load and program. *Unit head:* Dr. Richard A. Parsells, Program Director/Associate Professor of Organizational Studies, 512-637-1978, E-mail: richp@stedwards.edu. *Application contact:* Dave Bralower, Director of Graduate Admission, 512-233-1424, Fax: 512-464-8877, E-mail: davidcb@stedwards.edu.
Website: http://www.stedwards.edu

Saint Louis University, Graduate Education, College of Education and Public Service and Graduate Education, Department of Educational Leadership and Higher Education, St. Louis, MO 63103. Offers Catholic school leadership (MA); educational administration (MA, Ed D, PhD, Ed S); higher education (MA, Ed D, PhD); student personnel administration (MA). *Accreditation:* NCATE. *Program availability:* Part-time. *Degree requirements:* For master's, comprehensive written and oral exam; for doctorate, comprehensive exam, thesis/dissertation, preliminary oral and written exams. *Entrance requirements:* For master's, GRE General Test, MAT, LSAT, GMAT or MCAT, letters of recommendation, resume; for doctorate and Ed S, GRE General Test, LSAT, GMAT or MCAT, letters of recommendation, resumé, goal statement, transcripts. Additional exam requirements/recommendations for international students: Required—TOEFL (minimum score 525 paper-based). Electronic applications accepted. *Faculty research:* Superintendent of schools, school finance, school facilities, student personal administration, building leadership.

Seton Hall University, College of Education and Human Services, Department of Education Leadership, Management and Policy, Program in College Student Personnel Administration, South Orange, NJ 07079-2697. Offers MA. *Program availability:* Part-time, evening/weekend. *Faculty:* 12 full-time (4 women), 1 part-time/adjunct (0 women). *Students:* 3 full-time (1 woman), 7 part-time (4 women); includes 5 minority (2 Black or African American, non-Hispanic/Latino; 1 Asian, non-Hispanic/Latino; 2 Hispanic/Latino). Average age 33. 12 applicants, 100% accepted, 4 enrolled. In 2016, 2 master's awarded. *Entrance requirements:* For master's, GRE or MAT (within past 5 years), minimum GPA of 3.0. Additional exam requirements/recommendations for international students: Required—TOEFL. *Application deadline:* Applications are processed on a rolling basis. Application fee: $75. *Unit head:* Dr. Enyoung Kim, Program Director, 973-275-2156, E-mail: eunyoung.kim@shu.edu. *Application contact:* Diana Minakakis, Director of Graduate Admissions, 973-761-9668, Fax: 973-275-2187, E-mail: diana.minakakis@shu.edu.
Website: http://www.shu.edu/academics/education/ma-college-administration/index.cfm

Shippensburg University of Pennsylvania, School of Graduate Studies, College of Education and Human Services, Department of Counseling, Shippensburg, PA 17257-2299. Offers clinical mental health (MS); college counseling (MS); college student personnel (MS); counselor education and supervision (Ed D); couple and family counseling (Certificate); school counseling (M Ed). *Accreditation:* ACA (one or more programs are accredited); NCATE. *Program availability:* Part-time, evening/weekend, blended/hybrid learning. *Faculty:* 8 full-time (3 women), 6 part-time/adjunct (4 women). *Students:* 90 full-time (76 women), 57 part-time (45 women); includes 35 minority (21 Black or African American, non-Hispanic/Latino; 1 Asian, non-Hispanic/Latino; 10 Hispanic/Latino; 3 Two or more races, non-Hispanic/Latino), 5 international. Average age 28. 115 applicants, 44% accepted, 34 enrolled. In 2016, 51 master's awarded. *Degree requirements:* For master's, fieldwork, research project, internship, candidacy; for doctorate, thesis/dissertation, practicum, internship. *Entrance requirements:* For master's, GRE or MAT (for MS if GPA is less than 2.75), minimum GPA of 2.75 (3.0 for M Ed), resume, 3 letter of recommendation forms, one year of relevant work experience, on-campus interview, autobiographical statement; for doctorate, master's degree in counseling or related discipline; resume; three recommendation letters (1 from employer; 1 from clinical supervisor, 1 from prior graduate school faculty member); personal essay; interview with department chair. Additional exam requirements/recommendations for international students: Required—TOEFL (minimum score 550 paper-based, 68 iBT) or IELTS (minimum score 6). *Application deadline:* Applications are processed on a rolling basis. Application fee: $45. Electronic applications accepted. *Expenses:* Tuition, state resident: part-time $483 per credit. Tuition, nonresident: part-time $725 per credit. *Required fees:* $141 per credit. *Financial support:* In 2016–17, 62 students received support. Career-related internships or fieldwork, scholarships/grants, unspecified assistantships, and resident hall director and student payroll positions available. Support available to part-time students. Financial award application deadline: 3/1; financial award applicants required to submit FAFSA. *Unit head:* Dr. Kurt L. Kraus, Departmental Chair and Program Coordinator, 717-477-1603, Fax: 717-477-4016, E-mail: klkrau@ship.edu. *Application contact:* Megan N. Luft, Assistant Dean of Graduate Admissions, 717-477-1231, Fax: 717-477-4016, E-mail: mnluft@ship.edu.
Website: http://www.ship.edu/counsel/

Slippery Rock University of Pennsylvania, Graduate Studies (Recruitment), College of Education, Department of Counseling and Development, Slippery Rock, PA 16057-1383. Offers clinical mental health (MA); school counseling (M Ed); student affairs in higher education (MA); student affairs in higher education with college counseling (MA). *Accreditation:* ACA (one or more programs are accredited); NCATE. *Program availability:* Part-time, evening/weekend. *Faculty:* 7 full-time (5 women), 1 (woman) part-time/adjunct. *Students:* 86 full-time (55 women), 23 part-time (18 women); includes 13 minority (7 Black or African American, non-Hispanic/Latino; 4 Hispanic/Latino; 2 Two or more races, non-Hispanic/Latino), 1 international. Average age 28. 107 applicants, 57% accepted, 42 enrolled. In 2016, 39 master's awarded. *Degree requirements:* For master's, comprehensive exam, thesis (for some programs). *Entrance requirements:* For master's, GRE General Test or MAT, official transcripts, personal statement, three letters of recommendation, interview. Additional exam requirements/recommendations for international students: Required—TOEFL (minimum score 550 paper-based; 80 iBT). *Application deadline:* For fall admission, 1/15 priority date for domestic and international students. Applications are processed on a rolling basis. Application fee: $25 ($30 for international students). Electronic applications accepted. *Expenses:* $646.50 per credit in-state, $936.80 per credit out-of-state; $581.45 per online credit in-state, $648.65 per online credit out-of-state. *Financial support:* In 2016–17, 58 students received support. Career-related internships or fieldwork, Federal Work-Study, institutionally sponsored loans, scholarships/grants, tuition waivers (partial), and unspecified assistantships available. Support available to part-time students. Financial award application deadline: 5/1; financial award applicants required to submit FAFSA. *Unit head:* Dr. Stacy Jacob, Graduate Coordinator, 724-738-2758, Fax: 724-738-4859, E-mail: stacy.jacob@sru.edu. *Application contact:* Brandi Weber-Mortimer, Director of Graduate Admissions, 724-738-2051, Fax: 724-738-2146, E-mail: graduate.admissions@sru.edu.
Website: http://www.sru.edu/academics/colleges-and-departments/coe/departments/counseling-and-development

Southern Arkansas University–Magnolia, School of Graduate Studies, Magnolia, AR 71753. Offers agriculture (MS); business administration (MBA), including agri-business, social entrepreneurship, supply chain management; clinical and mental health counseling (MS); computer and information sciences (MS), including cyber security and privacy, data science, information technology; gifted and talented (M Ed), including curriculum and instruction, educational administration and supervision, gifted and talented P-8/7-12, instructional specialist P-4; higher, adult and lifelong education (M Ed); kinesiology (M Ed), including coaching; library media and information specialist (M Ed); public administration (MPA); school counseling K-12 (M Ed); student affairs and college counseling (M Ed); teaching (MAT). *Accreditation:* NCATE. *Program availability:* Part-time, 100% online, blended/hybrid learning. *Faculty:* 36 full-time (19 women), 33 part-time/adjunct (14 women). *Students:* 605 full-time (143 women), 879 part-time (352 women); includes 130 minority (113 Black or African American, non-Hispanic/Latino; 7 American Indian or Alaska Native, non-Hispanic/Latino; 2 Asian, non-Hispanic/Latino; 2 Hispanic/Latino; 6 Two or more races, non-Hispanic/Latino), 1,048 international. Average age 28. 904 applicants, 81% accepted, 262 enrolled. In 2016, 278 master's awarded. *Degree requirements:* For master's, comprehensive exam (for some programs), thesis optional. *Entrance requirements:* For master's, GRE, MAT or GMAT, minimum GPA of 2.5. Additional exam requirements/recommendations for international students: Required—TOEFL (minimum score 550 paper-based), IELTS (minimum score 6). *Application deadline:* For fall admission, 7/20 for domestic students, 7/10 for international students; for spring admission, 12/1 for domestic students, 11/15 for international students; for summer admission, 4/1 for domestic students, 5/1 for international students. Applications are processed on a rolling basis. Application fee: $25 ($50 for international students). Electronic applications accepted. *Expenses:* Tuition, state resident: full-time $2511; part-time $279 per credit hour. Tuition, nonresident: full-time $3726; part-time $414 per credit hour. *Required fees:* $307 per semester. Tuition and fees vary according to course load and program. *Financial support:* Career-related internships or fieldwork, Federal Work-Study, scholarships/grants, tuition waivers (full), and unspecified assistantships available. Financial award applicants required to submit FAFSA. *Faculty research:* Alternative certification for teachers, supervision of instruction, instructional leadership, counseling. *Unit head:* Dr. Kim Bloss, Dean, School of Graduate Studies, 870-235-4150, Fax: 870-235-5227, E-mail: kkbloss@saumag.edu. *Application contact:* Shrijana Malakar, Admissions Specialist, 870-235-4150, Fax: 870-235-5227, E-mail: smalakar@saumag.edu.
Website: http://www.saumag.edu/graduate

Southern Illinois University Edwardsville, Graduate School, School of Education, Health, and Human Behavior, Department of Educational Leadership, Program in College Student Personnel Administration, Edwardsville, IL 62026. Offers MS Ed. *Program availability:* Part-time, evening/weekend. *Degree requirements:* For master's, thesis or alternative, research project. *Entrance requirements:* Additional exam requirements/recommendations for international students: Required—TOEFL (minimum score 550 paper-based; 79 iBT), IELTS (minimum score 6.5). Electronic applications accepted.

Springfield College, Graduate Programs, Programs in Psychology, Springfield, MA 01109-3797. Offers athletic counseling (MS, CAGS); clinical mental health counseling (M Ed, CAGS); counseling psychology (Psy D); industrial and organizational psychology (M Ed, CAGS); school guidance counseling (M Ed, CAGS); student personnel administration in higher education (M Ed). *Accreditation:* APA. *Program availability:* Part-time. *Degree requirements:* For master's, research project, portfolio; for doctorate, dissertation project, 1500 hours of counseling psychology practicum, full-year internship. *Entrance requirements:* Additional exam requirements/recommendations for international students: Required—TOEFL (minimum score 550 paper-based). Electronic applications accepted. *Expenses: Tuition:* Full-time $29,640; part-time $988 per credit. *Required fees:* $195.

State University of New York at Plattsburgh, School of Education, Health, and Human Services, Department of Counselor Education, Plattsburgh, NY 12901-2681. Offers clinical mental health counseling (MS, Advanced Certificate); school counselor (MS Ed, CAS); student affairs counseling (MS). *Accreditation:* ACA (one or more programs are accredited); TEAC. *Program availability:* Part-time. *Entrance requirements:* For master's, GRE General Test or MAT, minimum GPA of 2.8. Additional exam requirements/recommendations for international students: Required—TOEFL. *Faculty research:* Campus violence, program accreditation, substance abuse, vocational assessment, group counseling, divorce.

Student Affairs

Syracuse University, School of Education, MS Program in Student Affairs Counseling, Syracuse, NY 13244. Offers MS. *Program availability:* Part-time. *Students:* Average age 28. *Entrance requirements:* For master's, GRE or MAT, baccalaureate degree from regionally-accredited college/university, three letters of recommendation, personal statement, transcripts, interview. Additional exam requirements/recommendations for international students: Required—TOEFL (minimum score 100 iBT). *Application deadline:* For fall admission, 6/15 priority date for domestic and international students; for spring admission, 10/15 priority date for domestic and international students; for summer admission, 1/15 priority date for domestic and international students. Applications are processed on a rolling basis. Application fee: $75. Electronic applications accepted. *Expenses: Tuition:* Full-time $25,974; part-time $1443 per credit hour. *Required fees:* $802; $50 per course. Tuition and fees vary according to course load and program. *Financial support:* Fellowships with full tuition reimbursements, research assistantships, teaching assistantships with tuition reimbursements, career-related internships or fieldwork, and scholarships/grants available. Financial award application deadline: 1/15. *Faculty research:* Group work in counseling, theories of counseling and psychotherapy, social and cultural dimensions of counseling, life-span human development, assessment in counseling. *Unit head:* Dr. Nicole Hill, Professor/Chair of the Department of Counseling and Human Service, 315-443-2266, E-mail: nrhill@syr.edu. *Application contact:* Speranza Migliore, Graduate Admissions Recruiter, 315-443-2505, E-mail: gradrcrt@syr.edu.
Website: http://soe.syr.edu/academic/counseling_and_human_services/graduate/masters/student_affairs_counseling/default.aspx

Texas State University, The Graduate College, College of Education, Program of Student Affairs in Higher Education, San Marcos, TX 78666. Offers M Ed. *Accreditation:* ACA. *Program availability:* Part-time, evening/weekend. *Faculty:* 3 full-time (2 women), 6 part-time/adjunct (2 women). *Students:* 34 full-time (28 women), 4 part-time (all women); includes 19 minority (3 Black or African American, non-Hispanic/Latino; 2 Asian, non-Hispanic/Latino; 12 Hispanic/Latino; 2 Two or more races, non-Hispanic/Latino), 1 international. Average age 24. 49 applicants, 61% accepted, 18 enrolled. In 2016, 14 master's awarded. *Degree requirements:* For master's, comprehensive exam. *Entrance requirements:* For master's, GRE General Test (minimum preferred score of 295 [150 verbal, 145 quantitative], 4 analytical writing), baccalaureate degree from regionally-accredited institution with minimum GPA of 3.0 in last 60 hours of undergraduate course work, resume, statement of purpose, 3 letters of recommendation. Additional exam requirements/recommendations for international students: Required—TOEFL (minimum score 550 paper-based; 78 iBT), IELTS (minimum score 6.5). *Application deadline:* For fall admission, 1/15 for domestic and international students. Applications are processed on a rolling basis. Application fee: $40 ($90 for international students). Electronic applications accepted. *Expenses:* $4,851 per semester. *Financial support:* In 2016–17, 28 students received support, including 35 teaching assistantships (averaging $12,754 per year); research assistantships, career-related internships or fieldwork, Federal Work-Study, institutionally sponsored loans, and scholarships/grants also available. Support available to part-time students. Financial award application deadline: 3/1; financial award applicants required to submit FAFSA. *Unit head:* Dr. Paige Haber-Curran, Graduate Advisor, 512-245-7628, Fax: 512-245-8872, E-mail: ph31@txstate.edu. *Application contact:* Dr. Andrea Golato, Dean of Graduate School, 512-245-2581, Fax: 512-245-8365, E-mail: gradcollege@txstate.edu.
Website: http://www.txstate.edu/clas/Student-Affairs/student-affairs-in-higher-ed2.html

University of Arkansas at Little Rock, Graduate School, College of Education and Health Professions, Department of Educational Leadership, Program in Higher Education, Little Rock, AR 72204-1099. Offers administration (MA); college student affairs (MA); health professions teaching and learning (MA); higher education (Ed D); two-year college teaching (MA). *Degree requirements:* For doctorate, comprehensive exam, oral defense of dissertation, residency. *Entrance requirements:* For master's, GRE General Test or MAT, interview, minimum graduate GPA of 3.0; for doctorate, GRE General Test, interview, minimum graduate GPA of 3.5, teaching certificate, three years of work experience.

University of Bridgeport, School of Arts and Sciences, Department of Counseling, Bridgeport, CT 06604. Offers clinical mental health counseling (MS); college student personnel (MS); community counseling (MS); human resource development (MS); human service (MS). *Program availability:* Part-time, evening/weekend. *Degree requirements:* For master's, thesis, project. *Entrance requirements:* Additional exam requirements/recommendations for international students: Recommended—TOEFL (minimum score 550 paper-based; 80 iBT), IELTS (minimum score 6.5). Electronic applications accepted. *Expenses:* Contact institution.

University of Central Arkansas, Graduate School, College of Education, Department of Leadership Studies, Program in College Student Personnel, Conway, AR 72035-0001. Offers MS. *Degree requirements:* For master's, comprehensive exam, thesis. *Entrance requirements:* For master's, GRE General Test, minimum GPA of 2.7. Additional exam requirements/recommendations for international students: Required—TOEFL (minimum score 550 paper-based). Electronic applications accepted. *Expenses:* Contact institution.

University of Central Florida, College of Education and Human Performance, Department of Educational and Human Sciences, Program in Educational Leadership, Orlando, FL 32816. Offers educational leadership (MA, Ed D, Ed S), including community college education (MA), higher education (Ed D), student personnel (MA). *Program availability:* Part-time, evening/weekend. *Students:* 121 full-time (78 women), 274 part-time (203 women); includes 147 minority (69 Black or African American, non-Hispanic/Latino; 7 Asian, non-Hispanic/Latino; 65 Hispanic/Latino; 6 Two or more races, non-Hispanic/Latino), 1 international. Average age 31. 258 applicants, 69% accepted, 101 enrolled. In 2016, 84 master's, 24 doctorates awarded. *Degree requirements:* For master's, thesis or alternative; for doctorate, thesis/dissertation, candidacy exam; for Ed S, thesis or alternative, final exam. *Entrance requirements:* For master's, GRE General Test; for doctorate, GRE General Test, GRE Subject Test, minimum GPA of 3.0, resume; for Ed S, GRE General Test, minimum GPA of 3.0, resume. Additional exam requirements/recommendations for international students: Required—TOEFL. *Application deadline:* For fall admission, 2/20 for domestic students; for spring admission, 9/20 for domestic students. Application fee: $30. Electronic applications accepted. *Expenses:* Tuition, state resident: part-time $288.16 per credit hour. Tuition, nonresident: part-time $1071.31 per credit hour. *Financial support:* In 2016–17, 22 students received support, including 1 fellowship with partial tuition reimbursement available (averaging $2,500 per year), 21 research assistantships with partial tuition reimbursements available (averaging $8,064 per year), 2 teaching assistantships with partial tuition reimbursements available (averaging $11,154 per year); career-related internships or fieldwork, Federal Work-Study, institutionally sponsored loans, tuition waivers (partial), and unspecified assistantships also available. Financial award application deadline: 3/1; financial award applicants required to submit FAFSA. *Unit head:* Dr. Kenneth Murray, Program Coordinator, 407-832-1468, E-mail: kenneth.murray@ucf.edu. *Application contact:* Assistant Director, Graduate Admissions, 407-823-2766, Fax: 407-823-6442, E-mail: gradadmissions@ucf.edu.
Website: http://education.ucf.edu/highered/index.cfm

University of Central Missouri, The Graduate School, Warrensburg, MO 64093. Offers accountancy (MA); accounting (MBA); applied mathematics (MS); aviation safety (MA); biology (MS); business administration (MBA); career and technical education leadership (MS); college student personnel administration (MS); communication (MA); computer science (MS); counseling (MS); criminal justice (MS); educational leadership (Ed D); educational technology (MS); elementary and early childhood education (MSE); English (MA); environmental studies (MA); finance (MBA); history (MA); human services/educational technology (Ed S); human services/learning resources (Ed S); human services/professional counseling (Ed S); industrial hygiene (MS); industrial management (MS); information systems (MBA); information technology (MS); kinesiology (MS); library science and information services (MS); literacy education (MSE); marketing (MBA); mathematics (MS); music (MA); occupational safety management (MS); psychology (MS); rural family nursing (MS); school administration (MSE); social gerontology (MS); sociology (MA); special education (MSE); speech language pathology (MS); superintendency (Ed S); teaching (MAT); teaching English as a second language (MA); technology (MS); technology management (PhD); theatre (MA). *Program availability:* Part-time, 100% online, blended/hybrid learning. *Degree requirements:* For master's and Ed S, comprehensive exam (for some programs), thesis (for some programs). *Entrance requirements:* Additional exam requirements/recommendations for international students: Required—TOEFL (minimum score 550 paper-based; 79 iBT). Electronic applications accepted.

University of Central Oklahoma, The Jackson College of Graduate Studies, College of Education and Professional Studies, Department of Adult Education and Safety Science, Edmond, OK 73034-5209. Offers adult and higher education (M Ed), including adult and higher education, interdisciplinary studies, student personnel, training. *Program availability:* Part-time. *Degree requirements:* For master's, comprehensive exam (for some programs), thesis (for some programs). *Entrance requirements:* For master's, GRE General Test. Additional exam requirements/recommendations for international students: Required—TOEFL (minimum score 550 paper-based; 79 iBT), IELTS (minimum score 6.5). Electronic applications accepted. *Faculty research:* Violence in the workplace/schools, aging issues, trade and industrial education.

University of Dayton, Department of Counselor Education and Human Services, Dayton, OH 45469. Offers clinical mental health counseling (MS Ed); college student personnel (MS Ed); higher education administration (MS Ed); human services (MS Ed); school counseling (MS Ed); school psychology (MS Ed, Ed S). *Accreditation:* ACA; NCATE. *Program availability:* Part-time, evening/weekend. *Faculty:* 10 full-time (6 women), 24 part-time/adjunct (15 women). *Students:* 198 full-time (155 women), 95 part-time (75 women); includes 15 minority (8 Black or African American, non-Hispanic/Latino; 2 Asian, non-Hispanic/Latino; 2 Hispanic/Latino; 3 Two or more races, non-Hispanic/Latino), 3 international. Average age 36. 426 applicants, 28% accepted. In 2016, 115 master's, 9 Ed Ss awarded. *Degree requirements:* For Ed S, thesis. *Entrance requirements:* For master's, MAT or GRE (if GPA less than 2.75), essays (for some programs). Additional exam requirements/recommendations for international students: Required—TOEFL (minimum score 550 paper-based; 80 iBT); Recommended—IELTS. *Application deadline:* For fall admission, 3/10 priority date for domestic and international students; for spring admission, 9/10 priority date for domestic and international students; for summer admission, 12/1 priority date for domestic and international students. Application fee: $0 ($50 for international students). Electronic applications accepted. *Expenses:* $620 per credit hour (for master's degree programs); $740 per credit hour (for Ed S). *Financial support:* In 2016–17, 7 research assistantships with partial tuition reimbursements (averaging $8,038 per year), 4 teaching assistantships with partial tuition reimbursements (averaging $9,390 per year) were awarded; career-related internships or fieldwork, institutionally sponsored loans, health care benefits, and unspecified assistantships also available. Financial award application deadline: 1/9; financial award applicants required to submit FAFSA. *Faculty research:* School bonding, traumatic brain injuries, second-year student experience, impact of physical space on learning, integrative health and mental health care. *Total annual research expenditures:* $1,500. *Unit head:* Dr. Alan Demmitt, Chair, 937-229-3644, Fax: 937-229-1055, E-mail: ademmitt1@udayton.edu. *Application contact:* Kathleen Brown, Administrative Assistant, 937-229-3644, Fax: 937-229-1055, E-mail: kbrown1@udayton.edu.
Website: https://www.udayton.edu/education/departments_and_programs/edc/

University of Florida, Graduate School, College of Education, School of Human Development and Organizational Studies in Education, Gainesville, FL 32611. Offers counseling and counselor education (Ed D, PhD), including counseling and counselor education, marriage and family counseling, mental health counseling, school counseling and guidance; educational leadership (M Ed, MAE, Ed D, PhD, Ed S), including educational leadership (Ed D, PhD), educational policy (Ed D, PhD); higher education administration (Ed D, PhD), including education policy (Ed D), educational policy, higher education administration; marriage and family counseling (M Ed, MAE, Ed D, PhD, Ed S); mental health counseling (M Ed, MAE, Ed D, PhD, Ed S); research and evaluation methodology (M Ed, MAE, Ed D, PhD); school counseling and guidance (M Ed, MAE, Ed D, PhD, Ed S); student personnel in higher education (M Ed, MAE). *Accreditation:* ACA (one or more programs are accredited); NCATE. *Program availability:* Part-time, online learning. Terminal master's awarded for partial completion of doctoral program. *Degree requirements:* For master's, thesis optional; for doctorate, comprehensive exam, thesis/dissertation. *Entrance requirements:* For master's and doctorate, GRE General Test, minimum GPA of 3.0 (undergraduate), 3.5 (graduate); for Ed S, GRE General Test. Additional exam requirements/recommendations for international students: Required—TOEFL (minimum score 550 paper-based; 80 iBT), IELTS (minimum score 6). Electronic applications accepted.

University of Georgia, College of Education, Department of Counseling and Human Development Services, Athens, GA 30602. Offers college student affairs administration (M Ed, PhD); professional school counseling (Ed S). *Accreditation:* ACA (one or more programs are accredited); APA (one or more programs are accredited); NCATE. *Degree requirements:* For master's, thesis (MA); for doctorate, variable foreign language requirement, thesis/dissertation. *Entrance requirements:* For master's, GRE General Test or MAT; for doctorate, GRE General Test. *Application deadline:* For fall admission, 7/1 priority date for domestic students; for spring admission, 11/15 for domestic students. Application fee: $50. Electronic applications accepted. *Financial support:* Fellowships, research assistantships, teaching assistantships, and unspecified assistantships available. *Unit head:* Dr. Rosemary E. Phelps, Head, 706-542-4221, Fax: 706-542-4130, E-mail: rephelps@uga.edu. *Application contact:* Merrilyn Dunn, Graduate Coordinator, 706-542-1812, E-mail: chdsgrad@uga.edu.
Website: http://www.coe.uga.edu/chds/

The University of Iowa, Graduate College, College of Education, Department of Educational Policy and Leadership Studies, Program in Higher Education and Student Affairs, Iowa City, IA 52242-1316. Offers MA, PhD. *Degree requirements:* For master's, exam; for doctorate, comprehensive exam, thesis/dissertation. *Entrance requirements:* For master's and doctorate, GRE General Test, minimum GPA of 3.0. Additional exam requirements/recommendations for international students: Required—TOEFL (minimum score 550 paper-based; 81 iBT). Electronic applications accepted.

University of Louisville, Graduate School, College of Education and Human Development, Department of Counseling and Human Development, Louisville, KY

40292-0001. Offers counseling and personnel services (M Ed, PhD), including art therapy (M Ed), clinical mental health counseling (M Ed), college student personnel, counseling psychology, counselor education and supervision (PhD), educational psychology, measurement, and evaluation (PhD), school counseling (M Ed). *Accreditation:* APA; NCATE. *Program availability:* Part-time, evening/weekend. *Students:* 148 full-time (115 women), 58 part-time (42 women); includes 52 minority (36 Black or African American, non-Hispanic/Latino; 1 American Indian or Alaska Native, non-Hispanic/Latino; 4 Asian, non-Hispanic/Latino; 7 Hispanic/Latino; 4 Two or more races, non-Hispanic/Latino), 2 international. Average age 28. 206 applicants, 56% accepted, 73 enrolled. In 2016, 38 master's, 1 doctorate awarded. *Degree requirements:* For doctorate, comprehensive exam, thesis/dissertation. *Entrance requirements:* For master's and doctorate, GRE General Test. Application fee: $60. *Expenses:* Tuition, state resident: full-time $12,246; part-time $681 per credit hour. Tuition, nonresident: full-time $25,486; part-time $1417 per credit hour. *Required fees:* $196. Tuition and fees vary according to program and reciprocity agreements. *Financial support:* Fellowships, research assistantships, teaching assistantships, career-related internships or fieldwork, Federal Work-Study, scholarships/grants, health care benefits, and unspecified assistantships available. Financial award application deadline: 6/1; financial award applicants required to submit FAFSA. *Faculty research:* Mental health services and under-served populations; health disparities and outcomes; well-being identity development; measurement and evaluation. *Total annual research expenditures:* $295,684. *Unit head:* Dr. Mark M. Leach, Interim Chair/Professor, 502-852-0588, Fax: 502-852-0629, E-mail: m.leach@louisville.edu. *Application contact:* Betty Hampton, Director of Graduate Student Services, 502-852-5597, Fax: 502-852-1465, E-mail: edadvise@louisville.edu.
Website: http://www.louisville.edu/education/departments/ecpy

University of Maryland, College Park, Academic Affairs, College of Education, Department of Counseling, Higher Education and Special Education, College Park, MD 20742. Offers college student personnel (M Ed, MA); college student personnel administration (PhD); community counseling (CAGS); community/career counseling (M Ed, MA); counseling and personnel services (M Ed, MA, PhD), including art therapy (M Ed), college student personnel (M Ed), counseling and personnel services (PhD), counseling psychology (M Ed), mental health counseling (M Ed), school counseling (M Ed); counseling psychology (PhD); counselor education (PhD); rehabilitation counseling (M Ed, MA, AGSC); school counseling (M Ed, MA); school psychology (M Ed, MA, PhD). *Accreditation:* ACA (one or more programs are accredited); APA (one or more programs are accredited); NCATE. *Program availability:* Part-time, evening/weekend, online learning. *Degree requirements:* For master's, thesis (for some programs); for doctorate, thesis/dissertation. *Entrance requirements:* For master's, GRE General Test or MAT, minimum GPA of 3.0, 3 letters of recommendation; for doctorate, GRE General Test or MAT, minimum GPA of 3.5, 3 letters of recommendation. Additional exam requirements/recommendations for international students: Required—TOEFL. Electronic applications accepted. *Faculty research:* Educational psychology, counseling, health.

University of Minnesota, Twin Cities Campus, Graduate School, College of Education and Human Development, Department of Educational Psychology, Program in Counseling and Student Personnel Psychology, Minneapolis, MN 55455-0213. Offers MA. *Students:* 77 full-time (58 women), 5 part-time (2 women); includes 11 minority (2 Asian, non-Hispanic/Latino; 5 Hispanic/Latino; 4 Two or more races, non-Hispanic/Latino), 6 international. Average age 27. 85 applicants, 42% accepted, 36 enrolled. In 2016, 33 master's awarded. Application fee: $75 ($95 for international students). *Unit head:* Dr. Geoffrey Maruyama, Chair, 612-624-1003, Fax: 612-625-5861, E-mail: geoff@umn.edu. *Application contact:* Dr. Ernest Davenport, Director of Graduate Studies, 612-624-1040, E-mail: lqr6576@umn.edu.
Website: http://www.cehd.umn.edu/EdPsych/Programs/CSPP/default.html

University of Nebraska at Kearney, College of Education, Department of Counseling and School Psychology, Kearney, NE 68849-0001. Offers clinical mental health counseling (MS Ed); school counseling (MS Ed), including elementary, secondary; school psychology (Ed S); student affairs (MS Ed). *Accreditation:* ACA; NCATE. *Program availability:* Part-time, evening/weekend, 100% online. *Faculty:* 7 full-time (3 women). *Students:* 69 full-time (56 women), 102 part-time (81 women); includes 21 minority (2 Black or African American, non-Hispanic/Latino; 2 Asian, non-Hispanic/Latino; 12 Hispanic/Latino; 5 Two or more races, non-Hispanic/Latino), 4 international. Average age 30. 43 applicants, 100% accepted, 37 enrolled. In 2016, 24 master's, 13 Ed Ss awarded. *Degree requirements:* For master's, comprehensive exam, thesis optional; for Ed S, thesis. *Entrance requirements:* For master's and Ed S, personal statement, recommendations, resume, interview. Additional exam requirements/recommendations for international students: Recommended—TOEFL (minimum score 550 paper-based; 79 iBT), IELTS (minimum score 6.5). *Application deadline:* For fall admission, 6/15 for domestic and international students; for spring admission, 10/15 for domestic and international students; for summer admission, 3/15 for domestic and international students. Application fee: $45. Electronic applications accepted. *Expenses:* Tuition, state resident: full-time $4064; part-time $225.75 per credit hour. Tuition, nonresident: full-time $8915; part-time $495.25 per credit hour. *Required fees:* $772; $23 per credit hour. Part-time tuition and fees vary according to course load, campus/location, program and reciprocity agreements. *Financial support:* In 2016–17, 7 students received support, including 7 research assistantships with full tuition reimbursements available (averaging $10,500 per year); fellowships, career-related internships or fieldwork, scholarships/grants, health care benefits, and unspecified assistantships also available. Support available to part-time students. Financial award application deadline: 2/28; financial award applicants required to submit FAFSA. *Faculty research:* Multicultural counseling and diversity issues, team decision-making, adult development, women's issues, brief therapy. *Unit head:* Dr. Grace Mims, Chair, Counseling and School Psychology, 308-865-8508, E-mail: mimsga@unk.edu. *Application contact:* Linda Johnson, Director, Graduate Admissions and Programs, 800-717-7881, Fax: 308-865-8837, E-mail: gradstudies@unk.edu.
Website: http://www.unk.edu/academics/csp/

University of Northern Colorado, Graduate School, College of Education and Behavioral Sciences, Department of Leadership, Policy and Development: Higher Education and P-12 Education, Program in Higher Education and Student Affairs Leadership, Greeley, CO 80639. Offers MA, PhD. *Program availability:* Part-time. *Entrance requirements:* For doctorate, GRE General Test, transcripts, 3 letters of recommendation. *Application deadline:* Applications are processed on a rolling basis. Application fee: $50 ($60 for international students). Electronic applications accepted. *Financial support:* Research assistantships and teaching assistantships available. Financial award application deadline: 3/1; financial award applicants required to submit FAFSA. *Unit head:* Katrina Rodriguez, Program Coordinator, 970-351-2861, E-mail: hesal@unco.edu. *Application contact:* Linda Sisson, Graduate Student Admission Coordinator, 970-351-1807, Fax: 970-351-2371, E-mail: linda.sisson@unco.edu.
Website: http://www.unco.edu/cebs/HESAL/contact.htm

University of Northern Iowa, Graduate College, College of Education, Department of Educational Leadership and Postsecondary Education, MA Program in Postsecondary Education: Student Affairs, Cedar Falls, IA 50614. Offers MA. *Degree requirements:* For master's, comprehensive exam, thesis or alternative. *Entrance requirements:* For master's, minimum GPA of 3.0. Additional exam requirements/recommendations for international students: Required—TOEFL (minimum score 500 paper-based; 61 iBT). Electronic applications accepted.

University of Oklahoma, Jeannine Rainbolt College of Education, Department of Educational Leadership and Policy Studies, Program in Adult and Higher Education, Norman, OK 73019. Offers adult and higher education (M Ed), including community college administration, higher education administration, institutional research, intercollegiate athletics administration, student affairs, workforce, adult and continuing education. *Accreditation:* NCATE. *Program availability:* Part-time, evening/weekend. *Students:* 115 full-time (66 women), 81 part-time (54 women); includes 62 minority (31 Black or African American, non-Hispanic/Latino; 11 American Indian or Alaska Native, non-Hispanic/Latino; 8 Hispanic/Latino; 1 Native Hawaiian or other Pacific Islander, non-Hispanic/Latino; 11 Two or more races, non-Hispanic/Latino), 5 international. Average age 30. 83 applicants, 67% accepted, 43 enrolled. In 2016, 72 degrees awarded. *Degree requirements:* For master's, comprehensive exam, thesis optional. *Entrance requirements:* Additional exam requirements/recommendations for international students: Required—TOEFL (minimum score 79 iBT) or IELTS (minimum score 6.5). *Application deadline:* For fall admission, 2/1 for domestic and international students; for spring admission, 10/1 for domestic and international students; for summer admission, 4/1 for domestic and international students. Application fee: $50 ($100 for international students). Electronic applications accepted. *Expenses:* Tuition, state resident: full-time $4886; part-time $203.60 per credit hour. Tuition, nonresident: full-time $18,989; part-time $791.20 per credit hour. *Required fees:* $3283; $126.25 per credit hour. $126.50 per semester. *Financial support:* In 2016–17, 166 students received support. Fellowships, research assistantships, teaching assistantships, career-related internships or fieldwork, Federal Work-Study, institutionally sponsored loans, scholarships/grants, traineeships, health care benefits, tuition waivers, and unspecified assistantships available. Support available to part-time students. Financial award application deadline: 6/1; financial award applicants required to submit FAFSA. *Faculty research:* Education and social policy; gender and equity; collegiate athletics; higher education and student affairs; adult learning and workforce development. *Unit head:* Doo Hun Lim, Associate Professor, 405-325-7941, E-mail: dhlim@ou.edu.
Website: http://www.ou.edu/education/elps/graduate-programs/adult-and-higher-education-masters.html

University of Rhode Island, Graduate School, College of Health Sciences, Department of Human Development and Family Studies, Kingston, RI 02881. Offers college student personnel (MS); human development and family studies (MS); marriage and family therapy (MS). *Accreditation:* AAMFT/COAMFTE. *Program availability:* Part-time. *Faculty:* 15 full-time (10 women). *Students:* 43 full-time (28 women), 14 part-time (10 women); includes 11 minority (7 Black or African American, non-Hispanic/Latino; 1 Asian, non-Hispanic/Latino; 1 Hispanic/Latino; 2 Two or more races, non-Hispanic/Latino). In 2016, 26 master's awarded. *Degree requirements:* For master's, comprehensive exam (for some programs), thesis optional. *Entrance requirements:* For master's, GRE or MAT, 2 letters of recommendation; resume (for college student personnel specialization). Additional exam requirements/recommendations for international students: Required—TOEFL. *Application deadline:* For fall admission, 1/15 for domestic and international students. Application fee: $65. Electronic applications accepted. *Expenses:* Tuition, state resident: full-time $11,796; part-time $655 per credit. Tuition, nonresident: full-time $24,206; part-time $1345 per credit. *Required fees:* $1546; $44 per credit. One-time fee: $155 full-time; $35 part-time. *Financial support:* In 2016–17, 2 research assistantships (averaging $8,592 per year), 4 teaching assistantships (averaging $11,456 per year) were awarded. Financial award application deadline: 1/15; financial award applicants required to submit FAFSA. *Unit head:* Dr. Karen McCurdy, Chair, 401-874-5960, Fax: 401-874-4020, E-mail: kmccurdy@uri.edu. *Application contact:* Graduate Admissions, 401-874-2872, E-mail: gradadm@etal.uri.edu.
Website: http://www.uri.edu/hss/hdf/

University of Rochester, Margaret Warner Graduate School of Education and Human Development, Master's Program in Higher Education, Rochester, NY 14627. Offers higher education (MS); higher education student affairs (MS). *Expenses: Tuition:* Full-time $47,450; part-time $1482 per credit hour. *Required fees:* $528. Tuition and fees vary according to program.

University of St. Thomas, Graduate Studies, College of Education, Leadership and Counseling, Department of Leadership, Policy and Administration, St. Paul, MN 55105-1096. Offers education leadership and administration (MA); educational leadership and learning (Ed D); executive coaching (Certificate); K-12 administration (Ed S); leadership in student affairs (MA). *Program availability:* Part-time, evening/weekend. Terminal master's awarded for partial completion of doctoral program. *Degree requirements:* For master's, thesis (for some programs); for doctorate, thesis/dissertation; for other advanced degree, thesis or alternative. *Entrance requirements:* For master's, minimum GPA of 3.0 or MAT; for doctorate, MAT, minimum graduate GPA of 3.5; for other advanced degree, minimum graduate GPA of 3.25 or MAT. Additional exam requirements/recommendations for international students: Required—TOEFL (minimum score 550 paper-based). *Application deadline:* For fall admission, 7/15 priority date for domestic and international students; for spring admission, 12/9 priority date for domestic and international students; for summer admission, 4/3 priority date for domestic and international students. Applications are processed on a rolling basis. Electronic applications accepted. *Expenses:* Contact institution. *Financial support:* Fellowships, research assistantships, institutionally sponsored loans, and scholarships/grants available. Support available to part-time students. Financial award application deadline: 8/1; financial award applicants required to submit FAFSA. *Application contact:* Jackie Grossklaus, Department Assistant, 651-962-4885, Fax: 651-962-4169, E-mail: jmgrossklaus@stthomas.edu.

University of South Carolina, The Graduate School, College of Education, Department of Educational Leadership and Policies, Program in Higher Education and Student Affairs, Columbia, SC 29208. Offers M Ed. *Accreditation:* NCATE. *Program availability:* Part-time. *Degree requirements:* For master's, comprehensive exam, thesis (for some programs). *Entrance requirements:* For master's, GRE General Test or MAT, letters of reference. Electronic applications accepted. *Faculty research:* Minorities in higher education, community college transfer problem, federal role in educational research.

University of Southern California, Graduate School, Rossier School of Education, Master's Programs in Education, Los Angeles, CA 90089-4038. Offers educational counseling (ME); marriage, family and child counseling (MMFT); postsecondary administration and student affairs [PASA] (ME); school counseling (ME); teaching (online) (MAT); teaching and teaching credential (MAT); teaching English to speakers of other languages (MAT). *Program availability:* Part-time, evening/weekend, online learning. *Degree requirements:* For master's, thesis optional. *Entrance requirements:* For master's, GRE (for all programs except MAT). Additional exam requirements/recommendations for international students: Required—TOEFL (minimum score 100 iBT). Electronic applications accepted. *Faculty research:* College access and equity, preparing teachers for culturally diverse populations, sociocultural basis of learning as mediated by instruction with focus on reading and literacy in English learners, social and political aspects of teaching and learning English, school counselor development and training.

University of Southern Mississippi, Graduate School, College of Education and Psychology, Department of Educational Research and Administration, Hattiesburg, MS 39406. Offers educational administration (M Ed, Ed D, PhD, Ed S); educational administration and supervision (M Ed); educational studies and research (MS); higher education (Ed D); higher education administration (PhD); higher education: student affairs (M Ed); research, evaluation, statistics, assessment (PhD). *Degree requirements:* For master's and Ed S, comprehensive exam, thesis (for some programs); for doctorate, comprehensive exam, thesis/dissertation. *Entrance requirements:* For master's and doctorate, GRE General Test, minimum GPA of 2.75. Additional exam requirements/recommendations for international students: Required—TOEFL. *Application deadline:* For fall admission, 2/1 for domestic students, 3/1 for international students. Applications are processed on a rolling basis. Application fee: $60. *Expenses: Tuition, area resident:* Full-time $15,708; part-time $437 per credit hour. *Financial support:* Career-related internships or fieldwork, Federal Work-Study, and institutionally sponsored loans available. Financial award application deadline: 3/15; financial award applicants required to submit FAFSA. *Unit head:* Dr. Lilian Hill, Co-Chair, 601-266-4622. *Application contact:* Shonna Breland, Manager of Graduate Admissions, 601-266-6563, Fax: 601-266-5138.
Website: https://www.usm.edu/educational-research-administration

University of South Florida, College of Education, Department of Educational and Psychological Studies, Tampa, FL 33620-9951. Offers college student affairs (M Ed); counselor education (MA, PhD, Ed S); interdisciplinary (PhD, Ed S); school psychology (PhD, Ed S). *Faculty:* 25 full-time (12 women). *Students:* 97 full-time (66 women), 94 part-time (62 women); includes 52 minority (22 Black or African American, non-Hispanic/Latino; 8 Asian, non-Hispanic/Latino; 19 Hispanic/Latino; 3 Two or more races, non-Hispanic/Latino), 25 international. Average age 34. 132 applicants, 45% accepted, 46 enrolled. In 2016, 94 master's, 7 doctorates, 8 other advanced degrees awarded. Application fee: $30. *Expenses:* Tuition, state resident: full-time $7766; part-time $431.43 per credit hour. Tuition, nonresident: full-time $15,789; part-time $877.17 per credit hour. *Required fees:* $37 per term. *Faculty research:* College student affairs, counselor education, educational psychology, school psychology, social foundations. *Total annual research expenditures:* $11.1 million. *Unit head:* Dr. Barabara Shircliff, Chair, 813-974-4001, E-mail: shirclif@usf.edu.
Website: http://www.coedu.usf.edu/main/departments/psf/psf.html

The University of Tennessee, Graduate School, College of Education, Health and Human Sciences, Department of Educational Psychology and Counseling, Program in College Student Personnel, Knoxville, TN 37996. Offers MS. *Accreditation:* NCATE. *Program availability:* Part-time. *Degree requirements:* For master's, thesis optional. *Entrance requirements:* For master's, GRE General Test, minimum GPA of 2.7. Additional exam requirements/recommendations for international students: Required—TOEFL. Electronic applications accepted.

The University of Tennessee at Martin, Graduate Programs, College of Education, Health and Behavioral Sciences, Program in Counseling, Martin, TN 38238. Offers addictions counseling (MS Ed); community counseling (MS Ed); school counseling (MS Ed); student affairs and college counseling (MS Ed). *Accreditation:* NCATE. *Program availability:* Part-time, online only, 100% online. *Students:* 14 full-time (12 women), 62 part-time (59 women); includes 10 minority (6 Black or African American, non-Hispanic/Latino; 3 Hispanic/Latino; 1 Two or more races, non-Hispanic/Latino). Average age 35. 40 applicants, 48% accepted, 18 enrolled. In 2016, 17 master's awarded. *Degree requirements:* For master's, comprehensive exam. *Entrance requirements:* For master's, GRE General Test, minimum GPA of 2.5, resume, letters of reference. Additional exam requirements/recommendations for international students: Required—TOEFL (minimum score 525 paper-based; 71 iBT). *Application deadline:* For fall admission, 7/27 priority date for domestic and international students; for spring admission, 12/17 priority date for domestic and international students; for summer admission, 5/10 priority date for domestic and international students. Applications are processed on a rolling basis. Application fee: $30 ($130 for international students). Electronic applications accepted. *Expenses:* Tuition, state resident: full-time $8254; part-time $459 per credit hour. Tuition, nonresident: full-time $22,198; part-time $1234 per credit hour. *Required fees:* $79 per credit hour. Part-time tuition and fees vary according to course load and campus/location. *Financial support:* Scholarships/grants and unspecified assistantships available. Financial award application deadline: 2/1; financial award applicants required to submit FAFSA. *Unit head:* Cynthia West, Dean, 731-881-7125, Fax: 731-881-7975, E-mail: cwest@utm.edu. *Application contact:* Jolene L. Cunningham, Student Services Specialist, 731-881-7012, Fax: 731-881-7499, E-mail: jcunningham@utm.edu.

University of the Cumberlands, Graduate Programs in Education, Williamsburg, KY 40769-1372. Offers all grades (P-12) (M Ed); business and marketing (MA Ed, MAT); counselor education and supervision (Ed D); director of pupil personnel (Certificate); director of special education (Certificate); educational administration and supervision (Ed S); educational leadership (Ed D); elementary education (MA Ed, MAT); instructional leadership - principalship (MA Ed); instructional leadership - school principal (Certificate); middle school education (MA Ed, MAT); reading and writing (MA Ed); school counseling (MA Ed); school superintendent (Certificate); secondary education (MA Ed, MAT); special education (MAT); supervisor of instruction (Certificate); teacher leader (MA Ed). *Program availability:* Part-time, evening/weekend, online learning. *Degree requirements:* For master's, comprehensive exam. Electronic applications accepted.

University of Utah, Graduate School, College of Education, Department of Educational Leadership and Policy, Salt Lake City, UT 84084. Offers educational leadership and policy (Ed D, PhD), including higher education administration (Ed D), K-12 (Ed D); K-12 school administration (M Ed); K-12 teacher instructional leadership (M Ed); student affairs (M Ed); MPA/PhD. *Program availability:* Part-time, evening/weekend. *Faculty:* 11 full-time (7 women), 3 part-time/adjunct (all women). *Students:* 79 full-time (47 women), 134 part-time (95 women); includes 63 minority (7 Black or African American, non-Hispanic/Latino; 2 American Indian or Alaska Native, non-Hispanic/Latino; 7 Asian, non-Hispanic/Latino; 38 Hispanic/Latino; 9 Two or more races, non-Hispanic/Latino), 1 international. Average age 35. 154 applicants, 67% accepted, 86 enrolled. In 2016, 42 master's, 8 doctorates awarded. *Degree requirements:* For master's, comprehensive exam (for some programs), internship, capstone; for doctorate, thesis/dissertation, qualifying exam. *Entrance requirements:* For master's, minimum undergraduate GPA of 3.0, valid bachelor's degree, 3 years' teaching or leadership experience, Level 1 or 2 UT educator's license (for K-12 programs only); for doctorate, GRE General Test (taken with five years of applying), minimum undergraduate GPA of 3.0, valid master's degree. Additional exam requirements/recommendations for international students: Required—TOEFL (minimum score 500 paper-based). *Application deadline:* For fall admission, 1/15 priority date for domestic and international students; for winter admission, 2/1 for domestic and international students; for spring admission, 11/1 priority date for domestic and international students; for summer admission, 3/1 priority date for domestic and international students. Applications are processed on a rolling basis. Application fee: $55 ($65 for international students). Electronic applications accepted. *Expenses:* Contact institution. *Financial support:* In 2016–17, 47 students received support, including 1 fellowship with full tuition reimbursement available (averaging $14,500 per year), 2 research assistantships with full tuition reimbursements available (averaging $15,000 per year), 6 teaching assistantships with full tuition reimbursements available (averaging $15,000 per year); career-related internships or fieldwork, scholarships/grants, health care benefits, and unspecified assistantships also available. Support available to part-time students. Financial award application deadline: 3/1; financial award applicants required to submit FAFSA. *Faculty research:* Education accountability, college student diversity, K-12 educational administration and school leadership, student affairs, higher education. *Unit head:* Dr. Gerardo Lopez, Chair, 801-581-6627, Fax: 801-585-6756, E-mail: gerardo.lopez@utah.edu. *Application contact:* Marilynn S. Howard, Academic Coordinator, 801-581-6714, Fax: 801-585-6756, E-mail: marilynn.howard@utah.edu.
Website: http://elp.utah.edu/

University of Virginia, Curry School of Education, Department of Leadership, Foundations and Policy, Program in Higher Education, Charlottesville, VA 22903. Offers higher education (Ed S); student affairs practice (M Ed). *Students:* 49 full-time (32 women), 21 part-time (9 women); includes 19 minority (10 Black or African American, non-Hispanic/Latino; 1 Asian, non-Hispanic/Latino; 6 Hispanic/Latino; 2 Two or more races, non-Hispanic/Latino), 1 international. Average age 27. 17 applicants, 76% accepted, 13 enrolled. In 2016, 46 master's, 5 doctorates awarded. *Entrance requirements:* For master's, doctorate, and Ed S, GRE General Test, 2 letters of recommendation. Additional exam requirements/recommendations for international students: Required—TOEFL (minimum score 600 paper-based; 90 iBT), IELTS (minimum score 7). *Application deadline:* Applications are processed on a rolling basis. Application fee: $60. Electronic applications accepted. *Expenses:* Tuition, state resident: full-time $15,026; part-time $834 per credit hour. Tuition, nonresident: full-time $25,168; part-time $1378 per credit hour. *Required fees:* $2654. *Financial support:* Fellowships, research assistantships, and teaching assistantships available. Financial award applicants required to submit FAFSA. *Unit head:* Brian Pusser, Program Coordinator, 434-924-7731, E-mail: highered@virginia.edu. *Application contact:* Eric Molnar, Assistant Director, Admissions and Enrollment Reporting, 434-243-2085, E-mail: eric.molnar@virginia.edu.
Website: http://curry.virginia.edu/academics/areas-of-study/higher-education

University of West Florida, College of Education and Professional Studies, Department of Research and Advanced Studies, Program in College Student Affairs Administration, Pensacola, FL 32514-5750. Offers M Ed. *Program availability:* Part-time, evening/weekend. *Degree requirements:* For master's, internship. *Entrance requirements:* For master's, GRE General Test, minimum GPA of 3.0. Additional exam requirements/recommendations for international students: Required—TOEFL (minimum score 550 paper-based). *Application deadline:* For fall admission, 6/1 for domestic and international students; for spring admission, 11/1 for domestic students, 10/1 for international students. Application fee: $30. *Expenses:* Tuition, state resident: full-time $5316.12. Tuition, nonresident: full-time $11,308. *Required fees:* $583.92. Tuition and fees vary according to course load and program. *Financial support:* Application deadline: 4/15; applicants required to submit FAFSA. *Unit head:* Dr. Thomas J. Kramer, Chairperson, 850-474-2949, Fax: 850-857-6288. *Application contact:* Terry McCray, Assistant Director of Graduate Admissions, 850-473-7718, Fax: 850-473-7714, E-mail: gradadmissions@uwf.edu.

University of Wisconsin–La Crosse, College of Liberal Studies, Department of Student Affairs Administration, La Crosse, WI 54601-3742. Offers MS Ed, Ed D. *Program availability:* Part-time, evening/weekend, 100% online, blended/hybrid learning. *Faculty:* 3 full-time (all women), 5 part-time/adjunct (2 women). *Students:* 41 full-time (30 women), 47 part-time (39 women); includes 13 minority (1 Black or African American, non-Hispanic/Latino; 3 Asian, non-Hispanic/Latino; 6 Hispanic/Latino; 3 Two or more races, non-Hispanic/Latino), 1 international. Average age 26. 54 applicants, 83% accepted, 18 enrolled. In 2016, 38 master's awarded. *Degree requirements:* For master's, comprehensive exam (for some programs), thesis optional, electronic portfolio, applied research project. *Entrance requirements:* For master's, bachelor's degree from accredited institution, minimum GPA of 2.85, resume, essay, 2 references. Additional exam requirements/recommendations for international students: Required—TOEFL (minimum score 550 paper-based; 79 iBT). *Application deadline:* For fall admission, 2/1 priority date for domestic and international students. Electronic applications accepted. *Financial support:* Research assistantships with partial tuition reimbursements, Federal Work-Study, scholarships/grants, and health care benefits available. Support available to part-time students. Financial award application deadline: 3/15; financial award applicants required to submit FAFSA. *Faculty research:* Persistence; developing positive social justice behaviors in heterosexual white college men; equity; diversity; inclusion in higher education at both interpersonal and institutional levels; expanding student affairs administration research and practice beyond the traditional, majority, or dominant student experience; underrepresented students at historically white institutions; college men and masculinities; Latina/o college student leadership; ethnic cultural centers at HWIs. *Unit head:* Dr. Jodie Rindt, Department Chair, 608-785-6450, E-mail: jrindt@uwlax.edu. *Application contact:* Brandon Schaller, Senior Graduate Student Status Examiner, 608-785-8941, E-mail: admissions@uwlax.edu.
Website: http://www.uwlax.edu/saa/

University of Wyoming, College of Education, Programs in Counselor Education, Laramie, WY 82071. Offers community mental health (MS); counselor education and supervision (PhD); school counseling (MS); student affairs (MS). *Accreditation:* ACA (one or more programs are accredited). *Degree requirements:* For master's, comprehensive exam (for some programs), thesis optional; for doctorate, thesis/dissertation, video demonstration. *Entrance requirements:* For master's, interview, background check; for doctorate, video tape session, interview, writing sample, master's degree, background check. Additional exam requirements/recommendations for international students: Required—TOEFL. *Faculty research:* Wyoming SAGE photovoice project; accountable school counseling programs; GLBT issues; addictions; play therapy-early childhood mental health.

Virginia Commonwealth University, Graduate School, School of Education, Program in Counselor Education, Richmond, VA 23284-9005. Offers college student development and counseling (M Ed); school counseling (M Ed). *Accreditation:* ACA; NCATE. *Entrance requirements:* For master's, GRE General Test or MAT. Additional exam requirements/recommendations for international students: Required—TOEFL (minimum score 600 paper-based; 100 iBT). *Application deadline:* For fall admission, 3/15 for domestic students; for spring admission, 11/1 for domestic students. Application fee: $50. Electronic applications accepted. *Financial support:* Career-related internships or fieldwork and tuition waivers (full and partial) available. Support available to part-time students. Financial award application deadline: 3/1; financial award applicants required to submit FAFSA. *Unit head:* Dr. Mary A. Hermann, Chair, 804-827-2626, E-mail: mahermann@vcu.edu. *Application contact:* Dr. Donna Gibson, Graduate Program Director, 804-828-1333, E-mail: dgibson7@vcu.edu.
Website: http://www.soe.vcu.edu/departments/ce/index.html

Virginia Polytechnic Institute and State University, Graduate School, College of Liberal Arts and Human Sciences, Blacksburg, VA 24061. Offers career and technical education (MS Ed, Ed D, PhD, Ed S); communication (MA); counselor education

(MA Ed, Ed D, PhD, Ed S); creative writing (MFA); curriculum and instruction (MA Ed, Ed D, PhD, Ed S); educational leadership and policy studies (MA Ed, Ed D, PhD, Ed S); educational research and evaluation (PhD); English (MA); foreign languages, cultures, and literatures (MA); higher education (PhD); higher education and student affairs (MA Ed); history (MA); human development (MS, PhD); material culture and public humanities (MA); philosophy (MA); political science (MA); rhetoric and writing (PhD); science and technology studies (MS, PhD); social, political, ethical, and cultural thought (PhD); sociology (MS, PhD); theater arts (MFA). *Faculty:* 408 full-time (204 women), 3 part-time/adjunct (2 women). *Students:* 657 full-time (446 women), 457 part-time (292 women); includes 213 minority (114 Black or African American, non-Hispanic/Latino; 3 American Indian or Alaska Native, non-Hispanic/Latino; 29 Asian, non-Hispanic/Latino; 44 Hispanic/Latino; 23 Two or more races, non-Hispanic/Latino), 93 international. Average age 33. 805 applicants, 55% accepted, 328 enrolled. In 2016, 270 master's, 91 doctorates awarded. *Degree requirements:* For master's, comprehensive exam (for some programs), thesis (for some programs); for doctorate, comprehensive exam (for some programs), thesis/dissertation (for some programs). *Entrance requirements:* For master's and doctorate, GRE/GMAT. Additional exam requirements/recommendations for international students: Required—TOEFL (minimum score 80 iBT). *Application deadline:* For fall admission, 8/1 for domestic students, 4/1 for international students; for spring admission, 1/1 for domestic students, 9/1 for international students. Applications are processed on a rolling basis. Application fee: $75. Electronic applications accepted. *Expenses:* Tuition, state resident: full-time $12,467; part-time $692.50 per credit hour. Tuition, nonresident: full-time $25,095; part-time $1394.25 per credit hour. *Required fees:* $2669; $491.50 per semester. Tuition and fees vary according to course load, campus/location and program. *Financial support:* In 2016–17, 21 research assistantships with full tuition reimbursements (averaging $19,817 per year), 237 teaching assistantships with full tuition reimbursements (averaging $15,497 per year) were awarded. Financial award application deadline: 3/1; financial award applicants required to submit FAFSA. *Total annual research expenditures:* $6.6 million. *Unit head:* Rosemary Blieszner, Interim Dean, 540-231-6779, Fax: 540-231-7157, E-mail: liberalartsdean@vt.edu. *Application contact:* Chelsea Blanchet, Executive Assistant, 540-231-6779, Fax: 540-231-7157, E-mail: bchels1@vt.edu.
Website: http://www.liberalarts.vt.edu/

Walsh University, Graduate Programs, Program in Counseling and Human Development, North Canton, OH 44720-3396. Offers clinical mental health counseling (MA); school counseling (MA); student affairs in higher education (MA). *Accreditation:* ACA. *Program availability:* Part-time, evening/weekend. *Faculty:* 5 full-time (4 women), 10 part-time/adjunct (8 women). *Students:* 34 full-time (24 women), 66 part-time (51 women); includes 11 minority (6 Black or African American, non-Hispanic/Latino; 2 American Indian or Alaska Native, non-Hispanic/Latino; 2 Hispanic/Latino; 1 Two or more races, non-Hispanic/Latino), 1 international. Average age 30. 58 applicants, 69% accepted, 27 enrolled. In 2016, 24 master's awarded. *Degree requirements:* For master's, comprehensive exam, internship, practicum. *Entrance requirements:* For master's, GRE (minimum score of 145 verbal and 146 quantitative) or MAT (minimum score of 397), interview, minimum GPA of 3.0, writing sample, reference forms, notarized affidavit of good moral conduct. Additional exam requirements/recommendations for international students: Required—TOEFL (minimum score 500 paper-based; 61 iBT). *Application deadline:* For fall admission, 7/15 priority date for domestic students. Applications are processed on a rolling basis. Application fee: $25. Electronic applications accepted. Application fee is waived when completed online. *Expenses:* $665 per credit hour. *Financial support:* In 2016–17, 11 students received support, including 11 research assistantships with partial tuition reimbursements available (averaging $8,442 per year). Financial award application deadline: 12/31. *Faculty research:* Supervision of clinical mental health, clinical mental health practice/issues, clinical mental health skills development, advocacy, teaching and professional development, career development, refugee development in US, supervision in student affairs, offender treatment, domestic violence issues, alcohol and drug treatment issues, Professional identity and advocacy in school counseling, Efficacy in counseling clinic. *Unit head:* Dr. Ruthann Anderson, Program Director, 330-490-7338, Fax: 330-490-7323, E-mail: randerson@walsh.edu. *Application contact:* Audra Dice, Graduate and Transfer Admissions Counselor, 330-490-7181, Fax: 330-244-4925, E-mail: adice@walsh.edu.
Website: http://www.walsh.edu/counseling-graduate-program

West Chester University of Pennsylvania, College of Education and Social Work, Department of Counselor Education, West Chester, PA 19383. Offers clinical mental health counseling (MS); counseling (Certificate); higher education counseling (Post Master's Certificate); higher education counseling/student affairs (MS, Certificate); school counseling (M Ed). *Accreditation:* ACA; NCATE. *Program availability:* Part-time, evening/weekend. *Faculty:* 10 full-time (6 women), 5 part-time/adjunct (3 women). *Students:* 130 full-time (100 women), 65 part-time (55 women); includes 48 minority (27 Black or African American, non-Hispanic/Latino; 2 Asian, non-Hispanic/Latino; 13 Hispanic/Latino; 6 Two or more races, non-Hispanic/Latino), 1 international. Average age 27. 199 applicants, 56% accepted, 66 enrolled. In 2016, 78 master's, 3 other advanced degrees awarded. *Degree requirements:* For master's, comprehensive exam. *Entrance requirements:* For master's, minimum GPA of 3.0, three letters of reference. Additional exam requirements/recommendations for international students: Required—TOEFL or IELTS. *Application deadline:* For fall admission, 5/15 for international students; for spring admission, 10/15 for international students. Applications are processed on a rolling basis. Application fee: $50. Electronic applications accepted. *Expenses:* Tuition, state resident: full-time $8694; part-time $483 per credit. Tuition, nonresident: full-time $13,050; part-time $725 per credit. *Required fees:* $2399; $119.05 per credit. Tuition and fees vary according to campus/location and program. *Financial support:* Scholarships/grants and unspecified assistantships available. Financial award application deadline: 2/15; financial award applicants required to submit FAFSA. *Faculty research:* Teacher and student cognition, adolescent cognitive development, college counseling, motivational interviewing. *Unit head:* Dr. Eric Owens, Chair, 610-436-2559, Fax: 610-425-7432, E-mail: eowens@wcupa.edu. *Application contact:* Dr. Cheryl Neale-McFall, Graduate Coordinator, 610-436-2559, Fax: 610-425-7432, E-mail: cneale-mcfall@wcupa.edu.
Website: http://www.wcupa.edu/education-socialWork/counselorEducation/

Western Illinois University, School of Graduate Studies, College of Education and Human Services, Department of Educational Studies, Program in College Student Personnel, Macomb, IL 61455-1390. Offers college student personnel (MS), including higher education leadership, student affairs. *Accreditation:* NCATE. *Program availability:* Part-time. *Students:* 56 full-time (37 women), 19 part-time (15 women); includes 19 minority (7 Black or African American, non-Hispanic/Latino; 1 Asian, non-Hispanic/Latino; 8 Hispanic/Latino; 3 Two or more races, non-Hispanic/Latino), 2 international. Average age 27. 110 applicants, 79% accepted, 28 enrolled. In 2016, 27 master's awarded. *Degree requirements:* For master's, thesis or alternative. *Entrance requirements:* For master's, interview. Additional exam requirements/recommendations for international students: Required—TOEFL (minimum score 550 paper-based; 80 iBT). *Application deadline:* For fall admission, 1/5 priority date for domestic students. Application fee: $30. Electronic applications accepted. *Financial support:* In 2016–17, 55 students received support. Unspecified assistantships available. Financial award applicants required to submit FAFSA. *Unit head:* Dr. Tracy Davis, Coordinator, 309-298-1183. *Application contact:* Dr. Nancy Parsons, Associate Provost and Director of Graduate Studies, 309-298-1806, Fax: 309-298-2345, E-mail: grad-office@wiu.edu.
Website: http://wiu.edu/csp/

Western Kentucky University, Graduate Studies, College of Education and Behavioral Sciences, Department of Counseling and Student Affairs, Bowling Green, KY 42101. Offers counseling (MA Ed), including marriage and family therapy, mental health counseling; school counseling (P-12) (MA Ed); student affairs in higher education (MA Ed). *Accreditation:* ACA; NCATE. *Program availability:* Part-time, evening/weekend. *Degree requirements:* For master's, comprehensive exam, thesis optional. *Entrance requirements:* For master's, GRE General Test. Additional exam requirements/recommendations for international students: Required—TOEFL (minimum score 555 paper-based; 79 iBT). *Faculty research:* Counselor education, research for residential workers.

William James College, Graduate Programs, Newton, MA 02459. Offers applied psychology in higher education student personnel administration (MA); clinical psychology (Psy D); counseling psychology (MA); counseling psychology and community mental health (MA); counseling psychology and global mental health (MA); executive coaching (Graduate Certificate); forensic and counseling psychology (MA); leadership psychology (Psy D); organizational psychology (MA); primary care psychology (MA); respecialization in clinical psychology (Certificate); school psychology (Psy D); MA/CAGS. *Accreditation:* APA. *Degree requirements:* For master's, comprehensive exam (for some programs); for doctorate, thesis/dissertation (for some programs). Electronic applications accepted.

SOKA UNIVERSITY OF AMERICA

Graduate School, Masters of Arts in Educational Leadership and Societal Changes

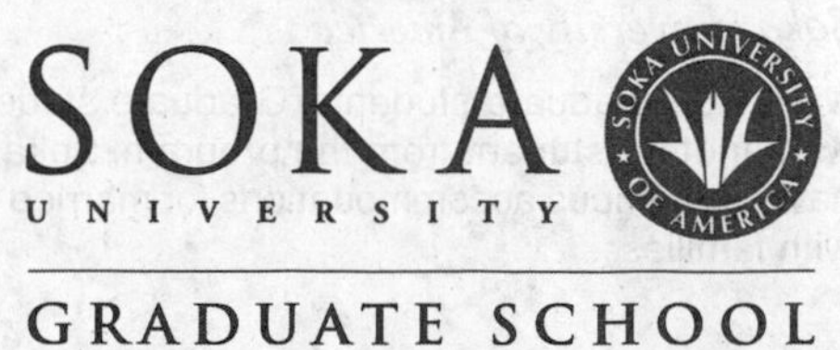

Programs of Study

The educational leader of tomorrow requires a new kind of preparation for a new kind of world, global in scope, all-inclusive in depth and breadth, calling out for meaningful, broad-based societal change focused on harnessing the values of peace.

Soka University of America's (SUA) Master of Arts (M.A.) program in Educational Leadership and Societal Change examines the broad landscape of modern institutions and structures, including but not limited to schools and colleges. It casts a wide interdisciplinary net to bring new light to bear on the symbiotic relationship between value-creating educational leadership and the transformation of society itself. Embedded in the curriculum are also the practical skills and abilities as well as the professional research tools needed by effective educational leaders to develop the knowledge, skills, and dispositions necessary to create learning environments that value diversity, continual knowledge acquisition, instructional leadership, innovative and ethical decision-making, and the successful achievement of all school-aged youth.

In the course of their studies, students will analyze past and present models of administrative leadership for their effectiveness in promoting equality of educational opportunity and greater workplace democracy and gain foundational knowledge of the historical and philosophical underpinnings of education. Students will learn to utilize networks and coalitions for broad-based initiative and reforms in addition to promoting meaningful collaboration among and between parents, and school administrators.

A Master of Arts in Educational Leadership and Societal Change is a degree with international and comparative dimensions that provides broad knowledge, cultural sensitivity, and perspective that is in demand. A Soka graduate-level education can help prepare and place students in a variety of industries. The desire to pursue a doctorate, become an educational leader, work in civil service or for a nonprofit organization, work in government, make a difference in the growing for-profit sector in education, or desire to start a school are some of the reasons students choose this program.

The M.A. in Educational Leadership and Societal Change is a full-time, two-year program (39 semester credits). The University's full-time learning environment provides students support for professional development opportunities, engagement with visiting distinguished scholars and practitioners, a summer research grant providing a field experience in a real-world leadership setting, and a residential living and learning experience including off-campus housing opportunities for students with dependents or special circumstances.

Students study and conduct research into the historical roots of educational policies and problems as well as on the relationship between educational philosophies and practices and contemporary social, political, economic and cultural developments. Related areas of study include comparative and international education, multicultural education, educational psychology, gender and education, school administration policy and practice, and educational law.

Regular semester-long courses are taught in a traditional graduate seminar format in which students read and discuss both common and individual readings, pursue a research project under the direction of a professor/mentor, and provide regular progress reports to the class as a whole for commentary and input. Courses include a fieldwork component, including a summer-long research internship that provides students with hands-on opportunities to shadow administrators, analyze organizational dynamics, and evaluate curriculum. Under the supervision of a principal professor, students integrate their fieldwork and educational research to produce a master's thesis for graduation.

Financial Aid

Soka University of America is committed to being a partner in helping students meet the costs of their education and investing its resources to ensure the success of its students. The Office of Financial Aid works with students to ensure that a Soka education is accessible to all students who are admitted. In an effort to promote greater diversity and access, SUA has designed a comprehensive merit and need-based financial aid program that ensures the fair distribution of institutional, state, and federal funds.

Soka's M.A. program is affordable. Financial aid in the form of grants and scholarships is available up to the full cost of tuition. Loan programs are also available to domestic and international students.

Cost of Study

For the 2017–18 academic year, the cost of tuition for domestic students is $30,106. Books and supplies are estimated at $1,854. Costs for transportation and personal expenses vary by student.

Living and Housing Costs

Soka University of America recognizes the value of establishing a culture of learning throughout the university campus. As a residential campus, Soka students are provided with distinctive accommodations within a unique setting. Soka's residence halls are a dynamic environment offering living and learning opportunities for residents to share intellectual and educational goals and grow through community engagement, interpersonal relationships, and social interaction within a diverse community.

Single graduate students may live in suite-style housing accommodations in the residence hall community. Graduate student housing is a designated floor in a residence hall community shared with undergraduate students. Graduate students will be matched with another student from the program. Soka University does not have on-campus accommodations for married students or students with families.

The cost of on-campus room and board is $12,166 for the 2017–18 academic year.

Student Group

The program offers a small, select, international community of inquiry, diverse in age and experience with a student/faculty ratio of 7:1.

Location

Soka University of America is a 103 acre campus located in south Orange County, California in the City of Aliso Viejo (between San Diego and Los Angeles). The campus is just 9 miles from the beach and located in the heart of Southern California's abundance of cultural, educational, sporting, and adventure opportunities.

The University

The Soka University of America Graduate School strives to provide an academic setting that nurtures men and women from a variety of cultures and national backgrounds, who seek to learn from shared experiences. The School also seeks to develop critical thinking and learning and to foster a commitment to lifelong learning. To this end, the School emphasizes small class sizes that cultivate close and informal relationship between teachers and students, rigorous academic endeavors, free and open dialogue, and an appreciation for human diversity.

Faculty

Soka University's high-caliber faculty enjoys working closely with students. With a low student/faculty ratio, the faculty can work individually with students to see how far they can go in exploring new concepts and learning opportunities.

Program Director John H. Heffron, Ph.D., is a Professor of Educational History and Culture. He is also the author of Leadership for Development: What Globalization Demands of Leaders Seeking Change and Toward a Cybernetic Pedagogy: The Cognitive Revolution and the Classroom, 1948–Present.

Applying

The student seeking admission to the M.A. program is expected to have completed a bachelor's degree from an accredited college or university with at least a B average or the equivalent of an undergraduate level education (normally 16 years of pre- and postsecondary education) from a foreign institution. The Graduate School Faculty Admission Committee will review applications to the program. Applicants will be admitted to the program based on ability to complete a rigorous program of academic study successfully; strong writing skills; clear professional and scholarly goals; and strong evidence of the ability to work cooperatively, influence group opinion, and facilitate task completion. There are some differences in the application process for domestic and international applicants. Additional information and a complete admission checklist is available at http://www.soka.edu/gradadmission.

The application deadline for the M.A. program is February 15. Students can apply by visiting http://admissions.soka.edu/apply.

Correspondence and Information

Soka University of America
Office of Graduate Admission
1 University Drive
Aliso Viejo, California 92656
Phone: 949-480-4111
E-mail: grad_admissions@soka.edu
Website: www.soka.edu
www.soka.edu/gradadmission
www.soka.edu/maprogram

Section 24
Instructional Levels

This section contains a directory of institutions offering graduate work in instructional levels. Additional information about programs listed in the directory may be obtained by writing directly to the dean of a graduate school or chair of a department at the address given in the directory.

For programs offering related work, see also in this book *Administration, Instruction, and Theory; Education; Leisure Studies and Recreation; Physical Education and Kinesiology; Special Focus;* and *Subject Areas.* In other guides in this series:

Graduate Programs in the Humanities, Arts & Social Sciences
See *Psychology and Counseling (School Psychology)*

Graduate Programs in the Biological/Biomedical Sciences and Health-Related Medical Professions
See *Health-Related Professions*

CONTENTS

Program Directories

Featured School: Display and Close-Up

See:

Adult Education

Alverno College, School of Education, Milwaukee, WI 53234-3922. Offers adaptive education (MA); administrative leadership (MA); adult education and organizational development (MA); adult educational and instructional design (MA); adult educational and instructional technology (MA); global connections in the humanities (MA); instructional leadership (MA); instructional technology for K-12 settings (MA); professional development (MA); reading education (MA); reading education with adaptive education (MA); science education (MA); special education (MA); teaching in alternative schools (MA). *Accreditation:* NCATE. *Program availability:* Part-time, evening/weekend. *Faculty:* 4 full-time (3 women), 23 part-time/adjunct (17 women). *Students:* 58 full-time (57 women), 62 part-time (54 women); includes 32 minority (22 Black or African American, non-Hispanic/Latino; 2 Asian, non-Hispanic/Latino; 8 Hispanic/Latino), 1 international. Average age 39. 77 applicants, 99% accepted, 61 enrolled. In 2016, 85 master's awarded. *Degree requirements:* For master's, presentation/defense of proposal, conference presentation of inquiry projects. *Entrance requirements:* For master's, bachelor's degree in related field, communication samples from work setting, 3 letters of recommendation. Additional exam requirements/recommendations for international students: Required—TOEFL. *Application deadline:* For fall admission, 7/15 priority date for domestic and international students; for spring admission, 12/15 priority date for domestic and international students. Applications are processed on a rolling basis. Application fee: $0. Electronic applications accepted. *Expenses:* Contact institution. *Financial support:* In 2016–17, 17 students received support. Federal Work-Study and scholarships/grants available. Support available to part-time students. Financial award applicants required to submit FAFSA. *Faculty research:* Student self-assessment, self-reflection, integration of curriculum, identifying needs of students in strategic situations and designing appropriate classroom strategies. *Unit head:* Dr. Desiree Pointer Mace, Associate Dean, Graduate Program, 414-382-6345, Fax: 414-382-6332, E-mail: desiree.pointer-mace@alverno.edu. *Application contact:* Katie Kipp, Graduate Admissions Counselor, 414-382-6045, Fax: 414-382-6354, E-mail: katie.kipp@alverno.edu.

Antioch University Seattle, Graduate Programs, Program in Education, Seattle, WA 98121-1814. Offers adult education (MA); drama therapy (MA); individualized studies (MA); leadership in edible education (MA); teaching (MAT); urban environmental education (MA). *Program availability:* Part-time, evening/weekend. *Degree requirements:* For master's, comprehensive exam (for some programs), thesis. *Entrance requirements:* For master's, WEST-B, WEST-E, current resume, transcripts of undergraduate degree and coursework (or for highest degree completed), two letters of recommendation, proof of fingerprinting and background check, moral character with fitness statement of understanding, documentation of 40 hours' experience in school classroom(s). *Application deadline:* Applications are processed on a rolling basis. *Expenses:* Contact institution. *Financial support:* Research assistantships, Federal Work-Study, scholarships/grants, and unspecified assistantships available. Financial award application deadline: 6/15. *Faculty research:* Visual thinking and science education, K-8 equity and engaged pedagogy in science education, K-12 inquiry-based mathematics education, education in prisons and other institutions of confinement. *Unit head:* Ed Mikel, Interim Dean, 206-268-4617, E-mail: emikel@antioch.edu. *Application contact:* Eileen Knight, Recruitment and Admissions Director, 206-268-4200, E-mail: eknight@antioch.edu.
Website: https://www.antioch.edu/seattle/degrees-programs/education-degrees/

Argosy University, Chicago, College of Education, Chicago, IL 60601. Offers adult education and training (MA Ed); community college executive leadership (Ed D); educational leadership (MA Ed, Ed D, Ed S), including district leadership (Ed D), higher education administration (Ed D), K-12 education (Ed D); instructional leadership (Ed D, Ed S), including higher education (Ed D), K-12 education (Ed D). *Program availability:* Online learning.

Argosy University, Hawai`i, College of Education, Honolulu, HI 96813. Offers adult education and training (MAEd); educational leadership (Ed D), including higher education administration, K-12 education; instructional leadership (Ed D), including higher education, K-12 education; school psychology (MA).

Argosy University, Phoenix, College of Education, Phoenix, AZ 85021. Offers adult education and training (MA Ed); advanced educational administration (Ed D, Ed S); community college executive leadership (Ed D); educational administration (MA Ed); educational leadership (MA Ed, Ed D, Ed S), including education technology (Ed D), higher education administration (Ed D), K-12 education (Ed D); higher and postsecondary education (MA Ed); initial educational administration (Ed D, Ed S); school psychology (MA); teaching and learning (MA Ed, Ed D, Ed S), including education technology (Ed D), higher education (Ed D), K-12 education (Ed D).

Argosy University, Seattle, College of Education, Seattle, WA 98121. Offers adult education and training (MA Ed); community college executive leadership (Ed D); educational leadership (MA Ed, Ed D), including higher education administration (Ed D), K-12 education (Ed D); higher and postsecondary education (MA Ed); instructional leadership (MA Ed, Ed D), including education technology (Ed D), higher education (Ed D), K-12 education (Ed D).

Armstrong State University, School of Graduate Studies, Department of Secondary, Adult, and Physical Education, Savannah, GA 31419-1997. Offers adolescent and adult education (Certificate); adult education and community leadership (M Ed); curriculum and instruction (M Ed); secondary education (MAT). *Program availability:* Part-time, evening/weekend, online learning. *Faculty:* 9 full-time (all women), 3 part-time/adjunct (all women). *Students:* 23 full-time (16 women), 103 part-time (68 women); includes 47 minority (40 Black or African American, non-Hispanic/Latino; 1 Asian, non-Hispanic/Latino; 2 Hispanic/Latino; 4 Two or more races, non-Hispanic/Latino), 1 international. Average age 32. 77 applicants, 52% accepted, 28 enrolled. In 2016, 36 master's, 1 other advanced degree awarded. *Degree requirements:* For master's, comprehensive exam (for some programs), thesis (for some programs), capstone project (for M Ed). *Entrance requirements:* For master's, edTPA (for MAT). Additional exam requirements/recommendations for international students: Required—TOEFL (minimum score 523 paper-based). *Application deadline:* For fall admission, 6/30 priority date for domestic students, 5/1 priority date for international students; for spring admission, 11/15 priority date for domestic students, 9/15 priority date for international students; for summer admission, 4/15 priority date for domestic students, 9/15 for international students. Applications are processed on a rolling basis. Application fee: $30. Electronic applications accepted. *Expenses:* Tuition, state resident: full-time $1781; part-time $161.93 per credit hour. Tuition, nonresident: full-time $6482; part-time $589.27 per credit hour. *Required fees:* $1224 per unit. $612 per semester. Tuition and fees vary according to course load, campus/location and program. *Financial support:* In 2016–17, research assistantships with full tuition reimbursements (averaging $5,000 per year) were awarded; career-related internships or fieldwork, Federal Work-Study, scholarships/grants, and unspecified assistantships also available. Support available to part-time students. Financial award application deadline: 3/15; financial award applicants required to submit FAFSA. *Faculty research:* Quality of teacher leadership, classroom management and first year teachers; edTPA preparation and success of candidates; social justice issues related to educational preparation; recruitment of STEM teachers. *Unit head:* Dr. Regina Rahimi, Interim Department Head, 912-344-2562, E-mail: regina.rahimi@armstrong.edu. *Application contact:* McKenzie Peterman, Assistant Director of Graduate Admissions, 912-344-2503, Fax: 912-344-3417, E-mail: graduate@armstrong.edu.
Website: http://www.armstrong.edu/Education/adolescent_adult_education2/aaed_welcome

Athabasca University, Centre for Interdisciplinary Studies, Athabasca, AB T9S 3A3, Canada. Offers adult education (MA); community studies (MA); cultural studies (MA); educational studies (MA); global change (MA); heritage resource management (Postbaccalaureate Certificate); legislative drafting (Postbaccalaureate Certificate); work, organization, and leadership (MA). *Program availability:* Part-time, evening/weekend, online learning. *Degree requirements:* For master's, project. *Entrance requirements:* Additional exam requirements/recommendations for international students: Required—TOEFL (minimum score 560 paper-based). Electronic applications accepted. *Faculty research:* Women's history, literature and culture studies, sustainable development, labor and education.

Auburn University, Graduate School, College of Education, Department of Educational Foundations, Leadership, and Technology, Auburn University, AL 36849. Offers adult education (PhD, Ed S); curriculum supervision (M Ed, PhD); higher education administration (PhD); library media (Ed S); school administration (M Ed, PhD). *Accreditation:* NCATE. *Program availability:* Part-time. *Faculty:* 29 full-time (15 women), 4 part-time/adjunct (3 women). *Students:* 119 full-time (72 women), 273 part-time (170 women); includes 132 minority (114 Black or African American, non-Hispanic/Latino; 2 American Indian or Alaska Native, non-Hispanic/Latino; 4 Asian, non-Hispanic/Latino; 6 Hispanic/Latino; 1 Native Hawaiian or other Pacific Islander, non-Hispanic/Latino; 5 Two or more races, non-Hispanic/Latino), 14 international. Average age 37. 220 applicants, 71% accepted, 78 enrolled. In 2016, 67 master's, 44 doctorates, 41 other advanced degrees awarded. *Degree requirements:* For master's, thesis (for some programs); for doctorate, thesis/dissertation; for Ed S, field project. *Entrance requirements:* For master's, doctorate, and Ed S, GRE General Test. *Application deadline:* Applications are processed on a rolling basis. Application fee: $50 ($60 for international students). Electronic applications accepted. *Expenses:* Tuition, state resident: full-time $9072; part-time $504 per credit hour. Tuition, nonresident: full-time $27,216; part-time $1512 per credit hour. *Required fees:* $812 per semester. Tuition and fees vary according to degree level and program. *Financial support:* Teaching assistantships and Federal Work-Study available. Support available to part-time students. Financial award application deadline: 3/15; financial award applicants required to submit FAFSA. *Unit head:* Dr. Sherida Downer, Head, 334-844-4460. *Application contact:* Dr. George Flowers, Dean of the Graduate School, 334-844-4700.
Website: http://www.education.auburn.edu/academic_departments/eflt/

Aurora University, School of Education and Human Performance, Aurora, IL 60506-4892. Offers bilingual-ESL education (MA); educational leadership (MA); educational technology (MA); leadership in administration (Ed D); leadership in adult learning and higher education (Ed D); leadership in curriculum and instruction (Ed D); reading instruction (MA); special education (MA). *Accreditation:* NCATE. *Program availability:* Part-time, evening/weekend. *Faculty:* 22 full-time (12 women), 46 part-time/adjunct (27 women). *Students:* 36 full-time (30 women), 559 part-time (372 women); includes 68 minority (27 Black or African American, non-Hispanic/Latino; 1 American Indian or Alaska Native, non-Hispanic/Latino; 6 Asian, non-Hispanic/Latino; 29 Hispanic/Latino; 2 Native Hawaiian or other Pacific Islander, non-Hispanic/Latino; 3 Two or more races, non-Hispanic/Latino). Average age 37. 126 applicants, 98% accepted, 72 enrolled. In 2016, 178 master's, 27 doctorates awarded. *Degree requirements:* For master's, student teaching; for doctorate, comprehensive exam, thesis/dissertation. *Entrance requirements:* For master's, 2 years of teaching experience, valid teaching certificate; for doctorate, appropriate master's degree, two references, curriculum vitae, personal statement, professional project, reflective essay. Additional exam requirements/recommendations for international students: Required—TOEFL (minimum score 550 paper-based; 79 iBT). *Application deadline:* For fall admission, 6/1 for international students; for spring admission, 10/1 for international students. Applications are processed on a rolling basis. Application fee: $0. Electronic applications accepted. *Expenses:* Contact institution. *Financial support:* In 2016–17, 10 students received support. Federal Work-Study, scholarships/grants, and unspecified assistantships available. Support available to part-time students. Financial award applicants required to submit FAFSA. *Unit head:* Dr. Jen Buckley, Executive Director of the School of Education and Human Performance, 630-844-1542, Fax: 630-844-6155, E-mail: jbuckley@aurora.edu. *Application contact:* Elizabeth Botica, Graduate Education Recruiter, 630-947-8918, E-mail: ebotica@aurora.edu.
Website: http://aurora.edu/education

Ball State University, Graduate School, Teachers College, Department of Educational Studies, Program in Adult Education, Muncie, IN 47306. Offers adult and community education (MA); adult, higher and community education (Ed D). *Accreditation:* NCATE. *Program availability:* Part-time, 100% online, blended/hybrid learning. *Degree requirements:* For doctorate, thesis/dissertation. *Entrance requirements:* For master's, minimum baccalaureate GPA of 2.75 or 3.0 in latter half of baccalauareate; for doctorate, GRE General Test, minimum graduate GPA of 3.2. Additional exam requirements/recommendations for international students: Required—TOEFL (minimum score 550 paper-based; 79 iBT), IELTS (minimum score 6.5). Electronic applications accepted. *Faculty research:* Community education, executive development for public services.

Buffalo State College, State University of New York, The Graduate School, Faculty of Applied Science and Education, Department of Educational Foundations, Program in Adult Education, Buffalo, NY 14222-1095. Offers adult education (MS, Certificate); human resources development (Certificate). *Program availability:* Part-time, evening/weekend, online learning. *Degree requirements:* For master's, comprehensive exam. *Entrance requirements:* Additional exam requirements/recommendations for international students: Required—TOEFL (minimum score 550 paper-based).

California Baptist University, Program in Education, Riverside, CA 92504-3206. Offers educational leadership (MS); educational leadership for faith-based institutions (MS); educational leadership for public institutions (MS); educational technology (MS); instructional computer applications (MS); international education (MS); leadership and adult learning (MS); leadership and organizational studies (MS); online teaching and

learning (MS); reading (MS); science education (MA); special education in mild/moderate disabilities (MS); special education in moderate/severe disabilities (MS); teacher leadership (MS); teaching (MS); teaching and learning (MS). *Program availability:* Part-time, evening/weekend, 100% online, blended/hybrid learning. *Faculty:* 20 full-time (8 women), 11 part-time/adjunct (7 women). *Students:* 191 full-time (148 women), 234 part-time (178 women); includes 194 minority (23 Black or African American, non-Hispanic/Latino; 5 American Indian or Alaska Native, non-Hispanic/Latino; 15 Asian, non-Hispanic/Latino; 131 Hispanic/Latino; 4 Native Hawaiian or other Pacific Islander, non-Hispanic/Latino; 16 Two or more races, non-Hispanic/Latino), 2 international. Average age 31. 277 applicants, 61% accepted, 150 enrolled. In 2016, 280 master's awarded. *Degree requirements:* For master's, comprehensive exam, project, or thesis. *Entrance requirements:* For master's, minimum undergraduate GPA of 2.75; 500-word essay; three letters of recommendation; two prerequisite courses completed with minimum C grade. Additional exam requirements/recommendations for international students: Required—TOEFL (minimum score 80 iBT). *Application deadline:* For fall admission, 8/1 priority date for domestic students, 7/1 for international students; for spring admission, 12/1 priority date for domestic students, 11/1 for international students. Applications are processed on a rolling basis. Application fee: $45. Electronic applications accepted. *Expenses:* Contact institution. *Financial support:* In 2016–17, 162 students received support. Federal Work-Study and scholarships/grants available. Financial award applicants required to submit CSS PROFILE or FAFSA. *Faculty research:* Leadership development, complexity theory, faith and learning, special education, social and philosophical contexts of education. *Unit head:* Dr. John Shoup, Dean, School of Education, 951-343-4516, E-mail: jshoup@calbaptist.edu.
Website: http://www.calbaptist.edu/mastersined/

California Baptist University, Program in Leadership and Adult Learning, Riverside, CA 92504-3206. Offers MA. *Program availability:* Part-time, evening/weekend. *Degree requirements:* For master's, CCCAOE professional training or leadership tactics. *Entrance requirements:* For master's, minimum undergraduate GPA of 2.75, bachelor's degree transcripts, three letters of recommendation, essay, resume. Additional exam requirements/recommendations for international students: Required—TOEFL (minimum score 80 iBT). *Application deadline:* For fall admission, 8/1 priority date for domestic students, 7/1 priority date for international students; for spring admission, 12/1 priority date for domestic students, 11/1 priority date for international students. Applications are processed on a rolling basis. Application fee: $45. Electronic applications accepted. *Expenses:* Contact institution. *Financial support:* Applicants required to submit CSS PROFILE or FAFSA. *Unit head:* Dr. John Shoup, Dean, School of Education, 951-343-4205, E-mail: jshoup@calbaptist.edu.

Capella University, School of Education, Doctoral Programs in Education, Minneapolis, MN 55402. Offers curriculum and instruction (PhD); educational leadership and management (Ed D); instructional design for online learning (PhD); K-12 studies in education (PhD); leadership for higher education (PhD); leadership in educational administration (PhD); postsecondary and adult education (PhD); professional studies in education (PhD); reading and literacy (Ed D); special education leadership (PhD); training and performance improvement (PhD).

Capella University, School of Education, Master's Programs in Education, Minneapolis, MN 55402. Offers adult education (MS); curriculum and instruction (MS); early childhood education (MS); enrollment management (MS); higher education leadership and management (MS); instructional design for online learning (MS); integrative studies (MS); K-12 studies in education (MS); leadership in educational administration (MS); reading and literacy (MS); special education teaching (MS).

Carroll University, Graduate Programs in Education, Waukesha, WI 53186-5593. Offers adult and continuing education (M Ed); educational leadership (MS); pk-12 (M Ed). *Program availability:* Part-time, evening/weekend. *Faculty:* 7 full-time (5 women), 14 part-time/adjunct (all women). *Students:* 11 full-time (10 women), 163 part-time (125 women); includes 11 minority (3 Black or African American, non-Hispanic/Latino; 3 American Indian or Alaska Native, non-Hispanic/Latino; 2 Asian, non-Hispanic/Latino; 3 Hispanic/Latino), 1 international. Average age 34. 96 applicants, 38% accepted, 18 enrolled. In 2016, 43 master's awarded. *Degree requirements:* For master's, thesis. *Entrance requirements:* For master's, minimum undergraduate GPA of 2.5 in related field. Additional exam requirements/recommendations for international students: Required—TOEFL. *Application deadline:* For fall admission, 8/15 priority date for domestic students. Applications are processed on a rolling basis. Application fee: $0. Electronic applications accepted. *Expenses: Tuition:* Full-time $10,548; part-time $586 per credit. *Required fees:* $520 per semester. Tuition and fees vary according to course load, degree level and program. *Financial support:* Available to part-time students. Application deadline: 3/15; applicants required to submit FAFSA. *Faculty research:* Qualitative research methods, whole language approaches to teaching, the writing process, multicultural education, gifted/talented learners. *Unit head:* Dr. Kathrine Kramer, Director of Graduate Studies, 262-650-4917, E-mail: kkramer@carrollu.edu. *Application contact:* Lori Aliota, Graduate Admission Counselor, 262-524-7226, E-mail: laliota@carrollu.edu.
Website: http://www.carrollu.edu/gradprograms/education/default.asp

Cleveland State University, College of Graduate Studies, College of Education and Human Services, Department of Counseling, Administration, Supervision and Adult Learning (CASAL), Cleveland, OH 44115. Offers adult learning and development (M Ed); counselor education (PhD); early childhood mental health counseling (Certificate); educational administration and supervision (M Ed). *Accreditation:* ACA (one or more programs are accredited). *Program availability:* Part-time, evening/weekend. *Faculty:* 15 full-time (8 women), 19 part-time/adjunct (10 women). *Students:* 104 full-time (85 women), 259 part-time (197 women); includes 138 minority (115 Black or African American, non-Hispanic/Latino; 1 American Indian or Alaska Native, non-Hispanic/Latino; 3 Asian, non-Hispanic/Latino; 16 Hispanic/Latino; 3 Two or more races, non-Hispanic/Latino), 8 international. Average age 34. 57 applicants, 93% accepted, 51 enrolled. In 2016, 102 master's awarded. *Degree requirements:* For master's, comprehensive exam (for some programs), thesis optional, internship. *Entrance requirements:* For master's, GRE General Test or MAT, letter of recommendation and minimum GPA of 2.75 (for counseling); 2 letters of recommendation and interviews (for organizational leadership). Additional exam requirements/recommendations for international students: Required—TOEFL (minimum score 550 paper-based; 78 iBT), IELTS (minimum score 6). *Application deadline:* For fall admission, 6/21 for domestic students, 5/15 for international students; for spring admission, 8/31 for domestic students, 11/1 for international students. Application fee: $40. Electronic applications accepted. *Expenses:* Tuition, state resident: full-time $9565. Tuition, nonresident: full-time $17,980. Tuition and fees vary according to program. *Financial support:* In 2016–17, 19 students received support, including 10 research assistantships with tuition reimbursements available (averaging $11,882 per year), 5 teaching assistantships with tuition reimbursements available (averaging $11,882 per year); scholarships/grants and unspecified assistantships also available. Support available to part-time students. *Faculty research:* Education law, career development, bullying, psychopharmacology, counseling and spirituality. *Total annual research expenditures:* $225,821. *Unit head:* Dr. Ann L. Bauer, Chairperson, 216-687-4582, Fax: 216-687-5378, E-mail: a.l.bauer@csuohio.edu. *Application contact:* Deborah L. Brown, Interim Assistant Director, Graduate Admissions, 216-523-7572, Fax: 216-687-5400, E-mail: d.l.brown@csuohio.edu.
Website: http://www.csuohio.edu/cehs/departments/CASAL/casal_dept.html

Cleveland State University, College of Graduate Studies, College of Education and Human Services, Program in Urban Education, Specialization in Adult, Continuing, and Higher Education, Cleveland, OH 44115. Offers PhD. *Program availability:* Part-time. *Faculty:* 4 full-time (3 women). *Students:* 1 full-time (0 women), 9 part-time (8 women); includes 1 minority (Black or African American, non-Hispanic/Latino). Average age 40. In 2016, 1 doctorate awarded. *Degree requirements:* For doctorate, one foreign language, comprehensive exam, thesis/dissertation. *Entrance requirements:* For doctorate, GRE General Test (minimum score of 297 for combined Verbal and Quantitative exams, 4.0 preferred for Analytical Writing), minimum graduate GPA of 3.25, curriculum vitae or resume, personal statement, 2 letters of recommendation. Additional exam requirements/recommendations for international students: Required—TOEFL (minimum score 550 paper-based; 78 iBT), IELTS (minimum score 6). *Application deadline:* For fall admission, 7/1 for domestic students, 5/15 for international students; for spring admission, 11/15 for domestic students, 11/1 for international students; for summer admission, 4/1 for domestic students, 3/15 for international students. Application fee: $40. Electronic applications accepted. *Expenses:* Tuition, state resident: full-time $9565. Tuition, nonresident: full-time $17,980. Tuition and fees vary according to program. *Financial support:* In 2016–17, 2 students received support, including 1 research assistantship with full tuition reimbursement available, 1 teaching assistantship with full tuition reimbursement available (averaging $11,800 per year); tuition waivers (full) also available. Support available to part-time students. Financial award application deadline: 4/1; financial award applicants required to submit FAFSA. *Faculty research:* Adult education research, practice in diverse contexts. *Unit head:* Dr. Graham Stead, Director, Doctoral Studies, 216-875-9869, E-mail: g.b.stead@csuohio.edu. *Application contact:* Rita M. Grabowski, Administrative Coordinator, 216-687-4697, Fax: 216-875-9697, E-mail: r.grabowski@csuohio.edu.
Website: http://www.csuohio.edu/cehs/departments/DOC/lll_doc.html

Colorado State University, College of Health and Human Sciences, School of Education, Fort Collins, CO 80523-1588. Offers adult education and training (M Ed); counseling and career development (M Ed); education sciences (PhD); higher education leadership (PhD); organization learning, performance, and change (PhD); organizational learning, performance, and change (M Ed); student affairs in higher education (MS); teaching and learning (M Ed), including principal licensure, teacher licensure. *Accreditation:* ACA; TEAC. *Program availability:* Part-time, online only, 100% online, blended/hybrid learning, face-to-face off-campus courses. *Faculty:* 29 full-time (21 women), 23 part-time/adjunct (11 women). *Students:* 80 full-time (56 women), 541 part-time (353 women); includes 142 minority (26 Black or African American, non-Hispanic/Latino; 2 American Indian or Alaska Native, non-Hispanic/Latino; 22 Asian, non-Hispanic/Latino; 71 Hispanic/Latino; 21 Two or more races, non-Hispanic/Latino), 18 international. Average age 37. 483 applicants, 31% accepted, 137 enrolled. In 2016, 183 master's, 33 doctorates awarded. *Degree requirements:* For master's, thesis optional, professional portfolio; for doctorate, comprehensive exam, thesis/dissertation. *Entrance requirements:* For master's, bachelor's degree; minimum GPA of 3.0 in last degree earned; for doctorate, GRE or GMAT (depending upon specialization), master's degree; minimum GPA of 3.0 in last degree earned. Additional exam requirements/recommendations for international students: Required—TOEFL (minimum score 550 paper-based; 80 iBT), IELTS (minimum score 6.5), PTE (minimum score 58). *Application deadline:* Applications are processed on a rolling basis. Application fee: $60 ($70 for international students). Electronic applications accepted. *Expenses:* Contact institution. *Financial support:* In 2016–17, 3 students received support, including 7 research assistantships with full tuition reimbursements available (averaging $11,749 per year), 5 teaching assistantships with full tuition reimbursements available (averaging $15,886 per year); fellowships with full tuition reimbursements available, scholarships/grants, and unspecified assistantships also available. Financial award application deadline: 3/1; financial award applicants required to submit FAFSA. *Faculty research:* Higher education leadership; research methods; human resource development; K-16 education; diversity, equity, and inclusion. *Total annual research expenditures:* $499,898. *Unit head:* Dr. Louise Jennings, Co-Director, 970-491-6317, Fax: 970-491-1317, E-mail: louise.jennings@colostate.edu. *Application contact:* Kelli Clark, Graduate Programs Coordinator, 970-491-2093, Fax: 970-491-1317, E-mail: kelli.clark@colostate.edu.
Website: http://www.soe.chhs.colostate.edu/

Concordia University, School of Graduate Studies, Faculty of Arts and Science, Department of Education, Program in Adult Education, Montréal, QC H3G 1M8, Canada. Offers Certificate, Diploma. *Degree requirements:* For other advanced degree, internship. *Entrance requirements:* For degree, interview. *Faculty research:* Staff development, human relations training, adult learning, professional development, learning in the workplace.

Concordia University, School of Graduate Studies, Faculty of Arts and Science, Department of Education, Program in Educational Studies, Montréal, QC H3G 1M8, Canada. Offers MA. *Degree requirements:* For master's, one foreign language, thesis optional. *Faculty research:* Social aspects of microtechnology, gender and education, minorities and immigrants in Canadian education, professional development, political education.

Coppin State University, Division of Graduate Studies, Division of Education, Department of Adult and General Education, Baltimore, MD 21216-3698. Offers MS. *Program availability:* Part-time, evening/weekend. *Degree requirements:* For master's, thesis optional, research paper, internship. *Entrance requirements:* For master's, GRE or PRAXIS, minimum GPA of 2.5, interview, resume, references.

Cornell University, Graduate School, Graduate Fields of Agriculture and Life Sciences, Field of Education, Ithaca, NY 14853. Offers adult and extension education (MPS, MS, PhD); learning, teaching, and social policy (MPS, MS, PhD); mathematics 7-12 (MS). Terminal master's awarded for partial completion of doctoral program. *Degree requirements:* For master's, thesis (MS); for doctorate, comprehensive exam, thesis/dissertation. *Entrance requirements:* For master's and doctorate, GRE General Test, sample of written work (recommended), 2 letters of recommendation. Additional exam requirements/recommendations for international students: Required—TOEFL (minimum score 550 paper-based; 77 iBT). Electronic applications accepted. *Faculty research:* Moral development and professional ethics, public issues education and community development, socio/political issues in public education, teacher education and curriculum in agricultural science and mathematics, extension research.

Dallas Theological Seminary, Graduate Programs, Dallas, TX 75204-6499. Offers adult education (Th M); apologetics (Th M); Bible backgrounds (Th M); Bible translation (Th M); Biblical and theological studies (Certificate); biblical counseling (MA); biblical exegesis and linguistics (MA); biblical exposition (PhD); biblical studies (MA); Biblical theology (Th M); children's education (Th M); Christian education (MA, D Min); Christian leadership (MA); cross-cultural ministries (MA); educational administration (Th M); educational leadership (Th M); evangelism and discipleship (Th M); exposition of Biblical books (Th M); family life education (Th M); general studies (Th M); Hebrew and cognate studies (Th M); hermeneutics (Th M); historical theology (Th M); homiletics (Th M);

intercultural ministries (Th M); Jesus studies (Th M); leadership studies (Th M); media and communication (MA); media arts (Th M); ministry (D Min); ministry with women (Th M); New Testament studies (Th M, PhD); Old Testament studies (Th M, PhD); parachurch ministries (Th M); pastoral care and counseling (Th M); pastoral theology and practice (Th M); philosophy (Th M); sacred theology (STM); spiritual formation (Th M); systematic theology (Th M); teaching in Christian institutions (Th M); theological studies (PhD); urban ministries (Th M); worship studies (Th M); youth education (Th M). *Program availability:* Part-time, online learning. *Degree requirements:* For master's, variable foreign language requirement, thesis (for some programs); for doctorate, 2 foreign languages, thesis/dissertation. *Entrance requirements:* For master's, GRE or MAT (if minimum undergraduate cumulative GPA is below 2.5 or undergraduate degree is unaccredited). Additional exam requirements/recommendations for international students: Required—TOEFL (minimum score 575 paper-based; 85 iBT), TWE. Electronic applications accepted.

Delaware State University, Graduate Programs, College of Education, Health and Public Policy, Program in Adult Literacy and Basic Education, Dover, DE 19901-2277. Offers MA. *Entrance requirements:* Additional exam requirements/recommendations for international students: Required—TOEFL (minimum score 550 paper-based). Electronic applications accepted.

DePaul University, College of Education, Chicago, IL 60614. Offers bilingual bicultural education (M Ed, MA); counseling (M Ed, MA), including clinical mental health counseling, college student development, school counseling; curriculum studies (M Ed, MA, Ed D); early childhood education (M Ed, MA, Ed D); educating adults (MA); educational leadership (M Ed, MA, Ed D), including administration and supervision (M Ed, MA), principal preparation (M Ed, MA); elementary education (MA); mathematics education (MA); mathematics for teaching (MS); middle school mathematics education (MS); reading specialist (M Ed, MA); secondary education (M Ed); social and cultural foundations in education (MA); special education (M Ed, MA); world languages education (M Ed, MA). *Program availability:* Part-time, evening/weekend, online learning. *Degree requirements:* For doctorate, thesis/dissertation. Electronic applications accepted.

DePaul University, School for New Learning, Chicago, IL 60604. Offers applied professional studies (MA); applied technology (MS); educating adults (MA). *Program availability:* Part-time, evening/weekend. *Degree requirements:* For master's, thesis or alternative. Electronic applications accepted.

East Carolina University, Graduate School, College of Education, Department of Interdisciplinary Professions, Greenville, NC 27858-4353. Offers adult education (MA Ed); business and marketing education (MA); career and technical education (MA Ed); counselor education (MS); library science (MLS); vocational education (MS). *Accreditation:* ACA; NCATE. *Program availability:* Part-time, evening/weekend. *Students:* 95 full-time (79 women), 427 part-time (374 women); includes 106 minority (68 Black or African American, non-Hispanic/Latino; 13 American Indian or Alaska Native, non-Hispanic/Latino; 4 Asian, non-Hispanic/Latino; 13 Hispanic/Latino; 8 Two or more races, non-Hispanic/Latino). Average age 37. 225 applicants, 93% accepted, 174 enrolled. In 2016, 86 master's awarded. *Degree requirements:* For master's, comprehensive exam, thesis optional. *Entrance requirements:* For master's, GRE General Test or MAT, interview, minimum GPA of 2.5, bachelor's degree in related field, teaching license (MA Ed). Additional exam requirements/recommendations for international students: Required—TOEFL. *Application deadline:* For fall admission, 5/15 priority date for domestic students. Applications are processed on a rolling basis. Application fee: $50. *Financial support:* Research assistantships with partial tuition reimbursements, teaching assistantships with partial tuition reimbursements, and Federal Work-Study available. Support available to part-time students. Financial award application deadline: 6/1. *Unit head:* Dr. Vivian W. Mott, Chair, 252-328-6177, Fax: 252-328-4368, E-mail: mottv@ecu.edu. *Application contact:* Dean of Graduate School, 252-328-6012, Fax: 252-328-6071, E-mail: gradschool@ecu.edu.
Website: http://www.ecu.edu/cs-educ/idp/index.cfm

Eastern Washington University, Graduate Studies, College of Arts, Letters and Education, Department of Education, Program in Adult Education, Cheney, WA 99004-2431. Offers M Ed. *Faculty:* 13 full-time (8 women), 12 part-time/adjunct (6 women). *Students:* 2 full-time (both women), 7 part-time (6 women). Average age 47. 6 applicants, 83% accepted, 4 enrolled. In 2016, 3 master's awarded. *Degree requirements:* For master's, comprehensive exam, thesis or alternative. *Entrance requirements:* For master's, minimum GPA of 3.0. Additional exam requirements/recommendations for international students: Required—PTE (minimum score 63), TOEFL (minimum score 580 paper-based, 92 iBT) or IELTS (7). *Application deadline:* For fall admission, 4/1 priority date for domestic students; for spring admission, 1/15 for domestic students. Applications are processed on a rolling basis. Application fee: $75. *Expenses:* Contact institution. *Financial support:* In 2016–17, teaching assistantships with partial tuition reimbursements (averaging $7,000 per year) were awarded; career-related internships or fieldwork, Federal Work-Study, institutionally sponsored loans, scholarships/grants, health care benefits, tuition waivers (partial), and unspecified assistantships also available. Support available to part-time students. Financial award application deadline: 2/1; financial award applicants required to submit FAFSA. *Unit head:* Robin Showalter, Program Coordinator, 509-359-6492, E-mail: rshowalter@mail.ewu.edu.

Edgewood College, Program in Education, Madison, WI 53711-1997. Offers adult learning (MA Ed); director of special education and pupil services (Certificate); education (MA Ed); teaching and learning (MA Ed). *Accreditation:* NCATE (one or more programs are accredited). *Program availability:* Part-time, evening/weekend. *Faculty:* 13 full-time (9 women), 15 part-time/adjunct (10 women). *Students:* 137 full-time (91 women), 215 part-time (150 women); includes 51 minority (23 Black or African American, non-Hispanic/Latino; 3 American Indian or Alaska Native, non-Hispanic/Latino; 5 Asian, non-Hispanic/Latino; 17 Hispanic/Latino; 3 Two or more races, non-Hispanic/Latino), 18 international. Average age 37. In 2016, 74 master's, 18 doctorates awarded. *Degree requirements:* For master's, practicum, research project; for doctorate, comprehensive exam, thesis/dissertation. *Entrance requirements:* For master's, minimum GPA of 2.75, 2 letters of recommendation, personal statement; for doctorate, resume, letter of intent, 2 letters of recommendation, interview, writing sample. Additional exam requirements/recommendations for international students: Required—TOEFL (minimum score 525 paper-based; 72 iBT). *Application deadline:* For fall admission, 8/15 for domestic students, 5/1 for international students; for spring admission, 1/8 for domestic students, 11/1 for international students. Applications are processed on a rolling basis. Application fee: $30. Electronic applications accepted. *Expenses: Tuition:* Part-time $898 per credit. Tuition and fees vary according to course load. *Financial support:* Applicants required to submit FAFSA. *Faculty research:* Urban high schools, transgender students, literacy pedagogy, funds of knowledge, English language learners. *Unit head:* Dr. Timothy D. Slekar, Dean, E-mail: tslekar@edgewood.edu. *Application contact:* Joann Eastman, Admissions Counselor, 608-663-3250, Fax: 608-663-2214, E-mail: gps@edgewood.edu.
Website: https://www.edgewood.edu/academics/schools/school-of-education

Florida Agricultural and Mechanical University, Division of Graduate Studies, Research, and Continuing Education, College of Education, Department of Educational Leadership and Human Services, Tallahassee, FL 32307-3200. Offers administration and supervision (M Ed, MS, PhD); adult education (M Ed, MS); educational leadership (PhD); guidance and counseling (M Ed, MS). *Accreditation:* NCATE. *Degree requirements:* For master's, thesis (for some programs); for doctorate, thesis/dissertation. *Entrance requirements:* For master's, GRE General Test, minimum GPA of 3.0. Additional exam requirements/recommendations for international students: Required—TOEFL.

Florida Atlantic University, College of Education, Department of Educational Leadership and Research Methodology, Boca Raton, FL 33431-0991. Offers adult and community education (M Ed, PhD, Ed S); educational leadership (M Ed, PhD, Ed S); higher education (M Ed, PhD); K-12 school leadership (M Ed, PhD, Ed S). *Accreditation:* NCATE. *Program availability:* Part-time, evening/weekend, online learning. *Faculty:* 24 full-time (12 women), 20 part-time/adjunct (9 women). *Students:* 110 full-time (71 women), 221 part-time (155 women); includes 166 minority (100 Black or African American, non-Hispanic/Latino; 6 Asian, non-Hispanic/Latino; 49 Hispanic/Latino; 1 Native Hawaiian or other Pacific Islander, non-Hispanic/Latino; 10 Two or more races, non-Hispanic/Latino), 6 international. Average age 36. 186 applicants, 65% accepted, 97 enrolled. In 2016, 66 master's, 19 doctorates, 8 other advanced degrees awarded. *Degree requirements:* For doctorate, comprehensive exam, thesis/dissertation, departmental qualifying exam; for Ed S, departmental qualifying exam. *Entrance requirements:* For master's, GRE General Test, minimum GPA of 3.0 during previous 2 years; for doctorate, GRE General Test, minimum GPA of 3.5; for Ed S, GRE General Test. Additional exam requirements/recommendations for international students: Required—TOEFL (minimum score 500 paper-based; 61 iBT), IELTS (minimum score 6). *Application deadline:* For fall admission, 7/1 for domestic students, 2/15 for international students; for spring admission, 9/15 for domestic students, 7/15 for international students. Applications are processed on a rolling basis. Application fee: $30. Electronic applications accepted. *Expenses:* Tuition, state resident: full-time $7392; part-time $369.82 per credit hour. Tuition, nonresident: full-time $19,432; part-time $1024.81 per credit hour. *Financial support:* Fellowships, research assistantships, teaching assistantships, career-related internships or fieldwork, and tuition waivers (partial) available. *Faculty research:* Self-directed learning, school reform issues, legal issues, mentoring, school leadership. *Unit head:* Dr. Robert E. Shockley, Chair, 561-297-3550, Fax: 561-297-3618, E-mail: shockley@fau.edu. *Application contact:* Kathy DuBois, Senior Secretary, 561-297-3550, Fax: 561-297-3618, E-mail: edleadership@fau.edu.
Website: http://www.coe.fau.edu/academicdepartments/el/

Florida International University, College of Arts, Sciences, and Education, Department of Leadership and Professional Studies, Miami, FL 33199. Offers adult education and human resource development (MS, Ed D); counseling (MS), including rehabilitation counseling, school counseling; counselor education (MS), including clinical mental health counseling; educational administration and supervision (Ed D); educational leadership (MS, Certificate, Ed S); higher education (Ed D); higher education administration (MS); international and comparative education (MS); recreation and sport management (MS), including recreation and sport management, recreational therapy; school psychology (Ed S); urban education (MS), including instruction in urban settings, learning technologies, multicultural/bilingual, multicultural/TESOL, urban education. *Program availability:* Part-time, evening/weekend. *Faculty:* 27 full-time (19 women), 38 part-time/adjunct (25 women). *Students:* 253 full-time (191 women), 306 part-time (241 women); includes 444 minority (129 Black or African American, non-Hispanic/Latino; 3 Asian, non-Hispanic/Latino; 304 Hispanic/Latino; 8 Two or more races, non-Hispanic/Latino), 18 international. Average age 31. 366 applicants, 60% accepted, 115 enrolled. In 2016, 193 master's, 8 doctorates awarded. *Degree requirements:* For doctorate, thesis/dissertation. *Entrance requirements:* For master's, minimum GPA of 3.0; for doctorate and other advanced degree, GRE General Test. Additional exam requirements/recommendations for international students: Required—TOEFL (minimum score 550 paper-based; 80 iBT), IELTS (minimum score 6.3). *Application deadline:* For fall admission, 6/1 priority date for domestic students, 4/1 for international students; for winter admission, 10/1 priority date for domestic students, 9/1 for international students; for spring admission, 3/1 priority date for domestic students, 2/1 for international students. Applications are processed on a rolling basis. Application fee: $30. Electronic applications accepted. *Expenses:* Tuition, state resident: full-time $8912; part-time $446 per credit hour. Tuition, nonresident: full-time $21,393; part-time $992 per credit hour. *Required fees:* $2185; $195 per semester. Tuition and fees vary according to program. *Financial support:* Fellowships, research assistantships with tuition reimbursements, teaching assistantships with tuition reimbursements, Federal Work-Study, and tuition waivers (full and partial) available. Support available to part-time students. Financial award applicants required to submit FAFSA. *Unit head:* Dr. Benjamin Baez, Chair, 305-348-3214, Fax: 305-348-1515, E-mail: benjamin.baez@fiu.edu. *Application contact:* Nanett Rojas, Assistant Director, Graduate Admissions, 305-348-7464, Fax: 305-348-7441, E-mail: gradadm@fiu.edu.
Website: http://education.fiu.edu

The George Washington University, Graduate School of Education and Human Development, Department of Human and Organizational Learning, Program in Design and Assessment of Adult Learning, Washington, DC 20052. Offers Graduate Certificate. *Entrance requirements:* For degree, two letters of recommendation, resume, statement of purpose. Electronic applications accepted. *Unit head:* Michael Feuer, Dean, 202-994-6161, E-mail: mjfeuer@gwu.edu. *Application contact:* Sarah Lang, Director of Graduate Admissions, 202-994-1447, Fax: 202-994-7207, E-mail: slang@gwu.edu.
Website: http://gsehd.gwu.edu/

Grand Valley State University, College of Education, Programs in General Education, Allendale, MI 49401-9403. Offers adult and higher education (M Ed); early childhood education (M Ed); educational differentiation (M Ed); educational leadership (M Ed); educational technology integration (M Ed); elementary education (M Ed); middle level education (M Ed); school library media services (M Ed); secondary level education (M Ed); teaching English to speakers of other languages (M Ed). *Program availability:* Part-time, evening/weekend, 100% online, blended/hybrid learning. *Students:* 28 part-time (20 women); includes 6 minority (4 Black or African American, non-Hispanic/Latino; 1 American Indian or Alaska Native, non-Hispanic/Latino; 1 Hispanic/Latino). Average age 42. In 2016, 17 master's awarded. *Degree requirements:* For master's, project or thesis. *Entrance requirements:* For master's, GRE General Test or minimum GPA of 3.0, last 60 credits from regionally-accredited college/university, 3 letters of recommendation. Additional exam requirements/recommendations for international students: Required—TOEFL (minimum score 550 paper-based, 80 iBT), IELTS (6.5), or Michigan English Language Assessment Battery. *Application deadline:* Applications are processed on a rolling basis. Application fee: $30. Electronic applications accepted. *Expenses:* $628 per credit hour. *Financial support:* In 2016–17, 2 students received support. Career-related internships or fieldwork, Federal Work-Study, scholarships/grants, and unspecified assistantships available. *Faculty research:* Effectiveness of technology in education, parental involvement, effective teaching, effective schools research. *Unit head:* Dr. Doug Busman, Graduate Program Director, 616-331-6250, E-mail: busmando@gvsu.edu. *Application contact:* Thomas Owens, Director, Student

Information and Services Center, 616-331-6282, Fax: 616-331-6217, E-mail: owenst@gvsu.edu.
Website: http://www.gvsu.edu/coe/

Indiana University of Pennsylvania, School of Graduate Studies and Research, College of Education and Educational Technology, Department of Adult and Community Education, Program in Adult and Community Education, Indiana, PA 15705. Offers MA. *Program availability:* Part-time, online learning. *Faculty:* 2 full-time (1 woman). *Students:* 2 full-time (both women), 7 part-time (6 women). Average age 29. 5 applicants, 60% accepted, 3 enrolled. In 2016, 11 master's awarded. *Degree requirements:* For master's, thesis optional. *Entrance requirements:* For master's, goal statement, letters of recommendation, official transcripts. Additional exam requirements/recommendations for international students: Required—TOEFL (minimum score 540 paper-based; 76 iBT). *Application deadline:* Applications are processed on a rolling basis. Application fee: $50. Electronic applications accepted. *Expenses:* Tuition, state resident: full-time $8694; part-time $483 per credit. Tuition, nonresident: full-time $13,050; part-time $725 per credit. *Required fees:* $157 per credit. $50 per term. Tuition and fees vary according to course load and program. *Financial support:* In 2016–17, 3 research assistantships with tuition reimbursements (averaging $1,000 per year) were awarded; career-related internships or fieldwork, Federal Work-Study, scholarships/grants, and unspecified assistantships also available. Support available to part-time students. Financial award application deadline: 4/15; financial award applicants required to submit FAFSA. *Unit head:* Dr. Gary Dean, Chairperson, 724-357-2470, E-mail: gjdean@iup.edu.
Website: http://www.iup.edu/grad/ace/default.aspx

Indiana University of Pennsylvania, School of Graduate Studies and Research, College of Education and Educational Technology, Department of Adult and Community Education, Program in Adult and Community Education/Communications Technology, Indiana, PA 15705. Offers MA. *Program availability:* Part-time, evening/weekend. *Faculty:* 2 full-time (1 woman). *Students:* 12 full-time (4 women), 6 part-time (4 women); includes 6 minority (3 Black or African American, non-Hispanic/Latino; 2 Hispanic/Latino; 1 Two or more races, non-Hispanic/Latino), 8 international. Average age 27. 28 applicants, 71% accepted, 13 enrolled. In 2016, 21 master's awarded. *Degree requirements:* For master's, thesis optional. *Entrance requirements:* For master's, 2 letters of recommendation, resume. Additional exam requirements/recommendations for international students: Required—TOEFL (minimum score 540 paper-based; 76 iBT). *Application deadline:* Applications are processed on a rolling basis. Application fee: $50. Electronic applications accepted. *Expenses:* Tuition, state resident: full-time $8694; part-time $483 per credit. Tuition, nonresident: full-time $13,050; part-time $725 per credit. *Required fees:* $157 per credit. $50 per term. Tuition and fees vary according to course load and program. *Financial support:* In 2016–17, 11 research assistantships with tuition reimbursements (averaging $4,698 per year) were awarded; fellowships, teaching assistantships, career-related internships or fieldwork, Federal Work-Study, scholarships/grants, and unspecified assistantships also available. Support available to part-time students. Financial award application deadline: 4/15; financial award applicants required to submit FAFSA. *Unit head:* Dr. Gary Dean, Graduate Coordinator, 724-357-2470, E-mail: gjdean@iup.edu.
Website: http://www.iup.edu/aec

Instituto Tecnologico de Santo Domingo, Graduate School, Area of Humanities and Social Sciences, Santo Domingo, Dominican Republic. Offers accounting (Certificate); adult education (Certificate); applied linguistics (MA); economics (MA); education (M Ed); educational psychology (MA, Certificate); gender and development (MA, Certificate); humanistic studies (MA); international marketing management (Certificate); international relations in the Caribbean basin (Certificate); intervention systems in family therapy (MA); linguistic and literary communication (Certificate); pedagogical support (MA); social science education (M Ed); sustainable human development (MA); terminal illness and death psychology (Certificate); youth and adult education (M Ed).

Kansas State University, Graduate School, College of Education, Department of Educational Leadership, Manhattan, KS 66506. Offers adult learning (Certificate); educational leadership (MS, Ed D, PhD); leadership dynamics for adult learners (Certificate); qualitative research (Certificate); social justice education (Certificate); teaching English as a second language for adult learners (Certificate). *Accreditation:* NCATE. *Program availability:* Online learning. *Faculty:* 14 full-time (9 women), 3 part-time/adjunct (2 women). *Students:* 42 full-time (20 women), 300 part-time (187 women); includes 65 minority (24 Black or African American, non-Hispanic/Latino; 6 American Indian or Alaska Native, non-Hispanic/Latino; 3 Asian, non-Hispanic/Latino; 21 Hispanic/Latino; 1 Native Hawaiian or other Pacific Islander, non-Hispanic/Latino; 10 Two or more races, non-Hispanic/Latino), 1 international. Average age 38. 180 applicants, 84% accepted, 126 enrolled. In 2016, 110 master's, 2 doctorates, 2 other advanced degrees awarded. *Degree requirements:* For master's, comprehensive exam; for doctorate, comprehensive exam, thesis/dissertation. *Entrance requirements:* For master's, minimum undergraduate GPA of 3.0; for doctorate, MAT (for educational administration); GRE General Test (for adult education), minimum GPA of 3.0 in last 60 hours. Additional exam requirements/recommendations for international students: Required—TOEFL. *Application deadline:* For fall admission, 2/1 priority date for domestic and international students; for spring admission, 8/1 priority date for domestic and international students. Applications are processed on a rolling basis. Application fee: $50 ($75 for international students). Electronic applications accepted. *Expenses:* Tuition, state resident: full-time $9670. Tuition, nonresident: full-time $21,828. *Required fees:* $862. *Financial support:* Research assistantships, institutionally sponsored loans, and scholarships/grants available. Financial award application deadline: 3/1; financial award applicants required to submit FAFSA. *Faculty research:* Educational law, school finance, school facilities, organizational leadership, adult learning, distance learning/education. *Total annual research expenditures:* $21,235. *Unit head:* Dr. David C. Thompson, Head, 785-532-5535, Fax: 785-532-7304, E-mail: thomsond@ksu.edu. *Application contact:* Jody Ellis, Applications Contact, 785-532-5535, E-mail: foxksu@ksu.edu.
Website: http://www.coe.k-state.edu/departments/edlea/index.html

Lesley University, Graduate School of Education, Cambridge, MA 02138-2790. Offers arts, community, and education (M Ed); autism studies (Certificate); curriculum and instruction (M Ed, CAGS); early childhood education (M Ed); ecological teaching and learning (MS); educational studies (PhD), including adult learning, educational leadership, individually designed; elementary education (M Ed); emergent technologies for educators (Certificate); ESLArts: language learning through the arts (M Ed); high school education (M Ed); individually designed (M Ed); integrated teaching through the arts (M Ed); literacy for K-8 classroom teachers (M Ed); mathematics education (M Ed); middle school education (M Ed); moderate disabilities (M Ed); online learning (Certificate); reading (CAGS); science in education (M Ed); severe disabilities (M Ed); special needs (CAGS); specialist teacher of reading (M Ed); teacher of visual art (M Ed); technology in education (M Ed, CAGS). *Accreditation:* TEAC. *Program availability:* Part-time, evening/weekend, online learning. *Degree requirements:* For master's, practicum; for doctorate, thesis/dissertation. *Entrance requirements:* For master's, Massachusetts Tests for Educator Licensure (MTEL), transcripts, statement of purpose, recommendations; interview (for special education); for doctorate, GRE General Test, transcripts, statement of purpose, recommendations, interview, master's degree, resume; for other advanced degree, interview, master's degree. Additional exam requirements/recommendations for international students: Required—TOEFL (minimum score 550 paper-based; 80 iBT). Electronic applications accepted. *Faculty research:* Assessment in literacy, mathematics and science; autism spectrum disorders; instructional technology and online learning; multicultural education and English language learners.

Marshall University, Academic Affairs Division, College of Education and Professional Development, Programs in Adult and Technical Education, Huntington, WV 25755. Offers MS. *Accreditation:* NCATE. *Program availability:* Evening/weekend. *Degree requirements:* For master's, thesis optional, comprehensive assessment.

Memorial University of Newfoundland, School of Graduate Studies, Faculty of Education, St. John's, NL A1C 5S7, Canada. Offers counseling psychology (M Ed); curriculum, teaching, and learning studies (M Ed); education (PhD); educational leadership studies (M Ed, Graduate Diploma); information technology (M Ed); post-secondary studies (M Ed, Diploma), including health professional education (Diploma). *Program availability:* Part-time. *Degree requirements:* For master's, thesis optional, internship, paper folio, project; for doctorate, comprehensive exam, thesis/dissertation, thesis seminar, oral defense of thesis. *Entrance requirements:* For master's, undergraduate degree with at least 2nd class standing, 1-2 years of work experience; for doctorate, minimum A average in graduate course work, MA in education, 2 years of professional experience; for other advanced degree, 2nd class degree, 2 years of work experience with adult learners, appropriate academic qualifications and work experience in a health-related field. Electronic applications accepted. *Faculty research:* Critical thinking, literacy, cognitive studies and counseling, educational change, technology in instruction.

Merrimack College, School of Education and Social Policy, North Andover, MA 01845-5800. Offers community engagement (M Ed), including community organizations, higher education, K-12 education; criminology and criminal justice (MS); curriculum and instruction (M Ed); early childhood education (M Ed); educational leadership (CAGS), including instructional leadership; elementary education (M Ed); English as a second language (PreK-6) (M Ed); high school education (M Ed); higher education (M Ed), including leadership and organizational development, student affairs; middle school education (M Ed); moderate disabilities (PreK-8) (M Ed); school counseling (M Ed). *Program availability:* Part-time, evening/weekend, 100% online courses with immersion events and in-classroom practicum close to home. *Faculty:* 17 full-time, 34 part-time/adjunct. *Students:* 204 full-time (172 women), 83 part-time (67 women); includes 32 minority (4 Black or African American, non-Hispanic/Latino; 2 Asian, non-Hispanic/Latino; 23 Hispanic/Latino; 3 Two or more races, non-Hispanic/Latino), 1 international. Average age 27. 261 applicants, 89% accepted, 200 enrolled. In 2016, 153 master's, 2 other advanced degrees awarded. *Degree requirements:* For master's, practicum, portfolio, and state test (for licensure track); capstone (for higher education, curriculum and instruction, and community engagement tracks). *Entrance requirements:* For master's, Massachusetts Teacher Education Licensure (MTEL), official transcripts from other colleges, resume, personal statement, 2 letters of recommendation. Additional exam requirements/recommendations for international students: Required—TOEFL (minimum score 84 iBT), IELTS (minimum score 6.5), PTE (minimum score 56). *Application deadline:* For fall admission, 8/14 for domestic students, 7/14 for international students; for spring admission, 1/10 for domestic students, 12/10 for international students; for summer admission, 5/10 for domestic students, 4/10 for international students. Applications are processed on a rolling basis. Application fee: $0. Electronic applications accepted. *Expenses:* Contact institution. *Financial support:* Fellowships with full tuition reimbursements, career-related internships or fieldwork, scholarships/grants, and health care benefits available. Support available to part-time students. Financial award application deadline: 5/1; financial award applicants required to submit FAFSA. *Faculty research:* Feminist praxis in higher education, transgender student agency and belonging, campus sexual violence prevention, the scholarship of engagement; community engagement; service learning; diversity education; community-university partnerships, college going behaviors and indicators of success for inner city youth, strategies to increase students pursuit and success in STEM higher education, effective workforce development for displaced or under employed individuals, police reform, e.g. surveillance. *Application contact:* Alyssa Frey, Graduate Admissions Counselor, 978-837-3563, E-mail: freya@merrimack.edu.
Website: http://www.merrimack.edu/academics/graduate/education/

Michigan State University, The Graduate School, College of Education, Department of Educational Administration, East Lansing, MI 48824. Offers higher, adult and lifelong education (MA, PhD); K–12 educational administration (MA, PhD, Ed S); student affairs administration (MA). *Program availability:* Part-time. *Entrance requirements:* Additional exam requirements/recommendations for international students: Required—TOEFL. Electronic applications accepted.

Montana State University, The Graduate School, College of Education, Health, and Human Development, Department of Education, Bozeman, MT 59717. Offers adult and higher education (Ed D); curriculum and instruction (M Ed, Ed D), including professional educator (M Ed), technology education (M Ed); education (M Ed), including adult and higher education, educational leadership, school counseling; educational leadership (Ed D, Ed S). *Accreditation:* TEAC. *Program availability:* Part-time, online learning. *Degree requirements:* For master's, comprehensive exam; for doctorate, comprehensive exam, thesis/dissertation. *Entrance requirements:* For master's, GRE, 3 letters of reference, essays, BA transcripts; for doctorate, GRE, MAT, 3 letters of reference, essay, BA and M Ed transcripts; for Ed S, PRAXIS. Additional exam requirements/recommendations for international students: Required—TOEFL (minimum score 550 paper-based). Electronic applications accepted. *Faculty research:* Critical literacy; standards-based education; school Improvement, organizational change, leadership in rural education, leadership in Indian education; student Learning; multicultural/culturally responsive education for social justice Native American indigenous education, community-centered education teacher preparation.

Morehead State University, Graduate Programs, College of Education, Department of Foundational and Graduate Studies in Education, Morehead, KY 40351. Offers adult and higher education (MA, Ed S); certified professional counselor (Ed S); counseling P-12 (MA); curriculum and instruction (Ed S); educational technology (MA Ed); instructional leadership (Ed S); school administration (MA); school counseling (Ed S); teacher leader business and marketing content (MA Ed); teacher leader business and marketing technology (MA Ed); teacher leader educational technology (MA Ed); teacher leader English (MA Ed); teacher leader gifted education (MA Ed); teacher leader IECE certification (MA Ed); teacher leader interdisciplinary education P-5 (MA Ed); teacher leader middle grades (MA Ed); teacher leader non IECE certification (MA Ed); teacher leader reading/writing - non-certification (MA Ed); teacher leader reading/writing certification (MA Ed); teacher leader school communication - certification (MA Ed); teacher leader school communication - non-certification (MA Ed); teacher leader social studies (MA Ed); teacher leader special education (MA Ed). *Accreditation:* NCATE. *Program availability:* Part-time, evening/weekend. *Degree requirements:* For master's, thesis optional, oral and/or written comprehensive exams; for Ed S, thesis, oral exam. *Entrance requirements:* For master's, GRE General Test, minimum overall undergraduate GPA of 2.5; for Ed S, GRE General Test, interview, master's degree, minimum GPA of 3.5, work experience. Additional exam requirements/recommendations for international students: Required—TOEFL (minimum score 500 paper-based). Electronic applications accepted. *Faculty research:* Character education, school accountability, computer applications for school administrators.

Mount Saint Vincent University, Graduate Programs, Faculty of Education, Program in Adult Education, Halifax, NS B3M 2J6, Canada. Offers M Ed, MA Ed, MA-R. *Program availability:* Part-time, evening/weekend, online learning. *Degree requirements:* For master's, thesis (for some programs), practicum. *Entrance requirements:* For master's, bachelor's degree in related field, minimum B average. Electronic applications accepted.

National Louis University, College of Arts and Sciences, Chicago, IL 60603. Offers adult education (Ed D); counseling and human services (MS); language and academic development (M Ed, Certificate); psychology (MA, PhD, Certificate); public policy (MA); written communication (MS, Certificate). *Program availability:* Part-time, evening/weekend, online learning. *Degree requirements:* For master's and Certificate, comprehensive exam (for some programs), thesis (for some programs); for doctorate, thesis/dissertation. *Entrance requirements:* For master's, MAT or GRE, 3 professional or academic references, interview, minimum GPA of 3.0; for doctorate, GRE General Test, MAT, or Watson-Glaser Critical Thinking Appraisal, three professional or academic references, statement of academic and professional goals, 3 years of experience in field, interview, master's degree, resume, writing sample; for Certificate, GRE, MAT, or Watson-Glaser Critical Thinking Appraisal, three professional or academic references, statement of academic and professional goals, interview, minimum GPA of 3.0. Additional exam requirements/recommendations for international students: Required—Department of Language Studies Assessment or TOEFL (minimum score 550 paper-based; 79 iBT). Electronic applications accepted.

North Carolina Agricultural and Technical State University, School of Graduate Studies, School of Education, Department of Human Development and Services, Greensboro, NC 27411. Offers adult education (MS); counseling (MS); school administration (MS). *Accreditation:* ACA. *Program availability:* Part-time, evening/weekend. *Degree requirements:* For master's, comprehensive exam, thesis, qualifying exam. *Entrance requirements:* For master's, GRE General Test, minimum GPA of 3.0.

North Carolina State University, Graduate School, College of Education, Department of Adult and Higher Education, Program in Adult and Community College Education, Raleigh, NC 27695. Offers M Ed, MS, Ed D. *Degree requirements:* For master's, thesis (for some programs); for doctorate, thesis/dissertation. *Entrance requirements:* For master's and doctorate, GRE or MAT. Electronic applications accepted.

North Dakota State University, College of Graduate and Interdisciplinary Studies, College of Human Development and Education, School of Education, Fargo, ND 58102. Offers agricultural education (M Ed, MS), including agricultural education; counselor education (M Ed, MS, PhD), including clinical mental health counseling (M Ed, MS), counselor education and supervision (PhD), school counseling (M Ed, MS); curriculum and instruction (M Ed, MS); education (PhD); educational leadership (M Ed, MS, Ed S); family and consumer sciences education (M Ed, MS); history education (M Ed, MS); institutional analysis (Ed D); mathematics education (M Ed, MS); music education (M Ed, MS); occupational and adult education (Ed D); science education (M Ed, MS). *Accreditation:* NCATE. *Program availability:* Part-time, evening/weekend, online learning. *Degree requirements:* For master's, comprehensive exam; for doctorate, thesis/dissertation; for Ed S, thesis. *Entrance requirements:* For degree, GRE General Test, master's degree, minimum GPA of 3.25. Additional exam requirements/recommendations for international students: Required—TOEFL.

Northern Illinois University, Graduate School, College of Education, Department of Counseling, Adult and Higher Education, De Kalb, IL 60115-2854. Offers adult and higher education (MS Ed, Ed D); counseling (MS Ed, Ed D). *Accreditation:* ACA. *Program availability:* Part-time, evening/weekend. *Faculty:* 19 full-time (11 women), 2 part-time/adjunct (1 woman). *Students:* 108 full-time (74 women), 205 part-time (146 women); includes 123 minority (68 Black or African American, non-Hispanic/Latino; 2 American Indian or Alaska Native, non-Hispanic/Latino; 10 Asian, non-Hispanic/Latino; 34 Hispanic/Latino; 9 Two or more races, non-Hispanic/Latino), 8 international. Average age 35. 126 applicants, 59% accepted, 36 enrolled. In 2016, 66 master's, 24 doctorates awarded. Terminal master's awarded for partial completion of doctoral program. *Degree requirements:* For master's, comprehensive exam, thesis optional; for doctorate, thesis/dissertation, candidacy exam, dissertation defense. *Entrance requirements:* For master's, GRE General Test or MAT, minimum undergraduate GPA of 2.75, interview (for counseling); for doctorate, GRE General Test, minimum undergraduate GPA of 2.75, 3.2 graduate; interview (for counseling). Additional exam requirements/recommendations for international students: Required—TOEFL (minimum score 550 paper-based). *Application deadline:* For fall admission, 6/1 for domestic students, 5/1 for international students; for spring admission, 11/1 for domestic students, 10/1 for international students. Applications are processed on a rolling basis. Application fee: $40. Electronic applications accepted. *Financial support:* In 2016–17, 12 research assistantships with full tuition reimbursements, 7 teaching assistantships with full tuition reimbursements were awarded; fellowships with full tuition reimbursements, career-related internships or fieldwork, Federal Work-Study, scholarships/grants, tuition waivers (full), and staff assistantships also available. Support available to part-time students. Financial award applicants required to submit FAFSA. *Unit head:* Dr. Suzanne Degges-White, Interim Chair, 815-753-1448, E-mail: cahe@niu.edu. *Application contact:* Graduate School Office, 815-753-0395, E-mail: gradsch@niu.edu.
Website: http://www.cedu.niu.edu/cahe/index.html

Northwestern Oklahoma State University, School of Professional Studies, Program in Adult Education Management and Administration, Alva, OK 73717-2799. Offers M Ed. *Program availability:* Part-time. *Degree requirements:* For master's, thesis optional, portfolio. *Entrance requirements:* For master's, GRE or MAT, minimum GPA of 2.75.

Northwestern State University of Louisiana, Graduate Studies and Research, College of Education and Human Development, Program in Adult and Continuing Education, Natchitoches, LA 71497. Offers MA. *Degree requirements:* For master's, comprehensive exam, thesis or alternative. *Entrance requirements:* For master's, GRE General Test, minimum undergraduate GPA of 2.5. Additional exam requirements/recommendations for international students: Required—TOEFL. Electronic applications accepted.

Oregon State University, College of Education, Program in Adult and Higher Education, Corvallis, OR 97331. Offers Ed M, Ed D, PhD. *Accreditation:* NCATE. *Program availability:* Part-time, blended/hybrid learning. *Faculty:* 5 full-time (all women), 4 part-time/adjunct (2 women). *Students:* 2 full-time (both women), 34 part-time (25 women); includes 8 minority (2 Black or African American, non-Hispanic/Latino; 2 Asian, non-Hispanic/Latino; 2 Hispanic/Latino; 2 Two or more races, non-Hispanic/Latino). Average age 43. 36 applicants, 72% accepted, 22 enrolled. *Degree requirements:* For master's, thesis or alternative. *Entrance requirements:* For master's, minimum GPA of 3.0 in last 90 hours. Additional exam requirements/recommendations for international students: Required—TOEFL (minimum score 575 paper-based). *Application deadline:* For fall admission, 3/15 for domestic students. Applications are processed on a rolling basis. Application fee: $75 ($85 for international students). *Expenses:* Tuition, state resident: full-time $12,150; part-time $450 per credit. Tuition, nonresident: full-time $21,789; part-time $807 per credit. *Required fees:* $1651; $1507 per credit. One-time fee: $350. Tuition and fees vary according to course load, campus/location and program. *Financial support:* Research assistantships, teaching assistantships, career-related internships or fieldwork, Federal Work-Study, and institutionally sponsored loans available. Support available to part-time students. *Unit head:* Dr. Shelley Dubkin-Lee, Adult and Higher Education Graduate Programs Coordinator and Instructor, E-mail: shelley.dubkin-lee@oregonstate.edu.
Website: http://education.oregonstate.edu/adult-education-masters-degree-program

Penn State Harrisburg, Graduate School, School of Behavioral Sciences and Education, Middletown, PA 17057. Offers adult education in the health and medical professions (Certificate); applied behavior analysis (MA); applied clinical psychology (MA); applied psychological research (MA); community psychology and social change (MA); English as a second language (ESL) program specialist and leadership (Certificate); folklore and ethnography (Certificate); health education (M Ed); lifelong learning and adult education (M Ed, D Ed); literacy education (M Ed); literacy leadership (Certificate); psychology: applications in clinical psychology (Certificate); psychology: health psychology (Certificate); teaching and curriculum (M Ed); training and development (M Ed, Certificate). *Program availability:* Part-time, evening/weekend. *Unit head:* Dr. Mukund S. Kulkarni, Chancellor, 717-948-6105, Fax: 717-948-6452. *Application contact:* Robert W. Coffman, Jr., Director of Enrollment Management, Recruitment and Admissions, 717-948-6250, Fax: 717-948-6325, E-mail: hbgadmit@psu.edu.
Website: https://harrisburg.psu.edu/behavioral-sciences-and-education/

Penn State University Park, Graduate School, College of Education, Department of Learning and Performance Systems, University Park, PA 16802. Offers adult education (M Ed, D Ed, PhD, Certificate); corporate training (MPS); learning, design, and technology (M Ed, MS, PhD, Certificate); lifelong learning and adult education (M Ed, D Ed, PhD, Certificate); organization development and change (MPS); workforce education and development (M Ed, MS, PhD). *Unit head:* Dr. David H. Monk, Dean, 814-865-2523, Fax: 814-865-0555. *Application contact:* Lori Hawn, Director, Graduate Student Services, 814-865-1795, Fax: 814-863-4627, E-mail: l-gswww@lists.psu.edu.
Website: http://ed.psu.edu/lps/dept-lps

Plymouth State University, College of Graduate Studies, Graduate Studies in Education, Program in Learning, Leadership and Community, Plymouth, NH 03264-1595. Offers Ed D. *Degree requirements:* For doctorate, thesis/dissertation.

Regent University, Graduate School, School of Education, Virginia Beach, VA 23464-9800. Offers adult education (Ed D, PhD, Ed S); advanced educational leadership (Ed D, PhD, Ed S); career switcher (M Ed); character education (Ed D, PhD, Ed S); Christian education leadership (Ed D, PhD, Ed S); Christian school administration (M Ed); curriculum and instruction (M Ed), including adult education, Christian school, gifted and talented education, STEM education, teacher leader; educational leadership (M Ed); educational psychology (Ed D, PhD, Ed S); educational technology and online learning (Ed D, PhD, Ed S); elementary education (M Ed); exceptional education executive leadership (Ed D, PhD, Ed S); higher education (Ed D, PhD, Ed S); higher education leadership and management (Ed D, PhD, Ed S); individualized degree plan (M Ed); K-12 school leadership (Ed D, PhD, Ed S); K-12 special education (M Ed); K-8 leadership in mathematics education (M Ed); leadership in mathematics education (Ed S); reading specialist (M Ed); special education (Ed D, PhD, Ed S); student affairs (M Ed); TESOL (M Ed), including adult education - collegiate, K-12. *Accreditation:* TEAC. *Program availability:* Part-time, evening/weekend, 100% online, blended/hybrid learning. *Faculty:* 22 full-time (10 women), 42 part-time/adjunct (31 women). *Students:* 89 full-time (62 women), 1,035 part-time (823 women); includes 466 minority (381 Black or African American, non-Hispanic/Latino; 3 American Indian or Alaska Native, non-Hispanic/Latino; 19 Asian, non-Hispanic/Latino; 50 Hispanic/Latino; 13 Two or more races, non-Hispanic/Latino), 11 international. Average age 39. 976 applicants, 59% accepted, 449 enrolled. In 2016, 241 master's, 22 doctorates, 4 other advanced degrees awarded. *Degree requirements:* For master's, thesis or alternative; for doctorate, comprehensive exam, thesis/dissertation. *Entrance requirements:* For master's, Virginia Communication and Literacy Assessment (VCLA), PRAXIS, college transcripts, writing sample, interview; for doctorate, GRE, writing sample, resume, transcripts, interview. Additional exam requirements/recommendations for international students: Required—TOEFL (minimum score 577 paper-based). *Application deadline:* For fall admission, 4/1 priority date for domestic students; for spring admission, 10/15 priority date for domestic students. Applications are processed on a rolling basis. Application fee: $50. Electronic applications accepted. *Expenses:* Contact institution. *Financial support:* In 2016–17, 622 students received support, including 1 fellowship (averaging $5,000 per year); career-related internships or fieldwork, scholarships/grants, and unspecified assistantships also available. Support available to part-time students. *Faculty research:* Christian school administration, curriculum and instruction, educational technology and online learning, higher education, special education. *Unit head:* Dr. Donald Finn, Dean, 757-352-4278, Fax: 757-352-4318, E-mail: dfinn@regent.edu. *Application contact:* Heidi Cece, Assistant Vice President of Enrollment Management, 800-373-5504, Fax: 757-352-4381, E-mail: admissions@regent.edu.
Website: http://www.regent.edu/soe/

St. Francis Xavier University, Graduate Studies, Department of Adult Education, Antigonish, NS B2G 2W5, Canada. Offers adult education (M Ad Ed); community development (M Ad Ed). *Program availability:* Part-time, online learning. *Degree requirements:* For master's, thesis. *Entrance requirements:* For master's, minimum undergraduate B average, 2 years of work experience in field. Additional exam requirements/recommendations for international students: Required—TOEFL (minimum score 580 paper-based). *Application deadline:* Applications are processed on a rolling basis. Application fee: $40. *Expenses: Tuition:* Full-time $9060 Canadian dollars; part-time $725 Canadian dollars per credit. *Required fees:* $789 Canadian dollars; $78.84 Canadian dollars per credit. Tuition and fees vary according to course load, degree level and program. *Faculty research:* Adult learning and development, religious education, women's issues, literacy, action research. *Unit head:* Dr. Maureen Coady, Chair, 902-867-3244, Fax: 902-867-3765, E-mail: mjcoady@stfx.ca. *Application contact:* 902-867-2219, Fax: 902-867-2329, E-mail: admit@stfx.ca.
Website: http://sites.stfx.ca/adult_education_graduate_studies/

Saint Joseph's College of Maine, Master of Science in Education Program, Standish, ME 04084. Offers adult education and training (MS Ed); Catholic school leadership (MS Ed); health care educator (MS Ed); school educator (MS Ed). Program available by correspondence. *Program availability:* Part-time, online learning. Electronic applications accepted.

San Francisco State University, Division of Graduate Studies, College of Education, Department of Equity, Leadership Studies, and Instructional Technologies, Program in Adult Education, San Francisco, CA 94132-1722. Offers MA. *Accreditation:* NCATE. *Expenses:* Tuition, state resident: full-time $6738. Tuition, nonresident: full-time $15,666. *Required fees:* $1012. Tuition and fees vary according to degree level and program. *Unit head:* Dr. Doris Flowers, Chair, 415-338-2614, Fax: 415-338-0568, E-mail: dflowers@sfsu.edu. *Application contact:* Dr. Ming Yeh Lee, Graduate Coordinator, 415-338-1081, Fax: 415-338-0568, E-mail: mylee@sfsu.edu.
Website: http://elsit.sfsu.edu/

Seattle University, College of Education, Program in Adult Education and Training, Seattle, WA 98122-1090. Offers M Ed, MA, Certificate. *Accreditation:* NCATE. *Program availability:* Part-time, evening/weekend. *Faculty:* 1 (woman) full-time, 2 part-time/adjunct (1 woman). *Students:* 26 part-time (20 women); includes 9 minority (1 American Indian or Alaska Native, non-Hispanic/Latino; 2 Asian, non-Hispanic/Latino; 6 Hispanic/Latino). Average age 39. 9 applicants, 100% accepted, 8 enrolled. In 2016, 9 master's awarded. *Degree requirements:* For master's, comprehensive exam. *Entrance requirements:* For master's, GRE, MAT, or minimum GPA of 3.0; 1 year of related experience. Additional exam requirements/recommendations for international students: Required—TOEFL. *Application deadline:* For fall admission, 8/20 priority date for domestic students; for winter admission, 11/20 for domestic students; for spring admission, 2/20 for domestic students. Applications are processed on a rolling basis. Application fee: $55. *Financial support:* In 2016–17, 4 students received support. Career-related internships or fieldwork and Federal Work-Study available. Support available to part-time students. Financial award applicants required to submit FAFSA. *Unit head:* Dr. Carol Weaver, Director, 206-296-5908, E-mail: cweaver@seattleu.edu. *Application contact:* Janet Shandley, Associate Dean of Graduate Admissions, 206-296-5900, Fax: 206-298-5656, E-mail: grad_admissions@seattleu.edu.
Website: https://www.seattleu.edu/education/adulted/

Southern Arkansas University–Magnolia, School of Graduate Studies, Magnolia, AR 71753. Offers agriculture (MS); business administration (MBA), including agri-business, social entrepreneurship, supply chain management; clinical and mental health counseling (MS); computer and information sciences (MS), including cyber security and privacy, data science, information technology; gifted and talented (M Ed), including curriculum and instruction, educational administration and supervision, gifted and talented P-8/7-12, instructional specialist P-4; higher, adult and lifelong education (M Ed); kinesiology (M Ed), including coaching; library media and information specialist (M Ed); public administration (MPA); school counseling K-12 (M Ed); student affairs and college counseling (M Ed); teaching (MAT). *Accreditation:* NCATE. *Program availability:* Part-time, 100% online, blended/hybrid learning. *Faculty:* 36 full-time (19 women), 33 part-time/adjunct (14 women). *Students:* 605 full-time (143 women), 879 part-time (352 women); includes 130 minority (113 Black or African American, non-Hispanic/Latino; 7 American Indian or Alaska Native, non-Hispanic/Latino; 2 Asian, non-Hispanic/Latino; 2 Hispanic/Latino; 6 Two or more races, non-Hispanic/Latino), 1,048 international. Average age 28. 904 applicants, 81% accepted, 262 enrolled. In 2016, 278 master's awarded. *Degree requirements:* For master's, comprehensive exam (for some programs), thesis optional. *Entrance requirements:* For master's, GRE, MAT or GMAT, minimum GPA of 2.5. Additional exam requirements/recommendations for international students: Required—TOEFL (minimum score 550 paper-based), IELTS (minimum score 6). *Application deadline:* For fall admission, 7/20 for domestic students, 7/10 for international students; for spring admission, 12/1 for domestic students, 11/15 for international students; for summer admission, 4/1 for domestic students, 5/1 for international students. Applications are processed on a rolling basis. Application fee: $25 ($50 for international students). Electronic applications accepted. *Expenses:* Tuition, state resident: full-time $2511; part-time $279 per credit hour. Tuition, nonresident: full-time $3726; part-time $414 per credit hour. *Required fees:* $307 per semester. Tuition and fees vary according to course load and program. *Financial support:* Career-related internships or fieldwork, Federal Work-Study, scholarships/grants, tuition waivers (full), and unspecified assistantships available. Financial award applicants required to submit FAFSA. *Faculty research:* Alternative certification for teachers, supervision of instruction, instructional leadership, counseling. *Unit head:* Dr. Kim Bloss, Dean, School of Graduate Studies, 870-235-4150, Fax: 870-235-5227, E-mail: kkbloss@saumag.edu. *Application contact:* Shrijana Malakar, Admissions Specialist, 870-235-4150, Fax: 870-235-5227, E-mail: smalakar@saumag.edu.
Website: http://www.saumag.edu/graduate

State University of New York Empire State College, School for Graduate Studies, Programs in Education, Saratoga Springs, NY 12866-4391. Offers adult learning (MA); learning and emerging technologies (MA); teaching (MAT); teaching and learning (M Ed). *Program availability:* Online learning.

Teachers College, Columbia University, Department of Organization and Leadership, New York, NY 10027-6696. Offers adult education guided intensive study (Ed D); adult learning and leadership (Ed M, MA, Ed D); educational leadership (Ed D); higher and postsecondary education (MA, Ed D); leadership, policy and politics (Ed D); nurse executive (MA, Ed D), including administration studies (MA), professorial studies (MA); private school leadership (Ed M, MA); public school building leadership (Ed M, MA); social and organizational psychology (MA); urban education leaders (Ed D); MA/MBA. *Program availability:* Part-time, evening/weekend. *Students:* 310 full-time (214 women), 390 part-time (250 women); includes 276 minority (116 Black or African American, non-Hispanic/Latino; 3 American Indian or Alaska Native, non-Hispanic/Latino; 61 Asian, non-Hispanic/Latino; 79 Hispanic/Latino; 17 Two or more races, non-Hispanic/Latino), 93 international. 624 applicants, 57% accepted, 172 enrolled. *Degree requirements:* For doctorate, thesis/dissertation. *Expenses: Tuition:* Full-time $36,288; part-time $1512 per credit. *Required fees:* $438 per semester. One-time fee: $510 full-time. Full-time tuition and fees vary according to course load. *Unit head:* Prof. Anna Neumann, Chair, 212-678-3272, Fax: 212-678-3036, E-mail: neumann@tc.columbia.edu. *Application contact:* David Estrella, Director of Admission, 212-678-3305, E-mail: estrella@tc.columbia.edu.

Texas A&M University–Kingsville, College of Graduate Studies, College of Education and Human Performance, Department of Educational Leadership and Counseling, Kingsville, TX 78363. Offers adult education (M Ed); counseling and guidance (MA, MS); educational administration (MA, MS); educational leadership (Ed D); instructional technology (MS). *Program availability:* Part-time, evening/weekend, 100% online, blended/hybrid learning. *Entrance requirements:* Additional exam requirements/recommendations for international students: Required—TOEFL (minimum score 550 paper-based; 79 iBT); Recommended—IELTS. Electronic applications accepted.

Texas A&M University–Kingsville, College of Graduate Studies, College of Education and Human Performance, Program in Adult Education, Kingsville, TX 78363. Offers M Ed. Program offered jointly with Texas A&M University. *Program availability:* Part-time, evening/weekend. *Degree requirements:* For master's, variable foreign language requirement, comprehensive exam, thesis (for some programs). *Entrance requirements:* For master's, GRE, MAT, GMAT. Additional exam requirements/recommendations for international students: Required—TOEFL (minimum score 550 paper-based; 79 iBT). Electronic applications accepted. *Faculty research:* Continuing education efforts in south Texas, adult education methodologies.

Texas A&M University–Texarkana, Graduate Studies and Research, College of Education and Liberal Arts, Texarkana, TX 75505-5518. Offers adult education (MS); curriculum and instruction (M Ed); education (MS); educational administration (M Ed); English (MA); instructional technology (MS); interdisciplinary studies (MA, MS); special education (MS). *Program availability:* Part-time, evening/weekend. *Degree requirements:* For master's, comprehensive exam (for some programs), thesis optional. *Entrance requirements:* For master's, minimum GPA of 2.5 on last 60 hours of bachelor's degree. Additional exam requirements/recommendations for international students: Required—TOEFL. Electronic applications accepted.

Texas State University, The Graduate College, College of Education, Program in Adult Education, San Marcos, TX 78666. Offers MA. *Program availability:* Part-time. *Faculty:* 2 full-time (1 woman), 2 part-time/adjunct (1 woman). *Students:* 9 full-time (5 women), 9 part-time (6 women); includes 11 minority (2 Black or African American, non-Hispanic/Latino; 1 Asian, non-Hispanic/Latino; 7 Hispanic/Latino; 1 Two or more races, non-Hispanic/Latino). Average age 36. 9 applicants, 44% accepted, 4 enrolled. In 2016, 4 master's awarded. *Degree requirements:* For master's, comprehensive exam, thesis optional, internship practicum. *Entrance requirements:* For master's, baccalaureate degree from regionally-accredited university; minimum GPA of 2.75 on last 60 undergraduate semester hours of letter-grade work earned at four-year college or university before receipt of bachelor's degree (plus any previously completed graduate work). Additional exam requirements/recommendations for international students: Required—TOEFL (minimum score 78 iBT), IELTS (minimum score 6.5). *Application deadline:* For fall admission, 2/15 priority date for domestic and international students; for spring admission, 10/15 for domestic students, 10/1 for international students; for summer admission, 4/15 for domestic and international students. Applications are processed on a rolling basis. Application fee: $40 ($90 for international students). Electronic applications accepted. *Expenses:* $4,851 per semester. *Financial support:* In 2016–17, 10 students received support, including 2 research assistantships (averaging $13,337 per year); teaching assistantships and scholarships/grants also available. Financial award application deadline: 3/1; financial award applicants required to submit FAFSA. *Unit head:* Dr. Clarena Larrotta, Graduate Advisor, 512-245-2531, E-mail: cl24@txstate.edu. *Application contact:* Dr. Andrea Golato, Dean of Graduate School, 512-245-2581, Fax: 512-245-8365, E-mail: gradcollege@txstate.edu.

Texas State University, The Graduate College, College of Education, Program in Adult, Professional and Community Education, San Marcos, TX 78666. Offers PhD. *Program availability:* Part-time. *Faculty:* 5 full-time (4 women). *Students:* 15 full-time (8 women), 40 part-time (30 women); includes 34 minority (12 Black or African American, non-Hispanic/Latino; 2 Asian, non-Hispanic/Latino; 19 Hispanic/Latino; 1 Two or more races, non-Hispanic/Latino), 2 international. Average age 42. 38 applicants, 53% accepted, 13 enrolled. In 2016, 8 degrees awarded. *Median time to degree:* Of those who began their doctoral program in fall 2008, 67% received their degree in 8 years or less. *Degree requirements:* For doctorate, comprehensive exam, thesis/dissertation. *Entrance requirements:* For doctorate, GRE (preferred), baccalaureate and master's degrees from regionally-accredited institution with minimum GPA of 3.5 in all related graduate course work; 3 complete recommendation forms addressing professional and academic background; statement of purpose including rationale for doctoral degree; interview with program faculty. Additional exam requirements/recommendations for international students: Required—TOEFL (minimum score 550 paper-based; 78 iBT). *Application deadline:* For fall admission, 2/1 for domestic and international students. Applications are processed on a rolling basis. Application fee: $40 ($90 for international students). Electronic applications accepted. *Expenses:* $4,851 per semester. *Financial support:* In 2016–17, 30 students received support, including 6 research assistantships (averaging $29,615 per year); teaching assistantships, career-related internships or fieldwork, Federal Work-Study, institutionally sponsored loans, and scholarships/grants also available. Support available to part-time students. Financial award application deadline: 3/1; financial award applicants required to submit FAFSA. *Faculty research:* Systems of learning, work organization, international cross cultural adult and higher education, informal learning among skilled workers, STEM education, issues of diversity and equity in adult higher education and continuing professional education. *Unit head:* Dr. Joellen Coryell, PhD Program Director, 512-245-2531, Fax: 512-245-8872, E-mail: jc59@txstate.edu. *Application contact:* Dr. Andrea Golato, Dean of Graduate School, 512-245-2531, Fax: 512-245-8365, E-mail: gradcollege@txstate.edu.

Trident University International, College of Education, Program in Education, Cypress, CA 90630. Offers adult education (MA Ed); aviation education (MA Ed); children's literacy development (MA Ed); e-learning (MA Ed); early childhood education (MA Ed); enrollment management (MA Ed); higher education (MA Ed); teaching and instruction (MA Ed); training and development (MA Ed). *Program availability:* Part-time, evening/weekend, online learning. *Degree requirements:* For master's, capstone project with integrative paper. *Entrance requirements:* For master's, minimum GPA of 2.5 (students with GPA 3.0 or greater may transfer up to 30% of graduate level credits). Additional exam requirements/recommendations for international students: Required—TOEFL (minimum score 525 paper-based). Electronic applications accepted.

Troy University, Graduate School, College of Education, Program in Adult Education, Troy, AL 36082. Offers MS. *Program availability:* Part-time, evening/weekend. *Faculty:* 5 full-time (3 women), 3 part-time/adjunct (1 woman). *Students:* 15 full-time (11 women), 86 part-time (57 women); includes 46 minority (43 Black or African American, non-Hispanic/Latino; 1 Hispanic/Latino; 2 Two or more races, non-Hispanic/Latino). Average age 40. 55 applicants, 100% accepted, 14 enrolled. In 2016, 48 master's awarded. *Degree requirements:* For master's, comprehensive exam, capstone course or thesis. *Entrance requirements:* For master's, GRE (minimum score of 850 on old exam or 290 on new exam), GMAT (minimum score of 380), or MAT (minimum score of 385), bachelor's degree; minimum undergraduate GPA of 2.5 or 3.0 on last 30 semester hours, letter of recommendation. Additional exam requirements/recommendations for international students: Required—TOEFL (minimum score 523 paper-based; 70 iBT), IELTS (minimum score 6). *Application deadline:* Applications are processed on a rolling basis. Application fee: $50. Electronic applications accepted. *Expenses:* Tuition, state resident: full-time $7146; part-time $397 per credit hour. Tuition, nonresident: full-time $14,292; part-time $794 per credit hour. *Required fees:* $802; $50 per semester. Tuition and fees vary according to campus/location and program. *Financial support:* Fellowships, career-related internships or fieldwork, and scholarships/grants available. Support available to part-time students. Financial award applicants required to submit FAFSA. *Unit head:* Dr. Jan Oliver, Chair, Leadership Development and Professional Studies, 334-670-3546, Fax: 670-808-6666, E-mail: oliverj@troy.edu. *Application contact:* Jessica A. Kimbro, Director of Graduate Admissions, 334-670-3178, E-mail: jacord@troy.edu.

Troy University, Graduate School, College of Education, Program in Postsecondary Education, Troy, AL 36082. Offers MS Ed. *Accreditation:* NCATE. *Program availability:* Part-time, evening/weekend. *Faculty:* 12 full-time (3 women), 2 part-time/adjunct (1 woman). *Students:* 5 full-time (1 woman). Average age 43. In 2016, 28 master's awarded. *Degree requirements:* For master's, comprehensive exam (for some programs), thesis (for some programs), thesis or comprehensive exam. *Entrance requirements:* For master's, GRE (minimum score of 850 on old exam or 290 on new exam), GMAT (minimum score of 380), or MAT (minimum score of 385), bachelor's degree; minimum undergraduate GPA of 2.5 or 3.0 on last 30 semester hours, letter of recommendation. Additional exam requirements/recommendations for international students: Required—TOEFL (minimum score 523 paper-based; 70 iBT), IELTS (minimum score 6). *Application deadline:* Applications are processed on a rolling basis. Application fee: $50. Electronic applications accepted. *Expenses:* Tuition, state resident: full-time $7146; part-time $397 per credit hour. Tuition, nonresident: full-time $14,292; part-time $794 per credit hour. *Required fees:* $802; $50 per semester. Tuition and fees vary according to campus/location and program. *Financial support:* Fellowships, career-related internships or fieldwork, and scholarships/grants available. Support available to part-time students. Financial award applicants required to submit

Adult Education

FAFSA. *Unit head:* Dr. Ruth Busby, Chair, Teacher Education, 334-670-3546, Fax: 334-808-6666, E-mail: rsbusby@troy.edu. *Application contact:* Jessica A. Kimbro, Director of Graduate Admissions, 334-670-3178, E-mail: jacord@troy.edu.

Universidad del Este, Graduate School, Carolina, PR 00984. Offers accounting (MBA); adult education (M Ed); agribusiness (MBA); criminal justice and criminology (MA); curriculum and instruction - early education (M Ed); curriculum and instruction - elementary (M Ed); curriculum and instruction - English (M Ed); curriculum and instruction - Spanish (M Ed); human resources (MBA); information security management (MBA); information technology and Web business development (MBA); management (MBA); public policy (MPA); social work (MA), including clinical social work; special education (M Ed); strategic leadership (MBA).

Universidad Metropolitana, School of Education, Program in Teaching of Physical Education, San Juan, PR 00928-1150. Offers teaching of adult physical education (M Ed); teaching of elementary physical education (M Ed); teaching of secondary physical education (M Ed). *Degree requirements:* For master's, thesis or alternative. *Entrance requirements:* For master's, EXADEP, interview. Electronic applications accepted.

University of Alberta, Faculty of Graduate Studies and Research, Department of Educational Policy Studies, Edmonton, AB T6G 2E1, Canada. Offers adult education (M Ed, Ed D, PhD); educational administration and leadership (M Ed, Ed D, PhD, Postgraduate Diploma); First Nations education (M Ed, Ed D, PhD); theoretical, cultural and international studies in education (M Ed, Ed D, PhD). *Degree requirements:* For master's, thesis (for some programs); for doctorate, thesis/dissertation. *Entrance requirements:* For master's, minimum GPA of 6.5 on a 9.0 scale; for doctorate, minimum GPA of 7.5 on a 9.0 scale. Additional exam requirements/recommendations for international students: Required—TOEFL (minimum score 580 paper-based). Electronic applications accepted.

University of Arkansas, Graduate School, College of Education and Health Professions, Department of Rehabilitation, Human Resources and Communication Disorders, Adult and Lifelong Learning Program, Fayetteville, AR 72701. Offers M Ed, Ed D. *Program availability:* Part-time, evening/weekend, online learning. In 2016, 5 master's, 2 doctorates awarded. *Application deadline:* For fall admission, 4/1 for international students; for spring admission, 10/1 for international students. Applications are processed on a rolling basis. Electronic applications accepted. *Financial support:* Fellowships, research assistantships, teaching assistantships, career-related internships or fieldwork, and Federal Work-Study available. Support available to part-time students. Financial award application deadline: 4/1; financial award applicants required to submit FAFSA. *Unit head:* Dr. Kate Mamiseishvili, Departmental Chairperson, 479-575-4758, Fax: 479-575-3319, E-mail: kmamisei@uark.edu. *Application contact:* Dr. Kenda Grover, Graduate Coordinator, 479-575-4758, E-mail: kgrover@uark.edu.
Website: http://rhrc.uark.edu

University of Arkansas at Little Rock, Graduate School, College of Education and Health Professions, Department of Counseling, Adult and Rehabilitation Education, Program in Adult Education, Little Rock, AR 72204-1099. Offers M Ed. *Accreditation:* NCATE. *Program availability:* Part-time, online learning. *Degree requirements:* For master's, comprehensive exam. *Entrance requirements:* For master's, minimum GPA of 2.75. *Faculty research:* Adult literacy, volunteer training, in-services education.

The University of British Columbia, Faculty of Education, Department of Educational Studies, Vancouver, BC V6T 1Z1, Canada. Offers adult learning and education (M Ed); adult learning and global change (M Ed); curriculum and leadership (M Ed); educational administration and leadership (M Ed); educational leadership and policy (Ed D); educational studies (M Ed, MA, PhD); higher education (M Ed); society, culture and politics in education (M Ed). *Program availability:* Part-time, evening/weekend. *Faculty:* 25 full-time (14 women), 3 part-time/adjunct (2 women). *Students:* 222 full-time (157 women), 62 part-time (44 women). Average age 35. 166 applicants, 66% accepted, 74 enrolled. In 2016, 103 master's, 13 doctorates awarded. Terminal master's awarded for partial completion of doctoral program. *Degree requirements:* For master's, thesis; for doctorate, comprehensive exam, thesis/dissertation. *Entrance requirements:* For master's, minimum B+ average, 4-year undergraduate degree, field-related experience; for doctorate, minimum B+ average, 4-year undergraduate degree, master's degree, field-related experience. Additional exam requirements/recommendations for international students: Required—TOEFL (minimum score 600 paper-based; 100 iBT) or IELTS (minimum score 6.5). Application fee: $90 ($150 for international students). Electronic applications accepted. *Expenses:* Contact institution. *Financial support:* In 2016–17, 7 fellowships with tuition reimbursements (averaging $17,000 per year), 12 research assistantships (averaging $4,000 per year), 8 teaching assistantships (averaging $5,000 per year) were awarded. *Faculty research:* Educational leadership educational administration adult education politics in education, global change and adult learning. *Total annual research expenditures:* $632,000. *Unit head:* Dr. Tara Fenwick, Head, 604-822-5359, Fax: 604-822-4244. *Application contact:* Christine Adams, Graduate Secretary, 604-822-6647, Fax: 604-822-4244, E-mail: grad.edst@ubc.ca.
Website: http://www.edst.educ.ubc.ca/

University of Calgary, Faculty of Graduate Studies, Werklund School of Education, Graduate Division of Educational Research, Calgary, AB T2N 1N4, Canada. Offers adult learning (M Ed, MA, Ed D, PhD); curriculum and learning (M Ed, MA, Ed D, PhD); educational leadership (M Ed, MA, Ed D, PhD); languages and diversity (M Ed, MA, Ed D, PhD); learning sciences (M Ed, MA, Ed D, PhD). Ed D in educational leadership offered via distance delivery. *Program availability:* Part-time, evening/weekend, online learning. *Degree requirements:* For master's, thesis (for some programs); for doctorate, thesis/dissertation, candidacy exam. *Entrance requirements:* For master's, minimum GPA of 3.0, 3 letters of reference; for doctorate, minimum GPA of 3.5, 3 letters of reference. Additional exam requirements/recommendations for international students: Required—TOEFL, IELTS. Electronic applications accepted. *Faculty research:* Curriculum, leadership, technology, contexts, gifted, second language teaching, work place and adult learning.

University of Central Arkansas, Graduate School, College of Education, Department of Leadership Studies, Conway, AR 72035-0001. Offers college student personnel (MS); district-level administration (PMC); educational leadership - district level (Ed S); instructional technology (MS); library media and information technology (MS); school counseling (MS); school leadership (MS); school-based leadership adult education program administration (PMC); school-based leadership building administration (PMC); school-based leadership curriculum administration (PMC); school-based leadership gifted and talented program administration (PMC); school-based leadership special education program administration (PMC). *Accreditation:* NCATE. *Program availability:* Part-time, evening/weekend, online learning. *Degree requirements:* For master's and other advanced degree, comprehensive exam. *Entrance requirements:* For master's, GRE. Additional exam requirements/recommendations for international students: Required—TOEFL (minimum score 80 iBT). Electronic applications accepted. *Expenses:* Contact institution.

University of Central Oklahoma, The Jackson College of Graduate Studies, College of Education and Professional Studies, Department of Adult Education and Safety Science, Edmond, OK 73034-5209. Offers adult and higher education (M Ed), including adult and higher education, interdisciplinary studies, student personnel, training. *Program availability:* Part-time. *Degree requirements:* For master's, comprehensive exam (for some programs), thesis (for some programs). *Entrance requirements:* For master's, GRE General Test. Additional exam requirements/recommendations for international students: Required—TOEFL (minimum score 550 paper-based; 79 iBT), IELTS (minimum score 6.5). Electronic applications accepted. *Faculty research:* Violence in the workplace/schools, aging issues, trade and industrial education.

University of Cincinnati, Graduate School, College of Education, Criminal Justice, and Human Services, Division of Teacher Education, Cincinnati, OH 45221. Offers curriculum and instruction (M Ed, Ed D); deaf studies (Certificate); early childhood education (M Ed); middle childhood education (M Ed); postsecondary literacy instruction (Certificate); reading/literacy (M Ed, Ed D); secondary education (M Ed); special education (M Ed, Ed D); teaching English as a second language (Ed D, Certificate); teaching science (MS). *Program availability:* Part-time. *Degree requirements:* For doctorate, thesis/dissertation. *Entrance requirements:* For master's, GRE General Test. Additional exam requirements/recommendations for international students: Required—TOEFL (minimum score 550 paper-based). Electronic applications accepted. *Expenses: Tuition, area resident:* Full-time $12,790; part-time $389 per credit hour. Tuition, state resident: full-time $13,290; part-time $419 per credit hour. Tuition, nonresident: full-time $24,532; part-time $976 per credit hour. *International tuition:* $24,832 full-time. *Required fees:* $3958; $140 per credit hour. Tuition and fees vary according to course load, degree level, program and reciprocity agreements.

University of Colorado Denver, School of Education and Human Development, Information and Learning Technologies Program, Denver, CO 80217. Offers e-learning design and implementation (MA); instructional design and adult learning (MA); K-12 teaching (MA). *Program availability:* Part-time, evening/weekend, online learning. *Students:* 68 full-time (56 women), 50 part-time (37 women); includes 16 minority (4 Black or African American, non-Hispanic/Latino; 5 Asian, non-Hispanic/Latino; 5 Hispanic/Latino; 1 Native Hawaiian or other Pacific Islander, non-Hispanic/Latino; 1 Two or more races, non-Hispanic/Latino), 2 international. Average age 38. 24 applicants, 88% accepted, 13 enrolled. In 2016, 45 master's awarded. *Degree requirements:* For master's, comprehensive exam (for some programs), comprehensive exam or online portfolio; 30 credit hours. *Entrance requirements:* For master's, GRE or MAT (if GPA is below 2.75), resume, statement of intent, three letters of recommendation, transcripts from all colleges/universities previously attended. Additional exam requirements/recommendations for international students: Required—TOEFL (minimum score 537 paper-based; 75 iBT); Recommended—IELTS (minimum score 6.5). *Application deadline:* For fall admission, 5/15 for domestic students, 5/1 for international students; for spring admission, 11/15 for domestic students, 11/1 for international students; for summer admission, 3/15 for domestic students, 3/1 for international students. Application fee: $50 ($75 for international students). Electronic applications accepted. *Expenses:* Contact institution. *Financial support:* In 2016–17, 7 students received support. Fellowships, research assistantships, teaching assistantships, Federal Work-Study, institutionally sponsored loans, scholarships/grants, and traineeships available. Financial award application deadline: 4/1; financial award applicants required to submit FAFSA. *Faculty research:* Technology for educational management, instructional design foundations, e-learning, educational design. *Unit head:* Brent Wilson, Professor, 303-720-7765, E-mail: brent.wilson@ucdenver.edu. *Application contact:* 303-315-6300, E-mail: education@ucdenver.edu.
Website: http://www.ucdenver.edu/academics/colleges/SchoolOfEducation/Academics/MASTERS/ILT/Pages/default.aspx

University of Connecticut, Graduate School, Neag School of Education, Department of Educational Leadership, Field of Adult Learning, Storrs, CT 06269. Offers MA, Certificate. *Accreditation:* NCATE. Terminal master's awarded for partial completion of doctoral program. *Degree requirements:* For master's, comprehensive exam, thesis or alternative. *Entrance requirements:* For master's, GRE General Test. Additional exam requirements/recommendations for international students: Required—TOEFL (minimum score 550 paper-based). Electronic applications accepted.

University of Georgia, College of Education, Department of Lifelong Education, Administration and Policy, Athens, GA 30602. Offers adult education (Ed D, Ed S); lifelong education, administration and policy (PhD). *Accreditation:* NCATE. *Faculty:* 25 full-time (18 women), 1 part-time/adjunct (0 women). *Students:* 74 full-time (56 women), 216 part-time (136 women); includes 73 minority (62 Black or African American, non-Hispanic/Latino; 4 Asian, non-Hispanic/Latino; 3 Hispanic/Latino; 4 Two or more races, non-Hispanic/Latino), 23 international. Average age 37. 123 applicants, 64% accepted, 45 enrolled. In 2016, 19 doctorates, 14 other advanced degrees awarded. *Entrance requirements:* For doctorate, GRE General Test; for Ed S, GRE General Test or MAT. *Application deadline:* For fall admission, 7/1 priority date for domestic students; for spring admission, 11/15 for domestic students. Application fee: $50. Electronic applications accepted. *Unit head:* Dr. Janette Hill, Head, 706-542-4035, Fax: 706-542-5873, E-mail: janette@.uga.edu. *Application contact:* Dr. Robert B. Hill, Graduate Coordinator, 706-542-4016, Fax: 706-542-5873, E-mail: bobhill@uga.edu.
Website: http://www.coe.uga.edu/leap/

University of Houston–Victoria, School of Education, Health Professions and Human Development, Victoria, TX 77901-4450. Offers administration and supervision (M Ed); adult and higher education (M Ed); counselor education (M Ed); curriculum and instruction (M Ed); educational technology (M Ed); special education (M Ed). *Program availability:* Part-time, evening/weekend, online learning. *Degree requirements:* For master's, comprehensive exam, project or thesis. *Entrance requirements:* For master's, GRE General Test. Additional exam requirements/recommendations for international students: Required—TOEFL. Electronic applications accepted. *Faculty research:* Reading and language arts education, evaluation and diagnosis of special children's abilities.

University of Manitoba, Faculty of Graduate Studies, Faculty of Education, Department of Educational Administration, Foundations and Psychology, Winnipeg, MB R3T 2N2, Canada. Offers adult and post-secondary education (M Ed); educational administration (M Ed); guidance and counseling (M Ed); inclusive special education (M Ed); social foundations of education (M Ed). *Degree requirements:* For master's, thesis or alternative.

University of Memphis, Graduate School, College of Education, Department of Leadership, Memphis, TN 38152. Offers adult education (Ed D); community college teaching and leadership (Graduate Certificate); community education (Ed D); educational leadership (Ed D); higher education (Ed D); leadership (MS); policy studies (Ed D); school administration and supervision (MS); student personnel (MS). *Accreditation:* NCATE. *Program availability:* Part-time, evening/weekend, online learning. *Faculty:* 8 full-time (4 women), 5 part-time/adjunct (2 women). *Students:* 20 full-time (12 women), 155 part-time (99 women); includes 84 minority (75 Black or African American, non-Hispanic/Latino; 1 Asian, non-Hispanic/Latino; 4 Hispanic/Latino; 4 Two or more races, non-Hispanic/Latino), 2 international. Average age 40. 59 applicants, 92% accepted, 49 enrolled. In 2016, 11 master's, 14 doctorates, 3 other advanced degrees awarded. *Degree requirements:* For master's, comprehensive exam, thesis optional; for doctorate, comprehensive exam, thesis/dissertation. *Entrance*

requirements: For master's, GRE, resume, letters of reference, statement of professional goals, current teacher certification, sample work, interview; for doctorate, GRE, resume, letters of reference, statement of professional goals, interview. Additional exam requirements/recommendations for international students: Required—TOEFL (minimum score 550 paper-based; 79 iBT). *Application deadline:* For fall admission, 6/15 for domestic students; for spring admission, 9/15 for domestic students; for summer admission, 2/15 for domestic students. Application fee: $35 ($60 for international students). Electronic applications accepted. *Expenses:* $5,231.50 per semester full-time in-state, $9,623.50 full-time out-of-state. *Financial support:* In 2016–17, 70 students received support, including 3 research assistantships with full tuition reimbursements available (averaging $16,800 per year); teaching assistantships, Federal Work-Study, scholarships/grants, and unspecified assistantships also available. Financial award application deadline: 2/1; financial award applicants required to submit FAFSA. *Faculty research:* School improvement, social justice, online learning, adult learning, diversity. *Unit head:* Dr. Reginald Green, Interim Chair, 901-678-3445, E-mail: rlgreen1@memphis.edu.
Website: http://www.memphis.edu/lead

University of Minnesota, Twin Cities Campus, Graduate School, College of Education and Human Development, Department of Organizational Leadership, Policy and Development, Program in Adult Education, Minneapolis, MN 55455-0213. Offers M Ed, Certificate. *Students:* 10 full-time (all women), 13 part-time (7 women); includes 6 minority (4 Black or African American, non-Hispanic/Latino; 1 Hispanic/Latino; 1 Two or more races, non-Hispanic/Latino), 1 international. Average age 40. 20 applicants, 75% accepted, 10 enrolled. In 2016, 11 master's, 8 Certificates awarded. Application fee: $75 ($95 for international students). *Unit head:* Dr. Heidi Barajas, Chair, 612-625-4823, E-mail: hbarajas@umn.edu. *Application contact:* Dr. Jeremy J. Hernandez, Coordinator of Graduate Studies, 612-626-9377, E-mail: herna220@umn.edu.
Website: http://www.cehd.umn.edu/OLPD/grad-programs/AdEd/med-ps.html

University of Missouri, Office of Research and Graduate Studies, College of Education, Department of Educational Leadership and Policy Analysis, Columbia, MO 65211. Offers education administration (M Ed, MA, Ed D, PhD, Ed S); higher and adult education (M Ed, MA, Ed D, PhD, Ed S). *Program availability:* Part-time. *Faculty:* 14 full-time (9 women), 1 part-time/adjunct (0 women). *Students:* 185 full-time (105 women), 143 part-time (86 women). *Degree requirements:* For doctorate, variable foreign language requirement, comprehensive exam (for some programs), thesis/dissertation. *Entrance requirements:* For master's, doctorate, and Ed S, minimum GPA of 3.0. Additional exam requirements/recommendations for international students: Required—TOEFL (minimum score 500 paper-based; 61 iBT), IELTS (minimum score 5.5). *Application deadline:* For fall admission, 1/15 priority date for domestic and international students; for winter admission, 9/15 priority date for domestic and international students; for spring admission, 10/15 for domestic students. Applications are processed on a rolling basis. Application fee: $75 ($90 for international students). Electronic applications accepted. *Expenses:* Tuition, state resident: full-time $6347; part-time $352.60 per credit hour. Tuition, nonresident: full-time $17,379; part-time $965.50 per credit hour. *Required fees:* $1035. Tuition and fees vary according to course load, campus/location and program. *Financial support:* Fellowships with full tuition reimbursements, research assistantships with full tuition reimbursements, teaching assistantships with full tuition reimbursements, institutionally sponsored loans, scholarships/grants, health care benefits, and unspecified assistantships available.
Website: http://elpa.missouri.edu/

University of Missouri–St. Louis, College of Education, Department of Education Sciences and Professional Programs, St. Louis, MO 63121. Offers adult and higher education (M Ed); educational leadership and policy studies (PhD); educational psychology (M Ed), including character and citizenship education, research and program evaluation; program evaluation (Certificate); school psychology (Ed S). *Faculty:* 36 full-time (25 women), 53 part-time/adjunct (40 women). *Students:* 47 full-time (34 women), 247 part-time (175 women); includes 107 minority (86 Black or African American, non-Hispanic/Latino; 2 American Indian or Alaska Native, non-Hispanic/Latino; 5 Asian, non-Hispanic/Latino; 10 Hispanic/Latino; 4 Two or more races, non-Hispanic/Latino), 7 international. 106 applicants, 92% accepted, 70 enrolled. *Degree requirements:* For other advanced degree, comprehensive exam, thesis or alternative, internship. *Entrance requirements:* For degree, GRE General Test, 2-4 letters of recommendation, personal interview. Additional exam requirements/recommendations for international students: Required—IELTS (minimum score 6.5); Recommended—TOEFL (minimum score 550 paper-based; 79 iBT). *Application deadline:* For fall admission, 2/15 priority date for domestic students, 2/15 for international students. Application fee: $50 ($40 for international students). Electronic applications accepted. *Financial support:* Application deadline: 4/1; applicants required to submit FAFSA. *Faculty research:* Child/adolescent psychology, quantitative and qualitative methodology, evaluation processes, measurement and assessment. *Unit head:* Dr. Donald Gouwens, Chairperson, 314-516-4773, Fax: 314-516 5784, E-mail: gouwensd@umsl.edu. *Application contact:* 314-516-5458, Fax: 314-516-6996, E-mail: gradadm@umsl.edu.
Website: https://coe.umsl.edu/dept/espp.html

University of Nebraska–Lincoln, Graduate College, College of Education and Human Sciences, Department of Teaching, Learning and Teacher Education, Lincoln, NE 68588. Offers adult and continuing education (MA); educational studies (Ed D, PhD), including special education (Ed D); teaching, learning and teacher education (M Ed, MA, MST, Ed D, PhD); vocational and adult education (M Ed, MA). *Accreditation:* NCATE. *Degree requirements:* For master's, thesis optional. *Entrance requirements:* Additional exam requirements/recommendations for international students: Required—TOEFL (minimum score 550 paper-based). Electronic applications accepted. *Faculty research:* Teacher education, instructional leadership, literacy education, technology, improvement of school curriculum.

The University of North Carolina at Greensboro, Graduate School, School of Education, Department of Teacher Education and Higher Education, Greensboro, NC 27412-5001. Offers college teaching and adult learning (Certificate); curriculum and instruction (M Ed), including chemistry education, elementary education, English as a second language, French education, instructional technology, mathematics education, middle grades education, reading education, science education, social studies education, Spanish education; curriculum and teaching (PhD), including higher education, teacher education and development; English as a second language (Certificate); higher education (M Ed); supervision (M Ed). *Accreditation:* NCATE. *Program availability:* Part-time. *Degree requirements:* For doctorate, thesis/dissertation. *Entrance requirements:* For master's and doctorate, GRE General Test. Additional exam requirements/recommendations for international students: Required—TOEFL. Electronic applications accepted. *Faculty research:* Community college literacy program, middle school mathematics/computer mathematics.

University of North Florida, College of Education and Human Services, Department of Foundations and Secondary Education, Jacksonville, FL 32224. Offers adult learning (M Ed); professional education (M Ed). *Accreditation:* NCATE. *Program availability:* Part-time, evening/weekend. *Faculty:* 12 full-time (5 women). *Students:* 30 part-time (20 women); includes 14 minority (6 Black or African American, non-Hispanic/Latino; 3 Asian, non-Hispanic/Latino; 2 Hispanic/Latino; 3 Two or more races, non-Hispanic/Latino). Average age 32. In 2016, 16 master's awarded. *Entrance requirements:* For master's, GRE General Test, minimum GPA of 3.0 in last 60 hours, interview, 3 letters of recommendation. Additional exam requirements/recommendations for international students: Required—TOEFL (minimum score 500 paper-based; 61 iBT). *Application deadline:* For fall admission, 5/1 for international students; for spring admission, 10/1 for international students. Application fee: $30. Electronic applications accepted. Tuition and fees vary according to course load, campus/location and program. *Financial support:* Research assistantships, teaching assistantships, career-related internships or fieldwork, Federal Work-Study, and tuition waivers (partial) available. Support available to part-time students. Financial award application deadline: 4/1; financial award applicants required to submit FAFSA. *Faculty research:* Using children's literature to enhance metalinguistic awareness, education, oral language diagnosis of middle-schoolers, science inquiry teaching and learning. *Total annual research expenditures:* $57,679. *Unit head:* Dr. Jeffery Cornett, Chair, 904-620-2610, Fax: 904-620-1821, E-mail: jcornett@unf.edu. *Application contact:* Dr. Amanda Pascale, Director, The Graduate School, 904-620-1360, Fax: 904-620-1362, E-mail: graduateschool@unf.edu.
Website: http://www.unf.edu/coehs/fse/

University of Oklahoma, Jeannine Rainbolt College of Education, Department of Educational Leadership and Policy Studies, Program in Adult and Higher Education, Norman, OK 73019. Offers adult and higher education (M Ed), including community college administration, higher education administration, institutional research, intercollegiate athletics administration, student affairs, workforce, adult and continuing education. *Accreditation:* NCATE. *Program availability:* Part-time, evening/weekend. *Students:* 115 full-time (66 women), 81 part-time (54 women); includes 62 minority (31 Black or African American, non-Hispanic/Latino; 11 American Indian or Alaska Native, non-Hispanic/Latino; 8 Hispanic/Latino; 1 Native Hawaiian or other Pacific Islander, non-Hispanic/Latino; 11 Two or more races, non-Hispanic/Latino), 5 international. Average age 30. 83 applicants, 67% accepted, 43 enrolled. In 2016, 72 degrees awarded. *Degree requirements:* For master's, comprehensive exam, thesis optional. *Entrance requirements:* Additional exam requirements/recommendations for international students: Required—TOEFL (minimum score 79 iBT) or IELTS (minimum score 6.5). *Application deadline:* For fall admission, 2/1 for domestic and international students; for spring admission, 10/1 for domestic and international students; for summer admission, 4/1 for domestic and international students. Application fee: $50 ($100 for international students). Electronic applications accepted. *Expenses:* Tuition, state resident: full-time $4886; part-time $203.60 per credit hour. Tuition, nonresident: full-time $18,989; part-time $791.20 per credit hour. *Required fees:* $3283; $126.25 per credit hour. $126.50 per semester. *Financial support:* In 2016–17, 166 students received support. Fellowships, research assistantships, teaching assistantships, career-related internships or fieldwork, Federal Work-Study, institutionally sponsored loans, scholarships/grants, traineeships, health care benefits, tuition waivers, and unspecified assistantships available. Support available to part-time students. Financial award application deadline: 6/1; financial award applicants required to submit FAFSA. *Faculty research:* Education and social policy; gender and equity; collegiate athletics; higher education and student affairs; adult learning and workforce development. *Unit head:* Doo Hun Lim, Associate Professor, 405-325-7941, E-mail: dhlim@ou.edu.
Website: http://www.ou.edu/education/elps/graduate-programs/adult-and-higher-education-masters.html

University of Phoenix–Bay Area Campus, College of Education, San Jose, CA 95134-1805. Offers administration and supervision (MA Ed); adult education and training (MA Ed); early childhood education (MA Ed); education (Ed S); educational leadership (Ed D); elementary teacher education (MA Ed); higher education administration (PhD); secondary teacher education (MA Ed); special education (MA Ed); teacher leadership (MA Ed). *Program availability:* Evening/weekend, online learning. *Degree requirements:* For master's, thesis (for some programs). *Entrance requirements:* For master's, minimum undergraduate GPA of 2.5, 3 years of work experience. Additional exam requirements/recommendations for international students: Required—TOEFL (minimum score 550 paper-based; 79 iBT). Electronic applications accepted.

University of Phoenix–Online Campus, College of Education, Phoenix, AZ 85034-7209. Offers administration and supervision (MAEd, Certificate); adult education and training (MAEd); curriculum and instruction (MAEd), including computer education, curriculum and instruction, English as a second language, language arts, mathematics, reading; early childhood education (MAEd); educational studies (MAEd); elementary teacher education (MAEd), including early childhood, elementary teacher education, high school middle level, middle level; principal licensure (Certificate); secondary teacher education (MAEd); special education (MAEd, Certificate); teacher education (MAEd), including middle level generalist; teacher education middle level mathematics (MAEd), including middle level mathematics; teacher education middle level science (MAEd), including middle level science; teacher education secondary mathematics (MAEd); teacher education secondary science (MAEd); teacher leadership (MAEd); teachers of English learners (Certificate); transition to teaching (Certificate), including elementary education, secondary education. *Program availability:* Evening/weekend, online learning. *Entrance requirements:* Additional exam requirements/recommendations for international students: Required—TOEFL, TOEIC (Test of English as an International Communication), Berlitz Online English Proficiency Exam, PTE, or IELTS. Electronic applications accepted. *Expenses:* Contact institution.

University of Phoenix–Phoenix Campus, College of Education, Tempe, AZ 85282-2371. Offers administration and supervision (MA Ed); adult education and training (MA Ed); curriculum and instruction reading (MA Ed); early childhood education (MA Ed); education studies (MA Ed); elementary teacher education (MA Ed); secondary teacher education (MA Ed); special education (MA Ed); teacher leadership (MA Ed). *Program availability:* Evening/weekend, online learning. *Entrance requirements:* Additional exam requirements/recommendations for international students: Required—TOEFL, TOEIC (Test of English as an International Communication), Berlitz Online English Proficiency Exam, PTE, or IELTS. Electronic applications accepted. *Expenses:* Contact institution.

University of Phoenix–Sacramento Valley Campus, College of Education, Sacramento, CA 95833-4334. Offers adult education (MA Ed); curriculum instruction (MA Ed); elementary teacher education (MA Ed); secondary teacher education (MA Ed); teacher education (Certificate). *Program availability:* Evening/weekend. *Degree requirements:* For master's, thesis (for some programs). *Entrance requirements:* For master's, 3 years of work experience, minimum undergraduate GPA of 2.5. Additional exam requirements/recommendations for international students: Required—TOEFL (minimum score 550 paper-based; 79 iBT). Electronic applications accepted.

University of Phoenix–Southern Arizona Campus, College of Education, Tucson, AZ 85711. Offers administration and supervision (MA Ed); adult education and training (MA Ed); curriculum instruction (MA Ed); educational counseling (MA Ed); elementary teacher education (MA Ed); school counseling (MSC); secondary teacher education (MA Ed); special education (MA Ed, Certificate). *Program availability:* Evening/weekend. *Degree requirements:* For master's, thesis (for some programs). *Entrance requirements:* For master's, minimum undergraduate GPA of 2.5, 3 years of work experience.

Adult Education

Additional exam requirements/recommendations for international students: Required—TOEFL (minimum score 550 paper-based; 79 iBT). Electronic applications accepted.

University of Phoenix–Southern California Campus, College of Education, Costa Mesa, CA 92626. Offers administration and supervision (MA Ed, Certificate); adult education and training (MA Ed); educational studies (MA Ed); elementary teacher education (MA Ed); secondary teacher education (MA Ed); teacher leadership (MA Ed); teachers of English learners (Certificate). *Program availability:* Evening/weekend, online learning. *Entrance requirements:* Additional exam requirements/recommendations for international students: Required—TOEFL, TOEIC (Test of English as an International Communication), Berlitz Online English Proficiency Exam, PTE, or IELTS. Electronic applications accepted. *Expenses:* Contact institution.

University of Phoenix–Washington D.C. Campus, College of Education, Washington, DC 20001. Offers administration and supervision (MA Ed); adult education and training (MA Ed); computer education (MA Ed); curriculum and instruction (MA Ed, Ed D); early childhood education (MA Ed); education (Ed S); educational leadership (Ed D); educational technology (Ed D); elementary teacher education (MA Ed); English and language arts education (MA Ed); English as a second language (MA Ed); higher education administration (PhD); mathematics education (MA Ed); secondary teacher education (MA Ed); special education (MA Ed); teacher leadership (MA Ed).

University of Regina, Faculty of Graduate Studies and Research, Faculty of Education, Department of Adult Education, Regina, SK S4S 0A2, Canada. Offers MA Ed. *Program availability:* Part-time. *Faculty:* 3 full-time (2 women). *Students:* 7 full-time (6 women), 19 part-time (17 women). 8 applicants, 50% accepted. In 2016, 3 master's awarded. *Degree requirements:* For master's, thesis (for some programs), practicum, project, or thesis. *Entrance requirements:* For master's, bachelor's degree in education, 2 years of teaching or other relevant professional experience. Additional exam requirements/recommendations for international students: Required—TOEFL (minimum score 580 paper-based; 80 iBT), IELTS (minimum score 6.5), PTE (minimum score 59). *Application deadline:* For fall admission, 2/15 for domestic and international students; for winter admission, 10/15 for domestic and international students; for spring admission, 2/15 for domestic students. Application fee: $100. Electronic applications accepted. *Financial support:* In 2016–17, 2 fellowships (averaging $6,000 per year), 2 teaching assistantships (averaging $2,501 per year) were awarded; scholarships/grants also available. Financial award application deadline: 6/15. *Unit head:* Dr. Ken Montgomery, Associate Dean, Research and Graduate Programs in Education, 306-585-5031, Fax: 306-585-5387, E-mail: ken.montgomery@uregina.ca. *Application contact:* Tania Gates, Graduate Program Coordinator, 306-585-4506, Fax: 306-585-5387, E-mail: edgrad@uregina.ca.
Website: http://www.uregina.ca/education/

University of South Africa, College of Human Sciences, Pretoria, South Africa. Offers adult education (M Ed); African languages (MA, PhD); African politics (MA, PhD); Afrikaans (MA, PhD); ancient history (MA, PhD); ancient Near Eastern studies (MA, PhD); anthropology (MA, PhD); applied linguistics (MA); Arabic (MA, PhD); archaeology (MA); art history (MA); Biblical archaeology (MA); Biblical studies (M Th, D Th, PhD); Christian spirituality (M Th, D Th); church history (M Th, D Th); classical studies (MA, PhD); clinical psychology (MA); communication (MA, PhD); comparative education (M Ed, Ed D); consulting psychology (D Admin, D Com, PhD); curriculum studies (M Ed, Ed D); development studies (M Admin, MA, D Admin, PhD); didactics (M Ed, Ed D); education (M Tech); education management (M Ed, Ed D); educational psychology (M Ed); English (MA); environmental education (M Ed); French (MA, PhD); German (MA, PhD); Greek (MA); guidance and counseling (M Ed); health studies (MA, PhD), including health sciences education (MA), health services management (MA), medical and surgical nursing science (critical care general) (MA), midwifery and neonatal nursing science (MA), trauma and emergency care (MA); history (MA, PhD); history of education (Ed D); inclusive education (M Ed, Ed D); information and communications technology policy and regulation (MA); information science (MA, MIS, PhD); international politics (MA, PhD); Islamic studies (MA, PhD); Italian (MA, PhD); Judaica (MA, PhD); linguistics (MA, PhD); mathematical education (M Ed); mathematics education (MA); missiology (M Th, D Th); modern Hebrew (MA, PhD); musicology (MA, MMus, D Mus, PhD); natural science education (M Ed); New Testament (M Th, D Th); Old Testament (D Th); pastoral therapy (M Th, D Th); philosophy (MA); philosophy of education (M Ed, Ed D); politics (MA, PhD); Portuguese (MA, PhD); practical theology (M Th, D Th); psychology (MA, MS, PhD); psychology of education (M Ed, Ed D); public health (MA); religious studies (MA, D Th, PhD); Romance languages (MA); Russian (MA, PhD); Semitic languages (MA, PhD); social behavior studies in HIV/AIDS (MA); social science (mental health) (MA); social science in development studies (MA); social science in psychology (MA); social science in social work (MA); social science in sociology (MA); social work (MSW, DSW, PhD); socio-education (M Ed, Ed D); sociolinguistics (MA); sociology (MA, PhD); Spanish (MA, PhD); systematic theology (M Th, D Th); TESOL (teaching English to speakers of other languages) (MA); theological ethics (M Th, D Th); theory of literature (MA, PhD); urban ministries (D Th); urban ministry (M Th).

The University of South Dakota, Graduate School, School of Education, Division of Educational Administration, Vermillion, SD 57069. Offers educational administration (MA, Ed D, Ed S), including adult and higher education (MA, Ed D), curriculum director, director of special education (Ed D, Ed S), preK-12 principal, school district superintendent. *Accreditation:* NCATE. *Program availability:* Part-time, evening/weekend, 100% online, blended/hybrid learning. *Degree requirements:* For master's and Ed S, comprehensive exam, thesis or alternative; for doctorate, comprehensive exam, thesis/dissertation. *Entrance requirements:* For master's and doctorate, GRE General Test, MAT, minimum GPA of 2.7. Additional exam requirements/recommendations for international students: Required—TOEFL (minimum score 550 paper-based; 79 iBT). Electronic applications accepted.

University of Southern Maine, College of Management and Human Service, School of Education and Human Development, Program in Adult Education, Portland, ME 04103. Offers adult and higher education (MS); adult learning (CAS). *Accreditation:* TEAC. *Program availability:* Part-time, evening/weekend, online learning. *Degree requirements:* For master's and CAS, thesis or alternative. *Entrance requirements:* For master's, interview; for CAS, master's degree. Additional exam requirements/recommendations for international students: Required—TOEFL (minimum score 550 paper-based; 79 iBT). Electronic applications accepted. *Faculty research:* Older learners, lifelong learning institutes, teaching and learning in later age.

University of South Florida, College of Education, Department of Leadership, Counseling, Adult, Career and Higher Education, Tampa, FL 33620-9951. Offers adult education (MA, Ed D, PhD, Ed S); career and technical education (MA); career and workforce education (PhD); higher education/community college teaching (MA, Ed D, PhD); vocational education (Ed S). *Faculty:* 17 full-time (10 women). *Students:* 137 full-time (96 women), 331 part-time (237 women); includes 170 minority (75 Black or African American, non-Hispanic/Latino; 2 American Indian or Alaska Native, non-Hispanic/Latino; 12 Asian, non-Hispanic/Latino; 71 Hispanic/Latino; 2 Native Hawaiian or other Pacific Islander, non-Hispanic/Latino; 8 Two or more races, non-Hispanic/Latino), 18 international. Average age 35. 175 applicants, 66% accepted, 93 enrolled. In 2016, 111 master's, 22 doctorates, 1 other advanced degree awarded. Application fee: $30. *Expenses:* Tuition, state resident: full-time $7766; part-time $431.43 per credit hour. Tuition, nonresident: full-time $15,789; part-time $877.17 per credit hour. *Required fees:* $37 per term. *Total annual research expenditures:* $545,936. *Unit head:* Dr. Judith Ponticell, Chair, 813-974-4897, Fax: 813-974-5423, E-mail: jponticell@usf.edu.
Website: http://www.coedu.usf.edu/main/departments/ache/ache.html

University of South Florida, Innovative Education, Tampa, FL 33620-9951. Offers adult, career and higher education (Graduate Certificate), including college teaching, leadership in developing human resources, leadership in higher education; Africana studies (Graduate Certificate), including diasporas and health disparities, genocide and human rights; aging studies (Graduate Certificate), including gerontology; art research (Graduate Certificate), including museum studies; business foundations (Graduate Certificate); chemical and biomedical engineering (Graduate Certificate), including materials science and engineering, water, health and sustainability; child and family studies (Graduate Certificate), including positive behavior support; civil and industrial engineering (Graduate Certificate), including transportation systems analysis; community and family health (Graduate Certificate), including maternal and child health, social marketing and public health, violence and injury: prevention and intervention, women's health; criminology (Graduate Certificate), including criminal justice administration; educational measurement and research (Graduate Certificate), including evaluation; English (Graduate Certificate), including comparative literary studies, creative writing, professional and technical communication; entrepreneurship (Graduate Certificate); environmental health (Graduate Certificate), including safety management; epidemiology and biostatistics (Graduate Certificate), including applied biostatistics, biostatistics, concepts and tools of epidemiology, epidemiology, epidemiology of infectious diseases; geography, environment and planning (Graduate Certificate), including community development, environmental policy and management, geographical information systems; geology (Graduate Certificate), including hydrogeology; global health (Graduate Certificate), including disaster management, global health and Latin American and Caribbean studies, global health practice, humanitarian assistance, infection control; government and international affairs (Graduate Certificate), including Cuban studies, globalization studies; health policy and management (Graduate Certificate), including health management and leadership, public health policy and programs; hearing specialist: early intervention (Graduate Certificate); industrial and management systems engineering (Graduate Certificate), including systems engineering, technology management; information studies (Graduate Certificate), including school library media specialist; information systems/decision sciences (Graduate Certificate), including analytics and business intelligence; instructional technology (Graduate Certificate), including distance education, Florida digital/virtual educator, instructional design, multimedia design, Web design; internal medicine, bioethics and medical humanities (Graduate Certificate), including biomedical ethics; Latin American and Caribbean studies (Graduate Certificate); mass communications (Graduate Certificate), including multimedia journalism; mathematics and statistics (Graduate Certificate), including mathematics; medicine (Graduate Certificate), including aging and neuroscience, bioinformatics, biotechnology, brain fitness and memory management, clinical investigation, health informatics, health sciences, integrative weight management, intellectual property, medicine and gender, metabolic and nutritional medicine, metabolic cardiology, pharmacy sciences; national and competitive intelligence (Graduate Certificate); psychological and social foundations (Graduate Certificate), including career counseling, college teaching, diversity in education, mental health counseling, school counseling; public affairs (Graduate Certificate), including nonprofit management, public management, research administration; public health (Graduate Certificate), including environmental health, health equity, public health generalist, translational research in adolescent behavioral health; public health practices (Graduate Certificate), including planning for healthy communities; rehabilitation and mental health counseling (Graduate Certificate), including integrative mental health care, marriage and family therapy, rehabilitation technology; secondary education (Graduate Certificate), including ESOL, foreign language education: culture and content, foreign language education: professional; social work (Graduate Certificate), including geriatric social work/clinical gerontology; special education (Graduate Certificate), including autism spectrum disorder, disabilities education: severe/profound; world languages (Graduate Certificate), including teaching English as a second language (TESL) or foreign language. *Expenses:* Tuition, state resident: full-time $7766; part-time $431.43 per credit hour. Tuition, nonresident: full-time $15,789; part-time $877.17 per credit hour. *Required fees:* $37 per term. *Unit head:* Kathy Barnes, Interdisciplinary Programs Coordinator, 813-974-8031, Fax: 813-974-7061, E-mail: barnesk@usf.edu. *Application contact:* Karen Tylinski, Metro Initiatives, 813-974-9943, Fax: 813-974-7061, E-mail: ktylinsk@usf.edu.
Website: http://www.usf.edu/innovative-education/

The University of Tennessee, Graduate School, College of Education, Health and Human Sciences, Department of Educational Psychology and Counseling, Knoxville, TN 37996. Offers adult education (MS); applied educational psychology (MS); collaborative learning (Ed D); college student personnel (MS); mental health counseling (MS); rehabilitation counseling (MS); school counseling (MS). *Accreditation:* ACA (one or more programs are accredited); CORE (one or more programs are accredited); NCATE. *Program availability:* Part-time, evening/weekend. *Degree requirements:* For master's, thesis optional. *Entrance requirements:* For master's, GRE General Test, minimum GPA of 2.7. Additional exam requirements/recommendations for international students: Required—TOEFL. Electronic applications accepted.

University of the District of Columbia, College of Arts and Sciences, Program in Adult Education, Washington, DC 20008-1175. Offers Graduate Certificate.

The University of West Alabama, School of Graduate Studies, College of Education, Departments of Instructional Leadership and Support/Curriculum and Instruction, Program in Continuing Education, Livingston, AL 35470. Offers counseling and psychology (MSCE); family counseling (MSCE); general (MSCE); guidance and counseling (MSCE); library media (MSCE); student affairs in higher education (MSCE). *Accreditation:* NCATE. *Program availability:* Part-time, evening/weekend, 100% online. *Faculty:* 14 full-time (11 women), 45 part-time/adjunct (31 women). *Students:* 352 (295 women); includes 247 minority (234 Black or African American, non-Hispanic/Latino; 3 American Indian or Alaska Native, non-Hispanic/Latino; 1 Asian, non-Hispanic/Latino; 3 Hispanic/Latino; 1 Native Hawaiian or other Pacific Islander, non-Hispanic/Latino; 5 Two or more races, non-Hispanic/Latino). Average age 34. 92 applicants, 90% accepted, 72 enrolled. In 2016, 117 master's awarded. *Degree requirements:* For master's, comprehensive exam, thesis optional. *Entrance requirements:* For master's, GRE General Test, MAT, minimum GPA of 2.75. Additional exam requirements/recommendations for international students: Required—TOEFL (minimum score 500 paper-based; 61 iBT). *Application deadline:* Applications are processed on a rolling basis. Application fee: $40. Electronic applications accepted. *Expenses:* Tuition, state resident: part-time $355 per credit hour. Tuition, nonresident: part-time $710 per credit hour. *Required fees:* $130 per semester. *Financial support:* Teaching assistantships, Federal Work-Study, scholarships/grants, and unspecified assistantships available. Support available to part-time students. Financial award applicants required to submit FAFSA. *Unit head:* Dr. Reenay Rogers, Chair of Instructional Leadership and Support, 205-652-5423, Fax: 205-652-3706, E-mail: rrogers@uwa.edu. *Application contact:* Dr. B. J. Kimbrough, Dean of Graduate Studies, 205-652-3647, Fax: 205-652-3670, E-mail: bkimbrough@uwa.edu.

University of Wisconsin–Milwaukee, Graduate School, College of Letters and Science, Department of Linguistics, Milwaukee, WI 53201-0413. Offers linguistics (MA, PhD), including teaching English to speakers of other languages (MA); teaching English to speakers of other languages, adult- and university-level (Graduate Certificate). *Students:* 19 full-time (10 women), 6 part-time (5 women), 15 international. Average age 34. 75 applicants, 36% accepted, 10 enrolled. In 2016, 6 master's, 4 doctorates, 4 other advanced degrees awarded. *Unit head:* Hamid Ouali, Department Chair, 414-229-1113, E-mail: ouali@uwm.edu. *Application contact:* General Information Contact, 414-229-4982, Fax: 414-229-6967, E-mail: gradschool@uwm.edu.
Website: http://www4.uwm.edu/letsci/linguistics/

University of Wisconsin–Milwaukee, Graduate School, School of Education, Department of Administrative Leadership, Milwaukee, WI 53201-0413. Offers administrative leadership (MS, Graduate Certificate), including adult and continuing education leadership (MS), educational administration and supervision (MS), higher education administration (MS); support services for online students in higher education (Graduate Certificate); teaching and learning in higher education (Graduate Certificate). *Program availability:* Part-time. *Students:* 22 full-time (16 women), 157 part-time (102 women); includes 52 minority (21 Black or African American, non-Hispanic/Latino; 4 Asian, non-Hispanic/Latino; 2 Hispanic/Latino; 25 Two or more races, non-Hispanic/Latino), 2 international. Average age 34. 108 applicants, 72% accepted, 48 enrolled. In 2016, 72 master's, 19 other advanced degrees awarded. *Degree requirements:* For master's, comprehensive exam, thesis or alternative. *Entrance requirements:* For master's, GRE General Test. Additional exam requirements/recommendations for international students: Required—TOEFL (minimum score 550 paper-based; 79 iBT), IELTS (minimum score 6.5). *Application deadline:* For fall admission, 1/1 priority date for domestic students; for spring admission, 9/1 for domestic students. Applications are processed on a rolling basis. Application fee: $56 ($96 for international students). Electronic applications accepted. *Financial support:* In 2016–17, 2 fellowships were awarded; research assistantships, teaching assistantships, career-related internships or fieldwork, health care benefits, unspecified assistantships, and project assistantships also available. Support available to part-time students. Financial award application deadline: 4/15; financial award applicants required to submit FAFSA. *Unit head:* Alan Shoho, Dean, 414-229-4181, E-mail: shoho@uwm.edu. *Application contact:* General Contact, 414-229-4721, E-mail: soeinfo@uwm.edu.
Website: http://uwm.edu/education/academics/administrative-leadership-department/

University of Wisconsin–Milwaukee, Graduate School, School of Education, Department of Exceptional Education, Milwaukee, WI 53201-0413. Offers autism spectrum disorders (Graduate Certificate); exceptional education (MS); transition for students with disabilities (Graduate Certificate); urban education (PhD), including adult, continuing and higher education leadership, art education, curriculum and instruction, exceptional education, mathematics education, multicultural studies, social foundations of education. *Program availability:* Part-time. *Students:* 50 full-time (41 women), 66 part-time (51 women); includes 42 minority (24 Black or African American, non-Hispanic/Latino; 6 Asian, non-Hispanic/Latino; 1 Hispanic/Latino; 11 Two or more races, non-Hispanic/Latino), 4 international. Average age 39. 55 applicants, 51% accepted, 22 enrolled. In 2016, 14 master's, 10 doctorates, 3 other advanced degrees awarded. *Degree requirements:* For master's, thesis. *Entrance requirements:* Additional exam requirements/recommendations for international students: Required—TOEFL (minimum score 550 paper-based; 79 iBT), IELTS (minimum score 6.5). *Application deadline:* For fall admission, 1/1 priority date for domestic students; for spring admission, 9/1 for domestic students. Applications are processed on a rolling basis. Application fee: $56 ($96 for international students). Electronic applications accepted. *Financial support:* Fellowships, research assistantships, teaching assistantships, career-related internships or fieldwork, health care benefits, and unspecified assistantships available. Support available to part-time students. Financial award application deadline: 4/15; financial award applicants required to submit FAFSA. *Faculty research:* Emotional disturbance, hearing impairment, learning disabilities, mental retardation. *Application contact:* General Information Contact, 414-229-4721, E-mail: soeinfo@uwm.edu.
Website: http://uwm.edu/education/academics/exceptional-edu-department/

University of Wisconsin–Platteville, School of Graduate Studies, College of Liberal Arts and Education, School of Education, Platteville, WI 53818-3099. Offers adult education (MSE). *Accreditation:* NCATE. *Program availability:* Part-time, evening/weekend. *Students:* 42 full-time (30 women), 72 part-time (54 women); includes 20 minority (18 Black or African American, non-Hispanic/Latino; 1 American Indian or Alaska Native, non-Hispanic/Latino; 1 Hispanic/Latino). 37 applicants, 86% accepted, 25 enrolled. In 2016, 59 master's awarded. *Degree requirements:* For master's, comprehensive exam, thesis or alternative. *Entrance requirements:* Additional exam requirements/recommendations for international students: Required—TOEFL (minimum score 550 paper-based; 79 iBT), IELTS (minimum score 6.5). *Application deadline:* For fall admission, 9/1 for domestic students, 7/1 for international students; for spring admission, 1/1 for domestic students, 11/15 for international students. Applications are processed on a rolling basis. Application fee: $56. Electronic applications accepted. *Financial support:* Research assistantships with partial tuition reimbursements, career-related internships or fieldwork, Federal Work-Study, institutionally sponsored loans, scholarships/grants, and unspecified assistantships available. Support available to part-time students. Financial award applicants required to submit FAFSA. *Unit head:* Dr. Dominic Barraclough, Interim Director, 608-342-1131, Fax: 608-342-1133, E-mail: education@uwplatt.edu. *Application contact:* Dee Dunbar, School of Graduate Studies, 608-342-1322, Fax: 608-342-1389, E-mail: gradstudies@uwplatt.edu.
Website: http://www.uwplatt.edu/

Virginia Commonwealth University, Graduate School, School of Education, Program in Adult Learning, Richmond, VA 23284-9005. Offers adult literacy (M Ed); human resource development (M Ed); teaching and learning with technology (M Ed). *Accreditation:* NCATE. *Program availability:* Part-time. *Entrance requirements:* For master's, GRE General Test or MAT. Additional exam requirements/recommendations for international students: Required—TOEFL (minimum score 600 paper-based; 100 iBT). *Application deadline:* For fall admission, 3/15 for domestic students; for spring admission, 11/1 for domestic students. Applications are processed on a rolling basis. Application fee: $50. Electronic applications accepted. *Financial support:* Career-related internships or fieldwork and Federal Work-Study available. Financial award application deadline: 3/1; financial award applicants required to submit FAFSA. *Faculty research:* Adult development and learning, program planning and evaluation. *Unit head:* Dr. Leila Christenbury, Interim Department Chair, 804-828-1306, Fax: 804-827-0676, E-mail: lchriste@vcu.edu. *Application contact:* Dr. Robin R. Hurst, Graduate Program Director, 804-828-8021, E-mail: rrhurst@vcu.edu.
Website: http://www.soe.vcu.edu/programs.html#graduate

Walden University, Graduate Programs, Richard W. Riley College of Education and Leadership, Minneapolis, MN 55401. Offers adult education (Post-Master's Certificate); adult learning (Graduate Certificate); college teaching and learning (Graduate Certificate); community college leadership (Ed D); curriculum, instruction and assessment (Ed D, Ed S, Graduate Certificate); developmental education (Graduate Certificate); early childhood administration, management, and leadership (Graduate Certificate); early childhood education (Ed D, Ed S); early childhood public policy and advocacy (Graduate Certificate); early childhood studies (MS), including administration, management and leadership, early childhood public policy and advocacy, teaching adults in the early childhood field, teaching and diversity in early childhood education; education (MS, PhD), including adolescent literacy and learning (MS), curriculum, instruction, and assessment (grades K-12) (MS), curriculum, instruction, assessment, and evaluation (PhD), early childhood leadership and advocacy (PhD), early childhood special education (PhD), educational leadership (MS), educational leadership and administration (principal preparation) (MS), educational technology and design (PhD), elementary reading and literacy (PreK-6) (MS), elementary reading and mathematics (grades K-6) (MS), global and comparative education (PhD), higher education leadership management and policy (PhD), integrating technology in the classroom (grades K-12) (MS), learning, instruction and innovation (PhD), mathematics (grades 5-8) (MS), mathematics (grades K-6) (MS), mathematics and science (grades K-8) (MS), organizational research, assessment, and evaluation (PhD), reading and literacy with a reading K-12 endorsement (MS), reading literacy assessment and evaluation (PhD), science (grades K-8) (MS), special education (non-licensure) (grades K-12) (MS), teacher leadership (grades K-12) (MS), teaching English language learners (grades K-12) (MS); educational administration and leadership (Ed D); educational leadership and administration (principal preparation) (Ed S); educational technology (Ed D, Ed S, Post Master's Certificate); elementary reading and literacy (Graduate Certificate); engaging culturally diverse learners (Graduate Certificate); enrollment management and institutional marketing (Graduate Certificate); higher education (MS), including adult learning, college teaching and learning, enrollment management and institutional marketing, global higher education, leadership for student success, online and distance learning; higher education and adult learning (Ed D); higher education leadership and management (Ed D); higher education leadership for student success (Graduate Certificate); instructional design and technology (MS, Postbaccalaureate Certificate), including general program (MS), online learning (MS), training and performance improvement (MS); integrating technology in the classroom (Graduate Certificate); mathematics 5-8 (Graduate Certificate); mathematics K-6 (Graduate Certificate); online teaching for adult educators (Graduate Certificate); reading, literacy, and assessment (Ed D, Ed S); science K-8 (Graduate Certificate); special education (Ed D, Ed S, Graduate Certificate); special education (K-age 21) (MAT); teacher leadership (Graduate Certificate); teaching adults English as a second language (Graduate Certificate); teaching adults in the early childhood field (Graduate Certificate); teaching and diversity in early childhood education (Graduate Certificate); teaching English language learners (grades K-12) (Graduate Certificate); teaching K-12 students online (Graduate Certificate). *Accreditation:* NCATE. *Program availability:* Part-time, evening/weekend, online only, 100% online. *Degree requirements:* For doctorate, thesis/dissertation (for some programs), residency; for other advanced degree, residency (for some programs). *Entrance requirements:* For master's, bachelor's degree or higher; minimum GPA of 2.5; official transcripts; goal statement (for some programs); access to computer and Internet; for doctorate, master's degree or higher; three years of related professional or academic experience (preferred); minimum GPA of 3.0; goal statement and current resume (for select programs); official transcripts; access to computer and Internet; for other advanced degree, relevant work experience; access to computer and Internet. Additional exam requirements/recommendations for international students: Required—TOEFL (minimum score 550 paper-based, 79 iBT), IELTS (minimum score 6.5), Michigan English Language Assessment Battery (minimum score 82), or PTE (minimum score 53). Electronic applications accepted.

Western Kentucky University, Graduate Studies, College of Education and Behavioral Sciences, Department of Educational Administration, Leadership, and Research, Bowling Green, KY 42101. Offers adult education (MAE); educational leadership (Ed D); school administration (Ed S); school principal (MAE). *Accreditation:* NCATE. *Program availability:* Part-time, evening/weekend. *Degree requirements:* For master's, comprehensive exam, thesis or applied project and oral defense; for Ed S, thesis. *Entrance requirements:* For master's, GRE General Test, minimum GPA of 2.75. Additional exam requirements/recommendations for international students: Required—TOEFL (minimum score 555 paper-based; 79 iBT). *Faculty research:* Principal internship, superintendent assessment, administrative leadership, group training for residential workers.

Western Washington University, Graduate School, Woodring College of Education, Department of Educational Leadership, Program in Continuing and College Education, Bellingham, WA 98225-5996. Offers M Ed. *Program availability:* Part-time, evening/weekend, online learning. *Degree requirements:* For master's, comprehensive exam, thesis optional. *Entrance requirements:* For master's, GRE General Test or MAT, minimum GPA of 3.0 in last 60 semester hours or last 90 quarter hours. Additional exam requirements/recommendations for international students: Required—TOEFL (minimum score 567 paper-based). Electronic applications accepted. *Faculty research:* Transfer of learning, postsecondary faculty development, action research as professional development, literacy education in community colleges, adult education in the Middle East, distance learning tools for graduate students.

Widener University, School of Education, Hospitality, and Continuing Studies, Chester, PA 19013-5792. Offers adult education (M Ed); counseling in higher education (M Ed); counselor education (M Ed); early childhood education (M Ed); educational foundations (M Ed); educational leadership (M Ed); educational psychology (M Ed); elementary education (M Ed); English and language arts (M Ed); health education (M Ed); higher education leadership (Ed D); home and school visitor (M Ed); human sexuality (M Ed, PhD); mathematics education (M Ed); middle school education (M Ed); principalship (M Ed); reading and language arts (Ed D); reading education (M Ed); school administration (Ed D); science education (M Ed); social studies education (M Ed); special education (M Ed); technology education (M Ed). *Accreditation:* NCATE. *Program availability:* Part-time, evening/weekend. *Faculty:* 34 full-time (22 women), 37 part-time/adjunct (14 women). *Students:* 97 full-time (64 women), 201 part-time (143 women); includes 56 minority (44 Black or African American, non-Hispanic/Latino; 1 American Indian or Alaska Native, non-Hispanic/Latino; 2 Asian, non-Hispanic/Latino; 8 Hispanic/Latino; 1 Two or more races, non-Hispanic/Latino), 32 international. Average age 39. 139 applicants, 88% accepted. In 2016, 45 master's, 21 doctorates awarded. Terminal master's awarded for partial completion of doctoral program. *Degree requirements:* For doctorate, thesis/dissertation. *Entrance requirements:* For master's, minimum GPA of 2.5; for doctorate, GRE or MAT, minimum GPA of 2.0 (undergraduate), 3.5 (graduate). *Application deadline:* Applications are processed on a rolling basis. Application fee: $25 ($300 for international students). Electronic applications accepted. *Expenses:* Contact institution. *Financial support:* Career-related internships or fieldwork, tuition waivers (full and partial), and unspecified assistantships available. Support available to part-time students. Financial award application deadline: 5/1. *Faculty research:* Reading and cognition, adult education, technology education, educational leadership, special education. *Unit head:* Dr. Shawn Fitzgerald, Dean, 610-499-4294, Fax: 610-499-4623, E-mail: smfitzgerald@widener.edu. *Application contact:* Dr. Roberta Nolan, Director of Graduate Admissions, 610-499-4125, E-mail: rdnolan@widener.edu.
Website: http://www.widener.edu/academics/schools/eics

Community College Education

Argosy University, Chicago, College of Education, Chicago, IL 60601. Offers adult education and training (MA Ed); community college executive leadership (Ed D); educational leadership (MA Ed, Ed D, Ed S), including district leadership (Ed D), higher education administration (Ed D), K-12 education (Ed D); instructional leadership (Ed D, Ed S), including higher education (Ed D), K-12 education (Ed D). *Program availability:* Online learning.

Argosy University, Denver, College of Education, Denver, CO 80231. Offers community college executive leadership (Ed D); educational leadership (MA Ed, Ed D), including higher education (Ed D), K-12 education (Ed D); instructional leadership (MA Ed, Ed D), including higher education administration (Ed D), K-12 education (Ed D).

Argosy University, Inland Empire, College of Education, Ontario, CA 91761. Offers community college executive leadership (Ed D); educational leadership (MA Ed, Ed D), including higher education administration (Ed D), K-12 education (Ed D); instructional leadership (MA Ed, Ed D), including higher education (Ed D), K-12 education (Ed D), multiple subject teacher preparation (MA Ed), single subject teacher preparation (MA Ed).

Argosy University, Los Angeles, College of Education, Santa Monica, CA 90045. Offers community college executive leadership (Ed D); educational leadership (MA Ed, Ed D), including higher education administration (Ed D), K-12 education (Ed D); instructional leadership (MA Ed, Ed D), including higher education (Ed D), K-12 education (Ed D), multiple subject teacher preparation (MA Ed), single subject teacher preparation (MA Ed).

Argosy University, Northern Virginia, College of Education, Arlington, VA 22209. Offers community college executive leadership (Ed D); educational leadership (MA Ed, Ed D, Ed S), including higher education administration (Ed D), K-12 education (Ed D); instructional leadership (MA Ed, Ed D, Ed S), including higher education (Ed D), K-12 education (Ed D).

Argosy University, Orange County, College of Education, Orange, CA 92868. Offers community college executive leadership (Ed D); educational leadership (MA Ed, Ed D), including higher education administration (Ed D), K-12 education (Ed D); instructional leadership (MA Ed, Ed D), including education technology (Ed D), higher education (Ed D), K-12 education (Ed D), multiple subject teacher preparation (MA Ed), single subject teacher preparation (MA Ed).

Argosy University, Phoenix, College of Education, Phoenix, AZ 85021. Offers adult education and training (MA Ed); advanced educational administration (Ed D, Ed S); community college executive leadership (Ed D); educational administration (MA Ed); educational leadership (MA Ed, Ed D, Ed S), including education technology (Ed D), higher education administration (Ed D), K-12 education (Ed D); higher and postsecondary education (MA Ed); initial educational administration (Ed D, Ed S); school psychology (MA); teaching and learning (MA Ed, Ed D, Ed S), including education technology (Ed D), higher education (Ed D), K-12 education (Ed D).

Argosy University, San Diego, College of Education, San Diego, CA 92108. Offers community college executive leadership (Ed D); educational leadership (MA Ed, Ed D), including higher education administration (Ed D), K-12 education (Ed D); instructional leadership (MA Ed, Ed D), including higher education (Ed D), K-12 education (Ed D).

Argosy University, San Francisco Bay Area, College of Education, Alameda, CA 94501. Offers community college executive leadership (Ed D); educational leadership (MA Ed, Ed D), including education technology (Ed D), higher education administration (Ed D), K-12 education (Ed D); instructional leadership (MA Ed, Ed D), including education technology (Ed D), higher education (Ed D), K-12 education (Ed D), multiple subject teacher preparation (MA Ed), single subject teacher preparation (MA Ed).

Argosy University, Seattle, College of Education, Seattle, WA 98121. Offers adult education and training (MA Ed); community college executive leadership (Ed D); educational leadership (MA Ed, Ed D), including higher education administration (Ed D), K-12 education (Ed D); higher and postsecondary education (MA Ed); instructional leadership (MA Ed, Ed D), including education technology (Ed D), higher education (Ed D), K-12 education (Ed D).

Argosy University, Tampa, College of Education, Tampa, FL 33607. Offers community college executive leadership (Ed D); educational leadership (MA Ed, Ed D, Ed S), including higher education administration (Ed D), K-12 education (Ed D); school counseling (MA); teaching and learning (MA Ed, Ed D, Ed S), including higher education (Ed D), K-12 education (Ed D).

Arkansas State University, Graduate School, College of Education and Behavioral Science, School of Teacher Education and Leadership, State University, AR 72467. Offers community college administration (SCCT); curriculum and instruction (MSE); early childhood education (MSE); early childhood services (MS); educational leadership (MSE, Ed D, Ed S); educational theory and practice (MSE); middle level education (MAT, MSE); reading (MSE, Ed S); special education - gifted, talented, and creative (MSE); special education - instructional specialist grades 4-12 (MSE); special education - instructional specialist grades P-4 (MSE); special education, K-12 (MSE). *Accreditation:* NCATE. *Program availability:* Part-time, online learning. *Degree requirements:* For master's, comprehensive exam, thesis or alternative; for doctorate, comprehensive exam, thesis/dissertation; for other advanced degree, comprehensive exam. *Entrance requirements:* For master's, GRE General Test or MAT, appropriate bachelor's degree, official transcripts, immunization records, letters of reference, interview; for doctorate, GRE General Test or MAT, interview, master's degree, letters of reference, official transcript, personal statement, writing sample, immunization records; for other advanced degree, GRE General Test or MAT, interview, master's degree, official transcript, immunization records, letters of reference, 3 years of teaching experience, teaching license. Additional exam requirements/recommendations for international students: Required—TOEFL (minimum score 550 paper-based; 79 iBT), IELTS (minimum score 6), PTE (minimum score 56). Electronic applications accepted.

California State University, San Bernardino, Graduate Studies, College of Education, Program in Educational Leadership: Community College Specialization, San Bernardino, CA 92407. Offers MA. *Program availability:* Part-time, evening/weekend. *Students:* 2 full-time (both women), 16 part-time (6 women); includes 10 minority (1 Asian, non-Hispanic/Latino; 8 Hispanic/Latino; 1 Two or more races, non-Hispanic/Latino), 1 international. 24 applicants, 67% accepted, 15 enrolled. *Degree requirements:* For master's, thesis optional. *Entrance requirements:* Additional exam requirements/recommendations for international students: Required—TOEFL. *Application deadline:* For fall admission, 7/17 for domestic students. Application fee: $55. *Expenses:* Tuition, state resident: full-time $7843; part-time $5011.20 per year. Tuition and fees vary according to course load, degree level, program and reciprocity agreements. *Unit head:* Dr. Jay Fiene, Dean, 909-537-7621, E-mail: jfiene@csusb.edu. *Application contact:* Dr. Francisca Beer, Dean of Graduate Studies, 909-537-5058, E-mail: fbeer@csusb.edu.

California State University, Stanislaus, College of Education, Programs in Educational Leadership (Ed D), Turlock, CA 95382. Offers community college leadership (Ed D); P-12 leadership (Ed D). *Program availability:* Part-time, evening/weekend. *Degree requirements:* For doctorate, thesis/dissertation. *Entrance requirements:* For doctorate, GRE, minimum GPA of 3.0, 3 letters of reference, interview, personal statement. Additional exam requirements/recommendations for international students: Required—TOEFL (minimum score 550 paper-based). Electronic applications accepted.

Central Michigan University, Central Michigan University Global Campus, Program in Education, Mount Pleasant, MI 48859. Offers college teaching (Graduate Certificate); community college (MA); curriculum and instruction (MA); educational technology (MA, DET); reading and literacy K-12 (MA); school principalship (MA), including charter school leadership; training and development (MA). *Accreditation:* TEAC. *Program availability:* Part-time, evening/weekend. *Faculty:* 24 full-time (14 women), 24 part-time/adjunct (8 women). *Students:* 888 (620 women); includes 225 minority (142 Black or African American, non-Hispanic/Latino; 8 American Indian or Alaska Native, non-Hispanic/Latino; 16 Asian, non-Hispanic/Latino; 13 Hispanic/Latino; 46 Two or more races, non-Hispanic/Latino). Average age 37. In 2016, 76 master's awarded. *Entrance requirements:* For master's, minimum GPA of 2.7 in major. Additional exam requirements/recommendations for international students: Required—TOEFL. *Application deadline:* Applications are processed on a rolling basis. Application fee: $50. Electronic applications accepted. *Financial support:* Scholarships/grants available. Support available to part-time students. *Unit head:* Kaleb Patrick, Director, 989-774-3144, E-mail: patri1kg@cmich.edu. *Application contact:* 877-268-4636, E-mail: cmuglobal@cmich.edu.

Drew University, Caspersen School of Graduate Studies, Madison, NJ 07940-1493. Offers conflict resolution and leadership (Certificate), including community leadership, moderation, peace building; history and culture (MA, PhD), including American history, book history, British history, European history, Holocaust and genocide (M Litt, MA, D Litt, PhD), intellectual history, Irish history, print culture, public history; K-12 education (MAT), including art, biology, chemistry, elementary education, English, French, Italian, math, secondary education, special education, teacher of students with disabilities; liberal studies (M Litt, D Litt), including history, Holocaust and genocide (M Litt, MA, D Litt, PhD), Irish/Irish-American studies, literature (M Litt, MMH, D Litt, DMH, CMH), religion, spirituality, teaching in the two-year college, writing; medical humanities (MMH, DMH, CMH), including arts, health, healthcare, literature (M Litt, MMH, D Litt, DMH, CMH), scientific research; poetry (MFA). *Program availability:* Part-time, evening/weekend. *Faculty:* 4 full-time (2 women), 31 part-time/adjunct (16 women). *Students:* 62 full-time (41 women), 199 part-time (130 women); includes 38 minority (17 Black or African American, non-Hispanic/Latino; 3 Asian, non-Hispanic/Latino; 17 Hispanic/Latino; 1 Two or more races, non-Hispanic/Latino), 3 international. Average age 27. 93 applicants, 81% accepted, 46 enrolled. In 2016, 39 master's, 27 doctorates, 26 other advanced degrees awarded. Terminal master's awarded for partial completion of doctoral program. *Degree requirements:* For master's and other advanced degree, thesis (for some programs); for doctorate, one foreign language, comprehensive exam (for some programs), thesis/dissertation. *Entrance requirements:* For master's, PRAXIS Core and Subject Area tests (for MAT), resume, transcripts, writing sample, personal statement, letters of recommendation; for doctorate, GRE (PhD in history and culture), resume, transcripts, writing sample, personal statement, letters of recommendation. Additional exam requirements/recommendations for international students: Required—TOEFL (minimum score 587 paper-based; 94 iBT), IELTS (minimum score 7), TWE (minimum score 4). *Application deadline:* For fall admission, 8/1 for domestic students, 6/1 for international students; for spring admission, 12/1 for domestic students, 10/1 for international students. Applications are processed on a rolling basis. Application fee: $35. Electronic applications accepted. Tuition and fees vary according to program. *Financial support:* Fellowships, research assistantships, teaching assistantships, career-related internships or fieldwork, Federal Work-Study, scholarships/grants, and unspecified assistantships available. Support available to part-time students. Financial award applicants required to submit FAFSA. *Application contact:* Leanne Horinko, Director of Caspersen Admissions, 973-408-3280, E-mail: gradm@drew.edu. Website: http://www.drew.edu/caspersen

East Carolina University, Graduate School, Thomas Harriot College of Arts and Sciences, Department of English, Greenville, NC 27858-4353. Offers creative writing (MA); English studies (MA); linguistics (MA); literature (MA); multicultural and transnational literatures (MA, Certificate); rhetoric and composition (MA); rhetoric, writing, and professional communication (PhD); teaching English in the two-year college (Certificate); teaching English to speakers of other languages (MA, Certificate); technical and professional communication (MA). *Program availability:* Part-time, evening/weekend. *Students:* 54 full-time (36 women), 95 part-time (77 women); includes 32 minority (19 Black or African American, non-Hispanic/Latino; 3 Asian, non-Hispanic/Latino; 6 Hispanic/Latino; 4 Two or more races, non-Hispanic/Latino), 1 international. Average age 35. 78 applicants, 96% accepted, 50 enrolled. In 2016, 34 master's, 1 doctorate awarded. *Degree requirements:* For master's, one foreign language, comprehensive exam, thesis optional. *Entrance requirements:* For master's, GRE General Test, MAT (for MA Ed). Additional exam requirements/recommendations for international students: Required—TOEFL. *Application deadline:* For fall admission, 6/1 priority date for domestic students; for spring admission, 10/15 for domestic students. Applications are processed on a rolling basis. Application fee: $50. *Financial support:* Research assistantships with partial tuition reimbursements, teaching assistantships with partial tuition reimbursements, and Federal Work-Study available. Support available to part-time students. Financial award application deadline: 6/1. *Unit head:* Dr. Jeffrey Johnson, Chair, 252-328-6041, E-mail: johnsonj@ecu.edu. *Application contact:* Dean of Graduate School, 252-328-6012, Fax: 252-328-6071, E-mail: gradschool@ecu.edu. Website: http://www.ecu.edu/cs-cas/engl/graduate/

East Carolina University, Graduate School, Thomas Harriot College of Arts and Sciences, Department of Mathematics, Greenville, NC 27858-4353. Offers mathematics (MA); mathematics in the community college (MA); statistics (MA, Certificate). *Program availability:* Part-time, evening/weekend. *Students:* 10 full-time (3 women), 3 part-time (all women); includes 3 minority (1 Black or African American, non-Hispanic/Latino; 1 Asian, non-Hispanic/Latino; 1 Hispanic/Latino), 2 international. Average age 27. 10 applicants, 100% accepted, 8 enrolled. In 2016, 7 master's awarded. *Degree requirements:* For master's, comprehensive exam. *Entrance requirements:* For master's, GRE General Test, MAT. Additional exam requirements/recommendations for international students: Required—TOEFL. *Application deadline:* For fall admission, 6/1 for domestic students; for spring admission, 10/15 for domestic students. Applications

are processed on a rolling basis. Application fee: $50. *Financial support:* Research assistantships with partial tuition reimbursements and teaching assistantships with partial tuition reimbursements available. Financial award application deadline: 6/1. *Unit head:* Dr. Johannes H. Hattingh, Chair, 252-328-6461, E-mail: hattinghj@ecu.edu. *Application contact:* Dean of Graduate School, 252-328-6012, Fax: 252-328-6071, E-mail: gradschool@ecu.edu.
Website: http://www.ecu.edu/cs-cas/math/graduateprogram.cfm

Eastern Illinois University, Graduate School, College of Arts and Humanities, Department of Communication Studies, Charleston, IL 61920. Offers community college pedagogy (MA). *Program availability:* Part-time, evening/weekend. *Degree requirements:* For master's, comprehensive exam (for some programs), thesis (for some programs). *Entrance requirements:* For master's, GMAT or GRE. Additional exam requirements/recommendations for international students: Required—TOEFL (minimum score 500 paper-based; 61 iBT), IELTS (minimum score 6). Electronic applications accepted.

Eastern Michigan University, Graduate School, College of Education, Department of Leadership and Counseling, Programs in Educational Leadership, Ypsilanti, MI 48197. Offers community college leadership (Graduate Certificate); educational leadership (MA, Ed D, SPA); higher education/general administration (MA); higher education/student affairs (MA); K-12 administration (MA); K-12 basic administration (Post Master's Certificate). *Program availability:* Part-time, evening/weekend, online learning. *Students:* 52 full-time (39 women), 298 part-time (198 women); includes 103 minority (81 Black or African American, non-Hispanic/Latino; 3 American Indian or Alaska Native, non-Hispanic/Latino; 4 Asian, non-Hispanic/Latino; 10 Hispanic/Latino; 5 Two or more races, non-Hispanic/Latino), 2 international. Average age 35. 185 applicants, 70% accepted, 67 enrolled. In 2016, 85 master's, 28 doctorates, 23 other advanced degrees awarded. *Degree requirements:* For master's, portfolio. *Entrance requirements:* For doctorate, GRE. Additional exam requirements/recommendations for international students: Required—TOEFL. *Application deadline:* For winter admission, 2/1 for domestic and international students. Applications are processed on a rolling basis. Application fee: $45. *Financial support:* Fellowships, research assistantships with full tuition reimbursements, teaching assistantships with full tuition reimbursements, career-related internships or fieldwork, Federal Work-Study, institutionally sponsored loans, scholarships/grants, tuition waivers (partial), and unspecified assistantships available. Support available to part-time students. *Application contact:* Dr. Jaclynn Tracy, Coordinator of Advising, Programs in Educational Leadership, 734-487-0255, Fax: 734-487-4608, E-mail: jtracy@emich.edu.

Elizabeth City State University, School of Mathematics, Science and Technology, Master of Science in Mathematics Program, Elizabeth City, NC 27909-7806. Offers applied mathematics (MS); community college teaching (MS); mathematics education (MS); remote sensing (MS). *Program availability:* Part-time, evening/weekend. *Degree requirements:* For master's, thesis. *Entrance requirements:* For master's, MAT and/or GRE, minimum GPA of 3.0, 3 letters of recommendation, two official transcripts from all undergraduate/graduate schools attended, typewritten one-page request for entry into program that includes description of student's educational preparation. Additional exam requirements/recommendations for international students: Required—TOEFL (minimum score 550 paper-based, 80 iBT) or IELTS (minimum score 6.5). Electronic applications accepted. *Faculty research:* Oceanic temperature effects, mathematics strategies in elementary schools, multimedia, Antarctic temperature mapping, computer networks, water quality, remote sensing, polar ice, satellite imagery.

Ferris State University, Extended and International Operations, Big Rapids, MI 49307. Offers community college leadership (Ed D). *Program availability:* Evening/weekend, blended/hybrid learning. *Faculty:* 23 part-time/adjunct (14 women). *Students:* 94 full-time (70 women), 4 part-time (1 woman); includes 21 minority (16 Black or African American, non-Hispanic/Latino; 5 Hispanic/Latino). Average age 46. 28 applicants, 75% accepted, 19 enrolled. In 2016, 11 doctorates awarded. *Degree requirements:* For doctorate, thesis/dissertation, e-portfolio demonstrating completion of program outcomes. *Entrance requirements:* For doctorate, master's degree with minimum GPA of 3.25, fierce commitment to the mission of community colleges, essay, writing samples. *Application deadline:* For fall admission, 12/15 for domestic and international students; for winter admission, 1/27 for domestic and international students; for spring admission, 4/15 for domestic students, 4/18 for international students. Applications are processed on a rolling basis. Application fee: $0. Electronic applications accepted. *Expenses:* Contact institution. *Financial support:* In 2016–17, 4 teaching assistantships (averaging $1,000 per year) were awarded. Financial award application deadline: 5/1; financial award applicants required to submit FAFSA. *Unit head:* Dr. Roberta Teahen, Director, 231-591-3805, E-mail: robertateahen@ferris.edu. *Application contact:* Megan Biller, Coordinator, 231-591-2710, Fax: 231-591-3539, E-mail: meganbiller@ferris.edu.

Florida State University, The Graduate School, College of Arts and Sciences, Department of Biological Science, Master's in Science Teaching Program, Tallahassee, FL 32306. Offers community college science teaching (MST). *Faculty:* 2 full-time (both women). *Students:* 8 full-time (7 women); includes 2 minority (1 American Indian or Alaska Native, non-Hispanic/Latino; 1 Hispanic/Latino), 1 international. Average age 27. In 2016, 2 master's awarded. *Degree requirements:* For master's, thesis or alternative, teacher work sample (action research). *Entrance requirements:* For master's, GRE, minimum upper-level undergraduate GPA of 3.0. *Application deadline:* For fall admission, 7/1 for domestic students; for spring admission, 11/1 for domestic students; for summer admission, 3/1 for domestic students. Applications are processed on a rolling basis. Application fee: $30. Electronic applications accepted. *Expenses:* Tuition, state resident: full-time $7263; part-time $403.51 per credit hour. Tuition, nonresident: full-time $18,087; part-time $1004.85 per credit hour. *Required fees:* $1365; $75.81 per credit hour. $20 per semester. Tuition and fees vary according to campus/location. *Faculty research:* Science and mathematics education, science and mathematics teacher preparation. *Unit head:* Dr. D. Ellen Granger, Director, Office of Science Teaching Activities, 850-644-6747, Fax: 850-644-0643, E-mail: granger@bio.fsu.edu. *Application contact:* Dr. Erica M. Staehling, Director, Master's in Science Teaching Program, 850-644-6747, Fax: 850-644-0643, E-mail: staehling@bio.fsu.edu.
Website: http://bio.fsu.edu/osta/tpp.php

George Mason University, College of Humanities and Social Sciences, Higher Education Program, Fairfax, VA 22030. Offers community college education (DA); higher education (Certificate). *Faculty:* 5 full-time (all women), 1 part-time/adjunct (0 women). *Students:* 3 full-time (1 woman), 20 part-time (12 women); includes 5 minority (3 Black or African American, non-Hispanic/Latino; 1 Asian, non-Hispanic/Latino; 1 Hispanic/Latino), 1 international. Average age 46. 3 applicants, 100% accepted, 2 enrolled. In 2016, 7 doctorates, 4 Certificates awarded. *Degree requirements:* For doctorate, thesis/dissertation, internship. *Entrance requirements:* For doctorate, GRE, 3 letters of recommendation; writing sample; resume; master's degree; expanded goals statement; official transcripts; for Certificate, official transcripts; expanded goals statement; 3 letters of recommendation; resume; writing sample. Additional exam requirements/recommendations for international students: Required—TOEFL (minimum score 575 paper-based; 88 iBT), IELTS (minimum score 6.5), PTE (minimum score 59). Application fee: $75 ($80 for international students). Electronic applications accepted. *Expenses:* Tuition, state resident: full-time $10,628; part-time $443 per credit. Tuition, nonresident: full-time $29,306; part-time $1221 per credit. *Required fees:* $3096; $129 per credit. Tuition and fees vary according to program. *Financial support:* Career-related internships or fieldwork, Federal Work-Study, and scholarships/grants available. Support available to part-time students. Financial award application deadline: 3/1; financial award applicants required to submit FAFSA. *Faculty research:* Leadership, the scholarship of teaching, learning, and assessment; ethical leadership; assessment; information technology; diversity. *Total annual research expenditures:* $24,021. *Unit head:* Jan Arminio, Director, 703-993-2064, Fax: 703-993-2307, E-mail: jarminio@gmu.edu. *Application contact:* Katie Richards, Administrative Coordinator, 703-993-2310, Fax: 703-993-2307, E-mail: kricha22@gmu.edu.
Website: http://highered.gmu.edu/

George Mason University, College of Humanities and Social Sciences, Interdisciplinary Studies Program, Fairfax, VA 22030. Offers community college teaching (MAIS); computational social science (MAIS); energy and sustainability (MAIS); folklore studies (MAIS); individualized studies (MAIS); neuroethics (MAIS); religion, culture, and values (MAIS); social entrepreneurship (MAIS); social justice and human rights (MAIS); war and the military in society (MAIS); women and gender studies (MAIS). *Faculty:* 10 full-time (3 women), 9 part-time/adjunct (4 women). *Students:* 25 full-time (21 women), 70 part-time (48 women); includes 31 minority (15 Black or African American, non-Hispanic/Latino; 5 Asian, non-Hispanic/Latino; 7 Hispanic/Latino; 4 Two or more races, non-Hispanic/Latino), 3 international. Average age 33. 52 applicants, 92% accepted, 23 enrolled. In 2016, 40 master's awarded. *Degree requirements:* For master's, project or thesis. *Entrance requirements:* For master's, 3 letters of recommendation; writing sample; official transcript; resume. Additional exam requirements/recommendations for international students: Required—TOEFL (minimum score 575 paper-based; 88 iBT), IELTS (minimum score 6.5), PTE (minimum score 59). *Application deadline:* For fall admission, 3/1 for domestic students. Application fee: $75 ($80 for international students). Electronic applications accepted. *Expenses:* Tuition, state resident: full-time $10,628; part-time $443 per credit. Tuition, nonresident: full-time $29,306; part-time $1221 per credit. *Required fees:* $3096; $129 per credit. Tuition and fees vary according to program. *Financial support:* In 2016–17, 8 students received support, including 3 research assistantships with tuition reimbursements available (averaging $9,629 per year), 5 teaching assistantships with tuition reimbursements available (averaging $12,814 per year); career-related internships or fieldwork, Federal Work-Study, scholarships/grants, unspecified assistantships, and health care benefits (for full-time research or teaching assistantship recipients) also available. Support available to part-time students. Financial award application deadline: 3/1; financial award applicants required to submit FAFSA. *Faculty research:* Combined English and folklore, religious and cultural studies (Christianity and Muslim society). *Unit head:* Meredith H. Lair, Director, 703-993-2159, Fax: 703-993-1251, E-mail: mlair@gmu.edu. *Application contact:* Morgan Fisher, Graduate Coordinator, 703-993-8762, E-mail: mfisherb@gmu.edu.
Website: http://mais.gmu.edu

Lenoir-Rhyne University, Graduate Programs, School of Education, Program in Community College Administration, Hickory, NC 28601. Offers MA. *Program availability:* Online learning. *Entrance requirements:* For master's, GRE or MAT, official transcripts, essay, resume. Electronic applications accepted. *Expenses:* Contact institution.

Marymount University, School of Arts and Sciences, Program in English and the Humanities, Arlington, VA 22207-4299. Offers English and humanities (MA); teaching English at the community college (Certificate). *Program availability:* Part-time, evening/weekend. *Faculty:* 5 full-time (2 women). *Students:* 1 (woman) full-time, 7 part-time (4 women); includes 2 minority (both Two or more races, non-Hispanic/Latino), 1 international. Average age 28. 4 applicants, 75% accepted, 2 enrolled. In 2016, 2 master's, 2 other advanced degrees awarded. *Degree requirements:* For master's, thesis, capstone (final project, practicum). *Entrance requirements:* For master's, 2 letters of recommendation, resume, minimum undergraduate GPA of 3.0 with major in English or other humanities discipline, writing samples of 8-10 pages. Additional exam requirements/recommendations for international students: Required—TOEFL (minimum score 600 paper-based; 96 iBT), IELTS (minimum score 6.5). *Application deadline:* Applications are processed on a rolling basis. Application fee: $40. Electronic applications accepted. *Expenses: Tuition:* Full-time $8460; part-time $940 per credit hour. *Required fees:* $10 per credit hour. One-time fee: $240 part-time. Tuition and fees vary according to program. *Financial support:* In 2016–17, 1 student received support, including 1 teaching assistantship with tuition reimbursement available; career-related internships or fieldwork, Federal Work-Study, scholarships/grants, and unspecified assistantships also available. Support available to part-time students. Financial award applicants required to submit FAFSA. *Unit head:* Dr. David Brown, Director, English and the Humanities, 703-284-5762, Fax: 703-284-3859, E-mail: david.brown@marymount.edu. *Application contact:* Francesca Reed, Director, Graduate Admissions, 703-284-5901, Fax: 703-527-3815, E-mail: grad.admissions@marymount.edu.
Website: http://www.marymount.edu/Academics/School-of-Arts-Sciences/Graduate-Programs/English-Humanities-(M-A-)

Mississippi State University, College of Education, Educational Leadership Program, Mississippi State, MS 39762. Offers community college education (MAT, PhD); elementary, middle and secondary education administration (PhD); school administration (MS, Ed S); workforce education leadership (MS). MS in workforce education leadership held jointly with Alcorn State University. *Faculty:* 16 full-time (10 women). *Students:* 32 full-time (16 women), 158 part-time (101 women); includes 82 minority (80 Black or African American, non-Hispanic/Latino; 1 Hispanic/Latino; 1 Two or more races, non-Hispanic/Latino). Average age 38. 60 applicants, 58% accepted, 34 enrolled. In 2016, 24 master's, 15 doctorates, 5 other advanced degrees awarded. *Degree requirements:* For master's and Ed S, comprehensive exam, thesis; for doctorate, comprehensive exam, thesis/dissertation. *Entrance requirements:* For master's, GRE, minimum GPA of 2.75 in junior and senior courses; for doctorate, GRE, minimum GPA of 3.4 on previous graduate work; for Ed S, GRE, minimum GPA of 3.2, master's degree. Additional exam requirements/recommendations for international students: Required—TOEFL (minimum score 550 paper-based; 79 iBT); Recommended—IELTS (minimum score 6.5). *Application deadline:* For fall admission, 7/1 for domestic students, 5/1 for international students; for spring admission, 11/1 for domestic students, 9/1 for international students. Application fee: $60. Electronic applications accepted. *Expenses:* Tuition, state resident: full-time $7670; part-time $852.50 per credit hour. Tuition, nonresident: full-time $20,790; part-time $2310.50 per credit hour. Part-time tuition and fees vary according to course load. *Financial support:* In 2016–17, 2 research assistantships with full tuition reimbursements (averaging $12,940 per year) were awarded; Federal Work-Study, institutionally sponsored loans, and unspecified assistantships also available. Financial award application deadline: 4/1; financial award applicants required to submit FAFSA. *Unit head:* Dr. Ed Davis, Interim Department Head/Professor, 662-325-0969, Fax: 662-325-0975, E-mail: jed11@colled.msstate.edu. *Application contact:* Linda Bonner, Senior Admissions Assistant, 662-325-3363, E-mail: lbonner@grad.msstate.edu.
Website: http://www.educationalleadership.msstate.edu/

Morgan State University, School of Graduate Studies, School of Education and Urban Studies, Department of Advanced Studies, Leadership and Policy, Program in

Community College Leadership, Baltimore, MD 21251. Offers Ed D. *Accreditation:* NCATE. *Program availability:* Part-time, evening/weekend. *Degree requirements:* For doctorate, comprehensive exam, thesis/dissertation. *Entrance requirements:* For doctorate, GRE General Test or MAT. Additional exam requirements/recommendations for international students: Required—TOEFL (minimum score 550 paper-based). *Faculty research:* Multicultural education, cooperative learning, psychology of cognition.

North Carolina State University, Graduate School, College of Education, Department of Adult and Higher Education, Program in Adult and Community College Education, Raleigh, NC 27695. Offers M Ed, MS, Ed D. *Degree requirements:* For master's, thesis (for some programs); for doctorate, thesis/dissertation. *Entrance requirements:* For master's and doctorate, GRE or MAT. Electronic applications accepted.

Northern Arizona University, Graduate College, College of Education, Department of Educational Leadership, Flagstaff, AZ 86011. Offers community college teaching and learning (Certificate); community college/higher education (M Ed); educational foundations (M Ed); educational leadership (M Ed, Ed D); principal (Certificate); principal K-12 (M Ed); school leadership K-12 (M Ed); superintendent (Certificate). *Program availability:* Part-time. *Degree requirements:* For master's, comprehensive exam, thesis (for some programs); for doctorate, comprehensive exam, thesis/ dissertation. *Entrance requirements:* For master's, minimum GPA of 3.0; for doctorate, GRE or MAT, minimum GPA of 3.5. Additional exam requirements/recommendations for international students: Required—TOEFL (minimum score 550 paper-based; 80 iBT), IELTS (minimum score 7). Electronic applications accepted. *Expenses:* Tuition, state resident: full-time $8971; part-time $444 per credit hour. Tuition, nonresident: full-time $20,958; part-time $1164 per credit hour. *Required fees:* $1018; $644 per credit hour. Tuition and fees vary according to course load, campus/location and program.

Old Dominion University, Darden College of Education, Doctoral Program in Community College Leadership, Norfolk, VA 23529. Offers PhD. *Program availability:* Evening/weekend, online only, 100% online, blended/hybrid learning. *Faculty:* 6 full-time (2 women), 1 (woman) part-time/adjunct. *Students:* 2 full-time (1 woman), 52 part-time (34 women); includes 18 minority (16 Black or African American, non-Hispanic/Latino; 1 Hispanic/Latino; 1 Two or more races, non-Hispanic/Latino). Average age 44. 32 applicants, 56% accepted, 16 enrolled. In 2016, 12 doctorates awarded. *Degree requirements:* For doctorate, comprehensive exam, thesis/dissertation, internship. *Entrance requirements:* For doctorate, GRE, master's degree, writing sample, 3 letters of reference, resume, essay, interview with faculty. Additional exam requirements/ recommendations for international students: Required—TOEFL (minimum score 600 paper-based). *Application deadline:* For spring admission, 2/1 for domestic students, 2/1 priority date for international students. Application fee: $50. Electronic applications accepted. *Expenses:* Tuition, state resident: full-time $8604; part-time $478 per credit hour. Tuition, nonresident: full-time $21,510; part-time $1195 per credit hour. *Required fees:* $66 per semester. Tuition and fees vary according to campus/location, program and reciprocity agreements. *Financial support:* In 2016–17, 12 fellowships with partial tuition reimbursements (averaging $1,500 per year), 1 research assistantship with full tuition reimbursement (averaging $15,000 per year) were awarded; career-related internships or fieldwork and unspecified assistantships also available. Financial award application deadline: 4/15. *Faculty research:* Rural community colleges, inter-institutional collaboration in higher education. *Unit head:* Dr. Chris Glass, Graduate Program Director, 757-683-4118, Fax: 757-683-5756, E-mail: cglass@odu.edu. *Application contact:* Sarah Noble, Office Manager, 757-683-4375, Fax: 757-683-5756, E-mail: snoble@odu.edu.
Website: http://education.odu.edu/efl/academics/commcollege/

Old Dominion University, Darden College of Education, Programs in STEM Education and Professional Studies, Norfolk, VA 23529. Offers community college teaching (MS); human resources training (PhD); technology education (PhD). *Accreditation:* NCATE (one or more programs are accredited). *Program availability:* Part-time, evening/ weekend, blended/hybrid learning, mix of synchronous and asynchronous study. *Faculty:* 6 full-time (2 women). *Students:* 12 full-time (7 women), 33 part-time (20 women); includes 16 minority (15 Black or African American, non-Hispanic/Latino; 1 Two or more races, non-Hispanic/Latino), 2 international. Average age 42. 3 applicants, 100% accepted, 3 enrolled. In 2016, 6 master's, 6 doctorates awarded. Terminal master's awarded for partial completion of doctoral program. *Degree requirements:* For master's, comprehensive exam, thesis optional, writing exam, candidacy exam; for doctorate, comprehensive exam, thesis/dissertation, writing exam, candidacy exam. *Entrance requirements:* For master's, GRE General Test or MAT, minimum GPA of 2.8, 2 letters of reference; for doctorate, GRE, minimum GPA of 3.0, 3 letters of reference. Additional exam requirements/recommendations for international students: Required—TOEFL. *Application deadline:* For fall admission, 6/1 priority date for domestic students, 6/1 for international students; for winter admission, 11/1 priority date for domestic students, 11/1 for international students; for spring admission, 3/1 priority date for domestic students, 3/1 for international students. Applications are processed on a rolling basis. Application fee: $50. Electronic applications accepted. *Expenses:* Tuition, state resident: full-time $8604; part-time $478 per credit hour. Tuition, nonresident: full-time $21,510; part-time $1195 per credit hour. *Required fees:* $66 per semester. Tuition and fees vary according to campus/location, program and reciprocity agreements. *Financial support:* In 2016–17, 3 students received support, including 2 teaching assistantships with partial tuition reimbursements available (averaging $15,000 per year). Financial award application deadline: 2/15; financial award applicants required to submit FAFSA. *Faculty research:* Training and development, STEM education, visualization, leadership, technology literacy. *Total annual research expenditures:* $1 million. *Unit head:* Dr. Petros Katsioloudis, Graduate Program Director, 757-683-5323, E-mail: pkatsiol@odu.edu.
Website: http://education.odu.edu/ots/

University of Arkansas at Little Rock, Graduate School, College of Education and Health Professions, Department of Educational Leadership, Program in Higher Education, Little Rock, AR 72204-1099. Offers administration (MA); college student affairs (MA); health professions teaching and learning (MA); higher education (Ed D); two-year college teaching (MA). *Degree requirements:* For doctorate, comprehensive exam, oral defense of dissertation, residency. *Entrance requirements:* For master's, GRE General Test or MAT, interview, minimum graduate GPA of 3.0; for doctorate, GRE General Test, interview, minimum graduate GPA of 3.5, teaching certificate, three years of work experience.

University of Central Florida, College of Education and Human Performance, Department of Educational and Human Sciences, Program in Educational Leadership, Orlando, FL 32816. Offers educational leadership (MA, Ed D, Ed S), including community college education (MA), higher education (Ed D), student personnel (MA). *Program availability:* Part-time, evening/weekend. *Students:* 121 full-time (78 women), 274 part-time (203 women); includes 147 minority (69 Black or African American, non-Hispanic/Latino; 7 Asian, non-Hispanic/Latino; 65 Hispanic/Latino; 6 Two or more races, non-Hispanic/Latino), 1 international. Average age 31. 258 applicants, 69% accepted, 101 enrolled. In 2016, 84 master's, 24 doctorates awarded. *Degree requirements:* For master's, thesis or alternative; for doctorate, thesis/dissertation, candidacy exam; for Ed S, thesis or alternative, final exam. *Entrance requirements:* For master's, GRE General Test; for doctorate, GRE General Test, GRE Subject Test, minimum GPA of 3.0, resume; for Ed S, GRE General Test, minimum GPA of 3.0, resume. Additional exam requirements/recommendations for international students: Required—TOEFL. *Application deadline:* For fall admission, 2/20 for domestic students; for spring admission, 9/20 for domestic students. Application fee: $30. Electronic applications accepted. *Expenses:* Tuition, state resident: part-time $288.16 per credit hour. Tuition, nonresident: part-time $1071.31 per credit hour. *Financial support:* In 2016–17, 22 students received support, including 1 fellowship with partial tuition reimbursement available (averaging $2,500 per year), 21 research assistantships with partial tuition reimbursements available (averaging $8,064 per year), 2 teaching assistantships with partial tuition reimbursements available (averaging $11,154 per year); career-related internships or fieldwork, Federal Work-Study, institutionally sponsored loans, tuition waivers (partial), and unspecified assistantships also available. Financial award application deadline: 3/1; financial award applicants required to submit FAFSA. *Unit head:* Dr. Kenneth Murray, Program Coordinator, 407-832-1468, E-mail: kenneth.murray@ucf.edu. *Application contact:* Assistant Director, Graduate Admissions, 407-823-2766, Fax: 407-823-6442, E-mail: gradadmissions@ucf.edu.
Website: http://education.ucf.edu/highered/index.cfm

University of Memphis, Graduate School, College of Education, Department of Leadership, Memphis, TN 38152. Offers adult education (Ed D); community college teaching and leadership (Graduate Certificate); community education (Ed D); educational leadership (Ed D); higher education (Ed D); leadership (MS); policy studies (Ed D); school administration and supervision (MS); student personnel (MS). *Accreditation:* NCATE. *Program availability:* Part-time, evening/weekend, online learning. *Faculty:* 8 full-time (4 women), 5 part-time/adjunct (2 women). *Students:* 20 full-time (12 women), 155 part-time (99 women); includes 84 minority (75 Black or African American, non-Hispanic/Latino; 1 Asian, non-Hispanic/Latino; 4 Hispanic/Latino; 4 Two or more races, non-Hispanic/Latino), 2 international. Average age 40. 59 applicants, 92% accepted, 49 enrolled. In 2016, 11 master's, 14 doctorates, 3 other advanced degrees awarded. *Degree requirements:* For master's, comprehensive exam, thesis optional; for doctorate, comprehensive exam, thesis/dissertation. *Entrance requirements:* For master's, GRE, resume, letters of reference, statement of professional goals, current teacher certification, sample work, interview; for doctorate, GRE, resume, letters of reference, statement of professional goals, interview. Additional exam requirements/recommendations for international students: Required—TOEFL (minimum score 550 paper-based; 79 iBT). *Application deadline:* For fall admission, 6/15 for domestic students; for spring admission, 9/15 for domestic students; for summer admission, 2/15 for domestic students. Application fee: $35 ($60 for international students). Electronic applications accepted. *Expenses:* $5,231.50 per semester full-time in-state, $9,623.50 full-time out-of-state. *Financial support:* In 2016–17, 70 students received support, including 3 research assistantships with full tuition reimbursements available (averaging $16,800 per year); teaching assistantships, Federal Work-Study, scholarships/grants, and unspecified assistantships also available. Financial award application deadline: 2/1; financial award applicants required to submit FAFSA. *Faculty research:* School improvement, social justice, online learning, adult learning, diversity. *Unit head:* Dr. Reginald Green, Interim Chair, 901-678-3445, E-mail: rlgreen1@memphis.edu.
Website: http://www.memphis.edu/lead

University of Northern Iowa, Graduate College, College of Humanities, Arts and Sciences, Department of Mathematics, MA Program in Mathematics, Cedar Falls, IA 50614. Offers community college teaching (MA); mathematics (MA); secondary teaching (MA).

University of South Florida, College of Education, Department of Leadership, Counseling, Adult, Career and Higher Education, Tampa, FL 33620-9951. Offers adult education (MA, Ed D, PhD, Ed S); career and technical education (MA); career and workforce education (PhD); higher education/community college teaching (MA, Ed D, PhD); vocational education (Ed S). *Faculty:* 17 full-time (10 women). *Students:* 137 full-time (96 women), 331 part-time (237 women); includes 170 minority (75 Black or African American, non-Hispanic/Latino; 2 American Indian or Alaska Native, non-Hispanic/ Latino; 12 Asian, non-Hispanic/Latino; 71 Hispanic/Latino; 2 Native Hawaiian or other Pacific Islander, non-Hispanic/Latino; 8 Two or more races, non-Hispanic/Latino), 18 international. Average age 35. 175 applicants, 66% accepted, 93 enrolled. In 2016, 111 master's, 22 doctorates, 1 other advanced degree awarded. Application fee: $30. *Expenses:* Tuition, state resident: full-time $7766; part-time $431.43 per credit hour. Tuition, nonresident: full-time $15,789; part-time $877.17 per credit hour. *Required fees:* $37 per term. *Total annual research expenditures:* $545,936. *Unit head:* Dr. Judith Ponticell, Chair, 813-974-4897, Fax: 813-974-5423, E-mail: jponticell@usf.edu.
Website: http://www.coedu.usf.edu/main/departments/ache/ache.html

Wingate University, Thayer School of Education, Wingate, NC 28174. Offers community college executive leadership (Ed D); educational leadership (MA Ed, Ed S); elementary education (MA Ed, MAT). *Accreditation:* NCATE. *Program availability:* Part-time, evening/weekend. *Degree requirements:* For master's, portfolio. *Entrance requirements:* For master's, GRE General Test or MAT, teaching certificate (MA Ed). *Application deadline:* For fall admission, 8/15 priority date for domestic students; for spring admission, 12/15 for domestic students. Applications are processed on a rolling basis. Application fee: $0. *Financial support:* Scholarships/grants available. Support available to part-time students. Financial award applicants required to submit FAFSA. *Unit head:* Dr. Annette D. Digby, Interim Dean, 704-233-8473, E-mail: a.digby@wingate.edu. *Application contact:* Theresa Gibson, Director of the Graduate Education Program, 980-359-1023, E-mail: t.gibson@wingate.edu.

Early Childhood Education

Alabama Agricultural and Mechanical University, School of Graduate Studies, College of Education, Humanities, and Behavioral Sciences, Department of Reading, Elementary, Early Childhood and Special Education, Huntsville, AL 35811. Offers early childhood education (MS Ed, Ed S); elementary education (MS Ed, Ed S); reading/

literacy (PhD); special education collaborative teacher training (MS Ed, Ed S). *Accreditation:* NCATE. *Program availability:* Evening/weekend. *Degree requirements:* For master's, comprehensive exam; for Ed S, thesis. *Entrance requirements:* For master's, GRE General Test. Additional exam requirements/recommendations for international students: Required—TOEFL (minimum score 500 paper-based; 61 iBT). *Application deadline:* For fall admission, 5/1 for domestic students. Applications are processed on a rolling basis. Application fee: $25. Electronic applications accepted. *Expenses:* Tuition, nonresident: part-time $826 per credit hour. Full-time tuition and fees vary according to course load and program. *Financial support:* Research assistantships with tuition reimbursements and career-related internships or fieldwork available. Financial award application deadline: 4/1. *Faculty research:* Multicultural education, learning styles, diagnostic-prescriptive instruction. *Unit head:* Dr. Derrick Davis, Interim Chair, 256-372-4047.

Alabama State University, College of Education, Department of Curriculum and Instruction, Montgomery, AL 36101-0271. Offers early childhood education (M Ed, Ed S); elementary education (M Ed, Ed S); secondary education (M Ed, Ed S), including biology education, English language arts education (M Ed), history education, math education, music education (M Ed), reading education (M Ed), social science education; special education (M Ed). *Program availability:* Part-time. *Faculty:* 7 full-time (4 women), 7 part-time/adjunct (4 women). *Students:* 37 full-time (30 women), 82 part-time (69 women); includes 117 minority (115 Black or African American, non-Hispanic/Latino; 2 Two or more races, non-Hispanic/Latino). Average age 33. 65 applicants, 55% accepted, 22 enrolled. In 2016, 25 master's, 5 Ed Ss awarded. *Degree requirements:* For master's, comprehensive exam, thesis optional; for Ed S, comprehensive exam, thesis. *Entrance requirements:* For master's, GRE General Test, MAT, writing competency test; for Ed S, writing competency test, GRE, MAT. Additional exam requirements/recommendations for international students: Required—TOEFL (minimum score 500 paper-based). *Application deadline:* For fall admission, 4/15 for domestic and international students; for spring admission, 11/15 for domestic and international students; for summer admission, 3/15 for domestic and international students. Applications are processed on a rolling basis. Application fee: $25. Electronic applications accepted. *Expenses:* Tuition, state resident: full-time $3087; part-time $2744 per credit. Tuition, nonresident: full-time $6174; part-time $5488 per credit. *Required fees:* $2284; $1142 per credit. $571 per semester. Tuition and fees vary according to class time, course level, course load, degree level, program and student level. *Financial support:* Research assistantships available. Financial award application deadline: 6/30; financial award applicants required to submit FAFSA. *Unit head:* Dr. Joyce Johnson, Acting Chairperson, 334-229-4485, Fax: 334-229-5603, E-mail: jjohnson@alasu.edu. *Application contact:* Dr. William Person, Dean of Graduate Studies, 334-229-4274, Fax: 334-229-4928, E-mail: wperson@alasu.edu.
Website: http://www.alasu.edu/academics/colleges—departments/college-of-education/curriculum—instruction/index.aspx

Albany State University, College of Education, Albany, GA 31705-2717. Offers early childhood education (M Ed); educational leadership (Ed S); health and physical education (M Ed); middle grades education (M Ed); school counseling (M Ed); special education (M Ed). *Accreditation:* NCATE. *Program availability:* Part-time, evening/weekend, online learning. *Degree requirements:* For master's, comprehensive exam, internship, GACE Content Exam. *Entrance requirements:* For master's, GRE or MAT. *Application deadline:* For fall admission, 6/1 for domestic students, 5/1 for international students; for spring admission, 11/1 for domestic students, 10/1 for international students. Applications are processed on a rolling basis. Application fee: $20. Electronic applications accepted. *Financial support:* Scholarships/grants available. Financial award application deadline: 4/15; financial award applicants required to submit FAFSA. *Faculty research:* GACE preparation, STEM (science, technology, engineering, and mathematics), technology education, special education, professional teacher development, health implications liberation philosophy, NET-Q, learning community, disabled or at-risk students. *Unit head:* Dr. Rhonda C. Porter, Interim Dean, 229-430-1718, Fax: 229-430-4993. *Application contact:* Jeffrey Pierce, II, Graduate Admissions Counselor, 229-430-4646, Fax: 229-430-4105, E-mail: jeffrey.pierce@asurams.edu.
Website: https://www.asurams.edu/Academics/collegeofeducation/

Albright College, Graduate Division, Reading, PA 19612-5234. Offers early childhood education (MS); elementary education (MS); English as a second language (MA); general education (MA); special education (MS). *Program availability:* Part-time, evening/weekend. *Degree requirements:* For master's, thesis. *Entrance requirements:* For master's, GRE General Test or MAT, minimum undergraduate GPA of 3.0, 2 letters of recommendation, interview. Additional exam requirements/recommendations for international students: Recommended—TOEFL (minimum score 525 paper-based). Electronic applications accepted.

American International College, School of Education, Springfield, MA 01109-3189. Offers early childhood education (M Ed, CAGS); elementary education (M Ed, CAGS); middle education/secondary education (M Ed, CAGS); moderate disabilities (M Ed, CAGS); reading specialist (M Ed, CAGS); school adjustment counseling (MAEP, CAGS); school guidance counseling (MAEP, CAGS); school leadership (M Ed, CAGS). *Program availability:* Evening/weekend. *Faculty:* 1 (woman) full-time, 90 part-time/adjunct (63 women). *Students:* 1,194 full-time (970 women), 118 part-time (83 women); includes 108 minority (15 Black or African American, non-Hispanic/Latino; 4 American Indian or Alaska Native, non-Hispanic/Latino; 12 Asian, non-Hispanic/Latino; 55 Hispanic/Latino; 2 Native Hawaiian or other Pacific Islander, non-Hispanic/Latino; 20 Two or more races, non-Hispanic/Latino). Average age 34. 517 applicants, 417 enrolled. In 2016, 879 master's, 194 CAGSs awarded. Terminal master's awarded for partial completion of doctoral program. *Degree requirements:* For master's, comprehensive exam (for some programs), thesis (for some programs), practicum/culminating experience; for CAGS, practicum/culminating experience. *Entrance requirements:* For master's, Communication and Literacy portion of the Massachusetts Tests for Education Licensure, graduate of accredited four-year college with minimum B- average in undergraduate course work; for CAGS, M Ed or master's degree in field related to licensure from accredited institution. *Application deadline:* Applications are processed on a rolling basis. Application fee: $50. Electronic applications accepted. *Expenses:* $439 per credit. *Financial support:* Applicants required to submit FAFSA. *Unit head:* Sylvia Mason, Dean, 413-205-1743, Fax: 413-205-3943, E-mail: sylvia.mason@aic.edu. *Application contact:* Kerry Barnes, Dean of Graduate Admissions, 413-205-3703, Fax: 413-205-3051, E-mail: kerry.barnes@aic.edu.
Website: http://www.aic.edu/school-of-education/

Anna Maria College, Graduate Division, Program in Education, Paxton, MA 01612. Offers early childhood education (M Ed); education (CAGS); elementary education (M Ed); English language arts (M Ed); visual arts (M Ed). *Program availability:* Part-time, evening/weekend. *Entrance requirements:* For master's, bachelor's degree in liberal arts or sciences, minimum GPA of 3.0. Additional exam requirements/recommendations for international students: Required—TOEFL (minimum score 500 paper-based). Electronic applications accepted.

Antioch University Midwest, Graduate Programs, School of Education, Yellow Springs, OH 45387-1609. Offers conflict management (M Ed); dyslexia (M Ed); early childhood education (M Ed); educational leadership (M Ed); intervention specialist, mild to moderate (M Ed); middle childhood education (M Ed); trauma informed education (M Ed). *Accreditation:* NCATE. *Program availability:* Part-time, evening/weekend. *Degree requirements:* For master's, thesis or alternative. *Entrance requirements:* For master's, resume, goal statement, interview. *Application deadline:* For fall admission, 9/7 for domestic students; for winter admission, 12/10 for domestic students; for spring admission, 3/10 for domestic students. Applications are processed on a rolling basis. Application fee: $50. Electronic applications accepted. *Expenses:* $675 per credit hour. *Financial support:* Federal Work-Study available. Financial award applicants required to submit FAFSA. *Unit head:* Dr. Marian Glancy, Director, 937-769-1880, Fax: 937-769-1805, E-mail: mglancy@antioch.edu. *Application contact:* Deena Kent-Hummel, Director of Admissions, 937-769-1823, Fax: 937-769-1804, E-mail: dkent@antioch.edu.
Website: https://www.antioch.edu/midwest/degrees-programs/education-degree/

Antioch University New England, Graduate School, Department of Education, Integrated Learning Program, Keene, NH 03431-3552. Offers early childhood education (M Ed); elementary education (M Ed), including arts and humanities, science and environmental education; special education (M Ed). *Degree requirements:* For master's, internship. *Entrance requirements:* For master's, previous course work or work experience in education. Additional exam requirements/recommendations for international students: Required—TOEFL (minimum score 550 paper-based). Electronic applications accepted. *Expenses:* Contact institution. *Faculty research:* Problem-based learning, place-based education, mathematics education, democratic classrooms, art education.

Arcadia University, School of Education, Glenside, PA 19038-3295. Offers art education (M Ed); computer education (CAS); curriculum (CAS); curriculum studies (M Ed); early childhood education (M Ed), including individualized, master teacher, research in child development; educational leadership (M Ed, Ed D, CAS); elementary education (M Ed); English education (MA Ed); environmental education (MA Ed); instructional technology (M Ed); language arts (M Ed); library science (M Ed); mathematics education (M Ed, MA Ed); music education (MA Ed); psychology (MA Ed); reading (M Ed, CAS); science education (M Ed, CAS); secondary education (M Ed, CAS); special education (M Ed, Ed D, CAS); theater arts (MA Ed); written communication (MA Ed). *Accreditation:* NASAD. *Program availability:* Part-time, evening/weekend, online learning. *Faculty:* 19 full-time (13 women), 3 part-time/adjunct (all women). *Students:* 22 full-time (16 women), 356 part-time (284 women); includes 84 minority (55 Black or African American, non-Hispanic/Latino; 2 American Indian or Alaska Native, non-Hispanic/Latino; 13 Asian, non-Hispanic/Latino; 11 Hispanic/Latino; 3 Two or more races, non-Hispanic/Latino), 4 international. Average age 34. 145 applicants, 73% accepted, 80 enrolled. In 2016, 95 master's, 11 doctorates awarded. *Application deadline:* Applications are processed on a rolling basis. Application fee: $50. Electronic applications accepted. *Expenses:* Contact institution. *Financial support:* Career-related internships or fieldwork, tuition waivers (partial), and unspecified assistantships available. *Unit head:* John T Groves, Interim Dean of the School of Education, 215-572-2940. *Application contact:* 215-572-2925, Fax: 215-572-2126, E-mail: grad@arcadia.edu.

Arkansas State University, Graduate School, College of Education and Behavioral Science, School of Teacher Education and Leadership, State University, AR 72467. Offers community college administration (SCCT); curriculum and instruction (MSE); early childhood education (MSE); early childhood services (MS); educational leadership (MSE, Ed D, Ed S); educational theory and practice (MSE); middle level education (MAT, MSE); reading (MSE, Ed S); special education - gifted, talented, and creative (MSE); special education - instructional specialist grades 4-12 (MSE); special education - instructional specialist grades P-4 (MSE); special education, K-12 (MSE). *Accreditation:* NCATE. *Program availability:* Part-time, online learning. *Degree requirements:* For master's, comprehensive exam, thesis or alternative; for doctorate, comprehensive exam, thesis/dissertation; for other advanced degree, comprehensive exam. *Entrance requirements:* For master's, GRE General Test or MAT, appropriate bachelor's degree, official transcripts, immunization records, letters of reference, interview; for doctorate, GRE General Test or MAT, interview, master's degree, letters of reference, official transcript, personal statement, writing sample, immunization records; for other advanced degree, GRE General Test or MAT, interview, master's degree, official transcript, immunization records, letters of reference, 3 years of teaching experience, teaching license. Additional exam requirements/recommendations for international students: Required—TOEFL (minimum score 550 paper-based; 79 iBT), IELTS (minimum score 6), PTE (minimum score 56). Electronic applications accepted.

Armstrong State University, School of Graduate Studies, Department of Childhood and Exceptional Student Education, Savannah, GA 31419-1997. Offers early childhood education (M Ed, MAT); reading (Certificate); special education (M Ed, MAT); special education transition specialist (Certificate). *Accreditation:* NCATE. *Program availability:* Part-time, evening/weekend. *Faculty:* 14 full-time (12 women), 1 (woman) part-time/adjunct. *Students:* 10 full-time (9 women), 199 part-time (177 women); includes 67 minority (55 Black or African American, non-Hispanic/Latino; 1 Asian, non-Hispanic/Latino; 5 Hispanic/Latino; 6 Two or more races, non-Hispanic/Latino). Average age 34. 131 applicants, 42% accepted, 45 enrolled. In 2016, 72 master's, 24 other advanced degrees awarded. *Degree requirements:* For master's, portfolio. *Entrance requirements:* For master's, MAT, Georgia Assessment for the Certification of Educators. Additional exam requirements/recommendations for international students: Required—TOEFL (minimum score 523 paper-based; 70 iBT). *Application deadline:* For fall admission, 7/1 priority date for domestic students, 5/1 priority date for international students; for spring admission, 11/15 priority date for domestic students, 9/15 priority date for international students; for summer admission, 4/15 priority date for domestic students, 9/15 for international students. Applications are processed on a rolling basis. Application fee: $30. Electronic applications accepted. *Expenses:* Tuition, state resident: full-time $1781; part-time $161.93 per credit hour. Tuition, nonresident: full-time $6482; part-time $589.27 per credit hour. *Required fees:* $1224 per unit. $612 per semester. Tuition and fees vary according to course load, campus/location and program. *Financial support:* In 2016–17, research assistantships with full tuition reimbursements (averaging $5,000 per year) were awarded; career-related internships or fieldwork, Federal Work-Study, and scholarships/grants also available. Support available to part-time students. Financial award application deadline: 3/15; financial award applicants required to submit FAFSA. *Faculty research:* Literacy, instructional design, poetry, working with local schools. *Unit head:* Dr. John Hobe, Department Head, 912-344-2619, Fax: 912-344-3443, E-mail: john.hobe@armstrong.edu. *Application contact:* McKenzie Peterman, Assistant Director of Graduate Admissions, 912-344-2503, Fax: 912-344-3417, E-mail: graduate@armstrong.edu.
Website: https://www.armstrong.edu/academic-departments/education-ceed

Auburn University at Montgomery, College of Education, Department of Counselor, Leadership, and Special Education, Montgomery, AL 36124-4023. Offers counselor education (M Ed, Ed S), including clinical mental health counseling, school counseling; early childhood special education (M Ed); instructional leadership (M Ed, Ed S); special education/collaborative teacher (M Ed, Ed S). *Accreditation:* ACA; NCATE. *Program availability:* Part-time, evening/weekend. *Faculty:* 9 full-time (7 women), 3 part-time/adjunct (all women). *Students:* 7 full-time (5 women), 28 part-time (all women); includes 11 minority (10 Black or African American, non-Hispanic/Latino; 1 Asian, non-Hispanic/

Early Childhood Education

Latino). Average age 35. In 2016, 35 master's, 9 Ed Ss awarded. *Degree requirements:* For master's and Ed S, comprehensive exam. *Entrance requirements:* For master's, GRE General Test or MAT, certification, BS in teaching; for Ed S, GRE General Test or MAT, certification. Additional exam requirements/recommendations for international students: Recommended—TOEFL (minimum score 500 paper-based; 61 iBT), IELTS (minimum score 5.5), TSE (minimum score 44). *Application deadline:* Applications are processed on a rolling basis. Electronic applications accepted. *Expenses:* Tuition, state resident: full-time $6462; part-time $359 per credit hour. Tuition, nonresident: full-time $14,526; part-time $807 per credit hour. *Required fees:* $554. *Financial support:* Career-related internships or fieldwork and scholarships/grants available. Support available to part-time students. Financial award application deadline: 3/1; financial award applicants required to submit FAFSA. *Unit head:* Dr. Samuel Flynt, Head, 334-244-3835, Fax: 334-244-3101, E-mail: sflynt@aum.edu. *Application contact:* Dr. Rhonda Morton, Associate Dean/Graduate Coordinator, 334-244-3287, Fax: 334-244-3978, E-mail: rmorton@aum.edu.
Website: http://education.aum.edu/academic-departments/counselor-leadership-and-special-education

Bank Street College of Education, Graduate School, Program in Early Childhood Education, New York, NY 10025. Offers MS Ed. *Degree requirements:* For master's, thesis. *Entrance requirements:* For master's, interview, essays. Additional exam requirements/recommendations for international students: Required—TOEFL (minimum score 600 paper-based; 100 iBT), IELTS (minimum score 7). Electronic applications accepted. *Faculty research:* Play in early childhood settings, early childhood learning environments, family-teacher interaction, child-centered education, developmental interaction.

Bank Street College of Education, Graduate School, Program in Infant and Family Development and Early Intervention, New York, NY 10025. Offers infant and family development (MS Ed); infant and family early childhood special and general education (MS Ed); infant and family/early childhood special education (Ed M). *Degree requirements:* For master's, thesis. *Entrance requirements:* For master's, interview, essays. Additional exam requirements/recommendations for international students: Required—TOEFL (minimum score 600 paper-based; 100 iBT), IELTS (minimum score 7). Electronic applications accepted. *Faculty research:* Early intervention, early attachment practice in infant and toddler childcare, parenting skills in adolescents.

Bank Street College of Education, Graduate School, Program in Reading and Literacy, New York, NY 10025. Offers advanced literacy specialization (Ed M); reading and literacy (MS Ed); teaching literacy (MS Ed); teaching literacy and childhood general education (MS Ed). *Degree requirements:* For master's, thesis. *Entrance requirements:* For master's, interview, essays. Additional exam requirements/recommendations for international students: Required—TOEFL (minimum score 600 paper-based; 100 iBT), IELTS (minimum score 7). Electronic applications accepted. *Faculty research:* Language development, children's literature, whole language, the reading and writing processes, reading difficulties in multicultural classrooms.

Bank Street College of Education, Graduate School, Programs in Educational Leadership, New York, NY 10025. Offers early childhood leadership (MS Ed); educational leadership (MS Ed); leadership for educational change (Ed M, MS Ed); leadership in community-based learning (MS Ed); leadership in mathematics education (MS Ed); leadership in museum education (MS Ed); leadership in the arts: creative writing (MS Ed); leadership in the arts: visual arts (MS Ed). *Degree requirements:* For master's, thesis. *Entrance requirements:* For master's, interview, essays, minimum of 2 years experience as a classroom teacher. Additional exam requirements/recommendations for international students: Required—TOEFL (minimum score 600 paper-based; 100 iBT), IELTS (minimum score 7). Electronic applications accepted. *Faculty research:* Leadership in urban schools, leadership in small schools, mathematics in elementary schools, professional development in early childhood, leadership in arts education, leadership in special education, museum leadership, community-based leadership.

Barry University, School of Education, Program in Curriculum and Instruction, Miami Shores, FL 33161-6695. Offers accomplished teacher (Ed S); culture, language and literacy (TESOL) (PhD); curriculum evaluation and research (PhD); early childhood (Ed S); early childhood education (PhD); elementary (Ed S); elementary education (PhD); ESOL (Ed S); gifted (Ed S); Montessori (Ed S); PKP/elementary (Ed S); reading (Ed S); reading, language and cognition (PhD). *Entrance requirements:* For doctorate, GRE, minimum GPA of 3.25.

Barry University, School of Education, Program in Montessori Education, Miami Shores, FL 33161-6695. Offers MS, Ed S. *Program availability:* Part-time, evening/weekend. *Degree requirements:* For master's, comprehensive exam, practicum; for Ed S, practicum. *Entrance requirements:* For master's, GRE General Test or MAT, minimum GPA of 3.0; for Ed S, GRE General Test, minimum GPA of 3.0. Electronic applications accepted.

Barry University, School of Education, Program in Pre-Kindergarten and Primary Education, Miami Shores, FL 33161-6695. Offers pre-k/primary (MS); pre-k/primary/ESOL (MS). *Program availability:* Part-time, evening/weekend. *Degree requirements:* For master's, comprehensive exam, practicum. *Entrance requirements:* For master's, GRE General Test or MAT, minimum GPA of 3.0. Electronic applications accepted.

Bayamón Central University, Graduate Programs, Program in Education, Bayamón, PR 00960-1725. Offers administration and supervision (MA Ed); commercial education (MA Ed); elementary education (K–3) (MA Ed); family counseling (Graduate Certificate); guidance and counseling (MA Ed); pre-elementary teacher (MA Ed); rehabilitation counseling (MA Ed); special education (MA Ed), including attention deficit disorder, education of the autistic, learning disabilities. *Program availability:* Part-time, evening/weekend. *Degree requirements:* For master's, comprehensive exam. *Entrance requirements:* For master's, EXADEP, bachelor's degree in education or related field.

Berry College, Graduate Programs, Graduate Programs in Education, Program in Early Childhood Education, Mount Berry, GA 30149-0159. Offers M Ed, MAT. *Accreditation:* NCATE. *Program availability:* Part-time. *Faculty:* 5 part-time/adjunct (3 women). *Students:* 2 part-time (1 woman). Average age 28. In 2016, 4 master's awarded. *Degree requirements:* For master's, thesis, portfolio, oral exams. *Entrance requirements:* For master's, GRE General Test or MAT, minimum GPA of 2.5. Additional exam requirements/recommendations for international students: Required—TOEFL (minimum score 550 paper-based). *Application deadline:* For fall admission, 7/21 for domestic students, 5/1 for international students; for spring admission, 12/1 for domestic students, 10/1 for international students. Applications are processed on a rolling basis. Application fee: $25 ($30 for international students). *Expenses:* Contact institution. *Financial support:* Research assistantships with full tuition reimbursements, scholarships/grants, and unspecified assistantships available. Support available to part-time students. Financial award application deadline: 3/1; financial award applicants required to submit FAFSA. *Unit head:* Dr. Jacqueline McDowell, Dean, 706-236-1717, Fax: 706-238-5827, E-mail: jmcdowell@berry.edu. *Application contact:* Brett Kennedy, Assistant Vice President of Enrollment Management, 706-236-2215, Fax: 706-290-2178, E-mail: admissions@berry.edu.
Website: http://www.berry.edu/academics/education/graduate/

Binghamton University, State University of New York, Graduate School, Graduate School of Education, Program in Childhood Education, Binghamton, NY 13902-6000. Offers MS Ed. *Accreditation:* TEAC. *Program availability:* Part-time, evening/weekend. *Students:* 6 applicants, 67% accepted. *Entrance requirements:* For master's, GRE General Test. Additional exam requirements/recommendations for international students: Required—TOEFL (minimum score 550 paper-based; 80 iBT). *Application deadline:* For fall admission, 2/1 priority date for domestic and international students. Application fee: $75. Electronic applications accepted. *Financial support:* Career-related internships or fieldwork, Federal Work-Study, institutionally sponsored loans, scholarships/grants, health care benefits, tuition waivers (full and partial), and unspecified assistantships available. Financial award applicants required to submit FAFSA. *Unit head:* Dr. Susan Strehle, Dean, 607-777-7329, E-mail: sstrehle@binghamton.edu. *Application contact:* Ben Balkaya, Assistant Dean and Director, 607-777-2151, Fax: 607-777-2501, E-mail: balkaya@binghamton.edu.

Biola University, School of Education, La Mirada, CA 90639-0001. Offers curriculum and instruction (Certificate); early childhood (MA Ed, MAT); multiple subject (MAT); single subject (MAT); special education (MA Ed, MAT, Certificate). *Program availability:* Part-time, evening/weekend, online learning. *Entrance requirements:* For master's, CBEST, CSET, GRE (waived if cumulative GPA is 3.5 or above or if CBEST and all CSET subtests are passed). Additional exam requirements/recommendations for international students: Required—TOEFL (minimum score 100 iBT). Electronic applications accepted. *Faculty research:* Early childhood education, elementary education, special education, curriculum development, teacher preparation.

Bloomsburg University of Pennsylvania, School of Graduate Studies, College of Education, Department of Teaching and Learning, Program in Early Childhood Education, Bloomsburg, PA 17815-1301. Offers M Ed. *Accreditation:* NCATE. *Faculty:* 6 full-time (1 woman). *Students:* 3 full-time (all women), 6 part-time (5 women). Average age 31. 8 applicants, 63% accepted, 5 enrolled. In 2016, 2 master's awarded. *Degree requirements:* For master's, thesis, practicum, student teaching. *Entrance requirements:* For master's, MAT, GRE, minimum QPA of 3.0, valid teaching certificate, U.S. citizenship. Additional exam requirements/recommendations for international students: Required—TOEFL, IELTS. *Application deadline:* Applications are processed on a rolling basis. Application fee: $35 ($60 for international students). Electronic applications accepted. *Expenses:* Tuition, state resident: full-time $9660; part-time $483 per credit. Tuition, nonresident: full-time $14,500; part-time $725 per credit. *Required fees:* $2410; $107 per credit. $75 per term. Tuition and fees vary according to course load, degree level and program. *Financial support:* Federal Work-Study and unspecified assistantships available. Financial award applicants required to submit FAFSA. *Unit head:* Dr. Ingrid Everett, Program Coordinator, 570-389-5120, Fax: 570-389-3030, E-mail: ieverett@bloomu.edu. *Application contact:* Jennifer Kessler, Administrative Assistant, 570-389-4015, Fax: 570-389-3054, E-mail: jkessler@bloomu.edu.
Website: http://www.bloomu.edu/gradschool/early-childhood-education

Boise State University, College of Education, Department of Early and Special Education, Boise, ID 83725-1725. Offers early and special education (M Ed). *Accreditation:* NCATE. *Program availability:* Part-time. *Faculty:* 14. *Students:* 29 full-time (27 women), 13 part-time (10 women); includes 4 minority (2 Asian, non-Hispanic/Latino; 1 Hispanic/Latino; 1 Native Hawaiian or other Pacific Islander, non-Hispanic/Latino). Average age 38. 18 applicants, 33% accepted, 3 enrolled. In 2016, 10 master's awarded. *Degree requirements:* For master's, thesis optional. *Entrance requirements:* For master's, minimum GPA of 3.0. Additional exam requirements/recommendations for international students: Required—TOEFL (minimum score 587 paper-based; 95 iBT), IELTS (minimum score 6.5). *Application deadline:* For fall admission, 3/31 for domestic and international students. Application fee: $65 ($95 for international students). Electronic applications accepted. *Expenses:* Tuition, state resident: full-time $6058; part-time $358 per credit hour. Tuition, nonresident: full-time $20,108; part-time $608 per credit hour. *Required fees:* $2108. Tuition and fees vary according to program. *Financial support:* In 2016–17, 4 students received support. Scholarships/grants and unspecified assistantships available. Financial award application deadline: 3/31; financial award applicants required to submit FAFSA. *Unit head:* Dr. Deb Carter, Department Chair, 208-426-2804, E-mail: debcarter@boisestate.edu. *Application contact:* Dr. Carrie Semmelroth, Graduate Coordinator, 208-426-2818, E-mail: carriesemmelroth@boisestate.edu.
Website: http://education.boisestate.edu/spedecs/

Brenau University, Sydney O. Smith Graduate School, College of Education, Gainesville, GA 30501. Offers early childhood (Ed S); early childhood education (M Ed, MAT); middle grades (Ed S); middle grades education (M Ed, MAT); secondary education (MAT); special education (M Ed, MAT). *Accreditation:* NCATE. *Program availability:* Part-time, evening/weekend, online learning. *Degree requirements:* For master's, thesis optional, comprehensive exam or applied research project, effective portfolio; for Ed S, thesis, applied research project. *Entrance requirements:* For master's, GRE, MAT, interview, minimum GPA of 3.0, 3 references, writing samples; for Ed S, GRE, MAT, master's degree, minimum GPA of 3.0, writing sample, letters of reference. Additional exam requirements/recommendations for international students: Required—TOEFL (minimum score 500 paper-based; 61 iBT); Recommended—IELTS (minimum score 5). Electronic applications accepted. *Expenses:* Contact institution.

Bridgewater State University, College of Graduate Studies, College of Education and Allied Studies, Department of Elementary and Early Childhood Education, Program in Early Childhood Education, Bridgewater, MA 02325. Offers M Ed. *Accreditation:* NCATE. *Program availability:* Part-time, evening/weekend. *Entrance requirements:* For master's, GRE General Test or Massachusetts Test for Educator Licensure.

Brooklyn College of the City University of New York, School of Education, Program in Early Childhood Education, Brooklyn, NY 11210-2889. Offers art teacher (K-12) (MA); birth-grade 2 (MS Ed). *Program availability:* Part-time, evening/weekend. *Entrance requirements:* For master's, LAST, bachelor's degree in early childhood education, resume, 2 letters of recommendation, essay. Additional exam requirements/recommendations for international students: Required—TOEFL (minimum score 500 paper-based; 61 iBT). Electronic applications accepted. *Faculty research:* Children's narrations, language acquisition, culture and education.

Brooklyn College of the City University of New York, School of Education, Program in Special Education, Brooklyn, NY 11210-2889. Offers autism spectrum disorders (AC); teacher of students with disabilities (MS Ed), including adolescence education, childhood education, early childhood education. *Program availability:* Part-time. *Entrance requirements:* For master's, LAST, interview; previous course work in education and psychology; minimum GPA of 3.0 in education, 2.8 overall; resume, 2 letters of recommendation; essay. Additional exam requirements/recommendations for international students: Required—TOEFL (minimum score 500 paper-based; 61 iBT). Electronic applications accepted. *Faculty research:* School reform, conflict resolution, curriculum for inclusive settings, urban issues in special education.

Buffalo State College, State University of New York, The Graduate School, Faculty of Applied Science and Education, Department of Elementary Education and Reading, Program in Elementary Education, Buffalo, NY 14222-1095. Offers childhood education (grades 1-6) (MS Ed); early childhood and childhood curriculum and instruction (MS Ed);

early childhood education (birth-grade 2) (MS Ed). *Accreditation:* NCATE. *Program availability:* Part-time. *Degree requirements:* For master's, thesis or project. *Entrance requirements:* For master's, minimum GPA of 2.5 in last 60 hours, New York teaching certificate. Additional exam requirements/recommendations for international students: Required—TOEFL (minimum score 550 paper-based).

California State University, Dominguez Hills, College of Education, Division of Teacher Education, Program in Special Education, Carson, CA 90747-0001. Offers early childhood special education (MA); mild/moderate disabilities (MA); moderate/severe disabilities (MA). *Program availability:* Part-time, evening/weekend. *Degree requirements:* For master's, comprehensive exam, thesis or alternative. *Entrance requirements:* For master's, minimum GPA of 2.75 in last 60 units, 3 letters of recommendation. Additional exam requirements/recommendations for international students: Required—TOEFL.

California State University, East Bay, Office of Graduate Studies, College of Education and Allied Studies, Department of Teacher Education, Hayward, CA 94542-3000. Offers education (MS), including curriculum, early childhood education, educational technology and leadership, reading instruction. *Program availability:* Online learning. *Students:* 55 full-time (43 women), 21 part-time (15 women); includes 34 minority (5 Black or African American, non-Hispanic/Latino; 1 American Indian or Alaska Native, non-Hispanic/Latino; 14 Asian, non-Hispanic/Latino; 10 Hispanic/Latino; 1 Native Hawaiian or other Pacific Islander, non-Hispanic/Latino; 3 Two or more races, non-Hispanic/Latino), 6 international. Average age 33. 65 applicants, 91% accepted, 11 enrolled. In 2016, 67 master's awarded. *Degree requirements:* For master's, project or thesis. *Entrance requirements:* For master's, minimum GPA of 3.0 in field, 2.5 overall; teaching experience; baccalaureate degree; 3 letters of recommendation. Additional exam requirements/recommendations for international students: Required—TOEFL (minimum score 550 paper-based), IELTS. *Application deadline:* For fall admission, 6/30 for domestic and international students. Application fee: $55. Electronic applications accepted. *Financial support:* Career-related internships or fieldwork, Federal Work-Study, and institutionally sponsored loans available. Support available to part-time students. Financial award application deadline: 3/2; financial award applicants required to submit FAFSA. *Faculty research:* Online, pedagogy, writing, learning, teaching. *Unit head:* Dr. Eric Engdahl, Chair, 510-885-4599, E-mail: eric.engdahl@csueastbay.edu. *Application contact:* Prof. Valerie Helgren-Lempesis, Education Graduate Advisor, 510-885-3006, Fax: 510-885-4632, E-mail: valerie.helgren-lempesis@csueastbay.edu.
Website: http://www20.csueastbay.edu/ceas/departments/ted/index.html

California State University, Fresno, Division of Research and Graduate Studies, Kremen School of Education and Human Development, Department of Literacy, Early, Bilingual, and Special Education, Fresno, CA 93740-8027. Offers education (MA), including early childhood education, reading/language arts; special education (MA). *Accreditation:* NCATE. *Program availability:* Part-time, evening/weekend. *Degree requirements:* For master's, thesis or alternative. *Entrance requirements:* For master's, GRE General Test, MAT, minimum GPA of 2.75. Additional exam requirements/recommendations for international students: Required—TOEFL. *Application deadline:* For fall admission, 5/1 for domestic and international students; for spring admission, 10/1 for domestic and international students. Applications are processed on a rolling basis. Application fee: $55. Electronic applications accepted. *Financial support:* Career-related internships or fieldwork, Federal Work-Study, scholarships/grants, and research awards available. Support available to part-time students. Financial award application deadline: 3/1; financial award applicants required to submit FAFSA. *Faculty research:* Reading recovery, monitoring/tutoring programs, character and academics, professional ethics, low-performing partnership schools. *Unit head:* Dr. Laura Alamillo, Chair, 559-278-0250, Fax: 559-278-0107. *Application contact:* Dr. Monica Billen, Coordinator, Early Childhood Education, 559-278-0267, E-mail: mbillen@csufresno.edu.
Website: http://www.fresnostate.edu/kremen/departments/lebse.html

California State University, Northridge, Graduate Studies, Michael D. Eisner College of Education, Department of Educational Psychology and Counseling, Northridge, CA 91330. Offers counseling (MS), including career counseling, college counseling and student services, marriage and family therapy, school counseling, school psychology; educational psychology (MA Ed), including development, learning, and instruction, early childhood education. *Accreditation:* ACA (one or more programs are accredited); NCATE. *Program availability:* Part-time, evening/weekend. *Faculty:* 17 full-time (4 women), 46 part-time/adjunct (15 women). *Students:* 283 full-time (235 women), 79 part-time (72 women); includes 180 minority (8 Black or African American, non-Hispanic/Latino; 22 Asian, non-Hispanic/Latino; 132 Hispanic/Latino; 18 Two or more races, non-Hispanic/Latino), 13 international. Average age 29. 411 applicants, 36% accepted, 129 enrolled. *Entrance requirements:* For master's, GRE General Test or minimum GPA of 3.0. Additional exam requirements/recommendations for international students: Required—TOEFL. *Application deadline:* For fall admission, 11/30 for domestic students. Application fee: $55. *Expenses:* Tuition, state resident: full-time $4152. *Financial support:* Scholarships/grants available. Support available to part-time students. Financial award application deadline: 3/1. *Unit head:* Dr. Shari Tarver-Behring, Chair, 818-677-2599. *Application contact:* 818-677-3755.
Website: http://www.csun.edu/eisner-education/educational-psychology-counseling

Cambridge College, School of Education, Cambridge, MA 02138-5304. Offers autism specialist (M Ed); autism/behavior analyst (M Ed); behavior analyst (Post-Master's Certificate); behavioral management (M Ed); early childhood teacher (M Ed); education specialist in curriculum and instruction (CAGS); educational leadership (Ed D); elementary teacher (M Ed); English as a second language (M Ed, Certificate); general science (M Ed); health education (Post-Master's Certificate); health/family and consumer sciences (M Ed); history (M Ed); individualized (M Ed); information technology literacy (M Ed); instructional technology (M Ed); interdisciplinary studies (M Ed); library teacher (M Ed); literacy education (M Ed); mathematics (M Ed); mathematics specialist (Certificate); middle school mathematics and science (M Ed); school administration (M Ed, CAGS); school guidance counselor (M Ed), school nurse education (M Ed); school social worker/school adjustment counselor (M Ed); special education administrator (CAGS); special education/moderate disabilities (M Ed); teaching skills and methodologies (M Ed). *Program availability:* Part-time, evening/weekend, online learning. *Degree requirements:* For master's, thesis, internship/practicum (licensure program only); for doctorate, thesis/dissertation; for other advanced degree, thesis. *Entrance requirements:* For master's, interview, resume, documentation of licensure, 2 professional references; for doctorate, official transcripts, interview, resume, documentation of licensure (if any), written personal statement/essay, portfolio of scholarly and professional work, qualifying assessment, 2 professional references, health insurance, immunizations form; for other advanced degree, official transcripts, interview, resume, documentation of licensure (if any), written personal statement/essay, 2 professional references, health insurance, immunizations form. Additional exam requirements/recommendations for international students: Required—TOEFL (minimum score 550 paper-based; 79 iBT), Michigan English Language Assessment Battery (minimum score 85); Recommended—IELTS (minimum score 6). Electronic applications accepted. *Expenses:* Contact institution. *Faculty research:* Adult education, accelerated learning, mathematics education, brain compatible learning, special education and law.

Canisius College, Graduate Division, School of Education and Human Services, Department of Teacher Education, Buffalo, NY 14208-1098. Offers adolescence education (MS Ed); childhood education (MS Ed); general education (MS Ed); special education (MS), including adolescence special education, advanced special education, childhood education grade 1-6, childhood special education. *Program availability:* Part-time, evening/weekend, 100% online, blended/hybrid learning. *Faculty:* 10 full-time (9 women), 7 part-time/adjunct (all women). *Students:* 46 full-time (33 women), 22 part-time (17 women); includes 7 minority (4 Black or African American, non-Hispanic/Latino; 1 American Indian or Alaska Native, non-Hispanic/Latino; 1 Hispanic/Latino; 1 Two or more races, non-Hispanic/Latino), 3 international. Average age 27. 74 applicants, 74% accepted, 43 enrolled. In 2016, 57 master's awarded. *Degree requirements:* For master's, research project or thesis, project internship. *Entrance requirements:* For master's, GRE (if cumulative GPA less than 2.7), transcripts, letters of recommendation. Additional exam requirements/recommendations for international students: Required—TOEFL (minimum score 550 paper-based, 79 iBT), IELTS (minimum score 6.5), or CAEL (minimum score 70). *Application deadline:* Applications are processed on a rolling basis. Application fee: $25. Electronic applications accepted. Application fee is waived when completed online. *Expenses: Tuition:* Full-time $14,742. *Required fees:* $724. *Financial support:* Career-related internships or fieldwork, Federal Work-Study, scholarships/grants, tuition waivers (partial), and unspecified assistantships available. Support available to part-time students. Financial award application deadline: 4/30; financial award applicants required to submit FAFSA. *Unit head:* Dr. Julie Henry, Chair/Professor, 716-888-3729, E-mail: henry1@canisius.edu. *Application contact:* Kathleen B. Davis, Director of Graduate Admissions, 716-888-2500, Fax: 716-888-3195, E-mail: daviskb@canisius.edu.
Website: http://www.canisius.edu/academics/graduate/

Capella University, School of Education, Master's Programs in Education, Minneapolis, MN 55402. Offers adult education (MS); curriculum and instruction (MS); early childhood education (MS); enrollment management (MS); higher education leadership and management (MS); instructional design for online learning (MS); integrative studies (MS); K-12 studies in education (MS); leadership in educational administration (MS); reading and literacy (MS); special education teaching (MS).

Caribbean University, Graduate School, Bayamón, PR 00960-0493. Offers administration and supervision (MA Ed); criminal justice (MA); curriculum and instruction (MA Ed, PhD), including elementary education (MA Ed), English education (MA Ed), history education (MA Ed), mathematics education (MA Ed), primary education (MA Ed), science education (MA Ed), Spanish education (MA Ed); educational technology in instructional systems (MA Ed); gerontology (MSN); human resources (MBA); museology, archiving and art history (MA Ed); neonatal pediatrics (MSN); physical education (MA Ed); special education (MA Ed). *Entrance requirements:* For master's, interview, minimum GPA of 2.5.

Carlow University, College of Learning and Innovation, Program in Early Childhood Education, Pittsburgh, PA 15213-3165. Offers M Ed. *Program availability:* Part-time, evening/weekend. *Students:* 2 full-time (both women), 4 part-time (all women); includes 1 minority (Black or African American, non-Hispanic/Latino). Average age 39. 2 applicants, 100% accepted, 2 enrolled. In 2016, 4 master's awarded. *Degree requirements:* For master's, thesis or alternative. *Entrance requirements:* For master's, personal essay; resume or curriculum vitae; two recommendations; official transcripts; interview; minimum undergraduate GPA of 3.0. Additional exam requirements/recommendations for international students: Required—TOEFL (minimum score 550 paper-based). *Application deadline:* Applications are processed on a rolling basis. Electronic applications accepted. *Expenses: Tuition:* Full-time $11,855; part-time $801 per credit. *Required fees:* $182; $13 per credit. Tuition and fees vary according to course load, degree level and program. *Financial support:* Application deadline: 4/1; applicants required to submit FAFSA. *Faculty research:* Understanding children's play, infant and toddler development, effects of violence on children, supervision and staff development. *Unit head:* Dr. Rae Ann Hirsh, Program Director, 412-578-6014, E-mail: rahirsh@carlow.edu.
Website: http://www.carlow.edu/Early_Childhood_MEd.aspx

Carlow University, College of Learning and Innovation, Program in Education, Pittsburgh, PA 15213-3165. Offers early childhood education (M Ed); special education (M Ed), including early childhood. *Program availability:* Part-time, evening/weekend, 100% online, blended/hybrid learning. *Students:* 47 full-time (43 women), 19 part-time (18 women); includes 10 minority (7 Black or African American, non-Hispanic/Latino; 3 Two or more races, non-Hispanic/Latino). Average age 31. 27 applicants, 81% accepted, 19 enrolled. In 2016, 14 master's awarded. *Entrance requirements:* For master's, personal essay; resume or curriculum vitae; two recommendations; official transcripts; interview; minimum undergraduate GPA of 3.0. Additional exam requirements/recommendations for international students: Required—TOEFL (minimum score 550 paper-based). *Application deadline:* Applications are processed on a rolling basis. Electronic applications accepted. *Expenses: Tuition:* Full-time $11,855; part-time $801 per credit. *Required fees:* $182; $13 per credit. Tuition and fees vary according to course load, degree level and program. *Financial support:* Application deadline: 4/1; applicants required to submit FAFSA. *Unit head:* Dr. Judith Toure, Chair, Department of Education, 412-578-6215, Fax: 412-578-8816, E-mail: jltoure@carlow.edu.
Website: http://www.carlow.edu/education.aspx

Carroll University, Graduate Programs in Education, Waukesha, WI 53186-5593. Offers adult and continuing education (M Ed); educational leadership (MS); pk-12 (M Ed). *Program availability:* Part-time, evening/weekend. *Faculty:* 7 full-time (5 women), 14 part-time/adjunct (all women). *Students:* 11 full-time (10 women), 163 part-time (125 women); includes 11 minority (3 Black or African American, non-Hispanic/Latino; 3 American Indian or Alaska Native, non-Hispanic/Latino; 2 Asian, non-Hispanic/Latino; 3 Hispanic/Latino), 1 international. Average age 34. 96 applicants, 38% accepted, 18 enrolled. In 2016, 43 master's awarded. *Degree requirements:* For master's, thesis. *Entrance requirements:* For master's, minimum undergraduate GPA of 2.5 in related field. Additional exam requirements/recommendations for international students: Required—TOEFL. *Application deadline:* For fall admission, 8/15 priority date for domestic students. Applications are processed on a rolling basis. Application fee: $0. Electronic applications accepted. *Expenses: Tuition:* Full-time $10,548; part-time $586 per credit. *Required fees:* $520 per semester. Tuition and fees vary according to course load, degree level and program. *Financial support:* Available to part-time students. Application deadline: 3/15; applicants required to submit FAFSA. *Faculty research:* Qualitative research methods, whole language approaches to teaching, the writing process, multicultural education, gifted/talented learners. *Unit head:* Dr. Kathrine Kramer, Director of Graduate Studies, 262-650-4917, E-mail: kkramer@carrollu.edu. *Application contact:* Lori Aliota, Graduate Admission Counselor, 262-524-7226, E-mail: laliota@carrollu.edu.
Website: http://www.carrollu.edu/gradprograms/education/default.asp

The Catholic University of America, School of Arts and Sciences, Department of Education, Washington, DC 20064. Offers Catholic school leadership (MA); education (Certificate); secondary education (MA); special education (MA), including early childhood, non-categorical. *Accreditation:* NCATE. *Program availability:* Part-time. *Faculty:* 8 full-time (7 women), 2 part-time/adjunct (both women). *Students:* 7 full-time (6

women), 21 part-time (13 women); includes 5 minority (2 Black or African American, non-Hispanic/Latino; 3 Hispanic/Latino), 3 international. Average age 38. 22 applicants, 45% accepted, 3 enrolled. In 2016, 14 master's awarded. *Degree requirements:* For master's, comprehensive exam, thesis or alternative; for Certificate, action research project. *Entrance requirements:* For master's, GRE General Test or MAT, statement of purpose, official copies of academic transcripts, three letters of recommendation, interview; for Certificate, PRAXIS I, statement of purpose, official copies of academic transcripts, three letters of recommendation, interview. Additional exam requirements/recommendations for international students: Required—TOEFL (minimum score 550 paper-based; 80 iBT). *Application deadline:* For fall admission, 7/15 priority date for domestic students, 7/1 for international students; for spring admission, 11/15 priority date for domestic students, 11/1 for international students. Applications are processed on a rolling basis. Application fee: $55. Electronic applications accepted. *Expenses:* $42,850 per year; $1,170 per credit; $200 per semester part-time fees. *Financial support:* Fellowships, research assistantships, teaching assistantships, Federal Work-Study, scholarships/grants, tuition waivers (full and partial), and unspecified assistantships available. Financial award application deadline: 2/1; financial award applicants required to submit FAFSA. *Faculty research:* Special education, early childhood education, educational psychology, Catholic school administration, leadership and policy studies, counseling, curriculum and instruction. *Total annual research expenditures:* $54,518. *Unit head:* Dr. John Convey, Chair, 202-319-5810, Fax: 202-319-5815, E-mail: convey@cua.edu. *Application contact:* Director of Graduate Admissions, 202-319-5057, Fax: 202-319-6533, E-mail: cua-admissions@cua.edu.
Website: http://education.cua.edu/

Central Connecticut State University, School of Graduate Studies, School of Education and Professional Studies, Department of Literacy, Elementary, and Early Childhood Education, New Britain, CT 06050-4010. Offers MS, AC, Sixth Year Certificate. *Program availability:* Part-time, evening/weekend. *Faculty:* 5 full-time (3 women), 2 part-time/adjunct (both women). *Students:* 11 full-time (8 women), 120 part-time (114 women); includes 9 minority (2 Black or African American, non-Hispanic/Latino; 5 Hispanic/Latino; 2 Two or more races, non-Hispanic/Latino), 1 international. Average age 30. 47 applicants, 81% accepted, 25 enrolled. In 2016, 44 master's, 11 other advanced degrees awarded. *Degree requirements:* For master's, comprehensive exam, thesis or alternative; for other advanced degree, qualifying exam. *Entrance requirements:* For master's, minimum undergraduate GPA of 2.7, teacher certification, interview, essay, letters of recommendation; for other advanced degree, master's degree, essay, teacher certification, interview, letters of recommendation. Additional exam requirements/recommendations for international students: Required—TOEFL (minimum score 550 paper-based; 79 iBT). *Application deadline:* For fall admission, 5/1 for domestic and international students; for spring admission, 11/1 for domestic and international students. Applications are processed on a rolling basis. Application fee: $50. Electronic applications accepted. *Expenses: Tuition, area resident:* Full-time $6497; part-time $606 per credit. Tuition, state resident: full-time $9748; part-time $622 per credit. Tuition, nonresident: full-time $18,102; part-time $622 per credit. *Required fees:* $4459; $246 per credit. *Financial support:* In 2016–17, 4 students received support. Career-related internships or fieldwork, Federal Work-Study, and scholarships/grants available. Support available to part-time students. Financial award application deadline: 3/1. *Faculty research:* Developmental, clinical, and administrative aspects of reading and language arts instruction. *Unit head:* Dr. Helen Abadiano, Chair, 860-832-2175, E-mail: abadiano@ccsu.edu. *Application contact:* Patricia Gardner, Associate Director of Graduate Studies, 860-832-2350, Fax: 860-832-2362.
Website: http://www.ccsu.edu/leece/index.html

Central Michigan University, College of Graduate Studies, College of Education and Human Services, Department of Teacher Education and Professional Development, Mount Pleasant, MI 48859. Offers educational technology (MA, Graduate Certificate); elementary education (MA), including classroom teaching, early childhood; reading and literacy K-12 (MA); secondary education (MA). *Program availability:* Part-time, evening/weekend. *Degree requirements:* For master's, thesis or alternative. Electronic applications accepted. *Faculty research:* Integrating literacy across the curriculum, science teaching and aesthetic learning in science, diversity education, educational technology, educational psychology and child development.

Chaminade University of Honolulu, Office of Professional and Continuing Education, Program in Education, Honolulu, HI 96816-1578. Offers child development (M Ed); early childhood education (MAT); educational leadership (M Ed); elementary education (MAT); instructional leadership (M Ed); Montessori (M Ed); secondary education (MAT); special education (MAT). *Program availability:* Part-time, evening/weekend, 100% online, blended/hybrid learning. *Faculty:* 7 full-time (4 women), 8 part-time/adjunct (6 women). *Students:* 98 full-time (80 women), 82 part-time (62 women); includes 110 minority (6 Black or African American, non-Hispanic/Latino; 2 American Indian or Alaska Native, non-Hispanic/Latino; 51 Asian, non-Hispanic/Latino; 9 Hispanic/Latino; 41 Native Hawaiian or other Pacific Islander, non-Hispanic/Latino; 1 Two or more races, non-Hispanic/Latino), 1 international. Average age 35. 38 applicants, 100% accepted, 29 enrolled. In 2016, 79 master's awarded. *Degree requirements:* For master's, thesis or alternative. *Entrance requirements:* For master's, PRAXIS (for MAT), minimum GPA of 2.75 (for M Ed), 3.0 (for MAT); 2 letters of recommendation, resume, writing sample (for MAT). Additional exam requirements/recommendations for international students: Required—TOEFL (minimum score 550 paper-based; 79 iBT). *Application deadline:* Applications are processed on a rolling basis. Application fee: $40. Electronic applications accepted. *Expenses:* $740 per credit hour plus $93 fee per online course. *Financial support:* Applicants required to submit FAFSA. *Unit head:* Dr. Dale Fryxell, Interim Dean, 808-739-4684, Fax: 808-739-4607, E-mail: edu-advising@chaminade.edu. *Application contact:* 808-735-4755, E-mail: gradserv@chaminade.edu.
Website: http://www.chaminade.edu/education

Champlain College, Graduate Studies, Burlington, VT 05402-0670. Offers business (MBA); digital forensic science (MS); early childhood education (M Ed); emergent media (MFA, MS); executive leadership (MS); health care administration (MS); information security operations (MS); law (MS); mediation and applied conflict studies (MS). MS in emergent media program held in Shanghai. *Program availability:* Part-time, online learning. *Degree requirements:* For master's, capstone project. *Entrance requirements:* Additional exam requirements/recommendations for international students: Required—TOEFL (minimum score 550 paper-based; 80 iBT). Electronic applications accepted.

Chatham University, Program in Education, Pittsburgh, PA 15232-2826. Offers early childhood education (MAT); elementary education (MAT); environmental education (K-12) (MAT); secondary art (MAT); secondary biology education (MAT); secondary chemistry education (MAT); secondary English education (MAT); secondary math education (MAT); secondary physics education (MAT); secondary social studies education (MAT); special education (MAT). *Degree requirements:* For master's, thesis, teaching experience. *Entrance requirements:* For master's, minimum GPA of 3.0, sample of written work, recommendation letters. Additional exam requirements/recommendations for international students: Required—TOEFL (minimum score 600 paper-based; 100 iBT), IELTS (minimum score 7), TWE. Electronic applications accepted. Application fee is waived when completed online. *Expenses: Tuition:* Full-time $16,254; part-time $903 per credit hour. *Required fees:* $468; $26 per credit hour. *Faculty research:* Gifted education, environmental education, technology in education, writing as learning, class size and achievement.

Chestnut Hill College, School of Graduate Studies, Department of Education, Program in Early Education, Philadelphia, PA 19118-2693. Offers early education (M Ed), including Montessori certificate preparation, preK-4 education, preK-4 education and special education preK-8. *Program availability:* Part-time, evening/weekend. *Degree requirements:* For master's, thesis optional. *Entrance requirements:* For master's, PRAXIS I or proof of teaching certification, writing sample, letters of recommendation, 6 graduate credits with minimum B grade or minimum undergraduate GPA of 3.0. Additional exam requirements/recommendations for international students: Required—TOEFL (minimum score 500 paper-based), IELTS (minimum score 6.0), or TWE (minimum score 22). Electronic applications accepted. *Expenses:* Contact institution. *Faculty research:* Gender issues, early childhood education standardized testing.

Chestnut Hill College, School of Graduate Studies, Department of Education, Program in Reading, Philadelphia, PA 19118-2693. Offers reading specialist (M Ed), including K-12, special education 7-12, special education PreK-8. *Program availability:* Part-time, evening/weekend. *Degree requirements:* For master's, thesis optional. *Entrance requirements:* Additional exam requirements/recommendations for international students: Required—TOEFL (minimum score 500 paper-based) or IELTS (minimum score 6). Electronic applications accepted. *Expenses:* Contact institution. *Faculty research:* Inclusive education, cultural issues in education.

Chicago State University, School of Graduate and Professional Studies, College of Education, Department of Special Education, Early Childhood Education and Bilingual Education, Program in Early Childhood Education, Chicago, IL 60628. Offers MAT, MS Ed. *Accreditation:* NCATE. *Degree requirements:* For master's, thesis optional. *Entrance requirements:* For master's, minimum GPA of 2.75.

The Citadel, The Military College of South Carolina, Citadel Graduate College, Zucker Family School of Education, Charleston, SC 29409. Offers elementary/secondary school administration and supervision (M Ed); elementary/secondary school counseling (M Ed); interdisciplinary STEM education (M Ed); literacy education (M Ed, Graduate Certificate); middle grades (MAT), including English, mathematics, science, social studies; physical education (grades K-12) (MAT); school superintendency (Ed S); secondary education (MAT), including biology, English, mathematics, social studies; student affairs (Graduate Certificate); student affairs and college counseling (M Ed). *Accreditation:* NCATE. *Program availability:* Part-time, evening/weekend, 100% online, blended/hybrid learning. *Faculty:* 9 full-time (4 women), 9 part-time/adjunct (5 women). *Students:* 70 full-time (58 women), 249 part-time (200 women); includes 87 minority (70 Black or African American, non-Hispanic/Latino; 1 Asian, non-Hispanic/Latino; 9 Hispanic/Latino; 7 Two or more races, non-Hispanic/Latino), 2 international. 146 applicants, 98% accepted, 105 enrolled. In 2016, 85 master's, 7 other advanced degrees awarded. *Degree requirements:* For master's, comprehensive exam (for some programs). *Entrance requirements:* For master's, GRE (minimum combined verbal and quantitative score of 290) or MAT (minimum score 396). Additional exam requirements/recommendations for international students: Required—TOEFL (minimum score 550 paper-based; 79 iBT). *Application deadline:* Applications are processed on a rolling basis. Application fee: $40. Electronic applications accepted. *Expenses:* Tuition, state resident: full-time $5121; part-time $569 per credit hour. Tuition, nonresident: full-time $8613; part-time $957 per credit hour. *Required fees:* $90 per term. *Financial support:* Fellowships and unspecified assistantships available. Support available to part-time students. Financial award application deadline: 7/1; financial award applicants required to submit FAFSA. *Unit head:* Dr. Larry G. Daniel, Dean, 843-953-5097, E-mail: ldaniel@citadel.edu. *Application contact:* Dr. Tammy J. Graham, Associate Professor, 843-953-6854, E-mail: tammy.graham@citadel.edu.
Website: http://www.citadel.edu/root/education-graduate-programs

City College of the City University of New York, Graduate School, School of Education, Department of Teaching, Learning and Culture, New York, NY 10031-9198. Offers bilingual education (MS); childhood education (MS); early childhood education (MS); educational theatre (MS); literacy (MS); TESOL (MS). *Accreditation:* NCATE. *Degree requirements:* For master's, thesis. *Entrance requirements:* For master's, Liberal Arts and Sciences Test (LAST), Content Specialty Test (CST). Additional exam requirements/recommendations for international students: Required—TOEFL. Tuition and fees vary according to course load, degree level and program.

Clarion University of Pennsylvania, Office of Transfer, Adult and Graduate Admissions, Master of Education Program, Clarion, PA 16214. Offers curriculum and instruction (M Ed); early childhood (M Ed); math education (M Ed); reading (M Ed); science education (M Ed); special education (M Ed); technology (M Ed). *Accreditation:* NCATE. *Program availability:* Part-time, evening/weekend, 100% online, blended/hybrid learning. *Faculty:* 12 full-time (8 women), 5 part-time/adjunct (all women). *Students:* 17 full-time (15 women), 97 part-time (78 women); includes 1 minority (Two or more races, non-Hispanic/Latino). Average age 29. 76 applicants, 99% accepted, 48 enrolled. In 2016, 34 master's awarded. *Degree requirements:* For master's, comprehensive exam, thesis, or portfolio. *Entrance requirements:* For master's, minimum QPA of 3.0. Additional exam requirements/recommendations for international students: Required—TOEFL (minimum score 550 paper-based; 80 iBT), IELTS (minimum score 7). *Application deadline:* For fall admission, 8/1 for domestic students, 4/15 for international students; for spring admission, 8/1 for domestic students, 9/15 for international students. Applications are processed on a rolling basis. Application fee: $40. Electronic applications accepted. *Expenses:* $632.35 per credit. *Financial support:* Career-related internships or fieldwork, Federal Work-Study, scholarships/grants, and unspecified assistantships available. Support available to part-time students. Financial award application deadline: 3/1; financial award applicants required to submit FAFSA. *Unit head:* Dr. John McCullough, Chair, Department of Education, 814-393-2104, Fax: 814-393-2446, E-mail: gradstudies@clarion.edu. *Application contact:* Dana Bearer, Associate Director for Transfer, Adult, and Graduate Programs, 814-393-2337, Fax: 814-393-2722, E-mail: gradstudies@clarion.edu.

Clarkson University, Program in Education, Schenectady, NY 12308. Offers adolescence education 7-12 (MAT); technology education K-12 (MAT). *Accreditation:* TEAC. *Faculty:* 8 full-time (all women), 31 part-time/adjunct (17 women). *Students:* 38 full-time (23 women), 2 part-time (0 women); includes 6 minority (3 Asian, non-Hispanic/Latino; 2 Hispanic/Latino; 1 Two or more races, non-Hispanic/Latino), 7 international. 39 applicants, 79% accepted, 26 enrolled. In 2016, 15 master's awarded. *Degree requirements:* For master's, thesis (for some programs), thesis or project. *Entrance requirements:* For master's, GRE, minimum undergraduate GPA of 3.0. Additional exam requirements/recommendations for international students: Required—TOEFL (minimum score 550 paper-based, 80 iBT) or IELTS (6.5). *Application deadline:* Applications are processed on a rolling basis. Application fee: $50. Electronic applications accepted. *Expenses:* $900 per credit. *Financial support:* Scholarships/grants available. *Unit head:* Dr. Catherine Snyder, Chair of Education, 518-631-9870, E-mail: csnyder@clarkson.edu. *Application contact:* Dan Capogna, Graduate Admissions Contact, 518-631-9910, E-mail: graduate@clarkson.edu.
Website: http://graduate.clarkson.edu

Clemson University, Graduate School, College of Education, Department of Teaching and Learning, Program in Teaching and Learning, Clemson, SC 29634. Offers science, technology, engineering, arts and mathematics education (Certificate); teaching and learning (M Ed), including early childhood, instructional coaching, science, technology, engineering, arts and mathematics. *Program availability:* Part-time, evening/weekend, online only, 100% online. *Faculty:* 24 full-time (19 women). *Students:* 19 part-time (17 women); includes 1 minority (Hispanic/Latino). Average age 32. 4 applicants, 50% accepted, 2 enrolled. In 2016, 27 master's awarded. *Entrance requirements:* For master's, GRE General Test, unofficial transcripts, teaching certificate, letters of recommendation. Additional exam requirements/recommendations for international students: Required—TOEFL (minimum score 80 iBT), IELTS (minimum score 7). *Application deadline:* Applications are processed on a rolling basis. Application fee: $80 ($90 for international students). Electronic applications accepted. *Expenses:* $394 per credit hour; $10 per credit hour information technology fee; $17 fee per session for matriculation and software; $22 fee for activities and career services for students taking over 6 credit hours. *Unit head:* Dr. Jeff Marshall, Department Head, Fax: 864-656-0311, E-mail: soedean@clemson.edu. *Application contact:* Julie Jones, Student Services Program Coordinator, 864-656-5096, E-mail: jgambre@clemson.edu.
Website: http://www.clemson.edu/education/academics/masters-specialist-programs/masters-education-teaching-learning/index.html

Cleveland State University, College of Graduate Studies, College of Education and Human Services, Department of Curriculum and Foundations, Cleveland, OH 44115. Offers art education (M Ed); early childhood education (M Ed); foreign language education (M Ed); middle childhood mathematics and science education (M Ed); special education (M Ed), including mild/moderate disabilities, moderate/intensive disabilities; teaching English to speakers of other languages (M Ed). *Program availability:* Part-time, evening/weekend. *Faculty:* 19 full-time (14 women), 32 part-time/adjunct (27 women). *Students:* 86 full-time (65 women), 369 part-time (301 women); includes 119 minority (89 Black or African American, non-Hispanic/Latino; 1 American Indian or Alaska Native, non-Hispanic/Latino; 2 Asian, non-Hispanic/Latino; 16 Hispanic/Latino; 11 Two or more races, non-Hispanic/Latino), 35 international. Average age 34. 177 applicants, 55% accepted, 68 enrolled. In 2016, 179 master's awarded. *Degree requirements:* For master's, comprehensive exam (for some programs), thesis or alternative. *Entrance requirements:* For master's, GRE General Test or MAT, minimum GPA of 2.75. Additional exam requirements/recommendations for international students: Required—TOEFL (minimum score 550 paper-based; 78 iBT), IELTS (minimum score 6). *Application deadline:* For fall admission, 7/1 priority date for domestic students, 5/15 for international students; for spring admission, 11/15 for domestic students, 11/1 for international students; for summer admission, 4/1 for domestic students, 3/15 for international students. Applications are processed on a rolling basis. Application fee: $30. *Expenses:* Tuition, state resident: full-time $9565. Tuition, nonresident: full-time $17,980. Tuition and fees vary according to program. *Financial support:* In 2016–17, 13 research assistantships with full tuition reimbursements (averaging $15,845 per year) were awarded; tuition waivers (partial) and unspecified assistantships also available. Financial award application deadline: 2/15; financial award applicants required to submit FAFSA. *Faculty research:* Early childhood education, literacy education, special education: mild/moderate, moderate/intensive, early childhood intervention specialist), teaching English to speakers of other languages (TESOL). *Total annual research expenditures:* $275,907. *Unit head:* Dr. Tachelle I. Banks, Chairperson, 216-687-4608, Fax: 216-687-5379, E-mail: t.i.banks@csuohio.edu. *Application contact:* Michael Almony, Senior Student Services Specialist, 216-875-9929, Fax: 216-687-5491, E-mail: m.almony@csuohio.edu.
Website: http://www.csuohio.edu/cehs/te/te

The College at Brockport, State University of New York, School of Education, Health, and Human Services, Department of Education and Human Development, Program in Childhood Curriculum Specialist, Brockport, NY 14420-2997. Offers MS Ed. *Accreditation:* NCATE. *Program availability:* Part-time. *Students:* 1 part-time (0 women). In 2016, 1 master's awarded. *Degree requirements:* For master's, thesis or alternative. *Entrance requirements:* For master's, minimum GPA of 3.0, letters of recommendation, statement of objectives, current resume. Additional exam requirements/recommendations for international students: Required—TOEFL (minimum score 550 paper-based; 79 iBT), IELTS (minimum score 6.5). *Application deadline:* For fall admission, 3/15 priority date for domestic and international students; for spring admission, 10/15 priority date for domestic and international students. Application fee: $80. Electronic applications accepted. *Expenses:* Contact institution. *Financial support:* Federal Work-Study, scholarships/grants, and unspecified assistantships available. Support available to part-time students. Financial award application deadline: 3/15; financial award applicants required to submit FAFSA. *Unit head:* Dr. Sue Robb, Chairperson, 585-395-5935, Fax: 585-395-2172, E-mail: awalton@brockport.edu. *Application contact:* Anne Walton, Coordinator of Certification and Graduate Advisement, 585-395-2326, Fax: 585-395-2172, E-mail: awalton@brockport.edu.
Website: http://www.brockport.edu/ehd

College of Charleston, Graduate School, School of Education, Health, and Human Performance, Department of Elementary and Early Childhood Education, Program in Early Childhood Education, Charleston, SC 29424-0001. Offers MAT. *Accreditation:* NCATE. *Program availability:* Part-time, evening/weekend. *Degree requirements:* For master's, thesis or alternative, written qualifying exam, student teaching experience (MAT). *Entrance requirements:* For master's, GRE, minimum GPA of 2.5, 2 letters of recommendation. Additional exam requirements/recommendations for international students: Required—TOEFL (minimum score 81 iBT). *Application deadline:* For fall admission, 4/1 for domestic students; for spring admission, 11/1 for domestic students. Applications are processed on a rolling basis. Application fee: $45. Electronic applications accepted. *Financial support:* Research assistantships, teaching assistantships, Federal Work-Study, and unspecified assistantships available. Support available to part-time students. Financial award application deadline: 4/1; financial award applicants required to submit FAFSA. *Faculty research:* Teacher education and creative arts, integrated curriculum, multicultural awareness, teaching models, cooperative learning. *Unit head:* Dr. Angela Cozart, Director, 843-953-6353, E-mail: cozarta@cofc.edu. *Application contact:* Susan Hallatt, Director of Graduate Admissions, 843-953-5614, Fax: 843-953-1434, E-mail: hallatts@cofc.edu.
Website: http://teachered.cofc.edu/grad-progs/edec.php

The College of New Jersey, Office of Graduate and Advancing Education, School of Education, Department of Elementary and Early Childhood Education, Program in Early Childhood Education, Ewing, NJ 08628. Offers M Ed, MAT. *Program availability:* Part-time. *Entrance requirements:* For master's, GRE, minimum GPA of 3.0 in field or 2.75 overall. Additional exam requirements/recommendations for international students: Required—TOEFL. Electronic applications accepted.

The College of New Rochelle, Graduate School, Division of Education, Program in Childhood Education/Early Childhood Education, New Rochelle, NY 10805-2308. Offers childhood education (MS Ed); early childhood education (MS Ed). *Program availability:* Part-time. *Degree requirements:* For master's, comprehensive exam (for some programs), thesis (for some programs), practicum. *Entrance requirements:* For master's, interview, minimum GPA of 3.0 in field, 2.7 overall.

The College of Saint Rose, Graduate Studies, Thelma P. Lally School of Education, Programs in Special Education, Albany, NY 12203-1419. Offers adolescence education and special education (MS Ed); childhood education and special education (MS Ed); childhood special education (MS Ed); early childhood special education (MS Ed); special education (Certificate); special education professional (MS Ed). *Accreditation:* NCATE. *Students:* 11 full-time (9 women), 19 part-time (17 women), 2 international. Average age 28. 17 applicants, 76% accepted, 7 enrolled. In 2016, 19 master's, 4 Certificates awarded. *Degree requirements:* For master's, comprehensive exam (for some programs), thesis or alternative, research project. *Entrance requirements:* For master's, minimum undergraduate GPA of 3.0. Additional exam requirements/recommendations for international students: Required—TOEFL (minimum score 550 paper-based; 80 iBT), IELTS (minimum score 6), PTE (minimum score 56). *Application deadline:* For fall admission, 4/1 priority date for domestic and international students; for spring admission, 10/15 priority date for domestic and international students; for summer admission, 3/15 priority date for domestic and international students. Applications are processed on a rolling basis. Application fee: $40. Electronic applications accepted. *Expenses: Tuition:* Full-time $14,382; part-time $799 per credit. *Required fees:* $814; $32 per credit. $88 per semester. Tuition and fees vary according to course load. *Financial support:* Career-related internships or fieldwork, scholarships/grants, tuition waivers (partial), and unspecified assistantships available. Support available to part-time students. Financial award application deadline: 4/15. *Unit head:* Susan DeLuke, Chair, 518-454-5194, E-mail: delukes@strose.edu. *Application contact:* Cris Murray, Assistant Vice President for Graduate Recruitment and Enrollment, 518-485-3390, E-mail: grad@strose.edu.
Website: https://www.strose.edu/special-education/

The College of Saint Rose, Graduate Studies, Thelma P. Lally School of Education, Teacher Education Programs, Albany, NY 12203-1419. Offers adolescence education (MS Ed, Advanced Certificate); adolescence education/special education (Advanced Certificate); childhood education (MS Ed); curriculum and instruction (MS Ed); early childhood education (MS Ed). *Students:* 72 full-time (59 women), 32 part-time (26 women); includes 6 minority (4 Black or African American, non-Hispanic/Latino; 2 Hispanic/Latino), 2 international. Average age 28. 60 applicants, 78% accepted, 25 enrolled. In 2016, 37 master's awarded. *Entrance requirements:* For master's, minimum undergraduate GPA of 3.0. Additional exam requirements/recommendations for international students: Required—TOEFL (minimum score 550 paper-based; 80 iBT), IELTS (minimum score 6), PTE (minimum score 56). *Application deadline:* For fall admission, 4/1 priority date for domestic and international students; for spring admission, 10/15 priority date for domestic and international students; for summer admission, 3/15 priority date for domestic and international students. Applications are processed on a rolling basis. Application fee: $40. Electronic applications accepted. *Expenses: Tuition:* Full-time $14,382; part-time $799 per credit. *Required fees:* $814; $32 per credit. $88 per semester. Tuition and fees vary according to course load. *Financial support:* Career-related internships or fieldwork, scholarships/grants, tuition waivers (partial), and unspecified assistantships available. Support available to part-time students. Financial award application deadline: 4/15. *Unit head:* Dr. Drey Martone, Chair, 518-454-5262, E-mail: martoned@strose.edu. *Application contact:* Cris Murray, Assistant Vice President for Graduate Recruitment and Enrollment, 518-485-3390, Fax: 518-458-5479, E-mail: grad@strose.edu.
Website: https://www.strose.edu/academics/schools/school-of-education/

Colorado Christian University, Program in Curriculum and Instruction, Lakewood, CO 80226. Offers corporate education (MACI); early childhood educator (MACI); elementary educator (MACI); instructional technology (MACI); master educator (MACI); online course developer (MACI); online teaching and learning (MACI); special education generalist (MACI). *Program availability:* Part-time, evening/weekend. *Degree requirements:* For master's, thesis optional, practicum. *Entrance requirements:* For master's, interviews, letters of recommendation. Additional exam requirements/recommendations for international students: Required—TOEFL. Electronic applications accepted. *Expenses:* Contact institution.

Columbia International University, Columbia Graduate School, Columbia, SC 29230-3122. Offers Bible teaching (MABT); counseling (MACN); early childhood and elementary education (MAT); educational administration (M Ed); educational leadership (PhD); instruction and learning (M Ed); teaching English as a foreign language (Certificate); teaching English as a foreign language and intercultural studies (MATF). *Program availability:* Part-time, evening/weekend, online learning. *Degree requirements:* For master's, internships, professional project. *Entrance requirements:* For master's, MAT; GRE (for some programs), minimum GPA of 2.7. Additional exam requirements/recommendations for international students: Required—TOEFL. Electronic applications accepted.

Columbus State University, Graduate Studies, College of Education and Health Professions, Department of Teacher Education, Columbus, GA 31907-5645. Offers curriculum and instruction in accomplished teaching (M Ed); early childhood education (M Ed, MAT, Ed S); middle grades education (M Ed, MAT, Ed S); secondary education (M Ed, MAT, Ed S), including biology (MAT), chemistry (MAT), earth and space science (MAT), English/language arts, general science (M Ed), history (MAT), mathematics, science (Ed S), social science (M Ed, Ed S); special education (M Ed, MAT, Ed S), including general curriculum (M Ed, MAT); teacher leadership (M Ed). *Accreditation:* NCATE. *Program availability:* Part-time, evening/weekend, 100% online, blended/hybrid learning. *Faculty:* 20 full-time (13 women), 19 part-time/adjunct (16 women). *Students:* 92 full-time (66 women), 212 part-time (179 women); includes 113 minority (104 Black or African American, non-Hispanic/Latino; 1 American Indian or Alaska Native, non-Hispanic/Latino; 2 Asian, non-Hispanic/Latino; 4 Hispanic/Latino; 2 Two or more races, non-Hispanic/Latino), 5 international. Average age 34. 209 applicants, 56% accepted, 79 enrolled. In 2016, 111 master's, 18 other advanced degrees awarded. *Degree requirements:* For Ed S, thesis or alternative. *Entrance requirements:* For master's, GRE General Test, minimum undergraduate GPA of 2.75; for Ed S, GRE General Test, minimum undergraduate GPA of 2.75, graduate 3.0. Additional exam requirements/recommendations for international students: Required—TOEFL (minimum score 550 paper-based; 79 iBT). *Application deadline:* For fall admission, 6/30 for domestic students, 5/1 for international students; for spring admission, 11/1 for domestic and international students; for summer admission, 3/1 for domestic and international students. Applications are processed on a rolling basis. Application fee: $50. Electronic applications accepted. *Expenses:* Tuition, state resident: full-time $4804; part-time $2412 per semester hour. Tuition, nonresident: full-time $19,218; part-time $9612 per semester hour. *Required fees:* $1850; $1850 per semester hour. Tuition and fees vary according to program. *Financial support:* In 2016–17, 60 students received support, including 12 research assistantships with partial tuition reimbursements available (averaging $3,000 per year); career-related internships or fieldwork, Federal Work-Study, institutionally sponsored loans, scholarships/grants, tuition waivers (partial), and unspecified assistantships also available. Support available to part-time students. Financial award application deadline: 5/1; financial award applicants required to submit FAFSA. *Unit head:* Dr. Jan Burcham, Department Chair, 706-507-8519, Fax: 706-568-3134, E-mail: burcham_jan@columbusstate.edu. *Application contact:* Kristin Williams,

Director of International and Graduate Recruitment, 706-507-8848, Fax: 706-568-5091, E-mail: williams_kristin@columbusstate.edu.
Website: http://te.columbusstate.edu/

Concordia University, College of Education, Portland, OR 97211-6099. Offers career and technical education (M Ed); curriculum and instruction (M Ed), including adolescent literacy, career and technical education, e-learning/technology education, early childhood education, English for speakers of other languages, English language development, environmental education, mathematics, methods and curriculum, reading, science, teacher leadership, the inclusive classroom; early childhood (MAT); education leadership (Ed D); educational administration (M Ed); elementary education (MAT); secondary education (MAT); special education (M Ed); teacher leadership (Ed D). *Program availability:* Part-time, online learning. *Degree requirements:* For master's, comprehensive exam, work samples/portfolio. *Entrance requirements:* For master's, California Basic Educational Skills Test or PRAXIS I, minimum undergraduate GPA of 2.8, graduate 3.0; 2 letters of recommendation. Additional exam requirements/ recommendations for international students: Required—TOEFL (minimum score 525 paper-based). Electronic applications accepted. *Faculty research:* Learner-centered classroom, brain-based learning, future of online learning.

Concordia University Chicago, College of Education, Program in Early Childhood Education, River Forest, IL 60305-1499. Offers MA, Ed D. *Program availability:* Part-time, evening/weekend. *Degree requirements:* For master's, comprehensive exam, thesis. *Entrance requirements:* For master's, minimum GPA of 2.9; for doctorate, MAT or GRE, minimum graduate GPA of 3.5. Additional exam requirements/ recommendations for international students: Required—TOEFL (minimum score 550 paper-based). Electronic applications accepted. *Faculty research:* Child care training project, "Children in Worship" project, ethical development of children.

Concordia University Chicago, College of Education, Program in Teaching, River Forest, IL 60305-1499. Offers early childhood education (MAT); elementary education (MAT); secondary education (MAT). *Degree requirements:* For master's, thesis or alternative. *Entrance requirements:* For master's, minimum GPA of 2.9. Additional exam requirements/recommendations for international students: Required—TOEFL (minimum score 550 paper-based). Electronic applications accepted.

Concordia University, Nebraska, Graduate Programs in Education, Program in Early Childhood Education, Seward, NE 68434-1556. Offers M Ed. *Accreditation:* NCATE. *Program availability:* Part-time. *Degree requirements:* For master's, comprehensive exam, thesis or alternative. *Entrance requirements:* For master's, GRE, MAT, or NTE, minimum GPA of 3.0, BS in education or equivalent. Additional exam requirements/ recommendations for international students: Required—TOEFL.

Concordia University Wisconsin, Graduate Programs, Department of Education, Program in Early Childhood, Mequon, WI 53097-2402. Offers MS Ed. *Degree requirements:* For master's, comprehensive exam, thesis or alternative. *Entrance requirements:* For master's, minimum GPA of 3.0, teaching license. Additional exam requirements/recommendations for international students: Required—TOEFL. Application fee: $35. *Financial support:* Application deadline: 8/1. *Unit head:* Amy Lindgren, Chair, 262-243-2714, E-mail: amy.lindgren@cuw.edu.

Daemen College, Education Department, Amherst, NY 14226-3592. Offers adolescence education (MS); childhood education (MS); childhood special education (MS); childhood special-alternative certification (MS); early childhood special-alternative certification (MS). *Accreditation:* TEAC. *Program availability:* Part-time. *Degree requirements:* For master's, thesis optional, research thesis in lieu of comprehensive exam; completion of degree within 5 years. *Entrance requirements:* For master's, 2 letters of recommendation (professional and character), proof of initial certificate of license for professional programs, resume. Additional exam requirements/ recommendations for international students: Required—TOEFL (minimum score 500 paper-based; 63 iBT), IELTS (minimum score 5.5). Electronic applications accepted. *Faculty research:* Transition for students with disabilities, early childhood special education, traumatic brain injury (TBI), reading assessment.

Dallas Baptist University, Dorothy M. Bush College of Education, Program in Educational Leadership, Dallas, TX 75211-9299. Offers charter school administration (M Ed); educational leadership K-12 (Ed D); principal certification (M Ed). *Program availability:* Part-time, evening/weekend, 100% online, blended/hybrid learning. *Application deadline:* Applications are processed on a rolling basis. Application fee: $25. Electronic applications accepted. Application fee is waived when completed online. *Expenses: Tuition:* Full-time $15,408; part-time $856 per credit hour. *Required fees:* $400 per semester. Tuition and fees vary according to course load and degree level. *Unit head:* Dr. Tam Jones, Program Administrator, 214-333-6841, E-mail: tamj@dbu.edu. *Application contact:* Bobby Soto, Director of Admissions, 214-333-5242, E-mail: graduate@dbu.edu.
Website: http://www3.dbu.edu/graduate/education.asp

Dallas Baptist University, Dorothy M. Bush College of Education, Teaching Program, Dallas, TX 75211-9299. Offers distance learning (MAT); early childhood through grade 6 certification (MAT); early childhood-12 (MAT); elementary (MAT); English as a second language (MAT); Montessori (MAT); multisensory (MAT); secondary (MAT). *Program availability:* Part-time, evening/weekend, 100% online, blended/hybrid learning. *Application deadline:* Applications are processed on a rolling basis. Application fee: $25. Electronic applications accepted. Application fee is waived when completed online. *Expenses: Tuition:* Full-time $15,408; part-time $856 per credit hour. *Required fees:* $400 per semester. Tuition and fees vary according to course load and degree level. *Unit head:* Dr. Carolyn Spain, Director, 214-333-5217, E-mail: carolyns@dbu.edu. *Application contact:* Bobby Soto, Director of Admissions, 214-333-5242, E-mail: graduate@dbu.edu.
Website: http://www3.dbu.edu/graduate/mat.asp

DePaul University, College of Education, Chicago, IL 60614. Offers bilingual bicultural education (M Ed, MA); counseling (M Ed, MA), including clinical mental health counseling, college student development, school counseling; curriculum studies (M Ed, MA, Ed D); early childhood education (M Ed, MA, Ed D); educating adults (MA); educational leadership (M Ed, MA, Ed D), including administration and supervision (M Ed, MA), principal preparation (M Ed, MA); elementary education (MA); mathematics education (MA); mathematics for teaching (MS); middle school mathematics education (MS); reading specialist (M Ed, MA); secondary education (M Ed); social and cultural foundations in education (MA); special education (M Ed, MA); world languages education (M Ed, MA). *Program availability:* Part-time, evening/weekend, online learning. *Degree requirements:* For doctorate, thesis/dissertation. Electronic applications accepted.

Dominican University, School of Education, River Forest, IL 60305-1099. Offers early childhood education (MS); education (MAT); elementary education (MA Ed); English as a second language (MA Ed); reading (MA Ed); special education (MS). *Accreditation:* NCATE. *Program availability:* Part-time, evening/weekend, 100% online, blended/hybrid learning. *Faculty:* 12 full-time (8 women), 64 part-time/adjunct (57 women). *Students:* 13 full-time (all women), 500 part-time (385 women); includes 88 minority (40 Black or African American, non-Hispanic/Latino; 3 American Indian or Alaska Native, non-Hispanic/Latino; 18 Asian, non-Hispanic/Latino; 11 Hispanic/Latino; 2 Native Hawaiian or other Pacific Islander, non-Hispanic/Latino; 14 Two or more races, non-Hispanic/ Latino), 1 international. Average age 32. 162 applicants, 96% accepted, 104 enrolled. In 2016, 200 master's awarded. *Entrance requirements:* For master's, Illinois Test of Basic Skills. Additional exam requirements/recommendations for international students: Required—TOEFL (minimum score 550 paper-based; 79 iBT). *Application deadline:* Applications are processed on a rolling basis. Application fee: $25. *Expenses:* $550 per credit hour. *Financial support:* Career-related internships or fieldwork, scholarships/ grants, tuition waivers (partial), and unspecified assistantships available. Support available to part-time students. Financial award application deadline: 8/15; financial award applicants required to submit FAFSA. *Faculty research:* Governance of private education institutions, reading and language arts, inclusion, organizational planning, leadership and vision. *Unit head:* Dr. Colleen Reardon, Interim Executive Director, School of Education, 708-524-6643, Fax: 708-524-6665, E-mail: creardon@dom.edu. *Application contact:* Keven Hansen, Coordinator of Recruitment and Admissions, 708-524-6921, Fax: 708-524-6665, E-mail: educate@dom.edu.
Website: http://educate.dom.edu/

Duquesne University, School of Education, Department of Instruction and Leadership, Program in Early Level (PreK-4) Education, Pittsburgh, PA 15282-0001. Offers MS Ed. *Program availability:* Part-time, evening/weekend. *Faculty:* 3 full-time (2 women). *Students:* 18 full-time (all women), 5 part-time (all women); includes 4 minority (2 Black or African American, non-Hispanic/Latino; 1 Asian, non-Hispanic/Latino; 1 Two or more races, non-Hispanic/Latino). Average age 30. 18 applicants, 100% accepted, 4 enrolled. In 2016, 18 master's awarded. *Degree requirements:* For master's, thesis optional. *Entrance requirements:* For master's, bachelor's degree. Additional exam requirements/ recommendations for international students: Required—TOEFL (minimum score 550 paper-based), IELTS (minimum score 7). *Application deadline:* For fall admission, 9/1 for domestic students; for spring admission, 1/1 for domestic students. Applications are processed on a rolling basis. Application fee: $0. Electronic applications accepted. *Expenses: Tuition:* Full-time $22,212; part-time $1234 per credit. Tuition and fees vary according to program. *Unit head:* Dr. Julia Williams, Assistant Professor, 412-396-6098, Fax: 412-396-5388, E-mail: williamsj@duq.edu. *Application contact:* Michael Dolinger, Director of Student and Academic Services, 412-396-6647, Fax: 412-396-5585, E-mail: dolingerm@duq.edu.
Website: http://www.duq.edu/academics/schools/education/graduate-programs/ms-early-level-prek-4

East Carolina University, Graduate School, College of Health and Human Performance, Department of Human Development and Family Science, Greenville, NC 27858-4353. Offers birth through kindergarten education (MA Ed); child development and family relations (MS); marriage and family therapy (MS); medical family therapy (PhD). *Accreditation:* AAMFT/COAMFTE. *Program availability:* Part-time. *Students:* 67 full-time (62 women), 25 part-time (23 women); includes 22 minority (13 Black or African American, non-Hispanic/Latino; 2 American Indian or Alaska Native, non-Hispanic/ Latino; 1 Asian, non-Hispanic/Latino; 3 Hispanic/Latino; 1 Native Hawaiian or other Pacific Islander, non-Hispanic/Latino; 2 Two or more races, non-Hispanic/Latino), 1 international. Average age 29. 126 applicants, 49% accepted, 43 enrolled. In 2016, 24 master's, 4 doctorates awarded. *Degree requirements:* For master's, comprehensive exam, thesis optional. *Application deadline:* For fall admission, 1/15 for domestic students; for spring admission, 10/15 for domestic students. Applications are processed on a rolling basis. Application fee: $50. *Financial support:* Research assistantships, teaching assistantships, career-related internships or fieldwork, Federal Work-Study, institutionally sponsored loans, and scholarships/grants available. Support available to part-time students. Financial award application deadline: 6/1. *Faculty research:* Child care quality, mental health delivery systems for children, family violence. *Unit head:* Dr. Sharon Ballard, Interim Chair, 252-328-1356, E-mail: ballards@ecu.edu. *Application contact:* Dean of Graduate School, 252-328-6012, Fax: 252-328-6071, E-mail: gradschool@ecu.edu.
Website: http://www.ecu.edu/cs-hhp/hdfs/

Eastern Connecticut State University, School of Education and Professional Studies/ Graduate Division, Program in Early Childhood Education, Willimantic, CT 06226-2295. Offers MS. *Accreditation:* NCATE. *Program availability:* Part-time, evening/weekend. *Faculty:* 12 full-time (7 women), 21 part-time/adjunct (17 women). *Students:* 4 full-time (all women), 14 part-time (all women); includes 3 minority (1 Asian, non-Hispanic/Latino; 1 Native Hawaiian or other Pacific Islander, non-Hispanic/Latino; 1 Two or more races, non-Hispanic/Latino). Average age 31. 7 applicants, 86% accepted, 6 enrolled. In 2016, 7 master's awarded. *Degree requirements:* For master's, comprehensive exam or thesis. *Entrance requirements:* For master's, PRAXIS I, PRAXIS II, GRE, minimum GPA of 3.0, bachelor's degree from accredited institution. Additional exam requirements/ recommendations for international students: Required—TOEFL (minimum score 550 paper-based; 79 iBT); Recommended—IELTS (minimum score 6). *Application deadline:* For fall admission, 7/6 priority date for domestic and international students; for spring admission, 11/3 priority date for domestic and international students. Applications are processed on a rolling basis. Application fee: $50. Electronic applications accepted. *Expenses: Tuition, area resident:* Full-time $11,781; part-time $560 per credit. Tuition, state resident: full-time $15,031; part-time $568 per credit. Tuition, nonresident: full-time $24,581; part-time $568 per credit. *Required fees:* $40 per semester. Full-time tuition and fees vary according to course level, course load and reciprocity agreements. *Financial support:* In 2016–17, 1 student received support. Research assistantships, teaching assistantships, career-related internships or fieldwork, institutionally sponsored loans, and unspecified assistantships available. Financial award application deadline: 3/ 1; financial award applicants required to submit FAFSA. *Unit head:* Dr. Jeffrey Trawick-Smith, Advisor, 860-465-5232, Fax: 860-465-5099, E-mail: trawick@easternct.edu. *Application contact:* Paula Goyette, Graduate Division, School of Education and Professional Studies, 860-465-5292, Fax: 860-465-4538, E-mail: graduateadmissions@easternct.edu.

Eastern Illinois University, Graduate School, College of Education and Professional Studies, Department of Early Childhood, Elementary and Middle Level Education, Charleston, IL 61920. Offers elementary education (MS Ed). *Accreditation:* NCATE. *Program availability:* Part-time, evening/weekend. *Degree requirements:* For master's, comprehensive exam (for some programs), thesis (for some programs). *Entrance requirements:* For master's, GMAT or GRE. Additional exam requirements/ recommendations for international students: Required—TOEFL (minimum score 500 paper-based; 61 iBT), IELTS (minimum score 6). Electronic applications accepted.

Eastern Michigan University, Graduate School, College of Education, Department of Teacher Education, Program in Early Childhood Education, Ypsilanti, MI 48197. Offers MA. *Accreditation:* NCATE. *Program availability:* Part-time, evening/weekend. *Students:* 29 part-time (all women); includes 4 minority (1 Black or African American, non-Hispanic/Latino; 2 Hispanic/Latino; 1 Two or more races, non-Hispanic/Latino). Average age 31. 8 applicants, 88% accepted, 6 enrolled. In 2016, 20 master's awarded. *Degree requirements:* For master's, thesis optional. *Entrance requirements:* For master's, GRE. Additional exam requirements/recommendations for international students: Required—TOEFL. *Application deadline:* Applications are processed on a rolling basis. Application fee: $45. *Financial support:* Fellowships and teaching assistantships available. Support available to part-time students. Financial award applicants required to submit FAFSA.

Application contact: Dr. Brigid Beaubien, Coordinator, 734-487-3260, Fax: 734-487-2101, E-mail: brigid.beaubien@emich.edu.

Eastern Nazarene College, Adult and Graduate Studies, Division of Teacher Education, Quincy, MA 02170. Offers administration (M Ed); early childhood education (M Ed, Certificate); elementary education (M Ed, Certificate); English as a second language (Certificate); instructional enrichment and development (Certificate); middle school education (M Ed, Certificate); moderate special needs education (Certificate); principal (Certificate); program development and supervision (Certificate); secondary education (M Ed, Certificate); special education administrator (Certificate); special needs (M Ed); supervisor (Certificate); teacher of reading (M Ed, Certificate). M Ed also available through weekend program for administration, special needs, and teacher of reading only. *Program availability:* Part-time, evening/weekend. *Entrance requirements:* Additional exam requirements/recommendations for international students: Required—TOEFL (minimum score 550 paper-based).

Eastern New Mexico University, Graduate School, College of Education and Technology, Department of Educational Studies, Program in Special Education, Portales, NM 88130. Offers early childhood special education (M Sp Ed); general (M Sp Ed). *Program availability:* Part-time. *Degree requirements:* For master's, comprehensive exam, thesis optional. *Entrance requirements:* For master's, minimum GPA of 3.0, letter of recommendation, photocopy of teaching license or confirmation of entrance into alternative licensure program, writing assessment, 2 letters of application, special education license or minimum 30 hours of undergraduate course work. Additional exam requirements/recommendations for international students: Required—TOEFL (minimum score 550 paper-based; 79 iBT), IELTS (minimum score 6). Electronic applications accepted.

Eastern University, Loeb School of Education, St. Davids, PA 19087-3696. Offers ESL program specialist (K-12) (Certificate); general supervisor (PreK-12) (Certificate); health and physical education (K-12) (Certificate); middle level (4-8) (Certificate); multicultural education (M Ed); organizational leadership with education (PhD); Pre K-4 (Certificate); Pre K-4 with special education (Certificate); reading (M Ed); reading specialist (K-12) (Certificate); reading supervisor (K-12) (Certificate); school health supervisor (Certificate); school nurse (K-12) (Certificate); secondary biology education (7-12) (Certificate); secondary chemistry education (7-12) (Certificate); secondary communication education (7-12) (Certificate); secondary education (7-12) (Certificate); secondary English education (7-12) (Certificate); secondary math education (7-12) (Certificate); secondary social studies education (7-12) (Certificate); special education (M Ed); special education (7-12) (Certificate); special education (Pre K-8) (Certificate); special education supervisor (N-12) (Certificate); TESOL (M Ed); world language (Certificate), including French, Spanish. *Program availability:* Part-time, evening/weekend, online learning. *Students:* 41 full-time (32 women), 89 part-time (68 women); includes 54 minority (38 Black or African American, non-Hispanic/Latino; 3 Asian, non-Hispanic/Latino; 11 Hispanic/Latino; 2 Two or more races, non-Hispanic/Latino), 2 international. Average age 37. In 2016, 64 master's awarded. *Entrance requirements:* Additional exam requirements/recommendations for international students: Required—TOEFL. *Application deadline:* Applications are processed on a rolling basis. Application fee: $35. Electronic applications accepted. Application fee is waived when completed online. *Expenses:* $690 per credit. *Unit head:* Michael Dziedziak, Executive Director of Enrollment, 800-452-0996, E-mail: gpsadmissions@eastern.edu.
Website: http://www.eastern.edu/academics/programs/loeb-school-education-0

Eastern Washington University, Graduate Studies, College of Arts, Letters and Education, Department of Education, Program in Early Childhood Education, Cheney, WA 99004-2431. Offers M Ed. *Students:* 6 full-time (3 women); includes 4 minority (1 Asian, non-Hispanic/Latino; 3 Hispanic/Latino). Average age 32. 10 applicants, 70% accepted, 5 enrolled. In 2016, 3 master's awarded. *Degree requirements:* For master's, comprehensive exam, thesis (for some programs). *Entrance requirements:* For master's, GRE, minimum GPA of 3.0. Additional exam requirements/recommendations for international students: Required—TOEFL (minimum score 580 paper-based; 92 iBT), IELTS (minimum score 7), PTE (minimum score 63). *Application deadline:* Applications are processed on a rolling basis. Application fee: $75. Electronic applications accepted. *Expenses:* Tuition, state resident: full-time $11,000; part-time $5500 per credit. Tuition, nonresident: full-time $24,000; part-time $12,000 per credit. *Required fees:* $1300. One-time fee: $50 full-time. Part-time tuition and fees vary according to course load, campus/location and program. *Financial support:* Application deadline: 2/1; applicants required to submit FAFSA. *Unit head:* Robin Showalter, Program Coordinator, 509-359-6492, E-mail: rshowalter@mail.ewu.edu.

East Stroudsburg University of Pennsylvania, Graduate and Extended Studies, College of Education, Department of Early Childhood and Elementary Education, East Stroudsburg, PA 18301-2999. Offers M Ed. *Program availability:* Part-time, evening/weekend, online learning. *Students:* 6 part-time (5 women). *Degree requirements:* For master's, comprehensive exam, professional portfolio, curriculum project or action research. *Entrance requirements:* For master's, PRAXIS/teacher certification, letter of recommendation, Pennsylvania Department of Education requirements. Additional exam requirements/recommendations for international students: Recommended—TOEFL (minimum score 560 paper-based; 83 iBT), IELTS. *Application deadline:* For fall admission, 7/31 priority date for domestic students, 6/30 priority date for international students; for spring admission, 11/30 for domestic students, 10/31 for international students. Applications are processed on a rolling basis. Application fee: $50. Electronic applications accepted. *Expenses:* Tuition, state resident: full-time $8694; part-time $5796 per year. Tuition, nonresident: full-time $13,050; part-time $8700 per year. *Required fees:* $2550; $1690 per unit. $845 per semester. Tuition and fees vary according to course load, campus/location and program. *Financial support:* Research assistantships with tuition reimbursements, Federal Work-Study, and unspecified assistantships available. Support available to part-time students. Financial award application deadline: 3/1; financial award applicants required to submit FAFSA. *Unit head:* Andrew Whitehead, Chair, 570-422-3356, Fax: 570-422-3942, E-mail: awhitehead@esu.edu. *Application contact:* Kevin Quintero, Associate Director, Graduate and Extended Studies, 570-422-3890, Fax: 570-422-2711, E-mail: kquintero@esu.edu.

East Tennessee State University, School of Graduate Studies, College of Education, Department of Teaching and Learning, Johnson City, TN 37614. Offers early childhood education (MA, PhD); early childhood education emergent inquiry (Post-Master's Certificate); special education (M Ed), including advanced practitioner, early childhood special education, special education. *Program availability:* Part-time. *Degree requirements:* For master's, thesis (for some programs), practicum, residency, or thesis; for doctorate, comprehensive exam, thesis/dissertation, apprenticeship. *Entrance requirements:* For master's, PRAXIS I or Tennessee teaching license (for special education only), minimum GPA of 3.0 (or complete probationary period with no grade lower than B for first 9 graduate hours for early childhood education); for doctorate, GRE General Test, professional resume; master's degree in early childhood or related field; interview; four letters of recommendation; for Post-Master's Certificate, bachelor's or master's degree in early childhood or related field; two years of experience working with young children (preferred). Additional exam requirements/recommendations for international students: Required—TOEFL (minimum score 550 paper-based; 79 iBT). *Faculty research:* Teaching students with significant disabilities, problem-solving in toddlers, children and their development and learning, connecting classroom environment to student engagement in PreK-3, bilingual education in Ecuador, positive discipline/behavior support programs, early childhood relationships, international and comparative special education.

Edinboro University of Pennsylvania, Department of Early Childhood and Reading, Edinboro, PA 16444. Offers arts infusion (Graduate Certificate); early childhood education (M Ed); reading (M Ed); reading specialist (Graduate Certificate). *Program availability:* Part-time, evening/weekend. *Degree requirements:* For master's, thesis or alternative, competency exam; for Graduate Certificate, thesis or alternative. *Entrance requirements:* For master's and Graduate Certificate, GRE or MAT, minimum QPA of 2.5. Electronic applications accepted.

Elms College, Division of Education, Chicopee, MA 01013-2839. Offers early childhood education (MAT); education (M Ed, CAGS); elementary education (MAT); English as a second language (MAT); reading (MAT); secondary education (MAT), including biology education, English education, Spanish education; special education (MAT). *Program availability:* Part-time, evening/weekend. *Faculty:* 5 full-time (all women), 7 part-time/adjunct (6 women). *Students:* 6 full-time (all women), 136 part-time (111 women); includes 6 minority (1 Asian, non-Hispanic/Latino; 5 Hispanic/Latino). Average age 33. 27 applicants, 89% accepted, 20 enrolled. In 2016, 47 master's, 3 other advanced degrees awarded. *Degree requirements:* For master's, thesis (for some programs). *Entrance requirements:* For master's, Massachusetts Educators Certification Test, minimum GPA of 3.0; for CAGS, master's degree in education. Additional exam requirements/recommendations for international students: Required—TOEFL. *Application deadline:* For fall admission, 7/1 priority date for domestic students; for spring admission, 11/1 priority date for domestic students. Applications are processed on a rolling basis. Application fee: $30. *Expenses: Tuition:* Full-time $13,392. *Required fees:* $200. *Financial support:* In 2016–17, 2 teaching assistantships with partial tuition reimbursements were awarded; tuition waivers (partial) also available. Support available to part-time students. Financial award applicants required to submit FAFSA. *Unit head:* Dr. Mary Janeczek, Chair, Division of Education, 413-594-2761, Fax: 413-592-4871, E-mail: janeczeke@elms.edu. *Application contact:* Dr. Elizabeth Teahan Hukowicz, Dean, School of Graduate and Professional Studies, 413-265-2360, Fax: 413-265-2459, E-mail: hukowicze@elms.edu.

Emporia State University, Program in Early Childhood Education, Emporia, KS 66801-5415. Offers MS. *Accreditation:* NCATE. *Program availability:* Part-time, online learning. *Faculty:* 29 full-time (21 women), 3 part-time/adjunct (2 women). *Students:* 2 full-time (both women), 52 part-time (50 women); includes 5 minority (all Hispanic/Latino). 13 applicants, 100% accepted, 9 enrolled. In 2016, 14 master's awarded. *Degree requirements:* For master's, comprehensive exam or thesis, practicum. *Entrance requirements:* For master's, GRE General Test or MAT, essay exam, appropriate bachelor's degree, letters of recommendation. Additional exam requirements/recommendations for international students: Required—TOEFL (minimum score 520 paper-based; 68 iBT). *Application deadline:* For fall admission, 8/15 priority date for domestic students. Applications are processed on a rolling basis. Application fee: $30 ($75 for international students). Electronic applications accepted. *Expenses:* Tuition, state resident: full-time $5922; part-time $246.75 per credit hour. Tuition, nonresident: full-time $18,414; part-time $767.25 per credit hour. *Required fees:* $1884; $78.50 per credit hour. *Financial support:* Federal Work-Study, institutionally sponsored loans, health care benefits, and unspecified assistantships available. Financial award application deadline: 3/15; financial award applicants required to submit FAFSA. *Unit head:* Dr. Matt Siemears, Chair, 620-341-6057, E-mail: mseimear@emporia.edu. *Application contact:* Mary Sewell, Admissions Coordinator, 800-950-GRAD, Fax: 620-341-5909, E-mail: msewell@emporia.edu.

Endicott College, Van Loan School of Graduate and Professional Studies, Program in Early Childhood and Elementary Education, Beverly, MA 01915-2096. Offers M Ed. *Program availability:* Part-time, evening/weekend, 100% online, blended/hybrid learning. *Faculty:* 3 full-time (2 women), 9 part-time/adjunct (8 women). *Students:* 9 full-time (8 women), 14 part-time (13 women). Average age 30. 10 applicants, 100% accepted, 10 enrolled. In 2016, 11 master's awarded. *Degree requirements:* For master's, comprehensive exam, thesis, practicum. *Entrance requirements:* For master's, MAT or GRE, Massachusetts Test for Educators Licensure, Massachusetts teaching certificate, 2 professional letters of recommendation, personal statement. Additional exam requirements/recommendations for international students: Required—TOEFL. *Application deadline:* Applications are processed on a rolling basis. Application fee: $50. Electronic applications accepted. *Expenses:* Contact institution. *Financial support:* Career-related internships or fieldwork available. Financial award applicants required to submit FAFSA. *Unit head:* Dr. Aubry Threlkeld, Director of Graduate Licensure Programs, 978-232-2408, E-mail: athrelke@endicott.edu. *Application contact:* Ian Menchini, Director, Graduate Enrollment and Advising, 978-232-5292, E-mail: imenchin@endicott.edu.
Website: http://www.endicott.edu/VanLoan/Graduate-Studies/Master-Education.aspx

Endicott College, Van Loan School of Graduate and Professional Studies, Program in Integrative Education, Beverly, MA 01915-2096. Offers M Ed. Program offered in conjunction with The Institute for Educational Studies (TIES). *Program availability:* Part-time, online only, 100% online. *Faculty:* 1 full-time (0 women). *Students:* 29 full-time (27 women). Average age 37. 13 applicants, 100% accepted, 12 enrolled. In 2016, 15 master's awarded. *Degree requirements:* For master's, thesis. *Entrance requirements:* For master's, undergraduate transcript. Additional exam requirements/recommendations for international students: Required—TOEFL. *Application deadline:* Applications are processed on a rolling basis. Application fee: $50. Electronic applications accepted. *Expenses:* Contact institution. *Financial support:* Tuition waivers (partial) available. Financial award applicants required to submit FAFSA. *Faculty research:* Neurophenomonology, autopoiesis, systems view. *Unit head:* Dr. Phil Snow Gang, Academic Dean, 888-722-4547, Fax: 978-232-3000, E-mail: ties@endicott.edu. *Application contact:* Ian Menchini, Director, Graduate Enrollment and Advising, 978-232-5292, E-mail: imenchin@endicott.edu.
Website: http://www.endicott.edu/VanLoan/Graduate-Studies/Master-Education/Integrative-Education.aspx

Erikson Institute, Erikson Institute, Chicago, IL 60654. Offers child development (MS); early childhood education (M Ed, MS, PhD). PhD offered through the Graduate School. *Accreditation:* NCA. *Degree requirements:* For master's, comprehensive exam, internship; for doctorate, one foreign language, comprehensive exam, thesis/dissertation. *Entrance requirements:* For master's, experience working with young children, interview; for doctorate, GRE General Test, interview. *Faculty research:* Early childhood development, cognitive development, sociocultural contexts, early childhood education, family and culture, early literacy.

Erikson Institute, Academic Programs, Program in Early Childhood Education, Chicago, IL 60654. Offers MS. *Degree requirements:* For master's, comprehensive exam. *Entrance requirements:* For master's, 3 letters of recommendation, minimum GPA of 2.75. Additional exam requirements/recommendations for international students: Required—TOEFL.

Early Childhood Education

Fairleigh Dickinson University, College at Florham, University College: Arts, Sciences, and Professional Studies, Peter Sammartino School of Education, Program in Education for Certified Teachers, Madison, NJ 07940-1099. Offers PreK - 3 certification (MA).

Fairleigh Dickinson University, College at Florham, University College: Arts, Sciences, and Professional Studies, Peter Sammartino School of Education, Program in Teaching, Madison, NJ 07940-1099. Offers PreK - 3 certification (MAT).

Fairleigh Dickinson University, Metropolitan Campus, University College: Arts, Sciences, and Professional Studies, Peter Sammartino School of Education, Program in Education for Certified Teachers, Teaneck, NJ 07666-1914. Offers PreK - 3 certification (MA).

Fairleigh Dickinson University, Metropolitan Campus, University College: Arts, Sciences, and Professional Studies, Peter Sammartino School of Education, Program in Teaching, Teaneck, NJ 07666-1914. Offers PreK - 3 certification (MAT).

Fitchburg State University, Division of Graduate and Continuing Education, Program in Early Childhood Education, Fitchburg, MA 01420-2697. Offers M Ed. *Accreditation:* NCATE. *Program availability:* Part-time, evening/weekend. *Entrance requirements:* Additional exam requirements/recommendations for international students: Recommended—TOEFL (minimum score 550 paper-based; 79 iBT). Electronic applications accepted. *Expenses:* Tuition, state resident: full-time $2871; part-time $1914 per year. Tuition, nonresident: full-time $2871; part-time $1914 per year. *Required fees:* $3828. Tuition and fees vary according to program.

Five Towns College, Graduate Programs, Dix Hills, NY 11746-6055. Offers childhood education (MS Ed); composition and arranging (DMA); jazz/commercial music (MM); music education (MM, DMA); music history and literature (DMA); music performance (DMA). *Program availability:* Part-time. *Faculty:* 12 full-time (3 women), 6 part-time/adjunct (0 women). *Students:* 18 full-time (7 women), 6 part-time (2 women); includes 9 minority (3 Black or African American, non-Hispanic/Latino; 4 Asian, non-Hispanic/Latino; 1 Hispanic/Latino; 1 Two or more races, non-Hispanic/Latino), 1 international. Average age 35. 63 applicants, 11% accepted, 7 enrolled. In 2016, 4 master's, 2 doctorates awarded. *Degree requirements:* For master's, thesis, exams, major composition or capstone project, recital; for doctorate, comprehensive exam, thesis/dissertation, final oral exam. *Entrance requirements:* For master's, audition (for MM); New York state teaching certification (for MS Ed); personal statement, two letters of recommendation; for doctorate, 3 letters of recommendation, audition, essay. Additional exam requirements/recommendations for international students: Required—TOEFL (minimum score 520 paper-based; 85 iBT); Recommended—IELTS (minimum score 7). *Application deadline:* For fall admission, 9/1 for domestic and international students; for spring admission, 1/25 for domestic and international students. Applications are processed on a rolling basis. Application fee: $50. Electronic applications accepted. *Expenses: Tuition:* Full-time $15,000; part-time $625 per credit. *Required fees:* $600; $150 per semester. Tuition and fees vary according to degree level. *Financial support:* Fellowships with tuition reimbursements, teaching assistantships with tuition reimbursements, and tuition waivers (partial) available. Financial award applicants required to submit FAFSA. *Faculty research:* Teaching methods, teaching strategies and techniques, analysis of modern music, jazz. *Application contact:* Ronnie MacDonald, Director of Admissions, 631-656-2110, Fax: 631-656-2172, E-mail: admissions@ftc.edu.
Website: http://www.ftc.edu

Florida Atlantic University, College of Education, Department of Curriculum, Culture, and Educational Inquiry, Boca Raton, FL 33431-0991. Offers curriculum and instruction (M Ed, PhD, Ed S); early childhood education (M Ed); multicultural education (M Ed); TESOL and bilingual education (MA). *Program availability:* Part-time, evening/weekend. *Faculty:* 12 full-time (9 women), 1 (woman) part-time/adjunct. *Students:* 31 full-time (27 women), 93 part-time (68 women); includes 37 minority (17 Black or African American, non-Hispanic/Latino; 4 Asian, non-Hispanic/Latino; 15 Hispanic/Latino; 1 Two or more races, non-Hispanic/Latino), 2 international. Average age 35. 65 applicants, 60% accepted, 25 enrolled. In 2016, 17 master's, 18 doctorates, 3 other advanced degrees awarded. *Entrance requirements:* Additional exam requirements/recommendations for international students: Required—TOEFL (minimum score 500 paper-based; 61 iBT), IELTS (minimum score 6). *Application deadline:* For fall admission, 7/1 for domestic students, 2/15 for international students; for spring admission, 11/1 for domestic students, 7/15 for international students. Application fee: $30. *Expenses:* Tuition, state resident: full-time $7392; part-time $369.82 per credit hour. Tuition, nonresident: full-time $19,432; part-time $1024.81 per credit hour. *Faculty research:* Multicultural education, early intervention strategies, family literacy, religious diversity in schools, early childhood curriculum. *Unit head:* Dr. Dilys Schoorman, Chair, 561-297-3965, E-mail: dschoorm@fau.edu. *Application contact:* Dr. Eliah Watlington, Associate Dean, 561-296-8520, Fax: 261-297-2991, E-mail: ewatling@fau.edu.
Website: http://www.coe.fau.edu/academicdepartments/ccei/

Florida Atlantic University, College of Education, Department of Teaching and Learning, Boca Raton, FL 33431-0991. Offers curriculum and instruction (M Ed), including art, biology, chemistry, English, French, German, mathematics, music, physics, Pre-K and primary education, reading, social sciences, Spanish; elementary education (M Ed); environmental education (M Ed); reading education (M Ed); social foundations of education (M Ed), including educational psychology, educational technology, multilingual education. *Accreditation:* NCATE. *Program availability:* Part-time, evening/weekend. *Faculty:* 15 full-time (12 women), 2 part-time/adjunct (1 woman). *Students:* 25 full-time (20 women), 41 part-time (37 women); includes 18 minority (9 Black or African American, non-Hispanic/Latino; 2 Asian, non-Hispanic/Latino; 7 Hispanic/Latino), 7 international. Average age 32. 54 applicants, 59% accepted, 18 enrolled. In 2016, 36 master's awarded. *Entrance requirements:* For master's, GRE General Test, minimum GPA of 3.0 in last 2 years of undergraduate course work. Additional exam requirements/recommendations for international students: Required—TOEFL (minimum score 500 paper-based; 61 iBT), IELTS (minimum score 6). *Application deadline:* For fall admission, 7/1 for domestic students, 2/15 for international students; for spring admission, 11/1 for domestic students, 7/15 for international students. Applications are processed on a rolling basis. Application fee: $30. *Expenses:* Tuition, state resident: full-time $7392; part-time $369.82 per credit hour. Tuition, nonresident: full-time $19,432; part-time $1024.81 per credit hour. *Financial support:* Fellowships with partial tuition reimbursements, research assistantships with partial tuition reimbursements, teaching assistantships with partial tuition reimbursements, career-related internships or fieldwork, scholarships/grants, and unspecified assistantships available. *Faculty research:* Technology, teaching English to speakers of other languages, math teaching, electronic portfolio assessment, global perspectives through social studies. *Unit head:* Dr. Barbara Ridener, Chairperson, 561-297-3588, E-mail: bridener@fau.edu. *Application contact:* Dr. Eliah Watlington, Associate Dean, 561-296-8520, Fax: 261-297-2991, E-mail: ewatling@fau.edu.
Website: http://www.coe.fau.edu/academicdepartments/tl/

Florida International University, College of Arts, Sciences, and Education, Department of Teaching and Learning, Miami, FL 33199. Offers art education (MA, MS); curriculum and instruction (MS, Ed D, PhD, Ed S), including curriculum development (MS), elementary education (MS), English education (MS), learning technologies (MS), mathematics education (MS), modern language education (MS), physical education (MS), science education (MS), social studies education (MS), special education (MS); early childhood education (MS); exceptional student education (Ed D); foreign language education (MS), including foreign language education, teaching English to speakers of other languages (TESOL); international/intercultural education (MS); language, literacy and culture (PhD); mathematics, science, and learning technologies (PhD); physical education (MS), including sport and fitness; reading education (MS). *Program availability:* Part-time, evening/weekend. *Faculty:* 34 full-time (23 women), 64 part-time/adjunct (48 women). *Students:* 182 full-time (154 women), 231 part-time (190 women); includes 323 minority (69 Black or African American, non-Hispanic/Latino; 10 Asian, non-Hispanic/Latino; 237 Hispanic/Latino; 7 Two or more races, non-Hispanic/Latino), 19 international. Average age 34. 282 applicants, 58% accepted, 113 enrolled. In 2016, 184 master's, 12 doctorates awarded. *Degree requirements:* For doctorate, comprehensive exam, thesis/dissertation. *Entrance requirements:* For master's, GRE General Test, Florida General Knowledge Test or Florida College Level Academic Skills Test; for doctorate and Ed S, GRE General Test. Additional exam requirements/recommendations for international students: Required—TOEFL (minimum score 550 paper-based; 80 iBT), IELTS (minimum score 6.3). *Application deadline:* For fall admission, 6/1 priority date for domestic students, 4/1 for international students; for winter admission, 10/1 priority date for domestic students, 9/1 for international students; for spring admission, 3/1 priority date for domestic students, 2/1 for international students. Applications are processed on a rolling basis. Application fee: $30. Electronic applications accepted. *Expenses:* Tuition, state resident: full-time $8912; part-time $446 per credit hour. Tuition, nonresident: full-time $21,393; part-time $992 per credit hour. *Required fees:* $2185; $195 per semester. Tuition and fees vary according to program. *Financial support:* Research assistantships with tuition reimbursements and teaching assistantships with tuition reimbursements available. *Unit head:* Dr. Lynn Miller, Chair, 305-348-2005, Fax: 305-348-2086, E-mail: lynne.miller@fiu.edu. *Application contact:* Nanett Rojas, Assistant Director, Graduate Admissions, 305-348-7464, Fax: 305-348-7441, E-mail: gradadm@fiu.edu.
Website: http://education.fiu.edu

Florida State University, The Graduate School, College of Education, Program in Curriculum and Instruction, Tallahassee, FL 32306. Offers curriculum and instruction (MS, PhD, Ed S), including early childhood education, elementary education, English education, English teaching (MS), exceptional student education (MS), foreign and second language education, foreign and second language teaching (MS), mathematics education, mathematics teaching (MS), reading education and language arts, science education, social science education, social science teaching (MS), special education, special education studies (MS), visual disabilities (MS, Ed S). *Program availability:* Part-time, evening/weekend. Terminal master's awarded for partial completion of doctoral program. *Degree requirements:* For master's and Ed S, comprehensive exam, thesis optional; for doctorate, comprehensive exam, thesis/dissertation, diagnostic exam, preliminary exam, prospectus defense, dissertation defense. *Entrance requirements:* For master's, doctorate, and Ed S, GRE General Test, minimum upper-division GPA of 3.0. Additional exam requirements/recommendations for international students: Required—TOEFL (minimum score 550 paper-based, 80 iBT), IELTS (minimum score 6.5), Michigan English Language Assessment Battery (minimum score 77), or PTE (minimum score 55). Application fee: $30. Electronic applications accepted. *Expenses:* Tuition, state resident: full-time $7263; part-time $403.51 per credit hour. Tuition, nonresident: full-time $18,087; part-time $1004.85 per credit hour. *Required fees:* $1365; $75.81 per credit hour. $20 per semester. Tuition and fees vary according to campus/location. *Financial support:* Fellowships, research assistantships, teaching assistantships, scholarships/grants, tuition waivers (full and partial), and unspecified assistantships available. Financial award application deadline: 1/15; financial award applicants required to submit FAFSA. *Faculty research:* Identifying effective intervention strategies to improve reading skills; improving literacy teaching and learning through technology; understanding of student sense making, problem solving, the history and structure of STEM disciplines, and teacher education to support the development of ambitious instruction that supports the STEM learning of all students; examining practices of international education; identifying ways to support the professional development of teachers. *Unit head:* Dr. Sherry Southerland, Professor/Department Chair, 850-644-4880, Fax: 850-644-7736, E-mail: ssoutherland@admin.fsu.edu. *Application contact:* Libbie Crowley, Academic Support Specialist, 850-644-2122, Fax: 850-644-7736, E-mail: ecrowley@fsu.edu.
Website: http://education.fsu.edu/degrees-and-programs/graduate-programs

Fontbonne University, Graduate Programs, St. Louis, MO 63105-3098. Offers accounting (MBA, MS); art (MA); art (K-12) (MAT); business (MBA); computer science (MS); deaf education (MA); early intervention in deaf education (MA); education (MA), including autism spectrum disorders, curriculum and instruction, diverse learners, early childhood education, reading, special education; elementary education (MAT); family and consumer sciences (MA), including multidisciplinary health communication studies; fine arts (MFA); instructional design and technology (MS); management and leadership (MM); middle school education (MAT); secondary education (MAT); special education (MAT); speech-language pathology (MS); supply chain management (MS); theatre (MA). *Program availability:* Part-time, evening/weekend, online learning. *Faculty:* 32 full-time (24 women), 43 part-time/adjunct (26 women). *Students:* 456 full-time (313 women), 102 part-time (77 women); includes 138 minority (118 Black or African American, non-Hispanic/Latino; 1 American Indian or Alaska Native, non-Hispanic/Latino; 7 Asian, non-Hispanic/Latino; 9 Hispanic/Latino; 3 Two or more races, non-Hispanic/Latino), 37 international. *Degree requirements:* For master's, comprehensive exam (for some programs), thesis (for some programs). *Entrance requirements:* Additional exam requirements/recommendations for international students: Required—TOEFL (minimum score 500 paper-based; 65 iBT). *Application deadline:* For fall admission, 8/1 for international students; for spring admission, 12/1 for international students. Applications are processed on a rolling basis. Application fee: $25 ($30 for international students). Electronic applications accepted. *Expenses: Tuition:* Full-time $8436; part-time $703 per credit hour. *Required fees:* $18 per credit hour. Tuition and fees vary according to course load. *Financial support:* Teaching assistantships with partial tuition reimbursements and scholarships/grants available. Support available to part-time students. Financial award application deadline: 4/1; financial award applicants required to submit FAFSA. *Unit head:* Dr. Carey Adams, Vice President for Academic Affairs, 314-719-3609, E-mail: cadams@fontbonne.edu. *Application contact:* Lauryn Filip, Coordinator, Graduate Admission and Professional Studies, 314-889-4650, E-mail: admissions@fontbonne.edu.
Website: https://www.fontbonne.edu/academics/graduate-programs/

Fordham University, Graduate School of Education, Division of Curriculum and Teaching, New York, NY 10023. Offers curriculum and teaching (MSE); early childhood education (MSE); elementary education (MST); special education (MSE, Adv C); teaching English as a second language (MSE). *Accreditation:* NCATE. *Program availability:* Part-time, evening/weekend. *Degree requirements:* For Adv C, thesis. *Entrance requirements:* Additional exam requirements/recommendations for international students: Required—TOEFL (minimum score 577 paper-based; 90 iBT), IELTS (minimum score 7). Electronic applications accepted.

Framingham State University, Continuing Education, Program in Early Childhood Education, Framingham, MA 01701-9101. Offers M Ed.

Furman University, Graduate Division, Department of Education, Greenville, SC 29613. Offers curriculum and instruction (MA); early childhood education (MA); educational leadership (Ed S); English as a second language (MA); literacy (MA); school leadership (MA); special education (MA). *Accreditation:* NCATE. *Program availability:* Part-time, online learning. *Degree requirements:* For master's, comprehensive exam (for some programs), thesis or alternative. *Entrance requirements:* For master's, PRAXIS II. *Faculty research:* Literacy, pedagogy and practice, social justice, advanced leadership, achievement in high poverty schools.

Gallaudet University, The Graduate School, Washington, DC 20002-3625. Offers American Sign Language/English bilingual early childhood deaf education: birth to 5 (Certificate); audiology (Au D); clinical psychology (PhD); deaf and hard of hearing infants, toddlers, and their families (Certificate); deaf education (MA, Ed S); deaf history (Certificate); deaf studies (Certificate); educating deaf students with disabilities (Certificate); education: teacher preparation (MA), including deaf education, early childhood education and deaf education, elementary education and deaf education, secondary education and deaf education; educational neuroscience (PhD); hearing, speech and language sciences (MS, PhD); international development (MA); interpretation (MA, PhD), including combined interpreting practice and research (MA), interpreting research (MA); linguistics (MA, PhD); mental health counseling (MA); peer mentoring (Certificate); public administration (MPA); school counseling (MA); school psychology (Psy S); sign language teaching (MA); social work (MSW); speech-language pathology (MS). *Program availability:* Part-time. *Students:* 297 full-time (231 women), 129 part-time (97 women); includes 105 minority (35 Black or African American, non-Hispanic/Latino; 20 Asian, non-Hispanic/Latino; 39 Hispanic/Latino; 11 Two or more races, non-Hispanic/Latino), 22 international. Average age 30. 471 applicants, 52% accepted, 147 enrolled. In 2016, 138 master's, 25 doctorates, 14 other advanced degrees awarded. Terminal master's awarded for partial completion of doctoral program. *Degree requirements:* For master's, comprehensive exam (for some programs), thesis optional; for doctorate, comprehensive exam, thesis/dissertation. *Entrance requirements:* For master's and doctorate, GRE General Test or MAT, letters of recommendation, interviews, goals statement, American Sign Language proficiency interview, written English competency. Additional exam requirements/recommendations for international students: Required—TOEFL. *Application deadline:* For fall admission, 2/15 for domestic students. Applications are processed on a rolling basis. Application fee: $75. Electronic applications accepted. *Expenses: Tuition:* Full-time $17,100; part-time $950 per credit hour. *Required fees:* $3725; $276 per semester. *Financial support:* Fellowships, research assistantships, teaching assistantships, career-related internships or fieldwork, Federal Work-Study, scholarships/grants, tuition waivers (partial), and unspecified assistantships available. Support available to part-time students. Financial award application deadline: 7/1; financial award applicants required to submit FAFSA. *Faculty research:* Signing math dictionaries, telecommunications access, cancer genetics, linguistics, visual language and visual learning, integrated quantum materials, deaf legal discourse, advance recruitment and retention in geosciences. *Unit head:* Dr. Gaurav Mathur, Dean, Graduate School and Continuing Studies, 202-250-2380, Fax: 202-651-5027, E-mail: gaurav.mathur@gallaudet.edu. *Application contact:* Wednesday Luria, Coordinator of Prospective Graduate Student Services, 202-651-5400, Fax: 202-651-5295, E-mail: graduate.school@gallaudet.edu.

Gateway Seminary, Graduate and Professional Programs, Ontario, CA 91761-8642. Offers divinity (M Div); early childhood education (Certificate); education leadership (MAEL, Diploma); ministry (D Min); theological studies (MTS); theology (Th M); youth ministry (Certificate). *Accreditation:* ACIPE. *Program availability:* Part-time, evening/weekend. *Degree requirements:* For master's, thesis (for some programs); for doctorate, 2 foreign languages, thesis/dissertation. *Entrance requirements:* For doctorate, MAT. Additional exam requirements/recommendations for international students: Required—TOEFL (minimum score 550 paper-based). Electronic applications accepted.

George Mason University, College of Education and Human Development, Programs in Curriculum and Instruction, Fairfax, VA 22030. Offers advanced international baccalaureate (M Ed); assistive technology (M Ed); designing digital learning in schools (M Ed); early childhood education (M Ed); early childhood education for diverse learners (M Ed); elementary education (M Ed); English as a second language (M Ed); gifted child education (M Ed); history (M Ed); literacy (M Ed), including PK-12 classroom teachers, reading specialist; literacy leadership for diverse schools (M Ed), including K-12 reading; physical education (M Ed); science K-12 (M Ed); secondary education (M Ed), including biology, chemistry, earth science, English, history/social science, math, physics; special education (M Ed); teacher leadership (M Ed); teaching culturally, linguistically diverse and exceptional learners (M Ed); transformative teaching (M Ed). *Faculty:* 41 full-time (35 women), 53 part-time/adjunct (46 women). *Students:* 155 full-time (127 women), 821 part-time (697 women); includes 267 minority (82 Black or African American, non-Hispanic/Latino; 5 American Indian or Alaska Native, non-Hispanic/Latino; 75 Asian, non-Hispanic/Latino; 88 Hispanic/Latino; 1 Native Hawaiian or other Pacific Islander, non-Hispanic/Latino; 16 Two or more races, non-Hispanic/Latino), 19 international. Average age 33. 513 applicants, 90% accepted, 352 enrolled. In 2016, 347 master's awarded. *Degree requirements:* For master's, comprehensive exam, thesis (for some programs). *Entrance requirements:* For master's, PRAXIS Core (for some programs), minimum GPA of 3.0 in last 60 hours, licensed as teacher or educational administrator, official transcripts, goals statement, 3 recommendation letters, interview or writing sample (depending on program), up to 3 years' teaching experience (depending on program). Additional exam requirements/recommendations for international students: Required—TOEFL (minimum score 575 paper-based; 88 iBT), IELTS (minimum score 6.5), PTE (minimum score 59). *Application deadline:* For spring admission, 11/1 priority date for domestic and international students. Application fee: $75 ($80 for international students). Electronic applications accepted. *Expenses:* Tuition, state resident: full-time $10,628; part-time $443 per credit. Tuition, nonresident: full-time $29,306; part-time $1221 per credit. *Required fees:* $3096; $129 per credit. Tuition and fees vary according to program. *Financial support:* In 2016–17, 1 student received support, including 1 teaching assistantship (averaging $4,060 per year); career-related internships or fieldwork, Federal Work-Study, scholarships/grants, unspecified assistantships, and health care benefits (for full-time research or teaching assistantship recipients) also available. Support available to part-time students. Financial award application deadline: 3/1; financial award applicants required to submit FAFSA. *Faculty research:* Achievement gaps and superintendent decisions, constructivist view of classroom teaching, cost of cheating, creating a critical literacy milieu in kindergarten. *Unit head:* Rebecca Fox, Professor and Academic Program Coordinator, 703-993-4123, E-mail: rfox@gmu.edu.
Website: http://gse.gmu.edu/programs/gsemasters

The George Washington University, Graduate School of Education and Human Development, Department of Special Education and Disability Studies, Program in Early Childhood Special Education, Washington, DC 20052. Offers infant special education (MA Ed/HD). *Accreditation:* NCATE. *Students:* 13 full-time (all women), 11 part-time (all women); includes 6 minority (3 Black or African American, non-Hispanic/Latino; 1 Hispanic/Latino; 2 Two or more races, non-Hispanic/Latino), 7 international. Average age 32. 30 applicants, 87% accepted, 12 enrolled. In 2016, 12 master's awarded. *Degree requirements:* For master's, comprehensive exam. *Entrance requirements:* For master's, GRE General Test or MAT, minimum GPA of 2.75. *Application deadline:* For fall admission, 1/15 priority date for domestic students; for spring admission, 10/1 for domestic students. Applications are processed on a rolling basis. Application fee: $75. *Financial support:* In 2016–17, 19 students received support. Fellowships, career-related internships or fieldwork, Federal Work-Study, and tuition waivers (full) available. Financial award application deadline: 1/15; financial award applicants required to submit FAFSA. *Faculty research:* Computer-assisted instruction and learning, disabled learner assessment of preschool, handicapped children. *Unit head:* Dr. Marian H. Jarrett, Faculty Coordinator, 202-994-1509, E-mail: mjarrett@gwu.edu. *Application contact:* Sarah Lang, Director of Graduate Admissions, 202-994-1447, Fax: 202-994-7207, E-mail: slang@gwu.edu.

Georgia College & State University, Graduate School, The John H. Lounsbury College of Education, Program in Early Childhood Education, Milledgeville, GA 31061. Offers M Ed. *Accreditation:* NCATE. *Program availability:* Part-time, evening/weekend. *Students:* 7 full-time (5 women), 4 part-time (all women); includes 3 minority (all Black or African American, non-Hispanic/Latino). Average age 30. *Degree requirements:* For master's, minimum GPA of 3.0, complete program within 6 years. *Entrance requirements:* For master's, on-site writing assessment, GRE General Test taken within six years (minimum scores 1,000 verbal and quantitative combined if taken before August 1, 2011; 305 if taken on or after August 1, 2011), or MAT, 2 professional recommendations, level 4 teaching certificate, transcript, immunization verification. *Application deadline:* For fall admission, 7/1 priority date for domestic students; for spring admission, 11/1 priority date for domestic students; for summer admission, 4/1 priority date for domestic students. Applications are processed on a rolling basis. Application fee: $40. Electronic applications accepted. *Expenses:* $288 per credit hour in-state tuition; $1,027 per credit hour out-of-state; fees vary by hours enrolled. *Financial support:* In 2016–17, 1 student received support. Unspecified assistantships available. Support available to part-time students. Financial award application deadline: 3/1; financial award applicants required to submit FAFSA. *Unit head:* Dr. Joseph Peters, Dean, College of Education, 478-445-2518, Fax: 478-445-6582, E-mail: joseph.peters@gcsu.edu. *Application contact:* Shanda Brand, Graduate Coordinator, 478-445-1383, E-mail: shanda.brand@gcsu.edu.
Website: http://gcsu.edu/education/teached/early-childhood-education-med

Georgia Southern University, Jack N. Averitt College of Graduate Studies, College of Education, Department of Teaching and Learning, Program in Early Childhood Education, Statesboro, GA 30460. Offers M Ed, MAT, Ed S. *Accreditation:* NCATE. *Program availability:* Part-time, evening/weekend. *Students:* 30 full-time (all women), 37 part-time (all women); includes 10 minority (9 Black or African American, non-Hispanic/Latino; 1 Hispanic/Latino). Average age 28. 18 applicants, 94% accepted, 12 enrolled. In 2016, 30 master's, 4 other advanced degrees awarded. *Degree requirements:* For master's, portfolio, transition point assessments, exit assessment. *Entrance requirements:* For master's, GRE General Test or MAT, minimum cumulative GPA of 2.5. Additional exam requirements/recommendations for international students: Required—TOEFL (minimum score 550 paper-based; 80 iBT), IELTS (minimum score 6). *Application deadline:* For fall admission, 3/15 priority date for domestic and international students; for spring admission, 10/1 priority date for domestic students, 10/1 for international students; for summer admission, 3/1 priority date for domestic students, 3/1 for international students. Applications are processed on a rolling basis. Application fee: $50. Electronic applications accepted. *Expenses:* Tuition, state resident: full-time $7236; part-time $277 per semester hour. Tuition, nonresident: full-time $27,118; part-time $1105 per semester hour. *Required fees:* $2092. *Financial support:* In 2016–17, 3 students received support, including 4 fellowships with full tuition reimbursements available (averaging $7,750 per year); career-related internships or fieldwork, Federal Work-Study, scholarships/grants, tuition waivers (full), and unspecified assistantships also available. Support available to part-time students. Financial award application deadline: 4/15; financial award applicants required to submit FAFSA. *Faculty research:* Technology, effective instructional strategies, multiculturalism, children's literature, school violence. *Unit head:* Dr. Bruce Field, Department Chair, 912-478-0210, Fax: 912-478-0026. *Application contact:* Lydia Cross, Coordinator for Graduate Academic Services Center, 912-478-8664, E-mail: lcross@georgiasouthern.edu.
Website: http://coe.georgiasouthern.edu/eced/

Georgia Southwestern State University, School of Education, Americus, GA 31709-4693. Offers early childhood education (M Ed, Ed S); middle grades education (Ed S); middle grades language arts (M Ed); middle grades mathematics (M Ed); special education (M Ed). *Accreditation:* NCATE. *Faculty:* 13 full-time (8 women), 7 part-time/adjunct (6 women). *Students:* 209 full-time (199 women), 6 part-time (all women); includes 52 minority (45 Black or African American, non-Hispanic/Latino; 6 Hispanic/Latino; 1 Two or more races, non-Hispanic/Latino). Average age 33. In 2016, 57 master's awarded. *Degree requirements:* For master's, minimum cumulative GPA of 3.0; for Ed S, minimum GPA of 3.25 in all courses with no grade less than a B; degree must be completed within 7 calendar years from date of initial enrollment in graduate work. *Entrance requirements:* For master's, undergraduate degree from accredited institution; professional Georgia Teaching Certificate or eligibility; minimum undergraduate GPA of 2.75 as reported on official final transcripts from all accredited institutions attended; 2 confidential Administrative Recommendation Forms; for Ed S, master's degree from accredited college or university; professional Georgia Teaching Certificate or eligibility; minimum graduate GPA of 3.0 as reported on official final graduate transcripts from all accredited institutions attended; 2 confidential Administrative Recommendation Forms. *Application deadline:* For summer admission, 4/15 for domestic students. Application fee: $25. Electronic applications accepted. *Expenses:* $257 per credit hour for online program courses, plus fees, which vary according to enrolled credit hours. *Financial support:* Application deadline: 6/1; applicants required to submit FAFSA. *Unit head:* Dr. Rachel Abbott, Dean, 229-931-2145. *Application contact:* Whitnoy Ford, Admissions Specialist, Office of Graduate Admissions, 800-338-0082, Fax: 229-931-2983.
Website: https://gsw.edu/Academics/Schools-and-Departments/School-of-Education/index

Georgia State University, College of Education and Human Development, Department of Early Childhood Education, Atlanta, GA 30302-3083. Offers early childhood and elementary education (PhD); early childhood education (M Ed, Ed S); mathematics education (M Ed); urban education (M Ed). *Accreditation:* NCATE. *Program availability:* Part-time, evening/weekend. *Faculty:* 27 full-time (22 women). *Students:* 68 full-time (60 women), 7 part-time (all women); includes 40 minority (33 Black or African American, non-Hispanic/Latino; 1 Asian, non-Hispanic/Latino; 4 Hispanic/Latino; 2 Two or more races, non-Hispanic/Latino), 3 international. Average age 32. 16 applicants, 44% accepted, 6 enrolled. In 2016, 35 master's, 4 doctorates awarded. *Degree requirements:* For master's, comprehensive exam (for some programs), thesis (for some programs); for doctorate, comprehensive exam, thesis/dissertation (for some programs); for Ed S, comprehensive exam (for some programs). *Entrance requirements:* For master's, GRE, undergraduate diploma; for doctorate and Ed S, GRE, master's degree. Additional exam requirements/recommendations for international students: Required—TOEFL (minimum score 550 paper-based; 79 iBT) or IELTS (minimum score 6.5). *Application deadline:*

Applications are processed on a rolling basis. Application fee: $50. Electronic applications accepted. *Expenses:* Tuition, state resident: full-time $6876; part-time $382 per credit hour. Tuition, nonresident: full-time $22,374; part-time $1243 per credit hour. *Required fees:* $2128; $1064 per term. Part-time tuition and fees vary according to course load and program. *Financial support:* In 2016–17, fellowships with full tuition reimbursements (averaging $24,000 per year), research assistantships with tuition reimbursements (averaging $4,000 per year), teaching assistantships with full tuition reimbursements (averaging $2,000 per year) were awarded; career-related internships or fieldwork, Federal Work-Study, institutionally sponsored loans, scholarships/grants, traineeships, health care benefits, tuition waivers (partial), and unspecified assistantships also available. Support available to part-time students. Financial award applicants required to submit FAFSA. *Faculty research:* Teacher development; language arts/literacy education; mathematics education; intersection of science, urban, and multicultural education; diversity in education. *Unit head:* Dr. Barbara Meyers, Department Chair, 404-413-8021, Fax: 404-413-8023, E-mail: barbara@gsu.edu. *Application contact:* Elaine King Jones, Administrative Curriculum Specialist, 404-413-8234, Fax: 404-413-8023, E-mail: ekjones@gsu.edu.
Website: http://ecee.education.gsu.edu/

Georgia State University, College of Education and Human Development, Department of Educational Psychology, Special Education, and Communication Disorders, Program in Education of Students with Exceptionalities, Atlanta, GA 30302-3083. Offers autism spectrum disorders (PhD); behavior disorders (PhD); communication disorders (PhD); early childhood special education (PhD); learning disabilities (PhD); mental retardation (PhD); orthopedic impairments (PhD); sensory impairments (PhD). *Accreditation:* NCATE. *Program availability:* Part-time, evening/weekend. *Degree requirements:* For doctorate, comprehensive exam, thesis/dissertation. *Entrance requirements:* Additional exam requirements/recommendations for international students: Required—TOEFL (minimum score 550 paper-based; 79 iBT) or IELTS (minimum score 6.5). *Application deadline:* For fall admission, 6/1 for domestic and international students; for winter admission, 11/1 for domestic and international students; for spring admission, 5/1 for domestic and international students. Application fee: $50. Electronic applications accepted. *Expenses:* Tuition, state resident: full-time $6876; part-time $382 per credit hour. Tuition, nonresident: full-time $22,374; part-time $1243 per credit hour. *Required fees:* $2128; $1064 per term. Part-time tuition and fees vary according to course load and program. *Financial support:* In 2016–17, fellowships with full tuition reimbursements (averaging $28,000 per year), research assistantships with full tuition reimbursements (averaging $2,000 per year) were awarded; scholarships/grants, health care benefits, and unspecified assistantships also available. *Faculty research:* Academic and behavioral supports for students with emotional/behavior disorders; academic interventions for learning disabilities; cultural, socioeconomic, and linguistic diversity; language and literacy development, disorders, and instruction. *Unit head:* Dr. Kristine Jolivette, Associate Professor, 404-413-8040, Fax: 404-413-8043, E-mail: kjolivette@gsu.edu. *Application contact:* Sandy Vaughn, Senior Administrative Coordinator, 404-413-8318, Fax: 404-413-8043, E-mail: svaughn@gsu.edu.
Website: http://esc.education.gsu.edu/academics-and-admissions/special-education/education-of-students-with-exceptionalities-ph-d/

Georgia State University, College of Education and Human Development, Department of Educational Psychology, Special Education, and Communication Disorders, Program in Multiple and Severe Disabilities, Atlanta, GA 30302-3083. Offers early childhood special education (M Ed); special education adapted curriculum (intellectual disabilities) (M Ed); special education deaf education (M Ed); special education general and adapted curriculum (autism spectrum disorders) (M Ed); special education physical and health disabilities (orthopedic impairments) (M Ed). *Accreditation:* NCATE. *Program availability:* Part-time. *Degree requirements:* For master's, variable foreign language requirement, comprehensive exam, thesis (for some programs). *Entrance requirements:* For master's, GRE. Additional exam requirements/recommendations for international students: Required—TOEFL (minimum score 550 paper-based; 79 iBT) or IELTS (minimum score 6.5). *Application deadline:* For fall admission, 6/1 for domestic and international students; for winter admission, 11/1 for domestic and international students; for spring admission, 5/1 for domestic and international students. Application fee: $50. Electronic applications accepted. *Expenses:* Tuition, state resident: full-time $6876; part-time $382 per credit hour. Tuition, nonresident: full-time $22,374; part-time $1243 per credit hour. *Required fees:* $2128; $1064 per term. Part-time tuition and fees vary according to course load and program. *Financial support:* In 2016–17, fellowships with full tuition reimbursements (averaging $25,000 per year), research assistantships with full tuition reimbursements (averaging $2,000 per year) were awarded; teaching assistantships with full tuition reimbursements, scholarships/grants, health care benefits, and unspecified assistantships also available. *Faculty research:* Literacy, language, behavioral supports. *Unit head:* Dr. Kathryn Wolff Heller, Professor, 404-413-8040, E-mail: kheller@gsu.edu. *Application contact:* Sandy Vaughn, Senior Administrative Coordinator, 404-413-8318, Fax: 404-413-8043, E-mail: svaughn@gsu.edu.

Gordon College, Graduate Education Program, Wenham, MA 01984-1899. Offers early childhood (M Ed); educational leadership (M Ed, Ed S); elementary education (M Ed); English as a second language (M Ed, Ed S); math specialist (M Ed); mathematics specialist (Ed S); middle school education (M Ed); moderate disabilities (M Ed); Montessori education (M Ed); reading (M Ed, Ed S); secondary education (M Ed). *Program availability:* Part-time, evening/weekend. *Faculty:* 17 full-time (9 women), 41 part-time/adjunct (34 women). *Students:* 81 full-time (61 women), 109 part-time (87 women); includes 28 minority (2 Black or African American, non-Hispanic/Latino; 11 Asian, non-Hispanic/Latino; 13 Hispanic/Latino; 2 Two or more races, non-Hispanic/Latino), 12 international. Average age 34. 190 applicants, 100% accepted, 141 enrolled. In 2016, 110 master's, 16 Ed Ss awarded. *Degree requirements:* For master's, action research or clinical experience (for most programs); for Ed S, action research or clinical experience (for some programs). *Entrance requirements:* For master's, minimum undergraduate GPA of 3.0; 2 official undergraduate transcripts; professional resume; 3 recommendation letters (one professional reference, one academic reference, one personal reference); 500-700 word statement of purpose; for Ed S, minimum master's GPA of 3.3; 2 official transcripts from undergraduate and graduate schools; professional resume; 3 recommendation letters (one professional reference, one academic reference, one personal reference); 500-700 word statement of purpose. Additional exam requirements/recommendations for international students: Required—TOEFL (minimum score 550 paper-based, 80 iBT) or IELTS (minimum score 6.5). *Application deadline:* Applications are processed on a rolling basis. Application fee: $75. *Expenses:* $325 per credit tuition, $75 per term fee. *Financial support:* Applicants required to submit FAFSA. *Faculty research:* Reading, early childhood development, English language learners, universal design for learning. *Unit head:* Dr. Janet Arndt, Director of Graduate Studies, 978-867-4355, Fax: 978-867-4663. *Application contact:* Julie Lenocker, Program Administrator, 978-867-4322, Fax: 978-867-4663, E-mail: graduate-education@gordon.edu.
Website: http://www.gordon.edu/graduate

Governors State University, College of Education, Program in Early Childhood Education, University Park, IL 60484. Offers MA. *Accreditation:* NCATE. *Program availability:* Part-time. *Faculty:* 47 full-time (31 women), 49 part-time/adjunct (39 women). *Students:* 1 (woman) full-time, 3 part-time (all women); includes 3 minority (all Black or African American, non-Hispanic/Latino). Average age 36. 7 applicants, 86% accepted, 3 enrolled. In 2016, 2 master's awarded. *Entrance requirements:* Additional exam requirements/recommendations for international students: Required—TOEFL (minimum score 550 paper-based; 80 iBT), IELTS. *Application deadline:* For fall admission, 4/1 for domestic students. Application fee: $50. Electronic applications accepted. *Expenses:* $307 per credit hour; $38 per term or $76 per credit hour fees. *Financial support:* Application deadline: 5/1; applicants required to submit FAFSA. *Unit head:* Timothy Harrington, Chair, Division of Education, 708-534-4361, E-mail: tharrington2@govst.edu. *Application contact:* Yakeea Daniels, Assistant Vice President for Enrollment Services/Director of Admission, 708-534-4510, E-mail: ydaniels@govst.edu.

Grand Canyon University, College of Education, Phoenix, AZ 85017-1097. Offers autism spectrum disorders (MA); curriculum and instruction (MA); early childhood education (M Ed); educational administration (M Ed); educational leadership (M Ed); elementary education (M Ed); gifted education (MA); instructional technology (MS); K-12 leadership (Ed S); reading (MA); secondary education (M Ed); secondary humanities education (M Ed); secondary STEM education (M Ed); special education (M Ed); teaching and learning (Ed D); teaching English to speakers of other languages (MA). *Program availability:* Part-time, evening/weekend, online learning. *Degree requirements:* For master's, publishable research paper (M Ed), e-portfolio. *Entrance requirements:* For master's, undergraduate degree from accredited, GCU-approved college, university, or program with minimum GPA 2.8. Additional exam requirements/recommendations for international students: Required—TOEFL (minimum score 550 paper-based; 79 iBT), IELTS (minimum score 6). *Application deadline:* For fall admission, 8/21 for domestic students, 7/2 for international students; for spring admission, 12/24 for domestic students, 11/1 for international students. Applications are processed on a rolling basis. Application fee: $100. Electronic applications accepted. *Financial support:* Federal Work-Study available. Support available to part-time students. Financial award applicants required to submit FAFSA. *Unit head:* Dr. Kimberly L. LaPrade, Dean, 602-639-6360, E-mail: kimberly.laprade@gcu.edu. *Application contact:* Dr. Kimberly L. LaPrade, Dean, 602-639-6360, E-mail: kimberly.laprade@gcu.edu.
Website: https://www.gcu.edu/college-of-education.php

Grand Valley State University, College of Education, Program in Special Education, Allendale, MI 49401-9403. Offers cognitive impairment (M Ed); early childhood developmental delay (M Ed); emotional impairment (M Ed); learning disabilities (M Ed); special education (M Ed). *Accreditation:* NCATE. *Program availability:* Part-time, evening/weekend. *Students:* 2 full-time (1 woman), 71 part-time (57 women); includes 3 minority (1 Hispanic/Latino; 2 Two or more races, non-Hispanic/Latino), 2 international. Average age 33. 9 applicants, 89% accepted, 2 enrolled. In 2016, 33 master's awarded. *Degree requirements:* For master's, project or thesis. *Entrance requirements:* For master's, GRE General Test or minimum GPA of 3.0, last 60 credits from regionally-accredited college/university, 3 letters of recommendation. Additional exam requirements/recommendations for international students: Required—TOEFL. *Application deadline:* Applications are processed on a rolling basis. Application fee: $30. Electronic applications accepted. *Expenses:* $628 per credit hour. *Financial support:* In 2016–17, 15 students received support. Career-related internships or fieldwork, Federal Work-Study, scholarships/grants, and unspecified assistantships available. *Faculty research:* Evaluation of special education program effects, adaptive behavior assessment, language development, writing disorders, comparative effects of presentation methods. *Unit head:* Dr. Amy Schelling, Director, 616-331-6243, Fax: 616-331-6294, E-mail: schellia@gvsu.edu. *Application contact:* Thomas Owens, Director, Student Information and Services Center, 616-331-6282, Fax: 616-331-6217, E-mail: owenst@gvsu.edu.

Grand Valley State University, College of Education, Programs in General Education, Allendale, MI 49401-9403. Offers adult and higher education (M Ed); early childhood education (M Ed); educational differentiation (M Ed); educational leadership (M Ed); educational technology integration (M Ed); elementary education (M Ed); middle level education (M Ed); school library media services (M Ed); secondary level education (M Ed); teaching English to speakers of other languages (M Ed). *Program availability:* Part-time, evening/weekend, 100% online, blended/hybrid learning. *Students:* 28 part-time (20 women); includes 6 minority (4 Black or African American, non-Hispanic/Latino; 1 American Indian or Alaska Native, non-Hispanic/Latino; 1 Hispanic/Latino). Average age 42. In 2016, 17 master's awarded. *Degree requirements:* For master's, project or thesis. *Entrance requirements:* For master's, GRE General Test or minimum GPA of 3.0, last 60 credits from regionally-accredited college/university, 3 letters of recommendation. Additional exam requirements/recommendations for international students: Required—TOEFL (minimum score 550 paper-based, 80 iBT), IELTS (6.5), or Michigan English Language Assessment Battery. *Application deadline:* Applications are processed on a rolling basis. Application fee: $30. Electronic applications accepted. *Expenses:* $628 per credit hour. *Financial support:* In 2016–17, 2 students received support. Career-related internships or fieldwork, Federal Work-Study, scholarships/grants, and unspecified assistantships available. *Faculty research:* Effectiveness of technology in education, parental involvement, effective teaching, effective schools research. *Unit head:* Dr. Doug Busman, Graduate Program Director, 616-331-6250, E-mail: busmando@gvsu.edu. *Application contact:* Thomas Owens, Director, Student Information and Services Center, 616-331-6282, Fax: 616-331-6217, E-mail: owenst@gvsu.edu.
Website: http://www.gvsu.edu/coe/

Harding University, Cannon-Clary College of Education, Searcy, AR 72149-0001. Offers advanced studies in teaching and learning (M Ed); art (MSE); behavioral science (MSE); counseling (MS, Ed S); early childhood special education (M Ed, MSE); education (MSE); educational leadership (M Ed, Ed S); elementary education (M Ed); English (MSE); French (MSE); history/social science (MSE); kinesiology (MSE); math (MSE); reading (M Ed); secondary education (M Ed); Spanish (MSE); teaching (MAT); teaching English as a second language (MSE). *Accreditation:* NCATE. *Program availability:* Part-time, evening/weekend. *Faculty:* 22 full-time (9 women), 51 part-time/adjunct (37 women). *Students:* 130 full-time (94 women), 321 part-time (234 women); includes 83 minority (50 Black or African American, non-Hispanic/Latino; 4 American Indian or Alaska Native, non-Hispanic/Latino; 6 Asian, non-Hispanic/Latino; 13 Hispanic/Latino; 10 Two or more races, non-Hispanic/Latino), 11 international. Average age 35. 125 applicants, 88% accepted, 110 enrolled. In 2016, 124 master's, 27 other advanced degrees awarded. *Degree requirements:* For master's, comprehensive exam (for some programs), thesis optional, portfolio(s); for Ed S, comprehensive exam, portfolio, project. *Entrance requirements:* For master's, GRE, MAT, PRAXIS; for Ed S, MAT or GRE. Additional exam requirements/recommendations for international students: Required—TOEFL (minimum score 550 paper-based; 79 iBT). *Application deadline:* For fall admission, 8/1 for domestic and international students; for spring admission, 1/1 for domestic and international students. Applications are processed on a rolling basis. Application fee: $35. Tuition and fees vary according to degree level and program. *Financial support:* In 2016–17, 31 students received support. Unspecified assistantships available. *Faculty research:* Reading, comprehension, school violence, educational technology, behavior, college choice, differentiated instruction, brain-based teaching. *Unit head:* Dr. Clara Carroll, Chair, 501-279-4501, Fax: 501-279-4083, E-mail:

ccarroll@harding.edu. *Application contact:* Information Contact, 501-279-4315, E-mail: gradstudiesedu@harding.edu.
Website: http://www.harding.edu/education

Hebrew College, Shoolman Graduate School of Jewish Education, Newton Centre, MA 02459. Offers early childhood Jewish education (Certificate); Jewish day school education (Certificate); Jewish education (MJ Ed); Jewish family education (Certificate); Jewish special education (Certificate); Jewish youth education, informal education and camping (Certificate). *Program availability:* Part-time, evening/weekend, online learning. *Degree requirements:* For master's, one foreign language. *Entrance requirements:* For master's, GRE, interview. Additional exam requirements/recommendations for international students: Required—TOEFL.

Henderson State University, Graduate Studies, Teachers College, Department of Advanced Instructional Studies, Arkadelphia, AR 71999-0001. Offers developmental therapy (MSE); dyslexia therapy (Graduate Certificate); education (MAT); educational technology leadership (Graduate Certificate); English as a second language (MSE, Graduate Certificate); instructional facilitator (MSE, Graduate Certificate); middle level education (MAT); special education (K-12) (MAT, MSE); special education/early childhood (MAT). *Accreditation:* NCATE. *Program availability:* Part-time. *Faculty:* 12 full-time (9 women), 5 part-time/adjunct (4 women). *Students:* 13 full-time (8 women), 79 part-time (66 women); includes 14 minority (8 Black or African American, non-Hispanic/Latino; 2 American Indian or Alaska Native, non-Hispanic/Latino; 2 Hispanic/Latino; 2 Two or more races, non-Hispanic/Latino). Average age 33. 21 applicants, 100% accepted, 21 enrolled. In 2016, 29 master's awarded. *Entrance requirements:* For master's, GRE General Test or MAT, minimum GPA of 2.7, teacher certification. Additional exam requirements/recommendations for international students: Required—TOEFL (minimum score 600 paper-based); Recommended—IELTS (minimum score 6.5). *Application deadline:* For fall admission, 8/1 priority date for domestic students, 6/30 priority date for international students; for spring admission, 1/1 priority date for domestic students, 11/30 priority date for international students. Applications are processed on a rolling basis. Application fee: $25 ($75 for international students). *Expenses:* Tuition, state resident: full-time $6288; part-time $3144 per credit hour. Tuition, nonresident: full-time $12,888; part-time $6444 per credit hour. *Required fees:* $1429; $1024 per credit hour. Tuition and fees vary according to course load and student level. *Financial support:* In 2016–17, 1 teaching assistantship with partial tuition reimbursement (averaging $4,000 per year) was awarded; scholarships/grants and unspecified assistantships also available. Financial award application deadline: 4/15; financial award applicants required to submit FAFSA. *Unit head:* Dr. Gary Smithey, Coordinator, 870-230-5361, Fax: 870-230-5455, E-mail: smitheg@hsu.edu. *Application contact:* Dr. Ken Taylor, Graduate Dean, 870-230-5126, Fax: 870-230-5479, E-mail: taylorke@hsu.edu.
Website: http://www.hsu.edu/Academics/TeachersCollege/AIS/index.html

Hofstra University, School of Education, Programs in Teacher Education, Hempstead, NY 11549. Offers bilingual education (MA, Advanced Certificate); bilingual extension (Advanced Certificate), including education/speech language pathology; business education (MS Ed); early childhood and childhood education (MS Ed); early childhood education (MA, MS Ed); education technology (Advanced Certificate); elementary education (MA, MS Ed), including science, technology, engineering, and mathematics (STEM) (MA); English education (MS Ed); family and consumer science (MS Ed); fine arts and music education (Advanced Certificate); fine arts education (MS Ed); foreign language and TESOL (MS Ed); foreign language education (MS Ed), including French, German, Russian, Spanish; learning and teaching (Ed D), including applied linguistics, art education, arts and humanities, early childhood education, English education, human development, math education, math, science, and technology, multicultural education, physical education, science education, social studies education, special education; mathematics education (MA, MS Ed); middle school extension (Advanced Certificate), including grades 5-6, grades 7-9; music education (MA, MS Ed); science education (MA, MS Ed), including biology, chemistry, earth science, geology, physics; secondary education (Advanced Certificate); social studies education (MA, MS Ed); teaching languages other than English and TESOL (MS Ed); TESOL (MS Ed, Advanced Certificate). *Program availability:* Part-time, evening/weekend, blended/hybrid learning. *Students:* 139 full-time (97 women), 145 part-time (106 women); includes 60 minority (15 Black or African American, non-Hispanic/Latino; 1 American Indian or Alaska Native, non-Hispanic/Latino; 12 Asian, non-Hispanic/Latino; 31 Hispanic/Latino; 1 Two or more races, non-Hispanic/Latino), 21 international. Average age 29. 255 applicants, 86% accepted, 122 enrolled. In 2016, 101 master's, 4 doctorates, 43 other advanced degrees awarded. *Degree requirements:* For master's, comprehensive exam, thesis (for some programs), exit project, student teaching, fieldwork, electronic portfolio, curriculum project, minimum GPA of 3.0; for doctorate, thesis/dissertation; for Advanced Certificate, 3 foreign languages, comprehensive exam (for some programs), thesis project. *Entrance requirements:* For master's, GRE, MAT, 2 letters of recommendation, portfolio, teacher certification (MA), interview, essay; for doctorate, GMAT, GRE, LSAT, or MAT; for Advanced Certificate, 2 letters of recommendation, essay, interview and/or portfolio, teaching certificate. Additional exam requirements/recommendations for international students: Required—TOEFL (minimum score 550 paper-based; 80 iBT). *Application deadline:* Applications are processed on a rolling basis. Application fee: $75. Electronic applications accepted. *Expenses: Tuition:* Full-time $1240. *Required fees:* $970. Tuition and fees vary according to program. *Financial support:* In 2016–17, 149 students received support, including 58 fellowships with full and partial tuition reimbursements available (averaging $5,309 per year), 5 research assistantships with full and partial tuition reimbursements available (averaging $7,073 per year); career-related internships or fieldwork, Federal Work-Study, institutionally sponsored loans, scholarships/grants, traineeships, tuition waivers (full and partial), and unspecified assistantships also available. Support available to part-time students. Financial award applicants required to submit FAFSA. *Faculty research:* Educational interventions that foster critical-thinking skills; teachers' attitudes about professional development; threats to teacher quality. *Unit head:* Dr. Eustace Thompson, Chairperson, 516-463-5749, Fax: 516-463-6275, E-mail: eustace.g.thompson@hofstra.edu. *Application contact:* Sunil Samuel, Assistant Vice President of Admissions, 516-463-4723, Fax: 516-463-4664, E-mail: graduateadmission@hofstra.edu.
Website: http://www.hofstra.edu/education/

Hofstra University, School of Education, Specialized Programs in Education, Hempstead, NY 11549. Offers applied behavior analysis (Advanced Certificate); early childhood special education (MS Ed, Advanced Certificate); educational and policy leadership (Ed D); educational leadership (Advanced Certificate), including school building leader/school district business leader; educational leadership and policy studies (MS Ed), including K-12; gifted education (Advanced Certificate), including school building leader/school district business leader; health education PK-12 teaching certification (MS); inclusive early childhood special education (MS Ed); inclusive elementary special education (MS Ed); inclusive secondary special education (MS Ed); literacy studies (MS Ed, Ed D, PhD, Advanced Certificate), including birth-grade 6 (MS Ed, Advanced Certificate), birth-grade 6 and special education (birth-grade2) (MS Ed), grades 5-12 (MS Ed, Advanced Certificate); physical education (MS); secondary education generalist (MS Ed), including students with disabilities 7-12; special education (MS Ed, Advanced Certificate); special education assessment and diagnosis (Advanced Certificate); special education generalist (MS Ed), including extension in secondary education; sport science (MS), including strength and conditioning; teaching students with severe or multiple disabilities (Advanced Certificate). *Program availability:* Part-time, evening/weekend, 100% online, blended/hybrid learning. *Students:* 149 full-time (115 women), 258 part-time (187 women); includes 97 minority (50 Black or African American, non-Hispanic/Latino; 1 American Indian or Alaska Native, non-Hispanic/Latino; 11 Asian, non-Hispanic/Latino; 34 Hispanic/Latino; 1 Native Hawaiian or other Pacific Islander, non-Hispanic/Latino), 5 international. Average age 32. 250 applicants, 88% accepted, 146 enrolled. In 2016, 85 master's, 13 doctorates, 35 other advanced degrees awarded. *Degree requirements:* For master's, one foreign language, comprehensive exam (for some programs), thesis (for some programs), electronic portfolio, capstone course, internship, practicum, student teaching, seminars, minimum GPA of 3.0; for doctorate, one foreign language, comprehensive exam, thesis/dissertation, qualifying hearing. *Entrance requirements:* For master's, GRE, interview, letters of recommendation, portfolio, essay, certification; for doctorate, GRE or MAT, interview, resume, essay, master's degree, 3 letters of recommendation, writing sample; for Advanced Certificate, GRE, interview, letters of recommendation, essay, professional experience, resume, master's degree. Additional exam requirements/recommendations for international students: Required—TOEFL (minimum score 550 paper-based; 80 iBT). *Application deadline:* Applications are processed on a rolling basis. Application fee: $75. Electronic applications accepted. *Expenses: Tuition:* Full-time $1240. *Required fees:* $970. Tuition and fees vary according to program. *Financial support:* In 2016–17, 244 students received support, including 117 fellowships with full and partial tuition reimbursements available (averaging $3,705 per year), 12 research assistantships with full and partial tuition reimbursements available (averaging $6,490 per year); career-related internships or fieldwork, Federal Work-Study, institutionally sponsored loans, scholarships/grants, traineeships, tuition waivers (full and partial), and unspecified assistantships also available. Support available to part-time students. Financial award applicants required to submit FAFSA. *Faculty research:* Collaborative teaching and learning; language and culture; new media literacies; applied behavior analysis; K-12 leadership development. *Unit head:* Dr. Elfreda Blue, Chairperson, 516-463-5762, Fax: 516-463-6184, E-mail: elfreda.blue@hofstra.edu. *Application contact:* Sunil Samuel, Assistant Vice President of Admissions, 516-463-4723, Fax: 516-463-4664, E-mail: graduateadmission@hofstra.edu. Website: http://www.hofstra.edu/education/

Holy Family University, Graduate and Professional Programs, School of Education, Master of Education Programs, Philadelphia, PA 19114. Offers early elementary education (PreK-Grade 4) (M Ed); education leadership (M Ed); general education (M Ed); reading specialist (M Ed); special education (M Ed); TESOL and literacy (M Ed). *Program availability:* Part-time. *Students:* 202 full-time, 58 part-time. 209 applicants, 77% accepted, 140 enrolled. In 2016, 123 master's awarded. *Degree requirements:* For master's, thesis optional. *Application deadline:* Applications are processed on a rolling basis. Application fee: $25. Electronic applications accepted. *Expenses: Tuition:* Part-time $751 per hour. *Required fees:* $140 per semester. One-time fee: $165 part-time. Part-time tuition and fees vary according to degree level and program. *Unit head:* Dr. Kevin Zook, Dean, 267-341-3246, Fax: 215-824-2438, E-mail: kzook@holyfamily.edu. *Application contact:* Donald Reimold, Director of Graduate Admissions, 267-341-5001, Fax: 215-637-1478, E-mail: dreimold@holyfamily.edu.

Hunter College of the City University of New York, Graduate School, School of Education, Department of Curriculum and Teaching, New York, NY 10065-5085. Offers bilingual education (MS); early childhood education (MS); educational supervision and administration (Ed D, AC), including administration and supervision (AC), instructional leadership (Ed D); elementary education (MS); teaching English as a second language (MA). *Students:* 133 full-time (102 women), 1,657 part-time (1,325 women); includes 691 minority (189 Black or African American, non-Hispanic/Latino; 2 American Indian or Alaska Native, non-Hispanic/Latino; 168 Asian, non-Hispanic/Latino; 332 Hispanic/Latino), 53 international. Average age 31. 963 applicants, 77% accepted, 529 enrolled. In 2016, 452 master's, 163 other advanced degrees awarded. *Degree requirements:* For master's, thesis; for AC, portfolio review. *Entrance requirements:* For degree, minimum B average in graduate course work, teaching certificate, minimum 3 years of full-time teaching experience, interview, 2 letters of support. Additional exam requirements/recommendations for international students: Required—TOEFL, TWE. *Application deadline:* For fall admission, 4/1 for domestic students; for spring admission, 11/1 for domestic students. Applications are processed on a rolling basis. *Financial support:* Federal Work-Study, scholarships/grants, and tuition waivers (partial) available. Support available to part-time students. *Faculty research:* Teacher opportunity corps (mentor program for first-year teachers), adult literacy, student literacy corporation. *Unit head:* Dr. Yang Hu, Chairperson, 212-772-4686. *Application contact:* Milena Solo, Director for Graduate Admissions, 212-772-4482, E-mail: milena.solo@hunter.cuny.edu.
Website: http://www.hunter.cuny.edu/school-of-education/departments/curriculum-teaching

Indiana University–Purdue University Indianapolis, School of Education, Indianapolis, IN 46202-5155. Offers curriculum and instruction (MS); early childhood (MS); educational leadership (MS, Certificate); English as a second language (Certificate); kindergarten (Certificate); language education (MS); reading (Certificate); school counseling (MS); special education (MS, Certificate). *Program availability:* Part-time, evening/weekend. *Faculty:* 35 full-time (27 women), 56 part-time/adjunct (42 women). *Students:* 125 full-time (86 women), 181 part-time (139 women); includes 106 minority (78 Black or African American, non-Hispanic/Latino; 9 Asian, non-Hispanic/Latino; 12 Hispanic/Latino; 7 Two or more races, non-Hispanic/Latino), 3 international. Average age 32. 73 applicants, 93% accepted, 68 enrolled. In 2016, 73 master's awarded. Terminal master's awarded for partial completion of doctoral program. *Degree requirements:* For master's, thesis optional. *Entrance requirements:* For master's, GRE General Test, minimum GPA of 2.5; for Certificate, official transcripts. Additional exam requirements/recommendations for international students: Required—TOEFL (minimum score 60 iBT), IELTS (minimum score 5.5). *Application deadline:* For fall admission, 5/1 for domestic students; for spring admission, 11/1 for domestic students. Application fee: $60 ($65 for international students). Electronic applications accepted. *Expenses:* $1,262 tuition, $213 general fee. *Financial support:* Applicants required to submit FAFSA. *Faculty research:* Educational policies and school leaders' responses to these; issues of intersectionality in the experiences of African American lesbian, gay, and bisexual students attending historically black colleges and universities and those who belong to black Greek-letter organizations; students' experiential knowledge and their evolving disciplinary-specific literacy and understanding; innovative program development; urban ESL teacher preparation; target-based instructional coaching. *Total annual research expenditures:* $2.1 million. *Unit head:* Dr. Robin Hughes, Executive Associate Dean, 317-274-6817, E-mail: roblhugh@iupui.edu. *Application contact:* Ky Shaw, Graduate Admissions Coordinator, 317-278-6778, E-mail: kycshaw@iupui.edu.
Website: http://education.iupui.edu/

Inter American University of Puerto Rico, Guayama Campus, Department of Education and Social Sciences, Guayama, PR 00785. Offers early childhood education (0-4 years) (M Ed); elementary education (M Ed). *Program availability:* Part-time. *Entrance requirements:* For master's, GRE, MAT, EXADEP, letters of recommendation, minimum GPA of 2.5. Electronic applications accepted.

Early Childhood Education

Iona College, School of Arts and Science, Department of Education, New Rochelle, NY 10801-1890. Offers adolescence education: biology (MS Ed, MST); adolescence education: English (MS Ed); adolescence education: mathematics (MST); adolescence education: social studies (MS Ed, MST); adolescence education: Spanish (MS Ed); adolescence special education 5-12 (MST); childhood and special education (MST); early childhood and childhood (MST); educational leadership (MS Ed). *Accreditation:* NCATE. *Program availability:* Part-time, evening/weekend. *Faculty:* 7 full-time (6 women), 4 part-time/adjunct (2 women). *Students:* 27 full-time (19 women), 27 part-time (18 women); includes 18 minority (4 Black or African American, non-Hispanic/Latino; 1 Asian, non-Hispanic/Latino; 12 Hispanic/Latino; 1 Two or more races, non-Hispanic/Latino). Average age 26. 6 applicants, 67% accepted, 3 enrolled. In 2016, 25 master's awarded. *Degree requirements:* For master's, thesis or alternative. *Entrance requirements:* For master's, minimum GPA of 3.0, NY State teaching certificate and bachelor's degree (for MS Ed). Additional exam requirements/recommendations for international students: Required—TOEFL (minimum score 550 paper-based; 80 iBT), IELTS (minimum score 6.5). *Application deadline:* For fall admission, 8/1 priority date for domestic students, 5/1 priority date for international students; for spring admission, 1/1 priority date for domestic students, 9/1 priority date for international students. Applications are processed on a rolling basis. Application fee: $50. Electronic applications accepted. *Expenses: Tuition:* Full-time $19,692; part-time $1094 per credit. *Required fees:* $245 per term. Tuition and fees vary according to program. *Financial support:* In 2016–17, 3 students received support. Unspecified assistantships available. Support available to part-time students. Financial award application deadline: 4/15; financial award applicants required to submit FAFSA. *Faculty research:* Engaging teacher educators in scientific process, cross-national comparisons of mathematics teaching, questioning strategies in the classroom, research methods, literacy development. *Unit head:* Margaret Smith, PhD, Chair, 914-633-2210, Fax: 914-633-2608, E-mail: msmith@iona.edu. *Application contact:* Richard McMahon, Coordinator, Graduate School of Education, 914-633-2552, E-mail: rmcmahon@iona.edu.
Website: http://www.iona.edu/Academics/School-of-Arts-Science/Departments/Education/Graduate-Programs.aspx

Jackson State University, Graduate School, College of Education and Human Development, Department of Elementary and Early Childhood Education, Jackson, MS 39217. Offers early childhood education (MS Ed, Ed D); elementary education (MS Ed, Ed S); reading education (MS Ed). *Accreditation:* NCATE. *Program availability:* Part-time, evening/weekend, 100% online, blended/hybrid learning. *Faculty:* 10 full-time (4 women). *Students:* 90 full-time (86 women), 132 part-time (123 women); includes 210 minority (207 Black or African American, non-Hispanic/Latino; 2 Hispanic/Latino; 1 Two or more races, non-Hispanic/Latino), 9 international. Average age 37. 137 applicants, 72% accepted, 58 enrolled. In 2016, 41 master's, 9 doctorates, 2 other advanced degrees awarded. Terminal master's awarded for partial completion of doctoral program. *Degree requirements:* For master's, comprehensive exam, thesis or alternative; for doctorate, comprehensive exam, thesis/dissertation. *Entrance requirements:* For master's, GRE General Test; for doctorate, MAT, teaching experience. Additional exam requirements/recommendations for international students: Required—TOEFL (minimum score 520 paper-based; 67 iBT). *Application deadline:* For fall admission, 3/1 priority date for domestic students, 3/1 for international students; for spring admission, 10/1 for domestic and international students. Applications are processed on a rolling basis. Application fee: $25. Electronic applications accepted. *Expenses:* Contact institution. *Financial support:* Career-related internships or fieldwork, Federal Work-Study, scholarships/grants, and unspecified assistantships available. Support available to part-time students. Financial award application deadline: 3/1; financial award applicants required to submit FAFSA. *Unit head:* Dr. Thea Williams-Black, Chair, 601-979-2341, E-mail: thea.h.williams-black@jsums.edu. *Application contact:* Dr. Thea Williams-Black, Chair, 601-979-2341, E-mail: thea.h.williams-black@jsums.edu.
Website: http://www.jsums.edu/earlyeducation/

Jacksonville State University, College of Graduate Studies and Continuing Education, College of Education and Professional Studies, Program in Early Childhood Education, Jacksonville, AL 36265-1602. Offers MS Ed. *Accreditation:* NCATE. *Program availability:* Part-time, evening/weekend. *Faculty:* 11 full-time (9 women), 1 (woman) part-time/adjunct. *Students:* 5 full-time (all women), 12 part-time (all women); includes 3 minority (all Black or African American, non-Hispanic/Latino). Average age 30. 16 applicants, 63% accepted, 5 enrolled. In 2016, 9 master's awarded. *Degree requirements:* For master's, comprehensive exam, thesis (for some programs). *Entrance requirements:* For master's, GRE General Test or MAT. Additional exam requirements/recommendations for international students: Required—TOEFL (minimum score 500 paper-based; 61 iBT). *Application deadline:* Applications are processed on a rolling basis. Application fee: $35. Electronic applications accepted. *Financial support:* In 2016–17, 1 student received support. Available to part-time students. Application deadline: 4/1; applicants required to submit FAFSA. *Unit head:* Dr. Janet Bavonese, Head, 256-782-8340, E-mail: jbavonese@jsu.edu. *Application contact:* Dr. Jean Pugliese, Associate Dean, 256-782-8279, Fax: 256-782-5321, E-mail: pugliese@jsu.edu.

James Madison University, The Graduate School, College of Education, Program in Early Childhood Education, Harrisonburg, VA 22807. Offers MAT. *Accreditation:* NCATE. *Program availability:* Part-time. *Students:* Average age 27. *Entrance requirements:* For master's, GRE General Test or MAT, PRAXIS I and II, 2-3 page written statement, faculty interview, minimum undergraduate GPA of 2.75. Additional exam requirements/recommendations for international students: Required—TOEFL. *Application deadline:* For fall admission, 5/1 priority date for domestic students; for spring admission, 9/1 priority date for domestic students. Applications are processed on a rolling basis. Application fee: $55. Electronic applications accepted. *Financial support:* Career-related internships or fieldwork and unspecified assistantships available. Financial award application deadline: 3/1; financial award applicants required to submit FAFSA. *Unit head:* Dr. Martha Ross, Academic Unit Head, 540-568-6255. *Application contact:* Lynette M. Bible, Director of Graduate Admissions, 540-568-6395, Fax: 540-568-7860, E-mail: biblelm@jmu.edu.

James Madison University, The Graduate School, College of Education, Program in Education, Harrisonburg, VA 22807. Offers early childhood education (preK-3) (MAT); educational leadership (M Ed); educational technology (M Ed); elementary education (MAT); equity and cultural diversity (M Ed); inclusive early childhood education (MAT); K-8 mathematics specialist (M Ed); middle education (MAT); reading education (M Ed); secondary education (MAT); Spanish language and culture for educators (M Ed); TESOL (MAT). *Accreditation:* NCATE. *Program availability:* Part-time, evening/weekend. *Faculty:* 21 full-time (12 women), 5 part-time/adjunct (2 women). *Students:* 249 full-time (220 women), 123 part-time (86 women); includes 43 minority (7 Black or African American, non-Hispanic/Latino; 7 Asian, non-Hispanic/Latino; 17 Hispanic/Latino; 12 Two or more races, non-Hispanic/Latino), 2 international. Average age 30. 355 applicants, 98% accepted, 312 enrolled. In 2016, 247 master's awarded. Application fee: $55. Electronic applications accepted. *Financial support:* In 2016–17, 16 students received support. Career-related internships or fieldwork, Federal Work-Study, and 22 assistantships (averaging $7911) available. Financial award application deadline: 3/1; financial award applicants required to submit FAFSA. *Unit head:* Dr. Phillip M. Wishon, Dean, 540-568-6572, E-mail: wishonpm@jmu.edu. *Application contact:* Lynette D. Michael, Director of Graduate Admissions, 540-568-6131 Ext. 6395, Fax: 540-568-7860, E-mail: michaeld@jmu.edu.
Website: http://www.jmu.edu/coe/index.shtml

Johns Hopkins University, School of Education, Master's Programs in Education, Baltimore, MD 21218. Offers counseling (MS), including clinical mental health counseling, school counseling; education (MS), including educational studies, gifted education, reading, school administration and supervision, technology for educators; elementary education (MAT); health professions (M Ed); intelligence analysis (MS); organizational leadership (MS); secondary education (MAT), including biology, chemistry, earth/space science, English, physics, social studies; special education (MS), including early childhood special education, general special education studies, mild to moderate disabilities, severe disabilities. *Program availability:* Part-time, evening/weekend, 100% online, blended/hybrid learning. *Students:* 345 full-time (265 women), 1,601 part-time (1,245 women); includes 837 minority (392 Black or African American, non-Hispanic/Latino; 7 American Indian or Alaska Native, non-Hispanic/Latino; 141 Asian, non-Hispanic/Latino; 207 Hispanic/Latino; 7 Native Hawaiian or other Pacific Islander, non-Hispanic/Latino; 83 Two or more races, non-Hispanic/Latino), 55 international. Average age 27. 1,352 applicants, 76% accepted, 819 enrolled. In 2016, 642 master's awarded. *Degree requirements:* For master's, comprehensive exam (for some programs), portfolio, capstone project and/or internship; PRAXIS II (subject area assessments) for initial teacher preparation programs that lead to licensure. *Entrance requirements:* For master's, GRE (for full-time programs only); PRAXIS I/core or state-approved alternative (for initial teacher preparation programs that lead to licensure), minimum of bachelor's degree from regionally- or nationally-accredited institution; minimum GPA of 3.0 in all previous programs of study; official transcripts from all post-secondary institutions attended; essay; curriculum vitae/resume; letters of recommendation (3 for full-time programs, 2 for part-time programs); dispositions survey. Additional exam requirements/recommendations for international students: Required—TOEFL (minimum score 600 paper-based; 100 iBT), IELTS (minimum score 7). *Application deadline:* For fall admission, 4/1 priority date for domestic students, 4/1 for international students; for spring admission, 10/1 priority date for domestic students, 10/1 for international students; for summer admission, 2/1 priority date for domestic students, 2/1 for international students. Applications are processed on a rolling basis. Application fee: $80. Electronic applications accepted. *Expenses:* Contact institution. *Financial support:* Application deadline: 4/1; applicants required to submit FAFSA. *Unit head:* Dr. Christopher C. Morphew, Dean. *Application contact:* Elisabeth Woodward, Director of Admissions, 410-516-9796, Fax: 410-516-9817, E-mail: soe.info@jhu.edu.
Website: http://education.jhu.edu

Jose Maria Vargas University, Program in Preschool Education, Pembroke Pines, FL 33026. Offers MS.

Kansas State University, Graduate School, College of Human Ecology, School of Family Studies and Human Services, Manhattan, KS 66506-1403. Offers applied family sciences (MS); communication sciences and disorders (MS); conflict resolution (Graduate Certificate); couple and family therapy (MS); early childhood education (MS); family and community service (MS); life-span human development (MS); personal financial planning (MS, PhD, Graduate Certificate); youth development (MS, Graduate Certificate). *Accreditation:* AAMFT/COAMFTE; ASHA. *Program availability:* Part-time, online learning. *Faculty:* 43 full-time (30 women), 4 part-time/adjunct (3 women). *Students:* 55 full-time (45 women), 87 part-time (73 women); includes 30 minority (9 Black or African American, non-Hispanic/Latino; 1 American Indian or Alaska Native, non-Hispanic/Latino; 1 Asian, non-Hispanic/Latino; 14 Hispanic/Latino; 1 Native Hawaiian or other Pacific Islander, non-Hispanic/Latino; 4 Two or more races, non-Hispanic/Latino), 6 international. Average age 29. 182 applicants, 29% accepted, 38 enrolled. In 2016, 39 master's, 17 other advanced degrees awarded. *Degree requirements:* For master's, comprehensive exam (for some programs), thesis optional. *Entrance requirements:* For master's, GRE, minimum GPA of 3.0 in last 2 years (60 semester hours) of undergraduate study; for doctorate, GRE. Additional exam requirements/recommendations for international students: Required—TOEFL (minimum score 600 paper-based). *Application deadline:* For fall admission, 2/1 priority date for domestic students, 1/1 priority date for international students; for spring admission, 10/1 priority date for domestic students, 8/1 priority date for international students; for summer admission, 2/1 priority date for domestic students, 12/1 priority date for international students. Applications are processed on a rolling basis. Application fee: $50 ($75 for international students). Electronic applications accepted. *Expenses:* Tuition, state resident: full-time $9670. Tuition, nonresident: full-time $21,828. *Required fees:* $862. *Financial support:* In 2016–17, 35 students received support, including 25 research assistantships (averaging $10,000 per year), 9 teaching assistantships with full tuition reimbursements available (averaging $10,000 per year); unspecified assistantships also available. Financial award application deadline: 3/1. *Faculty research:* Health and security of military families, training in and evaluation of professional human services (marriage and couple therapy, family life education, treatment of speech and swallowing disorders, financial therapy), disorders of communication and swallowing, family and relationship development and health, financial decision-making. *Total annual research expenditures:* $8.4 million. *Unit head:* Dr. Dottie Durband, Director, 785-532-5510, Fax: 785-532-5505, E-mail: dottie@ksu.edu. *Application contact:* Kristi Hageman, Administrative Specialist, 785-532-5510, Fax: 785-532-5505, E-mail: klsmith@ksu.edu.
Website: http://www.he.k-state.edu/fshs/

Kean University, College of Education, Program in Early Childhood Education, Union, NJ 07083. Offers administration in early childhood and family studies (MA); advanced curriculum and teaching (MA); classroom instruction - P-3 certification (MA). *Accreditation:* NCATE. *Program availability:* Part-time. *Faculty:* 15 full-time (9 women). *Students:* 1 full-time (0 women), 13 part-time (12 women); includes 7 minority (3 Black or African American, non-Hispanic/Latino; 3 Asian, non-Hispanic/Latino; 1 Hispanic/Latino). Average age 37. 42 applicants, 71% accepted, 30 enrolled. In 2016, 3 master's awarded. *Entrance requirements:* For master's, GRE General Test, PRAXIS Early Childhood Content Knowledge (for some programs), minimum GPA of 3.0, 2 letters of recommendation, teacher certification (for some programs), personal statement, official transcripts, resume. Additional exam requirements/recommendations for international students: Required—TOEFL (minimum score 550 paper-based; 79 iBT), IELTS (minimum score 6.5). *Application deadline:* For fall admission, 6/1 for domestic and international students; for spring admission, 12/1 for domestic and international students. Applications are processed on a rolling basis. Application fee: $75. Electronic applications accepted. *Expenses:* Tuition, state resident: full-time $13,156; part-time $640 per credit. Tuition, nonresident: full-time $17,831; part-time $785 per credit. *Required fees:* $3316; $151 per credit. Tuition and fees vary according to course level, course load, degree level and program. *Financial support:* Scholarships/grants and unspecified assistantships available. Financial award applicants required to submit FAFSA. *Unit head:* Dr. Polly Ashelman, Program Coordinator, 908-737-3785, E-mail: pashelma@kean.edu. *Application contact:* Brittany Gerstenhaber, Admissions Counselor, 908-737-7100, E-mail: grad-adm@kean.edu.
Website: http://grad.kean.edu/masters-programs/administration-early-childhood-family-studies

Kennesaw State University, Leland and Clarice C. Bagwell College of Education, Program in Graduate Education, Kennesaw, GA 30144. Offers educational leadership (M Ed); educational leadership technology (M Ed); elementary and early childhood education (M Ed); instructional technology (M Ed); middle grades education (M Ed); reading (M Ed); secondary education (M Ed); special education (M Ed); teaching English to speakers of other languages (M Ed). *Accreditation:* NCATE. *Program availability:* Part-time. *Degree requirements:* For master's, thesis or alternative. *Entrance requirements:* For master's, GRE General Test, T-4 state certification, minimum GPA of 2.75. Additional exam requirements/recommendations for international students: Required—TOEFL (minimum score 550 paper-based; 80 iBT), IELTS (minimum score 6.5). Electronic applications accepted.

Kent State University, College of Education, Health and Human Services, School of Lifespan Development and Educational Sciences, Program in Special Education, Kent, OH 44242-0001. Offers deaf education (M Ed); early childhood education (M Ed); educational interpreter K-12 (M Ed); general special education (M Ed); mild/moderate intervention (M Ed); special education (PhD, Ed S); transition to work (M Ed). *Accreditation:* NCATE. *Degree requirements:* For doctorate, comprehensive exam, thesis/dissertation. *Entrance requirements:* For master's, minimum undergraduate GPA of 2.75, moral character form, 2 letters of reference, goals statement; for doctorate and Ed S, GRE General Test, goals statement, 2 letters of reference, interview, resume. Additional exam requirements/recommendations for international students: Required—TOEFL (minimum score 550 paper-based; 80 iBT). Electronic applications accepted. *Expenses:* Tuition, state resident: full-time $10,864; part-time $495 per credit hour. Tuition, nonresident: full-time $18,380; part-time $837 per credit hour. *Faculty research:* Social/emotional needs of gifted, inclusion transition services, early intervention/ecobehavioral assessments, applied behavioral analysis.

Kent State University, College of Education, Health and Human Services, School of Teaching, Learning and Curriculum Studies, Program in Early Childhood Education, Kent, OH 44242-0001. Offers M Ed, MA, MAT. *Accreditation:* NCATE. *Degree requirements:* For master's, thesis (for some programs). *Entrance requirements:* For master's, GRE General Test (for licensure), 2 letters of reference, goals statement. Additional exam requirements/recommendations for international students: Required—TOEFL (minimum score 550 paper-based; 80 iBT). Electronic applications accepted. *Expenses:* Tuition, state resident: full-time $10,864; part-time $495 per credit hour. Tuition, nonresident: full-time $18,380; part-time $837 per credit hour. *Faculty research:* Parent-child relationships, professional preparation, curriculum and assessment.

Keuka College, Program in Childhood Education/Literacy, Keuka Park, NY 14478. Offers literacy 5-12 (MS); literacy B-6 (MS). *Faculty:* 7 full-time (5 women). *Students:* 9 full-time (8 women); includes 1 minority (Hispanic/Latino). Average age 23. 9 applicants, 100% accepted, 9 enrolled. In 2016, 8 master's awarded. *Degree requirements:* For master's, thesis, capstone project/student-led research project. *Entrance requirements:* For master's, GRE, minimum GPA of 3.0; 3 letters of recommendation (2 academic and one from cooperating teacher from student teaching or other professional). Additional exam requirements/recommendations for international students: Required—TOEFL (minimum score 550 paper-based). *Application deadline:* For fall admission, 8/15 priority date for domestic students; for winter admission, 12/15 priority date for domestic students; for spring admission, 4/15 priority date for domestic students. Applications are processed on a rolling basis. Application fee: $50. Electronic applications accepted. *Expenses:* Contact institution. *Financial support:* In 2016–17, 8 students received support. Scholarships/grants and tuition waivers (full and partial) available. Financial award applicants required to submit FAFSA. *Faculty research:* Marginalized populations, international literacy, teacher assessment. *Unit head:* Dr. Andrew Beigel, Director of Graduate Program in Education, 315-279-5442 Ext. 5662, E-mail: abeigel@keuka.edu. *Application contact:* Anna Decker, Secretary, Graduate Education, 315-279-5510, E-mail: adecker@keuka.edu.

Keystone College, Program in Early Childhood Education Leadership, La Plume, PA 18440. Offers M Ed. *Program availability:* Part-time, blended/hybrid learning. *Faculty:* 3 full-time (all women), 2 part-time/adjunct (both women). *Students:* 44 part-time (37 women). 35 applicants, 77% accepted, 23 enrolled. *Degree requirements:* For master's, internship, professional contribution, or addressing a grant initiative. *Entrance requirements:* For master's, GRE, college transcripts, resume or curriculum vitae, current clearances. Additional exam requirements/recommendations for international students: Required—TOEFL (minimum score 80 iBT) or IELTS (minimum score 6.5). *Application deadline:* For fall admission, 8/1 for domestic students; for spring admission, 12/1 for domestic students; for summer admission, 5/1 for domestic students. Applications are processed on a rolling basis. Application fee: $50. Electronic applications accepted. *Expenses:* Contact institution. *Financial support:* Unspecified assistantships available. Financial award application deadline: 5/1; financial award applicants required to submit FAFSA. *Unit head:* Fran Langan, PhD, Dean, School of Professional Studies, 570-945-8472, E-mail: fran.langan@keystone.edu. *Application contact:* Jennifer Sekol, Director of Admissions, 570-945-8117, Fax: 570-945-7916, E-mail: jennifer.sekol@keystone.edu.

Lander University, Graduate Studies, Greenwood, SC 29649-2099. Offers clinical nurse leader (MSN); emergency management (MS); Montessori education (M Ed); teaching and learning (M Ed). *Accreditation:* NCATE. *Program availability:* Part-time, online learning. *Degree requirements:* For master's, comprehensive exam, thesis or alternative. *Entrance requirements:* For master's, GRE General Test. Additional exam requirements/recommendations for international students: Required—TOEFL (minimum score 550 paper-based). Electronic applications accepted.

La Salle University, School of Arts and Sciences, Program in Education, Philadelphia, PA 19141-1199. Offers autism spectrum disorders (MA, Certificate); bilingual/bicultural studies (MA); classroom management (MA); dual early childhood and special education (MA); dual middle-level science and math and special education (MA); education (MA); English (MA); English as a second language (Certificate); history (MA); instructional coach (Certificate); instructional leadership (MA); reading specialist (MA, Certificate); secondary education (MA); special education (MA, Certificate). *Program availability:* Part-time, evening/weekend. *Faculty:* 5 full-time (4 women), 12 part-time/adjunct (8 women). *Students:* 10 full-time (all women), 98 part-time (74 women); includes 28 minority (13 Black or African American, non-Hispanic/Latino; 1 American Indian or Alaska Native, non-Hispanic/Latino; 1 Asian, non-Hispanic/Latino; 10 Hispanic/Latino; 3 Two or more races, non-Hispanic/Latino). Average age 34. 128 applicants, 84% accepted, 69 enrolled. In 2016, 53 master's awarded. *Degree requirements:* For master's, comprehensive exam. *Entrance requirements:* For master's, MAT or GRE, 2 letters of recommendation; for Certificate, GMAT or GRE, 2 letters of recommendation. Additional exam requirements/recommendations for international students: Required—TOEFL. *Application deadline:* For fall admission, 8/15 priority date for domestic students, 7/15 for international students; for spring admission, 12/15 priority date for domestic students, 11/15 for international students; for summer admission, 4/15 priority date for domestic students, 3/15 for international students. Applications are processed on a rolling basis. Application fee: $35. Electronic applications accepted. Application fee is waived when completed online. *Expenses:* Contact institution. *Financial support:* In 2016–17, 27 students received support. Scholarships/grants available. Support available to part-time students. Financial award application deadline: 8/31; financial award applicants required to submit FAFSA. *Unit head:* Dr. Greer Richardson, Director, 215-951-1806, Fax: 215-951-1843, E-mail: graded@lasalle.edu. *Application contact:* Elizabeth Heenan, Director, Graduate and Adult Enrollment, 215-951-1100, Fax: 215-951-1462, E-mail: heenan@lasalle.edu.
Website: http://www.lasalle.edu/grad-education-programs/

Lee University, Program in Education, Cleveland, TN 37320-3450. Offers art (MAT); curriculum and instruction (M Ed, Ed S); early childhood (MAT); educational leadership (M Ed, Ed S); elementary education (MAT); English and math (MAT); English and science (MAT); English and social studies (MAT); higher education administration (MS); history (MAT); history and economics (MAT); math and science (MAT); math and social studies (MAT); middle grades (MAT); science and social studies (MASW); secondary education (MAT); Spanish (MAT); special education (M Ed, MAT); TESOL (MAT). *Accreditation:* NCATE. *Program availability:* Part-time. *Faculty:* 13 full-time (6 women), 9 part-time/adjunct (4 women). *Students:* 35 full-time (27 women), 50 part-time (32 women); includes 12 minority (5 Black or African American, non-Hispanic/Latino; 5 Hispanic/Latino; 2 Two or more races, non-Hispanic/Latino), 4 international. Average age 30. 43 applicants, 79% accepted, 28 enrolled. In 2016, 42 master's, 6 other advanced degrees awarded. *Degree requirements:* For master's, variable foreign language requirement, thesis optional, internship. *Entrance requirements:* For master's, MAT or GRE General Test, minimum undergraduate GPA of 2.75, 3 letters of recommendation, interview, writing sample, official transcripts, background check; for Ed S, minimum undergraduate and master's GPA of 2.75, official transcripts for undergraduate and master's degrees. Additional exam requirements/recommendations for international students: Required—TOEFL (minimum score 61 iBT). *Application deadline:* For fall admission, 6/1 priority date for domestic and international students; for spring admission, 11/1 priority date for domestic and international students; for summer admission, 4/1 priority date for domestic and international students. Applications are processed on a rolling basis. Application fee: $25. Electronic applications accepted. *Expenses: Tuition:* Full-time $11,367; part-time $632 per credit hour. *Required fees:* $35 per term. One-time fee: $25. Tuition and fees vary according to program. *Financial support:* In 2016–17, 42 students received support. Career-related internships or fieldwork, Federal Work-Study, institutionally sponsored loans, scholarships/grants, and unspecified assistantships available. Financial award application deadline: 3/1; financial award applicants required to submit FAFSA. *Unit head:* Dr. William Kamm, Director, 423-614-8544, E-mail: wkamm@leeuniversity.edu. *Application contact:* Crystal Keeter, Graduate Education Secretary, 423-614-8544, E-mail: ckeeter@leeuniversity.edu.
Website: http://www.leeuniversity.edu/academics/graduate/education

Lehman College of the City University of New York, School of Education, Department of Early Childhood and Elementary Education, Program in Early Childhood Education, Bronx, NY 10468-1589. Offers MS Ed. *Accreditation:* NCATE. *Program availability:* Part-time, evening/weekend. *Entrance requirements:* For master's, minimum GPA of 2.7. *Faculty research:* TV programming, literacy, children's trauma conceptualization.

Le Moyne College, Department of Education, Syracuse, NY 13214. Offers adolescent education (MS Ed, MST); adolescent education/special education (MS Ed, MST); adolescent English (MST), including grades 7-12; adolescent English/special education (MST), including grades 7-12; adolescent foreign language (MST), including grades 7-12; adolescent history (MST), including grades 7-12; childhood education (MS Ed); childhood education/special education (MS Ed); elementary education (MS Ed); general education (MS Ed); inclusive childhood education (MST); literacy education (MS Ed), including birth to grade 6, grades 5-12; school building leader (MS Ed); school building leadership (CAS); school district business leader (MS Ed, CAS); school district leader (MS Ed); school district leadership (CAS); secondary education (MS Ed); special education (MS Ed); teaching English to speakers of other languages (MS Ed); urban studies (MS Ed). *Accreditation:* TEAC. *Program availability:* Part-time, evening/weekend. *Faculty:* 8 full-time (5 women), 20 part-time/adjunct (12 women). *Students:* 66 full-time (40 women), 155 part-time (117 women); includes 13 minority (4 Black or African American, non-Hispanic/Latino; 2 American Indian or Alaska Native, non-Hispanic/Latino; 2 Asian, non-Hispanic/Latino; 5 Hispanic/Latino), 3 international. Average age 30. 74 applicants, 99% accepted, 66 enrolled. In 2016, 81 master's, 53 CASs awarded. *Degree requirements:* For master's, thesis. *Entrance requirements:* For master's, bachelor's degree with minimum undergraduate GPA of 3.0, 2 letters of recommendation, transcripts. Additional exam requirements/recommendations for international students: Required—TOEFL (minimum score 550 paper-based; 79 iBT); Recommended—IELTS (minimum score 6.5). *Application deadline:* For fall admission, 4/1 priority date for domestic and international students; for spring admission, 10/1 priority date for domestic and international students; for summer admission, 3/1 priority date for domestic and international students. Applications are processed on a rolling basis. Application fee: $50. Electronic applications accepted. *Expenses:* $700 per credit hour. *Financial support:* In 2016–17, 21 students received support. Career-related internships or fieldwork, scholarships/grants, and health care benefits available. Support available to part-time students. Financial award applicants required to submit FAFSA. *Faculty research:* Minority teachers, special education, multiculturalism, literacy, technology, media literacy learning, autism, school district organization, service-learning, higher level problem solving, teacher leadership. *Unit head:* Dr. Stephen C. Fleury, Chair, Department of Education, 315-445-4376, Fax: 315-445-4744, E-mail: fleurysc@lemoyne.edu. *Application contact:* Kristen P. Richards, Senior Director of Enrollment Management, 315-445-5444, Fax: 315-445-6092, E-mail: trapaskp@lemoyne.edu.
Website: http://www.lemoyne.edu/education

Lesley University, Graduate School of Education, Cambridge, MA 02138-2790. Offers arts, community, and education (M Ed); autism studies (Certificate); curriculum and instruction (M Ed, CAGS); early childhood education (M Ed); ecological teaching and learning (MS); educational studies (PhD), including adult learning, educational leadership, individually designed; elementary education (M Ed); emergent technologies for educators (Certificate); ESLArts: language learning through the arts (M Ed); high school education (M Ed); individually designed (M Ed); integrated teaching through the arts (M Ed); literacy for K-8 classroom teachers (M Ed); mathematics education (M Ed); middle school education (M Ed); moderate disabilities (M Ed); online learning (Certificate); reading (CAGS); science in education (M Ed); severe disabilities (M Ed); special needs (CAGS); specialist teacher of reading (M Ed); teacher of visual art (M Ed); technology in education (M Ed, CAGS). *Accreditation:* TEAC. *Program availability:* Part-time, evening/weekend, online learning. *Degree requirements:* For master's, practicum; for doctorate, thesis/dissertation. *Entrance requirements:* For master's, Massachusetts Tests for Educator Licensure (MTEL), transcripts, statement of purpose, recommendations; interview (for special education); for doctorate, GRE General Test, transcripts, statement of purpose, recommendations, interview, master's degree, resume; for other advanced degree, interview, master's degree. Additional exam requirements/recommendations for international students: Required—TOEFL (minimum score 550 paper-based; 80 iBT). Electronic applications accepted. *Faculty research:* Assessment in literacy, mathematics and science; autism spectrum disorders; instructional technology and online learning; multicultural education and English language learners.

Lincoln University, Graduate Programs, Philadelphia, PA 19104. Offers counseling (MSC); early childhood education (M Ed), including PreK-4; early childhood education and special education (M Ed); educational leadership (M Ed), including principal certification; finance (MSB); human resources management (MSB); human services (MAHS). *Program availability:* Part-time, evening/weekend. *Faculty:* 11 full-time (5 women), 45 part-time/adjunct (24 women). *Students:* 191 full-time (131 women), 77 part-time (60 women); includes 245 minority (236 Black or African American, non-Hispanic/Latino; 1 American Indian or Alaska Native, non-Hispanic/Latino; 7 Hispanic/Latino; 1 Two or more races, non-Hispanic/Latino), 4 international. Average age 34. 221 applicants, 58% accepted, 55 enrolled. In 2016, 97 master's awarded. *Degree requirements:* For master's, thesis or alternative. *Entrance requirements:* For master's, official academic transcript from accredited institution presenting conferred bachelor's degree. *Application deadline:* For fall admission, 6/1 priority date for domestic and international students. Applications are processed on a rolling basis. Application fee: $50. Electronic applications accepted. *Expenses:* Tuition, state resident: full-time $12,264; part-time $511 per credit hour. Tuition, nonresident: full-time $21,264; part-time $886 per credit hour. *Required fees:* $1344; $56 per credit hour. Tuition and fees vary according to course load. *Financial support:* In 2016–17, 9 students received support. Scholarships/grants available. Financial award application deadline: 8/1; financial award applicants required to submit FAFSA. *Unit head:* Dr. Patricia Joseph, Dean, College of Professional, Graduate and Extended Studies, 484-365-7659, E-mail: joseph@lincoln.edu. *Application contact:* Jernice Lea, Director of Graduate Admissions, 215-590-8231, Fax: 215-387-3859, E-mail: jlea@lincoln.edu.
Website: http://www.lincoln.edu/academics/graduate-programs

London Metropolitan University, Graduate Programs, London, United Kingdom. Offers applied psychology (M Sc); architecture (MA); biomedical science (M Sc); blood science (M Sc); cancer pharmacology (M Sc); computer networking and cyber security (M Sc); computing and information systems (M Sc); conference interpreting (MA); counter-terrorism studies (M Sc); creative, digital and professional writing (MA); crime, violence and prevention (M Sc); criminology (M Sc); curating contemporary art (MA); data analytics (M Sc); digital media (MA); early childhood studies (MA); education (MA, Ed D); financial services law, regulation and compliance (LL M); food science (M Sc); forensic psychology (M Sc); health and social care management and policy (M Sc); human nutrition (M Sc); human resource management (MA); human rights and international conflict (MA); information technology (M Sc); intelligence and security studies (M Sc); international oil, gas and energy law (LL M); international relations (MA); interpreting (MA); learning and teaching in higher education (MA); legal practice (LL M); media and entertainment law (LL M); organizational and consumer psychology (M Sc); psychological therapy (M Sc); psychology of mental health (M Sc); public health (M Sc); public policy and management (MPA); security studies (M Sc); social work (M Sc); spatial planning and urban design (MA); sports therapy (M Sc); supporting older children and young people with dyslexia (MA); teaching languages (MA), including Arabic, English; translation (MA); woman and child abuse (MA).

Long Island University–Brentwood Campus, Graduate Programs, Brentwood, NY 11717. Offers childhood education (grades 1-6) (MS), including grades 1-6; childhood education/literacy (grades 1-6) (MS); childhood education/special education (grades 1-6) (MS); clinical mental health counseling (MS, Advanced Certificate); early childhood education (B-2) (MS); literacy (B-6) (MS Ed); school counselor (MS); special education (grades 1-6) (MS Ed); students with disabilities generalist (grades 7-12) (Advanced Certificate). *Program availability:* Part-time. *Faculty:* 54 part-time/adjunct (30 women). *Students:* 98 full-time (80 women), 57 part-time (47 women); includes 28 minority (7 Black or African American, non-Hispanic/Latino; 1 Asian, non-Hispanic/Latino; 20 Hispanic/Latino). 85 applicants, 89% accepted, 43 enrolled. In 2016, 99 master's, 11 other advanced degrees awarded. *Degree requirements:* For master's, comprehensive exam (for some programs), thesis optional. *Entrance requirements:* For master's and Advanced Certificate, GRE. Additional exam requirements/recommendations for international students: Required—TOEFL or IELTS. *Application deadline:* Applications are processed on a rolling basis. Application fee: $50. Electronic applications accepted. Application fee is waived when completed online. *Expenses: Tuition:* Full-time $28,272; part-time $1178 per credit. *Required fees:* $451 per term. *Financial support:* Scholarships/grants and unspecified assistantships available. Support available to part-time students. Financial award applicants required to submit FAFSA. *Unit head:* Donna Di Donato, Dean and Chief Operating Officer, 631-287-8010, Fax: 631-287-8575, E-mail: donna.didonato@liu.edu. *Application contact:* Scott Aug, Associate Director of Enrollment Management, 631-287-8500, Fax: 631-287-8575, E-mail: scott.aug@liu.edu.
Website: http://liu.edu/brentwood

Long Island University–Hudson, Graduate School, Purchase, NY 10577. Offers autism (Advanced Certificate); childhood education (MS Ed); early childhood education (MS Ed); educational leadership (MS Ed); finance (MBA); health administration (MPA); healthcare sector management (MBA); literacy (MS Ed); management (MBA); marriage and family therapy (MS); mental health counseling (MS), including credentialed alcoholism and substance abuse counselor; middle childhood and adolescence education (MS Ed); pharmaceutics (MS), including cosmetic science, industrial pharmacy; public administration (MPA); school counseling (MS Ed, Advanced Certificate); school psychology (MS Ed); special education (MS Ed); TESOL (all grades) (Advanced Certificate); TESOL and bilingual education (MS Ed); the business of pharmaceutics and biotechnology (MBA). *Program availability:* Part-time, evening/weekend, online learning. *Faculty:* 7 full-time (5 women), 42 part-time/adjunct (25 women). *Students:* 55 full-time (41 women), 158 part-time (123 women); includes 40 minority (8 Black or African American, non-Hispanic/Latino; 1 Asian, non-Hispanic/Latino; 31 Hispanic/Latino). Average age 35. *Entrance requirements:* Additional exam requirements/recommendations for international students: Required—TOEFL (minimum score 550 paper-based; 79 iBT). *Application deadline:* Applications are processed on a rolling basis. Application fee: $50. Electronic applications accepted. *Expenses:* Contact institution. *Unit head:* Dr. Sylvia Blake, Dean and Chief Operating Officer, 914-831-2700, E-mail: westchester@liu.edu. *Application contact:* Cindy Pagnotta, Director of Marketing and Enrollment, 914-831-2701, Fax: 914-251-5959, E-mail: cindy.pagnotta@liu.edu.

Long Island University–LIU Brooklyn, School of Education, Brooklyn, NY 11201-8423. Offers adolescence urban education (MS Ed); applied behavior analysis (Advanced Certificate); bilingual education (Advanced Certificate); bilingual school counselor (MS Ed, Advanced Certificate); childhood urban education (MS Ed); childhood/early childhood urban education (MS Ed); early childhood urban education (MS Ed, Advanced Certificate); educational leadership (Advanced Certificate); marriage and family therapy (MS, Advanced Certificate); mental health counseling (MS, Advanced Certificate); school building district leader (Advanced Certificate); school counselor (MS Ed, Advanced Certificate); school psychologist (MS Ed); teaching urban children/adolescents with disabilities (MS Ed); TESOL (MS Ed). *Accreditation:* TEAC. *Program availability:* Part-time, evening/weekend. *Faculty:* 23 full-time (17 women), 44 part-time/adjunct (32 women). *Students:* 161 full-time (144 women), 594 part-time (461 women); includes 493 minority (229 Black or African American, non-Hispanic/Latino; 1 American Indian or Alaska Native, non-Hispanic/Latino; 30 Asian, non-Hispanic/Latino; 218 Hispanic/Latino; 2 Native Hawaiian or other Pacific Islander, non-Hispanic/Latino; 13 Two or more races, non-Hispanic/Latino), 9 international. 513 applicants, 73% accepted, 272 enrolled. In 2016, 262 master's, 18 other advanced degrees awarded. *Degree requirements:* For master's, thesis optional, electronic portfolio. *Entrance requirements:* For master's, GRE (for MS Ed). Additional exam requirements/recommendations for international students: Required—TOEFL (minimum score 527 paper-based; 75 iBT). *Application deadline:* Applications are processed on a rolling basis. Application fee: $50. Electronic applications accepted. *Expenses: Tuition:* Full-time $28,272; part-time $1178 per credit. *Required fees:* $451 per term. Tuition and fees vary according to degree level, program and student level. *Financial support:* In 2016–17, 81 students received support. Career-related internships or fieldwork, Federal Work-Study, institutionally sponsored loans, scholarships/grants, and unspecified assistantships available. Support available to part-time students. Financial award application deadline: 2/15; financial award applicants required to submit FAFSA. *Faculty research:* Technology in education, teaching civics and sustainability, biliteracy and dual language instruction, diversity in organizations and leadership, counseling diverse couples and families. *Unit head:* Dr. Amy Ginsberg, Dean, 718-246-6308, E-mail: amy.ginsberg@liu.edu. *Application contact:* Gabrielle Gannon, Director of Graduate Admissions, 718-488-1011, Fax: 718-780-6110, E-mail: bkln-admissions@liu.edu.
Website: http://www.liu.edu/Brooklyn/Academics/School-of-Education

Long Island University–LIU Post, College of Education, Information and Technology, Brookville, NY 11548-1300. Offers adolescence education (MS); adolescence education 7-12 (MS); archives and records management (AC); art education (MS); childhood education (MS); childhood teaching literacy B-6 (MS); childhood/special education (MS); clinical mental health counseling (MS, AC); early childhood education (MS); early childhood education/childhood education (MS); educational leadership (AC); educational technology (MS); information studies (PhD); interdisciplinary educational studies (Ed D); middle childhood education (MS); music education (MS); school counselor (MS); special education (MS Ed); speech-language pathology (MA); students with disabilities, 7-12 generalist (AC); TESOL (MA). *Accreditation:* TEAC. *Program availability:* Part-time, 100% online, blended/hybrid learning. *Faculty:* 55 full-time (35 women), 104 part-time/adjunct (57 women). *Students:* 464 full-time (390 women), 740 part-time (580 women); includes 265 minority (99 Black or African American, non-Hispanic/Latino; 45 Asian, non-Hispanic/Latino; 113 Hispanic/Latino; 1 Native Hawaiian or other Pacific Islander, non-Hispanic/Latino; 7 Two or more races, non-Hispanic/Latino), 33 international. 928 applicants, 76% accepted, 406 enrolled. In 2016, 334 master's, 10 doctorates, 137 other advanced degrees awarded. Terminal master's awarded for partial completion of doctoral program. *Degree requirements:* For master's, variable foreign language requirement, comprehensive exam (for some programs), thesis optional; for doctorate, comprehensive exam, thesis/dissertation. *Entrance requirements:* For master's and AC, GRE. Additional exam requirements/recommendations for international students: Required—PTE, TOEFL (minimum score 550 paper-based, 75 iBT) or IELTS. *Application deadline:* Applications are processed on a rolling basis. Application fee: $50. Electronic applications accepted. *Expenses: Tuition:* Full-time $28,272; part-time $1178 per credit. *Required fees:* $451 per term. Tuition and fees vary according to degree level and program. *Financial support:* Career-related internships or fieldwork, Federal Work-Study, institutionally sponsored loans, scholarships/grants, tuition waivers (partial), and unspecified assistantships available. Support available to part-time students. Financial award application deadline: 2/15; financial award applicants required to submit FAFSA. *Faculty research:* English language learners, early childhood literacy development through play, sleep, social justice through education, using a structured protocol for discussing bad news. *Total annual research expenditures:* $575,000. *Unit head:* Dr. Albert Inserra, Dean, 516-299-2210, E-mail: albert.inserra@liu.edu. *Application contact:* Carol Zerah, Director of Graduate Admissions, 516-299-2900, Fax: 516-299-2137, E-mail: post-enroll@liu.edu.
Website: http://liu.edu/CWPost/Academics/College-of-Education-Information-and-Technology

Long Island University–Riverhead, Graduate Programs, Riverhead, NY 11901. Offers childhood education (MS), including grades 1-6; homeland security management (MS); literacy education (MS); teaching students with disabilities (MS), including grades 1-6, grades 7-12; TESOL (Advanced Certificate). *Accreditation:* TEAC. *Program availability:* Part-time. *Degree requirements:* For master's, thesis (for some programs); for Advanced Certificate, comprehensive exam (for some programs). *Entrance requirements:* Additional exam requirements/recommendations for international students: Required—TOEFL (minimum score 550 paper-based; 79 iBT), IELTS (minimum score 6). *Application deadline:* Applications are processed on a rolling basis. Application fee: $50. Electronic applications accepted. *Expenses:* Contact institution. *Financial support:* Institutionally sponsored loans, scholarships/grants, tuition waivers (partial), and unspecified assistantships available. Support available to part-time students. Financial award application deadline: 2/15; financial award applicants required to submit FAFSA. *Unit head:* Donna Di Donato, Dean and Chief Operating Officer, LIU Brentwood and LIU Riverhead, 631-287-8010, Fax: 631-287-8575, E-mail: donna.didonato@liu.edu. *Application contact:* Christina Seifert, Director of Admission, LIU Brentwood and LIU Riverhead, 631-287-8505, Fax: 631-287-8253, E-mail: christina.seifert@liu.edu.

Louisiana Tech University, Graduate School, College of Education, Department of Curriculum, Instruction and Leadership, Ruston, LA 71272. Offers curriculum and instruction (M Ed), including research, theory, and design, visually impaired; educational leadership (M Ed, Ed D), including higher education administration (Ed D), P-12 educational leadership (Ed D). *Accreditation:* NCATE. *Program availability:* Part-time. *Degree requirements:* For doctorate, thesis/dissertation. *Entrance requirements:* For master's and doctorate, GRE General Test. *Application deadline:* For fall admission, 7/29 for domestic students; for spring admission, 2/3 for domestic students. Application fee: $20 ($30 for international students). *Financial support:* Fellowships, research assistantships, and teaching assistantships available. Financial award application deadline: 2/1. *Unit head:* Dr. Bryan McCoy, Chair, 318-257-4609, Fax: 318-257-2379, E-mail: bmccoy@latech.edu. *Application contact:* Dr. John Harrison, Associate Dean of Graduate Studies, 318-257-3229, Fax: 318-257-2379, E-mail: johnharrison@latech.edu.
Website: http://education.latech.edu/departments/cil/

Loyola University Maryland, Graduate Programs, School of Education, Program in Montessori Education, Baltimore, MD 21210-2699. Offers elementary education (M Ed); Montessori education (CAS). *Accreditation:* NCATE. *Faculty:* 34 full-time (22 women), 30 part-time/adjunct (24 women). *Students:* 4,607 full-time (2,770 women), 1,477 part-time (986 women); includes 1,471 minority (557 Black or African American, non-Hispanic/Latino; 9 American Indian or Alaska Native, non-Hispanic/Latino; 222 Asian, non-Hispanic/Latino; 495 Hispanic/Latino; 8 Native Hawaiian or other Pacific Islander, non-Hispanic/Latino; 180 Two or more races, non-Hispanic/Latino), 68 international. Average age 24. 42 applicants, 93% accepted, 30 enrolled. In 2016, 105 master's awarded. *Degree requirements:* For master's, thesis. *Entrance requirements:* For master's, essay, transcripts. Additional exam requirements/recommendations for international students: Required—TOEFL (minimum score 550 paper-based), IELTS (minimum score 7). *Application deadline:* For fall admission, 5/1 priority date for domestic students, 5/1 for international students. Applications are processed on a rolling basis. Application fee: $60. *Expenses:* Contact institution. *Financial support:* In 2016–17, 5 students received support. Scholarships/grants available. Financial award application deadline: 4/15; financial award applicants required to submit FAFSA.

Application contact: Mechelle Palmer, Senior Associate Director of Graduate Admission, 410-617-7741, E-mail: mjpalmer@loyola.edu.
Website: http://www.loyola.edu/soe/academics/graduate/montessori.aspx

Lynn University, Donald E. and Helen L. Ross College of Education, Boca Raton, FL 33431-5598. Offers educational leadership (M Ed, Ed D), including K-12 (Ed D); exceptional student education (M Ed), including school administration K-12. *Program availability:* Part-time, evening/weekend, online learning. *Faculty:* 5 full-time (4 women), 8 part-time/adjunct (all women). *Students:* 85 full-time (63 women), 10 part-time (6 women); includes 27 minority (19 Black or African American, non-Hispanic/Latino; 7 Hispanic/Latino; 1 Two or more races, non-Hispanic/Latino), 4 international. Average age 36. 17 applicants, 94% accepted, 11 enrolled. In 2016, 24 master's, 22 doctorates awarded. *Degree requirements:* For master's, comprehensive exam, thesis (for some programs); for doctorate, thesis/dissertation, mid-program review. *Entrance requirements:* For master's, bachelor's degree from accredited institution, letter of recommendation, statement of professional goals, official transcripts; for doctorate, master's degree from accredited institution, resume, 2 letters of recommendation, professional practice statement, official transcripts. Additional exam requirements/recommendations for international students: Required—TOEFL (minimum score 550 paper-based; 80 iBT), IELTS (minimum score 6.5). *Application deadline:* For fall admission, 8/18 for domestic students, 8/4 for international students; for spring admission, 12/15 for domestic students, 12/1 for international students; for summer admission, 4/17 for domestic students, 4/3 for international students. Applications are processed on a rolling basis. Application fee: $45. Electronic applications accepted. *Expenses:* $850 per credit hour, $44,200 per year tuition and fees (for Ed D); $725 per credit hour, $29,000 per year tuition and fees (for master's). *Financial support:* In 2016–17, 74 students received support. Career-related internships or fieldwork, Federal Work-Study, scholarships/grants, tuition waivers (partial), and unspecified assistantships available. Support available to part-time students. Financial award application deadline: 3/1; financial award applicants required to submit FAFSA. *Unit head:* Dr. Kathleen Weigel, Dean, College of Education, 561-237-7441, E-mail: kweigel@lynn.edu. *Application contact:* Steven Pruitt, Director of Graduate and Undergraduate Evening Admission, 561-237-7834, Fax: 561-237-7100, E-mail: spruitt@lynn.edu.
Website: http://www.lynn.edu/academics/colleges/education

Manhattan College, Graduate Programs, School of Education and Health, Program in Special Education, Riverdale, NY 10471. Offers adolescence education students with disabilities generalist extension in English or math or social studies - grades 7-12 (MS Ed); bilingual education (Advanced Certificate); dual childhood/students with disabilities - grades 1-6 (MS Ed); students with disabilities - grades 1-6 (MS Ed). *Program availability:* Part-time, evening/weekend. *Faculty:* 3 full-time (all women), 11 part-time/adjunct (7 women). *Students:* 62 full-time (59 women), 4 part-time (all women). Average age 24. 34 applicants, 79% accepted, 24 enrolled. In 2016, 32 master's awarded. *Degree requirements:* For master's, thesis, internship (if not certified). *Entrance requirements:* For master's, GRE, minimum GPA of 3.0. Additional exam requirements/recommendations for international students: Required—TOEFL (minimum score 550 paper-based; 80 iBT), IELTS (minimum score 6). *Application deadline:* For fall admission, 8/10 priority date for domestic students; for spring admission, 1/7 priority date for domestic students. Applications are processed on a rolling basis. Application fee: $75. Electronic applications accepted. Application fee is waived when completed online. *Expenses:* $900 per credit, $105 registration fee, $175 information service fee. *Financial support:* In 2016–17, 52 students received support. Federal Work-Study, scholarships/grants, and unspecified assistantships available. Financial award application deadline: 2/1; financial award applicants required to submit FAFSA. *Unit head:* Dr. Elizabeth Mary Kosky, Director of Childhood and Adolescent Special Education Programs, 718-862-7969, Fax: 718-862-7816, E-mail: elizabeth.kosky@manhattan.edu. *Application contact:* William Bisset, Information Contact, 718-862-8000, E-mail: william.bisset@manhattan.edu.

Manhattanville College, School of Education, Jump Start Program, Purchase, NY 10577-2132. Offers childhood and special education (MPS); education (Advanced Certificate); secondary subject areas and special education (MPS); TESOL (MPS). *Program availability:* Part-time, evening/weekend. *Students:* 26 applicants, 46% accepted, 7 enrolled. In 2016, 17 master's awarded. *Degree requirements:* For master's, comprehensive exam (for some programs), thesis (for some programs), student teaching, research seminars, portfolios, internships, writing assessment; for Advanced Certificate, comprehensive exam (for some programs). *Entrance requirements:* For master's, GRE or MAT, minimum undergraduate GPA of 3.0, 2 letters of recommendation, interview. Additional exam requirements/recommendations for international students: Required—TOEFL (minimum score 85 iBT); Recommended—IELTS. *Application deadline:* For fall admission, 7/1 priority date for domestic and international students; for spring admission, 11/1 priority date for domestic and international students; for summer admission, 4/1 priority date for domestic and international students. Applications are processed on a rolling basis. Application fee: $75. Electronic applications accepted. *Expenses: Tuition:* Full-time $16,470; part-time $915 per credit. *Required fees:* $60 per semester. Part-time tuition and fees vary according to course load and program. *Financial support:* Teaching assistantships, career-related internships or fieldwork, Federal Work-Study, institutionally sponsored loans, scholarships/grants, and unspecified assistantships available. Financial award applicants required to submit FAFSA. *Unit head:* Robert Cooper, Program Director, 914-323-5368, E-mail: robert.cooper@mville.edu. *Application contact:* Jeanine Pardey-Levine, Director of Graduate Enrollment Management, 914-323-3208, Fax: 914-694-1732, E-mail: edschool@mville.edu.
Website: http://www.mville.edu/programs/jump-start

Manhattanville College, School of Education, Program in Early Childhood Education, Purchase, NY 10577-2132. Offers childhood education (grades 1-6) (MAT); early childhood and special education (birth-grade 2) (MPS); early childhood education (birth-grade 2) (MAT); special education (birth-grade 2) (MPS); special education (birth-grade 6) (MPS). *Program availability:* Part-time, evening/weekend. *Students:* 22 applicants, 64% accepted, 10 enrolled. In 2016, 10 master's awarded. *Degree requirements:* For master's, comprehensive exam (for some programs), thesis (for some programs), student teaching, research seminars, portfolios, internships, writing assessment. *Entrance requirements:* For master's, GRE or MAT, minimum undergraduate GPA of 3.0, 2 letters of recommendation. Additional exam requirements/recommendations for international students: Required—TOEFL (minimum score 85 iBT); Recommended—IELTS. *Application deadline:* For fall admission, 7/1 priority date for domestic and international students; for spring admission, 11/1 priority date for domestic and international students; for summer admission, 4/1 priority date for domestic and international students. Applications are processed on a rolling basis. Application fee: $75. Electronic applications accepted. *Expenses: Tuition:* Full-time $16,470; part-time $915 per credit. *Required fees:* $60 per semester. Part-time tuition and fees vary according to course load and program. *Financial support:* Teaching assistantships, career-related internships or fieldwork, Federal Work-Study, institutionally sponsored loans, scholarships/grants, and unspecified assistantships available. Financial award applicants required to submit FAFSA. *Faculty research:* Technology support for emergent literacies and storytelling in preschool; technology, teacher and reader identities in preservice teacher education; student teacher and mentor relationship; curriculum history and historiography of John Dewey and the Dewey School. *Unit head:* Dr. Patricia Vardin, Chairperson, Department of Early Childhood, 914-798-2714, Fax: 914-694-2386, E-mail: patricia.vardin@mville.edu. *Application contact:* Jeanine Pardey-Levine, Director of Graduate Enrollment Management, 914-323-3208, Fax: 914-694-1732, E-mail: edschool@mville.edu.
Website: http://www.mville.edu/programs/early-childhood-education

Manhattanville College, School of Education, Program in Special Education, Purchase, NY 10577-2132. Offers childhood education (MPS); early childhood education (MPS); secondary education (MPS). *Program availability:* Part-time, evening/weekend. *Students:* 45 applicants, 69% accepted, 28 enrolled. In 2016, 26 master's, 1 Advanced Certificate awarded. *Degree requirements:* For master's, comprehensive exam (for some programs), thesis (for some programs), student teaching, research seminars, portfolios, internships, writing assessment; for Advanced Certificate, comprehensive exam (for some programs). *Entrance requirements:* For master's, GRE or MAT, minimum undergraduate GPA of 3.0, 2 letters of recommendation. Additional exam requirements/recommendations for international students: Required—TOEFL (minimum score 85 iBT); Recommended—IELTS. *Application deadline:* For fall admission, 7/1 priority date for domestic and international students; for spring admission, 11/1 priority date for domestic and international students; for summer admission, 4/1 priority date for domestic and international students. Applications are processed on a rolling basis. Application fee: $75. Electronic applications accepted. *Expenses: Tuition:* Full-time $16,470; part-time $915 per credit. *Required fees:* $60 per semester. Part-time tuition and fees vary according to course load and program. *Financial support:* Teaching assistantships, career-related internships or fieldwork, Federal Work-Study, institutionally sponsored loans, scholarships/grants, and unspecified assistantships available. Financial award applicants required to submit FAFSA. *Faculty research:* Aspects of verbal behavior and communication skills in autistic children, PBIS systems and their implementation, effective instructional practices for students with E/BDs, effective pedagogical practices that improve student behavioral and academic performance, increasing communication skills of young non-vocal children with autism. *Unit head:* Vance Austin, Chairperson, Department of Special Education, 914-323-7262, E-mail: vance.austin@mville.edu. *Application contact:* Jeanine Pardey-Levine, Director of Admissions, 914-323-3208, Fax: 914-694-1732, E-mail: edschool@mville.edu.
Website: http://www.mville.edu/programs/special-education

Marshall University, Academic Affairs Division, College of Education and Professional Development, Program in Early Childhood Education, Huntington, WV 25755. Offers MA. *Accreditation:* NCATE. *Program availability:* Evening/weekend. *Degree requirements:* For master's, thesis optional, comprehensive or oral assessment. *Entrance requirements:* For master's, GRE General Test or MAT.

Martin Luther College, Graduate Studies, New Ulm, MN 56073. Offers early childhood director (MS Ed Admin); educational technology (MS Ed); instruction (MS Ed); leadership (MS Ed); principal (MS Ed Admin); special education (MS Ed). *Program availability:* Part-time, evening/weekend. *Faculty:* 9 full-time (1 woman), 21 part-time/adjunct (10 women). *Students:* 1 (woman) full-time, 77 part-time (30 women); includes 2 minority (1 Asian, non-Hispanic/Latino; 1 Two or more races, non-Hispanic/Latino), 4 international. Average age 37. 6 applicants, 100% accepted, 6 enrolled. In 2016, 15 master's awarded. *Degree requirements:* For master's, capstone project or comprehensive exam. *Entrance requirements:* For master's, undergraduate degree in education from an accredited college or university, minimum undergraduate GPA of 3.0. Additional exam requirements/recommendations for international students: Required—TOEFL (minimum score 550 paper-based; 80 iBT); Recommended—IELTS (minimum score 6.5). *Application deadline:* Applications are processed on a rolling basis. Application fee: $35. Electronic applications accepted. *Expenses:* $11,220 tuition, $140 graduation fee. *Financial support:* In 2016–17, 2 students received support. Scholarships/grants available. Financial award application deadline: 9/1. *Faculty research:* Principal effectiveness, principal support, cognitive load in math instruction, reading strategies in multigrade classrooms, mentor provided professional development for new teachers. *Unit head:* John E. Meyer, Director of Graduate Studies, 507-354-8221 Ext. 398, E-mail: meyerjd@mlc-wels.edu.
Website: https://mlc-wels.edu/graduate-studies/

Maryville University of Saint Louis, School of Education, St. Louis, MO 63141-7299. Offers early childhood education (MA Ed); educational leadership (Ed D); educational leadership: principal certification (MA Ed); elementary education (MA Ed); gifted education (MA Ed); higher education leadership (Ed D); literacy specialist (MA Ed); middle grades education (MA Ed); secondary teaching and inquiry (MA Ed); teacher as leader (MA Ed); teacher leadership (Ed D). *Accreditation:* NCATE. *Program availability:* Part-time, evening/weekend. *Faculty:* 17 full-time (11 women), 21 part-time/adjunct (17 women). *Students:* 12 full-time (11 women), 297 part-time (208 women); includes 92 minority (79 Black or African American, non-Hispanic/Latino; 4 Asian, non-Hispanic/Latino; 4 Hispanic/Latino; 5 Two or more races, non-Hispanic/Latino), 4 international. Average age 38. In 2016, 32 master's, 61 doctorates awarded. *Degree requirements:* For master's, thesis, project. *Entrance requirements:* For master's, minimum cumulative GPA of 3.0, 3 professional recommendations, essays, interview with program faculty; for doctorate, minimum GPA of 3.0, 3 professional recommendations, essay, interview, on-site writing sample. Additional exam requirements/recommendations for international students: Required—TOEFL (minimum score 550 paper-based). *Application deadline:* Applications are processed on a rolling basis. Electronic applications accepted. *Expenses:* $879 per credit (for Ed D); $781 per credit (for master's). *Financial support:* Career-related internships or fieldwork, Federal Work-Study, tuition waivers (partial), and professional educator discounts available. Financial award application deadline: 3/1; financial award applicants required to submit FAFSA. *Faculty research:* Collaboration with public schools, pre-service program development, mathematics, diversity, literacy. *Unit head:* Dr. Cathy Bear, Dean, 314-529-9692, Fax: 314-529-9921, E-mail: cbear@maryville.edu. *Application contact:* Stacey Ruffin, Coordinator of Clinical Experiences and Graduate Programs, 314-529-9542, Fax: 314-529-9921, E-mail: teachered@maryville.edu.
Website: http://www.maryville.edu/ed/graduate-programs/

Marywood University, Academic Affairs, Reap College of Education and Human Development, Department of Education, Program in Early Childhood Intervention, Scranton, PA 18509-1598. Offers MS. *Accreditation:* NCATE. *Program availability:* Part-time. Electronic applications accepted. *Faculty research:* Montessori education, developmentally-appropriate practice, child care environment.

McNeese State University, Doré School of Graduate Studies, Burton College of Education, Office of Graduate Education Programs, Program in Curriculum and Instruction, Lake Charles, LA 70609. Offers early childhood education (M Ed); elementary education (M Ed); reading (M Ed); secondary education (M Ed). *Program availability:* Evening/weekend. *Entrance requirements:* For master's, GRE, teaching certificate.

McNeese State University, Doré School of Graduate Studies, Burton College of Education, Office of Student Teaching and Professional Education Services, Program in Early Childhood Education Grades PK-3, Lake Charles, LA 70609. Offers Postbaccalaureate Certificate. *Entrance requirements:* For degree, PRAXIS, 2 letters of recommendation, autobiography.

Early Childhood Education

Mercer University, Graduate Studies, Cecil B. Day Campus, Tift College of Education (Atlanta), Macon, GA 31207. Offers curriculum and instruction (PhD); early childhood education (M Ed, MAT, Ed S); educational leadership (PhD), including higher education leadership, P-12 school leadership; educational leadership P-12 (M Ed, Ed S); higher education leadership (M Ed); independent and charter school leadership (M Ed); middle grades education (M Ed, MAT); reading specialist (M Ed); secondary education (M Ed, MAT); teacher leadership (Ed S). *Accreditation:* NCATE. *Program availability:* Part-time, evening/weekend. *Faculty:* 28 full-time (15 women), 30 part-time/adjunct (27 women). *Students:* 177 full-time (150 women), 324 part-time (264 women); includes 288 minority (256 Black or African American, non-Hispanic/Latino; 1 American Indian or Alaska Native, non-Hispanic/Latino; 7 Asian, non-Hispanic/Latino; 17 Hispanic/Latino; 1 Native Hawaiian or other Pacific Islander, non-Hispanic/Latino; 6 Two or more races, non-Hispanic/Latino), 1 international. Average age 35. In 2016, 173 master's, 34 doctorates, 54 other advanced degrees awarded. *Degree requirements:* For master's and Ed S, research project; for doctorate, comprehensive exam, thesis/dissertation. *Entrance requirements:* For master's, GRE or MAT, minimum undergraduate GPA of 2.75; for doctorate, GRE; for Ed S, GRE or MAT, minimum GPA of 3.25; 3 years of certified teaching experience (for educational leadership and teacher leadership). Additional exam requirements/recommendations for international students: Required—TOEFL (minimum score 80 iBT). *Application deadline:* For fall admission, 8/1 for domestic and international students; for spring admission, 12/1 for domestic and international students; for summer admission, 5/1 for domestic and international students. Applications are processed on a rolling basis. Application fee: $25 ($50 for international students). Electronic applications accepted. *Expenses:* $590 per credit, $1,770 per course (for M Ed); $595 per credit, $1,785 per course (for MAT); $615 per credit, $1,845 per course (for Ed S); $717 per credit, $2,151 per course (for PhD); $150 per semester technology fee. *Financial support:* Federal Work-Study and unspecified assistantships available. Support available to part-time students. Financial award application deadline: 5/1; financial award applicants required to submit FAFSA. *Faculty research:* Educational technology, multicultural and minority issues in education, educational leadership (P-12 and higher education), school discipline and school bullying, standards-based mathematics education. *Unit head:* Dr. James Barta, Dean, 478-301-5355, Fax: 478-301-2280, E-mail: barta_jj@mercer.edu. *Application contact:* Renee Slaton, Associate Director of Graduate Admissions, 678-547-6084, Fax: 678-547-6055, E-mail: mercereducation@mercer.edu.
Website: http://education.mercer.edu/

Mercer University, Graduate Studies, Macon Campus, Tift College of Education (Macon), Macon, GA 31207. Offers early childhood education (M Ed, Ed S); educational leadership (M Ed, PhD, Ed S), including higher education (PhD), P-12; higher education leadership (M Ed); teacher leadership (Ed S). *Accreditation:* NCATE. *Program availability:* Part-time, evening/weekend, 100% online, blended/hybrid learning. *Faculty:* 14 full-time (11 women), 1 part-time/adjunct (0 women). *Students:* 61 full-time (39 women), 39 part-time (30 women); includes 39 minority (34 Black or African American, non-Hispanic/Latino; 1 Asian, non-Hispanic/Latino; 2 Hispanic/Latino; 1 Native Hawaiian or other Pacific Islander, non-Hispanic/Latino; 1 Two or more races, non-Hispanic/Latino), 3 international. Average age 33. In 2016, 23 master's, 13 doctorates awarded. *Degree requirements:* For master's, research project report; for doctorate, comprehensive exam, thesis/dissertation. *Entrance requirements:* For master's, GRE or MAT, minimum GPA of 2.75; for doctorate, GRE, minimum GPA of 3.5; interview; writing sample; 3 recommendations; for Ed S, GRE or MAT, minimum GPA of 3.5 (for teacher leadership), 3.0 (for educational leadership). Additional exam requirements/recommendations for international students: Required—TOEFL (minimum score 80 iBT). *Application deadline:* For fall admission, 8/1 for domestic and international students; for spring admission, 12/1 for domestic and international students. Applications are processed on a rolling basis. Application fee: $35. Electronic applications accepted. *Expenses:* Contact institution. *Financial support:* Federal Work-Study, institutionally sponsored loans, and unspecified assistantships available. Support available to part-time students. Financial award application deadline: 5/1; financial award applicants required to submit FAFSA. *Faculty research:* Teacher effectiveness, specific learning disabilities, inclusion. *Unit head:* Dr. James Barta, Dean, 478-301-5397, Fax: 478-301-2280, E-mail: barta_jj@mercer.edu. *Application contact:* Tracey M. Wofford, Associate Director of Admissions, 678-547-6422, Fax: 678-547-6367, E-mail: wofford_tm@mercer.edu.
Website: http://education.mercer.edu/

Mercy College, School of Education, Program in Early Childhood Education, Dobbs Ferry, NY 10522-1189. Offers MS. *Program availability:* Part-time, evening/weekend, blended/hybrid learning. *Students:* 316 full-time (308 women), 235 part-time (226 women); includes 191 minority (95 Black or African American, non-Hispanic/Latino; 1 American Indian or Alaska Native, non-Hispanic/Latino; 7 Asian, non-Hispanic/Latino; 82 Hispanic/Latino; 6 Two or more races, non-Hispanic/Latino). Average age 32. 296 applicants, 83% accepted, 182 enrolled. In 2016, 342 master's awarded. *Degree requirements:* For master's, comprehensive exam (for some programs). *Entrance requirements:* For master's, GRE, resume, undergraduate transcript. Additional exam requirements/recommendations for international students: Required—TOEFL (minimum score 600 paper-based; 100 iBT), IELTS (minimum score 8). *Application deadline:* For fall admission, 8/1 for international students. Applications are processed on a rolling basis. Application fee: $40. Electronic applications accepted. *Expenses: Tuition:* Full-time $15,156; part-time $842 per credit hour. *Required fees:* $620; $155 per term. Tuition and fees vary according to course load and program. *Financial support:* Career-related internships or fieldwork, Federal Work-Study, scholarships/grants, and unspecified assistantships available. Support available to part-time students. Financial award applicants required to submit FAFSA. *Unit head:* Dr. Rose Rudnitski, Dean for the School of Education, 914-674-7447, Fax: 914-674-7352, E-mail: rrudnitski@mercy.edu. *Application contact:* Allison Gurdineer, Senior Director of Admissions, 877-637-2946, Fax: 914-674-7382, E-mail: admissions@mercy.edu.
Website: https://www.mercy.edu/degrees-programs/ms-early-childhood-education-birth-grade-2

Merrimack College, School of Education and Social Policy, North Andover, MA 01845-5800. Offers community engagement (M Ed), including community organizations, higher education, K-12 education; criminology and criminal justice (MS); curriculum and instruction (M Ed); early childhood education (M Ed); educational leadership (CAGS), including instructional leadership; elementary education (M Ed); English as a second language (PreK-6) (M Ed); high school education (M Ed); higher education (M Ed), including leadership and organizational development, student affairs; middle school education (M Ed); moderate disabilities (PreK-8) (M Ed); school counseling (M Ed). *Program availability:* Part-time, evening/weekend, 100% online courses with immersion events and in-classroom practicum close to home. *Faculty:* 17 full-time, 34 part-time/adjunct. *Students:* 204 full-time (172 women), 83 part-time (67 women); includes 32 minority (4 Black or African American, non-Hispanic/Latino; 2 Asian, non-Hispanic/Latino; 23 Hispanic/Latino; 3 Two or more races, non-Hispanic/Latino), 1 international. Average age 27. 261 applicants, 89% accepted, 200 enrolled. In 2016, 153 master's, 2 other advanced degrees awarded. *Degree requirements:* For master's, practicum, portfolio, and state test (for licensure track); capstone (for higher education, curriculum and instruction, and community engagement tracks). *Entrance requirements:* For master's, Massachusetts Teacher Education Licensure (MTEL), official transcripts from other colleges, resume, personal statement, 2 letters of recommendation. Additional exam requirements/recommendations for international students: Required—TOEFL (minimum score 84 iBT), IELTS (minimum score 6.5), PTE (minimum score 56). *Application deadline:* For fall admission, 8/14 for domestic students, 7/14 for international students; for spring admission, 1/10 for domestic students, 12/10 for international students; for summer admission, 5/10 for domestic students, 4/10 for international students. Applications are processed on a rolling basis. Application fee: $0. Electronic applications accepted. *Expenses:* Contact institution. *Financial support:* Fellowships with full tuition reimbursements, career-related internships or fieldwork, scholarships/grants, and health care benefits available. Support available to part-time students. Financial award application deadline: 5/1; financial award applicants required to submit FAFSA. *Faculty research:* Feminist praxis in higher education, transgender student agency and belonging, campus sexual violence prevention, the scholarship of engagement; community engagement; service learning; diversity education; community-university partnerships, college going behaviors and indicators of success for inner city youth, strategies to increase students pursuit and success in STEM higher education, effective workforce development for displaced or under employed individuals, police reform, e.g. surveillance. *Application contact:* Alyssa Frey, Graduate Admissions Counselor, 978-837-3563, E-mail: freya@merrimack.edu.
Website: http://www.merrimack.edu/academics/graduate/education/

Middle Tennessee State University, College of Graduate Studies, College of Education, Department of Elementary and Special Education, Major in Curriculum and Instruction, Murfreesboro, TN 37132. Offers early childhood education (M Ed); elementary education (M Ed, Ed S); middle school education (M Ed). *Accreditation:* NCATE. *Program availability:* Part-time, evening/weekend, online learning. *Degree requirements:* For master's, comprehensive exam; for Ed S, comprehensive exam, thesis or alternative. *Entrance requirements:* For master's and Ed S, GRE, MAT or PRAXIS. Additional exam requirements/recommendations for international students: Required—TOEFL (minimum score 525 paper-based; 71 iBT) or IELTS (minimum score 6). Electronic applications accepted.

Millersville University of Pennsylvania, College of Graduate Studies and Adult Learning, College of Education and Human Services, Department of Early, Middle, and Exceptional Education, Program in Early Childhood Education, Millersville, PA 17551-0302. Offers M Ed. *Program availability:* Part-time, evening/weekend. *Faculty:* 14 full-time (9 women). *Students:* 10 full-time (all women), 17 part-time (13 women); includes 2 minority (1 Black or African American, non-Hispanic/Latino; 1 Hispanic/Latino), 1 international. Average age 30. 10 applicants, 100% accepted, 5 enrolled. In 2016, 9 master's awarded. *Degree requirements:* For master's, comprehensive exam, thesis optional. *Entrance requirements:* For master's, teaching certificate (unless enrolled in post baccalaureate certification concurrently). Additional exam requirements/recommendations for international students: Required—TOEFL (minimum score 600 paper-based), IELTS (minimum score 6). *Application deadline:* Applications are processed on a rolling basis. Application fee: $40. Electronic applications accepted. *Expenses:* $483 per credit resident tuition; $725 per credit non-resident tuition. *Financial support:* In 2016–17, 3 students received support. Unspecified assistantships available. Financial award application deadline: 3/15; financial award applicants required to submit FAFSA. *Faculty research:* Early childhood education, play, diversity, teacher education, curriculum. *Unit head:* Dr. Elizabeth Powers, Coordinator, 717-871-4248, E-mail: elizabeth.powers@millersville.edu. *Application contact:* Dr. Victor S. DeSantis, Dean of College of Graduate Studies and Adult Learning/Associate Provost for Civic and Community Engagement, 717-871-7619, Fax: 717-871-7954, E-mail: victor.desantis@millersville.edu.
Website: http://www.millersville.edu/academics/educ/eled/graduate.php

Milligan College, Area of Education, Milligan College, TN 37682. Offers combined preK-3/K-5 education (M Ed); educational leadership (Ed D, Ed S); K-5 education (M Ed); middle grades education (M Ed); preK-3 education (M Ed); preK-3 special education (M Ed); secondary education (M Ed). *Accreditation:* NCATE. *Program availability:* Part-time. *Faculty:* 5 full-time (3 women), 3 part-time/adjunct (1 woman). *Students:* 26 full-time (19 women), 20 part-time (10 women); includes 2 minority (1 Black or African American, non-Hispanic/Latino; 1 Hispanic/Latino), 2 international. Average age 28. 16 applicants, 81% accepted, 11 enrolled. In 2016, 19 master's awarded. *Degree requirements:* For master's, thesis, portfolio, research project; for doctorate, thesis/dissertation, portfolio, research project. *Entrance requirements:* For master's, MAT, GRE General Test, ACT, SAT, or PRAXIS, undergraduate degree and supporting transcripts, professional recommendations, interview; for doctorate, MAT or GRE, master's degree and supporting transcripts, demonstrated scholastic ability, recognized leadership role within education, professional recommendations, essay/personal statement, portfolio (professional development plan, evidence of ability, knowledge and qualities), interview. Additional exam requirements/recommendations for international students: Required—TOEFL (minimum score 550 paper-based, 79 iBT) or IELTS (6.5). *Application deadline:* For fall admission, 8/1 priority date for domestic students, 6/1 for international students; for spring admission, 11/15 priority date for domestic students, 12/1 for international students; for summer admission, 4/1 for domestic students. Applications are processed on a rolling basis. Application fee: $30. Electronic applications accepted. *Expenses:* $360 per hour tuition (for M Ed); $475 per hour tuition (for Ed D and Ed S); $325 per semester tech/activity fees. *Financial support:* Scholarships/grants available. Financial award application deadline: 12/1; financial award applicants required to submit FAFSA. *Faculty research:* Assessment; school mental health; literacy; technology; educator preparation. *Unit head:* Dr. Angela Hilton-Prillhart, Area Chair of Education, 423-461-8769, Fax: 423-461-3103, E-mail: anhilton-prillhart@milligan.edu. *Application contact:* Melissa Dillow, Graduate Admissions Recruiter, Education, 423-461-8306, Fax: 423-461-8982, E-mail: msdillow@milligan.edu.
Website: http://www.Milligan.edu/GPS

Mills College, Graduate Studies, Program in Infant Mental Health, Oakland, CA 94613-1000. Offers MA. *Program availability:* Part-time. *Faculty:* 1 (woman) full-time. *Students:* 11 full-time (all women); includes 3 minority (1 Black or African American, non-Hispanic/Latino; 2 Hispanic/Latino). Average age 28. 13 applicants, 77% accepted, 6 enrolled. In 2016, 6 master's awarded. *Entrance requirements:* For master's, bachelor's degree, preferably in psychology, and the following prerequisite courses: fundamentals of psychology, developmental psychology, psychopathology, analytical methods/statistics, and research methods; three letters of recommendation; statement of purpose essay. Additional exam requirements/recommendations for international students: Required—TOEFL (minimum score 550 paper-based; 80 iBT) or IELTS (minimum score 6). *Application deadline:* For fall admission, 12/31 priority date for domestic students, 12/15 for international students. Applications are processed on a rolling basis. Electronic applications accepted. *Expenses: Tuition:* Full-time $31,620. *Required fees:* $1118. Tuition and fees vary according to course load, degree level and program. *Financial support:* In 2016–17, 14 students received support, including 11 fellowships with tuition reimbursements available (averaging $9,987 per year), 3 teaching assistantships with tuition reimbursements available (averaging $5,721 per year); scholarships/grants also available. Financial award application deadline: 2/1; financial award applicants required to submit FAFSA. *Faculty research:* Development and sequelae of attachment in

children and adults in normative and clinical/risk populations, identifying the mental health needs of young children who have experienced extraordinary traumatic situations during critical points in their early development, examining the effects of early childhood trauma, work on helping professionals' psychological well-being. *Unit head:* Linda Perez, Professor of Education, 510-430-2328, Fax: 510-430-2159, E-mail: lperez@mills.edu. *Application contact:* Robynne Lofton, Director of Admissions, 510-430-3295, Fax: 510-430-2159, E-mail: grad-admission@mills.edu.
Website: http://www.mills.edu/imh/

Mississippi State University, College of Education, Department of Curriculum, Instruction and Special Education, Mississippi State, MS 39762. Offers early childhood education (PhD); elementary education (MS, PhD, Ed S), including early childhood education (MS), general elementary education (MS), middle level education (MS); general curriculum and instruction (PhD); middle level (MAT); reading education (PhD); secondary education (MAT, MS, PhD, Ed S); special education (MAT, MS, PhD, Ed S). *Accreditation:* NCATE. *Program availability:* Part-time, evening/weekend. *Faculty:* 21 full-time (16 women), 1 (woman) part-time/adjunct. *Students:* 39 full-time (26 women), 168 part-time (128 women); includes 49 minority (43 Black or African American, non-Hispanic/Latino; 2 American Indian or Alaska Native, non-Hispanic/Latino; 1 Hispanic/Latino; 1 Native Hawaiian or other Pacific Islander, non-Hispanic/Latino; 2 Two or more races, non-Hispanic/Latino), 4 international. Average age 33. 98 applicants, 56% accepted, 47 enrolled. In 2016, 69 master's, 6 doctorates, 10 other advanced degrees awarded. *Degree requirements:* For master's, comprehensive exam; for doctorate, thesis/dissertation; for Ed S, comprehensive exam, thesis or alternative. *Entrance requirements:* For master's, GRE, minimum GPA of 2.75 in junior and senior year, eligibility for initial teacher certification; for doctorate, GRE, minimum GPA of 3.4 on previous graduate work; for Ed S, GRE, minimum GPA of 3.2 on master's degree. Additional exam requirements/recommendations for international students: Required—TOEFL (minimum score 550 paper-based; 79 iBT); Recommended—IELTS (minimum score 6.5). *Application deadline:* For fall admission, 3/1 priority date for domestic students, 5/1 for international students; for spring admission, 9/1 priority date for domestic students, 9/1 for international students. Applications are processed on a rolling basis. Application fee: $60. Electronic applications accepted. *Expenses:* Tuition, state resident: full-time $7670; part-time $852.50 per credit hour. Tuition, nonresident: full-time $20,790; part-time $2310.50 per credit hour. Part-time tuition and fees vary according to course load. *Financial support:* In 2016–17, 8 research assistantships with partial tuition reimbursements (averaging $11,381 per year) were awarded; Federal Work-Study, institutionally sponsored loans, scholarships/grants, and unspecified assistantships also available. Financial award application deadline: 4/1; financial award applicants required to submit FAFSA. *Faculty research:* Early childhood education, reading, rural schools, multicultural education, use of technology in instruction. *Unit head:* Dr. Janice Nicholson, Interim Department Head, 662-325-3704, Fax: 662-325-7857, E-mail: jin4@msstate.edu. *Application contact:* Linda Bonner, Senior Admissions Assistant, 662-325-3363, E-mail: lbonner@grad.msstate.edu.
Website: http://www.cise.msstate.edu/

Missouri Southern State University, Program in Early Childhood Education, Joplin, MO 64801-1595. Offers MS Ed. Program offered jointly with Northwest Missouri State University. *Accreditation:* NCATE. *Entrance requirements:* For master's, GRE, minimum cumulative undergraduate GPA of 2.5.

Missouri State University, Graduate College, College of Education, Department of Childhood Education and Family Studies, Springfield, MO 65897. Offers early childhood and family development (MS); elementary education (MS Ed). *Program availability:* Part-time. *Faculty:* 11 full-time (8 women), 2 part-time/adjunct (both women). *Students:* 16 full-time (15 women), 104 part-time (101 women); includes 9 minority (5 Black or African American, non-Hispanic/Latino; 1 Asian, non-Hispanic/Latino; 1 Hispanic/Latino; 2 Two or more races, non-Hispanic/Latino), 3 international. Average age 31. 57 applicants, 75% accepted, 35 enrolled. In 2016, 48 master's awarded. *Degree requirements:* For master's, comprehensive exam. *Entrance requirements:* For master's, GRE, minimum GPA of 3.0. Additional exam requirements/recommendations for international students: Required—TOEFL (minimum score 550 paper-based; 79 iBT), IELTS (minimum score 6). *Application deadline:* For fall admission, 7/20 priority date for domestic students, 5/1 for international students; for spring admission, 12/20 priority date for domestic students, 9/1 for international students; for summer admission, 5/20 priority date for domestic students. Applications are processed on a rolling basis. Application fee: $35 ($50 for international students). Electronic applications accepted. *Expenses:* Tuition, state resident: full-time $5830. Tuition, nonresident: full-time $10,708. *Required fees:* $1130. Tuition and fees vary according to class time, course level, course load and program. *Financial support:* Federal Work-Study, institutionally sponsored loans, scholarships/grants, and unspecified assistantships available. Financial award application deadline: 3/31; financial award applicants required to submit FAFSA. *Faculty research:* Infant development, play advocacy, building mathematical concepts. *Unit head:* Dr. Denise Cunningham, Department Head, 417-836-8915, Fax: 417-836-8900, E-mail: cefs@missouristate.edu. *Application contact:* Michael Edwards, Coordinator of Graduate Admissions, 417-836-5330, Fax: 417-836-6200, E-mail: michaeledwards@missouristate.edu.
Website: http://education.missouristate.edu/cefs/

Molloy College, Graduate Education Program, Rockville Centre, NY 11571-5002. Offers adolescent education in biology (MS Ed); adolescent special education (Advanced Certificate); bilingual extension (Advanced Certificate); childhood education (MS Ed); childhood special education (Advanced Certificate); early childhood education (MS Ed); educational technology (MS Ed); English (MS Ed); mathematics (MS Ed); social studies (MS Ed); Spanish (MS Ed); special education on both childhood and adolescent levels (MS Ed); teaching English to speakers of other languages (TESOL) in grades Pre-K to 12 (MS Ed); TESOL (Advanced Certificate). *Accreditation:* NCATE. *Program availability:* Part-time, evening/weekend. *Faculty:* 17 full-time (16 women), 23 part-time/adjunct (19 women). *Students:* 95 full-time (75 women), 221 part-time (177 women); includes 59 minority (14 Black or African American, non-Hispanic/Latino; 6 Asian, non-Hispanic/Latino; 38 Hispanic/Latino; 1 Two or more races, non-Hispanic/Latino), 1 international. Average age 42. 214 applicants, 66% accepted, 125 enrolled. In 2016, 95 master's, 4 Advanced Certificates awarded. *Entrance requirements:* Additional exam requirements/recommendations for international students: Required—TOEFL (minimum score 550 paper-based; 79 iBT). *Application deadline:* Applications are processed on a rolling basis. Application fee: $60. Electronic applications accepted. *Expenses: Tuition:* Full-time $19,170; part-time $1065 per credit. *Required fees:* $950; $790 per credit. Tuition and fees vary according to course load. *Financial support:* Applicants required to submit FAFSA. *Faculty research:* ESL - general education teacher collaboration; special education; school desegregation; American intellectual and social history; families and schools. *Unit head:* Joanne O'Brien, Associate Dean/Director, 516-323-3116, E-mail: jobrien@molloy.edu. *Application contact:* Jaclyn Machowicz, Assistant Director for Admissions, 516-323-4010, E-mail: jmachowicz@molloy.edu.

Monmouth University, Graduate Studies, School of Education, West Long Branch, NJ 07764-1898. Offers applied behavior analysis (Certificate); autism (Certificate); director of school counseling services (Post-Master's Certificate); early childhood (M Ed); educational leadership (Ed D); elementary education (MAT), including elementary level, secondary level; English as a second language (M Ed); learning disabilities teacher-consultant (Post-Master's Certificate); literacy (MS Ed); school counseling (MS Ed); special education (MS Ed), including autism, learning disabilities teacher-consultant, teacher of students with disabilities, teaching in inclusive settings; speech-language pathology (MS Ed); student affairs and college counseling (MS Ed); supervisor (Post-Master's Certificate); teaching English to speakers of other languages (Certificate). *Accreditation:* NCATE. *Program availability:* Part-time, evening/weekend, 100% online, blended/hybrid learning. *Faculty:* 23 full-time (19 women), 33 part-time/adjunct (25 women). *Students:* 191 full-time (172 women), 141 part-time (122 women); includes 56 minority (10 Black or African American, non-Hispanic/Latino; 9 Asian, non-Hispanic/Latino; 31 Hispanic/Latino; 6 Two or more races, non-Hispanic/Latino). Average age 26. 423 applicants, 53% accepted, 139 enrolled. In 2016, 148 master's, 4 other advanced degrees awarded. *Entrance requirements:* For master's, GRE taken within last 5 years (for MS Ed in speech-language pathology); SAT (minimum combined score of 1660 in 3 sections), ACT (23), GRE (minimum score of 4.0 on analytical writing section and minimum combined score of 310 on quantitative and verbal sections), or passing scores on 3 parts of Core Academic Skills Educators, minimum GPA of 3.0 in major; 2 letters of recommendation (for some programs); resume, personal statement or essay (depending on program). Additional exam requirements/recommendations for international students: Required—TOEFL (minimum score 550 paper-based; 79 iBT), IELTS (minimum score 6), Michigan English Language Assessment Battery (minimum score 77) or Certificate of Advanced English (minimum score B2). *Application deadline:* For fall admission, 7/15 priority date for domestic students, 7/1 for international students; for spring admission, 12/1 priority date for domestic students, 11/1 for international students; for summer admission, 5/1 for domestic students. Applications are processed on a rolling basis. Application fee: $50. Electronic applications accepted. *Expenses: Tuition, area resident:* Full-time $19,764; part-time $1098 per credit hour. *Required fees:* $175 per semester. Tuition and fees vary according to program. *Financial support:* In 2016–17, 349 students received support, including 305 fellowships (averaging $3,558 per year), 48 teaching assistantships (averaging $9,619 per year); research assistantships, institutionally sponsored loans, scholarships/grants, and unspecified assistantships also available. Support available to part-time students. Financial award application deadline: 2/1; financial award applicants required to submit FAFSA. *Faculty research:* Multicultural literacy, science and mathematics teaching strategies, teacher as reflective practitioner, children with disabilities. *Unit head:* Dr. John E. Henning, Dean, 732-263-5513, Fax: 732-263-5277. *Application contact:* Laurie Kuhn, Associate Director of Graduate Admission, 732-571-3452, Fax: 732-263-5123, E-mail: gradadm@monmouth.edu.
Website: http://www.monmouth.edu/academics/schools/education/default.asp

Mount St. Joseph University, Graduate Education Program, Cincinnati, OH 45233-1670. Offers adolescent to young adult education (MA); dyslexia (Certificate); inclusive early childhood education (MA); middle childhood education (MA); multicultural special education (MA); reading science (MA). *Accreditation:* TEAC. *Program availability:* Part-time, evening/weekend, online learning. *Faculty:* 7 full-time (5 women), 12 part-time/adjunct (10 women). *Students:* 44 full-time (33 women), 112 part-time (104 women); includes 16 minority (15 Black or African American, non-Hispanic/Latino; 1 Two or more races, non-Hispanic/Latino). Average age 34. In 2016, 60 master's awarded. *Degree requirements:* For master's, comprehensive exam, thesis, research project, student teaching, clinical and field-based experiences. *Entrance requirements:* For master's, GRE (if GPA is below 3.0), letter of intent, 2 referrals, background check, interview, resume, minimum undergraduate GPA of 3.0. Additional exam requirements/recommendations for international students: Required—TOEFL (minimum score 560 paper-based; 83 iBT). *Application deadline:* Applications are processed on a rolling basis. Application fee: $50. Electronic applications accepted. *Expenses:* $580 per credit hour. *Financial support:* Applicants required to submit FAFSA. *Faculty research:* Foreign and second language learning problems/reading disabilities, multicultural/bilingual special education, science education, pedagogical content knowledge, early childhood, response to intervention. *Unit head:* Dr. Laura Saylor, Dean, 513-244-3263, E-mail: laura.saylor@msj.edu. *Application contact:* Mary Brigham, Assistant Director of Graduate Recruitment, 513-244-4233, Fax: 513-244-4629, E-mail: mary.brigham@msj.edu.
Website: http://www.msj.edu/academics/graduate-programs/master-of-arts-initial-teacher-licensure-programs/

Murray State University, College of Education, Department of Early Childhood and Elementary Education, Program in Interdisciplinary Early Childhood Education, Murray, KY 42071. Offers MA Ed. *Program availability:* Part-time. *Degree requirements:* For master's, portfolio. *Entrance requirements:* For master's, minimum GPA of 2.5 for conditional admittance, 3.0 for unconditional.

National Louis University, National College of Education, Chicago, IL 60603. Offers administration and supervision (M Ed, Ed D, CAS, Ed S); curriculum and instruction (M Ed, MS Ed, CAS); early childhood administration (M Ed, CAS); early childhood education (M Ed, MAT, MS Ed, CAS); education (Ed D); educational psychology/human learning and development (M Ed, MS Ed, CAS, Ed S); elementary education (MAT); interdisciplinary curriculum and instruction (M Ed); mathematics education (M Ed, MS Ed, CAS); middle grades education (MAT); reading and language (M Ed, MS Ed, CAS); school psychology (M Ed, Ed S); science education (M Ed, MS Ed, CAS); secondary education (MAT); special education (M Ed, MAT, CAS); technology in education (M Ed, CAS). *Accreditation:* NCATE. *Program availability:* Part-time, evening/weekend. *Degree requirements:* For doctorate, comprehensive exam, thesis/dissertation. *Entrance requirements:* For master's, MAT or GRE, minimum GPA of 3.0; for doctorate, GRE General Test, minimum GPA of 3.25, interview, resume, writing sample, 4 recommendations. Additional exam requirements/recommendations for international students: Required—TOEFL (minimum score 550 paper-based; 79 iBT).

Nazareth College of Rochester, Graduate Studies, Department of Education, Program in Inclusive Early Childhood Education, Rochester, NY 14618. Offers MS Ed. *Accreditation:* TEAC. *Program availability:* Part-time, evening/weekend. *Entrance requirements:* For master's, minimum GPA of 3.0. Additional exam requirements/recommendations for international students: Required—TOEFL or IELTS. *Application deadline:* For fall admission, 4/1 priority date for domestic students; for spring admission, 10/1 priority date for domestic students. Application fee: $40. *Expenses: Tuition:* Part-time $880 per credit hour. Part-time tuition and fees vary according to course load, degree level and program. *Financial support:* Unspecified assistantships available. Financial award application deadline: 3/1; financial award applicants required to submit FAFSA. *Unit head:* Dr. Ellen Contopidis, Director, 585-389-2916, E-mail: econtop4@naz.edu. *Application contact:* Judith Baker, Director, Transfer and Graduate Admissions, 585-531-1154, Fax: 585-389-2826, E-mail: gradadmissions@naz.edu.

New Jersey City University, Debra Cannon Partridge Wolfe College of Education, Department of Early Childhood Education, Jersey City, NJ 07305-1597. Offers MAT. *Accreditation:* TEAC. *Program availability:* Part-time, evening/weekend. *Entrance requirements:* Additional exam requirements/recommendations for international students: Required—TOEFL (minimum score 79 iBT).

New Mexico State University, College of Education, Department of Curriculum and Instruction, Las Cruces, NM 88003. Offers bilingual education (MA); curriculum and

instruction (Ed D); early childhood education (MA); educational diagnostics (Ed S); language, literacy and culture (MA); learning design and technologies (MA); teaching (MAT), including Spanish; teaching English to speakers of other languages (MA). *Accreditation:* NCATE. *Program availability:* Part-time, evening/weekend, 100% online. *Faculty:* 23 full-time (17 women), 7 part-time/adjunct (5 women). *Students:* 114 full-time (81 women), 219 part-time (159 women); includes 190 minority (16 Black or African American, non-Hispanic/Latino; 2 American Indian or Alaska Native, non-Hispanic/Latino; 5 Asian, non-Hispanic/Latino; 160 Hispanic/Latino; 7 Two or more races, non-Hispanic/Latino), 33 international. Average age 37. 126 applicants, 75% accepted, 65 enrolled. In 2016, 92 master's, 19 doctorates awarded. *Degree requirements:* For master's, comprehensive exam, thesis optional; for doctorate, comprehensive exam, thesis/dissertation. *Entrance requirements:* For master's, minimum cumulative GPA of 3.0; for doctorate, portfolio, minimum cumulative GPA of 3.0. Additional exam requirements/recommendations for international students: Required—TOEFL (minimum score 550 paper-based; 79 iBT), IELTS (minimum score 6.5). *Application deadline:* For fall admission, 12/15 priority date for domestic and international students; for spring admission, 11/1 for domestic students. Applications are processed on a rolling basis. Application fee: $40 ($50 for international students). Electronic applications accepted. *Expenses:* Tuition, state resident: full-time $4086. Tuition, nonresident: full-time $14,254. *Required fees:* $853. Tuition and fees vary according to course load. *Financial support:* In 2016–17, 102 students received support, including 2 fellowships (averaging $4,076 per year), 2 research assistantships (averaging $18,070 per year), 16 teaching assistantships (averaging $16,454 per year); career-related internships or fieldwork, Federal Work-Study, scholarships/grants, traineeships, health care benefits, and unspecified assistantships also available. Support available to part-time students. Financial award application deadline: 3/1. *Faculty research:* STEM education, bilingual and English as a second language education, critical pedagogy/multicultural education, learning design and technology, early childhood education. *Total annual research expenditures:* $29,926. *Unit head:* Dr. David Rutledge, Department Head, 575-646-5411, Fax: 575-646-5436, E-mail: rutledge@nmsu.edu. *Application contact:* Dr. David Rutledge, Associate Department Head for Graduate Programs, 575-646-5411, Fax: 575-646-5436, E-mail: rutledge@nmsu.edu.
Website: http://ci.education.nmsu.edu

New Mexico State University, College of Education, Department of Educational Leadership and Administration, Las Cruces, NM 88003. Offers educational administration (MA), including community college and university administration, PK-12 public school administration; educational leadership (Ed D, PhD). *Accreditation:* NCATE. *Program availability:* Part-time-only, evening/weekend, blended/hybrid learning. *Faculty:* 7 full-time (5 women), 1 part-time/adjunct (0 women). *Students:* 18 full-time (15 women), 110 part-time (82 women); includes 83 minority (2 Black or African American, non-Hispanic/Latino; 7 American Indian or Alaska Native, non-Hispanic/Latino; 4 Asian, non-Hispanic/Latino; 68 Hispanic/Latino; 1 Native Hawaiian or other Pacific Islander, non-Hispanic/Latino; 1 Two or more races, non-Hispanic/Latino), 3 international. Average age 41. 22 applicants, 27% accepted, 6 enrolled. In 2016, 24 master's, 6 doctorates awarded. *Degree requirements:* For master's, comprehensive exam, thesis optional, internship; for doctorate, comprehensive exam, thesis/dissertation, internship. *Entrance requirements:* For master's, minimum GPA of 3.0, current U.S. teaching license, and minimum 3 years of teaching in PK-12 sector (for PK-12 public school administration); minimum bachelor's degree GPA of 3.0 (for community college and university administration); for doctorate, minimum GPA of 3.0, master's degree. Additional exam requirements/recommendations for international students: Required—TOEFL (minimum score 550 paper-based; 79 iBT), IELTS (minimum score 6.5). *Application deadline:* For spring admission, 11/15 for domestic and international students. Application fee: $40 ($50 for international students). Electronic applications accepted. *Expenses:* Tuition, state resident: full-time $4086. Tuition, nonresident: full-time $14,254. *Required fees:* $853. Tuition and fees vary according to course load. *Financial support:* In 2016–17, 14 students received support, including 1 research assistantship (averaging $17,368 per year), 2 teaching assistantships (averaging $17,166 per year); career-related internships or fieldwork, Federal Work-Study, scholarships/grants, traineeships, health care benefits, and unspecified assistantships also available. Support available to part-time students. Financial award application deadline: 3/1. *Faculty research:* Leadership in PK-12 and postsecondary education, community college administration, distance education administration, leadership for social justice, educational change. *Total annual research expenditures:* $2,656. *Unit head:* Dr. Azadeh Osanloo, Department Head, 575-646-5976, Fax: 575-646-4767, E-mail: azadeh@nmsu.edu. *Application contact:* Denise Rodgiguez-Strawn, 575-646-3825, Fax: 575-646-4767, E-mail: edmandev@nmsu.edu.
Website: http://ela.nmsu.edu/

New York Institute of Technology, School of Interdisciplinary Studies and Education, Department of Teacher Education, Old Westbury, NY 11568-8000. Offers adolescence education (MS), including mathematics, science; childhood education (MS); early childhood (MS). *Program availability:* Part-time, evening/weekend, 100% online, blended/hybrid learning. *Faculty:* 2 full-time (both women), 7 part-time/adjunct (3 women). *Students:* 19 full-time (15 women), 41 part-time (35 women); includes 18 minority (5 Black or African American, non-Hispanic/Latino; 4 Asian, non-Hispanic/Latino; 8 Hispanic/Latino; 1 Two or more races, non-Hispanic/Latino). Average age 33. 57 applicants, 74% accepted, 29 enrolled. In 2016, 12 master's awarded. *Entrance requirements:* For master's, GRE (minimum combined score of 300 from any two tests), MAT (minimum score 400), LAST (taken within past five years), BS or equivalent; minimum cumulative undergraduate GPA of 3.0; NY state provisional or initial certification (for adolescence education); BS with major in biology, chemistry, economics, English, history, life sciences, math, physics, or psychology (for childhood and early childhood education). Additional exam requirements/recommendations for international students: Required—TOEFL (minimum score 79 iBT), IELTS (minimum score 6). *Application deadline:* Applications are processed on a rolling basis. Application fee: $50. Electronic applications accepted. *Expenses:* $1,215 per credit. *Financial support:* Career-related internships or fieldwork, Federal Work-Study, scholarships/grants, tuition waivers (full and partial), and unspecified assistantships available. Support available to part-time students. Financial award application deadline: 3/1; financial award applicants required to submit FAFSA. *Faculty research:* Evolving definition of new literacies and its impact on teaching and learning (twenty-first century skills), new literacies practices in teacher education, teachers' professional development, English language and literacy learning through mobile learning, teaching reading to culturally and linguistically diverse children. *Unit head:* Dr. Hui-Yin Hsu, Department Chair, 516-686-1322, Fax: 516-686-7655, E-mail: hhsu02@nyit.edu. *Application contact:* Alice Dolitsky, Director, Graduate Admissions, 516-686-7520, Fax: 516-686-1116, E-mail: nyitgrad@nyit.edu.
Website: http://www.nyit.edu/interdisciplinary/department_teacher_education

New York University, Steinhardt School of Culture, Education, and Human Development, Department of Teaching and Learning, Program in Early Childhood and Childhood Education, New York, NY 10003. Offers childhood education (MA); early childhood education (MA); early childhood education/early childhood special education (MA). *Accreditation:* TEAC. *Program availability:* Part-time. *Degree requirements:* For master's, thesis (for some programs). *Entrance requirements:* Additional exam requirements/recommendations for international students: Required—TOEFL (minimum score 100 iBT). Electronic applications accepted. *Faculty research:* Teacher evaluation and beliefs about teaching, early literacy development, language arts, child development and education, cultural differences.

New York University, Steinhardt School of Culture, Education, and Human Development, Department of Teaching and Learning, Program in Special Education, New York, NY 10012-1019. Offers childhood (MA); early childhood (MA). *Accreditation:* TEAC. *Program availability:* Part-time. *Degree requirements:* For master's, thesis (for some programs). *Entrance requirements:* Additional exam requirements/recommendations for international students: Required—TOEFL (minimum score 100 iBT). Electronic applications accepted. *Faculty research:* Special education referrals, attention deficit disorders in children, mainstreaming, curriculum-based assessment and program implementation, special education policy.

Niagara University, Graduate Division of Education, Concentration in Teacher Education, Niagara University, NY 14109. Offers early childhood and childhood education (MS Ed, Certificate); early childhood special education (MS); middle and adolescence education (MS Ed); special education (MS Ed), including 1-6, 7-12; special education (grades 1-12) (Certificate); teaching English to speakers of other languages (MS Ed, Certificate). *Accreditation:* NCATE. *Students:* 101 full-time (83 women), 123 part-time (101 women); includes 14 minority (6 Black or African American, non-Hispanic/Latino; 1 American Indian or Alaska Native, non-Hispanic/Latino; 6 Hispanic/Latino; 1 Two or more races, non-Hispanic/Latino), 28 international. Average age 28. In 2016, 86 master's, 18 other advanced degrees awarded. *Entrance requirements:* For master's, GRE General Test or Academic Literacy Skills Test (ALST). Additional exam requirements/recommendations for international students: Required—TOEFL (minimum score 550 paper-based; 79 iBT), IELTS (minimum score 6). *Application deadline:* For fall admission, 8/1 for domestic students. Applications are processed on a rolling basis. Application fee: $30. *Expenses:* Contact institution. *Financial support:* Research assistantships with tuition reimbursements, teaching assistantships with tuition reimbursements, career-related internships or fieldwork, Federal Work-Study, scholarships/grants, and unspecified assistantships available. Financial award application deadline: 4/15; financial award applicants required to submit FAFSA. *Unit head:* Dr. Chandra Foote, Dean, College of Education, 716-286-8549, E-mail: cjf@niagara.edu. *Application contact:* Evan Pierce, Associate Director, Graduate Studies, 716-286-8327, E-mail: epierce@niagara.edu.
Website: http://www.niagara.edu/teacher-education

Norfolk State University, School of Graduate Studies, School of Education, Department of Early Childhood and Elementary Education, Norfolk, VA 23504. Offers early childhood education (MAT); pre-elementary education (MA). *Accreditation:* NCATE. *Program availability:* Part-time. *Degree requirements:* For master's, comprehensive exam, thesis or alternative. *Entrance requirements:* For master's, PRAXIS I and II, minimum GPA of 2.5, letters of recommendation, interview. *Faculty research:* Parent involvement in education.

North Carolina Agricultural and Technical State University, School of Graduate Studies, School of Agriculture and Environmental Sciences, Department of Family and Consumer Sciences, Greensboro, NC 27411. Offers child development early education and family studies (MAT); family and consumer sciences (MAT); food and nutrition (MS). *Program availability:* Part-time, evening/weekend. *Degree requirements:* For master's, comprehensive exam, thesis or alternative, qualifying exam. *Entrance requirements:* For master's, GRE General Test, minimum GPA of 2.6.

Northeastern Illinois University, College of Graduate Studies and Research, College of Education, Program in Early Childhood Education, Chicago, IL 60625-4699. Offers MAT. *Degree requirements:* For master's, practicum, internship, research project. *Entrance requirements:* For master's, bachelor's degree from accredited college or university; minimum undergraduate GPA of 3.0; three professional references. Electronic applications accepted.

Northeastern State University, College of Education, Department of Curriculum and Instruction, Program in Early Childhood Education, Tahlequah, OK 74464-2399. Offers M Ed. *Program availability:* Part-time, evening/weekend. *Faculty:* 12 full-time (9 women). *Students:* 1 (woman) full-time, 11 part-time (all women); includes 6 minority (1 Black or African American, non-Hispanic/Latino; 2 American Indian or Alaska Native, non-Hispanic/Latino; 1 Hispanic/Latino; 2 Two or more races, non-Hispanic/Latino). Average age 38. In 2016, 10 master's awarded. *Degree requirements:* For master's, thesis. *Entrance requirements:* For master's, GRE or MAT, minimum GPA of 2.5. Additional exam requirements/recommendations for international students: Required—TOEFL. *Application deadline:* For fall admission, 6/1 priority date for domestic students. Applications are processed on a rolling basis. Application fee: $25. Electronic applications accepted. *Expenses:* Tuition, state resident: full-time $2816; part-time $216.60 per credit hour. Tuition, nonresident: full-time $6365; part-time $489.60 per credit hour. *Required fees:* $37.40 per credit hour. *Financial support:* Teaching assistantships and Federal Work-Study available. Financial award application deadline: 3/1. *Unit head:* Dr. Anita Ede, Chair, 918-449-6523, E-mail: edear@nsuok.edu. *Application contact:* Josh McCollum, Graduate Coordinator, 918-444-2093, E-mail: mccolluj@nsuok.edu.
Website: https://academics.nsuok.edu/education/EducationHome/COEDepartments/CurriculumInstruction.aspx

Northern Arizona University, Graduate College, College of Education, Department of Teaching and Learning, Flagstaff, AZ 86011. Offers curriculum and instruction (Ed D); early childhood education (M Ed); elementary education (M Ed); secondary education (M Ed). *Program availability:* Part-time. *Degree requirements:* For master's, comprehensive exam (for some programs), thesis (for some programs). *Entrance requirements:* For master's, minimum GPA of 3.0. Additional exam requirements/recommendations for international students: Required—TOEFL (minimum score 550 paper-based; 80 iBT), IELTS (minimum score 7). Electronic applications accepted. *Expenses:* Tuition, state resident: full-time $8971; part-time $444 per credit hour. Tuition, nonresident: full-time $20,958; part-time $1164 per credit hour. *Required fees:* $1018; $644 per credit hour. Tuition and fees vary according to course load, campus/location and program.

Northern Illinois University, Graduate School, College of Education, Department of Special and Early Education, De Kalb, IL 60115-2854. Offers curriculum and instruction (MS Ed, Ed D), including curriculum leadership (Ed D), elementary education (Ed D), secondary education (Ed D); early childhood education (MS Ed); elementary education (MS Ed); special education (MS Ed). *Program availability:* Part-time, evening/weekend. *Faculty:* 22 full-time (14 women), 2 part-time/adjunct (both women). *Students:* 42 full-time (34 women), 85 part-time (68 women); includes 16 minority (4 Black or African American, non-Hispanic/Latino; 3 Asian, non-Hispanic/Latino; 6 Hispanic/Latino; 3 Two or more races, non-Hispanic/Latino), 6 international. Average age 33. 70 applicants, 73% accepted, 30 enrolled. In 2016, 19 master's, 1 doctorate awarded. *Degree requirements:* For master's, comprehensive exam, thesis optional; for doctorate, thesis/dissertation, candidacy exam, dissertation defense. *Entrance requirements:* For master's, GRE General Test or MAT, minimum undergraduate GPA of 2.75; for doctorate, GRE General Test or MAT, minimum undergraduate GPA of 2.75, graduate

3.2. Additional exam requirements/recommendations for international students: Required—TOEFL (minimum score 550 paper-based). *Application deadline:* For fall admission, 6/1 for domestic students, 5/1 for international students; for spring admission, 11/1 for domestic students, 10/1 for international students. Applications are processed on a rolling basis. Application fee: $40. Electronic applications accepted. *Financial support:* In 2016–17, 14 research assistantships with full tuition reimbursements were awarded; fellowships with full tuition reimbursements, teaching assistantships with full tuition reimbursements, career-related internships or fieldwork, Federal Work-Study, scholarships/grants, tuition waivers (full), and unspecified assistantships also available. Support available to part-time students. Financial award applicants required to submit FAFSA. *Faculty research:* Teacher certification, stress reduction during student teaching, teaching history, portfolios in student teaching. *Unit head:* Gregory Conderman, Chair, 815-753-1619, E-mail: seed@niu.edu. *Application contact:* Gail Myers, Clerk, Graduate Advising, 815-753-0381, E-mail: gmyers@niu.edu.
Website: http://www.cedu.niu.edu/seed/

Northwestern College, Program in Education, Orange City, IA 51041-1996. Offers early childhood (M Ed); master teacher (M Ed); teacher leadership (M Ed, Graduate Certificate). *Program availability:* Online learning.

Northwestern State University of Louisiana, Graduate Studies and Research, College of Education and Human Development, Program in Early Childhood Education, Natchitoches, LA 71497. Offers early childhood education and teaching (M Ed, MAT). *Degree requirements:* For master's, comprehensive exam, thesis or alternative. *Entrance requirements:* For master's, GRE General Test. Additional exam requirements/ recommendations for international students: Required—TOEFL. Electronic applications accepted.

Northwest Missouri State University, Graduate School, School of Education, Maryville, MO 64468-6001. Offers early childhood education (MS Ed); education leadership (MS Ed), including elementary, K-12, secondary; educational leadership (Ed S), including elementary school principalship, secondary school principalship, superintendency; educational leadership and policy analysis (Ed D); elementary education (MS Ed); elementary mathematics (MS Ed); higher education leadership (MS); middle school education (MS Ed); reading (MS Ed); special education (MS Ed); teacher leadership (MS Ed); teaching English language learners (MS Ed). *Accreditation:* NCATE. *Program availability:* Part-time. *Students:* 15 full-time (11 women), 150 part-time (103 women). In 2016, 46 master's awarded. *Degree requirements:* For master's, comprehensive exam; for Ed S, comprehensive exam, thesis. *Entrance requirements:* For master's, GRE General Test, writing sample; for Ed S, minimum graduate GPA of 3.25. Additional exam requirements/recommendations for international students: Required—TOEFL (minimum score 550 paper-based). *Application deadline:* For fall admission, 7/1 for domestic and international students; for spring admission, 11/15 for domestic and international students. Applications are processed on a rolling basis. Application fee: $0 ($50 for international students). Electronic applications accepted. *Expenses:* Tuition, state resident: full-time $3447; part-time $383 per credit hour. Tuition, nonresident: full-time $5724; part-time $636 per credit hour. *Required fees:* $130 per credit hour. *Financial support:* Research assistantships with full tuition reimbursements, teaching assistantships with full tuition reimbursements, and unspecified assistantships available. Financial award application deadline: 4/1; financial award applicants required to submit FAFSA. *Faculty research:* Great books of educational administration. *Unit head:* Dr. Tim Wall, Dean, 660-562-1179, E-mail: timwall@nwmissouri.edu.
Website: http://www.nwmissouri.edu/academics/ed/

Oakland University, Graduate Study and Lifelong Learning, School of Education and Human Services, Department of Human Development and Child Studies, Program in Early Childhood Education, Rochester, MI 48309-4401. Offers early childhood education (M Ed, PhD); early education and intervention (Ed S). *Accreditation:* TEAC. *Degree requirements:* For doctorate, thesis/dissertation. *Entrance requirements:* For master's, minimum GPA of 3.0; for doctorate, GRE General Test, minimum GPA of 3.0. Additional exam requirements/recommendations for international students: Required—TOEFL (minimum score 550 paper-based).

Oklahoma City University, Petree College of Arts and Sciences, Oklahoma City, OK 73106-1402. Offers applied behavioral studies (M Ed); applied sociology: nonprofit leadership (MA); creative writing (MFA); criminology (MS); early childhood education (M Ed); elementary education (M Ed); general studies (MLA); leadership/management (MLA); moving image arts (MFA); professional counseling (M Ed); teaching (MA); teaching English to speakers of other languages (MA). *Program availability:* Part-time, evening/weekend. *Faculty:* 11 full-time (5 women), 15 part-time/adjunct (6 women). *Students:* 77 full-time (55 women), 46 part-time (30 women); includes 32 minority (13 Black or African American, non-Hispanic/Latino; 1 American Indian or Alaska Native, non-Hispanic/Latino; 2 Asian, non-Hispanic/Latino; 12 Hispanic/Latino; 4 Two or more races, non-Hispanic/Latino), 37 international. Average age 34. 92 applicants, 74% accepted, 46 enrolled. In 2016, 72 master's awarded. *Degree requirements:* For master's, capstone/practicum. *Entrance requirements:* For master's, bachelor's degree from accredited institution with minimum GPA of 3.0, essay, recommendation letters. Additional exam requirements/recommendations for international students: Required—TOEFL (minimum score 550 paper-based; 80 iBT). *Application deadline:* Applications are processed on a rolling basis. Application fee: $50. Electronic applications accepted. *Expenses:* Contact institution. *Financial support:* In 2016–17, 16 students received support. Federal Work-Study, institutionally sponsored loans, scholarships/grants, and tuition waivers (full and partial) available. Support available to part-time students. Financial award application deadline: 6/1; financial award applicants required to submit FAFSA. *Unit head:* Dr. Amy Cataldi, Dean, 405-208-5446, Fax: 405-208-5447, E-mail: acataldi@okcu.edu. *Application contact:* Michael Harrington, Director of Graduate Admissions, 800-633-7242, Fax: 405-208-5356, E-mail: gadmissions@okcu.edu.
Website: http://www.okcu.edu/petree/

Old Dominion University, Darden College of Education, Program in Early Childhood Education, Norfolk, VA 23529. Offers MS Ed, PhD. *Accreditation:* NCATE. *Program availability:* Part-time, evening/weekend. *Faculty:* 5 full-time (3 women), 2 part-time/ adjunct (1 woman). *Students:* 2 full-time (both women), 3 part-time (all women); includes 2 minority (both Black or African American, non-Hispanic/Latino). Average age 37. 5 applicants, 80% accepted, 4 enrolled. In 2016, 6 master's, 1 doctorate awarded. *Degree requirements:* For master's, comprehensive exam, written exams; for doctorate, comprehensive exam, thesis/dissertation. *Entrance requirements:* For master's, GRE General Test, PRAXIS I, minimum undergraduate GPA of 2.8; for doctorate, GRE General Test. Additional exam requirements/recommendations for international students: Required—TOEFL. *Application deadline:* For fall admission, 6/1 for domestic students; for winter admission, 11/1 for domestic students; for spring admission, 3/1 for domestic students. Applications are processed on a rolling basis. Application fee: $50. *Expenses:* Tuition, state resident: full-time $8604; part-time $478 per credit hour. Tuition, nonresident: full-time $21,510; part-time $1195 per credit hour. *Required fees:* $66 per semester. Tuition and fees vary according to campus/location, program and reciprocity agreements. *Financial support:* In 2016–17, fellowships with full tuition reimbursements (averaging $15,000 per year), 2 research assistantships (averaging $9,000 per year), 2 teaching assistantships with full tuition reimbursements (averaging $15,000 per year) were awarded. Financial award application deadline: 2/15; financial award applicants required to submit FAFSA. *Faculty research:* Creativity, informal learning environment, children's thinking, early childhood teacher professional development, integrated curriculum. *Unit head:* Dr. Angela Eckhoff, Graduate Program Director, 757-683-3284, Fax: 757-683-5862, E-mail: aeckhoff@odu.edu. *Application contact:* William Heffelfinger, Director of Graduate Admissions, 757-683-5554, Fax: 757-683-3255, E-mail: gradadmit@odu.edu.
Website: http://www.odu.edu/academics/programs/masters/early-childhood-education

Old Dominion University, Darden College of Education, Program in Special Education, Norfolk, VA 23529. Offers adapted curriculum K-12 (MS Ed); early childhood special education (MS Ed); general curriculum K-12 (MS Ed); special education (PhD). *Accreditation:* NCATE. *Program availability:* Part-time, evening/weekend, 100% online, blended/hybrid learning. *Faculty:* 12 full-time (9 women), 13 part-time/adjunct (9 women). *Students:* 42 full-time (38 women), 65 part-time (56 women); includes 25 minority (18 Black or African American, non-Hispanic/Latino; 3 Asian, non-Hispanic/ Latino; 1 Hispanic/Latino; 3 Two or more races, non-Hispanic/Latino), 7 international. Average age 34. 78 applicants, 85% accepted, 61 enrolled. In 2016, 24 master's awarded. *Degree requirements:* For master's, comprehensive exam, thesis or alternative; for doctorate, comprehensive exam, thesis/dissertation. *Entrance requirements:* For master's, GRE General Test or MAT, PRAXIS Core Academic Skills for Educator Tests, minimum GPA of 2.8; for doctorate, GRE. Additional exam requirements/recommendations for international students: Recommended—TOEFL (minimum score 550 paper-based). *Application deadline:* For fall admission, 6/1 priority date for domestic and international students; for winter admission, 11/1 priority date for domestic and international students; for spring admission, 3/1 priority date for domestic and international students. Applications are processed on a rolling basis. Application fee: $50. Electronic applications accepted. *Expenses:* Contact institution. *Financial support:* In 2016–17, 70 students received support, including 1 teaching assistantship with full tuition reimbursement available (averaging $15,000 per year); fellowships, research assistantships with tuition reimbursements available, scholarships/grants, and unspecified assistantships also available. Support available to part-time students. Financial award application deadline: 2/15; financial award applicants required to submit FAFSA. *Faculty research:* Inclusion, autism spectrum disorder, functional behavioral assessment, infant, preschool, and school-age children and youth with disabilities, distance learning. *Total annual research expenditures:* $3.6 million. *Unit head:* Dr. Sabra Gear, Graduate Program Director, 757-683-4383, Fax: 757-683-4129, E-mail: sgear@odu.edu. *Application contact:* William Heffelfinger, Director of Graduate Admissions, 757-683-5554, Fax: 757-683-3255, E-mail: gradadmit@odu.edu.
Website: https://www.odu.edu/cdse/academics/sped

Oregon State University, College of Education, Program in Education, Corvallis, OR 97331. Offers advanced science and mathematics education (Ed M); agricultural education (PhD); education (Ed D); free-choice learning (Ed M); language equity and educational policy (PhD); mathematics education (MS); pre-K-12 English to speakers of other languages (ESOL) (Ed M); science education (MS); science/mathematics education (PhD); social justice in education (Ed M). *Program availability:* Part-time, 100% online, blended/hybrid learning. *Faculty:* 9 full-time (8 women), 6 part-time/adjunct (2 women). *Students:* 14 full-time (8 women), 76 part-time (53 women); includes 25 minority (6 Black or African American, non-Hispanic/Latino; 2 American Indian or Alaska Native, non-Hispanic/Latino; 5 Asian, non-Hispanic/Latino; 10 Hispanic/Latino; 2 Two or more races, non-Hispanic/Latino), 3 international. Average age 38. 72 applicants, 69% accepted, 40 enrolled. In 2016, 14 master's, 21 doctorates awarded. Terminal master's awarded for partial completion of doctoral program. *Degree requirements:* For master's, variable foreign language requirement, thesis (for some programs); for doctorate, variable foreign language requirement, thesis/dissertation. *Entrance requirements:* Additional exam requirements/recommendations for international students: Required—TOEFL (minimum score 575 paper-based). Application fee: $75 ($85 for international students). *Expenses:* Tuition, state resident: full-time $12,150; part-time $450 per credit. Tuition, nonresident: full-time $21,789; part-time $807 per credit. *Required fees:* $1651; $1507 per credit. One-time fee: $350. Tuition and fees vary according to course load, campus/location and program. *Financial support:* Fellowships, research assistantships, teaching assistantships, career-related internships or fieldwork, Federal Work-Study, and institutionally sponsored loans available. Support available to part-time students. *Faculty research:* School administration, educational foundations, research methodology, education policy development, higher education administration. *Unit head:* Dr. Larry Flick, Dean. *Application contact:* E-mail: askcoed@oregonstate.edu.

Ottawa University, Graduate Studies-Arizona, Program in Education, Ottawa, KS 66067-3399. Offers community college counseling (MA); curriculum and instruction (MA); early childhood (MA); education intervention (MA); education leadership (MA); education technology (MA); Montessori early childhood education (MA); Montessori elementary education (MA); professional development (MA); school guidance counseling (MA); special education - cross categorical (MA). Programs offered in Mesa, Phoenix, Tempe and West Valley, AZ. *Accreditation:* NCATE. *Program availability:* Part-time. *Degree requirements:* For master's, thesis or alternative. *Entrance requirements:* For master's, minimum undergraduate GPA of 3.0, copy of current state certification or teaching license. Additional exam requirements/recommendations for international students: Required—TOEFL (minimum score 550 paper-based). Electronic applications accepted. *Expenses:* Contact institution.

Pace University, School of Education, New York, NY 10038. Offers adolescent education (MST), including biology, business education, chemistry, earth science, English, foreign languages, mathematics, physics, social studies, visual arts; childhood education (MST); early childhood development, learning and intervention (MST); educational technology studies (MS); inclusive adolescent education (MST), including biology, business education, chemistry, earth science, English, foreign languages, mathematics, physics, social studies, visual arts; integrated instruction for educational technology (Certificate); integrated instruction for literacy and technology (Certificate); literacy (MS Ed); special education (MS Ed). *Accreditation:* NCATE. *Program availability:* Part-time, evening/weekend, blended/hybrid learning. *Faculty:* 19 full-time (13 women), 86 part-time/adjunct (49 women). *Students:* 115 full-time (97 women), 543 part-time (381 women); includes 280 minority (137 Black or African American, non-Hispanic/Latino; 1 American Indian or Alaska Native, non-Hispanic/Latino; 40 Asian, non-Hispanic/Latino; 87 Hispanic/Latino; 15 Two or more races, non-Hispanic/Latino), 13 international. Average age 30. 181 applicants, 78% accepted, 72 enrolled. In 2016, 193 master's, 9 other advanced degrees awarded. *Degree requirements:* For master's, certification exams. *Entrance requirements:* For master's, GRE, interview, teaching certificate (except for MST). Additional exam requirements/recommendations for international students: Required—TOEFL (minimum score 88 iBT), IELTS or PTE. *Application deadline:* For fall admission, 8/1 priority date for domestic students, 6/1 for international students; for spring admission, 12/1 priority date for domestic students, 10/ 1 for international students. Applications are processed on a rolling basis. Application fee: $70. Electronic applications accepted. *Expenses:* Contact institution. *Financial support:* In 2016–17, 17 students received support, including 17 research assistantships with partial tuition reimbursements available (averaging $6,020 per year); career-related internships or fieldwork and Federal Work-Study also available. Financial award application deadline: 9/1; financial award applicants required to submit FAFSA.

Early Childhood Education

Faculty research: STEM education, TESOL, teacher education, special education, language and literary development. *Total annual research expenditures:* $290,153. *Unit head:* Dr. Xiao-Lei Wang, Dean, School of Education, 914-773-3876, E-mail: xwang@pace.edu. *Application contact:* Susan Ford-Goldschein, Director of Graduate Admissions, 212-346-1531, Fax: 212-346-1585, E-mail: graduateadmission@pace.edu.
Website: http://www.pace.edu/school-of-education

Pacific Oaks College, Graduate School, Program in Early Childhood Education, Pasadena, CA 91103. Offers MA. *Program availability:* Part-time, online learning.

Pacific University, College of Education, Forest Grove, OR 97116-1797. Offers early childhood education (MAT); education (MAE); elementary education (MAT); ESOL (MAT); high school education (MAT); middle school education (MAT); special education (MAT); speech-language pathology (MS); STEM education (MAT); talented and gifted (M Ed); visual function in learning (M Ed). *Accreditation:* NCATE. *Program availability:* Part-time, evening/weekend. *Degree requirements:* For master's, research project. *Entrance requirements:* For master's, California Basic Educational Skills Test, PRAXIS II, minimum undergraduate GPA of 2.75, 3.0 graduate. Additional exam requirements/recommendations for international students: Required—TOEFL. Electronic applications accepted. *Expenses:* Contact institution. *Faculty research:* Defining a culturally competent classroom, technology in the k-12 classroom, Socratic seminars, social studies education.

Piedmont College, School of Education, Demorest, GA 30535. Offers art education (MAT); curriculum and instruction (Ed S); early childhood education (MA, MAT); instructional technology (MAT); middle grades education (MA, MAT); music education (MAT); secondary education (MA, MAT); special education (MA, MAT). *Program availability:* Part-time, evening/weekend. *Students:* 290 full-time (217 women), 614 part-time (508 women); includes 131 minority (97 Black or African American, non-Hispanic/Latino; 4 American Indian or Alaska Native, non-Hispanic/Latino; 5 Asian, non-Hispanic/Latino; 11 Hispanic/Latino; 6 Native Hawaiian or other Pacific Islander, non-Hispanic/Latino; 8 Two or more races, non-Hispanic/Latino), 6 international. Average age 37. 257 applicants, 64% accepted, 160 enrolled. In 2016, 288 master's, 243 other advanced degrees awarded. *Degree requirements:* For master's, thesis, field experience in the classroom teaching. *Entrance requirements:* For master's, GRE General Test, MAT, minimum undergraduate GPA of 2.5; for Ed S, minimum graduate GPA of 3.5, valid teaching certificate. Additional exam requirements/recommendations for international students: Required—TOEFL (minimum score 550 paper-based). *Application deadline:* For fall admission, 7/15 for domestic students; for spring admission, 12/1 for domestic students. Applications are processed on a rolling basis. Electronic applications accepted. *Expenses: Tuition:* Full-time $8910. *Financial support:* Career-related internships or fieldwork, Federal Work-Study, and unspecified assistantships available. Support available to part-time students. Financial award applicants required to submit FAFSA. *Unit head:* Dr. Don Gnecco, Dean, 706-778-3000 Ext. 1201, Fax: 706-776-9608, E-mail: dgnecco@piedmont.edu. *Application contact:* Kathleen Anderson, Director of Graduate Enrollment Management, 706-778-8500 Ext. 1181, Fax: 706-778-0150, E-mail: kanderson@piedmont.edu.

Pontificia Universidad Catolica Madre y Maestra, Graduate School, Faculty of Sciences and Humanities, Santiago, Dominican Republic. Offers architecture (M Arch), including architecture of interiors, architecture of tourist lodgings, landscaping; early childhood education (M Ed).

Prescott College, Graduate Programs, Program in Education, Prescott, AZ 86301. Offers early childhood education (MA); early childhood special education (MA); education (MA); elementary education (MA); environmental education leadership and administration (MA); equine-assisted learning (MA); school guidance counseling (MA); secondary education (MA); special education: learning disabilities (MA); special education: mental retardation (MA); special education: serious emotional disabilities (MA); student-directed independent study (MA); sustainability education (PhD). *Program availability:* Part-time, online learning. *Faculty:* 9 full-time (all women). *Students:* 9 full-time (8 women), 30 part-time (20 women); includes 11 minority (3 Black or African American, non-Hispanic/Latino; 2 American Indian or Alaska Native, non-Hispanic/Latino; 6 Hispanic/Latino). Average age 36. 66 applicants, 82% accepted, 32 enrolled. In 2016, 12 master's, 8 doctorates awarded. *Degree requirements:* For master's, thesis, fieldwork or internship, practicum; for doctorate, thesis/dissertation. *Entrance requirements:* For master's, 2 letters of recommendation, resume; for doctorate, 3 letters of recommendation, resume, official transcripts, personal statement, program proposal. Additional exam requirements/recommendations for international students: Required—TOEFL (minimum score 500 paper-based). *Application deadline:* For fall admission, 4/15 priority date for domestic and international students; for spring admission, 9/15 priority date for domestic and international students. Applications are processed on a rolling basis. Application fee: $40. Electronic applications accepted. *Expenses: Tuition:* Full-time $19,680. One-time fee: $260 part-time. *Financial support:* Fellowships, research assistantships, teaching assistantships, career-related internships or fieldwork, Federal Work-Study, institutionally sponsored loans, scholarships/grants, traineeships, health care benefits, tuition waivers, and unspecified assistantships available. Support available to part-time students. Financial award applicants required to submit FAFSA. *Unit head:* Bob Ellis, 928-350-2217, E-mail: bellis@prescott.edu. *Application contact:* Melanie Lefever, Assistant Director, Limited-residency Programs, 928-350-2106, Fax: 928-776-5242, E-mail: mlefever@prescott.edu.

Queens College of the City University of New York, Arts and Humanities Division, Department of English, Queens, NY 11367-1597. Offers creative writing and literary translation (MFA); early childhood birth-2nd grade (Advanced Certificate); English (MA). *Program availability:* Part-time. *Faculty:* 51 full-time (26 women), 74 part-time/adjunct (47 women). *Students:* 66 part-time (39 women); includes 29 minority (8 Black or African American, non-Hispanic/Latino; 4 Asian, non-Hispanic/Latino; 14 Hispanic/Latino; 3 Two or more races, non-Hispanic/Latino), 2 international. Average age 31. 88 applicants, 55% accepted, 21 enrolled. In 2016, 29 master's awarded. *Degree requirements:* For master's, thesis, oral exam (English language and literature). *Entrance requirements:* For master's, manuscript (creative writing), minimum GPA of 3.0. Additional exam requirements/recommendations for international students: Required—TOEFL (minimum score 100 iBT), IELTS (minimum score 7). *Application deadline:* For fall admission, 4/1 for domestic students; for spring admission, 11/1 for domestic students. Applications are processed on a rolling basis. Application fee: $125. Electronic applications accepted. *Expenses:* Tuition, state resident: full-time $5065; part-time $425 per credit. Tuition, nonresident: part-time $780 per credit. *Required fees:* $522; $397 per credit. Part-time tuition and fees vary according to course load and program. *Financial support:* Career-related internships or fieldwork available. Financial award application deadline: 4/1; financial award applicants required to submit FAFSA. *Unit head:* Prof. Glenn Burger, Chairperson, 718-997-4600, E-mail: glenn.burger@qc.cuny.edu.

Queens College of the City University of New York, Division of Education, Department of Educational and Community Programs, Queens, NY 11367-1597. Offers bilingual pupil personnel (AC); counselor education (MS Ed); mental health counseling (MS); school building leader (AC); school district leader (AC); school psychologist (MS Ed); special education-childhood education (AC); special education-early childhood (MS Ed); teacher of special education 1-6 (MS Ed); teacher of special education birth-2 (MS Ed); teaching students with disabilities, grades 7-12 (MS Ed, AC). *Program availability:* Part-time. *Faculty:* 20 full-time (14 women), 50 part-time/adjunct (26 women). *Students:* 101 full-time (85 women), 459 part-time (383 women); includes 230 minority (44 Black or African American, non-Hispanic/Latino; 3 American Indian or Alaska Native, non-Hispanic/Latino; 46 Asian, non-Hispanic/Latino; 128 Hispanic/Latino; 1 Native Hawaiian or other Pacific Islander, non-Hispanic/Latino; 8 Two or more races, non-Hispanic/Latino), 3 international. Average age 28. 515 applicants, 57% accepted, 230 enrolled. In 2016, 158 master's, 68 other advanced degrees awarded. *Degree requirements:* For master's, research project; for AC, internship. *Entrance requirements:* For master's, minimum GPA of 3.0. Additional exam requirements/recommendations for international students: Required—TOEFL, IELTS. *Application deadline:* For fall admission, 3/1 for domestic students. Applications are processed on a rolling basis. Application fee: $125. Electronic applications accepted. *Expenses:* Tuition, state resident: full-time $5065; part-time $425 per credit. Tuition, nonresident: part-time $780 per credit. *Required fees:* $522; $397 per credit. Part-time tuition and fees vary according to course load and program. *Financial support:* Career-related internships or fieldwork available. Financial award application deadline: 4/1; financial award applicants required to submit FAFSA. *Unit head:* Dr. Lynn Howell, Chairperson, 718-997-5250, E-mail: lynn.howell@qc.cuny.edu.

Queens College of the City University of New York, Division of Education, Department of Elementary and Early Childhood Education, Queens, NY 11367-1597. Offers bilingual education (MS Ed); child development psychology (AC); childhood education (MAT, MS Ed); childhood education and special education (MAT); childhood education-bilingual education (MAT, MS Ed, AC); children's literacy (AC); early childhood education (MAT); early childhood education birth-2 (MS Ed, AC); elementary education (MS Ed); literacy birth-grade 6 (AC); literacy technology birth-grade 6 (MS Ed); social studies education grades 1-6 (AC). *Program availability:* Part-time, evening/weekend. *Faculty:* 25 full-time (19 women), 33 part-time/adjunct (28 women). *Students:* 134 full-time (119 women), 374 part-time (349 women); includes 251 minority (55 Black or African American, non-Hispanic/Latino; 1 American Indian or Alaska Native, non-Hispanic/Latino; 82 Asian, non-Hispanic/Latino; 103 Hispanic/Latino; 10 Two or more races, non-Hispanic/Latino), 12 international. Average age 29. 364 applicants, 72% accepted, 224 enrolled. In 2016, 184 master's, 62 other advanced degrees awarded. *Degree requirements:* For master's, research project. *Entrance requirements:* For master's, minimum GPA of 3.0. Additional exam requirements/recommendations for international students: Required—TOEFL, IELTS. *Application deadline:* For fall admission, 4/1 for domestic students. Applications are processed on a rolling basis. Application fee: $125. Electronic applications accepted. *Expenses:* Tuition, state resident: full-time $5065; part-time $425 per credit. Tuition, nonresident: part-time $780 per credit. *Required fees:* $522; $397 per credit. Part-time tuition and fees vary according to course load and program. *Financial support:* Career-related internships or fieldwork available. Financial award application deadline: 4/1; financial award applicants required to submit FAFSA. *Unit head:* Dr. Mary Bushnell Greiner, Chairperson, 718-997-5328, E-mail: mary.greiner@qc.cuny.edu.

Radford University, College of Graduate Studies and Research, Program in Education, Radford, VA 24142. Offers early childhood education (MS); math education content area studies (MS). *Accreditation:* NCATE. *Program availability:* Part-time, evening/weekend. *Faculty:* 12 full-time (8 women). *Students:* 39 full-time (33 women), 53 part-time (39 women); includes 7 minority (3 Black or African American, non-Hispanic/Latino; 2 Hispanic/Latino; 2 Two or more races, non-Hispanic/Latino). Average age 30. 32 applicants, 94% accepted, 26 enrolled. In 2016, 46 master's awarded. *Degree requirements:* For master's, comprehensive exam. *Entrance requirements:* For master's, GRE (waived for any applicant with advanced degree), minimum GPA of 3.0, 2 letters of professional reference, personal statement, resume, official transcripts. Additional exam requirements/recommendations for international students: Required—TOEFL (minimum score 550 paper-based; 79 iBT), IELTS (minimum score 6.5). *Application deadline:* For fall admission, 2/15 priority date for domestic students, 12/1 for international students; for spring admission, 7/1 for international students. Applications are processed on a rolling basis. Application fee: $50. Electronic applications accepted. *Expenses:* Tuition, state resident: full-time $7868; part-time $328 per credit hour. Tuition, nonresident: full-time $16,394; part-time $683 per credit hour. *Required fees:* $3090; $130 per credit hour. Tuition and fees vary according to course load and program. *Financial support:* In 2016–17, 15 students received support. Career-related internships or fieldwork, scholarships/grants, and unspecified assistantships available. Support available to part-time students. Financial award application deadline: 3/1; financial award applicants required to submit FAFSA. *Unit head:* Dr. Wendy Eckenrod-Green, Coordinator, 540-831-5302, E-mail: stel@radford.edu.
Website: http://www.radford.edu/content/cehd/home/teacher-ed/programs/education-master.html

Regent University, Graduate School, School of Education, Virginia Beach, VA 23464-9800. Offers adult education (Ed D, PhD, Ed S); advanced educational leadership (Ed D, PhD, Ed S); career switcher (M Ed); character education (Ed D, PhD, Ed S); Christian education leadership (Ed D, PhD, Ed S); Christian school administration (M Ed); curriculum and instruction (M Ed), including adult education, Christian school, gifted and talented education, STEM education, teacher leader; educational leadership (M Ed); educational psychology (Ed D, PhD, Ed S); educational technology and online learning (Ed D, PhD, Ed S); elementary education (M Ed); exceptional education executive leadership (Ed D, PhD, Ed S); higher education (Ed D, PhD, Ed S); higher education leadership and management (Ed D, PhD, Ed S); individualized degree plan (M Ed); K-12 school leadership (Ed D, PhD, Ed S); K-12 special education (M Ed); K-8 leadership in mathematics education (M Ed); leadership in mathematics education (Ed S); reading specialist (M Ed); special education (Ed D, PhD, Ed S); student affairs (M Ed); TESOL (M Ed), including adult education - collegiate, K-12. *Accreditation:* TEAC. *Program availability:* Part-time, evening/weekend, 100% online, blended/hybrid learning. *Faculty:* 22 full-time (10 women), 42 part-time/adjunct (31 women). *Students:* 89 full-time (62 women), 1,035 part-time (823 women); includes 466 minority (381 Black or African American, non-Hispanic/Latino; 3 American Indian or Alaska Native, non-Hispanic/Latino; 19 Asian, non-Hispanic/Latino; 50 Hispanic/Latino; 13 Two or more races, non-Hispanic/Latino), 11 international. Average age 39. 976 applicants, 59% accepted, 449 enrolled. In 2016, 241 master's, 22 doctorates, 4 other advanced degrees awarded. *Degree requirements:* For master's, thesis or alternative; for doctorate, comprehensive exam, thesis/dissertation. *Entrance requirements:* For master's, Virginia Communication and Literacy Assessment (VCLA), PRAXIS, college transcripts, writing sample, interview; for doctorate, GRE, writing sample, resume, transcripts, interview. Additional exam requirements/recommendations for international students: Required—TOEFL (minimum score 577 paper-based). *Application deadline:* For fall admission, 4/1 priority date for domestic students; for spring admission, 10/15 priority date for domestic students. Applications are processed on a rolling basis. Application fee: $50. Electronic applications accepted. *Expenses:* Contact institution. *Financial support:* In 2016–17, 622 students received support, including 1 fellowship (averaging $5,000 per year); career-related internships or fieldwork, scholarships/grants, and unspecified assistantships also available. Support available to part-time students. *Faculty research:* Christian school administration, curriculum and instruction, educational technology and online learning, higher education, special education. *Unit head:* Dr. Donald Finn, Dean, 757-352-4278, Fax: 757-352-4318, E-mail: dfinn@regent.edu. *Application contact:* Heidi

Cece, Assistant Vice President of Enrollment Management, 800-373-5504, Fax: 757-352-4381, E-mail: admissions@regent.edu.
Website: http://www.regent.edu/soe/

Reinhardt University, Price School of Education, Waleska, GA 30183-2981. Offers M Ed, MAT. *Program availability:* Part-time, evening/weekend, online learning. *Degree requirements:* For master's, comprehensive exam. *Entrance requirements:* For master's, GACE, background check. Additional exam requirements/recommendations for international students: Required—TOEFL. *Application deadline:* For fall admission, 5/7 for domestic and international students. Applications are processed on a rolling basis. Application fee: $25. Electronic applications accepted. *Expenses: Tuition:* Part-time $475 per credit hour. *Required fees:* $100 per semester. Part-time tuition and fees vary according to program. *Financial support:* Application deadline: 5/1; applicants required to submit FAFSA. *Unit head:* Dr. Nancy Marsh, Interim Dean, 770-720-5657, Fax: 770-720-9173, E-mail: njm@reinhardt.edu. *Application contact:* Dr. Nancy Marsh, Interim Dean, 770-720-5657, Fax: 770-720-9173, E-mail: njm@reinhardt.edu.

Rhode Island College, School of Graduate Studies, Feinstein School of Education and Human Development, Department of Elementary Education, Providence, RI 02908-1991. Offers early childhood education (M Ed); elementary education (M Ed, MAT); reading (M Ed). *Accreditation:* NCATE. *Program availability:* Part-time, evening/weekend. *Faculty:* 11 full-time (9 women), 1 (woman) part-time/adjunct. *Students:* 14 full-time (all women), 24 part-time (22 women); includes 3 minority (all Hispanic/Latino). Average age 32. In 2016, 16 master's awarded. *Degree requirements:* For master's, comprehensive exam (for some programs), comprehensive assessment. *Entrance requirements:* For master's, GRE General Test or MAT, PRAXIS II (elementary content knowledge), undergraduate transcripts; minimum undergraduate GPA of 3.0; 3 letters of recommendation. Additional exam requirements/recommendations for international students: Recommended—TOEFL (minimum score 550 paper-based; 79 iBT). *Application deadline:* For fall admission, 3/1 for domestic students; for spring admission, 11/1 for domestic students. Applications are processed on a rolling basis. Application fee: $50. Electronic applications accepted. *Expenses:* Tuition, state resident: full-time $8928; part-time $372 per credit. Tuition, nonresident: full-time $17,376; part-time $724 per credit. *Required fees:* $604; $22 per credit. One-time fee: $74. *Financial support:* Teaching assistantships with full tuition reimbursements, Federal Work-Study, scholarships/grants, and health care benefits available. Support available to part-time students. Financial award application deadline: 5/15; financial award applicants required to submit FAFSA. *Unit head:* Dr. Patricia Cordeiro, Chair, 401-456-8016. *Application contact:* Graduate Studies, 401-456-8700.
Website: http://www.ric.edu/elementaryEducation/

Rivier University, School of Graduate Studies, Department of Education, Nashua, NH 03060. Offers curriculum and instruction (M Ed); early childhood education (M Ed); educational administration (M Ed); educational studies (M Ed); elementary education (M Ed); elementary education and general special education (M Ed); emotional and behavioral disorders (M Ed); general social education (M Ed); leadership and learning (Ed D, CAGS); learning disabilities (M Ed); learning disabilities and reading (M Ed); mental health counseling (MA); reading (M Ed); school counseling (M Ed). *Program availability:* Part-time, evening/weekend. *Degree requirements:* For master's, comprehensive exam (for some programs), internships. *Entrance requirements:* For master's, GRE General Test or MAT.

Roberts Wesleyan College, Graduate Teacher Education Programs, Rochester, NY 14624-1997. Offers adolescence and special education (M Ed); childhood and special education (M Ed); literacy education (M Ed); special education (M Ed). *Program availability:* Part-time, evening/weekend. *Degree requirements:* For master's, thesis. Electronic applications accepted.

Rockford University, Graduate Studies, Department of Education, Program in Early Childhood Education, Rockford, IL 61108-2393. Offers MAT. *Program availability:* Part-time, evening/weekend. *Degree requirements:* For master's, thesis optional. *Entrance requirements:* For master's, GRE General Test, basic skills test (for students seeking certification), 3 letters of recommendation. Additional exam requirements/recommendations for international students: Required—TOEFL. *Application deadline:* Applications are processed on a rolling basis. Application fee: $50. Electronic applications accepted. *Expenses: Tuition:* Part-time $710 per credit. *Required fees:* $50 per semester. *Financial support:* Unspecified assistantships available. *Application contact:* Michele Mehren, Assistant Director, Office of Graduate Studies, 815-226-4040, Fax: 815-394-3706, E-mail: mmehren@rockford.edu.
Website: https://www.rockford.edu/admission/graduate/mat/

Roosevelt University, Graduate Division, College of Education, Program in Teaching and Learning, Chicago, IL 60605. Offers early childhood education (MA). *Students:* 23 part-time (20 women); includes 6 minority (3 Black or African American, non-Hispanic/Latino; 1 Asian, non-Hispanic/Latino; 2 Hispanic/Latino). Average age 30. 8 applicants, 100% accepted, 3 enrolled. In 2016, 6 master's awarded. *Expenses: Tuition, area resident:* Full-time $19,566; part-time $880 per credit hour. *Required fees:* $175 per semester. One-time fee: $200. Part-time tuition and fees vary according to course load, degree level and program. *Unit head:* Laura Lag, Director, 312-853-4753. *Application contact:* Angela Ryan, Director of Graduate Enrollment, 312-341-2420, Fax: 312-281-3356, E-mail: aryan@roosevelt.edu.
Website: https://www.roosevelt.edu/academics/programs/masters-in-teaching-and-learning-ma

Rudolf Steiner College, Waldorf Teacher Education Programs, Fair Oaks, CA 95628-6811. Offers early childhood education (MA); elementary education (MA).

Rutgers University–New Brunswick, Graduate School of Education, Department of Learning and Teaching, Program in Early Childhood/Elementary Education, Piscataway, NJ 08854-8097. Offers Ed M, Ed D. *Program availability:* Part-time. Terminal master's awarded for partial completion of doctoral program. *Degree requirements:* For master's, comprehensive exam (for some programs); for doctorate, thesis/dissertation, qualifying exam. *Entrance requirements:* For master's, GRE General Test, minimum GPA of 3.0; for doctorate, GRE General Test, minimum GPA of 3.5. Additional exam requirements/recommendations for international students: Required—TOEFL. Electronic applications accepted.

Saginaw Valley State University, College of Education, Program in Early Childhood Education, University Center, MI 48710. Offers MAT. *Accreditation:* NCATE. *Program availability:* Part-time, evening/weekend. *Students:* 3 full-time (all women), 43 part-time (all women); includes 2 minority (both Black or African American, non-Hispanic/Latino), 1 international. Average age 32. 10 applicants, 80% accepted, 8 enrolled. In 2016, 35 master's awarded. *Degree requirements:* For master's, capstone course. *Entrance requirements:* For master's, minimum GPA of 3.0, teaching certificate. Additional exam requirements/recommendations for international students: Required—TOEFL (minimum score 550 paper-based; 79 iBT). *Application deadline:* For fall admission, 7/15 for international students; for winter admission, 11/15 for international students; for spring admission, 4/15 for international students. Applications are processed on a rolling basis. Application fee: $30 ($90 for international students). Electronic applications accepted. *Expenses:* Tuition, state resident: full-time $9652; part-time $536 per credit hour. Tuition, nonresident: full-time $12,259; part-time $1022 per credit hour. *Required fees:* $263; $14.60 per credit hour. Tuition and fees vary according to degree level. *Financial support:* Federal Work-Study and scholarships/grants available. Support available to part-time students. Financial award applicants required to submit FAFSA. *Unit head:* Dr. Mary Harmon, Dean, 989-964-4057, Fax: 989-964-4563, E-mail: coeconnect@svsu.edu. *Application contact:* Jenna Briggs, Director, Graduate and International Admissions, 989-964-6096, Fax: 989-964-2788, E-mail: gradadm@svsu.edu.

St. Bonaventure University, School of Graduate Studies, School of Education, Literacy Programs, St. Bonaventure, NY 14778-2284. Offers adolescent literacy 5-12 (MS Ed); childhood literacy B-6 (MS Ed). *Accreditation:* NCATE. *Program availability:* Part-time, evening/weekend. *Faculty:* 2 full-time (both women), 2 part-time/adjunct (both women). *Students:* 7 full-time (all women), 6 part-time (all women); includes 1 minority (Hispanic/Latino). Average age 25. 10 applicants, 70% accepted, 4 enrolled. In 2016, 14 master's awarded. *Degree requirements:* For master's, comprehensive exam, thesis optional, minimum cumulative GPA of 3.0, clinical practicum, literacy coaching internship, electronic portfolio. *Entrance requirements:* For master's, GRE or MAT, teaching certificate in matching area in-hand or pending, transcripts from all previous colleges, minimum GPA of 3.0, 2 references, interview, writing sample. Additional exam requirements/recommendations for international students: Required—TOEFL (minimum score 550 paper-based; 80 iBT). *Application deadline:* For fall admission, 6/15 priority date for domestic students, 2/1 for international students; for spring admission, 11/15 priority date for domestic students, 7/1 for international students. Applications are processed on a rolling basis. Application fee: $0. Electronic applications accepted. *Expenses:* $733 per credit, $100 graduation fee. *Financial support:* Federal Work-Study, scholarships/grants, health care benefits, and unspecified assistantships available. Support available to part-time students. Financial award application deadline: 4/15; financial award applicants required to submit FAFSA. *Faculty research:* Gifted education, curriculum and instruction, theory and language. *Unit head:* Kayla Zimmer, Program Director, 716-375-2167, Fax: 716-375-2360, E-mail: kzimmer@sbu.edu. *Application contact:* Bruce Campbell, Director of Graduate Admissions, 716-375-2429, Fax: 716-375-4015, E-mail: gradsch@sbu.edu.
Website: http://www.sbu.edu/academics/schools/education/graduate-degrees-certificates/msed-in-childhood-literacy

St. Catherine University, Graduate Programs, Program in Education - Montessori Education, St. Paul, MN 55105. Offers MA. *Program availability:* Part-time, evening/weekend, online learning. Tuition and fees vary according to program.

St. John's University, The School of Education, Department of Curriculum and Instruction, Program in Early Childhood Education, Queens, NY 11439. Offers MS Ed. *Program availability:* Part-time, evening/weekend. *Degree requirements:* For master's, comprehensive exam. *Entrance requirements:* For master's, minimum GPA of 3.0, 2 letters of recommendation, qualification for the New York State provisional (initial) teaching certificate, transcript, personal statement. Additional exam requirements/recommendations for international students: Required—TOEFL (minimum score 600 paper-based; 100 iBT), IELTS (minimum score 7). Electronic applications accepted. *Faculty research:* Improving children's learning in math, science and technology; health and nutrition education to prevent obesity; oral language and literacy development in diverse populations; home-school collaborations in literacy among young ELLS; multicultural and international education; bilingual education; at-risk children; arts education; parent, home and community partnership; special needs and inclusive education.

St. Joseph's College, Long Island Campus, Programs in Education, Field of Infant/Toddler Early Childhood Special Education, Patchogue, NY 11772-2399. Offers MA. *Program availability:* Part-time, evening/weekend. *Degree requirements:* For master's, thesis, full-time practicum experience. *Entrance requirements:* For master's, 1 course in child development, 2 courses in special education, minimum undergraduate GPA of 3.0, New York state teaching certificate, writing sample, resume, 2 letters of recommendation, interview. Additional exam requirements/recommendations for international students: Recommended—TOEFL (minimum score 550 paper-based; 79 iBT), IELTS (minimum score 7). Electronic applications accepted. *Expenses: Tuition:* Full-time $16,182; part-time $899 per credit. *Required fees:* $440.

Saint Joseph's University, College of Arts and Sciences, Graduate Programs in Education, Philadelphia, PA 19131-1395. Offers curriculum supervisor (Certificate); educational leadership (MS, Ed D); elementary education (MS, Certificate); elementary/middle school education (Certificate); instructional technology (MS, Certificate); organizational development and leadership (MS); principal (Certificate); professional education (MS); reading specialist (MS, Certificate); reading supervisor (Certificate); secondary education (MS, Certificate); special education (MS); special education 7-12 (Certificate); special education PK-8 (Certificate); superintendent's letter of eligibility (Certificate); supervisor of special education (Certificate); teacher of the deaf and hard of hearing (Certificate). *Program availability:* Part-time, evening/weekend, blended/hybrid learning. *Faculty:* 26 full-time (21 women), 74 part-time/adjunct (45 women). *Students:* 107 full-time (88 women), 826 part-time (622 women); includes 170 minority (115 Black or African American, non-Hispanic/Latino; 2 American Indian or Alaska Native, non-Hispanic/Latino; 11 Asian, non-Hispanic/Latino; 31 Hispanic/Latino; 1 Native Hawaiian or other Pacific Islander, non-Hispanic/Latino; 10 Two or more races, non-Hispanic/Latino), 18 international. Average age 33. 338 applicants, 76% accepted, 173 enrolled. In 2016, 419 master's, 16 doctorates, 24 other advanced degrees awarded. *Degree requirements:* For master's, thesis or alternative; for doctorate, comprehensive exam, thesis/dissertation. *Entrance requirements:* For master's, 2 letters of recommendation, minimum GPA of 3.0, official transcripts, personal statement; for doctorate, GRE, master's degree from accredited institution, minimum graduate GPA of 3.5, computer competence, interview with program director. Additional exam requirements/recommendations for international students: Required—TOEFL (minimum score 550 paper-based; 80 iBT), IELTS (minimum score 6.5), PTE (minimum score 60). *Application deadline:* For fall admission, 7/15 for international students; for spring admission, 11/1 for international students. Applications are processed on a rolling basis. Application fee: $35. Electronic applications accepted. *Expenses:* $750 per credit, $100 education fee, $360 online organization development and leadership residency fee. *Financial support:* In 2016–17, 25 students received support. Unspecified assistantships available. Financial award application deadline: 5/1; financial award applicants required to submit FAFSA. *Faculty research:* Factors predicting early mathematics skills for low income children, early child care and development, preschool quality, parent communication and home-school collaboration issues, education of terminally ill children, preparing literacy teachers for urban schools. *Total annual research expenditures:* $18,118. *Unit head:* Dr. John Vacca, Associate Dean, Education, 610-660-3131, E-mail: gradcas@sju.edu. *Application contact:* Graduate Admissions, College of Arts and Sciences, 610-660-3131, E-mail: gradcas@sju.edu.
Website: http://sju.edu/int/academics/cas/grad/education/index.html

Saint Mary's College of California, Kalmanovitz School of Education, Program in Early Childhood Education, Moraga, CA 94575. Offers supervision and leadership (MA). *Program availability:* Part-time, evening/weekend. *Degree requirements:* For master's, thesis or alternative. *Entrance requirements:* For master's, interview, minimum GPA of 3.0.

Early Childhood Education

Saint Mary's College of California, Kalmanovitz School of Education, Program in Montessori Education, Moraga, CA 94575. Offers MA. *Degree requirements:* For master's, thesis or project. *Entrance requirements:* For master's, writing proficiency exam.

Saint Xavier University, Graduate Studies, School of Education, Chicago, IL 60655-3105. Offers counseling (MA); curriculum and instruction (MA); early childhood education (MA); educational administration (MA); elementary education (MA); individualized studies (MA), including educational technology, English as a second language (ESL), ISTEM (integrative science, technology, engineering, and math), science education; music education (MA); reading (MA); secondary education (MA); Spanish education (MA); special education (MA); teaching and leadership (MA). *Accreditation:* NCATE. *Program availability:* Part-time, evening/weekend. *Degree requirements:* For master's, thesis or project. *Entrance requirements:* For master's, minimum GPA of 3.0. *Expenses:* Contact institution.

Salem State University, School of Graduate Studies, Program in Early Childhood Education, Salem, MA 01970-5353. Offers M Ed. *Accreditation:* NCATE. *Program availability:* Part-time, evening/weekend. *Entrance requirements:* For master's, GRE or MAT. Additional exam requirements/recommendations for international students: Required—TOEFL (minimum score 550 paper-based; 80 iBT) or IELTS (minimum score 5.5).

Samford University, Orlean Beeson School of Education, Birmingham, AL 35229. Offers education (Ed D, Certificate); educational leadership: policy, organizations, leadership (MSE); elementary education (MS Ed); gifted certification (MSE); instructional design and technology (MSE); instructional leadership (MSE, Ed S); K-12 collaborative special education (MSE); teacher leader (Ed S). *Accreditation:* NCATE. *Program availability:* Part-time, evening/weekend, 100% online, blended/hybrid learning. *Faculty:* 15 full-time (9 women), 17 part-time/adjunct (12 women). *Students:* 219 full-time (161 women), 86 part-time (55 women); includes 97 minority (86 Black or African American, non-Hispanic/Latino; 5 American Indian or Alaska Native, non-Hispanic/Latino; 1 Asian, non-Hispanic/Latino; 1 Hispanic/Latino; 4 Two or more races, non-Hispanic/Latino), 2 international. Average age 38. 244 applicants, 52% accepted, 112 enrolled. In 2016, 84 master's, 22 doctorates, 12 Certificates awarded. *Degree requirements:* For master's, comprehensive exam (for some programs); for doctorate, comprehensive exam, thesis/dissertation; for other advanced degree, comprehensive exam. *Entrance requirements:* For master's, GRE or MAT; Alabama Educator Certification Testing Program (AECTP), transcripts, essays, recommendations; for doctorate, professional resume, recommendations, transcripts, interview, essays; for other advanced degree, recommendations, transcripts. Additional exam requirements/recommendations for international students: Required—TOEFL (minimum score 90 iBT), IELTS (minimum score 6.5). *Application deadline:* For fall admission, 7/15 for domestic students, 7/1 for international students; for spring admission, 11/15 for domestic and international students; for summer admission, 4/15 for domestic and international students. Application fee: $35. Electronic applications accepted. *Expenses: Tuition:* Full-time $18,530; part-time $789 per credit hour. *Required fees:* $610. Tuition and fees vary according to course load, degree level, program and student level. *Financial support:* In 2016–17, 246 students received support. Scholarships/grants available. Financial award application deadline: 3/1; financial award applicants required to submit FAFSA. *Faculty research:* Standards-based grading in K-12 schools, effective school principal leadership, effective educational leadership preparation programs, teacher/administrator shortages and job retention, instructional strategies to maximize student learning. *Total annual research expenditures:* $254,360. *Unit head:* Dr. Jean Box, Dean, 205-726-2565, Fax: 205-726-4233, E-mail: jabox@samford.edu. *Application contact:* Brooke Karr, Graduate Admissions Coordinator, 205-729-2783, Fax: 205-726-4233, E-mail: kbgilrea@samford.edu.
Website: http://www.samford.edu/education/

San Francisco State University, Division of Graduate Studies, College of Education, Department of Elementary Education, Program in Early Childhood Education, San Francisco, CA 94132-1722. Offers MA. *Accreditation:* NCATE. *Expenses:* Tuition, state resident: full-time $6738. Tuition, nonresident: full-time $15,666. *Required fees:* $1012. Tuition and fees vary according to degree level and program. *Unit head:* Dr. Josephine Arce, Chair, 415-338-7636, Fax: 415-338-0567, E-mail: jarce@sfsu.edu. *Application contact:* Dr. Barbara Henderson, MA Program Coordinator, 415-338-1319, Fax: 415-338-0567, E-mail: barbarah@sfsu.edu.
Website: http://gcoe.sfsu.edu/

San Francisco State University, Division of Graduate Studies, College of Education, Department of Special Education and Communicative Disorders, San Francisco, CA 94132-1722. Offers augmentative and alternative communication (AC); autism spectrum (AC); communicative disorders (MS); early childhood special education (AC); education specialist (Credential); orientation and mobility (MA, Credential), including orientation and mobility (Credential), special education (MA); special education (MA, PhD), including early childhood special education (MA), mild to moderate disabilities (MA), moderate to severe disabilities (MA), visual impairment (MA). PhD offered jointly with University of California, Berkeley. *Accreditation:* NCATE. *Expenses:* Tuition, state resident: full-time $6738. Tuition, nonresident: full-time $15,666. *Required fees:* $1012. Tuition and fees vary according to degree level and program. *Unit head:* Dr. Yvonne Bui, Chair, 415-338-2503, Fax: 415-338-0566, E-mail: ybui@sfsu.edu. *Application contact:* Anna Kozubek, Academic Office Coordinator, 415-338-2501, Fax: 415-338-0566, E-mail: annak@sfsu.edu.
Website: http://www.sfsu.edu/~spedcd/

San Jose State University, Graduate Studies and Research, Connie L. Lurie College of Education, San Jose, CA 95192-0001. Offers child and adolescent development (MA); common core mathematics (K-8) (Certificate, Credential); education (MA, Credential), including counseling and student personnel (MA), speech pathology (MA); educational leadership (MA, Ed D, Credential), including administration and supervision (MA), higher education (MA), preliminary administrative services (Credential), professional administrative services (Credential); elementary education (MA), including curriculum and instruction; K-12 school counseling (Credential); K-12 school counseling internship (Credential); school child welfare attendance (Credential); single subject (Credential). *Accreditation:* NCATE. *Program availability:* Evening/weekend. Electronic applications accepted.

Shaw University, Department of Education, Raleigh, NC 27601-2399. Offers curriculum and instruction (MS), including early childhood education. *Program availability:* Part-time, evening/weekend. *Degree requirements:* For master's, comprehensive exam, thesis, practicum/internship, PRAXIS II. *Entrance requirements:* For master's, GRE General Test, letters of recommendation. Additional exam requirements/recommendations for international students: Required—TOEFL (minimum score 500 paper-based). Electronic applications accepted. *Faculty research:* Multicultural education, instructional technology.

Shippensburg University of Pennsylvania, School of Graduate Studies, College of Education and Human Services, Department of Teacher Education, Shippensburg, PA 17257-2299. Offers curriculum and instruction (M Ed), including biology, early childhood education, elementary and middle level education, elementary education, geography/earth science, history, mathematics, middle school education, modern languages; literacy studies (Certificate); online instruction, learning, and technology (Certificate); reading (M Ed); teaching English as a second language (Certificate). *Accreditation:* NCATE. *Program availability:* Part-time, evening/weekend, 100% online, blended/hybrid learning. *Faculty:* 14 full-time (9 women), 5 part-time/adjunct (all women). *Students:* 11 full-time (10 women), 88 part-time (81 women); includes 8 minority (3 Black or African American, non-Hispanic/Latino; 2 Asian, non-Hispanic/Latino; 3 Hispanic/Latino), 4 international. Average age 32. 57 applicants, 60% accepted, 28 enrolled. In 2016, 18 master's awarded. *Degree requirements:* For master's, comprehensive exam (for some programs), thesis optional, practicum or internship; capstone seminar (for some programs). *Entrance requirements:* For master's, MAT or GRE (if GPA less than 2.75), interview, 3 letters of reference, questionnaire of teaching background and future goals, resume. Additional exam requirements/recommendations for international students: Required—TOEFL (minimum score 550 paper-based, 68 iBT) or IELTS (minimum score 6). *Application deadline:* For fall admission, 4/1 priority date for domestic students, 4/30 for international students; for spring admission, 9/1 priority date for domestic students, 9/30 for international students; for summer admission, 2/1 priority date for domestic students. Applications are processed on a rolling basis. Application fee: $45. Electronic applications accepted. *Expenses:* Tuition, state resident: part-time $483 per credit. Tuition, nonresident: part-time $725 per credit. *Required fees:* $141 per credit. *Financial support:* In 2016–17, 3 students received support. Career-related internships or fieldwork, scholarships/grants, unspecified assistantships, and resident hall director and student payroll positions available. Support available to part-time students. Financial award application deadline: 3/1; financial award applicants required to submit FAFSA. *Unit head:* Dr. Christine A. Royce, Chairperson, 717-477-1688, Fax: 717-477-4046, E-mail: caroyc@ship.edu. *Application contact:* Megan N. Luft, Assistant Dean of Graduate Admissions, 717-477-1231, Fax: 717-477-4016, E-mail: mnluft@ship.edu.
Website: http://www.ship.edu/teacher/

Siena Heights University, Graduate College, Adrian, MI 49221-1796. Offers clinical mental health counseling (MA); educational leadership (Specialist); leadership (MA), including health care leadership, organizational leadership; teacher education (MA), including early childhood education, early childhood education: Montessori, education leadership: principal, elementary education: reading K-12, leadership: higher education, secondary education: reading K-12, special education: cognitive impairment, special education: learning disabilities. *Program availability:* Part-time, evening/weekend. *Degree requirements:* For master's, thesis, presentation. *Entrance requirements:* For master's, minimum GPA of 3.0, current resume, essay, all post-secondary transcripts, 3 letters of reference, conviction disclosure form; copy of teaching certificate (for some education programs); for Specialist, master's degree, minimum GPA of 3.0, current resume, essay, all post-secondary transcripts, 3 letters of reference, conviction disclosure form; copy of teaching certificate (for some education programs). Electronic applications accepted.

Sonoma State University, School of Education, Rohnert Park, CA 94928-3609. Offers administrative services (Credential); curriculum, teaching, and learning (MA); early childhood education (MA); education specialist (Credential); educational leadership (MA); multiple subject (Credential); reading and literacy (MA, Credential); single subject (Credential); special education (MA). *Accreditation:* NCATE. *Program availability:* Part-time, evening/weekend. *Degree requirements:* For master's, thesis or alternative. *Entrance requirements:* For master's, minimum GPA of 2.5. Additional exam requirements/recommendations for international students: Required—TOEFL (minimum score 500 paper-based). Application fee: $55. *Expenses:* Tuition, state resident: full-time $6738; part-time $3906 per unit. *Required fees:* $1916; $1916 per year. Tuition and fees vary according to course load, degree level and program. *Financial support:* Fellowships, research assistantships, career-related internships or fieldwork, and Federal Work-Study available. Support available to part-time students. Financial award application deadline: 3/2; financial award applicants required to submit FAFSA. *Unit head:* Dr. Carlos Ayala, Dean, 707-664-4412, E-mail: carlos.ayala@sonoma.edu. *Application contact:* Dr. Jennifer Mahdavi, Coordinator of Graduate Studies, 707-664-3311, E-mail: jennifer.mahdavi@sonoma.edu.
Website: http://www.sonoma.edu/education/

South Carolina State University, College of Graduate and Professional Studies, Department of Education, Orangeburg, SC 29117-0001. Offers early childhood education (MAT); education (M Ed); elementary education (M Ed, MAT); English (MAT); general science/biology (MAT); mathematics (MAT); secondary education (M Ed), including biology education, business education, counselor education, English education, home economics education, industrial education, mathematics education, science education, social studies education; special education (M Ed), including emotionally handicapped, learning disabilities, mentally handicapped. *Accreditation:* NCATE. *Program availability:* Part-time, evening/weekend. *Faculty:* 12 full-time (8 women), 3 part-time/adjunct (1 woman). *Students:* 28 full-time (20 women), 20 part-time (17 women); includes 45 minority (44 Black or African American, non-Hispanic/Latino; 1 Two or more races, non-Hispanic/Latino). Average age 31. 22 applicants, 100% accepted, 16 enrolled. In 2016, 9 master's awarded. *Degree requirements:* For master's, thesis optional, departmental qualifying exam. *Entrance requirements:* For master's, GRE General Test, NTE, interview, teaching certificate. *Application deadline:* For fall admission, 6/15 priority date for domestic students, 6/15 for international students; for spring admission, 11/1 for domestic and international students. Application fee: $25. Electronic applications accepted. *Expenses:* Tuition, state resident: full-time $8938; part-time $579 per credit hour. Tuition, nonresident: full-time $19,018; part-time $1139 per credit hour. *Required fees:* $1482; $82 per credit hour. *Financial support:* Fellowships, career-related internships or fieldwork, Federal Work-Study, and scholarships/grants available. Financial award application deadline: 6/1. *Unit head:* Dr. Charlie Spell, Interim Chair, Department of Education, 803-536-8963, Fax: 803-516-4568, E-mail: cspell@scsu.edu. *Application contact:* Curtis Foskey, Coordinator of Graduate Studies, 803-536-8419, Fax: 803-536-8812, E-mail: cfoskey@scsu.edu.

Southern Oregon University, Graduate Studies, School of Education, Ashland, OR 97520. Offers elementary education (MA Ed, MS Ed), including classroom teacher, early childhood, handicapped learner, reading, supervision; secondary education (MA Ed, MS Ed), including classroom teacher, handicapped learner, reading, supervision; teaching (MAT). *Program availability:* Online learning. *Faculty:* 15 full-time (10 women), 27 part-time/adjunct (21 women). *Students:* 116 full-time (82 women), 86 part-time (68 women); includes 22 minority (1 American Indian or Alaska Native, non-Hispanic/Latino; 4 Asian, non-Hispanic/Latino; 8 Hispanic/Latino; 9 Two or more races, non-Hispanic/Latino). Average age 34. 81 applicants, 80% accepted, 49 enrolled. In 2016, 107 master's awarded. *Degree requirements:* For master's, thesis optional. *Entrance requirements:* For master's, GRE General Test, minimum cumulative GPA of 3.0 in the last 90 quarter credits (60 semester credits) of undergraduate coursework. Additional exam requirements/recommendations for international students: Required—TOEFL (minimum score 540 paper-based; 76 iBT), IELTS (minimum score 6), ELPT (minimum score 964) or ELS (minimum score 112). *Application deadline:* For fall admission, 7/31 priority date for domestic and international students; for winter admission, 11/15 priority date for domestic and international students; for spring admission, 1/7 priority date for domestic and international students. Applications are processed on a rolling basis. Application fee: $60. Electronic applications accepted. *Expenses:* Tuition, state

resident: full-time $10,719; part-time $397 per credit. Tuition, nonresident: full-time $13,419; part-time $497 per credit. *Required fees:* $548. *Financial support:* In 2016–17, 2 students received support. Career-related internships or fieldwork, institutionally sponsored loans, scholarships/grants, and unspecified assistantships available. *Unit head:* Dr. Gerry McCain, Graduate Program Coordinator, 541-552-6934, E-mail: mccaing@sou.edu. *Application contact:* Kelly Moutsatson, Director of Admissions, 541-552-6411, Fax: 541-552-8403, E-mail: admissions@sou.edu.
Website: http://www.sou.edu/education/

Southwestern College, Education Programs, Winfield, KS 67156-2499. Offers curriculum and instruction (M Ed); early childhood education (M Ed); educational leadership (Ed D); special education (M Ed), including adaptive, functional; teaching (MA). *Accreditation:* NCATE. *Program availability:* Part-time, evening/weekend, 100% online, blended/hybrid learning. *Faculty:* 7 full-time (5 women), 15 part-time/adjunct (12 women). *Students:* 27 full-time (18 women), 102 part-time (77 women); includes 17 minority (8 Black or African American, non-Hispanic/Latino; 1 American Indian or Alaska Native, non-Hispanic/Latino; 1 Asian, non-Hispanic/Latino; 6 Hispanic/Latino; 1 Native Hawaiian or other Pacific Islander, non-Hispanic/Latino), 32 international. Average age 38. 36 applicants, 64% accepted, 16 enrolled. In 2016, 71 master's, 10 doctorates awarded. *Degree requirements:* For master's, practicum, portfolio; for doctorate, thesis/dissertation, professional portfolio. *Entrance requirements:* For master's, baccalaureate degree, minimum GPA of 3.0, valid teaching certificate (for special education); for doctorate, GRE if no master's degree, baccalaureate degree with minimum GPA of 3.25 and current teaching experience, or master's degree with minimum GPA of 3.5. Additional exam requirements/recommendations for international students: Required—TOEFL (minimum score 550 paper-based; 80 iBT). *Application deadline:* Applications are processed on a rolling basis. Application fee: $40. Electronic applications accepted. *Expenses:* $550 per credit; $485 per credit (online); $580 per credit (doctorate program). *Financial support:* In 2016–17, 8 students received support. Scholarships/grants available. Financial award applicants required to submit FAFSA. *Unit head:* Dana Thomson, Director of Education Operations, 800-846-1543 Ext. 6253, Fax: 620-229-6253, E-mail: dana.thomson@sckans.edu. *Application contact:* Dennis Russell, Director of Admissions and Student Services, 888-684-5335 Ext. 3372, Fax: 888-684-5218, E-mail: dennis.russell@sckans.edu.
Website: http://www.sckans.edu/graduate/education-med/

Southwestern Oklahoma State University, College of Professional and Graduate Studies, School of Behavioral Sciences and Education, Specialization in Early Childhood Education, Weatherford, OK 73096-3098. Offers M Ed. M Ed distance learning degree program offered to Oklahoma residents only. *Accreditation:* NCATE. *Program availability:* Part-time, evening/weekend. *Degree requirements:* For master's, exam. *Entrance requirements:* For master's, GRE General Test or minimum undergraduate GPA of 3.0. Additional exam requirements/recommendations for international students: Required—TOEFL.

Southwest Minnesota State University, Department of Education, Marshall, MN 56258. Offers ESL (MS); math (MS); reading (MS); special education (MS), including developmental disabilities, early childhood education, emotional behavioral disorders, learning disabilities; teaching, learning and leadership (MS). *Program availability:* Part-time, evening/weekend, online learning. *Entrance requirements:* Additional exam requirements/recommendations for international students: Required—TOEFL or IELTS; Recommended—TOEFL (minimum score 550 paper-based; 80 iBT), IELTS.

Spring Hill College, Graduate Programs, Program in Education, Mobile, AL 36608-1791. Offers early childhood education (MAT, MS Ed); educational theory (MS Ed); elementary education (MAT, MS Ed); secondary education (MAT, MS Ed). *Program availability:* Part-time. *Faculty:* 3 full-time (all women). *Students:* 3 full-time (all women), 7 part-time (5 women); includes 1 minority (Black or African American, non-Hispanic/Latino). Average age 26. In 2016, 10 master's awarded. *Degree requirements:* For master's, comprehensive exam, completion of program within 6 calendar years of entrance into graduate studies at Spring Hill; documentation of course field assignments (MS) or completion of internship (MAT). *Entrance requirements:* For master's, GRE, MAT, or PRAXIS (varies by program), bachelor's degree with minimum undergraduate GPA of 3.0; class B certificate (for MS); minimum number of hours in specific fields (for MAT). Additional exam requirements/recommendations for international students: Required—TOEFL (minimum score 550 paper-based; 80 iBT), IELTS (minimum score 6.5), CPE or CAE (minimum score C), Michigan English Language Assessment Battery (minimum score 90). *Application deadline:* For fall admission, 8/1 priority date for domestic and international students; for spring admission, 12/1 priority date for domestic and international students. Applications are processed on a rolling basis. Application fee: $25 ($35 for international students). Electronic applications accepted. *Expenses:* Contact institution. *Financial support:* Applicants required to submit FAFSA. *Unit head:* Dr. Lori P. Aultman, Chair of Education, 251-380-3473, Fax: 251-460-2184, E-mail: laultman@shc.edu. *Application contact:* Robert Stewart, Vice President of Enrollment, 251-380-3030, Fax: 251-460-2186, E-mail: rstewart@shc.edu.
Website: http://ug.shc.edu/graduate-degrees/master-science-education/

State University of New York at Fredonia, College of Education, Fredonia, NY 14063. Offers curriculum and instruction (MS Ed); literacy education (MS Ed), including birth-grade 12, grades 5-12; TESOL (MS Ed). *Accreditation:* NCATE. *Program availability:* Part-time. *Faculty:* 21 full-time (17 women), 11 part-time/adjunct (9 women). *Students:* 39 full-time (32 women), 54 part-time (33 women); includes 8 minority (1 Black or African American, non-Hispanic/Latino; 4 Asian, non-Hispanic/Latino; 2 Hispanic/Latino; 1 Two or more races, non-Hispanic/Latino). Average age 29. 60 applicants, 97% accepted, 39 enrolled. In 2016, 56 master's awarded. *Degree requirements:* For master's, thesis. *Entrance requirements:* For master's, GRE, minimum undergraduate GPA of 3.0. Additional exam requirements/recommendations for international students: Required—TOEFL (minimum score 79 iBT), IELTS (minimum score 6.5). *Application deadline:* For fall admission, 4/1 priority date for domestic and international students; for spring admission, 11/1 priority date for domestic students, 11/1 for international students. Applications are processed on a rolling basis. Application fee: $75. Electronic applications accepted. *Expenses:* Tuition, state resident: full-time $10,370; part-time $453 per credit. Tuition, nonresident: full-time $20,190; part-time $925 per credit. *Required fees:* $1619; $67.30 per credit hour. $403.80 per semester. *Financial support:* In 2016–17, 4 teaching assistantships with full and partial tuition reimbursements (averaging $7,075 per year) were awarded. Financial award application deadline: 3/15; financial award applicants required to submit FAFSA. *Faculty research:* Positive behavioral intervention and support (PBIS), place-based science education, peer support for education, primary source material for social studies education, policies and practices in learning English language. *Unit head:* Dr. Christine Givner, Dean, 716-673-3311, E-mail: christine.givner@fredonia.edu. *Application contact:* Wendy S. Dunst, Interim Graduate Recruitment and Admissions Associate, 716-673-3808, Fax: 716-673-3712, E-mail: wendy.dunst@fredonia.edu.
Website: http://www.fredonia.edu/coe/

State University of New York at New Paltz, Graduate School, School of Education, Department of Educational Studies, Program in Special Education, New Paltz, NY 12561. Offers adolescence special education (7-12) (MS Ed); adolescence special education and literacy (MS Ed); childhood special education (1-6) (MS Ed); childhood special education and literacy (MS Ed); early childhood special education (B-2) (MS Ed). *Accreditation:* NCATE. *Program availability:* Part-time, evening/weekend. *Students:* 25 full-time (19 women), 39 part-time (29 women); includes 9 minority (2 Asian, non-Hispanic/Latino; 7 Hispanic/Latino). 13 applicants, 85% accepted, 10 enrolled. In 2016, 36 master's awarded. *Entrance requirements:* For master's, minimum GPA of 3.0 (3.2 for special education and literacy programs), New York state teaching certificate. Additional exam requirements/recommendations for international students: Required—TOEFL (minimum score 550 paper-based; 80 iBT), IELTS (minimum score 6.5). *Application deadline:* For fall admission, 3/15 priority date for domestic students, 3/15 for international students; for spring admission, 11/1 for domestic and international students. Application fee: $50. Electronic applications accepted. *Financial support:* Application deadline: 8/1. *Unit head:* Dr. Jane Sileo, Coordinator, 845-257-2835, E-mail: sileoj@newpaltz.edu. *Application contact:* Vika Shock, Director of Graduate Admissions, 845-257-3286, E-mail: gradschool@newpaltz.edu.
Website: http://www.newpaltz.edu/schoolofed/department-of-teaching—learning/special_ed.html

State University of New York at New Paltz, Graduate School, School of Education, Department of Elementary Education, New Paltz, NY 12561. Offers childhood education 1-6 (MS Ed, MST), including childhood education 1-6 (MST), early childhood B-2 (MS Ed), mathematics, science and technology (MS Ed), reading/literacy (MS Ed); literacy education 5-12 (MS Ed); literacy education and childhood special education (MS Ed); literacy education B-6 (MS Ed). *Accreditation:* NCATE. *Program availability:* Part-time, evening/weekend. *Students:* 32 full-time (29 women), 100 part-time (91 women); includes 22 minority (5 Black or African American, non-Hispanic/Latino; 1 American Indian or Alaska Native, non-Hispanic/Latino; 2 Asian, non-Hispanic/Latino; 10 Hispanic/Latino; 4 Two or more races, non-Hispanic/Latino). 30 applicants, 73% accepted, 14 enrolled. In 2016, 70 master's awarded. *Degree requirements:* For master's, comprehensive exam (for some programs), portfolio. *Entrance requirements:* For master's, GRE or MAT (for MST), minimum GPA of 3.0 (3.2 for literacy and special education), New York state teaching certificate (for MS Ed). Additional exam requirements/recommendations for international students: Required—TOEFL (minimum score 550 paper-based; 80 iBT), IELTS (minimum score 6.5). *Application deadline:* For fall admission, 4/1 for domestic and international students; for spring admission, 11/1 priority date for domestic and international students; for summer admission, 4/15 priority date for domestic and international students. Applications are processed on a rolling basis. Application fee: $50. Electronic applications accepted. *Financial support:* Application deadline: 8/1. *Faculty research:* Multi-sensory teaching methods, volunteer tutoring programs for struggling readers, school readiness and transition, math/science/technology, university-school partnerships. *Unit head:* Dr. Aaron Isabelle, Chair, 845-257-2837, E-mail: isabella@newpaltz.edu. *Application contact:* Vika Shock, Assistant Director of Graduate Admissions, 845-257-3285, Fax: 845-257-3284, E-mail: gradschool@newpaltz.edu.
Website: http://www.newpaltz.edu/elementaryed/

State University of New York at Oswego, Graduate Studies, School of Education, Department of Curriculum and Instruction, Oswego, NY 13126. Offers adolescence education (MST); art education (MAT); childhood education (MST); curriculum and instruction (MS Ed); literacy education (MS Ed); special education (MS Ed). *Program availability:* Part-time, evening/weekend. *Degree requirements:* For master's, comprehensive exam (for some programs), thesis optional. *Entrance requirements:* For master's, GRE General Test, minimum GPA of 2.7, provisional teaching certificate. Additional exam requirements/recommendations for international students: Required—TOEFL (minimum score 560 paper-based). *Faculty research:* Classroom applications for microcomputers; classroom questioning, wait-time, and achievement; values clarification and academic achievement.

State University of New York at Plattsburgh, School of Education, Health, and Human Services, Program in Early Childhood Education, Plattsburgh, NY 12901-2681. Offers early childhood birth-grade 6 (Advanced Certificate).

State University of New York College at Cortland, Graduate Studies, School of Education, Program in Childhood Education, Cortland, NY 13045. Offers MST. *Accreditation:* NCATE.

State University of New York College at Geneseo, Graduate Studies, School of Education, Program in Early Childhood Education, Geneseo, NY 14454-1401. Offers MS Ed. *Program availability:* Part-time. *Degree requirements:* For master's, comprehensive exam (for some programs), comprehensive exam, research project, or thesis. *Entrance requirements:* For master's, initial certification to teach in New York state. Additional exam requirements/recommendations for international students: Required—TOEFL, IELTS, PTE. *Application deadline:* For fall admission, 4/1 priority date for domestic students; for spring admission, 11/1 priority date for domestic students. Applications are processed on a rolling basis. Application fee: $50. Electronic applications accepted. *Expenses:* Tuition, state resident: full-time $10,870; part-time $453 per credit. Tuition, nonresident: full-time $22,210; part-time $925 per credit. *Required fees:* $865; $35.85 per credit hour. *Financial support:* Fellowships, scholarships/grants, health care benefits, tuition waivers (full), and unspecified assistantships available. Support available to part-time students. Financial award application deadline: 4/1; financial award applicants required to submit FAFSA. *Unit head:* Dr. Anjoo Sikka, Dean of School of Education, 585-245-5151, Fax: 585-245-5220, E-mail: sikka@geneseo.edu. *Application contact:* Michael R. George, Graduate Enrollment Coordinator, 585-245-5040, Fax: 585-245-5550.

State University of New York College at Potsdam, School of Education and Professional Studies, Program in Special Education, Potsdam, NY 13676. Offers adolescence (grades 7-12) (MS Ed); childhood (grades 1-6) (MS Ed); early childhood (birth-grade 2) (MS Ed). *Accreditation:* NCATE. *Program availability:* Part-time. *Degree requirements:* For master's, culminating experience. *Entrance requirements:* For master's, minimum GPA of 3.0 in last 60 hours of course work. Additional exam requirements/recommendations for international students: Required—TOEFL (minimum score 550 paper-based; 80 iBT), IELTS (minimum score 6). Electronic applications accepted.

Stephen F. Austin State University, Graduate School, College of Education, Department of Elementary Education, Program in Early Childhood Education, Nacogdoches, TX 75962. Offers M Ed. *Accreditation:* NCATE. *Degree requirements:* For master's, comprehensive exam. *Entrance requirements:* For master's, GRE General Test. Additional exam requirements/recommendations for international students: Required—TOEFL (minimum score 550 paper-based).

Syracuse University, School of Education, MS Program in Early Childhood Special Education, Syracuse, NY 13244. Offers MS. *Program availability:* Part-time. *Entrance requirements:* For master's, GRE, baccalaureate degree from regionally-accredited college/university, strong teacher and/or employer recommendations, personal statement, experience working with children. Additional exam requirements/recommendations for international students: Required—TOEFL (minimum score 100 iBT). *Application deadline:* For fall admission, 1/15 priority date for domestic and international students; for spring admission, 10/15 priority date for domestic and international students; for summer admission, 1/15 priority date for domestic and

international students. Applications are processed on a rolling basis. Application fee: $75. Electronic applications accepted. *Expenses: Tuition:* Full-time $25,974; part-time $1443 per credit hour. *Required fees:* $802; $50 per course. Tuition and fees vary according to course load and program. *Financial support:* Fellowships with full tuition reimbursements, research assistantships, teaching assistantships with tuition reimbursements, career-related internships or fieldwork, and scholarships/grants available. Financial award application deadline: 1/15; financial award applicants required to submit FAFSA. *Faculty research:* Teaching children with diverse backgrounds and abilities, home-based itinerant teaching, early childhood special education, general preschool teaching, teacher consulting. *Unit head:* Dr. Gail Ensher, Program Coordinator, 315-443-9650, E-mail: glensher@syr.edu. *Application contact:* Speranza Migliore, Graduate Admissions Recruiter, 315-443-2505, E-mail: gradrcrt@syr.edu.
Website: http://soe.syr.edu/academic/teaching_and_leadership/graduate/masters/early_childhood_special_education/default.aspx

Teachers College, Columbia University, Department of Curriculum and Teaching, New York, NY 10027-6696. Offers curriculum and teaching (Ed M, MA, Ed D); curriculum and teaching: elementary education (MA); curriculum and teaching: secondary education (MA); early childhood education (MA, Ed D); early childhood education: special education (MA); elementary education-gifted extension (MA); elementary inclusive education (MA); gifted education (MA); literacy specialist (MA); secondary inclusive education (MA); special inclusive elementary education (MA). *Program availability:* Part-time, evening/weekend. *Students:* 236 full-time (219 women), 198 part-time (176 women); includes 160 minority (53 Black or African American, non-Hispanic/Latino; 1 American Indian or Alaska Native, non-Hispanic/Latino; 43 Asian, non-Hispanic/Latino; 41 Hispanic/Latino; 22 Two or more races, non-Hispanic/Latino), 38 international. 399 applicants, 66% accepted, 104 enrolled. Terminal master's awarded for partial completion of doctoral program. *Degree requirements:* For doctorate, thesis/dissertation. *Expenses: Tuition:* Full-time $36,288; part-time $1512 per credit. *Required fees:* $438 per semester. One-time fee: $510 full-time. Full-time tuition and fees vary according to course load. *Unit head:* Prof. Nancy Lesko, Chair, 212-678-3264, E-mail: lesko@tc.columbia.edu. *Application contact:* David Estrella, Director of Admission, 212-678-3305, Fax: 212-678-4171, E-mail: estrella@tc.columbia.edu.

Tennessee Technological University, College of Graduate Studies, College of Education, Department of Curriculum and Instruction, Program in Early Childhood Education, Cookeville, TN 38505. Offers MA, Ed S. *Accreditation:* NCATE. *Program availability:* Part-time, evening/weekend. *Faculty:* 2 full-time (both women). *Students:* 1 (woman) full-time, 5 part-time (all women), 2 international. Average age 27. 8 applicants, 25% accepted, 2 enrolled. In 2016, 2 master's awarded. *Degree requirements:* For master's and Ed S, comprehensive exam, thesis or alternative. *Entrance requirements:* For master's and Ed S, MAT or GRE. Additional exam requirements/recommendations for international students: Required—TOEFL (minimum score 527 paper-based; 71 iBT), IELTS (minimum score 5.5), PTE (minimum score 48), or TOEIC (Test of English as an International Communication). *Application deadline:* For fall admission, 8/1 priority date for domestic students, 5/1 for international students; for spring admission, 12/1 for domestic students, 10/1 for international students; for summer admission, 5/1 for domestic students, 2/1 for international students. Application fee: $35 ($40 for international students). Electronic applications accepted. *Expenses:* Tuition, state resident: full-time $9375; part-time $534 per credit hour. Tuition, nonresident: full-time $22,443; part-time $1260 per credit hour. *Financial support:* In 2016–17, teaching assistantships (averaging $4,000 per year) were awarded; fellowships, research assistantships, and career-related internships or fieldwork also available. Financial award application deadline: 4/1. *Unit head:* Dr. Jeremy Wendt, Interim Chairperson, 931-372-3181, Fax: 931-372-6270, E-mail: jwendt@tntech.edu. *Application contact:* Shelia K. Kendrick, Coordinator of Graduate Studies, 931-372-3808, Fax: 931-372-3497, E-mail: skendrick@tntech.edu.

Texas A&M University–Commerce, College of Education and Human Services, Commerce, TX 75429-3011. Offers counseling (MS); curriculum and instruction (M Ed, MS); early childhood education (M Ed, MS); educational administration (M Ed, Ed D); educational psychology (PhD); educational technology leadership (MS); educational technology library science (MS); health, kinesiology and sports studies (MS); higher education (MS, Ed D); organization, learning, and technology (MS); psychology (MS); reading (M Ed, MS); school psychology (SSP); secondary education (M Ed, MS); social work (MSW); special education (M Ed); supervision, curriculum and instruction-elementary education (Ed D). *Program availability:* Part-time, 100% online, blended/hybrid learning. *Faculty:* 88 full-time (52 women), 31 part-time/adjunct (24 women). *Students:* 341 full-time (276 women), 1,495 part-time (1,156 women); includes 762 minority (429 Black or African American, non-Hispanic/Latino; 4 American Indian or Alaska Native, non-Hispanic/Latino; 27 Asian, non-Hispanic/Latino; 247 Hispanic/Latino; 1 Native Hawaiian or other Pacific Islander, non-Hispanic/Latino; 54 Two or more races, non-Hispanic/Latino), 18 international. Average age 37. 1,070 applicants, 54% accepted, 452 enrolled. In 2016, 579 master's, 31 doctorates awarded. *Degree requirements:* For master's, one foreign language, comprehensive exam, thesis optional, departmental qualifying exams (for some programs); for doctorate, comprehensive exam, thesis/dissertation, departmental qualifying exam; for SSP, comprehensive exam, thesis optional. *Entrance requirements:* For master's and doctorate, GRE General Test. Additional exam requirements/recommendations for international students: Required—TOEFL (minimum score 550 paper-based; 79 iBT), IELTS (minimum score 6). *Application deadline:* For fall admission, 6/1 priority date for international students; for spring admission, 10/15 priority date for international students; for summer admission, 3/15 priority date for international students. Applications are processed on a rolling basis. Application fee: $50. Electronic applications accepted. *Expenses:* $2,254 resident; $4,744 non-resident. *Financial support:* In 2016–17, 301 students received support, including 39 research assistantships with partial tuition reimbursements available (averaging $9,000 per year), 17 teaching assistantships with partial tuition reimbursements available (averaging $9,000 per year); career-related internships or fieldwork, Federal Work-Study, institutionally sponsored loans, scholarships/grants, health care benefits, and unspecified assistantships also available. Financial award application deadline: 5/1; financial award applicants required to submit FAFSA. *Faculty research:* Cognitive and bilingual education, positive behavioral intervention, literacy, math readiness. *Total annual research expenditures:* $470,963. *Unit head:* Dr. Timothy Letzring, Dean, 903-886-5181, Fax: 903-886-5905, E-mail: tim.letzring@tamuc.edu. *Application contact:* Jennifer Faunce, Graduate Recruiter, 903-886-5030, Fax: 903-886-5905, E-mail: jennifer.faunce@tamuc.edu.
Website: http://www.tamuc.edu/academics/graduateSchool/programs/education/default.aspx

Texas A&M University–Commerce, College of Humanities, Social Sciences and Arts, Commerce, TX 75429-3011. Offers applied criminology (MS); applied linguistics (MA, MS); art (MA, MFA); Christianity in history (Graduate Certificate); computational linguistics (Graduate Certificate); creative writing (Graduate Certificate); English (MA, MS, PhD); film studies (Graduate Certificate); history (MA, MS); music (MM); political science (MA, MS); public history (Graduate Certificate); sociology (MS); Spanish (MA); studies in children's and adolescent literature and culture (Graduate Certificate); teaching English to speakers of other languages (Graduate Certificate); theater (MA, MS). *Program availability:* Part-time. *Faculty:* 53 full-time (26 women), 7 part-time/adjunct (2 women). *Students:* 87 full-time (55 women), 528 part-time (362 women); includes 198 minority (86 Black or African American, non-Hispanic/Latino; 2 American Indian or Alaska Native, non-Hispanic/Latino; 8 Asian, non-Hispanic/Latino; 84 Hispanic/Latino; 18 Two or more races, non-Hispanic/Latino), 27 international. Average age 37. 333 applicants, 56% accepted, 149 enrolled. In 2016, 66 master's, 8 doctorates awarded. *Degree requirements:* For master's, one foreign language, comprehensive exam, thesis (for some programs); for doctorate, one foreign language, comprehensive exam, thesis/dissertation, departmental qualifying exam. *Entrance requirements:* For master's and doctorate, GRE General Test. Additional exam requirements/recommendations for international students: Required—TOEFL (minimum score 550 paper-based; 79 iBT), IELTS (minimum score 6). *Application deadline:* Applications are processed on a rolling basis. Application fee: $50. Electronic applications accepted. *Expenses:* Contact institution. *Financial support:* In 2016–17, 255 students received support, including 9 research assistantships with partial tuition reimbursements available (averaging $9,000 per year), 68 teaching assistantships with partial tuition reimbursements available (averaging $9,000 per year); Federal Work-Study, institutionally sponsored loans, scholarships/grants, health care benefits, and unspecified assistantships also available. Financial award application deadline: 5/1; financial award applicants required to submit FAFSA. *Unit head:* Dr. Salvatore Attardo, Dean, 903-886-5166, Fax: 903-886-5774, E-mail: salvatore.attardo@tamuc.edu. *Application contact:* Shelby Miller, Graduate Recruiter, 903-468-8123, Fax: 903-886-5774, E-mail: shelby.miller@tamuc.edu.
Website: http://www.tamuc.edu/academics/graduateSchool/programs/humanitiesSocialScienceArts/default.aspx

Texas A&M University–Corpus Christi, College of Graduate Studies, College of Education, Corpus Christi, TX 78412-5503. Offers counseling (MS), including counseling; counselor education (PhD); curriculum and instruction (MS, PhD); early childhood education (MS); educational administration (MS); educational leadership (Ed D); elementary education (MS); instructional design and educational technology (MS); kinesiology (MS); reading (MS); secondary education (MS); special education (MS). *Program availability:* Part-time, evening/weekend, online learning. *Faculty:* 50 full-time (29 women), 29 part-time/adjunct (18 women). *Students:* 158 full-time (130 women), 344 part-time (281 women); includes 288 minority (28 Black or African American, non-Hispanic/Latino; 2 American Indian or Alaska Native, non-Hispanic/Latino; 8 Asian, non-Hispanic/Latino; 246 Hispanic/Latino; 4 Two or more races, non-Hispanic/Latino), 22 international. Average age 35. 273 applicants, 60% accepted, 142 enrolled. In 2016, 67 master's, 13 doctorates awarded. *Degree requirements:* For master's, comprehensive exam, capstone; for doctorate, thesis/dissertation. *Entrance requirements:* For master's, GRE General Test, essay (300 words); for doctorate, GRE, essay, resume, 3-4 reference forms. *Application deadline:* For fall admission, 7/15 priority date for domestic students, 5/1 priority date for international students; for spring admission, 11/15 priority date for domestic students, 9/1 priority date for international students. Applications are processed on a rolling basis. Application fee: $50 ($70 for international students). Electronic applications accepted. *Financial support:* Research assistantships, teaching assistantships, career-related internships or fieldwork, Federal Work-Study, institutionally sponsored loans, scholarships/grants, health care benefits, and unspecified assistantships available. Support available to part-time students. Financial award application deadline: 3/15; financial award applicants required to submit FAFSA. *Unit head:* Dr. Arthur Hernandez, Dean, 361-825-2660, E-mail: art.hernandez@tamucc.edu. *Application contact:* Graduate Admissions Coordinator, 361-825-2177, Fax: 361-825-2755, E-mail: gradweb@tamucc.edu.
Website: http://education.tamucc.edu/

Texas A&M University–Kingsville, College of Graduate Studies, College of Education and Human Performance, Department of Teacher and Bilingual Education, Program in Early Childhood Education, Kingsville, TX 78363. Offers M Ed. *Program availability:* Part-time, evening/weekend. *Degree requirements:* For master's, variable foreign language requirement, comprehensive exam, thesis (for some programs). *Entrance requirements:* For master's, GRE, MAT, GMAT. Additional exam requirements/recommendations for international students: Required—TOEFL (minimum score 550 paper-based; 79 iBT). Electronic applications accepted.

Texas A&M University–San Antonio, Department of Curriculum and Kinesiology, San Antonio, TX 78224. Offers bilingual education (MA); early childhood education (M Ed); kinesiology (MS); reading (MS); special education (M Ed), including educational diagnostician, instructional specialist. *Program availability:* Part-time, evening/weekend. *Degree requirements:* For master's, comprehensive exam, thesis or alternative. *Entrance requirements:* For master's, MAT. Additional exam requirements/recommendations for international students: Required—TOEFL (minimum score 550 paper-based; 80 iBT), IELTS (minimum score 6). Electronic applications accepted.

Texas Woman's University, Graduate School, College of Professional Education, Department of Family Sciences, Denton, TX 76204-5769. Offers child development (MS); counseling and development (MS); early childhood development and education (PhD); early childhood education (M Ed); family studies (MS, PhD); family therapy (MS, PhD). *Accreditation:* ACA (one or more programs are accredited). *Program availability:* Part-time, evening/weekend. *Students:* Average age 34. In 2016, 99 master's, 9 doctorates awarded. Terminal master's awarded for partial completion of doctoral program. *Degree requirements:* For master's, comprehensive exam (for some programs), thesis (for some programs); for doctorate, comprehensive exam, thesis/dissertation. *Entrance requirements:* Additional exam requirements/recommendations for international students: Required—TOEFL (minimum score 550 paper-based; 79 iBT). *Application deadline:* For fall admission, 7/1 priority date for domestic students, 2/15 for international students; for spring admission, 9/15 priority date for domestic students, 7/1 for international students. Applications are processed on a rolling basis. Application fee: $50 ($75 for international students). Electronic applications accepted. *Expenses:* Tuition, state resident: full-time $9046; part-time $251 per credit hour. Tuition, nonresident: full-time $22,922; part-time $614 per credit hour. *International tuition:* $23,046 full-time. *Required fees:* $2690; $1285 per credit hour. One-time fee: $50. Tuition and fees vary according to course level, course load, program and reciprocity agreements. *Financial support:* Research assistantships, teaching assistantships, career-related internships or fieldwork, Federal Work-Study, institutionally sponsored loans, scholarships/grants, traineeships, health care benefits, and unspecified assistantships available. Support available to part-time students. Financial award application deadline: 3/1; financial award applicants required to submit FAFSA. *Faculty research:* Parenting/parent education, military families, play therapy, family sexuality, diversity, healthy relationships/healthy marriages, childhood obesity, male communication. *Unit head:* Dr. Karen Petty, Chair, 940-898-2685, Fax: 940-898-2676, E-mail: famsci@twu.edu. *Application contact:* Dr. Samuel Wheeler, Assistant Director of Admissions, 940-898-3188, Fax: 940-898-3081, E-mail: wheelersr@twu.edu.
Website: http://www.twu.edu/family-sciences/

Theological University of the Caribbean, Graduate Programs, Saint Just, PR 00978-0901. Offers childhood and adolescent education (MA); counseling and pastoral care (MA); ministry (D Min); missions (MA).

Towson University, Program in Early Childhood Education, Towson, MD 21252-0001. Offers M Ed, CAS. *Accreditation:* NCATE. *Program availability:* Part-time, evening/

weekend. *Students:* 3 full-time (2 women), 107 part-time (all women); includes 15 minority (7 Black or African American, non-Hispanic/Latino; 2 Asian, non-Hispanic/Latino; 5 Hispanic/Latino; 1 Native Hawaiian or other Pacific Islander, non-Hispanic/Latino), 1 international. *Degree requirements:* For master's, thesis optional. *Entrance requirements:* For master's, bachelor's degree with minimum GPA of 3.0, resume, teacher certification, work experience or course work in early childhood education; for CAS, master's degree in early childhood education or related field from nationally-accredited institution; minimum overall GPA of 3.75 for graduate work; resume; 3 letters of recommendation. *Application deadline:* Applications are processed on a rolling basis. Application fee: $45. Electronic applications accepted. *Expenses:* Tuition, state resident: full-time $7580; part-time $379 per unit. Tuition, nonresident: full-time $15,700; part-time $785 per unit. *Required fees:* $2480. *Financial support:* Application deadline: 4/1. *Unit head:* Dr. Janese Daniels, Graduate Program Director, 410-704-4832, E-mail: ecedgrad@towson.edu. *Application contact:* Coverley Beidleman, Assistant Director of Graduate Admissions, 410-704-2113, Fax: 410-704-3030, E-mail: grads@towson.edu. Website: http://www.towson.edu/coe/departments/earlychildhood/grad/earlychildhood/index.html

Trident University International, College of Education, Program in Education, Cypress, CA 90630. Offers adult education (MA Ed); aviation education (MA Ed); children's literacy development (MA Ed); e-learning (MA Ed); early childhood education (MA Ed); enrollment management (MA Ed); higher education (MA Ed); teaching and instruction (MA Ed); training and development (MA Ed). *Program availability:* Part-time, evening/weekend, online learning. *Degree requirements:* For master's, capstone project with integrative paper. *Entrance requirements:* For master's, minimum GPA of 2.5 (students with GPA 3.0 or greater may transfer up to 30% of graduate level credits). Additional exam requirements/recommendations for international students: Required—TOEFL (minimum score 525 paper-based). Electronic applications accepted.

Trinity Washington University, School of Education, Washington, DC 20017-1094. Offers clinical mental health counseling (MA); early childhood education (MAT); educating for change (M Ed); educational administration (MSA); elementary education (MAT); reading (M Ed); school counseling (MA); secondary education (MAT), including English, social studies; special education (MAT). *Accreditation:* NCATE. *Program availability:* Part-time, evening/weekend. *Degree requirements:* For master's, thesis (for some programs), capstone project(s). *Entrance requirements:* For master's, PRAXIS I, minimum GPA of 2.8. Additional exam requirements/recommendations for international students: Required—TOEFL (minimum score 550 paper-based). *Faculty research:* Technology, literacy, special education, organizations, inclusion models.

Troy University, Graduate School, College of Education, Program in Early Childhood Education, Troy, AL 36082. Offers MS, Ed S. *Program availability:* Part-time, evening/weekend, 100% online, blended/hybrid learning. *Faculty:* 1 (woman) part-time/adjunct. *Students:* 1 (woman) full-time, 4 part-time (all women); includes 1 minority (Black or African American, non-Hispanic/Latino). Average age 29. In 2016, 2 master's awarded. *Entrance requirements:* For master's, GRE (minimum score of 850 on old exam or 290 on new exam), GMAT (minimum score of 380), or MAT (minimum score of 385), bachelor's degree; minimum undergraduate GPA of 2.5 or 3.0 on last 30 semester hours, letter of recommendation. Additional exam requirements/recommendations for international students: Required—TOEFL (minimum score 523 paper-based; 70 iBT), IELTS (minimum score 6). *Application deadline:* Applications are processed on a rolling basis. Application fee: $50. Electronic applications accepted. *Expenses:* Tuition, state resident: full-time $7146; part-time $397 per credit hour. Tuition, nonresident: full-time $14,292; part-time $794 per credit hour. *Required fees:* $802; $50 per semester. Tuition and fees vary according to campus/location and program. *Financial support:* Fellowships, career-related internships or fieldwork, and scholarships/grants available. Support available to part-time students. Financial award applicants required to submit FAFSA. *Unit head:* Dr. Ruth Busby, Chair, Teacher Education, 334-670-3546, Fax: 334-808-6666, E-mail: rsbusby@troy.edu. *Application contact:* Jessica A. Kimbro, Director of Graduate Admissions, 334-670-3178, E-mail: jacord@troy.edu.

Tufts University, Graduate School of Arts and Sciences, Eliot-Pearson Department of Child Study and Human Development, Medford, MA 02155. Offers child study and human development (MA, PhD); early childhood education (MAT). *Program availability:* Part-time. *Faculty:* 21 full-time (16 women), 15 part-time/adjunct (13 women). *Students:* 81 full-time (70 women), 6 part-time (5 women); includes 19 minority (6 Black or African American, non-Hispanic/Latino; 7 Asian, non-Hispanic/Latino; 3 Hispanic/Latino; 3 Two or more races, non-Hispanic/Latino), 16 international. Average age 27. 129 applicants, 59% accepted, 37 enrolled. In 2016, 19 master's, 5 doctorates awarded. *Degree requirements:* For master's, thesis (for some programs); for doctorate, comprehensive exam, thesis/dissertation. *Entrance requirements:* For master's and doctorate, GRE General Test. Additional exam requirements/recommendations for international students: Required—TOEFL (minimum score 550 paper-based; 80 iBT), IELTS (minimum score 6.5). *Application deadline:* For fall admission, 12/1 priority date for domestic and international students. Applications are processed on a rolling basis. Application fee: $85. Electronic applications accepted. *Expenses:* $49,982 full-time tuition (for MA); $29,936 full-time tuition (for PhD). *Financial support:* In 2016–17, 78 students received support. Fellowships, research assistantships, teaching assistantships, Federal Work-Study, scholarships/grants, tuition waivers (full and partial), and unspecified assistantships available. Support available to part-time students. Financial award application deadline: 1/15. *Faculty research:* Reading and language, developmental technologies, cognitive and social development, policy and program evaluation. *Unit head:* Dr. David Henry Feldman, Graduate Program Director. *Application contact:* Office of Graduate Admissions, 617-627-3395, E-mail: gradadmissions@tufts.edu.
Website: http://ase.tufts.edu/epcd

Universidad del Turabo, Graduate Programs, Programs in Education, Program in Teaching at Primary Level, Gurabo, PR 00778-3030. Offers M Ed. *Students:* 1 (woman) part-time; minority (Hispanic/Latino). Average age 43. In 2016, 2 master's awarded. *Entrance requirements:* For master's, GRE, EXADEP, GMAT, interview, official transcript, essay, recommendation letters. *Application deadline:* Applications are processed on a rolling basis. Application fee: $25. Electronic applications accepted. *Financial support:* Institutionally sponsored loans available. Financial award applicants required to submit FAFSA. *Unit head:* Israel Rodríguez, Dean, 787-743-7979. *Application contact:* Diriee Rodríguez, Admissions Director, 787-743-7979 Ext. 4453, E-mail: admisiones-ut@suagm.edu.
Website: http://ut.suagm.edu/es/educacion

University at Buffalo, the State University of New York, Graduate School, Graduate School of Education, Department of Learning and Instruction, Buffalo, NY 14260. Offers biology education (Ed M, Certificate); chemistry education (Ed M, Certificate); childhood education (Ed M); childhood education with bilingual extension (Ed M), college teaching (Advanced Certificate); curriculum, instruction and the science of learning (PhD); early childhood education (Ed M); early childhood education with bilingual extension (Ed M); earth science education (Ed M, Certificate); education and technology (Ed M); education studies (Ed M); educational technology and new literacies (Certificate); educational technology and new literacies (Advanced Certificate); elementary education (Ed D); English education (Ed M, Certificate); English education studies (Ed M); English for speakers of other languages (Ed M); foreign and second language education (PhD); French education (Ed M, Certificate); German education (Ed M, Certificate); gifted education (Certificate); Latin education (Ed M, Certificate); literacy education studies (Ed M); literacy specialist (Ed M); literacy teaching and learning (Certificate); mathematics education (Ed M, Certificate); music education (Ed M, Certificate); music education studies (Ed M); music learning theory (Advanced Certificate); online education (Advanced Certificate); physics education (Ed M, Certificate); science and the public (Ed M); social studies education (Ed M, Certificate); Spanish education (Ed M, Certificate); special education (PhD); teaching English to speakers of other languages (Ed M). *Program availability:* Part-time, evening/weekend, 100% online. *Faculty:* 28 full-time (21 women), 67 part-time/adjunct (49 women). *Students:* 198 full-time (153 women), 312 part-time (220 women); includes 48 minority (28 Black or African American, non-Hispanic/Latino; 4 American Indian or Alaska Native, non-Hispanic/Latino; 15 Asian, non-Hispanic/Latino; 1 Hispanic/Latino), 66 international. Average age 33. 336 applicants, 86% accepted, 178 enrolled. In 2016, 137 master's, 24 doctorates, 25 other advanced degrees awarded. *Degree requirements:* For master's, comprehensive exam; for doctorate, thesis/dissertation, research analysis exam, research experience. *Entrance requirements:* For master's, letters of reference; for doctorate, GRE General Test or MAT, interview, writing sample, letters of recommendation. Additional exam requirements/recommendations for international students: Required—TOEFL (minimum score 600 paper-based; 96 iBT). *Application deadline:* For fall admission, 2/1 priority date for domestic and international students; for spring admission, 11/15 priority date for domestic students, 10/1 for international students. Applications are processed on a rolling basis. Application fee: $50. Electronic applications accepted. *Financial support:* In 2016–17, 44 fellowships (averaging $4,010 per year), 39 research assistantships with tuition reimbursements (averaging $9,897 per year) were awarded; teaching assistantships, career-related internships or fieldwork, Federal Work-Study, institutionally sponsored loans, scholarships/grants, tuition waivers (full and partial), and unspecified assistantships also available. Financial award application deadline: 2/28; financial award applicants required to submit FAFSA. *Faculty research:* Science assessment, foreign language teaching and learning, early learning, new literacies, gender and education. *Total annual research expenditures:* $534,880. *Unit head:* Dr. Deborah Moore-Russo, Chair, 716-645-4069, Fax: 716-645-3161, E-mail: dam29@buffalo.edu. *Application contact:* Luann Zak, Admissions Assistant, 716-645-2110, Fax: 716-645-7937, E-mail: luannzak@buffalo.edu.
Website: http://gse.buffalo.edu/lai

The University of Alabama at Birmingham, School of Education, Program in Early Childhood Education, Birmingham, AL 35294. Offers MA Ed, PhD. *Accreditation:* NCATE. *Degree requirements:* For master's, comprehensive exam, thesis optional; for doctorate, thesis/dissertation. *Entrance requirements:* For master's, GRE General Test or MAT; for doctorate, GRE General Test, MAT, minimum GPA of 3.25, at least 3 years' teaching experience, essay, recommendations, interview. Electronic applications accepted. Full-time tuition and fees vary according to course load and program.

University of Alaska Anchorage, College of Education, Program in Special Education, Anchorage, AK 99508. Offers early childhood special education (M Ed); special education (M Ed, Certificate). *Program availability:* Part-time. *Degree requirements:* For master's, comprehensive exam (for some programs), thesis or alternative. *Entrance requirements:* For master's, GRE or MAT, interview, minimum GPA of 2.75. Additional exam requirements/recommendations for international students: Required—TOEFL (minimum score 550 paper-based). *Faculty research:* Mild disabilities, substance abuse issues for educators, partnerships to improve at-risk youth, analysis of planning models for teachers in special education.

University of Arkansas, Graduate School, College of Education and Health Professions, Department of Curriculum and Instruction, Program in Childhood Education, Fayetteville, AR 72701. Offers MAT. *Accreditation:* NCATE. In 2016, 68 master's awarded. *Application deadline:* For fall admission, 4/1 for international students; for spring admission, 10/1 for international students. Applications are processed on a rolling basis. Application fee: $40 ($50 for international students). Electronic applications accepted. *Financial support:* Fellowships, research assistantships, and teaching assistantships available. *Unit head:* Dr. Michael Daugherty, Unit Head, 479-575-4201, E-mail: mkd03@uark.edu. *Application contact:* Dr. Heather Kindall, Graduate Coordinator, 479-575-2516, Fax: 479-575-6676, E-mail: hkindall@uark.edu.
Website: http://cied.uark.edu/

University of Bridgeport, School of Education, Department of Education, Bridgeport, CT 06604. Offers education (MS); educational management (Ed D, Diploma), including intermediate administrator or supervisor (Diploma), leadership (Ed D); elementary education (MS, Diploma), including early childhood education, elementary education; middle school education (MS); music education (MS); remedial reading and language arts (Diploma); secondary education (MS, Diploma), including computer specialist (Diploma), international education (Diploma), reading specialist, secondary education. *Program availability:* Part-time, evening/weekend. *Degree requirements:* For master's, final exam, final project, or thesis; for doctorate, comprehensive exam, thesis/dissertation; for Diploma, thesis or alternative, final project. *Entrance requirements:* For master's, minimum undergraduate QPA of 2.67; for doctorate, GRE, MAT; for Diploma, GRE General Test or MAT, minimum graduate QPA of 3.0. Additional exam requirements/recommendations for international students: Recommended—TOEFL (minimum score 550 paper-based; 80 iBT), IELTS (minimum score 6.5). Electronic applications accepted. *Expenses:* Contact institution.

University of Central Florida, College of Education and Human Performance, Education Doctoral Programs, Orlando, FL 32816. Offers communication sciences and disorders (PhD); curriculum and instruction (Ed D); early childhood education (PhD); educational leadership (Ed D); elementary education (PhD); exceptional education (PhD); exercise physiology (PhD); higher education (PhD); instructional technology (PhD); mathematics education (PhD); methodology, measurement and analysis (PhD); reading education (PhD); science education (PhD); social science education (PhD); TESOL (PhD). *Students:* 127 full-time (91 women), 43 part-time (29 women); includes 33 minority (17 Black or African American, non-Hispanic/Latino; 5 Asian, non-Hispanic/Latino; 7 Hispanic/Latino; 4 Two or more races, non-Hispanic/Latino), 26 international. Average age 37. 163 applicants, 40% accepted, 52 enrolled. In 2016, 57 doctorates awarded. Application fee: $30. Electronic applications accepted. *Expenses:* Tuition, state resident: part-time $288.16 per credit hour. Tuition, nonresident: part-time $1071.31 per credit hour. *Financial support:* In 2016–17, 78 students received support, including 41 fellowships with partial tuition reimbursements available (averaging $5,916 per year), 44 research assistantships with partial tuition reimbursements available (averaging $7,637 per year), 48 teaching assistantships with partial tuition reimbursements available (averaging $9,633 per year). Financial award application deadline: 3/1; financial award applicants required to submit FAFSA. *Unit head:* Dr. Edward Robinson, Director of Doctoral Programs, 407-823-6106, E-mail: edward.robinson@ucf.edu. *Application contact:* Assistant Director, Graduate Admissions, 407-823-2766, Fax: 407-823-6442, E-mail: gradadmissions@ucf.edu.
Website: http://education.ucf.edu/programs.cfm?pid=g&cat=2

Early Childhood Education

University of Central Missouri, The Graduate School, Warrensburg, MO 64093. Offers accountancy (MA); accounting (MBA); applied mathematics (MS); aviation safety (MA); biology (MS); business administration (MBA); career and technical education leadership (MS); college student personnel administration (MS); communication (MA); computer science (MS); counseling (MS); criminal justice (MS); educational leadership (Ed D); educational technology (MS); elementary and early childhood education (MSE); English (MA); environmental studies (MA); finance (MBA); history (MA); human services/ educational technology (Ed S); human services/learning resources (Ed S); human services/professional counseling (Ed S); industrial hygiene (MS); industrial management (MS); information systems (MBA); information technology (MS); kinesiology (MS); library science and information services (MS); literacy education (MSE); marketing (MBA); mathematics (MS); music (MA); occupational safety management (MS); psychology (MS); rural family nursing (MS); school administration (MSE); social gerontology (MS); sociology (MA); special education (MSE); speech language pathology (MS); superintendency (Ed S); teaching (MAT); teaching English as a second language (MA); technology (MS); technology management (PhD); theatre (MA). *Program availability:* Part-time, 100% online, blended/hybrid learning. *Degree requirements:* For master's and Ed S, comprehensive exam (for some programs), thesis (for some programs). *Entrance requirements:* Additional exam requirements/recommendations for international students: Required—TOEFL (minimum score 550 paper-based; 79 iBT). Electronic applications accepted.

University of Central Oklahoma, The Jackson College of Graduate Studies, College of Education and Professional Studies, Department of Curriculum and Instruction, Edmond, OK 73034-5209. Offers bilingual education/teaching English as a second language (M Ed); early childhood education (M Ed); elementary education (M Ed). *Program availability:* Part-time. *Degree requirements:* For master's, comprehensive exam (for some programs), thesis optional. *Entrance requirements:* For master's, GRE General Test. Additional exam requirements/recommendations for international students: Required—TOEFL (minimum score 550 paper-based; 79 iBT), IELTS (minimum score 6.5). Electronic applications accepted. *Faculty research:* Tourette's syndrome, bilingual education, science education, language development/disorders.

University of Cincinnati, Graduate School, College of Education, Criminal Justice, and Human Services, Division of Teacher Education, Program in Early Childhood Education, Cincinnati, OH 45221. Offers M Ed. *Accreditation:* NCATE. *Program availability:* Part-time. *Degree requirements:* For master's, thesis or alternative. *Entrance requirements:* For master's, GRE General Test. Additional exam requirements/recommendations for international students: Required—TOEFL (minimum score 610 paper-based), TWE (minimum score 5), OEPT. Electronic applications accepted. *Expenses: Tuition, area resident:* Full-time $12,790; part-time $389 per credit hour. Tuition, state resident: full-time $13,290; part-time $419 per credit hour. Tuition, nonresident: full-time $24,532; part-time $976 per credit hour. *International tuition:* $24,832 full-time. *Required fees:* $3958; $140 per credit hour. Tuition and fees vary according to course load, degree level, program and reciprocity agreements.

University of Colorado Denver, School of Education and Human Development, Early Childhood Education Program, Denver, CO 80217. Offers early childhood education (MA); special education (MA). *Accreditation:* NCATE. *Program availability:* Part-time, evening/weekend, online learning. *Students:* 56 full-time (55 women), 33 part-time (29 women); includes 16 minority (4 Black or African American, non-Hispanic/Latino; 1 Asian, non-Hispanic/Latino; 7 Hispanic/Latino; 4 Two or more races, non-Hispanic/ Latino), 4 international. Average age 34. 26 applicants, 65% accepted, 12 enrolled. In 2016, 38 master's awarded. *Degree requirements:* For master's, comprehensive exam, fieldwork, practica, 40 credit hours. *Entrance requirements:* For master's, GRE or MAT (if GPA is below 2.75), minimum GPA of 2.75, resume, three letters of recommendation, documented experience with young children, transcripts from all previous colleges/ universities attended. Additional exam requirements/recommendations for international students: Required—TOEFL (minimum score 537 paper-based; 75 iBT); Recommended—IELTS (minimum score 6.5). *Application deadline:* For fall admission, 4/15 for domestic students, 4/1 for international students; for spring admission, 9/15 for domestic students, 9/1 for international students; for summer admission, 2/15 for domestic and international students. Application fee: $50 ($75 for international students). Electronic applications accepted. *Expenses:* Contact institution. *Financial support:* In 2016–17, 43 students received support. Research assistantships, teaching assistantships, Federal Work-Study, institutionally sponsored loans, scholarships/ grants, and traineeships available. Financial award application deadline: 4/1; financial award applicants required to submit FAFSA. *Faculty research:* Early childhood growth and development, faculty development, adult learning, gender and equity issues, research methodology. *Unit head:* Lori Ryan, Professor, 303-315-2578, E-mail: lori.ryan@ucdenver.edu. *Application contact:* 303-315-6351, E-mail: education@ ucdenver.edu.
Website: http://www.ucdenver.edu/academics/colleges/SchoolOfEducation/Academics/ MASTERS/ECE/Pages/EarlyChildhoodEducation.aspx

University of Colorado Denver, School of Education and Human Development, Program in Educational Leadership and Innovation, Denver, CO 80217. Offers educational studies and research (PhD), including administrative leadership and policy, early childhood special education, math education, research, assessment and evaluation, science education, urban ecologies. *Program availability:* Part-time, evening/ weekend. *Students:* 30 full-time (25 women), 14 part-time (11 women); includes 16 minority (7 Black or African American, non-Hispanic/Latino; 1 American Indian or Alaska Native, non-Hispanic/Latino; 1 Asian, non-Hispanic/Latino; 6 Hispanic/Latino; 1 Two or more races, non-Hispanic/Latino), 5 international. Average age 40. 21 applicants, 67% accepted, 8 enrolled. In 2016, 3 doctorates awarded. *Degree requirements:* For doctorate, comprehensive exam, thesis/dissertation, 75 credit hours (for PhD). *Entrance requirements:* For doctorate, GRE or equivalent, resume or curriculum vitae, letters of recommendation, master's degree or equivalent, completion of basic or advanced statistics course with minimum B grade. Additional exam requirements/ recommendations for international students: Required—TOEFL (minimum score 537 paper-based; 75 iBT); Recommended—IELTS (minimum score 6.5). *Application deadline:* For fall admission, 12/1 priority date for domestic students, 11/1 priority date for international students. Applications are processed on a rolling basis. Application fee: $50 ($75 for international students). Electronic applications accepted. *Expenses:* Contact institution. *Financial support:* In 2016–17, 45 students received support. Fellowships, research assistantships, teaching assistantships, Federal Work-Study, institutionally sponsored loans, scholarships/grants, and traineeships available. Financial award application deadline: 4/1; financial award applicants required to submit FAFSA. *Faculty research:* Administrative leadership and policy studies, early childhood education, research in diversity, paraprofessionals in education, urban schools lab. *Unit head:* 303-315-6300, E-mail: education@ucdenver.edu. *Application contact:* 303-315-6300, E-mail: education@ucdenver.edu.
Website: http://www.ucdenver.edu/academics/colleges/SchoolOfEducation/Academics/ Doctorate/Pages/PhD%20in%20Education%20and%20Human%20Development.aspx

University of Dayton, Department of Teacher Education, Dayton, OH 45469. Offers early childhood leadership and advocacy (MS Ed); interdisciplinary education studies (MS Ed); leadership in educational systems (MS Ed); literacy (MS Ed); mathematics education (MS Ed); music education (MS Ed); teacher as leader (MS Ed); teacher education (MS Ed); technology-enhanced learning (MS Ed); trans-disciplinary early childhood education (MS Ed). *Program availability:* Part-time, evening/weekend, blended/hybrid learning. *Faculty:* 23 full-time (18 women), 49 part-time/adjunct (42 women). *Students:* 52 full-time (47 women), 89 part-time (76 women); includes 6 minority (2 Black or African American, non-Hispanic/Latino; 2 Hispanic/Latino; 2 Two or more races, non-Hispanic/Latino), 24 international. Average age 31. 106 applicants, 28% accepted. In 2016, 69 master's awarded. *Degree requirements:* For master's, variable foreign language requirement, thesis optional. *Entrance requirements:* For master's, GRE (minimum score of 149 verbal, 4 on writing) or MAT (minimum score of 396) if undergraduate GPA was under 2.75, minimum GPA of 2.75, 3 letters of recommendation, personal statement or resume, official transcripts. Additional exam requirements/recommendations for international students: Required—TOEFL (minimum score 550 paper-based; 80 iBT); Recommended—IELTS (minimum score 6.5). *Application deadline:* Applications are processed on a rolling basis. Application fee: $0 ($50 for international students). Electronic applications accepted. *Expenses:* $620 per credit hour, $25 registration fee per term. *Financial support:* Institutionally sponsored loans available. Financial award application deadline: 3/1; financial award applicants required to submit FAFSA. *Faculty research:* Educational technology; facilitating teacher reflection; teacher preparation in dyslexia. *Unit head:* Dr. Connie L. Bowman, Chair, 937-229-3305, E-mail: cbowman1@udayton.edu. *Application contact:* Gina Seiter, Graduate Program Advisor, 937-229-3103, E-mail: gseiter1@udayton.edu.
Website: https://www.udayton.edu/education/departments_and_programs/edt

University of Denver, Morgridge College of Education, Denver, CO 80208. Offers child, family and school psychology (MA, PhD, Ed S); counseling psychology (MA, PhD); curriculum and instruction (MA, Ed D, PhD); curriculum instruction and teaching (Certificate); early childhood special education (MA, Certificate); educational leadership and policy studies (MA, Ed D, PhD, Certificate); higher education (Ed D, PhD); library and information science (MLIS); research methods and statistics (MA, PhD). *Accreditation:* ALA; APA (one or more programs are accredited). *Program availability:* Part-time, evening/weekend, online learning. *Faculty:* 39 full-time (29 women), 60 part-time/adjunct (42 women). *Students:* 498 full-time (392 women), 362 part-time (282 women); includes 223 minority (63 Black or African American, non-Hispanic/Latino; 6 American Indian or Alaska Native, non-Hispanic/Latino; 20 Asian, non-Hispanic/Latino; 102 Hispanic/Latino; 1 Native Hawaiian or other Pacific Islander, non-Hispanic/Latino; 31 Two or more races, non-Hispanic/Latino), 40 international. Average age 32. 1,027 applicants, 69% accepted, 386 enrolled. In 2016, 252 master's, 36 doctorates, 141 other advanced degrees awarded. Terminal master's awarded for partial completion of doctoral program. *Degree requirements:* For master's, comprehensive exam; for doctorate, 2 foreign languages, comprehensive exam, thesis/dissertation. *Entrance requirements:* For master's and doctorate, GRE General Test or GMAT. Additional exam requirements/recommendations for international students: Required—TOEFL (minimum score 550 paper-based; 80 iBT). *Application deadline:* Applications are processed on a rolling basis. Application fee: $65. Electronic applications accepted. *Expenses:* $29,022 per year full-time. *Financial support:* In 2016–17, 697 students received support, including 37 research assistantships with tuition reimbursements available (averaging $11,209 per year), 66 teaching assistantships with tuition reimbursements available (averaging $3,742 per year); career-related internships or fieldwork, Federal Work-Study, institutionally sponsored loans, scholarships/grants, and unspecified assistantships also available. Support available to part-time students. Financial award application deadline: 2/15; financial award applicants required to submit FAFSA. *Faculty research:* Early childhood education, access and equity, educational leadership, family and school partnerships, neurodevelopmental disorders. *Total annual research expenditures:* $3.3 million. *Unit head:* Dr. Karen Riley, Dean, 303-871-3665, Fax: 303-871-4456, E-mail: karen.riley@du.edu. *Application contact:* Jodi Dye, Director of Admissions, 303-871-2510, Fax: 303-871-4456, E-mail: jodi.dye@du.edu.
Website: http://morgridge.du.edu

University of Florida, Graduate School, College of Education, School of Special Education, School Psychology and Early Childhood Studies, Gainesville, FL 32611. Offers early childhood education (M Ed, MAE); school psychology (M Ed, MAE, Ed D, PhD, Ed S); special education (M Ed, MAE, Ed D, PhD, Ed S). *Accreditation:* NCATE. *Program availability:* Part-time, evening/weekend, online learning. *Degree requirements:* For master's, comprehensive exam (for some programs), thesis (MAE); for doctorate, comprehensive exam, thesis/dissertation. *Entrance requirements:* For master's and doctorate, GRE General Test, minimum GPA of 3.0; for Ed S, GRE General Test. Additional exam requirements/recommendations for international students: Required—TOEFL (minimum score 550 paper-based; 80 iBT), IELTS (minimum score 6). Electronic applications accepted. *Faculty research:* Teacher quality/teacher education, early childhood, autism, academic and behavioral assessment and interventions.

University of Hartford, College of Education, Nursing, and Health Professions, Program in Early Childhood Education, West Hartford, CT 06117-1599. Offers M Ed. *Accreditation:* NCATE. *Program availability:* Part-time, evening/weekend. *Degree requirements:* For master's, comprehensive exam. *Entrance requirements:* For master's, PRAXIS I or waiver, interview, 2 letters of recommendation. Additional exam requirements/recommendations for international students: Required—TOEFL (minimum score 550 paper-based). Electronic applications accepted.

University of Hawaii at Manoa, Graduate Division, College of Education, Department of Curriculum Studies, Program in Early Childhood Education, Honolulu, HI 96822. Offers M Ed. *Accreditation:* NCATE. *Program availability:* Part-time. *Degree requirements:* For master's, thesis optional. *Entrance requirements:* Additional exam requirements/recommendations for international students: Required—TOEFL (minimum score 580 paper-based; 92 iBT), IELTS (minimum score 5).

University of Houston–Clear Lake, School of Education, Program in Curriculum and Instruction, Houston, TX 77058-1002. Offers curriculum and instruction (MS); early childhood education (MS); reading (MS); school library and information science (MS). *Program availability:* Part-time, evening/weekend. *Degree requirements:* For master's, thesis (for some programs). *Entrance requirements:* For master's, GRE or minimum GPA of 3.0 in last 60 hours. Additional exam requirements/recommendations for international students: Required—TOEFL (minimum score 550 paper-based). Electronic applications accepted.

University of Illinois at Chicago, College of Education, Department of Educational Psychology, Chicago, IL 60607-7128. Offers early childhood education (M Ed); educational psychology (PhD); measurement, evaluation, statistics, and assessment (M Ed); youth development (M Ed). *Program availability:* Part-time, online learning. *Faculty research:* Children's construction of morality, development of resilience in the face of enduring economical difficulties, cognition and cognitive development, test fairness.

The University of Kansas, Graduate Studies, School of Education, Department of Special Education, Lawrence, KS 66045. Offers autism spectrum disorder (MS Ed, Certificate); early childhood unified (MS Ed); high incidence disabilities (MS Ed); leadership in special and inclusive education (Certificate); low incidence disabilities (MS Ed); secondary special education and transition (MS Ed); special education (PhD). *Accreditation:* NCATE. *Program availability:* Part-time, online learning. *Students:* 91 full-

time (82 women), 293 part-time (255 women); includes 50 minority (19 Black or African American, non-Hispanic/Latino; 4 American Indian or Alaska Native, non-Hispanic/Latino; 6 Asian, non-Hispanic/Latino; 7 Hispanic/Latino; 14 Two or more races, non-Hispanic/Latino), 28 international. Average age 33. 759 applicants, 27% accepted, 166 enrolled. In 2016, 51 master's, 3 doctorates awarded. *Median time to degree:* Of those who began their doctoral program in fall 2008, 90% received their degree in 8 years or less. *Entrance requirements:* For master's, minimum GPA of 3.0, official transcripts, 3 letters of reference, professional resume; for doctorate, GRE General Test, official transcripts, 3 letters of reference, professional resume, professional writing sample. Additional exam requirements/recommendations for international students: Required—TOEFL or IELTS. Application fee: $65 ($85 for international students). Electronic applications accepted. *Financial support:* Fellowships, research assistantships, teaching assistantships, Federal Work-Study, scholarships/grants, and unspecified assistantships available. Support available to part-time students. Financial award application deadline: 2/21; financial award applicants required to submit FAFSA. *Faculty research:* Autism spectrum disorders, learning disabilities research, leadership development, qualitative research and evaluation. *Unit head:* Elizabeth B. Kozleski, Chair, 785-864-0556, E-mail: elizabeth.kozleski@ku.edu. *Application contact:* Graduate Admission Contact, 785-864-4342, E-mail: specialeduadm@ku.edu.
Website: http://specialedu.ku.edu/

University of Kentucky, Graduate School, College of Education, Program in Special Education, Lexington, KY 40506-0032. Offers early childhood (MS Ed); rehabilitation counseling (MRC, PhD); special education (MS Ed, PhD). *Accreditation:* CORE; NCATE. Terminal master's awarded for partial completion of doctoral program. *Degree requirements:* For master's, comprehensive exam, thesis optional; for doctorate, comprehensive exam, thesis/dissertation. *Entrance requirements:* For master's, GRE General Test, minimum undergraduate GPA of 2.75; for doctorate, GRE General Test, minimum graduate GPA of 3.0. Additional exam requirements/recommendations for international students: Required—TOEFL (minimum score 550 paper-based). Electronic applications accepted. *Faculty research:* Applied behavior analysis applications in special education, single subject research design in classroom settings, transition research across life span, rural special education personnel.

University of Louisiana at Monroe, Graduate School, College of Arts, Education, and Sciences, School of Education, Program in Curriculum and Instruction, Monroe, LA 71209-0001. Offers art education (M Ed); biology education (M Ed); chemistry education (M Ed); curriculum and instruction (Ed D); early childhood education (M Ed); earth science education (M Ed); educational leadership (M Ed); elementary education (1-5) (M Ed); English as a second language (M Ed); English education (M Ed); family and consumer education (M Ed); French education (M Ed); history education (M Ed); math education (M Ed); middle school education (M Ed); music education (M Ed); reading education (K-12) (M Ed); Spanish education (M Ed); special education - academically gifted (M Ed); special education - early intervention (M Ed); special education - educational diagnostician (M Ed); special education - mild/moderate disabilities (M Ed); speech education (M Ed). *Accreditation:* NCATE. *Faculty:* 8 full-time (4 women), 4 part-time/adjunct (3 women). *Students:* 13 full-time (11 women), 80 part-time (65 women); includes 25 minority (19 Black or African American, non-Hispanic/Latino; 1 Asian, non-Hispanic/Latino; 3 Hispanic/Latino; 2 Two or more races, non-Hispanic/Latino). Average age 37. 118 applicants, 30% accepted, 16 enrolled. In 2016, 23 master's, 4 doctorates awarded. *Degree requirements:* For master's, comprehensive exam (for some programs), thesis; for doctorate, thesis/dissertation, internships. *Entrance requirements:* For master's, GRE General Test; for doctorate, GRE General Test, minimum undergraduate GPA of 2.75, graduate 3.25. Additional exam requirements/recommendations for international students: Required—TOEFL (minimum score 500 paper-based; 61 iBT). *Application deadline:* For fall admission, 8/24 priority date for domestic students, 7/1 for international students; for winter admission, 12/14 priority date for domestic students; for spring admission, 1/19 for domestic students, 11/1 for international students. Applications are processed on a rolling basis. Application fee: $20 ($30 for international students). Electronic applications accepted. *Expenses:* Tuition, state resident: full-time $6489. Tuition, nonresident: full-time $18,589. *Required fees:* $8984. Tuition and fees vary according to course level, course load, degree level and program. *Financial support:* Research assistantships, career-related internships or fieldwork, Federal Work-Study, and unspecified assistantships available. Financial award application deadline: 4/1; financial award applicants required to submit FAFSA. *Unit head:* Dr. Dorothy Schween, Director, 318-342-1268, Fax: 318-342-3131, E-mail: schween@ulm.edu.

University of Louisville, Graduate School, College of Education and Human Development, Department of Teaching and Learning, Louisville, KY 40292-0001. Offers art education (MAT); autism and applied behavior analysis (Certificate); curriculum and instruction (PhD); early elementary education (MAT); exercise physiology (MS); health and physical education (MAT); health professions education (Certificate); higher education (MA); human resources and organization development (MS); instructional technology (M Ed); interdisciplinary early childhood education (MAT); middle school education (MAT); music education (MAT); secondary education (MAT); special education (MAT); sport administration (MS); teacher leadership (M Ed). *Program availability:* Part-time, evening/weekend. *Students:* 116 full-time (68 women), 158 part-time (112 women); includes 46 minority (24 Black or African American, non-Hispanic/Latino; 8 Asian, non-Hispanic/Latino; 5 Hispanic/Latino; 9 Two or more races, non-Hispanic/Latino), 6 international. Average age 30. 114 applicants, 71% accepted, 57 enrolled. In 2016, 59 master's, 3 doctorates awarded. *Application deadline:* For spring admission, 1/1 priority date for international students. Application fee: $60. *Expenses:* Tuition, state resident: full-time $12,246; part-time $681 per credit hour. Tuition, nonresident: full-time $25,486; part-time $1417 per credit hour. *Required fees:* $196. Tuition and fees vary according to program and reciprocity agreements. *Financial support:* Application deadline: 6/1; applicants required to submit FAFSA. *Faculty research:* STEM teaching and learning; content literacy for English language learners; social justice in teacher education; adolescent literacy; mathematics teacher development. *Total annual research expenditures:* $1.7 million. *Unit head:* Dr. Ann E. Larson, Dean, College of Education and Human Development, 502-852-6411, Fax: 502-852-1464, E-mail: ann@louisville.edu. *Application contact:* Betty Hampton, Director of Graduate Student Services, 502-852-5597, Fax: 502-852-1465, E-mail: edadvise@louisville.edu.
Website: http://louisville.edu/delphi

University of Maine, Graduate School, College of Education and Human Development, School of Learning and Teaching, Orono, ME 04469. Offers counselor education (M Ed, MA, MS, CAS); early childhood teacher (CGS); education (PhD), including counselor education, literacy education, prevention and intervention studies; elementary education (M Ed, CAS); individualized education (M Ed); literacy education (CAS); response to intervention for behavior (CGS); secondary education (M Ed, CAS); social studies education (M Ed); special education (M Ed, CAS). *Program availability:* Part-time. *Students:* 89 full-time (82 women), 184 part-time (162 women); includes 13 minority (8 American Indian or Alaska Native, non-Hispanic/Latino; 3 Hispanic/Latino; 1 Native Hawaiian or other Pacific Islander, non-Hispanic/Latino; 1 Two or more races, non-Hispanic/Latino), 4 international. Average age 37. 132 applicants, 97% accepted, 100 enrolled. In 2016, 50 master's, 3 doctorates, 19 other advanced degrees awarded. *Degree requirements:* For master's, thesis (for some programs); for doctorate, comprehensive exam, thesis/dissertation. *Entrance requirements:* For master's, GRE General Test, MAT. Additional exam requirements/recommendations for international students: Required—TOEFL. *Application deadline:* For fall admission, 2/1 priority date for domestic students. Applications are processed on a rolling basis. Application fee: $65. Electronic applications accepted. *Expenses:* Tuition, state resident: full-time $7524; part-time $2508 per credit. Tuition, nonresident: full-time $24,498; part-time $8166 per credit. *Required fees:* $1148; $571 per credit. *Financial support:* In 2016–17, 20 students received support, including 12 teaching assistantships (averaging $14,600 per year); Federal Work-Study, scholarships/grants, and unspecified assistantships also available. Financial award application deadline: 3/1. *Unit head:* Dr. Jim Artesani, Associate Dean of Accreditation and Graduate Affairs, 207-581-4061. *Application contact:* Scott G. Delcourt, Assistant Vice President for Graduate Studies and Senior Associate Dean, 207-581-3291, Fax: 207-581-3232, E-mail: graduate@maine.edu.
Website: http://umaine.edu/edhd/

University of Maine at Farmington, Graduate Programs in Education, Farmington, ME 04938. Offers early childhood education (MS Ed); educational leadership (MS Ed); instructional technology (M Ed). M Ed offered in collaboration with University of Maine and University of Southern Maine. *Accreditation:* NCATE. *Program availability:* Part-time-only, evening/weekend, 100% online, blended/hybrid learning. *Faculty:* 7 full-time (6 women), 6 part-time/adjunct (3 women). *Students:* 90 part-time (76 women). Average age 36. 30 applicants, 100% accepted, 29 enrolled. In 2016, 14 master's awarded. *Degree requirements:* For master's, thesis, capstone project (for educational leadership). *Entrance requirements:* For master's, baccalaureate degree from accredited institution, valid teaching certificate or professional experience in education. Additional exam requirements/recommendations for international students: Required—TOEFL. *Application deadline:* For fall admission, 8/10 for domestic students; for spring admission, 1/5 for domestic students; for summer admission, 4/10 for domestic students. Applications are processed on a rolling basis. Application fee: $60. Electronic applications accepted. *Expenses:* Contact institution. *Financial support:* Applicants required to submit FAFSA. *Faculty research:* Teacher leadership, school improvement strategies, technology integration. *Unit head:* Dr. Johanna Prince, Director of Graduate Programs in Education, 207-778-7066, E-mail: gradstudies@maine.edu. *Application contact:* Valerie Soucie, Administrative Specialist, 207-778-7502, Fax: 207-778-8134, E-mail: gradstudies@maine.edu.
Website: http://www2.umf.maine.edu/gradstudies/

University of Maryland, Baltimore County, The Graduate School, College of Arts, Humanities and Social Sciences, Department of Education, Program in Teaching, Baltimore, MD 21250. Offers early childhood education (MAT); elementary education (MAT); teaching (MAT), including art, biology, chemistry, choral music, classical foreign language, dance, earth/space science, English, instrumental music, mathematics, modern foreign language, physical science, physics, social studies, theatre. *Program availability:* Part-time, evening/weekend. *Faculty:* 24 full-time (18 women), 25 part-time/adjunct (19 women). *Students:* 41 full-time (34 women), 27 part-time (18 women); includes 26 minority (6 Black or African American, non-Hispanic/Latino; 9 Asian, non-Hispanic/Latino; 7 Hispanic/Latino; 1 Native Hawaiian or other Pacific Islander, non-Hispanic/Latino; 3 Two or more races, non-Hispanic/Latino), 2 international. Average age 30. 54 applicants, 83% accepted, 35 enrolled. In 2016, 50 master's awarded. *Degree requirements:* For master's, comprehensive exam (for some programs), thesis (for some programs). *Entrance requirements:* For master's, PRAXIS Core Examination or GRE (minimum score of 1000), minimum GPA of 3.0. Additional exam requirements/recommendations for international students: Required—TOEFL. *Application deadline:* For fall admission, 6/1 for domestic and international students; for spring admission, 11/1 for domestic and international students. Applications are processed on a rolling basis. Application fee: $50. Electronic applications accepted. *Expenses:* Tuition, state resident: full-time $13,294. Tuition, nonresident: full-time $20,286. *Financial support:* In 2016–17, 8 students received support, including teaching assistantships with tuition reimbursements available (averaging $12,000 per year); career-related internships or fieldwork, Federal Work-Study, scholarships/grants, tuition waivers, and unspecified assistantships also available. Financial award application deadline: 3/15. *Faculty research:* STEM teacher education, culturally sensitive pedagogy, ESOL/bilingual education, early childhood education, language, literacy and culture. *Total annual research expenditures:* $100,000. *Unit head:* Dr. Susan M. Blunck, Graduate Program Director, 410-455-2869, Fax: 410-455-3986, E-mail: blunck@umbc.edu. *Application contact:* Cheryl Johnson, MAT Program Specialist, 410-455-3388, E-mail: blackwel@umbc.edu.
Website: http://www.umbc.edu/education/

University of Massachusetts Amherst, Graduate School, College of Education, Program in Education, Amherst, MA 01003. Offers bilingual, English as a second language, and multicultural education (M Ed, Ed S); child study and early education (M Ed); children, families and schools (Ed D, Ed S); early childhood and elementary teacher education (M Ed); educational leadership (M Ed); educational policy and leadership (Ed D); higher education (M Ed); international education (M Ed); language, literacy and culture (Ed D); learning, media and technology (M Ed, Ed S); mathematics, science, and learning technologies (Ed D); reading and writing (M Ed); research, educational measurement and psychometrics (Ed D); school counselor education (M Ed, Ed S); school psychology (Ed S); science education (Ed S); secondary teacher education (M Ed); social justice education (M Ed, Ed D, Ed S); special education (M Ed, Ed D, Ed S); teacher education and school improvement (Ed D, Ed S). *Accreditation:* NCATE. *Program availability:* Part-time, online learning. Terminal master's awarded for partial completion of doctoral program. *Degree requirements:* For doctorate, comprehensive exam, thesis/dissertation. *Entrance requirements:* Additional exam requirements/recommendations for international students: Required—TOEFL (minimum score 550 paper-based; 80 iBT), IELTS (minimum score 6.5). Electronic applications accepted.

University of Massachusetts Boston, College of Education and Human Development, Program in Early Childhood Education and Care, Boston, MA 02125-3393. Offers PhD. *Students:* 5 full-time (4 women); includes 1 minority (Hispanic/Latino), 2 international. Average age 34. 12 applicants, 42% accepted, 5 enrolled. *Degree requirements:* For doctorate, thesis/dissertation. *Application deadline:* For fall admission, 2/1 for domestic students. *Expenses:* Tuition, state resident: full-time $16,863. Tuition, nonresident: full-time $32,913. *Required fees:* $177. *Unit head:* Dr. Peter Langer, Interim Dean, 617-287-7600. *Application contact:* Peggy Roldan Patel, Graduate Admissions Coordinator, 617-287-6400, Fax: 617-287-6236, E-mail: bos.gadm@dpc.umassp.edu.

University of Massachusetts Dartmouth, Graduate School, College of Arts and Sciences, School of Education, Department of STEM Education and Teacher Development, North Dartmouth, MA 02747-2300. Offers education ESL preK-12 (Postbaccalaureate Certificate); mathematics education (PhD); middle school education (MAT); secondary school education (Postbaccalaureate Certificate); teaching secondary school education (MAT). *Program availability:* Part-time. *Faculty:* 9 full-time (6 women), 6 part-time/adjunct (3 women). *Students:* 25 full-time (12 women), 87 part-time (55 women); includes 15 minority (3 Black or African American, non-Hispanic/Latino; 2 Asian, non-Hispanic/Latino; 7 Hispanic/Latino; 3 Two or more races, non-Hispanic/

Latino), 3 international. Average age 32. 53 applicants, 91% accepted, 38 enrolled. In 2016, 67 master's awarded. *Degree requirements:* For doctorate, thesis/dissertation. *Entrance requirements:* For master's, Massachusetts Tests for Educator Licensure (MTEL) Communication and Literacy Test and Subject Matter Test, statement of purpose (minimum of 300 words), resume, 2 letters of recommendation, official transcripts; for doctorate, GRE, statement of purpose (minimum of 300 words), resume, official transcripts, 3 letters of recommendation; for Postbaccalaureate Certificate, statement of purpose (minimum of 300 words), resume, 2 letters of recommendation, official transcripts. Additional exam requirements/recommendations for international students: Required—TOEFL (minimum score 533 paper-based; 72 iBT). *Application deadline:* For fall admission, 2/15 priority date for domestic students, 1/15 priority date for international students; for spring admission, 12/15 priority date for domestic students, 11/15 priority date for international students. Application fee: $60. Electronic applications accepted. *Expenses:* Tuition, state resident: full-time $14,994; part-time $624.75 per credit. Tuition, nonresident: full-time $27,068; part-time $1127.83 per credit. *Required fees:* $405; $25.88 per credit. Tuition and fees vary according to course load and reciprocity agreements. *Financial support:* In 2016–17, 3 fellowships (averaging $6,250 per year), 3 research assistantships (averaging $5,027 per year), 2 teaching assistantships (averaging $8,000 per year) were awarded; institutionally sponsored loans, scholarships/grants, unspecified assistantships, and instructional assistants, Fulbright scholarships also available. Financial award application deadline: 3/1; financial award applicants required to submit FAFSA. *Faculty research:* Reading/special education, education reform, English education, literacy, language arts K-12. *Total annual research expenditures:* $1.3 million. *Unit head:* Traci Almeida, Graduate Program Director, 508-999-8098, Fax: 508-910-8183, E-mail: talmeida@umassd.edu. *Application contact:* Steven Briggs, Director of Marketing and Recruitment for Graduate Studies, 508-999-8604, Fax: 508-999-8183, E-mail: graduate@umassd.edu.
Website: http://www.umassd.edu/cas/schoolofeducation/departments/stemeducationandteacherdevelopment/

University of Memphis, Graduate School, College of Education, Department of Instruction and Curriculum Leadership, Memphis, TN 38152. Offers advanced studies in teaching and learning (M Ed); applied behavior analysis (Graduate Certificate); autism studies (Graduate Certificate); early childhood education (MAT, MS, Ed D); elementary education (MAT); instruction and curriculum (MS, Ed D); instruction design and technology (MS, Ed D); instructional design and technology (Graduate Certificate); literacy, leadership, and coaching (Graduate Certificate); reading (MS, Ed D); school library information specialist (Graduate Certificate); secondary education (MAT); special education (MAT, MS, Ed D); STEM teacher leadership (Graduate Certificate); urban education (Graduate Certificate). *Accreditation:* NCATE (one or more programs are accredited). *Program availability:* Part-time. *Faculty:* 24 full-time (14 women), 17 part-time/adjunct (12 women). *Students:* 66 full-time (52 women), 315 part-time (243 women); includes 163 minority (132 Black or African American, non-Hispanic/Latino; 1 American Indian or Alaska Native, non-Hispanic/Latino; 6 Asian, non-Hispanic/Latino; 13 Hispanic/Latino; 1 Native Hawaiian or other Pacific Islander, non-Hispanic/Latino; 10 Two or more races, non-Hispanic/Latino), 4 international. Average age 35. 215 applicants, 78% accepted, 120 enrolled. In 2016, 111 master's, 21 doctorates, 8 other advanced degrees awarded. Terminal master's awarded for partial completion of doctoral program. *Degree requirements:* For master's, comprehensive exam, thesis or alternative; for doctorate, comprehensive exam, thesis/dissertation. *Entrance requirements:* For master's, GRE General Test, PRAXIS, minimum GPA of 2.5, letters of reference; for doctorate, GRE General Test, GRE Subject Test, 2 years of teaching experience, letters of reference, statement of purpose, interview. Additional exam requirements/recommendations for international students: Required—TOEFL (minimum score 550 paper-based; 79 iBT). *Application deadline:* For fall admission, 4/1 priority date for domestic students; for spring admission, 10/1 priority date for domestic students; for summer admission, 2/1 priority date for domestic students. Applications are processed on a rolling basis. Application fee: $35 ($60 for international students). Electronic applications accepted. *Expenses:* $5,231.50 per semester full-time in-state, $9,623.50 full-time out-of-state. *Financial support:* In 2016–17, 2 research assistantships with full tuition reimbursements (averaging $10,000 per year), 3 teaching assistantships with full tuition reimbursements (averaging $10,666 per year) were awarded; career-related internships or fieldwork, Federal Work-Study, institutionally sponsored loans, scholarships/grants, traineeships, and unspecified assistantships also available. Support available to part-time students. Financial award application deadline: 2/1; financial award applicants required to submit FAFSA. *Faculty research:* Effective urban teachers, preparation and retention of urban teachers, technology utilization in schools, field-based teacher preparation programs, effective use of online instruction. *Unit head:* Dr. Angiline Powell, Interim Chair, 901-678-3310, E-mail: apowell3@memphis.edu. *Application contact:* Dr. James Meindl, Coordinator of Graduate Studies, 901-678-3310, E-mail: jnmeindl@memphis.edu.
Website: http://www.memphis.edu/icl/

University of Miami, Graduate School, School of Education and Human Development, Department of Teaching and Learning, Program in Early Childhood Special Education, Coral Gables, FL 33124. Offers MS Ed, Ed S. *Program availability:* Part-time, evening/weekend. *Faculty:* 4 full-time (3 women), 6 part-time/adjunct (all women). *Students:* 14 part-time (13 women); all minorities (4 Black or African American, non-Hispanic/Latino; 1 American Indian or Alaska Native, non-Hispanic/Latino; 9 Hispanic/Latino). Average age 33. *Degree requirements:* For master's, electronic portfolio. *Entrance requirements:* For master's, GRE General Test. Additional exam requirements/recommendations for international students: Required—TOEFL (minimum score 550 paper-based; 80 iBT); Recommended—IELTS (minimum score 6.5). *Application deadline:* For fall admission, 6/30 for domestic students. Application fee: $65. Electronic applications accepted. *Financial support:* Scholarships/grants available. Financial award application deadline: 3/1; financial award applicants required to submit FAFSA. *Unit head:* Dr. Elizabeth Harry, Professor, 305-284-4961, Fax: 305-284-6998, E-mail: bharry@miami.edu. *Application contact:* Lois Heffernan, Graduate Admissions Coordinator, 305-284-2167, E-mail: lheffernan@miami.edu.
Website: http://www.education.miami.edu

University of Michigan–Dearborn, College of Education, Health, and Human Services, Master of Arts Program in Early Childhood Education, Dearborn, MI 48126. Offers MA. *Program availability:* Part-time, evening/weekend. *Faculty:* 3 full-time (2 women), 5 part-time/adjunct (all women). *Students:* 1 (woman) full-time, 20 part-time (all women); includes 5 minority (3 Black or African American, non-Hispanic/Latino; 1 Asian, non-Hispanic/Latino; 1 Hispanic/Latino). Average age 34. 14 applicants, 86% accepted, 10 enrolled. In 2016, 8 master's awarded. *Entrance requirements:* Additional exam requirements/recommendations for international students: Required—TOEFL (minimum score 560 paper-based; 84 iBT), IELTS (minimum score 6.5). *Application deadline:* For fall admission, 8/1 priority date for domestic students, 5/1 for international students; for winter admission, 12/1 priority date for domestic students, 9/1 for international students; for spring admission, 4/1 priority date for domestic students, 1/1 for international students. Applications are processed on a rolling basis. Application fee: $60. Electronic applications accepted. *Expenses:* Contact institution. *Financial support:* In 2016–17, 6 students received support. Career-related internships or fieldwork and scholarships/grants available. Financial award application deadline: 3/1; financial award applicants required to submit FAFSA. *Faculty research:* Early childhood education, constructivist education, assessment. *Unit head:* Dr. Stein Brunvand, Director, Master's Programs, 313-583-6415, E-mail: sbrunvan@umich.edu. *Application contact:* Elizabeth Morden, Graduate Programs Assistant, 313-593-5090, E-mail: emorden@umich.edu.
Website: http://umdearborn.edu/cehhs/cehhs_maeced/

University of Michigan–Flint, School of Education and Human Services, Department of Education, Flint, MI 48502. Offers curriculum and instruction (Ed S); early childhood education (MA); education (Ed D); educational leadership (Ed S); educational technology (MA), including curriculum and instruction, developer; literacy education (MA); secondary education with certification (MA). *Program availability:* Part-time, evening/weekend, 100% online, mixed mode format (for some programs). *Faculty:* 14 full-time (9 women), 30 part-time/adjunct (17 women). *Students:* 31 full-time (18 women), 199 part-time (144 women); includes 61 minority (48 Black or African American, non-Hispanic/Latino; 1 Asian, non-Hispanic/Latino; 6 Hispanic/Latino; 1 Native Hawaiian or other Pacific Islander, non-Hispanic/Latino; 5 Two or more races, non-Hispanic/Latino), 2 international. Average age 39. 124 applicants, 86% accepted, 75 enrolled. In 2016, 77 master's, 1 doctorate awarded. *Degree requirements:* For master's, thesis optional; for doctorate, thesis/dissertation. *Entrance requirements:* For master's, bachelor's degree from regionally-accredited institution, minimum overall undergraduate GPA of 3.0; for doctorate, Ed S; minimum overall graduate GPA of 3.3 (6.0 on a 9.0 scale) or equivalent; at least 3 years of work experience in a P-16 educational institution or in an education-related position; for Ed S, MA or MS in education-related field from accredited institution; minimum overall graduate GPA of 3.0 (6.0 on a 9.0 scale) or equivalent; at least 3 years of work experience in an educational setting. Additional exam requirements/recommendations for international students: Required—TOEFL (minimum score 84 iBT), IELTS (minimum score 6.5). *Application deadline:* For fall admission, 8/1 for domestic students, 5/1 for international students; for winter admission, 11/15 for domestic students, 9/15 for international students; for spring admission, 3/15 for domestic students, 1/15 for international students; for summer admission, 5/15 for domestic students. Applications are processed on a rolling basis. Application fee: $55. Electronic applications accepted. *Expenses:* Contact institution. *Financial support:* Federal Work-Study, scholarships/grants, and unspecified assistantships available. Support available to part-time students. Financial award application deadline: 3/1; financial award applicants required to submit FAFSA. *Unit head:* Dr. Mary Jo Finney, Department Chair/Associate Professor, 810-766-6617, E-mail: mjfinney@umflint.edu. *Application contact:* Bradley T. Maki, Director of Graduate Admissions, 810-762-3171, Fax: 810-766-6789, E-mail: bmaki@umflint.edu.
Website: https://www.umflint.edu/education/graduate-programs

University of Minnesota, Twin Cities Campus, Graduate School, College of Education and Human Development, Department of Educational Psychology, Minneapolis, MN 55455-0213. Offers autism spectrum disorder (Certificate); counseling and student personnel psychology (MA); early childhood special education (M Ed); psychological foundations of education (MA, PhD); quantitative methods in education (MA, PhD); school psychology (MA, PhD, Ed S); special education (M Ed, MA, PhD); talent development and gifted education (Certificate). *Accreditation:* APA (one or more programs are accredited). *Faculty:* 31 full-time (16 women). *Students:* 261 full-time (197 women), 63 part-time (47 women); includes 46 minority (6 Black or African American, non-Hispanic/Latino; 19 Asian, non-Hispanic/Latino; 12 Hispanic/Latino; 9 Two or more races, non-Hispanic/Latino), 27 international. Average age 29. 285 applicants, 42% accepted, 110 enrolled. In 2016, 153 master's, 35 doctorates, 10 other advanced degrees awarded. Application fee: $75 ($95 for international students). *Financial support:* In 2016–17, 26 fellowships, 61 research assistantships (averaging $14,168 per year), 31 teaching assistantships (averaging $12,522 per year) were awarded. *Faculty research:* Achievement gap; autism; behavioral and social-emotional development; improving skills in mathematics, reading, and comprehension; measuring and analyzing student change. *Total annual research expenditures:* $5.3 million. *Unit head:* Dr. Geoffrey Maruyama, Chair, 612-624-1003, Fax: 612-625-5861, E-mail: geoff@umn.edu. *Application contact:* Dr. Ernest Davenport, Director of Graduate Studies, 612-624-1040, E-mail: lqr6576@umn.edu.
Website: http://www.cehd.umn.edu/EdPsych

University of Minnesota, Twin Cities Campus, Graduate School, College of Education and Human Development, Institute of Child Development, Minneapolis, MN 55455-0213. Offers applied child and adolescent development (MA); child psychology (PhD); early childhood education (M Ed). *Faculty:* 17 full-time (8 women). *Students:* 65 full-time (59 women), 16 part-time (15 women); includes 19 minority (5 Black or African American, non-Hispanic/Latino; 4 Asian, non-Hispanic/Latino; 7 Hispanic/Latino; 3 Two or more races, non-Hispanic/Latino), 2 international. Average age 28. 132 applicants, 23% accepted, 30 enrolled. In 2016, 26 master's, 9 doctorates awarded. Application fee: $75 ($95 for international students). *Financial support:* In 2016–17, 26 fellowships, 21 research assistantships with full tuition reimbursements (averaging $13,750 per year), 20 teaching assistantships with full tuition reimbursements (averaging $10,832 per year) were awarded. *Faculty research:* Developmental affective and cognitive neuroscience; developmental psychopathology; intervention and prevention science; social and emotional development; cognitive, language, and perceptual development. *Total annual research expenditures:* $7.2 million. *Unit head:* Dr. Megan Gunnar, Director, 612-624-2713, E-mail: gunnar@umn.edu. *Application contact:* Dr. Kathleen Thomas, Director of Graduate Studies, 612-625-3389, E-mail: thoma114@umn.edu.
Website: http://www.cehd.umn.edu/ICD

University of Missouri, Office of Research and Graduate Studies, College of Education, Department of Learning, Teaching and Curriculum, Columbia, MO 65211. Offers agricultural education (M Ed, PhD, Ed S); art education (M Ed, PhD, Ed S); business and office education (M Ed, PhD, Ed S); early childhood education (M Ed, PhD, Ed S); elementary education (M Ed, PhD, Ed S); English education (M Ed, PhD, Ed S); foreign language education (M Ed, PhD, Ed S); health education and promotion (M Ed, PhD); learning and instruction (M Ed); marketing education (M Ed, PhD, Ed S); mathematics education (M Ed, PhD, Ed S); music education (M Ed, PhD, Ed S); reading education (M Ed, PhD, Ed S); science education (M Ed, PhD, Ed S); social studies education (M Ed, PhD, Ed S); vocational education (M Ed, PhD, Ed S). *Program availability:* Part-time. *Faculty:* 30 full-time (18 women), 1 (woman) part-time/adjunct. *Students:* 157 full-time (124 women), 157 part-time (125 women). Terminal master's awarded for partial completion of doctoral program. *Degree requirements:* For doctorate, thesis/dissertation. *Entrance requirements:* For master's and Ed S, GRE General Test or MAT, minimum GPA of 3.0; for doctorate, GRE General Test, minimum GPA of 3.0. Additional exam requirements/recommendations for international students: Required—TOEFL (minimum score 600 paper-based; 100 iBT). *Application deadline:* For fall admission, 12/1 priority date for domestic and international students. Applications are processed on a rolling basis. Application fee: $75 ($90 for international students). Electronic applications accepted. *Expenses:* Tuition, state resident: full-time $6347; part-time $352.60 per credit hour. Tuition, nonresident: full-time $17,379; part-time $965.50 per credit hour. *Required fees:* $1035. Tuition and fees vary according to course load, campus/location and program. *Financial support:* Fellowships, research assistantships, teaching assistantships, institutionally sponsored loans, traineeships,

health care benefits, and unspecified assistantships available. Support available to part-time students.
Website: http://education.missouri.edu/LTC/index.php

University of Missouri–St. Louis, College of Education, Department of Educator Preparation, Innovation and Research, St. Louis, MO 63121. Offers elementary education (M Ed), including early childhood, general, reading; secondary education (M Ed), including curriculum and instruction, general, middle level education, reading, teaching English to speakers of other languages (TESOL); special education (M Ed), including autism and developmental disabilities, early childhood special education. *Program availability:* Part-time, evening/weekend. *Faculty:* 26 full-time (14 women), 22 part-time/adjunct (14 women). *Students:* 151 full-time (127 women), 728 part-time (564 women); includes 222 minority (165 Black or African American, non-Hispanic/Latino; 1 American Indian or Alaska Native, non-Hispanic/Latino; 16 Asian, non-Hispanic/Latino; 31 Hispanic/Latino; 1 Native Hawaiian or other Pacific Islander, non-Hispanic/Latino; 8 Two or more races, non-Hispanic/Latino), 6 international. Average age 29. 363 applicants, 84% accepted, 211 enrolled. *Degree requirements:* For master's, comprehensive exam. *Entrance requirements:* Additional exam requirements/recommendations for international students: Recommended—TOEFL (minimum score 550 paper-based; 79 iBT), IELTS (minimum score 6.5). *Application deadline:* For fall admission, 7/1 priority date for domestic and international students; for spring admission, 12/1 priority date for domestic and international students. Application fee: $50 ($40 for international students). Electronic applications accepted. *Financial support:* Application deadline: 4/1; applicants required to submit FAFSA. *Unit head:* Dr. Gayle Wilkinson, Chair, 314-516-5791. *Application contact:* 314-516-5458, Fax: 314-516-6996, E-mail: gadadm@umsl.edu.
Website: https://coe.umsl.edu/dept/epir.html

University of Montana, Graduate School, Phyllis J. Washington College of Education and Human Sciences, Department of Teaching and Learning, Missoula, MT 59812-0002. Offers curriculum and instruction (M Ed, Ed D); early childhood education (M Ed); education (MA); teaching and learning (PhD). *Program availability:* Part-time. *Degree requirements:* For doctorate, thesis/dissertation. *Entrance requirements:* For master's, GRE General Test. Additional exam requirements/recommendations for international students: Required—TOEFL.

University of Nebraska at Kearney, College of Education, Department of Teacher Education, Kearney, NE 68849-0001. Offers curriculum and instruction (MA Ed), including early childhood education, elementary education, English as a second language, instructional effectiveness, reading/special education, secondary education; instructional technology (MS Ed), including information technology, instructional technology, school librarian; reading PK-12 (MA Ed); special education (MA Ed), including advanced practitioner: assistive technology specialist, advanced practitioner: behavioral interventionist, advanced practitioner: inclusive collaboration specialist, gifted, teacher education. *Program availability:* Part-time, evening/weekend, online only, 100% online. *Faculty:* 18 full-time (13 women). *Students:* 21 full-time (15 women), 296 part-time (240 women); includes 21 minority (3 Black or African American, non-Hispanic/Latino; 1 Asian, non-Hispanic/Latino; 14 Hispanic/Latino; 1 Native Hawaiian or other Pacific Islander, non-Hispanic/Latino; 2 Two or more races, non-Hispanic/Latino), 1 international. Average age 32. 81 applicants, 100% accepted, 61 enrolled. In 2016, 129 master's awarded. *Degree requirements:* For master's, comprehensive exam, thesis optional. *Entrance requirements:* For master's, portfolio or GRE. Additional exam requirements/recommendations for international students: Recommended—TOEFL (minimum score 550 paper-based; 79 iBT), IELTS (minimum score 6.5). *Application deadline:* For fall admission, 6/15 for domestic students, 5/15 for international students; for spring admission, 10/15 for domestic and international students; for summer admission, 3/15 for domestic and international students. Application fee: $45. Electronic applications accepted. *Expenses:* $285 per credit hour resident tuition, $415 per credit hour non-resident tuition (online). *Financial support:* In 2016–17, 6 students received support, including 6 research assistantships with full tuition reimbursements available (averaging $10,500 per year); career-related internships or fieldwork, scholarships/grants, health care benefits, and unspecified assistantships also available. Support available to part-time students. Financial award application deadline: 2/28; financial award applicants required to submit FAFSA. *Unit head:* Sarah Bartling, Administrative Assistant, 308-865-8513, E-mail: bartlingseg@unk.edu. *Application contact:* Linda Johnson, Director, Graduate Admissions and Programs, 308-865-8841, Fax: 308-865-8837, E-mail: johnsonli@unk.edu.
Website: http://www.unk.edu/academics/ted/index.php

University of Nebraska–Lincoln, Graduate College, College of Education and Human Sciences, Department of Child, Youth and Family Studies, Lincoln, NE 68588. Offers child development/early childhood education (MS, PhD); child, youth and family studies (MS); family and consumer sciences education (MS, PhD); family financial planning (MS); family science (MS, PhD); gerontology (PhD); human sciences (PhD), including child, youth and family studies, gerontology, medical family therapy; marriage and family therapy (MS); medical family therapy (PhD); youth development (MS). *Accreditation:* AAMFT/COAMFTE (one or more programs are accredited). *Program availability:* Online learning. *Degree requirements:* For master's, thesis optional. *Entrance requirements:* For master's, GRE. Additional exam requirements/recommendations for international students: Required—TOEFL (minimum score 550 paper-based). Electronic applications accepted. *Faculty research:* Marriage and family therapy, child development/early childhood education, family financial management.

University of Nevada, Las Vegas, Graduate College, College of Education, Department of Educational and Clinical Studies, Las Vegas, NV 89154-3066. Offers addiction studies (Advanced Certificate); counselor education (M Ed, MS), including clinical mental health (MS), school counseling (M Ed); early childhood education (M Ed); early childhood special education (Certificate), including infancy, preschool; English language learning (M Ed); mental health counseling (Advanced Certificate); special education (M Ed, PhD); PhD/JD. *Program availability:* Part-time, evening/weekend. *Faculty:* 17 full-time (8 women), 28 part-time/adjunct (20 women). *Students:* 269 full-time (219 women), 174 part-time (138 women); includes 181 minority (51 Black or African American, non-Hispanic/Latino; 2 American Indian or Alaska Native, non-Hispanic/Latino; 15 Asian, non-Hispanic/Latino; 81 Hispanic/Latino; 3 Native Hawaiian or other Pacific Islander, non-Hispanic/Latino; 29 Two or more races, non-Hispanic/Latino), 23 international. Average age 34. 256 applicants, 72% accepted, 145 enrolled. In 2016, 178 master's, 3 doctorates awarded. *Degree requirements:* For master's, comprehensive exam (for some programs); for doctorate, comprehensive exam, thesis/dissertation; for other advanced degree, final project. *Entrance requirements:* For master's, bachelor's degree; letter of recommendation; statement of purpose; for doctorate, GRE General Test, statement of purpose; writing sample; 3 letters of recommendation. Additional exam requirements/recommendations for international students: Required—TOEFL (minimum score 550 paper-based; 80 iBT), IELTS (minimum score 7). *Application deadline:* For fall admission, 7/15 for domestic students, 5/1 for international students; for spring admission, 11/15 for domestic students, 10/1 for international students; for summer admission, 4/15 for domestic students. Application fee: $60 ($95 for international students). Electronic applications accepted. *Expenses:* $269.25 per credit, $792 per 3-credit course; $9,634 per year resident; $23,274 per year non-resident; $7,094 fees non-resident (7 credits or more); $1,307 annual health insurance fee. *Financial support:* In 2016–17, 12 research assistantships with partial tuition reimbursements (averaging $12,569 per year), 27 teaching assistantships with partial tuition reimbursements (averaging $13,759 per year) were awarded; institutionally sponsored loans, scholarships/grants, health care benefits, and unspecified assistantships also available. Financial award application deadline: 3/15. *Faculty research:* Multicultural issues in counseling, academic interventions for students with disabilities, establishment of pro-social skills in young children with severe disabilities, inclusive strategies for students with disabilities, language and literacy for English language learners. *Total annual research expenditures:* $768,906. *Unit head:* Dr. Monica Brown, Interim Department Chair/Professor, 702-895-3167, Fax: 702-895-3205, E-mail: monica.brown@unlv.edu. *Application contact:* Dr. Cori More, Graduate Coordinator, 702-895-3271, Fax: 702-895-3205, E-mail: cori.more@unlv.edu.
Website: http://education.unlv.edu/ecs/

University of New England, College of Graduate and Professional Studies, Portland, ME 04103. Offers applied nutrition (MS); career and technical education (MS Ed); curriculum and instruction (MS Ed); education (CAGS, Post-Master's Certificate); education leadership (Ed D); educational leadership (MS Ed); generalist (MS Ed); health informatics (MS, Graduate Certificate); inclusion education (MS Ed); literacy K-12 (MS Ed); medical education leadership (MMEL); public health (Graduate Certificate); reading specialist (MS Ed); social work (MSW). *Program availability:* Part-time, evening/weekend, online only, 100% online. *Faculty:* 67 part-time/adjunct (46 women). *Students:* 891 full-time (667 women), 359 part-time (261 women); includes 309 minority (215 Black or African American, non-Hispanic/Latino; 2 American Indian or Alaska Native, non-Hispanic/Latino; 63 Asian, non-Hispanic/Latino; 18 Hispanic/Latino; 2 Native Hawaiian or other Pacific Islander, non-Hispanic/Latino; 9 Two or more races, non-Hispanic/Latino). Average age 36. 777 applicants, 50% accepted, 316 enrolled. In 2016, 292 master's, 34 doctorates, 130 other advanced degrees awarded. *Application deadline:* Applications are processed on a rolling basis. Electronic applications accepted. Tuition and fees vary according to degree level, program and student level. *Financial support:* Application deadline: 5/1; applicants required to submit FAFSA. *Unit head:* Dr. Martha Wilson, Associate Provost for Online Worldwide Learning/Dean of the College of Graduate and Professional Studies, 207-221-4985, E-mail: mwilson13@une.edu.
Website: http://online.une.edu

University of New Hampshire, Graduate School, College of Liberal Arts, Department of Education, Durham, NH 03824. Offers early childhood education (M Ed); education (PhD); educational administration and supervision (Ed S); elementary education (M Ed); secondary education (MAT); special education (M Ed). *Accreditation:* TEAC. *Program availability:* Part-time. *Degree requirements:* For doctorate, thesis/dissertation. *Entrance requirements:* For master's, doctorate, and Ed S, GRE General Test. Additional exam requirements/recommendations for international students: Required—TOEFL (minimum score 550 paper-based; 80 iBT). Electronic applications accepted.

University of New Mexico, Graduate Studies, College of Education, Program in Multicultural Teacher and Childhood Education, Albuquerque, NM 87131-2039. Offers Ed D, PhD. *Accreditation:* NCATE. *Program availability:* Part-time. *Faculty:* 1 (woman) full-time. *Students:* 4 full-time (3 women), 9 part-time (6 women); includes 6 minority (5 Hispanic/Latino; 1 Two or more races, non-Hispanic/Latino). Average age 48. 1 applicant. In 2016, 1 doctorate awarded. *Degree requirements:* For doctorate, comprehensive exam, thesis/dissertation. *Entrance requirements:* For doctorate, GRE, master's degree, minimum GPA of 3.0, 3 years of teaching experience, 3-5 letters of reference, letter of intent, professional writing sample. Additional exam requirements/recommendations for international students: Required—TOEFL (minimum score 550 paper-based). *Application deadline:* For fall admission, 1/15 priority date for domestic students, 1/15 for international students; for spring admission, 10/30 for domestic and international students. Application fee: $50. Electronic applications accepted. *Financial support:* Fellowships, research assistantships, teaching assistantships with partial tuition reimbursements, scholarships/grants, and unspecified assistantships available. Financial award application deadline: 3/1; financial award applicants required to submit FAFSA. *Faculty research:* Teacher education, clinical preparation, reflective practice, science education, mathematics education, social justice, technology education, media literacy. *Unit head:* Dr. Cheryl Torrez, Department Chair, 505-277-9611, Fax: 505-277-0455, E-mail: ted@unm.edu. *Application contact:* Robert Romero, Program Coordinator, 505-277-0513, Fax: 505-277-0455, E-mail: ted@unm.edu.
Website: https://coe.unm.edu/departments-programs/ifce/ecme/

The University of North Carolina at Chapel Hill, Graduate School, School of Education, Master of Education Program for Experienced Teachers: Early Childhood Intervention and Family Support, Chapel Hill, NC 27599. Offers M Ed. *Accreditation:* NCATE. *Program availability:* Part-time. *Degree requirements:* For master's, comprehensive exam. *Entrance requirements:* For master's, minimum GPA of 3.0 during last 2 years of undergraduate course work. Electronic applications accepted.

The University of North Carolina at Chapel Hill, Graduate School, School of Education, Program in Education, Chapel Hill, NC 27599. Offers culture, curriculum and change (MA, PhD); early childhood, intervention and literacy (MA, PhD); educational psychology, measurement and evaluation (MA, PhD). *Accreditation:* NCATE. *Degree requirements:* For master's, thesis; for doctorate, comprehensive exam, thesis/dissertation. *Entrance requirements:* For master's, GRE General Test, minimum GPA of 3.0 during last 2 years of undergraduates course work; for doctorate, GRE General Test, minimum GPA of 3.0 during last 2 years of undergraduate course work. Additional exam requirements/recommendations for international students: Required—TOEFL (minimum score 550 paper-based). Electronic applications accepted.

The University of North Carolina at Charlotte, Cato College of Education, Interdisciplinary Education Programs, Charlotte, NC 28223-0001. Offers art education (Graduate Certificate); child and family development: early childhood education (MAT); curriculum and instruction (PhD); elementary education (MAT); foreign language education (MAT); middle grades education (MAT); secondary education (MAT), special education (MAT); teaching (Graduate Certificate); teaching English as a second language (MAT); theatre education (Graduate Certificate). *Program availability:* Part-time, 100% online, blended/hybrid learning. *Students:* 78 full-time (59 women), 619 part-time (484 women); includes 255 minority (186 Black or African American, non-Hispanic/Latino; 1 American Indian or Alaska Native, non-Hispanic/Latino; 16 Asian, non-Hispanic/Latino; 37 Hispanic/Latino; 15 Two or more races, non-Hispanic/Latino), 10 international. Average age 33. 380 applicants, 92% accepted, 264 enrolled. In 2016, 93 master's, 8 doctorates, 176 other advanced degrees awarded. *Degree requirements:* For master's, thesis or alternative, research project/portfolio. *Entrance requirements:* For master's, GRE or MAT, bachelor's degree, or its U.S. equivalent, from regionally-accredited college or university; minimum overall GPA of 3.0 on all previous work beyond high school; statement of purpose (essay); at least three recommendation forms; for doctorate, GRE or MAT, bachelor's degree (or its U.S. equivalent) from regionally-accredited college or university; minimum overall GPA of 3.5 in master's degree program; for Graduate Certificate, bachelor's degree from regionally-accredited university; minimum GPA of 2.75 on all post-secondary work attempted; transcripts; personal statement outlining why the applicant seeks admission to the program. Additional exam requirements/recommendations for international students: Required—

TOEFL (minimum score 523 paper-based, 70 iBT) or IELTS (6.5). *Application deadline:* For fall admission, 3/1 priority date for domestic and international students; for spring admission, 10/1 priority date for domestic and international students; for summer admission, 4/1 priority date for domestic and international students. Applications are processed on a rolling basis. Application fee: $75. Electronic applications accepted. *Expenses:* Tuition, state resident: full-time $4252. Tuition, nonresident: full-time $17,423. *Required fees:* $3026. Tuition and fees vary according to course load and program. *Financial support:* Career-related internships or fieldwork, institutionally sponsored loans, scholarships/grants, and unspecified assistantships available. Support available to part-time students. Financial award application deadline: 3/1; financial award applicants required to submit FAFSA. *Unit head:* Dr. Ellen McIntyre, Dean, 704-687-8722, E-mail: ellen.mcintyre@uncc.edu. *Application contact:* Kathy B. Giddings, Director of Graduate Admissions, 704-687-5503, Fax: 704-687-1668, E-mail: gradadm@uncc.edu.
Website: http://education.uncc.edu/academic-programs

The University of North Carolina at Greensboro, Graduate School, School of Education, Department of Specialized Education Services, Greensboro, NC 27412-5001. Offers cross-categorical special education (M Ed); interdisciplinary studies in special education (M Ed); leadership early care and education (Certificate); special education (M Ed, PhD). *Degree requirements:* For master's, thesis or alternative. *Entrance requirements:* For master's, GRE General Test. Additional exam requirements/recommendations for international students: Required—TOEFL. Electronic applications accepted.

The University of North Carolina Wilmington, Watson College of Education, Department of Early Childhood, Elementary, Middle, Literacy and Special Education, Wilmington, NC 28403-3297. Offers educational leadership, policy, and advocacy (M Ed); elementary education (M Ed, MAT); language and literacy (M Ed); middle grades education (M Ed, MAT). *Accreditation:* NCATE. *Program availability:* Part-time. *Faculty:* 26 full-time (19 women). *Students:* 121 full-time (89 women), 139 part-time (135 women); includes 70 minority (47 Black or African American, non-Hispanic/Latino; 1 Asian, non-Hispanic/Latino; 14 Hispanic/Latino; 8 Two or more races, non-Hispanic/Latino). Average age 34. 109 applicants, 78% accepted, 65 enrolled. In 2016, 83 master's awarded. *Degree requirements:* For master's, comprehensive exam, capstone experience. *Entrance requirements:* For master's, GRE General Test, MAT, minimum GPA of 3.0 in undergraduate work, 3 letters of recommendations, NC Class A teacher license in related field, statement of interest. *Application deadline:* For fall admission, 5/15 for domestic students; for spring admission, 10/15 for domestic students; for summer admission, 3/15 for domestic students. Applications are processed on a rolling basis. Application fee: $60. Electronic applications accepted. *Expenses:* Contact institution. *Financial support:* Scholarships/grants and unspecified assistantships available. Support available to part-time students. Financial award application deadline: 3/15; financial award applicants required to submit FAFSA. *Unit head:* Dr. Kathy Fox, Chair, 910-962-3240, Fax: 910-962-3988, E-mail: foxk@uncw.edu. *Application contact:* Dr. Elizabeth Crawford, Graduate Program Coordinator, 910-962-2916, Fax: 910-962-3988, E-mail: crawforde@uncw.edu.
Website: http://www.uncw.edu/ed/eemls/index.html

University of North Dakota, Graduate School, College of Education and Human Development, Program in Early Childhood Education, Grand Forks, ND 58202. Offers MS. *Accreditation:* NCATE. *Program availability:* Part-time. *Degree requirements:* For master's, comprehensive exam, thesis or alternative. *Entrance requirements:* For master's, minimum GPA of 3.0. Additional exam requirements/recommendations for international students: Required—TOEFL (minimum score 550 paper-based; 79 iBT), IELTS (minimum score 6.5). *Application deadline:* For fall admission, 8/1 priority date for domestic students, 5/1 priority date for international students; for spring admission, 12/1 priority date for domestic students, 9/1 priority date for international students. Applications are processed on a rolling basis. Application fee: $35. Electronic applications accepted. *Financial support:* Fellowships with full and partial tuition reimbursements, research assistantships with full and partial tuition reimbursements, teaching assistantships with full and partial tuition reimbursements, Federal Work-Study, institutionally sponsored loans, scholarships/grants, health care benefits, tuition waivers (full and partial), and unspecified assistantships available. Support available to part-time students. Financial award application deadline: 3/15; financial award applicants required to submit FAFSA. *Unit head:* Dr. Glenn Olson, Director, 701-777-3145, Fax: 701-777-4393, E-mail: glennolsen@mail.und.edu. *Application contact:* Staci Wells, Admissions Associate, 701-777-2945, Fax: 701-777-3619, E-mail: staci.wells@gradschool.und.edu.
Website: http://education.und.edu/teaching-and-learning/grad-early-childhood.cfm

University of Northern Iowa, Graduate College, College of Education, Department of Curriculum and Instruction, MAE Program in Early Childhood Education, Cedar Falls, IA 50614. Offers MAE. *Degree requirements:* For master's, comprehensive exam, thesis or alternative. *Entrance requirements:* For master's, minimum GPA of 3.0. Additional exam requirements/recommendations for international students: Required—TOEFL (minimum score 500 paper-based; 61 iBT). Electronic applications accepted.

University of North Georgia, College of Education, Dahlonega, GA 30597. Offers early childhood education (M Ed); middle grades education (M Ed, MAT); physical education (MS); school leadership (Ed S); secondary education (M Ed), including English education, history education, mathematics education, physical education. *Accreditation:* NCATE. *Program availability:* Part-time, evening/weekend, online learning. *Faculty:* 16 full-time (12 women), 3 part-time/adjunct (all women). *Students:* 11 full-time (8 women), 146 part-time (107 women); includes 19 minority (10 Black or African American, non-Hispanic/Latino; 2 Asian, non-Hispanic/Latino; 6 Hispanic/Latino; 1 Two or more races, non-Hispanic/Latino). Average age 28. 77 applicants, 83% accepted, 47 enrolled. In 2016, 79 master's awarded. *Degree requirements:* For master's, comprehensive exam, thesis optional. *Entrance requirements:* For master's, GRE or MAT, GACE, minimum GPA of 2.75; for Ed S, GRE General Test or MAT, 3 years of teaching experience, master's degree, minimum graduate GPA of 3.25, leadership position in the school. Additional exam requirements/recommendations for international students: Required—TOEFL (minimum score 550 paper-based; 79 iBT), IELTS (minimum score 6.5). *Application deadline:* For fall admission, 8/1 priority date for domestic students, 7/1 priority date for international students; for spring admission, 12/1 priority date for domestic students, 11/1 priority date for international students. Applications are processed on a rolling basis. Application fee: $40. Electronic applications accepted. *Expenses:* Contact institution. *Financial support:* Teaching assistantships, career-related internships or fieldwork, scholarships/grants, and unspecified assistantships available. Financial award application deadline: 5/1; financial award applicants required to submit CSS PROFILE or FAFSA. *Unit head:* Dr. Susan Ayers, Dean, College of Education, 706-864-1998, E-mail: susan.ayres@ung.edu. *Application contact:* Regina Boling, Teacher Education Graduate Admissions, 706-864-1533, E-mail: regina.boling@ung.edu.
Website: http://ung.edu/college-of-education/

University of North Texas, Robert B. Toulouse School of Graduate Studies, Denton, TX 76203-5459. Offers accounting (MS); applied anthropology (MA, MS); applied behavior analysis (Certificate); applied geography (MA); applied technology and performance improvement (M Ed, MS); art education (MA); art history (MA); art museum education (Certificate); arts leadership (Certificate); audiology (Au D); behavior analysis (MS); behavioral science (PhD); biochemistry and molecular biology (MS); biology (MA, MS); biomedical engineering (MS); business analysis (MS); chemistry (MS); clinical health psychology (PhD); communication studies (MA, MS); computer engineering (MS); computer science (MS); counseling (M Ed, MS), including clinical mental health counseling (MS), college and university counseling, elementary school counseling, secondary school counseling; creative writing (MA); criminal justice (MS); curriculum and instruction (M Ed); decision sciences (MBA); design (MA, MFA), including fashion design (MFA), innovation studies, interior design (MFA); early childhood studies (MS); economics (MS); educational leadership (M Ed, Ed D); educational psychology (MS, PhD), including family studies (MS), gifted and talented (MS), human development (MS), learning and cognition (MS), research, measurement and evaluation (MS); electrical engineering (MS); emergency management (MPA); engineering technology (MS); English (MA); English as a second language (MA); environmental science (MS); finance (MBA, MS); financial management (MPA); French (MA); health services management (MBA); higher education (M Ed, Ed D); history (MA, MS); hospitality management (MS); human resources management (MPA); information science (MS); information systems (PhD); information technologies (MBA); interdisciplinary studies (MA, MS); international studies (MA); international sustainable tourism (MS); jazz studies (MM); journalism (MA, MJ, Graduate Certificate), including interactive and virtual digital communication (Graduate Certificate), narrative journalism (Graduate Certificate), public relations (Graduate Certificate); kinesiology (MS); linguistics (MA); local government management (MPA); logistics (PhD); logistics and supply chain management (MBA); long-term care, senior housing, and aging services (MA); management (PhD); marketing (MBA); mathematics (MA, MS); mechanical and energy engineering (MS, PhD); music (MA), including ethnomusicology, music theory, musicology, performance; music composition (PhD); music education (MM Ed, PhD); nonprofit management (MPA); operations and supply chain management (MBA); performance (MM, DMA); philosophy (MA); political science (MA); professional and technical communication (MA); radio, television and film (MA, MFA); rehabilitation counseling (Certificate); sociology (MA); Spanish (MA); special education (M Ed); speech-language pathology (MA); strategic management (MBA); studio art (MFA); teaching (M Ed); MBA/MS. *Program availability:* Part-time, evening/weekend, online learning. Terminal master's awarded for partial completion of doctoral program. *Degree requirements:* For master's, variable foreign language requirement, comprehensive exam (for some programs), thesis (for some programs); for doctorate, variable foreign language requirement, comprehensive exam (for some programs), thesis/dissertation; for other advanced degree, variable foreign language requirement, comprehensive exam (for some programs). *Entrance requirements:* For master's and doctorate, GRE, GMAT. Additional exam requirements/recommendations for international students: Required—TOEFL (minimum score 550 paper-based; 79 iBT). Electronic applications accepted.

University of Oklahoma, Jeannine Rainbolt College of Education, Department of Instructional Leadership and Academic Curriculum, Norman, OK 73019. Offers instructional leadership and academic curriculum (M Ed, PhD), including biomedical education (PhD), early childhood education, elementary education (M Ed), English education, instructional leadership, mathematics education, reading education, science education, social studies education, world languages education (M Ed). *Accreditation:* NCATE. *Program availability:* Part-time. *Faculty:* 19 full-time (15 women), 1 (woman) part-time/adjunct. *Students:* 66 full-time (49 women), 116 part-time (88 women); includes 49 minority (12 Black or African American, non-Hispanic/Latino; 6 American Indian or Alaska Native, non-Hispanic/Latino; 6 Asian, non-Hispanic/Latino; 11 Hispanic/Latino; 1 Native Hawaiian or other Pacific Islander, non-Hispanic/Latino; 13 Two or more races, non-Hispanic/Latino), 13 international. Average age 35. 38 applicants, 97% accepted, 28 enrolled. In 2016, 33 master's, 10 doctorates awarded. Terminal master's awarded for partial completion of doctoral program. *Degree requirements:* For master's, comprehensive exam (for some programs), thesis (for some programs); for doctorate, comprehensive exam (for some programs), thesis/dissertation. *Entrance requirements:* For doctorate, GRE. Additional exam requirements/recommendations for international students: Required—TOEFL (minimum score 79 iBT) or IELTS (minimum score 6.5). Application fee: $50 ($100 for international students). Electronic applications accepted. *Expenses:* Tuition, state resident: full-time $4886; part-time $203.60 per credit hour. Tuition, nonresident: full-time $18,989; part-time $791.20 per credit hour. *Required fees:* $3283; $126.25 per credit hour. $126.50 per semester. *Financial support:* In 2016–17, 112 students received support, including 7 research assistantships with partial tuition reimbursements available (averaging $10,373 per year), 6 teaching assistantships with partial tuition reimbursements available (averaging $11,446 per year); fellowships, scholarships/grants, and unspecified assistantships also available. Financial award application deadline: 6/1; financial award applicants required to submit FAFSA. *Faculty research:* Teacher preparation; instruction; curriculum; learning; constructivist theory. *Total annual research expenditures:* $165,297. *Unit head:* Dr. Stacy Reeder, Chair, 405-325-1498, Fax: 405-325-4061, E-mail: reeder@ou.edu. *Application contact:* Anna Steele, Graduate Programs Officer, 405-325-4525, E-mail: anna.steele@ou.edu.
Website: http://www.ou.edu/education/ilac

University of Phoenix–Bay Area Campus, College of Education, San Jose, CA 95134-1805. Offers administration and supervision (MA Ed); adult education and training (MA Ed); early childhood education (MA Ed); education (Ed S); educational leadership (Ed D); elementary teacher education (MA Ed); higher education administration (PhD); secondary teacher education (MA Ed); special education (MA Ed); teacher leadership (MA Ed). *Program availability:* Evening/weekend, online learning. *Degree requirements:* For master's, thesis (for some programs). *Entrance requirements:* For master's, minimum undergraduate GPA of 2.5, 3 years of work experience. Additional exam requirements/recommendations for international students: Required—TOEFL (minimum score 550 paper-based; 79 iBT). Electronic applications accepted.

University of Phoenix–North Florida Campus, College of Education, Jacksonville, FL 32216-0959. Offers administration and supervision (MA Ed); curriculum and instruction (MA Ed), including computer education, mathematics education; early childhood education (MA Ed); elementary teacher education (MA Ed); secondary teacher education (MA Ed). *Program availability:* Evening/weekend. *Degree requirements:* For master's, thesis (for some programs). *Entrance requirements:* For master's, 3 years of work experience, minimum undergraduate GPA of 2.5. Additional exam requirements/recommendations for international students: Required—TOEFL (minimum score 550 paper-based; 49 iBT). Electronic applications accepted.

University of Phoenix–Online Campus, College of Education, Phoenix, AZ 85034-7209. Offers administration and supervision (MAEd, Certificate); adult education and training (MAEd); curriculum and instruction (MAEd), including computer education, curriculum and instruction, English as a second language, language arts, mathematics, reading; early childhood education (MAEd); educational studies (MAEd); elementary teacher education (MAEd), including early childhood, elementary teacher education, high school middle level, middle level; principal licensure (Certificate); secondary teacher education (MAEd); special education (MAEd, Certificate); teacher education (MAEd), including middle level generalist; teacher education middle level mathematics (MAEd), including middle level mathematics; teacher education middle level science (MAEd), including middle level science; teacher education secondary mathematics (MAEd); teacher education secondary science (MAEd); teacher leadership (MAEd);

teachers of English learners (Certificate); transition to teaching (Certificate), including elementary education, secondary education. *Program availability:* Evening/weekend, online learning. *Entrance requirements:* Additional exam requirements/ recommendations for international students: Required—TOEFL, TOEIC (Test of English as an International Communication), Berlitz Online English Proficiency Exam, PTE, or IELTS. Electronic applications accepted. *Expenses:* Contact institution.

University of Phoenix–Phoenix Campus, College of Education, Tempe, AZ 85282-2371. Offers administration and supervision (MA Ed); adult education and training (MA Ed); curriculum and instruction reading (MA Ed); early childhood education (MA Ed); education studies (MA Ed); elementary teacher education (MA Ed); secondary teacher education (MA Ed); special education (MA Ed); teacher leadership (MA Ed). *Program availability:* Evening/weekend, online learning. *Entrance requirements:* Additional exam requirements/recommendations for international students: Required—TOEFL, TOEIC (Test of English as an International Communication), Berlitz Online English Proficiency Exam, PTE, or IELTS. Electronic applications accepted. *Expenses:* Contact institution.

University of Phoenix–South Florida Campus, College of Education, Miramar, FL 33027-4145. Offers administration and supervision (MA Ed); curriculum and instruction (MA Ed), including computer education, curriculum and instruction, mathematics education; early childhood education (MA Ed); elementary teacher education (MA Ed); secondary teacher education (MA Ed). *Program availability:* Evening/weekend. *Degree requirements:* For master's, thesis (for some programs). *Entrance requirements:* For master's, 3 years of work experience, minimum undergraduate GPA of 2.5. Additional exam requirements/recommendations for international students: Required—TOEFL (minimum score 550 paper-based; 79 iBT). Electronic applications accepted.

University of Phoenix–Washington D.C. Campus, College of Education, Washington, DC 20001. Offers administration and supervision (MA Ed); adult education and training (MA Ed); computer education (MA Ed); curriculum and instruction (MA Ed, Ed D); early childhood education (MA Ed); education (Ed S); educational leadership (Ed D); educational technology (Ed D); elementary teacher education (MA Ed); English and language arts education (MA Ed); English as a second language (MA Ed); higher education administration (PhD); mathematics education (MA Ed); secondary teacher education (MA Ed); special education (MA Ed); teacher leadership (MA Ed).

University of Pittsburgh, School of Education, Department of Instruction and Learning, Program in Early Childhood Education, Pittsburgh, PA 15260. Offers M Ed. *Program availability:* Part-time, evening/weekend. *Degree requirements:* For master's, thesis. *Entrance requirements:* For master's, PRAXIS I. Additional exam requirements/ recommendations for international students: Required—TOEFL. Electronic applications accepted. Tuition and fees vary according to program.

University of Puerto Rico, Río Piedras Campus, College of Education, Program in Early Child Education, San Juan, PR 00931-3300. Offers M Ed. *Program availability:* Part-time. *Degree requirements:* For master's, thesis. *Entrance requirements:* For master's, EXADEP, GRE General Test or PAEG, interview, minimum GPA of 3.0, letter of recommendation.

University of South Alabama, College of Education and Professional Studies, Department of Leadership and Teacher Education, Mobile, AL 36688. Offers art education (M Ed); early childhood education (M Ed); educational leadership (M Ed, Ed D); elementary education (M Ed); reading education (M Ed); science education (M Ed); secondary education (M Ed); special education (M Ed). *Accreditation:* NCATE. *Program availability:* Part-time, 100% online, blended/hybrid learning. *Faculty:* 16 full-time (12 women), 6 part-time/adjunct (3 women). *Students:* 198 full-time (150 women), 77 part-time (58 women); includes 77 minority (61 Black or African American, non-Hispanic/Latino; 2 American Indian or Alaska Native, non-Hispanic/Latino; 2 Asian, non-Hispanic/Latino; 7 Hispanic/Latino; 1 Native Hawaiian or other Pacific Islander, non-Hispanic/Latino; 4 Two or more races, non-Hispanic/Latino). Average age 34. 153 applicants, 53% accepted, 69 enrolled. In 2016, 80 master's, 1 doctorate awarded. *Degree requirements:* For master's, comprehensive exam, thesis (for some programs); for doctorate, comprehensive exam, thesis/dissertation. *Entrance requirements:* For master's, GRE General Test or MAT, minimum GPA of 3.0; for doctorate, GRE, minimum graduate GPA of 3.25, 3 years of experience in field, 3 letters of recommendation, interview, official transcripts. Additional exam requirements/ recommendations for international students: Required—TOEFL. *Application deadline:* For fall admission, 7/15 for domestic students; for spring admission, 11/15 for domestic students; for summer admission, 4/15 for domestic students. Applications are processed on a rolling basis. Application fee: $35. Electronic applications accepted. *Expenses:* Tuition, state resident: full-time $9768; part-time $407 per credit hour. Tuition, nonresident: full-time $19,536; part-time $814 per credit hour. *Financial support:* Fellowships, research assistantships, teaching assistantships, career-related internships or fieldwork, Federal Work-Study, institutionally sponsored loans, scholarships/grants, and unspecified assistantships available. Support available to part-time students. Financial award application deadline: 5/31; financial award applicants required to submit FAFSA. *Unit head:* Dr. Susan Santoli, Department Chair, 251-380-2836, Fax: 251-380-2758, E-mail: ssantoli@southalabama.edu. *Application contact:* Dr. Susan Santoli, Director of Graduate Studies, 251-380-2836, Fax: 251-380-2758, E-mail: ssantoli@southalabama.edu.
Website: http://www.southalabama.edu/colleges/coe/lte/index.html

University of South Carolina, The Graduate School, College of Education, Department of Instruction and Teacher Education, Program in Early Childhood Education, Columbia, SC 29208. Offers M Ed, Ed D, PhD. *Accreditation:* NCATE. *Degree requirements:* For master's, comprehensive exam; for doctorate, one foreign language, comprehensive exam, thesis/dissertation. *Entrance requirements:* For master's, GRE General Test, MAT, interview; for doctorate, GRE General Test, MAT, interview, teaching experience. *Faculty research:* Parent involvement, play, multicultural education, global education.

University of South Carolina Upstate, Graduate Programs, Spartanburg, SC 29303-4999. Offers early childhood education (M Ed); elementary education (M Ed); informatics (MS); special education: visual impairment (M Ed). *Accreditation:* NCATE. *Program availability:* Part-time, evening/weekend. *Degree requirements:* For master's, professional portfolio. *Entrance requirements:* For master's, GRE General Test or MAT, interview, minimum undergraduate GPA of 2.5, teaching certificate, 2 letters of recommendation. *Faculty research:* Promoting university diversity awareness, rough and tumble play, social justice education, American Indian literatures and cultures, diversity and multicultural education, science teaching strategy.

The University of South Dakota, Graduate School, School of Education, Division of Curriculum and Instruction, Program in Elementary Education, Vermillion, SD 57069. Offers elementary education (MA), including early childhood education, English language learning, reading specialist/literacy coach, science, technology or math (STM). *Accreditation:* NCATE. *Program availability:* Part-time, 100% online, blended/hybrid learning. *Degree requirements:* For master's, comprehensive exam, thesis or alternative. *Entrance requirements:* For master's, GRE General Test, MAT, minimum GPA of 2.7. Additional exam requirements/recommendations for international students: Required—TOEFL (minimum score 550 paper-based; 79 iBT). Electronic applications accepted.

The University of South Dakota, Graduate School, School of Education, Division of Curriculum and Instruction, Program in Special Education, Vermillion, SD 57069. Offers special education (MA), including advanced specialist in disabilities, early childhood special education, multicategorical special education K-12. *Accreditation:* NCATE. *Program availability:* Part-time, online learning. *Degree requirements:* For master's, comprehensive exam, thesis or alternative. *Entrance requirements:* For master's, GRE General Test, MAT, minimum GPA of 2.7. Additional exam requirements/ recommendations for international students: Required—TOEFL (minimum score 550 paper-based; 79 iBT). Electronic applications accepted.

The University of South Dakota, Graduate School, School of Education, Division of Educational Administration, Vermillion, SD 57069. Offers educational administration (MA, Ed D, Ed S), including adult and higher education (MA, Ed D), curriculum director, director of special education (Ed D, Ed S), preK-12 principal, school district superintendent. *Accreditation:* NCATE. *Program availability:* Part-time, evening/ weekend, 100% online, blended/hybrid learning. *Degree requirements:* For master's and Ed S, comprehensive exam, thesis or alternative; for doctorate, comprehensive exam, thesis/dissertation. *Entrance requirements:* For master's and doctorate, GRE General Test, MAT, minimum GPA of 2.7. Additional exam requirements/recommendations for international students: Required—TOEFL (minimum score 550 paper-based; 79 iBT). Electronic applications accepted.

University of South Florida, College of Education, Department of Teaching and Learning, Tampa, FL 33620-9951. Offers early childhood education (M Ed, MA, PhD); elementary education (MA, MAT, PhD); reading/language arts (MA, PhD, Ed S). *Accreditation:* NCATE. *Faculty:* 40 full-time (29 women), 2 part-time/adjunct (both women). *Students:* 205 full-time (143 women), 263 part-time (207 women); includes 108 minority (45 Black or African American, non-Hispanic/Latino; 10 Asian, non-Hispanic/ Latino; 48 Hispanic/Latino; 5 Two or more races, non-Hispanic/Latino), 62 international. Average age 34. 153 applicants, 78% accepted, 100 enrolled. In 2016, 142 master's, 22 doctorates, 1 other advanced degree awarded. Application fee: $30. *Expenses:* Tuition, state resident: full-time $7766; part-time $431.43 per credit hour. Tuition, nonresident: full-time $15,789; part-time $877.17 per credit hour. *Required fees:* $37 per term. *Total annual research expenditures:* $2.8 million. *Unit head:* Dr. Denisse Thompson, Chair, 813-974-4110.
Website: http://www.coedu.usf.edu/main/departments/ce/ce.html

The University of Tennessee, Graduate School, College of Education, Health and Human Sciences, Department of Child and Family Studies, Knoxville, TN 37996. Offers child and family studies (MS); early childhood education (MS). *Program availability:* Part-time. *Degree requirements:* For master's, thesis or alternative. *Entrance requirements:* For master's, GRE General Test, minimum GPA of 2.7. Additional exam requirements/ recommendations for international students: Required—TOEFL. Electronic applications accepted.

The University of Tennessee, Graduate School, College of Education, Health and Human Sciences, Program in Education, Knoxville, TN 37996. Offers art education (MS); counseling education (PhD); cultural studies in education (PhD); curriculum (MS, Ed S); curriculum, educational research and evaluation (Ed D, PhD); early childhood education (PhD); early childhood special education (MS); education of deaf and hard of hearing (MS); educational administration and policy studies (Ed D, PhD); educational administration and supervision (Ed S); educational psychology (Ed D, PhD); elementary education (MS, Ed S); elementary teaching (MS); English education (MS, Ed S); exercise science (PhD); foreign language/ESL education (MS, Ed S); instructional technology (MS, Ed D, PhD, Ed S); literacy, language and ESL education (PhD); literacy, language education, and ESL education (Ed D); mathematics education (MS, Ed S); modified and comprehensive special education (MS); reading education (MS, Ed S); school counseling (Ed S); school psychology (PhD, Ed S); science education (MS, Ed S); secondary teaching (MS); social foundations (MS); social science education (MS, Ed S); socio-cultural foundations of sports and education (PhD); special education (Ed S); teacher education (Ed D, PhD). *Accreditation:* NCATE. *Program availability:* Part-time, evening/weekend. *Degree requirements:* For master's and Ed S, thesis optional; for doctorate, variable foreign language requirement, thesis/dissertation. *Entrance requirements:* For master's, minimum GPA of 2.7; for doctorate and Ed S, GRE General Test, minimum GPA of 2.7. Additional exam requirements/ recommendations for international students: Required—TOEFL. Electronic applications accepted.

The University of Texas at Austin, Graduate School, College of Education, Department of Curriculum and Instruction, Austin, TX 78712-1111. Offers bilingual/ bicultural education (M Ed, MA, PhD); cultural studies in education (M Ed, MA, PhD); early childhood education (M Ed, MA, PhD); language and literacy studies (M Ed, PhD); learning technologies (M Ed, MA, PhD); physical education (M Ed, MA, PhD). Terminal master's awarded for partial completion of doctoral program. *Degree requirements:* For doctorate, thesis/dissertation. *Entrance requirements:* For master's and doctorate, GRE General Test. Electronic applications accepted.

The University of Texas at Austin, Graduate School, College of Education, Department of Special Education, Austin, TX 78712-1111. Offers autism and developmental disabilities (Ed D, PhD); autism and developmental disability (M Ed, MA); early childhood special education (M Ed, MA, Ed D, PhD); learning disabilities (Ed D, PhD); learning disabilities/behavior disorders (M Ed, MA); multicultural special education (M Ed, MA, Ed D, PhD); rehabilitation counselor (M Ed); rehabilitation counselor education (Ed D, PhD); special education administration (Ed D, PhD). *Accreditation:* CORE. *Program availability:* Part-time, evening/weekend, online learning. *Degree requirements:* For master's, thesis or alternative; for doctorate, thesis/dissertation. *Entrance requirements:* For master's and doctorate, GRE General Test. *Faculty research:* Anchored instruction, reading disabilities, multicultural/bilingual.

The University of Texas at San Antonio, College of Education and Human Development, Department of Interdisciplinary Learning and Teaching, San Antonio, TX 78249-0617. Offers education (MA), including curriculum and instruction, early childhood and elementary education, instructional technology, reading and literacy, special education; interdisciplinary learning and teaching (PhD). *Program availability:* Part-time, evening/weekend. *Faculty:* 25 full-time (18 women), 4 part-time/adjunct (2 women). *Students:* 70 full-time (53 women), 256 part-time (222 women); includes 185 minority (22 Black or African American, non-Hispanic/Latino; 10 Asian, non-Hispanic/ Latino; 148 Hispanic/Latino; 1 Native Hawaiian or other Pacific Islander, non-Hispanic/ Latino; 4 Two or more races, non-Hispanic/Latino), 4 international. Average age 34. 145 applicants, 88% accepted, 100 enrolled. In 2016, 90 master's, 4 doctorates awarded. *Degree requirements:* For master's, comprehensive exam, thesis optional, 36 hours of course work without thesis (33 with thesis); for doctorate, comprehensive exam, thesis/ dissertation, minimum of 60 semester credit hours. *Entrance requirements:* For master's, bachelor's degree with minimum GPA of 3.0 in last 60 hours of coursework; 18 hours of undergraduate coursework in education or related field; for doctorate, GRE, transcripts from all colleges and universities attended, professional vitae demonstrating experience in work environment where education was primary professional emphasis, 3 letters of recommendation, statement of purpose, minimum GPA of 3.5. Additional exam requirements/recommendations for international students: Required—TOEFL (minimum score 550 paper-based; 79 iBT), IELTS (minimum score 6.5). *Application deadline:* For

fall admission, 7/1 for domestic students, 4/1 for international students; for spring admission, 11/1 for domestic students, 9/1 for international students. Applications are processed on a rolling basis. Application fee: $45 ($80 for international students). Electronic applications accepted. *Financial support:* Career-related internships or fieldwork, Federal Work-Study, and scholarships/grants available. Support available to part-time students. *Faculty research:* Explorations of science, learning and teaching, family involvement in early childhood, culturally-responsive literacy instruction in diverse settings, STEM education, autism spectrum disorder. *Total annual research expenditures:* $766,662. *Unit head:* Dr. Maria R. Cortez, Department Chair, 210-458-4413, Fax: 210-458-7281, E-mail: mari.cortez@utsa.edu. *Application contact:* Elizabeth Narvaes, Student Development Specialist, 210-458-7443, Fax: 210-458-7281, E-mail: elizabeth.narvaez@utsa.edu.
Website: http://education.utsa.edu/interdisciplinary_learning_and_teaching/

The University of Texas at Tyler, College of Education and Psychology, School of Education, Tyler, TX 75799-0001. Offers early childhood education (M Ed, MA); reading (M Ed, MA); special education (M Ed, MA). *Program availability:* Part-time, evening/weekend. *Degree requirements:* For master's, comprehensive exam, thesis (for some programs), research project. *Entrance requirements:* For master's, GRE General Test. Additional exam requirements/recommendations for international students: Required—TOEFL. Electronic applications accepted. *Faculty research:* Improving quality in childcare settings, play and creativity, teacher interactions, effects of modeling on early childhood teachers, biofeedback, literacy instruction.

The University of Texas of the Permian Basin, Office of Graduate Studies, School of Education, Program in Early Childhood Education, Odessa, TX 79762-0001. Offers MA. *Degree requirements:* For master's, comprehensive exam (for some programs), thesis (for some programs). *Entrance requirements:* For master's, GRE General Test. Additional exam requirements/recommendations for international students: Required—TOEFL (minimum score 550 paper-based).

The University of Texas Rio Grande Valley, College of Education and P-16 Integration, Department of Human Development and School Services, Edinburg, TX 78539. Offers early childhood education (M Ed); early childhood special education (M Ed); educational diagnostician (M Ed); school psychology (MA). *Program availability:* Part-time, evening/weekend. *Degree requirements:* For master's, comprehensive exam (for some programs), thesis (for some programs). *Entrance requirements:* For master's, GRE General Test, interview. Tuition and fees vary according to course load and program. *Faculty research:* Reading instruction, assessment practice, behavior interventions consultation, mental retardation.

University of the District of Columbia, College of Arts and Sciences, Program in Early Childhood Education, Washington, DC 20008-1175. Offers MA. *Accreditation:* NCATE. *Program availability:* Part-time. *Degree requirements:* For master's, comprehensive exam, research paper. *Entrance requirements:* For master's, GRE General Test, writing proficiency exam, minimum GPA of 3.0.

University of the Sacred Heart, Graduate Programs, Department of Education, San Juan, PR 00914-0383. Offers early childhood education (M Ed); information technology and multimedia (Certificate); instruction systems and education technology (M Ed), including English, information technology and multimedia, instructional design, mathematics, Spanish. *Program availability:* Part-time, evening/weekend. *Degree requirements:* For master's, thesis. *Entrance requirements:* For master's, EXADEP, minimum undergraduate GPA of 2.75, interview.

University of the Southwest, Graduate Programs, Hobbs, NM 88240-9129. Offers business administration (MBA); curriculum and instruction (MSE); curriculum and instruction: bilingual (MSE); curriculum and instruction: TESOL (MSE); early childhood education (MSE); educational administration (MSE); mental health counseling (MSE); school counseling (MSE); special education (MSE); sports management (MBA). *Program availability:* Part-time, evening/weekend, online learning. *Degree requirements:* For master's, comprehensive exam, thesis (for some programs). *Entrance requirements:* Additional exam requirements/recommendations for international students: Recommended—TOEFL. Electronic applications accepted.

The University of Toledo, College of Graduate Studies, Judith Herb College of Education, Department of Curriculum and Instruction, Toledo, OH 43606-3390. Offers art education (ME); career and technical education (ME, Ed S); curriculum and instruction (ME, PhD, Ed S); early childhood education (Ed S); education and anthropology (MAE); education and biology (MES); education and chemistry (MES); education and classics (MAE); education and economics (MAE); education and English (MAE); education and French (MAE); education and geology (MES); education and German (MAE); education and history (MAE); education and mathematics (MAE, MES); education and physics (MES); education and political science (MAE); education and sociology (MAE); education and Spanish (MAE); educational media (PhD); educational technology (ME); educational technology: virtual educator (Certificate); elementary education (PhD); English as a second language (MAE); gifted and talented education (PhD); middle childhood education (ME); secondary education (ME, PhD); special education (PhD). *Accreditation:* NCATE. *Program availability:* Part-time, evening/weekend. *Degree requirements:* For master's, comprehensive exam, thesis or alternative; for doctorate, comprehensive exam, thesis/dissertation; for other advanced degree, thesis optional. *Entrance requirements:* For master's, doctorate, and other advanced degree, minimum cumulative GPA of 2.7 for all previous academic work, letters of recommendation. Additional exam requirements/recommendations for international students: Required—TOEFL (minimum score 550 paper-based; 80 iBT). Electronic applications accepted.

The University of Toledo, College of Graduate Studies, Judith Herb College of Education, Department of Early Childhood, Physical and Special Education, Toledo, OH 43606-3390. Offers early childhood education (ME); physical education (ME); special education (ME). *Program availability:* Part-time. *Degree requirements:* For master's, thesis. *Entrance requirements:* For master's, minimum cumulative GPA of 2.7 for all previous academic work, letters of recommendation. Additional exam requirements/recommendations for international students: Required—TOEFL (minimum score 550 paper-based; 80 iBT). Electronic applications accepted.

University of Utah, Graduate School, College of Education, Department of Special Education, Salt Lake City, UT 84112. Offers deaf and hard of hearing (M Ed); deaf/blind (M Ed, MS); early childhood deaf and hard of hearing (MS); early childhood special education (M Ed, MS, PhD); early childhood vision impairments (M Ed); mild/moderate disabilities (M Ed, MS, PhD); severe disabilities (M Ed, MS, PhD); visual impairment (M Ed, MS). *Program availability:* Part-time, evening/weekend, 100% online, blended/hybrid learning. *Faculty:* 14 full-time (11 women), 26 part-time/adjunct (19 women). *Students:* 52 full-time (45 women), 20 part-time (15 women); includes 6 minority (2 Asian, non-Hispanic/Latino; 3 Hispanic/Latino; 1 Two or more races, non-Hispanic/Latino). Average age 34. 30 applicants, 97% accepted, 28 enrolled. In 2016, 17 master's, 2 doctorates awarded. Terminal master's awarded for partial completion of doctoral program. *Degree requirements:* For master's, comprehensive exam, thesis (for some programs), qualifying exam; for doctorate, thesis/dissertation, qualifying exam. *Entrance requirements:* For master's, GRE, minimum GPA of 3.0; for doctorate, GRE General Test, minimum GPA of 3.5. Additional exam requirements/recommendations for international students: Required—TOEFL (minimum score 600 paper-based; 100 iBT); Recommended—IELTS (minimum score 7). *Application deadline:* For fall admission, 3/1 for domestic and international students; for spring admission, 11/1 for domestic and international students; for summer admission, 5/16 for domestic and international students. Application fee: $55 ($65 for international students). Electronic applications accepted. *Expenses:* $4,270 per semester. *Financial support:* In 2016–17, 22 students received support, including 33 fellowships with partial tuition reimbursements available (averaging $4,350 per year), 3 teaching assistantships with tuition reimbursements available (averaging $10,000 per year); career-related internships or fieldwork and health care benefits also available. Support available to part-time students. Financial award application deadline: 3/1; financial award applicants required to submit FAFSA. *Faculty research:* Inclusive education, positive behavior support, reading, instruction and intervention strategies. *Total annual research expenditures:* $139,750. *Unit head:* Dr. Robert E. O'Neill, Chair, 801-581-8121, Fax: 801-585-6476, E-mail: rob.oneill@utah.edu. *Application contact:* Patty Davis, Academic Advisor, 801-581-4764, Fax: 801-585-6476, E-mail: patty.davis@utah.edu.
Website: http://special-ed.utah.edu/

University of Victoria, Faculty of Graduate Studies, Faculty of Education, Department of Curriculum and Instruction, Victoria, BC V8W 2Y2, Canada. Offers art education (M Ed, PhD); curriculum studies (M Ed, MA, PhD); early childhood education (M Ed, PhD); educational studies (PhD); language and literacy (M Ed, MA, PhD); mathematics (M Ed, MA, PhD); music education (M Ed, MA, PhD); science (M Ed, MA, PhD); social studies (M Ed, MA); social, cultural and foundational studies (MA, PhD); technology and environmental education (PhD). *Program availability:* Part-time. *Degree requirements:* For master's, thesis, project (M Ed); for doctorate, comprehensive exam, thesis/dissertation. *Entrance requirements:* For master's, minimum B average. Additional exam requirements/recommendations for international students: Required—TOEFL (minimum score 575 paper-based), IELTS (minimum score 7). Electronic applications accepted. *Faculty research:* Elementary and secondary English, language arts, curriculum theory and practice, educational media and technology, educational administration and leadership, history and philosophy of education.

University of Virginia, Curry School of Education, Program in Education, Charlottesville, VA 22903. Offers administration and supervision (PhD); applied developmental science (PhD); counselor education (PhD); curriculum and instruction (PhD); early childhood special education (MT); education evaluation (PhD); educational psychology (PhD); educational research (PhD); elementary education (MT); English education (MT, PhD); foreign language education (MT); higher education (PhD); instructional technology (PhD); kinesiology (MT, PhD); math education (PhD); reading education (PhD); research, statistics and evaluation (PhD); school psychology (PhD); science education (PhD); social studies education (MT, PhD); special education (PhD); world languages education (MT). *Students:* 452 full-time (357 women), 18 part-time (13 women); includes 100 minority (28 Black or African American, non-Hispanic/Latino; 39 Asian, non-Hispanic/Latino; 18 Hispanic/Latino; 15 Two or more races, non-Hispanic/Latino), 14 international. Average age 25. 309 applicants, 51% accepted, 87 enrolled. In 2016, 144 master's, 31 doctorates awarded. *Degree requirements:* For master's, comprehensive exam (for some programs), field project; for doctorate, comprehensive exam, thesis/dissertation. *Entrance requirements:* For doctorate, GRE General Test. Additional exam requirements/recommendations for international students: Required—TOEFL (minimum score 600 paper-based; 90 iBT), IELTS (minimum score 7). *Application deadline:* Applications are processed on a rolling basis. Application fee: $60. Electronic applications accepted. *Expenses:* Tuition, state resident: full-time $15,026; part-time $834 per credit hour. Tuition, nonresident: full-time $25,168; part-time $1378 per credit hour. *Required fees:* $2654. *Financial support:* Fellowships, research assistantships, and teaching assistantships available. Financial award application deadline: 1/5; financial award applicants required to submit FAFSA. *Unit head:* Robert C. Pianta, Dean, 434-924-3334, E-mail: pianta@virginia.edu. *Application contact:* Eric Molnar, Assistant Director, Admissions and Enrollment Reporting, 434-243-2085, E-mail: eric.molnar@virginia.edu.
Website: http://curry.virginia.edu/teacher-education

The University of West Alabama, School of Graduate Studies, College of Education, Departments of Instructional Leadership and Support/Curriculum and Instruction, Program in Early Childhood Education, Livingston, AL 35470. Offers early childhood development (M Ed); early childhood education (Ed S); early childhood education P-3 (M Ed). *Accreditation:* NCATE. *Program availability:* Part-time, evening/weekend, 100% online. *Faculty:* 5 full-time (all women), 22 part-time/adjunct (16 women). *Students:* 72 (70 women); includes 23 minority (all Black or African American, non-Hispanic/Latino). Average age 34. 27 applicants, 85% accepted, 18 enrolled. In 2016, 7 master's, 4 Ed Ss awarded. *Degree requirements:* For master's, comprehensive exam, thesis optional; for Ed S, comprehensive exam. *Entrance requirements:* For master's, GRE General Test, MAT, minimum GPA of 2.75. Additional exam requirements/recommendations for international students: Required—TOEFL (minimum score 500 paper-based; 61 iBT). *Application deadline:* Applications are processed on a rolling basis. Application fee: $40. Electronic applications accepted. *Expenses:* Tuition, state resident: part-time $355 per credit hour. Tuition, nonresident: part-time $710 per credit hour. *Required fees:* $130 per semester. *Financial support:* Teaching assistantships, Federal Work-Study, scholarships/grants, and unspecified assistantships available. Support available to part-time students. Financial award applicants required to submit FAFSA. *Unit head:* Dr. Jodie Winship, Chair of Curriculum and Instruction, 205-652-5415, Fax: 205-652-3706, E-mail: jwinship@uwa.edu. *Application contact:* Dr. B. J. Kimbrough, Dean of Graduate Studies, 205-652-3647, Fax: 205-652-3706, E-mail: bkimbrough@uwa.edu.
Website: http://www.uwa.edu/earlychildhoodeducationp3.aspx

University of West Georgia, College of Education, Carrollton, GA 30118. Offers business education (M Ed); early childhood education (M Ed, Ed S); educational leadership (M Ed, Ed S); media (M Ed, Ed S); professional counseling (M Ed, Ed S); professional counseling and supervision (Ed D); reading instruction (M Ed); school improvement (Ed D); secondary education (M Ed); special education (M Ed, Ed S), including teaching (M Ed); speech language pathology (M Ed); teaching (MAT). *Accreditation:* NCATE. *Program availability:* Part-time, evening/weekend, 100% online, blended/hybrid learning. *Faculty:* 46 full-time (31 women). *Students:* 321 full-time (266 women), 1,007 part-time (813 women); includes 456 minority (389 Black or African American, non-Hispanic/Latino; 1 American Indian or Alaska Native, non-Hispanic/Latino; 13 Asian, non-Hispanic/Latino; 43 Hispanic/Latino; 10 Two or more races, non-Hispanic/Latino), 12 international. Average age 33. 541 applicants, 79% accepted, 305 enrolled. In 2016, 286 master's, 20 doctorates, 156 other advanced degrees awarded. *Entrance requirements:* Additional exam requirements/recommendations for international students: Required—TOEFL (minimum score 523 paper-based; 69 iBT); Recommended—IELTS (minimum score 6.5). *Application deadline:* For fall admission, 7/21 for domestic students, 6/1 for international students; for spring admission, 11/30 for domestic students, 10/15 for international students; for summer admission, 4/15 for domestic students, 3/30 for international students. Applications are processed on a rolling basis. Application fee: $40. Electronic applications accepted. *Expenses:* Tuition, state resident: full-time $5316; part-time $222 per semester hour. Tuition, nonresident: full-time $20,658; part-time $861 per semester hour. *Required fees:* $1962. Tuition and fees vary according to course load, degree level and program. *Financial support:*

Fellowships, research assistantships, teaching assistantships, career-related internships or fieldwork, Federal Work-Study, institutionally sponsored loans, scholarships/grants, and unspecified assistantships available. Support available to part-time students. Financial award application deadline: 4/1; financial award applicants required to submit FAFSA. *Unit head:* Dr. Diane Hoff, Dean, College of Education, 678-839-6570, Fax: 678-839-6098, E-mail: dhoff@westga.edu. *Application contact:* Dr. Toby Ziglar, Assistant Dean of the Graduate School, 678-839-1394, Fax: 678-839-1395, E-mail: graduate@westga.edu.
Website: http://www.westga.edu/education/

University of Wisconsin–Milwaukee, Graduate School, School of Education, Department of Curriculum and Instruction, Milwaukee, WI 53201-0413. Offers curriculum and instruction (MS), including cross-curricular focus, early childhood education, English education, mathematics education, middle childhood/early adolescence education, reading education, science education, urban social studies education. *Program availability:* Part-time. *Students:* 21 full-time (13 women), 44 part-time (42 women); includes 10 minority (1 Black or African American, non-Hispanic/Latino; 1 Asian, non-Hispanic/Latino; 2 Hispanic/Latino; 6 Two or more races, non-Hispanic/Latino), 2 international. Average age 33. 42 applicants, 71% accepted, 20 enrolled. In 2016, 45 master's awarded. *Degree requirements:* For master's, thesis or alternative. *Entrance requirements:* Additional exam requirements/recommendations for international students: Required—TOEFL (minimum score 550 paper-based; 79 iBT), IELTS (minimum score 6.5). *Application deadline:* For fall admission, 1/1 priority date for domestic students; for spring admission, 9/1 for domestic students. Applications are processed on a rolling basis. Application fee: $56 ($96 for international students). Electronic applications accepted. *Financial support:* In 2016–17, 1 fellowship was awarded; research assistantships, teaching assistantships, career-related internships or fieldwork, health care benefits, unspecified assistantships, and project assistantships also available. Support available to part-time students. Financial award application deadline: 4/15; financial award applicants required to submit FAFSA. *Application contact:* General Information Contact, 414-229-4721, E-mail: soeinfo@uwm.edu.
Website: http://uwm.edu/education/academics/curriculum-instruction-department/

University of Wisconsin–Oshkosh, Graduate Studies, College of Education and Human Services, Department of Special Education, Oshkosh, WI 54901. Offers cross-categorical (MSE); early childhood: exceptional education needs (MSE); non-licensure (MSE). *Program availability:* Part-time, evening/weekend. *Degree requirements:* For master's, comprehensive exam (for some programs), thesis or alternative, field report. *Entrance requirements:* For master's, interview, minimum GPA of 3.0, teaching license, letters of recommendation. Additional exam requirements/recommendations for international students: Required—TOEFL (minimum score 550 paper-based; 79 iBT). Electronic applications accepted. *Faculty research:* Private agency contributions to the disabled, graduation requirements for exceptional education needs students, direct instruction in spelling for learning disabled, effects of behavioral parent training, secondary education programming issues.

Upper Iowa University, Master of Education Program, Fayette, IA 52142-1857. Offers early childhood (M Ed); English as a second language (M Ed); higher education (M Ed); instructional strategist (M Ed); reading (M Ed); teacher leadership (M Ed).

Ursuline College, School of Graduate Studies, Master Apprenticeship Program, Pepper Pike, OH 44124-4398. Offers adolescent to young adult education (MA); early childhood education (MA); middle childhood education (MA); special education (MA). *Accreditation:* NCATE. *Degree requirements:* For master's, comprehensive exam. *Entrance requirements:* For master's, minimum undergraduate GPA of 3.0. Additional exam requirements/recommendations for international students: Required—TOEFL (minimum score 500 paper-based). *Application deadline:* For fall admission, 8/1 priority date for domestic students. Applications are processed on a rolling basis. Application fee: $25. Electronic applications accepted. *Expenses:* Contact institution. *Financial support:* Application deadline: 3/1; applicants required to submit FAFSA. *Unit head:* Dr. Mary Jo Cherry, Director, 440-646-8147, Fax: 440-646-8328, E-mail: mcherry@ursuline.edu. *Application contact:* Stephanie Pratt McRoberts, Graduate Admission Coordinator, 440-646-8119, Fax: 440-684-6138, E-mail: graduateadmissions@ursuline.edu.
Website: http://www.ursuline.edu/Academics/Graduate_Professional/Masters_Programs/MAP/index.html

Valdosta State University, Department of Early Childhood and Special Education, Valdosta, GA 31698. Offers early childhood (M Ed); special education (M Ed, MAT, Ed S). *Accreditation:* ASHA (one or more programs are accredited); NCATE. *Program availability:* Part-time, evening/weekend, blended/hybrid learning. *Degree requirements:* For master's, thesis (for some programs), comprehensive written and/or oral exams; for Ed S, thesis. *Entrance requirements:* For master's, GRE General Test or MAT, minimum GPA of 2.75; for Ed S, GRE General Test or MAT, minimum GPA of 3.0. Additional exam requirements/recommendations for international students: Required—TOEFL (minimum score 523 paper-based); Recommended—IELTS. Electronic applications accepted. *Expenses:* Contact institution.

Virginia Commonwealth University, Graduate School, School of Education, Program in Special Education, Richmond, VA 23284-9005. Offers early childhood (M Ed); general education (M Ed); severe disabilities (M Ed). *Accreditation:* NCATE. *Degree requirements:* For master's, comprehensive exam. *Entrance requirements:* For master's, GRE General Test or MAT. Additional exam requirements/recommendations for international students: Required—TOEFL (minimum score 600 paper-based; 100 iBT). *Application deadline:* For fall admission, 3/15 for domestic students; for spring admission, 11/1 for domestic students. Applications are processed on a rolling basis. Application fee: $50. Electronic applications accepted. *Financial support:* Tuition waivers (partial) available. Financial award application deadline: 3/1; financial award applicants required to submit FAFSA. *Unit head:* Dr. Evelyn Reed, Department Chair, 804-827-2653, E-mail: mereed@vcu.edu. *Application contact:* Dr. Mary Ellen Huennekens, Graduate Studies Specialist, 804-827-2663, E-mail: huennekensme@vcu.edu.
Website: http://www.soe.vcu.edu/departments/sedp/programs.html

Virginia Commonwealth University, Graduate School, School of Education, Program in Teaching and Learning, Richmond, VA 23284-9005. Offers early and elementary education (MT). *Accreditation:* NCATE. *Program availability:* Part-time. *Entrance requirements:* For master's, GRE General Test or MAT. Additional exam requirements/recommendations for international students: Required—TOEFL (minimum score 600 paper-based; 100 iBT). *Application deadline:* For fall admission, 3/15 for domestic students; for spring admission, 11/1 for domestic students. Applications are processed on a rolling basis. Application fee: $50. Electronic applications accepted. *Financial support:* Application deadline: 3/1; applicants required to submit FAFSA. *Unit head:* Dr. Leila Christenbury, Interim Chair, 804-828-1305, E-mail: lchriste@vcu.edu. *Application contact:* Laura Domalik, Graduate Program Coordinator, 804-828-1305, E-mail: lsdomalik@vcu.edu.
Website: http://www.soe.vcu.edu/departments/tl/programs.html

Viterbo University, Graduate Programs in Education, La Crosse, WI 54601-4797. Offers cross-categorical special education (Certificate); director of instruction (Certificate); director of special education and pupil services (Certificate); early childhood (Certificate); education (MAE); literacy coaching (Certificate); PreK-12 principal/supervisor of special education (Certificate); principal (Certificate); reading specialist endorsement (Certificate); reading teacher (Certificate); reading teacher 5-12 endorsement (Certificate); reading teacher K-8 endorsement (Certificate); superintendent (Certificate); talented and gifted endorsement (Certificate); Wisconsin school business administrator (Certificate). Weekend courses available in summer. *Accreditation:* NCATE. *Program availability:* Part-time, evening/weekend. *Degree requirements:* For master's, comprehensive exam, thesis, 30 credits of course work. *Entrance requirements:* For master's, BS, transcripts, teaching license, written narrative. Electronic applications accepted. *Expenses:* Contact institution.

Wagner College, Division of Graduate Studies, Education Department, Program in Early Childhood Education/Students with Disabilities (Birth-Grade 2), Staten Island, NY 10301-4495. Offers MS Ed. *Program availability:* Part-time, evening/weekend. *Degree requirements:* For master's, thesis. *Entrance requirements:* For master's, minimum GPA of 3.0, valid initial NY State Certificate or equivalent, interview, recommendations. Electronic applications accepted. Tuition and fees vary according to degree level.

Walden University, Graduate Programs, Richard W. Riley College of Education and Leadership, Minneapolis, MN 55401. Offers adult education (Post-Master's Certificate); adult learning (Graduate Certificate); college teaching and learning (Graduate Certificate); community college leadership (Ed D); curriculum, instruction and assessment (Ed D, Ed S, Graduate Certificate); developmental education (Graduate Certificate); early childhood administration, management, and leadership (Graduate Certificate); early childhood education (Ed D, Ed S); early childhood public policy and advocacy (Graduate Certificate); early childhood studies (MS), including administration, management and leadership, early childhood public policy and advocacy, teaching adults in the early childhood field, teaching and diversity in early childhood education; education (MS, PhD), including adolescent literacy and learning (MS), curriculum, instruction, and assessment (grades K-12) (MS), curriculum, instruction, assessment, and evaluation (PhD), early childhood leadership and advocacy (PhD), early childhood special education (PhD), educational leadership (MS), educational leadership and administration (principal preparation) (MS), educational technology and design (PhD), elementary reading and literacy (PreK-6) (MS), elementary reading and mathematics (grades K-6) (MS), global and comparative education (PhD), higher education leadership management and policy (PhD), integrating technology in the classroom (grades K-12) (MS), learning, instruction and innovation (PhD), mathematics (grades 5-8) (MS), mathematics (grades K-6) (MS), mathematics and science (grades K-8) (MS), organizational research, assessment, and evaluation (PhD), reading and literacy with a reading K-12 endorsement (MS), reading literacy assessment and evaluation (PhD), science (grades K-8) (MS), special education (non-licensure) (grades K-12) (MS), teacher leadership (grades K-12) (MS), teaching English language learners (grades K-12) (MS); educational administration and leadership (Ed D); educational leadership and administration (principal preparation) (Ed S); educational technology (Ed D, Ed S, Post Master's Certificate); elementary reading and literacy (Graduate Certificate); engaging culturally diverse learners (Graduate Certificate); enrollment management and institutional marketing (Graduate Certificate); higher education (MS), including adult learning, college teaching and learning, enrollment management and institutional marketing, global higher education, leadership for student success, online and distance learning; higher education and adult learning (Ed D); higher education leadership and management (Ed D); higher education leadership for student success (Graduate Certificate); instructional design and technology (MS, Postbaccalaureate Certificate), including general program (MS), online learning (MS), training and performance improvement (MS); integrating technology in the classroom (Graduate Certificate); mathematics 5-8 (Graduate Certificate); mathematics K-6 (Graduate Certificate); online teaching for adult educators (Graduate Certificate); reading, literacy, and assessment (Ed D, Ed S); science K-8 (Graduate Certificate); special education (Ed D, Ed S, Graduate Certificate); special education (K-age 21) (MAT); teacher leadership (Graduate Certificate); teaching adults English as a second language (Graduate Certificate); teaching adults in the early childhood field (Graduate Certificate); teaching and diversity in early childhood education (Graduate Certificate); teaching English language learners (grades K-12) (Graduate Certificate); teaching K-12 students online (Graduate Certificate). *Accreditation:* NCATE. *Program availability:* Part-time, evening/weekend, online only, 100% online. *Degree requirements:* For doctorate, thesis/dissertation (for some programs), residency; for other advanced degree, residency (for some programs). *Entrance requirements:* For master's, bachelor's degree or higher; minimum GPA of 2.5; official transcripts; goal statement (for some programs); access to computer and Internet; for doctorate, master's degree or higher; three years of related professional or academic experience (preferred); minimum GPA of 3.0; goal statement and current resume (for select programs); official transcripts; access to computer and Internet; for other advanced degree, relevant work experience; access to computer and Internet. Additional exam requirements/recommendations for international students: Required—TOEFL (minimum score 550 paper-based, 79 iBT), IELTS (minimum score 6.5), Michigan English Language Assessment Battery (minimum score 82), or PTE (minimum score 53). Electronic applications accepted.

Wayne State College, School of Education and Counseling, Department of Educational Foundations and Leadership, Program in Curriculum and Instruction, Wayne, NE 68787. Offers alternative education (MSE); business and information technology education (MSE); communication arts education (MSE); early childhood education (MSE); elementary education (MSE); English as a second language (MSE); English education (MSE); family and consumer sciences education (MSE); industrial technology and vocational education (MSE); learning communities (MSE); mathematics education (MSE); music education (MSE); science education (MSE); social science education (MSE). *Accreditation:* NCATE. *Program availability:* Part-time, evening/weekend. *Degree requirements:* For master's, comprehensive exam, thesis optional. *Entrance requirements:* For master's, GRE General Test. Additional exam requirements/recommendations for international students: Required—TOEFL (minimum score 550 paper-based).

Wayne State University, College of Education, Division of Teacher Education, Detroit, MI 48202. Offers art education (M Ed); bilingual/bicultural education (M Ed, Certificate); career and technical education (M Ed); curriculum and instruction (Ed D, PhD, Ed S), including art education (Ed D, PhD), bilingual education (Ed D, Ed S), career and technical education (MAT, Ed D, PhD, Ed S), early childhood education (MAT, Ed D, PhD, Ed S), elementary education, English as a second language (MAT, Ed D, Ed S), English education (MAT, Ed D, PhD, Ed S), foreign language education (MAT, Ed D, PhD), K-12 curriculum, mathematics education (MAT, Ed D, PhD, Ed S), science education (MAT, Ed D, PhD, Ed S), secondary education, social studies education (MAT, Ed D, PhD, Ed S); early childhood education (M Ed); elementary education (M Ed, MAT), including bilingual/bicultural education (MAT), early childhood education (MAT, Ed D, PhD, Ed S), English as a second language (MAT, Ed D, Ed S), general elementary education (MAT), mathematics education (MAT, Ed D, PhD, Ed S), science education (MAT, Ed D, PhD, Ed S), social studies education (MAT, Ed D, PhD, Ed S); English as a second language (Certificate); English education (M Ed); foreign language education (M Ed); mathematics education (M Ed); reading (M Ed, Ed S); reading, language and literature (Ed D); science education (M Ed); secondary education (MAT),

including art education (K-12), bilingual/bicultural education, career and technical education (MAT, Ed D, PhD, Ed S), English as a second language (MAT, Ed D, Ed S), English education (MAT, Ed D, PhD, Ed S), foreign language education (MAT, Ed D, PhD), kinesiology, mathematics education (MAT, Ed D, PhD, Ed S); social studies education (M Ed); special education (M Ed, MAT, Ed D, PhD, Ed S), including autism spectrum disorders (MAT), cognitive development (MAT), emotional impairment (MAT), learning disabilities (MAT). *Program availability:* Part-time, blended/hybrid learning. *Faculty:* 29. *Students:* 106 full-time (73 women), 351 part-time (276 women); includes 115 minority (76 Black or African American, non-Hispanic/Latino; 10 Asian, non-Hispanic/Latino; 20 Hispanic/Latino; 1 Native Hawaiian or other Pacific Islander, non-Hispanic/Latino; 8 Two or more races, non-Hispanic/Latino), 12 international. Average age 37. 242 applicants, 37% accepted, 72 enrolled. In 2016, 178 master's, 19 doctorates, 17 other advanced degrees awarded. *Degree requirements:* For master's, essay or project (for some M Ed programs), professional field experience (for MAT programs); for doctorate, thesis/dissertation. *Entrance requirements:* For master's, Michigan Test for Teacher Certification, verification of participation in group work with children, Michigan State Police criminal background check; for doctorate, minimum undergraduate GPA of 3.0, graduate 3.5; interview; curriculum vitae; references. Additional exam requirements/recommendations for international students: Required—TOEFL (minimum score 550 paper-based; 79 iBT), TWE (minimum score 5.5), Michigan English Language Assessment Battery (minimum score 85); Recommended—IELTS (minimum score 6.5). *Application deadline:* For fall admission, 6/1 priority date for domestic students, 5/1 priority date for international students; for winter admission, 10/1 priority date for domestic students, 9/1 priority date for international students; for spring admission, 2/1 priority date for domestic students, 1/1 priority date for international students. Applications are processed on a rolling basis. Application fee: $50. Electronic applications accepted. *Expenses:* $16,503 per year resident tuition and fees, $33,697 per year non-resident tuition and fees. *Financial support:* In 2016–17, 101 students received support, including 3 fellowships (averaging $11,409 per year); research assistantships with tuition reimbursements available, Federal Work-Study, scholarships/grants, and unspecified assistantships also available. Support available to part-time students. Financial award applicants required to submit FAFSA. *Faculty research:* Improving students' skill achievement in mathematics, improving elementary children's understanding of informational text, teachers' use of their pedagogical and mathematical knowledge in the interactive work of teaching, the intersection of identity construction in teaching and learning, identifying effective methods of literacy instruction and assessments for bilingual students in elementary language arts classrooms. *Unit head:* Dr. Kathleen Crawford-McKinney, Assistant Dean, 313-577-0122. *Application contact:* Janice Green, Assistant Dean, 313-577-1605, E-mail: jwgreen@wayne.edu.
Website: http://coe.wayne.edu/ted/index.php

Webster University, School of Education, Department of Multidisciplinary Studies, St. Louis, MO 63119-3194. Offers applied educational psychology (MA, Ed S); communication arts (MA); early childhood education (MA, MAT); education and innovation (MA); educational technology (MET); elementary education (MAT); mathematics for educators (MA); middle school education (MAT); multidisciplinary studies (MAT); multimodal literacy for global impact (MA); reading (MA); secondary school education (MAT); special education (MA, MAT); teaching English as a second language (MA); transformative learning in the global community (Ed S). *Program availability:* Part-time. *Entrance requirements:* For master's, minimum GPA of 2.5. Additional exam requirements/recommendations for international students: Required—TOEFL. *Application deadline:* Applications are processed on a rolling basis. Application fee: $35 ($50 for international students). *Expenses: Tuition:* Full-time $21,900; part-time $730 per credit hour. Tuition and fees vary according to campus/location and program. *Financial support:* Federal Work-Study available. Support available to part-time students. Financial award application deadline: 4/1; financial award applicants required to submit FAFSA. *Unit head:* Dr. Deborah Stiles, Chair, 314-968-7056, Fax: 314-968-7118, E-mail: stilesda@webster.edu.

Wesleyan College, Department of Education, Program in Early Childhood Education, Macon, GA 31210-4462. Offers MA. *Program availability:* Part-time. *Degree requirements:* For master's, thesis or alternative, practicum, professional portfolio. *Entrance requirements:* For master's, GRE or MAT, interview, teaching certificate, 3 letters of recommendation. Additional exam requirements/recommendations for international students: Required—TOEFL.

West Chester University of Pennsylvania, College of Education and Social Work, Department of Early and Middle Grades Education, West Chester, PA 19383. Offers applied studies in teaching and learning (M Ed); early childhood education (M Ed), including accomplished teacher, program administrators; grades 4-8 (Teaching Certificate); grades preK-4 (Teaching Certificate). *Accreditation:* NCATE. *Program availability:* Part-time, 100% online. *Faculty:* 7 full-time (6 women), 1 (woman) part-time/adjunct. *Students:* 14 full-time (13 women), 97 part-time (83 women); includes 21 minority (14 Black or African American, non-Hispanic/Latino; 2 Asian, non-Hispanic/Latino; 4 Hispanic/Latino; 1 Two or more races, non-Hispanic/Latino), 1 international. Average age 30. 31 applicants, 87% accepted, 17 enrolled. In 2016, 24 master's, 21 other advanced degrees awarded. *Degree requirements:* For master's, teacher research project, portfolio. *Entrance requirements:* For master's, one year of full time teaching, minimum GPA of 3.0; for Teaching Certificate, math, social studies, or science concentration exams (for middle grades preparation), minimum GPA of 3.0. Additional exam requirements/recommendations for international students: Required—TOEFL or IELTS. *Application deadline:* For fall admission, 5/15 for international students; for spring admission, 10/15 for international students. Applications are processed on a rolling basis. Application fee: $50. Electronic applications accepted. *Expenses:* Tuition, state resident: full-time $8694; part-time $483 per credit. Tuition, nonresident: full-time $13,050; part-time $725 per credit. *Required fees:* $2399; $119.05 per credit. Tuition and fees vary according to campus/location and program. *Financial support:* Scholarships/grants and unspecified assistantships available. Financial award application deadline: 2/15; financial award applicants required to submit FAFSA. *Faculty research:* Cooperative learning, creative expression and critical thinking, teacher research, learning styles, middle school education. *Unit head:* Dr. Heather Leaman, Chair, 610-436-2944, Fax: 610-436-3102, E-mail: hleaman@wcupa.edu. *Application contact:* Office of Graduate Studies and Extended Education, 610-436-2943, Fax: 610-436-2763, E-mail: gradstudy@wcupa.edu.
Website: http://www.wcupa.edu/education-socialWork/earlyMiddleGrades/

Western Kentucky University, Graduate Studies, College of Education and Behavioral Sciences, School of Teacher Education, Bowling Green, KY 42101. Offers elementary education (MAE, Ed S); exceptional education: learning and behavioral disorders (MAE); exceptional education: moderate and severe disabilities (MAE); instructional design (MS); interdisciplinary early childhood education (MAE); library media education (MS); literacy education (MAE); middle grades education (MAE); secondary education (MAE, Ed S). *Program availability:* Part-time, evening/weekend, online learning. *Degree requirements:* For master's, comprehensive exam. *Entrance requirements:* For master's, GRE General Test. Additional exam requirements/recommendations for international students: Required—TOEFL (minimum score 555 paper-based; 79 iBT). *Faculty research:* Teacher preparation in moderate/severe disabilities.

Western Oregon University, Graduate Programs, College of Education, Division of Special Education, Program in Early Childhood Special Education, Monmouth, OR 97361. Offers MS Ed. *Accreditation:* NCATE. *Program availability:* Part-time, evening/weekend. *Degree requirements:* For master's, thesis optional, written exam, portfolio. *Entrance requirements:* For master's, CBEST, PRAXIS or GRE General Test, minimum GPA of 3.0, teaching license. Additional exam requirements/recommendations for international students: Required—TOEFL (minimum score 550 paper-based; 79 iBT), IELTS (minimum score 6.5). *Faculty research:* High school through university articulation, career development for early childhood educators professional collaboration/cooperation.

Westfield State University, College of Graduate and Continuing Education, Department of Education, Program in Early Childhood Education, Westfield, MA 01086. Offers M Ed. *Accreditation:* NCATE. *Program availability:* Part-time, evening/weekend. *Students:* 4 full-time (all women), 25 part-time (23 women). Average age 30. 10 applicants, 90% accepted, 5 enrolled. In 2016, 5 master's awarded. *Degree requirements:* For master's, comprehensive exam, practicum. *Entrance requirements:* For master's, GRE General Test or MAT, minimum undergraduate GPA of 2.8. Additional exam requirements/recommendations for international students: Recommended—TOEFL (minimum score 550 paper-based; 79 iBT). *Application deadline:* For fall admission, 6/30 for domestic students; for spring admission, 10/31 for domestic students; for summer admission, 3/31 for domestic students. Applications are processed on a rolling basis. Application fee: $50. Electronic applications accepted. *Expenses:* Tuition, state resident: part-time $318 per semester hour. Tuition, nonresident: part-time $318 per semester hour. *Required fees:* $75 per semester. Tuition and fees vary according to course load and program. *Financial support:* Unspecified assistantships and SOS scholarships for education majors only available. Financial award application deadline: 3/1; financial award applicants required to submit FAFSA. *Unit head:* Dr. Sandra Berkowitz, Department Chair, 413-572-5323, E-mail: sberkowitz@westfield.ma.edu. *Application contact:* Shelly Henrichon, Coordinator of DGCE Admissions, 413-572-8022, Fax: 413-572-5227, E-mail: mhenrichon@westfield.ma.edu.
Website: http://www.westfield.ma.edu/academics/degrees/education-graduate-programs

Westminster College, Graduate School, Program in Educational Administration, New Wilmington, PA 16172-0001. Offers school principal K-12 (M Ed); school superintendent (Certificate). *Expenses: Tuition:* Full-time $1362; part-time $454 per semester hour. One-time fee: $235.50 full-time. *Unit head:* Dr. Robert L. Zorn, Graduate School Director, 724-946-7031, Fax: 724-946-6158. *Application contact:* Dr. Darwin W. Huey, Graduate Education Director, 724-946-7186, Fax: 724-946-6158, E-mail: hueydw@westminster.edu.

West Virginia University, College of Education and Human Services, Department of Special Education, Morgantown, WV 26506. Offers autism spectrum disorder (5-adult) (MA); autism spectrum disorder (K-6) (MA); early intervention/early childhood special education (MA); gifted education (1-12) (MA); low vision (PreK-adult) (MA); multicategorical special education (5-adult) (MA); multicategorical special education (K-6) (MA); severe/multiple disabilities (K-adult) (MA); special education (MA, Ed D); vision impairments (PreK-adult) (MA). *Accreditation:* NCATE. *Program availability:* Part-time, evening/weekend, online learning. *Degree requirements:* For master's, thesis optional; for doctorate, comprehensive exam, thesis/dissertation. *Entrance requirements:* For master's, minimum GPA of 2.75 passing scores on PRAXIS PPST; for doctorate, GRE General Test or MAT. Additional exam requirements/recommendations for international students: Required—TOEFL.

Wheelock College, Graduate Programs, Division of Education, Boston, MA 02215. Offers early childhood education (MS); education leadership (MS); elementary education (MS); language, literacy, and reading (MS); teaching students with moderate disabilities (MS). *Accreditation:* NCATE. *Program availability:* Online learning. *Degree requirements:* For master's, comprehensive exam. *Entrance requirements:* Additional exam requirements/recommendations for international students: Required—TOEFL. Electronic applications accepted. *Faculty research:* Symbolic learning, emergent literacy, diversity inclusion, beginning reading language and culture, math education.

Wichita State University, Graduate School, College of Education, Department of Curriculum and Instruction, Wichita, KS 67260. Offers learning and instructional design (M Ed); special education (M Ed), including early childhood (M Ed, MAT), gifted, high incidence, low incidence; teaching (MAT), including early childhood (M Ed, MAT), middle level/secondary, transition to teaching. *Accreditation:* NCATE. *Program availability:* Part-time, evening/weekend, 100% online, blended/hybrid learning. *Entrance requirements:* For master's, MAT, minimum GPA of 2.75. *Unit head:* Dr. Kimberly McDowell, Department Head, 316-978-3322, E-mail: kim.mcdowell@wichita.edu. *Application contact:* Jordan Oleson, Admission Coordinator, 316-978-3095, Fax: 316-978-3253, E-mail: jordan.oleson@wichita.edu.

Widener University, School of Education, Hospitality, and Continuing Studies, Chester, PA 19013-5792. Offers adult education (M Ed); counseling in higher education (M Ed); counselor education (M Ed); early childhood education (M Ed); educational foundations (M Ed); educational leadership (M Ed); educational psychology (M Ed); elementary education (M Ed); English and language arts (M Ed); health education (M Ed); higher education leadership (Ed D); home and school visitor (M Ed); human sexuality (M Ed, PhD); mathematics education (M Ed); middle school education (M Ed); principalship (M Ed); reading and language arts (Ed D); reading education (M Ed); school administration (Ed D); science education (M Ed); social studies education (M Ed); special education (M Ed); technology education (M Ed). *Accreditation:* NCATE. *Program availability:* Part-time, evening/weekend. *Faculty:* 34 full-time (22 women), 37 part-time/adjunct (14 women). *Students:* 97 full-time (64 women), 201 part-time (143 women); includes 56 minority (44 Black or African American, non-Hispanic/Latino; 1 American Indian or Alaska Native, non-Hispanic/Latino; 2 Asian, non-Hispanic/Latino; 8 Hispanic/Latino; 1 Two or more races, non-Hispanic/Latino), 32 international. Average age 39. 139 applicants, 88% accepted. In 2016, 45 master's, 21 doctorates awarded. Terminal master's awarded for partial completion of doctoral program. *Degree requirements:* For doctorate, thesis/dissertation. *Entrance requirements:* For master's, minimum GPA of 2.5; for doctorate, GRE or MAT, minimum GPA of 2.0 (undergraduate), 3.5 (graduate). *Application deadline:* Applications are processed on a rolling basis. Application fee: $25 ($300 for international students). Electronic applications accepted. *Expenses:* Contact institution. *Financial support:* Career-related internships or fieldwork, tuition waivers (full and partial), and unspecified assistantships available. Support available to part-time students. Financial award application deadline: 5/1. *Faculty research:* Reading and cognition, adult education, technology education, educational leadership, special education. *Unit head:* Dr. Shawn Fitzgerald, Dean, 610-499-4294, Fax: 610-499-4623, E-mail: smfitzgerald@widener.edu. *Application contact:* Dr. Roberta Nolan, Director of Graduate Admissions, 610-499-4125, E-mail: rdnolan@widener.edu.
Website: http://www.widener.edu/academics/schools/eics

Wilkes University, College of Graduate and Professional Studies, School of Education, Wilkes-Barre, PA 18766-0002. Offers 21st century teaching and learning (MS Ed); art and science of teaching (MS Ed); classroom technology (MS Ed); early childhood literacy (MS Ed); educational development and strategies (MS Ed); educational

leadership (MS Ed, Ed D); effective teaching (MS Ed); instructional media (MS Ed); instructional technology (MS Ed); international school leadership (MS Ed); international teaching and learning (MS Ed); middle level education (MS Ed); online teaching (MS Ed); reading (MS Ed); school business leadership (MS Ed); special education (MS Ed); teaching English to speakers of other languages (MS Ed). *Program availability:* Part-time, evening/weekend, 100% online, blended/hybrid learning. *Students:* 87 full-time (70 women), 1,496 part-time (1,111 women); includes 77 minority (11 Black or African American, non-Hispanic/Latino; 2 American Indian or Alaska Native, non-Hispanic/Latino; 12 Asian, non-Hispanic/Latino; 28 Hispanic/Latino; 3 Native Hawaiian or other Pacific Islander, non-Hispanic/Latino; 21 Two or more races, non-Hispanic/Latino). Average age 33. In 2016, 524 master's, 21 doctorates awarded. *Entrance requirements:* Additional exam requirements/recommendations for international students: Required—TOEFL (minimum score 550 paper-based; 79 iBT). *Application deadline:* Applications are processed on a rolling basis. Application fee: $45. Electronic applications accepted. *Expenses:* Contact institution. *Financial support:* Unspecified assistantships available. Financial award application deadline: 3/1; financial award applicants required to submit FAFSA. *Unit head:* Dr. Rhonda Rabbitt, Dean, 570-408-4680, Fax: 570-408-7872, E-mail: rhonda.rabbitt@wilkes.edu. *Application contact:* Director of Graduate Education, 570-408-4234, Fax: 570-408-7846.
Website: http://www.wilkes.edu/academics/graduate-programs/masters-programs/graduate-education/index.aspx

Worcester State University, Graduate Studies, Department of Education, Program in Early Childhood Education, Worcester, MA 01602-2597. Offers M Ed. *Program availability:* Part-time, evening/weekend. *Faculty:* 13 full-time (12 women), 16 part-time/adjunct (7 women). *Students:* 1 (woman) full-time, 18 part-time (all women); includes 1 minority (Hispanic/Latino). Average age 38. 15 applicants, 60% accepted, 9 enrolled. In 2016, 2 master's awarded. *Degree requirements:* For master's, comprehensive exam (for some programs), thesis optional, research project. *Entrance requirements:* For master's, GRE General Test or MAT, initial license or its equivalent in early childhood education. Additional exam requirements/recommendations for international students: Required—TOEFL (minimum score 550 paper-based; 79 iBT), IELTS. *Application deadline:* For fall admission, 6/15 for domestic and international students; for spring admission, 11/1 for domestic and international students; for summer admission, 4/1 for domestic and international students. Applications are processed on a rolling basis. Application fee: $50. Electronic applications accepted. *Expenses:* Tuition, state resident: part-time $150 per credit. Tuition, nonresident: part-time $150 per credit. *Financial support:* Career-related internships or fieldwork, scholarships/grants, and unspecified assistantships available. Financial award application deadline: 3/1; financial award applicants required to submit FAFSA. *Unit head:* Dr. Carol Donnelly, Coordinator, 508-929-8667, Fax: 508-929-8164, E-mail: cdonnelly@worcester.edu. *Application contact:* Sara Grady, Associate Dean of Graduate Studies and Professional Development, 508-929-8787, Fax: 508-929-8100, E-mail: sara.grady@worcester.edu.

Xavier University, College of Social Sciences, Health and Education, School of Education, Department of Childhood Education and Literacy, Cincinnati, OH 45207. Offers children's multicultural literature (M Ed); elementary education (M Ed); Montessori education (M Ed); reading (M Ed). *Program availability:* Part-time. *Degree requirements:* For master's, comprehensive exam, thesis, 30 semester hours. *Entrance requirements:* For master's, GRE, MAT, official transcript; 3 letters of recommendation (for Montessori education); resume; statement of purpose. Additional exam requirements/recommendations for international students: Required—TOEFL (minimum score 550 paper-based; 79 iBT). Electronic applications accepted. Application fee is waived when completed online. *Expenses:* Contact institution. *Faculty research:* Multicultural literacy/fluency, early literacy development, writing/creative and across curriculum, assessment of reading abilities.

Youngstown State University, Graduate School, Beeghly College of Education, Department of Teacher Education, Program in Early Childhood Education, Youngstown, OH 44555-0001. Offers MS Ed. *Accreditation:* NCATE. *Program availability:* Part-time, evening/weekend. *Degree requirements:* For master's, comprehensive exam. *Entrance requirements:* For master's, GRE, MAT, or teaching certificate; minimum GPA of 2.7. Additional exam requirements/recommendations for international students: Required—TOEFL.

Elementary Education

Acacia University, American Graduate School of Education, Tempe, AZ 85284. Offers educational administration (M Ed); elementary education (MA); English as a second language (M Ed); secondary education (MA); special education (M Ed).

Adelphi University, Ruth S. Ammon School of Education, Program in Childhood Education, Garden City, NY 11530-0701. Offers MA. *Program availability:* Part-time, evening/weekend. *Students:* 61 full-time (56 women), 6 part-time (5 women); includes 10 minority (2 Black or African American, non-Hispanic/Latino; 5 Asian, non-Hispanic/Latino; 3 Hispanic/Latino). Average age 24. 31 applicants, 35% accepted, 7 enrolled. In 2016, 39 master's awarded. *Entrance requirements:* For master's, 2 letters of recommendation, resume. Additional exam requirements/recommendations for international students: Required—TOEFL (minimum score 550 paper-based; 80 iBT), IELTS (minimum score 6.5). *Application deadline:* For fall admission, 4/1 for international students; for spring admission, 11/1 for international students. Application fee: $50. Electronic applications accepted. *Expenses:* Contact institution. *Financial support:* Research assistantships, teaching assistantships, career-related internships or fieldwork, institutionally sponsored loans, scholarships/grants, traineeships, and unspecified assistantships available. Support available to part-time students. Financial award application deadline: 2/15; financial award applicants required to submit FAFSA. *Faculty research:* Diversity; parental involvement; teacher education; psychoanalytic understanding of racial formation; relationships between ideology, language, culture and individual subject formation. *Unit head:* Dr. Carl Mirra, Director, 516-877-4137, E-mail: mirra@adelphi.edu. *Application contact:* Christine Murphy, Director of Admissions, 516-877-3050, Fax: 516-877-3039, E-mail: graduateadmissions@adelphi.edu.

Alabama Agricultural and Mechanical University, School of Graduate Studies, College of Education, Humanities, and Behavioral Sciences, Department of Reading, Elementary, Early Childhood and Special Education, Huntsville, AL 35811. Offers early childhood education (MS Ed, Ed S); elementary education (MS Ed, Ed S); reading/literacy (PhD); special education collaborative teacher training (MS Ed, Ed S). *Accreditation:* NCATE. *Program availability:* Evening/weekend. *Degree requirements:* For master's, comprehensive exam; for Ed S, thesis. *Entrance requirements:* For master's, GRE General Test. Additional exam requirements/recommendations for international students: Required—TOEFL (minimum score 500 paper-based; 61 iBT). *Application deadline:* For fall admission, 5/1 for domestic students. Applications are processed on a rolling basis. Application fee: $25. Electronic applications accepted. *Expenses:* Tuition, nonresident: part-time $826 per credit hour. Full-time tuition and fees vary according to course load and program. *Financial support:* Research assistantships with tuition reimbursements and career-related internships or fieldwork available. Financial award application deadline: 4/1. *Faculty research:* Multicultural education, learning styles, diagnostic-prescriptive instruction. *Unit head:* Dr. Derrick Davis, Interim Chair, 256-372-4047.

Alabama State University, College of Education, Department of Curriculum and Instruction, Montgomery, AL 36101-0271. Offers early childhood education (M Ed, Ed S); elementary education (M Ed, Ed S), secondary education (M Ed, Ed S), including biology education, English language arts education (M Ed), history education, math education, music education (M Ed), reading education (M Ed), social science education; special education (M Ed). *Program availability:* Part-time. *Faculty:* 7 full-time (4 women), 7 part-time/adjunct (4 women). *Students:* 37 full-time (30 women), 82 part-time (69 women); includes 117 minority (115 Black or African American, non-Hispanic/Latino; 2 Two or more races, non-Hispanic/Latino). Average age 33. 65 applicants, 55% accepted, 22 enrolled. In 2016, 25 master's, 5 Ed Ss awarded. *Degree requirements:* For master's, comprehensive exam, thesis optional; for Ed S, comprehensive exam, thesis. *Entrance requirements:* For master's, GRE General Test, MAT, writing competency test; for Ed S, writing competency test, GRE, MAT. Additional exam requirements/recommendations for international students: Required—TOEFL (minimum score 500 paper-based). *Application deadline:* For fall admission, 4/15 for domestic and international students; for spring admission, 11/15 for domestic and international students; for summer admission, 3/15 for domestic and international students. Applications are processed on a rolling basis. Application fee: $25. Electronic applications accepted. *Expenses:* Tuition, state resident: full-time $3087; part-time $2744 per credit. Tuition, nonresident: full-time $6174; part-time $5488 per credit. *Required fees:* $2284; $1142 per credit. $571 per semester. Tuition and fees vary according to class time, course level, course load, degree level, program and student level. *Financial support:* Research assistantships available. Financial award application deadline: 6/30; financial award applicants required to submit FAFSA. *Unit head:* Dr. Joyce Johnson, Acting Chairperson, 334-229-4485, Fax: 334-229-5603, E-mail: jjohnson@alasu.edu. *Application contact:* Dr. William Person, Dean of Graduate Studies, 334-229-4274, Fax: 334-229-4928, E-mail: wperson@alasu.edu.
Website: http://www.alasu.edu/academics/colleges—departments/college-of-education/curriculum—instruction/index.aspx

Alaska Pacific University, Graduate Programs, Education Department, Program in Teaching, Anchorage, AK 99508-4672. Offers teaching (K-8) (MAT). *Degree requirements:* For master's, research project. *Entrance requirements:* For master's, GRE or MAT, PRAXIS, minimum GPA of 3.0.

Albright College, Graduate Division, Reading, PA 19612-5234. Offers early childhood education (MS); elementary education (MS); English as a second language (MA); general education (MA); special education (MS). *Program availability:* Part-time, evening/weekend. *Degree requirements:* For master's, thesis. *Entrance requirements:* For master's, GRE General Test or MAT, minimum undergraduate GPA of 3.0, 2 letters of recommendation, interview. Additional exam requirements/recommendations for international students: Recommended—TOEFL (minimum score 525 paper-based). Electronic applications accepted.

Alcorn State University, School of Graduate Studies, School of Psychology and Education, Lorman, MS 39096-7500. Offers agricultural education (MS Ed); elementary education (MS Ed, Ed S); guidance and counseling (MS Ed); industrial education (MS Ed); secondary education (MS Ed), including health and physical education; special education (MS Ed). *Accreditation:* NCATE. *Degree requirements:* For master's, thesis optional.

American International College, School of Education, Springfield, MA 01109-3189. Offers early childhood education (M Ed, CAGS); elementary education (M Ed, CAGS); middle education/secondary education (M Ed, CAGS); moderate disabilities (M Ed, CAGS); reading specialist (M Ed, CAGS); school adjustment counseling (MAEP, CAGS); school guidance counseling (MAEP, CAGS); school leadership (M Ed, CAGS). *Program availability:* Evening/weekend. *Faculty:* 1 (woman) full-time, 90 part-time/adjunct (63 women). *Students:* 1,194 full-time (970 women), 118 part-time (83 women); includes 108 minority (15 Black or African American, non-Hispanic/Latino; 4 American Indian or Alaska Native, non-Hispanic/Latino; 12 Asian, non-Hispanic/Latino; 55 Hispanic/Latino; 2 Native Hawaiian or other Pacific Islander, non-Hispanic/Latino; 20 Two or more races, non-Hispanic/Latino). Average age 34. 517 applicants, 417 enrolled. In 2016, 879 master's, 194 CAGSs awarded. Terminal master's awarded for partial completion of doctoral program. *Degree requirements:* For master's, comprehensive exam (for some programs), thesis (for some programs), practicum/culminating experience; for CAGS, practicum/culminating experience. *Entrance requirements:* For master's, Communication and Literacy portion of the Massachusetts Tests for Education Licensure, graduate of accredited four-year college with minimum B- average in undergraduate course work; for CAGS, M Ed or master's degree in field related to licensure from accredited institution. *Application deadline:* Applications are processed on a rolling basis. Application fee: $50. Electronic applications accepted. *Expenses:* $439 per credit. *Financial support:* Applicants required to submit FAFSA. *Unit head:* Sylvia Mason, Dean, 413-205-1743, Fax: 413-205-3943, E-mail: sylvia.mason@aic.edu. *Application contact:* Kerry Barnes, Dean of Graduate Admissions, 413-205-3703, Fax: 413-205-3051, E-mail: kerry.barnes@aic.edu.
Website: http://www.aic.edu/school-of-education/

American Public University System, AMU/APU Graduate Programs, Charles Town, WV 25414. Offers accounting (MBA, MS); applied business analytics (MBA, MS); criminal justice (MA), including business administration, emergency and disaster management, general (MA, MS); educational leadership (M Ed); emergency and disaster management (MA); entrepreneurship (MBA); environmental policy and management (MS), including environmental planning, environmental sustainability, fish and wildlife management, general (MA, MS), global environmental management; finance (MBA); general (MBA); government contracting and acquisition (MBA); health care administration (MBA); health information management (MS); history (MA), including American history, ancient and classical history, European history, global history, public history; homeland security (MA), including business administration, counterterrorism studies, criminal justice, cyber, emergency management and public health, intelligence

studies, transportation security; homeland security resource allocation (MBA); humanities (MA); information technology (MS), including digital forensics, enterprise software development, information assurance and security, IT project management; information technology management (MBA); intelligence studies (MA), including criminal intelligence, cyber, general (MA, MS), homeland security, intelligence analysis, intelligence collection, intelligence management, intelligence operations, terrorism studies; international relations and conflict resolution (MA), including comparative and security issues, conflict resolution, international and transnational security issues, peacekeeping; legal studies (MA); management (MA), including strategic consulting; marketing (MBA); military history (MA), including American military history, American Revolution, civil war, war since 1945, World War II; military studies (MA), including joint warfare, strategic leadership; national security studies (MA), including cyber, general (MA, MS), homeland security, regional security studies, security and intelligence analysis, terrorism studies; nonprofit management (MBA); political science (MA), including American politics and government, comparative government and development, general (MA, MS), international relations, public policy; psychology (MA); public administration (MPA), including disaster management, environmental policy, health policy, human resources, national security, organizational management, security management; public health (MPH); reverse logistics management (MA); security management (MA); space studies (MS), including aerospace science, general (MA, MS), planetary science; sports and health sciences (MS); sports management (MBA); teaching (M Ed), including autism spectrum disorder, curriculum and instruction for elementary teachers, elementary reading, English language learners, instructional leadership, online learning, special education, STEAM (STEM plus the arts); transportation and logistics management (MA). *Program availability:* Part-time, evening/weekend, online only, 100% online. *Faculty:* 401 full-time (228 women), 1,678 part-time/adjunct (781 women). *Students:* 378 full-time (184 women), 8,455 part-time (3,484 women); includes 2,972 minority (1,552 Black or African American, non-Hispanic/Latino; 52 American Indian or Alaska Native, non-Hispanic/Latino; 211 Asian, non-Hispanic/Latino; 791 Hispanic/Latino; 70 Native Hawaiian or other Pacific Islander, non-Hispanic/Latino; 296 Two or more races, non-Hispanic/Latino), 109 international. Average age 37. In 2016, 3,185 master's awarded. *Degree requirements:* For master's, comprehensive exam or practicum. *Entrance requirements:* For master's, official transcript showing earned bachelor's degree from institution accredited by recognized accrediting body. Additional exam requirements/recommendations for international students: Required—TOEFL (minimum score 550 paper-based), IELTS (minimum score 6.5). *Application deadline:* Applications are processed on a rolling basis. Application fee: $0. Electronic applications accepted. *Expenses: Tuition:* Part-time $350 per credit hour. *Required fees:* $50 per course. *Financial support:* Scholarships/grants available. Financial award applicants required to submit FAFSA. *Unit head:* Dr. Karan Powell, President, 877-468-6268, Fax: 304-724-3780. *Application contact:* Terry Grant, Vice President of Enrollment Management, 877-468-6268, Fax: 304-724-3780, E-mail: info@apus.edu.
Website: http://www.apus.edu

American University of Puerto Rico, Program in Education, Bayamon, PR 00960-2037. Offers art education (M Ed); elementary education 4-6 (M Ed); elementary education K-3 (M Ed); general science education (M Ed); physical education (M Ed); special education (M Ed). *Program availability:* Part-time, evening/weekend. *Faculty:* 17 part-time/adjunct (7 women). *Students:* 22 full-time (18 women), 54 part-time (42 women); all minorities (all Hispanic/Latino). Average age 33. 22 applicants, 86% accepted, 19 enrolled. In 2016, 53 master's awarded. *Entrance requirements:* For master's, EXADEP, GRE, or MAT, 2 letters of recommendation, minimum GPA of 2.5. *Application deadline:* For fall admission, 8/1 for domestic students; for winter admission, 10/18 for domestic students; for spring admission, 3/15 for domestic students. Applications are processed on a rolling basis. Application fee: $25. *Financial support:* In 2016–17, 79 students received support, including 76 fellowships (averaging $400 per year), 55 teaching assistantships (averaging $1,741 per year). Financial award applicants required to submit FAFSA. *Unit head:* Prof. Bolivar Ramirez-Carlo, III, Dean of Faculty, 787-620-2040 Ext. 2010, Fax: 787-620-2958, E-mail: bramirez@aupr.edu. *Application contact:* Keren I. Llanos-Figueroa, Information Contact, 787-620-2040 Ext. 2021, Fax: 787-785-7377, E-mail: oficnaadmisiones@aupr.edu.

Anderson University, College of Education, Anderson, SC 29621-4035. Offers administration and supervision (M Ed); education (M Ed); elementary education (MAT). *Accreditation:* NCATE. *Program availability:* 100% online. *Expenses:* Contact institution. *Financial support:* Tuition waivers available. Financial award application deadline: 3/1; financial award applicants required to submit FAFSA. *Unit head:* Dr. Mark Butler, Dean, 864-231-2042. *Application contact:* Mallory Knight, Graduate Admission Counselor, 864-231-2182, Fax: 864-231-2115, E-mail: malloryknight@andersonuniversity.edu.
Website: https://www.andersonuniversity.edu/education

Andrews University, School of Graduate Studies, School of Education, Department of Teaching, Learning, and Curriculum, Berrien Springs, MI 49104. Offers curriculum and instruction (MA, Ed D, PhD, Ed S); elementary education (MAT); secondary education (MAT), including biology, education, English, English as a second language, French, history, physics; teacher education (MAT). *Faculty:* 7 full-time (5 women). *Students:* 17 full-time (12 women), 10 part-time (all women); includes 11 minority (6 Black or African American, non-Hispanic/Latino; 5 Hispanic/Latino), 7 international. Average age 38. In 2016, 9 master's, 7 doctorates awarded. *Entrance requirements:* For master's, GRE Subject Test. Additional exam requirements/recommendations for international students: Required—TOEFL (minimum score 550 paper-based). *Application deadline:* For fall admission, 8/15 for domestic students. Applications are processed on a rolling basis. Application fee: $40. *Unit head:* Dr. Lee C. Davidson, Chair, 269-471-6364. *Application contact:* Justina Clayburn, Supervisor of Graduate Admission, 800-253-2874, Fax: 269-471-6321, E-mail: graduate@andrews.edu.

Anna Maria College, Graduate Division, Program in Education, Paxton, MA 01612. Offers early childhood education (M Ed); education (CAGS); elementary education (M Ed); English language arts (M Ed); visual arts (M Ed). *Program availability:* Part-time, evening/weekend. *Entrance requirements:* For master's, bachelor's degree in liberal arts or sciences, minimum GPA of 3.0. Additional exam requirements/recommendations for international students: Required—TOEFL (minimum score 500 paper-based). Electronic applications accepted.

Antioch University New England, Graduate School, Department of Education, Integrated Learning Program, Keene, NH 03431-3552. Offers early childhood education (M Ed); elementary education (M Ed), including arts and humanities, science and environmental education; special education (M Ed). *Degree requirements:* For master's, internship. *Entrance requirements:* For master's, previous course work or work experience in education. Additional exam requirements/recommendations for international students: Required—TOEFL (minimum score 550 paper-based). Electronic applications accepted. *Expenses:* Contact institution. *Faculty research:* Problem-based learning, place-based education, mathematics education, democratic classrooms, art education.

Antioch University New England, Graduate School, Department of Education, Waldorf Teacher Training Program, Keene, NH 03431-3552. Offers elementary education (M Ed, Certificate). *Degree requirements:* For master's, thesis (for some programs), internship. *Entrance requirements:* For master's, foundation studies in anthroposophy or equivalent. Additional exam requirements/recommendations for international students: Required—TOEFL (minimum score 550 paper-based). Electronic applications accepted. *Expenses:* Contact institution. *Faculty research:* Teacher renewal, early childhood education, collaborative leadership.

Appalachian State University, Cratis D. Williams Graduate School, Department of Curriculum and Instruction, Boone, NC 28608. Offers curriculum specialist (MA); educational media (MA); elementary education (MA); middle grades education (MA), including language arts, mathematics, science, social studies. *Accreditation:* NCATE. *Program availability:* Part-time, evening/weekend, online learning. *Degree requirements:* For master's, comprehensive exam, thesis or alternative. *Entrance requirements:* For master's, GRE General Test or MAT, 3 letters of recommendation. Additional exam requirements/recommendations for international students: Required—TOEFL (minimum score 570 paper-based; 79 iBT), IELTS (minimum score 6.5). *Application deadline:* For fall admission, 3/14 for domestic students, 2/1 for international students; for spring admission, 11/1 for domestic students, 7/1 for international students. Applications are processed on a rolling basis. Application fee: $55. Electronic applications accepted. *Expenses:* Tuition, state resident: full-time $4744. Tuition, nonresident: full-time $17,913. Full-time tuition and fees vary according to program. *Financial support:* Fellowships, research assistantships, teaching assistantships, career-related internships or fieldwork, Federal Work-Study, scholarships/grants, and unspecified assistantships available. Financial award application deadline: 4/1; financial award applicants required to submit FAFSA. *Faculty research:* Media literacy, elementary teaching, curriculum development, online learning environments. *Unit head:* Dr. Michael Jacobson, Chairperson, 828-262-2224. *Application contact:* Dr. Chrystal Dean, Program Director, 828-262-8009, E-mail: deanco@appstate.edu.
Website: http://www.ced.appstate.edu/departments/ci

Aquinas College, School of Education, Nashville, TN 37205-2005. Offers elementary education (MAT); secondary education (MAT); teaching and learning (M Ed). *Unit head:* Sr. Mary Anne Zuberbueler, OP, Dean, 615-297-7545 Ext. 282, Fax: 615-279-3892, E-mail: srmanne@aquinascollege.edu.

Arcadia University, School of Education, Glenside, PA 19038-3295. Offers art education (M Ed); computer education (CAS); curriculum (CAS); curriculum studies (M Ed); early childhood education (M Ed), including individualized, master teacher, research in child development; educational leadership (M Ed, Ed D, CAS); elementary education (M Ed); English education (MA Ed); environmental education (MA Ed); instructional technology (M Ed); language arts (M Ed); library science (M Ed); mathematics education (M Ed, MA Ed); music education (MA Ed); psychology (MA Ed); reading (M Ed, CAS); science education (M Ed, CAS); secondary education (M Ed, CAS); special education (M Ed, Ed D, CAS); theater arts (MA Ed); written communication (MA Ed). *Accreditation:* NASAD. *Program availability:* Part-time, evening/weekend, online learning. *Faculty:* 19 full-time (13 women), 3 part-time/adjunct (all women). *Students:* 22 full-time (16 women), 356 part-time (284 women); includes 84 minority (55 Black or African American, non-Hispanic/Latino; 2 American Indian or Alaska Native, non-Hispanic/Latino; 13 Asian, non-Hispanic/Latino; 11 Hispanic/Latino; 3 Two or more races, non-Hispanic/Latino), 4 international. Average age 34. 145 applicants, 73% accepted, 80 enrolled. In 2016, 95 master's, 11 doctorates awarded. *Application deadline:* Applications are processed on a rolling basis. Application fee: $50. Electronic applications accepted. *Expenses:* Contact institution. *Financial support:* Career-related internships or fieldwork, tuition waivers (partial), and unspecified assistantships available. *Unit head:* John T Groves, Interim Dean of the School of Education, 215-572-2940. *Application contact:* 215-572-2925, Fax: 215-572-2126, E-mail: grad@arcadia.edu.

Argosy University, Atlanta, College of Education, Atlanta, GA 30328. Offers educational leadership (MAEd, Ed D, Ed S), including higher education administration (Ed D), K-12 education (Ed D); teaching and learning (MAEd, Ed D, Ed S), including education technology (Ed D), higher education (Ed D), K-12 education (Ed D).

Argosy University, Chicago, College of Education, Chicago, IL 60601. Offers adult education and training (MA Ed); community college executive leadership (Ed D); educational leadership (MA Ed, Ed D, Ed S), including district leadership (Ed D), higher education administration (Ed D), K-12 education (Ed D); instructional leadership (Ed D, Ed S), including higher education (Ed D), K-12 education (Ed D). *Program availability:* Online learning.

Argosy University, Denver, College of Education, Denver, CO 80231. Offers community college executive leadership (Ed D); educational leadership (MA Ed, Ed D), including higher education (Ed D), K-12 education (Ed D); instructional leadership (MA Ed, Ed D), including higher education administration (Ed D), K-12 education (Ed D).

Argosy University, Hawai`i, College of Education, Honolulu, HI 96813. Offers adult education and training (MAEd); educational leadership (Ed D), including higher education administration, K-12 education; instructional leadership (Ed D), including higher education, K-12 education; school psychology (MA).

Argosy University, Inland Empire, College of Education, Ontario, CA 91761. Offers community college executive leadership (Ed D); educational leadership (MA Ed, Ed D), including higher education administration (Ed D), K-12 education (Ed D); instructional leadership (MA Ed, Ed D), including higher education (Ed D), K-12 education (Ed D), multiple subject teacher preparation (MA Ed), single subject teacher preparation (MA Ed).

Argosy University, Los Angeles, College of Education, Santa Monica, CA 90045. Offers community college executive leadership (Ed D); educational leadership (MA Ed, Ed D), including higher education administration (Ed D), K-12 education (Ed D); instructional leadership (MA Ed, Ed D), including higher education (Ed D), K-12 education (Ed D), multiple subject teacher preparation (MA Ed), single subject teacher preparation (MA Ed).

Argosy University, Nashville, College of Education, Program in Educational Leadership, Nashville, TN 37214. Offers educational leadership (MA Ed, Ed S); higher education administration (Ed D); K-12 education (Ed D).

Argosy University, Nashville, College of Education, Program in Instructional Leadership, Nashville, TN 37214. Offers education technology (Ed D); higher education administration (Ed D); instructional leadership (MA Ed, Ed S); K-12 education (Ed D).

Argosy University, Northern Virginia, College of Education, Arlington, VA 22209. Offers community college executive leadership (Ed D); educational leadership (MA Ed, Ed D, Ed S), including higher education administration (Ed D), K-12 education (Ed D); instructional leadership (MA Ed, Ed D, Ed S), including higher education (Ed D), K-12 education (Ed D).

Argosy University, Orange County, College of Education, Orange, CA 92868. Offers community college executive leadership (Ed D); educational leadership (MA Ed, Ed D), including higher education administration (Ed D), K-12 education (Ed D); instructional leadership (MA Ed, Ed D), including education technology (Ed D), higher education (Ed D), K-12 education (Ed D), multiple subject teacher preparation (MA Ed), single subject teacher preparation (MA Ed).

Argosy University, Phoenix, College of Education, Phoenix, AZ 85021. Offers adult education and training (MA Ed); advanced educational administration (Ed D, Ed S); community college executive leadership (Ed D); educational administration (MA Ed); educational leadership (MA Ed, Ed D, Ed S), including education technology (Ed D), higher education administration (Ed D), K-12 education (Ed D); higher and postsecondary education (MA Ed); initial educational administration (Ed D, Ed S); school psychology (MA); teaching and learning (MA Ed, Ed D, Ed S), including education technology (Ed D), higher education (Ed D), K-12 education (Ed D).

Argosy University, San Diego, College of Education, San Diego, CA 92108. Offers community college executive leadership (Ed D); educational leadership (MA Ed, Ed D), including higher education administration (Ed D), K-12 education (Ed D); instructional leadership (MA Ed, Ed D), including higher education (Ed D), K-12 education (Ed D).

Argosy University, San Francisco Bay Area, College of Education, Alameda, CA 94501. Offers community college executive leadership (Ed D); educational leadership (MA Ed, Ed D), including education technology (Ed D), higher education administration (Ed D), K-12 education (Ed D); instructional leadership (MA Ed, Ed D), including education technology (Ed D), higher education (Ed D), K-12 education (Ed D), multiple subject teacher preparation (MA Ed), single subject teacher preparation (MA Ed).

Argosy University, Sarasota, College of Education, Sarasota, FL 34235. Offers community college executive leadership (Ed D); educational leadership (MA Ed, Ed D, Ed S), including higher education administration (Ed D), K-12 education (Ed D); school counseling (MA, Ed S); school psychology (MA); teaching and learning (MA Ed, Ed D, Ed S), including education technology (Ed D), higher education (Ed D), K-12 education (Ed D).

Argosy University, Seattle, College of Education, Seattle, WA 98121. Offers adult education and training (MA Ed); community college executive leadership (Ed D); educational leadership (MA Ed, Ed D), including higher education administration (Ed D), K-12 education (Ed D); higher and postsecondary education (MA Ed); instructional leadership (MA Ed, Ed D), including education technology (Ed D), higher education (Ed D), K-12 education (Ed D).

Argosy University, Tampa, College of Education, Tampa, FL 33607. Offers community college executive leadership (Ed D); educational leadership (MA Ed, Ed D, Ed S), including higher education administration (Ed D), K-12 education (Ed D); school counseling (MA); teaching and learning (MA Ed, Ed D, Ed S), including higher education (Ed D), K-12 education (Ed D).

Argosy University, Twin Cities, College of Education, Eagan, MN 55121. Offers advanced educational administration (Ed D, Ed S); educational leadership (MA Ed, Ed D, Ed S), including higher education administration (Ed D), K-12 education (Ed D); higher and postsecondary education (MA Ed); initial educational administration (Ed D, Ed S); instructional leadership (MA Ed, Ed D, Ed S), including education technology (Ed D), higher education (Ed D), K-12 education (Ed D).

Arizona State University at the Tempe campus, Mary Lou Fulton Teachers College, Program in Curriculum and Instruction, Phoenix, AZ 85069. Offers curriculum and instruction (M Ed, MA); elementary education (M Ed); physical education (MPE); secondary education (M Ed). *Program availability:* Part-time, evening/weekend, online learning. Terminal master's awarded for partial completion of doctoral program. *Degree requirements:* For master's, thesis or alternative, applied project, interactive Program of Study (iPOS) submitted before completing 50 percent of required credit hours. *Entrance requirements:* For master's, GRE or GMAT (for some programs), minimum GPA of 3.0 or equivalent in last 2 years of work leading to bachelor's degree, 3 letters of recommendation, personal statement describing research and career goals, curriculum vitae or resume, IVP fingerprint clearance card (for those seeking Arizona certification). Additional exam requirements/recommendations for international students: Required—TOEFL, IELTS, or PTE. Electronic applications accepted. *Expenses:* Contact institution. *Faculty research:* Early childhood, media and computers, elementary education, secondary education, English education, bilingual education, language and literacy, science education, engineering education, exercise and wellness education.

Arkansas State University, Graduate School, College of Education and Behavioral Science, School of Teacher Education and Leadership, State University, AR 72467. Offers community college administration (SCCT); curriculum and instruction (MSE); early childhood education (MSE); early childhood services (MS); educational leadership (MSE, Ed D, Ed S); educational theory and practice (MSE); middle level education (MAT, MSE); reading (MSE, Ed S); special education - gifted, talented, and creative (MSE); special education - instructional specialist grades 4-12 (MSE); special education - instructional specialist grades P-4 (MSE); special education, K-12 (MSE). *Accreditation:* NCATE. *Program availability:* Part-time, online learning. *Degree requirements:* For master's, comprehensive exam, thesis or alternative; for doctorate, comprehensive exam, thesis/dissertation; for other advanced degree, comprehensive exam. *Entrance requirements:* For master's, GRE General Test or MAT, appropriate bachelor's degree, official transcripts, immunization records, letters of reference, interview; for doctorate, GRE General Test or MAT, interview, master's degree, letters of reference, official transcript, personal statement, writing sample, immunization records; for other advanced degree, GRE General Test or MAT, interview, master's degree, official transcript, immunization records, letters of reference, 3 years of teaching experience, teaching license. Additional exam requirements/recommendations for international students: Required—TOEFL (minimum score 550 paper-based; 79 iBT), IELTS (minimum score 6), PTE (minimum score 56). Electronic applications accepted.

Arkansas Tech University, College of Education, Russellville, AR 72801. Offers college student personnel (MS); educational leadership (M Ed, Ed S); elementary education (M Ed); instructional improvement (M Ed); instructional technology (M Ed); school counseling and leadership (M Ed); school leadership (Ed D); strength and conditioning studies (MS); teaching (MAT); teaching, learning, and leadership (M Ed). *Accreditation:* NCATE. *Program availability:* Part-time, evening/weekend, online learning. *Students:* 72 full-time (43 women), 371 part-time (283 women); includes 108 minority (80 Black or African American, non-Hispanic/Latino; 1 American Indian or Alaska Native, non-Hispanic/Latino; 4 Asian, non-Hispanic/Latino; 13 Hispanic/Latino; 10 Two or more races, non-Hispanic/Latino), 6 international. Average age 33. In 2016, 181 master's, 1 other advanced degree awarded. *Degree requirements:* For master's, comprehensive exam, thesis optional, action research project. *Entrance requirements:* Additional exam requirements/recommendations for international students: Required—TOEFL (minimum score 550 paper-based; 79 iBT), IELTS (minimum score 6.5). *Application deadline:* For fall admission, 3/1 priority date for domestic students, 5/1 priority date for international students; for spring admission, 10/1 priority date for domestic and international students. Applications are processed on a rolling basis. Application fee: $25 ($75 for international students). Electronic applications accepted. *Expenses:* Tuition, state resident: full-time $4932; part-time $274 per credit hour. Tuition, nonresident: full-time $9864; part-time $548 per credit hour. *Required fees:* $513 per semester. Tuition and fees vary according to course load. *Financial support:* In 2016–17, research assistantships with full tuition reimbursements (averaging $4,800 per year), teaching assistantships with full tuition reimbursements (averaging $4,800 per year) were awarded; career-related internships or fieldwork, Federal Work-Study, scholarships/grants, health care benefits, and unspecified assistantships also available. Support available to part-time students. Financial award application deadline: 4/15; financial award applicants required to submit FAFSA. *Unit head:* Dr. Mary Gunter, Dean, 479-964-3217, E-mail: mgunter@atu.edu.
Website: http://www.atu.edu/education/

Auburn University, Graduate School, College of Education, Department of Curriculum and Teaching, Auburn University, AL 36849. Offers elementary education (Ed S). *Accreditation:* NASM (one or more programs are accredited); NCATE. *Program availability:* Part-time. *Faculty:* 29 full-time (20 women), 5 part-time/adjunct (3 women). *Students:* 85 full-time (61 women), 141 part-time (105 women); includes 50 minority (31 Black or African American, non-Hispanic/Latino; 2 American Indian or Alaska Native, non-Hispanic/Latino; 1 Asian, non-Hispanic/Latino; 12 Hispanic/Latino; 4 Two or more races, non-Hispanic/Latino), 11 international. Average age 32. 173 applicants, 47% accepted, 63 enrolled. In 2016, 68 master's, 11 doctorates, 20 other advanced degrees awarded. *Degree requirements:* For master's, thesis (for some programs); for doctorate, thesis/dissertation; for Ed S, field project. *Entrance requirements:* For master's, doctorate, and Ed S, GRE General Test. *Application deadline:* Applications are processed on a rolling basis. Application fee: $50 ($60 for international students). Electronic applications accepted. *Expenses:* Tuition, state resident: full-time $9072; part-time $504 per credit hour. Tuition, nonresident: full-time $27,216; part-time $1512 per credit hour. *Required fees:* $812 per semester. Tuition and fees vary according to degree level and program. *Financial support:* Fellowships, teaching assistantships, career-related internships or fieldwork, and Federal Work-Study available. Support available to part-time students. Financial award application deadline: 3/15; financial award applicants required to submit FAFSA. *Faculty research:* Emerging literacy, reading attitudes, music for at-risk youth, portfolio assessment. *Unit head:* Dr. Kimberly Walls, Head, 334-844-4434. *Application contact:* Dr. George Flowers, Dean of the Graduate School, 334-844-2125.
Website: http://education.auburn.edu/academic_departments/curr/

Auburn University at Montgomery, College of Education, Department of Curriculum, Instruction, and Technology, Montgomery, AL 36124-4023. Offers elementary education (M Ed, Ed S); instructional technology (Ed S); secondary education (M Ed). *Faculty:* 10 full-time (6 women), 6 part-time/adjunct (4 women). *Students:* 18 full-time (15 women), 23 part-time (22 women); includes 11 minority (10 Black or African American, non-Hispanic/Latino; 1 Asian, non-Hispanic/Latino), 1 international. *Entrance requirements:* Additional exam requirements/recommendations for international students: Recommended—TOEFL (minimum score 500 paper-based; 61 iBT), IELTS (minimum score 5.5), TSE (minimum score 44). *Expenses:* Tuition, state resident: full-time $6462; part-time $359 per credit hour. Tuition, nonresident: full-time $14,526; part-time $807 per credit hour. *Required fees:* $554. *Financial support:* Application deadline: 3/1; applicants required to submit FAFSA. *Unit head:* Dr. Kellie Shumack, Head, 334-244-3737, Fax: 334-244-3835, E-mail: kshumack@aum.edu. *Application contact:* Dr. Rhonda Morton, Associate Dean/Graduate Coordinator, 334-224-3287, Fax: 334-244-3978, E-mail: rmorton@aum.edu.
Website: http://education.aum.edu/academic-departments/curriculum-instruction-technology

Augusta University, The Graduate School, College of Education, Program in Curriculum and Instruction, Augusta, GA 30912. Offers curriculum and instruction (Ed S); elementary education (MAT); foreign language education (MAT); instruction (M Ed); middle grades education (MAT); music education (MAT); secondary education (MAT); special education (MAT). *Degree requirements:* For master's, thesis, portfolio. *Entrance requirements:* For master's, GRE, MAT, minimum GPA of 2.5. Application fee: $20. *Financial support:* Career-related internships or fieldwork, Federal Work-Study, institutionally sponsored loans, and unspecified assistantships available. Support available to part-time students. Financial award application deadline: 4/15; financial award applicants required to submit FAFSA. *Unit head:* Dr. Gordon Eisenman, Director, 706-737-1496, Fax: 706-667-4706, E-mail: geisenman@augusta.edu. *Application contact:* Dr. Gordon Eisenman, Director, 706-737-1496, Fax: 706-667-4706, E-mail: geisenman@augusta.edu.

Austin Peay State University, College of Graduate Studies, College of Education, Department of Educational Specialties, Clarksville, TN 37044. Offers administration and supervision (Ed S); counseling and guidance (Ed S); curriculum and instruction (MA Ed); education leadership (MA Ed); elementary education (Ed S); reading (MA Ed); secondary education (Ed S). *Program availability:* Part-time, evening/weekend, online learning. *Faculty:* 7 full-time (4 women), 4 part-time/adjunct (3 women). *Students:* 4 full-time (3 women), 77 part-time (60 women); includes 13 minority (8 Black or African American, non-Hispanic/Latino; 1 Asian, non-Hispanic/Latino; 3 Hispanic/Latino; 1 Two or more races, non-Hispanic/Latino). Average age 37. 18 applicants, 89% accepted, 14 enrolled. In 2016, 34 master's, 9 Ed Ss awarded. *Degree requirements:* For master's, comprehensive exam, thesis optional. *Entrance requirements:* For master's, GRE General Test, MAT, minimum undergraduate GPA of 2.75. Additional exam requirements/recommendations for international students: Required—TOEFL (minimum score 500 paper-based). *Application deadline:* For fall admission, 8/9 priority date for domestic students. Applications are processed on a rolling basis. Application fee: $45 ($50 for international students). Electronic applications accepted. *Expenses:* Tuition, state resident: full-time $8300; part-time $415 per credit hour. Tuition, nonresident: full-time $22,280; part-time $1114 per credit hour. *Required fees:* $1473; $73.65 per credit hour. *Financial support:* Research assistantships with full tuition reimbursements, career-related internships or fieldwork, Federal Work-Study, institutionally sponsored loans, scholarships/grants, and unspecified assistantships available. Support available to part-time students. Financial award application deadline: 4/1; financial award applicants required to submit FAFSA. *Unit head:* Dr. Moniqueka Gold, Chair, 931-221-7696, Fax: 931-221-1292, E-mail: goldm@apsu.edu. *Application contact:* Brad Averitt, Coordinator of Graduate Admissions, 800-859-4723, Fax: 931-221-7641, E-mail: gradadmissions@apsu.edu.

Austin Peay State University, College of Graduate Studies, College of Education, Department of Teaching and Learning, Clarksville, TN 37044. Offers elementary education K-6 (MAT); reading (MA Ed); secondary education 7-12 (MAT); special education K-12 (MAT). *Program availability:* Part-time, evening/weekend, online learning. *Faculty:* 12 full-time (8 women), 1 (woman) part-time/adjunct. *Students:* 62 full-time (39 women), 79 part-time (72 women); includes 31 minority (16 Black or African American, non-Hispanic/Latino; 1 Asian, non-Hispanic/Latino; 8 Hispanic/Latino; 6 Two or more races, non-Hispanic/Latino), 2 international. Average age 33. 60 applicants, 80% accepted, 33 enrolled. In 2016, 53 master's awarded. *Degree requirements:* For master's, comprehensive exam, thesis optional. *Entrance requirements:* For master's, GRE General Test, minimum undergraduate GPA of 2.75. Additional exam requirements/recommendations for international students: Required—TOEFL (minimum score 500 paper-based). *Application deadline:* For fall admission, 8/9 priority date for domestic students. Applications are processed on a rolling basis. Application fee: $45 ($50 for international students). Electronic applications accepted. *Expenses:* Tuition, state resident: full-time $8300; part-time $415 per credit hour. Tuition, nonresident: full-time $22,280; part-time $1114 per credit hour. *Required fees:* $1473; $73.65 per credit hour. *Financial support:* Research assistantships, career-related internships or fieldwork, Federal Work-Study, institutionally sponsored loans, scholarships/grants, and unspecified assistantships available. Support available to part-time students. Financial award application deadline: 4/1; financial award applicants required to submit FAFSA. *Unit head:* Dr. Benita Bruster, Interim Chair, 931-221-6491, Fax: 931-221-1292, E-mail: brusterb@apsu.edu. *Application contact:* Brad Averitt, Coordinator of Graduate Admissions, 800-859-4723, Fax: 931-221-7641, E-mail: gradadmissions@apsu.edu.

Ball State University, Graduate School, College of Sciences and Humanities, Department of Mathematical Sciences, Muncie, IN 47306. Offers actuarial science (MA); elementary mathematics teacher leadership (Certificate); mathematics (MA, MS), including mathematics; mathematics education (MA), including mathematics education; middle school mathematics education (Certificate); post-secondary foundational mathematics teaching (MA, Certificate); statistical modeling (Certificate); statistics (MA, MS), including statistics. *Program availability:* Part-time, 100% online, blended/hybrid learning. *Degree requirements:* For master's, thesis (for some programs). *Entrance requirements:* For master's, minimum baccalaureate GPA of 2.75 or 3.0 in latter half of baccalauareate. Additional exam requirements/recommendations for international students: Required—TOEFL (minimum score 550 paper-based; 79 iBT), IELTS (minimum score 6.5). Electronic applications accepted. *Faculty research:* Differential equations.

Ball State University, Graduate School, Teachers College, Department of Elementary Education, Muncie, IN 47306. Offers early childhood administration (Certificate); elementary education (MAE, Ed D, PhD); enhanced teaching practice for elementary teachers (Certificate); literacy instruction (Certificate); response to intervention (Certificate). *Accreditation:* NCATE. *Program availability:* Part-time, 100% online. *Degree requirements:* For doctorate, thesis/dissertation. *Entrance requirements:* For master's, minimum baccalaureate GPA of 2.75 or 3.0 in latter half of baccalaureate; for doctorate, GRE General Test, minimum graduate GPA of 3.2. Additional exam requirements/recommendations for international students: Required—TOEFL (minimum score 550 paper-based; 79 iBT), IELTS (minimum score 6.5). Electronic applications accepted.

Bank Street College of Education, Graduate School, Program in Elementary/Childhood Education, New York, NY 10025. Offers early childhood and elementary/childhood education (MS Ed); elementary/childhood education (MS Ed). *Degree requirements:* For master's, thesis. *Entrance requirements:* For master's, interview, essays. Additional exam requirements/recommendations for international students: Required—TOEFL (minimum score 600 paper-based; 100 iBT), IELTS (minimum score 7). Electronic applications accepted. *Faculty research:* Social studies in the elementary grades, urban education, experiential learning, child-centered classrooms.

Barry University, School of Education, Program in Curriculum and Instruction, Miami Shores, FL 33161-6695. Offers accomplished teacher (Ed S); culture, language and literacy (TESOL) (PhD); curriculum evaluation and research (PhD); early childhood (Ed S); early childhood education (PhD); elementary (Ed S); elementary education (PhD); ESOL (Ed S); gifted (Ed S); Montessori (Ed S); PKP/elementary (Ed S); reading (Ed S); reading, language and cognition (PhD). *Entrance requirements:* For doctorate, GRE, minimum GPA of 3.25.

Barry University, School of Education, Program in Elementary Education, Miami Shores, FL 33161-6695. Offers elementary education (MS); elementary education/ESOL (MS). *Program availability:* Part-time, evening/weekend. *Degree requirements:* For master's, comprehensive exam, practicum. *Entrance requirements:* For master's, GRE General Test or MAT, minimum GPA of 3.0. Electronic applications accepted.

Barton College, Program in Elementary Education, Wilson, NC 27893-7000. Offers M Ed. *Entrance requirements:* For master's, MAT or GRE taken within last five years, bachelor's degree from accredited college or university, minimum GPA of 3.0 for undergraduate work (recommended), official transcript, one year of teaching experience, copy of recognized teaching license in elementary education, personal statement, recommendation form from current employer or administrator, interview. Additional exam requirements/recommendations for international students: Required—TOEFL (minimum score 550 paper-based). Electronic applications accepted.

Bayamón Central University, Graduate Programs, Program in Education, Bayamón, PR 00960-1725. Offers administration and supervision (MA Ed); commercial education (MA Ed); elementary education (K–3) (MA Ed); family counseling (Graduate Certificate); guidance and counseling (MA Ed); pre-elementary teacher (MA Ed); rehabilitation counseling (MA Ed); special education (MA Ed), including attention deficit disorder, education of the autistic, learning disabilities. *Program availability:* Part-time, evening/weekend. *Degree requirements:* For master's, comprehensive exam. *Entrance requirements:* For master's, EXADEP, bachelor's degree in education or related field.

Belhaven University, School of Education, Jackson, MS 39202-1789. Offers educational technology (M Ed); elementary education (M Ed, MAT); reading literacy (M Ed); secondary education (M Ed, MAT). *Program availability:* Part-time, evening/weekend, 100% online, blended/hybrid learning. *Faculty:* 36 full-time (27 women), 9 part-time/adjunct (6 women). *Students:* 319 full-time (270 women), 403 part-time (318 women); includes 502 minority (486 Black or African American, non-Hispanic/Latino; 2 Asian, non-Hispanic/Latino; 3 Hispanic/Latino; 11 Two or more races, non-Hispanic/Latino). Average age 35. In 2016, 78 master's awarded. *Degree requirements:* For master's, comprehensive exam, portfolio. *Entrance requirements:* For master's, PRAXIS I and II, minimum GPA of 2.8. *Application deadline:* Applications are processed on a rolling basis. Application fee: $25. Electronic applications accepted. *Expenses:* $495 per credit hour plus $75 technology fee per course. *Financial support:* Applicants required to submit FAFSA. *Unit head:* Dr. David Hand, Dean, 601-965-7020, E-mail: dhand@belhaven.edu. *Application contact:* Sean Kirnan, Assistant Vice President for Adult and Graduate Enrollment and Student Services, 601-968-8727, Fax: 601-968-5953, E-mail: gradadmission@belhaven.edu.
Website: http://graduateed.belhaven.edu

Bellarmine University, Annsley Frazier Thornton School of Education, Louisville, KY 40205. Offers education and district leadership (Ed D); education and social change (PhD); elementary education (MA Ed, MAT); leadership in higher education (PhD); learning and behavior disorders (MA Ed, MAT); middle grades education (MA Ed, MAT); principalship (Ed S); reading and writing (MA Ed); secondary education (MAT); teacher leadership (MA Ed). *Accreditation:* NCATE. *Program availability:* Part-time, evening/weekend. *Faculty:* 15 full-time (7 women), 44 part-time/adjunct (36 women). *Students:* 39 full-time (28 women), 211 part-time (164 women); includes 46 minority (35 Black or African American, non-Hispanic/Latino; 3 Asian, non-Hispanic/Latino; 5 Hispanic/Latino; 3 Two or more races, non-Hispanic/Latino). Average age 34. In 2016, 66 master's, 3 doctorates, 43 other advanced degrees awarded. *Degree requirements:* For master's, thesis (for some programs); for doctorate, thesis/dissertation. *Entrance requirements:* For master's, GRE, baccalaureate degree from accredited institution; minimum cumulative GPA of 2.75; recommendations from employers, supervisors, or professors attesting to applicant's potential as graduate student; statement of intent to pursue graduate degree; for doctorate, GRE, minimum GPA of 3.5 in all graduate coursework; baccalaureate and master's degrees in education or fields directly relevant to education; three letters of recommendation; two essays (no more than 1,000 words each); interview. Additional exam requirements/recommendations for international students: Required—TOEFL (minimum score 550 paper-based, 68 iBT), IELTS (minimum score 6), or Michigan English Language Assessment Battery. *Application deadline:* For fall admission, 8/1 priority date for domestic and international students; for spring admission, 12/1 priority date for domestic and international students; for summer admission, 4/10 priority date for domestic and international students. Applications are processed on a rolling basis. Application fee: $40. Electronic applications accepted. Tuition and fees vary according to program. *Financial support:* Scholarships/grants available. Financial award applicants required to submit FAFSA. *Faculty research:* Literacy, service-learning, dispositions, educational technology, special education. *Unit head:* Dr. Robert Cooter, Dean, 502-272-8191, Fax: 502-272-8189, E-mail: rcooter@bellarmine.edu. *Application contact:* Sarah Shumway Schuble, Senior Graduate Recruiter, 502-272-8271, Fax: 502-272-8002, E-mail: sshumway@bellarmine.edu.
Website: http://www.bellarmine.edu/education/graduate

Benedictine University, Graduate Programs, Program in Education, Lisle, IL 60532. Offers curriculum and instruction and collaborative teaching (M Ed); elementary education (MA Ed); leadership and administration (M Ed); reading and literacy (M Ed); secondary education (MA Ed); special education (MA Ed). *Program availability:* Part-time, evening/weekend. *Students:* 17 full-time (16 women), 30 part-time (26 women); includes 2 minority (both Black or African American, non-Hispanic/Latino). 21 applicants, 62% accepted, 8 enrolled. In 2016, 68 master's awarded. *Degree requirements:* For master's, comprehensive exam, thesis (for some programs). *Entrance requirements:* For master's, GRE or MAT. Additional exam requirements/recommendations for international students: Required—TOEFL (minimum score 550 paper-based). *Application deadline:* For fall admission, 9/1 for domestic students; for winter admission, 12/1 for domestic students; for spring admission, 2/15 for domestic students. Applications are processed on a rolling basis. Application fee: $40. Electronic applications accepted. *Expenses:* Contact institution. *Financial support:* Career-related internships or fieldwork and health care benefits available. Support available to part-time students. *Unit head:* MeShelda Jackson, Director, 630-829-6282, E-mail: mjackson@ben.edu. *Application contact:* Kari Gibbons, Associate Vice President, Enrollment Center, 630-829-6200, Fax: 630-829-6584, E-mail: kgibbons@ben.edu.

Bethel University, Graduate School, St. Paul, MN 55112-6999. Offers business administration (MBA); classroom management (Certificate); counseling (MA); international baccalaureate teaching and learning (Certificate); K-12 education (MA); leadership (Ed D); leadership foundations (Certificate); nurse educator (MS, Certificate); nurse-midwifery (MS); physician assistant (MS); special education (MA); strategic leadership (MA); teaching (MA). *Program availability:* Part-time, evening/weekend, 100% online, blended/hybrid learning. *Faculty:* 19 full-time (15 women), 57 part-time/adjunct (37 women). *Students:* 674 full-time (466 women), 378 part-time (256 women); includes 188 minority (94 Black or African American, non-Hispanic/Latino; 3 American Indian or Alaska Native, non-Hispanic/Latino; 43 Asian, non-Hispanic/Latino; 31 Hispanic/Latino; 1 Native Hawaiian or other Pacific Islander, non-Hispanic/Latino; 16 Two or more races, non-Hispanic/Latino), 33 international. *Degree requirements:* For master's, comprehensive exam (for some programs), thesis (for some programs); for doctorate, comprehensive exam, thesis/dissertation. *Entrance requirements:* Additional exam requirements/recommendations for international students: Required—TOEFL (minimum score 550 paper-based, 80 iBT) or IELTS. *Application deadline:* Applications are processed on a rolling basis. Application fee: $0. Electronic applications accepted. *Expenses:* Contact institution. *Financial support:* Teaching assistantships, career-related internships or fieldwork, and scholarships/grants available. Support available to part-time students. Financial award applicants required to submit FAFSA. *Unit head:* Dick Crombie, Vice-President/Dean, 651-635-8000, Fax: 651-635-8004, E-mail: gs@bethel.edu. *Application contact:* Director of Admissions, 651-635-8000, Fax: 651-635-8004, E-mail: gs@bethel.edu.
Website: https://www.bethel.edu/graduate/

Blue Mountain College, Program in Elementary Education, Blue Mountain, MS 38610. Offers M Ed. *Program availability:* Part-time, evening/weekend. *Degree requirements:* For master's, comprehensive exam. *Entrance requirements:* For master's, PRAXIS, GRE or MAT, official transcripts; bachelor's degree in a field of education from accredited university or college; teaching certificate; three recommendations. Additional exam requirements/recommendations for international students: Required—TOEFL (minimum score 550 paper-based). Electronic applications accepted.

Bob Jones University, Graduate Programs, Greenville, SC 29614. Offers accountancy (MS); Bible (MA); Bible translation (MA); Biblical studies (Certificate); broadcast management (MS); business administration (MBA); church history (MA, PhD); church ministries (MA); church music (MM); cinema and video production (MA); counseling (MS); curriculum and instruction (Ed D); divinity (M Div); dramatic production (MA); educational leadership (MS, Ed D, Ed S); elementary education (M Ed, MAT); English (M Ed, MA, MAT); fine arts (MA); graphic design (MA); history (M Ed, MA); illustration (MA); interpretative speech (MA); mathematics (M Ed, MAT); medical missions (Certificate); ministry (MM, D Min); multi-categorical special education (M Ed, MAT); music (M Ed); New Testament interpretation (PhD); Old Testament interpretation (PhD); orchestral instrument performance (MM); organ performance (MM); pastoral studies (MA); personnel services (MS, Ed S); piano pedagogy (MM); piano performance (MM); platform arts (MA); radio and television broadcasting (MS); rhetoric and public address (MA); secondary education (M Ed); studio art (MA); teaching Bible (MA); theology (MA, PhD); voice performance (MM); youth ministries (MA); M Div/MM.

Boston College, Lynch School of Education, Program in Elementary Education, Chestnut Hill, MA 02467-3800. Offers M Ed, MAT. *Accreditation:* TEAC. *Program availability:* Part-time, evening/weekend. *Faculty:* 9 full-time (5 women). *Students:* 19 full-time (16 women), 7 part-time (6 women); includes 8 minority (5 Black or African American, non-Hispanic/Latino; 1 Asian, non-Hispanic/Latino; 2 Hispanic/Latino), 2 international. Average age 24. 19 applicants, 79% accepted, 2 enrolled. In 2016, 14 master's awarded. *Degree requirements:* For master's, comprehensive exam. *Entrance requirements:* For master's, GRE General Test or MAT. Additional exam requirements/recommendations for international students: Required—TOEFL (minimum score 100 iBT). *Application deadline:* For fall admission, 12/1 priority date for domestic and international students; for spring admission, 11/1 priority date for domestic and international students. Application fee: $65. Electronic applications accepted. Tuition and fees vary according to program. *Financial support:* Federal Work-Study, scholarships/grants, and tuition waivers (full and partial) available. Financial award applicants required to submit FAFSA. *Unit head:* Dr. Susan Bruce, Chairperson, 617-552-4214, Fax: 617-552-0398. *Application contact:* Kimberly Rose, Graduate Admission Assistant, 617-552-4214, Fax: 617-552-0398, E-mail: roseki@bc.edu.

Bowie State University, Graduate Programs, Program in Elementary Education, Bowie, MD 20715-9465. Offers M Ed. *Accreditation:* NCATE. *Program availability:* Part-time, evening/weekend. *Degree requirements:* For master's, comprehensive exam, thesis optional, research paper. *Entrance requirements:* For master's, minimum GPA of 2.5, teaching certificate, teaching experience. Electronic applications accepted.

Brandeis University, Graduate School of Arts and Sciences, Teaching Program, Waltham, MA 02454-9110. Offers Jewish day school (MAT); public elementary education (MAT); secondary education (MAT), including Bible, biology, chemistry, Chinese, English, history, math, physics; teacher leadership (Ed M, CAGS). *Faculty:* 4 full-time (2 women), 11 part-time/adjunct (10 women). *Students:* 26 full-time (19

women), 32 part-time (26 women); includes 3 minority (all Hispanic/Latino), 10 international. 106 applicants, 70% accepted, 53 enrolled. In 2016, 39 master's awarded. *Degree requirements:* For master's, internship; research project. *Entrance requirements:* For master's, GRE General Test or MAT, official transcript(s), 2 letters of recommendation, resume, statement of purpose. Additional exam requirements/recommendations for international students: Required—TOEFL (minimum score 600 paper-based; 100 iBT); Recommended—IELTS (minimum score 7), TSE (minimum score 68). *Application deadline:* Applications are processed on a rolling basis. Application fee: $75. Electronic applications accepted. *Expenses:* Contact institution. *Financial support:* Scholarships/grants and tuition waivers (partial) available. Financial award application deadline: 4/15; financial award applicants required to submit FAFSA. *Faculty research:* Teacher education, education, teaching, elementary education, secondary education, Jewish education, English, history, biology, chemistry, physics, math, Chinese, Bible/Tanakh. *Unit head:* Prof. Marya Levenson, Director, 781-736-2002, Fax: 781-736-5020, E-mail: mlevenso@brandeis.edu. *Application contact:* Manuel Tuan, Department Coordinator, 781-736-2002, Fax: 781-736-5020, E-mail: tuan@brandeis.edu.
Website: http://www.brandeis.edu/programs/mat

Brandman University, School of Education, Irvine, CA 92618. Offers education (MA); elementary education (MAT); organizational leadership (Ed D); school counseling (MA); secondary education (MAT); special education (MA). *Expenses: Tuition:* Full-time $14,880; part-time $620 per credit hour. Tuition and fees vary according to degree level and program. *Unit head:* Dr. Christine G. Zeppos, Dean, 949-341-9948, E-mail: zeppos@brandman.edu.
Website: http://www.brandman.edu/education/

Bridgewater State University, College of Graduate Studies, College of Education and Allied Studies, Department of Elementary and Early Childhood Education, Program in Elementary Education, Bridgewater, MA 02325. Offers M Ed. *Accreditation:* NCATE. *Program availability:* Part-time, evening/weekend. *Entrance requirements:* For master's, GRE General Test or Massachusetts Test for Educator Licensure.

Brooklyn College of the City University of New York, School of Education, Program in Childhood Education, Brooklyn, NY 11210-2889. Offers bilingual education (MS Ed); liberal arts (MS Ed); mathematics (MS Ed); science and environmental education (MS Ed). *Program availability:* Part-time, evening/weekend. *Entrance requirements:* For master's, LAST, interview, previous course work in education, writing sample, resume, 2 letters of recommendation. Additional exam requirements/recommendations for international students: Required—TOEFL (minimum score 500 paper-based; 61 iBT). Electronic applications accepted. *Faculty research:* Emotional intelligence, multiculturalism, arts immersion, the Holocaust.

Brooklyn College of the City University of New York, School of Education, Program in Special Education, Brooklyn, NY 11210-2889. Offers autism spectrum disorders (AC); teacher of students with disabilities (MS Ed), including adolescence education, childhood education, early childhood education. *Program availability:* Part-time. *Entrance requirements:* For master's, LAST, interview; previous course work in education and psychology; minimum GPA of 3.0 in education, 2.8 overall; resume, 2 letters of recommendation; essay. Additional exam requirements/recommendations for international students: Required—TOEFL (minimum score 500 paper-based; 61 iBT). Electronic applications accepted. *Faculty research:* School reform, conflict resolution, curriculum for inclusive settings, urban issues in special education.

Brown University, Graduate School, Department of Education, Providence, RI 02912. Offers teaching (MAT), including elementary education, English, history/social studies, science, secondary education; urban education policy (AM). *Degree requirements:* For master's, student teaching, portfolio. *Entrance requirements:* For master's, GRE General Test, letters of recommendation, interview. Additional exam requirements/recommendations for international students: Recommended—TOEFL.

Buffalo State College, State University of New York, The Graduate School, Faculty of Applied Science and Education, Department of Elementary Education and Reading, Program in Elementary Education, Buffalo, NY 14222-1095. Offers childhood education (grades 1-6) (MS Ed); early childhood and childhood curriculum and instruction (MS Ed); early childhood education (birth-grade 2) (MS Ed). *Accreditation:* NCATE. *Program availability:* Part-time. *Degree requirements:* For master's, thesis or project. *Entrance requirements:* For master's, minimum GPA of 2.5 in last 60 hours, New York teaching certificate. Additional exam requirements/recommendations for international students: Required—TOEFL (minimum score 550 paper-based).

California Lutheran University, Graduate Studies, Graduate School of Education, Thousand Oaks, CA 91360-2787. Offers counseling and guidance (MS), including college student personnel, counseling and guidance; educational leadership (MA, Ed D), including educational leadership (K-12) (Ed D), higher education leadership (Ed D); special education (MS); teacher leadership (M Ed); teaching (M Ed). *Accreditation:* NCATE. *Program availability:* Part-time, evening/weekend. *Faculty:* 23 full-time (17 women), 39 part-time/adjunct (26 women). *Students:* 518 full-time (411 women), 79 part-time (67 women); includes 252 minority (12 Black or African American, non-Hispanic/Latino; 3 American Indian or Alaska Native, non-Hispanic/Latino; 17 Asian, non-Hispanic/Latino; 108 Hispanic/Latino; 1 Native Hawaiian or other Pacific Islander, non-Hispanic/Latino; 111 Two or more races, non-Hispanic/Latino), 14 international. Average age 35. 319 applicants, 74% accepted, 192 enrolled. In 2016, 93 master's, 13 doctorates awarded. *Degree requirements:* For master's, comprehensive exam or thesis; for doctorate, thesis/dissertation. *Entrance requirements:* For master's, GRE General Test, interview, minimum GPA of 3.0. *Application deadline:* For fall admission, 7/1 priority date for domestic students; for spring admission, 11/1 priority date for domestic students; for summer admission, 4/1 priority date for domestic students. Applications are processed on a rolling basis. Application fee: $50. Electronic applications accepted. *Unit head:* Dr. Michael Hillis, Dean, 805-493-3421. *Application contact:* 805-493-3325, Fax: 805-493-3861, E-mail: clugrad@callutheran.edu.

California State University, Fullerton, Graduate Studies, College of Education, Department of Elementary and Bilingual Education, Fullerton, CA 92834-9480. Offers bilingual/bicultural education (MS); educational technology (MS); elementary curriculum and instruction (MS). *Accreditation:* NCATE. *Program availability:* Part-time. *Degree requirements:* For master's, comprehensive exam, project or thesis. *Entrance requirements:* For master's, minimum GPA of 2.5, teaching certificate. Application fee: $55. *Expenses:* Tuition, state resident: full-time $3369; part-time $1953 per unit. Tuition, nonresident: full-time $3915; part-time $2499 per unit. Tuition and fees vary according to course load, degree level and program. *Financial support:* Career-related internships or fieldwork, Federal Work-Study, institutionally sponsored loans, and scholarships/grants available. Support available to part-time students. Financial award application deadline: 3/1; financial award applicants required to submit FAFSA. *Faculty research:* Teacher training and tracking, model for improvement of teaching. *Unit head:* Lisa Kirtman, Chair, 657-278-4731. *Application contact:* Admissions/Applications, 657-278-2371.
Website: http://ed.fullerton.edu/EDEL/

California State University, Long Beach, Graduate Studies, College of Education, Department of Teacher Education, Long Beach, CA 90840. Offers elementary education (MA); secondary education (MA). *Program availability:* Part-time, evening/weekend. *Degree requirements:* For master's, comprehensive exam or thesis. *Entrance requirements:* For master's, GRE General Test, minimum GPA of 2.75. *Application deadline:* For fall admission, 7/1 for domestic students; for spring admission, 12/1 for domestic students. Applications are processed on a rolling basis. Application fee: $55. Electronic applications accepted. *Financial support:* Federal Work-Study, institutionally sponsored loans, and scholarships/grants available. Financial award application deadline: 3/2. *Faculty research:* Teacher stress and burnout, new teacher induction. *Unit head:* Paul Boyde-Batstone, Chair, 562-985-4506.

California State University, Los Angeles, Graduate Studies, Charter College of Education, Division of Curriculum and Instruction, Los Angeles, CA 90032-8530. Offers elementary teaching (MA). *Program availability:* Part-time, evening/weekend. *Entrance requirements:* For master's, minimum GPA of 2.75 in last 90 units of course work, teaching certificate. Additional exam requirements/recommendations for international students: Required—TOEFL (minimum score 500 paper-based). Electronic applications accepted. *Faculty research:* Media, language arts, mathematics, computers, drug-free schools.

California State University, Northridge, Graduate Studies, Michael D. Eisner College of Education, Department of Elementary Education, Northridge, CA 91330. Offers curriculum and instruction (MA); language and literacy (MA); multilingual/multicultural education (MA). *Accreditation:* NCATE. *Program availability:* Part-time, evening/weekend. *Faculty:* 12 full-time (4 women), 17 part-time/adjunct (7 women). *Students:* 37 part-time (33 women); includes 21 minority (1 Asian, non-Hispanic/Latino; 17 Hispanic/Latino; 3 Two or more races, non-Hispanic/Latino). Average age 29. 44 applicants, 55% accepted, 20 enrolled. *Degree requirements:* For master's, comprehensive exam. *Entrance requirements:* For master's, GRE General Test or minimum GPA of 3.0. Additional exam requirements/recommendations for international students: Required—TOEFL. *Application deadline:* For fall admission, 11/30 for domestic students. Application fee: $55. *Expenses:* Tuition, state resident: full-time $4152. *Financial support:* Federal Work-Study available. Financial award application deadline: 3/1. *Unit head:* Dr. Joyce Burstein, Chair, 818-677-2621.
Website: http://www.csun.edu/eisner-education/elementary-education

California State University, Stanislaus, College of Education, Program in Education (MA), Turlock, CA 95382. Offers curriculum and instruction (MA), including education technology, elementary education, multilingual education, physical education, reading, secondary education, special education; school administration (MA); school counseling (MA). *Program availability:* Part-time, evening/weekend. *Degree requirements:* For master's, comprehensive exam (for some programs), thesis (for some programs). *Entrance requirements:* For master's, MAT, GRE, or CBEST (varies by concentration), 3 letters of recommendation, personal statement. Additional exam requirements/recommendations for international students: Required—TOEFL (minimum score 550 paper-based). Electronic applications accepted. *Faculty research:* Children's perspectives on historical events, method elementary schools dual language education, K-12 reading programs.

California University of Pennsylvania, School of Graduate Studies and Research, College of Education and Human Services, Program in Elementary Education, California, PA 15419-1394. Offers M Ed. *Accreditation:* NCATE. *Program availability:* Part-time, evening/weekend. *Degree requirements:* For master's, comprehensive exam, thesis optional. *Entrance requirements:* For master's, MAT, PRAXIS, minimum GPA of 3.0, state police clearances. Additional exam requirements/recommendations for international students: Required—TOEFL (minimum score 550 paper-based; 80 iBT). Electronic applications accepted. *Expenses:* Tuition, state resident: full-time $11,592; part-time $483 per credit. Tuition, nonresident: full-time $17,400; part-time $725 per credit. *Required fees:* $3916. Tuition and fees vary according to course load, degree level, campus/location and reciprocity agreements. *Faculty research:* English as a second language, adult literacy, emerging literacy, diagnosis and remediation, phonemic awareness.

Calvary University, Graduate School and Seminary, Kansas City, MO 64147. Offers Bible and theology (MS); Biblical counseling (MA); education (MS), including administration and leadership, Christian education, curriculum and instruction, elementary education; organization development (MS); pastoral studies (M Div). *Program availability:* Part-time, evening/weekend. *Faculty:* 6 full-time (2 women), 2 part-time/adjunct (1 woman). *Students:* 11 full-time (3 women), 29 part-time (15 women); includes 12 minority (4 Black or African American, non-Hispanic/Latino; 1 American Indian or Alaska Native, non-Hispanic/Latino; 6 Asian, non-Hispanic/Latino; 1 Native Hawaiian or other Pacific Islander, non-Hispanic/Latino). Average age 39. In 2016, 19 master's awarded. *Degree requirements:* For master's, variable foreign language requirement, comprehensive exam, thesis or alternative. *Entrance requirements:* For master's, minimum GPA of 2.5, BA or BS, doctrine agreement. Additional exam requirements/recommendations for international students: Required—TOEFL (minimum score 550 paper-based). *Application deadline:* Applications are processed on a rolling basis. Application fee: $0. Electronic applications accepted. *Expenses: Tuition:* Full-time $7200; part-time $4800 per credit. *Required fees:* $640; $520 per credit. $140 per semester. One-time fee: $100. Tuition and fees vary according to program. *Financial support:* In 2016–17, 8 students received support. Scholarships/grants available. Financial award application deadline: 11/5; financial award applicants required to submit FAFSA. *Unit head:* Dr. Thomas Baurain, Director of Seminary, 816-322-0110 Ext. 1502, Fax: 816-331-4474, E-mail: thomas.baurain@calvary.edu. *Application contact:* Ann Rogers, Admissions Office Assistant, 800-326-3960 Ext. 1321, Fax: 816-331-4474, E-mail: admissions@calvary.edu.
Website: http://www.calvary.edu

Cambridge College, School of Education, Cambridge, MA 02138-5304. Offers autism specialist (M Ed); autism/behavior analyst (M Ed); behavior analyst (Post-Master's Certificate); behavioral management (M Ed); early childhood teacher (M Ed); education specialist in curriculum and instruction (CAGS); educational leadership (Ed D); elementary teacher (M Ed); English as a second language (M Ed, Certificate); general science (M Ed); health education (Post-Master's Certificate); health/family and consumer sciences (M Ed); history (M Ed); individualized (M Ed); information technology literacy (M Ed); instructional technology (M Ed); interdisciplinary studies (M Ed); library teacher (M Ed); literacy education (M Ed); mathematics (M Ed); mathematics specialist (Certificate); middle school mathematics and science (M Ed); school administration (M Ed, CAGS); school guidance counselor (M Ed); school nurse education (M Ed); school social worker/school adjustment counselor (M Ed); special education administrator (CAGS); special education/moderate disabilities (M Ed); teaching skills and methodologies (M Ed). *Program availability:* Part-time, evening/weekend, online learning. *Degree requirements:* For master's, thesis, internship/practicum (licensure program only); for doctorate, thesis/dissertation; for other advanced degree, thesis. *Entrance requirements:* For master's, interview, resume, documentation of licensure, 2 professional references; for doctorate, official transcripts, interview, resume, documentation of licensure (if any), written personal statement/essay, portfolio of scholarly and professional work, qualifying assessment, 2 professional references, health insurance, immunizations form; for other advanced degree, official transcripts, interview, resume, documentation of licensure (if any), written personal statement/

essay, 2 professional references, health insurance, immunizations form. Additional exam requirements/recommendations for international students: Required—TOEFL (minimum score 550 paper-based; 79 iBT), Michigan English Language Assessment Battery (minimum score 85); Recommended—IELTS (minimum score 6). Electronic applications accepted. *Expenses:* Contact institution. *Faculty research:* Adult education, accelerated learning, mathematics education, brain compatible learning, special education and law.

Campbell University, Graduate and Professional Programs, School of Education, Buies Creek, NC 27506. Offers elementary education (M Ed); interdisciplinary studies (M Ed); middle grades education (M Ed); physical education (M Ed); school administration (MSA); school counseling (M Ed); secondary education (M Ed). *Accreditation:* NCATE. *Program availability:* Part-time, evening/weekend. *Degree requirements:* For master's, comprehensive exam. *Entrance requirements:* For master's, GRE General Test, minimum GPA of 2.7. *Faculty research:* Spiritual values and wellness issues in counseling, stress and professional burnout among counselors, thinking strategies, leadership, adaptive technology.

Canisius College, Graduate Division, School of Education and Human Services, Department of Graduate Education and Leadership, Buffalo, NY 14208-1098. Offers business and marketing education (MS Ed); college student personnel (MS Ed); deaf education (MS Ed); deaf/adolescent education, grades 7-12 (MS Ed); deaf/childhood education, grades 1-6 (MS Ed); differentiated instruction (MS Ed); education administration (MS); educational administration (MS Ed); educational technologies (Certificate); gifted education extension (Certificate); literacy (MS Ed); reading (Certificate); school building leadership (MS Ed, Certificate); school district leadership (Certificate); teacher leader (Certificate); TESOL (MS Ed). *Accreditation:* NCATE. *Program availability:* Part-time, evening/weekend, 100% online, blended/hybrid learning. *Faculty:* 5 full-time (all women), 23 part-time/adjunct (16 women). *Students:* 95 full-time (78 women), 223 part-time (177 women); includes 31 minority (15 Black or African American, non-Hispanic/Latino; 2 American Indian or Alaska Native, non-Hispanic/Latino; 4 Asian, non-Hispanic/Latino; 9 Hispanic/Latino; 1 Two or more races, non-Hispanic/Latino), 1 international. Average age 30. 162 applicants, 89% accepted, 135 enrolled. In 2016, 135 master's, 39 other advanced degrees awarded. *Entrance requirements:* For master's, GRE (if cumulative GPA less than 2.7), transcripts, two letters of recommendation. Additional exam requirements/recommendations for international students: Required—TOEFL (minimum score 550 paper-based, 79 iBT), IELTS (minimum score 6.5), or CAEL (minimum score 70). *Application deadline:* Applications are processed on a rolling basis. Application fee: $25. Electronic applications accepted. Application fee is waived when completed online. *Expenses: Tuition:* Full-time $14,742. *Required fees:* $724. *Financial support:* Career-related internships or fieldwork, Federal Work-Study, scholarships/grants, tuition waivers (partial), and unspecified assistantships available. Support available to part-time students. Financial award application deadline: 4/30; financial award applicants required to submit FAFSA. *Faculty research:* Asperger's disease, autism, private higher education, reading strategies. *Unit head:* Dr. Rosemary K. Murray, Chair/Associate Professor of Graduate Education and Leadership, 716-888-3723, E-mail: murray1@canisius.edu. *Application contact:* Kathleen B. Davis, Vice President of Enrollment Management, 716-888-2500, Fax: 716-888-3195, E-mail: daviskb@canisius.edu.
Website: http://www.canisius.edu/graduate/

Capella University, School of Education, Doctoral Programs in Education, Minneapolis, MN 55402. Offers curriculum and instruction (PhD); educational leadership and management (Ed D); instructional design for online learning (PhD); K-12 studies in education (PhD); leadership for higher education (PhD); leadership in educational administration (PhD); postsecondary and adult education (PhD); professional studies in education (PhD); reading and literacy (Ed D); special education leadership (PhD); training and performance improvement (PhD).

Capella University, School of Education, Master's Programs in Education, Minneapolis, MN 55402. Offers adult education (MS); curriculum and instruction (MS); early childhood education (MS); enrollment management (MS); higher education leadership and management (MS); instructional design for online learning (MS); integrative studies (MS); K-12 studies in education (MS); leadership in educational administration (MS); reading and literacy (MS); special education teaching (MS).

Caribbean University, Graduate School, Bayamón, PR 00960-0493. Offers administration and supervision (MA Ed); criminal justice (MA); curriculum and instruction (MA Ed, PhD), including elementary education (MA Ed), English education (MA Ed), history education (MA Ed), mathematics education (MA Ed), primary education (MA Ed), science education (MA Ed), Spanish education (MA Ed); educational technology in instructional systems (MA Ed); gerontology (MSN); human resources (MBA); museology, archiving and art history (MA Ed); neonatal pediatrics (MSN); physical education (MA Ed); special education (MA Ed). *Entrance requirements:* For master's, interview, minimum GPA of 2.5.

Carroll University, Graduate Programs in Education, Waukesha, WI 53186-5593. Offers adult and continuing education (M Ed); educational leadership (MS); pk-12 (M Ed). *Program availability:* Part-time, evening/weekend. *Faculty:* 7 full-time (5 women), 14 part-time/adjunct (all women). *Students:* 11 full-time (10 women), 163 part-time (125 women); includes 11 minority (3 Black or African American, non-Hispanic/Latino; 3 American Indian or Alaska Native, non-Hispanic/Latino; 2 Asian, non-Hispanic/Latino; 3 Hispanic/Latino), 1 international. Average age 34. 96 applicants, 38% accepted, 18 enrolled. In 2016, 43 master's awarded. *Degree requirements:* For master's, thesis. *Entrance requirements:* For master's, minimum undergraduate GPA of 2.5 in related field. Additional exam requirements/recommendations for international students: Required—TOEFL. *Application deadline:* For fall admission, 8/15 priority date for domestic students. Applications are processed on a rolling basis. Application fee: $0. Electronic applications accepted. *Expenses: Tuition:* Full-time $10,548; part-time $586 per credit. *Required fees:* $520 per semester. Tuition and fees vary according to course load, degree level and program. *Financial support:* Available to part-time students. Application deadline: 3/15; applicants required to submit FAFSA. *Faculty research:* Qualitative research methods, whole language approaches to teaching, the writing process, multicultural education, gifted/talented learners. *Unit head:* Dr. Kathrine Kramer, Director of Graduate Studies, 262-650-4917, E-mail: kkramer@carrollu.edu. *Application contact:* Lori Aliota, Graduate Admission Counselor, 262-524-7226, E-mail: laliota@carrollu.edu.
Website: http://www.carrollu.edu/gradprograms/education/default.asp

Carson-Newman University, Graduate Program in Education, Jefferson City, TN 37760. Offers curriculum and instruction (M Ed); educational leadership (M Ed); elementary education (MAT); school counseling (MS); secondary education (MAT); teaching English as a second language (MATESL). *Accreditation:* NCATE. *Program availability:* Part-time, evening/weekend, 100% online, blended/hybrid learning. *Degree requirements:* For master's, thesis or alternative. *Entrance requirements:* For master's, PRAXIS II or GRE with minimum score of 290 on the verbal and quantitative components (for MAT), minimum GPA of 3.0 in major, 2.5 overall. Additional exam requirements/recommendations for international students: Recommended—TOEFL (minimum score 79 iBT), IELTS (minimum score 6.5), TSE (minimum score 53). *Expenses: Tuition:* Full-time $10,142; part-time $461 per credit hour. *Required fees:* $300; $150 per semester. One-time fee: $150.

Catawba College, Department of Teacher Education, Salisbury, NC 28144-2488. Offers elementary education (M Ed); STEM education (M Ed). *Accreditation:* NCATE. *Program availability:* Part-time-only. *Faculty:* 4 full-time (3 women), 1 part-time/adjunct (0 women). *Students:* 9 part-time (all women). Average age 30. 9 applicants, 100% accepted, 9 enrolled. In 2016, 3 master's awarded. *Degree requirements:* For master's, portfolio. *Entrance requirements:* For master's, NTE, PRAXIS II, minimum undergraduate GPA of 3.0, valid teaching license, official transcripts, 3 references, essay, interview, practicing teacher. *Application deadline:* For spring admission, 10/1 for domestic students. Applications are processed on a rolling basis. Application fee: $25. Electronic applications accepted. *Expenses:* $185 per semester hour; $25 per semester parking fee. *Financial support:* In 2016–17, 9 students received support. Scholarships/grants and free tuition (for Rowan-Salisbury teachers only) available. Financial award application deadline: 10/1. *Unit head:* Dr. Kimberly Creamer, Director, Graduate Program, 704-637-4462, Fax: 704-637-4732, E-mail: kcreamer14@catawba.edu. *Application contact:* Jane V. Snider, Administrative Assistant, 704-637-4461, Fax: 704-637-4732, E-mail: jvsnider@catawba.edu.
Website: http://catawba.edu/academics/schools/education/teacher-education/

Centenary College of Louisiana, Graduate Programs, Department of Education, Shreveport, LA 71104. Offers elementary education (MAT); secondary education (MAT). *Program availability:* Part-time, evening/weekend. *Faculty:* 2 full-time (1 woman), 3 part-time/adjunct (all women). *Students:* 1 (woman) full-time, 47 part-time (30 women). In 2016, 25 master's awarded. *Degree requirements:* For master's, comprehensive exam. *Entrance requirements:* For master's, PRAXIS I and II (for MAT), undergraduate degree, minimum GPA of 2.5. *Application deadline:* For fall admission, 7/1 for domestic and international students; for spring admission, 11/1 for domestic and international students; for summer admission, 4/1 for domestic and international students. Application fee: $50. *Expenses:* Contact institution. *Financial support:* Unspecified assistantships available. *Faculty research:* Teachers as advocates for teachers, portfolio assessment, disabled readers. *Unit head:* Dr. Dominic Salinas, Director, 318-869-5225, Fax: 318-869-5795, E-mail: dsalinas@centenary.edu. *Application contact:* Lori Payne, Administrative Assistant, 318-869-5223, Fax: 318-869-5795, E-mail: lpayne@centenary.edu.

Central Connecticut State University, School of Graduate Studies, School of Education and Professional Studies, Department of Literacy, Elementary, and Early Childhood Education, New Britain, CT 06050-4010. Offers MS, AC, Sixth Year Certificate. *Program availability:* Part-time, evening/weekend. *Faculty:* 5 full-time (3 women), 2 part-time/adjunct (both women). *Students:* 11 full-time (8 women), 120 part-time (114 women); includes 9 minority (2 Black or African American, non-Hispanic/Latino; 5 Hispanic/Latino; 2 Two or more races, non-Hispanic/Latino), 1 international. Average age 30. 47 applicants, 81% accepted, 25 enrolled. In 2016, 44 master's, 11 other advanced degrees awarded. *Degree requirements:* For master's, comprehensive exam, thesis or alternative; for other advanced degree, qualifying exam. *Entrance requirements:* For master's, minimum undergraduate GPA of 2.7, teacher certification, interview, essay, letters of recommendation; for other advanced degree, master's degree, essay, teacher certification, interview, letters of recommendation. Additional exam requirements/recommendations for international students: Required—TOEFL (minimum score 550 paper-based; 79 iBT). *Application deadline:* For fall admission, 5/1 for domestic and international students; for spring admission, 11/1 for domestic and international students. Applications are processed on a rolling basis. Application fee: $50. Electronic applications accepted. *Expenses: Tuition, area resident:* Full-time $6497; part-time $606 per credit. Tuition, state resident: full-time $9748; part-time $622 per credit. Tuition, nonresident: full-time $18,102; part-time $622 per credit. *Required fees:* $4459; $246 per credit. *Financial support:* In 2016–17, 4 students received support. Career-related internships or fieldwork, Federal Work-Study, and scholarships/grants available. Support available to part-time students. Financial award application deadline: 3/1. *Faculty research:* Developmental, clinical, and administrative aspects of reading and language arts instruction. *Unit head:* Dr. Helen Abadiano, Chair, 860-832-2175, E-mail: abadiano@ccsu.edu. *Application contact:* Patricia Gardner, Associate Director of Graduate Studies, 860-832-2350, Fax: 860-832-2362.
Website: http://www.ccsu.edu/leece/index.html

Central Michigan University, Central Michigan University Global Campus, Program in Educational Leadership, Mount Pleasant, MI 48859. Offers K-12 leadership (Ed D). *Program availability:* Part-time, evening/weekend. *Faculty:* 14 full-time (5 women), 17 part-time/adjunct (7 women). *Students:* 43 (27 women); includes 13 minority (11 Black or African American, non-Hispanic/Latino; 2 Two or more races, non-Hispanic/Latino). Average age 43. In 2016, 3 doctorates awarded. *Entrance requirements:* Additional exam requirements/recommendations for international students: Required—TOEFL. *Application deadline:* Applications are processed on a rolling basis. Application fee: $50. Electronic applications accepted. *Financial support:* Scholarships/grants available. Support available to part-time students. *Unit head:* Patrick Graham, Coordinator, New Program and Cohort Enrollment Support, 989-774-1661, E-mail: graha1pm@cmich.edu. *Application contact:* 877-268-4636, E-mail: cmuglobal@cmich.edu.

Central Michigan University, College of Graduate Studies, College of Education and Human Services, Department of Teacher Education and Professional Development, Mount Pleasant, MI 48859. Offers educational technology (MA, Graduate Certificate); elementary education (MA), including classroom teaching, early childhood; reading and literacy K-12 (MA); secondary education (MA). *Program availability:* Part-time, evening/weekend. *Degree requirements:* For master's, thesis or alternative. Electronic applications accepted. *Faculty research:* Integrating literacy across the curriculum, science teaching and aesthetic learning in science, diversity education, educational technology, educational psychology and child development.

Chadron State College, School of Professional and Graduate Studies, Department of Education, Chadron, NE 69337. Offers business (MA Ed); community counseling (MA Ed); educational administration (MS Ed, Sp Ed); elementary education (MS Ed); history (MA Ed); language and literature (MA Ed); secondary administration (MS Ed); secondary education (MS Ed). *Accreditation:* NCATE. *Program availability:* Part-time, evening/weekend, online learning. *Degree requirements:* For master's, thesis optional. *Entrance requirements:* For master's, GRE General Test, GRE Writing Test, minimum GPA of 2.75 or 12 graduate hours at CSC with minimum GPA of 3.25. Additional exam requirements/recommendations for international students: Required—TOEFL. Electronic applications accepted. *Faculty research:* Rural education, technology, mental health.

Chaminade University of Honolulu, Office of Professional and Continuing Education, Program in Education, Honolulu, HI 96816-1578. Offers child development (M Ed); early childhood education (MAT); educational leadership (M Ed); elementary education (MAT); instructional leadership (M Ed); Montessori (M Ed); secondary education (MAT); special education (MAT). *Program availability:* Part-time, evening/weekend, 100% online, blended/hybrid learning. *Faculty:* 7 full-time (4 women), 8 part-time/adjunct (6 women). *Students:* 98 full-time (80 women), 82 part-time (62 women); includes 110 minority (6 Black or African American, non-Hispanic/Latino; 2 American Indian or Alaska Native, non-Hispanic/Latino; 51 Asian, non-Hispanic/Latino; 9 Hispanic/Latino; 41

Native Hawaiian or other Pacific Islander, non-Hispanic/Latino; 1 Two or more races, non-Hispanic/Latino), 1 international. Average age 35. 38 applicants, 100% accepted, 29 enrolled. In 2016, 79 master's awarded. *Degree requirements:* For master's, thesis or alternative. *Entrance requirements:* For master's, PRAXIS (for MAT), minimum GPA of 2.75 (for M Ed), 3.0 (for MAT); 2 letters of recommendation, resume, writing sample (for MAT). Additional exam requirements/recommendations for international students: Required—TOEFL (minimum score 550 paper-based; 79 iBT). *Application deadline:* Applications are processed on a rolling basis. Application fee: $40. Electronic applications accepted. *Expenses:* $740 per credit hour plus $93 fee per online course. *Financial support:* Applicants required to submit FAFSA. *Unit head:* Dr. Dale Fryxell, Interim Dean, 808-739-4684, Fax: 808-739-4607, E-mail: edu-advising@chaminade.edu. *Application contact:* 808-735-4755, E-mail: gradserv@chaminade.edu.
Website: http://www.chaminade.edu/education

Chapman University, College of Educational Studies, Orange, CA 92866. Offers counseling (MA), including school counseling (MA, Credential); education (PhD), including cultural and curricular studies, disability studies, leadership studies, school psychology (PhD, Credential); educational psychology (MA); leadership development (MA); multiple subjects (Credential), including Spanish/English bilingual; pupil personnel services (Credential), including school counseling (MA, Credential), school psychology (PhD, Credential); school psychology (Ed S); single subject (Credential); special education (MA, Credential), including mild/moderate (Credential), moderate/severe (Credential); teaching (MA), including elementary education, secondary education, secondary music education. *Accreditation:* TEAC. *Program availability:* Part-time, evening/weekend. *Faculty:* 29 full-time (14 women), 36 part-time/adjunct (28 women). *Students:* 186 full-time (148 women), 186 part-time (134 women); includes 144 minority (9 Black or African American, non-Hispanic/Latino; 39 Asian, non-Hispanic/Latino; 78 Hispanic/Latino; 2 Native Hawaiian or other Pacific Islander, non-Hispanic/Latino; 16 Two or more races, non-Hispanic/Latino), 8 international. Average age 29. 143 applicants, 63% accepted, 64 enrolled. In 2016, 111 master's, 24 doctorates awarded. *Degree requirements:* For doctorate, thesis/dissertation. *Entrance requirements:* Additional exam requirements/recommendations for international students: Required—TOEFL (minimum score 550 paper-based, 80 iBT), IELTS (6.5), PTE Academic (53), or CAE. *Application deadline:* Applications are processed on a rolling basis. Application fee: $60. Electronic applications accepted. *Expenses:* Contact institution. *Financial support:* Fellowships and scholarships/grants available. Financial award application deadline: 3/2; financial award applicants required to submit FAFSA. *Unit head:* Dr. Margaret Grogan, Dean, 714-516-5968, E-mail: grogan@chapman.edu. *Application contact:* Sara Simon, Graduate Admission Counselor, 714-997-6770, E-mail: simon@chapman.edu.
Website: http://www.chapman.edu/CES/

Charleston Southern University, School of Education, Charleston, SC 29423-8087. Offers elementary administration and supervision (M Ed); elementary education (M Ed); secondary administration and supervision (M Ed). *Accreditation:* NCATE. *Program availability:* Part-time, evening/weekend. *Degree requirements:* For master's, thesis optional. *Entrance requirements:* For master's, GRE or MAT. Additional exam requirements/recommendations for international students: Required—TOEFL (minimum score 550 paper-based; 79 iBT). *Application deadline:* Applications are processed on a rolling basis. Application fee: $40. *Expenses:* Contact institution. *Financial support:* Research assistantships with full tuition reimbursements, career-related internships or fieldwork, and Federal Work-Study available. Financial award application deadline: 4/15; financial award applicants required to submit FAFSA. *Unit head:* Dr. Melanie G. Reynolds-Murphy, Interim Dean, 843-863-7765, Fax: 843-863-7784, E-mail: mmurphy@csuniv.edu. *Application contact:* Dr. Melanie G. Reynolds-Murphy, Interim Dean, 843-863-7765, Fax: 843-863-7784, E-mail: mmurphy@csuniv.edu.
Website: http://www.csuniv.edu/education/

Chatham University, Program in Education, Pittsburgh, PA 15232-2826. Offers early childhood education (MAT); elementary education (MAT); environmental education (K-12) (MAT); secondary art (MAT); secondary biology education (MAT); secondary chemistry education (MAT); secondary English education (MAT); secondary math education (MAT); secondary physics education (MAT); secondary social studies education (MAT); special education (MAT). *Degree requirements:* For master's, thesis, teaching experience. *Entrance requirements:* For master's, minimum GPA of 3.0, sample of written work, recommendation letters. Additional exam requirements/recommendations for international students: Required—TOEFL (minimum score 600 paper-based; 100 iBT), IELTS (minimum score 7), TWE. Electronic applications accepted. Application fee is waived when completed online. *Expenses: Tuition:* Full-time $16,254; part-time $903 per credit hour. *Required fees:* $468; $26 per credit hour. *Faculty research:* Gifted education, environmental education, technology in education, writing as learning, class size and achievement.

Chestnut Hill College, School of Graduate Studies, Department of Education, Program in Elementary/Middle Education, Philadelphia, PA 19118-2693. Offers M Ed. *Program availability:* Part-time, evening/weekend. *Degree requirements:* For master's, thesis optional. *Entrance requirements:* For master's, PRAXIS I or proof of teaching certification, letters of recommendation, writing sample, 6 graduate credits with minimum B grade if undergraduate GPA less than 3.0. Additional exam requirements/recommendations for international students: Required—TOEFL (minimum score 500 paper-based), IELTS (minimum score 6.0), or TWE (minimum score 22). Electronic applications accepted. *Expenses:* Contact institution. *Faculty research:* Inclusive education, cultural issues in education.

Cheyney University of Pennsylvania, Graduate Programs, Program in Elementary Education, Cheyney, PA 19319. Offers M Ed. *Program availability:* Part-time, evening/weekend. *Degree requirements:* For master's, thesis. *Entrance requirements:* For master's, GRE General Test, MAT, minimum GPA of 2.75. Electronic applications accepted.

Chicago State University, School of Graduate and Professional Studies, College of Education, Department of Reading, Elementary Education, Library Information and Media Studies, Program in Elementary Education, Chicago, IL 60628. Offers MAT. *Accreditation:* NCATE. *Degree requirements:* For master's, comprehensive exam, thesis optional. *Entrance requirements:* For master's, minimum GPA of 3.0 in last 60 hours.

City University of Seattle, Graduate Division, Albright School of Education, Seattle, WA 98121. Offers administrator certification (Certificate); curriculum and instruction (M Ed); elementary education (MIT); guidance and counseling (M Ed); leadership (M Ed); reading and literacy (M Ed); school counseling (M Ed); special education (MIT); superintendent certification (Certificate). *Program availability:* Part-time, evening/weekend, online learning. *Degree requirements:* For master's, comprehensive exam (for some programs), thesis (for some programs). *Entrance requirements:* For master's, baccalaureate degree or equivalent from an accredited or otherwise recognized institution. Additional exam requirements/recommendations for international students: Required—TOEFL (minimum score 567 paper-based; 87 iBT); Recommended—IELTS. Electronic applications accepted. *Expenses:* Contact institution.

College of Charleston, Graduate School, School of Education, Health, and Human Performance, Department of Elementary and Early Childhood Education, Program in Elementary Education, Charleston, SC 29424-0001. Offers MAT. *Accreditation:* NCATE. *Program availability:* Part-time, evening/weekend. *Degree requirements:* For master's, thesis or alternative, written qualifying exam, student teaching experience. *Entrance requirements:* For master's, GRE, 2 letters of recommendation. Additional exam requirements/recommendations for international students: Required—TOEFL (minimum score 81 iBT). *Application deadline:* For fall admission, 4/1 for domestic students; for spring admission, 11/1 for domestic students. Applications are processed on a rolling basis. Application fee: $45. Electronic applications accepted. *Financial support:* Research assistantships, teaching assistantships, Federal Work-Study, scholarships/grants, and unspecified assistantships available. Support available to part-time students. Financial award application deadline: 4/1; financial award applicants required to submit FAFSA. *Unit head:* Dr. Angela Cozart, Director, 843-953-6353, Fax: 843-953-5407, E-mail: cozarta@cofc.edu. *Application contact:* Susan Hallatt, Director of Graduate Admissions, 843-953-5614, Fax: 843-953-1434, E-mail: hallatts@cofc.edu.

The College of New Jersey, Office of Graduate and Advancing Education, School of Education, Department of Elementary and Early Childhood Education, Program in Elementary Education, Ewing, NJ 08628. Offers M Ed, MAT. *Accreditation:* NCATE. *Program availability:* Part-time. *Degree requirements:* For master's, comprehensive exam. *Entrance requirements:* For master's, GRE General Test, minimum GPA of 3.0 in field or 2.75 overall. Additional exam requirements/recommendations for international students: Required—TOEFL. Electronic applications accepted.

The College of New Rochelle, Graduate School, Division of Education, Program in Childhood Education/Early Childhood Education, New Rochelle, NY 10805-2308. Offers childhood education (MS Ed); early childhood education (MS Ed). *Program availability:* Part-time. *Degree requirements:* For master's, comprehensive exam (for some programs), thesis (for some programs), practicum. *Entrance requirements:* For master's, interview, minimum GPA of 3.0 in field, 2.7 overall.

College of St. Joseph, Graduate Programs, Division of Education, Program in Elementary Education, Rutland, VT 05701-3899. Offers M Ed. *Program availability:* Part-time, evening/weekend. *Degree requirements:* For master's, comprehensive exam. *Entrance requirements:* For master's, PRAXIS I (for initial licensure), official college transcripts; 2 letters of reference; minimum GPA of 3.0 (initial licensure) or 2.7 (nonlicensure); interview. Additional exam requirements/recommendations for international students: Required—TOEFL (minimum score 550 paper-based). *Application deadline:* Applications are processed on a rolling basis. Application fee: $35. Electronic applications accepted. *Expenses: Tuition:* Full-time $13,800; part-time $560 per credit. *Required fees:* $75 per semester. Full-time tuition and fees vary according to course load. *Financial support:* Career-related internships or fieldwork, Federal Work-Study, and unspecified assistantships available. Support available to part-time students. Financial award application deadline: 3/1. *Unit head:* Dr. Maria Bove, Chair, 802-773-5900 Ext. 3243, Fax: 802-776-5258, E-mail: mbove@csj.edu. *Application contact:* Alan Young, Dean of Admissions, 802-773-5900 Ext. 3227, Fax: 802-776-5310, E-mail: alanyoung@csj.edu.

College of Staten Island of the City University of New York, Graduate Programs, School of Education, Program in Childhood Education, Staten Island, NY 10314-6600. Offers learning and development (MS Ed); literacy education (MS Ed); mathematics education (MS Ed); music education (MS Ed); science education (MS Ed); social foundations of education (MS Ed); social studies education (MS Ed). *Program availability:* Part-time, evening/weekend. *Faculty:* 2 full-time, 11 part-time/adjunct. *Students:* 16 full-time, 53 part-time. Average age 30. 40 applicants, 53% accepted, 13 enrolled. In 2016, 20 master's awarded. *Degree requirements:* For master's, educational research project; ten courses and a minimum of 32-38 credits in five required areas of study or minimum of 45-49 credits in six required core courses before selecting from array of advanced courses. *Entrance requirements:* For master's, GRE General Test or an approved equivalent examination, relevant bachelor's degree, letters of recommendation, one- or two-page personal statement. Additional exam requirements/recommendations for international students: Required—TOEFL (minimum score 550 paper-based; 79 iBT), IELTS (minimum score 6.5). *Application deadline:* For fall admission, 4/25 for domestic and international students; for spring admission, 11/25 for domestic and international students. Applications are processed on a rolling basis. Application fee: $125. Electronic applications accepted. *Expenses:* Tuition, state resident: full-time $10,130; part-time $425 per credit. Tuition, nonresident: full-time $18,720; part-time $780 per credit. *Required fees:* $181.10 per semester. Tuition and fees vary according to program. *Faculty research:* Preservice teacher preparation, music integration, music education through children's songs, literacy, emergent bilingual. *Unit head:* Dr. Vivian Shulman, Graduate Faculty Advisor, 718-982-4086, E-mail: vivian.shulman@csi.cuny.edu. *Application contact:* Sasha Spence, Associate Director for Graduate Admissions, 718-982-2019, Fax: 718-982-2500, E-mail: sasha.spence@csi.cuny.edu.
Website: http://www.csi.cuny.edu/admissions/grad/pdf/Education%20Fact%20Sheet.pdf

The College of William and Mary, School of Education, Program in Curriculum and Instruction, Williamsburg, VA 23187-8795. Offers elementary education (MA Ed); gifted education (MA Ed); literacy leadership (MA Ed); math specialist (MA Ed); secondary education (MA Ed), including English, foreign language, math, science, social studies; special education (MA Ed). *Accreditation:* NCATE. *Program availability:* Part-time. *Faculty:* 30 full-time (21 women), 48 part-time/adjunct (38 women). *Students:* 60 full-time (47 women), 14 part-time (all women); includes 13 minority (1 Black or African American, non-Hispanic/Latino; 1 American Indian or Alaska Native, non-Hispanic/Latino; 2 Asian, non-Hispanic/Latino; 7 Hispanic/Latino; 2 Two or more races, non-Hispanic/Latino). Average age 26. 134 applicants, 79% accepted, 66 enrolled. In 2016, 77 master's awarded. *Degree requirements:* For master's, project. *Entrance requirements:* For master's, GRE, MAT, PRAXIS Core Academic Skills for Educators, minimum GPA of 2.5. Additional exam requirements/recommendations for international students. Required—TOEFL (minimum score 100 iBT), IELTS (minimum score 7). *Application deadline:* For fall admission, 1/15 for domestic and international students; for spring admission, 10/1 for domestic and international students. Application fee: $50. Electronic applications accepted. *Expenses:* $14,258 per year in-state full-time, $275 per credit in-state part-time; $30,500 per year out-of-state full-time, $1,200 per credit out-of-state part-time. *Financial support:* In 2016–17, 30 students received support, including 3 research assistantships (averaging $14,259 per year); scholarships/grants and unspecified assistantships also available. Financial award application deadline: 1/15; financial award applicants required to submit FAFSA. *Faculty research:* Educational technology, professional development and evaluation, inclusive education, rural education, education policy. *Unit head:* Dr. Jeremy D. Stoddard, Department Chair, 757-221-2348, E-mail: jdstod@wm.edu. *Application contact:* Dorothy Smith Osborne, Assistant Dean for Academic Programs and Student Services, 757-221-2317, E-mail: dsosbo@wm.edu.
Website: http://education.wm.edu

Colorado Christian University, Program in Curriculum and Instruction, Lakewood, CO 80226. Offers corporate education (MACI); early childhood educator (MACI); elementary educator (MACI); instructional technology (MACI); master educator (MACI); online course developer (MACI); online teaching and learning (MACI); special education generalist (MACI). *Program availability:* Part-time, evening/weekend. *Degree requirements:* For master's, thesis optional, practicum. *Entrance requirements:* For master's, interviews, letters of recommendation. Additional exam requirements/recommendations for international students: Required—TOEFL. Electronic applications accepted. *Expenses:* Contact institution.

The Colorado College, Education Department, Program in Elementary Education, Colorado Springs, CO 80903-3294. Offers elementary school teaching (MAT). *Degree requirements:* For master's, thesis, internship. Electronic applications accepted.

Columbia College, Graduate Programs, Education Division, Columbia, SC 29203-5998. Offers divergent learning (M Ed); higher education administration (M Ed). *Accreditation:* NCATE. *Program availability:* Part-time, evening/weekend, online learning. *Degree requirements:* For master's, thesis. *Entrance requirements:* For master's, GRE General Test, MAT, 2 recommendations, current South Carolina teaching certificate, minimum GPA of 3.2. Electronic applications accepted. *Expenses:* Contact institution.

Columbia International University, Columbia Graduate School, Columbia, SC 29230-3122. Offers Bible teaching (MABT); counseling (MACN); early childhood and elementary education (MAT); educational administration (M Ed); educational leadership (PhD); instruction and learning (M Ed); teaching English as a foreign language (Certificate); teaching English as a foreign language and intercultural studies (MATF). *Program availability:* Part-time, evening/weekend, online learning. *Degree requirements:* For master's, internships, professional project. *Entrance requirements:* For master's, MAT; GRE (for some programs), minimum GPA of 2.7. Additional exam requirements/recommendations for international students: Required—TOEFL. Electronic applications accepted.

Concordia University, College of Education, Portland, OR 97211-6099. Offers career and technical education (M Ed); curriculum and instruction (M Ed), including adolescent literacy, career and technical education, e-learning/technology education, early childhood education, English for speakers of other languages, English language development, environmental education, mathematics, methods and curriculum, reading, science, teacher leadership, the inclusive classroom; early childhood (MAT); education leadership (Ed D); educational administration (M Ed); elementary education (MAT); secondary education (MAT); special education (M Ed); teacher leadership (Ed D). *Program availability:* Part-time, online learning. *Degree requirements:* For master's, comprehensive exam, work samples/portfolio. *Entrance requirements:* For master's, California Basic Educational Skills Test or PRAXIS I, minimum undergraduate GPA of 2.8, graduate 3.0; 2 letters of recommendation. Additional exam requirements/recommendations for international students: Required—TOEFL (minimum score 525 paper-based). Electronic applications accepted. *Faculty research:* Learner-centered classroom, brain-based learning, future of online learning.

Concordia University Chicago, College of Education, Program in Teaching, River Forest, IL 60305-1499. Offers early childhood education (MAT); elementary education (MAT); secondary education (MAT). *Degree requirements:* For master's, thesis or alternative. *Entrance requirements:* For master's, minimum GPA of 2.9. Additional exam requirements/recommendations for international students: Required—TOEFL (minimum score 550 paper-based). Electronic applications accepted.

Concordia University, Nebraska, Graduate Programs in Education, Program in Educational Administration, Seward, NE 68434-1556. Offers elementary and secondary education (M Ed); elementary education (M Ed); secondary education (M Ed). *Accreditation:* NCATE. *Program availability:* Part-time. *Degree requirements:* For master's, thesis or alternative. *Entrance requirements:* For master's, GRE, MAT, or NTE, BS in education or equivalent, minimum GPA of 3.0.

Converse College, School of Education and Graduate Studies, Program in Elementary Education, Spartanburg, SC 29302. Offers M Ed, MAT. *Program availability:* Part-time. *Degree requirements:* For master's, capstone paper. *Entrance requirements:* For master's, NTE or PRAXIS II (M Ed), minimum GPA of 2.75, 2 recommendations. *Application deadline:* For fall admission, 8/1 for domestic and international students; for winter admission, 11/15 for domestic and international students; for spring admission, 1/15 for domestic and international students. Applications are processed on a rolling basis. Application fee: $40. Electronic applications accepted. *Expenses: Tuition:* Full-time $3600; part-time $400 per credit hour. *Required fees:* $70 per term. *Financial support:* Available to part-time students. Applicants required to submit FAFSA. *Unit head:* Dr. Kelly Harrison-Maguire, Director of Elementary Education Programs, 864-596-9081, E-mail: kelly.harrison-maguire@converse.edu. *Application contact:* 864-596-9404, E-mail: graduate@converse.edu.

Creighton University, Graduate School, College of Arts and Sciences, Department of Education, Program in Teaching, Omaha, NE 68178-0001. Offers elementary teaching (M Ed); secondary teaching (M Ed). *Program availability:* Part-time, evening/weekend. *Faculty:* 10 full-time (5 women). *Students:* 14 full-time (11 women), 17 part-time (11 women); includes 4 minority (3 Black or African American, non-Hispanic/Latino; 1 Two or more races, non-Hispanic/Latino). Average age 26. In 2016, 18 master's awarded. *Degree requirements:* For master's, portfolio. *Entrance requirements:* For master's, 3 letters of recommendation, 2 writing samples. Additional exam requirements/recommendations for international students: Required—TOEFL (minimum score 90 iBT). *Application deadline:* For fall admission, 7/1 priority date for domestic students, 3/1 priority date for international students; for winter admission, 12/1 priority date for domestic students, 6/1 priority date for international students; for spring admission, 3/1 priority date for domestic and international students; for summer admission, 3/1 for domestic and international students. Application fee: $50. Electronic applications accepted. *Expenses: Tuition:* Full-time $14,400; part-time $800 per credit hour. *Required fees:* $158 per semester. Tuition and fees vary according to course load, campus/location, program, reciprocity agreements and student's religious affiliation. *Financial support:* Scholarships/grants and tuition waivers (partial) available. Support available to part-time students. Financial award applicants required to submit FAFSA. *Unit head:* Dr. Debra Ponec, Director, 402-280-2557, E-mail: dlponec@creighton.edu. *Application contact:* Lindsay Johnson, Director of Graduate and Adult Recruitment, 402-280-2703, Fax: 402-280-2423, E-mail: gradschool@creighton.edu.

Curry College, Graduate Studies, Program in Education, Milton, MA 02186-9984. Offers elementary education (M Ed); foundations (non-license) (M Ed); reading (M Ed, Certificate); special education (M Ed). *Program availability:* Part-time, evening/weekend. *Degree requirements:* For master's, project or thesis. *Entrance requirements:* For master's, interview, recommendations, resume, written statement. Additional exam requirements/recommendations for international students: Required—TOEFL (minimum score 550 paper-based; 80 iBT). *Expenses:* Contact institution. *Faculty research:* Classroom trauma, therapeutic writing, inclusionary practices.

Dallas Baptist University, Dorothy M. Bush College of Education, Teaching Program, Dallas, TX 75211-9299. Offers distance learning (MAT); early childhood through grade 6 certification (MAT); early childhood-12 (MAT); elementary (MAT); English as a second language (MAT); Montessori (MAT); multisensory (MAT); secondary (MAT). *Program availability:* Part-time, evening/weekend, 100% online, blended/hybrid learning. *Application deadline:* Applications are processed on a rolling basis. Application fee: $25. Electronic applications accepted. Application fee is waived when completed online. *Expenses: Tuition:* Full-time $15,408; part-time $856 per credit hour. *Required fees:* $400 per semester. Tuition and fees vary according to course load and degree level. *Unit head:* Dr. Carolyn Spain, Director, 214-333-5217, E-mail: carolyns@dbu.edu. *Application contact:* Bobby Soto, Director of Admissions, 214-333-5242, E-mail: graduate@dbu.edu.
Website: http://www3.dbu.edu/graduate/mat.asp

Delta State University, Graduate Programs, College of Education, Division of Teacher Education, Leadership, and Research, Program in Professional Studies, Cleveland, MS 38733-0001. Offers counselor education (Ed D); elementary education (Ed D); higher education (Ed D). *Program availability:* Part-time, evening/weekend. *Degree requirements:* For doctorate, thesis/dissertation. *Entrance requirements:* For doctorate, GRE General Test.

Delta State University, Graduate Programs, College of Education, Division of Teacher Education, Leadership, and Research, Programs in Elementary Education, Cleveland, MS 38733-0001. Offers M Ed, MAT, Ed S. *Accreditation:* NCATE. *Program availability:* Part-time, evening/weekend. *Degree requirements:* For master's, thesis optional. *Entrance requirements:* For master's, GRE General Test; for Ed S, master's degree, teaching certificate.

DePaul University, College of Education, Chicago, IL 60614. Offers bilingual bicultural education (M Ed, MA); counseling (M Ed, MA), including clinical mental health counseling, college student development, school counseling; curriculum studies (M Ed, MA, Ed D); early childhood education (M Ed, MA, Ed D); educating adults (MA); educational leadership (M Ed, MA, Ed D), including administration and supervision (M Ed, MA), principal preparation (M Ed, MA); elementary education (MA); mathematics education (MA); mathematics for teaching (MS); middle school mathematics education (MS); reading specialist (M Ed, MA); secondary education (M Ed); social and cultural foundations in education (MA); special education (M Ed, MA); world languages education (M Ed, MA). *Program availability:* Part-time, evening/weekend, online learning. *Degree requirements:* For doctorate, thesis/dissertation. Electronic applications accepted.

Dominican College, Division of Teacher Education, Orangeburg, NY 10962-1210. Offers education/teaching of individuals with multiple disabilities (MS Ed). *Program availability:* Part-time, evening/weekend, online learning. *Faculty:* 6 full-time (4 women), 4 part-time/adjunct (all women). *Students:* 3 full-time (all women), 53 part-time (41 women); includes 13 minority (3 Black or African American, non-Hispanic/Latino; 10 Hispanic/Latino). In 2016, 28 master's awarded. *Degree requirements:* For master's, comprehensive exam (for some programs), thesis. *Entrance requirements:* For master's, 3 letters of recommendation (written by former or current work supervisors or instructors), interview. Additional exam requirements/recommendations for international students: Required—TOEFL (minimum score 90 iBT). *Application deadline:* Applications are processed on a rolling basis. *Expenses: Tuition:* Part-time $900 per credit. One-time fee: $200 full-time. *Financial support:* Application deadline: 2/1; applicants required to submit FAFSA. *Unit head:* Dr. Mike Kelly, Director, 845-848-4090, Fax: 845-359-7802, E-mail: mike.kelly@dc.edu. *Application contact:* Christina Lifshey, Assistant Director of Graduate Admissions, 845-848-7908 Ext. 15, Fax: 845-365-3150, E-mail: admissions@dc.edu.

Dominican University, School of Education, River Forest, IL 60305-1099. Offers early childhood education (MS); education (MAT); elementary education (MA Ed); English as a second language (MA Ed); reading (MA Ed); special education (MS). *Accreditation:* NCATE. *Program availability:* Part-time, evening/weekend, 100% online, blended/hybrid learning. *Faculty:* 12 full-time (8 women), 64 part-time/adjunct (57 women). *Students:* 13 full-time (all women), 500 part-time (385 women); includes 88 minority (40 Black or African American, non-Hispanic/Latino; 3 American Indian or Alaska Native, non-Hispanic/Latino; 18 Asian, non-Hispanic/Latino; 11 Hispanic/Latino; 2 Native Hawaiian or other Pacific Islander, non-Hispanic/Latino; 14 Two or more races, non-Hispanic/Latino), 1 international. Average age 32. 162 applicants, 96% accepted, 104 enrolled. In 2016, 200 master's awarded. *Entrance requirements:* For master's, Illinois Test of Basic Skills. Additional exam requirements/recommendations for international students: Required—TOEFL (minimum score 550 paper-based; 79 iBT). *Application deadline:* Applications are processed on a rolling basis. Application fee: $25. *Expenses:* $550 per credit hour. *Financial support:* Career-related internships or fieldwork, scholarships/grants, tuition waivers (partial), and unspecified assistantships available. Support available to part-time students. Financial award application deadline: 8/15; financial award applicants required to submit FAFSA. *Faculty research:* Governance of private education institutions, reading and language arts, inclusion, organizational planning, leadership and vision. *Unit head:* Dr. Colleen Reardon, Interim Executive Director, School of Education, 708-524-6643, Fax: 708-524-6665, E-mail: creardon@dom.edu. *Application contact:* Keven Hansen, Coordinator of Recruitment and Admissions, 708-524-6921, Fax: 708-524-6665, E-mail: educate@dom.edu.
Website: http://educate.dom.edu/

Drew University, Caspersen School of Graduate Studies, Madison, NJ 07940-1493. Offers conflict resolution and leadership (Certificate), including community leadership, moderation, peace building; history and culture (MA, PhD), including American history, book history, British history, European history, Holocaust and genocide (M Litt, MA, D Litt, PhD), intellectual history, Irish history, print culture, public history; K-12 education (MAT), including art, biology, chemistry, elementary education, English, French, Italian, math, secondary education, special education, teacher of students with disabilities; liberal studies (M Litt, D Litt), including history, Holocaust and genocide (M Litt, MA, D Litt, PhD), Irish/Irish-American studies, literature (M Litt, MMH, D Litt, DMH, CMH), religion, spirituality, teaching in the two-year college, writing; medical humanities (MMH, DMH, CMH), including arts, health, healthcare, literature (M Litt, MMH, D Litt, DMH, CMH), scientific research; poetry (MFA). *Program availability:* Part-time, evening/weekend. *Faculty:* 4 full-time (2 women), 31 part-time/adjunct (16 women). *Students:* 62 full-time (41 women), 199 part-time (130 women); includes 38 minority (17 Black or African American, non-Hispanic/Latino; 3 Asian, non-Hispanic/Latino; 17 Hispanic/Latino; 1 Two or more races, non-Hispanic/Latino), 3 international. Average age 27. 93 applicants, 81% accepted, 46 enrolled. In 2016, 39 master's, 27 doctorates, 26 other advanced degrees awarded. Terminal master's awarded for partial completion of doctoral program. *Degree requirements:* For master's and other advanced degree, thesis (for some programs); for doctorate, one foreign language, comprehensive exam (for some programs), thesis/dissertation. *Entrance requirements:* For master's, PRAXIS Core and Subject Area tests (for MAT), resume, transcripts, writing sample, personal statement, letters of recommendation; for doctorate, GRE (PhD in history and culture), resume, transcripts, writing sample, personal statement, letters of recommendation. Additional exam requirements/recommendations for international students: Required—TOEFL (minimum score 587 paper-based; 94 iBT), IELTS (minimum score 7), TWE (minimum score 4). *Application deadline:* For fall admission, 8/1 for domestic students, 6/1 for international students; for spring admission, 12/1 for domestic students, 10/1 for international students. Applications are processed on a rolling basis. Application fee: $35. Electronic applications accepted. Tuition and fees vary according to program. *Financial support:* Fellowships, research assistantships, teaching assistantships, career-related internships or fieldwork, Federal Work-Study, scholarships/grants, and unspecified assistantships available. Support available to part-time students. Financial

award applicants required to submit FAFSA. *Application contact:* Leanne Horinko, Director of Caspersen Admissions, 973-408-3280, E-mail: gradm@drew.edu.
Website: http://www.drew.edu/caspersen

Drury University, Master in Education Program, Springfield, MO 5802. Offers curriculum and instruction (M Ed), including elementary, middle school, secondary; gifted education (M Ed); instructional leadership (M Ed); instructional technology (M Ed); integrated learning (M Ed); online teaching (M Ed); special education (M Ed); special reading (M Ed). *Accreditation:* NCATE. *Program availability:* Part-time, evening/weekend, 100% online, blended/hybrid learning. *Students:* 146 full-time (111 women); includes 6 minority (1 Asian, non-Hispanic/Latino; 3 Hispanic/Latino; 2 Two or more races, non-Hispanic/Latino), 1 international. Average age 34. 42 applicants, 74% accepted. In 2016, 74 master's awarded. *Entrance requirements:* For master's, GRE, bachelor's degree with minimum GPA of 2.75. Additional exam requirements/recommendations for international students: Recommended—TOEFL (minimum score 80 iBT), IELTS (minimum score 6.5). *Application deadline:* For fall admission, 8/4 priority date for domestic and international students; for spring admission, 1/5 priority date for domestic and international students; for summer admission, 5/26 priority date for domestic and international students. Applications are processed on a rolling basis. Application fee: $25 ($50 for international students). Electronic applications accepted. *Expenses:* $352 tuition per credit hour; $7 per credit hour technology fee; $100 graduation fee; $59 portfolio fee (one-time). *Financial support:* In 2016–17, 20 students received support. Career-related internships or fieldwork, scholarships/grants, tuition waivers (partial), and unspecified assistantships available. Financial award application deadline: 6/30; financial award applicants required to submit FAFSA. *Faculty research:* Gifted students, instructional technology, autism, diversity and social justice. *Unit head:* Dr. Asikaa Cosgrove, Director, Master in Education, 417-873-7806, E-mail: acosgrov@drury.edu.
Website: http://www.drury.edu/education-masters

Duquesne University, School of Education, Department of Instruction and Leadership, Program in Secondary Education, Pittsburgh, PA 15282-0001. Offers biology (MS Ed); chemistry (MS Ed); English (MS Ed); K-12 education (MS Ed), including Latin; mathematics (MS Ed); physics (MS Ed); social studies (MS Ed). *Program availability:* Part-time, evening/weekend. *Faculty:* 5 full-time (4 women). *Students:* 21 full-time (8 women), 4 part-time (0 women); includes 3 minority (2 Black or African American, non-Hispanic/Latino; 1 Two or more races, non-Hispanic/Latino). Average age 28. 12 applicants, 100% accepted, 7 enrolled. In 2016, 19 master's awarded. *Degree requirements:* For master's, thesis optional. *Entrance requirements:* For master's, letters of recommendation, letter of intent, interview, bachelor's degree. Additional exam requirements/recommendations for international students: Required—TOEFL (minimum score 550 paper-based), IELTS (minimum score 7). *Application deadline:* For fall admission, 9/1 for domestic students; for spring admission, 1/1 for domestic students. Applications are processed on a rolling basis. Application fee: $0. Electronic applications accepted. *Expenses: Tuition:* Full-time $22,212; part-time $1234 per credit. Tuition and fees vary according to program. *Financial support:* Research assistantships and Federal Work-Study available. Support available to part-time students. *Unit head:* Dr. Melissa Boston, Associate Professor and Director, 412-396-6109, E-mail: bostonm@duq.edu. *Application contact:* Michael Dolinger, Director of Student and Academic Services, 412-396-6647, Fax: 412-396-5585, E-mail: dolingerm@duq.edu.
Website: http://www.duq.edu/academics/schools/education/graduate-programs-education/ms-ed-secondary-education

D'Youville College, Department of Education, Buffalo, NY 14201-1084. Offers educational leadership (Ed D); elementary education (MS Ed); secondary education (MS Ed); special education (MS Ed). *Program availability:* Part-time, evening/weekend. *Degree requirements:* For master's, one foreign language, comprehensive exam, project or thesis. *Entrance requirements:* For master's, GRE (if GPA less than 2.75), minimum GPA of 3.0. Additional exam requirements/recommendations for international students: Required—TOEFL (minimum score 500 paper-based). Electronic applications accepted. *Faculty research:* Developmental disabilities, multiculturalism, early childhood education.

East Carolina University, Graduate School, College of Education, Department of Elementary and Middle Grades Education, Greenville, NC 27858-4353. Offers elementary education (MA Ed, MAT); English education (MAT); family and consumer science (MAT); health education (MAT); Hispanic studies (MAT); history education (MAT); middle grades education (MA Ed, MAT); music education (MAT); science education (MAT); special education (MAT), including general curriculum; vocational education (MAT). *Accreditation:* NCATE. *Program availability:* Part-time, evening/weekend, online learning. *Students:* 5 full-time (4 women), 18 part-time (16 women); includes 4 minority (3 Black or African American, non-Hispanic/Latino; 1 Hispanic/Latino). Average age 31. 19 applicants, 95% accepted, 13 enrolled. In 2016, 8 master's awarded. *Degree requirements:* For master's, comprehensive exam, thesis optional. *Entrance requirements:* For master's, GRE or MAT, minimum GPA of 2.5, bachelor's degree in related field, teaching license (MA Ed). Additional exam requirements/recommendations for international students: Required—TOEFL. *Application deadline:* For fall admission, 6/1 priority date for domestic students. Applications are processed on a rolling basis. Application fee: $70. *Financial support:* Federal Work-Study available. Support available to part-time students. Financial award application deadline: 6/1. *Unit head:* Dr. Ann Bullock, Chair, 252-328-1126, E-mail: bullockv@ecu.edu. *Application contact:* Dean of Graduate School, 252-328-6012, Fax: 252-328-6071, E-mail: gradschool@ecu.edu.
Website: http://www.ecu.edu/cs-educ/elmid/index.cfm

East Carolina University, Graduate School, College of Education, Department of Mathematics, Science, and Instructional Technology Education, Greenville, NC 27858-4353. Offers elementary mathematics (Certificate); instructional technology (MA Ed, MS); mathematics education (MA Ed); science education (MA Ed, MAT). *Program availability:* Part-time, evening/weekend. *Students:* 15 full-time (10 women), 266 part-time (213 women); includes 52 minority (34 Black or African American, non-Hispanic/Latino; 3 American Indian or Alaska Native, non-Hispanic/Latino; 4 Asian, non-Hispanic/Latino; 9 Hispanic/Latino; 2 Two or more races, non-Hispanic/Latino), 1 international. Average age 37. 131 applicants, 100% accepted, 116 enrolled. In 2016, 30 master's awarded. *Degree requirements:* For master's, comprehensive exam, thesis optional. *Entrance requirements:* For master's, GRE General Test or MAT, interview, minimum GPA of 2.5, bachelor's degree in related field, teaching license (MA Ed). Additional exam requirements/recommendations for international students: Required—TOEFL. *Application deadline:* For fall admission, 6/1 priority date for domestic students. Applications are processed on a rolling basis. Application fee: $50. *Financial support:* Research assistantships, teaching assistantships, and Federal Work-Study available. Support available to part-time students. Financial award application deadline: 6/1. *Unit head:* Susan Ganter, Chair, 252-737-3001, E-mail: ganters@ecu.edu. *Application contact:* Dean of Graduate School, 252-328-6012, Fax: 252-328-6071, E-mail: gradschool@ecu.edu.
Website: http://www.ecu.edu/cs-educ/msite/

Eastern Connecticut State University, School of Education and Professional Studies/Graduate Division, Program in Elementary Education, Willimantic, CT 06226-2295. Offers MS. *Accreditation:* NCATE. *Program availability:* Part-time, evening/weekend. *Faculty:* 12 full-time (7 women), 21 part-time/adjunct (17 women). *Students:* 21 full-time (17 women), 10 part-time (8 women); includes 4 minority (all Hispanic/Latino). Average age 27. 17 applicants, 65% accepted, 11 enrolled. In 2016, 9 master's awarded. *Degree requirements:* For master's, comprehensive exam or thesis. *Entrance requirements:* For master's, PRAXIS I, PRAXIS II, GRE, minimum GPA of 3.0, bachelor's degree from accredited institution. Additional exam requirements/recommendations for international students: Required—TOEFL (minimum score 550 paper-based; 79 iBT); Recommended—IELTS (minimum score 6). *Application deadline:* For fall admission, 7/6 priority date for domestic and international students; for spring admission, 11/3 priority date for domestic and international students. Applications are processed on a rolling basis. Application fee: $50. Electronic applications accepted. *Expenses: Tuition, area resident:* Full-time $11,781; part-time $560 per credit. Tuition, state resident: full-time $15,031; part-time $568 per credit. Tuition, nonresident: full-time $24,581; part-time $568 per credit. *Required fees:* $40 per semester. Full-time tuition and fees vary according to course level, course load and reciprocity agreements. *Financial support:* Research assistantships, teaching assistantships, career-related internships or fieldwork, institutionally sponsored loans, and unspecified assistantships available. Financial award application deadline: 3/1; financial award applicants required to submit FAFSA. *Unit head:* Dr. Ann Anderberg, Advisor, 860-465-0109, Fax: 860-465-4538, E-mail: anderberga@easternct.edu. *Application contact:* Paula Goyette, Graduate Division, School of Education and Professional Studies, 860-465-5292, Fax: 860-465-4538, E-mail: graduateadmissions@easternct.edu.

Eastern Illinois University, Graduate School, College of Education and Professional Studies, Department of Early Childhood, Elementary and Middle Level Education, Charleston, IL 61920. Offers elementary education (MS Ed). *Accreditation:* NCATE. *Program availability:* Part-time, evening/weekend. *Degree requirements:* For master's, comprehensive exam (for some programs), thesis (for some programs). *Entrance requirements:* For master's, GMAT or GRE. Additional exam requirements/recommendations for international students: Required—TOEFL (minimum score 500 paper-based; 61 iBT), IELTS (minimum score 6). Electronic applications accepted.

Eastern Illinois University, Graduate School, College of Sciences, Department of Mathematics and Computer Science, Charleston, IL 61920. Offers elementary/middle school mathematics education (MA); mathematics (MA). *Program availability:* Part-time, evening/weekend. *Degree requirements:* For master's, comprehensive exam (for some programs), thesis (for some programs). *Entrance requirements:* For master's, GMAT or GRE. Additional exam requirements/recommendations for international students: Required—TOEFL (minimum score 500 paper-based; 61 iBT), IELTS (minimum score 6). Electronic applications accepted.

Eastern Kentucky University, The Graduate School, College of Education, Department of Curriculum and Instruction, Richmond, KY 40475-3102. Offers elementary education (MA Ed), including early elementary education, reading; library science (MA Ed); music education (MA Ed); secondary and higher education (MA Ed), including secondary education; teaching (MAT). *Accreditation:* NCATE. *Program availability:* Part-time. *Degree requirements:* For master's, portfolio is part of exam. *Entrance requirements:* For master's, GRE General Test, PRAXIS II (KY), minimum GPA of 2.5. *Faculty research:* Technology in education, reading instruction, e-portfolios, induction to teacher education, dispositions of teachers.

Eastern Nazarene College, Adult and Graduate Studies, Division of Teacher Education, Quincy, MA 02170. Offers administration (M Ed); early childhood education (M Ed, Certificate); elementary education (M Ed, Certificate); English as a second language (Certificate); instructional enrichment and development (Certificate); middle school education (M Ed, Certificate); moderate special needs education (Certificate); principal (Certificate); program development and supervision (Certificate); secondary education (M Ed, Certificate); special education administrator (Certificate); special needs (M Ed); supervisor (Certificate); teacher of reading (M Ed, Certificate). M Ed also available through weekend program for administration, special needs, and teacher of reading only. *Program availability:* Part-time, evening/weekend. *Entrance requirements:* Additional exam requirements/recommendations for international students: Required—TOEFL (minimum score 550 paper-based).

Eastern New Mexico University, Graduate School, College of Education and Technology, Department of Curriculum and Instruction, Portales, NM 88130. Offers bilingual education (M Ed); educational technology (M Ed); elementary education (M Ed); English as a second language (M Ed); pedagogy and learning (M Ed); professional technical education (M Ed); reading/literacy (M Ed). *Program availability:* Part-time, online learning. *Degree requirements:* For master's, comprehensive exam, thesis optional. *Entrance requirements:* For master's, minimum GPA of 3.0, photocopy of teaching license, writing assessment, letter of recommendation. Additional exam requirements/recommendations for international students: Required—TOEFL (minimum score 550 paper-based; 79 iBT), IELTS (minimum score 6). Electronic applications accepted.

Eastern Oregon University, Master of Arts in Teaching Program, La Grande, OR 97850-2899. Offers elementary education (MAT); secondary education (MAT). *Program availability:* Online learning. *Faculty:* 9 full-time (6 women), 5 part-time/adjunct (2 women). *Students:* 43 full-time (31 women), 1 (woman) part-time; includes 8 minority (1 Black or African American, non-Hispanic/Latino; 1 American Indian or Alaska Native, non-Hispanic/Latino; 2 Asian, non-Hispanic/Latino; 4 Hispanic/Latino). Average age 31. In 2016, 40 master's awarded. *Degree requirements:* For master's, thesis. *Entrance requirements:* For master's, NTE. *Application deadline:* For fall admission, 1/1 priority date for domestic students. Applications are processed on a rolling basis. Application fee: $50. Electronic applications accepted. *Expenses:* $353.50 per credit plus campus fees for portion of degree delivered on-campus. *Financial support:* In 2016–17, 13 students received support. Federal Work-Study, scholarships/grants, and tuition waivers (full and partial) available. Support available to part-time students. *Unit head:* Dr. Danny Ray Mielke, Dean of College of Business and Education, 541-962-3399, Fax: 541-962-3701, E-mail: dmeilke@eou.edu. *Application contact:* Janet Frye, Administrative Support, MAT/MS Graduate Admission, 541-962-3772, Fax: 541-962-3701, E-mail: jfrye@eou.edu.

Eastern University, Loeb School of Education, St. Davids, PA 19087-3696. Offers ESL program specialist (K-12) (Certificate); general supervisor (PreK-12) (Certificate); health and physical education (K-12) (Certificate); middle level (4-8) (Certificate); multicultural education (M Ed); organizational leadership with education (PhD); Pre K-4 (Certificate); Pre K-4 with special education (Certificate); reading (M Ed); reading specialist (K-12) (Certificate); reading supervisor (K-12) (Certificate); school health supervisor (Certificate); school nurse (K-12) (Certificate); secondary biology education (7-12) (Certificate); secondary chemistry education (7-12) (Certificate); secondary communication education (7-12) (Certificate); secondary education (7-12) (Certificate); secondary English education (7-12) (Certificate); secondary math education (7-12) (Certificate); secondary social studies education (7-12) (Certificate); special education (M Ed); special education (7-12) (Certificate); special education (Pre K-8) (Certificate); special education supervisor (N-12) (Certificate); TESOL (M Ed); world language (Certificate), including French, Spanish. *Program availability:* Part-time, evening/weekend, online learning. *Students:* 41 full-time (32 women), 89 part-time (68 women);

includes 54 minority (38 Black or African American, non-Hispanic/Latino; 3 Asian, non-Hispanic/Latino; 11 Hispanic/Latino; 2 Two or more races, non-Hispanic/Latino), 2 international. Average age 37. In 2016, 64 master's awarded. *Entrance requirements:* Additional exam requirements/recommendations for international students: Required—TOEFL. *Application deadline:* Applications are processed on a rolling basis. Application fee: $35. Electronic applications accepted. Application fee is waived when completed online. *Expenses:* $690 per credit. *Unit head:* Michael Dziedziak, Executive Director of Enrollment, 800-452-0996, E-mail: gpsadmissions@eastern.edu.
Website: http://www.eastern.edu/academics/programs/loeb-school-education-0

Eastern Washington University, Graduate Studies, College of Arts, Letters and Education, Department of Education, Program in Elementary Teaching, Cheney, WA 99004-2431. Offers M Ed. *Students:* 16 full-time (13 women); includes 1 minority (Asian, non-Hispanic/Latino). Average age 30. In 2016, 11 master's awarded. *Degree requirements:* For master's, comprehensive exam. *Entrance requirements:* For master's, minimum GPA of 3.0. Additional exam requirements/recommendations for international students: Required—TOEFL (minimum score 580 paper-based; 92 iBT), IELTS (minimum score 7), PTE (minimum score 63). *Application deadline:* For fall admission, 4/1 priority date for domestic students; for spring admission, 1/15 for domestic students. Applications are processed on a rolling basis. Application fee: $75. Electronic applications accepted. *Expenses:* Tuition, state resident: full-time $11,000; part-time $5500 per credit. Tuition, nonresident: full-time $24,000; part-time $12,000 per credit. *Required fees:* $1300. One-time fee: $50 full-time. Part-time tuition and fees vary according to course load, campus/location and program. *Financial support:* In 2016–17, teaching assistantships with partial tuition reimbursements (averaging $10,000 per year) were awarded; career-related internships or fieldwork, Federal Work-Study, institutionally sponsored loans, scholarships/grants, health care benefits, tuition waivers (partial), and unspecified assistantships also available. Support available to part-time students. Financial award application deadline: 2/1; financial award applicants required to submit FAFSA. *Unit head:* Robin Showalter, Program Coordinator, 509-359-6492, E-mail: rshowalter@mail.ewu.edu.

East Stroudsburg University of Pennsylvania, Graduate and Extended Studies, College of Education, Department of Early Childhood and Elementary Education, East Stroudsburg, PA 18301-2999. Offers M Ed. *Program availability:* Part-time, evening/weekend, online learning. *Students:* 6 part-time (5 women). *Degree requirements:* For master's, comprehensive exam, professional portfolio, curriculum project or action research. *Entrance requirements:* For master's, PRAXIS/teacher certification, letter of recommendation, Pennsylvania Department of Education requirements. Additional exam requirements/recommendations for international students: Recommended—TOEFL (minimum score 560 paper-based; 83 iBT), IELTS. *Application deadline:* For fall admission, 7/31 priority date for domestic students, 6/30 priority date for international students; for spring admission, 11/30 for domestic students, 10/31 for international students. Applications are processed on a rolling basis. Application fee: $50. Electronic applications accepted. *Expenses:* Tuition, state resident: full-time $8694; part-time $5796 per year. Tuition, nonresident: full-time $13,050; part-time $8700 per year. *Required fees:* $2550; $1690 per unit. $845 per semester. Tuition and fees vary according to course load, campus/location and program. *Financial support:* Research assistantships with tuition reimbursements, Federal Work-Study, and unspecified assistantships available. Support available to part-time students. Financial award application deadline: 3/1; financial award applicants required to submit FAFSA. *Unit head:* Andrew Whitehead, Chair, 570-422-3356, Fax: 570-422-3942, E-mail: awhitehead@esu.edu. *Application contact:* Kevin Quintero, Associate Director, Graduate and Extended Studies, 570-422-3890, Fax: 570-422-2711, E-mail: kquintero@esu.edu.

East Tennessee State University, School of Graduate Studies, College of Education, Department of Curriculum and Instruction, Johnson City, TN 37614. Offers educational technology (M Ed), including educational communications and technology, school library media; elementary education (M Ed); reading (MA), including reading education; school library professional (Post-Master's Certificate); secondary education (M Ed), including classroom technology; teacher education with multiple levels (MAT), including elementary education, middle grades education, secondary education. *Accreditation:* NCATE. *Program availability:* Part-time, evening/weekend, online learning. *Degree requirements:* For master's, comprehensive exam, thesis optional, student teaching, practicum; for Post-Master's Certificate, field work (school library); culminating experience (storytelling). *Entrance requirements:* For master's, GRE, SAT, ACT, PRAXIS, minimum GPA of 3.0; for Post-Master's Certificate, master's degree, TN teaching license. Additional exam requirements/recommendations for international students: Required—TOEFL (minimum score 550 paper-based; 79 iBT). Electronic applications accepted. *Faculty research:* Critical thinking; curriculum development in reading, math, and science education; cultural diversity; cognitive processes; effective teaching strategies.

Elizabeth City State University, School of Education and Psychology, Master of Education in Elementary Education Program, Elizabeth City, NC 27909-7806. Offers M Ed. *Accreditation:* NCATE. *Program availability:* Part-time, evening/weekend. *Degree requirements:* For master's, comprehensive exam, thesis or alternative, electronic transformational teaching project. *Entrance requirements:* For master's, GRE and/or MAT, minimum GPA of 3.0, 3 letters of recommendation, 2 official transcripts from all undergraduate/graduate schools attended, teacher license, typewritten 2-page essay specifying educational philosophy. Additional exam requirements/recommendations for international students: Required—TOEFL (minimum score 550 paper-based, 80 iBT) or IELTS (minimum score 6.5). Electronic applications accepted. *Faculty research:* Diverse learners, disproportionality, inclusionary classrooms, international curriculum development.

Elms College, Division of Education, Chicopee, MA 01013-2839. Offers early childhood education (MAT); education (M Ed, CAGS); elementary education (MAT); English as a second language (MAT); reading (MAT); secondary education (MAT), including biology education, English education, Spanish education; special education (MAT). *Program availability:* Part-time, evening/weekend. *Faculty:* 5 full-time (all women), 7 part-time/adjunct (6 women). *Students:* 6 full-time (all women), 136 part-time (111 women); includes 6 minority (1 Asian, non-Hispanic/Latino; 5 Hispanic/Latino). Average age 33. 27 applicants, 89% accepted, 20 enrolled. In 2016, 47 master's, 3 other advanced degrees awarded. *Degree requirements:* For master's, thesis (for some programs). *Entrance requirements:* For master's, Massachusetts Educators Certification Test, minimum GPA of 3.0; for CAGS, master's degree in education. Additional exam requirements/recommendations for international students: Required—TOEFL. *Application deadline:* For fall admission, 7/1 priority date for domestic students; for spring admission, 11/1 priority date for domestic students. Applications are processed on a rolling basis. Application fee: $30. *Expenses: Tuition:* Full-time $13,392. *Required fees:* $200. *Financial support:* In 2016–17, 2 teaching assistantships with partial tuition reimbursements were awarded; tuition waivers (partial) also available. Support available to part-time students. Financial award applicants required to submit FAFSA. *Unit head:* Dr. Mary Janeczek, Chair, Division of Education, 413-594-2761, Fax: 413-592-4871, E-mail: janeczeke@elms.edu. *Application contact:* Dr. Elizabeth Teahan Hukowicz, Dean, School of Graduate and Professional Studies, 413-265-2360, Fax: 413-265-2459, E-mail: hukowicze@elms.edu.

Elon University, Program in Education, Elon, NC 27244-2010. Offers elementary education (M Ed); gifted education (M Ed); special education (M Ed). *Accreditation:* NCATE. *Program availability:* Part-time. *Faculty:* 9 full-time (7 women), 2 part-time/adjunct (both women). *Students:* 17 part-time (all women); includes 7 minority (3 Black or African American, non-Hispanic/Latino; 1 American Indian or Alaska Native, non-Hispanic/Latino; 2 Hispanic/Latino; 1 Two or more races, non-Hispanic/Latino). Average age 33. 24 applicants, 50% accepted, 8 enrolled. In 2016, 24 master's awarded. *Entrance requirements:* For master's, GRE, MAT. Additional exam requirements/recommendations for international students: Required—TOEFL (minimum score 550 paper-based; 79 iBT). *Application deadline:* For fall admission, 5/1 for domestic students. Applications are processed on a rolling basis. Application fee: $50. Electronic applications accepted. *Financial support:* Federal Work-Study and scholarships/grants available. Support available to part-time students. Financial award application deadline: 6/1; financial award applicants required to submit FAFSA. *Faculty research:* Teaching reading to low-achieving second and third graders, pre- and post-student teaching attitudes, children's writing, whole language methodology, critical creative thinking. *Unit head:* Dr. Ann Bullock, Dean of the School of Education/Professor, 336-278-5900, E-mail: abullock9@elon.edu. *Application contact:* Art Fadde, Director of Graduate Admissions, 800-334-8448 Ext. 3, Fax: 336-278-7699, E-mail: afadde@elon.edu.
Website: http://www.elon.edu/med

Emporia State University, Program in Instructional Specialist, Emporia, KS 66801-5415. Offers elementary subject matter (MS); reading (MS). *Accreditation:* NCATE. *Program availability:* Part-time. *Faculty:* 29 full-time (21 women), 3 part-time/adjunct (2 women). *Students:* 7 full-time (all women), 65 part-time (58 women). 23 applicants, 100% accepted, 16 enrolled. In 2016, 27 master's awarded. *Degree requirements:* For master's, comprehensive exam or thesis, practicum. *Entrance requirements:* For master's, GRE General Test or MAT, essay exam, appropriate bachelor's degree, letters of recommendation. Additional exam requirements/recommendations for international students: Required—TOEFL (minimum score 520 paper-based; 68 iBT). *Application deadline:* For fall admission, 8/15 priority date for domestic students. Applications are processed on a rolling basis. Application fee: $30 ($75 for international students). Electronic applications accepted. *Expenses:* Tuition, state resident: full-time $5922; part-time $246.75 per credit hour. Tuition, nonresident: full-time $18,414; part-time $767.25 per credit hour. *Required fees:* $1884; $78.50 per credit hour. *Financial support:* Federal Work-Study, institutionally sponsored loans, health care benefits, and unspecified assistantships available. Financial award application deadline: 3/15; financial award applicants required to submit FAFSA. *Unit head:* Dr. Matt Siemears, Chair, 620-341-6057, E-mail: msiemear@emporia.edu. *Application contact:* Mary Sewell, Admissions Coordinator, 800-950-GRAD, Fax: 620-341-5909, E-mail: msewell@emporia.edu.

Endicott College, Van Loan School of Graduate and Professional Studies, Program in Early Childhood and Elementary Education, Beverly, MA 01915-2096. Offers M Ed. *Program availability:* Part-time, evening/weekend, 100% online, blended/hybrid learning. *Faculty:* 3 full-time (2 women), 9 part-time/adjunct (8 women). *Students:* 9 full-time (6 women), 14 part-time (13 women). Average age 30. 10 applicants, 100% accepted, 10 enrolled. In 2016, 11 master's awarded. *Degree requirements:* For master's, comprehensive exam, thesis, practicum. *Entrance requirements:* For master's, MAT or GRE, Massachusetts Test for Educators Licensure, Massachusetts teaching certificate, 2 professional letters of recommendation, personal statement. Additional exam requirements/recommendations for international students: Required—TOEFL. *Application deadline:* Applications are processed on a rolling basis. Application fee: $50. Electronic applications accepted. *Expenses:* Contact institution. *Financial support:* Career-related internships or fieldwork available. Financial award applicants required to submit FAFSA. *Unit head:* Dr. Aubry Threlkeld, Director of Graduate Licensure Programs, 978-232-2408, E-mail: athrelke@endicott.edu. *Application contact:* Ian Menchini, Director, Graduate Enrollment and Advising, 978-232-5292, E-mail: imenchin@endicott.edu.
Website: http://www.endicott.edu/VanLoan/Graduate-Studies/Master-Education.aspx

Fairfield University, Graduate School of Education and Allied Professions, Fairfield, CT 06824. Offers applied behavior analysis (ATC); applied psychology (MA); clinical mental health counseling (MA, CAS); educational technology (MA); elementary education (MA, CAS); family studies (MA); integration of spirituality and religion in counseling (ATC); marriage and family therapy (MA); reading and language development (Sixth Year Certificate); school counseling (MA, CAS); school psychology (MA, CAS); school-based marriage and family therapy (ATC); secondary education (MA); special education (MA, CAS); substance abuse counseling (ATC); teaching (Certificate); teaching and foundations (MA, CAS); TESOL, world languages, and bilingual education (MA, CAS). *Accreditation:* NCATE. *Program availability:* Part-time, evening/weekend. *Faculty:* 19 full-time (15 women), 38 part-time/adjunct (26 women). *Students:* 153 full-time (132 women), 302 part-time (252 women); includes 97 minority (24 Black or African American, non-Hispanic/Latino; 12 Asian, non-Hispanic/Latino; 55 Hispanic/Latino; 6 Two or more races, non-Hispanic/Latino), 6 international. Average age 32. 283 applicants, 61% accepted, 97 enrolled. In 2016, 130 master's awarded. *Degree requirements:* For master's, comprehensive exam. *Entrance requirements:* For master's, minimum GPA of 3.0, 2 recommendations, resume. Additional exam requirements/recommendations for international students: Required—TOEFL (minimum score 550 paper-based; 84 iBT) or IELTS (minimum score 7.5). *Application deadline:* For fall admission, 2/15 for international students; for spring admission, 10/1 for international students. Application fee: $60. Electronic applications accepted. *Expenses:* $725 per credit hour. *Financial support:* In 2016–17, 42 students received support. Career-related internships or fieldwork and unspecified assistantships available. Support available to part-time students. Financial award applicants required to submit FAFSA. *Faculty research:* Reading and literacy, writing, social justice and inequality in education, addictions and mental health issues, therapeutic relationships and clinical supervision. *Unit head:* Dr. Robert D. Hannafin, Dean, 203-254-4250, Fax: 203-254-4241, E-mail: rhannafin@fairfield.edu. *Application contact:* Marianne Gumpper, Director of Graduate Admission, 203-254-4184, Fax: 203-254-4073, E-mail: gradadmis@fairfield.edu.
Website: http://www.fairfield.edu/gseap

Fayetteville State University, Graduate School, Programs in Middle Grades, Secondary, Special and Elementary Education, Fayetteville, NC 28301-4298. Offers middle grades (MA Ed); sociology (MA Ed); special education (MA Ed), including behavioral-emotional handicaps, mentally handicapped, specific training disability. *Accreditation:* NCATE. *Program availability:* Part-time, evening/weekend. *Faculty:* 12 full-time (8 women), 4 part-time/adjunct (3 women). *Students:* 9 full-time (6 women), 11 part-time (10 women); includes 12 minority (11 Black or African American, non-Hispanic/Latino; 1 Asian, non-Hispanic/Latino). Average age 35. 20 applicants, 100% accepted, 1 enrolled. In 2016, 11 master's awarded. *Degree requirements:* For master's, comprehensive exam, internship. *Entrance requirements:* Additional exam requirements/recommendations for international students: Required—TOEFL. *Application deadline:* For fall admission, 4/15 for domestic students; for spring admission, 10/15 for domestic students. Applications are processed on a rolling basis. Application fee: $40. Electronic applications accepted. *Financial support:* Application deadline: 3/1; applicants required to submit FAFSA. *Faculty research:* Students with disabilities and selected leadership behaviors, new vision for professional development, gifted and talented students, emotional and behavioral disabilities, professional development for high school biology teachers. *Unit head:* Dr. Kimberly Smith-Burton, Chairperson, 910-672-1181, Fax: 910-672-1941, E-mail: ksmith@uncfsu.edu. *Application contact:* Debra D. Brown, Administrative Support Associate, 910-672-1181, Fax: 910-672-1596, E-mail: ddbrown@uncfsu.edu.

Fitchburg State University, Division of Graduate and Continuing Education, Program in Elementary Education, Fitchburg, MA 01420-2697. Offers M Ed. *Accreditation:* NCATE. *Program availability:* Part-time, evening/weekend. *Entrance requirements:* Additional exam requirements/recommendations for international students: Required—TOEFL (minimum score 550 paper-based; 79 iBT). Electronic applications accepted. *Expenses:* Tuition, state resident: full-time $2871; part-time $1914 per year. Tuition, nonresident: full-time $2871; part-time $1914 per year. *Required fees:* $3828. Tuition and fees vary according to program.

Florida Agricultural and Mechanical University, Division of Graduate Studies, Research, and Continuing Education, College of Education, Department of Elementary Education, Tallahassee, FL 32307-3200. Offers M Ed, MS. *Accreditation:* NCATE. *Degree requirements:* For master's, thesis (for some programs). *Entrance requirements:* For master's, GRE General Test, minimum GPA of 3.0. Additional exam requirements/recommendations for international students: Required—TOEFL.

Florida Atlantic University, College of Education, Department of Teaching and Learning, Boca Raton, FL 33431-0991. Offers curriculum and instruction (M Ed), including art, biology, chemistry, English, French, German, mathematics, music, physics, Pre-K and primary education, reading, social sciences, Spanish; elementary education (M Ed); environmental education (M Ed); reading education (M Ed); social foundations of education (M Ed), including educational psychology, educational technology, multilingual education. *Accreditation:* NCATE. *Program availability:* Part-time, evening/weekend. *Faculty:* 15 full-time (12 women), 2 part-time/adjunct (1 woman). *Students:* 25 full-time (20 women), 41 part-time (37 women); includes 18 minority (9 Black or African American, non-Hispanic/Latino; 2 Asian, non-Hispanic/Latino; 7 Hispanic/Latino), 7 international. Average age 32. 54 applicants, 59% accepted, 18 enrolled. In 2016, 36 master's awarded. *Entrance requirements:* For master's, GRE General Test, minimum GPA of 3.0 in last 2 years of undergraduate course work. Additional exam requirements/recommendations for international students: Required—TOEFL (minimum score 500 paper-based; 61 iBT), IELTS (minimum score 6). *Application deadline:* For fall admission, 7/1 for domestic students, 2/15 for international students; for spring admission, 11/1 for domestic students, 7/15 for international students. Applications are processed on a rolling basis. Application fee: $30. *Expenses:* Tuition, state resident: full-time $7392; part-time $369.82 per credit hour. Tuition, nonresident: full-time $19,432; part-time $1024.81 per credit hour. *Financial support:* Fellowships with partial tuition reimbursements, research assistantships with partial tuition reimbursements, teaching assistantships with partial tuition reimbursements, career-related internships or fieldwork, scholarships/grants, and unspecified assistantships available. *Faculty research:* Technology, teaching English to speakers of other languages, math teaching, electronic portfolio assessment, global perspectives through social studies. *Unit head:* Dr. Barbara Ridener, Chairperson, 561-297-3588, E-mail: bridener@fau.edu. *Application contact:* Dr. Eliah Watlington, Associate Dean, 561-296-8520, Fax: 261-297-2991, E-mail: ewatling@fau.edu.
Website: http://www.coe.fau.edu/academicdepartments/tl/

Florida Gulf Coast University, College of Education, Program in Curriculum and Instruction, Fort Myers, FL 33965-6565. Offers elementary education (M Ed); English education (M Ed); gifted education (M Ed); mathematics education (M Ed); middle school education (M Ed); science education (M Ed); social science education (M Ed). *Program availability:* Part-time, evening/weekend, online learning. *Faculty:* 26 full-time (18 women), 44 part-time/adjunct (32 women). *Students:* 1 (woman) full-time, 22 part-time (20 women); includes 49 minority (19 Black or African American, non-Hispanic/Latino; 4 Asian, non-Hispanic/Latino; 24 Hispanic/Latino; 2 Two or more races, non-Hispanic/Latino), 2 international. Average age 28. 9 applicants, 78% accepted, 2 enrolled. In 2016, 9 master's awarded. *Degree requirements:* For master's, final project or portfolio. *Entrance requirements:* For master's, GRE General Test, MAT, minimum undergraduate GPA of 3.0 in last 2 years. Additional exam requirements/recommendations for international students: Required—TOEFL (minimum score 550 paper-based). *Application deadline:* For fall admission, 7/1 priority date for domestic students; for spring admission, 10/15 for domestic students. Applications are processed on a rolling basis. Application fee: $30. Electronic applications accepted. *Expenses:* Tuition, state resident: full-time $6721. Tuition, nonresident: full-time $28,170. *Required fees:* $1987. Tuition and fees vary according to course load and degree level. *Financial support:* In 2016–17, 1 student received support. Application deadline: 3/1; applicants required to submit FAFSA. *Faculty research:* Internet in schools, technology in pre-service and in-service teacher training. *Unit head:* Dr. Diane Schmidt, Department Chair, 239-590-7741, Fax: 239-590-7801, E-mail: dschmidt@fgcu.edu. *Application contact:* Keiana Desmore, Adviser/Counselor, 239-590-7759, Fax: 239-590-7801, E-mail: kdesmore@fgcu.edu.
Website: http://coe.fgcu.edu/c-imed/

Florida Institute of Technology, College of Science, Program in Elementary Science Education, Melbourne, FL 32901-6975. Offers M Ed. *Program availability:* Part-time. *Students:* 1 (woman) full-time. Average age 25. 2 applicants. *Degree requirements:* For master's, comprehensive exam, thesis or alternative, 30 credit hours, minimum GPA of 3.0. *Entrance requirements:* For master's, minimum GPA of 3.0, 3 letters of recommendation, resume, statement of objectives. Additional exam requirements/recommendations for international students: Required—TOEFL (minimum score 550 paper-based; 79 iBT). *Application deadline:* Applications are processed on a rolling basis. Electronic applications accepted. *Expenses: Tuition:* Full-time $22,338; part-time $1241 per credit hour. *Required fees:* $250. Tuition and fees vary according to degree level, campus/location and program. *Financial support:* Applicants required to submit FAFSA. *Unit head:* Dr. Kastro Hamed, Department Head, 321-674-7206, E-mail: khamed@fit.edu. *Application contact:* Cheryl A. Brown, Associate Director of Graduate Admissions, 321-674-7581, Fax: 321-723-9468, E-mail: cbrown@fit.edu.
Website: http://www.fit.edu/programs/8118/med-elementary-science-education#.VT_jlU10ypo

Florida International University, College of Arts, Sciences, and Education, Department of Teaching and Learning, Miami, FL 33199. Offers art education (MA, MS); curriculum and instruction (MS, Ed D, PhD, Ed S), including curriculum development (MS), elementary education (MS), English education (MS), learning technologies (MS), mathematics education (MS), modern language education (MS), physical education (MS), science education (MS), social studies education (MS), special education (MS); early childhood education (MS); exceptional student education (Ed D); foreign language education (MS), including foreign language education, teaching English to speakers of other languages (TESOL); international/intercultural education (MS); language, literacy and culture (PhD); mathematics, science, and learning technologies (PhD); physical education (MS), including sport and fitness; reading education (MS). *Program availability:* Part-time, evening/weekend. *Faculty:* 34 full-time (23 women), 64 part-time/adjunct (48 women). *Students:* 182 full-time (154 women), 231 part-time (190 women); includes 323 minority (69 Black or African American, non-Hispanic/Latino; 10 Asian, non-Hispanic/Latino; 237 Hispanic/Latino; 7 Two or more races, non-Hispanic/Latino), 19 international. Average age 34. 282 applicants, 58% accepted, 113 enrolled. In 2016, 184 master's, 12 doctorates awarded. *Degree requirements:* For doctorate, comprehensive exam, thesis/dissertation. *Entrance requirements:* For master's, GRE General Test, Florida General Knowledge Test or Florida College Level Academic Skills Test; for doctorate and Ed S, GRE General Test. Additional exam requirements/recommendations for international students: Required—TOEFL (minimum score 550 paper-based; 80 iBT), IELTS (minimum score 6.3). *Application deadline:* For fall admission, 6/1 priority date for domestic students, 4/1 for international students; for winter admission, 10/1 priority date for domestic students, 9/1 for international students; for spring admission, 3/1 priority date for domestic students, 2/1 for international students. Applications are processed on a rolling basis. Application fee: $30. Electronic applications accepted. *Expenses:* Tuition, state resident: full-time $8912; part-time $446 per credit hour. Tuition, nonresident: full-time $21,393; part-time $992 per credit hour. *Required fees:* $2185; $195 per semester. Tuition and fees vary according to program. *Financial support:* Research assistantships with tuition reimbursements and teaching assistantships with tuition reimbursements available. *Unit head:* Dr. Lynn Miller, Chair, 305-348-2005, Fax: 305-348-2086, E-mail: lynne.miller@fiu.edu. *Application contact:* Nanett Rojas, Assistant Director, Graduate Admissions, 305-348-7464, Fax: 305-348-7441, E-mail: gradadm@fiu.edu.
Website: http://education.fiu.edu

Florida Memorial University, School of Education, Miami-Dade, FL 33054. Offers elementary education (MS); exceptional student education (MS); reading (MS). *Degree requirements:* For master's, comprehensive exam or thesis, field and clinical experiences, exit exam. *Entrance requirements:* For master's, GRE, CLAST, PRAXIS I, baccalaureate or graduate degree with minimum GPA of 3.0 in last 60 hours, 3 recommendations. Additional exam requirements/recommendations for international students: Recommended—TOEFL.

Florida State University, The Graduate School, College of Education, Program in Curriculum and Instruction, Tallahassee, FL 32306. Offers curriculum and instruction (MS, PhD, Ed S), including early childhood education, elementary education, English education, English teaching (MS), exceptional student education (MS), foreign and second language education, foreign and second language teaching (MS), mathematics education, mathematics teaching (MS), reading education and language arts, science education, social science education, social science teaching (MS), special education, special education studies (MS), visual disabilities (MS, Ed S). *Program availability:* Part-time, evening/weekend. Terminal master's awarded for partial completion of doctoral program. *Degree requirements:* For master's and Ed S, comprehensive exam, thesis optional; for doctorate, comprehensive exam, thesis/dissertation, diagnostic exam, preliminary exam, prospectus defense, dissertation defense. *Entrance requirements:* For master's, doctorate, and Ed S, GRE General Test, minimum upper-division GPA of 3.0. Additional exam requirements/recommendations for international students: Required—TOEFL (minimum score 550 paper-based, 80 iBT), IELTS (minimum score 6.5), Michigan English Language Assessment Battery (minimum score 77), or PTE (minimum score 55). Application fee: $30. Electronic applications accepted. *Expenses:* Tuition, state resident: full-time $7263; part-time $403.51 per credit hour. Tuition, nonresident: full-time $18,087; part-time $1004.85 per credit hour. *Required fees:* $1365; $75.81 per credit hour. $20 per semester. Tuition and fees vary according to campus/location. *Financial support:* Fellowships, research assistantships, teaching assistantships, scholarships/grants, tuition waivers (full and partial), and unspecified assistantships available. Financial award application deadline: 1/15; financial award applicants required to submit FAFSA. *Faculty research:* Identifying effective intervention strategies to improve reading skills; improving literacy teaching and learning through technology; understanding of student sense making, problem solving, the history and structure of STEM disciplines, and teacher education to support the development of ambitious instruction that supports the STEM learning of all students; examining practices of international education; identifying ways to support the professional development of teachers. *Unit head:* Dr. Sherry Southerland, Professor/Department Chair, 850-644-4880, Fax: 850-644-7736, E-mail: ssoutherland@admin.fsu.edu. *Application contact:* Libbie Crowley, Academic Support Specialist, 850-644-2122, Fax: 850-644-7736, E-mail: ecrowley@fsu.edu.
Website: http://education.fsu.edu/degrees-and-programs/graduate-programs

Fontbonne University, Graduate Programs, St. Louis, MO 63105-3098. Offers accounting (MBA, MS); art (MA); art (K-12) (MAT); business (MBA); computer science (MS); deaf education (MA); early intervention in deaf education (MA); education (MA), including autism spectrum disorders, curriculum and instruction, diverse learners, early childhood education, reading, special education; elementary education (MAT); family and consumer sciences (MA), including multidisciplinary health communication studies; fine arts (MFA); instructional design and technology (MS); management and leadership (MM); middle school education (MAT); secondary education (MAT); special education (MAT); speech-language pathology (MS); supply chain management (MS); theatre (MA). *Program availability:* Part-time, evening/weekend, online learning. *Faculty:* 32 full-time (24 women), 43 part-time/adjunct (26 women). *Students:* 456 full-time (313 women), 102 part-time (77 women); includes 138 minority (118 Black or African American, non-Hispanic/Latino; 1 American Indian or Alaska Native, non-Hispanic/Latino; 7 Asian, non-Hispanic/Latino; 9 Hispanic/Latino; 3 Two or more races, non-Hispanic/Latino), 37 international. *Degree requirements:* For master's, comprehensive exam (for some programs), thesis (for some programs). *Entrance requirements:* Additional exam requirements/recommendations for international students: Required—TOEFL (minimum score 500 paper-based; 65 iBT). *Application deadline:* For fall admission, 8/1 for international students; for spring admission, 12/1 for international students. Applications are processed on a rolling basis. Application fee: $25 ($30 for international students). Electronic applications accepted. *Expenses: Tuition:* Full-time $8436; part-time $703 per credit hour. *Required fees:* $18 per credit hour. Tuition and fees vary according to course load. *Financial support:* Teaching assistantships with partial tuition reimbursements and scholarships/grants available. Support available to part-time students. Financial award application deadline: 4/1; financial award applicants required to submit FAFSA. *Unit head:* Dr. Carey Adams, Vice President for Academic Affairs, 314-719-3609, E-mail: cadams@fontbonne.edu. *Application contact:* Lauryn Filip, Coordinator, Graduate Admission and Professional Studies, 314-889-4650, E-mail: admissions@fontbonne.edu.
Website: https://www.fontbonne.edu/academics/graduate-programs/

Fordham University, Graduate School of Education, Division of Curriculum and Teaching, New York, NY 10023. Offers curriculum and teaching (MSE); early childhood education (MSE); elementary education (MST); special education (MSE, Adv C); teaching English as a second language (MSE). *Accreditation:* NCATE. *Program availability:* Part-time, evening/weekend. *Degree requirements:* For Adv C, thesis. *Entrance requirements:* Additional exam requirements/recommendations for international students: Required—TOEFL (minimum score 577 paper-based; 90 iBT), IELTS (minimum score 7). Electronic applications accepted.

Elementary Education

Framingham State University, Continuing Education, Program in Elementary Education, Framingham, MA 01701-9101. Offers M Ed.

Franklin Pierce University, Graduate and Professional Studies, Rindge, NH 03461-0060. Offers curriculum and instruction (M Ed); elementary education (MS Ed); emerging network technologies (Graduate Certificate); energy and sustainability studies (MBA, Graduate Certificate); health administration (MBA, Graduate Certificate); human resource management (MBA, Graduate Certificate); information technology (MBA); leadership (MBA); nursing education (MS); nursing leadership (MS); physical therapy (DPT); physician assistant studies (MPAS); special education (M Ed); sports management (MBA). *Accreditation:* APTA. *Program availability:* Part-time, 100% online, blended/hybrid learning. *Faculty:* 47 full-time (36 women), 165 part-time/adjunct (108 women). *Students:* 380 full-time (226 women), 245 part-time (158 women); includes 52 minority (13 Black or African American, non-Hispanic/Latino; 2 American Indian or Alaska Native, non-Hispanic/Latino; 14 Asian, non-Hispanic/Latino; 22 Hispanic/Latino; 1 Native Hawaiian or other Pacific Islander, non-Hispanic/Latino), 13 international. Average age 29. 1,995 applicants, 28% accepted, 267 enrolled. In 2016, 120 master's, 86 doctorates awarded. *Degree requirements:* For master's, concentrated original research projects; student teaching; fieldwork and/or internship; leadership project; PRAXIS I and II (for M Ed); for doctorate, concentrated original research projects, clinical fieldwork and/or internship, leadership project. *Entrance requirements:* For master's, minimum GPA of 2.5, 3 letters of recommendation; competencies in accounting, economics, statistics, and computer skills through life experience or undergraduate coursework (for MBA); certification/e-portfolio, minimum C grade in all education courses (for M Ed); license to practice as RN (for MS); for doctorate, GRE, 80 hours of observation/work in PT settings; completion of anatomy, chemistry, physics, and statistics; minimum GPA of 3.0. Additional exam requirements/recommendations for international students: Required—TOEFL (minimum score 550 paper-based; 61 iBT). *Application deadline:* Applications are processed on a rolling basis. Application fee: $0. Electronic applications accepted. *Expenses: Tuition:* Full-time $15,960; part-time $665 per credit hour. Tuition and fees vary according to program. *Financial support:* Teaching assistantships with tuition reimbursements, career-related internships or fieldwork, and unspecified assistantships available. Support available to part-time students. Financial award applicants required to submit FAFSA. *Faculty research:* Evidence-based practice in sports physical therapy, human resource management in economic crisis, leadership in nursing, innovation in sports facility management, differentiated learning and understanding by design. *Unit head:* Dr. Maria Altobello, Dean, 603-647-3509, Fax: 603-229-4580, E-mail: altobellom@franklinpierce.edu. *Application contact:* Graduate Studies, 800-325-1090, Fax: 603-626-4815, E-mail: cgps@franklinpierce.edu.
Website: http://www.franklinpierce.edu/academics/gradstudies/index.htm

Frostburg State University, Graduate School, College of Education, Department of Educational Professions, Program in Curriculum and Instruction, Frostburg, MD 21532-1099. Offers educational technology (M Ed); elementary education (M Ed); secondary education (M Ed). *Program availability:* Part-time, evening/weekend. *Degree requirements:* For master's, thesis or alternative. *Entrance requirements:* For master's, teaching certificate. Additional exam requirements/recommendations for international students: Required—TOEFL. Electronic applications accepted.

Frostburg State University, Graduate School, College of Education, Department of Educational Professions, Program in Elementary Teaching, Frostburg, MD 21532-1099. Offers MAT. *Accreditation:* NCATE. *Degree requirements:* For master's, thesis or alternative, PRAXIS II. *Entrance requirements:* For master's, PRAXIS I, entry portfolio. Additional exam requirements/recommendations for international students: Required—TOEFL. Electronic applications accepted.

Gallaudet University, The Graduate School, Washington, DC 20002-3625. Offers American Sign Language/English bilingual early childhood deaf education: birth to 5 (Certificate); audiology (Au D); clinical psychology (PhD); deaf and hard of hearing infants, toddlers, and their families (Certificate); deaf education (MA, Ed S); deaf history (Certificate); deaf studies (Certificate); educating deaf students with disabilities (Certificate); education: teacher preparation (MA), including deaf education, early childhood education and deaf education, elementary education and deaf education, secondary education and deaf education; educational neuroscience (PhD); hearing, speech and language sciences (MS, PhD); international development (MA); interpretation (MA, PhD), including combined interpreting practice and research (MA), interpreting research (MA); linguistics (MA, PhD); mental health counseling (MA); peer mentoring (Certificate); public administration (MPA); school counseling (MA); school psychology (Psy S); sign language teaching (MA); social work (MSW); speech-language pathology (MS). *Program availability:* Part-time. *Students:* 297 full-time (231 women), 129 part-time (97 women); includes 105 minority (35 Black or African American, non-Hispanic/Latino; 20 Asian, non-Hispanic/Latino; 39 Hispanic/Latino; 11 Two or more races, non-Hispanic/Latino), 22 international. Average age 30. 471 applicants, 52% accepted, 147 enrolled. In 2016, 138 master's, 25 doctorates, 14 other advanced degrees awarded. Terminal master's awarded for partial completion of doctoral program. *Degree requirements:* For master's, comprehensive exam (for some programs), thesis optional; for doctorate, comprehensive exam, thesis/dissertation. *Entrance requirements:* For master's and doctorate, GRE General Test or MAT, letters of recommendation, interviews, goals statement, American Sign Language proficiency interview, written English competency. Additional exam requirements/recommendations for international students: Required—TOEFL. *Application deadline:* For fall admission, 2/15 for domestic students. Applications are processed on a rolling basis. Application fee: $75. Electronic applications accepted. *Expenses: Tuition:* Full-time $17,100; part-time $950 per credit hour. *Required fees:* $3725; $276 per semester. *Financial support:* Fellowships, research assistantships, teaching assistantships, career-related internships or fieldwork, Federal Work-Study, scholarships/grants, tuition waivers (partial), and unspecified assistantships available. Support available to part-time students. Financial award application deadline: 7/1; financial award applicants required to submit FAFSA. *Faculty research:* Signing math dictionaries, telecommunications access, cancer genetics, linguistics, visual language and visual learning, integrated quantum materials, deaf legal discourse, advance recruitment and retention in geosciences. *Unit head:* Dr. Gaurav Mathur, Dean, Graduate School and Continuing Studies, 202-250-2380, Fax: 202-651-5027, E-mail: gaurav.mathur@gallaudet.edu. *Application contact:* Wednesday Luria, Coordinator of Prospective Graduate Student Services, 202-651-5400, Fax: 202-651-5295, E-mail: graduate.school@gallaudet.edu.

George Mason University, College of Education and Human Development, Programs in Curriculum and Instruction, Fairfax, VA 22030. Offers advanced international baccalaureate (M Ed); assistive technology (M Ed); designing digital learning in schools (M Ed); early childhood education (M Ed); early childhood education for diverse learners (M Ed); elementary education (M Ed); English as a second language (M Ed); gifted child education (M Ed); history (M Ed); literacy (M Ed), including PK-12 classroom teachers, reading specialist; literacy leadership for diverse schools (M Ed), including K-12 reading; physical education (M Ed); science K-12 (M Ed); secondary education (M Ed), including biology, chemistry, earth science, English, history/social science, math, physics; special education (M Ed); teacher leadership (M Ed); teaching culturally, linguistically diverse and exceptional learners (M Ed); transformative teaching (M Ed). *Faculty:* 41 full-time (35 women), 53 part-time/adjunct (46 women). *Students:* 155 full-time (127 women), 821 part-time (697 women); includes 267 minority (82 Black or African American, non-Hispanic/Latino; 5 American Indian or Alaska Native, non-Hispanic/Latino; 75 Asian, non-Hispanic/Latino; 88 Hispanic/Latino; 1 Native Hawaiian or other Pacific Islander, non-Hispanic/Latino; 16 Two or more races, non-Hispanic/Latino), 19 international. Average age 33. 513 applicants, 90% accepted, 352 enrolled. In 2016, 347 master's awarded. *Degree requirements:* For master's, comprehensive exam, thesis (for some programs). *Entrance requirements:* For master's, PRAXIS Core (for some programs), minimum GPA of 3.0 in last 60 hours, licensed as teacher or educational administrator, official transcripts, goals statement, 3 recommendation letters, interview or writing sample (depending on program), up to 3 years' teaching experience (depending on program). Additional exam requirements/recommendations for international students: Required—TOEFL (minimum score 575 paper-based; 88 iBT), IELTS (minimum score 6.5), PTE (minimum score 59). *Application deadline:* For spring admission, 11/1 priority date for domestic and international students. Application fee: $75 ($80 for international students). Electronic applications accepted. *Expenses:* Tuition, state resident: full-time $10,628; part-time $443 per credit. Tuition, nonresident: full-time $29,306; part-time $1221 per credit. *Required fees:* $3096; $129 per credit. Tuition and fees vary according to program. *Financial support:* In 2016–17, 1 student received support, including 1 teaching assistantship (averaging $4,060 per year); career-related internships or fieldwork, Federal Work-Study, scholarships/grants, unspecified assistantships, and health care benefits (for full-time research or teaching assistantship recipients) also available. Support available to part-time students. Financial award application deadline: 3/1; financial award applicants required to submit FAFSA. *Faculty research:* Achievement gaps and superintendent decisions, constructivist view of classroom teaching, cost of cheating, creating a critical literacy milieu in kindergarten. *Unit head:* Rebecca Fox, Professor and Academic Program Coordinator, 703-993-4123, E-mail: rfox@gmu.edu. Website: http://gse.gmu.edu/programs/gsemasters

The George Washington University, Graduate School of Education and Human Development, Department of Curriculum and Pedagogy, Program in Elementary Education, Washington, DC 20052. Offers MA Ed/HD. *Accreditation:* NCATE. *Program availability:* Part-time. *Students:* 14 full-time (12 women), 4 part-time (all women); includes 8 minority (4 Black or African American, non-Hispanic/Latino; 1 American Indian or Alaska Native, non-Hispanic/Latino; 2 Asian, non-Hispanic/Latino; 1 Two or more races, non-Hispanic/Latino), 2 international. Average age 34. 39 applicants, 85% accepted, 15 enrolled. In 2016, 20 master's awarded. *Degree requirements:* For master's, comprehensive exam. *Entrance requirements:* For master's, GRE General Test or MAT, minimum GPA of 2.75. *Application deadline:* For fall admission, 1/15 priority date for domestic students; for spring admission, 10/1 for domestic students. Applications are processed on a rolling basis. Application fee: $75. *Financial support:* In 2016–17, 20 students received support. Fellowships, career-related internships or fieldwork, Federal Work-Study, and tuition waivers (partial) available. Financial award application deadline: 1/15; financial award applicants required to submit FAFSA. *Faculty research:* Issues in teacher training. *Unit head:* Dr. Sylven S. Beck, Director, 202-994-3365, E-mail: sbeck@gwu.edu. *Application contact:* Sarah Lang, Director of Graduate Admissions, 202-994-1447, Fax: 202-994-7207, E-mail: slang@gwu.edu.

Georgia State University, College of Education and Human Development, Department of Early Childhood Education, Atlanta, GA 30302-3083. Offers early childhood and elementary education (PhD); early childhood education (M Ed, Ed S); mathematics education (M Ed); urban education (M Ed). *Accreditation:* NCATE. *Program availability:* Part-time, evening/weekend. *Faculty:* 27 full-time (22 women). *Students:* 68 full-time (60 women), 7 part-time (all women); includes 40 minority (33 Black or African American, non-Hispanic/Latino; 1 Asian, non-Hispanic/Latino; 4 Hispanic/Latino; 2 Two or more races, non-Hispanic/Latino), 3 international. Average age 32. 16 applicants, 44% accepted, 6 enrolled. In 2016, 35 master's, 4 doctorates awarded. *Degree requirements:* For master's, comprehensive exam (for some programs), thesis (for some programs); for doctorate, comprehensive exam, thesis/dissertation (for some programs); for Ed S, comprehensive exam (for some programs). *Entrance requirements:* For master's, GRE, undergraduate diploma; for doctorate and Ed S, GRE, master's degree. Additional exam requirements/recommendations for international students: Required—TOEFL (minimum score 550 paper-based; 79 iBT) or IELTS (minimum score 6.5). *Application deadline:* Applications are processed on a rolling basis. Application fee: $50. Electronic applications accepted. *Expenses:* Tuition, state resident: full-time $6876; part-time $382 per credit hour. Tuition, nonresident: full-time $22,374; part-time $1243 per credit hour. *Required fees:* $2128; $1064 per term. Part-time tuition and fees vary according to course load and program. *Financial support:* In 2016–17, fellowships with full tuition reimbursements (averaging $24,000 per year), research assistantships with tuition reimbursements (averaging $4,000 per year), teaching assistantships with full tuition reimbursements (averaging $2,000 per year) were awarded; career-related internships or fieldwork, Federal Work-Study, institutionally sponsored loans, scholarships/grants, traineeships, health care benefits, tuition waivers (partial), and unspecified assistantships also available. Support available to part-time students. Financial award applicants required to submit FAFSA. *Faculty research:* Teacher development; language arts/literacy education; mathematics education; intersection of science, urban, and multicultural education; diversity in education. *Unit head:* Dr. Barbara Meyers, Department Chair, 404-413-8021, Fax: 404-413-8023, E-mail: barbara@gsu.edu. *Application contact:* Elaine King Jones, Administrative Curriculum Specialist, 404-413-8234, Fax: 404-413-8023, E-mail: ekjones@gsu.edu.
Website: http://ecee.education.gsu.edu/

Gonzaga University, School of Education, Spokane, WA 99258. Offers clinical mental health counseling (MA); elementary education (MIT); leadership and administration (MA); marriage and family counseling (MA); school counseling (MA); secondary education (MIT); special education (M Ed, MIT); sport and athletic administration (MA). *Accreditation:* NCATE. *Program availability:* Part-time, evening/weekend, 100% online. *Faculty:* 22 full-time (17 women), 38 part-time/adjunct (22 women). *Students:* 104 full-time (73 women), 275 part-time (184 women); includes 31 minority (5 Black or African American, non-Hispanic/Latino; 1 American Indian or Alaska Native, non-Hispanic/Latino; 3 Asian, non-Hispanic/Latino; 18 Hispanic/Latino; 4 Two or more races, non-Hispanic/Latino), 163 international. Average age 32. 419 applicants, 67% accepted, 165 enrolled. In 2016, 39 master's awarded. *Degree requirements:* For master's, comprehensive exam. *Entrance requirements:* For master's, GRE, MAT, and/or Washington Educators Skills Test-Basic (WEST-B), official transcripts from all colleges or universities attended, interview, two letters of recommendation, resume, essay, minimum GPA of 3.0. Additional exam requirements/recommendations for international students: Required—TOEFL (minimum score 580 paper-based, 88 iBT) or IELTS (minimum score 6.5). *Application deadline:* Applications are processed on a rolling basis. Application fee: $50. Electronic applications accepted. *Expenses:* Contact institution. *Financial support:* In 2016–17, 28 students received support. Scholarships/grants and tuition waivers available. Support available to part-time students. Financial award applicants required to submit FAFSA. *Unit head:* Dr. Vincent Alfonso, Dean, 509-313-3594, Fax: 509-313-5821, E-mail: alfonso@gonzaga.edu. *Application contact:* Luke Cairney, Graduate Admissions Program Specialist, 509-313-3821, E-mail: cairney@gonzaga.edu.
Website: http://www.gonzaga.edu/Academics/Colleges-and-Schools/School-of-Education

Gordon College, Graduate Education Program, Wenham, MA 01984-1899. Offers early childhood (M Ed); educational leadership (M Ed, Ed S); elementary education (M Ed); English as a second language (M Ed, Ed S); math specialist (M Ed); mathematics specialist (Ed S); middle school education (M Ed); moderate disabilities (M Ed); Montessori education (M Ed); reading (M Ed, Ed S); secondary education (M Ed). *Program availability:* Part-time, evening/weekend. *Faculty:* 17 full-time (9 women), 41 part-time/adjunct (34 women). *Students:* 81 full-time (61 women), 109 part-time (87 women); includes 28 minority (2 Black or African American, non-Hispanic/Latino; 11 Asian, non-Hispanic/Latino; 13 Hispanic/Latino; 2 Two or more races, non-Hispanic/ Latino), 12 international. Average age 34. 190 applicants, 100% accepted, 141 enrolled. In 2016, 110 master's, 16 Ed Ss awarded. *Degree requirements:* For master's, action research or clinical experience (for most programs); for Ed S, action research or clinical experience (for some programs). *Entrance requirements:* For master's, minimum undergraduate GPA of 3.0; 2 official undergraduate transcripts; professional resume; 3 recommendation letters (one professional reference, one academic reference, one personal reference); 500-700 word statement of purpose; for Ed S, minimum master's GPA of 3.3; 2 official transcripts from undergraduate and graduate schools; professional resume; 3 recommendation letters (one professional reference, one academic reference, one personal reference); 500-700 word statement of purpose. Additional exam requirements/recommendations for international students: Required—TOEFL (minimum score 550 paper-based, 80 iBT) or IELTS (minimum score 6.5). *Application deadline:* Applications are processed on a rolling basis. Application fee: $75. *Expenses:* $325 per credit tuition, $75 per term fee. *Financial support:* Applicants required to submit FAFSA. *Faculty research:* Reading, early childhood development, English language learners, universal design for learning. *Unit head:* Dr. Janet Arndt, Director of Graduate Studies, 978-867-4355, Fax: 978-867-4663. *Application contact:* Julie Lenocker, Program Administrator, 978-867-4322, Fax: 978-867-4663, E-mail: graduate-education@gordon.edu.
Website: http://www.gordon.edu/graduate

Goucher College, Graduate Programs in Education, Baltimore, MD 21204-2794. Offers at-risk and diverse learners (M Ed, Certificate); athletic program leadership and administration (M Ed, Certificate); elementary and special education (MAT); elementary education (MAT); literacy strategies for content learning (M Ed, Certificate); middle school (M Ed, Certificate); Montessori studies (M Ed); reading instruction (M Ed, Certificate); school improvement leadership (M Ed, Certificate); school mediation (M Ed, Certificate); secondary and special education (MAT); secondary education (MAT); special education (MAT), including elementary education, secondary education; special education for certified teachers (M Ed, Certificate); teacher as leader in technology (M Ed, Certificate). *Program availability:* Part-time, evening/weekend. *Faculty:* 3 full-time (all women), 52 part-time/adjunct (40 women). *Students:* 29 full-time (20 women), 285 part-time (217 women); includes 54 minority (41 Black or African American, non-Hispanic/Latino; 3 Asian, non-Hispanic/Latino; 7 Hispanic/Latino; 3 Two or more races, non-Hispanic/Latino), 1 international. Average age 34. 85 applicants, 100% accepted, 61 enrolled. In 2016, 207 master's awarded. *Degree requirements:* For master's, thesis (M Ed), final presentation (MAT). *Entrance requirements:* For master's, minimum GPA of 3.0. Additional exam requirements/recommendations for international students: Required—TOEFL (minimum score 560 paper-based). *Application deadline:* For fall admission, 9/1 for domestic students; for spring admission, 1/15 for domestic students. Applications are processed on a rolling basis. Application fee: $75. Electronic applications accepted. *Expenses:* Contact institution. *Financial support:* Career-related internships or fieldwork and unspecified assistantships available. Support available to part-time students. Financial award application deadline: 4/15; financial award applicants required to submit FAFSA. *Faculty research:* Urban education, middle school, school improvement, teacher education, at-risk student achievement. *Unit head:* Dr. Phyllis Sunshine, Assistant Provost, 410-337-6047, Fax: 410-337-6394, E-mail: psunshin@goucher.edu. *Application contact:* Shelby Hillers, Admissions Coordinator, 410-337-6200, Fax: 410-337-6085, E-mail: shelby.hillers@goucher.edu.
Website: http://www.goucher.edu/graduate-programs/graduate-programs-in-education

Grand Canyon University, College of Education, Phoenix, AZ 85017-1097. Offers autism spectrum disorders (MA); curriculum and instruction (MA); early childhood education (M Ed); educational administration (M Ed); educational leadership (M Ed); elementary education (M Ed); gifted education (MA); instructional technology (MS); K-12 leadership (Ed S); reading (MA); secondary education (M Ed); secondary humanities education (M Ed); secondary STEM education (M Ed); special education (M Ed); teaching and learning (Ed D); teaching English to speakers of other languages (MA). *Program availability:* Part-time, evening/weekend, online learning. *Degree requirements:* For master's, publishable research paper (M Ed), e-portfolio. *Entrance requirements:* For master's, undergraduate degree from accredited, GCU-approved college, university, or program with minimum GPA 2.8. Additional exam requirements/recommendations for international students: Required—TOEFL (minimum score 550 paper-based; 79 iBT), IELTS (minimum score 6). *Application deadline:* For fall admission, 8/21 for domestic students, 7/2 for international students; for spring admission, 12/24 for domestic students, 11/1 for international students. Applications are processed on a rolling basis. Application fee: $100. Electronic applications accepted. *Financial support:* Federal Work-Study available. Support available to part-time students. Financial award applicants required to submit FAFSA. *Unit head:* Dr. Kimberly L. LaPrade, Dean, 602-639-6360, E-mail: kimberly.laprade@gcu.edu. *Application contact:* Dr. Kimberly L. LaPrade, Dean, 602-639-6360, E-mail: kimberly.laprade@gcu.edu.
Website: https://www.gcu.edu/college-of-education.php

Grand Valley State University, College of Education, Programs in General Education, Allendale, MI 49401-9403. Offers adult and higher education (M Ed); early childhood education (M Ed); educational differentiation (M Ed); educational leadership (M Ed); educational technology integration (M Ed); elementary education (M Ed); middle level education (M Ed); school library media services (M Ed); secondary level education (M Ed); teaching English to speakers of other languages (M Ed). *Program availability:* Part-time, evening/weekend, 100% online, blended/hybrid learning. *Students:* 28 part-time (20 women); includes 6 minority (4 Black or African American, non-Hispanic/Latino; 1 American Indian or Alaska Native, non-Hispanic/Latino; 1 Hispanic/Latino). Average age 42. In 2016, 17 master's awarded. *Degree requirements:* For master's, project or thesis. *Entrance requirements:* For master's, GRE General Test or minimum GPA of 3.0, last 60 credits from regionally-accredited college/university, 3 letters of recommendation. Additional exam requirements/recommendations for international students: Required—TOEFL (minimum score 550 paper-based, 80 iBT), IELTS (6.5), or Michigan English Language Assessment Battery. *Application deadline:* Applications are processed on a rolling basis. Application fee: $30. Electronic applications accepted. *Expenses:* $628 per credit hour. *Financial support:* In 2016–17, 2 students received support. Career-related internships or fieldwork, Federal Work-Study, scholarships/ grants, and unspecified assistantships available. *Faculty research:* Effectiveness of technology in education, parental involvement, effective teaching, effective schools research. *Unit head:* Dr. Doug Busman, Graduate Program Director, 616-331-6250, E-mail: busmando@gvsu.edu. *Application contact:* Thomas Owens, Director, Student Information and Services Center, 616-331-6282, Fax: 616-331-6217, E-mail: owenst@gvsu.edu.
Website: http://www.gvsu.edu/coe/

Greensboro College, Program in Education, Greensboro, NC 27401-1875. Offers elementary education (M Ed); special education (M Ed). *Program availability:* Part-time, evening/weekend. *Degree requirements:* For master's, thesis. *Entrance requirements:* For master's, GRE, teacher license, 2 years of teaching experience, 2 letters of recommendation. Additional exam requirements/recommendations for international students: Required—TOEFL (minimum score 550 paper-based). Electronic applications accepted.

Greenville College, Program in Education, Greenville, IL 62246-0159. Offers education (MAT); elementary education (MAE); secondary education (MAE). *Degree requirements:* For master's, thesis (for some programs). *Entrance requirements:* For master's, GRE, Illinois Basic Skills Test, teacher certification. Electronic applications accepted.

Hampton University, School of Education and Human Development, Program in Elementary Education, Hampton, VA 23668. Offers MA. *Accreditation:* NCATE. *Program availability:* Part-time, evening/weekend. *Faculty:* 5 full-time (all women), 2 part-time/ adjunct (both women). *Students:* 4 full-time (3 women), 8 part-time (6 women); all minorities (10 Black or African American, non-Hispanic/Latino; 1 Asian, non-Hispanic/ Latino; 1 Hispanic/Latino). In 2016, 6 master's awarded. *Entrance requirements:* For master's, GRE General Test. Additional exam requirements/recommendations for international students: Required—TOEFL (minimum score 525 paper-based) or IELTS (6.5). *Application deadline:* For fall admission, 6/1 priority date for domestic students, 4/ 1 priority date for international students; for winter admission, 11/1 priority date for domestic students, 9/1 priority date for international students; for spring admission, 11/1 for domestic students, 9/1 for international students; for summer admission, 4/1 priority date for domestic students, 2/1 priority date for international students. Applications are processed on a rolling basis. Application fee: $35. Electronic applications accepted. *Expenses: Tuition:* Full-time $10,776; part-time $548 per credit hour. *Required fees:* $35; $35 per credit hour. Tuition and fees vary according to course load and program. *Financial support:* Fellowships, research assistantships, teaching assistantships, career-related internships or fieldwork, Federal Work-Study, institutionally sponsored loans, and scholarships/grants available. Support available to part-time students. Financial award application deadline: 6/30; financial award applicants required to submit FAFSA. *Unit head:* Dr. Ava Marrow, Program Coordinator, 757-727-2072.

Harding University, Cannon-Clary College of Education, Searcy, AR 72149-0001. Offers advanced studies in teaching and learning (M Ed); art (MSE); behavioral science (MSE); counseling (MS, Ed S); early childhood special education (M Ed, MSE); education (MSE); educational leadership (M Ed, Ed S); elementary education (M Ed); English (MSE); French (MSE); history/social science (MSE); kinesiology (MSE); math (MSE); reading (M Ed); secondary education (M Ed); Spanish (MSE); teaching (MAT); teaching English as a second language (MSE). *Accreditation:* NCATE. *Program availability:* Part-time, evening/weekend. *Faculty:* 22 full-time (9 women), 51 part-time/ adjunct (37 women). *Students:* 130 full-time (94 women), 321 part-time (234 women); includes 83 minority (50 Black or African American, non-Hispanic/Latino; 4 American Indian or Alaska Native, non-Hispanic/Latino; 6 Asian, non-Hispanic/Latino; 13 Hispanic/ Latino; 10 Two or more races, non-Hispanic/Latino), 11 international. Average age 35. 125 applicants, 88% accepted, 110 enrolled. In 2016, 124 master's, 27 other advanced degrees awarded. *Degree requirements:* For master's, comprehensive exam (for some programs), thesis optional, portfolio(s); for Ed S, comprehensive exam, portfolio, project. *Entrance requirements:* For master's, GRE, MAT, PRAXIS; for Ed S, MAT or GRE. Additional exam requirements/recommendations for international students: Required—TOEFL (minimum score 550 paper-based; 79 iBT). *Application deadline:* For fall admission, 8/1 for domestic and international students; for spring admission, 1/1 for domestic and international students. Applications are processed on a rolling basis. Application fee: $35. Tuition and fees vary according to degree level and program. *Financial support:* In 2016–17, 31 students received support. Unspecified assistantships available. *Faculty research:* Reading, comprehension, school violence, educational technology, behavior, college choice, differentiated instruction, brain-based teaching. *Unit head:* Dr. Clara Carroll, Chair, 501-279-4501, Fax: 501-279-4083, E-mail: ccarroll@harding.edu. *Application contact:* Information Contact, 501-279-4315, E-mail: gradstudiesedu@harding.edu.
Website: http://www.harding.edu/education

Hawai`i Pacific University, College of Extended and Interdisciplinary Education, Program in Elementary Education, Honolulu, HI 96813. Offers M Ed. *Accreditation:* TEAC. *Program availability:* Part-time, evening/weekend. *Faculty:* 3 full-time (2 women), 6 part-time/adjunct (3 women). *Students:* 11 full-time (8 women), 1 (woman) part-time; includes 4 minority (1 Asian, non-Hispanic/Latino; 2 Hispanic/Latino; 1 Two or more races, non-Hispanic/Latino). Average age 32. 11 applicants, 82% accepted, 6 enrolled. In 2016, 6 master's awarded. *Entrance requirements:* For master's, minimum undergraduate GPA of 3.0, background check, interview. Additional exam requirements/ recommendations for international students: Recommended—TOEFL (minimum score 550 paper-based; 80 iBT), IELTS (minimum score 6), TWE (minimum score 5). *Application deadline:* For fall admission, 2/15 priority date for domestic students; for spring admission, 10/15 priority date for domestic students. Applications are processed on a rolling basis. Application fee: $50. Electronic applications accepted. *Expenses: Tuition:* Full-time $17,190; part-time $955 per credit. *Required fees:* $150; $26 per credit. Tuition and fees vary according to course load and program. *Financial support:* In 2016–17, 6 students received support. Career-related internships or fieldwork, Federal Work-Study, scholarships/grants, tuition waivers, and unspecified assistantships available. Financial award application deadline: 3/1; financial award applicants required to submit FAFSA. *Unit head:* Gustavo Martines-Padilla, Program Director, 808-566-2432, E-mail: gmartinezpadilla@hpu.edu. *Application contact:* Danny Lam, Assistant Director of Graduate Admissions, 808-544-1135, E-mail: graduate@hpu.edu.
Website: http://www.hpu.edu/CHSS/Education/MEDEE/index.html

High Point University, Norcross Graduate School, High Point, NC 27268. Offers business administration (MBA); educational leadership (M Ed); elementary education (M Ed); history (MA); nonprofit management (MA); secondary math (M Ed); special education (M Ed); strategic communication (MA); teaching elementary education k-6 (MAT); teaching secondary mathematics 9-12 (MAT). *Accreditation:* NCATE. *Program availability:* Part-time, evening/weekend. *Degree requirements:* For master's, comprehensive exam (for some programs), thesis (for some programs). *Entrance requirements:* For master's, GMAT (MBA), GRE, MAT, minimum GPA of 3.0. Additional exam requirements/recommendations for international students: Required—TOEFL (minimum score 550 paper-based). Electronic applications accepted.

Hofstra University, School of Education, Programs in Teacher Education, Hempstead, NY 11549. Offers bilingual education (MA, Advanced Certificate); bilingual extension (Advanced Certificate), including education/speech language pathology; business education (MS Ed); early childhood and childhood education (MS Ed); early childhood education (MA, MS Ed); education technology (Advanced Certificate); elementary education (MA, MS Ed), including science, technology, engineering, and mathematics (STEM) (MA); English education (MS Ed); family and consumer science (MS Ed); fine arts and music education (Advanced Certificate); fine arts education (MS Ed); foreign language and TESOL (MS Ed); foreign language education (MS Ed), including French,

Elementary Education

German, Russian, Spanish; learning and teaching (Ed D), including applied linguistics, art education, arts and humanities, early childhood education, English education, human development, math education, math, science, and technology, multicultural education, physical education, science education, social studies education, special education; mathematics education (MA, MS Ed); middle school extension (Advanced Certificate), including grades 5-6, grades 7-9; music education (MA, MS Ed); science education (MA, MS Ed), including biology, chemistry, earth science, geology, physics; secondary education (Advanced Certificate); social studies education (MA, MS Ed); teaching languages other than English and TESOL (MS Ed); TESOL (MS Ed, Advanced Certificate). *Program availability:* Part-time, evening/weekend, blended/hybrid learning. *Students:* 139 full-time (97 women), 145 part-time (106 women); includes 60 minority (15 Black or African American, non-Hispanic/Latino; 1 American Indian or Alaska Native, non-Hispanic/Latino; 12 Asian, non-Hispanic/Latino; 31 Hispanic/Latino; 1 Two or more races, non-Hispanic/Latino), 21 international. Average age 29. 255 applicants, 86% accepted, 122 enrolled. In 2016, 101 master's, 4 doctorates, 43 other advanced degrees awarded. *Degree requirements:* For master's, comprehensive exam, thesis (for some programs), exit project, student teaching, fieldwork, electronic portfolio, curriculum project, minimum GPA of 3.0; for doctorate, thesis/dissertation; for Advanced Certificate, 3 foreign languages, comprehensive exam (for some programs), thesis project. *Entrance requirements:* For master's, GRE, MAT, 2 letters of recommendation, portfolio, teacher certification (MA), interview, essay; for doctorate, GMAT, GRE, LSAT, or MAT; for Advanced Certificate, 2 letters of recommendation, essay, interview and/or portfolio, teaching certificate. Additional exam requirements/recommendations for international students: Required—TOEFL (minimum score 550 paper-based; 80 iBT). *Application deadline:* Applications are processed on a rolling basis. Application fee: $75. Electronic applications accepted. *Expenses: Tuition:* Full-time $1240. *Required fees:* $970. Tuition and fees vary according to program. *Financial support:* In 2016–17, 149 students received support, including 58 fellowships with full and partial tuition reimbursements available (averaging $5,309 per year), 5 research assistantships with full and partial tuition reimbursements available (averaging $7,073 per year); career-related internships or fieldwork, Federal Work-Study, institutionally sponsored loans, scholarships/grants, traineeships, tuition waivers (full and partial), and unspecified assistantships also available. Support available to part-time students. Financial award applicants required to submit FAFSA. *Faculty research:* Educational interventions that foster critical-thinking skills; teachers' attitudes about professional development; threats to teacher quality. *Unit head:* Dr. Eustace Thompson, Chairperson, 516-463-5749, Fax: 516-463-6275, E-mail: eustace.g.thompson@hofstra.edu. *Application contact:* Sunil Samuel, Assistant Vice President of Admissions, 516-463-4723, Fax: 516-463-4664, E-mail: graduateadmission@hofstra.edu.
Website: http://www.hofstra.edu/education/

Hofstra University, School of Education, Specialized Programs in Education, Hempstead, NY 11549. Offers applied behavior analysis (Advanced Certificate); early childhood special education (MS Ed, Advanced Certificate); educational and policy leadership (Ed D); educational leadership (Advanced Certificate), including school building leader/school district business leader; educational leadership and policy studies (MS Ed), including K-12; gifted education (Advanced Certificate), including school building leader/school district business leader; health education PK-12 teaching certification (MS); inclusive early childhood special education (MS Ed); inclusive elementary special education (MS Ed); inclusive secondary special education (MS Ed); literacy studies (MS Ed, Ed D, PhD, Advanced Certificate), including birth-grade 6 (MS Ed, Advanced Certificate), birth-grade 6 and special education (birth-grade2) (MS Ed), grades 5-12 (MS Ed, Advanced Certificate); physical education (MS); secondary education generalist (MS Ed), including students with disabilities 7-12; special education (MS Ed, Advanced Certificate); special education assessment and diagnosis (Advanced Certificate); special education generalist (MS Ed), including extension in secondary education; sport science (MS), including strength and conditioning; teaching students with severe or multiple disabilities (Advanced Certificate). *Program availability:* Part-time, evening/weekend, 100% online, blended/hybrid learning. *Students:* 149 full-time (115 women), 258 part-time (187 women); includes 97 minority (50 Black or African American, non-Hispanic/Latino; 1 American Indian or Alaska Native, non-Hispanic/Latino; 11 Asian, non-Hispanic/Latino; 34 Hispanic/Latino; 1 Native Hawaiian or other Pacific Islander, non-Hispanic/Latino), 5 international. Average age 32. 250 applicants, 88% accepted, 146 enrolled. In 2016, 85 master's, 13 doctorates, 35 other advanced degrees awarded. *Degree requirements:* For master's, one foreign language, comprehensive exam (for some programs), thesis (for some programs), electronic portfolio, capstone course, internship, practicum, student teaching, seminars, minimum GPA of 3.0; for doctorate, one foreign language, comprehensive exam, thesis/dissertation, qualifying hearing. *Entrance requirements:* For master's, GRE, interview, letters of recommendation, portfolio, essay, certification; for doctorate, GRE or MAT, interview, resume, essay, master's degree, 3 letters of recommendation, writing sample; for Advanced Certificate, GRE, interview, letters of recommendation, essay, professional experience, resume, master's degree. Additional exam requirements/recommendations for international students: Required—TOEFL (minimum score 550 paper-based; 80 iBT). *Application deadline:* Applications are processed on a rolling basis. Application fee: $75. Electronic applications accepted. *Expenses: Tuition:* Full-time $1240. *Required fees:* $970. Tuition and fees vary according to program. *Financial support:* In 2016–17, 244 students received support, including 117 fellowships with full and partial tuition reimbursements available (averaging $3,705 per year), 12 research assistantships with full and partial tuition reimbursements available (averaging $6,490 per year); career-related internships or fieldwork, Federal Work-Study, institutionally sponsored loans, scholarships/grants, traineeships, tuition waivers (full and partial), and unspecified assistantships also available. Support available to part-time students. Financial award applicants required to submit FAFSA. *Faculty research:* Collaborative teaching and learning; language and culture; new media literacies; applied behavior analysis; K-12 leadership development. *Unit head:* Dr. Elfreda Blue, Chairperson, 516-463-5762, Fax: 516-463-6184, E-mail: elfreda.blue@hofstra.edu. *Application contact:* Sunil Samuel, Assistant Vice President of Admissions, 516-463-4723, Fax: 516-463-4664, E-mail: graduateadmission@hofstra.edu.
Website: http://www.hofstra.edu/education/

Holy Family University, Graduate and Professional Programs, School of Education, Master of Education Programs, Philadelphia, PA 19114. Offers early elementary education (PreK-Grade 4) (M Ed); education leadership (M Ed); general education (M Ed); reading specialist (M Ed); special education (M Ed); TESOL and literacy (M Ed). *Program availability:* Part-time. *Students:* 202 full-time, 58 part-time. 209 applicants, 77% accepted, 140 enrolled. In 2016, 123 master's awarded. *Degree requirements:* For master's, thesis optional. *Application deadline:* Applications are processed on a rolling basis. Application fee: $25. Electronic applications accepted. *Expenses: Tuition:* Part-time $751 per hour. *Required fees:* $140 per semester. One-time fee: $165 part-time. Part-time tuition and fees vary according to degree level and program. *Unit head:* Dr. Kevin Zook, Dean, 267-341-3246, Fax: 215-824-2438, E-mail: kzook@holyfamily.edu. *Application contact:* Donald Reimold, Director of Graduate Admissions, 267-341-5001, Fax: 215-637-1478, E-mail: dreimold@holyfamily.edu.

Hood College, Graduate School, Department of Education, Frederick, MD 21701-8575. Offers curriculum and instruction (MS), including elementary education, elementary science and mathematics education, secondary education, special education; educational leadership (MS); reading specialization (MS); STEM education (Certificate). *Accreditation:* NCATE. *Program availability:* Part-time-only, evening/weekend. *Faculty:* 3 full-time, 37 part-time/adjunct. *Students:* 1 (woman) full-time, 357 part-time (283 women); includes 71 minority (41 Black or African American, non-Hispanic/Latino; 6 Asian, non-Hispanic/Latino; 15 Hispanic/Latino; 9 Two or more races, non-Hispanic/Latino). Average age 33. 96 applicants, 95% accepted, 83 enrolled. In 2016, 47 master's awarded. *Degree requirements:* For master's, action research project, portfolio (for reading specialization); for Certificate, STEM capstone activity. *Entrance requirements:* For master's, minimum GPA of 2.75, teaching certification, writing sample during interview, letter of recommendation from principal (for educational leadership program only). Additional exam requirements/recommendations for international students: Required—TOEFL (minimum score 575 paper-based; 89 iBT), IELTS (minimum score 6.5). *Application deadline:* For fall admission, 8/15 priority date for domestic students, 8/5 for international students; for spring admission, 12/1 priority date for domestic students, 12/1 for international students; for summer admission, 5/1 priority date for domestic students, 4/15 for international students. Applications are processed on a rolling basis. Application fee: $35. Electronic applications accepted. *Expenses:* $450 per credit; $105 comprehensive fee per semester. *Financial support:* Tuition waivers (partial) and unspecified assistantships available. Financial award applicants required to submit FAFSA. *Faculty research:* Leadership, action research, brain research, learning styles. *Unit head:* April Boulton, Interim Dean of the Graduate School, E-mail: gofurther@hood.edu. *Application contact:* Jan Marcus, Assistant Director of Graduate Admissions, 301-696-3600, E-mail: gofurther@hood.edu.
Website: http://www.hood.edu/academics/education/index.html

Hope International University, School of Graduate and Professional Studies, Program in Education, Fullerton, CA 92831-3138. Offers education administration (MA); elementary education (ME); secondary education (ME). *Program availability:* Part-time, evening/weekend. *Degree requirements:* For master's, comprehensive exam (for some programs), thesis. *Entrance requirements:* For master's, minimum GPA of 3.0, 2 references. Additional exam requirements/recommendations for international students: Required—TOEFL (minimum score 550 paper-based; 86 iBT); Recommended—IELTS (minimum score 6.5). Electronic applications accepted. *Expenses:* Contact institution. *Faculty research:* Distance education.

Howard University, School of Education, Department of Curriculum and Instruction, Program in Elementary Education, Washington, DC 20059-0002. Offers M Ed. *Accreditation:* NCATE. *Degree requirements:* For master's, comprehensive exam, expository writing exam, internships, seminar paper. *Entrance requirements:* For master's, PRAXIS I, GRE, minimum GPA of 2.7. Additional exam requirements/recommendations for international students: Required—TOEFL (minimum score 550 paper-based; 79 iBT). Electronic applications accepted.

Hunter College of the City University of New York, Graduate School, School of Education, Department of Curriculum and Teaching and Department of Educational Foundations and Counseling, Program in Elementary Education, New York, NY 10065-5085. Offers MS. *Accreditation:* NCATE. *Degree requirements:* For master's, thesis, integrative seminar, New York State Teacher Certification Exams, student teaching. *Entrance requirements:* For master's, minimum undergraduate GPA of 2.8, writing sample. Additional exam requirements/recommendations for international students: Required—TOEFL, TWE. *Application deadline:* For fall admission, 4/1 for domestic students, 2/1 for international students; for spring admission, 11/1 for domestic students, 9/1 for international students. *Financial support:* Federal Work-Study, scholarships/grants, and tuition waivers (partial) available. Support available to part-time students. *Faculty research:* Urban education, multicultural education, gifted education, educational technology, cultural cognition. *Unit head:* Dr. Christina Taharally, Coordinator, 212-772-4679, E-mail: christina.taharally@hunter.cuny.edu. *Application contact:* Milena Solo, Director for Graduate Admissions, 212-772-4480, E-mail: admissions@hunter.cuny.edu.

Idaho State University, Office of Graduate Studies, College of Education, Department of Educational Foundations, Pocatello, ID 83209-8059. Offers child and family studies (M Ed); curriculum leadership (M Ed); education (M Ed); educational administration (M Ed); educational foundations (5th Year Certificate); elementary education (M Ed), including K-12 education, literacy, secondary education. *Program availability:* Part-time. *Degree requirements:* For master's, comprehensive exam, thesis optional, oral exam, written exam; for 5th Year Certificate, comprehensive exam, thesis (for some programs), oral exam, written exam. *Entrance requirements:* For master's, GRE General Test or MAT, minimum undergraduate GPA of 3.0; for 5th Year Certificate, GRE General Test, minimum undergraduate GPA of 3.0, master's degree. Additional exam requirements/recommendations for international students: Required—TOEFL (minimum score 550 paper-based; 80 iBT). Electronic applications accepted. *Faculty research:* Child and families studies; business education; special education; math, science, and technology education.

Indiana University Bloomington, School of Education, Department of Curriculum and Instruction, Bloomington, IN 47405-7000. Offers art education (MS, Ed D, PhD); curriculum studies (Ed D, PhD); elementary education (MS, Ed D, PhD, Ed S); mathematics education (MS, Ed D, PhD); science education (MS, Ed D, PhD); secondary education (MS, Ed D, PhD); social studies education (MS, PhD); special education (PhD, Ed S). *Accreditation:* NCATE. *Program availability:* Part-time, evening/weekend. Terminal master's awarded for partial completion of doctoral program. *Degree requirements:* For doctorate, thesis/dissertation; for Ed S, comprehensive exam or project. *Entrance requirements:* For master's, doctorate, and Ed S, GRE General Test. Electronic applications accepted.

Indiana University Northwest, School of Education, Gary, IN 46408. Offers educational leadership (MS Ed); elementary education (MS Ed); K-12 online teaching (Graduate Certificate); secondary education (MS Ed). *Accreditation:* NCATE. *Program availability:* Part-time, evening/weekend. *Faculty:* 10 full-time (5 women), 2 part-time/adjunct (both women). *Students:* 11 full-time (8 women), 67 part-time (47 women); includes 32 minority (25 Black or African American, non-Hispanic/Latino; 7 Hispanic/Latino). Average age 38. 24 applicants, 96% accepted, 14 enrolled. In 2016, 22 master's awarded. *Entrance requirements:* For master's, GRE General Test or MAT, minimum GPA of 3.0. *Application deadline:* For fall admission, 7/15 priority date for domestic students; for spring admission, 11/15 for domestic students. Application fee: $40 ($60 for international students). Electronic applications accepted. *Expenses:* $276.98 per credit hour in-state; $652.54 per credit hour out-of-state. *Financial support:* Applicants required to submit FAFSA. *Unit head:* Dr. Charles Hobsen, Interim Dean, 219-980-6903, Fax: 219-680-4208, E-mail: chobson@iun.edu. *Application contact:* Kelly Zieba, Director of Enrollment Management, Finance, and Operations, 219-980-6879, Fax: 219-980-4208, E-mail: kmzieba@iun.edu.
Website: http://www.iun.edu/education/degrees/masters.htm

Indiana University–Purdue University Fort Wayne, College of Education and Public Policy, Department of Educational Studies, Fort Wayne, IN 46805-1499. Offers elementary education (MS Ed); secondary education (MS Ed). *Accreditation:* NCATE.

Program availability: Part-time. *Entrance requirements:* For master's, minimum GPA of 2.5, three professional letters of recommendation. Additional exam requirements/recommendations for international students: Required—TOEFL (minimum score 550 paper-based; 79 iBT). *Faculty research:* International faculty, gender in Burmese refugee narratives, planning effective instruction.

Indiana University South Bend, School of Education, South Bend, IN 46634-7111. Offers addiction counseling (MS Ed); alcohol and drug counseling (Graduate Certificate); clinical mental health counseling (MS Ed); educational leadership (MS Ed); elementary education (MS Ed); marriage, couple, and family counseling (MS Ed); school counseling (MS Ed); secondary education (MS Ed); special education (MAT, MS Ed), including intense intervention (MS Ed), mild intervention (MS Ed). *Accreditation:* NCATE. *Program availability:* Part-time, evening/weekend. *Faculty:* 21 full-time (11 women), 9 part-time/adjunct (3 women). *Students:* 26 full-time (19 women), 104 part-time (80 women); includes 22 minority (13 Black or African American, non-Hispanic/Latino; 5 Hispanic/Latino; 4 Two or more races, non-Hispanic/Latino). Average age 35. 51 applicants, 69% accepted, 22 enrolled. In 2016, 31 master's, 2 other advanced degrees awarded. *Degree requirements:* For master's, thesis or alternative, exit project. *Entrance requirements:* For master's, letters of recommendation, GRE or minimum GPA of 3.0. Additional exam requirements/recommendations for international students: Required—TOEFL. *Application deadline:* For fall admission, 7/1 for domestic students; for spring admission, 11/1 for domestic students. Applications are processed on a rolling basis. Application fee: $40 ($60 for international students). Electronic applications accepted. *Expenses:* $276.98 per credit hour in-state; $652.54 per credit hour out-of-state. *Financial support:* Career-related internships or fieldwork available. Support available to part-time students. Financial award application deadline: 3/1; financial award applicants required to submit FAFSA. *Faculty research:* Professional dispositions, early childhood literacy, online learning, program assessments, problem-based learning. *Unit head:* Dr. Marvin Lynn, Dean, 574-520-4339, E-mail: lynnm@iusb.edu. *Application contact:* Yvonne Walker, Student Services Representative, 574-520-4185, E-mail: ydwalker@iusb.edu.
Website: https://www.iusb.edu/education/index.php

Indiana University Southeast, School of Education, New Albany, IN 47150. Offers counselor education (MS Ed); elementary education (MS Ed); secondary education (MS Ed). *Accreditation:* NCATE. *Program availability:* Part-time, evening/weekend. *Students:* 13 full-time (10 women), 190 part-time (150 women); includes 29 minority (21 Black or African American, non-Hispanic/Latino; 5 Hispanic/Latino; 3 Two or more races, non-Hispanic/Latino). Average age 33. 61 applicants, 84% accepted, 43 enrolled. In 2016, 70 master's awarded. *Entrance requirements:* For master's, minimum undergraduate GPA of 2.5, graduate 3.0. *Application deadline:* Applications are processed on a rolling basis. Application fee: $40 ($60 for international students). Electronic applications accepted. *Financial support:* Career-related internships or fieldwork, Federal Work-Study, and institutionally sponsored loans available. Support available to part-time students. Financial award applicants required to submit FAFSA. *Faculty research:* Learning styles, technology, constructivism, group process, innovative math strategies. *Unit head:* Dr. Faye Marsha Camahalan, Director of Graduate Studies, 812-941-2136, Fax: 812-941-2667, E-mail: fcamahal@ius.edu. *Application contact:* Admissions Counselor, 812-941-2212, Fax: 812-941-2595, E-mail: admissions@ius.edu.
Website: http://www.ius.edu/education/graduate-programs/

Inter American University of Puerto Rico, Aguadilla Campus, Graduate School, Aguadilla, PR 00605. Offers accounting (MBA); counseling psychology specializing in family (MS); criminal justice (MA); educative management and leadership (MA); elementary education (M Ed); finance (MBA); human resources (MBA); industrial management (MBA); management information systems (MBA); marketing (MBA). *Program availability:* Part-time, evening/weekend. *Degree requirements:* For master's, comprehensive exam. *Entrance requirements:* For master's, EXADEP, 2 letters of recommendation, minimum GPA of 2.5. Electronic applications accepted.

Inter American University of Puerto Rico, Arecibo Campus, Programs in Education, Arecibo, PR 00614-4050. Offers administration and educational supervision (MA Ed); counseling and guidance (MA Ed); curriculum and teaching (MA Ed), including biology education, English as a second language, history education, math education, Spanish; elementary education (MA Ed). *Accreditation:* TEAC. *Degree requirements:* For master's, comprehensive exam, thesis optional. *Entrance requirements:* For master's, GRE, EXADEP, bachelor's degree in education or teaching license (administration and supervision) or courses in education and psychology (counseling and guidance), minimum GPA of 2.5 in last 60 credits.

Inter American University of Puerto Rico, Barranquitas Campus, Program in Education, Barranquitas, PR 00794. Offers curriculum and teaching (M Ed), including biology education, English as a second language, history education, mathematics education, Spanish; educational leadership and management (MA); elementary education (M Ed); information and library service technology (M Ed); special education (MA). *Accreditation:* TEAC. *Degree requirements:* For master's, comprehensive exam, thesis optional. *Entrance requirements:* For master's, EXADEP, letter of recommendation. Electronic applications accepted.

Inter American University of Puerto Rico, Fajardo Campus, Graduate Programs, Fajardo, PR 00738-7003. Offers computer science (MS); educational management and leadership (MA Ed); elementary education (MA Ed); general business (MBA); management information systems (MBA); marketing (MBA); special education (MA Ed).

Inter American University of Puerto Rico, Guayama Campus, Department of Education and Social Sciences, Guayama, PR 00785. Offers early childhood education (0-4 years) (M Ed); elementary education (M Ed). *Program availability:* Part-time. *Entrance requirements:* For master's, GRE, MAT, EXADEP, letters of recommendation, minimum GPA of 2.5. Electronic applications accepted.

Inter American University of Puerto Rico, Metropolitan Campus, Graduate Programs, Program in Elementary Education, San Juan, PR 00919-1293. Offers MA. *Degree requirements:* For master's, comprehensive exam. *Entrance requirements:* For master's, GRE or EXADEP, interview. Electronic applications accepted.

Inter American University of Puerto Rico, Ponce Campus, Graduate School, Mercedita, PR 00715-1602. Offers accounting (MBA); biology (M Ed); chemistry (M Ed); criminal justice (MA); elementary education (M Ed); English as a Second Language (M Ed); finance (MBA); history (M Ed); human resources (MBA); marketing (MBA); mathematics (M Ed); Spanish (M Ed). *Entrance requirements:* For master's, minimum GPA of 2.5.

Inter American University of Puerto Rico, San Germán Campus, Graduate Studies Center, Program in Elementary Education, San Germán, PR 00683-5008. Offers MA. *Program availability:* Part-time, evening/weekend. *Degree requirements:* For master's, comprehensive exam. *Entrance requirements:* For master's, GRE General Test or EXADEP, minimum GPA of 3.0.

Iowa State University of Science and Technology, Department of Education, Ames, IA 50011. Offers curriculum and instructional technology (M Ed, MS, PhD); elementary education (M Ed, MS); historical, philosophical, and comparative studies in education (M Ed, MS); special education (M Ed, MS, PhD). *Degree requirements:* For master's, thesis or alternative; for doctorate, thesis/dissertation. *Entrance requirements:* For master's and doctorate, GRE General Test. Additional exam requirements/recommendations for international students: Required—TOEFL (minimum score 560 paper-based; 83 iBT), IELTS (minimum score 6.5). *Application deadline:* For fall admission, 1/1 priority date for domestic and international students; for spring admission, 9/1 for domestic and international students. Application fee: $60 ($90 for international students). Electronic applications accepted. *Application contact:* Robyn Goldy, Application Contact, 515-294-1241, Fax: 515-294-4942, E-mail: rgoldy@iastate.edu. Website: http://www.ci.hs.iastate.edu

Ithaca College, School of Humanities and Sciences, Program in Childhood Education, Ithaca, NY 14850. Offers MS. *Program availability:* Part-time. *Faculty:* 26 full-time (12 women). *Students:* 9 full-time (7 women); includes 2 minority (both Hispanic/Latino). Average age 25. 19 applicants, 74% accepted, 9 enrolled. *Degree requirements:* For master's, thesis or alternative. *Entrance requirements:* Additional exam requirements/recommendations for international students: Required—TOEFL (minimum score 550 paper-based; 80 iBT). *Application deadline:* For fall admission, 2/15 for domestic and international students; for spring admission, 12/1 for domestic and international students. Applications are processed on a rolling basis. Application fee: $40. Electronic applications accepted. *Expenses:* Contact institution. *Financial support:* In 2016–17, 7 students received support, including 7 research assistantships (averaging $13,736 per year); career-related internships or fieldwork, Federal Work-Study, scholarships/grants, and unspecified assistantships also available. Support available to part-time students. Financial award application deadline: 2/15; financial award applicants required to submit CSS PROFILE or FAFSA. *Unit head:* Peter Martin, Chair, 607-274-1076, Fax: 607-274-1263, E-mail: pmartin@ithaca.edu. *Application contact:* Nicole Eversley Bradwell, Director, Office of Admission, 607-274-3124, Fax: 607-274-1263, E-mail: admission@ithaca.edu.
Website: http://www.ithaca.edu/gradprograms/education/programs/childhooded/

Jackson State University, Graduate School, College of Education and Human Development, Department of Elementary and Early Childhood Education, Jackson, MS 39217. Offers early childhood education (MS Ed, Ed D); elementary education (MS Ed, Ed S); reading education (MS Ed). *Accreditation:* NCATE. *Program availability:* Part-time, evening/weekend, 100% online, blended/hybrid learning. *Faculty:* 10 full-time (4 women). *Students:* 90 full-time (86 women), 132 part-time (123 women); includes 210 minority (207 Black or African American, non-Hispanic/Latino; 2 Hispanic/Latino; 1 Two or more races, non-Hispanic/Latino), 9 international. Average age 37. 137 applicants, 72% accepted, 58 enrolled. In 2016, 41 master's, 9 doctorates, 2 other advanced degrees awarded. Terminal master's awarded for partial completion of doctoral program. *Degree requirements:* For master's, comprehensive exam, thesis or alternative; for doctorate, comprehensive exam, thesis/dissertation. *Entrance requirements:* For master's, GRE General Test; for doctorate, MAT, teaching experience. Additional exam requirements/recommendations for international students: Required—TOEFL (minimum score 520 paper-based; 67 iBT). *Application deadline:* For fall admission, 3/1 priority date for domestic students, 3/1 for international students; for spring admission, 10/1 for domestic and international students. Applications are processed on a rolling basis. Application fee: $25. Electronic applications accepted. *Expenses:* Contact institution. *Financial support:* Career-related internships or fieldwork, Federal Work-Study, scholarships/grants, and unspecified assistantships available. Support available to part-time students. Financial award application deadline: 3/1; financial award applicants required to submit FAFSA. *Unit head:* Dr. Thea Williams-Black, Chair, 601-979-2341, E-mail: thea.h.williams-black@jsums.edu. *Application contact:* Dr. Thea Williams-Black, Chair, 601-979-2341, E-mail: thea.h.williams-black@jsums.edu.
Website: http://www.jsums.edu/earlyeducation/

Jacksonville State University, College of Graduate Studies and Continuing Education, College of Education and Professional Studies, Program in Elementary Education, Jacksonville, AL 36265-1602. Offers MS Ed. *Accreditation:* NCATE. *Program availability:* Part-time, evening/weekend. *Faculty:* 10 full-time (9 women), 1 (woman) part-time/adjunct. *Students:* 21 full-time (17 women), 20 part-time (19 women); includes 7 minority (6 Black or African American, non-Hispanic/Latino; 1 Hispanic/Latino), 1 international. Average age 30. 21 applicants, 67% accepted, 7 enrolled. In 2016, 23 master's awarded. *Degree requirements:* For master's, comprehensive exam, thesis (for some programs). *Entrance requirements:* For master's, GRE General Test or MAT. Additional exam requirements/recommendations for international students: Required—TOEFL (minimum score 500 paper-based; 61 iBT). *Application deadline:* Applications are processed on a rolling basis. Application fee: $35. Electronic applications accepted. *Financial support:* In 2016–17, 7 students received support. Available to part-time students. Application deadline: 4/1; applicants required to submit FAFSA. *Unit head:* Dr. Janet Bavonese, Head, 256-782-8340, E-mail: jbavonses@jsu.edu. *Application contact:* Dr. Jean Pugliese, Associate Dean, 256-782-8278, Fax: 256-782-5321, E-mail: pugliese@jsu.edu.

James Madison University, The Graduate School, College of Education, Program in Education, Harrisonburg, VA 22807. Offers early childhood education (preK-3) (MAT); educational leadership (M Ed); educational technology (M Ed); elementary education (MAT); equity and cultural diversity (M Ed); inclusive early childhood education (MAT); K-8 mathematics specialist (M Ed); middle education (MAT); reading education (M Ed); secondary education (MAT); Spanish language and culture for educators (M Ed); TESOL (MAT). *Accreditation:* NCATE. *Program availability:* Part-time, evening/weekend. *Faculty:* 21 full-time (12 women), 5 part-time/adjunct (2 women). *Students:* 249 full-time (220 women), 123 part-time (86 women); includes 43 minority (7 Black or African American, non-Hispanic/Latino; 7 Asian, non-Hispanic/Latino; 17 Hispanic/Latino; 12 Two or more races, non-Hispanic/Latino), 2 international. Average age 30. 355 applicants, 98% accepted, 312 enrolled. In 2016, 247 master's awarded. Application fee: $55. Electronic applications accepted. *Financial support:* In 2016–17, 16 students received support. Career-related internships or fieldwork, Federal Work-Study, and 22 assistantships (averaging $7911) available. Financial award application deadline: 3/1; financial award applicants required to submit FAFSA. *Unit head:* Dr. Phillip M. Wishon, Dean, 540-568-6572, E-mail: wishonpm@jmu.edu. *Application contact:* Lynette D. Michael, Director of Graduate Admissions, 540-568-6131 Ext. 6395, Fax: 540-568-7860, E-mail: michaeld@jmu.edu.
Website: http://www.jmu.edu/coe/index.shtml

James Madison University, The Graduate School, College of Education, Program in Elementary Education, Harrisonburg, VA 22807. Offers MAT. *Students:* Average age 27. *Entrance requirements:* For master's, GRE General Test, PRAXIS II, minimum undergraduate GPA of 2.75, 2-page essay, interview. Additional exam requirements/recommendations for international students: Required—TOEFL. *Application deadline:* For fall admission, 5/1 for domestic students; for spring admission, 9/1 for domestic students. Applications are processed on a rolling basis. Application fee: $55. Electronic applications accepted. *Unit head:* Dr. Martha Ross, Academic Unit Head, 540-568-6255. *Application contact:* Lynette M. Bible, Director of Graduate Admissions, 540-568-6395, Fax: 540-568-7860, E-mail: biblelm@jmu.edu.

Johns Hopkins University, School of Education, Master's Programs in Education, Baltimore, MD 21218. Offers counseling (MS), including clinical mental health counseling, school counseling; education (MS), including educational studies, gifted education, reading, school administration and supervision, technology for educators; elementary education (MAT); health professions (M Ed); intelligence analysis (MS); organizational leadership (MS); secondary education (MAT), including biology, chemistry, earth/space science, English, physics, social studies; special education (MS), including early childhood special education, general special education studies, mild to moderate disabilities, severe disabilities. *Program availability:* Part-time, evening/weekend, 100% online, blended/hybrid learning. *Students:* 345 full-time (265 women), 1,601 part-time (1,245 women); includes 837 minority (392 Black or African American, non-Hispanic/Latino; 7 American Indian or Alaska Native, non-Hispanic/Latino; 141 Asian, non-Hispanic/Latino; 207 Hispanic/Latino; 7 Native Hawaiian or other Pacific Islander, non-Hispanic/Latino; 83 Two or more races, non-Hispanic/Latino), 55 international. Average age 27. 1,352 applicants, 76% accepted, 819 enrolled. In 2016, 642 master's awarded. *Degree requirements:* For master's, comprehensive exam (for some programs), portfolio, capstone project and/or internship; PRAXIS II (subject area assessments) for initial teacher preparation programs that lead to licensure. *Entrance requirements:* For master's, GRE (for full-time programs only); PRAXIS I/core or state-approved alternative (for initial teacher preparation programs that lead to licensure), minimum of bachelor's degree from regionally- or nationally-accredited institution; minimum GPA of 3.0 in all previous programs of study; official transcripts from all post-secondary institutions attended; essay; curriculum vitae/resume; letters of recommendation (3 for full-time programs, 2 for part-time programs); dispositions survey. Additional exam requirements/recommendations for international students: Required—TOEFL (minimum score 600 paper-based; 100 iBT), IELTS (minimum score 7). *Application deadline:* For fall admission, 4/1 priority date for domestic students, 4/1 for international students; for spring admission, 10/1 priority date for domestic students, 10/1 for international students; for summer admission, 2/1 priority date for domestic students, 2/1 for international students. Applications are processed on a rolling basis. Application fee: $80. Electronic applications accepted. *Expenses:* Contact institution. *Financial support:* Application deadline: 4/1; applicants required to submit FAFSA. *Unit head:* Dr. Christopher C. Morphew, Dean. *Application contact:* Elisabeth Woodward, Director of Admissions, 410-516-9796, Fax: 410-516-9817, E-mail: soe.info@jhu.edu.
Website: http://education.jhu.edu

Johnson & Wales University, Graduate Studies, MAT Program in Teacher Education, Providence, RI 02903-3703. Offers business education and secondary special education (MAT); culinary arts education (MAT); elementary education and elementary special education (MAT); elementary education and elementary/secondary special education (MAT); elementary education and secondary special education (MAT); food service education (MAT). *Program availability:* Part-time, evening/weekend. *Entrance requirements:* For master's, MAT, minimum GPA of 2.75. Additional exam requirements/recommendations for international students: Required—TOEFL (minimum score 550 paper-based) or IELTS (recommended). *Faculty research:* Secondary education, student teaching, educational reform, evaluation procedures.

Kansas State University, Graduate School, College of Education, Department of Curriculum and Instruction, Manhattan, KS 66506. Offers curriculum and instruction (Ed D, PhD); digital teaching and learning (MS); educational computing, design and online learning (MS); elementary/middle level curriculum and instruction (MS); online learning (Certificate); reading specialist endorsement (MS); reading/language arts (MS); teacher leader/school improvement (MS); teaching and learning (Certificate). *Accreditation:* NCATE. *Program availability:* Part-time, online learning. *Faculty:* 36 full-time (22 women), 18 part-time/adjunct (9 women). *Students:* 59 full-time (40 women), 94 part-time (72 women); includes 21 minority (5 Black or African American, non-Hispanic/Latino; 3 Asian, non-Hispanic/Latino; 11 Hispanic/Latino; 2 Two or more races, non-Hispanic/Latino), 20 international. Average age 35. 70 applicants, 71% accepted, 36 enrolled. In 2016, 61 master's, 12 doctorates, 9 other advanced degrees awarded. *Degree requirements:* For master's, comprehensive exam, portfolio, project, report or thesis; for doctorate, comprehensive exam, thesis/dissertation, preliminary exam; for Certificate, comprehensive exam, portfolio. *Entrance requirements:* For master's, minimum GPA of 3.0, 3 letters of recommendation; for doctorate, GRE, minimum GPA of 3.0, 3 letters of recommendation, evidence of scholarly writing; for Certificate, minimum GPA of 3.0, letters of recommendation. Additional exam requirements/recommendations for international students: Required—TOEFL (minimum score 550 paper-based; 80 iBT) or IELTS. *Application deadline:* For fall admission, 3/1 priority date for domestic students, 2/1 priority date for international students; for spring admission, 10/1 priority date for domestic students, 8/1 priority date for international students. Applications are processed on a rolling basis. Application fee: $50 ($75 for international students). Electronic applications accepted. *Expenses:* Tuition, state resident: full-time $9670. Tuition, nonresident: full-time $21,828. *Required fees:* $862. *Financial support:* In 2016–17, 1 research assistantship (averaging $19,980 per year), 8 teaching assistantships (averaging $12,620 per year) were awarded; career-related internships or fieldwork, institutionally sponsored loans, scholarships/grants, and unspecified assistantships also available. Support available to part-time students. Financial award application deadline: 3/1; financial award applicants required to submit FAFSA. *Faculty research:* Literacy and technology, critical race theory and diversity, achievement gaps, school improvement, teacher education. *Total annual research expenditures:* $647,057. *Unit head:* Dr. F. Todd Goodson, Department Chair, 785-532-5904, Fax: 785-532-7304, E-mail: tgoodson@ksu.edu. *Application contact:* Dr. Kay Ann Taylor, Director, Curriculum and Instruction Graduate Programs, 785-532-6974, Fax: 785-532-7304, E-mail: ktaylor@ksu.edu.
Website: http://www.coe.ksu.edu/edci/index.html

Kennesaw State University, Leland and Clarice C. Bagwell College of Education, Program in Graduate Education, Kennesaw, GA 30144. Offers educational leadership (M Ed); educational leadership technology (M Ed); elementary and early childhood education (M Ed); instructional technology (M Ed); middle grades education (M Ed); reading (M Ed); secondary education (M Ed); special education (M Ed); teaching English to speakers of other languages (M Ed). *Accreditation:* NCATE. *Program availability:* Part-time. *Degree requirements:* For master's, thesis or alternative. *Entrance requirements:* For master's, GRE General Test, T-4 state certification, minimum GPA of 2.75. Additional exam requirements/recommendations for international students: Required—TOEFL (minimum score 550 paper-based; 80 iBT), IELTS (minimum score 6.5). Electronic applications accepted.

Keuka College, Program in Childhood Education/Literacy, Keuka Park, NY 14478. Offers literacy 5-12 (MS); literacy B-6 (MS). *Faculty:* 7 full-time (5 women). *Students:* 9 full-time (8 women); includes 1 minority (Hispanic/Latino). Average age 23. 9 applicants, 100% accepted, 9 enrolled. In 2016, 8 master's awarded. *Degree requirements:* For master's, thesis, capstone project/student-led research project. *Entrance requirements:* For master's, GRE, minimum GPA of 3.0; 3 letters of recommendation (2 academic and one from cooperating teacher from student teaching or other professional). Additional exam requirements/recommendations for international students: Required—TOEFL (minimum score 550 paper-based). *Application deadline:* For fall admission, 8/15 priority date for domestic students; for winter admission, 12/15 priority date for domestic students; for spring admission, 4/15 priority date for domestic students. Applications are processed on a rolling basis. Application fee: $50. Electronic applications accepted. *Expenses:* Contact institution. *Financial support:* In 2016–17, 8 students received support. Scholarships/grants and tuition waivers (full and partial) available. Financial award applicants required to submit FAFSA. *Faculty research:* Marginalized populations, international literacy, teacher assessment. *Unit head:* Dr. Andrew Beigel, Director of Graduate Program in Education, 315-279-5442 Ext. 5662, E-mail: abeigel@keuka.edu. *Application contact:* Anna Decker, Secretary, Graduate Education, 315-279-5510, E-mail: adecker@keuka.edu.

Kutztown University of Pennsylvania, College of Education, Program in Elementary Education, Kutztown, PA 19530-0730. Offers M Ed. *Accreditation:* NCATE. *Program availability:* Part-time, evening/weekend. *Faculty:* 5 full-time (4 women). *Students:* 1 (woman) full-time, 42 part-time (38 women); includes 2 minority (1 Asian, non-Hispanic/Latino; 1 Two or more races, non-Hispanic/Latino). Average age 31. 38 applicants, 89% accepted, 24 enrolled. In 2016, 11 master's awarded. *Degree requirements:* For master's, comprehensive exam, thesis optional, comprehensive project. *Entrance requirements:* For master's, GRE General Test, PA teaching certificate in elementary education, 3 letters of recommendation. Additional exam requirements/recommendations for international students: Required—TOEFL (minimum score 550 paper-based, 79 iBT) or IELTS (minimum score 6.5). *Application deadline:* For fall admission, 8/1 for domestic and international students; for spring admission, 12/1 for domestic and international students. Application fee: $35. Electronic applications accepted. *Expenses:* Tuition, state resident: full-time $4347; part-time $483 per credit. Tuition, nonresident: full-time $6525; part-time $725 per credit. *Required fees:* $88 per credit. One-time fee: $50 full-time. *Financial support:* Career-related internships or fieldwork, Federal Work-Study, scholarships/grants, and unspecified assistantships available. Financial award application deadline: 3/1; financial award applicants required to submit FAFSA. *Faculty research:* Whole language, middle schools, cooperative learning discussion techniques, oral reading techniques, hemisphericity. *Unit head:* Dr. Jeanie Burnett, Chairperson, 610-683-4286, Fax: 610-683-1327, E-mail: burnett@kutztown.edu.
Website: https://www.kutztown.edu/academics/graduate-programs/elementary-education.htm

Lake Forest College, Master of Arts in Teaching Program, Lake Forest, IL 60045. Offers elementary education (MAT); K-12 French (MAT); K-12 music (MAT); K-12 Spanish (MAT); K-12 visual art (MAT); secondary biology (MAT); secondary chemistry (MAT); secondary English (MAT); secondary history (MAT); secondary mathematics (MAT). *Degree requirements:* For master's, comprehensive exam, portfolio. *Entrance requirements:* For master's, GRE.

Lancaster Bible College, Graduate School, Lancaster, PA 17601-5036. Offers adult ministries (MA); Bible (MA); children and family ministry (MA); church planting (MA); consulting resource teacher (M Ed); elementary school counseling (M Ed); leadership (PhD); leadership studies (MA); marriage and family counseling (MA); mental health counseling (MA); pastoral studies (MA); secondary school counseling (M Ed); sports ministry (MA); student ministry (MA); town and country ministry (MA). *Program availability:* Part-time, evening/weekend. *Degree requirements:* For master's, comprehensive exam (for some programs), thesis (for some programs). *Entrance requirements:* For master's, bachelor's degree with a minimum of 30 credits of course work in Bible, minimum undergraduate GPA of 3.0, interview. Additional exam requirements/recommendations for international students: Required—TOEFL.

Langston University, School of Education and Behavioral Sciences, Langston, OK 73050. Offers bilingual/multicultural (M Ed); elementary education (M Ed); English as a second language (M Ed); rehabilitation counseling (M Sc); urban education (M Ed). *Accreditation:* CORE; NCATE (one or more programs are accredited). *Program availability:* Part-time. *Degree requirements:* For master's, comprehensive exam, thesis optional. *Entrance requirements:* For master's, GRE, writing skills test, minimum GPA of 2.5, 3 letters of recommendation. Additional exam requirements/recommendations for international students: Required—TOEFL, TWE. *Faculty research:* Bilingual/multicultural education, financing post-secondary education.

Lasell College, Graduate and Professional Studies in Education, Newton, MA 02466. Offers elementary education (M Ed); special education (M Ed), including moderate disabilities. *Program availability:* Part-time-only, evening/weekend, blended/hybrid learning. *Faculty:* 3 full-time (all women), 6 part-time/adjunct (5 women). *Students:* 4 full-time (3 women), 45 part-time (40 women); includes 2 minority (1 Hispanic/Latino; 1 Two or more races, non-Hispanic/Latino). Average age 28. 31 applicants, 58% accepted, 9 enrolled. In 2016, 12 master's awarded. *Degree requirements:* For master's, minimum GPA of 3.0; practicum. *Entrance requirements:* For master's, Massachusetts Tests for Educator Licensure (MTEL) Curriculum and Literacy foundations of reading and writing subtest, one-page personal statement, 2 letters of recommendation, resume, bachelor's degree transcript. Additional exam requirements/recommendations for international students: Required—TOEFL (minimum score 550 paper-based, 79 iBT) or IELTS (minimum score 6). *Application deadline:* For fall admission, 8/31 priority date for domestic students, 6/30 priority date for international students; for spring admission, 12/31 priority date for domestic students, 10/31 priority date for international students. Applications are processed on a rolling basis. Electronic applications accepted. *Expenses:* $600 per credit. *Financial support:* In 2016–17, 13 students received support. Federal Work-Study, scholarships/grants, and tuition discounts available. Support available to part-time students. Financial award application deadline: 8/31; financial award applicants required to submit FAFSA. *Faculty research:* Inclusion, English language learners, literacy, and urban education; teacher inquiry; universal design for learning, deaf-blindness, and visual impairments; social and emotional learning; educational law, applied behavior analysis, and classroom management. *Unit head:* Dr. Joan Dolamore, Dean of Graduate and Professional Studies, 617-243-2485, Fax: 617-243-2450, E-mail: gradinfo@lasell.edu. *Application contact:* Adrienne Franciosi, Director of Graduate Enrollment, 617-243-2214, Fax: 617-243-2450, E-mail: gradinfo@lasell.edu.
Website: http://www.lasell.edu/academics/graduate-and-professional-studies/programs-of-study/master-of-education.html

Lee University, Program in Education, Cleveland, TN 37320-3450. Offers art (MAT); curriculum and instruction (M Ed, Ed S); early childhood (MAT); educational leadership (M Ed, Ed S); elementary education (MAT); English and math (MAT); English and science (MAT); English and social studies (MAT); higher education administration (MS); history (MAT); history and economics (MAT); math and science (MAT); math and social studies (MAT); middle grades (MAT); science and social studies (MASW); secondary education (MAT); Spanish (MAT); special education (M Ed, MAT); TESOL (MAT). *Accreditation:* NCATE. *Program availability:* Part-time. *Faculty:* 13 full-time (6 women), 9 part-time/adjunct (4 women). *Students:* 35 full-time (27 women), 50 part-time (32 women); includes 12 minority (5 Black or African American, non-Hispanic/Latino; 5 Hispanic/Latino; 2 Two or more races, non-Hispanic/Latino), 4 international. Average age 30. 43 applicants, 79% accepted, 28 enrolled. In 2016, 42 master's, 6 other advanced degrees awarded. *Degree requirements:* For master's, variable foreign language requirement, thesis optional, internship. *Entrance requirements:* For master's, MAT or GRE General Test, minimum undergraduate GPA of 2.75, 3 letters of recommendation, interview, writing sample, official transcripts, background check; for

Ed S, minimum undergraduate and master's GPA of 2.75, official transcripts for undergraduate and master's degrees. Additional exam requirements/recommendations for international students: Required—TOEFL (minimum score 61 iBT). *Application deadline:* For fall admission, 6/1 priority date for domestic and international students; for spring admission, 11/1 priority date for domestic and international students; for summer admission, 4/1 priority date for domestic and international students. Applications are processed on a rolling basis. Application fee: $25. Electronic applications accepted. *Expenses: Tuition:* Full-time $11,367; part-time $632 per credit hour. *Required fees:* $35 per term. One-time fee: $25. Tuition and fees vary according to program. *Financial support:* In 2016–17, 42 students received support. Career-related internships or fieldwork, Federal Work-Study, institutionally sponsored loans, scholarships/grants, and unspecified assistantships available. Financial award application deadline: 3/1; financial award applicants required to submit FAFSA. *Unit head:* Dr. William Kamm, Director, 423-614-8544, E-mail: wkamm@leeuniversity.edu. *Application contact:* Crystal Keeter, Graduate Education Secretary, 423-614-8544, E-mail: ckeeter@leeuniversity.edu.
Website: http://www.leeuniversity.edu/academics/graduate/education

Lehigh University, College of Education, Program in Teaching, Learning and Technology, Bethlehem, PA 18015. Offers elementary education (M Ed); instructional technology (MS); teaching, learning and technology (PhD); technology use in the schools (Graduate Certificate); M Ed/MA. *Program availability:* Part-time. *Faculty:* 7 full-time (3 women), 4 part-time/adjunct (2 women). *Students:* 29 full-time (22 women), 61 part-time (48 women); includes 10 minority (1 Black or African American, non-Hispanic/Latino; 4 Asian, non-Hispanic/Latino; 3 Hispanic/Latino; 1 Native Hawaiian or other Pacific Islander, non-Hispanic/Latino; 1 Two or more races, non-Hispanic/Latino), 7 international. Average age 31. 65 applicants, 82% accepted, 12 enrolled. In 2016, 25 master's, 1 doctorate awarded. Terminal master's awarded for partial completion of doctoral program. *Degree requirements:* For doctorate, comprehensive exam, thesis/dissertation, qualifying exam. *Entrance requirements:* For master's, minimum GPA of 3.0, 2 letters of recommendation, essay, transcript; for doctorate, GRE General Test, minimum graduate GPA of 3.0, writing sample, 2 letters of recommendation, essay, transcript. Additional exam requirements/recommendations for international students: Required—TOEFL (minimum score 600 paper-based; 93 iBT). *Application deadline:* For fall admission, 4/1 for domestic and international students; for summer admission, 4/1 for domestic and international students. Applications are processed on a rolling basis. Application fee: $65. Electronic applications accepted. *Expenses:* $565 per credit. *Financial support:* In 2016–17, 2 research assistantships (averaging $21,473 per year) were awarded; fellowships also available. Financial award application deadline: 1/31. *Faculty research:* Teaching and learning, K-16 curriculum development, Web-based learning, teaching and technology, language and literacy. *Unit head:* Dr. Lynn Columba, Director, 610-758-3237, Fax: 610-758-3243, E-mail: hlc0@lehigh.edu. *Application contact:* Donna Toothman, Coordinator, 610-758-3230, Fax: 610-758-3243, E-mail: djt2@lehigh.edu.
Website: http://ed.lehigh.edu/academics/degrees

Lehman College of the City University of New York, School of Education, Department of Early Childhood and Elementary Education, Program in Elementary Education, Bronx, NY 10468-1589. Offers MS Ed. *Accreditation:* NCATE. *Program availability:* Part-time, evening/weekend. *Degree requirements:* For master's, thesis. *Entrance requirements:* For master's, minimum GPA of 3.0. *Faculty research:* POS network, emotional and intellectual learning, realistic picture books.

Le Moyne College, Department of Education, Syracuse, NY 13214. Offers adolescent education (MS Ed, MST); adolescent education/special education (MS Ed, MST); adolescent English (MST), including grades 7-12; adolescent English/special education (MST), including grades 7-12; adolescent foreign language (MST), including grades 7-12; adolescent history (MST), including grades 7-12; childhood education (MS Ed); childhood education/special education (MS Ed); elementary education (MS Ed); general education (MS Ed); inclusive childhood education (MST); literacy education (MS Ed), including birth to grade 6, grades 5-12; school building leader (MS Ed); school building leadership (CAS); school district business leader (MS Ed, CAS); school district leader (MS Ed); school district leadership (CAS); secondary education (MS Ed); special education (MS Ed); teaching English to speakers of other languages (MS Ed); urban studies (MS Ed). *Accreditation:* TEAC. *Program availability:* Part-time, evening/weekend. *Faculty:* 8 full-time (5 women), 20 part-time/adjunct (12 women). *Students:* 66 full-time (40 women), 155 part-time (117 women); includes 13 minority (4 Black or African American, non-Hispanic/Latino; 2 American Indian or Alaska Native, non-Hispanic/Latino; 2 Asian, non-Hispanic/Latino; 5 Hispanic/Latino), 3 international. Average age 30. 74 applicants, 99% accepted, 66 enrolled. In 2016, 81 master's, 53 CASs awarded. *Degree requirements:* For master's, thesis. *Entrance requirements:* For master's, bachelor's degree with minimum undergraduate GPA of 3.0, 2 letters of recommendation, transcripts. Additional exam requirements/recommendations for international students: Required—TOEFL (minimum score 550 paper-based; 79 iBT); Recommended—IELTS (minimum score 6.5). *Application deadline:* For fall admission, 4/1 priority date for domestic and international students; for spring admission, 10/1 priority date for domestic and international students; for summer admission, 3/1 priority date for domestic and international students. Applications are processed on a rolling basis. Application fee: $50. Electronic applications accepted. *Expenses:* $700 per credit hour. *Financial support:* In 2016–17, 21 students received support. Career-related internships or fieldwork, scholarships/grants, and health care benefits available. Support available to part-time students. Financial award applicants required to submit FAFSA. *Faculty research:* Minority teachers, special education, multiculturalism, literacy, technology, media literacy learning, autism, school district organization, service-learning, higher level problem solving, teacher leadership. *Unit head:* Dr. Stephen C. Fleury, Chair, Department of Education, 315-445-4376, Fax: 315-445-4744, E-mail: fleurysc@lemoyne.edu. *Application contact:* Kristen P. Richards, Senior Director of Enrollment Management, 315-445-5444, Fax: 315-445-6092, E-mail: trapaskp@lemoyne.edu.
Website: http://www.lemoyne.edu/education

Lesley University, Graduate School of Education, Cambridge, MA 02138-2790. Offers arts, community, and education (M Ed); autism studies (Certificate); curriculum and instruction (M Ed, CAGS); early childhood education (M Ed); ecological teaching and learning (MS); educational studies (PhD), including adult learning, educational leadership, individually designed; elementary education (M Ed); emergent technologies for educators (Certificate); ESLArts: language learning through the arts (M Ed); high school education (M Ed); individually designed (M Ed); integrated teaching through the arts (M Ed); literacy for K-8 classroom teachers (M Ed); mathematics education (M Ed); middle school education (M Ed); moderate disabilities (M Ed); online learning (Certificate); reading (CAGS); science in education (M Ed); severe disabilities (M Ed); special needs (CAGS); specialist teacher of reading (M Ed); teacher of visual art (M Ed); technology in education (M Ed, CAGS). *Accreditation:* TEAC. *Program availability:* Part-time, evening/weekend, online learning. *Degree requirements:* For master's, practicum; for doctorate, thesis/dissertation. *Entrance requirements:* For master's, Massachusetts Tests for Educator Licensure (MTEL), transcripts, statement of purpose, recommendations; interview (for special education); for doctorate, GRE General Test, transcripts, statement of purpose, recommendations, interview, master's degree, resume; for other advanced degree, interview, master's degree. Additional exam requirements/recommendations for international students: Required—TOEFL (minimum score 550 paper-based; 80 iBT). Electronic applications accepted. *Faculty research:* Assessment in literacy, mathematics and science; autism spectrum disorders; instructional technology and online learning; multicultural education and English language learners.

Lewis & Clark College, Graduate School of Education and Counseling, Department of Teacher Education, Program in Elementary Education, Portland, OR 97219-7899. Offers MAT. *Accreditation:* NCATE. *Entrance requirements:* For master's, minimum undergraduate GPA of 2.75; history of work, either volunteer or paid, with children in grades K-6. Additional exam requirements/recommendations for international students: Required—TOEFL (minimum score 575 paper-based). *Application deadline:* For fall admission, 12/1 priority date for domestic and international students. Application fee: $50. Electronic applications accepted. *Financial support:* Career-related internships or fieldwork, Federal Work-Study, institutionally sponsored loans, scholarships/grants, health care benefits, and tuition waivers (partial) available. Support available to part-time students. Financial award application deadline: 3/1; financial award applicants required to submit FAFSA. *Faculty research:* Classroom ethnography, assessing student learning, reading, moral development, language arts. *Unit head:* Dr. Linda Griffin, Coordinator, 503-768-6100, Fax: 503-768-6115, E-mail: lcteach@lclark.edu. *Application contact:* Becky Haas, Director of Admissions, 503-768-6200, Fax: 503-768-6205, E-mail: gseadmit@lclark.edu.
Website: http://graduate.lclark.edu/departments/teacher_education/prospective_teachers/early_childhood_elementary/

Lewis University, College of Education, Program in Elementary Education, Romeoville, IL 60446. Offers MA. *Students:* 11 full-time (8 women), 21 part-time (19 women); includes 8 minority (2 Black or African American, non-Hispanic/Latino; 6 Hispanic/Latino). Average age 30. *Degree requirements:* For master's, departmental qualifying exam. *Entrance requirements:* For master's, writing exam, minimum GPA of 2.75, 2 letters of recommendation, interview. Additional exam requirements/recommendations for international students: Required—TOEFL (minimum score 550 paper-based; 80 iBT). *Application deadline:* For fall admission, 5/1 priority date for international students. Application fee: $40. Electronic applications accepted. *Expenses: Tuition:* Full-time $13,860; part-time $770 per credit hour. *Required fees:* $75 per semester. Tuition and fees vary according to degree level and program. *Financial support:* Federal Work-Study, scholarships/grants, and unspecified assistantships available. Financial award application deadline: 5/1; financial award applicants required to submit FAFSA. *Unit head:* Dr. Suzanne O'Brien, Program Director, 815-836-5632, E-mail: obriensu@lewisu.edu. *Application contact:* Linda Campbell, Graduate Admission Counselor, 815-838-5610 Ext. 5704, E-mail: campbeli@lewisu.edu.

Lincoln University, Graduate Studies, Jefferson City, MO 65101. Offers business administration (MBA), including accounting, management, management information systems, public administration/policy; elementary teaching (M Ed); environmental science (MS); guidance and counseling (M Ed), including community/agency counseling, elementary school, secondary school; higher education (MA); history (MA); integrated agricultural systems (MS); middle school (M Ed); natural sciences (MS); secondary teaching (M Ed); sociology (MA); sociology/criminal justice (MA). *Program availability:* Part-time, evening/weekend, 100% online, blended/hybrid learning. *Students:* 50 full-time (29 women), 68 part-time (39 women); includes 40 minority (37 Black or African American, non-Hispanic/Latino; 1 Asian, non-Hispanic/Latino; 2 Two or more races, non-Hispanic/Latino), 14 international. Average age 33. 75 applicants, 80% accepted, 34 enrolled. In 2016, 51 master's awarded. *Degree requirements:* For master's, comprehensive exam, thesis optional. *Entrance requirements:* For master's, GRE, MAT or GMAT, minimum GPA of 2.75 overall, 3.0 in courses related to specialization; 3 letters of recommendation; minimum C average in English composition; personal statement of purpose. Additional exam requirements/recommendations for international students: Required—TOEFL (minimum score 500 paper-based; 61 iBT), IELTS (minimum score 5.5), Michigan English Language Assessment Battery (minimum score 80). *Application deadline:* For fall admission, 7/1 priority date for domestic students, 5/1 priority date for international students; for spring admission, 11/1 priority date for domestic students, 10/1 priority date for international students; for summer admission, 6/1 priority date for domestic students. Applications are processed on a rolling basis. Application fee: $30. Electronic applications accepted. *Expenses:* Tuition, state resident: full-time $6840; part-time $5130 per year. Tuition, nonresident: full-time $12,720; part-time $9540 per year. *Required fees:* $852; $811 per unit. Tuition and fees vary according to course load. *Financial support:* In 2016–17, 2 fellowships with tuition reimbursements, 8 research assistantships with tuition reimbursements were awarded; Federal Work-Study, scholarships/grants, and unspecified assistantships also available. Support available to part-time students. Financial award application deadline: 3/1; financial award applicants required to submit FAFSA. *Unit head:* Dr. Rolundus R. Rice, Dean, 573-681-5247, Fax: 573-681-5106, E-mail: gradschool@lincolnu.edu. *Application contact:* Irasema Steck, Administrative Assistant, 573-681-5247, Fax: 573-681-5106, E-mail: gradschool@lincolnu.edu.
Website: http://www.lincolnu.edu/web/graduate-studies/graduate-studies

Lock Haven University of Pennsylvania, College of Liberal Arts and Education, Lock Haven, PA 17745-2390. Offers alternative education (M Ed); educational leadership (M Ed); teaching and learning (M Ed). *Accreditation:* NCATE. *Program availability:* Part-time, evening/weekend, online learning. *Degree requirements:* For master's, thesis. *Entrance requirements:* For master's, minimum undergraduate GPA of 3.0. Additional exam requirements/recommendations for international students: Required—TOEFL. Electronic applications accepted.

Long Island University–Brentwood Campus, Graduate Programs, Brentwood, NY 11717. Offers childhood education (grades 1-6) (MS), including grades 1-6; childhood education/literacy (grades 1-6) (MS); childhood education/special education (grades 1-6) (MS); clinical mental health counseling (MS, Advanced Certificate); early childhood education (B-2) (MS); literacy (B-6) (MS Ed); school counselor (MS); special education (grades 1-6) (MS Ed); students with disabilities generalist (grades 7-12) (Advanced Certificate). *Program availability:* Part-time. *Faculty:* 54 part-time/adjunct (30 women). *Students:* 98 full-time (80 women), 57 part-time (47 women); includes 28 minority (7 Black or African American, non-Hispanic/Latino; 1 Asian, non-Hispanic/Latino; 20 Hispanic/Latino). 85 applicants, 89% accepted, 43 enrolled. In 2016, 99 master's, 11 other advanced degrees awarded. *Degree requirements:* For master's, comprehensive exam (for some programs), thesis optional. *Entrance requirements:* For master's and Advanced Certificate, GRE. Additional exam requirements/recommendations for international students: Required—TOEFL or IELTS. *Application deadline:* Applications are processed on a rolling basis. Application fee: $50. Electronic applications accepted. Application fee is waived when completed online. *Expenses: Tuition:* Full-time $28,272; part-time $1178 per credit. *Required fees:* $451 per term. *Financial support:* Scholarships/grants and unspecified assistantships available. Support available to part-time students. Financial award applicants required to submit FAFSA. *Unit head:* Donna Di Donato, Dean and Chief Operating Officer, 631-287-8010, Fax: 631-287-8575, E-mail: donna.didonato@liu.edu. *Application contact:* Scott Aug, Associate Director of Enrollment Management, 631-287-8500, Fax: 631-287-8575, E-mail: scott.aug@liu.edu.
Website: http://liu.edu/brentwood

Elementary Education

Long Island University–Hudson, Graduate School, Purchase, NY 10577. Offers autism (Advanced Certificate); childhood education (MS Ed); early childhood education (MS Ed); educational leadership (MS Ed); finance (MBA); health administration (MPA); healthcare sector management (MBA); literacy (MS Ed); management (MBA); marriage and family therapy (MS); mental health counseling (MS), including credentialed alcoholism and substance abuse counselor; middle childhood and adolescence education (MS Ed); pharmaceutics (MS), including cosmetic science, industrial pharmacy; public administration (MPA); school counseling (MS Ed, Advanced Certificate); school psychology (MS Ed); special education (MS Ed); TESOL (all grades) (Advanced Certificate); TESOL and bilingual education (MS Ed); the business of pharmaceutics and biotechnology (MBA). *Program availability:* Part-time, evening/weekend, online learning. *Faculty:* 7 full-time (5 women), 42 part-time/adjunct (25 women). *Students:* 55 full-time (41 women), 158 part-time (123 women); includes 40 minority (8 Black or African American, non-Hispanic/Latino; 1 Asian, non-Hispanic/Latino; 31 Hispanic/Latino). Average age 35. *Entrance requirements:* Additional exam requirements/recommendations for international students: Required—TOEFL (minimum score 550 paper-based; 79 iBT). *Application deadline:* Applications are processed on a rolling basis. Application fee: $50. Electronic applications accepted. *Expenses:* Contact institution. *Unit head:* Dr. Sylvia Blake, Dean and Chief Operating Officer, 914-831-2700, E-mail: westchester@liu.edu. *Application contact:* Cindy Pagnotta, Director of Marketing and Enrollment, 914-831-2701, Fax: 914-251-5959, E-mail: cindy.pagnotta@liu.edu.

Long Island University–Riverhead, Graduate Programs, Riverhead, NY 11901. Offers childhood education (MS), including grades 1-6; homeland security management (MS); literacy education (MS); teaching students with disabilities (MS), including grades 1-6, grades 7-12; TESOL (Advanced Certificate). *Accreditation:* TEAC. *Program availability:* Part-time. *Degree requirements:* For master's, thesis (for some programs); for Advanced Certificate, comprehensive exam (for some programs). *Entrance requirements:* Additional exam requirements/recommendations for international students: Required—TOEFL (minimum score 550 paper-based; 79 iBT), IELTS (minimum score 6). *Application deadline:* Applications are processed on a rolling basis. Application fee: $50. Electronic applications accepted. *Expenses:* Contact institution. *Financial support:* Institutionally sponsored loans, scholarships/grants, tuition waivers (partial), and unspecified assistantships available. Support available to part-time students. Financial award application deadline: 2/15; financial award applicants required to submit FAFSA. *Unit head:* Donna Di Donato, Dean and Chief Operating Officer, LIU Brentwood and LIU Riverhead, 631-287-8010, Fax: 631-287-8575, E-mail: donna.didonato@liu.edu. *Application contact:* Christina Seifert, Director of Admission, LIU Brentwood and LIU Riverhead, 631-287-8505, Fax: 631-287-8253, E-mail: christina.seifert@liu.edu.

Longwood University, College of Graduate and Professional Studies, College of Education and Human Services, Farmville, VA 23909. Offers education (MS), including algebra and middle school mathematics, counselor education, elementary and middle school mathematics, elementary education, elementary education initial licensure, health and physical education, special education general curriculum, special education initial licensure; reading, literacy and learning (M Ed); school librarianship (M Ed); social work and communication sciences and disorders (MS), including communication sciences and disorders. *Accreditation:* NCATE. *Program availability:* Part-time, evening/weekend. *Degree requirements:* For master's, comprehensive exam (for some programs), thesis optional, professional portfolio, internship, clinical experience, or practicum. *Entrance requirements:* For master's, PRAXIS I (for initial teaching licensure programs); GRE (for some programs), bachelor's degree from regionally-accredited institution, 2 recommendations (3 for some programs), minimum 500-word personal essay, official transcripts, minimum GPA of 2.75, valid teaching license (for some programs). Additional exam requirements/recommendations for international students: Required—TOEFL (minimum score 570 paper-based), IELTS (minimum score 6.5). Electronic applications accepted. *Expenses:* Contact institution.

Louisiana State University and Agricultural & Mechanical College, Graduate School, College of Human Sciences and Education, Department of Educational Theory, Policy and Practice, Baton Rouge, LA 70803. Offers counseling (M Ed, MA, Ed S); educational administration (M Ed, MA, PhD, Ed S); educational technology (MA); elementary education (M Ed, MAT); higher education (PhD); research methodology (PhD); secondary education (M Ed, MAT). *Accreditation:* ACA (one or more programs are accredited); NCATE.

Loyola Marymount University, School of Education, Department of Elementary and Secondary Education, Program in Elementary Education, Los Angeles, CA 90045-2659. Offers MA. *Program availability:* Part-time, evening/weekend. *Students:* 127 full-time (107 women), 13 part-time (9 women); includes 88 minority (3 Black or African American, non-Hispanic/Latino; 18 Asian, non-Hispanic/Latino; 59 Hispanic/Latino; 8 Two or more races, non-Hispanic/Latino), 4 international. Average age 30. 72 applicants, 92% accepted, 62 enrolled. In 2016, 42 master's awarded. *Entrance requirements:* For master's, CBEST, CSET, RICA, 3 letters of recommendation. Additional exam requirements/recommendations for international students: Required—TOEFL (minimum score 600 paper-based; 100 iBT). *Application deadline:* For fall admission, 6/15 for domestic students; for spring admission, 11/15 for domestic students. Application fee: $50. Electronic applications accepted. *Financial support:* In 2016–17, 101 students received support. Scholarships/grants and unspecified assistantships available. Support available to part-time students. Financial award application deadline: 6/30; financial award applicants required to submit FAFSA. *Unit head:* Dr. Irene Oliver, Chair, 310-338-7302, E-mail: ioliver@lmu.edu. *Application contact:* Chake H. Kouyoumjian, Associate Dean of Graduate Studies, 310-338-2721, E-mail: ckouyoum@lmu.edu.
Website: http://soe.lmu.edu/admissions/programs/tcp/elementaryeducation/

Loyola University Chicago, School of Education, Program in Teaching and Learning, Chicago, IL 60660. Offers elementary education (M Ed); English language teaching and learning (M Ed); secondary education (M Ed). *Accreditation:* NCATE. *Faculty:* 22 full-time (16 women), 38 part-time/adjunct (30 women). *Students:* 31 full-time (25 women), 20 part-time (15 women); includes 6 minority (5 Hispanic/Latino; 1 Two or more races, non-Hispanic/Latino), 3 international. Average age 27. 113 applicants, 52% accepted, 37 enrolled. In 2016, 35 master's awarded. *Degree requirements:* For master's, comprehensive exam. *Entrance requirements:* For master's, Illinois Basic Skills Test, 3 letters of recommendation, minimum GPA of 3.0, resume. Additional exam requirements/recommendations for international students: Required—TOEFL (minimum score 550 paper-based; 79 iBT). *Application deadline:* For fall admission, 7/1 for domestic and international students; for spring admission, 11/1 priority date for domestic and international students; for summer admission, 3/1 priority date for domestic and international students. Applications are processed on a rolling basis. Application fee: $50. Electronic applications accepted. Application fee is waived when completed online. *Expenses:* $949 per hour; $2,847 per course; $8,541-$11,388 per semester plus fees $432 per semester and $225 the first semester. *Financial support:* In 2016–17, 19 students received support, including 19 fellowships with partial tuition reimbursements available; institutionally sponsored loans, scholarships/grants, and unspecified assistantships also available. Support available to part-time students. Financial award application deadline: 2/1; financial award applicants required to submit FAFSA. *Faculty research:* Positive behavior support, school reform, school improvement. *Unit head:* Dr. David Ensminger, Program Chair, 312-915-7257, E-mail: densmin@luc.edu. *Application contact:* Thomas Ott, Information Contact, 312-915-8907, E-mail: tott@luc.edu.

Loyola University Maryland, Graduate Programs, School of Education, Master of Arts in Teaching Program, Baltimore, MD 21210-2699. Offers elementary education (MAT); secondary education (MAT). *Program availability:* Part-time. *Faculty:* 34 full-time (22 women), 30 part-time/adjunct (24 women). *Students:* 23 full-time (17 women), 167 part-time (149 women); includes 57 minority (35 Black or African American, non-Hispanic/Latino; 6 Asian, non-Hispanic/Latino; 8 Hispanic/Latino; 1 Native Hawaiian or other Pacific Islander, non-Hispanic/Latino; 7 Two or more races, non-Hispanic/Latino), 1 international. Average age 30. 34 applicants, 41% accepted, 13 enrolled. In 2016, 39 master's awarded. *Entrance requirements:* For master's, essay, 2 letters of recommendation, resume, transcipt. Additional exam requirements/recommendations for international students: Required—TOEFL (minimum score 550 paper-based), IELTS (minimum score 7). *Application deadline:* For spring admission, 11/1 for domestic students. Applications are processed on a rolling basis. Application fee: $60. Electronic applications accepted. *Expenses:* Contact institution. *Financial support:* In 2016–17, 12 students received support. Scholarships/grants available. Financial award application deadline: 4/15; financial award applicants required to submit FAFSA. *Application contact:* Brandon Gumabon, 410-617-2559, E-mail: bggumabon@loyola.edu.
Website: http://www.loyola.edu/soe/academics/graduate/mat.aspx

Loyola University Maryland, Graduate Programs, School of Education, Program in Montessori Education, Baltimore, MD 21210-2699. Offers elementary education (M Ed); Montessori education (CAS). *Accreditation:* NCATE. *Faculty:* 34 full-time (22 women), 30 part-time/adjunct (24 women). *Students:* 4,607 full-time (2,770 women), 1,477 part-time (986 women); includes 1,471 minority (557 Black or African American, non-Hispanic/Latino; 9 American Indian or Alaska Native, non-Hispanic/Latino; 222 Asian, non-Hispanic/Latino; 495 Hispanic/Latino; 8 Native Hawaiian or other Pacific Islander, non-Hispanic/Latino; 180 Two or more races, non-Hispanic/Latino), 68 international. Average age 24. 42 applicants, 93% accepted, 30 enrolled. In 2016, 105 master's awarded. *Degree requirements:* For master's, thesis. *Entrance requirements:* For master's, essay, transcripts. Additional exam requirements/recommendations for international students: Required—TOEFL (minimum score 550 paper-based), IELTS (minimum score 7). *Application deadline:* For fall admission, 5/1 priority date for domestic students, 5/1 for international students. Applications are processed on a rolling basis. Application fee: $60. *Expenses:* Contact institution. *Financial support:* In 2016–17, 5 students received support. Scholarships/grants available. Financial award application deadline: 4/15; financial award applicants required to submit FAFSA. *Application contact:* Mechelle Palmer, Senior Associate Director of Graduate Admission, 410-617-7741, E-mail: mjpalmer@loyola.edu.
Website: http://www.loyola.edu/soe/academics/graduate/montessori.aspx

Manhattan College, Graduate Programs, School of Education and Health, Program in Special Education, Riverdale, NY 10471. Offers adolescence education students with disabilities generalist extension in English or math or social studies - grades 7-12 (MS Ed); bilingual education (Advanced Certificate); dual childhood/students with disabilities - grades 1-6 (MS Ed); students with disabilities - grades 1-6 (MS Ed). *Program availability:* Part-time, evening/weekend. *Faculty:* 3 full-time (all women), 11 part-time/adjunct (7 women). *Students:* 62 full-time (59 women), 4 part-time (all women). Average age 24. 34 applicants, 79% accepted, 24 enrolled. In 2016, 32 master's awarded. *Degree requirements:* For master's, thesis, internship (if not certified). *Entrance requirements:* For master's, GRE, minimum GPA of 3.0. Additional exam requirements/recommendations for international students: Required—TOEFL (minimum score 550 paper-based; 80 iBT), IELTS (minimum score 6). *Application deadline:* For fall admission, 8/10 priority date for domestic students; for spring admission, 1/7 priority date for domestic students. Applications are processed on a rolling basis. Application fee: $75. Electronic applications accepted. Application fee is waived when completed online. *Expenses:* $900 per credit, $105 registration fee, $175 information service fee. *Financial support:* In 2016–17, 52 students received support. Federal Work-Study, scholarships/grants, and unspecified assistantships available. Financial award application deadline: 2/1; financial award applicants required to submit FAFSA. *Unit head:* Dr. Elizabeth Mary Kosky, Director of Childhood and Adolescent Special Education Programs, 718-862-7969, Fax: 718-862-7816, E-mail: elizabeth.kosky@manhattan.edu. *Application contact:* William Bisset, Information Contact, 718-862-8000, E-mail: william.bisset@manhattan.edu.

Manhattanville College, School of Education, Program in Childhood Education, Purchase, NY 10577-2132. Offers MAT, MPS. *Program availability:* Part-time, evening/weekend. *Students:* 46 applicants, 63% accepted, 20 enrolled. In 2016, 35 master's awarded. *Degree requirements:* For master's, comprehensive exam (for some programs), thesis (for some programs), student teaching, research seminars, portfolios, internships, writing assessment. *Entrance requirements:* For master's, GRE or MAT, minimum undergraduate GPA of 3.0, 2 letters of recommendation. Additional exam requirements/recommendations for international students: Required—TOEFL (minimum score 85 iBT); Recommended—IELTS. *Application deadline:* For fall admission, 7/1 priority date for domestic and international students; for spring admission, 11/1 priority date for domestic and international students; for summer admission, 4/1 priority date for domestic and international students. Applications are processed on a rolling basis. Application fee: $75. Electronic applications accepted. *Expenses: Tuition:* Full-time $16,470; part-time $915 per credit. *Required fees:* $60 per semester. Part-time tuition and fees vary according to course load and program. *Financial support:* Teaching assistantships, career-related internships or fieldwork, Federal Work-Study, institutionally sponsored loans, scholarships/grants, and unspecified assistantships available. Financial award applicants required to submit FAFSA. *Unit head:* Victoria Fantozzi, Chairperson, Department of Curriculum and Instruction, 914-323-7138, E-mail: victoria.fantozzi@mville.edu. *Application contact:* Jeanine Pardey-Levine, Director of Graduate Enrollment Management, 914-323-3208, Fax: 914-694-1732, E-mail: edschool@mville.edu.
Website: http://www.mville.edu/programs/childhood-education

Manhattanville College, School of Education, Program in Special Education, Purchase, NY 10577-2132. Offers childhood education (MPS); early childhood education (MPS); secondary education (MPS). *Program availability:* Part-time, evening/weekend. *Students:* 45 applicants, 69% accepted, 28 enrolled. In 2016, 26 master's, 1 Advanced Certificate awarded. *Degree requirements:* For master's, comprehensive exam (for some programs), thesis (for some programs), student teaching, research seminars, portfolios, internships, writing assessment; for Advanced Certificate, comprehensive exam (for some programs). *Entrance requirements:* For master's, GRE or MAT, minimum undergraduate GPA of 3.0, 2 letters of recommendation. Additional exam requirements/recommendations for international students: Required—TOEFL (minimum score 85 iBT); Recommended—IELTS. *Application deadline:* For fall admission, 7/1 priority date for domestic and international students; for spring admission, 11/1 priority date for domestic and international students; for summer admission, 4/1 priority date for domestic and international students. Applications are processed on a rolling basis. Application fee: $75. Electronic applications accepted. *Expenses: Tuition:* Full-time $16,470; part-time $915 per credit. *Required fees:* $60 per semester. Part-time tuition and fees vary according to course load and program. *Financial support:* Teaching

assistantships, career-related internships or fieldwork, Federal Work-Study, institutionally sponsored loans, scholarships/grants, and unspecified assistantships available. Financial award applicants required to submit FAFSA. *Faculty research:* Aspects of verbal behavior and communication skills in autistic children, PBIS systems and their implementation, effective instructional practices for students with E/BDs, effective pedagogical practices that improve student behavioral and academic performance, increasing communication skills of young non-vocal children with autism. *Unit head:* Vance Austin, Chairperson, Department of Special Education, 914-323-7262, E-mail: vance.austin@mville.edu. *Application contact:* Jeanine Pardey-Levine, Director of Admissions, 914-323-3208, Fax: 914-694-1732, E-mail: edschool@mville.edu.
Website: http://www.mville.edu/programs/special-education

Mansfield University of Pennsylvania, Graduate Studies, Department of Education and Special Education, Mansfield, PA 16933. Offers elementary education (M Ed); secondary education (MS); special education (M Ed). *Accreditation:* NCATE (one or more programs are accredited). *Program availability:* Part-time, evening/weekend, online learning. *Degree requirements:* For master's, comprehensive exam, thesis optional. *Entrance requirements:* For master's, minimum GPA of 3.0. Additional exam requirements/recommendations for international students: Required—TOEFL (minimum score 550 paper-based). Electronic applications accepted.

Marquette University, Graduate School, College of Education, Department of Educational Policy and Leadership, Milwaukee, WI 53201-1881. Offers college student personnel administration (M Ed); curriculum and instruction (MA); education (MA); educational administration (M Ed); educational policy and foundations (MA); elementary education (Certificate); literacy (MA); principal (Certificate); reading specialist (Certificate); reading teacher (Certificate); secondary education (Certificate); superintendent (Certificate). *Program availability:* Part-time, evening/weekend. *Faculty:* 17 full-time (14 women), 28 part-time/adjunct (23 women). *Students:* 31 full-time (23 women), 103 part-time (66 women); includes 22 minority (7 Black or African American, non-Hispanic/Latino; 1 American Indian or Alaska Native, non-Hispanic/Latino; 6 Asian, non-Hispanic/Latino; 6 Hispanic/Latino; 2 Two or more races, non-Hispanic/Latino). Average age 31. 96 applicants, 92% accepted, 67 enrolled. In 2016, 47 master's, 3 other advanced degrees awarded. Terminal master's awarded for partial completion of doctoral program. *Degree requirements:* For master's, comprehensive exam, thesis (for some programs); for doctorate, thesis/dissertation, qualifying exam. *Entrance requirements:* For master's, GRE General Test or MAT, official transcripts from all current and previous colleges/universities except Marquette, three letters of recommendation, statement of purpose; for doctorate, GRE General Test, MAT, sample of written work, official transcripts from all current and previous colleges/universities except Marquette, three letters of recommendation, statement of purpose, resume/curriculum vitae; for Certificate, GRE General Test or MAT, master's degree. Additional exam requirements/recommendations for international students: Required—TOEFL (minimum score 530 paper-based). *Application deadline:* For fall admission, 1/15 for domestic and international students. Application fee: $50. *Expenses:* Contact institution. *Financial support:* Fellowships, research assistantships, health care benefits, tuition waivers (partial), and unspecified assistantships available. Support available to part-time students. Financial award application deadline: 2/15. *Faculty research:* Leadership; social justice in education; development of lifelong learners; race, class, and schooling in historical perspective; urban teacher education. *Unit head:* Dr. Ellen Eckman, Chair, 414-288-1561. *Application contact:* Dr. Cynthia Ellwood.

Marshall University, Academic Affairs Division, College of Education and Professional Development, Program in Elementary Education, Huntington, WV 25755. Offers MA, Graduate Certificate. *Accreditation:* NCATE. *Program availability:* Part-time, evening/weekend. *Degree requirements:* For master's, thesis optional, comprehensive or oral assessment, research project. *Entrance requirements:* For master's, GRE General Test or MAT.

Mars Hill University, Adult and Graduate Studies, Mars Hill, NC 28754. Offers elementary education (K-6) (M Ed). *Degree requirements:* For master's, project.

Mary Baldwin University, Graduate Studies, Program in Teaching, Staunton, VA 24401-3610. Offers elementary education (MAT); middle grades education (MAT). *Accreditation:* TEAC.

Marygrove College, Graduate Division, Sage Program, Detroit, MI 48221-2599. Offers M Ed. *Accreditation:* TEAC. *Entrance requirements:* For master's, Michigan Teacher Test for Certification.

Marylhurst University, Department of Education, Marylhurst, OR 97036-0261. Offers education (M Ed); teaching (MA). *Program availability:* Part-time. *Students:* 46 (39 women); includes 10 minority (1 Asian, non-Hispanic/Latino; 5 Hispanic/Latino; 4 Two or more races, non-Hispanic/Latino), 1 international. Average age 35. In 2016, 21 master's awarded. *Degree requirements:* For master's, comprehensive exam. *Entrance requirements:* For master's, PRAXIS I or CBEST (for MA), official transcript from regionally-accredited institution, recommendations, personal statement of intent, essay or writing sample, fingerprint verification; copy of current teaching license (for M Ed). Additional exam requirements/recommendations for international students: Required—TOEFL (minimum score 79 iBT), IELTS (minimum score 6.5). *Application deadline:* Applications are processed on a rolling basis. Application fee: $0. Electronic applications accepted. *Expenses:* Contact institution. *Financial support:* Career-related internships or fieldwork and scholarships/grants available. Support available to part-time students. Financial award applicants required to submit FAFSA. *Faculty research:* ESOL, reading education. *Unit head:* Dr. Jan Carpenter, Chair, 503-675-3975, E-mail: jcarpenter@marylhurst.edu. *Application contact:* Maruska Lynch, Graduate Admissions Counselor, 800-699-6322, E-mail: admissions@marylhurst.edu.
Website: https://www.marylhurst.edu

Marymount University, School of Education and Human Services, Program in Education, Arlington, VA 22207-4299. Offers elementary education (M Ed); English as a second language (M Ed); professional studies (M Ed); secondary education (M Ed); special education: general curriculum (M Ed). *Accreditation:* NCATE. *Program availability:* Part-time, evening/weekend. *Faculty:* 28 full-time (all women), 8 part-time/adjunct (5 women). *Students:* 42 full-time (33 women), 94 part-time (72 women); includes 25 minority (6 Black or African American, non-Hispanic/Latino; 6 Asian, non-Hispanic/Latino; 8 Hispanic/Latino; 5 Two or more races, non-Hispanic/Latino), 12 international. Average age 32. 32 applicants, 100% accepted, 24 enrolled. In 2016, 79 master's awarded. *Degree requirements:* For master's, thesis or alternative, capstone/internship. *Entrance requirements:* For master's, GRE or MAT and PRAXIS I or SAT/ACT and Virginia Communication and Literacy Assessment (VCLA), 2 letters of recommendation, resume, interview, minimum undergraduate GPA of 2.75 or 3.25 in the last 60 hours. Additional exam requirements/recommendations for international students: Required—TOEFL (minimum score 600 paper-based; 96 iBT), IELTS (minimum score 6.5). *Application deadline:* Applications are processed on a rolling basis. Application fee: $40. Electronic applications accepted. *Expenses:* $690 per credit hour. *Financial support:* In 2016–17, 6 students received support, including 2 teaching assistantships with tuition reimbursements available; career-related internships or fieldwork, Federal Work-Study, scholarships/grants, and unspecified assistantships also available. Support available to part-time students. Financial award applicants required to submit FAFSA. *Unit head:* Dr. Lisa Turissini, Chair, Education, 703-526-1668, Fax: 703-284-1631, E-mail: lisa.turissini@marymount.edu. *Application contact:* Francesca Reed, Director, Graduate Admissions, 703-284-5901, Fax: 703-527-3815, E-mail: grad.admissions@marymount.edu.
Website: http://www.marymount.edu/Academics/School-of-Education-Human-Services/Graduate-Programs/Education-(M-Ed-)

Maryville University of Saint Louis, School of Education, St. Louis, MO 63141-7299. Offers early childhood education (MA Ed); educational leadership (Ed D); educational leadership: principal certification (MA Ed); elementary education (MA Ed); gifted education (MA Ed); higher education leadership (Ed D); literacy specialist (MA Ed); middle grades education (MA Ed); secondary teaching and inquiry (MA Ed); teacher as leader (MA Ed); teacher leadership (Ed D). *Accreditation:* NCATE. *Program availability:* Part-time, evening/weekend. *Faculty:* 17 full-time (11 women), 21 part-time/adjunct (17 women). *Students:* 12 full-time (11 women), 297 part-time (208 women); includes 92 minority (79 Black or African American, non-Hispanic/Latino; 4 Asian, non-Hispanic/Latino; 4 Hispanic/Latino; 5 Two or more races, non-Hispanic/Latino), 4 international. Average age 38. In 2016, 32 master's, 61 doctorates awarded. *Degree requirements:* For master's, thesis, project. *Entrance requirements:* For master's, minimum cumulative GPA of 3.0, 3 professional recommendations, essays, interview with program faculty; for doctorate, minimum GPA of 3.0, 3 professional recommendations, essay, interview, on-site writing sample. Additional exam requirements/recommendations for international students: Required—TOEFL (minimum score 550 paper-based). *Application deadline:* Applications are processed on a rolling basis. Electronic applications accepted. *Expenses:* $879 per credit (for Ed D); $781 per credit (for master's). *Financial support:* Career-related internships or fieldwork, Federal Work-Study, tuition waivers (partial), and professional educator discounts available. Financial award application deadline: 3/1; financial award applicants required to submit FAFSA. *Faculty research:* Collaboration with public schools, pre-service program development, mathematics, diversity, literacy. *Unit head:* Dr. Cathy Bear, Dean, 314-529-9692, Fax: 314-529-9921, E-mail: cbear@maryville.edu. *Application contact:* Stacey Ruffin, Coordinator of Clinical Experiences and Graduate Programs, 314-529-9542, Fax: 314-529-9921, E-mail: teachered@maryville.edu.
Website: http://www.maryville.edu/ed/graduate-programs/

Marywood University, Academic Affairs, Reap College of Education and Human Development, Department of Education, Program in PK-4 Education, Scranton, PA 18509-1598. Offers MAT. *Accreditation:* NCATE. *Program availability:* Part-time. Electronic applications accepted.

McDaniel College, Graduate and Professional Studies, Program in Elementary and Secondary Education, Westminster, MD 21157-4390. Offers elementary education (MS); elementary STEM instructional leader (Postbaccalaureate Certificate); equity and excellence in education (Postbaccalaureate Certificate); learning technology specialist (Postbaccalaureate Certificate); secondary education (MS). *Accreditation:* NCATE. *Program availability:* Part-time, evening/weekend. *Faculty:* 3 full-time (2 women), 27 part-time/adjunct (22 women). *Students:* 8 full-time (5 women), 179 part-time (143 women); includes 60 minority (31 Black or African American, non-Hispanic/Latino; 3 American Indian or Alaska Native, non-Hispanic/Latino; 13 Asian, non-Hispanic/Latino; 11 Hispanic/Latino; 2 Two or more races, non-Hispanic/Latino), 1 international. Average age 36. 79 applicants, 94% accepted. In 2016, 23 master's, 48 other advanced degrees awarded. *Degree requirements:* For master's, comprehensive exam (for some programs), thesis optional. *Entrance requirements:* For master's, PRAXIS, 2 references. Additional exam requirements/recommendations for international students: Required—TOEFL (minimum score 79 iBT), IELTS (minimum score 6). *Application deadline:* For fall admission, 6/1 priority date for domestic students; for spring admission, 11/1 priority date for domestic students; for summer admission, 3/1 priority date for domestic students. Applications are processed on a rolling basis. Application fee: $75. Electronic applications accepted. *Expenses: Tuition:* Full-time $8370; part-time $465 per credit. *Required fees:* $75 per semester. Tuition and fees vary according to course load, program and reciprocity agreements. *Financial support:* Application deadline: 3/1; applicants required to submit FAFSA. *Unit head:* Fax: 410-857-2515, E-mail: gradadms@mcdaniel.edu. *Application contact:* Penny Pfeiffer, Senior Graduate Enrollment Management Specialist, 410-857-2513, Fax: 410-857-2515, E-mail: ppfeiffer@mcdaniel.edu.

McNeese State University, Doré School of Graduate Studies, Burton College of Education, Office of Graduate Education Programs, Program in Curriculum and Instruction, Lake Charles, LA 70609. Offers early childhood education (M Ed); elementary education (M Ed); reading (M Ed); secondary education (M Ed). *Program availability:* Evening/weekend. *Entrance requirements:* For master's, GRE, teaching certificate.

McNeese State University, Doré School of Graduate Studies, Burton College of Education, Office of Graduate Education Programs, Program in Elementary Education, Lake Charles, LA 70609. Offers MAT. *Program availability:* Evening/weekend. *Degree requirements:* For master's, comprehensive exam, field experiences. *Entrance requirements:* For master's, GRE General Test, PRAXIS I and II, autobiography, two letters of recommendation.

McNeese State University, Doré School of Graduate Studies, Burton College of Education, Office of Student Teaching and Professional Education Services, Program in Elementary Education Grades 1-5, Lake Charles, LA 70609. Offers Postbaccalaureate Certificate. *Entrance requirements:* For degree, PRAXIS, 2 letters of recommendation, autobiography.

Medaille College, Program in Education, Buffalo, NY 14214-2695. Offers adolescent education (MS Ed); curriculum and instruction (MS Ed); education preparation (MS Ed); literacy (MS Ed); special education (MS). *Accreditation:* TEAC. *Program availability:* Part-time, evening/weekend. *Degree requirements:* For master's, comprehensive exam (for some programs), thesis or alternative. *Entrance requirements:* For master's, minimum undergraduate GPA of 2.7. Additional exam requirements/recommendations for international students: Required—TOEFL (minimum score 550 paper-based). Electronic applications accepted. *Faculty research:* Curriculum planning, truancy, tracking minority students, curriculum design, mentoring students.

Mercy College, School of Education, Program in Childhood Education, Dobbs Ferry, NY 10522-1189. Offers MS. *Program availability:* Part-time, evening/weekend, blended/hybrid learning. *Students:* 260 full-time (248 women), 340 part-time (316 women); includes 278 minority (123 Black or African American, non-Hispanic/Latino; 6 American Indian or Alaska Native, non-Hispanic/Latino; 16 Asian, non-Hispanic/Latino; 128 Hispanic/Latino; 1 Native Hawaiian or other Pacific Islander, non-Hispanic/Latino; 4 Two or more races, non-Hispanic/Latino). Average age 32. 195 applicants, 41% accepted, 40 enrolled. In 2016, 271 master's awarded. *Degree requirements:* For master's, comprehensive exam (for some programs), thesis (for some programs). *Entrance requirements:* For master's, GRE, resume, undergraduate transcript. Additional exam requirements/recommendations for international students: Required—TOEFL (minimum score 600 paper-based; 100 iBT), IELTS (minimum score 8). *Application deadline:* For fall admission, 8/1 for international students. Applications are processed on a rolling basis. Application fee: $40. Electronic applications accepted. *Expenses: Tuition:* Full-

time $15,156; part-time $842 per credit hour. *Required fees:* $620; $155 per term. Tuition and fees vary according to course load and program. *Financial support:* Career-related internships or fieldwork, Federal Work-Study, scholarships/grants, and unspecified assistantships available. Financial award applicants required to submit FAFSA. *Unit head:* Dr. Rose Rudnitski, Dean for the School of Education, 914-674-7447 Ext. 914, Fax: 914-674-7352, E-mail: rrudnitski@mercy.edu. *Application contact:* Allison Gurdineer, Senior Director of Admissions, 877-637-2946, Fax: 914-674-7382, E-mail: admissions@mercy.edu.
Website: https://www.mercy.edu/degrees-programs/ms-childhood-education-grade-1-6

Meredith College, School of Education, Health and Human Sciences, Raleigh, NC 27607-5298. Offers academically and intellectually gifted (M Ed); curriculum instruction specialist (M Ed); elementary education (M Ed, MAT); English as a second language (M Ed, MAT); health and physical education (MAT); nutrition, health and human performance (MS, Postbaccalaureate Certificate), including dietetic internship (Postbaccalaureate Certificate), nutrition (MS); reading (M Ed); special education (MAT). *Accreditation:* NCATE. *Program availability:* Part-time, evening/weekend. *Degree requirements:* For master's, thesis optional. *Entrance requirements:* For master's, GRE General Test or MAT, minimum GPA of 2.5, teaching license, recommendations. Additional exam requirements/recommendations for international students: Required—TOEFL. Electronic applications accepted. *Expenses:* Contact institution.

Merrimack College, School of Education and Social Policy, North Andover, MA 01845-5800. Offers community engagement (M Ed), including community organizations, higher education, K-12 education; criminology and criminal justice (MS); curriculum and instruction (M Ed); early childhood education (M Ed); educational leadership (CAGS), including instructional leadership; elementary education (M Ed); English as a second language (PreK-6) (M Ed); high school education (M Ed); higher education (M Ed), including leadership and organizational development, student affairs; middle school education (M Ed); moderate disabilities (PreK-8) (M Ed); school counseling (M Ed). *Program availability:* Part-time, evening/weekend, 100% online courses with immersion events and in-classroom practicum close to home. *Faculty:* 17 full-time, 34 part-time/adjunct. *Students:* 204 full-time (172 women), 83 part-time (67 women); includes 32 minority (4 Black or African American, non-Hispanic/Latino; 2 Asian, non-Hispanic/Latino; 23 Hispanic/Latino; 3 Two or more races, non-Hispanic/Latino), 1 international. Average age 27. 261 applicants, 89% accepted, 200 enrolled. In 2016, 153 master's, 2 other advanced degrees awarded. *Degree requirements:* For master's, practicum, portfolio, and state test (for licensure track); capstone (for higher education, curriculum and instruction, and community engagement tracks). *Entrance requirements:* For master's, Massachusetts Teacher Education Licensure (MTEL), official transcripts from other colleges, resume, personal statement, 2 letters of recommendation. Additional exam requirements/recommendations for international students: Required—TOEFL (minimum score 84 iBT), IELTS (minimum score 6.5), PTE (minimum score 56). *Application deadline:* For fall admission, 8/14 for domestic students, 7/14 for international students; for spring admission, 1/10 for domestic students, 12/10 for international students; for summer admission, 5/10 for domestic students, 4/10 for international students. Applications are processed on a rolling basis. Application fee: $0. Electronic applications accepted. *Expenses:* Contact institution. *Financial support:* Fellowships with full tuition reimbursements, career-related internships or fieldwork, scholarships/grants, and health care benefits available. Support available to part-time students. Financial award application deadline: 5/1; financial award applicants required to submit FAFSA. *Faculty research:* Feminist praxis in higher education, transgender student agency and belonging, campus sexual violence prevention, the scholarship of engagement; community engagement; service learning; diversity education; community-university partnerships, college going behaviors and indicators of success for inner city youth, strategies to increase students pursuit and success in STEM higher education, effective workforce development for displaced or under employed individuals, police reform, e.g. surveillance. *Application contact:* Alyssa Frey, Graduate Admissions Counselor, 978-837-3563, E-mail: freya@merrimack.edu.
Website: http://www.merrimack.edu/academics/graduate/education/

Metropolitan College of New York, Program in Childhood/Special Education, New York, NY 10006. Offers dual childhood 1-6 special education (MS). *Accreditation:* NCATE. *Students:* 21 full-time (19 women), 1 (woman) part-time; includes 15 minority (13 Black or African American, non-Hispanic/Latino; 2 Hispanic/Latino), 1 international. Average age 32. In 2016, 21 master's awarded. *Entrance requirements:* For master's, GRE or MAT, minimum GPA of 3.0, 2 letters of reference, interview, resume. Additional exam requirements/recommendations for international students: Required—TOEFL (minimum score 550 paper-based; 80 iBT), IELTS (minimum score 6.5). *Application deadline:* Applications are processed on a rolling basis. Application fee: $45. Electronic applications accepted. *Expenses:* Contact institution. *Financial support:* Career-related internships or fieldwork, Federal Work-Study, institutionally sponsored loans, and scholarships/grants available. Financial award application deadline: 8/15; financial award applicants required to submit FAFSA. *Faculty research:* Classroom management, learner autonomy, teacher research, math and gender, intelligence. *Unit head:* Dr. Patrick Ianniello, Director, 212-343-1234 Ext. 2424, E-mail: pianniello@metropolitan.edu. *Application contact:* Sylvia Cameron, Graduate Admissions Coordinator, 212-343-1234 Ext. 2704, Fax: 212-343-7900, E-mail: scameron@mcny.edu.
Website: http://www.mcny.edu/human_serv/msedc.php

Metropolitan State University of Denver, School of Education, Denver, CO 80204. Offers elementary education (MAT); special education (MAT). *Faculty:* 20 full-time (16 women), 1 part-time/adjunct (0 women). *Students:* 115 full-time (90 women), 14 part-time (11 women); includes 23 minority (7 Black or African American, non-Hispanic/Latino; 2 American Indian or Alaska Native, non-Hispanic/Latino; 1 Asian, non-Hispanic/Latino; 9 Hispanic/Latino; 4 Two or more races, non-Hispanic/Latino). Average age 32. In 2016, 59 master's awarded. *Application deadline:* For fall admission, 2/1 for domestic and international students; for spring admission, 10/1 for domestic and international students; for summer admission, 2/1 for domestic and international students. Application fee: $50. *Expenses:* $6,429.60 for full-time residents, $8,881.20 for full-time non-residents; $357.20 per credit hour for part-time residents, $493.40 per credit hour for part-time non-residents. *Unit head:* Kathy Heyl, Interim Dean, 303-556-2978, E-mail: heyl@msudenver.edu. *Application contact:* Ellen Sunbury, Graduate Admissions Coordinator, 303-556-6228, E-mail: esunbury@msudenver.edu.
Website: http://www.msudenver.edu/scops/

Middle Tennessee State University, College of Graduate Studies, College of Education, Department of Elementary and Special Education, Major in Curriculum and Instruction, Murfreesboro, TN 37132. Offers early childhood education (M Ed); elementary education (M Ed, Ed S); middle school education (M Ed). *Accreditation:* NCATE. *Program availability:* Part-time, evening/weekend, online learning. *Degree requirements:* For master's, comprehensive exam; for Ed S, comprehensive exam, thesis or alternative. *Entrance requirements:* For master's and Ed S, GRE, MAT or PRAXIS. Additional exam requirements/recommendations for international students: Required—TOEFL (minimum score 525 paper-based; 71 iBT) or IELTS (minimum score 6). Electronic applications accepted.

Milligan College, Area of Education, Milligan College, TN 37682. Offers combined preK-3/K-5 education (M Ed); educational leadership (Ed D, Ed S); K-5 education (M Ed); middle grades education (M Ed); preK-3 education (M Ed); preK-3 special education (M Ed); secondary education (M Ed). *Accreditation:* NCATE. *Program availability:* Part-time. *Faculty:* 5 full-time (3 women), 3 part-time/adjunct (1 woman). *Students:* 26 full-time (19 women), 20 part-time (10 women); includes 2 minority (1 Black or African American, non-Hispanic/Latino; 1 Hispanic/Latino), 2 international. Average age 28. 16 applicants, 81% accepted, 11 enrolled. In 2016, 19 master's awarded. *Degree requirements:* For master's, thesis, portfolio, research project; for doctorate, thesis/dissertation, portfolio, research project. *Entrance requirements:* For master's, MAT, GRE General Test, ACT, SAT, or PRAXIS, undergraduate degree and supporting transcripts, professional recommendations, interview; for doctorate, MAT or GRE, master's degree and supporting transcripts, demonstrated scholastic ability, recognized leadership role within education, professional recommendations, essay/personal statement, portfolio (professional development plan, evidence of ability, knowledge and qualities), interview. Additional exam requirements/recommendations for international students: Required—TOEFL (minimum score 550 paper-based, 79 iBT) or IELTS (6.5). *Application deadline:* For fall admission, 8/1 priority date for domestic students, 6/1 for international students; for spring admission, 11/15 priority date for domestic students, 12/1 for international students; for summer admission, 4/1 for domestic students. Applications are processed on a rolling basis. Application fee: $30. Electronic applications accepted. *Expenses:* $360 per hour tuition (for M Ed); $475 per hour tuition (for Ed D and Ed S); $325 per semester tech/activity fees. *Financial support:* Scholarships/grants available. Financial award application deadline: 12/1; financial award applicants required to submit FAFSA. *Faculty research:* Assessment; school mental health; literacy; technology; educator preparation. *Unit head:* Dr. Angela Hilton-Prillhart, Area Chair of Education, 423-461-8769, Fax: 423-461-3103, E-mail: anhilton-prillhart@milligan.edu. *Application contact:* Melissa Dillow, Graduate Admissions Recruiter, Education, 423-461-8306, Fax: 423-461-8982, E-mail: msdillow@milligan.edu. Website: http://www.Milligan.edu/GPS

Minot State University, Graduate School, Teacher Education and Human Performance Department, Minot, ND 58707-0002. Offers elementary education (M Ed). *Accreditation:* NCATE. *Degree requirements:* For master's, thesis. *Entrance requirements:* For master's, 2 years of teaching experience, bachelor's degree in education, minimum GPA of 2.75. Additional exam requirements/recommendations for international students: Required—TOEFL (minimum score 79 iBT), IELTS (minimum score 6).

Mississippi College, Graduate School, School of Education, Department of Teacher Education and Leadership, Clinton, MS 39058. Offers art (M Ed); biological science (M Ed); business education (M Ed); computer science (M Ed); dyslexia therapy (M Ed); educational leadership (M Ed, Ed D, Ed S); elementary education (M Ed, Ed S); English (M Ed); higher education administration (MS); mathematics (M Ed); secondary education (M Ed); social studies (history) (M Ed); teaching arts (M Ed). *Program availability:* Part-time, online learning. *Degree requirements:* For master's, comprehensive exam, thesis optional. *Entrance requirements:* For master's, NTE. Additional exam requirements/recommendations for international students: Recommended—TOEFL, IELTS. Electronic applications accepted.

Mississippi State University, College of Education, Department of Curriculum, Instruction and Special Education, Mississippi State, MS 39762. Offers early childhood education (PhD); elementary education (MS, PhD, Ed S), including early childhood education (MS), general elementary education (MS), middle level education (MS); general curriculum and instruction (PhD); middle level (MAT); reading education (PhD); secondary education (MAT, MS, PhD, Ed S); special education (MAT, MS, PhD, Ed S). *Accreditation:* NCATE. *Program availability:* Part-time, evening/weekend. *Faculty:* 21 full-time (16 women), 1 (woman) part-time/adjunct. *Students:* 39 full-time (26 women), 168 part-time (128 women); includes 49 minority (43 Black or African American, non-Hispanic/Latino; 2 American Indian or Alaska Native, non-Hispanic/Latino; 1 Hispanic/Latino; 1 Native Hawaiian or other Pacific Islander, non-Hispanic/Latino; 2 Two or more races, non-Hispanic/Latino), 4 international. Average age 33. 98 applicants, 56% accepted, 47 enrolled. In 2016, 69 master's, 6 doctorates, 10 other advanced degrees awarded. *Degree requirements:* For master's, comprehensive exam; for doctorate, thesis/dissertation; for Ed S, comprehensive exam, thesis or alternative. *Entrance requirements:* For master's, GRE, minimum GPA of 2.75 in junior and senior year, eligibility for initial teacher certification; for doctorate, GRE, minimum GPA of 3.4 on previous graduate work; for Ed S, GRE, minimum GPA of 3.2 on master's degree. Additional exam requirements/recommendations for international students: Required—TOEFL (minimum score 550 paper-based; 79 iBT); Recommended—IELTS (minimum score 6.5). *Application deadline:* For fall admission, 3/1 priority date for domestic students, 5/1 for international students; for spring admission, 9/1 priority date for domestic students, 9/1 for international students. Applications are processed on a rolling basis. Application fee: $60. Electronic applications accepted. *Expenses:* Tuition, state resident: full-time $7670; part-time $852.50 per credit hour. Tuition, nonresident: full-time $20,790; part-time $2310.50 per credit hour. Part-time tuition and fees vary according to course load. *Financial support:* In 2016–17, 8 research assistantships with partial tuition reimbursements (averaging $11,381 per year) were awarded; Federal Work-Study, institutionally sponsored loans, scholarships/grants, and unspecified assistantships also available. Financial award application deadline: 4/1; financial award applicants required to submit FAFSA. *Faculty research:* Early childhood education, reading, rural schools, multicultural education, use of technology in instruction. *Unit head:* Dr. Janice Nicholson, Interim Department Head, 662-325-3704, Fax: 662-325-7857, E-mail: jin4@msstate.edu. *Application contact:* Linda Bonner, Senior Admissions Assistant, 662-325-3363, E-mail: lbonner@grad.msstate.edu.
Website: http://www.cise.msstate.edu/

Mississippi State University, College of Education, Educational Leadership Program, Mississippi State, MS 39762. Offers community college education (MAT, PhD); elementary, middle and secondary education administration (PhD); school administration (MS, Ed S); workforce education leadership (MS). MS in workforce education leadership held jointly with Alcorn State University. *Faculty:* 16 full-time (10 women). *Students:* 32 full-time (16 women), 158 part-time (101 women); includes 82 minority (80 Black or African American, non-Hispanic/Latino; 1 Hispanic/Latino; 1 Two or more races, non-Hispanic/Latino). Average age 38. 60 applicants, 58% accepted, 34 enrolled. In 2016, 24 master's, 15 doctorates, 5 other advanced degrees awarded. *Degree requirements:* For master's and Ed S, comprehensive exam, thesis; for doctorate, comprehensive exam, thesis/dissertation. *Entrance requirements:* For master's, GRE, minimum GPA of 2.75 in junior and senior courses; for doctorate, GRE, minimum GPA of 3.4 on previous graduate work; for Ed S, GRE, minimum GPA of 3.2, master's degree. Additional exam requirements/recommendations for international students: Required—TOEFL (minimum score 550 paper-based; 79 iBT); Recommended—IELTS (minimum score 6.5). *Application deadline:* For fall admission, 7/1 for domestic students, 5/1 for international students; for spring admission, 11/1 for domestic students, 9/1 for international students. Application fee: $60. Electronic applications accepted. *Expenses:* Tuition, state resident: full-time $7670; part-time $852.50 per credit hour. Tuition, nonresident: full-time $20,790; part-time $2310.50 per credit hour. Part-time tuition and fees vary according to course load. *Financial support:* In 2016–17, 2 research assistantships with full tuition reimbursements (averaging

$12,940 per year) were awarded; Federal Work-Study, institutionally sponsored loans, and unspecified assistantships also available. Financial award application deadline: 4/1; financial award applicants required to submit FAFSA. *Unit head:* Dr. Ed Davis, Interim Department Head/Professor, 662-325-0969, Fax: 662-325-0975, E-mail: jed11@colled.msstate.edu. *Application contact:* Linda Bonner, Senior Admissions Assistant, 662-325-3363, E-mail: lbonner@grad.msstate.edu.
Website: http://www.educationalleadership.msstate.edu/

Missouri State University, Graduate College, College of Education, Department of Childhood Education and Family Studies, Program in Elementary Education, Springfield, MO 65897. Offers MS Ed. *Program availability:* Part-time, evening/weekend, 100% online, blended/hybrid learning. *Students:* 4 full-time (all women), 63 part-time (60 women); includes 3 minority (2 Black or African American, non-Hispanic/Latino; 1 Two or more races, non-Hispanic/Latino). Average age 32. 26 applicants, 77% accepted, 19 enrolled. In 2016, 27 master's awarded. *Degree requirements:* For master's, comprehensive exam, thesis or alternative. *Entrance requirements:* For master's, GRE (if GPA less than 3.0), minimum GPA of 2.75, teaching certificate. Additional exam requirements/recommendations for international students: Required—TOEFL (minimum score 550 paper-based; 79 iBT), IELTS (minimum score 6). *Application deadline:* For fall admission, 7/20 priority date for domestic students, 5/1 for international students; for spring admission, 12/20 priority date for domestic students, 9/1 for international students; for summer admission, 5/20 priority date for domestic students. Applications are processed on a rolling basis. Application fee: $35 ($50 for international students). Electronic applications accepted. *Expenses:* Tuition, state resident: full-time $5830. Tuition, nonresident: full-time $10,708. *Required fees:* $1130. Tuition and fees vary according to class time, course level, course load and program. *Financial support:* Federal Work-Study, institutionally sponsored loans, and scholarships/grants available. Financial award application deadline: 3/31; financial award applicants required to submit FAFSA. *Unit head:* Dr. Denise Cunningham, Department Head, 417-836-8915, E-mail: cefs@missouristate.edu. *Application contact:* Michael Edwards, Coordinator of Graduate Admissions, 417-836-5300, Fax: 417-836-6200, E-mail: michaeledwards@missouristate.edu.
Website: http://education.missouristate.edu/ele/

Missouri State University, Graduate College, College of Education, Department of Counseling, Leadership, and Special Education, Program in Counseling, Springfield, MO 65897. Offers elementary school counseling (MS); mental health counseling (MS); secondary school counseling (MS). *Accreditation:* ACA. *Program availability:* Part-time, evening/weekend. *Students:* 67 full-time (51 women), 43 part-time (39 women); includes 16 minority (4 Black or African American, non-Hispanic/Latino; 7 Hispanic/Latino; 5 Two or more races, non-Hispanic/Latino), 3 international. Average age 30. 46 applicants, 50% accepted, 18 enrolled. In 2016, 35 master's awarded. *Degree requirements:* For master's, comprehensive exam, thesis or alternative. *Entrance requirements:* For master's, GRE or MAT, minimum GPA of 2.75. Additional exam requirements/recommendations for international students: Required—TOEFL (minimum score 550 paper-based; 79 iBT), IELTS (minimum score 6). *Application deadline:* For fall admission, 2/1 priority date for domestic students, 1/1 priority date for international students; for spring admission, 10/1 priority date for domestic students, 9/1 priority date for international students. Application fee: $35 ($50 for international students). Electronic applications accepted. *Expenses:* Tuition, state resident: full-time $5830. Tuition, nonresident: full-time $10,708. *Required fees:* $1130. Tuition and fees vary according to class time, course level, course load and program. *Financial support:* Federal Work-Study, institutionally sponsored loans, scholarships/grants, and unspecified assistantships available. Financial award application deadline: 3/31; financial award applicants required to submit FAFSA. *Unit head:* Dr. James Satterfield, Department Head, 417-836-5392, Fax: 417-836-4918, E-mail: clse@missouristate.edu. *Application contact:* Michael Edwards, Coordinator of Graduate Admissions, 417-836-5300, Fax: 417-836-6200, E-mail: michaeledwards@missouristate.edu.
Website: http://education.missouristate.edu/clse/

Missouri State University, Graduate College, College of Education, Department of Counseling, Leadership, and Special Education, Program in Educational Administration, Springfield, MO 65897. Offers elementary principal (MS Ed, Ed S); secondary principal (MS Ed, Ed S); superintendent (Ed S). *Program availability:* Part-time, evening/weekend. *Students:* 2 full-time (0 women), 60 part-time (40 women); includes 6 minority (2 Black or African American, non-Hispanic/Latino; 1 American Indian or Alaska Native, non-Hispanic/Latino; 2 Hispanic/Latino; 1 Two or more races, non-Hispanic/Latino). Average age 34. 6 applicants, 67% accepted, 3 enrolled. In 2016, 34 master's, 15 Ed Ss awarded. *Degree requirements:* For master's and Ed S, comprehensive exam, thesis or alternative. *Entrance requirements:* For master's, minimum GPA of 2.75; for Ed S, GRE General Test, MAT, minimum GPA of 2.75. Additional exam requirements/recommendations for international students: Required—TOEFL (minimum score 550 paper-based; 79 iBT), IELTS (minimum score 6). *Application deadline:* For fall admission, 7/20 priority date for domestic students, 5/1 for international students; for spring admission, 12/20 priority date for domestic students, 9/1 for international students; for summer admission, 5/20 priority date for domestic students. Applications are processed on a rolling basis. Application fee: $35 ($50 for international students). Electronic applications accepted. *Expenses:* Tuition, state resident: full-time $5830. Tuition, nonresident: full-time $10,708. *Required fees:* $1130. Tuition and fees vary according to class time, course level, course load and program. *Financial support:* Career-related internships or fieldwork, Federal Work-Study, institutionally sponsored loans, scholarships/grants, and unspecified assistantships available. Financial award application deadline: 3/31; financial award applicants required to submit FAFSA. *Unit head:* Dr. James Satterfield, Department Head, 417-836-5392, Fax: 417-836-4918, E-mail: clse@missouristate.edu. *Application contact:* Michael Edwards, Coordinator of Graduate Admissions, 417-836-5330, Fax: 417-836-6200, E-mail: michaeledwards@missouristate.edu.
Website: http://education.missouristate.edu/edadmin/

Monmouth University, Graduate Studies, School of Education, West Long Branch, NJ 07764-1898. Offers applied behavior analysis (Certificate); autism (Certificate); director of school counseling services (Post-Master's Certificate); early childhood (M Ed); educational leadership (Ed D); elementary education (MAT), including elementary level, secondary level; English as a second language (M Ed); learning disabilities teacher-consultant (Post-Master's Certificate); literacy (MS Ed); school counseling (MS Ed); special education (MS Ed), including autism, learning disabilities teacher-consultant, teacher of students with disabilities, teaching in inclusive settings; speech-language pathology (MS Ed); student affairs and college counseling (MS Ed); supervisor (Post-Master's Certificate); teaching English to speakers of other languages (Certificate). *Accreditation:* NCATE. *Program availability:* Part-time, evening/weekend, 100% online, blended/hybrid learning. *Faculty:* 23 full-time (19 women), 33 part-time/adjunct (25 women). *Students:* 191 full-time (172 women), 141 part-time (122 women); includes 56 minority (10 Black or African American, non-Hispanic/Latino; 9 Asian, non-Hispanic/Latino; 31 Hispanic/Latino; 6 Two or more races, non-Hispanic/Latino). Average age 26. 423 applicants, 53% accepted, 139 enrolled. In 2016, 148 master's, 4 other advanced degrees awarded. *Entrance requirements:* For master's, GRE taken within last 5 years (for MS Ed in speech-language pathology); SAT (minimum combined score of 1660 in 3 sections), ACT (23), GRE (minimum score of 4.0 on analytical writing section and minimum combined score of 310 on quantitative and verbal sections), or passing scores on 3 parts of Core Academic Skills Educators, minimum GPA of 3.0 in major; 2 letters of recommendation (for some programs); resume, personal statement or essay (depending on program). Additional exam requirements/recommendations for international students: Required—TOEFL (minimum score 550 paper-based; 79 iBT), IELTS (minimum score 6), Michigan English Language Assessment Battery (minimum score 77) or Certificate of Advanced English (minimum score B2). *Application deadline:* For fall admission, 7/15 priority date for domestic students, 7/1 for international students; for spring admission, 12/1 priority date for domestic students, 11/1 for international students; for summer admission, 5/1 for domestic students. Applications are processed on a rolling basis. Application fee: $50. Electronic applications accepted. *Expenses: Tuition, area resident:* Full-time $19,764; part-time $1098 per credit hour. *Required fees:* $175 per semester. Tuition and fees vary according to program. *Financial support:* In 2016–17, 349 students received support, including 305 fellowships (averaging $3,558 per year), 48 teaching assistantships (averaging $9,619 per year); research assistantships, institutionally sponsored loans, scholarships/grants, and unspecified assistantships also available. Support available to part-time students. Financial award application deadline: 2/1; financial award applicants required to submit FAFSA. *Faculty research:* Multicultural literacy, science and mathematics teaching strategies, teacher as reflective practitioner, children with disabilities. *Unit head:* Dr. John E. Henning, Dean, 732-263-5513, Fax: 732-263-5277. *Application contact:* Laurie Kuhn, Associate Director of Graduate Admission, 732-571-3452, Fax: 732-263-5123, E-mail: gradadm@monmouth.edu.
Website: http://www.monmouth.edu/academics/schools/education/default.asp

Montana State University Billings, College of Education, Department of Educational Theory and Practice, Option in General Curriculum, Billings, MT 59101. Offers K-8 (M Ed); secondary (M Ed). *Accreditation:* NCATE. *Program availability:* Part-time. *Faculty:* 15 full-time (10 women), 1 (woman) part-time/adjunct. *Students:* 62. *Degree requirements:* For master's, thesis or professional paper and/or field experience. *Entrance requirements:* For master's, GRE General Test or MAT, minimum GPA of 3.0. Additional exam requirements/recommendations for international students: Required—TOEFL (minimum score 79 iBT), IELTS (minimum score 6.5). *Application deadline:* Applications are processed on a rolling basis. Application fee: $40. Electronic applications accepted. *Expenses:* Tuition, state resident: full-time $5265; part-time $3436 per year. Tuition, nonresident: full-time $14,030; part-time $9280 per year. *International tuition:* $19,295 full-time. Tuition and fees vary according to degree level, campus/location and program. *Financial support:* Teaching assistantships with partial tuition reimbursements, career-related internships or fieldwork, Federal Work-Study, institutionally sponsored loans, scholarships/grants, tuition waivers (partial), and unspecified assistantships available. Support available to part-time students. Financial award application deadline: 5/1; financial award applicants required to submit FAFSA. *Faculty research:* Social studies education, science education. *Unit head:* Dr. Ken Miller, Chair, 406-657-2034, Fax: 406-657-2807, E-mail: kmiller@msubillings.edu. *Application contact:* David M. Sullivan, Graduate Studies Counselor, 406-657-2053, Fax: 406-657-2299, E-mail: dsullivan@msubillings.edu.

Morehead State University, Graduate Programs, College of Education, Department of Curriculum and Instruction, Morehead, KY 40351. Offers curriculum and instruction (Ed S); elementary education (MA Ed), including elementary education, international education, middle school education, reading; secondary education (MA Ed); special education (MA Ed); teaching (MAT). *Program availability:* Part-time, evening/weekend. *Degree requirements:* For master's, comprehensive exam, thesis optional; for Ed S, thesis, oral exam. *Entrance requirements:* For master's, GRE General Test, minimum GPA of 2.75, teaching certificate; for Ed S, GRE General Test, interview, master's degree, minimum GPA of 3.5, work experience. Additional exam requirements/recommendations for international students: Required—TOEFL (minimum score 500 paper-based). Electronic applications accepted. *Faculty research:* Communicative competence of learning-disabled students, teaching social studies in elementary schools, ungraded primary school organization, study skills.

Morehead State University, Graduate Programs, College of Education, Department of Foundational and Graduate Studies in Education, Morehead, KY 40351. Offers adult and higher education (MA, Ed S); certified professional counselor (Ed S); counseling P-12 (MA); curriculum and instruction (Ed S); educational technology (MA Ed); instructional leadership (Ed S); school administration (MA); school counseling (Ed S); teacher leader business and marketing content (MA Ed); teacher leader business and marketing technology (MA Ed); teacher leader educational technology (MA Ed); teacher leader English (MA Ed); teacher leader gifted education (MA Ed); teacher leader IECE certification (MA Ed); teacher leader interdisciplinary education P-5 (MA Ed); teacher leader middle grades (MA Ed); teacher leader non IECE certification (MA Ed); teacher leader reading/writing - non-certification (MA Ed); teacher leader reading/writing certification (MA Ed); teacher leader school communication - certification (MA Ed); teacher leader school communication - non-certification (MA Ed); teacher leader social studies (MA Ed); teacher leader special education (MA Ed). *Accreditation:* NCATE. *Program availability:* Part-time, evening/weekend. *Degree requirements:* For master's, thesis optional, oral and/or written comprehensive exams; for Ed S, thesis, oral exam. *Entrance requirements:* For master's, GRE General Test, minimum overall undergraduate GPA of 2.5; for Ed S, GRE General Test, interview, master's degree, minimum GPA of 3.5, work experience. Additional exam requirements/recommendations for international students: Required—TOEFL (minimum score 500 paper-based). Electronic applications accepted. *Faculty research:* Character education, school accountability, computer applications for school administrators.

Morgan State University, School of Graduate Studies, School of Education and Urban Studies, MAT Program, Baltimore, MD 21251. Offers elementary education (MAT); high school education (MAT); middle school education (MAT). *Program availability:* Part-time. *Degree requirements:* For master's, comprehensive exam. *Entrance requirements:* For master's, GRE General Test or MAT. *Faculty research:* Multicultural education, cooperative learning, psychology of cognition.

Mount Saint Vincent University, Graduate Programs, Faculty of Education, Program in Elementary Education, Halifax, NS B3M 2J6, Canada. Offers M Ed, MA Ed, MA-R. *Program availability:* Part-time, evening/weekend, online learning. *Degree requirements:* For master's, thesis (for some programs). *Entrance requirements:* For master's, bachelor's degree in education, 1 year of teaching experience. Electronic applications accepted. *Faculty research:* Curriculum theory, mathematics education, philosophy in teacher education, science education, literacy education.

Murray State University, College of Education, Department of Early Childhood and Elementary Education, Programs in Elementary Education/Reading and Writing, Murray, KY 42071. Offers elementary education (MA Ed, Ed S); reading and writing (MA Ed). *Accreditation:* NCATE. *Program availability:* Part-time. *Degree requirements:* For master's, comprehensive exam, thesis optional; for Ed S, comprehensive exam. *Entrance requirements:* For master's, minimum GPA of 2.5 for conditional admittance, 3.0 for unconditional; for Ed S, GRE General Test or MAT. Additional exam requirements/recommendations for international students: Required—TOEFL.

National Louis University, National College of Education, Chicago, IL 60603. Offers administration and supervision (M Ed, Ed D, CAS, Ed S); curriculum and instruction (M Ed, MS Ed, CAS); early childhood administration (M Ed, CAS); early childhood education (M Ed, MAT, MS Ed, CAS); education (Ed D); educational psychology/human learning and development (M Ed, MS Ed, CAS, Ed S); elementary education (MAT); interdisciplinary curriculum and instruction (M Ed); mathematics education (M Ed, MS Ed, CAS); middle grades education (MAT); reading and language (M Ed, MS Ed, CAS); school psychology (M Ed, Ed S); science education (M Ed, MS Ed, CAS); secondary education (MAT); special education (M Ed, MAT, CAS); technology in education (M Ed, CAS). *Accreditation:* NCATE. *Program availability:* Part-time, evening/weekend. *Degree requirements:* For doctorate, comprehensive exam, thesis/dissertation. *Entrance requirements:* For master's, MAT or GRE, minimum GPA of 3.0; for doctorate, GRE General Test, minimum GPA of 3.25, interview, resume, writing sample, 4 recommendations. Additional exam requirements/recommendations for international students: Required—TOEFL (minimum score 550 paper-based; 79 iBT).

Nazareth College of Rochester, Graduate Studies, Department of Education, Program in Inclusive Childhood Education, Rochester, NY 14618. Offers MS Ed. *Accreditation:* TEAC. *Program availability:* Part-time, evening/weekend. *Entrance requirements:* For master's, minimum GPA of 3.0. Additional exam requirements/recommendations for international students: Required—TOEFL or IELTS. *Application deadline:* For fall admission, 4/1 priority date for domestic students; for spring admission, 10/1 priority date for domestic students. Application fee: $40. *Expenses: Tuition:* Part-time $880 per credit hour. Part-time tuition and fees vary according to course load, degree level and program. *Financial support:* Unspecified assistantships available. Financial award application deadline: 3/1; financial award applicants required to submit FAFSA. *Unit head:* Dr. Ellen Contopidis, Director, 585-389-2916, E-mail: econtop4@naz.edu. *Application contact:* Judith Baker, Director, Transfer and Graduate Admissions, 585-531-1154, Fax: 585-389-2826, E-mail: gradadmissions@naz.edu.

Neumann University, Graduate Program in Education, Aston, PA 19014-1298. Offers education (MS), including administrative (principal K-12), autism, early elementary education, secondary education, special education. *Program availability:* Part-time, evening/weekend, 100% online, blended/hybrid learning. *Faculty:* 6 full-time (5 women), 18 part-time/adjunct (7 women). *Students:* 80 full-time (64 women), 108 part-time (91 women); includes 40 minority (30 Black or African American, non-Hispanic/Latino; 6 Hispanic/Latino; 4 Two or more races, non-Hispanic/Latino), 1 international. Average age 34. 152 applicants, 67% accepted, 82 enrolled. In 2016, 42 master's awarded. *Entrance requirements:* For master's, official transcripts from all institutions attended, letter of intent, three professional references, copy of any teaching certifications. Additional exam requirements/recommendations for international students: Required—TOEFL (minimum score 70 iBT). *Application deadline:* Applications are processed on a rolling basis. Application fee: $0. Electronic applications accepted. *Expenses:* $700 per credit on-campus tuition; $480 per credit online or off-campus tuition; additional $320 for student teaching course. *Financial support:* Scholarships/grants and health care benefits available. Support available to part-time students. Financial award application deadline: 3/15; financial award applicants required to submit FAFSA. *Unit head:* Dr. Stephanie Smith-Budhai, Director of Graduate Education, 610-358-4249, E-mail: budhais@neumann.edu. *Application contact:* Dr. Erika Davis, Director of Adult and Graduate Admissions, 800-9-NEUMANN Ext. 5208, Fax: 610-361-2548, E-mail: GradAdultAdmiss@neumann.edu.
Website: https://www.neumann.edu/academics/grad/education/index.asp

New Jersey City University, Debra Cannon Partridge Wolfe College of Education, Department of Elementary and Secondary Education, Jersey City, NJ 07305-1597. Offers elementary education (MAT); secondary education (MAT). *Program availability:* Part-time, evening/weekend. *Entrance requirements:* Additional exam requirements/recommendations for international students: Required—TOEFL (minimum score 79 iBT).

New York Institute of Technology, School of Interdisciplinary Studies and Education, Department of Teacher Education, Old Westbury, NY 11568-8000. Offers adolescence education (MS), including mathematics, science; childhood education (MS); early childhood (MS). *Program availability:* Part-time, evening/weekend, 100% online, blended/hybrid learning. *Faculty:* 2 full-time (both women), 7 part-time/adjunct (3 women). *Students:* 19 full-time (15 women), 41 part-time (35 women); includes 18 minority (5 Black or African American, non-Hispanic/Latino; 4 Asian, non-Hispanic/Latino; 8 Hispanic/Latino; 1 Two or more races, non-Hispanic/Latino). Average age 33. 57 applicants, 74% accepted, 29 enrolled. In 2016, 12 master's awarded. *Entrance requirements:* For master's, GRE (minimum combined score of 300 from any two tests), MAT (minimum score 400), LAST (taken within past five years), BS or equivalent; minimum cumulative undergraduate GPA of 3.0; NY state provisional or initial certification (for adolescence education); BS with major in biology, chemistry, economics, English, history, life sciences, math, physics, or psychology (for childhood and early childhood education). Additional exam requirements/recommendations for international students: Required—TOEFL (minimum score 79 iBT), IELTS (minimum score 6). *Application deadline:* Applications are processed on a rolling basis. Application fee: $50. Electronic applications accepted. *Expenses:* $1,215 per credit. *Financial support:* Career-related internships or fieldwork, Federal Work-Study, scholarships/grants, tuition waivers (full and partial), and unspecified assistantships available. Support available to part-time students. Financial award application deadline: 3/1; financial award applicants required to submit FAFSA. *Faculty research:* Evolving definition of new literacies and its impact on teaching and learning (twenty-first century skills), new literacies practices in teacher education, teachers' professional development, English language and literacy learning through mobile learning, teaching reading to culturally and linguistically diverse children. *Unit head:* Dr. Hui-Yin Hsu, Department Chair, 516-686-1322, Fax: 516-686-7655, E-mail: hhsu02@nyit.edu. *Application contact:* Alice Dolitsky, Director, Graduate Admissions, 516-686-7520, Fax: 516-686-1116, E-mail: nyitgrad@nyit.edu.
Website: http://www.nyit.edu/interdisciplinary/department_teacher_education

New York University, Steinhardt School of Culture, Education, and Human Development, Department of Teaching and Learning, Program in Early Childhood and Childhood Education, New York, NY 10003. Offers childhood education (MA); early childhood education (MA); early childhood education/early childhood special education (MA). *Accreditation:* TEAC. *Program availability:* Part-time. *Degree requirements:* For master's, thesis (for some programs). *Entrance requirements:* Additional exam requirements/recommendations for international students: Required—TOEFL (minimum score 100 iBT). Electronic applications accepted. *Faculty research:* Teacher evaluation and beliefs about teaching, early literacy development, language arts, child development and education, cultural differences.

Niagara University, Graduate Division of Education, Concentration in Teacher Education, Niagara University, NY 14109. Offers early childhood and childhood education (MS Ed, Certificate); early childhood special education (MS); middle and adolescence education (MS Ed); special education (MS Ed), including 1-6, 7-12; special education (grades 1-12) (Certificate); teaching English to speakers of other languages (MS Ed, Certificate). *Accreditation:* NCATE. *Students:* 101 full-time (83 women), 123 part-time (101 women); includes 14 minority (6 Black or African American, non-Hispanic/Latino; 1 American Indian or Alaska Native, non-Hispanic/Latino; 6 Hispanic/Latino; 1 Two or more races, non-Hispanic/Latino), 28 international. Average age 28. In 2016, 86 master's, 18 other advanced degrees awarded. *Entrance requirements:* For master's, GRE General Test or Academic Literacy Skills Test (ALST). Additional exam requirements/recommendations for international students: Required—TOEFL (minimum score 550 paper-based; 79 iBT), IELTS (minimum score 6). *Application deadline:* For fall admission, 8/1 for domestic students. Applications are processed on a rolling basis. Application fee: $30. *Expenses:* Contact institution. *Financial support:* Research assistantships with tuition reimbursements, teaching assistantships with tuition reimbursements, career-related internships or fieldwork, Federal Work-Study, scholarships/grants, and unspecified assistantships available. Financial award application deadline: 4/15; financial award applicants required to submit FAFSA. *Unit head:* Dr. Chandra Foote, Dean, College of Education, 716-286-8549, E-mail: cjf@niagara.edu. *Application contact:* Evan Pierce, Associate Director, Graduate Studies, 716-286-8327, E-mail: epierce@niagara.edu.
Website: http://www.niagara.edu/teacher-education

Nicholls State University, Graduate Studies, College of Education, Department of Teacher Education, Thibodaux, LA 70310. Offers curriculum and instruction (M Ed); educational leadership (M Ed); elementary education (MAT); human performance education (MAT); middle school education (MAT); secondary education (MAT). *Accreditation:* NCATE. *Program availability:* Part-time, evening/weekend, online learning. *Degree requirements:* For master's, comprehensive exam, portfolio. *Entrance requirements:* For master's, GRE General Test, teaching license. Electronic applications accepted.

North Carolina Agricultural and Technical State University, School of Graduate Studies, School of Education, Department of Curriculum and Instruction, Program in Elementary Education, Greensboro, NC 27411. Offers MA Ed. *Accreditation:* NCATE. *Program availability:* Part-time, evening/weekend. *Degree requirements:* For master's, comprehensive exam, research project or comprehensive portfolio. *Entrance requirements:* For master's, GRE General Test, minimum GPA of 3.0.

North Carolina State University, Graduate School, College of Education, Department of Elementary Education, Raleigh, NC 27695. Offers M Ed. *Entrance requirements:* For master's, MAT or GRE, 3 letters of reference.

Northeastern Illinois University, College of Graduate Studies and Research, College of Education, MAT Program in Language Arts - Elementary Education, Chicago, IL 60625-4699. Offers MAT.

Northeastern Illinois University, College of Graduate Studies and Research, College of Education, MSI Program in Language Arts - Elementary Education, Chicago, IL 60625-4699. Offers MSI. *Entrance requirements:* For master's, minimum undergraduate GPA of 2.75; current valid state teaching certificate; 18 credit hours of undergraduate coursework in English literature and composition, linguistics, and/or speech; 15 credit hours of undergraduate coursework in education; two letters of recommendation; official transcripts.

Northeastern University, College of Professional Studies, Boston, MA 02115-5096. Offers applied nutrition (MS); college athletics administration (MSL); commerce and economic development (MS); corporate and organizational communication (MS); criminal justice (MS); digital media (MPS); elearning and instructional design (M Ed); elementary education (MAT); geographic information technology (MPS); global studies and international relations (MS); higher education administration (M Ed); homeland security (MA); human services (MS); informatics (MPS); leadership (MS); learning analytics (M Ed); learning and instruction (M Ed); nonprofit management (MS); professional sports administration (MSL); project management (MS); regulatory affairs for drugs, biologics, and medical devices (MS); respiratory care leadership (MS); special education (M Ed); technical communication (MS). *Program availability:* Part-time, evening/weekend, 100% online, blended/hybrid learning. *Faculty:* 82 full-time (51 women), 853 part-time/adjunct (366 women). *Students:* 4,947 part-time (3,076 women). In 2016, 1,456 master's awarded. *Application deadline:* Applications are processed on a rolling basis. Application fee: $0. Electronic applications accepted. *Expenses:* Contact institution. *Financial support:* Applicants required to submit FAFSA. *Unit head:* Dr. Mary Loeffelholz, Interim Dean of the College of Professional Studies.
Website: http://www.cps.neu.edu/

Northern Arizona University, Graduate College, College of Education, Department of Teaching and Learning, Flagstaff, AZ 86011. Offers curriculum and instruction (Ed D); early childhood education (M Ed); elementary education (M Ed); secondary education (M Ed). *Program availability:* Part-time. *Degree requirements:* For master's, comprehensive exam (for some programs), thesis (for some programs). *Entrance requirements:* For master's, minimum GPA of 3.0. Additional exam requirements/recommendations for international students: Required—TOEFL (minimum score 550 paper-based; 80 iBT), IELTS (minimum score 7). Electronic applications accepted. *Expenses:* Tuition, state resident: full-time $8971; part-time $444 per credit hour. Tuition, nonresident: full-time $20,958; part-time $1164 per credit hour. *Required fees:* $1018; $644 per credit hour. Tuition and fees vary according to course load, campus/location and program.

Northern Illinois University, Graduate School, College of Education, Department of Special and Early Education, De Kalb, IL 60115-2854. Offers curriculum and instruction (MS Ed, Ed D), including curriculum leadership (Ed D), elementary education (Ed D), secondary education (Ed D); early childhood education (MS Ed); elementary education (MS Ed); special education (MS Ed). *Program availability:* Part-time, evening/weekend. *Faculty:* 22 full-time (14 women), 2 part-time/adjunct (both women). *Students:* 42 full-time (34 women), 85 part-time (68 women); includes 16 minority (4 Black or African American, non-Hispanic/Latino; 3 Asian, non-Hispanic/Latino; 6 Hispanic/Latino; 3 Two or more races, non-Hispanic/Latino), 6 international. Average age 33. 70 applicants, 73% accepted, 30 enrolled. In 2016, 19 master's, 1 doctorate awarded. *Degree requirements:* For master's, comprehensive exam, thesis optional; for doctorate, thesis/dissertation, candidacy exam, dissertation defense. *Entrance requirements:* For master's, GRE General Test or MAT, minimum undergraduate GPA of 2.75; for doctorate, GRE General Test or MAT, minimum undergraduate GPA of 2.75, graduate 3.2. Additional exam requirements/recommendations for international students: Required—TOEFL (minimum score 550 paper-based). *Application deadline:* For fall admission, 6/1 for domestic students, 5/1 for international students; for spring admission, 11/1 for domestic students, 10/1 for international students. Applications are processed on a rolling basis. Application fee: $40. Electronic applications accepted. *Financial support:* In 2016–17, 14 research assistantships with full tuition reimbursements were awarded; fellowships with full tuition reimbursements, teaching assistantships with full tuition reimbursements, career-related internships or fieldwork, Federal Work-Study, scholarships/grants, tuition waivers (full), and unspecified assistantships also available. Support available to part-time students. Financial award applicants required to submit FAFSA. *Faculty research:* Teacher certification, stress reduction during student teaching, teaching history, portfolios in student teaching. *Unit head:* Gregory Conderman, Chair, 815-753-1619, E-mail: seed@niu.edu. *Application contact:* Gail Myers, Clerk, Graduate Advising, 815-753-0381, E-mail: gmyers@niu.edu.
Website: http://www.cedu.niu.edu/seed/

Northern Michigan University, Office of Graduate Education and Research, College of Health Sciences and Professional Studies, School of Education, Leadership and Public Service, Marquette, MI 49855-5301. Offers administration and supervision (MAE);

elementary education (MAE); higher education in student affairs (MA); instruction (MAE); learning disabilities (MAE); public administration (MPA), including criminal justice administration, human resource administration, public administration, public management, state and local government; reading education (MAE), including reading, reading specialist; science education (MS); secondary education (MAE). *Accreditation:* TEAC. *Program availability:* Part-time, online learning. *Degree requirements:* For master's, thesis (for some programs). *Entrance requirements:* For master's, minimum GPA of 3.0. Additional exam requirements/recommendations for international students: Required—TOEFL (minimum score 550 paper-based; 79 iBT), IELTS (minimum score 6.5). Electronic applications accepted.

Northwest Christian University, School of Education and Counseling, Eugene, OR 97401-3745. Offers clinical mental health counseling (MA); elementary teaching (MAT); English for speakers of other languages (ESOL) (MAT); school counseling (MA); secondary teaching (MAT). *Program availability:* Part-time, evening/weekend, online learning. *Faculty:* 9 full-time (5 women), 21 part-time/adjunct (14 women). *Students:* 87 full-time (64 women), 52 part-time (40 women); includes 22 minority (5 Black or African American, non-Hispanic/Latino; 2 American Indian or Alaska Native, non-Hispanic/Latino; 2 Asian, non-Hispanic/Latino; 7 Hispanic/Latino; 2 Native Hawaiian or other Pacific Islander, non-Hispanic/Latino; 4 Two or more races, non-Hispanic/Latino). Average age 36. In 2016, 76 master's awarded. *Degree requirements:* For master's, thesis (for some programs). *Entrance requirements:* For master's, MAT, minimum undergraduate GPA of 3.0, interview, 2-3 page statement of purpose, two letters of recommendation, resume, background check. Additional exam requirements/recommendations for international students: Required—TOEFL (minimum score 550 paper-based; 80 iBT). *Application deadline:* Applications are processed on a rolling basis. Electronic applications accepted. *Expenses:* Contact institution. *Unit head:* Gene James, Dean of Counseling, 541-684-7261, Fax: 541-684-7310, E-mail: gjames@nwcu.edu. *Application contact:* Billy Dorsch, Admission Counselor for Graduate Studies, 541-684-7279, Fax: 541-349-5281, E-mail: wdorsch@nwcu.edu.

Northwestern Oklahoma State University, School of Professional Studies, Program in Elementary Education, Alva, OK 73717-2799. Offers M Ed. *Accreditation:* NCATE. *Program availability:* Part-time. *Degree requirements:* For master's, thesis optional, portfolio. *Entrance requirements:* For master's, GRE General Test or MAT, minimum GPA of 2.75.

Northwestern State University of Louisiana, Graduate Studies and Research, College of Education and Human Development, Program in Elementary Education, Natchitoches, LA 71497. Offers MAT. *Degree requirements:* For master's, comprehensive exam, thesis or alternative. *Entrance requirements:* For master's, GRE General Test, minimum undergraduate GPA of 2.5. Additional exam requirements/recommendations for international students: Required—TOEFL. Electronic applications accepted.

Northwestern State University of Louisiana, Graduate Studies and Research, College of Education and Human Development, Programs in Educational Leadership and Instruction, Natchitoches, LA 71497. Offers counseling (Ed S); educational leadership (M Ed, Ed S); educational technology (Ed S); elementary teaching (Ed S); reading (Ed S); secondary teaching (Ed S); special education (Ed S). *Accreditation:* NASAD. *Degree requirements:* For master's, comprehensive exam, thesis (for some programs). *Entrance requirements:* For master's and Ed S, GRE General Test. Additional exam requirements/recommendations for international students: Required—TOEFL. Electronic applications accepted.

Northwestern University, The Graduate School, School of Education and Social Policy, Education and Social Policy Program, Evanston, IL 60035. Offers elementary teaching (MS); secondary teaching (MS); teacher leadership (MS). *Program availability:* Part-time, evening/weekend. *Degree requirements:* For master's, research project. *Entrance requirements:* For master's, GRE General Test, Illinois State Board of Education Basic Skills Exam (secondary and elementary), bachelor's degree. Additional exam requirements/recommendations for international students: Recommended—TOEFL. Electronic applications accepted. *Faculty research:* Cultural context and literacy, philosophy of education and interpretive discussion, productivity, enhancing research and teaching, motivation, new and junior faculty issues, professional development for K-12 teachers to improve math and science teaching, female/underrepresented students/faculty in STEM disciplines.

Northwest Missouri State University, Graduate School, School of Education, Maryville, MO 64468-6001. Offers early childhood education (MS Ed); education leadership (MS Ed), including elementary, K-12, secondary; educational leadership (Ed S), including elementary school principalship, secondary school principalship, superintendency; educational leadership and policy analysis (Ed D); elementary education (MS Ed); elementary mathematics (MS Ed); higher education leadership (MS); middle school education (MS Ed); reading (MS Ed); special education (MS Ed); teacher leadership (MS Ed); teaching English language learners (MS Ed). *Accreditation:* NCATE. *Program availability:* Part-time. *Students:* 15 full-time (11 women), 150 part-time (103 women). In 2016, 46 master's awarded. *Degree requirements:* For master's, comprehensive exam; for Ed S, comprehensive exam, thesis. *Entrance requirements:* For master's, GRE General Test, writing sample; for Ed S, minimum graduate GPA of 3.25. Additional exam requirements/recommendations for international students: Required—TOEFL (minimum score 550 paper-based). *Application deadline:* For fall admission, 7/1 for domestic and international students; for spring admission, 11/15 for domestic and international students. Applications are processed on a rolling basis. Application fee: $0 ($50 for international students). Electronic applications accepted. *Expenses:* Tuition, state resident: full-time $3447; part-time $383 per credit hour. Tuition, nonresident: full-time $5724; part-time $636 per credit hour. *Required fees:* $130 per credit hour. *Financial support:* Research assistantships with full tuition reimbursements, teaching assistantships with full tuition reimbursements, and unspecified assistantships available. Financial award application deadline: 4/1; financial award applicants required to submit FAFSA. *Faculty research:* Great books of educational administration. *Unit head:* Dr. Tim Wall, Dean, 660-562-1179, E-mail: timwall@nwmissouri.edu.
Website: http://www.nwmissouri.edu/academics/ed/

Nyack College, School of Education, Nyack, NY 10960. Offers childhood education (MS); childhood special education (MS); inclusive education (MA); TESOL (MAT, MS). *Program availability:* Part-time, 100% online, blended/hybrid learning. *Students:* 21 full-time (20 women), 36 part-time (31 women); includes 34 minority (7 Black or African American, non-Hispanic/Latino; 3 Asian, non-Hispanic/Latino; 22 Hispanic/Latino; 1 Native Hawaiian or other Pacific Islander, non-Hispanic/Latino; 1 Two or more races, non-Hispanic/Latino), 5 international. Average age 33. In 2016, 23 master's awarded. *Degree requirements:* For master's, comprehensive exam, clinical experience. *Entrance requirements:* For master's, GRE, transcripts, autobiography and statement on reasons for pursuing graduate study in education, recommendations, 6 credits of language, evidence of computer literacy, introductory course in psychology. Additional exam requirements/recommendations for international students: Required—TOEFL (minimum score 550 paper-based; 80 iBT), GRE. *Application deadline:* For fall admission, 8/4 for domestic students, 7/4 for international students; for spring admission, 12/15 for domestic students, 11/15 for international students; for summer admission, 4/7 for domestic students, 3/7 for international students. Applications are processed on a rolling basis. Application fee: $30. Electronic applications accepted. *Expenses:* $700 per credit. *Financial support:* Scholarships/grants available. Financial award applicants required to submit FAFSA. *Unit head:* Dr. JoAnn Looney, Dean, 845-675-4538, Fax: 845-358-0874. *Application contact:* Joseph Kim, Admissions Associate, 845-675-4400 Ext. 5708, Fax: 845-348-3912, E-mail: admissions.grad@nyack.edu.
Website: http://www.nyack.edu/edu

Oakland University, Graduate Study and Lifelong Learning, School of Education and Human Services, Department of Teacher Development and Educational Studies, Rochester, MI 48309-4401. Offers educational studies (M Ed); elementary education (MAT); secondary education (MAT); teaching and learning (Graduate Certificate). *Entrance requirements:* For master's, minimum GPA of 3.0. Electronic applications accepted.

Oklahoma City University, Petree College of Arts and Sciences, Oklahoma City, OK 73106-1402. Offers applied behavioral studies (M Ed); applied sociology: nonprofit leadership (MA); creative writing (MFA); criminology (MS); early childhood education (M Ed); elementary education (M Ed); general studies (MLA); leadership/management (MLA); moving image arts (MFA); professional counseling (M Ed); teaching (MA); teaching English to speakers of other languages (MA). *Program availability:* Part-time, evening/weekend. *Faculty:* 11 full-time (5 women), 15 part-time/adjunct (6 women). *Students:* 77 full-time (55 women), 46 part-time (30 women); includes 32 minority (13 Black or African American, non-Hispanic/Latino; 1 American Indian or Alaska Native, non-Hispanic/Latino; 2 Asian, non-Hispanic/Latino; 12 Hispanic/Latino; 4 Two or more races, non-Hispanic/Latino), 37 international. Average age 34. 92 applicants, 74% accepted, 46 enrolled. In 2016, 72 master's awarded. *Degree requirements:* For master's, capstone/practicum. *Entrance requirements:* For master's, bachelor's degree from accredited institution with minimum GPA of 3.0, essay, recommendation letters. Additional exam requirements/recommendations for international students: Required—TOEFL (minimum score 550 paper-based; 80 iBT). *Application deadline:* Applications are processed on a rolling basis. Application fee: $50. Electronic applications accepted. *Expenses:* Contact institution. *Financial support:* In 2016–17, 16 students received support. Federal Work-Study, institutionally sponsored loans, scholarships/grants, and tuition waivers (full and partial) available. Support available to part-time students. Financial award application deadline: 6/1; financial award applicants required to submit FAFSA. *Unit head:* Dr. Amy Cataldi, Dean, 405-208-5446, Fax: 405-208-5447, E-mail: acataldi@okcu.edu. *Application contact:* Michael Harrington, Director of Graduate Admissions, 800-633-7242, Fax: 405-208-5356, E-mail: gadmissions@okcu.edu.
Website: http://www.okcu.edu/petree/

Old Dominion University, Darden College of Education, Program in Elementary/Middle Education, Norfolk, VA 23529. Offers elementary education (Postbaccalaureate Certificate); instructional technology (MS Ed); library science (MS Ed). *Accreditation:* NCATE. *Program availability:* Part-time, evening/weekend, 100% online, blended/hybrid learning. *Faculty:* 21 full-time (19 women), 24 part-time/adjunct (22 women). *Students:* 120 full-time (112 women), 138 part-time (125 women); includes 60 minority (36 Black or African American, non-Hispanic/Latino; 1 American Indian or Alaska Native, non-Hispanic/Latino; 5 Asian, non-Hispanic/Latino; 12 Hispanic/Latino; 6 Two or more races, non-Hispanic/Latino). Average age 33. 213 applicants, 88% accepted, 172 enrolled. In 2016, 127 master's awarded. *Degree requirements:* For master's, comprehensive exam. *Entrance requirements:* For master's, GRE General Test or MAT; PRAXIS I, SAT or ACT, minimum GPA of 2.8. Additional exam requirements/recommendations for international students: Required—TOEFL (minimum score 600 paper-based). *Application deadline:* For fall admission, 6/1 priority date for domestic students; for winter admission, 11/1 priority date for domestic students; for spring admission, 3/1 priority date for domestic students. Applications are processed on a rolling basis. Application fee: $50. Electronic applications accepted. *Expenses:* $478 per credit hour in-state; $1,195 per credit hour out-of-state. *Financial support:* In 2016–17, 180 students received support. Unspecified assistantships available. Financial award application deadline: 2/15; financial award applicants required to submit FAFSA. *Faculty research:* Education pre-K to 6, school librarianship, reading, TESOL, literacy. *Unit head:* Dr. KaaVonia Hinton, Chair, Department of Teaching and Learning, 757-683-3284, Fax: 757-683-5862, E-mail: khintonj@odu.edu. *Application contact:* William Heffelfinger, Director of Graduate Admissions, 757-683-5554, Fax: 757-683-3255, E-mail: gradadmit@odu.edu.
Website: http://education.odu.edu/eci/

Olivet Nazarene University, Graduate School, Division of Education, Program in Elementary Education, Bourbonnais, IL 60914. Offers MAT. *Accreditation:* NCATE. *Program availability:* Evening/weekend. *Degree requirements:* For master's, thesis or alternative.

Oregon State University, College of Education, Program in Teaching, Corvallis, OR 97331. Offers clinically based elementary education (MAT); elementary education (MAT); language arts (MAT); mathematics (MAT); music education (MAT); science (MAT); social studies (MAT). *Program availability:* Part-time, blended/hybrid learning. *Faculty:* 17 full-time (8 women), 2 part-time/adjunct (both women). *Students:* 57 full-time (39 women), 22 part-time (18 women); includes 11 minority (2 Hispanic/Latino; 1 Native Hawaiian or other Pacific Islander, non-Hispanic/Latino; 8 Two or more races, non-Hispanic/Latino). Average age 29. 131 applicants, 76% accepted, 76 enrolled. In 2016, 92 master's awarded. *Entrance requirements:* For master's, CBEST. Additional exam requirements/recommendations for international students: Required—TOEFL (minimum score 575 paper-based). *Application deadline:* For fall admission, 12/1 for domestic students. Application fee: $60. *Expenses:* Contact institution. *Unit head:* Dr. Larry Flick, Dean. *Application contact:* E-mail: askcoed@oregonstate.edu.
Website: http://education.oregonstate.edu/mat

Ottawa University, Graduate Studies-Arizona, Program in Education, Ottawa, KS 66067-3399. Offers community college counseling (MA); curriculum and instruction (MA); early childhood (MA); education intervention (MA), education leadership (MA); education technology (MA); Montessori early childhood education (MA); Montessori elementary education (MA); professional development (MA); school guidance counseling (MA); special education - cross categorical (MA). Programs offered in Mesa, Phoenix, Tempe and West Valley, AZ. *Accreditation:* NCATE. *Program availability:* Part-time. *Degree requirements:* For master's, thesis or alternative. *Entrance requirements:* For master's, minimum undergraduate GPA of 3.0, copy of current state certification or teaching license. Additional exam requirements/recommendations for international students: Required—TOEFL (minimum score 550 paper-based). Electronic applications accepted. *Expenses:* Contact institution.

Pace University, School of Education, New York, NY 10038. Offers adolescent education (MST), including biology, business education, chemistry, earth science, English, foreign languages, mathematics, physics, social studies, visual arts; childhood education (MST); early childhood development, learning and intervention (MST); educational technology studies (MS); inclusive adolescent education (MST), including biology, business education, chemistry, earth science, English, foreign languages, mathematics, physics, social studies, visual arts; integrated instruction for educational technology (Certificate); integrated instruction for literacy and technology (Certificate); literacy (MS Ed); special education (MS Ed). *Accreditation:* NCATE. *Program*

availability: Part-time, evening/weekend, blended/hybrid learning. *Faculty:* 19 full-time (13 women), 86 part-time/adjunct (49 women). *Students:* 115 full-time (97 women), 543 part-time (381 women); includes 280 minority (137 Black or African American, non-Hispanic/Latino; 1 American Indian or Alaska Native, non-Hispanic/Latino; 40 Asian, non-Hispanic/Latino; 87 Hispanic/Latino; 15 Two or more races, non-Hispanic/Latino), 13 international. Average age 30. 181 applicants, 78% accepted, 72 enrolled. In 2016, 193 master's, 9 other advanced degrees awarded. *Degree requirements:* For master's, certification exams. *Entrance requirements:* For master's, GRE, interview, teaching certificate (except for MST). Additional exam requirements/recommendations for international students: Required—TOEFL (minimum score 88 iBT), IELTS or PTE. *Application deadline:* For fall admission, 8/1 priority date for domestic students, 6/1 for international students; for spring admission, 12/1 priority date for domestic students, 10/1 for international students. Applications are processed on a rolling basis. Application fee: $70. Electronic applications accepted. *Expenses:* Contact institution. *Financial support:* In 2016–17, 17 students received support, including 17 research assistantships with partial tuition reimbursements available (averaging $6,020 per year); career-related internships or fieldwork and Federal Work-Study also available. Financial award application deadline: 9/1; financial award applicants required to submit FAFSA. *Faculty research:* STEM education, TESOL, teacher education, special education, language and literary development. *Total annual research expenditures:* $290,153. *Unit head:* Dr. Xiao-Lei Wang, Dean, School of Education, 914-773-3876, E-mail: xwang@pace.edu. *Application contact:* Susan Ford-Goldschein, Director of Graduate Admissions, 212-346-1531, Fax: 212-346-1585, E-mail: graduateadmission@pace.edu.
Website: http://www.pace.edu/school-of-education

Pacific Union College, Education Department, Angwin, CA 94508-9707. Offers education (M Ed); elementary teaching (MAT); secondary teaching (MAT). *Program availability:* Part-time. *Faculty:* 3 full-time (1 woman), 1 (woman) part-time/adjunct. *Students:* 1 (woman) full-time, 5 part-time (3 women); includes 1 minority (Hispanic/Latino). Average age 41. In 2016, 1 master's awarded. *Degree requirements:* For master's, thesis, action research project, field experiences. *Entrance requirements:* For master's, GRE General Test, two interviews, teaching credential, letters of recommendation, essay. *Application deadline:* For summer admission, 6/1 for domestic students. Applications are processed on a rolling basis. Application fee: $0. *Expenses: Tuition:* Part-time $405 per quarter hour. *Required fees:* $210 per quarter. Tuition and fees vary according to student's religious affiliation. *Financial support:* Scholarships/grants available. Support available to part-time students. *Unit head:* Prof. Thomas Lee, Department Chair, 707-965-6646, Fax: 707-965-6645, E-mail: tdlee@puc.edu. *Application contact:* Cherith Mundy, Credential Analyst, 707-965-6643, Fax: 707-965-6645, E-mail: teachingcredentials@puc.edu.
Website: http://www.puc.edu/academics/departments/education/

Pacific University, College of Education, Forest Grove, OR 97116-1797. Offers early childhood education (MAT); education (MAE); elementary education (MAT); ESOL (MAT); high school education (MAT); middle school education (MAT); special education (MAT); speech-language pathology (MS); STEM education (MAT); talented and gifted (M Ed); visual function in learning (M Ed). *Accreditation:* NCATE. *Program availability:* Part-time, evening/weekend. *Degree requirements:* For master's, research project. *Entrance requirements:* For master's, California Basic Educational Skills Test, PRAXIS II, minimum undergraduate GPA of 2.75, 3.0 graduate. Additional exam requirements/recommendations for international students: Required—TOEFL. Electronic applications accepted. *Expenses:* Contact institution. *Faculty research:* Defining a culturally competent classroom, technology in the k-12 classroom, Socratic seminars, social studies education.

Pfeiffer University, Program in Elementary Education, Misenheimer, NC 28109-0960. Offers MAT, MS. *Accreditation:* NCATE. *Entrance requirements:* For master's, GRE, MAT, minimum GPA of 2.75.

Plymouth State University, College of Graduate Studies, Graduate Studies in Education, Program in Elementary Education, Plymouth, NH 03264-1595. Offers M Ed. *Accreditation:* NCATE. *Program availability:* Part-time, evening/weekend. *Degree requirements:* For master's, capstone project. *Entrance requirements:* For master's, MAT, minimum GPA of 3.0.

Prescott College, Graduate Programs, Program in Education, Prescott, AZ 86301. Offers early childhood education (MA); early childhood special education (MA); education (MA); elementary education (MA); environmental education leadership and administration (MA); equine-assisted learning (MA); school guidance counseling (MA); secondary education (MA); special education: learning disabilities (MA); special education: mental retardation (MA); special education: serious emotional disabilities (MA); student-directed independent study (MA); sustainability education (PhD). *Program availability:* Part-time, online learning. *Faculty:* 3 full-time (all women). *Students:* 9 full-time (8 women), 30 part-time (20 women); includes 11 minority (3 Black or African American, non-Hispanic/Latino; 2 American Indian or Alaska Native, non-Hispanic/Latino; 6 Hispanic/Latino). Average age 36. 66 applicants, 82% accepted, 32 enrolled. In 2016, 12 master's, 8 doctorates awarded. *Degree requirements:* For master's, thesis, fieldwork or internship, practicum; for doctorate, thesis/dissertation. *Entrance requirements:* For master's, 2 letters of recommendation, resume; for doctorate, 3 letters of recommendation, resume, official transcripts, personal statement, program proposal. Additional exam requirements/recommendations for international students: Required—TOEFL (minimum score 500 paper-based). *Application deadline:* For fall admission, 4/15 priority date for domestic and international students; for spring admission, 9/15 priority date for domestic and international students. Applications are processed on a rolling basis. Application fee: $40. Electronic applications accepted. *Expenses: Tuition:* Full-time $19,680. One-time fee: $260 part-time. *Financial support:* Fellowships, research assistantships, teaching assistantships, career-related internships or fieldwork, Federal Work-Study, institutionally sponsored loans, scholarships/grants, traineeships, health care benefits, tuition waivers, and unspecified assistantships available. Support available to part-time students. Financial award applicants required to submit FAFSA. *Unit head:* Bob Ellis, 928-350-2217, E-mail: bellis@prescott.edu. *Application contact:* Melanie Lefever, Assistant Director, Limited-residency Programs, 928-350-2106, Fax: 928-776-5242, E-mail: mlefever@prescott.edu.

Providence College, Program in Special Education, Providence, RI 02918. Offers special education (M Ed), including elementary teaching, secondary teaching. *Program availability:* Part-time, evening/weekend. *Faculty:* 6 full-time (4 women), 33 part-time/adjunct (21 women). *Students:* 3 full-time (2 women), 25 part-time (22 women); includes 2 minority (1 Asian, non-Hispanic/Latino; 1 Hispanic/Latino). Average age 28. 13 applicants, 100% accepted, 12 enrolled. In 2016, 14 master's awarded. *Degree requirements:* For master's, comprehensive exam, portfolio. *Entrance requirements:* Additional exam requirements/recommendations for international students: Required—TOEFL (minimum score 577 paper-based; 90 iBT). *Application deadline:* For fall admission, 7/15 priority date for domestic and international students; for spring admission, 11/15 priority date for domestic and international students; for summer admission, 3/15 priority date for domestic students, 3/15 for international students. Application fee: $55. *Expenses: Tuition:* Part-time $1260 per course. One-time fee: $265. Tuition and fees vary according to course load and program. *Financial support:* Career-related internships or fieldwork, institutionally sponsored loans, and unspecified assistantships available. Support available to part-time students. Financial award application deadline: 8/1; financial award applicants required to submit FAFSA.
Website: http://www.providence.edu/professional-studies/graduate-degrees

Providence College, Programs in Administration, Providence, RI 02918. Offers elementary administration (M Ed); secondary administration (M Ed). *Program availability:* Part-time, evening/weekend. *Faculty:* 6 full-time (4 women), 33 part-time/adjunct (21 women). *Students:* 2 full-time (both women), 47 part-time (30 women); includes 3 minority (1 Asian, non-Hispanic/Latino; 2 Hispanic/Latino). Average age 37. 23 applicants, 100% accepted, 13 enrolled. In 2016, 16 master's awarded. *Degree requirements:* For master's, comprehensive exam, portfolio. *Entrance requirements:* Additional exam requirements/recommendations for international students: Required—TOEFL (minimum score 577 paper-based; 90 iBT). *Application deadline:* For fall admission, 7/15 priority date for domestic and international students; for spring admission, 11/15 priority date for domestic and international students; for summer admission, 3/15 priority date for domestic students, 3/15 for international students. Application fee: $55. *Expenses: Tuition:* Part-time $1260 per course. One-time fee: $265. Tuition and fees vary according to course load and program. *Financial support:* Career-related internships or fieldwork, institutionally sponsored loans, and unspecified assistantships available. Support available to part-time students. Financial award application deadline: 8/1; financial award applicants required to submit FAFSA. *Application contact:* Rev. Mark D. Nowel, Dean of Undergraduate and Graduate Studies, 401-865-2649, Fax: 401-865-1496, E-mail: mnowel@providence.edu.
Website: http://www.providence.edu/professional-studies/graduate-degrees/Pages/master-education-administration.aspx

Purdue University, Graduate School, College of Education, Department of Curriculum and Instruction, West Lafayette, IN 47907. Offers agricultural and extension education (MS, MS Ed, PhD, Ed S); art education (PhD); career and technical education (MS Ed, PhD, Ed S); curriculum studies (MS Ed, PhD, Ed S); educational technology (MS Ed, PhD, Ed S); elementary education (MS Ed); family and consumer sciences education (MS Ed, PhD, Ed S); foreign language education (MS Ed, PhD, Ed S); industrial technology (PhD, Ed S); language arts (MS Ed, PhD, Ed S); literacy (MS Ed, PhD, Ed S); mathematics education (MS, MS Ed, PhD, Ed S); science education (MS, MS Ed, PhD, Ed S); social studies education (MS Ed, PhD, Ed S). *Accreditation:* NCATE. *Program availability:* Part-time, evening/weekend. *Faculty:* 37 full-time (27 women), 1 (woman) part-time/adjunct. *Students:* 78 full-time (50 women), 286 part-time (195 women); includes 68 minority (25 Black or African American, non-Hispanic/Latino; 3 American Indian or Alaska Native, non-Hispanic/Latino; 10 Asian, non-Hispanic/Latino; 22 Hispanic/Latino; 1 Native Hawaiian or other Pacific Islander, non-Hispanic/Latino; 7 Two or more races, non-Hispanic/Latino), 44 international. Average age 36. 150 applicants, 79% accepted, 73 enrolled. In 2016, 107 master's, 20 doctorates, 2 other advanced degrees awarded. *Degree requirements:* For master's, thesis optional; for doctorate, thesis/dissertation, oral and written exams; for Ed S, oral presentation, project. *Entrance requirements:* For master's, GRE General Test (if undergraduate GPA is below 3.0), minimum undergraduate GPA of 3.0 or equivalent; for doctorate, GRE General Test (minimum combined verbal and quantitative score of 1000, 300 for new scoring), minimum undergraduate GPA of 3.0 or equivalent; master's degree with minimum GPA of 3.0 or equivalent; for Ed S, GRE General Test (minimum combined verbal and quantitative score of 1000, 300 for new scoring), minimum undergraduate GPA of 3.0 or equivalent; master's degree. Additional exam requirements/recommendations for international students: Required—TOEFL (minimum score 550 paper-based; 77 iBT). *Application deadline:* For fall admission, 12/15 for domestic students, 3/1 for international students; for spring admission, 9/15 for domestic students, 8/1 for international students. Application fee: $60 ($75 for international students). Electronic applications accepted. *Financial support:* Fellowships with full tuition reimbursements, research assistantships with full tuition reimbursements, teaching assistantships with full tuition reimbursements, career-related internships or fieldwork, and tuition waivers (full) available. Support available to part-time students. Financial award application deadline: 3/1; financial award applicants required to submit FAFSA. *Faculty research:* Literacy acquisition and development, teacher beliefs and knowledge, recruitment and retention of underrepresented students, economic education, literacy discourse. *Unit head:* Janet M. Alsup, Head, 765-494-9667, E-mail: alsupj@purdue.edu. *Application contact:* Heather Brinkman, Graduate Contact, 765-494-2345, E-mail: hbrinkma@purdue.edu.
Website: http://www.edci.purdue.edu/

Queens College of the City University of New York, Division of Education, Department of Elementary and Early Childhood Education, Queens, NY 11367-1597. Offers bilingual education (MS Ed); child development psychology (AC); childhood education (MAT, MS Ed); childhood education and special education (MAT); childhood education-bilingual education (MAT, MS Ed, AC); children's literacy (AC); early childhood education (MAT); early childhood education birth-2 (MS Ed, AC); elementary education (MS Ed); literacy birth-grade 6 (AC); literacy technology birth-grade 6 (MS Ed); social studies education grades 1-6 (AC). *Program availability:* Part-time, evening/weekend. *Faculty:* 25 full-time (19 women), 33 part-time/adjunct (28 women). *Students:* 134 full-time (119 women), 374 part-time (349 women); includes 251 minority (55 Black or African American, non-Hispanic/Latino; 1 American Indian or Alaska Native, non-Hispanic/Latino; 82 Asian, non-Hispanic/Latino; 103 Hispanic/Latino; 10 Two or more races, non-Hispanic/Latino), 12 international. Average age 29. 364 applicants, 72% accepted, 224 enrolled. In 2016, 184 master's, 62 other advanced degrees awarded. *Degree requirements:* For master's, research project. *Entrance requirements:* For master's, minimum GPA of 3.0. Additional exam requirements/recommendations for international students: Required—TOEFL, IELTS. *Application deadline:* For fall admission, 4/1 for domestic students. Applications are processed on a rolling basis. Application fee: $125. Electronic applications accepted. *Expenses:* Tuition, state resident: full-time $5065; part-time $425 per credit. Tuition, nonresident: part-time $780 per credit. *Required fees:* $522; $397 per credit. Part-time tuition and fees vary according to course load and program. *Financial support:* Career-related internships or fieldwork available. Financial award application deadline: 4/1; financial award applicants required to submit FAFSA. *Unit head:* Dr. Mary Bushnell Greiner, Chairperson, 718-997-5328, E-mail: mary.greiner@qc.cuny.edu.

Queens University of Charlotte, Wayland H. Cato, Jr. School of Education, Charlotte, NC 28274-0002. Offers educational leadership (MA); K-6 (MAT); literacy K-12 (M Ed). *Accreditation:* NCATE. *Program availability:* Part-time, evening/weekend, online learning. *Degree requirements:* For master's, comprehensive exam. *Entrance requirements:* For master's, GRE General Test. *Expenses:* Contact institution.

Quinnipiac University, School of Education, Program in Elementary Education, Hamden, CT 06518-1940. Offers MAT. *Accreditation:* NCATE. *Faculty:* 6 full-time (2 women), 24 part-time/adjunct (16 women). *Students:* 47 full-time (45 women), 1 (woman) part-time; includes 4 minority (1 American Indian or Alaska Native, non-Hispanic/Latino; 2 Hispanic/Latino; 1 Two or more races, non-Hispanic/Latino). 47 applicants, 94% accepted, 38 enrolled. In 2016, 28 master's awarded. *Entrance requirements:* For master's, PRAXIS I or PRAXIS Core Academic Skills Exam, minimum GPA of 3.0, interview. *Application deadline:* For fall admission, 5/1 priority date for domestic students. Applications are processed on a rolling basis. Application fee: $45.

Electronic applications accepted. *Expenses: Tuition:* Part-time $985 per credit. *Required fees:* $40 per credit. $150 per semester. Tuition and fees vary according to program. *Financial support:* Career-related internships or fieldwork, Federal Work-Study, and unspecified assistantships available. Financial award application deadline: 6/1; financial award applicants required to submit FAFSA. *Faculty research:* Multicultural and urban education/leadership, challenges of teaching diverse learners, scholarship of teaching and learning, technology and teaching, humor and education. *Unit head:* Mordechai Gordon, Program Director, 203-582-8442, E-mail: mordechai.gordon@qu.edu. *Application contact:* Office of Graduate Admissions, 203-582-8672, Fax: 203-582-3443, E-mail: graduate@qu.edu.
Website: http://www.qu.edu/gradeducation

Regent University, Graduate School, School of Education, Virginia Beach, VA 23464-9800. Offers adult education (Ed D, PhD, Ed S); advanced educational leadership (Ed D, PhD, Ed S); career switcher (M Ed); character education (Ed D, PhD, Ed S); Christian education leadership (Ed D, PhD, Ed S); Christian school administration (M Ed); curriculum and instruction (M Ed), including adult education, Christian school, gifted and talented education, STEM education, teacher leader; educational leadership (M Ed); educational psychology (Ed D, PhD, Ed S); educational technology and online learning (Ed D, PhD, Ed S); elementary education (M Ed); exceptional education executive leadership (Ed D, PhD, Ed S); higher education (Ed D, PhD, Ed S); higher education leadership and management (Ed D, PhD, Ed S); individualized degree plan (M Ed); K-12 school leadership (Ed D, PhD, Ed S); K-12 special education (M Ed); K-8 leadership in mathematics education (M Ed); leadership in mathematics education (Ed S); reading specialist (M Ed); special education (Ed D, PhD, Ed S); student affairs (M Ed); TESOL (M Ed), including adult education - collegiate, K-12. *Accreditation:* TEAC. *Program availability:* Part-time, evening/weekend, 100% online, blended/hybrid learning. *Faculty:* 22 full-time (10 women), 42 part-time/adjunct (31 women). *Students:* 89 full-time (62 women), 1,035 part-time (823 women); includes 466 minority (381 Black or African American, non-Hispanic/Latino; 3 American Indian or Alaska Native, non-Hispanic/Latino; 19 Asian, non-Hispanic/Latino; 50 Hispanic/Latino; 13 Two or more races, non-Hispanic/Latino), 11 international. Average age 39. 976 applicants, 59% accepted, 449 enrolled. In 2016, 241 master's, 22 doctorates, 4 other advanced degrees awarded. *Degree requirements:* For master's, thesis or alternative; for doctorate, comprehensive exam, thesis/dissertation. *Entrance requirements:* For master's, Virginia Communication and Literacy Assessment (VCLA), PRAXIS, college transcripts, writing sample, interview; for doctorate, GRE, writing sample, resume, transcripts, interview. Additional exam requirements/recommendations for international students: Required—TOEFL (minimum score 577 paper-based). *Application deadline:* For fall admission, 4/1 priority date for domestic students; for spring admission, 10/15 priority date for domestic students. Applications are processed on a rolling basis. Application fee: $50. Electronic applications accepted. *Expenses:* Contact institution. *Financial support:* In 2016–17, 622 students received support, including 1 fellowship (averaging $5,000 per year); career-related internships or fieldwork, scholarships/grants, and unspecified assistantships also available. Support available to part-time students. *Faculty research:* Christian school administration, curriculum and instruction, educational technology and online learning, higher education, special education. *Unit head:* Dr. Donald Finn, Dean, 757-352-4278, Fax: 757-352-4318, E-mail: dfinn@regent.edu. *Application contact:* Heidi Cece, Assistant Vice President of Enrollment Management, 800-373-5504, Fax: 757-352-4381, E-mail: admissions@regent.edu.
Website: http://www.regent.edu/soe/

Regis College, Department of Education, Weston, MA 02493. Offers elementary teacher (MAT); higher education leadership (Ed D); reading (MAT); special education (MAT). *Program availability:* Part-time, evening/weekend, blended/hybrid learning. *Degree requirements:* For master's, thesis. *Entrance requirements:* For master's, GRE or MAT. Additional exam requirements/recommendations for international students: Required—TOEFL; Recommended—IELTS. *Application deadline:* Applications are processed on a rolling basis. Application fee: $50. Electronic applications accepted. *Financial support:* Federal Work-Study, scholarships/grants, and unspecified assistantships available. Financial award applicants required to submit FAFSA. *Unit head:* Dr. Priscilla Boerger, Department Chair/Graduate Program Director, 781-768-7422, E-mail: priscilla.boerger@regiscollege.edu.

Regis University, College of Contemporary Liberal Studies, Denver, CO 80221-1099. Offers creative writing (MFA); criminology (M Sc); curriculum, instruction and assessment (M Ed); education - teacher leadership (M Ed); educational leadership (M Ed); elementary education (M Ed); literacy (Certificate); reading (M Ed); secondary education (M Ed); special education (M Ed); teacher academic leadership (Certificate); teacher leadership (MA); teacher/educational leadership (M Ed); teaching the linguistically diverse (M Ed). *Program availability:* Part-time, evening/weekend, 100% online, blended/hybrid learning. *Faculty:* 18 full-time (12 women), 42 part-time/adjunct (26 women). *Students:* 302 full-time (234 women), 270 part-time (218 women); includes 148 minority (33 Black or African American, non-Hispanic/Latino; 3 American Indian or Alaska Native, non-Hispanic/Latino; 13 Asian, non-Hispanic/Latino; 83 Hispanic/Latino; 16 Two or more races, non-Hispanic/Latino), 3 international. Average age 36. 431 applicants, 90% accepted, 110 enrolled. In 2016, 308 master's awarded. *Degree requirements:* For master's, thesis (for some programs). *Entrance requirements:* For master's, official transcript reflecting baccalaureate degree awarded from regionally-accredited college or university, work experience, resume, letters of recommendation. Additional exam requirements/recommendations for international students: Required—TOEFL (minimum score 550 paper-based; 82 iBT). *Application deadline:* For fall admission, 8/15 priority date for domestic students, 7/13 for international students; for winter admission, 10/10 priority date for domestic students, 9/8 for international students; for spring admission, 1/10 priority date for domestic students, 11/17 for international students; for summer admission, 5/1 priority date for domestic students. Applications are processed on a rolling basis. Application fee: $75. Electronic applications accepted. *Expenses:* $485 per credit hour. *Financial support:* Scholarships/grants available. Financial award application deadline: 4/15; financial award applicants required to submit FAFSA. *Unit head:* Dr. Elisa Robyn, Academic Dean. *Application contact:* Cate Clark, Director of Admissions, 303-458-4900, Fax: 303-964-5534, E-mail: ruadmissions@regis.edu.
Website: http://www.regis.edu/CCLS.aspx

Rhode Island College, School of Graduate Studies, Feinstein School of Education and Human Development, Department of Elementary Education, Providence, RI 02908-1991. Offers early childhood education (M Ed); elementary education (M Ed, MAT); reading (M Ed). *Accreditation:* NCATE. *Program availability:* Part-time, evening/weekend. *Faculty:* 11 full-time (9 women), 1 (woman) part-time/adjunct. *Students:* 14 full-time (all women), 24 part-time (22 women); includes 3 minority (all Hispanic/Latino). Average age 32. In 2016, 16 master's awarded. *Degree requirements:* For master's, comprehensive exam (for some programs), comprehensive assessment. *Entrance requirements:* For master's, GRE General Test or MAT, PRAXIS II (elementary content knowledge), undergraduate transcripts; minimum undergraduate GPA of 3.0; 3 letters of recommendation. Additional exam requirements/recommendations for international students: Recommended—TOEFL (minimum score 550 paper-based; 79 iBT). *Application deadline:* For fall admission, 3/1 for domestic students; for spring admission, 11/1 for domestic students. Applications are processed on a rolling basis. Application fee: $50. Electronic applications accepted. *Expenses:* Tuition, state resident: full-time $8928; part-time $372 per credit. Tuition, nonresident: full-time $17,376; part-time $724 per credit. *Required fees:* $604; $22 per credit. One-time fee: $74. *Financial support:* Teaching assistantships with full tuition reimbursements, Federal Work-Study, scholarships/grants, and health care benefits available. Support available to part-time students. Financial award application deadline: 5/15; financial award applicants required to submit FAFSA. *Unit head:* Dr. Patricia Cordeiro, Chair, 401-456-8016. *Application contact:* Graduate Studies, 401-456-8700.
Website: http://www.ric.edu/elementaryEducation/

Rider University, Department of Graduate Education, Leadership and Counseling, Teacher Certification Program, Lawrenceville, NJ 08648-3001. Offers business education (Certificate); elementary education (Certificate); English as a second language (Certificate); English education (Certificate); mathematics education (Certificate); preschool to grade 3 (Certificate); science education (Certificate); social studies education (Certificate); world languages (Certificate), including French, German, Spanish. *Program availability:* Part-time. *Degree requirements:* For Certificate, internship, professional portfolio. *Entrance requirements:* For degree, PRAXIS, resume. Additional exam requirements/recommendations for international students: Required—TOEFL (minimum score 550 paper-based). Electronic applications accepted. *Faculty research:* Conceptual foundations for optimal development of creativity; creative theory, cognitive processes in mathematics learning, teacher collaboration.

Rivier University, School of Graduate Studies, Department of Education, Nashua, NH 03060. Offers curriculum and instruction (M Ed); early childhood education (M Ed); educational administration (M Ed); educational studies (M Ed); elementary education (M Ed); elementary education and general special education (M Ed); emotional and behavioral disorders (M Ed); general social education (M Ed); leadership and learning (Ed D, CAGS); learning disabilities (M Ed); learning disabilities and reading (M Ed); mental health counseling (MA); reading (M Ed); school counseling (M Ed). *Program availability:* Part-time, evening/weekend. *Degree requirements:* For master's, comprehensive exam (for some programs), internships. *Entrance requirements:* For master's, GRE General Test or MAT.

Rockford University, Graduate Studies, Department of Education, Program in Elementary Education, Rockford, IL 61108-2393. Offers MAT. *Program availability:* Part-time, evening/weekend. *Degree requirements:* For master's, thesis optional. *Entrance requirements:* For master's, GRE General Test, basic skills test (for students seeking certification), 3 letters of recommendation. Additional exam requirements/recommendations for international students: Required—TOEFL (minimum score 550 paper-based; 79 iBT). *Application deadline:* Applications are processed on a rolling basis. Application fee: $50. Electronic applications accepted. *Expenses: Tuition:* Part-time $710 per credit. *Required fees:* $50 per semester. *Financial support:* Scholarships/grants and unspecified assistantships available. Support available to part-time students. Financial award application deadline: 3/1; financial award applicants required to submit FAFSA. *Unit head:* Dr. Michelle McReynolds, MAT Director, 815-226-3390, Fax: 815-394-3706, E-mail: mmcreynolds@rockford.edu. *Application contact:* Michele Mehren, Office Manager for Graduate Studies, 815-226-4041, Fax: 815-394-3706, E-mail: mmehren@rockford.edu.

Rollins College, Hamilton Holt School, Graduate Education Programs, Winter Park, FL 32789-4499. Offers elementary education (M Ed, MAT). *Program availability:* Part-time, evening/weekend. *Faculty:* 4 full-time (2 women), 1 part-time/adjunct (0 women). *Students:* 5 full-time (4 women), 10 part-time (6 women); includes 3 minority (1 Black or African American, non-Hispanic/Latino; 2 American Indian or Alaska Native, non-Hispanic/Latino). Average age 34. 10 applicants, 70% accepted, 7 enrolled. In 2016, 5 master's awarded. *Degree requirements:* For master's, comprehensive exam, Professional Education Test (PED) and Subject Area Examination (SAE) of the Florida Teacher Certification Examinations (FTCE), successful review of the Expanded Teacher Education Portfolio (ETEP). *Entrance requirements:* For master's, General Knowledge Test of the Florida Teacher Certification Examination (FTCE), official transcripts, letter(s) of recommendation, essay. Additional exam requirements/recommendations for international students: Required—TOEFL (minimum score 550 paper-based; 80 iBT). *Application deadline:* For fall admission, 8/11 for domestic students; for spring admission, 12/10 for domestic students. Applications are processed on a rolling basis. Application fee: $50. *Expenses:* $525 per credit hour. *Financial support:* In 2016–17, 5 students received support. Federal Work-Study, scholarships/grants, and unspecified assistantships available. Support available to part-time students. Financial award applicants required to submit FAFSA. *Unit head:* Dr. Scott J. Hewit, Faculty Director, 407-646-2300, E-mail: shewit@rollins.edu. *Application contact:* 407-646-1568, Fax: 407-975-6430.

Roosevelt University, Graduate Division, College of Education, Program in Elementary Education, Chicago, IL 60605. Offers MA. *Students:* 11 full-time (9 women), 6 part-time (4 women); includes 6 minority (5 Black or African American, non-Hispanic/Latino; 1 Hispanic/Latino). Average age 31. 17 applicants, 88% accepted, 5 enrolled. In 2016, 22 master's awarded. *Expenses: Tuition, area resident:* Full-time $19,566; part-time $880 per credit hour. *Required fees:* $175 per semester. One-time fee: $200. Part-time tuition and fees vary according to course load, degree level and program. *Application contact:* Angela Ryan, Director of Graduate Enrollment, 312-341-2420, Fax: 312-281-3356, E-mail: aryan@roosevelt.edu.
Website: https://www.roosevelt.edu/academics/programs/masters-in-elementary-education-ma

Rosemont College, Schools of Graduate and Professional Studies, Graduate Education PreK-4 Program, Rosemont, PA 19010-1699. Offers elementary certification (MA); PreK-4 (MA). *Program availability:* Part-time, evening/weekend. *Degree requirements:* For master's, thesis optional. *Entrance requirements:* For master's, minimum college GPA of 3.0, 3 letters of recommendation. Additional exam requirements/recommendations for international students: Required—TOEFL. Electronic applications accepted. Application fee is waived when completed online.

Rowan University, Graduate School, College of Education, Department of Interdisciplinary and Inclusive Education, Program in Elementary Education, Glassboro, NJ 08028-1701. Offers MST. Electronic applications accepted.

Rudolf Steiner College, Waldorf Teacher Education Programs, Fair Oaks, CA 95628-6811. Offers early childhood education (MA); elementary education (MA).

Rutgers University–New Brunswick, Graduate School of Education, Department of Learning and Teaching, Program in Early Childhood/Elementary Education, Piscataway, NJ 08854-8097. Offers Ed M, Ed D. *Program availability:* Part-time. Terminal master's awarded for partial completion of doctoral program. *Degree requirements:* For master's, comprehensive exam (for some programs); for doctorate, thesis/dissertation, qualifying exam. *Entrance requirements:* For master's, GRE General Test, minimum GPA of 3.0; for doctorate, GRE General Test, minimum GPA of 3.5. Additional exam requirements/recommendations for international students: Required—TOEFL. Electronic applications accepted.

Sage Graduate School, Esteves School of Education, Program in Childhood Education/Literacy, Troy, NY 12180-4115. Offers MS. *Program availability:* Part-time, evening/weekend. *Faculty:* 17 full-time (13 women), 18 part-time/adjunct (12 women).

Students: 6 full-time (all women), 3 part-time (all women). Average age 25. 8 applicants, 88% accepted, 5 enrolled. In 2016, 1 master's awarded. *Degree requirements:* For master's, thesis optional. *Entrance requirements:* For master's, GRE (minimum scores: Verbal Reasoning 145, Quantitative Reasoning 145, Analytical Writing 3.5) or MAT (minimum score: 350), bachelor's degree in a liberal arts or science area, minimum cumulative GPA of 3.0. Additional exam requirements/recommendations for international students: Required—TOEFL (minimum score 550 paper-based). *Application deadline:* Applications are processed on a rolling basis. Application fee: $40. Electronic applications accepted. *Expenses: Tuition:* Full-time $12,240; part-time $680 per credit hour. Tuition and fees vary according to degree level and program. *Financial support:* Fellowships, research assistantships, Federal Work-Study, scholarships/grants, and unspecified assistantships available. Support available to part-time students. Financial award application deadline: 3/1; financial award applicants required to submit FAFSA. *Unit head:* Dr. John Pelizza, Interim Dean, Esteves School of Education, 518-244-2051, Fax: 518-244-2334, E-mail: pelizj@sage.edu. *Application contact:* Dr. Kathleen Gormley, Chair and Professor of Education, 518-244-2403, Fax: 518-244-2334, E-mail: gormlk@sage.edu.

Sage Graduate School, Esteves School of Education, Program in Childhood Special Education, Troy, NY 12180-4115. Offers MS Ed. *Accreditation:* NCATE. *Program availability:* Part-time, evening/weekend. *Faculty:* 17 full-time (13 women), 18 part-time/adjunct (12 women). *Students:* 1 (woman) full-time. Average age 22. 3 applicants, 67% accepted, 1 enrolled. In 2016, 1 master's awarded. *Degree requirements:* For master's, thesis optional. *Entrance requirements:* For master's, bachelor's degree in a liberal arts or sciences area or the equivalent. Additional exam requirements/recommendations for international students: Required—TOEFL (minimum score 550 paper-based). *Application deadline:* Applications are processed on a rolling basis. Application fee: $40. Electronic applications accepted. *Expenses: Tuition:* Full-time $12,240; part-time $680 per credit hour. Tuition and fees vary according to degree level and program. *Financial support:* Fellowships, research assistantships, Federal Work-Study, scholarships/grants, and unspecified assistantships available. Support available to part-time students. Financial award application deadline: 3/1; financial award applicants required to submit FAFSA. *Faculty research:* Effective behavioral strategies for classroom instruction. *Unit head:* Dr. John Pelizza, Interim Dean, Esteves School of Education, 518-244-2051, Fax: 518-244-2334, E-mail: pelizj@sage.edu. *Application contact:* Tracey McLeod, Chair and Assistant Professor, 518-244-3132, Fax: 518-244-2334, E-mail: mcleot@sage.edu.

Saginaw Valley State University, College of Education, Program in Elementary Classroom Teaching, University Center, MI 48710. Offers MAT. *Accreditation:* NCATE. *Program availability:* Part-time, evening/weekend. *Degree requirements:* For master's, capstone course. *Entrance requirements:* For master's, minimum GPA of 3.0, teaching certificate. Additional exam requirements/recommendations for international students: Required—TOEFL (minimum score 550 paper-based; 79 iBT). *Application deadline:* For fall admission, 7/15 for international students; for winter admission, 11/15 for international students; for spring admission, 4/15 for international students. Applications are processed on a rolling basis. Application fee: $30 ($90 for international students). Electronic applications accepted. *Expenses:* Tuition, state resident: full-time $9652; part-time $536 per credit hour. Tuition, nonresident: full-time $12,259; part-time $1022 per credit hour. *Required fees:* $263; $14.60 per credit hour. Tuition and fees vary according to degree level. *Financial support:* Federal Work-Study and scholarships/grants available. Support available to part-time students. Financial award applicants required to submit FAFSA. *Unit head:* Dr. Mary Harmon, Dean, 989-964-4057, Fax: 989-964-4563, E-mail: coeconnect@svsu.edu. *Application contact:* Jenna Briggs, Director, Graduate and International Admissions, 989-964-6096, Fax: 989-964-2788, E-mail: gradadm@svsu.edu.

St. John Fisher College, Ralph C. Wilson Jr. School of Education, Program in Childhood Education/Special Education, Rochester, NY 14618-3597. Offers childhood education (MS); childhood education/special education (Certificate). *Program availability:* Part-time, evening/weekend. *Faculty:* 8 full-time (6 women), 4 part-time/adjunct (all women). *Students:* 19 full-time (16 women), 10 part-time (9 women); includes 2 minority (1 Black or African American, non-Hispanic/Latino; 1 Two or more races, non-Hispanic/Latino). Average age 27. 30 applicants, 67% accepted, 15 enrolled. In 2016, 17 master's awarded. *Degree requirements:* For master's, field experience, student teaching, LAST. *Entrance requirements:* For master's, 2 letters of recommendation, personal statement, current resume. Additional exam requirements/recommendations for international students: Required—TOEFL (minimum score 575 paper-based; 80 iBT). *Application deadline:* Applications are processed on a rolling basis. Application fee: $30. Electronic applications accepted. *Expenses:* $885 per credit hour. *Financial support:* Scholarships/grants available. Financial award applicants required to submit FAFSA. *Faculty research:* Professional development, science assessment, multi-cultural, educational technology. *Unit head:* Dr. Susan Hildenbrand, Program Director, 585-385-7297, E-mail: shildenbrand@sjfc.edu. *Application contact:* Michelle Gosier, Associate Director of Transfer and Graduate Admissions, 585-385-8064, E-mail: mgosier@sjfc.edu.
Website: https://www.sjfc.edu/graduate-programs/ms-in-childhood-educationspecial-education/

St. John's University, The School of Education, Department of Curriculum and Instruction, Program in Childhood Education, Queens, NY 11439. Offers MS Ed. *Program availability:* Part-time, evening/weekend. *Degree requirements:* For master's, comprehensive exam. *Entrance requirements:* For master's, minimum GPA of 3.0, qualification for New York State provisional (initial) teaching certificate, 2 letters of recommendation, transcript, personal statement. Additional exam requirements/recommendations for international students: Required—TOEFL (minimum score 600 paper-based; 100 iBT), IELTS (minimum score 7). Electronic applications accepted. *Faculty research:* Self determination in the special education setting; parent, teacher, and student views on testing in elementary school.

Saint Joseph's University, College of Arts and Sciences, Graduate Programs in Education, Philadelphia, PA 19131-1395. Offers curriculum supervisor (Certificate); educational leadership (MS, Ed D); elementary education (MS, Certificate); elementary/middle school education (Certificate); instructional technology (MS, Certificate); organizational development and leadership (MS); principal (Certificate); professional education (MS); reading specialist (MS, Certificate); reading supervisor (Certificate); secondary education (MS, Certificate); special education (MS); special education 7-12 (Certificate); special education PK-8 (Certificate); superintendent's letter of eligibility (Certificate); supervisor of special education (Certificate); teacher of the deaf and hard of hearing (Certificate). *Program availability:* Part-time, evening/weekend, blended/hybrid learning. *Faculty:* 26 full-time (21 women), 74 part-time/adjunct (45 women). *Students:* 107 full-time (88 women), 826 part-time (622 women); includes 170 minority (115 Black or African American, non-Hispanic/Latino; 2 American Indian or Alaska Native, non-Hispanic/Latino; 11 Asian, non-Hispanic/Latino; 31 Hispanic/Latino; 1 Native Hawaiian or other Pacific Islander, non-Hispanic/Latino; 10 Two or more races, non-Hispanic/Latino), 18 international. Average age 33. 338 applicants, 76% accepted, 173 enrolled. In 2016, 419 master's, 16 doctorates, 24 other advanced degrees awarded. *Degree requirements:* For master's, thesis or alternative; for doctorate, comprehensive exam, thesis/dissertation. *Entrance requirements:* For master's, 2 letters of recommendation, minimum GPA of 3.0, official transcripts, personal statement; for doctorate, GRE, master's degree from accredited institution, minimum graduate GPA of 3.5, computer competence, interview with program director. Additional exam requirements/recommendations for international students: Required—TOEFL (minimum score 550 paper-based; 80 iBT), IELTS (minimum score 6.5), PTE (minimum score 60). *Application deadline:* For fall admission, 7/15 for international students; for spring admission, 11/1 for international students. Applications are processed on a rolling basis. Application fee: $35. Electronic applications accepted. *Expenses:* $750 per credit, $100 education fee, $360 online organization development and leadership residency fee. *Financial support:* In 2016–17, 25 students received support. Unspecified assistantships available. Financial award application deadline: 5/1; financial award applicants required to submit FAFSA. *Faculty research:* Factors predicting early mathematics skills for low income children, early child care and development, preschool quality, parent communication and home-school collaboration issues, education of terminally ill children, preparing literacy teachers for urban schools. *Total annual research expenditures:* $18,118. *Unit head:* Dr. John Vacca, Associate Dean, Education, 610-660-3131, E-mail: gradcas@sju.edu. *Application contact:* Graduate Admissions, College of Arts and Sciences, 610-660-3131, E-mail: gradcas@sju.edu.
Website: http://sju.edu/int/academics/cas/grad/education/index.html

Saint Mary's University of Minnesota, Schools of Graduate and Professional Programs, Graduate School of Education, Instruction Program, Winona, MN 55987-1399. Offers MA. Tuition and fees vary according to degree level and program. *Unit head:* Delores Roethke, Director, 612-238-4511, E-mail: droethke@smumn.edu. *Application contact:* James Callinan, Director of Admissions for Graduate and Professional Programs, 612-728-5185, Fax: 612-728-5121, E-mail: jcallina@smumn.edu.
Website: http://www.smumn.edu/graduate-home/areas-of-study/graduate-school-of-education/ma-in-instruction

Saint Peter's University, Graduate Programs in Education, Program in Teaching, Jersey City, NJ 07306-5997. Offers 6-8 middle school education (MA Ed, Certificate); K-12 secondary education (MA Ed, Certificate); K-5 elementary education (MA Ed, Certificate). *Program availability:* Part-time, evening/weekend. *Degree requirements:* For master's, comprehensive exam. *Entrance requirements:* For master's, GRE or MAT. Additional exam requirements/recommendations for international students: Required—TOEFL. Electronic applications accepted.

St. Thomas Aquinas College, Division of Teacher Education, Sparkill, NY 10976. Offers adolescence education (MST); childhood and special education (MST); childhood education (MST); educational leadership (MS Ed); reading (MS Ed, PMC); special education (MS Ed, PMC); teaching (MS Ed), including elementary education, middle school education, secondary education. *Accreditation:* NCATE. *Program availability:* Part-time, evening/weekend. *Degree requirements:* For master's, comprehensive exam, comprehensive professional portfolio; for PMC, action research project. *Entrance requirements:* For master's, New York State Qualifying Exam, GRE General Test or minimum GPA of 3.0, teaching certificate; for PMC, GRE General Test or minimum GPA of 3.0. Electronic applications accepted. *Faculty research:* Computer applications in education, adolescent special education students, literacy development, inclusive practices for special education students.

St. Thomas University, School of Leadership Studies, Institute for Education, Miami Gardens, FL 33054-6459. Offers earth/space science (Certificate); educational administration (MS, Certificate); educational leadership (Ed D); elementary education (MS); ESOL (Certificate); gifted education (Certificate); instructional technology (MS, Certificate); professional/studies (Certificate); reading (MS, Certificate); special education (MS). *Program availability:* Part-time, evening/weekend. *Degree requirements:* For master's, comprehensive exam; for doctorate, comprehensive exam, thesis/dissertation. *Entrance requirements:* For master's, interview, minimum GPA of 3.0 or GRE; for doctorate, GRE or MAT. Additional exam requirements/recommendations for international students: Required—TOEFL (minimum score 550 paper-based; 79 iBT). Electronic applications accepted.

Saint Xavier University, Graduate Studies, School of Education, Chicago, IL 60655-3105. Offers counseling (MA); curriculum and instruction (MA); early childhood education (MA); educational administration (MA); elementary education (MA); individualized studies (MA), including educational technology, English as a second language (ESL), ISTEM (integrative science, technology, engineering, and math), science education; music education (MA); reading (MA); secondary education (MA); Spanish education (MA); special education (MA); teaching and leadership (MA). *Accreditation:* NCATE. *Program availability:* Part-time, evening/weekend. *Degree requirements:* For master's, thesis or project. *Entrance requirements:* For master's, minimum GPA of 3.0. *Expenses:* Contact institution.

Salem College, Department of Education, Winston-Salem, NC 27101. Offers art education (MAT); elementary education (M Ed, MAT); language and literacy (M Ed); middle school education (MAT); school counseling (M Ed); second language studies (MAT); secondary education (MAT); special education (M Ed, MAT). *Accreditation:* NCATE. *Program availability:* Part-time, evening/weekend, online learning. *Degree requirements:* For master's, practicum (MAT), project (M Ed), oral and written comprehensive exams. *Entrance requirements:* For master's, minimum GPA of 2.5. *Faculty research:* Content area reading strategies, literacy development, brain compatible instruction.

Salem State University, School of Graduate Studies, Program in Elementary Education, Salem, MA 01970-5353. Offers M Ed. *Accreditation:* NCATE. *Program availability:* Part-time, evening/weekend. *Entrance requirements:* For master's, GRE or MAT. Additional exam requirements/recommendations for international students: Required—TOEFL (minimum score 550 paper-based; 80 iBT) or IELTS (minimum score 5.5).

Salem State University, School of Graduate Studies, Program in Spanish, Salem, MA 01970-5353. Offers MAT. *Program availability:* Part-time, evening/weekend. *Entrance requirements:* For master's, GRE or MAT. Additional exam requirements/recommendations for international students: Required—TOEFL (minimum score 550 paper-based; 80 iBT) or IELTS (minimum score 5.5).

Samford University, Orlean Beeson School of Education, Birmingham, AL 35229. Offers education (Ed D, Certificate); educational leadership: policy, organizations, leadership (MSE); elementary education (MS Ed); gifted certification (MSE); instructional design and technology (MSE); instructional leadership (MSE, Ed S); K-12 collaborative special education (MSE); teacher leader (Ed S). *Accreditation:* NCATE. *Program availability:* Part-time, evening/weekend, 100% online, blended/hybrid learning. *Faculty:* 15 full-time (9 women), 17 part-time/adjunct (12 women). *Students:* 219 full-time (161 women), 86 part-time (55 women); includes 97 minority (86 Black or African American, non-Hispanic/Latino; 5 American Indian or Alaska Native, non-Hispanic/Latino; 1 Asian, non-Hispanic/Latino; 1 Hispanic/Latino; 4 Two or more races, non-Hispanic/Latino), 2 international. Average age 38. 244 applicants, 52% accepted, 112 enrolled. In 2016, 84 master's, 22 doctorates, 12 Certificates awarded. *Degree requirements:* For master's, comprehensive exam (for some programs); for doctorate, comprehensive exam, thesis/dissertation; for other advanced degree, comprehensive

exam. *Entrance requirements:* For master's, GRE or MAT; Alabama Educator Certification Testing Program (AECTP), transcripts, essays, recommendations; for doctorate, professional resume, recommendations, transcripts, interview, essays; for other advanced degree, recommendations, transcripts. Additional exam requirements/recommendations for international students: Required—TOEFL (minimum score 90 iBT), IELTS (minimum score 6.5). *Application deadline:* For fall admission, 7/15 for domestic students, 7/1 for international students; for spring admission, 11/15 for domestic and international students; for summer admission, 4/15 for domestic and international students. Application fee: $35. Electronic applications accepted. *Expenses: Tuition:* Full-time $18,530; part-time $789 per credit hour. *Required fees:* $610. Tuition and fees vary according to course load, degree level, program and student level. *Financial support:* In 2016–17, 246 students received support. Scholarships/grants available. Financial award application deadline: 3/1; financial award applicants required to submit FAFSA. *Faculty research:* Standards-based grading in K-12 schools, effective school principal leadership, effective educational leadership preparation programs, teacher/administrator shortages and job retention, instructional strategies to maximize student learning. *Total annual research expenditures:* $254,360. *Unit head:* Dr. Jean Box, Dean, 205-726-2565, Fax: 205-726-4233, E-mail: jabox@samford.edu. *Application contact:* Brooke Karr, Graduate Admissions Coordinator, 205-729-2783, Fax: 205-726-4233, E-mail: kbgilrea@samford.edu.
Website: http://www.samford.edu/education/

San Diego State University, Graduate and Research Affairs, College of Education, School of Teacher Education, Program in Elementary Curriculum and Instruction, San Diego, CA 92182. Offers MA. *Accreditation:* NCATE. *Program availability:* Evening/weekend. *Entrance requirements:* For master's, GRE General Test, letters of reference. Additional exam requirements/recommendations for international students: Required—TOEFL. Electronic applications accepted.

San Francisco State University, Division of Graduate Studies, College of Education, Department of Elementary Education, Program in Elementary Education, San Francisco, CA 94132-1722. Offers MA. *Accreditation:* NCATE. *Expenses:* Tuition, state resident: full-time $6738. Tuition, nonresident: full-time $15,666. *Required fees:* $1012. Tuition and fees vary according to degree level and program. *Unit head:* Dr. Josephine Arce, Chair, 415-338-7636, Fax: 415-338-0567, E-mail: jarce@sfsu.edu. *Application contact:* Dr. Stephanie Sisk-Hilton, MA Program Coordinator, 415-338-1747, Fax: 415-338-0567, E-mail: stephsh@sfsu.edu.
Website: http://gcoe.sfsu.edu/

San Jose State University, Graduate Studies and Research, Connie L. Lurie College of Education, San Jose, CA 95192-0001. Offers child and adolescent development (MA); common core mathematics (K-8) (Certificate, Credential); education (MA, Credential), including counseling and student personnel (MA), speech pathology (MA); educational leadership (MA, Ed D, Credential), including administration and supervision (MA), higher education (MA), preliminary administrative services (Credential), professional administrative services (Credential); elementary education (MA), including curriculum and instruction; K-12 school counseling (Credential); K-12 school counseling internship (Credential); school child welfare attendance (Credential); single subject (Credential). *Accreditation:* NCATE. *Program availability:* Evening/weekend. Electronic applications accepted.

Seton Hill University, Program in Elementary Education/Middle Level Education, Greensburg, PA 15601. Offers MA, Certificate. *Program availability:* Part-time, evening/weekend, online learning. *Entrance requirements:* For master's, teacher's certification, 3 letters of recommendation, personal statement, transcripts, resume. Additional exam requirements/recommendations for international students: Required—TOEFL (minimum score 600 paper-based; 100 iBT), IELTS (minimum score 6.5). Electronic applications accepted.

Shippensburg University of Pennsylvania, School of Graduate Studies, College of Education and Human Services, Department of Teacher Education, Shippensburg, PA 17257-2299. Offers curriculum and instruction (M Ed), including biology, early childhood education, elementary and middle level education, elementary education, geography/earth science, history, mathematics, middle school education, modern languages; literacy studies (Certificate); online instruction, learning, and technology (Certificate); reading (M Ed); teaching English as a second language (Certificate). *Accreditation:* NCATE. *Program availability:* Part-time, evening/weekend, 100% online, blended/hybrid learning. *Faculty:* 14 full-time (9 women), 5 part-time/adjunct (all women). *Students:* 11 full-time (10 women), 88 part-time (81 women); includes 8 minority (3 Black or African American, non-Hispanic/Latino; 2 Asian, non-Hispanic/Latino; 3 Hispanic/Latino), 4 international. Average age 32. 57 applicants, 60% accepted, 28 enrolled. In 2016, 18 master's awarded. *Degree requirements:* For master's, comprehensive exam (for some programs), thesis optional, practicum or internship; capstone seminar (for some programs). *Entrance requirements:* For master's, MAT or GRE (if GPA less than 2.75), interview, 3 letters of reference, questionnaire of teaching background and future goals, resume. Additional exam requirements/recommendations for international students: Required—TOEFL (minimum score 550 paper-based, 68 iBT) or IELTS (minimum score 6). *Application deadline:* For fall admission, 4/1 priority date for domestic students, 4/30 for international students; for spring admission, 9/1 priority date for domestic students, 9/30 for international students; for summer admission, 2/1 priority date for domestic students. Applications are processed on a rolling basis. Application fee: $45. Electronic applications accepted. *Expenses:* Tuition, state resident: part-time $483 per credit. Tuition, nonresident: part-time $725 per credit. *Required fees:* $141 per credit. *Financial support:* In 2016–17, 3 students received support. Career-related internships or fieldwork, scholarships/grants, unspecified assistantships, and resident hall director and student payroll positions available. Support available to part-time students. Financial award application deadline: 3/1; financial award applicants required to submit FAFSA. *Unit head:* Dr. Christine A. Royce, Chairperson, 717-477-1688, Fax: 717-477-4046, E-mail: caroyc@ship.edu. *Application contact:* Megan N. Luft, Assistant Dean of Graduate Admissions, 717-477-1231, Fax: 717-477-4016, E-mail: mnluft@ship.edu.
Website: http://www.ship.edu/teacher/

Siena Heights University, Graduate College, Adrian, MI 49221-1796. Offers clinical mental health counseling (MA); educational leadership (Specialist); leadership (MA), including health care leadership, organizational leadership; teacher education (MA), including early childhood education, early childhood education: Montessori, education leadership: principal, elementary education: reading K-12, leadership: higher education, secondary education: reading K-12, special education: cognitive impairment, special education: learning disabilities. *Program availability:* Part-time, evening/weekend. *Degree requirements:* For master's, thesis, presentation. *Entrance requirements:* For master's, minimum GPA of 3.0, current resume, essay, all post-secondary transcripts, 3 letters of reference, conviction disclosure form; copy of teaching certificate (for some education programs); for Specialist, master's degree, minimum GPA of 3.0, current resume, essay, all post-secondary transcripts, 3 letters of reference, conviction disclosure form; copy of teaching certificate (for some education programs). Electronic applications accepted.

Sierra Nevada College, Teacher Education Program, Incline Village, NV 89451. Offers advanced teaching and leadership (M Ed); elementary education (MAT); secondary education (MAT). *Program availability:* Part-time, evening/weekend, online learning. *Degree requirements:* For master's, comprehensive exam, thesis, PRAXIS I and II. *Entrance requirements:* For master's, 2 letters of recommendation, minimum GPA of 3.0. Electronic applications accepted.

Simmons College, College of Arts and Sciences, Boston, MA 02115. Offers elementary education (MAT); English (MA); gender/cultural studies (MA); history (MA); public health (MPH); public policy (MPP). *Program availability:* Part-time. *Faculty:* 19 full-time (12 women), 1 (woman) part-time/adjunct. *Students:* 6 full-time (all women), 38 part-time (27 women); includes 10 minority (4 Black or African American, non-Hispanic/Latino; 1 Asian, non-Hispanic/Latino; 2 Hispanic/Latino; 3 Two or more races, non-Hispanic/Latino), 1 international. Average age 26. 50 applicants, 88% accepted, 17 enrolled. In 2016, 19 master's awarded. Terminal master's awarded for partial completion of doctoral program. *Degree requirements:* For master's, thesis (for some programs). *Entrance requirements:* For master's, GRE. Additional exam requirements/recommendations for international students: Required—TOEFL (minimum score 600 paper-based; 100 iBT). *Application deadline:* For fall admission, 8/1 for domestic and international students; for spring admission, 12/15 for domestic and international students; for summer admission, 5/1 for domestic and international students. Applications are processed on a rolling basis. Application fee: $35. Electronic applications accepted. *Expenses:* $1,050 per credit, $4,200 per course, $52 activity fee per semester. *Financial support:* In 2016–17, 4 fellowships with partial tuition reimbursements, 22 teaching assistantships with partial tuition reimbursements were awarded; scholarships/grants and unspecified assistantships also available. Support available to part-time students. Financial award applicants required to submit FAFSA. *Unit head:* Dr. Renee White, Dean, 617-521-2079. *Application contact:* Patricia Flaherty, Director, Graduate Studies Admission, 617-521-3902, Fax: 617-521-3058, E-mail: gsa@simmons.edu.
Website: http://www.simmons.edu/gradstudies/

Simmons College, School of Social Work, Boston, MA 02115. Offers behavior analysis (MS, PhD, Ed S); education (MS Ed); social work (MSW, PhD); special education (MS Ed), including moderate and severe disabilities; teaching (MAT), including elementary education; MSW/MBA. *Accreditation:* CSWE (one or more programs are accredited). *Program availability:* Part-time, 100% online. *Faculty:* 37 full-time (28 women), 62 part-time/adjunct (44 women). *Students:* 797 full-time (705 women), 951 part-time (829 women); includes 420 minority (200 Black or African American, non-Hispanic/Latino; 5 American Indian or Alaska Native, non-Hispanic/Latino; 46 Asian, non-Hispanic/Latino; 122 Hispanic/Latino; 4 Native Hawaiian or other Pacific Islander, non-Hispanic/Latino; 43 Two or more races, non-Hispanic/Latino), 13 international. Average age 31. 1,356 applicants, 78% accepted, 592 enrolled. In 2016, 342 master's, 2 doctorates, 1 other advanced degree awarded. Terminal master's awarded for partial completion of doctoral program. *Degree requirements:* For master's, thesis (for some programs); for doctorate, comprehensive exam (for some programs), thesis/dissertation (for some programs). *Entrance requirements:* For master's, GRE, MAT, Massachusetts Tests for Education Licensure (for different programs); for doctorate, GRE, BCBA Analyst Exam. Additional exam requirements/recommendations for international students: Required—TOEFL (minimum score 600 paper-based; 100 iBT). *Application deadline:* For fall admission, 8/1 for domestic students; for spring admission, 12/15 for domestic students; for summer admission, 5/1 for domestic students. Applications are processed on a rolling basis. Application fee: $35. Electronic applications accepted. *Expenses:* $1,010 per credit; $52 activity fee per semester. *Financial support:* In 2016–17, 12 fellowships with partial tuition reimbursements were awarded; scholarships/grants and unspecified assistantships also available. Support available to part-time students. *Unit head:* Dr. Cheryl Parks, Dean, 617-521-3293, E-mail: cheryl.parks@simmons.edu. *Application contact:* Carlos D. Frontado, Director of Admissions, 617-521-3920, Fax: 617-521-3980, E-mail: ssw@simmons.edu.
Website: http://www.simmons.edu/ssw/

Sinte Gleska University, Graduate Education Program, Mission, SD 57555. Offers elementary education (M Ed). *Program availability:* Part-time, evening/weekend. *Degree requirements:* For master's, thesis. *Entrance requirements:* For master's, 2 years of experience in elementary education, minimum GPA of 2.5, South Dakota elementary education certification. *Faculty research:* American Indian graduate education, teaching of Native American students.

Slippery Rock University of Pennsylvania, Graduate Studies (Recruitment), College of Education, Department of Elementary Education and Early Childhood, Slippery Rock, PA 16057-1383. Offers instructional coach (M Ed); K-12 reading (M Ed); K-12 science and math (M Ed); reading specialist (M Ed). *Accreditation:* NCATE. *Program availability:* Part-time, evening/weekend, online only, 100% online. *Faculty:* 9 full-time (8 women). *Students:* 6 full-time (all women), 128 part-time (124 women); includes 1 minority (Two or more races, non-Hispanic/Latino). Average age 28. 100 applicants, 77% accepted, 54 enrolled. In 2016, 49 master's awarded. *Degree requirements:* For master's, comprehensive exam (for some programs), thesis optional. *Entrance requirements:* For master's, minimum GPA of 3.0, resume, teaching certification, transcripts, letters of recommendation (depending on program). Additional exam requirements/recommendations for international students: Required—TOEFL (minimum score 550 paper-based; 80 iBT). *Application deadline:* For fall admission, 3/1 priority date for domestic students, 5/1 priority date for international students; for spring admission, 10/1 priority date for domestic students, 9/1 priority date for international students. Applications are processed on a rolling basis. Application fee: $25 ($30 for international students). Electronic applications accepted. *Expenses:* $646.50 per credit in-state, $936.80 per credit out-of-state; $581.45 per online credit in-state, $648.65 per online credit out-of-state. *Financial support:* Career-related internships or fieldwork, Federal Work-Study, institutionally sponsored loans, scholarships/grants, tuition waivers (partial), and unspecified assistantships available. Support available to part-time students. Financial award application deadline: 5/1; financial award applicants required to submit FAFSA. *Unit head:* Dr. Suzanne Rose, Graduate Coordinator, 724-738-2042, Fax: 724-738-2779, E-mail: suzanne.rose@sru.edu. *Application contact:* Brandi Weber-Mortimer, Director of Graduate Admissions, 724-738-2051, Fax: 724-738-2146, E-mail: graduate.admissions@sru.edu.
Website: http://www.sru.edu/academics/colleges-and-departments/coe/departments/elementary-education-/-early-childhood/graduate-programs

Smith College, Graduate and Special Programs, Department of Education and Child Study, Program in Elementary Education, Northampton, MA 01063. Offers MAT. *Program availability:* Part-time. *Students:* 11 full-time (8 women); includes 1 minority (Two or more races, non-Hispanic/Latino). Average age 25. 22 applicants, 77% accepted, 10 enrolled. In 2016, 10 master's awarded. *Entrance requirements:* Additional exam requirements/recommendations for international students: Required—TOEFL (minimum score 595 paper-based; 97 iBT), IELTS. *Application deadline:* For fall admission, 4/1 for domestic students, 1/15 priority date for international students; for spring admission, 12/1 for domestic students. Application fee: $60. *Expenses: Tuition:* Full-time $34,560; part-time $1440 per credit. Tuition and fees vary according to course load and program. *Financial support:* In 2016–17, 11 students received support, including 5 fellowships with full tuition reimbursements available; scholarships/grants also available. Support available to part-time students. Financial award application deadline: 4/1; financial award applicants required to submit FAFSA. *Unit head:* Alan

Elementary Education

Rudnitsky, Graduate Student Adviser, 413-585-3261, E-mail: arudnits@smith.edu. *Application contact:* Ruth Morgan, Program Assistant, 413-585-3050, Fax: 413-585-3054, E-mail: gradstdy@smith.edu.
Website: http://www.smith.edu/educ/

South Carolina State University, College of Graduate and Professional Studies, Department of Education, Orangeburg, SC 29117-0001. Offers early childhood education (MAT); education (M Ed); elementary education (M Ed, MAT); English (MAT); general science/biology (MAT); mathematics (MAT); secondary education (M Ed), including biology education, business education, counselor education, English education, home economics education, industrial education, mathematics education, science education, social studies education; special education (M Ed), including emotionally handicapped, learning disabilities, mentally handicapped. *Accreditation:* NCATE. *Program availability:* Part-time, evening/weekend. *Faculty:* 12 full-time (8 women), 3 part-time/adjunct (1 woman). *Students:* 28 full-time (20 women), 20 part-time (17 women); includes 45 minority (44 Black or African American, non-Hispanic/Latino; 1 Two or more races, non-Hispanic/Latino). Average age 31. 22 applicants, 100% accepted, 16 enrolled. In 2016, 9 master's awarded. *Degree requirements:* For master's, thesis optional, departmental qualifying exam. *Entrance requirements:* For master's, GRE General Test, NTE, interview, teaching certificate. *Application deadline:* For fall admission, 6/15 priority date for domestic students, 6/15 for international students; for spring admission, 11/1 for domestic and international students. Application fee: $25. Electronic applications accepted. *Expenses:* Tuition, state resident: full-time $8938; part-time $579 per credit hour. Tuition, nonresident: full-time $19,018; part-time $1139 per credit hour. *Required fees:* $1482; $82 per credit hour. *Financial support:* Fellowships, career-related internships or fieldwork, Federal Work-Study, and scholarships/grants available. Financial award application deadline: 6/1. *Unit head:* Dr. Charlie Spell, Interim Chair, Department of Education, 803-536-8963, Fax: 803-516-4568, E-mail: cspell@scsu.edu. *Application contact:* Curtis Foskey, Coordinator of Graduate Studies, 803-536-8419, Fax: 803-536-8812, E-mail: cfoskey@scsu.edu.

Southeastern Louisiana University, College of Education, Department of Teaching and Learning, Hammond, LA 70402. Offers curriculum and instruction (M Ed); elementary education (MAT); special education (M Ed); special education: early interventionist (MAT). *Accreditation:* NCATE. *Program availability:* Part-time, evening/weekend. *Faculty:* 14 full-time (all women), 2 part-time/adjunct (1 woman). *Students:* 8 full-time (all women), 48 part-time (46 women); includes 7 minority (6 Black or African American, non-Hispanic/Latino; 1 Hispanic/Latino). Average age 32. 79 applicants, 49% accepted, 21 enrolled. In 2016, 34 master's awarded. *Degree requirements:* For master's, comprehensive exam (for some programs), thesis (for some programs), action research project, oral defense of research project, portfolio, teaching certificate, minimum cumulative GPA of 3.0. *Entrance requirements:* For master's, GRE (verbal and quantitative), PRAXIS (for MAT). Additional exam requirements/recommendations for international students: Required—TOEFL (minimum score 500 paper-based; 61 iBT). *Application deadline:* For fall admission, 7/15 priority date for domestic students, 6/1 priority date for international students; for spring admission, 12/1 priority date for domestic students, 10/1 priority date for international students. Applications are processed on a rolling basis. Application fee: $20 ($30 for international students). Electronic applications accepted. *Expenses:* Tuition, state resident: full-time $6540; part-time $465 per credit hour. Tuition, nonresident: full-time $19,017; part-time $1158 per credit hour. *Required fees:* $1829. *Financial support:* In 2016–17, 13 students received support. Research assistantships, career-related internships or fieldwork, Federal Work-Study, institutionally sponsored loans, scholarships/grants, and unspecified assistantships available. Support available to part-time students. Financial award application deadline: 5/1; financial award applicants required to submit FAFSA. *Faculty research:* Teacher in services, STEM, educational technology, pre-service teacher education. *Unit head:* Dr. Colleen Klein-Ezell, Department Head, 985-549-2221, Fax: 985-549-5009, E-mail: colleen.klein-ezell@southeastern.edu. *Application contact:* Amanda Harper, Graduate Admissions Analyst, 985-549-5620, Fax: 985-549-5632, E-mail: admissions@southeastern.edu.
Website: http://www.southeastern.edu/acad_research/depts/teach_lrn/index.html

Southeastern University, College of Education, Lakeland, FL 33801-6099. Offers curriculum and instruction (Ed D); educational leadership (M Ed); elementary education (M Ed); exceptional student education (M Ed); exceptional student education/educational therapy (M Ed); organizational leadership (Ed D); reading education (M Ed); teaching English to speakers of other languages (M Ed). *Expenses: Tuition:* Full-time $9450; part-time $6300 per credit. *Required fees:* $500; $250 per semester. One-time fee: $150. Tuition and fees vary according to degree level, campus/location and program. *Unit head:* Amy N. Bratten, Dean, 863-667-5238, E-mail: anbratten@seu.edu.
Website: http://www.seu.edu/education/

Southeast Missouri State University, School of Graduate Studies, Department of Educational Leadership and Counseling, Cape Girardeau, MO 63701-4799. Offers counseling (MA, Ed S), including career counseling (MA), counseling education (Ed S), mental health counseling (MA), school counseling (MA); educational administration (MA, Ed D, Ed S), including educational administration (Ed S), educational leadership (Ed D), elementary administration (MA), higher education administration (MA), secondary administration (MA), teacher leadership (MA, Ed S). *Accreditation:* NCATE. *Program availability:* Part-time, evening/weekend, online only, 100% online, blended/hybrid learning. *Faculty:* 11 full-time (7 women), 6 part-time/adjunct (3 women). *Students:* 81 full-time (55 women), 205 part-time (143 women); includes 29 minority (23 Black or African American, non-Hispanic/Latino; 2 American Indian or Alaska Native, non-Hispanic/Latino; 2 Asian, non-Hispanic/Latino; 2 Hispanic/Latino), 15 international. Average age 33. 110 applicants, 100% accepted, 110 enrolled. In 2016, 71 master's, 43 other advanced degrees awarded. *Degree requirements:* For master's and Ed S, comprehensive exam, thesis or alternative, paper; for doctorate, comprehensive exam, thesis/dissertation. *Entrance requirements:* For master's, minimum GPA of 3.5; for doctorate, minimum GPA of 3.7. Additional exam requirements/recommendations for international students: Required—TOEFL (minimum score 550 paper-based; 79 iBT), IELTS (minimum score 6), PTE (minimum score 53). *Application deadline:* For fall admission, 8/1 for domestic students, 6/1 for international students; for spring admission, 11/21 for domestic students, 10/1 for international students; for summer admission, 5/15 for domestic students. Applications are processed on a rolling basis. Application fee: $30 ($40 for international students). Electronic applications accepted. *Expenses:* Tuition, state resident: full-time $3130; part-time $260.80 per credit hour. Tuition, nonresident: full-time $5842; part-time $486.80 per credit hour. *Required fees:* $33.70 per credit hour. *Financial support:* In 2016–17, 41 students received support. Career-related internships or fieldwork, Federal Work-Study, scholarships/grants, traineeships, tuition waivers (full), and unspecified assistantships available. Financial award application deadline: 6/30; financial award applicants required to submit FAFSA. *Faculty research:* Mental health counseling, technology in the classroom, administration and student success, school counseling, social justice in leadership and higher education, career counseling, leadership, equity, and social justice in p-12 schools and higher education. gender Identity and queer youth, building level and district level leadership, school culture and climate. *Unit head:* Dr. C. P. Gause, Professor/Department Chair, 573-651-2137, Fax: 573-986-6512, E-mail: cgause@semo.edu.
Website: http://www.semo.edu/eduleadcounsel/

Southeast Missouri State University, School of Graduate Studies, Department of Elementary, Early and Special Education, Program in Elementary Education, Cape Girardeau, MO 63701-4799. Offers MA. *Accreditation:* NCATE. *Program availability:* Part-time, evening/weekend, online only, 100% online. *Faculty:* 12 full-time (10 women), 4 part-time/adjunct (3 women). *Students:* 1 (woman) full-time, 44 part-time (41 women); includes 2 minority (1 Black or African American, non-Hispanic/Latino; 1 Hispanic/Latino). Average age 32. 18 applicants, 100% accepted, 18 enrolled. In 2016, 16 master's awarded. *Degree requirements:* For master's, comprehensive exam, action research project and presentation. *Entrance requirements:* For master's, state licensure exam or GRE, minimum GPA of 2.75; teaching certificate. Additional exam requirements/recommendations for international students: Required—TOEFL (minimum score 95 iBT), IELTS (minimum score 7), PTE. *Application deadline:* For fall admission, 8/1 for domestic students, 6/1 for international students; for spring admission, 11/21 for domestic students, 10/1 for international students; for summer admission, 5/15 for domestic students. Applications are processed on a rolling basis. Application fee: $30 ($40 for international students). Electronic applications accepted. *Expenses:* Tuition, state resident: full-time $3130; part-time $260.80 per credit hour. Tuition, nonresident: full-time $5842; part-time $486.80 per credit hour. *Required fees:* $33.70 per credit hour. *Financial support:* In 2016–17, 3 students received support. Career-related internships or fieldwork, Federal Work-Study, scholarships/grants, traineeships, tuition waivers (full), and unspecified assistantships available. Financial award application deadline: 6/30; financial award applicants required to submit FAFSA. *Faculty research:* Instructional technology, field and clinical experiences, student professional dispositions, family engagement in P-12 schools, applied behavior analysis. *Unit head:* Dr. Julie Ray, Department of Elementary, Early, and Special Education Chair/Professor, 573-651-2444, E-mail: jaray@semo.edu. *Application contact:* Dr. Min Zou, Assistant Professor, 573-651-2122, E-mail: mzou@semo.edu.
Website: http://www.semo.edu/eese/

Southern Connecticut State University, School of Graduate Studies, School of Education, Department of Elementary Education, New Haven, CT 06515-1355. Offers classroom teacher specialist (Diploma); educational coach (Diploma); elementary education (MS). *Accreditation:* NCATE. *Program availability:* Part-time, evening/weekend. *Faculty:* 6 full-time (3 women), 3 part-time/adjunct (2 women). *Students:* 41 full-time (31 women), 45 part-time (36 women); includes 15 minority (5 Black or African American, non-Hispanic/Latino; 3 Asian, non-Hispanic/Latino; 7 Hispanic/Latino), 3 international. Average age 31. 72 applicants, 39% accepted, 25 enrolled. In 2016, 53 master's, 6 other advanced degrees awarded. *Degree requirements:* For master's, thesis or alternative. *Entrance requirements:* For master's, interview, minimum QPA of 2.5; for Diploma, master's degree. *Application deadline:* For fall admission, 7/15 priority date for domestic students. Applications are processed on a rolling basis. Application fee: $50. Electronic applications accepted. *Expenses:* Tuition, state resident: full-time $6497; part-time $519 per credit hour. Tuition, nonresident: full-time $18,102; part-time $535 per credit hour. *Required fees:* $4722; $55 per semester. Tuition and fees vary according to program. *Financial support:* Career-related internships or fieldwork, scholarships/grants, and unspecified assistantships available. Financial award application deadline: 4/15; financial award applicants required to submit FAFSA. *Unit head:* Dr. Steven Greengross, Chairperson, 203-392-6430, Fax: 203-392-6473, E-mail: greengrosss1@southernct.edu. *Application contact:* Lisa Galvin, Director of Graduate Admissions, 203-392-5240, Fax: 203-392-5235, E-mail: galvinl1@southernct.edu.
Website: http://www.southernct.edu/academics/schools/education/departments/elementaryeducation/

Southern New Hampshire University, School of Education, Manchester, NH 03106-1045. Offers business education (M Ed); child development (M Ed); curriculum and instruction (M Ed), including education leadership, reading, special education, technology integration; education (M Ed); educational leadership (M Ed, Ed D); educational studies (M Ed); elementary education (M Ed); English (MAT); English for speakers of other languages (M Ed); reading and writing specialist (M Ed); school business administration (Certificate); secondary education (M Ed); special education (M Ed); technology integration specialist (M Ed). *Program availability:* Part-time, evening/weekend, online learning. *Degree requirements:* For master's, comprehensive exam (for some programs), thesis or alternative. *Entrance requirements:* For master's, PRAXIS I, minimum GPA of 2.75. Additional exam requirements/recommendations for international students: Required—TOEFL (minimum score 550 paper-based). Electronic applications accepted. *Expenses:* Contact institution.

Southern Oregon University, Graduate Studies, School of Education, Ashland, OR 97520. Offers elementary education (MA Ed, MS Ed), including classroom teacher, early childhood, handicapped learner, reading, supervision; secondary education (MA Ed, MS Ed), including classroom teacher, handicapped learner, reading, supervision; teaching (MAT). *Program availability:* Online learning. *Faculty:* 15 full-time (10 women), 27 part-time/adjunct (21 women). *Students:* 116 full-time (82 women), 86 part-time (68 women); includes 22 minority (1 American Indian or Alaska Native, non-Hispanic/Latino; 4 Asian, non-Hispanic/Latino; 8 Hispanic/Latino; 9 Two or more races, non-Hispanic/Latino). Average age 34. 81 applicants, 80% accepted, 49 enrolled. In 2016, 107 master's awarded. *Degree requirements:* For master's, thesis optional. *Entrance requirements:* For master's, GRE General Test, minimum cumulative GPA of 3.0 in the last 90 quarter credits (60 semester credits) of undergraduate coursework. Additional exam requirements/recommendations for international students: Required—TOEFL (minimum score 540 paper-based; 76 iBT), IELTS (minimum score 6), ELPT (minimum score 964) or ELS (minimum score 112). *Application deadline:* For fall admission, 7/31 priority date for domestic and international students; for winter admission, 11/15 priority date for domestic and international students; for spring admission, 1/7 priority date for domestic and international students. Applications are processed on a rolling basis. Application fee: $60. Electronic applications accepted. *Expenses:* Tuition, state resident: full-time $10,719; part-time $397 per credit. Tuition, nonresident: full-time $13,419; part-time $497 per credit. *Required fees:* $548. *Financial support:* In 2016–17, 2 students received support. Career-related internships or fieldwork, institutionally sponsored loans, scholarships/grants, and unspecified assistantships available. *Unit head:* Dr. Gerry McCain, Graduate Program Coordinator, 541-552-6934, E-mail: mccaing@sou.edu. *Application contact:* Kelly Moutsatson, Director of Admissions, 541-552-6411, Fax: 541-552-8403, E-mail: admissions@sou.edu.
Website: http://www.sou.edu/education/

Southern University and Agricultural and Mechanical College, Graduate School, College of Education, Department of Curriculum and Instruction, Baton Rouge, LA 70813. Offers elementary education (M Ed); media (M Ed); secondary education (M Ed). *Degree requirements:* For master's, comprehensive exam, thesis optional. *Entrance requirements:* For master's, GMAT or GRE General Test. Additional exam requirements/recommendations for international students: Required—TOEFL (minimum score 525 paper-based).

Southwestern Oklahoma State University, College of Professional and Graduate Studies, School of Behavioral Sciences and Education, Specialization in Elementary Education, Weatherford, OK 73096-3098. Offers M Ed. M Ed distance learning degree program offered to Oklahoma residents only. *Accreditation:* NCATE. *Program availability:* Part-time, evening/weekend. *Degree requirements:* For master's, exam.

Entrance requirements: For master's, GRE General Test or minimum undergraduate GPA of 3.0. Additional exam requirements/recommendations for international students: Required—TOEFL.

Spalding University, Graduate Studies, College of Education, Programs in Education, Louisville, KY 40203-2188. Offers art teacher education (MAT); business teacher education (MAT); elementary school education (MAT); foreign language (MAT); high school education (MAT); middle school education (MAT); secondary education (MAT); special education (learning and behavioral disorders) (MAT); student guidance counselor (MA); teacher leader (M Ed). *Accreditation:* NCATE. *Program availability:* Part-time, evening/weekend. *Faculty:* 39 full-time (26 women), 13 part-time/adjunct (4 women). *Students:* 97 full-time (76 women), 31 part-time (23 women); includes 39 minority (33 Black or African American, non-Hispanic/Latino; 1 Asian, non-Hispanic/Latino; 3 Hispanic/Latino; 2 Two or more races, non-Hispanic/Latino). Average age 35. 62 applicants, 55% accepted, 33 enrolled. In 2016, 49 master's awarded. *Entrance requirements:* For master's, GRE General Test or MAT, interview, letters of recommendation, resume. Additional exam requirements/recommendations for international students: Required—TOEFL (minimum score 535 paper-based). *Application deadline:* Applications are processed on a rolling basis. Application fee: $30. Electronic applications accepted. *Expenses: Tuition:* Full-time $15,300. *Financial support:* Scholarships/grants, traineeships, and unspecified assistantships available. Financial award applicants required to submit FAFSA. *Faculty research:* Instructional technology, achievement gap, classroom management, assessment. *Unit head:* Dr. Chris Walsh, Associate Dean, 502-873-4272, Fax: 502-585-7123, E-mail: cwalsh@spalding.edu. *Application contact:* Valerie Anderson, Administrative Assistant, 502-873-4260, E-mail: vanderson@spalding.edu.

Spring Hill College, Graduate Programs, Program in Education, Mobile, AL 36608-1791. Offers early childhood education (MAT, MS Ed); educational theory (MS Ed); elementary education (MAT, MS Ed); secondary education (MAT, MS Ed). *Program availability:* Part-time. *Faculty:* 3 full-time (all women). *Students:* 3 full-time (all women), 7 part-time (5 women); includes 1 minority (Black or African American, non-Hispanic/Latino). Average age 26. In 2016, 10 master's awarded. *Degree requirements:* For master's, comprehensive exam, completion of program within 6 calendar years of entrance into graduate studies at Spring Hill; documentation of course field assignments (MS) or completion of internship (MAT). *Entrance requirements:* For master's, GRE, MAT, or PRAXIS (varies by program), bachelor's degree with minimum undergraduate GPA of 3.0; class B certificate (for MS); minimum number of hours in specific fields (for MAT). Additional exam requirements/recommendations for international students: Required—TOEFL (minimum score 550 paper-based; 80 iBT), IELTS (minimum score 6.5), CPE or CAE (minimum score C), Michigan English Language Assessment Battery (minimum score 90). *Application deadline:* For fall admission, 8/1 priority date for domestic and international students; for spring admission, 12/1 priority date for domestic and international students. Applications are processed on a rolling basis. Application fee: $25 ($35 for international students). Electronic applications accepted. *Expenses:* Contact institution. *Financial support:* Applicants required to submit FAFSA. *Unit head:* Dr. Lori P. Aultman, Chair of Education, 251-380-3473, Fax: 251-460-2184, E-mail: laultman@shc.edu. *Application contact:* Robert Stewart, Vice President of Enrollment, 251-380-3030, Fax: 251-460-2186, E-mail: rstewart@shc.edu.
Website: http://ug.shc.edu/graduate-degrees/master-science-education/

Stanford University, Graduate School of Education, Teacher Education Program, Stanford, CA 94305-2004. Offers elementary education (MAE); secondary education (MAE). *Degree requirements:* For master's, thesis. *Entrance requirements:* For master's, GRE General Test. Electronic applications accepted. *Expenses: Tuition:* Full-time $47,331. *Required fees:* $609.

State University of New York at New Paltz, Graduate School, School of Education, Department of Elementary Education, New Paltz, NY 12561. Offers childhood education 1-6 (MS Ed, MST), including childhood education 1-6 (MST), early childhood B-2 (MS Ed), mathematics, science and technology (MS Ed), reading/literacy (MS Ed); literacy education 5-12 (MS Ed); literacy education and childhood special education (MS Ed); literacy education B-6 (MS Ed). *Accreditation:* NCATE. *Program availability:* Part-time, evening/weekend. *Students:* 32 full-time (29 women), 100 part-time (91 women); includes 22 minority (5 Black or African American, non-Hispanic/Latino; 1 American Indian or Alaska Native, non-Hispanic/Latino; 2 Asian, non-Hispanic/Latino; 10 Hispanic/Latino; 4 Two or more races, non-Hispanic/Latino). 30 applicants, 73% accepted, 14 enrolled. In 2016, 70 master's awarded. *Degree requirements:* For master's, comprehensive exam (for some programs), portfolio. *Entrance requirements:* For master's, GRE or MAT (for MST), minimum GPA of 3.0 (3.2 for literacy and special education), New York state teaching certificate (for MS Ed). Additional exam requirements/recommendations for international students: Required—TOEFL (minimum score 550 paper-based; 80 iBT), IELTS (minimum score 6.5). *Application deadline:* For fall admission, 4/1 for domestic and international students; for spring admission, 11/1 priority date for domestic and international students; for summer admission, 4/15 priority date for domestic and international students. Applications are processed on a rolling basis. Application fee: $50. Electronic applications accepted. *Financial support:* Application deadline: 8/1. *Faculty research:* Multi-sensory teaching methods, volunteer tutoring programs for struggling readers, school readiness and transition, math/science/technology, university-school partnerships. *Unit head:* Dr. Aaron Isabelle, Chair, 845-257-2837, E-mail: isabella@newpaltz.edu. *Application contact:* Vika Shock, Assistant Director of Graduate Admissions, 845-257-3285, Fax: 845-257-3284, E-mail: gradschool@newpaltz.edu.
Website: http://www.newpaltz.edu/elementaryed/

State University of New York at Oswego, Graduate Studies, School of Education, Department of Curriculum and Instruction, Oswego, NY 13126. Offers adolescence education (MST); art education (MAT); childhood education (MST); curriculum and instruction (MS Ed); literacy education (MS Ed); special education (MS Ed). *Program availability:* Part-time, evening/weekend. *Degree requirements:* For master's, comprehensive exam (for some programs), thesis optional. *Entrance requirements:* For master's, GRE General Test, minimum GPA of 2.7, provisional teaching certificate. Additional exam requirements/recommendations for international students: Required—TOEFL (minimum score 560 paper-based). *Faculty research:* Classroom applications for microcomputers; classroom questioning, wait-time, and achievement; values clarification and academic achievement.

State University of New York at Plattsburgh, School of Education, Health, and Human Services, Program in Early Childhood Education, Plattsburgh, NY 12901-2681. Offers early childhood birth-grade 6 (Advanced Certificate).

State University of New York at Plattsburgh, School of Education, Health, and Human Services, Program in Teacher Education: Adolescence Education, Plattsburgh, NY 12901-2681. Offers adolescence education (MST); biology 7-12 (MST); chemistry 7-12 (MST); earth science 7-12 (MST); English 7-12 (MST); French 7-12 (MST); mathematics 7-12 (MST); physics 7-12 (MST); social studies 7-12 (MST); Spanish 7-12 (MST). *Accreditation:* TEAC. *Program availability:* Part-time, evening/weekend. *Entrance requirements:* For master's, minimum GPA of 2.75. Additional exam requirements/recommendations for international students: Required—TOEFL.

State University of New York at Plattsburgh, School of Education, Health, and Human Services, Program in Teacher Education: Childhood Education, Plattsburgh, NY 12901-2681. Offers childhood education (grades 1-6) (MST). *Accreditation:* TEAC. *Program availability:* Part-time, evening/weekend. *Entrance requirements:* For master's, minimum GPA of 2.75. Additional exam requirements/recommendations for international students: Required—TOEFL.

State University of New York College at Oneonta, Graduate Programs, Division of Education, Department of Elementary Education and Reading, Oneonta, NY 13820-4015. Offers childhood education (MS Ed); literacy education (MS Ed). *Accreditation:* NCATE. *Program availability:* Part-time, evening/weekend. *Entrance requirements:* For master's, GRE General Test. *Application deadline:* For fall admission, 3/25 priority date for domestic students; for spring admission, 10/1 priority date for domestic students. Applications are processed on a rolling basis. Application fee: $50. *Unit head:* Dr. Cindy Lassonde, Chair, 607-436-3176, Fax: 607-436-2554, E-mail: lassonc@oneonta.edu. *Application contact:* Patrick J. Mente, Director of Graduate Studies, 607-436-2523, Fax: 607-436-3084, E-mail: gradstudies@oneonta.edu.
Website: http://www.oneonta.edu/academics/ed/eled/

State University of New York College at Potsdam, School of Education and Professional Studies, Program in Curriculum and Instruction, Potsdam, NY 13676. Offers childhood education (MST); curriculum and instruction (MS Ed). *Accreditation:* NCATE. *Program availability:* Online learning. *Degree requirements:* For master's, thesis (for some programs). *Entrance requirements:* For master's, minimum GPA of 2.75 in last 60 credit hours of undergraduate study. Additional exam requirements/recommendations for international students: Required—TOEFL (minimum score 550 paper-based; 80 iBT), IELTS (minimum score 6). Electronic applications accepted.

State University of New York College at Potsdam, School of Education and Professional Studies, Program in Special Education, Potsdam, NY 13676. Offers adolescence (grades 7-12) (MS Ed); childhood (grades 1-6) (MS Ed); early childhood (birth-grade 2) (MS Ed). *Accreditation:* NCATE. *Program availability:* Part-time. *Degree requirements:* For master's, culminating experience. *Entrance requirements:* For master's, minimum GPA of 3.0 in last 60 hours of course work. Additional exam requirements/recommendations for international students: Required—TOEFL (minimum score 550 paper-based; 80 iBT), IELTS (minimum score 6). Electronic applications accepted.

Stephen F. Austin State University, Graduate School, College of Education, Department of Elementary Education, Program in Elementary Education, Nacogdoches, TX 75962. Offers M Ed. *Accreditation:* NCATE. *Degree requirements:* For master's, comprehensive exam. *Entrance requirements:* For master's, GRE General Test. Additional exam requirements/recommendations for international students: Required—TOEFL.

Sul Ross State University, Rio Grande College of Sul Ross State University, Alpine, TX 79832. Offers business administration (MBA); teacher education (M Ed), including bilingual education, counseling, educational diagnostics, elementary education, general education, reading, school administration, secondary education. *Program availability:* Part-time, evening/weekend, online learning. *Degree requirements:* For master's, comprehensive exam, thesis optional, minimum GPA of 3.0. *Entrance requirements:* For master's, GMAT or GRE General Test, minimum GPA of 2.5 in last 60 hours of undergraduate work. Additional exam requirements/recommendations for international students: Required—TOEFL.

Tarleton State University, College of Graduate Studies, College of Education, Department of Curriculum and Instruction, Stephenville, TX 76402. Offers educational diagnostician (M Ed); elementary education (M Ed); instructional design and technology (M Ed); instructional leadership (M Ed); professional reading specialist (M Ed); secondary education (M Ed); special education (M Ed); technology applications (M Ed); technology director (M Ed). *Program availability:* Part-time, evening/weekend. *Faculty:* 9 full-time (7 women), 6 part-time/adjunct (4 women). *Students:* 17 full-time (0 women), 104 part-time (101 women); includes 28 minority (5 Black or African American, non-Hispanic/Latino; 1 American Indian or Alaska Native, non-Hispanic/Latino; 19 Hispanic/Latino; 3 Two or more races, non-Hispanic/Latino). 62 applicants, 94% accepted, 35 enrolled. In 2016, 34 master's awarded. *Degree requirements:* For master's, comprehensive exam. *Entrance requirements:* For master's, GRE General Test, minimum GPA of 3.0. Additional exam requirements/recommendations for international students: Required—TOEFL (minimum score 550 paper-based; 80 iBT). *Application deadline:* For fall admission, 8/15 priority date for domestic students; for spring admission, 1/7 for domestic students. Applications are processed on a rolling basis. Application fee: $45 ($145 for international students). Electronic applications accepted. *Expenses:* $3,672 tuition; $2,437 fees. *Financial support:* Research assistantships, teaching assistantships, career-related internships or fieldwork, Federal Work-Study, and institutionally sponsored loans available. Support available to part-time students. Financial award application deadline: 5/1; financial award applicants required to submit FAFSA. *Unit head:* Dr. Jordan Barkley, Department Head, 254-968-9089, E-mail: jbarkley@tarleton.edu. *Application contact:* Information Contact, 254-968-9104, Fax: 254-968-9670, E-mail: gradoffice@tarleton.edu.
Website: http://www.tarleton.edu/cimasters/

Teachers College, Columbia University, Department of Curriculum and Teaching, New York, NY 10027-6696. Offers curriculum and teaching (Ed M, MA, Ed D); curriculum and teaching: elementary education (MA); curriculum and teaching: secondary education (MA); early childhood education (MA, Ed D); early childhood education: special education (MA); elementary education-gifted extension (MA); elementary inclusive education (MA); gifted education (MA); literacy specialist (MA); secondary inclusive education (MA); special inclusive elementary education (MA). *Program availability:* Part-time, evening/weekend. *Students:* 236 full-time (219 women), 198 part-time (176 women); includes 160 minority (53 Black or African American, non-Hispanic/Latino; 1 American Indian or Alaska Native, non-Hispanic/Latino; 43 Asian, non-Hispanic/Latino; 41 Hispanic/Latino; 22 Two or more races, non-Hispanic/Latino), 38 international. 399 applicants, 66% accepted, 104 enrolled. Terminal master's awarded for partial completion of doctoral program. *Degree requirements:* For doctorate, thesis/dissertation. *Expenses: Tuition:* Full-time $36,288; part-time $1512 per credit. *Required fees:* $438 per semester. One-time fee: $510 full-time. Full-time tuition and fees vary according to course load. *Unit head:* Prof. Nancy Lesko, Chair, 212-678-3264, E-mail: lesko@tc.columbia.edu. *Application contact:* David Estrella, Director of Admission, 212-678-3305, Fax: 212-678-4171, E-mail: estrella@tc.columbia.edu.

Tennessee State University, The School of Graduate Studies and Research, College of Education, Department of Teaching and Learning, Nashville, TN 37209-1561. Offers curriculum and instruction (M Ed, Ed D); elementary education (M Ed); special education (M Ed). *Accreditation:* NCATE. *Degree requirements:* For doctorate, thesis/dissertation. *Entrance requirements:* For master's, GRE General Test, GRE Subject Test, or MAT, minimum GPA of 2.5; for doctorate, GRE General Test, GRE Subject Test, or MAT, minimum GPA of 3.25. Electronic applications accepted. *Faculty research:* Multicultural education, teacher education reform, whole language, interactive video teaching, English as a second language.

Elementary Education

Tennessee Technological University, College of Graduate Studies, College of Education, Department of Curriculum and Instruction, Program in Elementary Education, Cookeville, TN 38505. Offers MA, Ed S. *Accreditation:* NCATE. *Program availability:* Part-time, evening/weekend. *Faculty:* 8 full-time (2 women). *Students:* 11 full-time (10 women), 15 part-time (14 women); includes 2 minority (both Black or African American, non-Hispanic/Latino). Average age 27. 10 applicants, 80% accepted, 7 enrolled. In 2016, 9 master's awarded. *Degree requirements:* For master's and Ed S, comprehensive exam, thesis or alternative. *Entrance requirements:* For master's and Ed S, MAT or GRE. Additional exam requirements/recommendations for international students: Required—TOEFL (minimum score 527 paper-based; 71 iBT), IELTS (minimum score 5.5), PTE (minimum score 48), or TOEIC (Test of English as an International Communication). *Application deadline:* For fall admission, 8/1 for domestic students, 5/1 for international students; for spring admission, 12/1 for domestic students, 10/1 for international students; for summer admission, 5/1 for domestic students, 2/1 for international students. Applications are processed on a rolling basis. Application fee: $35 ($40 for international students). Electronic applications accepted. *Expenses:* Tuition, state resident: full-time $9375; part-time $534 per credit hour. Tuition, nonresident: full-time $22,443; part-time $1260 per credit hour. *Financial support:* In 2016–17, 1 fellowship (averaging $8,000 per year) was awarded; research assistantships, teaching assistantships, and career-related internships or fieldwork also available. Financial award application deadline: 4/1. *Faculty research:* Educational television art program. *Unit head:* Dr. Jeremy Wendt, Interim Chairperson, 931-372-3181, Fax: 931-372-6270, E-mail: jwendt@tntech.edu. *Application contact:* Shelia K. Kendrick, Coordinator of Graduate Studies, 931-372-3808, Fax: 931-372-3497, E-mail: skendrick@tntech.edu.

Tennessee Technological University, College of Graduate Studies, College of Education, Department of Exercise Science, Physical Education and Wellness, Cookeville, TN 38505. Offers adapted physical education (MA); elementary/middle school physical education (MA); lifetime wellness (MA); sport management (MA). *Accreditation:* NCATE. *Program availability:* Part-time, online learning. *Faculty:* 7 full-time (0 women). *Students:* 17 full-time (5 women), 32 part-time (17 women); includes 6 minority (4 Black or African American, non-Hispanic/Latino; 1 Hispanic/Latino; 1 Two or more races, non-Hispanic/Latino). Average age 27. 29 applicants, 59% accepted, 15 enrolled. In 2016, 24 master's awarded. *Degree requirements:* For master's, comprehensive exam, thesis or alternative. *Entrance requirements:* For master's, MAT or GRE. Additional exam requirements/recommendations for international students: Required—TOEFL (minimum score 527 paper-based; 71 iBT), IELTS (minimum score 5.5), PTE (minimum score 48), or TOEIC (Test of English as an International Communication). *Application deadline:* For fall admission, 8/1 for domestic students, 5/1 for international students; for spring admission, 12/1 for domestic students, 10/1 for international students; for summer admission, 5/1 for domestic students, 2/1 for international students. Applications are processed on a rolling basis. Application fee: $35 ($40 for international students). Electronic applications accepted. *Expenses:* Tuition, state resident: full-time $9375; part-time $534 per credit hour. Tuition, nonresident: full-time $22,443; part-time $1260 per credit hour. *Financial support:* In 2016–17, 2 research assistantships (averaging $4,400 per year), 9 teaching assistantships (averaging $4,400 per year) were awarded; fellowships and career-related internships or fieldwork also available. Financial award application deadline: 4/1. *Unit head:* Dr. Christy Killman, Chairperson, 931-372-3467, Fax: 931-372-6319, E-mail: ckillman@tntech.edu. *Application contact:* Shelia K. Kendrick, Coordinator of Graduate Studies, 931-372-3808, Fax: 931-372-3497, E-mail: skendrick@tntech.edu.

Texas A&M University–Commerce, College of Education and Human Services, Commerce, TX 75429-3011. Offers counseling (MS); curriculum and instruction (M Ed, MS); early childhood education (M Ed, MS); educational administration (M Ed, Ed D); educational psychology (PhD); educational technology leadership (MS); educational technology library science (MS); health, kinesiology and sports studies (MS); higher education (MS, Ed D); organization, learning, and technology (MS); psychology (MS); reading (M Ed, MS); school psychology (SSP); secondary education (M Ed, MS); social work (MSW); special education (M Ed); supervision, curriculum and instruction-elementary education (Ed D). *Program availability:* Part-time, 100% online, blended/hybrid learning. *Faculty:* 88 full-time (52 women), 31 part-time/adjunct (24 women). *Students:* 341 full-time (276 women), 1,495 part-time (1,156 women); includes 762 minority (429 Black or African American, non-Hispanic/Latino; 4 American Indian or Alaska Native, non-Hispanic/Latino; 27 Asian, non-Hispanic/Latino; 247 Hispanic/Latino; 1 Native Hawaiian or other Pacific Islander, non-Hispanic/Latino; 54 Two or more races, non-Hispanic/Latino), 18 international. Average age 37. 1,070 applicants, 54% accepted, 452 enrolled. In 2016, 579 master's, 31 doctorates awarded. *Degree requirements:* For master's, one foreign language, comprehensive exam, thesis optional, departmental qualifying exams (for some programs); for doctorate, comprehensive exam, thesis/dissertation, departmental qualifying exam; for SSP, comprehensive exam, thesis optional. *Entrance requirements:* For master's and doctorate, GRE General Test. Additional exam requirements/recommendations for international students: Required—TOEFL (minimum score 550 paper-based; 79 iBT), IELTS (minimum score 6). *Application deadline:* For fall admission, 6/1 priority date for international students; for spring admission, 10/15 priority date for international students; for summer admission, 3/15 priority date for international students. Applications are processed on a rolling basis. Application fee: $50. Electronic applications accepted. *Expenses:* $2,254 resident; $4,744 non-resident. *Financial support:* In 2016–17, 301 students received support, including 39 research assistantships with partial tuition reimbursements available (averaging $9,000 per year), 17 teaching assistantships with partial tuition reimbursements available (averaging $9,000 per year); career-related internships or fieldwork, Federal Work-Study, institutionally sponsored loans, scholarships/grants, health care benefits, and unspecified assistantships also available. Financial award application deadline: 5/1; financial award applicants required to submit FAFSA. *Faculty research:* Cognitive and bilingual education, positive behavioral intervention, literacy, math readiness. *Total annual research expenditures:* $470,963. *Unit head:* Dr. Timothy Letzring, Dean, 903-886-5181, Fax: 903-886-5905, E-mail: tim.letzring@tamuc.edu. *Application contact:* Jennifer Faunce, Graduate Recruiter, 903-886-5030, Fax: 903-886-5905, E-mail: jennifer.faunce@tamuc.edu.
Website: http://www.tamuc.edu/academics/graduateSchool/programs/education/default.aspx

Texas A&M University–Commerce, College of Humanities, Social Sciences and Arts, Commerce, TX 75429-3011. Offers applied criminology (MS); applied linguistics (MA, MS); art (MA, MFA); Christianity in history (Graduate Certificate); computational linguistics (Graduate Certificate); creative writing (Graduate Certificate); English (MA, MS, PhD); film studies (Graduate Certificate); history (MA, MS); music (MM); political science (MA, MS); public history (Graduate Certificate); sociology (MS); Spanish (MA); studies in children's and adolescent literature and culture (Graduate Certificate); teaching English to speakers of other languages (Graduate Certificate); theater (MA, MS). *Program availability:* Part-time. *Faculty:* 53 full-time (26 women), 7 part-time/adjunct (2 women). *Students:* 87 full-time (55 women), 528 part-time (362 women); includes 198 minority (86 Black or African American, non-Hispanic/Latino; 2 American Indian or Alaska Native, non-Hispanic/Latino; 8 Asian, non-Hispanic/Latino; 84 Hispanic/Latino; 18 Two or more races, non-Hispanic/Latino), 27 international. Average age 37. 333 applicants, 56% accepted, 149 enrolled. In 2016, 66 master's, 8 doctorates awarded. *Degree requirements:* For master's, one foreign language, comprehensive exam, thesis (for some programs); for doctorate, one foreign language, comprehensive exam, thesis/dissertation, departmental qualifying exam. *Entrance requirements:* For master's and doctorate, GRE General Test. Additional exam requirements/recommendations for international students: Required—TOEFL (minimum score 550 paper-based; 79 iBT), IELTS (minimum score 6). *Application deadline:* Applications are processed on a rolling basis. Application fee: $50. Electronic applications accepted. *Expenses:* Contact institution. *Financial support:* In 2016–17, 255 students received support, including 9 research assistantships with partial tuition reimbursements available (averaging $9,000 per year), 68 teaching assistantships with partial tuition reimbursements available (averaging $9,000 per year); Federal Work-Study, institutionally sponsored loans, scholarships/grants, health care benefits, and unspecified assistantships also available. Financial award application deadline: 5/1; financial award applicants required to submit FAFSA. *Unit head:* Dr. Salvatore Attardo, Dean, 903-886-5166, Fax: 903-886-5774, E-mail: salvatore.attardo@tamuc.edu. *Application contact:* Shelby Miller, Graduate Recruiter, 903-468-8123, Fax: 903-886-5774, E-mail: shelby.miller@tamuc.edu.
Website: http://www.tamuc.edu/academics/graduateSchool/programs/humanitiesSocialScienceArts/default.aspx

Texas A&M University–Corpus Christi, College of Graduate Studies, College of Education, Program in Elementary Education, Corpus Christi, TX 78412-5503. Offers MS. *Program availability:* Part-time, evening/weekend, online learning. *Students:* 8 full-time (all women), 11 part-time (10 women); includes 12 minority (11 Hispanic/Latino; 1 Two or more races, non-Hispanic/Latino). Average age 35. 8 applicants, 50% accepted, 3 enrolled. In 2016, 6 master's awarded. *Degree requirements:* For master's, capstone experience. *Entrance requirements:* For master's, minimum GPA of 3.0 in last 60 hours. Additional exam requirements/recommendations for international students: Required—TOEFL (minimum score 550 paper-based; 79 iBT), IELTS (minimum score 6.5). *Application deadline:* For fall admission, 8/19 priority date for domestic students, 7/26 priority date for international students; for spring admission, 1/13 priority date for domestic students, 12/20 priority date for international students; for summer admission, 5/25 priority date for domestic students, 5/1 priority date for international students. Applications are processed on a rolling basis. Application fee: $50 ($70 for international students). Electronic applications accepted. *Financial support:* Research assistantships, teaching assistantships, career-related internships or fieldwork, Federal Work-Study, institutionally sponsored loans, scholarships/grants, health care benefits, and unspecified assistantships available. Support available to part-time students. Financial award application deadline: 3/15; financial award applicants required to submit FAFSA. *Unit head:* Dr. Linda Kelly, Clinical Assistant Professor, 361-825-2437, E-mail: linda.kelly@tamucc.edu. *Application contact:* Graduate Admissions Coordinator, 361-825-2177, Fax: 361-825-2755, E-mail: gradweb@tamucc.edu.
Website: http://macprogram.tamucc.edu/

Texas State University, The Graduate College, College of Education, Program in Elementary Education, San Marcos, TX 78666. Offers M Ed, MA. *Program availability:* Part-time, evening/weekend. *Faculty:* 21 full-time (12 women), 9 part-time/adjunct (7 women). *Students:* 82 full-time (75 women), 77 part-time (70 women); includes 57 minority (16 Black or African American, non-Hispanic/Latino; 2 American Indian or Alaska Native, non-Hispanic/Latino; 1 Asian, non-Hispanic/Latino; 36 Hispanic/Latino; 1 Native Hawaiian or other Pacific Islander, non-Hispanic/Latino; 1 Two or more races, non-Hispanic/Latino), 1 international. Average age 31. 72 applicants, 88% accepted, 42 enrolled. In 2016, 87 master's awarded. *Degree requirements:* For master's, comprehensive exam, thesis (for some programs). *Entrance requirements:* For master's, GRE (preferred), baccalaureate degree from regionally-accredited institution with minimum GPA of 2.75 in last 60 hours of course work. Additional exam requirements/recommendations for international students: Required—TOEFL (minimum score 550 paper-based; 78 iBT), IELTS (minimum score 6.5). *Application deadline:* For fall admission, 2/15 priority date for domestic and international students; for spring admission, 10/15 for domestic students, 10/1 for international students; for summer admission, 4/15 for domestic students, 3/15 for international students. Applications are processed on a rolling basis. Application fee: $40 ($90 for international students). Electronic applications accepted. *Expenses:* $4,851 per semester. *Financial support:* In 2016–17, 92 students received support, including 2 research assistantships (averaging $13,600 per year), 20 teaching assistantships (averaging $14,888 per year); career-related internships or fieldwork, Federal Work-Study, institutionally sponsored loans, and scholarships/grants also available. Support available to part-time students. Financial award application deadline: 3/1; financial award applicants required to submit FAFSA. *Faculty research:* Novice teacher induction, developmental education research, college and career initiative, teacher preparation academy, creative science, responsive interactive parent training, developing science, technology, engineering, and math curriculum. *Total annual research expenditures:* $4.2 million. *Unit head:* Dr. Cheryll Dennis, Graduate Advisor, 512-716-4533, Fax: 512-245-7911, E-mail: elemedgrad@txstate.edu. *Application contact:* Dr. Andrea Golato, Dean of Graduate School, 512-245-2581, Fax: 512-245-8365, E-mail: gradcollege@txstate.edu.
Website: http://www.education.txstate.edu/ci/degrees-programs/graduate/elementary-education.html

Texas State University, The Graduate College, College of Education, Program in Elementary Education - Bilingual/Bicultural, San Marcos, TX 78666. Offers M Ed, MA. *Program availability:* Part-time. *Faculty:* 5 full-time (all women), 2 part-time/adjunct (both women). *Students:* 3 full-time (all women), 9 part-time (all women); includes 9 minority (all Hispanic/Latino), 2 international. Average age 33. 6 applicants, 67% accepted, 2 enrolled. In 2016, 4 master's awarded. *Degree requirements:* For master's, comprehensive exam, thesis (for some programs). *Entrance requirements:* For master's, GRE (preferred), baccalaureate degree from regionally-accredited institution with minimum GPA of 2.75 in last 60 hours of course work; meeting with bilingual coordinator to ensure proficiency in written and spoken Spanish. Additional exam requirements/recommendations for international students: Required—TOEFL (minimum score 550 paper-based; 78 iBT), IELTS (minimum score 6.5). *Application deadline:* For fall admission, 2/15 priority date for domestic and international students; for spring admission, 10/15 for domestic students, 10/1 for international students; for summer admission, 4/15 for domestic students, 3/15 for international students. Applications are processed on a rolling basis. Application fee: $40 ($90 for international students). Electronic applications accepted. *Expenses:* $4,851 per semester. *Financial support:* In 2016–17, 10 students received support. Research assistantships, teaching assistantships, career-related internships or fieldwork, Federal Work-Study, institutionally sponsored loans, scholarships/grants, and unspecified assistantships available. Support available to part-time students. Financial award application deadline: 3/1; financial award applicants required to submit FAFSA. *Unit head:* Dr. Mary Esther Huerta, Graduate Advisor, 512-245-3099, Fax: 512-245-7911, E-mail: mh75@txstate.edu. *Application contact:* Dr. Andrea Golato, Dean of Graduate School, 512-245-2581, Fax: 512-245-8365, E-mail: gradcollege@txstate.edu.
Website: http://www.education.txstate.edu/ci/degrees-programs/graduate/elementary-education.html

Texas Tech University, Graduate School, College of Education, Department of Curriculum and Instruction, Lubbock, TX 79409-1071. Offers bilingual education (M Ed); curriculum and instruction (M Ed); elementary education (M Ed); language/literacy education (M Ed); multidisciplinary science (MS); secondary education (M Ed). *Accreditation:* NCATE. *Program availability:* Part-time, evening/weekend, online learning. *Faculty:* 24 full-time (17 women), 1 part-time/adjunct (0 women). *Students:* 65 full-time (52 women), 237 part-time (191 women); includes 97 minority (30 Black or African American, non-Hispanic/Latino; 1 American Indian or Alaska Native, non-Hispanic/Latino; 10 Asian, non-Hispanic/Latino; 47 Hispanic/Latino; 9 Two or more races, non-Hispanic/Latino), 41 international. Average age 39. 181 applicants, 54% accepted, 78 enrolled. In 2016, 20 master's, 28 doctorates awarded. Terminal master's awarded for partial completion of doctoral program. *Degree requirements:* For master's, comprehensive exam (for some programs), thesis optional; for doctorate, comprehensive exam, thesis/dissertation. *Entrance requirements:* For master's, bachelor's degree; resume; letter of intent; academic writing sample; 2 letters of recommendation; for doctorate, GRE, master's degree; resume; letter of intent; academic writing sample; 3 letters of recommendation. Additional exam requirements/recommendations for international students: Required—TOEFL (minimum score 550 paper-based; 79 iBT). *Application deadline:* For fall admission, 6/1 priority date for domestic students, 1/15 priority date for international students; for spring admission, 9/1 priority date for domestic students, 6/15 priority date for international students. Applications are processed on a rolling basis. Application fee: $75. Electronic applications accepted. *Expenses:* $285 per credit hour full-time resident tuition, $693 per credit hour full-time non-resident tuition; $50.50 per credit hour fee plus $608 per term fee. *Financial support:* In 2016–17, 110 students received support, including 110 fellowships (averaging $3,132 per year); research assistantships, Federal Work-Study, institutionally sponsored loans, scholarships/grants, health care benefits, and unspecified assistantships also available. Support available to part-time students. Financial award application deadline: 2/1; financial award applicants required to submit FAFSA. *Faculty research:* Teacher education, curriculum studies, bilingual education, science and math education, language and literacy education. *Total annual research expenditures:* $120,552. *Unit head:* Dr. Jian Wang, Department Chair, Curriculum and Instruction, 806-834-5165, Fax: 806-742-2179, E-mail: jian.wang@ttu.edu. *Application contact:* Brianna Sanchez, Coordinator, 806-834-2353, Fax: 806-742-2179, E-mail: brianna.sanchez@ttu.edu.
Website: http://www.educ.ttu.edu

Towson University, Program in Elementary Education, Towson, MD 21252-0001. Offers M Ed. *Accreditation:* NCATE. *Program availability:* Part-time, evening/weekend. *Students:* 5 part-time (4 women); includes 2 minority (both Black or African American, non-Hispanic/Latino). *Entrance requirements:* For master's, minimum GPA of 3.0, bachelor's degree in education, teaching certification or eligibility for certification. Application fee: $45. Electronic applications accepted. *Expenses:* Tuition, state resident: full-time $7580; part-time $379 per unit. Tuition, nonresident: full-time $15,700; part-time $785 per unit. *Required fees:* $2480. *Financial support:* Application deadline: 4/1. *Unit head:* Dr. Todd Kenreich, Graduate Program Director, 410-704-4956, E-mail: scedmed@towson.edu. *Application contact:* Coverley Beidleman, Assistant Director of Graduate Admissions, 410-704-2113, Fax: 410-704-3030, E-mail: grads@towson.edu.
Website: http://www.towson.edu/coe/departments/grad/elementary/

Trevecca Nazarene University, Graduate Education Program, Nashville, TN 37210-2877. Offers accountability and instructional leadership (Ed S); curriculum and instruction for Christian school educators (M Ed); curriculum and instruction K-12 (M Ed); educational leadership (M Ed); English second language (M Ed); library and information science (MLI Sc); special education: visual impairments (M Ed); teaching (MAT), including teaching 6-12, teaching K-5. *Accreditation:* NCATE. *Program availability:* Part-time, evening/weekend, online learning. *Faculty:* 5 full-time (3 women), 18 part-time/adjunct (12 women). *Students:* 80 full-time (64 women), 16 part-time (13 women); includes 19 minority (17 Black or African American, non-Hispanic/Latino; 2 Hispanic/Latino). Average age 35. In 2016, 68 master's, 7 other advanced degrees awarded. *Degree requirements:* For master's, comprehensive exam, exit assessment/e-portfolio. *Entrance requirements:* For master's, GRE (minimum score of 290) or MAT (minimum score of 378); PRAXIS (for MAT), minimum GPA of 3.0, official transcript from regionally-accredited institution, at least 3 years' successful teaching experience (for M Ed in educational leadership major). Additional exam requirements/recommendations for international students: Required—TOEFL (minimum score 550 paper-based). *Application deadline:* Applications are processed on a rolling basis. Electronic applications accepted. *Expenses:* Contact institution. *Financial support:* Applicants required to submit FAFSA. *Unit head:* Dr. Suzie Harris, Dean, School of Education/Director of Graduate Education Programs, 615-248-1201, Fax: 615-248-1597, E-mail: admissions_ged@trevecca.edu. *Application contact:* 844-TNU-GRAD, E-mail: sgcsadmissions@trevecca.edu.
Website: http://www.trevecca.edu/soe

Trinity Washington University, School of Education, Washington, DC 20017-1094. Offers clinical mental health counseling (MA); early childhood education (MAT); educating for change (M Ed); educational administration (MSA); elementary education (MAT); reading (M Ed); school counseling (MA); secondary education (MAT), including English, social studies; special education (MAT). *Accreditation:* NCATE. *Program availability:* Part-time, evening/weekend. *Degree requirements:* For master's, thesis (for some programs), capstone project(s). *Entrance requirements:* For master's, PRAXIS I, minimum GPA of 2.8. Additional exam requirements/recommendations for international students: Required—TOEFL (minimum score 550 paper-based). *Faculty research:* Technology, literacy, special education, organizations, inclusion models.

Troy University, Graduate School, College of Education, Program in K–6 Elementary and Collaborative Education, Troy, AL 36082. Offers MS, Ed S. *Accreditation:* NCATE. *Program availability:* Part-time, evening/weekend. *Faculty:* 15 full-time (9 women), 6 part-time/adjunct (5 women). *Students:* 42 full-time (40 women), 43 part-time (36 women); includes 27 minority (25 Black or African American, non-Hispanic/Latino; 1 American Indian or Alaska Native, non-Hispanic/Latino; 1 Hispanic/Latino). Average age 33. 92 applicants, 98% accepted, 8 enrolled. In 2016, 47 master's, 1 other advanced degree awarded. *Degree requirements:* For master's, comprehensive exam, thesis. *Entrance requirements:* For master's, GRE (minimum score of 850 on old exam or 290 on new exam), GMAT (minimum score of 380), or MAT (minimum score of 385), bachelor's degree; minimum undergraduate GPA of 2.5 or 3.0 on last 30 semester hours, letter of recommendation; for Ed S, GRE (minimum score of 850 on old exam or 286 on new exam) or GMAT (minimum score of 380), Alabama Class A certificate or equivalent, master's degree, minimum graduate GPA of 3.0. Additional exam requirements/recommendations for international students: Required—TOEFL (minimum score 523 paper-based; 70 iBT), IELTS (minimum score 5.5). *Application deadline:* Applications are processed on a rolling basis. Application fee: $50. Electronic applications accepted. *Expenses:* Tuition, state resident: full-time $7146; part-time $397 per credit hour. Tuition, nonresident: full-time $14,292; part-time $794 per credit hour. *Required fees:* $802; $50 per semester. Tuition and fees vary according to campus/location and program. *Financial support:* Fellowships, career-related internships or fieldwork, and scholarships/grants available. Support available to part-time students. Financial award applicants required to submit FAFSA. *Unit head:* Dr. Ruth Busby, Chair, Teacher Education, 334-670-3546, Fax: 334-670-6666, E-mail: rbusby@troy.edu. *Application contact:* Jessica A. Kimbro, Director of Graduate Admissions, 334-670-3178, E-mail: jacord@troy.edu.

Tufts University, Graduate School of Arts and Sciences, Department of Education, Program in Education, Medford, MA 02155. Offers educational studies (MA); elementary education (MAT); middle and secondary education (MAT); museum education (MA); secondary education (MA); STEM education (MS, PhD). *Program availability:* Part-time. *Students:* 67 full-time (49 women), 14 part-time (12 women); includes 17 minority (4 Black or African American, non-Hispanic/Latino; 6 Asian, non-Hispanic/Latino; 6 Hispanic/Latino; 1 Two or more races, non-Hispanic/Latino), 6 international. Average age 28. 120 applicants, 71% accepted, 49 enrolled. In 2016, 25 master's awarded. *Degree requirements:* For master's, thesis optional. *Entrance requirements:* For master's, GRE General Test, portfolio (for art education only); for doctorate, GRE General Test, writing sample. Additional exam requirements/recommendations for international students: Required—TOEFL (minimum score 550 paper-based; 80 iBT), IELTS (minimum score 6.5). *Application deadline:* For fall admission, 1/2 for domestic and international students; for spring admission, 10/15 for domestic and international students. Applications are processed on a rolling basis. Application fee: $85. Electronic applications accepted. *Expenses:* Contact institution. *Financial support:* In 2016–17, 69 students received support. Research assistantships, teaching assistantships, Federal Work-Study, scholarships/grants, and tuition waivers (full and partial) available. Support available to part-time students. Financial award application deadline: 1/2. *Unit head:* Dr. Sabina Vaught, Graduate Program Director. *Application contact:* Office of Graduate Admissions, 617-627-3395, E-mail: gradadmissions@tufts.edu.

Union College, Graduate Programs, Department of Education, Program in Elementary Education, Barbourville, KY 40906-1499. Offers MA. *Degree requirements:* For master's, thesis optional. *Entrance requirements:* For master's, GRE General Test, NTE.

Universidad del Este, Graduate School, Carolina, PR 00984. Offers accounting (MBA); adult education (M Ed); agribusiness (MBA); criminal justice and criminology (MA); curriculum and instruction - early education (M Ed); curriculum and instruction - elementary (M Ed); curriculum and instruction - English (M Ed); curriculum and instruction - Spanish (M Ed); human resources (MBA); information security management (MBA); information technology and Web business development (MBA); management (MBA); public policy (MPA); social work (MA), including clinical social work; special education (M Ed); strategic leadership (MBA).

Universidad Metropolitana, School of Education, Program in Teaching of Physical Education, San Juan, PR 00928-1150. Offers teaching of adult physical education (M Ed); teaching of elementary physical education (M Ed); teaching of secondary physical education (M Ed). *Degree requirements:* For master's, thesis or alternative. *Entrance requirements:* For master's, EXADEP, interview. Electronic applications accepted.

Université de Sherbrooke, Faculty of Education, Program in Elementary Education, Sherbrooke, QC J1K 2R1, Canada. Offers M Ed, Diploma. *Program availability:* Part-time, evening/weekend. *Degree requirements:* For master's, thesis.

University at Buffalo, the State University of New York, Graduate School, Graduate School of Education, Department of Learning and Instruction, Buffalo, NY 14260. Offers biology education (Ed M, Certificate); chemistry education (Ed M, Certificate); childhood education (Ed M); childhood education with bilingual extension (Ed M); college teaching (Advanced Certificate); curriculum, instruction and the science of learning (PhD); early childhood education (Ed M); early childhood education with bilingual extension (Ed M); earth science education (Ed M, Certificate); education and technology (Ed M); education studies (Ed M); educational technology and new literacies (Certificate); educational technology and new literacies (Advanced Certificate); elementary education (Ed D); English education (Ed M, Certificate); English education studies (Ed M); English for speakers of other languages (Ed M); foreign and second language education (PhD); French education (Ed M, Certificate); German education (Ed M, Certificate); gifted education (Certificate); Latin education (Ed M, Certificate); literacy education studies (Ed M); literacy specialist (Ed M); literacy teaching and learning (Certificate); mathematics education (Ed M, Certificate); music education (Ed M, Certificate); music education studies (Ed M); music learning theory (Advanced Certificate); online education (Advanced Certificate); physics education (Ed M, Certificate); science and the public (Ed M); social studies education (Ed M, Certificate); Spanish education (Ed M, Certificate); special education (PhD); teaching English to speakers of other languages (Ed M). *Program availability:* Part-time, evening/weekend, 100% online. *Faculty:* 28 full-time (21 women), 67 part-time/adjunct (49 women). *Students:* 198 full-time (153 women), 312 part-time (220 women); includes 48 minority (28 Black or African American, non-Hispanic/Latino; 4 American Indian or Alaska Native, non-Hispanic/Latino; 15 Asian, non-Hispanic/Latino; 1 Hispanic/Latino), 66 international. Average age 33. 336 applicants, 86% accepted, 178 enrolled. In 2016, 137 master's, 24 doctorates, 25 other advanced degrees awarded. *Degree requirements:* For master's, comprehensive exam; for doctorate, thesis/dissertation, research analysis exam, research experience. *Entrance requirements:* For master's, letters of reference; for doctorate, GRE General Test or MAT, interview, writing sample, letters of recommendation. Additional exam requirements/recommendations for international students: Required—TOEFL (minimum score 600 paper-based; 96 iBT). *Application deadline:* For fall admission, 2/1 priority date for domestic and international students; for spring admission, 11/15 priority date for domestic students, 10/1 for international students. Applications are processed on a rolling basis. Application fee: $50. Electronic applications accepted. *Financial support:* In 2016–17, 44 fellowships (averaging $4,010 per year), 39 research assistantships with tuition reimbursements (averaging $9,897 per year) were awarded; teaching assistantships, career-related internships or fieldwork, Federal Work-Study, institutionally sponsored loans, scholarships/grants, tuition waivers (full and partial), and unspecified assistantships also available. Financial award application deadline: 2/28; financial award applicants required to submit FAFSA. *Faculty research:* Science assessment, foreign language teaching and learning, early learning, new literacies, gender and education. *Total annual research expenditures:* $534,880. *Unit head:* Dr. Deborah Moore-Russo, Chair, 716-645-4069, Fax: 716-645-3161, E-mail: dam29@buffalo.edu. *Application contact:* Luann Zak, Admissions Assistant, 716-645-2110, Fax: 716-645-7937, E-mail: luannzak@buffalo.edu.
Website: http://gse.buffalo.edu/lai

The University of Akron, Graduate School, College of Education, Department of Curricular and Instructional Studies, Program in Elementary Education - Literacy Option, Akron, OH 44325. Offers MA. *Accreditation:* NCATE. *Students:* 7 full-time (4 women), 36 part-time (31 women); includes 6 minority (4 Black or African American, non-Hispanic/Latino; 1 Hispanic/Latino; 1 Two or more races, non-Hispanic/Latino), 6 international. Average age 35. 12 applicants, 100% accepted, 7 enrolled. In 2016, 14 master's awarded. *Degree requirements:* For master's, comprehensive exam, thesis optional. *Entrance requirements:* For master's, valid teaching license. Additional exam requirements/recommendations for international students: Required—TOEFL (minimum score 550 paper-based; 79 iBT), IELTS (minimum score 6.5). *Application deadline:* Applications are processed on a rolling basis. Application fee: $45 ($70 for international students). Electronic applications accepted. *Expenses:* Tuition, state resident: full-time

$8618; part-time $359 per credit hour. Tuition, nonresident: full-time $17,149; part-time $715 per credit hour. *Required fees:* $1652. *Unit head:* Dr. Susan Clark, Interim Chair, 330-972-7780, E-mail: sclark1@uakron.edu. *Application contact:* Kelly Chaff, College Program Specialist, 330-972-7028, E-mail: klchaff@uakron.edu.

The University of Alabama, Graduate School, College of Education, Department of Curriculum and Instruction, Tuscaloosa, AL 35487. Offers elementary education (MA, Ed D, PhD, Ed S); secondary education (MA, Ed D, PhD, Ed S). *Program availability:* Part-time, evening/weekend, 100% online, blended/hybrid learning. *Faculty:* 20 full-time (13 women), 2 part-time/adjunct (both women). *Students:* 66 full-time (45 women), 105 part-time (83 women); includes 28 minority (14 Black or African American, non-Hispanic/Latino; 2 American Indian or Alaska Native, non-Hispanic/Latino; 1 Asian, non-Hispanic/Latino; 6 Hispanic/Latino; 1 Native Hawaiian or other Pacific Islander, non-Hispanic/Latino; 4 Two or more races, non-Hispanic/Latino), 17 international. Average age 35. 93 applicants, 53% accepted, 40 enrolled. In 2016, 55 master's, 7 doctorates, 13 other advanced degrees awarded. *Degree requirements:* For master's, comprehensive exam, thesis (for some programs); for doctorate, comprehensive exam, thesis/dissertation; for Ed S, comprehensive exam, thesis. *Entrance requirements:* For master's and Ed S, MAT and/or GRE; for doctorate, GRE. Additional exam requirements/recommendations for international students: Recommended—TOEFL (minimum score 550 paper-based), IELTS (minimum score 6.5). *Application deadline:* For fall admission, 7/15 priority date for domestic students, 1/15 priority date for international students; for spring admission, 11/15 priority date for domestic students, 6/1 priority date for international students; for summer admission, 5/1 priority date for domestic students, 3/1 priority date for international students. Applications are processed on a rolling basis. Application fee: $50 ($60 for international students). Electronic applications accepted. *Expenses:* Tuition, state resident: full-time $10,470. Tuition, nonresident: full-time $26,950. *Financial support:* In 2016–17, 14 students received support, including 19 research assistantships with tuition reimbursements available (averaging $13,140 per year), 5 teaching assistantships with tuition reimbursements available (averaging $13,140 per year); institutionally sponsored loans, traineeships, and unspecified assistantships also available. Financial award application deadline: 12/31; financial award applicants required to submit FAFSA. *Faculty research:* Teacher education, diversity, integration of curriculum, technology, pedagogical content knowledge. *Total annual research expenditures:* $226,200. *Unit head:* Dr. Cynthia Camille Sunal, Chair, 205-348-8264, Fax: 205-348-9863, E-mail: cvsunal@ua.edu. *Application contact:* Dr. Kathy S. Wetzel, Assistant Dean for Student Services, 205-348-1154, Fax: 205-348-0080, E-mail: kwetzel@bamaed.ua.edu.
Website: http://courseleaf.ua.edu/education/curriculumandinstruction/

The University of Alabama at Birmingham, School of Education, Program in Elementary Education, Birmingham, AL 35294. Offers MA Ed. *Accreditation:* NCATE. *Program availability:* Part-time, online learning. *Degree requirements:* For master's, thesis optional. *Entrance requirements:* For master's, GRE General Test or MAT. Electronic applications accepted. Full-time tuition and fees vary according to course load and program.

University of Alaska Southeast, Graduate Programs, Program in Education, Juneau, AK 99801. Offers educational leadership (M Ed); elementary education (MAT); learning design and technology (M Ed); mathematics education (M Ed); reading specialist (M Ed); secondary education (MAT); special education (M Ed, MAT). *Accreditation:* NCATE. *Program availability:* Part-time, evening/weekend, online learning. *Degree requirements:* For master's, comprehensive exam or project, portfolio. *Entrance requirements:* For master's, PRAXIS, minimum GPA of 3.0, writing sample, letters of recommendation. *Application deadline:* For fall admission, 3/8 for domestic students. Applications are processed on a rolling basis. Application fee: $60. Electronic applications accepted. *Expenses:* Tuition, state resident: part-time $466 per credit. Tuition, nonresident: part-time $979 per credit. *Required fees:* $19 per credit. Part-time tuition and fees vary according to course level, campus/location and reciprocity agreements. *Financial support:* Federal Work-Study, scholarships/grants, and tuition waivers (full and partial) available. Support available to part-time students. Financial award applicants required to submit FAFSA. *Faculty research:* Applied classroom research, culturally responsive practices, action research, teaching effectiveness. *Unit head:* Dr. Larry Harris, Dean, 907-796-6551, Fax: 907-796-6550, E-mail: larry.harris@uas.alaska.edu. *Application contact:* Susan A. Stuck, Administrative Assistant, 866-465-6424, Fax: 866-465-5159, E-mail: jnsas@uas.alaska.edu.

University of Alberta, Faculty of Graduate Studies and Research, Department of Elementary Education, Edmonton, AB T6G 2E1, Canada. Offers M Ed, Ed D, PhD. *Program availability:* Part-time, evening/weekend, online learning. *Degree requirements:* For master's, thesis (for some programs); for doctorate, thesis/dissertation. *Entrance requirements:* For master's and doctorate, 1 year of teaching experience, minimum GPA of 6.5 on a 9.0 scale. *Faculty research:* Literacy education, early childhood education, teacher education, curriculum studies, instructional studies.

The University of Arizona, College of Education, Department of Teaching, Learning and Sociocultural Studies, Program in Teaching and Teacher Education, Tucson, AZ 85721. Offers M Ed, MA, PhD. *Program availability:* Part-time, evening/weekend. *Degree requirements:* For master's, thesis optional; for doctorate, comprehensive exam, thesis/dissertation. *Entrance requirements:* For master's, writing sample, 1 year of teaching experience, 3 letters of recommendation; for doctorate, GRE General Test (minimum score 1000), minimum GPA of 3.5, 2 years of teaching experience, 3 letters of recommendation, writing sample. Additional exam requirements/recommendations for international students: Required—TOEFL (minimum score 550 paper-based; 79 iBT). Electronic applications accepted. *Faculty research:* Staff development, science education, environmental education, math education.

University of Arkansas at Pine Bluff, School of Education, Pine Bluff, AR 71601-2799. Offers elementary education (M Ed); secondary education (M Ed), including English education, mathematics education, science education, social studies education; teaching (MAT). *Accreditation:* NCATE. *Program availability:* Part-time, evening/weekend. *Degree requirements:* For master's, comprehensive exam. *Entrance requirements:* For master's, GRE, minimum GPA of 2.75, NTE or Standard Arkansas Teaching Certificate. Application fee: $25. *Expenses:* Tuition, state resident: full-time $4776. Tuition, nonresident: full-time $10,824. *Required fees:* $1612. Tuition and fees vary according to course load. *Financial support:* Research assistantships with full and partial tuition reimbursements, teaching assistantships with full and partial tuition reimbursements, institutionally sponsored loans, and scholarships/grants available. Support available to part-time students. *Faculty research:* Teacher certification, accreditation, assessment, standards, portfolio development, rehabilitation, technology. *Unit head:* Dr. George Herts, Dean, 870-575-8000, E-mail: johnson_c@uapb.edu.
Website: http://www.uapb.edu/academics/school_of_education.aspx

University of Bridgeport, School of Education, Department of Education, Bridgeport, CT 06604. Offers education (MS); educational management (Ed D, Diploma), including intermediate administrator or supervisor (Diploma), leadership (Ed D); elementary education (MS, Diploma), including early childhood education, elementary education; middle school education (MS); music education (MS); remedial reading and language arts (Diploma); secondary education (MS, Diploma), including computer specialist (Diploma), international education (Diploma), reading specialist, secondary education. *Program availability:* Part-time, evening/weekend. *Degree requirements:* For master's, final exam, final project, or thesis; for doctorate, comprehensive exam, thesis/dissertation; for Diploma, thesis or alternative, final project. *Entrance requirements:* For master's, minimum undergraduate QPA of 2.67; for doctorate, GRE, MAT; for Diploma, GRE General Test or MAT, minimum graduate QPA of 3.0. Additional exam requirements/recommendations for international students: Recommended—TOEFL (minimum score 550 paper-based; 80 iBT), IELTS (minimum score 6.5). Electronic applications accepted. *Expenses:* Contact institution.

University of California, Irvine, School of Education, Irvine, CA 92697. Offers educational administration (Ed D); educational administration and leadership (Ed D); elementary and secondary education (MAT). *Program availability:* Part-time, evening/weekend. *Students:* 189 full-time (139 women), 1 part-time (0 women); includes 101 minority (44 Asian, non-Hispanic/Latino; 40 Hispanic/Latino; 1 Native Hawaiian or other Pacific Islander, non-Hispanic/Latino; 16 Two or more races, non-Hispanic/Latino), 16 international. Average age 27. 456 applicants, 54% accepted, 131 enrolled. In 2016, 139 master's, 16 doctorates awarded. *Degree requirements:* For doctorate, thesis/dissertation. *Entrance requirements:* For master's, GRE, minimum GPA of 3.0; for doctorate, GRE General Test, minimum GPA of 3.0. Additional exam requirements/recommendations for international students: Required—TOEFL (minimum score 550 paper-based). *Application deadline:* For fall admission, 1/2 priority date for domestic students, 1/2 for international students. Application fee: $105 ($125 for international students). Electronic applications accepted. *Financial support:* Fellowships, research assistantships with full tuition reimbursements, institutionally sponsored loans, traineeships, health care benefits, and unspecified assistantships available. Financial award application deadline: 3/1; financial award applicants required to submit FAFSA. *Faculty research:* Education technology, learning theory, social theory, cultural diversity, postmodernism. *Unit head:* Richard Arum, Dean, 949-824-2534, E-mail: richard.arum@uci.edu. *Application contact:* Denise Earley, Assistant Director of Student Affairs, 949-824-4022, E-mail: denise.earley@uci.edu.
Website: http://education.uci.edu/

University of Central Florida, College of Education and Human Performance, Education Doctoral Programs, Orlando, FL 32816. Offers communication sciences and disorders (PhD); curriculum and instruction (Ed D); early childhood education (PhD); educational leadership (Ed D); elementary education (PhD); exceptional education (PhD); exercise physiology (PhD); higher education (PhD); instructional technology (PhD); mathematics education (PhD); methodology, measurement and analysis (PhD); reading education (PhD); science education (PhD); social science education (PhD); TESOL (PhD). *Students:* 127 full-time (91 women), 43 part-time (29 women); includes 33 minority (17 Black or African American, non-Hispanic/Latino; 5 Asian, non-Hispanic/Latino; 7 Hispanic/Latino; 4 Two or more races, non-Hispanic/Latino), 26 international. Average age 37. 163 applicants, 40% accepted, 52 enrolled. In 2016, 57 doctorates awarded. Application fee: $30. Electronic applications accepted. *Expenses:* Tuition, state resident: part-time $288.16 per credit hour. Tuition, nonresident: part-time $1071.31 per credit hour. *Financial support:* In 2016–17, 78 students received support, including 41 fellowships with partial tuition reimbursements available (averaging $5,916 per year), 44 research assistantships with partial tuition reimbursements available (averaging $7,637 per year), 48 teaching assistantships with partial tuition reimbursements available (averaging $9,633 per year). Financial award application deadline: 3/1; financial award applicants required to submit FAFSA. *Unit head:* Dr. Edward Robinson, Director of Doctoral Programs, 407-823-6106, E-mail: edward.robinson@ucf.edu. *Application contact:* Assistant Director, Graduate Admissions, 407-823-2766, Fax: 407-823-6442, E-mail: gradadmissions@ucf.edu.
Website: http://education.ucf.edu/programs.cfm?pid=g&cat=2

University of Central Florida, College of Education and Human Performance, School of Teaching, Learning, and Leadership, Program in Elementary Education, Orlando, FL 32816. Offers M Ed, MA. *Accreditation:* NCATE. *Students:* 19 full-time (all women), 39 part-time (37 women); includes 17 minority (5 Black or African American, non-Hispanic/Latino; 3 Asian, non-Hispanic/Latino; 8 Hispanic/Latino; 1 Two or more races, non-Hispanic/Latino). Average age 27. 38 applicants, 55% accepted, 16 enrolled. In 2016, 27 master's awarded. *Degree requirements:* For master's, thesis or alternative. *Entrance requirements:* For master's, Florida Teacher Certification Exam/General Knowledge Test or GRE. Additional exam requirements/recommendations for international students: Required—TOEFL. *Application deadline:* For fall admission, 7/15 for domestic students; for spring admission, 12/1 for domestic students. Application fee: $30. Electronic applications accepted. *Expenses:* Tuition, state resident: part-time $288.16 per credit hour. Tuition, nonresident: part-time $1071.31 per credit hour. *Financial support:* Career-related internships or fieldwork, Federal Work-Study, institutionally sponsored loans, tuition waivers (partial), and unspecified assistantships available. Financial award application deadline: 3/1; financial award applicants required to submit FAFSA. *Unit head:* Dr. Robert Everett, Program Coordinator, 407-823-5788, E-mail: robert.everett@ucf.edu. *Application contact:* Assistant Director, Graduate Admissions, 321-823-2766, Fax: 407-823-6442, E-mail: gradadmissions@ucf.edu.
Website: http://education.ucf.edu/elemed/

University of Central Missouri, The Graduate School, Warrensburg, MO 64093. Offers accountancy (MA); accounting (MBA); applied mathematics (MS); aviation safety (MA); biology (MS); business administration (MBA); career and technical education leadership (MS); college student personnel administration (MS); communication (MA); computer science (MS); counseling (MS); criminal justice (MS); educational leadership (Ed D); educational technology (MS); elementary and early childhood education (MSE); English (MA); environmental studies (MA); finance (MBA); history (MA); human services/educational technology (Ed S); human services/learning resources (Ed S); human services/professional counseling (Ed S); industrial hygiene (MS); industrial management (MS); information systems (MBA); information technology (MS); kinesiology (MS); library science and information services (MS); literacy education (MSE); marketing (MBA); mathematics (MS); music (MA); occupational safety management (MS); psychology (MS); rural family nursing (MS); school administration (MSE); social gerontology (MS); sociology (MA); special education (MSE); speech language pathology (MS); superintendency (Ed S); teaching (MAT); teaching English as a second language (MA); technology (MS); technology management (PhD); theatre (MA). *Program availability:* Part-time, 100% online, blended/hybrid learning. *Degree requirements:* For master's and Ed S, comprehensive exam (for some programs), thesis (for some programs). *Entrance requirements:* Additional exam requirements/recommendations for international students: Required—TOEFL (minimum score 550 paper-based; 79 iBT). Electronic applications accepted.

University of Central Oklahoma, The Jackson College of Graduate Studies, College of Education and Professional Studies, Department of Curriculum and Instruction, Edmond, OK 73034-5209. Offers bilingual education/teaching English as a second language (M Ed); early childhood education (M Ed); elementary education (M Ed). *Program availability:* Part-time. *Degree requirements:* For master's, comprehensive exam (for some programs), thesis optional. *Entrance requirements:* For master's, GRE General Test. Additional exam requirements/recommendations for international students: Required—TOEFL (minimum score 550 paper-based; 79 iBT), IELTS (minimum score 6.5). Electronic applications accepted. *Faculty research:* Tourette's syndrome, bilingual education, science education, language development/disorders.

University of Cincinnati, Graduate School, College of Education, Criminal Justice, and Human Services, Division of Teacher Education, Program in Middle Childhood Education, Cincinnati, OH 45221. Offers M Ed. *Accreditation:* NCATE. *Program availability:* Part-time. *Degree requirements:* For master's, thesis or alternative. *Entrance requirements:* For master's, GRE General Test. Additional exam requirements/recommendations for international students: Required—TOEFL (minimum score 550 paper-based), TWE (minimum score 4.5), OEPT. Electronic applications accepted. *Expenses: Tuition, area resident:* Full-time $12,790; part-time $389 per credit hour. Tuition, state resident: full-time $13,290; part-time $419 per credit hour. Tuition, nonresident: full-time $24,532; part-time $976 per credit hour. *International tuition:* $24,832 full-time. *Required fees:* $3958; $140 per credit hour. Tuition and fees vary according to course load, degree level, program and reciprocity agreements.

University of Colorado Denver, School of Education and Human Development, Information and Learning Technologies Program, Denver, CO 80217. Offers e-learning design and implementation (MA); instructional design and adult learning (MA); K-12 teaching (MA). *Program availability:* Part-time, evening/weekend, online learning. *Students:* 68 full-time (56 women), 50 part-time (37 women); includes 16 minority (4 Black or African American, non-Hispanic/Latino; 5 Asian, non-Hispanic/Latino; 5 Hispanic/Latino; 1 Native Hawaiian or other Pacific Islander, non-Hispanic/Latino; 1 Two or more races, non-Hispanic/Latino), 2 international. Average age 38. 24 applicants, 88% accepted, 13 enrolled. In 2016, 45 master's awarded. *Degree requirements:* For master's, comprehensive exam (for some programs), comprehensive exam or online portfolio; 30 credit hours. *Entrance requirements:* For master's, GRE or MAT (if GPA is below 2.75), resume, statement of intent, three letters of recommendation, transcripts from all colleges/universities previously attended. Additional exam requirements/recommendations for international students: Required—TOEFL (minimum score 537 paper-based; 75 iBT); Recommended—IELTS (minimum score 6.5). *Application deadline:* For fall admission, 5/15 for domestic students, 5/1 for international students; for spring admission, 11/15 for domestic students, 11/1 for international students; for summer admission, 3/15 for domestic students, 3/1 for international students. Application fee: $50 ($75 for international students). Electronic applications accepted. *Expenses:* Contact institution. *Financial support:* In 2016–17, 7 students received support. Fellowships, research assistantships, teaching assistantships, Federal Work-Study, institutionally sponsored loans, scholarships/grants, and traineeships available. Financial award application deadline: 4/1; financial award applicants required to submit FAFSA. *Faculty research:* Technology for educational management, instructional design foundations, e-learning, educational design. *Unit head:* Brent Wilson, Professor, 303-720-7765, E-mail: brent.wilson@ucdenver.edu. *Application contact:* 303-315-6300, E-mail: education@ucdenver.edu.
Website: http://www.ucdenver.edu/academics/colleges/SchoolOfEducation/Academics/MASTERS/ILT/Pages/default.aspx

University of Colorado Denver, School of Education and Human Development, Teacher Education Programs, Denver, CO 80217. Offers elementary linguistically diverse education (MA); elementary math and science education (MA); elementary math education (MA); elementary reading and writing (MA); elementary science education (MA); secondary English education (MA); secondary linguistically diverse education (MA); secondary math education (MA); secondary reading and writing (MA); secondary science education (MA); special education (MA). *Accreditation:* NCATE. *Program availability:* Part-time, evening/weekend. *Students:* 142 full-time (117 women), 184 part-time (159 women); includes 56 minority (6 Black or African American, non-Hispanic/Latino; 1 American Indian or Alaska Native, non-Hispanic/Latino; 4 Asian, non-Hispanic/Latino; 38 Hispanic/Latino; 1 Native Hawaiian or other Pacific Islander, non-Hispanic/Latino; 6 Two or more races, non-Hispanic/Latino), 1 international. Average age 30. 18 applicants, 67% accepted, 9 enrolled. In 2016, 134 master's awarded. *Degree requirements:* For master's, comprehensive exam. *Entrance requirements:* For master's, GRE or MAT (for those with GPA below 2.75), transcripts, resume, letters of recommendation. Additional exam requirements/recommendations for international students: Required—TOEFL (minimum score 537 paper-based; 75 iBT); Recommended—IELTS (minimum score 6.5). *Application deadline:* For fall admission, 4/15 for domestic students, 4/1 for international students; for spring admission, 9/15 for domestic students, 9/1 for international students; for summer admission, 2/15 for domestic students, 2/1 for international students. Applications are processed on a rolling basis. Application fee: $50 ($75 for international students). Electronic applications accepted. *Expenses:* Contact institution. *Financial support:* In 2016–17, 26 students received support. Fellowships, research assistantships, teaching assistantships, Federal Work-Study, institutionally sponsored loans, scholarships/grants, and traineeships available. Financial award application deadline: 4/1; financial award applicants required to submit FAFSA. *Faculty research:* Linguistically diverse education/ESL, elementary reading and writing, elementary teacher education, secondary teacher education, special education. *Unit head:* Cindy Gutierrez, Director, 303-315-4982, E-mail: cindy.gutierrez@ucdenver.edu. *Application contact:* 303-315-6300, E-mail: education@ucdenver.edu.
Website: http://www.ucdenver.edu/academics/colleges/SchoolOfEducation/Academics/MASTERS/Pages/default.aspx

University of Connecticut, Graduate School, Neag School of Education, Department of Curriculum and Instruction, Program in Elementary Education, Storrs, CT 06269. Offers MA, PhD. *Accreditation:* NCATE. Terminal master's awarded for partial completion of doctoral program. *Degree requirements:* For master's, comprehensive exam, thesis or alternative; for doctorate, thesis/dissertation. *Entrance requirements:* For doctorate, GRE General Test. Additional exam requirements/recommendations for international students: Required—TOEFL (minimum score 550 paper-based). Electronic applications accepted.

University of Florida, Graduate School, College of Education, School of Teaching and Learning, Gainesville, FL 32611. Offers curriculum and instruction (M Ed, MAE, Ed D, PhD, Ed S); elementary education (M Ed, MAE); English education (M Ed, MAE); mathematics education (M Ed, MAE); reading education (M Ed, MAE); science education (M Ed, MAE); social studies education (M Ed, MAE). *Accreditation:* NCATE. *Program availability:* Part-time, evening/weekend, online learning. Terminal master's awarded for partial completion of doctoral program. *Degree requirements:* For master's, comprehensive exam (for some programs), thesis (for some programs); for doctorate, comprehensive exam (for some programs), thesis/dissertation (for some programs). *Entrance requirements:* For master's and doctorate, GRE General Test, minimum GPA of 3.0; for Ed S, GRE General Test. Additional exam requirements/recommendations for international students: Required—TOEFL (minimum score 550 paper-based; 80 iBT), IELTS (minimum score 6). Electronic applications accepted. *Faculty research:* STEM education; curriculum; teaching and teacher education; languages and literacy; schools, culture, and society; theories and processes of learning.

University of Hartford, College of Education, Nursing, and Health Professions, Program in Elementary and Special Education, West Hartford, CT 06117-1599. Offers elementary education (M Ed). *Accreditation:* NCATE. *Program availability:* Part-time, evening/weekend. *Degree requirements:* For master's, comprehensive exam. *Entrance requirements:* For master's, PRAXIS I or waiver, interview, 2 letters of recommendation. Additional exam requirements/recommendations for international students: Required—TOEFL (minimum score 550 paper-based). Electronic applications accepted.

University of Illinois at Chicago, College of Education, Department of Curriculum and Instruction, Chicago, IL 60607-7128. Offers curriculum studies (PhD); elementary education (M Ed); secondary education (M Ed). *Program availability:* Part-time, evening/weekend. *Degree requirements:* For doctorate, thesis/dissertation. *Entrance requirements:* For master's, minimum GPA of 2.75; for doctorate, GRE General Test, minimum GPA of 2.75. Additional exam requirements/recommendations for international students: Required—TOEFL. Electronic applications accepted. *Faculty research:* Curriculum theory, curriculum development, research on teaching, curriculum and context, reading/literacy.

University of Indianapolis, Graduate Programs, School of Education, Indianapolis, IN 46227-3697. Offers art education (MAT); biology (MAT); chemistry (MAT); curriculum and instruction (MA); earth sciences (MAT); education (MA, MAT); educational leadership (MA); elementary education (MA); English (MAT); French (MAT); math (MAT); physical education (MAT); physics (MAT); secondary education (MA), including art education, education, English education, social studies education; social studies (MAT); Spanish (MAT). *Accreditation:* NCATE. *Program availability:* Part-time, evening/weekend. *Entrance requirements:* For master's, GRE Subject Test, PRAXIS I, minimum GPA of 2.5, 3 letters of recommendation, interview. Additional exam requirements/recommendations for international students: Required—TOEFL (minimum score 550 paper-based). *Faculty research:* Assessment of teacher education, perceptions of prospective teachers by parents.

The University of Iowa, Graduate College, College of Education, Department of Teaching and Learning, Program in Education, Iowa City, IA 52242-1316. Offers art education (MA); developmental reading (MA); elementary education (MA); English education (MA, MAT); foreign and second language education (MAT); foreign language education (MA); foreign language/ESL education (PhD); language, literacy and culture (PhD); mathematics education (MA, MAT, PhD); music education (MM, PhD); science education (MA); secondary education (MA); social studies (MA, PhD). *Degree requirements:* For master's, thesis optional, exam; for doctorate, comprehensive exam, thesis/dissertation. *Entrance requirements:* For master's and doctorate, GRE General Test, minimum GPA of 3.0. Additional exam requirements/recommendations for international students: Required—TOEFL (minimum score 550 paper-based; 81 iBT). Electronic applications accepted.

University of Kentucky, Graduate School, College of Education, Program in Curriculum and Instruction, Lexington, KY 40506-0032. Offers curriculum and instruction (Ed D, PhD); elementary education (MA Ed); instructional system design (MS Ed); literacy (MA Ed); middle school education (MA Ed, MS Ed); secondary education (MA Ed, MS Ed). *Accreditation:* NCATE. *Degree requirements:* For master's, comprehensive exam, thesis optional; for doctorate, comprehensive exam, thesis/dissertation. *Entrance requirements:* For master's, GRE General Test, minimum undergraduate GPA of 2.75; for doctorate, GRE General Test, minimum graduate GPA of 3.0. Additional exam requirements/recommendations for international students: Required—TOEFL (minimum score 550 paper-based). Electronic applications accepted. *Faculty research:* Educational reform, multicultural education, classroom instructional practices, performance based assessment, primary school programs.

University of La Verne, Regional and Online Campuses, Graduate Programs, Central Coast/Vandenberg Air Force Base Campuses, La Verne, CA 91750-4443. Offers business administration for experienced professionals (MBA), including health services management, information technology; education (special emphasis) (M Ed); educational counseling (MS); educational leadership (M Ed); multiple subject (elementary) (Credential); preliminary administrative services (Credential); pupil personnel services (Credential); single subject (secondary) (Credential). *Program availability:* Part-time. *Expenses:* Contact institution.

University of La Verne, Regional and Online Campuses, Graduate Programs, High Desert Campus, Victorville, CA 92392. Offers business administration for experienced professionals (MBA); educational counseling (MS); educational leadership (M Ed); multiple subject (elementary) (Credential); preliminary administrative services (Credential); pupil personnel services (Credential); single subject (secondary) (Credential). *Expenses:* Contact institution.

University of La Verne, Regional and Online Campuses, Graduate Programs, Kern County Campus, Bakersfield, CA 93301. Offers business administration for experienced professionals (MBA-EP); education (special emphasis) (M Ed); educational counseling (MS); educational leadership (M Ed); health administration (MHA); leadership and management (MS); mild/moderate education specialist (Credential); multiple subject (elementary) (Credential); organizational leadership (Ed D); preliminary administrative services (Credential); single subject (secondary) (Credential); special education studies (MS). *Program availability:* Part-time, evening/weekend. *Expenses:* Contact institution.

University of La Verne, Regional and Online Campuses, Graduate Programs, Ventura County/Point Mugu Naval Air Station Campuses, Oxnard, CA 93036. Offers business administration for experienced professionals (MS); educational counseling (MS); educational leadership (M Ed); leadership and management (MS); multiple subject (elementary) (Credential); pupil personnel services (Credential); single subject (secondary) (Credential). *Program availability:* Part-time, evening/weekend. *Expenses:* Contact institution.

University of Louisiana at Monroe, Graduate School, College of Arts, Education, and Sciences, School of Education, Program in Curriculum and Instruction, Monroe, LA 71209-0001. Offers art education (M Ed); biology education (M Ed); chemistry education (M Ed); curriculum and instruction (Ed D); early childhood education (M Ed); earth science education (M Ed); educational leadership (M Ed); elementary education (1-5) (M Ed), English as a second language (M Ed); English education (M Ed); family and consumer education (M Ed); French education (M Ed); history education (M Ed), math education (M Ed); middle school education (M Ed); music education (M Ed); reading education (K-12) (M Ed); Spanish education (M Ed); special education - academically gifted (M Ed); special education - early intervention (M Ed); special education - educational diagnostician (M Ed); special education - mild/moderate disabilities (M Ed); speech education (M Ed). *Accreditation:* NCATE. *Faculty:* 8 full-time (4 women), 4 part-time/adjunct (3 women). *Students:* 13 full-time (11 women), 80 part-time (65 women); includes 25 minority (19 Black or African American, non-Hispanic/Latino; 1 Asian, non-Hispanic/Latino; 3 Hispanic/Latino; 2 Two or more races, non-Hispanic/Latino). Average age 37. 118 applicants, 30% accepted, 16 enrolled. In 2016, 23 master's, 4 doctorates awarded. *Degree requirements:* For master's, comprehensive exam (for some programs), thesis; for doctorate, thesis/dissertation, internships. *Entrance requirements:* For master's, GRE General Test; for doctorate, GRE General Test, minimum undergraduate GPA of 2.75, graduate 3.25. Additional exam requirements/recommendations for international students: Required—TOEFL (minimum score 500 paper-based; 61 iBT). *Application deadline:* For fall admission, 8/24 priority date for domestic students, 7/1 for international students; for winter admission, 12/14 priority date for domestic students; for spring admission, 1/19 for domestic students, 11/1 for international students. Applications are processed on a rolling basis. Application fee:

$20 ($30 for international students). Electronic applications accepted. *Expenses:* Tuition, state resident: full-time $6489. Tuition, nonresident: full-time $18,589. *Required fees:* $8984. Tuition and fees vary according to course level, course load, degree level and program. *Financial support:* Research assistantships, career-related internships or fieldwork, Federal Work-Study, and unspecified assistantships available. Financial award application deadline: 4/1; financial award applicants required to submit FAFSA. *Unit head:* Dr. Dorothy Schween, Director, 318-342-1268, Fax: 318-342-3131, E-mail: schween@ulm.edu.

University of Louisiana at Monroe, Graduate School, College of Arts, Education, and Sciences, School of Education, Program in Elementary Education, Monroe, LA 71209-0001. Offers MAT. *Accreditation:* NCATE. *Program availability:* Part-time, evening/weekend. *Faculty:* 8 full-time (4 women), 4 part-time/adjunct (3 women). *Students:* 12 full-time (all women), 25 part-time (all women); includes 5 minority (3 Black or African American, non-Hispanic/Latino; 2 Two or more races, non-Hispanic/Latino). Average age 33. 64 applicants, 36% accepted, 10 enrolled. In 2016, 19 master's awarded. *Degree requirements:* For master's, thesis optional. *Entrance requirements:* For master's, GRE General Test, minimum GPA of 2.5. Additional exam requirements/recommendations for international students: Required—TOEFL (minimum score 500 paper-based; 61 iBT). *Application deadline:* For fall admission, 8/24 for domestic students, 7/1 for international students; for winter admission, 12/14 priority date for domestic students; for spring admission, 1/19 for domestic students, 11/1 for international students. Applications are processed on a rolling basis. Application fee: $20 ($30 for international students). Electronic applications accepted. *Expenses:* Tuition, state resident: full-time $6489. Tuition, nonresident: full-time $18,589. *Required fees:* $8984. Tuition and fees vary according to course level, course load, degree level and program. *Financial support:* Career-related internships or fieldwork, Federal Work-Study, and unspecified assistantships available. Financial award application deadline: 4/1; financial award applicants required to submit FAFSA. *Faculty research:* Student attitudes. *Unit head:* Dr. Dorothy Schween, Director, 318-342-1268, E-mail: schween@ulm.edu.

University of Louisville, Graduate School, College of Education and Human Development, Department of Teaching and Learning, Louisville, KY 40292-0001. Offers art education (MAT); autism and applied behavior analysis (Certificate); curriculum and instruction (PhD); early elementary education (MAT); exercise physiology (MS); health and physical education (MAT); health professions education (Certificate); higher education (MA); human resources and organization development (MS); instructional technology (M Ed); interdisciplinary early childhood education (MAT); middle school education (MAT); music education (MAT); secondary education (MAT); special education (MAT); sport administration (MS); teacher leadership (M Ed). *Program availability:* Part-time, evening/weekend. *Students:* 116 full-time (68 women), 158 part-time (112 women); includes 46 minority (24 Black or African American, non-Hispanic/Latino; 8 Asian, non-Hispanic/Latino; 5 Hispanic/Latino; 9 Two or more races, non-Hispanic/Latino), 6 international. Average age 30. 114 applicants, 71% accepted, 57 enrolled. In 2016, 59 master's, 3 doctorates awarded. *Application deadline:* For spring admission, 1/1 priority date for international students. Application fee: $60. *Expenses:* Tuition, state resident: full-time $12,246; part-time $681 per credit hour. Tuition, nonresident: full-time $25,486; part-time $1417 per credit hour. *Required fees:* $196. Tuition and fees vary according to program and reciprocity agreements. *Financial support:* Application deadline: 6/1; applicants required to submit FAFSA. *Faculty research:* STEM teaching and learning; content literacy for English language learners; social justice in teacher education; adolescent literacy; mathematics teacher development. *Total annual research expenditures:* $1.7 million. *Unit head:* Dr. Ann E. Larson, Dean, College of Education and Human Development, 502-852-6411, Fax: 502-852-1464, E-mail: ann@louisville.edu. *Application contact:* Betty Hampton, Director of Graduate Student Services, 502-852-5597, Fax: 502-852-1465, E-mail: edadvise@louisville.edu.
Website: http://louisville.edu/delphi

University of Mary Hardin-Baylor, Graduate Studies in Education, Belton, TX 76513. Offers curriculum and instruction (M Ed); educational administration (M Ed, Ed D), including higher education (Ed D), leadership in nursing education (Ed D), P-12 (Ed D). *Program availability:* Part-time, evening/weekend. *Faculty:* 15 full-time (11 women), 9 part-time/adjunct (5 women). *Students:* 55 full-time (40 women), 79 part-time (60 women); includes 50 minority (29 Black or African American, non-Hispanic/Latino; 1 Asian, non-Hispanic/Latino; 18 Hispanic/Latino; 2 Two or more races, non-Hispanic/Latino), 3 international. Average age 38. 20 applicants, 95% accepted, 19 enrolled. In 2016, 23 master's, 19 doctorates awarded. *Degree requirements:* For master's, comprehensive exam; for doctorate, thesis/dissertation. *Entrance requirements:* For master's, minimum GPA of 3.0, interview; for doctorate, minimum GPA of 3.5, interview, essay, resume, employment verification, 3 letters of recommendation. Additional exam requirements/recommendations for international students: Required—TOEFL (minimum score 60 iBT), IELTS (minimum score 4.5). *Application deadline:* For fall admission, 6/1 for domestic students, 4/30 priority date for international students; for spring admission, 11/1 for domestic students, 9/30 priority date for international students. Applications are processed on a rolling basis. Application fee: $35 ($135 for international students). Electronic applications accepted. *Expenses:* $885 per credit hour. *Financial support:* In 2016–17, 99 students received support. Federal Work-Study and scholarships for some active duty military personnel available. Support available to part-time students. Financial award application deadline: 6/1; financial award applicants required to submit FAFSA. *Faculty research:* Motivational orientation of preservice teachers. *Unit head:* Dr. Craig Hammonds, Director, Graduate Programs in Education, 254-295-4189, E-mail: rhammonds@umhb.edu. *Application contact:* Sharon Aguilera, Assistant Director, Graduate Admissions, 254-295-4835, Fax: 254-295-5038, E-mail: saguilera@umhb.edu.
Website: http://graduate.umhb.edu/education/

University of Maryland, Baltimore County, The Graduate School, College of Arts, Humanities and Social Sciences, Department of Education, Program in Teaching, Baltimore, MD 21250. Offers early childhood education (MAT); elementary education (MAT); teaching (MAT), including art, biology, chemistry, choral music, classical foreign language, dance, earth/space science, English, instrumental music, mathematics, modern foreign language, physical science, physics, social studies, theatre. *Program availability:* Part-time, evening/weekend. *Faculty:* 24 full-time (18 women), 25 part-time/adjunct (19 women). *Students:* 41 full-time (34 women), 27 part-time (18 women); includes 26 minority (6 Black or African American, non-Hispanic/Latino; 9 Asian, non-Hispanic/Latino; 7 Hispanic/Latino; 1 Native Hawaiian or other Pacific Islander, non-Hispanic/Latino; 3 Two or more races, non-Hispanic/Latino), 2 international. Average age 30. 54 applicants, 83% accepted, 35 enrolled. In 2016, 50 master's awarded. *Degree requirements:* For master's, comprehensive exam (for some programs), thesis (for some programs). *Entrance requirements:* For master's, PRAXIS Core Examination or GRE (minimum score of 1000), minimum GPA of 3.0. Additional exam requirements/recommendations for international students: Required—TOEFL. *Application deadline:* For fall admission, 6/1 for domestic and international students; for spring admission, 11/1 for domestic and international students. Applications are processed on a rolling basis. Application fee: $50. Electronic applications accepted. *Expenses:* Tuition, state resident: full-time $13,294. Tuition, nonresident: full-time $20,286. *Financial support:* In 2016–17, 8 students received support, including teaching assistantships with tuition reimbursements available (averaging $12,000 per year); career-related internships or fieldwork, Federal Work-Study, scholarships/grants, tuition waivers, and unspecified assistantships also available. Financial award application deadline: 3/15. *Faculty research:* STEM teacher education, culturally sensitive pedagogy, ESOL/bilingual education, early childhood education, language, literacy and culture. *Total annual research expenditures:* $100,000. *Unit head:* Dr. Susan M. Blunck, Graduate Program Director, 410-455-2869, Fax: 410-455-3986, E-mail: blunck@umbc.edu. *Application contact:* Cheryl Johnson, MAT Program Specialist, 410-455-3388, E-mail: blackwel@umbc.edu.
Website: http://www.umbc.edu/education/

University of Mary Washington, College of Education, Fredericksburg, VA 22401. Offers education (M Ed); elementary education (MS). *Program availability:* Part-time, evening/weekend. *Faculty:* 12 full-time (9 women), 18 part-time/adjunct (12 women). *Students:* 102 full-time (90 women), 106 part-time (89 women); includes 34 minority (11 Black or African American, non-Hispanic/Latino; 2 Asian, non-Hispanic/Latino; 12 Hispanic/Latino; 9 Two or more races, non-Hispanic/Latino). Average age 29. 231 applicants, 59% accepted, 79 enrolled. In 2016, 107 master's awarded. *Degree requirements:* For master's, one foreign language, comprehensive exam (for some programs). *Entrance requirements:* For master's, PRAXIS Core Academic Skills for Educators (Reading; Writing; Math or Virginia Department of Education accepted equivalent). Additional exam requirements/recommendations for international students: Required—TOEFL (minimum score 570 paper-based; 88 iBT), IELTS (minimum score 6.5). *Application deadline:* For fall admission, 4/15 for domestic and international students; for spring admission, 9/15 for domestic and international students. Applications are processed on a rolling basis. Application fee: $50. Electronic applications accepted. Application fee is waived when completed online. *Expenses:* Contact institution. *Financial support:* In 2016–17, 29 students received support, including 3 fellowships with partial tuition reimbursements available (averaging $9,000 per year); research assistantships, teaching assistantships, and scholarships/grants also available. Financial award application deadline: 4/25; financial award applicants required to submit FAFSA. *Unit head:* Dr. Marie Sheckels, Dean, 540-654-1334. *Application contact:* Deanna C. Pack, Director of Graduate Admissions, 540-286-8030, Fax: 540-286-8085, E-mail: dpack@umw.edu.
Website: http://www.umw.edu/education/

University of Massachusetts Amherst, Graduate School, College of Education, Program in Education, Amherst, MA 01003. Offers bilingual, English as a second language, and multicultural education (M Ed, Ed S); child study and early education (M Ed); children, families and schools (Ed D, Ed S); early childhood and elementary teacher education (M Ed); educational leadership (M Ed); educational policy and leadership (Ed D); higher education (M Ed); international education (M Ed); language, literacy and culture (Ed D); learning, media and technology (M Ed, Ed S); mathematics, science, and learning technologies (Ed D); reading and writing (M Ed); research, educational measurement and psychometrics (Ed D); school counselor education (M Ed, Ed S); school psychology (Ed S); science education (Ed S); secondary teacher education (M Ed); social justice education (M Ed, Ed D, Ed S); special education (M Ed, Ed D, Ed S); teacher education and school improvement (Ed D, Ed S). *Accreditation:* NCATE. *Program availability:* Part-time, online learning. Terminal master's awarded for partial completion of doctoral program. *Degree requirements:* For doctorate, comprehensive exam, thesis/dissertation. *Entrance requirements:* Additional exam requirements/recommendations for international students: Required—TOEFL (minimum score 550 paper-based; 80 iBT), IELTS (minimum score 6.5). Electronic applications accepted.

University of Memphis, Graduate School, College of Education, Department of Instruction and Curriculum Leadership, Memphis, TN 38152. Offers advanced studies in teaching and learning (M Ed); applied behavior analysis (Graduate Certificate); autism studies (Graduate Certificate); early childhood education (MAT, MS, Ed D); elementary education (MAT); instruction and curriculum (MS, Ed D); instruction design and technology (MS, Ed D); instructional design and technology (Graduate Certificate); literacy, leadership, and coaching (Graduate Certificate); reading (MS, Ed D); school library information specialist (Graduate Certificate); secondary education (MAT); special education (MAT, MS, Ed D); STEM teacher leadership (Graduate Certificate); urban education (Graduate Certificate). *Accreditation:* NCATE (one or more programs are accredited). *Program availability:* Part-time. *Faculty:* 24 full-time (14 women), 17 part-time/adjunct (12 women). *Students:* 66 full-time (52 women), 315 part-time (243 women); includes 163 minority (132 Black or African American, non-Hispanic/Latino; 1 American Indian or Alaska Native, non-Hispanic/Latino; 6 Asian, non-Hispanic/Latino; 13 Hispanic/Latino; 1 Native Hawaiian or other Pacific Islander, non-Hispanic/Latino; 10 Two or more races, non-Hispanic/Latino), 4 international. Average age 35. 215 applicants, 78% accepted, 120 enrolled. In 2016, 111 master's, 21 doctorates, 8 other advanced degrees awarded. Terminal master's awarded for partial completion of doctoral program. *Degree requirements:* For master's, comprehensive exam, thesis or alternative; for doctorate, comprehensive exam, thesis/dissertation. *Entrance requirements:* For master's, GRE General Test, PRAXIS, minimum GPA of 2.5, letters of reference; for doctorate, GRE General Test, GRE Subject Test, 2 years of teaching experience, letters of reference, statement of purpose, interview. Additional exam requirements/recommendations for international students: Required—TOEFL (minimum score 550 paper-based; 79 iBT). *Application deadline:* For fall admission, 4/1 priority date for domestic students; for spring admission, 10/1 priority date for domestic students; for summer admission, 2/1 priority date for domestic students. Applications are processed on a rolling basis. Application fee: $35 ($60 for international students). Electronic applications accepted. *Expenses:* $5,231.50 per semester full-time in-state, $9,623.50 full-time out-of-state. *Financial support:* In 2016–17, 2 research assistantships with full tuition reimbursements (averaging $10,000 per year), 3 teaching assistantships with full tuition reimbursements (averaging $10,666 per year) were awarded; career-related internships or fieldwork, Federal Work-Study, institutionally sponsored loans, scholarships/grants, traineeships, and unspecified assistantships also available. Support available to part-time students. Financial award application deadline: 2/1; financial award applicants required to submit FAFSA. *Faculty research:* Effective urban teachers, preparation and retention of urban teachers, technology utilization in schools, field-based teacher preparation programs, effective use of online instruction. *Unit head:* Dr. Angiline Powell, Interim Chair, 901-678-3310, E-mail: apowell3@memphis.edu. *Application contact:* Dr. James Meindl, Coordinator of Graduate Studies, 901-678-3310, E-mail: jnmeindl@memphis.edu.
Website: http://www.memphis.edu/icl/

University of Minnesota, Twin Cities Campus, Graduate School, College of Education and Human Development, Department of Curriculum and Instruction, Program in Teaching, Minneapolis, MN 55455-0213. Offers teaching (M Ed), including arts in education, elementary education, English education, mathematics, science, second language education, social studies. *Students:* 237 full-time (169 women), 171 part-time (112 women); includes 91 minority (23 Black or African American, non-Hispanic/Latino; 3 American Indian or Alaska Native, non-Hispanic/Latino; 19 Asian, non-Hispanic/Latino; 25 Hispanic/Latino; 21 Two or more races, non-Hispanic/Latino), 10 international. Average age 27. 421 applicants, 72% accepted, 275 enrolled. In 2016,

584 master's awarded. Application fee: $75 ($95 for international students). *Unit head:* Dr. Cynthia Lewis, Chair, 612-625-6313, Fax: 612-624-8277, E-mail: lewis@umn.edu. *Application contact:* Dr. Kendall King, Director of Graduate Studies, 612-625-3692, E-mail: roehr013@umn.edu.
Website: http://www.cehd.umn.edu/ci/

University of Missouri, Office of Research and Graduate Studies, College of Education, Department of Learning, Teaching and Curriculum, Columbia, MO 65211. Offers agricultural education (M Ed, PhD, Ed S); art education (M Ed, PhD, Ed S); business and office education (M Ed, PhD, Ed S); early childhood education (M Ed, PhD, Ed S); elementary education (M Ed, PhD, Ed S); English education (M Ed, PhD, Ed S); foreign language education (M Ed, PhD, Ed S); health education and promotion (M Ed, PhD); learning and instruction (M Ed); marketing education (M Ed, PhD, Ed S); mathematics education (M Ed, PhD, Ed S); music education (M Ed, PhD, Ed S); reading education (M Ed, PhD, Ed S); science education (M Ed, PhD, Ed S); social studies education (M Ed, PhD, Ed S); vocational education (M Ed, PhD, Ed S). *Program availability:* Part-time. *Faculty:* 30 full-time (18 women), 1 (woman) part-time/adjunct. *Students:* 157 full-time (124 women), 157 part-time (125 women). Terminal master's awarded for partial completion of doctoral program. *Degree requirements:* For doctorate, thesis/dissertation. *Entrance requirements:* For master's and Ed S, GRE General Test or MAT, minimum GPA of 3.0; for doctorate, GRE General Test, minimum GPA of 3.0. Additional exam requirements/recommendations for international students: Required—TOEFL (minimum score 600 paper-based; 100 iBT). *Application deadline:* For fall admission, 12/1 priority date for domestic and international students. Applications are processed on a rolling basis. Application fee: $75 ($90 for international students). Electronic applications accepted. *Expenses:* Tuition, state resident: full-time $6347; part-time $352.60 per credit hour. Tuition, nonresident: full-time $17,379; part-time $965.50 per credit hour. *Required fees:* $1035. Tuition and fees vary according to course load, campus/location and program. *Financial support:* Fellowships, research assistantships, teaching assistantships, institutionally sponsored loans, traineeships, health care benefits, and unspecified assistantships available. Support available to part-time students.
Website: http://education.missouri.edu/LTC/index.php

University of Missouri–St. Louis, College of Education, Department of Counseling and Family Therapy, St. Louis, MO 63121. Offers clinical mental health counseling (M Ed); counseling (PhD); elementary school counseling (M Ed); secondary school counseling (M Ed). *Accreditation:* ACA; NCATE. *Program availability:* Part-time, evening/weekend. *Faculty:* 8 full-time (4 women), 7 part-time/adjunct (6 women). *Students:* 58 full-time (48 women), 164 part-time (129 women); includes 61 minority (48 Black or African American, non-Hispanic/Latino; 2 American Indian or Alaska Native, non-Hispanic/Latino; 3 Asian, non-Hispanic/Latino; 4 Hispanic/Latino; 4 Two or more races, non-Hispanic/Latino), 4 international. Average age 32. 74 applicants, 72% accepted, 44 enrolled. *Degree requirements:* For master's, comprehensive exam. *Entrance requirements:* For master's, 3 letters of recommendation; for doctorate, GRE General Test, 3 letters of recommendation. Additional exam requirements/recommendations for international students: Recommended—TOEFL (minimum score 550 paper-based; 79 iBT), IELTS (minimum score 6.5). *Application deadline:* For fall admission, 5/1 for domestic and international students; for spring admission, 10/1 for domestic and international students. Application fee: $50 ($40 for international students). Electronic applications accepted. *Financial support:* Teaching assistantships with tuition reimbursements available. Financial award application deadline: 4/1; financial award applicants required to submit FAFSA. *Faculty research:* Vocational interests, self-concept, decision-making factors, developmental differences. *Unit head:* Dr. Mark Pope, Chair, 314-516-5782. *Application contact:* 314-516-5458, Fax: 314-516-6996, E-mail: gradadm@umsl.edu.

University of Missouri–St. Louis, College of Education, Department of Educator Preparation, Innovation and Research, St. Louis, MO 63121. Offers elementary education (M Ed), including early childhood, general, reading; secondary education (M Ed), including curriculum and instruction, general, middle level education, reading, teaching English to speakers of other languages (TESOL); special education (M Ed), including autism and developmental disabilities, early childhood special education. *Program availability:* Part-time, evening/weekend. *Faculty:* 26 full-time (14 women), 22 part-time/adjunct (14 women). *Students:* 151 full-time (127 women), 728 part-time (564 women); includes 222 minority (165 Black or African American, non-Hispanic/Latino; 1 American Indian or Alaska Native, non-Hispanic/Latino; 16 Asian, non-Hispanic/Latino; 31 Hispanic/Latino; 1 Native Hawaiian or other Pacific Islander, non-Hispanic/Latino; 8 Two or more races, non-Hispanic/Latino), 6 international. Average age 29. 363 applicants, 84% accepted, 211 enrolled. *Degree requirements:* For master's, comprehensive exam. *Entrance requirements:* Additional exam requirements/recommendations for international students: Recommended—TOEFL (minimum score 550 paper-based; 79 iBT), IELTS (minimum score 6.5). *Application deadline:* For fall admission, 7/1 priority date for domestic and international students; for spring admission, 12/1 priority date for domestic and international students. Application fee: $50 ($40 for international students). Electronic applications accepted. *Financial support:* Application deadline: 4/1; applicants required to submit FAFSA. *Unit head:* Dr. Gayle Wilkinson, Chair, 314-516-5791. *Application contact:* 314-516-5458, Fax: 314-516-6996, E-mail: gadadm@umsl.edu.
Website: https://coe.umsl.edu/dept/epir.html

University of Montevallo, College of Education, Program in Elementary Education, Montevallo, AL 35115. Offers M Ed. *Accreditation:* NCATE. *Program availability:* Part-time. *Students:* 9 full-time (all women), 22 part-time (20 women); includes 4 minority (3 Black or African American, non-Hispanic/Latino; 1 Asian, non-Hispanic/Latino). In 2016, 21 master's awarded. *Degree requirements:* For master's, comprehensive exam. *Entrance requirements:* For master's, GRE General Test, MAT, minimum undergraduate GPA of 2.5. Additional exam requirements/recommendations for international students: Required—TOEFL (minimum score 550 paper-based). *Application deadline:* For fall admission, 7/15 for domestic students; for spring admission, 11/15 for domestic students. Application fee: $25. *Expenses:* Tuition, state resident: full-time $9936. Tuition, nonresident: full-time $20,592. *Required fees:* $640. *Financial support:* Federal Work-Study, scholarships/grants, and unspecified assistantships available. *Unit head:* Dr. Anna E. McEwan, Dean, 205-665-6360, E-mail: mcewanae@montevallo.edu. *Application contact:* Kevin Thornthwaite, Director, Graduate Admissions and Records, 205-665-6350, E-mail: graduate@montevallo.edu.
Website: http://www.montevallo.edu/education/college-of-education/traditional-masters-degrees/elementary-secondary-p-12-education/

University of Nebraska at Kearney, College of Education, Department of Teacher Education, Kearney, NE 68849-0001. Offers curriculum and instruction (MA Ed), including early childhood education, elementary education, English as a second language, instructional effectiveness, reading/special education, secondary education; instructional technology (MS Ed), including information technology, instructional technology, school librarian; reading PK-12 (MA Ed); special education (MA Ed), including advanced practitioner: assistive technology specialist, advanced practitioner: behavioral interventionist, advanced practitioner: inclusive collaboration specialist, gifted, teacher education. *Program availability:* Part-time, evening/weekend, online only, 100% online. *Faculty:* 18 full-time (13 women). *Students:* 21 full-time (15 women), 296 part-time (240 women); includes 21 minority (3 Black or African American, non-Hispanic/Latino; 1 Asian, non-Hispanic/Latino; 14 Hispanic/Latino; 1 Native Hawaiian or other Pacific Islander, non-Hispanic/Latino; 2 Two or more races, non-Hispanic/Latino), 1 international. Average age 32. 81 applicants, 100% accepted, 61 enrolled. In 2016, 129 master's awarded. *Degree requirements:* For master's, comprehensive exam, thesis optional. *Entrance requirements:* For master's, portfolio or GRE. Additional exam requirements/recommendations for international students: Recommended—TOEFL (minimum score 550 paper-based; 79 iBT), IELTS (minimum score 6.5). *Application deadline:* For fall admission, 6/15 for domestic students, 5/15 for international students; for spring admission, 10/15 for domestic and international students; for summer admission, 3/15 for domestic and international students. Application fee: $45. Electronic applications accepted. *Expenses:* $285 per credit hour resident tuition, $415 per credit hour non-resident tuition (online). *Financial support:* In 2016–17, 6 students received support, including 6 research assistantships with full tuition reimbursements available (averaging $10,500 per year); career-related internships or fieldwork, scholarships/grants, health care benefits, and unspecified assistantships also available. Support available to part-time students. Financial award application deadline: 2/28; financial award applicants required to submit FAFSA. *Unit head:* Sarah Bartling, Administrative Assistant, 308-865-8513, E-mail: bartlingseg@unk.edu. *Application contact:* Linda Johnson, Director, Graduate Admissions and Programs, 308-865-8841, Fax: 308-865-8837, E-mail: johnsonli@unk.edu.
Website: http://www.unk.edu/academics/ted/index.php

University of Nebraska at Omaha, Graduate Studies, College of Education, Department of Teacher Education, Program in Elementary Education, Omaha, NE 68182. Offers MS. *Accreditation:* NCATE. *Program availability:* Part-time, evening/weekend. *Faculty:* 8 full-time (all women). *Students:* 9 full-time (all women), 113 part-time (107 women); includes 8 minority (2 Black or African American, non-Hispanic/Latino; 2 Asian, non-Hispanic/Latino; 3 Hispanic/Latino; 1 Two or more races, non-Hispanic/Latino), 1 international. Average age 34. 31 applicants, 74% accepted, 22 enrolled. In 2016, 43 master's awarded. *Degree requirements:* For master's, comprehensive exam (for some programs), thesis (for some programs). *Entrance requirements:* For master's, minimum GPA of 3.0, transcripts. Additional exam requirements/recommendations for international students: Required—TOEFL, IELTS, PTE. *Application deadline:* For fall admission, 8/1 priority date for domestic and international students; for spring admission, 12/1 priority date for domestic and international students; for summer admission, 6/1 for domestic and international students. Applications are processed on a rolling basis. Application fee: $45. Electronic applications accepted. *Financial support:* In 2016–17, 3 students received support, including 3 research assistantships with tuition reimbursements available; fellowships, teaching assistantships with tuition reimbursements available, Federal Work-Study, institutionally sponsored loans, scholarships/grants, health care benefits, tuition waivers (full), and unspecified assistantships also available. Support available to part-time students. Financial award application deadline: 3/1. *Unit head:* Dr. Sarah Edwards, Chairperson, 402-554-2341, E-mail: graduate@unomaha.edu. *Application contact:* Dr. Kathleen Danielson, Graduate Program Chair, 402-554-2341, E-mail: graduate@unomaha.edu.

University of Nevada, Las Vegas, Graduate College, College of Education, Department of Teaching and Learning, Las Vegas, NV 89154-3005. Offers curriculum and instruction (M Ed, MS, Ed D, PhD, Ed S), including teacher education (PhD); elementary teaching (Certificate); online teaching and training (Certificate); secondary teaching (Certificate); social justice studies (Certificate); teaching and learning (PhD). *Program availability:* Part-time, evening/weekend. *Faculty:* 26 full-time (12 women), 10 part-time/adjunct (8 women). *Students:* 280 full-time (202 women), 206 part-time (131 women); includes 188 minority (51 Black or African American, non-Hispanic/Latino; 4 American Indian or Alaska Native, non-Hispanic/Latino; 23 Asian, non-Hispanic/Latino; 72 Hispanic/Latino; 4 Native Hawaiian or other Pacific Islander, non-Hispanic/Latino; 34 Two or more races, non-Hispanic/Latino), 18 international. Average age 35. 178 applicants, 89% accepted, 142 enrolled. In 2016, 156 master's, 14 doctorates, 1 other advanced degree awarded. *Degree requirements:* For master's, comprehensive exam (for some programs), thesis (for some programs); for doctorate, comprehensive exam, thesis/dissertation, defense of dissertation; for other advanced degree, comprehensive exam (for some programs), oral presentation of special project or professional paper. *Entrance requirements:* For master's, bachelor's degree with minimum GPA 2.75; for doctorate, GRE General Test, master's degree with minimum GPA of 3.0; statement of purpose; demonstration of oral communication skills; 3 letters of recommendation; for other advanced degree, PRAXIS Core (for some programs); PRAXIS II (for some programs), bachelor's degree (for some programs). Additional exam requirements/recommendations for international students: Required—TOEFL (minimum score 550 paper-based; 80 iBT), IELTS (minimum score 7). *Application deadline:* For fall admission, 6/1 for domestic students, 5/1 for international students; for spring admission, 11/1 for domestic students, 10/1 for international students; for summer admission, 3/15 for domestic students. Application fee: $60 ($95 for international students). Electronic applications accepted. *Expenses:* $269.25 per credit, $792 per 3-credit course; $9,634 per year resident; $23,274 per year non-resident; $7,094 fees non-resident (7 credits or more); $1,307 annual health insurance fee. *Financial support:* In 2016–17, 8 research assistantships with partial tuition reimbursements (averaging $16,719 per year), 28 teaching assistantships with partial tuition reimbursements (averaging $17,023 per year) were awarded; institutionally sponsored loans, scholarships/grants, health care benefits, and unspecified assistantships also available. Financial award application deadline: 3/15. *Faculty research:* Content area and critical literacy, education in content areas, teacher education, STEM education, technology education. *Total annual research expenditures:* $652,413. *Unit head:* Dr. Emily Lin, Chair/Professor, 702-895-6407, Fax: 702-895-4898, E-mail: emily.lin@unlv.edu. *Application contact:* Dr. Travis Olson, Graduate Coordinator, 702-895-0471, Fax: 702-895-4000, E-mail: travis.olson@unlv.edu.
Website: http://tl.unlv.edu/

University of Nevada, Reno, Graduate School, College of Education, Department of Curriculum, Teaching and Learning, Program in Elementary Education, Reno, NV 89557. Offers M Ed, MA, MS. *Degree requirements:* For master's, thesis optional. *Entrance requirements:* For master's, GRE General Test, minimum GPA of 2.75. Additional exam requirements/recommendations for international students: Required—TOEFL (minimum score 500 paper-based; 61 iBT), IELTS (minimum score 6). Electronic applications accepted. *Faculty research:* Child development, educational trends.

University of New Hampshire, Graduate School, College of Liberal Arts, Department of Education, Program in Elementary Education, Durham, NH 03824. Offers M Ed. *Program availability:* Part-time. *Degree requirements:* For master's, thesis or alternative. *Entrance requirements:* For master's, GRE General Test. Additional exam requirements/recommendations for international students: Required—TOEFL (minimum score 550 paper-based; 80 iBT). *Application deadline:* For fall admission, 4/1 priority date for domestic students, 4/1 for international students; for spring admission, 11/1 for domestic students. Applications are processed on a rolling basis. Application fee: $65. Electronic applications accepted. *Financial support:* Fellowships, research assistantships, teaching assistantships, career-related internships or fieldwork, Federal Work-Study,

scholarships/grants, and tuition waivers (full and partial) available. Support available to part-time students. Financial award application deadline: 2/15. *Faculty research:* Pre-service teacher education. *Unit head:* Leslie Couse, Chair, 603-862-0638, E-mail: education.department@unh.edu. *Application contact:* Lisa Wilder, Administrative Assistant, 603-862-2381, E-mail: education.department@unh.edu.
Website: http://cola.unh.edu/education

University of New Hampshire, Graduate School Manchester Campus, Manchester, NH 03101. Offers business administration (MBA); educational administration and supervision (Ed S); educational studies (M Ed); elementary teacher education (M Ed); information technology (MS); public administration (MPA); public health (MPH, Certificate); secondary teacher education (M Ed, MAT); social work (MSW); substance use disorders (Certificate). *Program availability:* Part-time, evening/weekend. *Degree requirements:* For master's, thesis or alternative. *Entrance requirements:* Additional exam requirements/recommendations for international students: Required—TOEFL (minimum score 550 paper-based; 80 iBT). Electronic applications accepted.

University of New Mexico, Graduate Studies, College of Education, Program in Elementary Education, Albuquerque, NM 87131-2039. Offers math, science, and educational technology (MA). *Program availability:* Part-time. *Faculty:* 9 full-time (all women), 2 part-time/adjunct (both women). *Students:* 16 full-time (14 women), 62 part-time (54 women); includes 43 minority (2 Black or African American, non-Hispanic/Latino; 11 American Indian or Alaska Native, non-Hispanic/Latino; 2 Asian, non-Hispanic/Latino; 26 Hispanic/Latino; 2 Two or more races, non-Hispanic/Latino). Average age 33. 39 applicants, 79% accepted, 26 enrolled. In 2016, 71 master's awarded. *Degree requirements:* For master's, comprehensive exam, thesis optional. *Entrance requirements:* For master's, minimum overall GPA of 3.0, some experience working with students, NMTA or teacher's license, 3 letters of reference, letter of intent. Additional exam requirements/recommendations for international students: Required—TOEFL (minimum score 550 paper-based). *Application deadline:* For fall admission, 2/15 for domestic students; for spring admission, 10/1 for domestic students. Application fee: $50. Electronic applications accepted. *Financial support:* Fellowships, career-related internships or fieldwork, scholarships/grants, and unspecified assistantships available. Financial award application deadline: 4/15; financial award applicants required to submit FAFSA. *Faculty research:* Elementary education, science education, technology education, reflective practice, teacher education. *Unit head:* Dr. Cheryl Torrez, Chair, 505-277-0911, Fax: 505-277-0455, E-mail: ted@unm.edu. *Application contact:* Lea Briggs, Administrative Assistant, 505-277-9439, Fax: 505-277-0455, E-mail: ted@unm.edu.
Website: http://coe.unm.edu/departments-programs/teelp/elementary-education/index.html

University of North Alabama, College of Education, Department of Elementary Education, Program in Elementary Education, Florence, AL 35632-0001. Offers MA Ed, Ed S. *Accreditation:* NCATE. *Program availability:* Part-time. *Faculty:* 5 full-time (all women), 1 part-time/adjunct (0 women). *Students:* 4 full-time (all women), 57 part-time (56 women); includes 4 minority (3 Black or African American, non-Hispanic/Latino; 1 American Indian or Alaska Native, non-Hispanic/Latino). Average age 33. 24 applicants, 92% accepted, 14 enrolled. In 2016, 30 master's, 1 Ed S awarded. *Degree requirements:* For master's, comprehensive exam. *Entrance requirements:* For master's, GRE, MAT, or NTE, minimum GPA of 2.5, Alabama Class B Certificate or equivalent, teaching experience. Additional exam requirements/recommendations for international students: Required—TOEFL (minimum score 79 iBT), IELTS (minimum score 6), PTE (minimum score 54). *Application deadline:* Applications are processed on a rolling basis. Application fee: $50 ($100 for international students). Electronic applications accepted. *Expenses:* Tuition, state resident: full-time $2799; part-time $1866 per semester. Tuition, nonresident: full-time $5598; part-time $3732 per semester. *Required fees:* $915; $642 per semester. Tuition and fees vary according to course load. *Financial support:* In 2016–17, 3 students received support. Scholarships/grants available. Financial award application deadline: 2/1; financial award applicants required to submit FAFSA. *Unit head:* Dr. Donna Lefort, Dean, College of Education and Human Sciences, 256-765-4252, E-mail: dpjacobs@una.edu. *Application contact:* Hillary N. Coats, Graduate Admissions Coordinator, 256-765-4447, E-mail: graduate@una.edu.

The University of North Carolina at Charlotte, Cato College of Education, Department of Reading and Elementary Education, Charlotte, NC 28223-0001. Offers elementary education (M Ed, Graduate Certificate); elementary mathematics education (Graduate Certificate); reading education (M Ed). *Program availability:* Part-time, evening/weekend, 100% online, blended/hybrid learning. *Faculty:* 25 full-time (13 women), 3 part-time/adjunct (all women). *Students:* 5 full-time (all women), 72 part-time (69 women); includes 13 minority (8 Black or African American, non-Hispanic/Latino; 4 Hispanic/Latino; 1 Two or more races, non-Hispanic/Latino), 1 international. Average age 30. 55 applicants, 98% accepted, 51 enrolled. In 2016, 24 master's awarded. *Degree requirements:* For master's, thesis or alternative, capstone project. *Entrance requirements:* For master's, GRE or MAT, three letters of recommendation, official transcripts, academic and professional goals statement, valid teacher's license, bachelor's degree in elementary education; NC A-level license or its equivalent in another state (for reading education). Additional exam requirements/recommendations for international students: Required—TOEFL (minimum score 523 paper-based, 70 iBT) or IELTS (6.5). *Application deadline:* For fall admission, 3/1 priority date for domestic students, 3/1 for international students; for spring admission, 10/1 priority date for domestic students, 10/1 for international students; for summer admission, 4/1 priority date for domestic students, 4/1 for international students. Applications are processed on a rolling basis. Application fee: $75. Electronic applications accepted. *Expenses:* Tuition, state resident: full-time $4252. Tuition, nonresident: full-time $17,423. *Required fees:* $3026. Tuition and fees vary according to course load and program. *Financial support:* In 2016–17, 4 students received support, including 4 research assistantships (averaging $16,437 per year); career-related internships or fieldwork, institutionally sponsored loans, scholarships/grants, and unspecified assistantships also available. Support available to part-time students. Financial award application deadline: 3/1; financial award applicants required to submit FAFSA. *Total annual research expenditures:* $44,142. *Unit head:* Dr. Mike Putman, Chair, 704-687-8019, E-mail: michael.putman@uncc.edu. *Application contact:* Kathy B. Giddings, Director of Graduate Admissions, 704-687-5503, Fax: 704-687-1668, E-mail: gradadm@uncc.edu.
Website: http://reel.uncc.edu/

The University of North Carolina at Greensboro, Graduate School, School of Education, Department of Teacher Education and Higher Education, Program in Curriculum and Teaching, Greensboro, NC 27412-5001. Offers higher education (PhD); teacher education and development (PhD). *Accreditation:* NCATE. *Degree requirements:* For doctorate, comprehensive exam, thesis/dissertation. *Entrance requirements:* For doctorate, GRE General Test. Additional exam requirements/recommendations for international students: Required—TOEFL. Electronic applications accepted.

The University of North Carolina at Pembroke, The Graduate School, School of Education, Program in Elementary Education, Pembroke, NC 28372-1510. Offers MA Ed. *Accreditation:* NCATE. *Program availability:* Part-time, evening/weekend, online learning. *Degree requirements:* For master's, comprehensive exam, thesis optional. *Entrance requirements:* For master's, GRE General Test or MAT, minimum GPA of 3.0 in major, 2.5 overall; teaching license; two years of full-time teaching experience (recommended). Additional exam requirements/recommendations for international students: Required—TOEFL.

The University of North Carolina Wilmington, Watson College of Education, Department of Early Childhood, Elementary, Middle, Literacy and Special Education, Wilmington, NC 28403-3297. Offers educational leadership, policy, and advocacy (M Ed); elementary education (M Ed, MAT); language and literacy (M Ed); middle grades education (M Ed, MAT). *Accreditation:* NCATE. *Program availability:* Part-time. *Faculty:* 26 full-time (19 women). *Students:* 121 full-time (89 women), 139 part-time (135 women); includes 70 minority (47 Black or African American, non-Hispanic/Latino; 1 Asian, non-Hispanic/Latino; 14 Hispanic/Latino; 8 Two or more races, non-Hispanic/Latino). Average age 34. 109 applicants, 78% accepted, 65 enrolled. In 2016, 83 master's awarded. *Degree requirements:* For master's, comprehensive exam, capstone experience. *Entrance requirements:* For master's, GRE General Test, MAT, minimum GPA of 3.0 in undergraduate work, 3 letters of recommendations, NC Class A teacher license in related field, statement of interest. *Application deadline:* For fall admission, 5/15 for domestic students; for spring admission, 10/15 for domestic students; for summer admission, 3/15 for domestic students. Applications are processed on a rolling basis. Application fee: $60. Electronic applications accepted. *Expenses:* Contact institution. *Financial support:* Scholarships/grants and unspecified assistantships available. Support available to part-time students. Financial award application deadline: 3/15; financial award applicants required to submit FAFSA. *Unit head:* Dr. Kathy Fox, Chair, 910-962-3240, Fax: 910-962-3988, E-mail: foxk@uncw.edu. *Application contact:* Dr. Elizabeth Crawford, Graduate Program Coordinator, 910-962-2916, Fax: 910-962-3988, E-mail: crawforde@uncw.edu.
Website: http://www.uncw.edu/ed/eemls/index.html

University of North Dakota, Graduate School, College of Education and Human Development, Program in Elementary Education, Grand Forks, ND 58202. Offers M Ed, MS. *Accreditation:* NCATE. *Program availability:* Part-time, online learning. *Degree requirements:* For master's, comprehensive exam, thesis or alternative. *Entrance requirements:* For master's, minimum GPA of 3.0. Additional exam requirements/recommendations for international students: Required—TOEFL (minimum score 550 paper-based; 79 iBT), IELTS (minimum score 6.5). *Application deadline:* For fall admission, 8/1 priority date for domestic students, 5/1 priority date for international students; for spring admission, 12/1 priority date for domestic students, 9/1 priority date for international students. Applications are processed on a rolling basis. Application fee: $35. Electronic applications accepted. *Financial support:* Fellowships with full and partial tuition reimbursements, research assistantships with full tuition reimbursements, teaching assistantships with full and partial tuition reimbursements, career-related internships or fieldwork, Federal Work-Study, institutionally sponsored loans, scholarships/grants, health care benefits, tuition waivers (full and partial), and unspecified assistantships available. Support available to part-time students. Financial award application deadline: 3/15; financial award applicants required to submit FAFSA. *Faculty research:* Whole language, multicultural education, child-focused learning, experiential science, cooperative learning. *Unit head:* Dr. Mary Baker, Graduate Director, 701-777-6759, Fax: 701-777-4393, E-mail: mary.baker@und.edu. *Application contact:* Staci Wells, Admissions Associate, 701-777-2945, Fax: 701-777-3619, E-mail: staci.wells@gradschool.und.edu.
Website: http://www.und.edu/dept/tl/elemed/

University of Northern Colorado, Graduate School, College of Education and Behavioral Sciences, School of Teacher Education, Greeley, CO 80639. Offers curriculum studies (MAT); educational studies (Ed D); elementary education (MAT); English education (MAT); literacy (MA); multilingual education (MA), including TESOL, world languages; teaching diverse learners (MA). *Accreditation:* NCATE. *Program availability:* Part-time, evening/weekend. *Degree requirements:* For master's, comprehensive exam, thesis or alternative; for doctorate, comprehensive exam, thesis/dissertation. *Entrance requirements:* For master's and doctorate, GRE General Test, 3 letters of recommendation. *Application deadline:* Applications are processed on a rolling basis. Application fee: $50 ($60 for international students). Electronic applications accepted. *Financial support:* Fellowships, research assistantships, teaching assistantships, and unspecified assistantships available. Financial award application deadline: 3/1; financial award applicants required to submit FAFSA. *Unit head:* Dr. Alexander Sidorkin, Director, 970-351-2908, Fax: 970-351-1877. *Application contact:* Linda Sisson, Graduate Student Admission Coordinator, 970-351-1807, Fax: 970-351-2371, E-mail: linda.sisson@unco.edu.
Website: http://www.unco.edu/cebs/teachered/

University of Northern Iowa, Graduate College, College of Education, Department of Curriculum and Instruction, MAE Program in Elementary Education, Cedar Falls, IA 50614. Offers MAE. *Program availability:* Part-time, evening/weekend. *Degree requirements:* For master's, comprehensive exam, thesis or alternative. *Entrance requirements:* For master's, minimum GPA of 3.0. Additional exam requirements/recommendations for international students: Required—TOEFL (minimum score 500 paper-based; 61 iBT).

University of North Florida, College of Education and Human Services, Department of Childhood Education, Literacy, and TESOL, Jacksonville, FL 32224. Offers literacy (M Ed); professional education (M Ed); TESOL (M Ed). *Accreditation:* NCATE. *Program availability:* Part-time, evening/weekend. *Faculty:* 10 full-time (8 women). *Students:* 9 full-time (7 women), 27 part-time (all women); includes 14 minority (7 Black or African American, non-Hispanic/Latino; 2 Asian, non-Hispanic/Latino; 2 Hispanic/Latino; 3 Two or more races, non-Hispanic/Latino), 2 international. Average age 31. 34 applicants, 50% accepted, 12 enrolled. In 2016, 22 master's awarded. *Entrance requirements:* For master's, GRE General Test, minimum GPA of 3.0 in last 60 hours, 3 letters of recommendation, interview. Additional exam requirements/recommendations for international students: Required—TOEFL (minimum score 500 paper-based). *Application deadline:* For fall admission, 8/1 priority date for domestic students, 5/1 for international students; for spring admission, 12/1 priority date for domestic students, 10/1 for international students; for summer admission, 3/15 priority date for domestic students, 2/1 for international students. Application fee: $30. Electronic applications accepted. Tuition and fees vary according to course load, campus/location and program. *Financial support:* In 2016–17, 3 students received support. Research assistantships, Federal Work-Study, tuition waivers (partial), and unspecified assistantships available. Support available to part-time students. Financial award application deadline: 4/1; financial award applicants required to submit FAFSA. *Faculty research:* Social context of and processes in learning, inter-disciplinary instruction, cross-cultural conflict resolution, the Vygotskian perspective on literacy diagnosis and instruction, performance poetry and teaching the language arts through drama. *Total annual research expenditures:* $2,531. *Unit head:* Dr. Paul Parkison, Chair, 904-620-5352, Fax: 904-620-1025, E-mail: n01230143@unf.edu. *Application contact:* Dr. Amanda Pascale, Director, The Graduate School, 904-620-1360, Fax: 904-620-1362, E-mail: graduateschool@unf.edu.
Website: http://www.unf.edu/coehs/celt/

University of Oklahoma, Jeannine Rainbolt College of Education, Department of Instructional Leadership and Academic Curriculum, Norman, OK 73019. Offers instructional leadership and academic curriculum (M Ed, PhD), including biomedical education (PhD), early childhood education, elementary education (M Ed), English education, instructional leadership, mathematics education, reading education, science education, social studies education, world languages education (M Ed). *Accreditation:* NCATE. *Program availability:* Part-time. *Faculty:* 19 full-time (15 women), 1 (woman) part-time/adjunct. *Students:* 66 full-time (49 women), 116 part-time (88 women); includes 49 minority (12 Black or African American, non-Hispanic/Latino; 6 American Indian or Alaska Native, non-Hispanic/Latino; 6 Asian, non-Hispanic/Latino; 11 Hispanic/Latino; 1 Native Hawaiian or other Pacific Islander, non-Hispanic/Latino; 13 Two or more races, non-Hispanic/Latino), 13 international. Average age 35. 38 applicants, 97% accepted, 28 enrolled. In 2016, 33 master's, 10 doctorates awarded. Terminal master's awarded for partial completion of doctoral program. *Degree requirements:* For master's, comprehensive exam (for some programs), thesis (for some programs); for doctorate, comprehensive exam (for some programs), thesis/dissertation. *Entrance requirements:* For doctorate, GRE. Additional exam requirements/recommendations for international students: Required—TOEFL (minimum score 79 iBT) or IELTS (minimum score 6.5). Application fee: $50 ($100 for international students). Electronic applications accepted. *Expenses:* Tuition, state resident: full-time $4886; part-time $203.60 per credit hour. Tuition, nonresident: full-time $18,989; part-time $791.20 per credit hour. *Required fees:* $3283; $126.25 per credit hour. $126.50 per semester. *Financial support:* In 2016–17, 112 students received support, including 7 research assistantships with partial tuition reimbursements available (averaging $10,373 per year), 6 teaching assistantships with partial tuition reimbursements available (averaging $11,446 per year); fellowships, scholarships/grants, and unspecified assistantships also available. Financial award application deadline: 6/1; financial award applicants required to submit FAFSA. *Faculty research:* Teacher preparation; instruction; curriculum; learning; constructivist theory. *Total annual research expenditures:* $165,297. *Unit head:* Dr. Stacy Reeder, Chair, 405-325-1498, Fax: 405-325-4061, E-mail: reeder@ou.edu. *Application contact:* Anna Steele, Graduate Programs Officer, 405-325-4525, E-mail: anna.steele@ou.edu.
Website: http://www.ou.edu/education/ilac

University of Pennsylvania, Graduate School of Education, Division of Teaching, Learning, and Leadership, Teacher Education Program, Philadelphia, PA 19104. Offers elementary education (MS Ed); secondary education (MS Ed). *Students:* 43 full-time (32 women), 1 (woman) part-time; includes 15 minority (4 Black or African American, non-Hispanic/Latino; 7 Asian, non-Hispanic/Latino; 3 Hispanic/Latino; 1 Two or more races, non-Hispanic/Latino). Average age 25. 123 applicants, 81% accepted, 45 enrolled. In 2016, 60 master's awarded. *Degree requirements:* For master's, thesis or alternative, student teaching, portfolio. *Entrance requirements:* For master's, GRE, bachelor's degree. Additional exam requirements/recommendations for international students: Required—TOEFL, IELTS. *Application deadline:* For summer admission, 6/1 priority date for domestic students, 6/1 for international students. Applications are processed on a rolling basis. Application fee: $75. Electronic applications accepted. *Expenses: Tuition:* Full-time $31,068; part-time $5762 per course. *Required fees:* $3200; $336 per course. Full-time tuition and fees vary according to degree level, program and student level. Part-time tuition and fees vary according to course load, degree level and program. *Financial support:* In 2016–17, 53 students received support. Federal Work-Study and scholarships/grants available. Financial award applicants required to submit FAFSA. *Faculty research:* Teacher competencies, social justice teaching, teacher practitioner inquiry. *Unit head:* Maureen Cotterill, Program Manager, 215-898-7364.
Website: http://www2.gse.upenn.edu/tep/

University of Phoenix–Bay Area Campus, College of Education, San Jose, CA 95134-1805. Offers administration and supervision (MA Ed); adult education and training (MA Ed); early childhood education (MA Ed); education (Ed S); educational leadership (Ed D); elementary teacher education (MA Ed); higher education administration (PhD); secondary teacher education (MA Ed); special education (MA Ed); teacher leadership (MA Ed). *Program availability:* Evening/weekend, online learning. *Degree requirements:* For master's, thesis (for some programs). *Entrance requirements:* For master's, minimum undergraduate GPA of 2.5, 3 years of work experience. Additional exam requirements/recommendations for international students: Required—TOEFL (minimum score 550 paper-based; 79 iBT). Electronic applications accepted.

University of Phoenix–Central Valley Campus, College of Education, Fresno, CA 93720-1552. Offers curriculum and instruction (MA Ed); curriculum and instruction-computer education (MA Ed); elementary teacher education (MA Ed); secondary teacher education (MA Ed).

University of Phoenix–Colorado Campus, College of Education, Lone Tree, CO 80124-5453. Offers administration and supervision (MAEd); curriculum instruction (MAEd); elementary teacher education (MAEd); school counseling (MSC); secondary teacher education (MAEd). *Program availability:* Evening/weekend. *Degree requirements:* For master's, thesis (for some programs). *Entrance requirements:* For master's, minimum undergraduate GPA of 2.5, 3 years work experience. Additional exam requirements/recommendations for international students: Required—TOEFL (minimum score 550 paper-based; 79 iBT). Electronic applications accepted.

University of Phoenix–Colorado Springs Downtown Campus, College of Education, Colorado Springs, CO 80903. Offers administration and supervision (MA Ed); curriculum and instruction (MA Ed); elementary teacher education (MA Ed); principal licensure certification (Certificate); school counseling (MSC); secondary teacher education (MA Ed). *Program availability:* Evening/weekend. *Degree requirements:* For master's, thesis (for some programs). *Entrance requirements:* For master's, minimum undergraduate GPA of 2.5, 3 years of work experience. Additional exam requirements/recommendations for international students: Required—TOEFL (minimum score 550 paper-based; 79 iBT). Electronic applications accepted.

University of Phoenix–Hawaii Campus, College of Education, Honolulu, HI 96813-3800. Offers administration and supervision (MA Ed); curriculum and instruction (MA Ed); elementary education (MA Ed); secondary education (MA Ed); special education (MA Ed); teacher education for elementary licensure (MA Ed). *Program availability:* Evening/weekend. *Degree requirements:* For master's, thesis (for some programs). *Entrance requirements:* For master's, minimum undergraduate GPA of 2.5, 3 years of work experience. Additional exam requirements/recommendations for international students: Required—TOEFL (minimum score 550 paper-based; 79 iBT). Electronic applications accepted.

University of Phoenix–Las Vegas Campus, College of Education, Las Vegas, NV 89135. Offers administration and supervision (MA Ed); curriculum and instruction (MA Ed); school counseling (MSC); teacher education-elementary licensure (MA Ed). *Program availability:* Evening/weekend. *Degree requirements:* For master's, thesis (for some programs). *Entrance requirements:* For master's, minimum undergraduate GPA of 2.5, 3 years of work experience. Additional exam requirements/recommendations for international students: Required—TOEFL (minimum score 550 paper-based; 79 iBT). Electronic applications accepted.

University of Phoenix–New Mexico Campus, College of Education, Albuquerque, NM 87113-1570. Offers administration and supervision (MAEd); curriculum and instruction (MAEd); elementary teacher education (MAEd); school counseling (MSC); secondary teacher education (MAEd). *Program availability:* Evening/weekend. *Degree requirements:* For master's, thesis (for some programs). *Entrance requirements:* For master's, minimum undergraduate GPA of 2.5, 3 years of work experience. Additional exam requirements/recommendations for international students: Required—TOEFL (minimum score 550 paper-based; 79 iBT). Electronic applications accepted.

University of Phoenix–North Florida Campus, College of Education, Jacksonville, FL 32216-0959. Offers administration and supervision (MA Ed); curriculum and instruction (MA Ed), including computer education, mathematics education; early childhood education (MA Ed); elementary teacher education (MA Ed); secondary teacher education (MA Ed). *Program availability:* Evening/weekend. *Degree requirements:* For master's, thesis (for some programs). *Entrance requirements:* For master's, 3 years of work experience, minimum undergraduate GPA of 2.5. Additional exam requirements/recommendations for international students: Required—TOEFL (minimum score 550 paper-based; 49 iBT). Electronic applications accepted.

University of Phoenix–Online Campus, College of Education, Phoenix, AZ 85034-7209. Offers administration and supervision (MAEd, Certificate); adult education and training (MAEd); curriculum and instruction (MAEd), including computer education, curriculum and instruction, English as a second language, language arts, mathematics, reading; early childhood education (MAEd); educational studies (MAEd); elementary teacher education (MAEd), including early childhood, elementary teacher education, high school middle level, middle level; principal licensure (Certificate); secondary teacher education (MAEd); special education (MAEd, Certificate); teacher education (MAEd), including middle level generalist; teacher education middle level mathematics (MAEd), including middle level mathematics; teacher education middle level science (MAEd), including middle level science; teacher education secondary mathematics (MAEd); teacher education secondary science (MAEd); teacher leadership (MAEd); teachers of English learners (Certificate); transition to teaching (Certificate), including elementary education, secondary education. *Program availability:* Evening/weekend, online learning. *Entrance requirements:* Additional exam requirements/recommendations for international students: Required—TOEFL, TOEIC (Test of English as an International Communication), Berlitz Online English Proficiency Exam, PTE, or IELTS. Electronic applications accepted. *Expenses:* Contact institution.

University of Phoenix–Phoenix Campus, College of Education, Tempe, AZ 85282-2371. Offers administration and supervision (MA Ed); adult education and training (MA Ed); curriculum and instruction reading (MA Ed); early childhood education (MA Ed); education studies (MA Ed); elementary teacher education (MA Ed); secondary teacher education (MA Ed); special education (MA Ed); teacher leadership (MA Ed). *Program availability:* Evening/weekend, online learning. *Entrance requirements:* Additional exam requirements/recommendations for international students: Required—TOEFL, TOEIC (Test of English as an International Communication), Berlitz Online English Proficiency Exam, PTE, or IELTS. Electronic applications accepted. *Expenses:* Contact institution.

University of Phoenix–Sacramento Valley Campus, College of Education, Sacramento, CA 95833-4334. Offers adult education (MA Ed); curriculum instruction (MA Ed); elementary teacher education (MA Ed); secondary teacher education (MA Ed); teacher education (Certificate). *Program availability:* Evening/weekend. *Degree requirements:* For master's, thesis (for some programs). *Entrance requirements:* For master's, 3 years of work experience, minimum undergraduate GPA of 2.5. Additional exam requirements/recommendations for international students: Required—TOEFL (minimum score 550 paper-based; 79 iBT). Electronic applications accepted.

University of Phoenix–San Diego Campus, College of Education, San Diego, CA 92123. Offers curriculum and instruction (MA Ed), including computer education, curriculum and instruction, English as a second language; elementary teacher education (MA Ed); secondary teacher education (MA Ed). *Program availability:* Evening/weekend. *Degree requirements:* For master's, thesis (for some programs). *Entrance requirements:* For master's, 3 years of work experience, minimum undergraduate GPA of 3.0. Additional exam requirements/recommendations for international students: Required—TOEFL (minimum score 550 paper-based; 79 iBT). Electronic applications accepted.

University of Phoenix–Southern Arizona Campus, College of Education, Tucson, AZ 85711. Offers administration and supervision (MA Ed); adult education and training (MA Ed); curriculum instruction (MA Ed); educational counseling (MA Ed); elementary teacher education (MA Ed); school counseling (MSC); secondary teacher education (MA Ed); special education (MA Ed, Certificate). *Program availability:* Evening/weekend. *Degree requirements:* For master's, thesis (for some programs). *Entrance requirements:* For master's, minimum undergraduate GPA of 2.5, 3 years of work experience. Additional exam requirements/recommendations for international students: Required—TOEFL (minimum score 550 paper-based; 79 iBT). Electronic applications accepted.

University of Phoenix–Southern California Campus, College of Education, Costa Mesa, CA 92626. Offers administration and supervision (MA Ed, Certificate); adult education and training (MA Ed); educational studies (MA Ed); elementary teacher education (MA Ed); secondary teacher education (MA Ed); teacher leadership (MA Ed); teachers of English learners (Certificate). *Program availability:* Evening/weekend, online learning. *Entrance requirements:* Additional exam requirements/recommendations for international students: Required—TOEFL, TOEIC (Test of English as an International Communication), Berlitz Online English Proficiency Exam, PTE, or IELTS. Electronic applications accepted. *Expenses:* Contact institution.

University of Phoenix–South Florida Campus, College of Education, Miramar, FL 33027-4145. Offers administration and supervision (MA Ed); curriculum and instruction (MA Ed), including computer education, curriculum and instruction, mathematics education; early childhood education (MA Ed); elementary teacher education (MA Ed); secondary teacher education (MA Ed). *Program availability:* Evening/weekend. *Degree requirements:* For master's, thesis (for some programs). *Entrance requirements:* For master's, 3 years of work experience, minimum undergraduate GPA of 2.5. Additional exam requirements/recommendations for international students: Required—TOEFL (minimum score 550 paper-based; 79 iBT). Electronic applications accepted.

University of Phoenix–Utah Campus, College of Education, Salt Lake City, UT 84123-4642. Offers administration and supervision (MA Ed); curriculum and instruction (MA Ed); elementary teacher education (MA Ed); school counseling (MSC); secondary teacher education (MA Ed); special education (MA Ed). *Program availability:* Evening/weekend. *Degree requirements:* For master's, thesis (for some programs). *Entrance requirements:* For master's, minimum undergraduate GPA of 2.5, 3 years work experience. Additional exam requirements/recommendations for international students: Required—TOEFL (minimum score 550 paper-based; 79 iBT). Electronic applications accepted.

University of Phoenix–Washington D.C. Campus, College of Education, Washington, DC 20001. Offers administration and supervision (MA Ed); adult education and training (MA Ed); computer education (MA Ed); curriculum and instruction (MA Ed, Ed D); early childhood education (MA Ed); education (Ed S); educational leadership (Ed D); educational technology (Ed D); elementary teacher education (MA Ed); English and language arts education (MA Ed); English as a second language (MA Ed); higher education administration (PhD); mathematics education (MA Ed); secondary teacher education (MA Ed); special education (MA Ed); teacher leadership (MA Ed).

University of Pittsburgh, School of Education, Department of Instruction and Learning, Program in Elementary Education, Pittsburgh, PA 15260. Offers M Ed, MAT. *Degree requirements:* For master's, thesis. *Entrance requirements:* For master's, PRAXIS I. Additional exam requirements/recommendations for international students: Required—TOEFL. Electronic applications accepted. Tuition and fees vary according to program.

University of Puget Sound, School of Education, Program in Teaching, Tacoma, WA 98416. Offers elementary education (MAT); secondary education (MAT). *Accreditation:* NASM. *Faculty:* 6 full-time (3 women), 1 (woman) part-time/adjunct. *Students:* 26 full-time (20 women), 2 part-time (both women); includes 6 minority (1 American Indian or Alaska Native, non-Hispanic/Latino; 2 Asian, non-Hispanic/Latino; 3 Two or more races, non-Hispanic/Latino). Average age 26. 60 applicants, 68% accepted, 27 enrolled. In 2016, 33 master's awarded. *Degree requirements:* For master's, project. *Entrance requirements:* For master's, WEST-E or NES, WEST-B or ACT/SAT, two education foundation prerequisite courses; minor in content area (for secondary education). Additional exam requirements/recommendations for international students: Required—TOEFL (minimum score 550 paper-based; 90 iBT). *Application deadline:* For fall admission, 3/1 priority date for domestic and international students. Applications are processed on a rolling basis. Application fee: $60. Electronic applications accepted. *Expenses:* $3,575 per unit. *Financial support:* In 2016–17, 23 students received support. Scholarships/grants available. Financial award application deadline: 3/31; financial award applicants required to submit FAFSA. *Faculty research:* Pre-service teacher learning, public school partnerships and professional development, creating equitable classrooms, literacy development, teaching social studies. *Unit head:* Amy Ryken, Dean, 253-879-2810, Fax: 253-879-3926, E-mail: aryken@pugetsound.edu. *Application contact:* Karen Stump, Certification Officer/Admission Coordinator, 253-879-3382, Fax: 253-879-3926, E-mail: kstump@pugetsound.edu.
Website: http://www.pugetsound.edu/academics/departments-and-programs/graduate/school-of-education/mat/

University of St. Francis, College of Education, Joliet, IL 60435-6169. Offers educational leadership (MS, Ed D); elementary education (M Ed); reading (MS); secondary education (M Ed), including English education, math education, science education, social studies education, visual arts education; special education (M Ed); teaching and learning (MS); TESOL (Certificate). *Accreditation:* NCATE. *Program availability:* Part-time, evening/weekend, 100% online, blended/hybrid learning. *Faculty:* 11 full-time (8 women), 60 part-time/adjunct (42 women). *Students:* 34 full-time (26 women), 420 part-time (318 women); includes 92 minority (51 Black or African American, non-Hispanic/Latino; 5 Asian, non-Hispanic/Latino; 31 Hispanic/Latino; 5 Two or more races, non-Hispanic/Latino), 4 international. Average age 36. 242 applicants, 48% accepted, 96 enrolled. In 2016, 229 master's, 44 doctorates, 10 other advanced degrees awarded. *Degree requirements:* For master's, comprehensive exam; for doctorate, thesis/dissertation. *Entrance requirements:* Additional exam requirements/recommendations for international students: Required—TOEFL (minimum score 550 paper-based; 79 iBT), IELTS (minimum score 6). *Application deadline:* Applications are processed on a rolling basis. Application fee: $30. Electronic applications accepted. Application fee is waived when completed online. *Expenses:* Contact institution. *Financial support:* In 2016–17, 48 students received support. Career-related internships or fieldwork and unspecified assistantships available. Support available to part-time students. Financial award applicants required to submit FAFSA. *Unit head:* Dr. John Gambro, Dean, 815-740-3829, Fax: 815-740-2264, E-mail: jgambro@stfrancis.edu. *Application contact:* Sandra Sloka, Director of Admissions for Graduate and Degree Completion Programs, 800-735-7500, Fax: 815-740-3431, E-mail: ssloka@stfrancis.edu.
Website: http://www.stfrancis.edu/academics/college-of-education/

University of Saint Mary, Graduate Programs, Program in Elementary Education, Leavenworth, KS 66048-5082. Offers MA. *Program availability:* Part-time, evening/weekend. *Students:* 32 full-time (25 women), 2 part-time (both women); includes 3 minority (1 Black or African American, non-Hispanic/Latino; 1 American Indian or Alaska Native, non-Hispanic/Latino; 1 Hispanic/Latino). Average age 33. In 2016, 12 master's awarded. *Entrance requirements:* For master's, PPST, minimum GPA of 2.75, interview, essay, two letters of reference. Application fee: $25. Electronic applications accepted. *Expenses:* $395 per hour. *Unit head:* Dr. Gwen Landever, Chair of Education, 913-758-6159, E-mail: gwen.landever@stmary.edu.
Website: http://www.stmary.edu/success/Grad-Program/Master-of-Arts-Elementary-Education.aspx

University of St. Thomas, School of Education and Human Services, Houston, TX 77006-4696. Offers all level education (M Ed); bilingual/dual language (M Ed); Catholic school teaching (M Ed); Catholic/private school leadership (M Ed); counselor education (M Ed); curriculum and instruction (M Ed); education (Ed D); educational leadership (M Ed); elementary teaching (M Ed); English as a second language (M Ed); exceptionality/educational diagnostician (M Ed); exceptionality/special education (M Ed); generalist (M Ed); reading (M Ed); secondary teaching (M Ed); teaching (MAT). *Accreditation:* TEAC. *Program availability:* Part-time, evening/weekend, online learning. *Faculty:* 44 full-time (29 women), 31 part-time/adjunct (17 women). *Students:* 65 full-time (61 women), 719 part-time (645 women); includes 515 minority (169 Black or African American, non-Hispanic/Latino; 25 Asian, non-Hispanic/Latino; 315 Hispanic/Latino; 2 Native Hawaiian or other Pacific Islander, non-Hispanic/Latino; 4 Two or more races, non-Hispanic/Latino), 24 international. Average age 36. 297 applicants, 92% accepted, 211 enrolled. In 2016, 403 master's awarded. *Degree requirements:* For master's, thesis, field experience. *Entrance requirements:* For master's, GRE or MAT if GPA is below 3.0, bachelor's degree; minimum GPA of 2.75 in bachelor's degree or last 60 credit hours; official transcripts from all institutions; goal statement of 250-300 words; 1 reference. Additional exam requirements/recommendations for international students: Required—TOEFL (minimum score 94 iBT), IELTS (minimum score 7), PTE (minimum score 53). *Application deadline:* Applications are processed on a rolling basis. Application fee: $35. Electronic applications accepted. *Expenses:* Contact institution. *Financial support:* In 2016–17, 52 students received support. Federal Work-Study, scholarships/grants, and state work-study, institutional employment available. Support available to part-time students. Financial award application deadline: 4/15; financial award applicants required to submit FAFSA. *Faculty research:* Leadership, diversity, personality traits, second language acquisition. *Unit head:* Dr. Robert LeBlanc, Dean, 713-525-3540, Fax: 713-525-3871, E-mail: education@stthom.edu. *Application contact:* Rita Paredes, Administrative Assistant, 713-525-3442, Fax: 713-525-3871, E-mail: rparede@stthom.edu.
Website: http://www.stthom.edu/Academics/School_of_Education_and_Human_Services/Index.aqf

University of South Alabama, College of Education and Professional Studies, Department of Leadership and Teacher Education, Mobile, AL 36688. Offers art education (M Ed); early childhood education (M Ed); educational leadership (M Ed, Ed D); elementary education (M Ed); reading education (M Ed); science education (M Ed); secondary education (M Ed); special education (M Ed). *Accreditation:* NCATE. *Program availability:* Part-time, 100% online, blended/hybrid learning. *Faculty:* 16 full-time (12 women), 6 part-time/adjunct (3 women). *Students:* 198 full-time (150 women), 77 part-time (58 women); includes 77 minority (61 Black or African American, non-Hispanic/Latino; 2 American Indian or Alaska Native, non-Hispanic/Latino; 2 Asian, non-Hispanic/Latino; 7 Hispanic/Latino; 1 Native Hawaiian or other Pacific Islander, non-Hispanic/Latino; 4 Two or more races, non-Hispanic/Latino). Average age 34. 153 applicants, 53% accepted, 69 enrolled. In 2016, 80 master's, 1 doctorate awarded. *Degree requirements:* For master's, comprehensive exam, thesis (for some programs); for doctorate, comprehensive exam, thesis/dissertation. *Entrance requirements:* For master's, GRE General Test or MAT, minimum GPA of 3.0; for doctorate, GRE, minimum graduate GPA of 3.25, 3 years of experience in field, 3 letters of recommendation, interview, official transcripts. Additional exam requirements/recommendations for international students: Required—TOEFL. *Application deadline:* For fall admission, 7/15 for domestic students; for spring admission, 11/15 for domestic students; for summer admission, 4/15 for domestic students. Applications are processed on a rolling basis. Application fee: $35. Electronic applications accepted. *Expenses:* Tuition, state resident: full-time $9768; part-time $407 per credit hour. Tuition, nonresident: full-time $19,536; part-time $814 per credit hour. *Financial support:* Fellowships, research assistantships, teaching assistantships, career-related internships or fieldwork, Federal Work-Study, institutionally sponsored loans, scholarships/grants, and unspecified assistantships available. Support available to part-time students. Financial award application deadline: 5/31; financial award applicants required to submit FAFSA. *Unit head:* Dr. Susan Santoli, Department Chair, 251-380-2836, Fax: 251-380-2758, E-mail: ssantoli@southalabama.edu. *Application contact:* Dr. Susan Santoli, Director of Graduate Studies, 251-380-2836, Fax: 251-380-2758, E-mail: ssantoli@southalabama.edu.
Website: http://www.southalabama.edu/colleges/coe/lte/index.html

University of South Carolina, The Graduate School, College of Education, Department of Instruction and Teacher Education, Program in Elementary Education, Columbia, SC 29208. Offers MAT, Ed D, PhD. *Accreditation:* NCATE. *Degree requirements:* For master's, comprehensive exam; for doctorate, one foreign language, comprehensive exam, thesis/dissertation. *Entrance requirements:* For master's, GRE General Test, MAT, interview, letters of reference, resume; for doctorate, GRE General Test, MAT, interview, letters of reference, letters of intent, resum&e, transcript. *Faculty research:* Children's conception of science, whole language, middle school curriculum.

University of South Carolina Upstate, Graduate Programs, Spartanburg, SC 29303-4999. Offers early childhood education (M Ed); elementary education (M Ed); informatics (MS); special education: visual impairment (M Ed). *Accreditation:* NCATE. *Program availability:* Part-time, evening/weekend. *Degree requirements:* For master's, professional portfolio. *Entrance requirements:* For master's, GRE General Test or MAT, interview, minimum undergraduate GPA of 2.5, teaching certificate, 2 letters of recommendation. *Faculty research:* Promoting university diversity awareness, rough and tumble play, social justice education, American Indian literatures and cultures, diversity and multicultural education, science teaching strategy.

The University of South Dakota, Graduate School, School of Education, Division of Curriculum and Instruction, Program in Elementary Education, Vermillion, SD 57069. Offers elementary education (MA), including early childhood education, English language learning, reading specialist/literacy coach, science, technology or math (STM). *Accreditation:* NCATE. *Program availability:* Part-time, 100% online, blended/hybrid learning. *Degree requirements:* For master's, comprehensive exam, thesis or alternative. *Entrance requirements:* For master's, GRE General Test, MAT, minimum GPA of 2.7. Additional exam requirements/recommendations for international students: Required—TOEFL (minimum score 550 paper-based; 79 iBT). Electronic applications accepted.

University of Southern Indiana, Graduate Studies, Pott College of Science, Engineering, and Education, Department of Teacher Education, Program in Elementary Education, Evansville, IN 47712-3590. Offers MSE. *Accreditation:* NCATE. *Program availability:* Part-time, evening/weekend. *Faculty:* 5 full-time (4 women), 2 part-time/adjunct (1 woman). *Students:* 1 (woman) full-time, 7 part-time (all women). Average age 29. In 2016, 10 master's awarded. *Entrance requirements:* For master's, PRAXIS II, bachelor's degree with minimum cumulative GPA of 2.75 from college or university accredited by NCATE or comparable association; minimum GPA of 3.0 in all courses taken at graduate level at all schools attended; teaching license. Additional exam requirements/recommendations for international students: Required—TOEFL (minimum score 550 paper-based; 79 iBT), IELTS (minimum score 6). *Application deadline:* For fall admission, 7/1 priority date for domestic students. Applications are processed on a rolling basis. Application fee: $40. Electronic applications accepted. *Expenses:* Tuition, state resident: full-time $8497. Tuition, nonresident: full-time $16,691. *Required fees:* $500. *Financial support:* Fellowships, Federal Work-Study, scholarships/grants, tuition waivers (full and partial), and unspecified assistantships available. Financial award application deadline: 3/1; financial award applicants required to submit FAFSA. *Unit head:* Dr. Bonnie Beach, Associate Dean, 812-465-1620, E-mail: blbeach@usi.edu. *Application contact:* Dr. Mayola Rowser, Director, Graduate Studies, 812-465-7015, Fax: 812-464-1956, E-mail: mrowser@usi.edu.
Website: http://www.usi.edu/science/teacher-education/programs/mse

University of Southern Mississippi, Graduate School, College of Education and Psychology, Department of Curriculum, Instruction and Special Education, Hattiesburg, MS 39406. Offers elementary education (M Ed, PhD); instructional technology (MS); instructional technology and design (PhD); secondary education (MAT); special education (M Ed, PhD). *Program availability:* Part-time, online learning. *Degree requirements:* For master's, comprehensive exam, thesis (for some programs); for doctorate, comprehensive exam, thesis/dissertation. *Entrance requirements:* For master's, GRE General Test, MAT, minimum GPA of 3.0; for doctorate, GRE General Test, minimum GPA of 3.5. Additional exam requirements/recommendations for international students: Required—TOEFL, IELTS. *Application deadline:* For fall admission, 3/1 priority date for domestic students, 3/1 for international students; for spring admission, 1/10 priority date for domestic and international students. Applications are processed on a rolling basis. Application fee: $60. *Expenses: Tuition, area resident:* Full-time $15,708; part-time $437 per credit hour. *Financial support:* Research assistantships with tuition reimbursements, teaching assistantships with full tuition reimbursements, Federal Work-Study, institutionally sponsored loans, scholarships/grants, health care benefits, tuition waivers (partial), and unspecified assistantships available. Financial award application deadline: 3/15; financial award applicants required to submit FAFSA. *Faculty research:* Mathematical problem solving, integrative curriculum, writing process, teacher education models. *Unit head:* Dr. Mary Ariail, Chair, 601-266-5247, Fax: 601-266-4548.
Website: https://www.usm.edu/elementary-special-technology-education

University of South Florida, College of Education, Department of Teaching and Learning, Tampa, FL 33620-9951. Offers early childhood education (M Ed, MA, PhD); elementary education (MA, MAT, PhD); reading/language arts (MA, PhD, Ed S). *Accreditation:* NCATE. *Faculty:* 40 full-time (29 women), 2 part-time/adjunct (both women). *Students:* 205 full-time (143 women), 263 part-time (207 women); includes 108 minority (45 Black or African American, non-Hispanic/Latino; 10 Asian, non-Hispanic/Latino; 48 Hispanic/Latino; 5 Two or more races, non-Hispanic/Latino), 62 international.

Average age 34. 153 applicants, 78% accepted, 100 enrolled. In 2016, 142 master's, 22 doctorates, 1 other advanced degree awarded. Application fee: $30. *Expenses:* Tuition, state resident: full-time $7766; part-time $431.43 per credit hour. Tuition, nonresident: full-time $15,789; part-time $877.17 per credit hour. *Required fees:* $37 per term. *Total annual research expenditures:* $2.8 million. *Unit head:* Dr. Denisse Thompson, Chair, 813-974-4110.
Website: http://www.coedu.usf.edu/main/departments/ce/ce.html

University of South Florida, St. Petersburg, College of Education, St. Petersburg, FL 33701. Offers educational leadership development (M Ed); elementary education (MA), including math/science; English education (MA); middle grades STEM education (MS); reading education (MA). *Program availability:* Part-time. *Degree requirements:* For master's, comprehensive exam, practicum, internship, comprehensive portfolio. *Entrance requirements:* For master's, State of Florida General Knowledge Test (GKT), Florida Teaching Certificate (for non-initial certification programs), letters of recommendation. Additional exam requirements/recommendations for international students: Required—TOEFL (minimum score 550 paper-based; 79 iBT); Recommended—IELTS. Electronic applications accepted.

University of South Florida Sarasota-Manatee, College of Liberal Arts and Social Sciences, Sarasota, FL 34243. Offers criminal justice (MA); education (MA); educational leadership (M Ed), including curriculum leadership, K-12 public school leadership, non-public/charter school leadership; elementary education (MAT); English education (MA); social work (MSW). *Program availability:* Part-time, 100% online, blended/hybrid learning. *Faculty:* 11 full-time (9 women), 7 part-time/adjunct (5 women). *Students:* 11 full-time (all women), 55 part-time (41 women); includes 18 minority (5 Black or African American, non-Hispanic/Latino; 1 American Indian or Alaska Native, non-Hispanic/Latino; 2 Asian, non-Hispanic/Latino; 10 Hispanic/Latino). Average age 36. 40 applicants, 43% accepted, 17 enrolled. In 2016, 28 master's awarded. *Degree requirements:* For master's, comprehensive exam (for some programs). *Entrance requirements:* Additional exam requirements/recommendations for international students: Required—TOEFL (minimum score 550 paper-based; 79 iBT), IELTS (minimum score 6.5). *Application deadline:* For fall admission, 3/1 priority date for domestic students, 3/1 for international students; for spring admission, 10/1 priority date for domestic students, 10/1 for international students. Applications are processed on a rolling basis. Application fee: $30. Electronic applications accepted. *Expenses:* Contact institution. *Financial support:* In 2016–17, 9 students received support. Career-related internships or fieldwork, institutionally sponsored loans, scholarships/grants, health care benefits, and unspecified assistantships available. Support available to part-time students. Financial award application deadline: 3/1; financial award applicants required to submit FAFSA. *Faculty research:* Educational leadership, secondary education, elementary education, criminal justice, social work. *Unit head:* Dr. Jane Rose, Dean, 941-359-4469, Fax: 941-359-4778, E-mail: jane.rose@sar.usf.edu. *Application contact:* Brandon Avery, Assistant Director, Admissions, 941-359-4331, E-mail: bavery@sar.usf.edu.
Website: http://usfsm.edu/college-of-liberal-arts-sciences/

The University of Tennessee, Graduate School, College of Education, Health and Human Sciences, Program in Education, Knoxville, TN 37996. Offers art education (MS); counseling education (PhD); cultural studies in education (PhD); curriculum (MS, Ed S); curriculum, educational research and evaluation (Ed D, PhD); early childhood education (PhD); early childhood special education (MS); education of deaf and hard of hearing (MS); educational administration and policy studies (Ed D, PhD); educational administration and supervision (Ed S); educational psychology (Ed D, PhD); elementary education (MS, Ed S); elementary teaching (MS); English education (MS, Ed S); exercise science (PhD); foreign language/ESL education (MS, Ed S); instructional technology (MS, Ed D, PhD, Ed S); literacy, language and ESL education (PhD); literacy, language education, and ESL education (Ed D); mathematics education (MS, Ed S); modified and comprehensive special education (MS); reading education (MS, Ed S); school counseling (Ed S); school psychology (PhD, Ed S); science education (MS, Ed S); secondary teaching (MS); social foundations (MS); social science education (MS, Ed S); socio-cultural foundations of sports and education (PhD); special education (Ed S); teacher education (Ed D, PhD). *Accreditation:* NCATE. *Program availability:* Part-time, evening/weekend. *Degree requirements:* For master's and Ed S, thesis optional; for doctorate, variable foreign language requirement, thesis/dissertation. *Entrance requirements:* For master's, minimum GPA of 2.7; for doctorate and Ed S, GRE General Test, minimum GPA of 2.7. Additional exam requirements/recommendations for international students: Required—TOEFL. Electronic applications accepted.

The University of Tennessee at Chattanooga, School of Education, Chattanooga, TN 37403. Offers counseling (M Ed), including community counseling, school counseling; education (M Ed, Post-Master's Certificate), including elementary education (M Ed), school leadership, secondary education (M Ed), special education (M Ed); educational specialist (Ed S), including educational technology, school psychology; learning and leadership (Ed D), including educational leadership. *Accreditation:* ACA; NCATE. *Program availability:* Part-time. *Faculty:* 13 full-time (8 women), 2 part-time/adjunct (both women). *Students:* 50 full-time (32 women), 157 part-time (107 women); includes 42 minority (28 Black or African American, non-Hispanic/Latino; 4 Asian, non-Hispanic/Latino; 2 Hispanic/Latino; 8 Two or more races, non-Hispanic/Latino), 1 international. Average age 36. 169 applicants, 76% accepted, 49 enrolled. In 2016, 77 master's, 5 other advanced degrees awarded. *Degree requirements:* For master's, comprehensive exam, thesis optional, culminating experience; for doctorate, comprehensive exam, thesis/dissertation; for other advanced degree, internship. *Entrance requirements:* For master's, GRE General Test, PPST 1, teaching certificate; for doctorate, GRE General Test, master's degree, two years of practical work experience in organizational environment; for other advanced degree, GRE General Test, letters of reference. Additional exam requirements/recommendations for international students: Required—TOEFL (minimum score 550 paper-based; 79 iBT), IELTS (minimum score 6). *Application deadline:* For fall admission, 6/15 for domestic students, 7/1 for international students; for spring admission, 11/1 for domestic and international students. Applications are processed on a rolling basis. Application fee: $35 ($40 for international students). Electronic applications accepted. *Expenses:* $9,876 full-time in-state; $25,994 full-time out-of-state; $450 per credit part-time in-state; $1,345 per credit part-time out-of-state. *Financial support:* In 2016–17, 18 research assistantships, 5 teaching assistantships were awarded; career-related internships or fieldwork, institutionally sponsored loans, scholarships/grants, and unspecified assistantships also available. Support available to part-time students. Financial award application deadline: 7/1; financial award applicants required to submit FAFSA. *Faculty research:* School counseling, community counseling, elementary and secondary education, school leadership and administration. *Total annual research expenditures:* $247,231. *Unit head:* Dr. Renee Murley, Director, 423-425-4684, Fax: 423-425-5380, E-mail: renee-murley@utc.edu. *Application contact:* Dr. Joanne Romagni, Dean of the Graduate School, 423-425-4478, Fax: 423-425-5223, E-mail: joanne-romagni@utc.edu.
Website: http://www.utc.edu/school-education/abouttheschool/gradprograms.php

The University of Tennessee at Martin, Graduate Programs, College of Education, Health and Behavioral Sciences, Program in Teaching, Martin, TN 38238. Offers curriculum and instruction (MS Ed), including 7-12, K-6; initial licensure (MS Ed), including elementary education, secondary education; initial licensure K-12 (MS Ed), including physical education, special education; interdisciplinary (MS Ed). *Students:* 21 full-time (14 women), 125 part-time (87 women); includes 22 minority (18 Black or African American, non-Hispanic/Latino; 3 Hispanic/Latino; 1 Two or more races, non-Hispanic/Latino). 115 applicants, 81% accepted, 51 enrolled. In 2016, 26 master's awarded. *Expenses:* Tuition, state resident: full-time $8254; part-time $459 per credit hour. Tuition, nonresident: full-time $22,198; part-time $1234 per credit hour. *Required fees:* $79 per credit hour. Part-time tuition and fees vary according to course load and campus/location. *Faculty research:* Special education, science/math/technology, school reform, reading. *Unit head:* Cynthia West, Dean, 731-881-7125, Fax: 731-881-7975, E-mail: cwest@utm.edu. *Application contact:* Jolene L. Cunningham, Student Services Specialist, 731-881-7012, Fax: 731-881-7499, E-mail: jcunningham@utm.edu.

The University of Texas Rio Grande Valley, College of Education and P-16 Integration, Department of Teaching and Learning, Edinburg, TX 78539. Offers curriculum and instruction (M Ed, Ed D); educational technology (M Ed). *Program availability:* Part-time. *Degree requirements:* For master's, comprehensive exam, thesis optional. *Entrance requirements:* For master's, GRE. Additional exam requirements/recommendations for international students: Required—TOEFL, IELTS. Tuition and fees vary according to course load and program. *Faculty research:* Dual language instruction, literacy and technology, teacher education in diverse populations, mathematics and science education.

University of the Cumberlands, Graduate Programs in Education, Williamsburg, KY 40769-1372. Offers all grades (P-12) (M Ed); business and marketing (MA Ed, MAT); counselor education and supervision (Ed D); director of pupil personnel (Certificate); director of special education (Certificate); educational administration and supervision (Ed S); educational leadership (Ed D); elementary education (MA Ed, MAT); instructional leadership - principalship (MA Ed); instructional leadership - school principal (Certificate); middle school education (MA Ed, MAT); reading and writing (MA Ed); school counseling (MA Ed); school superintendent (Certificate); secondary education (MA Ed, MAT); special education (MAT); supervisor of instruction (Certificate); teacher leader (MA Ed). *Program availability:* Part-time, evening/weekend, online learning. *Degree requirements:* For master's, comprehensive exam. Electronic applications accepted.

University of the District of Columbia, College of Arts and Sciences, Program in Teaching, Washington, DC 20008-1175. Offers elementary education (MAT); middle school mathematics (MAT); secondary English language arts (MAT); secondary social studies (MAT).

The University of Toledo, College of Graduate Studies, Judith Herb College of Education, Department of Curriculum and Instruction, Toledo, OH 43606-3390. Offers art education (ME); career and technical education (ME, Ed S); curriculum and instruction (ME, PhD, Ed S); early childhood education (Ed S); education and anthropology (MAE); education and biology (MES); education and chemistry (MES); education and classics (MAE); education and economics (MAE); education and English (MAE); education and French (MAE); education and geology (MES); education and German (MAE); education and history (MAE); education and mathematics (MAE, MES); education and physics (MES); education and political science (MAE); education and sociology (MAE); education and Spanish (MAE); educational media (PhD); educational technology (ME); educational technology: virtual educator (Certificate); elementary education (PhD); English as a second language (MAE); gifted and talented education (PhD); middle childhood education (ME); secondary education (ME, PhD); special education (PhD). *Accreditation:* NCATE. *Program availability:* Part-time, evening/weekend. *Degree requirements:* For master's, comprehensive exam, thesis or alternative; for doctorate, comprehensive exam, thesis/dissertation; for other advanced degree, thesis optional. *Entrance requirements:* For master's, doctorate, and other advanced degree, minimum cumulative GPA of 2.7 for all previous academic work, letters of recommendation. Additional exam requirements/recommendations for international students: Required—TOEFL (minimum score 550 paper-based; 80 iBT). Electronic applications accepted.

The University of Tulsa, Graduate School, Kendall College of Arts and Sciences, School of Urban Education, Program in Education, Tulsa, OK 74104-3189. Offers elementary certification (M Ed); secondary certification (M Ed). *Program availability:* Part-time. *Students:* 1 full-time (0 women), all international. Average age 24. 9 applicants. *Degree requirements:* For master's, thesis optional. *Entrance requirements:* For master's, GRE General Test. Additional exam requirements/recommendations for international students: Required—TOEFL (minimum score 577 paper-based; 91 iBT), IELTS (minimum score 6.5). *Application deadline:* Applications are processed on a rolling basis. Application fee: $55. Electronic applications accepted. *Expenses: Tuition:* Full-time $22,230; part-time $1235 per credit hour. *Required fees:* $990 per semester. Tuition and fees vary according to course load. *Financial support:* In 2016–17, 1 student received support, including 1 fellowship with tuition reimbursement available (averaging $2,235 per year), 1 teaching assistantship with full tuition reimbursement available (averaging $13,410 per year); Federal Work-Study, scholarships/grants, health care benefits, tuition waivers (full and partial), and unspecified assistantships also available. Support available to part-time students. Financial award application deadline: 2/1; financial award applicants required to submit FAFSA. *Faculty research:* Elementary and secondary education. *Unit head:* Dr. Sharon Baker, Chair, 918-631-2541, Fax: 918-631-2238, E-mail: sharon-baker@utulsa.edu. *Application contact:* Dr. David Brown, Advisor, 918-631-2719, Fax: 918-631-2133, E-mail: david-brown@utulsa.edu.

University of Utah, Graduate School, College of Education, Department of Educational Leadership and Policy, Salt Lake City, UT 84084. Offers educational leadership and policy (Ed D, PhD), including higher education administration (Ed D), K-12 (Ed D); K-12 school administration (M Ed); K-12 teacher instructional leadership (M Ed); student affairs (M Ed); MPA/PhD. *Program availability:* Part-time, evening/weekend. *Faculty:* 11 full-time (7 women), 0 part-time/adjunct (all women). *Students:* 70 full time (47 women), 134 part-time (95 women); includes 63 minority (7 Black or African American, non-Hispanic/Latino; 2 American Indian or Alaska Native, non-Hispanic/Latino; 7 Asian, non-Hispanic/Latino; 38 Hispanic/Latino; 9 Two or more races, non-Hispanic/Latino), 1 international. Average age 35. 154 applicants, 67% accepted, 86 enrolled. In 2016, 42 master's, 8 doctorates awarded. *Degree requirements:* For master's, comprehensive exam (for some programs), internship, capstone; for doctorate, thesis/dissertation, qualifying exam. *Entrance requirements:* For master's, minimum undergraduate GPA of 3.0, valid bachelor's degree, 3 years' teaching or leadership experience, Level 1 or 2 UT educator's license (for K-12 programs only); for doctorate, GRE General Test (taken with five years of applying), minimum undergraduate GPA of 3.0, valid master's degree. Additional exam requirements/recommendations for international students: Required—TOEFL (minimum score 500 paper-based). *Application deadline:* For fall admission, 1/15 priority date for domestic and international students; for winter admission, 2/1 for domestic and international students; for spring admission, 11/1 priority date for domestic and international students; for summer admission, 3/1 priority date for domestic and international students. Applications are processed on a rolling basis. Application fee: $55 ($65 for international students). Electronic applications accepted. *Expenses:* Contact institution. *Financial support:* In 2016–17, 47 students received support,

including 1 fellowship with full tuition reimbursement available (averaging $14,500 per year), 2 research assistantships with full tuition reimbursements available (averaging $15,000 per year), 6 teaching assistantships with full tuition reimbursements available (averaging $15,000 per year); career-related internships or fieldwork, scholarships/grants, health care benefits, and unspecified assistantships also available. Support available to part-time students. Financial award application deadline: 3/1; financial award applicants required to submit FAFSA. *Faculty research:* Education accountability, college student diversity, K-12 educational administration and school leadership, student affairs, higher education. *Unit head:* Dr. Gerardo Lopez, Chair, 801-581-6627, Fax: 801-585-6756, E-mail: gerardo.lopez@utah.edu. *Application contact:* Marilynn S. Howard, Academic Coordinator, 801-581-6714, Fax: 801-585-6756, E-mail: marilynn.howard@utah.edu.
Website: http://elp.utah.edu/

University of Utah, Graduate School, College of Education, Department of Educational Psychology, Salt Lake City, UT 84112. Offers clinical mental health counseling (M Ed); counseling psychology (PhD); elementary education (M Ed); instructional design and educational technology (M Ed); instructional design and technology (MS); learning and cognition (MS, PhD); reading and literacy (M Ed, PhD); school counseling (M Ed); school psychology (M Ed, PhD, Ed S); statistics (M Stat). *Accreditation:* APA (one or more programs are accredited). *Faculty:* 23 full-time (12 women), 15 part-time/adjunct (10 women). *Students:* 119 full-time (95 women), 106 part-time (74 women); includes 37 minority (2 Black or African American, non-Hispanic/Latino; 6 Asian, non-Hispanic/Latino; 22 Hispanic/Latino; 7 Two or more races, non-Hispanic/Latino), 6 international. Average age 31. 296 applicants, 27% accepted, 73 enrolled. In 2016, 47 master's, 8 doctorates awarded. Terminal master's awarded for partial completion of doctoral program. *Degree requirements:* For master's, variable foreign language requirement, comprehensive exam (for some programs), thesis (for some programs), projects; for doctorate, variable foreign language requirement, comprehensive exam, thesis/dissertation, oral exam. *Entrance requirements:* For master's and doctorate, GRE General Test, minimum GPA of 3.0. Additional exam requirements/recommendations for international students: Required—TOEFL (minimum score 80 iBT). *Application deadline:* For fall admission, 12/15 for domestic and international students; for winter admission, 11/1 for domestic and international students; for spring admission, 3/15 for domestic and international students. Application fee: $55 ($65 for international students). Electronic applications accepted. *Expenses:* Contact institution. *Financial support:* In 2016–17, 84 students received support, including 12 fellowships with full and partial tuition reimbursements available (averaging $18,000 per year), 21 research assistantships with full and partial tuition reimbursements available (averaging $14,500 per year), 57 teaching assistantships with full and partial tuition reimbursements available (averaging $14,500 per year); career-related internships or fieldwork, Federal Work-Study, institutionally sponsored loans, scholarships/grants, traineeships, health care benefits, and unspecified assistantships also available. Financial award application deadline: 4/1; financial award applicants required to submit FAFSA. *Faculty research:* Autism, computer technology and instruction, cognitive behavior, aging, group counseling. *Total annual research expenditures:* $620,935. *Unit head:* Dr. Anne E. Cook, Chair, 801-581-7148, Fax: 801-581-5566, E-mail: anne.cook@utah.edu. *Application contact:* JoLynn N. Yates, Academic Coordinator, 801-581-7148, Fax: 801-581-5566, E-mail: jo.yates@utah.edu.
Website: http://www.ed.utah.edu/edps/

University of Virginia, Curry School of Education, Department of Curriculum, Instruction, and Special Education, Program in Curriculum and Instruction, Charlottesville, VA 22903. Offers curriculum and instruction (M Ed, Ed S); elementary education (M Ed, Ed D); English education (M Ed, Ed D); foreign language education (M Ed); mathematics education (M Ed, Ed D); science education (Ed D); social studies education (M Ed); MBA/M Ed. *Students:* 43 full-time (35 women), 24 part-time (16 women); includes 7 minority (1 Black or African American, non-Hispanic/Latino; 1 Asian, non-Hispanic/Latino; 2 Hispanic/Latino; 3 Two or more races, non-Hispanic/Latino), 4 international. Average age 33. 93 applicants, 78% accepted, 54 enrolled. In 2016, 52 master's, 14 other advanced degrees awarded. *Degree requirements:* For master's, comprehensive exam (for some programs); for doctorate, comprehensive exam, thesis/dissertation; for Ed S, comprehensive exam. *Entrance requirements:* For master's, doctorate, and Ed S, GRE General Test, 2 letters of recommendation. Additional exam requirements/recommendations for international students: Required—TOEFL (minimum score 600 paper-based; 90 iBT), IELTS (minimum score 7). *Application deadline:* Applications are processed on a rolling basis. Application fee: $60. Electronic applications accepted. *Expenses:* Tuition, state resident: full-time $15,026; part-time $834 per credit hour. Tuition, nonresident: full-time $25,168; part-time $1378 per credit hour. *Required fees:* $2654. *Financial support:* Fellowships with tuition reimbursements, research assistantships with tuition reimbursements, and teaching assistantships with tuition reimbursements available. Financial award application deadline: 1/5; financial award applicants required to submit FAFSA. *Unit head:* Susan Mintz, Program Area Director, 434-924-3128, E-mail: slm4r@virginia.edu. *Application contact:* Eric Molnar, Assistant Director, Admissions and Enrollment Reporting, 434-243-2085, E-mail: eric.molnar@virginia.edu.
Website: http://curry.virginia.edu/academics/areas-of-study/curriculum-teaching-learning

University of Virginia, Curry School of Education, Program in Education, Charlottesville, VA 22903. Offers administration and supervision (PhD); applied developmental science (PhD); counselor education (PhD); curriculum and instruction (PhD); early childhood special education (MT); education evaluation (PhD); educational psychology (PhD); educational research (PhD); elementary education (MT); English education (MT, PhD); foreign language education (MT); higher education (PhD); instructional technology (PhD); kinesiology (MT, PhD); math education (PhD); reading education (PhD); research, statistics and evaluation (PhD); school psychology (PhD); science education (PhD); social studies education (MT, PhD); special education (PhD); world languages education (MT). *Students:* 452 full-time (357 women), 18 part-time (13 women); includes 100 minority (28 Black or African American, non-Hispanic/Latino; 39 Asian, non-Hispanic/Latino; 18 Hispanic/Latino; 15 Two or more races, non-Hispanic/Latino), 14 international. Average age 25. 309 applicants, 51% accepted, 87 enrolled. In 2016, 144 master's, 31 doctorates awarded. *Degree requirements:* For master's, comprehensive exam (for some programs), field project; for doctorate, comprehensive exam, thesis/dissertation. *Entrance requirements:* For doctorate, GRE General Test. Additional exam requirements/recommendations for international students: Required—TOEFL (minimum score 600 paper-based; 90 iBT), IELTS (minimum score 7). *Application deadline:* Applications are processed on a rolling basis. Application fee: $60. Electronic applications accepted. *Expenses:* Tuition, state resident: full-time $15,026; part-time $834 per credit hour. Tuition, nonresident: full-time $25,168; part-time $1378 per credit hour. *Required fees:* $2654. *Financial support:* Fellowships, research assistantships, and teaching assistantships available. Financial award application deadline: 1/5; financial award applicants required to submit FAFSA. *Unit head:* Robert C. Pianta, Dean, 434-924-3334, E-mail: pianta@virginia.edu. *Application contact:* Eric Molnar, Assistant Director, Admissions and Enrollment Reporting, 434-243-2085, E-mail: eric.molnar@virginia.edu.
Website: http://curry.virginia.edu/teacher-education

University of Washington, Tacoma, Graduate Programs, Program in Education, Tacoma, WA 98402-3100. Offers education (M Ed); educational administration (principal or program administrator certification) (M Ed); elementary education teacher certification (M Ed); elementary education/special education teacher certification (M Ed); secondary science or math teacher certification (M Ed). *Program availability:* Part-time, evening/weekend. *Degree requirements:* For master's, culminating project. *Entrance requirements:* For master's, WEST-B, WEST-E (teacher certification programs only), official sealed transcript from every college/university attended, personal goal statement, letters of recommendation, copy of valid teaching certificate. Additional exam requirements/recommendations for international students: Required—TOEFL (minimum score 580 paper-based; 92 iBT). Electronic applications accepted. *Faculty research:* Global learning communities for English/Chinese languages, evaluation of mathematics and reading intervention programs, response to intervention, school-wide behavioral and emotional support, mathematics education and culturally responsive mathematics education.

The University of West Alabama, School of Graduate Studies, College of Education, Departments of Instructional Leadership and Support/Curriculum and Instruction, Program in Elementary Education, Livingston, AL 35470. Offers elementary education (Ed S); elementary education K-6 (M Ed). *Accreditation:* NCATE. *Program availability:* Part-time, evening/weekend, 100% online. *Faculty:* 9 full-time (all women), 25 part-time/adjunct (18 women). *Students:* 249 (240 women); includes 74 minority (69 Black or African American, non-Hispanic/Latino; 2 American Indian or Alaska Native, non-Hispanic/Latino; 3 Two or more races, non-Hispanic/Latino). Average age 33. 97 applicants, 87% accepted, 70 enrolled. In 2016, 74 master's, 29 Ed Ss awarded. *Degree requirements:* For master's, comprehensive exam, thesis optional; for Ed S, comprehensive exam. *Entrance requirements:* For master's, GRE General Test, MAT, minimum GPA of 2.75. Additional exam requirements/recommendations for international students: Required—TOEFL (minimum score 500 paper-based; 61 iBT). *Application deadline:* Applications are processed on a rolling basis. Application fee: $40. Electronic applications accepted. *Expenses:* Tuition, state resident: part-time $355 per credit hour. Tuition, nonresident: part-time $710 per credit hour. *Required fees:* $130 per semester. *Financial support:* Teaching assistantships, Federal Work-Study, and unspecified assistantships available. Support available to part-time students. Financial award application deadline: 3/1; financial award applicants required to submit FAFSA. *Unit head:* Dr. Jodie Winship, Chair of Curriculum and Instruction, 205-652-5415, Fax: 205-652-3706, E-mail: jwinship@uwa.edu. *Application contact:* Dr. B. J. Kimbrough, Dean of Graduate Studies, 205-652-3647, Fax: 205-652-3706, E-mail: bkimbrough@uwa.edu.
Website: http://www.uwa.edu/elementaryeducationk6.aspx

University of West Florida, College of Education and Professional Studies, Department of Teacher Education and Educational Leadership, Program in Curriculum and Instruction, Pensacola, FL 32514-5750. Offers elementary education (M Ed); middle level education (M Ed); secondary education (M Ed). *Program availability:* Part-time, evening/weekend. *Entrance requirements:* For master's, GRE (minimum score 450 verbal) or MAT (minimum score 396) if bachelor's GPA less than 3.0, state teaching certification; letter of intent; two professional references. Additional exam requirements/recommendations for international students: Required—TOEFL (minimum score 550 paper-based). *Application deadline:* For fall admission, 6/1 for domestic and international students; for spring admission, 10/1 for domestic and international students. Applications are processed on a rolling basis. Application fee: $30. *Expenses:* Tuition, state resident: full-time $5316.12. Tuition, nonresident: full-time $11,308. *Required fees:* $583.92. Tuition and fees vary according to course load and program. *Financial support:* Career-related internships or fieldwork, Federal Work-Study, scholarships/grants, and tuition waivers (partial) available. Support available to part-time students. Financial award application deadline: 4/15; financial award applicants required to submit FAFSA. *Unit head:* Dr. William H. Evans, Acting Director, 850-474-2892, Fax: 850-474-2844, E-mail: wevans@uwf.edu. *Application contact:* Terry McCray, Assistant Director of Graduate Admissions, 850-473-7718, Fax: 850-473-7714, E-mail: gradadmissions@uwf.edu.

University of Wisconsin–Milwaukee, Graduate School, School of Education, Department of Curriculum and Instruction, Milwaukee, WI 53201-0413. Offers curriculum and instruction (MS), including cross-curricular focus, early childhood education, English education, mathematics education, middle childhood/early adolescence education, reading education, science education, urban social studies education. *Program availability:* Part-time. *Students:* 21 full-time (13 women), 44 part-time (42 women); includes 10 minority (1 Black or African American, non-Hispanic/Latino; 1 Asian, non-Hispanic/Latino; 2 Hispanic/Latino; 6 Two or more races, non-Hispanic/Latino), 2 international. Average age 33. 42 applicants, 71% accepted, 20 enrolled. In 2016, 45 master's awarded. *Degree requirements:* For master's, thesis or alternative. *Entrance requirements:* Additional exam requirements/recommendations for international students: Required—TOEFL (minimum score 550 paper-based; 79 iBT), IELTS (minimum score 6.5). *Application deadline:* For fall admission, 1/1 priority date for domestic students; for spring admission, 9/1 for domestic students. Applications are processed on a rolling basis. Application fee: $56 ($96 for international students). Electronic applications accepted. *Financial support:* In 2016–17, 1 fellowship was awarded; research assistantships, teaching assistantships, career-related internships or fieldwork, health care benefits, unspecified assistantships, and project assistantships also available. Support available to part-time students. Financial award application deadline: 4/15; financial award applicants required to submit FAFSA. *Application contact:* General Information Contact, 414-229-4721, E-mail: soeinfo@uwm.edu.
Website: http://uwm.edu/education/academics/curriculum-instruction-department/

University of Wisconsin–River Falls, Outreach and Graduate Studies, College of Education and Professional Studies, Department of Teacher Education, River Falls, WI 54022. Offers elementary education (MSE); professional development shared inquiry communities (MSE); reading (MSE). *Program availability:* Part-time. *Degree requirements:* For master's, comprehensive exam, thesis or alternative. *Entrance requirements:* For master's, minimum GPA of 2.75. Additional exam requirements/recommendations for international students: Required—TOEFL (minimum score 500 paper-based; 65 iBT), IELTS (minimum score 5.5). Electronic applications accepted.

University of Wisconsin–Stevens Point, College of Fine Arts and Communication, Department of Music, Stevens Point, WI 54481-3897. Offers elementary/secondary (MM Ed); studio pedagogy (MM Ed); Suzuki talent education (MM Ed). *Accreditation:* NASM. *Program availability:* Part-time. *Degree requirements:* For master's, thesis or alternative. *Entrance requirements:* For master's, teaching certificate. *Faculty research:* Music education, music composition, music performance.

University of Wisconsin–Stevens Point, College of Professional Studies, School of Education, Program in Elementary Education, Stevens Point, WI 54481-3897. Offers MSE. *Program availability:* Part-time. *Degree requirements:* For master's, comprehensive exam, thesis or alternative. *Entrance requirements:* For master's, teacher certification, minimum undergraduate GPA of 3.0. Additional exam requirements/recommendations for international students: Required—TOEFL (minimum score 523 paper-based). *Faculty research:* Gifted education, early childhood special education, curriculum and instruction, standards-based education.

Utah State University, School of Graduate Studies, Emma Eccles Jones College of Education and Human Services, Program in Elementary Education, Logan, UT 84322. Offers M Ed, MA, MS. *Program availability:* Part-time, online learning. *Degree requirements:* For master's, comprehensive exam (for some programs), thesis (for some programs). *Entrance requirements:* For master's, GRE General Test or MAT, minimum GPA of 3.0, teaching certificate, 3 recommendations, 1 year teaching department record. Additional exam requirements/recommendations for international students: Required—TOEFL. *Faculty research:* Teacher education, supervision, gifted and talented education, language arts/writing, early childhood education.

Utah Valley University, Program in Education, Orem, UT 84058-5999. Offers educational technology (M Ed); elementary mathematics (M Ed); elementary STEM (M Ed); English as a second language (M Ed); reading (M Ed); teachers as leaders (M Ed). *Accreditation:* TEAC. *Program availability:* Part-time. *Degree requirements:* For master's, project. *Entrance requirements:* For master's, GRE, 3 letters of recommendation, interview, essay. Additional exam requirements/recommendations for international students: Required—TOEFL (minimum score 83 iBT). Electronic applications accepted. *Expenses:* Contact institution.

Valley City State University, Online Master of Education Program, Valley City, ND 58072. Offers elementary education (M Ed); English education (M Ed); library and information technologies (M Ed); teaching (MAT); teaching and technology (M Ed); teaching English language learners (M Ed); technology education (M Ed). *Accreditation:* NCATE. *Program availability:* Part-time, evening/weekend, online only, 100% online. *Faculty:* 21 full-time (12 women), 15 part-time/adjunct (11 women). *Students:* 4 full-time (3 women), 133 part-time (92 women); includes 9 minority (1 American Indian or Alaska Native, non-Hispanic/Latino; 4 Hispanic/Latino; 4 Two or more races, non-Hispanic/Latino), 1 international. Average age 34. 35 applicants, 91% accepted, 28 enrolled. In 2016, 45 master's awarded. *Degree requirements:* For master's, action research report, comprehensive portfolio. *Entrance requirements:* For master's, GRE, MAT, PRAXIS II or National Teaching Board for Professional Standards (if GPA is less than 3.0). Additional exam requirements/recommendations for international students: Required—TOEFL (minimum score 525 paper-based; 71 iBT); Recommended—IELTS (minimum score 5.5). *Application deadline:* For fall admission, 7/21 priority date for domestic and international students; for spring admission, 12/8 priority date for domestic and international students; for summer admission, 5/5 priority date for domestic and international students. Applications are processed on a rolling basis. Application fee: $35. Electronic applications accepted. *Expenses:* $373 per credit. *Financial support:* In 2016–17, 23 students received support. Scholarships/grants, tuition waivers (full and partial), and unspecified assistantships available. Financial award application deadline: 6/14; financial award applicants required to submit FAFSA. *Faculty research:* Universal accessibility, instructional design and technology, gender communication, STEM education in K-12. *Unit head:* Dr. Gary Thompson, Dean, 701-845-7197, E-mail: gary.thompson@vcsu.edu. *Application contact:* Misty Lindgren, Graduate Studies, 701-845-7303, Fax: 701-845-7190, E-mail: misty.lindgren@vcsu.edu.
Website: http://www.vcsu.edu/graduate

Vanderbilt University, Peabody College, Department of Teaching and Learning, Nashville, TN 37240-1001. Offers elementary education (M Ed); English language learners (M Ed); learning and design (M Ed); learning, diversity, and urban studies (M Ed); reading education (M Ed); secondary education (M Ed). *Accreditation:* NCATE. *Program availability:* Part-time. *Faculty:* 44 full-time (34 women), 26 part-time/adjunct (21 women). *Students:* 120 full-time (106 women), 26 part-time (18 women); includes 22 minority (9 Black or African American, non-Hispanic/Latino; 6 Asian, non-Hispanic/Latino; 6 Hispanic/Latino; 1 Two or more races, non-Hispanic/Latino), 44 international. Average age 24. 328 applicants, 73% accepted, 76 enrolled. In 2016, 110 master's awarded. *Degree requirements:* For master's, comprehensive exam, thesis optional. *Entrance requirements:* For master's, GRE General Test, MAT. Additional exam requirements/recommendations for international students: Required—TOEFL (minimum score 550 paper-based; 80 iBT). *Application deadline:* For fall admission, 12/31 priority date for domestic and international students; for spring admission, 11/1 priority date for domestic and international students. Applications are processed on a rolling basis. Application fee: $0. Electronic applications accepted. *Expenses: Tuition:* Part-time $1854 per credit hour. *Financial support:* Fellowships with partial tuition reimbursements, research assistantships with partial tuition reimbursements, teaching assistantships with partial tuition reimbursements, Federal Work-Study, institutionally sponsored loans, scholarships/grants, tuition waivers (partial), and unspecified assistantships available. Support available to part-time students. Financial award application deadline: 1/15; financial award applicants required to submit FAFSA. *Faculty research:* Children's learning and development in core conceptual domains (STEM, English language arts, social studies); classroom discourse structures that teachers can learn and use to support students' learning and development K-6; intervention and design-based research on educational improvement at classroom, school, and district levels; design-based and learning sciences research on relations between learning in schools and other settings. *Unit head:* Dr. Rogers Hall, Chair, 615-322-8100, Fax: 615-322-8999, E-mail: rogers.hall@vanderbilt.edu. *Application contact:* Angela Saylor, Educational Coordinator, 615-322-8092, Fax: 615-322-8999, E-mail: angela.saylor@vanderbilt.edu.

Virginia Commonwealth University, Graduate School, School of Education, Program in Teaching and Learning, Richmond, VA 23284-9005. Offers early and elementary education (MT). *Accreditation:* NCATE. *Program availability:* Part-time. *Entrance requirements:* For master's, GRE General Test or MAT. Additional exam requirements/recommendations for international students: Required—TOEFL (minimum score 600 paper-based; 100 iBT). *Application deadline:* For fall admission, 3/15 for domestic students; for spring admission, 11/1 for domestic students. Applications are processed on a rolling basis. Application fee: $50. Electronic applications accepted. *Financial support:* Application deadline: 3/1; applicants required to submit FAFSA. *Unit head:* Dr. Leila Christenbury, Interim Chair, 804-828-1305, E-mail: lchriste@vcu.edu. *Application contact:* Laura Domalik, Graduate Program Coordinator, 804-828-1305, E-mail: lsdomalik@vcu.edu.
Website: http://www.soe.vcu.edu/departments/tl/programs.html

Wagner College, Division of Graduate Studies, Education Department, Program in Childhood Education/Students with Disabilities, Staten Island, NY 10301-4495. Offers MS Ed. *Program availability:* Part-time, evening/weekend. *Degree requirements:* For master's, thesis (for some programs), passage of New York State certification exams before student teaching. *Entrance requirements:* For master's, minimum GPA of 3.0, interview, recommendations. Additional exam requirements/recommendations for international students: Required—TOEFL. Electronic applications accepted. Tuition and fees vary according to degree level.

Walden University, Graduate Programs, Richard W. Riley College of Education and Leadership, Minneapolis, MN 55401. Offers adult education (Post-Master's Certificate); adult learning (Graduate Certificate); college teaching and learning (Graduate Certificate); community college leadership (Ed D); curriculum, instruction and assessment (Ed D, Ed S, Graduate Certificate); developmental education (Graduate Certificate); early childhood administration, management, and leadership (Graduate Certificate); early childhood education (Ed D, Ed S); early childhood public policy and advocacy (Graduate Certificate); early childhood studies (MS), including administration, management and leadership, early childhood public policy and advocacy, teaching adults in the early childhood field, teaching and diversity in early childhood education; education (MS, PhD), including adolescent literacy and learning (MS), curriculum, instruction, and assessment (grades K-12) (MS), curriculum, instruction, assessment, and evaluation (PhD), early childhood leadership and advocacy (PhD), early childhood special education (PhD), educational leadership (MS), educational leadership and administration (principal preparation) (MS), educational technology and design (PhD), elementary reading and literacy (PreK-6) (MS), elementary reading and mathematics (grades K-6) (MS), global and comparative education (PhD), higher education leadership management and policy (PhD), integrating technology in the classroom (grades K-12) (MS), learning, instruction and innovation (PhD), mathematics (grades 5-8) (MS), mathematics (grades K-6) (MS), mathematics and science (grades K-8) (MS), organizational research, assessment, and evaluation (PhD), reading and literacy with a reading K-12 endorsement (MS), reading literacy assessment and evaluation (PhD), science (grades K-8) (MS), special education (non-licensure) (grades K-12) (MS), teacher leadership (grades K-12) (MS), teaching English language learners (grades K-12) (MS); educational administration and leadership (Ed D); educational leadership and administration (principal preparation) (Ed S); educational technology (Ed D, Ed S, Post Master's Certificate); elementary reading and literacy (Graduate Certificate); engaging culturally diverse learners (Graduate Certificate); enrollment management and institutional marketing (Graduate Certificate); higher education (MS), including adult learning, college teaching and learning, enrollment management and institutional marketing, global higher education, leadership for student success, online and distance learning; higher education and adult learning (Ed D); higher education leadership and management (Ed D); higher education leadership for student success (Graduate Certificate); instructional design and technology (MS, Postbaccalaureate Certificate), including general program (MS), online learning (MS), training and performance improvement (MS); integrating technology in the classroom (Graduate Certificate); mathematics 5-8 (Graduate Certificate); mathematics K-6 (Graduate Certificate); online teaching for adult educators (Graduate Certificate); reading, literacy, and assessment (Ed D, Ed S); science K-8 (Graduate Certificate); special education (Ed D, Ed S, Graduate Certificate); special education (K-age 21) (MAT); teacher leadership (Graduate Certificate); teaching adults English as a second language (Graduate Certificate); teaching adults in the early childhood field (Graduate Certificate); teaching and diversity in early childhood education (Graduate Certificate); teaching English language learners (grades K-12) (Graduate Certificate); teaching K-12 students online (Graduate Certificate). *Accreditation:* NCATE. *Program availability:* Part-time, evening/weekend, online only, 100% online. *Degree requirements:* For doctorate, thesis/dissertation (for some programs), residency; for other advanced degree, residency (for some programs). *Entrance requirements:* For master's, bachelor's degree or higher; minimum GPA of 2.5; official transcripts; goal statement (for some programs); access to computer and Internet; for doctorate, master's degree or higher; three years of related professional or academic experience (preferred); minimum GPA of 3.0; goal statement and current resume (for select programs); official transcripts; access to computer and Internet; for other advanced degree, relevant work experience; access to computer and Internet. Additional exam requirements/recommendations for international students: Required—TOEFL (minimum score 550 paper-based, 79 iBT), IELTS (minimum score 6.5), Michigan English Language Assessment Battery (minimum score 82), or PTE (minimum score 53). Electronic applications accepted.

Warner University, School of Education, Lake Wales, FL 33859. Offers curriculum and instruction (MAEd); elementary education (MAEd); science, technology, engineering, and mathematics (STEM) (MAEd). *Program availability:* Part-time, evening/weekend, online learning. *Degree requirements:* For master's, thesis, accomplished practices portfolio. *Entrance requirements:* For master's, minimum GPA of 3.0 in last 60 hours of undergraduate coursework; 2 letters of recommendation. Additional exam requirements/recommendations for international students: Required—TOEFL (minimum score 550 paper-based). *Application deadline:* Applications are processed on a rolling basis. Application fee: $50. Electronic applications accepted. *Financial support:* Scholarships/grants available. Financial award applicants required to submit FAFSA. *Unit head:* Dr. Bill Rigel, Dean, 863-638-7207, Fax: 863-638-4907, E-mail: bill.rigel@warner.edu. *Application contact:* Torshanda Howard, Admissions Advisor, 863-638-7501, Fax: 863-638-4907, E-mail: admissons@warner.edu.
Website: http://warner.edu/graduate/degrees-offered/arts-in-education/

Washington State University, College of Education, Department of Teaching and Learning, Pullman, WA 99164-2132. Offers cultural studies and social thought in education (PhD); curriculum and instruction (Ed M, MA); English language learners (Ed M, MA); language, literacy and technology (PhD); literacy education (Ed M, MA); mathematics education (PhD); special education (Ed M, MA, PhD); teacher leadership (Ed D); teaching (MIT), including elementary education, secondary education. Programs offered at the Pullman, Spokane, Tri-cities, Vancouver and Global (online) campuses. *Program availability:* Part-time, online learning. *Degree requirements:* For master's, comprehensive exam, thesis, oral or written exam; for doctorate, comprehensive exam, thesis/dissertation, oral and written exam. *Entrance requirements:* For master's, GRE General Test, minimum GPA of 3.0, 3 letters of recommendation, letter of intent, transcripts, resume/curriculum vitae; for doctorate, GRE General Test, minimum GPA of 3.0, 3 letters of recommendation, letter of intent, transcripts, writing sample, resume/curriculum vitae. Additional exam requirements/recommendations for international students: Required—TOEFL (minimum score 550 paper-based; 80 iBT). Electronic applications accepted. *Faculty research:* Intersection of gender, youth cultures and schooling; examination of ideology of power in children's literature; early childhood special education; analyzing pre-service and in-service teacher development; second language acquisition.

Washington University in St. Louis, The Graduate School, Department of Education, Program in Elementary Education, St. Louis, MO 63130-4899. Offers MA Ed. *Degree requirements:* For master's, thesis or alternative. *Entrance requirements:* For master's, GRE General Test or MAT. Additional exam requirements/recommendations for international students: Required—TOEFL. Electronic applications accepted.

Wayland Baptist University, Graduate Programs, Program in Education, Plainview, TX 79072-6998. Offers education administration (M Ed); education diagnostics (M Ed); education literacy (M Ed); elementary certification (M Ed); English (M Ed); English as a second language (M Ed); higher education administration (M Ed); human resources (M Ed); instructional leadership (M Ed); instructional technology (M Ed); leadership training and development (M Ed); science education (M Ed); secondary certification (M Ed); social studies (M Ed); special education (M Ed); sports administration and management (M Ed). *Program availability:* Part-time, evening/weekend, online learning. *Degree requirements:* For master's, comprehensive exam, capstone course. *Entrance requirements:* For master's, GRE, GMAT or MAT. Additional exam requirements/recommendations for international students: Required—TOEFL (minimum score 500 paper-based; 61 iBT). Electronic applications accepted.

Wayne State College, School of Education and Counseling, Department of Educational Foundations and Leadership, Program in Curriculum and Instruction, Wayne, NE 68787. Offers alternative education (MSE); business and information technology education

(MSE); communication arts education (MSE); early childhood education (MSE); elementary education (MSE); English as a second language (MSE); English education (MSE); family and consumer sciences education (MSE); industrial technology and vocational education (MSE); learning communities (MSE); mathematics education (MSE); music education (MSE); science education (MSE); social science education (MSE). *Accreditation:* NCATE. *Program availability:* Part-time, evening/weekend. *Degree requirements:* For master's, comprehensive exam, thesis optional. *Entrance requirements:* For master's, GRE General Test. Additional exam requirements/ recommendations for international students: Required—TOEFL (minimum score 550 paper-based).

Wayne State University, College of Education, Division of Teacher Education, Detroit, MI 48202. Offers art education (M Ed); bilingual/bicultural education (M Ed, Certificate); career and technical education (M Ed); curriculum and instruction (Ed D, PhD, Ed S), including art education (Ed D, PhD), bilingual education (Ed D, Ed S), career and technical education (MAT, Ed D, PhD, Ed S), early childhood education (MAT, Ed D, PhD, Ed S), elementary education, English as a second language (MAT, Ed D, Ed S), English education (MAT, Ed D, PhD, Ed S), foreign language education (MAT, Ed D, PhD), K-12 curriculum, mathematics education (MAT, Ed D, PhD, Ed S), science education (MAT, Ed D, PhD, Ed S), secondary education, social studies education (MAT, Ed D, PhD, Ed S); early childhood education (M Ed); elementary education (M Ed, MAT), including bilingual/bicultural education (MAT), early childhood education (MAT, Ed D, PhD, Ed S), English as a second language (MAT, Ed D, Ed S), general elementary education (MAT), mathematics education (MAT, Ed D, PhD, Ed S), science education (MAT, Ed D, PhD, Ed S), social studies education (MAT, Ed D, PhD, Ed S); English as a second language (Certificate); English education (M Ed); foreign language education (M Ed); mathematics education (M Ed); reading (M Ed, Ed S); reading, language and literature (Ed D); science education (M Ed); secondary education (MAT), including art education (K-12), bilingual/bicultural education, career and technical education (MAT, Ed D, PhD, Ed S), English as a second language (MAT, Ed D, Ed S), English education (MAT, Ed D, PhD, Ed S), foreign language education (MAT, Ed D, PhD), kinesiology, mathematics education (MAT, Ed D, PhD, Ed S); social studies education (M Ed); special education (M Ed, MAT, Ed D, PhD, Ed S), including autism spectrum disorders (MAT), cognitive development (MAT), emotional impairment (MAT), learning disabilities (MAT). *Program availability:* Part-time, blended/hybrid learning. *Faculty:* 29. *Students:* 106 full-time (73 women), 351 part-time (276 women); includes 115 minority (76 Black or African American, non-Hispanic/Latino; 10 Asian, non-Hispanic/Latino; 20 Hispanic/Latino; 1 Native Hawaiian or other Pacific Islander, non-Hispanic/Latino; 8 Two or more races, non-Hispanic/Latino), 12 international. Average age 37. 242 applicants, 37% accepted, 72 enrolled. In 2016, 178 master's, 19 doctorates, 17 other advanced degrees awarded. *Degree requirements:* For master's, essay or project (for some M Ed programs), professional field experience (for MAT programs); for doctorate, thesis/dissertation. *Entrance requirements:* For master's, Michigan Test for Teacher Certification, verification of participation in group work with children, Michigan State Police criminal background check; for doctorate, minimum undergraduate GPA of 3.0, graduate 3.5; interview; curriculum vitae; references. Additional exam requirements/recommendations for international students: Required—TOEFL (minimum score 550 paper-based; 79 iBT), TWE (minimum score 5.5), Michigan English Language Assessment Battery (minimum score 85); Recommended—IELTS (minimum score 6.5). *Application deadline:* For fall admission, 6/1 priority date for domestic students, 5/1 priority date for international students; for winter admission, 10/1 priority date for domestic students, 9/1 priority date for international students; for spring admission, 2/1 priority date for domestic students, 1/1 priority date for international students. Applications are processed on a rolling basis. Application fee: $50. Electronic applications accepted. *Expenses:* $16,503 per year resident tuition and fees, $33,697 per year non-resident tuition and fees. *Financial support:* In 2016–17, 101 students received support, including 3 fellowships (averaging $11,409 per year); research assistantships with tuition reimbursements available, Federal Work-Study, scholarships/ grants, and unspecified assistantships also available. Support available to part-time students. Financial award applicants required to submit FAFSA. *Faculty research:* Improving students' skill achievement in mathematics, improving elementary children's understanding of informational text, teachers' use of their pedagogical and mathematical knowledge in the interactive work of teaching, the intersection of identity construction in teaching and learning, identifying effective methods of literacy instruction and assessments for bilingual students in elementary language arts classrooms. *Unit head:* Dr. Kathleen Crawford-McKinney, Assistant Dean, 313-577-0122. *Application contact:* Janice Green, Assistant Dean, 313-577-1605, E-mail: jwgreen@wayne.edu.
Website: http://coe.wayne.edu/ted/index.php

Webster University, School of Education, Department of Multidisciplinary Studies, St. Louis, MO 63119-3194. Offers applied educational psychology (MA, Ed S); communication arts (MA); early childhood education (MA, MAT); education and innovation (MA); educational technology (MET); elementary education (MAT); mathematics for educators (MA); middle school education (MAT); multidisciplinary studies (MAT); multimodal literacy for global impact (MA); reading (MA); secondary school education (MAT); special education (MA, MAT); teaching English as a second language (MA); transformative learning in the global community (Ed S). *Program availability:* Part-time. *Entrance requirements:* For master's, minimum GPA of 2.5. Additional exam requirements/recommendations for international students: Required—TOEFL. *Application deadline:* Applications are processed on a rolling basis. Application fee: $35 ($50 for international students). *Expenses: Tuition:* Full-time $21,900; part-time $730 per credit hour. Tuition and fees vary according to campus/location and program. *Financial support:* Federal Work-Study available. Support available to part-time students. Financial award application deadline: 4/1; financial award applicants required to submit FAFSA. *Unit head:* Dr. Deborah Stiles, Chair, 314-968-7056, Fax: 314-968-7118, E-mail: stilesda@webster.edu.

Western Governors University, Teachers College, Salt Lake City, UT 84107. Offers curriculum and instruction (MS); educational leadership (MS); educational studies (MA); educational studies (5-12) (MA), including mathematics; elementary education (K-8) (MAT, Postbaccalaureate Certificate); elementary education (PreK-8) (MAT); English language learning (K-12) (MA); instructional design (MAT); learning and technology (M Ed, MA); management and innovation (M Ed); mathematics (5-12) (MAT, Postbaccalaureate Certificate); mathematics (5-9) (MAT, Postbaccalaureate Certificate); mathematics education (5-12) (MA); mathematics education (5-9) (MA); mathematics education (K-6) (MA); measurement and evaluation (M Ed); science (5-12) (Postbaccalaureate Certificate); science (5-9) (MAT, Postbaccalaureate Certificate); science education (5-12) (MA), including biology, chemistry, geology, physics; science education (5-9) (MA); social science (5-12) (MAT, Postbaccalaureate Certificate); special education (MAT, MS). *Accreditation:* NCATE. *Program availability:* Evening/ weekend, online learning. *Degree requirements:* For master's, capstone project. *Entrance requirements:* For master's and Postbaccalaureate Certificate, Readiness Assessment, transcripts. Additional exam requirements/recommendations for international students: Required—TOEFL (minimum score 450 paper-based; 80 iBT). Electronic applications accepted. *Expenses:* Contact institution.

Western Kentucky University, Graduate Studies, College of Education and Behavioral Sciences, School of Teacher Education, Bowling Green, KY 42101. Offers elementary education (MAE, Ed S); exceptional education: learning and behavioral disorders (MAE); exceptional education: moderate and severe disabilities (MAE); instructional design (MS); interdisciplinary early childhood education (MAE); library media education (MS); literacy education (MAE); middle grades education (MAE); secondary education (MAE, Ed S). *Program availability:* Part-time, evening/weekend, online learning. *Degree requirements:* For master's, comprehensive exam. *Entrance requirements:* For master's, GRE General Test. Additional exam requirements/recommendations for international students: Required—TOEFL (minimum score 555 paper-based; 79 iBT). *Faculty research:* Teacher preparation in moderate/severe disabilities.

Western New Mexico University, Graduate Division, School of Education, Silver City, NM 88062-0680. Offers bilingual education (MAT); educational leadership (MA); elementary education (MAT); reading (MAT); secondary education (MAT); special education (MAT); TESOL (teaching English to speakers of other languages) (MAT). *Accreditation:* NCATE. *Program availability:* Part-time, online learning. *Degree requirements:* For master's, comprehensive exam. *Entrance requirements:* For master's, minimum GPA of 3.0 in last 64 hours of undergraduate study. Additional exam requirements/recommendations for international students: Required—TOEFL (minimum score 550 paper-based; 79 iBT). Electronic applications accepted. *Faculty research:* International education, electronic reading assessment, developing STEM teachers.

Western Washington University, Graduate School, Woodring College of Education, Department of Elementary Education, Bellingham, WA 98225-5996. Offers M Ed. *Accreditation:* NCATE. *Program availability:* Part-time. *Degree requirements:* For master's, comprehensive exam, thesis optional. *Entrance requirements:* For master's, GRE General Test or MAT, minimum GPA of 3.0 in last 60 semester hours or last 90 quarter hours, elementary teaching certificate. Additional exam requirements/ recommendations for international students: Required—TOEFL (minimum score 567 paper-based). Electronic applications accepted. *Faculty research:* Teacher learning through National Board certification.

Westfield State University, College of Graduate and Continuing Education, Department of Education, Program in Elementary Education, Westfield, MA 01086. Offers M Ed. *Accreditation:* NCATE. *Program availability:* Part-time, evening/weekend. *Students:* 2 full-time (1 woman), 33 part-time (26 women); includes 1 minority (Hispanic/ Latino), 1 international. Average age 30. 9 applicants, 78% accepted, 7 enrolled. In 2016, 6 master's awarded. *Degree requirements:* For master's, comprehensive exam, practicum. *Entrance requirements:* For master's, GRE General Test or MAT, minimum undergraduate GPA of 2.8. Additional exam requirements/recommendations for international students: Recommended—TOEFL (minimum score 550 paper-based; 79 iBT). *Application deadline:* For fall admission, 6/30 for domestic students; for spring admission, 10/31 for domestic students; for summer admission, 3/31 for domestic students. Applications are processed on a rolling basis. Application fee: $50. Electronic applications accepted. *Expenses:* Tuition, state resident: part-time $318 per semester hour. Tuition, nonresident: part-time $318 per semester hour. *Required fees:* $75 per semester. Tuition and fees vary according to course load and program. *Financial support:* Unspecified assistantships and SOS scholarships for education majors only available. Financial award application deadline: 3/1; financial award applicants required to submit FAFSA. *Unit head:* Dr. Sandra Berkowitz, Department Chair, 413-572-5323, E-mail: sberkowitz@westfield.ma.edu. *Application contact:* Shelly Henrichon, Coordinator of DGCE Admissions, 413-572-8022, Fax: 413-572-5227, E-mail: mhenrichon@westfield.ma.edu.
Website: http://www.westfield.ma.edu/academics/degrees/education-graduate-programs

West Virginia University, College of Education and Human Services, Department of Curriculum and Instruction/Literacy Studies, Program in Elementary Education, Morgantown, WV 26506. Offers MA. Students enter program as undergraduates. *Accreditation:* NCATE. *Program availability:* Part-time. *Degree requirements:* For master's, thesis optional, content exams. *Entrance requirements:* For master's, minimum GPA of 2.75. Additional exam requirements/recommendations for international students: Required—TOEFL. Electronic applications accepted. *Faculty research:* Teacher education, school reform, teacher and student attitudes, curriculum development, education technology.

Wheaton College, Graduate School, Department of Education, Wheaton, IL 60187-5593. Offers elementary education (MAT); secondary education (MAT). *Accreditation:* NCATE. *Faculty:* 1 full-time (0 women). *Students:* 14 full-time (10 women); includes 2 minority (both Asian, non-Hispanic/Latino). Average age 25. 11 applicants, 100% accepted, 8 enrolled. In 2016, 10 master's awarded. *Degree requirements:* For master's, thesis or alternative. *Entrance requirements:* For master's, GRE General Test or MAT. Additional exam requirements/recommendations for international students: Required—TOEFL (minimum score 550 paper-based; 80 iBT), IELTS (minimum score 6.5). *Application deadline:* For fall admission, 5/1 for domestic students, 1/1 for international students; for spring admission, 11/1 for domestic students. Applications are processed on a rolling basis. Application fee: $30. Electronic applications accepted. *Expenses: Tuition:* Full-time $19,080; part-time $795 per credit hour. Tuition and fees vary according to degree level and program. *Financial support:* Career-related internships or fieldwork and Federal Work-Study available. Financial award application deadline: 3/1; financial award applicants required to submit FAFSA. *Unit head:* Dr. Paul Egeland, Chair, 630-752-5041. *Application contact:* Dusty Di Santo, Director of Graduate Admissions, 630-752-5195, Fax: 630-752-7047, E-mail: graduate.admissions@ wheaton.edu.
Website: http://www.wheaton.edu/academics/departments/education

Wheelock College, Graduate Programs, Division of Education, Boston, MA 02215. Offers early childhood education (MS); education leadership (MS); elementary education (MS); language, literacy, and reading (MS); teaching students with moderate disabilities (MS). *Accreditation:* NCATE. *Program availability:* Online learning. *Degree requirements:* For master's, comprehensive exam. *Entrance requirements:* Additional exam requirements/recommendations for international students: Required—TOEFL. Electronic applications accepted. *Faculty research:* Symbolic learning, emergent literacy, diversity inclusion, beginning reading language and culture, math education.

Whittier College, Graduate Programs, Department of Education and Child Development, Program in Elementary Education, Whittier, CA 90608-0634. Offers MA Ed. *Program availability:* Part-time, evening/weekend. *Degree requirements:* For master's, thesis. *Entrance requirements:* For master's, GRE General Test, MAT.

Whitworth University, School of Education, Graduate Studies in Education, Spokane, WA 99251-0001. Offers administration (M Ed); counseling (M Ed), including school counselors, social agency/church setting; elementary education (M Ed); gifted and talented (MAT); secondary education (M Ed); special education (MAT); teaching (MIT). *Accreditation:* NCATE. *Program availability:* Part-time, evening/weekend. *Degree requirements:* For master's, comprehensive exam, thesis (for some programs). *Entrance requirements:* For master's, GRE General Test, MAT. Additional exam requirements/ recommendations for international students: Required—TOEFL. *Faculty research:* Rural program development, mainstreaming, special needs learners.

Widener University, School of Education, Hospitality, and Continuing Studies, Chester, PA 19013-5792. Offers adult education (M Ed); counseling in higher education (M Ed);

counselor education (M Ed); early childhood education (M Ed); educational foundations (M Ed); educational leadership (M Ed); educational psychology (M Ed); elementary education (M Ed); English and language arts (M Ed); health education (M Ed); higher education leadership (Ed D); home and school visitor (M Ed); human sexuality (M Ed, PhD); mathematics education (M Ed); middle school education (M Ed); principalship (M Ed); reading and language arts (Ed D); reading education (M Ed); school administration (Ed D); science education (M Ed); social studies education (M Ed); special education (M Ed); technology education (M Ed). *Accreditation:* NCATE. *Program availability:* Part-time, evening/weekend. *Faculty:* 34 full-time (22 women), 37 part-time/adjunct (14 women). *Students:* 97 full-time (64 women), 201 part-time (143 women); includes 56 minority (44 Black or African American, non-Hispanic/Latino; 1 American Indian or Alaska Native, non-Hispanic/Latino; 2 Asian, non-Hispanic/Latino; 8 Hispanic/Latino; 1 Two or more races, non-Hispanic/Latino), 32 international. Average age 39. 139 applicants, 88% accepted. In 2016, 45 master's, 21 doctorates awarded. Terminal master's awarded for partial completion of doctoral program. *Degree requirements:* For doctorate, thesis/dissertation. *Entrance requirements:* For master's, minimum GPA of 2.5; for doctorate, GRE or MAT, minimum GPA of 2.0 (undergraduate), 3.5 (graduate). *Application deadline:* Applications are processed on a rolling basis. Application fee: $25 ($300 for international students). Electronic applications accepted. *Expenses:* Contact institution. *Financial support:* Career-related internships or fieldwork, tuition waivers (full and partial), and unspecified assistantships available. Support available to part-time students. Financial award application deadline: 5/1. *Faculty research:* Reading and cognition, adult education, technology education, educational leadership, special education. *Unit head:* Dr. Shawn Fitzgerald, Dean, 610-499-4294, Fax: 610-499-4623, E-mail: smfitzgerald@widener.edu. *Application contact:* Dr. Roberta Nolan, Director of Graduate Admissions, 610-499-4125, E-mail: rdnolan@widener.edu.
Website: http://www.widener.edu/academics/schools/eics

William Carey University, School of Education, Hattiesburg, MS 39401-5499. Offers art education (M Ed); art of teaching (M Ed); elementary education (M Ed, Ed S); English education (M Ed); gifted education (M Ed); history and social science (M Ed); mild/moderate disabilities (M Ed); secondary education (M Ed). *Accreditation:* NCATE. *Program availability:* Part-time. *Degree requirements:* For master's, comprehensive exam. *Entrance requirements:* For master's, GRE, MAT, minimum GPA of 2.5, Class A teacher's license. Additional exam requirements/recommendations for international students: Required—TOEFL (minimum score 550 paper-based).

William Paterson University of New Jersey, College of Education, Wayne, NJ 07470-8420. Offers curriculum and learning (M Ed); educational leadership (M Ed); elementary education (MAT); literacy (M Ed); professional counseling (M Ed); secondary education (MAT); special education (M Ed). *Accreditation:* NCATE. *Program availability:* Part-time, evening/weekend. *Faculty:* 36 full-time (25 women), 32 part-time/adjunct (27 women). *Students:* 74 full-time (51 women), 607 part-time (515 women); includes 194 minority (42 Black or African American, non-Hispanic/Latino; 21 Asian, non-Hispanic/Latino; 116 Hispanic/Latino; 15 Two or more races, non-Hispanic/Latino), 1 international. Average age 35. 390 applicants, 83% accepted, 263 enrolled. In 2016, 170 master's awarded. *Degree requirements:* For master's, comprehensive exam, thesis (for some programs), exit interview (for some programs); practicum/internship; minimum GPA of 3.0 (for some programs); exit portfolio (for some programs). *Entrance requirements:* For master's, GRE/MAT, minimum GPA of 2.75; teaching certificate; essay; interview; 2 letters of recommendation; personal statement. Additional exam requirements/recommendations for international students: Required—TOEFL (minimum score 550 paper-based; 79 iBT), IELTS (minimum score 6). *Application deadline:* For fall admission, 8/1 for domestic students, 4/1 for international students; for spring admission, 12/1 for domestic students, 11/1 for international students; for summer admission, 5/1 for domestic students, 2/1 for international students. Applications are processed on a rolling basis. Application fee: $50. Electronic applications accepted. *Expenses:* Tuition, state resident: full-time $12,480; part-time $611 per credit. Tuition, nonresident: full-time $20,263; part-time $992 per credit. *Required fees:* $1573; $77 per credit. Tuition and fees vary according to course load, degree level and program. *Financial support:* Career-related internships or fieldwork, Federal Work-Study, scholarships/grants, and unspecified assistantships available. Support available to part-time students. Financial award application deadline: 4/1; financial award applicants required to submit FAFSA. *Faculty research:* History of education, social media in classrooms and education, integrating environmental lessons into urban classrooms, minority student self-advocacy in higher education, factors affecting high school teacher retention. *Total annual research expenditures:* $289,197. *Unit head:* Dr. Candace Burns, Dean, 973-720-2137, Fax: 973-720-3467, E-mail: burnsc@wpunj.edu. *Application contact:* Liana Fornarotto, Director of Education Enrollment and Certification, 973-720-2206, Fax: 973-720-2989, E-mail: fornarottol@wpunj.edu.
Website: http://www.wpunj.edu/coe

Wilmington University, College of Education, New Castle, DE 19720-6491. Offers applied technology in education (M Ed); career and technical education (M Ed); educational leadership (Ed D); elementary and secondary school counseling (M Ed); elementary studies (M Ed); ESOL literacy (M Ed); higher education leadership (Ed D); instruction: gifted and talented (M Ed); instruction: teacher of reading (M Ed); instruction: teaching and learning (M Ed); organizational leadership (Ed D); school leadership (M Ed); secondary education (MAT); special education (M Ed). *Accreditation:* NCATE. *Program availability:* Part-time, evening/weekend. *Faculty:* 19 full-time (11 women), 178 part-time/adjunct (99 women). *Students:* 248 full-time (176 women), 999 part-time (738 women); includes 244 minority (193 Black or African American, non-Hispanic/Latino; 17 American Indian or Alaska Native, non-Hispanic/Latino; 9 Asian, non-Hispanic/Latino; 19 Hispanic/Latino; 2 Native Hawaiian or other Pacific Islander, non-Hispanic/Latino; 4 Two or more races, non-Hispanic/Latino), 7 international. Average age 34. 672 applicants, 96% accepted, 348 enrolled. In 2016, 529 master's, 87 doctorates awarded. *Entrance requirements:* For master's, 2 letters of recommendation, interview. Additional exam requirements/recommendations for international students: Required—TOEFL (minimum score 500 paper-based). *Application deadline:* For fall admission, 4/30 for domestic students. Applications are processed on a rolling basis. Application fee: $35. Electronic applications accepted. *Expenses: Tuition:* Full-time $8388; part-time $466 per credit. *Required fees:* $25 per semester. Tuition and fees vary according to degree level. *Financial support:* Applicants required to submit FAFSA. *Unit head:* Dr. John C. Gray, Dean. *Application contact:* Laura Morris, Director of Admissions, 877-967-5464, E-mail: infocenter@wilmu.edu.
Website: http://www.wilmu.edu/education/

Wilson College, Graduate Programs, Chambersburg, PA 17201-1285. Offers accounting (M Acc); choreography and visual art (MFA); education (M Ed); healthcare management for sustainability (MHM); humanities (MA), including art and culture, critical/cultural theory, English language and literature, women's studies; management (MSM); nursing (MSN), including nursing education, nursing leadership and management. *Program availability:* Evening/weekend. *Degree requirements:* For master's, project. *Entrance requirements:* For master's, PRAXIS, minimum undergraduate cumulative GPA of 3.0, 2 letters of recommendation, current certification for eligibility to teach in grades K-12, resume, personal interview. Electronic applications accepted.

Wingate University, Thayer School of Education, Wingate, NC 28174. Offers community college executive leadership (Ed D); educational leadership (MA Ed, Ed S); elementary education (MA Ed, MAT). *Accreditation:* NCATE. *Program availability:* Part-time, evening/weekend. *Degree requirements:* For master's, portfolio. *Entrance requirements:* For master's, GRE General Test or MAT, teaching certificate (MA Ed). *Application deadline:* For fall admission, 8/15 priority date for domestic students; for spring admission, 12/15 for domestic students. Applications are processed on a rolling basis. Application fee: $0. *Financial support:* Scholarships/grants available. Support available to part-time students. Financial award applicants required to submit FAFSA. *Unit head:* Dr. Annette D. Digby, Interim Dean, 704-233-8473, E-mail: a.digby@wingate.edu. *Application contact:* Theresa Gibson, Director of the Graduate Education Program, 980-359-1023, E-mail: t.gibson@wingate.edu.

Worcester State University, Graduate Studies, Department of Education, Program in Elementary Education, Worcester, MA 01602-2597. Offers M Ed. *Program availability:* Part-time, evening/weekend. *Faculty:* 13 full-time (12 women), 16 part-time/adjunct (7 women). *Students:* 3 full-time (all women), 21 part-time (all women); includes 1 minority (American Indian or Alaska Native, non-Hispanic/Latino). Average age 29. 12 applicants, 100% accepted, 10 enrolled. In 2016, 7 master's awarded. *Degree requirements:* For master's, comprehensive exam (for some programs), thesis optional. *Entrance requirements:* For master's, GRE General Test or MAT, elementary teaching certificate. Additional exam requirements/recommendations for international students: Required—TOEFL (minimum score 550 paper-based; 79 iBT). *Application deadline:* For fall admission, 6/15 for domestic and international students; for spring admission, 11/1 for domestic and international students; for summer admission, 4/1 for domestic and international students. Applications are processed on a rolling basis. Application fee: $50. Electronic applications accepted. *Expenses:* Tuition, state resident: part-time $150 per credit. Tuition, nonresident: part-time $150 per credit. *Financial support:* Career-related internships or fieldwork, scholarships/grants, and unspecified assistantships available. Financial award application deadline: 3/1; financial award applicants required to submit FAFSA. *Faculty research:* Contemporary elementary education, social studies in the elementary school. *Unit head:* Dr. Christine Bebas, Coordinator, 508-929-8753, Fax: 508-929-8164, E-mail: cbebas@worcester.edu. *Application contact:* Sara Grady, Associate Dean of Graduate Studies and Professional Development, 508-929-8787, Fax: 508-929-8100, E-mail: sara.grady@worcester.edu.

Wright State University, Graduate School, College of Education and Human Services, Department of Teacher Education, Programs in Classroom Teacher Education, Dayton, OH 45435. Offers M Ed, MA. *Accreditation:* NCATE. *Degree requirements:* For master's, thesis (for some programs). *Entrance requirements:* For master's, GRE General Test, MAT, PRAXIS II. Additional exam requirements/recommendations for international students: Required—TOEFL. Application fee: $25. *Expenses:* Tuition, state resident: full-time $9952; part-time $622 per credit hour. Tuition, nonresident: full-time $16,960; part-time $1060 per credit hour. *Financial support:* Available to part-time students. Applicants required to submit FAFSA. *Unit head:* Dr. Colleen A. Finegan, Chair, 937-775-2332, Fax: 937-775-3308, E-mail: colleen.finegan@wright.edu. *Application contact:* John Kimble, Associate Director of Graduate Admissions and Records, 937-775-2957, Fax: 937-775-2453, E-mail: john.kimble@wright.edu.

Xavier University, College of Social Sciences, Health and Education, School of Education, Department of Childhood Education and Literacy, Cincinnati, OH 45207. Offers children's multicultural literature (M Ed); elementary education (M Ed); Montessori education (M Ed); reading (M Ed). *Program availability:* Part-time. *Degree requirements:* For master's, comprehensive exam, thesis, 30 semester hours. *Entrance requirements:* For master's, GRE, MAT, official transcript; 3 letters of recommendation (for Montessori education); resume; statement of purpose. Additional exam requirements/recommendations for international students: Required—TOEFL (minimum score 550 paper-based; 79 iBT). Electronic applications accepted. Application fee is waived when completed online. *Expenses:* Contact institution. *Faculty research:* Multicultural literacy/fluency, early literacy development, writing/creative and across curriculum, assessment of reading abilities.

Higher Education

Abilene Christian University, College of Graduate and Professional Studies, Program in Higher Education, Abilene, TX 79699. Offers M Ed. *Program availability:* Part-time, online learning. *Faculty:* 1 full-time (0 women). *Students:* 46 full-time (31 women), 24 part-time (20 women); includes 35 minority (21 Black or African American, non-Hispanic/Latino; 1 American Indian or Alaska Native, non-Hispanic/Latino; 2 Asian, non-Hispanic/Latino; 9 Hispanic/Latino; 2 Two or more races, non-Hispanic/Latino). 23 applicants, 96% accepted, 18 enrolled. In 2016, 21 master's awarded. *Degree requirements:* For master's, internship capstone. *Entrance requirements:* Additional exam requirements/recommendations for international students: Required—TOEFL (minimum score 80 iBT), IELTS (minimum score 6), PTE. *Application deadline:* For fall admission, 8/15 priority date for domestic students; for winter admission, 10/1 priority date for domestic students; for spring admission, 12/15 priority date for domestic students; for summer admission, 4/15 for domestic students. Applications are processed on a rolling basis. Application fee: $50. Electronic applications accepted. *Expenses:* $726 per credit hour. *Financial support:* In 2016–17, 1 student received support. Scholarships/grants available. Financial award application deadline: 4/1; financial award applicants required to submit FAFSA. *Unit head:* Dr. Jason Morris, Graduate Director, 325-674-2830, Fax: 325-674-2123, E-mail: morrisj@acu.edu. *Application contact:* Graduate Admissions, 855-219-7000, E-mail: gradonline@acu.edu.
Website: http://www.acu.edu/online/academics/higher-education.html

Alliant International University–San Diego, Shirley M. Hufstedler School of Education, Educational Leadership Programs, San Diego, CA 92131. Offers educational administration (MA); educational leadership and management (K-12) (Ed D); higher education (Ed D, Certificate); preliminary administrative services (Credential). *Program availability:* Part-time. *Degree requirements:* For doctorate, comprehensive exam, thesis/dissertation. *Entrance requirements:* For master's, minimum GPA of 2.5, letters of recommendation; for doctorate, minimum GPA of 3.0, letters of recommendation. Additional exam requirements/recommendations for international students: Required—TOEFL (minimum score 550 paper-based; 80 iBT), TWE (minimum score 5). Electronic applications accepted. *Faculty research:* Global education, women and international educational opportunities.

Alliant International University–San Francisco, Shirley M. Hufstedler School of Education, Educational Leadership Programs, San Francisco, CA 94133. Offers community college administration (Ed D); educational administration (MA); educational leadership and management (K-12) (Ed D); higher education (Ed D); preliminary administrative services (Credential). *Program availability:* Part-time. *Degree requirements:* For doctorate, comprehensive exam, thesis/dissertation. *Entrance requirements:* For master's and doctorate, minimum GPA of 3.0, letters of recommendation. Additional exam requirements/recommendations for international students: Required—TOEFL (minimum score 550 paper-based; 80 iBT), TWE (minimum score 5). Electronic applications accepted. *Faculty research:* Leadership in higher education, community colleges.

Andrews University, School of Graduate Studies, School of Education, Department of Leadership and Educational Administration, Berrien Springs, MI 49104. Offers educational administration and leadership (MA, Ed D, PhD, Ed S); higher education administration (MA, Ed D, PhD, Ed S); leadership (MA, Ed D, PhD, Ed S). *Faculty:* 6 full-time (2 women). *Students:* 43 full-time (21 women), 51 part-time (27 women); includes 36 minority (17 Black or African American, non-Hispanic/Latino; 3 Asian, non-Hispanic/Latino; 14 Hispanic/Latino; 2 Two or more races, non-Hispanic/Latino), 18 international. Average age 47. In 2016, 4 master's, 6 doctorates awarded. *Degree requirements:* For doctorate, thesis/dissertation. *Entrance requirements:* For master's, GRE. Additional exam requirements/recommendations for international students: Required—TOEFL (minimum score 550 paper-based). *Application deadline:* Applications are processed on a rolling basis. Application fee: $40. *Unit head:* Dr. Robson Marinho, Chair, 269-471-3487. *Application contact:* Justina Clayburn, Supervisor of Graduate Admission, 800-253-2874, Fax: 269-471-6321, E-mail: graduate@andrews.edu.

Angelo State University, College of Graduate Studies and Research, College of Education, Department of Curriculum and Instruction, San Angelo, TX 76909. Offers curriculum and instruction (MA); educational administration (M Ed); guidance and counseling (M Ed); student development and leadership in higher education (M Ed). *Program availability:* Part-time, evening/weekend, online learning. *Students:* 400 full-time (328 women), 396 part-time (325 women); includes 242 minority (80 Black or African American, non-Hispanic/Latino; 2 American Indian or Alaska Native, non-Hispanic/Latino; 6 Asian, non-Hispanic/Latino; 148 Hispanic/Latino; 6 Two or more races, non-Hispanic/Latino), 1 international. Average age 35. *Application deadline:* For fall admission, 7/15 priority date for domestic students, 6/10 for international students; for spring admission, 12/1 priority date for domestic students, 11/1 for international students. Application fee: $40 ($50 for international students). *Expenses:* Tuition, state resident: full-time $3726; part-time $2484 per year. Tuition, nonresident: full-time $10,746; part-time $7164 per year. *Required fees:* $2538; $1702 per unit. *Unit head:* Dr. Jim Summerlin, Chair, 325-942-2647, Fax: 325-942-2039, E-mail: james.summerlin@angelo.edu. *Application contact:* Lesley Casarez, Graduate Advisor, 325-486-6775, E-mail: lesley.casarez@angelo.edu.
Website: http://www.angelo.edu/dept/ci/

Appalachian State University, Cratis D. Williams Graduate School, Department of Leadership and Educational Studies, Boone, NC 28608. Offers educational administration (Ed S); educational media (MA); higher education (MA, Ed S); library science (MLS); school administration (MSA). *Program availability:* Part-time, evening/weekend, online learning. *Degree requirements:* For master's and Ed S, comprehensive exam, thesis optional. *Entrance requirements:* For master's and Ed S, GRE or MAT, 3 letters of recommendation. Additional exam requirements/recommendations for international students: Required—TOEFL (minimum score 570 paper-based; 79 iBT), IELTS (minimum score 6.5). *Application deadline:* For fall admission, 3/14 priority date for domestic students, 2/1 for international students; for spring admission, 11/1 for domestic students, 7/1 for international students. Applications are processed on a rolling basis. Application fee: $55. Electronic applications accepted. *Expenses:* Tuition, state resident: full-time $4744. Tuition, nonresident: full-time $17,913. Full-time tuition and fees vary according to program. *Financial support:* Research assistantships, career-related internships or fieldwork, scholarships/grants, and unspecified assistantships available. Financial award application deadline: 4/1; financial award applicants required to submit FAFSA. *Faculty research:* Brain, learning and meditation; leadership of teaching and learning. *Unit head:* Dr. Robert Sanders, Interim Director, 828-262-3112, E-mail: sandersrl@appstate.edu. *Application contact:* Dr. Vachel Miller, Program Director, 828-262-2287, E-mail: millervw@appstate.edu.
Website: http://www.les.appstate.edu

Argosy University, Atlanta, College of Education, Atlanta, GA 30328. Offers educational leadership (MAEd, Ed D, Ed S), including higher education administration (Ed D), K-12 education (Ed D); teaching and learning (MAEd, Ed D, Ed S), including education technology (Ed D), higher education (Ed D), K-12 education (Ed D).

Argosy University, Chicago, College of Education, Chicago, IL 60601. Offers adult education and training (MA Ed); community college executive leadership (Ed D); educational leadership (MA Ed, Ed D, Ed S), including district leadership (Ed D), higher education administration (Ed D), K-12 education (Ed D); instructional leadership (Ed D, Ed S), including higher education (Ed D), K-12 education (Ed D). *Program availability:* Online learning.

Argosy University, Dallas, College of Education, Farmers Branch, TX 75244. Offers educational administration (MA Ed); educational leadership (Ed D); higher and postsecondary education (MA Ed); instructional leadership (MA Ed); school psychology (MA).

Argosy University, Denver, College of Education, Denver, CO 80231. Offers community college executive leadership (Ed D); educational leadership (MA Ed, Ed D), including higher education (Ed D), K-12 education (Ed D); instructional leadership (MA Ed, Ed D), including higher education administration (Ed D), K-12 education (Ed D).

Argosy University, Hawai`i, College of Education, Honolulu, HI 96813. Offers adult education and training (MAEd); educational leadership (Ed D), including higher education administration, K-12 education; instructional leadership (Ed D), including higher education, K-12 education; school psychology (MA).

Argosy University, Inland Empire, College of Education, Ontario, CA 91761. Offers community college executive leadership (Ed D); educational leadership (MA Ed, Ed D), including higher education administration (Ed D), K-12 education (Ed D); instructional leadership (MA Ed, Ed D), including higher education (Ed D), K-12 education (Ed D), multiple subject teacher preparation (MA Ed), single subject teacher preparation (MA Ed).

Argosy University, Los Angeles, College of Education, Santa Monica, CA 90045. Offers community college executive leadership (Ed D); educational leadership (MA Ed, Ed D), including higher education administration (Ed D), K-12 education (Ed D); instructional leadership (MA Ed, Ed D), including higher education (Ed D), K-12 education (Ed D), multiple subject teacher preparation (MA Ed), single subject teacher preparation (MA Ed).

Argosy University, Nashville, College of Education, Program in Educational Leadership, Nashville, TN 37214. Offers educational leadership (MA Ed, Ed S); higher education administration (Ed D); K-12 education (Ed D).

Argosy University, Nashville, College of Education, Program in Instructional Leadership, Nashville, TN 37214. Offers education technology (Ed D); higher education administration (Ed D); instructional leadership (MA Ed, Ed S); K-12 education (Ed D).

Argosy University, Northern Virginia, College of Education, Arlington, VA 22209. Offers community college executive leadership (Ed D); educational leadership (MA Ed, Ed D, Ed S), including higher education administration (Ed D), K-12 education (Ed D); instructional leadership (MA Ed, Ed D, Ed S), including higher education (Ed D), K-12 education (Ed D).

Argosy University, Orange County, College of Education, Orange, CA 92868. Offers community college executive leadership (Ed D); educational leadership (MA Ed, Ed D), including higher education administration (Ed D), K-12 education (Ed D); instructional leadership (MA Ed, Ed D), including education technology (Ed D), higher education (Ed D), K-12 education (Ed D), multiple subject teacher preparation (MA Ed), single subject teacher preparation (MA Ed).

Argosy University, Phoenix, College of Education, Phoenix, AZ 85021. Offers adult education and training (MA Ed); advanced educational administration (Ed D, Ed S); community college executive leadership (Ed D); educational administration (MA Ed); educational leadership (MA Ed, Ed D, Ed S), including education technology (Ed D), higher education administration (Ed D), K-12 education (Ed D); higher and postsecondary education (MA Ed); initial educational administration (Ed D, Ed S); school psychology (MA); teaching and learning (MA Ed, Ed D, Ed S), including education technology (Ed D), higher education (Ed D), K-12 education (Ed D).

Argosy University, San Diego, College of Education, San Diego, CA 92108. Offers community college executive leadership (Ed D); educational leadership (MA Ed, Ed D), including higher education administration (Ed D), K-12 education (Ed D); instructional leadership (MA Ed, Ed D), including higher education (Ed D), K-12 education (Ed D).

Argosy University, San Francisco Bay Area, College of Education, Alameda, CA 94501. Offers community college executive leadership (Ed D); educational leadership (MA Ed, Ed D), including education technology (Ed D), higher education administration (Ed D), K-12 education (Ed D); instructional leadership (MA Ed, Ed D), including education technology (Ed D), higher education (Ed D), K-12 education (Ed D), multiple subject teacher preparation (MA Ed), single subject teacher preparation (MA Ed).

Argosy University, Sarasota, College of Education, Sarasota, FL 34235. Offers community college executive leadership (Ed D); educational leadership (MA Ed, Ed D, Ed S), including higher education administration (Ed D), K-12 education (Ed D); school counseling (MA, Ed S); school psychology (MA); teaching and learning (MA Ed, Ed D, Ed S), including education technology (Ed D), higher education (Ed D), K-12 education (Ed D).

Argosy University, Seattle, College of Education, Seattle, WA 98121. Offers adult education and training (MA Ed); community college executive leadership (Ed D); educational leadership (MA Ed, Ed D), including higher education administration (Ed D), K-12 education (Ed D); higher and postsecondary education (MA Ed); instructional leadership (MA Ed, Ed D), including education technology (Ed D), higher education (Ed D), K-12 education (Ed D).

Argosy University, Tampa, College of Education, Tampa, FL 33607. Offers community college executive leadership (Ed D); educational leadership (MA Ed, Ed D, Ed S), including higher education administration (Ed D), K-12 education (Ed D); school counseling (MA); teaching and learning (MA Ed, Ed D, Ed S), including higher education (Ed D), K-12 education (Ed D).

Argosy University, Twin Cities, College of Education, Eagan, MN 55121. Offers advanced educational administration (Ed D, Ed S); educational leadership (MA Ed, Ed D, Ed S), including higher education administration (Ed D), K-12 education (Ed D); higher and postsecondary education (MA Ed); initial educational administration (Ed D, Ed S); instructional leadership (MA Ed, Ed D, Ed S), including education technology (Ed D), higher education (Ed D), K-12 education (Ed D).

Arizona State University at the Tempe campus, Mary Lou Fulton Teachers College, Program in Higher and Post-Secondary Education, Phoenix, AZ 85069. Offers M Ed. *Program availability:* Part-time, evening/weekend. *Degree requirements:* For master's, thesis or alternative, applied project, interactive Program of Study (iPOS) submitted before completing 50 percent of required credit hours. *Entrance requirements:* For master's, minimum GPA of 3.0 or equivalent in last 2 years of work leading to bachelor's degree, 3 letters of recommendation, personal statement describing research and career goals, curriculum vitae or resume. Additional exam requirements/recommendations for international students: Required—TOEFL, IELTS, or PTE. Electronic applications accepted.

Auburn University, Graduate School, College of Education, Department of Educational Foundations, Leadership, and Technology, Auburn University, AL 36849. Offers adult education (PhD, Ed S); curriculum supervision (M Ed, PhD); higher education administration (PhD); library media (Ed S); school administration (M Ed, PhD). *Accreditation:* NCATE. *Program availability:* Part-time. *Faculty:* 29 full-time (15 women), 4 part-time/adjunct (3 women). *Students:* 119 full-time (72 women), 273 part-time (170 women); includes 132 minority (114 Black or African American, non-Hispanic/Latino; 2 American Indian or Alaska Native, non-Hispanic/Latino; 4 Asian, non-Hispanic/Latino; 6 Hispanic/Latino; 1 Native Hawaiian or other Pacific Islander, non-Hispanic/Latino; 5 Two or more races, non-Hispanic/Latino), 14 international. Average age 37. 220 applicants, 71% accepted, 78 enrolled. In 2016, 67 master's, 44 doctorates, 41 other advanced degrees awarded. *Degree requirements:* For master's, thesis (for some programs); for doctorate, thesis/dissertation; for Ed S, field project. *Entrance requirements:* For master's, doctorate, and Ed S, GRE General Test. *Application deadline:* Applications are processed on a rolling basis. Application fee: $50 ($60 for international students). Electronic applications accepted. *Expenses:* Tuition, state resident: full-time $9072; part-time $504 per credit hour. Tuition, nonresident: full-time $27,216; part-time $1512 per credit hour. *Required fees:* $812 per semester. Tuition and fees vary according to degree level and program. *Financial support:* Teaching assistantships and Federal Work-Study available. Support available to part-time students. Financial award application deadline: 3/15; financial award applicants required to submit FAFSA. *Unit head:* Dr. Sherida Downer, Head, 334-844-4460. *Application contact:* Dr. George Flowers, Dean of the Graduate School, 334-844-4700.
Website: http://www.education.auburn.edu/academic_departments/eflt/

Aurora University, School of Education and Human Performance, Aurora, IL 60506-4892. Offers bilingual-ESL education (MA); educational leadership (MA); educational technology (MA); leadership in administration (Ed D); leadership in adult learning and higher education (Ed D); leadership in curriculum and instruction (Ed D); reading instruction (MA); special education (MA). *Accreditation:* NCATE. *Program availability:*

Part-time, evening/weekend. *Faculty:* 22 full-time (12 women), 46 part-time/adjunct (27 women). *Students:* 36 full-time (30 women), 559 part-time (372 women); includes 68 minority (27 Black or African American, non-Hispanic/Latino; 1 American Indian or Alaska Native, non-Hispanic/Latino; 6 Asian, non-Hispanic/Latino; 29 Hispanic/Latino; 2 Native Hawaiian or other Pacific Islander, non-Hispanic/Latino; 3 Two or more races, non-Hispanic/Latino). Average age 37. 126 applicants, 98% accepted, 72 enrolled. In 2016, 178 master's, 27 doctorates awarded. *Degree requirements:* For master's, student teaching; for doctorate, comprehensive exam, thesis/dissertation. *Entrance requirements:* For master's, 2 years of teaching experience, valid teaching certificate; for doctorate, appropriate master's degree, two references, curriculum vitae, personal statement, professional project, reflective essay. Additional exam requirements/recommendations for international students: Required—TOEFL (minimum score 550 paper-based; 79 iBT). *Application deadline:* For fall admission, 6/1 for international students; for spring admission, 10/1 for international students. Applications are processed on a rolling basis. Application fee: $0. Electronic applications accepted. *Expenses:* Contact institution. *Financial support:* In 2016–17, 10 students received support. Federal Work-Study, scholarships/grants, and unspecified assistantships available. Support available to part-time students. Financial award applicants required to submit FAFSA. *Unit head:* Dr. Jen Buckley, Executive Director of the School of Education and Human Performance, 630-844-1542, Fax: 630-844-6155, E-mail: jbuckley@aurora.edu. *Application contact:* Elizabeth Botica, Graduate Education Recruiter, 630-947-8918, E-mail: ebotica@aurora.edu.
Website: http://aurora.edu/education

Azusa Pacific University, School of Behavioral and Applied Sciences, Department of Higher Education, Azusa, CA 91702-7000. Offers educational leadership (Ed D); higher education leadership (Ed D).

Azusa Pacific University, School of Behavioral and Applied Sciences, Department of Leadership and Organizational Psychology, Program in College Student Affairs, Azusa, CA 91702-7000. Offers M Ed. *Program availability:* Part-time, evening/weekend. *Degree requirements:* For master's, exam. *Entrance requirements:* For master's, 12 units of course work in social science, minimum GPA of 3.0.

Ball State University, Graduate School, Teachers College, Department of Educational Studies, Program in Adult Education, Muncie, IN 47306. Offers adult and community education (MA); adult, higher and community education (Ed D). *Accreditation:* NCATE. *Program availability:* Part-time, 100% online, blended/hybrid learning. *Degree requirements:* For doctorate, thesis/dissertation. *Entrance requirements:* For master's, minimum baccalaureate GPA of 2.75 or 3.0 in latter half of baccalauareate; for doctorate, GRE General Test, minimum graduate GPA of 3.2. Additional exam requirements/recommendations for international students: Required—TOEFL (minimum score 550 paper-based; 79 iBT), IELTS (minimum score 6.5). Electronic applications accepted. *Faculty research:* Community education, executive development for public services.

Ball State University, Graduate School, Teachers College, Department of Educational Studies, Program in Student Affairs Administration in Higher Education, Muncie, IN 47306. Offers MA. *Accreditation:* NCATE. *Entrance requirements:* For master's, GRE General Test, minimum baccalaureate GPA of 2.75 or 3.0 in latter half of baccalauareate, resume, three professional references. Additional exam requirements/recommendations for international students: Required—TOEFL (minimum score 550 paper-based; 79 iBT), IELTS (minimum score 6.5). Electronic applications accepted.

Barry University, School of Education, Program in Higher Education Administration, Miami Shores, FL 33161-6695. Offers MS. *Program availability:* Part-time, evening/weekend. *Degree requirements:* For master's, comprehensive exam. *Entrance requirements:* For master's, GRE General Test or MAT, minimum GPA of 3.0. Electronic applications accepted.

Barry University, School of Education, Program in Leadership and Education, Miami Shores, FL 33161-6695. Offers educational technology (PhD); exceptional student education (PhD); higher education administration (PhD); human resource development (PhD); leadership (PhD). *Program availability:* Part-time, evening/weekend. *Degree requirements:* For doctorate, thesis/dissertation. *Entrance requirements:* For doctorate, GRE General Test, minimum GPA of 3.25. Electronic applications accepted.

Baruch College of the City University of New York, Austin W. Marxe School of Public and International Affairs, Program in Higher Education Administration, New York, NY 10010-5585. Offers MS Ed. *Program availability:* Part-time, evening/weekend. *Entrance requirements:* For master's, GRE General Test. Additional exam requirements/recommendations for international students: Required—TOEFL. Electronic applications accepted. *Expenses:* Contact institution.

Bay Path University, Program in Higher Education Administration, Longmeadow, MA 01106-2292. Offers enrollment management (MS); general administration (MS); institutional advancement (MS); online teaching and program administration (MS). *Program availability:* Part-time, online only, 100% online. *Students:* 9 full-time (8 women), 50 part-time (39 women); includes 18 minority (8 Black or African American, non-Hispanic/Latino; 1 American Indian or Alaska Native, non-Hispanic/Latino; 7 Hispanic/Latino; 2 Two or more races, non-Hispanic/Latino). Average age 36. 27 applicants, 67% accepted, 14 enrolled. In 2016, 15 master's awarded. *Degree requirements:* For master's, 8 core courses (24 credits) and 4 elective courses (12 credits) for a total of 36 credits. *Application deadline:* Applications are processed on a rolling basis. Application fee: $45. Electronic applications accepted. Application fee is waived when completed online. *Expenses:* $20,385. *Financial support:* Unspecified assistantships available. Financial award applicants required to submit FAFSA. *Unit head:* Dr. Lauren Way, Program Director, 413-565-1193, E-mail: lway@baypath.edu. *Application contact:* Diane Ranaldi, Dean of Graduate Admissions, 413-565-1332, Fax: 413-565-1250, E-mail: dranaldi@baypath.edu.
Website: http://graduate.baypath.edu/Graduate-Programs/Programs-Online/MS-Programs/Higher-Education-Administration

Bay Path University, Program in Strategic Fundraising and Philanthropy, Longmeadow, MA 01106-2292. Offers higher education fundraising (MS); nonprofit fundraising (MS). *Program availability:* Part-time, 100% online. *Students:* 1 full-time (0 women), 15 part-time (14 women); includes 2 minority (both Black or African American, non-Hispanic/Latino). Average age 35. 7 applicants, 71% accepted, 5 enrolled. In 2016, 4 master's awarded. *Degree requirements:* For master's, 36 hours of coursework including portfolio. *Application deadline:* Applications are processed on a rolling basis. Application fee: $45. Electronic applications accepted. Application fee is waived when completed online. *Expenses:* $18,225. *Financial support:* Unspecified assistantships available. Financial award applicants required to submit FAFSA. *Unit head:* Silvia de Haas-Phillips, Program Director, E-mail: sdphillips@baypath.edu. *Application contact:* Diane Ranaldi, Dean of Graduate Admissions, 413-565-1332, Fax: 413-565-1250, E-mail: dranaldi@baypath.edu.
Website: http://graduate.baypath.edu/Graduate-Programs/Programs-On-Campus/MS-Programs/Strategic-Fundraising-and-Philanthropy

Bellarmine University, Annsley Frazier Thornton School of Education, Louisville, KY 40205. Offers education and district leadership (Ed D); education and social change (PhD); elementary education (MA Ed, MAT); leadership in higher education (PhD); learning and behavior disorders (MA Ed, MAT); middle grades education (MA Ed, MAT); principalship (Ed S); reading and writing (MA Ed); secondary education (MAT); teacher leadership (MA Ed). *Accreditation:* NCATE. *Program availability:* Part-time, evening/weekend. *Faculty:* 15 full-time (7 women), 44 part-time/adjunct (36 women). *Students:* 39 full-time (28 women), 211 part-time (164 women); includes 46 minority (35 Black or African American, non-Hispanic/Latino; 3 Asian, non-Hispanic/Latino; 5 Hispanic/Latino; 3 Two or more races, non-Hispanic/Latino). Average age 34. In 2016, 66 master's, 3 doctorates, 43 other advanced degrees awarded. *Degree requirements:* For master's, thesis (for some programs); for doctorate, thesis/dissertation. *Entrance requirements:* For master's, GRE, baccalaureate degree from accredited institution; minimum cumulative GPA of 2.75; recommendations from employers, supervisors, or professors attesting to applicant's potential as graduate student; statement of intent to pursue graduate degree; for doctorate, GRE, minimum GPA of 3.5 in all graduate coursework; baccalaureate and master's degrees in education or fields directly relevant to education; three letters of recommendation; two essays (no more than 1,000 words each); interview. Additional exam requirements/recommendations for international students: Required—TOEFL (minimum score 550 paper-based, 68 iBT), IELTS (minimum score 6), or Michigan English Language Assessment Battery. *Application deadline:* For fall admission, 8/1 priority date for domestic and international students; for spring admission, 12/1 priority date for domestic and international students; for summer admission, 4/10 priority date for domestic and international students. Applications are processed on a rolling basis. Application fee: $40. Electronic applications accepted. Tuition and fees vary according to program. *Financial support:* Scholarships/grants available. Financial award applicants required to submit FAFSA. *Faculty research:* Literacy, service-learning, dispositions, educational technology, special education. *Unit head:* Dr. Robert Cooter, Dean, 502-272-8191, Fax: 502-272-8189, E-mail: rcooter@bellarmine.edu. *Application contact:* Sarah Shumway Schuble, Senior Graduate Recruiter, 502-272-8271, Fax: 502-272-8002, E-mail: sshumway@bellarmine.edu.
Website: http://www.bellarmine.edu/education/graduate

Benedictine University, Graduate Programs, Program in Higher Education and Organizational Change, Lisle, IL 60532. Offers Ed D. *Students:* 15 full-time (10 women), 34 part-time (21 women); includes 16 minority (12 Black or African American, non-Hispanic/Latino; 4 Hispanic/Latino). 32 applicants, 94% accepted, 26 enrolled. In 2016, 21 doctorates awarded. Application fee: $40. *Expenses: Tuition:* Full-time $15,600; part-time $650 per hour. *Required fees:* $300. One-time fee: $125 part-time. Tuition and fees vary according to class time, course load, campus/location and program. *Unit head:* Dr. Sunil Chand, Director, 630-829-1930, E-mail: schand@ben.edu. *Application contact:* Kari Gibbons, Associate Vice President, Enrollment Center, 630-829-6200, Fax: 630-829-6584, E-mail: kgibbons@ben.edu.

Boston College, Lynch School of Education, Program in Higher Education, Chestnut Hill, MA 02467-3800. Offers MA, PhD, JD/MA, MBA/MA. *Accreditation:* TEAC. *Program availability:* Part-time, evening/weekend. *Faculty:* 9 full-time (5 women). *Students:* 25 full-time (20 women), 95 part-time (68 women); includes 27 minority (4 Black or African American, non-Hispanic/Latino; 7 Asian, non-Hispanic/Latino; 12 Hispanic/Latino; 4 Two or more races, non-Hispanic/Latino), 6 international. Average age 28. 77 applicants, 48% accepted, 13 enrolled. In 2016, 39 master's, 9 doctorates awarded. Terminal master's awarded for partial completion of doctoral program. *Degree requirements:* For master's, comprehensive exam; for doctorate, comprehensive exam, thesis/dissertation. *Entrance requirements:* For master's, GRE General Test or MAT; for doctorate, GRE General Test. Additional exam requirements/recommendations for international students: Required—TOEFL (minimum score 100 iBT). *Application deadline:* For fall admission, 12/1 priority date for domestic and international students; for spring admission, 11/1 priority date for domestic and international students. Application fee: $65. Electronic applications accepted. Tuition and fees vary according to program. *Financial support:* Research assistantships with full tuition reimbursements, Federal Work-Study, scholarships/grants, tuition waivers (full and partial), and unspecified assistantships available. Support available to part-time students. Financial award applicants required to submit FAFSA. *Application contact:* Kimberly Rose, Graduate Admission Assistant, 617-552-4214, Fax: 617-552-0398, E-mail: roseki@bc.edu.

Boston College, Lynch School of Education, Program in International Higher Education, Chestnut Hill, MA 02467-3800. Offers MA. *Students:* 4 full-time (2 women), 4 part-time (3 women); includes 2 minority (both Asian, non-Hispanic/Latino), 3 international. Average age 27. 11 applicants, 91% accepted, 9 enrolled. *Application deadline:* Applications are processed on a rolling basis. Application fee: $65. Tuition and fees vary according to program. *Unit head:* Hans de Wit, Director. *Application contact:* Laura E. Rumbley, Coordinator, 617-552-4185.
Website: http://www.bc.edu/schools/lsoe/academics/departments/eahe/graduate/maihe

Bowling Green State University, Graduate College, College of Education and Human Development, Department of Higher Education and Student Affairs, Program in Higher Education Administration, Bowling Green, OH 43403. Offers PhD. *Accreditation:* NCATE. *Program availability:* Part-time. *Degree requirements:* For doctorate, comprehensive exam, thesis/dissertation. *Entrance requirements:* For doctorate, GRE General Test. Additional exam requirements/recommendations for international students: Required—TOEFL. *Application deadline:* For fall admission, 1/15 for domestic students. Application fee: $30. Electronic applications accepted. *Financial support:* Research assistantships with full tuition reimbursements, teaching assistantships, career-related internships or fieldwork, Federal Work-Study, institutionally sponsored loans, and unspecified assistantships available. Support available to part-time students. Financial award applicants required to submit FAFSA. *Faculty research:* Adult learners, legal issues, intellectual development. *Unit head:* Dr. Craig Mertler, Director, 419-372-9357. *Application contact:* Dr. Michael Coomes, Graduate Coordinator, 419-372-7157.

California Baptist University, Program in Higher Education Leadership and Student Development, Riverside, CA 92504-3206. Offers MS. *Program availability:* Part-time, evening/weekend. *Faculty:* 5 full-time (2 women), 2 part-time/adjunct (1 woman). *Students:* 23 part-time (16 women); includes 11 minority (4 Black or African American, non-Hispanic/Latino; 7 Hispanic/Latino), 2 international. Average age 29. 24 applicants, 67% accepted, 16 enrolled. In 2016, 11 master's awarded. *Entrance requirements:* For master's, minimum cumulative GPA of 2.75, three letters of recommendation, current resume, 500-word comprehensive essay. Additional exam requirements/recommendations for international students: Required—TOEFL (minimum score 80 iBT). *Application deadline:* For fall admission, 8/1 priority date for domestic students, 7/1 for international students; for spring admission, 12/1 priority date for domestic students, 11/1 for international students. Applications are processed on a rolling basis. Application fee: $45. Electronic applications accepted. *Expenses:* Contact institution. *Financial support:* In 2016–17, 5 students received support. Federal Work-Study and scholarships/grants available. Financial award applicants required to submit CSS PROFILE or FAFSA. *Faculty research:* Sociology of education, student retention, women in academic leadership, curriculum and instruction, global education. *Unit head:* Dr. John Shoup, Dean, School of Education, 951-343-4205, E-mail: jshoup@calbaptist.edu. *Application contact:* Dr. Shana Matamala, Associate Dean, School of Education, 951-343-4760, E-mail: smatamala@calbaptist.edu.
Website: http://www.calbaptist.edu/academics/schools-colleges/school-education/programs/graduate/master-science-higher-education-leadership-and-student-develop

Higher Education

California Lutheran University, Graduate Studies, Graduate School of Education, Thousand Oaks, CA 91360-2787. Offers counseling and guidance (MS), including college student personnel, counseling and guidance; educational leadership (MA, Ed D), including educational leadership (K-12) (Ed D), higher education leadership (Ed D); special education (MS); teacher leadership (M Ed); teaching (M Ed). *Accreditation:* NCATE. *Program availability:* Part-time, evening/weekend. *Faculty:* 23 full-time (17 women), 39 part-time/adjunct (26 women). *Students:* 518 full-time (411 women), 79 part-time (67 women); includes 252 minority (12 Black or African American, non-Hispanic/Latino; 3 American Indian or Alaska Native, non-Hispanic/Latino; 17 Asian, non-Hispanic/Latino; 108 Hispanic/Latino; 1 Native Hawaiian or other Pacific Islander, non-Hispanic/Latino; 111 Two or more races, non-Hispanic/Latino), 14 international. Average age 35. 319 applicants, 74% accepted, 192 enrolled. In 2016, 93 master's, 13 doctorates awarded. *Degree requirements:* For master's, comprehensive exam or thesis; for doctorate, thesis/dissertation. *Entrance requirements:* For master's, GRE General Test, interview, minimum GPA of 3.0. *Application deadline:* For fall admission, 7/1 priority date for domestic students; for spring admission, 11/1 priority date for domestic students; for summer admission, 4/1 priority date for domestic students. Applications are processed on a rolling basis. Application fee: $50. Electronic applications accepted. *Unit head:* Dr. Michael Hillis, Dean, 805-493-3421. *Application contact:* 805-493-3325, Fax: 805-493-3861, E-mail: clugrad@callutheran.edu.

California State University, Long Beach, Graduate Studies, College of Education, Department of Advanced Studies in Education and Counseling, Long Beach, CA 90840. Offers counseling (MS), including marriage and family therapy, school counseling, student development in higher education; education (MA, Ed D); educational administration (MA, Ed D); educational psychology (MA); special education (MS). *Program availability:* Part-time, evening/weekend. *Entrance requirements:* For master's, GRE General Test, minimum GPA of 2.75. *Application deadline:* For fall admission, 3/1 for domestic students. Applications are processed on a rolling basis. Application fee: $55. Electronic applications accepted. *Financial support:* Federal Work-Study, institutionally sponsored loans, and scholarships/grants available. Financial award application deadline: 3/2. *Unit head:* Dr. Hiromi Masunaga, Chair, 562-985-4517, E-mail: asec@csulb.edu.

California State University, Sacramento, Office of Graduate Studies, College of Education, Graduate and Professional Studies in Education, Sacramento, CA 95819. Offers child development (MA); counseling (MS); curriculum and instruction (MA); education (Ed D); education leadership and policy studies (MA), including higher education, PreK-12; educational technology (MA); gender equity (MA); language and literacy (MA); multicultural education (MA); school psychology (MA); special education (MA); workforce development advocacy (MA). *Program availability:* Part-time. *Students:* 446 full-time (335 women), 125 part-time (97 women); includes 298 minority (39 Black or African American, non-Hispanic/Latino; 3 American Indian or Alaska Native, non-Hispanic/Latino; 97 Asian, non-Hispanic/Latino; 153 Hispanic/Latino; 6 Native Hawaiian or other Pacific Islander, non-Hispanic/Latino). Average age 32. 540 applicants, 76% accepted, 250 enrolled. In 2016, 107 master's, 7 doctorates awarded. *Degree requirements:* For master's, thesis or project; writing proficiency exam. *Entrance requirements:* For master's, minimum GPA of 2.5, 3.0 in last 60 units. Additional exam requirements/recommendations for international students: Required—TOEFL (minimum score 550 paper-based; 80 iBT). *Application deadline:* For fall admission, 2/15 for domestic students, 1/15 for international students. Applications are processed on a rolling basis. Application fee: $55. Electronic applications accepted. *Expenses:* $4,302 full-time tuition and fees per semester, $2,796 part-time. *Financial support:* Career-related internships or fieldwork and Federal Work-Study available. Support available to part-time students. Financial award application deadline: 3/1; financial award applicants required to submit FAFSA. *Unit head:* Dr. Susan Heredia, Chair, 916-278-5942, E-mail: coe@csus.edu. *Application contact:* Jose Martinez, Graduate Admissions Supervisor, 916-278-7871, E-mail: martinj@skymail.csus.edu.
Website: http://www.csus.edu/coe/academics/graduate/index.html

Capella University, School of Education, Doctoral Programs in Education, Minneapolis, MN 55402. Offers curriculum and instruction (PhD); educational leadership and management (Ed D); instructional design for online learning (PhD); K-12 studies in education (PhD); leadership for higher education (PhD); leadership in educational administration (PhD); postsecondary and adult education (PhD); professional studies in education (PhD); reading and literacy (Ed D); special education leadership (PhD); training and performance improvement (PhD).

Capella University, School of Education, Master's Programs in Education, Minneapolis, MN 55402. Offers adult education (MS); curriculum and instruction (MS); early childhood education (MS); enrollment management (MS); higher education leadership and management (MS); instructional design for online learning (MS); integrative studies (MS); K-12 studies in education (MS); leadership in educational administration (MS); reading and literacy (MS); special education teaching (MS).

Cardinal Stritch University, College of Education and Leadership, Department of Education, Milwaukee, WI 53217-3985. Offers educational leadership (MS); higher education student affairs leadership (MS); leadership for the advancement of learning and service (Ed D, PhD); leadership for the advancement of learning and service in higher education (Ed D, PhD); teaching (MAT); urban education (MA). *Accreditation:* NCATE. *Program availability:* Evening/weekend. *Degree requirements:* For master's, comprehensive exam, thesis (for some programs), research project, faculty recommendation; for doctorate, thesis/dissertation, practica, field experience. *Entrance requirements:* For master's, 3 letters of recommendation, minimum GPA of 3.0; for doctorate, minimum GPA of 3.5 in master's coursework, 3 letters of recommendation. *Application deadline:* For fall admission, 7/15 priority date for domestic students; for spring admission, 12/15 priority date for domestic students. Applications are processed on a rolling basis. Application fee: $25. *Expenses: Tuition:* Full-time $11,890; part-time $765 per credit hour. Tuition and fees vary according to class time, course load, degree level, program and student's religious affiliation. *Financial support:* Fellowships, research assistantships with partial tuition reimbursements, career-related internships or fieldwork, Federal Work-Study, and scholarships/grants available. Financial award applicants required to submit FAFSA. *Unit head:* Dr. Nancy Blair, Chair, 414-410-4367. *Application contact:* 800-347-8822 Ext. 4042, E-mail: gradadm@stritch.edu.

Central Michigan University, Central Michigan University Global Campus, Program in Education, Mount Pleasant, MI 48859. Offers college teaching (Graduate Certificate); community college (MA); curriculum and instruction (MA); educational technology (MA, DET); reading and literacy K-12 (MA); school principalship (MA), including charter school leadership; training and development (MA). *Accreditation:* TEAC. *Program availability:* Part-time, evening/weekend. *Faculty:* 24 full-time (14 women), 24 part-time/adjunct (8 women). *Students:* 888 (620 women); includes 225 minority (142 Black or African American, non-Hispanic/Latino; 8 American Indian or Alaska Native, non-Hispanic/Latino; 16 Asian, non-Hispanic/Latino; 13 Hispanic/Latino; 46 Two or more races, non-Hispanic/Latino). Average age 37. In 2016, 76 master's awarded. *Entrance requirements:* For master's, minimum GPA of 2.7 in major. Additional exam requirements/recommendations for international students: Required—TOEFL. *Application deadline:* Applications are processed on a rolling basis. Application fee: $50. Electronic applications accepted. *Financial support:* Scholarships/grants available. Support available to part-time students. *Unit head:* Kaleb Patrick, Director, 989-774-3144, E-mail: patri1kg@cmich.edu. *Application contact:* 877-268-4636, E-mail: cmuglobal@cmich.edu.

Central Michigan University, College of Graduate Studies, College of Education and Human Services, Department of Educational Leadership, Mount Pleasant, MI 48859. Offers educational leadership (Ed D), including educational technology (Ed D, Ed S), higher education leadership, K-12 curriculum, K-12 leadership; general educational administration (Ed S), including administrative leadership K-12, educational technology (Ed D, Ed S), higher education administration, instructional leadership K-12; school principalship (MA), including charter school leadership, site-based leadership; student affairs administration (MA); teacher leadership (MA). *Program availability:* Part-time, evening/weekend. *Degree requirements:* For master's and Ed S, thesis or alternative; for doctorate, thesis/dissertation. *Entrance requirements:* For doctorate, GRE or MAT, master's degree, minimum GPA of 3.5, 3 years of professional education experience. Electronic applications accepted. *Faculty research:* Elementary administration, secondary administration, student achievement, in-service training, internships in administration.

Chicago State University, School of Graduate and Professional Studies, College of Education, Department of Educational Leadership, Curriculum and Foundations, Program in Educational Leadership, Chicago, IL 60628. Offers educational leadership (Ed D); general administration (MA); higher education administration (MA). *Accreditation:* NCATE. *Degree requirements:* For master's, comprehensive exam, thesis optional. *Entrance requirements:* For master's, minimum GPA of 2.75.

Claremont Graduate University, Graduate Programs, School of Educational Studies, Claremont, CA 91711-6160. Offers Africana education (Certificate); education and policy (MA, PhD); higher education/student affairs (MA, PhD); human development (MA, PhD); public school administration (MA, PhD); quantitative evaluation (MA, PhD); special education (MA, PhD); teacher education (MA); teaching and learning (MA, PhD); urban leadership (PhD); MBA/PhD. PhD program offered jointly with San Diego State University. *Program availability:* Part-time. *Faculty:* 14 full-time (9 women), 1 part-time/adjunct (0 women). *Students:* 195 full-time (143 women), 196 part-time (137 women); includes 217 minority (43 Black or African American, non-Hispanic/Latino; 4 American Indian or Alaska Native, non-Hispanic/Latino; 32 Asian, non-Hispanic/Latino; 117 Hispanic/Latino; 2 Native Hawaiian or other Pacific Islander, non-Hispanic/Latino; 19 Two or more races, non-Hispanic/Latino), 14 international. Average age 38. In 2016, 48 master's, 39 doctorates, 7 other advanced degrees awarded. Terminal master's awarded for partial completion of doctoral program. *Entrance requirements:* For master's and doctorate, GRE General Test. Additional exam requirements/recommendations for international students: Required—TOEFL (minimum score 75 iBT). *Application deadline:* For fall admission, 3/1 priority date for domestic and international students. Applications are processed on a rolling basis. Application fee: $80. Electronic applications accepted. *Expenses: Tuition:* Full-time $44,328; part-time $1847 per unit. *Required fees:* $600; $300 per semester. Tuition and fees vary according to course load and program. *Financial support:* Fellowships, research assistantships, Federal Work-Study, institutionally sponsored loans, and scholarships/grants available. Support available to part-time students. Financial award application deadline: 2/15; financial award applicants required to submit FAFSA. *Faculty research:* Education administration, K-12 and higher education, multicultural education, education policy, diversity in higher education, faculty issues. *Unit head:* Allen Omoto, Dean, 909-607-3786, E-mail: allen.omoto@cgu.edu. *Application contact:* Rachel Camacho, Senior Assistant Director of Admission, 909-607-9418, E-mail: camacho@cgu.edu.
Website: https://www.cgu.edu/school/school-of-educational-studies/

Clemson University, Graduate School, College of Education, Department of Educational and Organizational Leadership Development, Program in Educational Leadership, Clemson, SC 29634. Offers educational leadership (PhD), including higher education, P-12. *Accreditation:* NCATE. *Program availability:* Part-time, evening/weekend. *Faculty:* 12 full-time (5 women). *Students:* 29 full-time (20 women), 76 part-time (44 women); includes 24 minority (22 Black or African American, non-Hispanic/Latino; 2 Hispanic/Latino), 3 international. Average age 39. 31 applicants, 32% accepted, 6 enrolled. In 2016, 13 doctorates awarded. *Degree requirements:* For doctorate, comprehensive exam, thesis/dissertation, preliminary exam. *Entrance requirements:* For doctorate, GRE General Test, unofficial transcripts, letters of recommendation. Additional exam requirements/recommendations for international students: Required—TOEFL (minimum score 80 iBT), IELTS (minimum score 7). *Application deadline:* For fall admission, 3/1 priority date for domestic and international students; for spring admission, 10/1 priority date for domestic and international students. Application fee: $80 ($90 for international students). Electronic applications accepted. *Expenses:* $4,264 per semester full-time resident, $8,485 per semester full-time non-resident, $471 per credit hour part-time resident, $942 per credit hour part-time non-resident. *Financial support:* In 2016–17, 29 students received support, including 5 fellowships with partial tuition reimbursements available (averaging $5,000 per year), 7 research assistantships with partial tuition reimbursements available (averaging $14,596 per year), 1 teaching assistantship with partial tuition reimbursement available (averaging $18,000 per year); unspecified assistantships also available. Financial award application deadline: 3/1. *Faculty research:* Higher education leadership, P-12 educational leadership. *Unit head:* Dr. George Petersen, Dean, 864-656-4444, Fax: 864-656-0311, E-mail: soedean@clemson.edu. *Application contact:* Dr. Frederick Buskey, Program Coordinator, 864-656-4777, E-mail: bbuskey@clemson.edu.
Website: http://www.clemson.edu/education/departments/educational-organizational-leadership-development/academics/index.html

Cleveland State University, College of Graduate Studies, College of Education and Human Services, Program in Urban Education, Specialization in Adult, Continuing, and Higher Education, Cleveland, OH 44115. Offers PhD. *Program availability:* Part-time. *Faculty:* 4 full-time (3 women). *Students:* 1 full-time (0 women), 9 part-time (8 women); includes 1 minority (Black or African American, non-Hispanic/Latino). Average age 40. In 2016, 1 doctorate awarded. *Degree requirements:* For doctorate, one foreign language, comprehensive exam, thesis/dissertation. *Entrance requirements:* For doctorate, GRE General Test (minimum score of 297 for combined Verbal and Quantitative exams, 4.0 preferred for Analytical Writing), minimum graduate GPA of 3.25, curriculum vitae or resume, personal statement, 2 letters of recommendation. Additional exam requirements/recommendations for international students: Required—TOEFL (minimum score 550 paper-based; 78 iBT), IELTS (minimum score 6). *Application deadline:* For fall admission, 7/1 for domestic students, 5/15 for international students; for spring admission, 11/15 for domestic students, 11/1 for international students; for summer admission, 4/1 for domestic students, 3/15 for international students. Application fee: $40. Electronic applications accepted. *Expenses:* Tuition, state resident: full-time $9565. Tuition, nonresident: full-time $17,980. Tuition and fees vary according to program. *Financial support:* In 2016–17, 2 students received support, including 1 research assistantship with full tuition reimbursement available, 1 teaching assistantship with full tuition reimbursement available (averaging $11,800 per year); tuition waivers (full) also available. Support available to part-time students. Financial award application deadline: 4/1; financial award applicants required to submit FAFSA. *Faculty research:* Adult education research, practice in diverse contexts. *Unit head:* Dr. Graham Stead,

Director, Doctoral Studies, 216-875-9869, E-mail: g.b.stead@csuohio.edu. *Application contact:* Rita M. Grabowski, Administrative Coordinator, 216-687-4697, Fax: 216-875-9697, E-mail: r.grabowski@csuohio.edu.
Website: http://www.csuohio.edu/cehs/departments/DOC/lll_doc.html

College of Saint Elizabeth, Department of Psychology, Morristown, NJ 07960-6989. Offers counseling psychology (MA); forensic psychology (MA); mental health counseling (Certificate); psychology (Psy D); student affairs in higher education (Certificate). *Program availability:* Part-time. *Degree requirements:* For master's, thesis or alternative. *Entrance requirements:* For master's, minimum GPA of 3.0, BA in psychology (preferred), 12 credits of course work in psychology; for doctorate, GRE, 3 letters of recommendation from professionals who can comment on the applicant's qualifications for doctoral study; master's degree in counseling psychology, forensic psychology and counseling, or its equivalent. Additional exam requirements/recommendations for international students: Required—TOEFL (minimum score 550 paper-based; 79 iBT), IELTS (minimum score 6.5). Electronic applications accepted. *Expenses:* Contact institution.

The College of Saint Rose, Graduate Studies, Thelma P. Lally School of Education, Programs in Higher Education Leadership and Administration, Albany, NY 12203-1419. Offers MS Ed, Advanced Certificate. *Program availability:* Part-time, evening/weekend. *Students:* 17 part-time (7 women); includes 3 minority (2 Black or African American, non-Hispanic/Latino; 1 Hispanic/Latino), 1 international. Average age 31. 13 applicants, 85% accepted, 5 enrolled. In 2016, 11 master's, 1 Advanced Certificate awarded. *Degree requirements:* For master's, capstone seminar. *Entrance requirements:* For master's, resume, letter of recommendation. Additional exam requirements/recommendations for international students: Required—TOEFL (minimum score 550 paper-based; 80 iBT), IELTS (minimum score 6), PTE (minimum score 56). *Application deadline:* For fall admission, 4/1 priority date for domestic and international students; for spring admission, 10/15 priority date for domestic and international students; for summer admission, 3/15 priority date for domestic and international students. Applications are processed on a rolling basis. Application fee: $40. Electronic applications accepted. *Expenses: Tuition:* Full-time $14,382; part-time $799 per credit. *Required fees:* $814; $32 per credit. $88 per semester. Tuition and fees vary according to course load. *Financial support:* Scholarships/grants, tuition waivers (partial), and unspecified assistantships available. Support available to part-time students. Financial award application deadline: 4/15. *Unit head:* Dr. R. Mark Sullivan, Director, 518-454-5122, E-mail: sullivam@strose.edu. *Application contact:* Cris Murray, Assistant Vice President for Graduate Recruitment and Enrollment, 518-454-5136, Fax: 518-458-5479, E-mail: grad@strose.edu.
Website: https://www.strose.edu/higher-education-leadership-and-administration/

Colorado State University, College of Health and Human Sciences, School of Education, Fort Collins, CO 80523-1588. Offers adult education and training (M Ed); counseling and career development (M Ed); education sciences (PhD); higher education leadership (PhD); organization learning, performance, and change (PhD); organizational learning, performance, and change (M Ed); student affairs in higher education (MS); teaching and learning (M Ed), including principal licensure, teacher licensure. *Accreditation:* ACA; TEAC. *Program availability:* Part-time, online only, 100% online, blended/hybrid learning, face-to-face off-campus courses. *Faculty:* 29 full-time (21 women), 23 part-time/adjunct (11 women). *Students:* 80 full-time (56 women), 541 part-time (353 women); includes 142 minority (26 Black or African American, non-Hispanic/Latino; 2 American Indian or Alaska Native, non-Hispanic/Latino; 22 Asian, non-Hispanic/Latino; 71 Hispanic/Latino; 21 Two or more races, non-Hispanic/Latino), 18 international. Average age 37. 483 applicants, 31% accepted, 137 enrolled. In 2016, 183 master's, 33 doctorates awarded. *Degree requirements:* For master's, thesis optional, professional portfolio; for doctorate, comprehensive exam, thesis/dissertation. *Entrance requirements:* For master's, bachelor's degree; minimum GPA of 3.0 in last degree earned; for doctorate, GRE or GMAT (depending upon specialization), master's degree; minimum GPA of 3.0 in last degree earned. Additional exam requirements/recommendations for international students: Required—TOEFL (minimum score 550 paper-based; 80 iBT), IELTS (minimum score 6.5), PTE (minimum score 58). *Application deadline:* Applications are processed on a rolling basis. Application fee: $60 ($70 for international students). Electronic applications accepted. *Expenses:* Contact institution. *Financial support:* In 2016–17, 3 students received support, including 7 research assistantships with full tuition reimbursements available (averaging $11,749 per year), 5 teaching assistantships with full tuition reimbursements available (averaging $15,886 per year); fellowships with full tuition reimbursements available, scholarships/grants, and unspecified assistantships also available. Financial award application deadline: 3/1; financial award applicants required to submit FAFSA. *Faculty research:* Higher education leadership; research methods; human resource development; K-16 education; diversity, equity, and inclusion. *Total annual research expenditures:* $499,898. *Unit head:* Dr. Louise Jennings, Co-Director, 970-491-6317, Fax: 970-491-1317, E-mail: louise.jennings@colostate.edu. *Application contact:* Kelli Clark, Graduate Programs Coordinator, 970-491-2093, Fax: 970-491-1317, E-mail: kelli.clark@colostate.edu.
Website: http://www.soe.chhs.colostate.edu/

Columbia College, Graduate Programs, Education Division, Columbia, SC 29203-5998. Offers divergent learning (M Ed); higher education administration (M Ed). *Accreditation:* NCATE. *Program availability:* Part-time, evening/weekend, online learning. *Degree requirements:* For master's, thesis. *Entrance requirements:* For master's, GRE General Test, MAT, 2 recommendations, current South Carolina teaching certificate, minimum GPA of 3.2. Electronic applications accepted. *Expenses:* Contact institution.

Columbus State University, Graduate Studies, College of Education and Health Professions, Department of Counseling, Foundations, and Leadership, Columbus, GA 31907-5645. Offers clinical mental health counseling (MS); curriculum and leadership (Ed D), including curriculum, educational leadership, higher education (M Ed, Ed D); educational leadership (M Ed, Ed S), including higher education (M Ed, Ed D); school counseling (M Ed, Ed S). *Accreditation:* ACA; NCATE. *Program availability:* Part-time, evening/weekend, 100% online, blended/hybrid learning. *Faculty:* 14 full-time (4 women), 25 part-time/adjunct (14 women). *Students:* 226 full-time (159 women), 294 part-time (219 women); includes 298 minority (270 Black or African American, non-Hispanic/Latino; 1 American Indian or Alaska Native, non-Hispanic/Latino; 5 Asian, non-Hispanic/Latino; 13 Hispanic/Latino; 9 Two or more races, non-Hispanic/Latino), 1 international. Average age 39. 367 applicants, 57% accepted, 162 enrolled. In 2016, 20 master's, 7 doctorates, 121 other advanced degrees awarded. *Degree requirements:* For master's, thesis, exit exam; for doctorate, comprehensive exam, thesis/dissertation; for Ed S, thesis or alternative. *Entrance requirements:* For master's, GRE General Test, minimum undergraduate GPA of 2.75; for doctorate, GRE General Test, minimum graduate GPA of 3.5, four years of professional service; for Ed S, GRE General Test, minimum undergraduate GPA of 2.75, graduate 3.0. Additional exam requirements/recommendations for international students: Required—TOEFL (minimum score 550 paper-based; 79 iBT). *Application deadline:* For fall admission, 6/30 for domestic and international students; for spring admission, 11/1 for domestic and international students; for summer admission, 3/1 for domestic and international students. Applications are processed on a rolling basis. Application fee: $50. Electronic applications accepted. *Expenses:* Tuition, state resident: full-time $4804; part-time $2412 per semester hour. Tuition, nonresident: full-time $19,218; part-time $9612 per semester hour. *Required fees:* $1850; $1850 per semester hour. Tuition and fees vary according to program. *Financial support:* In 2016–17, 43 students received support, including 9 research assistantships with partial tuition reimbursements available (averaging $3,000 per year); career-related internships or fieldwork, Federal Work-Study, institutionally sponsored loans, scholarships/grants, tuition waivers (partial), and unspecified assistantships also available. Support available to part-time students. Financial award application deadline: 5/1; financial award applicants required to submit FAFSA. *Unit head:* Dr. Tom Hackett, Department Chair, 706-507-8968, Fax: 706-569-3134, E-mail: hackett_paul@columbusstate.edu. *Application contact:* Kristin Williams, Director of International and Graduate Recruitment, 706-507-8848, Fax: 706-568-5091, E-mail: williams_kristin@columbusstate.edu.
Website: http://cfl.columbusstate.edu/

Dallas Baptist University, Gary Cook School of Leadership, Program in Educational Leadership, Dallas, TX 75211-9299. Offers educational leadership (Ed D), including educational ministry leadership, general leadership, higher education leadership. *Program availability:* Part-time. *Degree requirements:* For doctorate, thesis/dissertation. *Application deadline:* Applications are processed on a rolling basis. Application fee: $25. Electronic applications accepted. Application fee is waived when completed online. *Expenses: Tuition:* Full-time $15,408; part-time $856 per credit hour. *Required fees:* $400 per semester. Tuition and fees vary according to course load and degree level. *Unit head:* Dr. Ozzie Ingram, Academic Director, 214-333-6875, E-mail: ozzie@dbu.edu. *Application contact:* Bobby Soto, Director of Admissions, 214-333-5242, E-mail: graduate@dbu.edu.
Website: http://www4.dbu.edu/leadership/education-leadership-ed-d

Dallas Baptist University, Gary Cook School of Leadership, Program in Higher Education, Dallas, TX 75211-9299. Offers administration (M Ed), including community college leadership, distance learning, interdisciplinary studies, student affairs leadership; instructional (M Ed). *Program availability:* Part-time, evening/weekend, 100% online, blended/hybrid learning. *Application deadline:* Applications are processed on a rolling basis. Application fee: $25. Electronic applications accepted. Application fee is waived when completed online. *Expenses: Tuition:* Full-time $15,408; part-time $856 per credit hour. *Required fees:* $400 per semester. Tuition and fees vary according to course load and degree level. *Faculty research:* Enrollment management, portfolio assessment, servant leadership. *Unit head:* Mamo Ishida, Director, 214-333-5812, E-mail: mamo@dbu.edu. *Application contact:* Bobby Soto, Director of Admissions, 214-333-5242, E-mail: graduate@dbu.edu.
Website: http://www3.dbu.edu/leadership/hied/

Dallas Baptist University, Gary Cook School of Leadership, Program in Leadership Studies, Dallas, TX 75211-9299. Offers leadership studies (PhD), including business, general leadership, higher education, ministry. *Program availability:* Part-time. *Degree requirements:* For doctorate, thesis/dissertation. *Application deadline:* Applications are processed on a rolling basis. Application fee: $25. Electronic applications accepted. Application fee is waived when completed online. *Expenses: Tuition:* Full-time $15,408; part-time $856 per credit hour. *Required fees:* $400 per semester. Tuition and fees vary according to course load and degree level. *Unit head:* Dr. Jack Goodyear, Director, 214-333-5595, E-mail: jackg@dbu.edu. *Application contact:* Bobby Soto, Director of Admissions, 214-333-5242, E-mail: graduate@dbu.edu.
Website: http://www3.dbu.edu/leadership/phdLeadership.asp

Dallas Baptist University, Professional Development Program, Dallas, TX 75211-9299. Offers accounting (MA); church leadership (MA); communication (MA); counseling (MA); criminal justice (MA); English as a second language (MA); finance (MA); higher education (MA); leadership studies (MA); management (MA); management information systems (MA); marketing (MA); missions (MA); professional life coaching (MA); training and development (MA). *Program availability:* Part-time, evening/weekend, 100% online, blended/hybrid learning. *Application deadline:* Applications are processed on a rolling basis. Application fee: $25. Electronic applications accepted. Application fee is waived when completed online. *Expenses: Tuition:* Full-time $15,408; part-time $856 per credit hour. *Required fees:* $400 per semester. Tuition and fees vary according to course load and degree level. *Unit head:* Jared Ingram, Director, 214-333-5584, E-mail: jaredi@dbu.edu. *Application contact:* Bobby Soto, Director of Admissions, 214-333-5242, E-mail: graduate@dbu.edu.
Website: http://www3.dbu.edu/graduate/mapd.asp

Delta State University, Graduate Programs, College of Education, Division of Teacher Education, Leadership, and Research, Program in Professional Studies, Cleveland, MS 38733-0001. Offers counselor education (Ed D); elementary education (Ed D); higher education (Ed D). *Program availability:* Part-time, evening/weekend. *Degree requirements:* For doctorate, thesis/dissertation. *Entrance requirements:* For doctorate, GRE General Test.

DeVry University–Folsom Campus, Graduate Programs, Folsom, CA 95630. Offers accounting (M Acc); accounting and financial management (MAFM); business administration (MBA); curriculum leadership (M Ed); educational leadership (M Ed); educational technology (M Ed); higher education leadership (M Ed); human resource management (MHRM); information systems management (MISM); network and communications management (MNCM); project management (MPM); public administration (MPA).

Drexel University, Goodwin College of Professional Studies, School of Education, Philadelphia, PA 19104-2875. Offers applied behavior analysis (MS); creativity and innovation (MS); education improvement and transformation (MS); educational administration (MS); educational leadership and management (Ed D); educational leadership development and learning technologies (PhD); global and international education (MS); higher education (MS); human resources development (MS); learning technologies (MS); mathematics, learning and teaching (MS); special education (MS); teaching, learning and curriculum (MS). *Program availability:* Part-time, evening/weekend, online learning. *Degree requirements:* For doctorate, thesis/dissertation. *Entrance requirements:* For doctorate, GRE or GMAT. Additional exam requirements/recommendations for international students: Required—TOEFL, IELTS. Electronic applications accepted. Application fee is waived when completed online. *Expenses:* Contact institution. *Faculty research:* Leadership development, mathematics education, literacy, autism, educational technology.

See Display on page 660 and Close-Up on page 727.

Eastern Kentucky University, The Graduate School, College of Education, Department of Curriculum and Instruction, Program in Secondary and Higher Education, Richmond, KY 40475-3102. Offers secondary education (MA Ed), including agricultural education, art education, biological sciences education, business education, English education, geography education, history education, home economics education, industrial education, mathematical sciences education, physical education, school health education. *Accreditation:* NCATE. *Program availability:* Part-time. *Entrance requirements:* For master's, GRE General Test, minimum GPA of 2.5.

Higher Education

Eastern Michigan University, Graduate School, College of Education, Department of Leadership and Counseling, Programs in Educational Leadership, Ypsilanti, MI 48197. Offers community college leadership (Graduate Certificate); educational leadership (MA, Ed D, SPA); higher education/general administration (MA); higher education/student affairs (MA); K-12 administration (MA); K-12 basic administration (Post Master's Certificate). *Program availability:* Part-time, evening/weekend, online learning. *Students:* 52 full-time (39 women), 298 part-time (198 women); includes 103 minority (81 Black or African American, non-Hispanic/Latino; 3 American Indian or Alaska Native, non-Hispanic/Latino; 4 Asian, non-Hispanic/Latino; 10 Hispanic/Latino; 5 Two or more races, non-Hispanic/Latino), 2 international. Average age 35. 185 applicants, 70% accepted, 67 enrolled. In 2016, 85 master's, 28 doctorates, 23 other advanced degrees awarded. *Degree requirements:* For master's, portfolio. *Entrance requirements:* For doctorate, GRE. Additional exam requirements/recommendations for international students: Required—TOEFL. *Application deadline:* For winter admission, 2/1 for domestic and international students. Applications are processed on a rolling basis. Application fee: $45. *Financial support:* Fellowships, research assistantships with full tuition reimbursements, teaching assistantships with full tuition reimbursements, career-related internships or fieldwork, Federal Work-Study, institutionally sponsored loans, scholarships/grants, tuition waivers (partial), and unspecified assistantships available. Support available to part-time students. *Application contact:* Dr. Jaclynn Tracy, Coordinator of Advising, Programs in Educational Leadership, 734-487-0255, Fax: 734-487-4608, E-mail: jtracy@emich.edu.

Florida Atlantic University, College of Education, Department of Educational Leadership and Research Methodology, Boca Raton, FL 33431-0991. Offers adult and community education (M Ed, PhD, Ed S); educational leadership (M Ed, PhD, Ed S); higher education (M Ed, PhD); K-12 school leadership (M Ed, PhD, Ed S). *Accreditation:* NCATE. *Program availability:* Part-time, evening/weekend, online learning. *Faculty:* 24 full-time (12 women), 20 part-time/adjunct (9 women). *Students:* 110 full-time (71 women), 221 part-time (155 women); includes 166 minority (100 Black or African American, non-Hispanic/Latino; 6 Asian, non-Hispanic/Latino; 49 Hispanic/Latino; 1 Native Hawaiian or other Pacific Islander, non-Hispanic/Latino; 10 Two or more races, non-Hispanic/Latino), 6 international. Average age 36. 186 applicants, 65% accepted, 97 enrolled. In 2016, 66 master's, 19 doctorates, 8 other advanced degrees awarded. *Degree requirements:* For doctorate, comprehensive exam, thesis/dissertation, departmental qualifying exam; for Ed S, departmental qualifying exam. *Entrance requirements:* For master's, GRE General Test, minimum GPA of 3.0 during previous 2 years; for doctorate, GRE General Test, minimum GPA of 3.5; for Ed S, GRE General Test. Additional exam requirements/recommendations for international students: Required—TOEFL (minimum score 500 paper-based; 61 iBT), IELTS (minimum score 6). *Application deadline:* For fall admission, 7/1 for domestic students, 2/15 for international students; for spring admission, 9/15 for domestic students, 7/15 for international students. Applications are processed on a rolling basis. Application fee: $30. Electronic applications accepted. *Expenses:* Tuition, state resident: full-time $7392; part-time $369.82 per credit hour. Tuition, nonresident: full-time $19,432; part-time $1024.81 per credit hour. *Financial support:* Fellowships, research assistantships, teaching assistantships, career-related internships or fieldwork, and tuition waivers (partial) available. *Faculty research:* Self-directed learning, school reform issues, legal issues, mentoring, school leadership. *Unit head:* Dr. Robert E. Shockley, Chair, 561-297-3550, Fax: 561-297-3618, E-mail: shockley@fau.edu. *Application contact:* Kathy DuBois, Senior Secretary, 561-297-3550, Fax: 561-297-3618, E-mail: edleadership@fau.edu.
Website: http://www.coe.fau.edu/academicdepartments/el/

Florida International University, College of Arts, Sciences, and Education, Department of Leadership and Professional Studies, Miami, FL 33199. Offers adult education and human resource development (MS, Ed D); counseling (MS), including rehabilitation counseling, school counseling; counselor education (MS), including clinical mental health counseling; educational administration and supervision (Ed D); educational leadership (MS, Certificate, Ed S); higher education (Ed D); higher education administration (MS); international and comparative education (MS); recreation and sport management (MS), including recreation and sport management, recreational therapy; school psychology (Ed S); urban education (MS), including instruction in urban settings, learning technologies, multicultural/bilingual, multicultural/TESOL, urban education. *Program availability:* Part-time, evening/weekend. *Faculty:* 27 full-time (19 women), 38 part-time/adjunct (25 women). *Students:* 253 full-time (191 women), 306 part-time (241 women); includes 444 minority (129 Black or African American, non-Hispanic/Latino; 3 Asian, non-Hispanic/Latino; 304 Hispanic/Latino; 8 Two or more races, non-Hispanic/Latino), 18 international. Average age 31. 366 applicants, 60% accepted, 115 enrolled. In 2016, 193 master's, 8 doctorates awarded. *Degree requirements:* For doctorate, thesis/dissertation. *Entrance requirements:* For master's, minimum GPA of 3.0; for doctorate and other advanced degree, GRE General Test. Additional exam requirements/recommendations for international students: Required—TOEFL (minimum score 550 paper-based; 80 iBT), IELTS (minimum score 6.3). *Application deadline:* For fall admission, 6/1 priority date for domestic students, 4/1 for international students; for winter admission, 10/1 priority date for domestic students, 9/1 for international students; for spring admission, 3/1 priority date for domestic students, 2/1 for international students. Applications are processed on a rolling basis. Application fee: $30. Electronic applications accepted. *Expenses:* Tuition, state resident: full-time $8912; part-time $446 per credit hour. Tuition, nonresident: full-time $21,393; part-time $992 per credit hour. *Required fees:* $2185; $195 per semester. Tuition and fees vary according to program. *Financial support:* Fellowships, research assistantships with tuition reimbursements, teaching assistantships with tuition reimbursements, Federal Work-Study, and tuition waivers (full and partial) available. Support available to part-time students. Financial award applicants required to submit FAFSA. *Unit head:* Dr. Benjamin Baez, Chair, 305-348-3214, Fax: 305-348-1515, E-mail: benjamin.baez@fiu.edu. *Application contact:* Nanett Rojas, Assistant Director, Graduate Admissions, 305-348-7464, Fax: 305-348-7441, E-mail: gradadm@fiu.edu.
Website: http://education.fiu.edu

Florida State University, The Graduate School, College of Education, Program in Higher Education, Tallahassee, FL 32306. Offers MS, Ed D, PhD. Terminal master's awarded for partial completion of doctoral program. *Degree requirements:* For master's, comprehensive exam, thesis optional; for doctorate, comprehensive exam, thesis/dissertation, diagnostic exam, preliminary exam, prospectus defense, dissertation defense. *Entrance requirements:* For master's and doctorate, GRE General Test, minimum upper-division GPA of 3.0. Additional exam requirements/recommendations for international students: Required—TOEFL (minimum score 550 paper-based, 80 iBT), IELTS (minimum score 6.5), Michigan English Language Assessment Battery (minimum score 77), or PTE (minimum score 55). Application fee: $30. Electronic applications accepted. *Expenses:* Tuition, state resident: full-time $7263; part-time $403.51 per credit hour. Tuition, nonresident: full-time $18,087; part-time $1004.85 per credit hour. *Required fees:* $1365; $75.81 per credit hour. $20 per semester. Tuition and fees vary according to campus/location. *Financial support:* Fellowships, research assistantships, teaching assistantships, scholarships/grants, tuition waivers (full and partial), and unspecified assistantships available. Financial award application deadline: 1/15; financial award applicants required to submit FAFSA. *Faculty research:* Student engagement, success, and outcomes; equity and access for underserved students; learning and outcomes of leadership and civic education; policy and politics of higher education; race, ethnicity, and gender disparities through sociological/historical perspectives. *Unit head:* Dr. Tamara Bertrand-Jones, Associate Professor/Program Coordinator, 850-645-9558, Fax: 850-644-1258, E-mail: tbertrand@admin.fsu.edu. *Application contact:* Linda J. Lyons, Academic Support Assistant, 850-644-7077, Fax: 850-644-1258, E-mail: ljlyons@fsu.edu.
Website: http://education.fsu.edu/degrees-and-programs/graduate-programs

Geneva College, Master of Arts in Higher Education Program, Beaver Falls, PA 15010-3599. Offers campus ministry (MA); college teaching (MA); educational leadership (MA); student affairs administration (MA). *Program availability:* Part-time, evening/weekend, blended/hybrid learning. *Faculty:* 2 full-time (0 women), 11 part-time/adjunct (4 women). *Students:* 49 full-time (30 women), 7 part-time (2 women); includes 6 minority (3 Black or African American, non-Hispanic/Latino; 1 Hispanic/Latino; 2 Two or more races, non-Hispanic/Latino), 1 international. Average age 26. 47 applicants, 74% accepted, 23 enrolled. In 2016, 23 master's awarded. *Degree requirements:* For master's, 36 hours (27 in core courses) including a capstone research project. *Entrance requirements:* For master's, minimum GPA of 3.0, writing sample, 3 letters of recommendation, essay on motivation for participation in the program. Additional exam requirements/recommendations for international students: Required—TOEFL. *Application deadline:* For fall admission, 9/1 priority date for domestic students; for winter admission, 1/2 priority date for domestic students; for spring admission, 3/11 priority date for domestic students. Applications are processed on a rolling basis. Electronic applications accepted. *Expenses:* $655 per credit. *Financial support:* In 2016–17, 37 students received support. Unspecified assistantships available. Financial award application deadline: 8/1; financial award applicants required to submit FAFSA. *Faculty research:* Learning theories, church-related higher education, organizational culture, sexual assault and transgender students at Christian colleges, emerging technology in higher education. *Unit head:* Dr. Keith Martel, Program Director, 724-847-6884, Fax: 724-847-6107, E-mail: hed@geneva.edu. *Application contact:* Jerryn S. Carson, Program Coordinator, 724-847-6510, Fax: 724-847-6696, E-mail: hed@geneva.edu.
Website: http://www.geneva.edu/page/higher_ed

George Mason University, College of Education and Human Development, Program in Education, Fairfax, VA 22030. Offers higher education (PhD). *Faculty:* 61 full-time (44 women), 2 part-time/adjunct (1 woman). *Students:* 89 full-time (76 women), 246 part-time (178 women); includes 90 minority (45 Black or African American, non-Hispanic/Latino; 1 American Indian or Alaska Native, non-Hispanic/Latino; 16 Asian, non-Hispanic/Latino; 19 Hispanic/Latino; 1 Native Hawaiian or other Pacific Islander, non-Hispanic/Latino; 8 Two or more races, non-Hispanic/Latino), 24 international. Average age 39. 92 applicants, 64% accepted, 37 enrolled. In 2016, 45 doctorates awarded. *Entrance requirements:* For doctorate, GRE (no more than 5 years old), official transcripts from graduate and undergraduate institutions; 3 letters of recommendation; goal statement of 750-1000 words. Additional exam requirements/recommendations for international students: Required—TOEFL (minimum score 575 paper-based; 88 iBT), IELTS, PTE (minimum score 59). *Application deadline:* For spring admission, 9/15 for domestic and international students. Application fee: $75 ($80 for international students). Electronic applications accepted. *Expenses:* Tuition, state resident: full-time $10,628; part-time $443 per credit. Tuition, nonresident: full-time $29,306; part-time $1221 per credit. *Required fees:* $3096; $129 per credit. Tuition and fees vary according to program. *Financial support:* In 2016–17, 88 students received support, including 10 fellowships (averaging $7,300 per year), 68 research assistantships with tuition reimbursements available (averaging $14,134 per year), 33 teaching assistantships with tuition reimbursements available (averaging $7,500 per year); career-related internships or fieldwork, Federal Work-Study, unspecified assistantships, and health care benefits (for full-time research or teaching assistantship recipients) also available. Support available to part-time students. Financial award application deadline: 3/1; financial award applicants required to submit FAFSA. *Unit head:* Anastasia Kitsantis, Director, 703-993-2688, E-mail: akitsant@gmu.edu. *Application contact:* Nicole Mariam, Graduate Admissions Coordinator, 703-993-3832, Fax: 703-993-2020, E-mail: nwhite5@gmu.edu.

George Mason University, College of Humanities and Social Sciences, Higher Education Program, Fairfax, VA 22030. Offers community college education (DA); higher education (Certificate). *Faculty:* 5 full-time (all women), 1 part-time/adjunct (0 women). *Students:* 3 full-time (1 woman), 20 part-time (12 women); includes 5 minority (3 Black or African American, non-Hispanic/Latino; 1 Asian, non-Hispanic/Latino; 1 Hispanic/Latino), 1 international. Average age 46. 3 applicants, 100% accepted, 2 enrolled. In 2016, 7 doctorates, 4 Certificates awarded. *Degree requirements:* For doctorate, thesis/dissertation, internship. *Entrance requirements:* For doctorate, GRE, 3 letters of recommendation; writing sample; resume; master's degree; expanded goals statement; official transcripts; for Certificate, official transcripts; expanded goals statement; 3 letters of recommendation; resume; writing sample. Additional exam requirements/recommendations for international students: Required—TOEFL (minimum score 575 paper-based; 88 iBT), IELTS (minimum score 6.5), PTE (minimum score 59). Application fee: $75 ($80 for international students). Electronic applications accepted. *Expenses:* Tuition, state resident: full-time $10,628; part-time $443 per credit. Tuition, nonresident: full-time $29,306; part-time $1221 per credit. *Required fees:* $3096; $129 per credit. Tuition and fees vary according to program. *Financial support:* Career-related internships or fieldwork, Federal Work-Study, and scholarships/grants available. Support available to part-time students. Financial award application deadline: 3/1; financial award applicants required to submit FAFSA. *Faculty research:* Leadership, the scholarship of teaching, learning, and assessment; ethical leadership; assessment; information technology; diversity. *Total annual research expenditures:* $24,021. *Unit head:* Jan Arminio, Director, 703-993-2064, Fax: 703-993-2307, E-mail: jarminio@gmu.edu. *Application contact:* Katie Richards, Administrative Coordinator, 703-993-2310, Fax: 703-993-2307, E-mail: kricha22@gmu.edu.
Website: http://highered.gmu.edu/

The George Washington University, Graduate School of Education and Human Development, Department of Educational Leadership, Program in Higher Education Administration, Washington, DC 20052. Offers college teaching and academic leadership (MA Ed/HD, Ed S); general administration (MA Ed/HD, Ed S); higher education administration (Ed D); higher education finance (MA Ed/HD, Ed S); international education (MA Ed/HD, Ed S); policy (MA Ed/HD, Ed S); student affairs administration (MA Ed/HD, Ed S). *Accreditation:* NCATE. *Students:* 23 full-time (18 women), 70 part-time (51 women); includes 35 minority (20 Black or African American, non-Hispanic/Latino; 8 Asian, non-Hispanic/Latino; 6 Hispanic/Latino; 1 Two or more races, non-Hispanic/Latino), 3 international. Average age 31. 148 applicants, 74% accepted, 37 enrolled. In 2016, 30 master's, 9 doctorates, 1 other advanced degree awarded. *Degree requirements:* For master's and Ed S, comprehensive exam; for doctorate, comprehensive exam, thesis/dissertation. *Entrance requirements:* For master's, GRE General Test or MAT, minimum GPA of 2.75; for doctorate, GRE General Test or MAT, interview, minimum GPA of 3.3; for Ed S, GRE General Test or MAT, minimum GPA of 3.3. *Application deadline:* For fall admission, 1/15 priority date for domestic students; for spring admission, 10/1 for domestic students. Applications are processed on a rolling basis. Application fee: $75. *Financial support:* In 2016–17, 17 students received support. Fellowships, research assistantships, career-related internships or fieldwork, Federal Work-Study, and tuition waivers (partial) available. Financial award application deadline: 1/15; financial award applicants required to submit FAFSA. *Faculty research:* Technology in higher education administration. *Unit head:* Michael Feuer, Dean, 202-994-6161, E-mail: mjfeuer@gwu.edu. *Application contact:* Sarah Lang, Director of Graduate Admissions, 202-994-1447, Fax: 202-994-7207, E-mail: slang@gwu.edu.

Georgia Southern University, Jack N. Averitt College of Graduate Studies, College of Education, Department of Leadership, Technology, and Human Development, Program in Higher Education, Statesboro, GA 30460. Offers M Ed. *Accreditation:* NCATE. *Program availability:* Part-time, evening/weekend. *Students:* 5 part-time (4 women); includes 2 minority (both Black or African American, non-Hispanic/Latino). Average age 37. In 2016, 23 master's awarded. *Degree requirements:* For master's, portfolio, practicum, transition point assessments. *Entrance requirements:* For master's, GRE General Test or MAT, minimum GPA of 2.5. Additional exam requirements/ recommendations for international students: Required—TOEFL (minimum score 550 paper-based; 80 iBT), IELTS (minimum score 6). *Application deadline:* For fall admission, 4/1 priority date for domestic students, 3/1 for international students; for spring admission, 10/1 for domestic and international students. Applications are processed on a rolling basis. Application fee: $50. Electronic applications accepted. *Expenses:* Tuition, state resident: full-time $7236; part-time $277 per semester hour. Tuition, nonresident: full-time $27,118; part-time $1105 per semester hour. *Required fees:* $2092. *Financial support:* In 2016–17, 3 fellowships with full tuition reimbursements (averaging $7,750 per year) were awarded; research assistantships with partial tuition reimbursements, teaching assistantships with partial tuition reimbursements, career-related internships or fieldwork, Federal Work-Study, scholarships/grants, tuition waivers (full), and unspecified assistantships also available. Support available to part-time students. Financial award application deadline: 4/15; financial award applicants required to submit FAFSA. *Faculty research:* Global issues in higher education, leadership and identity development in higher education. *Unit head:* Dr. Daniel Calhoun, Program Coordinator, 912-478-1428, Fax: 912-478-7140, E-mail: dwcalhoun@georgiasouthern.edu. *Application contact:* Lydia Cross, Coordinator for Graduate Academic Services Center, 912-478-8664, E-mail: lcross@georgiasouthern.edu.
Website: http://coe.georgiasouthern.edu/edld/

Georgia Southern University, Jack N. Averitt College of Graduate Studies, College of Education, Department of Leadership, Technology, and Human Development, Program in Higher Education Administration, Statesboro, GA 30458. Offers M Ed. *Program availability:* Part-time, evening/weekend. *Students:* 45 full-time (30 women), 108 part-time (78 women); includes 69 minority (57 Black or African American, non-Hispanic/Latino; 2 Asian, non-Hispanic/Latino; 9 Hispanic/Latino; 1 Two or more races, non-Hispanic/Latino). Average age 30. 61 applicants, 98% accepted, 46 enrolled. In 2016, 35 master's awarded. *Entrance requirements:* For master's, GRE, minimum GPA of 2.5. Additional exam requirements/recommendations for international students: Required—TOEFL (minimum score 550 paper-based; 80 iBT), IELTS (minimum score 6). *Application deadline:* For fall admission, 4/1 for domestic students; for spring admission, 11/1 for domestic students. Application fee: $50. Electronic applications accepted. *Expenses:* Tuition, state resident: full-time $7236; part-time $277 per semester hour. Tuition, nonresident: full-time $27,118; part-time $1105 per semester hour. *Required fees:* $2092. *Financial support:* In 2016–17, 4 students received support, including 3 fellowships with full tuition reimbursements available (averaging $7,750 per year). Financial award application deadline: 4/20; financial award applicants required to submit FAFSA. *Faculty research:* Higher education administration, student affairs. *Unit head:* Dr. Daniel Calhoun, Program Director, 912-478-1428, Fax: 912-478-7104, E-mail: dwcalhoun@georgiasouthern.edu.

Grambling State University, School of Graduate Studies and Research, College of Education, Department of Educational Leadership, Grambling, LA 71245. Offers developmental education (MS, Ed D, PMC), including curriculum and instructional design (Ed D), English (MS), guidance and counseling (MS), higher education administration and management (Ed D), mathematics (MS), reading (MS), science (MS), student development and personnel services (Ed D); educational leadership (M Ed). *Program availability:* Part-time, evening/weekend. *Degree requirements:* For master's, comprehensive exam, thesis (for some programs); for doctorate, comprehensive exam, thesis/dissertation. *Entrance requirements:* For master's, GRE, minimum GPA of 2.5 on last degree; for doctorate, GRE (minimum score 1000, 500 on Verbal), master's degree, minimum GPA of 3.0 on last degree. Additional exam requirements/recommendations for international students: Required—TOEFL (minimum score 500 paper-based; 62 iBT). Electronic applications accepted.

Grand Valley State University, College of Education, Program in College Student Affairs Leadership, Allendale, MI 49401-9403. Offers M Ed. *Students:* 71 full-time (50 women), 7 part-time (5 women); includes 22 minority (12 Black or African American, non-Hispanic/Latino; 1 American Indian or Alaska Native, non-Hispanic/Latino; 1 Asian, non-Hispanic/Latino; 5 Hispanic/Latino; 3 Two or more races, non-Hispanic/Latino), 2 international. Average age 24. In 2016, 33 master's awarded. *Degree requirements:* For master's, project or thesis. *Entrance requirements:* For master's, GRE General Test or minimum GPA of 3.0, last 60 credits from regionally-accredited college/university, 3 letters of recommendation. Additional exam requirements/recommendations for international students: Required—TOEFL (minimum score 550 paper-based, 80 iBT), IELTS (6.5), or Michigan English Language Assessment Battery. *Application deadline:* Applications are processed on a rolling basis. Application fee: $30. Electronic applications accepted. *Expenses:* $628 per credit hour. *Financial support:* In 2016–17, 63 students received support. Unspecified assistantships available. *Faculty research:* Adult learners, diversity and multiculturalism. *Unit head:* Dr. Donald Mitchell, Graduate Program Director, 616-331-6250, E-mail: mitchedo@gvsu.edu. *Application contact:* Thomas Owens, Director, Student Information and Services Center, 616-331-6282, E-mail: owenst@gvsu.edu.

Grand Valley State University, College of Education, Program in Higher Education, Allendale, MI 49401-9403. Offers M Ed. *Program availability:* Part-time. *Students:* 11 full-time (7 women), 37 part-time (26 women); includes 15 minority (6 Black or African American, non-Hispanic/Latino; 2 Asian, non-Hispanic/Latino; 4 Hispanic/Latino; 3 Two or more races, non-Hispanic/Latino), 1 international. Average age 34. 116 applicants, 95% accepted, 9 enrolled. In 2016, 24 master's awarded. *Degree requirements:* For master's, project or thesis. *Entrance requirements:* For master's, minimum undergraduate GPA of 3.0 or GRE General Test, last 60 credits from regionally-accredited college/university, 3 letters of recommendation. Additional exam requirements/recommendations for international students: Required—TOEFL (minimum score 550 paper-based, 80 iBT), IELTS (6.5), or Michigan English Language Assessment Battery. *Application deadline:* Applications are processed on a rolling basis. Application fee: $30. Electronic applications accepted. *Expenses:* $628 per credit hour. *Financial support:* In 2016–17, 8 students received support. Unspecified assistantships available. *Unit head:* Dr. Donald Mitchell, Director/Student Application and Recruiting Contact, 616-331-6292, Fax: 616-331-6515, E-mail: mitchedo@gvsu.edu. *Application contact:* Thomas Owens, Director, Student Information and Services Center, 616-331-6282, E-mail: owenst@gvsu.edu.
Website: http://www.gvsu.edu/grad/highered/

Grand Valley State University, College of Education, Programs in General Education, Allendale, MI 49401-9403. Offers adult and higher education (M Ed); early childhood education (M Ed); educational differentiation (M Ed); educational leadership (M Ed); educational technology integration (M Ed); elementary education (M Ed); middle level education (M Ed); school library media services (M Ed); secondary level education (M Ed); teaching English to speakers of other languages (M Ed). *Program availability:* Part-time, evening/weekend, 100% online, blended/hybrid learning. *Students:* 28 part-time (20 women); includes 6 minority (4 Black or African American, non-Hispanic/Latino; 1 American Indian or Alaska Native, non-Hispanic/Latino; 1 Hispanic/Latino). Average age 42. In 2016, 17 master's awarded. *Degree requirements:* For master's, project or thesis. *Entrance requirements:* For master's, GRE General Test or minimum GPA of 3.0, last 60 credits from regionally-accredited college/university, 3 letters of recommendation. Additional exam requirements/recommendations for international students: Required—TOEFL (minimum score 550 paper-based, 80 iBT), IELTS (6.5), or Michigan English Language Assessment Battery. *Application deadline:* Applications are processed on a rolling basis. Application fee: $30. Electronic applications accepted. *Expenses:* $628 per credit hour. *Financial support:* In 2016–17, 2 students received support. Career-related internships or fieldwork, Federal Work-Study, scholarships/grants, and unspecified assistantships available. *Faculty research:* Effectiveness of technology in education, parental involvement, effective teaching, effective schools research. *Unit head:* Dr. Doug Busman, Graduate Program Director, 616-331-6250, E-mail: busmando@gvsu.edu. *Application contact:* Thomas Owens, Director, Student Information and Services Center, 616-331-6282, Fax: 616-331-6217, E-mail: owenst@gvsu.edu.
Website: http://www.gvsu.edu/coe/

Illinois State University, Graduate School, College of Education, Department of Curriculum and Instruction, Normal, IL 61790-2200. Offers curriculum and instruction (MS, MS Ed, Ed D); educational policies (Ed D); postsecondary education (Ed D); reading (MS Ed); supervision (Ed D). *Accreditation:* NCATE. *Degree requirements:* For master's, variable foreign language requirement, thesis or alternative; for doctorate, variable foreign language requirement, thesis/dissertation, 2 terms of residency, internship. *Entrance requirements:* For master's, GRE General Test, minimum GPA of 3.0 in last 60 hours of course work; for doctorate, GRE General Test. *Faculty research:* In-service and pre-service teacher education for teachers of English language learners; teachers for all children: developing a model for alternative, bilingual elementary certification for paraprofessionals in Illinois; Illinois Geographic Alliance, Connections Project.

Indiana State University, College of Graduate and Professional Studies, Bayh College of Education, Department of Educational Leadership, Terre Haute, IN 47809. Offers educational administration (PhD); higher education leadership (PhD); K-12 district leadership (PhD); school administration (Ed S); school administration and supervision (M Ed); student affairs and higher education (MS). *Accreditation:* NCATE. *Program availability:* Part-time, evening/weekend. Terminal master's awarded for partial completion of doctoral program. *Degree requirements:* For master's, thesis; for doctorate, thesis/dissertation. *Entrance requirements:* For master's, GRE General Test, minimum undergraduate GPA of 2.5; for doctorate, GRE General Test, minimum undergraduate GPA of 3.5; for Ed S, GRE General Test, minimum graduate GPA of 3.25. Electronic applications accepted.

Indiana University Bloomington, School of Education, Department of Educational Leadership and Policy Studies, Bloomington, IN 47405. Offers educational leadership (MS, Ed D, Ed S); higher education (Ed D, PhD); higher education and student affairs (MS); history and philosophy of education (MS); history, philosophy, and policy in education (PhD), including education policy studies, history of education, philosophy of education; international and comparative education (MS). *Accreditation:* NCATE. *Faculty:* 32 full-time (18 women). *Students:* 223 full-time (140 women), 94 part-time (50 women); includes 80 minority (44 Black or African American, non-Hispanic/Latino; 13 Asian, non-Hispanic/Latino; 18 Hispanic/Latino; 1 Native Hawaiian or other Pacific Islander, non-Hispanic/Latino; 4 Two or more races, non-Hispanic/Latino), 29 international. Average age 34. 309 applicants, 40% accepted, 57 enrolled. In 2016, 60 master's, 18 doctorates, 5 other advanced degrees awarded. *Degree requirements:* For master's, thesis optional; for doctorate, comprehensive exam, thesis/dissertation; for Ed S, comprehensive exam or project. *Entrance requirements:* For master's, doctorate, and Ed S, GRE General Test. Additional exam requirements/recommendations for international students: Required—TOEFL (minimum score 79 iBT). *Application deadline:* For fall admission, 1/15 priority date for domestic students, 12/1 priority date for international students; for spring admission, 9/1 priority date for domestic and international students. Applications are processed on a rolling basis. Application fee: $55 ($65 for international students). Electronic applications accepted. *Financial support:* Fellowships with full and partial tuition reimbursements, research assistantships with full and partial tuition reimbursements, teaching assistantships with full and partial tuition reimbursements, career-related internships or fieldwork, scholarships/grants, health care benefits, and unspecified assistantships available. *Faculty research:* Culturally engaging campus environments, school choice policy analysis, democracy and education in the national and international context, and principal leadership. *Unit head:* Dr. Dionne Danns, Interim Chair, 812-856-8398. *Application contact:* Maria Jensen, Department Administrator, 812-856-8370, Fax: 812-856-8394, E-mail: jensen5@indiana.edu.
Website: http://education.indiana.edu/about/departments/leadership/index.html

Indiana University of Pennsylvania, School of Graduate Studies and Research, College of Education and Educational Technology, Department of Student Affairs in Higher Education, Indiana, PA 15705. Offers MA. *Accreditation:* NCATE. *Program availability:* Part-time. *Faculty:* 4 full-time (2 women), 1 part-time/adjunct (0 women). *Students:* 45 full-time (37 women), 5 part-time (4 women); includes 11 minority (6 Black or African American, non-Hispanic/Latino; 3 Hispanic/Latino; 1 Native Hawaiian or other Pacific Islander, non-Hispanic/Latino; 1 Two or more races, non-Hispanic/Latino). Average age 24. 101 applicants, 61% accepted, 26 enrolled. In 2016, 21 master's awarded. *Degree requirements:* For master's, comprehensive exam, thesis optional. *Entrance requirements:* For master's, resume, interview, 2 letters of recommendation, writing sample, minimum GPA of 2.8. Additional exam requirements/recommendations for international students: Required—TOEFL (minimum score 540 paper-based). *Application deadline:* For fall admission, 1/15 priority date for domestic students. Application fee: $50. Electronic applications accepted. *Expenses:* Contact institution. *Financial support:* In 2016–17, 21 research assistantships with tuition reimbursements (averaging $5,445 per year) were awarded; fellowships, career-related internships or fieldwork, Federal Work-Study, scholarships/grants, and unspecified assistantships also available. Support available to part-time students. Financial award application deadline: 4/15; financial award applicants required to submit FAFSA. *Unit head:* Dr. John Wesley Lowery, Chairperson, 724-357-4545, E-mail: jlowery@iup.edu.
Website: http://www.iup.edu/sahe

Indiana Wesleyan University, Graduate School, College of Arts and Sciences, Marion, IN 46953. Offers addictions counseling (MS); clinical mental health counseling (MS);

community counseling (MS); marriage and family therapy (MS); school counseling (MS); student development counseling and administration (MS). *Accreditation:* ACA. *Program availability:* Part-time. *Degree requirements:* For master's, thesis or alternative. *Entrance requirements:* For master's, GRE General Test. Additional exam requirements/recommendations for international students: Required—TOEFL. Electronic applications accepted. *Expenses:* Contact institution. *Faculty research:* Community counseling, multicultural counseling, addictions.

Inter American University of Puerto Rico, Metropolitan Campus, Graduate Programs, Program in Higher Education Administration, San Juan, PR 00919-1293. Offers MA. *Degree requirements:* For master's, comprehensive exam. *Entrance requirements:* For master's, GRE or EXADEP, interview. Electronic applications accepted.

Iowa State University of Science and Technology, Department of Educational Leadership and Policy Studies, Ames, IA 50011. Offers counselor education (M Ed, MS); educational administration (M Ed, MS); educational leadership (PhD); higher education (M Ed, MS); organizational learning and human resource development (M Ed, MS); research and evaluation (MS); student affairs (MS). *Degree requirements:* For master's, thesis or alternative; for doctorate, thesis/dissertation. *Entrance requirements:* For master's and doctorate, GRE General Test. Additional exam requirements/recommendations for international students: Required—TOEFL (minimum score 560 paper-based; 83 iBT), IELTS (minimum score 6.5). *Application deadline:* For fall admission, 1/1 priority date for domestic and international students. Application fee: $60 ($90 for international students). Electronic applications accepted. *Application contact:* Robyn Goldy, Application Contact, 515-294-1241, Fax: 515-294-4942, E-mail: rgoldy@iastate.edu.
Website: http://www.elps.hs.iastate.edu/

Jackson State University, Graduate School, College of Education and Human Development, Department of Educational Leadership, Jackson, MS 39217. Offers education administration and supervision (Ed S); educational administration and supervision (MS Ed, PhD); higher education (Ed S). *Accreditation:* NCATE. *Program availability:* Part-time, evening/weekend, online only, 100% online, blended/hybrid learning. *Faculty:* 12 full-time (9 women), 3 part-time/adjunct (0 women). *Students:* 44 full-time (8 women), 238 part-time (181 women); includes 255 minority (all Black or African American, non-Hispanic/Latino). Average age 38. 158 applicants, 60% accepted, 64 enrolled. In 2016, 8 master's, 18 doctorates, 13 other advanced degrees awarded. *Degree requirements:* For master's and Ed S, comprehensive exam, thesis; for doctorate, comprehensive exam, thesis/dissertation. *Entrance requirements:* For master's, GRE General Test; for doctorate, MAT, GRE, teaching experience. Additional exam requirements/recommendations for international students: Required—TOEFL (minimum score 520 paper-based; 67 iBT). *Application deadline:* For fall admission, 3/1 priority date for domestic students, 3/1 for international students; for spring admission, 10/1 for domestic and international students. Applications are processed on a rolling basis. Application fee: $25. Electronic applications accepted. *Expenses:* Contact institution. *Financial support:* Career-related internships or fieldwork, Federal Work-Study, scholarships/grants, and unspecified assistantships available. Support available to part-time students. Financial award application deadline: 3/1; financial award applicants required to submit FAFSA. *Unit head:* Dr. Benjamin Ngwudike, Chair, 601-979-2351, Fax: 601-979-7048, E-mail: benjamin.c.ngwudike@jsums.edu. *Application contact:* Dr. Benjamin Ngwudike, Chair, 601-979-2351, Fax: 601-979-7048, E-mail: benjamin.c.ngwudike@jsums.edu.
Website: http://www.jsums.edu/eduleadership/

James Madison University, The Graduate School, College of Education, Program in Adult Education and Human Resource Development, Harrisonburg, VA 22802. Offers higher education (MS Ed); human resource management (MS Ed); individualized (MS Ed); instructional design (MS Ed); leadership and facilitation (MS Ed); program evaluation and measurement (MS Ed). *Accreditation:* NCATE. *Program availability:* Part-time, evening/weekend. *Students:* 10 full-time (8 women), 11 part-time (10 women); includes 7 minority (4 Black or African American, non-Hispanic/Latino; 1 Hispanic/Latino; 2 Two or more races, non-Hispanic/Latino), 1 international. Average age 30. 23 applicants, 91% accepted, 18 enrolled. In 2016, 17 master's awarded. Application fee: $55. Electronic applications accepted. *Financial support:* In 2016–17, 15 students received support. Teaching assistantships, Federal Work-Study, and 8 assistantships (averaging $7911), 1 athletic assistantship (averaging $9284) available. Financial award application deadline: 3/1; financial award applicants required to submit FAFSA. *Unit head:* Dr. Jane B. Thall, Department Head, 540-568-5531, E-mail: thalljb@jmu.edu. *Application contact:* Lynette D. Michael, Director of Graduate Admissions, 540-568-6131 Ext. 6395, Fax: 540-568-7860, E-mail: michaeld@jmu.edu.

Johnson University, Graduate and Professional Programs, Knoxville, TN 37998-1001. Offers biblical interpretation (Graduate Certificate); business administration (MBA); Christian ministries (Graduate Certificate); clinical mental health counseling (MA); educational technology (MA); intercultural studies (MA); leadership (MBA); leadership studies (PhD); New Testament (MA); nonprofit management (MBA); school counseling (MA); spiritual formation and leadership (Graduate Certificate); strategic ministry (MA); teacher education (MA). *Program availability:* Part-time, evening/weekend, 100% online, blended/hybrid learning. *Faculty:* 26 full-time (10 women), 32 part-time/adjunct (9 women). *Students:* 126 full-time (46 women), 170 part-time (65 women); includes 33 minority (13 Black or African American, non-Hispanic/Latino; 1 American Indian or Alaska Native, non-Hispanic/Latino; 4 Asian, non-Hispanic/Latino; 8 Hispanic/Latino; 7 Two or more races, non-Hispanic/Latino), 21 international. Average age 35. In 2016, 106 master's, 3 doctorates awarded. *Degree requirements:* For master's, variable foreign language requirement, comprehensive exam, thesis (for some programs), internships; for doctorate, variable foreign language requirement, comprehensive exam, thesis/dissertation, internships. *Entrance requirements:* For master's, PRAXIS (for MA in teacher education); MAT (for counseling); GRE or GMAT (for MBA), interview, 3 references, transcripts, essay, minimum GPA of 2.5 or 3.0 (depending on program); for doctorate, GRE or MAT (taken not less than 5 years prior), interview, 3 references, transcripts, essay, minimum GPA of 3.0; for Graduate Certificate, interview, 3 references, transcripts, essay, minimum GPA of 3.0. Additional exam requirements/recommendations for international students: Required—TOEFL (minimum score 527 paper-based; 71 iBT). *Application deadline:* For fall admission, 7/1 for domestic students; for spring admission, 11/1 for domestic students; for summer admission, 4/1 for domestic students. Application fee: $50. Electronic applications accepted. *Expenses:* Contact institution. *Financial support:* Scholarships/grants available. Financial award application deadline: 4/15; financial award applicants required to submit FAFSA. *Unit head:* Richard Clark, Vice President for External Relations, 865-251-2327, E-mail: rclark@johnsonu.edu. *Application contact:* Lisa Tarwater, Director of Graduate Admissions, 865-251-3400, E-mail: ltarwater@johnsonu.edu.

Kaplan University, Davenport Campus, School of Higher Education Studies, Davenport, IA 52807. Offers college administration and leadership (MS); college teaching and learning (MS); student services (MS). *Program availability:* Part-time, evening/weekend, online learning. *Entrance requirements:* Additional exam requirements/recommendations for international students: Required—TOEFL (minimum score 550 paper-based; 80 iBT).

Kent State University, College of Education, Health and Human Services, School of Foundations, Leadership and Administration, Program in Higher Education, Kent, OH 44242-0001. Offers PhD, Ed S. *Accreditation:* NCATE. *Program availability:* Part-time, evening/weekend. *Degree requirements:* For doctorate, comprehensive exam, thesis/dissertation. *Entrance requirements:* For doctorate, GRE General Test, 2 letters of reference, resume, interview, goals statement. Additional exam requirements/recommendations for international students: Required—TOEFL (minimum score 550 paper-based; 80 iBT). Electronic applications accepted. *Expenses:* Tuition, state resident: full-time $10,864; part-time $495 per credit hour. Tuition, nonresident: full-time $18,380; part-time $837 per credit hour. *Faculty research:* Leadership.

Kent State University, College of Education, Health and Human Services, School of Foundations, Leadership and Administration, Program in Higher Education and Student Personnel, Kent, OH 44242-0001. Offers M Ed. *Accreditation:* NCATE. *Program availability:* Part-time, evening/weekend. *Entrance requirements:* For master's, GRE if undergraduate GPA is below 3.0, resume, interview, 2 letters of recommendation, goals statement. Additional exam requirements/recommendations for international students: Required—TOEFL (minimum score 550 paper-based; 80 iBT). Electronic applications accepted. *Expenses:* Tuition, state resident: full-time $10,864; part-time $495 per credit hour. Tuition, nonresident: full-time $18,380; part-time $837 per credit hour. *Faculty research:* History/sociology of higher education, organization and administration in higher education.

Lee University, Program in Education, Cleveland, TN 37320-3450. Offers art (MAT); curriculum and instruction (M Ed, Ed S); early childhood (MAT); educational leadership (M Ed, Ed S); elementary education (MAT); English and math (MAT); English and science (MAT); English and social studies (MAT); higher education administration (MS); history (MAT); history and economics (MAT); math and science (MAT); math and social studies (MAT); middle grades (MAT); science and social studies (MASW); secondary education (MAT); Spanish (MAT); special education (M Ed, MAT); TESOL (MAT). *Accreditation:* NCATE. *Program availability:* Part-time. *Faculty:* 13 full-time (6 women), 9 part-time/adjunct (4 women). *Students:* 35 full-time (27 women), 50 part-time (32 women); includes 12 minority (5 Black or African American, non-Hispanic/Latino; 5 Hispanic/Latino; 2 Two or more races, non-Hispanic/Latino), 4 international. Average age 30. 43 applicants, 79% accepted, 28 enrolled. In 2016, 42 master's, 6 other advanced degrees awarded. *Degree requirements:* For master's, variable foreign language requirement, thesis optional, internship. *Entrance requirements:* For master's, MAT or GRE General Test, minimum undergraduate GPA of 2.75, 3 letters of recommendation, interview, writing sample, official transcripts, background check; for Ed S, minimum undergraduate and master's GPA of 2.75, official transcripts for undergraduate and master's degrees. Additional exam requirements/recommendations for international students: Required—TOEFL (minimum score 61 iBT). *Application deadline:* For fall admission, 6/1 priority date for domestic and international students; for spring admission, 11/1 priority date for domestic and international students; for summer admission, 4/1 priority date for domestic and international students. Applications are processed on a rolling basis. Application fee: $25. Electronic applications accepted. *Expenses: Tuition:* Full-time $11,367; part-time $632 per credit hour. *Required fees:* $35 per term. One-time fee: $25. Tuition and fees vary according to program. *Financial support:* In 2016–17, 42 students received support. Career-related internships or fieldwork, Federal Work-Study, institutionally sponsored loans, scholarships/grants, and unspecified assistantships available. Financial award application deadline: 3/1; financial award applicants required to submit FAFSA. *Unit head:* Dr. William Kamm, Director, 423-614-8544, E-mail: wkamm@leeuniversity.edu. *Application contact:* Crystal Keeter, Graduate Education Secretary, 423-614-8544, E-mail: ckeeter@leeuniversity.edu.
Website: http://www.leeuniversity.edu/academics/graduate/education

Lewis University, College of Arts and Sciences, Program in Organizational Leadership, Romeoville, IL 60446. Offers higher education/student services (MA); non-profit management (MA); organizational management (MA); professional and executive coaching (MA); training and development (MA). *Program availability:* Part-time, evening/weekend, 100% online. *Students:* 15 full-time (12 women), 176 part-time (130 women); includes 75 minority (51 Black or African American, non-Hispanic/Latino; 2 American Indian or Alaska Native, non-Hispanic/Latino; 2 Asian, non-Hispanic/Latino; 16 Hispanic/Latino; 4 Two or more races, non-Hispanic/Latino), 2 international. Average age 36. *Entrance requirements:* For master's, bachelor's degree, at least 24 years of age, minimum of 3 years of work experience, minimum GPA of 3.0, letter of recommendation. Additional exam requirements/recommendations for international students: Required—TOEFL (minimum score 550 paper-based; 80 iBT). *Application deadline:* For fall admission, 5/1 priority date for international students; for spring admission, 11/15 priority date for international students. Applications are processed on a rolling basis. Application fee: $40. Electronic applications accepted. *Expenses: Tuition:* Full-time $13,860; part-time $770 per credit hour. *Required fees:* $75 per semester. Tuition and fees vary according to degree level and program. *Financial support:* Tuition waivers and unspecified assistantships available. Financial award application deadline: 5/1; financial award applicants required to submit FAFSA. *Unit head:* Dr. Keith Lavine, Chair of Organizational Leadership, 815-838-0500, E-mail: lavineke@lewisu.edu. *Application contact:* Nancy Wiksten, Graduate Admission Counselor, 815-836-5628, Fax: 815-836-5578, E-mail: grad@lewisu.edu.

Lincoln Memorial University, Carter and Moyers School of Education, Harrogate, TN 37752-1901. Offers administration and supervision (M Ed, Ed S); counseling and guidance (M Ed); curriculum and instruction (M Ed, Ed D, Ed S); English (M Ed); executive leadership (Ed D); higher education administration (Ed D); human resource development (Ed D); leadership and administration (Ed D). *Program availability:* Part-time, evening/weekend, online learning. *Degree requirements:* For master's, comprehensive exam, thesis optional; for Ed S, comprehensive exam. *Entrance requirements:* For master's, PRAXIS, NTE, GRE, MAT, letters of recommendation; for Ed S, graduate transcripts. Additional exam requirements/recommendations for international students: Recommended—TOEFL. *Faculty research:* Brain compatible teaching and learning; poverty in Appalachia; leadership for change; ethics, moral responsibility and social justice; human and organizational learning.

Lincoln University, Graduate Studies, Jefferson City, MO 65101. Offers business administration (MBA), including accounting, management, management information systems, public administration/policy; elementary teaching (M Ed); environmental science (MS); guidance and counseling (M Ed), including community/agency counseling, elementary school, secondary school; higher education (MA); history (MA); integrated agricultural systems (MS); middle school (M Ed); natural sciences (MS); secondary teaching (M Ed); sociology (MA); sociology/criminal justice (MA). *Program availability:* Part-time, evening/weekend, 100% online, blended/hybrid learning. *Students:* 50 full-time (29 women), 68 part-time (39 women); includes 40 minority (37 Black or African American, non-Hispanic/Latino; 1 Asian, non-Hispanic/Latino; 2 Two or more races, non-Hispanic/Latino), 14 international. Average age 33. 75 applicants, 80% accepted, 34 enrolled. In 2016, 51 master's awarded. *Degree requirements:* For master's, comprehensive exam, thesis optional. *Entrance requirements:* For master's, GRE, MAT or GMAT, minimum GPA of 2.75 overall, 3.0 in courses related to specialization; 3 letters of recommendation; minimum C average in English composition; personal statement of purpose. Additional exam requirements/recommendations for

international students: Required—TOEFL (minimum score 500 paper-based; 61 iBT), IELTS (minimum score 5.5), Michigan English Language Assessment Battery (minimum score 80). *Application deadline:* For fall admission, 7/1 priority date for domestic students, 5/1 priority date for international students; for spring admission, 11/1 priority date for domestic students, 10/1 priority date for international students; for summer admission, 6/1 priority date for domestic students. Applications are processed on a rolling basis. Application fee: $30. Electronic applications accepted. *Expenses:* Tuition, state resident: full-time $6840; part-time $5130 per year. Tuition, nonresident: full-time $12,720; part-time $9540 per year. *Required fees:* $852; $811 per unit. Tuition and fees vary according to course load. *Financial support:* In 2016–17, 2 fellowships with tuition reimbursements, 8 research assistantships with tuition reimbursements were awarded; Federal Work-Study, scholarships/grants, and unspecified assistantships also available. Support available to part-time students. Financial award application deadline: 3/1; financial award applicants required to submit FAFSA. *Unit head:* Dr. Rolundus R. Rice, Dean, 573-681-5247, Fax: 573-681-5106, E-mail: gradschool@lincolnu.edu. *Application contact:* Irasema Steck, Administrative Assistant, 573-681-5247, Fax: 573-681-5106, E-mail: gradschool@lincolnu.edu.
Website: http://www.lincolnu.edu/web/graduate-studies/graduate-studies

London Metropolitan University, Graduate Programs, London, United Kingdom. Offers applied psychology (M Sc); architecture (MA); biomedical science (M Sc); blood science (M Sc); cancer pharmacology (M Sc); computer networking and cyber security (M Sc); computing and information systems (M Sc); conference interpreting (MA); counter-terrorism studies (M Sc); creative, digital and professional writing (MA); crime, violence and prevention (M Sc); criminology (M Sc); curating contemporary art (MA); data analytics (M Sc); digital media (MA); early childhood studies (MA); education (MA, Ed D); financial services law, regulation and compliance (LL M); food science (M Sc); forensic psychology (M Sc); health and social care management and policy (M Sc); human nutrition (M Sc); human resource management (MA); human rights and international conflict (MA); information technology (M Sc); intelligence and security studies (M Sc); international oil, gas and energy law (LL M); international relations (MA); interpreting (MA); learning and teaching in higher education (MA); legal practice (LL M); media and entertainment law (LL M); organizational and consumer psychology (M Sc); psychological therapy (M Sc); psychology of mental health (M Sc); public health (M Sc); public policy and management (MPA); security studies (M Sc); social work (M Sc); spatial planning and urban design (MA); sports therapy (M Sc); supporting older children and young people with dyslexia (MA); teaching languages (MA), including Arabic, English; translation (MA); woman and child abuse (MA).

Louisiana State University and Agricultural & Mechanical College, Graduate School, College of Human Sciences and Education, Department of Educational Theory, Policy and Practice, Baton Rouge, LA 70803. Offers counseling (M Ed, MA, Ed S); educational administration (M Ed, MA, PhD, Ed S); educational technology (MA); elementary education (M Ed, MAT); higher education (PhD); research methodology (PhD); secondary education (M Ed, MAT). *Accreditation:* ACA (one or more programs are accredited); NCATE.

Louisiana Tech University, Graduate School, College of Education, Department of Curriculum, Instruction and Leadership, Ruston, LA 71272. Offers curriculum and instruction (M Ed), including research, theory, and design, visually impaired; educational leadership (M Ed, Ed D), including higher education administration (Ed D), P-12 educational leadership (Ed D). *Accreditation:* NCATE. *Program availability:* Part-time. *Degree requirements:* For doctorate, thesis/dissertation. *Entrance requirements:* For master's and doctorate, GRE General Test. *Application deadline:* For fall admission, 7/29 for domestic students; for spring admission, 2/3 for domestic students. Application fee: $20 ($30 for international students). *Financial support:* Fellowships, research assistantships, and teaching assistantships available. Financial award application deadline: 2/1. *Unit head:* Dr. Bryan McCoy, Chair, 318-257-4609, Fax: 318-257-2379, E-mail: bmccoy@latech.edu. *Application contact:* Dr. John Harrison, Associate Dean of Graduate Studies, 318-257-3229, Fax: 318-257-2379, E-mail: johnharrison@latech.edu.
Website: http://education.latech.edu/departments/cil/

Loyola Marymount University, School of Education, Department of Educational Leadership, Program in Higher Education Administration, Los Angeles, CA 90045-2659. Offers MA. *Students:* 19 full-time (17 women); includes 14 minority (2 Black or African American, non-Hispanic/Latino; 1 Asian, non-Hispanic/Latino; 10 Hispanic/Latino; 1 Two or more races, non-Hispanic/Latino). Average age 29. 24 applicants, 63% accepted, 11 enrolled. *Entrance requirements:* For master's, two letters of recommendation, letter of intent. Additional exam requirements/recommendations for international students: Required—TOEFL (minimum score 600 paper-based; 100 iBT). *Application deadline:* For summer admission, 4/8 for domestic students. Application fee: $50. Electronic applications accepted. *Financial support:* In 2016–17, 7 students received support, including 1 research assistantship. *Unit head:* Dr. Elizabeth Stoddard, Director, 310-338-1967, E-mail: elizabeth.stoddard@lmu.edu. *Application contact:* Chake H. Kouyoumjian, Associate Dean of Graduate Studies, 310-338-2721, E-mail: ckouyoum@lmu.edu.
Website: http://soe.lmu.edu/academics/highereducationadministration/

Loyola University Chicago, School of Education, Program in Higher Education, Chicago, IL 60660. Offers M Ed, PhD. PhD offered through the Graduate School. *Accreditation:* NCATE. *Program availability:* Part-time, blended/hybrid learning. *Faculty:* 6 full-time (3 women), 10 part-time/adjunct (6 women). *Students:* 80 full-time (50 women), 58 part-time (50 women); includes 65 minority (19 Black or African American, non-Hispanic/Latino; 1 American Indian or Alaska Native, non-Hispanic/Latino; 8 Asian, non-Hispanic/Latino; 29 Hispanic/Latino; 8 Two or more races, non-Hispanic/Latino), 2 international. Average age 28. 277 applicants, 66% accepted, 64 enrolled. In 2016, 52 master's, 2 doctorates awarded. *Degree requirements:* For master's, comprehensive exam; for doctorate, comprehensive exam, thesis/dissertation. *Entrance requirements:* For master's, letters of recommendation, minimum GPA of 3.0, resume, transcripts; for doctorate, GMAT, GRE General Test, or MAT, 5 years of higher education work experience, interview. Additional exam requirements/recommendations for international students: Required—TOEFL (minimum score 550 paper-based; 79 iBT). *Application deadline:* For fall admission, 12/1 for domestic and international students. Applications are processed on a rolling basis. Application fee: $50. Electronic applications accepted. Application fee is waived when completed online. *Expenses:* $949 per hour; $2,847 per course; $8,541-$11,388 per semester plus fees $432 per semester and $225 the first semester. *Financial support:* In 2016–17, 98 students received support, including 34 fellowships with partial tuition reimbursements available, 41 research assistantships with full tuition reimbursements available (averaging $14,000 per year), 23 teaching assistantships with full tuition reimbursements available (averaging $4,000 per year); career-related internships or fieldwork, institutionally sponsored loans, scholarships/grants, traineeships, health care benefits, and unspecified assistantships also available. Support available to part-time students. Financial award application deadline: 2/1; financial award applicants required to submit FAFSA. *Faculty research:* Church-affiliated higher education, enrollment management, academic programs, program evaluation/quality. *Unit head:* Dr. John Dugan, Director, 312-915-7637, Fax: 312-915-6660, E-mail: jdugan1@luc.edu. *Application contact:* Thomas Ott, Information Contact, 312-915-8907, E-mail: tott@luc.edu.

Lynchburg College, Graduate Studies, M Ed Program in Educational Leadership, Lynchburg, VA 24501-3199. Offers higher education (M Ed); PK-12 administrative and supervisory (M Ed). *Program availability:* Part-time, evening/weekend. *Students:* 16 full-time (10 women), 49 part-time (37 women); includes 5 minority (4 Black or African American, non-Hispanic/Latino; 1 Hispanic/Latino). In 2016, 34 master's awarded. *Degree requirements:* For master's, comprehensive exam (for some programs), internship; ISLLC exam or comprehensive exam. *Entrance requirements:* For master's, GRE, minimum GPA of 3.0 (preferred), official transcripts (bachelor's, others as relevant), three letters of recommendation, career goals statement. Additional exam requirements/recommendations for international students: Required—TOEFL (minimum score 550 paper-based; 79 iBT), IELTS (minimum score 6.5). *Application deadline:* For fall admission, 7/31 for domestic students, 6/1 for international students; for spring admission, 11/30 for domestic students, 10/5 for international students. Applications are processed on a rolling basis. Application fee: $30. Electronic applications accepted. Application fee is waived when completed online. *Expenses:* Contact institution. *Financial support:* Career-related internships or fieldwork, Federal Work-Study, scholarships/grants, health care benefits, and unspecified assistantships available. Support available to part-time students. Financial award application deadline: 7/31; financial award applicants required to submit FAFSA. *Unit head:* Dr. John Walker, Professor/Director, Leadership Studies, 434-544-8032, E-mail: walker.jc@lynchburg.edu.
Website: http://www.lynchburg.edu/graduate/master-of-education-in-educational-leadership/

Maryville University of Saint Louis, School of Education, St. Louis, MO 63141-7299. Offers early childhood education (MA Ed); educational leadership (Ed D); educational leadership: principal certification (MA Ed); elementary education (MA Ed); gifted education (MA Ed); higher education leadership (Ed D); literacy specialist (MA Ed); middle grades education (MA Ed); secondary teaching and inquiry (MA Ed); teacher as leader (MA Ed); teacher leadership (Ed D). *Accreditation:* NCATE. *Program availability:* Part-time, evening/weekend. *Faculty:* 17 full-time (11 women), 21 part-time/adjunct (17 women). *Students:* 12 full-time (11 women), 297 part-time (208 women); includes 92 minority (79 Black or African American, non-Hispanic/Latino; 4 Asian, non-Hispanic/Latino; 4 Hispanic/Latino; 5 Two or more races, non-Hispanic/Latino), 4 international. Average age 38. In 2016, 32 master's, 61 doctorates awarded. *Degree requirements:* For master's, thesis, project. *Entrance requirements:* For master's, minimum cumulative GPA of 3.0, 3 professional recommendations, essays, interview with program faculty; for doctorate, minimum GPA of 3.0, 3 professional recommendations, essay, interview, on-site writing sample. Additional exam requirements/recommendations for international students: Required—TOEFL (minimum score 550 paper-based). *Application deadline:* Applications are processed on a rolling basis. Electronic applications accepted. *Expenses:* $879 per credit (for Ed D); $781 per credit (for master's). *Financial support:* Career-related internships or fieldwork, Federal Work-Study, tuition waivers (partial), and professional educator discounts available. Financial award application deadline: 3/1; financial award applicants required to submit FAFSA. *Faculty research:* Collaboration with public schools, pre-service program development, mathematics, diversity, literacy. *Unit head:* Dr. Cathy Bear, Dean, 314-529-9692, Fax: 314-529-9921, E-mail: cbear@maryville.edu. *Application contact:* Stacey Ruffin, Coordinator of Clinical Experiences and Graduate Programs, 314-529-9542, Fax: 314-529-9921, E-mail: teachered@maryville.edu.
Website: http://www.maryville.edu/ed/graduate-programs/

Marywood University, Academic Affairs, Center for Interdisciplinary Studies, Scranton, PA 18509-1598. Offers human development (PhD), including educational administration, health promotion, higher education administration, instructional leadership, social work. *Program availability:* Part-time. Electronic applications accepted. *Expenses:* Contact institution.

Marywood University, Academic Affairs, Reap College of Education and Human Development, Department of Education, Program in Higher Education Administration, Scranton, PA 18509-1598. Offers MS. *Program availability:* Part-time, evening/weekend. Electronic applications accepted. *Faculty research:* Integrated thematic instruction.

McKendree University, Graduate Programs, Programs in Education, Lebanon, IL 62254-1299. Offers curriculum design and instruction (Ed D, Ed S); educational administration and leadership (MA Ed); educational studies (MA Ed); higher education administrative services (MA Ed); music education (MA Ed); reading (MA Ed); special education (MA Ed); teacher leadership (MA Ed); teaching certification (MA Ed). *Accreditation:* NCATE. *Program availability:* Part-time, evening/weekend, online learning. *Entrance requirements:* For master's, official transcripts from all institutions previously attended, minimum GPA of 3.0, resume, references; for doctorate, GRE (within the past 5 years), master's degree in education and Ed S, or the equivalent, from regionally-accredited institution; official transcripts from all institutions previously attended; curriculum vitae/resume; essay/personal statement; two years of teaching/professional experience; for Ed S, GRE (within the past 5 years), master's degree in education from regionally-accredited institution of higher education; official transcripts from all institutions previously attended; curriculum vitae/resume; essay/personal statement; two years of teaching/professional experience. Additional exam requirements/recommendations for international students: Required—TOEFL. Electronic applications accepted.

Mercer University, Graduate Studies, Cecil B. Day Campus, Tift College of Education (Atlanta), Macon, GA 31207. Offers curriculum and instruction (PhD); early childhood education (M Ed, MAT, Ed S); educational leadership (PhD), including higher education leadership, P-12 school leadership; educational leadership P-12 (M Ed, Ed S); higher education leadership (M Ed); independent and charter school leadership (M Ed); middle grades education (M Ed, MAT); reading specialist (M Ed); secondary education (M Ed, MAT); teacher leadership (Ed S). *Accreditation:* NCATE. *Program availability:* Part-time, evening/weekend. *Faculty:* 28 full-time (15 women), 30 part-time/adjunct (27 women). *Students:* 177 full time (150 women), 324 part-time (264 women); includes 288 minority (256 Black or African American, non-Hispanic/Latino; 1 American Indian or Alaska Native, non-Hispanic/Latino; 7 Asian, non-Hispanic/Latino; 17 Hispanic/Latino; 1 Native Hawaiian or other Pacific Islander, non-Hispanic/Latino; 6 Two or more races, non-Hispanic/Latino), 1 international. Average age 35. In 2016, 173 master's, 34 doctorates, 54 other advanced degrees awarded. *Degree requirements:* For master's and Ed S, research project; for doctorate, comprehensive exam, thesis/dissertation. *Entrance requirements:* For master's, GRE or MAT, minimum undergraduate GPA of 2.75; for doctorate, GRE; for Ed S, GRE or MAT, minimum GPA of 3.25; 3 years of certified teaching experience (for educational leadership and teacher leadership). Additional exam requirements/recommendations for international students: Required—TOEFL (minimum score 80 iBT). *Application deadline:* For fall admission, 8/1 for domestic and international students; for spring admission, 12/1 for domestic and international students; for summer admission, 5/1 for domestic and international students. Applications are processed on a rolling basis. Application fee: $25 ($50 for international students). Electronic applications accepted. *Expenses:* $590 per credit, $1,770 per course (for M Ed); $595 per credit, $1,785 per course (for MAT); $615 per credit, $1,845 per course (for Ed S); $717 per credit, $2,151 per course (for PhD); $150 per semester

technology fee. *Financial support:* Federal Work-Study and unspecified assistantships available. Support available to part-time students. Financial award application deadline: 5/1; financial award applicants required to submit FAFSA. *Faculty research:* Educational technology, multicultural and minority issues in education, educational leadership (P-12 and higher education), school discipline and school bullying, standards-based mathematics education. *Unit head:* Dr. James Barta, Dean, 478-301-5355, Fax: 478-301-2280, E-mail: barta_jj@mercer.edu. *Application contact:* Renee Slaton, Associate Director of Graduate Admissions, 678-547-6084, Fax: 678-547-6055, E-mail: mercereducation@mercer.edu.
Website: http://education.mercer.edu/

Mercer University, Graduate Studies, Macon Campus, Tift College of Education (Macon), Macon, GA 31207. Offers early childhood education (M Ed, Ed S); educational leadership (M Ed, PhD, Ed S), including higher education (PhD), P-12; higher education leadership (M Ed); teacher leadership (Ed S). *Accreditation:* NCATE. *Program availability:* Part-time, evening/weekend, 100% online, blended/hybrid learning. *Faculty:* 14 full-time (11 women), 1 part-time/adjunct (0 women). *Students:* 61 full-time (39 women), 39 part-time (30 women); includes 39 minority (34 Black or African American, non-Hispanic/Latino; 1 Asian, non-Hispanic/Latino; 2 Hispanic/Latino; 1 Native Hawaiian or other Pacific Islander, non-Hispanic/Latino; 1 Two or more races, non-Hispanic/Latino), 3 international. Average age 33. In 2016, 23 master's, 13 doctorates awarded. *Degree requirements:* For master's, research project report; for doctorate, comprehensive exam, thesis/dissertation. *Entrance requirements:* For master's, GRE or MAT, minimum GPA of 2.75; for doctorate, GRE, minimum GPA of 3.5; interview; writing sample; 3 recommendations; for Ed S, GRE or MAT, minimum GPA of 3.5 (for teacher leadership), 3.0 (for educational leadership). Additional exam requirements/recommendations for international students: Required—TOEFL (minimum score 80 iBT). *Application deadline:* For fall admission, 8/1 for domestic and international students; for spring admission, 12/1 for domestic and international students. Applications are processed on a rolling basis. Application fee: $35. Electronic applications accepted. *Expenses:* Contact institution. *Financial support:* Federal Work-Study, institutionally sponsored loans, and unspecified assistantships available. Support available to part-time students. Financial award application deadline: 5/1; financial award applicants required to submit FAFSA. *Faculty research:* Teacher effectiveness, specific learning disabilities, inclusion. *Unit head:* Dr. James Barta, Dean, 478-301-5397, Fax: 478-301-2280, E-mail: barta_jj@mercer.edu. *Application contact:* Tracey M. Wofford, Associate Director of Admissions, 678-547-6422, Fax: 678-547-6367, E-mail: wofford_tm@mercer.edu.
Website: http://education.mercer.edu/

Mercyhurst University, Graduate Studies, Program in Organizational Leadership, Erie, PA 16546. Offers accounting (MS); higher education administration (MS); human resources (MS); organizational leadership (MS, Certificate); sports leadership (MS); strategy and innovation (MS). *Program availability:* Part-time, evening/weekend. *Degree requirements:* For master's, thesis. *Entrance requirements:* For master's, GRE General Test or MAT, interview, resume, essay, three professional references, transcripts. Additional exam requirements/recommendations for international students: Required—TOEFL (minimum score 80 iBT), IELTS (minimum score 6.5). Electronic applications accepted. *Faculty research:* Leadership training, organizational communication, leadership pedagogy.

Merrimack College, School of Education and Social Policy, North Andover, MA 01845-5800. Offers community engagement (M Ed), including community organizations, higher education, K-12 education; criminology and criminal justice (MS); curriculum and instruction (M Ed); early childhood education (M Ed); educational leadership (CAGS), including instructional leadership; elementary education (M Ed); English as a second language (PreK-6) (M Ed); high school education (M Ed); higher education (M Ed), including leadership and organizational development, student affairs; middle school education (M Ed); moderate disabilities (PreK-8) (M Ed); school counseling (M Ed). *Program availability:* Part-time, evening/weekend, 100% online courses with immersion events and in-classroom practicum close to home. *Faculty:* 17 full-time, 34 part-time/adjunct. *Students:* 204 full-time (172 women), 83 part-time (67 women); includes 32 minority (4 Black or African American, non-Hispanic/Latino; 2 Asian, non-Hispanic/Latino; 23 Hispanic/Latino; 3 Two or more races, non-Hispanic/Latino), 1 international. Average age 27. 261 applicants, 89% accepted, 200 enrolled. In 2016, 153 master's, 2 other advanced degrees awarded. *Degree requirements:* For master's, practicum, portfolio, and state test (for licensure track); capstone (for higher education, curriculum and instruction, and community engagement tracks). *Entrance requirements:* For master's, Massachusetts Teacher Education Licensure (MTEL), official transcripts from other colleges, resume, personal statement, 2 letters of recommendation. Additional exam requirements/recommendations for international students: Required—TOEFL (minimum score 84 iBT), IELTS (minimum score 6.5), PTE (minimum score 56). *Application deadline:* For fall admission, 8/14 for domestic students, 7/14 for international students; for spring admission, 1/10 for domestic students, 12/10 for international students; for summer admission, 5/10 for domestic students, 4/10 for international students. Applications are processed on a rolling basis. Application fee: $0. Electronic applications accepted. *Expenses:* Contact institution. *Financial support:* Fellowships with full tuition reimbursements, career-related internships or fieldwork, scholarships/grants, and health care benefits available. Support available to part-time students. Financial award application deadline: 5/1; financial award applicants required to submit FAFSA. *Faculty research:* Feminist praxis in higher education, transgender student agency and belonging, campus sexual violence prevention, the scholarship of engagement; community engagement; service learning; diversity education; community-university partnerships, college going behaviors and indicators of success for inner city youth, strategies to increase students pursuit and success in STEM higher education, effective workforce development for displaced or under employed individuals, police reform, e.g. surveillance. *Application contact:* Alyssa Frey, Graduate Admissions Counselor, 978-837-3563, E-mail: freya@merrimack.edu.
Website: http://www.merrimack.edu/academics/graduate/education/

Messiah College, Program in Higher Education, Mechanicsburg, PA 17055. Offers college athletics management (MA); self-designed concentration (MA); student affairs (MA). *Program availability:* Part-time. Electronic applications accepted. *Faculty research:* College athletics management, assessment and student learning outcomes, the life and legacy of Ernest L. Boyer, common learning, student affairs practice.

Michigan State University, The Graduate School, College of Education, Department of Educational Administration, East Lansing, MI 48824. Offers higher, adult and lifelong education (MA, PhD); K–12 educational administration (MA, PhD, Ed S); student affairs administration (MA). *Program availability:* Part-time. *Entrance requirements:* Additional exam requirements/recommendations for international students: Required—TOEFL. Electronic applications accepted.

Minnesota State University Mankato, College of Graduate Studies and Research, College of Social and Behavioral Sciences, Department of Sociology and Corrections, Mankato, MN 56001. Offers sociology (MA); sociology: college teaching (MA); sociology: corrections (MS); sociology: human services planning and administration (MS). *Program availability:* Part-time. *Students:* 9 full-time (5 women), 19 part-time (16 women). *Degree requirements:* For master's, comprehensive exam, thesis or alternative. *Entrance requirements:* For master's, minimum GPA of 3.0 during previous 2 years, 3 letters of reference, resume. Additional exam requirements/recommendations for international students: Required—TOEFL. *Application deadline:* For fall admission, 7/1 priority date for domestic students; for spring admission, 11/1 for domestic students. Applications are processed on a rolling basis. Application fee: $40. Electronic applications accepted. *Financial support:* Research assistantships with full tuition reimbursements, teaching assistantships with full tuition reimbursements, career-related internships or fieldwork, Federal Work-Study, institutionally sponsored loans, and unspecified assistantships available. Support available to part-time students. Financial award application deadline: 3/15; financial award applicants required to submit FAFSA. *Unit head:* Dr. Luis Posas, Chair, 507-389-2257, E-mail: luis.posas@mnsu.edu. *Application contact:* Donald Ebel, Graduate Studies Coordinator, 507-389-5188, Fax: 507-389-5615, E-mail: donald.ebel@mnsu.edu.
Website: http://sbs.mnsu.edu/soccorr/

Mississippi College, Graduate School, School of Education, Department of Teacher Education and Leadership, Clinton, MS 39058. Offers art (M Ed); biological science (M Ed); business education (M Ed); computer science (M Ed); dyslexia therapy (M Ed); educational leadership (M Ed, Ed D, Ed S); elementary education (M Ed, Ed S); English (M Ed); higher education administration (MS); mathematics (M Ed); secondary education (M Ed); social studies (history) (M Ed); teaching arts (M Ed). *Program availability:* Part-time, online learning. *Degree requirements:* For master's, comprehensive exam, thesis optional. *Entrance requirements:* For master's, NTE. Additional exam requirements/recommendations for international students: Recommended—TOEFL, IELTS. Electronic applications accepted.

Mississippi College, Graduate School, School of Education, Program in Higher Education Administration, Clinton, MS 39058. Offers MS. *Program availability:* Part-time, online learning. *Degree requirements:* For master's, comprehensive exam, thesis optional. *Entrance requirements:* For master's, GRE or GMAT, minimum GPA of 3.0. Additional exam requirements/recommendations for international students: Recommended—TOEFL, IELTS.

Missouri State University, Graduate College, College of Education, Department of Counseling, Leadership, and Special Education, Program in Student Affairs in Higher Education, Springfield, MO 65897. Offers MS. *Program availability:* Part-time. *Students:* 32 full-time (26 women), 4 part-time (3 women); includes 6 minority (3 Black or African American, non-Hispanic/Latino; 1 Hispanic/Latino; 2 Two or more races, non-Hispanic/Latino), 3 international. Average age 26. 39 applicants, 69% accepted, 13 enrolled. In 2016, 10 master's awarded. *Degree requirements:* For master's, comprehensive exam, thesis or alternative. *Entrance requirements:* For master's, GRE, statement of purpose; three references. Additional exam requirements/recommendations for international students: Required—TOEFL (minimum score 550 paper-based; 79 iBT), IELTS (minimum score 6). *Application deadline:* For fall admission, 2/1 priority date for domestic students, 2/1 for international students. Applications are processed on a rolling basis. Application fee: $35 ($50 for international students). Electronic applications accepted. *Expenses:* Tuition, state resident: full-time $5830. Tuition, nonresident: full-time $10,708. *Required fees:* $1130. Tuition and fees vary according to class time, course level, course load and program. *Financial support:* Federal Work-Study, institutionally sponsored loans, scholarships/grants, and unspecified assistantships available. Financial award application deadline: 3/31; financial award applicants required to submit FAFSA. *Unit head:* Dr. James Satterfield, Department Head, 417-836-5392, E-mail: clse@missouristate.edu. *Application contact:* Michael Edwards, Coordinator of Graduate Admissions, 417-836-5330, Fax: 417-836-6200, E-mail: michaeledwards@missouristate.edu.
Website: http://education.missouristate.edu/edadmin/MSEDSA.htm

Montana State University, The Graduate School, College of Education, Health, and Human Development, Department of Education, Bozeman, MT 59717. Offers adult and higher education (Ed D); curriculum and instruction (M Ed, Ed D), including professional educator (M Ed), technology education (M Ed); education (M Ed), including adult and higher education, educational leadership, school counseling; educational leadership (Ed D, Ed S). *Accreditation:* TEAC. *Program availability:* Part-time, online learning. *Degree requirements:* For master's, comprehensive exam; for doctorate, comprehensive exam, thesis/dissertation. *Entrance requirements:* For master's, GRE, 3 letters of reference, essays, BA transcripts; for doctorate, GRE, MAT, 3 letters of reference, essay, BA and M Ed transcripts; for Ed S, PRAXIS. Additional exam requirements/recommendations for international students: Required—TOEFL (minimum score 550 paper-based). Electronic applications accepted. *Faculty research:* Critical literacy; standards-based education; school Improvement, organizational change, leadership in rural education, leadership in Indian education; student Learning; multicultural/culturally responsive education for social justice Native American indigenous education, community-centered education teacher preparation.

Morehead State University, Graduate Programs, College of Education, Department of Foundational and Graduate Studies in Education, Morehead, KY 40351. Offers adult and higher education (MA, Ed S); certified professional counselor (Ed S); counseling P-12 (MA); curriculum and instruction (Ed S); educational technology (MA Ed); instructional leadership (Ed S); school administration (MA); school counseling (Ed S); teacher leader business and marketing content (MA Ed); teacher leader business and marketing technology (MA Ed); teacher leader educational technology (MA Ed); teacher leader English (MA Ed); teacher leader gifted education (MA Ed); teacher leader IECE certification (MA Ed); teacher leader interdisciplinary education P-5 (MA Ed); teacher leader middle grades (MA Ed); teacher leader non IECE certification (MA Ed); teacher leader reading/writing - non-certification (MA Ed); teacher leader reading/writing certification (MA Ed); teacher leader school communication - certification (MA Ed); teacher leader school communication - non-certification (MA Ed); teacher leader social studies (MA Ed); teacher leader special education (MA Ed). *Accreditation:* NCATE. *Program availability:* Part-time, evening/weekend. *Degree requirements:* For master's, thesis optional, oral and/or written comprehensive exams; for Ed S, thesis, oral exam. *Entrance requirements:* For master's, GRE General Test, minimum overall undergraduate GPA of 2.5; for Ed S, GRE General Test, interview, master's degree, minimum GPA of 3.5, work experience. Additional exam requirements/recommendations for international students: Required—TOEFL (minimum score 500 paper-based). Electronic applications accepted. *Faculty research:* Character education, school accountability, computer applications for school administrators.

Morgan State University, School of Graduate Studies, School of Education and Urban Studies, Department of Advanced Studies, Leadership and Policy, Program in Community College Leadership, Baltimore, MD 21251. Offers Ed D. *Accreditation:* NCATE. *Program availability:* Part-time, evening/weekend. *Degree requirements:* For doctorate, comprehensive exam, thesis/dissertation. *Entrance requirements:* For doctorate, GRE General Test or MAT. Additional exam requirements/recommendations for international students: Required—TOEFL (minimum score 550 paper-based). *Faculty research:* Multicultural education, cooperative learning, psychology of cognition.

Morgan State University, School of Graduate Studies, School of Education and Urban Studies, Department of Advanced Studies, Leadership and Policy, Program in Higher Education Administration, Baltimore, MD 21251. Offers higher education (PhD); higher education administration (MA). *Degree requirements:* For doctorate, comprehensive exam, thesis/dissertation. *Entrance requirements:* For doctorate, GRE General Test or MAT, minimum GPA of 3.0.

New England College, Program in Education, Henniker, NH 03242-3293. Offers higher education administration (MS, Ed D); K-12 leadership (Ed D); literacy and language arts (M Ed); meeting the needs of all learners/special education (M Ed); teacher leadership/school reform (M Ed). *Program availability:* Part-time, evening/weekend.

New Mexico State University, College of Education, Department of Educational Leadership and Administration, Las Cruces, NM 88003. Offers educational administration (MA), including community college and university administration, PK-12 public school administration; educational leadership (Ed D, PhD). *Accreditation:* NCATE. *Program availability:* Part-time-only, evening/weekend, blended/hybrid learning. *Faculty:* 7 full-time (5 women), 1 part-time/adjunct (0 women). *Students:* 18 full-time (15 women), 110 part-time (82 women); includes 83 minority (2 Black or African American, non-Hispanic/Latino; 7 American Indian or Alaska Native, non-Hispanic/Latino; 4 Asian, non-Hispanic/Latino; 68 Hispanic/Latino; 1 Native Hawaiian or other Pacific Islander, non-Hispanic/Latino; 1 Two or more races, non-Hispanic/Latino), 3 international. Average age 41. 22 applicants, 27% accepted, 6 enrolled. In 2016, 24 master's, 6 doctorates awarded. *Degree requirements:* For master's, comprehensive exam, thesis optional, internship; for doctorate, comprehensive exam, thesis/dissertation, internship. *Entrance requirements:* For master's, minimum GPA of 3.0, current U.S. teaching license, and minimum 3 years of teaching in PK-12 sector (for PK-12 public school administration); minimum bachelor's degree GPA of 3.0 (for community college and university administration); for doctorate, minimum GPA of 3.0, master's degree. Additional exam requirements/recommendations for international students: Required—TOEFL (minimum score 550 paper-based; 79 iBT), IELTS (minimum score 6.5). *Application deadline:* For spring admission, 11/15 for domestic and international students. Application fee: $40 ($50 for international students). Electronic applications accepted. *Expenses:* Tuition, state resident: full-time $4086. Tuition, nonresident: full-time $14,254. *Required fees:* $853. Tuition and fees vary according to course load. *Financial support:* In 2016–17, 14 students received support, including 1 research assistantship (averaging $17,368 per year), 2 teaching assistantships (averaging $17,166 per year); career-related internships or fieldwork, Federal Work-Study, scholarships/grants, traineeships, health care benefits, and unspecified assistantships also available. Support available to part-time students. Financial award application deadline: 3/1. *Faculty research:* Leadership in PK-12 and postsecondary education, community college administration, distance education administration, leadership for social justice, educational change. *Total annual research expenditures:* $2,656. *Unit head:* Dr. Azadeh Osanloo, Department Head, 575-646-5976, Fax: 575-646-4767, E-mail: azadeh@nmsu.edu. *Application contact:* Denise Rodgiguez-Strawn, 575-646-3825, Fax: 575-646-4767, E-mail: edmandev@nmsu.edu.
Website: http://ela.nmsu.edu/

New York University, Steinhardt School of Culture, Education, and Human Development, Department of Administration, Leadership, and Technology, Program in Higher Education, New York, NY 10012. Offers higher and postsecondary education (PhD); higher education administration (Ed D); higher education and student affairs (MA). *Accreditation:* TEAC. *Program availability:* Part-time. *Degree requirements:* For master's, thesis (for some programs); for doctorate, thesis/dissertation. *Entrance requirements:* For master's, interview, 2 letters of recommendation; for doctorate, GRE General Test, interview. Additional exam requirements/recommendations for international students: Required—TOEFL (minimum score 100 iBT). Electronic applications accepted. *Faculty research:* Organizational theory and culture, systemic change, leadership development, access, equity and diversity.

New York University, Steinhardt School of Culture, Education, and Human Development, Department of Music and Performing Arts Professions, Program in Educational Theatre, New York, NY 10012. Offers educational theatre and English 7-12 (MA); educational theatre and social studies 7-12 (MA); educational theatre in colleges and communities (MA, Ed D, PhD); educational theatre, all grades (MA). *Program availability:* Part-time. *Degree requirements:* For master's, thesis (for some programs); for doctorate, thesis/dissertation. *Entrance requirements:* For master's, audition; for doctorate, GRE General Test, interview. Additional exam requirements/recommendations for international students: Required—TOEFL (minimum score 100 iBT). Electronic applications accepted. *Faculty research:* Theatre for young audiences, drama in education, applied theatre, arts education assessment, reflective praxis.

North Carolina State University, Graduate School, College of Education, Department of Adult and Higher Education, Program in Higher Education Administration, Raleigh, NC 27695. Offers M Ed, MS, Ed D. *Degree requirements:* For master's, thesis (for some programs); for doctorate, thesis/dissertation. *Entrance requirements:* For master's and doctorate, GRE General Test or MAT, minimum GPA of 3.0 in major. Electronic applications accepted.

North Dakota State University, College of Graduate and Interdisciplinary Studies, Program in College Teaching, Fargo, ND 58102. Offers Certificate. *Entrance requirements:* For degree, minimum cumulative GPA of 3.0. Electronic applications accepted.

Northeastern University, College of Professional Studies, Boston, MA 02115-5096. Offers applied nutrition (MS); college athletics administration (MSL); commerce and economic development (MS); corporate and organizational communication (MS); criminal justice (MS); digital media (MPS); elearning and instructional design (M Ed); elementary education (MAT); geographic information technology (MPS); global studies and international relations (MS); higher education administration (M Ed); homeland security (MA); human services (MS); informatics (MPS); leadership (MS); learning analytics (M Ed); learning and instruction (M Ed); nonprofit management (MS); professional sports administration (MSL); project management (MS); regulatory affairs for drugs, biologics, and medical devices (MS); respiratory care leadership (MS); special education (M Ed); technical communication (MS). *Program availability:* Part-time, evening/weekend, 100% online, blended/hybrid learning. *Faculty:* 82 full-time (51 women), 853 part-time/adjunct (366 women). *Students:* 4,917 part time (3,070 women). In 2016, 1,456 master's awarded. *Application deadline:* Applications are processed on a rolling basis. Application fee: $0. Electronic applications accepted. *Expenses:* Contact institution. *Financial support:* Applicants required to submit FAFSA. *Unit head:* Dr. Mary Loeffelholz, Interim Dean of the College of Professional Studies.
Website: http://www.cps.neu.edu/

Northern Arizona University, Graduate College, College of Education, Department of Educational Leadership, Flagstaff, AZ 86011. Offers community college teaching and learning (Certificate); community college/higher education (M Ed); educational foundations (M Ed); educational leadership (M Ed, Ed D); principal (Certificate); principal K-12 (M Ed); school leadership K-12 (M Ed); superintendent (Certificate). *Program availability:* Part-time. *Degree requirements:* For master's, comprehensive exam, thesis (for some programs); for doctorate, comprehensive exam, thesis/dissertation. *Entrance requirements:* For master's, minimum GPA of 3.0; for doctorate, GRE or MAT, minimum GPA of 3.5. Additional exam requirements/recommendations for international students: Required—TOEFL (minimum score 550 paper-based; 80 iBT), IELTS (minimum score 7). Electronic applications accepted. *Expenses:* Tuition, state resident: full-time $8971; part-time $444 per credit hour. Tuition, nonresident: full-time $20,958; part-time $1164 per credit hour. *Required fees:* $1018; $644 per credit hour. Tuition and fees vary according to course load, campus/location and program.

Northern Illinois University, Graduate School, College of Education, Department of Counseling, Adult and Higher Education, De Kalb, IL 60115-2854. Offers adult and higher education (MS Ed, Ed D); counseling (MS Ed, Ed D). *Accreditation:* ACA. *Program availability:* Part-time, evening/weekend. *Faculty:* 19 full-time (11 women), 2 part-time/adjunct (1 woman). *Students:* 108 full-time (74 women), 205 part-time (146 women); includes 123 minority (68 Black or African American, non-Hispanic/Latino; 2 American Indian or Alaska Native, non-Hispanic/Latino; 10 Asian, non-Hispanic/Latino; 34 Hispanic/Latino; 9 Two or more races, non-Hispanic/Latino), 8 international. Average age 35. 126 applicants, 59% accepted, 36 enrolled. In 2016, 66 master's, 24 doctorates awarded. Terminal master's awarded for partial completion of doctoral program. *Degree requirements:* For master's, comprehensive exam, thesis optional; for doctorate, thesis/dissertation, candidacy exam, dissertation defense. *Entrance requirements:* For master's, GRE General Test or MAT, minimum undergraduate GPA of 2.75, interview (for counseling); for doctorate, GRE General Test, minimum undergraduate GPA of 2.75, 3.2 graduate; interview (for counseling). Additional exam requirements/recommendations for international students: Required—TOEFL (minimum score 550 paper-based). *Application deadline:* For fall admission, 6/1 for domestic students, 5/1 for international students; for spring admission, 11/1 for domestic students, 10/1 for international students. Applications are processed on a rolling basis. Application fee: $40. Electronic applications accepted. *Financial support:* In 2016–17, 12 research assistantships with full tuition reimbursements, 7 teaching assistantships with full tuition reimbursements were awarded; fellowships with full tuition reimbursements, career-related internships or fieldwork, Federal Work-Study, scholarships/grants, tuition waivers (full), and staff assistantships also available. Support available to part-time students. Financial award applicants required to submit FAFSA. *Unit head:* Dr. Suzanne Degges-White, Interim Chair, 815-753-1448, E-mail: cahe@niu.edu. *Application contact:* Graduate School Office, 815-753-0395, E-mail: gradsch@niu.edu.
Website: http://www.cedu.niu.edu/cahe/index.html

Northern Michigan University, Office of Graduate Education and Research, College of Health Sciences and Professional Studies, School of Education, Leadership and Public Service, Marquette, MI 49855-5301. Offers administration and supervision (MAE); elementary education (MAE); higher education in student affairs (MA); instruction (MAE); learning disabilities (MAE); public administration (MPA), including criminal justice administration, human resource administration, public administration, public management, state and local government; reading education (MAE), including reading, reading specialist; science education (MS); secondary education (MAE). *Accreditation:* TEAC. *Program availability:* Part-time, online learning. *Degree requirements:* For master's, thesis (for some programs). *Entrance requirements:* For master's, minimum GPA of 3.0. Additional exam requirements/recommendations for international students: Required—TOEFL (minimum score 550 paper-based; 79 iBT), IELTS (minimum score 6.5). Electronic applications accepted.

Northwest Missouri State University, Graduate School, School of Education, Maryville, MO 64468-6001. Offers early childhood education (MS Ed); education leadership (MS Ed), including elementary, K-12, secondary; educational leadership (Ed S), including elementary school principalship, secondary school principalship, superintendency; educational leadership and policy analysis (Ed D); elementary education (MS Ed); elementary mathematics (MS Ed); higher education leadership (MS); middle school education (MS Ed); reading (MS Ed); special education (MS Ed); teacher leadership (MS Ed); teaching English language learners (MS Ed). *Accreditation:* NCATE. *Program availability:* Part-time. *Students:* 15 full-time (11 women), 150 part-time (103 women). In 2016, 46 master's awarded. *Degree requirements:* For master's, comprehensive exam; for Ed S, comprehensive exam, thesis. *Entrance requirements:* For master's, GRE General Test, writing sample; for Ed S, minimum graduate GPA of 3.25. Additional exam requirements/recommendations for international students: Required—TOEFL (minimum score 550 paper-based). *Application deadline:* For fall admission, 7/1 for domestic and international students; for spring admission, 11/15 for domestic and international students. Applications are processed on a rolling basis. Application fee: $0 ($50 for international students). Electronic applications accepted. *Expenses:* Tuition, state resident: full-time $3447; part-time $383 per credit hour. Tuition, nonresident: full-time $5724; part-time $636 per credit hour. *Required fees:* $130 per credit hour. *Financial support:* Research assistantships with full tuition reimbursements, teaching assistantships with full tuition reimbursements, and unspecified assistantships available. Financial award application deadline: 4/1; financial award applicants required to submit FAFSA. *Faculty research:* Great books of educational administration. *Unit head:* Dr. Tim Wall, Dean, 660-562-1179, E-mail: timwall@nwmissouri.edu.
Website: http://www.nwmissouri.edu/academics/ed/

Oakland University, Graduate Study and Lifelong Learning, School of Education and Human Services, Department of Organizational Leadership, Rochester, MI 48309-4401. Offers educational leadership (M Ed, PhD); higher education (Certificate); school administration (Ed S). *Entrance requirements:* Additional exam requirements/recommendations for international students: Required—TOEFL (minimum score 550 paper-based).

Ohio University, Graduate College, Gladys W. and David H. Patton College of Education and Human Services, Department of Counseling and Higher Education, Athens, OH 45701-2979. Offers college student personnel (M Ed); community/agency counseling (M Ed); counselor education (PhD); higher education (PhD); rehabilitation counseling (M Ed); school counseling (M Ed). *Accreditation:* ACA; CORE. *Program availability:* Part-time, evening/weekend. *Degree requirements:* For master's, comprehensive exam (for some programs), thesis or alternative; for doctorate, comprehensive exam, thesis/dissertation. *Entrance requirements:* For master's, GRE General Test or MAT (if GPA less than 2.9), 3 letters of reference; for doctorate, GRE General Test, work experience, minimum GPA of 3.4. Additional exam requirements/recommendations for international students: Required—TOEFL (minimum score 550 paper-based; 80 iBT) or IELTS (minimum score 6.5). *Application deadline:* For fall admission, 1/15 for domestic and international students. Application fee: $50 ($55 for international students). Electronic applications accepted. *Financial support:* Research assistantships with full tuition reimbursements, teaching assistantships with full tuition reimbursements, Federal Work-Study, institutionally sponsored loans, tuition waivers (partial), and unspecified assistantships available. Financial award application deadline: 1/15. *Faculty research:* Youth violence, gender studies, student affairs, chemical dependency, disabilities issues. *Unit head:* Dr. Tracy Leinbaugh, Chair, 740-593-0846, Fax: 740-593-0477, E-mail: leinbaug@ohio.edu. *Application contact:* Floyd J. Doney, Director of Student Affairs, 740-593-4400, Fax: 740-593-9310, E-mail: doney@ohio.edu.
Website: http://www.cehs.ohio.edu/academics/che/

Oklahoma State University, College of Education, School of Educational Studies, Stillwater, OK 74078. Offers higher education (Ed D). *Program availability:* Part-time. *Faculty:* 26 full-time (15 women), 34 part-time/adjunct (10 women). *Students:* 56 full-time (28 women), 224 part-time (122 women); includes 77 minority (21 Black or African American, non-Hispanic/Latino; 19 American Indian or Alaska Native, non-Hispanic/

Latino; 7 Asian, non-Hispanic/Latino; 18 Hispanic/Latino; 1 Native Hawaiian or other Pacific Islander, non-Hispanic/Latino; 11 Two or more races, non-Hispanic/Latino), 5 international. Average age 38. 117 applicants, 67% accepted, 70 enrolled. In 2016, 39 master's, 24 doctorates awarded. *Degree requirements:* For master's, thesis (for some programs); for doctorate, comprehensive exam, thesis/dissertation. *Entrance requirements:* For master's and doctorate, GRE or GMAT. Additional exam requirements/recommendations for international students: Required—TOEFL (minimum score 550 paper-based; 79 iBT). *Application deadline:* For fall admission, 3/1 priority date for international students; for spring admission, 8/1 priority date for international students. Applications are processed on a rolling basis. Application fee: $40 ($75 for international students). Electronic applications accepted. *Expenses:* Tuition, state resident: full-time $3775; part-time $209.70 per credit hour. Tuition, nonresident: full-time $14,851; part-time $825.05 per credit hour. *Required fees:* $2027; $112.60 per credit hour. Tuition and fees vary according to campus/location. *Financial support:* In 2016–17, 19 research assistantships (averaging $8,716 per year), 7 teaching assistantships (averaging $9,086 per year) were awarded; career-related internships or fieldwork, Federal Work-Study, scholarships/grants, health care benefits, tuition waivers (partial), and unspecified assistantships also available. Support available to part-time students. Financial award application deadline: 3/1; financial award applicants required to submit FAFSA. *Unit head:* Dr. Jesse Mendez, Head, 405-744-9447, Fax: 405-744-7758, E-mail: jesse.perez.mendez@okstate.edu.
Website: http://education.okstate.edu/ses

Old Dominion University, Darden College of Education, Doctoral Program in Higher Education, Norfolk, VA 23529. Offers PhD. *Program availability:* Part-time, online learning. *Faculty:* 3 full-time (0 women), 8 part-time/adjunct (2 women). *Students:* 5 full-time (4 women), 28 part-time (19 women); includes 14 minority (8 Black or African American, non-Hispanic/Latino; 1 American Indian or Alaska Native, non-Hispanic/Latino; 3 Hispanic/Latino; 2 Two or more races, non-Hispanic/Latino), 1 international. Average age 36. 13 applicants, 54% accepted, 5 enrolled. In 2016, 3 doctorates awarded. *Degree requirements:* For doctorate, comprehensive exam, thesis/dissertation. *Entrance requirements:* For doctorate, GRE, master's degree, minimum graduate GPA of 3.5. Additional exam requirements/recommendations for international students: Required—TOEFL. *Application deadline:* For spring admission, 2/1 for domestic and international students. Application fee: $50. Electronic applications accepted. *Expenses:* Tuition, state resident: full-time $8604; part-time $478 per credit hour. Tuition, nonresident: full-time $21,510; part-time $1195 per credit hour. *Required fees:* $66 per semester. Tuition and fees vary according to campus/location, program and reciprocity agreements. *Financial support:* In 2016–17, 2 fellowships with tuition reimbursements (averaging $15,000 per year), research assistantships with full tuition reimbursements (averaging $15,000 per year), 6 teaching assistantships with full tuition reimbursements (averaging $15,000 per year) were awarded; career-related internships or fieldwork, tuition waivers (full), and unspecified assistantships also available. Financial award application deadline: 2/1. *Faculty research:* Law leadership, student development, research administration, international higher education administration, academic integrity, leadership. *Unit head:* Dr. Chris Glass, Graduate Program Director, 757-683-4118, E-mail: cglass@odu.edu. *Application contact:* William Heffelfinger, Director of Graduate Admissions, 757-683-5554, Fax: 757-683-3255, E-mail: gradadmit@odu.edu.

Old Dominion University, Darden College of Education, Programs in Higher Education, Norfolk, VA 23529. Offers MS Ed, Ed S. *Program availability:* Part-time. *Faculty:* 6 full-time (2 women), 6 part-time/adjunct (3 women). *Students:* 34 full-time (23 women), 14 part-time (6 women); includes 18 minority (9 Black or African American, non-Hispanic/Latino; 5 Hispanic/Latino; 4 Two or more races, non-Hispanic/Latino), 4 international. Average age 28. 59 applicants, 64% accepted, 18 enrolled. In 2016, 25 master's, 4 Ed Ss awarded. *Degree requirements:* For master's, comprehensive exam. *Entrance requirements:* For master's, GRE, minimum undergraduate GPA of 2.8; for Ed S, GRE, 2 letters of reference, minimum GPA of 3.5, master's degree. Additional exam requirements/recommendations for international students: Required—TOEFL. *Application deadline:* For fall admission, 3/1 priority date for domestic and international students; for winter admission, 10/1 for domestic and international students; for spring admission, 3/1 for domestic and international students. Applications are processed on a rolling basis. Application fee: $50. Electronic applications accepted. *Expenses:* Tuition, state resident: full-time $8604; part-time $478 per credit hour. Tuition, nonresident: full-time $21,510; part-time $1195 per credit hour. *Required fees:* $66 per semester. Tuition and fees vary according to campus/location, program and reciprocity agreements. *Financial support:* Research assistantships with partial tuition reimbursements, career-related internships or fieldwork, scholarships/grants, and unspecified assistantships available. *Faculty research:* Law leadership, student development, research administration, international higher education administration. *Unit head:* Dr. Chris Glass, Graduate Program Director, 757-683-4118, E-mail: hied@odu.edu. *Application contact:* William Heffelfinger, Director of Graduate Admissions, 757-683-5554, Fax: 757-683-3255, E-mail: gradadmit@odu.edu.
Website: http://education.odu.edu/efl/academics/highered/msed/msed_international_2.shtml

Oral Roberts University, School of Education, Tulsa, OK 74171. Offers Christian school administration (K-12) (MA Ed, Ed D); Christian school curriculum development (MA Ed); college and higher education administration (Ed D); public school administration (K-12) (MA Ed, Ed D); public school teaching (MA Ed). *Accreditation:* NCATE. *Program availability:* Part-time, online learning. *Degree requirements:* For master's, comprehensive exam, thesis optional; for doctorate, comprehensive exam, thesis/dissertation. *Entrance requirements:* For master's, GRE General Test or MAT, minimum GPA of 3.0; for doctorate, minimum GPA of 3.0. Additional exam requirements/recommendations for international students: Required—TOEFL (minimum score 500 paper-based). *Expenses:* Contact institution. *Faculty research:* Teacher effectiveness, college success in high achieving African-Americans, professional development practices.

Oregon State University, College of Education, Program in Adult and Higher Education, Corvallis, OR 97331. Offers Ed M, Ed D, PhD. *Accreditation:* NCATE. *Program availability:* Part-time, blended/hybrid learning. *Faculty:* 5 full-time (all women), 4 part-time/adjunct (2 women). *Students:* 2 full-time (both women), 34 part-time (25 women); includes 8 minority (2 Black or African American, non-Hispanic/Latino; 2 Asian, non-Hispanic/Latino; 2 Hispanic/Latino; 2 Two or more races, non-Hispanic/Latino). Average age 43. 36 applicants, 72% accepted, 22 enrolled. *Degree requirements:* For master's, thesis or alternative. *Entrance requirements:* For master's, minimum GPA of 3.0 in last 90 hours. Additional exam requirements/recommendations for international students: Required—TOEFL (minimum score 575 paper-based). *Application deadline:* For fall admission, 3/15 for domestic students. Applications are processed on a rolling basis. Application fee: $75 ($85 for international students). *Expenses:* Tuition, state resident: full-time $12,150; part-time $450 per credit. Tuition, nonresident: full-time $21,789; part-time $807 per credit. *Required fees:* $1651; $1507 per credit. One-time fee: $350. Tuition and fees vary according to course load, campus/location and program. *Financial support:* Research assistantships, teaching assistantships, career-related internships or fieldwork, Federal Work-Study, and institutionally sponsored loans available. Support available to part-time students. *Unit head:* Dr. Shelley Dubkin-Lee, Adult and Higher Education Graduate Programs Coordinator and Instructor, E-mail: shelley.dubkin-lee@oregonstate.edu.
Website: http://education.oregonstate.edu/adult-education-masters-degree-program

Penn State University Park, Graduate School, College of Education, Department of Education Policy Studies, University Park, PA 16802. Offers educational leadership (M Ed, D Ed, PhD, Certificate); educational theory and policy (MA, PhD); higher education (M Ed, MS, D Ed, PhD). *Accreditation:* NCATE. *Program availability:* Online learning. *Unit head:* Dr. David H. Monk, Dean, 814-865-2523, Fax: 814-865-0555. *Application contact:* Lori Hawn, Director, Graduate Student Services, 814-865-1795, Fax: 814-863-4627, E-mail: l-gswww@lists.psu.edu.
Website: http://ed.psu.edu/eps

Phillips Theological Seminary, Programs in Theology, Tulsa, OK 74116. Offers administration of church agencies (M Div); campus ministry (M Div); church-related social work (M Div); college and seminary teaching (M Div); global mission work (M Div); institutional chaplaincy (M Div); ministerial vocations in Christian education (M Div); ministry (D Min), including parish ministry, pastoral counseling, practices of ministry; ministry and culture (MAMC), including Christian education, congregational leadership, history and practice of Christian spirituality, theology, ethics, and culture; ministry of music (M Div); pastoral care and counseling (M Div); pastoral ministry (M Div); theological studies (MTS). *Accreditation:* ATS. *Program availability:* Part-time, online learning. *Degree requirements:* For master's, thesis (for some programs); for doctorate, thesis/dissertation. *Entrance requirements:* For master's, minimum GPA of 2.5; for doctorate, M Div, minimum GPA of 3.0. *Faculty research:* Biblical studies, historical studies, theology and culture, practical theology, theology and film.

Plymouth State University, College of Graduate Studies, Graduate Studies in Education, Certificate of Advanced Graduate Studies Programs, Plymouth, NH 03264-1595. Offers clinical mental health counseling (CAGS); educational leadership (CAGS); higher education (CAGS); school psychology (CAGS). *Program availability:* Part-time, evening/weekend.

Plymouth State University, College of Graduate Studies, Graduate Studies in Education, Program in Higher Education, Plymouth, NH 03264-1595. Offers Ed D.

Purdue University, Graduate School, College of Education, Department of Educational Studies, West Lafayette, IN 47907. Offers administration (MS Ed, PhD, Ed S); counseling and development (MS Ed, PhD); education of the gifted (MS Ed); educational psychology (MS Ed, PhD); foundations of education (MS Ed, PhD); higher education administration (MS Ed, PhD); special education (MS Ed, PhD). *Accreditation:* ACA (one or more programs are accredited); NCATE (one or more programs are accredited). *Program availability:* Part-time, evening/weekend. *Faculty:* 29 full-time (22 women), 1 part-time/adjunct (0 women). *Students:* 78 full-time (60 women), 226 part-time (162 women); includes 45 minority (16 Black or African American, non-Hispanic/Latino; 8 Asian, non-Hispanic/Latino; 15 Hispanic/Latino; 6 Two or more races, non-Hispanic/Latino), 45 international. Average age 32. 214 applicants, 53% accepted, 70 enrolled. In 2016, 38 master's, 20 doctorates, 4 other advanced degrees awarded. *Degree requirements:* For master's, thesis optional; for doctorate, thesis/dissertation, oral and written exams; for Ed S, oral presentation, project. *Entrance requirements:* For master's, GRE General Test (except for special education if undergraduate GPA is higher than a 3.0), minimum undergraduate GPA of 3.0; for doctorate and Ed S, GRE General Test (minimum combined score of 1000, 300 for new scoring), minimum undergraduate GPA of 3.0. Additional exam requirements/recommendations for international students: Required—TOEFL (minimum score 550 paper-based; 77 iBT), TWE (minimum score 5). *Application deadline:* Applications are processed on a rolling basis. Application fee: $60 ($75 for international students). Electronic applications accepted. *Financial support:* Fellowships with full tuition reimbursements, research assistantships with full tuition reimbursements, teaching assistantships with full tuition reimbursements, career-related internships or fieldwork, and tuition waivers (full) available. Support available to part-time students. Financial award application deadline: 3/1; financial award applicants required to submit FAFSA. *Faculty research:* Motivation, learning disabilities, school learning, group processes, cognitive development. *Unit head:* F. Richard Olenchak, Head, 765-494-9170, E-mail: olenchak@purdue.edu. *Application contact:* Heather Brinkman, Graduate Contact, 765-494-2345, Fax: 765-494-5832, E-mail: hbrinkma@purdue.edu.
Website: http://www.edst.purdue.edu/

Regent University, Graduate School, School of Education, Virginia Beach, VA 23464-9800. Offers adult education (Ed D, PhD, Ed S); advanced educational leadership (Ed D, PhD, Ed S); career switcher (M Ed); character education (Ed D, PhD, Ed S); Christian education leadership (Ed D, PhD, Ed S); Christian school administration (M Ed); curriculum and instruction (M Ed), including adult education, Christian school, gifted and talented education, STEM education, teacher leader; educational leadership (M Ed); educational psychology (Ed D, PhD, Ed S); educational technology and online learning (Ed D, PhD, Ed S); elementary education (M Ed); exceptional education executive leadership (Ed D, PhD, Ed S); higher education (Ed D, PhD, Ed S); higher education leadership and management (Ed D, PhD, Ed S); individualized degree plan (M Ed); K-12 school leadership (Ed D, PhD, Ed S); K-12 special education (M Ed); K-8 leadership in mathematics education (M Ed); leadership in mathematics education (Ed S); reading specialist (M Ed); special education (Ed D, PhD, Ed S); student affairs (M Ed); TESOL (M Ed), including adult education - collegiate, K-12. *Accreditation:* TEAC. *Program availability:* Part-time, evening/weekend, 100% online, blended/hybrid learning. *Faculty:* 22 full-time (10 women), 42 part-time/adjunct (31 women). *Students:* 89 full-time (62 women), 1,035 part-time (823 women); includes 466 minority (381 Black or African American, non-Hispanic/Latino; 3 American Indian or Alaska Native, non-Hispanic/Latino; 19 Asian, non-Hispanic/Latino; 50 Hispanic/Latino; 13 Two or more races, non-Hispanic/Latino), 11 international. Average age 39. 976 applicants, 59% accepted, 449 enrolled. In 2016, 241 master's, 22 doctorates, 4 other advanced degrees awarded. *Degree requirements:* For master's, thesis or alternative; for doctorate, comprehensive exam, thesis/dissertation. *Entrance requirements:* For master's, Virginia Communication and Literacy Assessment (VCLA), PRAXIS, college transcripts, writing sample, interview; for doctorate, GRE, writing sample, resume, transcripts, interview. Additional exam requirements/recommendations for international students: Required—TOEFL (minimum score 577 paper-based). *Application deadline:* For fall admission, 4/1 priority date for domestic students; for spring admission, 10/15 priority date for domestic students. Applications are processed on a rolling basis. Application fee: $50. Electronic applications accepted. *Expenses:* Contact institution. *Financial support:* In 2016–17, 622 students received support, including 1 fellowship (averaging $5,000 per year); career-related internships or fieldwork, scholarships/grants, and unspecified assistantships also available. Support available to part-time students. *Faculty research:* Christian school administration, curriculum and instruction, educational technology and online learning, higher education, special education. *Unit head:* Dr. Donald Finn, Dean, 757-352-4278, Fax: 757-352-4318, E-mail: dfinn@regent.edu. *Application contact:* Heidi Cece, Assistant Vice President of Enrollment Management, 800-373-5504, Fax: 757-352-4381, E-mail: admissions@regent.edu.
Website: http://www.regent.edu/soe/

Regis College, Department of Education, Weston, MA 02493. Offers elementary teacher (MAT); higher education leadership (Ed D); reading (MAT); special education

(MAT). *Program availability:* Part-time, evening/weekend, blended/hybrid learning. *Degree requirements:* For master's, thesis. *Entrance requirements:* For master's, GRE or MAT. Additional exam requirements/recommendations for international students: Required—TOEFL; Recommended—IELTS. *Application deadline:* Applications are processed on a rolling basis. Application fee: $50. Electronic applications accepted. *Financial support:* Federal Work-Study, scholarships/grants, and unspecified assistantships available. Financial award applicants required to submit FAFSA. *Unit head:* Dr. Priscilla Boerger, Department Chair/Graduate Program Director, 781-768-7422, E-mail: priscilla.boerger@regiscollege.edu.

Robert Morris University, School of Education and Social Sciences, Moon Township, PA 15108-1189. Offers business education (MS); counseling psychology (MS); education (Postbaccalaureate Certificate); higher education (MS); instructional leadership (MS), including education; instructional management and leadership (PhD); literacy (MS); special education (MS). *Accreditation:* TEAC. *Program availability:* Part-time, evening/weekend, online learning. *Faculty:* 17 full-time (9 women), 4 part-time/adjunct (3 women). *Students:* 154 part-time (104 women); includes 18 minority (11 Black or African American, non-Hispanic/Latino; 2 Hispanic/Latino; 5 Two or more races, non-Hispanic/Latino), 1 international. Average age 26. 69 applicants, 26% accepted, 18 enrolled. In 2016, 40 master's, 15 doctorates awarded. *Degree requirements:* For doctorate, thesis/dissertation. *Entrance requirements:* Additional exam requirements/recommendations for international students: Required—TOEFL (minimum score 550 paper-based; 79 iBT). *Application deadline:* For fall admission, 7/1 priority date for domestic and international students; for spring admission, 11/1 priority date for domestic and international students. Applications are processed on a rolling basis. Application fee: $35. Electronic applications accepted. *Expenses:* $840 per credit (for master's degree). *Unit head:* Dr. Mary Ann Rafoth, Dean, 412-397-6020, Fax: 412-397-6044, E-mail: rafoth@rmu.edu.
Website: http://www.rmu.edu/web/cms/schools/sess/

Robert Morris University Illinois, Morris Graduate School of Management, Chicago, IL 60605. Offers accounting (MBA); accounting/finance (MBA); business analytics (MIS); design and media (MM); design management (MM); educational technology (MM); health care administration (MM); higher education administration (MM); human resource management (MBA); information security (MIS); information systems (MBA, MIS); law enforcement administration (MM); management (MBA); management/finance (MBA); management/human resource management (MBA); mobile computing (MIS); sports administration (MM). *Program availability:* Part-time, evening/weekend. *Faculty:* 4 full-time (1 woman), 25 part-time/adjunct (5 women). *Students:* 196 full-time (98 women), 151 part-time (85 women); includes 200 minority (114 Black or African American, non-Hispanic/Latino; 17 Asian, non-Hispanic/Latino; 67 Hispanic/Latino; 2 Two or more races, non-Hispanic/Latino), 23 international. Average age 33. 174 applicants, 61% accepted, 97 enrolled. In 2016, 190 master's awarded. *Entrance requirements:* For master's, official transcripts and letters of recommendation (for some programs); written personal statement. Additional exam requirements/recommendations for international students: Required—TOEFL (minimum score 550 paper-based). *Application deadline:* Applications are processed on a rolling basis. Application fee: $20 ($100 for international students). Electronic applications accepted. *Expenses: Tuition:* Full-time $16,500; part-time $2750 per course. *Financial support:* In 2016–17, 444 students received support. Federal Work-Study, scholarships/grants, and unspecified assistantships available. Support available to part-time students. Financial award applicants required to submit FAFSA. *Unit head:* Kayed Akkawi, Dean, 312-935-6050, Fax: 312-935-6020, E-mail: kakkawi@robertmorris.edu. *Application contact:* Danielle Naffziger, Vice President of Marketing and Enrollment, 312-935-4812, Fax: 312-935-6020, E-mail: dnaffziger@robertmorris.edu.

Rowan University, Graduate School, College of Education, Department of Educational Services and Leadership, Program in Higher Education Administration, Glassboro, NJ 08028-1701. Offers MA. *Accreditation:* NCATE. *Program availability:* Part-time, evening/weekend. *Degree requirements:* For master's, comprehensive exam, thesis. *Entrance requirements:* For master's, GRE General Test, minimum GPA of 2.8, 2 years of teaching experience. Additional exam requirements/recommendations for international students: Required—TOEFL. Electronic applications accepted.

St. Cloud State University, School of Graduate Studies, School of Education, Department of Educational Leadership and Higher Education, Program in Higher Education Administration, St. Cloud, MN 56301-4498. Offers MS, Ed D.

Saint Louis University, Graduate Education, College of Education and Public Service and Graduate Education, Department of Educational Leadership and Higher Education, St. Louis, MO 63103. Offers Catholic school leadership (MA); educational administration (MA, Ed D, PhD, Ed S); higher education (MA, Ed D, PhD); student personnel administration (MA). *Accreditation:* NCATE. *Program availability:* Part-time. *Degree requirements:* For master's, comprehensive written and oral exam; for doctorate, comprehensive exam, thesis/dissertation, preliminary oral and written exams. *Entrance requirements:* For master's, GRE General Test, MAT, LSAT, GMAT or MCAT, letters of recommendation, resume; for doctorate and Ed S, GRE General Test, LSAT, GMAT or MCAT, letters of recommendation, resumé, goal statement, transcripts. Additional exam requirements/recommendations for international students: Required—TOEFL (minimum score 525 paper-based). Electronic applications accepted. *Faculty research:* Superintendent of schools, school finance, school facilities, student personal administration, building leadership.

Saint Peter's University, Graduate Programs in Education, Program in Higher Education, Jersey City, NJ 07306-5997. Offers Ed D. *Degree requirements:* For doctorate, comprehensive exam, thesis/dissertation, qualifying examination, internship. *Entrance requirements:* For doctorate, GRE or MAT (taken within the last 5 years), official transcripts from all previously attended postsecondary institutions; bachelor's degree; master's degree; three letters of recommendation; essay; current resume; personal interview.

Salem State University, School of Graduate Studies, Program in Higher Education in Student Affairs, Salem, MA 01970-5353. Offers M Ed. *Program availability:* Part-time, evening/weekend. *Entrance requirements:* For master's, GRE or MAT. Additional exam requirements/recommendations for international students: Required—TOEFL (minimum score 550 paper-based; 80 iBT) or IELTS (minimum score 5.5).

Sam Houston State University, College of Education, Department of Educational Leadership, Huntsville, TX 77341. Offers administration (M Ed); developmental education administration (Ed D); educational leadership (Ed D); higher education administration (MA); instructional leadership (M Ed, MA). *Program availability:* Part-time, evening/weekend, online learning. *Degree requirements:* For master's, comprehensive exam (for some programs), thesis (for some programs); for doctorate, comprehensive exam, thesis/dissertation. *Entrance requirements:* For master's, GRE General Test, references, personal essay, resume, professional statement; for doctorate, GRE General Test, master's degree, references, personal essay, resume. Additional exam requirements/recommendations for international students: Required—TOEFL (minimum score 550 paper-based; 79 iBT), IELTS (minimum score 6.5). Electronic applications accepted.

San Diego State University, Graduate and Research Affairs, College of Education, Department of Administration, Rehabilitation and Post-Secondary Education, San Diego, CA 92182. Offers educational leadership in post-secondary education (MA); rehabilitation counseling (MS), including deafness. *Program availability:* Evening/weekend, online learning. *Degree requirements:* For master's, comprehensive exam (for some programs), thesis (for some programs). *Entrance requirements:* For master's, GRE General Test, letters of reference. Additional exam requirements/recommendations for international students: Required—TOEFL. Electronic applications accepted. *Faculty research:* Rehabilitation in cultural diversity, distance learning technology.

San Jose State University, Graduate Studies and Research, Connie L. Lurie College of Education, San Jose, CA 95192-0001. Offers child and adolescent development (MA); common core mathematics (K-8) (Certificate, Credential); education (MA, Credential), including counseling and student personnel (MA), speech pathology (MA); educational leadership (MA, Ed D, Credential), including administration and supervision (MA), higher education (MA), preliminary administrative services (Credential), professional administrative services (Credential); elementary education (MA), including curriculum and instruction; K-12 school counseling (Credential); K-12 school counseling internship (Credential); school child welfare attendance (Credential); single subject (Credential). *Accreditation:* NCATE. *Program availability:* Evening/weekend. Electronic applications accepted.

Seton Hall University, College of Education and Human Services, Department of Education Leadership, Management and Policy, Program in Higher Education Administration, South Orange, NJ 07079-2697. Offers Ed D, PhD. *Accreditation:* NCATE. *Program availability:* Part-time, evening/weekend. *Faculty:* 12 full-time (4 women), 1 part-time/adjunct (0 women). *Students:* 20 full-time (12 women), 78 part-time (50 women); includes 39 minority (26 Black or African American, non-Hispanic/Latino; 5 Asian, non-Hispanic/Latino; 8 Hispanic/Latino), 2 international. Average age 41. 37 applicants, 84% accepted, 15 enrolled. In 2016, 8 doctorates awarded. *Degree requirements:* For doctorate, comprehensive exam, thesis/dissertation, internship. *Entrance requirements:* For doctorate, GRE or MAT, interview, minimum GPA of 3.5. Additional exam requirements/recommendations for international students: Required—TOEFL. *Application deadline:* For fall admission, 2/1 priority date for domestic students; for spring admission, 10/1 for domestic students. Applications are processed on a rolling basis. Application fee: $75. *Financial support:* In 2016–17, 7 research assistantships with tuition reimbursements (averaging $4,500 per year) were awarded. Financial award application deadline: 2/1. *Unit head:* Dr. Elaine Walker, Chair, 973-275-2307, E-mail: elaine.walker@shu.edu. *Application contact:* Diana Minakakis, Associate Dean, 973-275-2824, Fax: 973-275-2187, E-mail: diana.minakakis@shu.edu.
Website: http://www.shu.edu/academics/education/edd-higher-ed/index.cfm

Shippensburg University of Pennsylvania, School of Graduate Studies, College of Arts and Sciences, Department of Sociology and Anthropology, Shippensburg, PA 17257-2299. Offers organizational development and leadership (MS), including business, higher education structure and policy, historical administration, leadership in society, management information systems, public organizations. *Program availability:* Part-time, evening/weekend. *Faculty:* 4 full-time (3 women). *Students:* 11 full-time (6 women), 29 part-time (18 women); includes 9 minority (7 Black or African American, non-Hispanic/Latino; 1 Hispanic/Latino; 1 Two or more races, non-Hispanic/Latino). Average age 29. 58 applicants, 67% accepted, 21 enrolled. In 2016, 24 master's awarded. *Degree requirements:* For master's, capstone experience including internship. *Entrance requirements:* For master's, interview (if GPA less than 2.75), current resume, personal goals statement. Additional exam requirements/recommendations for international students: Required—TOEFL (minimum score 550 paper-based, 68 iBT) or IELTS (minimum score 6). *Application deadline:* For fall admission, 4/30 for international students; for spring admission, 9/30 for international students. Applications are processed on a rolling basis. Application fee: $45. Electronic applications accepted. *Expenses:* Tuition, state resident: part-time $483 per credit. Tuition, nonresident: part-time $725 per credit. *Required fees:* $141 per credit. *Financial support:* In 2016–17, 9 students received support. Career-related internships or fieldwork, scholarships/grants, unspecified assistantships, and resident hall director and student payroll positions available. Support available to part-time students. Financial award application deadline: 3/1; financial award applicants required to submit FAFSA. *Unit head:* Dr. Barbara J. Denison, Departmental Chair and Program Coordinator, 717-477-1735, Fax: 717-477-4011, E-mail: bjdeni@ship.edu. *Application contact:* Megan N. Luft, Assistant Dean of Graduate Admissions, 717-477-1231, Fax: 717-477-4016, E-mail: mnluft@ship.edu.
Website: http://www.ship.edu/odl/

Siena Heights University, Graduate College, Adrian, MI 49221-1796. Offers clinical mental health counseling (MA); educational leadership (Specialist); leadership (MA), including health care leadership, organizational leadership; teacher education (MA), including early childhood education, early childhood education: Montessori, education leadership: principal, elementary education: reading K-12, leadership: higher education, secondary education: reading K-12, special education: cognitive impairment, special education: learning disabilities. *Program availability:* Part-time, evening/weekend. *Degree requirements:* For master's, thesis, presentation. *Entrance requirements:* For master's, minimum GPA of 3.0, current resume, essay, all post-secondary transcripts, 3 letters of reference, conviction disclosure form; copy of teaching certificate (for some education programs); for Specialist, master's degree, minimum GPA of 3.0, current resume, essay, all post-secondary transcripts, 3 letters of reference, conviction disclosure form; copy of teaching certificate (for some education programs). Electronic applications accepted.

Southeast Missouri State University, School of Graduate Studies, Department of Educational Leadership and Counseling, Program in Educational Administration, Cape Girardeau, MO 63701-4799. Offers educational leadership (Ed D); higher education administration (MA); secondary administration (MA); teacher leadership (MA, Ed S). *Accreditation:* NCATE. *Program availability:* Part-time, evening/weekend, online only, 100% online. *Faculty:* 7 full-time (4 women), 4 part-time/adjunct (1 woman). *Students:* 48 full-time (31 women), 166 part-time (107 women); includes 23 minority (19 Black or African American, non-Hispanic/Latino; 2 Asian, non-Hispanic/Latino; 2 Hispanic/Latino), 14 international. Average age 33. 79 applicants, 100% accepted, 79 enrolled. In 2016, 27 master's, 36 other advanced degrees awarded. *Degree requirements:* For master's and Ed S, comprehensive exam, thesis or alternative, paper; for doctorate, comprehensive exam, thesis/dissertation. *Entrance requirements:* For master's, minimum GPA of 3.5; for doctorate, GRE, interview; for Ed S, minimum GPA of 3.7. Additional exam requirements/recommendations for international students: Required—TOEFL (minimum score 550 paper-based; 79 iBT), IELTS (minimum score 6), PTE (minimum score 53). *Application deadline:* For fall admission, 8/1 for domestic students, 6/1 for international students; for spring admission, 11/21 for domestic students, 10/1 for international students; for summer admission, 5/15 for domestic students. Applications are processed on a rolling basis. Application fee: $30 ($40 for international students). Electronic applications accepted. *Expenses:* Tuition, state resident: full-time $3130; part-time $260.80 per credit hour. Tuition, nonresident: full-time $5842; part-time $486.80 per credit hour. *Required fees:* $33.70 per credit hour. *Financial support:* In 2016–17, 31 students received support. Career-related internships or fieldwork, Federal

Work-Study, scholarships/grants, traineeships, tuition waivers (full), and unspecified assistantships available. Financial award application deadline: 6/30; financial award applicants required to submit FAFSA. *Faculty research:* Learning and technology; leadership, equity and social justice in P-12 schools and higher education; school culture; leadership and academic achievement; school leadership and student success. *Unit head:* Dr. C. P. Gause, Professor/Chair, 573-651-2137, Fax: 573-986-6512, E-mail: cgause@semo.edu. *Application contact:* Dr. Lisa Bertrand, Professor/Coordinator, 573-651-5080, Fax: 573-986-6512, E-mail: lbertrand@semo.edu.
Website: http://www.semo.edu/eduleadcounsel/

Southern Arkansas University–Magnolia, School of Graduate Studies, Magnolia, AR 71753. Offers agriculture (MS); business administration (MBA), including agri-business, social entrepreneurship, supply chain management; clinical and mental health counseling (MS); computer and information sciences (MS), including cyber security and privacy, data science, information technology; gifted and talented (M Ed), including curriculum and instruction, educational administration and supervision, gifted and talented P-8/7-12, instructional specialist P-4; higher, adult and lifelong education (M Ed); kinesiology (M Ed), including coaching; library media and information specialist (M Ed); public administration (MPA); school counseling K-12 (M Ed); student affairs and college counseling (M Ed); teaching (MAT). *Accreditation:* NCATE. *Program availability:* Part-time, 100% online, blended/hybrid learning. *Faculty:* 36 full-time (19 women), 33 part-time/adjunct (14 women). *Students:* 605 full-time (143 women), 879 part-time (352 women); includes 130 minority (113 Black or African American, non-Hispanic/Latino; 7 American Indian or Alaska Native, non-Hispanic/Latino; 2 Asian, non-Hispanic/Latino; 2 Hispanic/Latino; 6 Two or more races, non-Hispanic/Latino), 1,048 international. Average age 28. 904 applicants, 81% accepted, 262 enrolled. In 2016, 278 master's awarded. *Degree requirements:* For master's, comprehensive exam (for some programs), thesis optional. *Entrance requirements:* For master's, GRE, MAT or GMAT, minimum GPA of 2.5. Additional exam requirements/recommendations for international students: Required—TOEFL (minimum score 550 paper-based), IELTS (minimum score 6). *Application deadline:* For fall admission, 7/20 for domestic students, 7/10 for international students; for spring admission, 12/1 for domestic students, 11/15 for international students; for summer admission, 4/1 for domestic students, 5/1 for international students. Applications are processed on a rolling basis. Application fee: $25 ($50 for international students). Electronic applications accepted. *Expenses:* Tuition, state resident: full-time $2511; part-time $279 per credit hour. Tuition, nonresident: full-time $3726; part-time $414 per credit hour. *Required fees:* $307 per semester. Tuition and fees vary according to course load and program. *Financial support:* Career-related internships or fieldwork, Federal Work-Study, scholarships/grants, tuition waivers (full), and unspecified assistantships available. Financial award applicants required to submit FAFSA. *Faculty research:* Alternative certification for teachers, supervision of instruction, instructional leadership, counseling. *Unit head:* Dr. Kim Bloss, Dean, School of Graduate Studies, 870-235-4150, Fax: 870-235-5227, E-mail: kkbloss@saumag.edu. *Application contact:* Shrijana Malakar, Admissions Specialist, 870-235-4150, Fax: 870-235-5227, E-mail: smalakar@saumag.edu.
Website: http://www.saumag.edu/graduate

Southern Illinois University Carbondale, Graduate School, College of Education and Human Services, Department of Educational Administration and Higher Education, Program in Higher Education, Carbondale, IL 62901-4701. Offers education (MS Ed). *Accreditation:* NCATE. *Program availability:* Part-time. *Degree requirements:* For master's, thesis. *Entrance requirements:* For master's, GRE General Test or MAT, minimum GPA of 2.7. Additional exam requirements/recommendations for international students: Required—TOEFL. *Faculty research:* Student affairs administration, international education, community college teaching.

Southern Illinois University Edwardsville, Graduate School, College of Arts and Sciences, Department of Mathematics and Statistics, Program in Postsecondary Mathematics Education, Edwardsville, IL 62026. Offers MS. *Program availability:* Part-time. *Degree requirements:* For master's, thesis (for some programs), special project. *Entrance requirements:* Additional exam requirements/recommendations for international students: Required—TOEFL (minimum score 550 paper-based, 79 iBT), IELTS (minimum score 6.5), Michigan Test of English Language Proficiency or PTE. Electronic applications accepted.

Stony Brook University, State University of New York, School of Professional Development, Stony Brook, NY 11794-443. Offers biology (MAT); chemistry (MAT); coaching (Graduate Certificate); earth science (MAT); educational computing (Graduate Certificate); educational leadership (Advanced Certificate); English (MAT); environmental management (MPS, Graduate Certificate); French (MAT); German (MAT); higher education administration (MA, Certificate); human resource management (MS, Graduate Certificate); industrial management (Graduate Certificate); information systems management (Graduate Certificate); Italian (MAT); liberal studies (MA); mathematics (MAT); operations research (Graduate Certificate); physics (MAT); school district business leadership (Advanced Certificate); social studies (MAT); Spanish (MAT). *Program availability:* Part-time, evening/weekend, online learning. *Faculty:* 4 full-time (3 women), 77 part-time/adjunct (34 women). *Students:* 197 full-time (125 women), 965 part-time (674 women); includes 222 minority (79 Black or African American, non-Hispanic/Latino; 2 American Indian or Alaska Native, non-Hispanic/Latino; 35 Asian, non-Hispanic/Latino; 87 Hispanic/Latino; 1 Native Hawaiian or other Pacific Islander, non-Hispanic/Latino; 18 Two or more races, non-Hispanic/Latino), 5 international. Average age 33. 462 applicants, 87% accepted, 317 enrolled. In 2016, 348 master's, 159 other advanced degrees awarded. *Degree requirements:* For master's, one foreign language, thesis or alternative. *Entrance requirements:* Additional exam requirements/recommendations for international students: Required—TOEFL (minimum score 85 iBT). *Application deadline:* For fall admission, 1/15 for domestic students, 6/1 for international students; for spring admission, 10/1 for domestic and international students. Applications are processed on a rolling basis. Application fee: $100. *Expenses:* Contact institution. *Financial support:* Fellowships, research assistantships, teaching assistantships, and career-related internships or fieldwork available. Support available to part-time students. *Unit head:* Dr. Ken Lindblom, Dean, 631-632-7049, Fax: 631-632-9046, E-mail: kenneth.lindblom@stonybrook.edu. *Application contact:* Melissa Jordan, Assistant Dean, 631-632-7751, E-mail: melissa.jordan@stonybrook.edu.
Website: http://www.stonybrook.edu/spd/

Syracuse University, College of Arts and Sciences, Program in College Science Teaching, Syracuse, NY 13244. Offers PhD. *Program availability:* Part-time. *Degree requirements:* For doctorate, comprehensive exam, thesis/dissertation. *Entrance requirements:* For doctorate, GRE General Test, three letters of recommendation, personal statement, transcripts. Additional exam requirements/recommendations for international students: Required—TOEFL (minimum score 100 iBT). *Application deadline:* For fall admission, 2/1 priority date for domestic and international students. Applications are processed on a rolling basis. Application fee: $75. Electronic applications accepted. *Expenses: Tuition:* Full-time $25,974; part-time $1443 per credit hour. *Required fees:* $802; $50 per course. Tuition and fees vary according to course load and program. *Financial support:* Fellowships with full tuition reimbursements, research assistantships with tuition reimbursements, teaching assistantships with tuition reimbursements, and scholarships/grants available. Financial award application deadline: 1/15; financial award applicants required to submit FAFSA. *Faculty research:* Philosophy of science, methods of teaching science in higher education, research focused on the problems of college teaching, curriculum development. *Unit head:* Dr. Sharon Dotger, Program Coordinator, 315-443-9138. *Application contact:* Michelle Mondo, Office Coordinator, 315-443-2685, E-mail: mrmondo@syr.edu.
Website: http://sciteach.syr.edu/

Syracuse University, School of Education, Programs in Higher Education, Syracuse, NY 13244. Offers MS, PhD. *Program availability:* Part-time. *Students:* Average age 30. *Degree requirements:* For master's, thesis or alternative; for doctorate, comprehensive exam, thesis/dissertation. *Entrance requirements:* For master's, baccalaureate degree from regionally-accredited college/university, experience in student affairs or higher education, personal statement, resume, transcripts, three letters of recommendation; for doctorate, GRE, master's degree in higher education, student affairs, or related area; three years of work experience in higher education, student affairs, related area, or college teaching; strong writing skills; transcripts; three letters of recommendation. Additional exam requirements/recommendations for international students: Required—TOEFL (minimum score 100 iBT). *Application deadline:* For fall admission, 2/1 priority date for domestic and international students; for spring admission, 10/15 priority date for domestic and international students. Applications are processed on a rolling basis. Application fee: $75. Electronic applications accepted. *Expenses: Tuition:* Full-time $25,974; part-time $1443 per credit hour. *Required fees:* $802; $50 per course. Tuition and fees vary according to course load and program. *Financial support:* Fellowships with full tuition reimbursements, research assistantships with tuition reimbursements, teaching assistantships with tuition reimbursements, career-related internships or fieldwork, and scholarships/grants available. Financial award application deadline: 1/15. *Faculty research:* Student culture, college student personnel development, programming advising, policy-making, faculty roles on behalf of students from diverse groups. *Unit head:* Dr. Dawn Johnson, Associate Professor/Chair, 315-443-3130, E-mail: drjohn02@syr.edu. *Application contact:* Speranza Migliore, Graduate Admissions Recruiter, 315-443-2505, E-mail: gradrcrt@syr.edu.
Website: http://soeweb.syr.edu/highered/HIGHEREDU/

Taylor University, Master of Arts in Higher Education and Student Development Program, Upland, IN 46989-1001. Offers MA. *Accreditation:* NCATE. *Program availability:* Part-time. *Degree requirements:* For master's, thesis.

Teachers College, Columbia University, Department of Organization and Leadership, New York, NY 10027-6696. Offers adult education guided intensive study (Ed D); adult learning and leadership (Ed M, MA, Ed D); educational leadership (Ed D); higher and postsecondary education (MA, Ed D); leadership, policy and politics (Ed D); nurse executive (MA, Ed D), including administration studies (MA), professorial studies (MA); private school leadership (Ed M, MA); public school building leadership (Ed M, MA); social and organizational psychology (MA); urban education leaders (Ed D); MA/MBA. *Program availability:* Part-time, evening/weekend. *Students:* 310 full-time (214 women), 390 part-time (250 women); includes 276 minority (116 Black or African American, non-Hispanic/Latino; 3 American Indian or Alaska Native, non-Hispanic/Latino; 61 Asian, non-Hispanic/Latino; 79 Hispanic/Latino; 17 Two or more races, non-Hispanic/Latino), 93 international. 624 applicants, 57% accepted, 172 enrolled. *Degree requirements:* For doctorate, thesis/dissertation. *Expenses: Tuition:* Full-time $36,288; part-time $1512 per credit. *Required fees:* $438 per semester. One-time fee: $510 full-time. Full-time tuition and fees vary according to course load. *Unit head:* Prof. Anna Neumann, Chair, 212-678-3272, Fax: 212-678-3036, E-mail: neumann@tc.columbia.edu. *Application contact:* David Estrella, Director of Admission, 212-678-3305, E-mail: estrella@tc.columbia.edu.

Texas A&M University–Commerce, College of Education and Human Services, Commerce, TX 75429-3011. Offers counseling (MS); curriculum and instruction (M Ed, MS); early childhood education (M Ed, MS); educational administration (M Ed, Ed D); educational psychology (PhD); educational technology leadership (MS); educational technology library science (MS); health, kinesiology and sports studies (MS); higher education (MS, Ed D); organization, learning, and technology (MS); psychology (MS); reading (M Ed, MS); school psychology (SSP); secondary education (M Ed, MS); social work (MSW); special education (M Ed); supervision, curriculum and instruction-elementary education (Ed D). *Program availability:* Part-time, 100% online, blended/hybrid learning. *Faculty:* 88 full-time (52 women), 31 part-time/adjunct (24 women). *Students:* 341 full-time (276 women), 1,495 part-time (1,156 women); includes 762 minority (429 Black or African American, non-Hispanic/Latino; 4 American Indian or Alaska Native, non-Hispanic/Latino; 27 Asian, non-Hispanic/Latino; 247 Hispanic/Latino; 1 Native Hawaiian or other Pacific Islander, non-Hispanic/Latino; 54 Two or more races, non-Hispanic/Latino), 18 international. Average age 37. 1,070 applicants, 54% accepted, 452 enrolled. In 2016, 579 master's, 31 doctorates awarded. *Degree requirements:* For master's, one foreign language, comprehensive exam, thesis optional, departmental qualifying exams (for some programs); for doctorate, comprehensive exam, thesis/dissertation, departmental qualifying exam; for SSP, comprehensive exam, thesis optional. *Entrance requirements:* For master's and doctorate, GRE General Test. Additional exam requirements/recommendations for international students: Required—TOEFL (minimum score 550 paper-based; 79 iBT), IELTS (minimum score 6). *Application deadline:* For fall admission, 6/1 priority date for international students; for spring admission, 10/15 priority date for international students; for summer admission, 3/15 priority date for international students. Applications are processed on a rolling basis. Application fee: $50. Electronic applications accepted. *Expenses:* $2,254 resident; $4,744 non-resident. *Financial support:* In 2016–17, 301 students received support, including 39 research assistantships with partial tuition reimbursements available (averaging $9,000 per year), 17 teaching assistantships with partial tuition reimbursements available (averaging $9,000 per year); career-related internships or fieldwork, Federal Work-Study, institutionally sponsored loans, scholarships/grants, health care benefits, and unspecified assistantships also available. Financial award application deadline: 5/1; financial award applicants required to submit FAFSA. *Faculty research:* Cognitive and bilingual education, positive behavioral intervention, literacy, math readiness. *Total annual research expenditures:* $470,963. *Unit head:* Dr. Timothy Letzring, Dean, 903-886-5181, Fax: 903-886-5905, E-mail: tim.letzring@tamuc.edu. *Application contact:* Jennifer Faunce, Graduate Recruiter, 903-886-5030, Fax: 903-886-5905, E-mail: jennifer.faunce@tamuc.edu.
Website: http://www.tamuc.edu/academics/graduateSchool/programs/education/default.aspx

Texas Southern University, College of Education, Department of Educational Administration and Foundation, Houston, TX 77004-4584. Offers educational administration (M Ed, Ed D). *Program availability:* Part-time, evening/weekend. *Degree requirements:* For master's, comprehensive exam; for doctorate, comprehensive exam, thesis/dissertation. *Entrance requirements:* For master's, GRE General Test, minimum GPA of 2.5; for doctorate, GRE General Test or MAT, master's degree, minimum B+ average. Additional exam requirements/recommendations for international students: Required—TOEFL. Electronic applications accepted.

Texas State University, The Graduate College, College of Education, Program of Student Affairs in Higher Education, San Marcos, TX 78666. Offers M Ed. *Accreditation:* ACA. *Program availability:* Part-time, evening/weekend. *Faculty:* 3 full-time (2 women), 6 part-time/adjunct (2 women). *Students:* 34 full-time (28 women), 4 part-time (all women);

includes 19 minority (3 Black or African American, non-Hispanic/Latino; 2 Asian, non-Hispanic/Latino; 12 Hispanic/Latino; 2 Two or more races, non-Hispanic/Latino), 1 international. Average age 24. 49 applicants, 61% accepted, 18 enrolled. In 2016, 14 master's awarded. *Degree requirements:* For master's, comprehensive exam. *Entrance requirements:* For master's, GRE General Test (minimum preferred score of 295 [150 verbal, 145 quantitative], 4 analytical writing), baccalaureate degree from regionally-accredited institution with minimum GPA of 3.0 in last 60 hours of undergraduate course work, resume, statement of purpose, 3 letters of recommendation. Additional exam requirements/recommendations for international students: Required—TOEFL (minimum score 550 paper-based; 78 iBT), IELTS (minimum score 6.5). *Application deadline:* For fall admission, 1/15 for domestic and international students. Applications are processed on a rolling basis. Application fee: $40 ($90 for international students). Electronic applications accepted. *Expenses:* $4,851 per semester. *Financial support:* In 2016–17, 28 students received support, including 35 teaching assistantships (averaging $12,754 per year); research assistantships, career-related internships or fieldwork, Federal Work-Study, institutionally sponsored loans, and scholarships/grants also available. Support available to part-time students. Financial award application deadline: 3/1; financial award applicants required to submit FAFSA. *Unit head:* Dr. Paige Haber-Curran, Graduate Advisor, 512-245-7628, Fax: 512-245-8872, E-mail: ph31@txstate.edu. *Application contact:* Dr. Andrea Golato, Dean of Graduate School, 512-245-2581, Fax: 512-245-8365, E-mail: gradcollege@txstate.edu.
Website: http://www.txstate.edu/clas/Student-Affairs/student-affairs-in-higher-ed2.html

Texas Tech University, Graduate School, College of Education, Department of Educational Psychology and Leadership, Lubbock, TX 79409-1071. Offers counselor education (M Ed, PhD); distance education (M Ed); educational leadership (M Ed, Ed D, PhD); educational psychology (M Ed, PhD); higher education (M Ed, Ed D); higher education research (PhD); instructional technology (M Ed, Ed D); special education (M Ed, Ed D, PhD). *Accreditation:* ACA; NCATE. *Program availability:* Part-time, evening/weekend. *Faculty:* 59 full-time (29 women), 3 part-time/adjunct (all women). *Students:* 300 full-time (218 women), 656 part-time (482 women); includes 320 minority (87 Black or African American, non-Hispanic/Latino; 5 American Indian or Alaska Native, non-Hispanic/Latino; 5 Asian, non-Hispanic/Latino; 200 Hispanic/Latino; 23 Two or more races, non-Hispanic/Latino), 51 international. Average age 36. 668 applicants, 56% accepted, 285 enrolled. In 2016, 171 master's, 47 doctorates awarded. Terminal master's awarded for partial completion of doctoral program. *Degree requirements:* For master's, comprehensive exam, thesis optional; for doctorate, comprehensive exam, thesis/dissertation. *Entrance requirements:* For master's, GRE (for some programs); for doctorate, GRE. Additional exam requirements/recommendations for international students: Required—TOEFL (minimum score 550 paper-based; 79 iBT). *Application deadline:* For fall admission, 6/1 priority date for domestic students, 1/15 priority date for international students; for spring admission, 9/1 priority date for domestic students, 6/15 priority date for international students. Applications are processed on a rolling basis. Application fee: $75. Electronic applications accepted. *Expenses:* $285 per credit hour full-time resident tuition, $693 per credit hour full-time non-resident tuition; $50.50 per credit hour fee plus $608 per term fee. *Financial support:* In 2016–17, 384 students received support, including 384 fellowships (averaging $3,632 per year); scholarships/grants and unspecified assistantships also available. Support available to part-time students. Financial award application deadline: 1/3; financial award applicants required to submit FAFSA. *Faculty research:* Cognitive, motivational, and developmental processes in learning; counseling education; instructional technology; generic special education and sensory impairment; community college administration; K-12 school administration. *Total annual research expenditures:* $1,371. *Unit head:* Dr. Hansel Burley, Chair, 806-834-5135, Fax: 806-742-2179, E-mail: hansel.burley@ttu.edu. *Application contact:* Pam Smith, Admissions Advisor, 806-834-2969, Fax: 806-742-2179, E-mail: pam.smith@ttu.edu.
Website: http://www.educ.ttu.edu/

Tiffin University, Program in Education, Tiffin, OH 44883-2161. Offers educational technology management (M Ed); higher education administration (M Ed). *Program availability:* Part-time, evening/weekend, online only, 100% online, blended/hybrid learning. *Students:* 99 part-time (75 women); includes 26 minority (20 Black or African American, non-Hispanic/Latino; 1 Asian, non-Hispanic/Latino; 4 Hispanic/Latino; 1 Two or more races, non-Hispanic/Latino). Average age 32. 31 applicants, 90% accepted, 24 enrolled. In 2016, 45 master's awarded. *Entrance requirements:* Additional exam requirements/recommendations for international students: Required—TOEFL. *Application deadline:* Applications are processed on a rolling basis. Electronic applications accepted. *Expenses:* Contact institution. *Financial support:* Unspecified assistantships available. *Application contact:* Nikki Hintze, Director of Graduate Admissions and Student Services, 800-968-6446 Ext. 3445, Fax: 419-443-5002, E-mail: hintzenm@tiffin.edu.

Trident University International, College of Education, Program in Education, Cypress, CA 90630. Offers adult education (MA Ed); aviation education (MA Ed); children's literacy development (MA Ed); e-learning (MA Ed); early childhood education (MA Ed); enrollment management (MA Ed); higher education (MA Ed); teaching and instruction (MA Ed); training and development (MA Ed). *Program availability:* Part-time, evening/weekend, online learning. *Degree requirements:* For master's, capstone project with integrative paper. *Entrance requirements:* For master's, minimum GPA of 2.5 (students with GPA 3.0 or greater may transfer up to 30% of graduate level credits). Additional exam requirements/recommendations for international students: Required—TOEFL (minimum score 525 paper-based). Electronic applications accepted.

Trident University International, College of Education, Program in Educational Leadership, Cypress, CA 90630. Offers e-learning leadership (MA Ed, PhD); educational leadership (MA Ed); higher education leadership (PhD); K-12 leadership (PhD). *Program availability:* Part-time, evening/weekend, online learning. *Degree requirements:* For doctorate, comprehensive exam, thesis/dissertation, defense of dissertation. *Entrance requirements:* For master's, minimum GPA of 2.5 (students with GPA 3.0 or greater may transfer up to 30% of graduate level credits); for doctorate, minimum GPA of 3.4, course work in research methods or statistics. Additional exam requirements/recommendations for international students: Required—TOEFL. Electronic applications accepted.

Union University, School of Education, Jackson, TN 38305-3697. Offers education (M Ed, MA Ed); education administration generalist (Ed S); educational leadership (Ed D); educational supervision (Ed S); higher education (Ed D). M Ed also available at Germantown campus. *Accreditation:* NCATE. *Program availability:* Part-time, evening/weekend, online learning. *Degree requirements:* For master's, thesis (for some programs), capstone research course (for MA Ed); performance exhibition (for M Ed); for doctorate, comprehensive exam, thesis/dissertation; for Ed S, thesis or alternative. *Entrance requirements:* For master's, MAT, PRAXIS II or GRE, minimum GPA of 3.0, teaching license (for M Ed only), writing sample; for doctorate, GRE, minimum graduate GPA of 3.2, writing sample; for Ed S, PRAXIS II, minimum graduate GPA of 3.2, writing sample. Additional exam requirements/recommendations for international students: Required—TOEFL (minimum score 560 paper-based; 80 iBT). Electronic applications accepted. *Expenses:* Contact institution. *Faculty research:* Mathematics education, brain compatible learning, transformational teaching, cognitive strategy development, instructional technology.

Universidad Central del Este, Graduate School, San Pedro de Macoris, Dominican Republic. Offers environmental engineering (ME); financial management (M Ad); higher education (M Ed), including higher education management, higher education pedagogy; human resources (M Ad). *Entrance requirements:* For master's, letters of recommendation.

Université de Sherbrooke, Faculty of Education, Program in Postsecondary Education Training, Sherbrooke, QC J1K 2R1, Canada. Offers M Ed, Diploma. *Degree requirements:* For master's, thesis.

University at Albany, State University of New York, School of Education, Department of Educational Policy and Leadership, Albany, NY 12222-0001. Offers educational policy and leadership (MS, PhD); higher education (MS); international education management (CAS). *Program availability:* Evening/weekend. *Faculty:* 10 full-time (4 women), 7 part-time/adjunct (6 women). *Students:* 27 full-time (11 women), 103 part-time (53 women); includes 24 minority (14 Black or African American, non-Hispanic/Latino; 1 Asian, non-Hispanic/Latino; 9 Hispanic/Latino), 15 international. Average age 31. 48 applicants, 75% accepted, 33 enrolled. In 2016, 16 master's, 9 doctorates, 11 other advanced degrees awarded. *Degree requirements:* For doctorate, one foreign language, thesis/dissertation. *Entrance requirements:* For doctorate, GRE General Test, GRE Subject Test. Additional exam requirements/recommendations for international students: Required—TOEFL (minimum score 550 paper-based). *Application deadline:* For fall admission, 2/1 for domestic students, 5/1 for international students; for spring admission, 9/1 for domestic students, 11/1 for international students. Applications are processed on a rolling basis. Application fee: $75. Electronic applications accepted. *Expenses:* Tuition, state resident: full-time $10,870; part-time $453 per credit hour. Tuition, nonresident: full-time $22,210; part-time $925 per credit hour. *International tuition:* $21,550 full-time. *Required fees:* $1864; $96 per credit hour. *Financial support:* Fellowships and career-related internships or fieldwork available. Financial award application deadline: 3/15. *Total annual research expenditures:* $273,985. *Unit head:* Kevin Kinser, Chair, 518-442-5092, E-mail: kkinser@albany.edu.
Website: http://www.albany.edu/epl/

University at Buffalo, the State University of New York, Graduate School, Graduate School of Education, Department of Educational Leadership and Policy, Buffalo, NY 14260. Offers economics and education policy analysis (MA); education studies (Ed M); educational administration (Ed M, Ed D, PhD); educational culture, policy and society (PhD); higher education administration (Ed M, PhD); school building leadership (Certificate); school business and human resource administration (Certificate); school district business leadership (Certificate); school district leadership (Certificate). *Program availability:* Part-time, evening/weekend. *Faculty:* 15 full-time (9 women), 8 part-time/adjunct (6 women). *Students:* 77 full-time (51 women), 122 part-time (76 women); includes 30 minority (23 Black or African American, non-Hispanic/Latino; 4 Asian, non-Hispanic/Latino; 3 Hispanic/Latino), 22 international. Average age 34. 144 applicants, 75% accepted, 63 enrolled. In 2016, 59 master's, 11 doctorates, 29 other advanced degrees awarded. *Degree requirements:* For master's, comprehensive exam (for some programs), thesis optional; for doctorate, comprehensive exam, thesis/dissertation. *Entrance requirements:* For master's, interview, letters of reference; for doctorate, GRE General Test or MAT, writing sample, letters of reference. Additional exam requirements/recommendations for international students: Required—TOEFL (minimum score 550 paper-based; 79 iBT). *Application deadline:* For fall admission, 2/1 priority date for domestic students, 2/1 for international students; for spring admission, 11/15 priority date for domestic students, 10/1 for international students. Applications are processed on a rolling basis. Application fee: $50. Electronic applications accepted. *Financial support:* In 2016–17, 13 fellowships (averaging $6,862 per year), 32 research assistantships with tuition reimbursements (averaging $10,496 per year) were awarded; career-related internships or fieldwork, Federal Work-Study, institutionally sponsored loans, scholarships/grants, health care benefits, tuition waivers (full and partial), and unspecified assistantships also available. Financial award application deadline: 3/15; financial award applicants required to submit FAFSA. *Faculty research:* College access and choice, school leadership preparation and practice, public policy, curriculum and pedagogy, comparative and international education. *Total annual research expenditures:* $435,404. *Unit head:* Dr. Janina C. Brutt-Griffler, Chair, 716-645-2471, Fax: 716-645-2481, E-mail: bruttg@buffalo.edu. *Application contact:* Veronica Kase, Admission Assistant, 716-645-2110, Fax: 716-645-7937, E-mail: vakase@buffalo.edu.
Website: http://gse.buffalo.edu/elp

The University of Akron, Graduate School, College of Education, Department of Educational Foundations and Leadership, Program in Higher Education Administration, Akron, OH 44325. Offers MA, MS. *Accreditation:* NCATE. *Students:* 16 full-time (10 women), 21 part-time (15 women); includes 8 minority (4 Black or African American, non-Hispanic/Latino; 1 Hispanic/Latino; 3 Two or more races, non-Hispanic/Latino), 1 international. Average age 32. 26 applicants, 50% accepted, 9 enrolled. In 2016, 21 master's awarded. *Degree requirements:* For master's, comprehensive exam. *Entrance requirements:* For master's, GRE, minimum GPA of 2.75, declaration of intent that includes statement of professional goals and reasons for choosing the field of higher education administration and The University of Akron. Additional exam requirements/recommendations for international students: Required—TOEFL (minimum score 550 paper-based; 79 iBT), IELTS (minimum score 6.5). *Application deadline:* Applications are processed on a rolling basis. Application fee: $45 ($70 for international students). Electronic applications accepted. *Expenses:* Tuition, state resident: full-time $8618; part-time $359 per credit hour. Tuition, nonresident: full-time $17,149; part-time $715 per credit hour. *Required fees:* $1652. *Financial support:* Research assistantships and teaching assistantships available. *Unit head:* Dr. Susan Clark, Interim Chair, 330-972-7780, E-mail: sclark1@uakron.edu. *Application contact:* Kelly Chaff, College Program Specialist, 330-972-7028, E-mail: klchaff@uakron.edu.

The University of Alabama, Graduate School, College of Education, Department of Educational Leadership, Policy, and Technology Studies, Higher Education Administration Program, Tuscaloosa, AL 35487. Offers MA, Ed D, PhD. *Program availability:* Evening/weekend, 100% online. *Students:* 60 full-time (38 women), 86 part-time (36 women); includes 54 minority (42 Black or African American, non-Hispanic/Latino; 2 Asian, non-Hispanic/Latino; 5 Hispanic/Latino; 5 Two or more races, non-Hispanic/Latino). Average age 38. 77 applicants, 49% accepted, 27 enrolled. In 2016, 14 master's, 15 doctorates awarded. Terminal master's awarded for partial completion of doctoral program. *Degree requirements:* For master's, capstone seminar; for doctorate, comprehensive exam, thesis/dissertation. *Entrance requirements:* For master's, GRE or MAT, minimum GPA of 3.0; for doctorate, GRE (for PhD), GRE or MAT (for Ed D), master's degree, minimum GPA of 3.0. Additional exam requirements/recommendations for international students: Required—TOEFL. *Application deadline:* For fall admission, 1/15 priority date for domestic and international students. Application fee: $60 ($75 for international students). Electronic applications accepted. *Expenses:* Tuition, state resident: full-time $10,470. Tuition, nonresident: full-time $26,950. *Financial support:* In 2016–17, 5 students received support, including 2 research assistantships with full tuition reimbursements available (averaging $11,900 per year); career-related internships or fieldwork, scholarships/grants, health care benefits, and

unspecified assistantships also available. *Faculty research:* College teaching and learning, faculty-administration relations, community colleges, organizational change, student affairs. *Unit head:* Dr. Karri Holley, Coordinator and Associate Professor, 205-348-7825, Fax: 205-348-2161, E-mail: kaholley@ua.edu. *Application contact:* Donna Smith, Administrative Assistant, 205-348-6871, Fax: 205-348-2161, E-mail: dbsmith@ua.edu.
Website: http://education.ua.edu/academics/elpts/hea/

The University of Arizona, College of Education, Department of Educational Policy Studies and Practice, Program in Higher Education, Tucson, AZ 85721. Offers MA, PhD. *Program availability:* Part-time. Terminal master's awarded for partial completion of doctoral program. *Degree requirements:* For master's, comprehensive exam, thesis; for doctorate, comprehensive exam, thesis/dissertation. *Entrance requirements:* For master's, GRE General Test or MAT, minimum undergraduate GPA of 3.0; for doctorate, GRE General Test or MAT, minimum undergraduate GPA of 3.0, graduate 3.5. Additional exam requirements/recommendations for international students: Required—TOEFL (minimum score 550 paper-based; 79 iBT). Electronic applications accepted. *Faculty research:* Technology transfer, higher education policy, finance, curricular change.

University of Arkansas, Graduate School, College of Education and Health Professions, Department of Rehabilitation, Human Resources and Communication Disorders, Program in Higher Education, Fayetteville, AR 72701. Offers M Ed, Ed D, Ed S. *Accreditation:* NCATE. *Program availability:* Part-time, evening/weekend. In 2016, 26 master's, 5 doctorates awarded. *Degree requirements:* For master's, thesis optional; for doctorate, thesis/dissertation. *Entrance requirements:* For master's, GRE General Test, MAT or minimum GPA of 3.0; for doctorate, GRE General Test or MAT. *Application deadline:* For fall admission, 4/1 for international students; for spring admission, 10/1 for international students. Applications are processed on a rolling basis. Application fee: $40 ($50 for international students). Electronic applications accepted. *Financial support:* In 2016–17, 30 research assistantships, 1 teaching assistantship were awarded; fellowships with tuition reimbursements, career-related internships or fieldwork, and Federal Work-Study also available. Support available to part-time students. Financial award application deadline: 4/1; financial award applicants required to submit FAFSA. *Unit head:* Dr. Kate Mamiseishvili, Departmental Chairperson, 479-575-4758, Fax: 479-575-3319, E-mail: kmamisei@uark.edu. *Application contact:* Dr. John Murry, Graduate Coordinator, 479-575-7332, E-mail: jmurry@uark.edu.
Website: http://hied.uark.edu

University of Arkansas at Little Rock, Graduate School, College of Education and Health Professions, Department of Educational Leadership, Program in Higher Education, Little Rock, AR 72204-1099. Offers administration (MA); college student affairs (MA); health professions teaching and learning (MA); higher education (Ed D); two-year college teaching (MA). *Degree requirements:* For doctorate, comprehensive exam, oral defense of dissertation, residency. *Entrance requirements:* For master's, GRE General Test or MAT, interview, minimum graduate GPA of 3.0; for doctorate, GRE General Test, interview, minimum graduate GPA of 3.5, teaching certificate, three years of work experience.

The University of British Columbia, Faculty of Education, Department of Educational Studies, Vancouver, BC V6T 1Z1, Canada. Offers adult learning and education (M Ed); adult learning and global change (M Ed); curriculum and leadership (M Ed); educational administration and leadership (M Ed); educational leadership and policy (Ed D); educational studies (M Ed, MA, PhD); higher education (M Ed); society, culture and politics in education (M Ed). *Program availability:* Part-time, evening/weekend. *Faculty:* 25 full-time (14 women), 3 part-time/adjunct (2 women). *Students:* 222 full-time (157 women), 62 part-time (44 women). Average age 35. 166 applicants, 66% accepted, 74 enrolled. In 2016, 103 master's, 13 doctorates awarded. Terminal master's awarded for partial completion of doctoral program. *Degree requirements:* For master's, thesis; for doctorate, comprehensive exam, thesis/dissertation. *Entrance requirements:* For master's, minimum B+ average, 4-year undergraduate degree, field-related experience; for doctorate, minimum B+ average, 4-year undergraduate degree, master's degree, field-related experience. Additional exam requirements/recommendations for international students: Required—TOEFL (minimum score 600 paper-based; 100 iBT) or IELTS (minimum score 6.5). Application fee: $90 ($150 for international students). Electronic applications accepted. *Expenses:* Contact institution. *Financial support:* In 2016–17, 7 fellowships with tuition reimbursements (averaging $17,000 per year), 12 research assistantships (averaging $4,000 per year), 8 teaching assistantships (averaging $5,000 per year) were awarded. *Faculty research:* Educational leadership educational administration adult education politics in education, global change and adult learning. *Total annual research expenditures:* $632,000. *Unit head:* Dr. Tara Fenwick, Head, 604-822-5359, Fax: 604-822-4244. *Application contact:* Christine Adams, Graduate Secretary, 604-822-6647, Fax: 604-822-4244, E-mail: grad.edst@ubc.ca.
Website: http://www.edst.educ.ubc.ca/

University of California, Riverside, Graduate Division, Graduate School of Education, Riverside, CA 92521-0102. Offers autism (M Ed); diversity and equity (M Ed); education specialist (Credential); education, society, and culture (MA, PhD); educational psychology (MA, PhD); general education (M Ed); higher education administration and policy (M Ed, PhD); multiple subject (Credential); reading (M Ed); school psychology (PhD); single subject (Credential); special education (M Ed, MA, PhD); TESOL (M Ed). Terminal master's awarded for partial completion of doctoral program. *Degree requirements:* For master's, thesis optional, comprehensive exams or thesis (MA), case study or analytical report (M Ed); for doctorate, thesis/dissertation, written and oral qualifying exams, college teaching practicum. *Entrance requirements:* For master's, GRE General Test (for MA); CBEST and CSET (for M Ed in general education only), UCR Extension TESOL certificate (for M Ed with TESOL emphasis only); for doctorate, GRE General Test, writing sample; for Credential, CBEST, CSET. Additional exam requirements/recommendations for international students: Required—TOEFL (minimum score 550 paper-based; 80 iBT), IELTS (minimum score 7). Electronic applications accepted. *Expenses:* Tuition, state resident: full-time $16,666. Tuition, nonresident: full-time $31,768. *Required fees:* $11,055.54 per quarter. $3685.18 per quarter. Tuition and fees vary according to campus/location and program. *Faculty research:* Responsiveness to intervention, faculty core, response to intervention of English language learners, advanced modeling techniques, study on social capital, trust, and motivation.

University of Central Florida, College of Education and Human Performance, Department of Educational and Human Sciences, Program in Educational Leadership, Orlando, FL 32816. Offers educational leadership (MA, Ed D, Ed S), including community college education (MA), higher education (Ed D), student personnel (MA). *Program availability:* Part-time, evening/weekend. *Students:* 121 full-time (78 women), 274 part-time (203 women); includes 147 minority (69 Black or African American, non-Hispanic/Latino; 7 Asian, non-Hispanic/Latino; 65 Hispanic/Latino; 6 Two or more races, non-Hispanic/Latino), 1 international. Average age 31. 258 applicants, 69% accepted, 101 enrolled. In 2016, 84 master's, 24 doctorates awarded. *Degree requirements:* For master's, thesis or alternative; for doctorate, thesis/dissertation, candidacy exam; for Ed S, thesis or alternative, final exam. *Entrance requirements:* For master's, GRE General Test; for doctorate, GRE General Test, GRE Subject Test, minimum GPA of 3.0, resume; for Ed S, GRE General Test, minimum GPA of 3.0, resume. Additional exam requirements/recommendations for international students: Required—TOEFL. *Application deadline:* For fall admission, 2/20 for domestic students; for spring admission, 9/20 for domestic students. Application fee: $30. Electronic applications accepted. *Expenses:* Tuition, state resident: part-time $288.16 per credit hour. Tuition, nonresident: part-time $1071.31 per credit hour. *Financial support:* In 2016–17, 22 students received support, including 1 fellowship with partial tuition reimbursement available (averaging $2,500 per year), 21 research assistantships with partial tuition reimbursements available (averaging $8,064 per year), 2 teaching assistantships with partial tuition reimbursements available (averaging $11,154 per year); career-related internships or fieldwork, Federal Work-Study, institutionally sponsored loans, tuition waivers (partial), and unspecified assistantships also available. Financial award application deadline: 3/1; financial award applicants required to submit FAFSA. *Unit head:* Dr. Kenneth Murray, Program Coordinator, 407-832-1468, E-mail: kenneth.murray@ucf.edu. *Application contact:* Assistant Director, Graduate Admissions, 407-823-2766, Fax: 407-823-6442, E-mail: gradadmissions@ucf.edu.
Website: http://education.ucf.edu/highered/index.cfm

University of Central Florida, College of Education and Human Performance, Education Doctoral Programs, Orlando, FL 32816. Offers communication sciences and disorders (PhD); curriculum and instruction (Ed D); early childhood education (PhD); educational leadership (Ed D); elementary education (PhD); exceptional education (PhD); exercise physiology (PhD); higher education (PhD); instructional technology (PhD); mathematics education (PhD); methodology, measurement and analysis (PhD); reading education (PhD); science education (PhD); social science education (PhD); TESOL (PhD). *Students:* 127 full-time (91 women), 43 part-time (29 women); includes 33 minority (17 Black or African American, non-Hispanic/Latino; 5 Asian, non-Hispanic/Latino; 7 Hispanic/Latino; 4 Two or more races, non-Hispanic/Latino), 26 international. Average age 37. 163 applicants, 40% accepted, 52 enrolled. In 2016, 57 doctorates awarded. Application fee: $30. Electronic applications accepted. *Expenses:* Tuition, state resident: part-time $288.16 per credit hour. Tuition, nonresident: part-time $1071.31 per credit hour. *Financial support:* In 2016–17, 78 students received support, including 41 fellowships with partial tuition reimbursements available (averaging $5,916 per year), 44 research assistantships with partial tuition reimbursements available (averaging $7,637 per year), 48 teaching assistantships with partial tuition reimbursements available (averaging $9,633 per year). Financial award application deadline: 3/1; financial award applicants required to submit FAFSA. *Unit head:* Dr. Edward Robinson, Director of Doctoral Programs, 407-823-6106, E-mail: edward.robinson@ucf.edu. *Application contact:* Assistant Director, Graduate Admissions, 407-823-2766, Fax: 407-823-6442, E-mail: gradadmissions@ucf.edu.
Website: http://education.ucf.edu/programs.cfm?pid=g&cat=2

University of Central Oklahoma, The Jackson College of Graduate Studies, College of Education and Professional Studies, Department of Adult Education and Safety Science, Edmond, OK 73034-5209. Offers adult and higher education (M Ed), including adult and higher education, interdisciplinary studies, student personnel, training. *Program availability:* Part-time. *Degree requirements:* For master's, comprehensive exam (for some programs), thesis (for some programs). *Entrance requirements:* For master's, GRE General Test. Additional exam requirements/recommendations for international students: Required—TOEFL (minimum score 550 paper-based; 79 iBT), IELTS (minimum score 6.5). Electronic applications accepted. *Faculty research:* Violence in the workplace/schools, aging issues, trade and industrial education.

University of Connecticut, Graduate School, Neag School of Education, Department of Educational Leadership, Field of Higher Education and Student Affairs, Storrs, CT 06269. Offers MA. *Accreditation:* NCATE. *Degree requirements:* For master's, comprehensive exam, thesis or alternative. *Entrance requirements:* Additional exam requirements/recommendations for international students: Required—TOEFL (minimum score 550 paper-based). Electronic applications accepted.

University of Dayton, PhD Program in Educational Leadership, Dayton, OH 45469-2963. Offers educational leadership (PhD); higher education administration (PhD); PreK-12 school administration (PhD). *Program availability:* Part-time, blended/hybrid learning. *Faculty:* 5 full-time (3 women), 1 part-time/adjunct (0 women). *Students:* 50 full-time (26 women); includes 6 minority (4 Black or African American, non-Hispanic/Latino; 1 Hispanic/Latino; 1 Two or more races, non-Hispanic/Latino), 2 international. Average age 41. 59 applicants, 17% accepted. In 2016, 6 doctorates awarded. *Degree requirements:* For doctorate, comprehensive exam, thesis/dissertation. *Entrance requirements:* For doctorate, GRE (minimum score of 149 in verbal and 4.0 in analytical writing), official transcripts, 3 letters of recommendation, 500-700 word essay, current resume, interview. Additional exam requirements/recommendations for international students: Required—TOEFL (minimum score 550 paper-based; 80 iBT), GRE. *Application deadline:* Applications are processed on a rolling basis. Application fee: $0 ($50 for international students). Electronic applications accepted. *Expenses:* $808 per credit hour, $25 registration fee per term. *Financial support:* In 2016–17, 1 fellowship (averaging $2,400 per year) was awarded; institutionally sponsored loans also available. Financial award application deadline: 3/1; financial award applicants required to submit FAFSA. *Faculty research:* School law; principalship; school finance; leadership. *Unit head:* Dr. Charles J. Russo, Director, 937-229-3722, Fax: 937-229-4824, E-mail: crusso1@udayton.edu. *Application contact:* Elizabeth Pearn, Administrative Assistant, 937-229-4003, Fax: 937-229-4729, E-mail: epearn1@udayton.edu.
Website: https://www.udayton.edu/education/departments_and_programs/phd/index.php

University of Delaware, College of Education and Human Development, School of Education, Newark, DE 19716. Offers education (PhD); educational leadership (Ed D); higher education (M Ed); instruction (MI); reading (M Ed); school leadership (M Ed); school psychology (MA, Ed S); teaching English as a second language (TESL) (MA). *Accreditation:* NCATE. *Program availability:* Part-time, evening/weekend. Terminal master's awarded for partial completion of doctoral program. *Degree requirements:* For master's, comprehensive exam (for some programs), thesis (for some programs); for doctorate, comprehensive exam (for some programs), thesis/dissertation. *Entrance requirements:* For master's and doctorate, GRE, 3 letters of recommendation. Additional exam requirements/recommendations for international students: Required—TOEFL (minimum score 600 paper-based). Electronic applications accepted. *Faculty research:* Teacher education; curriculum theory and development; community based education models, educational leadership.

University of Denver, Morgridge College of Education, Denver, CO 80208. Offers child, family and school psychology (MA, PhD, Ed S); counseling psychology (MA, PhD); curriculum and instruction (MA, Ed D, PhD); curriculum instruction and teaching (Certificate); early childhood special education (MA, Certificate); educational leadership and policy studies (MA, Ed D, PhD, Certificate); higher education (Ed D, PhD); library and information science (MLIS); research methods and statistics (MA, PhD). *Accreditation:* ALA; APA (one or more programs are accredited). *Program availability:* Part-time, evening/weekend, online learning. *Faculty:* 39 full-time (29 women), 60 part-time/adjunct (42 women). *Students:* 498 full-time (392 women), 362 part-time (282 women); includes 223 minority (63 Black or African American, non-Hispanic/Latino; 6 American Indian or Alaska Native, non-Hispanic/Latino; 20 Asian, non-Hispanic/Latino; 102 Hispanic/Latino; 1 Native Hawaiian or other Pacific Islander, non-Hispanic/Latino;

31 Two or more races, non-Hispanic/Latino), 40 international. Average age 32. 1,027 applicants, 69% accepted, 386 enrolled. In 2016, 252 master's, 36 doctorates, 141 other advanced degrees awarded. Terminal master's awarded for partial completion of doctoral program. *Degree requirements:* For master's, comprehensive exam; for doctorate, 2 foreign languages, comprehensive exam, thesis/dissertation. *Entrance requirements:* For master's and doctorate, GRE General Test or GMAT. Additional exam requirements/recommendations for international students: Required—TOEFL (minimum score 550 paper-based; 80 iBT). *Application deadline:* Applications are processed on a rolling basis. Application fee: $65. Electronic applications accepted. *Expenses:* $29,022 per year full-time. *Financial support:* In 2016–17, 697 students received support, including 37 research assistantships with tuition reimbursements available (averaging $11,209 per year), 66 teaching assistantships with tuition reimbursements available (averaging $3,742 per year); career-related internships or fieldwork, Federal Work-Study, institutionally sponsored loans, scholarships/grants, and unspecified assistantships also available. Support available to part-time students. Financial award application deadline: 2/15; financial award applicants required to submit FAFSA. *Faculty research:* Early childhood education, access and equity, educational leadership, family and school partnerships, neurodevelopmental disorders. *Total annual research expenditures:* $3.3 million. *Unit head:* Dr. Karen Riley, Dean, 303-871-3665, Fax: 303-871-4456, E-mail: karen.riley@du.edu. *Application contact:* Jodi Dye, Director of Admissions, 303-871-2510, Fax: 303-871-4456, E-mail: jodi.dye@du.edu.
Website: http://morgridge.du.edu

University of Florida, Graduate School, College of Education, School of Human Development and Organizational Studies in Education, Gainesville, FL 32611. Offers counseling and counselor education (Ed D, PhD), including counseling and counselor education, marriage and family counseling, mental health counseling, school counseling and guidance; educational leadership (M Ed, MAE, Ed D, PhD, Ed S), including educational leadership (Ed D, PhD), educational policy (Ed D, PhD); higher education administration (Ed D, PhD), including education policy (Ed D), educational policy, higher education administration; marriage and family counseling (M Ed, MAE, Ed D, PhD, Ed S); mental health counseling (M Ed, MAE, Ed D, PhD, Ed S); research and evaluation methodology (M Ed, MAE, Ed D, PhD); school counseling and guidance (M Ed, MAE, Ed D, PhD, Ed S); student personnel in higher education (M Ed, MAE). *Accreditation:* ACA (one or more programs are accredited); NCATE. *Program availability:* Part-time, online learning. Terminal master's awarded for partial completion of doctoral program. *Degree requirements:* For master's, thesis optional; for doctorate, comprehensive exam, thesis/dissertation. *Entrance requirements:* For master's and doctorate, GRE General Test, minimum GPA of 3.0 (undergraduate), 3.5 (graduate); for Ed S, GRE General Test. Additional exam requirements/recommendations for international students: Required—TOEFL (minimum score 550 paper-based; 80 iBT), IELTS (minimum score 6). Electronic applications accepted.

University of Georgia, College of Education, Program in Higher Education, Athens, GA 30602. Offers M Ed, Ed D, PhD. *Accreditation:* NCATE. *Degree requirements:* For doctorate, thesis/dissertation. *Entrance requirements:* For doctorate, GRE General Test. *Application deadline:* For fall admission, 7/1 priority date for domestic students; for spring admission, 11/15 for domestic students. Application fee: $50. Electronic applications accepted. *Financial support:* Fellowships, research assistantships, teaching assistantships, and unspecified assistantships available. *Unit head:* Dr. Libby V. Morris, Director, 706-542-3464, E-mail: lvmorris@uga.edu. *Application contact:* Dr. Eric C. Ness, Graduate Coordinator, 706-542-0573, E-mail: eness@uga.edu.
Website: http://www.uga.edu/ihe

University of Houston, College of Education, Department of Educational Leadership and Cultural Studies, Houston, TX 77204. Offers administration and supervision (M Ed, Ed D); higher education (M Ed); historical, social, and cultural foundations of education (M Ed). *Accreditation:* NCATE. *Program availability:* Part-time, evening/weekend. *Degree requirements:* For master's, comprehensive exam or thesis; for doctorate, comprehensive exam, thesis/dissertation. *Entrance requirements:* For master's, GRE General Test, minimum cumulative GPA of 2.6, 3 letters of recommendation, resume/vitae, goal statement; for doctorate, GRE General Test, minimum cumulative GPA of 2.6, 3 letters of recommendation, resume/vitae, goal statement, writing sample, interview. Additional exam requirements/recommendations for international students: Required—TOEFL (minimum score 550 paper-based; 79 iBT). Electronic applications accepted. *Faculty research:* Change, supervision, multiculturalism, evaluation, policy.

University of Houston, College of Education, Department of Educational Psychology, Houston, TX 77204. Offers administration and supervision - higher education (M Ed); counseling (M Ed); counseling psychology (PhD); educational psychology (M Ed); school psychology (PhD); school psychology and individual differences (PhD); special education (M Ed). *Accreditation:* NCATE. *Program availability:* Part-time, evening/weekend, online learning. *Degree requirements:* For master's, comprehensive exam or thesis; for doctorate, comprehensive exam, thesis/dissertation. *Entrance requirements:* For master's, GRE, transcripts, 3 letters of recommendation, curriculum vita, goal statement; for doctorate, GRE, transcripts, 3 letters of recommendation, curriculum vita, goal statement, writing sample, interview. Additional exam requirements/recommendations for international students: Required—TOEFL (minimum score 550 paper-based; 79 iBT), IELTS (minimum score 6.5). Electronic applications accepted. *Faculty research:* Evidence-based assessment and intervention, multicultural issues in psychology, social and cultural context of learning, systemic barriers to college, motivational aspects of self-regulated learning.

University of Houston–Victoria, School of Education, Health Professions and Human Development, Victoria, TX 77901-4450. Offers administration and supervision (M Ed); adult and higher education (M Ed); counselor education (M Ed); curriculum and instruction (M Ed); educational technology (M Ed); special education (M Ed). *Program availability:* Part-time, evening/weekend, online learning. *Degree requirements:* For master's, comprehensive exam, project or thesis. *Entrance requirements:* For master's, GRE General Test. Additional exam requirements/recommendations for international students: Required—TOEFL. Electronic applications accepted. *Faculty research:* Reading and language arts education, evaluation and diagnosis of special children's abilities.

University of Illinois at Springfield, Graduate Programs, College of Education and Human Services, Department of Educational Leadership, Springfield, IL 62703-5407. Offers chief school business official (CAS); educational leadership (MA); educational technology (Graduate Certificate); English as a second language (Graduate Certificate); higher education online pedagogy (Graduate Certificate); leadership and learning (Graduate Certificate); legal aspects of education (Graduate Certificate); superintendent (CAS); teacher leadership (MA). *Program availability:* Part-time, evening/weekend, 100% online, blended/hybrid learning. *Faculty:* 5 full-time (2 women), 8 part-time/adjunct (7 women). *Students:* 4 full-time (2 women), 113 part-time (68 women); includes 20 minority (15 Black or African American, non-Hispanic/Latino, 1 American Indian or Alaska Native, non-Hispanic/Latino; 4 Hispanic/Latino), 1 international. Average age 36. 45 applicants, 62% accepted, 19 enrolled. In 2016, 22 master's, 2 other advanced degrees awarded. *Degree requirements:* For master's, capstone course. *Entrance requirements:* For master's, minimum undergraduate GPA of 3.0, valid Illinois Teaching License, minimum of two years of successful teaching experience, portfolio, interview. Additional exam requirements/recommendations for international students: Required—TOEFL (minimum score 500 paper-based; 61 iBT). *Application deadline:* Applications are processed on a rolling basis. Application fee: $60 ($75 for international students). Electronic applications accepted. *Expenses:* Tuition, state resident: part-time $329 per credit hour. Tuition, nonresident: part-time $675 per credit hour. *Financial support:* In 2016–17, fellowships with full tuition reimbursements (averaging $9,900 per year), research assistantships with full tuition reimbursements (averaging $9,991 per year), teaching assistantships with full tuition reimbursements (averaging $10,059 per year) were awarded; career-related internships or fieldwork, Federal Work-Study, scholarships/grants, health care benefits, and unspecified assistantships also available. Support available to part-time students. Financial award application deadline: 11/15; financial award applicants required to submit FAFSA. *Unit head:* Dr. Scott Day, Program Administrator, 217-206-7520, Fax: 217-206-6775, E-mail: day.scott@uis.edu. *Application contact:* Dr. Cecelia Cornell, Associate Vice Chancellor for Graduate Education, 217-206-7230, E-mail: ccorn1@uis.edu.
Website: http://www.uis.edu/edl/

The University of Iowa, Graduate College, College of Education, Department of Educational Policy and Leadership Studies, Program in Higher Education and Student Affairs, Iowa City, IA 52242-1316. Offers MA, PhD. *Degree requirements:* For master's, exam; for doctorate, comprehensive exam, thesis/dissertation. *Entrance requirements:* For master's and doctorate, GRE General Test, minimum GPA of 3.0. Additional exam requirements/recommendations for international students: Required—TOEFL (minimum score 550 paper-based; 81 iBT). Electronic applications accepted.

The University of Kansas, Graduate Studies, School of Education, Department of Educational Leadership and Policy Studies, Program in Higher Education Administration, Lawrence, KS 66045-3101. Offers MS Ed, Ed D, PhD. *Program availability:* Part-time, evening/weekend. *Students:* 49 full-time (34 women), 16 part-time (15 women); includes 14 minority (6 Black or African American, non-Hispanic/Latino; 1 Asian, non-Hispanic/Latino; 2 Hispanic/Latino; 5 Two or more races, non-Hispanic/Latino), 1 international. Average age 25. 64 applicants, 81% accepted, 28 enrolled. In 2016, 32 master's awarded. *Entrance requirements:* For master's, minimum GPA of 3.0, resume, statement of purpose, official transcript, three letters of recommendation; for doctorate, GRE General Test, minimum graduate GPA of 3.5, resume, statement of purpose, official transcripts, three letters of recommendation, writing sample; minimum of three years of professional experience in higher education or related organization and master's degree (preferred for Ed D). Additional exam requirements/recommendations for international students: Required—TOEFL or IELTS. *Application deadline:* For fall admission, 7/1 for domestic and international students; for spring admission, 11/1 for domestic and international students; for summer admission, 3/1 for domestic and international students. Application fee: $65 ($85 for international students). Electronic applications accepted. *Financial support:* Fellowships, career-related internships or fieldwork, scholarships/grants, and unspecified assistantships available. Financial award application deadline: 1/3; financial award applicants required to submit FAFSA. *Faculty research:* Higher education policy, faculty issues, research on college students, financial aid, access to higher education. *Unit head:* Dr. Susan B. Twombly, Chair, 785-864-9721, Fax: 785-864-4697, E-mail: stwombly@ku.edu. *Application contact:* Denise Brubaker, Admissions Coordinator, 785-864-7973, Fax: 785-864-4697, E-mail: brubaker@ku.edu.

University of Kentucky, Graduate School, College of Education, Program in Educational Policy Studies and Evaluation, Lexington, KY 40506-0032. Offers educational policy studies and evaluation (Ed D); higher education (MS Ed, PhD); social and philosophical studies (MS Ed). *Accreditation:* NCATE. Terminal master's awarded for partial completion of doctoral program. *Degree requirements:* For master's, comprehensive exam, thesis optional; for doctorate, comprehensive exam, thesis/dissertation. *Entrance requirements:* For master's, GRE General Test, minimum undergraduate GPA of 2.75; for doctorate, GRE General Test, minimum graduate GPA of 3.0. Additional exam requirements/recommendations for international students: Required—TOEFL (minimum score 550 paper-based). Electronic applications accepted. *Faculty research:* Studies in higher education; comparative and international education; evaluation of educational programs, policies, and reform; student, teacher, and faculty cultures; gender and education.

University of Louisville, Graduate School, College of Education and Human Development, Department of Educational Leadership, Evaluation and Organizational Development, Louisville, KY 40292-0001. Offers educational leadership and organizational development (Ed D, PhD), including evaluation (PhD), human resource development (PhD), P-12 administration (PhD), post-secondary administration (PhD), sport administration (PhD); health professions education (Certificate); higher education administration (MA); human resources and organization development (MS), including health professions education, human resource leadership, workplace learning and performance; P-12 educational administration (Ed S), including principalship, supervisor of instruction. *Accreditation:* NCATE. *Program availability:* Part-time, evening/weekend, online learning. *Students:* 278 full-time (65 women), 409 part-time (260 women); includes 202 minority (121 Black or African American, non-Hispanic/Latino; 1 American Indian or Alaska Native, non-Hispanic/Latino; 13 Asian, non-Hispanic/Latino; 44 Hispanic/Latino; 3 Native Hawaiian or other Pacific Islander, non-Hispanic/Latino; 20 Two or more races, non-Hispanic/Latino), 5 international. Average age 36. 233 applicants, 78% accepted, 129 enrolled. In 2016, 58 master's, 4 doctorates, 17 other advanced degrees awarded. Application fee: $60. *Expenses:* Tuition, state resident: full-time $12,246; part-time $681 per credit hour. Tuition, nonresident: full-time $25,486; part-time $1417 per credit hour. *Required fees:* $196. Tuition and fees vary according to program and reciprocity agreements. *Financial support:* Application deadline: 6/1; applicants required to submit FAFSA. *Faculty research:* Urban educational leadership and policy, human resources, organizational development, program evaluation, military education, community partnerships, higher education administration. *Total annual research expenditures:* $256,111. *Unit head:* Dr. Jeffrey Sun, Chair and Professor, 502-852-0618, E-mail: jeffrey.sun@louisville.edu. *Application contact:* Betty Hampton, Director of Graduate Student Services, 502-852-5597, Fax: 502-852-1465, E-mail: edadvise@louisville.edu.
Website: http://louisville.edu/education/departments/eleod

University of Louisville, Graduate School, College of Education and Human Development, Department of Teaching and Learning, Louisville, KY 40292-0001. Offers art education (MAT); autism and applied behavior analysis (Certificate); curriculum and instruction (PhD); early elementary education (MAT); exercise physiology (MS); health and physical education (MAT); health professions education (Certificate); higher education (MA); human resources and organization development (MS); instructional technology (M Ed); interdisciplinary early childhood education (MAT); middle school education (MAT); music education (MAT); secondary education (MAT); special education (MAT); sport administration (MS); teacher leadership (M Ed). *Program availability:* Part-time, evening/weekend. *Students:* 116 full-time (68 women), 158 part-time (112 women); includes 46 minority (24 Black or African American, non-Hispanic/Latino; 8 Asian, non-Hispanic/Latino; 5 Hispanic/Latino; 9 Two or more races, non-Hispanic/Latino), 6 international. Average age 30. 114 applicants, 71% accepted, 57 enrolled. In 2016, 59 master's, 3 doctorates awarded. *Application deadline:* For spring admission, 1/1 priority date for international students. Application fee: $60. *Expenses:*

Tuition, state resident: full-time $12,246; part-time $681 per credit hour. Tuition, nonresident: full-time $25,486; part-time $1417 per credit hour. *Required fees:* $196. Tuition and fees vary according to program and reciprocity agreements. *Financial support:* Application deadline: 6/1; applicants required to submit FAFSA. *Faculty research:* STEM teaching and learning; content literacy for English language learners; social justice in teacher education; adolescent literacy; mathematics teacher development. *Total annual research expenditures:* $1.7 million. *Unit head:* Dr. Ann E. Larson, Dean, College of Education and Human Development, 502-852-6411, Fax: 502-852-1464, E-mail: ann@louisville.edu. *Application contact:* Betty Hampton, Director of Graduate Student Services, 502-852-5597, Fax: 502-852-1465, E-mail: edadvise@louisville.edu.
Website: http://louisville.edu/delphi

University of Maine, Graduate School, College of Education and Human Development, School of Educational Leadership, Higher Education, and Human Development, Orono, ME 04469. Offers educational leadership (M Ed, CAS); higher education (CAS); human development (MS). *Program availability:* Part-time. *Students:* 48 full-time (32 women), 84 part-time (62 women); includes 10 minority (3 Black or African American, non-Hispanic/Latino; 2 American Indian or Alaska Native, non-Hispanic/Latino; 3 Hispanic/Latino; 2 Two or more races, non-Hispanic/Latino), 2 international. Average age 38. 85 applicants, 93% accepted, 61 enrolled. In 2016, 28 master's, 2 doctorates, 10 other advanced degrees awarded. *Degree requirements:* For master's, thesis (for some programs); for doctorate, comprehensive exam, thesis/dissertation. *Entrance requirements:* For master's, GRE General Test, MAT; for doctorate, GRE. Additional exam requirements/recommendations for international students: Required—TOEFL. *Application deadline:* For fall admission, 2/1 priority date for domestic students. Applications are processed on a rolling basis. Application fee: $65. Electronic applications accepted. *Expenses:* Tuition, state resident: full-time $7524; part-time $2508 per credit. Tuition, nonresident: full-time $24,498; part-time $8166 per credit. *Required fees:* $1148; $571 per credit. *Financial support:* In 2016–17, 22 students received support, including 4 teaching assistantships (averaging $14,600 per year); career-related internships or fieldwork, Federal Work-Study, institutionally sponsored loans, tuition waivers (full and partial), and unspecified assistantships also available. Financial award application deadline: 3/1. *Faculty research:* Leadership formation, school organization, collective efficacy and collaborative climate of high schools, change process in high schools, principalship; equity policy; gender and education; doctoral student development, retention, and attrition; faculty development and socialization; sexuality education and curriculum development; family/domestic violence; friendship/kin relationships; early childhood education; support for families with members with disabilities. *Unit head:* Dr. Jim Artesani, Associate Dean of Accreditation and Graduate Affairs, 207-581-4061, Fax: 207-581-3120. *Application contact:* Scott G. Delcourt, Senior Associate Dean of the Graduate School, 207-581-3291, Fax: 207-581-3232, E-mail: graduate@maine.edu.
Website: http://www.umaine.edu/edhd/

University of Manitoba, Faculty of Graduate Studies, Faculty of Education, Department of Educational Administration, Foundations and Psychology, Winnipeg, MB R3T 2N2, Canada. Offers adult and post-secondary education (M Ed); educational administration (M Ed); guidance and counseling (M Ed); inclusive special education (M Ed); social foundations of education (M Ed). *Degree requirements:* For master's, thesis or alternative.

University of Mary Hardin-Baylor, Graduate Studies in Education, Belton, TX 76513. Offers curriculum and instruction (M Ed); educational administration (M Ed, Ed D), including higher education (Ed D), leadership in nursing education (Ed D), P-12 (Ed D). *Program availability:* Part-time, evening/weekend. *Faculty:* 15 full-time (11 women), 9 part-time/adjunct (5 women). *Students:* 55 full-time (40 women), 79 part-time (60 women); includes 50 minority (29 Black or African American, non-Hispanic/Latino; 1 Asian, non-Hispanic/Latino; 18 Hispanic/Latino; 2 Two or more races, non-Hispanic/Latino), 3 international. Average age 38. 20 applicants, 95% accepted, 19 enrolled. In 2016, 23 master's, 19 doctorates awarded. *Degree requirements:* For master's, comprehensive exam; for doctorate, thesis/dissertation. *Entrance requirements:* For master's, minimum GPA of 3.0, interview; for doctorate, minimum GPA of 3.5, interview, essay, resume, employment verification, 3 letters of recommendation. Additional exam requirements/recommendations for international students: Required—TOEFL (minimum score 60 iBT), IELTS (minimum score 4.5). *Application deadline:* For fall admission, 6/1 for domestic students, 4/30 priority date for international students; for spring admission, 11/1 for domestic students, 9/30 priority date for international students. Applications are processed on a rolling basis. Application fee: $35 ($135 for international students). Electronic applications accepted. *Expenses:* $885 per credit hour. *Financial support:* In 2016–17, 99 students received support. Federal Work-Study and scholarships for some active duty military personnel available. Support available to part-time students. Financial award application deadline: 6/1; financial award applicants required to submit FAFSA. *Faculty research:* Motivational orientation of preservice teachers. *Unit head:* Dr. Craig Hammonds, Director, Graduate Programs in Education, 254-295-4189, E-mail: rhammonds@umhb.edu. *Application contact:* Sharon Aguilera, Assistant Director, Graduate Admissions, 254-295-4835, Fax: 254-295-5038, E-mail: saguilera@umhb.edu.
Website: http://graduate.umhb.edu/education/

University of Massachusetts Amherst, Graduate School, College of Education, Program in Education, Amherst, MA 01003. Offers bilingual, English as a second language, and multicultural education (M Ed, Ed S); child study and early education (M Ed); children, families and schools (Ed D, Ed S); early childhood and elementary teacher education (M Ed); educational leadership (M Ed); educational policy and leadership (Ed D); higher education (M Ed); international education (M Ed); language, literacy and culture (Ed D); learning, media and technology (M Ed, Ed S); mathematics, science, and learning technologies (Ed D); reading and writing (M Ed); research, educational measurement and psychometrics (Ed D); school counselor education (M Ed, Ed S); school psychology (Ed S); science education (Ed S); secondary teacher education (M Ed); social justice education (M Ed, Ed D, Ed S); special education (M Ed, Ed D, Ed S); teacher education and school improvement (Ed D, Ed S). *Accreditation:* NCATE. *Program availability:* Part-time, online learning. Terminal master's awarded for partial completion of doctoral program. *Degree requirements:* For doctorate, comprehensive exam, thesis/dissertation. *Entrance requirements:* Additional exam requirements/recommendations for international students: Required—TOEFL (minimum score 550 paper-based; 80 iBT), IELTS (minimum score 6.5). Electronic applications accepted.

University of Massachusetts Amherst, Graduate School, Interdisciplinary Programs, Dual Degree Program in Education and Public Policy and Administration, Amherst, MA 01003. Offers MPPA/M Ed. *Entrance requirements:* Additional exam requirements/recommendations for international students: Required—TOEFL (minimum score 550 paper-based; 80 iBT), IELTS (minimum score 6.5). Electronic applications accepted.

University of Massachusetts Boston, College of Education and Human Development, Program in Higher Education, Boston, MA 02125-3393. Offers Ed D, PhD. *Expenses:* Tuition, state resident: full-time $16,863. Tuition, nonresident: full-time $32,913. *Required fees:* $177.

University of Memphis, Graduate School, College of Education, Department of Leadership, Memphis, TN 38152. Offers adult education (Ed D); community college teaching and leadership (Graduate Certificate); community education (Ed D); educational leadership (Ed D); higher education (Ed D); leadership (MS); policy studies (Ed D); school administration and supervision (MS); student personnel (MS). *Accreditation:* NCATE. *Program availability:* Part-time, evening/weekend, online learning. *Faculty:* 8 full-time (4 women), 5 part-time/adjunct (2 women). *Students:* 20 full-time (12 women), 155 part-time (99 women); includes 84 minority (75 Black or African American, non-Hispanic/Latino; 1 Asian, non-Hispanic/Latino; 4 Hispanic/Latino; 4 Two or more races, non-Hispanic/Latino), 2 international. Average age 40. 59 applicants, 92% accepted, 49 enrolled. In 2016, 11 master's, 14 doctorates, 3 other advanced degrees awarded. *Degree requirements:* For master's, comprehensive exam, thesis optional; for doctorate, comprehensive exam, thesis/dissertation. *Entrance requirements:* For master's, GRE, resume, letters of reference, statement of professional goals, current teacher certification, sample work, interview; for doctorate, GRE, resume, letters of reference, statement of professional goals, interview. Additional exam requirements/recommendations for international students: Required—TOEFL (minimum score 550 paper-based; 79 iBT). *Application deadline:* For fall admission, 6/15 for domestic students; for spring admission, 9/15 for domestic students; for summer admission, 2/15 for domestic students. Application fee: $35 ($60 for international students). Electronic applications accepted. *Expenses:* $5,231.50 per semester full-time in-state, $9,623.50 full-time out-of-state. *Financial support:* In 2016–17, 70 students received support, including 3 research assistantships with full tuition reimbursements available (averaging $16,800 per year); teaching assistantships, Federal Work-Study, scholarships/grants, and unspecified assistantships also available. Financial award application deadline: 2/1; financial award applicants required to submit FAFSA. *Faculty research:* School improvement, social justice, online learning, adult learning, diversity. *Unit head:* Dr. Reginald Green, Interim Chair, 901-678-3445, E-mail: rlgreen1@memphis.edu.
Website: http://www.memphis.edu/lead

University of Miami, Graduate School, School of Education and Human Development, Department of Educational and Psychological Studies, Program in Higher Education Administration, Coral Gables, FL 33124. Offers enrollment management (MS Ed, Certificate); higher education leadership (Ed D); student life and development (MS Ed, Certificate). *Program availability:* Part-time, evening/weekend. *Faculty:* 2 full-time (1 woman), 9 part-time/adjunct (3 women). *Students:* 47 full-time (28 women), 24 part-time (16 women); includes 45 minority (9 Black or African American, non-Hispanic/Latino; 1 American Indian or Alaska Native, non-Hispanic/Latino; 2 Asian, non-Hispanic/Latino; 31 Hispanic/Latino; 2 Two or more races, non-Hispanic/Latino), 6 international. Average age 32. 37 applicants, 84% accepted, 19 enrolled. In 2016, 9 master's, 6 doctorates, 3 Certificates awarded. Terminal master's awarded for partial completion of doctoral program. *Degree requirements:* For master's, comprehensive exam; for doctorate, thesis/dissertation, qualifying exam. *Entrance requirements:* For master's and doctorate, GRE General Test. Additional exam requirements/recommendations for international students: Required—TOEFL (minimum score 550 paper-based; 80 iBT); Recommended—IELTS (minimum score 6.5). *Application deadline:* Applications are processed on a rolling basis. Application fee: $65. Electronic applications accepted. *Financial support:* Institutionally sponsored loans, scholarships/grants, health care benefits, and tuition waivers (full and partial) available. Support available to part-time students. Financial award application deadline: 3/1; financial award applicants required to submit FAFSA. *Unit head:* Dr. Carol Anne Phekoo, Associate Professor of Professional Practice/Program Director, 305-284-5013, E-mail: cphekoo@miami.edu. *Application contact:* Lois Heffernan, Graduate Admissions Coordinator, 305-284-2167, Fax: 305-284-9395, E-mail: lheffernan@miami.edu.
Website: http://www.education.miami.edu

University of Minnesota, Twin Cities Campus, Graduate School, College of Education and Human Development, Department of Organizational Leadership, Policy and Development, Program in Higher Education, Minneapolis, MN 55455-0213. Offers higher education (MA, PhD); multicultural college teaching and learning (MA). *Students:* 50 full-time (37 women), 62 part-time (35 women); includes 27 minority (8 Black or African American, non-Hispanic/Latino; 1 American Indian or Alaska Native, non-Hispanic/Latino; 7 Asian, non-Hispanic/Latino; 7 Hispanic/Latino; 4 Two or more races, non-Hispanic/Latino), 2 international. Average age 37. 66 applicants, 50% accepted, 33 enrolled. In 2016, 18 master's, 16 doctorates awarded. Application fee: $75 ($95 for international students). *Unit head:* Dr. Heidi Barajas, Chair, 612-625-4823, E-mail: hbarajas@umn.edu. *Application contact:* Dr. Jeremy J. Hernandez, Director of Graduate Studies, 612-626-9377, E-mail: herna220@umn.edu.
Website: http://www.cehd.umn.edu/olpd/grad-programs/HiEd/

University of Missouri, Office of Research and Graduate Studies, College of Education, Department of Educational Leadership and Policy Analysis, Columbia, MO 65211. Offers education administration (M Ed, MA, Ed D, PhD, Ed S); higher and adult education (M Ed, MA, Ed D, PhD, Ed S). *Program availability:* Part-time. *Faculty:* 14 full-time (9 women), 1 part-time/adjunct (0 women). *Students:* 185 full-time (105 women), 143 part-time (86 women). *Degree requirements:* For doctorate, variable foreign language requirement, comprehensive exam (for some programs), thesis/dissertation. *Entrance requirements:* For master's, doctorate, and Ed S, minimum GPA of 3.0. Additional exam requirements/recommendations for international students: Required—TOEFL (minimum score 500 paper-based; 61 iBT), IELTS (minimum score 5.5). *Application deadline:* For fall admission, 1/15 priority date for domestic and international students; for winter admission, 9/15 priority date for domestic and international students; for spring admission, 10/15 for domestic students. Applications are processed on a rolling basis. Application fee: $75 ($90 for international students). Electronic applications accepted. *Expenses:* Tuition, state resident: full-time $6347; part-time $352.60 per credit hour. Tuition, nonresident: full-time $17,379; part-time $965.50 per credit hour. *Required fees:* $1035. Tuition and fees vary according to course load, campus/location and program. *Financial support:* Fellowships with full tuition reimbursements, research assistantships with full tuition reimbursements, teaching assistantships with full tuition reimbursements, institutionally sponsored loans, scholarships/grants, health care benefits, and unspecified assistantships available.
Website: http://elpa.missouri.edu/

University of Missouri–Kansas City, School of Education, Kansas City, MO 64110-2499. Offers administration (Ed D); counseling and guidance (MA, Ed S), including mental health counseling (Ed S), school counseling (Ed S); counseling psychology (PhD); curriculum and instruction (MA, Ed S), including language and literacy (Ed S); education (PhD), including higher education administration, PK-12 education administration; educational administration (MA, Ed S), including advanced principal (Ed S), beginning principal (Ed S), district-level administration (Ed S); reading education (MA); special education (MA). PhD in education offered through the School of Graduate Studies. *Accreditation:* NCATE. *Program availability:* Part-time, evening/weekend. *Faculty:* 33 full-time (26 women), 51 part-time/adjunct (39 women). *Students:* 136 full-time (103 women), 275 part-time (194 women); includes 110 minority (71 Black or African American, non-Hispanic/Latino; 3 American Indian or Alaska Native, non-Hispanic/Latino; 8 Asian, non-Hispanic/Latino; 22 Hispanic/Latino; 6 Two or more races, non-Hispanic/Latino), 20 international. Average age 32. 324 applicants, 45% accepted,

108 enrolled. In 2016, 152 master's, 13 doctorates, 50 other advanced degrees awarded. *Degree requirements:* For doctorate, thesis/dissertation, internship, practicum. *Entrance requirements:* For master's, GRE, minimum GPA of 2.75, 2 letters of reference, written statement of purpose; for doctorate, GRE, minimum GPA of 3.0; for Ed S, minimum GPA of 3.0. Additional exam requirements/recommendations for international students: Required—TOEFL (minimum score 550 paper-based; 80 iBT). *Application deadline:* For fall admission, 4/1 priority date for domestic and international students; for spring admission, 11/1 priority date for domestic and international students. Applications are processed on a rolling basis. Application fee: $45 ($50 for international students). *Financial support:* In 2016–17, 12 research assistantships with partial tuition reimbursements (averaging $12,476 per year) were awarded; career-related internships or fieldwork, Federal Work-Study, institutionally sponsored loans, and tuition waivers (full and partial) also available. Support available to part-time students. Financial award application deadline: 3/1; financial award applicants required to submit FAFSA. *Faculty research:* Urban education, inquiry-based field study, theories of counseling and psychotherapy, school literacy, educational technology. *Unit head:* Justin Perry, Dean, 816-235-5663, Fax: 816-235-5270, E-mail: education@umkc.edu.
Website: http://education.umkc.edu

University of Missouri–St. Louis, College of Education, Department of Education Sciences and Professional Programs, St. Louis, MO 63121. Offers adult and higher education (M Ed); educational leadership and policy studies (PhD); educational psychology (M Ed), including character and citizenship education, research and program evaluation; program evaluation (Certificate); school psychology (Ed S). *Faculty:* 36 full-time (25 women), 53 part-time/adjunct (40 women). *Students:* 47 full-time (34 women), 247 part-time (175 women); includes 107 minority (86 Black or African American, non-Hispanic/Latino; 2 American Indian or Alaska Native, non-Hispanic/Latino; 5 Asian, non-Hispanic/Latino; 10 Hispanic/Latino; 4 Two or more races, non-Hispanic/Latino), 7 international. 106 applicants, 92% accepted, 70 enrolled. *Degree requirements:* For other advanced degree, comprehensive exam, thesis or alternative, internship. *Entrance requirements:* For degree, GRE General Test, 2-4 letters of recommendation, personal interview. Additional exam requirements/recommendations for international students: Required—IELTS (minimum score 6.5); Recommended—TOEFL (minimum score 550 paper-based; 79 iBT). *Application deadline:* For fall admission, 2/15 priority date for domestic students, 2/15 for international students. Application fee: $50 ($40 for international students). Electronic applications accepted. *Financial support:* Application deadline: 4/1; applicants required to submit FAFSA. *Faculty research:* Child/adolescent psychology, quantitative and qualitative methodology, evaluation processes, measurement and assessment. *Unit head:* Dr. Donald Gouwens, Chairperson, 314-516-4773, Fax: 314-516-5784, E-mail: gouwensd@umsl.edu. *Application contact:* 314-516-5458, Fax: 314-516-6996, E-mail: gradadm@umsl.edu.
Website: https://coe.umsl.edu/dept/espp.html

University of Nevada, Las Vegas, Graduate College, College of Education, Department of Educational Psychology and Higher Education, Las Vegas, NV 89154-3002. Offers chief diversity officer in higher education (Certificate); college sport leadership (Certificate); educational psychology (M Ed, MS, PhD, Ed S); higher education (M Ed, PhD, Certificate); psychology/learning and technology (PhD), including learning and technology; workforce development/educational leadership (PhD); PhD/JD. *Program availability:* Part-time, evening/weekend, 100% online, blended/hybrid learning. *Faculty:* 20 full-time (14 women), 5 part-time/adjunct (3 women). *Students:* 74 full-time (55 women), 100 part-time (69 women); includes 60 minority (17 Black or African American, non-Hispanic/Latino; 11 Asian, non-Hispanic/Latino; 26 Hispanic/Latino; 6 Two or more races, non-Hispanic/Latino), 5 international. Average age 36. 121 applicants, 58% accepted, 46 enrolled. In 2016, 22 master's, 14 doctorates, 8 other advanced degrees awarded. *Degree requirements:* For master's, comprehensive exam (for some programs), thesis (for some programs); for doctorate, comprehensive exam, thesis/dissertation. *Entrance requirements:* For master's, GRE General Test or GMAT (for some programs), letters of recommendation; writing sample; bachelor's degree; for doctorate, GMAT or GRE General Test, writing exam; for other advanced degree, GRE General Test (for some programs). Additional exam requirements/recommendations for international students: Required—TOEFL (minimum score 550 paper-based; 80 iBT), IELTS (minimum score 7). *Application deadline:* For fall admission, 3/15 for domestic students, 5/1 for international students. Application fee: $60 ($95 for international students). Electronic applications accepted. *Expenses:* $269.25 per credit, $792 per 3-credit course; $9,634 per year resident; $23,274 per year non-resident; $7,094 fees non-resident (7 credits or more); $1,307 annual health insurance fee. *Financial support:* In 2016–17, 24 research assistantships with partial tuition reimbursements (averaging $14,790 per year), 21 teaching assistantships with partial tuition reimbursements (averaging $15,631 per year) were awarded; institutionally sponsored loans, scholarships/grants, health care benefits, and unspecified assistantships also available. Financial award application deadline: 3/15. *Faculty research:* Innovation and change in educational settings; educational policy, finance, and marketing; psycho-educational assessment; student retention, persistence, development, language, and culture; statistical modeling, program evaluation, and quantitative and qualitative research methods. *Total annual research expenditures:* $158,780. *Unit head:* Dr. LeAnn Putney, Chair/Professor, 702-895-4879, Fax: 702-895-1658, E-mail: leann.putney@unlv.edu. *Application contact:* Dr. Steve McCafferty, Graduate Coordinator, 702-895-3245, Fax: 702-895-1658, E-mail: mccaffes@unlv.nevada.edu.
Website: http://education.unlv.edu/ephe/

University of New Hampshire, Graduate School, Interdisciplinary Programs, Program in College Teaching, Durham, NH 03824. Offers Postbaccalaureate Certificate. Program offered in summer only. *Program availability:* Part-time. *Entrance requirements:* Additional exam requirements/recommendations for international students: Required—TOEFL (minimum score 550 paper-based; 80 iBT). *Application deadline:* For fall admission, 6/1 priority date for domestic students, 4/1 for international students; for spring admission, 12/1 for domestic students. Applications are processed on a rolling basis. Application fee: $65. Electronic applications accepted. *Financial support:* Fellowships, research assistantships, and teaching assistantships available. Financial award application deadline: 2/15. *Unit head:* Cair J. Moorhead, Interim Dean, 603-862-3007. *Application contact:* Dovev Levine, 603-862-2234, E-mail: college.teaching@unh.edu.
Website: http://www.unh.edu/cetl/certificate/

University of New Mexico, School of Medicine, Program in University Science Teaching, Albuquerque, NM 87131-2039. Offers Certificate. In 2016, 1 Certificate awarded. *Unit head:* Dr. Sherry Rogers, Program Director, 505-272-0007, E-mail: srogers@salud.unm.edu. *Application contact:* Dr. Angela Wandinger-Ness, Coordinator, 505-272-1459, Fax: 505-272-8738, E-mail: awandinger@salud.unm.edu.

The University of North Carolina at Greensboro, Graduate School, School of Education, Department of Teacher Education and Higher Education, Program in Curriculum and Teaching, Greensboro, NC 27412-5001. Offers higher education (PhD); teacher education and development (PhD). *Accreditation:* NCATE. *Degree requirements:* For doctorate, comprehensive exam, thesis/dissertation. *Entrance requirements:* For doctorate, GRE General Test. Additional exam requirements/recommendations for international students: Required—TOEFL. Electronic applications accepted.

The University of North Carolina Wilmington, Watson College of Education, Department of Educational Leadership, Wilmington, NC 28403-3297. Offers curriculum, instruction and supervision (M Ed); educational leadership and administration (Ed D), including curriculum and instruction; higher education (M Ed); school administration (MSA), including school administration. *Program availability:* Part-time. *Faculty:* 25 full-time (14 women), 5 part-time/adjunct (3 women). *Students:* 49 full-time (31 women), 151 part-time (106 women); includes 55 minority (42 Black or African American, non-Hispanic/Latino; 7 American Indian or Alaska Native, non-Hispanic/Latino; 3 Asian, non-Hispanic/Latino; 1 Hispanic/Latino; 1 Native Hawaiian or other Pacific Islander, non-Hispanic/Latino; 1 Two or more races, non-Hispanic/Latino), 1 international. Average age 36. 113 applicants, 70% accepted, 57 enrolled. In 2016, 32 master's, 19 doctorates awarded. *Degree requirements:* For master's, comprehensive exam, thesis or alternative, e-portfolio defense; for doctorate, comprehensive exam, thesis/dissertation. *Entrance requirements:* For master's, GRE General Test, MAT, minimum B average in undergraduate work, 3 letters of recommendation, statement of interest, NC Class A teacher licensure in related field, minimum of 3 years' teaching experience; for doctorate, GRE, statement of interest, master's degree in education field, 3 years of leadership experience, minimum GPA of 3.0 in undergraduate and graduate work. Additional exam requirements/recommendations for international students: Required—TOEFL (minimum score 79 iBT), IELTS (minimum score 6.5). *Application deadline:* For fall admission, 5/15 for domestic students; for spring admission, 10/15 for domestic students; for summer admission, 3/15 for domestic students. Applications are processed on a rolling basis. Application fee: $60. Electronic applications accepted. *Expenses:* Contact institution. *Financial support:* Scholarships/grants and unspecified assistantships available. Support available to part-time students. Financial award application deadline: 3/15; financial award applicants required to submit FAFSA. *Unit head:* Dr. Tamara Walser, Interim Chair, 910-962-2290, Fax: 910-962-3609, E-mail: walsert@uncw.edu. *Application contact:* Dr. William Sterrett, Graduate Program Coordinator, 910-962-7995, E-mail: stewettw@uncw.edu.
Website: http://uncw.edu/ed/el/

University of Northern Colorado, Graduate School, College of Education and Behavioral Sciences, Department of Leadership, Policy and Development: Higher Education and P-12 Education, Program in Higher Education and Student Affairs Leadership, Greeley, CO 80639. Offers MA, PhD. *Program availability:* Part-time. *Entrance requirements:* For doctorate, GRE General Test, transcripts, 3 letters of recommendation. *Application deadline:* Applications are processed on a rolling basis. Application fee: $50 ($60 for international students). Electronic applications accepted. *Financial support:* Research assistantships and teaching assistantships available. Financial award application deadline: 3/1; financial award applicants required to submit FAFSA. *Unit head:* Katrina Rodriguez, Program Coordinator, 970-351-2861, E-mail: hesal@unco.edu. *Application contact:* Linda Sisson, Graduate Student Admission Coordinator, 970-351-1807, Fax: 970-351-2371, E-mail: linda.sisson@unco.edu.
Website: http://www.unco.edu/cebs/HESAL/contact.htm

University of Northern Iowa, Graduate College, College of Education, Department of Educational Leadership and Postsecondary Education, MA Program in Postsecondary Education: Student Affairs, Cedar Falls, IA 50614. Offers MA. *Degree requirements:* For master's, comprehensive exam, thesis or alternative. *Entrance requirements:* For master's, minimum GPA of 3.0. Additional exam requirements/recommendations for international students: Required—TOEFL (minimum score 500 paper-based; 61 iBT). Electronic applications accepted.

University of North Texas, Robert B. Toulouse School of Graduate Studies, Denton, TX 76203-5459. Offers accounting (MS); applied anthropology (MA, MS); applied behavior analysis (Certificate); applied geography (MA); applied technology and performance improvement (M Ed, MS); art education (MA); art history (MA); art museum education (Certificate); arts leadership (Certificate); audiology (Au D); behavior analysis (MS); behavioral science (PhD); biochemistry and molecular biology (MS); biology (MA, MS); biomedical engineering (MS); business analysis (MS); chemistry (MS); clinical health psychology (PhD); communication studies (MA, MS); computer engineering (MS); computer science (MS); counseling (M Ed, MS), including clinical mental health counseling (MS), college and university counseling, elementary school counseling, secondary school counseling; creative writing (MA); criminal justice (MS); curriculum and instruction (M Ed); decision sciences (MBA); design (MA, MFA), including fashion design (MFA), innovation studies, interior design (MFA); early childhood studies (MS); economics (MS); educational leadership (M Ed, Ed D); educational psychology (MS, PhD), including family studies (MS), gifted and talented (MS), human development (MS), learning and cognition (MS), research, measurement and evaluation (MS); electrical engineering (MS); emergency management (MPA); engineering technology (MS); English (MA); English as a second language (MA); environmental science (MS); finance (MBA, MS); financial management (MPA); French (MA); health services management (MBA); higher education (M Ed, Ed D); history (MA, MS); hospitality management (MS); human resources management (MPA); information science (MS); information systems (PhD); information technologies (MBA); interdisciplinary studies (MA, MS); international studies (MA); international sustainable tourism (MS); jazz studies (MM); journalism (MA, MJ, Graduate Certificate), including interactive and virtual digital communication (Graduate Certificate), narrative journalism (Graduate Certificate), public relations (Graduate Certificate); kinesiology (MS); linguistics (MA); local government management (MPA); logistics (PhD); logistics and supply chain management (MBA); long-term care, senior housing, and aging services (MA); management (PhD); marketing (MBA); mathematics (MA, MS); mechanical and energy engineering (MS, PhD); music (MA), including ethnomusicology, music theory, musicology, performance; music composition (PhD); music education (MM Ed, PhD); nonprofit management (MPA); operations and supply chain management (MBA); performance (MM, DMA); philosophy (MA); political science (MA); professional and technical communication (MA); radio, television and film (MA, MFA); rehabilitation counseling (Certificate); sociology (MA); Spanish (MA); special education (M Ed); speech-language pathology (MA); strategic management (MBA); studio art (MFA); teaching (M Ed); MBA/MS. *Program availability:* Part-time, evening/weekend, online learning. Terminal master's awarded for partial completion of doctoral program. *Degree requirements:* For master's, variable foreign language requirement, comprehensive exam (for some programs), thesis (for some programs); for doctorate, variable foreign language requirement, comprehensive exam (for some programs), thesis/dissertation; for other advanced degree, variable foreign language requirement, comprehensive exam (for some programs). *Entrance requirements:* For master's and doctorate, GRE, GMAT. Additional exam requirements/recommendations for international students: Required—TOEFL (minimum score 550 paper-based; 79 iBT). Electronic applications accepted.

University of Oklahoma, Jeannine Rainbolt College of Education, Department of Educational Leadership and Policy Studies, Program in Adult and Higher Education, Norman, OK 73019. Offers adult and higher education (M Ed), including community college administration, higher education administration, institutional research, intercollegiate athletics administration, student affairs, workforce, adult and continuing education. *Accreditation:* NCATE. *Program availability:* Part-time, evening/weekend.

Higher Education

Students: 115 full-time (66 women), 81 part-time (54 women); includes 62 minority (31 Black or African American, non-Hispanic/Latino; 11 American Indian or Alaska Native, non-Hispanic/Latino; 8 Hispanic/Latino; 1 Native Hawaiian or other Pacific Islander, non-Hispanic/Latino; 11 Two or more races, non-Hispanic/Latino), 5 international. Average age 30. 83 applicants, 67% accepted, 43 enrolled. In 2016, 72 degrees awarded. *Degree requirements:* For master's, comprehensive exam, thesis optional. *Entrance requirements:* Additional exam requirements/recommendations for international students: Required—TOEFL (minimum score 79 iBT) or IELTS (minimum score 6.5). *Application deadline:* For fall admission, 2/1 for domestic and international students; for spring admission, 10/1 for domestic and international students; for summer admission, 4/1 for domestic and international students. Application fee: $50 ($100 for international students). Electronic applications accepted. *Expenses:* Tuition, state resident: full-time $4886; part-time $203.60 per credit hour. Tuition, nonresident: full-time $18,989; part-time $791.20 per credit hour. *Required fees:* $3283; $126.25 per credit hour. $126.50 per semester. *Financial support:* In 2016–17, 166 students received support. Fellowships, research assistantships, teaching assistantships, career-related internships or fieldwork, Federal Work-Study, institutionally sponsored loans, scholarships/grants, traineeships, health care benefits, tuition waivers, and unspecified assistantships available. Support available to part-time students. Financial award application deadline: 6/1; financial award applicants required to submit FAFSA. *Faculty research:* Education and social policy; gender and equity; collegiate athletics; higher education and student affairs; adult learning and workforce development. *Unit head:* Doo Hun Lim, Associate Professor, 405-325-7941, E-mail: dhlim@ou.edu.
Website: http://www.ou.edu/education/elps/graduate-programs/adult-and-higher-education-masters.html

University of Oklahoma, Jeannine Rainbolt College of Education, Department of Educational Psychology, Program in Special Education, Norman, OK 73019. Offers applied behavior analysis (M Ed); higher education and community support (PhD); higher education professor (PhD); school instructional leaders (PhD); secondary transition (M Ed). *Accreditation:* NCATE. *Program availability:* Part-time, 100% online, blended/hybrid learning. *Students:* 23 full-time (18 women), 57 part-time (49 women); includes 23 minority (6 Black or African American, non-Hispanic/Latino; 5 American Indian or Alaska Native, non-Hispanic/Latino; 1 Asian, non-Hispanic/Latino; 6 Hispanic/Latino; 5 Two or more races, non-Hispanic/Latino), 4 international. Average age 39. 74 applicants, 42% accepted, 21 enrolled. In 2016, 20 master's, 1 doctorate awarded. Terminal master's awarded for partial completion of doctoral program. *Degree requirements:* For master's, thesis optional; for doctorate, comprehensive exam, thesis/dissertation. *Entrance requirements:* For doctorate, GRE. Additional exam requirements/recommendations for international students: Required—TOEFL (minimum score 79 iBT) or IELTS (minimum score 6.5). *Application deadline:* For fall admission, 2/1 for domestic and international students. Application fee: $50 ($100 for international students). Electronic applications accepted. *Expenses:* Tuition, state resident: full-time $4886; part-time $203.60 per credit hour. Tuition, nonresident: full-time $18,989; part-time $791.20 per credit hour. *Required fees:* $3283; $126.25 per credit hour. $126.50 per semester. *Financial support:* In 2016–17, 44 students received support. Teaching assistantships with full and partial tuition reimbursements available and scholarships/grants available. Financial award application deadline: 6/1; financial award applicants required to submit FAFSA. *Faculty research:* Attitudes toward students with cultural and linguistic diversity; grandparents of students with disabilities; K-12 literacy instruction for struggling readers; behavior management; disability awareness and self-advocacy. *Unit head:* Dr. Nancy E. Marchand-Martella, Chair, Department of Educational Psychology, 405-325-0624, Fax: 405-325-6655, E-mail: nmarchand-martella@ou.edu. *Application contact:* Anna Steele, Graduate Programs Specialist, 405-325-4525, Fax: 405-325-7390, E-mail: jrcoe_gps@ou.edu.
Website: http://www.ou.edu/education/edpy

University of Oklahoma, Jeannine Rainbolt College of Education, Department of General Education, Norman, OK 73019. Offers college teaching (Graduate Certificate). *Program availability:* Part-time, evening/weekend, online learning. *Students:* 3 full-time (all women), 21 part-time (16 women); includes 5 minority (1 Black or African American, non-Hispanic/Latino; 3 American Indian or Alaska Native, non-Hispanic/Latino; 1 Two or more races, non-Hispanic/Latino). Average age 39. 10 applicants, 40% accepted, 3 enrolled. In 2016, 12 Graduate Certificates awarded. *Degree requirements:* For Graduate Certificate, program evaluation class taken during last semester. *Entrance requirements:* Additional exam requirements/recommendations for international students: Required—TOEFL (minimum score 79 iBT) or IELTS (minimum score 6.5). *Application deadline:* For fall admission, 3/15 for domestic and international students; for spring admission, 10/1 for domestic and international students. Application fee: $50 ($100 for international students). Electronic applications accepted. *Expenses:* Tuition, state resident: full-time $4886; part-time $203.60 per credit hour. Tuition, nonresident: full-time $18,989; part-time $791.20 per credit hour. *Required fees:* $3283; $126.25 per credit hour. $126.50 per semester. *Financial support:* Scholarships/grants available. Financial award application deadline: 6/1; financial award applicants required to submit FAFSA. *Faculty research:* Teacher beliefs and efficacy; assessment; motivation and academic engagement; political and moral beliefs; statistics. *Unit head:* Dr. Nancy E. Marchand-Martella, Chair, Department of Educational Psychology, 405-325-5973, Fax: 405-325-6655, E-mail: nmarchand-martella@ou.edu. *Application contact:* Barbara Green, Professor of Education, 405-325-1534, Fax: 405-325-6655, E-mail: barbara@ou.edu.
Website: http://www.ou.edu/education

University of Pennsylvania, Graduate School of Education, Division of Higher Education, Executive Doctorate Program in Higher Education Management, Philadelphia, PA 19104. Offers Ed D. *Program availability:* Evening/weekend. *Students:* 32 full-time (19 women), 20 part-time (15 women); includes 17 minority (9 Black or African American, non-Hispanic/Latino; 1 Asian, non-Hispanic/Latino; 5 Hispanic/Latino; 2 Two or more races, non-Hispanic/Latino). Average age 44. 86 applicants, 31% accepted, 25 enrolled. In 2016, 21 doctorates awarded. *Degree requirements:* For doctorate, comprehensive exam. *Entrance requirements:* For doctorate, bachelor's degree. Additional exam requirements/recommendations for international students: Required—TOEFL, IELTS. *Application deadline:* For summer admission, 3/1 priority date for domestic and international students. Application fee: $75. Electronic applications accepted. *Expenses: Tuition:* Full-time $31,068; part-time $5762 per course. *Required fees:* $3200; $336 per course. Full-time tuition and fees vary according to degree level, program and student level. Part-time tuition and fees vary according to course load, degree level and program. *Faculty research:* Access, choice, and equity in higher education, college finance and affordability, academic governance and leadership. *Unit head:* Eric Kaplan, Director. *Application contact:* Jessica Lundeen, Program Coordinator, 215-573-0588, E-mail: mlundeen@upenn.edu.
Website: http://www2.gse.upenn.edu/execdoc/

University of Pennsylvania, Graduate School of Education, Division of Higher Education, Program in Higher Education, Philadelphia, PA 19104. Offers MS Ed, Ed D, PhD. *Program availability:* Part-time. *Students:* 65 full-time (40 women), 34 part-time (28 women); includes 44 minority (23 Black or African American, non-Hispanic/Latino; 7 Asian, non-Hispanic/Latino; 12 Hispanic/Latino; 2 Two or more races, non-Hispanic/Latino), 2 international. Average age 31. 315 applicants, 50% accepted, 65 enrolled. In 2016, 45 master's, 8 doctorates awarded. *Expenses: Tuition:* Full-time $31,068; part-time $5762 per course. *Required fees:* $3200; $336 per course. Full-time tuition and fees vary according to degree level, program and student level. Part-time tuition and fees vary according to course load, degree level and program.

University of Phoenix–Bay Area Campus, College of Education, San Jose, CA 95134-1805. Offers administration and supervision (MA Ed); adult education and training (MA Ed); early childhood education (MA Ed); education (Ed S); educational leadership (Ed D); elementary teacher education (MA Ed); higher education administration (PhD); secondary teacher education (MA Ed); special education (MA Ed); teacher leadership (MA Ed). *Program availability:* Evening/weekend, online learning. *Degree requirements:* For master's, thesis (for some programs). *Entrance requirements:* For master's, minimum undergraduate GPA of 2.5, 3 years of work experience. Additional exam requirements/recommendations for international students: Required—TOEFL (minimum score 550 paper-based; 79 iBT). Electronic applications accepted.

University of Phoenix–Online Campus, School of Advanced Studies, Phoenix, AZ 85034-7209. Offers business administration (DBA); education (Ed S); educational leadership (Ed D), including curriculum and instruction, education technology, educational leadership; health administration (DHA); higher education administration (PhD); industrial/organizational psychology (PhD); nursing (PhD); organizational leadership (DM), including information systems and technology, organizational leadership. *Program availability:* Evening/weekend, online learning. *Degree requirements:* For doctorate, thesis/dissertation. *Entrance requirements:* Additional exam requirements/recommendations for international students: Required—TOEFL, TOEIC (Test of English as an International Communication), Berlitz Online English Proficiency Exam, PTE, or IELTS. Electronic applications accepted. *Expenses:* Contact institution.

University of Phoenix–Washington D.C. Campus, College of Education, Washington, DC 20001. Offers administration and supervision (MA Ed); adult education and training (MA Ed); computer education (MA Ed); curriculum and instruction (MA Ed, Ed D); early childhood education (MA Ed); education (Ed S); educational leadership (Ed D); educational technology (Ed D); elementary teacher education (MA Ed); English and language arts education (MA Ed); English as a second language (MA Ed); higher education administration (PhD); mathematics education (MA Ed); secondary teacher education (MA Ed); special education (MA Ed); teacher leadership (MA Ed).

University of Pittsburgh, School of Education, Department of Administrative and Policy Studies, Program in Higher Education Management, Pittsburgh, PA 15260. Offers M Ed, Ed D, PhD. *Program availability:* Part-time, evening/weekend. *Degree requirements:* For master's, thesis; for doctorate, thesis/dissertation. *Entrance requirements:* For doctorate, GRE General Test. Additional exam requirements/recommendations for international students: Required—TOEFL (minimum score 80 iBT). Electronic applications accepted. Tuition and fees vary according to program.

University of Puerto Rico, Mayagüez Campus, Graduate Studies, College of Arts and Sciences, Department of Mathematical Sciences, Mayagüez, PR 00681-9000. Offers applied mathematics (MS); pre-college math education (MS); pure mathematics (MS); scientific computing (MS); statistics (MS). *Program availability:* Part-time. *Faculty:* 39 full-time (6 women). *Students:* 62 full-time (18 women), 2 part-time (0 women); includes 37 minority (all Hispanic/Latino), 22 international. Average age 27. 29 applicants, 45% accepted, 11 enrolled. In 2016, 3 master's awarded. *Degree requirements:* For master's, one foreign language, comprehensive exam, thesis. *Entrance requirements:* For master's, undergraduate degree in mathematics or its equivalent. *Application deadline:* For fall admission, 2/15 for domestic and international students; for spring admission, 9/15 for domestic and international students. Applications are processed on a rolling basis. Application fee: $25. Electronic applications accepted. *Expenses: Tuition, area resident:* Full-time $2466. *International tuition:* $7166 full-time. *Required fees:* $210. Tuition and fees vary according to course level, campus/location, program and student level. *Financial support:* In 2016–17, 71 students received support, including 8 research assistantships with full and partial tuition reimbursements available (averaging $2,642 per year), 68 teaching assistantships with full and partial tuition reimbursements available (averaging $4,775 per year); unspecified assistantships also available. *Faculty research:* Automata theory, linear algebra, logic. *Unit head:* Olgamary Rivera, PhD, Director, 787-832-4040 Ext. 3848, Fax: 787-265-5454, E-mail: olgamary.rivera@upr.edu. *Application contact:* Carmen L. Gonzlez, Secretary, 787-832-4040 Ext. 3285, Fax: 787-265-5454, E-mail: carmen.gonzalez23@upr.edu.
Website: http://math.uprm.edu/

University of Rochester, Margaret Warner Graduate School of Education and Human Development, Doctoral Programs in Education, Rochester, NY 14627. Offers counseling (Ed D); educational administration (Ed D); educational policy and theory (PhD); higher education (PhD); human development in educational context (PhD); teaching, curriculum, and change (PhD). *Expenses: Tuition:* Full-time $47,450; part-time $1482 per credit hour. *Required fees:* $528. Tuition and fees vary according to program.

University of Rochester, Margaret Warner Graduate School of Education and Human Development, Master's Program in Higher Education, Rochester, NY 14627. Offers higher education (MS); higher education student affairs (MS). *Expenses: Tuition:* Full-time $47,450; part-time $1482 per credit hour. *Required fees:* $528. Tuition and fees vary according to program.

University of San Diego, School of Leadership and Education Sciences, Department of Leadership Studies, San Diego, CA 92110-2492. Offers higher education leadership (MA); leadership studies (MA, PhD, Certificate); nonprofit leadership and management (MA). *Program availability:* Part-time, evening/weekend. *Faculty:* 11 full-time (5 women), 17 part-time/adjunct (9 women). *Students:* 40 full-time (26 women), 219 part-time (149 women); includes 120 minority (28 Black or African American, non-Hispanic/Latino; 15 Asian, non-Hispanic/Latino; 62 Hispanic/Latino; 2 Native Hawaiian or other Pacific Islander, non-Hispanic/Latino; 13 Two or more races, non-Hispanic/Latino), 21 international. Average age 33. 312 applicants, 75% accepted, 110 enrolled. In 2016, 57 master's, 21 doctorates awarded. *Degree requirements:* For master's, thesis (for some programs), international experience; for doctorate, comprehensive exam, thesis/dissertation, international experience. *Entrance requirements:* For master's, GRE (recommended with GPA less than 3.25), minimum GPA of 3.0, interview; for doctorate, GRE (less than 5 years old), master's degree, minimum GPA of 3.5 (recommended), resume. Additional exam requirements/recommendations for international students: Required—TOEFL (minimum score 580 paper-based; 83 iBT), TWE. Application fee: $45. Electronic applications accepted. *Financial support:* In 2016–17, 186 students received support. Career-related internships or fieldwork, Federal Work-Study, institutionally sponsored loans, unspecified assistantships, and stipends available. Support available to part-time students. Financial award application deadline: 4/1; financial award applicants required to submit FAFSA. *Faculty research:* Higher education administration policy and relations, organizational leadership, nonprofits and philanthropy, student affairs leadership. *Unit head:* Dr. Lea Hubbard, Graduate Program Director, 619-260-7818, E-mail: lhubbard@sandiego.edu. *Application contact:* Monica Mahon, Associate Director of Graduate Admissions, 619-260-4524, Fax: 619-260-4158, E-mail: grads@sandiego.edu.
Website: https://www.sandiego.edu/soles/departments/leadership-studies/

University of South Carolina, The Graduate School, College of Education, Department of Educational Leadership and Policies, Program in Higher Education and Student Affairs, Columbia, SC 29208. Offers M Ed. *Accreditation:* NCATE. *Program availability:* Part-time. *Degree requirements:* For master's, comprehensive exam, thesis (for some programs). *Entrance requirements:* For master's, GRE General Test or MAT, letters of reference. Electronic applications accepted. *Faculty research:* Minorities in higher education, community college transfer problem, federal role in educational research.

The University of South Dakota, Graduate School, School of Education, Division of Educational Administration, Vermillion, SD 57069. Offers educational administration (MA, Ed D, Ed S), including adult and higher education (MA, Ed D), curriculum director, director of special education (Ed D, Ed S), preK-12 principal, school district superintendent. *Accreditation:* NCATE. *Program availability:* Part-time, evening/weekend, 100% online, blended/hybrid learning. *Degree requirements:* For master's and Ed S, comprehensive exam, thesis or alternative; for doctorate, comprehensive exam, thesis/dissertation. *Entrance requirements:* For master's and doctorate, GRE General Test, MAT, minimum GPA of 2.7. Additional exam requirements/recommendations for international students: Required—TOEFL (minimum score 550 paper-based; 79 iBT). Electronic applications accepted.

University of Southern California, Graduate School, Rossier School of Education, Doctor of Education Programs, Los Angeles, CA 90089. Offers educational psychology (Ed D); higher education administration (Ed D); K-12 leadership in urban school settings (Ed D); teacher education in multicultural societies (Ed D). *Program availability:* Part-time, evening/weekend. *Degree requirements:* For doctorate, thesis/dissertation. *Entrance requirements:* For doctorate, GRE. Additional exam requirements/recommendations for international students: Required—TOEFL (minimum score 100 iBT). Electronic applications accepted. *Faculty research:* Data-driven decision-making in K-12 schools and districts; examination of college and university leadership and management in U. S. and Asia; studies in facilitating student learning; organizational change and the role of leaders; leadership, diversity, learning and accountability.

University of Southern California, Graduate School, Rossier School of Education, Doctor of Philosophy in Education Programs, Los Angeles, CA 90089. Offers educational psychology (PhD); higher education administration and policy (PhD); K-12 policy and practice (PhD). *Degree requirements:* For doctorate, thesis/dissertation, 63 units; qualifying exam; dissertation proposal and defense. *Entrance requirements:* For doctorate, GRE. Additional exam requirements/recommendations for international students: Required—TOEFL (minimum score 100 iBT). Electronic applications accepted. *Faculty research:* Diversity in higher education, organizational change, educational psychology, policy and politics of educational reform, economics of education and education policy.

University of Southern Maine, College of Management and Human Service, School of Education and Human Development, Program in Adult Education, Portland, ME 04103. Offers adult and higher education (MS); adult learning (CAS). *Accreditation:* TEAC. *Program availability:* Part-time, evening/weekend, online learning. *Degree requirements:* For master's and CAS, thesis or alternative. *Entrance requirements:* For master's, interview; for CAS, master's degree. Additional exam requirements/recommendations for international students: Required—TOEFL (minimum score 550 paper-based; 79 iBT). Electronic applications accepted. *Faculty research:* Older learners, lifelong learning institutes, teaching and learning in later age.

University of Southern Mississippi, Graduate School, College of Education and Psychology, Department of Educational Research and Administration, Hattiesburg, MS 39406. Offers educational administration (M Ed, Ed D, PhD, Ed S); educational administration and supervision (M Ed); educational studies and research (MS); higher education (Ed D); higher education administration (PhD); higher education: student affairs (M Ed); research, evaluation, statistics, assessment (PhD). *Degree requirements:* For master's and Ed S, comprehensive exam, thesis (for some programs); for doctorate, comprehensive exam, thesis/dissertation. *Entrance requirements:* For master's and doctorate, GRE General Test, minimum GPA of 2.75. Additional exam requirements/recommendations for international students: Required—TOEFL. *Application deadline:* For fall admission, 2/1 for domestic students, 3/1 for international students. Applications are processed on a rolling basis. Application fee: $60. *Expenses: Tuition, area resident:* Full-time $15,708; part-time $437 per credit hour. *Financial support:* Career-related internships or fieldwork, Federal Work-Study, and institutionally sponsored loans available. Financial award application deadline: 3/15; financial award applicants required to submit FAFSA. *Unit head:* Dr. Lilian Hill, Co-Chair, 601-266-4622. *Application contact:* Shonna Breland, Manager of Graduate Admissions, 601-266-6563, Fax: 601-266-5138.
Website: https://www.usm.edu/educational-research-administration

University of South Florida, College of Education, Department of Leadership, Counseling, Adult, Career and Higher Education, Tampa, FL 33620-9951. Offers adult education (MA, Ed D, PhD, Ed S); career and technical education (MA); career and workforce education (PhD); higher education/community college teaching (MA, Ed D, PhD); vocational education (Ed S). *Faculty:* 17 full-time (10 women). *Students:* 137 full-time (96 women), 331 part-time (237 women); includes 170 minority (75 Black or African American, non-Hispanic/Latino; 2 American Indian or Alaska Native, non-Hispanic/Latino; 12 Asian, non-Hispanic/Latino; 71 Hispanic/Latino; 2 Native Hawaiian or other Pacific Islander, non-Hispanic/Latino; 8 Two or more races, non-Hispanic/Latino), 18 international. Average age 35. 175 applicants, 66% accepted, 93 enrolled. In 2016, 111 master's, 22 doctorates, 1 other advanced degree awarded. Application fee: $30. *Expenses:* Tuition, state resident: full-time $7766; part-time $431.43 per credit hour. Tuition, nonresident: full-time $15,789; part-time $877.17 per credit hour. *Required fees:* $37 per term. *Total annual research expenditures:* $545,936. *Unit head:* Dr. Judith Ponticell, Chair, 813-974-4897, Fax: 813-974-5423, E-mail: jponticell@usf.edu.
Website: http://www.coedu.usf.edu/main/departments/ache/ache.html

University of South Florida, Innovative Education, Tampa, FL 33620-9951. Offers adult, career and higher education (Graduate Certificate), including college teaching, leadership in developing human resources, leadership in higher education; Africana studies (Graduate Certificate), including diasporas and health disparities, genocide and human rights; aging studies (Graduate Certificate), including gerontology; art research (Graduate Certificate), including museum studies; business foundations (Graduate Certificate); chemical and biomedical engineering (Graduate Certificate), including materials science and engineering, water, health and sustainability; child and family studies (Graduate Certificate), including positive behavior support; civil and industrial engineering (Graduate Certificate), including transportation systems analysis; community and family health (Graduate Certificate), including maternal and child health, social marketing and public health, violence and injury: prevention and intervention, women's health; criminology (Graduate Certificate), including criminal justice administration; educational measurement and research (Graduate Certificate), including evaluation; English (Graduate Certificate), including comparative literary studies, creative writing, professional and technical communication; entrepreneurship (Graduate Certificate); environmental health (Graduate Certificate), including safety management; epidemiology and biostatistics (Graduate Certificate), including applied biostatistics, biostatistics, concepts and tools of epidemiology, epidemiology, epidemiology of infectious diseases; geography, environment and planning (Graduate Certificate), including community development, environmental policy and management, geographical information systems; geology (Graduate Certificate), including hydrogeology; global health (Graduate Certificate), including disaster management, global health and Latin American and Caribbean studies, global health practice, humanitarian assistance, infection control; government and international affairs (Graduate Certificate), including Cuban studies, globalization studies; health policy and management (Graduate Certificate), including health management and leadership, public health policy and programs; hearing specialist: early intervention (Graduate Certificate); industrial and management systems engineering (Graduate Certificate), including systems engineering, technology management; information studies (Graduate Certificate), including school library media specialist; information systems/decision sciences (Graduate Certificate), including analytics and business intelligence; instructional technology (Graduate Certificate), including distance education, Florida digital/virtual educator, instructional design, multimedia design, Web design; internal medicine, bioethics and medical humanities (Graduate Certificate), including biomedical ethics; Latin American and Caribbean studies (Graduate Certificate); mass communications (Graduate Certificate), including multimedia journalism; mathematics and statistics (Graduate Certificate), including mathematics; medicine (Graduate Certificate), including aging and neuroscience, bioinformatics, biotechnology, brain fitness and memory management, clinical investigation, health informatics, health sciences, integrative weight management, intellectual property, medicine and gender, metabolic and nutritional medicine, metabolic cardiology, pharmacy sciences; national and competitive intelligence (Graduate Certificate); psychological and social foundations (Graduate Certificate), including career counseling, college teaching, diversity in education, mental health counseling, school counseling; public affairs (Graduate Certificate), including nonprofit management, [illegible] management, research administration; public health (Graduate Certificate), including environmental health, health equity, public health generalist, translational research in adolescent behavioral health; public health practices (Graduate Certificate), including planning for healthy communities; rehabilitation and mental health counseling (Graduate Certificate), including integrative mental health care, marriage and family therapy, rehabilitation technology; secondary education (Graduate Certificate), including ESOL, foreign language education: culture and content, foreign language education: professional; social work (Graduate Certificate), including geriatric social work/clinical gerontology; special education (Graduate Certificate), including autism spectrum disorder, disabilities education: severe/profound; world languages (Graduate Certificate), including teaching English as a second language (TESL) or foreign language. *Expenses:* Tuition, state resident: full-time $7766; part-time $431.43 per credit hour. Tuition, nonresident: full-time $15,789; part-time $877.17 per credit hour. *Required fees:* $37 per term. *Unit head:* Kathy Barnes, Interdisciplinary Programs Coordinator, 813-974-8031, Fax: 813-974-7061, E-mail: barnesk@usf.edu. *Application contact:* Karen Tylinski, Metro Initiatives, 813-974-9943, Fax: 813-974-7061, E-mail: ktylinsk@usf.edu.
Website: http://www.usf.edu/innovative-education/

The University of Texas at Arlington, Graduate School, College of Education, Department of Educational Leadership and Policy Studies, Arlington, TX 76019. Offers educational leadership (PhD); higher education (M Ed); principal certification (M Ed). *Program availability:* Part-time, evening/weekend, online learning. *Degree requirements:* For master's, 2 field-based practica; for doctorate, comprehensive exam, thesis/dissertation, 2 research-based practica. *Entrance requirements:* For master's, GRE, 3 references forms, minimum undergraduate GPA of 3.0 in the last 60 hours of course work; for doctorate, GRE, resume, statement of intent, 3 reference forms, applicable master's degree. Application fee: $50. *Financial support:* Fellowships and research assistantships available. Financial award applicants required to submit FAFSA. *Faculty research:* Lived realities of students of color in K-16 contexts, K-16 faculty, K-16 policy and law, K-16 student access, K-16 student success. *Unit head:* Dr. Adrienne E. Hyle, Chair, 817-272-2841, Fax: 817-272-2127, E-mail: ahyle@uta.edu. *Application contact:* Paige Cordor, Graduate Advisor, 817-272-5051, Fax: 817-272-2127, E-mail: paigec@uta.edu.
Website: http://www.uta.edu/coehp/educleadership/

The University of Texas at San Antonio, College of Education and Human Development, Department of Educational Leadership and Policy Studies, San Antonio, TX 78249-0617. Offers educational leadership (Ed D); educational leadership and policy studies (M Ed), including educational leadership, higher education administration. *Program availability:* Part-time. *Faculty:* 19 full-time (6 women), 15 part-time/adjunct (7 women). *Students:* 64 full-time (46 women), 274 part-time (189 women); includes 220 minority (36 Black or African American, non-Hispanic/Latino; 2 Asian, non-Hispanic/Latino; 176 Hispanic/Latino; 6 Two or more races, non-Hispanic/Latino), 3 international. Average age 36. 103 applicants, 79% accepted, 54 enrolled. In 2016, 95 master's, 21 doctorates awarded. *Degree requirements:* For master's, comprehensive exam, thesis or alternative; for doctorate, comprehensive exam, thesis/dissertation. *Entrance requirements:* For master's, transcripts, statement of purpose, resume or curriculum vitae; for doctorate, GRE General Test, minimum GPA of 3.5 in a master's program, resume, three letters of recommendation, statement of purpose. Additional exam requirements/recommendations for international students: Required—TOEFL (minimum score 550 paper-based; 79 iBT), IELTS (minimum score 6.5). *Application deadline:* For fall admission, 7/1 for domestic students, 4/1 for international students; for spring admission, 11/1 for domestic students, 9/1 for international students. Application fee: $45 ($80 for international students). *Financial support:* In 2016–17, 6 students received support, including 6 fellowships (averaging $41,666 per year). Financial award application deadline: 2/1. *Faculty research:* Urban and international school leadership, student success, college access, higher education policy, multiculturalism, minority student achievement. *Total annual research expenditures:* $9,119. *Unit head:* Dr. Enrique Aleman, Department Chair, 210-458-5411, E-mail: enrique.aleman@utsa.edu. *Application contact:* Elisha Reynolds, Student Development Specialist, 210-458-6620, Fax: 210-458-5848, E-mail: elisha.reynolds@utsa.edu.
Website: http://education.utsa.edu/educational_leadership_and_policy_studies/

The University of Toledo, College of Graduate Studies, College of Social Justice and Human Service, Department of School Psychology, Higher Education and Counselor Education, Toledo, OH 43606-3390. Offers counselor education (MA, PhD); higher education (ME, PhD, Certificate); school psychology (MA, Ed S). *Program availability:* Part-time. *Degree requirements:* For master's, comprehensive exam, thesis or alternative; for doctorate, comprehensive exam, thesis/dissertation; for other advanced degree, thesis optional. *Entrance requirements:* For master's, doctorate, and other advanced degree, minimum cumulative GPA of 2.7 for all previous academic work, letters of recommendation. Additional exam requirements/recommendations for international students: Required—TOEFL (minimum score 550 paper-based; 80 iBT). Electronic applications accepted.

University of Utah, Graduate School, College of Education, Department of Educational Leadership and Policy, Salt Lake City, UT 84084. Offers educational leadership and policy (Ed D, PhD), including higher education administration (Ed D), K-12 (Ed D); K-12 school administration (M Ed); K-12 teacher instructional leadership (M Ed); student affairs (M Ed); MPA/PhD. *Program availability:* Part-time, evening/weekend. *Faculty:* 11 full-time (7 women), 3 part-time/adjunct (all women). *Students:* 79 full-time (47 women), 134 part-time (95 women); includes 63 minority (7 Black or African American, non-Hispanic/Latino; 2 American Indian or Alaska Native, non-Hispanic/Latino; 7 Asian, non-

Hispanic/Latino; 38 Hispanic/Latino; 9 Two or more races, non-Hispanic/Latino), 1 international. Average age 35. 154 applicants, 67% accepted, 86 enrolled. In 2016, 42 master's, 8 doctorates awarded. *Degree requirements:* For master's, comprehensive exam (for some programs), internship, capstone; for doctorate, thesis/dissertation, qualifying exam. *Entrance requirements:* For master's, minimum undergraduate GPA of 3.0, valid bachelor's degree, 3 years' teaching or leadership experience, Level 1 or 2 UT educator's license (for K-12 programs only); for doctorate, GRE General Test (taken with five years of applying), minimum undergraduate GPA of 3.0, valid master's degree. Additional exam requirements/recommendations for international students: Required—TOEFL (minimum score 500 paper-based). *Application deadline:* For fall admission, 1/15 priority date for domestic and international students; for winter admission, 2/1 for domestic and international students; for spring admission, 11/1 priority date for domestic and international students; for summer admission, 3/1 priority date for domestic and international students. Applications are processed on a rolling basis. Application fee: $55 ($65 for international students). Electronic applications accepted. *Expenses:* Contact institution. *Financial support:* In 2016–17, 47 students received support, including 1 fellowship with full tuition reimbursement available (averaging $14,500 per year), 2 research assistantships with full tuition reimbursements available (averaging $15,000 per year), 6 teaching assistantships with full tuition reimbursements available (averaging $15,000 per year); career-related internships or fieldwork, scholarships/grants, health care benefits, and unspecified assistantships also available. Support available to part-time students. Financial award application deadline: 3/1; financial award applicants required to submit FAFSA. *Faculty research:* Education accountability, college student diversity, K-12 educational administration and school leadership, student affairs, higher education. *Unit head:* Dr. Gerardo Lopez, Chair, 801-581-6627, Fax: 801-585-6756, E-mail: gerardo.lopez@utah.edu. *Application contact:* Marilynn S. Howard, Academic Coordinator, 801-581-6714, Fax: 801-585-6756, E-mail: marilynn.howard@utah.edu.
Website: http://elp.utah.edu/

University of Virginia, Curry School of Education, Department of Leadership, Foundations and Policy, Program in Higher Education, Charlottesville, VA 22903. Offers higher education (Ed S); student affairs practice (M Ed). *Students:* 49 full-time (32 women), 21 part-time (9 women); includes 19 minority (10 Black or African American, non-Hispanic/Latino; 1 Asian, non-Hispanic/Latino; 6 Hispanic/Latino; 2 Two or more races, non-Hispanic/Latino), 1 international. Average age 27. 17 applicants, 76% accepted, 13 enrolled. In 2016, 46 master's, 5 doctorates awarded. *Entrance requirements:* For master's, doctorate, and Ed S, GRE General Test, 2 letters of recommendation. Additional exam requirements/recommendations for international students: Required—TOEFL (minimum score 600 paper-based; 90 iBT), IELTS (minimum score 7). *Application deadline:* Applications are processed on a rolling basis. Application fee: $60. Electronic applications accepted. *Expenses:* Tuition, state resident: full-time $15,026; part-time $834 per credit hour. Tuition, nonresident: full-time $25,168; part-time $1378 per credit hour. *Required fees:* $2654. *Financial support:* Fellowships, research assistantships, and teaching assistantships available. Financial award applicants required to submit FAFSA. *Unit head:* Brian Pusser, Program Coordinator, 434-924-7731, E-mail: highered@virginia.edu. *Application contact:* Eric Molnar, Assistant Director, Admissions and Enrollment Reporting, 434-243-2085, E-mail: eric.molnar@virginia.edu.
Website: http://curry.virginia.edu/academics/areas-of-study/higher-education

University of Virginia, Curry School of Education, Program in Education, Charlottesville, VA 22903. Offers administration and supervision (PhD); applied developmental science (PhD); counselor education (PhD); curriculum and instruction (PhD); early childhood special education (MT); education evaluation (PhD); educational psychology (PhD); educational research (PhD); elementary education (MT); English education (MT, PhD); foreign language education (MT); higher education (PhD); instructional technology (PhD); kinesiology (MT, PhD); math education (PhD); reading education (PhD); research, statistics and evaluation (PhD); school psychology (PhD); science education (PhD); social studies education (MT, PhD); special education (PhD); world languages education (MT). *Students:* 452 full-time (357 women), 18 part-time (13 women); includes 100 minority (28 Black or African American, non-Hispanic/Latino; 39 Asian, non-Hispanic/Latino; 18 Hispanic/Latino; 15 Two or more races, non-Hispanic/Latino), 14 international. Average age 25. 309 applicants, 51% accepted, 87 enrolled. In 2016, 144 master's, 31 doctorates awarded. *Degree requirements:* For master's, comprehensive exam (for some programs), field project; for doctorate, comprehensive exam, thesis/dissertation. *Entrance requirements:* For doctorate, GRE General Test. Additional exam requirements/recommendations for international students: Required—TOEFL (minimum score 600 paper-based; 90 iBT), IELTS (minimum score 7). *Application deadline:* Applications are processed on a rolling basis. Application fee: $60. Electronic applications accepted. *Expenses:* Tuition, state resident: full-time $15,026; part-time $834 per credit hour. Tuition, nonresident: full-time $25,168; part-time $1378 per credit hour. *Required fees:* $2654. *Financial support:* Fellowships, research assistantships, and teaching assistantships available. Financial award application deadline: 1/5; financial award applicants required to submit FAFSA. *Unit head:* Robert C. Pianta, Dean, 434-924-3334, E-mail: pianta@virginia.edu. *Application contact:* Eric Molnar, Assistant Director, Admissions and Enrollment Reporting, 434-243-2085, E-mail: eric.molnar@virginia.edu.
Website: http://curry.virginia.edu/teacher-education

University of Washington, Graduate School, College of Education, Seattle, WA 98195. Offers curriculum and instruction (M Ed, Ed D, PhD), including educational technology, general curriculum (Ed D, PhD), language, literacy, and culture, mathematics education, multicultural education, reading and language arts education (Ed D), science education, social studies education, teaching and curriculum (M Ed); educational leadership and policy studies (M Ed, Ed D, PhD), including administration (Ed D), educational policy, organization, and leadership (M Ed, PhD), higher education, leadership for learning (Ed D), social and cultural foundations of education (M Ed, PhD); educational psychology (M Ed, PhD), including educational psychology (PhD), human development and cognition (M Ed), learning sciences, measurement, statistics and research design (M Ed), school psychology (M Ed); instructional leadership (M Ed); intercollegiate athletic leadership (M Ed); special education (M Ed, Ed D, PhD), including early childhood special education (M Ed), emotional and behavioral disabilities (M Ed), learning disabilities (M Ed), low-incidence disabilities (M Ed), severe disabilities (M Ed), special education (Ed D, PhD); teacher education (MIT). *Accreditation:* APA. *Program availability:* Part-time, evening/weekend. *Degree requirements:* For master's, thesis optional; for doctorate, thesis/dissertation. *Entrance requirements:* For master's and doctorate, GRE General Test, minimum GPA of 3.0. Additional exam requirements/recommendations for international students: Required—TOEFL. Electronic applications accepted. *Faculty research:* School restructuring/effective schools, special education interventions, literacy and writing, technology, school partnerships, teacher preparation.

The University of West Alabama, School of Graduate Studies, College of Education, Departments of Instructional Leadership and Support/Curriculum and Instruction, Program in Continuing Education, Livingston, AL 35470. Offers counseling and psychology (MSCE); family counseling (MSCE); general (MSCE); guidance and counseling (MSCE); library media (MSCE); student affairs in higher education (MSCE). *Accreditation:* NCATE. *Program availability:* Part-time, evening/weekend, 100% online. *Faculty:* 14 full-time (11 women), 45 part-time/adjunct (31 women). *Students:* 352 (295 women); includes 247 minority (234 Black or African American, non-Hispanic/Latino; 3 American Indian or Alaska Native, non-Hispanic/Latino; 1 Asian, non-Hispanic/Latino; 3 Hispanic/Latino; 1 Native Hawaiian or other Pacific Islander, non-Hispanic/Latino; 5 Two or more races, non-Hispanic/Latino). Average age 34. 92 applicants, 90% accepted, 72 enrolled. In 2016, 117 master's awarded. *Degree requirements:* For master's, comprehensive exam, thesis optional. *Entrance requirements:* For master's, GRE General Test, MAT, minimum GPA of 2.75. Additional exam requirements/recommendations for international students: Required—TOEFL (minimum score 500 paper-based; 61 iBT). *Application deadline:* Applications are processed on a rolling basis. Application fee: $40. Electronic applications accepted. *Expenses:* Tuition, state resident: part-time $355 per credit hour. Tuition, nonresident: part-time $710 per credit hour. *Required fees:* $130 per semester. *Financial support:* Teaching assistantships, Federal Work-Study, scholarships/grants, and unspecified assistantships available. Support available to part-time students. Financial award applicants required to submit FAFSA. *Unit head:* Dr. Reenay Rogers, Chair of Instructional Leadership and Support, 205-652-5423, Fax: 205-652-3706, E-mail: rrogers@uwa.edu. *Application contact:* Dr. B. J. Kimbrough, Dean of Graduate Studies, 205-652-3647, Fax: 205-652-3670, E-mail: bkimbrough@uwa.edu.

University of Wisconsin–La Crosse, College of Liberal Studies, Department of Student Affairs Administration, La Crosse, WI 54601-3742. Offers MS Ed, Ed D. *Program availability:* Part-time, evening/weekend, 100% online, blended/hybrid learning. *Faculty:* 3 full-time (all women), 5 part-time/adjunct (2 women). *Students:* 41 full-time (30 women), 47 part-time (39 women); includes 13 minority (1 Black or African American, non-Hispanic/Latino; 3 Asian, non-Hispanic/Latino; 6 Hispanic/Latino; 3 Two or more races, non-Hispanic/Latino), 1 international. Average age 26. 54 applicants, 83% accepted, 18 enrolled. In 2016, 38 master's awarded. *Degree requirements:* For master's, comprehensive exam (for some programs), thesis optional, electronic portfolio, applied research project. *Entrance requirements:* For master's, bachelor's degree from accredited institution, minimum GPA of 2.85, resume, essay, 2 references. Additional exam requirements/recommendations for international students: Required—TOEFL (minimum score 550 paper-based; 79 iBT). *Application deadline:* For fall admission, 2/1 priority date for domestic and international students. Electronic applications accepted. *Financial support:* Research assistantships with partial tuition reimbursements, Federal Work-Study, scholarships/grants, and health care benefits available. Support available to part-time students. Financial award application deadline: 3/15; financial award applicants required to submit FAFSA. *Faculty research:* Persistence; developing positive social justice behaviors in heterosexual white college men; equity; diversity; inclusion in higher education at both interpersonal and institutional levels; expanding student affairs administration research and practice beyond the traditional, majority, or dominant student experience; underrepresented students at historically white institutions; college men and masculinities; Latina/o college student leadership; ethnic cultural centers at HWIs. *Unit head:* Dr. Jodie Rindt, Department Chair, 608-785-6450, E-mail: jrindt@uwlax.edu. *Application contact:* Brandon Schaller, Senior Graduate Student Status Examiner, 608-785-8941, E-mail: admissions@uwlax.edu.
Website: http://www.uwlax.edu/saa/

University of Wisconsin–Madison, Graduate School, School of Education, Department of Educational Leadership and Policy Analysis, Madison, WI 53706-1380. Offers administration (Certificate); educational policy (MS, PhD); global higher education (MS). *Degree requirements:* For doctorate, thesis/dissertation. *Entrance requirements:* For master's and doctorate, GRE General Test. Electronic applications accepted.

University of Wisconsin–Milwaukee, Graduate School, School of Education, Department of Administrative Leadership, Milwaukee, WI 53201-0413. Offers administrative leadership (MS, Graduate Certificate), including adult and continuing education leadership (MS), educational administration and supervision (MS), higher education administration (MS); support services for online students in higher education (Graduate Certificate); teaching and learning in higher education (Graduate Certificate). *Program availability:* Part-time. *Students:* 22 full-time (16 women), 157 part-time (102 women); includes 52 minority (21 Black or African American, non-Hispanic/Latino; 4 Asian, non-Hispanic/Latino; 2 Hispanic/Latino; 25 Two or more races, non-Hispanic/Latino), 2 international. Average age 34. 108 applicants, 72% accepted, 48 enrolled. In 2016, 72 master's, 19 other advanced degrees awarded. *Degree requirements:* For master's, comprehensive exam, thesis or alternative. *Entrance requirements:* For master's, GRE General Test. Additional exam requirements/recommendations for international students: Required—TOEFL (minimum score 550 paper-based; 79 iBT), IELTS (minimum score 6.5). *Application deadline:* For fall admission, 1/1 priority date for domestic students; for spring admission, 9/1 for domestic students. Applications are processed on a rolling basis. Application fee: $56 ($96 for international students). Electronic applications accepted. *Financial support:* In 2016–17, 2 fellowships were awarded; research assistantships, teaching assistantships, career-related internships or fieldwork, health care benefits, unspecified assistantships, and project assistantships also available. Support available to part-time students. Financial award application deadline: 4/15; financial award applicants required to submit FAFSA. *Unit head:* Alan Shoho, Dean, 414-229-4181, E-mail: shoho@uwm.edu. *Application contact:* General Contact, 414-229-4721, E-mail: soeinfo@uwm.edu.
Website: http://uwm.edu/education/academics/administrative-leadership-department/

Upper Iowa University, Master of Education Program, Fayette, IA 52142-1857. Offers early childhood (M Ed); English as a second language (M Ed); higher education (M Ed); instructional strategist (M Ed); reading (M Ed); teacher leadership (M Ed).

Vanderbilt University, Peabody College, Department of Leadership, Policy, and Organizations, Nashville, TN 37240-1001. Offers education policy (MPP); educational leadership and policy (Ed D); higher education (M Ed); higher education leadership and policy (Ed D); independent school leadership (M Ed); international education policy and management (M Ed); leadership and organizational performance (M Ed). *Program availability:* Part-time. *Faculty:* 29 full-time (14 women), 21 part-time/adjunct (5 women). *Students:* 166 full-time (124 women), 107 part-time (63 women); includes 50 minority (25 Black or African American, non-Hispanic/Latino; 7 Asian, non-Hispanic/Latino; 9 Hispanic/Latino; 1 Native Hawaiian or other Pacific Islander, non-Hispanic/Latino; 8 Two or more races, non-Hispanic/Latino), 32 international. Average age 29. 543 applicants, 63% accepted, 133 enrolled. In 2016, 109 master's, 22 doctorates awarded. *Degree requirements:* For master's, comprehensive exam, thesis optional; for doctorate, thesis/dissertation, qualifying exams, residency. *Entrance requirements:* For master's and doctorate, GRE General Test. Additional exam requirements/recommendations for international students: Required—TOEFL (minimum score 550 paper-based; 80 iBT). *Application deadline:* For fall admission, 12/31 priority date for domestic and international students; for spring admission, 11/1 priority date for domestic and international students. Applications are processed on a rolling basis. Application fee: $0. Electronic applications accepted. *Expenses: Tuition:* Part-time $1854 per credit hour. *Financial support:* Fellowships with partial tuition reimbursements, research assistantships with partial tuition reimbursements, teaching assistantships with partial tuition reimbursements, Federal Work-Study, institutionally sponsored loans, scholarships/grants, tuition waivers (partial), and unspecified assistantships available. Support available to part-time students. Financial award application deadline: 1/15;

financial award applicants required to submit FAFSA. *Faculty research:* Higher education, educational leadership, education policy, international education, educator effectiveness. *Unit head:* Dr. Ellen B. Goldring, Chair, 615-322-8000, Fax: 615-343-7094, E-mail: ellen.b.goldring@vanderbilt.edu. *Application contact:* Rosie Moody, Educational Coordinator, 615-322-8019, Fax: 615-343-7094, E-mail: rosie.moody@vanderbilt.edu.
Website: http://peabody.vanderbilt.edu/departments/lpo/index.php

Virginia Polytechnic Institute and State University, Graduate School, College of Liberal Arts and Human Sciences, Blacksburg, VA 24061. Offers career and technical education (MS Ed, Ed D, PhD, Ed S); communication (MA); counselor education (MA Ed, Ed D, PhD, Ed S); creative writing (MFA); curriculum and instruction (MA Ed, Ed D, PhD, Ed S); educational leadership and policy studies (MA Ed, Ed D, PhD, Ed S); educational research and evaluation (PhD); English (MA); foreign languages, cultures, and literatures (MA); higher education (PhD); higher education and student affairs (MA Ed); history (MA); human development (MS, PhD); material culture and public humanities (MA); philosophy (MA); political science (MA); rhetoric and writing (PhD); science and technology studies (MS, PhD); social, political, ethical, and cultural thought (PhD); sociology (MS, PhD); theater arts (MFA). *Faculty:* 408 full-time (204 women), 3 part-time/adjunct (2 women). *Students:* 657 full-time (446 women), 457 part-time (292 women); includes 213 minority (114 Black or African American, non-Hispanic/Latino; 3 American Indian or Alaska Native, non-Hispanic/Latino; 29 Asian, non-Hispanic/Latino; 44 Hispanic/Latino; 23 Two or more races, non-Hispanic/Latino), 93 international. Average age 33. 805 applicants, 55% accepted, 328 enrolled. In 2016, 270 master's, 91 doctorates awarded. *Degree requirements:* For master's, comprehensive exam (for some programs), thesis (for some programs); for doctorate, comprehensive exam (for some programs), thesis/dissertation (for some programs). *Entrance requirements:* For master's and doctorate, GRE/GMAT. Additional exam requirements/recommendations for international students: Required—TOEFL (minimum score 80 iBT). *Application deadline:* For fall admission, 8/1 for domestic students, 4/1 for international students; for spring admission, 1/1 for domestic students, 9/1 for international students. Applications are processed on a rolling basis. Application fee: $75. Electronic applications accepted. *Expenses:* Tuition, state resident: full-time $12,467; part-time $692.50 per credit hour. Tuition, nonresident: full-time $25,095; part-time $1394.25 per credit hour. *Required fees:* $2669; $491.50 per semester. Tuition and fees vary according to course load, campus/location and program. *Financial support:* In 2016–17, 21 research assistantships with full tuition reimbursements (averaging $19,817 per year), 237 teaching assistantships with full tuition reimbursements (averaging $15,497 per year) were awarded. Financial award application deadline: 3/1; financial award applicants required to submit FAFSA. *Total annual research expenditures:* $6.6 million. *Unit head:* Rosemary Blieszner, Interim Dean, 540-231-6779, Fax: 540-231-7157, E-mail: liberalartsdean@vt.edu. *Application contact:* Chelsea Blanchet, Executive Assistant, 540-231-6779, Fax: 540-231-7157, E-mail: bchels1@vt.edu.
Website: http://www.liberalarts.vt.edu/

Walden University, Graduate Programs, Richard W. Riley College of Education and Leadership, Minneapolis, MN 55401. Offers adult education (Post-Master's Certificate); adult learning (Graduate Certificate); college teaching and learning (Graduate Certificate); community college leadership (Ed D); curriculum, instruction and assessment (Ed D, Ed S, Graduate Certificate); developmental education (Graduate Certificate); early childhood administration, management, and leadership (Graduate Certificate); early childhood education (Ed D, Ed S); early childhood public policy and advocacy (Graduate Certificate); early childhood studies (MS), including administration, management and leadership, early childhood public policy and advocacy, teaching adults in the early childhood field, teaching and diversity in early childhood education; education (MS, PhD), including adolescent literacy and learning (MS), curriculum, instruction, and assessment (grades K-12) (MS), curriculum, instruction, assessment, and evaluation (PhD), early childhood leadership and advocacy (PhD), early childhood special education (PhD), educational leadership (MS), educational leadership and administration (principal preparation) (MS), educational technology and design (PhD), elementary reading and literacy (PreK-6) (MS), elementary reading and mathematics (grades K-6) (MS), global and comparative education (PhD), higher education leadership management and policy (PhD), integrating technology in the classroom (grades K-12) (MS), learning, instruction and innovation (PhD), mathematics (grades 5-8) (MS), mathematics (grades K-6) (MS), mathematics and science (grades K-8) (MS), organizational research, assessment, and evaluation (PhD), reading and literacy with a reading K-12 endorsement (MS), reading literacy assessment and evaluation (PhD), science (grades K-8) (MS), special education (non-licensure) (grades K-12) (MS), teacher leadership (grades K-12) (MS), teaching English language learners (grades K-12) (MS); educational administration and leadership (Ed D); educational leadership and administration (principal preparation) (Ed S); educational technology (Ed D, Ed S, Post Master's Certificate); elementary reading and literacy (Graduate Certificate); engaging culturally diverse learners (Graduate Certificate); enrollment management and institutional marketing (Graduate Certificate); higher education (MS), including adult learning, college teaching and learning, enrollment management and institutional marketing, global higher education, leadership for student success, online and distance learning; higher education and adult learning (Ed D); higher education leadership and management (Ed D); higher education leadership for student success (Graduate Certificate); instructional design and technology (MS, Postbaccalaureate Certificate), including general program (MS), online learning (MS), training and performance improvement (MS); integrating technology in the classroom (Graduate Certificate); mathematics 5-8 (Graduate Certificate); mathematics K-6 (Graduate Certificate); online teaching for adult educators (Graduate Certificate); reading, literacy, and assessment (Ed D, Ed S); science K-8 (Graduate Certificate); special education (Ed D, Ed S, Graduate Certificate); special education (K-age 21) (MAT); teacher leadership (Graduate Certificate); teaching adults English as a second language (Graduate Certificate); teaching adults in the early childhood field (Graduate Certificate); teaching and diversity in early childhood education (Graduate Certificate); teaching English language learners (grades K-12) (Graduate Certificate); teaching K-12 students online (Graduate Certificate). *Accreditation:* NCATE. *Program availability:* Part-time, evening/weekend, online only, 100% online. *Degree requirements:* For doctorate, thesis/dissertation (for some programs), residency; for other advanced degree, residency (for some programs). *Entrance requirements:* For master's, bachelor's degree or higher; minimum GPA of 2.5; official transcripts; goal statement (for some programs); access to computer and Internet; for doctorate, master's degree or higher; three years of related professional or academic experience (preferred); minimum GPA of 3.0; goal statement and current resume (for select programs); official transcripts; access to computer and Internet; for other advanced degree, relevant work experience; access to computer and Internet. Additional exam requirements/recommendations for international students: Required—TOEFL (minimum score 550 paper-based, 79 iBT), IELTS (minimum score 6.5), Michigan English Language Assessment Battery (minimum score 82), or PTE (minimum score 53). Electronic applications accepted.

Walden University, Graduate Programs, School of Social Work and Human Services, Minneapolis, MN 55401. Offers addictions and social work (DSW); advanced clinical practice (MSW); clinical expertise (DSW); criminal justice (DSW); disaster, crisis, and intervention (DSW); family studies and interventions (DSW); human and social services (PhD), including advanced research, community and social services, community intervention and leadership, conflict management, criminal justice, disaster crisis and intervention, family studies and intervention, gerontology, global social services, higher education, human services and nonprofit administration, mental health facilitation; medical social work (DSW); military social work (MSW); policy practice (DSW); social work (PhD), including addictions and social work, clinical expertise, criminal justice, disaster, crisis and intervention, family studies and interventions, medical social work, policy practice, social work administration; social work administration (DSW); social work in healthcare (MSW); social work with children and families (MSW). *Accreditation:* CSWE. *Program availability:* Part-time, evening/weekend, online only, 100% online. *Degree requirements:* For master's, residency (for some programs); for doctorate, thesis/dissertation, residency. *Entrance requirements:* For master's, bachelor's degree or higher; minimum GPA of 2.5; official transcripts; goal statement (for some programs); access to computer and Internet; for doctorate, master's degree or higher; three years of related professional or academic experience (preferred); minimum GPA of 3.0; goal statement and current resume (for select programs); official transcripts; access to computer and Internet. Additional exam requirements/recommendations for international students: Required—TOEFL (minimum score 550 paper-based, 79 iBT), IELTS (minimum score 6.5), Michigan English Language Assessment Battery (minimum score 82), or PTE (minimum score 53). Electronic applications accepted.

Walsh University, Graduate Programs, Program in Counseling and Human Development, North Canton, OH 44720-3396. Offers clinical mental health counseling (MA); school counseling (MA); student affairs in higher education (MA). *Accreditation:* ACA. *Program availability:* Part-time, evening/weekend. *Faculty:* 5 full-time (4 women), 10 part-time/adjunct (8 women). *Students:* 34 full-time (24 women), 66 part-time (51 women); includes 11 minority (6 Black or African American, non-Hispanic/Latino; 2 American Indian or Alaska Native, non-Hispanic/Latino; 2 Hispanic/Latino; 1 Two or more races, non-Hispanic/Latino), 1 international. Average age 30. 58 applicants, 69% accepted, 27 enrolled. In 2016, 24 master's awarded. *Degree requirements:* For master's, comprehensive exam, internship, practicum. *Entrance requirements:* For master's, GRE (minimum score of 145 verbal and 146 quantitative) or MAT (minimum score of 397), interview, minimum GPA of 3.0, writing sample, reference forms, notarized affidavit of good moral conduct. Additional exam requirements/recommendations for international students: Required—TOEFL (minimum score 500 paper-based; 61 iBT). *Application deadline:* For fall admission, 7/15 priority date for domestic students. Applications are processed on a rolling basis. Application fee: $25. Electronic applications accepted. Application fee is waived when completed online. *Expenses:* $665 per credit hour. *Financial support:* In 2016–17, 11 students received support, including 11 research assistantships with partial tuition reimbursements available (averaging $8,442 per year). Financial award application deadline: 12/31. *Faculty research:* Supervision of clinical mental health, clinical mental health practice/issues, clinical mental health skills development, advocacy, teaching and professional development, career development, refugee development in US, supervision in student affairs, offender treatment, domestic violence issues, alcohol and drug treatment issues, Professional identity and advocacy in school counseling, Efficacy in counseling clinic. *Unit head:* Dr. Ruthann Anderson, Program Director, 330-490-7338, Fax: 330-490-7323, E-mail: randerson@walsh.edu. *Application contact:* Audra Dice, Graduate and Transfer Admissions Counselor, 330-490-7181, Fax: 330-244-4925, E-mail: adice@walsh.edu.
Website: http://www.walsh.edu/counseling-graduate-program

Wayland Baptist University, Graduate Programs, Program in Education, Plainview, TX 79072-6998. Offers education administration (M Ed); education diagnostics (M Ed); education literacy (M Ed); elementary certification (M Ed); English (M Ed); English as a second language (M Ed); higher education administration (M Ed); human resources (M Ed); instructional leadership (M Ed); instructional technology (M Ed); leadership training and development (M Ed); science education (M Ed); secondary certification (M Ed); social studies (M Ed); special education (M Ed); sports administration and management (M Ed). *Program availability:* Part-time, evening/weekend, online learning. *Degree requirements:* For master's, comprehensive exam, capstone course. *Entrance requirements:* For master's, GRE, GMAT or MAT. Additional exam requirements/recommendations for international students: Required—TOEFL (minimum score 500 paper-based; 61 iBT). Electronic applications accepted.

Wayne State University, College of Education, Division of Administrative and Organizational Studies, Detroit, MI 48202. Offers college and university teaching (Certificate); educational administration and supervision (Ed S); educational leadership (M Ed); educational leadership and policy studies (Ed D, PhD); educational technology (Certificate); learning design and technology (M Ed, Ed D, PhD, Ed S); online teaching (Certificate). *Program availability:* Part-time, 100% online, blended/hybrid learning. *Faculty:* 11. *Students:* 83 full-time (58 women), 223 part-time (148 women); includes 151 minority (126 Black or African American, non-Hispanic/Latino; 3 American Indian or Alaska Native, non-Hispanic/Latino; 4 Asian, non-Hispanic/Latino; 8 Hispanic/Latino; 10 Two or more races, non-Hispanic/Latino), 14 international. Average age 39. 143 applicants, 43% accepted, 38 enrolled. In 2016, 53 master's, 9 doctorates, 34 other advanced degrees awarded. *Degree requirements:* For doctorate, thesis/dissertation. *Entrance requirements:* For master's, baccalaureate degree from accredited U.S. institution or equivalent from college or university of government-recognized standing; minimum undergraduate GPA of 2.75 in upper-division coursework; personal statement; for doctorate, GRE (instructional design and technology), interview; curriculum vitae; three references (two professional and one academic); master's degree; minimum graduate GPA of 3.5; autobiographical statement; research experience. Additional exam requirements/recommendations for international students: Required—TOEFL (minimum score 550 paper-based; 79 iBT), Michigan English Language Assessment Battery (minimum score 85); Recommended—IELTS (minimum score 6.5), TWE (minimum score 5.5). *Application deadline:* For fall admission, 6/1 priority date for domestic students, 5/1 priority date for international students; for winter admission, 10/1 priority date for domestic students, 9/1 priority date for international students; for spring admission, 2/1 priority date for domestic students, 1/1 priority date for international students. Applications are processed on a rolling basis. Application fee: $50. Electronic applications accepted. *Expenses:* $16,503 per year resident tuition and fees, $33,697 per year non-resident tuition and fees. *Financial support:* In 2016–17, 96 students received support, including 1 fellowship with tuition reimbursement available (averaging $11,000 per year), 4 research assistantships with tuition reimbursements available (averaging $17,949 per year); scholarships/grants and unspecified assistantships also available. Support available to part-time students. Financial award applicants required to submit FAFSA. *Faculty research:* Total quality management, participatory management, administering educational technology, school improvement, principalship. *Unit head:* Dr. William Hill, Assistant Dean, 313-577-9316, E-mail: ad2107@wayne.edu. *Application contact:* Janice Green, Assistant Dean, 313-577-1605, E-mail: jwgreen@wayne.edu.
Website: http://coe.wayne.edu/aos/index.php

West Chester University of Pennsylvania, College of Education and Social Work, Department of Counselor Education, West Chester, PA 19383. Offers clinical mental health counseling (MS); counseling (Certificate); higher education counseling (Post Master's Certificate); higher education counseling/student affairs (MS, Certificate); school counseling (M Ed). *Accreditation:* ACA; NCATE. *Program availability:* Part-time, evening/weekend. *Faculty:* 10 full-time (6 women), 5 part-time/adjunct (3 women).

Students: 130 full-time (100 women), 65 part-time (55 women); includes 48 minority (27 Black or African American, non-Hispanic/Latino; 2 Asian, non-Hispanic/Latino; 13 Hispanic/Latino; 6 Two or more races, non-Hispanic/Latino), 1 international. Average age 27. 199 applicants, 56% accepted, 66 enrolled. In 2016, 78 master's, 3 other advanced degrees awarded. *Degree requirements:* For master's, comprehensive exam. *Entrance requirements:* For master's, minimum GPA of 3.0, three letters of reference. Additional exam requirements/recommendations for international students: Required—TOEFL or IELTS. *Application deadline:* For fall admission, 5/15 for international students; for spring admission, 10/15 for international students. Applications are processed on a rolling basis. Application fee: $50. Electronic applications accepted. *Expenses:* Tuition, state resident: full-time $8694; part-time $483 per credit. Tuition, nonresident: full-time $13,050; part-time $725 per credit. *Required fees:* $2399; $119.05 per credit. Tuition and fees vary according to campus/location and program. *Financial support:* Scholarships/grants and unspecified assistantships available. Financial award application deadline: 2/15; financial award applicants required to submit FAFSA. *Faculty research:* Teacher and student cognition, adolescent cognitive development, college counseling, motivational interviewing. *Unit head:* Dr. Eric Owens, Chair, 610-436-2559, Fax: 610-425-7432, E-mail: eowens@wcupa.edu. *Application contact:* Dr. Cheryl Neale-McFall, Graduate Coordinator, 610-436-2559, Fax: 610-425-7432, E-mail: cneale-mcfall@wcupa.edu.
Website: http://www.wcupa.edu/education-socialWork/counselorEducation/

Western Governors University, Teachers College, Salt Lake City, UT 84107. Offers curriculum and instruction (MS); educational leadership (MS); educational studies (MA); educational studies (5-12) (MA), including mathematics; elementary education (K-8) (MAT, Postbaccalaureate Certificate); elementary education (PreK-8) (MAT); English language learning (K-12) (MA); instructional design (MAT); learning and technology (M Ed, MA); management and innovation (M Ed); mathematics (5-12) (MAT, Postbaccalaureate Certificate); mathematics (5-9) (MAT, Postbaccalaureate Certificate); mathematics education (5-12) (MA); mathematics education (5-9) (MA); mathematics education (K-6) (MA); measurement and evaluation (M Ed); science (5-12) (Postbaccalaureate Certificate); science (5-9) (MAT, Postbaccalaureate Certificate); science education (5-12) (MA), including biology, chemistry, geology, physics; science education (5-9) (MA); social science (5-12) (MAT, Postbaccalaureate Certificate); special education (MAT, MS). *Accreditation:* NCATE. *Program availability:* Evening/weekend, online learning. *Degree requirements:* For master's, capstone project. *Entrance requirements:* For master's and Postbaccalaureate Certificate, Readiness Assessment, transcripts. Additional exam requirements/recommendations for international students: Required—TOEFL (minimum score 450 paper-based; 80 iBT). Electronic applications accepted. *Expenses:* Contact institution.

Western Illinois University, School of Graduate Studies, College of Education and Human Services, Department of Educational Studies, Program in College Student Personnel, Macomb, IL 61455-1390. Offers college student personnel (MS), including higher education leadership, student affairs. *Accreditation:* NCATE. *Program availability:* Part-time. *Students:* 56 full-time (37 women), 19 part-time (15 women); includes 19 minority (7 Black or African American, non-Hispanic/Latino; 1 Asian, non-Hispanic/Latino; 8 Hispanic/Latino; 3 Two or more races, non-Hispanic/Latino), 2 international. Average age 27. 110 applicants, 79% accepted, 28 enrolled. In 2016, 27 master's awarded. *Degree requirements:* For master's, thesis or alternative. *Entrance requirements:* For master's, interview. Additional exam requirements/recommendations for international students: Required—TOEFL (minimum score 550 paper-based; 80 iBT). *Application deadline:* For fall admission, 1/5 priority date for domestic students. Application fee: $30. Electronic applications accepted. *Financial support:* In 2016–17, 55 students received support. Unspecified assistantships available. Financial award applicants required to submit FAFSA. *Unit head:* Dr. Tracy Davis, Coordinator, 309-298-1183. *Application contact:* Dr. Nancy Parsons, Associate Provost and Director of Graduate Studies, 309-298-1806, Fax: 309-298-2345, E-mail: grad-office@wiu.edu.
Website: http://wiu.edu/csp/

Western Kentucky University, Graduate Studies, College of Education and Behavioral Sciences, Department of Counseling and Student Affairs, Bowling Green, KY 42101. Offers counseling (MA Ed), including marriage and family therapy, mental health counseling; school counseling (P-12) (MA Ed); student affairs in higher education (MA Ed). *Accreditation:* ACA; NCATE. *Program availability:* Part-time, evening/weekend. *Degree requirements:* For master's, comprehensive exam, thesis optional. *Entrance requirements:* For master's, GRE General Test. Additional exam requirements/recommendations for international students: Required—TOEFL (minimum score 555 paper-based; 79 iBT). *Faculty research:* Counselor education, research for residential workers.

Western Michigan University, Graduate College, College of Arts and Sciences, Department of Mathematics, Kalamazoo, MI 49008. Offers applied and computational mathematics (MS); mathematics education (MA, PhD), including collegiate mathematics education (PhD). *Degree requirements:* For doctorate, one foreign language, thesis/dissertation.

Western Washington University, Graduate School, Woodring College of Education, Department of Educational Leadership, Program in Continuing and College Education, Bellingham, WA 98225-5996. Offers M Ed. *Program availability:* Part-time, evening/weekend, online learning. *Degree requirements:* For master's, comprehensive exam, thesis optional. *Entrance requirements:* For master's, GRE General Test or MAT, minimum GPA of 3.0 in last 60 semester hours or last 90 quarter hours. Additional exam requirements/recommendations for international students: Required—TOEFL (minimum score 567 paper-based). Electronic applications accepted. *Faculty research:* Transfer of learning, postsecondary faculty development, action research as professional development, literacy education in community colleges, adult education in the Middle East, distance learning tools for graduate students.

West Virginia University, College of Education and Human Services, Department of Curriculum and Instruction/Literacy Studies, Program in Secondary Education, Morgantown, WV 26506. Offers higher education curriculum and teaching (MA); secondary education (MA). Students enter program as undergraduates. *Accreditation:* NCATE. *Program availability:* Part-time. *Degree requirements:* For master's, thesis optional, content exams. *Entrance requirements:* For master's, minimum GPA of 2.75. Additional exam requirements/recommendations for international students: Required—TOEFL. Electronic applications accepted. *Faculty research:* Teacher education, school reform, curriculum development, education technology.

West Virginia University, College of Education and Human Services, Department of Educational Leadership Studies, Morgantown, WV 26506. Offers educational leadership (Ed D); higher education administration (MA); public school administration (MA). *Accreditation:* NCATE. *Program availability:* Part-time. *Degree requirements:* For master's, content exams; for doctorate, comprehensive exam, thesis/dissertation. *Entrance requirements:* For master's, minimum GPA of 2.75 or MA Degree or MAT of 4107; for doctorate, GRE General Test or MAT, minimum GPA of 3.25. Additional exam requirements/recommendations for international students: Required—TOEFL. Electronic applications accepted. *Faculty research:* Evaluation, collective bargaining, educational law, international higher education, superintendency.

Wilmington University, College of Education, New Castle, DE 19720-6491. Offers applied technology in education (M Ed); career and technical education (M Ed); educational leadership (Ed D); elementary and secondary school counseling (M Ed); elementary studies (M Ed); ESOL literacy (M Ed); higher education leadership (Ed D); instruction: gifted and talented (M Ed); instruction: teacher of reading (M Ed); instruction: teaching and learning (M Ed); organizational leadership (Ed D); school leadership (M Ed); secondary education (MAT); special education (M Ed). *Accreditation:* NCATE. *Program availability:* Part-time, evening/weekend. *Faculty:* 19 full-time (11 women), 178 part-time/adjunct (99 women). *Students:* 248 full-time (176 women), 999 part-time (738 women); includes 244 minority (193 Black or African American, non-Hispanic/Latino; 17 American Indian or Alaska Native, non-Hispanic/Latino; 9 Asian, non-Hispanic/Latino; 19 Hispanic/Latino; 2 Native Hawaiian or other Pacific Islander, non-Hispanic/Latino; 4 Two or more races, non-Hispanic/Latino), 7 international. Average age 34. 672 applicants, 96% accepted, 348 enrolled. In 2016, 529 master's, 87 doctorates awarded. *Entrance requirements:* For master's, 2 letters of recommendation, interview. Additional exam requirements/recommendations for international students: Required—TOEFL (minimum score 500 paper-based). *Application deadline:* For fall admission, 4/30 for domestic students. Applications are processed on a rolling basis. Application fee: $35. Electronic applications accepted. *Expenses: Tuition:* Full-time $8388; part-time $466 per credit. *Required fees:* $25 per semester. Tuition and fees vary according to degree level. *Financial support:* Applicants required to submit FAFSA. *Unit head:* Dr. John C. Gray, Dean. *Application contact:* Laura Morris, Director of Admissions, 877-967-5464, E-mail: infocenter@wilmu.edu.
Website: http://www.wilmu.edu/education/

Middle School Education

Alaska Pacific University, Graduate Programs, Education Department, Program in Teaching, Anchorage, AK 99508-4672. Offers teaching (K-8) (MAT). *Degree requirements:* For master's, research project. *Entrance requirements:* For master's, GRE or MAT, PRAXIS, minimum GPA of 3.0.

Albany State University, College of Education, Albany, GA 31705-2717. Offers early childhood education (M Ed); educational leadership (Ed S); health and physical education (M Ed); middle grades education (M Ed); school counseling (M Ed); special education (M Ed). *Accreditation:* NCATE. *Program availability:* Part-time, evening/weekend, online learning. *Degree requirements:* For master's, comprehensive exam, internship, GACE Content Exam. *Entrance requirements:* For master's, GRE or MAT. *Application deadline:* For fall admission, 6/1 for domestic students, 5/1 for international students; for spring admission, 11/1 for domestic students, 10/1 for international students. Applications are processed on a rolling basis. Application fee: $20. Electronic applications accepted. *Financial support:* Scholarships/grants available. Financial award application deadline: 4/15; financial award applicants required to submit FAFSA. *Faculty research:* GACE preparation, STEM (science, technology, engineering, and mathematics), technology education, special education, professional teacher development, health implications liberation philosophy, NET-Q, learning community, disabled or at-risk students. *Unit head:* Dr. Rhonda C. Porter, Interim Dean, 229-430-1718, Fax: 229-430-4993. *Application contact:* Jeffrey Pierce, II, Graduate Admissions Counselor, 229-430-4646, Fax: 229-430-4105, E-mail: jeffrey.pierce@asurams.edu.
Website: https://www.asurams.edu/Academics/collegeofeducation/

American International College, School of Education, Springfield, MA 01109-3189. Offers early childhood education (M Ed, CAGS); elementary education (M Ed, CAGS); middle education/secondary education (M Ed, CAGS); moderate disabilities (M Ed, CAGS); reading specialist (M Ed, CAGS); school adjustment counseling (MAEP, CAGS); school guidance counseling (MAEP, CAGS); school leadership (M Ed, CAGS). *Program availability:* Evening/weekend. *Faculty:* 1 (woman) full-time, 90 part-time/adjunct (63 women). *Students:* 1,194 full-time (970 women), 118 part-time (83 women); includes 108 minority (15 Black or African American, non-Hispanic/Latino; 4 American Indian or Alaska Native, non-Hispanic/Latino; 12 Asian, non-Hispanic/Latino; 55 Hispanic/Latino; 2 Native Hawaiian or other Pacific Islander, non-Hispanic/Latino; 20 Two or more races, non-Hispanic/Latino). Average age 34. 517 applicants, 417 enrolled. In 2016, 879 master's, 194 CAGSs awarded. Terminal master's awarded for partial completion of doctoral program. *Degree requirements:* For master's, comprehensive exam (for some programs), thesis (for some programs), practicum/culminating experience; for CAGS, practicum/culminating experience. *Entrance requirements:* For master's, Communication and Literacy portion of the Massachusetts Tests for Education Licensure, graduate of accredited four-year college with minimum B- average in undergraduate course work; for CAGS, M Ed or master's degree in field related to licensure from accredited institution. *Application deadline:* Applications are processed on a rolling basis. Application fee: $50. Electronic applications accepted. *Expenses:* $439 per credit. *Financial support:* Applicants required to submit FAFSA. *Unit head:* Sylvia Mason, Dean, 413-205-1743, Fax: 413-205-3943, E-mail: sylvia.mason@aic.edu. *Application contact:* Kerry Barnes, Dean of Graduate Admissions, 413-205-3703, Fax: 413-205-3051, E-mail: kerry.barnes@aic.edu.
Website: http://www.aic.edu/school-of-education/

Antioch University Midwest, Graduate Programs, School of Education, Yellow Springs, OH 45387-1609. Offers conflict management (M Ed); dyslexia (M Ed); early childhood education (M Ed); educational leadership (M Ed); intervention specialist, mild to moderate (M Ed); middle childhood education (M Ed); trauma informed education (M Ed). *Accreditation:* NCATE. *Program availability:* Part-time, evening/weekend. *Degree requirements:* For master's, thesis or alternative. *Entrance requirements:* For master's, resume, goal statement, interview. *Application deadline:* For fall admission, 9/7 for domestic students; for winter admission, 12/10 for domestic students; for spring admission, 3/10 for domestic students. Applications are processed on a rolling basis. Application fee: $50. Electronic applications accepted. *Expenses:* $675 per credit hour. *Financial support:* Federal Work-Study available. Financial award applicants required to

submit FAFSA. *Unit head:* Dr. Marian Glancy, Director, 937-769-1880, Fax: 937-769-1805, E-mail: mglancy@antioch.edu. *Application contact:* Deena Kent-Hummel, Director of Admissions, 937-769-1823, Fax: 937-769-1804, E-mail: dkent@antioch.edu.
Website: https://www.antioch.edu/midwest/degrees-programs/education-degree/

Appalachian State University, Cratis D. Williams Graduate School, Department of Curriculum and Instruction, Boone, NC 28608. Offers curriculum specialist (MA); educational media (MA); elementary education (MA); middle grades education (MA), including language arts, mathematics, science, social studies. *Accreditation:* NCATE. *Program availability:* Part-time, evening/weekend, online learning. *Degree requirements:* For master's, comprehensive exam, thesis or alternative. *Entrance requirements:* For master's, GRE General Test or MAT, 3 letters of recommendation. Additional exam requirements/recommendations for international students: Required—TOEFL (minimum score 570 paper-based; 79 iBT), IELTS (minimum score 6.5). *Application deadline:* For fall admission, 3/14 for domestic students, 2/1 for international students; for spring admission, 11/1 for domestic students, 7/1 for international students. Applications are processed on a rolling basis. Application fee: $55. Electronic applications accepted. *Expenses:* Tuition, state resident: full-time $4744. Tuition, nonresident: full-time $17,913. Full-time tuition and fees vary according to program. *Financial support:* Fellowships, research assistantships, teaching assistantships, career-related internships or fieldwork, Federal Work-Study, scholarships/grants, and unspecified assistantships available. Financial award application deadline: 4/1; financial award applicants required to submit FAFSA. *Faculty research:* Media literacy, elementary teaching, curriculum development, online learning environments. *Unit head:* Dr. Michael Jacobson, Chairperson, 828-262-2224. *Application contact:* Dr. Chrystal Dean, Program Director, 828-262-8009, E-mail: deanco@appstate.edu.
Website: http://www.ced.appstate.edu/departments/ci

Arkansas State University, Graduate School, College of Education and Behavioral Science, School of Teacher Education and Leadership, State University, AR 72467. Offers community college administration (SCCT); curriculum and instruction (MSE); early childhood education (MSE); early childhood services (MS); educational leadership (MSE, Ed D, Ed S); educational theory and practice (MSE); middle level education (MAT, MSE); reading (MSE, Ed S); special education - gifted, talented, and creative (MSE); special education - instructional specialist grades 4-12 (MSE); special education - instructional specialist grades P-4 (MSE); special education, K-12 (MSE). *Accreditation:* NCATE. *Program availability:* Part-time, online learning. *Degree requirements:* For master's, comprehensive exam, thesis or alternative; for doctorate, comprehensive exam, thesis/dissertation; for other advanced degree, comprehensive exam. *Entrance requirements:* For master's, GRE General Test or MAT, appropriate bachelor's degree, official transcripts, immunization records, letters of reference, interview; for doctorate, GRE General Test or MAT, interview, master's degree, letters of reference, official transcript, personal statement, writing sample, immunization records; for other advanced degree, GRE General Test or MAT, interview, master's degree, official transcript, immunization records, letters of reference, 3 years of teaching experience, teaching license. Additional exam requirements/recommendations for international students: Required—TOEFL (minimum score 550 paper-based; 79 iBT), IELTS (minimum score 6), PTE (minimum score 56). Electronic applications accepted.

Augusta University, The Graduate School, College of Education, Program in Curriculum and Instruction, Augusta, GA 30912. Offers curriculum and instruction (Ed S); elementary education (MAT); foreign language education (MAT); instruction (M Ed); middle grades education (MAT); music education (MAT); secondary education (MAT); special education (MAT). *Degree requirements:* For master's, thesis, portfolio. *Entrance requirements:* For master's, GRE, MAT, minimum GPA of 2.5. Application fee: $20. *Financial support:* Career-related internships or fieldwork, Federal Work-Study, institutionally sponsored loans, and unspecified assistantships available. Support available to part-time students. Financial award application deadline: 4/15; financial award applicants required to submit FAFSA. *Unit head:* Dr. Gordon Eisenman, Director, 706-737-1496, Fax: 706-667-4706, E-mail: geisenman@augusta.edu. *Application contact:* Dr. Gordon Eisenman, Director, 706-737-1496, Fax: 706-667-4706, E-mail: geisenman@augusta.edu.

Ball State University, Graduate School, College of Sciences and Humanities, Department of Mathematical Sciences, Muncie, IN 47306. Offers actuarial science (MA); elementary mathematics teacher leadership (Certificate); mathematics (MA, MS), including mathematics; mathematics education (MA), including mathematics education; middle school mathematics education (Certificate); post-secondary foundational mathematics teaching (MA, Certificate); statistical modeling (Certificate); statistics (MA, MS), including statistics. *Program availability:* Part-time, 100% online, blended/hybrid learning. *Degree requirements:* For master's, thesis (for some programs). *Entrance requirements:* For master's, minimum baccalaureate GPA of 2.75 or 3.0 in latter half of baccalauareate. Additional exam requirements/recommendations for international students: Required—TOEFL (minimum score 550 paper-based; 79 iBT), IELTS (minimum score 6.5). Electronic applications accepted. *Faculty research:* Differential equations.

Bellarmine University, Annsley Frazier Thornton School of Education, Louisville, KY 40205. Offers education and district leadership (Ed D); education and social change (PhD); elementary education (MA Ed, MAT); leadership in higher education (PhD); learning and behavior disorders (MA Ed, MAT); middle grades education (MA Ed, MAT); principalship (Ed S); reading and writing (MA Ed); secondary education (MAT); teacher leadership (MA Ed). *Accreditation:* NCATE. *Program availability:* Part-time, evening/weekend. *Faculty:* 15 full-time (7 women), 44 part-time/adjunct (36 women). *Students:* 39 full-time (28 women), 211 part-time (164 women); includes 46 minority (35 Black or African American, non-Hispanic/Latino; 3 Asian, non-Hispanic/Latino; 5 Hispanic/Latino; 3 Two or more races, non-Hispanic/Latino). Average age 34. In 2016, 66 master's, 3 doctorates, 43 other advanced degrees awarded. *Degree requirements:* For master's, thesis (for some programs); for doctorate, thesis/dissertation. *Entrance requirements:* For master's, GRE, baccalaureate degree from accredited institution; minimum cumulative GPA of 2.75; recommendations from employers, supervisors, or professors attesting to applicant's potential as graduate student; statement of intent to pursue graduate degree; for doctorate, GRE, minimum GPA of 3.5 in all graduate coursework; baccalaureate and master's degrees in education or fields directly relevant to education; three letters of recommendation; two essays (no more than 1,000 words each); interview. Additional exam requirements/recommendations for international students: Required—TOEFL (minimum score 550 paper-based, 68 iBT), IELTS (minimum score 6), or Michigan English Language Assessment Battery. *Application deadline:* For fall admission, 8/1 priority date for domestic and international students; for spring admission, 12/1 priority date for domestic and international students; for summer admission, 4/10 priority date for domestic and international students. Applications are processed on a rolling basis. Application fee: $40. Electronic applications accepted. Tuition and fees vary according to program. *Financial support:* Scholarships/grants available. Financial award applicants required to submit FAFSA. *Faculty research:* Literacy, service-learning, dispositions, educational technology, special education. *Unit head:* Dr. Robert Cooter, Dean, 502-272-8191, Fax: 502-272-8189, E-mail: rcooter@bellarmine.edu. *Application contact:* Sarah Shumway Schuble, Senior Graduate Recruiter, 502-272-8271, Fax: 502-272-8002, E-mail: sshumway@bellarmine.edu.
Website: http://www.bellarmine.edu/education/graduate

Berry College, Graduate Programs, Graduate Programs in Education, Program in Middle-Grades Education and Reading, Mount Berry, GA 30149-0159. Offers middle grades education (MAT); middle-grades education (M Ed); reading (M Ed). *Accreditation:* NCATE. *Program availability:* Part-time. *Faculty:* 6 part-time/adjunct (4 women). *Students:* 1 part-time (0 women). Average age 40. *Degree requirements:* For master's, thesis, portfolio, oral exams. *Entrance requirements:* For master's, GRE General Test or MAT, minimum GPA of 2.5. Additional exam requirements/recommendations for international students: Required—TOEFL (minimum score 550 paper-based). *Application deadline:* For fall admission, 7/21 for domestic students, 5/1 for international students; for spring admission, 12/1 for domestic students, 10/1 for international students. Applications are processed on a rolling basis. Application fee: $25 ($30 for international students). Electronic applications accepted. *Expenses:* Contact institution. *Financial support:* In 2016–17, 1 student received support. Research assistantships with full tuition reimbursements available, scholarships/grants, tuition waivers (partial), and unspecified assistantships available. Support available to part-time students. Financial award application deadline: 3/1; financial award applicants required to submit FAFSA. *Unit head:* Dr. Jacqueline McDowell, Dean, 706-236-1717, Fax: 706-238-5827, E-mail: jmcdowell@berry.edu. *Application contact:* Brett Kennedy, Assistant Vice President of Enrollment Management, 706-236-2215, Fax: 706-290-2178, E-mail: admissions@berry.edu.
Website: http://www.berry.edu/academics/education/graduate/

Bloomsburg University of Pennsylvania, School of Graduate Studies, College of Education, Department of Teaching and Learning, Program in Middle Level Education Grades 4-8, Bloomsburg, PA 17815-1301. Offers language arts (M Ed); math (M Ed); science (M Ed); social studies (M Ed). *Accreditation:* NCATE. *Faculty:* 6 full-time (1 woman). *Students:* 3 applicants, 67% accepted. In 2016, 2 master's awarded. *Degree requirements:* For master's, thesis optional, practicum, student teaching. *Entrance requirements:* For master's, MAT, GRE, or PRAXIS, minimum QPA of 3.0, teaching certificate, U.S. citizenship, related undergraduate coursework, professional liability insurance, recent TB test. Additional exam requirements/recommendations for international students: Required—TOEFL (minimum score 550 paper-based), IELTS. *Application deadline:* Applications are processed on a rolling basis. Application fee: $35 ($60 for international students). Electronic applications accepted. *Expenses:* Tuition, state resident: full-time $9660; part-time $483 per credit. Tuition, nonresident: full-time $14,500; part-time $725 per credit. *Required fees:* $2410; $107 per credit. $75 per term. Tuition and fees vary according to course load, degree level and program. *Financial support:* Federal Work-Study and unspecified assistantships available. Financial award applicants required to submit FAFSA. *Unit head:* Dr. Ingrid Everett, Program Coordinator, 570-389-5120, Fax: 570-389-3030, E-mail: ieverett@bloomu.edu. *Application contact:* Jennifer Kessler, Administrative Assistant, 570-389-4015, Fax: 570-389-3054, E-mail: jkessler@bloomu.edu.
Website: http://www.bloomu.edu/gradschool/middle-level-education

Brenau University, Sydney O. Smith Graduate School, College of Education, Gainesville, GA 30501. Offers early childhood (Ed S); early childhood education (M Ed, MAT); middle grades (Ed S); middle grades education (M Ed, MAT); secondary education (MAT); special education (M Ed, MAT). *Accreditation:* NCATE. *Program availability:* Part-time, evening/weekend, online learning. *Degree requirements:* For master's, thesis optional, comprehensive exam or applied research project, effective portfolio; for Ed S, thesis, applied research project. *Entrance requirements:* For master's, GRE, MAT, interview, minimum GPA of 3.0, 3 references, writing samples; for Ed S, GRE, MAT, master's degree, minimum GPA of 3.0, writing sample, letters of reference. Additional exam requirements/recommendations for international students: Required—TOEFL (minimum score 500 paper-based; 61 iBT); Recommended—IELTS (minimum score 5). Electronic applications accepted. *Expenses:* Contact institution.

Brooklyn College of the City University of New York, School of Education, Program in Middle Childhood Mathematics Education, Brooklyn, NY 11210-2889. Offers MS Ed. *Entrance requirements:* For master's, LAST, 2 letters of recommendation, essay, resume. Additional exam requirements/recommendations for international students: Required—TOEFL (minimum score 500 paper-based; 61 iBT). Electronic applications accepted.

Brooklyn College of the City University of New York, School of Education, Program in Middle Childhood Science Education, Brooklyn, NY 11210-2889. Offers biology (MA); chemistry (MA); earth science (MA); general science (MA); physics (MA). *Program availability:* Part-time, evening/weekend. *Entrance requirements:* For master's, LAST, interview, previous course work in education and mathematics, resume, 2 letters of recommendation, essay. Additional exam requirements/recommendations for international students: Required—TOEFL (minimum score 500 paper-based; 61 iBT). Electronic applications accepted. *Faculty research:* Geometric thinking, mastery of basic facts, problem-solving strategies, history of mathematics.

Brooklyn College of the City University of New York, School of Education, Program in Special Education, Brooklyn, NY 11210-2889. Offers autism spectrum disorders (AC); teacher of students with disabilities (MS Ed), including adolescence education, childhood education, early childhood education. *Program availability:* Part-time. *Entrance requirements:* For master's, LAST, interview; previous course work in education and psychology; minimum GPA of 3.0 in education, 2.8 overall; resume, 2 letters of recommendation; essay. Additional exam requirements/recommendations for international students: Required—TOEFL (minimum score 500 paper-based; 61 iBT). Electronic applications accepted. *Faculty research:* School reform, conflict resolution, curriculum for inclusive settings, urban issues in special education.

California Lutheran University, Graduate Studies, Graduate School of Education, Thousand Oaks, CA 91360-2787. Offers counseling and guidance (MS), including college student personnel, counseling and guidance; educational leadership (MA, Ed D), including educational leadership (K-12) (Ed D), higher education leadership (Ed D); special education (MS); teacher leadership (M Ed); teaching (M Ed). *Accreditation:* NCATE. *Program availability:* Part-time, evening/weekend. *Faculty:* 23 full-time (17 women), 39 part-time/adjunct (26 women). *Students:* 518 full-time (411 women), 79 part-time (67 women); includes 252 minority (12 Black or African American, non-Hispanic/Latino; 3 American Indian or Alaska Native, non-Hispanic/Latino; 17 Asian, non-Hispanic/Latino; 108 Hispanic/Latino; 1 Native Hawaiian or other Pacific Islander, non-Hispanic/Latino; 111 Two or more races, non-Hispanic/Latino), 14 international. Average age 35. 319 applicants, 74% accepted, 192 enrolled. In 2016, 93 master's, 13 doctorates awarded. *Degree requirements:* For master's, comprehensive exam or thesis; for doctorate, thesis/dissertation. *Entrance requirements:* For master's, GRE General Test, interview, minimum GPA of 3.0. *Application deadline:* For fall admission, 7/1 priority date for domestic students; for spring admission, 11/1 priority date for domestic students; for summer admission, 4/1 priority date for domestic students. Applications are processed on a rolling basis. Application fee: $50. Electronic applications accepted. *Unit head:* Dr. Michael Hillis, Dean, 805-493-3421. *Application contact:* 805-493-3325, Fax: 805-493-3861, E-mail: clugrad@callutheran.edu.

Middle School Education

California State University, Bakersfield, Division of Graduate Studies, School of Natural Sciences, Mathematics, and Engineering, Program in Teaching Mathematics, Bakersfield, CA 93311. Offers MA. *Students:* 1 full-time (0 women); minority (Hispanic/Latino). *Entrance requirements:* For master's, minimum GPA of 2.5 for last 90 quarter units. *Expenses:* Tuition, state resident: full-time $2246; part-time $1302 per semester. *Unit head:* Sophia Raczkowski, Chair, 661-654-3151, Fax: 661-664-2039. *Application contact:* Debbie Blowers, Assistant Director of Admissions and Evaluations, 661-664-3381, E-mail: dblowers@csub.edu.
Website: https://www.csub.edu/math/info/index.html

Cambridge College, School of Education, Cambridge, MA 02138-5304. Offers autism specialist (M Ed); autism/behavior analyst (M Ed); behavior analyst (Post-Master's Certificate); behavioral management (M Ed); early childhood teacher (M Ed); education specialist in curriculum and instruction (CAGS); educational leadership (Ed D); elementary teacher (M Ed); English as a second language (M Ed, Certificate); general science (M Ed); health education (Post-Master's Certificate); health/family and consumer sciences (M Ed); history (M Ed); individualized (M Ed); information technology literacy (M Ed); instructional technology (M Ed); interdisciplinary studies (M Ed); library teacher (M Ed); literacy education (M Ed); mathematics (M Ed); mathematics specialist (Certificate); middle school mathematics and science (M Ed); school administration (M Ed, CAGS); school guidance counselor (M Ed); school nurse education (M Ed); school social worker/school adjustment counselor (M Ed); special education administrator (CAGS); special education/moderate disabilities (M Ed); teaching skills and methodologies (M Ed). *Program availability:* Part-time, evening/weekend, online learning. *Degree requirements:* For master's, thesis, internship/practicum (licensure program only); for doctorate, thesis/dissertation; for other advanced degree, thesis. *Entrance requirements:* For master's, interview, resume, documentation of licensure, 2 professional references; for doctorate, official transcripts, interview, resume, documentation of licensure (if any), written personal statement/essay, portfolio of scholarly and professional work, qualifying assessment, 2 professional references, health insurance, immunizations form; for other advanced degree, official transcripts, interview, resume, documentation of licensure (if any), written personal statement/essay, 2 professional references, health insurance, immunizations form. Additional exam requirements/recommendations for international students: Required—TOEFL (minimum score 550 paper-based; 79 iBT), Michigan English Language Assessment Battery (minimum score 85); Recommended—IELTS (minimum score 6). Electronic applications accepted. *Expenses:* Contact institution. *Faculty research:* Adult education, accelerated learning, mathematics education, brain compatible learning, special education and law.

Campbell University, Graduate and Professional Programs, School of Education, Buies Creek, NC 27506. Offers elementary education (M Ed); interdisciplinary studies (M Ed); middle grades education (M Ed); physical education (M Ed); school administration (MSA); school counseling (M Ed); secondary education (M Ed). *Accreditation:* NCATE. *Program availability:* Part-time, evening/weekend. *Degree requirements:* For master's, comprehensive exam. *Entrance requirements:* For master's, GRE General Test, minimum GPA of 2.7. *Faculty research:* Spiritual values and wellness issues in counseling, stress and professional burnout among counselors, thinking strategies, leadership, adaptive technology.

Canisius College, Graduate Division, School of Education and Human Services, Department of Teacher Education, Buffalo, NY 14208-1098. Offers adolescence education (MS Ed); childhood education (MS Ed); general education (MS Ed); special education (MS), including adolescence special education, advanced special education, childhood education grade 1-6, childhood special education. *Program availability:* Part-time, evening/weekend, 100% online, blended/hybrid learning. *Faculty:* 10 full-time (9 women), 7 part-time/adjunct (all women). *Students:* 46 full-time (33 women), 22 part-time (17 women); includes 7 minority (4 Black or African American, non-Hispanic/Latino; 1 American Indian or Alaska Native, non-Hispanic/Latino; 1 Hispanic/Latino; 1 Two or more races, non-Hispanic/Latino), 3 international. Average age 27. 74 applicants, 74% accepted, 43 enrolled. In 2016, 57 master's awarded. *Degree requirements:* For master's, research project or thesis, project internship. *Entrance requirements:* For master's, GRE (if cumulative GPA less than 2.7), transcripts, letters of recommendation. Additional exam requirements/recommendations for international students: Required—TOEFL (minimum score 550 paper-based, 79 iBT), IELTS (minimum score 6.5), or CAEL (minimum score 70). *Application deadline:* Applications are processed on a rolling basis. Application fee: $25. Electronic applications accepted. Application fee is waived when completed online. *Expenses:* *Tuition:* Full-time $14,742. *Required fees:* $724. *Financial support:* Career-related internships or fieldwork, Federal Work-Study, scholarships/grants, tuition waivers (partial), and unspecified assistantships available. Support available to part-time students. Financial award application deadline: 4/30; financial award applicants required to submit FAFSA. *Unit head:* Dr. Julie Henry, Chair/Professor, 716-888-3729, E-mail: henry1@canisius.edu. *Application contact:* Kathleen B. Davis, Director of Graduate Admissions, 716-888-2500, Fax: 716-888-3195, E-mail: daviskb@canisius.edu.
Website: http://www.canisius.edu/academics/graduate/

Capella University, School of Education, Doctoral Programs in Education, Minneapolis, MN 55402. Offers curriculum and instruction (PhD); educational leadership and management (Ed D); instructional design for online learning (PhD); K-12 studies in education (PhD); leadership for higher education (PhD); leadership in educational administration (PhD); postsecondary and adult education (PhD); professional studies in education (PhD); reading and literacy (Ed D); special education leadership (PhD); training and performance improvement (PhD).

Capella University, School of Education, Master's Programs in Education, Minneapolis, MN 55402. Offers adult education (MS); curriculum and instruction (MS); early childhood education (MS); enrollment management (MS); higher education leadership and management (MS); instructional design for online learning (MS); integrative studies (MS); K-12 studies in education (MS); leadership in educational administration (MS); reading and literacy (MS); special education teaching (MS).

Chestnut Hill College, School of Graduate Studies, Department of Education, Program in Elementary/Middle Education, Philadelphia, PA 19118-2693. Offers M Ed. *Program availability:* Part-time, evening/weekend. *Degree requirements:* For master's, thesis optional. *Entrance requirements:* For master's, PRAXIS I or proof of teaching certification, letters of recommendation, writing sample, 6 graduate credits with minimum B grade if undergraduate GPA less than 3.0. Additional exam requirements/recommendations for international students: Required—TOEFL (minimum score 500 paper-based), IELTS (minimum score 6.0), or TWE (minimum score 22). Electronic applications accepted. *Expenses:* Contact institution. *Faculty research:* Inclusive education, cultural issues in education.

Chestnut Hill College, School of Graduate Studies, Department of Education, Program in Reading, Philadelphia, PA 19118-2693. Offers reading specialist (M Ed), including K-12, special education 7-12, special education PreK-8. *Program availability:* Part-time, evening/weekend. *Degree requirements:* For master's, thesis optional. *Entrance requirements:* Additional exam requirements/recommendations for international students: Required—TOEFL (minimum score 500 paper-based) or IELTS (minimum score 6). Electronic applications accepted. *Expenses:* Contact institution. *Faculty research:* Inclusive education, cultural issues in education.

Chicago State University, School of Graduate and Professional Studies, College of Education, Department of Reading, Elementary Education, Library Information and Media Studies, Program in Middle School Education, Chicago, IL 60628. Offers MAT.

The Citadel, The Military College of South Carolina, Citadel Graduate College, Zucker Family School of Education, Charleston, SC 29409. Offers elementary/secondary school administration and supervision (M Ed); elementary/secondary school counseling (M Ed); interdisciplinary STEM education (M Ed); literacy education (M Ed, Graduate Certificate); middle grades (MAT), including English, mathematics, science, social studies; physical education (grades K-12) (MAT); school superintendency (Ed S); secondary education (MAT), including biology, English, mathematics, social studies; student affairs (Graduate Certificate); student affairs and college counseling (M Ed). *Accreditation:* NCATE. *Program availability:* Part-time, evening/weekend, 100% online, blended/hybrid learning. *Faculty:* 9 full-time (4 women), 9 part-time/adjunct (5 women). *Students:* 70 full-time (58 women), 249 part-time (200 women); includes 87 minority (70 Black or African American, non-Hispanic/Latino; 1 Asian, non-Hispanic/Latino; 9 Hispanic/Latino; 7 Two or more races, non-Hispanic/Latino), 2 international. 146 applicants, 98% accepted, 105 enrolled. In 2016, 85 master's, 7 other advanced degrees awarded. *Degree requirements:* For master's, comprehensive exam (for some programs). *Entrance requirements:* For master's, GRE (minimum combined verbal and quantitative score of 290) or MAT (minimum score 396). Additional exam requirements/recommendations for international students: Required—TOEFL (minimum score 550 paper-based; 79 iBT). *Application deadline:* Applications are processed on a rolling basis. Application fee: $40. Electronic applications accepted. *Expenses:* Tuition, state resident: full-time $5121; part-time $569 per credit hour. Tuition, nonresident: full-time $8613; part-time $957 per credit hour. *Required fees:* $90 per term. *Financial support:* Fellowships and unspecified assistantships available. Support available to part-time students. Financial award application deadline: 7/1; financial award applicants required to submit FAFSA. *Unit head:* Dr. Larry G. Daniel, Dean, 843-953-5097, E-mail: ldaniel@citadel.edu. *Application contact:* Dr. Tammy J. Graham, Associate Professor, 843-953-6854, E-mail: tammy.graham@citadel.edu.
Website: http://www.citadel.edu/root/education-graduate-programs

City College of the City University of New York, Graduate School, School of Education, Department of Secondary Education, New York, NY 10031-9198. Offers adolescent mathematics education (MA, AC); English education (MA); middle school mathematics education (MS); science education (MA); social studies education (AC). *Accreditation:* NCATE. *Entrance requirements:* For master's, Liberal Arts and Sciences Test (LAST), Content Specialty Test (CST). Additional exam requirements/recommendations for international students: Required—TOEFL. Tuition and fees vary according to course load, degree level and program.

Clarkson University, Program in Education, Schenectady, NY 12308. Offers adolescence education 7-12 (MAT); technology education K-12 (MAT). *Accreditation:* TEAC. *Faculty:* 8 full-time (all women), 31 part-time/adjunct (17 women). *Students:* 38 full-time (23 women), 2 part-time (0 women); includes 6 minority (3 Asian, non-Hispanic/Latino; 2 Hispanic/Latino; 1 Two or more races, non-Hispanic/Latino), 7 international. 39 applicants, 79% accepted, 26 enrolled. In 2016, 15 master's awarded. *Degree requirements:* For master's, thesis (for some programs), thesis or project. *Entrance requirements:* For master's, GRE, minimum undergraduate GPA of 3.0. Additional exam requirements/recommendations for international students: Required—TOEFL (minimum score 550 paper-based, 80 iBT) or IELTS (6.5). *Application deadline:* Applications are processed on a rolling basis. Application fee: $50. Electronic applications accepted. *Expenses:* $900 per credit. *Financial support:* Scholarships/grants available. *Unit head:* Dr. Catherine Snyder, Chair of Education, 518-631-9870, E-mail: csnyder@clarkson.edu. *Application contact:* Dan Capogna, Graduate Admissions Contact, 518-631-9910, E-mail: graduate@clarkson.edu.
Website: http://graduate.clarkson.edu

Clemson University, Graduate School, College of Education, Clemson, SC 29634-0702. Offers administration and supervision (K-12) (M Ed, Ed S); education and organizational leadership (MS), including athletic leadership; educational leadership (PhD), including P-12; human resource development (MHRD); middle-level education (MAT). *Program availability:* Part-time, evening/weekend, 100% online. *Faculty:* 75 full-time (54 women), 1 part-time/adjunct (0 women). *Students:* 120 full-time (84 women), 309 part-time (206 women); includes 96 minority (68 Black or African American, non-Hispanic/Latino; 1 American Indian or Alaska Native, non-Hispanic/Latino; 3 Asian, non-Hispanic/Latino; 19 Hispanic/Latino; 5 Two or more races, non-Hispanic/Latino), 11 international. Average age 34. 417 applicants, 50% accepted, 133 enrolled. In 2016, 239 master's, 21 doctorates, 59 other advanced degrees awarded. *Degree requirements:* For master's, comprehensive exam (for some programs), thesis (for some programs); for doctorate, comprehensive exam, thesis/dissertation. *Entrance requirements:* For master's, doctorate, and other advanced degree, GRE General Test, unofficial transcripts, letters of recommendation. Additional exam requirements/recommendations for international students: Required—TOEFL (minimum score 80 iBT), IELTS (minimum score 7). *Application deadline:* Applications are processed on a rolling basis. Application fee: $80 ($90 for international students). Electronic applications accepted. *Expenses:* Contact institution. *Financial support:* In 2016–17, 75 students received support, including 22 fellowships with partial tuition reimbursements available (averaging $6,316 per year), 28 research assistantships with partial tuition reimbursements available (averaging $15,399 per year), 5 teaching assistantships with partial tuition reimbursements available (averaging $30,000 per year); unspecified assistantships also available. *Faculty research:* Early literacy and motivation, STEAM education, legal/policy issues in education, leadership, special education interventions/assessment/policy. *Total annual research expenditures:* $2.8 million. *Unit head:* Dr. George Petersen, Dean, 864-656-4444, Fax: 864-656-0311, E-mail: soedean@clemson.edu. *Application contact:* Dr. David Fleming, Graduate Programs Coordinator, 864-656-1881, Fax: 864-656-0311, E-mail: dflemin@clemson.edu.
Website: http://www.clemson.edu/education/

Clemson University, Graduate School, College of Education, Department of Teaching and Learning, Program in Middle Level Education, Clemson, SC 29634. Offers MAT. *Faculty:* 15 full-time (12 women). *Students:* 27 full-time (18 women), 3 part-time (2 women); includes 5 minority (4 Black or African American, non-Hispanic/Latino; 1 Two or more races, non-Hispanic/Latino), 25 international. Average age 29. 4 applicants, 50% accepted, 2 enrolled. In 2016, 30 master's awarded. *Degree requirements:* For master's, comprehensive exam, student teaching. *Entrance requirements:* For master's, GRE General Test, unofficial transcripts, letters of recommendation. Additional exam requirements/recommendations for international students: Required—TOEFL (minimum score 540 paper-based; 80 iBT). *Application deadline:* For fall admission, 4/1 for domestic and international students. Applications are processed on a rolling basis. Application fee: $80 ($90 for international students). Electronic applications accepted. *Expenses:* $4,841 per semester full-time resident, $9,640 per semester full-time non-resident, $612 per credit hour part-time resident, $1,223 per credit hour part-time non-resident. *Financial support:* In 2016–17, 2 students received support, including 1 fellowship with partial tuition reimbursement available (averaging $2,000 per year);

unspecified assistantships also available. Financial award application deadline: 4/1. *Faculty research:* Career changers in education, equity and ethics in science classrooms, equitable teaching practices, religious literacy and American schooling, inquiry-based instruction. *Unit head:* Dr. Jeff Marshall, Department Chair, 864-656-2059, E-mail: marsha9@clemson.edu. *Application contact:* Alison Search, Student Services Coordinator, 864-250-8880, E-mail: alisonp@clemson.edu.
Website: http://www.clemson.edu/education/academics/masters-specialist-programs/masters-education-arts-teaching-mat-middle-grades/index.html

The College at Brockport, State University of New York, School of Education, Health, and Human Services, Department of Education and Human Development, Program in Adolescence Education, Brockport, NY 14420-2997. Offers adolescence biology education (MS Ed); adolescence chemistry education (MS Ed); adolescence earth science education (MS Ed); adolescence English education (MS Ed); adolescence mathematics education (MS Ed); adolescence physics education (MS Ed); adolescence social studies education (MS Ed). *Accreditation:* NCATE. *Program availability:* Part-time. *Students:* 4 full-time (1 woman), 35 part-time (23 women); includes 3 minority (2 Black or African American, non-Hispanic/Latino; 1 Two or more races, non-Hispanic/Latino). 21 applicants, 71% accepted, 11 enrolled. In 2016, 18 master's awarded. *Degree requirements:* For master's, thesis or alternative. *Entrance requirements:* For master's, minimum GPA of 3.0, letters of recommendation, statement of objectives, current resume. Additional exam requirements/recommendations for international students: Required—TOEFL (minimum score 550 paper-based; 79 iBT), IELTS (minimum score 6.5). *Application deadline:* For fall admission, 3/15 priority date for domestic and international students; for spring admission, 10/15 priority date for domestic and international students; for summer admission, 3/15 priority date for domestic students, 3/13 priority date for international students. Application fee: $80. Electronic applications accepted. *Expenses:* Contact institution. *Financial support:* Federal Work-Study, scholarships/grants, and unspecified assistantships available. Support available to part-time students. Financial award application deadline: 3/15; financial award applicants required to submit FAFSA. *Unit head:* Dr. Sue Robb, Chairperson, 585-395-5935, Fax: 585-395-2172, E-mail: srobb@brockport.edu. *Application contact:* Anne Walton, Coordinator of Certification and Graduate Advisement, 585-395-2326, Fax: 585-395-2172, E-mail: awalton@brockport.edu.
Website: http://www.brockport.edu/ehd/

College of Mount Saint Vincent, School of Professional and Graduate Studies, Department of Teacher Education, Riverdale, NY 10471-1093. Offers instructional technology and global perspectives (Certificate); middle level education (Certificate); multicultural studies (Certificate); teaching English to speakers of other languages (MS Ed); urban and multicultural education (MS Ed). *Accreditation:* TEAC. *Program availability:* Part-time. *Degree requirements:* For master's, comprehensive exam. *Entrance requirements:* For master's, interview, New York teaching certificate. Additional exam requirements/recommendations for international students: Required—TOEFL.

The College of Saint Rose, Graduate Studies, Thelma P. Lally School of Education, Teacher Education Programs, Albany, NY 12203-1419. Offers adolescence education (MS Ed, Advanced Certificate); adolescence education/special education (Advanced Certificate); childhood education (MS Ed); curriculum and instruction (MS Ed); early childhood education (MS Ed). *Students:* 72 full-time (59 women), 32 part-time (26 women); includes 6 minority (4 Black or African American, non-Hispanic/Latino; 2 Hispanic/Latino), 2 international. Average age 28. 60 applicants, 78% accepted, 25 enrolled. In 2016, 37 master's awarded. *Entrance requirements:* For master's, minimum undergraduate GPA of 3.0. Additional exam requirements/recommendations for international students: Required—TOEFL (minimum score 550 paper-based; 80 iBT), IELTS (minimum score 6), PTE (minimum score 56). *Application deadline:* For fall admission, 4/1 priority date for domestic and international students; for spring admission, 10/15 priority date for domestic and international students; for summer admission, 3/15 priority date for domestic and international students. Applications are processed on a rolling basis. Application fee: $40. Electronic applications accepted. *Expenses: Tuition:* Full-time $14,382; part-time $799 per credit. *Required fees:* $814; $32 per credit. $88 per semester. Tuition and fees vary according to course load. *Financial support:* Career-related internships or fieldwork, scholarships/grants, tuition waivers (partial), and unspecified assistantships available. Support available to part-time students. Financial award application deadline: 4/15. *Unit head:* Dr. Drey Martone, Chair, 518-454-5262, E-mail: martoned@strose.edu. *Application contact:* Cris Murray, Assistant Vice President for Graduate Recruitment and Enrollment, 518-485-3390, Fax: 518-458-5479, E-mail: grad@strose.edu.
Website: https://www.strose.edu/academics/schools/school-of-education/

Columbus State University, Graduate Studies, College of Education and Health Professions, Department of Teacher Education, Columbus, GA 31907-5645. Offers curriculum and instruction in accomplished teaching (M Ed); early childhood education (M Ed, MAT, Ed S); middle grades education (M Ed, MAT, Ed S); secondary education (M Ed, MAT, Ed S), including biology (MAT), chemistry (MAT), earth and space science (MAT), English/language arts, general science (M Ed), history (MAT), mathematics, science (Ed S), social science (M Ed, Ed S); special education (M Ed, MAT, Ed S), including general curriculum (M Ed, MAT); teacher leadership (M Ed). *Accreditation:* NCATE. *Program availability:* Part-time, evening/weekend, 100% online, blended/hybrid learning. *Faculty:* 20 full-time (13 women), 19 part-time/adjunct (16 women). *Students:* 92 full-time (66 women), 212 part-time (179 women); includes 113 minority (104 Black or African American, non-Hispanic/Latino; 1 American Indian or Alaska Native, non-Hispanic/Latino; 2 Asian, non-Hispanic/Latino; 4 Hispanic/Latino; 2 Two or more races, non-Hispanic/Latino), 5 international. Average age 34. 209 applicants, 56% accepted, 79 enrolled. In 2016, 111 master's, 18 other advanced degrees awarded. *Degree requirements:* For Ed S, thesis or alternative. *Entrance requirements:* For master's, GRE General Test, minimum undergraduate GPA of 2.75; for Ed S, GRE General Test, minimum undergraduate GPA of 2.75, graduate 3.0. Additional exam requirements/recommendations for international students: Required—TOEFL (minimum score 550 paper-based; 79 iBT). *Application deadline:* For fall admission, 6/30 for domestic students, 5/1 for international students; for spring admission, 11/1 for domestic and international students; for summer admission, 3/1 for domestic and international students. Applications are processed on a rolling basis. Application fee: $50. Electronic applications accepted. *Expenses:* Tuition, state resident: full-time $4804; part-time $2412 per semester hour. Tuition, nonresident: full-time $19,218; part-time $9612 per semester hour. *Required fees:* $1850; $1850 per semester hour. Tuition and fees vary according to program. *Financial support:* In 2016–17, 60 students received support, including 12 research assistantships with partial tuition reimbursements available (averaging $3,000 per year); career-related internships or fieldwork, Federal Work-Study, institutionally sponsored loans, scholarships/grants, tuition waivers (partial), and unspecified assistantships also available. Support available to part-time students. Financial award application deadline: 5/1; financial award applicants required to submit FAFSA. *Unit head:* Dr. Jan Burcham, Department Chair, 706-507-8519, Fax: 706-568-3134, E-mail: burcham_jan@columbusstate.edu. *Application contact:* Kristin Williams, Director of International and Graduate Recruitment, 706-507-8848, Fax: 706-568-5091, E-mail: williams_kristin@columbusstate.edu.
Website: http://te.columbusstate.edu/

Converse College, School of Education and Graduate Studies, Program in Middle Level Education, Spartanburg, SC 29302. Offers language arts/English (MAT); mathematics (MAT); middle level education (M Ed); science (MAT); social studies (MAT). *Expenses: Tuition:* Full-time $3600; part-time $400 per credit hour. *Required fees:* $70 per term. *Application contact:* 864-596-9404, E-mail: graduate@converse.edu.

Daemen College, Education Department, Amherst, NY 14226-3592. Offers adolescence education (MS); childhood education (MS); childhood special education (MS); childhood special-alternative certification (MS); early childhood special-alternative certification (MS). *Accreditation:* TEAC. *Program availability:* Part-time. *Degree requirements:* For master's, thesis optional, research thesis in lieu of comprehensive exam; completion of degree within 5 years. *Entrance requirements:* For master's, 2 letters of recommendation (professional and character), proof of initial certificate of license for professional programs, resume. Additional exam requirements/recommendations for international students: Required—TOEFL (minimum score 500 paper-based; 63 iBT), IELTS (minimum score 5.5). Electronic applications accepted. *Faculty research:* Transition for students with disabilities, early childhood special education, traumatic brain injury (TBI), reading assessment.

Drury University, Master in Education Program, Springfield, MO 5802. Offers curriculum and instruction (M Ed), including elementary, middle school, secondary; gifted education (M Ed); instructional leadership (M Ed); instructional technology (M Ed); integrated learning (M Ed); online teaching (M Ed); special education (M Ed); special reading (M Ed). *Accreditation:* NCATE. *Program availability:* Part-time, evening/weekend, 100% online, blended/hybrid learning. *Students:* 146 full-time (111 women); includes 6 minority (1 Asian, non-Hispanic/Latino; 3 Hispanic/Latino; 2 Two or more races, non-Hispanic/Latino), 1 international. Average age 34. 42 applicants, 74% accepted. In 2016, 74 master's awarded. *Entrance requirements:* For master's, GRE, bachelor's degree with minimum GPA of 2.75. Additional exam requirements/recommendations for international students: Recommended—TOEFL (minimum score 80 iBT), IELTS (minimum score 6.5). *Application deadline:* For fall admission, 8/4 priority date for domestic and international students; for spring admission, 1/5 priority date for domestic and international students; for summer admission, 5/26 priority date for domestic and international students. Applications are processed on a rolling basis. Application fee: $25 ($50 for international students). Electronic applications accepted. *Expenses:* $352 tuition per credit hour; $7 per credit hour technology fee; $100 graduation fee; $59 portfolio fee (one-time). *Financial support:* In 2016–17, 20 students received support. Career-related internships or fieldwork, scholarships/grants, tuition waivers (partial), and unspecified assistantships available. Financial award application deadline: 6/30; financial award applicants required to submit FAFSA. *Faculty research:* Gifted students, instructional technology, autism, diversity and social justice. *Unit head:* Dr. Asikaa Cosgrove, Director, Master in Education, 417-873-7806, E-mail: acosgrov@drury.edu.
Website: http://www.drury.edu/education-masters

Duquesne University, School of Education, Department of Instruction and Leadership, Program in Middle Level (4-8) Education, Pittsburgh, PA 15282-0001. Offers MS Ed. *Program availability:* Part-time, evening/weekend. *Faculty:* 1 (woman) full-time. *Students:* 3 full-time (1 woman); includes 1 minority (Two or more races, non-Hispanic/Latino). Average age 32. 3 applicants, 100% accepted, 1 enrolled. In 2016, 1 master's awarded. *Entrance requirements:* For master's, bachelor's degree. Additional exam requirements/recommendations for international students: Required—TOEFL (minimum score 550 paper-based). *Application deadline:* For fall admission, 9/1 for domestic students; for spring admission, 1/1 for domestic students. Applications are processed on a rolling basis. Application fee: $0. Electronic applications accepted. *Expenses: Tuition:* Full-time $22,212; part-time $1234 per credit. Tuition and fees vary according to program. *Financial support:* Research assistantships with tuition reimbursements available. *Unit head:* Dr. Carla Meyer, Assistant Professor, 412-396-5838, Fax: 412-396-5388, E-mail: meyer2@duq.edu. *Application contact:* Michael Dolinger, Director of Student and Academic Services, 412-396-6647, Fax: 412-396-5585, E-mail: dolingerm@duq.edu.
Website: http://www.duq.edu/academics/schools/education/graduate-programs-education/ms-middle-level-4-8

East Carolina University, Graduate School, College of Education, Department of Elementary and Middle Grades Education, Greenville, NC 27858-4353. Offers elementary education (MA Ed, MAT); English education (MAT); family and consumer science (MAT); health education (MAT); Hispanic studies (MAT); history education (MAT); middle grades education (MA Ed, MAT); music education (MAT); science education (MAT); special education (MAT), including general curriculum; vocational education (MAT). *Accreditation:* NCATE. *Program availability:* Part-time, evening/weekend, online learning. *Students:* 5 full-time (4 women), 18 part-time (16 women); includes 4 minority (3 Black or African American, non-Hispanic/Latino; 1 Hispanic/Latino). Average age 31. 19 applicants, 95% accepted, 13 enrolled. In 2016, 8 master's awarded. *Degree requirements:* For master's, comprehensive exam, thesis optional. *Entrance requirements:* For master's, GRE or MAT, minimum GPA of 2.5, bachelor's degree in related field, teaching license (MA Ed). Additional exam requirements/recommendations for international students: Required—TOEFL. *Application deadline:* For fall admission, 6/1 priority date for domestic students. Applications are processed on a rolling basis. Application fee: $70. *Financial support:* Federal Work-Study available. Support available to part-time students. Financial award application deadline: 6/1. *Unit head:* Dr. Ann Bullock, Chair, 252-328-1126, E-mail: bullockv@ecu.edu. *Application contact:* Dean of Graduate School, 252-328-6012, Fax: 252-328-6071, E-mail: gradschool@ecu.edu.
Website: http://www.ecu.edu/cs-educ/elmid/index.cfm

Eastern Illinois University, Graduate School, College of Education and Professional Studies, Department of Early Childhood, Elementary and Middle Level Education, Charleston, IL 61920. Offers elementary education (MS Ed). *Accreditation:* NCATE. *Program availability:* Part-time, evening/weekend. *Degree requirements:* For master's, comprehensive exam (for some programs), thesis (for some programs). *Entrance requirements:* For master's, GMAT or GRE. Additional exam requirements/recommendations for international students: Required—TOEFL (minimum score 500 paper-based; 61 iBT), IELTS (minimum score 6). Electronic applications accepted.

Eastern Illinois University, Graduate School, College of Sciences, Department of Mathematics and Computer Science, Charleston, IL 61920. Offers elementary/middle school mathematics education (MA); mathematics (MA). *Program availability:* Part-time, evening/weekend. *Degree requirements:* For master's, comprehensive exam (for some programs), thesis (for some programs). *Entrance requirements:* For master's, GMAT or GRE. Additional exam requirements/recommendations for international students: Required—TOEFL (minimum score 500 paper-based; 61 iBT), IELTS (minimum score 6). Electronic applications accepted.

Eastern Michigan University, Graduate School, College of Education, Department of Teacher Education, Programs in K–12 Education, Ypsilanti, MI 48197. Offers middle school education (MA); secondary school education (MA). *Accreditation:* NCATE. *Program availability:* Part-time, evening/weekend, online learning. *Students:* 9 full-time (8 women), 34 part-time (27 women); includes 3 minority (1 Black or African American, non-Hispanic/Latino; 1 Asian, non-Hispanic/Latino; 1 Hispanic/Latino), 4 international.

Average age 35. 35 applicants, 83% accepted, 18 enrolled. In 2016, 13 master's awarded. *Entrance requirements:* For master's, GRE. Additional exam requirements/recommendations for international students: Required—TOEFL. *Application deadline:* Applications are processed on a rolling basis. Application fee: $45. *Financial support:* Fellowships, research assistantships with full tuition reimbursements, teaching assistantships with full tuition reimbursements, career-related internships or fieldwork, Federal Work-Study, institutionally sponsored loans, scholarships/grants, tuition waivers (partial), and unspecified assistantships available. Support available to part-time students. Financial award applicants required to submit FAFSA. *Application contact:* Dr. Martha Kinney-Sedgwick, Department Head, 734-487-3260, Fax: 734-487-2101, E-mail: mkinneys@emich.edu.

Eastern Nazarene College, Adult and Graduate Studies, Division of Teacher Education, Quincy, MA 02170. Offers administration (M Ed); early childhood education (M Ed, Certificate); elementary education (M Ed, Certificate); English as a second language (Certificate); instructional enrichment and development (Certificate); middle school education (M Ed, Certificate); moderate special needs education (Certificate); principal (Certificate); program development and supervision (Certificate); secondary education (M Ed, Certificate); special education administrator (Certificate); special needs (M Ed); supervisor (Certificate); teacher of reading (M Ed, Certificate). M Ed also available through weekend program for administration, special needs, and teacher of reading only. *Program availability:* Part-time, evening/weekend. *Entrance requirements:* Additional exam requirements/recommendations for international students: Required—TOEFL (minimum score 550 paper-based).

Eastern University, Loeb School of Education, St. Davids, PA 19087-3696. Offers ESL program specialist (K-12) (Certificate); general supervisor (PreK-12) (Certificate); health and physical education (K-12) (Certificate); middle level (4-8) (Certificate); multicultural education (M Ed); organizational leadership with education (PhD); Pre K-4 (Certificate); Pre K-4 with special education (Certificate); reading (M Ed); reading specialist (K-12) (Certificate); reading supervisor (K-12) (Certificate); school health supervisor (Certificate); school nurse (K-12) (Certificate); secondary biology education (7-12) (Certificate); secondary chemistry education (7-12) (Certificate); secondary communication education (7-12) (Certificate); secondary education (7-12) (Certificate); secondary English education (7-12) (Certificate); secondary math education (7-12) (Certificate); secondary social studies education (7-12) (Certificate); special education (M Ed); special education (7-12) (Certificate); special education (Pre K-8) (Certificate); special education supervisor (N-12) (Certificate); TESOL (M Ed); world language (Certificate), including French, Spanish. *Program availability:* Part-time, evening/weekend, online learning. *Students:* 41 full-time (32 women), 89 part-time (68 women); includes 54 minority (38 Black or African American, non-Hispanic/Latino; 3 Asian, non-Hispanic/Latino; 11 Hispanic/Latino; 2 Two or more races, non-Hispanic/Latino), 2 international. Average age 37. In 2016, 64 master's awarded. *Entrance requirements:* Additional exam requirements/recommendations for international students: Required—TOEFL. *Application deadline:* Applications are processed on a rolling basis. Application fee: $35. Electronic applications accepted. Application fee is waived when completed online. *Expenses:* $690 per credit. *Unit head:* Michael Dziedziak, Executive Director of Enrollment, 800-452-0996, E-mail: gpsadmissions@eastern.edu.
Website: http://www.eastern.edu/academics/programs/loeb-school-education-0

East Tennessee State University, School of Graduate Studies, College of Education, Department of Curriculum and Instruction, Johnson City, TN 37614. Offers educational technology (M Ed), including educational communications and technology, school library media; elementary education (M Ed); reading (MA), including reading education; school library professional (Post-Master's Certificate); secondary education (M Ed), including classroom technology; teacher education with multiple levels (MAT), including elementary education, middle grades education, secondary education. *Accreditation:* NCATE. *Program availability:* Part-time, evening/weekend, online learning. *Degree requirements:* For master's, comprehensive exam, thesis optional, student teaching, practicum; for Post-Master's Certificate, field work (school library); culminating experience (storytelling). *Entrance requirements:* For master's, GRE, SAT, ACT, PRAXIS, minimum GPA of 3.0; for Post-Master's Certificate, master's degree, TN teaching license. Additional exam requirements/recommendations for international students: Required—TOEFL (minimum score 550 paper-based; 79 iBT). Electronic applications accepted. *Faculty research:* Critical thinking; curriculum development in reading, math, and science education; cultural diversity; cognitive processes; effective teaching strategies.

Edinboro University of Pennsylvania, Department of Middle and Secondary Education and Educational Leadership, Edinboro, PA 16444. Offers educational leadership (M Ed); middle and secondary instruction (M Ed). *Program availability:* Part-time, evening/weekend. *Degree requirements:* For master's, comprehensive exam, thesis or alternative, project. *Entrance requirements:* For master's, GRE or MAT, minimum QPA of 2.5. Electronic applications accepted.

Emory University, Laney Graduate School, Division of Educational Studies, Atlanta, GA 30322-1100. Offers educational studies (MA, PhD); middle grades teaching (MAT); secondary teaching (MAT). *Accreditation:* NCATE. Terminal master's awarded for partial completion of doctoral program. *Degree requirements:* For master's, thesis; for doctorate, comprehensive exam, thesis/dissertation. *Entrance requirements:* For master's and doctorate, GRE General Test, minimum GPA of 3.0. Additional exam requirements/recommendations for international students: Required—TOEFL. Electronic applications accepted. *Faculty research:* Educational policy, educational measurement, urban and multicultural education, mathematics and science education, comparative education.

Fayetteville State University, Graduate School, Programs in Middle Grades, Secondary, Special and Elementary Education, Fayetteville, NC 28301-4298. Offers middle grades (MA Ed); sociology (MA Ed); special education (MA Ed), including behavioral-emotional handicaps, mentally handicapped, specific training disability. *Accreditation:* NCATE. *Program availability:* Part-time, evening/weekend. *Faculty:* 12 full-time (8 women), 4 part-time/adjunct (3 women). *Students:* 9 full-time (6 women), 11 part-time (10 women); includes 12 minority (11 Black or African American, non-Hispanic/Latino; 1 Asian, non-Hispanic/Latino). Average age 35. 20 applicants, 100% accepted, 1 enrolled. In 2016, 11 master's awarded. *Degree requirements:* For master's, comprehensive exam, internship. *Entrance requirements:* Additional exam requirements/recommendations for international students: Required—TOEFL. *Application deadline:* For fall admission, 4/15 for domestic students; for spring admission, 10/15 for domestic students. Applications are processed on a rolling basis. Application fee: $40. Electronic applications accepted. *Financial support:* Application deadline: 3/1; applicants required to submit FAFSA. *Faculty research:* Students with disabilities and selected leadership behaviors, new vision for professional development, gifted and talented students, emotional and behavioral disabilities, professional development for high school biology teachers. *Unit head:* Dr. Kimberly Smith-Burton, Chairperson, 910-672-1181, Fax: 910-672-1941, E-mail: ksmith@uncfsu.edu. *Application contact:* Debra D. Brown, Administrative Support Associate, 910-672-1181, Fax: 910-672-1596, E-mail: ddbrown@uncfsu.edu.

Fitchburg State University, Division of Graduate and Continuing Education, Program in Middle School Education, Fitchburg, MA 01420-2697. Offers M Ed. *Accreditation:* NCATE. *Program availability:* Part-time, evening/weekend. *Entrance requirements:* Additional exam requirements/recommendations for international students: Required—TOEFL (minimum score 550 paper-based; 79 iBT). Electronic applications accepted. *Expenses:* Tuition, state resident: full-time $2871; part-time $1914 per year. Tuition, nonresident: full-time $2871; part-time $1914 per year. *Required fees:* $3828. Tuition and fees vary according to program.

Florida Gulf Coast University, College of Education, Program in Curriculum and Instruction, Fort Myers, FL 33965-6565. Offers elementary education (M Ed); English education (M Ed); gifted education (M Ed); mathematics education (M Ed); middle school education (M Ed); science education (M Ed); social science education (M Ed). *Program availability:* Part-time, evening/weekend, online learning. *Faculty:* 26 full-time (18 women), 44 part-time/adjunct (32 women). *Students:* 1 (woman) full-time, 22 part-time (20 women); includes 49 minority (19 Black or African American, non-Hispanic/Latino; 4 Asian, non-Hispanic/Latino; 24 Hispanic/Latino; 2 Two or more races, non-Hispanic/Latino), 2 international. Average age 28. 9 applicants, 78% accepted, 2 enrolled. In 2016, 9 master's awarded. *Degree requirements:* For master's, final project or portfolio. *Entrance requirements:* For master's, GRE General Test, MAT, minimum undergraduate GPA of 3.0 in last 2 years. Additional exam requirements/recommendations for international students: Required—TOEFL (minimum score 550 paper-based). *Application deadline:* For fall admission, 7/1 priority date for domestic students; for spring admission, 10/15 for domestic students. Applications are processed on a rolling basis. Application fee: $30. Electronic applications accepted. *Expenses:* Tuition, state resident: full-time $6721. Tuition, nonresident: full-time $28,170. *Required fees:* $1987. Tuition and fees vary according to course load and degree level. *Financial support:* In 2016–17, 1 student received support. Application deadline: 3/1; applicants required to submit FAFSA. *Faculty research:* Internet in schools, technology in pre-service and in-service teacher training. *Unit head:* Dr. Diane Schmidt, Department Chair, 239-590-7741, Fax: 239-590-7801, E-mail: dschmidt@fgcu.edu. *Application contact:* Keiana Desmore, Adviser/Counselor, 239-590-7759, Fax: 239-590-7801, E-mail: kdesmore@fgcu.edu.
Website: http://coe.fgcu.edu/c-imed/

Fontbonne University, Graduate Programs, St. Louis, MO 63105-3098. Offers accounting (MBA, MS); art (MA); art (K-12) (MAT); business (MBA); computer science (MS); deaf education (MA); early intervention in deaf education (MA); education (MA), including autism spectrum disorders, curriculum and instruction, diverse learners, early childhood education, reading, special education; elementary education (MAT); family and consumer sciences (MA), including multidisciplinary health communication studies; fine arts (MFA); instructional design and technology (MS); management and leadership (MM); middle school education (MAT); secondary education (MAT); special education (MAT); speech-language pathology (MS); supply chain management (MS); theatre (MA). *Program availability:* Part-time, evening/weekend, online learning. *Faculty:* 32 full-time (24 women), 43 part-time/adjunct (26 women). *Students:* 456 full-time (313 women), 102 part-time (77 women); includes 138 minority (118 Black or African American, non-Hispanic/Latino; 1 American Indian or Alaska Native, non-Hispanic/Latino; 7 Asian, non-Hispanic/Latino; 9 Hispanic/Latino; 3 Two or more races, non-Hispanic/Latino), 37 international. *Degree requirements:* For master's, comprehensive exam (for some programs), thesis (for some programs). *Entrance requirements:* Additional exam requirements/recommendations for international students: Required—TOEFL (minimum score 500 paper-based; 65 iBT). *Application deadline:* For fall admission, 8/1 for international students; for spring admission, 12/1 for international students. Applications are processed on a rolling basis. Application fee: $25 ($30 for international students). Electronic applications accepted. *Expenses: Tuition:* Full-time $8436; part-time $703 per credit hour. *Required fees:* $18 per credit hour. Tuition and fees vary according to course load. *Financial support:* Teaching assistantships with partial tuition reimbursements and scholarships/grants available. Support available to part-time students. Financial award application deadline: 4/1; financial award applicants required to submit FAFSA. *Unit head:* Dr. Carey Adams, Vice President for Academic Affairs, 314-719-3609, E-mail: cadams@fontbonne.edu. *Application contact:* Lauryn Filip, Coordinator, Graduate Admission and Professional Studies, 314-889-4650, E-mail: admissions@fontbonne.edu.
Website: https://www.fontbonne.edu/academics/graduate-programs/

Georgia Southern University, Jack N. Averitt College of Graduate Studies, College of Education, Department of Teaching and Learning, Program in Middle Grades Education, Statesboro, GA 30460. Offers M Ed, MAT, Ed S. *Accreditation:* NCATE. *Program availability:* Part-time, evening/weekend. *Students:* 13 full-time (11 women), 17 part-time (16 women); includes 8 minority (7 Black or African American, non-Hispanic/Latino; 1 Two or more races, non-Hispanic/Latino). Average age 30. 13 applicants, 92% accepted, 9 enrolled. In 2016, 8 master's, 8 other advanced degrees awarded. *Degree requirements:* For master's, portfolio, transition point assessments, exit assessment. *Entrance requirements:* For master's, GRE General Test or MAT; GACE Basic Skills and Content Assessments (for MAT), minimum cumulative GPA of 2.5. Additional exam requirements/recommendations for international students: Required—TOEFL (minimum score 550 paper-based; 80 iBT), IELTS (minimum score 6). *Application deadline:* For fall admission, 3/15 priority date for domestic students, 3/14 priority date for international students; for spring admission, 10/1 priority date for domestic students, 10/1 for international students; for summer admission, 3/1 for domestic and international students. Applications are processed on a rolling basis. Application fee: $50. Electronic applications accepted. *Expenses:* Tuition, state resident: full-time $7236; part-time $277 per semester hour. Tuition, nonresident: full-time $27,118; part-time $1105 per semester hour. *Required fees:* $2092. *Financial support:* In 2016–17, 4 students received support, including 4 fellowships with full tuition reimbursements available (averaging $7,750 per year); career-related internships or fieldwork, Federal Work-Study, and tuition waivers (full) also available. Support available to part-time students. Financial award application deadline: 4/15; financial award applicants required to submit FAFSA. *Faculty research:* Gender, technology applications, early and young adolescent literature, content subjects and literacy, integrated curriculum, content subject learning. *Unit head:* Dr. Greg Chamblee, Program Coordinator, 912-478-5701, Fax: 912-478-0026, E-mail: gchamblee@georgiasouthern.edu. *Application contact:* Lydia Cross, Coordinator for Graduate Academic Services Center, 912-478-8664, E-mail: lcross@georgiasouthern.edu.
Website: http://coe.georgiasouthern.edu/ger/

Georgia Southwestern State University, School of Education, Americus, GA 31709-4693. Offers early childhood education (M Ed, Ed S); middle grades education (Ed S); middle grades language arts (M Ed); middle grades mathematics (M Ed); special education (M Ed). *Accreditation:* NCATE. *Faculty:* 13 full-time (8 women), 7 part-time/adjunct (6 women). *Students:* 209 full-time (199 women), 6 part-time (all women); includes 52 minority (45 Black or African American, non-Hispanic/Latino; 6 Hispanic/Latino; 1 Two or more races, non-Hispanic/Latino). Average age 33. In 2016, 57 master's awarded. *Degree requirements:* For master's, minimum cumulative GPA of 3.0; for Ed S, minimum GPA of 3.25 in all courses with no grade less than a B; degree must be completed within 7 calendar years from date of initial enrollment in graduate work. *Entrance requirements:* For master's, undergraduate degree from accredited institution; professional Georgia Teaching Certificate or eligibility; minimum undergraduate GPA of 2.75 as reported on official final transcripts from all accredited institutions attended; 2

confidential Administrative Recommendation Forms; for Ed S, master's degree from accredited college or university; professional Georgia Teaching Certificate or eligibility; minimum graduate GPA of 3.0 as reported on official final graduate transcripts from all accredited institutions attended; 2 confidential Administrative Recommendation Forms. *Application deadline:* For summer admission, 4/15 for domestic students. Application fee: $25. Electronic applications accepted. *Expenses:* $257 per credit hour for online program courses, plus fees, which vary according to enrolled credit hours. *Financial support:* Application deadline: 6/1; applicants required to submit FAFSA. *Unit head:* Dr. Rachel Abbott, Dean, 229-931-2145. *Application contact:* Whitney Ford, Admissions Specialist, Office of Graduate Admissions, 800-338-0082, Fax: 229-931-2983.
Website: https://gsw.edu/Academics/Schools-and-Departments/School-of-Education/index

Georgia State University, College of Education and Human Development, Department of Middle and Secondary Education, Atlanta, GA 30302-3083. Offers curriculum and instruction (Ed D); English education (MAT); mathematics education (M Ed, MAT); middle level education (MAT); reading, language and literacy education (M Ed, MAT), including reading instruction (M Ed); science education (M Ed, MAT), including biology (MAT), broad field science (MAT), chemistry (MAT), earth science (MAT), physics (MAT); social studies education (M Ed, MAT), including economics (MAT), geography (MAT), history (MAT), political science (MAT); teaching and learning (PhD), including language and literacy, mathematics education, music education, science education, social studies education, teaching and teacher education. *Accreditation:* NCATE. *Program availability:* Part-time, evening/weekend, online learning. *Faculty:* 24 full-time (18 women). *Students:* 145 full-time (91 women), 151 part-time (102 women); includes 141 minority (104 Black or African American, non-Hispanic/Latino; 1 American Indian or Alaska Native, non-Hispanic/Latino; 16 Asian, non-Hispanic/Latino; 12 Hispanic/Latino; 8 Two or more races, non-Hispanic/Latino), 10 international. Average age 36. 115 applicants, 50% accepted, 41 enrolled. In 2016, 94 master's, 22 doctorates awarded. *Degree requirements:* For master's, comprehensive exam (for some programs), thesis or alternative, exit portfolio; for doctorate, comprehensive exam, thesis/dissertation. *Entrance requirements:* For master's, GRE; GACE I (for initial teacher preparation programs), baccalaureate degree or equivalent, resume, goals statement, two letters of recommendation, minimum undergraduate GPA of 2.5; proof of initial teacher certification in the content area (for M Ed); for doctorate, GRE, resume, goals statement, writing sample, two letters of recommendation, minimum graduate GPA of 3.3, interview. Additional exam requirements/recommendations for international students: Required—TOEFL (minimum score 550 paper-based; 79 iBT) or IELTS (minimum score 6.5). *Application deadline:* For fall admission, 1/15 priority date for domestic and international students; for spring admission, 10/1 for domestic and international students. Application fee: $50. Electronic applications accepted. *Expenses:* Tuition, state resident: full-time $6876; part-time $382 per credit hour. Tuition, nonresident: full-time $22,374; part-time $1243 per credit hour. *Required fees:* $2128; $1064 per term. Part-time tuition and fees vary according to course load and program. *Financial support:* In 2016–17, fellowships with full tuition reimbursements (averaging $19,667 per year), research assistantships with full tuition reimbursements (averaging $5,436 per year), teaching assistantships with full tuition reimbursements (averaging $2,779 per year) were awarded; career-related internships or fieldwork, Federal Work-Study, scholarships/grants, health care benefits, tuition waivers (full and partial), and unspecified assistantships also available. Financial award application deadline: 3/15. *Faculty research:* Teacher education in language and literacy, mathematics, science, and social studies in urban middle and secondary school settings; learning technologies in school, community, and corporate settings; multicultural education and education for social justice; urban education; international education. *Unit head:* Dr. Dana L. Fox, Chair, 404-413-8060, Fax: 404-413-8063, E-mail: dfox@gsu.edu. *Application contact:* Bobbie Turner, Administrative Coordinator I, 404-413-8405, Fax: 404-413-8063, E-mail: bnturner@gsu.edu.
Website: http://mse.education.gsu.edu/

Gordon College, Graduate Education Program, Wenham, MA 01984-1899. Offers early childhood (M Ed); educational leadership (M Ed, Ed S); elementary education (M Ed); English as a second language (M Ed, Ed S); math specialist (M Ed); mathematics specialist (Ed S); middle school education (M Ed); moderate disabilities (M Ed); Montessori education (M Ed); reading (M Ed, Ed S); secondary education (M Ed). *Program availability:* Part-time, evening/weekend. *Faculty:* 17 full-time (9 women), 41 part-time/adjunct (34 women). *Students:* 81 full-time (61 women), 109 part-time (87 women); includes 28 minority (2 Black or African American, non-Hispanic/Latino; 11 Asian, non-Hispanic/Latino; 13 Hispanic/Latino; 2 Two or more races, non-Hispanic/Latino), 12 international. Average age 34. 190 applicants, 100% accepted, 141 enrolled. In 2016, 110 master's, 16 Ed Ss awarded. *Degree requirements:* For master's, action research or clinical experience (for most programs); for Ed S, action research or clinical experience (for some programs). *Entrance requirements:* For master's, minimum undergraduate GPA of 3.0; 2 official undergraduate transcripts; professional resume; 3 recommendation letters (one professional reference, one academic reference, one personal reference); 500-700 word statement of purpose; for Ed S, minimum master's GPA of 3.3; 2 official transcripts from undergraduate and graduate schools; professional resume; 3 recommendation letters (one professional reference, one academic reference, one personal reference); 500-700 word statement of purpose. Additional exam requirements/recommendations for international students: Required—TOEFL (minimum score 550 paper-based, 80 iBT) or IELTS (minimum score 6.5). *Application deadline:* Applications are processed on a rolling basis. Application fee: $75. *Expenses:* $325 per credit tuition, $75 per term fee. *Financial support:* Applicants required to submit FAFSA. *Faculty research:* Reading, early childhood development, English language learners, universal design for learning. *Unit head:* Dr. Janet Arndt, Director of Graduate Studies, 978-867-4355, Fax: 978-867-4663. *Application contact:* Julie Lenocker, Program Administrator, 978-867-4322, Fax: 978-867-4663, E-mail: graduate-education@gordon.edu.
Website: http://www.gordon.edu/graduate

Goucher College, Graduate Programs in Education, Baltimore, MD 21204-2794. Offers at-risk and diverse learners (M Ed, Certificate); athletic program leadership and administration (M Ed, Certificate); elementary and special education (MAT); elementary education (MAT); literacy strategies for content learning (M Ed, Certificate); middle school (M Ed, Certificate); Montessori studies (M Ed); reading instruction (M Ed, Certificate); school improvement leadership (M Ed, Certificate); school mediation (M Ed, Certificate); secondary and special education (MAT); secondary education (MAT); special education (MAT), including elementary education, secondary education; special education for certified teachers (M Ed, Certificate); teacher as leader in technology (M Ed, Certificate). *Program availability:* Part-time, evening/weekend. *Faculty:* 3 full-time (all women), 52 part-time/adjunct (40 women). *Students:* 29 full-time (20 women), 285 part-time (217 women); includes 54 minority (41 Black or African American, non-Hispanic/Latino; 3 Asian, non-Hispanic/Latino; 7 Hispanic/Latino; 3 Two or more races, non-Hispanic/Latino), 1 international. Average age 34. 85 applicants, 100% accepted, 61 enrolled. In 2016, 207 master's awarded. *Degree requirements:* For master's, thesis (M Ed), final presentation (MAT). *Entrance requirements:* For master's, minimum GPA of 3.0. Additional exam requirements/recommendations for international students: Required—TOEFL (minimum score 560 paper-based). *Application deadline:* For fall admission, 9/1 for domestic students; for spring admission, 1/15 for domestic students. Applications are processed on a rolling basis. Application fee: $75. Electronic applications accepted. *Expenses:* Contact institution. *Financial support:* Career-related internships or fieldwork and unspecified assistantships available. Support available to part-time students. Financial award application deadline: 4/15; financial award applicants required to submit FAFSA. *Faculty research:* Urban education, middle school, school improvement, teacher education, at-risk student achievement. *Unit head:* Dr. Phyllis Sunshine, Assistant Provost, 410-337-6047, Fax: 410-337-6394, E-mail: psunshin@goucher.edu. *Application contact:* Shelby Hillers, Admissions Coordinator, 410-337-6200, Fax: 410-337-6085, E-mail: shelby.hillers@goucher.edu.
Website: http://www.goucher.edu/graduate-programs/graduate-programs-in-education

Grand Valley State University, College of Education, Programs in General Education, Allendale, MI 49401-9403. Offers adult and higher education (M Ed); early childhood education (M Ed); educational differentiation (M Ed); educational leadership (M Ed); educational technology integration (M Ed); elementary education (M Ed); middle level education (M Ed); school library media services (M Ed); secondary level education (M Ed); teaching English to speakers of other languages (M Ed). *Program availability:* Part-time, evening/weekend, 100% online, blended/hybrid learning. *Students:* 28 part-time (20 women); includes 6 minority (4 Black or African American, non-Hispanic/Latino; 1 American Indian or Alaska Native, non-Hispanic/Latino; 1 Hispanic/Latino). Average age 42. In 2016, 17 master's awarded. *Degree requirements:* For master's, project or thesis. *Entrance requirements:* For master's, GRE General Test or minimum GPA of 3.0, last 60 credits from regionally-accredited college/university, 3 letters of recommendation. Additional exam requirements/recommendations for international students: Required—TOEFL (minimum score 550 paper-based, 80 iBT), IELTS (6.5), or Michigan English Language Assessment Battery. *Application deadline:* Applications are processed on a rolling basis. Application fee: $30. Electronic applications accepted. *Expenses:* $628 per credit hour. *Financial support:* In 2016–17, 2 students received support. Career-related internships or fieldwork, Federal Work-Study, scholarships/grants, and unspecified assistantships available. *Faculty research:* Effectiveness of technology in education, parental involvement, effective teaching, effective schools research. *Unit head:* Dr. Doug Busman, Graduate Program Director, 616-331-6250, E-mail: busmando@gvsu.edu. *Application contact:* Thomas Owens, Director, Student Information and Services Center, 616-331-6282, Fax: 616-331-6217, E-mail: owenst@gvsu.edu.
Website: http://www.gvsu.edu/coe/

Hebrew College, Shoolman Graduate School of Jewish Education, Newton Centre, MA 02459. Offers early childhood Jewish education (Certificate); Jewish day school education (Certificate); Jewish education (MJ Ed); Jewish family education (Certificate); Jewish special education (Certificate); Jewish youth education, informal education and camping (Certificate). *Program availability:* Part-time, evening/weekend, online learning. *Degree requirements:* For master's, one foreign language. *Entrance requirements:* For master's, GRE, interview. Additional exam requirements/recommendations for international students: Required—TOEFL.

Henderson State University, Graduate Studies, Teachers College, Department of Advanced Instructional Studies, Arkadelphia, AR 71999-0001. Offers developmental therapy (MSE); dyslexia therapy (Graduate Certificate); education (MAT); educational technology leadership (Graduate Certificate); English as a second language (MSE, Graduate Certificate); instructional facilitator (MSE, Graduate Certificate); middle level education (MAT); special education (K-12) (MAT, MSE); special education/early childhood (MAT). *Accreditation:* NCATE. *Program availability:* Part-time. *Faculty:* 12 full-time (9 women), 5 part-time/adjunct (4 women). *Students:* 13 full-time (8 women), 79 part-time (66 women); includes 14 minority (8 Black or African American, non-Hispanic/Latino; 2 American Indian or Alaska Native, non-Hispanic/Latino; 2 Hispanic/Latino; 2 Two or more races, non-Hispanic/Latino). Average age 33. 21 applicants, 100% accepted, 21 enrolled. In 2016, 29 master's awarded. *Entrance requirements:* For master's, GRE General Test or MAT, minimum GPA of 2.7, teacher certification. Additional exam requirements/recommendations for international students: Required—TOEFL (minimum score 600 paper-based); Recommended—IELTS (minimum score 6.5). *Application deadline:* For fall admission, 8/1 priority date for domestic students, 6/30 priority date for international students; for spring admission, 1/1 priority date for domestic students, 11/30 priority date for international students. Applications are processed on a rolling basis. Application fee: $25 ($75 for international students). *Expenses:* Tuition, state resident: full-time $6288; part-time $3144 per credit hour. Tuition, nonresident: full-time $12,888; part-time $6444 per credit hour. *Required fees:* $1429; $1024 per credit hour. Tuition and fees vary according to course load and student level. *Financial support:* In 2016–17, 1 teaching assistantship with partial tuition reimbursement (averaging $4,000 per year) was awarded; scholarships/grants and unspecified assistantships also available. Financial award application deadline: 4/15; financial award applicants required to submit FAFSA. *Unit head:* Dr. Gary Smithey, Coordinator, 870-230-5361, Fax: 870-230-5455, E-mail: smitheg@hsu.edu. *Application contact:* Dr. Ken Taylor, Graduate Dean, 870-230-5126, Fax: 870-230-5479, E-mail: taylorke@hsu.edu.
Website: http://www.hsu.edu/Academics/TeachersCollege/AIS/index.html

Hofstra University, School of Education, Programs in Teacher Education, Hempstead, NY 11549. Offers bilingual education (MA, Advanced Certificate); bilingual extension (Advanced Certificate), including education/speech language pathology; business education (MS Ed); early childhood and childhood education (MS Ed); early childhood education (MA, MS Ed); education technology (Advanced Certificate); elementary education (MA, MS Ed), including science, technology, engineering, and mathematics (STEM) (MA); English education (MS Ed); family and consumer science (MS Ed); fine arts and music education (Advanced Certificate); fine arts education (MS Ed); foreign language and TESOL (MS Ed); foreign language education (MS Ed), including French, German, Russian, Spanish; learning and teaching (Ed D), including applied linguistics, art education, arts and humanities, early childhood education, English education, human development, math education, math, science, and technology, multicultural education, physical education, science education, social studies education, special education; mathematics education (MA, MS Ed); middle school extension (Advanced Certificate), including grades 5-6, grades 7-9; music education (MA, MS Ed); science education (MA, MS Ed), including biology, chemistry, earth science, geology, physics; secondary education (Advanced Certificate); social studies education (MA, MS Ed); teaching languages other than English and TESOL (MS Ed); TESOL (MS Ed, Advanced Certificate). *Program availability:* Part-time, evening/weekend, blended/hybrid learning. *Students:* 139 full-time (97 women), 145 part-time (106 women); includes 60 minority (15 Black or African American, non-Hispanic/Latino; 1 American Indian or Alaska Native, non-Hispanic/Latino; 12 Asian, non-Hispanic/Latino; 31 Hispanic/Latino; 1 Two or more races, non-Hispanic/Latino), 21 international. Average age 29. 255 applicants, 86% accepted, 122 enrolled. In 2016, 101 master's, 4 doctorates, 43 other advanced degrees awarded. *Degree requirements:* For master's, comprehensive exam, thesis (for some programs), exit project, student teaching, fieldwork, electronic portfolio, curriculum project, minimum GPA of 3.0; for doctorate, thesis/dissertation; for Advanced Certificate, 3 foreign languages, comprehensive exam (for some programs), thesis project. *Entrance requirements:* For master's, GRE, MAT, 2 letters of recommendation, portfolio, teacher certification (MA), interview, essay; for doctorate, GMAT, GRE, LSAT, or MAT; for Advanced Certificate, 2 letters of recommendation, essay, interview and/or portfolio,

teaching certificate. Additional exam requirements/recommendations for international students: Required—TOEFL (minimum score 550 paper-based; 80 iBT). *Application deadline:* Applications are processed on a rolling basis. Application fee: $75. Electronic applications accepted. *Expenses: Tuition:* Full-time $1240. *Required fees:* $970. Tuition and fees vary according to program. *Financial support:* In 2016–17, 149 students received support, including 58 fellowships with full and partial tuition reimbursements available (averaging $5,309 per year), 5 research assistantships with full and partial tuition reimbursements available (averaging $7,073 per year); career-related internships or fieldwork, Federal Work-Study, institutionally sponsored loans, scholarships/grants, traineeships, tuition waivers (full and partial), and unspecified assistantships also available. Support available to part-time students. Financial award applicants required to submit FAFSA. *Faculty research:* Educational interventions that foster critical-thinking skills; teachers' attitudes about professional development; threats to teacher quality. *Unit head:* Dr. Eustace Thompson, Chairperson, 516-463-5749, Fax: 516-463-6275, E-mail: eustace.g.thompson@hofstra.edu. *Application contact:* Sunil Samuel, Assistant Vice President of Admissions, 516-463-4723, Fax: 516-463-4664, E-mail: graduateadmission@hofstra.edu.
Website: http://www.hofstra.edu/education/

Hofstra University, School of Education, Specialized Programs in Education, Hempstead, NY 11549. Offers applied behavior analysis (Advanced Certificate); early childhood special education (MS Ed, Advanced Certificate); educational and policy leadership (Ed D); educational leadership (Advanced Certificate), including school building leader/school district business leader; educational leadership and policy studies (MS Ed), including K-12; gifted education (Advanced Certificate), including school building leader/school district business leader; health education PK-12 teaching certification (MS); inclusive early childhood special education (MS Ed); inclusive elementary special education (MS Ed); inclusive secondary special education (MS Ed); literacy studies (MS Ed, Ed D, PhD, Advanced Certificate), including birth-grade 6 (MS Ed, Advanced Certificate), birth-grade 6 and special education (birth-grade2) (MS Ed), grades 5-12 (MS Ed, Advanced Certificate); physical education (MS); secondary education generalist (MS Ed), including students with disabilities 7-12; special education (MS Ed, Advanced Certificate); special education assessment and diagnosis (Advanced Certificate); special education generalist (MS Ed), including extension in secondary education; sport science (MS), including strength and conditioning; teaching students with severe or multiple disabilities (Advanced Certificate). *Program availability:* Part-time, evening/weekend, 100% online, blended/hybrid learning. *Students:* 149 full-time (115 women), 258 part-time (187 women); includes 97 minority (50 Black or African American, non-Hispanic/Latino; 1 American Indian or Alaska Native, non-Hispanic/Latino; 11 Asian, non-Hispanic/Latino; 34 Hispanic/Latino; 1 Native Hawaiian or other Pacific Islander, non-Hispanic/Latino), 5 international. Average age 32. 250 applicants, 88% accepted, 146 enrolled. In 2016, 85 master's, 13 doctorates, 35 other advanced degrees awarded. *Degree requirements:* For master's, one foreign language, comprehensive exam (for some programs), thesis (for some programs), electronic portfolio, capstone course, internship, practicum, student teaching, seminars, minimum GPA of 3.0; for doctorate, one foreign language, comprehensive exam, thesis/dissertation, qualifying hearing. *Entrance requirements:* For master's, GRE, interview, letters of recommendation, portfolio, essay, certification; for doctorate, GRE or MAT, interview, resume, essay, master's degree, 3 letters of recommendation, writing sample; for Advanced Certificate, GRE, interview, letters of recommendation, essay, professional experience, resume, master's degree. Additional exam requirements/recommendations for international students: Required—TOEFL (minimum score 550 paper-based; 80 iBT). *Application deadline:* Applications are processed on a rolling basis. Application fee: $75. Electronic applications accepted. *Expenses: Tuition:* Full-time $1240. *Required fees:* $970. Tuition and fees vary according to program. *Financial support:* In 2016–17, 244 students received support, including 117 fellowships with full and partial tuition reimbursements available (averaging $3,705 per year), 12 research assistantships with full and partial tuition reimbursements available (averaging $6,490 per year); career-related internships or fieldwork, Federal Work-Study, institutionally sponsored loans, scholarships/grants, traineeships, tuition waivers (full and partial), and unspecified assistantships also available. Support available to part-time students. Financial award applicants required to submit FAFSA. *Faculty research:* Collaborative teaching and learning; language and culture; new media literacies; applied behavior analysis; K-12 leadership development. *Unit head:* Dr. Elfreda Blue, Chairperson, 516-463-5762, Fax: 516-463-6184, E-mail: elfreda.blue@hofstra.edu. *Application contact:* Sunil Samuel, Assistant Vice President of Admissions, 516-463-4723, Fax: 516-463-4664, E-mail: graduateadmission@hofstra.edu.
Website: http://www.hofstra.edu/education/

Huntington University, Graduate School, Huntington, IN 46750-1299. Offers counseling (MA), including licensed mental health counselor; early adolescent education (M Ed); education (M Ed); global missions leadership (MA); global youth ministry (MA); TESOL education (M Ed); youth ministry leadership (MA). *Program availability:* Part-time, online learning. *Degree requirements:* For master's, comprehensive exam (for some programs), thesis (for some programs). *Entrance requirements:* For master's, GRE (for counseling and education students only); for doctorate, GRE (for occupational therapy students). Additional exam requirements/recommendations for international students: Required—TOEFL (minimum score 85 iBT), IELTS (minimum score 6.5). Electronic applications accepted. *Faculty research:* Leadership, educational technology trends, evangelism, youth ministry, mental health.

James Madison University, The Graduate School, College of Education, Program in Education, Harrisonburg, VA 22807. Offers early childhood education (preK-3) (MAT); educational leadership (M Ed); educational technology (M Ed); elementary education (MAT); equity and cultural diversity (M Ed); inclusive early childhood education (MAT); K-8 mathematics specialist (M Ed); middle education (MAT); reading education (M Ed); secondary education (MAT); Spanish language and culture for educators (M Ed); TESOL (MAT). *Accreditation:* NCATE. *Program availability:* Part-time, evening/weekend. *Faculty:* 21 full-time (12 women), 5 part-time/adjunct (2 women). *Students:* 249 full-time (220 women), 123 part-time (86 women); includes 43 minority (7 Black or African American, non-Hispanic/Latino; 7 Asian, non-Hispanic/Latino; 17 Hispanic/Latino; 12 Two or more races, non-Hispanic/Latino), 2 international. Average age 30. 355 applicants, 98% accepted, 312 enrolled. In 2016, 247 master's awarded. Application fee: $55. Electronic applications accepted. *Financial support:* In 2016–17, 16 students received support. Career-related internships or fieldwork, Federal Work-Study, and 22 assistantships (averaging $7911) available. Financial award application deadline: 3/1; financial award applicants required to submit FAFSA. *Unit head:* Dr. Phillip M. Wishon, Dean, 540-568-6572, E-mail: wishonpm@jmu.edu. *Application contact:* Lynette D. Michael, Director of Graduate Admissions, 540-568-6131 Ext. 6395, Fax: 540-568-7860, E-mail: michaeld@jmu.edu.
Website: http://www.jmu.edu/coe/index.shtml

James Madison University, The Graduate School, College of Education, Program in Middle Education, Harrisonburg, VA 22807. Offers MAT. *Accreditation:* NCATE. *Program availability:* Part-time, evening/weekend. *Students:* Average age 27. *Entrance requirements:* For master's, GRE General Test, minimum undergraduate GPA of 2.5. Additional exam requirements/recommendations for international students: Required—TOEFL. *Application deadline:* For fall admission, 5/1 priority date for domestic students; for spring admission, 9/1 priority date for domestic students. Applications are processed on a rolling basis. Application fee: $55. Electronic applications accepted. *Financial support:* Federal Work-Study and unspecified assistantships available. Financial award application deadline: 3/1; financial award applicants required to submit FAFSA. *Unit head:* Dr. Steven L. Purcell, Academic Unit Head, 540-568-6793. *Application contact:* Lynette M. Bible, Director of Graduate Admissions, 540-568-6395, Fax: 540-568-7860, E-mail: biblelm@jmu.edu.

Kansas State University, Graduate School, College of Education, Department of Curriculum and Instruction, Manhattan, KS 66506. Offers curriculum and instruction (Ed D, PhD); digital teaching and learning (MS); educational computing, design and online learning (MS); elementary/middle level curriculum and instruction (MS); online learning (Certificate); reading specialist endorsement (MS); reading/language arts (MS); teacher leader/school improvement (MS); teaching and learning (Certificate). *Accreditation:* NCATE. *Program availability:* Part-time, online learning. *Faculty:* 36 full-time (22 women), 18 part-time/adjunct (9 women). *Students:* 59 full-time (40 women), 94 part-time (72 women); includes 21 minority (5 Black or African American, non-Hispanic/Latino; 3 Asian, non-Hispanic/Latino; 11 Hispanic/Latino; 2 Two or more races, non-Hispanic/Latino), 20 international. Average age 35. 70 applicants, 71% accepted, 36 enrolled. In 2016, 61 master's, 12 doctorates, 9 other advanced degrees awarded. *Degree requirements:* For master's, comprehensive exam, portfolio, project, report or thesis; for doctorate, comprehensive exam, thesis/dissertation, preliminary exam; for Certificate, comprehensive exam, portfolio. *Entrance requirements:* For master's, minimum GPA of 3.0, 3 letters of recommendation; for doctorate, GRE, minimum GPA of 3.0, 3 letters of recommendation, evidence of scholarly writing; for Certificate, minimum GPA of 3.0, letters of recommendation. Additional exam requirements/recommendations for international students: Required—TOEFL (minimum score 550 paper-based; 80 iBT) or IELTS. *Application deadline:* For fall admission, 3/1 priority date for domestic students, 2/1 priority date for international students; for spring admission, 10/1 priority date for domestic students, 8/1 priority date for international students. Applications are processed on a rolling basis. Application fee: $50 ($75 for international students). Electronic applications accepted. *Expenses:* Tuition, state resident: full-time $9670. Tuition, nonresident: full-time $21,828. *Required fees:* $862. *Financial support:* In 2016–17, 1 research assistantship (averaging $19,980 per year), 8 teaching assistantships (averaging $12,620 per year) were awarded; career-related internships or fieldwork, institutionally sponsored loans, scholarships/grants, and unspecified assistantships also available. Support available to part-time students. Financial award application deadline: 3/1; financial award applicants required to submit FAFSA. *Faculty research:* Literacy and technology, critical race theory and diversity, achievement gaps, school improvement, teacher education. *Total annual research expenditures:* $647,057. *Unit head:* Dr. F. Todd Goodson, Department Chair, 785-532-5904, Fax: 785-532-7304, E-mail: tgoodson@ksu.edu. *Application contact:* Dr. Kay Ann Taylor, Director, Curriculum and Instruction Graduate Programs, 785-532-6974, Fax: 785-532-7304, E-mail: ktaylor@ksu.edu.
Website: http://www.coe.ksu.edu/edci/index.html

Kennesaw State University, Leland and Clarice C. Bagwell College of Education, Program in Graduate Education, Kennesaw, GA 30144. Offers educational leadership (M Ed); educational leadership technology (M Ed); elementary and early childhood education (M Ed); instructional technology (M Ed); middle grades education (M Ed); reading (M Ed); secondary education (M Ed); special education (M Ed); teaching English to speakers of other languages (M Ed). *Accreditation:* NCATE. *Program availability:* Part-time. *Degree requirements:* For master's, thesis or alternative. *Entrance requirements:* For master's, GRE General Test, T-4 state certification, minimum GPA of 2.75. Additional exam requirements/recommendations for international students: Required—TOEFL (minimum score 550 paper-based; 80 iBT), IELTS (minimum score 6.5). Electronic applications accepted.

Kent State University, College of Education, Health and Human Services, School of Teaching, Learning and Curriculum Studies, Program in Junior High/Middle School, Kent, OH 44242-0001. Offers M Ed, MA. *Program availability:* Part-time. *Degree requirements:* For master's, thesis (for some programs). *Entrance requirements:* For master's, 2 letters of reference, goals statement. Additional exam requirements/recommendations for international students: Required—TOEFL (minimum score 550 paper-based; 80 iBT). Electronic applications accepted. *Expenses:* Tuition, state resident: full-time $10,864; part-time $495 per credit hour. Tuition, nonresident: full-time $18,380; part-time $837 per credit hour. *Faculty research:* Middle school reform, teacher action research.

Kutztown University of Pennsylvania, College of Education, Program in Secondary Education, Kutztown, PA 19530-0730. Offers biology (M Ed); curriculum and instruction (M Ed); English (M Ed); mathematics (M Ed); middle level (M Ed); social studies (M Ed); teaching (M Ed). *Accreditation:* NCATE. *Program availability:* Part-time, evening/weekend. *Faculty:* 4 full-time (2 women), 2 part-time/adjunct (0 women). *Students:* 35 full-time (23 women), 58 part-time (37 women); includes 4 minority (2 Black or African American, non-Hispanic/Latino; 2 Hispanic/Latino). Average age 31. 96 applicants, 86% accepted, 43 enrolled. In 2016, 35 master's awarded. *Degree requirements:* For master's, comprehensive exam, thesis optional. *Entrance requirements:* For master's, GRE General Test, minimum undergraduate major GPA of 3.0, 3 letters of recommendation, copy of PRAXIS II or valid instructional I or II teaching certificate. Additional exam requirements/recommendations for international students: Required—TOEFL (minimum score 550 paper-based, 79 iBT) or IELTS (minimum score 6.5). *Application deadline:* For fall admission, 8/1 for domestic and international students; for spring admission, 12/1 for domestic and international students. Application fee: $35. Electronic applications accepted. *Expenses:* Tuition, state resident: full-time $4347; part-time $483 per credit. Tuition, nonresident: full-time $6525; part-time $725 per credit. *Required fees:* $88 per credit. One-time fee: $50 full-time. *Financial support:* Career-related internships or fieldwork, Federal Work-Study, scholarships/grants, and unspecified assistantships available. Financial award application deadline: 3/1; financial award applicants required to submit FAFSA. *Unit head:* Dr. Theresa Stahler, Chairperson, 610-683-4259, Fax: 610-683-1338, E-mail: stahler@kutztown.edu. *Application contact:* Dr. Patricia Walsh Coates, Graduate Coordinator, 610-638-4289, Fax: 610-683-1338, E-mail: coates@kutztown.edu.
Website: https://www.kutztown.edu/academcs/graduate-programs/secondary-education.htm

LaGrange College, Graduate Programs, Department of Education, LaGrange, GA 30240-2999. Offers curriculum and instruction (M Ed, Ed S); middle grades (MAT); secondary education (MAT). *Program availability:* Part-time, evening/weekend. *Degree requirements:* For master's, comprehensive exam. *Entrance requirements:* For master's, GRE, MAT, minimum GPA of 2.5. Additional exam requirements/recommendations for international students: Required—TOEFL (minimum score 550 paper-based).

La Salle University, School of Arts and Sciences, Program in Education, Philadelphia, PA 19141-1199. Offers autism spectrum disorders (MA, Certificate); bilingual/bicultural studies (MA); classroom management (MA); dual early childhood and special education (MA); dual middle-level science and math and special education (MA); education (MA);

English (MA); English as a second language (Certificate); history (MA); instructional coach (Certificate); instructional leadership (MA); reading specialist (MA, Certificate); secondary education (MA); special education (MA, Certificate). *Program availability:* Part-time, evening/weekend. *Faculty:* 5 full-time (4 women), 12 part-time/adjunct (8 women). *Students:* 10 full-time (all women), 98 part-time (74 women); includes 28 minority (13 Black or African American, non-Hispanic/Latino; 1 American Indian or Alaska Native, non-Hispanic/Latino; 1 Asian, non-Hispanic/Latino; 10 Hispanic/Latino; 3 Two or more races, non-Hispanic/Latino). Average age 34. 128 applicants, 84% accepted, 69 enrolled. In 2016, 53 master's awarded. *Degree requirements:* For master's, comprehensive exam. *Entrance requirements:* For master's, MAT or GRE, 2 letters of recommendation; for Certificate, GMAT or GRE, 2 letters of recommendation. Additional exam requirements/recommendations for international students: Required—TOEFL. *Application deadline:* For fall admission, 8/15 priority date for domestic students, 7/15 for international students; for spring admission, 12/15 priority date for domestic students, 11/15 for international students; for summer admission, 4/15 priority date for domestic students, 3/15 for international students. Applications are processed on a rolling basis. Application fee: $35. Electronic applications accepted. Application fee is waived when completed online. *Expenses:* Contact institution. *Financial support:* In 2016–17, 27 students received support. Scholarships/grants available. Support available to part-time students. Financial award application deadline: 8/31; financial award applicants required to submit FAFSA. *Unit head:* Dr. Greer Richardson, Director, 215-951-1806, Fax: 215-951-1843, E-mail: graded@lasalle.edu. *Application contact:* Elizabeth Heenan, Director, Graduate and Adult Enrollment, 215-951-1100, Fax: 215-951-1462, E-mail: heenan@lasalle.edu.
Website: http://www.lasalle.edu/grad-education-programs/

Lee University, Program in Education, Cleveland, TN 37320-3450. Offers art (MAT); curriculum and instruction (M Ed, Ed S); early childhood (MAT); educational leadership (M Ed, Ed S); elementary education (MAT); English and math (MAT); English and science (MAT); English and social studies (MAT); higher education administration (MS); history (MAT); history and economics (MAT); math and science (MAT); math and social studies (MAT); middle grades (MAT); science and social studies (MASW); secondary education (MAT); Spanish (MAT); special education (M Ed, MAT); TESOL (MAT). *Accreditation:* NCATE. *Program availability:* Part-time. *Faculty:* 13 full-time (6 women), 9 part-time/adjunct (4 women). *Students:* 35 full-time (27 women), 50 part-time (32 women); includes 12 minority (5 Black or African American, non-Hispanic/Latino; 5 Hispanic/Latino; 2 Two or more races, non-Hispanic/Latino), 4 international. Average age 30. 43 applicants, 79% accepted, 28 enrolled. In 2016, 42 master's, 6 other advanced degrees awarded. *Degree requirements:* For master's, variable foreign language requirement, thesis optional, internship. *Entrance requirements:* For master's, MAT or GRE General Test, minimum undergraduate GPA of 2.75, 3 letters of recommendation, interview, writing sample, official transcripts, background check; for Ed S, minimum undergraduate and master's GPA of 2.75, official transcripts for undergraduate and master's degrees. Additional exam requirements/recommendations for international students: Required—TOEFL (minimum score 61 iBT). *Application deadline:* For fall admission, 6/1 priority date for domestic and international students; for spring admission, 11/1 priority date for domestic and international students; for summer admission, 4/1 priority date for domestic and international students. Applications are processed on a rolling basis. Application fee: $25. Electronic applications accepted. *Expenses: Tuition:* Full-time $11,367; part-time $632 per credit hour. *Required fees:* $35 per term. One-time fee: $25. Tuition and fees vary according to program. *Financial support:* In 2016–17, 42 students received support. Career-related internships or fieldwork, Federal Work-Study, institutionally sponsored loans, scholarships/grants, and unspecified assistantships available. Financial award application deadline: 3/1; financial award applicants required to submit FAFSA. *Unit head:* Dr. William Kamm, Director, 423-614-8544, E-mail: wkamm@leeuniversity.edu. *Application contact:* Crystal Keeter, Graduate Education Secretary, 423-614-8544, E-mail: ckeeter@leeuniversity.edu.
Website: http://www.leeuniversity.edu/academics/graduate/education

Le Moyne College, Department of Education, Syracuse, NY 13214. Offers adolescent education (MS Ed, MST); adolescent education/special education (MS Ed, MST); adolescent English (MST), including grades 7-12; adolescent English/special education (MST), including grades 7-12; adolescent foreign language (MST), including grades 7-12; adolescent history (MST), including grades 7-12; childhood education (MS Ed); childhood education/special education (MS Ed); elementary education (MS Ed); general education (MS Ed); inclusive childhood education (MST); literacy education (MS Ed), including birth to grade 6, grades 5-12; school building leader (MS Ed); school building leadership (CAS); school district business leader (MS Ed, CAS); school district leader (MS Ed); school district leadership (CAS); secondary education (MS Ed); special education (MS Ed); teaching English to speakers of other languages (MS Ed); urban studies (MS Ed). *Accreditation:* TEAC. *Program availability:* Part-time, evening/weekend. *Faculty:* 8 full-time (5 women), 20 part-time/adjunct (12 women). *Students:* 66 full-time (40 women), 155 part-time (117 women); includes 13 minority (4 Black or African American, non-Hispanic/Latino; 2 American Indian or Alaska Native, non-Hispanic/Latino; 2 Asian, non-Hispanic/Latino; 5 Hispanic/Latino), 3 international. Average age 30. 74 applicants, 99% accepted, 66 enrolled. In 2016, 81 master's, 53 CASs awarded. *Degree requirements:* For master's, thesis. *Entrance requirements:* For master's, bachelor's degree with minimum undergraduate GPA of 3.0, 2 letters of recommendation, transcripts. Additional exam requirements/recommendations for international students: Required—TOEFL (minimum score 550 paper-based; 79 iBT); Recommended—IELTS (minimum score 6.5). *Application deadline:* For fall admission, 4/1 priority date for domestic and international students; for spring admission, 10/1 priority date for domestic and international students; for summer admission, 3/1 priority date for domestic and international students. Applications are processed on a rolling basis. Application fee: $50. Electronic applications accepted. *Expenses:* $700 per credit hour. *Financial support:* In 2016–17, 21 students received support. Career-related internships or fieldwork, scholarships/grants, and health care benefits available. Support available to part-time students. Financial award applicants required to submit FAFSA. *Faculty research:* Minority teachers, special education, multiculturalism, literacy, technology, media literacy learning, autism, school district organization, service-learning, higher level problem solving, teacher leadership. *Unit head:* Dr. Stephen C. Fleury, Chair, Department of Education, 315-445-4376, Fax: 315-445-4744, E-mail: fleurysc@lemoyne.edu. *Application contact:* Kristen P. Richards, Senior Director of Enrollment Management, 315-445-5444, Fax: 315-445-6092, E-mail: trapaskp@lemoyne.edu.
Website: http://www.lemoyne.edu/education

Lesley University, Graduate School of Education, Cambridge, MA 02138-2790. Offers arts, community, and education (M Ed); autism studies (Certificate); curriculum and instruction (M Ed, CAGS); early childhood education (M Ed); ecological teaching and learning (MS); educational studies (PhD), including adult learning, educational leadership, individually designed; elementary education (M Ed); emergent technologies for educators (Certificate); ESLArts: language learning through the arts (M Ed); high school education (M Ed); individually designed (M Ed); integrated teaching through the arts (M Ed); literacy for K-8 classroom teachers (M Ed); mathematics education (M Ed); middle school education (M Ed); moderate disabilities (M Ed); online learning (Certificate); reading (CAGS); science in education (M Ed); severe disabilities (M Ed); special needs (CAGS); specialist teacher of reading (M Ed); teacher of visual art (M Ed); technology in education (M Ed, CAGS). *Accreditation:* TEAC. *Program availability:* Part-time, evening/weekend, online learning. *Degree requirements:* For master's, practicum; for doctorate, thesis/dissertation. *Entrance requirements:* For master's, Massachusetts Tests for Educator Licensure (MTEL), transcripts, statement of purpose, recommendations; interview (for special education); for doctorate, GRE General Test, transcripts, statement of purpose, recommendations, interview, master's degree, resume; for other advanced degree, interview, master's degree. Additional exam requirements/recommendations for international students: Required—TOEFL (minimum score 550 paper-based; 80 iBT). Electronic applications accepted. *Faculty research:* Assessment in literacy, mathematics and science; autism spectrum disorders; instructional technology and online learning; multicultural education and English language learners.

Liberty University, School of Education, Lynchburg, VA 24515. Offers educational leadership (Ed D); gifted education (Certificate); math specialist (M Ed); middle grades (MAT, Certificate); reading specialist (M Ed); school leadership (Certificate); secondary education (MAT); sport management (MS), including administration, outdoor recreation, sport management, tourism. *Accreditation:* NCATE. *Program availability:* Part-time, online learning. *Students:* 1,910 full-time (1,427 women), 4,420 part-time (3,311 women); includes 1,451 minority (1,182 Black or African American, non-Hispanic/Latino; 33 American Indian or Alaska Native, non-Hispanic/Latino; 44 Asian, non-Hispanic/Latino; 46 Hispanic/Latino; 11 Native Hawaiian or other Pacific Islander, non-Hispanic/Latino; 135 Two or more races, non-Hispanic/Latino), 87 international. Average age 37. 5,120 applicants, 44% accepted, 1193 enrolled. In 2016, 1,378 master's, 151 doctorates, 497 other advanced degrees awarded. *Degree requirements:* For doctorate, comprehensive exam, thesis/dissertation. *Entrance requirements:* For master's, GRE General Test or MAT (if taken in or before 1999), 2 letters of recommendation, minimum undergraduate GPA of 3.0, curriculum vitae; for doctorate and Certificate, GRE General Test or MAT (if taken before 1999), minimum master's GPA of 3.0, 3 years of teaching experience. Additional exam requirements/recommendations for international students: Required—TOEFL (minimum score 600 paper-based; 100 iBT). *Application deadline:* For fall admission, 6/1 for domestic students; for spring admission, 11/1 for domestic students. Applications are processed on a rolling basis. Application fee: $50. Electronic applications accepted. *Expenses:* Contact institution. *Financial support:* Federal Work-Study and tuition waivers (partial) available. *Faculty research:* Self-determination, character education, bibliotherapy, learning styles, distance education. *Unit head:* Dr. Heather Schoffstall, Dean, 434-582-2445, Fax: 434-582-2468, E-mail: awgunter@liberty.edu. *Application contact:* Jay Bridge, Director of Graduate Admissions, 800-424-9595, Fax: 800-628-7977, E-mail: gradadmissions@liberty.edu.
Website: http://www.liberty.edu/academics/education/graduate/

Lincoln University, Graduate Studies, Jefferson City, MO 65101. Offers business administration (MBA), including accounting, management, management information systems, public administration/policy; elementary teaching (M Ed); environmental science (MS); guidance and counseling (M Ed), including community/agency counseling, elementary school, secondary school; higher education (MA); history (MA); integrated agricultural systems (MS); middle school (M Ed); natural sciences (MS); secondary teaching (M Ed); sociology (MA); sociology/criminal justice (MA). *Program availability:* Part-time, evening/weekend, 100% online, blended/hybrid learning. *Students:* 50 full-time (29 women), 68 part-time (39 women); includes 40 minority (37 Black or African American, non-Hispanic/Latino; 1 Asian, non-Hispanic/Latino; 2 Two or more races, non-Hispanic/Latino), 14 international. Average age 33. 75 applicants, 80% accepted, 34 enrolled. In 2016, 51 master's awarded. *Degree requirements:* For master's, comprehensive exam, thesis optional. *Entrance requirements:* For master's, GRE, MAT or GMAT, minimum GPA of 2.75 overall, 3.0 in courses related to specialization; 3 letters of recommendation; minimum C average in English composition; personal statement of purpose. Additional exam requirements/recommendations for international students: Required—TOEFL (minimum score 500 paper-based; 61 iBT), IELTS (minimum score 5.5), Michigan English Language Assessment Battery (minimum score 80). *Application deadline:* For fall admission, 7/1 priority date for domestic students, 5/1 priority date for international students; for spring admission, 11/1 priority date for domestic students, 10/1 priority date for international students; for summer admission, 6/1 priority date for domestic students. Applications are processed on a rolling basis. Application fee: $30. Electronic applications accepted. *Expenses:* Tuition, state resident: full-time $6840; part-time $5130 per year. Tuition, nonresident: full-time $12,720; part-time $9540 per year. *Required fees:* $852; $811 per unit. Tuition and fees vary according to course load. *Financial support:* In 2016–17, 2 fellowships with tuition reimbursements, 8 research assistantships with tuition reimbursements were awarded; Federal Work-Study, scholarships/grants, and unspecified assistantships also available. Support available to part-time students. Financial award application deadline: 3/1; financial award applicants required to submit FAFSA. *Unit head:* Dr. Rolundus R. Rice, Dean, 573-681-5247, Fax: 573-681-5106, E-mail: gradschool@lincolnu.edu. *Application contact:* Irasema Steck, Administrative Assistant, 573-681-5247, Fax: 573-681-5106, E-mail: gradschool@lincolnu.edu.
Website: http://www.lincolnu.edu/web/graduate-studies/graduate-studies

Long Island University–Hudson, Graduate School, Purchase, NY 10577. Offers autism (Advanced Certificate); childhood education (MS Ed); early childhood education (MS Ed); educational leadership (MS Ed); finance (MBA); health administration (MPA); healthcare sector management (MBA); literacy (MS Ed); management (MBA); marriage and family therapy (MS); mental health counseling (MS), including credentialed alcoholism and substance abuse counselor; middle childhood and adolescence education (MS Ed); pharmaceutics (MS), including cosmetic science, industrial pharmacy; public administration (MPA); school counseling (MS Ed, Advanced Certificate); school psychology (MS Ed); special education (MS Ed); TESOL (all grades) (Advanced Certificate); TESOL and bilingual education (MS Ed); the business of pharmaceutics and biotechnology (MBA). *Program availability:* Part-time, evening/weekend, online learning. *Faculty:* 7 full-time (5 women), 42 part-time/adjunct (25 women). *Students:* 55 full-time (41 women), 158 part-time (123 women); includes 40 minority (8 Black or African American, non-Hispanic/Latino; 1 Asian, non-Hispanic/Latino; 31 Hispanic/Latino). Average age 35. *Entrance requirements:* Additional exam requirements/recommendations for international students: Required—TOEFL (minimum score 550 paper-based; 79 iBT). *Application deadline:* Applications are processed on a rolling basis. Application fee: $50. Electronic applications accepted. *Expenses:* Contact institution. *Unit head:* Dr. Sylvia Blake, Dean and Chief Operating Officer, 914-831-2700, E-mail: westchester@liu.edu. *Application contact:* Cindy Pagnotta, Director of Marketing and Enrollment, 914-831-2701, Fax: 914-251-5959, E-mail: cindy.pagnotta@liu.edu.

Long Island University–LIU Post, College of Education, Information and Technology, Brookville, NY 11548-1300. Offers adolescence education (MS); adolescence education 7-12 (MS); archives and records management (AC); art education (MS); childhood education (MS); childhood teaching literacy B-6 (MS); childhood/special education (MS); clinical mental health counseling (MS, AC); early childhood education (MS); early childhood education/childhood education (MS); educational leadership (AC); educational technology (MS); information studies (PhD); interdisciplinary educational studies (Ed D); middle childhood education (MS); music education (MS); school counselor (MS); special education (MS Ed); speech-language pathology (MA); students

with disabilities, 7-12 generalist (AC); TESOL (MA). *Accreditation:* TEAC. *Program availability:* Part-time, 100% online, blended/hybrid learning. *Faculty:* 55 full-time (35 women), 104 part-time/adjunct (57 women). *Students:* 464 full-time (390 women), 740 part-time (580 women); includes 265 minority (99 Black or African American, non-Hispanic/Latino; 45 Asian, non-Hispanic/Latino; 113 Hispanic/Latino; 1 Native Hawaiian or other Pacific Islander, non-Hispanic/Latino; 7 Two or more races, non-Hispanic/Latino), 33 international. 928 applicants, 76% accepted, 406 enrolled. In 2016, 334 master's, 10 doctorates, 137 other advanced degrees awarded. Terminal master's awarded for partial completion of doctoral program. *Degree requirements:* For master's, variable foreign language requirement, comprehensive exam (for some programs), thesis optional; for doctorate, comprehensive exam, thesis/dissertation. *Entrance requirements:* For master's and AC, GRE. Additional exam requirements/recommendations for international students: Required—PTE, TOEFL (minimum score 550 paper-based, 75 iBT) or IELTS. *Application deadline:* Applications are processed on a rolling basis. Application fee: $50. Electronic applications accepted. *Expenses: Tuition:* Full-time $28,272; part-time $1178 per credit. *Required fees:* $451 per term. Tuition and fees vary according to degree level and program. *Financial support:* Career-related internships or fieldwork, Federal Work-Study, institutionally sponsored loans, scholarships/grants, tuition waivers (partial), and unspecified assistantships available. Support available to part-time students. Financial award application deadline: 2/15; financial award applicants required to submit FAFSA. *Faculty research:* English language learners, early childhood literacy development through play, sleep, social justice through education, using a structured protocol for discussing bad news. *Total annual research expenditures:* $575,000. *Unit head:* Dr. Albert Inserra, Dean, 516-299-2210, E-mail: albert.inserra@liu.edu. *Application contact:* Carol Zerah, Director of Graduate Admissions, 516-299-2900, Fax: 516-299-2137, E-mail: post-enroll@liu.edu.
Website: http://liu.edu/CWPost/Academics/College-of-Education-Information-and-Technology

Long Island University–Riverhead, Graduate Programs, Riverhead, NY 11901. Offers childhood education (MS), including grades 1-6; homeland security management (MS); literacy education (MS); teaching students with disabilities (MS), including grades 1-6, grades 7-12; TESOL (Advanced Certificate). *Accreditation:* TEAC. *Program availability:* Part-time. *Degree requirements:* For master's, thesis (for some programs); for Advanced Certificate, comprehensive exam (for some programs). *Entrance requirements:* Additional exam requirements/recommendations for international students: Required—TOEFL (minimum score 550 paper-based; 79 iBT), IELTS (minimum score 6). *Application deadline:* Applications are processed on a rolling basis. Application fee: $50. Electronic applications accepted. *Expenses:* Contact institution. *Financial support:* Institutionally sponsored loans, scholarships/grants, tuition waivers (partial), and unspecified assistantships available. Support available to part-time students. Financial award application deadline: 2/15; financial award applicants required to submit FAFSA. *Unit head:* Donna Di Donato, Dean and Chief Operating Officer, LIU Brentwood and LIU Riverhead, 631-287-8010, Fax: 631-287-8575, E-mail: donna.didonato@liu.edu. *Application contact:* Christina Seifert, Director of Admission, LIU Brentwood and LIU Riverhead, 631-287-8505, Fax: 631-287-8253, E-mail: christina.seifert@liu.edu.

Longwood University, College of Graduate and Professional Studies, College of Education and Human Services, Farmville, VA 23909. Offers education (MS), including algebra and middle school mathematics, counselor education, elementary and middle school mathematics, elementary education, elementary education initial licensure, health and physical education, special education general curriculum, special education initial licensure; reading, literacy and learning (M Ed); school librarianship (M Ed); social work and communication sciences and disorders (MS), including communication sciences and disorders. *Accreditation:* NCATE. *Program availability:* Part-time, evening/weekend. *Degree requirements:* For master's, comprehensive exam (for some programs), thesis optional, professional portfolio, internship, clinical experience, or practicum. *Entrance requirements:* For master's, PRAXIS I (for initial teaching licensure programs); GRE (for some programs), bachelor's degree from regionally-accredited institution, 2 recommendations (3 for some programs), minimum 500-word personal essay, official transcripts, minimum GPA of 2.75, valid teaching license (for some programs). Additional exam requirements/recommendations for international students: Required—TOEFL (minimum score 570 paper-based), IELTS (minimum score 6.5). Electronic applications accepted. *Expenses:* Contact institution.

Louisiana Tech University, Graduate School, College of Education, Department of Curriculum, Instruction and Leadership, Ruston, LA 71272. Offers curriculum and instruction (M Ed), including research, theory, and design, visually impaired; educational leadership (M Ed, Ed D), including higher education administration (Ed D), P-12 educational leadership (Ed D). *Accreditation:* NCATE. *Program availability:* Part-time. *Degree requirements:* For doctorate, thesis/dissertation. *Entrance requirements:* For master's and doctorate, GRE General Test. *Application deadline:* For fall admission, 7/29 for domestic students; for spring admission, 2/3 for domestic students. Application fee: $20 ($30 for international students). *Financial support:* Fellowships, research assistantships, and teaching assistantships available. Financial award application deadline: 2/1. *Unit head:* Dr. Bryan McCoy, Chair, 318-257-4609, Fax: 318-257-2379, E-mail: bmccoy@latech.edu. *Application contact:* Dr. John Harrison, Associate Dean of Graduate Studies, 318-257-3229, Fax: 318-257-2379, E-mail: johnharrison@latech.edu.
Website: http://education.latech.edu/departments/cil/

Lynn University, Donald E. and Helen L. Ross College of Education, Boca Raton, FL 33431-5598. Offers educational leadership (M Ed, Ed D), including K-12 (Ed D); exceptional student education (M Ed), including school administration K-12. *Program availability:* Part-time, evening/weekend, online learning. *Faculty:* 5 full-time (4 women), 8 part-time/adjunct (all women). *Students:* 85 full-time (63 women), 10 part-time (6 women); includes 27 minority (19 Black or African American, non-Hispanic/Latino; 7 Hispanic/Latino; 1 Two or more races, non-Hispanic/Latino), 4 international. Average age 36. 17 applicants, 94% accepted, 11 enrolled. In 2016, 24 master's, 22 doctorates awarded. *Degree requirements:* For master's, comprehensive exam, thesis (for some programs); for doctorate, thesis/dissertation, mid-program review. *Entrance requirements:* For master's, bachelor's degree from accredited institution, letter of recommendation, statement of professional goals, official transcripts; for doctorate, master's degree from accredited institution, resume, 2 letters of recommendation, professional practice statement, official transcripts. Additional exam requirements/recommendations for international students: Required—TOEFL (minimum score 550 paper-based; 80 iBT), IELTS (minimum score 6.5). *Application deadline:* For fall admission, 8/18 for domestic students, 8/4 for international students; for spring admission, 12/15 for domestic students, 12/1 for international students; for summer admission, 4/17 for domestic students, 4/3 for international students. Applications are processed on a rolling basis. Application fee: $45. Electronic applications accepted. *Expenses:* $850 per credit hour, $44,200 per year tuition and fees (for Ed D); $725 per credit hour, $29,000 per year tuition and fees (for master's). *Financial support:* In 2016–17, 74 students received support. Career-related internships or fieldwork, Federal Work-Study, scholarships/grants, tuition waivers (partial), and unspecified assistantships available. Support available to part-time students. Financial award application deadline: 3/1; financial award applicants required to submit FAFSA. *Unit head:* Dr. Kathleen Weigel, Dean, College of Education, 561-237-7441, E-mail: kweigel@lynn.edu. *Application contact:* Steven Pruitt, Director of Graduate and Undergraduate Evening Admission, 561-237-7834, Fax: 561-237-7100, E-mail: spruitt@lynn.edu.
Website: http://www.lynn.edu/academics/colleges/education

Manhattanville College, School of Education, Program in Middle Childhood/Adolescence Education (Grades 5-12), Purchase, NY 10577-2132. Offers biology (MAT); biology and special education (MPS); chemistry (MAT); chemistry and special education (MPS); English (MAT); English and special education (MPS); literacy and special education (MPS); literacy specialist (MPS); math and special education (MPS); mathematics (MAT); physics (MAT); social studies (MAT); social studies and special education (MPS); special education generalist (MPS); teaching languages other than English (MAT), including French, Italian, Latin, Spanish. *Program availability:* Part-time, evening/weekend. *Students:* 28 applicants, 86% accepted, 21 enrolled. In 2016, 23 master's awarded. *Degree requirements:* For master's, comprehensive exam (for some programs), thesis (for some programs), student teaching, research seminars, portfolios, internships, writing assessment. *Entrance requirements:* For master's, GRE or MAT, minimum undergraduate GPA of 3.0, 2 letters of recommendation. Additional exam requirements/recommendations for international students: Required—TOEFL (minimum score 85 iBT); Recommended—IELTS. *Application deadline:* For fall admission, 7/1 priority date for domestic and international students; for spring admission, 11/1 priority date for domestic and international students; for summer admission, 4/1 priority date for domestic and international students. Applications are processed on a rolling basis. Application fee: $75. Electronic applications accepted. *Expenses: Tuition:* Full-time $16,470; part-time $915 per credit. *Required fees:* $60 per semester. Part-time tuition and fees vary according to course load and program. *Financial support:* Teaching assistantships, career-related internships or fieldwork, Federal Work-Study, institutionally sponsored loans, scholarships/grants, and unspecified assistantships available. Financial award applicants required to submit FAFSA. *Unit head:* Victoria Fantozzi, Chairperson, Department of Curriculum and Instruction, 914-323-7138, E-mail: victoria.fantozzi@mville.edu. *Application contact:* Jeanine Pardey-Levine, Director of Graduate Enrollment Management, 914-323-3208, Fax: 914-694-1732, E-mail: edschool@mville.edu.
Website: http://www.mville.edu/programs#/search/19

Mary Baldwin University, Graduate Studies, Program in Teaching, Staunton, VA 24401-3610. Offers elementary education (MAT); middle grades education (MAT). *Accreditation:* TEAC.

Maryville University of Saint Louis, School of Education, St. Louis, MO 63141-7299. Offers early childhood education (MA Ed); educational leadership (Ed D); educational leadership: principal certification (MA Ed); elementary education (MA Ed); gifted education (MA Ed); higher education leadership (Ed D); literacy specialist (MA Ed); middle grades education (MA Ed); secondary teaching and inquiry (MA Ed); teacher as leader (MA Ed); teacher leadership (Ed D). *Accreditation:* NCATE. *Program availability:* Part-time, evening/weekend. *Faculty:* 17 full-time (11 women), 21 part-time/adjunct (17 women). *Students:* 12 full-time (11 women), 297 part-time (208 women); includes 92 minority (79 Black or African American, non-Hispanic/Latino; 4 Asian, non-Hispanic/Latino; 4 Hispanic/Latino; 5 Two or more races, non-Hispanic/Latino), 4 international. Average age 38. In 2016, 32 master's, 61 doctorates awarded. *Degree requirements:* For master's, thesis, project. *Entrance requirements:* For master's, minimum cumulative GPA of 3.0, 3 professional recommendations, essays, interview with program faculty; for doctorate, minimum GPA of 3.0, 3 professional recommendations, essay, interview, on-site writing sample. Additional exam requirements/recommendations for international students: Required—TOEFL (minimum score 550 paper-based). *Application deadline:* Applications are processed on a rolling basis. Electronic applications accepted. *Expenses:* $879 per credit (for Ed D); $781 per credit (for master's). *Financial support:* Career-related internships or fieldwork, Federal Work-Study, tuition waivers (partial), and professional educator discounts available. Financial award application deadline: 3/1; financial award applicants required to submit FAFSA. *Faculty research:* Collaboration with public schools, pre-service program development, mathematics, diversity, literacy. *Unit head:* Dr. Cathy Bear, Dean, 314-529-9692, Fax: 314-529-9921, E-mail: cbear@maryville.edu. *Application contact:* Stacey Ruffin, Coordinator of Clinical Experiences and Graduate Programs, 314-529-9542, Fax: 314-529-9921, E-mail: teachered@maryville.edu.
Website: http://www.maryville.edu/ed/graduate-programs/

McNeese State University, Doré School of Graduate Studies, Burton College of Education, Office of Student Teaching and Professional Education Services, Program in Middle School Education Grades 4-8, Lake Charles, LA 70609. Offers Postbaccalaureate Certificate. *Entrance requirements:* For degree, PRAXIS, 2 letters of recommendation, autobiography.

Mercer University, Graduate Studies, Cecil B. Day Campus, Tift College of Education (Atlanta), Macon, GA 31207. Offers curriculum and instruction (PhD); early childhood education (M Ed, MAT, Ed S); educational leadership (PhD), including higher education leadership, P-12 school leadership; educational leadership P-12 (M Ed, Ed S); higher education leadership (M Ed); independent and charter school leadership (M Ed); middle grades education (M Ed, MAT); reading specialist (M Ed); secondary education (M Ed, MAT); teacher leadership (Ed S). *Accreditation:* NCATE. *Program availability:* Part-time, evening/weekend. *Faculty:* 28 full-time (15 women), 30 part-time/adjunct (27 women). *Students:* 177 full-time (150 women), 324 part-time (264 women); includes 288 minority (256 Black or African American, non-Hispanic/Latino; 1 American Indian or Alaska Native, non-Hispanic/Latino; 7 Asian, non-Hispanic/Latino; 17 Hispanic/Latino; 1 Native Hawaiian or other Pacific Islander, non-Hispanic/Latino; 6 Two or more races, non-Hispanic/Latino), 1 international. Average age 35. In 2016, 173 master's, 34 doctorates, 54 other advanced degrees awarded. *Degree requirements:* For master's and Ed S, research project; for doctorate, comprehensive exam, thesis/dissertation. *Entrance requirements:* For master's, GRE or MAT, minimum undergraduate GPA of 2.75; for doctorate, GRE; for Ed S, GRE or MAT, minimum GPA of 3.25; 3 years of certified teaching experience (for educational leadership and teacher leadership). Additional exam requirements/recommendations for international students: Required—TOEFL (minimum score 80 iBT). *Application deadline:* For fall admission, 8/1 for domestic and international students; for spring admission, 12/1 for domestic and international students; for summer admission, 5/1 for domestic and international students. Applications are processed on a rolling basis. Application fee: $25 ($50 for international students). Electronic applications accepted. *Expenses:* $590 per credit, $1,770 per course (for M Ed); $595 per credit, $1,785 per course (for MAT); $615 per credit, $1,845 per course (for Ed S); $717 per credit, $2,151 per course (for PhD); $150 per semester technology fee. *Financial support:* Federal Work-Study and unspecified assistantships available. Support available to part-time students. Financial award application deadline: 5/1; financial award applicants required to submit FAFSA. *Faculty research:* Educational technology, multicultural and minority issues in education, educational leadership (P-12 and higher education), school discipline and school bullying, standards-based mathematics education. *Unit head:* Dr. James Barta, Dean, 478-301-5355, Fax: 478-301-2280, E-mail: barta_jj@mercer.edu. *Application contact:* Renee Slaton, Associate Director of Graduate Admissions, 678-547-6084, Fax: 678-547-6055, E-mail: mercereducation@mercer.edu.
Website: http://education.mercer.edu/

Mercy College, School of Education, Program in Teaching Literacy, Dobbs Ferry, NY 10522-1189. Offers teaching literacy (Advanced Certificate); teaching literacy, birth-6 (MS); teaching literacy, grades 5-12 (MS). *Program availability:* Part-time, evening/weekend, blended/hybrid learning. *Students:* 7 full-time (6 women), 92 part-time (82 women); includes 51 minority (12 Black or African American, non-Hispanic/Latino; 3 Asian, non-Hispanic/Latino; 35 Hispanic/Latino; 1 Two or more races, non-Hispanic/Latino). Average age 32. 28 applicants, 43% accepted, 8 enrolled. In 2016, 25 master's awarded. *Degree requirements:* For master's, comprehensive exam (for some programs), thesis (for some programs). *Entrance requirements:* For master's, GRE, resume, undergraduate transcript. Additional exam requirements/recommendations for international students: Required—TOEFL (minimum score 600 paper-based; 100 iBT), IELTS (minimum score 8). *Application deadline:* For fall admission, 8/1 for international students. Applications are processed on a rolling basis. Application fee: $40. Electronic applications accepted. *Expenses: Tuition:* Full-time $15,156; part-time $842 per credit hour. *Required fees:* $620; $155 per term. Tuition and fees vary according to course load and program. *Financial support:* Career-related internships or fieldwork, Federal Work-Study, scholarships/grants, and unspecified assistantships available. Support available to part-time students. Financial award applicants required to submit FAFSA. *Unit head:* Dr. Rose Rudnitski, Dean for the School of Education, 914-674-7447, Fax: 914-674-7352, E-mail: rrudnitski@mercy.edu. *Application contact:* Allison Gurdineer, Senior Director of Admissions, 877-637-2946, Fax: 914-674-7382, E-mail: admissions@mercy.edu.
Website: https://www.mercy.edu/education/literacy-and-multilingual-studies

Merrimack College, School of Education and Social Policy, North Andover, MA 01845-5800. Offers community engagement (M Ed), including community organizations, higher education, K-12 education; criminology and criminal justice (MS); curriculum and instruction (M Ed); early childhood education (M Ed); educational leadership (CAGS), including instructional leadership; elementary education (M Ed); English as a second language (PreK-6) (M Ed); high school education (M Ed); higher education (M Ed), including leadership and organizational development, student affairs; middle school education (M Ed); moderate disabilities (PreK-8) (M Ed); school counseling (M Ed). *Program availability:* Part-time, evening/weekend, 100% online courses with immersion events and in-classroom practicum close to home. *Faculty:* 17 full-time, 34 part-time/adjunct. *Students:* 204 full-time (172 women), 83 part-time (67 women); includes 32 minority (4 Black or African American, non-Hispanic/Latino; 2 Asian, non-Hispanic/Latino; 23 Hispanic/Latino; 3 Two or more races, non-Hispanic/Latino), 1 international. Average age 27. 261 applicants, 89% accepted, 200 enrolled. In 2016, 153 master's, 2 other advanced degrees awarded. *Degree requirements:* For master's, practicum, portfolio, and state test (for licensure track); capstone (for higher education, curriculum and instruction, and community engagement tracks). *Entrance requirements:* For master's, Massachusetts Teacher Education Licensure (MTEL), official transcripts from other colleges, resume, personal statement, 2 letters of recommendation. Additional exam requirements/recommendations for international students: Required—TOEFL (minimum score 84 iBT), IELTS (minimum score 6.5), PTE (minimum score 56). *Application deadline:* For fall admission, 8/14 for domestic students, 7/14 for international students; for spring admission, 1/10 for domestic students, 12/10 for international students; for summer admission, 5/10 for domestic students, 4/10 for international students. Applications are processed on a rolling basis. Application fee: $0. Electronic applications accepted. *Expenses:* Contact institution. *Financial support:* Fellowships with full tuition reimbursements, career-related internships or fieldwork, scholarships/grants, and health care benefits available. Support available to part-time students. Financial award application deadline: 5/1; financial award applicants required to submit FAFSA. *Faculty research:* Feminist praxis in higher education, transgender student agency and belonging, campus sexual violence prevention, the scholarship of engagement; community engagement; service learning; diversity education; community-university partnerships, college going behaviors and indicators of success for inner city youth, strategies to increase students pursuit and success in STEM higher education, effective workforce development for displaced or under employed individuals, police reform, e.g. surveillance. *Application contact:* Alyssa Frey, Graduate Admissions Counselor, 978-837-3563, E-mail: freya@merrimack.edu.
Website: http://www.merrimack.edu/academics/graduate/education/

Middle Tennessee State University, College of Graduate Studies, College of Education, Department of Elementary and Special Education, Major in Curriculum and Instruction, Murfreesboro, TN 37132. Offers early childhood education (M Ed); elementary education (M Ed, Ed S); middle school education (M Ed). *Accreditation:* NCATE. *Program availability:* Part-time, evening/weekend, online learning. *Degree requirements:* For master's, comprehensive exam; for Ed S, comprehensive exam, thesis or alternative. *Entrance requirements:* For master's and Ed S, GRE, MAT or PRAXIS. Additional exam requirements/recommendations for international students: Required—TOEFL (minimum score 525 paper-based; 71 iBT) or IELTS (minimum score 6). Electronic applications accepted.

Milligan College, Area of Education, Milligan College, TN 37682. Offers combined preK-3/K-5 education (M Ed); educational leadership (Ed D, Ed S); K-5 education (M Ed); middle grades education (M Ed); preK-3 education (M Ed); preK-3 special education (M Ed); secondary education (M Ed). *Accreditation:* NCATE. *Program availability:* Part-time. *Faculty:* 5 full-time (3 women), 3 part-time/adjunct (1 woman). *Students:* 26 full-time (19 women), 20 part-time (10 women); includes 2 minority (1 Black or African American, non-Hispanic/Latino; 1 Hispanic/Latino), 2 international. Average age 28. 16 applicants, 81% accepted, 11 enrolled. In 2016, 19 master's awarded. *Degree requirements:* For master's, thesis, portfolio, research project; for doctorate, thesis/dissertation, portfolio, research project. *Entrance requirements:* For master's, MAT, GRE General Test, ACT, SAT, or PRAXIS, undergraduate degree and supporting transcripts, professional recommendations, interview; for doctorate, MAT or GRE, master's degree and supporting transcripts, demonstrated scholastic ability, recognized leadership role within education, professional recommendations, essay/personal statement, portfolio (professional development plan, evidence of ability, knowledge and qualities), interview. Additional exam requirements/recommendations for international students: Required—TOEFL (minimum score 550 paper-based, 79 iBT) or IELTS (6.5). *Application deadline:* For fall admission, 8/1 priority date for domestic students, 6/1 for international students; for spring admission, 11/15 priority date for domestic students, 12/1 for international students; for summer admission, 4/1 for domestic students. Applications are processed on a rolling basis. Application fee: $30. Electronic applications accepted. *Expenses:* $360 per hour tuition (for M Ed); $475 per hour tuition (for Ed D and Ed S); $325 per semester tech/activity fees. *Financial support:* Scholarships/grants available. Financial award application deadline: 12/1; financial award applicants required to submit FAFSA. *Faculty research:* Assessment; school mental health; literacy; technology; educator preparation. *Unit head:* Dr. Angela Hilton-Prillhart, Area Chair of Education, 423-461-8769, Fax: 423-461-3103, E-mail: anhilton-prillhart@milligan.edu. *Application contact:* Melissa Dillow, Graduate Admissions Recruiter, Education, 423-461-8306, Fax: 423-461-8982, E-mail: msdillow@milligan.edu.
Website: http://www.Milligan.edu/GPS

Minot State University, Graduate School, Teacher Education and Human Performance Department, Minot, ND 58707-0002. Offers elementary education (M Ed). *Accreditation:* NCATE. *Degree requirements:* For master's, thesis. *Entrance requirements:* For master's, 2 years of teaching experience, bachelor's degree in education, minimum GPA of 2.75. Additional exam requirements/recommendations for international students: Required—TOEFL (minimum score 79 iBT), IELTS (minimum score 6).

Mississippi State University, College of Education, Department of Curriculum, Instruction and Special Education, Mississippi State, MS 39762. Offers early childhood education (PhD); elementary education (MS, PhD, Ed S), including early childhood education (MS), general elementary education (MS), middle level education (MS); general curriculum and instruction (PhD); middle level (MAT); reading education (PhD); secondary education (MAT, MS, PhD, Ed S); special education (MAT, MS, PhD, Ed S). *Accreditation:* NCATE. *Program availability:* Part-time, evening/weekend. *Faculty:* 21 full-time (16 women), 1 (woman) part-time/adjunct. *Students:* 39 full-time (26 women), 168 part-time (128 women); includes 49 minority (43 Black or African American, non-Hispanic/Latino; 2 American Indian or Alaska Native, non-Hispanic/Latino; 1 Hispanic/Latino; 1 Native Hawaiian or other Pacific Islander, non-Hispanic/Latino; 2 Two or more races, non-Hispanic/Latino), 4 international. Average age 33. 98 applicants, 56% accepted, 47 enrolled. In 2016, 69 master's, 6 doctorates, 10 other advanced degrees awarded. *Degree requirements:* For master's, comprehensive exam; for doctorate, thesis/dissertation; for Ed S, comprehensive exam, thesis or alternative. *Entrance requirements:* For master's, GRE, minimum GPA of 2.75 in junior and senior year, eligibility for initial teacher certification; for doctorate, GRE, minimum GPA of 3.4 on previous graduate work; for Ed S, GRE, minimum GPA of 3.2 on master's degree. Additional exam requirements/recommendations for international students: Required—TOEFL (minimum score 550 paper-based; 79 iBT); Recommended—IELTS (minimum score 6.5). *Application deadline:* For fall admission, 3/1 priority date for domestic students, 5/1 for international students; for spring admission, 9/1 priority date for domestic students, 9/1 for international students. Applications are processed on a rolling basis. Application fee: $60. Electronic applications accepted. *Expenses:* Tuition, state resident: full-time $7670; part-time $852.50 per credit hour. Tuition, nonresident: full-time $20,790; part-time $2310.50 per credit hour. Part-time tuition and fees vary according to course load. *Financial support:* In 2016–17, 8 research assistantships with partial tuition reimbursements (averaging $11,381 per year) were awarded; Federal Work-Study, institutionally sponsored loans, scholarships/grants, and unspecified assistantships also available. Financial award application deadline: 4/1; financial award applicants required to submit FAFSA. *Faculty research:* Early childhood education, reading, rural schools, multicultural education, use of technology in instruction. *Unit head:* Dr. Janice Nicholson, Interim Department Head, 662-325-3704, Fax: 662-325-7857, E-mail: jin4@msstate.edu. *Application contact:* Linda Bonner, Senior Admissions Assistant, 662-325-3363, E-mail: lbonner@grad.msstate.edu.
Website: http://www.cise.msstate.edu/

Morehead State University, Graduate Programs, College of Education, Department of Curriculum and Instruction, Morehead, KY 40351. Offers curriculum and instruction (Ed S); elementary education (MA Ed), including elementary education, international education, middle school education, reading; secondary education (MA Ed); special education (MA Ed); teaching (MAT). *Program availability:* Part-time, evening/weekend. *Degree requirements:* For master's, comprehensive exam, thesis optional; for Ed S, thesis, oral exam. *Entrance requirements:* For master's, GRE General Test, minimum GPA of 2.75, teaching certificate; for Ed S, GRE General Test, interview, master's degree, minimum GPA of 3.5, work experience. Additional exam requirements/recommendations for international students: Required—TOEFL (minimum score 500 paper-based). Electronic applications accepted. *Faculty research:* Communicative competence of learning-disabled students, teaching social studies in elementary schools, ungraded primary school organization, study skills.

Morehead State University, Graduate Programs, College of Education, Department of Foundational and Graduate Studies in Education, Morehead, KY 40351. Offers adult and higher education (MA, Ed S); certified professional counselor (Ed S); counseling P-12 (MA); curriculum and instruction (Ed S); educational technology (MA Ed); instructional leadership (Ed S); school administration (MA); school counseling (Ed S); teacher leader business and marketing content (MA Ed); teacher leader business and marketing technology (MA Ed); teacher leader educational technology (MA Ed); teacher leader English (MA Ed); teacher leader gifted education (MA Ed); teacher leader IECE certification (MA Ed); teacher leader interdisciplinary education P-5 (MA Ed); teacher leader middle grades (MA Ed); teacher leader non IECE certification (MA Ed); teacher leader reading/writing - non-certification (MA Ed); teacher leader reading/writing certification (MA Ed); teacher leader school communication - certification (MA Ed); teacher leader school communication - non-certification (MA Ed); teacher leader social studies (MA Ed); teacher leader special education (MA Ed). *Accreditation:* NCATE. *Program availability:* Part-time, evening/weekend. *Degree requirements:* For master's, thesis optional, oral and/or written comprehensive exams; for Ed S, thesis, oral exam. *Entrance requirements:* For master's, GRE General Test, minimum overall undergraduate GPA of 2.5; for Ed S, GRE General Test, interview, master's degree, minimum GPA of 3.5, work experience. Additional exam requirements/recommendations for international students: Required—TOEFL (minimum score 500 paper-based). Electronic applications accepted. *Faculty research:* Character education, school accountability, computer applications for school administrators.

Morehead State University, Graduate Programs, College of Education, Department of Middle Grades and Secondary Education, Morehead, KY 40351. Offers business and marketing education (MAT); English/language arts 5-9 (MAT); French (MAT); health P-12 (MAT); mathematics 5-9 (MAT); physical education P-12 (MAT); science 5-9 (MAT); secondary biology (MAT); secondary chemistry (MAT); secondary earth science (MAT); secondary English (MAT); secondary math (MAT); secondary physics (MAT); secondary social studies (MAT); social studies 5-9 (MAT); Spanish (MAT). *Program availability:* Part-time, evening/weekend. *Degree requirements:* For master's, portfolio. *Entrance requirements:* For master's, GRE or PRAXIS II content exam, minimum overall undergraduate GPA of 2.5. Additional exam requirements/recommendations for international students: Required—TOEFL (minimum score 500 paper-based). Electronic applications accepted.

Morgan State University, School of Graduate Studies, School of Education and Urban Studies, MAT Program, Baltimore, MD 21251. Offers elementary education (MAT); high school education (MAT); middle school education (MAT). *Program availability:* Part-time. *Degree requirements:* For master's, comprehensive exam. *Entrance requirements:* For master's, GRE General Test or MAT. *Faculty research:* Multicultural education, cooperative learning, psychology of cognition.

Mount St. Joseph University, Graduate Education Program, Cincinnati, OH 45233-1670. Offers adolescent to young adult education (MA); dyslexia (Certificate); inclusive early childhood education (MA); middle childhood education (MA); multicultural special education (MA); reading science (MA). *Accreditation:* TEAC. *Program availability:* Part-time, evening/weekend, online learning. *Faculty:* 7 full-time (5 women), 12 part-time/adjunct (10 women). *Students:* 44 full-time (33 women), 112 part-time (104 women); includes 16 minority (15 Black or African American, non-Hispanic/Latino; 1 Two or more races, non-Hispanic/Latino). Average age 34. In 2016, 60 master's awarded. *Degree requirements:* For master's, comprehensive exam, thesis, research project, student teaching, clinical and field-based experiences. *Entrance requirements:* For master's,

GRE (if GPA is below 3.0), letter of intent, 2 referrals, background check, interview, resume, minimum undergraduate GPA of 3.0. Additional exam requirements/recommendations for international students: Required—TOEFL (minimum score 560 paper-based; 83 iBT). *Application deadline:* Applications are processed on a rolling basis. Application fee: $50. Electronic applications accepted. *Expenses:* $580 per credit hour. *Financial support:* Applicants required to submit FAFSA. *Faculty research:* Foreign and second language learning problems/reading disabilities, multicultural/bilingual special education, science education, pedagogical content knowledge, early childhood, response to intervention. *Unit head:* Dr. Laura Saylor, Dean, 513-244-3263, E-mail: laura.saylor@msj.edu. *Application contact:* Mary Brigham, Assistant Director of Graduate Recruitment, 513-244-4233, Fax: 513-244-4629, E-mail: mary.brigham@msj.edu.
Website: http://www.msj.edu/academics/graduate-programs/master-of-arts-initial-teacher-licensure-programs/

Mount Saint Mary College, Division of Education, Newburgh, NY 12550-3494. Offers adolescence and special education (MS Ed); childhood education (MS Ed); literacy education (MS Ed); middle school (7-9) (MS Ed). *Accreditation:* NCATE. *Program availability:* Part-time, evening/weekend. *Faculty:* 12 full-time (10 women), 3 part-time/adjunct (all women). *Students:* 27 full-time (19 women), 78 part-time (59 women); includes 12 minority (1 Black or African American, non-Hispanic/Latino; 1 Asian, non-Hispanic/Latino; 7 Hispanic/Latino; 3 Two or more races, non-Hispanic/Latino). Average age 28. 30 applicants, 100% accepted, 16 enrolled. In 2016, 62 master's awarded. *Entrance requirements:* Additional exam requirements/recommendations for international students: Required—TOEFL (minimum score 80 iBT). *Application deadline:* Applications are processed on a rolling basis. Application fee: $45. Electronic applications accepted. Application fee is waived when completed online. *Expenses: Tuition:* Full-time $13,914; part-time $773 per credit. *Required fees:* $82 per semester. *Financial support:* In 2016–17, 18 students received support. Unspecified assistantships available. Financial award application deadline: 4/15; financial award applicants required to submit FAFSA. *Faculty research:* Learning and teaching styles, computers in special education, language development. *Unit head:* Dr. Monica Merritt, Graduate Coordinator, 845-569-3430, Fax: 845-569-3535, E-mail: monica.merritt@msmc.edu. *Application contact:* Lisa Gallina, Director of Admissions for Graduate Programs and Adult Degree Completion, 845-569-3166, Fax: 845-569-3450, E-mail: lisa.gallina@msmc.edu.
Website: http://www.msmc.edu/Academics/Graduate_Programs/Master_of_Science_in_Education

Mount Saint Vincent University, Graduate Programs, Faculty of Education, Program in Curriculum Studies, Halifax, NS B3M 2J6, Canada. Offers education of young adolescents (M Ed, MA Ed, MA-R); general studies (M Ed, MA Ed, MA-R); teaching English as a second language (M Ed, MA Ed, MA-R). *Program availability:* Part-time, evening/weekend, online learning. *Degree requirements:* For master's, thesis (for some programs). *Entrance requirements:* For master's, bachelor's degree in related field, minimum B average, 1 year of teaching experience. Electronic applications accepted. *Faculty research:* Science education, cultural studies, international education, curriculum development.

Murray State University, College of Education, Department of Adolescent, Career and Special Education, Program in Middle School Education, Murray, KY 42071. Offers MA Ed, Ed S. *Accreditation:* NCATE. *Degree requirements:* For master's, comprehensive exam, thesis optional. *Entrance requirements:* Additional exam requirements/recommendations for international students: Required—TOEFL.

National Louis University, National College of Education, Chicago, IL 60603. Offers administration and supervision (M Ed, Ed D, CAS, Ed S); curriculum and instruction (M Ed, MS Ed, CAS); early childhood administration (M Ed, CAS); early childhood education (M Ed, MAT, MS Ed, CAS); education (Ed D); educational psychology/human learning and development (M Ed, MS Ed, CAS, Ed S); elementary education (MAT); interdisciplinary curriculum and instruction (M Ed); mathematics education (M Ed, MS Ed, CAS); middle grades education (MAT); reading and language (M Ed, MS Ed, CAS); school psychology (M Ed, Ed S); science education (M Ed, MS Ed, CAS); secondary education (MAT); special education (M Ed, MAT, CAS); technology in education (M Ed, CAS). *Accreditation:* NCATE. *Program availability:* Part-time, evening/weekend. *Degree requirements:* For doctorate, comprehensive exam, thesis/dissertation. *Entrance requirements:* For master's, MAT or GRE, minimum GPA of 3.0; for doctorate, GRE General Test, minimum GPA of 3.25, interview, resume, writing sample, 4 recommendations. Additional exam requirements/recommendations for international students: Required—TOEFL (minimum score 550 paper-based; 79 iBT).

Nazareth College of Rochester, Graduate Studies, Department of Education, Program in Inclusive Adolescence Education, Rochester, NY 14618. Offers MS Ed. *Accreditation:* TEAC. *Entrance requirements:* For master's, minimum GPA of 3.0. Additional exam requirements/recommendations for international students: Required—TOEFL or IELTS. *Application deadline:* For fall admission, 4/1 priority date for domestic students; for spring admission, 10/1 priority date for domestic students. Application fee: $40. *Expenses: Tuition:* Part-time $880 per credit hour. Part-time tuition and fees vary according to course load, degree level and program. *Financial support:* Career-related internships or fieldwork and unspecified assistantships available. Financial award application deadline: 3/1; financial award applicants required to submit FAFSA. *Unit head:* Dr. James W. Black, Director, 585-389-2619, E-mail: jblack8@naz.edu. *Application contact:* Judith Baker, Director, Transfer and Graduate Admissions, 585-531-1154, Fax: 585-389-2826, E-mail: gradadmissions@naz.edu.

New York Institute of Technology, School of Interdisciplinary Studies and Education, Department of Teacher Education, Old Westbury, NY 11568-8000. Offers adolescence education (MS), including mathematics, science; childhood education (MS); early childhood (MS). *Program availability:* Part-time, evening/weekend, 100% online, blended/hybrid learning. *Faculty:* 2 full-time (both women), 7 part-time/adjunct (3 women). *Students:* 19 full-time (15 women), 41 part-time (35 women); includes 18 minority (5 Black or African American, non-Hispanic/Latino; 4 Asian, non-Hispanic/Latino; 8 Hispanic/Latino; 1 Two or more races, non-Hispanic/Latino). Average age 33. 57 applicants, 74% accepted, 29 enrolled. In 2016, 12 master's awarded. *Entrance requirements:* For master's, GRE (minimum combined score of 300 from any two tests), MAT (minimum score 400), LAST (taken within past five years), BS or equivalent; minimum cumulative undergraduate GPA of 3.0; NY state provisional or initial certification (for adolescence education); BS with major in biology, chemistry, economics, English, history, life sciences, math, physics, or psychology (for childhood and early childhood education). Additional exam requirements/recommendations for international students: Required—TOEFL (minimum score 79 iBT), IELTS (minimum score 6). *Application deadline:* Applications are processed on a rolling basis. Application fee: $50. Electronic applications accepted. *Expenses:* $1,215 per credit. *Financial support:* Career-related internships or fieldwork, Federal Work-Study, scholarships/grants, tuition waivers (full and partial), and unspecified assistantships available. Support available to part-time students. Financial award application deadline: 3/1; financial award applicants required to submit FAFSA. *Faculty research:* Evolving definition of new literacies and its impact on teaching and learning (twenty-first century skills), new literacies practices in teacher education, teachers' professional development, English language and literacy learning through mobile learning, teaching reading to culturally and linguistically diverse children. *Unit head:* Dr. Hui-Yin Hsu, Department Chair, 516-686-1322, Fax: 516-686-7655, E-mail: hhsu02@nyit.edu. *Application contact:* Alice Dolitsky, Director, Graduate Admissions, 516-686-7520, Fax: 516-686-1116, E-mail: nyitgrad@nyit.edu.
Website: http://www.nyit.edu/interdisciplinary/department_teacher_education

New York University, Steinhardt School of Culture, Education, and Human Development, Department of Teaching and Learning, New York, NY 10003. Offers clinically rich integrated science (MA), including clinically rich integrated science, teaching biology grades 7-12, teaching chemistry 7-12, teaching physics 7-12; early childhood and childhood education (MA), including childhood education, early childhood education, early childhood education/early childhood special education; English education (MA, PhD, Advanced Certificate), including clinically-based English education, grades 7-12 (MA), English education (PhD, Advanced Certificate), English education, grades 7-12 (MA); environmental conservation education (MA); literacy education (MA), including literacy 5-12, literacy B-6; mathematics education (MA), including teachers of mathematics 7-12; multilingual/multicultural studies (MA, PhD, Advanced Certificate), including bilingual education, foreign language education (MA), teaching English to speakers of other languages (MA, PhD), teaching foreign languages, 7-12 (MA), teaching French as a foreign language (MA), teaching Spanish as a foreign language (MA); social studies education (MA), including teaching art/social studies 7-12, teaching social studies 7-12; special education (MA), including childhood, early childhood; teaching and learning (Ed D, PhD). *Program availability:* Part-time. *Degree requirements:* For doctorate, thesis/dissertation. *Entrance requirements:* For doctorate, GRE General Test, interview; for Advanced Certificate, master's degree. Additional exam requirements/recommendations for international students: Required—TOEFL (minimum score 100 iBT). Electronic applications accepted. *Faculty research:* Cultural contexts for literacy learning, school restructuring, parenting and education, teacher learning, language assessment.

Niagara University, Graduate Division of Education, Concentration in Teacher Education, Niagara University, NY 14109. Offers early childhood and childhood education (MS Ed, Certificate); early childhood special education (MS); middle and adolescence education (MS Ed); special education (MS Ed), including 1-6, 7-12; special education (grades 1-12) (Certificate); teaching English to speakers of other languages (MS Ed, Certificate). *Accreditation:* NCATE. *Students:* 101 full-time (83 women), 123 part-time (101 women); includes 14 minority (6 Black or African American, non-Hispanic/Latino; 1 American Indian or Alaska Native, non-Hispanic/Latino; 6 Hispanic/Latino; 1 Two or more races, non-Hispanic/Latino), 28 international. Average age 28. In 2016, 86 master's, 18 other advanced degrees awarded. *Entrance requirements:* For master's, GRE General Test or Academic Literacy Skills Test (ALST). Additional exam requirements/recommendations for international students: Required—TOEFL (minimum score 550 paper-based; 79 iBT), IELTS (minimum score 6). *Application deadline:* For fall admission, 8/1 for domestic students. Applications are processed on a rolling basis. Application fee: $30. *Expenses:* Contact institution. *Financial support:* Research assistantships with tuition reimbursements, teaching assistantships with tuition reimbursements, career-related internships or fieldwork, Federal Work-Study, scholarships/grants, and unspecified assistantships available. Financial award application deadline: 4/15; financial award applicants required to submit FAFSA. *Unit head:* Dr. Chandra Foote, Dean, College of Education, 716-286-8549, E-mail: cjf@niagara.edu. *Application contact:* Evan Pierce, Associate Director, Graduate Studies, 716-286-8327, E-mail: epierce@niagara.edu.
Website: http://www.niagara.edu/teacher-education

Nicholls State University, Graduate Studies, College of Education, Department of Teacher Education, Thibodaux, LA 70310. Offers curriculum and instruction (M Ed); educational leadership (M Ed); elementary education (MAT); human performance education (MAT); middle school education (MAT); secondary education (MAT). *Accreditation:* NCATE. *Program availability:* Part-time, evening/weekend, online learning. *Degree requirements:* For master's, comprehensive exam, portfolio. *Entrance requirements:* For master's, GRE General Test, teaching license. Electronic applications accepted.

North Carolina State University, Graduate School, College of Education, Department of Curriculum and Instruction, Program in Middle Grades Education, Raleigh, NC 27695. Offers M Ed, MS. *Accreditation:* NCATE. *Degree requirements:* For master's, thesis optional. *Entrance requirements:* For master's, GRE General Test or MAT, minimum GPA of 3.0 in major.

Northwestern State University of Louisiana, Graduate Studies and Research, College of Education and Human Development, Program in Middle School Education, Natchitoches, LA 71497. Offers MAT. *Degree requirements:* For master's, comprehensive exam, thesis or alternative. *Entrance requirements:* For master's, GRE General Test, minimum undergraduate GPA of 2.5. Additional exam requirements/recommendations for international students: Required—TOEFL. Electronic applications accepted.

Northwest Missouri State University, Graduate School, School of Education, Maryville, MO 64468-6001. Offers early childhood education (MS Ed); education leadership (MS Ed), including elementary, K-12, secondary; educational leadership (Ed S), including elementary school principalship, secondary school principalship, superintendency; educational leadership and policy analysis (Ed D); elementary education (MS Ed); elementary mathematics (MS Ed); higher education leadership (MS); middle school education (MS Ed); reading (MS Ed); special education (MS Ed); teacher leadership (MS Ed); teaching English language learners (MS Ed). *Accreditation:* NCATE. *Program availability:* Part-time. *Students:* 15 full-time (11 women), 150 part-time (103 women). In 2016, 46 master's awarded. *Degree requirements:* For master's, comprehensive exam; for Ed S, comprehensive exam, thesis. *Entrance requirements:* For master's, GRE General Test, writing sample; for Ed S, minimum graduate GPA of 3.25. Additional exam requirements/recommendations for international students: Required—TOEFL (minimum score 550 paper-based). *Application deadline:* For fall admission, 7/1 for domestic and international students; for spring admission, 11/15 for domestic and international students. Applications are processed on a rolling basis. Application fee: $0 ($50 for international students). Electronic applications accepted. *Expenses:* Tuition, state resident: full-time $3447; part-time $383 per credit hour. Tuition, nonresident: full-time $5724; part-time $636 per credit hour. *Required fees:* $130 per credit hour. *Financial support:* Research assistantships with full tuition reimbursements, teaching assistantships with full tuition reimbursements, and unspecified assistantships available. Financial award application deadline: 4/1; financial award applicants required to submit FAFSA. *Faculty research:* Great books of educational administration. *Unit head:* Dr. Tim Wall, Dean, 660-562-1179, E-mail: timwall@nwmissouri.edu.
Website: http://www.nwmissouri.edu/academics/ed/

Ohio University, Graduate College, Gladys W. and David H. Patton College of Education and Human Services, Department of Teacher Education, Athens, OH 45701-2979. Offers adolescent to young adult education (M Ed); curriculum and instruction (M Ed, PhD); early childhood/special education (M Ed); intervention specialist/mild-moderate needs (M Ed); intervention specialist/moderate-intensive needs (M Ed);

middle childhood education (M Ed); reading education (M Ed). *Program availability:* Part-time, evening/weekend. *Degree requirements:* For master's, thesis or alternative; for doctorate, comprehensive exam, thesis/dissertation. *Entrance requirements:* For master's, GRE General Test or MAT (if GPA is below 2.9); for doctorate, GRE General Test, minimum GPA of 3.4, work experience. Additional exam requirements/ recommendations for international students: Required—TOEFL (minimum score 550 paper-based; 80 iBT) or IELTS (minimum score 6.5). *Application deadline:* For fall admission, 5/1 priority date for domestic students, 4/1 priority date for international students; for winter admission, 11/1 priority date for domestic students, 10/1 priority date for international students; for spring admission, 2/15 priority date for domestic students, 1/1 priority date for international students. Applications are processed on a rolling basis. Application fee: $50 ($55 for international students). Electronic applications accepted. *Financial support:* Research assistantships with full tuition reimbursements, teaching assistantships with full tuition reimbursements, Federal Work-Study, institutionally sponsored loans, tuition waivers (partial), and unspecified assistantships available. Financial award application deadline: 3/1. *Faculty research:* Cognition literacy, character education, teacher's education reform, disabilities. *Unit head:* Dr. John Henning, Chair, 740-597-1830, Fax: 740-593-0477, E-mail: henningj@ohio.edu. *Application contact:* Floyd J. Doney, Director of Student Affairs, 740-593-4400, Fax: 740-593-9310, E-mail: doney@ohio.edu.
Website: http://www.cehs.ohio.edu/academics/te/index.htm

Old Dominion University, Darden College of Education, Program in Elementary/Middle Education, Norfolk, VA 23529. Offers elementary education (Postbaccalaureate Certificate); instructional technology (MS Ed); library science (MS Ed). *Accreditation:* NCATE. *Program availability:* Part-time, evening/weekend, 100% online, blended/hybrid learning. *Faculty:* 21 full-time (19 women), 24 part-time/adjunct (22 women). *Students:* 120 full-time (112 women), 138 part-time (125 women); includes 60 minority (36 Black or African American, non-Hispanic/Latino; 1 American Indian or Alaska Native, non-Hispanic/Latino; 5 Asian, non-Hispanic/Latino; 12 Hispanic/Latino; 6 Two or more races, non-Hispanic/Latino). Average age 33. 213 applicants, 88% accepted, 172 enrolled. In 2016, 127 master's awarded. *Degree requirements:* For master's, comprehensive exam. *Entrance requirements:* For master's, GRE General Test or MAT; PRAXIS I, SAT or ACT, minimum GPA of 2.8. Additional exam requirements/recommendations for international students: Required—TOEFL (minimum score 600 paper-based). *Application deadline:* For fall admission, 6/1 priority date for domestic students; for winter admission, 11/1 priority date for domestic students; for spring admission, 3/1 priority date for domestic students. Applications are processed on a rolling basis. Application fee: $50. Electronic applications accepted. *Expenses:* $478 per credit hour in-state; $1,195 per credit hour out-of-state. *Financial support:* In 2016–17, 180 students received support. Unspecified assistantships available. Financial award application deadline: 2/15; financial award applicants required to submit FAFSA. *Faculty research:* Education pre-K to 6, school librarianship, reading, TESOL, literacy. *Unit head:* Dr. KaaVonia Hinton, Chair, Department of Teaching and Learning, 757-683-3284, Fax: 757-683-5862, E-mail: khintonj@odu.edu. *Application contact:* William Heffelfinger, Director of Graduate Admissions, 757-683-5554, Fax: 757-683-3255, E-mail: gradadmit@odu.edu.
Website: http://education.odu.edu/eci/

Pacific University, College of Education, Forest Grove, OR 97116-1797. Offers early childhood education (MAT); education (MAE); elementary education (MAT); ESOL (MAT); high school education (MAT); middle school education (MAT); special education (MAT); speech-language pathology (MS); STEM education (MAT); talented and gifted (M Ed); visual function in learning (M Ed). *Accreditation:* NCATE. *Program availability:* Part-time, evening/weekend. *Degree requirements:* For master's, research project. *Entrance requirements:* For master's, California Basic Educational Skills Test, PRAXIS II, minimum undergraduate GPA of 2.75, 3.0 graduate. Additional exam requirements/ recommendations for international students: Required—TOEFL. Electronic applications accepted. *Expenses:* Contact institution. *Faculty research:* Defining a culturally competent classroom, technology in the k-12 classroom, Socratic seminars, social studies education.

Piedmont College, School of Education, Demorest, GA 30535. Offers art education (MAT); curriculum and instruction (Ed S); early childhood education (MA, MAT); instructional technology (MAT); middle grades education (MA, MAT); music education (MAT); secondary education (MA, MAT); special education (MA, MAT). *Program availability:* Part-time, evening/weekend. *Students:* 290 full-time (217 women), 614 part-time (508 women); includes 131 minority (97 Black or African American, non-Hispanic/ Latino; 4 American Indian or Alaska Native, non-Hispanic/Latino; 5 Asian, non-Hispanic/ Latino; 11 Hispanic/Latino; 6 Native Hawaiian or other Pacific Islander, non-Hispanic/ Latino; 8 Two or more races, non-Hispanic/Latino), 6 international. Average age 37. 257 applicants, 64% accepted, 160 enrolled. In 2016, 288 master's, 243 other advanced degrees awarded. *Degree requirements:* For master's, thesis, field experience in the classroom teaching. *Entrance requirements:* For master's, GRE General Test, MAT, minimum undergraduate GPA of 2.5; for Ed S, minimum graduate GPA of 3.5, valid teaching certificate. Additional exam requirements/recommendations for international students: Required—TOEFL (minimum score 550 paper-based). *Application deadline:* For fall admission, 7/15 for domestic students; for spring admission, 12/1 for domestic students. Applications are processed on a rolling basis. Electronic applications accepted. *Expenses: Tuition:* Full-time $8910. *Financial support:* Career-related internships or fieldwork, Federal Work-Study, and unspecified assistantships available. Support available to part-time students. Financial award applicants required to submit FAFSA. *Unit head:* Dr. Don Gnecco, Dean, 706-778-3000 Ext. 1201, Fax: 706-776-9608, E-mail: dgnecco@piedmont.edu. *Application contact:* Kathleen Anderson, Director of Graduate Enrollment Management, 706-778-8500 Ext. 1181, Fax: 706-778-0150, E-mail: kanderson@piedmont.edu.

Queens College of the City University of New York, Division of Education, Department of Educational and Community Programs, Queens, NY 11367-1597. Offers bilingual pupil personnel (AC); counselor education (MS Ed); mental health counseling (MS); school building leader (AC); school district leader (AC); school psychologist (MS Ed); special education-childhood education (AC); special education-early childhood (MS Ed); teacher of special education 1-6 (MS Ed); teacher of special education birth-2 (MS Ed); teaching students with disabilities, grades 7-12 (MS Ed, AC). *Program availability:* Part-time. *Faculty:* 20 full-time (14 women), 50 part-time/adjunct (26 women). *Students:* 101 full-time (85 women), 459 part-time (383 women); includes 230 minority (44 Black or African American, non-Hispanic/Latino; 3 American Indian or Alaska Native, non-Hispanic/Latino; 46 Asian, non-Hispanic/Latino; 128 Hispanic/Latino; 1 Native Hawaiian or other Pacific Islander, non-Hispanic/Latino; 8 Two or more races, non-Hispanic/Latino), 3 international. Average age 28. 515 applicants, 57% accepted, 230 enrolled. In 2016, 158 master's, 68 other advanced degrees awarded. *Degree requirements:* For master's, research project; for AC, internship. *Entrance requirements:* For master's, minimum GPA of 3.0. Additional exam requirements/recommendations for international students: Required—TOEFL, IELTS. *Application deadline:* For fall admission, 3/1 for domestic students. Applications are processed on a rolling basis. Application fee: $125. Electronic applications accepted. *Expenses:* Tuition, state resident: full-time $5065; part-time $425 per credit. Tuition, nonresident: part-time $780 per credit. *Required fees:* $522; $397 per credit. Part-time tuition and fees vary according to course load and program. *Financial support:* Career-related internships or fieldwork available. Financial award application deadline: 4/1; financial award applicants required to submit FAFSA. *Unit head:* Dr. Lynn Howell, Chairperson, 718-997-5250, E-mail: lynn.howell@qc.cuny.edu.

Queens College of the City University of New York, Division of Education, Department of Elementary and Early Childhood Education, Queens, NY 11367-1597. Offers bilingual education (MS Ed); child development psychology (AC); childhood education (MAT, MS Ed); childhood education and special education (MAT); childhood education-bilingual education (MAT, MS Ed, AC); children's literacy (AC); early childhood education (MAT); early childhood education birth-2 (MS Ed, AC); elementary education (MS Ed); literacy birth-grade 6 (AC); literacy technology birth-grade 6 (MS Ed); social studies education grades 1-6 (AC). *Program availability:* Part-time, evening/weekend. *Faculty:* 25 full-time (19 women), 33 part-time/adjunct (28 women). *Students:* 134 full-time (119 women), 374 part-time (349 women); includes 251 minority (55 Black or African American, non-Hispanic/Latino; 1 American Indian or Alaska Native, non-Hispanic/Latino; 82 Asian, non-Hispanic/Latino; 103 Hispanic/Latino; 10 Two or more races, non-Hispanic/Latino), 12 international. Average age 29. 364 applicants, 72% accepted, 224 enrolled. In 2016, 184 master's, 62 other advanced degrees awarded. *Degree requirements:* For master's, research project. *Entrance requirements:* For master's, minimum GPA of 3.0. Additional exam requirements/recommendations for international students: Required—TOEFL, IELTS. *Application deadline:* For fall admission, 4/1 for domestic students. Applications are processed on a rolling basis. Application fee: $125. Electronic applications accepted. *Expenses:* Tuition, state resident: full-time $5065; part-time $425 per credit. Tuition, nonresident: part-time $780 per credit. *Required fees:* $522; $397 per credit. Part-time tuition and fees vary according to course load and program. *Financial support:* Career-related internships or fieldwork available. Financial award application deadline: 4/1; financial award applicants required to submit FAFSA. *Unit head:* Dr. Mary Bushnell Greiner, Chairperson, 718-997-5328, E-mail: mary.greiner@qc.cuny.edu.

Quinnipiac University, School of Education, Program in Secondary Education, Hamden, CT 06518-1940. Offers biology (MAT); English (MAT); history/social studies (MAT); mathematics (MAT); Spanish (MAT). *Accreditation:* NCATE. *Faculty:* 6 full-time (2 women), 24 part-time/adjunct (16 women). *Students:* 43 full-time (29 women), 1 part-time (0 women); includes 6 minority (1 Asian, non-Hispanic/Latino; 4 Hispanic/Latino; 1 Two or more races, non-Hispanic/Latino). 43 applicants, 98% accepted, 36 enrolled. In 2016, 32 master's awarded. *Entrance requirements:* For master's, PRAXIS I or PRAXIS Core Academic Skills Exam, minimum GPA of 3.0, interview. *Application deadline:* For fall admission, 5/1 priority date for domestic students. Applications are processed on a rolling basis. Application fee: $45. Electronic applications accepted. *Expenses: Tuition:* Part-time $985 per credit. *Required fees:* $40 per credit. $150 per semester. Tuition and fees vary according to program. *Financial support:* Career-related internships or fieldwork, Federal Work-Study, and unspecified assistantships available. Financial award application deadline: 6/1; financial award applicants required to submit FAFSA. *Faculty research:* Multicultural and urban education/leadership, challenges of teaching diverse learners, scholarship of teaching and learning, technology and teaching, humor and education. *Unit head:* Mordechai Gordon, Program Director, 203-582-8442, E-mail: mordechai.gordon@qu.edu. *Application contact:* Office of Graduate Admissions, 203-582-8672, Fax: 203-582-3443, E-mail: graduate@qu.edu.
Website: http://www.qu.edu/gradeducation

Roberts Wesleyan College, Graduate Teacher Education Programs, Rochester, NY 14624-1997. Offers adolescence and special education (M Ed); childhood and special education (M Ed); literacy education (M Ed); special education (M Ed). *Program availability:* Part-time, evening/weekend. *Degree requirements:* For master's, thesis. Electronic applications accepted.

Rowan University, Graduate School, College of Science and Mathematics, Department of Mathematics, Program in Middle Grades Math Education, Glassboro, NJ 08028-1701. Offers CGS. Electronic applications accepted.

Saginaw Valley State University, College of Education, Program in Middle School Classroom Teaching, University Center, MI 48710. Offers MAT. *Accreditation:* NCATE. *Program availability:* Part-time, evening/weekend. *Degree requirements:* For master's, capstone course. *Entrance requirements:* For master's, minimum GPA of 3.0, teaching certificate. Additional exam requirements/recommendations for international students: Required—TOEFL (minimum score 550 paper-based; 79 iBT). *Application deadline:* For fall admission, 7/15 for international students; for winter admission, 11/15 for international students; for spring admission, 4/15 for international students. Applications are processed on a rolling basis. Application fee: $30 ($90 for international students). Electronic applications accepted. *Expenses:* Tuition, state resident: full-time $9652; part-time $536 per credit hour. Tuition, nonresident: full-time $12,259; part-time $1022 per credit hour. *Required fees:* $263; $14.60 per credit hour. Tuition and fees vary according to degree level. *Financial support:* Federal Work-Study and scholarships/ grants available. Support available to part-time students. Financial award applicants required to submit FAFSA. *Unit head:* Dr. Craig Douglas, Dean, 989-964-4057, Fax: 989-964-4385, E-mail: coeconnect@svsu.edu. *Application contact:* Jenna Briggs, Director, Graduate and International Programs, 989-964-6096, Fax: 989-964-2788, E-mail: gradadm@svsu.edu.

St. Bonaventure University, School of Graduate Studies, School of Education, Adolescence Education Program, St. Bonaventure, NY 14778-2284. Offers MS Ed. *Program availability:* Part-time. *Faculty:* 1 (woman) full-time, 1 (woman) part-time/ adjunct. *Students:* 10 full-time (6 women), 8 part-time (3 women). Average age 24. 3 applicants, 100% accepted, 3 enrolled. In 2016, 3 master's awarded. *Degree requirements:* For master's, comprehensive exam, minimum cumulative GPA of 3.0, electronic portfolio, student teaching. *Entrance requirements:* For master's, New York State Teacher Certification Exams, CST in subject area, bachelor's degree or thirty semester hours in an arts or sciences major in the subject area of teaching certification from an accredited college or university; official transcripts showing proof of degree and all college and university courses taken; at least six semester hours of university-level credit. Additional exam requirements/recommendations for international students: Required—TOEFL (minimum score 550 paper-based; 79 iBT). *Application deadline:* For fall admission, 6/15 priority date for domestic students, 2/1 priority date for international students; for spring admission, 10/1 for domestic students, 7/1 for international students. Applications are processed on a rolling basis. Application fee: $0. Electronic applications accepted. *Expenses:* $733 per credit, $100 graduation fee. *Financial support:* Federal Work-Study, scholarships/grants, health care benefits, and unspecified assistantships available. Support available to part-time students. Financial award application deadline: 4/15; financial award applicants required to submit FAFSA. *Faculty research:* Critical and media literacy, gifted education. *Unit head:* Dr. Amanda Winkelsas, Director, 716-375-2177, Fax: 716-375-2360, E-mail: awinkels@sbu.edu. *Application contact:* Bruce Campbell, Director of Graduate Admissions, 716-375-2429, Fax: 716-375-4015, E-mail: gradsch@sbu.edu.
Website: http://www.sbu.edu/academics/schools/education/graduate-degrees-certificates/msed-in-adolescence-education

St. Bonaventure University, School of Graduate Studies, School of Education, Literacy Programs, St. Bonaventure, NY 14778-2284. Offers adolescent literacy 5-12 (MS Ed);

childhood literacy B-6 (MS Ed). *Accreditation:* NCATE. *Program availability:* Part-time, evening/weekend. *Faculty:* 2 full-time (both women), 2 part-time/adjunct (both women). *Students:* 7 full-time (all women), 6 part-time (all women); includes 1 minority (Hispanic/Latino). Average age 25. 10 applicants, 70% accepted, 4 enrolled. In 2016, 14 master's awarded. *Degree requirements:* For master's, comprehensive exam, thesis optional, minimum cumulative GPA of 3.0, clinical practicum, literacy coaching internship, electronic portfolio. *Entrance requirements:* For master's, GRE or MAT, teaching certificate in matching area in-hand or pending, transcripts from all previous colleges, minimum GPA of 3.0, 2 references, interview, writing sample. Additional exam requirements/recommendations for international students: Required—TOEFL (minimum score 550 paper-based; 80 iBT). *Application deadline:* For fall admission, 6/15 priority date for domestic students, 2/1 for international students; for spring admission, 11/15 priority date for domestic students, 7/1 for international students. Applications are processed on a rolling basis. Application fee: $0. Electronic applications accepted. *Expenses:* $733 per credit, $100 graduation fee. *Financial support:* Federal Work-Study, scholarships/grants, health care benefits, and unspecified assistantships available. Support available to part-time students. Financial award application deadline: 4/15; financial award applicants required to submit FAFSA. *Faculty research:* Gifted education, curriculum and instruction, theory and language. *Unit head:* Kayla Zimmer, Program Director, 716-375-2167, Fax: 716-375-2360, E-mail: kzimmer@sbu.edu. *Application contact:* Bruce Campbell, Director of Graduate Admissions, 716-375-2429, Fax: 716-375-4015, E-mail: gradsch@sbu.edu.
Website: http://www.sbu.edu/academics/schools/education/graduate-degrees-certificates/msed-in-childhood-literacy

St. John Fisher College, Ralph C. Wilson Jr. School of Education, Program in Adolescence Education and Special Education, Rochester, NY 14618-3597. Offers adolescence education: biology with special education (MS Ed); adolescence education: chemistry with special education (MS Ed); adolescence education: English with special education (MS Ed); adolescence education: French with special education (MS Ed); adolescence education: math with special education (MS Ed); adolescence education: physics with special education (MS Ed); adolescence education: social studies with special education (MS Ed); adolescence education: Spanish with special education (MS Ed). *Program availability:* Part-time, evening/weekend. *Faculty:* 7 full-time (6 women), 5 part-time/adjunct (all women). *Students:* 15 full-time (6 women), 9 part-time (6 women); includes 3 minority (2 Black or African American, non-Hispanic/Latino; 1 Hispanic/Latino). Average age 28. 16 applicants, 56% accepted, 6 enrolled. In 2016, 8 master's awarded. *Degree requirements:* For master's, field experiences, student teaching, LAST. *Entrance requirements:* For master's, 2 letters of recommendation, personal statement, current resume. Additional exam requirements/recommendations for international students: Required—TOEFL (minimum score 575 paper-based; 80 iBT). *Application deadline:* Applications are processed on a rolling basis. Application fee: $30. Electronic applications accepted. *Expenses:* $885 per credit hour. *Financial support:* Scholarships/grants available. Financial award applicants required to submit FAFSA. *Faculty research:* Arts and humanities, urban schools, constructivist learning, at-risk students, mentoring. *Unit head:* Dr. Susan Hildenbrand, Program Director, 585-385-7297, E-mail: shildenbrand@sjfc.edu. *Application contact:* Michelle Gosier, Associate Director of Transfer and Graduate Admissions, 585-385-8064, E-mail: mgosier@sjfc.edu.

St. John's University, The School of Education, Department of Curriculum and Instruction, Queens, NY 11439. Offers adolescent education (MS Ed, Certificate); childhood education (MS Ed); early childhood education (MS Ed); middle school education (Certificate). *Program availability:* Part-time, evening/weekend. *Degree requirements:* For master's, comprehensive exam. *Entrance requirements:* For master's, minimum GPA of 3.0, 2 letters of recommendation, qualification for the New York State provisional (initial) teaching certificate, transcript, personal statement. Additional exam requirements/recommendations for international students: Required—TOEFL (minimum score 600 paper-based; 100 iBT), IELTS (minimum score 7). Electronic applications accepted. *Faculty research:* Student learning and satisfaction in online courses, online collaboration needs, female education in south and east Asia, e-portfolio assessment, pedagogical practices in mathematics education.

Saint Joseph's University, College of Arts and Sciences, Graduate Programs in Education, Philadelphia, PA 19131-1395. Offers curriculum supervisor (Certificate); educational leadership (MS, Ed D); elementary education (MS, Certificate); elementary/middle school education (Certificate); instructional technology (MS, Certificate); organizational development and leadership (MS); principal (Certificate); professional education (MS); reading specialist (MS, Certificate); reading supervisor (Certificate); secondary education (MS, Certificate); special education (MS); special education 7-12 (Certificate); special education PK-8 (Certificate); superintendent's letter of eligibility (Certificate); supervisor of special education (Certificate); teacher of the deaf and hard of hearing (Certificate). *Program availability:* Part-time, evening/weekend, blended/hybrid learning. *Faculty:* 26 full-time (21 women), 74 part-time/adjunct (45 women). *Students:* 107 full-time (88 women), 826 part-time (622 women); includes 170 minority (115 Black or African American, non-Hispanic/Latino; 2 American Indian or Alaska Native, non-Hispanic/Latino; 11 Asian, non-Hispanic/Latino; 31 Hispanic/Latino; 1 Native Hawaiian or other Pacific Islander, non-Hispanic/Latino; 10 Two or more races, non-Hispanic/Latino), 18 international. Average age 33. 338 applicants, 76% accepted, 173 enrolled. In 2016, 419 master's, 16 doctorates, 24 other advanced degrees awarded. *Degree requirements:* For master's, thesis or alternative; for doctorate, comprehensive exam, thesis/dissertation. *Entrance requirements:* For master's, 2 letters of recommendation, minimum GPA of 3.0, official transcripts, personal statement; for doctorate, GRE, master's degree from accredited institution, minimum graduate GPA of 3.5, computer competence, interview with program director. Additional exam requirements/recommendations for international students: Required—TOEFL (minimum score 550 paper-based; 80 iBT), IELTS (minimum score 6.5), PTE (minimum score 60). *Application deadline:* For fall admission, 7/15 for international students; for spring admission, 11/1 for international students. Applications are processed on a rolling basis. Application fee: $35. Electronic applications accepted. *Expenses:* $750 per credit, $100 education fee, $360 online organization development and leadership residency fee. *Financial support:* In 2016–17, 25 students received support. Unspecified assistantships available. Financial award application deadline: 5/1; financial award applicants required to submit FAFSA. *Faculty research:* Factors predicting early mathematics skills for low income children, early child care and development, preschool quality, parent communication and home-school collaboration issues, education of terminally ill children, preparing literacy teachers for urban schools. *Total annual research expenditures:* $18,118. *Unit head:* Dr. John Vacca, Associate Dean, Education, 610-660-3131, E-mail: gradcas@sju.edu. *Application contact:* Graduate Admissions, College of Arts and Sciences, 610-660-3131, E-mail: gradcas@sju.edu.
Website: http://sju.edu/int/academics/cas/grad/education/index.html

Saint Peter's University, Graduate Programs in Education, Program in Teaching, Jersey City, NJ 07306-5997. Offers 6-8 middle school education (MA Ed, Certificate); K-12 secondary education (MA Ed, Certificate); K-5 elementary education (MA Ed, Certificate). *Program availability:* Part-time, evening/weekend. *Degree requirements:* For master's, comprehensive exam. *Entrance requirements:* For master's, GRE or MAT. Additional exam requirements/recommendations for international students: Required—TOEFL. Electronic applications accepted.

St. Thomas Aquinas College, Division of Teacher Education, Sparkill, NY 10976. Offers adolescence education (MST); childhood and special education (MST); childhood education (MST); educational leadership (MS Ed); reading (MS Ed, PMC); special education (MS Ed, PMC); teaching (MS Ed), including elementary education, middle school education, secondary education. *Accreditation:* NCATE. *Program availability:* Part-time, evening/weekend. *Degree requirements:* For master's, comprehensive exam, comprehensive professional portfolio; for PMC, action research project. *Entrance requirements:* For master's, New York State Qualifying Exam, GRE General Test or minimum GPA of 3.0, teaching certificate; for PMC, GRE General Test or minimum GPA of 3.0. Electronic applications accepted. *Faculty research:* Computer applications in education, adolescent special education students, literacy development, inclusive practices for special education students.

Salem College, Department of Education, Winston-Salem, NC 27101. Offers art education (MAT); elementary education (M Ed, MAT); language and literacy (M Ed); middle school education (MAT); school counseling (M Ed); second language studies (MAT); secondary education (MAT); special education (M Ed, MAT). *Accreditation:* NCATE. *Program availability:* Part-time, evening/weekend, online learning. *Degree requirements:* For master's, practicum (MAT), project (M Ed), oral and written comprehensive exams. *Entrance requirements:* For master's, minimum GPA of 2.5. *Faculty research:* Content area reading strategies, literacy development, brain compatible instruction.

Salem State University, School of Graduate Studies, Program in Middle School Education, Salem, MA 01970-5353. Offers humanities (M Ed); math/science (MAT). *Program availability:* Part-time, evening/weekend. *Entrance requirements:* For master's, GRE or MAT. Additional exam requirements/recommendations for international students: Required—TOEFL (minimum score 550 paper-based; 80 iBT) or IELTS (minimum score 5.5).

Salem State University, School of Graduate Studies, Program in Middle School General Science, Salem, MA 01970-5353. Offers MAT. *Program availability:* Part-time, evening/weekend. *Entrance requirements:* For master's, GRE or MAT. Additional exam requirements/recommendations for international students: Required—TOEFL (minimum score 550 paper-based; 80 iBT) or IELTS (minimum score 5.5).

Salem State University, School of Graduate Studies, Program in Middle School Math, Salem, MA 01970-5353. Offers MAT. *Program availability:* Part-time, evening/weekend. *Entrance requirements:* For master's, GRE or MAT. Additional exam requirements/recommendations for international students: Required—TOEFL (minimum score 550 paper-based; 80 iBT) or IELTS (minimum score 5.5).

Salisbury University, Program in Mathematics Education, Salisbury, MD 21801-6837. Offers mathematics (MSME), including high school, middle school. *Program availability:* Part-time. *Faculty:* 3 full-time (1 woman). *Students:* 2 full-time (1 woman), 8 part-time (5 women); includes 1 minority (Two or more races, non-Hispanic/Latino). Average age 27. 2 applicants, 100% accepted, 2 enrolled. In 2016, 2 master's awarded. *Entrance requirements:* Additional exam requirements/recommendations for international students: Required—TOEFL (minimum score 550 paper-based, 79 iBT) or IELTS (6.5). *Application deadline:* For fall admission, 5/15 priority date for domestic and international students; for spring admission, 10/1 priority date for domestic and international students. Applications are processed on a rolling basis. Application fee: $65. Electronic applications accepted. *Expenses:* $381 per credit hour resident tuition, $670 per credit hour non-resident tuition; $84 per credit hour fees. *Financial support:* In 2016–17, 1 teaching assistantship with full tuition reimbursement (averaging $8,000 per year) was awarded; career-related internships or fieldwork and scholarships/grants also available. Support available to part-time students. Financial award application deadline: 3/1; financial award applicants required to submit FAFSA. *Faculty research:* Conceptual development of multiplicative reasoning; early childhood mathematics; teachers' attitudes towards mathematics. *Unit head:* Dr. Jennifer Bergner, Graduate Program Director, Mathematics Education, 410-677-5429, E-mail: jabergner@salisbury.edu.
Website: http://www.salisbury.edu/gsr/gradstudies/MSMEpage.html

Seton Hill University, Program in Elementary Education/Middle Level Education, Greensburg, PA 15601. Offers MA, Certificate. *Program availability:* Part-time, evening/weekend, online learning. *Entrance requirements:* For master's, teacher's certification, 3 letters of recommendation, personal statement, transcripts, resume. Additional exam requirements/recommendations for international students: Required—TOEFL (minimum score 600 paper-based; 100 iBT), IELTS (minimum score 6.5). Electronic applications accepted.

Shenandoah University, School of Education and Human Development, Winchester, VA 22601-5195. Offers administrative leadership (D Ed); educational administration (MSE); emphasis in teaching (MSE); health and physical education (Certificate); individual focus (MSE); literacy education (MS); middle school teacher education (Certificate); organizational leadership (MS, D Prof); secondary school teacher education (Certificate); special education (MSE). *Accreditation:* TEAC. *Program availability:* Part-time, evening/weekend. *Faculty:* 9 full-time (7 women), 43 part-time/adjunct (33 women). *Students:* 31 full-time (25 women), 236 part-time (160 women); includes 39 minority (19 Black or African American, non-Hispanic/Latino; 1 American Indian or Alaska Native, non-Hispanic/Latino; 10 Asian, non-Hispanic/Latino; 7 Hispanic/Latino; 1 Native Hawaiian or other Pacific Islander, non-Hispanic/Latino; 1 Two or more races, non-Hispanic/Latino), 4 international. Average age 37. 90 applicants, 97% accepted, 56 enrolled. In 2016, 113 master's, 13 doctorates, 38 other advanced degrees awarded. *Degree requirements:* For master's, comprehensive exam (for some programs), thesis (for some programs); for doctorate, comprehensive exam, thesis/dissertation. *Entrance requirements:* For degree, PRAXIS Academic Core, SAT/ACT, PRAXIS Academic Core Math, or VCLA, three letters of recommendation, writing sample, undergraduate degree. Additional exam requirements/recommendations for international students: Required—TOEFL (minimum score 550 paper-based; 79 iBT), IELTS (minimum score 6.5). *Application deadline:* For fall admission, 5/1 priority date for domestic students, 5/1 for international students; for spring admission, 10/15 priority date for domestic students, 10/15 for international students; for summer admission, 3/15 priority date for domestic students, 3/15 for international students. Application fee: $30. Electronic applications accepted. *Expenses:* Contact institution. *Financial support:* In 2016–17, 18 students received support. Scholarships/grants and unspecified assistantships available. Financial award applicants required to submit FAFSA. *Faculty research:* Exploring helplessness and anxiety in learning statistics, facilitating effective classroom group work, expert-novice dynamics in teaching, K-12 policy implementation and change, adult education, family-school-community relations, mentoring of first-year school principals. *Total annual research expenditures:* $2,000. *Unit head:* Dennis William Kellison, PhD, Director, 540-535-7324, Fax: 540-665-4726, E-mail: dkelliso@su.edu. *Application contact:* Andrew Woodall, Executive Director of Recruitment and Admissions, 540-665-4581, Fax: 540-665-4627, E-mail: admit@su.edu.
Website: http://www.su.edu/education/

Shippensburg University of Pennsylvania, School of Graduate Studies, College of Education and Human Services, Department of Teacher Education, Shippensburg, PA

17257-2299. Offers curriculum and instruction (M Ed), including biology, early childhood education, elementary and middle level education, elementary education, geography/earth science, history, mathematics, middle school education, modern languages; literacy studies (Certificate); online instruction, learning, and technology (Certificate); reading (M Ed); teaching English as a second language (Certificate). *Accreditation:* NCATE. *Program availability:* Part-time, evening/weekend, 100% online, blended/hybrid learning. *Faculty:* 14 full-time (9 women), 5 part-time/adjunct (all women). *Students:* 11 full-time (10 women), 88 part-time (81 women); includes 8 minority (3 Black or African American, non-Hispanic/Latino; 2 Asian, non-Hispanic/Latino; 3 Hispanic/Latino), 4 international. Average age 32. 57 applicants, 60% accepted, 28 enrolled. In 2016, 18 master's awarded. *Degree requirements:* For master's, comprehensive exam (for some programs), thesis optional, practicum or internship; capstone seminar (for some programs). *Entrance requirements:* For master's, MAT or GRE (if GPA less than 2.75), interview, 3 letters of reference, questionnaire of teaching background and future goals, resume. Additional exam requirements/recommendations for international students: Required—TOEFL (minimum score 550 paper-based, 68 iBT) or IELTS (minimum score 6). *Application deadline:* For fall admission, 4/1 priority date for domestic students, 4/30 for international students; for spring admission, 9/1 priority date for domestic students, 9/30 for international students; for summer admission, 2/1 priority date for domestic students. Applications are processed on a rolling basis. Application fee: $45. Electronic applications accepted. *Expenses:* Tuition, state resident: part-time $483 per credit. Tuition, nonresident: part-time $725 per credit. *Required fees:* $141 per credit. *Financial support:* In 2016–17, 3 students received support. Career-related internships or fieldwork, scholarships/grants, unspecified assistantships, and resident hall director and student payroll positions available. Support available to part-time students. Financial award application deadline: 3/1; financial award applicants required to submit FAFSA. *Unit head:* Dr. Christine A. Royce, Chairperson, 717-477-1688, Fax: 717-477-4046, E-mail: caroyc@ship.edu. *Application contact:* Megan N. Luft, Assistant Dean of Graduate Admissions, 717-477-1231, Fax: 717-477-4016, E-mail: mnluft@ship.edu.
Website: http://www.ship.edu/teacher/

Smith College, Graduate and Special Programs, Department of Education and Child Study, Northampton, MA 01063. Offers elementary education (MAT); middle school education (MAT); secondary education (MAT), including secondary education. *Program availability:* Part-time. *Students:* 14 full-time (10 women), 3 part-time (2 women); includes 1 minority (Two or more races, non-Hispanic/Latino). Average age 27. 36 applicants, 78% accepted, 14 enrolled. In 2016, 21 master's awarded. *Entrance requirements:* Additional exam requirements/recommendations for international students: Required—TOEFL (minimum score 595 paper-based; 97 iBT), IELTS. *Application deadline:* For fall admission, 4/1 for domestic students, 1/15 for international students; for spring admission, 12/1 for domestic students. Application fee: $60. *Expenses: Tuition:* Full-time $34,560; part-time $1440 per credit. Tuition and fees vary according to course load and program. *Financial support:* In 2016–17, 16 students received support, including 6 fellowships with full tuition reimbursements available; scholarships/grants also available. Support available to part-time students. Financial award application deadline: 4/1; financial award applicants required to submit CSS PROFILE or FAFSA. *Unit head:* Alan Rudnitsky, Chair, 413-585-3261, Fax: 413-585-3268, E-mail: arudnits@smith.edu. *Application contact:* Ruth Morgan, Program Assistant, 413-585-3050, Fax: 413-585-3054, E-mail: gradstdy@smith.edu.
Website: http://www.smith.edu/education

Southeast Missouri State University, School of Graduate Studies, Department of Middle and Secondary Education, Cape Girardeau, MO 63701-4799. Offers MA. *Accreditation:* NCATE. *Program availability:* Part-time, online only, 100% online. *Faculty:* 6 full-time (4 women), 1 (woman) part-time/adjunct. *Students:* 5 full-time (2 women), 45 part-time (36 women); includes 3 minority (1 Black or African American, non-Hispanic/Latino; 1 Asian, non-Hispanic/Latino; 1 Hispanic/Latino). Average age 31. 20 applicants, 90% accepted, 22 enrolled. In 2016, 20 master's awarded. *Degree requirements:* For master's, comprehensive exam, research paper. *Entrance requirements:* For master's, minimum undergraduate GPA of 2.75. Additional exam requirements/recommendations for international students: Required—TOEFL (minimum score 550 paper-based; 79 iBT), IELTS (minimum score 6), PTE (minimum score 53). *Application deadline:* For fall admission, 8/1 for domestic students, 6/1 for international students; for spring admission, 11/21 for domestic students, 10/1 for international students; for summer admission, 5/15 for domestic students. Applications are processed on a rolling basis. Application fee: $30 ($40 for international students). Electronic applications accepted. *Expenses:* Tuition, state resident: full-time $3130; part-time $260.80 per credit hour. Tuition, nonresident: full-time $5842; part-time $486.80 per credit hour. *Required fees:* $33.70 per credit hour. *Financial support:* In 2016–17, 4 students received support. Career-related internships or fieldwork, Federal Work-Study, scholarships/grants, traineeships, tuition waivers (full), and unspecified assistantships available. Financial award application deadline: 6/30; financial award applicants required to submit FAFSA. *Faculty research:* Assessment, technology, diversity. *Unit head:* Dr. Simin L. Cwick, Middle and Secondary Education Department Chair, 573-651-5965, E-mail: scwick@semo.edu. *Application contact:* Alisa Aleen McFerron, Assistant Director of Admissions for Operations, 573-651-5937, E-mail: amcferron@semo.edu.
Website: http://www.semo.edu/midsecondaryed/

Spalding University, Graduate Studies, College of Education, Programs in Education, Louisville, KY 40203-2188. Offers art teacher education (MAT); business teacher education (MAT); elementary school education (MAT); foreign language (MAT); high school education (MAT); middle school education (MAT); secondary education (MAT); special education (learning and behavioral disorders) (MAT); student guidance counselor (MA); teacher leader (M Ed). *Accreditation:* NCATE. *Program availability:* Part-time, evening/weekend. *Faculty:* 39 full-time (26 women), 13 part-time/adjunct (4 women). *Students:* 97 full-time (76 women), 31 part-time (23 women); includes 39 minority (33 Black or African American, non-Hispanic/Latino; 1 Asian, non-Hispanic/Latino; 3 Hispanic/Latino; 2 Two or more races, non-Hispanic/Latino). Average age 35. 62 applicants, 55% accepted, 33 enrolled. In 2016, 49 master's awarded. *Entrance requirements:* For master's, GRE General Test or MAT, interview, letters of recommendation, resume. Additional exam requirements/recommendations for international students: Required—TOEFL (minimum score 535 paper-based). *Application deadline:* Applications are processed on a rolling basis. Application fee: $30. Electronic applications accepted. *Expenses: Tuition:* Full-time $15,300. *Financial support:* Scholarships/grants, traineeships, and unspecified assistantships available. Financial award applicants required to submit FAFSA. *Faculty research:* Instructional technology, achievement gap, classroom management, assessment. *Unit head:* Dr. Chris Walsh, Associate Dean, 502-873-4272, Fax: 502-585-7123, E-mail: cwalsh@spalding.edu. *Application contact:* Valerie Anderson, Administrative Assistant, 502-873-4260, E-mail: vanderson@spalding.edu.

State University of New York at Fredonia, College of Education, Fredonia, NY 14063. Offers curriculum and instruction (MS Ed); literacy education (MS Ed), including birth-grade 12, grades 5-12; TESOL (MS Ed). *Accreditation:* NCATE. *Program availability:* Part-time. *Faculty:* 21 full-time (17 women), 11 part-time/adjunct (9 women). *Students:* 39 full-time (32 women), 54 part-time (33 women); includes 8 minority (1 Black or African American, non-Hispanic/Latino; 4 Asian, non-Hispanic/Latino; 2 Hispanic/Latino; 1 Two or more races, non-Hispanic/Latino). Average age 29. 60 applicants, 97% accepted, 39 enrolled. In 2016, 56 master's awarded. *Degree requirements:* For master's, thesis. *Entrance requirements:* For master's, GRE, minimum undergraduate GPA of 3.0. Additional exam requirements/recommendations for international students: Required—TOEFL (minimum score 79 iBT), IELTS (minimum score 6.5). *Application deadline:* For fall admission, 4/1 priority date for domestic and international students; for spring admission, 11/1 priority date for domestic students, 11/1 for international students. Applications are processed on a rolling basis. Application fee: $75. Electronic applications accepted. *Expenses:* Tuition, state resident: full-time $10,370; part-time $453 per credit. Tuition, nonresident: full-time $20,190; part-time $925 per credit. *Required fees:* $1619; $67.30 per credit hour. $403.80 per semester. *Financial support:* In 2016–17, 4 teaching assistantships with full and partial tuition reimbursements (averaging $7,075 per year) were awarded. Financial award application deadline: 3/15; financial award applicants required to submit FAFSA. *Faculty research:* Positive behavioral intervention and support (PBIS), place-based science education, peer support for education, primary source material for social studies education, policies and practices in learning English language. *Unit head:* Dr. Christine Givner, Dean, 716-673-3311, E-mail: christine.givner@fredonia.edu. *Application contact:* Wendy S. Dunst, Interim Graduate Recruitment and Admissions Associate, 716-673-3808, Fax: 716-673-3712, E-mail: wendy.dunst@fredonia.edu.
Website: http://www.fredonia.edu/coe/

State University of New York at Oswego, Graduate Studies, School of Education, Department of Curriculum and Instruction, Oswego, NY 13126. Offers adolescence education (MST); art education (MAT); childhood education (MST); curriculum and instruction (MS Ed); literacy education (MS Ed); special education (MS Ed). *Program availability:* Part-time, evening/weekend. *Degree requirements:* For master's, comprehensive exam (for some programs), thesis optional. *Entrance requirements:* For master's, GRE General Test, minimum GPA of 2.7, provisional teaching certificate. Additional exam requirements/recommendations for international students: Required—TOEFL (minimum score 560 paper-based). *Faculty research:* Classroom applications for microcomputers; classroom questioning, wait-time, and achievement; values clarification and academic achievement.

State University of New York College at Potsdam, School of Education and Professional Studies, Program in Special Education, Potsdam, NY 13676. Offers adolescence (grades 7-12) (MS Ed); childhood (grades 1-6) (MS Ed); early childhood (birth-grade 2) (MS Ed). *Accreditation:* NCATE. *Program availability:* Part-time. *Degree requirements:* For master's, culminating experience. *Entrance requirements:* For master's, minimum GPA of 3.0 in last 60 hours of course work. Additional exam requirements/recommendations for international students: Required—TOEFL (minimum score 550 paper-based; 80 iBT), IELTS (minimum score 6). Electronic applications accepted.

Temple University, College of Education, Department of Teaching and Learning, Philadelphia, PA 19122-6096. Offers career and technical education (Ed M), including business, computing, and information technology, industrial education, marketing education; middle grades education (Ed M), including math and language arts, math and science, science and language arts; secondary education (Ed M), including English, math, social studies; teaching English to speakers of other languages (MS Ed); urban education (Ed M). *Program availability:* Part-time, evening/weekend. *Faculty:* 26 full-time (16 women), 74 part-time/adjunct (54 women). *Students:* 204 full-time (139 women), 320 part-time (201 women); includes 112 minority (66 Black or African American, non-Hispanic/Latino; 17 Asian, non-Hispanic/Latino; 18 Hispanic/Latino; 11 Two or more races, non-Hispanic/Latino), 18 international. 300 applicants, 55% accepted, 99 enrolled. In 2016, 93 master's awarded. Terminal master's awarded for partial completion of doctoral program. *Degree requirements:* For master's, thesis or alternative. *Entrance requirements:* Additional exam requirements/recommendations for international students: Required—TOEFL (minimum score 550 paper-based; 79 iBT). *Application deadline:* For fall admission, 4/1 for domestic students, 12/15 for international students; for spring admission, 10/1 for domestic students, 8/1 for international students. Application fee: $60. Electronic applications accepted. *Expenses:* Contact institution. *Financial support:* Fellowships, research assistantships, and teaching assistantships available. Financial award application deadline: 1/15; financial award applicants required to submit FAFSA. *Faculty research:* Workforce development, vocational education, technical education, industrial education, professional development, literacy, classroom management, school communities, curriculum development, instruction, applied linguistics, cross linguistic influence, bilingual education, oral proficiency, multilingualism. *Unit head:* Dr. Christine Woyshner, Chairperson, 215-204-6387, E-mail: christine.woyshner@temple.edu. *Application contact:* Sarah Stapleton, Assistant Director, Academic Operations, 215-204-8220, E-mail: sarah.stapleton@temple.edu.
Website: http://education.temple.edu/tl

Tennessee Technological University, College of Graduate Studies, College of Education, Department of Exercise Science, Physical Education and Wellness, Cookeville, TN 38505. Offers adapted physical education (MA); elementary/middle school physical education (MA); lifetime wellness (MA); sport management (MA). *Accreditation:* NCATE. *Program availability:* Part-time, online learning. *Faculty:* 7 full-time (0 women). *Students:* 17 full-time (5 women), 32 part-time (17 women); includes 6 minority (4 Black or African American, non-Hispanic/Latino; 1 Hispanic/Latino; 1 Two or more races, non-Hispanic/Latino). Average age 27. 29 applicants, 59% accepted, 15 enrolled. In 2016, 24 master's awarded. *Degree requirements:* For master's, comprehensive exam, thesis or alternative. *Entrance requirements:* For master's, MAT or GRE. Additional exam requirements/recommendations for international students: Required—TOEFL (minimum score 527 paper-based; 71 iBT), IELTS (minimum score 5.5), PTE (minimum score 48), or TOEIC (Test of English as an International Communication). *Application deadline:* For fall admission, 8/1 for domestic students, 5/1 for international students; for spring admission, 12/1 for domestic students, 10/1 for international students; for summer admission, 5/1 for domestic students, 2/1 for international students. Applications are processed on a rolling basis. Application fee: $35 ($40 for international students). Electronic applications accepted. *Expenses:* Tuition, state resident: full-time $9375; part-time $534 per credit hour. Tuition, nonresident: full-time $22,443; part-time $1260 per credit hour. *Financial support:* In 2016–17, 2 research assistantships (averaging $4,400 per year), 9 teaching assistantships (averaging $4,400 per year) were awarded; fellowships and career-related internships or fieldwork also available. Financial award application deadline: 4/1. *Unit head:* Dr. Christy Killman, Chairperson, 931-372-3467, Fax: 931-372-6319, E-mail: ckillman@tntech.edu. *Application contact:* Shelia K. Kendrick, Coordinator of Graduate Studies, 931-372-3808, Fax: 931-372-3497, E-mail: skendrick@tntech.edu.

Theological University of the Caribbean, Graduate Programs, Saint Just, PR 00978-0901. Offers childhood and adolescent education (MA); counseling and pastoral care (MA); ministry (D Min); missions (MA).

Tufts University, Graduate School of Arts and Sciences, Department of Education, Program in Education, Medford, MA 02155. Offers educational studies (MA); elementary education (MAT); middle and secondary education (MAT); museum education (MA); secondary education (MA); STEM education (MS, PhD). *Program availability:* Part-time. *Students:* 67 full-time (49 women), 14 part-time (12 women); includes 17 minority (4

Black or African American, non-Hispanic/Latino; 6 Asian, non-Hispanic/Latino; 6 Hispanic/Latino; 1 Two or more races, non-Hispanic/Latino), 6 international. Average age 28. 120 applicants, 71% accepted, 49 enrolled. In 2016, 25 master's awarded. *Degree requirements:* For master's, thesis optional. *Entrance requirements:* For master's, GRE General Test, portfolio (for art education only); for doctorate, GRE General Test, writing sample. Additional exam requirements/recommendations for international students: Required—TOEFL (minimum score 550 paper-based; 80 iBT), IELTS (minimum score 6.5). *Application deadline:* For fall admission, 1/2 for domestic and international students; for spring admission, 10/15 for domestic and international students. Applications are processed on a rolling basis. Application fee: $85. Electronic applications accepted. *Expenses:* Contact institution. *Financial support:* In 2016–17, 69 students received support. Research assistantships, teaching assistantships, Federal Work-Study, scholarships/grants, and tuition waivers (full and partial) available. Support available to part-time students. Financial award application deadline: 1/2. *Unit head:* Dr. Sabina Vaught, Graduate Program Director. *Application contact:* Office of Graduate Admissions, 617-627-3395, E-mail: gradadmissions@tufts.edu.

Union College, Graduate Programs, Department of Education, Program in Middle Grades, Barbourville, KY 40906-1499. Offers MA. *Degree requirements:* For master's, thesis optional. *Entrance requirements:* For master's, GRE General Test, NTE.

University of Arkansas, Graduate School, College of Education and Health Professions, Department of Curriculum and Instruction, Fayetteville, AR 72701. Offers childhood education (MAT); curriculum and instruction (M Ed, PhD, Ed S); educational leadership (M Ed, Ed D, Ed S); educational statistics and research methods (MS, PhD); educational technology (M Ed); middle-level education (MAT); secondary education (M Ed, MAT, Ed S); special education (M Ed, MAT). *Accreditation:* NCATE. In 2016, 230 master's, 16 doctorates awarded. *Degree requirements:* For doctorate, thesis/dissertation. *Entrance requirements:* For doctorate, GRE General Test or MAT. *Application deadline:* For fall admission, 4/1 for international students; for spring admission, 10/1 for international students. Applications are processed on a rolling basis. Application fee: $40 ($50 for international students). Electronic applications accepted. *Financial support:* In 2016–17, 41 research assistantships, 2 teaching assistantships were awarded; fellowships with tuition reimbursements, career-related internships or fieldwork, and Federal Work-Study also available. Support available to part-time students. Financial award application deadline: 4/1; financial award applicants required to submit FAFSA. *Unit head:* Dr. Michael Daugherty, Departmental Chairperson, 479-575-4209, Fax: 479-575-5119, E-mail: mkd03@uark.edu. *Application contact:* Dr. Derrick Mears, Graduate Coordinator, 479-575-6195, Fax: 479-575-6676, E-mail: dmears@uark.edu.
Website: http://cied.uark.edu/

University of Arkansas at Little Rock, Graduate School, College of Education and Health Professions, Department of Teacher Education, Program in Middle Childhood Education, Little Rock, AR 72204-1099. Offers M Ed. *Degree requirements:* For master's, electronic portfolio. *Entrance requirements:* For master's, PRAXIS, minimum undergraduate GPA of 2.75 overall or 3.0 in the last 60 hours of undergraduate work; interview.

University of Bridgeport, School of Education, Department of Education, Bridgeport, CT 06604. Offers education (MS); educational management (Ed D, Diploma), including intermediate administrator or supervisor (Diploma), leadership (Ed D); elementary education (MS, Diploma), including early childhood education, elementary education; middle school education (MS); music education (MS); remedial reading and language arts (Diploma); secondary education (MS, Diploma), including computer specialist (Diploma), international education (Diploma), reading specialist, secondary education. *Program availability:* Part-time, evening/weekend. *Degree requirements:* For master's, final exam, final project, or thesis; for doctorate, comprehensive exam, thesis/dissertation; for Diploma, thesis or alternative, final project. *Entrance requirements:* For master's, minimum undergraduate QPA of 2.67; for doctorate, GRE, MAT; for Diploma, GRE General Test or MAT, minimum graduate QPA of 3.0. Additional exam requirements/recommendations for international students: Recommended—TOEFL (minimum score 550 paper-based; 80 iBT), IELTS (minimum score 6.5). Electronic applications accepted. *Expenses:* Contact institution.

University of Central Florida, College of Education and Human Performance, School of Teaching, Learning, and Leadership, Program in Teacher Education, Orlando, FL 32816. Offers art education (MAT); English language (MAT); mathematics education (MAT); middle school mathematics (MAT); middle school science (MAT); science education (MAT), including biology, chemistry, physics; social science education (MAT). *Accreditation:* NCATE. *Program availability:* Part-time, evening/weekend. *Students:* 16 full-time (11 women), 28 part-time (23 women); includes 16 minority (6 Black or African American, non-Hispanic/Latino; 1 Asian, non-Hispanic/Latino; 8 Hispanic/Latino; 1 Two or more races, non-Hispanic/Latino), 1 international. Average age 31. 1 applicant, 100% accepted. In 2016, 33 master's awarded. *Entrance requirements:* For master's, GRE General Test. Additional exam requirements/recommendations for international students: Required—TOEFL. *Application deadline:* For spring admission, 12/1 for domestic students; for summer admission, 4/15 for domestic students. Application fee: $30. Electronic applications accepted. *Expenses:* Tuition, state resident: part-time $288.16 per credit hour. Tuition, nonresident: part-time $1071.31 per credit hour. *Financial support:* Fellowships, research assistantships, teaching assistantships, career-related internships or fieldwork, Federal Work-Study, institutionally sponsored loans, tuition waivers (partial), and unspecified assistantships available. Financial award application deadline: 3/1; financial award applicants required to submit FAFSA. *Unit head:* Dr. Michael Hynes, Director, 407-823-2005, E-mail: mychael.hynes@ucf.edu. *Application contact:* Assistant Director, Graduate Admissions, 407-823-2766, Fax: 407-823-6442, E-mail: gradadmissions@ucf.edu.
Website: http://education.ucf.edu/programs.cfm?pid=g&cat=2

University of Dayton, Department of Teacher Education, Dayton, OH 45469. Offers early childhood leadership and advocacy (MS Ed); interdisciplinary education studies (MS Ed); leadership in educational systems (MS Ed); literacy (MS Ed); mathematics education (MS Ed); music education (MS Ed); teacher as leader (MS Ed); teacher education (MS Ed); technology-enhanced learning (MS Ed); trans-disciplinary early childhood education (MS Ed). *Program availability:* Part-time, evening/weekend, blended/hybrid learning. *Faculty:* 23 full-time (18 women), 49 part-time/adjunct (42 women). *Students:* 52 full-time (47 women), 89 part-time (76 women); includes 6 minority (2 Black or African American, non-Hispanic/Latino; 2 Hispanic/Latino; 2 Two or more races, non-Hispanic/Latino), 24 international. Average age 31. 106 applicants, 28% accepted. In 2016, 69 master's awarded. *Degree requirements:* For master's, variable foreign language requirement, thesis optional. *Entrance requirements:* For master's, GRE (minimum score of 149 verbal, 4 on writing) or MAT (minimum score of 396) if undergraduate GPA was under 2.75, minimum GPA of 2.75, 3 letters of recommendation, personal statement or resume, official transcripts. Additional exam requirements/recommendations for international students: Required—TOEFL (minimum score 550 paper-based; 80 iBT); Recommended—IELTS (minimum score 6.5). *Application deadline:* Applications are processed on a rolling basis. Application fee: $0 ($50 for international students). Electronic applications accepted. *Expenses:* $620 per credit hour, $25 registration fee per term. *Financial support:* Institutionally sponsored loans available. Financial award application deadline: 3/1; financial award applicants required to submit FAFSA. *Faculty research:* Educational technology; facilitating teacher reflection; teacher preparation in dyslexia. *Unit head:* Dr. Connie L. Bowman, Chair, 937-229-3305, E-mail: cbowman1@udayton.edu. *Application contact:* Gina Seiter, Graduate Program Advisor, 937-229-3103, E-mail: gseiter1@udayton.edu.
Website: https://www.udayton.edu/education/departments_and_programs/edt

University of Houston–Downtown, College of Public Service, Department of Urban Education, Houston, TX 77002. Offers curriculum and instruction (MAT); elementary and secondary education (MAT). *Program availability:* Part-time, evening/weekend, 100% online. *Faculty:* 6 full-time (2 women), 2 part-time/adjunct (both women). *Students:* 7 full-time (3 women), 47 part-time (42 women); includes 45 minority (18 Black or African American, non-Hispanic/Latino; 6 Asian, non-Hispanic/Latino; 21 Hispanic/Latino). Average age 34. 36 applicants, 89% accepted, 28 enrolled. In 2016, 11 master's awarded. *Degree requirements:* For master's, capstone course with completed project, position paper, grant proposal, empirical study, curriculum development/revision, or advanced technology project presented at annual Graduate Project Exhibition. *Entrance requirements:* For master's, GRE, personal statement, 3 recommendation forms. Additional exam requirements/recommendations for international students: Required—TOEFL (minimum score 550 paper-based; 80 iBT). *Application deadline:* For fall admission, 7/15 for domestic and international students; for spring admission, 11/15 for domestic and international students. Application fee: $35 ($60 for international students). Electronic applications accepted. *Expenses:* $305.50 in-state, per credit; $663.50 out-of-state, per credit. *Financial support:* Federal Work-Study and scholarships/grants available. Financial award application deadline: 4/1; financial award applicants required to submit FAFSA. *Unit head:* Dr. Ron Beebe, Department Chair, 713-221-8689, Fax: 713-226-5294, E-mail: beeber@uhd.edu. *Application contact:* Ceshia Love, Director of Graduate and International Admissions, 713-221-8093, Fax: 713-223-7408, E-mail: gradadmissions@uhd.edu.
Website: https://www.uhd.edu/academics/public-service/urban-education/Pages/default.aspx

University of Kentucky, Graduate School, College of Education, Program in Curriculum and Instruction, Lexington, KY 40506-0032. Offers curriculum and instruction (Ed D, PhD); elementary education (MA Ed); instructional system design (MS Ed); literacy (MA Ed); middle school education (MA Ed, MS Ed); secondary education (MA Ed, MS Ed). *Accreditation:* NCATE. *Degree requirements:* For master's, comprehensive exam, thesis optional; for doctorate, comprehensive exam, thesis/dissertation. *Entrance requirements:* For master's, GRE General Test, minimum undergraduate GPA of 2.75; for doctorate, GRE General Test, minimum graduate GPA of 3.0. Additional exam requirements/recommendations for international students: Required—TOEFL (minimum score 550 paper-based). Electronic applications accepted. *Faculty research:* Educational reform, multicultural education, classroom instructional practices, performance based assessment, primary school programs.

University of Louisiana at Monroe, Graduate School, College of Arts, Education, and Sciences, School of Education, Program in Curriculum and Instruction, Monroe, LA 71209-0001. Offers art education (M Ed); biology education (M Ed); chemistry education (M Ed); curriculum and instruction (Ed D); early childhood education (M Ed); earth science education (M Ed); educational leadership (M Ed); elementary education (1-5) (M Ed); English as a second language (M Ed); English education (M Ed); family and consumer education (M Ed); French education (M Ed); history education (M Ed); math education (M Ed); middle school education (M Ed); music education (M Ed); reading education (K-12) (M Ed); Spanish education (M Ed); special education - academically gifted (M Ed); special education - early intervention (M Ed); special education - educational diagnostician (M Ed); special education - mild/moderate disabilities (M Ed); speech education (M Ed). *Accreditation:* NCATE. *Faculty:* 8 full-time (4 women), 4 part-time/adjunct (3 women). *Students:* 13 full-time (11 women), 80 part-time (65 women); includes 25 minority (19 Black or African American, non-Hispanic/Latino; 1 Asian, non-Hispanic/Latino; 3 Hispanic/Latino; 2 Two or more races, non-Hispanic/Latino). Average age 37. 118 applicants, 30% accepted, 16 enrolled. In 2016, 23 master's, 4 doctorates awarded. *Degree requirements:* For master's, comprehensive exam (for some programs), thesis; for doctorate, thesis/dissertation, internships. *Entrance requirements:* For master's, GRE General Test; for doctorate, GRE General Test, minimum undergraduate GPA of 2.75, graduate 3.25. Additional exam requirements/recommendations for international students: Required—TOEFL (minimum score 500 paper-based; 61 iBT). *Application deadline:* For fall admission, 8/24 priority date for domestic students, 7/1 for international students; for winter admission, 12/14 priority date for domestic students; for spring admission, 1/19 for domestic students, 11/1 for international students. Applications are processed on a rolling basis. Application fee: $20 ($30 for international students). Electronic applications accepted. *Expenses:* Tuition, state resident: full-time $6489. Tuition, nonresident: full-time $18,589. *Required fees:* $8984. Tuition and fees vary according to course level, course load, degree level and program. *Financial support:* Research assistantships, career-related internships or fieldwork, Federal Work-Study, and unspecified assistantships available. Financial award application deadline: 4/1; financial award applicants required to submit FAFSA. *Unit head:* Dr. Dorothy Schween, Director, 318-342-1268, Fax: 318-342-3131, E-mail: schween@ulm.edu.

University of Louisville, Graduate School, College of Education and Human Development, Department of Teaching and Learning, Louisville, KY 40292-0001. Offers art education (MAT); autism and applied behavior analysis (Certificate); curriculum and instruction (PhD); early elementary education (MAT); exercise physiology (MS); health and physical education (MAT); health professions education (Certificate); higher education (MA); human resources and organization development (MS); instructional technology (M Ed); interdisciplinary early childhood education (MAT); middle school education (MAT); music education (MAT); secondary education (MAT); special education (MAT); sport administration (MS); teacher leadership (M Ed). *Program availability:* Part-time, evening/weekend. *Students:* 116 full-time (68 women), 158 part-time (112 women); includes 46 minority (24 Black or African American, non-Hispanic/Latino; 8 Asian, non-Hispanic/Latino; 5 Hispanic/Latino; 9 Two or more races, non-Hispanic/Latino), 6 international. Average age 30. 114 applicants, 71% accepted, 57 enrolled. In 2016, 59 master's, 3 doctorates awarded. *Application deadline:* For spring admission, 1/1 priority date for international students. Application fee: $60. *Expenses:* Tuition, state resident: full-time $12,246; part-time $681 per credit hour. Tuition, nonresident: full-time $25,486; part-time $1417 per credit hour. *Required fees:* $196. Tuition and fees vary according to program and reciprocity agreements. *Financial support:* Application deadline: 6/1; applicants required to submit FAFSA. *Faculty research:* STEM teaching and learning; content literacy for English language learners; social justice in teacher education; adolescent literacy; mathematics teacher development. *Total annual research expenditures:* $1.7 million. *Unit head:* Dr. Ann E. Larson, Dean, College of Education and Human Development, 502-852-6411, Fax: 502-852-1464, E-mail: ann@louisville.edu. *Application contact:* Betty Hampton, Director of Graduate Student Services, 502-852-5597, Fax: 502-852-1465, E-mail: edadvise@louisville.edu.
Website: http://louisville.edu/delphi

University of Massachusetts Dartmouth, Graduate School, College of Arts and Sciences, School of Education, Department of STEM Education and Teacher Development, North Dartmouth, MA 02747-2300. Offers education ESL preK-12 (Postbaccalaureate Certificate); mathematics education (PhD); middle school education (MAT); secondary school education (Postbaccalaureate Certificate); teaching secondary school education (MAT). *Program availability:* Part-time. *Faculty:* 9 full-time (6 women), 6 part-time/adjunct (3 women). *Students:* 25 full-time (12 women), 87 part-time (55 women); includes 15 minority (3 Black or African American, non-Hispanic/Latino; 2 Asian, non-Hispanic/Latino; 7 Hispanic/Latino; 3 Two or more races, non-Hispanic/Latino), 3 international. Average age 32. 53 applicants, 91% accepted, 38 enrolled. In 2016, 67 master's awarded. *Degree requirements:* For doctorate, thesis/dissertation. *Entrance requirements:* For master's, Massachusetts Tests for Educator Licensure (MTEL) Communication and Literacy Test and Subject Matter Test, statement of purpose (minimum of 300 words), resume, 2 letters of recommendation, official transcripts; for doctorate, GRE, statement of purpose (minimum of 300 words), resume, official transcripts, 3 letters of recommendation; for Postbaccalaureate Certificate, statement of purpose (minimum of 300 words), resume, 2 letters of recommendation, official transcripts. Additional exam requirements/recommendations for international students: Required—TOEFL (minimum score 533 paper-based; 72 iBT). *Application deadline:* For fall admission, 2/15 priority date for domestic students, 1/15 priority date for international students; for spring admission, 12/15 priority date for domestic students, 11/15 priority date for international students. Application fee: $60. Electronic applications accepted. *Expenses:* Tuition, state resident: full-time $14,994; part-time $624.75 per credit. Tuition, nonresident: full-time $27,068; part-time $1127.83 per credit. *Required fees:* $405; $25.88 per credit. Tuition and fees vary according to course load and reciprocity agreements. *Financial support:* In 2016–17, 3 fellowships (averaging $6,250 per year), 3 research assistantships (averaging $5,027 per year), 2 teaching assistantships (averaging $8,000 per year) were awarded; institutionally sponsored loans, scholarships/grants, unspecified assistantships, and instructional assistants, Fulbright scholarships also available. Financial award application deadline: 3/1; financial award applicants required to submit FAFSA. *Faculty research:* Reading/special education, education reform, English education, literacy, language arts K-12. *Total annual research expenditures:* $1.3 million. *Unit head:* Traci Almeida, Graduate Program Director, 508-999-8098, Fax: 508-910-8183, E-mail: talmeida@umassd.edu. *Application contact:* Steven Briggs, Director of Marketing and Recruitment for Graduate Studies, 508-999-8604, Fax: 508-999-8183, E-mail: graduate@umassd.edu.
Website: http://www.umassd.edu/cas/schoolofeducation/departments/stemeducationandteacherdevelopment/

University of Missouri–St. Louis, College of Education, Department of Educator Preparation, Innovation and Research, St. Louis, MO 63121. Offers elementary education (M Ed), including early childhood, general, reading; secondary education (M Ed), including curriculum and instruction, general, middle level education, reading, teaching English to speakers of other languages (TESOL); special education (M Ed), including autism and developmental disabilities, early childhood special education. *Program availability:* Part-time, evening/weekend. *Faculty:* 26 full-time (14 women), 22 part-time/adjunct (14 women). *Students:* 151 full-time (127 women), 728 part-time (564 women); includes 222 minority (165 Black or African American, non-Hispanic/Latino; 1 American Indian or Alaska Native, non-Hispanic/Latino; 16 Asian, non-Hispanic/Latino; 31 Hispanic/Latino; 1 Native Hawaiian or other Pacific Islander, non-Hispanic/Latino; 8 Two or more races, non-Hispanic/Latino), 6 international. Average age 29. 363 applicants, 84% accepted, 211 enrolled. *Degree requirements:* For master's, comprehensive exam. *Entrance requirements:* Additional exam requirements/recommendations for international students: Recommended—TOEFL (minimum score 550 paper-based; 79 iBT), IELTS (minimum score 6.5). *Application deadline:* For fall admission, 7/1 priority date for domestic and international students; for spring admission, 12/1 priority date for domestic and international students. Application fee: $50 ($40 for international students). Electronic applications accepted. *Financial support:* Application deadline: 4/1; applicants required to submit FAFSA. *Unit head:* Dr. Gayle Wilkinson, Chair, 314-516-5791. *Application contact:* 314-516-5458, Fax: 314-516-6996, E-mail: gadadm@umsl.edu.
Website: https://coe.umsl.edu/dept/epir.html

The University of North Carolina at Charlotte, Cato College of Education, Department of Middle, Secondary and K-12 Education, Charlotte, NC 28223-0001. Offers middle grades and secondary education (M Ed); teaching English as a second language (M Ed, Graduate Certificate). *Program availability:* Part-time. *Faculty:* 17 full-time (9 women), 6 part-time/adjunct (5 women). *Students:* 6 full-time (5 women), 62 part-time (56 women); includes 9 minority (8 Black or African American, non-Hispanic/Latino; 1 Hispanic/Latino), 1 international. Average age 32. 32 applicants, 97% accepted, 28 enrolled. In 2016, 12 master's awarded. *Degree requirements:* For master's, thesis, comprehensive portfolio, or research project. *Entrance requirements:* For master's, GRE or MAT, bachelor's degree from accredited college or university; minimum GPA of 3.0 in undergraduate work; North Carolina Class A teaching license in appropriate middle grades or secondary education field; minimum of two years' teaching experience; written narrative providing statement of purpose for master's degree study; letters of recommendation; for Graduate Certificate, bachelor's degree from accredited institution; minimum undergraduate GPA of 2.5 overall or 3.0 in senior year, or 15 hours taken in the last 5 years; satisfactory recommendations from three persons knowledgeable of applicant's interactions with children or adolescents; statement of purpose. Additional exam requirements/recommendations for international students: Required—TOEFL (minimum score 523 paper-based, 70 iBT) or IELTS (6.5). *Application deadline:* For fall admission, 3/1 priority date for domestic and international students; for spring admission, 10/1 priority date for domestic and international students; for summer admission, 4/1 priority date for domestic and international students. Applications are processed on a rolling basis. Application fee: $75. Electronic applications accepted. *Expenses:* Tuition, state resident: full-time $4252. Tuition, nonresident: full-time $17,423. *Required fees:* $3026. Tuition and fees vary according to course load and program. *Financial support:* In 2016–17, 5 students received support, including 1 fellowship (averaging $02,780 per year), 4 research assistantships (averaging $14,309 per year); career-related internships or fieldwork, institutionally sponsored loans, scholarships/grants, and unspecified assistantships also available. Support available to part-time students. Financial award application deadline: 3/1; financial award applicants required to submit FAFSA. *Total annual research expenditures:* $58,472. *Unit head:* Scott Kissau, Chair, 704-687-8875, E-mail: spkissau@uncc.edu. *Application contact:* Kathy B. Giddings, Director of Graduate Admissions, 704-687-5503, Fax: 704-687-1668, E-mail: gradadm@uncc.edu.
Website: http://mdsk.uncc.edu/

The University of North Carolina at Charlotte, Cato College of Education, Interdisciplinary Education Programs, Charlotte, NC 28223-0001. Offers art education (Graduate Certificate); child and family development: early childhood education (MAT); curriculum and instruction (PhD); elementary education (MAT); foreign language education (MAT); middle grades education (MAT); secondary education (MAT); special education (MAT); teaching (Graduate Certificate); teaching English as a second language (MAT); theatre education (Graduate Certificate). *Program availability:* Part-time, 100% online, blended/hybrid learning. *Students:* 78 full-time (59 women), 619 part-time (484 women); includes 255 minority (186 Black or African American, non-Hispanic/Latino; 1 American Indian or Alaska Native, non-Hispanic/Latino; 16 Asian, non-Hispanic/Latino; 37 Hispanic/Latino; 15 Two or more races, non-Hispanic/Latino), 10 international. Average age 33. 380 applicants, 92% accepted, 264 enrolled. In 2016, 93 master's, 8 doctorates, 176 other advanced degrees awarded. *Degree requirements:* For master's, thesis or alternative, research project/portfolio. *Entrance requirements:* For master's, GRE or MAT, bachelor's degree, or its U.S. equivalent, from regionally-accredited college or university; minimum overall GPA of 3.0 on all previous work beyond high school; statement of purpose (essay); at least three recommendation forms; for doctorate, GRE or MAT, bachelor's degree (or its U.S. equivalent) from regionally-accredited college or university; minimum overall GPA of 3.5 in master's degree program; for Graduate Certificate, bachelor's degree from regionally-accredited university; minimum GPA of 2.75 on all post-secondary work attempted; transcripts; personal statement outlining why the applicant seeks admission to the program. Additional exam requirements/recommendations for international students: Required—TOEFL (minimum score 523 paper-based, 70 iBT) or IELTS (6.5). *Application deadline:* For fall admission, 3/1 priority date for domestic and international students; for spring admission, 10/1 priority date for domestic and international students; for summer admission, 4/1 priority date for domestic and international students. Applications are processed on a rolling basis. Application fee: $75. Electronic applications accepted. *Expenses:* Tuition, state resident: full-time $4252. Tuition, nonresident: full-time $17,423. *Required fees:* $3026. Tuition and fees vary according to course load and program. *Financial support:* Career-related internships or fieldwork, institutionally sponsored loans, scholarships/grants, and unspecified assistantships available. Support available to part-time students. Financial award application deadline: 3/1; financial award applicants required to submit FAFSA. *Unit head:* Dr. Ellen McIntyre, Dean, 704-687-8722, E-mail: ellen.mcintyre@uncc.edu. *Application contact:* Kathy B. Giddings, Director of Graduate Admissions, 704-687-5503, Fax: 704-687-1668, E-mail: gradadm@uncc.edu.
Website: http://education.uncc.edu/academic-programs

The University of North Carolina at Greensboro, Graduate School, School of Education, Department of Teacher Education and Higher Education, Greensboro, NC 27412-5001. Offers college teaching and adult learning (Certificate); curriculum and instruction (M Ed), including chemistry education, elementary education, English as a second language, French education, instructional technology, mathematics education, middle grades education, reading education, science education, social studies education, Spanish education; curriculum and teaching (PhD), including higher education, teacher education and development; English as a second language (Certificate); higher education (M Ed); supervision (M Ed). *Accreditation:* NCATE. *Program availability:* Part-time. *Degree requirements:* For doctorate, thesis/dissertation. *Entrance requirements:* For master's and doctorate, GRE General Test. Additional exam requirements/recommendations for international students: Required—TOEFL. Electronic applications accepted. *Faculty research:* Community college literacy program, middle school mathematics/computer mathematics.

The University of North Carolina Wilmington, Watson College of Education, Department of Early Childhood, Elementary, Middle, Literacy and Special Education, Wilmington, NC 28403-3297. Offers educational leadership, policy, and advocacy (M Ed); elementary education (M Ed, MAT); language and literacy (M Ed); middle grades education (M Ed, MAT). *Accreditation:* NCATE. *Program availability:* Part-time. *Faculty:* 26 full-time (19 women). *Students:* 121 full-time (89 women), 139 part-time (135 women); includes 70 minority (47 Black or African American, non-Hispanic/Latino; 1 Asian, non-Hispanic/Latino; 14 Hispanic/Latino; 8 Two or more races, non-Hispanic/Latino). Average age 34. 109 applicants, 78% accepted, 65 enrolled. In 2016, 83 master's awarded. *Degree requirements:* For master's, comprehensive exam, capstone experience. *Entrance requirements:* For master's, GRE General Test, MAT, minimum GPA of 3.0 in undergraduate work, 3 letters of recommendations, NC Class A teacher license in related field, statement of interest. *Application deadline:* For fall admission, 5/15 for domestic students; for spring admission, 10/15 for domestic students; for summer admission, 3/15 for domestic students. Applications are processed on a rolling basis. Application fee: $60. Electronic applications accepted. *Expenses:* Contact institution. *Financial support:* Scholarships/grants and unspecified assistantships available. Support available to part-time students. Financial award application deadline: 3/15; financial award applicants required to submit FAFSA. *Unit head:* Dr. Kathy Fox, Chair, 910-962-3240, Fax: 910-962-3988, E-mail: foxk@uncw.edu. *Application contact:* Dr. Elizabeth Crawford, Graduate Program Coordinator, 910-962-2916, Fax: 910-962-3988, E-mail: crawforde@uncw.edu.
Website: http://www.uncw.edu/ed/eemls/index.html

University of Northern Iowa, Graduate College, College of Humanities, Arts and Sciences, Department of Mathematics, MA Program in Mathematics for the Middle Grades, Cedar Falls, IA 50614. Offers MA.

University of North Georgia, College of Education, Dahlonega, GA 30597. Offers early childhood education (M Ed); middle grades education (M Ed, MAT); physical education (MS); school leadership (Ed S); secondary education (M Ed), including English education, history education, mathematics education, physical education. *Accreditation:* NCATE. *Program availability:* Part-time, evening/weekend, online learning. *Faculty:* 16 full-time (12 women), 3 part-time/adjunct (all women). *Students:* 11 full-time (8 women), 146 part-time (107 women); includes 19 minority (10 Black or African American, non-Hispanic/Latino; 2 Asian, non-Hispanic/Latino; 6 Hispanic/Latino; 1 Two or more races, non-Hispanic/Latino). Average age 28. 77 applicants, 83% accepted, 47 enrolled. In 2016, 79 master's awarded. *Degree requirements:* For master's, comprehensive exam, thesis optional. *Entrance requirements:* For master's, GRE or MAT, GACE, minimum GPA of 2.75; for Ed S, GRE General Test or MAT, 3 years of teaching experience, master's degree, minimum graduate GPA of 3.25, leadership position in the school. Additional exam requirements/recommendations for international students: Required—TOEFL (minimum score 550 paper-based; 79 iBT), IELTS (minimum score 6.5). *Application deadline:* For fall admission, 8/1 priority date for domestic students, 7/1 priority date for international students; for spring admission, 12/1 priority date for domestic students, 11/1 priority date for international students. Applications are processed on a rolling basis. Application fee: $40. Electronic applications accepted. *Expenses:* Contact institution. *Financial support:* Teaching assistantships, career-related internships or fieldwork, scholarships/grants, and unspecified assistantships available. Financial award application deadline: 5/1; financial award applicants required to submit CSS PROFILE or FAFSA. *Unit head:* Dr. Susan Ayers, Dean, College of Education, 706-864-1998, E-mail: susan.ayres@ung.edu. *Application contact:* Regina Boling, Teacher Education Graduate Admissions, 706-864-1533, E-mail: regina.boling@ung.edu.
Website: http://ung.edu/college-of-education/

University of Phoenix–Online Campus, College of Education, Phoenix, AZ 85034-7209. Offers administration and supervision (MAEd, Certificate); adult education and training (MAEd); curriculum and instruction (MAEd), including computer education, curriculum and instruction, English as a second language, language arts, mathematics, reading; early childhood education (MAEd); educational studies (MAEd); elementary teacher education (MAEd), including early childhood, elementary teacher education, high school middle level, middle level; principal licensure (Certificate); secondary teacher education (MAEd); special education (MAEd, Certificate); teacher education (MAEd), including middle level generalist; teacher education middle level mathematics (MAEd), including middle level mathematics; teacher education middle level science (MAEd), including middle level science; teacher education secondary mathematics (MAEd); teacher education secondary science (MAEd); teacher leadership (MAEd); teachers of English learners (Certificate); transition to teaching (Certificate), including elementary education, secondary education. *Program availability:* Evening/weekend, online learning. *Entrance requirements:* Additional exam requirements/recommendations for international students: Required—TOEFL, TOEIC (Test of English as an International Communication), Berlitz Online English Proficiency Exam, PTE, or IELTS. Electronic applications accepted. *Expenses:* Contact institution.

University of South Florida, St. Petersburg, College of Education, St. Petersburg, FL 33701. Offers educational leadership development (M Ed); elementary education (MA), including math/science; English education (MA); middle grades STEM education (MS); reading education (MA). *Program availability:* Part-time. *Degree requirements:* For master's, comprehensive exam, practicum, internship, comprehensive portfolio. *Entrance requirements:* For master's, State of Florida General Knowledge Test (GKT), Florida Teaching Certificate (for non-initial certification programs), letters of recommendation. Additional exam requirements/recommendations for international students: Required—TOEFL (minimum score 550 paper-based; 79 iBT); Recommended—IELTS. Electronic applications accepted.

University of the Cumberlands, Graduate Programs in Education, Williamsburg, KY 40769-1372. Offers all grades (P-12) (M Ed); business and marketing (MA Ed, MAT); counselor education and supervision (Ed D); director of pupil personnel (Certificate); director of special education (Certificate); educational administration and supervision (Ed S); educational leadership (Ed D); elementary education (MA Ed, MAT); instructional leadership - principalship (MA Ed); instructional leadership - school principal (Certificate); middle school education (MA Ed, MAT); reading and writing (MA Ed); school counseling (MA Ed); school superintendent (Certificate); secondary education (MA Ed, MAT); special education (MAT); supervisor of instruction (Certificate); teacher leader (MA Ed). *Program availability:* Part-time, evening/weekend, online learning. *Degree requirements:* For master's, comprehensive exam. Electronic applications accepted.

University of the District of Columbia, College of Arts and Sciences, Program in Teaching, Washington, DC 20008-1175. Offers elementary education (MAT); middle school mathematics (MAT); secondary English language arts (MAT); secondary social studies (MAT).

The University of Toledo, College of Graduate Studies, Judith Herb College of Education, Department of Curriculum and Instruction, Toledo, OH 43606-3390. Offers art education (ME); career and technical education (ME, Ed S); curriculum and instruction (ME, PhD, Ed S); early childhood education (Ed S); education and anthropology (MAE); education and biology (MES); education and chemistry (MES); education and classics (MAE); education and economics (MAE); education and English (MAE); education and French (MAE); education and geology (MES); education and German (MAE); education and history (MAE); education and mathematics (MAE, MES); education and physics (MES); education and political science (MAE); education and sociology (MAE); education and Spanish (MAE); educational media (PhD); educational technology (ME); educational technology: virtual educator (Certificate); elementary education (PhD); English as a second language (MAE); gifted and talented education (PhD); middle childhood education (ME); secondary education (ME, PhD); special education (PhD). *Accreditation:* NCATE. *Program availability:* Part-time, evening/weekend. *Degree requirements:* For master's, comprehensive exam, thesis or alternative; for doctorate, comprehensive exam, thesis/dissertation; for other advanced degree, thesis optional. *Entrance requirements:* For master's, doctorate, and other advanced degree, minimum cumulative GPA of 2.7 for all previous academic work, letters of recommendation. Additional exam requirements/recommendations for international students: Required—TOEFL (minimum score 550 paper-based; 80 iBT). Electronic applications accepted.

University of Washington, Bothell, Program in Education, Bothell, WA 98011. Offers education (M Ed); leadership development for educators (M Ed); secondary/middle level endorsement (M Ed). *Program availability:* Part-time, evening/weekend. *Degree requirements:* For master's, thesis. *Entrance requirements:* Additional exam requirements/recommendations for international students: Required—TOEFL. Electronic applications accepted. *Faculty research:* Multicultural education in citizenship education, intercultural education, knowledge and practice in the principalship, educational public policy, national board certification for teachers, teacher learning in literacy, technology and its impact on teaching and learning of mathematics, reading assessments, professional development in literacy education and mobility, digital media, education and class.

University of West Florida, College of Education and Professional Studies, Department of Teacher Education and Educational Leadership, Program in Curriculum and Instruction, Pensacola, FL 32514-5750. Offers elementary education (M Ed); middle level education (M Ed); secondary education (M Ed). *Program availability:* Part-time, evening/weekend. *Entrance requirements:* For master's, GRE (minimum score 450 verbal) or MAT (minimum score 396) if bachelor's GPA less than 3.0, state teaching certification; letter of intent; two professional references. Additional exam requirements/recommendations for international students: Required—TOEFL (minimum score 550 paper-based). *Application deadline:* For fall admission, 6/1 for domestic and international students; for spring admission, 10/1 for domestic and international students. Applications are processed on a rolling basis. Application fee: $30. *Expenses:* Tuition, state resident: full-time $5316.12. Tuition, nonresident: full-time $11,308. *Required fees:* $583.92. Tuition and fees vary according to course load and program. *Financial support:* Career-related internships or fieldwork, Federal Work-Study, scholarships/grants, and tuition waivers (partial) available. Support available to part-time students. Financial award application deadline: 4/15; financial award applicants required to submit FAFSA. *Unit head:* Dr. William H. Evans, Acting Director, 850-474-2892, Fax: 850-474-2844, E-mail: wevans@uwf.edu. *Application contact:* Terry McCray, Assistant Director of Graduate Admissions, 850-473-7718, Fax: 850-473-7714, E-mail: gradadmissions@uwf.edu.

University of Wisconsin–Milwaukee, Graduate School, School of Education, Department of Curriculum and Instruction, Milwaukee, WI 53201-0413. Offers curriculum and instruction (MS), including cross-curricular focus, early childhood education, English education, mathematics education, middle childhood/early adolescence education, reading education, science education, urban social studies education. *Program availability:* Part-time. *Students:* 21 full-time (13 women), 44 part-time (42 women); includes 10 minority (1 Black or African American, non-Hispanic/Latino; 1 Asian, non-Hispanic/Latino; 2 Hispanic/Latino; 6 Two or more races, non-Hispanic/Latino), 2 international. Average age 33. 42 applicants, 71% accepted, 20 enrolled. In 2016, 45 master's awarded. *Degree requirements:* For master's, thesis or alternative. *Entrance requirements:* Additional exam requirements/recommendations for international students: Required—TOEFL (minimum score 550 paper-based; 79 iBT), IELTS (minimum score 6.5). *Application deadline:* For fall admission, 1/1 priority date for domestic students; for spring admission, 9/1 for domestic students. Applications are processed on a rolling basis. Application fee: $56 ($96 for international students). Electronic applications accepted. *Financial support:* In 2016–17, 1 fellowship was awarded; research assistantships, teaching assistantships, career-related internships or fieldwork, health care benefits, unspecified assistantships, and project assistantships also available. Support available to part-time students. Financial award application deadline: 4/15; financial award applicants required to submit FAFSA. *Application contact:* General Information Contact, 414-229-4721, E-mail: soeinfo@uwm.edu.
Website: http://uwm.edu/education/academics/curriculum-instruction-department/

Ursuline College, School of Graduate Studies, Master Apprenticeship Program, Pepper Pike, OH 44124-4398. Offers adolescent to young adult education (MA); early childhood education (MA); middle childhood education (MA); special education (MA). *Accreditation:* NCATE. *Degree requirements:* For master's, comprehensive exam. *Entrance requirements:* For master's, minimum undergraduate GPA of 3.0. Additional exam requirements/recommendations for international students: Required—TOEFL (minimum score 500 paper-based). *Application deadline:* For fall admission, 8/1 priority date for domestic students. Applications are processed on a rolling basis. Application fee: $25. Electronic applications accepted. *Expenses:* Contact institution. *Financial support:* Application deadline: 3/1; applicants required to submit FAFSA. *Unit head:* Dr. Mary Jo Cherry, Director, 440-646-8147, Fax: 440-646-8328, E-mail: mcherry@ursuline.edu. *Application contact:* Stephanie Pratt McRoberts, Graduate Admission Coordinator, 440-646-8119, Fax: 440-684-6138, E-mail: graduateadmissions@ursuline.edu.
Website: http://www.ursuline.edu/Academics/Graduate_Professional/Masters_Programs/MAP/index.html

Wagner College, Division of Graduate Studies, Education Department, Program in Secondary Education/Students with Disabilities, Staten Island, NY 10301-4495. Offers secondary education 7-12 (MS Ed), including language arts, languages other than English, mathematics and technology, science and technology, social studies. *Program availability:* Part-time, evening/weekend. *Degree requirements:* For master's, thesis (for some programs), completion of state certification exams before student teaching. *Entrance requirements:* For master's, minimum GPA of 3.0, interview, recommendations. Electronic applications accepted. Tuition and fees vary according to degree level.

Webster University, School of Education, Department of Multidisciplinary Studies, St. Louis, MO 63119-3194. Offers applied educational psychology (MA, Ed S); communication arts (MA); early childhood education (MA, MAT); education and innovation (MA); educational technology (MET); elementary education (MAT); mathematics for educators (MA); middle school education (MAT); multidisciplinary studies (MAT); multimodal literacy for global impact (MA); reading (MA); secondary school education (MAT); special education (MA, MAT); teaching English as a second language (MA); transformative learning in the global community (Ed S). *Program availability:* Part-time. *Entrance requirements:* For master's, minimum GPA of 2.5. Additional exam requirements/recommendations for international students: Required—TOEFL. *Application deadline:* Applications are processed on a rolling basis. Application fee: $35 ($50 for international students). *Expenses: Tuition:* Full-time $21,900; part-time $730 per credit hour. Tuition and fees vary according to campus/location and program. *Financial support:* Federal Work-Study available. Support available to part-time students. Financial award application deadline: 4/1; financial award applicants required to submit FAFSA. *Unit head:* Dr. Deborah Stiles, Chair, 314-968-7056, Fax: 314-968-7118, E-mail: stilesda@webster.edu.

Western Kentucky University, Graduate Studies, College of Education and Behavioral Sciences, School of Teacher Education, Bowling Green, KY 42101. Offers elementary education (MAE, Ed S); exceptional education: learning and behavioral disorders (MAE); exceptional education: moderate and severe disabilities (MAE); instructional design (MS); interdisciplinary early childhood education (MAE); library media education (MS); literacy education (MAE); middle grades education (MAE); secondary education (MAE, Ed S). *Program availability:* Part-time, evening/weekend, online learning. *Degree requirements:* For master's, comprehensive exam. *Entrance requirements:* For master's, GRE General Test. Additional exam requirements/recommendations for international students: Required—TOEFL (minimum score 555 paper-based; 79 iBT). *Faculty research:* Teacher preparation in moderate/severe disabilities.

Wichita State University, Graduate School, College of Education, Department of Curriculum and Instruction, Wichita, KS 67260. Offers learning and instructional design (M Ed); special education (M Ed), including early childhood (M Ed, MAT), gifted, high incidence, low incidence; teaching (MAT), including early childhood (M Ed, MAT), middle level/secondary, transition to teaching. *Accreditation:* NCATE. *Program availability:* Part-time, evening/weekend, 100% online, blended/hybrid learning. *Entrance requirements:* For master's, MAT, minimum GPA of 2.75. *Unit head:* Dr. Kimberly McDowell, Department Head, 316-978-3322, E-mail: kim.mcdowell@wichita.edu. *Application contact:* Jordan Oleson, Admission Coordinator, 316-978-3095, Fax: 316-978-3253, E-mail: jordan.oleson@wichita.edu.

Widener University, School of Education, Hospitality, and Continuing Studies, Chester, PA 19013-5792. Offers adult education (M Ed); counseling in higher education (M Ed); counselor education (M Ed); early childhood education (M Ed); educational foundations (M Ed); educational leadership (M Ed); educational psychology (M Ed); elementary education (M Ed); English and language arts (M Ed); health education (M Ed); higher education leadership (Ed D); home and school visitor (M Ed); human sexuality (M Ed, PhD); mathematics education (M Ed); middle school education (M Ed); principalship (M Ed); reading and language arts (Ed D); reading education (M Ed); school administration (Ed D); science education (M Ed); social studies education (M Ed); special education (M Ed); technology education (M Ed). *Accreditation:* NCATE. *Program availability:* Part-time, evening/weekend. *Faculty:* 34 full-time (22 women), 37 part-time/adjunct (14 women). *Students:* 97 full-time (64 women), 201 part-time (143 women); includes 56 minority (44 Black or African American, non-Hispanic/Latino; 1 American Indian or Alaska Native, non-Hispanic/Latino; 2 Asian, non-Hispanic/Latino; 8 Hispanic/Latino; 1 Two or more races, non-Hispanic/Latino), 32 international. Average age 39. 139 applicants, 88% accepted. In 2016, 45 master's, 21 doctorates awarded. Terminal master's awarded for partial completion of doctoral program. *Degree requirements:* For doctorate, thesis/dissertation. *Entrance requirements:* For master's, minimum GPA of 2.5; for doctorate, GRE or MAT, minimum GPA of 2.0 (undergraduate), 3.5 (graduate). *Application deadline:* Applications are processed on a rolling basis. Application fee: $25 ($300 for international students). Electronic applications accepted. *Expenses:* Contact institution. *Financial support:* Career-related internships or fieldwork, tuition waivers (full and partial), and unspecified assistantships available. Support available to part-time students. Financial award application deadline: 5/1. *Faculty research:* Reading and cognition, adult education, technology education, educational leadership, special education. *Unit head:* Dr. Shawn Fitzgerald, Dean, 610-499-4294, Fax: 610-499-4623, E-mail: smfitzgerald@widener.edu. *Application contact:* Dr. Roberta Nolan, Director of Graduate Admissions, 610-499-4125, E-mail: rdnolan@widener.edu.
Website: http://www.widener.edu/academics/schools/eics

Wilkes University, College of Graduate and Professional Studies, School of Education, Wilkes-Barre, PA 18766-0002. Offers 21st century teaching and learning (MS Ed); art

and science of teaching (MS Ed); classroom technology (MS Ed); early childhood literacy (MS Ed); educational development and strategies (MS Ed); educational leadership (MS Ed, Ed D); effective teaching (MS Ed); instructional media (MS Ed); instructional technology (MS Ed); international school leadership (MS Ed); international teaching and learning (MS Ed); middle level education (MS Ed); online teaching (MS Ed); reading (MS Ed); school business leadership (MS Ed); special education (MS Ed); teaching English to speakers of other languages (MS Ed). *Program availability:* Part-time, evening/weekend, 100% online, blended/hybrid learning. *Students:* 87 full-time (70 women), 1,496 part-time (1,111 women); includes 77 minority (11 Black or African American, non-Hispanic/Latino; 2 American Indian or Alaska Native, non-Hispanic/Latino; 12 Asian, non-Hispanic/Latino; 28 Hispanic/Latino; 3 Native Hawaiian or other Pacific Islander, non-Hispanic/Latino; 21 Two or more races, non-Hispanic/Latino). Average age 33. In 2016, 524 master's, 21 doctorates awarded. *Entrance requirements:* Additional exam requirements/recommendations for international students: Required—TOEFL (minimum score 550 paper-based; 79 iBT). *Application deadline:* Applications are processed on a rolling basis. Application fee: $45. Electronic applications accepted. *Expenses:* Contact institution. *Financial support:* Unspecified assistantships available. Financial award application deadline: 3/1; financial award applicants required to submit FAFSA. *Unit head:* Dr. Rhonda Rabbitt, Dean, 570-408-4680, Fax: 570-408-7872, E-mail: rhonda.rabbitt@wilkes.edu. *Application contact:* Director of Graduate Education, 570-408-4234, Fax: 570-408-7846.
Website: http://www.wilkes.edu/academics/graduate-programs/masters-programs/graduate-education/index.aspx

Winston-Salem State University, MAT Program, Winston-Salem, NC 27110-0003. Offers middle grades education (MAT); special education (MAT). *Accreditation:* NCATE. *Program availability:* Part-time, evening/weekend, online learning. *Entrance requirements:* For master's, GRE, MAT, NC teacher licensure. Electronic applications accepted. *Faculty research:* Action research on issues in elementary classroom.

Worcester State University, Graduate Studies, Department of Education, Program in Middle School Education, Worcester, MA 01602-2597. Offers M Ed, Postbaccalaureate Certificate. *Program availability:* Part-time. *Faculty:* 13 full-time (12 women), 16 part-time/adjunct (7 women). *Students:* 3 full-time (2 women), 21 part-time (12 women); includes 3 minority (2 Hispanic/Latino; 1 Two or more races, non-Hispanic/Latino). Average age 35. 37 applicants, 68% accepted, 14 enrolled. In 2016, 9 master's, 8 other advanced degrees awarded. *Degree requirements:* For master's, comprehensive exam (for some programs), thesis optional, portfolio. *Entrance requirements:* For master's, GRE General Test or MAT, initial license in middle school education from Commonwealth of Massachusetts; evidence of undergraduate or graduate course in adolescent/developmental psychology with minimum B grade or CLEP exam in human growth and development (minimum score of 50); for Postbaccalaureate Certificate, MTEL (content area, Communication and Literacy Skills). Additional exam requirements/recommendations for international students: Required—TOEFL (minimum score 550 paper-based; 79 iBT). *Application deadline:* For fall admission, 6/15 for domestic and international students; for spring admission, 11/1 for domestic and international students; for summer admission, 4/1 for domestic and international students. Applications are processed on a rolling basis. Application fee: $50. Electronic applications accepted. *Expenses:* Tuition, state resident: part-time $150 per credit. Tuition, nonresident: part-time $150 per credit. *Financial support:* Career-related internships or fieldwork, scholarships/grants, and unspecified assistantships available. Financial award application deadline: 3/1; financial award applicants required to submit FAFSA. *Unit head:* Dr. Sara Young, Program Coordinator, 508-929-8246, E-mail: syoung3@worcester.edu. *Application contact:* Sara Grady, Associate Dean for Graduate Studies and Professional Development, 508-929-8787, Fax: 508-929-8100, E-mail: sara.grady@worcester.edu.

Youngstown State University, Graduate School, Beeghly College of Education, Department of Teacher Education, Program in Early Childhood Education, Youngstown, OH 44555-0001. Offers MS Ed. *Accreditation:* NCATE. *Program availability:* Part-time, evening/weekend. *Degree requirements:* For master's, comprehensive exam. *Entrance requirements:* For master's, GRE, MAT, or teaching certificate; minimum GPA of 2.7. Additional exam requirements/recommendations for international students: Required—TOEFL.

Youngstown State University, Graduate School, Beeghly College of Education, Department of Teacher Education, Program in Middle Childhood Education, Youngstown, OH 44555-0001. Offers MS Ed. *Accreditation:* NCATE. *Program availability:* Part-time, evening/weekend. *Degree requirements:* For master's, comprehensive exam, thesis optional. *Entrance requirements:* For master's, GRE, MAT, or teaching certificate; minimum GPA of 2.7. Additional exam requirements/recommendations for international students: Required—TOEFL. *Faculty research:* Critical reflectivity, gender issues in classroom instruction, collaborative research and analysis, literacy methodology.

Secondary Education

Acacia University, American Graduate School of Education, Tempe, AZ 85284. Offers educational administration (M Ed); elementary education (MA); English as a second language (M Ed); secondary education (MA); special education (M Ed).

Adelphi University, Ruth S. Ammon School of Education, Program in Adolescent Education, Garden City, NY 11530-0701. Offers MA. *Program availability:* Part-time, evening/weekend. *Students:* 47 full-time (35 women), 10 part-time (4 women); includes 15 minority (6 Black or African American, non-Hispanic/Latino; 1 American Indian or Alaska Native, non-Hispanic/Latino; 1 Asian, non-Hispanic/Latino; 5 Hispanic/Latino; 2 Two or more races, non-Hispanic/Latino). Average age 24. 43 applicants, 72% accepted, 14 enrolled. In 2016, 44 master's awarded. *Entrance requirements:* For master's, 2 letters of recommendation, resume. Additional exam requirements/recommendations for international students: Required—TOEFL (minimum score 550 paper-based; 80 iBT), IELTS (minimum score 6.5). *Application deadline:* For fall admission, 4/1 for international students; for spring admission, 11/1 for international students. Applications are processed on a rolling basis. Application fee: $50. Electronic applications accepted. *Expenses:* Contact institution. *Financial support:* Research assistantships with partial tuition reimbursements, teaching assistantships, career-related internships or fieldwork, institutionally sponsored loans, scholarships/grants, traineeships, and unspecified assistantships available. Support available to part-time students. Financial award application deadline: 2/15; financial award applicants required to submit FAFSA. *Faculty research:* Methods to enhance the development of teaching dispositions, ethical and moral issues in education. *Unit head:* Dr. Robert Linne, Director, 516-877-4411, E-mail: linne@adelphi.edu. *Application contact:* Christine Murphy, Director of Admissions, 516-877-3050, Fax: 516-877-3039, E-mail: graduateadmissions@adelphi.edu.

Alabama Agricultural and Mechanical University, School of Graduate Studies, College of Education, Humanities, and Behavioral Sciences, Department of Educational Leadership and Secondary Education, Huntsville, AL 35811. Offers biology (M Ed); business/marketing education (M Ed, Ed S); chemistry (M Ed); collaborative teacher secondary education (M Ed, Ed S); education (M Ed, Ed S); English language arts (M Ed); family/consumer science education (M Ed, Ed S); general science (M Ed); general social science (M Ed); mathematics (M Ed, Ed S); physics (M Ed, Ed S); technology education (M Ed). *Accreditation:* NCATE. *Program availability:* Evening/weekend. *Degree requirements:* For master's, comprehensive exam; for Ed S, thesis. *Entrance requirements:* For master's, GRE General Test. Additional exam requirements/recommendations for international students: Required—TOEFL (minimum score 500 paper-based; 61 iBT). *Application deadline:* For fall admission, 5/1 for domestic students. Applications are processed on a rolling basis. Application fee: $25. Electronic applications accepted. *Expenses:* Tuition, nonresident: part-time $826 per credit hour. Full-time tuition and fees vary according to course load and program. *Financial support:* Research assistantships, career-related internships or fieldwork, Federal Work-Study, institutionally sponsored loans, and traineeships available. Financial award application deadline: 4/1. *Faculty research:* World peace through education, computer-assisted instruction. *Unit head:* Dr. Derrick Davis, Chair, 256-372-4047, Fax: 256-372-5526.

Alabama State University, College of Education, Department of Curriculum and Instruction, Montgomery, AL 36101-0271. Offers early childhood education (M Ed, Ed S); elementary education (M Ed, Ed S); secondary education (M Ed, Ed S), including biology education, English language arts education (M Ed), history education, math education, music education (M Ed), reading education (M Ed), social science education; special education (M Ed). *Program availability:* Part-time. *Faculty:* 7 full-time (4 women), 7 part-time/adjunct (4 women). *Students:* 37 full-time (30 women), 82 part-time (69 women); includes 117 minority (115 Black or African American, non-Hispanic/Latino; 2 Two or more races, non-Hispanic/Latino). Average age 33. 65 applicants, 55% accepted, 22 enrolled. In 2016, 25 master's, 5 Ed Ss awarded. *Degree requirements:* For master's, comprehensive exam, thesis optional; for Ed S, comprehensive exam, thesis. *Entrance requirements:* For master's, GRE General Test, MAT, writing competency test; for Ed S, writing competency test, GRE, MAT. Additional exam requirements/recommendations for international students: Required—TOEFL (minimum score 500 paper-based). *Application deadline:* For fall admission, 4/15 for domestic and international students; for spring admission, 11/15 for domestic and international students; for summer admission, 3/15 for domestic and international students. Applications are processed on a rolling basis. Application fee: $25. Electronic applications accepted. *Expenses:* Tuition, state resident: full-time $3087; part-time $2744 per credit. Tuition, nonresident: full-time $6174; part-time $5488 per credit. *Required fees:* $2284; $1142 per credit. $571 per semester. Tuition and fees vary according to class time, course level, course load, degree level, program and student level. *Financial support:* Research assistantships available. Financial award application deadline: 6/30; financial award applicants required to submit FAFSA. *Unit head:* Dr. Joyce Johnson, Acting Chairperson, 334-229-4485, Fax: 334-229-5603, E-mail: jjohnson@alasu.edu. *Application contact:* Dr. William Person, Dean of Graduate Studies, 334-229-4274, Fax: 334-229-4928, E-mail: wperson@alasu.edu.
Website: http://www.alasu.edu/academics/colleges—departments/college-of-education/curriculum—instruction/index.aspx

Alcorn State University, School of Graduate Studies, School of Psychology and Education, Lorman, MS 39096-7500. Offers agricultural education (MS Ed); elementary education (MS Ed, Ed S); guidance and counseling (MS Ed); industrial education (MS Ed); secondary education (MS Ed), including health and physical education; special education (MS Ed). *Accreditation:* NCATE. *Degree requirements:* For master's, thesis optional.

American International College, School of Education, Springfield, MA 01109-3189. Offers early childhood education (M Ed, CAGS); elementary education (M Ed, CAGS); middle education/secondary education (M Ed, CAGS); moderate disabilities (M Ed, CAGS); reading specialist (M Ed, CAGS); school adjustment counseling (MAEP, CAGS); school guidance counseling (MAEP, CAGS); school leadership (M Ed, CAGS). *Program availability:* Evening/weekend. *Faculty:* 1 (woman) full-time, 90 part-time/adjunct (63 women). *Students:* 1,194 full-time (970 women), 118 part-time (83 women); includes 108 minority (15 Black or African American, non-Hispanic/Latino; 4 American Indian or Alaska Native, non-Hispanic/Latino; 12 Asian, non-Hispanic/Latino; 55 Hispanic/Latino; 2 Native Hawaiian or other Pacific Islander, non-Hispanic/Latino; 20 Two or more races, non-Hispanic/Latino). Average age 34. 517 applicants, 417 enrolled. In 2016, 879 master's, 194 CAGSs awarded. Terminal master's awarded for partial completion of doctoral program. *Degree requirements:* For master's, comprehensive exam (for some programs), thesis (for some programs), practicum/culminating experience; for CAGS, practicum/culminating experience. *Entrance requirements:* For master's, Communication and Literacy portion of the Massachusetts Tests for Education Licensure, graduate of accredited four-year college with minimum B- average in undergraduate course work; for CAGS, M Ed or master's degree in field related to licensure from accredited institution. *Application deadline:* Applications are processed on a rolling basis. Application fee: $50. Electronic applications accepted. *Expenses:* $439 per credit. *Financial support:* Applicants required to submit FAFSA. *Unit head:* Sylvia Mason, Dean, 413-205-1743, Fax: 413-205-3943, E-mail: sylvia.mason@aic.edu. *Application contact:* Kerry Barnes, Dean of Graduate Admissions, 413-205-3703, Fax: 413-205-3051, E-mail: kerry.barnes@aic.edu.
Website: http://www.aic.edu/school-of-education/

American Public University System, AMU/APU Graduate Programs, Charles Town, WV 25414. Offers accounting (MBA, MS); applied business analytics (MBA, MS); criminal justice (MA), including business administration, emergency and disaster management, general (MA, MS); educational leadership (M Ed); emergency and disaster management (MA); entrepreneurship (MBA); environmental policy and management (MS), including environmental planning, environmental sustainability, fish and wildlife management, general (MA, MS), global environmental management; finance (MBA); general (MBA); government contracting and acquisition (MBA); health care administration (MBA); health information management (MS); history (MA), including American history, ancient and classical history, European history, global history, public history; homeland security (MA), including business administration, counterterrorism studies, criminal justice, cyber, emergency management and public health, intelligence

studies, transportation security; homeland security resource allocation (MBA); humanities (MA); information technology (MS), including digital forensics, enterprise software development, information assurance and security, IT project management; information technology management (MBA); intelligence studies (MA), including criminal intelligence, cyber, general (MA, MS), homeland security, intelligence analysis, intelligence collection, intelligence management, intelligence operations, terrorism studies; international relations and conflict resolution (MA), including comparative and security issues, conflict resolution, international and transnational security issues, peacekeeping; legal studies (MA); management (MA), including strategic consulting; marketing (MBA); military history (MA), including American military history, American Revolution, civil war, war since 1945, World War II; military studies (MA), including joint warfare, strategic leadership; national security studies (MA), including cyber, general (MA, MS), homeland security, regional security studies, security and intelligence analysis, terrorism studies; nonprofit management (MBA); political science (MA), including American politics and government, comparative government and development, general (MA, MS), international relations, public policy; psychology (MA); public administration (MPA), including disaster management, environmental policy, health policy, human resources, national security, organizational management, security management; public health (MPH); reverse logistics management (MA); security management (MA); space studies (MS), including aerospace science, general (MA, MS), planetary science; sports and health sciences (MS); sports management (MBA); teaching (M Ed), including autism spectrum disorder, curriculum and instruction for elementary teachers, elementary reading, English language learners, instructional leadership, online learning, special education, STEAM (STEM plus the arts); transportation and logistics management (MA). *Program availability:* Part-time, evening/weekend, online only, 100% online. *Faculty:* 401 full-time (228 women), 1,678 part-time/adjunct (781 women). *Students:* 378 full-time (184 women), 8,455 part-time (3,484 women); includes 2,972 minority (1,552 Black or African American, non-Hispanic/Latino; 52 American Indian or Alaska Native, non-Hispanic/Latino; 211 Asian, non-Hispanic/Latino; 791 Hispanic/Latino; 70 Native Hawaiian or other Pacific Islander, non-Hispanic/Latino; 296 Two or more races, non-Hispanic/Latino), 109 international. Average age 37. In 2016, 3,185 master's awarded. *Degree requirements:* For master's, comprehensive exam or practicum. *Entrance requirements:* For master's, official transcript showing earned bachelor's degree from institution accredited by recognized accrediting body. Additional exam requirements/recommendations for international students: Required—TOEFL (minimum score 550 paper-based), IELTS (minimum score 6.5). *Application deadline:* Applications are processed on a rolling basis. Application fee: $0. Electronic applications accepted. *Expenses: Tuition:* Part-time $350 per credit hour. *Required fees:* $50 per course. *Financial support:* Scholarships/grants available. Financial award applicants required to submit FAFSA. *Unit head:* Dr. Karan Powell, President, 877-468-6268, Fax: 304-724-3780. *Application contact:* Terry Grant, Vice President of Enrollment Management, 877-468-6268, Fax: 304-724-3780, E-mail: info@apus.edu.
Website: http://www.apus.edu

Andrews University, School of Graduate Studies, School of Education, Department of Teaching, Learning, and Curriculum, Berrien Springs, MI 49104. Offers curriculum and instruction (MA, Ed D, PhD, Ed S); elementary education (MAT); secondary education (MAT), including biology, education, English, English as a second language, French, history, physics; teacher education (MAT). *Faculty:* 7 full-time (5 women). *Students:* 17 full-time (12 women), 10 part-time (all women); includes 11 minority (6 Black or African American, non-Hispanic/Latino; 5 Hispanic/Latino), 7 international. Average age 38. In 2016, 9 master's, 7 doctorates awarded. *Entrance requirements:* For master's, GRE Subject Test. Additional exam requirements/recommendations for international students: Required—TOEFL (minimum score 550 paper-based). *Application deadline:* For fall admission, 8/15 for domestic students. Applications are processed on a rolling basis. Application fee: $40. *Unit head:* Dr. Lee C. Davidson, Chair, 269-471-6364. *Application contact:* Justina Clayburn, Supervisor of Graduate Admission, 800-253-2874, Fax: 269-471-6321, E-mail: graduate@andrews.edu.

Aquinas College, School of Education, Nashville, TN 37205-2005. Offers elementary education (MAT); secondary education (MAT); teaching and learning (M Ed). *Unit head:* Sr. Mary Anne Zuberbueler, OP, Dean, 615-297-7545 Ext. 282, Fax: 615-279-3892, E-mail: srmanne@aquinascollege.edu.

Arcadia University, School of Education, Glenside, PA 19038-3295. Offers art education (M Ed); computer education (CAS); curriculum (CAS); curriculum studies (M Ed); early childhood education (M Ed), including individualized, master teacher, research in child development; educational leadership (M Ed, Ed D, CAS); elementary education (M Ed); English education (MA Ed); environmental education (MA Ed); instructional technology (M Ed); language arts (M Ed); library science (M Ed); mathematics education (M Ed, MA Ed); music education (MA Ed); psychology (MA Ed); reading (M Ed, CAS); science education (M Ed, CAS); secondary education (M Ed, CAS); special education (M Ed, Ed D, CAS); theater arts (MA Ed); written communication (MA Ed). *Accreditation:* NASAD. *Program availability:* Part-time, evening/weekend, online learning. *Faculty:* 19 full-time (13 women), 3 part-time/adjunct (all women). *Students:* 22 full-time (16 women), 356 part-time (284 women); includes 84 minority (55 Black or African American, non-Hispanic/Latino; 2 American Indian or Alaska Native, non-Hispanic/Latino; 13 Asian, non-Hispanic/Latino; 11 Hispanic/Latino; 3 Two or more races, non-Hispanic/Latino), 4 international. Average age 34. 145 applicants, 73% accepted, 80 enrolled. In 2016, 95 master's, 11 doctorates awarded. *Application deadline:* Applications are processed on a rolling basis. Application fee: $50. Electronic applications accepted. *Expenses:* Contact institution. *Financial support:* Career-related internships or fieldwork, tuition waivers (partial), and unspecified assistantships available. *Unit head:* John T Groves, Interim Dean of the School of Education, 215-572-2940. *Application contact:* 215-572-2925, Fax: 215-572-2126, E-mail: grad@arcadia.edu.

Argosy University, Atlanta, College of Education, Atlanta, GA 30328. Offers educational leadership (MAEd, Ed D, Ed S), including higher education administration (Ed D), K-12 education (Ed D); teaching and learning (MAEd, Ed D, Ed S), including education technology (Ed D), higher education (Ed D), K-12 education (Ed D).

Argosy University, Chicago, College of Education, Chicago, IL 60601. Offers adult education and training (MA Ed); community college executive leadership (Ed D); educational leadership (MA Ed, Ed D, Ed S), including district leadership (Ed D), higher education administration (Ed D), K-12 education (Ed D); instructional leadership (Ed D, Ed S), including higher education (Ed D), K-12 education (Ed D). *Program availability:* Online learning.

Argosy University, Hawai`i, College of Education, Honolulu, HI 96813. Offers adult education and training (MAEd); educational leadership (Ed D), including higher education administration, K-12 education; instructional leadership (Ed D), including higher education, K-12 education; school psychology (MA).

Argosy University, Inland Empire, College of Education, Ontario, CA 91761. Offers community college executive leadership (Ed D); educational leadership (MA Ed, Ed D), including higher education administration (Ed D), K-12 education (Ed D); instructional leadership (MA Ed, Ed D), including higher education (Ed D), K-12 education (Ed D), multiple subject teacher preparation (MA Ed), single subject teacher preparation (MA Ed).

Argosy University, Los Angeles, College of Education, Santa Monica, CA 90045. Offers community college executive leadership (Ed D); educational leadership (MA Ed, Ed D), including higher education administration (Ed D), K-12 education (Ed D); instructional leadership (MA Ed, Ed D), including higher education (Ed D), K-12 education (Ed D), multiple subject teacher preparation (MA Ed), single subject teacher preparation (MA Ed).

Argosy University, Nashville, College of Education, Program in Educational Leadership, Nashville, TN 37214. Offers educational leadership (MA Ed, Ed S); higher education administration (Ed D); K-12 education (Ed D).

Argosy University, Nashville, College of Education, Program in Instructional Leadership, Nashville, TN 37214. Offers education technology (Ed D); higher education administration (Ed D); instructional leadership (MA Ed, Ed S); K-12 education (Ed D).

Argosy University, Northern Virginia, College of Education, Arlington, VA 22209. Offers community college executive leadership (Ed D); educational leadership (MA Ed, Ed D, Ed S), including higher education administration (Ed D), K-12 education (Ed D); instructional leadership (MA Ed, Ed D, Ed S), including higher education (Ed D), K-12 education (Ed D).

Argosy University, Orange County, College of Education, Orange, CA 92868. Offers community college executive leadership (Ed D); educational leadership (MA Ed, Ed D), including higher education administration (Ed D), K-12 education (Ed D); instructional leadership (MA Ed, Ed D), including education technology (Ed D), higher education (Ed D), K-12 education (Ed D), multiple subject teacher preparation (MA Ed), single subject teacher preparation (MA Ed).

Argosy University, Phoenix, College of Education, Phoenix, AZ 85021. Offers adult education and training (MA Ed); advanced educational administration (Ed D, Ed S); community college executive leadership (Ed D); educational administration (MA Ed); educational leadership (MA Ed, Ed D, Ed S), including education technology (Ed D), higher education administration (Ed D), K-12 education (Ed D); higher and postsecondary education (MA Ed); initial educational administration (Ed D, Ed S); school psychology (MA); teaching and learning (MA Ed, Ed D, Ed S), including education technology (Ed D), higher education (Ed D), K-12 education (Ed D).

Argosy University, San Diego, College of Education, San Diego, CA 92108. Offers community college executive leadership (Ed D); educational leadership (MA Ed, Ed D), including higher education administration (Ed D), K-12 education (Ed D); instructional leadership (MA Ed, Ed D), including higher education (Ed D), K-12 education (Ed D).

Argosy University, San Francisco Bay Area, College of Education, Alameda, CA 94501. Offers community college executive leadership (Ed D); educational leadership (MA Ed, Ed D), including education technology (Ed D), higher education administration (Ed D), K-12 education (Ed D); instructional leadership (MA Ed, Ed D), including education technology (Ed D), higher education (Ed D), K-12 education (Ed D), multiple subject teacher preparation (MA Ed), single subject teacher preparation (MA Ed).

Argosy University, Sarasota, College of Education, Sarasota, FL 34235. Offers community college executive leadership (Ed D); educational leadership (MA Ed, Ed D, Ed S), including higher education administration (Ed D), K-12 education (Ed D); school counseling (MA, Ed S); school psychology (MA); teaching and learning (MA Ed, Ed D, Ed S), including education technology (Ed D), higher education (Ed D), K-12 education (Ed D).

Argosy University, Seattle, College of Education, Seattle, WA 98121. Offers adult education and training (MA Ed); community college executive leadership (Ed D); educational leadership (MA Ed, Ed D), including higher education administration (Ed D), K-12 education (Ed D); higher and postsecondary education (MA Ed); instructional leadership (MA Ed, Ed D), including education technology (Ed D), higher education (Ed D), K-12 education (Ed D).

Argosy University, Tampa, College of Education, Tampa, FL 33607. Offers community college executive leadership (Ed D); educational leadership (MA Ed, Ed D, Ed S), including higher education administration (Ed D), K-12 education (Ed D); school counseling (MA); teaching and learning (MA Ed, Ed D, Ed S), including higher education (Ed D), K-12 education (Ed D).

Argosy University, Twin Cities, College of Education, Eagan, MN 55121. Offers advanced educational administration (Ed D, Ed S); educational leadership (MA Ed, Ed D, Ed S), including higher education administration (Ed D), K-12 education (Ed D); higher and postsecondary education (MA Ed); initial educational administration (Ed D, Ed S); instructional leadership (MA Ed, Ed D, Ed S), including education technology (Ed D), higher education (Ed D), K-12 education (Ed D).

Arizona State University at the Tempe campus, Mary Lou Fulton Teachers College, Program in Curriculum and Instruction, Phoenix, AZ 85069. Offers curriculum and instruction (M Ed, MA); elementary education (M Ed); physical education (MPE); secondary education (M Ed). *Program availability:* Part-time, evening/weekend, online learning. Terminal master's awarded for partial completion of doctoral program. *Degree requirements:* For master's, thesis or alternative, applied project, interactive Program of Study (iPOS) submitted before completing 50 percent of required credit hours. *Entrance requirements:* For master's, GRE or GMAT (for some programs), minimum GPA of 3.0 or equivalent in last 2 years of work leading to bachelor's degree, 3 letters of recommendation, personal statement describing research and career goals, curriculum vitae or resume, IVP fingerprint clearance card (for those seeking Arizona certification). Additional exam requirements/recommendations for international students: Required—TOEFL, IELTS, or PTE. Electronic applications accepted. *Expenses:* Contact institution. *Faculty research:* Early childhood, media and computers, elementary education, secondary education, English education, bilingual education, language and literacy, science education, engineering education, exercise and wellness education.

Armstrong State University, School of Graduate Studies, Department of Secondary, Adult, and Physical Education, Savannah, GA 31419-1997. Offers adolescent and adult education (Certificate); adult education and community leadership (M Ed); curriculum and instruction (M Ed); secondary education (MAT). *Program availability:* Part-time, evening/weekend, online learning. *Faculty:* 9 full-time (all women), 3 part-time/adjunct (all women). *Students:* 23 full-time (16 women), 103 part-time (68 women); includes 47 minority (40 Black or African American, non-Hispanic/Latino; 1 Asian, non-Hispanic/Latino; 2 Hispanic/Latino; 4 Two or more races, non-Hispanic/Latino), 1 international. Average age 32. 77 applicants, 52% accepted, 28 enrolled. In 2016, 36 master's, 1 other advanced degree awarded. *Degree requirements:* For master's, comprehensive exam (for some programs), thesis (for some programs), capstone project (for M Ed). *Entrance requirements:* For master's, edTPA (for MAT). Additional exam requirements/recommendations for international students: Required—TOEFL (minimum score 523 paper-based). *Application deadline:* For fall admission, 6/30 priority date for domestic students, 5/1 priority date for international students; for spring admission, 11/15 priority date for domestic students, 9/15 priority date for international students; for summer admission, 4/15 priority date for domestic students, 9/15 for international students. Applications are processed on a rolling basis. Application fee: $30. Electronic applications accepted. *Expenses:* Tuition, state resident: full-time $1781; part-time $161.93 per credit hour. Tuition, nonresident: full-time $6482; part-time $589.27 per credit hour. *Required fees:* $1224 per unit. $612 per semester. Tuition and fees vary

according to course load, campus/location and program. *Financial support:* In 2016–17, research assistantships with full tuition reimbursements (averaging $5,000 per year) were awarded; career-related internships or fieldwork, Federal Work-Study, scholarships/grants, and unspecified assistantships also available. Support available to part-time students. Financial award application deadline: 3/15; financial award applicants required to submit FAFSA. *Faculty research:* Quality of teacher leadership, classroom management and first year teachers; edTPA preparation and success of candidates; social justice issues related to educational preparation; recruitment of STEM teachers. *Unit head:* Dr. Regina Rahimi, Interim Department Head, 912-344-2562, E-mail: regina.rahimi@armstrong.edu. *Application contact:* McKenzie Peterman, Assistant Director of Graduate Admissions, 912-344-2503, Fax: 912-344-3417, E-mail: graduate@armstrong.edu.
Website: http://www.armstrong.edu/Education/adolescent_adult_education2/aaed_welcome

Auburn University at Montgomery, College of Education, Department of Curriculum, Instruction, and Technology, Montgomery, AL 36124-4023. Offers elementary education (M Ed, Ed S); instructional technology (Ed S); secondary education (M Ed). *Faculty:* 10 full-time (6 women), 6 part-time/adjunct (4 women). *Students:* 18 full-time (15 women), 23 part-time (22 women); includes 11 minority (10 Black or African American, non-Hispanic/Latino; 1 Asian, non-Hispanic/Latino), 1 international. *Entrance requirements:* Additional exam requirements/recommendations for international students: Recommended—TOEFL (minimum score 500 paper-based; 61 iBT), IELTS (minimum score 5.5), TSE (minimum score 44). *Expenses:* Tuition, state resident: full-time $6462; part-time $359 per credit hour. Tuition, nonresident: full-time $14,526; part-time $807 per credit hour. *Required fees:* $554. *Financial support:* Application deadline: 3/1; applicants required to submit FAFSA. *Unit head:* Dr. Kellie Shumack, Head, 334-244-3737, Fax: 334-244-3835, E-mail: kshumack@aum.edu. *Application contact:* Dr. Rhonda Morton, Associate Dean/Graduate Coordinator, 334-224-3287, Fax: 334-244-3978, E-mail: rmorton@aum.edu.
Website: http://education.aum.edu/academic-departments/curriculum-instruction-technology

Augusta University, The Graduate School, College of Education, Program in Curriculum and Instruction, Augusta, GA 30912. Offers curriculum and instruction (Ed S); elementary education (MAT); foreign language education (MAT); instruction (M Ed); middle grades education (MAT); music education (MAT); secondary education (MAT); special education (MAT). *Degree requirements:* For master's, thesis, portfolio. *Entrance requirements:* For master's, GRE, MAT, minimum GPA of 2.5. Application fee: $20. *Financial support:* Career-related internships or fieldwork, Federal Work-Study, institutionally sponsored loans, and unspecified assistantships available. Support available to part-time students. Financial award application deadline: 4/15; financial award applicants required to submit FAFSA. *Unit head:* Dr. Gordon Eisenman, Director, 706-737-1496, Fax: 706-667-4706, E-mail: geisenman@augusta.edu. *Application contact:* Dr. Gordon Eisenman, Director, 706-737-1496, Fax: 706-667-4706, E-mail: geisenman@augusta.edu.

Austin Peay State University, College of Graduate Studies, College of Education, Department of Educational Specialties, Clarksville, TN 37044. Offers administration and supervision (Ed S); counseling and guidance (Ed S); curriculum and instruction (MA Ed); education leadership (MA Ed); elementary education (Ed S); reading (MA Ed); secondary education (Ed S). *Program availability:* Part-time, evening/weekend, online learning. *Faculty:* 7 full-time (4 women), 4 part-time/adjunct (3 women). *Students:* 4 full-time (3 women), 77 part-time (60 women); includes 13 minority (8 Black or African American, non-Hispanic/Latino; 1 Asian, non-Hispanic/Latino; 3 Hispanic/Latino; 1 Two or more races, non-Hispanic/Latino). Average age 37. 18 applicants, 89% accepted, 14 enrolled. In 2016, 34 master's, 9 Ed Ss awarded. *Degree requirements:* For master's, comprehensive exam, thesis optional. *Entrance requirements:* For master's, GRE General Test, MAT, minimum undergraduate GPA of 2.75. Additional exam requirements/recommendations for international students: Required—TOEFL (minimum score 500 paper-based). *Application deadline:* For fall admission, 8/9 priority date for domestic students. Applications are processed on a rolling basis. Application fee: $45 ($50 for international students). Electronic applications accepted. *Expenses:* Tuition, state resident: full-time $8300; part-time $415 per credit hour. Tuition, nonresident: full-time $22,280; part-time $1114 per credit hour. *Required fees:* $1473; $73.65 per credit hour. *Financial support:* Research assistantships with full tuition reimbursements, career-related internships or fieldwork, Federal Work-Study, institutionally sponsored loans, scholarships/grants, and unspecified assistantships available. Support available to part-time students. Financial award application deadline: 4/1; financial award applicants required to submit FAFSA. *Unit head:* Dr. Moniqueka Gold, Chair, 931-221-7696, Fax: 931-221-1292, E-mail: goldm@apsu.edu. *Application contact:* Brad Averitt, Coordinator of Graduate Admissions, 800-859-4723, Fax: 931-221-7641, E-mail: gradadmissions@apsu.edu.

Austin Peay State University, College of Graduate Studies, College of Education, Department of Teaching and Learning, Clarksville, TN 37044. Offers elementary education K-6 (MAT); reading (MA Ed); secondary education 7-12 (MAT); special education K-12 (MAT). *Program availability:* Part-time, evening/weekend, online learning. *Faculty:* 12 full-time (8 women), 1 (woman) part-time/adjunct. *Students:* 62 full-time (39 women), 79 part-time (72 women); includes 31 minority (16 Black or African American, non-Hispanic/Latino; 1 Asian, non-Hispanic/Latino; 8 Hispanic/Latino; 6 Two or more races, non-Hispanic/Latino), 2 international. Average age 33. 60 applicants, 80% accepted, 33 enrolled. In 2016, 53 master's awarded. *Degree requirements:* For master's, comprehensive exam, thesis optional. *Entrance requirements:* For master's, GRE General Test, minimum undergraduate GPA of 2.75. Additional exam requirements/recommendations for international students: Required—TOEFL (minimum score 500 paper-based). *Application deadline:* For fall admission, 8/9 priority date for domestic students. Applications are processed on a rolling basis. Application fee: $45 ($50 for international students). Electronic applications accepted. *Expenses:* Tuition, state resident: full-time $8300; part-time $415 per credit hour. Tuition, nonresident: full-time $22,280; part-time $1114 per credit hour. *Required fees:* $1473; $73.65 per credit hour. *Financial support:* Research assistantships, career-related internships or fieldwork, Federal Work-Study, institutionally sponsored loans, scholarships/grants, and unspecified assistantships available. Support available to part-time students. Financial award application deadline: 4/1; financial award applicants required to submit FAFSA. *Unit head:* Dr. Benita Bruster, Interim Chair, 931-221-6491, Fax: 931-221-1292, E-mail: brusterb@apsu.edu. *Application contact:* Brad Averitt, Coordinator of Graduate Admissions, 800-859-4723, Fax: 931-221-7641, E-mail: gradadmissions@apsu.edu.

Ball State University, Graduate School, Teachers College, Department of Educational Studies, Program in Secondary Education, Muncie, IN 47306. Offers MA. *Accreditation:* NCATE. *Program availability:* Part-time, online only, 100% online. *Entrance requirements:* For master's, minimum baccalaureate GPA of 2.75 or 3.0 in latter half of baccalaureate. Additional exam requirements/recommendations for international students: Required—TOEFL (minimum score 550 paper-based; 79 iBT), IELTS (minimum score 6.5). Electronic applications accepted.

Bard College, Master of Arts in Teaching Program, Annandale-on-Hudson, NY 12504. Offers secondary education (MAT), including biology, history, literature, mathematics, Spanish; MS/MAT. *Program availability:* Part-time. *Degree requirements:* For master's, year-long teaching residencies in area middle and high schools. *Entrance requirements:* For master's, GRE General Test, resume, 3 letters of recommendation, personal statement, official transcripts. Additional exam requirements/recommendations for international students: Required—TOEFL. *Application deadline:* For winter admission, 1/30 priority date for domestic students; for spring admission, 4/27 for domestic students, 4/30 for international students. Applications are processed on a rolling basis. Application fee: $65. Electronic applications accepted. Application fee is waived when completed online. *Financial support:* Fellowships, institutionally sponsored loans, and scholarships/grants available. Support available to part-time students. Financial award application deadline: 4/28; financial award applicants required to submit FAFSA. *Unit head:* Derek Furr, Director, 845-758-7136, Fax: 845-758-7149, E-mail: mat@bard.edu. *Application contact:* Cecilia Maple, Assistant Director for Admission and Student Affairs, 845-758-7145, E-mail: mat@bard.edu.
Website: http://www.bard.edu/mat/ny

Belhaven University, School of Education, Jackson, MS 39202-1789. Offers educational technology (M Ed); elementary education (M Ed, MAT); reading literacy (M Ed); secondary education (M Ed, MAT). *Program availability:* Part-time, evening/weekend, 100% online, blended/hybrid learning. *Faculty:* 36 full-time (27 women), 9 part-time/adjunct (6 women). *Students:* 319 full-time (270 women), 403 part-time (318 women); includes 502 minority (486 Black or African American, non-Hispanic/Latino; 2 Asian, non-Hispanic/Latino; 3 Hispanic/Latino; 11 Two or more races, non-Hispanic/Latino). Average age 35. In 2016, 78 master's awarded. *Degree requirements:* For master's, comprehensive exam, portfolio. *Entrance requirements:* For master's, PRAXIS I and II, minimum GPA of 2.8. *Application deadline:* Applications are processed on a rolling basis. Application fee: $25. Electronic applications accepted. *Expenses:* $495 per credit hour plus $75 technology fee per course. *Financial support:* Applicants required to submit FAFSA. *Unit head:* Dr. David Hand, Dean, 601-965-7020, E-mail: dhand@belhaven.edu. *Application contact:* Sean Kirnan, Assistant Vice President for Adult and Graduate Enrollment and Student Services, 601-968-8727, Fax: 601-968-5953, E-mail: gradadmission@belhaven.edu.
Website: http://graduateed.belhaven.edu

Bellarmine University, Annsley Frazier Thornton School of Education, Louisville, KY 40205. Offers education and district leadership (Ed D); education and social change (PhD); elementary education (MA Ed, MAT); leadership in higher education (PhD); learning and behavior disorders (MA Ed, MAT); middle grades education (MA Ed, MAT); principalship (Ed S); reading and writing (MA Ed); secondary education (MAT); teacher leadership (MA Ed). *Accreditation:* NCATE. *Program availability:* Part-time, evening/weekend. *Faculty:* 15 full-time (7 women), 44 part-time/adjunct (36 women). *Students:* 39 full-time (28 women), 211 part-time (164 women); includes 46 minority (35 Black or African American, non-Hispanic/Latino; 3 Asian, non-Hispanic/Latino; 5 Hispanic/Latino; 3 Two or more races, non-Hispanic/Latino). Average age 34. In 2016, 66 master's, 3 doctorates, 43 other advanced degrees awarded. *Degree requirements:* For master's, thesis (for some programs); for doctorate, thesis/dissertation. *Entrance requirements:* For master's, GRE, baccalaureate degree from accredited institution; minimum cumulative GPA of 2.75; recommendations from employers, supervisors, or professors attesting to applicant's potential as graduate student; statement of intent to pursue graduate degree; for doctorate, GRE, minimum GPA of 3.5 in all graduate coursework; baccalaureate and master's degrees in education or fields directly relevant to education; three letters of recommendation; two essays (no more than 1,000 words each); interview. Additional exam requirements/recommendations for international students: Required—TOEFL (minimum score 550 paper-based, 68 iBT), IELTS (minimum score 6), or Michigan English Language Assessment Battery. *Application deadline:* For fall admission, 8/1 priority date for domestic and international students; for spring admission, 12/1 priority date for domestic and international students; for summer admission, 4/10 priority date for domestic and international students. Applications are processed on a rolling basis. Application fee: $40. Electronic applications accepted. Tuition and fees vary according to program. *Financial support:* Scholarships/grants available. Financial award applicants required to submit FAFSA. *Faculty research:* Literacy, service-learning, dispositions, educational technology, special education. *Unit head:* Dr. Robert Cooter, Dean, 502-272-8191, Fax: 502-272-8189, E-mail: rcooter@bellarmine.edu. *Application contact:* Sarah Shumway Schuble, Senior Graduate Recruiter, 502-272-8271, Fax: 502-272-8002, E-mail: sshumway@bellarmine.edu.
Website: http://www.bellarmine.edu/education/graduate

Benedictine University, Graduate Programs, Program in Education, Lisle, IL 60532. Offers curriculum and instruction and collaborative teaching (M Ed); elementary education (MA Ed); leadership and administration (M Ed); reading and literacy (M Ed); secondary education (MA Ed); special education (MA Ed). *Program availability:* Part-time, evening/weekend. *Students:* 17 full-time (16 women), 30 part-time (26 women); includes 2 minority (both Black or African American, non-Hispanic/Latino). 21 applicants, 62% accepted, 8 enrolled. In 2016, 68 master's awarded. *Degree requirements:* For master's, comprehensive exam, thesis (for some programs). *Entrance requirements:* For master's, GRE or MAT. Additional exam requirements/recommendations for international students: Required—TOEFL (minimum score 550 paper-based). *Application deadline:* For fall admission, 9/1 for domestic students; for winter admission, 12/1 for domestic students; for spring admission, 2/15 for domestic students. Applications are processed on a rolling basis. Application fee: $40. Electronic applications accepted. *Expenses:* Contact institution. *Financial support:* Career-related internships or fieldwork and health care benefits available. Support available to part-time students. *Unit head:* MeShelda Jackson, Director, 630-829-6282, E-mail: mjackson@ben.edu. *Application contact:* Kari Gibbons, Associate Vice President, Enrollment Center, 630-829-6200, Fax: 630-829-6584, E-mail: kgibbons@ben.edu.

Berry College, Graduate Programs, Graduate Programs in Education, Program in Secondary Education, Mount Berry, GA 30149-0159. Offers MAT. *Faculty:* 5 part-time/adjunct (4 women). *Students:* 2 part-time (1 woman). Average age 27. In 2016, 2 master's awarded. *Degree requirements:* For master's, thesis, portfolio, oral exams. *Entrance requirements:* For master's, GRE General Test or MAT, minimum GPA of 2.5. Additional exam requirements/recommendations for international students: Required—TOEFL (minimum score 550 paper-based). *Application deadline:* For fall admission, 7/21 for domestic students, 5/1 for international students; for spring admission, 12/1 for domestic students, 10/1 for international students. Applications are processed on a rolling basis. Application fee: $25 ($30 for international students). Electronic applications accepted. *Expenses:* Contact institution. *Financial support:* In 2016–17, 1 student received support. Research assistantships with full tuition reimbursements available, scholarships/grants, tuition waivers (partial), and unspecified assistantships available. Support available to part-time students. Financial award application deadline: 3/1; financial award applicants required to submit FAFSA. *Unit head:* Dr. Jacqueline McDowell, Dean, Charter School of Education and Human Sciences, 706-236-1717, Fax: 706-238-5827, E-mail: jmcdowell@berry.edu. *Application contact:* Brett Kennedy, Assistant Vice President of Enrollment Management, 706-236-2215, Fax: 706-290-2178, E-mail: admissions@berry.edu.
Website: http://www.berry.edu/academics/education/graduate/

Secondary Education

Bethel University, Graduate School, St. Paul, MN 55112-6999. Offers business administration (MBA); classroom management (Certificate); counseling (MA); international baccalaureate teaching and learning (Certificate); K-12 education (MA); leadership (Ed D); leadership foundations (Certificate); nurse educator (MS, Certificate); nurse-midwifery (MS); physician assistant (MS); special education (MA); strategic leadership (MA); teaching (MA). *Program availability:* Part-time, evening/weekend, 100% online, blended/hybrid learning. *Faculty:* 19 full-time (15 women), 57 part-time/adjunct (37 women). *Students:* 674 full-time (466 women), 378 part-time (256 women); includes 188 minority (94 Black or African American, non-Hispanic/Latino; 3 American Indian or Alaska Native, non-Hispanic/Latino; 43 Asian, non-Hispanic/Latino; 31 Hispanic/Latino; 1 Native Hawaiian or other Pacific Islander, non-Hispanic/Latino; 16 Two or more races, non-Hispanic/Latino), 33 international. *Degree requirements:* For master's, comprehensive exam (for some programs), thesis (for some programs); for doctorate, comprehensive exam, thesis/dissertation. *Entrance requirements:* Additional exam requirements/recommendations for international students: Required—TOEFL (minimum score 550 paper-based, 80 iBT) or IELTS. *Application deadline:* Applications are processed on a rolling basis. Application fee: $0. Electronic applications accepted. *Expenses:* Contact institution. *Financial support:* Teaching assistantships, career-related internships or fieldwork, and scholarships/grants available. Support available to part-time students. Financial award applicants required to submit FAFSA. *Unit head:* Dick Crombie, Vice-President/Dean, 651-635-8000, Fax: 651-635-8004, E-mail: gs@bethel.edu. *Application contact:* Director of Admissions, 651-635-8000, Fax: 651-635-8004, E-mail: gs@bethel.edu.
Website: https://www.bethel.edu/graduate/

Binghamton University, State University of New York, Graduate School, Graduate School of Education, Program in Adolescence Education, Binghamton, NY 13902-6000. Offers biology education (MAT, MS Ed); chemistry education (MAT, MS Ed); earth science education (MAT, MS Ed); English education (MAT, MS Ed); French education (MAT, MS Ed); literacy education (MS Ed); mathematical sciences education (MAT, MS Ed); physics (MAT, MS Ed); social studies (MAT, MS Ed); Spanish education (MAT, MS Ed). *Accreditation:* TEAC. *Program availability:* Part-time, evening/weekend. *Students:* 59 full-time (36 women), 7 part-time (2 women); includes 10 minority (2 Black or African American, non-Hispanic/Latino; 1 American Indian or Alaska Native, non-Hispanic/Latino; 1 Asian, non-Hispanic/Latino; 5 Hispanic/Latino; 1 Two or more races, non-Hispanic/Latino). Average age 26. 46 applicants, 76% accepted, 25 enrolled. In 2016, 26 master's awarded. *Degree requirements:* For master's, portfolio. *Entrance requirements:* For master's, GRE General Test, teaching certification. Additional exam requirements/recommendations for international students: Required—TOEFL (minimum score 550 paper-based; 80 iBT). *Application deadline:* For fall admission, 2/1 priority date for domestic and international students; for spring admission, 10/15 priority date for domestic and international students. Application fee: $75. Electronic applications accepted. *Financial support:* In 2016–17, 6 students received support. Research assistantships, teaching assistantships, career-related internships or fieldwork, Federal Work-Study, institutionally sponsored loans, scholarships/grants, health care benefits, tuition waivers (full and partial), and unspecified assistantships available. Financial award applicants required to submit FAFSA. *Unit head:* Dr. Susan Strehle, Dean, 607-777-7329, E-mail: sstrehle@binghamton.edu. *Application contact:* Ben Balkaya, Assistant Dean and Director, 607-777-2151, Fax: 607-777-2501, E-mail: balkaya@binghamton.edu.

Bob Jones University, Graduate Programs, Greenville, SC 29614. Offers accountancy (MS); Bible (MA); Bible translation (MA); Biblical studies (Certificate); broadcast management (MS); business administration (MBA); church history (MA, PhD); church ministries (MA); church music (MM); cinema and video production (MA); counseling (MS); curriculum and instruction (Ed D); divinity (M Div); dramatic production (MA); educational leadership (MS, Ed D, Ed S); elementary education (M Ed, MAT); English (M Ed, MA, MAT); fine arts (MA); graphic design (MA); history (M Ed, MA); illustration (MA); interpretative speech (MA); mathematics (M Ed, MAT); medical missions (Certificate); ministry (MM, D Min); multi-categorical special education (M Ed, MAT); music (M Ed); New Testament interpretation (PhD); Old Testament interpretation (PhD); orchestral instrument performance (MM); organ performance (MM); pastoral studies (MA); personnel services (MS, Ed S); piano pedagogy (MM); piano performance (MM); platform arts (MA); radio and television broadcasting (MS); rhetoric and public address (MA); secondary education (M Ed); studio art (MA); teaching Bible (MA); theology (MA, PhD); voice performance (MM); youth ministries (MA); M Div/MM.

Boston College, Lynch School of Education, Program in Secondary Education, Chestnut Hill, MA 02467-3800. Offers M Ed, MAT, MST. *Accreditation:* TEAC. *Program availability:* Part-time, evening/weekend. *Faculty:* 6 full-time (4 women). *Students:* 21 full-time (12 women), 16 part-time (5 women); includes 9 minority (4 Black or African American, non-Hispanic/Latino; 1 Asian, non-Hispanic/Latino; 3 Hispanic/Latino; 1 Two or more races, non-Hispanic/Latino), 1 international. Average age 25. 54 applicants, 87% accepted, 6 enrolled. In 2016, 34 master's awarded. *Degree requirements:* For master's, comprehensive exam. *Entrance requirements:* For master's, GRE General Test or MAT. Additional exam requirements/recommendations for international students: Required—TOEFL (minimum score 100 iBT). *Application deadline:* For fall admission, 12/1 priority date for domestic students, 12/1 for international students; for spring admission, 11/1 priority date for domestic and international students. Application fee: $65. Electronic applications accepted. Tuition and fees vary according to program. *Financial support:* Fellowships with tuition reimbursements, research assistantships with tuition reimbursements, teaching assistantships with tuition reimbursements, Federal Work-Study, scholarships/grants, and tuition waivers (full and partial) available. Support available to part-time students. Financial award applicants required to submit FAFSA. *Unit head:* Dr. Susan Bruce, Chairperson, 617-552-4214, Fax: 617-552-0398. *Application contact:* Kimberly Rose, Graduate Admission Assistant, 617-552-4214, Fax: 617-552-0398, E-mail: roseki@bc.edu.

Bowie State University, Graduate Programs, Program in Secondary Education, Bowie, MD 20715-9465. Offers M Ed. *Accreditation:* NCATE. *Program availability:* Part-time, evening/weekend. *Degree requirements:* For master's, comprehensive exam, thesis optional, research paper. *Entrance requirements:* For master's, minimum undergraduate GPA of 3.0, bachelor's degree in education, teaching certificate, teaching experience. Electronic applications accepted.

Brandeis University, Graduate School of Arts and Sciences, Teaching Program, Waltham, MA 02454-9110. Offers Jewish day school (MAT); public elementary education (MAT); secondary education (MAT), including Bible, biology, chemistry, Chinese, English, history, math, physics; teacher leadership (Ed M, CAGS). *Faculty:* 4 full-time (2 women), 11 part-time/adjunct (10 women). *Students:* 26 full-time (19 women), 32 part-time (26 women); includes 3 minority (all Hispanic/Latino), 10 international. 106 applicants, 70% accepted, 53 enrolled. In 2016, 39 master's awarded. *Degree requirements:* For master's, internship; research project. *Entrance requirements:* For master's, GRE General Test or MAT, official transcript(s), 2 letters of recommendation, resume, statement of purpose. Additional exam requirements/recommendations for international students: Required—TOEFL (minimum score 600 paper-based; 100 iBT); Recommended—IELTS (minimum score 7), TSE (minimum score 68). *Application deadline:* Applications are processed on a rolling basis. Application fee: $75. Electronic applications accepted. *Expenses:* Contact institution. *Financial support:* Scholarships/grants and tuition waivers (partial) available. Financial award application deadline: 4/15; financial award applicants required to submit FAFSA. *Faculty research:* Teacher education, education, teaching, elementary education, secondary education, Jewish education, English, history, biology, chemistry, physics, math, Chinese, Bible/Tanakh. *Unit head:* Prof. Marya Levenson, Director, 781-736-2002, Fax: 781-736-5020, E-mail: mlevenso@brandeis.edu. *Application contact:* Manuel Tuan, Department Coordinator, 781-736-2002, Fax: 781-736-5020, E-mail: tuan@brandeis.edu.
Website: http://www.brandeis.edu/programs/mat

Brandman University, School of Education, Irvine, CA 92618. Offers education (MA); elementary education (MAT); organizational leadership (Ed D); school counseling (MA); secondary education (MAT); special education (MA). *Expenses: Tuition:* Full-time $14,880; part-time $620 per credit hour. Tuition and fees vary according to degree level and program. *Unit head:* Dr. Christine G. Zeppos, Dean, 949-341-9948, E-mail: zeppos@brandman.edu.
Website: http://www.brandman.edu/education/

Brenau University, Sydney O. Smith Graduate School, College of Education, Gainesville, GA 30501. Offers early childhood (Ed S); early childhood education (M Ed, MAT); middle grades (Ed S); middle grades education (M Ed, MAT); secondary education (MAT); special education (M Ed, MAT). *Accreditation:* NCATE. *Program availability:* Part-time, evening/weekend, online learning. *Degree requirements:* For master's, thesis optional, comprehensive exam or applied research project, effective portfolio; for Ed S, thesis, applied research project. *Entrance requirements:* For master's, GRE, MAT, interview, minimum GPA of 3.0, 3 references, writing samples; for Ed S, GRE, MAT, master's degree, minimum GPA of 3.0, writing sample, letters of reference. Additional exam requirements/recommendations for international students: Required—TOEFL (minimum score 500 paper-based; 61 iBT); Recommended—IELTS (minimum score 5). Electronic applications accepted. *Expenses:* Contact institution.

Bridgewater State University, College of Graduate Studies, College of Education and Allied Studies, Department of Secondary Education and Professional Programs, Program in Secondary Education, Bridgewater, MA 02325. Offers MAT. *Accreditation:* NCATE. *Program availability:* Part-time, evening/weekend. *Entrance requirements:* For master's, GRE General Test.

Brooklyn College of the City University of New York, School of Education, Program in Adolescence Science Education and Special Subjects, Brooklyn, NY 11210-2889. Offers adolescence science education (MAT); biology teacher (7-12) (MA); chemistry teacher (7-12) (MA); earth science teacher (7-12) (MAT); English teacher (7-12) (MA); French teacher (7-12) (MA); mathematics teacher (7-12) (MA); music teacher (MA); physics teacher (7-12) (MA); social studies teacher (7-12) (MA); Spanish teacher (7-12) (MA). *Program availability:* Part-time, evening/weekend. *Degree requirements:* For master's, comprehensive exam (for some programs), thesis (for some programs). *Entrance requirements:* For master's, LAST, previous course work in education, resume, 2 letters of recommendation, essay. Additional exam requirements/recommendations for international students: Required—TOEFL (minimum score 500 paper-based; 61 iBT). Electronic applications accepted. *Faculty research:* Interdisciplinary education, semiotics, discourse analysis, autobiography, teacher identity.

Brown University, Graduate School, Department of Education, Program in Teaching, Providence, RI 02912. Offers elementary education (MAT); English (MAT); history/social studies (MAT); science (MAT); secondary education (MAT). *Degree requirements:* For master's, student teaching, portfolio. *Entrance requirements:* For master's, GRE General Test, transcript, personal statement, 3 letters of recommendation, interview, writing sample (English applicants only). Additional exam requirements/recommendations for international students: Required—TOEFL (minimum score 577 paper-based). Electronic applications accepted. *Faculty research:* Literacy, English language learners, diversity, special education, biodiversity.

California State University, Bakersfield, Division of Graduate Studies, School of Natural Sciences, Mathematics, and Engineering, Program in Teaching Mathematics, Bakersfield, CA 93311. Offers MA. *Students:* 1 full-time (0 women); minority (Hispanic/Latino). *Entrance requirements:* For master's, minimum GPA of 2.5 for last 90 quarter units. *Expenses:* Tuition, state resident: full-time $2246; part-time $1302 per semester. *Unit head:* Sophia Raczkowski, Chair, 661-654-3151, Fax: 661-664-2039. *Application contact:* Debbie Blowers, Assistant Director of Admissions and Evaluations, 661-664-3381, E-mail: dblowers@csub.edu.
Website: https://www.csub.edu/math/info/index.html

California State University, Fullerton, Graduate Studies, College of Education, Department of Secondary Education, Fullerton, CA 92834-9480. Offers teacher instruction (MS); teaching foundational mathematics (MS). *Program availability:* Part-time. Application fee: $55. *Expenses:* Tuition, state resident: full-time $3369; part-time $1953 per unit. Tuition, nonresident: full-time $3915; part-time $2499 per unit. Tuition and fees vary according to course load, degree level and program. *Financial support:* Career-related internships or fieldwork, Federal Work-Study, institutionally sponsored loans, and scholarships/grants available. Support available to part-time students. Financial award application deadline: 3/1; financial award applicants required to submit FAFSA. *Unit head:* Dr. Grace Cho, Chair, 657-278-3283, E-mail: gcho@fullerton.edu. *Application contact:* Admissions/Applications, 657-278-2371.

California State University, Long Beach, Graduate Studies, College of Education, Department of Teacher Education, Long Beach, CA 90840. Offers elementary education (MA); secondary education (MA). *Program availability:* Part-time, evening/weekend. *Degree requirements:* For master's, comprehensive exam or thesis. *Entrance requirements:* For master's, GRE General Test, minimum GPA of 2.75. *Application deadline:* For fall admission, 7/1 for domestic students; for spring admission, 12/1 for domestic students. Applications are processed on a rolling basis. Application fee: $55. Electronic applications accepted. *Financial support:* Federal Work-Study, institutionally sponsored loans, and scholarships/grants available. Financial award application deadline: 3/2. *Faculty research:* Teacher stress and burnout, new teacher induction. *Unit head:* Paul Boyde-Batstone, Chair, 562-985-4506.

California State University, Long Beach, Graduate Studies, College of Natural Sciences and Mathematics, Department of Mathematics and Statistics, Long Beach, CA 90840. Offers mathematics (MS), including applied mathematics, applied statistics, mathematics education for secondary school teachers. *Program availability:* Part-time. *Degree requirements:* For master's, comprehensive exam or thesis. *Application deadline:* For fall admission, 7/1 for domestic students; for spring admission, 12/1 for domestic students. Applications are processed on a rolling basis. Application fee: $55. Electronic applications accepted. *Financial support:* Teaching assistantships, Federal Work-Study, institutionally sponsored loans, scholarships/grants, and traineeships available. Financial award application deadline: 3/2. *Faculty research:* Algebra, functional analysis, partial differential equations, operator theory, numerical analysis. *Unit head:* Dr. Robert Mena, Chair, 562-985-4721, Fax: 562-985-8227, E-mail: rmena@csulb.edu. *Application contact:* Dr. Ngo Viet, Graduate Associate Chair, 562-985-4721, Fax: 562-985-8227, E-mail: viet@csulb.edu.

California State University, Northridge, Graduate Studies, Michael D. Eisner College of Education, Department of Secondary Education, Northridge, CA 91330. Offers educational technology (MA); English education (MA); mathematics education (MA); secondary science education (MA); teaching and learning (MA). *Accreditation:* NCATE. *Program availability:* Part-time. *Faculty:* 10 full-time (5 women), 50 part-time/adjunct (24 women). *Students:* 17 full-time (10 women), 87 part-time (55 women); includes 41 minority (3 Black or African American, non-Hispanic/Latino; 11 Asian, non-Hispanic/Latino; 24 Hispanic/Latino; 1 Native Hawaiian or other Pacific Islander, non-Hispanic/Latino; 2 Two or more races, non-Hispanic/Latino), 4 international. Average age 37. 80 applicants, 80% accepted, 50 enrolled. *Degree requirements:* For master's, thesis optional. *Entrance requirements:* For master's, GRE General Test or minimum GPA of 3.0. Additional exam requirements/recommendations for international students: Required—TOEFL. *Application deadline:* For fall admission, 11/30 for domestic students. Application fee: $55. *Expenses:* Tuition, state resident: full-time $4152. *Financial support:* Application deadline: 3/1. *Unit head:* Dr. Julie Gainsburg, Chair, 818-677-2580. *Application contact:* Dr. Michael Rivas, Graduate Advisor, 818-677-6792, E-mail: michael.rivas@csun.edu.
Website: http://www.csun.edu/eisner-education/secondary-education

California State University, Stanislaus, College of Education, Program in Education (MA), Turlock, CA 95382. Offers curriculum and instruction (MA), including education technology, elementary education, multilingual education, physical education, reading, secondary education, special education; school administration (MA); school counseling (MA). *Program availability:* Part-time, evening/weekend. *Degree requirements:* For master's, comprehensive exam (for some programs), thesis (for some programs). *Entrance requirements:* For master's, MAT, GRE, or CBEST (varies by concentration), 3 letters of recommendation, personal statement. Additional exam requirements/recommendations for international students: Required—TOEFL (minimum score 550 paper-based). Electronic applications accepted. *Faculty research:* Children's perspectives on historical events, method elementary schools dual language education, K-12 reading programs.

California State University, Stanislaus, College of Humanities and Social Sciences, Program in History (MA), Turlock, CA 95382. Offers history (MA); international relations (MA); secondary school teachers (MA). *Program availability:* Part-time. *Degree requirements:* For master's, comprehensive exam, thesis or alternative. *Entrance requirements:* For master's, GRE, minimum GPA of 3.0, personal statement. Additional exam requirements/recommendations for international students: Required—TOEFL (minimum score 575 paper-based). Electronic applications accepted. *Faculty research:* History of Ancient Greece, history and ecology of the Central Valley, acculturation and gender.

California University of Pennsylvania, School of Graduate Studies and Research, College of Education and Human Services, Program in Secondary Education, California, PA 15419-1394. Offers MAT. *Program availability:* Part-time, evening/weekend, online learning. *Degree requirements:* For master's, comprehensive exam, thesis. *Entrance requirements:* For master's, PRAXIS, minimum GPA of 3.0. Additional exam requirements/recommendations for international students: Required—TOEFL (minimum score 550 paper-based; 80 iBT). Electronic applications accepted. *Expenses:* Tuition, state resident: full-time $11,592; part-time $483 per credit. Tuition, nonresident: full-time $17,400; part-time $725 per credit. *Required fees:* $3916. Tuition and fees vary according to course load, degree level, campus/location and reciprocity agreements. *Faculty research:* The effectiveness of online instruction, student-centered instruction strategies in secondary education, computer technology in education, environmental education, multi-media in education.

Campbell University, Graduate and Professional Programs, School of Education, Buies Creek, NC 27506. Offers elementary education (M Ed); interdisciplinary studies (M Ed); middle grades education (M Ed); physical education (M Ed); school administration (MSA); school counseling (M Ed); secondary education (M Ed). *Accreditation:* NCATE. *Program availability:* Part-time, evening/weekend. *Degree requirements:* For master's, comprehensive exam. *Entrance requirements:* For master's, GRE General Test, minimum GPA of 2.7. *Faculty research:* Spiritual values and wellness issues in counseling, stress and professional burnout among counselors, thinking strategies, leadership, adaptive technology.

Canisius College, Graduate Division, School of Education and Human Services, Department of Graduate Education and Leadership, Buffalo, NY 14208-1098. Offers business and marketing education (MS Ed); college student personnel (MS Ed); deaf education (MS Ed); deaf/adolescent education, grades 7-12 (MS Ed); deaf/childhood education, grades 1-6 (MS Ed); differentiated instruction (MS Ed); education administration (MS); educational administration (MS Ed); educational technologies (Certificate); gifted education extension (Certificate); literacy (MS Ed); reading (Certificate); school building leadership (MS Ed, Certificate); school district leadership (Certificate); teacher leader (Certificate); TESOL (MS Ed). *Accreditation:* NCATE. *Program availability:* Part-time, evening/weekend, 100% online, blended/hybrid learning. *Faculty:* 5 full-time (all women), 23 part-time/adjunct (16 women). *Students:* 95 full-time (78 women), 223 part-time (177 women); includes 31 minority (15 Black or African American, non-Hispanic/Latino; 2 American Indian or Alaska Native, non-Hispanic/Latino; 4 Asian, non-Hispanic/Latino; 9 Hispanic/Latino; 1 Two or more races, non-Hispanic/Latino), 1 international. Average age 30. 162 applicants, 89% accepted, 135 enrolled. In 2016, 135 master's, 39 other advanced degrees awarded. *Entrance requirements:* For master's, GRE (if cumulative GPA less than 2.7), transcripts, two letters of recommendation. Additional exam requirements/recommendations for international students: Required—TOEFL (minimum score 550 paper-based, 79 iBT), IELTS (minimum score 6.5), or CAEL (minimum score 70). *Application deadline:* Applications are processed on a rolling basis. Application fee: $25. Electronic applications accepted. Application fee is waived when completed online. *Expenses: Tuition:* Full-time $14,742. *Required fees:* $724. *Financial support:* Career-related internships or fieldwork, Federal Work-Study, scholarships/grants, tuition waivers (partial), and unspecified assistantships available. Support available to part-time students. Financial award application deadline: 4/30; financial award applicants required to submit FAFSA. *Faculty research:* Asperger's disease, autism, private higher education, reading strategies. *Unit head:* Dr. Rosemary K. Murray, Chair/Associate Professor of Graduate Education and Leadership, 716-888-3723, E-mail: murray1@canisius.edu. *Application contact:* Kathleen B. Davis, Vice President of Enrollment Management, 716-888-2500, Fax: 716-888-3195, E-mail: daviskb@canisius.edu.
Website: http://www.canisius.edu/graduate/

Carroll University, Graduate Programs in Education, Waukesha, WI 53186-5593. Offers adult and continuing education (M Ed); educational leadership (MS); pk-12 (M Ed). *Program availability:* Part-time, evening/weekend. *Faculty:* 7 full-time (5 women), 14 part-time/adjunct (all women). *Students:* 11 full-time (10 women), 163 part-time (125 women); includes 11 minority (3 Black or African American, non-Hispanic/Latino; 3 American Indian or Alaska Native, non-Hispanic/Latino; 2 Asian, non-Hispanic/Latino; 3 Hispanic/Latino), 1 international. Average age 34. 96 applicants, 38% accepted, 18 enrolled. In 2016, 43 master's awarded. *Degree requirements:* For master's, thesis. *Entrance requirements:* For master's, minimum undergraduate GPA of 2.5 in related field. Additional exam requirements/recommendations for international students: Required—TOEFL. *Application deadline:* For fall admission, 8/15 priority date for domestic students. Applications are processed on a rolling basis. Application fee: $0. Electronic applications accepted. *Expenses: Tuition:* Full-time $10,548; part-time $586 per credit. *Required fees:* $520 per semester. Tuition and fees vary according to course load, degree level and program. *Financial support:* Available to part-time students. Application deadline: 3/15; applicants required to submit FAFSA. *Faculty research:* Qualitative research methods, whole language approaches to teaching, the writing process, multicultural education, gifted/talented learners. *Unit head:* Dr. Kathrine Kramer, Director of Graduate Studies, 262-650-4917, E-mail: kkramer@carrollu.edu. *Application contact:* Lori Aliota, Graduate Admission Counselor, 262-524-7226, E-mail: laliota@carrollu.edu.
Website: http://www.carrollu.edu/gradprograms/education/default.asp

Carson-Newman University, Graduate Program in Education, Jefferson City, TN 37760. Offers curriculum and instruction (M Ed); educational leadership (M Ed); elementary education (MAT); school counseling (MS); secondary education (MAT); teaching English as a second language (MATESL). *Accreditation:* NCATE. *Program availability:* Part-time, evening/weekend, 100% online, blended/hybrid learning. *Degree requirements:* For master's, thesis or alternative. *Entrance requirements:* For master's, PRAXIS II or GRE with minimum score of 290 on the verbal and quantitative components (for MAT), minimum GPA of 3.0 in major, 2.5 overall. Additional exam requirements/recommendations for international students: Recommended—TOEFL (minimum score 79 iBT), IELTS (minimum score 6.5), TSE (minimum score 53). *Expenses: Tuition:* Full-time $10,142; part-time $461 per credit hour. *Required fees:* $300; $150 per semester. One-time fee: $150.

The Catholic University of America, School of Arts and Sciences, Department of Education, Washington, DC 20064. Offers Catholic school leadership (MA); education (Certificate); secondary education (MA); special education (MA), including early childhood, non-categorical. *Accreditation:* NCATE. *Program availability:* Part-time. *Faculty:* 8 full-time (7 women), 2 part-time/adjunct (both women). *Students:* 7 full-time (6 women), 21 part-time (13 women); includes 5 minority (2 Black or African American, non-Hispanic/Latino; 3 Hispanic/Latino), 3 international. Average age 38. 22 applicants, 45% accepted, 3 enrolled. In 2016, 14 master's awarded. *Degree requirements:* For master's, comprehensive exam, thesis or alternative; for Certificate, action research project. *Entrance requirements:* For master's, GRE General Test or MAT, statement of purpose, official copies of academic transcripts, three letters of recommendation, interview; for Certificate, PRAXIS I, statement of purpose, official copies of academic transcripts, three letters of recommendation, interview. Additional exam requirements/recommendations for international students: Required—TOEFL (minimum score 550 paper-based; 80 iBT). *Application deadline:* For fall admission, 7/15 priority date for domestic students, 7/1 for international students; for spring admission, 11/15 priority date for domestic students, 11/1 for international students. Applications are processed on a rolling basis. Application fee: $55. Electronic applications accepted. *Expenses:* $42,850 per year; $1,170 per credit; $200 per semester part-time fees. *Financial support:* Fellowships, research assistantships, teaching assistantships, Federal Work-Study, scholarships/grants, tuition waivers (full and partial), and unspecified assistantships available. Financial award application deadline: 2/1; financial award applicants required to submit FAFSA. *Faculty research:* Special education, early childhood education, educational psychology, Catholic school administration, leadership and policy studies, counseling, curriculum and instruction. *Total annual research expenditures:* $54,518. *Unit head:* Dr. John Convey, Chair, 202-319-5810, Fax: 202-319-5815, E-mail: convey@cua.edu. *Application contact:* Director of Graduate Admissions, 202-319-5057, Fax: 202-319-6533, E-mail: cua-admissions@cua.edu.
Website: http://education.cua.edu/

Centenary College of Louisiana, Graduate Programs, Department of Education, Shreveport, LA 71104. Offers elementary education (MAT); secondary education (MAT). *Program availability:* Part-time, evening/weekend. *Faculty:* 2 full-time (1 woman), 3 part-time/adjunct (all women). *Students:* 1 (woman) full-time, 47 part-time (30 women). In 2016, 25 master's awarded. *Degree requirements:* For master's, comprehensive exam. *Entrance requirements:* For master's, PRAXIS I and II (for MAT), undergraduate degree, minimum GPA of 2.5. *Application deadline:* For fall admission, 7/1 for domestic and international students; for spring admission, 11/1 for domestic and international students; for summer admission, 4/1 for domestic and international students. Application fee: $50. *Expenses:* Contact institution. *Financial support:* Unspecified assistantships available. *Faculty research:* Teachers as advocates for teachers, portfolio assessment, disabled readers. *Unit head:* Dr. Dominic Salinas, Director, 318-869-5225, Fax: 318-869-5795, E-mail: dsalinas@centenary.edu. *Application contact:* Lori Payne, Administrative Assistant, 318-869-5223, Fax: 318-869-5795, E-mail: lpayne@centenary.edu.

Central Connecticut State University, School of Graduate Studies, School of Engineering, Science and Technology, Department of Mathematical Sciences, New Britain, CT 06050-4010. Offers data mining (MS, Certificate); mathematics (MA, MS), including actuarial science (MA), computer science (MA), statistics (MA); mathematics education leadership (Sixth Year Certificate); mathematics for secondary education (Certificate). *Program availability:* Part-time, evening/weekend, 100% online. *Faculty:* 14 full-time (4 women). *Students:* 8 full-time (5 women), 73 part-time (37 women); includes 17 minority (4 Black or African American, non-Hispanic/Latino; 7 Asian, non-Hispanic/Latino; 4 Hispanic/Latino; 2 Two or more races, non-Hispanic/Latino), 4 international. Average age 37. 44 applicants, 68% accepted, 21 enrolled. In 2016, 23 master's, 1 other advanced degree awarded. *Degree requirements:* For master's, comprehensive exam, thesis or alternative, special project; for other advanced degree, qualifying exam. *Entrance requirements:* For master's, minimum undergraduate GPA of 2.7; for other advanced degree, minimum undergraduate GPA of 3.0, essay, letters of recommendation. Additional exam requirements/recommendations for international students: Required—TOEFL (minimum score 550 paper-based; 79 iBT). *Application deadline:* For fall admission, 5/1 for domestic and international students; for spring admission, 11/1 for domestic and international students. Applications are processed on a rolling basis. Application fee: $50. Electronic applications accepted. *Expenses: Tuition, area resident:* Full-time $6497; part-time $606 per credit. Tuition, state resident: full-time $9748; part-time $622 per credit. Tuition, nonresident: full-time $18,102; part-time $622 per credit. *Required fees:* $4459; $246 per credit. *Financial support:* In 2016–17, 18 students received support. Career-related internships or fieldwork, Federal Work-Study, and scholarships/grants available. Support available to part-time students. Financial award application deadline: 3/1; financial award applicants required to submit FAFSA. *Faculty research:* Statistics, actuarial mathematics, computer systems and engineering, computer programming techniques, operations research. *Unit head:* Dr. Philip Halloran, Chair, 860-832-2835, E-mail: halloranp@ccsu.edu. *Application contact:* Patricia Gardner, Associate Director of Graduate Studies, 860-832-2350, Fax: 860-832-2362.
Website: http://www.ccsu.edu/mathematics/

Central Michigan University, Central Michigan University Global Campus, Program in Educational Leadership, Mount Pleasant, MI 48859. Offers K-12 leadership (Ed D). *Program availability:* Part-time, evening/weekend. *Faculty:* 14 full-time (5 women), 17 part-time/adjunct (7 women). *Students:* 43 (27 women); includes 13 minority (11 Black or African American, non-Hispanic/Latino; 2 Two or more races, non-Hispanic/Latino). Average age 43. In 2016, 3 doctorates awarded. *Entrance requirements:* Additional exam requirements/recommendations for international students: Required—TOEFL. *Application deadline:* Applications are processed on a rolling basis. Application fee: $50. Electronic applications accepted. *Financial support:* Scholarships/grants available. Support available to part-time students. *Unit head:* Patrick Graham, Coordinator, New Program and Cohort Enrollment Support, 989-774-1661, E-mail: graha1pm@cmich.edu. *Application contact:* 877-268-4636, E-mail: cmuglobal@cmich.edu.

Central Michigan University, College of Graduate Studies, College of Education and Human Services, Department of Teacher Education and Professional Development, Mount Pleasant, MI 48859. Offers educational technology (MA, Graduate Certificate); elementary education (MA), including classroom teaching, early childhood; reading and literacy K-12 (MA); secondary education (MA). *Program availability:* Part-time, evening/weekend. *Degree requirements:* For master's, thesis or alternative. Electronic applications accepted. *Faculty research:* Integrating literacy across the curriculum, science teaching and aesthetic learning in science, diversity education, educational technology, educational psychology and child development.

Central Michigan University, College of Graduate Studies, College of Science and Technology, Department of Chemistry, Mount Pleasant, MI 48859. Offers chemistry (MS); teaching chemistry (MA), including teaching college chemistry, teaching high school chemistry. *Program availability:* Part-time. *Degree requirements:* For master's, comprehensive exam, thesis or alternative. *Entrance requirements:* For master's, GRE. Electronic applications accepted. *Faculty research:* Analytical and organic-inorganic chemistry, biochemistry, catalysis, dendrimer and polymer studies, nanotechnology.

Chadron State College, School of Professional and Graduate Studies, Department of Education, Chadron, NE 69337. Offers business (MA Ed); community counseling (MA Ed); educational administration (MS Ed, Sp Ed); elementary education (MS Ed); history (MA Ed); language and literature (MA Ed); secondary administration (MS Ed); secondary education (MS Ed). *Accreditation:* NCATE. *Program availability:* Part-time, evening/weekend, online learning. *Degree requirements:* For master's, thesis optional. *Entrance requirements:* For master's, GRE General Test, GRE Writing Test, minimum GPA of 2.75 or 12 graduate hours at CSC with minimum GPA of 3.25. Additional exam requirements/recommendations for international students: Required—TOEFL. Electronic applications accepted. *Faculty research:* Rural education, technology, mental health.

Chaminade University of Honolulu, Office of Professional and Continuing Education, Program in Education, Honolulu, HI 96816-1578. Offers child development (M Ed); early childhood education (MAT); educational leadership (M Ed); elementary education (MAT); instructional leadership (M Ed); Montessori (M Ed); secondary education (MAT); special education (MAT). *Program availability:* Part-time, evening/weekend, 100% online, blended/hybrid learning. *Faculty:* 7 full-time (4 women), 8 part-time/adjunct (6 women). *Students:* 98 full-time (80 women), 82 part-time (62 women); includes 110 minority (6 Black or African American, non-Hispanic/Latino; 2 American Indian or Alaska Native, non-Hispanic/Latino; 51 Asian, non-Hispanic/Latino; 9 Hispanic/Latino; 41 Native Hawaiian or other Pacific Islander, non-Hispanic/Latino; 1 Two or more races, non-Hispanic/Latino), 1 international. Average age 35. 38 applicants, 100% accepted, 29 enrolled. In 2016, 79 master's awarded. *Degree requirements:* For master's, thesis or alternative. *Entrance requirements:* For master's, PRAXIS (for MAT), minimum GPA of 2.75 (for M Ed), 3.0 (for MAT); 2 letters of recommendation, resume, writing sample (for MAT). Additional exam requirements/recommendations for international students: Required—TOEFL (minimum score 550 paper-based; 79 iBT). *Application deadline:* Applications are processed on a rolling basis. Application fee: $40. Electronic applications accepted. *Expenses:* $740 per credit hour plus $93 fee per online course. *Financial support:* Applicants required to submit FAFSA. *Unit head:* Dr. Dale Fryxell, Interim Dean, 808-739-4684, Fax: 808-739-4607, E-mail: edu-advising@chaminade.edu. *Application contact:* 808-735-4755, E-mail: gradserv@chaminade.edu.
Website: http://www.chaminade.edu/education

Chapman University, College of Educational Studies, Orange, CA 92866. Offers counseling (MA), including school counseling (MA, Credential); education (PhD), including cultural and curricular studies, disability studies, leadership studies, school psychology (PhD, Credential); educational psychology (MA); leadership development (MA); multiple subjects (Credential), including Spanish/English bilingual; pupil personnel services (Credential), including school counseling (MA, Credential), school psychology (PhD, Credential); school psychology (Ed S); single subject (Credential); special education (MA, Credential), including mild/moderate (Credential), moderate/severe (Credential); teaching (MA), including elementary education, secondary education, secondary music education. *Accreditation:* TEAC. *Program availability:* Part-time, evening/weekend. *Faculty:* 29 full-time (14 women), 36 part-time/adjunct (28 women). *Students:* 186 full-time (148 women), 186 part-time (134 women); includes 144 minority (9 Black or African American, non-Hispanic/Latino; 39 Asian, non-Hispanic/Latino; 78 Hispanic/Latino; 2 Native Hawaiian or other Pacific Islander, non-Hispanic/Latino; 16 Two or more races, non-Hispanic/Latino), 8 international. Average age 29. 143 applicants, 63% accepted, 64 enrolled. In 2016, 111 master's, 24 doctorates awarded. *Degree requirements:* For doctorate, thesis/dissertation. *Entrance requirements:* Additional exam requirements/recommendations for international students: Required—TOEFL (minimum score 550 paper-based, 80 iBT), IELTS (6.5), PTE Academic (53), or CAE. *Application deadline:* Applications are processed on a rolling basis. Application fee: $60. Electronic applications accepted. *Expenses:* Contact institution. *Financial support:* Fellowships and scholarships/grants available. Financial award application deadline: 3/2; financial award applicants required to submit FAFSA. *Unit head:* Dr. Margaret Grogan, Dean, 714-516-5968, E-mail: grogan@chapman.edu. *Application contact:* Sara Simon, Graduate Admission Counselor, 714-997-6770, E-mail: simon@chapman.edu.
Website: http://www.chapman.edu/CES/

Chatham University, Program in Education, Pittsburgh, PA 15232-2826. Offers early childhood education (MAT); elementary education (MAT); environmental education (K-12) (MAT); secondary art (MAT); secondary biology education (MAT); secondary chemistry education (MAT); secondary English education (MAT); secondary math education (MAT); secondary physics education (MAT); secondary social studies education (MAT); special education (MAT). *Degree requirements:* For master's, thesis, teaching experience. *Entrance requirements:* For master's, minimum GPA of 3.0, sample of written work, recommendation letters. Additional exam requirements/recommendations for international students: Required—TOEFL (minimum score 600 paper-based; 100 iBT), IELTS (minimum score 7), TWE. Electronic applications accepted. Application fee is waived when completed online. *Expenses: Tuition:* Full-time $16,254; part-time $903 per credit hour. *Required fees:* $468; $26 per credit hour. *Faculty research:* Gifted education, environmental education, technology in education, writing as learning, class size and achievement.

Chestnut Hill College, School of Graduate Studies, Department of Education, Program in Secondary Education, Philadelphia, PA 19118-2693. Offers M Ed. *Program availability:* Part-time, evening/weekend. *Degree requirements:* For master's, thesis optional. *Entrance requirements:* For master's, PRAXIS I or proof of teaching certification, letters of recommendation; writing sample; 6 graduate credits with minimum B grade if undergraduate GPA less than 3.0. Additional exam requirements/recommendations for international students: Required—TOEFL (minimum score 500 paper-based), IELTS (minimum score 6.0), or TWE (minimum score 22). Electronic applications accepted. *Expenses:* Contact institution. *Faculty research:* Science teaching.

Chicago State University, School of Graduate and Professional Studies, College of Education, Department of Technology and Education, Chicago, IL 60628. Offers secondary education (MAT); technology and education (MS Ed). *Program availability:* Online learning. *Degree requirements:* For master's, thesis optional. *Entrance requirements:* For master's, minimum GPA of 2.75.

The Citadel, The Military College of South Carolina, Citadel Graduate College, Zucker Family School of Education, Charleston, SC 29409. Offers elementary/secondary school administration and supervision (M Ed); elementary/secondary school counseling (M Ed); interdisciplinary STEM education (M Ed); literacy education (M Ed, Graduate Certificate); middle grades (MAT), including English, mathematics, science, social studies; physical education (grades K-12) (MAT); school superintendency (Ed S); secondary education (MAT), including biology, English, mathematics, social studies; student affairs (Graduate Certificate); student affairs and college counseling (M Ed). *Accreditation:* NCATE. *Program availability:* Part-time, evening/weekend, 100% online, blended/hybrid learning. *Faculty:* 9 full-time (4 women), 9 part-time/adjunct (5 women). *Students:* 70 full-time (58 women), 249 part-time (200 women); includes 87 minority (70 Black or African American, non-Hispanic/Latino; 1 Asian, non-Hispanic/Latino; 9 Hispanic/Latino; 7 Two or more races, non-Hispanic/Latino), 2 international. 146 applicants, 98% accepted, 105 enrolled. In 2016, 85 master's, 7 other advanced degrees awarded. *Degree requirements:* For master's, comprehensive exam (for some programs). *Entrance requirements:* For master's, GRE (minimum combined verbal and quantitative score of 290) or MAT (minimum score 396). Additional exam requirements/recommendations for international students: Required—TOEFL (minimum score 550 paper-based; 79 iBT). *Application deadline:* Applications are processed on a rolling basis. Application fee: $40. Electronic applications accepted. *Expenses:* Tuition, state resident: full-time $5121; part-time $569 per credit hour. Tuition, nonresident: full-time $8613; part-time $957 per credit hour. *Required fees:* $90 per term. *Financial support:* Fellowships and unspecified assistantships available. Support available to part-time students. Financial award application deadline: 7/1; financial award applicants required to submit FAFSA. *Unit head:* Dr. Larry G. Daniel, Dean, 843-953-5097, E-mail: ldaniel@citadel.edu. *Application contact:* Dr. Tammy J. Graham, Associate Professor, 843-953-6854, E-mail: tammy.graham@citadel.edu.
Website: http://www.citadel.edu/root/education-graduate-programs

City College of the City University of New York, Graduate School, School of Education, Department of Secondary Education, New York, NY 10031-9198. Offers adolescent mathematics education (MA, AC); English education (MA); middle school mathematics education (MS); science education (MA); social studies education (AC). *Accreditation:* NCATE. *Entrance requirements:* For master's, Liberal Arts and Sciences Test (LAST), Content Specialty Test (CST). Additional exam requirements/recommendations for international students: Required—TOEFL. Tuition and fees vary according to course load, degree level and program.

Clarkson University, Program in Education, Schenectady, NY 12308. Offers adolescence education 7-12 (MAT); technology education K-12 (MAT). *Accreditation:* TEAC. *Faculty:* 8 full-time (all women), 31 part-time/adjunct (17 women). *Students:* 38 full-time (23 women), 2 part-time (0 women); includes 6 minority (3 Asian, non-Hispanic/Latino; 2 Hispanic/Latino; 1 Two or more races, non-Hispanic/Latino), 7 international. 39 applicants, 79% accepted, 26 enrolled. In 2016, 15 master's awarded. *Degree requirements:* For master's, thesis (for some programs), thesis or project. *Entrance requirements:* For master's, GRE, minimum undergraduate GPA of 3.0. Additional exam requirements/recommendations for international students: Required—TOEFL (minimum score 550 paper-based, 80 iBT) or IELTS (6.5). *Application deadline:* Applications are processed on a rolling basis. Application fee: $50. Electronic applications accepted. *Expenses:* $900 per credit. *Financial support:* Scholarships/grants available. *Unit head:* Dr. Catherine Snyder, Chair of Education, 518-631-9870, E-mail: csnyder@clarkson.edu. *Application contact:* Dan Capogna, Graduate Admissions Contact, 518-631-9910, E-mail: graduate@clarkson.edu.
Website: http://graduate.clarkson.edu

Clemson University, Graduate School, College of Education, Department of Teaching and Learning, Program in Secondary Math and Science, Clemson, SC 29634. Offers MAT. *Accreditation:* NCATE. *Faculty:* 15 full-time (12 women). *Students:* 13 full-time (10 women); includes 1 minority (Black or African American, non-Hispanic/Latino). Average age 28. In 2016, 16 master's awarded. *Degree requirements:* For master's, comprehensive exam, student teaching. *Entrance requirements:* For master's, GRE General Test, unofficial transcripts, letters of recommendation. Additional exam requirements/recommendations for international students: Required—TOEFL (minimum score 540 paper-based; 80 iBT). *Application deadline:* For fall admission, 4/1 for domestic and international students. Applications are processed on a rolling basis. Application fee: $80 ($90 for international students). Electronic applications accepted. *Expenses:* $4,841 per semester full-time resident, $9,640 per semester full-time non-resident, $612 per credit hour part-time resident, $1,223 per credit hour part-time non-resident. *Financial support:* In 2016–17, 10 students received support, including 10 fellowships with partial tuition reimbursements available (averaging $6,862 per year). Financial award application deadline: 4/1. *Faculty research:* Hegemony, culture and mathematics; representations in science education, pre-service science teacher preparation, developing standards-based mathematics pedagogy, environmental sustainability perspectives. *Unit head:* Dr. Jeff Marshall, Department Chair, 864-656-2059, E-mail: marsha9@clemson.edu. *Application contact:* Alison Search, Student Services Coordinator, 864-250-8880, E-mail: alisonp@clemson.edu.
Website: http://www.clemson.edu/education/academics/masters-specialist-programs/masters-education-arts-teaching-mat-secondary-math-science/index.html

Colgate University, Master of Arts in Teaching Program, Hamilton, NY 13346-1386. Offers MAT. *Accreditation:* TEAC. *Degree requirements:* For master's, special project or thesis. *Entrance requirements:* For master's, GRE General Test, interview. *Faculty research:* Culturally-responsive teaching, comparative education, moral development in education, politics in education, educational psychology.

The College of New Jersey, Office of Graduate and Advancing Education, School of Education, Department of Educational Administration and Secondary Education, Program in Secondary Education, Ewing, NJ 08628. Offers MAT. *Degree requirements:* For master's, comprehensive exam. *Entrance requirements:* For master's, GRE, minimum GPA of 3.0 in field or 2.75 overall. Additional exam requirements/recommendations for international students: Required—TOEFL. Electronic applications accepted.

College of St. Joseph, Graduate Programs, Division of Education, Program in Secondary Education, Rutland, VT 05701-3899. Offers English (M Ed); social studies (M Ed). *Program availability:* Part-time, evening/weekend. *Degree requirements:* For master's, comprehensive exam. *Entrance requirements:* For master's, PRAXIS I, official college transcripts; 2 letters of reference; minimum GPA of 3.0 (initial licensure) or 2.7

(nonlicensure); interview. Additional exam requirements/recommendations for international students: Required—TOEFL (minimum score 550 paper-based). *Application deadline:* Applications are processed on a rolling basis. Application fee: $35. Electronic applications accepted. *Expenses: Tuition:* Full-time $13,800; part-time $560 per credit. *Required fees:* $75 per semester. Full-time tuition and fees vary according to course load. *Financial support:* Career-related internships or fieldwork, Federal Work-Study, and unspecified assistantships available. Support available to part-time students. Financial award application deadline: 3/1. *Unit head:* Dr. Maria Bove, Chair, 802-773-5900 Ext. 3243, Fax: 802-776-5258, E-mail: mbove@csj.edu. *Application contact:* Alan Young, Director of Admissions, 802-773-5900 Ext. 3227, Fax: 802-776-5310, E-mail: alanyoung@csj.edu.

The College of Saint Rose, Graduate Studies, Thelma P. Lally School of Education, Programs in Special Education, Albany, NY 12203-1419. Offers adolescence education and special education (MS Ed); childhood education and special education (MS Ed); childhood special education (MS Ed); early childhood special education (MS Ed); special education (Certificate); special education professional (MS Ed). *Accreditation:* NCATE. *Students:* 11 full-time (9 women), 19 part-time (17 women), 2 international. Average age 28. 17 applicants, 76% accepted, 7 enrolled. In 2016, 19 master's, 4 Certificates awarded. *Degree requirements:* For master's, comprehensive exam (for some programs), thesis or alternative, research project. *Entrance requirements:* For master's, minimum undergraduate GPA of 3.0. Additional exam requirements/recommendations for international students: Required—TOEFL (minimum score 550 paper-based; 80 iBT), IELTS (minimum score 6), PTE (minimum score 56). *Application deadline:* For fall admission, 4/1 priority date for domestic and international students; for spring admission, 10/15 priority date for domestic and international students; for summer admission, 3/15 priority date for domestic and international students. Applications are processed on a rolling basis. Application fee: $40. Electronic applications accepted. *Expenses: Tuition:* Full-time $14,382; part-time $799 per credit. *Required fees:* $814; $32 per credit. $88 per semester. Tuition and fees vary according to course load. *Financial support:* Career-related internships or fieldwork, scholarships/grants, tuition waivers (partial), and unspecified assistantships available. Support available to part-time students. Financial award application deadline: 4/15. *Unit head:* Susan DeLuke, Chair, 518-454-5194, E-mail: delukes@strose.edu. *Application contact:* Cris Murray, Assistant Vice President for Graduate Recruitment and Enrollment, 518-485-3390, E-mail: grad@strose.edu.
Website: https://www.strose.edu/special-education/

The College of Saint Rose, Graduate Studies, Thelma P. Lally School of Education, Teacher Education Programs, Albany, NY 12203-1419. Offers adolescence education (MS Ed, Advanced Certificate); adolescence education/special education (Advanced Certificate); childhood education (MS Ed); curriculum and instruction (MS Ed); early childhood education (MS Ed). *Students:* 72 full-time (59 women), 32 part-time (26 women); includes 6 minority (4 Black or African American, non-Hispanic/Latino; 2 Hispanic/Latino), 2 international. Average age 28. 60 applicants, 78% accepted, 25 enrolled. In 2016, 37 master's awarded. *Entrance requirements:* For master's, minimum undergraduate GPA of 3.0. Additional exam requirements/recommendations for international students: Required—TOEFL (minimum score 550 paper-based; 80 iBT), IELTS (minimum score 6), PTE (minimum score 56). *Application deadline:* For fall admission, 4/1 priority date for domestic and international students; for spring admission, 10/15 priority date for domestic and international students; for summer admission, 3/15 priority date for domestic and international students. Applications are processed on a rolling basis. Application fee: $40. Electronic applications accepted. *Expenses: Tuition:* Full-time $14,382; part-time $799 per credit. *Required fees:* $814; $32 per credit. $88 per semester. Tuition and fees vary according to course load. *Financial support:* Career-related internships or fieldwork, scholarships/grants, tuition waivers (partial), and unspecified assistantships available. Support available to part-time students. Financial award application deadline: 4/15. *Unit head:* Dr. Drey Martone, Chair, 518-454-5262, E-mail: martoned@strose.edu. *Application contact:* Cris Murray, Assistant Vice President for Graduate Recruitment and Enrollment, 518-485-3390, Fax: 518-458-5479, E-mail: grad@strose.edu.
Website: https://www.strose.edu/academics/schools/school-of-education/

College of Staten Island of the City University of New York, Graduate Programs, School of Education, Program in Adolescence Education, Staten Island, NY 10314-6600. Offers biology (MS Ed); English (MS Ed); mathematics (MS Ed); social studies (MS Ed). *Program availability:* Part-time, evening/weekend. *Faculty:* 18 full-time, 8 part-time/adjunct. *Students:* 4 full-time, 84 part-time. Average age 29. 40 applicants, 88% accepted, 14 enrolled. In 2016, 41 master's awarded. *Degree requirements:* For master's, thesis, educational research project supervised by faculty; minimum of 33-38 credits distributed among 11 courses or minimum of 46-53 credits. *Entrance requirements:* For master's, GRE General Test or an approved equivalent examination, relevant bachelor's degree, minimum overall GPA of 3.0, two letters of recommendation, one- or two-page personal statement. Additional exam requirements/recommendations for international students: Required—TOEFL (minimum score 550 paper-based; 79 iBT), IELTS (minimum score 6.5). *Application deadline:* For fall admission, 4/25 for domestic and international students; for spring admission, 11/25 for domestic and international students. Applications are processed on a rolling basis. Application fee: $125. Electronic applications accepted. *Expenses:* Tuition, state resident: full-time $10,130; part-time $425 per credit. Tuition, nonresident: full-time $18,720; part-time $780 per credit. *Required fees:* $181.10 per semester. Tuition and fees vary according to program. *Faculty research:* Development and assessment of TPACK (technological pedagogical content knowledge), technology and differentiation in stem classrooms, teacher effectiveness and student achievement, teacher knowledge, knowledge transfer from college to classroom. *Unit head:* Dr. Bethany Rogers, Graduate Faculty Advisor, 718-982-4247, E-mail: bethany.rogers@csi.cuny.edu. *Application contact:* Sasha Spence, Associate Director for Graduate Admissions, 718-982-2019, Fax: 718-982-2500, E-mail: sasha.spence@csi.cuny.edu.
Website: http://www.csi.cuny.edu/catalog/graduate/graduate-programs-in-education.htm#o2608

The College of William and Mary, School of Education, Program in Curriculum and Instruction, Williamsburg, VA 23187-8795. Offers elementary education (MA Ed); gifted education (MA Ed); literacy leadership (MA Ed); math specialist (MA Ed); secondary education (MA Ed), including English, foreign language, math, science, social studies; special education (MA Ed). *Accreditation:* NCATE. *Program availability:* Part-time. *Faculty:* 30 full-time (21 women), 48 part-time/adjunct (38 women). *Students:* 60 full-time (47 women), 14 part-time (all women); includes 13 minority (1 Black or African American, non-Hispanic/Latino; 1 American Indian or Alaska Native, non-Hispanic/Latino; 2 Asian, non-Hispanic/Latino; 7 Hispanic/Latino; 2 Two or more races, non-Hispanic/Latino). Average age 26. 134 applicants, 79% accepted, 60 enrolled. In 2016, 77 master's awarded. *Degree requirements:* For master's, project. *Entrance requirements:* For master's, GRE, MAT, PRAXIS Core Academic Skills for Educators, minimum GPA of 2.5. Additional exam requirements/recommendations for international students: Required—TOEFL (minimum score 100 iBT), IELTS (minimum score 7). *Application deadline:* For fall admission, 1/15 for domestic and international students; for spring admission, 10/1 for domestic and international students. Application fee: $50. Electronic applications accepted. *Expenses:* $14,258 per year in-state full-time, $275 per credit in-state part-time; $30,500 per year out-of-state full-time, $1,200 per credit out-of-state part-time. *Financial support:* In 2016–17, 30 students received support, including 3 research assistantships (averaging $14,259 per year); scholarships/grants and unspecified assistantships also available. Financial award application deadline: 1/15; financial award applicants required to submit FAFSA. *Faculty research:* Educational technology, professional development and evaluation, inclusive education, rural education, education policy. *Unit head:* Dr. Jeremy D. Stoddard, Department Chair, 757-221-2348, E-mail: jdstod@wm.edu. *Application contact:* Dorothy Smith Osborne, Assistant Dean for Academic Programs and Student Services, 757-221-2317, E-mail: dsosbo@wm.edu.
Website: http://education.wm.edu

The Colorado College, Education Department, Program in Secondary Education, Colorado Springs, CO 80903-3294. Offers art teaching (K-12) (MAT); English teaching (MAT); foreign language teaching (MAT); mathematics teaching (MAT); music teaching (MAT); science teaching (MAT); social studies teaching (MAT). *Degree requirements:* For master's, thesis, internship. Electronic applications accepted.

Columbus State University, Graduate Studies, College of Education and Health Professions, Department of Teacher Education, Columbus, GA 31907-5645. Offers curriculum and instruction in accomplished teaching (M Ed); early childhood education (M Ed, MAT, Ed S); middle grades education (M Ed, MAT, Ed S); secondary education (M Ed, MAT, Ed S), including biology (MAT), chemistry (MAT), earth and space science (MAT), English/language arts, general science (M Ed), history (MAT), mathematics, science (Ed S), social science (M Ed, Ed S); special education (M Ed, MAT, Ed S), including general curriculum (M Ed, MAT); teacher leadership (M Ed). *Accreditation:* NCATE. *Program availability:* Part-time, evening/weekend, 100% online, blended/hybrid learning. *Faculty:* 20 full-time (13 women), 19 part-time/adjunct (16 women). *Students:* 92 full-time (66 women), 212 part-time (179 women); includes 113 minority (104 Black or African American, non-Hispanic/Latino; 1 American Indian or Alaska Native, non-Hispanic/Latino; 2 Asian, non-Hispanic/Latino; 4 Hispanic/Latino; 2 Two or more races, non-Hispanic/Latino), 5 international. Average age 34. 209 applicants, 56% accepted, 79 enrolled. In 2016, 111 master's, 18 other advanced degrees awarded. *Degree requirements:* For Ed S, thesis or alternative. *Entrance requirements:* For master's, GRE General Test, minimum undergraduate GPA of 2.75; for Ed S, GRE General Test, minimum undergraduate GPA of 2.75, graduate 3.0. Additional exam requirements/recommendations for international students: Required—TOEFL (minimum score 550 paper-based; 79 iBT). *Application deadline:* For fall admission, 6/30 for domestic students, 5/1 for international students; for spring admission, 11/1 for domestic and international students; for summer admission, 3/1 for domestic and international students. Applications are processed on a rolling basis. Application fee: $50. Electronic applications accepted. *Expenses:* Tuition, state resident: full-time $4804; part-time $2412 per semester hour. Tuition, nonresident: full-time $19,218; part-time $9612 per semester hour. *Required fees:* $1850; $1850 per semester hour. Tuition and fees vary according to program. *Financial support:* In 2016–17, 60 students received support, including 12 research assistantships with partial tuition reimbursements available (averaging $3,000 per year); career-related internships or fieldwork, Federal Work-Study, institutionally sponsored loans, scholarships/grants, tuition waivers (partial), and unspecified assistantships also available. Support available to part-time students. Financial award application deadline: 5/1; financial award applicants required to submit FAFSA. *Unit head:* Dr. Jan Burcham, Department Chair, 706-507-8519, Fax: 706-568-3134, E-mail: burcham_jan@columbusstate.edu. *Application contact:* Kristin Williams, Director of International and Graduate Recruitment, 706-507-8848, Fax: 706-568-5091, E-mail: williams_kristin@columbusstate.edu.
Website: http://te.columbusstate.edu/

Concordia University, College of Education, Portland, OR 97211-6099. Offers career and technical education (M Ed); curriculum and instruction (M Ed), including adolescent literacy, career and technical education, e-learning/technology education, early childhood education, English for speakers of other languages, English language development, environmental education, mathematics, methods and curriculum, reading, science, teacher leadership, the inclusive classroom; early childhood (MAT); education leadership (Ed D); educational administration (M Ed); elementary education (MAT); secondary education (MAT); special education (M Ed); teacher leadership (Ed D). *Program availability:* Part-time, online learning. *Degree requirements:* For master's, comprehensive exam, work samples/portfolio. *Entrance requirements:* For master's, California Basic Educational Skills Test or PRAXIS I, minimum undergraduate GPA of 2.8, graduate 3.0; 2 letters of recommendation. Additional exam requirements/recommendations for international students: Required—TOEFL (minimum score 525 paper-based). Electronic applications accepted. *Faculty research:* Learner-centered classroom, brain-based learning, future of online learning.

Concordia University Chicago, College of Education, Program in Teaching, River Forest, IL 60305-1499. Offers early childhood education (MAT); elementary education (MAT); secondary education (MAT). *Degree requirements:* For master's, thesis or alternative. *Entrance requirements:* For master's, minimum GPA of 2.9. Additional exam requirements/recommendations for international students: Required—TOEFL (minimum score 550 paper-based). Electronic applications accepted.

Concordia University, Nebraska, Graduate Programs in Education, Program in Educational Administration, Seward, NE 68434-1556. Offers elementary and secondary education (M Ed); elementary education (M Ed); secondary education (M Ed). *Accreditation:* NCATE. *Program availability:* Part-time. *Degree requirements:* For master's, thesis or alternative. *Entrance requirements:* For master's, GRE, MAT, or NTE, BS in education or equivalent, minimum GPA of 3.0.

Converse College, School of Education and Graduate Studies, Program in Secondary Education, Spartanburg, SC 29302. Offers biology (MAT); chemistry (MAT); English (M Ed, MAT); mathematics (M Ed, MAT); natural sciences (M Ed); social sciences (M Ed, MAT). *Program availability:* Part-time. *Degree requirements:* For master's, capstone paper. *Entrance requirements:* For master's, NTE or PRAXIS II (M Ed), minimum GPA of 2.75, 2 recommendations. *Application deadline:* For fall admission, 8/1 for domestic and international students; for winter admission, 11/15 for domestic and international students; for spring admission, 1/15 for domestic and international students. Applications are processed on a rolling basis. Application fee: $40. Electronic applications accepted. *Expenses: Tuition:* Full-time $3600; part-time $400 per credit hour. *Required fees:* $70 per term. *Financial support:* Available to part-time students. Applicants required to submit FAFSA. *Application contact:* 864-596-9404, E-mail: graduate@converse.edu.

Cornell University, Graduate School, Graduate Fields of Agriculture and Life Sciences, Field of Education, Ithaca, NY 14853. Offers adult and extension education (MPS, MS, PhD); learning, teaching, and social policy (MPS, MS, PhD); mathematics 7-12 (MS). Terminal master's awarded for partial completion of doctoral program. *Degree requirements:* For master's, thesis (MS); for doctorate, comprehensive exam, thesis/dissertation. *Entrance requirements:* For master's and doctorate, GRE General Test, sample of written work (recommended), 2 letters of recommendation. Additional exam requirements/recommendations for international students: Required—TOEFL (minimum score 550 paper-based; 77 iBT). Electronic applications accepted. *Faculty research:* Moral development and professional ethics, public issues education and community development, socio/political issues in public education, teacher education and curriculum in agricultural science and mathematics, extension research.

Creighton University, Graduate School, College of Arts and Sciences, Department of Education, Program in Teaching, Omaha, NE 68178-0001. Offers elementary teaching (M Ed); secondary teaching (M Ed). *Program availability:* Part-time, evening/weekend. *Faculty:* 10 full-time (5 women). *Students:* 14 full-time (11 women), 17 part-time (11 women); includes 4 minority (3 Black or African American, non-Hispanic/Latino; 1 Two or more races, non-Hispanic/Latino). Average age 26. In 2016, 18 master's awarded. *Degree requirements:* For master's, portfolio. *Entrance requirements:* For master's, 3 letters of recommendation, 2 writing samples. Additional exam requirements/recommendations for international students: Required—TOEFL (minimum score 90 iBT). *Application deadline:* For fall admission, 7/1 priority date for domestic students, 3/1 priority date for international students; for winter admission, 12/1 priority date for domestic students, 6/1 priority date for international students; for spring admission, 3/1 priority date for domestic and international students; for summer admission, 3/1 for domestic and international students. Application fee: $50. Electronic applications accepted. *Expenses: Tuition:* Full-time $14,400; part-time $800 per credit hour. *Required fees:* $158 per semester. Tuition and fees vary according to course load, campus/location, program, reciprocity agreements and student's religious affiliation. *Financial support:* Scholarships/grants and tuition waivers (partial) available. Support available to part-time students. Financial award applicants required to submit FAFSA. *Unit head:* Dr. Debra Ponec, Director, 402-280-2557, E-mail: dlponec@creighton.edu. *Application contact:* Lindsay Johnson, Director of Graduate and Adult Recruitment, 402-280-2703, Fax: 402-280-2423, E-mail: gradschool@creighton.edu.

Dakota Wesleyan University, Program in Education, Mitchell, SD 57301-4398. Offers curriculum and instruction (MA Ed); educational policy and administration (MA Ed); preK-12 principal certification (MA Ed); secondary certification (MA Ed). *Program availability:* Part-time, evening/weekend. *Degree requirements:* For master's, comprehensive exam, thesis optional, electronic portfolio. *Entrance requirements:* For master's, minimum GPA of 2.7, elementary statistics course, statement of purpose, official transcripts, resume, three letters of recommendation. Additional exam requirements/recommendations for international students: Required—TOEFL (minimum score 500 paper-based), IELTS (minimum score 6.5). Electronic applications accepted. *Faculty research:* Math, political policy, technology in the classroom.

Dallas Baptist University, Dorothy M. Bush College of Education, Teaching Program, Dallas, TX 75211-9299. Offers distance learning (MAT); early childhood through grade 6 certification (MAT); early childhood-12 (MAT); elementary (MAT); English as a second language (MAT); Montessori (MAT); multisensory (MAT); secondary (MAT). *Program availability:* Part-time, evening/weekend, 100% online, blended/hybrid learning. *Application deadline:* Applications are processed on a rolling basis. Application fee: $25. Electronic applications accepted. Application fee is waived when completed online. *Expenses: Tuition:* Full-time $15,408; part-time $856 per credit hour. *Required fees:* $400 per semester. Tuition and fees vary according to course load and degree level. *Unit head:* Dr. Carolyn Spain, Director, 214-333-5217, E-mail: carolyns@dbu.edu. *Application contact:* Bobby Soto, Director of Admissions, 214-333-5242, E-mail: graduate@dbu.edu.
Website: http://www3.dbu.edu/graduate/mat.asp

Delta State University, Graduate Programs, College of Arts and Sciences, Division of Languages and Literature, Cleveland, MS 38733-0001. Offers secondary education (M Ed), including English. *Program availability:* Part-time. *Degree requirements:* For master's, thesis or alternative.

Delta State University, Graduate Programs, College of Arts and Sciences, Division of Social Sciences and History, Cleveland, MS 38733-0001. Offers community development (MS); social justice and criminology (MSJC); social science secondary education (M Ed), including history, social sciences. *Program availability:* Part-time, online learning. *Degree requirements:* For master's, thesis or alternative.

Delta State University, Graduate Programs, College of Education, Division of Teacher Education, Leadership, and Research, Cleveland, MS 38733-0001. Offers educational administration and supervision (M Ed, Ed S); elementary education (M Ed, MAT, Ed S); professional studies (Ed D), including counselor education, elementary education, higher education; secondary education (MAT); special education (M Ed). *Accreditation:* NCATE. *Program availability:* Part-time, evening/weekend. *Degree requirements:* For master's, thesis optional. *Entrance requirements:* For master's, GRE General Test; for Ed S, master's degree, teaching certificate. Electronic applications accepted. *Faculty research:* Thinking skills, writing across the curriculum, mathematics/science education.

DePaul University, College of Education, Chicago, IL 60614. Offers bilingual bicultural education (M Ed, MA); counseling (M Ed, MA), including clinical mental health counseling, college student development, school counseling; curriculum studies (M Ed, MA, Ed D); early childhood education (M Ed, MA, Ed D); educating adults (MA); educational leadership (M Ed, MA, Ed D), including administration and supervision (M Ed, MA), principal preparation (M Ed, MA); elementary education (MA); mathematics education (MA); mathematics for teaching (MS); middle school mathematics education (MS); reading specialist (M Ed, MA); secondary education (M Ed); social and cultural foundations in education (MA); special education (M Ed, MA); world languages education (M Ed, MA). *Program availability:* Part-time, evening/weekend, online learning. *Degree requirements:* For doctorate, thesis/dissertation. Electronic applications accepted.

DeSales University, Division of Liberal Arts and Social Sciences, Center Valley, PA 18034-9568. Offers criminal justice (MCJ); digital forensics (MCJ, Postbaccalaureate Certificate); education (M Ed), including instructional technology, secondary education, special education, teaching English to speakers of other languages; investigative forensics (MCJ, Postbaccalaureate Certificate). *Program availability:* Part-time, 100% online, blended/hybrid learning. *Faculty:* 5 full-time (3 women), 20 part-time/adjunct (13 women). *Students:* 55 full-time (36 women), 100 part-time (64 women); includes 25 minority (5 Black or African American, non-Hispanic/Latino; 14 Hispanic/Latino; 6 Two or more races, non-Hispanic/Latino). Average age 33. 145 applicants, 80% accepted, 103 enrolled. In 2016, 36 master's awarded. *Entrance requirements:* For master's, bachelor's degree from accredited institution, minimum undergraduate GPA of 3.0, personal statement showing potential of graduate work, three letters of recommendation, professional goal statement. Additional exam requirements/recommendations for international students: Required—TOEFL. *Application deadline:* Applications are processed on a rolling basis. Application fee: $50. Electronic applications accepted. *Expenses: Tuition:* Part-time $815 per credit hour. Tuition and fees vary according to degree level and program. *Financial support:* Applicants required to submit FAFSA. *Unit head:* Dr. Brain Kane, Division Head of Liberal Arts and Social Studies, 610-282-1100 Ext. 1274, E-mail: brian.kane@desales.edu. *Application contact:* Julia Ferraro, Director of Graduate Admissions, 610-282-1100 Ext. 1768, E-mail: gradadmissions@desales.edu.

Drew University, Caspersen School of Graduate Studies, Madison, NJ 07940-1493. Offers conflict resolution and leadership (Certificate), including community leadership, moderation, peace building; history and culture (MA, PhD), including American history, book history, British history, European history, Holocaust and genocide (M Litt, MA, D Litt, PhD), intellectual history, Irish history, print culture, public history; K-12 education (MAT), including art, biology, chemistry, elementary education, English, French, Italian, math, secondary education, special education, teacher of students with disabilities; liberal studies (M Litt, D Litt), including history, Holocaust and genocide (M Litt, MA, D Litt, PhD), Irish/Irish-American studies, literature (M Litt, MMH, D Litt, DMH, CMH), religion, spirituality, teaching in the two-year college, writing; medical humanities (MMH, DMH, CMH), including arts, health, healthcare, literature (M Litt, MMH, D Litt, DMH, CMH), scientific research; poetry (MFA). *Program availability:* Part-time, evening/weekend. *Faculty:* 4 full-time (2 women), 31 part-time/adjunct (16 women). *Students:* 62 full-time (41 women), 199 part-time (130 women); includes 38 minority (17 Black or African American, non-Hispanic/Latino; 3 Asian, non-Hispanic/Latino; 17 Hispanic/Latino; 1 Two or more races, non-Hispanic/Latino), 3 international. Average age 27. 93 applicants, 81% accepted, 46 enrolled. In 2016, 39 master's, 27 doctorates, 26 other advanced degrees awarded. Terminal master's awarded for partial completion of doctoral program. *Degree requirements:* For master's and other advanced degree, thesis (for some programs); for doctorate, one foreign language, comprehensive exam (for some programs), thesis/dissertation. *Entrance requirements:* For master's, PRAXIS Core and Subject Area tests (for MAT), resume, transcripts, writing sample, personal statement, letters of recommendation; for doctorate, GRE (PhD in history and culture), resume, transcripts, writing sample, personal statement, letters of recommendation. Additional exam requirements/recommendations for international students: Required—TOEFL (minimum score 587 paper-based; 94 iBT), IELTS (minimum score 7), TWE (minimum score 4). *Application deadline:* For fall admission, 8/1 for domestic students, 6/1 for international students; for spring admission, 12/1 for domestic students, 10/1 for international students. Applications are processed on a rolling basis. Application fee: $35. Electronic applications accepted. Tuition and fees vary according to program. *Financial support:* Fellowships, research assistantships, teaching assistantships, career-related internships or fieldwork, Federal Work-Study, scholarships/grants, and unspecified assistantships available. Support available to part-time students. Financial award applicants required to submit FAFSA. *Application contact:* Leanne Horinko, Director of Caspersen Admissions, 973-408-3280, E-mail: gradm@drew.edu.
Website: http://www.drew.edu/caspersen

Drury University, Master in Education Program, Springfield, MO 5802. Offers curriculum and instruction (M Ed), including elementary, middle school, secondary; gifted education (M Ed); instructional leadership (M Ed); instructional technology (M Ed); integrated learning (M Ed); online teaching (M Ed); special education (M Ed); special reading (M Ed). *Accreditation:* NCATE. *Program availability:* Part-time, evening/weekend, 100% online, blended/hybrid learning. *Students:* 146 full-time (111 women); includes 6 minority (1 Asian, non-Hispanic/Latino; 3 Hispanic/Latino; 2 Two or more races, non-Hispanic/Latino), 1 international. Average age 34. 42 applicants, 74% accepted. In 2016, 74 master's awarded. *Entrance requirements:* For master's, GRE, bachelor's degree with minimum GPA of 2.75. Additional exam requirements/recommendations for international students: Recommended—TOEFL (minimum score 80 iBT), IELTS (minimum score 6.5). *Application deadline:* For fall admission, 8/4 priority date for domestic and international students; for spring admission, 1/5 priority date for domestic and international students; for summer admission, 5/26 priority date for domestic and international students. Applications are processed on a rolling basis. Application fee: $25 ($50 for international students). Electronic applications accepted. *Expenses:* $352 tuition per credit hour; $7 per credit hour technology fee; $100 graduation fee; $59 portfolio fee (one-time). *Financial support:* In 2016–17, 20 students received support. Career-related internships or fieldwork, scholarships/grants, tuition waivers (partial), and unspecified assistantships available. Financial award application deadline: 6/30; financial award applicants required to submit FAFSA. *Faculty research:* Gifted students, instructional technology, autism, diversity and social justice. *Unit head:* Dr. Asikaa Cosgrove, Director, Master in Education, 417-873-7806, E-mail: acosgrov@drury.edu.
Website: http://www.drury.edu/education-masters

Duquesne University, School of Education, Department of Instruction and Leadership, Program in Secondary Education, Pittsburgh, PA 15282-0001. Offers biology (MS Ed); chemistry (MS Ed); English (MS Ed); K-12 education (MS Ed), including Latin; mathematics (MS Ed); physics (MS Ed); social studies (MS Ed). *Program availability:* Part-time, evening/weekend. *Faculty:* 5 full-time (4 women). *Students:* 21 full-time (8 women), 4 part-time (0 women); includes 3 minority (2 Black or African American, non-Hispanic/Latino; 1 Two or more races, non-Hispanic/Latino). Average age 28. 12 applicants, 100% accepted, 7 enrolled. In 2016, 19 master's awarded. *Degree requirements:* For master's, thesis optional. *Entrance requirements:* For master's, letters of recommendation, letter of intent, interview, bachelor's degree. Additional exam requirements/recommendations for international students: Required—TOEFL (minimum score 550 paper-based), IELTS (minimum score 7). *Application deadline:* For fall admission, 9/1 for domestic students; for spring admission, 1/1 for domestic students. Applications are processed on a rolling basis. Application fee: $0. Electronic applications accepted. *Expenses: Tuition:* Full-time $22,212; part-time $1234 per credit. Tuition and fees vary according to program. *Financial support:* Research assistantships and Federal Work-Study available. Support available to part-time students. *Unit head:* Dr. Melissa Boston, Associate Professor and Director, 412-396-6109, E-mail: bostonm@duq.edu. *Application contact:* Michael Dolinger, Director of Student and Academic Services, 412-396-6647, Fax: 412-396-5585, E-mail: dolingerm@duq.edu.
Website: http://www.duq.edu/academics/schools/education/graduate-programs-education/ms-ed-secondary-education

D'Youville College, Department of Education, Buffalo, NY 14201-1084. Offers educational leadership (Ed D); elementary education (MS Ed); secondary education (MS Ed); special education (MS Ed). *Program availability:* Part-time, evening/weekend. *Degree requirements:* For master's, one foreign language, comprehensive exam, project or thesis. *Entrance requirements:* For master's, GRE (if GPA less than 2.75), minimum GPA of 3.0. Additional exam requirements/recommendations for international students: Required—TOEFL (minimum score 500 paper-based). Electronic applications accepted. *Faculty research:* Developmental disabilities, multiculturalism, early childhood education.

Eastern Connecticut State University, School of Education and Professional Studies/Graduate Division, Program in Secondary Education, Willimantic, CT 06226-2295. Offers MS. *Accreditation:* NCATE. *Program availability:* Part-time, evening/weekend. *Faculty:* 12 full-time (7 women), 21 part-time/adjunct (17 women). *Students:* 26 full-time (13 women), 15 part-time (7 women); includes 5 minority (2 Black or African American, non-Hispanic/Latino; 1 Asian, non-Hispanic/Latino; 1 Hispanic/Latino; 1 Native Hawaiian or other Pacific Islander, non-Hispanic/Latino). Average age 28. 19 applicants, 89% accepted, 17 enrolled. In 2016, 22 master's awarded. *Degree requirements:* For master's, comprehensive exam or thesis. *Entrance requirements:* For master's, PRAXIS I, PRAXIS II, minimum GPA of 3.0, bachelor's degree from accredited institution. Additional exam requirements/recommendations for international students: Required—TOEFL (minimum score 550 paper-based; 79 iBT); Recommended—IELTS (minimum score 6). *Application deadline:* For fall admission, 7/6 priority date for domestic and international students; for spring admission, 11/3 priority date for domestic and international students. Applications are processed on a rolling basis. Application fee: $50. Electronic applications accepted. *Expenses: Tuition, area resident:* Full-time

$11,781; part-time $560 per credit. Tuition, state resident: full-time $15,031; part-time $568 per credit. Tuition, nonresident: full-time $24,581; part-time $568 per credit. *Required fees:* $40 per semester. Full-time tuition and fees vary according to course level, course load and reciprocity agreements. *Financial support:* Research assistantships, teaching assistantships, career-related internships or fieldwork, institutionally sponsored loans, and unspecified assistantships available. Financial award application deadline: 3/1; financial award applicants required to submit FAFSA. *Unit head:* Dr. Jeanelle Day, Advisor, 860-465-4532, Fax: 860-465-5099, E-mail: dayj@easternct.edu. *Application contact:* Paula Goyette, Graduate Division, School of Education and Professional Studies, 860-465-5292, Fax: 860-465-4538, E-mail: graduateadmissions@easternct.edu.

Eastern Kentucky University, The Graduate School, College of Education, Department of Curriculum and Instruction, Program in Secondary and Higher Education, Richmond, KY 40475-3102. Offers secondary education (MA Ed), including agricultural education, art education, biological sciences education, business education, English education, geography education, history education, home economics education, industrial education, mathematical sciences education, physical education, school health education. *Accreditation:* NCATE. *Program availability:* Part-time. *Entrance requirements:* For master's, GRE General Test, minimum GPA of 2.5.

Eastern Michigan University, Graduate School, College of Education, Department of Teacher Education, Programs in K–12 Education, Ypsilanti, MI 48197. Offers middle school education (MA); secondary school education (MA). *Accreditation:* NCATE. *Program availability:* Part-time, evening/weekend, online learning. *Students:* 9 full-time (8 women), 34 part-time (27 women); includes 3 minority (1 Black or African American, non-Hispanic/Latino; 1 Asian, non-Hispanic/Latino; 1 Hispanic/Latino), 4 international. Average age 35. 35 applicants, 83% accepted, 18 enrolled. In 2016, 13 master's awarded. *Entrance requirements:* For master's, GRE. Additional exam requirements/recommendations for international students: Required—TOEFL. *Application deadline:* Applications are processed on a rolling basis. Application fee: $45. *Financial support:* Fellowships, research assistantships with full tuition reimbursements, teaching assistantships with full tuition reimbursements, career-related internships or fieldwork, Federal Work-Study, institutionally sponsored loans, scholarships/grants, tuition waivers (partial), and unspecified assistantships available. Support available to part-time students. Financial award applicants required to submit FAFSA. *Application contact:* Dr. Martha Kinney-Sedgwick, Department Head, 734-487-3260, Fax: 734-487-2101, E-mail: mkinneys@emich.edu.

Eastern Nazarene College, Adult and Graduate Studies, Division of Teacher Education, Quincy, MA 02170. Offers administration (M Ed); early childhood education (M Ed, Certificate); elementary education (M Ed, Certificate); English as a second language (Certificate); instructional enrichment and development (Certificate); middle school education (M Ed, Certificate); moderate special needs education (Certificate); principal (Certificate); program development and supervision (Certificate); secondary education (M Ed, Certificate); special education administrator (Certificate); special needs (M Ed); supervisor (Certificate); teacher of reading (M Ed, Certificate). M Ed also available through weekend program for administration, special needs, and teacher of reading only. *Program availability:* Part-time, evening/weekend. *Entrance requirements:* Additional exam requirements/recommendations for international students: Required—TOEFL (minimum score 550 paper-based).

Eastern New Mexico University, Graduate School, College of Education and Technology, Department of Educational Studies, Portales, NM 88130. Offers counseling (MA); education (M Ed), including educational administration, secondary education; school counseling (M Ed); special education (M Sp Ed), including early childhood special education, general. *Accreditation:* NCATE. *Program availability:* Part-time, evening/weekend, online learning. *Degree requirements:* For master's, comprehensive exam, thesis optional. *Entrance requirements:* For master's, minimum GPA of 3.0, letter of recommendation, photocopy of teaching license, writing assessment, Level II teaching license (for M Ed in educational administration). Additional exam requirements/recommendations for international students: Required—TOEFL (minimum score 550 paper-based; 79 iBT), IELTS (minimum score 6). Electronic applications accepted.

Eastern Oregon University, Master of Arts in Teaching Program, La Grande, OR 97850-2899. Offers elementary education (MAT); secondary education (MAT). *Program availability:* Online learning. *Faculty:* 9 full-time (6 women), 5 part-time/adjunct (2 women). *Students:* 43 full-time (31 women), 1 (woman) part-time; includes 8 minority (1 Black or African American, non-Hispanic/Latino; 1 American Indian or Alaska Native, non-Hispanic/Latino; 2 Asian, non-Hispanic/Latino; 4 Hispanic/Latino). Average age 31. In 2016, 40 master's awarded. *Degree requirements:* For master's, thesis. *Entrance requirements:* For master's, NTE. *Application deadline:* For fall admission, 1/1 priority date for domestic students. Applications are processed on a rolling basis. Application fee: $50. Electronic applications accepted. *Expenses:* $353.50 per credit plus campus fees for portion of degree delivered on-campus. *Financial support:* In 2016–17, 13 students received support. Federal Work-Study, scholarships/grants, and tuition waivers (full and partial) available. Support available to part-time students. *Unit head:* Dr. Danny Ray Mielke, Dean of College of Business and Education, 541-962-3399, Fax: 541-962-3701, E-mail: dmeilke@eou.edu. *Application contact:* Janet Frye, Administrative Support, MAT/MS Graduate Admission, 541-962-3772, Fax: 541-962-3701, E-mail: jfrye@eou.edu.

Eastern University, Loeb School of Education, St. Davids, PA 19087-3696. Offers ESL program specialist (K-12) (Certificate); general supervisor (PreK-12) (Certificate); health and physical education (K-12) (Certificate); middle level (4-8) (Certificate); multicultural education (M Ed); organizational leadership with education (PhD); Pre K-4 (Certificate); Pre K-4 with special education (Certificate); reading (M Ed); reading specialist (K-12) (Certificate); reading supervisor (K-12) (Certificate); school health supervisor (Certificate); school nurse (K-12) (Certificate); secondary biology education (7-12) (Certificate); secondary chemistry education (7-12) (Certificate); secondary communication education (7-12) (Certificate); secondary education (7-12) (Certificate); secondary English education (7-12) (Certificate); secondary math education (7-12) (Certificate); secondary social studies education (7-12) (Certificate); special education (M Ed); special education (7-12) (Certificate); special education (Pre K-8) (Certificate); special education supervisor (N-12) (Certificate); TESOL (M Ed); world language (Certificate), including French, Spanish. *Program availability:* Part-time, evening/weekend, online learning. *Students:* 41 full-time (32 women), 89 part-time (68 women); includes 54 minority (38 Black or African American, non-Hispanic/Latino; 3 Asian, non-Hispanic/Latino; 11 Hispanic/Latino; 2 Two or more races, non-Hispanic/Latino), 2 international. Average age 37. In 2016, 64 master's awarded. *Entrance requirements:* Additional exam requirements/recommendations for international students: Required—TOEFL. *Application deadline:* Applications are processed on a rolling basis. Application fee: $35. Electronic applications accepted. Application fee is waived when completed online. *Expenses:* $690 per credit. *Unit head:* Michael Dziedziak, Executive Director of Enrollment, 800-452-0996, E-mail: gpsadmissions@eastern.edu.
Website: http://www.eastern.edu/academics/programs/loeb-school-education-0

Eastern Washington University, Graduate Studies, College of Arts, Letters and Education, Department of Education, Program in Secondary Teaching, Cheney, WA 99004-2431. Offers M Ed. *Expenses:* Tuition, state resident: full-time $11,000; part-time $5500 per credit. Tuition, nonresident: full-time $24,000; part-time $12,000 per credit. *Required fees:* $1300. One-time fee: $50 full-time. Part-time tuition and fees vary according to course load, campus/location and program. *Application contact:* Dr. Robin Showalter, Graduate Program Coordinator, 509-359-6492, E-mail: rshowalter@ewu.edu.

East Stroudsburg University of Pennsylvania, Graduate and Extended Studies, College of Education, Department of Professional and Secondary Education, East Stroudsburg, PA 18301-2999. Offers professional and secondary education (Ed D); secondary education (M Ed). *Accreditation:* NCATE. *Program availability:* Part-time, evening/weekend, online learning. *Students:* 19 full-time (9 women), 92 part-time (56 women); includes 20 minority (8 Black or African American, non-Hispanic/Latino; 11 Hispanic/Latino; 1 Two or more races, non-Hispanic/Latino), 1 international. *Degree requirements:* For master's, independent research problem or comprehensive assessment portfolio. *Entrance requirements:* For master's, PRAXIS/teacher certification, letter of recommendation, Pennsylvania Department of Education requirements. Additional exam requirements/recommendations for international students: Recommended—TOEFL (minimum score 560 paper-based; 83 iBT), IELTS. *Application deadline:* For fall admission, 7/31 priority date for domestic students, 5/30 priority date for international students; for spring admission, 11/30 for domestic students, 10/31 for international students. Applications are processed on a rolling basis. Application fee: $50. Electronic applications accepted. *Expenses:* Tuition, state resident: full-time $8694; part-time $5796 per year. Tuition, nonresident: full-time $13,050; part-time $8700 per year. *Required fees:* $2550; $1690 per unit. $845 per semester. Tuition and fees vary according to course load, campus/location and program. *Financial support:* Research assistantships with tuition reimbursements, career-related internships or fieldwork, Federal Work-Study, and unspecified assistantships available. Support available to part-time students. Financial award application deadline: 3/1; financial award applicants required to submit FAFSA. *Unit head:* Dr. Beth Sockman, Chair, 570-422-3374, Fax: 570-422-3506, E-mail: bsockman@esu.edu. *Application contact:* Kevin Quintero, Associate Director, Graduate and Extended Studies, 570-422-3890, Fax: 570-422-2711, E-mail: kquintero@esu.edu.

East Tennessee State University, School of Graduate Studies, College of Education, Department of Curriculum and Instruction, Johnson City, TN 37614. Offers educational technology (M Ed), including educational communications and technology, school library media; elementary education (M Ed); reading (MA), including reading education; school library professional (Post-Master's Certificate); secondary education (M Ed), including classroom technology; teacher education with multiple levels (MAT), including elementary education, middle grades education, secondary education. *Accreditation:* NCATE. *Program availability:* Part-time, evening/weekend, online learning. *Degree requirements:* For master's, comprehensive exam, thesis optional, student teaching, practicum; for Post-Master's Certificate, field work (school library); culminating experience (storytelling). *Entrance requirements:* For master's, GRE, SAT, ACT, PRAXIS, minimum GPA of 3.0; for Post-Master's Certificate, master's degree, TN teaching license. Additional exam requirements/recommendations for international students: Required—TOEFL (minimum score 550 paper-based; 79 iBT). Electronic applications accepted. *Faculty research:* Critical thinking; curriculum development in reading, math, and science education; cultural diversity; cognitive processes; effective teaching strategies.

Edinboro University of Pennsylvania, Department of Middle and Secondary Education and Educational Leadership, Edinboro, PA 16444. Offers educational leadership (M Ed); middle and secondary instruction (M Ed). *Program availability:* Part-time, evening/weekend. *Degree requirements:* For master's, comprehensive exam, thesis or alternative, project. *Entrance requirements:* For master's, GRE or MAT, minimum QPA of 2.5. Electronic applications accepted.

Elms College, Division of Education, Chicopee, MA 01013-2839. Offers early childhood education (MAT); education (M Ed, CAGS); elementary education (MAT); English as a second language (MAT); reading (MAT); secondary education (MAT), including biology education, English education, Spanish education; special education (MAT). *Program availability:* Part-time, evening/weekend. *Faculty:* 5 full-time (all women), 7 part-time/adjunct (6 women). *Students:* 6 full-time (all women), 136 part-time (111 women); includes 6 minority (1 Asian, non-Hispanic/Latino; 5 Hispanic/Latino). Average age 33. 27 applicants, 89% accepted, 20 enrolled. In 2016, 47 master's, 3 other advanced degrees awarded. *Degree requirements:* For master's, thesis (for some programs). *Entrance requirements:* For master's, Massachusetts Educators Certification Test, minimum GPA of 3.0; for CAGS, master's degree in education. Additional exam requirements/recommendations for international students: Required—TOEFL. *Application deadline:* For fall admission, 7/1 priority date for domestic students; for spring admission, 11/1 priority date for domestic students. Applications are processed on a rolling basis. Application fee: $30. *Expenses: Tuition:* Full-time $13,392. *Required fees:* $200. *Financial support:* In 2016–17, 2 teaching assistantships with partial tuition reimbursements were awarded; tuition waivers (partial) also available. Support available to part-time students. Financial award applicants required to submit FAFSA. *Unit head:* Dr. Mary Janeczek, Chair, Division of Education, 413-594-2761, Fax: 413-592-4871, E-mail: janeczeke@elms.edu. *Application contact:* Dr. Elizabeth Teahan Hukowicz, Dean, School of Graduate and Professional Studies, 413-265-2360, Fax: 413-265-2459, E-mail: hukowiczе@elms.edu.

Emory University, Laney Graduate School, Division of Educational Studies, Atlanta, GA 30322-1100. Offers educational studies (MA, PhD); middle grades teaching (MAT); secondary teaching (MAT). *Accreditation:* NCATE. Terminal master's awarded for partial completion of doctoral program. *Degree requirements:* For master's, thesis; for doctorate, comprehensive exam, thesis/dissertation. *Entrance requirements:* For master's and doctorate, GRE General Test, minimum GPA of 3.0. Additional exam requirements/recommendations for international students: Required—TOEFL. Electronic applications accepted. *Faculty research:* Educational policy, educational measurement, urban and multicultural education, mathematics and science education, comparative education.

Endicott College, Van Loan School of Graduate and Professional Studies, Program in Secondary Education, Beverly, MA 01915-2096. Offers M Ed. *Program availability:* Part-time, evening/weekend, 100% online, blended/hybrid learning. *Faculty:* 3 full-time (1 woman), 9 part-time/adjunct (4 women). *Students:* 29 full-time (15 women), 11 part-time (9 women); includes 1 minority (Hispanic/Latino). Average age 35. 19 applicants, 100% accepted, 16 enrolled. In 2016, 32 master's awarded. *Degree requirements:* For master's, thesis, practicum, seminar. *Entrance requirements:* For master's, Massachusetts Tests for Educator Licensure (MTEL) Communication and Literacy Test and Subject Matter Test, MAT or GRE, bachelor's degree from accredited college, transcript, two recommendations, essay. Additional exam requirements/recommendations for international students: Required—TOEFL. *Application deadline:* Applications are processed on a rolling basis. Application fee: $50. Electronic applications accepted. *Expenses:* Contact institution. *Financial support:* Applicants required to submit FAFSA. *Unit head:* Dr. Aubry Threlkeld, Director of Graduate Licensure Programs, 978-232-2408, Fax: 978-232-3000, E-mail: athrelke@endicott.edu. *Application contact:* Ian Menchini, Director, Graduate Enrollment and Advising, 978-232-

5292, Fax: 978-232-3000, E-mail: imenchin@endicott.edu.
Website: http://www.endicott.edu/VanLoan/Graduate-Studies/Master-Education.aspx

Evangel University, Department of Education, Springfield, MO 65802. Offers curriculum and instruction (M Ed); educational leadership (M Ed); literacy (M Ed); secondary teaching (M Ed). *Accreditation:* NCATE. *Program availability:* Part-time, evening/weekend, 100% online, blended/hybrid learning. *Faculty:* 3 full-time (2 women), 4 part-time/adjunct (2 women). *Students:* 2 full-time (1 woman), 33 part-time (29 women); includes 1 minority (Asian, non-Hispanic/Latino). Average age 30. 10 applicants, 90% accepted, 9 enrolled. In 2016, 28 master's awarded. *Degree requirements:* For master's, comprehensive exam, thesis optional. *Entrance requirements:* For master's, PRAXIS II (preferred) or GRE, minimum undergraduate GPA of 3.0. Additional exam requirements/recommendations for international students: Required—TOEFL (minimum score 550 paper-based). *Application deadline:* For fall admission, 7/15 priority date for domestic students, 8/1 for international students; for spring admission, 11/15 priority date for domestic students, 12/1 for international students. Applications are processed on a rolling basis. Application fee: $25. Electronic applications accepted. Application fee is waived when completed online. *Expenses: Tuition:* Part-time $400 per credit hour. *Required fees:* $148 per trimester. One-time fee: $25. Tuition and fees vary according to course load, degree level and program. *Financial support:* In 2016–17, 11 students received support. Scholarships/grants and unspecified assistantships available. Financial award application deadline: 4/1; financial award applicants required to submit FAFSA. *Unit head:* Dr. Susan Langston, Program Coordinator, 417-865-2815 Ext. 8552, E-mail: langstons@evangel.edu. *Application contact:* Karen Benitez, Admissions Representative, Graduate Studies, 417-865-2815 Ext. 7416, Fax: 417-575-5484, E-mail: benitezk@evangel.edu.
Website: http://www.evangel.edu/academics/graduate-studies/graduate-programs

Fairfield University, Graduate School of Education and Allied Professions, Fairfield, CT 06824. Offers applied behavior analysis (ATC); applied psychology (MA); clinical mental health counseling (MA, CAS); educational technology (MA); elementary education (MA, CAS); family studies (MA); integration of spirituality and religion in counseling (ATC); marriage and family therapy (MA); reading and language development (Sixth Year Certificate); school counseling (MA, CAS); school psychology (MA, CAS); school-based marriage and family therapy (ATC); secondary education (MA); special education (MA, CAS); substance abuse counseling (ATC); teaching (Certificate); teaching and foundations (MA, CAS); TESOL, world languages, and bilingual education (MA, CAS). *Accreditation:* NCATE. *Program availability:* Part-time, evening/weekend. *Faculty:* 19 full-time (15 women), 38 part-time/adjunct (26 women). *Students:* 153 full-time (132 women), 302 part-time (252 women); includes 97 minority (24 Black or African American, non-Hispanic/Latino; 12 Asian, non-Hispanic/Latino; 55 Hispanic/Latino; 6 Two or more races, non-Hispanic/Latino), 6 international. Average age 32. 283 applicants, 61% accepted, 97 enrolled. In 2016, 130 master's awarded. *Degree requirements:* For master's, comprehensive exam. *Entrance requirements:* For master's, minimum GPA of 3.0, 2 recommendations, resume. Additional exam requirements/recommendations for international students: Required—TOEFL (minimum score 550 paper-based; 84 iBT) or IELTS (minimum score 7.5). *Application deadline:* For fall admission, 2/15 for international students; for spring admission, 10/1 for international students. Application fee: $60. Electronic applications accepted. *Expenses:* $725 per credit hour. *Financial support:* In 2016–17, 42 students received support. Career-related internships or fieldwork and unspecified assistantships available. Support available to part-time students. Financial award applicants required to submit FAFSA. *Faculty research:* Reading and literacy, writing, social justice and inequality in education, addictions and mental health issues, therapeutic relationships and clinical supervision. *Unit head:* Dr. Robert D. Hannafin, Dean, 203-254-4250, Fax: 203-254-4241, E-mail: rhannafin@fairfield.edu. *Application contact:* Marianne Gumpper, Director of Graduate Admission, 203-254-4184, Fax: 203-254-4073, E-mail: gradadmis@fairfield.edu.
Website: http://www.fairfield.edu/gseap

Fayetteville State University, Graduate School, Programs in Middle Grades, Secondary, Special and Elementary Education, Fayetteville, NC 28301-4298. Offers middle grades (MA Ed); sociology (MA Ed); special education (MA Ed), including behavioral-emotional handicaps, mentally handicapped, specific training disability. *Accreditation:* NCATE. *Program availability:* Part-time, evening/weekend. *Faculty:* 12 full-time (8 women), 4 part-time/adjunct (3 women). *Students:* 9 full-time (6 women), 11 part-time (10 women); includes 12 minority (11 Black or African American, non-Hispanic/Latino; 1 Asian, non-Hispanic/Latino). Average age 35. 20 applicants, 100% accepted, 1 enrolled. In 2016, 11 master's awarded. *Degree requirements:* For master's, comprehensive exam, internship. *Entrance requirements:* Additional exam requirements/recommendations for international students: Required—TOEFL. *Application deadline:* For fall admission, 4/15 for domestic students; for spring admission, 10/15 for domestic students. Applications are processed on a rolling basis. Application fee: $40. Electronic applications accepted. *Financial support:* Application deadline: 3/1; applicants required to submit FAFSA. *Faculty research:* Students with disabilities and selected leadership behaviors, new vision for professional development, gifted and talented students, emotional and behavioral disabilities, professional development for high school biology teachers. *Unit head:* Dr. Kimberly Smith-Burton, Chairperson, 910-672-1181, Fax: 910-672-1941, E-mail: ksmith@uncfsu.edu. *Application contact:* Debra D. Brown, Administrative Support Associate, 910-672-1181, Fax: 910-672-1596, E-mail: ddbrown@uncfsu.edu.

Florida Agricultural and Mechanical University, Division of Graduate Studies, Research, and Continuing Education, College of Education, Program in Secondary Education and Foundation, Tallahassee, FL 32307-3200. Offers biology (M Ed); chemistry (MS Ed); English (MS Ed); history (MS Ed); math (MS Ed); physics (MS Ed). *Accreditation:* NCATE. *Degree requirements:* For master's, thesis (for some programs). *Entrance requirements:* For master's, GRE General Test, minimum GPA of 3.0. Additional exam requirements/recommendations for international students: Required—TOEFL.

Fontbonne University, Graduate Programs, St. Louis, MO 63105-3098. Offers accounting (MBA, MS); art (MA); art (K-12) (MAT); business (MBA); computer science (MS); deaf education (MA); early intervention in deaf education (MA); education (MA), including autism spectrum disorders, curriculum and instruction, diverse learners, early childhood education, reading, special education; elementary education (MAT); family and consumer sciences (MA), including multidisciplinary health communication studies; fine arts (MFA); instructional design and technology (MS); management and leadership (MM); middle school education (MAT); secondary education (MAT); special education (MAT); speech-language pathology (MS); supply chain management (MS); theatre (MA). *Program availability:* Part-time, evening/weekend, online learning. *Faculty:* 32 full-time (24 women), 43 part-time/adjunct (26 women). *Students:* 456 full-time (313 women), 102 part-time (77 women); includes 138 minority (118 Black or African American, non-Hispanic/Latino; 1 American Indian or Alaska Native, non-Hispanic/Latino; 7 Asian, non-Hispanic/Latino; 9 Hispanic/Latino; 3 Two or more races, non-Hispanic/Latino), 37 international. *Degree requirements:* For master's, comprehensive exam (for some programs), thesis (for some programs). *Entrance requirements:* Additional exam requirements/recommendations for international students: Required—TOEFL (minimum score 500 paper-based; 65 iBT). *Application deadline:* For fall admission, 8/1 for international students; for spring admission, 12/1 for international students. Applications are processed on a rolling basis. Application fee: $25 ($30 for international students). Electronic applications accepted. *Expenses: Tuition:* Full-time $8436; part-time $703 per credit hour. *Required fees:* $18 per credit hour. Tuition and fees vary according to course load. *Financial support:* Teaching assistantships with partial tuition reimbursements and scholarships/grants available. Support available to part-time students. Financial award application deadline: 4/1; financial award applicants required to submit FAFSA. *Unit head:* Dr. Carey Adams, Vice President for Academic Affairs, 314-719-3609, E-mail: cadams@fontbonne.edu. *Application contact:* Lauryn Filip, Coordinator, Graduate Admission and Professional Studies, 314-889-4650, E-mail: admissions@fontbonne.edu.
Website: https://www.fontbonne.edu/academics/graduate-programs/

Frostburg State University, Graduate School, College of Education, Department of Educational Professions, Program in Curriculum and Instruction, Frostburg, MD 21532-1099. Offers educational technology (M Ed); elementary education (M Ed); secondary education (M Ed). *Program availability:* Part-time, evening/weekend. *Degree requirements:* For master's, thesis or alternative. *Entrance requirements:* For master's, teaching certificate. Additional exam requirements/recommendations for international students: Required—TOEFL. Electronic applications accepted.

Frostburg State University, Graduate School, College of Education, Department of Educational Professions, Program in Secondary Teaching, Frostburg, MD 21532-1099. Offers MAT. *Entrance requirements:* For master's, PRAXIS I, entry portfolio. Additional exam requirements/recommendations for international students: Required—TOEFL.

Gallaudet University, The Graduate School, Washington, DC 20002-3625. Offers American Sign Language/English bilingual early childhood deaf education: birth to 5 (Certificate); audiology (Au D); clinical psychology (PhD); deaf and hard of hearing infants, toddlers, and their families (Certificate); deaf education (MA, Ed S); deaf history (Certificate); deaf studies (Certificate); educating deaf students with disabilities (Certificate); education: teacher preparation (MA), including deaf education, early childhood education and deaf education, elementary education and deaf education, secondary education and deaf education; educational neuroscience (PhD); hearing, speech and language sciences (MS, PhD); international development (MA); interpretation (MA, PhD), including combined interpreting practice and research (MA), interpreting research (MA); linguistics (MA, PhD); mental health counseling (MA); peer mentoring (Certificate); public administration (MPA); school counseling (MA); school psychology (Psy S); sign language teaching (MA); social work (MSW); speech-language pathology (MS). *Program availability:* Part-time. *Students:* 297 full-time (231 women), 129 part-time (97 women); includes 105 minority (35 Black or African American, non-Hispanic/Latino; 20 Asian, non-Hispanic/Latino; 39 Hispanic/Latino; 11 Two or more races, non-Hispanic/Latino), 22 international. Average age 30. 471 applicants, 52% accepted, 147 enrolled. In 2016, 138 master's, 25 doctorates, 14 other advanced degrees awarded. Terminal master's awarded for partial completion of doctoral program. *Degree requirements:* For master's, comprehensive exam (for some programs), thesis optional; for doctorate, comprehensive exam, thesis/dissertation. *Entrance requirements:* For master's and doctorate, GRE General Test or MAT, letters of recommendation, interviews, goals statement, American Sign Language proficiency interview, written English competency. Additional exam requirements/recommendations for international students: Required—TOEFL. *Application deadline:* For fall admission, 2/15 for domestic students. Applications are processed on a rolling basis. Application fee: $75. Electronic applications accepted. *Expenses: Tuition:* Full-time $17,100; part-time $950 per credit hour. *Required fees:* $3725; $276 per semester. *Financial support:* Fellowships, research assistantships, teaching assistantships, career-related internships or fieldwork, Federal Work-Study, scholarships/grants, tuition waivers (partial), and unspecified assistantships available. Support available to part-time students. Financial award application deadline: 7/1; financial award applicants required to submit FAFSA. *Faculty research:* Signing math dictionaries, telecommunications access, cancer genetics, linguistics, visual language and visual learning, integrated quantum materials, deaf legal discourse, advance recruitment and retention in geosciences. *Unit head:* Dr. Gaurav Mathur, Dean, Graduate School and Continuing Studies, 202-250-2380, Fax: 202-651-5027, E-mail: gaurav.mathur@gallaudet.edu. *Application contact:* Wednesday Luria, Coordinator of Prospective Graduate Student Services, 202-651-5400, Fax: 202-651-5295, E-mail: graduate.school@gallaudet.edu.

George Mason University, College of Education and Human Development, Programs in Curriculum and Instruction, Fairfax, VA 22030. Offers advanced international baccalaureate (M Ed); assistive technology (M Ed); designing digital learning in schools (M Ed); early childhood education (M Ed); early childhood education for diverse learners (M Ed); elementary education (M Ed); English as a second language (M Ed); gifted child education (M Ed); history (M Ed); literacy (M Ed), including PK-12 classroom teachers, reading specialist; literacy leadership for diverse schools (M Ed), including K-12 reading; physical education (M Ed); science K-12 (M Ed); secondary education (M Ed), including biology, chemistry, earth science, English, history/social science, math, physics; special education (M Ed); teacher leadership (M Ed); teaching culturally, linguistically diverse and exceptional learners (M Ed); transformative teaching (M Ed). *Faculty:* 41 full-time (35 women), 53 part-time/adjunct (46 women). *Students:* 155 full-time (127 women), 821 part-time (697 women); includes 267 minority (82 Black or African American, non-Hispanic/Latino; 5 American Indian or Alaska Native, non-Hispanic/Latino; 75 Asian, non-Hispanic/Latino; 88 Hispanic/Latino; 1 Native Hawaiian or other Pacific Islander, non-Hispanic/Latino; 16 Two or more races, non-Hispanic/Latino), 19 international. Average age 33. 513 applicants, 90% accepted, 352 enrolled. In 2016, 347 master's awarded. *Degree requirements:* For master's, comprehensive exam, thesis (for some programs). *Entrance requirements:* For master's, PRAXIS Core (for some programs), minimum GPA of 3.0 in last 60 hours, licensed as teacher or educational administrator, official transcripts, goals statement, 3 recommendation letters, interview or writing sample (depending on program), up to 3 years' teaching experience (depending on program). Additional exam requirements/recommendations for international students: Required—TOEFL (minimum score 575 paper-based; 88 iBT), IELTS (minimum score 6.5), PTE (minimum score 59). *Application deadline:* For spring admission, 11/1 priority date for domestic and international students. Application fee: $75 ($80 for international students). Electronic applications accepted. *Expenses:* Tuition, state resident: full-time $10,628; part-time $443 per credit. Tuition, nonresident: full-time $29,306; part-time $1221 per credit. *Required fees:* $3096; $129 per credit. Tuition and fees vary according to program. *Financial support:* In 2016–17, 1 student received support, including 1 teaching assistantship (averaging $4,060 per year); career-related internships or fieldwork, Federal Work-Study, scholarships/grants, unspecified assistantships, and health care benefits (for full-time research or teaching assistantship recipients) also available. Support available to part-time students. Financial award application deadline: 3/1; financial award applicants required to submit FAFSA. *Faculty research:* Achievement gaps and superintendent decisions, constructivist view of classroom teaching, cost of cheating, creating a critical literacy milieu in kindergarten. *Unit head:* Rebecca Fox, Professor and Academic Program Coordinator, 703-993-4123, E-mail: rfox@gmu.edu.
Website: http://gse.gmu.edu/programs/gsemasters

The George Washington University, Graduate School of Education and Human Development, Department of Curriculum and Pedagogy, Program in Secondary Education, Washington, DC 20052. Offers Arabic (M Ed); Italian (M Ed); math (M Ed); physics (M Ed); Russian (M Ed). Programs also offered in Arlington and Ashburn, VA. *Accreditation:* NCATE. *Students:* 13 full-time (11 women), 21 part-time (15 women); includes 12 minority (4 Black or African American, non-Hispanic/Latino; 2 Asian, non-Hispanic/Latino; 4 Hispanic/Latino; 2 Two or more races, non-Hispanic/Latino). Average age 32. 50 applicants, 82% accepted, 25 enrolled. In 2016, 22 master's awarded. *Degree requirements:* For master's, comprehensive exam. *Entrance requirements:* For master's, GRE General Test or MAT, interview, minimum GPA of 2.75. *Application deadline:* For fall admission, 1/15 priority date for domestic students; for spring admission, 10/1 for domestic students. Applications are processed on a rolling basis. Application fee: $75. *Financial support:* Fellowships, career-related internships or fieldwork, Federal Work-Study, tuition waivers (full and partial), and stipends available. Financial award application deadline: 1/15; financial award applicants required to submit FAFSA. *Unit head:* Prof. Curtis Pyke, Chair, 202-994-4516, E-mail: cpyke@gwu.edu. *Application contact:* Sarah Lang, Director of Graduate Admissions, 202-994-1447, Fax: 202-994-7207, E-mail: slang@gwu.edu.

Georgia College & State University, Graduate School, The John H. Lounsbury College of Education, Program in Secondary Education, Milledgeville, GA 31061. Offers MAT. *Program availability:* Part-time, evening/weekend. *Students:* 31 full-time (19 women), 17 part-time (8 women); includes 12 minority (9 Black or African American, non-Hispanic/Latino; 1 Asian, non-Hispanic/Latino; 1 Hispanic/Latino; 1 Two or more races, non-Hispanic/Latino). Average age 28. 6 applicants, 100% accepted, 6 enrolled. In 2016, 54 master's awarded. *Degree requirements:* For master's, comprehensive exam, minimum GPA of 3.0, complete program within 6 years. *Entrance requirements:* For master's, on-site writing assessment, GRE General Test taken within six years (minimum scores 1,000 verbal and quantitative combined if taken before August 1, 2011; 305 if taken on or after August 1, 2011), or MAT, 2 recommendations, transcripts, proof of immunization. *Application deadline:* For fall admission, 7/1 priority date for domestic students; for spring admission, 11/1 priority date for domestic students; for summer admission, 4/1 priority date for domestic students. Applications are processed on a rolling basis. Application fee: $40. Electronic applications accepted. *Expenses:* $288 per credit hour in-state, $1,027 out-of-state. *Financial support:* In 2016–17, 5 students received support. Unspecified assistantships available. Financial award application deadline: 3/1; financial award applicants required to submit FAFSA. *Unit head:* Dr. Joseph Peters, Dean, College of Education, 478-445-2518, Fax: 478-445-6582, E-mail: joseph.peters@gcsu.edu. *Application contact:* Shanda Brand, Graduate Admission Advisor, 478-445-1383, Fax: 478-445-6582, E-mail: shanda.brand@gcsu.edu.

Georgia Southern University, Jack N. Averitt College of Graduate Studies, College of Education, Department of Teaching and Learning, Program in Secondary Education, Statesboro, GA 30460. Offers M Ed, MAT, Ed S. *Program availability:* Part-time, evening/weekend. *Students:* 23 full-time (17 women), 60 part-time (41 women); includes 10 minority (6 Black or African American, non-Hispanic/Latino; 1 Asian, non-Hispanic/Latino; 2 Hispanic/Latino; 1 Two or more races, non-Hispanic/Latino), 1 international. Average age 30. 29 applicants, 97% accepted, 20 enrolled. In 2016, 38 master's, 11 other advanced degrees awarded. *Degree requirements:* For master's, portfolio, transition point assessments, exit assessment. *Entrance requirements:* For master's, GRE General Test or MAT, minimum cumulative GPA of 2.5. Additional exam requirements/recommendations for international students: Required—TOEFL (minimum score 550 paper-based; 80 iBT), IELTS (minimum score 6). *Application deadline:* For fall admission, 3/15 priority date for domestic and international students; for spring admission, 10/1 priority date for domestic students, 10/1 for international students; for summer admission, 3/1 for domestic and international students. Applications are processed on a rolling basis. Application fee: $50. Electronic applications accepted. *Expenses:* Tuition, state resident: full-time $7236; part-time $277 per semester hour. Tuition, nonresident: full-time $27,118; part-time $1105 per semester hour. *Required fees:* $2092. *Financial support:* In 2016–17, 11 students received support, including 4 fellowships with full tuition reimbursements available (averaging $7,750 per year); career-related internships or fieldwork, Federal Work-Study, and tuition waivers (full) also available. Support available to part-time students. Financial award application deadline: 4/15; financial award applicants required to submit FAFSA. *Faculty research:* Social studies education, mathematics education, science education, language arts education, dispositions. *Unit head:* Dr. Missy Bennett, Coordinator, 912-478-0356, Fax: 912-478-0026, E-mail: mbennett@georgiasouthern.edu. *Application contact:* Lydia Cross, Coordinator for Graduate Academic Services Center, 912-478-8664, E-mail: lcross@georgiasouthern.edu.

Georgia State University, College of Education and Human Development, Department of Middle and Secondary Education, Atlanta, GA 30302-3083. Offers curriculum and instruction (Ed D); English education (MAT); mathematics education (M Ed, MAT); middle level education (MAT); reading, language and literacy education (M Ed, MAT), including reading instruction (M Ed); science education (M Ed, MAT), including biology (MAT), broad field science (MAT), chemistry (MAT), earth science (MAT), physics (MAT); social studies education (M Ed, MAT), including economics (MAT), geography (MAT), history (MAT), political science (MAT); teaching and learning (PhD), including language and literacy, mathematics education, music education, science education, social studies education, teaching and teacher education. *Accreditation:* NCATE. *Program availability:* Part-time, evening/weekend, online learning. *Faculty:* 24 full-time (18 women). *Students:* 145 full-time (91 women), 151 part-time (102 women); includes 141 minority (104 Black or African American, non-Hispanic/Latino; 1 American Indian or Alaska Native, non-Hispanic/Latino; 16 Asian, non-Hispanic/Latino; 12 Hispanic/Latino; 8 Two or more races, non-Hispanic/Latino), 10 international. Average age 36. 115 applicants, 50% accepted, 41 enrolled. In 2016, 94 master's, 22 doctorates awarded. *Degree requirements:* For master's, comprehensive exam (for some programs), thesis or alternative, exit portfolio; for doctorate, comprehensive exam, thesis/dissertation. *Entrance requirements:* For master's, GRE; GACE I (for initial teacher preparation programs), baccalaureate degree or equivalent, resume, goals statement, two letters of recommendation, minimum undergraduate GPA of 2.5; proof of initial teacher certification in the content area (for M Ed); for doctorate, GRE, resume, goals statement, writing sample, two letters of recommendation, minimum graduate GPA of 3.3, interview. Additional exam requirements/recommendations for international students: Required—TOEFL (minimum score 550 paper-based; 79 iBT) or IELTS (minimum score 6.5). *Application deadline:* For fall admission, 1/15 priority date for domestic and international students; for spring admission, 10/1 for domestic and international students. Application fee: $50. Electronic applications accepted. *Expenses:* Tuition, state resident: full-time $6876; part-time $382 per credit hour. Tuition, nonresident: full-time $22,374; part-time $1243 per credit hour. *Required fees:* $2128; $1064 per term. Part-time tuition and fees vary according to course load and program. *Financial support:* In 2016–17, fellowships with full tuition reimbursements (averaging $19,667 per year), research assistantships with full tuition reimbursements (averaging $5,436 per year), teaching assistantships with full tuition reimbursements (averaging $2,779 per year) were awarded; career-related internships or fieldwork, Federal Work-Study, scholarships/grants, health care benefits, tuition waivers (full and partial), and unspecified assistantships also available. Financial award application deadline: 3/15. *Faculty research:* Teacher education in language and literacy, mathematics, science, and social studies in urban middle and secondary school settings; learning technologies in school, community, and corporate settings; multicultural education and education for social justice; urban education; international education. *Unit head:* Dr. Dana L. Fox, Chair, 404-413-8060, Fax: 404-413-8063, E-mail: dfox@gsu.edu. *Application contact:* Bobbie Turner, Administrative Coordinator I, 404-413-8405, Fax: 404-413-8063, E-mail: bnturner@gsu.edu.
Website: http://mse.education.gsu.edu/

Gonzaga University, School of Education, Spokane, WA 99258. Offers clinical mental health counseling (MA); elementary education (MIT); leadership and administration (MA); marriage and family counseling (MA); school counseling (MA); secondary education (MIT); special education (M Ed, MIT); sport and athletic administration (MA). *Accreditation:* NCATE. *Program availability:* Part-time, evening/weekend, 100% online. *Faculty:* 22 full-time (17 women), 38 part-time/adjunct (22 women). *Students:* 104 full-time (73 women), 275 part-time (184 women); includes 31 minority (5 Black or African American, non-Hispanic/Latino; 1 American Indian or Alaska Native, non-Hispanic/Latino; 3 Asian, non-Hispanic/Latino; 18 Hispanic/Latino; 4 Two or more races, non-Hispanic/Latino), 163 international. Average age 32. 419 applicants, 67% accepted, 165 enrolled. In 2016, 39 master's awarded. *Degree requirements:* For master's, comprehensive exam. *Entrance requirements:* For master's, GRE, MAT, and/or Washington Educators Skills Test-Basic (WEST-B), official transcripts from all colleges or universities attended, interview, two letters of recommendation, resume, essay, minimum GPA of 3.0. Additional exam requirements/recommendations for international students: Required—TOEFL (minimum score 580 paper-based, 88 iBT) or IELTS (minimum score 6.5). *Application deadline:* Applications are processed on a rolling basis. Application fee: $50. Electronic applications accepted. *Expenses:* Contact institution. *Financial support:* In 2016–17, 28 students received support. Scholarships/grants and tuition waivers available. Support available to part-time students. Financial award applicants required to submit FAFSA. *Unit head:* Dr. Vincent Alfonso, Dean, 509-313-3594, Fax: 509-313-5821, E-mail: alfonso@gonzaga.edu. *Application contact:* Luke Cairney, Graduate Admissions Program Specialist, 509-313-3821, E-mail: cairney@gonzaga.edu.
Website: http://www.gonzaga.edu/Academics/Colleges-and-Schools/School-of-Education

Gordon College, Graduate Education Program, Wenham, MA 01984-1899. Offers early childhood (M Ed); educational leadership (M Ed, Ed S); elementary education (M Ed); English as a second language (M Ed, Ed S); math specialist (M Ed); mathematics specialist (Ed S); middle school education (M Ed); moderate disabilities (M Ed); Montessori education (M Ed); reading (M Ed, Ed S); secondary education (M Ed). *Program availability:* Part-time, evening/weekend. *Faculty:* 17 full-time (9 women), 41 part-time/adjunct (34 women). *Students:* 81 full-time (61 women), 109 part-time (87 women); includes 28 minority (2 Black or African American, non-Hispanic/Latino; 11 Asian, non-Hispanic/Latino; 13 Hispanic/Latino; 2 Two or more races, non-Hispanic/Latino), 12 international. Average age 34. 190 applicants, 100% accepted, 141 enrolled. In 2016, 110 master's, 16 Ed Ss awarded. *Degree requirements:* For master's, action research or clinical experience (for most programs); for Ed S, action research or clinical experience (for some programs). *Entrance requirements:* For master's, minimum undergraduate GPA of 3.0; 2 official undergraduate transcripts; professional resume; 3 recommendation letters (one professional reference, one academic reference, one personal reference); 500-700 word statement of purpose; for Ed S, minimum master's GPA of 3.3; 2 official transcripts from undergraduate and graduate schools; professional resume; 3 recommendation letters (one professional reference, one academic reference, one personal reference); 500-700 word statement of purpose. Additional exam requirements/recommendations for international students: Required—TOEFL (minimum score 550 paper-based, 80 iBT) or IELTS (minimum score 6.5). *Application deadline:* Applications are processed on a rolling basis. Application fee: $75. *Expenses:* $325 per credit tuition, $75 per term fee. *Financial support:* Applicants required to submit FAFSA. *Faculty research:* Reading, early childhood development, English language learners, universal design for learning. *Unit head:* Dr. Janet Arndt, Director of Graduate Studies, 978-867-4355, Fax: 978-867-4663. *Application contact:* Julie Lenocker, Program Administrator, 978-867-4322, Fax: 978-867-4663, E-mail: graduate-education@gordon.edu.
Website: http://www.gordon.edu/graduate

Goucher College, Graduate Programs in Education, Baltimore, MD 21204-2794. Offers at-risk and diverse learners (M Ed, Certificate); athletic program leadership and administration (M Ed, Certificate); elementary and special education (MAT); elementary education (MAT); literacy strategies for content learning (M Ed, Certificate); middle school (M Ed, Certificate); Montessori studies (M Ed); reading instruction (M Ed, Certificate); school improvement leadership (M Ed, Certificate); school mediation (M Ed, Certificate); secondary and special education (MAT); secondary education (MAT); special education (MAT), including elementary education, secondary education; special education for certified teachers (M Ed, Certificate); teacher as leader in technology (M Ed, Certificate). *Program availability:* Part-time, evening/weekend. *Faculty:* 3 full-time (all women), 52 part-time/adjunct (40 women). *Students:* 29 full-time (20 women), 285 part-time (217 women); includes 54 minority (41 Black or African American, non-Hispanic/Latino; 3 Asian, non-Hispanic/Latino; 7 Hispanic/Latino; 3 Two or more races, non-Hispanic/Latino), 1 international. Average age 34. 85 applicants, 100% accepted, 61 enrolled. In 2016, 207 master's awarded. *Degree requirements:* For master's, thesis (M Ed), final presentation (MAT). *Entrance requirements:* For master's, minimum GPA of 3.0. Additional exam requirements/recommendations for international students: Required—TOEFL (minimum score 560 paper-based). *Application deadline:* For fall admission, 9/1 for domestic students; for spring admission, 1/15 for domestic students. Applications are processed on a rolling basis. Application fee: $75. Electronic applications accepted. *Expenses:* Contact institution. *Financial support:* Career-related internships or fieldwork and unspecified assistantships available. Support available to part-time students. Financial award application deadline: 4/15; financial award applicants required to submit FAFSA. *Faculty research:* Urban education, middle school, school improvement, teacher education, at-risk student achievement. *Unit head:* Dr. Phyllis Sunshine, Assistant Provost, 410-337-6047, Fax: 410-337-6394, E-mail: psunshin@goucher.edu. *Application contact:* Shelby Hillers, Admissions Coordinator, 410-337-6200, Fax: 410-337-6085, E-mail: shelby.hillers@goucher.edu.
Website: http://www.goucher.edu/graduate-programs/graduate-programs-in-education

Grand Canyon University, College of Education, Phoenix, AZ 85017-1097. Offers autism spectrum disorders (MA); curriculum and instruction (MA); early childhood education (M Ed); educational administration (M Ed); educational leadership (M Ed); elementary education (M Ed); gifted education (MA); instructional technology (MS); K-12 leadership (Ed S); reading (MA); secondary education (M Ed); secondary humanities education (M Ed); secondary STEM education (M Ed), special education (M Ed); teaching and learning (Ed D); teaching English to speakers of other languages (MA). *Program availability:* Part-time, evening/weekend, online learning. *Degree requirements:* For master's, publishable research paper (M Ed), e-portfolio. *Entrance requirements:* For master's, undergraduate degree from accredited, GCU-approved college, university, or program with minimum GPA 2.8. Additional exam requirements/recommendations for international students: Required—TOEFL (minimum score 550 paper-based; 79 iBT),

IELTS (minimum score 6). *Application deadline:* For fall admission, 8/21 for domestic students, 7/2 for international students; for spring admission, 12/24 for domestic students, 11/1 for international students. Applications are processed on a rolling basis. Application fee: $100. Electronic applications accepted. *Financial support:* Federal Work-Study available. Support available to part-time students. Financial award applicants required to submit FAFSA. *Unit head:* Dr. Kimberly L. LaPrade, Dean, 602-639-6360, E-mail: kimberly.laprade@gcu.edu. *Application contact:* Dr. Kimberly L. LaPrade, Dean, 602-639-6360, E-mail: kimberly.laprade@gcu.edu.
Website: https://www.gcu.edu/college-of-education.php

Grand Valley State University, College of Education, Programs in General Education, Allendale, MI 49401-9403. Offers adult and higher education (M Ed); early childhood education (M Ed); educational differentiation (M Ed); educational leadership (M Ed); educational technology integration (M Ed); elementary education (M Ed); middle level education (M Ed); school library media services (M Ed); secondary level education (M Ed); teaching English to speakers of other languages (M Ed). *Program availability:* Part-time, evening/weekend, 100% online, blended/hybrid learning. *Students:* 28 part-time (20 women); includes 6 minority (4 Black or African American, non-Hispanic/Latino; 1 American Indian or Alaska Native, non-Hispanic/Latino; 1 Hispanic/Latino). Average age 42. In 2016, 17 master's awarded. *Degree requirements:* For master's, project or thesis. *Entrance requirements:* For master's, GRE General Test or minimum GPA of 3.0, last 60 credits from regionally-accredited college/university, 3 letters of recommendation. Additional exam requirements/recommendations for international students: Required—TOEFL (minimum score 550 paper-based, 80 iBT), IELTS (6.5), or Michigan English Language Assessment Battery. *Application deadline:* Applications are processed on a rolling basis. Application fee: $30. Electronic applications accepted. *Expenses:* $628 per credit hour. *Financial support:* In 2016–17, 2 students received support. Career-related internships or fieldwork, Federal Work-Study, scholarships/grants, and unspecified assistantships available. *Faculty research:* Effectiveness of technology in education, parental involvement, effective teaching, effective schools research. *Unit head:* Dr. Doug Busman, Graduate Program Director, 616-331-6250, E-mail: busmando@gvsu.edu. *Application contact:* Thomas Owens, Director, Student Information and Services Center, 616-331-6282, Fax: 616-331-6217, E-mail: owenst@gvsu.edu.
Website: http://www.gvsu.edu/coe/

Greenville College, Program in Education, Greenville, IL 62246-0159. Offers education (MAT); elementary education (MAE); secondary education (MAE). *Degree requirements:* For master's, thesis (for some programs). *Entrance requirements:* For master's, GRE, Illinois Basic Skills Test, teacher certification. Electronic applications accepted.

Hampton University, School of Education and Human Development, Program in Teaching, Hampton, VA 23668. Offers music education (MT); secondary education (MT). *Program availability:* Part-time. *Faculty:* 5 full-time (4 women), 2 part-time/adjunct (both women). *Students:* 8 full-time (4 women); all minorities (all Black or African American, non-Hispanic/Latino). Average age 23. 7 applicants, 57% accepted, 4 enrolled. In 2016, 2 master's awarded. *Entrance requirements:* For master's, GRE General Test. Additional exam requirements/recommendations for international students: Required—TOEFL (minimum score 525 paper-based) or IELTS (6.5). *Application deadline:* For fall admission, 6/1 priority date for domestic students, 4/1 for international students; for spring admission, 11/1 priority date for domestic students, 9/1 for international students; for summer admission, 4/1 priority date for domestic students, 2/1 priority date for international students. Applications are processed on a rolling basis. Application fee: $35. Electronic applications accepted. *Expenses: Tuition:* Full-time $10,776; part-time $548 per credit hour. *Required fees:* $35; $35 per credit hour. Tuition and fees vary according to course load and program. *Financial support:* Application deadline: 6/30; applicants required to submit FAFSA. *Unit head:* Dr. Ava Marrow, Program Coordinator, 757-727-2072.

Harding University, Cannon-Clary College of Education, Searcy, AR 72149-0001. Offers advanced studies in teaching and learning (M Ed); art (MSE); behavioral science (MSE); counseling (MS, Ed S); early childhood special education (M Ed, MSE); education (MSE); educational leadership (M Ed, Ed S); elementary education (M Ed); English (MSE); French (MSE); history/social science (MSE); kinesiology (MSE); math (MSE); reading (M Ed); secondary education (M Ed); Spanish (MSE); teaching (MAT); teaching English as a second language (MSE). *Accreditation:* NCATE. *Program availability:* Part-time, evening/weekend. *Faculty:* 22 full-time (9 women), 51 part-time/adjunct (37 women). *Students:* 130 full-time (94 women), 321 part-time (234 women); includes 83 minority (50 Black or African American, non-Hispanic/Latino; 4 American Indian or Alaska Native, non-Hispanic/Latino; 6 Asian, non-Hispanic/Latino; 13 Hispanic/Latino; 10 Two or more races, non-Hispanic/Latino), 11 international. Average age 35. 125 applicants, 88% accepted, 110 enrolled. In 2016, 124 master's, 27 other advanced degrees awarded. *Degree requirements:* For master's, comprehensive exam (for some programs), thesis optional, portfolio(s); for Ed S, comprehensive exam, portfolio, project. *Entrance requirements:* For master's, GRE, MAT, PRAXIS; for Ed S, MAT or GRE. Additional exam requirements/recommendations for international students: Required—TOEFL (minimum score 550 paper-based; 79 iBT). *Application deadline:* For fall admission, 8/1 for domestic and international students; for spring admission, 1/1 for domestic and international students. Applications are processed on a rolling basis. Application fee: $35. Tuition and fees vary according to degree level and program. *Financial support:* In 2016–17, 31 students received support. Unspecified assistantships available. *Faculty research:* Reading, comprehension, school violence, educational technology, behavior, college choice, differentiated instruction, brain-based teaching. *Unit head:* Dr. Clara Carroll, Chair, 501-279-4501, Fax: 501-279-4083, E-mail: ccarroll@harding.edu. *Application contact:* Information Contact, 501-279-4315, E-mail: gradstudiesedu@harding.edu.
Website: http://www.harding.edu/education

Hawai`i Pacific University, College of Extended and Interdisciplinary Education, Program in Secondary Education, Honolulu, HI 96813. Offers M Ed. *Accreditation:* TEAC. *Program availability:* Part-time, evening/weekend. *Faculty:* 3 full-time (2 women), 6 part-time/adjunct (3 women). *Students:* 18 full-time (10 women), 2 part-time (1 woman); includes 14 minority (5 Asian, non-Hispanic/Latino; 2 Hispanic/Latino; 7 Two or more races, non-Hispanic/Latino). Average age 29. 21 applicants, 81% accepted, 15 enrolled. In 2016, 24 master's awarded. *Entrance requirements:* For master's, minimum undergraduate GPA of 3.0, background check. Additional exam requirements/recommendations for international students: Recommended—TOEFL (minimum score 550 paper-based; 80 iBT), IELTS (minimum score 6), TWE (minimum score 5). *Application deadline:* For fall admission, 2/15 priority date for domestic students; for spring admission, 10/15 priority date for domestic students. Applications are processed on a rolling basis. Application fee: $50. Electronic applications accepted. *Expenses: Tuition:* Full-time $17,190; part-time $955 per credit. *Required fees:* $150; $26 per credit. Tuition and fees vary according to course load and program. *Financial support:* In 2016–17, 8 students received support. Career-related internships or fieldwork, Federal Work-Study, scholarships/grants, tuition waivers, and unspecified assistantships available. Financial award application deadline: 3/1; financial award applicants required to submit FAFSA. *Unit head:* Dr. Linda Wheeler, Field Services Director, 808-356-5229, E-mail: lwheeler@hpu.edu. *Application contact:* Danny Lam, Assistant Director of Graduate Admissions, 808-544-1135, E-mail: graduate@hpu.edu.
Website: http://www.hpu.edu/CHSS/Education/MEDSE/index.html

High Point University, Norcross Graduate School, High Point, NC 27268. Offers business administration (MBA); educational leadership (M Ed); elementary education (M Ed); history (MA); nonprofit management (MA); secondary math (M Ed); special education (M Ed); strategic communication (MA); teaching elementary education k-6 (MAT); teaching secondary mathematics 9-12 (MAT). *Accreditation:* NCATE. *Program availability:* Part-time, evening/weekend. *Degree requirements:* For master's, comprehensive exam (for some programs), thesis (for some programs). *Entrance requirements:* For master's, GMAT (MBA), GRE, MAT, minimum GPA of 3.0. Additional exam requirements/recommendations for international students: Required—TOEFL (minimum score 550 paper-based). Electronic applications accepted.

Hofstra University, School of Education, Programs in Teacher Education, Hempstead, NY 11549. Offers bilingual education (MA, Advanced Certificate); bilingual extension (Advanced Certificate), including education/speech language pathology; business education (MS Ed); early childhood and childhood education (MS Ed); early childhood education (MA, MS Ed); education technology (Advanced Certificate); elementary education (MA, MS Ed), including science, technology, engineering, and mathematics (STEM) (MA); English education (MS Ed); family and consumer science (MS Ed); fine arts and music education (Advanced Certificate); fine arts education (MS Ed); foreign language and TESOL (MS Ed); foreign language education (MS Ed), including French, German, Russian, Spanish; learning and teaching (Ed D), including applied linguistics, art education, arts and humanities, early childhood education, English education, human development, math education, math, science, and technology, multicultural education, physical education, science education, social studies education, special education; mathematics education (MA, MS Ed); middle school extension (Advanced Certificate), including grades 5-6, grades 7-9; music education (MA, MS Ed); science education (MA, MS Ed), including biology, chemistry, earth science, geology, physics; secondary education (Advanced Certificate); social studies education (MA, MS Ed); teaching languages other than English and TESOL (MS Ed); TESOL (MS Ed, Advanced Certificate). *Program availability:* Part-time, evening/weekend, blended/hybrid learning. *Students:* 139 full-time (97 women), 145 part-time (106 women); includes 60 minority (15 Black or African American, non-Hispanic/Latino; 1 American Indian or Alaska Native, non-Hispanic/Latino; 12 Asian, non-Hispanic/Latino; 31 Hispanic/Latino; 1 Two or more races, non-Hispanic/Latino), 21 international. Average age 29. 255 applicants, 86% accepted, 122 enrolled. In 2016, 101 master's, 4 doctorates, 43 other advanced degrees awarded. *Degree requirements:* For master's, comprehensive exam, thesis (for some programs), exit project, student teaching, fieldwork, electronic portfolio, curriculum project, minimum GPA of 3.0; for doctorate, thesis/dissertation; for Advanced Certificate, 3 foreign languages, comprehensive exam (for some programs), thesis project. *Entrance requirements:* For master's, GRE, MAT, 2 letters of recommendation, portfolio, teacher certification (MA), interview, essay; for doctorate, GMAT, GRE, LSAT, or MAT; for Advanced Certificate, 2 letters of recommendation, essay, interview and/or portfolio, teaching certificate. Additional exam requirements/recommendations for international students: Required—TOEFL (minimum score 550 paper-based; 80 iBT). *Application deadline:* Applications are processed on a rolling basis. Application fee: $75. Electronic applications accepted. *Expenses: Tuition:* Full-time $1240. *Required fees:* $970. Tuition and fees vary according to program. *Financial support:* In 2016–17, 149 students received support, including 58 fellowships with full and partial tuition reimbursements available (averaging $5,309 per year), 5 research assistantships with full and partial tuition reimbursements available (averaging $7,073 per year); career-related internships or fieldwork, Federal Work-Study, institutionally sponsored loans, scholarships/grants, traineeships, tuition waivers (full and partial), and unspecified assistantships also available. Support available to part-time students. Financial award applicants required to submit FAFSA. *Faculty research:* Educational interventions that foster critical-thinking skills; teachers' attitudes about professional development; threats to teacher quality. *Unit head:* Dr. Eustace Thompson, Chairperson, 516-463-5749, Fax: 516-463-6275, E-mail: eustace.g.thompson@hofstra.edu. *Application contact:* Sunil Samuel, Assistant Vice President of Admissions, 516-463-4723, Fax: 516-463-4664, E-mail: graduateadmission@hofstra.edu.
Website: http://www.hofstra.edu/education/

Hofstra University, School of Education, Specialized Programs in Education, Hempstead, NY 11549. Offers applied behavior analysis (Advanced Certificate); early childhood special education (MS Ed, Advanced Certificate); educational and policy leadership (Ed D); educational leadership (Advanced Certificate), including school building leader/school district business leader; educational leadership and policy studies (MS Ed), including K-12; gifted education (Advanced Certificate), including school building leader/school district business leader; health education PK-12 teaching certification (MS); inclusive early childhood special education (MS Ed); inclusive elementary special education (MS Ed); inclusive secondary special education (MS Ed); literacy studies (MS Ed, Ed D, PhD, Advanced Certificate), including birth-grade 6 (MS Ed, Advanced Certificate), birth-grade 6 and special education (birth-grade2) (MS Ed), grades 5-12 (MS Ed, Advanced Certificate); physical education (MS); secondary education generalist (MS Ed), including students with disabilities 7-12; special education (MS Ed, Advanced Certificate); special education assessment and diagnosis (Advanced Certificate); special education generalist (MS Ed), including extension in secondary education; sport science (MS), including strength and conditioning; teaching students with severe or multiple disabilities (Advanced Certificate). *Program availability:* Part-time, evening/weekend, 100% online, blended/hybrid learning. *Students:* 149 full-time (115 women), 258 part-time (187 women); includes 97 minority (50 Black or African American, non-Hispanic/Latino; 1 American Indian or Alaska Native, non-Hispanic/Latino; 11 Asian, non-Hispanic/Latino; 34 Hispanic/Latino; 1 Native Hawaiian or other Pacific Islander, non-Hispanic/Latino), 5 international. Average age 32. 250 applicants, 88% accepted, 146 enrolled. In 2016, 85 master's, 13 doctorates, 35 other advanced degrees awarded. *Degree requirements:* For master's, one foreign language, comprehensive exam (for some programs), thesis (for some programs), electronic portfolio, capstone course, internship, practicum, student teaching, seminars, minimum GPA of 3.0; for doctorate, one foreign language, comprehensive exam, thesis/dissertation, qualifying hearing. *Entrance requirements:* For master's, GRE, interview, letters of recommendation, portfolio, essay, certification; for doctorate, GRE or MAT, interview, resume, essay, master's degree, 3 letters of recommendation, writing sample; for Advanced Certificate, GRE, interview, letters of recommendation, essay, professional experience, resume, master's degree. Additional exam requirements/recommendations for international students: Required—TOEFL (minimum score 550 paper-based; 80 iBT). *Application deadline:* Applications are processed on a rolling basis. Application fee: $75. Electronic applications accepted. *Expenses: Tuition:* Full-time $1240. *Required fees:* $970. Tuition and fees vary according to program. *Financial support:* In 2016–17, 244 students received support, including 117 fellowships with full and partial tuition reimbursements available (averaging $3,705 per year), 12 research assistantships with full and partial tuition reimbursements available (averaging $6,490 per year); career-related internships or fieldwork, Federal Work-Study, institutionally sponsored loans, scholarships/grants, traineeships, tuition waivers (full and partial), and unspecified assistantships also

available. Support available to part-time students. Financial award applicants required to submit FAFSA. *Faculty research:* Collaborative teaching and learning; language and culture; new media literacies; applied behavior analysis; K-12 leadership development. *Unit head:* Dr. Elfreda Blue, Chairperson, 516-463-5762, Fax: 516-463-6184, E-mail: elfreda.blue@hofstra.edu. *Application contact:* Sunil Samuel, Assistant Vice President of Admissions, 516-463-4723, Fax: 516-463-4664, E-mail: graduateadmission@hofstra.edu.
Website: http://www.hofstra.edu/education/

Hood College, Graduate School, Department of Education, Frederick, MD 21701-8575. Offers curriculum and instruction (MS), including elementary education, elementary science and mathematics education, secondary education, special education; educational leadership (MS); reading specialization (MS); STEM education (Certificate). *Accreditation:* NCATE. *Program availability:* Part-time-only, evening/weekend. *Faculty:* 3 full-time, 37 part-time/adjunct. *Students:* 1 (woman) full-time, 357 part-time (283 women); includes 71 minority (41 Black or African American, non-Hispanic/Latino; 6 Asian, non-Hispanic/Latino; 15 Hispanic/Latino; 9 Two or more races, non-Hispanic/Latino). Average age 33. 96 applicants, 95% accepted, 83 enrolled. In 2016, 47 master's awarded. *Degree requirements:* For master's, action research project, portfolio (for reading specialization); for Certificate, STEM capstone activity. *Entrance requirements:* For master's, minimum GPA of 2.75, teaching certification, writing sample during interview, letter of recommendation from principal (for educational leadership program only). Additional exam requirements/recommendations for international students: Required—TOEFL (minimum score 575 paper-based; 89 iBT), IELTS (minimum score 6.5). *Application deadline:* For fall admission, 8/15 priority date for domestic students, 8/5 for international students; for spring admission, 12/1 priority date for domestic students, 12/1 for international students; for summer admission, 5/1 priority date for domestic students, 4/15 for international students. Applications are processed on a rolling basis. Application fee: $35. Electronic applications accepted. *Expenses:* $450 per credit; $105 comprehensive fee per semester. *Financial support:* Tuition waivers (partial) and unspecified assistantships available. Financial award applicants required to submit FAFSA. *Faculty research:* Leadership, action research, brain research, learning styles. *Unit head:* April Boulton, Interim Dean of the Graduate School, E-mail: gofurther@hood.edu. *Application contact:* Jan Marcus, Assistant Director of Graduate Admissions, 301-696-3600, E-mail: gofurther@hood.edu.
Website: http://www.hood.edu/academics/education/index.html

Hope International University, School of Graduate and Professional Studies, Program in Education, Fullerton, CA 92831-3138. Offers education administration (MA); elementary education (ME); secondary education (ME). *Program availability:* Part-time, evening/weekend. *Degree requirements:* For master's, comprehensive exam (for some programs), thesis. *Entrance requirements:* For master's, minimum GPA of 3.0, 2 references. Additional exam requirements/recommendations for international students: Required—TOEFL (minimum score 550 paper-based; 86 iBT); Recommended—IELTS (minimum score 6.5). Electronic applications accepted. *Expenses:* Contact institution. *Faculty research:* Distance education.

Howard University, School of Education, Department of Curriculum and Instruction, Program in Secondary Education, Washington, DC 20059-0002. Offers M Ed. *Accreditation:* NCATE. *Degree requirements:* For master's, comprehensive exam, thesis (for some programs), expository writing exam, internships, practicum. *Entrance requirements:* For master's, PRAXIS I, GRE, minimum GPA of 2.7. Additional exam requirements/recommendations for international students: Required—TOEFL (minimum score 550 paper-based; 79 iBT). Electronic applications accepted.

Hunter College of the City University of New York, Graduate School, School of Arts and Sciences, Department of Mathematics and Statistics, New York, NY 10065-5085. Offers adolescent mathematics education (MA); applied mathematics (MA); bioinformatics (MA); pure mathematics (MA); statistics (MA). *Program availability:* Part-time, evening/weekend. *Students:* 1 full-time (0 women), 47 part-time (19 women); includes 14 minority (4 Black or African American, non-Hispanic/Latino; 8 Asian, non-Hispanic/Latino; 2 Hispanic/Latino), 8 international. Average age 32. 41 applicants, 73% accepted, 13 enrolled. In 2016, 8 master's awarded. *Degree requirements:* For master's, one foreign language, comprehensive exam, thesis (for some programs). *Entrance requirements:* For master's, GRE General Test, 24 credits in mathematics. Additional exam requirements/recommendations for international students: Required—TOEFL. *Application deadline:* For fall admission, 4/1 for domestic students, 2/1 for international students; for spring admission, 11/1 for domestic students, 9/1 for international students. *Financial support:* Federal Work-Study, institutionally sponsored loans, scholarships/grants, and tuition waivers (partial) available. Support available to part-time students. *Faculty research:* Data analysis, dynamical systems, computer graphics, topology, statistical decision theory. *Unit head:* Robert Thompson, Chair, 212-650-3831, Fax: 212-772-4858, E-mail: robert.thompson@hunter.cuny.edu. *Application contact:* Ada Peluso, Director for Graduate Admissions, 212-772-4632, Fax: 212-772-4858, E-mail: peluso@math.hunter.cuny.edu.
Website: http://math.hunter.cuny.edu/

Hunter College of the City University of New York, Graduate School, School of Education, Programs in Secondary Education, New York, NY 10065-5085. Offers biology education (MA); chemistry education (MA); earth science (MA); English education (MA); French education (MA); Italian education (MA); mathematics education (MA); physics education (MA); social studies education (MA); Spanish education (MA). *Accreditation:* NCATE. *Degree requirements:* For master's, thesis. *Entrance requirements:* Additional exam requirements/recommendations for international students: Required—TOEFL. *Application deadline:* For fall admission, 4/1 for domestic students, 2/1 for international students; for spring admission, 11/1 for domestic students, 9/1 for international students. Applications are processed on a rolling basis. *Financial support:* Fellowships and tuition waivers (full and partial) available. Support available to part-time students. *Unit head:* Dr. Kenney Robinson, Director of Adolescent Education Clinical Experiences, 212-772-4038, E-mail: krobi@hunter.cuny.edu. *Application contact:* Milena Solo, Director for Graduate Admissions, 212-772-4482, E-mail: milena.solo@hunter.cuny.edu.

Idaho State University, Office of Graduate Studies, College of Education, Department of Educational Foundations, Pocatello, ID 83209-8059. Offers child and family studies (M Ed); curriculum leadership (M Ed); education (M Ed); educational administration (M Ed); educational foundations (5th Year Certificate); elementary education (M Ed), including K-12 education, literacy, secondary education. *Program availability:* Part-time. *Degree requirements:* For master's, comprehensive exam, thesis optional, oral exam, written exam; for 5th Year Certificate, comprehensive exam, thesis (for some programs), oral exam, written exam. *Entrance requirements:* For master's, GRE General Test or MAT, minimum undergraduate GPA of 3.0; for 5th Year Certificate, GRE General Test, minimum undergraduate GPA of 3.0, master's degree. Additional exam requirements/recommendations for international students: Required—TOEFL (minimum score 550 paper-based; 80 iBT). Electronic applications accepted. *Faculty research:* Child and families studies; business education; special education; math, science, and technology education.

Immaculata University, College of Graduate Studies, Program in Educational Leadership, Immaculata, PA 19345. Offers educational leadership (MA, Ed D); principal (Certificate); secondary education (Certificate); supervisor of special education (Certificate). *Program availability:* Part-time, evening/weekend. *Degree requirements:* For master's, comprehensive exam, thesis optional; for doctorate, comprehensive exam, thesis/dissertation. *Entrance requirements:* For master's, GRE or MAT, minimum GPA of 3.0; for doctorate, GRE General Test or MAT, minimum GPA of 3.5. Additional exam requirements/recommendations for international students: Required—TOEFL. Electronic applications accepted. *Faculty research:* Cooperative learning, school-based management, whole language, performance assessment.

Indiana University Bloomington, School of Education, Department of Curriculum and Instruction, Bloomington, IN 47405-7000. Offers art education (MS, Ed D, PhD); curriculum studies (Ed D, PhD); elementary education (MS, Ed D, PhD, Ed S); mathematics education (MS, Ed D, PhD); science education (MS, Ed D, PhD); secondary education (MS, Ed D, PhD); social studies education (MS, PhD); special education (PhD, Ed S). *Accreditation:* NCATE. *Program availability:* Part-time, evening/weekend. Terminal master's awarded for partial completion of doctoral program. *Degree requirements:* For doctorate, thesis/dissertation; for Ed S, comprehensive exam or project. *Entrance requirements:* For master's, doctorate, and Ed S, GRE General Test. Electronic applications accepted.

Indiana University Northwest, School of Education, Gary, IN 46408. Offers educational leadership (MS Ed); elementary education (MS Ed); K-12 online teaching (Graduate Certificate); secondary education (MS Ed). *Accreditation:* NCATE. *Program availability:* Part-time, evening/weekend. *Faculty:* 10 full-time (5 women), 2 part-time/adjunct (both women). *Students:* 11 full-time (8 women), 67 part-time (47 women); includes 32 minority (25 Black or African American, non-Hispanic/Latino; 7 Hispanic/Latino). Average age 38. 24 applicants, 96% accepted, 14 enrolled. In 2016, 22 master's awarded. *Entrance requirements:* For master's, GRE General Test or MAT, minimum GPA of 3.0. *Application deadline:* For fall admission, 7/15 priority date for domestic students; for spring admission, 11/15 for domestic students. Application fee: $40 ($60 for international students). Electronic applications accepted. *Expenses:* $276.98 per credit hour in-state; $652.54 per credit hour out-of-state. *Financial support:* Applicants required to submit FAFSA. *Unit head:* Dr. Charles Hobsen, Interim Dean, 219-980-6903, Fax: 219-680-4208, E-mail: chobson@iun.edu. *Application contact:* Kelly Zieba, Director of Enrollment Management, Finance, and Operations, 219-980-6879, Fax: 219-980-4208, E-mail: kmzieba@iun.edu.
Website: http://www.iun.edu/education/degrees/masters.htm

Indiana University–Purdue University Fort Wayne, College of Education and Public Policy, Department of Educational Studies, Fort Wayne, IN 46805-1499. Offers elementary education (MS Ed); secondary education (MS Ed). *Accreditation:* NCATE. *Program availability:* Part-time. *Entrance requirements:* For master's, minimum GPA of 2.5, three professional letters of recommendation. Additional exam requirements/recommendations for international students: Required—TOEFL (minimum score 550 paper-based; 79 iBT). *Faculty research:* International faculty, gender in Burmese refugee narratives, planning effective instruction.

Indiana University South Bend, School of Education, South Bend, IN 46634-7111. Offers addiction counseling (MS Ed); alcohol and drug counseling (Graduate Certificate); clinical mental health counseling (MS Ed); educational leadership (MS Ed); elementary education (MS Ed); marriage, couple, and family counseling (MS Ed); school counseling (MS Ed); secondary education (MS Ed); special education (MAT, MS Ed), including intense intervention (MS Ed), mild intervention (MS Ed). *Accreditation:* NCATE. *Program availability:* Part-time, evening/weekend. *Faculty:* 21 full-time (11 women), 9 part-time/adjunct (3 women). *Students:* 26 full-time (19 women), 104 part-time (80 women); includes 22 minority (13 Black or African American, non-Hispanic/Latino; 5 Hispanic/Latino; 4 Two or more races, non-Hispanic/Latino). Average age 35. 51 applicants, 69% accepted, 22 enrolled. In 2016, 31 master's, 2 other advanced degrees awarded. *Degree requirements:* For master's, thesis or alternative, exit project. *Entrance requirements:* For master's, letters of recommendation, GRE or minimum GPA of 3.0. Additional exam requirements/recommendations for international students: Required—TOEFL. *Application deadline:* For fall admission, 7/1 for domestic students; for spring admission, 11/1 for domestic students. Applications are processed on a rolling basis. Application fee: $40 ($60 for international students). Electronic applications accepted. *Expenses:* $276.98 per credit hour in-state; $652.54 per credit hour out-of-state. *Financial support:* Career-related internships or fieldwork available. Support available to part-time students. Financial award application deadline: 3/1; financial award applicants required to submit FAFSA. *Faculty research:* Professional dispositions, early childhood literacy, online learning, program assessments, problem-based learning. *Unit head:* Dr. Marvin Lynn, Dean, 574-520-4339, E-mail: lynnm@iusb.edu. *Application contact:* Yvonne Walker, Student Services Representative, 574-520-4185, E-mail: ydwalker@iusb.edu.
Website: https://www.iusb.edu/education/index.php

Indiana University Southeast, School of Education, New Albany, IN 47150. Offers counselor education (MS Ed); elementary education (MS Ed); secondary education (MS Ed). *Accreditation:* NCATE. *Program availability:* Part-time, evening/weekend. *Students:* 13 full-time (10 women), 190 part-time (150 women); includes 29 minority (21 Black or African American, non-Hispanic/Latino; 5 Hispanic/Latino; 3 Two or more races, non-Hispanic/Latino). Average age 33. 61 applicants, 84% accepted, 43 enrolled. In 2016, 70 master's awarded. *Entrance requirements:* For master's, minimum undergraduate GPA of 2.5, graduate 3.0. *Application deadline:* Applications are processed on a rolling basis. Application fee: $40 ($60 for international students). Electronic applications accepted. *Financial support:* Career-related internships or fieldwork, Federal Work-Study, and institutionally sponsored loans available. Support available to part-time students. Financial award applicants required to submit FAFSA. *Faculty research:* Learning styles, technology, constructivism, group process, innovative math strategies. *Unit head:* Dr. Faye Marsha Camahalan, Director of Graduate Studies, 812-941-2136, Fax: 812-941-2667, E-mail: fcamahal@ius.edu. *Application contact:* Admissions Counselor, 812-941-2212, Fax: 812-941-2595, E-mail: admissions@ius.edu.
Website: http://www.ius.edu/education/graduate-programs/

Instituto Tecnologico de Santo Domingo, Graduate School, Area of Humanities and Social Sciences, Santo Domingo, Dominican Republic. Offers accounting (Certificate); adult education (Certificate); applied linguistics (MA); economics (MA); education (M Ed); educational psychology (MA, Certificate); gender and development (MA, Certificate); humanistic studies (MA); international marketing management (Certificate); international relations in the Caribbean basin (Certificate); intervention systems in family therapy (MA); linguistic and literary communication (Certificate); pedagogical support (MA); social science education (M Ed); sustainable human development (MA); terminal illness and death psychology (Certificate); youth and adult education (M Ed).

Ithaca College, School of Humanities and Sciences, Program in Adolescence Education, Ithaca, NY 14850. Offers biology (MAT); chemistry (MAT); earth science (MAT); English (MAT); French (MAT); mathematics (MAT); physics (MAT); social studies (MAT); Spanish (MAT). *Program availability:* Part-time. *Faculty:* 26 full-time (12 women). *Students:* 11 full-time (4 women). Average age 26. 17 applicants, 94% accepted, 10 enrolled. *Degree requirements:* For master's, thesis or alternative. *Entrance requirements:* Additional exam requirements/recommendations for

international students: Required—TOEFL (minimum score 550 paper-based; 80 iBT). *Application deadline:* For fall admission, 2/15 for domestic and international students; for spring admission, 12/1 for domestic and international students. Applications are processed on a rolling basis. Application fee: $40. Electronic applications accepted. *Expenses:* Contact institution. *Financial support:* In 2016–17, 5 students received support, including 5 research assistantships (averaging $13,259 per year); career-related internships or fieldwork, Federal Work-Study, scholarships/grants, and unspecified assistantships also available. Support available to part-time students. Financial award application deadline: 2/15; financial award applicants required to submit CSS PROFILE or FAFSA. *Unit head:* Peter Martin, Chair, 607-274-1076, E-mail: pmartin@ithaca.edu. *Application contact:* Nicole Eversley Bradwell, Director, Office of Admission, 607-274-3124, Fax: 607-274-1263, E-mail: admission@ithaca.edu.
Website: http://www.ithaca.edu/gradprograms/education/programs/aded

Jacksonville State University, College of Graduate Studies and Continuing Education, College of Education and Professional Studies, Program in Secondary Education, Jacksonville, AL 36265-1602. Offers MS Ed. *Accreditation:* NCATE. *Program availability:* Part-time, evening/weekend. *Faculty:* 8 full-time (4 women). *Students:* 11 full-time (10 women), 16 part-time (15 women); includes 2 minority (1 Black or African American, non-Hispanic/Latino; 1 American Indian or Alaska Native, non-Hispanic/ Latino). Average age 30. 23 applicants, 48% accepted, 6 enrolled. In 2016, 22 master's awarded. *Degree requirements:* For master's, comprehensive exam, thesis (for some programs). *Entrance requirements:* For master's, GRE General Test or MAT. Additional exam requirements/recommendations for international students: Required—TOEFL (minimum score 500 paper-based; 61 iBT). *Application deadline:* Applications are processed on a rolling basis. Application fee: $35. Electronic applications accepted. *Financial support:* In 2016–17, 7 students received support. Available to part-time students. Application deadline: 4/1; applicants required to submit FAFSA. *Unit head:* Dr. Janet Bavonese, Head, 256-782-5180, E-mail: jbarkley@jsu.edu. *Application contact:* Dr. Jean Pugliese, Associate Dean, 256-782-8278, Fax: 256-782-5321, E-mail: pugliese@jsu.edu.

James Madison University, The Graduate School, College of Education, Program in Education, Harrisonburg, VA 22807. Offers early childhood education (preK-3) (MAT); educational leadership (M Ed); educational technology (M Ed); elementary education (MAT); equity and cultural diversity (M Ed); inclusive early childhood education (MAT); K-8 mathematics specialist (M Ed); middle education (MAT); reading education (M Ed); secondary education (MAT); Spanish language and culture for educators (M Ed); TESOL (MAT). *Accreditation:* NCATE. *Program availability:* Part-time, evening/ weekend. *Faculty:* 21 full-time (12 women), 5 part-time/adjunct (2 women). *Students:* 249 full-time (220 women), 123 part-time (86 women); includes 43 minority (7 Black or African American, non-Hispanic/Latino; 7 Asian, non-Hispanic/Latino; 17 Hispanic/ Latino; 12 Two or more races, non-Hispanic/Latino), 2 international. Average age 30. 355 applicants, 98% accepted, 312 enrolled. In 2016, 247 master's awarded. Application fee: $55. Electronic applications accepted. *Financial support:* In 2016–17, 16 students received support. Career-related internships or fieldwork, Federal Work-Study, and 22 assistantships (averaging $7911) available. Financial award application deadline: 3/1; financial award applicants required to submit FAFSA. *Unit head:* Dr. Phillip M. Wishon, Dean, 540-568-6572, E-mail: wishonpm@jmu.edu. *Application contact:* Lynette D. Michael, Director of Graduate Admissions, 540-568-6131 Ext. 6395, Fax: 540-568-7860, E-mail: michaeld@jmu.edu.
Website: http://www.jmu.edu/coe/index.shtml

James Madison University, The Graduate School, College of Education, Program in Secondary Education, Harrisonburg, VA 22807. Offers MAT. *Accreditation:* NCATE. *Program availability:* Part-time, evening/weekend. *Students:* Average age 27. *Entrance requirements:* For master's, GRE General Test. Additional exam requirements/ recommendations for international students: Required—TOEFL. *Application deadline:* For fall admission, 5/1 priority date for domestic students; for spring admission, 9/1 priority date for domestic students. Applications are processed on a rolling basis. Application fee: $55. Electronic applications accepted. *Financial support:* Federal Work-Study and unspecified assistantships available. Financial award application deadline: 3/ 1; financial award applicants required to submit FAFSA. *Unit head:* Dr. Steven L. Purcell, Academic Unit Head, 540-568-6793. *Application contact:* Lynette M. Bible, Director of Graduate Admissions, 540-568-6395, Fax: 540-568-7860, E-mail: biblelm@jmu.edu.

John Brown University, Graduate Education Programs, Siloam Springs, AR 72761-2121. Offers curriculum and instruction (M Ed); secondary education (MAT). *Program availability:* Part-time, evening/weekend. *Faculty:* 1 (woman) full-time, 5 part-time/ adjunct (3 women). *Students:* 17 part-time (8 women). Average age 32. 11 applicants, 64% accepted, 5 enrolled. In 2016, 7 master's awarded. *Entrance requirements:* For master's, GRE (minimum score of 300). Additional exam requirements/ recommendations for international students: Required—TOEFL (minimum score 550 paper-based; 79 iBT). *Application deadline:* Applications are processed on a rolling basis. Application fee: $35 ($100 for international students). Electronic applications accepted. *Expenses: Tuition:* Full-time $13,000; part-time $6500 per credit hour. Part-time tuition and fees vary according to course load and program. *Financial support:* Scholarships/grants and unspecified assistantships available. *Unit head:* Dr. Connie Matchell, Graduate Program Director, 479-524-9500, E-mail: cmatchell@jbu.edu. *Application contact:* Mark Bjornsen, Graduate Education Representative, 479-631-4665, E-mail: mbjornsen@jbu.edu.
Website: http://www.jbu.edu/grad/education/

John Carroll University, Graduate Studies, Program in Child and Adolescent Health and Wellness, University Heights, OH 44118-4581. Offers M Ed. *Degree requirements:* For master's, comprehensive exam. *Entrance requirements:* For master's, GRE General Test or MAT, minimum GPA of 2.75, interview. *Application deadline:* For spring admission, 5/15 for domestic students. Applications are processed on a rolling basis. Application fee: $25 ($35 for international students). Electronic applications accepted. *Expenses: Tuition:* Full-time $10,425; part-time $695 per credit hour. One-time fee: $200 full-time. Tuition and fees vary according to course load, campus/location and program. *Financial support:* Application deadline: 3/1; applicants required to submit FAFSA. *Unit head:* Dr. Mark Storz, Coordinator, 216-397-3070, Fax: 216-397-3045, E-mail: mstorz@jcu.edu. *Application contact:* Jennifer L. Tucker, Records Management Assistant, 216-397-1925, Fax: 216-397-1835, E-mail: jtucker@jcu.edu.

John Carroll University, Graduate Studies, Program in Secondary Education, University Heights, OH 44118-4581. Offers M Ed. *Degree requirements:* For master's, comprehensive exam. *Entrance requirements:* For master's, GRE General Test or MAT, minimum GPA of 2.75, interview. Additional exam requirements/recommendations for international students: Required—TOEFL. *Application deadline:* For spring admission, 5/15 for domestic students. Applications are processed on a rolling basis. Application fee: $25 ($35 for international students). Electronic applications accepted. *Expenses: Tuition:* Full-time $10,425; part-time $695 per credit hour. One-time fee: $200 full-time. Tuition and fees vary according to course load, campus/location and program. *Financial support:* Application deadline: 3/1; applicants required to submit FAFSA. *Unit head:* Dr. Mark Storz, Coordinator, 216-397-3070, Fax: 216-397-3045, E-mail: mstorz@jcu.edu. *Application contact:* Jennifer L. Tucker, Records Management Assistant, 216-397-1925, Fax: 216-397-1835, E-mail: jtucker@jcu.edu.

Johns Hopkins University, School of Education, Master's Programs in Education, Baltimore, MD 21218. Offers counseling (MS), including clinical mental health counseling, school counseling; education (MS), including educational studies, gifted education, reading, school administration and supervision, technology for educators; elementary education (MAT); health professions (M Ed); intelligence analysis (MS); organizational leadership (MS); secondary education (MAT), including biology, chemistry, earth/space science, English, physics, social studies; special education (MS), including early childhood special education, general special education studies, mild to moderate disabilities, severe disabilities. *Program availability:* Part-time, evening/ weekend, 100% online, blended/hybrid learning. *Students:* 345 full-time (265 women), 1,601 part-time (1,245 women); includes 837 minority (392 Black or African American, non-Hispanic/Latino; 7 American Indian or Alaska Native, non-Hispanic/Latino; 141 Asian, non-Hispanic/Latino; 207 Hispanic/Latino; 7 Native Hawaiian or other Pacific Islander, non-Hispanic/Latino; 83 Two or more races, non-Hispanic/Latino), 55 international. Average age 27. 1,352 applicants, 76% accepted, 819 enrolled. In 2016, 642 master's awarded. *Degree requirements:* For master's, comprehensive exam (for some programs), portfolio, capstone project and/or internship; PRAXIS II (subject area assessments) for initial teacher preparation programs that lead to licensure. *Entrance requirements:* For master's, GRE (for full-time programs only); PRAXIS I/core or state-approved alternative (for initial teacher preparation programs that lead to licensure), minimum of bachelor's degree from regionally- or nationally-accredited institution; minimum GPA of 3.0 in all previous programs of study; official transcripts from all post-secondary institutions attended; essay; curriculum vitae/resume; letters of recommendation (3 for full-time programs, 2 for part-time programs); dispositions survey. Additional exam requirements/recommendations for international students: Required—TOEFL (minimum score 600 paper-based; 100 iBT), IELTS (minimum score 7). *Application deadline:* For fall admission, 4/1 priority date for domestic students, 4/1 for international students; for spring admission, 10/1 priority date for domestic students, 10/1 for international students; for summer admission, 2/1 priority date for domestic students, 2/1 for international students. Applications are processed on a rolling basis. Application fee: $80. Electronic applications accepted. *Expenses:* Contact institution. *Financial support:* Application deadline: 4/1; applicants required to submit FAFSA. *Unit head:* Dr. Christopher C. Morphew, Dean. *Application contact:* Elisabeth Woodward, Director of Admissions, 410-516-9796, Fax: 410-516-9817, E-mail: soe.info@jhu.edu.
Website: http://education.jhu.edu

Johnson & Wales University, Graduate Studies, MAT Program in Teacher Education, Providence, RI 02903-3703. Offers business education and secondary special education (MAT); culinary arts education (MAT); elementary education and elementary special education (MAT); elementary education and elementary/secondary special education (MAT); elementary education and secondary special education (MAT); food service education (MAT). *Program availability:* Part-time, evening/weekend. *Entrance requirements:* For master's, MAT, minimum GPA of 2.75. Additional exam requirements/ recommendations for international students: Required—TOEFL (minimum score 550 paper-based) or IELTS (recommended). *Faculty research:* Secondary education, student teaching, educational reform, evaluation procedures.

Kaplan University, Davenport Campus, School of Teacher Education, Davenport, IA 52807. Offers education (M Ed); secondary education (M Ed); teaching and learning (MA); teaching literacy and language: grades 6-12 (MA); teaching literacy and language: grades K-6 (MA); teaching mathematics: grades 6-8 (MA); teaching mathematics: grades 9-12 (MA); teaching mathematics: grades K-5 (MA); teaching science: grades 6-12 (MA); teaching science: grades K-6 (MA); teaching students with special needs (MA); teaching with technology (MA). *Program availability:* Part-time, evening/weekend, online learning. *Entrance requirements:* Additional exam requirements/recommendations for international students: Required—TOEFL (minimum score 550 paper-based; 80 iBT).

Kennesaw State University, Leland and Clarice C. Bagwell College of Education, Program in Graduate Education, Kennesaw, GA 30144. Offers educational leadership (M Ed); educational leadership technology (M Ed); elementary and early childhood education (M Ed); instructional technology (M Ed); middle grades education (M Ed); reading (M Ed); secondary education (M Ed); special education (M Ed); teaching English to speakers of other languages (M Ed). *Accreditation:* NCATE. *Program availability:* Part-time. *Degree requirements:* For master's, thesis or alternative. *Entrance requirements:* For master's, GRE General Test, T-4 state certification, minimum GPA of 2.75. Additional exam requirements/recommendations for international students: Required—TOEFL (minimum score 550 paper-based; 80 iBT), IELTS (minimum score 6.5). Electronic applications accepted.

Kennesaw State University, Leland and Clarice C. Bagwell College of Education, Program in Teaching, Kennesaw, GA 30144. Offers art education (MAT); biology (MAT); chemistry (MAT); foreign language education (Chinese and Spanish) (MAT); physics (MAT); secondary English (MAT); secondary mathematics (MAT); special education (MAT); teaching English to speakers of other languages (MAT). *Program availability:* Part-time, evening/weekend. *Entrance requirements:* For master's, GRE, GACE I (state certificate exam), minimum GPA of 2.75, 2 recommendations, resume. Additional exam requirements/recommendations for international students: Required—TOEFL (minimum score 550 paper-based; 80 iBT), IELTS (minimum score 6.5). Electronic applications accepted.

Kent State University, College of Arts and Sciences, Department of Mathematical Sciences, Kent, OH 44242-0001. Offers applied mathematics (MA, MS, PhD); mathematics for secondary teachers (MA); pure mathematics (MA, MS, PhD). *Program availability:* Part-time. *Faculty:* 41 full-time (16 women). *Students:* 69 full-time (24 women), 41 part-time (19 women); includes 6 minority (2 Black or African American, non-Hispanic/Latino; 4 Asian, non-Hispanic/Latino), 46 international. Average age 30. 86 applicants, 67% accepted, 17 enrolled. In 2016, 18 master's, 4 doctorates awarded. *Degree requirements:* For master's, comprehensive exam (for some programs), thesis (for some programs); for doctorate, comprehensive exam, thesis/dissertation. *Entrance requirements:* For master's, bachelor's degree in mathematics or similar field, minimum GPA of 3.0, personal statement, resume, 3 letters of recommendation; for doctorate, master's degree, minimum GPA of 3.0, personal statement, resume, 3 letters of recommendation. Additional exam requirements/recommendations for international students: Required—TOEFL (minimum score of 525 paper-based, 71 iBT), IELTS (minimum score of 6), Michigan English Language Assessment Battery (minimum score of 75), or PTE (minimum score of 48). *Application deadline:* For fall admission, 5/1 for domestic and international students; for spring admission, 10/1 for domestic and international students; for summer admission, 2/1 for domestic and international students. Applications are processed on a rolling basis. Application fee: $45 ($70 for international students). Electronic applications accepted. *Expenses:* Tuition, state resident: full-time $10,864; part-time $495 per credit hour. Tuition, nonresident: full-time $18,380; part-time $837 per credit hour. *Financial support:* Fellowships with full tuition reimbursements, research assistantships with full tuition reimbursements, teaching assistantships with full tuition reimbursements, scholarships/grants, and unspecified assistantships available. Financial award application deadline: 1/31. *Unit head:* Dr. Andrew Tonge, Professor and Chair, 330-672-9046, E-mail: tonge@math.kent.edu. *Application contact:* Artem Zvavitch, Professor and Graduate Coordinator, 330-672-

9054, E-mail: jackn@math.kent.edu.
Website: http://www.kent.edu/math/

Kent State University, College of Education, Health and Human Services, School of Teaching, Learning and Curriculum Studies, Program in Secondary Education, Kent, OH 44242-0001. Offers MAT. *Accreditation:* NCATE. *Entrance requirements:* For master's, GRE General Test, 2 letters of reference, moral character form. Additional exam requirements/recommendations for international students: Required—TOEFL (minimum score 550 paper-based; 80 iBT). Electronic applications accepted. *Expenses:* Tuition, state resident: full-time $10,864; part-time $495 per credit hour. Tuition, nonresident: full-time $18,380; part-time $837 per credit hour. *Faculty research:* Creativity in science, women in science, teaching of writing, curriculum theory, mathematical reasoning.

Keuka College, Program in Childhood Education/Literacy, Keuka Park, NY 14478. Offers literacy 5-12 (MS); literacy B-6 (MS). *Faculty:* 7 full-time (5 women). *Students:* 9 full-time (8 women); includes 1 minority (Hispanic/Latino). Average age 23. 9 applicants, 100% accepted, 9 enrolled. In 2016, 8 master's awarded. *Degree requirements:* For master's, thesis, capstone project/student-led research project. *Entrance requirements:* For master's, GRE, minimum GPA of 3.0; 3 letters of recommendation (2 academic and one from cooperating teacher from student teaching or other professional). Additional exam requirements/recommendations for international students: Required—TOEFL (minimum score 550 paper-based). *Application deadline:* For fall admission, 8/15 priority date for domestic students; for winter admission, 12/15 priority date for domestic students; for spring admission, 4/15 priority date for domestic students. Applications are processed on a rolling basis. Application fee: $50. Electronic applications accepted. *Expenses:* Contact institution. *Financial support:* In 2016–17, 8 students received support. Scholarships/grants and tuition waivers (full and partial) available. Financial award applicants required to submit FAFSA. *Faculty research:* Marginalized populations, international literacy, teacher assessment. *Unit head:* Dr. Andrew Beigel, Director of Graduate Program in Education, 315-279-5442 Ext. 5662, E-mail: abeigel@keuka.edu. *Application contact:* Anna Decker, Secretary, Graduate Education, 315-279-5510, E-mail: adecker@keuka.edu.

Kutztown University of Pennsylvania, College of Education, Program in Secondary Education, Kutztown, PA 19530-0730. Offers biology (M Ed); curriculum and instruction (M Ed); English (M Ed); mathematics (M Ed); middle level (M Ed); social studies (M Ed); teaching (M Ed). *Accreditation:* NCATE. *Program availability:* Part-time, evening/weekend. *Faculty:* 4 full-time (2 women), 2 part-time/adjunct (0 women). *Students:* 35 full-time (23 women), 58 part-time (37 women); includes 4 minority (2 Black or African American, non-Hispanic/Latino; 2 Hispanic/Latino). Average age 31. 96 applicants, 86% accepted, 43 enrolled. In 2016, 35 master's awarded. *Degree requirements:* For master's, comprehensive exam, thesis optional. *Entrance requirements:* For master's, GRE General Test, minimum undergraduate major GPA of 3.0, 3 letters of recommendation, copy of PRAXIS II or valid instructional I or II teaching certificate. Additional exam requirements/recommendations for international students: Required—TOEFL (minimum score 550 paper-based, 79 iBT) or IELTS (minimum score 6.5). *Application deadline:* For fall admission, 8/1 for domestic and international students; for spring admission, 12/1 for domestic and international students. Application fee: $35. Electronic applications accepted. *Expenses:* Tuition, state resident: full-time $4347; part-time $483 per credit. Tuition, nonresident: full-time $6525; part-time $725 per credit. *Required fees:* $88 per credit. One-time fee: $50 full-time. *Financial support:* Career-related internships or fieldwork, Federal Work-Study, scholarships/grants, and unspecified assistantships available. Financial award application deadline: 3/1; financial award applicants required to submit FAFSA. *Unit head:* Dr. Theresa Stahler, Chairperson, 610-683-4259, Fax: 610-683-1338, E-mail: stahler@kutztown.edu. *Application contact:* Dr. Patricia Walsh Coates, Graduate Coordinator, 610-638-4289, Fax: 610-683-1338, E-mail: coates@kutztown.edu.
Website: https://www.kutztown.edu/academcs/graduate-programs/secondary-education.htm

LaGrange College, Graduate Programs, Department of Education, LaGrange, GA 30240-2999. Offers curriculum and instruction (M Ed, Ed S); middle grades (MAT); secondary education (MAT). *Program availability:* Part-time, evening/weekend. *Degree requirements:* For master's, comprehensive exam. *Entrance requirements:* For master's, GRE, MAT, minimum GPA of 2.5. Additional exam requirements/recommendations for international students: Required—TOEFL (minimum score 550 paper-based).

Lake Forest College, Master of Arts in Teaching Program, Lake Forest, IL 60045. Offers elementary education (MAT); K-12 French (MAT); K-12 music (MAT); K-12 Spanish (MAT); K-12 visual art (MAT); secondary biology (MAT); secondary chemistry (MAT); secondary English (MAT); secondary history (MAT); secondary mathematics (MAT). *Degree requirements:* For master's, comprehensive exam, portfolio. *Entrance requirements:* For master's, GRE.

Lancaster Bible College, Graduate School, Lancaster, PA 17601-5036. Offers adult ministries (MA); Bible (MA); children and family ministry (MA); church planting (MA); consulting resource teacher (M Ed); elementary school counseling (M Ed); leadership (PhD); leadership studies (MA); marriage and family counseling (MA); mental health counseling (MA); pastoral studies (MA); secondary school counseling (M Ed); sports ministry (MA); student ministry (MA); town and country ministry (MA). *Program availability:* Part-time, evening/weekend. *Degree requirements:* For master's, comprehensive exam (for some programs), thesis (for some programs). *Entrance requirements:* For master's, bachelor's degree with a minimum of 30 credits of course work in Bible, minimum undergraduate GPA of 3.0, interview. Additional exam requirements/recommendations for international students: Required—TOEFL.

La Salle University, School of Arts and Sciences, Program in Education, Philadelphia, PA 19141 1100. Offers autism spectrum disorders (MA, Certificate); bilingual/bicultural studies (MA); classroom management (MA); dual early childhood and special education (MA); dual middle-level science and math and special education (MA); education (MA); English (MA); English as a second language (Certificate); history (MA); instructional coach (Certificate); instructional leadership (MA); reading specialist (MA, Certificate); secondary education (MA); special education (MA, Certificate). *Program availability:* Part-time, evening/weekend. *Faculty:* 5 full-time (4 women), 12 part-time/adjunct (8 women). *Students:* 10 full-time (all women), 98 part-time (74 women); includes 28 minority (13 Black or African American, non-Hispanic/Latino; 1 American Indian or Alaska Native, non-Hispanic/Latino; 1 Asian, non-Hispanic/Latino; 10 Hispanic/Latino; 3 Two or more races, non-Hispanic/Latino). Average age 34. 128 applicants, 84% accepted, 69 enrolled. In 2016, 53 master's awarded. *Degree requirements:* For master's, comprehensive exam. *Entrance requirements:* For master's, MAT or GRE, 2 letters of recommendation; for Certificate, GMAT or GRE, 2 letters of recommendation. Additional exam requirements/recommendations for international students: Required—TOEFL. *Application deadline:* For fall admission, 8/15 priority date for domestic students, 7/15 for international students; for spring admission, 12/15 priority date for domestic students, 11/15 for international students; for summer admission, 4/15 priority date for domestic students, 3/15 for international students. Applications are processed on a rolling basis. Application fee: $35. Electronic applications accepted. Application fee is waived when completed online. *Expenses:* Contact institution. *Financial support:* In 2016–17, 27 students received support. Scholarships/grants available. Support available to part-time students. Financial award application deadline: 8/31; financial award applicants required to submit FAFSA. *Unit head:* Dr. Greer Richardson, Director, 215-951-1806, Fax: 215-951-1843, E-mail: graded@lasalle.edu. *Application contact:* Elizabeth Heenan, Director, Graduate and Adult Enrollment, 215-951-1100, Fax: 215-951-1462, E-mail: heenan@lasalle.edu.
Website: http://www.lasalle.edu/grad-education-programs/

Lee University, Program in Education, Cleveland, TN 37320-3450. Offers art (MAT); curriculum and instruction (M Ed, Ed S); early childhood (MAT); educational leadership (M Ed, Ed S); elementary education (MAT); English and math (MAT); English and science (MAT); English and social studies (MAT); higher education administration (MS); history (MAT); history and economics (MAT); math and science (MAT); math and social studies (MAT); middle grades (MAT); science and social studies (MASW); secondary education (MAT); Spanish (MAT); special education (M Ed, MAT); TESOL (MAT). *Accreditation:* NCATE. *Program availability:* Part-time. *Faculty:* 13 full-time (6 women), 9 part-time/adjunct (4 women). *Students:* 35 full-time (27 women), 50 part-time (32 women); includes 12 minority (5 Black or African American, non-Hispanic/Latino; 5 Hispanic/Latino; 2 Two or more races, non-Hispanic/Latino), 4 international. Average age 30. 43 applicants, 79% accepted, 28 enrolled. In 2016, 42 master's, 6 other advanced degrees awarded. *Degree requirements:* For master's, variable foreign language requirement, thesis optional, internship. *Entrance requirements:* For master's, MAT or GRE General Test, minimum undergraduate GPA of 2.75, 3 letters of recommendation, interview, writing sample, official transcripts, background check; for Ed S, minimum undergraduate and master's GPA of 2.75, official transcripts for undergraduate and master's degrees. Additional exam requirements/recommendations for international students: Required—TOEFL (minimum score 61 iBT). *Application deadline:* For fall admission, 6/1 priority date for domestic and international students; for spring admission, 11/1 priority date for domestic and international students; for summer admission, 4/1 priority date for domestic and international students. Applications are processed on a rolling basis. Application fee: $25. Electronic applications accepted. *Expenses:* *Tuition:* Full-time $11,367; part-time $632 per credit hour. *Required fees:* $35 per term. One-time fee: $25. Tuition and fees vary according to program. *Financial support:* In 2016–17, 42 students received support. Career-related internships or fieldwork, Federal Work-Study, institutionally sponsored loans, scholarships/grants, and unspecified assistantships available. Financial award application deadline: 3/1; financial award applicants required to submit FAFSA. *Unit head:* Dr. William Kamm, Director, 423-614-8544, E-mail: wkamm@leeuniversity.edu. *Application contact:* Crystal Keeter, Graduate Education Secretary, 423-614-8544, E-mail: ckeeter@leeuniversity.edu.
Website: http://www.leeuniversity.edu/academics/graduate/education

Le Moyne College, Department of Education, Syracuse, NY 13214. Offers adolescent education (MS Ed, MST); adolescent education/special education (MS Ed, MST); adolescent English (MST), including grades 7-12; adolescent English/special education (MST), including grades 7-12; adolescent foreign language (MST), including grades 7-12; adolescent history (MST), including grades 7-12; childhood education (MS Ed); childhood education/special education (MS Ed); elementary education (MS Ed); general education (MS Ed); inclusive childhood education (MST); literacy education (MS Ed), including birth to grade 6, grades 5-12; school building leader (MS Ed); school building leadership (CAS); school district business leader (MS Ed, CAS); school district leader (MS Ed); school district leadership (CAS); secondary education (MS Ed); special education (MS Ed); teaching English to speakers of other languages (MS Ed); urban studies (MS Ed). *Accreditation:* TEAC. *Program availability:* Part-time, evening/weekend. *Faculty:* 8 full-time (5 women), 20 part-time/adjunct (12 women). *Students:* 66 full-time (40 women), 155 part-time (117 women); includes 13 minority (4 Black or African American, non-Hispanic/Latino; 2 American Indian or Alaska Native, non-Hispanic/Latino; 2 Asian, non-Hispanic/Latino; 5 Hispanic/Latino), 3 international. Average age 30. 74 applicants, 99% accepted, 66 enrolled. In 2016, 81 master's, 53 CASs awarded. *Degree requirements:* For master's, thesis. *Entrance requirements:* For master's, bachelor's degree with minimum undergraduate GPA of 3.0, 2 letters of recommendation, transcripts. Additional exam requirements/recommendations for international students: Required—TOEFL (minimum score 550 paper-based; 79 iBT); Recommended—IELTS (minimum 6.5). *Application deadline:* For fall admission, 4/1 priority date for domestic and international students; for spring admission, 10/1 priority date for domestic and international students; for summer admission, 3/1 priority date for domestic and international students. Applications are processed on a rolling basis. Application fee: $50. Electronic applications accepted. *Expenses:* $700 per credit hour. *Financial support:* In 2016–17, 21 students received support. Career-related internships or fieldwork, scholarships/grants, and health care benefits available. Support available to part-time students. Financial award applicants required to submit FAFSA. *Faculty research:* Minority teachers, special education, multiculturalism, literacy, technology, media literacy learning, autism, school district organization, service-learning, higher level problem solving, teacher leadership. *Unit head:* Dr. Stephen C. Fleury, Chair, Department of Education, 315-445-4376, Fax: 315-445-4744, E-mail: fleurysc@lemoyne.edu. *Application contact:* Kristen P. Richards, Senior Director of Enrollment Management, 315-445-5444, Fax: 315-445-6092, E-mail: trapaskp@lemoyne.edu.
Website: http://www.lemoyne.edu/education

Lenoir-Rhyne University, Graduate Programs, School of Education, Master of Arts in Teaching Secondary Education Program, Hickory, NC 28601. Offers MAT. *Entrance requirements:* For master's, GRE (minimum score of 147 on each of the verbal and quantitative sections and 3.5 on the analytical) or MAT (minimum score of 390); or PRAXIS I (minimum scores of Reading 176, Writing 173, and Math 173), official transcripts from all undergraduate and graduate institutions attended, resume, essay, criminal background check. *Expenses:* Contact institution.

Lesley University, Graduate School of Education, Cambridge, MA 02138-2790. Offers arts, community, and education (M Ed); autism studies (Certificate); curriculum and instruction (M Ed, CAGS); early childhood education (M Ed); ecological teaching and learning (MS); educational studies (PhD), including adult learning, educational leadership, individually designed; elementary education (M Ed); emergent technologies for educators (Certificate); ESLArts: language learning through the arts (M Ed); high school education (M Ed); individually designed (M Ed); integrated teaching through the arts (M Ed); literacy for K-8 classroom teachers (M Ed); mathematics education (M Ed); middle school education (M Ed); moderate disabilities (M Ed); online learning (Certificate); reading (CAGS); science in education (M Ed); severe disabilities (M Ed); special needs (CAGS); specialist teacher of reading (M Ed); teacher of visual art (M Ed); technology in education (M Ed, CAGS). *Accreditation:* TEAC. *Program availability:* Part-time, evening/weekend, online learning. *Degree requirements:* For master's, practicum; for doctorate, thesis/dissertation. *Entrance requirements:* For master's, Massachusetts Tests for Educator Licensure (MTEL), transcripts, statement of purpose, recommendations; interview (for special education); for doctorate, GRE General Test, transcripts, statement of purpose, recommendations, interview, master's degree, resume; for other advanced degree, interview, master's degree. Additional exam requirements/recommendations for international students: Required—TOEFL (minimum score 550 paper-based; 80 iBT). Electronic applications accepted. *Faculty research:* Assessment in literacy, mathematics and science; autism spectrum disorders;

instructional technology and online learning; multicultural education and English language learners.

Lewis & Clark College, Graduate School of Education and Counseling, Department of Teacher Education, Program in Secondary Education, Portland, OR 97219-7899. Offers MAT. *Accreditation:* NCATE. *Entrance requirements:* For master's, prior experience working with children and/or youth; minimum undergraduate GPA of 2.75. Additional exam requirements/recommendations for international students: Required—TOEFL (minimum score 575 paper-based). *Application deadline:* For fall admission, 12/1 priority date for domestic and international students. Application fee: $50. Electronic applications accepted. *Financial support:* Career-related internships or fieldwork, Federal Work-Study, institutionally sponsored loans, scholarships/grants, health care benefits, and tuition waivers (partial) available. Support available to part-time students. Financial award application deadline: 3/1; financial award applicants required to submit FAFSA. *Faculty research:* Classroom management, classroom assessment, science education, classroom ethnography, moral development. *Unit head:* Liza Finkel, Director, 503-768-6104, Fax: 503-768-7715, E-mail: lcteach@lclark.edu. *Application contact:* Becky Haas, Director of Admissions, 503-768-6200, Fax: 503-768-6205, E-mail: gseadmit@lclark.edu.
Website: http://graduate.lclark.edu/departments/teacher_education/prospective_teachers/middle_high_school/

Lewis University, College of Education, Program in Secondary Education, Romeoville, IL 60446. Offers biology (MA); chemistry (MA); English (MA); history (MA); math (MA); physics (MA); psychology and social science (MA). *Program availability:* Part-time. *Students:* 12 full-time (7 women), 16 part-time (12 women); includes 6 minority (2 Black or African American, non-Hispanic/Latino; 3 Hispanic/Latino; 1 Two or more races, non-Hispanic/Latino). Average age 27. *Degree requirements:* For master's, departmental qualifying exam. *Entrance requirements:* For master's, writing exam, minimum GPA of 2.75, 2 letters of recommendation, interview. Additional exam requirements/recommendations for international students: Required—TOEFL (minimum score 550 paper-based; 80 iBT). *Application deadline:* For fall admission, 5/1 priority date for international students; for spring admission, 11/15 priority date for international students. Applications are processed on a rolling basis. Application fee: $40. Electronic applications accepted. *Expenses: Tuition:* Full-time $13,860; part-time $770 per credit hour. *Required fees:* $75 per semester. Tuition and fees vary according to degree level and program. *Financial support:* Federal Work-Study, scholarships/grants, and unspecified assistantships available. Financial award application deadline: 5/1; financial award applicants required to submit FAFSA. *Unit head:* Dr. Dorene Huvaere, Program Director, 815-838-0500 Ext. 5885, E-mail: huvaersdo@lewisu.edu. *Application contact:* Linda Campbell, Graduate Admissions Counselor, 815-836-5610, E-mail: campbeld@lewisu.edu.

Liberty University, School of Education, Lynchburg, VA 24515. Offers educational leadership (Ed D); gifted education (Certificate); math specialist (M Ed); middle grades (MAT, Certificate); reading specialist (M Ed); school leadership (Certificate); secondary education (MAT); sport management (MS), including administration, outdoor recreation, sport management, tourism. *Accreditation:* NCATE. *Program availability:* Part-time, online learning. *Students:* 1,910 full-time (1,427 women), 4,420 part-time (3,311 women); includes 1,451 minority (1,182 Black or African American, non-Hispanic/Latino; 33 American Indian or Alaska Native, non-Hispanic/Latino; 44 Asian, non-Hispanic/Latino; 46 Hispanic/Latino; 11 Native Hawaiian or other Pacific Islander, non-Hispanic/Latino; 135 Two or more races, non-Hispanic/Latino), 87 international. Average age 37. 5,120 applicants, 44% accepted, 1193 enrolled. In 2016, 1,378 master's, 151 doctorates, 497 other advanced degrees awarded. *Degree requirements:* For doctorate, comprehensive exam, thesis/dissertation. *Entrance requirements:* For master's, GRE General Test or MAT (if taken in or before 1999), 2 letters of recommendation, minimum undergraduate GPA of 3.0, curriculum vitae; for doctorate and Certificate, GRE General Test or MAT (if taken before 1999), minimum master's GPA of 3.0, 3 years of teaching experience. Additional exam requirements/recommendations for international students: Required—TOEFL (minimum score 600 paper-based; 100 iBT). *Application deadline:* For fall admission, 6/1 for domestic students; for spring admission, 11/1 for domestic students. Applications are processed on a rolling basis. Application fee: $50. Electronic applications accepted. *Expenses:* Contact institution. *Financial support:* Federal Work-Study and tuition waivers (partial) available. *Faculty research:* Self-determination, character education, bibliotherapy, learning styles, distance education. *Unit head:* Dr. Heather Schoffstall, Dean, 434-582-2445, Fax: 434-582-2468, E-mail: awgunter@liberty.edu. *Application contact:* Jay Bridge, Director of Graduate Admissions, 800-424-9595, Fax: 800-628-7977, E-mail: gradadmissions@liberty.edu.
Website: http://www.liberty.edu/academics/education/graduate/

Lincoln University, Graduate Studies, Jefferson City, MO 65101. Offers business administration (MBA), including accounting, management, management information systems, public administration/policy; elementary teaching (M Ed); environmental science (MS); guidance and counseling (M Ed), including community/agency counseling, elementary school, secondary school; higher education (MA); history (MA); integrated agricultural systems (MS); middle school (M Ed); natural sciences (MS); secondary teaching (M Ed); sociology (MA); sociology/criminal justice (MA). *Program availability:* Part-time, evening/weekend, 100% online, blended/hybrid learning. *Students:* 50 full-time (29 women), 68 part-time (39 women); includes 40 minority (37 Black or African American, non-Hispanic/Latino; 1 Asian, non-Hispanic/Latino; 2 Two or more races, non-Hispanic/Latino), 14 international. Average age 33. 75 applicants, 80% accepted, 34 enrolled. In 2016, 51 master's awarded. *Degree requirements:* For master's, comprehensive exam, thesis optional. *Entrance requirements:* For master's, GRE, MAT or GMAT, minimum GPA of 2.75 overall, 3.0 in courses related to specialization; 3 letters of recommendation; minimum C average in English composition; personal statement of purpose. Additional exam requirements/recommendations for international students: Required—TOEFL (minimum score 500 paper-based; 61 iBT), IELTS (minimum score 5.5), Michigan English Language Assessment Battery (minimum score 80). *Application deadline:* For fall admission, 7/1 priority date for domestic students, 5/1 priority date for international students; for spring admission, 11/1 priority date for domestic students, 10/1 priority date for international students; for summer admission, 6/1 priority date for domestic students. Applications are processed on a rolling basis. Application fee: $30. Electronic applications accepted. *Expenses:* Tuition, state resident: full-time $6840; part-time $5130 per year. Tuition, nonresident: full-time $12,720; part-time $9540 per year. *Required fees:* $852; $811 per unit. Tuition and fees vary according to course load. *Financial support:* In 2016–17, 2 fellowships with tuition reimbursements, 8 research assistantships with tuition reimbursements were awarded; Federal Work-Study, scholarships/grants, and unspecified assistantships also available. Support available to part-time students. Financial award application deadline: 3/1; financial award applicants required to submit FAFSA. *Unit head:* Dr. Rolundus R. Rice, Dean, 573-681-5247, Fax: 573-681-5106, E-mail: gradschool@lincolnu.edu. *Application contact:* Irasema Steck, Administrative Assistant, 573-681-5247, Fax: 573-681-5106, E-mail: gradschool@lincolnu.edu.
Website: http://www.lincolnu.edu/web/graduate-studies/graduate-studies

Long Island University–LIU Post, College of Education, Information and Technology, Brookville, NY 11548-1300. Offers adolescence education (MS); adolescence education 7-12 (MS); archives and records management (AC); art education (MS); childhood education (MS); childhood teaching literacy B-6 (MS); childhood/special education (MS); clinical mental health counseling (MS, AC); early childhood education (MS); early childhood education/childhood education (MS); educational leadership (AC); educational technology (MS); information studies (PhD); interdisciplinary educational studies (Ed D); middle childhood education (MS); music education (MS); school counselor (MS); special education (MS Ed); speech-language pathology (MA); students with disabilities, 7-12 generalist (AC); TESOL (MA). *Accreditation:* TEAC. *Program availability:* Part-time, 100% online, blended/hybrid learning. *Faculty:* 55 full-time (35 women), 104 part-time/adjunct (57 women). *Students:* 464 full-time (390 women), 740 part-time (580 women); includes 265 minority (99 Black or African American, non-Hispanic/Latino; 45 Asian, non-Hispanic/Latino; 113 Hispanic/Latino; 1 Native Hawaiian or other Pacific Islander, non-Hispanic/Latino; 7 Two or more races, non-Hispanic/Latino), 33 international. 928 applicants, 76% accepted, 406 enrolled. In 2016, 334 master's, 10 doctorates, 137 other advanced degrees awarded. Terminal master's awarded for partial completion of doctoral program. *Degree requirements:* For master's, variable foreign language requirement, comprehensive exam (for some programs), thesis optional; for doctorate, comprehensive exam, thesis/dissertation. *Entrance requirements:* For master's and AC, GRE. Additional exam requirements/recommendations for international students: Required—PTE, TOEFL (minimum score 550 paper-based, 75 iBT) or IELTS. *Application deadline:* Applications are processed on a rolling basis. Application fee: $50. Electronic applications accepted. *Expenses: Tuition:* Full-time $28,272; part-time $1178 per credit. *Required fees:* $451 per term. Tuition and fees vary according to degree level and program. *Financial support:* Career-related internships or fieldwork, Federal Work-Study, institutionally sponsored loans, scholarships/grants, tuition waivers (partial), and unspecified assistantships available. Support available to part-time students. Financial award application deadline: 2/15; financial award applicants required to submit FAFSA. *Faculty research:* English language learners, early childhood literacy development through play, sleep, social justice through education, using a structured protocol for discussing bad news. *Total annual research expenditures:* $575,000. *Unit head:* Dr. Albert Inserra, Dean, 516-299-2210, E-mail: albert.inserra@liu.edu. *Application contact:* Carol Zerah, Director of Graduate Admissions, 516-299-2900, Fax: 516-299-2137, E-mail: post-enroll@liu.edu.
Website: http://liu.edu/CWPost/Academics/College-of-Education-Information-and-Technology

Long Island University–LIU Post, College of Liberal Arts and Sciences, Brookville, NY 11548-1300. Offers applied mathematics (MS); behavior analysis (MA); biology (MS); criminal justice (MS); earth science (MS); English (MA); environmental sustainability (MS); genetic counseling (MS); history (MA); interdisciplinary studies (MA, MS); mathematics for secondary school teachers (MS); mobile GIS application development (Advanced Certificate); political science (MA); psychology (MA). *Program availability:* Part-time, evening/weekend, blended/hybrid learning. *Faculty:* 68 full-time (30 women), 20 part-time/adjunct (13 women). *Students:* 155 full-time (117 women), 125 part-time (82 women); includes 65 minority (17 Black or African American, non-Hispanic/Latino; 14 Asian, non-Hispanic/Latino; 27 Hispanic/Latino; 7 Two or more races, non-Hispanic/Latino), 19 international. 485 applicants, 36% accepted, 77 enrolled. In 2016, 91 master's, 15 other advanced degrees awarded. *Degree requirements:* For master's, comprehensive exam (for some programs), thesis (for some programs). *Entrance requirements:* Additional exam requirements/recommendations for international students: Required—PTE, TOEFL (minimum score 550 paper-based, 75 iBT) or IELTS (6.5). *Application deadline:* Applications are processed on a rolling basis. Application fee: $50. Electronic applications accepted. *Expenses: Tuition:* Full-time $28,272; part-time $1178 per credit. *Required fees:* $451 per term. Tuition and fees vary according to degree level and program. *Financial support:* In 2016–17, 24 teaching assistantships with partial tuition reimbursements (averaging $410 per year) were awarded; fellowships, research assistantships, career-related internships or fieldwork, Federal Work-Study, institutionally sponsored loans, scholarships/grants, tuition waivers (partial), and unspecified assistantships also available. Support available to part-time students. Financial award application deadline: 2/15; financial award applicants required to submit FAFSA. *Faculty research:* Biology, criminal justice, environmental sustainability, mathematics, psychology. *Total annual research expenditures:* $218,000. *Unit head:* Dr. Jeffrey Belnap, Acting Dean, 516-299-2233, Fax: 516-299-4140, E-mail: jeffrey.belnap@liu.edu. *Application contact:* Carol Zerah, Director of Graduate Admissions, 516-299-2900, Fax: 516-299-2137, E-mail: post-enroll@liu.edu.
Website: http://liu.edu/CWPost/Academics/Schools/CLAS

Long Island University–Riverhead, Graduate Programs, Riverhead, NY 11901. Offers childhood education (MS), including grades 1-6; homeland security management (MS); literacy education (MS); teaching students with disabilities (MS), including grades 1-6, grades 7-12; TESOL (Advanced Certificate). *Accreditation:* TEAC. *Program availability:* Part-time. *Degree requirements:* For master's, thesis (for some programs); for Advanced Certificate, comprehensive exam (for some programs). *Entrance requirements:* Additional exam requirements/recommendations for international students: Required—TOEFL (minimum score 550 paper-based; 79 iBT), IELTS (minimum score 6). *Application deadline:* Applications are processed on a rolling basis. Application fee: $50. Electronic applications accepted. *Expenses:* Contact institution. *Financial support:* Institutionally sponsored loans, scholarships/grants, tuition waivers (partial), and unspecified assistantships available. Support available to part-time students. Financial award application deadline: 2/15; financial award applicants required to submit FAFSA. *Unit head:* Donna Di Donato, Dean and Chief Operating Officer, LIU Brentwood and LIU Riverhead, 631-287-8010, Fax: 631-287-8575, E-mail: donna.didonato@liu.edu. *Application contact:* Christina Seifert, Director of Admission, LIU Brentwood and LIU Riverhead, 631-287-8505, Fax: 631-287-8253, E-mail: christina.seifert@liu.edu.

Louisiana State University and Agricultural & Mechanical College, Graduate School, College of Human Sciences and Education, Department of Educational Theory, Policy and Practice, Baton Rouge, LA 70803. Offers counseling (M Ed, MA, Ed S); educational administration (M Ed, MA, PhD, Ed S); educational technology (MA); elementary education (M Ed, MAT); higher education (PhD); research methodology (PhD); secondary education (M Ed, MAT). *Accreditation:* ACA (one or more programs are accredited); NCATE.

Loyola Marymount University, School of Education, Department of Elementary and Secondary Education, Program in Secondary Education, Los Angeles, CA 90045-2659. Offers MA. *Program availability:* Part-time. *Students:* 89 full-time (53 women), 25 part-time (13 women); includes 68 minority (8 Black or African American, non-Hispanic/Latino; 10 Asian, non-Hispanic/Latino; 45 Hispanic/Latino; 5 Two or more races, non-Hispanic/Latino). Average age 29. 60 applicants, 82% accepted, 45 enrolled. In 2016, 37 master's awarded. *Entrance requirements:* For master's, CBEST, CSET, 3 letters of recommendation. Additional exam requirements/recommendations for international students: Required—TOEFL (minimum score 600 paper-based; 100 iBT). *Application deadline:* For fall admission, 6/15 for domestic students; for spring admission, 11/15 for domestic students. Application fee: $50. Electronic applications accepted. *Financial support:* In 2016–17, 79 students received support, including 1 teaching assistantship; scholarships/grants and unspecified assistantships also available. Support available to part-time students. Financial award application deadline: 6/30; financial award applicants required to submit FAFSA. *Unit head:* Dr. Irene Oliver, Director, 310-338-

7302, E-mail: ioliver@lmu.edu. *Application contact:* Chake H. Kouyoumjian, Associate Dean of Graduate Studies, 310-338-2721, E-mail: ckouyoum@lmu.edu.
Website: http://soe.lmu.edu/academics/secondaryeducation/

Loyola University Chicago, School of Education, Program in Teaching and Learning, Chicago, IL 60660. Offers elementary education (M Ed); English language teaching and learning (M Ed); secondary education (M Ed). *Accreditation:* NCATE. *Faculty:* 22 full-time (16 women), 38 part-time/adjunct (30 women). *Students:* 31 full-time (25 women), 20 part-time (15 women); includes 6 minority (5 Hispanic/Latino; 1 Two or more races, non-Hispanic/Latino), 3 international. Average age 27. 113 applicants, 52% accepted, 37 enrolled. In 2016, 35 master's awarded. *Degree requirements:* For master's, comprehensive exam. *Entrance requirements:* For master's, Illinois Basic Skills Test, 3 letters of recommendation, minimum GPA of 3.0, resume. Additional exam requirements/recommendations for international students: Required—TOEFL (minimum score 550 paper-based; 79 iBT). *Application deadline:* For fall admission, 7/1 for domestic and international students; for spring admission, 11/1 priority date for domestic and international students; for summer admission, 3/1 priority date for domestic and international students. Applications are processed on a rolling basis. Application fee: $50. Electronic applications accepted. Application fee is waived when completed online. *Expenses:* $949 per hour; $2,847 per course; $8,541-$11,388 per semester plus fees $432 per semester and $225 the first semester. *Financial support:* In 2016–17, 19 students received support, including 19 fellowships with partial tuition reimbursements available; institutionally sponsored loans, scholarships/grants, and unspecified assistantships also available. Support available to part-time students. Financial award application deadline: 2/1; financial award applicants required to submit FAFSA. *Faculty research:* Positive behavior support, school reform, school improvement. *Unit head:* Dr. David Ensminger, Program Chair, 312-915-7257, E-mail: densmin@luc.edu. *Application contact:* Thomas Ott, Information Contact, 312-915-8907, E-mail: tott@luc.edu.

Loyola University Maryland, Graduate Programs, School of Education, Master of Arts in Teaching Program, Baltimore, MD 21210-2699. Offers elementary education (MAT); secondary education (MAT). *Program availability:* Part-time. *Faculty:* 34 full-time (22 women), 30 part-time/adjunct (24 women). *Students:* 23 full-time (17 women), 167 part-time (149 women); includes 57 minority (35 Black or African American, non-Hispanic/Latino; 6 Asian, non-Hispanic/Latino; 8 Hispanic/Latino; 1 Native Hawaiian or other Pacific Islander, non-Hispanic/Latino; 7 Two or more races, non-Hispanic/Latino), 1 international. Average age 30. 34 applicants, 41% accepted, 13 enrolled. In 2016, 39 master's awarded. *Entrance requirements:* For master's, essay, 2 letters of recommendation, resume, transcipt. Additional exam requirements/recommendations for international students: Required—TOEFL (minimum score 550 paper-based), IELTS (minimum score 7). *Application deadline:* For spring admission, 11/1 for domestic students. Applications are processed on a rolling basis. Application fee: $60. Electronic applications accepted. *Expenses:* Contact institution. *Financial support:* In 2016–17, 12 students received support. Scholarships/grants available. Financial award application deadline: 4/15; financial award applicants required to submit FAFSA. *Application contact:* Brandon Gumabon, 410-617-2559, E-mail: bggumabon@loyola.edu.
Website: http://www.loyola.edu/soe/academics/graduate/mat.aspx

Loyola University New Orleans, College of Arts and Sciences, Master of Arts in Teaching Program, New Orleans, LA 70118-6195. Offers MAT. *Program availability:* Part-time. *Faculty:* 1 (woman) full-time, 2 part-time/adjunct (1 woman). *Students:* 9 part-time (5 women); includes 5 minority (2 Black or African American, non-Hispanic/Latino; 1 American Indian or Alaska Native, non-Hispanic/Latino; 1 Asian, non-Hispanic/Latino; 1 Hispanic/Latino). Average age 30. 10 applicants, 100% accepted, 9 enrolled. *Application deadline:* Applications are processed on a rolling basis. Electronic applications accepted. *Expenses:* Contact institution. *Financial support:* Applicants required to submit FAFSA. *Unit head:* Dr. Glenda Hembree, Office of Teacher Education, E-mail: gghembre@loyno.edu. *Application contact:* 800-4LOYOLA, Fax: 504-865-3383, E-mail: admit@loyno.edu.
Website: http://cas.loyno.edu/teacher-education/mat

Manhattanville College, School of Education, Program in Middle Childhood/Adolescence Education (Grades 5-12), Purchase, NY 10577-2132. Offers biology (MAT); biology and special education (MPS); chemistry (MAT); chemistry and special education (MPS); English (MAT); English and special education (MPS); literacy and special education (MPS); literacy specialist (MPS); math and special education (MPS); mathematics (MAT); physics (MAT); social studies (MAT); social studies and special education (MPS); special education generalist (MPS); teaching languages other than English (MAT), including French, Italian, Latin, Spanish. *Program availability:* Part-time, evening/weekend. *Students:* 28 applicants, 86% accepted, 21 enrolled. In 2016, 23 master's awarded. *Degree requirements:* For master's, comprehensive exam (for some programs), thesis (for some programs), student teaching, research seminars, portfolios, internships, writing assessment. *Entrance requirements:* For master's, GRE or MAT, minimum undergraduate GPA of 3.0, 2 letters of recommendation. Additional exam requirements/recommendations for international students: Required—TOEFL (minimum score 85 iBT); Recommended—IELTS. *Application deadline:* For fall admission, 7/1 priority date for domestic and international students; for spring admission, 11/1 priority date for domestic and international students; for summer admission, 4/1 priority date for domestic and international students. Applications are processed on a rolling basis. Application fee: $75. Electronic applications accepted. *Expenses: Tuition:* Full-time $16,470; part-time $915 per credit. *Required fees:* $60 per semester. Part-time tuition and fees vary according to course load and program. *Financial support:* Teaching assistantships, career-related internships or fieldwork, Federal Work-Study, institutionally sponsored loans, scholarships/grants, and unspecified assistantships available. Financial award applicants required to submit FAFSA. *Unit head:* Victoria Fantozzi, Chairperson, Department of Curriculum and Instruction, 914-323-7138, E-mail: victoria.fantozzi@mville.edu. *Application contact:* Jeanine Pardey-Levine, Director of Graduate Enrollment Management, 914-323-3200, Fax: 914-694-1732, E-mail: edschool@mville.edu.
Website: http://www.mville.edu/programs#/search/19

Manhattanville College, School of Education, Program in Special Education, Purchase, NY 10577-2132. Offers childhood education (MPS); early childhood education (MPS); secondary education (MPS). *Program availability:* Part-time, evening/weekend. *Students:* 45 applicants, 69% accepted, 28 enrolled. In 2016, 26 master's, 1 Advanced Certificate awarded. *Degree requirements:* For master's, comprehensive exam (for some programs), thesis (for some programs), student teaching, research seminars, portfolios, internships, writing assessment; for Advanced Certificate, comprehensive exam (for some programs). *Entrance requirements:* For master's, GRE or MAT, minimum undergraduate GPA of 3.0, 2 letters of recommendation. Additional exam requirements/recommendations for international students: Required—TOEFL (minimum score 85 iBT); Recommended—IELTS. *Application deadline:* For fall admission, 7/1 priority date for domestic and international students; for spring admission, 11/1 priority date for domestic and international students; for summer admission, 4/1 priority date for domestic and international students. Applications are processed on a rolling basis. Application fee: $75. Electronic applications accepted. *Expenses: Tuition:* Full-time $16,470; part-time $915 per credit. *Required fees:* $60 per semester. Part-time tuition and fees vary according to course load and program. *Financial support:* Teaching assistantships, career-related internships or fieldwork, Federal Work-Study, institutionally sponsored loans, scholarships/grants, and unspecified assistantships available. Financial award applicants required to submit FAFSA. *Faculty research:* Aspects of verbal behavior and communication skills in autistic children, PBIS systems and their implementation, effective instructional practices for students with E/BDs, effective pedagogical practices that improve student behavioral and academic performance, increasing communication skills of young non-vocal children with autism. *Unit head:* Vance Austin, Chairperson, Department of Special Education, 914-323-7262, E-mail: vance.austin@mville.edu. *Application contact:* Jeanine Pardey-Levine, Director of Admissions, 914-323-3208, Fax: 914-694-1732, E-mail: edschool@mville.edu.
Website: http://www.mville.edu/programs/special-education

Mansfield University of Pennsylvania, Graduate Studies, Department of Education and Special Education, Mansfield, PA 16933. Offers elementary education (M Ed); secondary education (MS); special education (M Ed). *Accreditation:* NCATE (one or more programs are accredited). *Program availability:* Part-time, evening/weekend, online learning. *Degree requirements:* For master's, comprehensive exam, thesis optional. *Entrance requirements:* For master's, minimum GPA of 3.0. Additional exam requirements/recommendations for international students: Required—TOEFL (minimum score 550 paper-based). Electronic applications accepted.

Marquette University, Graduate School, College of Education, Department of Educational Policy and Leadership, Milwaukee, WI 53201-1881. Offers college student personnel administration (M Ed); curriculum and instruction (MA); education (MA); educational administration (M Ed); educational policy and foundations (MA); elementary education (Certificate); literacy (MA); principal (Certificate); reading specialist (Certificate); reading teacher (Certificate); secondary education (Certificate); superintendent (Certificate). *Program availability:* Part-time, evening/weekend. *Faculty:* 17 full-time (14 women), 28 part-time/adjunct (23 women). *Students:* 31 full-time (23 women), 103 part-time (66 women); includes 22 minority (7 Black or African American, non-Hispanic/Latino; 1 American Indian or Alaska Native, non-Hispanic/Latino; 6 Asian, non-Hispanic/Latino; 6 Hispanic/Latino; 2 Two or more races, non-Hispanic/Latino). Average age 31. 96 applicants, 92% accepted, 67 enrolled. In 2016, 47 master's, 3 other advanced degrees awarded. Terminal master's awarded for partial completion of doctoral program. *Degree requirements:* For master's, comprehensive exam, thesis (for some programs); for doctorate, thesis/dissertation, qualifying exam. *Entrance requirements:* For master's, GRE General Test or MAT, official transcripts from all current and previous colleges/universities except Marquette, three letters of recommendation, statement of purpose; for doctorate, GRE General Test, MAT, sample of written work, official transcripts from all current and previous colleges/universities except Marquette, three letters of recommendation, statement of purpose, resume/curriculum vitae; for Certificate, GRE General Test or MAT, master's degree. Additional exam requirements/recommendations for international students: Required—TOEFL (minimum score 530 paper-based). *Application deadline:* For fall admission, 1/15 for domestic and international students. Application fee: $50. *Expenses:* Contact institution. *Financial support:* Fellowships, research assistantships, health care benefits, tuition waivers (partial), and unspecified assistantships available. Support available to part-time students. Financial award application deadline: 2/15. *Faculty research:* Leadership; social justice in education; development of lifelong learners; race, class, and schooling in historical perspective; urban teacher education. *Unit head:* Dr. Ellen Eckman, Chair, 414-288-1561. *Application contact:* Dr. Cynthia Ellwood.

Marshall University, Academic Affairs Division, College of Education and Professional Development, Program in Secondary Education, Huntington, WV 25755. Offers MA. *Accreditation:* NCATE. *Program availability:* Part-time, evening/weekend. *Degree requirements:* For master's, thesis optional, comprehensive or oral assessment. *Entrance requirements:* For master's, GRE General Test or MAT.

Marygrove College, Graduate Division, Sage Program, Detroit, MI 48221-2599. Offers M Ed. *Accreditation:* TEAC. *Entrance requirements:* For master's, Michigan Teacher Test for Certification.

Marymount University, School of Education and Human Services, Program in Education, Arlington, VA 22207-4299. Offers elementary education (M Ed); English as a second language (M Ed); professional studies (M Ed); secondary education (M Ed); special education: general curriculum (M Ed). *Accreditation:* NCATE. *Program availability:* Part-time, evening/weekend. *Faculty:* 28 full-time (all women), 8 part-time/adjunct (5 women). *Students:* 42 full-time (33 women), 94 part-time (72 women); includes 25 minority (6 Black or African American, non-Hispanic/Latino; 6 Asian, non-Hispanic/Latino; 8 Hispanic/Latino; 5 Two or more races, non-Hispanic/Latino), 12 international. Average age 32. 32 applicants, 100% accepted, 24 enrolled. In 2016, 79 master's awarded. *Degree requirements:* For master's, thesis or alternative, capstone/internship. *Entrance requirements:* For master's, GRE or MAT and PRAXIS I or SAT/ACT and Virginia Communication and Literacy Assessment (VCLA), 2 letters of recommendation, resume, interview, minimum undergraduate GPA of 2.75 or 3.25 in the last 60 hours. Additional exam requirements/recommendations for international students: Required—TOEFL (minimum score 600 paper-based; 96 iBT), IELTS (minimum score 6.5). *Application deadline:* Applications are processed on a rolling basis. Application fee: $40. Electronic applications accepted. *Expenses:* $690 per credit hour. *Financial support:* In 2016–17, 6 students received support, including 2 teaching assistantships with tuition reimbursements available; career-related internships or fieldwork, Federal Work-Study, scholarships/grants, and unspecified assistantships also available. Support available to part-time students. Financial award applicants required to submit FAFSA. *Unit head:* Dr. Lisa Turissini, Chair, Education, 703-526-1668, Fax: 703-284-1631, E-mail: lisa.turissini@marymount.edu. *Application contact:* Francesca Reed, Director, Graduate Admissions, 703-284-5901, Fax: 703-527-3815, E-mail: grad.admissions@marymount.edu.
Website: http://www.marymount.edu/Academics/School-of-Education-Human-Services/Graduate-Programs/Education-(M-Ed-)

Maryville University of Saint Louis, School of Education, St. Louis, MO 63141-7299. Offers early childhood education (MA Ed); educational leadership (Ed D); educational leadership: principal certification (MA Ed); elementary education (MA Ed); gifted education (MA Ed); higher education leadership (Ed D); literacy specialist (MA Ed); middle grades education (MA Ed); secondary teaching and inquiry (MA Ed); teacher as leader (MA Ed); teacher leadership (Ed D). *Accreditation:* NCATE. *Program availability:* Part-time, evening/weekend. *Faculty:* 17 full-time (11 women), 21 part-time/adjunct (17 women). *Students:* 12 full-time (11 women), 297 part-time (208 women); includes 92 minority (79 Black or African American, non-Hispanic/Latino; 4 Asian, non-Hispanic/Latino; 4 Hispanic/Latino; 5 Two or more races, non-Hispanic/Latino), 4 international. Average age 38. In 2016, 32 master's, 61 doctorates awarded. *Degree requirements:* For master's, thesis, project. *Entrance requirements:* For master's, minimum cumulative GPA of 3.0, 3 professional recommendations, essays, interview with program faculty; for doctorate, minimum GPA of 3.0, 3 professional recommendations, essay, interview, on-site writing sample. Additional exam requirements/recommendations for international students: Required—TOEFL (minimum score 550 paper-based). *Application deadline:* Applications are processed on a rolling basis. Electronic applications accepted. *Expenses:* $879 per credit (for Ed D); $781 per credit (for master's). *Financial support:* Career-related internships or fieldwork, Federal Work-Study, tuition waivers (partial),

and professional educator discounts available. Financial award application deadline: 3/1; financial award applicants required to submit FAFSA. *Faculty research:* Collaboration with public schools, pre-service program development, mathematics, diversity, literacy. *Unit head:* Dr. Cathy Bear, Dean, 314-529-9692, Fax: 314-529-9921, E-mail: cbear@maryville.edu. *Application contact:* Stacey Ruffin, Coordinator of Clinical Experiences and Graduate Programs, 314-529-9542, Fax: 314-529-9921, E-mail: teachered@maryville.edu.
Website: http://www.maryville.edu/ed/graduate-programs/

Marywood University, Academic Affairs, Reap College of Education and Human Development, Department of Education, Program in Secondary/K-12 Education, Scranton, PA 18509-1598. Offers MAT. *Program availability:* Part-time. Electronic applications accepted.

McDaniel College, Graduate and Professional Studies, Program in Elementary and Secondary Education, Westminster, MD 21157-4390. Offers elementary education (MS); elementary STEM instructional leader (Postbaccalaureate Certificate); equity and excellence in education (Postbaccalaureate Certificate); learning technology specialist (Postbaccalaureate Certificate); secondary education (MS). *Accreditation:* NCATE. *Program availability:* Part-time, evening/weekend. *Faculty:* 3 full-time (2 women), 27 part-time/adjunct (22 women). *Students:* 8 full-time (5 women), 179 part-time (143 women); includes 60 minority (31 Black or African American, non-Hispanic/Latino; 3 American Indian or Alaska Native, non-Hispanic/Latino; 13 Asian, non-Hispanic/Latino; 11 Hispanic/Latino; 2 Two or more races, non-Hispanic/Latino), 1 international. Average age 36. 79 applicants, 94% accepted. In 2016, 23 master's, 48 other advanced degrees awarded. *Degree requirements:* For master's, comprehensive exam (for some programs), thesis optional. *Entrance requirements:* For master's, PRAXIS, 2 references. Additional exam requirements/recommendations for international students: Required—TOEFL (minimum score 79 iBT), IELTS (minimum score 6). *Application deadline:* For fall admission, 6/1 priority date for domestic students; for spring admission, 11/1 priority date for domestic students; for summer admission, 3/1 priority date for domestic students. Applications are processed on a rolling basis. Application fee: $75. Electronic applications accepted. *Expenses: Tuition:* Full-time $8370; part-time $465 per credit. *Required fees:* $75 per semester. Tuition and fees vary according to course load, program and reciprocity agreements. *Financial support:* Application deadline: 3/1; applicants required to submit FAFSA. *Unit head:* Fax: 410-857-2515, E-mail: gradadms@mcdaniel.edu. *Application contact:* Penny Pfeiffer, Senior Graduate Enrollment Management Specialist, 410-857-2513, Fax: 410-857-2515, E-mail: ppfeiffer@mcdaniel.edu.

McNeese State University, Doré School of Graduate Studies, Burton College of Education, Office of Graduate Education Programs, Program in Curriculum and Instruction, Lake Charles, LA 70609. Offers early childhood education (M Ed); elementary education (M Ed); reading (M Ed); secondary education (M Ed). *Program availability:* Evening/weekend. *Entrance requirements:* For master's, GRE, teaching certificate.

McNeese State University, Doré School of Graduate Studies, Burton College of Education, Office of Graduate Education Programs, Program in Secondary Education, Lake Charles, LA 70609. Offers MAT. *Program availability:* Evening/weekend. *Degree requirements:* For master's, comprehensive exam, field experiences. *Entrance requirements:* For master's, GRE General Test, PRAXIS I and II, autobiography, two letters of recommendation.

McNeese State University, Doré School of Graduate Studies, Burton College of Education, Office of Student Teaching and Professional Education Services, Program in Secondary Education Grades 6-12, Lake Charles, LA 70609. Offers Postbaccalaureate Certificate. *Entrance requirements:* For degree, PRAXIS, 2 letters of recommendation, autobiography.

Medaille College, Program in Education, Buffalo, NY 14214-2695. Offers adolescent education (MS Ed); curriculum and instruction (MS Ed); education preparation (MS Ed); literacy (MS Ed); special education (MS). *Accreditation:* TEAC. *Program availability:* Part-time, evening/weekend. *Degree requirements:* For master's, comprehensive exam (for some programs), thesis or alternative. *Entrance requirements:* For master's, minimum undergraduate GPA of 2.7. Additional exam requirements/recommendations for international students: Required—TOEFL (minimum score 550 paper-based). Electronic applications accepted. *Faculty research:* Curriculum planning, truancy, tracking minority students, curriculum design, mentoring students.

Mercer University, Graduate Studies, Cecil B. Day Campus, Tift College of Education (Atlanta), Macon, GA 31207. Offers curriculum and instruction (PhD); early childhood education (M Ed, MAT, Ed S); educational leadership (PhD), including higher education leadership, P-12 school leadership; educational leadership P-12 (M Ed, Ed S); higher education leadership (M Ed); independent and charter school leadership (M Ed); middle grades education (M Ed, MAT); reading specialist (M Ed); secondary education (M Ed, MAT); teacher leadership (Ed S). *Accreditation:* NCATE. *Program availability:* Part-time, evening/weekend. *Faculty:* 28 full-time (15 women), 30 part-time/adjunct (27 women). *Students:* 177 full-time (150 women), 324 part-time (264 women); includes 288 minority (256 Black or African American, non-Hispanic/Latino; 1 American Indian or Alaska Native, non-Hispanic/Latino; 7 Asian, non-Hispanic/Latino; 17 Hispanic/Latino; 1 Native Hawaiian or other Pacific Islander, non-Hispanic/Latino; 6 Two or more races, non-Hispanic/Latino), 1 international. Average age 35. In 2016, 173 master's, 34 doctorates, 54 other advanced degrees awarded. *Degree requirements:* For master's and Ed S, research project; for doctorate, comprehensive exam, thesis/dissertation. *Entrance requirements:* For master's, GRE or MAT, minimum undergraduate GPA of 2.75; for doctorate, GRE; for Ed S, GRE or MAT, minimum GPA of 3.25; 3 years of certified teaching experience (for educational leadership and teacher leadership). Additional exam requirements/recommendations for international students: Required—TOEFL (minimum score 80 iBT). *Application deadline:* For fall admission, 8/1 for domestic and international students; for spring admission, 12/1 for domestic and international students; for summer admission, 5/1 for domestic and international students. Applications are processed on a rolling basis. Application fee: $25 ($50 for international students). Electronic applications accepted. *Expenses:* $590 per credit, $1,770 per course (for M Ed); $595 per credit, $1,785 per course (for MAT); $615 per credit, $1,845 per course (for Ed S); $717 per credit, $2,151 per course (for PhD); $150 per semester technology fee. *Financial support:* Federal Work-Study and unspecified assistantships available. Support available to part-time students. Financial award application deadline: 5/1; financial award applicants required to submit FAFSA. *Faculty research:* Educational technology, multicultural and minority issues in education, educational leadership (P-12 and higher education), school discipline and school bullying, standards-based mathematics education. *Unit head:* Dr. James Barta, Dean, 478-301-5355, Fax: 478-301-2280, E-mail: barta_jj@mercer.edu. *Application contact:* Renee Slaton, Associate Director of Graduate Admissions, 678-547-6084, Fax: 678-547-6055, E-mail: mercereducation@mercer.edu.
Website: http://education.mercer.edu/

Mercy College, School of Education, Program in Adolescence Education, Dobbs Ferry, NY 10522-1189. Offers MS. *Program availability:* Part-time, evening/weekend, blended/hybrid learning. *Students:* 46 full-time (32 women), 83 part-time (51 women); includes 48 minority (19 Black or African American, non-Hispanic/Latino; 1 American Indian or Alaska Native, non-Hispanic/Latino; 1 Asian, non-Hispanic/Latino; 22 Hispanic/Latino; 5 Two or more races, non-Hispanic/Latino). Average age 32. 45 applicants, 40% accepted, 10 enrolled. In 2016, 38 master's awarded. *Degree requirements:* For master's, comprehensive exam (for some programs), thesis (for some programs). *Entrance requirements:* For master's, GRE, resume, undergraduate transcript. Additional exam requirements/recommendations for international students: Required—TOEFL (minimum score 600 paper-based; 100 iBT), IELTS (minimum score 8). *Application deadline:* For fall admission, 8/1 for international students. Applications are processed on a rolling basis. Application fee: $40. Electronic applications accepted. *Expenses: Tuition:* Full-time $15,156; part-time $842 per credit hour. *Required fees:* $620; $155 per term. Tuition and fees vary according to course load and program. *Financial support:* Career-related internships or fieldwork, Federal Work-Study, scholarships/grants, and unspecified assistantships available. Support available to part-time students. Financial award applicants required to submit FAFSA. *Unit head:* Dr. Rose Rudnitski, Dean for the School of Education, 914-674-7447, Fax: 914-674-7352, E-mail: rrudnitski@mercy.edu. *Application contact:* Allison Gurdineer, Senior Director of Admissions, 877-637-2946, Fax: 914-674-7382, E-mail: admissions@mercy.edu.
Website: https://www.mercy.edu/education/secondary-education

Mercy College, School of Education, Program in Teaching Literacy, Dobbs Ferry, NY 10522-1189. Offers teaching literacy (Advanced Certificate); teaching literacy, birth-6 (MS); teaching literacy, grades 5-12 (MS). *Program availability:* Part-time, evening/weekend, blended/hybrid learning. *Students:* 7 full-time (6 women), 92 part-time (82 women); includes 51 minority (12 Black or African American, non-Hispanic/Latino; 3 Asian, non-Hispanic/Latino; 35 Hispanic/Latino; 1 Two or more races, non-Hispanic/Latino). Average age 32. 28 applicants, 43% accepted, 8 enrolled. In 2016, 25 master's awarded. *Degree requirements:* For master's, comprehensive exam (for some programs), thesis (for some programs). *Entrance requirements:* For master's, GRE, resume, undergraduate transcript. Additional exam requirements/recommendations for international students: Required—TOEFL (minimum score 600 paper-based; 100 iBT), IELTS (minimum score 8). *Application deadline:* For fall admission, 8/1 for international students. Applications are processed on a rolling basis. Application fee: $40. Electronic applications accepted. *Expenses: Tuition:* Full-time $15,156; part-time $842 per credit hour. *Required fees:* $620; $155 per term. Tuition and fees vary according to course load and program. *Financial support:* Career-related internships or fieldwork, Federal Work-Study, scholarships/grants, and unspecified assistantships available. Support available to part-time students. Financial award applicants required to submit FAFSA. *Unit head:* Dr. Rose Rudnitski, Dean for the School of Education, 914-674-7447, Fax: 914-674-7352, E-mail: rrudnitski@mercy.edu. *Application contact:* Allison Gurdineer, Senior Director of Admissions, 877-637-2946, Fax: 914-674-7382, E-mail: admissions@mercy.edu.
Website: https://www.mercy.edu/education/literacy-and-multilingual-studies

Mercyhurst University, Graduate Studies, Program in Secondary Education: Pedagogy and Practice, Erie, PA 16546. Offers MS. *Program availability:* Part-time, evening/weekend. *Entrance requirements:* For master's, GRE or PRAXIS I, resume, essay, three professional references, transcripts. Additional exam requirements/recommendations for international students: Required—TOEFL.

Merrimack College, School of Education and Social Policy, North Andover, MA 01845-5800. Offers community engagement (M Ed), including community organizations, higher education, K-12 education; criminology and criminal justice (MS); curriculum and instruction (M Ed); early childhood education (M Ed); educational leadership (CAGS), including instructional leadership; elementary education (M Ed); English as a second language (PreK-6) (M Ed); high school education (M Ed); higher education (M Ed), including leadership and organizational development, student affairs; middle school education (M Ed); moderate disabilities (PreK-8) (M Ed); school counseling (M Ed). *Program availability:* Part-time, evening/weekend, 100% online courses with immersion events and in-classroom practicum close to home. *Faculty:* 17 full-time, 34 part-time/adjunct. *Students:* 204 full-time (172 women), 83 part-time (67 women); includes 32 minority (4 Black or African American, non-Hispanic/Latino; 2 Asian, non-Hispanic/Latino; 23 Hispanic/Latino; 3 Two or more races, non-Hispanic/Latino), 1 international. Average age 27. 261 applicants, 89% accepted, 200 enrolled. In 2016, 153 master's, 2 other advanced degrees awarded. *Degree requirements:* For master's, practicum, portfolio, and state test (for licensure track); capstone (for higher education, curriculum and instruction, and community engagement tracks). *Entrance requirements:* For master's, Massachusetts Teacher Education Licensure (MTEL), official transcripts from other colleges, resume, personal statement, 2 letters of recommendation. Additional exam requirements/recommendations for international students: Required—TOEFL (minimum score 84 iBT), IELTS (minimum score 6.5), PTE (minimum score 56). *Application deadline:* For fall admission, 8/14 for domestic students, 7/14 for international students; for spring admission, 1/10 for domestic students, 12/10 for international students; for summer admission, 5/10 for domestic students, 4/10 for international students. Applications are processed on a rolling basis. Application fee: $0. Electronic applications accepted. *Expenses:* Contact institution. *Financial support:* Fellowships with full tuition reimbursements, career-related internships or fieldwork, scholarships/grants, and health care benefits available. Support available to part-time students. Financial award application deadline: 5/1; financial award applicants required to submit FAFSA. *Faculty research:* Feminist praxis in higher education, transgender student agency and belonging, campus sexual violence prevention, the scholarship of engagement; community engagement; service learning; diversity education; community-university partnerships, college going behaviors and indicators of success for inner city youth, strategies to increase students pursuit and success in STEM higher education, effective workforce development for displaced or under employed individuals, police reform, e.g. surveillance. *Application contact:* Alyssa Frey, Graduate Admissions Counselor, 978-837-3563, E-mail: freya@merrimack.edu.
Website: http://www.merrimack.edu/academics/graduate/education/

Middle Tennessee State University, College of Graduate Studies, College of Education, Department of Educational Leadership, Program in Curriculum and Instruction, Murfreesboro, TN 37132. Offers curriculum and instruction (M Ed, Ed S); English as a second language (M Ed, Ed S); secondary education (M Ed); technology and curriculum design (Ed S). *Accreditation:* NCATE. *Program availability:* Part-time, evening/weekend, online learning. *Degree requirements:* For master's, comprehensive exam; for Ed S, comprehensive exam, thesis or alternative. *Entrance requirements:* For master's and Ed S, GRE, MAT or PRAXIS. Additional exam requirements/recommendations for international students: Required—TOEFL (minimum score 525 paper-based; 71 iBT) or IELTS (minimum score 6). Electronic applications accepted.

Milligan College, Area of Education, Milligan College, TN 37682. Offers combined preK-3/K-5 education (M Ed); educational leadership (Ed D, Ed S); K-5 education (M Ed); middle grades education (M Ed); preK-3 education (M Ed); preK-3 special education (M Ed); secondary education (M Ed). *Accreditation:* NCATE. *Program availability:* Part-time. *Faculty:* 5 full-time (3 women), 3 part-time/adjunct (1 woman). *Students:* 26 full-time (19 women), 20 part-time (10 women); includes 2 minority (1 Black or African American, non-Hispanic/Latino; 1 Hispanic/Latino), 2 international. Average age 28. 16 applicants, 81% accepted, 11 enrolled. In 2016, 19 master's awarded.

Degree requirements: For master's, thesis, portfolio, research project; for doctorate, thesis/dissertation, portfolio, research project. *Entrance requirements:* For master's, MAT, GRE General Test, ACT, SAT, or PRAXIS, undergraduate degree and supporting transcripts, professional recommendations, interview; for doctorate, MAT or GRE, master's degree and supporting transcripts, demonstrated scholastic ability, recognized leadership role within education, professional recommendations, essay/personal statement, portfolio (professional development plan, evidence of ability, knowledge and qualities), interview. Additional exam requirements/recommendations for international students: Required—TOEFL (minimum score 550 paper-based, 79 iBT) or IELTS (6.5). *Application deadline:* For fall admission, 8/1 priority date for domestic students, 6/1 for international students; for spring admission, 11/15 priority date for domestic students, 12/1 for international students; for summer admission, 4/1 for domestic students. Applications are processed on a rolling basis. Application fee: $30. Electronic applications accepted. *Expenses:* $360 per hour tuition (for M Ed); $475 per hour tuition (for Ed D and Ed S); $325 per semester tech/activity fees. *Financial support:* Scholarships/grants available. Financial award application deadline: 12/1; financial award applicants required to submit FAFSA. *Faculty research:* Assessment; school mental health; literacy; technology; educator preparation. *Unit head:* Dr. Angela Hilton-Prillhart, Area Chair of Education, 423-461-8769, Fax: 423-461-3103, E-mail: anhilton-prillhart@milligan.edu. *Application contact:* Melissa Dillow, Graduate Admissions Recruiter, Education, 423-461-8306, Fax: 423-461-8982, E-mail: msdillow@milligan.edu.
Website: http://www.Milligan.edu/GPS

Mississippi College, Graduate School, School of Education, Department of Teacher Education and Leadership, Clinton, MS 39058. Offers art (M Ed); biological science (M Ed); business education (M Ed); computer science (M Ed); dyslexia therapy (M Ed); educational leadership (M Ed, Ed D, Ed S); elementary education (M Ed, Ed S); English (M Ed); higher education administration (MS); mathematics (M Ed); secondary education (M Ed); social studies (history) (M Ed); teaching arts (M Ed). *Program availability:* Part-time, online learning. *Degree requirements:* For master's, comprehensive exam, thesis optional. *Entrance requirements:* For master's, NTE. Additional exam requirements/recommendations for international students: Recommended—TOEFL, IELTS. Electronic applications accepted.

Mississippi State University, College of Education, Department of Curriculum, Instruction and Special Education, Mississippi State, MS 39762. Offers early childhood education (PhD); elementary education (MS, PhD, Ed S), including early childhood education (MS), general elementary education (MS), middle level education (MS); general curriculum and instruction (PhD); middle level (MAT); reading education (PhD); secondary education (MAT, MS, PhD, Ed S); special education (MAT, MS, PhD, Ed S). *Accreditation:* NCATE. *Program availability:* Part-time, evening/weekend. *Faculty:* 21 full-time (16 women), 1 (woman) part-time/adjunct. *Students:* 39 full-time (26 women), 168 part-time (128 women); includes 49 minority (43 Black or African American, non-Hispanic/Latino; 2 American Indian or Alaska Native, non-Hispanic/Latino; 1 Hispanic/Latino; 1 Native Hawaiian or other Pacific Islander, non-Hispanic/Latino; 2 Two or more races, non-Hispanic/Latino), 4 international. Average age 33. 98 applicants, 56% accepted, 47 enrolled. In 2016, 69 master's, 6 doctorates, 10 other advanced degrees awarded. *Degree requirements:* For master's, comprehensive exam; for doctorate, thesis/dissertation; for Ed S, comprehensive exam, thesis or alternative. *Entrance requirements:* For master's, GRE, minimum GPA of 2.75 in junior and senior year, eligibility for initial teacher certification; for doctorate, GRE, minimum GPA of 3.4 on previous graduate work; for Ed S, GRE, minimum GPA of 3.2 on master's degree. Additional exam requirements/recommendations for international students: Required—TOEFL (minimum score 550 paper-based; 79 iBT); Recommended—IELTS (minimum score 6.5). *Application deadline:* For fall admission, 3/1 priority date for domestic students, 5/1 for international students; for spring admission, 9/1 priority date for domestic students, 9/1 for international students. Applications are processed on a rolling basis. Application fee: $60. Electronic applications accepted. *Expenses:* Tuition, state resident: full-time $7670; part-time $852.50 per credit hour. Tuition, nonresident: full-time $20,790; part-time $2310.50 per credit hour. Part-time tuition and fees vary according to course load. *Financial support:* In 2016–17, 8 research assistantships with partial tuition reimbursements (averaging $11,381 per year) were awarded; Federal Work-Study, institutionally sponsored loans, scholarships/grants, and unspecified assistantships also available. Financial award application deadline: 4/1; financial award applicants required to submit FAFSA. *Faculty research:* Early childhood education, reading, rural schools, multicultural education, use of technology in instruction. *Unit head:* Dr. Janice Nicholson, Interim Department Head, 662-325-3704, Fax: 662-325-7857, E-mail: jin4@msstate.edu. *Application contact:* Linda Bonner, Senior Admissions Assistant, 662-325-3363, E-mail: lbonner@grad.msstate.edu.
Website: http://www.cise.msstate.edu/

Mississippi State University, College of Education, Educational Leadership Program, Mississippi State, MS 39762. Offers community college education (MAT, PhD); elementary, middle and secondary education administration (PhD); school administration (MS, Ed S); workforce education leadership (MS). MS in workforce education leadership held jointly with Alcorn State University. *Faculty:* 16 full-time (10 women). *Students:* 32 full-time (16 women), 158 part-time (101 women); includes 82 minority (80 Black or African American, non-Hispanic/Latino; 1 Hispanic/Latino; 1 Two or more races, non-Hispanic/Latino). Average age 38. 60 applicants, 58% accepted, 34 enrolled. In 2016, 24 master's, 15 doctorates, 5 other advanced degrees awarded. *Degree requirements:* For master's and Ed S, comprehensive exam, thesis; for doctorate, comprehensive exam, thesis/dissertation. *Entrance requirements:* For master's, GRE, minimum GPA of 2.75 in junior and senior courses; for doctorate, GRE, minimum GPA of 3.4 on previous graduate work; for Ed S, GRE, minimum GPA of 3.2, master's degree. Additional exam requirements/recommendations for international students: Required—TOEFL (minimum score 550 paper-based; 79 iBT); Recommended—IELTS (minimum score 6.5). *Application deadline:* For fall admission, 7/1 for domestic students, 5/1 for international students; for spring admission, 11/1 for domestic students, 9/1 for international students. Application fee: $60. Electronic applications accepted. *Expenses:* Tuition, state resident: full-time $7670; part-time $852.50 per credit hour. Tuition, nonresident: full-time $20,790; part-time $2310.50 per credit hour. Part-time tuition and fees vary according to course load. *Financial support:* In 2016–17, 2 research assistantships with full tuition reimbursements (averaging $12,940 per year) were awarded; Federal Work-Study, institutionally sponsored loans, and unspecified assistantships also available. Financial award application deadline: 4/1; financial award applicants required to submit FAFSA. *Unit head:* Dr. Ed Davis, Interim Department Head/Professor, 662-325-0969, Fax: 662-325-0975, E-mail: jed11@colled.msstate.edu. *Application contact:* Linda Bonner, Senior Admissions Assistant, 662-325-3363, E-mail: lbonner@grad.msstate.edu.
Website: http://www.educationalleadership.msstate.edu/

Missouri State University, Graduate College, College of Education, Department of Counseling, Leadership, and Special Education, Program in Counseling, Springfield, MO 65897. Offers elementary school counseling (MS); mental health counseling (MS); secondary school counseling (MS). *Accreditation:* ACA. *Program availability:* Part-time, evening/weekend. *Students:* 67 full-time (51 women), 43 part-time (39 women); includes 16 minority (4 Black or African American, non-Hispanic/Latino; 7 Hispanic/Latino; 5 Two or more races, non-Hispanic/Latino), 3 international. Average age 30. 46 applicants, 50% accepted, 18 enrolled. In 2016, 35 master's awarded. *Degree requirements:* For master's, comprehensive exam, thesis or alternative. *Entrance requirements:* For master's, GRE or MAT, minimum GPA of 2.75. Additional exam requirements/recommendations for international students: Required—TOEFL (minimum score 550 paper-based; 79 iBT), IELTS (minimum score 6). *Application deadline:* For fall admission, 2/1 priority date for domestic students, 1/1 priority date for international students; for spring admission, 10/1 priority date for domestic students, 9/1 priority date for international students. Application fee: $35 ($50 for international students). Electronic applications accepted. *Expenses:* Tuition, state resident: full-time $5830. Tuition, nonresident: full-time $10,708. *Required fees:* $1130. Tuition and fees vary according to class time, course level, course load and program. *Financial support:* Federal Work-Study, institutionally sponsored loans, scholarships/grants, and unspecified assistantships available. Financial award application deadline: 3/31; financial award applicants required to submit FAFSA. *Unit head:* Dr. James Satterfield, Department Head, 417-836-5392, Fax: 417-836-4918, E-mail: clse@missouristate.edu. *Application contact:* Michael Edwards, Coordinator of Graduate Admissions, 417-836-5300, Fax: 417-836-6200, E-mail: michaeledwards@missouristate.edu.
Website: http://education.missouristate.edu/clse/

Missouri State University, Graduate College, College of Education, Department of Counseling, Leadership, and Special Education, Program in Educational Administration, Springfield, MO 65897. Offers elementary principal (MS Ed, Ed S); secondary principal (MS Ed, Ed S); superintendent (Ed S). *Program availability:* Part-time, evening/weekend. *Students:* 2 full-time (0 women), 60 part-time (40 women); includes 6 minority (2 Black or African American, non-Hispanic/Latino; 1 American Indian or Alaska Native, non-Hispanic/Latino; 2 Hispanic/Latino; 1 Two or more races, non-Hispanic/Latino). Average age 34. 6 applicants, 67% accepted, 3 enrolled. In 2016, 34 master's, 15 Ed Ss awarded. *Degree requirements:* For master's and Ed S, comprehensive exam, thesis or alternative. *Entrance requirements:* For master's, minimum GPA of 2.75; for Ed S, GRE General Test, MAT, minimum GPA of 2.75. Additional exam requirements/recommendations for international students: Required—TOEFL (minimum score 550 paper-based; 79 iBT), IELTS (minimum score 6). *Application deadline:* For fall admission, 7/20 priority date for domestic students, 5/1 for international students; for spring admission, 12/20 priority date for domestic students, 9/1 for international students; for summer admission, 5/20 priority date for domestic students. Applications are processed on a rolling basis. Application fee: $35 ($50 for international students). Electronic applications accepted. *Expenses:* Tuition, state resident: full-time $5830. Tuition, nonresident: full-time $10,708. *Required fees:* $1130. Tuition and fees vary according to class time, course level, course load and program. *Financial support:* Career-related internships or fieldwork, Federal Work-Study, institutionally sponsored loans, scholarships/grants, and unspecified assistantships available. Financial award application deadline: 3/31; financial award applicants required to submit FAFSA. *Unit head:* Dr. James Satterfield, Department Head, 417-836-5392, Fax: 417-836-4918, E-mail: clse@missouristate.edu. *Application contact:* Michael Edwards, Coordinator of Graduate Admissions, 417-836-5330, Fax: 417-836-6200, E-mail: michaeledwards@missouristate.edu.
Website: http://education.missouristate.edu/edadmin/

Missouri State University, Graduate College, College of Education, Department of Reading, Foundations, and Technology, Master of Arts in Teaching Program, Springfield, MO 65897. Offers MAT. *Program availability:* Part-time. *Students:* 13 full-time (10 women), 69 part-time (50 women); includes 10 minority (8 Hispanic/Latino; 2 Two or more races, non-Hispanic/Latino), 1 international. Average age 33. 7 applicants, 100% accepted, 3 enrolled. In 2016, 19 master's awarded. *Degree requirements:* For master's, comprehensive exam, project. *Entrance requirements:* For master's, PRAXIS II. Additional exam requirements/recommendations for international students: Required—TOEFL (minimum score 550 paper-based; 79 iBT), IELTS (minimum score 6). *Application deadline:* For fall admission, 2/15 priority date for domestic and international students; for summer admission, 2/15 priority date for domestic students. Application fee: $35 ($50 for international students). Electronic applications accepted. *Expenses:* Tuition, state resident: full-time $5830. Tuition, nonresident: full-time $10,708. *Required fees:* $1130. Tuition and fees vary according to class time, course level, course load and program. *Financial support:* Federal Work-Study, institutionally sponsored loans, scholarships/grants, tuition waivers (full), and unspecified assistantships available. Financial award application deadline: 3/31; financial award applicants required to submit FAFSA. *Unit head:* Dr. Cathy Pearman, Department Head, 417-836-6769, E-mail: rft@missouristate.edu. *Application contact:* Michael Edwards, Coordinator of Graduate Admissions, 417-836-5330, Fax: 417-836-6200, E-mail: michaeledwards@missouristate.edu.

Missouri State University, Graduate College, College of Health and Human Services, Department of Kinesiology, Springfield, MO 65897. Offers health promotion and wellness management (MS); secondary education (MS Ed), including physical education. *Program availability:* Part-time. *Faculty:* 14 full-time (6 women). *Students:* 19 full-time (7 women), 8 part-time (4 women); includes 3 minority (1 Black or African American, non-Hispanic/Latino; 1 Asian, non-Hispanic/Latino; 1 Hispanic/Latino), 1 international. Average age 26. 19 applicants, 63% accepted, 7 enrolled. In 2016, 14 master's awarded. *Degree requirements:* For master's, comprehensive exam, thesis or alternative. *Entrance requirements:* For master's, GRE (for MS), minimum GPA of 2.8 (MS); 9-12 teaching certification (MS Ed). Additional exam requirements/recommendations for international students: Required—TOEFL (minimum score 550 paper-based; 79 iBT), IELTS (minimum score 6). *Application deadline:* For fall admission, 7/20 priority date for domestic students, 5/1 for international students; for spring admission, 12/20 priority date for domestic students, 9/1 for international students. Applications are processed on a rolling basis. Application fee: $35 ($50 for international students). Electronic applications accepted. *Expenses:* Tuition, state resident: full-time $5830. Tuition, nonresident: full-time $10,708. *Required fees:* $1130. Tuition and fees vary according to class time, course level, course load and program. *Financial support:* In 2016–17, 7 teaching assistantships with partial tuition reimbursements (averaging $8,772 per year) were awarded; Federal Work-Study, institutionally sponsored loans, scholarships/grants, and unspecified assistantships also available. Financial award application deadline: 3/31; financial award applicants required to submit FAFSA. *Unit head:* Dr. Sarah McCallister, Head, 417-836-6582, Fax: 417-836-5371, E-mail: sarahmccallister@missouristate.edu. *Application contact:* Michael Edwards, Coordinator of Graduate Admissions, 417-836-5330, Fax: 417-836-6200, E-mail: michaeledwards@missouristate.edu.
Website: http://www.missouristate.edu/kinesiology/

Missouri State University, Graduate College, College of Natural and Applied Sciences, Department of Biology, Springfield, MO 65897. Offers biology (MS); natural and applied science (MNAS), including biology (MNAS, MS Ed); secondary education (MS Ed), including biology (MNAS, MS Ed). *Faculty:* 18 full-time (3 women), 7 part-time/adjunct (2 women). *Students:* 11 full-time (7 women), 30 part-time (22 women); includes 4 minority (1 Asian, non-Hispanic/Latino; 2 Hispanic/Latino; 1 Two or more races, non-Hispanic/Latino), 7 international. Average age 26. 34 applicants, 41% accepted, 10 enrolled. In 2016, 23 master's awarded. *Degree requirements:* For master's, comprehensive exam, thesis or alternative. *Entrance requirements:* For master's, GRE (MS, MNAS), 24 hours

of course work in biology (MS); minimum GPA of 3.0 (MS, MNAS); 9-12 teacher certification (MS Ed). Additional exam requirements/recommendations for international students: Required—TOEFL (minimum score 550 paper-based; 79 iBT), IELTS (minimum score 6). *Application deadline:* For fall admission, 7/20 priority date for domestic students, 5/1 for international students; for spring admission, 12/20 priority date for domestic students, 9/1 for international students; for summer admission, 5/20 priority date for domestic students. Applications are processed on a rolling basis. Application fee: $35 ($50 for international students). Electronic applications accepted. *Expenses:* Tuition, state resident: full-time $5830. Tuition, nonresident: full-time $10,708. *Required fees:* $1130. Tuition and fees vary according to class time, course level, course load and program. *Financial support:* In 2016–17, 2 research assistantships with full tuition reimbursements (averaging $10,672 per year), 26 teaching assistantships with full tuition reimbursements (averaging $9,746 per year) were awarded; Federal Work-Study, institutionally sponsored loans, scholarships/grants, and unspecified assistantships also available. Financial award application deadline: 3/31; financial award applicants required to submit FAFSA. *Faculty research:* Hibernation physiology of bats, behavioral ecology of salamanders, mussel conservation, plant evolution and systematics, cellular/molecular mechanisms involved in migraine pathology. *Unit head:* Dr. S. Alicia Mathis, Department Head, 417-836-5126, Fax: 417-836-6934, E-mail: biology@missouristate.edu. *Application contact:* Michael Edwards, Coordinator of Graduate Admissions, 417-836-5330, Fax: 417-836-6200, E-mail: michaeledwards@missouristate.edu.
Website: http://biology.missouristate.edu/

Missouri State University, Graduate College, College of Natural and Applied Sciences, Department of Chemistry, Springfield, MO 65897. Offers chemistry (MS); natural and applied science (MNAS), including chemistry (MNAS, MS Ed); secondary education (MS Ed), including chemistry (MNAS, MS Ed). *Program availability:* Part-time. *Faculty:* 15 full-time (2 women). *Students:* 12 full-time (4 women), 7 part-time (1 woman), 4 international. Average age 27. 22 applicants, 18% accepted, 4 enrolled. In 2016, 8 master's awarded. *Degree requirements:* For master's, comprehensive exam, thesis. *Entrance requirements:* For master's, GRE General Test (MS, MNAS), minimum undergraduate GPA of 3.0 (MS and MNAS), 9-12 teacher certification (MS Ed). Additional exam requirements/recommendations for international students: Required—TOEFL (minimum score 550 paper-based; 79 iBT), IELTS (minimum score 6). *Application deadline:* For fall admission, 7/20 priority date for domestic students, 5/1 for international students; for spring admission, 12/20 priority date for domestic students, 9/1 for international students; for summer admission, 5/20 priority date for domestic students. Applications are processed on a rolling basis. Application fee: $35 ($50 for international students). Electronic applications accepted. *Expenses:* Tuition, state resident: full-time $5830. Tuition, nonresident: full-time $10,708. *Required fees:* $1130. Tuition and fees vary according to class time, course level, course load and program. *Financial support:* In 2016–17, 17 teaching assistantships with full tuition reimbursements (averaging $8,772 per year) were awarded; Federal Work-Study, institutionally sponsored loans, scholarships/grants, and unspecified assistantships also available. Financial award application deadline: 3/31; financial award applicants required to submit FAFSA. *Faculty research:* Polyethylene glycol derivatives, electrochemiluminescence of environmental systems, enzymology, environmental organic pollutants, DNA repair via nuclear magnetic resonance (NMR). *Unit head:* Dr. Bryan Breyfogle, Department Head, 417-836-5601, Fax: 417-836-5507, E-mail: chemistry@missouristate.edu. *Application contact:* Michael Edwards, Coordinator of Graduate Admissions, 417-836-5330, Fax: 417-836-6200, E-mail: michaeledwards@missouristate.edu.
Website: http://chemistry.missouristate.edu/

Missouri State University, Graduate College, College of Natural and Applied Sciences, Department of Geography, Geology, and Planning, Springfield, MO 65897. Offers natural and applied science (MNAS), including geography, geology and planning; secondary education (MS Ed), including earth science, physical geography. *Program availability:* Part-time, evening/weekend. *Faculty:* 18 full-time (4 women), 1 part-time/adjunct (0 women). *Students:* 18 full-time (6 women), 15 part-time (9 women); includes 2 minority (both Hispanic/Latino), 4 international. Average age 30. 36 applicants, 67% accepted, 19 enrolled. In 2016, 5 master's awarded. *Degree requirements:* For master's, comprehensive exam, thesis (for some programs). *Entrance requirements:* For master's, GRE General Test (MS, MNAS), minimum undergraduate GPA of 3.0 (MS, MNAS), 9-12 teacher certification (MS Ed). Additional exam requirements/recommendations for international students: Required—TOEFL (minimum score 550 paper-based; 79 iBT), IELTS (minimum score 6). *Application deadline:* For fall admission, 7/20 priority date for domestic students, 5/1 for international students; for spring admission, 12/20 priority date for domestic students, 9/1 for international students. Applications are processed on a rolling basis. Application fee: $35 ($50 for international students). Electronic applications accepted. *Expenses:* Tuition, state resident: full-time $5830. Tuition, nonresident: full-time $10,708. *Required fees:* $1130. Tuition and fees vary according to class time, course level, course load and program. *Financial support:* In 2016–17, 3 research assistantships with full tuition reimbursements (averaging $11,574 per year), 15 teaching assistantships with full tuition reimbursements (averaging $9,365 per year) were awarded; career-related internships or fieldwork, Federal Work-Study, institutionally sponsored loans, scholarships/grants, and unspecified assistantships also available. Financial award application deadline: 3/31; financial award applicants required to submit FAFSA. *Faculty research:* Stratigraphy and ancient meteorite impacts, environmental geochemistry of karst, hyperspectral image processing, water quality, small town planning. *Unit head:* Dr. Toby Dogwiler, Department Head, 417-836-5800, Fax: 417-836-6934, E-mail: tobydogwiler@missouristate.edu. *Application contact:* Michael Edwards, Coordinator of Graduate Admissions, 417-836-5330, Fax: 417-836-6200, E-mail: michaeledwards@missouristate.edu.
Website: http://geosciences.missouristate.edu/

Missouri State University, Graduate College, College of Natural and Applied Sciences, Department of Mathematics, Springfield, MO 65897. Offers mathematics (MS); natural and applied science (MNAS), including mathematics (MNAS, MS Ed); secondary education (MS Ed), including mathematics (MNAS, MS Ed). *Program availability:* Part-time. *Faculty:* 21 full-time (4 women). *Students:* 5 full-time (1 woman), 20 part-time (10 women), 7 international. Average age 27. 23 applicants, 43% accepted, 3 enrolled. In 2016, 17 master's awarded. *Degree requirements:* For master's, comprehensive exam, thesis or alternative. *Entrance requirements:* For master's, GRE (MS, MNAS), minimum undergraduate GPA of 3.0 (MS, MNAS), 9-12 teacher certification (MS Ed). Additional exam requirements/recommendations for international students: Required—TOEFL (minimum score 550 paper-based; 79 iBT), IELTS (minimum score 6). *Application deadline:* For fall admission, 7/20 priority date for domestic students, 5/1 for international students; for spring admission, 12/20 priority date for domestic students, 9/1 for international students. Applications are processed on a rolling basis. Application fee: $35 ($50 for international students). Electronic applications accepted. *Expenses:* Tuition, state resident: full-time $5830. Tuition, nonresident: full-time $10,708. *Required fees:* $1130. Tuition and fees vary according to class time, course level, course load and program. *Financial support:* In 2016–17, 11 teaching assistantships with full tuition reimbursements (averaging $10,672 per year) were awarded; Federal Work-Study, institutionally sponsored loans, scholarships/grants, and unspecified assistantships also available. Financial award application deadline: 3/31; financial award applicants required to submit FAFSA. *Faculty research:* Harmonic analysis, commutative algebra, number theory, K-theory, probability. *Unit head:* Dr. William Bray, Department Head, 417-836-5112, Fax: 417-836-6966, E-mail: mathematics@missouristate.edu. *Application contact:* Michael Edwards, Coordinator of Graduate Admissions, 417-836-5330, Fax: 417-836-6200, E-mail: michaeledwards@missouristate.edu.
Website: http://math.missouristate.edu/

Missouri State University, Graduate College, College of Natural and Applied Sciences, Department of Physics, Astronomy, and Materials Science, Springfield, MO 65897. Offers materials science (MS); natural and applied science (MNAS), including physics (MNAS, MS Ed); secondary education (MS Ed), including physics (MNAS, MS Ed). *Program availability:* Part-time. *Faculty:* 9 full-time (0 women). *Students:* 17 full-time (2 women), 3 part-time (0 women), 15 international. Average age 26. 36 applicants, 44% accepted, 7 enrolled. In 2016, 5 master's awarded. *Degree requirements:* For master's, comprehensive exam, thesis. *Entrance requirements:* For master's, GRE (MS, MNAS), minimum undergraduate GPA of 3.0 (MS and MNAS), 9-12 teaching certification (MS Ed). Additional exam requirements/recommendations for international students: Required—TOEFL (minimum score 550 paper-based; 79 iBT), IELTS (minimum score 6). *Application deadline:* For fall admission, 7/20 priority date for domestic students, 5/1 for international students; for spring admission, 12/20 priority date for domestic students, 9/1 for international students. Applications are processed on a rolling basis. Application fee: $35 ($50 for international students). Electronic applications accepted. *Expenses:* Tuition, state resident: full-time $5830. Tuition, nonresident: full-time $10,708. *Required fees:* $1130. Tuition and fees vary according to class time, course level, course load and program. *Financial support:* In 2016–17, 6 research assistantships with full tuition reimbursements (averaging $10,672 per year), 11 teaching assistantships with full tuition reimbursements (averaging $10,672 per year) were awarded; Federal Work-Study, institutionally sponsored loans, scholarships/grants, and unspecified assistantships also available. Financial award application deadline: 3/31; financial award applicants required to submit FAFSA. *Faculty research:* Nanocomposites, ferroelectricity, infrared focal plane array sensors, biosensors, pulsating stars. *Unit head:* Dr. David Cornelison, Department Head, 417-836-4467, Fax: 417-836-6226, E-mail: physics@missouristate.edu. *Application contact:* Michael Edwards, Coordinator of Graduate Admissions, 417-836-5330, Fax: 417-836-6200, E-mail: michaeledwards@missouristate.edu.
Website: http://physics.missouristate.edu/

Missouri State University, Graduate College, Darr College of Agriculture, Springfield, MO 65897. Offers plant science (MS); secondary education (MS Ed), including agriculture. *Program availability:* Part-time. *Faculty:* 16 full-time (5 women), 1 part-time/adjunct (0 women). *Students:* 20 full-time (16 women), 26 part-time (10 women); includes 4 minority (1 Black or African American, non-Hispanic/Latino; 3 Two or more races, non-Hispanic/Latino), 2 international. Average age 27. 28 applicants, 64% accepted, 17 enrolled. In 2016, 26 master's awarded. *Degree requirements:* For master's, comprehensive exam, thesis or alternative. *Entrance requirements:* For master's, GRE (MS in plant science, MNAS), 9-12 teacher certification (MS Ed), minimum GPA of 3.0 (MS plant science, MNAS). Additional exam requirements/recommendations for international students: Required—TOEFL (minimum score 550 paper-based; 79 iBT), IELTS (minimum score 6). *Application deadline:* For fall admission, 7/20 priority date for domestic students, 5/1 for international students; for spring admission, 12/20 priority date for domestic students, 9/1 for international students; for summer admission, 5/20 priority date for domestic students. Applications are processed on a rolling basis. Application fee: $35 ($50 for international students). Electronic applications accepted. *Expenses:* Tuition, state resident: full-time $5830. Tuition, nonresident: full-time $10,708. *Required fees:* $1130. Tuition and fees vary according to class time, course level, course load and program. *Financial support:* In 2016–17, 7 research assistantships with full tuition reimbursements (averaging $9,365 per year), 6 teaching assistantships with full tuition reimbursements (averaging $8,450 per year) were awarded; Federal Work-Study, institutionally sponsored loans, scholarships/grants, and unspecified assistantships also available. Financial award application deadline: 3/31; financial award applicants required to submit FAFSA. *Faculty research:* Grapevine biotechnology, agricultural marketing, Asian elephant reproduction, poultry science, integrated pest management. *Unit head:* Dr. Ronald Del Vecchio, Dean, 417-836-5050, E-mail: darr@missouristate.edu. *Application contact:* Michael Edwards, Coordinator of Graduate Admissions, 417-836-5330, Fax: 417-836-6200, E-mail: michaeledwards@missouristate.edu.
Website: http://ag.missouristate.edu/

Monmouth University, Graduate Studies, School of Education, West Long Branch, NJ 07764-1898. Offers applied behavior analysis (Certificate); autism (Certificate); director of school counseling services (Post-Master's Certificate); early childhood (M Ed); educational leadership (Ed D); elementary education (MAT), including elementary level, secondary level; English as a second language (M Ed); learning disabilities teacher-consultant (Post-Master's Certificate); literacy (MS Ed); school counseling (MS Ed); special education (MS Ed), including autism, learning disabilities teacher-consultant, teacher of students with disabilities, teaching in inclusive settings; speech-language pathology (MS Ed); student affairs and college counseling (MS Ed); supervisor (Post-Master's Certificate); teaching English to speakers of other languages (Certificate). *Accreditation:* NCATE. *Program availability:* Part-time, evening/weekend, 100% online, blended/hybrid learning. *Faculty:* 23 full-time (19 women), 33 part-time/adjunct (25 women). *Students:* 191 full-time (172 women), 141 part-time (122 women); includes 56 minority (10 Black or African American, non-Hispanic/Latino; 9 Asian, non-Hispanic/Latino; 31 Hispanic/Latino; 6 Two or more races, non-Hispanic/Latino). Average age 26. 423 applicants, 53% accepted, 139 enrolled. In 2016, 148 master's, 4 other advanced degrees awarded. *Entrance requirements:* For master's, GRE taken within last 5 years (for MS Ed in speech-language pathology); SAT (minimum combined score of 1660 in 3 sections), ACT (23), GRE (minimum score of 4.0 on analytical writing section and minimum combined score of 310 on quantitative and verbal sections), or passing scores on 3 parts of Core Academic Skills Educators, minimum GPA of 3.0 in major; 2 letters of recommendation (for some programs); resume, personal statement or essay (depending on program). Additional exam requirements/recommendations for international students: Required—TOEFL (minimum score 550 paper-based; 79 iBT), IELTS (minimum score 6), Michigan English Language Assessment Battery (minimum score 77) or Certificate of Advanced English (minimum score B2). *Application deadline:* For fall admission, 7/15 priority date for domestic students, 7/1 for international students; for spring admission, 12/1 priority date for domestic students, 11/1 for international students; for summer admission, 5/1 for domestic students. Applications are processed on a rolling basis. Application fee: $50. Electronic applications accepted. *Expenses: Tuition, area resident:* Full-time $19,764; part-time $1098 per credit hour. *Required fees:* $175 per semester. Tuition and fees vary according to program. *Financial support:* In 2016–17, 349 students received support, including 305 fellowships (averaging $3,558 per year), 48 teaching assistantships (averaging $9,619 per year); research assistantships, institutionally sponsored loans, scholarships/grants, and unspecified assistantships also available. Support available to part-time students. Financial award application deadline: 2/1; financial award applicants required to submit FAFSA. *Faculty research:* Multicultural literacy, science and mathematics teaching strategies, teacher as reflective practitioner,

children with disabilities. *Unit head:* Dr. John E. Henning, Dean, 732-263-5513, Fax: 732-263-5277. *Application contact:* Laurie Kuhn, Associate Director of Graduate Admission, 732-571-3452, Fax: 732-263-5123, E-mail: gradadm@monmouth.edu.
Website: http://www.monmouth.edu/academics/schools/education/default.asp

Montana State University Billings, College of Education, Department of Educational Theory and Practice, Option in General Curriculum, Billings, MT 59101. Offers K-8 (M Ed); secondary (M Ed). *Accreditation:* NCATE. *Program availability:* Part-time. *Faculty:* 15 full-time (10 women), 1 (woman) part-time/adjunct. *Students:* 62. *Degree requirements:* For master's, thesis or professional paper and/or field experience. *Entrance requirements:* For master's, GRE General Test or MAT, minimum GPA of 3.0. Additional exam requirements/recommendations for international students: Required—TOEFL (minimum score 79 iBT), IELTS (minimum score 6.5). *Application deadline:* Applications are processed on a rolling basis. Application fee: $40. Electronic applications accepted. *Expenses:* Tuition, state resident: full-time $5265; part-time $3436 per year. Tuition, nonresident: full-time $14,030; part-time $9280 per year. *International tuition:* $19,295 full-time. Tuition and fees vary according to degree level, campus/location and program. *Financial support:* Teaching assistantships with partial tuition reimbursements, career-related internships or fieldwork, Federal Work-Study, institutionally sponsored loans, scholarships/grants, tuition waivers (partial), and unspecified assistantships available. Support available to part-time students. Financial award application deadline: 5/1; financial award applicants required to submit FAFSA. *Faculty research:* Social studies education, science education. *Unit head:* Dr. Ken Miller, Chair, 406-657-2034, Fax: 406-657-2807, E-mail: kmiller@msubillings.edu. *Application contact:* David M. Sullivan, Graduate Studies Counselor, 406-657-2053, Fax: 406-657-2299, E-mail: dsullivan@msubillings.edu.

Morehead State University, Graduate Programs, College of Education, Department of Curriculum and Instruction, Morehead, KY 40351. Offers curriculum and instruction (Ed S); elementary education (MA Ed), including elementary education, international education, middle school education, reading; secondary education (MA Ed); special education (MA Ed); teaching (MAT). *Program availability:* Part-time, evening/weekend. *Degree requirements:* For master's, comprehensive exam, thesis optional; for Ed S, thesis, oral exam. *Entrance requirements:* For master's, GRE General Test, minimum GPA of 2.75, teaching certificate; for Ed S, GRE General Test, interview, master's degree, minimum GPA of 3.5, work experience. Additional exam requirements/recommendations for international students: Required—TOEFL (minimum score 500 paper-based). Electronic applications accepted. *Faculty research:* Communicative competence of learning-disabled students, teaching social studies in elementary schools, ungraded primary school organization, study skills.

Morehead State University, Graduate Programs, College of Education, Department of Middle Grades and Secondary Education, Morehead, KY 40351. Offers business and marketing education (MAT); English/language arts 5-9 (MAT); French (MAT); health P-12 (MAT); mathematics 5-9 (MAT); physical education P-12 (MAT); science 5-9 (MAT); secondary biology (MAT); secondary chemistry (MAT); secondary earth science (MAT); secondary English (MAT); secondary math (MAT); secondary physics (MAT); secondary social studies (MAT); social studies 5-9 (MAT); Spanish (MAT). *Program availability:* Part-time, evening/weekend. *Degree requirements:* For master's, portfolio. *Entrance requirements:* For master's, GRE or PRAXIS II content exam, minimum overall undergraduate GPA of 2.5. Additional exam requirements/recommendations for international students: Required—TOEFL (minimum score 500 paper-based). Electronic applications accepted.

Morgan State University, School of Graduate Studies, School of Education and Urban Studies, MAT Program, Baltimore, MD 21251. Offers elementary education (MAT); high school education (MAT); middle school education (MAT). *Program availability:* Part-time. *Degree requirements:* For master's, comprehensive exam. *Entrance requirements:* For master's, GRE General Test or MAT. *Faculty research:* Multicultural education, cooperative learning, psychology of cognition.

Mount St. Joseph University, Graduate Education Program, Cincinnati, OH 45233-1670. Offers adolescent to young adult education (MA); dyslexia (Certificate); inclusive early childhood education (MA); middle childhood education (MA); multicultural special education (MA); reading science (MA). *Accreditation:* TEAC. *Program availability:* Part-time, evening/weekend, online learning. *Faculty:* 7 full-time (5 women), 12 part-time/adjunct (10 women). *Students:* 44 full-time (33 women), 112 part-time (104 women); includes 16 minority (15 Black or African American, non-Hispanic/Latino; 1 Two or more races, non-Hispanic/Latino). Average age 34. In 2016, 60 master's awarded. *Degree requirements:* For master's, comprehensive exam, thesis, research project, student teaching, clinical and field-based experiences. *Entrance requirements:* For master's, GRE (if GPA is below 3.0), letter of intent, 2 referrals, background check, interview, resume, minimum undergraduate GPA of 3.0. Additional exam requirements/recommendations for international students: Required—TOEFL (minimum score 560 paper-based; 83 iBT). *Application deadline:* Applications are processed on a rolling basis. Application fee: $50. Electronic applications accepted. *Expenses:* $580 per credit hour. *Financial support:* Applicants required to submit FAFSA. *Faculty research:* Foreign and second language learning problems/reading disabilities, multicultural/bilingual special education, science education, pedagogical content knowledge, early childhood, response to intervention. *Unit head:* Dr. Laura Saylor, Dean, 513-244-3263, E-mail: laura.saylor@msj.edu. *Application contact:* Mary Brigham, Assistant Director of Graduate Recruitment, 513-244-4233, Fax: 513-244-4629, E-mail: mary.brigham@msj.edu.
Website: http://www.msj.edu/academics/graduate-programs/master-of-arts-initial-teacher-licensure-programs/

Murray State University, College of Education, Department of Adolescent, Career and Special Education, Program in Secondary Education, Murray, KY 42071. Offers MA Ed, Ed S. *Accreditation:* NCATE. *Program availability:* Part-time. *Degree requirements:* For master's, comprehensive exam, thesis optional; for Ed S, comprehensive exam. *Entrance requirements:* Additional exam requirements/recommendations for international students: Required—TOEFL.

National Louis University, National College of Education, Chicago, IL 60603. Offers administration and supervision (M Ed, Ed D, CAS, Ed S); curriculum and instruction (M Ed, MS Ed, CAS); early childhood administration (M Ed, CAS); early childhood education (M Ed, MAT, MS Ed, CAS); education (Ed D); educational psychology/human learning and development (M Ed, MS Ed, CAS, Ed S); elementary education (MAT); interdisciplinary curriculum and instruction (M Ed); mathematics education (M Ed, MS Ed, CAS); middle grades education (MAT); reading and language (M Ed, MS Ed, CAS); school psychology (M Ed, Ed S); science education (M Ed, MS Ed, CAS); secondary education (MAT); special education (M Ed, MAT, CAS); technology in education (M Ed, CAS). *Accreditation:* NCATE. *Program availability:* Part-time, evening/weekend. *Degree requirements:* For doctorate, comprehensive exam, thesis/dissertation. *Entrance requirements:* For master's, MAT or GRE, minimum GPA of 3.0; for doctorate, GRE General Test, minimum GPA of 3.25, interview, resume, writing sample, 4 recommendations. Additional exam requirements/recommendations for international students: Required—TOEFL (minimum score 550 paper-based; 79 iBT).

Neumann University, Graduate Program in Education, Aston, PA 19014-1298. Offers education (MS), including administrative (principal K-12), autism, early elementary education, secondary education, special education. *Program availability:* Part-time, evening/weekend, 100% online, blended/hybrid learning. *Faculty:* 6 full-time (5 women), 18 part-time/adjunct (7 women). *Students:* 80 full-time (64 women), 108 part-time (91 women); includes 40 minority (30 Black or African American, non-Hispanic/Latino; 6 Hispanic/Latino; 4 Two or more races, non-Hispanic/Latino), 1 international. Average age 34. 152 applicants, 67% accepted, 82 enrolled. In 2016, 42 master's awarded. *Entrance requirements:* For master's, official transcripts from all institutions attended, letter of intent, three professional references, copy of any teaching certifications. Additional exam requirements/recommendations for international students: Required—TOEFL (minimum score 70 iBT). *Application deadline:* Applications are processed on a rolling basis. Application fee: $0. Electronic applications accepted. *Expenses:* $700 per credit on-campus tuition; $480 per credit online or off-campus tuition; additional $320 for student teaching course. *Financial support:* Scholarships/grants and health care benefits available. Support available to part-time students. Financial award application deadline: 3/15; financial award applicants required to submit FAFSA. *Unit head:* Dr. Stephanie Smith-Budhai, Director of Graduate Education, 610-358-4249, E-mail: budhais@neumann.edu. *Application contact:* Dr. Erika Davis, Director of Adult and Graduate Admissions, 800-9-NEUMANN Ext. 5208, Fax: 610-361-2548, E-mail: GradAdultAdmiss@neumann.edu.
Website: https://www.neumann.edu/academics/grad/education/index.asp

New Jersey City University, Debra Cannon Partridge Wolfe College of Education, Department of Elementary and Secondary Education, Jersey City, NJ 07305-1597. Offers elementary education (MAT); secondary education (MAT). *Program availability:* Part-time, evening/weekend. *Entrance requirements:* Additional exam requirements/recommendations for international students: Required—TOEFL (minimum score 79 iBT).

New York Institute of Technology, School of Interdisciplinary Studies and Education, Department of Teacher Education, Old Westbury, NY 11568-8000. Offers adolescence education (MS), including mathematics, science; childhood education (MS); early childhood (MS). *Program availability:* Part-time, evening/weekend, 100% online, blended/hybrid learning. *Faculty:* 2 full-time (both women), 7 part-time/adjunct (3 women). *Students:* 19 full-time (15 women), 41 part-time (35 women); includes 18 minority (5 Black or African American, non-Hispanic/Latino; 4 Asian, non-Hispanic/Latino; 8 Hispanic/Latino; 1 Two or more races, non-Hispanic/Latino). Average age 33. 57 applicants, 74% accepted, 29 enrolled. In 2016, 12 master's awarded. *Entrance requirements:* For master's, GRE (minimum combined score of 300 from any two tests), MAT (minimum score 400), LAST (taken within past five years), BS or equivalent; minimum cumulative undergraduate GPA of 3.0; NY state provisional or initial certification (for adolescence education); BS with major in biology, chemistry, economics, English, history, life sciences, math, physics, or psychology (for childhood and early childhood education). Additional exam requirements/recommendations for international students: Required—TOEFL (minimum score 79 iBT), IELTS (minimum score 6). *Application deadline:* Applications are processed on a rolling basis. Application fee: $50. Electronic applications accepted. *Expenses:* $1,215 per credit. *Financial support:* Career-related internships or fieldwork, Federal Work-Study, scholarships/grants, tuition waivers (full and partial), and unspecified assistantships available. Support available to part-time students. Financial award application deadline: 3/1; financial award applicants required to submit FAFSA. *Faculty research:* Evolving definition of new literacies and its impact on teaching and learning (twenty-first century skills), new literacies practices in teacher education, teachers' professional development, English language and literacy learning through mobile learning, teaching reading to culturally and linguistically diverse children. *Unit head:* Dr. Hui-Yin Hsu, Department Chair, 516-686-1322, Fax: 516-686-7655, E-mail: hhsu02@nyit.edu. *Application contact:* Alice Dolitsky, Director, Graduate Admissions, 516-686-7520, Fax: 516-686-1116, E-mail: nyitgrad@nyit.edu.
Website: http://www.nyit.edu/interdisciplinary/department_teacher_education

New York University, Steinhardt School of Culture, Education, and Human Development, Department of Art and Art Professions, Program in Art Education, New York, NY 10003-5799. Offers art, education, and community practice (MA); teachers of art, all grades (MA); teaching art/social studies 7-12 (MA), including 5-6 extension. *Accreditation:* TEAC. *Program availability:* Part-time. *Degree requirements:* For master's, thesis (for some programs). *Entrance requirements:* For master's, portfolio. Additional exam requirements/recommendations for international students: Required—TOEFL (minimum score 100 iBT). Electronic applications accepted. *Faculty research:* Multicultural aesthetic inquiry, urban art education, feminism, equity and social justice.

New York University, Steinhardt School of Culture, Education, and Human Development, Department of Music and Performing Arts Professions, Program in Educational Theatre, New York, NY 10012. Offers educational theatre and English 7-12 (MA); educational theatre and social studies 7-12 (MA); educational theatre in colleges and communities (MA, Ed D, PhD); educational theatre, all grades (MA). *Program availability:* Part-time. *Degree requirements:* For master's, thesis (for some programs); for doctorate, thesis/dissertation. *Entrance requirements:* For master's, audition; for doctorate, GRE General Test, interview. Additional exam requirements/recommendations for international students: Required—TOEFL (minimum score 100 iBT). Electronic applications accepted. *Faculty research:* Theatre for young audiences, drama in education, applied theatre, arts education assessment, reflective praxis.

New York University, Steinhardt School of Culture, Education, and Human Development, Department of Teaching and Learning, Program in English Education, New York, NY 10012-1019. Offers clinically-based English education, grades 7-12 (MA); English education (PhD, Advanced Certificate); English education, grades 7-12 (MA). *Accreditation:* TEAC. *Program availability:* Part-time. *Degree requirements:* For master's, thesis (for some programs); for doctorate, thesis/dissertation. *Entrance requirements:* For doctorate, GRE General Test, interview; for Advanced Certificate, master's degree. Additional exam requirements/recommendations for international students: Required—TOEFL (minimum score 100 iBT). Electronic applications accepted. *Faculty research:* Making meaning of literature, teaching of literature, urban adolescent literacy and equity, literacy development and globalization, digital media and literacy.

New York University, Steinhardt School of Culture, Education, and Human Development, Department of Teaching and Learning, Program in Multilingual/Multicultural Studies, New York, NY 10003. Offers bilingual education (MA, PhD, Advanced Certificate); foreign language education (MA); teaching English to speakers of other languages (MA, PhD); teaching foreign languages, 7-12 (MA), including Chinese, French, Italian, Japanese, Spanish; teaching French as a foreign language (MA), including teaching English to speakers of other languages; teaching Spanish as a foreign language (MA), including teaching English to speakers of other languages. *Accreditation:* TEAC. *Program availability:* Part-time, evening/weekend. *Degree requirements:* For master's, thesis (for some programs); for doctorate, thesis/dissertation. *Entrance requirements:* For doctorate, GRE General Test, interview; for Advanced Certificate, master's degree. Additional exam requirements/recommendations for international students: Required—TOEFL (minimum score 100 iBT). Electronic applications accepted. *Faculty research:* Second language acquisition, cross-cultural communication, technology-enhanced language learning, language variation, action learning.

New York University, Steinhardt School of Culture, Education, and Human Development, Department of Teaching and Learning, Program in Social Studies Education, New York, NY 10003. Offers teaching art/social studies 7-12 (MA), including 5-6 extension; teaching social studies 7-12 (MA). *Accreditation:* TEAC. *Program availability:* Part-time, evening/weekend. *Degree requirements:* For master's, thesis (for some programs). *Entrance requirements:* Additional exam requirements/recommendations for international students: Required—TOEFL (minimum score 100 iBT). Electronic applications accepted. *Faculty research:* Social studies education reform, ethnography and oral history, civic education, labor history and social studies curriculum, material culture.

Niagara University, Graduate Division of Education, Concentration in Teacher Education, Niagara University, NY 14109. Offers early childhood and childhood education (MS Ed, Certificate); early childhood special education (MS); middle and adolescence education (MS Ed); special education (MS Ed), including 1-6, 7-12; special education (grades 1-12) (Certificate); teaching English to speakers of other languages (MS Ed, Certificate). *Accreditation:* NCATE. *Students:* 101 full-time (83 women), 123 part-time (101 women); includes 14 minority (6 Black or African American, non-Hispanic/Latino; 1 American Indian or Alaska Native, non-Hispanic/Latino; 6 Hispanic/Latino; 1 Two or more races, non-Hispanic/Latino), 28 international. Average age 28. In 2016, 86 master's, 18 other advanced degrees awarded. *Entrance requirements:* For master's, GRE General Test or Academic Literacy Skills Test (ALST). Additional exam requirements/recommendations for international students: Required—TOEFL (minimum score 550 paper-based; 79 iBT), IELTS (minimum score 6). *Application deadline:* For fall admission, 8/1 for domestic students. Applications are processed on a rolling basis. Application fee: $30. *Expenses:* Contact institution. *Financial support:* Research assistantships with tuition reimbursements, teaching assistantships with tuition reimbursements, career-related internships or fieldwork, Federal Work-Study, scholarships/grants, and unspecified assistantships available. Financial award application deadline: 4/15; financial award applicants required to submit FAFSA. *Unit head:* Dr. Chandra Foote, Dean, College of Education, 716-286-8549, E-mail: cjf@niagara.edu. *Application contact:* Evan Pierce, Associate Director, Graduate Studies, 716-286-8327, E-mail: epierce@niagara.edu.
Website: http://www.niagara.edu/teacher-education

Nicholls State University, Graduate Studies, College of Education, Department of Teacher Education, Thibodaux, LA 70310. Offers curriculum and instruction (M Ed); educational leadership (M Ed); elementary education (MAT); human performance education (MAT); middle school education (MAT); secondary education (MAT). *Accreditation:* NCATE. *Program availability:* Part-time, evening/weekend, online learning. *Degree requirements:* For master's, comprehensive exam, portfolio. *Entrance requirements:* For master's, GRE General Test, teaching license. Electronic applications accepted.

Norfolk State University, School of Graduate Studies, School of Education, Department of Secondary Education and School Leadership, Norfolk, VA 23504. Offers principal preparation (MA); secondary education (MAT); urban education/administration (MA), including teaching. *Accreditation:* NCATE. *Program availability:* Part-time. *Entrance requirements:* For master's, GRE General Test, PRAXIS I, minimum GPA of 3.0 in major, 2.5 overall. Additional exam requirements/recommendations for international students: Required—TOEFL (minimum score 500 paper-based).

North Carolina Agricultural and Technical State University, School of Graduate Studies, College of Arts and Sciences, Department of Mathematics, Greensboro, NC 27411. Offers applied mathematics (MS), including secondary education. *Accreditation:* NCATE. *Program availability:* Part-time, evening/weekend. *Degree requirements:* For master's, comprehensive exam, thesis or alternative, qualifying exam. *Entrance requirements:* For master's, GRE General Test, minimum GPA of 3.0.

North Carolina State University, Graduate School, College of Education, Department of Curriculum and Instruction, Program in Secondary English Education, Raleigh, NC 27695. Offers M Ed, MS Ed. *Degree requirements:* For master's, thesis optional.

Northeastern Illinois University, College of Graduate Studies and Research, College of Arts and Sciences, Program in Mathematics, Chicago, IL 60625-4699. Offers MS. *Program availability:* Part-time, evening/weekend. *Degree requirements:* For master's, comprehensive exam, thesis optional, project. *Entrance requirements:* For master's, minimum GPA of 2.75, 6 undergraduate courses in mathematics. Additional exam requirements/recommendations for international students: Required—TOEFL (minimum score 550 paper-based; 79 iBT). Electronic applications accepted. *Faculty research:* Numerical analysis, mathematical biology, operations research, statistics, geometry and mathematics of finance.

Northeastern Illinois University, College of Graduate Studies and Research, College of Education, MAT Program in Language Arts - Secondary Education, Chicago, IL 60625-4699. Offers MAT.

Northeastern Illinois University, College of Graduate Studies and Research, College of Education, MSI Program in Language Arts - Secondary Education, Chicago, IL 60625-4699. Offers MSI.

Northern Arizona University, Graduate College, College of Education, Department of Teaching and Learning, Flagstaff, AZ 86011. Offers curriculum and instruction (Ed D); early childhood education (M Ed); elementary education (M Ed); secondary education (M Ed). *Program availability:* Part-time. *Degree requirements:* For master's, comprehensive exam (for some programs), thesis (for some programs). *Entrance requirements:* For master's, minimum GPA of 3.0. Additional exam requirements/recommendations for international students: Required—TOEFL (minimum score 550 paper-based; 80 iBT), IELTS (minimum score 7). Electronic applications accepted. *Expenses:* Tuition, state resident: full-time $8971; part-time $444 per credit hour. Tuition, nonresident: full-time $20,958; part-time $1164 per credit hour. *Required fees:* $1018; $644 per credit hour. Tuition and fees vary according to course load, campus/location and program.

Northern Illinois University, Graduate School, College of Education, Department of Special and Early Education, De Kalb, IL 60115-2854. Offers curriculum and instruction (MS Ed, Ed D), including curriculum leadership (Ed D), elementary education (Ed D), secondary education (Ed D); early childhood education (MS Ed); elementary education (MS Ed); special education (MS Ed). *Program availability:* Part-time, evening/weekend. *Faculty:* 22 full-time (14 women), 2 part-time/adjunct (both women). *Students:* 42 full-time (34 women), 85 part-time (68 women); includes 16 minority (4 Black or African American, non-Hispanic/Latino; 3 Asian, non-Hispanic/Latino; 6 Hispanic/Latino; 3 Two or more races, non-Hispanic/Latino), 6 international. Average age 33. 70 applicants, 73% accepted, 30 enrolled. In 2016, 19 master's, 1 doctorate awarded. *Degree requirements:* For master's, comprehensive exam, thesis optional; for doctorate, thesis/dissertation, candidacy exam, dissertation defense. *Entrance requirements:* For master's, GRE General Test or MAT, minimum undergraduate GPA of 2.75; for doctorate, GRE General Test or MAT, minimum undergraduate GPA of 2.75, graduate 3.2. Additional exam requirements/recommendations for international students: Required—TOEFL (minimum score 550 paper-based). *Application deadline:* For fall admission, 6/1 for domestic students, 5/1 for international students; for spring admission, 11/1 for domestic students, 10/1 for international students. Applications are processed on a rolling basis. Application fee: $40. Electronic applications accepted. *Financial support:* In 2016–17, 14 research assistantships with full tuition reimbursements were awarded; fellowships with full tuition reimbursements, teaching assistantships with full tuition reimbursements, career-related internships or fieldwork, Federal Work-Study, scholarships/grants, tuition waivers (full), and unspecified assistantships also available. Support available to part-time students. Financial award applicants required to submit FAFSA. *Faculty research:* Teacher certification, stress reduction during student teaching, teaching history, portfolios in student teaching. *Unit head:* Gregory Conderman, Chair, 815-753-1619, E-mail: seed@niu.edu. *Application contact:* Gail Myers, Clerk, Graduate Advising, 815-753-0381, E-mail: gmyers@niu.edu.
Website: http://www.cedu.niu.edu/seed/

Northern Michigan University, Office of Graduate Education and Research, College of Health Sciences and Professional Studies, School of Education, Leadership and Public Service, Marquette, MI 49855-5301. Offers administration and supervision (MAE); elementary education (MAE); higher education in student affairs (MA); instruction (MAE); learning disabilities (MAE); public administration (MPA), including criminal justice administration, human resource administration, public administration, public management, state and local government; reading education (MAE), including reading, reading specialist; science education (MS); secondary education (MAE). *Accreditation:* TEAC. *Program availability:* Part-time, online learning. *Degree requirements:* For master's, thesis (for some programs). *Entrance requirements:* For master's, minimum GPA of 3.0. Additional exam requirements/recommendations for international students: Required—TOEFL (minimum score 550 paper-based; 79 iBT), IELTS (minimum score 6.5). Electronic applications accepted.

Northwest Christian University, School of Education and Counseling, Eugene, OR 97401-3745. Offers clinical mental health counseling (MA); elementary teaching (MAT); English for speakers of other languages (ESOL) (MAT); school counseling (MA); secondary teaching (MAT). *Program availability:* Part-time, evening/weekend, online learning. *Faculty:* 9 full-time (5 women), 21 part-time/adjunct (14 women). *Students:* 87 full-time (64 women), 52 part-time (40 women); includes 22 minority (5 Black or African American, non-Hispanic/Latino; 2 American Indian or Alaska Native, non-Hispanic/Latino; 2 Asian, non-Hispanic/Latino; 7 Hispanic/Latino; 2 Native Hawaiian or other Pacific Islander, non-Hispanic/Latino; 4 Two or more races, non-Hispanic/Latino). Average age 36. In 2016, 76 master's awarded. *Degree requirements:* For master's, thesis (for some programs). *Entrance requirements:* For master's, MAT, minimum undergraduate GPA of 3.0, interview, 2-3 page statement of purpose, two letters of recommendation, resume, background check. Additional exam requirements/recommendations for international students: Required—TOEFL (minimum score 550 paper-based; 80 iBT). *Application deadline:* Applications are processed on a rolling basis. Electronic applications accepted. *Expenses:* Contact institution. *Unit head:* Gene James, Dean of Counseling, 541-684-7261, Fax: 541-684-7310, E-mail: gjames@nwcu.edu. *Application contact:* Billy Dorsch, Admission Counselor for Graduate Studies, 541-684-7279, Fax: 541-349-5281, E-mail: wdorsch@nwcu.edu.

Northwestern Oklahoma State University, School of Professional Studies, Program in Secondary Education, Alva, OK 73717-2799. Offers M Ed. *Accreditation:* NCATE. *Program availability:* Part-time. *Degree requirements:* For master's, thesis optional, portfolio. *Entrance requirements:* For master's, GRE General Test or MAT, minimum GPA of 2.75. *Faculty research:* Teacher education, professional school models of pedagogy, competency exams for teachers, teacher accreditation/certification.

Northwestern State University of Louisiana, Graduate Studies and Research, College of Education and Human Development, Program in Secondary Education, Natchitoches, LA 71497. Offers MAT. *Degree requirements:* For master's, comprehensive exam, thesis or alternative. *Entrance requirements:* For master's, GRE General Test, minimum undergraduate GPA of 2.5. Additional exam requirements/recommendations for international students: Required—TOEFL. Electronic applications accepted.

Northwestern State University of Louisiana, Graduate Studies and Research, College of Education and Human Development, Programs in Educational Leadership and Instruction, Natchitoches, LA 71497. Offers counseling (Ed S); educational leadership (M Ed, Ed S); educational technology (Ed S); elementary teaching (Ed S); reading (Ed S); secondary teaching (Ed S); special education (Ed S). *Accreditation:* NASAD. *Degree requirements:* For master's, comprehensive exam, thesis (for some programs). *Entrance requirements:* For master's and Ed S, GRE General Test. Additional exam requirements/recommendations for international students: Required—TOEFL. Electronic applications accepted.

Northwestern University, The Graduate School, School of Education and Social Policy, Education and Social Policy Program, Evanston, IL 60035. Offers elementary teaching (MS); secondary teaching (MS); teacher leadership (MS). *Program availability:* Part-time, evening/weekend. *Degree requirements:* For master's, research project. *Entrance requirements:* For master's, GRE General Test, Illinois State Board of Education Basic Skills Exam (secondary and elementary), bachelor's degree. Additional exam requirements/recommendations for international students: Recommended—TOEFL. Electronic applications accepted. *Faculty research:* Cultural context and literacy, philosophy of education and interpretive discussion, productivity, enhancing research and teaching, motivation, new and junior faculty issues, professional development for K-12 teachers to improve math and science teaching, female/underrepresented students/faculty in STEM disciplines.

Oakland University, Graduate Study and Lifelong Learning, School of Education and Human Services, Department of Teacher Development and Educational Studies, Rochester, MI 48309-4401. Offers educational studies (M Ed); elementary education (MAT); secondary education (MAT); teaching and learning (Graduate Certificate). *Entrance requirements:* For master's, minimum GPA of 3.0. Electronic applications accepted.

Ohio University, Graduate College, Gladys W. and David H. Patton College of Education and Human Services, Department of Teacher Education, Athens, OH 45701-2979. Offers adolescent to young adult education (M Ed); curriculum and instruction (M Ed, PhD); early childhood/special education (M Ed); intervention specialist/mild-moderate needs (M Ed); intervention specialist/moderate-intensive needs (M Ed); middle childhood education (M Ed); reading education (M Ed). *Program availability:* Part-time, evening/weekend. *Degree requirements:* For master's, thesis or alternative; for doctorate, comprehensive exam, thesis/dissertation. *Entrance requirements:* For master's, GRE General Test or MAT (if GPA is below 2.9); for doctorate, GRE General Test, minimum GPA of 3.4, work experience. Additional exam requirements/recommendations for international students: Required—TOEFL (minimum score 550 paper-based; 80 iBT) or IELTS (minimum score 6.5). *Application deadline:* For fall admission, 5/1 priority date for domestic students, 4/1 priority date for international students; for winter admission, 11/1 priority date for domestic students, 10/1 priority date for international students; for spring admission, 2/15 priority date for domestic students,

1/1 priority date for international students. Applications are processed on a rolling basis. Application fee: $50 ($55 for international students). Electronic applications accepted. *Financial support:* Research assistantships with full tuition reimbursements, teaching assistantships with full tuition reimbursements, Federal Work-Study, institutionally sponsored loans, tuition waivers (partial), and unspecified assistantships available. Financial award application deadline: 3/1. *Faculty research:* Cognition literacy, character education, teacher's education reform, disabilities. *Unit head:* Dr. John Henning, Chair, 740-597-1830, Fax: 740-593-0477, E-mail: henningj@ohio.edu. *Application contact:* Floyd J. Doney, Director of Student Affairs, 740-593-4400, Fax: 740-593-9310, E-mail: doney@ohio.edu.
Website: http://www.cehs.ohio.edu/academics/te/index.htm

Old Dominion University, Darden College of Education, Programs in Secondary Education, Norfolk, VA 23529. Offers chemistry (MS Ed); English (MS Ed); secondary education (MS Ed). *Accreditation:* NCATE. *Program availability:* Part-time, evening/weekend, online learning. *Faculty:* 13 full-time (7 women), 10 part-time/adjunct (7 women). *Students:* 55 full-time (33 women), 70 part-time (56 women); includes 25 minority (11 Black or African American, non-Hispanic/Latino; 1 American Indian or Alaska Native, non-Hispanic/Latino; 3 Asian, non-Hispanic/Latino; 5 Hispanic/Latino; 5 Two or more races, non-Hispanic/Latino), 1 international. Average age 33. 75 applicants, 71% accepted, 53 enrolled. In 2016, 29 master's awarded. *Degree requirements:* For master's, comprehensive exam, thesis. *Entrance requirements:* For master's, GRE General Test or MAT, PRAXIS I (for licensure), minimum GPA of 2.8, teaching certificate. Additional exam requirements/recommendations for international students: Required—TOEFL. *Application deadline:* For fall admission, 6/1 for domestic and international students; for winter admission, 11/1 for domestic and international students; for spring admission, 3/1 for domestic and international students. Applications are processed on a rolling basis. Application fee: $50. Electronic applications accepted. *Expenses:* Tuition, state resident: full-time $8604; part-time $478 per credit hour. Tuition, nonresident: full-time $21,510; part-time $1195 per credit hour. *Required fees:* $66 per semester. Tuition and fees vary according to campus/location, program and reciprocity agreements. *Financial support:* In 2016–17, 56 students received support, including fellowships (averaging $15,000 per year), research assistantships with tuition reimbursements available (averaging $9,000 per year), teaching assistantships with tuition reimbursements available (averaging $15,000 per year). Financial award application deadline: 2/15; financial award applicants required to submit FAFSA. *Faculty research:* Use of technology, writing project for teachers, geography teaching, reading. *Unit head:* Dr. KaaVonia Hinton, Department Chair, 757-683-5958, Fax: 757-683-5862, E-mail: khintonj@odu.edu. *Application contact:* William Heffelfinger, Director of Graduate Admissions, 757-683-5554, Fax: 757-683-3255, E-mail: gradadmit@odu.edu.
Website: http://education.odu.edu/eci/secondary/

Olivet Nazarene University, Graduate School, Division of Education, Program in Secondary Education, Bourbonnais, IL 60914. Offers MAT. *Accreditation:* NCATE. *Program availability:* Evening/weekend. *Degree requirements:* For master's, thesis or alternative.

Pacific Union College, Education Department, Angwin, CA 94508-9707. Offers education (M Ed); elementary teaching (MAT); secondary teaching (MAT). *Program availability:* Part-time. *Faculty:* 3 full-time (1 woman), 1 (woman) part-time/adjunct. *Students:* 1 (woman) full-time, 5 part-time (3 women); includes 1 minority (Hispanic/Latino). Average age 41. In 2016, 1 master's awarded. *Degree requirements:* For master's, thesis, action research project, field experiences. *Entrance requirements:* For master's, GRE General Test, two interviews, teaching credential, letters of recommendation, essay. *Application deadline:* For summer admission, 6/1 for domestic students. Applications are processed on a rolling basis. Application fee: $0. *Expenses: Tuition:* Part-time $405 per quarter hour. *Required fees:* $210 per quarter. Tuition and fees vary according to student's religious affiliation. *Financial support:* Scholarships/grants available. Support available to part-time students. *Unit head:* Prof. Thomas Lee, Department Chair, 707-965-6646, Fax: 707-965-6645, E-mail: tdlee@puc.edu. *Application contact:* Cherith Mundy, Credential Analyst, 707-965-6643, Fax: 707-965-6645, E-mail: teachingcredentials@puc.edu.
Website: http://www.puc.edu/academics/departments/education/

Pacific University, College of Education, Forest Grove, OR 97116-1797. Offers early childhood education (MAT); education (MAE); elementary education (MAT), ESOL (MAT); high school education (MAT); middle school education (MAT); special education (MAT); speech-language pathology (MS); STEM education (MAT); talented and gifted (M Ed); visual function in learning (M Ed). *Accreditation:* NCATE. *Program availability:* Part-time, evening/weekend. *Degree requirements:* For master's, research project. *Entrance requirements:* For master's, California Basic Educational Skills Test, PRAXIS II, minimum undergraduate GPA of 2.75, 3.0 graduate. Additional exam requirements/recommendations for international students: Required—TOEFL. Electronic applications accepted. *Expenses:* Contact institution. *Faculty research:* Defining a culturally competent classroom, technology in the k-12 classroom, Socratic seminars, social studies education.

Piedmont College, School of Education, Demorest, GA 30535. Offers art education (MAT); curriculum and instruction (Ed S); early childhood education (MA, MAT); instructional technology (MAT); middle grades education (MA, MAT); music education (MAT); secondary education (MA, MAT); special education (MA, MAT). *Program availability:* Part-time, evening/weekend. *Students:* 290 full-time (217 women), 614 part-time (508 women); includes 131 minority (97 Black or African American, non-Hispanic/Latino; 4 American Indian or Alaska Native, non-Hispanic/Latino; 5 Asian, non-Hispanic/Latino; 11 Hispanic/Latino; 6 Native Hawaiian or other Pacific Islander, non-Hispanic/Latino; 8 Two or more races, non-Hispanic/Latino), 6 international. Average age 37. 257 applicants, 64% accepted, 160 enrolled. In 2016, 288 master's, 243 other advanced degrees awarded. *Degree requirements:* For master's, thesis, field experience in the classroom teaching. *Entrance requirements:* For master's, GRE General Test, MAT, minimum undergraduate GPA of 2.5; for Ed S, minimum graduate GPA of 3.5, valid teaching certificate. Additional exam requirements/recommendations for international students: Required—TOEFL (minimum score 550 paper-based). *Application deadline:* For fall admission, 7/15 for domestic students; for spring admission, 12/1 for domestic students. Applications are processed on a rolling basis. Electronic applications accepted. *Expenses: Tuition:* Full-time $8910. *Financial support:* Career-related internships or fieldwork, Federal Work-Study, and unspecified assistantships available. Support available to part-time students. Financial award applicants required to submit FAFSA. *Unit head:* Dr. Don Gnecco, Dean, 706-778-3000 Ext. 1201, Fax: 706-776-9608, E-mail: dgnecco@piedmont.edu. *Application contact:* Kathleen Anderson, Director of Graduate Enrollment Management, 706-778-8500 Ext. 1181, Fax: 706-778-0150, E-mail: kanderson@piedmont.edu.

Plymouth State University, College of Graduate Studies, Graduate Studies in Education, Program in Secondary Education, Plymouth, NH 03264-1595. Offers curriculum and instruction (M Ed); language education (M Ed); library media (M Ed); physical education (M Ed); social studies education (M Ed); special education (M Ed). *Program availability:* Part-time, evening/weekend. *Entrance requirements:* For master's, MAT.

Prescott College, Graduate Programs, Program in Education, Prescott, AZ 86301. Offers early childhood education (MA); early childhood special education (MA); education (MA); elementary education (MA); environmental education leadership and administration (MA); equine-assisted learning (MA); school guidance counseling (MA); secondary education (MA); special education: learning disabilities (MA); special education: mental retardation (MA); special education: serious emotional disabilities (MA); student-directed independent study (MA); sustainability education (PhD). *Program availability:* Part-time, online learning. *Faculty:* 3 full-time (all women). *Students:* 9 full-time (8 women), 30 part-time (20 women); includes 11 minority (3 Black or African American, non-Hispanic/Latino; 2 American Indian or Alaska Native, non-Hispanic/Latino; 6 Hispanic/Latino). Average age 36. 66 applicants, 82% accepted, 32 enrolled. In 2016, 12 master's, 8 doctorates awarded. *Degree requirements:* For master's, thesis, fieldwork or internship, practicum; for doctorate, thesis/dissertation. *Entrance requirements:* For master's, 2 letters of recommendation, resume; for doctorate, 3 letters of recommendation, resume, official transcripts, personal statement, program proposal. Additional exam requirements/recommendations for international students: Required—TOEFL (minimum score 500 paper-based). *Application deadline:* For fall admission, 4/15 priority date for domestic and international students; for spring admission, 9/15 priority date for domestic and international students. Applications are processed on a rolling basis. Application fee: $40. Electronic applications accepted. *Expenses: Tuition:* Full-time $19,680. One-time fee: $260 part-time. *Financial support:* Fellowships, research assistantships, teaching assistantships, career-related internships or fieldwork, Federal Work-Study, institutionally sponsored loans, scholarships/grants, traineeships, health care benefits, tuition waivers, and unspecified assistantships available. Support available to part-time students. Financial award applicants required to submit FAFSA. *Unit head:* Bob Ellis, 928-350-2217, E-mail: bellis@prescott.edu. *Application contact:* Melanie Lefever, Assistant Director, Limited-residency Programs, 928-350-2106, Fax: 928-776-5242, E-mail: mlefever@prescott.edu.

Providence College, Program in Special Education, Providence, RI 02918. Offers special education (M Ed), including elementary teaching, secondary teaching. *Program availability:* Part-time, evening/weekend. *Faculty:* 6 full-time (4 women), 33 part-time/adjunct (21 women). *Students:* 3 full-time (2 women), 25 part-time (22 women); includes 2 minority (1 Asian, non-Hispanic/Latino; 1 Hispanic/Latino). Average age 28. 13 applicants, 100% accepted, 12 enrolled. In 2016, 14 master's awarded. *Degree requirements:* For master's, comprehensive exam, portfolio. *Entrance requirements:* Additional exam requirements/recommendations for international students: Required—TOEFL (minimum score 577 paper-based; 90 iBT). *Application deadline:* For fall admission, 7/15 priority date for domestic and international students; for spring admission, 11/15 priority date for domestic and international students; for summer admission, 3/15 priority date for domestic students, 3/15 for international students. Application fee: $55. *Expenses: Tuition:* Part-time $1260 per course. One-time fee: $265. Tuition and fees vary according to course load and program. *Financial support:* Career-related internships or fieldwork, institutionally sponsored loans, and unspecified assistantships available. Support available to part-time students. Financial award application deadline: 8/1; financial award applicants required to submit FAFSA.
Website: http://www.providence.edu/professional-studies/graduate-degrees

Providence College, Programs in Administration, Providence, RI 02918. Offers elementary administration (M Ed); secondary administration (M Ed). *Program availability:* Part-time, evening/weekend. *Faculty:* 6 full-time (4 women), 33 part-time/adjunct (21 women). *Students:* 2 full-time (both women), 47 part-time (30 women); includes 3 minority (1 Asian, non-Hispanic/Latino; 2 Hispanic/Latino). Average age 37. 23 applicants, 100% accepted, 13 enrolled. In 2016, 16 master's awarded. *Degree requirements:* For master's, comprehensive exam, portfolio. *Entrance requirements:* Additional exam requirements/recommendations for international students: Required—TOEFL (minimum score 577 paper-based; 90 iBT). *Application deadline:* For fall admission, 7/15 priority date for domestic and international students; for spring admission, 11/15 priority date for domestic and international students; for summer admission, 3/15 priority date for domestic students, 3/15 for international students. Application fee: $55. *Expenses: Tuition:* Part-time $1260 per course. One-time fee: $265. Tuition and fees vary according to course load and program. *Financial support:* Career-related internships or fieldwork, institutionally sponsored loans, and unspecified assistantships available. Support available to part-time students. Financial award application deadline: 8/1; financial award applicants required to submit FAFSA. *Application contact:* Rev. Mark D. Nowel, Dean of Undergraduate and Graduate Studies, 401-865-2649, Fax: 401-865-1496, E-mail: mnowel@providence.edu.
Website: http://www.providence.edu/professional-studies/graduate-degrees/Pages/master-education-administration.aspx

Providence College, Providence Alliance for Catholic Teachers (PACT) Program, Providence, RI 02918. Offers secondary education (M Ed). *Faculty:* 6 full-time (4 women), 33 part-time/adjunct (21 women). *Students:* 28 full-time (15 women); includes 2 minority (1 Hispanic/Latino; 1 Native Hawaiian or other Pacific Islander, non-Hispanic/Latino). Average age 23. 25 applicants, 92% accepted, 15 enrolled. In 2016, 14 master's awarded. *Entrance requirements:* For master's, GRE/MAT/PRAXIS. Additional exam requirements/recommendations for international students: Required—TOEFL (minimum score 550 paper-based; 90 iBT). *Application deadline:* For fall admission, 3/10 priority date for domestic and international students. Applications are processed on a rolling basis. Application fee: $55. *Expenses: Tuition:* Part-time $1260 per course. One-time fee: $265. Tuition and fees vary according to course load and program. *Financial support:* Career-related internships or fieldwork, institutionally sponsored loans, and unspecified assistantships available. Support available to part-time students. Financial award application deadline: 8/1; financial award applicants required to submit FAFSA.
Website: http://www.providence.edu/pact/Pages/default.aspx

Queens College of the City University of New York, Division of Education, Department of Secondary Education and Youth Services, Queens, NY 11367-1597. Offers adolescent biology (MAT); art (MS Ed); biology (MS Ed, AC); chemistry (MS Ed, AC); earth sciences (MS Ed, AC); English (MS Ed, AC); French (MS Ed); Italian (MS Ed, AC); literacy education (MS Ed); mathematics (MS Ed, AC); music (MS Ed, AC); physics (MS Ed, AC); social studies (MS Ed, AC); Spanish (MS Ed, AC). *Program availability:* Part-time, evening/weekend. *Faculty:* 22 full-time (14 women), 40 part-time/adjunct (26 women). *Students:* 31 full-time (21 women), 356 part-time (211 women); includes 164 minority (22 Black or African American, non-Hispanic/Latino; 54 Asian, non-Hispanic/Latino; 81 Hispanic/Latino; 7 Two or more races, non-Hispanic/Latino), 11 international. Average age 29. 236 applicants, 88% accepted, 121 enrolled. In 2016, 119 master's, 51 other advanced degrees awarded. *Degree requirements:* For master's, research project. *Entrance requirements:* For master's, minimum GPA of 3.0. Additional exam requirements/recommendations for international students: Required—TOEFL, IELTS. *Application deadline:* For fall admission, 4/1 for domestic students; for spring admission, 11/1 for domestic students. Applications are processed on a rolling basis. Application fee: $125. Electronic applications accepted. *Expenses:* Tuition, state resident: full-time $5065; part-time $425 per credit. Tuition, nonresident: part-time $780 per credit. *Required fees:* $522; $397 per credit. Part-time tuition and fees vary according to course load and program. *Financial support:* Career-related internships or fieldwork available. Financial award application deadline: 4/1; financial award applicants required to submit

FAFSA. *Unit head:* Dr. Eleanor Armour-Thomas, Chairperson, 718-997-5150, E-mail: armourthomas@yahoo.com.

Quinnipiac University, School of Education, Program in Secondary Education, Hamden, CT 06518-1940. Offers biology (MAT); English (MAT); history/social studies (MAT); mathematics (MAT); Spanish (MAT). *Accreditation:* NCATE. *Faculty:* 6 full-time (2 women), 24 part-time/adjunct (16 women). *Students:* 43 full-time (29 women), 1 part-time (0 women); includes 6 minority (1 Asian, non-Hispanic/Latino; 4 Hispanic/Latino; 1 Two or more races, non-Hispanic/Latino). 43 applicants, 98% accepted, 36 enrolled. In 2016, 32 master's awarded. *Entrance requirements:* For master's, PRAXIS I or PRAXIS Core Academic Skills Exam, minimum GPA of 3.0, interview. *Application deadline:* For fall admission, 5/1 priority date for domestic students. Applications are processed on a rolling basis. Application fee: $45. Electronic applications accepted. *Expenses: Tuition:* Part-time $985 per credit. *Required fees:* $40 per credit. $150 per semester. Tuition and fees vary according to program. *Financial support:* Career-related internships or fieldwork, Federal Work-Study, and unspecified assistantships available. Financial award application deadline: 6/1; financial award applicants required to submit FAFSA. *Faculty research:* Multicultural and urban education/leadership, challenges of teaching diverse learners, scholarship of teaching and learning, technology and teaching, humor and education. *Unit head:* Mordechai Gordon, Program Director, 203-582-8442, E-mail: mordechai.gordon@qu.edu. *Application contact:* Office of Graduate Admissions, 203-582-8672, Fax: 203-582-3443, E-mail: graduate@qu.edu.
Website: http://www.qu.edu/gradeducation

Regis University, College of Contemporary Liberal Studies, Denver, CO 80221-1099. Offers creative writing (MFA); criminology (M Sc); curriculum, instruction and assessment (M Ed); education - teacher leadership (M Ed); educational leadership (M Ed); elementary education (M Ed); literacy (Certificate); reading (M Ed); secondary education (M Ed); special education (M Ed); teacher academic leadership (Certificate); teacher leadership (MA); teacher/educational leadership (M Ed); teaching the linguistically diverse (M Ed). *Program availability:* Part-time, evening/weekend, 100% online, blended/hybrid learning. *Faculty:* 18 full-time (12 women), 42 part-time/adjunct (26 women). *Students:* 302 full-time (234 women), 270 part-time (218 women); includes 148 minority (33 Black or African American, non-Hispanic/Latino; 3 American Indian or Alaska Native, non-Hispanic/Latino; 13 Asian, non-Hispanic/Latino; 83 Hispanic/Latino; 16 Two or more races, non-Hispanic/Latino), 3 international. Average age 36. 431 applicants, 90% accepted, 110 enrolled. In 2016, 308 master's awarded. *Degree requirements:* For master's, thesis (for some programs). *Entrance requirements:* For master's, official transcript reflecting baccalaureate degree awarded from regionally-accredited college or university, work experience, resume, letters of recommendation. Additional exam requirements/recommendations for international students: Required—TOEFL (minimum score 550 paper-based; 82 iBT). *Application deadline:* For fall admission, 8/15 priority date for domestic students, 7/13 for international students; for winter admission, 10/10 priority date for domestic students, 9/8 for international students; for spring admission, 1/10 priority date for domestic students, 11/17 for international students; for summer admission, 5/1 priority date for domestic students. Applications are processed on a rolling basis. Application fee: $75. Electronic applications accepted. *Expenses:* $485 per credit hour. *Financial support:* Scholarships/grants available. Financial award application deadline: 4/15; financial award applicants required to submit FAFSA. *Unit head:* Dr. Elisa Robyn, Academic Dean. *Application contact:* Cate Clark, Director of Admissions, 303-458-4900, Fax: 303-964-5534, E-mail: ruadmissions@regis.edu.
Website: http://www.regis.edu/CCLS.aspx

Rhode Island College, School of Graduate Studies, Feinstein School of Education and Human Development, Department of Educational Studies, Providence, RI 02908-1991. Offers advanced studies in teaching and learning (M Ed); English (MAT); French (MAT); history (MAT); math (MAT); secondary education (MAT); Spanish (MAT); teaching English as a second language (M Ed). *Accreditation:* NCATE. *Program availability:* Part-time, evening/weekend. *Faculty:* 6 full-time (5 women), 8 part-time/adjunct (6 women). *Students:* 5 full-time (2 women), 53 part-time (48 women); includes 8 minority (2 Black or African American, non-Hispanic/Latino; 2 Asian, non-Hispanic/Latino; 3 Hispanic/Latino; 1 Two or more races, non-Hispanic/Latino). Average age 39. In 2016, 29 master's awarded. *Degree requirements:* For master's, capstone or comprehensive assessment. *Entrance requirements:* For master's, GRE or MAT (for most programs), minimum undergraduate GPA of 3.0; baccalaureate degree in English, French, history, math or Spanish; 3 letters of recommendation; interview. Additional exam requirements/recommendations for international students: Recommended—TOEFL (minimum score 550 paper-based; 79 iBT). *Application deadline:* For fall admission, 3/1 for domestic students; for spring admission, 11/1 for domestic students. Applications are processed on a rolling basis. Application fee: $50. Electronic applications accepted. *Expenses:* Tuition, state resident: full-time $8928; part-time $372 per credit. Tuition, nonresident: full-time $17,376; part-time $724 per credit. *Required fees:* $604; $22 per credit. One-time fee: $74. *Financial support:* In 2016–17, 1 teaching assistantship with full tuition reimbursement (averaging $3,000 per year) was awarded; career-related internships or fieldwork, Federal Work-Study, scholarships/grants, health care benefits, and unspecified assistantships also available. Support available to part-time students. Financial award application deadline: 5/15; financial award applicants required to submit FAFSA. *Unit head:* Dr. Gerri August, Chair, 401-456-8170. *Application contact:* Graduate Studies, 401-456-8700.
Website: http://www.ric.edu/educationalStudies/

Roberts Wesleyan College, Graduate Teacher Education Programs, Rochester, NY 14624-1997. Offers adolescence and special education (M Ed); childhood and special education (M Ed); literacy education (M Ed); special education (M Ed). *Program availability:* Part-time, evening/weekend. *Degree requirements:* For master's, thesis. Electronic applications accepted.

Rochester Institute of Technology, Graduate Enrollment Services, National Technical Institute for the Deaf, Research and Teacher Education Department, MS Program in Secondary Education for the Deaf and Hard of Hearing, Rochester, NY 14623. Offers MS. *Program availability:* Part-time, evening/weekend, blended/hybrid learning. *Students:* 28 full-time (21 women), 2 part-time (both women); includes 7 minority (1 Black or African American, non-Hispanic/Latino; 4 Hispanic/Latino; 2 Two or more races, non-Hispanic/Latino), 6 international. Average age 28. 44 applicants, 43% accepted, 17 enrolled. In 2016, 20 master's awarded. *Degree requirements:* For master's, comprehensive exam, student teaching and observations. *Entrance requirements:* For master's, GRE, minimum cumulative GPA of 3.0. *Application deadline:* For fall admission, 6/1 priority date for domestic and international students. Applications are processed on a rolling basis. Electronic applications accepted. *Expenses:* $17,390. *Financial support:* Fellowships with partial tuition reimbursements, research assistantships with partial tuition reimbursements, teaching assistantships with partial tuition reimbursements, career-related internships or fieldwork, scholarships/grants, and unspecified assistantships available. Support available to part-time students. Financial award applicants required to submit FAFSA. *Faculty research:* Effective use of technology and online learning in teaching deaf students; strategies for inclusive instruction/deaf students with other disabilities; effective literacy instruction strategies for DHH readers; single case experimental design methods; STEM language, literacy and learning; deaf studies; international deaf education; stereotype threat effects on mathematical performance. *Unit head:* Dr. Gerald C. Bateman, Director, 585-475-6480, E-mail: gcbnmp@rit.edu. *Application contact:* Diane Ellison, Assistant Vice President, Graduate Enrollment Services, 585-475-2229, Fax: 585-475-7164, E-mail: gradinfo@rit.edu.
Website: http://www.ntid.rit.edu/msse/

Rockford University, Graduate Studies, Department of Education, Program in Secondary Education, Rockford, IL 61108-2393. Offers MAT. *Program availability:* Part-time, evening/weekend. *Degree requirements:* For master's, thesis optional. *Entrance requirements:* For master's, GRE General Test, basic skills test (for students seeking certification), 3 letters of recommendation. Additional exam requirements/recommendations for international students: Required—TOEFL (minimum score 550 paper-based; 79 iBT). *Application deadline:* Applications are processed on a rolling basis. Application fee: $50. Electronic applications accepted. *Expenses: Tuition:* Part-time $710 per credit. *Required fees:* $50 per semester. *Financial support:* Scholarships/grants and unspecified assistantships available. Support available to part-time students. Financial award application deadline: 3/1; financial award applicants required to submit FAFSA. *Unit head:* Dr. Michelle McReynolds, MAT Director, 815-226-3390, Fax: 815-394-3706, E-mail: mmcreynolds@rockford.edu. *Application contact:* Michele Mehren, Office Manager for Graduate Studies, 815-226-4041, Fax: 815-394-3706, E-mail: mmehren@rockford.edu.

Roosevelt University, Graduate Division, College of Education, Program in Secondary Education, Chicago, IL 60605. Offers MA. *Students:* 4 full-time (2 women), 16 part-time (11 women); includes 2 minority (1 Hispanic/Latino; 1 Two or more races, non-Hispanic/Latino). Average age 33. 19 applicants, 100% accepted, 7 enrolled. In 2016, 15 master's awarded. *Expenses: Tuition, area resident:* Full-time $19,566; part-time $880 per credit hour. *Required fees:* $175 per semester. One-time fee: $200. Part-time tuition and fees vary according to course load, degree level and program. *Unit head:* Dr. Linda Pincham, Chair, 312-853-4784. *Application contact:* Angela Ryan, Director of Graduate Enrollment, 312-341-2420, Fax: 312-281-3356, E-mail: aryan@roosevelt.edu.
Website: https://www.roosevelt.edu/academics/programs/masters-in-secondary-education-ma

Rowan University, Graduate School, College of Education, Department of Interdisciplinary and Inclusive Education, Program in Secondary Education, Glassboro, NJ 08028-1701. Offers MST. *Accreditation:* NCATE. *Program availability:* Part-time, evening/weekend. *Degree requirements:* For master's, comprehensive exam, thesis. *Entrance requirements:* For master's, GRE General Test, minimum GPA of 2.8. Additional exam requirements/recommendations for international students: Required—TOEFL. Electronic applications accepted.

Saginaw Valley State University, College of Education, Program in Secondary Classroom Teaching, University Center, MI 48710. Offers MAT. *Accreditation:* NCATE. *Program availability:* Part-time, evening/weekend. *Degree requirements:* For master's, capstone course. *Entrance requirements:* For master's, minimum GPA of 3.0, teaching certificate. Additional exam requirements/recommendations for international students: Required—TOEFL (minimum score 550 paper-based; 79 iBT). *Application deadline:* For fall admission, 7/15 for international students; for winter admission, 11/15 for international students; for spring admission, 4/15 for international students. Applications are processed on a rolling basis. Application fee: $30 ($90 for international students). Electronic applications accepted. *Expenses:* Tuition, state resident: full-time $9652; part-time $536 per credit hour. Tuition, nonresident: full-time $12,259; part-time $1022 per credit hour. *Required fees:* $263; $14.60 per credit hour. Tuition and fees vary according to degree level. *Financial support:* Federal Work-Study and scholarships/grants available. Support available to part-time students. Financial award applicants required to submit FAFSA. *Unit head:* Dr. Deborah Smith, Professor of Teacher Education, 989-964-4526, Fax: 989-964-4563, E-mail: coeconnect@svsu.edu. *Application contact:* Jenna Briggs, Director, Graduate and International Admissions, 989-964-6096, Fax: 989-964-2788, E-mail: gradadm@svsu.edu.

St. Bonaventure University, School of Graduate Studies, School of Education, Literacy Programs, St. Bonaventure, NY 14778-2284. Offers adolescent literacy 5-12 (MS Ed); childhood literacy B-6 (MS Ed). *Accreditation:* NCATE. *Program availability:* Part-time, evening/weekend. *Faculty:* 2 full-time (both women), 2 part-time/adjunct (both women). *Students:* 7 full-time (all women), 6 part-time (all women); includes 1 minority (Hispanic/Latino). Average age 25. 10 applicants, 70% accepted, 4 enrolled. In 2016, 14 master's awarded. *Degree requirements:* For master's, comprehensive exam, thesis optional, minimum cumulative GPA of 3.0, clinical practicum, literacy coaching internship, electronic portfolio. *Entrance requirements:* For master's, GRE or MAT, teaching certificate in matching area in-hand or pending, transcripts from all previous colleges, minimum GPA of 3.0, 2 references, interview, writing sample. Additional exam requirements/recommendations for international students: Required—TOEFL (minimum score 550 paper-based; 80 iBT). *Application deadline:* For fall admission, 6/15 priority date for domestic students, 2/1 for international students; for spring admission, 11/15 priority date for domestic students, 7/1 for international students. Applications are processed on a rolling basis. Application fee: $0. Electronic applications accepted. *Expenses:* $733 per credit, $100 graduation fee. *Financial support:* Federal Work-Study, scholarships/grants, health care benefits, and unspecified assistantships available. Support available to part-time students. Financial award application deadline: 4/15; financial award applicants required to submit FAFSA. *Faculty research:* Gifted education, curriculum and instruction, theory and language. *Unit head:* Kayla Zimmer, Program Director, 716-375-2167, Fax: 716-375-2360, E-mail: kzimmer@sbu.edu. *Application contact:* Bruce Campbell, Director of Graduate Admissions, 716-375-2429, Fax: 716-375-4015, E-mail: gradsch@sbu.edu.
Website: http://www.sbu.edu/academics/schools/education/graduate-degrees-certificates/msed-in-childhood-literacy

St. John's University, The School of Education, Department of Curriculum and Instruction, Program in Adolescent Education, Queens, NY 11439. Offers MS Ed, Certificate. *Program availability:* Part-time, evening/weekend. *Degree requirements:* For master's, variable foreign language requirement, comprehensive exam. *Entrance requirements:* For master's, minimum GPA of 3.0, 2 letters of recommendation, qualification for the New York State provisional (initial) teaching certificate, transcript, personal statement. Additional exam requirements/recommendations for international students: Required—TOEFL (minimum score 600 paper-based; 100 iBT), IELTS (minimum score 7). Electronic applications accepted. *Faculty research:* Investigating self-efficacy in literacy learning, using problem solving as an approach for math learning.

Saint Joseph's University, College of Arts and Sciences, Graduate Programs in Education, Philadelphia, PA 19131-1395. Offers curriculum supervisor (Certificate); educational leadership (MS, Ed D); elementary education (MS, Certificate); elementary/middle school education (Certificate); instructional technology (MS, Certificate); organizational development and leadership (MS); principal (Certificate); professional education (MS); reading specialist (MS, Certificate); reading supervisor (Certificate); secondary education (MS, Certificate); special education (MS); special education 7-12 (Certificate); special education PK-8 (Certificate); superintendent's letter of eligibility (Certificate); supervisor of special education (Certificate); teacher of the deaf and hard of hearing (Certificate). *Program availability:* Part-time, evening/weekend, blended/hybrid

learning. *Faculty:* 26 full-time (21 women), 74 part-time/adjunct (45 women). *Students:* 107 full-time (88 women), 826 part-time (622 women); includes 170 minority (115 Black or African American, non-Hispanic/Latino; 2 American Indian or Alaska Native, non-Hispanic/Latino; 11 Asian, non-Hispanic/Latino; 31 Hispanic/Latino; 1 Native Hawaiian or other Pacific Islander, non-Hispanic/Latino; 10 Two or more races, non-Hispanic/Latino), 18 international. Average age 33. 338 applicants, 76% accepted, 173 enrolled. In 2016, 419 master's, 16 doctorates, 24 other advanced degrees awarded. *Degree requirements:* For master's, thesis or alternative; for doctorate, comprehensive exam, thesis/dissertation. *Entrance requirements:* For master's, 2 letters of recommendation, minimum GPA of 3.0, official transcripts, personal statement; for doctorate, GRE, master's degree from accredited institution, minimum graduate GPA of 3.5, computer competence, interview with program director. Additional exam requirements/recommendations for international students: Required—TOEFL (minimum score 550 paper-based; 80 iBT), IELTS (minimum score 6.5), PTE (minimum score 60). *Application deadline:* For fall admission, 7/15 for international students; for spring admission, 11/1 for international students. Applications are processed on a rolling basis. Application fee: $35. Electronic applications accepted. *Expenses:* $750 per credit, $100 education fee, $360 online organization development and leadership residency fee. *Financial support:* In 2016–17, 25 students received support. Unspecified assistantships available. Financial award application deadline: 5/1; financial award applicants required to submit FAFSA. *Faculty research:* Factors predicting early mathematics skills for low income children, early child care and development, preschool quality, parent communication and home-school collaboration issues, education of terminally ill children, preparing literacy teachers for urban schools. *Total annual research expenditures:* $18,118. *Unit head:* Dr. John Vacca, Associate Dean, Education, 610-660-3131, E-mail: gradcas@sju.edu. *Application contact:* Graduate Admissions, College of Arts and Sciences, 610-660-3131, E-mail: gradcas@sju.edu.
Website: http://sju.edu/int/academics/cas/grad/education/index.html

Saint Mary's University of Minnesota, Schools of Graduate and Professional Programs, Graduate School of Education, Instruction Program, Winona, MN 55987-1399. Offers MA. Tuition and fees vary according to degree level and program. *Unit head:* Delores Roethke, Director, 612-238-4511, E-mail: droethke@smumn.edu. *Application contact:* James Callinan, Director of Admissions for Graduate and Professional Programs, 612-728-5185, Fax: 612-728-5121, E-mail: jcallina@smumn.edu.
Website: http://www.smumn.edu/graduate-home/areas-of-study/graduate-school-of-education/ma-in-instruction

Saint Peter's University, Graduate Programs in Education, Program in Teaching, Jersey City, NJ 07306-5997. Offers 6-8 middle school education (MA Ed, Certificate); K-12 secondary education (MA Ed, Certificate); K-5 elementary education (MA Ed, Certificate). *Program availability:* Part-time, evening/weekend. *Degree requirements:* For master's, comprehensive exam. *Entrance requirements:* For master's, GRE or MAT. Additional exam requirements/recommendations for international students: Required—TOEFL. Electronic applications accepted.

St. Thomas Aquinas College, Division of Teacher Education, Sparkill, NY 10976. Offers adolescence education (MST); childhood and special education (MST); childhood education (MST); educational leadership (MS Ed); reading (MS Ed, PMC); special education (MS Ed, PMC); teaching (MS Ed), including elementary education, middle school education, secondary education. *Accreditation:* NCATE. *Program availability:* Part-time, evening/weekend. *Degree requirements:* For master's, comprehensive exam, comprehensive professional portfolio; for PMC, action research project. *Entrance requirements:* For master's, New York State Qualifying Exam, GRE General Test or minimum GPA of 3.0, teaching certificate; for PMC, GRE General Test or minimum GPA of 3.0. Electronic applications accepted. *Faculty research:* Computer applications in education, adolescent special education students, literacy development, inclusive practices for special education students.

Saint Xavier University, Graduate Studies, School of Education, Chicago, IL 60655-3105. Offers counseling (MA); curriculum and instruction (MA); early childhood education (MA); educational administration (MA); elementary education (MA); individualized studies (MA), including educational technology, English as a second language (ESL), ISTEM (integrative science, technology, engineering, and math), science education; music education (MA); reading (MA); secondary education (MA); Spanish education (MA); special education (MA); teaching and leadership (MA). *Accreditation:* NCATE. *Program availability:* Part-time, evening/weekend. *Degree requirements:* For master's, thesis or project. *Entrance requirements:* For master's, minimum GPA of 3.0. *Expenses:* Contact institution.

Salem College, Department of Education, Winston-Salem, NC 27101. Offers art education (MAT); elementary education (M Ed, MAT); language and literacy (M Ed); middle school education (MAT); school counseling (M Ed); second language studies (MAT); secondary education (MAT); special education (M Ed, MAT). *Accreditation:* NCATE. *Program availability:* Part-time, evening/weekend, online learning. *Degree requirements:* For master's, practicum (MAT), project (M Ed), oral and written comprehensive exams. *Entrance requirements:* For master's, minimum GPA of 2.5. *Faculty research:* Content area reading strategies, literacy development, brain compatible instruction.

Salem State University, School of Graduate Studies, Program in Secondary Education, Salem, MA 01970-5353. Offers M Ed. *Program availability:* Part-time, evening/weekend. *Entrance requirements:* For master's, GRE or MAT. Additional exam requirements/recommendations for international students: Required—TOEFL (minimum score 550 paper-based; 80 iBT) or IELTS (minimum score 5.5).

Salem State University, School of Graduate Studies, Program in Spanish, Salem, MA 01970-5353. Offers MAT. *Program availability:* Part-time, evening/weekend. *Entrance requirements:* For master's, GRE or MAT. Additional exam requirements/recommendations for international students: Required—TOEFL (minimum score 550 paper-based; 80 iBT) or IELTS (minimum score 5.5).

Salisbury University, Department of English, Salisbury, MD 21801-6837. Offers English (MA), including creative writing, film, literature, secondary education, TESOL, writing and rhetoric. *Program availability:* Part-time. *Faculty:* 11 full-time (5 women), 1 (woman) part-time/adjunct. *Students:* 11 full-time (9 women), 24 part-time (19 women); includes 1 minority (Black or African American, non-Hispanic/Latino), 4 international. Average age 33. 18 applicants, 67% accepted, 9 enrolled. In 2016, 17 master's awarded. *Degree requirements:* For master's, comprehensive exam, thesis optional. *Entrance requirements:* Additional exam requirements/recommendations for international students: Required—TOEFL (minimum score 550 paper-based, 79 iBT) or IELTS (6.5). *Application deadline:* For fall admission, 8/1 for domestic and international students; for spring admission, 1/1 for domestic and international students. Application fee: $65. Electronic applications accepted. *Expenses:* $381 per credit hour resident tuition, $670 per credit hour non-resident tuition; $84 per credit hour fees. *Financial support:* In 2016–17, 2 students received support, including 11 teaching assistantships with full tuition reimbursements available (averaging $9,395 per year); career-related internships or fieldwork and scholarships/grants also available. Support available to part-time students. Financial award application deadline: 3/1; financial award applicants required to submit FAFSA. *Faculty research:* Literature; linguistics; film studies; rhetoric and composition; TESOL. *Unit head:* Dr. Christopher Vilmar, Graduate Program Director, English, 410-677-6511, E-mail: csvilmar@salisbury.edu.
Website: http://www.salisbury.edu/gsr/gradstudies/ENGpage.html

Salisbury University, Program in Mathematics Education, Salisbury, MD 21801-6837. Offers mathematics (MSME), including high school, middle school. *Program availability:* Part-time. *Faculty:* 3 full-time (1 woman). *Students:* 2 full-time (1 woman), 8 part-time (5 women); includes 1 minority (Two or more races, non-Hispanic/Latino). Average age 27. 2 applicants, 100% accepted, 2 enrolled. In 2016, 2 master's awarded. *Entrance requirements:* Additional exam requirements/recommendations for international students: Required—TOEFL (minimum score 550 paper-based, 79 iBT) or IELTS (6.5). *Application deadline:* For fall admission, 5/15 priority date for domestic and international students; for spring admission, 10/1 priority date for domestic and international students. Applications are processed on a rolling basis. Application fee: $65. Electronic applications accepted. *Expenses:* $381 per credit hour resident tuition, $670 per credit hour non-resident tuition; $84 per credit hour fees. *Financial support:* In 2016–17, 1 teaching assistantship with full tuition reimbursement (averaging $8,000 per year) was awarded; career-related internships or fieldwork and scholarships/grants also available. Support available to part-time students. Financial award application deadline: 3/1; financial award applicants required to submit FAFSA. *Faculty research:* Conceptual development of multiplicative reasoning; early childhood mathematics; teachers' attitudes towards mathematics. *Unit head:* Dr. Jennifer Bergner, Graduate Program Director, Mathematics Education, 410-677-5429, E-mail: jabergner@salisbury.edu.
Website: http://www.salisbury.edu/gsr/gradstudies/MSMEpage.html

Salisbury University, Program in Teaching, Salisbury, MD 21801-6837. Offers secondary education (MAT). *Faculty:* 3 full-time (2 women). *Students:* 6 full-time (3 women), 1 (woman) part-time. Average age 29. In 2016, 6 master's awarded. *Degree requirements:* For master's, comprehensive exam. *Entrance requirements:* Additional exam requirements/recommendations for international students: Required—TOEFL (minimum score 550 paper-based, 79 iBT) or IELTS (6.5). *Application deadline:* For winter admission, 12/15 priority date for domestic and international students. Application fee: $65. Electronic applications accepted. *Expenses:* $381 per credit hour resident tuition, $670 per credit hour non-resident tuition; $84 per credit hour fees. *Financial support:* Career-related internships or fieldwork and scholarships/grants available. Support available to part-time students. Financial award application deadline: 3/1; financial award applicants required to submit FAFSA. *Faculty research:* Technology; standards; classroom management. *Unit head:* Dr. Regina Royer, Graduate Program Director, Teaching, 410-548-3949, E-mail: rdroyer@salisbury.edu.
Website: http://www.salisbury.edu/gsr/gradstudies/MATpage.html

San Diego State University, Graduate and Research Affairs, College of Education, School of Teacher Education, Program in Secondary Curriculum and Instruction, San Diego, CA 92182. Offers MA. *Accreditation:* NCATE. *Entrance requirements:* For master's, GRE General Test, letters of reference. Additional exam requirements/recommendations for international students: Required—TOEFL. Electronic applications accepted.

San Francisco State University, Division of Graduate Studies, College of Education, Department of Secondary Education, San Francisco, CA 94132-1722. Offers mathematics education (MA); secondary education (MA, Credential). *Accreditation:* NCATE. *Expenses:* Tuition, state resident: full-time $6738. Tuition, nonresident: full-time $15,666. *Required fees:* $1012. Tuition and fees vary according to degree level and program. *Unit head:* Dr. Maika Watanabe, Chair, 415-338-1622, Fax: 415-338-0914, E-mail: watanabe@sfsu.edu. *Application contact:* Administrative Office Coordinator, 415-338-7649, Fax: 415-338-0914, E-mail: seced@sfsu.edu.
Website: http://secondaryed.sfsu.edu/

Seattle Pacific University, Master of Arts in Teaching Program, Seattle, WA 98119-1997. Offers MAT. *Accreditation:* NCATE. *Program availability:* Part-time, evening/weekend. *Degree requirements:* For master's, field experience, internship. *Entrance requirements:* For master's, GRE or MAT, WEST-B, WEST-E, official transcript(s) from each college/university attended, resume, personal statement (one to two pages), two to four letters of recommendation, endorsement verification form, moral character and personal fitness policy form. Electronic applications accepted. *Expenses:* Contact institution.

Shenandoah University, School of Education and Human Development, Winchester, VA 22601-5195. Offers administrative leadership (D Ed); educational administration (MSE); emphasis in teaching (MSE); health and physical education (Certificate); individual focus (MSE); literacy education (MS); middle school teacher education (Certificate); organizational leadership (MS, D Prof); secondary school teacher education (Certificate); special education (MSE). *Accreditation:* TEAC. *Program availability:* Part-time, evening/weekend. *Faculty:* 9 full-time (7 women), 43 part-time/adjunct (33 women). *Students:* 31 full-time (25 women), 236 part-time (160 women); includes 39 minority (19 Black or African American, non-Hispanic/Latino; 1 American Indian or Alaska Native, non-Hispanic/Latino; 10 Asian, non-Hispanic/Latino; 7 Hispanic/Latino; 1 Native Hawaiian or other Pacific Islander, non-Hispanic/Latino; 1 Two or more races, non-Hispanic/Latino), 4 international. Average age 37. 90 applicants, 97% accepted, 56 enrolled. In 2016, 113 master's, 13 doctorates, 38 other advanced degrees awarded. *Degree requirements:* For master's, comprehensive exam (for some programs), thesis (for some programs); for doctorate, comprehensive exam, thesis/dissertation. *Entrance requirements:* For degree, PRAXIS Academic Core, SAT/ACT, PRAXIS Academic Core Math, or VCLA, three letters of recommendation, writing sample, undergraduate degree. Additional exam requirements/recommendations for international students: Required—TOEFL (minimum score 550 paper-based; 79 iBT), IELTS (minimum score 6.5). *Application deadline:* For fall admission, 5/1 priority date for domestic students, 5/1 for international students; for spring admission, 10/15 priority date for domestic students, 10/15 for international students; for summer admission, 3/15 priority date for domestic students, 3/15 for international students. Application fee: $30. Electronic applications accepted. *Expenses:* Contact institution. *Financial support:* In 2016–17, 18 students received support. Scholarships/grants and unspecified assistantships available. Financial award applicants required to submit FAFSA. *Faculty research:* Exploring helplessness and anxiety in learning statistics, facilitating effective classroom group work, expert-novice dynamics in teaching, K-12 policy implementation and change, adult education, family-school-community relations, mentoring of first-year school principals. *Total annual research expenditures:* $2,000. *Unit head:* Dennis William Kellison, PhD, Director, 540-535-7324, Fax: 540-665-4726, E-mail: dkelliso@su.edu. *Application contact:* Andrew Woodall, Executive Director of Recruitment and Admissions, 540-665-4581, Fax: 540-665-4627, E-mail: admit@su.edu.
Website: http://www.su.edu/education/

Siena Heights University, Graduate College, Adrian, MI 49221-1796. Offers clinical mental health counseling (MA); educational leadership (Specialist); leadership (MA), including health care leadership, organizational leadership; teacher education (MA), including early childhood education, early childhood education: Montessori, education leadership: principal, elementary education: reading K-12, leadership: higher education, secondary education: reading K-12, special education: cognitive impairment, special education: learning disabilities. *Program availability:* Part-time, evening/weekend.

Degree requirements: For master's, thesis, presentation. *Entrance requirements:* For master's, minimum GPA of 3.0, current resume, essay, all post-secondary transcripts, 3 letters of reference, conviction disclosure form; copy of teaching certificate (for some education programs); for Specialist, master's degree, minimum GPA of 3.0, current resume, essay, all post-secondary transcripts, 3 letters of reference, conviction disclosure form; copy of teaching certificate (for some education programs). Electronic applications accepted.

Sierra Nevada College, Teacher Education Program, Incline Village, NV 89451. Offers advanced teaching and leadership (M Ed); elementary education (MAT); secondary education (MAT). *Program availability:* Part-time, evening/weekend, online learning. *Degree requirements:* For master's, comprehensive exam, thesis, PRAXIS I and II. *Entrance requirements:* For master's, 2 letters of recommendation, minimum GPA of 3.0. Electronic applications accepted.

Simpson College, Department of Education, Indianola, IA 50125-1297. Offers secondary education (MAT). *Degree requirements:* For master's, PRAXIS II, electronic portfolio. *Entrance requirements:* For master's, bachelor's degree; minimum cumulative GPA of 2.75, 3.0 in major; 3 letters of recommendation.

Slippery Rock University of Pennsylvania, Graduate Studies (Recruitment), College of Education, Department of Secondary Education/Foundations of Education, Slippery Rock, PA 16057-1383. Offers secondary education (M Ed), including English, math/science, social studies. *Accreditation:* NCATE. *Program availability:* Part-time, evening/weekend, 100% online. *Faculty:* 7 full-time (2 women), 1 part-time/adjunct (0 women). *Students:* 43 full-time (23 women), 36 part-time (23 women); includes 2 minority (1 Black or African American, non-Hispanic/Latino; 1 Two or more races, non-Hispanic/Latino). Average age 29. 77 applicants, 79% accepted, 35 enrolled. In 2016, 36 master's awarded. *Degree requirements:* For master's, comprehensive exam, thesis (for some programs). *Entrance requirements:* For master's, copy of teaching certification and two letters of recommendation (for some programs). Additional exam requirements/recommendations for international students: Required—TOEFL (minimum score 550 paper-based; 80 iBT). *Application deadline:* For fall admission, 3/1 priority date for domestic students, 5/1 priority date for international students; for spring admission, 10/1 priority date for domestic students, 9/1 priority date for international students. Applications are processed on a rolling basis. Application fee: $25 ($30 for international students). Electronic applications accepted. *Expenses:* $646.50 per credit in-state, $936.80 per credit out-of-state; $581.45 per online credit in-state, $648.65 per online credit out-of-state. *Financial support:* In 2016–17, 12 students received support. Career-related internships or fieldwork, Federal Work-Study, institutionally sponsored loans, scholarships/grants, tuition waivers (partial), and unspecified assistantships available. Support available to part-time students. Financial award application deadline: 5/1; financial award applicants required to submit FAFSA. *Unit head:* Dr. Jeffrey Lehman, Graduate Coordinator, 724-738-2311, Fax: 724-738-4987, E-mail: jeffrey.lehman@sru.edu. *Application contact:* Brandi Weber-Mortimer, Director of Graduate Studies, 724-738-2051, Fax: 724-738-2146, E-mail: graduate.admissions@sru.edu.
Website: http://www.sru.edu/academics/colleges-and-departments/coe/departments/secondary-education-/-foundations-of-education

Smith College, Graduate and Special Programs, Department of Biological Sciences, Northampton, MA 01063. Offers biological sciences (MS); secondary teaching (MAT), including biology teaching. *Program availability:* Part-time. *Students:* 5 part-time (4 women); includes 1 minority (Hispanic/Latino). Average age 32. 8 applicants, 38% accepted, 2 enrolled. In 2016, 7 master's awarded. *Degree requirements:* For master's, one foreign language, thesis (for some programs). *Entrance requirements:* For master's, GRE General Test (for MS). Additional exam requirements/recommendations for international students: Required—TOEFL (minimum score 595 paper-based; 97 iBT), IELTS. *Application deadline:* For fall admission, 1/15 for domestic and international students; for spring admission, 12/1 for domestic students. Application fee: $60. *Expenses: Tuition:* Full-time $34,560; part-time $1440 per credit. Tuition and fees vary according to course load and program. *Financial support:* In 2016–17, 5 students received support, including 5 research assistantships with full tuition reimbursements available (averaging $13,850 per year); fellowships and scholarships/grants also available. Support available to part-time students. Financial award application deadline: 1/15; financial award applicants required to submit CSS PROFILE or FAFSA. *Unit head:* Jesse Bellemare, Graduate Student Advisor, 413-585-3812, E-mail: jbellema@smith.edu. *Application contact:* Ruth Morgan, Program Assistant, 413-585-3050, Fax: 413-585-3054, E-mail: rmorgan@smith.edu.
Website: http://www.smith.edu/biology/

Smith College, Graduate and Special Programs, Department of Chemistry, Northampton, MA 01063. Offers secondary education (MAT), including chemistry. *Program availability:* Part-time. *Entrance requirements:* Additional exam requirements/recommendations for international students: Required—TOEFL (minimum score 595 paper-based; 97 iBT), IELTS. *Application deadline:* For fall admission, 4/1 for domestic students, 1/15 for international students; for spring admission, 12/1 for domestic students. Application fee: $60. *Expenses: Tuition:* Full-time $34,560; part-time $1440 per credit. Tuition and fees vary according to course load and program. *Financial support:* Scholarships/grants available. Support available to part-time students. Financial award application deadline: 1/15; financial award applicants required to submit CSS PROFILE or FAFSA. *Unit head:* Kevin Shea, Chair, 413-585-4687, E-mail: kshea@smith.edu. *Application contact:* Ruth Morgan, Program Assistant, 413-585-3050, Fax: 413-585-3054, E-mail: gradstdy@smith.edu.
Website: http://www.science.smith.edu/departments/chem/

Smith College, Graduate and Special Programs, Department of Education and Child Study, Program in Secondary Education, Northampton, MA 01063. Offers secondary education (MAT), including biological sciences education, chemistry education, English education, French education, geology education, government education, history education, mathematics education, physics education, Spanish education. *Program availability:* Part-time. *Students:* 3 full-time (2 women), 3 part-time (2 women). Average age 31. 14 applicants, 79% accepted, 4 enrolled. In 2016, 11 master's awarded. *Entrance requirements:* Additional exam requirements/recommendations for international students: Required—TOEFL (minimum score 595 paper-based; 97 iBT), IELTS. *Application deadline:* For fall admission, 4/1 for domestic students, 1/15 priority date for international students; for spring admission, 12/1 for domestic students. Application fee: $60. *Expenses: Tuition:* Full-time $34,560; part-time $1440 per credit. Tuition and fees vary according to course load and program. *Financial support:* In 2016–17, 5 students received support, including 1 fellowship with full tuition reimbursement available; scholarships/grants also available. Support available to part-time students. Financial award application deadline: 4/1; financial award applicants required to submit CSS PROFILE or FAFSA. *Unit head:* Rosetta Cohen, Graduate Student Advisor, 413-585-3266, E-mail: rcohen@smith.edu. *Application contact:* Ruth Morgan, Program Assistant, 413-585-3050, Fax: 413-585-3054, E-mail: gradstdy@smith.edu.
Website: http://www.smith.edu/educ/

Smith College, Graduate and Special Programs, Department of English Language and Literature, Northampton, MA 01063. Offers secondary education (MAT), including English education. *Program availability:* Part-time. *Students:* 1 (woman) full-time. Average age 23. 3 applicants, 67% accepted, 1 enrolled. In 2016, 6 master's awarded. *Entrance requirements:* Additional exam requirements/recommendations for international students: Required—TOEFL (minimum score 595 paper-based; 97 iBT), IELTS. *Application deadline:* For fall admission, 4/1 for domestic students, 1/15 for international students; for spring admission, 12/1 for domestic students. Application fee: $60. *Expenses: Tuition:* Full-time $34,560; part-time $1440 per credit. Tuition and fees vary according to course load and program. *Financial support:* In 2016–17, 1 student received support. Scholarships/grants available. Support available to part-time students. Financial award application deadline: 4/1; financial award applicants required to submit CSS PROFILE or FAFSA. *Unit head:* Craig Davis, Graduate Adviser, 413-585-3327, E-mail: crdavis@smith.edu. *Application contact:* Ruth Morgan, Program Assistant, 413-585-3050, Fax: 413-585-3054, E-mail: gradstdy@smith.edu.
Website: http://www.smith.edu/english/

Smith College, Graduate and Special Programs, Department of French Language and Literature, Northampton, MA 01063. Offers secondary education (MAT), including French education. *Program availability:* Part-time. In 2016, 1 master's awarded. *Degree requirements:* For master's, one foreign language. *Entrance requirements:* Additional exam requirements/recommendations for international students: Required—TOEFL (minimum score 595 paper-based; 97 iBT), IELTS. *Application deadline:* For fall admission, 4/1 for domestic students, 1/15 for international students; for spring admission, 12/1 for domestic students. Application fee: $60. *Expenses: Tuition:* Full-time $34,560; part-time $1440 per credit. Tuition and fees vary according to course load and program. *Financial support:* In 2016–17, 1 student received support. Scholarships/grants available. Support available to part-time students. Financial award application deadline: 4/1; financial award applicants required to submit CSS PROFILE or FAFSA. *Unit head:* Helene Visentin, Chair, 413-585-3359, E-mail: hvisenti@smith.edu. *Application contact:* Ruth Morgan, Program Assistant, 413-585-3050, Fax: 413-585-3054, E-mail: gradstdy@smith.edu.
Website: http://www.smith.edu/french

Smith College, Graduate and Special Programs, Department of Government, Northampton, MA 01063. Offers secondary education (MAT), including government education. *Program availability:* Part-time. *Students:* 1 applicant, 100% accepted, 1 enrolled. *Entrance requirements:* Additional exam requirements/recommendations for international students: Required—TOEFL (minimum score 595 paper-based; 97 iBT), IELTS. *Application deadline:* For fall admission, 4/1 for domestic students, 1/15 for international students; for spring admission, 12/1 for domestic students. Application fee: $60. *Expenses: Tuition:* Full-time $34,560; part-time $1440 per credit. Tuition and fees vary according to course load and program. *Financial support:* Scholarships/grants available. Support available to part-time students. Financial award application deadline: 4/1; financial award applicants required to submit CSS PROFILE or FAFSA. *Unit head:* Gregory White, Department Chair, 413-585-3542, E-mail: gwhite@smith.edu. *Application contact:* Ruth Morgan, Program Assistant, 413-585-3050, Fax: 413-585-3054, E-mail: gradstdy@smith.edu.
Website: http://www.smith.edu/gov/

Smith College, Graduate and Special Programs, Department of History, Northampton, MA 01063. Offers secondary education (MAT), including history education. *Program availability:* Part-time. *Students:* 2 full-time (1 woman), 1 part-time (0 women). Average age 28. 6 applicants, 83% accepted, 3 enrolled. In 2016, 2 master's awarded. *Entrance requirements:* Additional exam requirements/recommendations for international students: Required—TOEFL (minimum score 595 paper-based; 97 iBT), IELTS. *Application deadline:* For fall admission, 4/1 for domestic students, 1/15 for international students; for spring admission, 12/1 for domestic students. Application fee: $60. *Expenses: Tuition:* Full-time $34,560; part-time $1440 per credit. Tuition and fees vary according to course load and program. *Financial support:* In 2016–17, 2 students received support. Scholarships/grants available. Support available to part-time students. Financial award application deadline: 4/1; financial award applicants required to submit CSS PROFILE or FAFSA. *Unit head:* Joshua Birk, Graduate Student Adviser, 413-585-3740, E-mail: jbirk@smith.edu. *Application contact:* Ruth Morgan, Program Assistant, 413-585-3050, Fax: 413-585-3054, E-mail: gradstdy@smith.edu.
Website: http://www.smith.edu/history/

Smith College, Graduate and Special Programs, Department of Mathematics, Northampton, MA 01063. Offers secondary education (MAT), including mathematics education. *Program availability:* Part-time. *Students:* 1 (woman) part-time. Average age 52. *Entrance requirements:* Additional exam requirements/recommendations for international students: Required—TOEFL (minimum score 595 paper-based; 97 iBT), IELTS. *Application deadline:* For fall admission, 4/1 for domestic students, 1/15 for international students; for spring admission, 12/1 for domestic students. Application fee: $60. *Expenses: Tuition:* Full-time $34,560; part-time $1440 per credit. Tuition and fees vary according to course load and program. *Financial support:* Scholarships/grants available. Support available to part-time students. Financial award application deadline: 4/1; financial award applicants required to submit CSS PROFILE or FAFSA. *Unit head:* Julianna Tymoczko, Department Chair, 413-585-3775, E-mail: jtymoczko@smith.edu. *Application contact:* Ruth Morgan, Program Assistant, 413-585-3050, Fax: 413-585-3054, E-mail: gradstdy@smith.edu.
Website: http://www.math.smith.edu/

Smith College, Graduate and Special Programs, Department of Physics, Northampton, MA 01063. Offers secondary education (MAT), including physics education. *Program availability:* Part-time. *Students:* 1 (woman) part-time. Average age 24. 1 applicant, 100% accepted. *Entrance requirements:* Additional exam requirements/recommendations for international students: Required—TOEFL (minimum score 595 paper-based; 97 iBT), IELTS. *Application deadline:* For fall admission, 4/1 for domestic students, 1/15 for international students; for spring admission, 12/1 for domestic students. Application fee: $60. *Expenses: Tuition:* Full-time $34,560; part-time $1440 per credit. Tuition and fees vary according to course load and program. *Financial support:* Scholarships/grants available. Support available to part-time students. Financial award application deadline: 4/1; financial award applicants required to submit CSS PROFILE or FAFSA. *Unit head:* Gary Felder, Chair, 413-585-4489, E-mail: gfelder@smith.edu. *Application contact:* Ruth Morgan, Program Assistant, 413-585-3050, Fax: 413-585-3054, E-mail: gradstdy@smith.edu.

Smith College, Graduate and Special Programs, Department of Spanish and Portuguese, Northampton, MA 01063. Offers secondary education (MAT), including Spanish education. *Program availability:* Part-time. *Degree requirements:* For master's, one foreign language. *Entrance requirements:* Additional exam requirements/recommendations for international students: Required—TOEFL (minimum score 595 paper-based; 97 iBT), IELTS. *Application deadline:* For fall admission, 4/1 for domestic students, 1/15 for international students; for spring admission, 12/1 for domestic students. Application fee: $60. *Expenses: Tuition:* Full-time $34,560; part-time $1440 per credit. Tuition and fees vary according to course load and program. *Financial support:* Scholarships/grants available. Support available to part-time students. Financial award application deadline: 4/1; financial award applicants required to submit CSS PROFILE or FAFSA. *Unit head:* Maria Helena Rueda, Chair, 413-585-3451, E-mail: mrueda@smith.edu. *Application contact:* Ruth Morgan, Program Assistant, 413-

585-3050, Fax: 413-585-3054, E-mail: gradstdy@smith.edu.
Website: http://www.smith.edu/spp/

South Carolina State University, College of Graduate and Professional Studies, Department of Education, Orangeburg, SC 29117-0001. Offers early childhood education (MAT); education (M Ed); elementary education (M Ed, MAT); English (MAT); general science/biology (MAT); mathematics (MAT); secondary education (M Ed), including biology education, business education, counselor education, English education, home economics education, industrial education, mathematics education, science education, social studies education; special education (M Ed), including emotionally handicapped, learning disabilities, mentally handicapped. *Accreditation:* NCATE. *Program availability:* Part-time, evening/weekend. *Faculty:* 12 full-time (8 women), 3 part-time/adjunct (1 woman). *Students:* 28 full-time (20 women), 20 part-time (17 women); includes 45 minority (44 Black or African American, non-Hispanic/Latino; 1 Two or more races, non-Hispanic/Latino). Average age 31. 22 applicants, 100% accepted, 16 enrolled. In 2016, 9 master's awarded. *Degree requirements:* For master's, thesis optional, departmental qualifying exam. *Entrance requirements:* For master's, GRE General Test, NTE, interview, teaching certificate. *Application deadline:* For fall admission, 6/15 priority date for domestic students, 6/15 for international students; for spring admission, 11/1 for domestic and international students. Application fee: $25. Electronic applications accepted. *Expenses:* Tuition, state resident: full-time $8938; part-time $579 per credit hour. Tuition, nonresident: full-time $19,018; part-time $1139 per credit hour. *Required fees:* $1482; $82 per credit hour. *Financial support:* Fellowships, career-related internships or fieldwork, Federal Work-Study, and scholarships/grants available. Financial award application deadline: 6/1. *Unit head:* Dr. Charlie Spell, Interim Chair, Department of Education, 803-536-8963, Fax: 803-516-4568, E-mail: cspell@scsu.edu. *Application contact:* Curtis Foskey, Coordinator of Graduate Studies, 803-536-8419, Fax: 803-536-8812, E-mail: cfoskey@scsu.edu.

Southeast Missouri State University, School of Graduate Studies, Department of Educational Leadership and Counseling, Program in Educational Administration, Cape Girardeau, MO 63701-4799. Offers educational leadership (Ed D); higher education administration (MA); secondary administration (MA); teacher leadership (MA, Ed S). *Accreditation:* NCATE. *Program availability:* Part-time, evening/weekend, online only, 100% online. *Faculty:* 7 full-time (4 women), 4 part-time/adjunct (1 woman). *Students:* 48 full-time (31 women), 166 part-time (107 women); includes 23 minority (19 Black or African American, non-Hispanic/Latino; 2 Asian, non-Hispanic/Latino; 2 Hispanic/Latino), 14 international. Average age 33. 79 applicants, 100% accepted, 79 enrolled. In 2016, 27 master's, 36 other advanced degrees awarded. *Degree requirements:* For master's and Ed S, comprehensive exam, thesis or alternative, paper; for doctorate, comprehensive exam, thesis/dissertation. *Entrance requirements:* For master's, minimum GPA of 3.5; for doctorate, GRE, interview; for Ed S, minimum GPA of 3.7. Additional exam requirements/recommendations for international students: Required—TOEFL (minimum score 550 paper-based; 79 iBT), IELTS (minimum score 6), PTE (minimum score 53). *Application deadline:* For fall admission, 8/1 for domestic students, 6/1 for international students; for spring admission, 11/21 for domestic students, 10/1 for international students; for summer admission, 5/15 for domestic students. Applications are processed on a rolling basis. Application fee: $30 ($40 for international students). Electronic applications accepted. *Expenses:* Tuition, state resident: full-time $3130; part-time $260.80 per credit hour. Tuition, nonresident: full-time $5842; part-time $486.80 per credit hour. *Required fees:* $33.70 per credit hour. *Financial support:* In 2016–17, 31 students received support. Career-related internships or fieldwork, Federal Work-Study, scholarships/grants, traineeships, tuition waivers (full), and unspecified assistantships available. Financial award application deadline: 6/30; financial award applicants required to submit FAFSA. *Faculty research:* Learning and technology; leadership, equity and social justice in P-12 schools and higher education; school culture; leadership and academic achievement; school leadership and student success. *Unit head:* Dr. C. P. Gause, Professor/Chair, 573-651-2137, Fax: 573-986-6512, E-mail: cgause@semo.edu. *Application contact:* Dr. Lisa Bertrand, Professor/Coordinator, 573-651-5080, Fax: 573-986-6512, E-mail: lbertrand@semo.edu.
Website: http://www.semo.edu/eduleadcounsel/

Southeast Missouri State University, School of Graduate Studies, Department of Middle and Secondary Education, Cape Girardeau, MO 63701-4799. Offers MA. *Accreditation:* NCATE. *Program availability:* Part-time, online only, 100% online. *Faculty:* 6 full-time (4 women), 1 (woman) part-time/adjunct. *Students:* 5 full-time (2 women), 45 part-time (36 women); includes 3 minority (1 Black or African American, non-Hispanic/Latino; 1 Asian, non-Hispanic/Latino; 1 Hispanic/Latino). Average age 31. 20 applicants, 90% accepted, 22 enrolled. In 2016, 20 master's awarded. *Degree requirements:* For master's, comprehensive exam, research paper. *Entrance requirements:* For master's, minimum undergraduate GPA of 2.75. Additional exam requirements/recommendations for international students: Required—TOEFL (minimum score 550 paper-based; 79 iBT), IELTS (minimum score 6), PTE (minimum score 53). *Application deadline:* For fall admission, 8/1 for domestic students, 6/1 for international students; for spring admission, 11/21 for domestic students, 10/1 for international students; for summer admission, 5/15 for domestic students. Applications are processed on a rolling basis. Application fee: $30 ($40 for international students). Electronic applications accepted. *Expenses:* Tuition, state resident: full-time $3130; part-time $260.80 per credit hour. Tuition, nonresident: full-time $5842; part-time $486.80 per credit hour. *Required fees:* $33.70 per credit hour. *Financial support:* In 2016–17, 4 students received support. Career-related internships or fieldwork, Federal Work-Study, scholarships/grants, traineeships, tuition waivers (full), and unspecified assistantships available. Financial award application deadline: 6/30; financial award applicants required to submit FAFSA. *Faculty research:* Assessment, technology, diversity. *Unit head:* Dr. Simin L. Cwick, Middle and Secondary Education Department Chair, 573-651-5965, E-mail: scwick@semo.edu. *Application contact:* Alisa Aleen McFerron, Assistant Director of Admissions for Operations, 573-651-5937, E-mail: amcferron@semo.edu.
Website: http://www.semo.edu/midsecondaryed/

Southern New Hampshire University, School of Education, Manchester, NH 03106-1045. Offers business education (M Ed); child development (M Ed); curriculum and instruction (M Ed), including education leadership, reading, special education, technology integration; education (M Ed); educational leadership (M Ed, Ed D); educational studies (M Ed); elementary education (M Ed); English (MAT); English for speakers of other languages (M Ed); reading and writing specialist (M Ed); school business administration (Certificate); secondary education (M Ed); special education (M Ed); technology integration specialist (M Ed). *Program availability:* Part-time, evening/weekend, online learning. *Degree requirements:* For master's, comprehensive exam (for some programs), thesis or alternative. *Entrance requirements:* For master's, PRAXIS I, minimum GPA of 2.75. Additional exam requirements/recommendations for international students: Required—TOEFL (minimum score 550 paper-based). Electronic applications accepted. *Expenses:* Contact institution.

Southern Oregon University, Graduate Studies, School of Education, Ashland, OR 97520. Offers elementary education (MA Ed, MS Ed), including classroom teacher, early childhood, handicapped learner, reading, supervision; secondary education (MA Ed, MS Ed), including classroom teacher, handicapped learner, reading, supervision; teaching (MAT). *Program availability:* Online learning. *Faculty:* 15 full-time (10 women), 27 part-time/adjunct (21 women). *Students:* 116 full-time (82 women), 86 part-time (68 women); includes 22 minority (1 American Indian or Alaska Native, non-Hispanic/Latino; 4 Asian, non-Hispanic/Latino; 8 Hispanic/Latino; 9 Two or more races, non-Hispanic/Latino). Average age 34. 81 applicants, 80% accepted, 49 enrolled. In 2016, 107 master's awarded. *Degree requirements:* For master's, thesis optional. *Entrance requirements:* For master's, GRE General Test, minimum cumulative GPA of 3.0 in the last 90 quarter credits (60 semester credits) of undergraduate coursework. Additional exam requirements/recommendations for international students: Required—TOEFL (minimum score 540 paper-based; 76 iBT), IELTS (minimum score 6), ELPT (minimum score 964) or ELS (minimum score 112). *Application deadline:* For fall admission, 7/31 priority date for domestic and international students; for winter admission, 11/15 priority date for domestic and international students; for spring admission, 1/7 priority date for domestic and international students. Applications are processed on a rolling basis. Application fee: $60. Electronic applications accepted. *Expenses:* Tuition, state resident: full-time $10,719; part-time $397 per credit. Tuition, nonresident: full-time $13,419; part-time $497 per credit. *Required fees:* $548. *Financial support:* In 2016–17, 2 students received support. Career-related internships or fieldwork, institutionally sponsored loans, scholarships/grants, and unspecified assistantships available. *Unit head:* Dr. Gerry McCain, Graduate Program Coordinator, 541-552-6934, E-mail: mccaing@sou.edu. *Application contact:* Kelly Moutsatson, Director of Admissions, 541-552-6411, Fax: 541-552-8403, E-mail: admissions@sou.edu.
Website: http://www.sou.edu/education/

Southern University and Agricultural and Mechanical College, Graduate School, College of Education, Department of Curriculum and Instruction, Baton Rouge, LA 70813. Offers elementary education (M Ed); media (M Ed); secondary education (M Ed). *Degree requirements:* For master's, comprehensive exam, thesis optional. *Entrance requirements:* For master's, GMAT or GRE General Test. Additional exam requirements/recommendations for international students: Required—TOEFL (minimum score 525 paper-based).

Southwestern Assemblies of God University, Thomas F. Harrison School of Graduate Studies, Program in Education, Waxahachie, TX 75165-5735. Offers Christian school administration (MS); curriculum development (MS); early education administration (M Ed); middle and secondary education (M Ed). *Degree requirements:* For master's, comprehensive written and oral exams. *Entrance requirements:* For master's, GRE General Test, minimum GPA of 2.5. Electronic applications accepted.

Southwestern Oklahoma State University, College of Professional and Graduate Studies, School of Behavioral Sciences and Education, Weatherford, OK 73096-3098. Offers community counseling (M Ed); early childhood education (M Ed); educational administration (M Ed); elementary education (M Ed); health sciences and microbiology (M Ed); kinesiology (M Ed); parks and recreation management (M Ed); school counseling (M Ed); school psychology (MS); school psychometry (M Ed); secondary education (M Ed); special education (M Ed). *Accreditation:* NCATE. *Program availability:* Part-time, evening/weekend, online learning. *Degree requirements:* For master's, exam. *Entrance requirements:* For master's, GRE General Test or minimum undergraduate GPA of 3.0. Additional exam requirements/recommendations for international students: Required—TOEFL.

Spalding University, Graduate Studies, College of Education, Programs in Education, Louisville, KY 40203-2188. Offers art teacher education (MAT); business teacher education (MAT); elementary school education (MAT); foreign language (MAT); high school education (MAT); middle school education (MAT); secondary education (MAT); special education (learning and behavioral disorders) (MAT); student guidance counselor (MA); teacher leader (M Ed). *Accreditation:* NCATE. *Program availability:* Part-time, evening/weekend. *Faculty:* 39 full-time (26 women), 13 part-time/adjunct (4 women). *Students:* 97 full-time (76 women), 31 part-time (23 women); includes 39 minority (33 Black or African American, non-Hispanic/Latino; 1 Asian, non-Hispanic/Latino; 3 Hispanic/Latino; 2 Two or more races, non-Hispanic/Latino). Average age 35. 62 applicants, 55% accepted, 33 enrolled. In 2016, 49 master's awarded. *Entrance requirements:* For master's, GRE General Test or MAT, interview, letters of recommendation, resume. Additional exam requirements/recommendations for international students: Required—TOEFL (minimum score 535 paper-based). *Application deadline:* Applications are processed on a rolling basis. Application fee: $30. Electronic applications accepted. *Expenses: Tuition:* Full-time $15,300. *Financial support:* Scholarships/grants, traineeships, and unspecified assistantships available. Financial award applicants required to submit FAFSA. *Faculty research:* Instructional technology, achievement gap, classroom management, assessment. *Unit head:* Dr. Chris Walsh, Associate Dean, 502-873-4272, Fax: 502-585-7123, E-mail: cwalsh@spalding.edu. *Application contact:* Valerie Anderson, Administrative Assistant, 502-873-4260, E-mail: vanderson@spalding.edu.

Springfield College, Graduate Programs, Programs in Education, Springfield, MA 01109-3797. Offers educational studies (M Ed); school guidance counseling (M Ed); secondary education (M Ed); special education (M Ed). *Program availability:* Part-time, evening/weekend. *Entrance requirements:* Additional exam requirements/recommendations for international students: Required—TOEFL (minimum score 550 paper-based); Recommended—IELTS (minimum score 6). Electronic applications accepted. *Expenses: Tuition:* Full-time $29,640; part-time $988 per credit. *Required fees:* $195.

Spring Hill College, Graduate Programs, Program in Education, Mobile, AL 36608-1791. Offers early childhood education (MAT, MS Ed); educational theory (MS Ed); elementary education (MAT, MS Ed); secondary education (MAT, MS Ed). *Program availability:* Part-time. *Faculty:* 3 full-time (all women). *Students:* 3 full-time (all women), 7 part-time (5 women); includes 1 minority (Black or African American, non-Hispanic/Latino). Average age 26. In 2016, 10 master's awarded. *Degree requirements:* For master's, comprehensive exam, completion of program within 6 calendar years of entrance into graduate studies at Spring Hill; documentation of course field assignments (MS) or completion of internship (MAT). *Entrance requirements:* For master's, GRE, MAT, or PRAXIS (varies by program), bachelor's degree with minimum undergraduate GPA of 3.0; class B certificate (for MS); minimum number of hours in specific fields (for MAT). Additional exam requirements/recommendations for international students: Required—TOEFL (minimum score 550 paper-based; 80 iBT), IELTS (minimum score 6.5), CPE or CAE (minimum score C), Michigan English Language Assessment Battery (minimum score 90). *Application deadline:* For fall admission, 8/1 priority date for domestic and international students; for spring admission, 12/1 priority date for domestic and international students. Applications are processed on a rolling basis. Application fee: $25 ($35 for international students). Electronic applications accepted. *Expenses:* Contact institution. *Financial support:* Applicants required to submit FAFSA. *Unit head:* Dr. Lori P. Aultman, Chair of Education, 251-380-3473, Fax: 251-460-2184, E-mail: laultman@shc.edu. *Application contact:* Robert Stewart, Vice President of Enrollment, 251-380-3030, Fax: 251-460-2186, E-mail: rstewart@shc.edu.
Website: http://ug.shc.edu/graduate-degrees/master-science-education/

Stanford University, Graduate School of Education, Teacher Education Program, Stanford, CA 94305-2004. Offers elementary education (MAE); secondary education (MAE). *Degree requirements:* For master's, thesis. *Entrance requirements:* For master's, GRE General Test. Electronic applications accepted. *Expenses: Tuition:* Full-time $47,331. *Required fees:* $609.

State University of New York at Fredonia, College of Education, Fredonia, NY 14063. Offers curriculum and instruction (MS Ed); literacy education (MS Ed), including birth-grade 12, grades 5-12; TESOL (MS Ed). *Accreditation:* NCATE. *Program availability:* Part-time. *Faculty:* 21 full-time (17 women), 11 part-time/adjunct (9 women). *Students:* 39 full-time (32 women), 54 part-time (33 women); includes 8 minority (1 Black or African American, non-Hispanic/Latino; 4 Asian, non-Hispanic/Latino; 2 Hispanic/Latino; 1 Two or more races, non-Hispanic/Latino). Average age 29. 60 applicants, 97% accepted, 39 enrolled. In 2016, 56 master's awarded. *Degree requirements:* For master's, thesis. *Entrance requirements:* For master's, GRE, minimum undergraduate GPA of 3.0. Additional exam requirements/recommendations for international students: Required—TOEFL (minimum score 79 iBT), IELTS (minimum score 6.5). *Application deadline:* For fall admission, 4/1 priority date for domestic and international students; for spring admission, 11/1 priority date for domestic students, 11/1 for international students. Applications are processed on a rolling basis. Application fee: $75. Electronic applications accepted. *Expenses:* Tuition, state resident: full-time $10,370; part-time $453 per credit. Tuition, nonresident: full-time $20,190; part-time $925 per credit. *Required fees:* $1619; $67.30 per credit hour. $403.80 per semester. *Financial support:* In 2016–17, 4 teaching assistantships with full and partial tuition reimbursements (averaging $7,075 per year) were awarded. Financial award application deadline: 3/15; financial award applicants required to submit FAFSA. *Faculty research:* Positive behavioral intervention and support (PBIS), place-based science education, peer support for education, primary source material for social studies education, policies and practices in learning English language. *Unit head:* Dr. Christine Givner, Dean, 716-673-3311, E-mail: christine.givner@fredonia.edu. *Application contact:* Wendy S. Dunst, Interim Graduate Recruitment and Admissions Associate, 716-673-3808, Fax: 716-673-3712, E-mail: wendy.dunst@fredonia.edu.
Website: http://www.fredonia.edu/coe/

State University of New York at New Paltz, Graduate School, School of Education, Department of Educational Studies, Program in Special Education, New Paltz, NY 12561. Offers adolescence special education (7-12) (MS Ed); adolescence special education and literacy (MS Ed); childhood special education (1-6) (MS Ed); childhood special education and literacy (MS Ed); early childhood special education (B-2) (MS Ed). *Accreditation:* NCATE. *Program availability:* Part-time, evening/weekend. *Students:* 25 full-time (19 women), 39 part-time (29 women); includes 9 minority (2 Asian, non-Hispanic/Latino; 7 Hispanic/Latino). 13 applicants, 85% accepted, 10 enrolled. In 2016, 36 master's awarded. *Entrance requirements:* For master's, minimum GPA of 3.0 (3.2 for special education and literacy programs), New York state teaching certificate. Additional exam requirements/recommendations for international students: Required—TOEFL (minimum score 550 paper-based; 80 iBT), IELTS (minimum score 6.5). *Application deadline:* For fall admission, 3/15 priority date for domestic students, 3/15 for international students; for spring admission, 11/1 for domestic and international students. Application fee: $50. Electronic applications accepted. *Financial support:* Application deadline: 8/1. *Unit head:* Dr. Jane Sileo, Coordinator, 845-257-2835, E-mail: sileoj@newpaltz.edu. *Application contact:* Vika Shock, Director of Graduate Admissions, 845-257-3286, E-mail: gradschool@newpaltz.edu.
Website: http://www.newpaltz.edu/schoolofed/department-of-teaching—learning/special_ed.html

State University of New York at New Paltz, Graduate School, School of Education, Department of Secondary Education, New Paltz, NY 12561. Offers adolescence education: biology (MAT, MS Ed); adolescence education: chemistry (MAT, MS Ed); adolescence education: earth science (MAT, MS Ed); adolescence education: English (MAT, MS Ed); adolescence education: French (MAT, MS Ed); adolescence education: social studies (MAT, MS Ed); adolescence education: Spanish (MAT, MS Ed); second language education (MS Ed, AC), including second language education (MS Ed), teaching English language learners (AC). *Accreditation:* NCATE. *Program availability:* Part-time, evening/weekend. *Students:* 60 full-time (36 women), 59 part-time (48 women); includes 28 minority (2 Black or African American, non-Hispanic/Latino; 2 Asian, non-Hispanic/Latino; 22 Hispanic/Latino; 2 Two or more races, non-Hispanic/Latino). 96 applicants, 83% accepted, 54 enrolled. In 2016, 56 master's awarded. *Degree requirements:* For master's, comprehensive exam (for some programs), portfolio. *Entrance requirements:* For master's, minimum GPA of 3.0, New York state teaching certificate (MS Ed). Additional exam requirements/recommendations for international students: Required—TOEFL (minimum score 550 paper-based; 80 iBT), IELTS (minimum score 6.5). *Application deadline:* For fall admission, 3/1 priority date for domestic students, 3/1 for international students; for spring admission, 10/1 priority date for domestic students, 10/1 for international students. Application fee: $50. Electronic applications accepted. *Financial support:* Application deadline: 8/1. *Unit head:* Dr. Laura Dull, Chair, 845-257-2849, E-mail: dullj@newpaltz.edu. *Application contact:* Vika Shock, Director of Graduate Admissions, 845-257-3285, Fax: 845-257-3284, E-mail: gradschool@newpaltz.edu.
Website: http://www.newpaltz.edu/secondaryed/

State University of New York at Oswego, Graduate Studies, School of Education, Department of Curriculum and Instruction, Oswego, NY 13126. Offers adolescence education (MST); art education (MAT); childhood education (MST); curriculum and instruction (MS Ed); literacy education (MS Ed); special education (MS Ed). *Program availability:* Part-time, evening/weekend. *Degree requirements:* For master's, comprehensive exam (for some programs), thesis optional. *Entrance requirements:* For master's, GRE General Test, minimum GPA of 2.7, provisional teaching certificate. Additional exam requirements/recommendations for international students: Required—TOEFL (minimum score 560 paper-based). *Faculty research:* Classroom applications for microcomputers; classroom questioning, wait-time, and achievement; values clarification and academic achievement.

State University of New York at Plattsburgh, School of Education, Health, and Human Services, Program in Teacher Education: Adolescence Education, Plattsburgh, NY 12901-2681. Offers adolescence education (MST); biology 7-12 (MST); chemistry 7-12 (MST); earth science 7-12 (MST); English 7-12 (MST); French 7-12 (MST); mathematics 7-12 (MST); physics 7-12 (MST); social studies 7-12 (MST); Spanish 7-12 (MST). *Accreditation:* TEAC. *Program availability:* Part-time, evening/weekend. *Entrance requirements:* For master's, minimum GPA of 2.75. Additional exam requirements/recommendations for international students: Required—TOEFL.

State University of New York College at Cortland, Graduate Studies, School of Arts and Sciences, Programs in Adolescence Education, Cortland, NY 13045. Offers biology (MAT); chemistry (MAT); English (MAT, MS Ed); mathematics (MAT); mathematics and physics (MS Ed); physics (MAT, MS Ed). *Accreditation:* NCATE. *Program availability:* Part-time, evening/weekend. *Degree requirements:* For master's, one foreign language, comprehensive exam (for some programs), thesis (for some programs). *Entrance requirements:* For master's, GRE General Test.

State University of New York College at Geneseo, Graduate Studies, School of Education, Program in Adolescence Education, Geneseo, NY 14454-1401. Offers English 7-12 (MS Ed); math 7-12 (MS Ed); Spanish 7-12 (MS Ed). *Program availability:* Part-time. *Faculty:* 8 full-time (4 women). *Students:* 5 part-time (4 women). Average age 30. 8 applicants, 13% accepted. In 2016, 4 master's awarded. *Degree requirements:* For master's, 2 foreign languages. *Entrance requirements:* For master's, initial certification to teach in New York state. Additional exam requirements/recommendations for international students: Required—TOEFL, IELTS, PTE. *Application deadline:* For fall admission, 4/1 priority date for domestic students; for spring admission, 11/1 priority date for domestic students. Applications are processed on a rolling basis. Application fee: $50. Electronic applications accepted. *Expenses:* Tuition, state resident: full-time $10,870; part-time $453 per credit. Tuition, nonresident: full-time $22,210; part-time $925 per credit. *Required fees:* $865; $35.85 per credit hour. *Financial support:* In 2016–17, 1 student received support, including 1 fellowship with partial tuition reimbursement available (averaging $10,000 per year); scholarships/grants, health care benefits, tuition waivers (partial), and unspecified assistantships also available. Support available to part-time students. Financial award application deadline: 4/1; financial award applicants required to submit FAFSA. *Unit head:* Dr. Anjoo Sikka, Dean of School of Education, 585-245-5151, Fax: 585-245-5220, E-mail: sikka@geneseo.edu. *Application contact:* Michael R. George, Graduate Enrollment Coordinator, 585-245-5148, Fax: 585-245-5550, E-mail: georgem@geneseo.edu.

State University of New York College at Potsdam, School of Education and Professional Studies, Program in Secondary Education, Potsdam, NY 13676. Offers English education (MST); mathematics education (MST); science education (MST), including biology, chemistry, earth science, physics; social studies education (MST). *Accreditation:* NCATE. *Degree requirements:* For master's, culminating experience. *Entrance requirements:* For master's, minimum GPA of 2.75 in last 60 hours of course work (3.0 for English program). Additional exam requirements/recommendations for international students: Required—TOEFL (minimum score 550 paper-based; 80 iBT), IELTS (minimum score 6). Electronic applications accepted.

Stephen F. Austin State University, Graduate School, College of Education, Department of Secondary Education and Educational Leadership, Nacogdoches, TX 75962. Offers educational leadership (Ed D); secondary education (M Ed). *Accreditation:* NCATE. *Degree requirements:* For master's, comprehensive exam; for doctorate, thesis/dissertation. *Entrance requirements:* For master's, GRE General Test; for doctorate, GRE General Test, interview, writing sample. Additional exam requirements/recommendations for international students: Required—TOEFL. Electronic applications accepted.

Sul Ross State University, Rio Grande College of Sul Ross State University, Alpine, TX 79832. Offers business administration (MBA); teacher education (M Ed), including bilingual education, counseling, educational diagnostics, elementary education, general education, reading, school administration, secondary education. *Program availability:* Part-time, evening/weekend, online learning. *Degree requirements:* For master's, comprehensive exam, thesis optional, minimum GPA of 3.0. *Entrance requirements:* For master's, GMAT or GRE General Test, minimum GPA of 2.5 in last 60 hours of undergraduate work. Additional exam requirements/recommendations for international students: Required—TOEFL.

Tarleton State University, College of Graduate Studies, College of Education, Department of Curriculum and Instruction, Stephenville, TX 76402. Offers educational diagnostician (M Ed); elementary education (M Ed); instructional design and technology (M Ed); instructional leadership (M Ed); professional reading specialist (M Ed); secondary education (M Ed); special education (M Ed); technology applications (M Ed); technology director (M Ed). *Program availability:* Part-time, evening/weekend. *Faculty:* 9 full-time (7 women), 6 part-time/adjunct (4 women). *Students:* 17 full-time (0 women), 104 part-time (101 women); includes 28 minority (5 Black or African American, non-Hispanic/Latino; 1 American Indian or Alaska Native, non-Hispanic/Latino; 19 Hispanic/Latino; 3 Two or more races, non-Hispanic/Latino). 62 applicants, 94% accepted, 35 enrolled. In 2016, 34 master's awarded. *Degree requirements:* For master's, comprehensive exam. *Entrance requirements:* For master's, GRE General Test, minimum GPA of 3.0. Additional exam requirements/recommendations for international students: Required—TOEFL (minimum score 550 paper-based; 80 iBT). *Application deadline:* For fall admission, 8/15 priority date for domestic students; for spring admission, 1/7 for domestic students. Applications are processed on a rolling basis. Application fee: $45 ($145 for international students). Electronic applications accepted. *Expenses:* $3,672 tuition; $2,437 fees. *Financial support:* Research assistantships, teaching assistantships, career-related internships or fieldwork, Federal Work-Study, and institutionally sponsored loans available. Support available to part-time students. Financial award application deadline: 5/1; financial award applicants required to submit FAFSA. *Unit head:* Dr. Jordan Barkley, Department Head, 254-968-9089, E-mail: jbarkley@tarleton.edu. *Application contact:* Information Contact, 254-968-9104, Fax: 254-968-9670, E-mail: gradoffice@tarleton.edu.
Website: http://www.tarleton.edu/cimasters/

Teachers College, Columbia University, Department of Curriculum and Teaching, New York, NY 10027-6696. Offers curriculum and teaching (Ed M, MA, Ed D); curriculum and teaching: elementary education (MA); curriculum and teaching: secondary education (MA); early childhood education (MA, Ed D); early childhood education: special education (MA); elementary education-gifted extension (MA); elementary inclusive education (MA); gifted education (MA); literacy specialist (MA); secondary inclusive education (MA); special inclusive elementary education (MA). *Program availability:* Part-time, evening/weekend. *Students:* 236 full-time (219 women), 198 part-time (176 women); includes 160 minority (53 Black or African American, non-Hispanic/Latino; 1 American Indian or Alaska Native, non-Hispanic/Latino; 43 Asian, non-Hispanic/Latino; 41 Hispanic/Latino; 22 Two or more races, non-Hispanic/Latino), 38 international. 399 applicants, 66% accepted, 104 enrolled. Terminal master's awarded for partial completion of doctoral program. *Degree requirements:* For doctorate, thesis/dissertation. *Expenses: Tuition:* Full-time $36,288; part-time $1512 per credit. *Required fees:* $438 per semester. One-time fee: $510 full-time. Full-time tuition and fees vary according to course load. *Unit head:* Prof. Nancy Lesko, Chair, 212-678-3264, E-mail: lesko@tc.columbia.edu. *Application contact:* David Estrella, Director of Admission, 212-678-3305, Fax: 212-678-4171, E-mail: estrella@tc.columbia.edu.

Temple University, College of Education, Department of Teaching and Learning, Philadelphia, PA 19122-6096. Offers career and technical education (Ed M), including business, computing, and information technology, industrial education, marketing education; middle grades education (Ed M), including math and language arts, math and science, science and language arts; secondary education (Ed M), including English, math, social studies; teaching English to speakers of other languages (MS Ed); urban education (Ed M). *Program availability:* Part-time, evening/weekend. *Faculty:* 26 full-time (16 women), 74 part-time/adjunct (54 women). *Students:* 204 full-time (139 women), 320 part-time (201 women); includes 112 minority (66 Black or African American, non-Hispanic/Latino; 17 Asian, non-Hispanic/Latino; 18 Hispanic/Latino; 11 Two or more races, non-Hispanic/Latino), 18 international. 300 applicants, 55% accepted, 99 enrolled. In 2016, 93 master's awarded. Terminal master's awarded for partial completion of doctoral program. *Degree requirements:* For master's, thesis or alternative. *Entrance requirements:* Additional exam requirements/recommendations for international students: Required—TOEFL (minimum score 550 paper-based; 79 iBT). *Application deadline:* For fall admission, 4/1 for domestic students, 12/15 for international students; for spring admission, 10/1 for domestic students, 8/1 for

international students. Application fee: $60. Electronic applications accepted. *Expenses:* Contact institution. *Financial support:* Fellowships, research assistantships, and teaching assistantships available. Financial award application deadline: 1/15; financial award applicants required to submit FAFSA. *Faculty research:* Workforce development, vocational education, technical education, industrial education, professional development, literacy, classroom management, school communities, curriculum development, instruction, applied linguistics, cross linguistic influence, bilingual education, oral proficiency, multilingualism. *Unit head:* Dr. Christine Woyshner, Chairperson, 215-204-6387, E-mail: christine.woyshner@temple.edu. *Application contact:* Sarah Stapleton, Assistant Director, Academic Operations, 215-204-8220, E-mail: sarah.stapleton@temple.edu.
Website: http://education.temple.edu/tl

Tennessee Technological University, College of Graduate Studies, College of Education, Department of Curriculum and Instruction, Program in Secondary Education, Cookeville, TN 38505. Offers MA, Ed S. *Accreditation:* NCATE. *Program availability:* Part-time, evening/weekend. *Faculty:* 7 full-time (0 women). *Students:* 18 full-time (10 women), 25 part-time (14 women); includes 9 minority (4 Black or African American, non-Hispanic/Latino; 3 Hispanic/Latino; 2 Two or more races, non-Hispanic/Latino), 1 international. Average age 27. 23 applicants, 61% accepted, 14 enrolled. In 2016, 17 master's, 2 other advanced degrees awarded. *Degree requirements:* For master's and Ed S, comprehensive exam, thesis or alternative. *Entrance requirements:* For master's and Ed S, MAT or GRE. Additional exam requirements/recommendations for international students: Required—TOEFL (minimum score 527 paper-based; 71 iBT), IELTS (minimum score 5.5), PTE (minimum score 48), or TOEIC (Test of English as an International Communication). *Application deadline:* For fall admission, 8/1 for domestic students, 5/1 for international students; for spring admission, 12/1 for domestic students, 10/1 for international students; for summer admission, 5/1 for domestic students, 2/1 for international students. Applications are processed on a rolling basis. Application fee: $35 ($40 for international students). Electronic applications accepted. *Expenses:* Tuition, state resident: full-time $9375; part-time $534 per credit hour. Tuition, nonresident: full-time $22,443; part-time $1260 per credit hour. *Financial support:* Fellowships, research assistantships, teaching assistantships, and career-related internships or fieldwork available. Financial award application deadline: 4/1. *Unit head:* Dr. Jeremy Wendt, Interim Chairperson, 931-372-3181, Fax: 931-372-6270, E-mail: jwendt@tntech.edu. *Application contact:* Shelia K. Kendrick, Coordinator of Graduate Studies, 931-372-3808, Fax: 931-372-3497, E-mail: skendrick@tntech.edu.

Texas A&M University–Commerce, College of Education and Human Services, Commerce, TX 75429-3011. Offers counseling (MS); curriculum and instruction (M Ed, MS); early childhood education (M Ed, MS); educational administration (M Ed, Ed D); educational psychology (PhD); educational technology leadership (MS); educational technology library science (MS); health, kinesiology and sports studies (MS); higher education (MS, Ed D); organization, learning, and technology (MS); psychology (MS); reading (M Ed, MS); school psychology (SSP); secondary education (M Ed, MS); social work (MSW); special education (M Ed); supervision, curriculum and instruction-elementary education (Ed D). *Program availability:* Part-time, 100% online, blended/hybrid learning. *Faculty:* 88 full-time (52 women), 31 part-time/adjunct (24 women). *Students:* 341 full-time (276 women), 1,495 part-time (1,156 women); includes 762 minority (429 Black or African American, non-Hispanic/Latino; 4 American Indian or Alaska Native, non-Hispanic/Latino; 27 Asian, non-Hispanic/Latino; 247 Hispanic/Latino; 1 Native Hawaiian or other Pacific Islander, non-Hispanic/Latino; 54 Two or more races, non-Hispanic/Latino), 18 international. Average age 37. 1,070 applicants, 54% accepted, 452 enrolled. In 2016, 579 master's, 31 doctorates awarded. *Degree requirements:* For master's, one foreign language, comprehensive exam, thesis optional, departmental qualifying exams (for some programs); for doctorate, comprehensive exam, thesis/dissertation, departmental qualifying exam; for SSP, comprehensive exam, thesis optional. *Entrance requirements:* For master's and doctorate, GRE General Test. Additional exam requirements/recommendations for international students: Required—TOEFL (minimum score 550 paper-based; 79 iBT), IELTS (minimum score 6). *Application deadline:* For fall admission, 6/1 priority date for international students; for spring admission, 10/15 priority date for international students; for summer admission, 3/15 priority date for international students. Applications are processed on a rolling basis. Application fee: $50. Electronic applications accepted. *Expenses:* $2,254 resident; $4,744 non-resident. *Financial support:* In 2016–17, 301 students received support, including 39 research assistantships with partial tuition reimbursements available (averaging $9,000 per year), 17 teaching assistantships with partial tuition reimbursements available (averaging $9,000 per year); career-related internships or fieldwork, Federal Work-Study, institutionally sponsored loans, scholarships/grants, health care benefits, and unspecified assistantships also available. Financial award application deadline: 5/1; financial award applicants required to submit FAFSA. *Faculty research:* Cognitive and bilingual education, positive behavioral intervention, literacy, math readiness. *Total annual research expenditures:* $470,963. *Unit head:* Dr. Timothy Letzring, Dean, 903-886-5181, Fax: 903-886-5905, E-mail: tim.letzring@tamuc.edu. *Application contact:* Jennifer Faunce, Graduate Recruiter, 903-886-5030, Fax: 903-886-5905, E-mail: jennifer.faunce@tamuc.edu.
Website: http://www.tamuc.edu/academics/graduateSchool/programs/education/default.aspx

Texas A&M University–Corpus Christi, College of Graduate Studies, College of Education, Program in Secondary Education, Corpus Christi, TX 78412-5503. Offers MS. *Program availability:* Part-time, evening/weekend, online learning. *Students:* 8 full-time (6 women), 17 part-time (12 women); includes 19 minority (5 Black or African American, non-Hispanic/Latino; 14 Hispanic/Latino). Average age 32. 15 applicants, 73% accepted, 7 enrolled. In 2016, 2 master's awarded. *Degree requirements:* For master's, capstone experience. *Entrance requirements:* For master's, minimum GPA of 3.0 in last 60 hours. Additional exam requirements/recommendations for international students: Required—TOEFL (minimum score 550 paper-based; 79 iBT), IELTS (minimum score 6.5). *Application deadline:* For fall admission, 8/19 priority date for domestic students, 7/26 priority date for international students; for spring admission, 1/13 priority date for domestic students, 12/20 priority date for international students; for summer admission, 5/25 priority date for domestic students, 5/1 priority date for international students. Applications are processed on a rolling basis. Application fee: $50 ($70 for international students). Electronic applications accepted. *Financial support:* Research assistantships, teaching assistantships, career-related internships or fieldwork, Federal Work-Study, institutionally sponsored loans, scholarships/grants, health care benefits, and unspecified assistantships available. Support available to part-time students. Financial award application deadline: 3/15; financial award applicants required to submit FAFSA. *Unit head:* Dr. Linda Kelly, Clinical Assistant Professor, 361-825-2437, E-mail: linda.kelly@tamucc.edu. *Application contact:* Graduate Admissions Coordinator, 361-825-2177, Fax: 361-825-2755, E-mail: gradweb@tamucc.edu.
Website: http://macprogram.tamucc.edu/

Texas A&M University–Kingsville, College of Graduate Studies, College of Education and Human Performance, Department of Teacher and Bilingual Education, Program in Education, Kingsville, TX 78363. Offers MS. *Program availability:* Part-time, evening/weekend. *Degree requirements:* For master's, comprehensive exam, thesis or alternative, research report. *Entrance requirements:* For master's, GRE General Test, MAT, minimum GPA of 3.0. *Faculty research:* Professional development/technology, interdisciplinary teaming, educational restructuring.

Texas Southern University, College of Education, Area of Curriculum and Instruction, Houston, TX 77004-4584. Offers bilingual education (M Ed); curriculum and instruction (Ed D); secondary education (M Ed). *Program availability:* Part-time, evening/weekend. *Degree requirements:* For master's, comprehensive exam; for doctorate, comprehensive exam, thesis/dissertation. *Entrance requirements:* For master's, GRE General Test, minimum GPA of 2.5; for doctorate, GRE General Test or MAT, master's degree, minimum B+ average. Additional exam requirements/recommendations for international students: Required—TOEFL. Electronic applications accepted.

Texas State University, The Graduate College, College of Education, Program in Secondary Education, San Marcos, TX 78666. Offers M Ed, MA. *Program availability:* Part-time, evening/weekend. *Faculty:* 20 full-time (12 women), 8 part-time/adjunct (6 women). *Students:* 49 full-time (36 women), 31 part-time (20 women); includes 27 minority (3 Black or African American, non-Hispanic/Latino; 5 Asian, non-Hispanic/Latino; 14 Hispanic/Latino; 5 Two or more races, non-Hispanic/Latino), 3 international. Average age 30. 50 applicants, 86% accepted, 26 enrolled. In 2016, 38 master's awarded. *Degree requirements:* For master's, comprehensive exam, thesis (for some programs). *Entrance requirements:* For master's, GRE General Test (preferred), baccalaureate degree from regionally-accredited institution with minimum GPA of 2.75 in last 60 hours of course work (for M Ed), 3.4 (for MA); statement of purpose identifying research interest (for MA). Additional exam requirements/recommendations for international students: Required—TOEFL (minimum score 550 paper-based; 78 iBT), IELTS (minimum score 6.5). *Application deadline:* For fall admission, 2/15 priority date for domestic and international students; for spring admission, 10/15 for domestic students, 10/1 for international students; for summer admission, 4/15 for domestic students, 3/15 for international students. Applications are processed on a rolling basis. Application fee: $40 ($90 for international students). Electronic applications accepted. *Expenses:* $4,851 per semester. *Financial support:* In 2016–17, 52 students received support, including 2 research assistantships (averaging $9,962 per year), 3 teaching assistantships (averaging $13,618 per year); career-related internships or fieldwork, Federal Work-Study, institutionally sponsored loans, and scholarships/grants also available. Support available to part-time students. Financial award application deadline: 3/1; financial award applicants required to submit FAFSA. *Faculty research:* Positive behavioral intervention and support, guidance and consultation. *Unit head:* Dr. Nathan Bond, Graduate Advisor, 512-245-3098, Fax: 512-245-7911, E-mail: jb50@txstate.edu. *Application contact:* Dr. Andrea Golato, Dean of Graduate School, 512-245-2581, Fax: 512-245-8365, E-mail: gradcollege@txstate.edu.
Website: http://www.education.txstate.edu/ci/degrees-programs/graduate/secondary-education.html

Texas Tech University, Graduate School, College of Education, Department of Curriculum and Instruction, Lubbock, TX 79409-1071. Offers bilingual education (M Ed); curriculum and instruction (M Ed); elementary education (M Ed); language/literacy education (M Ed); multidisciplinary science (MS); secondary education (M Ed). *Accreditation:* NCATE. *Program availability:* Part-time, evening/weekend, online learning. *Faculty:* 24 full-time (17 women), 1 part-time/adjunct (0 women). *Students:* 65 full-time (52 women), 237 part-time (191 women); includes 97 minority (30 Black or African American, non-Hispanic/Latino; 1 American Indian or Alaska Native, non-Hispanic/Latino; 10 Asian, non-Hispanic/Latino; 47 Hispanic/Latino; 9 Two or more races, non-Hispanic/Latino), 41 international. Average age 39. 181 applicants, 54% accepted, 78 enrolled. In 2016, 20 master's, 28 doctorates awarded. Terminal master's awarded for partial completion of doctoral program. *Degree requirements:* For master's, comprehensive exam (for some programs), thesis optional; for doctorate, comprehensive exam, thesis/dissertation. *Entrance requirements:* For master's, bachelor's degree; resume; letter of intent; academic writing sample; 2 letters of recommendation; for doctorate, GRE, master's degree; resume; letter of intent; academic writing sample; 3 letters of recommendation. Additional exam requirements/recommendations for international students: Required—TOEFL (minimum score 550 paper-based; 79 iBT). *Application deadline:* For fall admission, 6/1 priority date for domestic students, 1/15 priority date for international students; for spring admission, 9/1 priority date for domestic students, 6/15 priority date for international students. Applications are processed on a rolling basis. Application fee: $75. Electronic applications accepted. *Expenses:* $285 per credit hour full-time resident tuition, $693 per credit hour full-time non-resident tuition; $50.50 per credit hour fee plus $608 per term fee. *Financial support:* In 2016–17, 110 students received support, including 110 fellowships (averaging $3,132 per year); research assistantships, Federal Work-Study, institutionally sponsored loans, scholarships/grants, health care benefits, and unspecified assistantships also available. Support available to part-time students. Financial award application deadline: 2/1; financial award applicants required to submit FAFSA. *Faculty research:* Teacher education, curriculum studies, bilingual education, science and math education, language and literacy education. *Total annual research expenditures:* $120,552. *Unit head:* Dr. Jian Wang, Department Chair, Curriculum and Instruction, 806-834-5165, Fax: 806-742-2179, E-mail: jian.wang@ttu.edu. *Application contact:* Brianna Sanchez, Coordinator, 806-834-2353, Fax: 806-742-2179, E-mail: brianna.sanchez@ttu.edu.
Website: http://www.educ.ttu.edu

Towson University, Program in Secondary Education, Towson, MD 21252-0001. Offers M Ed. *Accreditation:* NCATE. *Program availability:* Part-time, evening/weekend. *Students:* 1 (woman) full-time, 5 part-time (4 women); includes 1 minority (Black or African American, non-Hispanic/Latino). *Degree requirements:* For master's, thesis optional. *Entrance requirements:* For master's, Maryland teaching certification or permission of program director, minimum GPA of 3.0. *Application deadline:* Applications are processed on a rolling basis. Application fee: $45. Electronic applications accepted. *Expenses:* Tuition, state resident: full-time $7580; part-time $379 per unit. Tuition, nonresident: full-time $15,700; part-time $785 per unit. *Required fees:* $2480. *Financial support:* Application deadline: 4/1. *Unit head:* Dr. Todd Kenreich, Graduate Program Director, 410-704-4956, E-mail: scedmed@towson.edu. *Application contact:* Coverley Beidleman, Assistant Director of Graduate Admissions, 410-704-2113, Fax: 410-704-3030, E-mail: grads@towson.edu.
Website: http://www.towson.edu/coe/departments/secondary/gradsecondary/

Trevecca Nazarene University, Graduate Education Program, Nashville, TN 37210-2877. Offers accountability and instructional leadership (Ed S); curriculum and instruction for Christian school educators (M Ed); curriculum and instruction K-12 (M Ed); educational leadership (M Ed); English second language (M Ed); library and information science (MLI Sc); special education: visual impairments (M Ed); teaching (MAT), including teaching 6-12, teaching K-5. *Accreditation:* NCATE. *Program availability:* Part-time, evening/weekend, online learning. *Faculty:* 5 full-time (3 women), 18 part-time/adjunct (12 women). *Students:* 80 full-time (64 women), 16 part-time (13 women); includes 19 minority (17 Black or African American, non-Hispanic/Latino; 2 Hispanic/Latino). Average age 35. In 2016, 68 master's, 7 other advanced degrees awarded. *Degree requirements:* For master's, comprehensive exam, exit assessment/e-portfolio. *Entrance requirements:* For master's, GRE (minimum score of 290) or MAT (minimum score of 378); PRAXIS (for MAT), minimum GPA of 3.0, official transcript from

regionally-accredited institution, at least 3 years' successful teaching experience (for M Ed in educational leadership major). Additional exam requirements/recommendations for international students: Required—TOEFL (minimum score 550 paper-based). *Application deadline:* Applications are processed on a rolling basis. Electronic applications accepted. *Expenses:* Contact institution. *Financial support:* Applicants required to submit FAFSA. *Unit head:* Dr. Suzie Harris, Dean, School of Education/ Director of Graduate Education Programs, 615-248-1201, Fax: 615-248-1597, E-mail: admissions_ged@trevecca.edu. *Application contact:* 844-TNU-GRAD, E-mail: sgcsadmissions@trevecca.edu.
Website: http://www.trevecca.edu/soe

Trinity Washington University, School of Education, Washington, DC 20017-1094. Offers clinical mental health counseling (MA); early childhood education (MAT); educating for change (M Ed); educational administration (MSA); elementary education (MAT); reading (M Ed); school counseling (MA); secondary education (MAT), including English, social studies; special education (MAT). *Accreditation:* NCATE. *Program availability:* Part-time, evening/weekend. *Degree requirements:* For master's, thesis (for some programs), capstone project(s). *Entrance requirements:* For master's, PRAXIS I, minimum GPA of 2.8. Additional exam requirements/recommendations for international students: Required—TOEFL (minimum score 550 paper-based). *Faculty research:* Technology, literacy, special education, organizations, inclusion models.

Troy University, Graduate School, College of Education, Program in Secondary Education, Troy, AL 36082. Offers MS. *Accreditation:* NCATE. *Program availability:* Part-time, evening/weekend. *Faculty:* 2 full-time (1 woman). *Students:* 15 full-time (9 women), 6 part-time (5 women). Average age 31. 16 applicants, 88% accepted, 9 enrolled. In 2016, 9 master's awarded. *Degree requirements:* For master's, comprehensive exam, thesis. *Entrance requirements:* For master's, GRE (minimum score of 850 on old exam or 290 on new exam), GMAT (minimum score of 380), or MAT (minimum score of 385), bachelor's degree; minimum undergraduate GPA of 2.5 or 3.0 on last 30 semester hours, letter of recommendation. Additional exam requirements/ recommendations for international students: Required—TOEFL (minimum score 523 paper-based; 70 iBT), IELTS (minimum score 6). *Application deadline:* Applications are processed on a rolling basis. Application fee: $50. Electronic applications accepted. *Expenses:* Tuition, state resident: full-time $7146; part-time $397 per credit hour. Tuition, nonresident: full-time $14,292; part-time $794 per credit hour. *Required fees:* $802; $50 per semester. Tuition and fees vary according to campus/location and program. *Financial support:* Fellowships, career-related internships or fieldwork, and scholarships/grants available. Support available to part-time students. Financial award applicants required to submit FAFSA. *Unit head:* Dr. Ruth Busby, Chair, Teacher Education, 334-670-3546, Fax: 334-808-6666, E-mail: rsbusby@troy.edu. *Application contact:* Jessica A. Kimbro, Director of Graduate Admissions, 334-670-3178, E-mail: bcamp@troy.edu.

Tufts University, Graduate School of Arts and Sciences, Department of Education, Program in Education, Medford, MA 02155. Offers educational studies (MA); elementary education (MAT); middle and secondary education (MAT); museum education (MA); secondary education (MA); STEM education (MS, PhD). *Program availability:* Part-time. *Students:* 67 full-time (49 women), 14 part-time (12 women); includes 17 minority (4 Black or African American, non-Hispanic/Latino; 6 Asian, non-Hispanic/Latino; 6 Hispanic/Latino; 1 Two or more races, non-Hispanic/Latino), 6 international. Average age 28. 120 applicants, 71% accepted, 49 enrolled. In 2016, 25 master's awarded. *Degree requirements:* For master's, thesis optional. *Entrance requirements:* For master's, GRE General Test, portfolio (for art education only); for doctorate, GRE General Test, writing sample. Additional exam requirements/recommendations for international students: Required—TOEFL (minimum score 550 paper-based; 80 iBT), IELTS (minimum score 6.5). *Application deadline:* For fall admission, 1/2 for domestic and international students; for spring admission, 10/15 for domestic and international students. Applications are processed on a rolling basis. Application fee: $85. Electronic applications accepted. *Expenses:* Contact institution. *Financial support:* In 2016–17, 69 students received support. Research assistantships, teaching assistantships, Federal Work-Study, scholarships/grants, and tuition waivers (full and partial) available. Support available to part-time students. Financial award application deadline: 1/2. *Unit head:* Dr. Sabina Vaught, Graduate Program Director. *Application contact:* Office of Graduate Admissions, 617-627-3395, E-mail: gradadmissions@tufts.edu.

Union College, Graduate Programs, Department of Education, Program in Secondary Education, Barbourville, KY 40906-1499. Offers MA. *Degree requirements:* For master's, thesis optional. *Entrance requirements:* For master's, GRE General Test, NTE.

Universidad Metropolitana, School of Education, Program in Teaching of Physical Education, San Juan, PR 00928-1150. Offers teaching of adult physical education (M Ed); teaching of elementary physical education (M Ed); teaching of secondary physical education (M Ed). *Degree requirements:* For master's, thesis or alternative. *Entrance requirements:* For master's, EXADEP, interview. Electronic applications accepted.

The University of Akron, Graduate School, College of Education, Department of Curricular and Instructional Studies, Program in Adolescent to Young Adult Education, Akron, OH 44325. Offers chemistry (MS); chemistry and physics (MS); earth science (MS); earth science and chemistry (MS); earth science and physics (MS); integrated language arts (MS); integrated mathematics (MS); integrated social studies (MS); life science (MS); life science and chemistry (MS); life science and earth science (MS); life science and physics (MS); physics (MS). *Accreditation:* NCATE. *Degree requirements:* For master's, comprehensive exam, portfolio. *Entrance requirements:* Additional exam requirements/recommendations for international students: Required—TOEFL (minimum score 550 paper-based, 79 iBT) or IELTS (minimum score 6.5). *Application deadline:* For fall admission, 3/1 for domestic and international students; for spring admission, 10/1 for domestic and international students. Applications are processed on a rolling basis. Application fee: $45 ($70 for international students). Electronic applications accepted. *Expenses:* Tuition, state resident: full-time $8618; part-time $359 per credit hour. Tuition, nonresident: full-time $17,149; part-time $715 per credit hour. *Required fees:* $1652. *Unit head:* Dr. Peggy McCann, Interim Chair, 330-972-5742, E-mail: plm@uakron.edu.

The University of Alabama, Graduate School, College of Education, Department of Curriculum and Instruction, Tuscaloosa, AL 35487. Offers elementary education (MA, Ed D, PhD, Ed S); secondary education (MA, Ed D, PhD, Ed S). *Program availability:* Part-time, evening/weekend, 100% online, blended/hybrid learning. *Faculty:* 20 full-time (13 women), 2 part-time/adjunct (both women). *Students:* 66 full-time (45 women), 105 part-time (83 women); includes 28 minority (14 Black or African American, non-Hispanic/ Latino; 2 American Indian or Alaska Native, non-Hispanic/Latino; 1 Asian, non-Hispanic/ Latino; 6 Hispanic/Latino; 1 Native Hawaiian or other Pacific Islander, non-Hispanic/ Latino; 4 Two or more races, non-Hispanic/Latino), 17 international. Average age 35. 93 applicants, 53% accepted, 40 enrolled. In 2016, 55 master's, 7 doctorates, 13 other advanced degrees awarded. *Degree requirements:* For master's, comprehensive exam, thesis (for some programs); for doctorate, comprehensive exam, thesis/dissertation; for Ed S, comprehensive exam, thesis. *Entrance requirements:* For master's and Ed S, MAT and/or GRE; for doctorate, GRE. Additional exam requirements/recommendations for international students: Recommended—TOEFL (minimum score 550 paper-based), IELTS (minimum score 6.5). *Application deadline:* For fall admission, 7/15 priority date for domestic students, 1/15 priority date for international students; for spring admission, 11/15 priority date for domestic students, 6/1 priority date for international students; for summer admission, 5/1 priority date for domestic students, 3/1 priority date for international students. Applications are processed on a rolling basis. Application fee: $50 ($60 for international students). Electronic applications accepted. *Expenses:* Tuition, state resident: full-time $10,470. Tuition, nonresident: full-time $26,950. *Financial support:* In 2016–17, 14 students received support, including 19 research assistantships with tuition reimbursements available (averaging $13,140 per year), 5 teaching assistantships with tuition reimbursements available (averaging $13,140 per year); institutionally sponsored loans, traineeships, and unspecified assistantships also available. Financial award application deadline: 12/31; financial award applicants required to submit FAFSA. *Faculty research:* Teacher education, diversity, integration of curriculum, technology, pedagogical content knowledge. *Total annual research expenditures:* $226,200. *Unit head:* Dr. Cynthia Camille Sunal, Chair, 205-348-8264, Fax: 205-348-9863, E-mail: cvsunal@ua.edu. *Application contact:* Dr. Kathy S. Wetzel, Assistant Dean for Student Services, 205-348-1154, Fax: 205-348-0080, E-mail: kwetzel@bamaed.ua.edu.
Website: http://courseleaf.ua.edu/education/curriculumandinstruction/

The University of Alabama at Birmingham, School of Education, Program in High School Education, Birmingham, AL 35294. Offers MA Ed. *Accreditation:* NCATE. *Degree requirements:* For master's, thesis optional. *Entrance requirements:* For master's, GRE General Test, MAT, or NTE, minimum GPA of 3.0. Electronic applications accepted. Full-time tuition and fees vary according to course load and program.

The University of Alabama in Huntsville, School of Graduate Studies, College of Education, Huntsville, AL 35899. Offers autism spectrum disorders (M Ed, Graduate Certificate); biology (MAT); chemistry (MAT); differentiated instruction in elementary education (M Ed); English language arts (MAT); English speakers of other languages (M Ed, MAT); history (MAT); mathematics (MAT); physics (MAT); reading education (M Ed); secondary education (M Ed). *Expenses:* Tuition, state resident: full-time $9834; part-time $600 per credit hour. Tuition, nonresident: full-time $21,830; part-time $1325 per credit hour.

University of Alaska Southeast, Graduate Programs, Program in Education, Juneau, AK 99801. Offers educational leadership (M Ed); elementary education (MAT); learning design and technology (M Ed); mathematics education (M Ed); reading specialist (M Ed); secondary education (MAT); special education (M Ed, MAT). *Accreditation:* NCATE. *Program availability:* Part-time, evening/weekend, online learning. *Degree requirements:* For master's, comprehensive exam or project, portfolio. *Entrance requirements:* For master's, PRAXIS, minimum GPA of 3.0, writing sample, letters of recommendation. *Application deadline:* For fall admission, 3/8 for domestic students. Applications are processed on a rolling basis. Application fee: $60. Electronic applications accepted. *Expenses:* Tuition, state resident: part-time $466 per credit. Tuition, nonresident: part-time $979 per credit. *Required fees:* $19 per credit. Part-time tuition and fees vary according to course level, campus/location and reciprocity agreements. *Financial support:* Federal Work-Study, scholarships/grants, and tuition waivers (full and partial) available. Support available to part-time students. Financial award applicants required to submit FAFSA. *Faculty research:* Applied classroom research, culturally responsive practices, action research, teaching effectiveness. *Unit head:* Dr. Larry Harris, Dean, 907-796-6551, Fax: 907-796-6550, E-mail: larry.harris@uas.alaska.edu. *Application contact:* Susan A. Stuck, Administrative Assistant, 866-465-6424, Fax: 866-465-5159, E-mail: jnsas@uas.alaska.edu.

University of Alberta, Faculty of Graduate Studies and Research, Department of Secondary Education, Edmonton, AB T6G 2E1, Canada. Offers M Ed, Ed D, PhD. *Program availability:* Part-time. *Degree requirements:* For master's, thesis or alternative, 1 year of residency; for doctorate, thesis/dissertation, 2 years of residency (PhD), 1 year of residency (Ed D). *Entrance requirements:* For master's, teaching certificate, 2 years of teaching experience; for doctorate, master's degree. *Faculty research:* Curriculum studies, teacher education, subject area specializations.

The University of Arizona, College of Education, Department of Teaching, Learning and Sociocultural Studies, Program in Teaching and Teacher Education, Tucson, AZ 85721. Offers M Ed, MA, PhD. *Program availability:* Part-time, evening/weekend. *Degree requirements:* For master's, thesis optional; for doctorate, comprehensive exam, thesis/dissertation. *Entrance requirements:* For master's, writing sample, 1 year of teaching experience, 3 letters of recommendation; for doctorate, GRE General Test (minimum score 1000), minimum GPA of 3.5, 2 years of teaching experience, 3 letters of recommendation, writing sample. Additional exam requirements/recommendations for international students: Required—TOEFL (minimum score 550 paper-based; 79 iBT). Electronic applications accepted. *Faculty research:* Staff development, science education, environmental education, math education.

The University of Arizona, College of Science, Department of Mathematics, Program in Secondary Mathematics Education, Tucson, AZ 85721. Offers MA. *Program availability:* Part-time. *Degree requirements:* For master's, thesis, internships, colloquium, business courses. *Entrance requirements:* For master's, GRE, minimum GPA of 3.0, statement of purpose. Additional exam requirements/recommendations for international students: Required—TOEFL (minimum score 550 paper-based). *Faculty research:* Algebra, coding theory, graph theory, combinatorics, probability.

University of Arkansas, Graduate School, College of Education and Health Professions, Department of Curriculum and Instruction, Program in Secondary Education, Fayetteville, AR 72701. Offers M Ed, MAT, Ed S. *Accreditation:* NCATE. In 2016, 40 master's awarded. *Application deadline:* For fall admission, 4/1 for international students; for spring admission, 10/1 for international students. Applications are processed on a rolling basis. Application fee: $40 ($50 for international students). Electronic applications accepted. *Financial support:* Fellowships with tuition reimbursements, research assistantships, teaching assistantships, career-related internships or fieldwork, and Federal Work-Study available. Support available to part-time students. Financial award application deadline: 4/1; financial award applicants required to submit FAFSA. *Faculty research:* Mathematics. *Unit head:* Dr. Michael Daugherty, Unit Head, 479-575-4209, E-mail: mkd03@uark.edu. *Application contact:* Dr. Freddie Bowles, Graduate Coordinator, 479-575-3035, Fax: 479-575-6676, E-mail: fbowles@uark.edu.
Website: http://cied.uark.edu/

University of Arkansas at Little Rock, Graduate School, College of Education and Health Professions, Department of Teacher Education, Program in Secondary Education, Little Rock, AR 72204-1099. Offers M Ed. *Accreditation:* NCATE. *Program availability:* Part-time. *Degree requirements:* For master's, comprehensive exam. *Entrance requirements:* For master's, interview, minimum GPA of 2.75, GRE General Test or teaching certificate.

University of Arkansas at Pine Bluff, School of Education, Pine Bluff, AR 71601-2799. Offers elementary education (M Ed); secondary education (M Ed), including English education, mathematics education, science education, social studies education;

teaching (MAT). *Accreditation:* NCATE. *Program availability:* Part-time, evening/weekend. *Degree requirements:* For master's, comprehensive exam. *Entrance requirements:* For master's, GRE, minimum GPA of 2.75, NTE or Standard Arkansas Teaching Certificate. Application fee: $25. *Expenses:* Tuition, state resident: full-time $4776. Tuition, nonresident: full-time $10,824. *Required fees:* $1612. Tuition and fees vary according to course load. *Financial support:* Research assistantships with full and partial tuition reimbursements, teaching assistantships with full and partial tuition reimbursements, institutionally sponsored loans, and scholarships/grants available. Support available to part-time students. *Faculty research:* Teacher certification, accreditation, assessment, standards, portfolio development, rehabilitation, technology. *Unit head:* Dr. George Herts, Dean, 870-575-8000, E-mail: johnson_c@uapb.edu.
Website: http://www.uapb.edu/academics/school_of_education.aspx

University of Bridgeport, School of Education, Department of Education, Bridgeport, CT 06604. Offers education (MS); educational management (Ed D, Diploma), including intermediate administrator or supervisor (Diploma), leadership (Ed D); elementary education (MS, Diploma), including early childhood education, elementary education; middle school education (MS); music education (MS); remedial reading and language arts (Diploma); secondary education (MS, Diploma), including computer specialist (Diploma), international education (Diploma), reading specialist, secondary education. *Program availability:* Part-time, evening/weekend. *Degree requirements:* For master's, final exam, final project, or thesis; for doctorate, comprehensive exam, thesis/dissertation; for Diploma, thesis or alternative, final project. *Entrance requirements:* For master's, minimum undergraduate QPA of 2.67; for doctorate, GRE, MAT; for Diploma, GRE General Test or MAT, minimum graduate QPA of 3.0. Additional exam requirements/recommendations for international students: Recommended—TOEFL (minimum score 550 paper-based; 80 iBT), IELTS (minimum score 6.5). Electronic applications accepted. *Expenses:* Contact institution.

University of California, Irvine, School of Education, Irvine, CA 92697. Offers educational administration (Ed D); educational administration and leadership (Ed D); elementary and secondary education (MAT). *Program availability:* Part-time, evening/weekend. *Students:* 189 full-time (139 women), 1 part-time (0 women); includes 101 minority (44 Asian, non-Hispanic/Latino; 40 Hispanic/Latino; 1 Native Hawaiian or other Pacific Islander, non-Hispanic/Latino; 16 Two or more races, non-Hispanic/Latino), 16 international. Average age 27. 456 applicants, 54% accepted, 131 enrolled. In 2016, 139 master's, 16 doctorates awarded. *Degree requirements:* For doctorate, thesis/dissertation. *Entrance requirements:* For master's, GRE, minimum GPA of 3.0; for doctorate, GRE General Test, minimum GPA of 3.0. Additional exam requirements/recommendations for international students: Required—TOEFL (minimum score 550 paper-based). *Application deadline:* For fall admission, 1/2 priority date for domestic students, 1/2 for international students. Application fee: $105 ($125 for international students). Electronic applications accepted. *Financial support:* Fellowships, research assistantships with full tuition reimbursements, institutionally sponsored loans, traineeships, health care benefits, and unspecified assistantships available. Financial award application deadline: 3/1; financial award applicants required to submit FAFSA. *Faculty research:* Education technology, learning theory, social theory, cultural diversity, postmodernism. *Unit head:* Richard Arum, Dean, 949-824-2534, E-mail: richard.arum@uci.edu. *Application contact:* Denise Earley, Assistant Director of Student Affairs, 949-824-4022, E-mail: denise.earley@uci.edu.
Website: http://education.uci.edu/

University of Central Oklahoma, The Jackson College of Graduate Studies, College of Education and Professional Studies, Department of Educational Sciences, Foundations and Research, Edmond, OK 73034-5209. Offers secondary education (M Ed). *Program availability:* Part-time. *Degree requirements:* For master's, comprehensive exam (for some programs). *Entrance requirements:* For master's, GRE General Test. Additional exam requirements/recommendations for international students: Required—TOEFL (minimum score 550 paper-based; 79 iBT); Recommended—IELTS (minimum score 6.5). Electronic applications accepted. *Faculty research:* At-risk youth.

University of Cincinnati, Graduate School, College of Education, Criminal Justice, and Human Services, Division of Teacher Education, Program in Secondary Education, Cincinnati, OH 45221. Offers M Ed. *Accreditation:* NCATE. *Program availability:* Part-time. *Degree requirements:* For master's, thesis or alternative. *Entrance requirements:* For master's, GRE General Test. Additional exam requirements/recommendations for international students: Required—TOEFL (minimum score 550 paper-based), TWE (minimum score 4.5), OEPT. Electronic applications accepted. *Expenses: Tuition, area resident:* Full-time $12,790; part-time $389 per credit hour. Tuition, state resident: full-time $13,290; part-time $419 per credit hour. Tuition, nonresident: full-time $24,532; part-time $976 per credit hour. *International tuition:* $24,832 full-time. *Required fees:* $3958; $140 per credit hour. Tuition and fees vary according to course load, degree level, program and reciprocity agreements.

University of Colorado Denver, School of Education and Human Development, Information and Learning Technologies Program, Denver, CO 80217. Offers e-learning design and implementation (MA); instructional design and adult learning (MA); K-12 teaching (MA). *Program availability:* Part-time, evening/weekend, online learning. *Students:* 68 full-time (56 women), 50 part-time (37 women); includes 16 minority (4 Black or African American, non-Hispanic/Latino; 5 Asian, non-Hispanic/Latino; 5 Hispanic/Latino; 1 Native Hawaiian or other Pacific Islander, non-Hispanic/Latino; 1 Two or more races, non-Hispanic/Latino), 2 international. Average age 38. 24 applicants, 88% accepted, 13 enrolled. In 2016, 45 master's awarded. *Degree requirements:* For master's, comprehensive exam (for some programs), comprehensive exam or online portfolio; 30 credit hours. *Entrance requirements:* For master's, GRE or MAT (if GPA is below 2.75), resume, statement of intent, three letters of recommendation, transcripts from all colleges/universities previously attended. Additional exam requirements/recommendations for international students: Required—TOEFL (minimum score 537 paper-based; 75 iBT); Recommended—IELTS (minimum score 6.5). *Application deadline:* For fall admission, 5/15 for domestic students, 5/1 for international students; for spring admission, 11/15 for domestic students, 11/1 for international students; for summer admission, 3/15 for domestic students, 3/1 for international students. Application fee: $50 ($75 for international students). Electronic applications accepted. *Expenses:* Contact institution. *Financial support:* In 2016–17, 7 students received support. Fellowships, research assistantships, teaching assistantships, Federal Work-Study, institutionally sponsored loans, scholarships/grants, and traineeships available. Financial award application deadline: 4/1; financial award applicants required to submit FAFSA. *Faculty research:* Technology for educational management, instructional design foundations, e-learning, educational design. *Unit head:* Brent Wilson, Professor, 303-720-7765, E-mail: brent.wilson@ucdenver.edu. *Application contact:* 303-315-6300, E-mail: education@ucdenver.edu.
Website: http://www.ucdenver.edu/academics/colleges/SchoolOfEducation/Academics/MASTERS/ILT/Pages/default.aspx

University of Colorado Denver, School of Education and Human Development, Teacher Education Programs, Denver, CO 80217. Offers elementary linguistically diverse education (MA); elementary math and science education (MA); elementary math education (MA); elementary reading and writing (MA); elementary science education (MA); secondary English education (MA); secondary linguistically diverse education (MA); secondary math education (MA); secondary reading and writing (MA); secondary science education (MA); special education (MA). *Accreditation:* NCATE. *Program availability:* Part-time, evening/weekend. *Students:* 142 full-time (117 women), 184 part-time (159 women); includes 56 minority (6 Black or African American, non-Hispanic/Latino; 1 American Indian or Alaska Native, non-Hispanic/Latino; 4 Asian, non-Hispanic/Latino; 38 Hispanic/Latino; 1 Native Hawaiian or other Pacific Islander, non-Hispanic/Latino; 6 Two or more races, non-Hispanic/Latino), 1 international. Average age 30. 18 applicants, 67% accepted, 9 enrolled. In 2016, 134 master's awarded. *Degree requirements:* For master's, comprehensive exam. *Entrance requirements:* For master's, GRE or MAT (for those with GPA below 2.75), transcripts, resume, letters of recommendation. Additional exam requirements/recommendations for international students: Required—TOEFL (minimum score 537 paper-based; 75 iBT); Recommended—IELTS (minimum score 6.5). *Application deadline:* For fall admission, 4/15 for domestic students, 4/1 for international students; for spring admission, 9/15 for domestic students, 9/1 for international students; for summer admission, 2/15 for domestic students, 2/1 for international students. Applications are processed on a rolling basis. Application fee: $50 ($75 for international students). Electronic applications accepted. *Expenses:* Contact institution. *Financial support:* In 2016–17, 26 students received support. Fellowships, research assistantships, teaching assistantships, Federal Work-Study, institutionally sponsored loans, scholarships/grants, and traineeships available. Financial award application deadline: 4/1; financial award applicants required to submit FAFSA. *Faculty research:* Linguistically diverse education/ESL, elementary reading and writing, elementary teacher education, secondary teacher education, special education. *Unit head:* Cindy Gutierrez, Director, 303-315-4982, E-mail: cindy.gutierrez@ucdenver.edu. *Application contact:* 303-315-6300, E-mail: education@ucdenver.edu.
Website: http://www.ucdenver.edu/academics/colleges/SchoolOfEducation/Academics/MASTERS/Pages/default.aspx

University of Connecticut, Graduate School, Neag School of Education, Department of Curriculum and Instruction, Program in Secondary Education, Storrs, CT 06269. Offers MA, PhD. *Accreditation:* NCATE. Terminal master's awarded for partial completion of doctoral program. *Degree requirements:* For master's, comprehensive exam, thesis or alternative; for doctorate, thesis/dissertation. *Entrance requirements:* For doctorate, GRE General Test. Additional exam requirements/recommendations for international students: Required—TOEFL (minimum score 550 paper-based). Electronic applications accepted.

University of Dayton, Department of Teacher Education, Dayton, OH 45469. Offers early childhood leadership and advocacy (MS Ed); interdisciplinary education studies (MS Ed); leadership in educational systems (MS Ed); literacy (MS Ed); mathematics education (MS Ed); music education (MS Ed); teacher as leader (MS Ed); teacher education (MS Ed); technology-enhanced learning (MS Ed); trans-disciplinary early childhood education (MS Ed). *Program availability:* Part-time, evening/weekend, blended/hybrid learning. *Faculty:* 23 full-time (18 women), 49 part-time/adjunct (42 women). *Students:* 52 full-time (47 women), 89 part-time (76 women); includes 6 minority (2 Black or African American, non-Hispanic/Latino; 2 Hispanic/Latino; 2 Two or more races, non-Hispanic/Latino), 24 international. Average age 31. 106 applicants, 28% accepted. In 2016, 69 master's awarded. *Degree requirements:* For master's, variable foreign language requirement, thesis optional. *Entrance requirements:* For master's, GRE (minimum score of 149 verbal, 4 on writing) or MAT (minimum score of 396) if undergraduate GPA was under 2.75, minimum GPA of 2.75, 3 letters of recommendation, personal statement or resume, official transcripts. Additional exam requirements/recommendations for international students: Required—TOEFL (minimum score 550 paper-based; 80 iBT); Recommended—IELTS (minimum score 6.5). *Application deadline:* Applications are processed on a rolling basis. Application fee: $0 ($50 for international students). Electronic applications accepted. *Expenses:* $620 per credit hour, $25 registration fee per term. *Financial support:* Institutionally sponsored loans available. Financial award application deadline: 3/1; financial award applicants required to submit FAFSA. *Faculty research:* Educational technology; facilitating teacher reflection; teacher preparation in dyslexia. *Unit head:* Dr. Connie L. Bowman, Chair, 937-229-3305, E-mail: cbowman1@udayton.edu. *Application contact:* Gina Seiter, Graduate Program Advisor, 937-229-3103, E-mail: gseiter1@udayton.edu.
Website: https://www.udayton.edu/education/departments_and_programs/edt

University of Guam, Office of Graduate Studies, School of Education, Program in Secondary Education, Mangilao, GU 96923. Offers M Ed. *Degree requirements:* For master's, thesis, comprehensive oral and written exams. *Entrance requirements:* For master's, GRE General Test. Additional exam requirements/recommendations for international students: Required—TOEFL.

University of Houston–Downtown, College of Public Service, Department of Urban Education, Houston, TX 77002. Offers curriculum and instruction (MAT); elementary and secondary education (MAT). *Program availability:* Part-time, evening/weekend, 100% online. *Faculty:* 6 full-time (2 women), 2 part-time/adjunct (both women). *Students:* 7 full-time (3 women), 47 part-time (42 women); includes 45 minority (18 Black or African American, non-Hispanic/Latino; 6 Asian, non-Hispanic/Latino; 21 Hispanic/Latino). Average age 34. 36 applicants, 89% accepted, 28 enrolled. In 2016, 11 master's awarded. *Degree requirements:* For master's, capstone course with completed project, position paper, grant proposal, empirical study, curriculum development/revision, or advanced technology project presented at annual Graduate Project Exhibition. *Entrance requirements:* For master's, GRE, personal statement, 3 recommendation forms. Additional exam requirements/recommendations for international students: Required—TOEFL (minimum score 550 paper-based; 80 iBT). *Application deadline:* For fall admission, 7/15 for domestic and international students; for spring admission, 11/15 for domestic and international students. Application fee: $35 ($60 for international students). Electronic applications accepted. *Expenses:* $305.50 in-state, per credit; $663.50 out-of-state, per credit. *Financial support:* Federal Work-Study and scholarships/grants available. Financial award application deadline: 4/1; financial award applicants required to submit FAFSA. *Unit head:* Dr. Ron Beebe, Department Chair, 713-221-8689, Fax: 713-226-5294, E-mail: beeber@uhd.edu. *Application contact:* Ceshia Love, Director of Graduate and International Admissions, 713-221-8093, Fax: 713-223-7408, E-mail: gradadmissions@uhd.edu.
Website: https://www.uhd.edu/academics/public-service/urban-education/Pages/default.aspx

University of Illinois at Chicago, College of Education, Department of Curriculum and Instruction, Chicago, IL 60607-7128. Offers curriculum studies (PhD); elementary education (M Ed); secondary education (M Ed). *Program availability:* Part-time, evening/weekend. *Degree requirements:* For doctorate, thesis/dissertation. *Entrance requirements:* For master's, minimum GPA of 2.75; for doctorate, GRE General Test, minimum GPA of 2.75. Additional exam requirements/recommendations for international students: Required—TOEFL. Electronic applications accepted. *Faculty research:* Curriculum theory, curriculum development, research on teaching, curriculum and context, reading/literacy.

University of Indianapolis, Graduate Programs, School of Education, Indianapolis, IN 46227-3697. Offers art education (MAT); biology (MAT); chemistry (MAT); curriculum and instruction (MA); earth sciences (MAT); education (MA, MAT); educational leadership (MA); elementary education (MA); English (MAT); French (MAT); math (MAT); physical education (MAT); physics (MAT); secondary education (MA), including art education, education, English education, social studies education; social studies (MAT); Spanish (MAT). *Accreditation:* NCATE. *Program availability:* Part-time, evening/weekend. *Entrance requirements:* For master's, GRE Subject Test, PRAXIS I, minimum GPA of 2.5, 3 letters of recommendation, interview. Additional exam requirements/recommendations for international students: Required—TOEFL (minimum score 550 paper-based). *Faculty research:* Assessment of teacher education, perceptions of prospective teachers by parents.

The University of Iowa, Graduate College, College of Education, Department of Teaching and Learning, Program in Education, Iowa City, IA 52242-1316. Offers art education (MA); developmental reading (MA); elementary education (MA); English education (MA, MAT); foreign and second language education (MAT); foreign language education (MA); foreign language/ESL education (PhD); language, literacy and culture (PhD); mathematics education (MA, MAT, PhD); music education (MM, PhD); science education (MA); secondary education (MA); social studies (MA, PhD). *Degree requirements:* For master's, thesis optional, exam; for doctorate, comprehensive exam, thesis/dissertation. *Entrance requirements:* For master's and doctorate, GRE General Test, minimum GPA of 3.0. Additional exam requirements/recommendations for international students: Required—TOEFL (minimum score 550 paper-based; 81 iBT). Electronic applications accepted.

University of Kentucky, Graduate School, College of Education, Program in Curriculum and Instruction, Lexington, KY 40506-0032. Offers curriculum and instruction (Ed D, PhD); elementary education (MA Ed); instructional system design (MS Ed); literacy (MA Ed); middle school education (MA Ed, MS Ed); secondary education (MA Ed, MS Ed). *Accreditation:* NCATE. *Degree requirements:* For master's, comprehensive exam, thesis optional; for doctorate, comprehensive exam, thesis/dissertation. *Entrance requirements:* For master's, GRE General Test, minimum undergraduate GPA of 2.75; for doctorate, GRE General Test, minimum graduate GPA of 3.0. Additional exam requirements/recommendations for international students: Required—TOEFL (minimum score 550 paper-based). Electronic applications accepted. *Faculty research:* Educational reform, multicultural education, classroom instructional practices, performance based assessment, primary school programs.

University of La Verne, Regional and Online Campuses, Graduate Programs, Central Coast/Vandenberg Air Force Base Campuses, La Verne, CA 91750-4443. Offers business administration for experienced professionals (MBA), including health services management, information technology; education (special emphasis) (M Ed); educational counseling (MS); educational leadership (M Ed); multiple subject (elementary) (Credential); preliminary administrative services (Credential); pupil personnel services (Credential); single subject (secondary) (Credential). *Program availability:* Part-time. *Expenses:* Contact institution.

University of La Verne, Regional and Online Campuses, Graduate Programs, High Desert Campus, Victorville, CA 92392. Offers business administration for experienced professionals (MBA); educational counseling (MS); educational leadership (M Ed); multiple subject (elementary) (Credential); preliminary administrative services (Credential); pupil personnel services (Credential); single subject (secondary) (Credential). *Expenses:* Contact institution.

University of La Verne, Regional and Online Campuses, Graduate Programs, Kern County Campus, Bakersfield, CA 93301. Offers business administration for experienced professionals (MBA-EP); education (special emphasis) (M Ed); educational counseling (MS); educational leadership (M Ed); health administration (MHA); leadership and management (MS); mild/moderate education specialist (Credential); multiple subject (elementary) (Credential); organizational leadership (Ed D); preliminary administrative services (Credential); single subject (secondary) (Credential); special education studies (MS). *Program availability:* Part-time, evening/weekend. *Expenses:* Contact institution.

University of La Verne, Regional and Online Campuses, Graduate Programs, Ventura County/Point Mugu Naval Air Station Campuses, Oxnard, CA 93036. Offers business administration for experienced professionals (MS); educational counseling (MS); educational leadership (M Ed); leadership and management (MS); multiple subject (elementary) (Credential); pupil personnel services (Credential); single subject (secondary) (Credential). *Program availability:* Part-time, evening/weekend. *Expenses:* Contact institution.

University of Louisiana at Monroe, Graduate School, College of Arts, Education, and Sciences, School of Education, Program in Secondary Education, Monroe, LA 71209-0001. Offers MAT. *Accreditation:* NCATE. *Program availability:* Part-time, evening/weekend. *Faculty:* 10 full-time (6 women), 5 part-time/adjunct (4 women). *Students:* 5 full-time (3 women), 20 part-time (11 women); includes 6 minority (4 Black or African American, non-Hispanic/Latino; 2 Hispanic/Latino). Average age 29. 21 applicants, 71% accepted, 7 enrolled. In 2016, 7 master's awarded. *Entrance requirements:* For master's, GRE General Test, PRAXIS, minimum GPA of 2.5. Additional exam requirements/recommendations for international students: Required—TOEFL (minimum score 500 paper-based; 61 iBT). *Application deadline:* For fall admission, 8/24 priority date for domestic students, 7/1 for international students; for winter admission, 12/14 priority date for domestic students; for spring admission, 1/19 for domestic students, 11/1 for international students. Applications are processed on a rolling basis. Application fee: $20 ($30 for international students). Electronic applications accepted. *Expenses:* Tuition, state resident: full-time $6489. Tuition, nonresident: full-time $18,589. *Required fees:* $8984. Tuition and fees vary according to course level, course load, degree level and program. *Financial support:* Career-related internships or fieldwork, Federal Work-Study, and unspecified assistantships available. Financial award application deadline: 4/1; financial award applicants required to submit FAFSA. *Unit head:* Dr. Dorothy Schween, Director, 318-342-1268, E-mail: schween@ulm.edu.

University of Louisville, Graduate School, College of Education and Human Development, Department of Teaching and Learning, Louisville, KY 40292-0001. Offers art education (MAT); autism and applied behavior analysis (Certificate); curriculum and instruction (PhD); early elementary education (MAT); exercise physiology (MS); health and physical education (MAT); health professions education (Certificate); higher education (MA); human resources and organization development (MS); instructional technology (M Ed); interdisciplinary early childhood education (MAT); middle school education (MAT); music education (MAT); secondary education (MAT); special education (MAT); sport administration (MS); teacher leadership (M Ed). *Program availability:* Part-time, evening/weekend. *Students:* 116 full-time (68 women), 158 part-time (112 women); includes 46 minority (24 Black or African American, non-Hispanic/Latino; 8 Asian, non-Hispanic/Latino; 5 Hispanic/Latino; 9 Two or more races, non-Hispanic/Latino), 6 international. Average age 30. 114 applicants, 71% accepted, 57 enrolled. In 2016, 59 master's, 3 doctorates awarded. *Application deadline:* For spring admission, 1/1 priority date for international students. Application fee: $60. *Expenses:* Tuition, state resident: full-time $12,246; part-time $681 per credit hour. Tuition, nonresident: full-time $25,486; part-time $1417 per credit hour. *Required fees:* $196. Tuition and fees vary according to program and reciprocity agreements. *Financial support:* Application deadline: 6/1; applicants required to submit FAFSA. *Faculty research:* STEM teaching and learning; content literacy for English language learners; social justice in teacher education; adolescent literacy; mathematics teacher development. *Total annual research expenditures:* $1.7 million. *Unit head:* Dr. Ann E. Larson, Dean, College of Education and Human Development, 502-852-6411, Fax: 502-852-1464, E-mail: ann@louisville.edu. *Application contact:* Betty Hampton, Director of Graduate Student Services, 502-852-5597, Fax: 502-852-1465, E-mail: edadvise@louisville.edu.
Website: http://louisville.edu/delphi

University of Mary Hardin-Baylor, Graduate Studies in Education, Belton, TX 76513. Offers curriculum and instruction (M Ed); educational administration (M Ed, Ed D), including higher education (Ed D), leadership in nursing education (Ed D), P-12 (Ed D). *Program availability:* Part-time, evening/weekend. *Faculty:* 15 full-time (11 women), 9 part-time/adjunct (5 women). *Students:* 55 full-time (40 women), 79 part-time (60 women); includes 50 minority (29 Black or African American, non-Hispanic/Latino; 1 Asian, non-Hispanic/Latino; 18 Hispanic/Latino; 2 Two or more races, non-Hispanic/Latino), 3 international. Average age 38. 20 applicants, 95% accepted, 19 enrolled. In 2016, 23 master's, 19 doctorates awarded. *Degree requirements:* For master's, comprehensive exam; for doctorate, thesis/dissertation. *Entrance requirements:* For master's, minimum GPA of 3.0, interview; for doctorate, minimum GPA of 3.5, interview, essay, resume, employment verification, 3 letters of recommendation. Additional exam requirements/recommendations for international students: Required—TOEFL (minimum score 60 iBT), IELTS (minimum score 4.5). *Application deadline:* For fall admission, 6/1 for domestic students, 4/30 priority date for international students; for spring admission, 11/1 for domestic students, 9/30 priority date for international students. Applications are processed on a rolling basis. Application fee: $35 ($135 for international students). Electronic applications accepted. *Expenses:* $885 per credit hour. *Financial support:* In 2016–17, 99 students received support. Federal Work-Study and scholarships for some active duty military personnel available. Support available to part-time students. Financial award application deadline: 6/1; financial award applicants required to submit FAFSA. *Faculty research:* Motivational orientation of preservice teachers. *Unit head:* Dr. Craig Hammonds, Director, Graduate Programs in Education, 254-295-4189, E-mail: rhammonds@umhb.edu. *Application contact:* Sharon Aguilera, Assistant Director, Graduate Admissions, 254-295-4835, Fax: 254-295-5038, E-mail: saguilera@umhb.edu.
Website: http://graduate.umhb.edu/education/

University of Maryland, College Park, Academic Affairs, College of Education, Department of Teaching, Learning, Policy and Leadership, College Park, MD 20742. Offers reading (M Ed, MA, PhD, CAGS); secondary education (M Ed, MA, Ed D, PhD, CAGS); teaching English to speakers of other languages (M Ed). *Accreditation:* NCATE. *Program availability:* Part-time, evening/weekend, online learning. *Degree requirements:* For master's, comprehensive exam, seminar paper; for doctorate, comprehensive exam, thesis/dissertation, published paper, oral exam. *Entrance requirements:* For master's, GRE General Test or MAT, minimum GPA of 3.0, 3 letters of recommendation; for doctorate, GRE General Test or MAT, minimum undergraduate GPA of 3.0, graduate 3.5; 3 letters of recommendation. Electronic applications accepted. *Faculty research:* Teacher preparation, curriculum study, in-service education.

University of Massachusetts Amherst, Graduate School, College of Education, Program in Education, Amherst, MA 01003. Offers bilingual, English as a second language, and multicultural education (M Ed, Ed S); child study and early education (M Ed); children, families and schools (Ed D, Ed S); early childhood and elementary teacher education (M Ed); educational leadership (M Ed); educational policy and leadership (Ed D); higher education (M Ed); international education (M Ed); language, literacy and culture (Ed D); learning, media and technology (M Ed, Ed S); mathematics, science, and learning technologies (Ed D); reading and writing (M Ed); research, educational measurement and psychometrics (Ed D); school counselor education (M Ed, Ed S); school psychology (Ed S); science education (Ed S); secondary teacher education (M Ed); social justice education (M Ed, Ed D, Ed S); special education (M Ed, Ed D, Ed S); teacher education and school improvement (Ed D, Ed S). *Accreditation:* NCATE. *Program availability:* Part-time, online learning. Terminal master's awarded for partial completion of doctoral program. *Degree requirements:* For doctorate, comprehensive exam, thesis/dissertation. *Entrance requirements:* Additional exam requirements/recommendations for international students: Required—TOEFL (minimum score 550 paper-based; 80 iBT), IELTS (minimum score 6.5). Electronic applications accepted.

University of Massachusetts Dartmouth, Graduate School, College of Arts and Sciences, School of Education, Department of STEM Education and Teacher Development, North Dartmouth, MA 02747-2300. Offers education ESL preK-12 (Postbaccalaureate Certificate); mathematics education (PhD); middle school education (MAT); secondary school education (Postbaccalaureate Certificate); teaching secondary school education (MAT). *Program availability:* Part-time. *Faculty:* 9 full-time (6 women), 6 part-time/adjunct (3 women). *Students:* 25 full-time (12 women), 87 part-time (55 women); includes 15 minority (3 Black or African American, non-Hispanic/Latino; 2 Asian, non-Hispanic/Latino; 7 Hispanic/Latino; 3 Two or more races, non-Hispanic/Latino), 3 international. Average age 32. 53 applicants, 91% accepted, 38 enrolled. In 2016, 67 master's awarded. *Degree requirements:* For doctorate, thesis/dissertation. *Entrance requirements:* For master's, Massachusetts Tests for Educator Licensure (MTEL) Communication and Literacy Test and Subject Matter Test, statement of purpose (minimum of 300 words), resume, 2 letters of recommendation, official transcripts; for doctorate, GRE, statement of purpose (minimum of 300 words), resume, official transcripts, 3 letters of recommendation; for Postbaccalaureate Certificate, statement of purpose (minimum of 300 words), resume, 2 letters of recommendation, official transcripts. Additional exam requirements/recommendations for international students: Required—TOEFL (minimum score 533 paper-based; 72 iBT). *Application deadline:* For fall admission, 2/15 priority date for domestic students, 1/15 priority date for international students; for spring admission, 12/15 priority date for domestic students, 11/15 priority date for international students. Application fee: $60. Electronic applications accepted. *Expenses:* Tuition, state resident: full-time $14,994; part-time $624.75 per credit. Tuition, nonresident: full-time $27,068; part-time $1127.83 per credit. *Required fees:* $405; $25.88 per credit. Tuition and fees vary according to course load and reciprocity agreements. *Financial support:* In 2016–17, 3 fellowships (averaging $6,250 per year), 3 research assistantships (averaging $5,027 per year), 2 teaching assistantships (averaging $8,000 per year) were awarded; institutionally sponsored loans, scholarships/grants, unspecified assistantships, and instructional assistants, Fulbright scholarships also available. Financial award application deadline: 3/1; financial award applicants required to submit FAFSA. *Faculty research:* Reading/special education, education reform, English education, literacy, language arts K-12. *Total annual research expenditures:* $1.3 million. *Unit head:* Traci Almeida, Graduate Program Director, 508-999-8098, Fax: 508-910-8183, E-mail: talmeida@umassd.edu. *Application contact:* Steven Briggs, Director of Marketing and Recruitment for Graduate Studies, 508-999-8604, Fax: 508-999-8183, E-mail: graduate@umassd.edu.
Website: http://www.umassd.edu/cas/schoolofeducation/departments/stemeducationandteacherdevelopment/

University of Memphis, Graduate School, College of Education, Department of Instruction and Curriculum Leadership, Memphis, TN 38152. Offers advanced studies in

teaching and learning (M Ed); applied behavior analysis (Graduate Certificate); autism studies (Graduate Certificate); early childhood education (MAT, MS, Ed D); elementary education (MAT); instruction and curriculum (MS, Ed D); instruction design and technology (MS, Ed D); instructional design and technology (Graduate Certificate); literacy, leadership, and coaching (Graduate Certificate); reading (MS, Ed D); school library information specialist (Graduate Certificate); secondary education (MAT); special education (MAT, MS, Ed D); STEM teacher leadership (Graduate Certificate); urban education (Graduate Certificate). *Accreditation:* NCATE (one or more programs are accredited). *Program availability:* Part-time. *Faculty:* 24 full-time (14 women), 17 part-time/adjunct (12 women). *Students:* 66 full-time (52 women), 315 part-time (243 women); includes 163 minority (132 Black or African American, non-Hispanic/Latino; 1 American Indian or Alaska Native, non-Hispanic/Latino; 6 Asian, non-Hispanic/Latino; 13 Hispanic/Latino; 1 Native Hawaiian or other Pacific Islander, non-Hispanic/Latino; 10 Two or more races, non-Hispanic/Latino), 4 international. Average age 35. 215 applicants, 78% accepted, 120 enrolled. In 2016, 111 master's, 21 doctorates, 8 other advanced degrees awarded. Terminal master's awarded for partial completion of doctoral program. *Degree requirements:* For master's, comprehensive exam, thesis or alternative; for doctorate, comprehensive exam, thesis/dissertation. *Entrance requirements:* For master's, GRE General Test, PRAXIS, minimum GPA of 2.5, letters of reference; for doctorate, GRE General Test, GRE Subject Test, 2 years of teaching experience, letters of reference, statement of purpose, interview. Additional exam requirements/recommendations for international students: Required—TOEFL (minimum score 550 paper-based; 79 iBT). *Application deadline:* For fall admission, 4/1 priority date for domestic students; for spring admission, 10/1 priority date for domestic students; for summer admission, 2/1 priority date for domestic students. Applications are processed on a rolling basis. Application fee: $35 ($60 for international students). Electronic applications accepted. *Expenses:* $5,231.50 per semester full-time in-state, $9,623.50 full-time out-of-state. *Financial support:* In 2016–17, 2 research assistantships with full tuition reimbursements (averaging $10,000 per year), 3 teaching assistantships with full tuition reimbursements (averaging $10,666 per year) were awarded; career-related internships or fieldwork, Federal Work-Study, institutionally sponsored loans, scholarships/grants, traineeships, and unspecified assistantships also available. Support available to part-time students. Financial award application deadline: 2/1; financial award applicants required to submit FAFSA. *Faculty research:* Effective urban teachers, preparation and retention of urban teachers, technology utilization in schools, field-based teacher preparation programs, effective use of online instruction. *Unit head:* Dr. Angiline Powell, Interim Chair, 901-678-3310, E-mail: apowell3@memphis.edu. *Application contact:* Dr. James Meindl, Coordinator of Graduate Studies, 901-678-3310, E-mail: jnmeindl@memphis.edu.
Website: http://www.memphis.edu/icl/

University of Michigan–Flint, School of Education and Human Services, Department of Education, Flint, MI 48502. Offers curriculum and instruction (Ed S); early childhood education (MA); education (Ed D); educational leadership (Ed S); educational technology (MA), including curriculum and instruction, developer; literacy education (MA); secondary education with certification (MA). *Program availability:* Part-time, evening/weekend, 100% online, mixed mode format (for some programs). *Faculty:* 14 full-time (9 women), 30 part-time/adjunct (17 women). *Students:* 31 full-time (18 women), 199 part-time (144 women); includes 61 minority (48 Black or African American, non-Hispanic/Latino; 1 Asian, non-Hispanic/Latino; 6 Hispanic/Latino; 1 Native Hawaiian or other Pacific Islander, non-Hispanic/Latino; 5 Two or more races, non-Hispanic/Latino), 2 international. Average age 39. 124 applicants, 86% accepted, 75 enrolled. In 2016, 77 master's, 1 doctorate awarded. *Degree requirements:* For master's, thesis optional; for doctorate, thesis/dissertation. *Entrance requirements:* For master's, bachelor's degree from regionally-accredited institution, minimum overall undergraduate GPA of 3.0; for doctorate, Ed S; minimum overall graduate GPA of 3.3 (6.0 on a 9.0 scale) or equivalent; at least 3 years of work experience in a P-16 educational institution or in an education-related position; for Ed S, MA or MS in education-related field from accredited institution; minimum overall graduate GPA of 3.0 (6.0 on a 9.0 scale) or equivalent; at least 3 years of work experience in an educational setting. Additional exam requirements/recommendations for international students: Required—TOEFL (minimum score 84 iBT), IELTS (minimum score 6.5). *Application deadline:* For fall admission, 8/1 for domestic students, 5/1 for international students; for winter admission, 11/15 for domestic students, 9/15 for international students; for spring admission, 3/15 for domestic students, 1/15 for international students; for summer admission, 5/15 for domestic students. Applications are processed on a rolling basis. Application fee: $55. Electronic applications accepted. *Expenses:* Contact institution. *Financial support:* Federal Work-Study, scholarships/grants, and unspecified assistantships available. Support available to part-time students. Financial award application deadline: 3/1; financial award applicants required to submit FAFSA. *Unit head:* Dr. Mary Jo Finney, Department Chair/Associate Professor, 810-766-6617, E-mail: mjfinney@umflint.edu. *Application contact:* Bradley T. Maki, Director of Graduate Admissions, 810-762-3171, Fax: 810-766-6789, E-mail: bmaki@umflint.edu.
Website: https://www.umflint.edu/education/graduate-programs

University of Missouri–St. Louis, College of Education, Department of Counseling and Family Therapy, St. Louis, MO 63121. Offers clinical mental health counseling (M Ed); counseling (PhD); elementary school counseling (M Ed); secondary school counseling (M Ed). *Accreditation:* ACA; NCATE. *Program availability:* Part-time, evening/weekend. *Faculty:* 8 full-time (4 women), 7 part-time/adjunct (6 women). *Students:* 58 full-time (48 women), 164 part-time (129 women); includes 61 minority (48 Black or African American, non-Hispanic/Latino; 2 American Indian or Alaska Native, non-Hispanic/Latino; 3 Asian, non-Hispanic/Latino; 4 Hispanic/Latino; 4 Two or more races, non-Hispanic/Latino), 4 international. Average age 32. 74 applicants, 72% accepted, 44 enrolled. *Degree requirements:* For master's, comprehensive exam. *Entrance requirements:* For master's, 3 letters of recommendation; for doctorate, GRE General Test, 3 letters of recommendation. Additional exam requirements/recommendations for international students: Recommended—TOEFL (minimum score 550 paper-based; 79 iBT), IELTS (minimum score 6.5). *Application deadline:* For fall admission, 5/1 for domestic and international students; for spring admission, 10/1 for domestic and international students. Application fee: $50 ($40 for international students). Electronic applications accepted. *Financial support:* Teaching assistantships with tuition reimbursements available. Financial award application deadline: 4/1; financial award applicants required to submit FAFSA. *Faculty research:* Vocational interests, self-concept, decision-making factors, developmental differences. *Unit head:* Dr. Mark Pope, Chair, 314-516-5782. *Application contact:* 314-516-5458, Fax: 314-516-6996, E-mail: gradadm@umsl.edu.

University of Missouri–St. Louis, College of Education, Department of Educator Preparation, Innovation and Research, St. Louis, MO 63121. Offers elementary education (M Ed), including early childhood, general, reading; secondary education (M Ed), including curriculum and instruction, general, middle level education, reading, teaching English to speakers of other languages (TESOL); special education (M Ed), including autism and developmental disabilities, early childhood special education. *Program availability:* Part-time, evening/weekend. *Faculty:* 26 full-time (14 women), 22 part-time/adjunct (14 women). *Students:* 151 full-time (127 women), 728 part-time (564 women); includes 222 minority (165 Black or African American, non-Hispanic/Latino; 1 American Indian or Alaska Native, non-Hispanic/Latino; 16 Asian, non-Hispanic/Latino; 31 Hispanic/Latino; 1 Native Hawaiian or other Pacific Islander, non-Hispanic/Latino; 8 Two or more races, non-Hispanic/Latino), 6 international. Average age 29. 363 applicants, 84% accepted, 211 enrolled. *Degree requirements:* For master's, comprehensive exam. *Entrance requirements:* Additional exam requirements/recommendations for international students: Recommended—TOEFL (minimum score 550 paper-based; 79 iBT), IELTS (minimum score 6.5). *Application deadline:* For fall admission, 7/1 priority date for domestic and international students; for spring admission, 12/1 priority date for domestic and international students. Application fee: $50 ($40 for international students). Electronic applications accepted. *Financial support:* Application deadline: 4/1; applicants required to submit FAFSA. *Unit head:* Dr. Gayle Wilkinson, Chair, 314-516-5791. *Application contact:* 314-516-5458, Fax: 314-516-6996, E-mail: gadadm@umsl.edu.
Website: https://coe.umsl.edu/dept/epir.html

University of Montevallo, College of Education, Program in Secondary/High School Education, Montevallo, AL 35115. Offers M Ed. *Accreditation:* NCATE. *Students:* 24 full-time (13 women), 61 part-time (38 women); includes 16 minority (14 Black or African American, non-Hispanic/Latino; 1 Hispanic/Latino; 1 Two or more races, non-Hispanic/Latino). In 2016, 50 master's awarded. *Degree requirements:* For master's, comprehensive exam. *Entrance requirements:* For master's, GRE General Test, MAT, minimum undergraduate GPA of 2.5. Additional exam requirements/recommendations for international students: Required—TOEFL (minimum score 550 paper-based). *Application deadline:* For fall admission, 7/15 for domestic students; for spring admission, 11/15 for domestic students. Application fee: $25. *Expenses:* Tuition, state resident: full-time $9936. Tuition, nonresident: full-time $20,592. *Required fees:* $640. *Financial support:* Federal Work-Study, scholarships/grants, and unspecified assistantships available. *Unit head:* Dr. Anna E. McEwan, Dean, 205-665-6360, E-mail: mcewanae@montevallo.edu. *Application contact:* Kevin Thornthwaite, Director, Graduate Admissions and Records, 205-665-6350, E-mail: graduate@montevallo.edu.
Website: http://www.montevallo.edu/education/college-of-education/traditional-masters-degrees/elementary-secondary-p-12-education/

University of Nebraska at Kearney, College of Education, Department of Teacher Education, Kearney, NE 68849-0001. Offers curriculum and instruction (MA Ed), including early childhood education, elementary education, English as a second language, instructional effectiveness, reading/special education, secondary education; instructional technology (MS Ed), including information technology, instructional technology, school librarian; reading PK-12 (MA Ed); special education (MA Ed), including advanced practitioner: assistive technology specialist, advanced practitioner: behavioral interventionist, advanced practitioner: inclusive collaboration specialist, gifted, teacher education. *Program availability:* Part-time, evening/weekend, online only, 100% online. *Faculty:* 18 full-time (13 women). *Students:* 21 full-time (15 women), 296 part-time (240 women); includes 21 minority (3 Black or African American, non-Hispanic/Latino; 1 Asian, non-Hispanic/Latino; 14 Hispanic/Latino; 1 Native Hawaiian or other Pacific Islander, non-Hispanic/Latino; 2 Two or more races, non-Hispanic/Latino), 1 international. Average age 32. 81 applicants, 100% accepted, 61 enrolled. In 2016, 129 master's awarded. *Degree requirements:* For master's, comprehensive exam, thesis optional. *Entrance requirements:* For master's, portfolio or GRE. Additional exam requirements/recommendations for international students: Recommended—TOEFL (minimum score 550 paper-based; 79 iBT), IELTS (minimum score 6.5). *Application deadline:* For fall admission, 6/15 for domestic students, 5/15 for international students; for spring admission, 10/15 for domestic and international students; for summer admission, 3/15 for domestic and international students. Application fee: $45. Electronic applications accepted. *Expenses:* $285 per credit hour resident tuition, $415 per credit hour non-resident tuition (online). *Financial support:* In 2016–17, 6 students received support, including 6 research assistantships with full tuition reimbursements available (averaging $10,500 per year); career-related internships or fieldwork, scholarships/grants, health care benefits, and unspecified assistantships also available. Support available to part-time students. Financial award application deadline: 2/28; financial award applicants required to submit FAFSA. *Unit head:* Sarah Bartling, Administrative Assistant, 308-865-8513, E-mail: bartlingseg@unk.edu. *Application contact:* Linda Johnson, Director, Graduate Admissions and Programs, 308-865-8841, Fax: 308-865-8837, E-mail: johnsonli@unk.edu.
Website: http://www.unk.edu/academics/ted/index.php

University of Nebraska at Omaha, Graduate Studies, College of Education, Department of Teacher Education, Program in Secondary Education, Omaha, NE 68182. Offers instruction in urban schools (Certificate); secondary education (MS). *Accreditation:* NCATE. *Program availability:* Part-time, evening/weekend. *Faculty:* 8 full-time (all women). *Students:* 14 full-time (9 women), 61 part-time (45 women); includes 9 minority (3 Black or African American, non-Hispanic/Latino; 3 Asian, non-Hispanic/Latino; 2 Hispanic/Latino; 1 Two or more races, non-Hispanic/Latino), 1 international. Average age 34. 21 applicants, 71% accepted, 14 enrolled. In 2016, 22 master's awarded. *Degree requirements:* For master's, comprehensive exam, thesis (for some programs). *Entrance requirements:* For master's, minimum GPA of 3.0, transcripts. Additional exam requirements/recommendations for international students: Required—TOEFL, IELTS, PTE. *Application deadline:* For fall admission, 8/1 priority date for domestic and international students; for spring admission, 12/1 priority date for domestic and international students; for summer admission, 6/1 for domestic and international students. Applications are processed on a rolling basis. Application fee: $45. Electronic applications accepted. *Financial support:* In 2016–17, 2 students received support, including 2 research assistantships with tuition reimbursements available; fellowships, teaching assistantships with tuition reimbursements available, Federal Work-Study, institutionally sponsored loans, scholarships/grants, health care benefits, tuition waivers (full), and unspecified assistantships also available. Support available to part-time students. Financial award application deadline: 3/1. *Unit head:* Dr. Sarah Edwards, Chairperson, 402-554-2341, E-mail: graduate@unomaha.edu. *Application contact:* Dr. Rebecca Pasco, Graduate Program Chair, 402-554-2341, E-mail: graduate@unomaha.edu.

University of Nevada, Las Vegas, Graduate College, College of Education, Department of Teaching and Learning, Las Vegas, NV 89154-3005. Offers curriculum and instruction (M Ed, MS, Ed D, PhD, Ed S), including teacher education (PhD); elementary teaching (Certificate); online teaching and training (Certificate); secondary teaching (Certificate); social justice studies (Certificate); teaching and learning (PhD). *Program availability:* Part-time, evening/weekend. *Faculty:* 26 full-time (12 women), 10 part-time/adjunct (8 women). *Students:* 280 full-time (202 women), 206 part-time (131 women); includes 188 minority (51 Black or African American, non-Hispanic/Latino; 4 American Indian or Alaska Native, non-Hispanic/Latino; 23 Asian, non-Hispanic/Latino; 72 Hispanic/Latino; 4 Native Hawaiian or other Pacific Islander, non-Hispanic/Latino; 34 Two or more races, non-Hispanic/Latino), 18 international. Average age 35. 178 applicants, 89% accepted, 142 enrolled. In 2016, 156 master's, 14 doctorates, 1 other advanced degree awarded. *Degree requirements:* For master's, comprehensive exam (for some programs), thesis (for some programs); for doctorate, comprehensive exam, thesis/dissertation, defense of dissertation; for other advanced degree, comprehensive exam (for some programs), oral presentation of special project or professional paper. *Entrance requirements:* For master's, bachelor's degree with minimum GPA 2.75; for

doctorate, GRE General Test, master's degree with minimum GPA of 3.0; statement of purpose; demonstration of oral communication skills; 3 letters of recommendation; for other advanced degree, PRAXIS Core (for some programs); PRAXIS II (for some programs), bachelor's degree (for some programs). Additional exam requirements/recommendations for international students: Required—TOEFL (minimum score 550 paper-based; 80 iBT), IELTS (minimum score 7). *Application deadline:* For fall admission, 6/1 for domestic students, 5/1 for international students; for spring admission, 11/1 for domestic students, 10/1 for international students; for summer admission, 3/15 for domestic students. Application fee: $60 ($95 for international students). Electronic applications accepted. *Expenses:* $269.25 per credit, $792 per 3-credit course; $9,634 per year resident; $23,274 per year non-resident; $7,094 fees non-resident (7 credits or more); $1,307 annual health insurance fee. *Financial support:* In 2016–17, 8 research assistantships with partial tuition reimbursements (averaging $16,719 per year), 28 teaching assistantships with partial tuition reimbursements (averaging $17,023 per year) were awarded; institutionally sponsored loans, scholarships/grants, health care benefits, and unspecified assistantships also available. Financial award application deadline: 3/15. *Faculty research:* Content area and critical literacy, education in content areas, teacher education, STEM education, technology education. *Total annual research expenditures:* $652,413. *Unit head:* Dr. Emily Lin, Chair/Professor, 702-895-6407, Fax: 702-895-4898, E-mail: emily.lin@unlv.edu. *Application contact:* Dr. Travis Olson, Graduate Coordinator, 702-895-0471, Fax: 702-895-4898, E-mail: travis.olson@unlv.edu.
Website: http://tl.unlv.edu/

University of Nevada, Reno, Graduate School, College of Education, Department of Curriculum, Teaching and Learning, Program in Secondary Education, Reno, NV 89557. Offers M Ed, MA, MS. *Degree requirements:* For master's, thesis optional. *Entrance requirements:* For master's, GRE General Test, minimum GPA of 2.75. Additional exam requirements/recommendations for international students: Required—TOEFL (minimum score 500 paper-based; 61 iBT), IELTS (minimum score 6). Electronic applications accepted. *Faculty research:* Educational trends, pedagogy.

University of New Hampshire, Graduate School, College of Liberal Arts, Department of Education, Program in Secondary Education, Durham, NH 03824. Offers M Ed, MAT. *Program availability:* Part-time. *Degree requirements:* For master's, thesis or alternative. *Entrance requirements:* For master's, GRE General Test. Additional exam requirements/recommendations for international students: Required—TOEFL (minimum score 550 paper-based; 80 iBT). *Application deadline:* For fall admission, 6/1 priority date for domestic students, 4/1 for international students; for spring admission, 12/1 for domestic students. Applications are processed on a rolling basis. Application fee: $65. Electronic applications accepted. *Financial support:* Fellowships, research assistantships, teaching assistantships, career-related internships or fieldwork, Federal Work-Study, scholarships/grants, and tuition waivers (full and partial) available. Support available to part-time students. Financial award application deadline: 2/15. *Faculty research:* Pre-service teacher education. *Unit head:* Leslie Couse, Chair, 603-862-0638, E-mail: education.department@unh.edu. *Application contact:* Lisa Wilder, Administrative Assistant, 603-862-2381, E-mail: education.department@unh.edu.
Website: http://cola.unh.edu/education

University of New Hampshire, Graduate School Manchester Campus, Manchester, NH 03101. Offers business administration (MBA); educational administration and supervision (Ed S); educational studies (M Ed); elementary teacher education (M Ed); information technology (MS); public administration (MPA); public health (MPH, Certificate); secondary teacher education (M Ed, MAT); social work (MSW); substance use disorders (Certificate). *Program availability:* Part-time, evening/weekend. *Degree requirements:* For master's, thesis or alternative. *Entrance requirements:* Additional exam requirements/recommendations for international students: Required—TOEFL (minimum score 550 paper-based; 80 iBT). Electronic applications accepted.

University of New Mexico, Graduate Studies, College of Education, Program in Secondary Education, Albuquerque, NM 87131-2039. Offers math, science, and educational technology (MA). *Program availability:* Part-time. *Faculty:* 10 full-time (7 women), 1 (woman) part-time/adjunct. *Students:* 24 full-time (10 women), 35 part-time (19 women); includes 28 minority (1 American Indian or Alaska Native, non-Hispanic/Latino; 3 Asian, non-Hispanic/Latino; 21 Hispanic/Latino; 3 Two or more races, non-Hispanic/Latino). Average age 33. 35 applicants, 80% accepted, 22 enrolled. In 2016, 42 master's awarded. *Degree requirements:* For master's, comprehensive exam, thesis optional. *Entrance requirements:* For master's, minimum overall GPA of 3.0, some experience working with students, NMTA or teacher's licensure, 3 letters of reference, letter of intent. Additional exam requirements/recommendations for international students: Required—TOEFL (minimum score 550 paper-based). *Application deadline:* For fall admission, 2/1 for domestic students; for spring admission, 10/1 for domestic students. Application fee: $50. Electronic applications accepted. *Financial support:* Teaching assistantships with partial tuition reimbursements, career-related internships or fieldwork, scholarships/grants, and unspecified assistantships available. Financial award application deadline: 4/15. *Faculty research:* Secondary education, teacher education, reflective practice, teacher leadership, student learning. *Unit head:* Dr. Cheryl Torrez, Chair, 505-277-0911, Fax: 505-277-0455, E-mail: ted@unm.edu. *Application contact:* Robert Romero, Administrative Assistant, 505-277-0513, Fax: 505-277-0455, E-mail: ted@unm.edu.
Website: http://coe.unm.edu/departments-programs/teelp/secondary-education/index.html

University of North Alabama, College of Education, Department of Secondary Education, Program in Education Leadership, Florence, AL 35632-0001. Offers instructional leadership (MA Ed); secondary education (MA Ed); teacher education multiple levels (MA Ed). *Accreditation:* NCATE. *Program availability:* Part-time, 100% online, blended/hybrid learning. *Faculty:* 24 full-time (10 women), 2 part-time/adjunct (0 women). *Students:* 18 full-time (12 women), 62 part-time (43 women); includes 11 minority (8 Black or African American, non-Hispanic/Latino; 1 American Indian or Alaska Native, non-Hispanic/Latino; 1 Hispanic/Latino; 1 Two or more races, non-Hispanic/Latino). Average age 38. 32 applicants, 69% accepted, 20 enrolled. In 2016, 44 master's awarded. *Entrance requirements:* Additional exam requirements/recommendations for international students: Required—TOEFL (minimum score 79 iBT), IELTS (minimum score 6), PTE (minimum score 54). *Application deadline:* Applications are processed on a rolling basis. Application fee: $50 ($100 for international students). Electronic applications accepted. *Expenses:* Tuition, state resident: full-time $2799; part-time $1866 per semester. Tuition, nonresident: full-time $5598; part-time $3732 per semester. *Required fees:* $915; $642 per semester. Tuition and fees vary according to course load. *Financial support:* In 2016–17, 10 students received support. Application deadline: 2/1; applicants required to submit FAFSA. *Unit head:* Dr. Leah Whitten, Interim Chair, 256-765-4575, E-mail: lswhitten@una.edu. *Application contact:* Hillary N. Coats, Graduate Admissions Counselor, 256-765-4447, E-mail: graduate@una.edu.
Website: https://www.una.edu/education/departments/secondary-education.html

University of North Alabama, College of Education, Department of Secondary Education, Program in Secondary Education, Florence, AL 35632-0001. Offers secondary education (MA Ed); special education (MA Ed). *Accreditation:* NCATE. *Program availability:* Part-time, 100% online, blended/hybrid learning. *Faculty:* 14 full-time (5 women), 8 part-time/adjunct (6 women). *Students:* 47 full-time (25 women), 33 part-time (26 women); includes 12 minority (5 Black or African American, non-Hispanic/Latino; 3 American Indian or Alaska Native, non-Hispanic/Latino; 3 Hispanic/Latino; 1 Two or more races, non-Hispanic/Latino), 3 international. Average age 29. 46 applicants, 67% accepted, 25 enrolled. In 2016, 21 master's awarded. *Degree requirements:* For master's, comprehensive exam. *Entrance requirements:* For master's, GRE, MAT, or NTE, minimum GPA of 2.5, Alabama Class B Certificate or equivalent, teaching experience. Additional exam requirements/recommendations for international students: Required—TOEFL (minimum score 79 iBT), IELTS (minimum score 6), PTE (minimum score 54). *Application deadline:* Applications are processed on a rolling basis. Application fee: $50 ($100 for international students). Electronic applications accepted. *Expenses:* Tuition, state resident: full-time $2799; part-time $1866 per semester. Tuition, nonresident: full-time $5598; part-time $3732 per semester. *Required fees:* $915; $642 per semester. Tuition and fees vary according to course load. *Financial support:* In 2016–17, 9 students received support. Scholarships/grants and unspecified assistantships available. Financial award application deadline: 2/1; financial award applicants required to submit FAFSA. *Unit head:* Dr. Leah Whitten, Interim Chair, 256-765-4575, E-mail: lswhitten@una.edu. *Application contact:* Hillary N. Coats, Graduate Admissions Coordinator, 256-765-4447, E-mail: graduate@una.edu.
Website: https://www.una.edu/education/departments/secondary-education.html

The University of North Carolina at Chapel Hill, Graduate School, School of Education, Program in Secondary Education, Chapel Hill, NC 27599. Offers English (Grades 9-12) (MAT); English as a second language (MAT); French (Grades K-12) (MAT); German (Grades K-12) (MAT); Japanese (Grades K-12) (MAT); Latin (Grades 9-12) (MAT); mathematics (Grades 9-12) (MAT); music (Grades K-12) (MAT); science (Grades 9-12) (MAT); social studies (Grades 9-12) (MAT); Spanish (Grades K-12) (MAT). *Accreditation:* NCATE. *Degree requirements:* For master's, comprehensive exam. *Entrance requirements:* For master's, GRE General Test, minimum GPA of 3.0 during last 2 years of undergraduate course work. Additional exam requirements/recommendations for international students: Required—TOEFL (minimum score 550 paper-based). Electronic applications accepted.

The University of North Carolina at Charlotte, Cato College of Education, Department of Middle, Secondary and K-12 Education, Charlotte, NC 28223-0001. Offers middle grades and secondary education (M Ed); teaching English as a second language (M Ed, Graduate Certificate). *Program availability:* Part-time. *Faculty:* 17 full-time (9 women), 6 part-time/adjunct (5 women). *Students:* 6 full-time (5 women), 62 part-time (56 women); includes 9 minority (8 Black or African American, non-Hispanic/Latino; 1 Hispanic/Latino), 1 international. Average age 32. 32 applicants, 97% accepted, 28 enrolled. In 2016, 12 master's awarded. *Degree requirements:* For master's, thesis, comprehensive portfolio, or research project. *Entrance requirements:* For master's, GRE or MAT, bachelor's degree from accredited college or university; minimum GPA of 3.0 in undergraduate work; North Carolina Class A teaching license in appropriate middle grades or secondary education field; minimum of two years' teaching experience; written narrative providing statement of purpose for master's degree study; letters of recommendation; for Graduate Certificate, bachelor's degree from accredited institution; minimum undergraduate GPA of 2.5 overall or 3.0 in senior year, or 15 hours taken in the last 5 years; satisfactory recommendations from three persons knowledgeable of applicant's interactions with children or adolescents; statement of purpose. Additional exam requirements/recommendations for international students: Required—TOEFL (minimum score 523 paper-based, 70 iBT) or IELTS (6.5). *Application deadline:* For fall admission, 3/1 priority date for domestic and international students; for spring admission, 10/1 priority date for domestic and international students; for summer admission, 4/1 priority date for domestic and international students. Applications are processed on a rolling basis. Application fee: $75. Electronic applications accepted. *Expenses:* Tuition, state resident: full-time $4252. Tuition, nonresident: full-time $17,423. *Required fees:* $3026. Tuition and fees vary according to course load and program. *Financial support:* In 2016–17, 5 students received support, including 1 fellowship (averaging $32,786 per year), 4 research assistantships (averaging $14,309 per year); career-related internships or fieldwork, institutionally sponsored loans, scholarships/grants, and unspecified assistantships also available. Support available to part-time students. Financial award application deadline: 3/1; financial award applicants required to submit FAFSA. *Total annual research expenditures:* $58,472. *Unit head:* Scott Kissau, Chair, 704-687-8875, E-mail: spkissau@uncc.edu. *Application contact:* Kathy B. Giddings, Director of Graduate Admissions, 704-687-5503, Fax: 704-687-1668, E-mail: gradadm@uncc.edu.
Website: http://mdsk.uncc.edu/

The University of North Carolina at Charlotte, Cato College of Education, Interdisciplinary Education Programs, Charlotte, NC 28223-0001. Offers art education (Graduate Certificate); child and family development: early childhood education (MAT); curriculum and instruction (PhD); elementary education (MAT); foreign language education (MAT); middle grades education (MAT); secondary education (MAT); special education (MAT); teaching (Graduate Certificate); teaching English as a second language (MAT); theatre education (Graduate Certificate). *Program availability:* Part-time, 100% online, blended/hybrid learning. *Students:* 78 full-time (59 women), 619 part-time (484 women); includes 255 minority (186 Black or African American, non-Hispanic/Latino; 1 American Indian or Alaska Native, non-Hispanic/Latino; 16 Asian, non-Hispanic/Latino; 37 Hispanic/Latino; 15 Two or more races, non-Hispanic/Latino), 10 international. Average age 33. 380 applicants, 92% accepted, 264 enrolled. In 2016, 93 master's, 8 doctorates, 176 other advanced degrees awarded. *Degree requirements:* For master's, thesis or alternative, research project/portfolio. *Entrance requirements:* For master's, GRE or MAT, bachelor's degree, or its U.S. equivalent, from regionally-accredited college or university; minimum overall GPA of 3.0 on all previous work beyond high school; statement of purpose (essay); at least three recommendation forms; for doctorate, GRE or MAT, bachelor's degree (or its U.S. equivalent) from regionally-accredited college or university; minimum overall GPA of 3.5 in master's degree program; for Graduate Certificate, bachelor's degree from regionally-accredited university; minimum GPA of 2.75 on all post-secondary work attempted; transcripts; personal statement outlining why the applicant seeks admission to the program. Additional exam requirements/recommendations for international students: Required—TOEFL (minimum score 523 paper-based, 70 iBT) or IELTS (6.5). *Application deadline:* For fall admission, 3/1 priority date for domestic and international students; for spring admission, 10/1 priority date for domestic and international students; for summer admission, 4/1 priority date for domestic and international students. Applications are processed on a rolling basis. Application fee: $75. Electronic applications accepted. *Expenses:* Tuition, state resident: full-time $4252. Tuition, nonresident: full-time $17,423. *Required fees:* $3026. Tuition and fees vary according to course load and program. *Financial support:* Career-related internships or fieldwork, institutionally sponsored loans, scholarships/grants, and unspecified assistantships available. Support available to part-time students. Financial award application deadline: 3/1; financial award applicants required to submit FAFSA. *Unit head:* Dr. Ellen McIntyre, Dean, 704-687-8722, E-mail: ellen.mcintyre@uncc.edu. *Application contact:* Kathy B. Giddings, Director of Graduate Admissions, 704-687-5503, Fax: 704-687-1668, E-mail: gradadm@uncc.edu.
Website: http://education.uncc.edu/academic-programs

The University of North Carolina Wilmington, Watson College of Education, Department of Instructional Technology, Foundations and Secondary Education, Wilmington, NC 28403-3297. Offers academically or intellectually gifted (M Ed); English as a second language (M Ed, MAT); instructional technology (MS); physical education and health (M Ed, MAT); secondary education (M Ed, MAT); Spanish (MAT); Spanish education (MASS). *Program availability:* Part-time. *Faculty:* 17 full-time (11 women). *Students:* 36 full-time (22 women), 62 part-time (49 women); includes 17 minority (12 Black or African American, non-Hispanic/Latino; 3 Hispanic/Latino; 2 Two or more races, non-Hispanic/Latino), 5 international. Average age 34. 89 applicants, 89% accepted, 59 enrolled. In 2016, 36 master's awarded. *Degree requirements:* For master's, comprehensive exam (for some programs), thesis (for some programs), thesis or research project. *Entrance requirements:* For master's, GRE or MAT, statement of interest, 3 letters of recommendation, minimum GPA of 3.0 in undergraduate work. Additional exam requirements/recommendations for international students: Required—TOEFL (minimum score 79 iBT), IELTS (minimum score 6.5). *Application deadline:* For fall admission, 5/15 for domestic students; for spring admission, 10/15 for domestic students; for summer admission, 3/15 for domestic students. Applications are processed on a rolling basis. Application fee: $60. Electronic applications accepted. *Expenses:* Contact institution. *Financial support:* Scholarships/grants and unspecified assistantships available. Financial award application deadline: 3/15; financial award applicants required to submit FAFSA. *Unit head:* Dr. Donyell Roseboro, Chair, 910-962-2289, Fax: 910-962-3609, E-mail: roseborod@uncw.edu. *Application contact:* Dr. Mahnaz Moallem, Graduate Coordinator, 910-962-4183, E-mail: moallemm@uncw.edu. Website: http://www.uncw.edu/ed/itfse/

University of Northern Iowa, Graduate College, College of Humanities, Arts and Sciences, Department of Languages and Literatures, MA Program in Teaching English in Secondary Schools, Cedar Falls, IA 50614. Offers MA.

University of Northern Iowa, Graduate College, College of Humanities, Arts and Sciences, Department of Mathematics, MA Program in Mathematics, Cedar Falls, IA 50614. Offers community college teaching (MA); mathematics (MA); secondary teaching (MA).

University of North Florida, College of Education and Human Services, Department of Foundations and Secondary Education, Jacksonville, FL 32224. Offers adult learning (M Ed); professional education (M Ed). *Accreditation:* NCATE. *Program availability:* Part-time, evening/weekend. *Faculty:* 12 full-time (5 women). *Students:* 30 part-time (20 women); includes 14 minority (6 Black or African American, non-Hispanic/Latino; 3 Asian, non-Hispanic/Latino; 2 Hispanic/Latino; 3 Two or more races, non-Hispanic/Latino). Average age 32. In 2016, 16 master's awarded. *Entrance requirements:* For master's, GRE General Test, minimum GPA of 3.0 in last 60 hours, interview, 3 letters of recommendation. Additional exam requirements/recommendations for international students: Required—TOEFL (minimum score 500 paper-based; 61 iBT). *Application deadline:* For fall admission, 5/1 for international students; for spring admission, 10/1 for international students. Application fee: $30. Electronic applications accepted. Tuition and fees vary according to course load, campus/location and program. *Financial support:* Research assistantships, teaching assistantships, career-related internships or fieldwork, Federal Work-Study, and tuition waivers (partial) available. Support available to part-time students. Financial award application deadline: 4/1; financial award applicants required to submit FAFSA. *Faculty research:* Using children's literature to enhance metalinguistic awareness, education, oral language diagnosis of middle-schoolers, science inquiry teaching and learning. *Total annual research expenditures:* $57,679. *Unit head:* Dr. Jeffery Cornett, Chair, 904-620-2610, Fax: 904-620-1821, E-mail: jcornett@unf.edu. *Application contact:* Dr. Amanda Pascale, Director, The Graduate School, 904-620-1360, Fax: 904-620-1362, E-mail: graduateschool@unf.edu. Website: http://www.unf.edu/coehs/fse/

University of North Georgia, College of Education, Dahlonega, GA 30597. Offers early childhood education (M Ed); middle grades education (M Ed, MAT); physical education (MS); school leadership (Ed S); secondary education (M Ed), including English education, history education, mathematics education, physical education. *Accreditation:* NCATE. *Program availability:* Part-time, evening/weekend, online learning. *Faculty:* 16 full-time (12 women), 3 part-time/adjunct (all women). *Students:* 11 full-time (8 women), 146 part-time (107 women); includes 19 minority (10 Black or African American, non-Hispanic/Latino; 2 Asian, non-Hispanic/Latino; 6 Hispanic/Latino; 1 Two or more races, non-Hispanic/Latino). Average age 28. 77 applicants, 83% accepted, 47 enrolled. In 2016, 79 master's awarded. *Degree requirements:* For master's, comprehensive exam, thesis optional. *Entrance requirements:* For master's, GRE or MAT, GACE, minimum GPA of 2.75; for Ed S, GRE General Test or MAT, 3 years of teaching experience, master's degree, minimum graduate GPA of 3.25, leadership position in the school. Additional exam requirements/recommendations for international students: Required—TOEFL (minimum score 550 paper-based; 79 iBT), IELTS (minimum score 6.5). *Application deadline:* For fall admission, 8/1 priority date for domestic students, 7/1 priority date for international students; for spring admission, 12/1 priority date for domestic students, 11/1 priority date for international students. Applications are processed on a rolling basis. Application fee: $40. Electronic applications accepted. *Expenses:* Contact institution. *Financial support:* Teaching assistantships, career-related internships or fieldwork, scholarships/grants, and unspecified assistantships available. Financial award application deadline: 5/1; financial award applicants required to submit CSS PROFILE or FAFSA. *Unit head:* Dr. Susan Ayers, Dean, College of Education, 706-864-1998, E-mail: susan.ayres@ung.edu. *Application contact:* Regina Boling, Teacher Education Graduate Admissions, 706-864-1533, E-mail: regina.boling@ung.edu.
Website: http://ung.edu/college-of-education/

University of Pennsylvania, Graduate School of Education, Division of Teaching, Learning, and Leadership, Teacher Education Program, Philadelphia, PA 19104. Offers elementary education (MS Ed); secondary education (MS Ed). *Students:* 43 full-time (32 women), 1 (woman) part-time; includes 15 minority (4 Black or African American, non-Hispanic/Latino; 7 Asian, non-Hispanic/Latino; 3 Hispanic/Latino; 1 Two or more races, non-Hispanic/Latino). Average age 25. 123 applicants, 81% accepted, 45 enrolled. In 2016, 60 master's awarded. *Degree requirements:* For master's, thesis or alternative, student teaching, portfolio. *Entrance requirements:* For master's, GRE, bachelor's degree. Additional exam requirements/recommendations for international students: Required—TOEFL, IELTS. *Application deadline:* For summer admission, 6/1 priority date for domestic students, 6/1 for international students. Applications are processed on a rolling basis. Application fee: $75. Electronic applications accepted. *Expenses: Tuition:* Full-time $31,068; part-time $5762 per course. *Required fees:* $3200; $336 per course. Full-time tuition and fees vary according to degree level, program and student level. Part-time tuition and fees vary according to course load, degree level and program. *Financial support:* In 2016–17, 53 students received support. Federal Work-Study and scholarships/grants available. Financial award applicants required to submit FAFSA. *Faculty research:* Teacher competencies, social justice teaching, teacher practitioner inquiry. *Unit head:* Maureen Cotterill, Program Manager, 215-898-7364.
Website: http://www2.gse.upenn.edu/tep/

University of Phoenix–Bay Area Campus, College of Education, San Jose, CA 95134-1805. Offers administration and supervision (MA Ed); adult education and training (MA Ed); early childhood education (MA Ed); education (Ed S); educational leadership (Ed D); elementary teacher education (MA Ed); higher education administration (PhD); secondary teacher education (MA Ed); special education (MA Ed); teacher leadership (MA Ed). *Program availability:* Evening/weekend, online learning. *Degree requirements:* For master's, thesis (for some programs). *Entrance requirements:* For master's, minimum undergraduate GPA of 2.5, 3 years of work experience. Additional exam requirements/recommendations for international students: Required—TOEFL (minimum score 550 paper-based; 79 iBT). Electronic applications accepted.

University of Phoenix–Central Valley Campus, College of Education, Fresno, CA 93720-1552. Offers curriculum and instruction (MA Ed); curriculum and instruction-computer education (MA Ed); elementary teacher education (MA Ed); secondary teacher education (MA Ed).

University of Phoenix–Colorado Campus, College of Education, Lone Tree, CO 80124-5453. Offers administration and supervision (MAEd); curriculum instruction (MAEd); elementary teacher education (MAEd); school counseling (MSC); secondary teacher education (MAEd). *Program availability:* Evening/weekend. *Degree requirements:* For master's, thesis (for some programs). *Entrance requirements:* For master's, minimum undergraduate GPA of 2.5, 3 years work experience. Additional exam requirements/recommendations for international students: Required—TOEFL (minimum score 550 paper-based; 79 iBT). Electronic applications accepted.

University of Phoenix–Colorado Springs Downtown Campus, College of Education, Colorado Springs, CO 80903. Offers administration and supervision (MA Ed); curriculum and instruction (MA Ed); elementary teacher education (MA Ed); principal licensure certification (Certificate); school counseling (MSC); secondary teacher education (MA Ed). *Program availability:* Evening/weekend. *Degree requirements:* For master's, thesis (for some programs). *Entrance requirements:* For master's, minimum undergraduate GPA of 2.5, 3 years of work experience. Additional exam requirements/recommendations for international students: Required—TOEFL (minimum score 550 paper-based; 79 iBT). Electronic applications accepted.

University of Phoenix–Hawaii Campus, College of Education, Honolulu, HI 96813-3800. Offers administration and supervision (MA Ed); curriculum and instruction (MA Ed); elementary education (MA Ed); secondary education (MA Ed); special education (MA Ed); teacher education for elementary licensure (MA Ed). *Program availability:* Evening/weekend. *Degree requirements:* For master's, thesis (for some programs). *Entrance requirements:* For master's, minimum undergraduate GPA of 2.5, 3 years of work experience. Additional exam requirements/recommendations for international students: Required—TOEFL (minimum score 550 paper-based; 79 iBT). Electronic applications accepted.

University of Phoenix–New Mexico Campus, College of Education, Albuquerque, NM 87113-1570. Offers administration and supervision (MAEd); curriculum and instruction (MAEd); elementary teacher education (MAEd); school counseling (MSC); secondary teacher education (MAEd). *Program availability:* Evening/weekend. *Degree requirements:* For master's, thesis (for some programs). *Entrance requirements:* For master's, minimum undergraduate GPA of 2.5, 3 years of work experience. Additional exam requirements/recommendations for international students: Required—TOEFL (minimum score 550 paper-based; 79 iBT). Electronic applications accepted.

University of Phoenix–North Florida Campus, College of Education, Jacksonville, FL 32216-0959. Offers administration and supervision (MA Ed); curriculum and instruction (MA Ed), including computer education, mathematics education; early childhood education (MA Ed); elementary teacher education (MA Ed); secondary teacher education (MA Ed). *Program availability:* Evening/weekend. *Degree requirements:* For master's, thesis (for some programs). *Entrance requirements:* For master's, 3 years of work experience, minimum undergraduate GPA of 2.5. Additional exam requirements/recommendations for international students: Required—TOEFL (minimum score 550 paper-based; 49 iBT). Electronic applications accepted.

University of Phoenix–Online Campus, College of Education, Phoenix, AZ 85034-7209. Offers administration and supervision (MAEd, Certificate); adult education and training (MAEd); curriculum and instruction (MAEd), including computer education, curriculum and instruction, English as a second language, language arts, mathematics, reading; early childhood education (MAEd); educational studies (MAEd); elementary teacher education (MAEd), including early childhood, elementary teacher education, high school middle level, middle level; principal licensure (Certificate); secondary teacher education (MAEd); special education (MAEd, Certificate); teacher education (MAEd), including middle level generalist; teacher education middle level mathematics (MAEd), including middle level mathematics; teacher education middle level science (MAEd), including middle level science; teacher education secondary mathematics (MAEd); teacher education secondary science (MAEd); teacher leadership (MAEd); teachers of English learners (Certificate); transition to teaching (Certificate), including elementary education, secondary education. *Program availability:* Evening/weekend, online learning. *Entrance requirements:* Additional exam requirements/recommendations for international students: Required—TOEFL, TOEIC (Test of English as an International Communication), Berlitz Online English Proficiency Exam, PTE, or IELTS. Electronic applications accepted. *Expenses:* Contact Institution.

University of Phoenix–Phoenix Campus, College of Education, Tempe, AZ 85282-2371. Offers administration and supervision (MA Ed); adult education and training (MA Ed); curriculum and instruction reading (MA Ed); early childhood education (MA Ed); education studies (MA Ed); elementary teacher education (MA Ed); secondary teacher education (MA Ed); special education (MA Ed); teacher leadership (MA Ed). *Program availability:* Evening/weekend, online learning. *Entrance requirements:* Additional exam requirements/recommendations for international students: Required—TOEFL, TOEIC (Test of English as an International Communication), Berlitz Online English Proficiency Exam, PTE, or IELTS. Electronic applications accepted. *Expenses:* Contact institution.

University of Phoenix–Sacramento Valley Campus, College of Education, Sacramento, CA 95833-4334. Offers adult education (MA Ed); curriculum instruction (MA Ed); elementary teacher education (MA Ed); secondary teacher education (MA Ed); teacher education (Certificate). *Program availability:* Evening/weekend. *Degree requirements:* For master's, thesis (for some programs). *Entrance requirements:* For master's, 3 years of work experience, minimum undergraduate GPA of 2.5. Additional exam requirements/recommendations for international students: Required—TOEFL (minimum score 550 paper-based; 79 iBT). Electronic applications accepted.

University of Phoenix–San Diego Campus, College of Education, San Diego, CA 92123. Offers curriculum and instruction (MA Ed), including computer education, curriculum and instruction, English as a second language; elementary teacher education (MA Ed); secondary teacher education (MA Ed). *Program availability:* Evening/weekend. *Degree requirements:* For master's, thesis (for some programs). *Entrance requirements:* For master's, 3 years of work experience, minimum undergraduate GPA of 3.0. Additional exam requirements/recommendations for international students: Required—TOEFL (minimum score 550 paper-based; 79 iBT). Electronic applications accepted.

University of Phoenix–Southern Arizona Campus, College of Education, Tucson, AZ 85711. Offers administration and supervision (MA Ed); adult education and training

(MA Ed); curriculum instruction (MA Ed); educational counseling (MA Ed); elementary teacher education (MA Ed); school counseling (MSC); secondary teacher education (MA Ed); special education (MA Ed, Certificate). *Program availability:* Evening/weekend. *Degree requirements:* For master's, thesis (for some programs). *Entrance requirements:* For master's, minimum undergraduate GPA of 2.5, 3 years of work experience. Additional exam requirements/recommendations for international students: Required—TOEFL (minimum score 550 paper-based; 79 iBT). Electronic applications accepted.

University of Phoenix–Southern California Campus, College of Education, Costa Mesa, CA 92626. Offers administration and supervision (MA Ed, Certificate); adult education and training (MA Ed); educational studies (MA Ed); elementary teacher education (MA Ed); secondary teacher education (MA Ed); teacher leadership (MA Ed); teachers of English learners (Certificate). *Program availability:* Evening/weekend, online learning. *Entrance requirements:* Additional exam requirements/recommendations for international students: Required—TOEFL, TOEIC (Test of English as an International Communication), Berlitz Online English Proficiency Exam, PTE, or IELTS. Electronic applications accepted. *Expenses:* Contact institution.

University of Phoenix–South Florida Campus, College of Education, Miramar, FL 33027-4145. Offers administration and supervision (MA Ed); curriculum and instruction (MA Ed), including computer education, curriculum and instruction, mathematics education; early childhood education (MA Ed); elementary teacher education (MA Ed); secondary teacher education (MA Ed). *Program availability:* Evening/weekend. *Degree requirements:* For master's, thesis (for some programs). *Entrance requirements:* For master's, 3 years of work experience, minimum undergraduate GPA of 2.5. Additional exam requirements/recommendations for international students: Required—TOEFL (minimum score 550 paper-based; 79 iBT). Electronic applications accepted.

University of Phoenix–Utah Campus, College of Education, Salt Lake City, UT 84123-4642. Offers administration and supervision (MA Ed); curriculum and instruction (MA Ed); elementary teacher education (MA Ed); school counseling (MSC); secondary teacher education (MA Ed); special education (MA Ed). *Program availability:* Evening/weekend. *Degree requirements:* For master's, thesis (for some programs). *Entrance requirements:* For master's, minimum undergraduate GPA of 2.5, 3 years work experience. Additional exam requirements/recommendations for international students: Required—TOEFL (minimum score 550 paper-based; 79 iBT). Electronic applications accepted.

University of Phoenix–Washington D.C. Campus, College of Education, Washington, DC 20001. Offers administration and supervision (MA Ed); adult education and training (MA Ed); computer education (MA Ed); curriculum and instruction (MA Ed, Ed D); early childhood education (MA Ed); education (Ed S); educational leadership (Ed D); educational technology (Ed D); elementary teacher education (MA Ed); English and language arts education (MA Ed); English as a second language (MA Ed); higher education administration (PhD); mathematics education (MA Ed); secondary teacher education (MA Ed); special education (MA Ed); teacher leadership (MA Ed).

University of Pittsburgh, School of Education, Department of Instruction and Learning, Program in Secondary Education, Pittsburgh, PA 15260. Offers English and communications education (M Ed, MAT); foreign language education (M Ed, MAT); language, literacy and culture education (Ed D, PhD); mathematics education (M Ed, MAT, Ed D, PhD); science education (M Ed, MAT, Ed D, PhD); secondary education (PhD); social studies education (M Ed, MAT); STEM education (Ed D). *Program availability:* Part-time, evening/weekend. *Degree requirements:* For master's, thesis; for doctorate, thesis/dissertation. *Entrance requirements:* For master's, PRAXIS I; for doctorate, GRE General Test. Additional exam requirements/recommendations for international students: Required—TOEFL. Electronic applications accepted. Tuition and fees vary according to program.

University of Puget Sound, School of Education, Program in Teaching, Tacoma, WA 98416. Offers elementary education (MAT); secondary education (MAT). *Accreditation:* NASM. *Faculty:* 6 full-time (3 women), 1 (woman) part-time/adjunct. *Students:* 26 full-time (20 women), 2 part-time (both women); includes 6 minority (1 American Indian or Alaska Native, non-Hispanic/Latino; 2 Asian, non-Hispanic/Latino; 3 Two or more races, non-Hispanic/Latino). Average age 26. 60 applicants, 68% accepted, 27 enrolled. In 2016, 33 master's awarded. *Degree requirements:* For master's, project. *Entrance requirements:* For master's, WEST-E or NES, WEST-B or ACT/SAT, two education foundation prerequisite courses; minor in content area (for secondary education). Additional exam requirements/recommendations for international students: Required—TOEFL (minimum score 550 paper-based; 90 iBT). *Application deadline:* For fall admission, 3/1 priority date for domestic and international students. Applications are processed on a rolling basis. Application fee: $60. Electronic applications accepted. *Expenses:* $3,575 per unit. *Financial support:* In 2016–17, 23 students received support. Scholarships/grants available. Financial award application deadline: 3/31; financial award applicants required to submit FAFSA. *Faculty research:* Pre-service teacher learning, public school partnerships and professional development, creating equitable classrooms, literacy development, teaching social studies. *Unit head:* Amy Ryken, Dean, 253-879-2810, Fax: 253-879-3926, E-mail: aryken@pugetsound.edu. *Application contact:* Karen Stump, Certification Officer/Admission Coordinator, 253-879-3382, Fax: 253-879-3926, E-mail: kstump@pugetsound.edu.
Website: http://www.pugetsound.edu/academics/departments-and-programs/graduate/school-of-education/mat/

University of St. Francis, College of Education, Joliet, IL 60435-6169. Offers educational leadership (MS, Ed D); elementary education (M Ed); reading (MS); secondary education (M Ed), including English education, math education, science education, social studies education, visual arts education; special education (M Ed); teaching and learning (MS); TESOL (Certificate). *Accreditation:* NCATE. *Program availability:* Part-time, evening/weekend, 100% online, blended/hybrid learning. *Faculty:* 11 full-time (8 women), 60 part-time/adjunct (42 women). *Students:* 34 full-time (26 women), 420 part-time (318 women); includes 92 minority (51 Black or African American, non-Hispanic/Latino; 5 Asian, non-Hispanic/Latino; 31 Hispanic/Latino; 5 Two or more races, non-Hispanic/Latino), 4 international. Average age 36. 242 applicants, 48% accepted, 96 enrolled. In 2016, 229 master's, 44 doctorates, 10 other advanced degrees awarded. *Degree requirements:* For master's, comprehensive exam; for doctorate, thesis/dissertation. *Entrance requirements:* Additional exam requirements/recommendations for international students: Required—TOEFL (minimum score 550 paper-based; 79 iBT), IELTS (minimum score 6). *Application deadline:* Applications are processed on a rolling basis. Application fee: $30. Electronic applications accepted. Application fee is waived when completed online. *Expenses:* Contact institution. *Financial support:* In 2016–17, 48 students received support. Career-related internships or fieldwork and unspecified assistantships available. Support available to part-time students. Financial award applicants required to submit FAFSA. *Unit head:* Dr. John Gambro, Dean, 815-740-3829, Fax: 815-740-2264, E-mail: jgambro@stfrancis.edu. *Application contact:* Sandra Sloka, Director of Admissions for Graduate and Degree Completion Programs, 800-735-7500, Fax: 815-740-3431, E-mail: ssloka@stfrancis.edu.
Website: http://www.stfrancis.edu/academics/college-of-education/

University of Saint Francis, Graduate School, Department of Education, Fort Wayne, IN 46808-3994. Offers education (MAT); secondary education (MAT); special education (MS Ed), including intense intervention, mild intervention. *Accreditation:* NCATE. *Program availability:* Part-time, evening/weekend, online only, 100% online. *Faculty:* 1 (woman) full-time, 4 part-time/adjunct (2 women). *Students:* 4 full-time (3 women), 16 part-time (8 women); includes 2 minority (both Black or African American, non-Hispanic/Latino). Average age 29. 5 applicants, 100% accepted, 4 enrolled. In 2016, 2 master's awarded. *Degree requirements:* For master's, comprehensive exam. *Entrance requirements:* For master's, GRE (minimum composite score of 280 verbal and quantitative subtests) or MAT (minimum score of 389) if undergraduate GPA is below a 2.8 or prior graduate level GPA is below 3.0; GRE, ACT, SAT, or CASA exam if no license, minimum undergraduate GPA of 2.8; resume (if GPA is below 3.0); standard teaching license and/or bachelor's degree from regionally-accredited institution; background check; two professional recommendations. Additional exam requirements/recommendations for international students: Required—TOEFL (minimum score 550 paper-based) or IELTS (minimum score 6.5). *Application deadline:* Applications are processed on a rolling basis. Application fee: $0. Electronic applications accepted. *Expenses:* $475 per credit hour. *Financial support:* Federal Work-Study, scholarships/grants, and unspecified assistantships available. Financial award application deadline: 3/10; financial award applicants required to submit FAFSA. *Unit head:* Mary Riepenhoff, Assistant Professor/Department Chair, 260-399-7700 Ext. 8409, Fax: 260-399-8170, E-mail: mriepenhoff@sf.edu. *Application contact:* Kyle Richardson, Enrollment Specialist, 260-399-7700 Ext. 6310, Fax: 260-399-8152, E-mail: krichardson@sf.edu.
Website: http://education.sf.edu/

University of St. Thomas, School of Education and Human Services, Houston, TX 77006-4696. Offers all level education (M Ed); bilingual/dual language (M Ed); Catholic school teaching (M Ed); Catholic/private school leadership (M Ed); counselor education (M Ed); curriculum and instruction (M Ed); education (Ed D); educational leadership (M Ed); elementary teaching (M Ed); English as a second language (M Ed); exceptionality/educational diagnostician (M Ed); exceptionality/special education (M Ed); generalist (M Ed); reading (M Ed); secondary teaching (M Ed); teaching (MAT). *Accreditation:* TEAC. *Program availability:* Part-time, evening/weekend, online learning. *Faculty:* 44 full-time (29 women), 31 part-time/adjunct (17 women). *Students:* 65 full-time (61 women), 719 part-time (645 women); includes 515 minority (169 Black or African American, non-Hispanic/Latino; 25 Asian, non-Hispanic/Latino; 315 Hispanic/Latino; 2 Native Hawaiian or other Pacific Islander, non-Hispanic/Latino; 4 Two or more races, non-Hispanic/Latino), 24 international. Average age 36. 297 applicants, 92% accepted, 211 enrolled. In 2016, 403 master's awarded. *Degree requirements:* For master's, thesis, field experience. *Entrance requirements:* For master's, GRE or MAT if GPA is below 3.0, bachelor's degree; minimum GPA of 2.75 in bachelor's degree or last 60 credit hours; official transcripts from all institutions; goal statement of 250-300 words; 1 reference. Additional exam requirements/recommendations for international students: Required—TOEFL (minimum score 94 iBT), IELTS (minimum score 7), PTE (minimum score 53). *Application deadline:* Applications are processed on a rolling basis. Application fee: $35. Electronic applications accepted. *Expenses:* Contact institution. *Financial support:* In 2016–17, 52 students received support. Federal Work-Study, scholarships/grants, and state work-study, institutional employment available. Support available to part-time students. Financial award application deadline: 4/15; financial award applicants required to submit FAFSA. *Faculty research:* Leadership, diversity, personality traits, second language acquisition. *Unit head:* Dr. Robert LeBlanc, Dean, 713-525-3540, Fax: 713-525-3871, E-mail: education@stthom.edu. *Application contact:* Rita Paredes, Administrative Assistant, 713-525-3442, Fax: 713-525-3871, E-mail: rparede@stthom.edu.
Website: http://www.stthom.edu/Academics/School_of_Education_and_Human_Services/Index.aqf

The University of Scranton, Panuska College of Professional Studies, Department of Education, Program in Secondary Education, Scranton, PA 18510. Offers MS. *Accreditation:* NCATE. *Program availability:* Part-time, evening/weekend. *Degree requirements:* For master's, comprehensive exam (for some programs), thesis (for some programs), capstone experience. *Entrance requirements:* For master's, minimum GPA of 3.0, three letters of reference. Additional exam requirements/recommendations for international students: Required—TOEFL (minimum score 500 paper-based; 80 iBT), IELTS (minimum score 6.5). Electronic applications accepted.

University of South Alabama, College of Education and Professional Studies, Department of Leadership and Teacher Education, Mobile, AL 36688. Offers art education (M Ed); early childhood education (M Ed); educational leadership (M Ed, Ed D); elementary education (M Ed); reading education (M Ed); science education (M Ed); secondary education (M Ed); special education (M Ed). *Accreditation:* NCATE. *Program availability:* Part-time, 100% online, blended/hybrid learning. *Faculty:* 16 full-time (12 women), 6 part-time/adjunct (3 women). *Students:* 198 full-time (150 women), 77 part-time (58 women); includes 77 minority (61 Black or African American, non-Hispanic/Latino; 2 American Indian or Alaska Native, non-Hispanic/Latino; 2 Asian, non-Hispanic/Latino; 7 Hispanic/Latino; 1 Native Hawaiian or other Pacific Islander, non-Hispanic/Latino; 4 Two or more races, non-Hispanic/Latino). Average age 34. 153 applicants, 53% accepted, 69 enrolled. In 2016, 80 master's, 1 doctorate awarded. *Degree requirements:* For master's, comprehensive exam, thesis (for some programs); for doctorate, comprehensive exam, thesis/dissertation. *Entrance requirements:* For master's, GRE General Test or MAT, minimum GPA of 3.0; for doctorate, GRE, minimum graduate GPA of 3.25, 3 years of experience in field, 3 letters of recommendation, interview, official transcripts. Additional exam requirements/recommendations for international students: Required—TOEFL. *Application deadline:* For fall admission, 7/15 for domestic students; for spring admission, 11/15 for domestic students; for summer admission, 4/15 for domestic students. Applications are processed on a rolling basis. Application fee: $35. Electronic applications accepted. *Expenses:* Tuition, state resident: full-time $9768; part-time $407 per credit hour. Tuition, nonresident: full-time $19,536; part-time $814 per credit hour. *Financial support:* Fellowships, research assistantships, teaching assistantships, career-related internships or fieldwork, Federal Work-Study, institutionally sponsored loans, scholarships/grants, and unspecified assistantships available. Support available to part-time students. Financial award application deadline: 5/31; financial award applicants required to submit FAFSA. *Unit head:* Dr. Susan Santoli, Department Chair, 251-380-2836, Fax: 251-380-2758, E-mail: ssantoli@southalabama.edu. *Application contact:* Dr. Susan Santoli, Director of Graduate Studies, 251-380-2836, Fax: 251-380-2758, E-mail: ssantoli@southalabama.edu.
Website: http://www.southalabama.edu/colleges/coe/lte/index.html

University of South Carolina, The Graduate School, College of Education, Department of Instruction and Teacher Education, Program in Secondary Education, Columbia, SC 29208. Offers art education (IMA, MAT); business education (IMA, MAT); English (MAT); foreign language (MAT); health education (MAT); mathematics (MAT); science (IMA, MAT); secondary (Ed D); secondary education (MT, PhD); social studies (MAT); theatre and speech (MAT). IMA and MT offered jointly with the subject areas. *Accreditation:* NCATE. *Degree requirements:* For master's, comprehensive exam, thesis (for some programs), foreign language (MA); for doctorate, one foreign language, comprehensive exam, thesis/dissertation. *Entrance requirements:* For master's, GRE

General Test or MAT, teaching certificate (IMA, M Ed), interview; for doctorate, GRE General Test or MAT, interview. *Faculty research:* Middle school programs, professional development, school collaboration.

The University of South Dakota, Graduate School, School of Education, Division of Curriculum and Instruction, Program in Secondary Education, Vermillion, SD 57069. Offers secondary education (MA), including English language learning, science, technology or math (STM), secondary education plus certification. *Accreditation:* NCATE. *Program availability:* Part-time, online learning. *Degree requirements:* For master's, comprehensive exam, thesis or alternative. *Entrance requirements:* For master's, GRE General Test, MAT, minimum GPA of 2.7. Additional exam requirements/recommendations for international students: Required—TOEFL (minimum score 550 paper-based; 79 iBT). Electronic applications accepted.

University of Southern Indiana, Graduate Studies, Pott College of Science, Engineering, and Education, Department of Teacher Education, Program in Secondary Education, Evansville, IN 47712-3590. Offers MSE. *Accreditation:* NCATE. *Program availability:* Part-time, evening/weekend. *Faculty:* 5 full-time (4 women), 2 part-time/adjunct (1 woman). *Students:* 1 full-time (0 women), 1 (woman) part-time, 1 international. Average age 36. In 2016, 6 master's awarded. *Entrance requirements:* For master's, PRAXIS II, bachelor's degree with minimum cumulative GPA of 2.75 from college or university accredited by NCATE or comparable association; minimum GPA of 3.0 in all courses taken at graduate level at all schools attended; teaching license. Additional exam requirements/recommendations for international students: Required—TOEFL (minimum score 550 paper-based; 79 iBT), IELTS (minimum score 6). *Application deadline:* For fall admission, 7/1 priority date for domestic students, 1/1 priority date for international students. Applications are processed on a rolling basis. Application fee: $40. Electronic applications accepted. *Expenses:* Tuition, state resident: full-time $8497. Tuition, nonresident: full-time $16,691. *Required fees:* $500. *Financial support:* Federal Work-Study, institutionally sponsored loans, scholarships/grants, tuition waivers (full and partial), and unspecified assistantships available. Financial award application deadline: 3/1; financial award applicants required to submit FAFSA. *Unit head:* Dr. Bonnie Beach, Associate Dean, 812-465-1620, E-mail: blbeach@usi.edu. *Application contact:* Dr. Mayola Rowser, Director, Graduate Studies, 812-465-7015, Fax: 812-464-1956, E-mail: mrowser@usi.edu.
Website: http://www.usi.edu/science/teacher-education/programs/mse

University of Southern Mississippi, Graduate School, College of Education and Psychology, Department of Curriculum, Instruction and Special Education, Hattiesburg, MS 39406. Offers elementary education (M Ed, PhD); instructional technology (MS); instructional technology and design (PhD); secondary education (MAT); special education (M Ed, PhD). *Program availability:* Part-time, online learning. *Degree requirements:* For master's, comprehensive exam, thesis (for some programs); for doctorate, comprehensive exam, thesis/dissertation. *Entrance requirements:* For master's, GRE General Test, MAT, minimum GPA of 3.0; for doctorate, GRE General Test, minimum GPA of 3.5. Additional exam requirements/recommendations for international students: Required—TOEFL, IELTS. *Application deadline:* For fall admission, 3/1 priority date for domestic students, 3/1 for international students; for spring admission, 1/10 priority date for domestic and international students. Applications are processed on a rolling basis. Application fee: $60. *Expenses: Tuition, area resident:* Full-time $15,708; part-time $437 per credit hour. *Financial support:* Research assistantships with tuition reimbursements, teaching assistantships with full tuition reimbursements, Federal Work-Study, institutionally sponsored loans, scholarships/grants, health care benefits, tuition waivers (partial), and unspecified assistantships available. Financial award application deadline: 3/15; financial award applicants required to submit FAFSA. *Faculty research:* Mathematical problem solving, integrative curriculum, writing process, teacher education models. *Unit head:* Dr. Mary Ariail, Chair, 601-266-5247, Fax: 601-266-4548.
Website: https://www.usm.edu/elementary-special-technology-education

University of South Florida, Innovative Education, Tampa, FL 33620-9951. Offers adult, career and higher education (Graduate Certificate), including college teaching, leadership in developing human resources, leadership in higher education; Africana studies (Graduate Certificate), including diasporas and health disparities, genocide and human rights; aging studies (Graduate Certificate), including gerontology; art research (Graduate Certificate), including museum studies; business foundations (Graduate Certificate); chemical and biomedical engineering (Graduate Certificate), including materials science and engineering, water, health and sustainability; child and family studies (Graduate Certificate), including positive behavior support; civil and industrial engineering (Graduate Certificate), including transportation systems analysis; community and family health (Graduate Certificate), including maternal and child health, social marketing and public health, violence and injury: prevention and intervention, women's health; criminology (Graduate Certificate), including criminal justice administration; educational measurement and research (Graduate Certificate), including evaluation; English (Graduate Certificate), including comparative literary studies, creative writing, professional and technical communication; entrepreneurship (Graduate Certificate); environmental health (Graduate Certificate), including safety management; epidemiology and biostatistics (Graduate Certificate), including applied biostatistics, biostatistics, concepts and tools of epidemiology, epidemiology, epidemiology of infectious diseases; geography, environment and planning (Graduate Certificate), including community development, environmental policy and management, geographical information systems; geology (Graduate Certificate), including hydrogeology; global health (Graduate Certificate), including disaster management, global health and Latin American and Caribbean studies, global health practice, humanitarian assistance, infection control; government and international affairs (Graduate Certificate), including Cuban studies, globalization studies; health policy and management (Graduate Certificate), including health management and leadership, public health policy and programs; hearing specialist: early intervention (Graduate Certificate); industrial and management systems engineering (Graduate Certificate), including systems engineering, technology management; information studies (Graduate Certificate), including school library media specialist; information systems/decision sciences (Graduate Certificate), including analytics and business intelligence; instructional technology (Graduate Certificate), including distance education, Florida digital/virtual educator, instructional design, multimedia design, Web design; internal medicine, bioethics and medical humanities (Graduate Certificate), including biomedical ethics; Latin American and Caribbean studies (Graduate Certificate); mass communications (Graduate Certificate), including multimedia journalism; mathematics and statistics (Graduate Certificate), including mathematics; medicine (Graduate Certificate), including aging and neuroscience, bioinformatics, biotechnology, brain fitness and memory management, clinical investigation, health informatics, health sciences, integrative weight management, intellectual property, medicine and gender, metabolic and nutritional medicine, metabolic cardiology, pharmacy sciences; national and competitive intelligence (Graduate Certificate); psychological and social foundations (Graduate Certificate), including career counseling, college teaching, diversity in education, mental health counseling, school counseling; public affairs (Graduate Certificate), including nonprofit management, public management, research administration; public health (Graduate Certificate), including environmental health, health equity, public health generalist, translational research in adolescent behavioral health; public health practices (Graduate Certificate), including planning for healthy communities; rehabilitation and mental health counseling (Graduate Certificate), including integrative mental health care, marriage and family therapy, rehabilitation technology; secondary education (Graduate Certificate), including ESOL, foreign language education: culture and content, foreign language education: professional; social work (Graduate Certificate), including geriatric social work/clinical gerontology; special education (Graduate Certificate), including autism spectrum disorder, disabilities education: severe/profound; world languages (Graduate Certificate), including teaching English as a second language (TESL) or foreign language. *Expenses:* Tuition, state resident: full-time $7766; part-time $431.43 per credit hour. Tuition, nonresident: full-time $15,789; part-time $877.17 per credit hour. *Required fees:* $37 per term. *Unit head:* Kathy Barnes, Interdisciplinary Programs Coordinator, 813-974-8031, Fax: 813-974-7061, E-mail: barnesk@usf.edu. *Application contact:* Karen Tylinski, Metro Initiatives, 813-974-9943, Fax: 813-974-7061, E-mail: ktylinsk@usf.edu.
Website: http://www.usf.edu/innovative-education/

The University of Tennessee, Graduate School, College of Education, Health and Human Sciences, Program in Education, Knoxville, TN 37996. Offers art education (MS); counseling education (PhD); cultural studies in education (PhD); curriculum (MS, Ed S); curriculum, educational research and evaluation (Ed D, PhD); early childhood education (PhD); early childhood special education (MS); education of deaf and hard of hearing (MS); educational administration and policy studies (Ed D, PhD); educational administration and supervision (Ed S); educational psychology (Ed D, PhD); elementary education (MS, Ed S); elementary teaching (MS); English education (MS, Ed S); exercise science (PhD); foreign language/ESL education (MS, Ed S); instructional technology (MS, Ed D, PhD, Ed S); literacy, language and ESL education (PhD); literacy, language education, and ESL education (Ed D); mathematics education (MS, Ed S); modified and comprehensive special education (MS); reading education (MS, Ed S); school counseling (Ed S); school psychology (PhD, Ed S); science education (MS, Ed S); secondary teaching (MS); social foundations (MS); social science education (MS, Ed S); socio-cultural foundations of sports and education (PhD); special education (Ed S); teacher education (Ed D, PhD). *Accreditation:* NCATE. *Program availability:* Part-time, evening/weekend. *Degree requirements:* For master's and Ed S, thesis optional; for doctorate, variable foreign language requirement, thesis/dissertation. *Entrance requirements:* For master's, minimum GPA of 2.7; for doctorate and Ed S, GRE General Test, minimum GPA of 2.7. Additional exam requirements/recommendations for international students: Required—TOEFL. Electronic applications accepted.

The University of Tennessee at Chattanooga, School of Education, Chattanooga, TN 37403. Offers counseling (M Ed), including community counseling, school counseling; education (M Ed, Post-Master's Certificate), including elementary education (M Ed), school leadership, secondary education (M Ed), special education (M Ed); educational specialist (Ed S), including educational technology, school psychology; learning and leadership (Ed D), including educational leadership. *Accreditation:* ACA; NCATE. *Program availability:* Part-time. *Faculty:* 13 full-time (8 women), 2 part-time/adjunct (both women). *Students:* 50 full-time (32 women), 157 part-time (107 women); includes 42 minority (28 Black or African American, non-Hispanic/Latino; 4 Asian, non-Hispanic/Latino; 2 Hispanic/Latino; 8 Two or more races, non-Hispanic/Latino), 1 international. Average age 36. 169 applicants, 76% accepted, 49 enrolled. In 2016, 77 master's, 5 other advanced degrees awarded. *Degree requirements:* For master's, comprehensive exam, thesis optional, culminating experience; for doctorate, comprehensive exam, thesis/dissertation; for other advanced degree, internship. *Entrance requirements:* For master's, GRE General Test, PPST 1, teaching certificate; for doctorate, GRE General Test, master's degree, two years of practical work experience in organizational environment; for other advanced degree, GRE General Test, letters of reference. Additional exam requirements/recommendations for international students: Required—TOEFL (minimum score 550 paper-based; 79 iBT), IELTS (minimum score 6). *Application deadline:* For fall admission, 6/15 for domestic students, 7/1 for international students; for spring admission, 11/1 for domestic and international students. Applications are processed on a rolling basis. Application fee: $35 ($40 for international students). Electronic applications accepted. *Expenses:* $9,876 full-time in-state; $25,994 full-time out-of-state; $450 per credit part-time in-state; $1,345 per credit part-time out-of-state. *Financial support:* In 2016–17, 18 research assistantships, 5 teaching assistantships were awarded; career-related internships or fieldwork, institutionally sponsored loans, scholarships/grants, and unspecified assistantships also available. Support available to part-time students. Financial award application deadline: 7/1; financial award applicants required to submit FAFSA. *Faculty research:* School counseling, community counseling, elementary and secondary education, school leadership and administration. *Total annual research expenditures:* $247,231. *Unit head:* Dr. Renee Murley, Director, 423-425-4684, Fax: 423-425-5380, E-mail: renee-murley@utc.edu. *Application contact:* Dr. Joanne Romagni, Dean of the Graduate School, 423-425-4478, Fax: 423-425-5223, E-mail: joanne-romagni@utc.edu.
Website: http://www.utc.edu/school-education/abouttheschool/gradprograms.php

The University of Tennessee at Martin, Graduate Programs, College of Education, Health and Behavioral Sciences, Program in Teaching, Martin, TN 38238. Offers curriculum and instruction (MS Ed), including 7-12, K-6; initial licensure (MS Ed), including elementary education, secondary education; initial licensure K-12 (MS Ed), including physical education, special education; interdisciplinary (MS Ed). *Students:* 21 full-time (14 women), 125 part-time (87 women); includes 22 minority (18 Black or African American, non-Hispanic/Latino; 3 Hispanic/Latino; 1 Two or more races, non-Hispanic/Latino). 115 applicants, 81% accepted, 51 enrolled. In 2016, 26 master's awarded. *Expenses:* Tuition, state resident: full-time $8254; part-time $459 per credit hour. Tuition, nonresident: full-time $22,198; part-time $1234 per credit hour. *Required fees:* $79 per credit hour. Part-time tuition and fees vary according to course load and campus/location. *Faculty research:* Special education, science/math/technology, school reform, reading. *Unit head:* Cynthia West, Dean, 731-881-7125, Fax: 731-881-7975, E-mail: cwest@utm.edu. *Application contact:* Jolene L. Cunningham, Student Services Specialist, 731-881-7012, Fax: 731-881-7499, E-mail: jcunningham@utm.edu.

The University of Texas Rio Grande Valley, College of Education and P-16 Integration, Department of Teaching and Learning, Edinburg, TX 78539. Offers curriculum and instruction (M Ed, Ed D); educational technology (M Ed). *Program availability:* Part-time. *Degree requirements:* For master's, comprehensive exam, thesis optional. *Entrance requirements:* For master's, GRE. Additional exam requirements/recommendations for international students: Required—TOEFL, IELTS. Tuition and fees vary according to course load and program. *Faculty research:* Dual language instruction, literacy and technology, teacher education in diverse populations, mathematics and science education.

University of the Cumberlands, Graduate Programs in Education, Williamsburg, KY 40769-1372. Offers all grades (P-12) (M Ed); business and marketing (MA Ed, MAT); counselor education and supervision (Ed D); director of pupil personnel (Certificate); director of special education (Certificate); educational administration and supervision (Ed S); educational leadership (Ed D); elementary education (MA Ed, MAT); instructional leadership - principalship (MA Ed); instructional leadership - school principal (Certificate); middle school education (MA Ed, MAT); reading and writing

(MA Ed); school counseling (MA Ed); school superintendent (Certificate); secondary education (MA Ed, MAT); special education (MAT); supervisor of instruction (Certificate); teacher leader (MA Ed). *Program availability:* Part-time, evening/weekend, online learning. *Degree requirements:* For master's, comprehensive exam. Electronic applications accepted.

University of the District of Columbia, College of Arts and Sciences, Program in Teaching, Washington, DC 20008-1175. Offers elementary education (MAT); middle school mathematics (MAT); secondary English language arts (MAT); secondary social studies (MAT).

University of the Virgin Islands, College of Science and Mathematics, St. Thomas, VI 00802. Offers marine and environmental science (MS); mathematics for secondary teachers (MA). *Program availability:* Part-time, online learning. *Faculty:* 5 full-time (4 women), 7 part-time/adjunct (2 women). *Students:* 12 full-time (10 women), 26 part-time (19 women); includes 7 minority (6 Black or African American, non-Hispanic/Latino; 1 Hispanic/Latino). Average age 27. 25 applicants, 80% accepted, 11 enrolled. In 2016, 6 master's awarded. *Degree requirements:* For master's, comprehensive exam, thesis. *Entrance requirements:* For master's, GRE, minimum GPA of 2.5. Additional exam requirements/recommendations for international students: Required—TOEFL (minimum score 550 paper-based). *Application deadline:* For fall admission, 4/30 for domestic and international students; for spring admission, 10/30 for domestic and international students. Application fee: $30. Electronic applications accepted. *Expenses:* Tuition, state resident: part-time $386 per credit hour. Tuition, nonresident: part-time $735 per credit hour. *Financial support:* Career-related internships or fieldwork and scholarships/grants available. Financial award application deadline: 4/15; financial award applicants required to submit FAFSA. *Unit head:* Dr. Sandra Romano, Dean, 340-693-1230, Fax: 340-693-1245, E-mail: sromano@uvi.edu. *Application contact:* Dr. Xuri M. Allen, Director of Admissions, 340-693-1224, Fax: 340-693-1167, E-mail: xallen@uvi.edu.

The University of Toledo, College of Graduate Studies, Judith Herb College of Education, Department of Curriculum and Instruction, Toledo, OH 43606-3390. Offers art education (ME); career and technical education (ME, Ed S); curriculum and instruction (ME, PhD, Ed S); early childhood education (Ed S); education and anthropology (MAE); education and biology (MES); education and chemistry (MES); education and classics (MAE); education and economics (MAE); education and English (MAE); education and French (MAE); education and geology (MES); education and German (MAE); education and history (MAE); education and mathematics (MAE, MES); education and physics (MES); education and political science (MAE); education and sociology (MAE); education and Spanish (MAE); educational media (PhD); educational technology (ME); educational technology: virtual educator (Certificate); elementary education (PhD); English as a second language (MAE); gifted and talented education (PhD); middle childhood education (ME); secondary education (ME, PhD); special education (PhD). *Accreditation:* NCATE. *Program availability:* Part-time, evening/weekend. *Degree requirements:* For master's, comprehensive exam, thesis or alternative; for doctorate, comprehensive exam, thesis/dissertation; for other advanced degree, thesis optional. *Entrance requirements:* For master's, doctorate, and other advanced degree, minimum cumulative GPA of 2.7 for all previous academic work, letters of recommendation. Additional exam requirements/recommendations for international students: Required—TOEFL (minimum score 550 paper-based; 80 iBT). Electronic applications accepted.

The University of Tulsa, Graduate School, Kendall College of Arts and Sciences, School of Urban Education, Program in Education, Tulsa, OK 74104-3189. Offers elementary certification (M Ed); secondary certification (M Ed). *Program availability:* Part-time. *Students:* 1 full-time (0 women), all international. Average age 24. 9 applicants. *Degree requirements:* For master's, thesis optional. *Entrance requirements:* For master's, GRE General Test. Additional exam requirements/recommendations for international students: Required—TOEFL (minimum score 577 paper-based; 91 iBT), IELTS (minimum score 6.5). *Application deadline:* Applications are processed on a rolling basis. Application fee: $55. Electronic applications accepted. *Expenses: Tuition:* Full-time $22,230; part-time $1235 per credit hour. *Required fees:* $990 per semester. Tuition and fees vary according to course load. *Financial support:* In 2016–17, 1 student received support, including 1 fellowship with tuition reimbursement available (averaging $2,235 per year), 1 teaching assistantship with full tuition reimbursement available (averaging $13,410 per year); Federal Work-Study, scholarships/grants, health care benefits, tuition waivers (full and partial), and unspecified assistantships also available. Support available to part-time students. Financial award application deadline: 2/1; financial award applicants required to submit FAFSA. *Faculty research:* Elementary and secondary education. *Unit head:* Dr. Sharon Baker, Chair, 918-631-2541, Fax: 918-631-2238, E-mail: sharon-baker@utulsa.edu. *Application contact:* Dr. David Brown, Advisor, 918-631-2719, Fax: 918-631-2133, E-mail: david-brown@utulsa.edu.

University of Utah, Graduate School, College of Education, Department of Educational Leadership and Policy, Salt Lake City, UT 84084. Offers educational leadership and policy (Ed D, PhD), including higher education administration (Ed D), K-12 (Ed D); K-12 school administration (M Ed); K-12 teacher instructional leadership (M Ed); student affairs (M Ed); MPA/PhD. *Program availability:* Part-time, evening/weekend. *Faculty:* 11 full-time (7 women), 3 part-time/adjunct (all women). *Students:* 79 full-time (47 women), 134 part-time (95 women); includes 63 minority (7 Black or African American, non-Hispanic/Latino; 2 American Indian or Alaska Native, non-Hispanic/Latino; 7 Asian, non-Hispanic/Latino; 38 Hispanic/Latino; 9 Two or more races, non-Hispanic/Latino), 1 international. Average age 35. 154 applicants, 67% accepted, 86 enrolled. In 2016, 42 master's, 8 doctorates awarded. *Degree requirements:* For master's, comprehensive exam (for some programs), internship, capstone; for doctorate, thesis/dissertation, qualifying exam. *Entrance requirements:* For master's, minimum undergraduate GPA of 3.0, valid bachelor's degree, 3 years' teaching or leadership experience, Level 1 or 2 UT educator's license (for K-12 programs only); for doctorate, GRE General Test (taken with five years of applying), minimum undergraduate GPA of 3.0, valid master's degree. Additional exam requirements/recommendations for international students: Required—TOEFL (minimum score 500 paper-based). *Application deadline:* For fall admission, 1/15 priority date for domestic and international students; for winter admission, 2/1 for domestic and international students; for spring admission, 11/1 priority date for domestic and international students; for summer admission, 3/1 priority date for domestic and international students. Applications are processed on a rolling basis. Application fee: $55 ($65 for international students). Electronic applications accepted. *Expenses:* Contact institution. *Financial support:* In 2016–17, 47 students received support, including 1 fellowship with full tuition reimbursement available (averaging $14,500 per year), 2 research assistantships with full tuition reimbursements available (averaging $15,000 per year), 6 teaching assistantships with full tuition reimbursements available (averaging $15,000 per year); career-related internships or fieldwork, scholarships/grants, health care benefits, and unspecified assistantships also available. Support available to part-time students. Financial award application deadline: 3/1; financial award applicants required to submit FAFSA. *Faculty research:* Education accountability, college student diversity, K-12 educational administration and school leadership, student affairs, higher education. *Unit head:* Dr. Gerardo Lopez, Chair, 801-581-6627, Fax: 801-585-6756, E-mail: gerardo.lopez@utah.edu. *Application contact:* Marilynn S. Howard, Academic Coordinator, 801-581-6714, Fax: 801-585-6756, E-mail: marilynn.howard@utah.edu.
Website: http://elp.utah.edu/

University of Washington, Bothell, Program in Education, Bothell, WA 98011. Offers education (M Ed); leadership development for educators (M Ed); secondary/middle level endorsement (M Ed). *Program availability:* Part-time, evening/weekend. *Degree requirements:* For master's, thesis. *Entrance requirements:* Additional exam requirements/recommendations for international students: Required—TOEFL. Electronic applications accepted. *Faculty research:* Multicultural education in citizenship education, intercultural education, knowledge and practice in the principalship, educational public policy, national board certification for teachers, teacher learning in literacy, technology and its impact on teaching and learning of mathematics, reading assessments, professional development in literacy education and mobility, digital media, education and class.

The University of West Alabama, School of Graduate Studies, College of Education, Departments of Instructional Leadership and Support/Curriculum and Instruction, Program in Secondary Education, Livingston, AL 35470. Offers biology (MAT); English language arts (MAT); high school 6-12 (M Ed); history (MAT); mathematics (MAT); science (MAT); social science (MAT). *Program availability:* Part-time, evening/weekend, 100% online. *Faculty:* 19 full-time (7 women), 7 part-time/adjunct (3 women). *Students:* 236 (159 women); includes 59 minority (53 Black or African American, non-Hispanic/Latino; 2 American Indian or Alaska Native, non-Hispanic/Latino; 1 Asian, non-Hispanic/Latino; 1 Hispanic/Latino; 2 Two or more races, non-Hispanic/Latino). Average age 32. 85 applicants, 88% accepted, 52 enrolled. In 2016, 84 master's awarded. *Degree requirements:* For master's, comprehensive exam, thesis optional. *Entrance requirements:* For master's, GRE General Test, MAT, minimum GPA of 2.75. Additional exam requirements/recommendations for international students: Required—TOEFL (minimum score 500 paper-based; 61 iBT). *Application deadline:* Applications are processed on a rolling basis. Application fee: $40. Electronic applications accepted. *Expenses:* Tuition, state resident: part-time $355 per credit hour. Tuition, nonresident: part-time $710 per credit hour. *Required fees:* $130 per semester. *Financial support:* Teaching assistantships, Federal Work-Study, scholarships/grants, and unspecified assistantships available. Support available to part-time students. Financial award application deadline: 3/1; financial award applicants required to submit FAFSA. *Faculty research:* Integrated arts in the curriculum, moral development of children. *Unit head:* Dr. Jodie Winship, Chair of Curriculum and Instruction, 205-652-5415, Fax: 205-652-3706, E-mail: jwinship@uwa.edu. *Application contact:* Dr. B. J. Kimbrough, Dean of Graduate Studies, 205-652-3647, Fax: 205-652-3706, E-mail: bkimbrough@uwa.edu.
Website: http://www.uwa.edu/highschool612.aspx

University of West Florida, College of Education and Professional Studies, Department of Teacher Education and Educational Leadership, Program in Curriculum and Instruction, Pensacola, FL 32514-5750. Offers elementary education (M Ed); middle level education (M Ed); secondary education (M Ed). *Program availability:* Part-time, evening/weekend. *Entrance requirements:* For master's, GRE (minimum score 450 verbal) or MAT (minimum score 396) if bachelor's GPA less than 3.0, state teaching certification; letter of intent; two professional references. Additional exam requirements/recommendations for international students: Required—TOEFL (minimum score 550 paper-based). *Application deadline:* For fall admission, 6/1 for domestic and international students; for spring admission, 10/1 for domestic and international students. Applications are processed on a rolling basis. Application fee: $30. *Expenses:* Tuition, state resident: full-time $5316.12. Tuition, nonresident: full-time $11,308. *Required fees:* $583.92. Tuition and fees vary according to course load and program. *Financial support:* Career-related internships or fieldwork, Federal Work-Study, scholarships/grants, and tuition waivers (partial) available. Support available to part-time students. Financial award application deadline: 4/15; financial award applicants required to submit FAFSA. *Unit head:* Dr. William H. Evans, Acting Director, 850-474-2892, Fax: 850-474-2844, E-mail: wevans@uwf.edu. *Application contact:* Terry McCray, Assistant Director of Graduate Admissions, 850-473-7718, Fax: 850-473-7714, E-mail: gradadmissions@uwf.edu.

University of West Georgia, College of Education, Carrollton, GA 30118. Offers business education (M Ed); early childhood education (M Ed, Ed S); educational leadership (M Ed, Ed S); media (M Ed, Ed S); professional counseling (M Ed, Ed S); professional counseling and supervision (Ed D); reading instruction (M Ed); school improvement (Ed D); secondary education (M Ed); special education (M Ed, Ed S), including teaching (M Ed); speech language pathology (M Ed); teaching (MAT). *Accreditation:* NCATE. *Program availability:* Part-time, evening/weekend, 100% online, blended/hybrid learning. *Faculty:* 46 full-time (31 women). *Students:* 321 full-time (266 women), 1,007 part-time (813 women); includes 456 minority (389 Black or African American, non-Hispanic/Latino; 1 American Indian or Alaska Native, non-Hispanic/Latino; 13 Asian, non-Hispanic/Latino; 43 Hispanic/Latino; 10 Two or more races, non-Hispanic/Latino), 12 international. Average age 33. 541 applicants, 79% accepted, 305 enrolled. In 2016, 286 master's, 20 doctorates, 156 other advanced degrees awarded. *Entrance requirements:* Additional exam requirements/recommendations for international students: Required—TOEFL (minimum score 523 paper-based; 69 iBT); Recommended—IELTS (minimum score 6.5). *Application deadline:* For fall admission, 7/21 for domestic students, 6/1 for international students; for spring admission, 11/30 for domestic students, 10/15 for international students; for summer admission, 4/15 for domestic students, 3/30 for international students. Applications are processed on a rolling basis. Application fee: $40. Electronic applications accepted. *Expenses:* Tuition, state resident: full-time $5316; part-time $222 per semester hour. Tuition, nonresident: full-time $20,658; part-time $861 per semester hour. *Required fees:* $1962. Tuition and fees vary according to course load, degree level and program. *Financial support:* Fellowships, research assistantships, teaching assistantships, career-related internships or fieldwork, Federal Work-Study, institutionally sponsored loans, scholarships/grants, and unspecified assistantships available. Support available to part-time students. Financial award application deadline: 4/1; financial award applicants required to submit FAFSA. *Unit head:* Dr. Diane Hoff, Dean, College of Education, 678-839-6570, Fax: 678-839-6098, E-mail: dhoff@westga.edu. *Application contact:* Dr. Toby Ziglar, Assistant Dean of the Graduate School, 678-839-1394, Fax: 678-839-1395, E-mail: graduate@westga.edu.
Website: http://www.westga.edu/education/

University of Wisconsin–Eau Claire, College of Education and Human Sciences, Program in Secondary Education, Eau Claire, WI 54702-4004. Offers professional development (ME-PD), including library science, professional development. *Program availability:* Part-time, online learning. *Degree requirements:* For master's, comprehensive exam, thesis, research paper, portfolio or written exam; oral exam. *Entrance requirements:* For master's, certification to teach, minimum GPA of 2.75. Additional exam requirements/recommendations for international students: Required—TOEFL (minimum score 79 iBT).

University of Wisconsin–Stevens Point, College of Fine Arts and Communication, Department of Music, Stevens Point, WI 54481-3897. Offers elementary/secondary (MM Ed); studio pedagogy (MM Ed); Suzuki talent education (MM Ed). *Accreditation:* NASM. *Program availability:* Part-time. *Degree requirements:* For master's, thesis or alternative. *Entrance requirements:* For master's, teaching certificate. *Faculty research:* Music education, music composition, music performance.

Ursuline College, School of Graduate Studies, Master Apprenticeship Program, Pepper Pike, OH 44124-4398. Offers adolescent to young adult education (MA); early childhood education (MA); middle childhood education (MA); special education (MA). *Accreditation:* NCATE. *Degree requirements:* For master's, comprehensive exam. *Entrance requirements:* For master's, minimum undergraduate GPA of 3.0. Additional exam requirements/recommendations for international students: Required—TOEFL (minimum score 500 paper-based). *Application deadline:* For fall admission, 8/1 priority date for domestic students. Applications are processed on a rolling basis. Application fee: $25. Electronic applications accepted. *Expenses:* Contact institution. *Financial support:* Application deadline: 3/1; applicants required to submit FAFSA. *Unit head:* Dr. Mary Jo Cherry, Director, 440-646-8147, Fax: 440-646-8328, E-mail: mcherry@ ursuline.edu. *Application contact:* Stephanie Pratt McRoberts, Graduate Admission Coordinator, 440-646-8119, Fax: 440-684-6138, E-mail: graduateadmissions@ ursuline.edu.
Website: http://www.ursuline.edu/Academics/Graduate_Professional/ Masters_Programs/MAP/index.html

Utah State University, School of Graduate Studies, Emma Eccles Jones College of Education and Human Services, Program in Secondary Education, Logan, UT 84322. Offers M Ed, MA, MS. *Program availability:* Part-time, evening/weekend. *Degree requirements:* For master's, thesis (for some programs). *Entrance requirements:* For master's, GRE General Test or MAT, minimum GPA of 3.0, 1 year teaching, teaching license, letters of recommendation. Additional exam requirements/recommendations for international students: Required—TOEFL. Electronic applications accepted. *Faculty research:* Character education, science education, reading/writing skills, mathematics education, pre-service teacher education.

Valparaiso University, Graduate School and Continuing Education, Department of Education, Program in Initial Licensure, Valparaiso, IN 46383. Offers humane education (M Ed); instructional leadership (M Ed); primary education (M Ed); school psychology (M Ed, Ed S); secondary education (M Ed). *Program availability:* Part-time, evening/ weekend. *Entrance requirements:* For master's, GRE General Test, Pre-Professional Skills Test (PPST), minimum GPA of 3.0. Additional exam requirements/ recommendations for international students: Required—TOEFL (minimum score 550 paper-based; 80 iBT), IELTS (minimum score 6). Electronic applications accepted. *Expenses: Tuition:* Full-time $11,070; part-time $615 per credit hour. *Required fees:* $116 per semester. Tuition and fees vary according to course load, degree level and program.

Vanderbilt University, Peabody College, Department of Teaching and Learning, Nashville, TN 37240-1001. Offers elementary education (M Ed); English language learners (M Ed); learning and design (M Ed); learning, diversity, and urban studies (M Ed); reading education (M Ed); secondary education (M Ed). *Accreditation:* NCATE. *Program availability:* Part-time. *Faculty:* 44 full-time (34 women), 26 part-time/adjunct (21 women). *Students:* 120 full-time (106 women), 26 part-time (18 women); includes 22 minority (9 Black or African American, non-Hispanic/Latino; 6 Asian, non-Hispanic/ Latino; 6 Hispanic/Latino; 1 Two or more races, non-Hispanic/Latino), 44 international. Average age 24. 328 applicants, 73% accepted, 76 enrolled. In 2016, 110 master's awarded. *Degree requirements:* For master's, comprehensive exam, thesis optional. *Entrance requirements:* For master's, GRE General Test, MAT. Additional exam requirements/recommendations for international students: Required—TOEFL (minimum score 550 paper-based; 80 iBT). *Application deadline:* For fall admission, 12/31 priority date for domestic and international students; for spring admission, 11/1 priority date for domestic and international students. Applications are processed on a rolling basis. Application fee: $0. Electronic applications accepted. *Expenses: Tuition:* Part-time $1854 per credit hour. *Financial support:* Fellowships with partial tuition reimbursements, research assistantships with partial tuition reimbursements, teaching assistantships with partial tuition reimbursements, Federal Work-Study, institutionally sponsored loans, scholarships/grants, tuition waivers (partial), and unspecified assistantships available. Support available to part-time students. Financial award application deadline: 1/15; financial award applicants required to submit FAFSA. *Faculty research:* Children's learning and development in core conceptual domains (STEM, English language arts, social studies); classroom discourse structures that teachers can learn and use to support students' learning and development K-6; intervention and design-based research on educational improvement at classroom, school, and district levels; design-based and learning sciences research on relations between learning in schools and other settings. *Unit head:* Dr. Rogers Hall, Chair, 615-322-8100, Fax: 615-322-8999, E-mail: rogers.hall@vanderbilt.edu. *Application contact:* Angela Saylor, Educational Coordinator, 615-322-8092, Fax: 615-322-8999, E-mail: angela.saylor@ vanderbilt.edu.

Villanova University, Graduate School of Liberal Arts and Sciences, Department of Education and Counseling, Villanova, PA 19085-1699. Offers clinical mental health counseling (MS), including counseling and human relations; education (MA); education plus teacher certification (MA); elementary school counseling (MS), including counseling and human relations; secondary school counseling (MS), including counseling and human relations; teacher leadership (MA). *Program availability:* Part-time, evening/ weekend. *Faculty:* 20. *Students:* 81 full-time (67 women), 35 part-time (24 women); includes 18 minority (5 Black or African American, non-Hispanic/Latino; 7 Asian, non-Hispanic/Latino; 6 Hispanic/Latino), 2 international. Average age 30. 71 applicants, 72% accepted, 38 enrolled. In 2016, 47 master's awarded. *Degree requirements:* For master's, comprehensive exam. *Entrance requirements:* For master's, GRE or MAT, minimum GPA of 3.0, statement of goals. Additional exam requirements/ recommendations for international students: Required—TOEFL or IELTS. *Application deadline:* For fall admission, 3/1 priority date for domestic students, 5/1 for international students; for spring admission, 11/15 priority date for domestic students, 10/15 for international students; for summer admission, 5/1 for domestic students. Applications are processed on a rolling basis. Application fee: $50. Electronic applications accepted. *Financial support:* Research assistantships, teaching assistantships, scholarships/ grants, and unspecified assistantships available. Financial award applicants required to submit FAFSA. *Unit head:* Dr. Edward Fierros, Chairperson, 610-519-4625. *Application contact:* Dean, Graduate School of Liberal Arts and Sciences.
Website: http://www.education.villanova.edu/

Wagner College, Division of Graduate Studies, Education Department, Program in Secondary Education/Students with Disabilities, Staten Island, NY 10301-4495. Offers secondary education 7-12 (MS Ed), including language arts, languages other than English, mathematics and technology, science and technology, social studies. *Program availability:* Part-time, evening/weekend. *Degree requirements:* For master's, thesis (for some programs), completion of state certification exams before student teaching. *Entrance requirements:* For master's, minimum GPA of 3.0, interview, recommendations. Electronic applications accepted. Tuition and fees vary according to degree level.

Wake Forest University, Graduate School of Arts and Sciences, Department of Education, Winston-Salem, NC 27106. Offers secondary education (MA Ed). *Accreditation:* ACA; NCATE. *Faculty:* 8 full-time (4 women). *Students:* 12 full-time (5 women); includes 2 minority (1 Black or African American, non-Hispanic/Latino; 1 Native Hawaiian or other Pacific Islander, non-Hispanic/Latino). Average age 24. 24 applicants, 71% accepted, 12 enrolled. In 2016, 11 master's awarded. *Degree requirements:* For master's, thesis optional. *Entrance requirements:* For master's, GRE General Test. Additional exam requirements/recommendations for international students: Required—TOEFL (minimum score 550 paper-based). *Application deadline:* For fall admission, 1/ 15 for domestic students, 1/15 priority date for international students. Application fee: $75. Electronic applications accepted. *Expenses:* Contact institution. *Financial support:* In 2016–17, 12 students received support, including 8 fellowships with full tuition reimbursements available (averaging $49,000 per year), 3 teaching assistantships with full tuition reimbursements available (averaging $49,000 per year); scholarships/grants and tuition waivers (full and partial) also available. Financial award application deadline: 2/15. *Faculty research:* Teaching and learning. *Unit head:* Dr. Adam Friedman, Chair, 336-758-5507, Fax: 336-758-4591, E-mail: amfriedman@wfu.edu. *Application contact:* Dr. Leah McCoy, Program Director, 336-758-5498, Fax: 336-758-4591, E-mail: mccoy@ wfu.edu.
Website: http://college.wfu.edu/education/graduate-program/overview-of-graduate-programs/

Washington State University, College of Education, Department of Teaching and Learning, Pullman, WA 99164-2132. Offers cultural studies and social thought in education (PhD); curriculum and instruction (Ed M, MA); English language learners (Ed M, MA); language, literacy and technology (PhD); literacy education (Ed M, MA); mathematics education (PhD); special education (Ed M, MA, PhD); teacher leadership (Ed D); teaching (MIT), including elementary education, secondary education. Programs offered at the Pullman, Spokane, Tri-cities, Vancouver and Global (online) campuses. *Program availability:* Part-time, online learning. *Degree requirements:* For master's, comprehensive exam, thesis, oral or written exam; for doctorate, comprehensive exam, thesis/dissertation, oral and written exam. *Entrance requirements:* For master's, GRE General Test, minimum GPA of 3.0, 3 letters of recommendation, letter of intent, transcripts, resume/curriculum vitae; for doctorate, GRE General Test, minimum GPA of 3.0, 3 letters of recommendation, letter of intent, transcripts, writing sample, resume/ curriculum vitae. Additional exam requirements/recommendations for international students: Required—TOEFL (minimum score 550 paper-based; 80 iBT). Electronic applications accepted. *Faculty research:* Intersection of gender, youth cultures and schooling; examination of ideology of power in children's literature; early childhood special education; analyzing pre-service and in-service teacher development; second language acquisition.

Washington University in St. Louis, The Graduate School, Department of Education, Program in Secondary Education, St. Louis, MO 63130-4899. Offers MAT. *Degree requirements:* For master's, thesis or alternative. *Entrance requirements:* For master's, GRE General Test or MAT. Additional exam requirements/recommendations for international students: Required—TOEFL. Electronic applications accepted.

Wayland Baptist University, Graduate Programs, Program in Education, Plainview, TX 79072-6998. Offers education administration (M Ed); education diagnostics (M Ed); education literacy (M Ed); elementary certification (M Ed); English (M Ed); English as a second language (M Ed); higher education administration (M Ed); human resources (M Ed); instructional leadership (M Ed); instructional technology (M Ed); leadership training and development (M Ed); science education (M Ed); secondary certification (M Ed); social studies (M Ed); special education (M Ed); sports administration and management (M Ed). *Program availability:* Part-time, evening/weekend, online learning. *Degree requirements:* For master's, comprehensive exam, capstone course. *Entrance requirements:* For master's, GRE, GMAT or MAT. Additional exam requirements/ recommendations for international students: Required—TOEFL (minimum score 500 paper-based; 61 iBT). Electronic applications accepted.

Wayne State University, College of Education, Division of Teacher Education, Detroit, MI 48202. Offers art education (M Ed); bilingual/bicultural education (M Ed, Certificate); career and technical education (M Ed); curriculum and instruction (Ed D, PhD, Ed S), including art education (Ed D, PhD), bilingual education (Ed D, Ed S), career and technical education (MAT, Ed D, PhD, Ed S), early childhood education (MAT, Ed D, PhD, Ed S), elementary education, English as a second language (MAT, Ed D, Ed S), English education (MAT, Ed D, PhD, Ed S), foreign language education (MAT, Ed D, PhD), K-12 curriculum, mathematics education (MAT, Ed D, PhD, Ed S), science education (MAT, Ed D, PhD, Ed S), secondary education, social studies education (MAT, Ed D, PhD, Ed S); early childhood education (M Ed); elementary education (M Ed, MAT), including bilingual/bicultural education (MAT), early childhood education (MAT, Ed D, PhD, Ed S), English as a second language (MAT, Ed D, Ed S), general elementary education (MAT), mathematics education (MAT, Ed D, PhD, Ed S), science education (MAT, Ed D, PhD, Ed S), social studies education (MAT, Ed D, PhD, Ed S); English as a second language (Certificate); English education (M Ed); foreign language education (M Ed); mathematics education (M Ed); reading (M Ed, Ed S); reading, language and literature (Ed D); science education (M Ed); secondary education (MAT), including art education (K-12), bilingual/bicultural education, career and technical education (MAT, Ed D, PhD, Ed S), English as a second language (MAT, Ed D, Ed S), English education (MAT, Ed D, PhD, Ed S), foreign language education (MAT, Ed D, PhD), kinesiology, mathematics education (MAT, Ed D, PhD, Ed S); social studies education (M Ed); special education (M Ed, MAT, Ed D, PhD, Ed S), including autism spectrum disorders (MAT), cognitive development (MAT), emotional impairment (MAT), learning disabilities (MAT). *Program availability:* Part-time, blended/hybrid learning. *Faculty:* 29. *Students:* 106 full-time (73 women), 351 part-time (276 women); includes 115 minority (76 Black or African American, non-Hispanic/Latino; 10 Asian, non-Hispanic/Latino; 20 Hispanic/Latino; 1 Native Hawaiian or other Pacific Islander, non-Hispanic/Latino; 8 Two or more races, non-Hispanic/Latino), 12 international. Average age 37. 242 applicants, 37% accepted, 72 enrolled. In 2016, 178 master's, 19 doctorates, 17 other advanced degrees awarded. *Degree requirements:* For master's, essay or project (for some M Ed programs), professional field experience (for MAT programs); for doctorate, thesis/dissertation. *Entrance requirements:* For master's, Michigan Test for Teacher Certification, verification of participation in group work with children, Michigan State Police criminal background check; for doctorate, minimum undergraduate GPA of 3.0, graduate 3.5; interview; curriculum vitae; references. Additional exam requirements/recommendations for international students: Required—TOEFL (minimum score 550 paper-based; 79 iBT), TWE (minimum score 5.5), Michigan English Language Assessment Battery (minimum score 85); Recommended—IELTS (minimum score 6.5). *Application deadline:* For fall admission, 6/1 priority date for domestic students, 5/1 priority date for international students; for winter admission, 10/1 priority date for domestic students, 9/1 priority date for international students; for spring admission, 2/1 priority date for domestic students, 1/1 priority date for international students. Applications are processed on a rolling basis. Application fee: $50. Electronic applications accepted. *Expenses:* $16,503 per year resident tuition and fees, $33,697 per year non-resident tuition and fees. *Financial support:* In 2016–17, 101 students received support, including 3 fellowships (averaging $11,409 per year); research assistantships with tuition reimbursements available, Federal Work-Study, scholarships/ grants, and unspecified assistantships also available. Support available to part-time students. Financial award applicants required to submit FAFSA. *Faculty research:* Improving students' skill achievement in mathematics, improving elementary children's

understanding of informational text, teachers' use of their pedagogical and mathematical knowledge in the interactive work of teaching, the intersection of identity construction in teaching and learning, identifying effective methods of literacy instruction and assessments for bilingual students in elementary language arts classrooms. *Unit head:* Dr. Kathleen Crawford-McKinney, Assistant Dean, 313-577-0122. *Application contact:* Janice Green, Assistant Dean, 313-577-1605, E-mail: jwgreen@wayne.edu.
Website: http://coe.wayne.edu/ted/index.php

Webster University, School of Education, Department of Multidisciplinary Studies, St. Louis, MO 63119-3194. Offers applied educational psychology (MA, Ed S); communication arts (MA); early childhood education (MA, MAT); education and innovation (MA); educational technology (MET); elementary education (MAT); mathematics for educators (MA); middle school education (MAT); multidisciplinary studies (MAT); multimodal literacy for global impact (MA); reading (MA); secondary school education (MAT); special education (MA, MAT); teaching English as a second language (MA); transformative learning in the global community (Ed S). *Program availability:* Part-time. *Entrance requirements:* For master's, minimum GPA of 2.5. Additional exam requirements/recommendations for international students: Required—TOEFL. *Application deadline:* Applications are processed on a rolling basis. Application fee: $35 ($50 for international students). *Expenses: Tuition:* Full-time $21,900; part-time $730 per credit hour. Tuition and fees vary according to campus/location and program. *Financial support:* Federal Work-Study available. Support available to part-time students. Financial award application deadline: 4/1; financial award applicants required to submit FAFSA. *Unit head:* Dr. Deborah Stiles, Chair, 314-968-7056, Fax: 314-968-7118, E-mail: stilesda@webster.edu.

West Chester University of Pennsylvania, College of Education and Social Work, Department of Professional and Secondary Education, West Chester, PA 19383. Offers education for sustainability (Certificate); educational technology (Certificate); entrepreneurial education (Certificate); transformative education and social change (MS). *Program availability:* Part-time. *Faculty:* 10 full-time (3 women). *Students:* 6 full-time (5 women), 35 part-time (22 women); includes 2 minority (1 Hispanic/Latino; 1 Two or more races, non-Hispanic/Latino). Average age 30. 24 applicants, 88% accepted, 17 enrolled. In 2016, 7 master's, 3 other advanced degrees awarded. *Degree requirements:* For master's, comprehensive exam (for some programs), thesis, 36 credits. *Entrance requirements:* For master's, teaching certification (strongly recommended); for Certificate, minimum GPA of 3.0. Additional exam requirements/recommendations for international students: Required—TOEFL or IELTS. *Application deadline:* For fall admission, 5/15 for international students; for spring admission, 10/15 for international students. Applications are processed on a rolling basis. Application fee: $50. Electronic applications accepted. *Expenses:* Tuition, state resident: full-time $8694; part-time $483 per credit. Tuition, nonresident: full-time $13,050; part-time $725 per credit. *Required fees:* $2399; $119.05 per credit. Tuition and fees vary according to campus/location and program. *Financial support:* Scholarships/grants and unspecified assistantships available. Financial award application deadline: 2/15; financial award applicants required to submit FAFSA. *Faculty research:* Technology integration: preparing our teachers for the twenty-first century, critical pedagogy. *Unit head:* Dr. John Elmore, Chair, 610-436-6934, Fax: 610-436-3102, E-mail: jelmore@wcupa.edu. *Application contact:* Dr. Matthew Kruger-Ross, Graduate Coordinator, 610-436-2106, Fax: 610-436-3102, E-mail: mkruger-ross@wcupa.edu.
Website: http://www.wcupa.edu/education-socialWork/profsecedu/

Western Kentucky University, Graduate Studies, College of Education and Behavioral Sciences, School of Teacher Education, Bowling Green, KY 42101. Offers elementary education (MAE, Ed S); exceptional education: learning and behavioral disorders (MAE); exceptional education: moderate and severe disabilities (MAE); instructional design (MS); interdisciplinary early childhood education (MAE); library media education (MS); literacy education (MAE); middle grades education (MAE); secondary education (MAE, Ed S). *Program availability:* Part-time, evening/weekend, online learning. *Degree requirements:* For master's, comprehensive exam. *Entrance requirements:* For master's, GRE General Test. Additional exam requirements/recommendations for international students: Required—TOEFL (minimum score 555 paper-based; 79 iBT). *Faculty research:* Teacher preparation in moderate/severe disabilities.

Western New Mexico University, Graduate Division, School of Education, Silver City, NM 88062-0680. Offers bilingual education (MAT); educational leadership (MA); elementary education (MAT); reading (MAT); secondary education (MAT); special education (MAT); TESOL (teaching English to speakers of other languages) (MAT). *Accreditation:* NCATE. *Program availability:* Part-time, online learning. *Degree requirements:* For master's, comprehensive exam. *Entrance requirements:* For master's, minimum GPA of 3.0 in last 64 hours of undergraduate study. Additional exam requirements/recommendations for international students: Required—TOEFL (minimum score 550 paper-based; 79 iBT). Electronic applications accepted. *Faculty research:* International education, electronic reading assessment, developing STEM teachers.

Western Oregon University, Graduate Programs, College of Education, Division of Teacher Education, Program in Secondary Education, Monmouth, OR 97361. Offers bilingual education (MS Ed); health (MS Ed); humanities (MAT, MS Ed); initial licensure (MAT); mathematics (MAT, MS Ed); science (MAT, MS Ed); social science (MAT, MS Ed). *Accreditation:* NCATE. *Program availability:* Part-time, evening/weekend. *Degree requirements:* For master's, thesis optional, written exam. *Entrance requirements:* For master's, minimum GPA of 3.0, teaching license. Additional exam requirements/recommendations for international students: Required—TOEFL (minimum score 550 paper-based; 79 iBT), IELTS (minimum score 6.5). *Faculty research:* Literacy, science in primary grades, geography education, retention, teacher burnout.

Western Washington University, Graduate School, Woodring College of Education, Department of Secondary Education, Bellingham, WA 98225-5996. Offers MIT. *Accreditation:* NCATE. *Program availability:* Part-time. *Degree requirements:* For master's, comprehensive exam, thesis optional. *Entrance requirements:* For master's, GRE General Test or MAT, minimum GPA of 3.0 in last 60 semester hours or last 90 quarter hours, secondary teaching certification. Additional exam requirements/recommendations for international students: Required—TOEFL (minimum score 567 paper-based). Electronic applications accepted. *Faculty research:* Service learning, controversial issues in classroom, trauma-sensitive teaching-learning, measuring a teacher's "withitness".

Westfield State University, College of Graduate and Continuing Education, Department of Education, Programs in Secondary Education, Westfield, MA 01086. Offers biology teacher education (M Ed), including secondary education-biology; chemistry teacher education (M Ed), including secondary education-chemistry; general science teacher education (M Ed), including secondary education-general science; history teacher education (M Ed), including secondary education-history; mathematics teacher education (M Ed), including secondary education-mathematics; physical education teacher education (M Ed), including secondary education-physical education. *Accreditation:* NCATE. *Program availability:* Part-time, evening/weekend. *Students:* 12 full-time (2 women), 48 part-time (24 women); includes 2 minority (1 Black or African American, non-Hispanic/Latino; 1 Two or more races, non-Hispanic/Latino). Average age 27. 16 applicants, 88% accepted, 11 enrolled. In 2016, 17 master's awarded. *Degree requirements:* For master's, comprehensive exam, practicum. *Entrance requirements:* For master's, GRE General Test or MAT, minimum undergraduate GPA of 2.8. Additional exam requirements/recommendations for international students: Recommended—TOEFL (minimum score 550 paper-based; 79 iBT). *Application deadline:* For fall admission, 6/30 for domestic students; for spring admission, 10/31 for domestic students; for summer admission, 3/31 for domestic students. Applications are processed on a rolling basis. Application fee: $50. *Expenses:* Tuition, state resident: part-time $318 per semester hour. Tuition, nonresident: part-time $318 per semester hour. *Required fees:* $75 per semester. Tuition and fees vary according to course load and program. *Financial support:* Unspecified assistantships and SOS scholarships for education majors only available. Financial award application deadline: 3/1; financial award applicants required to submit FAFSA. *Unit head:* Dr. Sandra Berkowitz, Chair, 413-572-5323. *Application contact:* Shelly Henrichon, Coordinator of DGCE Admissions, 413-572-8022, Fax: 413-572-5227, E-mail: mhenrichon@westfield.ma.edu.

West Virginia University, College of Education and Human Services, Department of Curriculum and Instruction/Literacy Studies, Program in Secondary Education, Morgantown, WV 26506. Offers higher education curriculum and teaching (MA); secondary education (MA). Students enter program as undergraduates. *Accreditation:* NCATE. *Program availability:* Part-time. *Degree requirements:* For master's, thesis optional, content exams. *Entrance requirements:* For master's, minimum GPA of 2.75. Additional exam requirements/recommendations for international students: Required—TOEFL. Electronic applications accepted. *Faculty research:* Teacher education, school reform, curriculum development, education technology.

West Virginia University, Eberly College of Arts and Sciences, Department of Mathematics, Morgantown, WV 26506. Offers applied mathematics (MS, PhD); discrete mathematics (PhD); interdisciplinary mathematics (MS); mathematics for secondary education (MS); pure mathematics (MS). *Program availability:* Part-time. Terminal master's awarded for partial completion of doctoral program. *Degree requirements:* For master's, comprehensive exam (for some programs), thesis optional; for doctorate, one foreign language, comprehensive exam, thesis/dissertation. *Entrance requirements:* For master's, GRE Subject Test (recommended), minimum GPA of 2.5; for doctorate, GRE Subject Test (recommended), master's degree in mathematics. Additional exam requirements/recommendations for international students: Required—TOEFL (paper-based 550) or IELTS (6). *Faculty research:* Combinatorics and graph theory, differential equations, applied and computational mathematics.

Wheaton College, Graduate School, Department of Education, Wheaton, IL 60187-5593. Offers elementary education (MAT); secondary education (MAT). *Accreditation:* NCATE. *Faculty:* 1 full-time (0 women). *Students:* 14 full-time (10 women); includes 2 minority (both Asian, non-Hispanic/Latino). Average age 25. 11 applicants, 100% accepted, 8 enrolled. In 2016, 10 master's awarded. *Degree requirements:* For master's, thesis or alternative. *Entrance requirements:* For master's, GRE General Test or MAT. Additional exam requirements/recommendations for international students: Required—TOEFL (minimum score 550 paper-based; 80 iBT), IELTS (minimum score 6.5). *Application deadline:* For fall admission, 5/1 for domestic students, 1/1 for international students; for spring admission, 11/1 for domestic students. Applications are processed on a rolling basis. Application fee: $30. Electronic applications accepted. *Expenses: Tuition:* Full-time $19,080; part-time $795 per credit hour. Tuition and fees vary according to degree level and program. *Financial support:* Career-related internships or fieldwork and Federal Work-Study available. Financial award application deadline: 3/1; financial award applicants required to submit FAFSA. *Unit head:* Dr. Paul Egeland, Chair, 630-752-5041. *Application contact:* Dusty Di Santo, Director of Graduate Admissions, 630-752-5195, Fax: 630-752-7047, E-mail: graduate.admissions@wheaton.edu.
Website: http://www.wheaton.edu/academics/departments/education

Whittier College, Graduate Programs, Department of Education and Child Development, Program in Secondary Education, Whittier, CA 90608-0634. Offers MA Ed. *Program availability:* Part-time, evening/weekend. *Degree requirements:* For master's, thesis. *Entrance requirements:* For master's, GRE General Test, MAT.

Whitworth University, School of Education, Graduate Studies in Education, Spokane, WA 99251-0001. Offers administration (M Ed); counseling (M Ed), including school counselors, social agency/church setting; elementary education (M Ed); gifted and talented (MAT); secondary education (M Ed); special education (MAT); teaching (MIT). *Accreditation:* NCATE. *Program availability:* Part-time, evening/weekend. *Degree requirements:* For master's, comprehensive exam, thesis (for some programs). *Entrance requirements:* For master's, GRE General Test, MAT. Additional exam requirements/recommendations for international students: Required—TOEFL. *Faculty research:* Rural program development, mainstreaming, special needs learners.

Wichita State University, Graduate School, College of Education, Department of Curriculum and Instruction, Wichita, KS 67260. Offers learning and instructional design (M Ed); special education (M Ed), including early childhood (M Ed, MAT), gifted, high incidence, low incidence; teaching (MAT), including early childhood (M Ed, MAT), middle level/secondary, transition to teaching. *Accreditation:* NCATE. *Program availability:* Part-time, evening/weekend, 100% online, blended/hybrid learning. *Entrance requirements:* For master's, MAT, minimum GPA of 2.75. *Unit head:* Dr. Kimberly McDowell, Department Head, 316-978-3322, E-mail: kim.mcdowell@wichita.edu. *Application contact:* Jordan Oleson, Admission Coordinator, 316-978-3095, Fax: 316-978-3253, E-mail: jordan.oleson@wichita.edu.

William Carey University, School of Education, Hattiesburg, MS 39401-5499. Offers art education (M Ed); art of teaching (M Ed); elementary education (M Ed, Ed S); English education (M Ed); gifted education (M Ed); history and social science (M Ed); mild/moderate disabilities (M Ed); secondary education (M Ed). *Accreditation:* NCATE. *Program availability:* Part-time. *Degree requirements:* For master's, comprehensive exam. *Entrance requirements:* For master's, GRE, MAT, minimum GPA of 2.5, Class A teacher's license. Additional exam requirements/recommendations for international students: Required—TOEFL (minimum score 550 paper-based).

William Paterson University of New Jersey, College of Education, Wayne, NJ 07470-8420. Offers curriculum and learning (M Ed); educational leadership (M Ed); elementary education (MAT); literacy (M Ed); professional counseling (M Ed); secondary education (MAT); special education (M Ed). *Accreditation:* NCATE. *Program availability:* Part-time, evening/weekend. *Faculty:* 36 full-time (25 women), 32 part-time/adjunct (27 women). *Students:* 74 full-time (51 women), 607 part-time (515 women); includes 194 minority (42 Black or African American, non-Hispanic/Latino; 21 Asian, non-Hispanic/Latino; 116 Hispanic/Latino; 15 Two or more races, non-Hispanic/Latino), 1 international. Average age 35. 390 applicants, 83% accepted, 263 enrolled. In 2016, 170 master's awarded. *Degree requirements:* For master's, comprehensive exam, thesis (for some programs), exit interview (for some programs); practicum/internship; minimum GPA of 3.0 (for some programs); exit portfolio (for some programs). *Entrance requirements:* For master's, GRE/MAT, minimum GPA of 2.75; teaching certificate; essay; interview; 2 letters of recommendation; personal statement. Additional exam requirements/recommendations for international students: Required—TOEFL (minimum score 550 paper-based; 79 iBT), IELTS (minimum score 6). *Application deadline:* For fall admission, 8/1 for domestic students, 4/1 for international students; for spring admission, 12/1 for domestic students, 11/1 for international students; for summer admission, 5/1 for domestic students, 2/1 for

international students. Applications are processed on a rolling basis. Application fee: $50. Electronic applications accepted. *Expenses:* Tuition, state resident: full-time $12,480; part-time $611 per credit. Tuition, nonresident: full-time $20,263; part-time $992 per credit. *Required fees:* $1573; $77 per credit. Tuition and fees vary according to course load, degree level and program. *Financial support:* Career-related internships or fieldwork, Federal Work-Study, scholarships/grants, and unspecified assistantships available. Support available to part-time students. Financial award application deadline: 4/1; financial award applicants required to submit FAFSA. *Faculty research:* History of education, social media in classrooms and education, integrating environmental lessons into urban classrooms, minority student self-advocacy in higher education, factors affecting high school teacher retention. *Total annual research expenditures:* $289,197. *Unit head:* Dr. Candace Burns, Dean, 973-720-2137, Fax: 973-720-3467, E-mail: burnsc@wpunj.edu. *Application contact:* Liana Fornarotto, Director of Education Enrollment and Certification, 973-720-2206, Fax: 973-720-2989, E-mail: fornarottol@wpunj.edu.
Website: http://www.wpunj.edu/coe

Wilmington University, College of Education, New Castle, DE 19720-6491. Offers applied technology in education (M Ed); career and technical education (M Ed); educational leadership (Ed D); elementary and secondary school counseling (M Ed); elementary studies (M Ed); ESOL literacy (M Ed); higher education leadership (Ed D); instruction: gifted and talented (M Ed); instruction: teacher of reading (M Ed); instruction: teaching and learning (M Ed); organizational leadership (Ed D); school leadership (M Ed); secondary education (MAT); special education (M Ed). *Accreditation:* NCATE. *Program availability:* Part-time, evening/weekend. *Faculty:* 19 full-time (11 women), 178 part-time/adjunct (99 women). *Students:* 248 full-time (176 women), 999 part-time (738 women); includes 244 minority (193 Black or African American, non-Hispanic/Latino; 17 American Indian or Alaska Native, non-Hispanic/Latino; 9 Asian, non-Hispanic/Latino; 19 Hispanic/Latino; 2 Native Hawaiian or other Pacific Islander, non-Hispanic/Latino; 4 Two or more races, non-Hispanic/Latino), 7 international. Average age 34. 672 applicants, 96% accepted, 348 enrolled. In 2016, 529 master's, 87 doctorates awarded. *Entrance requirements:* For master's, 2 letters of recommendation, interview. Additional exam requirements/recommendations for international students: Required—TOEFL (minimum score 500 paper-based). *Application deadline:* For fall admission, 4/30 for domestic students. Applications are processed on a rolling basis. Application fee: $35. Electronic applications accepted. *Expenses: Tuition:* Full-time $8388; part-time $466 per credit. *Required fees:* $25 per semester. Tuition and fees vary according to degree level. *Financial support:* Applicants required to submit FAFSA. *Unit head:* Dr. John C. Gray, Dean. *Application contact:* Laura Morris, Director of Admissions, 877-967-5464, E-mail: infocenter@wilmu.edu.
Website: http://www.wilmu.edu/education/

Wilson College, Graduate Programs, Chambersburg, PA 17201-1285. Offers accounting (M Acc); choreography and visual art (MFA); education (M Ed); healthcare management for sustainability (MHM); humanities (MA), including art and culture, critical/cultural theory, English language and literature, women's studies; management (MSM); nursing (MSN), including nursing education, nursing leadership and management. *Program availability:* Evening/weekend. *Degree requirements:* For master's, project. *Entrance requirements:* For master's, PRAXIS, minimum undergraduate cumulative GPA of 3.0, 2 letters of recommendation, current certification for eligibility to teach in grades K-12, resume, personal interview. Electronic applications accepted.

Winthrop University, College of Education, Program in Secondary Education, Rock Hill, SC 29733. Offers M Ed. *Accreditation:* NCATE. *Program availability:* Part-time. *Entrance requirements:* For master's, PRAXIS, minimum GPA of 3.0, South Carolina Class III Teaching Certificate. Additional exam requirements/recommendations for international students: Required—TOEFL (minimum score 550 paper-based; 79 iBT), IELTS (minimum score 6). Electronic applications accepted. *Expenses:* Tuition, state resident: full-time $14,312; part-time $599 per credit hour. Tuition, nonresident: full-time $27,570; part-time $1153 per credit hour.

Worcester State University, Graduate Studies, Department of Education, Program in Secondary Education, Worcester, MA 01602-2597. Offers M Ed, CAGS, Ed S, Postbaccalaureate Certificate. *Program availability:* Part-time. *Faculty:* 13 full-time (12 women), 16 part-time/adjunct (7 women). *Students:* 4 full-time (3 women), 72 part-time (38 women); includes 9 minority (2 Black or African American, non-Hispanic/Latino; 1 Asian, non-Hispanic/Latino; 4 Hispanic/Latino; 2 Two or more races, non-Hispanic/Latino), 1 international. Average age 33. 68 applicants, 79% accepted, 29 enrolled. In 2016, 6 master's, 23 CAGSs awarded. *Degree requirements:* For master's, comprehensive exam, thesis, portfolio. *Entrance requirements:* For master's, GRE General Test or MAT, secondary school license (grades 8-12) from Commonwealth of Massachusetts in relevant field of licensure; evidence of undergraduate or graduate course in adolescent/developmental psychology with minimum B grade or CLEP exam in human growth and development (minimum score of 50); for other advanced degree, MTEL in content area (for Postbaccalaureate Certificate), M Ed or master's degree in related field with minimum GPA of 3.0 (for CAGS); evidence of an undergraduate or graduate course in adolescent/developmental psychology with minimum B grade or CLEP exam in human growth and development with minimum score of 50 (for Post-Baccalaureate Certificate). Additional exam requirements/recommendations for international students: Required—TOEFL (minimum score 550 paper-based; 79 iBT). *Application deadline:* For fall admission, 6/15 for domestic and international students; for spring admission, 11/1 for domestic and international students; for summer admission, 4/1 for domestic and international students. Applications are processed on a rolling basis. Application fee: $50. Electronic applications accepted. *Expenses:* Tuition, state resident: part-time $150 per credit. Tuition, nonresident: part-time $150 per credit. *Financial support:* Career-related internships or fieldwork, scholarships/grants, and unspecified assistantships available. Financial award application deadline: 3/1; financial award applicants required to submit FAFSA. *Unit head:* Dr. Sara Young, Coordinator, 508-929-8246, E-mail: syoung3@worcester.edu. *Application contact:* Sara Grady, Associate Dean for Graduate Studies and Professional Development, 508-929-8787, Fax: 508-929-8100, E-mail: sara.grady@worcester.edu.

Wright State University, Graduate School, College of Education and Human Services, Department of Teacher Education, Programs in Classroom Teacher Education, Dayton, OH 45435. Offers M Ed, MA. *Accreditation:* NCATE. *Degree requirements:* For master's, thesis (for some programs). *Entrance requirements:* For master's, GRE General Test, MAT, PRAXIS II. Additional exam requirements/recommendations for international students: Required—TOEFL. Application fee: $25. *Expenses:* Tuition, state resident: full-time $9952; part-time $622 per credit hour. Tuition, nonresident: full-time $16,960; part-time $1060 per credit hour. *Financial support:* Available to part-time students. Applicants required to submit FAFSA. *Unit head:* Dr. Colleen A. Finegan, Chair, 937-775-2332, Fax: 937-775-3308, E-mail: colleen.finegan@wright.edu. *Application contact:* John Kimble, Associate Director of Graduate Admissions and Records, 937-775-2957, Fax: 937-775-2453, E-mail: john.kimble@wright.edu.

Xavier University, College of Social Sciences, Health and Education, School of Education, Department of Secondary and Special Education, Cincinnati, OH 45207. Offers secondary education (M Ed); special education (M Ed). *Entrance requirements:* Additional exam requirements/recommendations for international students: Required—TOEFL (minimum score 550 paper-based; 79 iBT). Application fee is waived when completed online. *Expenses:* Contact institution.

Youngstown State University, Graduate School, Beeghly College of Education, Department of Teacher Education, Program in Middle Childhood Education, Youngstown, OH 44555-0001. Offers MS Ed. *Accreditation:* NCATE. *Program availability:* Part-time, evening/weekend. *Degree requirements:* For master's, comprehensive exam, thesis optional. *Entrance requirements:* For master's, GRE, MAT, or teaching certificate; minimum GPA of 2.7. Additional exam requirements/recommendations for international students: Required—TOEFL. *Faculty research:* Critical reflectivity, gender issues in classroom instruction, collaborative research and analysis, literacy methodology.

Section 25
Special Focus

This section contains a directory of institutions offering graduate work in special focus. Additional information about programs listed in the directory may be obtained by writing directly to the dean of a graduate school or chair of a department at the address given in the directory.

For programs offering related work, see also in this book *Administration, Instruction, and Theory; Education; Instructional Levels; Leisure Studies and Recreation; Physical Education and Kinesiology;* and *Subject Areas.* In other guides in this series:

Graduate Programs in the Humanities, Arts & Social Sciences
See *Psychology and Counseling (School Psychology)* and *Public, Regional, and Industrial Affairs (Urban Studies)*

Graduate Programs in the Biological/Biomedical Sciences and Health-Related Medical Professions
See *Health-Related Professions*

CONTENTS

Program Directories

Featured School: Display and Close-Up

See:

Education of Students with Severe/Multiple Disabilities

Cleveland State University, College of Graduate Studies, College of Education and Human Services, Department of Curriculum and Foundations, Cleveland, OH 44115. Offers art education (M Ed); early childhood education (M Ed); foreign language education (M Ed); middle childhood mathematics and science education (M Ed); special education (M Ed), including mild/moderate disabilities, moderate/intensive disabilities; teaching English to speakers of other languages (M Ed). *Program availability:* Part-time, evening/weekend. *Faculty:* 19 full-time (14 women), 32 part-time/adjunct (27 women). *Students:* 86 full-time (65 women), 369 part-time (301 women); includes 119 minority (89 Black or African American, non-Hispanic/Latino; 1 American Indian or Alaska Native, non-Hispanic/Latino; 2 Asian, non-Hispanic/Latino; 16 Hispanic/Latino; 11 Two or more races, non-Hispanic/Latino), 35 international. Average age 34. 177 applicants, 55% accepted, 68 enrolled. In 2016, 179 master's awarded. *Degree requirements:* For master's, comprehensive exam (for some programs), thesis or alternative. *Entrance requirements:* For master's, GRE General Test or MAT, minimum GPA of 2.75. Additional exam requirements/recommendations for international students: Required—TOEFL (minimum score 550 paper-based; 78 iBT), IELTS (minimum score 6). *Application deadline:* For fall admission, 7/1 priority date for domestic students, 5/15 for international students; for spring admission, 11/15 for domestic students, 11/1 for international students; for summer admission, 4/1 for domestic students, 3/15 for international students. Applications are processed on a rolling basis. Application fee: $30. *Expenses:* Tuition, state resident: full-time $9565. Tuition, nonresident: full-time $17,980. Tuition and fees vary according to program. *Financial support:* In 2016–17, 13 research assistantships with full tuition reimbursements (averaging $15,845 per year) were awarded; tuition waivers (partial) and unspecified assistantships also available. Financial award application deadline: 2/15; financial award applicants required to submit FAFSA. *Faculty research:* Early childhood education, literacy education, special education: mild/moderate, moderate/intensive, early childhood intervention specialist), teaching English to speakers of other languages (TESOL). *Total annual research expenditures:* $275,907. *Unit head:* Dr. Tachelle I. Banks, Chairperson, 216-687-4608, Fax: 216-687-5379, E-mail: t.i.banks@csuohio.edu. *Application contact:* Michael Almony, Senior Student Services Specialist, 216-875-9929, Fax: 216-687-5491, E-mail: m.almony@csuohio.edu.
Website: http://www.csuohio.edu/cehs/te/te

Georgia State University, College of Education and Human Development, Department of Educational Psychology, Special Education, and Communication Disorders, Program in Multiple and Severe Disabilities, Atlanta, GA 30302-3083. Offers early childhood special education (M Ed); special education adapted curriculum (intellectual disabilities) (M Ed); special education deaf education (M Ed); special education general and adapted curriculum (autism spectrum disorders) (M Ed); special education physical and health disabilities (orthopedic impairments) (M Ed). *Accreditation:* NCATE. *Program availability:* Part-time. *Degree requirements:* For master's, variable foreign language requirement, comprehensive exam, thesis (for some programs). *Entrance requirements:* For master's, GRE. Additional exam requirements/recommendations for international students: Required—TOEFL (minimum score 550 paper-based; 79 iBT) or IELTS (minimum score 6.5). *Application deadline:* For fall admission, 6/1 for domestic and international students; for winter admission, 11/1 for domestic and international students; for spring admission, 5/1 for domestic and international students. Application fee: $50. Electronic applications accepted. *Expenses:* Tuition, state resident: full-time $6876; part-time $382 per credit hour. Tuition, nonresident: full-time $22,374; part-time $1243 per credit hour. *Required fees:* $2128; $1064 per term. Part-time tuition and fees vary according to course load and program. *Financial support:* In 2016–17, fellowships with full tuition reimbursements (averaging $25,000 per year), research assistantships with full tuition reimbursements (averaging $2,000 per year) were awarded; teaching assistantships with full tuition reimbursements, scholarships/grants, health care benefits, and unspecified assistantships also available. *Faculty research:* Literacy, language, behavioral supports. *Unit head:* Dr. Kathryn Wolff Heller, Professor, 404-413-8040, E-mail: kheller@gsu.edu. *Application contact:* Sandy Vaughn, Senior Administrative Coordinator, 404-413-8318, Fax: 404-413-8043, E-mail: svaughn@gsu.edu.

Hunter College of the City University of New York, Graduate School, School of Education, Department of Special Education, New York, NY 10065-5085. Offers blind and visually impaired (MS Ed); severe/multiple disabilities (MS Ed). *Accreditation:* NCATE. *Students:* 57 full-time (47 women), 832 part-time (688 women); includes 357 minority (159 Black or African American, non-Hispanic/Latino; 1 American Indian or Alaska Native, non-Hispanic/Latino; 63 Asian, non-Hispanic/Latino; 134 Hispanic/Latino), 14 international. Average age 29. 504 applicants, 84% accepted, 311 enrolled. In 2016, 322 master's awarded. *Degree requirements:* For master's, comprehensive exam, thesis, student teaching practica, clinical teaching lab courses, New York State Teacher Certification Exams. *Entrance requirements:* For master's, minimum GPA of 2.8. Additional exam requirements/recommendations for international students: Required—TOEFL, TWE. *Application deadline:* For fall admission, 4/1 for domestic students, 2/1 for international students; for spring admission, 11/1 for domestic students, 9/1 for international students. Applications are processed on a rolling basis. *Financial support:* Career-related internships or fieldwork, Federal Work-Study, institutionally sponsored loans, and tuition waivers (partial) available. Support available to part-time students. *Faculty research:* Mathematics learning disabilities; street behavior; assessment; bilingual special education; families, diversity, and disabilities. *Unit head:* Prof. David Connor, Chairperson, 212-772-4700, E-mail: dconnor@hunter.cuny.edu. *Application contact:* Milena Solo, Director for Graduate Admissions, 212-772-4480, E-mail: admissions@hunter.cuny.edu.

Norfolk State University, School of Graduate Studies, School of Education, Department of Special Education, Program in Severe Disabilities, Norfolk, VA 23504. Offers MA. *Accreditation:* NCATE. *Program availability:* Part-time. *Degree requirements:* For master's, thesis or alternative. *Entrance requirements:* For master's, GRE, minimum GPA of 3.0 in major, 2.5 overall.

Syracuse University, School of Education, MS Program in Inclusive Special Education: Severe/Multiple Disabilities, Syracuse, NY 13244. Offers MS. *Program availability:* Part-time. *Students:* Average age 27. *Entrance requirements:* For master's, GRE, baccalaureate degree from regionally-accredited college/university, New York State initial certification in students with disabilities, strong professor and/or employer recommendations, personal statement, interview. Additional exam requirements/recommendations for international students: Required—TOEFL (minimum score 100 iBT). *Application deadline:* For fall admission, 1/15 priority date for domestic and international students; for spring admission, 10/15 priority date for domestic and international students. Applications are processed on a rolling basis. Application fee: $75. Electronic applications accepted. *Expenses: Tuition:* Full-time $25,974; part-time $1443 per credit hour. *Required fees:* $802; $50 per course. Tuition and fees vary according to course load and program. *Financial support:* Fellowships with full tuition reimbursements, research assistantships, teaching assistantships with tuition reimbursements, career-related internships or fieldwork, and scholarships/grants available. Financial award application deadline: 1/15. *Faculty research:* Teaching children and adolescents with autism, augmentation of communication in the inclusive classroom, families of students with disabilities, positive approaches to challenging behaviors, creating safe and peaceful schools. *Unit head:* Dr. Gail Ensher, Program Coordinator, 315-443-9650, E-mail: glensher@syr.edu. *Application contact:* Speranza Migliore, Graduate Admissions Recruiter, 315-443-2505, E-mail: gradrcrt@syr.edu.
Website: http://soe.syr.edu/academic/teaching_and_leadership/graduate/masters/inclusive_special_education_grades_1_6/admissions.aspx

Teachers College, Columbia University, Department of Health and Behavior Studies, New York, NY 10027-6696. Offers applied behavior analysis (MA, PhD); applied educational psychology: school psychology (Ed M, PhD); behavioral nutrition (PhD), including nutrition (Ed D, PhD); community health education (MS); community nutrition education (Ed M), including community nutrition education; education of deaf and hard of hearing (MA, PhD); health education (MA, Ed D); hearing impairment (Ed D); intellectual disability/autism (MA, Ed D, PhD); nursing education (Ed D, Advanced Certificate); nutrition and education (MS); nutrition and exercise physiology (MS); nutrition and public health (MS); nutrition education (Ed D), including nutrition (Ed D, PhD); physical disabilities (Ed D); reading specialist (MA); severe or multiple disabilities (MA); special education (Ed M, MA, Ed D); teaching of sign language (MA). *Program availability:* Part-time, evening/weekend. *Students:* 282 full-time (262 women), 262 part-time (222 women); includes 180 minority (54 Black or African American, non-Hispanic/Latino; 1 American Indian or Alaska Native, non-Hispanic/Latino; 56 Asian, non-Hispanic/Latino; 56 Hispanic/Latino; 1 Native Hawaiian or other Pacific Islander, non-Hispanic/Latino; 12 Two or more races, non-Hispanic/Latino), 55 international. 503 applicants, 57% accepted, 146 enrolled. Terminal master's awarded for partial completion of doctoral program. *Expenses: Tuition:* Full-time $36,288; part-time $1512 per credit. *Required fees:* $438 per semester. One-time fee: $510 full-time. Full-time tuition and fees vary according to course load. *Unit head:* Prof. Stephen T. Peverly, Chair, 212-678-3964, Fax: 212-678-8259, E-mail: stp4@columbia.edu. *Application contact:* David Estrella, Director of Admission, 212-678-3305, E-mail: estrella@tc.columbia.edu.
Website: http://www.tc.columbia.edu/health-and-behavior-studies/

University of Illinois at Urbana–Champaign, Graduate College, College of Education, Department of Special Education, Champaign, IL 61820. Offers Ed M, MS, Ed D, PhD, CAS. *Program availability:* Part-time, online learning.

West Virginia University, College of Education and Human Services, Department of Special Education, Morgantown, WV 26506. Offers autism spectrum disorder (5-adult) (MA); autism spectrum disorder (K-6) (MA); early intervention/early childhood special education (MA); gifted education (1-12) (MA); low vision (PreK-adult) (MA); multicategorical special education (5-adult) (MA); multicategorical special education (K-6) (MA); severe/multiple disabilities (K-adult) (MA); special education (MA, Ed D); vision impairments (PreK-adult) (MA). *Accreditation:* NCATE. *Program availability:* Part-time, evening/weekend, online learning. *Degree requirements:* For master's, thesis optional; for doctorate, comprehensive exam, thesis/dissertation. *Entrance requirements:* For master's, minimum GPA of 2.75 passing scores on PRAXIS PPST; for doctorate, GRE General Test or MAT. Additional exam requirements/recommendations for international students: Required—TOEFL.

Education of the Gifted

Arkansas State University, Graduate School, College of Education and Behavioral Science, School of Teacher Education and Leadership, State University, AR 72467. Offers community college administration (SCCT); curriculum and instruction (MSE); early childhood education (MSE); early childhood services (MS); educational leadership (MSE, Ed D, Ed S); educational theory and practice (MSE); middle level education (MAT, MSE); reading (MSE, Ed S); special education - gifted, talented, and creative (MSE); special education - instructional specialist grades 4-12 (MSE); special education - instructional specialist grades P-4 (MSE); special education, K-12 (MSE). *Accreditation:* NCATE. *Program availability:* Part-time, online learning. *Degree requirements:* For master's, comprehensive exam, thesis or alternative; for doctorate, comprehensive exam, thesis/dissertation; for other advanced degree, comprehensive exam. *Entrance requirements:* For master's, GRE General Test or MAT, appropriate bachelor's degree, official transcripts, immunization records, letters of reference, interview; for doctorate, GRE General Test or MAT, interview, master's degree, letters of reference, official transcript, personal statement, writing sample, immunization records; for other advanced degree, GRE General Test or MAT, interview, master's degree, official transcript, immunization records, letters of reference, 3 years of teaching experience, teaching license. Additional exam requirements/recommendations for international students: Required—TOEFL (minimum score 550 paper-based; 79 iBT), IELTS (minimum score 6), PTE (minimum score 56). Electronic applications accepted.

Ashland University, Dwight Schar College of Education, Department of Inclusive Services and Exceptional Learners, Ashland, OH 44805-3702. Offers intervention specialist, mild/moderate (M Ed); intervention specialist, moderate/intensive (M Ed); talented and gifted (M Ed). *Program availability:* Part-time, evening/weekend. *Degree requirements:* For master's, thesis or alternative, internship, practicum, inquiry seminar. *Entrance requirements:* Additional exam requirements/recommendations for international students: Required—TOEFL. *Application deadline:* For fall admission, 8/15 for domestic students; for spring admission, 1/15 for domestic students. Applications are processed on a rolling basis. Application fee: $30. Electronic applications accepted. *Financial support:* Teaching assistantships with partial tuition reimbursements and scholarships/grants available. Financial award application deadline: 4/15. *Unit head:* Dr. Allison Dickey, Chair, 419-289-5376, Fax: 419-207-4949, E-mail: adickey@ashland.edu. *Application contact:* Dr. Linda Billman, Associate Dean, 419-289-5369, Fax: 419-289-5331, E-mail: lbillman@ashland.edu.

Ball State University, Graduate School, Teachers College, Department of Educational Psychology, Muncie, IN 47306. Offers educational psychology (MA, MS), including educational psychology (MA, MS, PhD); educational psychology (PhD), including educational psychology (MA, MS, PhD); gifted and talented education (Certificate); human development and learning (Certificate); instructional design and assessment (Certificate); neuropsychology (Certificate); quantitative psychology (MS); response to intervention (Certificate); school psychology (MA, PhD), including school psychology (MA, PhD, Ed S); school psychology (Ed S), including school psychology (MA, PhD, Ed S). *Program availability:* 100% online. *Degree requirements:* For doctorate, thesis/dissertation; for other advanced degree, thesis. *Entrance requirements:* For master's, GRE General Test, minimum baccalaureate GPA of 2.75 or 3.0 in latter half of baccalauareate, professional goals and self-assessment; for doctorate, GRE General Test, minimum graduate GPA of 3.2; for other advanced degree, GRE General Test. Additional exam requirements/recommendations for international students: Required—TOEFL (minimum score 550 paper-based; 79 iBT), IELTS (minimum score 6.5). Electronic applications accepted.

Barry University, School of Education, Program in Curriculum and Instruction, Miami Shores, FL 33161-6695. Offers accomplished teacher (Ed S); culture, language and literacy (TESOL) (PhD); curriculum evaluation and research (PhD); early childhood (Ed S); early childhood education (PhD); elementary (Ed S); elementary education (PhD); ESOL (Ed S); gifted (Ed S); Montessori (Ed S); PKP/elementary (Ed S); reading (Ed S); reading, language and cognition (PhD). *Entrance requirements:* For doctorate, GRE, minimum GPA of 3.25.

Barry University, School of Education, Program in Exceptional Student Education, Miami Shores, FL 33161-6695. Offers MS, Ed S. *Program availability:* Part-time, evening/weekend. *Degree requirements:* For master's, comprehensive exam; for Ed S, practicum. *Entrance requirements:* For master's, GRE General Test or MAT, minimum GPA of 3.0; for Ed S, GRE General Test, minimum GPA of 3.0. Electronic applications accepted.

Barry University, School of Education, Program in Leadership and Education, Miami Shores, FL 33161-6695. Offers educational technology (PhD); exceptional student education (PhD); higher education administration (PhD); human resource development (PhD); leadership (PhD). *Program availability:* Part-time, evening/weekend. *Degree requirements:* For doctorate, thesis/dissertation. *Entrance requirements:* For doctorate, GRE General Test, minimum GPA of 3.25. Electronic applications accepted.

Canisius College, Graduate Division, School of Education and Human Services, Department of Graduate Education and Leadership, Buffalo, NY 14208-1098. Offers business and marketing education (MS Ed); college student personnel (MS Ed); deaf education (MS Ed); deaf/adolescent education, grades 7-12 (MS Ed); deaf/childhood education, grades 1-6 (MS Ed); differentiated instruction (MS Ed); education administration (MS); educational administration (MS Ed); educational technologies (Certificate); gifted education extension (Certificate); literacy (MS Ed); reading (Certificate); school building leadership (MS Ed, Certificate); school district leadership (Certificate); teacher leader (Certificate); TESOL (MS Ed). *Accreditation:* NCATE. *Program availability:* Part-time, evening/weekend, 100% online, blended/hybrid learning. *Faculty:* 5 full-time (all women), 23 part-time/adjunct (16 women). *Students:* 95 full-time (78 women), 223 part-time (177 women); includes 31 minority (15 Black or African American, non-Hispanic/Latino; 2 American Indian or Alaska Native, non-Hispanic/Latino; 4 Asian, non-Hispanic/Latino; 9 Hispanic/Latino; 1 Two or more races, non-Hispanic/Latino), 1 international. Average age 30. 162 applicants, 89% accepted, 135 enrolled. In 2016, 135 master's, 39 other advanced degrees awarded. *Entrance requirements:* For master's, GRE (if cumulative GPA less than 2.7), transcripts, two letters of recommendation. Additional exam requirements/recommendations for international students: Required—TOEFL (minimum score 550 paper-based, 79 iBT), IELTS (minimum score 6.5), or CAEL (minimum score 70). *Application deadline:* Applications are processed on a rolling basis. Application fee: $25. Electronic applications accepted. Application fee is waived when completed online. *Expenses: Tuition:* Full-time $14,742. *Required fees:* $724. *Financial support:* Career-related internships or fieldwork, Federal Work-Study, scholarships/grants, tuition waivers (partial), and unspecified assistantships available. Support available to part-time students. Financial award application deadline: 4/30; financial award applicants required to submit FAFSA. *Faculty research:* Asperger's disease, autism, private higher education, reading strategies. *Unit head:* Dr. Rosemary K. Murray, Chair/Associate Professor of Graduate Education and Leadership, 716-888-3723, E-mail: murray1@canisius.edu. *Application contact:* Kathleen B. Davis, Vice President of Enrollment Management, 716-888-2500, Fax: 716-888-3195, E-mail: daviskb@canisius.edu.
Website: http://www.canisius.edu/graduate/

Carlos Albizu University, Miami Campus, Graduate Programs, Miami, FL 33172-2209. Offers clinical psychology (PhD, Psy D); entrepreneurship (MBA); exceptional student education (MS); human services (PhD); industrial/organizational psychology (MS); marriage and family therapy (MS); mental health counseling (MS); nonprofit management (MBA); organizational management (MBA); psychology (MS); school counseling (MS); speech and language pathology (MS); teaching English for speakers of other languages (MS). *Accreditation:* APA. *Program availability:* Part-time, evening/weekend, 100% online. *Faculty:* 28 full-time (22 women), 31 part-time/adjunct (19 women). *Students:* 475 full-time (396 women), 191 part-time (161 women); includes 560 minority (56 Black or African American, non-Hispanic/Latino; 1 American Indian or Alaska Native, non-Hispanic/Latino; 4 Asian, non-Hispanic/Latino; 494 Hispanic/Latino; 5 Two or more races, non-Hispanic/Latino), 15 international. Average age 34. 335 applicants, 46% accepted, 122 enrolled. In 2016, 143 master's, 48 doctorates awarded. Terminal master's awarded for partial completion of doctoral program. *Degree requirements:* For master's, comprehensive exam, integrative project (for MBA); research project (for exceptional student education, teaching English as a second language); for doctorate, comprehensive exam, thesis/dissertation, internship, project. *Entrance requirements:* For master's, 3 letters of recommendation, interview, minimum GPA of 3.0, resume, statement of purpose, official transcripts; for doctorate, 3 letters of recommendation, minimum GPA of 3.0, resume, interview, statement of purpose, official transcripts. Additional exam requirements/recommendations for international students: Required—Michigan Test of English Language Proficiency. *Application deadline:* For fall admission, 4/1 priority date for domestic students, 5/1 priority date for international students; for spring admission, 11/1 priority date for domestic students, 9/1 priority date for international students. Applications are processed on a rolling basis. Application fee: $50. Electronic applications accepted. *Expenses:* Contact institution. *Financial support:* In 2016–17, 131 students received support. Federal Work-Study, scholarships/grants, unspecified assistantships, and tuition discounts available. Financial award application deadline: 6/1; financial award applicants required to submit FAFSA. *Faculty research:* Psychotherapy, forensic psychology, neuropsychology, marketing strategy, entrepreneurship, special education, speech-language pathology. *Unit head:* Dr. Etiony Aldarondo, Provost, 305-593-1223 Ext. 3138, Fax: 305-592-7930, E-mail: ealdarondo@albizu.edu. *Application contact:* Sonia Feliciano, Institutional Director of Student Recruitment, 305-593-1223 Ext. 3108, Fax: 305-477-8983, E-mail: sfeliciano@albizu.edu.

Carthage College, Division of Teacher Education, Kenosha, WI 53140. Offers classroom guidance and counseling (M Ed); creative arts (M Ed); gifted and talented children (M Ed); language arts (M Ed); modern language (M Ed); natural sciences (M Ed); reading (M Ed, Certificate); social sciences (M Ed); teacher leadership (M Ed). *Program availability:* Part-time, evening/weekend. *Degree requirements:* For master's, thesis optional. *Entrance requirements:* For master's, MAT, minimum B average, letters of reference.

The College of New Rochelle, Graduate School, Division of Education, Program in Gifted Education, New Rochelle, NY 10805-2308. Offers Certificate. *Program availability:* Part-time. *Degree requirements:* For Certificate, practicum.

The College of William and Mary, School of Education, Program in Curriculum and Instruction, Williamsburg, VA 23187-8795. Offers elementary education (MA Ed); gifted education (MA Ed); literacy leadership (MA Ed); math specialist (MA Ed); secondary education (MA Ed), including English, foreign language, math, science, social studies; special education (MA Ed). *Accreditation:* NCATE. *Program availability:* Part-time. *Faculty:* 30 full-time (21 women), 48 part-time/adjunct (38 women). *Students:* 60 full-time (47 women), 14 part-time (all women); includes 13 minority (1 Black or African American, non-Hispanic/Latino; 1 American Indian or Alaska Native, non-Hispanic/Latino; 2 Asian, non-Hispanic/Latino; 7 Hispanic/Latino; 2 Two or more races, non-Hispanic/Latino). Average age 26. 134 applicants, 79% accepted, 66 enrolled. In 2016, 77 master's awarded. *Degree requirements:* For master's, project. *Entrance requirements:* For master's, GRE, MAT, PRAXIS Core Academic Skills for Educators, minimum GPA of 2.5. Additional exam requirements/recommendations for international students: Required—TOEFL (minimum score 100 iBT), IELTS (minimum score 7). *Application deadline:* For fall admission, 1/15 for domestic and international students; for spring admission, 10/1 for domestic and international students. Application fee: $50. Electronic applications accepted. *Expenses:* $14,258 per year in-state full-time, $275 per credit in-state part-time; $30,500 per year out-of-state full-time, $1,200 per credit out-of-state part-time. *Financial support:* In 2016–17, 30 students received support, including 3 research assistantships (averaging $14,259 per year); scholarships/grants and unspecified assistantships also available. Financial award application deadline: 1/15; financial award applicants required to submit FAFSA. *Faculty research:* Educational technology, professional development and evaluation, inclusive education, rural education, education policy. *Unit head:* Dr. Jeremy D. Stoddard, Department Chair, 757-221-2348, E-mail: jdstod@wm.edu. *Application contact:* Dorothy Smith Osborne, Assistant Dean for Academic Programs and Student Services, 757-221-2317, E-mail: dsosbo@wm.edu.
Website: http://education.wm.edu

Colorado Mesa University, Center for Teacher Education, Grand Junction, CO 81501-3122. Offers educational leadership (MAEd); English for speakers of other languages (MAEd); exceptional learner/special education (MAEd); teacher education (Graduate Certificate); teacher leader (MAEd). *Accreditation:* NCATE. *Program availability:* Part-time. *Faculty:* 6 full-time (5 women), 12 part-time/adjunct (6 women). *Students:* 18 full-time (13 women), 35 part-time (28 women); includes 4 minority (1 American Indian or Alaska Native, non-Hispanic/Latino; 3 Hispanic/Latino), 1 international. Average age 34. 28 applicants, 25% accepted, 6 enrolled. In 2016, 26 master's, 36 other advanced degrees awarded. *Degree requirements:* For master's, comprehensive exam (for some programs), capstone presentation. *Entrance requirements:* For master's, 3 professional letters of recommendation, Colorado teaching license, minimum baccalaureate GPA of 3.0; for Graduate Certificate, minimum baccalaureate GPA of 3.0. Additional exam requirements/recommendations for international students: Required—TOEFL (minimum score 550 paper-based). *Application deadline:* For fall admission, 6/1 priority date for domestic and international students; for spring admission, 11/1 priority date for domestic and international students; for summer admission, 3/1 priority date for domestic and international students. Applications are processed on a rolling basis. Application fee: $50. Electronic applications accepted. *Expenses:* $406.43 per credit hour resident tuition and fees, $1,092.43 per credit hour non-resident tuition and fees. *Financial support:* In 2016–17, 2 students received support. Scholarships/grants available. Financial award applicants required to submit FAFSA. *Faculty research:* K-8 STEM instruction, special education inclusion, elementary math literacy, secondary literacy, elementary/early childhood education literacy. *Unit head:* Dr. Blake Bickham, Department Head, 970-248-1729, E-mail: bbickham@coloradomesa.edu. *Application contact:* Mary Kienietz, Administrative Assistant, 970-248-1786, E-mail: mkieniet@coloradomesa.edu.
Website: http://coloradomesa.edu/teachered/index.html

Converse College, School of Education and Graduate Studies, Program in Gifted Education, Spartanburg, SC 29302. Offers M Ed. *Program availability:* Part-time. *Degree requirements:* For master's, capstone paper. *Entrance requirements:* For master's, NTE or PRAXIS II, minimum GPA of 2.75, teaching certificate, 2 recommendations. *Application deadline:* For fall admission, 8/1 for domestic and international students; for winter admission, 11/15 for domestic and international students; for spring admission, 1/15 for domestic and international students. Applications are processed on a rolling basis. Application fee: $40. Electronic applications accepted. *Expenses: Tuition:* Full-time $3600; part-time $400 per credit hour. *Required fees:* $70 per term. *Financial support:* Career-related internships or fieldwork available. Support available to part-time students. Financial award applicants required to submit FAFSA. *Faculty research:* Identification of gifted minorities, arts in gifted education. *Unit head:* Ansley Boggs, 864-596-9084, E-mail: ansley.boggs@converse.edu. *Application contact:* E-mail: graduate@converse.edu.

Drury University, Master in Education Program, Springfield, MO 5802. Offers curriculum and instruction (M Ed), including elementary, middle school, secondary; gifted education (M Ed); instructional leadership (M Ed); instructional technology (M Ed); integrated learning (M Ed); online teaching (M Ed); special education (M Ed); special reading (M Ed). *Accreditation:* NCATE. *Program availability:* Part-time, evening/weekend, 100% online, blended/hybrid learning. *Students:* 146 full-time (111 women); includes 6 minority (1 Asian, non-Hispanic/Latino; 3 Hispanic/Latino; 2 Two or more races, non-Hispanic/Latino), 1 international. Average age 34. 42 applicants, 74% accepted. In 2016, 74 master's awarded. *Entrance requirements:* For master's, GRE,

bachelor's degree with minimum GPA of 2.75. Additional exam requirements/ recommendations for international students: Recommended—TOEFL (minimum score 80 iBT), IELTS (minimum score 6.5). *Application deadline:* For fall admission, 8/4 priority date for domestic and international students; for spring admission, 1/5 priority date for domestic and international students; for summer admission, 5/26 priority date for domestic and international students. Applications are processed on a rolling basis. Application fee: $25 ($50 for international students). Electronic applications accepted. *Expenses:* $352 tuition per credit hour; $7 per credit hour technology fee; $100 graduation fee; $59 portfolio fee (one-time). *Financial support:* In 2016–17, 20 students received support. Career-related internships or fieldwork, scholarships/grants, tuition waivers (partial), and unspecified assistantships available. Financial award application deadline: 6/30; financial award applicants required to submit FAFSA. *Faculty research:* Gifted students, instructional technology, autism, diversity and social justice. *Unit head:* Dr. Asikaa Cosgrove, Director, Master in Education, 417-873-7806, E-mail: acosgrov@drury.edu.
Website: http://www.drury.edu/education-masters

Elon University, Program in Education, Elon, NC 27244-2010. Offers elementary education (M Ed); gifted education (M Ed); special education (M Ed). *Accreditation:* NCATE. *Program availability:* Part-time. *Faculty:* 9 full-time (7 women), 2 part-time/ adjunct (both women). *Students:* 17 part-time (all women); includes 7 minority (3 Black or African American, non-Hispanic/Latino; 1 American Indian or Alaska Native, non-Hispanic/Latino; 2 Hispanic/Latino; 1 Two or more races, non-Hispanic/Latino). Average age 33. 24 applicants, 50% accepted, 8 enrolled. In 2016, 24 master's awarded. *Entrance requirements:* For master's, GRE, MAT. Additional exam requirements/ recommendations for international students: Required—TOEFL (minimum score 550 paper-based; 79 iBT). *Application deadline:* For fall admission, 5/1 for domestic students. Applications are processed on a rolling basis. Application fee: $50. Electronic applications accepted. *Financial support:* Federal Work-Study and scholarships/grants available. Support available to part-time students. Financial award application deadline: 6/1; financial award applicants required to submit FAFSA. *Faculty research:* Teaching reading to low-achieving second and third graders, pre- and post-student teaching attitudes, children's writing, whole language methodology, critical creative thinking. *Unit head:* Dr. Ann Bullock, Dean of the School of Education/Professor, 336-278-5900, E-mail: abullock9@elon.edu. *Application contact:* Art Fadde, Director of Graduate Admissions, 800-334-8448 Ext. 3, Fax: 336-278-7699, E-mail: afadde@elon.edu.
Website: http://www.elon.edu/med

Emporia State University, Program in Special Education, Emporia, KS 66801-5415. Offers behavior disorders (MS); gifted, talented, and creative (MS); interrelated special education (MS). *Accreditation:* NCATE. *Program availability:* Part-time. *Faculty:* 29 full-time (21 women), 3 part-time/adjunct (2 women). *Students:* 5 full-time (all women), 158 part-time (119 women); includes 6 minority (1 Asian, non-Hispanic/Latino; 4 Hispanic/ Latino; 1 Two or more races, non-Hispanic/Latino). 35 applicants, 100% accepted, 23 enrolled. In 2016, 40 master's awarded. *Degree requirements:* For master's, comprehensive exam or thesis, practicum. *Entrance requirements:* For master's, GRE General Test or MAT, essay exam, appropriate bachelor's degree, teacher certification, letters of recommendation. Additional exam requirements/recommendations for international students: Required—TOEFL (minimum score 520 paper-based; 68 iBT). *Application deadline:* For fall admission, 8/15 priority date for domestic students. Applications are processed on a rolling basis. Application fee: $30 ($75 for international students). Electronic applications accepted. *Expenses:* Tuition, state resident: full-time $5922; part-time $246.75 per credit hour. Tuition, nonresident: full-time $18,414; part-time $767.25 per credit hour. *Required fees:* $1884; $78.50 per credit hour. *Financial support:* In 2016–17, 1 teaching assistantship with full tuition reimbursement (averaging $7,335 per year) was awarded; Federal Work-Study, institutionally sponsored loans, health care benefits, and unspecified assistantships also available. Financial award application deadline: 3/15; financial award applicants required to submit FAFSA. *Unit head:* Dr. Matt Siemears, Chair, 620-341-6057, E-mail: msiemear@emporia.edu. *Application contact:* Mary Sewell, Admissions Coordinator, 800-950-GRAD, Fax: 620-341-5909, E-mail: msewell@emporia.edu.
Website: http://www.emporia.edu/elecse/sped/

Florida Gulf Coast University, College of Education, Program in Curriculum and Instruction, Fort Myers, FL 33965-6565. Offers elementary education (M Ed); English education (M Ed); gifted education (M Ed); mathematics education (M Ed); middle school education (M Ed); science education (M Ed); social science education (M Ed). *Program availability:* Part-time, evening/weekend, online learning. *Faculty:* 26 full-time (18 women), 44 part-time/adjunct (32 women). *Students:* 1 (woman) full-time, 22 part-time (20 women); includes 49 minority (19 Black or African American, non-Hispanic/ Latino; 4 Asian, non-Hispanic/Latino; 24 Hispanic/Latino; 2 Two or more races, non-Hispanic/Latino), 2 international. Average age 28. 9 applicants, 78% accepted, 2 enrolled. In 2016, 9 master's awarded. *Degree requirements:* For master's, final project or portfolio. *Entrance requirements:* For master's, GRE General Test, MAT, minimum undergraduate GPA of 3.0 in last 2 years. Additional exam requirements/ recommendations for international students: Required—TOEFL (minimum score 550 paper-based). *Application deadline:* For fall admission, 7/1 priority date for domestic students; for spring admission, 10/15 for domestic students. Applications are processed on a rolling basis. Application fee: $30. Electronic applications accepted. *Expenses:* Tuition, state resident: full-time $6721. Tuition, nonresident: full-time $28,170. *Required fees:* $1987. Tuition and fees vary according to course load and degree level. *Financial support:* In 2016–17, 1 student received support. Application deadline: 3/1; applicants required to submit FAFSA. *Faculty research:* Internet in schools, technology in pre-service and in-service teacher training. *Unit head:* Dr. Diane Schmidt, Department Chair, 239-590-7741, Fax: 239-590-7801, E-mail: dschmidt@fgcu.edu. *Application contact:* Keiana Desmore, Adviser/Counselor, 239-590-7759, Fax: 239-590-7801, E-mail: kdesmore@fgcu.edu.
Website: http://coe.fgcu.edu/c-imed/

George Mason University, College of Education and Human Development, Programs in Curriculum and Instruction, Fairfax, VA 22030. Offers advanced international baccalaureate (M Ed); assistive technology (M Ed); designing digital learning in schools (M Ed); early childhood education (M Ed); early childhood education for diverse learners (M Ed); elementary education (M Ed); English as a second language (M Ed); gifted child education (M Ed); history (M Ed); literacy (M Ed), including PK-12 classroom teachers, reading specialist; literacy leadership for diverse schools (M Ed), including K-12 reading; physical education (M Ed); science K-12 (M Ed); secondary education (M Ed), including biology, chemistry, earth science, English, history/social science, math, physics; special education (M Ed); teacher leadership (M Ed); teaching culturally, linguistically diverse and exceptional learners (M Ed); transformative teaching (M Ed). *Faculty:* 41 full-time (35 women), 53 part-time/adjunct (46 women). *Students:* 155 full-time (127 women), 821 part-time (697 women); includes 267 minority (82 Black or African American, non-Hispanic/Latino; 5 American Indian or Alaska Native, non-Hispanic/Latino; 75 Asian, non-Hispanic/Latino; 88 Hispanic/Latino; 1 Native Hawaiian or other Pacific Islander, non-Hispanic/Latino; 16 Two or more races, non-Hispanic/Latino), 19 international. Average age 33. 513 applicants, 90% accepted, 352 enrolled. In 2016, 347 master's awarded. *Degree requirements:* For master's, comprehensive exam, thesis (for some programs). *Entrance requirements:* For master's, PRAXIS Core (for some programs), minimum GPA of 3.0 in last 60 hours, licensed as teacher or educational administrator, official transcripts, goals statement, 3 recommendation letters, interview or writing sample (depending on program), up to 3 years' teaching experience (depending on program). Additional exam requirements/recommendations for international students: Required—TOEFL (minimum score 575 paper-based; 88 iBT), IELTS (minimum score 6.5), PTE (minimum score 59). *Application deadline:* For spring admission, 11/1 priority date for domestic and international students. Application fee: $75 ($80 for international students). Electronic applications accepted. *Expenses:* Tuition, state resident: full-time $10,628; part-time $443 per credit. Tuition, nonresident: full-time $29,306; part-time $1221 per credit. *Required fees:* $3096; $129 per credit. Tuition and fees vary according to program. *Financial support:* In 2016–17, 1 student received support, including 1 teaching assistantship (averaging $4,060 per year); career-related internships or fieldwork, Federal Work-Study, scholarships/grants, unspecified assistantships, and health care benefits (for full-time research or teaching assistantship recipients) also available. Support available to part-time students. Financial award application deadline: 3/1; financial award applicants required to submit FAFSA. *Faculty research:* Achievement gaps and superintendent decisions, constructivist view of classroom teaching, cost of cheating, creating a critical literacy milieu in kindergarten. *Unit head:* Rebecca Fox, Professor and Academic Program Coordinator, 703-993-4123, E-mail: rfox@gmu.edu.
Website: http://gse.gmu.edu/programs/gsemasters

Grand Canyon University, College of Education, Phoenix, AZ 85017-1097. Offers autism spectrum disorders (MA); curriculum and instruction (MA); early childhood education (M Ed); educational administration (M Ed); educational leadership (M Ed); elementary education (M Ed); gifted education (MA); instructional technology (MS); K-12 leadership (Ed S); reading (MA); secondary education (M Ed); secondary humanities education (M Ed); secondary STEM education (M Ed); special education (M Ed); teaching and learning (Ed D); teaching English to speakers of other languages (MA). *Program availability:* Part-time, evening/weekend, online learning. *Degree requirements:* For master's, publishable research paper (M Ed), e-portfolio. *Entrance requirements:* For master's, undergraduate degree from accredited, GCU-approved college, university, or program with minimum GPA 2.8. Additional exam requirements/recommendations for international students: Required—TOEFL (minimum score 550 paper-based; 79 iBT), IELTS (minimum score 6). *Application deadline:* For fall admission, 8/21 for domestic students, 7/2 for international students; for spring admission, 12/24 for domestic students, 11/1 for international students. Applications are processed on a rolling basis. Application fee: $100. Electronic applications accepted. *Financial support:* Federal Work-Study available. Support available to part-time students. Financial award applicants required to submit FAFSA. *Unit head:* Dr. Kimberly L. LaPrade, Dean, 602-639-6360, E-mail: kimberly.laprade@gcu.edu. *Application contact:* Dr. Kimberly L. LaPrade, Dean, 602-639-6360, E-mail: kimberly.laprade@gcu.edu.
Website: https://www.gcu.edu/college-of-education.php

Hardin-Simmons University, Graduate School, Irvin School of Education, Department of Educational Studies, Program in Gifted Education, Abilene, TX 79698-0001. Offers M Ed. *Program availability:* Part-time. *Faculty:* 2 full-time (both women), 1 (woman) part-time/adjunct. *Students:* 1 (woman) full-time, 39 part-time (35 women); includes 5 minority (2 Black or African American, non-Hispanic/Latino; 3 Hispanic/Latino). Average age 38. In 2016, 7 master's awarded. *Degree requirements:* For master's, comprehensive exam. *Entrance requirements:* For master's, minimum undergraduate GPA of 3.0 in major, 2.7 overall. Additional exam requirements/recommendations for international students: Required—TOEFL (minimum score 550 paper-based; 75 iBT). *Application deadline:* For fall admission, 8/15 priority date for domestic students, 4/1 for international students; for spring admission, 1/5 priority date for domestic students, 9/1 for international students. Applications are processed on a rolling basis. Application fee: $50. Electronic applications accepted. *Expenses: Tuition:* Full-time $12,510; part-time $695 per credit hour. *Required fees:* $325; $110 per semester. *Financial support:* In 2016–17, 10 students received support. Fellowships and scholarships/grants available. Support available to part-time students. Financial award application deadline: 6/30; financial award applicants required to submit FAFSA. *Faculty research:* Experiences of gifted learners in college, use of authentic assessment, brain research and how it works in learning, theories of multiple intelligence beyond Howard Gardner. *Unit head:* Dr. Mary Christopher, Director, 325-670-1510, Fax: 325-670-1397, E-mail: mchris@hsutx.edu. *Application contact:* Dr. Nancy Kucinski, Dean of Graduate Studies, 325-670-1298, Fax: 325-670-1564, E-mail: gradoff@hsutx.edu.
Website: http://www.hsutx.edu/academics/irvin/graduate/gifted

Hofstra University, School of Education, Specialized Programs in Education, Hempstead, NY 11549. Offers applied behavior analysis (Advanced Certificate); early childhood special education (MS Ed, Advanced Certificate); educational and policy leadership (Ed D); educational leadership (Advanced Certificate), including school building leader/school district business leader; educational leadership and policy studies (MS Ed), including K-12; gifted education (Advanced Certificate), including school building leader/school district business leader; health education PK-12 teaching certification (MS); inclusive early childhood special education (MS Ed); inclusive elementary special education (MS Ed); inclusive secondary special education (MS Ed); literacy studies (MS Ed, Ed D, PhD, Advanced Certificate), including birth-grade 6 (MS Ed, Advanced Certificate), birth-grade 6 and special education (birth-grade2) (MS Ed), grades 5-12 (MS Ed, Advanced Certificate); physical education (MS); secondary education generalist (MS Ed), including students with disabilities 7-12; special education (MS Ed, Advanced Certificate); special education assessment and diagnosis (Advanced Certificate); special education generalist (MS Ed), including extension in secondary education; sport science (MS), including strength and conditioning; teaching students with severe or multiple disabilities (Advanced Certificate). *Program availability:* Part-time, evening/weekend, 100% online, blended/ hybrid learning. *Students:* 149 full-time (115 women), 258 part-time (187 women); includes 97 minority (50 Black or African American, non-Hispanic/Latino; 1 American Indian or Alaska Native, non-Hispanic/Latino; 11 Asian, non-Hispanic/Latino; 34 Hispanic/Latino; 1 Native Hawaiian or other Pacific Islander, non-Hispanic/Latino), 5 international. Average age 32. 250 applicants, 88% accepted, 146 enrolled. In 2016, 85 master's, 13 doctorates, 35 other advanced degrees awarded. *Degree requirements:* For master's, one foreign language, comprehensive exam (for some programs), thesis (for some programs), electronic portfolio, capstone course, internship, practicum, student teaching, seminars, minimum GPA of 3.0; for doctorate, one foreign language, comprehensive exam, thesis/dissertation, qualifying hearing. *Entrance requirements:* For master's, GRE, interview, letters of recommendation, portfolio, essay, certification; for doctorate, GRE or MAT, interview, resume, essay, master's degree, 3 letters of recommendation, writing sample; for Advanced Certificate, GRE, interview, letters of recommendation, essay, professional experience, resume, master's degree. Additional exam requirements/recommendations for international students: Required—TOEFL (minimum score 550 paper-based; 80 iBT). *Application deadline:* Applications are processed on a rolling basis. Application fee: $75. Electronic applications accepted. *Expenses: Tuition:* Full-time $1240. *Required fees:* $970. Tuition and fees vary according to program. *Financial support:* In 2016–17, 244 students received support, including 117 fellowships with full and partial tuition reimbursements available (averaging $3,705 per year), 12 research assistantships with full and partial tuition

reimbursements available (averaging $6,490 per year); career-related internships or fieldwork, Federal Work-Study, institutionally sponsored loans, scholarships/grants, traineeships, tuition waivers (full and partial), and unspecified assistantships also available. Support available to part-time students. Financial award applicants required to submit FAFSA. *Faculty research:* Collaborative teaching and learning; language and culture; new media literacies; applied behavior analysis; K-12 leadership development. *Unit head:* Dr. Elfreda Blue, Chairperson, 516-463-5762, Fax: 516-463-6184, E-mail: elfreda.blue@hofstra.edu. *Application contact:* Sunil Samuel, Assistant Vice President of Admissions, 516-463-4723, Fax: 516-463-4664, E-mail: graduateadmission@hofstra.edu.
Website: http://www.hofstra.edu/education/

James Madison University, The Graduate School, College of Education, Program in Special Education, Harrisonburg, VA 22807. Offers adapted curriculum (MAT); autism (M Ed); behavior specialist (M Ed); early childhood special education (MAT); general curriculum K-12 special education (MAT); gifted education (M Ed); inclusive early childhood special education (MAT); instructional specialist (M Ed); K-12 special education (MAT); visual impairments (MAT). *Accreditation:* NCATE. *Program availability:* Part-time. *Students:* 31 full-time (30 women), 7 part-time (3 women); includes 2 minority (1 Hispanic/Latino; 1 Two or more races, non-Hispanic/Latino). Average age 30. In 2016, 67 master's awarded. Application fee: $55. Electronic applications accepted. *Financial support:* In 2016–17, 6 students received support, including 1 fellowship; Federal Work-Study and 6 assistantships (averaging $7911) also available. Financial award application deadline: 3/1; financial award applicants required to submit FAFSA. *Unit head:* Dr. David A. Slykhuis, Interim Department Head, 540-568-4314, E-mail: slykhuda@jmu.edu. *Application contact:* Lynette D. Michael, Director of Graduate Admissions, 540-568-6131 Ext. 6395, Fax: 540-568-7860, E-mail: michaeld@jmu.edu.
Website: http://www.jmu.edu/coe/efex/index.shtml

Johns Hopkins University, School of Education, Certificate Programs in Education, Baltimore, MD 21218. Offers advanced methods for differentiated instruction and inclusive education (Graduate Certificate); applied behavior analysis (Post-Master's Certificate); clinical mental health counseling (Post-Master's Certificate); counseling (Advanced Certificate); data-based decision making and organizational improvement (Graduate Certificate); early intervention/preschool special education specialist (Graduate Certificate); education of students with autism and other pervasive developmental disorders (Graduate Certificate); educational leadership for independent schools (Graduate Certificate); evidence-based teaching in the health professions (Post-Master's Certificate); gifted education (Graduate Certificate); leadership in technology integration (Graduate Certificate); mind, brain and teaching (Graduate Certificate); school administration and supervision (Graduate Certificate); urban education (Graduate Certificate). *Program availability:* Part-time-only, evening/weekend, 100% online, blended/hybrid learning. *Students:* 5 full-time (all women), 194 part-time (164 women); includes 46 minority (29 Black or African American, non-Hispanic/Latino; 2 American Indian or Alaska Native, non-Hispanic/Latino; 3 Asian, non-Hispanic/Latino; 8 Hispanic/Latino; 4 Two or more races, non-Hispanic/Latino), 7 international. Average age 37. 240 applicants, 75% accepted, 143 enrolled. In 2016, 167 Advanced Certificates awarded. *Entrance requirements:* For degree, minimum of bachelor's degree from regionally- or nationally-accredited institution (master's degree for some programs); minimum GPA of 3.0 in all previous programs of study; official transcripts from all post-secondary institutions attended; essay; curriculum vitae/resume; two letters of recommendation; dispositions survey. *Application deadline:* For fall admission, 4/1 priority date for domestic students; for spring admission, 10/1 priority date for domestic students; for summer admission, 2/1 priority date for domestic students. Applications are processed on a rolling basis. Application fee: $80. Electronic applications accepted. *Expenses:* Contact institution. *Financial support:* Application deadline: 4/1; applicants required to submit FAFSA. *Unit head:* Dr. Christopher C. Morphew, Dean. *Application contact:* Elisabeth Woodward, Director of Admissions, 410-516-9796, Fax: 410-516-9817, E-mail: soe.info@jhu.edu.
Website: http://education.jhu.edu

Johns Hopkins University, School of Education, Master's Programs in Education, Baltimore, MD 21218. Offers counseling (MS), including clinical mental health counseling, school counseling; education (MS), including educational studies, gifted education, reading, school administration and supervision, technology for educators; elementary education (MAT); health professions (M Ed); intelligence analysis (MS); organizational leadership (MS); secondary education (MAT), including biology, chemistry, earth/space science, English, physics, social studies; special education (MS), including early childhood special education, general special education studies, mild to moderate disabilities, severe disabilities. *Program availability:* Part-time, evening/weekend, 100% online, blended/hybrid learning. *Students:* 345 full-time (265 women), 1,601 part-time (1,245 women); includes 837 minority (392 Black or African American, non-Hispanic/Latino; 7 American Indian or Alaska Native, non-Hispanic/Latino; 141 Asian, non-Hispanic/Latino; 207 Hispanic/Latino; 7 Native Hawaiian or other Pacific Islander, non-Hispanic/Latino; 83 Two or more races, non-Hispanic/Latino), 55 international. Average age 27. 1,352 applicants, 76% accepted, 819 enrolled. In 2016, 642 master's awarded. *Degree requirements:* For master's, comprehensive exam (for some programs), portfolio, capstone project and/or internship; PRAXIS II (subject area assessments) for initial teacher preparation programs that lead to licensure. *Entrance requirements:* For master's, GRE (for full-time programs only); PRAXIS I/core or state-approved alternative (for initial teacher preparation programs that lead to licensure), minimum of bachelor's degree from regionally- or nationally-accredited institution; minimum GPA of 3.0 in all previous programs of study; official transcripts from all post-secondary institutions attended; essay; curriculum vitae/resume; letters of recommendation (3 for full-time programs, 2 for part-time programs); dispositions survey. Additional exam requirements/recommendations for international students: Required—TOEFL (minimum score 600 paper-based; 100 iBT), IELTS (minimum score 7). *Application deadline:* For fall admission, 4/1 priority date for domestic students, 4/1 for international students; for spring admission, 10/1 priority date for domestic students, 10/1 for international students; for summer admission, 2/1 priority date for domestic students, 2/1 for international students. Applications are processed on a rolling basis. Application fee: $80. Electronic applications accepted. *Expenses:* Contact institution. *Financial support:* Application deadline: 4/1; applicants required to submit FAFSA. *Unit head:* Dr. Christopher C. Morphew, Dean. *Application contact:* Elisabeth Woodward, Director of Admissions, 410-516-9796, Fax: 410-516-9817, E-mail: soe.info@jhu.edu.
Website: http://education.jhu.edu

Kent State University, College of Education, Health and Human Services, School of Lifespan Development and Educational Sciences, Kent, OH 44242-0001. Offers clinical mental health counseling (M Ed); counseling (Ed S); counseling and human development services (PhD); educational psychology (M Ed, MA); human development and family studies (MA); instructional technology (M Ed, PhD), including computer technology (M Ed), educational psychology (PhD), general instructional technology (M Ed); rehabilitation counseling (M Ed); school counseling (M Ed); school psychology (PhD, Ed S); special education (M Ed, PhD, Ed S), including deaf education (M Ed), early childhood education (M Ed), educational interpreter K-12 (M Ed), general special education (M Ed), gifted education (M Ed), mild/moderate intervention (M Ed), moderate/intensive intervention (M Ed), special education (PhD, Ed S), transition to work (M Ed). *Program availability:* Part-time, evening/weekend. *Degree requirements:* For master's, thesis optional; for doctorate, comprehensive exam, thesis/dissertation. *Entrance requirements:* For master's, doctorate, and Ed S, GRE General Test. Additional exam requirements/recommendations for international students: Required—TOEFL (minimum score 550 paper-based; 80 iBT). Electronic applications accepted. *Expenses:* Tuition, state resident: full-time $10,864; part-time $495 per credit hour. Tuition, nonresident: full-time $18,380; part-time $837 per credit hour.

Liberty University, School of Education, Lynchburg, VA 24515. Offers educational leadership (Ed D); gifted education (Certificate); math specialist (M Ed); middle grades (MAT, Certificate); reading specialist (M Ed); school leadership (Certificate); secondary education (MAT); sport management (MS), including administration, outdoor recreation, sport management, tourism. *Accreditation:* NCATE. *Program availability:* Part-time, online learning. *Students:* 1,910 full-time (1,427 women), 4,420 part-time (3,311 women); includes 1,451 minority (1,182 Black or African American, non-Hispanic/Latino; 33 American Indian or Alaska Native, non-Hispanic/Latino; 44 Asian, non-Hispanic/Latino; 46 Hispanic/Latino; 11 Native Hawaiian or other Pacific Islander, non-Hispanic/Latino; 135 Two or more races, non-Hispanic/Latino), 87 international. Average age 37. 5,120 applicants, 44% accepted, 1193 enrolled. In 2016, 1,378 master's, 151 doctorates, 497 other advanced degrees awarded. *Degree requirements:* For doctorate, comprehensive exam, thesis/dissertation. *Entrance requirements:* For master's, GRE General Test or MAT (if taken in or before 1999), 2 letters of recommendation, minimum undergraduate GPA of 3.0, curriculum vitae; for doctorate and Certificate, GRE General Test or MAT (if taken before 1999), minimum master's GPA of 3.0, 3 years of teaching experience. Additional exam requirements/recommendations for international students: Required—TOEFL (minimum score 600 paper-based; 100 iBT). *Application deadline:* For fall admission, 6/1 for domestic students; for spring admission, 11/1 for domestic students. Applications are processed on a rolling basis. Application fee: $50. Electronic applications accepted. *Expenses:* Contact institution. *Financial support:* Federal Work-Study and tuition waivers (partial) available. *Faculty research:* Self-determination, character education, bibliotherapy, learning styles, distance education. *Unit head:* Dr. Heather Schoffstall, Dean, 434-582-2445, Fax: 434-582-2468, E-mail: awgunter@liberty.edu. *Application contact:* Jay Bridge, Director of Graduate Admissions, 800-424-9595, Fax: 800-628-7977, E-mail: gradadmissions@liberty.edu.
Website: http://www.liberty.edu/academics/education/graduate/

Lindenwood University, Graduate Programs, School of Education, St. Charles, MO 63301-1695. Offers education (MA), including autism spectrum disorders, character education, early intervention in autism and sensory impairment, gifted, technology; educational administration (MA, Ed D, Ed S); English to speakers of other languages (MA); instructional leadership (Ed D, Ed S); library media (MA); professional counseling (MA); school administration (MA, Ed S); school counseling (MA); teaching (MA). *Program availability:* Part-time, evening/weekend, 100% online, blended/hybrid learning. *Faculty:* 39 full-time (27 women), 210 part-time/adjunct (136 women). *Students:* 292 full-time (227 women), 1,580 part-time (1,203 women); includes 404 minority (333 Black or African American, non-Hispanic/Latino; 4 American Indian or Alaska Native, non-Hispanic/Latino; 10 Asian, non-Hispanic/Latino; 36 Hispanic/Latino; 1 Native Hawaiian or other Pacific Islander, non-Hispanic/Latino; 20 Two or more races, non-Hispanic/Latino), 20 international. Average age 36. 558 applicants, 72% accepted, 353 enrolled. In 2016, 491 master's, 72 doctorates, 111 other advanced degrees awarded. *Degree requirements:* For master's, thesis (for some programs), minimum GPA of 3.0; for doctorate, thesis/dissertation, minimum GPA of 3.0; for Ed S, comprehensive exam, project, minimum GPA of 3.0. *Entrance requirements:* For master's, interview, minimum undergraduate cumulative GPA of 3.0, writing sample, letter of recommendation; for doctorate, GRE, minimum graduate GPA of 3.4, resume, interview, writing sample, 4 letters of recommendation; for Ed S, master's degree in education, relevant work experience. Additional exam requirements/recommendations for international students: Required—TOEFL (minimum score 550 paper-based; 80 iBT); Recommended—IELTS (minimum score 6.5). *Application deadline:* For fall admission, 8/28 priority date for domestic and international students; for spring admission, 1/8 priority date for domestic and international students; for summer admission, 6/5 priority date for domestic and international students. Applications are processed on a rolling basis. Application fee: $30 ($100 for international students). Electronic applications accepted. *Expenses: Tuition:* Full-time $15,672; part-time $453 per credit hour. *Required fees:* $205 per semester. Tuition and fees vary according to course level, course load and degree level. *Financial support:* In 2016–17, 334 students received support. Career-related internships or fieldwork, Federal Work-Study, institutionally sponsored loans, scholarships/grants, tuition waivers (partial), and unspecified assistantships available. Financial award application deadline: 6/30; financial award applicants required to submit FAFSA. *Unit head:* Dr. Cynthia Bice, Dean, School of Education, 636-949-4618, Fax: 636-949-4197, E-mail: cbice@lindenwood.edu. *Application contact:* Tyler Kostich, Director, Evening and Graduate Admissions, 636-949-4138, Fax: 636-949-4109, E-mail: adultadmissions@lindenwood.edu.
Website: http://www.lindenwood.edu/academics/academic-schools/school-of-education/

Lynn University, Donald E. and Helen L. Ross College of Education, Boca Raton, FL 33431-5598. Offers educational leadership (M Ed, Ed D), including K-12 (Ed D); exceptional student education (M Ed), including school administration K-12. *Program availability:* Part-time, evening/weekend, online learning. *Faculty:* 5 full-time (4 women), 8 part-time/adjunct (all women). *Students:* 85 full-time (63 women), 10 part-time (6 women); includes 27 minority (19 Black or African American, non-Hispanic/Latino; 7 Hispanic/Latino; 1 Two or more races, non-Hispanic/Latino), 4 international. Average age 36. 17 applicants, 94% accepted, 11 enrolled. In 2016, 24 master's, 22 doctorates awarded. *Degree requirements:* For master's, comprehensive exam, thesis (for some programs); for doctorate, thesis/dissertation, mid-program review. *Entrance requirements:* For master's, bachelor's degree from accredited institution, letter of recommendation, statement of professional goals, official transcripts; for doctorate, master's degree from accredited institution, resume, 2 letters of recommendation, professional practice statement, official transcripts. Additional exam requirements/recommendations for international students: Required—TOEFL (minimum score 550 paper-based; 80 iBT), IELTS (minimum score 6.5). *Application deadline:* For fall admission, 8/18 for domestic students, 8/4 for international students; for spring admission, 12/15 for domestic students, 12/1 for international students; for summer admission, 4/17 for domestic students, 4/3 for international students. Applications are processed on a rolling basis. Application fee: $45. Electronic applications accepted. *Expenses:* $850 per credit hour, $44,200 per year tuition and fees (for Ed D); $725 per credit hour, $29,000 per year tuition and fees (for master's). *Financial support:* In 2016–17, 74 students received support. Career-related internships or fieldwork, Federal Work-Study, scholarships/grants, tuition waivers (partial), and unspecified assistantships available. Support available to part-time students. Financial award application deadline: 3/1; financial award applicants required to submit FAFSA. *Unit head:* Dr. Kathleen Weigel, Dean, College of Education, 561-237-7441, E-mail: kweigel@lynn.edu. *Application contact:* Steven Pruitt, Director of Graduate and Undergraduate Evening Admission, 561-237-7834, Fax: 561-237-7100, E-mail: spruitt@lynn.edu.
Website: http://www.lynn.edu/academics/colleges/education

Maryville University of Saint Louis, School of Education, St. Louis, MO 63141-7299. Offers early childhood education (MA Ed); educational leadership (Ed D); educational leadership: principal certification (MA Ed); elementary education (MA Ed); gifted education (MA Ed); higher education leadership (Ed D); literacy specialist (MA Ed); middle grades education (MA Ed); secondary teaching and inquiry (MA Ed); teacher as leader (MA Ed); teacher leadership (Ed D). *Accreditation:* NCATE. *Program availability:* Part-time, evening/weekend. *Faculty:* 17 full-time (11 women), 21 part-time/adjunct (17 women). *Students:* 12 full-time (11 women), 297 part-time (208 women); includes 92 minority (79 Black or African American, non-Hispanic/Latino; 4 Asian, non-Hispanic/Latino; 4 Hispanic/Latino; 5 Two or more races, non-Hispanic/Latino), 4 international. Average age 38. In 2016, 32 master's, 61 doctorates awarded. *Degree requirements:* For master's, thesis, project. *Entrance requirements:* For master's, minimum cumulative GPA of 3.0, 3 professional recommendations, essays, interview with program faculty; for doctorate, minimum GPA of 3.0, 3 professional recommendations, essay, interview, on-site writing sample. Additional exam requirements/recommendations for international students: Required—TOEFL (minimum score 550 paper-based). *Application deadline:* Applications are processed on a rolling basis. Electronic applications accepted. *Expenses:* $879 per credit (for Ed D); $781 per credit (for master's). *Financial support:* Career-related internships or fieldwork, Federal Work-Study, tuition waivers (partial), and professional educator discounts available. Financial award application deadline: 3/1; financial award applicants required to submit FAFSA. *Faculty research:* Collaboration with public schools, pre-service program development, mathematics, diversity, literacy. *Unit head:* Dr. Cathy Bear, Dean, 314-529-9692, Fax: 314-529-9921, E-mail: cbear@maryville.edu. *Application contact:* Stacey Ruffin, Coordinator of Clinical Experiences and Graduate Programs, 314-529-9542, Fax: 314-529-9921, E-mail: teachered@maryville.edu.
Website: http://www.maryville.edu/ed/graduate-programs/

Meredith College, School of Education, Health and Human Sciences, Raleigh, NC 27607-5298. Offers academically and intellectually gifted (M Ed); curriculum instruction specialist (M Ed); elementary education (M Ed, MAT); English as a second language (M Ed, MAT); health and physical education (MAT); nutrition, health and human performance (MS, Postbaccalaureate Certificate), including dietetic internship (Postbaccalaureate Certificate), nutrition (MS); reading (M Ed); special education (MAT). *Accreditation:* NCATE. *Program availability:* Part-time, evening/weekend. *Degree requirements:* For master's, thesis optional. *Entrance requirements:* For master's, GRE General Test or MAT, minimum GPA of 2.5, teaching license, recommendations. Additional exam requirements/recommendations for international students: Required—TOEFL. Electronic applications accepted. *Expenses:* Contact institution.

Millersville University of Pennsylvania, College of Graduate Studies and Adult Learning, College of Education and Human Services, Department of Early, Middle, and Exceptional Education, Program in Gifted Education, Millersville, PA 17551-0302. Offers M Ed, Postbaccalaureate Certificate. *Program availability:* Part-time, evening/weekend, 100% online. *Faculty:* 14 full-time (9 women). *Students:* 15 part-time (11 women); includes 1 minority (Two or more races, non-Hispanic/Latino). Average age 34. 10 applicants, 100% accepted, 5 enrolled. In 2016, 3 master's awarded. *Degree requirements:* For master's, thesis optional, clinical practicum, evaluation of coursework. *Entrance requirements:* For master's, GRE or MAT (if GPA is lower than 3.0), teaching certificate. Additional exam requirements/recommendations for international students: Required—TOEFL (minimum score 600 paper-based), IELTS (minimum score 6). *Application deadline:* Applications are processed on a rolling basis. Application fee: $40. Electronic applications accepted. *Expenses:* $483 per credit resident tuition; $725 per credit non-resident tuition. *Financial support:* Unspecified assistantships available. Financial award application deadline: 3/15; financial award applicants required to submit FAFSA. *Faculty research:* Gifted education, STEM education, academic competition. *Unit head:* Dr. Charlton H. Wolfgang, Coordinator, 717-871-7338, E-mail: charlton.wolfgang@millersville.edu. *Application contact:* Dr. Victor S. DeSantis, Dean of College of Graduate Studies and Adult Learning/Associate Provost for Civic and Community Engagement, 717-871-7619, Fax: 717-871-7954, E-mail: victor.desantis@millersville.edu.
Website: http://www.millersville.edu/academics/educ/eled/graduate-programs/gifted-education.php#MasterofEducationDegreeinGiftedEducation

Mississippi University for Women, Graduate School, College of Education and Human Sciences, Columbus, MS 39701-9998. Offers differentiated instruction (M Ed); educational leadership (M Ed); gifted studies (M Ed); reading/literacy (M Ed); teaching (MAT). *Accreditation:* ASHA; NCATE. *Program availability:* Part-time. *Degree requirements:* For master's, comprehensive exam, thesis optional. *Entrance requirements:* For master's, GRE General Test or NTE (M Ed in gifted education or MS in speech/language pathology), MAT (M Ed in instructional management), minimum QPA of 3.0.

Morehead State University, Graduate Programs, College of Education, Department of Foundational and Graduate Studies in Education, Morehead, KY 40351. Offers adult and higher education (MA, Ed S); certified professional counselor (Ed S); counseling P-12 (MA); curriculum and instruction (Ed S); educational technology (MA Ed); instructional leadership (Ed S); school administration (MA); school counseling (Ed S); teacher leader business and marketing content (MA Ed); teacher leader business and marketing technology (MA Ed); teacher leader educational technology (MA Ed); teacher leader English (MA Ed); teacher leader gifted education (MA Ed); teacher leader IECE certification (MA Ed); teacher leader interdisciplinary education P-5 (MA Ed); teacher leader middle grades (MA Ed); teacher leader non IECE certification (MA Ed); teacher leader reading/writing - non-certification (MA Ed); teacher leader reading/writing certification (MA Ed); teacher leader school communication - certification (MA Ed); teacher leader school communication - non-certification (MA Ed); teacher leader social studies (MA Ed); teacher leader special education (MA Ed). *Accreditation:* NCATE. *Program availability:* Part-time, evening/weekend. *Degree requirements:* For master's, thesis optional, oral and/or written comprehensive exams; for Ed S, thesis, oral exam. *Entrance requirements:* For master's, GRE General Test, minimum overall undergraduate GPA of 2.5; for Ed S, GRE General Test, interview, master's degree, minimum GPA of 3.5, work experience. Additional exam requirements/recommendations for international students: Required—TOEFL (minimum score 500 paper-based). Electronic applications accepted. *Faculty research:* Character education, school accountability, computer applications for school administrators.

Northeastern Illinois University, College of Graduate Studies and Research, College of Education, Program in Gifted Education, Chicago, IL 60625-4699. Offers MA. *Program availability:* Part-time, evening/weekend. *Degree requirements:* For master's, comprehensive exam, thesis or alternative. *Entrance requirements:* For master's, teaching certificate or previous course work in history or philosophy of education, minimum GPA of 2.75. Additional exam requirements/recommendations for international students: Required—TOEFL (minimum score 550 paper-based; 79 iBT). Electronic applications accepted. *Faculty research:* Effect of inclusion in public school gifted programs, social and emotional needs of gifted children, problem-based learning strategies.

Pacific University, College of Education, Forest Grove, OR 97116-1797. Offers early childhood education (MAT); education (MAE); elementary education (MAT); ESOL (MAT); high school education (MAT); middle school education (MAT); special education (MAT); speech-language pathology (MS); STEM education (MAT); talented and gifted (M Ed); visual function in learning (M Ed). *Accreditation:* NCATE. *Program availability:* Part-time, evening/weekend. *Degree requirements:* For master's, research project. *Entrance requirements:* For master's, California Basic Educational Skills Test, PRAXIS II, minimum undergraduate GPA of 2.75, 3.0 graduate. Additional exam requirements/recommendations for international students: Required—TOEFL. Electronic applications accepted. *Expenses:* Contact institution. *Faculty research:* Defining a culturally competent classroom, technology in the k-12 classroom, Socratic seminars, social studies education.

Purdue University, Graduate School, College of Education, Department of Educational Studies, West Lafayette, IN 47907. Offers administration (MS Ed, PhD, Ed S); counseling and development (MS Ed, PhD); education of the gifted (MS Ed); educational psychology (MS Ed, PhD); foundations of education (MS Ed, PhD); higher education administration (MS Ed, PhD); special education (MS Ed, PhD). *Accreditation:* ACA (one or more programs are accredited); NCATE (one or more programs are accredited). *Program availability:* Part-time, evening/weekend. *Faculty:* 29 full-time (22 women), 1 part-time/adjunct (0 women). *Students:* 78 full-time (60 women), 226 part-time (162 women); includes 45 minority (16 Black or African American, non-Hispanic/Latino; 8 Asian, non-Hispanic/Latino; 15 Hispanic/Latino; 6 Two or more races, non-Hispanic/Latino), 45 international. Average age 32. 214 applicants, 53% accepted, 70 enrolled. In 2016, 38 master's, 20 doctorates, 4 other advanced degrees awarded. *Degree requirements:* For master's, thesis optional; for doctorate, thesis/dissertation, oral and written exams; for Ed S, oral presentation, project. *Entrance requirements:* For master's, GRE General Test (except for special education if undergraduate GPA is higher than a 3.0), minimum undergraduate GPA of 3.0; for doctorate and Ed S, GRE General Test (minimum combined score of 1000, 300 for new scoring), minimum undergraduate GPA of 3.0. Additional exam requirements/recommendations for international students: Required—TOEFL (minimum score 550 paper-based; 77 iBT), TWE (minimum score 5). *Application deadline:* Applications are processed on a rolling basis. Application fee: $60 ($75 for international students). Electronic applications accepted. *Financial support:* Fellowships with full tuition reimbursements, research assistantships with full tuition reimbursements, teaching assistantships with full tuition reimbursements, career-related internships or fieldwork, and tuition waivers (full) available. Support available to part-time students. Financial award application deadline: 3/1; financial award applicants required to submit FAFSA. *Faculty research:* Motivation, learning disabilities, school learning, group processes, cognitive development. *Unit head:* F. Richard Olenchak, Head, 765-494-9170, E-mail: olenchak@purdue.edu. *Application contact:* Heather Brinkman, Graduate Contact, 765-494-2345, Fax: 765-494-5832, E-mail: hbrinkma@purdue.edu.
Website: http://www.edst.purdue.edu/

Regent University, Graduate School, School of Education, Virginia Beach, VA 23464-9800. Offers adult education (Ed D, PhD, Ed S); advanced educational leadership (Ed D, PhD, Ed S); career switcher (M Ed); character education (Ed D, PhD, Ed S); Christian education leadership (Ed D, PhD, Ed S); Christian school administration (M Ed); curriculum and instruction (M Ed), including adult education, Christian school, gifted and talented education, STEM education, teacher leader; educational leadership (M Ed); educational psychology (Ed D, PhD, Ed S); educational technology and online learning (Ed D, PhD, Ed S); elementary education (M Ed); exceptional education executive leadership (Ed D, PhD, Ed S); higher education (Ed D, PhD, Ed S); higher education leadership and management (Ed D, PhD, Ed S); individualized degree plan (M Ed); K-12 school leadership (Ed D, PhD, Ed S); K-12 special education (M Ed); K-8 leadership in mathematics education (M Ed); leadership in mathematics education (Ed S); reading specialist (M Ed); special education (Ed D, PhD, Ed S); student affairs (M Ed); TESOL (M Ed), including adult education - collegiate, K-12. *Accreditation:* TEAC. *Program availability:* Part-time, evening/weekend, 100% online, blended/hybrid learning. *Faculty:* 22 full-time (10 women), 42 part-time/adjunct (31 women). *Students:* 89 full-time (62 women), 1,035 part-time (823 women); includes 466 minority (381 Black or African American, non-Hispanic/Latino; 3 American Indian or Alaska Native, non-Hispanic/Latino; 19 Asian, non-Hispanic/Latino; 50 Hispanic/Latino; 13 Two or more races, non-Hispanic/Latino), 11 international. Average age 39. 976 applicants, 59% accepted, 449 enrolled. In 2016, 241 master's, 22 doctorates, 4 other advanced degrees awarded. *Degree requirements:* For master's, thesis or alternative; for doctorate, comprehensive exam, thesis/dissertation. *Entrance requirements:* For master's, Virginia Communication and Literacy Assessment (VCLA), PRAXIS, college transcripts, writing sample, interview; for doctorate, GRE, writing sample, resume, transcripts, interview. Additional exam requirements/recommendations for international students: Required—TOEFL (minimum score 577 paper-based). *Application deadline:* For fall admission, 4/1 priority date for domestic students; for spring admission, 10/15 priority date for domestic students. Applications are processed on a rolling basis. Application fee: $50. Electronic applications accepted. *Expenses:* Contact institution. *Financial support:* In 2016–17, 622 students received support, including 1 fellowship (averaging $5,000 per year); career-related internships or fieldwork, scholarships/grants, and unspecified assistantships also available. Support available to part-time students. *Faculty research:* Christian school administration, curriculum and instruction, educational technology and online learning, higher education, special education. *Unit head:* Dr. Donald Finn, Dean, 757-352-4278, Fax: 757-352-4318, E-mail: dfinn@regent.edu. *Application contact:* Heidi Cece, Assistant Vice President of Enrollment Management, 800-373-5504, Fax: 757-352-4381, E-mail: admissions@regent.edu.
Website: http://www.regent.edu/soe/

St. Bonaventure University, School of Graduate Studies, School of Education, Differentiated Instruction Program, St. Bonaventure, NY 14778-2284. Offers gifted education (MS Ed, Adv C); gifted education and students with disabilities (MS Ed). *Program availability:* Part-time, evening/weekend. *Faculty:* 3 full-time (all women), 1 (woman) part-time/adjunct. *Students:* 20 full-time (17 women), 17 part-time (16 women); includes 1 minority (Two or more races, non-Hispanic/Latino). Average age 25. 7 applicants, 100% accepted, 6 enrolled. In 2016, 16 master's awarded. *Degree requirements:* For master's, comprehensive exam, internship, portfolio; for Adv C, practicum, portfolio. *Entrance requirements:* For master's, GRE or MAT, disabilities or special education teaching certification (or letter of eligibility); interview; transcripts from all colleges previously attended; 2 letters of recommendation; writing sample; for Adv C, teaching certification (or letter of eligibility); interview; transcripts from all colleges previously attended; 2 references; master's degree; writing sample. Additional exam requirements/recommendations for international students: Required—TOEFL (minimum score 550 paper-based; 79 iBT). *Application deadline:* For fall admission, 6/15 priority date for domestic students, 2/1 priority date for international students; for spring admission, 11/15 priority date for domestic students, 7/1 priority date for international students. Applications are processed on a rolling basis. Application fee: $0. Electronic applications accepted. *Expenses:* $733 per credit, $100 graduation fee. *Financial support:* Federal Work-Study, scholarships/grants, health care benefits, and unspecified assistantships available. Support available to part-time students. Financial award application deadline: 4/15; financial award applicants required to submit FAFSA. *Faculty*

research: Disproportionality in special education, gifted education, teacher education and curriculum, specializing in authentic and responsive pedagogy for diverse learners. *Unit head:* Dr. Rene' Hauser, Director, 716-375-4078, Fax: 716-375-2360, E-mail: rhauser@sbu.edu. *Application contact:* Bruce Campbell, Director of Graduate Admissions, 716-375-2429, Fax: 716-375-4015, E-mail: gradsch@sbu.edu.
Website: http://www.sbu.edu/academics/schools/education/graduate-degrees-certificates/msed-in-differentiated-instruction-gifted

St. John's University, The School of Education, Division of Administrative and Instructional Leadership, Queens, NY 11439. Offers educational administration and supervision (Ed D), including administration and supervision; gifted education (Certificate); instructional leadership (Ed D, Adv C); school building leadership (MS Ed, Adv C); school building leadership/school district leadership (Adv C); school district leadership (Adv C). *Program availability:* Part-time, evening/weekend, online learning. *Degree requirements:* For master's, comprehensive exam; for doctorate, thesis/dissertation. *Entrance requirements:* For master's, GRE, personal statement, official transcript, minimum GPA of 3.0, 2 letters of recommendation, NYC permanent teaching certificate, 3 years of teaching, bachelor's degree; for doctorate, GRE General Test, interview, personal statement, official transcript, minimum GPA of 3.2, 2 letters of recommendation; for other advanced degree, New York teaching certificate, minimum GPA of 3.2, 2 letters of recommendation. Additional exam requirements/recommendations for international students: Required—TOEFL (minimum score 600 paper-based; 100 iBT), IELTS (minimum score 7). Electronic applications accepted. *Faculty research:* Mathematics learning disabilities and difficulties with learning disabled or English language learner students, identification of mathematical giftedness in students who are English language learners, effects of parental participation and parenting behaviors on the science and mathematics academic achievement of school-age students, school administrators' accountability in response to N.Y. state and federal regulations and reforms, use of twenty-first century technology in today's schools.

Saint Leo University, Graduate Studies in Education, Saint Leo, FL 33574-6665. Offers educational leadership (M Ed), including Catholic school administration; exceptional student education (M Ed); instructional design (MS, Certificate); instructional leadership (M Ed); reading (M Ed, Certificate); school leadership (Ed S). *Program availability:* Part-time, evening/weekend, online learning. *Faculty:* 11 full-time (10 women), 22 part-time/adjunct (15 women). *Students:* 424 part-time (335 women); includes 94 minority (54 Black or African American, non-Hispanic/Latino; 2 Asian, non-Hispanic/Latino; 32 Hispanic/Latino; 6 Two or more races, non-Hispanic/Latino), 1 international. Average age 37. 260 applicants, 76% accepted, 107 enrolled. In 2016, 166 master's, 6 other advanced degrees awarded. *Degree requirements:* For master's, appropriate State of Florida certification tests. *Entrance requirements:* For master's, GRE (minimum score of 1000), MAT (minimum score of 410), or minimum undergraduate GPA of 3.0 in final 2 years, official transcripts, current resumé, 2 professional recommendations, personal statement, bachelor's degree from regionally-accredited university, valid professional teaching certificate; for other advanced degree, valid professional teaching certificate (for Ed S). Additional exam requirements/recommendations for international students: Required—TOEFL (minimum score 550 paper-based; 80 iBT). *Application deadline:* For fall admission, 7/1 priority date for domestic students, 7/1 for international students; for winter admission, 7/1 for international students; for spring admission, 11/1 priority date for domestic students. Applications are processed on a rolling basis. Application fee: $80. Electronic applications accepted. *Expenses:* $465 per semester hour (for MS); $480 per semester hour (for M Ed); $670 per semester hour (for Ed S). *Financial support:* In 2016–17, 17 students received support. Career-related internships or fieldwork, scholarships/grants, and health care benefits available. Financial award application deadline: 3/1; financial award applicants required to submit FAFSA. *Faculty research:* Student achievement in literacy, leadership, instructional technology. *Unit head:* Dr. Fern Aefsky, Director of Graduate Studies in Education, 352-588-8309, Fax: 352-588-8861, E-mail: kara.winkler@saintleo.edu. *Application contact:* Jennifer Shelley, Senior Associate Director of Graduate Admissions, 800-707-8846, Fax: 352-588-7873, E-mail: grad.admissions@saintleo.edu.
Website: http://www.saintleo.edu/academics/graduate.aspx

Saint Mary's University of Minnesota, Schools of Graduate and Professional Programs, Graduate School of Education, Education Program, Winona, MN 55987-1399. Offers culturally responsive teaching (Certificate); education (MA); gifted inclusive education (Certificate). Tuition and fees vary according to degree level and program. *Unit head:* Lynn Albee, Director, 612-728-5179, Fax: 612-728-5128, E-mail: lalbee@smumn.edu. *Application contact:* James Callinan, Director of Admissions for Graduate and Professional Programs, 612-728-5185, Fax: 612-728-5121, E-mail: jcallina@smumn.edu.
Website: http://www.smumn.edu/graduate-home/areas-of-study/graduate-school-of-education/ma-in-education

St. Thomas University, School of Leadership Studies, Institute for Education, Miami Gardens, FL 33054-6459. Offers earth/space science (Certificate); educational administration (MS, Certificate); educational leadership (Ed D); elementary education (MS); ESOL (Certificate); gifted education (Certificate); instructional technology (MS, Certificate); professional/studies (Certificate); reading (MS, Certificate); special education (MS). *Program availability:* Part-time, evening/weekend. *Degree requirements:* For master's, comprehensive exam; for doctorate, comprehensive exam, thesis/dissertation. *Entrance requirements:* For master's, interview, minimum GPA of 3.0 or GRE; for doctorate, GRE or MAT. Additional exam requirements/recommendations for international students: Required—TOEFL (minimum score 550 paper-based; 79 iBT). Electronic applications accepted.

Samford University, Orlean Beeson School of Education, Birmingham, AL 35229. Offers education (Ed D, Certificate); educational leadership: policy, organizations, leadership (MSE); elementary education (MS Ed); gifted certification (MSE); instructional design and technology (MSE); instructional leadership (MSE, Ed S); K-12 collaborative special education (MSE); teacher leader (Ed S). *Accreditation:* NCATE. *Program availability:* Part-time, evening/weekend, 100% online, blended/hybrid learning. *Faculty:* 15 full-time (9 women), 17 part-time/adjunct (12 women). *Students:* 219 full-time (161 women), 86 part-time (55 women); includes 97 minority (86 Black or African American, non-Hispanic/Latino; 5 American Indian or Alaska Native, non-Hispanic/Latino; 1 Asian, non-Hispanic/Latino; 1 Hispanic/Latino; 4 Two or more races, non-Hispanic/Latino), 2 international. Average age 38. 244 applicants, 52% accepted, 112 enrolled. In 2016, 84 master's, 22 doctorates, 12 Certificates awarded. *Degree requirements:* For master's, comprehensive exam (for some programs); for doctorate, comprehensive exam, thesis/dissertation; for other advanced degree, comprehensive exam. *Entrance requirements:* For master's, GRE or MAT; Alabama Educator Certification Testing Program (AECTP), transcripts, essays, recommendations; for doctorate, professional resume, recommendations, transcripts, interview, essays; for other advanced degree, recommendations, transcripts. Additional exam requirements/recommendations for international students: Required—TOEFL (minimum score 90 iBT), IELTS (minimum score 6.5). *Application deadline:* For fall admission, 7/15 for domestic students, 7/1 for international students; for spring admission, 11/15 for domestic and international students; for summer admission, 4/15 for domestic and international students. Application fee: $35. Electronic applications accepted. *Expenses:* *Tuition:* Full-time $18,530; part-time $789 per credit hour. *Required fees:* $610. Tuition and fees vary according to course load, degree level, program and student level. *Financial support:* In 2016–17, 246 students received support. Scholarships/grants available. Financial award application deadline: 3/1; financial award applicants required to submit FAFSA. *Faculty research:* Standards-based grading in K-12 schools, effective school principal leadership, effective educational leadership preparation programs, teacher/administrator shortages and job retention, instructional strategies to maximize student learning. *Total annual research expenditures:* $254,360. *Unit head:* Dr. Jean Box, Dean, 205-726-2565, Fax: 205-726-4233, E-mail: jabox@samford.edu. *Application contact:* Brooke Karr, Graduate Admissions Coordinator, 205-729-2783, Fax: 205-726-4233, E-mail: kbgilrea@samford.edu.
Website: http://www.samford.edu/education/

Southeastern University, College of Education, Lakeland, FL 33801-6099. Offers curriculum and instruction (Ed D); educational leadership (M Ed); elementary education (M Ed); exceptional student education (M Ed); exceptional student education/educational therapy (M Ed); organizational leadership (Ed D); reading education (M Ed); teaching English to speakers of other languages (M Ed). *Expenses: Tuition:* Full-time $9450; part-time $6300 per credit. *Required fees:* $500; $250 per semester. One-time fee: $150. Tuition and fees vary according to degree level, campus/location and program. *Unit head:* Amy N. Bratten, Dean, 863-667-5238, E-mail: anbratten@seu.edu.
Website: http://www.seu.edu/education/

Southern Arkansas University–Magnolia, School of Graduate Studies, Magnolia, AR 71753. Offers agriculture (MS); business administration (MBA), including agri-business, social entrepreneurship, supply chain management; clinical and mental health counseling (MS); computer and information sciences (MS), including cyber security and privacy, data science, information technology; gifted and talented (M Ed), including curriculum and instruction, educational administration and supervision, gifted and talented P-8/7-12, instructional specialist P-4; higher, adult and lifelong education (M Ed); kinesiology (M Ed), including coaching; library media and information specialist (M Ed); public administration (MPA); school counseling K-12 (M Ed); student affairs and college counseling (M Ed); teaching (MAT). *Accreditation:* NCATE. *Program availability:* Part-time, 100% online, blended/hybrid learning. *Faculty:* 36 full-time (19 women), 33 part-time/adjunct (14 women). *Students:* 605 full-time (143 women), 879 part-time (352 women); includes 130 minority (113 Black or African American, non-Hispanic/Latino; 7 American Indian or Alaska Native, non-Hispanic/Latino; 2 Asian, non-Hispanic/Latino; 2 Hispanic/Latino; 6 Two or more races, non-Hispanic/Latino), 1,048 international. Average age 28. 904 applicants, 81% accepted, 262 enrolled. In 2016, 278 master's awarded. *Degree requirements:* For master's, comprehensive exam (for some programs), thesis optional. *Entrance requirements:* For master's, GRE, MAT or GMAT, minimum GPA of 2.5. Additional exam requirements/recommendations for international students: Required—TOEFL (minimum score 550 paper-based), IELTS (minimum score 6). *Application deadline:* For fall admission, 7/20 for domestic students, 7/10 for international students; for spring admission, 12/1 for domestic students, 11/15 for international students; for summer admission, 4/1 for domestic students, 5/1 for international students. Applications are processed on a rolling basis. Application fee: $25 ($50 for international students). Electronic applications accepted. *Expenses:* Tuition, state resident: full-time $2511; part-time $279 per credit hour. Tuition, nonresident: full-time $3726; part-time $414 per credit hour. *Required fees:* $307 per semester. Tuition and fees vary according to course load and program. *Financial support:* Career-related internships or fieldwork, Federal Work-Study, scholarships/grants, tuition waivers (full), and unspecified assistantships available. Financial award applicants required to submit FAFSA. *Faculty research:* Alternative certification for teachers, supervision of instruction, instructional leadership, counseling. *Unit head:* Dr. Kim Bloss, Dean, School of Graduate Studies, 870-235-4150, Fax: 870-235-5227, E-mail: kkbloss@saumag.edu. *Application contact:* Shrijana Malakar, Admissions Specialist, 870-235-4150, Fax: 870-235-5227, E-mail: smalakar@saumag.edu.
Website: http://www.saumag.edu/graduate

Southern Methodist University, Annette Caldwell Simmons School of Education and Human Development, Department of Teaching and Learning, Dallas, TX 75275. Offers bilingual/ESL education (MBE); education (M Ed, PhD); gifted education (MBE); reading and writing (M Ed); special education (M Ed). *Program availability:* Part-time, evening/weekend. Terminal master's awarded for partial completion of doctoral program. *Degree requirements:* For master's, comprehensive exam, minimum GPA of 3.0; for doctorate, thesis/dissertation, qualifying exams, major area paper, evidence of teaching competency, dissemination of research (e.g., conference presentation), professional portfolio. *Entrance requirements:* For master's, minimum GPA of 3.0 or GRE, 3 letters of recommendation; for doctorate, GRE, minimum GPA of 3.3, 3 years of full-time teaching, 3 letters of recommendation, interview. Additional exam requirements/recommendations for international students: Required—TOEFL. Electronic applications accepted. *Faculty research:* Reading intervention, mathematics intervention, bilingual education, new literacies.

Teachers College, Columbia University, Department of Curriculum and Teaching, New York, NY 10027-6696. Offers curriculum and teaching (Ed M, MA, Ed D); curriculum and teaching: elementary education (MA); curriculum and teaching: secondary education (MA); early childhood education (MA, Ed D); early childhood education: special education (MA); elementary education-gifted extension (MA); elementary inclusive education (MA); gifted education (MA); literacy specialist (MA); secondary inclusive education (MA); special inclusive elementary education (MA). *Program availability:* Part-time, evening/weekend. *Students:* 236 full-time (219 women), 198 part-time (176 women); includes 160 minority (53 Black or African American, non-Hispanic/Latino; 1 American Indian or Alaska Native, non-Hispanic/Latino; 43 Asian, non-Hispanic/Latino; 41 Hispanic/Latino; 22 Two or more races, non-Hispanic/Latino), 38 international. 399 applicants, 66% accepted, 104 enrolled. Terminal master's awarded for partial completion of doctoral program. *Degree requirements:* For doctorate, thesis/dissertation. *Expenses: Tuition:* Full-time $36,288; part-time $1512 per credit. *Required fees:* $438 per semester. One-time fee: $510 full-time. Full-time tuition and fees vary according to course load. *Unit head:* Prof. Nancy Lesko, Chair, 212-678-3264, E-mail: lesko@tc.columbia.edu. *Application contact:* David Estrella, Director of Admission, 212-678-3305, Fax: 212-678-4171, E-mail: estrella@tc.columbia.edu.

Tennessee Technological University, College of Graduate Studies, College of Education, Department of Curriculum and Instruction, Program in Exceptional Learning, Cookeville, TN 38505. Offers applied behavior analysis (PhD); literacy (PhD); program planning and evaluation (PhD); STEM education (PhD). *Program availability:* Part-time, evening/weekend. *Students:* 10 full-time (6 women), 28 part-time (21 women); includes 2 minority (1 Black or African American, non-Hispanic/Latino; 1 Two or more races, non-Hispanic/Latino), 2 international. 15 applicants, 67% accepted, 7 enrolled. In 2016, 5 doctorates awarded. *Degree requirements:* For doctorate, comprehensive exam, thesis/dissertation. *Entrance requirements:* For doctorate, GRE, minimum GPA of 3.0. Additional exam requirements/recommendations for international students: Required—TOEFL (minimum score 550 paper-based; 79 iBT), IELTS (minimum score 5.5), PTE (minimum score 53), or TOEIC (Test of English as an International Communication). *Application deadline:* For fall admission, 8/1 for domestic students, 5/1 for international students; for spring admission, 12/1 for domestic students, 10/1 for international

students; for summer admission, 5/1 for domestic students, 2/1 for international students. Applications are processed on a rolling basis. Application fee: $35 ($40 for international students). Electronic applications accepted. *Expenses:* Tuition, state resident: full-time $9375; part-time $534 per credit hour. Tuition, nonresident: full-time $22,443; part-time $1260 per credit hour. *Financial support:* In 2016–17, 4 fellowships (averaging $8,000 per year), 9 research assistantships (averaging $12,000 per year), 2 teaching assistantships (averaging $12,000 per year) were awarded. Financial award application deadline: 4/1. *Unit head:* Dr. Lisa Zagumny, Director, 931-372-3078, Fax: 931-372-3517, E-mail: lzagumny@tntech.edu. *Application contact:* Shelia K. Kendrick, Coordinator of Graduate Studies, 931-372-3808, Fax: 931-372-3497, E-mail: skendrick@tntech.edu.
Website: https://www.tntech.edu/education/elphd/

University at Buffalo, the State University of New York, Graduate School, Graduate School of Education, Department of Learning and Instruction, Buffalo, NY 14260. Offers biology education (Ed M, Certificate); chemistry education (Ed M, Certificate); childhood education (Ed M); childhood education with bilingual extension (Ed M); college teaching (Advanced Certificate); curriculum, instruction and the science of learning (PhD); early childhood education (Ed M); early childhood education with bilingual extension (Ed M); earth science education (Ed M, Certificate); education and technology (Ed M); education studies (Ed M); educational technology and new literacies (Certificate); educational technology and new literacies (Advanced Certificate); elementary education (Ed D); English education (Ed M, Certificate); English education studies (Ed M); English for speakers of other languages (Ed M); foreign and second language education (PhD); French education (Ed M, Certificate); German education (Ed M, Certificate); gifted education (Certificate); Latin education (Ed M, Certificate); literacy education studies (Ed M); literacy specialist (Ed M); literacy teaching and learning (Certificate); mathematics education (Ed M, Certificate); music education (Ed M, Certificate); music education studies (Ed M); music learning theory (Advanced Certificate); online education (Advanced Certificate); physics education (Ed M, Certificate); science and the public (Ed M); social studies education (Ed M, Certificate); Spanish education (Ed M, Certificate); special education (PhD); teaching English to speakers of other languages (Ed M). *Program availability:* Part-time, evening/weekend, 100% online. *Faculty:* 28 full-time (21 women), 67 part-time/adjunct (49 women). *Students:* 198 full-time (153 women), 312 part-time (220 women); includes 48 minority (28 Black or African American, non-Hispanic/Latino; 4 American Indian or Alaska Native, non-Hispanic/Latino; 15 Asian, non-Hispanic/Latino; 1 Hispanic/Latino), 66 international. Average age 33. 336 applicants, 86% accepted, 178 enrolled. In 2016, 137 master's, 24 doctorates, 25 other advanced degrees awarded. *Degree requirements:* For master's, comprehensive exam; for doctorate, thesis/dissertation, research analysis exam, research experience. *Entrance requirements:* For master's, letters of reference; for doctorate, GRE General Test or MAT, interview, writing sample, letters of recommendation. Additional exam requirements/recommendations for international students: Required—TOEFL (minimum score 600 paper-based; 96 iBT). *Application deadline:* For fall admission, 2/1 priority date for domestic and international students; for spring admission, 11/15 priority date for domestic students, 10/1 for international students. Applications are processed on a rolling basis. Application fee: $50. Electronic applications accepted. *Financial support:* In 2016–17, 44 fellowships (averaging $4,010 per year), 39 research assistantships with tuition reimbursements (averaging $9,897 per year) were awarded; teaching assistantships, career-related internships or fieldwork, Federal Work-Study, institutionally sponsored loans, scholarships/grants, tuition waivers (full and partial), and unspecified assistantships also available. Financial award application deadline: 2/28; financial award applicants required to submit FAFSA. *Faculty research:* Science assessment, foreign language teaching and learning, early learning, new literacies, gender and education. *Total annual research expenditures:* $534,880. *Unit head:* Dr. Deborah Moore-Russo, Chair, 716-645-4069, Fax: 716-645-3161, E-mail: dam29@buffalo.edu. *Application contact:* Luann Zak, Admissions Assistant, 716-645-2110, Fax: 716-645-7937, E-mail: luannzak@buffalo.edu.
Website: http://gse.buffalo.edu/lai

The University of Alabama, Graduate School, College of Education, Department of Special Education and Multiple Abilities, Tuscaloosa, AL 35487. Offers collaborative special education (M Ed, Ed S); early intervention (M Ed, Ed S); gifted and talented education (M Ed, Ed S); multiple abilities (M Ed); special education (Ed D, PhD). *Program availability:* Part-time, evening/weekend. *Faculty:* 12 full-time (8 women). *Students:* 26 full-time (24 women), 34 part-time (33 women); includes 8 minority (5 Black or African American, non-Hispanic/Latino; 1 American Indian or Alaska Native, non-Hispanic/Latino; 1 Asian, non-Hispanic/Latino; 1 Hispanic/Latino). Average age 33. 50 applicants, 54% accepted, 24 enrolled. In 2016, 34 master's, 1 doctorate, 1 other advanced degree awarded. Terminal master's awarded for partial completion of doctoral program. *Degree requirements:* For master's, comprehensive exam, thesis optional; for doctorate, one foreign language, comprehensive exam, thesis/dissertation. *Entrance requirements:* For master's, GRE, minimum undergraduate GPA of 3.0, teaching certificate, 3 letters of recommendation; for doctorate, GRE, 3 years of teaching experience, minimum undergraduate GPA of 3.25. Additional exam requirements/recommendations for international students: Required—TOEFL. *Application deadline:* Applications are processed on a rolling basis. Application fee: $50 ($60 for international students). Electronic applications accepted. *Expenses:* Tuition, state resident: full-time $10,470. Tuition, nonresident: full-time $26,950. *Financial support:* In 2016–17, 10 students received support, including 5 research assistantships with tuition reimbursements available (averaging $9,000 per year), 5 teaching assistantships with tuition reimbursements available (averaging $9,000 per year); health care benefits and unspecified assistantships also available. Financial award application deadline: 7/1; financial award applicants required to submit FAFSA. *Faculty research:* Gifted education, mild disabilities, early intervention, severe disabilities, behavior disorders. *Unit head:* Dr. Robert Alexander McWilliam, Professor and Department Head, 205-348-6527, Fax: 205-348-6782, E-mail: ramcwilliam@ua.edu. *Application contact:* Bernice Ofori-Parku, Office Associate II, 205-348-6093, Fax: 205-348-6782, E-mail: bsoforiparku@ua.edu.
Website: http://education.ua.edu/departments/spema/

University of Arkansas at Little Rock, Graduate School, College of Education and Health Professions, Department of Educational Leadership, Program in Gifted and Talented Education, Little Rock, AR 72204-1099. Offers M Ed, Graduate Certificate. *Degree requirements:* For Graduate Certificate, comprehensive exam. *Entrance requirements:* For degree, teacher license.

University of Central Arkansas, Graduate School, College of Education, Department of Early Childhood and Special Education, Conway, AR 72035-0001. Offers gifted and talented education (Graduate Certificate); instructional facilitator (Graduate Certificate); reading education (MSE); special education (MSE, Graduate Certificate), including collaborative instructional specialist (ages 0-8) (MSE), collaborative instructional specialist (grades 4-12) (MSE), special education instructional specialist grades 4-12 (Graduate Certificate), special education instructional specialist P-4 (Graduate Certificate). *Program availability:* Part-time, evening/weekend, online learning. *Degree requirements:* For master's, comprehensive exam, thesis optional. *Entrance requirements:* For master's, GRE General Test, minimum GPA of 2.7. Additional exam requirements/recommendations for international students: Required—TOEFL (minimum score 550 paper-based; 80 iBT). Electronic applications accepted.

University of Central Arkansas, Graduate School, College of Education, Department of Leadership Studies, Conway, AR 72035-0001. Offers college student personnel (MS); district-level administration (PMC); educational leadership - district level (Ed S); instructional technology (MS); library media and information technology (MS); school counseling (MS); school leadership (MS); school-based leadership adult education program administration (PMC); school-based leadership building administration (PMC); school-based leadership curriculum administration (PMC); school-based leadership gifted and talented program administration (PMC); school-based leadership special education program administration (PMC). *Accreditation:* NCATE. *Program availability:* Part-time, evening/weekend, online learning. *Degree requirements:* For master's and other advanced degree, comprehensive exam. *Entrance requirements:* For master's, GRE. Additional exam requirements/recommendations for international students: Required—TOEFL (minimum score 80 iBT). Electronic applications accepted. *Expenses:* Contact institution.

University of Connecticut, Graduate School, Neag School of Education, Department of Educational Psychology, Program in Gifted and Talented Education, Storrs, CT 06269. Offers Graduate Certificate. *Accreditation:* NCATE. Terminal master's awarded for partial completion of doctoral program. *Entrance requirements:* Additional exam requirements/recommendations for international students: Required—TOEFL (minimum score 550 paper-based). Electronic applications accepted.

University of Louisiana at Lafayette, College of Education, Graduate Studies and Research in Education, Program in Education of the Gifted, Lafayette, LA 70504. Offers M Ed. *Accreditation:* NCATE. *Degree requirements:* For master's, thesis or alternative. *Entrance requirements:* For master's, GRE General Test, teaching certificate. Additional exam requirements/recommendations for international students: Required—TOEFL (minimum score 550 paper-based). Electronic applications accepted.

University of Louisiana at Monroe, Graduate School, College of Arts, Education, and Sciences, School of Education, Program in Curriculum and Instruction, Monroe, LA 71209-0001. Offers art education (M Ed); biology education (M Ed); chemistry education (M Ed); curriculum and instruction (Ed D); early childhood education (M Ed); earth science education (M Ed); educational leadership (M Ed); elementary education (1-5) (M Ed); English as a second language (M Ed); English education (M Ed); family and consumer education (M Ed); French education (M Ed); history education (M Ed); math education (M Ed); middle school education (M Ed); music education (M Ed); reading education (K-12) (M Ed); Spanish education (M Ed); special education - academically gifted (M Ed); special education - early intervention (M Ed); special education - educational diagnostician (M Ed); special education - mild/moderate disabilities (M Ed); speech education (M Ed). *Accreditation:* NCATE. *Faculty:* 8 full-time (4 women), 4 part-time/adjunct (3 women). *Students:* 13 full-time (11 women), 80 part-time (65 women); includes 25 minority (19 Black or African American, non-Hispanic/Latino; 1 Asian, non-Hispanic/Latino; 3 Hispanic/Latino; 2 Two or more races, non-Hispanic/Latino). Average age 37. 118 applicants, 30% accepted, 16 enrolled. In 2016, 23 master's, 4 doctorates awarded. *Degree requirements:* For master's, comprehensive exam (for some programs), thesis; for doctorate, thesis/dissertation, internships. *Entrance requirements:* For master's, GRE General Test; for doctorate, GRE General Test, minimum undergraduate GPA of 2.75, graduate 3.25. Additional exam requirements/recommendations for international students: Required—TOEFL (minimum score 500 paper-based; 61 iBT). *Application deadline:* For fall admission, 8/24 priority date for domestic students, 7/1 for international students; for winter admission, 12/14 priority date for domestic students; for spring admission, 1/19 for domestic students, 11/1 for international students. Applications are processed on a rolling basis. Application fee: $20 ($30 for international students). Electronic applications accepted. *Expenses:* Tuition, state resident: full-time $6489. Tuition, nonresident: full-time $18,589. *Required fees:* $8984. Tuition and fees vary according to course level, course load, degree level and program. *Financial support:* Research assistantships, career-related internships or fieldwork, Federal Work-Study, and unspecified assistantships available. Financial award application deadline: 4/1; financial award applicants required to submit FAFSA. *Unit head:* Dr. Dorothy Schween, Director, 318-342-1268, Fax: 318-342-3131, E-mail: schween@ulm.edu.

University of Minnesota, Twin Cities Campus, Graduate School, College of Education and Human Development, Department of Educational Psychology, Minneapolis, MN 55455-0213. Offers autism spectrum disorder (Certificate); counseling and student personnel psychology (MA); early childhood special education (M Ed); psychological foundations of education (MA, PhD); quantitative methods in education (MA, PhD); school psychology (MA, PhD, Ed S); special education (M Ed, MA, PhD); talent development and gifted education (Certificate). *Accreditation:* APA (one or more programs are accredited). *Faculty:* 31 full-time (16 women). *Students:* 261 full-time (197 women), 63 part-time (47 women); includes 46 minority (6 Black or African American, non-Hispanic/Latino; 19 Asian, non-Hispanic/Latino; 12 Hispanic/Latino; 9 Two or more races, non-Hispanic/Latino), 27 international. Average age 29. 285 applicants, 42% accepted, 110 enrolled. In 2016, 153 master's, 35 doctorates, 10 other advanced degrees awarded. Application fee: $75 ($95 for international students). *Financial support:* In 2016–17, 26 fellowships, 61 research assistantships (averaging $14,168 per year), 31 teaching assistantships (averaging $12,522 per year) were awarded. *Faculty research:* Achievement gap; autism; behavioral and social-emotional development; improving skills in mathematics, reading, and comprehension; measuring and analyzing student change. *Total annual research expenditures:* $5.3 million. *Unit head:* Dr. Geoffrey Maruyama, Chair, 612-624-1003, Fax: 612-625-5861, E-mail: geoff@umn.edu. *Application contact:* Dr. Ernest Davenport, Director of Graduate Studies, 612-624-1040, E-mail: lqr6576@umn.edu.
Website: http://www.cehd.umn.edu/EdPsych

University of Missouri, Office of Research and Graduate Studies, College of Education, Department of Special Education, Columbia, MO 65211. Offers administration and supervision of special education (PhD); behavior disorders (M Ed, PhD); curriculum development of exceptional students (M Ed, PhD); early childhood special education (M Ed, PhD); general special education (M Ed, MA, PhD); learning and instruction (M Ed); learning disabilities (M Ed, PhD); mental retardation (M Ed, PhD). *Accreditation:* TEAC. *Program availability:* Part-time, evening/weekend, online learning. *Faculty:* 13 full-time (11 women). *Students:* 22 full-time (20 women), 36 part-time (32 women). *Degree requirements:* For master's, comprehensive exam, thesis or alternative; for doctorate, comprehensive exam, thesis/dissertation. *Entrance requirements:* For master's and doctorate, GRE General Test, letters of recommendation. Additional exam requirements/recommendations for international students: Required—TOEFL (minimum score 500 paper-based; 61 iBT). *Application deadline:* For fall admission, 1/15 priority date for domestic and international students; for winter admission, 11/1 priority date for domestic and international students; for spring admission, 4/1 priority date for domestic and international students. Application fee: $75 ($90 for international students). Electronic applications accepted. *Expenses:* Tuition, state resident: full-time $6347; part-time $352.60 per credit hour. Tuition, nonresident: full-time $17,379; part-time $965.50 per credit hour. *Required fees:* $1035. Tuition and fees vary according to course load, campus/location and program. *Financial support:*

Fellowships with tuition reimbursements, research assistantships with tuition reimbursements, teaching assistantships with tuition reimbursements, career-related internships or fieldwork, scholarships/grants, health care benefits, and unspecified assistantships available.
Website: http://education.missouri.edu/SPED/

University of Nebraska at Kearney, College of Education, Department of Teacher Education, Kearney, NE 68849-0001. Offers curriculum and instruction (MA Ed), including early childhood education, elementary education, English as a second language, instructional effectiveness, reading/special education, secondary education; instructional technology (MS Ed), including information technology, instructional technology, school librarian; reading PK-12 (MA Ed); special education (MA Ed), including advanced practitioner: assistive technology specialist, advanced practitioner: behavioral interventionist, advanced practitioner: inclusive collaboration specialist, gifted, teacher education. *Program availability:* Part-time, evening/weekend, online only, 100% online. *Faculty:* 18 full-time (13 women). *Students:* 21 full-time (15 women), 296 part-time (240 women); includes 21 minority (3 Black or African American, non-Hispanic/Latino; 1 Asian, non-Hispanic/Latino; 14 Hispanic/Latino; 1 Native Hawaiian or other Pacific Islander, non-Hispanic/Latino; 2 Two or more races, non-Hispanic/Latino), 1 international. Average age 32. 81 applicants, 100% accepted, 61 enrolled. In 2016, 129 master's awarded. *Degree requirements:* For master's, comprehensive exam, thesis optional. *Entrance requirements:* For master's, portfolio or GRE. Additional exam requirements/recommendations for international students: Recommended—TOEFL (minimum score 550 paper-based; 79 iBT), IELTS (minimum score 6.5). *Application deadline:* For fall admission, 6/15 for domestic students, 5/15 for international students; for spring admission, 10/15 for domestic and international students; for summer admission, 3/15 for domestic and international students. Application fee: $45. Electronic applications accepted. *Expenses:* $285 per credit hour resident tuition, $415 per credit hour non-resident tuition (online). *Financial support:* In 2016–17, 6 students received support, including 6 research assistantships with full tuition reimbursements available (averaging $10,500 per year); career-related internships or fieldwork, scholarships/grants, health care benefits, and unspecified assistantships also available. Support available to part-time students. Financial award application deadline: 2/28; financial award applicants required to submit FAFSA. *Unit head:* Sarah Bartling, Administrative Assistant, 308-865-8513, E-mail: bartlingseg@unk.edu. *Application contact:* Linda Johnson, Director, Graduate Admissions and Programs, 308-865-8841, Fax: 308-865-8837, E-mail: johnsonli@unk.edu.
Website: http://www.unk.edu/academics/ted/index.php

The University of North Carolina at Charlotte, Cato College of Education, Department of Special Education and Child Development, Charlotte, NC 28223-0001. Offers academically or intellectually gifted (Graduate Certificate); autism spectrum disorders (Graduate Certificate); child and family development: birth through kindergarten (Graduate Certificate); child and family studies: early education (M Ed); special education (M Ed, PhD, Graduate Certificate), including academically or intellectually gifted (M Ed). *Program availability:* Part-time, 100% online, blended/hybrid learning. *Faculty:* 25 full-time (18 women), 8 part-time/adjunct (6 women). *Students:* 21 full-time (17 women), 106 part-time (101 women); includes 11 minority (8 Black or African American, non-Hispanic/Latino; 1 Hispanic/Latino; 2 Two or more races, non-Hispanic/Latino), 4 international. Average age 34. 83 applicants, 95% accepted, 66 enrolled. In 2016, 6 master's, 7 doctorates, 42 other advanced degrees awarded. *Degree requirements:* For master's, thesis or alternative, research project; for doctorate, thesis/dissertation, portfolio; for Graduate Certificate, internship. *Entrance requirements:* For master's, GRE or MAT, personal statement, letters of recommendation; for doctorate, GRE or MAT, 2 official transcripts of all academic work attempted since high school indicating minimum GPA of 3.5 in graduate degree program; at least 3 references of someone who knows applicant's current work and/or academic achievements in previous degree work; two-page essay; current resume or curriculum vitae; writing sample; documentation of teaching; for Graduate Certificate, undergraduate degree from regionally-accredited four-year institution; minimum cumulative undergraduate GPA of 3.0; three recommendations from persons knowledgeable of applicant's interaction with children and families; statement of purpose; clear criminal background check. Additional exam requirements/recommendations for international students: Required—TOEFL (minimum score 523 paper-based, 70 iBT) or IELTS (6.5). *Application deadline:* For fall admission, 12/1 for domestic and international students; for spring admission, 10/1 priority date for domestic and international students; for summer admission, 4/1 priority date for domestic and international students. Applications are processed on a rolling basis. Application fee: $75. Electronic applications accepted. *Expenses:* Tuition, state resident: full-time $4252. Tuition, nonresident: full-time $17,423. *Required fees:* $3026. Tuition and fees vary according to course load and program. *Financial support:* In 2016–17, 11 students received support, including 10 research assistantships (averaging $9,195 per year), 1 teaching assistantship (averaging $16,848 per year); career-related internships or fieldwork, institutionally sponsored loans, scholarships/grants, and unspecified assistantships also available. Support available to part-time students. Financial award application deadline: 3/1; financial award applicants required to submit FAFSA. *Total annual research expenditures:* $4 million. *Unit head:* Dr. Belva Collins, Chair, 704-687-8828, E-mail: belva.collins@uncc.edu. *Application contact:* Kathy B. Giddings, Director of Graduate Admissions, 704-687-5503, Fax: 704-687-1668, E-mail: gradadm@uncc.edu.
Website: http://spcd.uncc.edu/

The University of North Carolina Wilmington, Watson College of Education, Department of Instructional Technology, Foundations and Secondary Education, Wilmington, NC 28403-3297. Offers academically or intellectually gifted (M Ed); English as a second language (M Ed, MAT); instructional technology (MS); physical education and health (M Ed, MAT); secondary education (M Ed, MAT); Spanish (MAT); Spanish education (MASS). *Program availability:* Part-time. *Faculty:* 17 full-time (11 women). *Students:* 36 full-time (22 women), 62 part-time (49 women); includes 17 minority (12 Black or African American, non-Hispanic/Latino; 3 Hispanic/Latino; 2 Two or more races, non-Hispanic/Latino), 5 international. Average age 34. 89 applicants, 89% accepted, 59 enrolled. In 2016, 36 master's awarded. *Degree requirements:* For master's, comprehensive exam (for some programs), thesis (for some programs), thesis or research project. *Entrance requirements:* For master's, GRE or MAT, statement of interest, 3 letters of recommendation, minimum GPA of 3.0 in undergraduate work. Additional exam requirements/recommendations for international students: Required—TOEFL (minimum score 79 iBT), IELTS (minimum score 6.5). *Application deadline:* For fall admission, 5/15 for domestic students; for spring admission, 10/15 for domestic students; for summer admission, 3/15 for domestic students. Applications are processed on a rolling basis. Application fee: $60. Electronic applications accepted. *Expenses:* Contact institution. *Financial support:* Scholarships/grants and unspecified assistantships available. Financial award application deadline: 3/15; financial award applicants required to submit FAFSA. *Unit head:* Dr. Donyell Roseboro, Chair, 910-962-2289, Fax: 910-962-3609, E-mail: roseborod@uncw.edu. *Application contact:* Dr. Mahnaz Moallem, Graduate Coordinator, 910-962-4183, E-mail: moallemm@uncw.edu.
Website: http://www.uncw.edu/ed/itfse/

University of Northern Colorado, Graduate School, College of Education and Behavioral Sciences, School of Special Education, Greeley, CO 80639. Offers deaf/hard of hearing (MA); early childhood special education (MA); gifted and talented (MA); special education (MA, PhD); visual impairment (MA). *Program availability:* Part-time, evening/weekend, online learning. *Degree requirements:* For master's, comprehensive exam, thesis or alternative; for doctorate, comprehensive exam, thesis/dissertation. *Entrance requirements:* For master's, letters of recommendation, interview; for doctorate, GRE General Test, resume. *Application deadline:* Applications are processed on a rolling basis. Application fee: $50 ($60 for international students). Electronic applications accepted. *Financial support:* Fellowships, research assistantships, teaching assistantships, and unspecified assistantships available. Financial award application deadline: 3/1; financial award applicants required to submit FAFSA. *Unit head:* Dr. Harvey Rude, Director, 970-351-2691, Fax: 970-351-1061. *Application contact:* Linda Sisson, Graduate Student Admission Coordinator, 970-351-1807, Fax: 970-351-2371, E-mail: linda.sisson@unco.edu.
Website: http://www.unco.edu/cebs/sped/

University of North Texas, Robert B. Toulouse School of Graduate Studies, Denton, TX 76203-5459. Offers accounting (MS); applied anthropology (MA, MS); applied behavior analysis (Certificate); applied geography (MA); applied technology and performance improvement (M Ed, MS); art education (MA); art history (MA); art museum education (Certificate); arts leadership (Certificate); audiology (Au D); behavior analysis (MS); behavioral science (PhD); biochemistry and molecular biology (MS); biology (MA, MS); biomedical engineering (MS); business analysis (MS); chemistry (MS); clinical health psychology (PhD); communication studies (MA, MS); computer engineering (MS); computer science (MS); counseling (M Ed, MS), including clinical mental health counseling (MS), college and university counseling, elementary school counseling, secondary school counseling; creative writing (MA); criminal justice (MS); curriculum and instruction (M Ed); decision sciences (MBA); design (MA, MFA), including fashion design (MFA), innovation studies, interior design (MFA); early childhood studies (MS); economics (MS); educational leadership (M Ed, Ed D); educational psychology (MS, PhD), including family studies (MS), gifted and talented (MS), human development (MS), learning and cognition (MS), research, measurement and evaluation (MS); electrical engineering (MS); emergency management (MPA); engineering technology (MS); English (MA); English as a second language (MA); environmental science (MS); finance (MBA, MS); financial management (MPA); French (MA); health services management (MBA); higher education (M Ed, Ed D); history (MA, MS); hospitality management (MS); human resources management (MPA); information science (MS); information systems (PhD); information technologies (MBA); interdisciplinary studies (MA, MS); international studies (MA); international sustainable tourism (MS); jazz studies (MM); journalism (MA, MJ, Graduate Certificate), including interactive and virtual digital communication (Graduate Certificate), narrative journalism (Graduate Certificate), public relations (Graduate Certificate); kinesiology (MS); linguistics (MA); local government management (MPA); logistics (PhD); logistics and supply chain management (MBA); long-term care, senior housing, and aging services (MA); management (PhD); marketing (MBA); mathematics (MA, MS); mechanical and energy engineering (MS, PhD); music (MA), including ethnomusicology, music theory, musicology, performance; music composition (PhD); music education (MM Ed, PhD); nonprofit management (MPA); operations and supply chain management (MBA); performance (MM, DMA); philosophy (MA); political science (MA); professional and technical communication (MA); radio, television and film (MA, MFA); rehabilitation counseling (Certificate); sociology (MA); Spanish (MA); special education (M Ed); speech-language pathology (MA); strategic management (MBA); studio art (MFA); teaching (M Ed); MBA/MS. *Program availability:* Part-time, evening/weekend, online learning. Terminal master's awarded for partial completion of doctoral program. *Degree requirements:* For master's, variable foreign language requirement, comprehensive exam (for some programs), thesis (for some programs); for doctorate, variable foreign language requirement, comprehensive exam (for some programs), thesis/dissertation; for other advanced degree, variable foreign language requirement, comprehensive exam (for some programs). *Entrance requirements:* For master's and doctorate, GRE, GMAT. Additional exam requirements/recommendations for international students: Required—TOEFL (minimum score 550 paper-based; 79 iBT). Electronic applications accepted.

University of Southern Maine, College of Management and Human Service, School of Education and Human Development, Program in Special Education, Portland, ME 04103. Offers gifted and talented education (CGS); special education (MS); teaching all students (CGS); youth with moderate to severe disabilities (CGS). *Accreditation:* TEAC. *Program availability:* Part-time, evening/weekend. *Degree requirements:* For master's, thesis or alternative, portfolio. *Entrance requirements:* For master's, proof of teacher certification. Additional exam requirements/recommendations for international students: Required—TOEFL (minimum score 550 paper-based; 79 iBT). Electronic applications accepted. *Faculty research:* Special education, gifted and talented education, diversity education, positive behavioral interventions and supports.

The University of Toledo, College of Graduate Studies, Judith Herb College of Education, Department of Curriculum and Instruction, Toledo, OH 43606-3390. Offers art education (ME); career and technical education (ME, Ed S); curriculum and instruction (ME, PhD, Ed S); early childhood education (Ed S); education and anthropology (MAE); education and biology (MES); education and chemistry (MES); education and classics (MAE); education and economics (MAE); education and English (MAE); education and French (MAE); education and geology (MES); education and German (MAE); education and history (MAE); education and mathematics (MAE, MES); education and physics (MES); education and political science (MAE); education and sociology (MAE); education and Spanish (MAE); educational media (PhD); educational technology (ME); educational technology: virtual educator (Certificate); elementary education (PhD); English as a second language (MAE); gifted and talented education (PhD); middle childhood education (ME); secondary education (ME, PhD); special education (PhD). *Accreditation:* NCATE. *Program availability:* Part-time, evening/weekend. *Degree requirements:* For master's, comprehensive exam, thesis or alternative; for doctorate, comprehensive exam, thesis/dissertation; for other advanced degree, thesis optional. *Entrance requirements:* For master's, doctorate, and other advanced degree, minimum cumulative GPA of 2.7 for all previous academic work, letters of recommendation. Additional exam requirements/recommendations for international students: Required—TOEFL (minimum score 550 paper-based; 80 iBT). Electronic applications accepted.

University of Virginia, Curry School of Education, Department of Leadership, Foundations and Policy, Program in Educational Psychology, Charlottesville, VA 22903. Offers applied developmental science (M Ed); educational evaluation (M Ed); educational psychology (M Ed, Ed D, Ed S); educational research (Ed D); gifted education (M Ed); instructional technology (M Ed, Ed S); research statistics and evaluation (Ed D); school psychology (Ed D). *Students:* 28 full-time (15 women), 10 part-time (7 women); includes 8 minority (2 Black or African American, non-Hispanic/Latino; 2 Asian, non-Hispanic/Latino; 3 Hispanic/Latino; 1 Two or more races, non-Hispanic/Latino), 7 international. Average age 26. 85 applicants, 80% accepted, 33 enrolled. In 2016, 35 master's, 1 other advanced degree awarded. *Degree requirements:* For master's, comprehensive exam. *Entrance requirements:* For master's and doctorate, GRE General Test, 2 letters of recommendation. Additional exam requirements/recommendations for international students: Required—TOEFL (minimum score 600 paper-based; 90 iBT), IELTS (minimum score 7). *Application deadline:* Applications are

processed on a rolling basis. Application fee: $60. Electronic applications accepted. *Expenses:* Tuition, state resident: full-time $15,026; part-time $834 per credit hour. Tuition, nonresident: full-time $25,168; part-time $1378 per credit hour. *Required fees:* $2654. *Financial support:* Fellowships, research assistantships, and teaching assistantships available. Financial award application deadline: 1/5; financial award applicants required to submit FAFSA. *Unit head:* Sara Rimm-Kaufman, Program Director, 434-982-2863, E-mail: serk@virginia.edu. *Application contact:* Eric Molnar, Assistant Director, Admissions and Enrollment Reporting, 434-243-2085, E-mail: eric.molnar@virginia.edu.
Website: http://curry.virginia.edu/academics/areas-of-study/educational-psychology

Viterbo University, Graduate Programs in Education, La Crosse, WI 54601-4797. Offers cross-categorical special education (Certificate); director of instruction (Certificate); director of special education and pupil services (Certificate); early childhood (Certificate); education (MAE); literacy coaching (Certificate); PreK-12 principal/supervisor of special education (Certificate); principal (Certificate); reading specialist endorsement (Certificate); reading teacher (Certificate); reading teacher 5-12 endorsement (Certificate); reading teacher K-8 endorsement (Certificate); superintendent (Certificate); talented and gifted endorsement (Certificate); Wisconsin school business administrator (Certificate). Weekend courses available in summer. *Accreditation:* NCATE. *Program availability:* Part-time, evening/weekend. *Degree requirements:* For master's, comprehensive exam, thesis, 30 credits of course work. *Entrance requirements:* For master's, BS, transcripts, teaching license, written narrative. Electronic applications accepted. *Expenses:* Contact institution.

Western Washington University, Graduate School, Woodring College of Education, Department of Special Education, Bellingham, WA 98225-5996. Offers M Ed. *Accreditation:* NCATE. *Program availability:* Part-time. *Degree requirements:* For master's, comprehensive exam, thesis optional. *Entrance requirements:* For master's, GRE General Test or MAT, minimum GPA of 3.0 in last 60 semester hours or last 90 quarter hours. Additional exam requirements/recommendations for international students: Required—TOEFL (minimum score 567 paper-based). Electronic applications accepted. *Faculty research:* Applied behavioral analysis, controversial practices, infant/toddler social-emotional interventions, reflective practices in teacher education.

West Virginia University, College of Education and Human Services, Department of Special Education, Morgantown, WV 26506. Offers autism spectrum disorder (5-adult) (MA); autism spectrum disorder (K-6) (MA); early intervention/early childhood special education (MA); gifted education (1-12) (MA); low vision (PreK-adult) (MA); multicategorical special education (5-adult) (MA); multicategorical special education (K-6) (MA); severe/multiple disabilities (K-adult) (MA); special education (MA, Ed D); vision impairments (PreK-adult) (MA). *Accreditation:* NCATE. *Program availability:* Part-time, evening/weekend, online learning. *Degree requirements:* For master's, thesis optional; for doctorate, comprehensive exam, thesis/dissertation. *Entrance requirements:* For master's, minimum GPA of 2.75 passing scores on PRAXIS PPST; for doctorate, GRE General Test or MAT. Additional exam requirements/recommendations for international students: Required—TOEFL.

Whitworth University, School of Education, Graduate Studies in Education, Program in Gifted and Talented, Spokane, WA 99251-0001. Offers MAT. *Accreditation:* NCATE. *Program availability:* Part-time, evening/weekend. *Degree requirements:* For master's, comprehensive exam, thesis (for some programs). *Entrance requirements:* For master's, GRE General Test, MAT.

Wichita State University, Graduate School, College of Education, Department of Curriculum and Instruction, Wichita, KS 67260. Offers learning and instructional design (M Ed); special education (M Ed), including early childhood (M Ed, MAT), gifted, high incidence, low incidence; teaching (MAT), including early childhood (M Ed, MAT), middle level/secondary, transition to teaching. *Accreditation:* NCATE. *Program availability:* Part-time, evening/weekend, 100% online, blended/hybrid learning. *Entrance requirements:* For master's, MAT, minimum GPA of 2.75. *Unit head:* Dr. Kimberly McDowell, Department Head, 316-978-3322, E-mail: kim.mcdowell@wichita.edu. *Application contact:* Jordan Oleson, Admission Coordinator, 316-978-3095, Fax: 316-978-3253, E-mail: jordan.oleson@wichita.edu.

William Carey University, School of Education, Hattiesburg, MS 39401-5499. Offers art education (M Ed); art of teaching (M Ed); elementary education (M Ed, Ed S); English education (M Ed); gifted education (M Ed); history and social science (M Ed); mild/moderate disabilities (M Ed); secondary education (M Ed). *Accreditation:* NCATE. *Program availability:* Part-time. *Degree requirements:* For master's, comprehensive exam. *Entrance requirements:* For master's, GRE, MAT, minimum GPA of 2.5, Class A teacher's license. Additional exam requirements/recommendations for international students: Required—TOEFL (minimum score 550 paper-based).

Wilmington University, College of Education, New Castle, DE 19720-6491. Offers applied technology in education (M Ed); career and technical education (M Ed); educational leadership (Ed D); elementary and secondary school counseling (M Ed); elementary studies (M Ed); ESOL literacy (M Ed); higher education leadership (Ed D); instruction: gifted and talented (M Ed); instruction: teacher of reading (M Ed); instruction: teaching and learning (M Ed); organizational leadership (Ed D); school leadership (M Ed); secondary education (MAT); special education (M Ed). *Accreditation:* NCATE. *Program availability:* Part-time, evening/weekend. *Faculty:* 19 full-time (11 women), 178 part-time/adjunct (99 women). *Students:* 248 full-time (176 women), 999 part-time (738 women); includes 244 minority (193 Black or African American, non-Hispanic/Latino; 17 American Indian or Alaska Native, non-Hispanic/Latino; 9 Asian, non-Hispanic/Latino; 19 Hispanic/Latino; 2 Native Hawaiian or other Pacific Islander, non-Hispanic/Latino; 4 Two or more races, non-Hispanic/Latino), 7 international. Average age 34. 672 applicants, 96% accepted, 348 enrolled. In 2016, 529 master's, 87 doctorates awarded. *Entrance requirements:* For master's, 2 letters of recommendation, interview. Additional exam requirements/recommendations for international students: Required—TOEFL (minimum score 500 paper-based). *Application deadline:* For fall admission, 4/30 for domestic students. Applications are processed on a rolling basis. Application fee: $35. Electronic applications accepted. *Expenses: Tuition:* Full-time $8388; part-time $466 per credit. *Required fees:* $25 per semester. Tuition and fees vary according to degree level. *Financial support:* Applicants required to submit FAFSA. *Unit head:* Dr. John C. Gray, Dean. *Application contact:* Laura Morris, Director of Admissions, 877-967-5464, E-mail: infocenter@wilmu.edu.
Website: http://www.wilmu.edu/education/

Youngstown State University, Graduate School, Beeghly College of Education, Department of Teacher Education, Program in Special Education, Youngstown, OH 44555-0001. Offers gifted and talented education (MS Ed); special education (MS Ed). *Accreditation:* NCATE. *Program availability:* Part-time, evening/weekend. *Degree requirements:* For master's, comprehensive exam. *Entrance requirements:* For master's, GRE, MAT, or teaching certificate; interview; minimum GPA of 2.7. Additional exam requirements/recommendations for international students: Required—TOEFL. *Faculty research:* Learning disabilities, learning styles, developing self-esteem and social skills of severe behaviorally handicapped students, inclusion.

English as a Second Language

Acacia University, American Graduate School of Education, Tempe, AZ 85284. Offers educational administration (M Ed); elementary education (MA); English as a second language (M Ed); secondary education (MA); special education (M Ed).

Adelphi University, Ruth S. Ammon School of Education, Program in Teaching English to Speakers of Other Languages, Garden City, NY 11530-0701. Offers MA, Certificate. *Program availability:* Part-time, evening/weekend. *Students:* 33 full-time (28 women), 44 part-time (36 women); includes 28 minority (4 Black or African American, non-Hispanic/Latino; 3 Asian, non-Hispanic/Latino; 19 Hispanic/Latino; 2 Two or more races, non-Hispanic/Latino), 18 international. Average age 31. 59 applicants, 64% accepted, 14 enrolled. In 2016, 26 master's, 20 other advanced degrees awarded. *Entrance requirements:* For master's, 2 letters of recommendation, resume. Additional exam requirements/recommendations for international students: Required—TOEFL (minimum score 550 paper-based; 80 iBT), IELTS (minimum score 6.5). *Application deadline:* For fall admission, 4/1 priority date for domestic students; for spring admission, 11/1 priority date for domestic students. Applications are processed on a rolling basis. Application fee: $50. Electronic applications accepted. *Expenses:* Contact institution. *Financial support:* Research assistantships with partial tuition reimbursements, teaching assistantships, career-related internships or fieldwork, institutionally sponsored loans, scholarships/grants, traineeships, and unspecified assistantships available. Support available to part-time students. Financial award application deadline: 2/15; financial award applicants required to submit FAFSA. *Faculty research:* Theories of language acquisition, English as a second language in the content areas, apprenticeship in English as a second language instruction. *Unit head:* Eva Roca, Director, 516-877-4072, E-mail: rocaz@adelphi.edu. *Application contact:* Christine Murphy, Director of Admissions, 516-877-3050, Fax: 516-877-3039, E-mail: graduateadmissions@adelphi.edu.

Albright College, Graduate Division, Reading, PA 19612-5234. Offers early childhood education (MS); elementary education (MS); English as a second language (MA); general education (MA); special education (MS). *Program availability:* Part-time, evening/weekend. *Degree requirements:* For master's, thesis. *Entrance requirements:* For master's, GRE General Test or MAT, minimum undergraduate GPA of 3.0, 2 letters of recommendation, interview. Additional exam requirements/recommendations for international students: Recommended—TOEFL (minimum score 525 paper-based). Electronic applications accepted.

Alliant International University–San Diego, Shirley M. Hufstedler School of Education, Program in Teaching English to Speakers of Other Languages, San Diego, CA 92131. Offers MA, Ed D, Certificate. *Program availability:* Part-time. *Degree requirements:* For doctorate, thesis/dissertation. *Entrance requirements:* For master's, minimum GPA of 2.5, letters of recommendation; for doctorate, minimum GPA of 3.0, letters of recommendation. Additional exam requirements/recommendations for international students: Required—TOEFL (minimum score 575 paper-based; 83 iBT), TWE (minimum score 5). Electronic applications accepted. *Faculty research:* Global education, psycho-linguistics, bilingualism and education, curriculum and instruction.

Alliant International University–San Francisco, Shirley M. Hufstedler School of Education, Teacher Education Programs, San Francisco, CA 94133. Offers auditory oral education (Certificate); CLAD (Certificate); education specialist: mild/moderate disabilities (Credential); preliminary multiple subject (Credential); preliminary single subject (Credential); professional clear multiple subject (Credential); professional clear single subject (Credential); special education (MA); teaching (MA); TESOL (Certificate). *Program availability:* Part-time, evening/weekend. *Degree requirements:* For master's, thesis. *Entrance requirements:* For degree, California Basic Educational Skills Test, minimum GPA of 2.5. Additional exam requirements/recommendations for international students: Required—TOEFL (minimum score 550 paper-based), TWE (minimum score 5). Electronic applications accepted. *Faculty research:* Curriculum development, first year teachers, cross-cultural issues in teaching, biliteracy.

American College of Education, Graduate Programs, Indianapolis, IN 46204. Offers curriculum and instruction (M Ed), including bilingual, ESL; educational leadership (M Ed); educational technology (M Ed).

American Public University System, AMU/APU Graduate Programs, Charles Town, WV 25414. Offers accounting (MBA, MS); applied business analytics (MBA, MS); criminal justice (MA), including business administration, emergency and disaster management, general (MA, MS); educational leadership (M Ed); emergency and disaster management (MA); entrepreneurship (MBA); environmental policy and management (MS), including environmental planning, environmental sustainability, fish and wildlife management, general (MA, MS), global environmental management; finance (MBA); general (MBA); government contracting and acquisition (MBA); health care administration (MBA); health information management (MS); history (MA), including American history, ancient and classical history, European history, global history, public history; homeland security (MA), including business administration, counterterrorism studies, criminal justice, cyber, emergency management and public health, intelligence studies, transportation security; homeland security resource allocation (MBA); humanities (MA); information technology (MS), including digital forensics, enterprise software development, information assurance and security, IT project management; information technology management (MBA); intelligence studies (MA), including criminal intelligence, cyber, general (MA, MS), homeland security, intelligence analysis, intelligence collection, intelligence management, intelligence operations, terrorism studies; international relations and conflict resolution (MA), including comparative and security issues, conflict resolution, international and transnational security issues, peacekeeping; legal studies (MA); management (MA), including strategic consulting; marketing (MBA); military history (MA), including American military history, American Revolution, civil war, war since 1945, World War II; military studies (MA), including joint warfare, strategic leadership; national security studies (MA), including cyber, general (MA, MS), homeland security, regional security studies, security and intelligence

analysis, terrorism studies; nonprofit management (MBA); political science (MA), including American politics and government, comparative government and development, general (MA, MS), international relations, public policy; psychology (MA); public administration (MPA), including disaster management, environmental policy, health policy, human resources, national security, organizational management, security management; public health (MPH); reverse logistics management (MA); security management (MA); space studies (MS), including aerospace science, general (MA, MS), planetary science; sports and health sciences (MS); sports management (MBA); teaching (M Ed), including autism spectrum disorder, curriculum and instruction for elementary teachers, elementary reading, English language learners, instructional leadership, online learning, special education, STEAM (STEM plus the arts); transportation and logistics management (MA). *Program availability:* Part-time, evening/weekend, online only, 100% online. *Faculty:* 401 full-time (228 women), 1,678 part-time/adjunct (781 women). *Students:* 378 full-time (184 women), 8,455 part-time (3,484 women); includes 2,972 minority (1,552 Black or African American, non-Hispanic/Latino; 52 American Indian or Alaska Native, non-Hispanic/Latino; 211 Asian, non-Hispanic/Latino; 791 Hispanic/Latino; 70 Native Hawaiian or other Pacific Islander, non-Hispanic/Latino; 296 Two or more races, non-Hispanic/Latino), 109 international. Average age 37. In 2016, 3,185 master's awarded. *Degree requirements:* For master's, comprehensive exam or practicum. *Entrance requirements:* For master's, official transcript showing earned bachelor's degree from institution accredited by recognized accrediting body. Additional exam requirements/recommendations for international students: Required—TOEFL (minimum score 550 paper-based), IELTS (minimum score 6.5). *Application deadline:* Applications are processed on a rolling basis. Application fee: $0. Electronic applications accepted. *Expenses: Tuition:* Part-time $350 per credit hour. *Required fees:* $50 per course. *Financial support:* Scholarships/grants available. Financial award applicants required to submit FAFSA. *Unit head:* Dr. Karan Powell, President, 877-468-6268, Fax: 304-724-3780. *Application contact:* Terry Grant, Vice President of Enrollment Management, 877-468-6268, Fax: 304-724-3780, E-mail: info@apus.edu.
Website: http://www.apus.edu

American University, College of Arts and Sciences, Department of World Languages and Cultures, Washington, DC 20016-8045. Offers Spanish: Latin American studies (MA); teaching English as a foreign language (MA); teaching English to speakers of other languages (MA, Certificate); translation: French (Certificate); translation: Russian (Certificate); translation: Spanish (Certificate). *Program availability:* Part-time, evening/weekend. *Faculty:* 42 full-time (31 women), 27 part-time/adjunct (18 women). *Students:* 41 full-time (31 women), 31 part-time (23 women); includes 14 minority (3 Black or African American, non-Hispanic/Latino; 2 Asian, non-Hispanic/Latino; 7 Hispanic/Latino; 2 Two or more races, non-Hispanic/Latino), 9 international. Average age 32. 73 applicants, 92% accepted, 20 enrolled. In 2016, 24 master's, 6 other advanced degrees awarded. *Degree requirements:* For master's, one foreign language, comprehensive exam, thesis or alternative. *Entrance requirements:* For master's, GRE, writing sample, statement of purpose, transcripts, 2 letters of recommendation, resume; for Certificate, bachelor's degree, statement of purpose, transcripts, resume. Additional exam requirements/recommendations for international students: Required—TOEFL (minimum score 100 iBT), IELTS (minimum score 7), PTE (minimum score 68). *Application deadline:* For fall admission, 2/1 for domestic students; for spring admission, 11/1 for domestic students. Application fee: $55. *Expenses:* $1,579 per credit tuition; $690 mandatory fees. *Financial support:* Institutionally sponsored loans, scholarships/grants, and unspecified assistantships available. Financial award application deadline: 2/1; financial award applicants required to submit FAFSA. *Unit head:* Henry Gerfen, Chair, 202-885-2385, Fax: 202-885-1076, E-mail: gerfen@american.edu. *Application contact:* Kathleen Clowery, Director of Graduate Admissions, 202-885-3620, Fax: 202-885-1344, E-mail: clowery@american.edu.
Website: http://www.american.edu/cas/wlc/

The American University in Cairo, School of Humanities and Social Sciences, Cairo, Egypt. Offers Arab and Islamic civilizations (Graduate Diploma); Arabic studies (MA); comparative literary studies (Graduate Diploma); Egyptology and Coptology (MA); English and comparative literature (MA); humanities and social sciences (Graduate Diploma); philosophy (MA); psychology (MA); sociology and anthropology (MA); teaching Arabic as a foreign language (MA); teaching English to speakers of other languages (MA). *Program availability:* Part-time, evening/weekend. *Faculty:* 51 full-time (29 women), 4 part-time/adjunct (2 women). *Students:* 65 full-time (47 women), 179 part-time (138 women), 32 international. Average age 30. 221 applicants, 45% accepted, 54 enrolled. In 2016, 95 master's awarded. *Degree requirements:* For master's, comprehensive exam (for some programs), thesis (for some programs). *Entrance requirements:* Additional exam requirements/recommendations for international students: Required—TOEFL (minimum score 450 paper-based; 45 iBT), IELTS (minimum score 5). *Application deadline:* For fall admission, 2/1 priority date for domestic and international students; for spring admission, 10/15 priority date for domestic and international students. Applications are processed on a rolling basis. Application fee: $80. Electronic applications accepted. *Expenses:* Contact institution. *Financial support:* Fellowships with partial tuition reimbursements, scholarships/grants, tuition waivers (partial), and unspecified assistantships available. Financial award application deadline: 3/10. *Faculty research:* English literature, political science, psychology, sociology, anthropology and Egyptology, teaching English for non-speakers, teaching Arabic as a foreign language, philosophy, Arabic studies. *Unit head:* Dr. Nathaniel Bowditch, Dean, 20-2-2615-1788, E-mail: nbowditch@aucegypt.edu. *Application contact:* Maha Hegazi, Director for Graduate Admissions, 20-2-2615-1462, E-mail: mahahegazi@aucegypt.edu.
Website: http://www.aucegypt.edu/huss/Pages/default.aspx

American University of Armenia, Graduate Programs, Yerevan, Armenia. Offers business administration (MBA); computer and information science (MS), including business management, design and manufacturing, energy (ME, MS), industrial engineering and systems management; economics (MS); industrial engineering and systems management (ME), including business, computer aided design/manufacturing, energy (ME, MS), information technology; law (LL M); political science and international affairs (MPSIA); public health (MPH); teaching English as a foreign language (MA). *Program availability:* Part-time, evening/weekend. *Degree requirements:* For master's, thesis (for some programs), capstone/project. *Entrance requirements:* For master's, GRE, GMAT, or LSAT. Additional exam requirements/recommendations for international students: Recommended—TOEFL (minimum score 79 iBT), IELTS (minimum score 6.5). *Faculty research:* Microfinance, finance (rural/development, international, corporate), firm life cycle theory, TESOL, language proficiency testing, public policy, administrative law, economic development, cryptography, artificial intelligence, energy efficiency/renewable energy, computer-aided design/manufacturing, health financing, tuberculosis control, mother/child health, preventive ophthalmology, post-earthquake psychopathological investigations, tobacco control, environmental health risk assessments.

American University of Sharjah, Graduate Programs, Sharjah, United Arab Emirates. Offers accounting (MS); biomedical engineering (MSBME); business (MBA); chemical engineering (MS Ch E); civil engineering (MSCE); computer engineering (MS); electrical engineering (MSEE); engineering systems management (MS); mathematics (MS); mechanical engineering (MSME); mechatronics engineering (MS); teaching English to speakers of other languages (MA); translation and interpreting (MA); urban planning (MUP). *Program availability:* Part-time, evening/weekend. *Students:* 123 full-time (53 women), 306 part-time (151 women). Average age 27. 184 applicants, 83% accepted, 92 enrolled. In 2016, 97 master's awarded. *Degree requirements:* For master's, thesis (for some programs). *Entrance requirements:* For master's, GMAT (for MBA). Additional exam requirements/recommendations for international students: Required—TOEFL (minimum score 550 paper-based; 80 iBT), TWE (minimum score 5); Recommended—IELTS (minimum score 6.5). *Application deadline:* For fall admission, 8/28 priority date for domestic students, 8/14 priority date for international students; for spring admission, 1/22 priority date for domestic students, 1/8 for international students; for summer admission, 5/21 for domestic and international students. Applications are processed on a rolling basis. Application fee: $350. Electronic applications accepted. *Expenses: Tuition, area resident:* Part-time 4660 United Arab Emirates dirhams per credit hour. *Financial support:* In 2016–17, 63 students received support, including 28 research assistantships with full and partial tuition reimbursements available, 35 teaching assistantships with full and partial tuition reimbursements available; scholarships/grants also available. *Faculty research:* Water pollution, management and waste water treatment, energy and sustainability, air pollution, Islamic finance, family business and small and medium enterprises. *Unit head:* Ali Shuhaimy, Executive Director of Enrollment Management, 971-6515-1030. *Application contact:* Mona A. Mabrouk, Graduate Admissions/Office of Enrollment Management, 971-65151012, E-mail: graduateadmission@aus.edu.
Website: http://www.aus.edu/programs/graduate/

Anaheim University, Program in Teaching English to Speakers of Other Languages, Anaheim, CA 92806-5150. Offers MA, Ed D, Certificate, Diploma. *Program availability:* Part-time, evening/weekend, online only, 100% online. In 2016, 1 master's, 1 doctorate awarded. *Application deadline:* Applications are processed on a rolling basis. *Unit head:* Hayo Reinders, Director, Doctor of Education in TESOL Program, 714-771-3330, Fax: 714-772-3331, E-mail: admissions@anaheim.edu.

Andrews University, School of Graduate Studies, School of Education, Department of Teaching, Learning, and Curriculum, Berrien Springs, MI 49104. Offers curriculum and instruction (MA, Ed D, PhD, Ed S); elementary education (MAT); secondary education (MAT), including biology, education, English, English as a second language, French, history, physics; teacher education (MAT). *Faculty:* 7 full-time (5 women). *Students:* 17 full-time (12 women), 10 part-time (all women); includes 11 minority (6 Black or African American, non-Hispanic/Latino; 5 Hispanic/Latino), 7 international. Average age 38. In 2016, 9 master's, 7 doctorates awarded. *Entrance requirements:* For master's, GRE Subject Test. Additional exam requirements/recommendations for international students: Required—TOEFL (minimum score 550 paper-based). *Application deadline:* For fall admission, 8/15 for domestic students. Applications are processed on a rolling basis. Application fee: $40. *Unit head:* Dr. Lee C. Davidson, Chair, 269-471-6364. *Application contact:* Justina Clayburn, Supervisor of Graduate Admission, 800-253-2874, Fax: 269-471-6321, E-mail: graduate@andrews.edu.

Angelo State University, College of Graduate Studies and Research, College of Arts and Humanities, Department of English and Modern Languages, San Angelo, TX 76909. Offers English (MA); TESOL (MA). *Program availability:* Part-time, evening/weekend. *Students:* 4 full-time (3 women), 7 part-time (all women); includes 5 minority (1 American Indian or Alaska Native, non-Hispanic/Latino; 4 Hispanic/Latino), 1 international. Average age 27. *Degree requirements:* For master's, comprehensive exam. *Entrance requirements:* For master's, essay. Additional exam requirements/recommendations for international students: Required—TOEFL or IELTS. *Application deadline:* For fall admission, 7/15 priority date for domestic students, 6/10 for international students; for spring admission, 12/1 priority date for domestic students, 11/1 for international students. Applications are processed on a rolling basis. Application fee: $40 ($50 for international students). Electronic applications accepted. *Expenses:* Tuition, state resident: full-time $3726; part-time $2484 per year. Tuition, nonresident: full-time $10,746; part-time $7164 per year. *Required fees:* $2538; $1702 per unit. *Financial support:* Teaching assistantships, Federal Work-Study, scholarships/grants, and unspecified assistantships available. Support available to part-time students. Financial award application deadline: 3/1; financial award applicants required to submit FAFSA. *Unit head:* Dr. Laurence E. Musgrove, Chair, 325-486-6138, Fax: 325-942-2208, E-mail: laurence.musgrove@angelo.edu. *Application contact:* Dr. Laurence E. Musgrove, Chair, 325-486-6138, Fax: 325-942-2208, E-mail: laurence.musgrove@angelo.edu.
Website: http://www.angelo.edu/dept/english_modern_languages/

Arizona State University at the Tempe campus, College of Liberal Arts and Sciences, Department of English, Tempe, AZ 85287-0302. Offers applied linguistics (PhD); creative writing (MFA); English (MA, PhD), including comparative literature (MA), linguistics (MA), literature, rhetoric and composition (MA), rhetoric, composition, and linguistics (PhD); film and media studies (MAS), including American media and popular culture; linguistics (Graduate Certificate); teaching English to speakers of other languages (MTESOL); translation studies (Graduate Certificate). Terminal master's awarded for partial completion of doctoral program. *Degree requirements:* For master's, variable foreign language requirement, comprehensive exam (for some programs), thesis (for some programs), interactive Program of Study (iPOS) submitted before completing 50 percent of required credit hours; for doctorate, variable foreign language requirement, comprehensive exam, thesis/dissertation, interactive Program of Study (iPOS) submitted before completing 50 percent of required credit hours. *Entrance requirements:* For master's and doctorate, GRE, minimum GPA of 3.0 or equivalent in last 2 years of work leading to bachelor's degree. Additional exam requirements/recommendations for international students: Required—TOEFL, IELTS, or PTE. Electronic applications accepted.

Arkansas Tech University, College of Arts and Humanities, Russellville, AR 72801. Offers applied sociology (MS); English (M Ed, MA); history (MA); liberal arts (MLA); multi-media journalism (MA); psychology (MS); teaching English as a second language (MA). *Program availability:* Part-time. *Students:* 56 full-time (42 women), 121 part-time (85 women); includes 23 minority (7 Black or African American, non-Hispanic/Latino; 1 Asian, non-Hispanic/Latino; 11 Hispanic/Latino; 4 Two or more races, non-Hispanic/Latino), 34 international. Average age 32. In 2016, 90 master's awarded. *Degree requirements:* For master's, comprehensive exam (for some programs), thesis (for some programs), project. *Entrance requirements:* For master's, GRE General Test or GMAT. Additional exam requirements/recommendations for international students: Required—TOEFL (minimum score 550 paper-based; 79 iBT), IELTS (minimum score 6). *Application deadline:* For fall admission, 3/1 priority date for domestic students, 5/1 priority date for international students; for spring admission, 10/1 priority date for domestic and international students. Applications are processed on a rolling basis. Application fee: $25 ($75 for international students). Electronic applications accepted. *Expenses:* Tuition, state resident: full-time $4932; part-time $274 per credit hour. Tuition, nonresident: full-time $9864; part-time $548 per credit hour. *Required fees:* $513 per semester. Tuition and fees vary according to course load. *Financial support:* In 2016–17, research assistantships with full tuition reimbursements (averaging $4,800 per year), teaching assistantships with full tuition reimbursements (averaging $4,800 per year) were awarded; career-related internships or fieldwork, Federal Work-Study, scholarships/grants, health care benefits, and unspecified assistantships also available.

Support available to part-time students. Financial award application deadline: 4/15; financial award applicants required to submit FAFSA. *Unit head:* Dr. Jeffrey Woods, Dean, 479-968-0274, Fax: 479-964-0812, E-mail: jwoods@atu.edu. *Application contact:* Dr. Mary B. Gunter, Dean of Graduate College, 479-968-0398, Fax: 479-964-0542, E-mail: gradcollege@atu.edu.
Website: http://www.atu.edu/humanities/

Asbury University, School of Graduate and Professional Studies, Wilmore, KY 40390-1198. Offers biology: alternative certificate (MA Ed); chemistry: alternative certificate (MA Ed); English (MA Ed); English as a second language (MA Ed); ESL (MA Ed); French (MA Ed); Latin: alternative certificate (MA Ed); mathematics: alternative certificate (MA Ed); reading/writing endorsement (MA Ed); social studies (MA Ed); social work (MSW), including child and family services; Spanish (MA Ed); special education (MA Ed); special education: alternative certificate (MA Ed); teacher as leader endorsement (MA Ed). *Accreditation:* NCATE. *Program availability:* Part-time. *Degree requirements:* For master's, action research project, portfolio. *Entrance requirements:* For master's, PRAXIS/NTE, minimum GPA of 2.75, letters of recommendation. Additional exam requirements/recommendations for international students: Required—TOEFL (minimum score 550 paper-based). Electronic applications accepted.

Aurora University, School of Education and Human Performance, Aurora, IL 60506-4892. Offers bilingual-ESL education (MA); educational leadership (MA); educational technology (MA); leadership in administration (Ed D); leadership in adult learning and higher education (Ed D); leadership in curriculum and instruction (Ed D); reading instruction (MA); special education (MA). *Accreditation:* NCATE. *Program availability:* Part-time, evening/weekend. *Faculty:* 22 full-time (12 women), 46 part-time/adjunct (27 women). *Students:* 36 full-time (30 women), 559 part-time (372 women); includes 68 minority (27 Black or African American, non-Hispanic/Latino; 1 American Indian or Alaska Native, non-Hispanic/Latino; 6 Asian, non-Hispanic/Latino; 29 Hispanic/Latino; 2 Native Hawaiian or other Pacific Islander, non-Hispanic/Latino; 3 Two or more races, non-Hispanic/Latino). Average age 37. 126 applicants, 98% accepted, 72 enrolled. In 2016, 178 master's, 27 doctorates awarded. *Degree requirements:* For master's, student teaching; for doctorate, comprehensive exam, thesis/dissertation. *Entrance requirements:* For master's, 2 years of teaching experience, valid teaching certificate; for doctorate, appropriate master's degree, two references, curriculum vitae, personal statement, professional project, reflective essay. Additional exam requirements/recommendations for international students: Required—TOEFL (minimum score 550 paper-based; 79 iBT). *Application deadline:* For fall admission, 6/1 for international students; for spring admission, 10/1 for international students. Applications are processed on a rolling basis. Application fee: $0. Electronic applications accepted. *Expenses:* Contact institution. *Financial support:* In 2016–17, 10 students received support. Federal Work-Study, scholarships/grants, and unspecified assistantships available. Support available to part-time students. Financial award applicants required to submit FAFSA. *Unit head:* Dr. Jen Buckley, Executive Director of the School of Education and Human Performance, 630-844-1542, Fax: 630-844-6155, E-mail: jbuckley@aurora.edu. *Application contact:* Elizabeth Botica, Graduate Education Recruiter, 630-947-8918, E-mail: ebotica@aurora.edu.
Website: http://aurora.edu/education

Avila University, School of Education, Kansas City, MO 64145-1698. Offers English language learners (Advanced Certificate); international advocacy and leadership (MA, Certificate); literacy (MA); special reading (Advanced Certificate); teaching and learning (MA); TESL (MA). *Program availability:* Part-time, evening/weekend, online learning. *Faculty:* 6 full-time (5 women), 11 part-time/adjunct (6 women). *Students:* 65 full-time (50 women), 23 part-time (17 women); includes 12 minority (8 Black or African American, non-Hispanic/Latino; 2 Asian, non-Hispanic/Latino; 1 Hispanic/Latino; 1 Two or more races, non-Hispanic/Latino), 3 international. Average age 34. 135 applicants, 44% accepted, 33 enrolled. In 2016, 29 master's awarded. *Entrance requirements:* For master's, minimum GPA of 3.0, writing sample, recommendation, interview; for other advanced degree, foreign language. Additional exam requirements/recommendations for international students: Required—TOEFL (minimum score 580 paper-based; 92 iBT). *Application deadline:* Applications are processed on a rolling basis. Electronic applications accepted. *Expenses:* $483 per credit hour. *Financial support:* In 2016–17, 6 students received support. Unspecified assistantships available. Financial award applicants required to submit FAFSA. *Unit head:* Dr. Stacy Keith, Director of Graduate Education, 816-501-2446, Fax: 816-501-2915, E-mail: stacy.keith@avila.edu. *Application contact:* Cory Roup, Graduate Education Enrollment and Academic Advisor, 816-501-2464, E-mail: cory.roup@avila.edu.
Website: https://www.avila.edu/academics/graduate-studies/grad-education

Azusa Pacific University, College of Liberal Arts and Sciences, Program in Teaching English to Speakers of Other Languages, Azusa, CA 91702-7000. Offers MA.

Ball State University, Graduate School, College of Sciences and Humanities, Department of English, Program in Linguistics, Muncie, IN 47306. Offers linguistics (MA); teaching English to speakers of other languages (TESOL) and linguistics (MA). *Program availability:* Part-time. *Entrance requirements:* For master's, GRE General Test, minimum baccalaureate GPA of 2.75 or 3.0 in latter half of baccalauareate, statement of purpose, writing sample, three letters of recommendation. Additional exam requirements/recommendations for international students: Required—TOEFL (minimum score 550 paper-based; 79 iBT), IELTS (minimum score 6.5). Electronic applications accepted. *Faculty research:* Descriptive and theoretical linguistics.

Barry University, School of Education, Program in Curriculum and Instruction, Miami Shores, FL 33161-6695. Offers accomplished teacher (Ed S); culture, language and literacy (TESOL) (PhD); curriculum evaluation and research (PhD); early childhood (Ed S); early childhood education (PhD); elementary (Ed S); elementary education (PhD); ESOL (Ed S); gifted (Ed S); Montessori (Ed S); PKP/elementary (Ed S); reading (Ed S); reading, language and cognition (PhD). *Entrance requirements:* For doctorate, GRE, minimum GPA of 3.25.

Barry University, School of Education, Program in Technology and TESOL, Miami Shores, FL 33161-6695. Offers MS, Ed S.

Barry University, School of Education, Program in TESOL, Miami Shores, FL 33161-6695. Offers TESOL (MS); TESOL international (MS). *Entrance requirements:* For master's, GRE or MAT.

Binghamton University, State University of New York, Graduate School, Graduate School of Education, Program in TESOL Education, Binghamton, NY 13902-6000. Offers MS Ed. *Students:* 2 full-time (both women), 14 part-time (all women); includes 1 minority (Hispanic/Latino). Average age 39. 7 applicants, 100% accepted, 7 enrolled. *Degree requirements:* For master's, capstone project or thesis, practicum. *Application deadline:* Applications are processed on a rolling basis. *Unit head:* Tami Mann, Senior Staff Assistant, 607-777-5322, E-mail: tmann@binghamton.edu. *Application contact:* Ben Balkaya, Assistant Dean and Director, 607-777-2151, Fax: 607-777-2501, E-mail: balkaya@binghamton.edu.

Biola University, Cook School of Intercultural Studies, La Mirada, CA 90639-0001. Offers anthropology (MA); applied linguistics (MA); intercultural education (PhD); intercultural studies (MA, PhD); linguistics (Certificate); linguistics and Biblical languages (MA); missiology (D Miss); missions (MA); teaching English to speakers of other languages (MA, Certificate); teaching English to speakers of other languages (online) (MA). *Program availability:* Part-time, 100% online. *Entrance requirements:* For master's, minimum undergraduate GPA of 3.0; for doctorate, master's degree or equivalent, 3 years of cross-cultural experience, minimum graduate GPA of 3.3. Additional exam requirements/recommendations for international students: Required—TOEFL. Electronic applications accepted. *Faculty research:* Linguistics, anthropology, intercultural studies, teaching English to speakers of other languages, missions, missiology.

Bishop's University, School of Education, Sherbrooke, QC J1M 1Z7, Canada. Offers advanced studies in education (Diploma); education (M Ed, MA); teaching English as a second language (Certificate). *Program availability:* Part-time, online learning. *Degree requirements:* For master's, thesis (for some programs). *Entrance requirements:* For master's, teaching license, 2 years of teaching experience. *Faculty research:* Integration of special needs students, multigrade classes/small schools, leadership in organizational development, second language acquisition.

Boise State University, College of Education, Department of Literacy, Language and Culture, Boise, ID 83725-1725. Offers bilingual education (M Ed); English as a new language (M Ed); literacy (MA). *Accreditation:* NCATE. *Program availability:* Part-time, evening/weekend. *Faculty:* 11 full-time (6 women). *Students:* 10 full-time (9 women), 53 part-time (46 women); includes 9 minority (1 Black or African American, non-Hispanic/Latino; 2 Asian, non-Hispanic/Latino; 5 Hispanic/Latino; 1 Native Hawaiian or other Pacific Islander, non-Hispanic/Latino), 6 international. Average age 36. 20 applicants, 75% accepted, 12 enrolled. In 2016, 26 master's awarded. *Degree requirements:* For master's, thesis optional. *Entrance requirements:* For master's, minimum GPA of 3.0. Additional exam requirements/recommendations for international students: Required—TOEFL (minimum score 550 paper-based; 80 iBT), IELTS (minimum score 6). Application fee: $65 ($95 for international students). Electronic applications accepted. *Expenses:* Tuition, state resident: full-time $6058; part-time $358 per credit hour. Tuition, nonresident: full-time $20,108; part-time $608 per credit hour. *Required fees:* $2108. Tuition and fees vary according to program. *Financial support:* In 2016–17, 4 students received support. Scholarships/grants and unspecified assistantships available. Financial award applicants required to submit FAFSA. *Unit head:* Dr. Maggie Chase, Department Chair, 208-426-3206, E-mail: maggiechase@boisestate.edu. *Application contact:* Dr. Arturo Rodriguez, Program Coordinator, 208-426-2243, E-mail: arturorodriguez@boisestate.edu.
Website: http://education.boisestate.edu/literacy/graduate/

Boricua College, Program in TESOL Education (K-12), New York, NY 10032-1560. Offers MS. *Program availability:* Evening/weekend. *Degree requirements:* For master's, thesis. *Entrance requirements:* For master's, interview by the faculty. *Application deadline:* Applications are processed on a rolling basis. Application fee: $100. *Expenses: Tuition:* Full-time $13,000. *Required fees:* $100. *Financial support:* Career-related internships or fieldwork and Federal Work-Study available. Financial award applicants required to submit FAFSA. *Unit head:* Dr. Joseph H. Gaines, Co-Chairperson, 212-694-1000. *Application contact:* Dr. Shivaji Sengupta, Vice President, 212-694-1000 Ext. 650, Fax: 212-694-1015, E-mail: ssengupta@boricuacollege.edu.

Brigham Young University, Graduate Studies, College of Humanities, Department of Linguistics and English Language, Provo, UT 84602. Offers linguistics (MA); teaching English as a second language (MA). *Program availability:* Part-time. *Faculty:* 23 full-time (4 women), 8 part-time/adjunct (6 women). *Students:* 63 full-time (42 women), 21 part-time (13 women); includes 22 minority (1 American Indian or Alaska Native, non-Hispanic/Latino; 12 Asian, non-Hispanic/Latino; 8 Hispanic/Latino; 1 Native Hawaiian or other Pacific Islander, non-Hispanic/Latino), 14 international. Average age 32. 30 applicants, 77% accepted, 19 enrolled. In 2016, 18 master's awarded. *Degree requirements:* For master's, 2 foreign languages, thesis. *Entrance requirements:* For master's, GRE General Test, minimum GPA of 3.0 in last 60 hours of course work. Additional exam requirements/recommendations for international students: Required—TOEFL (minimum score 580 paper-based; 90 iBT), TWE. *Application deadline:* 1/15 for domestic and international students. Application fee: $50. Electronic applications accepted. *Expenses:* $6,680. *Financial support:* In 2016–17, 53 students received support, including 8 research assistantships with partial tuition reimbursements available (averaging $7,200 per year), 8 teaching assistantships with partial tuition reimbursements available (averaging $2,079 per year); fellowships with partial tuition reimbursements available, career-related internships or fieldwork, scholarships/grants, unspecified assistantships, and travel to conference presentations also available. Financial award application deadline: 7/1. *Faculty research:* Teaching English to speakers of other languages, second language acquisition, computational linguistics, semiotics and semantics, computer-assisted language instruction, forensic linguistics, endangered language documentation. *Unit head:* Dr. Norman Evans, Chair, 801-422-8472, E-mail: norm_evans@byu.edu. *Application contact:* LoriAnne Spear, Graduate Program Manager, 801-422-9010, Fax: 801-422-9010, E-mail: lorianne_spear@byu.edu.
Website: http://linguistics.byu.edu/

Brock University, Faculty of Graduate Studies, Faculty of Humanities, Program in Applied Linguistics, St. Catharines, ON L2S 3A1, Canada. Offers MA. *Program availability:* Part-time. *Degree requirements:* For master's, thesis optional. *Entrance requirements:* For master's, honours degree with a background in English, English linguistics, teaching English as a second language, or a comparable field. Additional exam requirements/recommendations for international students: Required—TOEFL (minimum score 630 paper-based; 109 iBT), IELTS (minimum score 8), TWE (minimum score 5.5). Electronic applications accepted. *Expenses:* Contact institution. *Faculty research:* Metalinguistic ability in subsequent language learning, language teaching methodology, forensic linguistics, philosophy of education, culturally appropriate pedagogy.

Brown University, Graduate School, Department of Portuguese and Brazilian Studies, Providence, RI 02912. Offers Brazilian studies (AM); English as a second language and cross-cultural studies (AM); Portuguese and Brazilian studies (AM, PhD); Portuguese bilingual education and cross-cultural studies (AM). *Degree requirements:* For doctorate, thesis/dissertation.

Buena Vista University, School of Education, Storm Lake, IA 50588. Offers curriculum and instruction (M Ed), including effective teaching, TESL; school guidance and counseling (MS Ed). Program offered in summer only. *Program availability:* Part-time, evening/weekend, online learning. *Degree requirements:* For master's, thesis, fieldwork/practicum, capstone portfolio. *Entrance requirements:* For master's, Analytical Writing Assessment (in-house), minimum undergraduate GPA of 2.75. Electronic applications accepted. *Faculty research:* Reading, curriculum, educational psychology, special education.

California Baptist University, Program in English, Riverside, CA 92504-3206. Offers English pedagogy (MA); literature (MA); teaching English to speakers of other languages (TESOL) (MA). *Program availability:* Part-time, evening/weekend. *Faculty:* 9 full-time (7 women), 1 (woman) part-time/adjunct. *Students:* 3 full-time (2 women), 26 part-time (19 women); includes 14 minority (4 Black or African American, non-Hispanic/Latino; 1 Asian, non-Hispanic/Latino; 9 Hispanic/Latino), 3 international. Average age

28. 8 applicants, 88% accepted, 6 enrolled. In 2016, 4 master's awarded. *Degree requirements:* For master's, comprehensive exam, project, or thesis. *Entrance requirements:* For master's, GRE (for applicants with a GPA below 2.75) or CSET, minimum undergraduate GPA of 2.75; 18 semester hours of course work in English beyond freshman level; three recommendations; essay; demonstration of writing; interview. Additional exam requirements/recommendations for international students: Required—TOEFL (minimum score 80 iBT). *Application deadline:* For fall admission, 8/1 priority date for domestic students, 7/1 for international students; for spring admission, 12/1 priority date for domestic students, 11/1 for international students. Applications are processed on a rolling basis. Application fee: $45. Electronic applications accepted. *Expenses:* Contact institution. *Financial support:* In 2016–17, 5 students received support. Federal Work-Study and scholarships/grants available. Financial award applicants required to submit CSS PROFILE or FAFSA. *Faculty research:* Classical mythology and folklore, multicultural literature, genre studies, science fiction and fantasy literature, intercultural rhetoric. *Unit head:* Dr. Gayne Anacker, Dean, College of Arts and Sciences, 951-343-4682, E-mail: ganacker@calbaptist.edu. *Application contact:* Dr. Laura Veltman, Director, Master of Arts Program in English, 951-343-4276, Fax: 951-343-4661, E-mail: lveltman@calbaptist.edu.
Website: http://www.calbaptist.edu/maenglish/

California State University, Dominguez Hills, College of Arts and Humanities, Department of English, Carson, CA 90747-0001. Offers English literature (MA); rhetoric and composition (Certificate); teaching English as a second language (MA, Certificate). *Program availability:* Part-time, evening/weekend. *Degree requirements:* For master's, comprehensive exam (for some programs), thesis or alternative. *Entrance requirements:* For master's, minimum GPA of 3.0 in last 60 units. Additional exam requirements/recommendations for international students: Required—TOEFL (minimum score 550 paper-based). Electronic applications accepted. *Faculty research:* Gender studies, transnationalism, discourse analysis, visual culture, Shakespeare.

California State University, East Bay, Office of Graduate Studies, College of Letters, Arts, and Social Sciences, Department of English, Hayward, CA 94542-3000. Offers creative writing (MA); literary studies (MA); teaching English to speakers of other languages (MA). *Program availability:* Part-time. *Students:* 10 full-time (8 women), 35 part-time (24 women); includes 19 minority (4 Black or African American, non-Hispanic/Latino; 3 Asian, non-Hispanic/Latino; 7 Hispanic/Latino; 5 Two or more races, non-Hispanic/Latino), 8 international. Average age 36. 35 applicants, 63% accepted, 13 enrolled. In 2016, 25 master's awarded. *Degree requirements:* For master's, one foreign language, comprehensive exam, thesis optional. *Entrance requirements:* For master's, minimum GPA of 3.0 in field; 2 letters of recommendation; academic or professional writing sample; teaching experience and some degree of bilingualism (preferred for TESOL). Additional exam requirements/recommendations for international students: Required—TOEFL (minimum score 550 paper-based); Recommended—IELTS (minimum score 6.5). *Application deadline:* For fall admission, 6/30 for domestic and international students. Applications are processed on a rolling basis. Application fee: $55. Electronic applications accepted. *Financial support:* Fellowships, teaching assistantships, career-related internships or fieldwork, Federal Work-Study, institutionally sponsored loans, and scholarships/grants available. Support available to part-time students. Financial award application deadline: 3/2; financial award applicants required to submit FAFSA. *Unit head:* Dr. Sarah Nielsen, Acting Chair, 510-885-3151, Fax: 510-885-4797. *Application contact:* Dr. Donna Wiley, Interim Associate Vice President for Academic Programs and Graduate Studies, 510-885-3716, Fax: 510-885-4777, E-mail: donna.wiley@csueastbay.edu.
Website: http://www20.csueastbay.edu/class/departments/english/index.html

California State University, Fresno, Division of Research and Graduate Studies, College of Arts and Humanities, Department of Linguistics, Fresno, CA 93740-8027. Offers linguistics (MA), including teaching English as a second language. *Program availability:* Part-time, evening/weekend. *Degree requirements:* For master's, comprehensive exam. *Entrance requirements:* For master's, GRE General Test, minimum GPA of 3.0. Additional exam requirements/recommendations for international students: Required—TOEFL. *Application deadline:* For fall admission, 5/1 for domestic and international students; for spring admission, 10/1 for domestic and international students. Applications are processed on a rolling basis. Application fee: $55. Electronic applications accepted. *Financial support:* Career-related internships or fieldwork, Federal Work-Study, and scholarships/grants available. Support available to part-time students. Financial award application deadline: 3/1; financial award applicants required to submit FAFSA. *Faculty research:* Communication systems, bilingual education, animal communication, conflict resolution, literacy programs. *Unit head:* Brian Agbayani, Chair, 559-278-2441, Fax: 559-278-7299, E-mail: bagbayan@csufresno.edu. *Application contact:* Jidong Chen, Graduate Coordinator, 559-278-2441, Fax: 559-278-7299, E-mail: jchen@csufresno.edu.
Website: http://www.fresnostate.edu/artshum/linguistics/

California State University, Long Beach, Graduate Studies, College of Liberal Arts, Department of Linguistics, Long Beach, CA 90840. Offers general linguistics (MA); language and culture (MA); special concentration (MA); teaching English to speakers of other languages (MA, Graduate Certificate). *Program availability:* Part-time, evening/weekend. *Degree requirements:* For master's, one foreign language, comprehensive exam, thesis optional. *Application deadline:* For fall admission, 5/1 for domestic students. Applications are processed on a rolling basis. Application fee: $55. Electronic applications accepted. *Financial support:* Teaching assistantships, career-related internships or fieldwork, Federal Work-Study, institutionally sponsored loans, and scholarships/grants available. Financial award application deadline: 3/2. *Faculty research:* Pedagogy of language instruction, role of language in society, Khmer language instruction. *Unit head:* Alexandra Jaffe, Chair, 562-985-5792, Fax: 562-985-2593.
Website: http://www.csulb.edu/colleges/cla/departments/linguistics/

California State University, Sacramento, Office of Graduate Studies, College of Arts and Letters, Department of English, Sacramento, CA 95819. Offers composition (MA); creative writing (MA); literature (MA); teaching English to speakers of other languages (MA). *Program availability:* Part-time. *Students:* 36 full-time (26 women), 47 part-time (35 women); includes 22 minority (5 Black or African American, non-Hispanic/Latino; 1 American Indian or Alaska Native, non-Hispanic/Latino; 8 Asian, non-Hispanic/Latino; 8 Hispanic/Latino). Average age 30. 54 applicants, 69% accepted, 26 enrolled. In 2016, 29 master's awarded. *Degree requirements:* For master's, thesis, project, or comprehensive exam; TESOL exam; writing proficiency exam. *Entrance requirements:* For master's, portfolio (creative writing); minimum GPA of 3.0 in English and overall during previous 2 years. Additional exam requirements/recommendations for international students: Required—TOEFL (minimum score 600 paper-based; 100 iBT). *Application deadline:* For fall admission, 2/15 for domestic students, 3/1 for international students; for spring admission, 9/30 for international students. Applications are processed on a rolling basis. Application fee: $55. Electronic applications accepted. *Expenses:* $4,302 full-time tuition and fees per semester, $2,796 part-time. *Financial support:* Research assistantships, teaching assistantships, career-related internships or fieldwork, and Federal Work-Study available. Support available to part-time students. Financial award application deadline: 3/1; financial award applicants required to submit FAFSA. *Faculty research:* Teaching composition, remedial writing. *Unit head:* Dr. David Toise, Chair, 916-278-6586, E-mail: dwtoise@csus.edu. *Application contact:* Jose Martinez, Graduate Admissions Supervisor, 916-278-7871, E-mail: martinj@skymail.csus.edu.
Website: http://www.csus.edu/engl

California State University, Stanislaus, College of Humanities and Social Sciences, Program in English (MA), Turlock, CA 95382. Offers literature (Certificate); rhetoric and teaching writing (MA); teaching English to speakers of other languages (MA). *Program availability:* Part-time. *Degree requirements:* For master's, comprehensive exam, thesis or alternative. *Entrance requirements:* For master's, GRE, minimum GPA of 3.0, 2 letters of reference, personal statement. Additional exam requirements/recommendations for international students: Required—TOEFL (minimum score 575 paper-based), TWE (minimum score 4). Electronic applications accepted. *Faculty research:* Transnational literacies, Renaissance and medieval literature, abolition writings and slave narratives, qualitative writing.

Cambridge College, School of Education, Cambridge, MA 02138-5304. Offers autism specialist (M Ed); autism/behavior analyst (M Ed); behavior analyst (Post-Master's Certificate); behavioral management (M Ed); early childhood teacher (M Ed); education specialist in curriculum and instruction (CAGS); educational leadership (Ed D); elementary teacher (M Ed); English as a second language (M Ed, Certificate); general science (M Ed); health education (Post-Master's Certificate); health/family and consumer sciences (M Ed); history (M Ed); individualized (M Ed); information technology literacy (M Ed); instructional technology (M Ed); interdisciplinary studies (M Ed); library teacher (M Ed); literacy education (M Ed); mathematics (M Ed); mathematics specialist (Certificate); middle school mathematics and science (M Ed); school administration (M Ed, CAGS); school guidance counselor (M Ed); school nurse education (M Ed); school social worker/school adjustment counselor (M Ed); special education administrator (CAGS); special education/moderate disabilities (M Ed); teaching skills and methodologies (M Ed). *Program availability:* Part-time, evening/weekend, online learning. *Degree requirements:* For master's, thesis, internship/practicum (licensure program only); for doctorate, thesis/dissertation; for other advanced degree, thesis. *Entrance requirements:* For master's, interview, resume, documentation of licensure, 2 professional references; for doctorate, official transcripts, interview, resume, documentation of licensure (if any), written personal statement/essay, portfolio of scholarly and professional work, qualifying assessment, 2 professional references, health insurance, immunizations form; for other advanced degree, official transcripts, interview, resume, documentation of licensure (if any), written personal statement/essay, 2 professional references, health insurance, immunizations form. Additional exam requirements/recommendations for international students: Required—TOEFL (minimum score 550 paper-based; 79 iBT), Michigan English Language Assessment Battery (minimum score 85); Recommended—IELTS (minimum score 6). Electronic applications accepted. *Expenses:* Contact institution. *Faculty research:* Adult education, accelerated learning, mathematics education, brain compatible learning, special education and law.

Canisius College, Graduate Division, School of Education and Human Services, Department of Graduate Education and Leadership, Buffalo, NY 14208-1098. Offers business and marketing education (MS Ed); college student personnel (MS Ed); deaf education (MS Ed); deaf/adolescent education, grades 7-12 (MS Ed); deaf/childhood education, grades 1-6 (MS Ed); differentiated instruction (MS Ed); education administration (MS); educational administration (MS Ed); educational technologies (Certificate); gifted education extension (Certificate); literacy (MS Ed); reading (Certificate); school building leadership (MS Ed, Certificate); school district leadership (Certificate); teacher leader (Certificate); TESOL (MS Ed). *Accreditation:* NCATE. *Program availability:* Part-time, evening/weekend, 100% online, blended/hybrid learning. *Faculty:* 5 full-time (all women), 23 part-time/adjunct (16 women). *Students:* 95 full-time (78 women), 223 part-time (177 women); includes 31 minority (15 Black or African American, non-Hispanic/Latino; 2 American Indian or Alaska Native, non-Hispanic/Latino; 4 Asian, non-Hispanic/Latino; 9 Hispanic/Latino; 1 Two or more races, non-Hispanic/Latino), 1 international. Average age 30. 162 applicants, 89% accepted, 135 enrolled. In 2016, 135 master's, 39 other advanced degrees awarded. *Entrance requirements:* For master's, GRE (if cumulative GPA less than 2.7), transcripts, two letters of recommendation. Additional exam requirements/recommendations for international students: Required—TOEFL (minimum score 550 paper-based, 79 iBT), IELTS (minimum score 6.5), or CAEL (minimum score 70). *Application deadline:* Applications are processed on a rolling basis. Application fee: $25. Electronic applications accepted. Application fee is waived when completed online. *Expenses:* *Tuition:* Full-time $14,742. *Required fees:* $724. *Financial support:* Career-related internships or fieldwork, Federal Work-Study, scholarships/grants, tuition waivers (partial), and unspecified assistantships available. Support available to part-time students. Financial award application deadline: 4/30; financial award applicants required to submit FAFSA. *Faculty research:* Asperger's disease, autism, private higher education, reading strategies. *Unit head:* Dr. Rosemary K. Murray, Chair/Associate Professor of Graduate Education and Leadership, 716-888-3723, E-mail: murray1@canisius.edu. *Application contact:* Kathleen B. Davis, Vice President of Enrollment Management, 716-888-2500, Fax: 716-888-3195, E-mail: daviskb@canisius.edu.
Website: http://www.canisius.edu/graduate/

Carlos Albizu University, Miami Campus, Graduate Programs, Miami, FL 33172-2209. Offers clinical psychology (PhD, Psy D); entrepreneurship (MBA); exceptional student education (MS); human services (PhD); industrial/organizational psychology (MS); marriage and family therapy (MS); mental health counseling (MS); nonprofit management (MBA); organizational management (MBA); psychology (MS); school counseling (MS); speech and language pathology (MS); teaching English for speakers of other languages (MS). *Accreditation:* APA. *Program availability:* Part-time, evening/weekend, 100% online. *Faculty:* 28 full-time (22 women), 31 part-time/adjunct (19 women). *Students:* 475 full-time (396 women), 191 part-time (161 women); includes 560 minority (56 Black or African American, non-Hispanic/Latino; 1 American Indian or Alaska Native, non-Hispanic/Latino; 4 Asian, non-Hispanic/Latino; 494 Hispanic/Latino; 5 Two or more races, non-Hispanic/Latino), 15 international. Average age 34. 335 applicants, 46% accepted, 122 enrolled. In 2016, 143 master's, 48 doctorates awarded. Terminal master's awarded for partial completion of doctoral program. *Degree requirements:* For master's, comprehensive exam, integrative project (for MBA); research project (for exceptional student education, teaching English as a second language); for doctorate, comprehensive exam, thesis/dissertation, internship, project. *Entrance requirements:* For master's, 3 letters of recommendation, interview, minimum GPA of 3.0, resume, statement of purpose, official transcripts; for doctorate, 3 letters of recommendation, minimum GPA of 3.0, resume, interview, statement of purpose, official transcripts. Additional exam requirements/recommendations for international students: Required—Michigan Test of English Language Proficiency. *Application deadline:* For fall admission, 4/1 priority date for domestic students, 5/1 priority date for international students; for spring admission, 11/1 priority date for domestic students, 9/1 priority date for international students. Applications are processed on a rolling basis. Application fee: $50. Electronic applications accepted. *Expenses:* Contact institution. *Financial support:* In 2016–17, 131 students received support. Federal Work-Study, scholarships/grants, unspecified assistantships, and tuition discounts available. Financial award application deadline: 6/1; financial award applicants required to submit FAFSA. *Faculty research:* Psychotherapy, forensic psychology, neuropsychology, marketing strategy, entrepreneurship, special education, speech-language pathology. *Unit head:* Dr. Etiony Aldarondo, Provost, 305-593-1223 Ext. 3138, Fax: 305-592-7930, E-mail: ealdarondo@albizu.edu. *Application contact:* Sonia Feliciano, Institutional Director of Student Recruitment, 305-593-1223 Ext. 3108, Fax: 305-477-8983, E-mail: sfeliciano@albizu.edu.

Carson-Newman University, Graduate Program in Education, Jefferson City, TN 37760. Offers curriculum and instruction (M Ed); educational leadership (M Ed); elementary education (MAT); school counseling (MS); secondary education (MAT); teaching English as a second language (MATESL). *Accreditation:* NCATE. *Program availability:* Part-time, evening/weekend, 100% online, blended/hybrid learning. *Degree requirements:* For master's, thesis or alternative. *Entrance requirements:* For master's, PRAXIS II or GRE with minimum score of 290 on the verbal and quantitative components (for MAT), minimum GPA of 3.0 in major, 2.5 overall. Additional exam requirements/recommendations for international students: Recommended—TOEFL (minimum score 79 iBT), IELTS (minimum score 6.5), TSE (minimum score 53). *Expenses: Tuition:* Full-time $10,142; part-time $461 per credit hour. *Required fees:* $300; $150 per semester. One-time fee: $150.

Central Michigan University, College of Graduate Studies, College of Humanities and Social and Behavioral Sciences, Department of English Language and Literature, Mount Pleasant, MI 48859. Offers English composition and communication (MA); English language and literature (MA), including children's and young adult literature, creative writing, English language and literature; TESOL: teaching English to speakers of other languages (MA). *Program availability:* Part-time, evening/weekend. *Degree requirements:* For master's, thesis or alternative. Electronic applications accepted. *Faculty research:* Composition theory, science fiction history and bibliography, children's and young adult literature, nineteenth century American literature, applied linguistics.

Central Washington University, Graduate Studies and Research, College of Arts and Humanities, Department of English, Ellensburg, WA 98926. Offers English (MA); teaching English as a second language (MA). *Program availability:* Part-time. *Degree requirements:* For master's, thesis or alternative. *Entrance requirements:* For master's, GRE General Test, minimum GPA of 3.0, writing sample. Additional exam requirements/recommendations for international students: Required—TOEFL (minimum score 550 paper-based; 79 iBT) or IELTS (minimum score 6.5). Electronic applications accepted.

City College of the City University of New York, Graduate School, School of Education, Department of Teaching, Learning and Culture, New York, NY 10031-9198. Offers bilingual education (MS); childhood education (MS); early childhood education (MS); educational theatre (MS); literacy (MS); TESOL (MS). *Accreditation:* NCATE. *Degree requirements:* For master's, thesis. *Entrance requirements:* For master's, Liberal Arts and Sciences Test (LAST), Content Specialty Test (CST). Additional exam requirements/recommendations for international students: Required—TOEFL. Tuition and fees vary according to course load, degree level and program.

Clarks Summit University, Graduate Studies, South Abington Township, PA 18411. Offers Bible (MA); counseling (MA, MS); curriculum and instruction (M Ed); educational administration (M Ed); intercultural studies (MA); literature (MA); missions (MA); organizational leadership (MA); reading specialist (M Ed); secondary English/communications (M Ed); social entrepreneurship (MA); worldview studies (MA). MA in missions program available only for Association of Baptists for World Evangelism missionary personnel. *Program availability:* Part-time, evening/weekend, online learning. *Entrance requirements:* Additional exam requirements/recommendations for international students: Required—TOEFL (minimum score 500 paper-based).

Cleveland State University, College of Graduate Studies, College of Education and Human Services, Department of Curriculum and Foundations, Cleveland, OH 44115. Offers art education (M Ed); early childhood education (M Ed); foreign language education (M Ed); middle childhood mathematics and science education (M Ed); special education (M Ed), including mild/moderate disabilities, moderate/intensive disabilities; teaching English to speakers of other languages (M Ed). *Program availability:* Part-time, evening/weekend. *Faculty:* 19 full-time (14 women), 32 part-time/adjunct (27 women). *Students:* 86 full-time (65 women), 369 part-time (301 women); includes 119 minority (89 Black or African American, non-Hispanic/Latino; 1 American Indian or Alaska Native, non-Hispanic/Latino; 2 Asian, non-Hispanic/Latino; 16 Hispanic/Latino; 11 Two or more races, non-Hispanic/Latino), 35 international. Average age 34. 177 applicants, 55% accepted, 68 enrolled. In 2016, 179 master's awarded. *Degree requirements:* For master's, comprehensive exam (for some programs), thesis or alternative. *Entrance requirements:* For master's, GRE General Test or MAT, minimum GPA of 2.75. Additional exam requirements/recommendations for international students: Required—TOEFL (minimum score 550 paper-based; 78 iBT), IELTS (minimum score 6). *Application deadline:* For fall admission, 7/1 priority date for domestic students, 5/15 for international students; for spring admission, 11/15 for domestic students, 11/1 for international students; for summer admission, 4/1 for domestic students, 3/15 for international students. Applications are processed on a rolling basis. Application fee: $30. *Expenses:* Tuition, state resident: full-time $9565. Tuition, nonresident: full-time $17,980. Tuition and fees vary according to program. *Financial support:* In 2016–17, 13 research assistantships with full tuition reimbursements (averaging $15,845 per year) were awarded; tuition waivers (partial) and unspecified assistantships also available. Financial award application deadline: 2/15; financial award applicants required to submit FAFSA. *Faculty research:* Early childhood education, literacy education, special education: mild/moderate, moderate/intensive, early childhood intervention specialist), teaching English to speakers of other languages (TESOL). *Total annual research expenditures:* $275,907. *Unit head:* Dr. Tachelle I. Banks, Chairperson, 216-687-4608, Fax: 216-687-5379, E-mail: t.i.banks@csuohio.edu. *Application contact:* Michael Almony, Senior Student Services Specialist, 216-875-9929, Fax: 216-687-5491, E-mail: m.almony@csuohio.edu.
Website: http://www.csuohio.edu/cehs/te/te

Coastal Carolina University, Spadoni College of Education, Conway, SC 29528-6054. Offers education (MAT); educational leadership (M Ed, Ed S); English for speakers of other languages (Certificate); instructional technology (M Ed, Ed S); learning and teaching (M Ed); online teaching and training (Certificate); special education (M Ed). *Accreditation:* NCATE. *Program availability:* Part-time, evening/weekend. *Faculty:* 16 full-time (8 women), 12 part-time/adjunct (7 women). *Students:* 74 full-time (48 women), 340 part-time (271 women); includes 78 minority (70 Black or African American, non-Hispanic/Latino; 1 American Indian or Alaska Native, non-Hispanic/Latino; 2 Asian, non-Hispanic/Latino; 4 Hispanic/Latino; 1 Two or more races, non-Hispanic/Latino), 2 international. Average age 33. 298 applicants, 93% accepted, 213 enrolled. In 2016, 167 master's, 8 other advanced degrees awarded. *Degree requirements:* For master's and other advanced degree, comprehensive exam. *Entrance requirements:* For master's, GRE, GMAT, 2 letters of recommendation, evidence of teacher certification, official transcripts; for other advanced degree, official transcripts, minimum of 3 years' teaching experience, statement of interest in the program, 3 letters of reference, master's degree in educational leadership or related field with minimum overall GPA of 3.0. Additional exam requirements/recommendations for international students: Required—TOEFL (minimum score 550 paper-based; 79 iBT), IELTS (minimum score 6.5). *Application deadline:* For fall admission, 7/1 priority date for domestic and international students; for spring admission, 11/1 priority date for domestic and international students; for summer admission, 3/1 priority date for domestic and international students. Applications are processed on a rolling basis. Application fee: $45. Electronic applications accepted. *Expenses:* Tuition, state resident: full-time $9990; part-time $555 per credit hour. Tuition, nonresident: full-time $18,108; part-time $1006 per credit hour. *Required fees:* $90; $5 per credit hour. *Financial support:* Fellowships, research assistantships, and unspecified assistantships available. Support available to part-time students. Financial award application deadline: 3/1; financial award applicants required to submit FAFSA. *Unit head:* Dr. Edward Jadallah, Dean, 843-349-2773, Fax: 843-349-2106, E-mail: ejadalla@coastal.edu. *Application contact:* Dr. James O. Luken, Associate Provost/Vice-Dean of the Coastal Environment, 843-349-2235, Fax: 843-349-6444, E-mail: joluken@coastal.edu.
Website: http://www.coastal.edu/education/

College of Charleston, Graduate School, School of Education, Health, and Human Performance, Program in English to Speakers of Other Languages, Charleston, SC 29424-0001. Offers Certificate. *Program availability:* Part-time, online learning. *Entrance requirements:* Additional exam requirements/recommendations for international students: Required—TOEFL (minimum score 81 iBT). *Application deadline:* For fall admission, 7/1 for domestic students; for spring admission, 11/1 for domestic students. Application fee: $45. Electronic applications accepted. *Unit head:* Dr. Angela Crespo Cozart, Director, 843-953-6353, E-mail: cozarta@cofc.edu. *Application contact:* Susan Hallatt, Director of Graduate Admissions, 843-953-5614, Fax: 843-953-1434, E-mail: hallatts@cofc.edu.
Website: http://teachered.cofc.edu/grad-progs/esol-cert.php

College of Mount Saint Vincent, School of Professional and Graduate Studies, Department of Teacher Education, Riverdale, NY 10471-1093. Offers instructional technology and global perspectives (Certificate); middle level education (Certificate); multicultural studies (Certificate); teaching English to speakers of other languages (MS Ed); urban and multicultural education (MS Ed). *Accreditation:* TEAC. *Program availability:* Part-time. *Degree requirements:* For master's, comprehensive exam. *Entrance requirements:* For master's, interview, New York teaching certificate. Additional exam requirements/recommendations for international students: Required—TOEFL.

The College of New Jersey, Office of Graduate and Advancing Education, School of Education, Department of Special Education, Language and Literacy, Program in Teaching English as a Second Language, Ewing, NJ 08628. Offers English as a second language (M Ed); teaching English as a second language (Certificate). *Accreditation:* NCATE. *Program availability:* Part-time. *Degree requirements:* For master's, comprehensive exam. *Entrance requirements:* For master's, GRE General Test, minimum GPA of 3.0 in field or 2.75 overall. Additional exam requirements/recommendations for international students: Required—TOEFL. Electronic applications accepted.

The College of New Rochelle, Graduate School, Division of Education, Program in Multilingual/Multicultural Education, New Rochelle, NY 10805-2308. Offers bilingual education (Certificate); multilingual/multicultural education (Certificate); teaching English to speakers of other languages (MS Ed, Certificate). *Program availability:* Part-time, evening/weekend. *Degree requirements:* For master's, student teaching or practicum. *Entrance requirements:* For master's, interview, minimum GPA of 3.0 in field, 2.7 overall.

College of Saint Mary, Program in Education, Omaha, NE 68106. Offers assessment leadership (MSE); English as a second language (MSE). *Program availability:* Part-time. *Entrance requirements:* For master's, technology competency test or equivalent, minimum cumulative GPA of 3.0, teaching certificate, 2 letters of reference, resume.

College of Staten Island of the City University of New York, Graduate Programs, School of Education, Program in Teaching of English to Speakers of Other Languages, Staten Island, NY 10314-6600. Offers MS Ed, Advanced Certificate. *Program availability:* Part-time, evening/weekend. *Faculty:* 4 part-time/adjunct. *Students:* 57 part-time. Average age 31. 27 applicants, 70% accepted, 14 enrolled. *Degree requirements:* For master's, comprehensive exam, fieldwork; twelve three-credit courses (36 credits); research project under faculty supervision; for Advanced Certificate, seven three-credit courses (21 credits). *Entrance requirements:* For master's, baccalaureate degree in liberal arts and sciences major or 36 approved credits in liberal arts and sciences, one year of college level foreign language, minimum overall GPA of 3.0, two letters of recommendation, one- or two-page personal statement; for Advanced Certificate, courses required for New York State initial certificate in early childhood, childhood or adolescence education or its equivalent from another state; baccalaureate degree in a liberal arts and sciences major, or 36 credits in a liberal arts and sciences concentration, with minimum overall GPA of 3.0. Additional exam requirements/recommendations for international students: Required—TOEFL (minimum score 550 paper-based; 79 iBT), IELTS (minimum score 6.5), PTE. *Application deadline:* For fall admission, 4/25 for domestic and international students; for spring admission, 11/25 for domestic and international students. Applications are processed on a rolling basis. Application fee: $125. Electronic applications accepted. *Expenses:* Tuition, state resident: full-time $10,130; part-time $425 per credit. Tuition, nonresident: full-time $18,720; part-time $780 per credit. *Required fees:* $181.10 per semester. Tuition and fees vary according to program. *Faculty research:* Application of critical pedagogies focusing on intersections of race, class, culture, and gender in first and second language literacies; urban education; second language acquisition in secondary education; cross-linguistic predictors in reading comprehension; students with interrupted or inconsistent formal education (SIFE). *Unit head:* Dr. Rachel Grant, Graduate Faculty Advisor, 718-982-3740, E-mail: rachel.grant@csi.cuny.edu. *Application contact:* Sasha Spence, Associate Director for Graduate Admissions, 718-982-2019, Fax: 718-982-2500, E-mail: sasha.spence@csi.cuny.edu.
Website: http://www.csi.cuny.edu/schoolofeducation/programs/graduate/tesol/

Colorado Mesa University, Center for Teacher Education, Grand Junction, CO 81501-3122. Offers educational leadership (MAEd); English for speakers of other languages (MAEd); exceptional learner/special education (MAEd); teacher education (Graduate Certificate); teacher leader (MAEd). *Accreditation:* NCATE. *Program availability:* Part-time. *Faculty:* 6 full-time (5 women), 12 part-time/adjunct (6 women). *Students:* 18 full-time (13 women), 35 part-time (28 women); includes 4 minority (1 American Indian or Alaska Native, non-Hispanic/Latino; 3 Hispanic/Latino), 1 international. Average age 34. 28 applicants, 25% accepted, 6 enrolled. In 2016, 26 master's, 36 other advanced degrees awarded. *Degree requirements:* For master's, comprehensive exam (for some programs), capstone presentation. *Entrance requirements:* For master's, 3 professional letters of recommendation, Colorado teaching license, minimum baccalaureate GPA of 3.0; for Graduate Certificate, minimum baccalaureate GPA of 3.0. Additional exam requirements/recommendations for international students: Required—TOEFL (minimum score 550 paper-based). *Application deadline:* For fall admission, 6/1 priority date for domestic and international students; for spring admission, 11/1 priority date for domestic and international students; for summer admission, 3/1 priority date for domestic and international students. Applications are processed on a rolling basis. Application fee: $50. Electronic applications accepted. *Expenses:* $406.43 per credit hour resident tuition and fees, $1,092.43 per credit hour non-resident tuition and fees. *Financial*

support: In 2016–17, 2 students received support. Scholarships/grants available. Financial award applicants required to submit FAFSA. *Faculty research:* K-8 STEM instruction, special education inclusion, elementary math literacy, secondary literacy, elementary/early childhood education literacy. *Unit head:* Dr. Blake Bickham, Department Head, 970-248-1729, E-mail: bbickham@coloradomesa.edu. *Application contact:* Mary Kienietz, Administrative Assistant, 970-248-1786, E-mail: mkieniet@coloradomesa.edu.
Website: http://coloradomesa.edu/teachered/index.html

Colorado State University, College of Liberal Arts, Department of English, Fort Collins, CO 80523-1773. Offers creative nonfiction (MA); creative writing (MFA); literature (MA); rhetoric and composition (MA); TESL/TEFL (MA). *Program availability:* Part-time. *Faculty:* 31 full-time (21 women), 25 part-time/adjunct (23 women). *Students:* 71 full-time (54 women), 30 part-time (21 women); includes 7 minority (1 Black or African American, non-Hispanic/Latino; 2 Asian, non-Hispanic/Latino; 2 Hispanic/Latino; 2 Two or more races, non-Hispanic/Latino), 13 international. Average age 29. 177 applicants, 42% accepted, 39 enrolled. In 2016, 33 master's awarded. *Degree requirements:* For master's, thesis (for some programs). *Entrance requirements:* For master's, BA/BS or equivalent with minimum cumulative undergraduate GPA of 3.0, transcripts, writing sample, statement of purpose, 3 letters of recommendation. Additional exam requirements/recommendations for international students: Recommended—TOEFL (minimum score 550 paper-based; 80 iBT), IELTS (minimum score 6.5). *Application deadline:* For spring admission, 9/15 for domestic and international students. Application fee: $60 ($70 for international students). Electronic applications accepted. *Expenses:* Tuition, state resident: full-time $9628. Tuition, nonresident: full-time $23,603. *Required fees:* $2253; $528.14 per credit hour. $264.07 per semester. Tuition and fees vary according to course load and program. *Financial support:* In 2016–17, 39 students received support, including 38 teaching assistantships with full and partial tuition reimbursements available (averaging $14,005 per year); scholarships/grants, health care benefits, and unspecified assistantships also available. Financial award application deadline: 1/1. *Faculty research:* Literary texts in historical and cultural contexts; creation and criticism of fiction, poetry, creative nonfiction and hybrid genres; critical literacies, multimodalities, and technologies including pedagogical theory and practice; linguistics, second language acquisition and TEFL/TESOL; rhetoric and social change. *Total annual research expenditures:* $154,039. *Unit head:* Louann Reid, Professor, 970-491-6428, E-mail: louann.reid@colostate.edu. *Application contact:* Marnie Leonard, Administrative Assistant, 970-491-2403, E-mail: marnie.leonard@colostate.edu.
Website: http://english.colostate.edu/

Columbia International University, Columbia Graduate School, Columbia, SC 29230-3122. Offers Bible teaching (MABT); counseling (MACN); early childhood and elementary education (MAT); educational administration (M Ed); educational leadership (PhD); instruction and learning (M Ed); teaching English as a foreign language (Certificate); teaching English as a foreign language and intercultural studies (MATF). *Program availability:* Part-time, evening/weekend, online learning. *Degree requirements:* For master's, internships, professional project. *Entrance requirements:* For master's, MAT; GRE (for some programs), minimum GPA of 2.7. Additional exam requirements/recommendations for international students: Required—TOEFL. Electronic applications accepted.

Columbus State University, Graduate Studies, College of Letters and Sciences, Program in Teaching English to Speakers of Other Languages, Columbus, GA 31907-5645. Offers teaching English to speakers of other languages (Certificate). *Students:* 1 full-time. Average age 30. *Entrance requirements:* Additional exam requirements/recommendations for international students: Required—TOEFL (minimum score 550 paper-based; 79 iBT). *Application deadline:* For fall admission, 6/30 for domestic and international students; for spring admission, 11/1 for domestic and international students; for summer admission, 5/1 for domestic and international students. Applications are processed on a rolling basis. Application fee: $50. Electronic applications accepted. *Expenses:* Tuition, state resident: full-time $4804; part-time $2412 per semester hour. Tuition, nonresident: full-time $19,218; part-time $9612 per semester hour. *Required fees:* $1850; $1850 per semester hour. Tuition and fees vary according to program. *Unit head:* Dr. Dennis Rome, Dean, 706-568-2056, E-mail: rome_dennis@columbusstate.edu. *Application contact:* Kristin Williams, Director of International and Graduate Recruitment, 706-507-8848, Fax: 706-568-5091, E-mail: williams_kristin@columbusstate.edu.

Concordia University, College of Education, Portland, OR 97211-6099. Offers career and technical education (M Ed); curriculum and instruction (M Ed), including adolescent literacy, career and technical education, e-learning/technology education, early childhood education, English for speakers of other languages, English language development, environmental education, mathematics, methods and curriculum, reading, science, teacher leadership, the inclusive classroom; early childhood (MAT); education leadership (Ed D); educational administration (M Ed); elementary education (MAT); secondary education (MAT); special education (M Ed); teacher leadership (Ed D). *Program availability:* Part-time, online learning. *Degree requirements:* For master's, comprehensive exam, work samples/portfolio. *Entrance requirements:* For master's, California Basic Educational Skills Test or PRAXIS I, minimum undergraduate GPA of 2.8, graduate 3.0; 2 letters of recommendation. Additional exam requirements/recommendations for international students: Required—TOEFL (minimum score 525 paper-based). Electronic applications accepted. *Faculty research:* Learner-centered classroom, brain-based learning, future of online learning.

Concordia University, School of Graduate Studies, Faculty of Arts and Science, Department of Education, Program in Applied Linguistics, Montréal, QC H3G 1M8, Canada. Offers applied linguistics (MA); teaching English as a second language (Certificate).

Cornerstone University, Graduate Programs, Grand Rapids, MI 49525-5897. Offers business administration (MBA); education (MA Ed); management (MSM); teaching English to speakers of other languages (MA, Graduate Certificate). Programs also offered at Holland, Kalamazoo, and Troy, MI campuses. *Program availability:* Part-time, online learning. *Degree requirements:* For master's, comprehensive exam (for some programs), thesis (for some programs). *Entrance requirements:* For master's, minimum GPA of 2.5, 2 letters of reference. Additional exam requirements/recommendations for international students: Required—TOEFL (minimum score 575 paper-based). Electronic applications accepted.

Dallas Baptist University, Dorothy M. Bush College of Education, Program in Bilingual Education, Dallas, TX 75211-9299. Offers dual language (M Ed); English as a second language/multilingual (M Ed). *Program availability:* Part-time, evening/weekend. *Application deadline:* Applications are processed on a rolling basis. Application fee: $25. Electronic applications accepted. Application fee is waived when completed online. *Expenses: Tuition:* Full-time $15,408; part-time $856 per credit hour. *Required fees:* $400 per semester. Tuition and fees vary according to course load and degree level. *Unit head:* Dr. Carolyn Spain, Director, 214-333-5413, E-mail: carolyns@dbu.edu. *Application contact:* Bobby Soto, Director of Admissions, 214-333-5242, E-mail: graduate@dbu.edu.
Website: http://www3.dbu.edu/graduate/bilingual_education.asp

Dallas Baptist University, Dorothy M. Bush College of Education, Program in Curriculum and Instruction, Dallas, TX 75211-9299. Offers Christian school administration (M Ed); distance learning (M Ed); English as a second language (M Ed); instructional technology (M Ed); professional life coaching (M Ed); special education (M Ed); supervision (M Ed). *Program availability:* Part-time, evening/weekend, 100% online, blended/hybrid learning. *Application deadline:* Applications are processed on a rolling basis. Application fee: $25. Electronic applications accepted. Application fee is waived when completed online. *Expenses: Tuition:* Full-time $15,408; part-time $856 per credit hour. *Required fees:* $400 per semester. Tuition and fees vary according to course load and degree level. *Unit head:* Dr. Deborah H. Tribble, Director, 214-333-5201, E-mail: debbiet@dbu.edu. *Application contact:* Bobby Soto, Director of Admissions, 214-333-5242, E-mail: graduate@dbu.edu.
Website: http://www3.dbu.edu/graduate/curriculum_instruction.asp

Dallas Baptist University, Dorothy M. Bush College of Education, Program in Reading and English as a Second Language, Dallas, TX 75211-9299. Offers bilingual education (M Ed); English as a second language (M Ed); master reading teacher (M Ed); reading specialist (M Ed). *Program availability:* Part-time, evening/weekend. *Application deadline:* Applications are processed on a rolling basis. Application fee: $25. Electronic applications accepted. Application fee is waived when completed online. *Expenses: Tuition:* Full-time $15,408; part-time $856 per credit hour. *Required fees:* $400 per semester. Tuition and fees vary according to course load and degree level. *Unit head:* Dr. Carolyn Spain, Director, 214-333-5200, E-mail: carolyns@dbu.edu. *Application contact:* Bobby Soto, Director of Admissions, 214-333-5242, E-mail: graduate@dbu.edu.
Website: http://www3.dbu.edu/graduate/english_reading.asp

Dallas Baptist University, Dorothy M. Bush College of Education, Teaching Program, Dallas, TX 75211-9299. Offers distance learning (MAT); early childhood through grade 6 certification (MAT); early childhood-12 (MAT); elementary (MAT); English as a second language (MAT); Montessori (MAT); multisensory (MAT); secondary (MAT). *Program availability:* Part-time, evening/weekend, 100% online, blended/hybrid learning. *Application deadline:* Applications are processed on a rolling basis. Application fee: $25. Electronic applications accepted. Application fee is waived when completed online. *Expenses: Tuition:* Full-time $15,408; part-time $856 per credit hour. *Required fees:* $400 per semester. Tuition and fees vary according to course load and degree level. *Unit head:* Dr. Carolyn Spain, Director, 214-333-5217, E-mail: carolyns@dbu.edu. *Application contact:* Bobby Soto, Director of Admissions, 214-333-5242, E-mail: graduate@dbu.edu.
Website: http://www3.dbu.edu/graduate/mat.asp

Dallas Baptist University, Graduate School of Ministry, Program in Global Leadership, Dallas, TX 75211-9299. Offers church planting (MA); East Asian Studies (MA); English as a second language (MA); general studies (MA); global communication (MA); global studies (MA); international business (MA); leading the nonprofit organization (MA); missions (MA); small group ministry (MA); urban ministry (MA). *Program availability:* Part-time, evening/weekend. *Application deadline:* Applications are processed on a rolling basis. Application fee: $25. Electronic applications accepted. Application fee is waived when completed online. *Expenses: Tuition:* Full-time $15,408; part-time $856 per credit hour. *Required fees:* $400 per semester. Tuition and fees vary according to course load and degree level. *Unit head:* Dr. Bob Garrett, Director, 214-333-5508, E-mail: bobg@dbu.edu. *Application contact:* Bobby Soto, Director of Admissions, 214-333-5242, E-mail: graduate@dbu.edu.
Website: http://www3.dbu.edu/gsom/global-leadership/

Dallas Baptist University, Liberal Arts Program, Dallas, TX 75211-9299. Offers art (MLA); Christian studies (MLA); commercial art (MLA); East Asian studies (MLA); English (MLA); English as a second language (MLA); fine arts (MLA); history (MLA); missions (MLA); political science (MLA). *Program availability:* Part-time, evening/weekend, 100% online, blended/hybrid learning. *Application deadline:* Applications are processed on a rolling basis. Application fee: $25. Electronic applications accepted. Application fee is waived when completed online. *Expenses: Tuition:* Full-time $15,408; part-time $856 per credit hour. *Required fees:* $400 per semester. Tuition and fees vary according to course load and degree level. *Faculty research:* Milton and seventeenth-century Puritans, inter-Biblical years, nineteenth-century literature, Latin American and Texas history. *Unit head:* Jared Ingram, Director, 214-333-5584, E-mail: jaredi@dbu.edu. *Application contact:* Bobby Soto, Director of Admissions, 214-333-5242, E-mail: graduate@dbu.edu.
Website: http://www3.dbu.edu/graduate/mla.asp

Dallas Baptist University, Professional Development Program, Dallas, TX 75211-9299. Offers accounting (MA); church leadership (MA); communication (MA); counseling (MA); criminal justice (MA); English as a second language (MA); finance (MA); higher education (MA); leadership studies (MA); management (MA); management information systems (MA); marketing (MA); missions (MA); professional life coaching (MA); training and development (MA). *Program availability:* Part-time, evening/weekend, 100% online, blended/hybrid learning. *Application deadline:* Applications are processed on a rolling basis. Application fee: $25. Electronic applications accepted. Application fee is waived when completed online. *Expenses: Tuition:* Full-time $15,408; part-time $856 per credit hour. *Required fees:* $400 per semester. Tuition and fees vary according to course load and degree level. *Unit head:* Jared Ingram, Director, 214-333-5584, E-mail: jaredi@dbu.edu. *Application contact:* Bobby Soto, Director of Admissions, 214-333-5242, E-mail: graduate@dbu.edu.
Website: http://www3.dbu.edu/graduate/mapd.asp

DeSales University, Division of Liberal Arts and Social Sciences, Center Valley, PA 18034-9568. Offers criminal justice (MCJ); digital forensics (MCJ, Postbaccalaureate Certificate); education (M Ed), including instructional technology, secondary education, special education, teaching English to speakers of other languages; investigative forensics (MCJ, Postbaccalaureate Certificate). *Program availability:* Part-time, 100% online, blended/hybrid learning. *Faculty:* 5 full-time (3 women), 20 part-time/adjunct (13 women). *Students:* 55 full-time (36 women), 100 part-time (64 women); includes 25 minority (5 Black or African American, non-Hispanic/Latino; 14 Hispanic/Latino; 6 Two or more races, non-Hispanic/Latino). Average age 33. 145 applicants, 80% accepted, 103 enrolled. In 2016, 36 master's awarded. *Entrance requirements:* For master's, bachelor's degree from accredited institution, minimum undergraduate GPA of 3.0, personal statement showing potential of graduate work, three letters of recommendation, professional goal statement. Additional exam requirements/recommendations for international students: Required—TOEFL. *Application deadline:* Applications are processed on a rolling basis. Application fee: $50. Electronic applications accepted. *Expenses: Tuition:* Part-time $815 per credit hour. Tuition and fees vary according to degree level and program. *Financial support:* Applicants required to submit FAFSA. *Unit head:* Dr. Brain Kane, Division Head of Liberal Arts and Social Studies, 610-282-1100 Ext. 1274, E-mail: brian.kane@desales.edu. *Application contact:* Julia Ferraro, Director of Graduate Admissions, 610-282-1100 Ext. 1768, E-mail: gradadmissions@desales.edu.

Dominican University, School of Education, River Forest, IL 60305-1099. Offers early childhood education (MS); education (MAT); elementary education (MA Ed); English as a second language (MA Ed); reading (MA Ed); special education (MS). *Accreditation:*

NCATE. *Program availability:* Part-time, evening/weekend, 100% online, blended/hybrid learning. *Faculty:* 12 full-time (8 women), 64 part-time/adjunct (57 women). *Students:* 13 full-time (all women), 500 part-time (385 women); includes 88 minority (40 Black or African American, non-Hispanic/Latino; 3 American Indian or Alaska Native, non-Hispanic/Latino; 18 Asian, non-Hispanic/Latino; 11 Hispanic/Latino; 2 Native Hawaiian or other Pacific Islander, non-Hispanic/Latino; 14 Two or more races, non-Hispanic/Latino), 1 international. Average age 32. 162 applicants, 96% accepted, 104 enrolled. In 2016, 200 master's awarded. *Entrance requirements:* For master's, Illinois Test of Basic Skills. Additional exam requirements/recommendations for international students: Required—TOEFL (minimum score 550 paper-based; 79 iBT). *Application deadline:* Applications are processed on a rolling basis. Application fee: $25. *Expenses:* $550 per credit hour. *Financial support:* Career-related internships or fieldwork, scholarships/grants, tuition waivers (partial), and unspecified assistantships available. Support available to part-time students. Financial award application deadline: 8/15; financial award applicants required to submit FAFSA. *Faculty research:* Governance of private education institutions, reading and language arts, inclusion, organizational planning, leadership and vision. *Unit head:* Dr. Colleen Reardon, Interim Executive Director, School of Education, 708-524-6643, Fax: 708-524-6665, E-mail: creardon@dom.edu. *Application contact:* Keven Hansen, Coordinator of Recruitment and Admissions, 708-524-6921, Fax: 708-524-6665, E-mail: educate@dom.edu.
Website: http://educate.dom.edu/

Duquesne University, School of Education, Department of Instruction and Leadership, Program in English as a Second Language, Pittsburgh, PA 15282-0001. Offers MS Ed. *Program availability:* Part-time, evening/weekend. *Faculty:* 3 full-time (2 women). *Students:* 14 full-time (9 women), 1 (woman) part-time; includes 4 minority (2 Black or African American, non-Hispanic/Latino; 2 Asian, non-Hispanic/Latino), 6 international. Average age 29. 34 applicants, 97% accepted, 11 enrolled. In 2016, 18 master's awarded. *Degree requirements:* For master's, thesis optional. *Entrance requirements:* For master's, bachelor's degree. Additional exam requirements/recommendations for international students: Required—TOEFL (minimum score 550 paper-based), IELTS (minimum score 7). *Application deadline:* For fall admission, 9/1 for domestic students; for spring admission, 1/1 for domestic students. Applications are processed on a rolling basis. Application fee: $0. Electronic applications accepted. *Expenses: Tuition:* Full-time $22,212; part-time $1234 per credit. Tuition and fees vary according to program. *Unit head:* Dr. Laura Mahalingappa, Associate Professor and Director, 412-396-6111, Fax: 412-396-1997, E-mail: mahalingappa1@duq.edu. *Application contact:* Michael Dolinger, Director of Student and Academic Services, 412-396-6647, Fax: 412-396-5585, E-mail: dolingerm@duq.edu.
Website: http://wwwtest.duq.edu/academics/schools/education/graduate-programs-education/english-second-language

East Carolina University, Graduate School, Thomas Harriot College of Arts and Sciences, Department of English, Greenville, NC 27858-4353. Offers creative writing (MA); English studies (MA); linguistics (MA); literature (MA); multicultural and transnational literatures (MA, Certificate); rhetoric and composition (MA); rhetoric, writing, and professional communication (PhD); teaching English in the two-year college (Certificate); teaching English to speakers of other languages (MA, Certificate); technical and professional communication (MA). *Program availability:* Part-time, evening/weekend. *Students:* 54 full-time (36 women), 95 part-time (77 women); includes 32 minority (19 Black or African American, non-Hispanic/Latino; 3 Asian, non-Hispanic/Latino; 6 Hispanic/Latino; 4 Two or more races, non-Hispanic/Latino), 1 international. Average age 35. 78 applicants, 96% accepted, 50 enrolled. In 2016, 34 master's, 1 doctorate awarded. *Degree requirements:* For master's, one foreign language, comprehensive exam, thesis optional. *Entrance requirements:* For master's, GRE General Test, MAT (for MA Ed). Additional exam requirements/recommendations for international students: Required—TOEFL. *Application deadline:* For fall admission, 6/1 priority date for domestic students; for spring admission, 10/15 for domestic students. Applications are processed on a rolling basis. Application fee: $50. *Financial support:* Research assistantships with partial tuition reimbursements, teaching assistantships with partial tuition reimbursements, and Federal Work-Study available. Support available to part-time students. Financial award application deadline: 6/1. *Unit head:* Dr. Jeffrey Johnson, Chair, 252-328-6041, E-mail: johnsonj@ecu.edu. *Application contact:* Dean of Graduate School, 252-328-6012, Fax: 252-328-6071, E-mail: gradschool@ecu.edu.
Website: http://www.ecu.edu/cs-cas/engl/graduate/

Eastern Michigan University, Graduate School, College of Arts and Sciences, Department of World Languages, Program in Teaching English to Speakers of Other Languages, Ypsilanti, MI 48197. Offers MA, Graduate Certificate. *Program availability:* Part-time, evening/weekend, online learning. *Students:* 2 full-time (both women), 27 part-time (21 women); includes 2 minority (both Asian, non-Hispanic/Latino), 6 international. Average age 33. 27 applicants, 74% accepted, 13 enrolled. In 2016, 10 master's awarded. *Degree requirements:* For master's, one foreign language. *Entrance requirements:* Additional exam requirements/recommendations for international students: Required—TOEFL. *Application deadline:* Applications are processed on a rolling basis. Application fee: $45. *Financial support:* Fellowships, research assistantships with full tuition reimbursements, teaching assistantships with full tuition reimbursements, career-related internships or fieldwork, Federal Work-Study, institutionally sponsored loans, scholarships/grants, tuition waivers (partial), and unspecified assistantships available. Support available to part-time students. Financial award applicants required to submit FAFSA. *Application contact:* Dr. Thom Cullen, Program Advisor, 734-487-0130, Fax: 734-487-3411, E-mail: tcullen@emich.edu.

Eastern Nazarene College, Adult and Graduate Studies, Division of Teacher Education, Quincy, MA 02170. Offers administration (M Ed); early childhood education (M Ed, Certificate); elementary education (M Ed, Certificate); English as a second language (Certificate); instructional enrichment and development (Certificate); middle school education (M Ed, Certificate); moderate special needs education (Certificate); principal (Certificate); program development and supervision (Certificate); secondary education (M Ed, Certificate); special education administrator (Certificate); special needs (M Ed); supervisor (Certificate); teacher of reading (M Ed, Certificate). M Ed also available through weekend program for administration, special needs, and teacher of reading only. *Program availability:* Part-time, evening/weekend. *Entrance requirements:* Additional exam requirements/recommendations for international students: Required—TOEFL (minimum score 550 paper-based).

Eastern New Mexico University, Graduate School, College of Education and Technology, Department of Curriculum and Instruction, Portales, NM 88130. Offers bilingual education (M Ed); educational technology (M Ed); elementary education (M Ed); English as a second language (M Ed); pedagogy and learning (M Ed); professional technical education (M Ed); reading/literacy (M Ed). *Program availability:* Part-time, online learning. *Degree requirements:* For master's, comprehensive exam, thesis optional. *Entrance requirements:* For master's, minimum GPA of 3.0, photocopy of teaching license, writing assessment, letter of recommendation. Additional exam requirements/recommendations for international students: Required—TOEFL (minimum score 550 paper-based; 79 iBT), IELTS (minimum score 6). Electronic applications accepted.

Eastern University, Loeb School of Education, St. Davids, PA 19087-3696. Offers ESL program specialist (K-12) (Certificate); general supervisor (PreK-12) (Certificate); health and physical education (K-12) (Certificate); middle level (4-8) (Certificate); multicultural education (M Ed); organizational leadership with education (PhD); Pre K-4 (Certificate); Pre K-4 with special education (Certificate); reading (M Ed); reading specialist (K-12) (Certificate); reading supervisor (K-12) (Certificate); school health supervisor (Certificate); school nurse (K-12) (Certificate); secondary biology education (7-12) (Certificate); secondary chemistry education (7-12) (Certificate); secondary communication education (7-12) (Certificate); secondary education (7-12) (Certificate); secondary English education (7-12) (Certificate); secondary math education (7-12) (Certificate); secondary social studies education (7-12) (Certificate); special education (M Ed); special education (7-12) (Certificate); special education (Pre K-8) (Certificate); special education supervisor (N-12) (Certificate); TESOL (M Ed); world language (Certificate), including French, Spanish. *Program availability:* Part-time, evening/weekend, online learning. *Students:* 41 full-time (32 women), 89 part-time (68 women); includes 54 minority (38 Black or African American, non-Hispanic/Latino; 3 Asian, non-Hispanic/Latino; 11 Hispanic/Latino; 2 Two or more races, non-Hispanic/Latino), 2 international. Average age 37. In 2016, 64 master's awarded. *Entrance requirements:* Additional exam requirements/recommendations for international students: Required—TOEFL. *Application deadline:* Applications are processed on a rolling basis. Application fee: $35. Electronic applications accepted. Application fee is waived when completed online. *Expenses:* $690 per credit. *Unit head:* Michael Dziedziak, Executive Director of Enrollment, 800-452-0996, E-mail: gpsadmissions@eastern.edu.
Website: http://www.eastern.edu/academics/programs/loeb-school-education-0

Eastern Washington University, Graduate Studies, College of Arts, Letters and Education, Department of English, Cheney, WA 99004-2431. Offers literature (MA); rhetoric, composition, and technical communication (MA); teaching English as a second language (MA). *Faculty:* 2 full-time (1 woman), 19 part-time/adjunct (9 women). *Students:* 23 full-time (16 women), 7 part-time (5 women); includes 4 minority (1 Black or African American, non-Hispanic/Latino; 2 Hispanic/Latino; 1 Native Hawaiian or other Pacific Islander, non-Hispanic/Latino), 6 international. Average age 35. 27 applicants, 67% accepted, 13 enrolled. In 2016, 20 master's awarded. *Degree requirements:* For master's, comprehensive exam, thesis or alternative. *Entrance requirements:* For master's, GRE General Test, minimum GPA of 3.0. Additional exam requirements/recommendations for international students: Required—TOEFL (minimum score 580 paper-based; 92 iBT), IELTS (minimum score 7), PTE (minimum score 6). *Application deadline:* For fall admission, 4/1 priority date for domestic students; for spring admission, 1/15 for domestic students. Applications are processed on a rolling basis. Application fee: $50. *Expenses:* Tuition, state resident: full-time $11,000; part-time $5500 per credit. Tuition, nonresident: full-time $24,000; part-time $12,000 per credit. *Required fees:* $1300. One-time fee: $50 full-time. Part-time tuition and fees vary according to course load, campus/location and program. *Financial support:* In 2016–17, 25 teaching assistantships with partial tuition reimbursements (averaging $7,000 per year) were awarded; career-related internships or fieldwork, Federal Work-Study, institutionally sponsored loans, scholarships/grants, health care benefits, tuition waivers (partial), and unspecified assistantships also available. Support available to part-time students. Financial award application deadline: 2/1; financial award applicants required to submit FAFSA. *Unit head:* Dr. Logan Greene, Chair, 509-359-2400, E-mail: lgreene@ewu.edu. *Application contact:* Kathy White, Advisor/Recruiter for Graduate Studies, 509-359-2491, E-mail: gradprograms@ewu.edu.
Website: http://www.ewu.edu/CALE/Programs/English.xml

Elms College, Division of Education, Chicopee, MA 01013-2839. Offers early childhood education (MAT); education (M Ed, CAGS); elementary education (MAT); English as a second language (MAT); reading (MAT); secondary education (MAT), including biology education, English education, Spanish education; special education (MAT). *Program availability:* Part-time, evening/weekend. *Faculty:* 5 full-time (all women), 7 part-time/adjunct (6 women). *Students:* 6 full-time (all women), 136 part-time (111 women); includes 6 minority (1 Asian, non-Hispanic/Latino; 5 Hispanic/Latino). Average age 33. 27 applicants, 89% accepted, 20 enrolled. In 2016, 47 master's, 3 other advanced degrees awarded. *Degree requirements:* For master's, thesis (for some programs). *Entrance requirements:* For master's, Massachusetts Educators Certification Test, minimum GPA of 3.0; for CAGS, master's degree in education. Additional exam requirements/recommendations for international students: Required—TOEFL. *Application deadline:* For fall admission, 7/1 priority date for domestic students; for spring admission, 11/1 priority date for domestic students. Applications are processed on a rolling basis. Application fee: $30. *Expenses: Tuition:* Full-time $13,392. *Required fees:* $200. *Financial support:* In 2016–17, 2 teaching assistantships with partial tuition reimbursements were awarded; tuition waivers (partial) also available. Support available to part-time students. Financial award applicants required to submit FAFSA. *Unit head:* Dr. Mary Janeczek, Chair, Division of Education, 413-594-2761, Fax: 413-592-4871, E-mail: janeczeke@elms.edu. *Application contact:* Dr. Elizabeth Teahan Hukowicz, Dean, School of Graduate and Professional Studies, 413-265-2360, Fax: 413-265-2459, E-mail: hukowiczе@elms.edu.

Emporia State University, Program in Teaching English to Speakers of Other Languages, Emporia, KS 66801-5415. Offers MA. *Program availability:* Part-time. *Faculty:* 7 full-time (3 women). *Students:* 4 full-time (3 women), 16 part-time (13 women); includes 2 minority (1 Black or African American, non-Hispanic/Latino; 1 Hispanic/Latino), 2 international. 10 applicants, 100% accepted, 4 enrolled. In 2016, 16 master's awarded. *Degree requirements:* For master's, comprehensive exam, thesis optional. *Entrance requirements:* For master's, minimum undergraduate GPA of 2.75 over last 60 hours. Additional exam requirements/recommendations for international students: Required—TOEFL (minimum score 520 paper-based; 68 iBT). *Application deadline:* For fall admission, 8/15 priority date for domestic students. Applications are processed on a rolling basis. Application fee: $30 ($75 for international students). Electronic applications accepted. *Expenses:* Tuition, state resident: full-time $5922; part-time $246.75 per credit hour. Tuition, nonresident: full-time $18,414; part-time $767.25 per credit hour. *Required fees:* $1884; $78.50 per credit hour. *Financial support:* In 2016–17, 1 research assistantship with full tuition reimbursement (averaging $7,353 per year) was awarded; Federal Work-Study, institutionally sponsored loans, health care benefits, and unspecified assistantships also available. Financial award application deadline: 2/15. *Unit head:* Dr. Abdelilah Salim Sehlaoui, Professor, 620-341-5237, E-mail: asehlaou@emporia.edu. *Application contact:* Mary Sewell, Admissions Coordinator, 800-950-GRAD, Fax: 620-341-5909, E-mail: msewell@emporia.edu.

Erikson Institute, Academic Programs, Chicago, IL 60654. Offers administration (Certificate); bilingual/ESL (Certificate); child development (MS); early childhood education (MS); infant mental health (Certificate); infant studies (Certificate); MS/MSW. MS/MSW offered jointly with Loyola University Chicago. *Program availability:* Part-time, evening/weekend. *Degree requirements:* For master's, comprehensive exam, internship; for Certificate, internship. *Entrance requirements:* For master's and Certificate, minimum GPA of 2.75. Additional exam requirements/recommendations for international students: Required—TOEFL. *Faculty research:* Assessment strategies from early childhood through elementary years; language, literacy, and the arts in children's development; inclusive special education; parent-child relationships; cognitive development.

Fairfield University, Graduate School of Education and Allied Professions, Fairfield, CT 06824. Offers applied behavior analysis (ATC); applied psychology (MA); clinical mental health counseling (MA, CAS); educational technology (MA); elementary education (MA, CAS); family studies (MA); integration of spirituality and religion in counseling (ATC); marriage and family therapy (MA); reading and language development (Sixth Year Certificate); school counseling (MA, CAS); school psychology (MA, CAS); school-based marriage and family therapy (ATC); secondary education (MA); special education (MA, CAS); substance abuse counseling (ATC); teaching (Certificate); teaching and foundations (MA, CAS); TESOL, world languages, and bilingual education (MA, CAS). *Accreditation:* NCATE. *Program availability:* Part-time, evening/weekend. *Faculty:* 19 full-time (15 women), 38 part-time/adjunct (26 women). *Students:* 153 full-time (132 women), 302 part-time (252 women); includes 97 minority (24 Black or African American, non-Hispanic/Latino; 12 Asian, non-Hispanic/Latino; 55 Hispanic/Latino; 6 Two or more races, non-Hispanic/Latino), 6 international. Average age 32. 283 applicants, 61% accepted, 97 enrolled. In 2016, 130 master's awarded. *Degree requirements:* For master's, comprehensive exam. *Entrance requirements:* For master's, minimum GPA of 3.0, 2 recommendations, resume. Additional exam requirements/recommendations for international students: Required—TOEFL (minimum score 550 paper-based; 84 iBT) or IELTS (minimum score 7.5). *Application deadline:* For fall admission, 2/15 for international students; for spring admission, 10/1 for international students. Application fee: $60. Electronic applications accepted. *Expenses:* $725 per credit hour. *Financial support:* In 2016–17, 42 students received support. Career-related internships or fieldwork and unspecified assistantships available. Support available to part-time students. Financial award applicants required to submit FAFSA. *Faculty research:* Reading and literacy, writing, social justice and inequality in education, addictions and mental health issues, therapeutic relationships and clinical supervision. *Unit head:* Dr. Robert D. Hannafin, Dean, 203-254-4250, Fax: 203-254-4241, E-mail: rhannafin@fairfield.edu. *Application contact:* Marianne Gumpper, Director of Graduate Admission, 203-254-4184, Fax: 203-254-4073, E-mail: gradadmis@fairfield.edu.
Website: http://www.fairfield.edu/gseap

Florida Atlantic University, College of Education, Department of Curriculum, Culture, and Educational Inquiry, Boca Raton, FL 33431-0991. Offers curriculum and instruction (M Ed, PhD, Ed S); early childhood education (M Ed); multicultural education (M Ed); TESOL and bilingual education (MA). *Program availability:* Part-time, evening/weekend. *Faculty:* 12 full-time (9 women), 1 (woman) part-time/adjunct. *Students:* 31 full-time (27 women), 93 part-time (68 women); includes 37 minority (17 Black or African American, non-Hispanic/Latino; 4 Asian, non-Hispanic/Latino; 15 Hispanic/Latino; 1 Two or more races, non-Hispanic/Latino), 2 international. Average age 35. 65 applicants, 60% accepted, 25 enrolled. In 2016, 17 master's, 18 doctorates, 3 other advanced degrees awarded. *Entrance requirements:* Additional exam requirements/recommendations for international students: Required—TOEFL (minimum score 500 paper-based; 61 iBT), IELTS (minimum score 6). *Application deadline:* For fall admission, 7/1 for domestic students, 2/15 for international students; for spring admission, 11/1 for domestic students, 7/15 for international students. Application fee: $30. *Expenses:* Tuition, state resident: full-time $7392; part-time $369.82 per credit hour. Tuition, nonresident: full-time $19,432; part-time $1024.81 per credit hour. *Faculty research:* Multicultural education, early intervention strategies, family literacy, religious diversity in schools, early childhood curriculum. *Unit head:* Dr. Dilys Schoorman, Chair, 561-297-3965, E-mail: dschoorm@fau.edu. *Application contact:* Dr. Eliah Watlington, Associate Dean, 561-296-8520, Fax: 261-297-2991, E-mail: ewatling@fau.edu.
Website: http://www.coe.fau.edu/academicdepartments/ccei/

Florida International University, College of Arts, Sciences, and Education, Department of Leadership and Professional Studies, Miami, FL 33199. Offers adult education and human resource development (MS, Ed D); counseling (MS), including rehabilitation counseling, school counseling; counselor education (MS), including clinical mental health counseling; educational administration and supervision (Ed D); educational leadership (MS, Certificate, Ed S); higher education (Ed D); higher education administration (MS); international and comparative education (MS); recreation and sport management (MS), including recreation and sport management, recreational therapy; school psychology (Ed S); urban education (MS), including instruction in urban settings, learning technologies, multicultural/bilingual, multicultural/TESOL, urban education. *Program availability:* Part-time, evening/weekend. *Faculty:* 27 full-time (19 women), 38 part-time/adjunct (25 women). *Students:* 253 full-time (191 women), 306 part-time (241 women); includes 444 minority (129 Black or African American, non-Hispanic/Latino; 3 Asian, non-Hispanic/Latino; 304 Hispanic/Latino; 8 Two or more races, non-Hispanic/Latino), 18 international. Average age 31. 366 applicants, 60% accepted, 115 enrolled. In 2016, 193 master's, 8 doctorates awarded. *Degree requirements:* For doctorate, thesis/dissertation. *Entrance requirements:* For master's, minimum GPA of 3.0; for doctorate and other advanced degree, GRE General Test. Additional exam requirements/recommendations for international students: Required—TOEFL (minimum score 550 paper-based; 80 iBT), IELTS (minimum score 6.3). *Application deadline:* For fall admission, 6/1 priority date for domestic students, 4/1 for international students; for winter admission, 10/1 priority date for domestic students, 9/1 for international students; for spring admission, 3/1 priority date for domestic students, 2/1 for international students. Applications are processed on a rolling basis. Application fee: $30. Electronic applications accepted. *Expenses:* Tuition, state resident: full-time $8912; part-time $446 per credit hour. Tuition, nonresident: full-time $21,393; part-time $992 per credit hour. *Required fees:* $2185; $195 per semester. Tuition and fees vary according to program. *Financial support:* Fellowships, research assistantships with tuition reimbursements, teaching assistantships with tuition reimbursements, Federal Work-Study, and tuition waivers (full and partial) available. Support available to part-time students. Financial award applicants required to submit FAFSA. *Unit head:* Dr. Benjamin Baez, Chair, 305-348-3214, Fax: 305-348-1515, E-mail: benjamin.baez@fiu.edu. *Application contact:* Nanett Rojas, Assistant Director, Graduate Admissions, 305-348-7464, Fax: 305-348-7441, E-mail: gradadm@fiu.edu.
Website: http://education.fiu.edu

Florida International University, College of Arts, Sciences, and Education, Department of Teaching and Learning, Miami, FL 33199. Offers art education (MA, MS); curriculum and instruction (MS, Ed D, PhD, Ed S), including curriculum development (MS), elementary education (MS), English education (MS), learning technologies (MS), mathematics education (MS), modern language education (MS), physical education (MS), science education (MS), social studies education (MS), special education (MS); early childhood education (MS); exceptional student education (Ed D); foreign language education (MS), including foreign language education, teaching English to speakers of other languages (TESOL); international/intercultural education (MS); language, literacy and culture (PhD); mathematics, science, and learning technologies (PhD); physical education (MS), including sport and fitness; reading education (MS). *Program availability:* Part-time, evening/weekend. *Faculty:* 34 full-time (23 women), 64 part-time/adjunct (48 women). *Students:* 182 full-time (154 women), 231 part-time (190 women); includes 323 minority (69 Black or African American, non-Hispanic/Latino; 10 Asian, non-Hispanic/Latino; 237 Hispanic/Latino; 7 Two or more races, non-Hispanic/Latino), 19 international. Average age 34. 282 applicants, 58% accepted, 113 enrolled. In 2016, 184 master's, 12 doctorates awarded. *Degree requirements:* For doctorate, comprehensive exam, thesis/dissertation. *Entrance requirements:* For master's, GRE General Test, Florida General Knowledge Test or Florida College Level Academic Skills Test; for doctorate and Ed S, GRE General Test. Additional exam requirements/recommendations for international students: Required—TOEFL (minimum score 550 paper-based; 80 iBT), IELTS (minimum score 6.3). *Application deadline:* For fall admission, 6/1 priority date for domestic students, 4/1 for international students; for winter admission, 10/1 priority date for domestic students, 9/1 for international students; for spring admission, 3/1 priority date for domestic students, 2/1 for international students. Applications are processed on a rolling basis. Application fee: $30. Electronic applications accepted. *Expenses:* Tuition, state resident: full-time $8912; part-time $446 per credit hour. Tuition, nonresident: full-time $21,393; part-time $992 per credit hour. *Required fees:* $2185; $195 per semester. Tuition and fees vary according to program. *Financial support:* Research assistantships with tuition reimbursements and teaching assistantships with tuition reimbursements available. *Unit head:* Dr. Lynn Miller, Chair, 305-348-2005, Fax: 305-348-2086, E-mail: lynne.miller@fiu.edu. *Application contact:* Nanett Rojas, Assistant Director, Graduate Admissions, 305-348-7464, Fax: 305-348-7441, E-mail: gradadm@fiu.edu.
Website: http://education.fiu.edu

Fordham University, Graduate School of Education, Division of Curriculum and Teaching, New York, NY 10023. Offers curriculum and teaching (MSE); early childhood education (MSE); elementary education (MST); special education (MSE, Adv C); teaching English as a second language (MSE). *Accreditation:* NCATE. *Program availability:* Part-time, evening/weekend. *Degree requirements:* For Adv C, thesis. *Entrance requirements:* Additional exam requirements/recommendations for international students: Required—TOEFL (minimum score 577 paper-based; 90 iBT), IELTS (minimum score 7). Electronic applications accepted.

Framingham State University, Continuing Education, Program in the Teaching of English as a Second Language, Framingham, MA 01701-9101. Offers M Ed.

Fresno Pacific University, Graduate Programs, School of Education, Program in Reading and Language Arts, Fresno, CA 93702-4709. Offers reading (Certificate); reading/English as a second language (MA Ed); reading/language arts (MA Ed). *Program availability:* Part-time, evening/weekend. *Degree requirements:* For master's, thesis or alternative. *Entrance requirements:* For master's, three references. Additional exam requirements/recommendations for international students: Required—TOEFL (minimum score 550 paper-based). Electronic applications accepted. *Expenses:* Contact institution.

Furman University, Graduate Division, Department of Education, Greenville, SC 29613. Offers curriculum and instruction (MA); early childhood education (MA); educational leadership (Ed S); English as a second language (MA); literacy (MA); school leadership (MA); special education (MA). *Accreditation:* NCATE. *Program availability:* Part-time, online learning. *Degree requirements:* For master's, comprehensive exam (for some programs), thesis or alternative. *Entrance requirements:* For master's, PRAXIS II. *Faculty research:* Literacy, pedagogy and practice, social justice, advanced leadership, achievement in high poverty schools.

Gannon University, School of Graduate Studies, College of Humanities, Education, and Social Sciences, School of Education, Program in English as a Second Language, Erie, PA 16541-0001. Offers Certificate. *Program availability:* Part-time, evening/weekend, 100% online. *Students:* 1 (woman) part-time. Average age 36. 1 applicant, 100% accepted, 1 enrolled. In 2016, 1 Certificate awarded. *Degree requirements:* For Certificate, comprehensive exam, practicum. *Entrance requirements:* For degree, 3 letters of recommendation, bachelor's degree from regionally-accredited college or university with minimum GPA of 3.0, valid Pennsylvania Instructional I or II teaching certificate. Additional exam requirements/recommendations for international students: Required—TOEFL (minimum score 79 iBT). *Application deadline:* Applications are processed on a rolling basis. Application fee: $25. Electronic applications accepted. Application fee is waived when completed online. *Expenses:* Contact institution. *Financial support:* Federal Work-Study available. Financial award application deadline: 7/1; financial award applicants required to submit FAFSA. *Unit head:* Dr. Robin Quick, Program Coordinator, 814-871-5399, E-mail: quick003@gannon.edu. *Application contact:* Bridget Philip, Director of Graduate Admissions, 814-871-7412, E-mail: graduate@gannon.edu.

George Fox University, College of Education, Graduate Teaching and Leading Program, Newberg, OR 97132-2697. Offers administrative leadership (Ed S); continuing administrator license (Certificate); educational leadership (M Ed); educational technology (M Ed); English for speakers of other languages (M Ed); ESOL (Certificate); initial administrator license (Certificate); reading (M Ed, Certificate); special education (M Ed); teaching (MAT). *Accreditation:* NCATE. *Program availability:* Part-time, evening/weekend, online learning. *Degree requirements:* For master's, thesis (for some programs). *Entrance requirements:* For master's, minimum undergraduate GPA of 3.0 during previous 2 years of course work, resume, 3 professional recommendations on university forms, official transcripts. Additional exam requirements/recommendations for international students: Required—TOEFL (minimum score 577 paper-based; 90 iBT). Electronic applications accepted. *Expenses:* Contact institution.

George Mason University, College of Education and Human Development, Programs in Curriculum and Instruction, Fairfax, VA 22030. Offers advanced international baccalaureate (M Ed); assistive technology (M Ed); designing digital learning in schools (M Ed); early childhood education (M Ed); early childhood education for diverse learners (M Ed); elementary education (M Ed); English as a second language (M Ed); gifted child education (M Ed); history (M Ed); literacy (M Ed), including PK-12 classroom teachers, reading specialist; literacy leadership for diverse schools (M Ed), including K-12 reading; physical education (M Ed); science K-12 (M Ed); secondary education (M Ed), including biology, chemistry, earth science, English, history/social science, math, physics; special education (M Ed); teacher leadership (M Ed); teaching culturally, linguistically diverse and exceptional learners (M Ed); transformative teaching (M Ed). *Faculty:* 41 full-time (35 women), 53 part-time/adjunct (46 women). *Students:* 155 full-time (127 women), 821 part-time (697 women); includes 267 minority (82 Black or African American, non-Hispanic/Latino; 5 American Indian or Alaska Native, non-Hispanic/Latino; 75 Asian, non-Hispanic/Latino; 88 Hispanic/Latino; 1 Native Hawaiian or other Pacific Islander, non-Hispanic/Latino; 16 Two or more races, non-Hispanic/Latino), 19 international. Average age 33. 513 applicants, 90% accepted, 352 enrolled. In 2016, 347 master's awarded. *Degree requirements:* For master's, comprehensive exam, thesis (for some programs). *Entrance requirements:* For master's, PRAXIS Core (for some programs), minimum GPA of 3.0 in last 60 hours, licensed as teacher or educational administrator, official transcripts, goals statement, 3 recommendation letters, interview or writing sample (depending on program), up to 3 years' teaching experience (depending on program). Additional exam requirements/recommendations for international students: Required—TOEFL (minimum score 575 paper-based; 88 iBT), IELTS (minimum score 6.5), PTE (minimum score 59). *Application deadline:* For spring admission, 11/1 priority date for domestic and international students. Application fee: $75 ($80 for international students). Electronic applications accepted. *Expenses:* Tuition, state resident: full-time $10,628; part-time $443 per credit. Tuition, nonresident: full-time $29,306; part-time $1221 per credit. *Required fees:* $3096; $129 per credit. Tuition and fees vary according to program. *Financial support:* In 2016–17, 1 student received support, including 1

teaching assistantship (averaging $4,060 per year); career-related internships or fieldwork, Federal Work-Study, scholarships/grants, unspecified assistantships, and health care benefits (for full-time research or teaching assistantship recipients) also available. Support available to part-time students. Financial award application deadline: 3/1; financial award applicants required to submit FAFSA. *Faculty research:* Achievement gaps and superintendent decisions, constructivist view of classroom teaching, cost of cheating, creating a critical literacy milieu in kindergarten. *Unit head:* Rebecca Fox, Professor and Academic Program Coordinator, 703-993-4123, E-mail: rfox@gmu.edu.
Website: http://gse.gmu.edu/programs/gsemasters

Gonzaga University, English Language Center, Spokane, WA 99258. Offers teaching English as a second language (MA); teaching English as a second language: studies in language and culture (MA). *Faculty:* 8 full-time (7 women), 6 part-time/adjunct (all women). *Students:* 6 full-time (5 women), 21 part-time (16 women); includes 2 minority (1 Asian, non-Hispanic/Latino; 1 Hispanic/Latino), 14 international. Average age 34. 29 applicants, 66% accepted, 12 enrolled. In 2016, 3 master's awarded. *Degree requirements:* For master's, research thesis or research project. *Entrance requirements:* For master's, two letters of recommendation, written statement of purpose, two official transcripts from each college or university attended. Additional exam requirements/recommendations for international students: Required—TOEFL. Application fee: $50. Electronic applications accepted. *Expenses:* $695 per credit. *Financial support:* In 2016–17, 6 students received support. Scholarships/grants available. Support available to part-time students. Financial award applicants required to submit FAFSA. *Unit head:* Melissa Heid, Manager of Student Services, 509-313-6560, E-mail: heid@gonzaga.edu.
Website: http://www.gonzaga.edu/Academics/International-Students/ELC

Gordon College, Graduate Education Program, Wenham, MA 01984-1899. Offers early childhood (M Ed); educational leadership (M Ed, Ed S); elementary education (M Ed); English as a second language (M Ed, Ed S); math specialist (M Ed); mathematics specialist (Ed S); middle school education (M Ed); moderate disabilities (M Ed); Montessori education (M Ed); reading (M Ed, Ed S); secondary education (M Ed). *Program availability:* Part-time, evening/weekend. *Faculty:* 17 full-time (9 women), 41 part-time/adjunct (34 women). *Students:* 81 full-time (61 women), 109 part-time (87 women); includes 28 minority (2 Black or African American, non-Hispanic/Latino; 11 Asian, non-Hispanic/Latino; 13 Hispanic/Latino; 2 Two or more races, non-Hispanic/Latino), 12 international. Average age 34. 190 applicants, 100% accepted, 141 enrolled. In 2016, 110 master's, 16 Ed Ss awarded. *Degree requirements:* For master's, action research or clinical experience (for most programs); for Ed S, action research or clinical experience (for some programs). *Entrance requirements:* For master's, minimum undergraduate GPA of 3.0; 2 official undergraduate transcripts; professional resume; 3 recommendation letters (one professional reference, one academic reference, one personal reference); 500-700 word statement of purpose; for Ed S, minimum master's GPA of 3.3; 2 official transcripts from undergraduate and graduate schools; professional resume; 3 recommendation letters (one professional reference, one academic reference, one personal reference); 500-700 word statement of purpose. Additional exam requirements/recommendations for international students: Required—TOEFL (minimum score 550 paper-based, 80 iBT) or IELTS (minimum score 6.5). *Application deadline:* Applications are processed on a rolling basis. Application fee: $75. *Expenses:* $325 per credit tuition, $75 per term fee. *Financial support:* Applicants required to submit FAFSA. *Faculty research:* Reading, early childhood development, English language learners, universal design for learning. *Unit head:* Dr. Janet Arndt, Director of Graduate Studies, 978-867-4355, Fax: 978-867-4663. *Application contact:* Julie Lenocker, Program Administrator, 978-867-4322, Fax: 978-867-4663, E-mail: graduate-education@gordon.edu.
Website: http://www.gordon.edu/graduate

Grand Canyon University, College of Education, Phoenix, AZ 85017-1097. Offers autism spectrum disorders (MA); curriculum and instruction (MA); early childhood education (M Ed); educational administration (M Ed); educational leadership (M Ed); elementary education (M Ed); gifted education (MA); instructional technology (MS); K-12 leadership (Ed S); reading (MA); secondary education (M Ed); secondary humanities education (M Ed); secondary STEM education (M Ed); special education (M Ed); teaching and learning (Ed D); teaching English to speakers of other languages (MA). *Program availability:* Part-time, evening/weekend, online learning. *Degree requirements:* For master's, publishable research paper (M Ed), e-portfolio. *Entrance requirements:* For master's, undergraduate degree from accredited, GCU-approved college, university, or program with minimum GPA 2.8. Additional exam requirements/recommendations for international students: Required—TOEFL (minimum score 550 paper-based; 79 iBT), IELTS (minimum score 6). *Application deadline:* For fall admission, 8/21 for domestic students, 7/2 for international students; for spring admission, 12/24 for domestic students, 11/1 for international students. Applications are processed on a rolling basis. Application fee: $100. Electronic applications accepted. *Financial support:* Federal Work-Study available. Support available to part-time students. Financial award applicants required to submit FAFSA. *Unit head:* Dr. Kimberly L. LaPrade, Dean, 602-639-6360, E-mail: kimberly.laprade@gcu.edu. *Application contact:* Dr. Kimberly L. LaPrade, Dean, 602-639-6360, E-mail: kimberly.laprade@gcu.edu.
Website: https://www.gcu.edu/college-of-education.php

Grand Valley State University, College of Education, Programs in General Education, Allendale, MI 49401-9403. Offers adult and higher education (M Ed); early childhood education (M Ed); educational differentiation (M Ed); educational leadership (M Ed); educational technology integration (M Ed); elementary education (M Ed); middle level education (M Ed); school library media services (M Ed); secondary level education (M Ed); teaching English to speakers of other languages (M Ed). *Program availability:* Part-time, evening/weekend, 100% online, blended/hybrid learning. *Students:* 28 part-time (20 women); includes 6 minority (4 Black or African American, non-Hispanic/Latino; 1 American Indian or Alaska Native, non-Hispanic/Latino; 1 Hispanic/Latino). Average age 42. In 2016, 17 master's awarded. *Degree requirements:* For master's, project or thesis. *Entrance requirements:* For master's, GRE General Test or minimum GPA of 3.0, last 60 credits from regionally-accredited college/university, 3 letters of recommendation. Additional exam requirements/recommendations for international students: Required—TOEFL (minimum score 550 paper-based, 80 iBT), IELTS (6.5), or Michigan English Language Assessment Battery. *Application deadline:* Applications are processed on a rolling basis. Application fee: $30. Electronic applications accepted. *Expenses:* $628 per credit hour. *Financial support:* In 2016–17, 2 students received support. Career-related internships or fieldwork, Federal Work-Study, scholarships/grants, and unspecified assistantships available. *Faculty research:* Effectiveness of technology in education, parental involvement, effective teaching, effective schools research. *Unit head:* Dr. Doug Busman, Graduate Program Director, 616-331-6250, E-mail: busmando@gvsu.edu. *Application contact:* Thomas Owens, Director, Student Information and Services Center, 616-331-6282, Fax: 616-331-6217, E-mail: owenst@gvsu.edu.
Website: http://www.gvsu.edu/coe/

Greensboro College, Program in Teaching English to Speakers of Other Languages, Greensboro, NC 27401-1875. Offers MA. *Accreditation:* NCATE. *Program availability:* Part-time, evening/weekend. *Degree requirements:* For master's, thesis, portfolio, project. *Entrance requirements:* For master's, GRE or MAT, 2 letters of recommendation, writing sample. Additional exam requirements/recommendations for international students: Required—TOEFL (minimum score 550 paper-based). Electronic applications accepted.

Hamline University, School of Education, St. Paul, MN 55104-1284. Offers education (MA Ed, Ed D); English as a second language (MA); literacy education (MA); natural science and environmental education (MA Ed); teaching (MAT); teaching English to speakers of other languages (MA). *Accreditation:* NCATE (one or more programs are accredited). *Program availability:* Part-time, evening/weekend, 100% online, blended/hybrid learning. *Faculty:* 29 full-time (23 women), 90 part-time/adjunct (70 women). *Students:* 277 full-time (201 women), 762 part-time (601 women); includes 122 minority (29 Black or African American, non-Hispanic/Latino; 1 American Indian or Alaska Native, non-Hispanic/Latino; 43 Asian, non-Hispanic/Latino; 29 Hispanic/Latino; 20 Two or more races, non-Hispanic/Latino), 12 international. Average age 34. 408 applicants, 77% accepted, 230 enrolled. In 2016, 279 master's, 14 doctorates awarded. *Degree requirements:* For master's, thesis (for some programs), thesis or capstone project; for doctorate, comprehensive exam, thesis/dissertation. *Entrance requirements:* For master's, official transcripts, essay, letters of recommendation, minimum GPA of 3.0 from bachelor's work; resume and/or writing samples (for some programs); for doctorate, personal statement, master's degree with minimum GPA of 3.0, letters of recommendation, writing sample. Additional exam requirements/recommendations for international students: Required—TOEFL. *Application deadline:* For fall admission, 6/1 for domestic and international students; for spring admission, 11/1 for domestic and international students; for summer admission, 3/1 for domestic and international students. Applications are processed on a rolling basis. Application fee: $0 ($100 for international students). Electronic applications accepted. *Expenses:* $466-$721 per credit. *Financial support:* Career-related internships or fieldwork, Federal Work-Study, and scholarships/grants available. Support available to part-time students. Financial award applicants required to submit FAFSA. *Faculty research:* Adult basic education, service-learning, teacher dispositions, diversity, technology. *Unit head:* Dr. Nancy Sorenson, Dean, 651-523-2600, Fax: 651-523-2489, E-mail: education@hamline.edu. *Application contact:* Shawn Skoog, Director of Graduate Recruitment and Admission, 651-523-2900, Fax: 651-523-3058, E-mail: gradprog@hamline.edu.
Website: http://www.hamline.edu/education

Harding University, Cannon-Clary College of Education, Searcy, AR 72149-0001. Offers advanced studies in teaching and learning (M Ed); art (MSE); behavioral science (MSE); counseling (MS, Ed S); early childhood special education (M Ed, MSE); education (MSE); educational leadership (M Ed, Ed S); elementary education (M Ed); English (MSE); French (MSE); history/social science (MSE); kinesiology (MSE); math (MSE); reading (M Ed); secondary education (M Ed); Spanish (MSE); teaching (MAT); teaching English as a second language (MSE). *Accreditation:* NCATE. *Program availability:* Part-time, evening/weekend. *Faculty:* 22 full-time (9 women), 51 part-time/adjunct (37 women). *Students:* 130 full-time (94 women), 321 part-time (234 women); includes 83 minority (50 Black or African American, non-Hispanic/Latino; 4 American Indian or Alaska Native, non-Hispanic/Latino; 6 Asian, non-Hispanic/Latino; 13 Hispanic/Latino; 10 Two or more races, non-Hispanic/Latino), 11 international. Average age 35. 125 applicants, 88% accepted, 110 enrolled. In 2016, 124 master's, 27 other advanced degrees awarded. *Degree requirements:* For master's, comprehensive exam (for some programs), thesis optional, portfolio(s); for Ed S, comprehensive exam, portfolio, project. *Entrance requirements:* For master's, GRE, MAT, PRAXIS; for Ed S, MAT or GRE. Additional exam requirements/recommendations for international students: Required—TOEFL (minimum score 550 paper-based; 79 iBT). *Application deadline:* For fall admission, 8/1 for domestic and international students; for spring admission, 1/1 for domestic and international students. Applications are processed on a rolling basis. Application fee: $35. Tuition and fees vary according to degree level and program. *Financial support:* In 2016–17, 31 students received support. Unspecified assistantships available. *Faculty research:* Reading, comprehension, school violence, educational technology, behavior, college choice, differentiated instruction, brain-based teaching. *Unit head:* Dr. Clara Carroll, Chair, 501-279-4501, Fax: 501-279-4083, E-mail: ccarroll@harding.edu. *Application contact:* Information Contact, 501-279-4315, E-mail: gradstudiesedu@harding.edu.
Website: http://www.harding.edu/education

Hawai`i Pacific University, College of Liberal Arts, Program in Teaching English to Speakers of Other Languages, Honolulu, HI 96813. Offers MA. *Program availability:* Part-time. *Faculty:* 3 full-time (2 women). *Students:* 16 full-time (10 women), 12 part-time (9 women); includes 11 minority (1 Black or African American, non-Hispanic/Latino; 3 Asian, non-Hispanic/Latino; 2 Hispanic/Latino; 5 Two or more races, non-Hispanic/Latino), 8 international. Average age 35. 23 applicants, 100% accepted, 14 enrolled. In 2016, 15 master's awarded. *Entrance requirements:* Additional exam requirements/recommendations for international students: Required—TOEFL (minimum score 550 paper-based; 80 iBT), IELTS (minimum score 6.5), TWE (minimum score 5). *Application deadline:* For fall admission, 2/15 priority date for domestic students; for spring admission, 10/15 priority date for domestic students. Applications are processed on a rolling basis. Application fee: $50. Electronic applications accepted. *Expenses: Tuition:* Full-time $17,190; part-time $955 per credit. *Required fees:* $150; $26 per credit. Tuition and fees vary according to course load and program. *Financial support:* In 2016–17, 5 students received support. Career-related internships or fieldwork, Federal Work-Study, scholarships/grants, tuition waivers, and unspecified assistantships available. Financial award application deadline: 3/1; financial award applicants required to submit FAFSA. *Unit head:* Dr. Laurie Leach, Department Chair, 808-544-1103, E-mail: lleach@hpu.edu. *Application contact:* Danny Lam, Assistant Director of Graduate Admissions, 808-544-1135, E-mail: graduate@hpu.edu.
Website: https://hpu.edu/CHSS/English/TESOL/index.html

Henderson State University, Graduate Studies, Teachers College, Department of Advanced Instructional Studies, Arkadelphia, AR 71999-0001. Offers developmental therapy (MSE); dyslexia therapy (Graduate Certificate); education (MAT); educational technology leadership (Graduate Certificate); English as a second language (MSE, Graduate Certificate); instructional facilitator (MSE, Graduate Certificate); middle level education (MAT); special education (K-12) (MAT, MSE); special education/early childhood (MAT). *Accreditation:* NCATE. *Program availability:* Part-time. *Faculty:* 12 full-time (9 women), 5 part-time/adjunct (4 women). *Students:* 13 full-time (8 women), 79 part-time (66 women); includes 14 minority (8 Black or African American, non-Hispanic/Latino; 2 American Indian or Alaska Native, non-Hispanic/Latino; 2 Hispanic/Latino; 2 Two or more races, non-Hispanic/Latino). Average age 33. 21 applicants, 100% accepted, 21 enrolled. In 2016, 29 master's awarded. *Entrance requirements:* For master's, GRE General Test or MAT, minimum GPA of 2.7, teacher certification. Additional exam requirements/recommendations for international students: Required—TOEFL (minimum score 600 paper-based); Recommended—IELTS (minimum score 6.5). *Application deadline:* For fall admission, 8/1 priority date for domestic students, 6/30 priority date for international students; for spring admission, 1/1 priority date for domestic students, 11/30 priority date for international students. Applications are processed on a rolling basis. Application fee: $25 ($75 for international students). *Expenses:* Tuition, state resident: full-time $6288; part-time $3144 per credit hour. Tuition, nonresident: full-time $12,888; part-time $6444 per credit hour. *Required fees:*

$1429; $1024 per credit hour. Tuition and fees vary according to course load and student level. *Financial support:* In 2016–17, 1 teaching assistantship with partial tuition reimbursement (averaging $4,000 per year) was awarded; scholarships/grants and unspecified assistantships also available. Financial award application deadline: 4/15; financial award applicants required to submit FAFSA. *Unit head:* Dr. Gary Smithey, Coordinator, 870-230-5361, Fax: 870-230-5455, E-mail: smitheg@hsu.edu. *Application contact:* Dr. Ken Taylor, Graduate Dean, 870-230-5126, Fax: 870-230-5479, E-mail: taylorke@hsu.edu.
Website: http://www.hsu.edu/Academics/TeachersCollege/AIS/index.html

Heritage University, Graduate Programs in Education, Program in Professional Studies, Toppenish, WA 98948-9599. Offers bilingual education/ESL (M Ed); biology (M Ed); English and literature (M Ed); reading/literacy (M Ed); special education (M Ed). *Program availability:* Part-time, evening/weekend. *Degree requirements:* For master's, comprehensive exam (for some programs), thesis (for some programs).

Hofstra University, College of Liberal Arts and Sciences, Programs in Forensic Linguistics and Applied Linguistics, Hempstead, NY 11549. Offers applied linguistics (TESOL) (MA); linguistics (MA), including forensic linguistics. *Program availability:* Part-time, blended/hybrid learning. *Students:* 34 full-time (26 women), 3 part-time (2 women); includes 7 minority (3 Black or African American, non-Hispanic/Latino; 4 Hispanic/ Latino), 5 international. Average age 26. 38 applicants, 89% accepted, 13 enrolled. In 2016, 26 master's awarded. *Degree requirements:* For master's, thesis, 36 credits, capstone, minimum GPA of 3.0. *Entrance requirements:* For master's, bachelor's degree in related area, interview, 2 letters of recommendation. Additional exam requirements/recommendations for international students: Required—TOEFL (minimum score 550 paper-based; 80 iBT). *Application deadline:* Applications are processed on a rolling basis. Application fee: $75. Electronic applications accepted. *Expenses: Tuition:* Full-time $1240. *Required fees:* $970. Tuition and fees vary according to program. *Financial support:* In 2016–17, 9 students received support, including 6 fellowships with full and partial tuition reimbursements available (averaging $5,942 per year); research assistantships with full and partial tuition reimbursements available, career-related internships or fieldwork, Federal Work-Study, institutionally sponsored loans, scholarships/grants, tuition waivers (full and partial), and unspecified assistantships also available. Support available to part-time students. Financial award applicants required to submit FAFSA. *Faculty research:* Stance in threatening communications, cross-examination techniques in cases of sexual assault, expressions of contrition in parole board hearings, analysis of ordinary meaning in laws using corpus techniques, manifestation of ideologies in immigration legislation; ancient rhetoric, second-language writing instruction, pedagogical grammar of English, English etymology, political oratory. *Unit head:* Dr. George L. Greaney, Program Director, 516-463-5651, E-mail: george.l.greaney@hofstra.edu. *Application contact:* Sunil Samuel, Assistant Vice President of Admissions, 516-463-4723, Fax: 516-463-4664, E-mail: graduateadmission@hofstra.edu.
Website: http://www.hofstra.edu/hclas

Hofstra University, School of Education, Programs in Teacher Education, Hempstead, NY 11549. Offers bilingual education (MA, Advanced Certificate); bilingual extension (Advanced Certificate), including education/speech language pathology; business education (MS Ed); early childhood and childhood education (MS Ed); early childhood education (MA, MS Ed); education technology (Advanced Certificate); elementary education (MA, MS Ed), including science, technology, engineering, and mathematics (STEM) (MA); English education (MS Ed); family and consumer science (MS Ed); fine arts and music education (Advanced Certificate); fine arts education (MS Ed); foreign language and TESOL (MS Ed); foreign language education (MS Ed), including French, German, Russian, Spanish; learning and teaching (Ed D), including applied linguistics, art education, arts and humanities, early childhood education, English education, human development, math education, math, science, and technology, multicultural education, physical education, science education, social studies education, special education; mathematics education (MA, MS Ed); middle school extension (Advanced Certificate), including grades 5-6, grades 7-9; music education (MA, MS Ed); science education (MA, MS Ed), including biology, chemistry, earth science, geology, physics; secondary education (Advanced Certificate); social studies education (MA, MS Ed); teaching languages other than English and TESOL (MS Ed); TESOL (MS Ed, Advanced Certificate). *Program availability:* Part-time, evening/weekend, blended/hybrid learning. *Students:* 139 full-time (97 women), 145 part-time (106 women); includes 60 minority (15 Black or African American, non-Hispanic/Latino; 1 American Indian or Alaska Native, non-Hispanic/Latino; 12 Asian, non-Hispanic/Latino; 31 Hispanic/Latino; 1 Two or more races, non-Hispanic/Latino), 21 international. Average age 29. 255 applicants, 86% accepted, 122 enrolled. In 2016, 101 master's, 4 doctorates, 43 other advanced degrees awarded. *Degree requirements:* For master's, comprehensive exam, thesis (for some programs), exit project, student teaching, fieldwork, electronic portfolio, curriculum project, minimum GPA of 3.0; for doctorate, thesis/dissertation; for Advanced Certificate, 3 foreign languages, comprehensive exam (for some programs), thesis project. *Entrance requirements:* For master's, GRE, MAT, 2 letters of recommendation, portfolio, teacher certification (MA), interview, essay; for doctorate, GMAT, GRE, LSAT, or MAT; for Advanced Certificate, 2 letters of recommendation, essay, interview and/or portfolio, teaching certificate. Additional exam requirements/recommendations for international students: Required—TOEFL (minimum score 550 paper-based; 80 iBT). *Application deadline:* Applications are processed on a rolling basis. Application fee: $75. Electronic applications accepted. *Expenses: Tuition:* Full-time $1240. *Required fees:* $970. Tuition and fees vary according to program. *Financial support:* In 2016–17, 149 students received support, including 58 fellowships with full and partial tuition reimbursements available (averaging $5,309 per year), 5 research assistantships with full and partial tuition reimbursements available (averaging $7,073 per year); career-related internships or fieldwork, Federal Work-Study, institutionally sponsored loans, scholarships/grants, traineeships, tuition waivers (full and partial), and unspecified assistantships also available. Support available to part-time students. Financial award applicants required to submit FAFSA. *Faculty research:* Educational interventions that foster critical-thinking skills; teachers' attitudes about professional development; threats to teacher quality. *Unit head:* Dr. Eustace Thompson, Chairperson, 516-463-5749, Fax: 516-463-6275, E-mail: eustace.g.thompson@hofstra.edu. *Application contact:* Sunil Samuel, Assistant Vice President of Admissions, 516-463-4723, Fax: 516-463-4664, E-mail: graduateadmission@hofstra.edu.
Website: http://www.hofstra.edu/education/

Holy Family University, Graduate and Professional Programs, School of Education, Master of Education Programs, Philadelphia, PA 19114. Offers early elementary education (PreK-Grade 4) (M Ed); education leadership (M Ed); general education (M Ed); reading specialist (M Ed); special education (M Ed); TESOL and literacy (M Ed). *Program availability:* Part-time. *Students:* 202 full-time, 58 part-time. 209 applicants, 77% accepted, 140 enrolled. In 2016, 123 master's awarded. *Degree requirements:* For master's, thesis optional. *Application deadline:* Applications are processed on a rolling basis. Application fee: $25. Electronic applications accepted. *Expenses: Tuition:* Part-time $751 per hour. *Required fees:* $140 per semester. One-time fee: $165 part-time. Part-time tuition and fees vary according to degree level and program. *Unit head:* Dr. Kevin Zook, Dean, 267-341-3246, Fax: 215-824-2438, E-mail: kzook@holyfamily.edu. *Application contact:* Donald Reimold, Director of Graduate Admissions, 267-341-5001, Fax: 215-637-1478, E-mail: dreimold@holyfamily.edu.

Houston Baptist University, College of Education and Behavioral Sciences, Programs in Education, Houston, TX 77074-3298. Offers bilingual education (M Ed); counselor education (M Ed); curriculum and instruction (M Ed); educational administration (M Ed); educational diagnostician (M Ed); executive educational leadership (Ed D); reading education (M Ed). *Program availability:* Part-time, evening/weekend, 100% online, blended/hybrid learning. *Students:* 45 full-time (35 women), 158 part-time (136 women); includes 141 minority (87 Black or African American, non-Hispanic/Latino; 1 American Indian or Alaska Native, non-Hispanic/Latino; 5 Asian, non-Hispanic/Latino; 47 Hispanic/ Latino; 1 Two or more races, non-Hispanic/Latino), 3 international. Average age 34. 320 applicants, 30% accepted, 61 enrolled. In 2016, 121 degrees awarded. *Degree requirements:* For master's, comprehensive exam; for doctorate, thesis/dissertation. *Entrance requirements:* For master's, minimum GPA of 2.75, two recommendations, resume, bachelor's degree conferred transcript; interview (for non-certified teachers); for doctorate, GRE, 3 letters of recommendation. Additional exam requirements/ recommendations for international students: Required—TOEFL (minimum score 80 iBT), IELTS (minimum score 6.5). *Application deadline:* For fall admission, 8/1 for domestic students, 6/1 for international students; for spring admission, 1/1 for domestic students, 11/1 for international students; for summer admission, 5/1 for domestic students, 3/1 for international students. Applications are processed on a rolling basis. Application fee: $0 ($100 for international students). Electronic applications accepted. Application fee is waived when completed online. *Expenses:* $1,650 per 3-hour course; $1,275 annual general fee; $1,060 annual technology fee. *Financial support:* In 2016–17, 2 students received support. Research assistantships, teaching assistantships, Federal Work-Study, and scholarships/grants available. Support available to part-time students. Financial award application deadline: 4/1; financial award applicants required to submit FAFSA. *Faculty research:* Autism and inclusion, integrating technology into instruction, school change and leadership trust. *Unit head:* Dr. Charlotte Fontenot, Director, Graduate Programs, 281-649-3078, Fax: 281-649-3361, E-mail: cfontenot@hbu.edu. *Application contact:* Kristy Wright, Administrative Assistant for Graduate Programs, 281-649-3094, Fax: 281-649-3361, E-mail: kwright@hbu.edu.
Website: http://www.hbu.edu/MED

Humboldt State University, Academic Programs, College of Arts, Humanities, and Social Sciences, Department of English, Arcata, CA 95521-8299. Offers English (MA), including composition studies and pedagogy, literary and cultural studies, teaching English as a second language. *Degree requirements:* For master's, variable foreign language requirement, thesis or alternative, qualifying exam. *Entrance requirements:* For master's, GRE, minimum GPA of 3.0, 3 letters of recommendation, sample of writing. Additional exam requirements/recommendations for international students: Required—TOEFL (minimum score 500 paper-based). *Expenses:* Tuition, state resident: full-time $6738; part-time $1953 per semester. Tuition, nonresident: full-time $13,434; part-time $3813 per semester. *Required fees:* $1738; $653 per semester. Tuition and fees vary according to program. *Faculty research:* Teaching of writing, literature.

Hunter College of the City University of New York, Graduate School, School of Education, Department of Curriculum and Teaching, Program in Teaching English as a Second Language, New York, NY 10065-5085. Offers MA. *Accreditation:* NCATE. *Degree requirements:* For master's, one foreign language, thesis, comprehensive exam or essay, New York state teacher certification exams. *Entrance requirements:* For master's, minimum GPA of 2.8, 2 letters of recommendation, interview. Additional exam requirements/recommendations for international students: Required—TOEFL (minimum score 600 paper-based), TWE (minimum score 5). *Application deadline:* For fall admission, 4/1 for domestic students, 2/1 for international students; for spring admission, 11/1 for domestic students, 9/1 for international students. Applications are processed on a rolling basis. *Financial support:* Federal Work-Study, scholarships/ grants, and tuition waivers (partial) available. Support available to part-time students. *Unit head:* Dr. Anne Ediger, Coordinator, 212-777-4665, E-mail: aediger@hunter.cuny.edu. *Application contact:* Milena Solo, Director for Graduate Admissions, 212-772-4480, E-mail: admissions@hunter.cuny.edu.

Huntington University, Graduate School, Huntington, IN 46750-1299. Offers counseling (MA), including licensed mental health counselor; early adolescent education (M Ed); education (M Ed); global missions leadership (MA); global youth ministry (MA); TESOL education (M Ed); youth ministry leadership (MA). *Program availability:* Part-time, online learning. *Degree requirements:* For master's, comprehensive exam (for some programs), thesis (for some programs). *Entrance requirements:* For master's, GRE (for counseling and education students only); for doctorate, GRE (for occupational therapy students). Additional exam requirements/recommendations for international students: Required—TOEFL (minimum score 85 iBT), IELTS (minimum score 6.5). Electronic applications accepted. *Faculty research:* Leadership, educational technology trends, evangelism, youth ministry, mental health.

Idaho State University, Office of Graduate Studies, College of Arts and Letters, Department of English, Pocatello, ID 83209-8056. Offers English (MA, DA); English and the teaching of English (PhD); TESOL (Post-Master's Certificate). *Program availability:* Part-time. *Degree requirements:* For master's, one foreign language, comprehensive exam, thesis optional; for doctorate, one foreign language, comprehensive exam, thesis/ dissertation, 2 papers, 2 teaching internships; for Post-Master's Certificate, 6 credits of elective linguistics, practicum. *Entrance requirements:* For master's, GRE General Test (minimum 50th percentile verbal), general literature exam, minimum GPA of 3.0, 3 letters of recommendation, 5-page writing sample; for doctorate, GRE General Test, GRE Subject Test, minimum GPA of 3.5, writing examples, 3 letters of recommendation, master's degree in English; for Post-Master's Certificate, GRE (minimum 35th percentile on verbal section), bachelor's degree, minimum undergraduate GPA of 3.0 in last 2 years, 3 letters of recommendation, knowledge of second language. Additional exam requirements/recommendations for international students: Required—TOEFL (minimum score 550 paper-based; 80 iBT). Electronic applications accepted. *Faculty research:* American literature, Renaissance literature, composition and rhetoric, Intermountain West studies, ethics.

Immaculata University, College of Graduate Studies, Program in Cultural and Linguistic Diversity, Immaculata, PA 19345. Offers bilingual studies (MA); TESOL (MA). *Program availability:* Part-time, evening/weekend. *Degree requirements:* For master's, one foreign language, comprehensive exam, thesis optional, professional experience. *Entrance requirements:* For master's, GRE or MAT, proficiency in Spanish or Asian language, minimum GPA of 3.0. Additional exam requirements/recommendations for international students: Required—TOEFL, IELTS. Electronic applications accepted. *Faculty research:* Cognitive learning, Caribbean literature and culture, English as a second language, teaching English to speakers of other languages.

Indiana State University, College of Graduate and Professional Studies, College of Arts and Sciences, Department of Languages, Literatures, and Linguistics, Terre Haute, IN 47809. Offers applied linguistics/teaching English as a second language (MA); language education (PhD); Spanish/teaching english as a second language (MA); TESL/TEFL (CAS). *Degree requirements:* For master's, comprehensive exam. Electronic applications accepted.

English as a Second Language

Indiana University Bloomington, University Graduate School, College of Arts and Sciences, Department of Second Language Studies, Bloomington, IN 47405-7000. Offers second language studies (MA, PhD); TESOL and applied linguistics (MA). *Faculty:* 10 full-time (4 women). *Students:* 40 full-time (25 women), 1 (woman) part-time; includes 4 minority (2 Asian, non-Hispanic/Latino; 1 Hispanic/Latino; 1 Two or more races, non-Hispanic/Latino), 14 international. Average age 33. 64 applicants, 52% accepted, 12 enrolled. In 2016, 11 master's, 1 doctorate awarded. *Entrance requirements:* Additional exam requirements/recommendations for international students: Required—TOEFL (minimum score 100 iBT). *Application deadline:* For fall admission, 1/15 for domestic students, 12/1 for international students. Application fee: $55 ($65 for international students). Electronic applications accepted. *Financial support:* Fellowships with tuition reimbursements, research assistantships, teaching assistantships with tuition reimbursements, health care benefits, and unspecified assistantships available. *Unit head:* Laurent Dekydtspotter, Chair, 812-855-7951, E-mail: ldekydts@indiana.edu. *Application contact:* Mandy Stewart, Graduate Secretary, 812-855-7951, E-mail: dsls@indiana.edu.
Website: http://dsls.indiana.edu

Indiana University of Pennsylvania, School of Graduate Studies and Research, College of Humanities and Social Sciences, Department of English, PhD Program in Composition and Teaching English to Speakers of Other Languages, Indiana, PA 15705. Offers PhD. *Program availability:* Part-time. *Faculty:* 20 full-time (9 women). *Students:* 28 full-time (13 women), 78 part-time (52 women); includes 9 minority (3 Black or African American, non-Hispanic/Latino; 1 Asian, non-Hispanic/Latino; 1 Hispanic/Latino; 4 Two or more races, non-Hispanic/Latino), 41 international. Average age 37. 113 applicants, 42% accepted, 13 enrolled. In 2016, 14 doctorates awarded. *Degree requirements:* For doctorate, one foreign language, comprehensive exam, thesis/dissertation. *Entrance requirements:* For doctorate, 2 letters of recommendation. Additional exam requirements/recommendations for international students: Required—TOEFL (minimum score 600 paper-based). *Application deadline:* For fall admission, 2/1 priority date for domestic students; for summer admission, 11/1 priority date for domestic students. Applications are processed on a rolling basis. Application fee: $50. Electronic applications accepted. *Expenses:* Contact institution. *Financial support:* In 2016–17, 18 research assistantships with tuition reimbursements (averaging $6,398 per year), 5 teaching assistantships with partial tuition reimbursements (averaging $11,652 per year) were awarded; fellowships with full tuition reimbursements, career-related internships or fieldwork, Federal Work-Study, scholarships/grants, and unspecified assistantships also available. Support available to part-time students. Financial award application deadline: 4/15; financial award applicants required to submit FAFSA. *Unit head:* Dr. Sharon Deckert, Graduate Coordinator, 724-357-2261, E-mail: sharon.deckert@iup.edu.
Website: http://www.iup.edu/english/grad/composition-tesol-phd/default.aspx

Indiana University of Pennsylvania, School of Graduate Studies and Research, College of Humanities and Social Sciences, Department of English, Program in English: TESOL, Indiana, PA 15705. Offers MA. *Program availability:* Part-time. *Faculty:* 20 full-time (9 women). *Students:* 21 full-time (13 women), 1 (woman) part-time; includes 2 minority (1 Black or African American, non-Hispanic/Latino; 1 Two or more races, non-Hispanic/Latino), 13 international. Average age 28. 49 applicants, 61% accepted, 12 enrolled. In 2016, 12 master's awarded. *Degree requirements:* For master's, thesis optional. *Entrance requirements:* For master's, two letters of recommendation. Additional exam requirements/recommendations for international students: Required—TOEFL (minimum score 580 paper-based). *Application deadline:* Applications are processed on a rolling basis. Application fee: $50. Electronic applications accepted. *Expenses:* Contact institution. *Financial support:* In 2016–17, 4 research assistantships with tuition reimbursements (averaging $2,628 per year) were awarded; fellowships with full tuition reimbursements, Federal Work-Study, scholarships/grants, and unspecified assistantships also available. Financial award application deadline: 4/15; financial award applicants required to submit FAFSA. *Unit head:* Dr. Gloria Park, Director, 724-357-3095, E-mail: gloria.park@iup.edu.
Website: http://www.iup.edu/english/grad/tesol-ma/default.aspx

Indiana University–Purdue University Fort Wayne, College of Arts and Sciences, Department of English and Linguistics, Fort Wayne, IN 46805-1499. Offers English (MA, MAT); TENL (teaching English as a new language) (Certificate). *Program availability:* Part-time. *Degree requirements:* For master's, one foreign language, thesis (for some programs), teaching certificate (for MAT). *Entrance requirements:* For master's, GRE General Test, minimum GPA of 3.0, major or minor in English, 3 letters of recommendation; for Certificate, bachelor's degree with minimum GPA of 2.5. Additional exam requirements/recommendations for international students: Required—TOEFL (minimum score 600 paper-based; 79 iBT). *Faculty research:* Hebrew names and the vernacular Savior in Anglo-Saxon England.

Indiana University–Purdue University Indianapolis, School of Education, Indianapolis, IN 46202-5155. Offers curriculum and instruction (MS); early childhood (MS); educational leadership (MS, Certificate); English as a second language (Certificate); kindergarten (Certificate); language education (MS); reading (Certificate); school counseling (MS); special education (MS, Certificate). *Program availability:* Part-time, evening/weekend. *Faculty:* 35 full-time (27 women), 56 part-time/adjunct (42 women). *Students:* 125 full-time (86 women), 181 part-time (139 women); includes 106 minority (78 Black or African American, non-Hispanic/Latino; 9 Asian, non-Hispanic/Latino; 12 Hispanic/Latino; 7 Two or more races, non-Hispanic/Latino), 3 international. Average age 32. 73 applicants, 93% accepted, 68 enrolled. In 2016, 73 master's awarded. Terminal master's awarded for partial completion of doctoral program. *Degree requirements:* For master's, thesis optional. *Entrance requirements:* For master's, GRE General Test, minimum GPA of 2.5; for Certificate, official transcripts. Additional exam requirements/recommendations for international students: Required—TOEFL (minimum score 60 iBT), IELTS (minimum score 5.5). *Application deadline:* For fall admission, 5/1 for domestic students; for spring admission, 11/1 for domestic students. Application fee: $60 ($65 for international students). Electronic applications accepted. *Expenses:* $1,262 tuition, $213 general fee. *Financial support:* Applicants required to submit FAFSA. *Faculty research:* Educational policies and school leaders' responses to these; issues of intersectionality in the experiences of African American lesbian, gay, and bisexual students attending historically black colleges and universities and those who belong to black Greek-letter organizations; students' experiential knowledge and their evolving disciplinary-specific literacy and understanding; innovative program development; urban ESL teacher preparation; target-based instructional coaching. *Total annual research expenditures:* $2.1 million. *Unit head:* Dr. Robin Hughes, Executive Associate Dean, 317-274-6817, E-mail: roblhugh@iupui.edu. *Application contact:* Ky Shaw, Graduate Admissions Coordinator, 317-278-6778, E-mail: kycshaw@iupui.edu.
Website: http://education.iupui.edu/

Indiana University–Purdue University Indianapolis, School of Liberal Arts, Department of English, Indianapolis, IN 46202. Offers English (MA); teaching English to speakers of other languages (TESOL) (Certificate); teaching writing (Certificate). *Entrance requirements:* For master's, GRE. Additional exam requirements/recommendations for international students: Required—TOEFL.

Inter American University of Puerto Rico, Arecibo Campus, Programs in Education, Arecibo, PR 00614-4050. Offers administration and educational supervision (MA Ed); counseling and guidance (MA Ed); curriculum and teaching (MA Ed), including biology education, English as a second language, history education, math education, Spanish; elementary education (MA Ed). *Accreditation:* TEAC. *Degree requirements:* For master's, comprehensive exam, thesis optional. *Entrance requirements:* For master's, GRE, EXADEP, bachelor's degree in education or teaching license (administration and supervision) or courses in education and psychology (counseling and guidance), minimum GPA of 2.5 in last 60 credits.

Inter American University of Puerto Rico, Barranquitas Campus, Program in Education, Barranquitas, PR 00794. Offers curriculum and teaching (M Ed), including biology education, English as a second language, history education, mathematics education, Spanish; educational leadership and management (MA); elementary education (M Ed); information and library service technology (M Ed); special education (MA). *Accreditation:* TEAC. *Degree requirements:* For master's, comprehensive exam, thesis optional. *Entrance requirements:* For master's, EXADEP, letter of recommendation. Electronic applications accepted.

Inter American University of Puerto Rico, Metropolitan Campus, Graduate Programs, Program in Teaching English as a Second Language, San Juan, PR 00919-1293. Offers MA. *Program availability:* Part-time, evening/weekend. *Degree requirements:* For master's, comprehensive exam, thesis or alternative. *Entrance requirements:* For master's, GRE General Test or EXADEP, interview, minimum GPA of 2.5. Electronic applications accepted.

Inter American University of Puerto Rico, Ponce Campus, Graduate School, Mercedita, PR 00715-1602. Offers accounting (MBA); biology (M Ed); chemistry (M Ed); criminal justice (MA); elementary education (M Ed); English as a Second Language (M Ed); finance (MBA); history (M Ed); human resources (MBA); marketing (MBA); mathematics (M Ed); Spanish (M Ed). *Entrance requirements:* For master's, minimum GPA of 2.5.

Inter American University of Puerto Rico, San Germán Campus, Graduate Studies Center, Program in Teaching English as a Second Language, San Germán, PR 00683-5008. Offers MA. *Accreditation:* TEAC. *Program availability:* Part-time, evening/weekend. *Degree requirements:* For master's, comprehensive exam. *Entrance requirements:* For master's, GRE General Test or EXADEP, minimum GPA of 3.0.

Iowa State University of Science and Technology, Program in Teaching English as a Second Language/Applied Linguistics, Ames, IA 50011. Offers MA. *Entrance requirements:* For master's, GRE, official academic transcripts, resume, three letters of recommendation, statement of personal goals, writing sample. Additional exam requirements/recommendations for international students: Required—TOEFL (minimum score 600 paper-based; 100 iBT), IELTS (minimum score 7). *Application deadline:* For fall admission, 1/5 for domestic students. Application fee: $60 ($90 for international students). Electronic applications accepted. *Application contact:* Teresa Smiley, Application Contact, 515-294-2477, Fax: 515-294-6814, E-mail: englgrad@iastate.edu.
Website: http://www.public.iastate.edu/~apling/TESL_cert.html

James Madison University, The Graduate School, College of Education, Program in Education, Harrisonburg, VA 22807. Offers early childhood education (preK-3) (MAT); educational leadership (M Ed); educational technology (M Ed); elementary education (MAT); equity and cultural diversity (M Ed); inclusive early childhood education (MAT); K-8 mathematics specialist (M Ed); middle education (MAT); reading education (M Ed); secondary education (MAT); Spanish language and culture for educators (M Ed); TESOL (MAT). *Accreditation:* NCATE. *Program availability:* Part-time, evening/weekend. *Faculty:* 21 full-time (12 women), 5 part-time/adjunct (2 women). *Students:* 249 full-time (220 women), 123 part-time (86 women); includes 43 minority (7 Black or African American, non-Hispanic/Latino; 7 Asian, non-Hispanic/Latino; 17 Hispanic/Latino; 12 Two or more races, non-Hispanic/Latino), 2 international. Average age 30. 355 applicants, 98% accepted, 312 enrolled. In 2016, 247 master's awarded. Application fee: $55. Electronic applications accepted. *Financial support:* In 2016–17, 16 students received support. Career-related internships or fieldwork, Federal Work-Study, and 22 assistantships (averaging $7911) available. Financial award application deadline: 3/1; financial award applicants required to submit FAFSA. *Unit head:* Dr. Phillip M. Wishon, Dean, 540-568-6572, E-mail: wishonpm@jmu.edu. *Application contact:* Lynette D. Michael, Director of Graduate Admissions, 540-568-6131 Ext. 6395, Fax: 540-568-7860, E-mail: michaeld@jmu.edu.
Website: http://www.jmu.edu/coe/index.shtml

Kansas State University, Graduate School, College of Education, Department of Educational Leadership, Manhattan, KS 66506. Offers adult learning (Certificate); educational leadership (MS, Ed D, PhD); leadership dynamics for adult learners (Certificate); qualitative research (Certificate); social justice education (Certificate); teaching English as a second language for adult learners (Certificate). *Accreditation:* NCATE. *Program availability:* Online learning. *Faculty:* 14 full-time (9 women), 3 part-time/adjunct (2 women). *Students:* 42 full-time (20 women), 300 part-time (187 women); includes 65 minority (24 Black or African American, non-Hispanic/Latino; 6 American Indian or Alaska Native, non-Hispanic/Latino; 3 Asian, non-Hispanic/Latino; 21 Hispanic/Latino; 1 Native Hawaiian or other Pacific Islander, non-Hispanic/Latino; 10 Two or more races, non-Hispanic/Latino), 1 international. Average age 38. 180 applicants, 84% accepted, 126 enrolled. In 2016, 110 master's, 2 doctorates, 2 other advanced degrees awarded. *Degree requirements:* For master's, comprehensive exam; for doctorate, comprehensive exam, thesis/dissertation. *Entrance requirements:* For master's, minimum undergraduate GPA of 3.0; for doctorate, MAT (for educational administration); GRE General Test (for adult education), minimum GPA of 3.0 in last 60 hours. Additional exam requirements/recommendations for international students: Required—TOEFL. *Application deadline:* For fall admission, 2/1 priority date for domestic and international students; for spring admission, 8/1 priority date for domestic and international students. Applications are processed on a rolling basis. Application fee: $50 ($75 for international students). Electronic applications accepted. *Expenses:* Tuition, state resident: full-time $9670. Tuition, nonresident: full-time $21,828. *Required fees:* $862. *Financial support:* Research assistantships, institutionally sponsored loans, and scholarships/grants available. Financial award application deadline: 3/1; financial award applicants required to submit FAFSA. *Faculty research:* Educational law, school finance, school facilities, organizational leadership, adult learning, distance learning/education. *Total annual research expenditures:* $21,235. *Unit head:* Dr. David C. Thompson, Head, 785-532-5535, Fax: 785-532-7304, E-mail: thomsond@ksu.edu. *Application contact:* Jody Ellis, Applications Contact, 785-532-5535, E-mail: foxksu@ksu.edu.
Website: http://www.coe.k-state.edu/departments/edlea/index.html

Kean University, College of Education, Program in Instruction and Curriculum, Union, NJ 07083. Offers bilingual/bicultural education (MA); teaching English as a second language (MA). *Accreditation:* NCATE. *Program availability:* Part-time. *Faculty:* 15 full-time (9 women). *Students:* 3 full-time (all women), 25 part-time (19 women); includes 21 minority (1 Black or African American, non-Hispanic/Latino; 20 Hispanic/Latino), 2 international. Average age 37. 21 applicants, 52% accepted, 10 enrolled. In 2016, 25 master's awarded. *Degree requirements:* For master's, comprehensive exam (for some programs), thesis optional, two-semester advanced seminar. *Entrance requirements:* For master's, GRE General Test or MAT; PRAXIS (for some programs), minimum GPA

of 3.0, personal statement, professional resume/curriculum vitae, commitment to working with children, certification (for some programs), two letters of recommendation. Additional exam requirements/recommendations for international students: Required—TOEFL (minimum score 550 paper-based; 79 iBT), IELTS (minimum score 6.5). *Application deadline:* For fall admission, 6/1 for domestic and international students; for spring admission, 12/1 for domestic and international students. Applications are processed on a rolling basis. Application fee: $75. Electronic applications accepted. *Expenses:* Tuition, state resident: full-time $13,156; part-time $640 per credit. Tuition, nonresident: full-time $17,831; part-time $785 per credit. *Required fees:* $3316; $151 per credit. Tuition and fees vary according to course level, course load, degree level and program. *Financial support:* Scholarships/grants and unspecified assistantships available. Financial award applicants required to submit FAFSA. *Unit head:* Dr. Gail Verdi, Program Coordinator, 908-737-3908, E-mail: gverdi@kean.edu. *Application contact:* Brittany Gerstenhaber, Admissions Counselor, 908-737-7100, E-mail: grad-adm@kean.edu.
Website: http://grad.kean.edu/masters-programs/bilingualbicultural-education-instruction-and-curriculum

Kennesaw State University, Leland and Clarice C. Bagwell College of Education, Program in Graduate Education, Kennesaw, GA 30144. Offers educational leadership (M Ed); educational leadership technology (M Ed); elementary and early childhood education (M Ed); instructional technology (M Ed); middle grades education (M Ed); reading (M Ed); secondary education (M Ed); special education (M Ed); teaching English to speakers of other languages (M Ed). *Accreditation:* NCATE. *Program availability:* Part-time. *Degree requirements:* For master's, thesis or alternative. *Entrance requirements:* For master's, GRE General Test, T-4 state certification, minimum GPA of 2.75. Additional exam requirements/recommendations for international students: Required—TOEFL (minimum score 550 paper-based; 80 iBT), IELTS (minimum score 6.5). Electronic applications accepted.

Kennesaw State University, Leland and Clarice C. Bagwell College of Education, Program in Teaching, Kennesaw, GA 30144. Offers art education (MAT); biology (MAT); chemistry (MAT); foreign language education (Chinese and Spanish) (MAT); physics (MAT); secondary English (MAT); secondary mathematics (MAT); special education (MAT); teaching English to speakers of other languages (MAT). *Program availability:* Part-time, evening/weekend. *Entrance requirements:* For master's, GRE, GACE I (state certificate exam), minimum GPA of 2.75, 2 recommendations, resume. Additional exam requirements/recommendations for international students: Required—TOEFL (minimum score 550 paper-based; 80 iBT), IELTS (minimum score 6.5). Electronic applications accepted.

Kent State University, College of Arts and Sciences, Department of English, Kent, OH 44242-0001. Offers creative writing (MFA); English (MA, PhD); English for teachers (MA); literature and writing (MA); rhetoric and composition (PhD); teaching English as a second language (MA). MFA program offered jointly with Cleveland State University, The University of Akron, and Youngstown State University. *Program availability:* Part-time. *Faculty:* 45 full-time (29 women). *Students:* 111 full-time (75 women), 19 part-time (13 women); includes 8 minority (3 Black or African American, non-Hispanic/Latino; 1 Asian, non-Hispanic/Latino; 2 Hispanic/Latino; 2 Two or more races, non-Hispanic/Latino), 27 international. Average age 30. 98 applicants, 61% accepted, 19 enrolled. In 2016, 30 master's, 8 doctorates awarded. *Degree requirements:* For master's, one foreign language, thesis (for some programs), final portfolio, final exam, or thesis (for MA in teaching English as a second language); for doctorate, one foreign language, comprehensive exam, thesis/dissertation. *Entrance requirements:* For master's and doctorate, GRE General Test, statement of purpose, 3 letters of recommendation, writing sample or undergraduate/graduate paper, transcripts. Additional exam requirements/recommendations for international students: Required—TOEFL (minimum score of 600 paper-based, 100 iBT), IELTS (minimum score of 7.0), Michigan English Language Assessment Battery (minimum score of 85), or PTE (minimum score of 68). *Application deadline:* For fall admission, 1/15 for domestic and international students. Applications are processed on a rolling basis. Application fee: $45 ($70 for international students). Electronic applications accepted. *Expenses:* Tuition, state resident: full-time $10,864; part-time $495 per credit hour. Tuition, nonresident: full-time $18,380; part-time $837 per credit hour. *Financial support:* Fellowships with full tuition reimbursements, teaching assistantships with full tuition reimbursements, and unspecified assistantships available. Financial award application deadline: 1/15. *Unit head:* Dr. Robert Trogdon, Chair, 330-672-2676, E-mail: rtrogdon@kent.edu. *Application contact:* Kevin Floyd, Professor and Graduate Coordinator, 330-672-1708, E-mail: kfloyd@kent.edu.
Website: http://www.kent.edu/english/

Langston University, School of Education and Behavioral Sciences, Langston, OK 73050. Offers bilingual/multicultural (M Ed); elementary education (M Ed); English as a second language (M Ed); rehabilitation counseling (M Sc); urban education (M Ed). *Accreditation:* CORE; NCATE (one or more programs are accredited). *Program availability:* Part-time. *Degree requirements:* For master's, comprehensive exam, thesis optional. *Entrance requirements:* For master's, GRE, writing skills test, minimum GPA of 2.5, 3 letters of recommendation. Additional exam requirements/recommendations for international students: Required—TOEFL, TWE. *Faculty research:* Bilingual/multicultural education, financing post-secondary education.

La Salle University, School of Arts and Sciences, Hispanic Institute, Philadelphia, PA 19141-1199. Offers bilingual/bicultural studies (MA); ESL program specialist (Certificate); interpretation: English/Spanish-Spanish/English (Certificate); teaching English to speakers of other languages (MA); translation and interpretation (MA); translation: English/Spanish-Spanish/English (Certificate). *Program availability:* Part-time, evening/weekend. *Faculty:* 2 full-time (1 woman), 6 part-time/adjunct (3 women). *Students:* 1 (woman) full-time, 26 part-time (18 women); includes 15 minority (5 Black or African American, non-Hispanic/Latino; 10 Hispanic/Latino), 1 international. Average age 37. 17 applicants, 76% accepted, 7 enrolled. In 2016, 7 master's, 4 other advanced degrees awarded. *Degree requirements:* For master's, one foreign language, project or thesis. *Entrance requirements:* For master's, GRE, MAT, or GMAT, professional resume; two letters of recommendation; for Certificate, GRE, MAT, or GMAT, professional resume; two letters of recommendation; evidence of an advanced level in Spanish. Additional exam requirements/recommendations for international students: Required—TOEFL. *Application deadline:* For fall admission, 8/15 priority date for domestic students, 7/15 for international students; for spring admission, 12/15 priority date for domestic students, 11/15 for international students; for summer admission, 4/15 priority date for domestic students, 3/15 for international students. Applications are processed on a rolling basis. Application fee: $35. Electronic applications accepted. Application fee is waived when completed online. *Expenses:* Contact institution. *Financial support:* In 2016–17, 3 students received support. Scholarships/grants available. Support available to part-time students. Financial award application deadline: 8/31; financial award applicants required to submit FAFSA. *Faculty research:* Puerto Rican literature, cross-cultural communication, English as a second language methodology, Spanish language. *Unit head:* Guadalupe Da Costa Montesinos, Director, 215-951-1209, Fax: 215-991-3506, E-mail: montesin@lasalle.edu. *Application contact:* Elizabeth Heenan, Director, Graduate and Adult Enrollment, 215-951-1100, Fax: 215-951-1462, E-mail: heenan@lasalle.edu.
Website: http://www.lasalle.edu/hispanic-institute/

La Salle University, School of Arts and Sciences, Program in Education, Philadelphia, PA 19141-1199. Offers autism spectrum disorders (MA, Certificate); bilingual/bicultural studies (MA); classroom management (MA); dual early childhood and special education (MA); dual middle-level science and math and special education (MA); education (MA); English (MA); English as a second language (Certificate); history (MA); instructional coach (Certificate); instructional leadership (MA); reading specialist (MA, Certificate); secondary education (MA); special education (MA, Certificate). *Program availability:* Part-time, evening/weekend. *Faculty:* 5 full-time (4 women), 12 part-time/adjunct (8 women). *Students:* 10 full-time (all women), 98 part-time (74 women); includes 28 minority (13 Black or African American, non-Hispanic/Latino; 1 American Indian or Alaska Native, non-Hispanic/Latino; 1 Asian, non-Hispanic/Latino; 10 Hispanic/Latino; 3 Two or more races, non-Hispanic/Latino). Average age 34. 128 applicants, 84% accepted, 69 enrolled. In 2016, 53 master's awarded. *Degree requirements:* For master's, comprehensive exam. *Entrance requirements:* For master's, MAT or GRE, 2 letters of recommendation; for Certificate, GMAT or GRE, 2 letters of recommendation. Additional exam requirements/recommendations for international students: Required—TOEFL. *Application deadline:* For fall admission, 8/15 priority date for domestic students, 7/15 for international students; for spring admission, 12/15 priority date for domestic students, 11/15 for international students; for summer admission, 4/15 priority date for domestic students, 3/15 for international students. Applications are processed on a rolling basis. Application fee: $35. Electronic applications accepted. Application fee is waived when completed online. *Expenses:* Contact institution. *Financial support:* In 2016–17, 27 students received support. Scholarships/grants available. Support available to part-time students. Financial award application deadline: 8/31; financial award applicants required to submit FAFSA. *Unit head:* Dr. Greer Richardson, Director, 215-951-1806, Fax: 215-951-1843, E-mail: graded@lasalle.edu. *Application contact:* Elizabeth Heenan, Director, Graduate and Adult Enrollment, 215-951-1100, Fax: 215-951-1462, E-mail: heenan@lasalle.edu.
Website: http://www.lasalle.edu/grad-education-programs/

Lee University, Program in Education, Cleveland, TN 37320-3450. Offers art (MAT); curriculum and instruction (M Ed, Ed S); early childhood (MAT); educational leadership (M Ed, Ed S); elementary education (MAT); English and math (MAT); English and science (MAT); English and social studies (MAT); higher education administration (MS); history (MAT); history and economics (MAT); math and science (MAT); math and social studies (MAT); middle grades (MAT); science and social studies (MASW); secondary education (MAT); Spanish (MAT); special education (M Ed, MAT); TESOL (MAT). *Accreditation:* NCATE. *Program availability:* Part-time. *Faculty:* 13 full-time (6 women), 9 part-time/adjunct (4 women). *Students:* 35 full-time (27 women), 50 part-time (32 women); includes 12 minority (5 Black or African American, non-Hispanic/Latino; 5 Hispanic/Latino; 2 Two or more races, non-Hispanic/Latino), 4 international. Average age 30. 43 applicants, 79% accepted, 28 enrolled. In 2016, 42 master's, 6 other advanced degrees awarded. *Degree requirements:* For master's, variable foreign language requirement, thesis optional, internship. *Entrance requirements:* For master's, MAT or GRE General Test, minimum undergraduate GPA of 2.75, 3 letters of recommendation, interview, writing sample, official transcripts, background check; for Ed S, minimum undergraduate and master's GPA of 2.75, official transcripts for undergraduate and master's degrees. Additional exam requirements/recommendations for international students: Required—TOEFL (minimum score 61 iBT). *Application deadline:* For fall admission, 6/1 priority date for domestic and international students; for spring admission, 11/1 priority date for domestic and international students; for summer admission, 4/1 priority date for domestic and international students. Applications are processed on a rolling basis. Application fee: $25. Electronic applications accepted. *Expenses: Tuition:* Full-time $11,367; part-time $632 per credit hour. *Required fees:* $35 per term. One-time fee: $25. Tuition and fees vary according to program. *Financial support:* In 2016–17, 42 students received support. Career-related internships or fieldwork, Federal Work-Study, institutionally sponsored loans, scholarships/grants, and unspecified assistantships available. Financial award application deadline: 3/1; financial award applicants required to submit FAFSA. *Unit head:* Dr. William Kamm, Director, 423-614-8544, E-mail: wkamm@leeuniversity.edu. *Application contact:* Crystal Keeter, Graduate Education Secretary, 423-614-8544, E-mail: ckeeter@leeuniversity.edu.
Website: http://www.leeuniversity.edu/academics/graduate/education

Lehman College of the City University of New York, School of Education, Department of Middle and High School Education, Program in Teaching English to Speakers of Other Languages, Bronx, NY 10468-1589. Offers MS Ed. *Accreditation:* NCATE. *Degree requirements:* For master's, thesis. *Entrance requirements:* For master's, minimum GPA of 3.0.

Le Moyne College, Department of Education, Syracuse, NY 13214. Offers adolescent education (MS Ed, MST); adolescent education/special education (MS Ed, MST); adolescent English (MST), including grades 7-12; adolescent English/special education (MST), including grades 7-12; adolescent foreign language (MST), including grades 7-12; adolescent history (MST), including grades 7-12; childhood education (MS Ed); childhood education/special education (MS Ed); elementary education (MS Ed); general education (MS Ed); inclusive childhood education (MST); literacy education (MS Ed), including birth to grade 6, grades 5-12; school building leader (MS Ed); school building leadership (CAS); school district business leader (MS Ed, CAS); school district leader (MS Ed); school district leadership (CAS); secondary education (MS Ed); special education (MS Ed); teaching English to speakers of other languages (MS Ed); urban studies (MS Ed). *Accreditation:* TEAC. *Program availability:* Part-time, evening/weekend. *Faculty:* 8 full-time (5 women), 20 part-time/adjunct (12 women). *Students:* 66 full-time (40 women), 155 part-time (117 women); includes 13 minority (4 Black or African American, non-Hispanic/Latino; 2 American Indian or Alaska Native, non-Hispanic/Latino; 2 Asian, non-Hispanic/Latino; 5 Hispanic/Latino), 3 international. Average age 30. 74 applicants, 90% accepted, 66 enrolled. In 2016, 81 master's, 53 CASs awarded. *Degree requirements:* For master's, thesis. *Entrance requirements:* For master's, bachelor's degree with minimum undergraduate GPA of 3.0, 2 letters of recommendation, transcripts. Additional exam requirements/recommendations for international students: Required—TOEFL (minimum score 550 paper-based; 79 iBT); Recommended—IELTS (minimum score 6.5). *Application deadline:* For fall admission, 4/1 priority date for domestic and international students; for spring admission, 10/1 priority date for domestic and international students; for summer admission, 3/1 priority date for domestic and international students. Applications are processed on a rolling basis. Application fee: $50. Electronic applications accepted. *Expenses:* $700 per credit hour. *Financial support:* In 2016–17, 21 students received support. Career-related internships or fieldwork, scholarships/grants, and health care benefits available. Support available to part-time students. Financial award applicants required to submit FAFSA. *Faculty research:* Minority teachers, special education, multiculturalism, literacy, technology, media literacy learning, autism, school district organization, service-learning, higher level problem solving, teacher leadership. *Unit head:* Dr. Stephen C. Fleury, Chair, Department of Education, 315-445-4376, Fax: 315-445-4744, E-mail: fleurysc@lemoyne.edu. *Application contact:* Kristen P. Richards, Senior Director of Enrollment Management, 315-445-5444, Fax: 315-445-6092, E-mail: trapaskp@

lemoyne.edu.
Website: http://www.lemoyne.edu/education

Lesley University, Graduate School of Education, Cambridge, MA 02138-2790. Offers arts, community, and education (M Ed); autism studies (Certificate); curriculum and instruction (M Ed, CAGS); early childhood education (M Ed); ecological teaching and learning (MS); educational studies (PhD), including adult learning, educational leadership, individually designed; elementary education (M Ed); emergent technologies for educators (Certificate); ESLArts: language learning through the arts (M Ed); high school education (M Ed); individually designed (M Ed); integrated teaching through the arts (M Ed); literacy for K-8 classroom teachers (M Ed); mathematics education (M Ed); middle school education (M Ed); moderate disabilities (M Ed); online learning (Certificate); reading (CAGS); science in education (M Ed); severe disabilities (M Ed); special needs (CAGS); specialist teacher of reading (M Ed); teacher of visual art (M Ed); technology in education (M Ed, CAGS). *Accreditation:* TEAC. *Program availability:* Part-time, evening/weekend, online learning. *Degree requirements:* For master's, practicum; for doctorate, thesis/dissertation. *Entrance requirements:* For master's, Massachusetts Tests for Educator Licensure (MTEL), transcripts, statement of purpose, recommendations; interview (for special education); for doctorate, GRE General Test, transcripts, statement of purpose, recommendations, interview, master's degree, resume; for other advanced degree, interview, master's degree. Additional exam requirements/recommendations for international students: Required—TOEFL (minimum score 550 paper-based; 80 iBT). Electronic applications accepted. *Faculty research:* Assessment in literacy, mathematics and science; autism spectrum disorders; instructional technology and online learning; multicultural education and English language learners.

Lewis University, College of Education, Program in English as a Second Language, Romeoville, IL 60446. Offers M Ed. *Program availability:* Part-time, evening/weekend. *Students:* 6 full-time (2 women), 19 part-time (18 women); includes 2 minority (both Hispanic/Latino), 6 international. Average age 35. *Degree requirements:* For master's, departmental qualifying exam. *Entrance requirements:* For master's, writing exam, minimum GPA of 2.75, 2 letters of recommendation, interview. Additional exam requirements/recommendations for international students: Required—TOEFL (minimum score 550 paper-based; 80 iBT). *Application deadline:* For fall admission, 5/1 priority date for international students; for spring admission, 11/15 priority date for international students. Application fee: $40. *Expenses: Tuition:* Full-time $13,860; part-time $770 per credit hour. *Required fees:* $75 per semester. Tuition and fees vary according to degree level and program. *Financial support:* Federal Work-Study, scholarships/grants, and unspecified assistantships available. Financial award application deadline: 5/1; financial award applicants required to submit FAFSA. *Unit head:* Dr. Barbara Mackey, Program Director, 815-838-0500 Ext. 5962, E-mail: mackeyba@lewisu.edu. *Application contact:* Linda Campbell, Graduate Admission Counselor, 815-838-0500 Ext. 5704, E-mail: campbeli@lewisu.edu.

Lindenwood University, Graduate Programs, School of Education, St. Charles, MO 63301-1695. Offers education (MA), including autism spectrum disorders, character education, early intervention in autism and sensory impairment, gifted, technology; educational administration (MA, Ed D, Ed S); English to speakers of other languages (MA); instructional leadership (Ed D, Ed S); library media (MA); professional counseling (MA); school administration (MA, Ed S); school counseling (MA); teaching (MA). *Program availability:* Part-time, evening/weekend, 100% online, blended/hybrid learning. *Faculty:* 39 full-time (27 women), 210 part-time/adjunct (136 women). *Students:* 292 full-time (227 women), 1,580 part-time (1,203 women); includes 404 minority (333 Black or African American, non-Hispanic/Latino; 4 American Indian or Alaska Native, non-Hispanic/Latino; 10 Asian, non-Hispanic/Latino; 36 Hispanic/Latino; 1 Native Hawaiian or other Pacific Islander, non-Hispanic/Latino; 20 Two or more races, non-Hispanic/Latino), 20 international. Average age 36. 558 applicants, 72% accepted, 353 enrolled. In 2016, 491 master's, 72 doctorates, 111 other advanced degrees awarded. *Degree requirements:* For master's, thesis (for some programs), minimum GPA of 3.0; for doctorate, thesis/dissertation, minimum GPA of 3.0; for Ed S, comprehensive exam, project, minimum GPA of 3.0. *Entrance requirements:* For master's, interview, minimum undergraduate cumulative GPA of 3.0, writing sample, letter of recommendation; for doctorate, GRE, minimum graduate GPA of 3.4, resume, interview, writing sample, 4 letters of recommendation; for Ed S, master's degree in education, relevant work experience. Additional exam requirements/recommendations for international students: Required—TOEFL (minimum score 550 paper-based; 80 iBT); Recommended—IELTS (minimum score 6.5). *Application deadline:* For fall admission, 8/28 priority date for domestic and international students; for spring admission, 1/8 priority date for domestic and international students; for summer admission, 6/5 priority date for domestic and international students. Applications are processed on a rolling basis. Application fee: $30 ($100 for international students). Electronic applications accepted. *Expenses: Tuition:* Full-time $15,672; part-time $453 per credit hour. *Required fees:* $205 per semester. Tuition and fees vary according to course level, course load and degree level. *Financial support:* In 2016–17, 334 students received support. Career-related internships or fieldwork, Federal Work-Study, institutionally sponsored loans, scholarships/grants, tuition waivers (partial), and unspecified assistantships available. Financial award application deadline: 6/30; financial award applicants required to submit FAFSA. *Unit head:* Dr. Cynthia Bice, Dean, School of Education, 636-949-4618, Fax: 636-949-4197, E-mail: cbice@lindenwood.edu. *Application contact:* Tyler Kostich, Director, Evening and Graduate Admissions, 636-949-4138, Fax: 636-949-4109, E-mail: adultadmissions@lindenwood.edu.
Website: http://www.lindenwood.edu/academics/academic-schools/school-of-education/

Long Island University–Hudson, Graduate School, Purchase, NY 10577. Offers autism (Advanced Certificate); childhood education (MS Ed); early childhood education (MS Ed); educational leadership (MS Ed); finance (MBA); health administration (MPA); healthcare sector management (MBA); literacy (MS Ed); management (MBA); marriage and family therapy (MS); mental health counseling (MS), including credentialed alcoholism and substance abuse counselor; middle childhood and adolescence education (MS Ed); pharmaceutics (MS), including cosmetic science, industrial pharmacy; public administration (MPA); school counseling (MS Ed, Advanced Certificate); school psychology (MS Ed); special education (MS Ed); TESOL (all grades) (Advanced Certificate); TESOL and bilingual education (MS Ed); the business of pharmaceutics and biotechnology (MBA). *Program availability:* Part-time, evening/weekend, online learning. *Faculty:* 7 full-time (5 women), 42 part-time/adjunct (25 women). *Students:* 55 full-time (41 women), 158 part-time (123 women); includes 40 minority (8 Black or African American, non-Hispanic/Latino; 1 Asian, non-Hispanic/Latino; 31 Hispanic/Latino). Average age 35. *Entrance requirements:* Additional exam requirements/recommendations for international students: Required—TOEFL (minimum score 550 paper-based; 79 iBT). *Application deadline:* Applications are processed on a rolling basis. Application fee: $50. Electronic applications accepted. *Expenses:* Contact institution. *Unit head:* Dr. Sylvia Blake, Dean and Chief Operating Officer, 914-831-2700, E-mail: westchester@liu.edu. *Application contact:* Cindy Pagnotta, Director of Marketing and Enrollment, 914-831-2701, Fax: 914-251-5959, E-mail: cindy.pagnotta@liu.edu.

Long Island University–LIU Brooklyn, School of Education, Brooklyn, NY 11201-8423. Offers adolescence urban education (MS Ed); applied behavior analysis (Advanced Certificate); bilingual education (Advanced Certificate); bilingual school counselor (MS Ed, Advanced Certificate); childhood urban education (MS Ed); childhood/early childhood urban education (MS Ed); early childhood urban education (MS Ed, Advanced Certificate); educational leadership (Advanced Certificate); marriage and family therapy (MS, Advanced Certificate); mental health counseling (MS, Advanced Certificate); school building district leader (Advanced Certificate); school counselor (MS Ed, Advanced Certificate); school psychologist (MS Ed); teaching urban children/adolescents with disabilities (MS Ed); TESOL (MS Ed). *Accreditation:* TEAC. *Program availability:* Part-time, evening/weekend. *Faculty:* 23 full-time (17 women), 44 part-time/adjunct (32 women). *Students:* 161 full-time (144 women), 594 part-time (461 women); includes 493 minority (229 Black or African American, non-Hispanic/Latino; 1 American Indian or Alaska Native, non-Hispanic/Latino; 30 Asian, non-Hispanic/Latino; 218 Hispanic/Latino; 2 Native Hawaiian or other Pacific Islander, non-Hispanic/Latino; 13 Two or more races, non-Hispanic/Latino), 9 international. 513 applicants, 73% accepted, 272 enrolled. In 2016, 262 master's, 18 other advanced degrees awarded. *Degree requirements:* For master's, thesis optional, electronic portfolio. *Entrance requirements:* For master's, GRE (for MS Ed). Additional exam requirements/recommendations for international students: Required—TOEFL (minimum score 527 paper-based; 75 iBT). *Application deadline:* Applications are processed on a rolling basis. Application fee: $50. Electronic applications accepted. *Expenses: Tuition:* Full-time $28,272; part-time $1178 per credit. *Required fees:* $451 per term. Tuition and fees vary according to degree level, program and student level. *Financial support:* In 2016–17, 81 students received support. Career-related internships or fieldwork, Federal Work-Study, institutionally sponsored loans, scholarships/grants, and unspecified assistantships available. Support available to part-time students. Financial award application deadline: 2/15; financial award applicants required to submit FAFSA. *Faculty research:* Technology in education, teaching civics and sustainability, biliteracy and dual language instruction, diversity in organizations and leadership, counseling diverse couples and families. *Unit head:* Dr. Amy Ginsberg, Dean, 718-246-6308, E-mail: amy.ginsberg@liu.edu. *Application contact:* Gabrielle Gannon, Director of Graduate Admissions, 718-488-1011, Fax: 718-780-6110, E-mail: bkln-admissions@liu.edu.
Website: http://www.liu.edu/Brooklyn/Academics/School-of-Education

Long Island University–LIU Post, College of Education, Information and Technology, Brookville, NY 11548-1300. Offers adolescence education (MS); adolescence education 7-12 (MS); archives and records management (AC); art education (MS); childhood education (MS); childhood teaching literacy B-6 (MS); childhood/special education (MS); clinical mental health counseling (MS, AC); early childhood education (MS); early childhood education/childhood education (MS); educational leadership (AC); educational technology (MS); information studies (PhD); interdisciplinary educational studies (Ed D); middle childhood education (MS); music education (MS); school counselor (MS); special education (MS Ed); speech-language pathology (MA); students with disabilities, 7-12 generalist (AC); TESOL (MA). *Accreditation:* TEAC. *Program availability:* Part-time, 100% online, blended/hybrid learning. *Faculty:* 55 full-time (35 women), 104 part-time/adjunct (57 women). *Students:* 464 full-time (390 women), 740 part-time (580 women); includes 265 minority (99 Black or African American, non-Hispanic/Latino; 45 Asian, non-Hispanic/Latino; 113 Hispanic/Latino; 1 Native Hawaiian or other Pacific Islander, non-Hispanic/Latino; 7 Two or more races, non-Hispanic/Latino), 33 international. 928 applicants, 76% accepted, 406 enrolled. In 2016, 334 master's, 10 doctorates, 137 other advanced degrees awarded. Terminal master's awarded for partial completion of doctoral program. *Degree requirements:* For master's, variable foreign language requirement, comprehensive exam (for some programs), thesis optional; for doctorate, comprehensive exam, thesis/dissertation. *Entrance requirements:* For master's and AC, GRE. Additional exam requirements/recommendations for international students: Required—PTE, TOEFL (minimum score 550 paper-based, 75 iBT) or IELTS. *Application deadline:* Applications are processed on a rolling basis. Application fee: $50. Electronic applications accepted. *Expenses: Tuition:* Full-time $28,272; part-time $1178 per credit. *Required fees:* $451 per term. Tuition and fees vary according to degree level and program. *Financial support:* Career-related internships or fieldwork, Federal Work-Study, institutionally sponsored loans, scholarships/grants, tuition waivers (partial), and unspecified assistantships available. Support available to part-time students. Financial award application deadline: 2/15; financial award applicants required to submit FAFSA. *Faculty research:* English language learners, early childhood literacy development through play, sleep, social justice through education, using a structured protocol for discussing bad news. *Total annual research expenditures:* $575,000. *Unit head:* Dr. Albert Inserra, Dean, 516-299-2210, E-mail: albert.inserra@liu.edu. *Application contact:* Carol Zerah, Director of Graduate Admissions, 516-299-2900, Fax: 516-299-2137, E-mail: post-enroll@liu.edu.
Website: http://liu.edu/CWPost/Academics/College-of-Education-Information-and-Technology

Long Island University–Riverhead, Graduate Programs, Riverhead, NY 11901. Offers childhood education (MS), including grades 1-6; homeland security management (MS); literacy education (MS); teaching students with disabilities (MS), including grades 1-6, grades 7-12; TESOL (Advanced Certificate). *Accreditation:* TEAC. *Program availability:* Part-time. *Degree requirements:* For master's, thesis (for some programs); for Advanced Certificate, comprehensive exam (for some programs). *Entrance requirements:* Additional exam requirements/recommendations for international students: Required—TOEFL (minimum score 550 paper-based; 79 iBT), IELTS (minimum score 6). *Application deadline:* Applications are processed on a rolling basis. Application fee: $50. Electronic applications accepted. *Expenses:* Contact institution. *Financial support:* Institutionally sponsored loans, scholarships/grants, tuition waivers (partial), and unspecified assistantships available. Support available to part-time students. Financial award application deadline: 2/15; financial award applicants required to submit FAFSA. *Unit head:* Donna Di Donato, Dean and Chief Operating Officer, LIU Brentwood and LIU Riverhead, 631-287-8010, Fax: 631-287-8575, E-mail: donna.didonato@liu.edu. *Application contact:* Christina Seifert, Director of Admission, LIU Brentwood and LIU Riverhead, 631-287-8505, Fax: 631-287-8253, E-mail: christina.seifert@liu.edu.

Madonna University, Program in Teaching English to Speakers of Other Languages, Livonia, MI 48150-1173. Offers MATESOL. *Program availability:* Part-time, evening/weekend. *Degree requirements:* For master's, one foreign language, thesis or alternative. Electronic applications accepted.

Manhattanville College, School of Education, Jump Start Program, Purchase, NY 10577-2132. Offers childhood and special education (MPS); education (Advanced Certificate); secondary subject areas and special education (MPS); TESOL (MPS). *Program availability:* Part-time, evening/weekend. *Students:* 26 applicants, 46% accepted, 7 enrolled. In 2016, 17 master's awarded. *Degree requirements:* For master's, comprehensive exam (for some programs), thesis (for some programs), student teaching, research seminars, portfolios, internships, writing assessment; for Advanced Certificate, comprehensive exam (for some programs). *Entrance requirements:* For master's, GRE or MAT, minimum undergraduate GPA of 3.0, 2 letters of recommendation, interview. Additional exam requirements/recommendations for international students: Required—TOEFL (minimum score 85 iBT); Recommended—IELTS. *Application deadline:* For fall admission, 7/1 priority date for domestic and international students; for spring admission, 11/1 priority date for domestic and international students; for summer admission, 4/1 priority date for domestic and

international students. Applications are processed on a rolling basis. Application fee: $75. Electronic applications accepted. *Expenses: Tuition:* Full-time $16,470; part-time $915 per credit. *Required fees:* $60 per semester. Part-time tuition and fees vary according to course load and program. *Financial support:* Teaching assistantships, career-related internships or fieldwork, Federal Work-Study, institutionally sponsored loans, scholarships/grants, and unspecified assistantships available. Financial award applicants required to submit FAFSA. *Unit head:* Robert Cooper, Program Director, 914-323-5368, E-mail: robert.cooper@mville.edu. *Application contact:* Jeanine Pardey-Levine, Director of Graduate Enrollment Management, 914-323-3208, Fax: 914-694-1732, E-mail: edschool@mville.edu.
Website: http://www.mville.edu/programs/jump-start

Manhattanville College, School of Education, Program in Teaching English to Speakers of Other Languages, Purchase, NY 10577-2132. Offers adult and international settings (MPS); teaching English as a second language (MPS). *Program availability:* Part-time, evening/weekend. *Students:* 11 applicants, 82% accepted, 7 enrolled. In 2016, 7 master's, 1 Advanced Certificate awarded. *Degree requirements:* For master's, comprehensive exam (for some programs), thesis (for some programs), student teaching, research seminars, portfolios, internships, writing assessment; for Advanced Certificate, comprehensive exam (for some programs). *Entrance requirements:* For master's, GRE or MAT, minimum undergraduate GPA of 3.0, 2 letters of recommendation. Additional exam requirements/recommendations for international students: Required—TOEFL (minimum score 85 iBT); Recommended—IELTS. *Application deadline:* For fall admission, 7/1 priority date for domestic and international students; for spring admission, 11/1 priority date for domestic and international students; for summer admission, 4/1 priority date for domestic and international students. Applications are processed on a rolling basis. Application fee: $75. Electronic applications accepted. *Expenses: Tuition:* Full-time $16,470; part-time $915 per credit. *Required fees:* $60 per semester. Part-time tuition and fees vary according to course load and program. *Financial support:* Teaching assistantships, career-related internships or fieldwork, Federal Work-Study, institutionally sponsored loans, scholarships/grants, and unspecified assistantships available. Financial award applicants required to submit FAFSA. *Faculty research:* Effective acquisition of vocabulary by English language learners, achievement of English language learners in full service community schools, leadership in schools in changing suburbs. *Unit head:* Diane Gomez, Chairperson, Department of Educational Leadership and Special Subjects, 914-323-5488, E-mail: diane.gomez@mville.edu. *Application contact:* Jeanine Pardey-Levine, Director of Graduate Enrollment Management, 914-323-3208, Fax: 914-694-1732, E-mail: edschool@mville.edu.
Website: http://www.mville.edu/programs/tesol-teaching-english-speakers-other-languages

Marlboro College, Graduate and Professional Studies, Program in Teaching English to Speakers of Other Languages, Marlboro, VT 05344. Offers MAT. *Faculty:* 1 (woman) full-time, 6 part-time/adjunct (4 women). *Students:* 5 part-time (2 women); includes 1 minority (Two or more races, non-Hispanic/Latino). Average age 39. 13 applicants, 62% accepted, 5 enrolled. In 2016, 8 master's awarded. *Degree requirements:* For master's, 36 credits, final learning portfolio. *Entrance requirements:* For master's, 2 letters of recommendation, letter of intent, transcripts, interview. Additional exam requirements/recommendations for international students: Required—TOEFL (minimum score 577 paper-based, 90 iBT) or IELTS (minimum score 7). *Application deadline:* For spring admission, 4/5 priority date for domestic students, 3/1 for international students. Applications are processed on a rolling basis. Application fee: $0. Electronic applications accepted. *Expenses:* $765 per credit. *Financial support:* In 2016–17, 5 students received support. Scholarships/grants available. Financial award application deadline: 4/5; financial award applicants required to submit FAFSA. *Unit head:* Beverley Burkett, Degree Chair, 802-451-7514, Fax: 802-258-9201, E-mail: bburkett@gradschool.marlboro.edu. *Application contact:* Kara Hamilton, Admissions Counselor, 802-451-7506, Fax: 802-258-9201, E-mail: graduateadmissions@marlboro.edu.
Website: https://www.marlboro.edu/academics/graduate/tesol

Marymount University, School of Education and Human Services, Program in Education, Arlington, VA 22207-4299. Offers elementary education (M Ed); English as a second language (M Ed); professional studies (M Ed); secondary education (M Ed); special education: general curriculum (M Ed). *Accreditation:* NCATE. *Program availability:* Part-time, evening/weekend. *Faculty:* 28 full-time (all women), 8 part-time/adjunct (5 women). *Students:* 42 full-time (33 women), 94 part-time (72 women); includes 25 minority (6 Black or African American, non-Hispanic/Latino; 6 Asian, non-Hispanic/Latino; 8 Hispanic/Latino; 5 Two or more races, non-Hispanic/Latino), 12 international. Average age 32. 32 applicants, 100% accepted, 24 enrolled. In 2016, 79 master's awarded. *Degree requirements:* For master's, thesis or alternative, capstone/internship. *Entrance requirements:* For master's, GRE or MAT and PRAXIS I or SAT/ACT and Virginia Communication and Literacy Assessment (VCLA), 2 letters of recommendation, resume, interview, minimum undergraduate GPA of 2.75 or 3.25 in the last 60 hours. Additional exam requirements/recommendations for international students: Required—TOEFL (minimum score 600 paper-based; 96 iBT), IELTS (minimum score 6.5). *Application deadline:* Applications are processed on a rolling basis. Application fee: $40. Electronic applications accepted. *Expenses:* $690 per credit hour. *Financial support:* In 2016–17, 6 students received support, including 2 teaching assistantships with tuition reimbursements available; career-related internships or fieldwork, Federal Work-Study, scholarships/grants, and unspecified assistantships also available. Support available to part-time students. Financial award applicants required to submit FAFSA. *Unit head:* Dr. Lisa Turissini, Chair, Education, 703-526-1668, Fax: 703-284-1631, E-mail: lisa.turissini@marymount.edu. *Application contact:* Francesca Reed, Director, Graduate Admissions, 703-284-5901, Fax: 703-527-3815, E-mail: grad.admissions@marymount.edu.
Website: http://www.marymount.edu/Academics/School-of-Education-Human-Services/Graduate-Programs/Education-(M-Ed-)

McDaniel College, Graduate and Professional Studies, Program in TESOL, Westminster, MD 21157-4390. Offers MS. *Program availability:* Part-time, evening/weekend, online only, 100% online. *Faculty:* 5 part-time/adjunct (3 women). *Students:* 2 full-time (1 woman), 23 part-time (20 women); includes 6 minority (1 Black or African American, non-Hispanic/Latino; 2 Asian, non-Hispanic/Latino; 3 Hispanic/Latino), 1 international. Average age 35. 8 applicants, 88% accepted. In 2016, 6 master's awarded. *Degree requirements:* For master's, thesis optional, portfolio. *Entrance requirements:* For master's, PRAXIS I, bachelor's degree from accredited institution with minimum cumulative GPA of 2.75; statement of intent; three references. Additional exam requirements/recommendations for international students: Required—TOEFL (minimum score 79 iBT), IELTS (minimum score 6). *Application deadline:* For fall admission, 6/1 priority date for domestic students; for spring admission, 11/1 priority date for domestic students; for summer admission, 3/1 priority date for domestic students. Applications are processed on a rolling basis. Application fee: $75. Electronic applications accepted. *Expenses: Tuition:* Full-time $8370; part-time $465 per credit. *Required fees:* $75 per semester. Tuition and fees vary according to course load, program and reciprocity agreements. *Financial support:* Application deadline: 3/1; applicants required to submit FAFSA. *Unit head:* E-mail: gradadms@mcdaniel.edu. *Application contact:* Crystal L. Perry, Assistant Director, Graduate Enrollment Management, 410-857-2516, Fax: 410-857-2515, E-mail: cperry@mcdaniel.edu.

Mercy College, School of Education, Program in Teaching English to Speakers of Other Languages (TESOL), Dobbs Ferry, NY 10522-1189. Offers MS, Advanced Certificate. *Program availability:* Part-time, evening/weekend, blended/hybrid learning. *Students:* 3 full-time (2 women), 31 part-time (27 women); includes 24 minority (3 Black or African American, non-Hispanic/Latino; 2 Asian, non-Hispanic/Latino; 19 Hispanic/Latino). Average age 32. 31 applicants, 29% accepted, 4 enrolled. In 2016, 23 master's awarded. *Degree requirements:* For master's, comprehensive exam (for some programs). *Entrance requirements:* For master's, GRE, resume, interview, undergraduate transcript. Additional exam requirements/recommendations for international students: Required—TOEFL (minimum score 600 paper-based; 100 iBT), IELTS (minimum score 8). *Application deadline:* For fall admission, 8/1 for international students. Applications are processed on a rolling basis. Application fee: $40. Electronic applications accepted. *Expenses: Tuition:* Full-time $15,156; part-time $842 per credit hour. *Required fees:* $620; $155 per term. Tuition and fees vary according to course load and program. *Financial support:* Career-related internships or fieldwork, Federal Work-Study, scholarships/grants, and unspecified assistantships available. Support available to part-time students. Financial award applicants required to submit FAFSA. *Unit head:* Dr. Rose Rudnitski, Dean for the School of Education, 914-674-7447, Fax: 914-674-7352, E-mail: rrudnitski@mercy.edu. *Application contact:* Allison Gurdineer, Senior Director of Admissions, 877-637-2946, Fax: 914-674-7382, E-mail: admissions@mercy.edu.
Website: https://www.mercy.edu/degrees-programs/ms-teaching-english-speakers-other-languages-tesol

Meredith College, School of Education, Health and Human Sciences, Raleigh, NC 27607-5298. Offers academically and intellectually gifted (M Ed); curriculum instruction specialist (M Ed); elementary education (M Ed, MAT); English as a second language (M Ed, MAT); health and physical education (MAT); nutrition, health and human performance (MS, Postbaccalaureate Certificate), including dietetic internship (Postbaccalaureate Certificate), nutrition (MS); reading (M Ed); special education (MAT). *Accreditation:* NCATE. *Program availability:* Part-time, evening/weekend. *Degree requirements:* For master's, thesis optional. *Entrance requirements:* For master's, GRE General Test or MAT, minimum GPA of 2.5, teaching license, recommendations. Additional exam requirements/recommendations for international students: Required—TOEFL. Electronic applications accepted. *Expenses:* Contact institution.

Merrimack College, School of Education and Social Policy, North Andover, MA 01845-5800. Offers community engagement (M Ed), including community organizations, higher education, K-12 education; criminology and criminal justice (MS); curriculum and instruction (M Ed); early childhood education (M Ed); educational leadership (CAGS), including instructional leadership; elementary education (M Ed); English as a second language (PreK-6) (M Ed); high school education (M Ed); higher education (M Ed), including leadership and organizational development, student affairs; middle school education (M Ed); moderate disabilities (PreK-8) (M Ed); school counseling (M Ed). *Program availability:* Part-time, evening/weekend, 100% online courses with immersion events and in-classroom practicum close to home. *Faculty:* 17 full-time, 34 part-time/adjunct. *Students:* 204 full-time (172 women), 83 part-time (67 women); includes 32 minority (4 Black or African American, non-Hispanic/Latino; 2 Asian, non-Hispanic/Latino; 23 Hispanic/Latino; 3 Two or more races, non-Hispanic/Latino), 1 international. Average age 27. 261 applicants, 89% accepted, 200 enrolled. In 2016, 153 master's, 2 other advanced degrees awarded. *Degree requirements:* For master's, practicum, portfolio, and state test (for licensure track); capstone (for higher education, curriculum and instruction, and community engagement tracks). *Entrance requirements:* For master's, Massachusetts Teacher Education Licensure (MTEL), official transcripts from other colleges, resume, personal statement, 2 letters of recommendation. Additional exam requirements/recommendations for international students: Required—TOEFL (minimum score 84 iBT), IELTS (minimum score 6.5), PTE (minimum score 56). *Application deadline:* For fall admission, 8/14 for domestic students, 7/14 for international students; for spring admission, 1/10 for domestic students, 12/10 for international students; for summer admission, 5/10 for domestic students, 4/10 for international students. Applications are processed on a rolling basis. Application fee: $0. Electronic applications accepted. *Expenses:* Contact institution. *Financial support:* Fellowships with full tuition reimbursements, career-related internships or fieldwork, scholarships/grants, and health care benefits available. Support available to part-time students. Financial award application deadline: 5/1; financial award applicants required to submit FAFSA. *Faculty research:* Feminist praxis in higher education, transgender student agency and belonging, campus sexual violence prevention, the scholarship of engagement; community engagement; service learning; diversity education; community-university partnerships, college going behaviors and indicators of success for inner city youth, strategies to increase students pursuit and success in STEM higher education, effective workforce development for displaced or under employed individuals, police reform, e.g. surveillance. *Application contact:* Alyssa Frey, Graduate Admissions Counselor, 978-837-3563, E-mail: freya@merrimack.edu.
Website: http://www.merrimack.edu/academics/graduate/education/

Messiah College, Program in Education, Mechanicsburg, PA 17055. Offers curriculum and instruction (M Ed); special education (M Ed); teaching English to speakers of other languages (M Ed). *Program availability:* Part-time, online learning. Electronic applications accepted. *Faculty research:* Socio-cultural perspectives on education, TESOL, autism, special education.

Michigan State University, The Graduate School, College of Arts and Letters, Department of Linguistics and Germanic, Slavic, Asian, and African Languages, East Lansing, MI 48824. Offers German studies (MA, PhD); linguistics (MA, PhD); teaching English to speakers of other languages (MA). *Program availability:* Part-time, evening/weekend. *Entrance requirements:* For master's, GRE General Test, minimum GPA of 3.2 in last 2 undergraduate years, 2 years of college-level foreign language, 3 letters of recommendation, portfolio (German studies); for doctorate, GRE General Test, minimum graduate GPA of 3.5, 3 letters of recommendation, master's degree or sufficient graduate course work in linguistics or language of study, master's thesis or major research paper. Additional exam requirements/recommendations for international students: Required—TOEFL. Electronic applications accepted.

MidAmerica Nazarene University, Professional and Graduate Studies in Education, Olathe, KS 66062-1899. Offers ESOL (M Ed); reading specialist (M Ed); technology enhanced teaching (M Ed). *Accreditation:* NCATE. *Program availability:* Part-time, evening/weekend, online only, 100% online. *Faculty:* 5 full-time (3 women), 12 part-time/adjunct (7 women). *Students:* 22 full-time (16 women), 43 part-time (38 women); includes 6 minority (3 Black or African American, non-Hispanic/Latino; 1 Asian, non-Hispanic/Latino; 2 Two or more races, non-Hispanic/Latino). Average age 32. 18 applicants, 22% accepted, 2 enrolled. In 2016, 41 master's awarded. *Entrance requirements:* For master's, bachelor's degree from an accredited college or university, minimum undergraduate GPA of 3.0, valid teaching license. Additional exam requirements/recommendations for international students: Required—TOEFL (minimum score 81 iBT), IELTS (minimum score 6). *Application deadline:* For fall admission, 8/6 for

domestic students; for spring admission, 12/15 for domestic students; for summer admission, 5/7 for domestic students. Applications are processed on a rolling basis. Electronic applications accepted. *Expenses:* Contact institution. *Financial support:* Scholarships/grants available. Financial award applicants required to submit FAFSA. *Unit head:* Dr. Ramona Stowe, Chair, 913-971-3524, Fax: 913-971-3407, E-mail: rsstowe@mnu.edu. *Application contact:* Glenna Murray, Administrative Assistant, 913-971-3292, Fax: 913-971-3002, E-mail: gkmurray@mnu.edu.
Website: http://www.mnu.edu/education.html

Middlebury Institute of International Studies at Monterey, Graduate School of Translation, Interpretation and Language Education, Program in Teaching English to Speakers of Other Languages, Monterey, CA 93940-2691. Offers MATESOL. *Degree requirements:* For master's, portfolio, oral defense. *Entrance requirements:* For master's, minimum GPA of 3.0. Additional exam requirements/recommendations for international students: Required—TOEFL (minimum score 600 paper-based; 100 iBT). Electronic applications accepted. *Expenses: Tuition:* Full-time $38,250; part-time $1820 per credit. *Required fees:* $78 per semester.

Middle Tennessee State University, College of Graduate Studies, College of Education, Department of Educational Leadership, Program in Curriculum and Instruction, Murfreesboro, TN 37132. Offers curriculum and instruction (M Ed, Ed S); English as a second language (M Ed, Ed S); secondary education (M Ed); technology and curriculum design (Ed S). *Accreditation:* NCATE. *Program availability:* Part-time, evening/weekend, online learning. *Degree requirements:* For master's, comprehensive exam; for Ed S, comprehensive exam, thesis or alternative. *Entrance requirements:* For master's and Ed S, GRE, MAT or PRAXIS. Additional exam requirements/recommendations for international students: Required—TOEFL (minimum score 525 paper-based; 71 iBT) or IELTS (minimum score 6). Electronic applications accepted.

Millersville University of Pennsylvania, College of Graduate Studies and Adult Learning, College of Education and Human Services, Department of Early, Middle, and Exceptional Education, Program in Language and Literacy: ESL, Millersville, PA 17551-0302. Offers M Ed. *Program availability:* Part-time, evening/weekend. *Faculty:* 14 full-time (9 women). *Students:* 1 (woman) full-time, 14 part-time (13 women); includes 4 minority (2 Black or African American, non-Hispanic/Latino; 1 Hispanic/Latino; 1 Two or more races, non-Hispanic/Latino). Average age 30. 3 applicants, 100% accepted, 2 enrolled. In 2016, 4 master's awarded. *Degree requirements:* For master's, thesis optional. *Entrance requirements:* For master's, GRE or MAT if undergraduate cumulative GPA is lower than 3.0, teaching certificate. Additional exam requirements/recommendations for international students: Required—TOEFL (minimum score 600 paper-based), IELTS (minimum score 6). *Application deadline:* Applications are processed on a rolling basis. Application fee: $40. Electronic applications accepted. *Expenses:* $483 per credit resident tuition; $725 per credit non-resident tuition. *Financial support:* In 2016–17, 2 students received support. Unspecified assistantships available. Financial award application deadline: 3/15; financial award applicants required to submit FAFSA. *Faculty research:* ELL education, total participation techniques. *Unit head:* Dr. Judith K. Wenrich, Coordinator, 717-871-7348, E-mail: judith.wenrich@millersville.edu. *Application contact:* Dr. Victor S. DeSantis, Dean of College of Graduate Studies and Adult Learning/Associate Provost for Civic and Community Engagement, 717-871-7619, Fax: 717-871-7954, E-mail: victor.desantis@millersville.edu.
Website: http://www.millersville.edu/academics/educ/eled/graduate-programs/language-and-literacy.php

Minnesota State University Mankato, College of Graduate Studies and Research, College of Arts and Humanities, Department of English, Mankato, MN 56001. Offers communication and composition (MA); creative writing (MFA); English studies (MA); teaching English as a second language (MA, Certificate); technical communication (MA, Certificate). *Program availability:* Part-time. *Students:* 59 full-time (44 women), 106 part-time (67 women). *Degree requirements:* For master's, one foreign language, comprehensive exam, thesis or alternative. *Entrance requirements:* For master's, minimum GPA of 3.0 during previous 2 years, writing sample (MFA). Additional exam requirements/recommendations for international students: Required—TOEFL (minimum score 500 paper-based; 61 iBT). *Application deadline:* For fall admission, 7/1 for domestic students, 5/1 for international students. Applications are processed on a rolling basis. Application fee: $40. Electronic applications accepted. *Financial support:* Research assistantships with full tuition reimbursements, teaching assistantships with full tuition reimbursements, career-related internships or fieldwork, Federal Work-Study, and unspecified assistantships available. Financial award application deadline: 3/15; financial award applicants required to submit FAFSA. *Unit head:* Matthew Sewell, Chair, 507-389-2117, E-mail: matthew.sewell@mnsu.edu.
Website: http://english.mnsu.edu/

Minnesota State University Moorhead, Graduate Studies, College of Humanities and Social Sciences, Moorhead, MN 56563. Offers teaching English as a second language (MA). *Program availability:* Part-time, evening/weekend. *Students:* 13 part-time (9 women). Average age 32. 4 applicants, 100% accepted. In 2016, 3 master's awarded. *Degree requirements:* For master's, comprehensive exam (for some programs), thesis. *Entrance requirements:* For master's, essay, writing sample, minimum GPA of 3.0. Additional exam requirements/recommendations for international students: Required—TOEFL (minimum score 550 paper-based). *Application deadline:* For fall admission, 4/15 for domestic students; for spring admission, 11/15 for domestic students. Applications are processed on a rolling basis. Application fee: $20. Electronic applications accepted. *Expenses:* Tuition, state resident: full-time $9000; part-time $4500 per credit. Tuition, nonresident: full-time $18,000; part-time $9000 per credit. *Required fees:* $942; $39.25 per credit. One-time fee: $90 full-time. Full-time tuition and fees vary according to course load, degree level, program and reciprocity agreements. *Financial support:* Federal Work-Study and unspecified assistantships available. Financial award application deadline: 10/1; financial award applicants required to submit FAFSA. *Unit head:* Dr. Randy Cagle, Dean, 218-477-2477, E-mail: caglera@mnstate.edu. *Application contact:* Karla Wenger, Graduate Studies Office Manager, 218-477-2344, Fax: 218-477-2482, E-mail: wengerk@mnstate.edu.
Website: http://www.mnstate.edu/chss/

Mississippi College, Graduate School, College of Arts and Sciences, School of Humanities and Social Sciences, Department of Modern Languages, Clinton, MS 39058. Offers teaching English to speakers of other languages (MA, MS). *Program availability:* Part-time. *Degree requirements:* For master's, thesis (for some programs). *Entrance requirements:* For master's, GRE or NTE. Additional exam requirements/recommendations for international students: Recommended—TOEFL, IELTS. Electronic applications accepted.

Missouri State University, Graduate College, College of Arts and Letters, Department of English, Springfield, MO 65897. Offers applied second language acquisition (MASLA); English (MA); English education (MS Ed); teaching English to speakers of other languages (Certificate); writing (MA). MASLA offered with the Department of Modern and Classical Languages. *Program availability:* Part-time, evening/weekend. *Faculty:* 25 full-time (18 women), 5 part-time/adjunct (2 women). *Students:* 47 full-time (34 women), 44 part-time (32 women); includes 4 minority (1 Asian, non-Hispanic/Latino; 3 Two or more races, non-Hispanic/Latino), 17 international. Average age 29. 79 applicants, 63% accepted, 27 enrolled. In 2016, 49 master's awarded. *Degree requirements:* For master's, one foreign language, comprehensive exam, thesis or alternative. *Entrance requirements:* For master's, GRE (for MA), 9-12 teacher certification (MS Ed); minimum GPA of 3.0 (MA); personal statement (200- to 250-word description of reasons and goals behind interest in English graduate studies); at least two letters of recommendation from individuals able to speak of the applicant's academic achievements and potential; writing sample. Additional exam requirements/recommendations for international students: Required—TOEFL (minimum score 550 paper-based; 79 iBT), IELTS (minimum score 6). *Application deadline:* For fall admission, 3/1 priority date for domestic students, 3/1 for international students; for spring admission, 10/1 priority date for domestic students, 10/1 for international students. Applications are processed on a rolling basis. Application fee: $35 ($50 for international students). Electronic applications accepted. *Expenses:* Tuition, state resident: full-time $5830. Tuition, nonresident: full-time $10,708. *Required fees:* $1130. Tuition and fees vary according to class time, course level, course load and program. *Financial support:* In 2016–17, 2 teaching assistantships with full tuition reimbursements (averaging $8,772 per year) were awarded; Federal Work-Study, institutionally sponsored loans, scholarships/grants, and unspecified assistantships also available. Financial award application deadline: 3/31; financial award applicants required to submit FAFSA. *Faculty research:* History of rhetoric, modern poetry, African-American literature, digital writing, teaching English to speakers of other languages. *Unit head:* Dr. W. D. Blackmon, Department Head, 417-836-5107, Fax: 417-836-6940, E-mail: english@missouristate.edu. *Application contact:* Michael Edwards, Coordinator of Graduate Admissions, 417-836-5330, Fax: 417-836-6200, E-mail: michaeledwards@missouristate.edu.
Website: http://english.missouristate.edu/

Missouri Western State University, Program in Assessment, St. Joseph, MO 64507-2294. Offers autism spectrum disorders (MAS, Graduate Certificate); TESOL (MAS, Graduate Certificate); writing (MAS). *Program availability:* Part-time. *Students:* 1 (woman) full-time, 33 part-time (25 women). Average age 37. 9 applicants, 100% accepted, 5 enrolled. In 2016, 6 master's, 1 other advanced degree awarded. *Entrance requirements:* For master's, minimum GPA of 2.75. Additional exam requirements/recommendations for international students: Recommended—TOEFL (minimum score 79 iBT), IELTS (minimum score 6). *Application deadline:* For fall admission, 7/15 for domestic and international students; for spring admission, 10/1 for domestic and international students; for summer admission, 3/15 for domestic students. Applications are processed on a rolling basis. Application fee: $50. Electronic applications accepted. *Expenses:* Tuition, state resident: full-time $6548; part-time $327.39 per credit hour. Tuition, nonresident: full-time $11,848; part-time $592.39 per credit hour. *Required fees:* $542; $99 per credit hour. $176 per semester. One-time fee: $50. Tuition and fees vary according to course load and program. *Financial support:* Scholarships/grants and unspecified assistantships available. Support available to part-time students. *Unit head:* Dr. Susan Bashinski, Director of Graduate Programs in Education, 816-271-5629, E-mail: sbashinski@missouriwestern.edu. *Application contact:* Dr. Benjamin D. Caldwell, Dean of the Graduate School, 816-271-4394, Fax: 816-271-4525, E-mail: graduate@missouriwestern.edu.
Website: https://www.missouriwestern.edu/masa/

Molloy College, Graduate Education Program, Rockville Centre, NY 11571-5002. Offers adolescent education in biology (MS Ed); adolescent special education (Advanced Certificate); bilingual extension (Advanced Certificate); childhood education (MS Ed); childhood special education (Advanced Certificate); early childhood education (MS Ed); educational technology (MS Ed); English (MS Ed); mathematics (MS Ed); social studies (MS Ed); Spanish (MS Ed); special education on both childhood and adolescent levels (MS Ed); teaching English to speakers of other languages (TESOL) in grades Pre-K to 12 (MS Ed); TESOL (Advanced Certificate). *Accreditation:* NCATE. *Program availability:* Part-time, evening/weekend. *Faculty:* 17 full-time (16 women), 23 part-time/adjunct (19 women). *Students:* 95 full-time (75 women), 221 part-time (177 women); includes 59 minority (14 Black or African American, non-Hispanic/Latino; 6 Asian, non-Hispanic/Latino; 38 Hispanic/Latino; 1 Two or more races, non-Hispanic/Latino), 1 international. Average age 42. 214 applicants, 66% accepted, 125 enrolled. In 2016, 95 master's, 4 Advanced Certificates awarded. *Entrance requirements:* Additional exam requirements/recommendations for international students: Required—TOEFL (minimum score 550 paper-based; 79 iBT). *Application deadline:* Applications are processed on a rolling basis. Application fee: $60. Electronic applications accepted. *Expenses: Tuition:* Full-time $19,170; part-time $1065 per credit. *Required fees:* $950; $790 per credit. Tuition and fees vary according to course load. *Financial support:* Applicants required to submit FAFSA. *Faculty research:* ESL - general education teacher collaboration; special education; school desegregation; American intellectual and social history; families and schools. *Unit head:* Joanne O'Brien, Associate Dean/Director, 516-323-3116, E-mail: jobrien@molloy.edu. *Application contact:* Jaclyn Machowicz, Assistant Director for Admissions, 516-323-4010, E-mail: jmachowicz@molloy.edu.

Monmouth University, Graduate Studies, School of Education, West Long Branch, NJ 07764-1898. Offers applied behavior analysis (Certificate); autism (Certificate); director of school counseling services (Post-Master's Certificate); early childhood (M Ed); educational leadership (Ed D); elementary education (MAT), including elementary level, secondary level; English as a second language (M Ed); learning disabilities teacher-consultant (Post-Master's Certificate); literacy (MS Ed); school counseling (MS Ed); special education (MS Ed), including autism, learning disabilities teacher-consultant, teacher of students with disabilities, teaching in inclusive settings; speech-language pathology (MS Ed); student affairs and college counseling (MS Ed); supervisor (Post-Master's Certificate); teaching English to speakers of other languages (Certificate). *Accreditation:* NCATE. *Program availability:* Part-time, evening/weekend, 100% online, blended/hybrid learning. *Faculty:* 23 full-time (19 women), 33 part-time/adjunct (25 women). *Students:* 191 full-time (172 women), 141 part-time (122 women); includes 56 minority (10 Black or African American, non-Hispanic/Latino; 9 Asian, non-Hispanic/Latino; 31 Hispanic/Latino; 6 Two or more races, non-Hispanic/Latino). Average age 26. 423 applicants, 53% accepted, 139 enrolled. In 2016, 148 master's, 4 other advanced degrees awarded. *Entrance requirements:* For master's, GRE taken within last 5 years (for MS Ed in speech-language pathology); SAT (minimum combined score of 1660 in 3 sections), ACT (23), GRE (minimum score of 4.0 on analytical writing section and minimum combined score of 310 on quantitative and verbal sections), or passing scores on 3 parts of Core Academic Skills Educators, minimum GPA of 3.0 in major; 2 letters of recommendation (for some programs); resume, personal statement or essay (depending on program). Additional exam requirements/recommendations for international students: Required—TOEFL (minimum score 550 paper-based; 79 iBT), IELTS (minimum score 6), Michigan English Language Assessment Battery (minimum score 77) or Certificate of Advanced English (minimum score B2). *Application deadline:* For fall admission, 7/15 priority date for domestic students, 7/1 for international students; for spring admission, 12/1 priority date for domestic students, 11/1 for international students; for summer admission, 5/1 for domestic students. Applications are processed on a rolling basis. Application fee: $50. Electronic applications accepted. *Expenses: Tuition, area resident:* Full-time $19,764; part-time $1098 per credit hour. *Required fees:* $175 per semester. Tuition and fees vary according to program. *Financial support:* In 2016–17, 349 students received support, including 305 fellowships (averaging $3,558 per year), 48

teaching assistantships (averaging $9,619 per year); research assistantships, institutionally sponsored loans, scholarships/grants, and unspecified assistantships also available. Support available to part-time students. Financial award application deadline: 2/1; financial award applicants required to submit FAFSA. *Faculty research:* Multicultural literacy, science and mathematics teaching strategies, teacher as reflective practitioner, children with disabilities. *Unit head:* Dr. John E. Henning, Dean, 732-263-5513, Fax: 732-263-5277. *Application contact:* Laurie Kuhn, Associate Director of Graduate Admission, 732-571-3452, Fax: 732-263-5123, E-mail: gradadm@monmouth.edu.
Website: http://www.monmouth.edu/academics/schools/education/default.asp

Montclair State University, The Graduate School, College of Education and Human Services, MAT Program in Teaching, Montclair, NJ 07043-1624. Offers art (MAT); biology (MAT); chemistry (MAT); earth science (MAT); English (MAT); French (MAT); health and physical education (MAT); health education (MAT); mathematics (MAT); music (MAT); physical education (MAT); physical science (MAT); social studies (MAT); Spanish (MAT); teacher of English as a second language (MAT). *Degree requirements:* For master's, comprehensive exam, thesis or alternative. *Entrance requirements:* For master's, interview, 2 letters of recommendation. Additional exam requirements/recommendations for international students: Required—TOEFL (minimum score 83 iBT), IELTS (minimum score 6.5). Electronic applications accepted. *Expenses:* Tuition, state resident: part-time $553 per credit. Tuition, nonresident: part-time $854 per credit. *Required fees:* $91 per credit. Tuition and fees vary according to program.

Montclair State University, The Graduate School, College of Humanities and Social Sciences, Teaching English to Speakers of Other Languages Certificate Program, Montclair, NJ 07043-1624. Offers Certificate. *Program availability:* Part-time, evening/weekend. *Degree requirements:* For Certificate, comprehensive exam. *Entrance requirements:* For degree, 2 letters of recommendation, essay. Additional exam requirements/recommendations for international students: Required—TOEFL (minimum score 83 iBT), IELTS (minimum score 6.5). Electronic applications accepted. *Expenses:* Tuition, state resident: part-time $553 per credit. Tuition, nonresident: part-time $854 per credit. *Required fees:* $91 per credit. Tuition and fees vary according to program. *Faculty research:* Language learning and technology research, interlanguage, bilingual pragmatics.

Mount Saint Vincent University, Graduate Programs, Faculty of Education, Program in Curriculum Studies, Halifax, NS B3M 2J6, Canada. Offers education of young adolescents (M Ed, MA Ed, MA-R); general studies (M Ed, MA Ed, MA-R); teaching English as a second language (M Ed, MA Ed, MA-R). *Program availability:* Part-time, evening/weekend, online learning. *Degree requirements:* For master's, thesis (for some programs). *Entrance requirements:* For master's, bachelor's degree in related field, minimum B average, 1 year of teaching experience. Electronic applications accepted. *Faculty research:* Science education, cultural studies, international education, curriculum development.

Multnomah University, Graduate Programs, Portland, OR 97220-5898. Offers counseling (MA); global development and justice (MA); teaching (MA); TESOL (MA). *Program availability:* Part-time, evening/weekend. *Faculty:* 6 full-time (4 women), 16 part-time/adjunct (10 women). *Students:* 120 full-time (80 women), 31 part-time (23 women); includes 35 minority (15 Black or African American, non-Hispanic/Latino; 2 Asian, non-Hispanic/Latino; 9 Hispanic/Latino; 1 Native Hawaiian or other Pacific Islander, non-Hispanic/Latino; 8 Two or more races, non-Hispanic/Latino), 3 international. Average age 30. 69 applicants, 55% accepted, 24 enrolled. In 2016, 55 degrees awarded. *Degree requirements:* For master's, variable foreign language requirement, comprehensive exam (for some programs), thesis (for some programs). *Entrance requirements:* For master's, CBEST or WEST-B (for MAT), interview; references (4 for teaching); writing sample (for counseling). Additional exam requirements/recommendations for international students: Required—TOEFL (minimum score 550 paper-based). *Application deadline:* For fall admission, 8/1 for domestic students, 12/1 for international students; for spring admission, 12/1 for domestic and international students. Application fee: $40. Electronic applications accepted. *Expenses: Tuition:* Full-time $10,000; part-time $6000 per semester. *Required fees:* $230; $120 per semester. Tuition and fees vary according to course load, degree level and program. *Financial support:* Career-related internships or fieldwork and scholarships/grants available. Support available to part-time students. Financial award application deadline: 7/1; financial award applicants required to submit FAFSA. *Unit head:* Dr. Daniel Scalberg, Academic Dean, 503-251-6441, E-mail: dscalberg@multnomah.edu. *Application contact:* Mindy Kate Hasenkamp, Director of Admissions, 503-251-6483, Fax: 503-254-1268, E-mail: admiss@multnomah.edu.

Murray State University, College of Humanities and Fine Arts, Department of English and Philosophy, Program in Teaching English to Speakers of Other Languages, Murray, KY 42071. Offers MA. *Program availability:* Part-time, online learning. *Degree requirements:* For master's, one foreign language, comprehensive exam, 12 hours for portfolio. *Entrance requirements:* For master's, minimum GPA of 2.25. Additional exam requirements/recommendations for international students: Required—TOEFL (minimum score 525 paper-based), IELTS (minimum score 5.5). *Faculty research:* Methods, integrated skills, intercultural communication, assessment.

Nazareth College of Rochester, Graduate Studies, Department of Education, Program in Teaching English to Speakers of Other Languages, Rochester, NY 14618. Offers MS Ed. *Accreditation:* TEAC. *Entrance requirements:* For master's, minimum GPA of 3.0. Additional exam requirements/recommendations for international students: Required—TOEFL or IELTS. *Application deadline:* For fall admission, 4/1 priority date for domestic students; for spring admission, 10/1 priority date for domestic students. Application fee: $40. *Expenses: Tuition:* Part-time $880 per credit hour. Part-time tuition and fees vary according to course load, degree level and program. *Financial support:* Unspecified assistantships available. Financial award application deadline: 3/1; financial award applicants required to submit FAFSA. *Unit head:* Dr. Cindy McPhail, Professor/ Director of TESOL Certification Programs and Bilingual Extension Program in Language, Literacy and Technology Education, 585-389-2607, E-mail: cmcphai2@naz.edu. *Application contact:* Judith Baker, Director, Transfer and Graduate Admissions, 585-531-1154, Fax: 585-389-2826, E-mail: gradadmissions@naz.edu.

New Jersey City University, Debra Cannon Partridge Wolfe College of Education, Department of Multicultural Education, Jersey City, NJ 07305-1597. Offers bilingual/ bicultural education (MA); English as a second language (MA). *Program availability:* Part-time, evening/weekend. *Entrance requirements:* For master's, GRE General Test or MAT. Additional exam requirements/recommendations for international students: Required—TOEFL.

Newman University, Master of Science in Education Program, Wichita, KS 67213-2097. Offers building leadership (MS Ed); curriculum and instruction (MS Ed), including English as a second language, reading specialist; organizational leadership (MS Ed). *Accreditation:* NCATE. *Program availability:* Part-time, evening/weekend, online learning. *Degree requirements:* For master's, thesis optional. *Entrance requirements:* For master's, 3 years' full-time teaching experience, minimum GPA of 3.0, writing sample, 2 letters of recommendation, evidence of teaching certification. Additional exam requirements/recommendations for international students: Required—TOEFL (minimum score 600 paper-based; 100 iBT). Electronic applications accepted. *Expenses:* Contact institution. *Faculty research:* Online course design and deliver, staff engagement, classroom action.

New Mexico State University, College of Education, Department of Curriculum and Instruction, Las Cruces, NM 88003. Offers bilingual education (MA); curriculum and instruction (Ed D); early childhood education (MA); educational diagnostics (Ed S); language, literacy and culture (MA); learning design and technologies (MA); teaching (MAT), including Spanish; teaching English to speakers of other languages (MA). *Accreditation:* NCATE. *Program availability:* Part-time, evening/weekend, 100% online. *Faculty:* 23 full-time (17 women), 7 part-time/adjunct (5 women). *Students:* 114 full-time (81 women), 219 part-time (159 women); includes 190 minority (16 Black or African American, non-Hispanic/Latino; 2 American Indian or Alaska Native, non-Hispanic/ Latino; 5 Asian, non-Hispanic/Latino; 160 Hispanic/Latino; 7 Two or more races, non-Hispanic/Latino), 33 international. Average age 37. 126 applicants, 75% accepted, 65 enrolled. In 2016, 92 master's, 19 doctorates awarded. *Degree requirements:* For master's, comprehensive exam, thesis optional; for doctorate, comprehensive exam, thesis/dissertation. *Entrance requirements:* For master's, minimum cumulative GPA of 3.0; for doctorate, portfolio, minimum cumulative GPA of 3.0. Additional exam requirements/recommendations for international students: Required—TOEFL (minimum score 550 paper-based; 79 iBT), IELTS (minimum score 6.5). *Application deadline:* For fall admission, 12/15 priority date for domestic and international students; for spring admission, 11/1 for domestic students. Applications are processed on a rolling basis. Application fee: $40 ($50 for international students). Electronic applications accepted. *Expenses:* Tuition, state resident: full-time $4086. Tuition, nonresident: full-time $14,254. *Required fees:* $853. Tuition and fees vary according to course load. *Financial support:* In 2016–17, 102 students received support, including 2 fellowships (averaging $4,076 per year), 2 research assistantships (averaging $18,070 per year), 16 teaching assistantships (averaging $16,454 per year); career-related internships or fieldwork, Federal Work-Study, scholarships/grants, traineeships, health care benefits, and unspecified assistantships also available. Support available to part-time students. Financial award application deadline: 3/1. *Faculty research:* STEM education, bilingual and English as a second language education, critical pedagogy/multicultural education, learning design and technology, early childhood education. *Total annual research expenditures:* $29,926. *Unit head:* Dr. David Rutledge, Department Head, 575-646-5411, Fax: 575-646-5436, E-mail: rutledge@nmsu.edu. *Application contact:* Dr. David Rutledge, Associate Department Head for Graduate Programs, 575-646-5411, Fax: 575-646-5436, E-mail: rutledge@nmsu.edu.
Website: http://ci.education.nmsu.edu

The New School, Schools of Public Engagement, Program in Teaching English to Speakers of Other Languages, New York, NY 10011. Offers teaching English to speakers of other languages (MA). *Program availability:* Part-time. *Faculty:* 9 part-time/ adjunct (3 women). *Students:* 8 full-time (6 women), 42 part-time (30 women); includes 11 minority (3 Black or African American, non-Hispanic/Latino; 2 Asian, non-Hispanic/ Latino; 5 Hispanic/Latino; 1 Two or more races, non-Hispanic/Latino), 5 international. Average age 38. 54 applicants, 81% accepted, 19 enrolled. In 2016, 27 master's awarded. *Degree requirements:* For master's, thesis optional. *Entrance requirements:* For master's, two letters of recommendation, statement of purpose, resume, transcripts, interview. Additional exam requirements/recommendations for international students: Required—TOEFL (minimum score 100 iBT), IELTS (minimum score 7), PTE (minimum score 68). *Application deadline:* For fall admission, 1/15 priority date for domestic and international students; for spring admission, 10/15 priority date for domestic and international students; for summer admission, 1/15 priority date for domestic and international students. Applications are processed on a rolling basis. Application fee: $50. Electronic applications accepted. *Expenses:* Contact institution. *Financial support:* Fellowships, research assistantships, teaching assistantships, career-related internships or fieldwork, Federal Work-Study, scholarships/grants, and unspecified assistantships available. Support available to part-time students. Financial award application deadline: 2/1; financial award applicants required to submit FAFSA. *Application contact:* Merida Gasbarro, Director, 212-229-5600 Ext. 1108, E-mail: escandom@newschool.edu.
Website: http://www.newschool.edu/

New York University, Steinhardt School of Culture, Education, and Human Development, Department of Teaching and Learning, Program in Multilingual/ Multicultural Studies, New York, NY 10003. Offers bilingual education (MA, PhD, Advanced Certificate); foreign language education (MA); teaching English to speakers of other languages (MA, PhD); teaching foreign languages, 7-12 (MA), including Chinese, French, Italian, Japanese, Spanish; teaching French as a foreign language (MA), including teaching English to speakers of other languages; teaching Spanish as a foreign language (MA), including teaching English to speakers of other languages. *Accreditation:* TEAC. *Program availability:* Part-time, evening/weekend. *Degree requirements:* For master's, thesis (for some programs); for doctorate, thesis/ dissertation. *Entrance requirements:* For doctorate, GRE General Test, interview; for Advanced Certificate, master's degree. Additional exam requirements/recommendations for international students: Required—TOEFL (minimum score 100 iBT). Electronic applications accepted. *Faculty research:* Second language acquisition, cross-cultural communication, technology-enhanced language learning, language variation, action learning.

Niagara University, Graduate Division of Education, Concentration in Teacher Education, Niagara University, NY 14109. Offers early childhood and childhood education (MS Ed, Certificate); early childhood special education (MS); middle and adolescence education (MS Ed); special education (MS Ed), including 1-6, 7-12; special education (grades 1-12) (Certificate); teaching English to speakers of other languages (MS Ed, Certificate). *Accreditation:* NCATE. *Students:* 101 full-time (83 women), 123 part-time (101 women); includes 14 minority (6 Black or African American, non-Hispanic/ Latino; 1 American Indian or Alaska Native, non-Hispanic/Latino; 6 Hispanic/Latino; 1 Two or more races, non-Hispanic/Latino), 28 international. Average age 28. In 2016, 86 master's, 18 other advanced degrees awarded. *Entrance requirements:* For master's, GRE General Test or Academic Literacy Skills Test (ALST). Additional exam requirements/recommendations for international students: Required—TOEFL (minimum score 550 paper-based; 79 iBT), IELTS (minimum score 6). *Application deadline:* For fall admission, 8/1 for domestic students. Applications are processed on a rolling basis. Application fee: $30. *Expenses:* Contact institution. *Financial support:* Research assistantships with tuition reimbursements, teaching assistantships with tuition reimbursements, career-related internships or fieldwork, Federal Work-Study, scholarships/grants, and unspecified assistantships available. Financial award application deadline: 4/15; financial award applicants required to submit FAFSA. *Unit head:* Dr. Chandra Foote, Dean, College of Education, 716-286-8549, E-mail: cjf@niagara.edu. *Application contact:* Evan Pierce, Associate Director, Graduate Studies, 716-286-8327, E-mail: epierce@niagara.edu.
Website: http://www.niagara.edu/teacher-education

Northeastern Illinois University, College of Graduate Studies and Research, College of Arts and Sciences, Program in Linguistics, Chicago, IL 60625-4699. Offers linguistics (MA); TESL (MA). *Program availability:* Part-time, evening/weekend. *Degree requirements:* For master's, one foreign language, comprehensive exam, thesis optional. *Entrance requirements:* For master's, 9 undergraduate hours in a foreign language or equivalent, minimum GPA of 2.75. Additional exam requirements/recommendations for international students: Required—TOEFL (minimum score 550 paper-based; 79 iBT). Electronic applications accepted. *Faculty research:* Acquisition of literacy, Mayan language, Rotuman language, English as a second language methodology, Farsi language.

Northeastern Illinois University, College of Graduate Studies and Research, College of Arts and Sciences, Program in Teaching English as a Second/Foreign Language, Chicago, IL 60625-4699. Offers MA.

Northern Arizona University, Graduate College, College of Arts and Letters, Department of English, Flagstaff, AZ 86011. Offers applied linguistics (PhD); creative writing (MFA), including creative writing; English (MA), including English education, literature, professional writing, rhetoric, writing, and digital media studies; professional writing (Certificate); teaching English as a second language (MA, Certificate). *Program availability:* Part-time. *Degree requirements:* For master's, comprehensive exam (for some programs), thesis (for some programs), departmental qualifying exam; for doctorate, comprehensive exam, thesis/dissertation, departmental qualifying exam. *Entrance requirements:* For master's, minimum GPA of 3.0 or GRE; for doctorate, GRE General Test. Additional exam requirements/recommendations for international students: Required—TOEFL (minimum score 550 paper-based; 80 iBT), IELTS (minimum score 7), TOEFL (minimum score 600 paper-based; 100 iBT) for PhD; TOEFL (minimum score 570 paper-based; 89 iBT) for MA. Electronic applications accepted. *Expenses:* Tuition, state resident: full-time $8971; part-time $444 per credit hour. Tuition, nonresident: full-time $20,958; part-time $1164 per credit hour. *Required fees:* $1018; $644 per credit hour. Tuition and fees vary according to course load, campus/location and program.

Northern Arizona University, Graduate College, College of Education, Department of Educational Specialties, Flagstaff, AZ 86011. Offers autism spectrum disorders (Certificate); bilingual/multicultural education (M Ed), including bilingual education, ESL education; career and technical education (M Ed, Certificate); culturally and linguistically diverse special education (Certificate); early childhood special education (M Ed); educational technology (M Ed, Certificate); English as a second language (Certificate); mild/moderate disabilities (M Ed); positive behavior support (Certificate); special education (M Ed). *Degree requirements:* For master's, comprehensive exam (for some programs), thesis (for some programs). *Entrance requirements:* For master's, minimum GPA of 3.0. Additional exam requirements/recommendations for international students: Required—TOEFL (minimum score 550 paper-based; 80 iBT), IELTS (minimum score 7). Electronic applications accepted. *Expenses:* Tuition, state resident: full-time $8971; part-time $444 per credit hour. Tuition, nonresident: full-time $20,958; part-time $1164 per credit hour. *Required fees:* $1018; $644 per credit hour. Tuition and fees vary according to course load, campus/location and program.

Northern Michigan University, Office of Graduate Education and Research, College of Arts and Sciences, Department of English, Marquette, MI 49855-5301. Offers creative writing (MFA); literature (MA); pedagogy (MA); teaching English to speakers of other languages (Graduate Certificate); theater (MA); writing (MA). *Program availability:* Part-time, evening/weekend. Terminal master's awarded for partial completion of doctoral program. *Degree requirements:* For master's, capstone project: thesis, practicum or portfolio (for MA); thesis (for MFA); for Graduate Certificate, one foreign language. *Entrance requirements:* For master's, minimum GPA of 3.0; bachelor's degree in English or minimum of 30 credit hours in undergraduate English; statement of purpose; resume; critical essay; 3 letters of recommendation; for Graduate Certificate, bachelor's degree. Additional exam requirements/recommendations for international students: Required—TOEFL (minimum score 550 paper-based; 79 iBT), IELTS (minimum score 6.5). Electronic applications accepted. *Faculty research:* Modern Arabic literature, British literature (medieval to contemporary), postcolonial literature, Native and African-American literature, creative writing, critical theory, pedagogy.

Northwest Christian University, School of Education and Counseling, Eugene, OR 97401-3745. Offers clinical mental health counseling (MA); elementary teaching (MAT); English for speakers of other languages (ESOL) (MAT); school counseling (MA); secondary teaching (MAT). *Program availability:* Part-time, evening/weekend, online learning. *Faculty:* 9 full-time (5 women), 21 part-time/adjunct (14 women). *Students:* 87 full-time (64 women), 52 part-time (40 women); includes 22 minority (5 Black or African American, non-Hispanic/Latino; 2 American Indian or Alaska Native, non-Hispanic/Latino; 2 Asian, non-Hispanic/Latino; 7 Hispanic/Latino; 2 Native Hawaiian or other Pacific Islander, non-Hispanic/Latino; 4 Two or more races, non-Hispanic/Latino). Average age 36. In 2016, 76 master's awarded. *Degree requirements:* For master's, thesis (for some programs). *Entrance requirements:* For master's, MAT, minimum undergraduate GPA of 3.0, interview, 2-3 page statement of purpose, two letters of recommendation, resume, background check. Additional exam requirements/recommendations for international students: Required—TOEFL (minimum score 550 paper-based; 80 iBT). *Application deadline:* Applications are processed on a rolling basis. Electronic applications accepted. *Expenses:* Contact institution. *Unit head:* Gene James, Dean of Counseling, 541-684-7261, Fax: 541-684-7310, E-mail: gjames@nwcu.edu. *Application contact:* Billy Dorsch, Admission Counselor for Graduate Studies, 541-684-7279, Fax: 541-349-5281, E-mail: wdorsch@nwcu.edu.

Northwest Missouri State University, Graduate School, School of Education, Maryville, MO 64468-6001. Offers early childhood education (MS Ed); education leadership (MS Ed), including elementary, K-12, secondary; educational leadership (Ed S), including elementary school principalship, secondary school principalship, superintendency; educational leadership and policy analysis (Ed D); elementary education (MS Ed); elementary mathematics (MS Ed); higher education leadership (MS); middle school education (MS Ed); reading (MS Ed); special education (MS Ed); teacher leadership (MS Ed); teaching English language learners (MS Ed). *Accreditation:* NCATE. *Program availability:* Part-time. *Students:* 15 full-time (11 women), 150 part-time (103 women). In 2016, 46 master's awarded. *Degree requirements:* For master's, comprehensive exam; for Ed S, comprehensive exam, thesis. *Entrance requirements:* For master's, GRE General Test, writing sample; for Ed S, minimum graduate GPA of 3.25. Additional exam requirements/recommendations for international students: Required—TOEFL (minimum score 550 paper-based). *Application deadline:* For fall admission, 7/1 for domestic and international students; for spring admission, 11/15 for domestic and international students. Applications are processed on a rolling basis. Application fee: $0 ($50 for international students). Electronic applications accepted. *Expenses:* Tuition, state resident: full-time $3447; part-time $383 per credit hour. Tuition, nonresident: full-time $5724; part-time $636 per credit hour. *Required fees:* $130 per credit hour. *Financial support:* Research assistantships with full tuition reimbursements, teaching assistantships with full tuition reimbursements, and unspecified assistantships available. Financial award application deadline: 4/1; financial award applicants required to submit FAFSA. *Faculty research:* Great books of educational administration. *Unit head:* Dr. Tim Wall, Dean, 660-562-1179, E-mail: timwall@nwmissouri.edu.
Website: http://www.nwmissouri.edu/academics/ed/

Notre Dame of Maryland University, Graduate Studies, Program in Teaching English to Speakers of Other Languages, Baltimore, MD 21210-2476. Offers MA. *Accreditation:* NCATE. *Program availability:* Part-time, evening/weekend. *Entrance requirements:* Additional exam requirements/recommendations for international students: Required—TOEFL (minimum score 500 paper-based; 61 iBT). Electronic applications accepted.

Nyack College, School of Education, Nyack, NY 10960. Offers childhood education (MS); childhood special education (MS); inclusive education (MA); TESOL (MAT, MS). *Program availability:* Part-time, 100% online, blended/hybrid learning. *Students:* 21 full-time (20 women), 36 part-time (31 women); includes 34 minority (7 Black or African American, non-Hispanic/Latino; 3 Asian, non-Hispanic/Latino; 22 Hispanic/Latino; 1 Native Hawaiian or other Pacific Islander, non-Hispanic/Latino; 1 Two or more races, non-Hispanic/Latino), 5 international. Average age 33. In 2016, 23 master's awarded. *Degree requirements:* For master's, comprehensive exam, clinical experience. *Entrance requirements:* For master's, GRE, transcripts, autobiography and statement on reasons for pursuing graduate study in education, recommendations, 6 credits of language, evidence of computer literacy, introductory course in psychology. Additional exam requirements/recommendations for international students: Required—TOEFL (minimum score 550 paper-based; 80 iBT), GRE. *Application deadline:* For fall admission, 8/4 for domestic students, 7/4 for international students; for spring admission, 12/15 for domestic students, 11/15 for international students; for summer admission, 4/7 for domestic students, 3/7 for international students. Applications are processed on a rolling basis. Application fee: $30. Electronic applications accepted. *Expenses:* $700 per credit. *Financial support:* Scholarships/grants available. Financial award applicants required to submit FAFSA. *Unit head:* Dr. JoAnn Looney, Dean, 845-675-4538, Fax: 845-358-0874. *Application contact:* Joseph Kim, Admissions Associate, 845-675-4400 Ext. 5708, Fax: 845-348-3912, E-mail: admissions.grad@nyack.edu.
Website: http://www.nyack.edu/edu

Oakland University, Graduate Study and Lifelong Learning, College of Arts and Sciences, Department of Linguistics, Rochester, MI 48309-4401. Offers linguistics (MA); teaching English as a second language (Certificate). *Program availability:* Part-time, evening/weekend. *Entrance requirements:* For master's, minimum GPA of 3.0. Additional exam requirements/recommendations for international students: Required—TOEFL (minimum score 550 paper-based).

Ohio Dominican University, Division of Education, Program in Teaching English to Speakers of Other Languages, Columbus, OH 43219-2099. Offers MA. *Program availability:* Part-time, evening/weekend. *Faculty:* 1 full-time, 1 (woman) part-time/adjunct. *Students:* 3 full-time (2 women), 25 part-time (16 women); includes 5 minority (1 Black or African American, non-Hispanic/Latino; 2 Asian, non-Hispanic/Latino; 2 Hispanic/Latino), 3 international. Average age 32. 14 applicants, 71% accepted, 9 enrolled. In 2016, 15 master's awarded. *Degree requirements:* For master's, thesis. *Entrance requirements:* For master's, bachelor's degree with minimum cumulative GPA of 3.0, 3 letters of recommendation. Additional exam requirements/recommendations for international students: Required—TOEFL (minimum score 550 paper-based), IELTS (minimum score 6.5). *Application deadline:* For fall admission, 9/15 for domestic students, 6/10 for international students; for spring admission, 1/4 for domestic students, 11/2 for international students; for summer admission, 5/30 for domestic students. Applications are processed on a rolling basis. Application fee: $25. Electronic applications accepted. *Expenses:* $590 per credit hour; $225 fees per semester. *Financial support:* Applicants required to submit FAFSA. *Unit head:* Dr. Timothy A. Micek, Director, 614-251-4675, E-mail: micekt@ohiodominican.edu. *Application contact:* John W. Naughton, Director for Graduate Admissions, 614-251-4721, Fax: 614-251-6654, E-mail: grad@ohiodominican.edu.
Website: http://www.ohiodominican.edu/academics/graduate/ma-tesol

Oklahoma City University, Petree College of Arts and Sciences, Oklahoma City, OK 73106-1402. Offers applied behavioral studies (M Ed); applied sociology: nonprofit leadership (MA); creative writing (MFA); criminology (MS); early childhood education (M Ed); elementary education (M Ed); general studies (MLA); leadership/management (MLA); moving image arts (MFA); professional counseling (M Ed); teaching (MA); teaching English to speakers of other languages (MA). *Program availability:* Part-time, evening/weekend. *Faculty:* 11 full-time (5 women), 15 part-time/adjunct (6 women). *Students:* 77 full-time (55 women), 46 part-time (30 women); includes 32 minority (13 Black or African American, non-Hispanic/Latino; 1 American Indian or Alaska Native, non-Hispanic/Latino; 2 Asian, non-Hispanic/Latino; 12 Hispanic/Latino; 4 Two or more races, non-Hispanic/Latino), 37 international. Average age 34. 92 applicants, 74% accepted, 46 enrolled. In 2016, 72 master's awarded. *Degree requirements:* For master's, capstone/practicum. *Entrance requirements:* For master's, bachelor's degree from accredited institution with minimum GPA of 3.0, essay, recommendation letters. Additional exam requirements/recommendations for international students: Required—TOEFL (minimum score 550 paper-based; 80 iBT). *Application deadline:* Applications are processed on a rolling basis. Application fee: $50. Electronic applications accepted. *Expenses:* Contact institution. *Financial support:* In 2016–17, 16 students received support. Federal Work-Study, institutionally sponsored loans, scholarships/grants, and tuition waivers (full and partial) available. Support available to part-time students. Financial award application deadline: 6/1; financial award applicants required to submit FAFSA. *Unit head:* Dr. Amy Cataldi, Dean, 405-208-5446, Fax: 405-208-5447, E-mail: acataldi@okcu.edu. *Application contact:* Michael Harrington, Director of Graduate Admissions, 800-633-7242, Fax: 405-208-5356, E-mail: gadmissions@okcu.edu.
Website: http://www.okcu.edu/petree/

Old Dominion University, College of Arts and Letters, Program in Applied Linguistics, Norfolk, VA 23529. Offers sociolinguistics (MA); TESOL (MA). *Program availability:* Part-time. *Faculty:* 4 full-time (all women). *Students:* 5 full-time (3 women), 12 part-time (9 women); includes 2 minority (1 Asian, non-Hispanic/Latino; 1 Two or more races, non-Hispanic/Latino), 1 international. Average age 32. 23 applicants, 91% accepted, 11 enrolled. In 2016, 10 master's awarded. *Degree requirements:* For master's, one foreign language, comprehensive exam, thesis optional, program portfolio. *Entrance requirements:* For master's, GRE General Test, sample of written work; 12 hours in English, 9 on the upper-level; minimum B average; letters of recommendation; resume; essay. Additional exam requirements/recommendations for international students: Required—TOEFL (minimum score 570 paper-based; 88 iBT). *Application deadline:* For fall admission, 3/15 priority date for domestic and international students; for spring admission, 10/1 priority date for domestic and international students. Applications are processed on a rolling basis. Application fee: $50. Electronic applications accepted. *Expenses:* Tuition, state resident: full-time $8604; part-time $478 per credit hour. Tuition, nonresident: full-time $21,510; part-time $1195 per credit hour. *Required fees:* $66 per semester. Tuition and fees vary according to campus/location, program and reciprocity agreements. *Financial support:* In 2016–17, 6 students received support. Career-related internships or fieldwork, institutionally sponsored loans, and unspecified assistantships available. Financial award application deadline: 2/15. *Faculty research:* Discourse analysis, phonology, syntax, second language acquisition, gender, sociolinguistics. *Unit head:* Dr. Bridget Anderson, Graduate Program Director, 757-683-4020, Fax: 757-683-3241, E-mail: linggpd@odu.edu. *Application contact:* Dr. David C. Earnest, Associate Dean, 757-683-6077, Fax: 757-683-5746, E-mail: dearnest@odu.edu.
Website: https://www.odu.edu/academics/programs/masters/applied-linguistics

Oregon State University, College of Education, Program in Education, Corvallis, OR 97331. Offers advanced science and mathematics education (Ed M); agricultural education (PhD); education (Ed D); free-choice learning (Ed M); language equity and educational policy (PhD); mathematics education (MS); pre-K-12 English to speakers of other languages (ESOL) (Ed M); science education (MS); science/mathematics education (PhD); social justice in education (Ed M). *Program availability:* Part-time, 100% online, blended/hybrid learning. *Faculty:* 9 full-time (8 women), 6 part-time/adjunct (2 women). *Students:* 14 full-time (8 women), 76 part-time (53 women); includes 25 minority (6 Black or African American, non-Hispanic/Latino; 2 American Indian or Alaska Native, non-Hispanic/Latino; 5 Asian, non-Hispanic/Latino; 10 Hispanic/Latino; 2 Two or more races, non-Hispanic/Latino), 3 international. Average age 38. 72 applicants, 69% accepted, 40 enrolled. In 2016, 14 master's, 21 doctorates awarded. Terminal master's awarded for partial completion of doctoral program. *Degree requirements:* For master's, variable foreign language requirement, thesis (for some programs); for doctorate, variable foreign language requirement, thesis/dissertation. *Entrance requirements:* Additional exam requirements/recommendations for international students: Required—TOEFL (minimum score 575 paper-based). Application fee: $75 ($85 for international students). *Expenses:* Tuition, state resident: full-time $12,150; part-time $450 per credit. Tuition, nonresident: full-time $21,789; part-time $807 per credit. *Required fees:* $1651; $1507 per credit. One-time fee: $350. Tuition and fees vary according to course load, campus/location and program. *Financial support:* Fellowships, research assistantships, teaching assistantships, career-related internships or fieldwork, Federal Work-Study, and institutionally sponsored loans available. Support available to part-time students. *Faculty research:* School administration, educational foundations, research methodology, education policy development, higher education administration. *Unit head:* Dr. Larry Flick, Dean. *Application contact:* E-mail: askcoed@oregonstate.edu.

Pacific University, College of Education, Forest Grove, OR 97116-1797. Offers early childhood education (MAT); education (MAE); elementary education (MAT); ESOL (MAT); high school education (MAT); middle school education (MAT); special education (MAT); speech-language pathology (MS); STEM education (MAT); talented and gifted (M Ed); visual function in learning (M Ed). *Accreditation:* NCATE. *Program availability:* Part-time, evening/weekend. *Degree requirements:* For master's, research project. *Entrance requirements:* For master's, California Basic Educational Skills Test, PRAXIS II, minimum undergraduate GPA of 2.75, 3.0 graduate. Additional exam requirements/ recommendations for international students: Required—TOEFL. Electronic applications accepted. *Expenses:* Contact institution. *Faculty research:* Defining a culturally competent classroom, technology in the k-12 classroom, Socratic seminars, social studies education.

Penn State Harrisburg, Graduate School, School of Behavioral Sciences and Education, Middletown, PA 17057. Offers adult education in the health and medical professions (Certificate); applied behavior analysis (MA); applied clinical psychology (MA); applied psychological research (MA); community psychology and social change (MA); English as a second language (ESL) program specialist and leadership (Certificate); folklore and ethnography (Certificate); health education (M Ed); lifelong learning and adult education (M Ed, D Ed); literacy education (M Ed); literacy leadership (Certificate); psychology: applications in clinical psychology (Certificate); psychology: health psychology (Certificate); teaching and curriculum (M Ed); training and development (M Ed, Certificate). *Program availability:* Part-time, evening/weekend. *Unit head:* Dr. Mukund S. Kulkarni, Chancellor, 717-948-6105, Fax: 717-948-6452. *Application contact:* Robert W. Coffman, Jr., Director of Enrollment Management, Recruitment and Admissions, 717-948-6250, Fax: 717-948-6325, E-mail: hbgadmit@psu.edu.
Website: https://harrisburg.psu.edu/behavioral-sciences-and-education/

Penn State University Park, Graduate School, College of the Liberal Arts, Department of Applied Linguistics, University Park, PA 16802. Offers applied linguistics (PhD); teaching English as a second language (MA). *Unit head:* Dr. Susan Welch, Dean, 814-865-7691, Fax: 814-863-2085. *Application contact:* Lori Hawn, Director, Graduate Student Services, 814-865-1795, Fax: 814-863-4627, E-mail: l-gswww@lists.psu.edu.
Website: http://aplng.la.psu.edu/

Penn State York, Graduate School, York, PA 17403. Offers ESL specialist (Certificate); teaching and curriculum (M Ed). *Students:* 6 part-time (all women). Average age 33. 3 applicants, 33% accepted, 1 enrolled. *Unit head:* Dr. Regina Vasilatos-Younken, Vice Provost for Graduate Education/Dean, Graduate School, 814-865-2516, Fax: 814-863-4627. *Application contact:* Lori Hawn, Director, Graduate Student Services, 814-865-1795, Fax: 814-863-4627, E-mail: l-gswww@lists.psu.edu.
Website: http://www.gradschool.psu.edu/

Pontifical Catholic University of Puerto Rico, College of Education, Program in English as a Second Language, Ponce, PR 00717-0777. Offers M Ed. *Degree requirements:* For master's, comprehensive exam, thesis (for some programs). *Entrance requirements:* For master's, GRE, 2 letters of recommendation, interview, minimum GPA of 2.75.

Portland State University, Graduate Studies, College of Liberal Arts and Sciences, Department of Applied Linguistics, Portland, OR 97207-0751. Offers teaching English to speakers of other languages (MA). *Program availability:* Part-time. *Faculty:* 11 full-time (7 women), 4 part-time/adjunct (3 women). *Students:* 29 full-time (21 women), 34 part-time (26 women); includes 9 minority (4 Asian, non-Hispanic/Latino; 4 Hispanic/Latino; 1 Two or more races, non-Hispanic/Latino), 4 international. Average age 34. 41 applicants, 59% accepted, 14 enrolled. In 2016, 17 master's awarded. *Degree requirements:* For master's, one foreign language, comprehensive exam, thesis, portfolio. *Entrance requirements:* For master's, bachelor's degree with minimum undergraduate GPA of 3.0, 2 letters of recommendation, personal statement, resume. Additional exam requirements/recommendations for international students: Required—TOEFL (minimum score 600 paper-based; 100 iBT), IELTS (minimum score 7). *Application deadline:* For fall admission, 2/1 priority date for domestic students, 2/1 for international students. Application fee: $65. Electronic applications accepted. *Expenses:* Contact institution. *Financial support:* In 2016–17, 2 research assistantships with tuition reimbursements (averaging $5,763 per year), 4 teaching assistantships with tuition reimbursements (averaging $6,390 per year) were awarded; career-related internships or fieldwork, Federal Work-Study, scholarships/grants, tuition waivers (partial), and unspecified assistantships also available. Support available to part-time students. Financial award application deadline: 3/1; financial award applicants required to submit FAFSA. *Faculty research:* Sociolinguistics, linguistics and cognitive science, language proficiency testing, lexical phrases and language teaching, teaching English as a second language methodology. *Total annual research expenditures:* $708,243. *Unit head:* Dr. Tucker Childs, Chair, 503-725-4099, Fax: 503-725-4139, E-mail: childst@pdx.edu. *Application contact:* 503-725-2040, Fax: 503-725-4139, E-mail: linginfo@pdx.edu.
Website: http://www.pdx.edu/linguistics/

Post University, Program in Education, Waterbury, CT 06723-2540. Offers education (M Ed); higher education administration (M Ed); instructional design and technology (M Ed); online teaching (M Ed); teaching and learning (M Ed); TESOL (teaching English to speakers of other languages) (M Ed). *Program availability:* Online learning.

Providence University College & Theological Seminary, Theological Seminary, Otterburne, MB R0A 1G0, Canada. Offers children's ministry (Certificate); Christian studies (MA, Certificate); counseling (MA); cross-cultural discipleship (Certificate); divinity (M Div); educational studies (MA), including counseling psychology, educational ministries, student development, teaching English to speakers of other languages, training teachers of English to speakers of other languages; global studies (MA); lay counseling (Diploma); ministry (D Min); teaching English to speakers of other languages (Certificate); theological studies (MA); training teacher of English to speakers of other languages (Certificate); youth ministry (Certificate). *Accreditation:* ATS. *Program availability:* Part-time. *Degree requirements:* For master's, variable foreign language requirement, thesis (for some programs); for doctorate, thesis/dissertation. *Entrance requirements:* Additional exam requirements/recommendations for international students: Recommended—TOEFL (minimum score 550 paper-based). *Faculty research:* Studies in Isaiah, theology of sin.

Queens College of the City University of New York, Arts and Humanities Division, Department of Linguistics and Communication Disorders, Queens, NY 11367-1597. Offers applied linguistics (MA); English language teaching (Advanced Certificate); speech-language pathology (MA); teaching English to speakers of other languages (MS Ed); TESOL (MS Ed); TESOL and bilingual education (MS Ed). *Accreditation:* ASHA. *Program availability:* Part-time. *Faculty:* 22 full-time (16 women), 19 part-time/ adjunct (13 women). *Students:* 44 full-time (42 women), 123 part-time (107 women); includes 64 minority (11 Black or African American, non-Hispanic/Latino; 20 Asian, non-Hispanic/Latino; 31 Hispanic/Latino; 2 Two or more races, non-Hispanic/Latino), 4 international. Average age 28. 390 applicants, 25% accepted, 81 enrolled. In 2016, 71 master's, 30 other advanced degrees awarded. *Entrance requirements:* For master's, minimum GPA of 3.0. Additional exam requirements/recommendations for international students: Required—TOEFL, IELTS. *Application deadline:* For fall admission, 4/1 for domestic students. Applications are processed on a rolling basis. Application fee: $125. Electronic applications accepted. *Expenses:* Tuition, state resident: full-time $5065; part-time $425 per credit. Tuition, nonresident: part-time $780 per credit. *Required fees:* $522; $397 per credit. Part-time tuition and fees vary according to course load and program. *Financial support:* Career-related internships or fieldwork available. Financial award application deadline: 4/1; financial award applicants required to submit FAFSA. *Unit head:* Dr. Robert Vago, Chairperson, 718-997-2875, E-mail: robert.vago@qc.cuny.edu.

Quincy University, Master of Science in Education Programs, Quincy, IL 62301-2699. Offers curriculum and instruction (MS Ed), including bilingual/English as a second language; leadership (MS Ed); reading education (MS Ed); special education (MS Ed); teacher leader (MS Ed). *Program availability:* Part-time, evening/weekend, online learning. *Degree requirements:* For master's, comprehensive exam (for some programs), thesis optional. *Entrance requirements:* For master's, MAT or GRE. Additional exam requirements/recommendations for international students: Required—TOEFL (minimum score 550 paper-based; 79 iBT). Electronic applications accepted. Application fee is waived when completed online.

Regent University, Graduate School, School of Education, Virginia Beach, VA 23464-9800. Offers adult education (Ed D, PhD, Ed S); advanced educational leadership (Ed D, PhD, Ed S); career switcher (M Ed); character education (Ed D, PhD, Ed S); Christian education leadership (Ed D, PhD, Ed S); Christian school administration (M Ed); curriculum and instruction (M Ed), including adult education, Christian school, gifted and talented education, STEM education, teacher leader; educational leadership (M Ed); educational psychology (Ed D, PhD, Ed S); educational technology and online learning (Ed D, PhD, Ed S); elementary education (M Ed); exceptional education executive leadership (Ed D, PhD, Ed S); higher education (Ed D, PhD, Ed S); higher education leadership and management (Ed D, PhD, Ed S); individualized degree plan (M Ed); K-12 school leadership (Ed D, PhD, Ed S); K-12 special education (M Ed); K-8 leadership in mathematics education (M Ed); leadership in mathematics education (Ed S); reading specialist (M Ed); special education (Ed D, PhD, Ed S); student affairs (M Ed); TESOL (M Ed), including adult education - collegiate, K-12. *Accreditation:* TEAC. *Program availability:* Part-time, evening/weekend, 100% online, blended/hybrid learning. *Faculty:* 22 full-time (10 women), 42 part-time/adjunct (31 women). *Students:* 89 full-time (62 women), 1,035 part-time (823 women); includes 466 minority (381 Black or African American, non-Hispanic/Latino; 3 American Indian or Alaska Native, non-Hispanic/Latino; 19 Asian, non-Hispanic/Latino; 50 Hispanic/Latino; 13 Two or more races, non-Hispanic/Latino), 11 international. Average age 39. 976 applicants, 59% accepted, 449 enrolled. In 2016, 241 master's, 22 doctorates, 4 other advanced degrees awarded. *Degree requirements:* For master's, thesis or alternative; for doctorate, comprehensive exam, thesis/dissertation. *Entrance requirements:* For master's, Virginia Communication and Literacy Assessment (VCLA), PRAXIS, college transcripts, writing sample, interview; for doctorate, GRE, writing sample, resume, transcripts, interview. Additional exam requirements/recommendations for international students: Required—TOEFL (minimum score 577 paper-based). *Application deadline:* For fall admission, 4/1 priority date for domestic students; for spring admission, 10/15 priority date for domestic students. Applications are processed on a rolling basis. Application fee: $50. Electronic applications accepted. *Expenses:* Contact institution. *Financial support:* In 2016–17, 622 students received support, including 1 fellowship (averaging $5,000 per year); career-related internships or fieldwork, scholarships/grants, and unspecified assistantships also available. Support available to part-time students. *Faculty research:* Christian school administration, curriculum and instruction, educational technology and online learning, higher education, special education. *Unit head:* Dr. Donald Finn, Dean, 757-352-4278, Fax: 757-352-4318, E-mail: dfinn@regent.edu. *Application contact:* Heidi Cece, Assistant Vice President of Enrollment Management, 800-373-5504, Fax: 757-352-4381, E-mail: admissions@regent.edu.
Website: http://www.regent.edu/soe/

Rhode Island College, School of Graduate Studies, Feinstein School of Education and Human Development, Department of Educational Studies, Providence, RI 02908-1991. Offers advanced studies in teaching and learning (M Ed); English (MAT); French (MAT); history (MAT); math (MAT); secondary education (MAT); Spanish (MAT); teaching English as a second language (M Ed). *Accreditation:* NCATE. *Program availability:* Part-time, evening/weekend. *Faculty:* 6 full-time (5 women), 8 part-time/adjunct (6 women). *Students:* 5 full-time (2 women), 53 part-time (48 women); includes 8 minority (2 Black or African American, non-Hispanic/Latino; 2 Asian, non-Hispanic/Latino; 3 Hispanic/Latino; 1 Two or more races, non-Hispanic/Latino). Average age 39. In 2016, 29 master's awarded. *Degree requirements:* For master's, capstone or comprehensive assessment. *Entrance requirements:* For master's, GRE or MAT (for most programs), minimum undergraduate GPA of 3.0; baccalaureate degree in English, French, history, math or Spanish; 3 letters of recommendation; interview. Additional exam requirements/ recommendations for international students: Recommended—TOEFL (minimum score 550 paper-based; 79 iBT). *Application deadline:* For fall admission, 3/1 for domestic students; for spring admission, 11/1 for domestic students. Applications are processed on a rolling basis. Application fee: $50. Electronic applications accepted. *Expenses:* Tuition, state resident: full-time $8928; part-time $372 per credit. Tuition, nonresident: full-time $17,376; part-time $724 per credit. *Required fees:* $604; $22 per credit. One-time fee: $74. *Financial support:* In 2016–17, 1 teaching assistantship with full tuition reimbursement (averaging $3,000 per year) was awarded; career-related internships or

fieldwork, Federal Work-Study, scholarships/grants, health care benefits, and unspecified assistantships also available. Support available to part-time students. Financial award application deadline: 5/15; financial award applicants required to submit FAFSA. *Unit head:* Dr. Gerri August, Chair, 401-456-8170. *Application contact:* Graduate Studies, 401-456-8700.
Website: http://www.ric.edu/educationalStudies/

Rider University, Department of Graduate Education, Leadership and Counseling, Teacher Certification Program, Lawrenceville, NJ 08648-3001. Offers business education (Certificate); elementary education (Certificate); English as a second language (Certificate); English education (Certificate); mathematics education (Certificate); preschool to grade 3 (Certificate); science education (Certificate); social studies education (Certificate); world languages (Certificate), including French, German, Spanish. *Program availability:* Part-time. *Degree requirements:* For Certificate, internship, professional portfolio. *Entrance requirements:* For degree, PRAXIS, resume. Additional exam requirements/recommendations for international students: Required—TOEFL (minimum score 550 paper-based). Electronic applications accepted. *Faculty research:* Conceptual foundations for optimal development of creativity; creative theory, cognitive processes in mathematics learning, teacher collaboration.

Rowan University, Graduate School, College of Education, Department of Language, Literacy, and Sociocultural Education, Program in ESL Education, Glassboro, NJ 08028-1701. Offers CGS. Electronic applications accepted.

Rutgers University–New Brunswick, Graduate School of Education, Department of Learning and Teaching, Program in Language Education, Piscataway, NJ 08854-8097. Offers English as a second language education (Ed M); language education (Ed M, Ed D). *Program availability:* Part-time. Terminal master's awarded for partial completion of doctoral program. *Degree requirements:* For master's, comprehensive exam; for doctorate, thesis/dissertation, concept paper, qualifying exam. *Entrance requirements:* For master's, GRE General Test, minimum GPA of 3.0; for doctorate, GRE General Test, minimum GPA of 3.5. Additional exam requirements/recommendations for international students: Required—TOEFL. Electronic applications accepted. *Faculty research:* Linguistics, sociolinguistics, cross-cultural/international communication.

Sacred Heart University, Graduate Programs, Isabelle Farrington College of Education, Department of Teacher Education, Fairfield, CT 06825. Offers advanced educational studies for teachers (CAS); teaching: education (MAT); TESOL (MAT). *Program availability:* Part-time, evening/weekend. *Faculty:* 13 full-time (8 women), 10 part-time/adjunct (5 women). *Students:* 203 full-time (155 women), 458 part-time (349 women); includes 99 minority (30 Black or African American, non-Hispanic/Latino; 1 American Indian or Alaska Native, non-Hispanic/Latino; 12 Asian, non-Hispanic/Latino; 50 Hispanic/Latino; 1 Native Hawaiian or other Pacific Islander, non-Hispanic/Latino; 5 Two or more races, non-Hispanic/Latino). Average age 34. 290 applicants, 97% accepted, 255 enrolled. In 2016, 241 master's, 66 other advanced degrees awarded. *Entrance requirements:* For master's, bachelor's degree, copy of official teaching certificate, background check. Additional exam requirements/recommendations for international students: Required—TOEFL (minimum score 570 paper-based, 80 iBT), TWE, or IELTS (6.5); Recommended—TSE. *Application deadline:* Applications are processed on a rolling basis. Application fee: $75. Electronic applications accepted. *Expenses:* $705 per credit. *Financial support:* Unspecified assistantships available. Financial award applicants required to submit FAFSA. *Unit head:* Dr. Jim Carl, Dean, 203-396-8454, E-mail: carlj@sacredheart.edu. *Application contact:* William Sweeney, Director of Graduate Admissions, 203-365-4827, E-mail: sweeneyw@sacredheart.edu.
Website: http://www.sacredheart.edu/academics/isabellefarringtoncollegeofeducation/programsoffered/masterofartsinteaching/

St. Cloud State University, School of Graduate Studies, College of Liberal Arts, Department of English, St. Cloud, MN 56301-4498. Offers English (MA, MS); teaching English as a second language (MA). *Program availability:* Part-time. *Degree requirements:* For master's, thesis or alternative. *Entrance requirements:* For master's, GRE General Test, minimum GPA of 2.75. Additional exam requirements/recommendations for international students: Required—Michigan English Language Assessment Battery; Recommended—TOEFL (minimum score 550 paper-based), IELTS (minimum score 6.5). Electronic applications accepted.

St. John's University, The School of Education, Department of Education Specialties, Program in Teaching English to Speakers of Other Languages and Bilingual Education, Queens, NY 11439. Offers MS Ed, Adv C. *Program availability:* Part-time, evening/weekend, online learning. *Degree requirements:* For master's, comprehensive exam, fieldwork. *Entrance requirements:* For master's, minimum GPA of 3.0, eligibility for teacher certification, 2 letters of recommendation, bachelor's degree; for Adv C, New York State initial teaching certification or eligibility. Additional exam requirements/recommendations for international students: Required—TOEFL (minimum score 600 paper-based; 100 iBT), IELTS (minimum score 7). Electronic applications accepted. *Faculty research:* Second language learning and academic achievement, heritage language education, assessing the progress of English language learners toward English acquisition, dual language acquisition, study of English Creoles and dialects of other Englishes.

Saint Michael's College, Graduate Programs, Program in Teaching English to Speakers of Other Languages, Colchester, VT 05439. Offers MATESOL, Certificate. *Program availability:* Part-time, evening/weekend. *Faculty:* 6 full-time (3 women), 2 part-time/adjunct (1 woman). *Students:* 17 full-time (11 women), 16 part-time (9 women). 22 applicants, 100% accepted, 10 enrolled. *Degree requirements:* For master's, one foreign language, comprehensive exam (for some programs), thesis or alternative, capstone paper or portfolio. *Entrance requirements:* For master's, minimum GPA of 3.0, resume, essay. Additional exam requirements/recommendations for international students: Required—TOEFL (minimum score 550 paper-based; 79 iBT); Recommended—IELTS. *Application deadline:* For fall admission, 7/1 for domestic students, 6/1 for international students; for spring admission, 12/1 for domestic students, 10/1 for international students; for summer admission, 4/1 for domestic students, 2/1 for international students. Applications are processed on a rolling basis. Application fee: $50. *Expenses: Tuition:* Full-time $10,620; part-time $590 per credit. Part-time tuition and fees vary according to course load and program. *Financial support:* Research assistantships, career-related internships or fieldwork, Federal Work-Study, institutionally sponsored loans, and scholarships/grants available. Financial award applicants required to submit FAFSA. *Faculty research:* Language teaching methodology, discourse analysis, second language acquisition, language assessment, sociolinguistics, K–12 English as a second language for children. *Unit head:* Dr. Elizabeth O'Dowd, Director, 802-654-2276, Fax: 802-654-2595, E-mail: eodowd@smcvt.edu. *Application contact:* Kirstin Van Luling, Administrative Assistant, 802-654-2684, Fax: 802-654-2595, E-mail: tesol@smcvt.edu.
Website: http://www.smcvt.edu/graduate-programs/academic-programs/teaching-english-to-speakers-of-other-languages.aspx

St. Thomas University, School of Leadership Studies, Institute for Education, Miami Gardens, FL 33054-6459. Offers earth/space science (Certificate); educational administration (MS, Certificate); educational leadership (Ed D); elementary education (MS); ESOL (Certificate); gifted education (Certificate); instructional technology (MS, Certificate); professional/studies (Certificate); reading (MS, Certificate); special education (MS). *Program availability:* Part-time, evening/weekend. *Degree requirements:* For master's, comprehensive exam; for doctorate, comprehensive exam, thesis/dissertation. *Entrance requirements:* For master's, interview, minimum GPA of 3.0 or GRE; for doctorate, GRE or MAT. Additional exam requirements/recommendations for international students: Required—TOEFL (minimum score 550 paper-based; 79 iBT). Electronic applications accepted.

Saint Xavier University, Graduate Studies, School of Education, Chicago, IL 60655-3105. Offers counseling (MA); curriculum and instruction (MA); early childhood education (MA); educational administration (MA); elementary education (MA); individualized studies (MA), including educational technology, English as a second language (ESL), ISTEM (integrative science, technology, engineering, and math), science education; music education (MA); reading (MA); secondary education (MA); Spanish education (MA); special education (MA); teaching and leadership (MA). *Accreditation:* NCATE. *Program availability:* Part-time, evening/weekend. *Degree requirements:* For master's, thesis or project. *Entrance requirements:* For master's, minimum GPA of 3.0. *Expenses:* Contact institution.

Salem College, Department of Education, Winston-Salem, NC 27101. Offers art education (MAT); elementary education (M Ed, MAT); language and literacy (M Ed); middle school education (MAT); school counseling (M Ed); second language studies (MAT); secondary education (MAT); special education (M Ed, MAT). *Accreditation:* NCATE. *Program availability:* Part-time, evening/weekend, online learning. *Degree requirements:* For master's, practicum (MAT), project (M Ed), oral and written comprehensive exams. *Entrance requirements:* For master's, minimum GPA of 2.5. *Faculty research:* Content area reading strategies, literacy development, brain compatible instruction.

Salem State University, School of Graduate Studies, Program in Teaching English as a Second Language, Salem, MA 01970-5353. Offers MAT. *Program availability:* Part-time, evening/weekend. *Entrance requirements:* Additional exam requirements/recommendations for international students: Required—TOEFL (minimum score 550 paper-based; 80 iBT) or IELTS (minimum score 5.5).

Salisbury University, Department of English, Salisbury, MD 21801-6837. Offers English (MA), including creative writing, film, literature, secondary education, TESOL, writing and rhetoric. *Program availability:* Part-time. *Faculty:* 11 full-time (5 women), 1 (woman) part-time/adjunct. *Students:* 11 full-time (9 women), 24 part-time (19 women); includes 1 minority (Black or African American, non-Hispanic/Latino), 4 international. Average age 33. 18 applicants, 67% accepted, 9 enrolled. In 2016, 17 master's awarded. *Degree requirements:* For master's, comprehensive exam, thesis optional. *Entrance requirements:* Additional exam requirements/recommendations for international students: Required—TOEFL (minimum score 550 paper-based, 79 iBT) or IELTS (6.5). *Application deadline:* For fall admission, 8/1 for domestic and international students; for spring admission, 1/1 for domestic and international students. Application fee: $65. Electronic applications accepted. *Expenses:* $381 per credit hour resident tuition, $670 per credit hour non-resident tuition; $84 per credit hour fees. *Financial support:* In 2016–17, 2 students received support, including 11 teaching assistantships with full tuition reimbursements available (averaging $9,395 per year); career-related internships or fieldwork and scholarships/grants also available. Support available to part-time students. Financial award application deadline: 3/1; financial award applicants required to submit FAFSA. *Faculty research:* Literature; linguistics; film studies; rhetoric and composition; TESOL. *Unit head:* Dr. Christopher Vilmar, Graduate Program Director, English, 410-677-6511, E-mail: csvilmar@salisbury.edu.
Website: http://www.salisbury.edu/gsr/gradstudies/ENGpage.html

San Diego State University, Graduate and Research Affairs, College of Arts and Letters, Department of Linguistics and Oriental Languages, San Diego, CA 92182. Offers applied linguistics and English as a second language (CAL); computational linguistics (MA); English as a second language/applied linguistics (MA); general linguistics (MA). *Degree requirements:* For master's, one foreign language, comprehensive exam, thesis optional. *Entrance requirements:* For master's, GRE General Test, 2 letters of recommendation. Additional exam requirements/recommendations for international students: Required—TOEFL (minimum score 570 paper-based). Electronic applications accepted. *Faculty research:* Cross-cultural linguistic studies of semantics.

San Francisco State University, Division of Graduate Studies, College of Liberal and Creative Arts, Department of English Language and Literature, Program in Teaching English to Speakers of Other Languages, San Francisco, CA 94132-1722. Offers MA. *Program availability:* Part-time. *Degree requirements:* For master's, comprehensive exam (for some programs), thesis (for some programs). *Application deadline:* Applications are processed on a rolling basis. Electronic applications accepted. *Expenses:* Tuition, state resident: full-time $6738. Tuition, nonresident: full-time $15,666. *Required fees:* $1012. Tuition and fees vary according to degree level and program. *Unit head:* Dr. Sugie Goen-Salter, Chair, 415-338-7582, Fax: 415-338-6159, E-mail: sgoen@sfsu.edu. *Application contact:* Dr. David Olsher, Professor and Graduate Coordinator, 415-338-2827, Fax: 415-338-6159, E-mail: olsher@sfsu.edu.
Website: http://english.sfsu.edu/graduate-matesol/

San Jose State University, Graduate Studies and Research, College of Humanities and the Arts, San Jose, CA 95192-0001. Offers art (MA, MFA), including art history and visual culture (MA), digital media art (MFA), photography (MFA), pictorial art (MFA), spatial art (MFA); computational linguistics (Certificate); English (MA, MFA), including creative writing (MFA); French (MA); humanities and arts (Certificate); linguistics (MA); music (MA); philosophy (MA); professional and technical communication (Certificate); Spanish (MA); teaching English to speakers of other languages (MA); TESOL (Certificate); theatre arts (MA). Electronic applications accepted.

Seattle Pacific University, MA in Teaching English to Speakers of Other Languages Program, Seattle, WA 98119-1997. Offers K-12 (MA); teaching English to speakers of other languages (MA). *Program availability:* Part-time. *Degree requirements:* For master's, one foreign language, practicum. *Entrance requirements:* For master's, GRE (minimum score of 155 verbal/500 old scoring, 3.5 analytical writing) or MAT (minimum score of 400), bachelor's degree; letters of recommendation; official copies of transcripts; minimum GPA of 3.0; personal statement; essay; resume. Additional exam requirements/recommendations for international students: Required—TOEFL (minimum score 600 paper-based). Electronic applications accepted. *Expenses:* Contact institution. *Faculty research:* Second language acquisition.

Seattle University, College of Education, Program in Teaching English to Speakers of Other Languages, Seattle, WA 98122-1090. Offers M Ed, MA, Certificate. *Accreditation:* NCATE. *Program availability:* Part-time. *Faculty:* 1 full-time (0 women), 1 part-time/adjunct (0 women). *Students:* 12 full-time (10 women), 27 part-time (17 women); includes 6 minority (3 Asian, non-Hispanic/Latino; 2 Hispanic/Latino; 1 Two or more races, non-Hispanic/Latino), 8 international. Average age 33. 28 applicants, 50% accepted, 7 enrolled. In 2016, 18 master's, 1 other advanced degree awarded. *Degree requirements:* For master's, comprehensive exam, thesis, internship. *Entrance requirements:* For master's, GRE, MAT, or minimum GPA of 3.0. Additional exam requirements/recommendations for international students: Required—TOEFL. *Application deadline:* For fall admission, 8/20 priority date for domestic students; for

winter admission, 11/20 for domestic students; for spring admission, 2/20 for domestic students. Applications are processed on a rolling basis. Application fee: $55. *Financial support:* In 2016–17, 1 student received support. Career-related internships or fieldwork and Federal Work-Study available. Support available to part-time students. Financial award applicants required to submit FAFSA. *Unit head:* Dr. Jian Yang, Coordinator, 209-296-5908, E-mail: tesol@seattleu.edu. *Application contact:* Janet Shandley, Associate Dean of Graduate Admissions, 206-296-5900, Fax: 206-298-5656, E-mail: grad_admissions@seattleu.edu.
Website: https://www.seattleu.edu/education/tesol/

Shippensburg University of Pennsylvania, School of Graduate Studies, College of Education and Human Services, Department of Teacher Education, Shippensburg, PA 17257-2299. Offers curriculum and instruction (M Ed), including biology, early childhood education, elementary and middle level education, elementary education, geography/earth science, history, mathematics, middle school education, modern languages; literacy studies (Certificate); online instruction, learning, and technology (Certificate); reading (M Ed); teaching English as a second language (Certificate). *Accreditation:* NCATE. *Program availability:* Part-time, evening/weekend, 100% online, blended/hybrid learning. *Faculty:* 14 full-time (9 women), 5 part-time/adjunct (all women). *Students:* 11 full-time (10 women), 88 part-time (81 women); includes 8 minority (3 Black or African American, non-Hispanic/Latino; 2 Asian, non-Hispanic/Latino; 3 Hispanic/Latino), 4 international. Average age 32. 57 applicants, 60% accepted, 28 enrolled. In 2016, 18 master's awarded. *Degree requirements:* For master's, comprehensive exam (for some programs), thesis optional, practicum or internship; capstone seminar (for some programs). *Entrance requirements:* For master's, MAT or GRE (if GPA less than 2.75), interview, 3 letters of reference, questionnaire of teaching background and future goals, resume. Additional exam requirements/recommendations for international students: Required—TOEFL (minimum score 550 paper-based, 68 iBT) or IELTS (minimum score 6). *Application deadline:* For fall admission, 4/1 priority date for domestic students, 4/30 for international students; for spring admission, 9/1 priority date for domestic students, 9/30 for international students; for summer admission, 2/1 priority date for domestic students. Applications are processed on a rolling basis. Application fee: $45. Electronic applications accepted. *Expenses:* Tuition, state resident: part-time $483 per credit. Tuition, nonresident: part-time $725 per credit. *Required fees:* $141 per credit. *Financial support:* In 2016–17, 3 students received support. Career-related internships or fieldwork, scholarships/grants, unspecified assistantships, and resident hall director and student payroll positions available. Support available to part-time students. Financial award application deadline: 3/1; financial award applicants required to submit FAFSA. *Unit head:* Dr. Christine A. Royce, Chairperson, 717-477-1688, Fax: 717-477-4046, E-mail: caroyc@ship.edu. *Application contact:* Megan N. Luft, Assistant Dean of Graduate Admissions, 717-477-1231, Fax: 717-477-4016, E-mail: mnluft@ship.edu.
Website: http://www.ship.edu/teacher/

Simon Fraser University, Office of Graduate Studies and Postdoctoral Fellows, Faculty of Education, Program in Teaching English as a Second/Foreign Language, Burnaby, BC V5A 1S6, Canada. Offers M Ed. *Program availability:* Part-time, evening/weekend. *Faculty:* 4 full-time (all women). *Degree requirements:* For master's, comprehensive exam. *Entrance requirements:* For master's, minimum GPA of 3.0 (on scale of 4.33) or 3.33 based on last 60 credits of undergraduate courses. Additional exam requirements/recommendations for international students: Recommended—TOEFL (minimum score 580 paper-based; 93 iBT), IELTS (minimum score 7), TWE (minimum score 5). *Application deadline:* For fall admission, 2/15 for domestic students. Application fee: $90 ($125 for international students). Electronic applications accepted. *Financial support:* In 2016–17, fellowships (averaging $6,250 per year) were awarded; scholarships/grants also available. *Faculty research:* Internationalization of higher education, international student experiences, language practices and language ideology in the globalized political economy, integration of immigrants, minorities and international students in educational settings, critical and psychoanalytical perspectives on second language learning, pedagogy, and curriculum. *Unit head:* Dr. Shawn Bullock, Graduate Chair, 778-782-4102, E-mail: educadgs@sfu.ca. *Application contact:* Amy Lau, Graduate Secretary, 778-782-3984, E-mail: intlmed@sfu.ca.

SIT Graduate Institute, Graduate Programs, Program in Teaching English as a Second Language, Brattleboro, VT 05302-0676. Offers MAT. *Degree requirements:* For master's, one foreign language, thesis, teaching practice. *Entrance requirements:* For master's, 3 letters of reference. Additional exam requirements/recommendations for international students: Required—TOEFL. *Faculty research:* Teaching English to speakers of other languages (TESOL).

Slippery Rock University of Pennsylvania, Graduate Studies (Recruitment), College of Liberal Arts, Department of Modern Languages and Cultures, Slippery Rock, PA 16057-1383. Offers teaching English to speakers of other languages (MA). *Program availability:* Part-time, evening/weekend, blended/hybrid learning, 1 evening class per week on campus. *Faculty:* 1 (woman) full-time. *Students:* 2 part-time (1 woman). Average age 36. 3 applicants, 67% accepted, 2 enrolled. *Degree requirements:* For master's, thesis (for some programs), practicum or end project. *Entrance requirements:* For master's, two letters of recommendation, statement of intent, official transcripts, minimum GPA of 2.75. Additional exam requirements/recommendations for international students: Required—TOEFL (minimum score 550 paper-based; 80 iBT). *Application deadline:* For fall admission, 5/1 priority date for domestic students, 3/1 priority date for international students; for spring admission, 9/1 priority date for domestic students, 10/1 priority date for international students. Applications are processed on a rolling basis. Application fee: $25 ($30 for international students). Electronic applications accepted. *Expenses:* $646.50 per credit in-state, $936.80 per credit out-of-state; $581.45 per online credit in-state, $648.65 per online credit out-of-state. *Financial support:* In 2016–17, 1 student received support. Career-related internships or fieldwork, Federal Work-Study, institutionally sponsored loans, scholarships/grants, tuition waivers (partial), and unspecified assistantships available. Support available to part-time students. Financial award application deadline: 5/1; financial award applicants required to submit FAFSA. *Unit head:* Dr. Marnie Petray-Covey, Graduate Coordinator, 724-738-4577, Fax: 724-738-2263, E-mail: marnie.petray-covey@sru.edu. *Application contact:* Brandi Weber-Mortimer, Director of Graduate Admissions, 724-738-4430, E-mail: graduate.admissions@sru.edu.
Website: http://www.sru.edu/academics/colleges-and-departments/cla/departments/modern-languages-and-cultures

Southeastern University, College of Education, Lakeland, FL 33801-6099. Offers curriculum and instruction (Ed D); educational leadership (M Ed); elementary education (M Ed); exceptional student education (M Ed); exceptional student education/educational therapy (M Ed); organizational leadership (Ed D); reading education (M Ed); teaching English to speakers of other languages (M Ed). *Expenses: Tuition:* Full-time $9450; part-time $6300 per credit. *Required fees:* $500; $250 per semester. One-time fee: $150. Tuition and fees vary according to degree level, campus/location and program. *Unit head:* Amy N. Bratten, Dean, 863-667-5238, E-mail: anbratten@seu.edu.
Website: http://www.seu.edu/education/

Southeast Missouri State University, School of Graduate Studies, Department of English, Cape Girardeau, MO 63701-4799. Offers teaching English to speakers of other languages (MA). *Program availability:* Part-time, evening/weekend, online learning. *Faculty:* 17 full-time (8 women). *Students:* 52 full-time (33 women), 50 part-time (40 women); includes 3 minority (2 Black or African American, non-Hispanic/Latino; 1 Hispanic/Latino), 33 international. Average age 32. 50 applicants, 84% accepted, 34 enrolled. In 2016, 39 master's awarded. *Degree requirements:* For master's, comprehensive exam (for some programs), thesis optional. *Entrance requirements:* Additional exam requirements/recommendations for international students: Required—TOEFL (minimum score 550 paper-based; 79 iBT), IELTS (minimum score 6), PTE (minimum score 53). *Application deadline:* For fall admission, 8/1 for domestic students, 6/1 for international students; for spring admission, 11/21 for domestic students, 10/1 for international students; for summer admission, 5/15 for domestic students. Applications are processed on a rolling basis. Application fee: $30 ($40 for international students). Electronic applications accepted. *Expenses:* Tuition, state resident: full-time $3130; part-time $260.80 per credit hour. Tuition, nonresident: full-time $5842; part-time $486.80 per credit hour. *Required fees:* $33.70 per credit hour. *Financial support:* In 2016–17, 24 students received support, including 17 teaching assistantships with full tuition reimbursements available; career-related internships or fieldwork, Federal Work-Study, scholarships/grants, traineeships, tuition waivers (full), and unspecified assistantships also available. Financial award application deadline: 6/30; financial award applicants required to submit FAFSA. *Faculty research:* Literature, creative writing, technical writing, secondary English education, teaching English as a second language. *Unit head:* Dr. Susan Kendrick, Department of English Chair, 573-651-2156, Fax: 573-651-5188, E-mail: skendrick@semo.edu. *Application contact:* 573-651-2590, E-mail: admissions@semo.edu.
Website: http://www.semo.edu/english/

Southern Connecticut State University, School of Graduate Studies, School of Arts and Sciences, Department of World Languages and Literatures, New Haven, CT 06515-1355. Offers multicultural-bilingual education/teaching English to speakers of other languages (MS); romance languages (MA). *Program availability:* Part-time, evening/weekend. *Faculty:* 8 full-time (6 women). *Students:* 10 full-time (8 women), 41 part-time (36 women); includes 16 minority (2 Black or African American, non-Hispanic/Latino; 1 Asian, non-Hispanic/Latino; 13 Hispanic/Latino), 2 international. Average age 36. 41 applicants, 51% accepted, 15 enrolled. In 2016, 18 master's awarded. *Degree requirements:* For master's, one foreign language, thesis or alternative. *Entrance requirements:* For master's, interview, minimum undergraduate GPA of 2.7. *Application deadline:* For fall admission, 7/15 priority date for domestic students. Applications are processed on a rolling basis. Application fee: $50. Electronic applications accepted. *Expenses:* Tuition, state resident: full-time $6497; part-time $519 per credit hour. Tuition, nonresident: full-time $18,102; part-time $535 per credit hour. *Required fees:* $4722; $55 per semester. Tuition and fees vary according to program. *Financial support:* Career-related internships or fieldwork, scholarships/grants, and unspecified assistantships available. Financial award application deadline: 4/15; financial award applicants required to submit FAFSA. *Unit head:* Dr. Resha Cardone, Chairperson, 203-392-7170, Fax: 203-392-6136, E-mail: cardoner1@southernct.edu. *Application contact:* Lisa Galvin, Director of Graduate Admissions, 203-392-5240, Fax: 203-392-5235, E-mail: galvinl1@southernct.edu.
Website: http://www.southernct.edu/academics/schools/arts/departments/world-languages/

Southern Illinois University Carbondale, Graduate School, College of Liberal Arts, Department of Linguistics, Program in Teaching English to Speakers of Other Languages, Carbondale, IL 62901-4701. Offers MA. *Entrance requirements:* Additional exam requirements/recommendations for international students: Required—TOEFL (minimum score 90 iBT).

Southern Illinois University Edwardsville, Graduate School, College of Arts and Sciences, Department of English Language and Literature, Program in Teaching English as a Second Language, Edwardsville, IL 62026-0001. Offers MA, Postbaccalaureate Certificate. *Program availability:* Part-time, evening/weekend. *Degree requirements:* For master's, one foreign language, thesis (for some programs), final exam. *Entrance requirements:* Additional exam requirements/recommendations for international students: Required—TOEFL (minimum score 550 paper-based, 79 iBT), IELTS (minimum score 6.5), Michigan Test of English Language Proficiency or PTE. Electronic applications accepted.

Southern New Hampshire University, School of Arts and Sciences, Manchester, NH 03106-1045. Offers community mental health (Graduate Certificate); community mental health and mental health counseling (MS); fiction and nonfiction (MFA); teaching English as a foreign language (MS). *Program availability:* Part-time, evening/weekend. *Degree requirements:* For master's, one foreign language, thesis. *Entrance requirements:* For master's, minimum GPA of 2.75 (for MS in teaching English as a foreign language), 3.0 (for MFA). Additional exam requirements/recommendations for international students: Required—TOEFL (minimum score 550 paper-based; 79 iBT), IELTS (minimum score 6.5), TWE (minimum score 5). Electronic applications accepted. *Expenses:* Contact institution. *Faculty research:* Action research, state of the art practice in behavioral health services, wraparound approaches to working with youth, learning styles.

Southern New Hampshire University, School of Education, Manchester, NH 03106-1045. Offers business education (M Ed); child development (M Ed); curriculum and instruction (M Ed), including education leadership, reading, special education, technology integration; education (M Ed); educational leadership (M Ed, Ed D); educational studies (M Ed); elementary education (M Ed); English (MAT); English for speakers of other languages (M Ed); reading and writing specialist (M Ed); school business administration (Certificate); secondary education (M Ed); special education (M Ed); technology integration specialist (M Ed). *Program availability:* Part-time, evening/weekend, online learning. *Degree requirements:* For master's, comprehensive exam (for some programs), thesis or alternative. *Entrance requirements:* For master's, PRAXIS I, minimum GPA of 2.75. Additional exam requirements/recommendations for international students: Required—TOEFL (minimum score 550 paper-based). Electronic applications accepted. *Expenses:* Contact institution.

Southwest Minnesota State University, Department of Education, Marshall, MN 56258. Offers ESL (MS); math (MS); reading (MS); special education (MS), including developmental disabilities, early childhood education, emotional behavioral disorders, learning disabilities; teaching, learning and leadership (MS). *Program availability:* Part-time, evening/weekend, online learning. *Entrance requirements:* Additional exam requirements/recommendations for international students: Required—TOEFL or IELTS; Recommended—TOEFL (minimum score 550 paper-based; 80 iBT), IELTS.

State University of New York at Fredonia, College of Education, Fredonia, NY 14063. Offers curriculum and instruction (MS Ed); literacy education (MS Ed), including birth-grade 12, grades 5-12; TESOL (MS Ed). *Accreditation:* NCATE. *Program availability:* Part-time. *Faculty:* 21 full-time (17 women), 11 part-time/adjunct (9 women). *Students:* 39 full-time (32 women), 54 part-time (33 women); includes 8 minority (1 Black or African American, non-Hispanic/Latino; 4 Asian, non-Hispanic/Latino; 2 Hispanic/Latino; 1 Two or more races, non-Hispanic/Latino). Average age 29. 60 applicants, 97% accepted, 39 enrolled. In 2016, 56 master's awarded. *Degree requirements:* For master's, thesis. *Entrance requirements:* For master's, GRE, minimum undergraduate GPA of 3.0. Additional exam requirements/recommendations for international students: Required—TOEFL (minimum score 79 iBT), IELTS (minimum score 6.5). *Application deadline:* For

fall admission, 4/1 priority date for domestic and international students; for spring admission, 11/1 priority date for domestic students, 11/1 for international students. Applications are processed on a rolling basis. Application fee: $75. Electronic applications accepted. *Expenses:* Tuition, state resident: full-time $10,370; part-time $453 per credit. Tuition, nonresident: full-time $20,190; part-time $925 per credit. *Required fees:* $1619; $67.30 per credit hour. $403.80 per semester. *Financial support:* In 2016–17, 4 teaching assistantships with full and partial tuition reimbursements (averaging $7,075 per year) were awarded. Financial award application deadline: 3/15; financial award applicants required to submit FAFSA. *Faculty research:* Positive behavioral intervention and support (PBIS), place-based science education, peer support for education, primary source material for social studies education, policies and practices in learning English language. *Unit head:* Dr. Christine Givner, Dean, 716-673-3311, E-mail: christine.givner@fredonia.edu. *Application contact:* Wendy S. Dunst, Interim Graduate Recruitment and Admissions Associate, 716-673-3808, Fax: 716-673-3712, E-mail: wendy.dunst@fredonia.edu.
Website: http://www.fredonia.edu/coe/

State University of New York at New Paltz, Graduate School, School of Education, Department of Secondary Education, Program in Second Language Education, New Paltz, NY 12561. Offers second language education (MS Ed); teaching English language learners (AC). *Accreditation:* NCATE. *Program availability:* Part-time, evening/weekend. *Students:* 14 full-time (13 women), 45 part-time (41 women); includes 16 minority (1 Black or African American, non-Hispanic/Latino; 14 Hispanic/Latino; 1 Two or more races, non-Hispanic/Latino). 33 applicants, 82% accepted, 19 enrolled. In 2016, 24 master's awarded. *Degree requirements:* For master's, practicum. *Entrance requirements:* For master's, minimum GPA of 3.0, 12 credits of a foreign language. Additional exam requirements/recommendations for international students: Required—TOEFL (minimum score 575 paper-based; 90 iBT), IELTS (minimum score 7). *Application deadline:* For fall admission, 4/15 priority date for domestic and international students. Application fee: $50. Electronic applications accepted. *Financial support:* Application deadline: 8/1. *Unit head:* Prof. Devon Duhaney, Coordinator, 845-257-2853, E-mail: duhaneyd@newpaltz.edu. *Application contact:* Vika Shock, Director of Graduate Admissions, 845-257-3286, Fax: 845-257-3284, E-mail: gradschool@newpaltz.edu.
Website: http://www.newpaltz.edu/secondaryed/sec_ed_msed_2nd_lang_ed.html

State University of New York College at Cortland, Graduate Studies, School of Arts and Sciences, Department of Modern Languages, Cortland, NY 13045. Offers second language education (MS Ed). *Accreditation:* NCATE.

Stony Brook University, State University of New York, Graduate School, College of Arts and Sciences, Department of Linguistics, Program in Teaching English to Speakers of Other Languages, Stony Brook, NY 11794. Offers MA. *Accreditation:* NCATE. *Students:* 27 full-time (19 women), 19 part-time (18 women); includes 9 minority (2 Black or African American, non-Hispanic/Latino; 1 Asian, non-Hispanic/Latino; 5 Hispanic/Latino; 1 Two or more races, non-Hispanic/Latino), 1 international. Average age 26. 103 applicants, 48% accepted, 25 enrolled. In 2016, 21 master's awarded. *Degree requirements:* For master's, minimum GPA of 3.0. *Entrance requirements:* For master's, GRE, statement of purpose, curriculum vitae, 3 letters of recommendation, official transcripts. Additional exam requirements/recommendations for international students: Required—TOEFL (minimum score 85 iBT). *Application deadline:* For fall admission, 6/20 for domestic students, 4/15 for international students; for spring admission, 10/1 for domestic students. Application fee: $100. Electronic applications accepted. *Expenses:* Contact institution. *Financial support:* Fellowships, research assistantships, and teaching assistantships available. *Unit head:* Dr. Richard Larson, Chair, 631-632-7776, E-mail: richard.larson@stonybrook.edu. *Application contact:* Michelle Carbone, Coordinator, 631-632-7774, Fax: 631-632-9789, E-mail: michelle.carbone@stonybrook.edu.
Website: https://linguistics.stonybrook.edu/programs/graduate/ma

Syracuse University, College of Arts and Sciences, CAS Program in Language Teaching: TESOL/TLOTE, Syracuse, NY 13244. Offers CAS. *Program availability:* Part-time. In 2016, 12 CASs awarded. *Entrance requirements:* Additional exam requirements/recommendations for international students: Required—TOEFL (minimum score 100 iBT). *Application deadline:* For fall admission, 1/10 priority date for domestic and international students. Applications are processed on a rolling basis. Application fee: $75. Electronic applications accepted. *Expenses: Tuition:* Full-time $25,974; part-time $1443 per credit hour. *Required fees:* $802; $50 per course. Tuition and fees vary according to course load and program. *Faculty research:* Linguistic analysis, methods for language teaching, teaching English. *Unit head:* Dr. Amanda Brown, Coordinator, 315-443-2244, E-mail: abrown08@syr.edu.
Website: http://lang.syr.edu/academics/CAS-TESOL-TLOTE/Teaching-Certificate-Linguistics.html

Syracuse University, College of Arts and Sciences, MA Program in Linguistic Studies, Syracuse, NY 13244. Offers linguistic studies (MA), including information representation and retrieval, language acquisition, language teaching (TESOL), language, culture, and society, linguistic theory, logic and language. *Program availability:* Part-time. *Students:* Average age 25. *Degree requirements:* For master's, comprehensive exam, thesis or alternative. *Entrance requirements:* For master's, GRE General Test, personal statement detailing interest in field of linguistics and possible concentration areas, transcripts, three recommendation letters. Additional exam requirements/recommendations for international students: Required—TOEFL (minimum score 100 iBT). *Application deadline:* For fall admission, 1/15 priority date for domestic and international students. Application fee: $75. Electronic applications accepted. *Expenses: Tuition:* Full-time $25,974; part-time $1443 per credit hour. *Required fees:* $802; $50 per course. Tuition and fees vary according to course load and program. *Financial support:* Fellowships with full tuition reimbursements, teaching assistantships with tuition reimbursements, and scholarships/grants available. Financial award application deadline: 1/1. *Faculty research:* Information representation and retrieval, language acquisition, linguistic theory, logic and language, teaching languages. *Unit head:* Dr. Gerald R. Greenberg, Director, 315-443-1414, E-mail: ggreenbe@syr.edu. *Application contact:* Amanda Brown, Linguistics Graduate Advisor, 315-443-2244, E-mail: abrown08@syr.edu.
Website: http://lang.syr.edu/academics/Linguistics/MA-Linguistics.html

Syracuse University, School of Education, MS Program in Teaching English Language Learners (Pre-K-12), Syracuse, NY 13244. Offers MS. *Program availability:* Part-time. *Students:* Average age 22. *Entrance requirements:* For master's, GRE or MAT, baccalaureate degree from regionally-accredited college/university, strong teacher and/or employer recommendations, 12 credits in a language other than English, personal statement. Additional exam requirements/recommendations for international students: Required—TOEFL (minimum score 100 iBT). *Application deadline:* For fall admission, 1/15 priority date for domestic and international students. Application fee: $75. Electronic applications accepted. *Expenses: Tuition:* Full-time $25,974; part-time $1443 per credit hour. *Required fees:* $802; $50 per course. Tuition and fees vary according to course load and program. *Financial support:* Fellowships with full tuition reimbursements, teaching assistantships with tuition reimbursements, career-related internships or fieldwork, scholarships/grants, and tuition waivers available. Financial award application deadline: 1/15; financial award applicants required to submit FAFSA. *Unit head:* Dr. Zaline Roy-Campbell, Program Coordinator, 315-443-8194, E-mail: zmroycam@syr.edu. *Application contact:* Speranza Migliore, Graduate Admissions Recruiter, 315-443-2505, E-mail: gradrcrt@syr.edu.
Website: http://soe.syr.edu/academic/reading_language_arts/graduate/masters/teaching_english_language_learners/default.aspx

Taylor College and Seminary, Graduate and Professional Programs, Edmonton, AB T6J 4T3, Canada. Offers Christian studies (Diploma); intercultural studies (MA, Diploma), including intercultural studies (Diploma), TESOL; theology (M Div, MTS). *Accreditation:* ATS. *Program availability:* Part-time, online learning. *Degree requirements:* For master's, thesis optional. *Entrance requirements:* Additional exam requirements/recommendations for international students: Required—TOEFL (minimum score 550 paper-based; 80 iBT), IELTS (minimum score 6.5). *Faculty research:* Biblical studies, administration and organization, world religions, ethics, missiology.

Teachers College, Columbia University, Department of Arts and Humanities, New York, NY 10027. Offers applied linguistics (MA, Ed D); art and art education (Ed M, MA, Ed D, Ed DCT); arts administration (MA); bilingual and bicultural education (MA); global competence (Certificate); history and education (Ed D, PhD); music and music education (Ed DCT); philosophy and education (MA, Ed D, PhD); social studies education (Ed M, PhD); teaching English to speakers of other languages (Ed M); teaching of English and English education (Ed M, MA, Ed D, PhD), including English education (Ed M, Ed D, PhD), teaching of English (MA); teaching of social studies (MA); TESOL (MA, Ed D). *Program availability:* Part-time, evening/weekend. *Students:* 429 full-time (329 women), 467 part-time (332 women); includes 268 minority (62 Black or African American, non-Hispanic/Latino; 1 American Indian or Alaska Native, non-Hispanic/Latino; 108 Asian, non-Hispanic/Latino; 76 Hispanic/Latino; 21 Two or more races, non-Hispanic/Latino), 212 international. 1,068 applicants, 53% accepted, 272 enrolled. Terminal master's awarded for partial completion of doctoral program. *Expenses: Tuition:* Full-time $36,288; part-time $1512 per credit. *Required fees:* $438 per semester. One-time fee: $510 full-time. Full-time tuition and fees vary according to course load. *Financial support:* Fellowships, research assistantships, teaching assistantships, career-related internships or fieldwork, Federal Work-Study, institutionally sponsored loans, tuition waivers (full and partial), and unspecified assistantships available. Support available to part-time students. *Unit head:* Prof. William Gaudelli, Department Chair, 212-678-3150, E-mail: wg74@columbia.edu. *Application contact:* David Estrella, Director of Admissions, 212-678-3305, Fax: 212-678-4171, E-mail: estrella@tc.columbia.edu.
Website: http://www.tc.edu/a%26h/

Temple University, College of Education, Department of Teaching and Learning, Philadelphia, PA 19122-6096. Offers career and technical education (Ed M), including business, computing, and information technology, industrial education, marketing education; middle grades education (Ed M), including math and language arts, math and science, science and language arts; secondary education (Ed M), including English, math, social studies; teaching English to speakers of other languages (MS Ed); urban education (Ed M). *Program availability:* Part-time, evening/weekend. *Faculty:* 26 full-time (16 women), 74 part-time/adjunct (54 women). *Students:* 204 full-time (139 women), 320 part-time (201 women); includes 112 minority (66 Black or African American, non-Hispanic/Latino; 17 Asian, non-Hispanic/Latino; 18 Hispanic/Latino; 11 Two or more races, non-Hispanic/Latino), 18 international. 300 applicants, 55% accepted, 99 enrolled. In 2016, 93 master's awarded. Terminal master's awarded for partial completion of doctoral program. *Degree requirements:* For master's, thesis or alternative. *Entrance requirements:* Additional exam requirements/recommendations for international students: Required—TOEFL (minimum score 550 paper-based; 79 iBT). *Application deadline:* For fall admission, 4/1 for domestic students, 12/15 for international students; for spring admission, 10/1 for domestic students, 8/1 for international students. Application fee: $60. Electronic applications accepted. *Expenses:* Contact institution. *Financial support:* Fellowships, research assistantships, and teaching assistantships available. Financial award application deadline: 1/15; financial award applicants required to submit FAFSA. *Faculty research:* Workforce development, vocational education, technical education, industrial education, professional development, literacy, classroom management, school communities, curriculum development, instruction, applied linguistics, cross linguistic influence, bilingual education, oral proficiency, multilingualism. *Unit head:* Dr. Christine Woyshner, Chairperson, 215-204-6387, E-mail: christine.woyshner@temple.edu. *Application contact:* Sarah Stapleton, Assistant Director, Academic Operations, 215-204-8220, E-mail: sarah.stapleton@temple.edu.
Website: http://education.temple.edu/tl

Texas A&M University–Commerce, College of Humanities, Social Sciences and Arts, Commerce, TX 75429-3011. Offers applied criminology (MS); applied linguistics (MA, MS); art (MA, MFA); Christianity in history (Graduate Certificate); computational linguistics (Graduate Certificate); creative writing (Graduate Certificate); English (MA, MS, PhD); film studies (Graduate Certificate); history (MA, MS); music (MM); political science (MA, MS); public history (Graduate Certificate); sociology (MS); Spanish (MA); studies in children's and adolescent literature and culture (Graduate Certificate); teaching English to speakers of other languages (Graduate Certificate); theater (MA, MS). *Program availability:* Part-time. *Faculty:* 53 full-time (26 women), 7 part-time/adjunct (2 women). *Students:* 87 full-time (55 women), 528 part-time (362 women); includes 198 minority (86 Black or African American, non-Hispanic/Latino; 2 American Indian or Alaska Native, non-Hispanic/Latino; 8 Asian, non-Hispanic/Latino; 84 Hispanic/Latino; 18 Two or more races, non-Hispanic/Latino), 27 international. Average age 37. 333 applicants, 56% accepted, 149 enrolled. In 2016, 66 master's, 8 doctorates awarded. *Degree requirements:* For master's, one foreign language, comprehensive exam, thesis (for some programs); for doctorate, one foreign language, comprehensive exam, thesis/dissertation, departmental qualifying exam. *Entrance requirements:* For master's and doctorate, GRE General Test. Additional exam requirements/recommendations for international students: Required—TOEFL (minimum score 550 paper-based; 79 iBT), IELTS (minimum score 6). *Application deadline:* Applications are processed on a rolling basis. Application fee: $50. Electronic applications accepted. *Expenses:* Contact institution. *Financial support:* In 2016–17, 255 students received support, including 9 research assistantships with partial tuition reimbursements available (averaging $9,000 per year), 68 teaching assistantships with partial tuition reimbursements available (averaging $9,000 per year); Federal Work-Study, institutionally sponsored loans, scholarships/grants, health care benefits, and unspecified assistantships also available. Financial award application deadline: 5/1; financial award applicants required to submit FAFSA. *Unit head:* Dr. Salvatore Attardo, Dean, 903-886-5166, Fax: 903-886-5774, E-mail: salvatore.attardo@tamuc.edu. *Application contact:* Shelby Miller, Graduate Recruiter, 903-468-8123, Fax: 903-886-5774, E-mail: shelby.miller@tamuc.edu.
Website: http://www.tamuc.edu/academics/graduateSchool/programs/humanitiesSocialScienceArts/default.aspx

Texas A&M University–Kingsville, College of Graduate Studies, College of Education and Human Performance, Department of Teacher and Bilingual Education, Program in Bilingual Education, Kingsville, TX 78363. Offers M Ed, Ed D. *Degree requirements:* For master's, comprehensive exam. *Entrance requirements:* For master's, GRE General Test, MAT, minimum GPA of 3.0.

Touro College, Graduate School of Education, New York, NY 10010. Offers education and special education (MS); education biology (MS); instructional technology (MS); mathematics education (MS); school leadership (MS); teaching English to speakers of other languages (MS); teaching literacy (MS). *Accreditation:* TEAC. *Program availability:* Part-time, evening/weekend, online learning. *Faculty:* 52 full-time (34 women), 199 part-time/adjunct (136 women). *Students:* 578 full-time (483 women), 1,932 part-time (1,626 women); includes 749 minority (318 Black or African American, non-Hispanic/Latino; 5 American Indian or Alaska Native, non-Hispanic/Latino; 108 Asian, non-Hispanic/Latino; 288 Hispanic/Latino; 2 Native Hawaiian or other Pacific Islander, non-Hispanic/Latino; 28 Two or more races, non-Hispanic/Latino), 17 international. Average age 32. 1,422 applicants, 50% accepted, 675 enrolled. In 2016, 6 master's awarded. *Entrance requirements:* Additional exam requirements/recommendations for international students: Required—TOEFL (minimum score 83 iBT), IELTS (minimum score 6.5). *Application deadline:* For fall admission, 8/26 for domestic students, 7/15 for international students; for spring admission, 12/31 for domestic students, 12/15 for international students. Applications are processed on a rolling basis. Application fee: $50. *Financial support:* Federal Work-Study available. Financial award applicants required to submit FAFSA. *Faculty research:* Equity assistance, language development, scholarly communications, Latin American studies and cultural sensitivity, behavior management techniques and strategies in special education. *Unit head:* Dr. Arnold Spinner, Dean, 212-463-0400 Ext. 5561, Fax: 212-462-4889, E-mail: aspinner@touro.edu. *Application contact:* Luna Feliciano, Admissions, 212-463-0400.

Trevecca Nazarene University, Graduate Education Program, Nashville, TN 37210-2877. Offers accountability and instructional leadership (Ed S); curriculum and instruction for Christian school educators (M Ed); curriculum and instruction K-12 (M Ed); educational leadership (M Ed); English second language (M Ed); library and information science (MLI Sc); special education: visual impairments (M Ed); teaching (MAT), including teaching 6-12, teaching K-5. *Accreditation:* NCATE. *Program availability:* Part-time, evening/weekend, online learning. *Faculty:* 5 full-time (3 women), 18 part-time/adjunct (12 women). *Students:* 80 full-time (64 women), 16 part-time (13 women); includes 19 minority (17 Black or African American, non-Hispanic/Latino; 2 Hispanic/Latino). Average age 35. In 2016, 68 master's, 7 other advanced degrees awarded. *Degree requirements:* For master's, comprehensive exam, exit assessment/e-portfolio. *Entrance requirements:* For master's, GRE (minimum score of 290) or MAT (minimum score of 378); PRAXIS (for MAT), minimum GPA of 3.0, official transcript from regionally-accredited institution, at least 3 years' successful teaching experience (for M Ed in educational leadership major). Additional exam requirements/recommendations for international students: Required—TOEFL (minimum score 550 paper-based). *Application deadline:* Applications are processed on a rolling basis. Electronic applications accepted. *Expenses:* Contact institution. *Financial support:* Applicants required to submit FAFSA. *Unit head:* Dr. Suzie Harris, Dean, School of Education/Director of Graduate Education Programs, 615-248-1201, Fax: 615-248-1597, E-mail: admissions_ged@trevecca.edu. *Application contact:* 844-TNU-GRAD, E-mail: sgcsadmissions@trevecca.edu.
Website: http://www.trevecca.edu/soe

Trinity Western University, School of Graduate Studies, Program in Teaching English to Speakers of Other Languages (TESOL), Langley, BC V2Y 1Y1, Canada. Offers MA. *Program availability:* Part-time, online learning. *Degree requirements:* For master's, project. *Entrance requirements:* For master's, minimum GPA of 3.0. Additional exam requirements/recommendations for international students: Required—TOEFL (minimum score 600 paper-based). *Faculty research:* ESL methodology, second language acquisition, computer assisted language learning.

Troy University, Graduate School, College of Education, Program in Second Language Instruction, Troy, AL 36082. Offers MS. *Program availability:* Part-time, evening/weekend. *Faculty:* 2 full-time (both women), 1 (woman) part-time/adjunct. *Students:* 10 full-time (9 women), 7 part-time (5 women); includes 4 minority (2 Black or African American, non-Hispanic/Latino; 1 Asian, non-Hispanic/Latino; 1 Hispanic/Latino). Average age 26. 16 applicants, 94% accepted. In 2016, 2 master's awarded. *Degree requirements:* For master's, thesis or capstone. *Entrance requirements:* For master's, GRE (minimum score of 850 on old exam or 290 on new exam), GMAT (minimum score of 380), or MAT (minimum score of 385), bachelor's degree; minimum undergraduate GPA of 2.5 or 3.0 on last 30 semester hours; letters of recommendation. Additional exam requirements/recommendations for international students: Required—TOEFL (minimum score 523 paper-based; 70 iBT), IELTS (minimum score 6). *Application deadline:* Applications are processed on a rolling basis. Application fee: $50. Electronic applications accepted. *Expenses:* Tuition, state resident: full-time $7146; part-time $397 per credit hour. Tuition, nonresident: full-time $14,292; part-time $794 per credit hour. *Required fees:* $802; $50 per semester. Tuition and fees vary according to campus/location and program. *Financial support:* Fellowships, career-related internships or fieldwork, and scholarships/grants available. Support available to part-time students. Financial award applicants required to submit FAFSA. *Unit head:* Dr. Jan Oliver, Chair, Leadership Development and Professional Studies, 334-670-3546, Fax: 334-808-6666, E-mail: oliverj@troy.edu. *Application contact:* Jessica A. Kimbro, Director of Graduate Admissions, 334-670-3178, E-mail: jacord@troy.edu.

Universidad del Este, Graduate School, Carolina, PR 00984. Offers accounting (MBA); adult education (M Ed); agribusiness (MBA); criminal justice and criminology (MA); curriculum and instruction - early education (M Ed); curriculum and instruction - elementary (M Ed); curriculum and instruction - English (M Ed); curriculum and instruction - Spanish (M Ed); human resources (MBA); information security management (MBA); information technology and Web business development (MBA); management (MBA); public policy (MPA); social work (MA), including clinical social work; special education (M Ed); strategic leadership (MBA).

Universidad del Turabo, Graduate Programs, Programs in Education, Program in Teaching English as a Second Language, Gurabo, PR 00778-3030. Offers M Ed. *Students:* 34 full-time (27 women), 34 part-time (26 women); all minorities (all Hispanic/Latino). Average age 37. 49 applicants, 51% accepted, 19 enrolled. In 2016, 29 master's awarded. *Entrance requirements:* For master's, GRE, EXADEP, GMAT, interview, official transcript, essay, recommendation letters. *Application deadline:* For fall admission, 8/5 for domestic students. Applications are processed on a rolling basis. Application fee: $25. Electronic applications accepted. *Financial support:* Institutionally sponsored loans available. Financial award applicants required to submit FAFSA. *Unit head:* Israel Rodríguez, Dean, 787-743-7979. *Application contact:* Diree Rodríguez, Admissions Director, 787-743-7979 Ext. 4453, E-mail: admisiones-ut@suagm.edu.
Website: http://ut.suagm.edu/es/educacion

University at Buffalo, the State University of New York, Graduate School, Graduate School of Education, Department of Learning and Instruction, Buffalo, NY 14260. Offers biology education (Ed M, Certificate); chemistry education (Ed M, Certificate); childhood education (Ed M); childhood education with bilingual extension (Ed M); college teaching (Advanced Certificate); curriculum, instruction and the science of learning (PhD); early childhood education (Ed M); early childhood education with bilingual extension (Ed M); earth science education (Ed M, Certificate); education and technology (Ed M); education studies (Ed M); educational technology and new literacies (Certificate); educational technology and new literacies (Advanced Certificate); elementary education (Ed D); English education (Ed M, Certificate); English education studies (Ed M); English for speakers of other languages (Ed M); foreign and second language education (PhD); French education (Ed M, Certificate); German education (Ed M, Certificate); gifted education (Certificate); Latin education (Ed M, Certificate); literacy education studies (Ed M); literacy specialist (Ed M); literacy teaching and learning (Certificate); mathematics education (Ed M, Certificate); music education (Ed M, Certificate); music education studies (Ed M); music learning theory (Advanced Certificate); online education (Advanced Certificate); physics education (Ed M, Certificate); science and the public (Ed M); social studies education (Ed M, Certificate); Spanish education (Ed M, Certificate); special education (PhD); teaching English to speakers of other languages (Ed M). *Program availability:* Part-time, evening/weekend, 100% online. *Faculty:* 28 full-time (21 women), 67 part-time/adjunct (49 women). *Students:* 198 full-time (153 women), 312 part-time (220 women); includes 48 minority (28 Black or African American, non-Hispanic/Latino; 4 American Indian or Alaska Native, non-Hispanic/Latino; 15 Asian, non-Hispanic/Latino; 1 Hispanic/Latino), 66 international. Average age 33. 336 applicants, 86% accepted, 178 enrolled. In 2016, 137 master's, 24 doctorates, 25 other advanced degrees awarded. *Degree requirements:* For master's, comprehensive exam; for doctorate, thesis/dissertation, research analysis exam, research experience. *Entrance requirements:* For master's, letters of reference; for doctorate, GRE General Test or MAT, interview, writing sample, letters of recommendation. Additional exam requirements/recommendations for international students: Required—TOEFL (minimum score 600 paper-based; 96 iBT). *Application deadline:* For fall admission, 2/1 priority date for domestic and international students; for spring admission, 11/15 priority date for domestic students, 10/1 for international students. Applications are processed on a rolling basis. Application fee: $50. Electronic applications accepted. *Financial support:* In 2016–17, 44 fellowships (averaging $4,010 per year), 39 research assistantships with tuition reimbursements (averaging $9,897 per year) were awarded; teaching assistantships, career-related internships or fieldwork, Federal Work-Study, institutionally sponsored loans, scholarships/grants, tuition waivers (full and partial), and unspecified assistantships also available. Financial award application deadline: 2/28; financial award applicants required to submit FAFSA. *Faculty research:* Science assessment, foreign language teaching and learning, early learning, new literacies, gender and education. *Total annual research expenditures:* $534,880. *Unit head:* Dr. Deborah Moore-Russo, Chair, 716-645-4069, Fax: 716-645-3161, E-mail: dam29@buffalo.edu. *Application contact:* Luann Zak, Admissions Assistant, 716-645-2110, Fax: 716-645-7937, E-mail: luannzak@buffalo.edu.
Website: http://gse.buffalo.edu/lai

The University of Alabama, Graduate School, College of Arts and Sciences, Department of English, Tuscaloosa, AL 35487. Offers composition and rhetoric (PhD); creative writing (MFA), including fiction, poetry; literature (MA, PhD); rhetoric and composition (MA); teaching English as a second language (MATESOL). *Faculty:* 38 full-time (20 women). *Students:* 129 full-time (69 women), 6 part-time (5 women); includes 23 minority (12 Black or African American, non-Hispanic/Latino; 1 Asian, non-Hispanic/Latino; 7 Hispanic/Latino; 3 Two or more races, non-Hispanic/Latino), 3 international. Average age 29. 406 applicants, 13% accepted, 35 enrolled. In 2016, 31 master's, 4 doctorates awarded. *Degree requirements:* For master's, one foreign language, comprehensive exam, thesis optional; for doctorate, 2 foreign languages, comprehensive exam, thesis/dissertation. *Entrance requirements:* For master's, GRE (minimum score of 300, except for MFA), minimum GPA of 3.0, critical writing sample; for doctorate, GRE (minimum score of 300), minimum GPA of 3.5 on master's or equivalent graduate work, critical writing sample. Additional exam requirements/recommendations for international students: Required—TOEFL (minimum score 550 paper-based; 79 iBT). *Application deadline:* For fall admission, 12/31 priority date for domestic and international students. Application fee: $50 ($60 for international students). Electronic applications accepted. *Expenses:* Tuition, state resident: full-time $10,470. Tuition, nonresident: full-time $26,950. *Financial support:* In 2016–17, 128 students received support, including 11 fellowships with full tuition reimbursements available (averaging $15,000 per year), 13 research assistantships with full tuition reimbursements available (averaging $13,500 per year), 100 teaching assistantships with full tuition reimbursements available (averaging $13,500 per year); career-related internships or fieldwork, scholarships/grants, health care benefits, and unspecified assistantships also available. Financial award application deadline: 12/31. *Faculty research:* American literature, British literature, composition/rhetoric, applied linguistics, creative writing. *Unit head:* Prof. Joel Brouwer, Department Chair, 205-348-5065, Fax: 205-348-1388, E-mail: joel.brouwer@ua.edu. *Application contact:* Jennifer Fuqua, Graduate Coordinator, 205-348-0766, Fax: 205-348-1388, E-mail: jfuqua@ua.edu.

The University of Alabama at Birmingham, School of Education, Program in English as a Second Language, Birmingham, AL 35294-1250. Offers MA Ed, Ed S. *Program availability:* Part-time, evening/weekend. *Degree requirements:* For master's, variable foreign language requirement, comprehensive exam. *Entrance requirements:* For master's, MAT (minimum score of 388 scaled, 35 raw) or GRE (minimum 290 on current test). Additional exam requirements/recommendations for international students: Required—TOEFL, IELTS. Electronic applications accepted. *Expenses:* Contact institution. *Faculty research:* How mainstream teachers learn to implement ESL best practices and how they help their colleagues through collaborative mentoring; language use, identity, and the relationship between school and community empowering K- 12 administrators to become EL advocates; oral English proficiency of non-native English speakers pursuing graduate degrees in education and factors related to their identity and perceptions of self-efficacy as teachers.

The University of Alabama in Huntsville, School of Graduate Studies, College of Arts, Humanities, and Social Sciences, Department of English, Huntsville, AL 35899. Offers education (MA); English (MA); technical writing (Certificate); TESOL (Certificate). *Program availability:* Part-time, evening/weekend. *Degree requirements:* For master's, one foreign language, comprehensive exam, thesis or alternative, oral and written exams. *Entrance requirements:* For master's and Certificate, GRE General Test, minimum GPA of 3.0. Additional exam requirements/recommendations for international students: Required—TOEFL (minimum score 500 paper-based; 80 iBT), IELTS (minimum score 6.5). Electronic applications accepted. *Expenses:* Tuition, state resident: full-time $9834; part-time $600 per credit hour. Tuition, nonresident: full-time $21,830; part-time $1325 per credit hour. *Faculty research:* Fiction and identity, Shakespeare, science fiction, eighteenth-century literature, technical writing.

The University of Alabama in Huntsville, School of Graduate Studies, College of Education, Huntsville, AL 35899. Offers autism spectrum disorders (M Ed, Graduate Certificate); biology (MAT); chemistry (MAT); differentiated instruction in elementary education (M Ed); English language arts (MAT); English speakers of other languages (M Ed, MAT); history (MAT); mathematics (MAT); physics (MAT); reading education (M Ed); secondary education (M Ed). *Expenses:* Tuition, state resident: full-time $9834; part-time $600 per credit hour. Tuition, nonresident: full-time $21,830; part-time $1325 per credit hour.

University of Alberta, Faculty of Graduate Studies and Research, Department of Educational Psychology, Edmonton, AB T6G 2E1, Canada. Offers counseling psychology (M Ed, PhD); educational psychology (M Ed, PhD); instructional technology (M Ed); school counseling (M Ed); school psychology (M Ed, PhD); special education (M Ed, PhD); special education-deafness studies (M Ed); teaching English as a second language (M Ed). *Program availability:* Part-time. *Degree requirements:* For master's, thesis optional; for doctorate, comprehensive exam, thesis/dissertation. *Entrance requirements:* For master's and doctorate, minimum GPA of 3.0. Additional exam requirements/recommendations for international students: Required—TOEFL. *Faculty research:* Human learning, development and assessment.

The University of Arizona, College of Humanities, Department of English, English Language/Linguistics Program, Tucson, AZ 85721. Offers English (MA, PhD); ESL (MA). *Entrance requirements:* Additional exam requirements/recommendations for international students: Required—TOEFL (minimum score 550 paper-based; 79 iBT); Recommended—IELTS (minimum score 7). Electronic applications accepted.

The University of Arizona, Graduate Interdisciplinary Programs, Graduate Interdisciplinary Program in Second Language Acquisition and Teaching, Tucson, AZ 85721. Offers PhD. *Degree requirements:* For doctorate, one foreign language, comprehensive exam, thesis/dissertation. *Entrance requirements:* For doctorate, GRE, 3 letters of recommendation, writing sample. Additional exam requirements/recommendations for international students: Required—TOEFL (minimum score 550 paper-based; 79 iBT); Recommended—TWE. Electronic applications accepted.

University of Arkansas at Little Rock, Graduate School, College of Arts, Letters, and Sciences, Department of International and Second Language Studies, Little Rock, AR 72204-1099. Offers second languages (MA). *Degree requirements:* For master's, comprehensive exam, thesis. *Entrance requirements:* For master's, GRE or MAT, bachelor's degree; 3 letters of reference; personal interview; minimum overall undergraduate GPA of 2.75, 3.0 in last 60 hours.

The University of British Columbia, Faculty of Education, Department of Language and Literacy Education, Vancouver, BC V6T 1Z2, Canada. Offers literacy education (M Ed, MA, PhD); modern languages education (M Ed, MA); teaching English as a second language (M Ed, MA, PhD). *Program availability:* Part-time, evening/weekend. *Degree requirements:* For master's, thesis (MA); for doctorate, thesis/dissertation. *Entrance requirements:* For master's and doctorate, minimum B+ average in last 2 years with minimum 2 courses at A standing. Additional exam requirements/recommendations for international students: Required—TOEFL, TWE. *Application deadline:* Applications are processed on a rolling basis. Application fee: $100 Canadian dollars ($162 Canadian dollars for international students). Electronic applications accepted. *Expenses:* $6,865 per year tuition and fees domestic, $10,938 per year international (for MA and M Ed); $4,802 per year tuition and fees, $8,436 per year international (for PhD). *Financial support:* Fellowships with partial tuition reimbursements, research assistantships, teaching assistantships, institutionally sponsored loans, scholarships/grants, tuition waivers (full and partial), and unspecified assistantships available. *Faculty research:* Language and literacy development, second language acquisition, Asia Pacific language curriculum, children's literature, whole language instruction. *Application contact:* Christopher Fernandez, Graduate Program Staff, 604-822-8259, Fax: 604-822-3154, E-mail: lled.educ@ubc.ca.
Website: http://www.lled.educ.ubc.ca/

University of California, Berkeley, UC Berkeley Extension, Certificate Programs in Education, Berkeley, CA 94720-1500. Offers college admissions and career planning (Certificate); teaching English as a second language (Certificate).

University of California, Los Angeles, Graduate Division, College of Letters and Science, Department of Applied Linguistics and Teaching English as a Second Language, Los Angeles, CA 90095. Offers applied linguistics (PhD); applied linguistics and teaching English as a second language (MA); teaching English as a second language (Certificate). *Degree requirements:* For master's, one foreign language, thesis; for doctorate, one foreign language, thesis/dissertation, oral and written qualifying exams. *Entrance requirements:* For master's and doctorate, bachelor's degree; minimum undergraduate GPA of 3.0 (or its equivalent if letter grade system not used). Additional exam requirements/recommendations for international students: Required—TOEFL. Electronic applications accepted.

University of California, Riverside, Graduate Division, Graduate School of Education, Riverside, CA 92521-0102. Offers autism (M Ed); diversity and equity (M Ed); education specialist (Credential); education, society, and culture (MA, PhD); educational psychology (MA, PhD); general education (M Ed); higher education administration and policy (M Ed, PhD); multiple subject (Credential); reading (M Ed); school psychology (PhD); single subject (Credential); special education (M Ed, MA, PhD); TESOL (M Ed). Terminal master's awarded for partial completion of doctoral program. *Degree requirements:* For master's, thesis optional, comprehensive exams or thesis (MA), case study or analytical report (M Ed); for doctorate, thesis/dissertation, written and oral qualifying exams, college teaching practicum. *Entrance requirements:* For master's, GRE General Test (for MA); CBEST and CSET (for M Ed in general education only), UCR Extension TESOL certificate (for M Ed with TESOL emphasis only); for doctorate, GRE General Test, writing sample; for Credential, CBEST, CSET. Additional exam requirements/recommendations for international students: Required—TOEFL (minimum score 550 paper-based; 80 iBT), IELTS (minimum score 7). Electronic applications accepted. *Expenses:* Tuition, state resident: full-time $16,666. Tuition, nonresident: full-time $31,768. *Required fees:* $11,055.54 per quarter. $3685.18 per quarter. Tuition and fees vary according to campus/location and program. *Faculty research:* Responsiveness to intervention, faculty core, response to intervention of English language learners, advanced modeling techniques, study on social capital, trust, and motivation.

University of Central Florida, College of Arts and Humanities, Department of Modern Languages and Literatures, Program in Teaching English to Speakers of Other Languages, Orlando, FL 32816. Offers ESOL endorsement K-12 (Certificate); teaching English as a foreign language (Certificate); teaching English to speakers of other languages (MA). *Accreditation:* NCATE. *Program availability:* Part-time, evening/weekend. *Students:* 19 full-time (10 women), 28 part-time (18 women); includes 12 minority (1 Black or African American, non-Hispanic/Latino; 11 Hispanic/Latino), 7 international. Average age 34. 43 applicants, 79% accepted, 18 enrolled. In 2016, 17 master's, 20 other advanced degrees awarded. *Degree requirements:* For master's, comprehensive exam, thesis or alternative. *Entrance requirements:* For master's, GRE General Test, minimum GPA of 3.0 in last 60 hours. Additional exam requirements/recommendations for international students: Required—TOEFL. *Application deadline:* For fall admission, 7/1 for domestic students; for spring admission, 12/1 for domestic students. Application fee: $30. Electronic applications accepted. *Expenses:* Tuition, state resident: part-time $288.16 per credit hour. Tuition, nonresident: part-time $1071.31 per credit hour. *Financial support:* In 2016–17, 5 students received support, including 3 fellowships (averaging $2,333 per year), 3 teaching assistantships with partial tuition reimbursements available (averaging $9,088 per year); career-related internships or fieldwork, Federal Work-Study, institutionally sponsored loans, tuition waivers (partial), and unspecified assistantships also available. Financial award application deadline: 3/1; financial award applicants required to submit FAFSA. *Unit head:* Dr. Keith Folse, Director, 407-823-0087, E-mail: keith.folse@ucf.edu. *Application contact:* Assistant Director, Graduate Admissions, 407-823-2766, Fax: 407-823-6442, E-mail: gradadmissions@ucf.edu.
Website: http://mll.cah.ucf.edu/graduate/index.php#TESOL

University of Central Florida, College of Education and Human Performance, Education Doctoral Programs, Orlando, FL 32816. Offers communication sciences and disorders (PhD); curriculum and instruction (Ed D); early childhood education (PhD); educational leadership (Ed D); elementary education (PhD); exceptional education (PhD); exercise physiology (PhD); higher education (PhD); instructional technology (PhD); mathematics education (PhD); methodology, measurement and analysis (PhD); reading education (PhD); science education (PhD); social science education (PhD); TESOL (PhD). *Students:* 127 full-time (91 women), 43 part-time (29 women); includes 33 minority (17 Black or African American, non-Hispanic/Latino; 5 Asian, non-Hispanic/Latino; 7 Hispanic/Latino; 4 Two or more races, non-Hispanic/Latino), 26 international. Average age 37. 163 applicants, 40% accepted, 52 enrolled. In 2016, 57 doctorates awarded. Application fee: $30. Electronic applications accepted. *Expenses:* Tuition, state resident: part-time $288.16 per credit hour. Tuition, nonresident: part-time $1071.31 per credit hour. *Financial support:* In 2016–17, 78 students received support, including 41 fellowships with partial tuition reimbursements available (averaging $5,916 per year), 44 research assistantships with partial tuition reimbursements available (averaging $7,637 per year), 48 teaching assistantships with partial tuition reimbursements available (averaging $9,633 per year). Financial award application deadline: 3/1; financial award applicants required to submit FAFSA. *Unit head:* Dr. Edward Robinson, Director of Doctoral Programs, 407-823-6106, E-mail: edward.robinson@ucf.edu. *Application contact:* Assistant Director, Graduate Admissions, 407-823-2766, Fax: 407-823-6442, E-mail: gradadmissions@ucf.edu.
Website: http://education.ucf.edu/programs.cfm?pid=g&cat=2

University of Central Missouri, The Graduate School, Warrensburg, MO 64093. Offers accountancy (MA); accounting (MBA); applied mathematics (MS); aviation safety (MA); biology (MS); business administration (MBA); career and technical education leadership (MS); college student personnel administration (MS); communication (MA); computer science (MS); counseling (MS); criminal justice (MS); educational leadership (Ed D); educational technology (MS); elementary and early childhood education (MSE); English (MA); environmental studies (MA); finance (MBA); history (MA); human services/educational technology (Ed S); human services/learning resources (Ed S); human services/professional counseling (Ed S); industrial hygiene (MS); industrial management (MS); information systems (MBA); information technology (MS); kinesiology (MS); library science and information services (MS); literacy education (MSE); marketing (MBA); mathematics (MS); music (MA); occupational safety management (MS); psychology (MS); rural family nursing (MS); school administration (MSE); social gerontology (MS); sociology (MA); special education (MSE); speech language pathology (MS); superintendency (Ed S); teaching (MAT); teaching English as a second language (MA); technology (MS); technology management (PhD); theatre (MA). *Program availability:* Part-time, 100% online, blended/hybrid learning. *Degree requirements:* For master's and Ed S, comprehensive exam (for some programs), thesis (for some programs). *Entrance requirements:* Additional exam requirements/recommendations for international students: Required—TOEFL (minimum score 550 paper-based; 79 iBT). Electronic applications accepted.

University of Central Oklahoma, The Jackson College of Graduate Studies, College of Education and Professional Studies, Department of Curriculum and Instruction, Edmond, OK 73034-5209. Offers bilingual education/teaching English as a second language (M Ed); early childhood education (M Ed); elementary education (M Ed). *Program availability:* Part-time. *Degree requirements:* For master's, comprehensive exam (for some programs), thesis optional. *Entrance requirements:* For master's, GRE General Test. Additional exam requirements/recommendations for international students: Required—TOEFL (minimum score 550 paper-based; 79 iBT), IELTS (minimum score 6.5). Electronic applications accepted. *Faculty research:* Tourette's syndrome, bilingual education, science education, language development/disorders.

University of Cincinnati, Graduate School, College of Education, Criminal Justice, and Human Services, Division of Teacher Education, Cincinnati, OH 45221. Offers curriculum and instruction (M Ed, Ed D); deaf studies (Certificate); early childhood education (M Ed); middle childhood education (M Ed); postsecondary literacy instruction (Certificate); reading/literacy (M Ed, Ed D); secondary education (M Ed); special education (M Ed, Ed D); teaching English as a second language (Ed D, Certificate); teaching science (MS). *Program availability:* Part-time. *Degree requirements:* For doctorate, thesis/dissertation. *Entrance requirements:* For master's, GRE General Test. Additional exam requirements/recommendations for international students: Required—TOEFL (minimum score 550 paper-based). Electronic applications accepted. *Expenses: Tuition, area resident:* Full-time $12,790; part-time $389 per credit hour. Tuition, state resident: full-time $13,290; part-time $419 per credit hour. Tuition, nonresident: full-time $24,532; part-time $976 per credit hour. *International tuition:* $24,832 full-time. *Required fees:* $3958; $140 per credit hour. Tuition and fees vary according to course load, degree level, program and reciprocity agreements.

University of Colorado Colorado Springs, College of Education, Colorado Springs, CO 80918. Offers counseling and human services (MA); curriculum and instruction (MA); educational leadership (MA); educational leadership, research and policy (PhD); special education (MA); teaching English to speakers of other languages (MA). *Accreditation:* ACA; NCATE. *Program availability:* Part-time, evening/weekend, 100% online, blended/hybrid learning. *Faculty:* 26 full-time (18 women), 33 part-time/adjunct (21 women). *Students:* 136 full-time (94 women), 264 part-time (177 women); includes 99 minority (17 Black or African American, non-Hispanic/Latino; 1 American Indian or Alaska Native, non-Hispanic/Latino; 8 Asian, non-Hispanic/Latino; 55 Hispanic/Latino; 18 Two or more races, non-Hispanic/Latino), 9 international. Average age 35. 152 applicants, 89% accepted, 88 enrolled. In 2016, 161 master's, 11 doctorates awarded. *Degree requirements:* For master's, comprehensive exam, thesis or alternative, microcomputer proficiency; for doctorate, comprehensive exam, thesis/dissertation, research lab. *Entrance requirements:* For master's and doctorate, GRE General Test. Additional exam requirements/recommendations for international students: Recommended—TOEFL (minimum score 550 paper-based; 80 iBT), IELTS (minimum score 6). *Application deadline:* For fall admission, 2/1 priority date for domestic students, 2/1 for international students; for spring admission, 10/15 for domestic students, 10/1 for international students. Applications are processed on a rolling basis. Application fee: $60 ($100 for international students). Electronic applications accepted. *Expenses:* Contact institution. *Financial support:* In 2016–17, 108 students received support. Career-related internships or fieldwork, Federal Work-Study, scholarships/grants, and unspecified assistantships available. Support available to part-time students. Financial award application deadline: 3/1; financial award applicants required to submit FAFSA. *Faculty research:* Linguistically diverse education (LDE), educational policy, evidence-based reading and writing instruction, relational and social aggression, positive behavior supports, inclusive schooling, K-12 education policy. *Total annual research expenditures:* $272,136. *Unit head:* Dr. Valerie Martin Conley, Dean, 719-255-4133, E-mail: vmconley@uccs.edu. *Application contact:* The College of Education Student Resource Office, 719-255-4996, E-mail: education@uccs.edu.
Website: http://www.uccs.edu/coe

University of Dayton, Department of English, Dayton, OH 45469. Offers literary and cultural studies (MA); teaching English to speakers of other languages (TESOL) (MA); writing and rhetoric (MA). *Program availability:* Part-time. *Faculty:* 22 full-time (11 women). *Students:* 15 full-time (10 women), 2 part-time (1 woman); includes 1 minority (Black or African American, non-Hispanic/Latino), 7 international. Average age 27. 55 applicants, 29% accepted. In 2016, 8 master's awarded. *Degree requirements:* For master's, thesis. *Entrance requirements:* For master's, 24 undergraduate-level semester hours in literature and/or writing; minimum GPA of 3.0; transcripts; personal statement; 8-10 page writing sample; three professional letters of recommendation. Additional exam requirements/recommendations for international students: Required—TOEFL (minimum score 550 paper-based, 80 iBT) or IELTS. *Application deadline:* For fall admission, 6/15 priority date for domestic and international students; for spring admission, 12/15 priority date for domestic and international students. Applications are processed on a rolling basis. Application fee: $0 ($50 for international students). Electronic applications accepted. *Expenses:* $890 per credit hour, $25 registration fee. *Financial support:* In 2016–17, 9 teaching assistantships with full tuition reimbursements (averaging $11,000 per year) were awarded; institutionally sponsored loans and health care benefits also available. Financial award application deadline: 12/15; financial award applicants required to submit FAFSA. *Faculty research:* Gender and Victorian periodicals; literature and human rights; Paul Lawrence Dunbar; the archetype of the Indian princess; Amish country. *Total annual research expenditures:* $35,000. *Unit head:* Dr. Andrew Slade, Chair, 937-229-3434, Fax: 937-229-3563, E-mail: aslade1@udayton.edu. *Application contact:* Dr. Tereza Szeghi, Director of Graduate Studies, 937-229-3443, E-mail: tszeghi1@udayton.edu.
Website: https://www.udayton.edu/artssciences/academics/english/welcome/index.php

University of Delaware, College of Education and Human Development, School of Education, Newark, DE 19716. Offers education (PhD); educational leadership (Ed D); higher education (M Ed); instruction (MI); reading (M Ed); school leadership (M Ed); school psychology (MA, Ed S); teaching English as a second language (TESL) (MA). *Accreditation:* NCATE. *Program availability:* Part-time, evening/weekend. Terminal master's awarded for partial completion of doctoral program. *Degree requirements:* For master's, comprehensive exam (for some programs), thesis (for some programs); for doctorate, comprehensive exam (for some programs), thesis/dissertation. *Entrance requirements:* For master's and doctorate, GRE, 3 letters of recommendation. Additional exam requirements/recommendations for international students: Required—TOEFL (minimum score 600 paper-based). Electronic applications accepted. *Faculty research:* Teacher education; curriculum theory and development; community based education models, educational leadership.

The University of Findlay, Office of Graduate Admissions, Findlay, OH 45840-3653. Offers applied security and analytics (MSAS); athletic training (MAT); business (MBA), including certified management accountant, certified public accountant, health care management, hospitality management; education (MA Ed, Ed D), including children's literature (MA Ed), curriculum and teaching (MA Ed), education (MA Ed), educational administration (MA Ed), human resource development (MA Ed), reading (MA Ed), science education (MA Ed), superintendent (Ed D), teaching (Ed D), technology (MA Ed); environmental, safety and health management (MSEM); health informatics (MS); occupational therapy (MOT); pharmacy (Pharm D); physical therapy (DPT); physician assistant (MPA); rhetoric and writing (MA); teaching English to speakers of other languages (TESOL) and bilingual education (MA). *Program availability:* Part-time, evening/weekend, 100% online, blended/hybrid learning. *Faculty:* 114 full-time (63 women), 44 part-time/adjunct (18 women). *Students:* 751 full-time (452 women), 573 part-time (323 women); includes 164 minority (82 Black or African American, non-Hispanic/Latino; 1 American Indian or Alaska Native, non-Hispanic/Latino; 27 Asian, non-Hispanic/Latino; 37 Hispanic/Latino; 17 Two or more races, non-Hispanic/Latino), 280 international. Average age 28. 661 applicants, 52% accepted, 288 enrolled. In 2016, 366 master's, 137 doctorates awarded. *Degree requirements:* For master's, comprehensive exam (for some programs), thesis, cumulative project, capstone project; for doctorate, thesis/dissertation. *Entrance requirements:* For master's, GRE (for some programs), bachelor's degree from accredited institution, minimum undergraduate GPA of 3.0 in last 64 hours of course work; for doctorate, MAT, minimum cumulative GPA of 3.0, master's degree. Additional exam requirements/recommendations for international students: Recommended—TOEFL (minimum score 79 iBT), IELTS (minimum score 7). *Application deadline:* For fall admission, 6/15 for international students; for spring admission, 12/1 for international students; for summer admission, 4/1 for international students. Applications are processed on a rolling basis. Electronic applications accepted. *Expenses:* Contact institution. *Financial support:* In 2016–17, 139 students received support, including 15 research assistantships with partial tuition reimbursements available (averaging $7,200 per year), 25 teaching assistantships with partial tuition reimbursements available (averaging $7,200 per year); Federal Work-Study, institutionally sponsored loans, and unspecified assistantships also available. Financial award application deadline: 4/1; financial award applicants required to submit FAFSA. *Unit head:* Christopher M. Harris, Director of Admissions, 419-434-4347, E-mail: harrisc1@findlay.edu. *Application contact:* Madeline Fauser Brennan, Graduate Admissions Counselor, 419-434-4636, Fax: 419-434-4898, E-mail: fauserbrennan@findlay.edu.
Website: http://www.findlay.edu/admissions/graduate/Pages/default.aspx

University of Florida, Graduate School, College of Liberal Arts and Sciences, Department of Linguistics, Gainesville, FL 32611. Offers linguistics (MA, PhD); teaching English as a second language (Certificate). *Program availability:* Part-time. Terminal master's awarded for partial completion of doctoral program. *Degree requirements:* For master's, one foreign language, comprehensive exam, thesis (for some programs); for doctorate, 2 foreign languages, comprehensive exam, thesis/dissertation. *Entrance requirements:* For master's and doctorate, GRE General Test, minimum GPA of 3.0. Additional exam requirements/recommendations for international students: Required—TOEFL (minimum score 550 paper-based, 80 iBT), IELTS (minimum score 6). Electronic applications accepted. *Faculty research:* Language documentation, psycholinguistics and neuro-linguistics, theoretical linguistics, sociolinguistics second language acquisition.

University of Guam, Office of Graduate Studies, School of Education, Program in Teaching English to Speakers of Other Languages, Mangilao, GU 96923. Offers M Ed. *Degree requirements:* For master's, comprehensive oral and written exams, special project or thesis. *Entrance requirements:* For master's, GRE General Test. Additional exam requirements/recommendations for international students: Required—TOEFL.

University of Hawaii at Manoa, Graduate Division, College of Languages, Linguistics and Literature, Department of Second Language Studies, Honolulu, HI 96822. Offers English as a second language (MA, Graduate Certificate); second language acquisition (PhD). *Program availability:* Part-time. *Degree requirements:* For master's, 2 foreign languages, thesis optional; for doctorate, 2 foreign languages, comprehensive exam, thesis/dissertation. *Entrance requirements:* For master's, GRE General Test, minimum GPA of 3.0; for doctorate, GRE General Test, MA, scholarly publications. Additional exam requirements/recommendations for international students: Required—TOEFL (minimum score 600 paper-based; 100 iBT), IELTS (minimum score 7). *Faculty research:* Second language use, second language analysis, second language pedagogy and testing, second language learning, qualitative and quantitative research methods for second languages.

University of Idaho, College of Graduate Studies, College of Letters, Arts and Social Sciences, Department of English, Moscow, ID 83844. Offers creative writing (MFA); English (MA, MAT); teaching English as a second language (MA). *Faculty:* 14 full-time (7 women). *Students:* 53 full-time, 10 part-time. Average age 31. In 2016, 40 master's awarded. *Entrance requirements:* For master's, minimum GPA of 3.0. Additional exam requirements/recommendations for international students: Required—TOEFL. *Application deadline:* For fall admission, 8/1 for domestic students; for spring admission, 12/15 for domestic students. Applications are processed on a rolling basis. Application fee: $60. Electronic applications accepted. *Expenses:* Tuition, state resident: full-time $6460; part-time $414 per credit hour. Tuition, nonresident: full-time $21,268; part-time $1237 per credit hour. *Required fees:* $2070; $60 per credit hour. Full-time tuition and fees vary according to course load and reciprocity agreements. *Financial support:* Research assistantships and teaching assistantships available. Financial award applicants required to submit FAFSA. *Unit head:* Dr. Scott Slovic, Chair, 208-885-6156, E-mail: englishdept@uidaho.edu. *Application contact:* Sean Scoggin, Graduate Recruitment Coordinator, 208-885-4723, Fax: 208-885-4406, E-mail: graduateadmissions@uidaho.edu.
Website: https://www.uidaho.edu/class/english

University of Illinois at Chicago, College of Liberal Arts and Sciences, School of Literatures, Cultural Studies and Linguistics, Chicago, IL 60607-7128. Offers French and Francophone studies (MA); Germanic studies (MA); Hispanic and Italian studies (MAT, PhD), including Hispanic linguistics (PhD), Hispanic literary and cultural studies (PhD), teaching of Spanish (MAT); linguistics (MA), including teaching English to speakers of other languages/applied linguistics; Slavic and Baltic languages and literatures (MA), including Slavic studies (MA, PhD); Slavic and Baltic languages and literatures (PhD), including Slavic studies (MA, PhD). *Program availability:* Part-time. Terminal master's awarded for partial completion of doctoral program. *Degree requirements:* For master's, one foreign language, exam. *Entrance requirements:* For master's, minimum GPA of 2.75. Additional exam requirements/recommendations for international students: Required—TOEFL. Electronic applications accepted. *Faculty research:* International studies, religious (Catholic, Jewish) studies, moving image arts.

University of Illinois at Springfield, Graduate Programs, College of Education and Human Services, Department of Educational Leadership, Springfield, IL 62703-5407. Offers chief school business official (CAS); educational leadership (MA); educational technology (Graduate Certificate); English as a second language (Graduate Certificate); higher education online pedagogy (Graduate Certificate); leadership and learning (Graduate Certificate); legal aspects of education (Graduate Certificate); superintendent (CAS); teacher leadership (MA). *Program availability:* Part-time, evening/weekend, 100% online, blended/hybrid learning. *Faculty:* 5 full-time (2 women), 8 part-time/adjunct (7 women). *Students:* 4 full-time (2 women), 113 part-time (68 women); includes 20 minority (15 Black or African American, non-Hispanic/Latino; 1 American Indian or Alaska Native, non-Hispanic/Latino; 4 Hispanic/Latino), 1 international. Average age 36. 45 applicants, 62% accepted, 19 enrolled. In 2016, 22 master's, 2 other advanced degrees awarded. *Degree requirements:* For master's, capstone course. *Entrance requirements:* For master's, minimum undergraduate GPA of 3.0, valid Illinois Teaching License, minimum of two years of successful teaching experience, portfolio, interview. Additional exam requirements/recommendations for international students: Required—TOEFL (minimum score 500 paper-based; 61 iBT). *Application deadline:* Applications are processed on a rolling basis. Application fee: $60 ($75 for international students). Electronic applications accepted. *Expenses:* Tuition, state resident: part-time $329 per credit hour. Tuition, nonresident: part-time $675 per credit hour. *Financial support:* In 2016–17, fellowships with full tuition reimbursements (averaging $9,900 per year), research assistantships with full tuition reimbursements (averaging $9,991 per year), teaching assistantships with full tuition reimbursements (averaging $10,059 per year) were awarded; career-related internships or fieldwork, Federal Work-Study, scholarships/grants, health care benefits, and unspecified assistantships also available. Support available to part-time students. Financial award application deadline: 11/15; financial award applicants required to submit FAFSA. *Unit head:* Dr. Scott Day, Program Administrator, 217-206-7520, Fax: 217-206-6775, E-mail: day.scott@uis.edu. *Application contact:* Dr. Cecelia Cornell, Associate Vice Chancellor for Graduate Education, 217-206-7230, E-mail: ccorn1@uis.edu.
Website: http://www.uis.edu/edl/

University of Illinois at Urbana–Champaign, Graduate College, College of Liberal Arts and Sciences, School of Literatures, Cultures and Linguistics, Department of Linguistics, Champaign, IL 61820. Offers linguistics (MA, PhD); teaching of English as a second language (MA).

University of Illinois at Urbana–Champaign, Graduate College, College of Liberal Arts and Sciences, School of Literatures, Cultures and Linguistics, Program in Second Language Acquisition and Teacher Education, Champaign, IL 61820. Offers PhD.

The University of Iowa, Graduate College, College of Education, Department of Teaching and Learning, Program in Education, Iowa City, IA 52242-1316. Offers art education (MA); developmental reading (MA); elementary education (MA); English education (MA, MAT); foreign and second language education (MAT); foreign language education (MA); foreign language/ESL education (PhD); language, literacy and culture (PhD); mathematics education (MA, MAT, PhD); music education (MM, PhD); science education (MA); secondary education (MA); social studies (MA, PhD). *Degree requirements:* For master's, thesis optional, exam; for doctorate, comprehensive exam, thesis/dissertation. *Entrance requirements:* For master's and doctorate, GRE General Test, minimum GPA of 3.0. Additional exam requirements/recommendations for international students: Required—TOEFL (minimum score 550 paper-based; 81 iBT). Electronic applications accepted.

University of Louisiana at Monroe, Graduate School, College of Arts, Education, and Sciences, School of Education, Program in Curriculum and Instruction, Monroe, LA 71209-0001. Offers art education (M Ed); biology education (M Ed); chemistry education (M Ed); curriculum and instruction (Ed D); early childhood education (M Ed); earth science education (M Ed); educational leadership (M Ed); elementary education (1-5) (M Ed); English as a second language (M Ed); English education (M Ed); family and consumer education (M Ed); French education (M Ed); history education (M Ed); math education (M Ed); middle school education (M Ed); music education (M Ed); reading education (K-12) (M Ed); Spanish education (M Ed); special education - academically gifted (M Ed); special education - early intervention (M Ed); special education - educational diagnostician (M Ed); special education - mild/moderate disabilities (M Ed); speech education (M Ed). *Accreditation:* NCATE. *Faculty:* 8 full-time (4 women), 4 part-time/adjunct (3 women). *Students:* 13 full-time (11 women), 80 part-time (65 women); includes 25 minority (19 Black or African American, non-Hispanic/Latino; 1 Asian, non-Hispanic/Latino; 3 Hispanic/Latino; 2 Two or more races, non-Hispanic/Latino). Average age 37. 118 applicants, 30% accepted, 16 enrolled. In 2016, 23 master's, 4 doctorates awarded. *Degree requirements:* For master's, comprehensive exam (for some programs), thesis; for doctorate, thesis/dissertation, internships. *Entrance requirements:* For master's, GRE General Test; for doctorate, GRE General Test, minimum undergraduate GPA of 2.75, graduate 3.25. Additional exam requirements/

recommendations for international students: Required—TOEFL (minimum score 500 paper-based; 61 iBT). *Application deadline:* For fall admission, 8/24 priority date for domestic students, 7/1 for international students; for winter admission, 12/14 priority date for domestic students; for spring admission, 1/19 for domestic students, 11/1 for international students. Applications are processed on a rolling basis. Application fee: $20 ($30 for international students). Electronic applications accepted. *Expenses:* Tuition, state resident: full-time $6489. Tuition, nonresident: full-time $18,589. *Required fees:* $8984. Tuition and fees vary according to course level, course load, degree level and program. *Financial support:* Research assistantships, career-related internships or fieldwork, Federal Work-Study, and unspecified assistantships available. Financial award application deadline: 4/1; financial award applicants required to submit FAFSA. *Unit head:* Dr. Dorothy Schween, Director, 318-342-1268, Fax: 318-342-3131, E-mail: schween@ulm.edu.

The University of Manchester, School of Languages, Linguistics and Cultures, Manchester, United Kingdom. Offers Arab world studies (PhD); Chinese studies (M Phil, PhD); East Asian studies (M Phil, PhD); English language (PhD); French studies (M Phil, PhD); German studies (M Phil, PhD); interpreting studies (PhD); Italian studies (M Phil, PhD); Japanese studies (M Phil, PhD); Latin American cultural studies (M Phil, PhD); linguistics (M Phil, PhD); Middle Eastern studies (M Phil, PhD); Polish studies (M Phil, PhD); Portuguese studies (M Phil, PhD); Russian studies (M Phil, PhD); Spanish studies (M Phil, PhD); translation and intercultural studies (M Phil, PhD).

University of Manitoba, Faculty of Graduate Studies, Faculty of Education, Department of Curriculum, Teaching and Learning, Winnipeg, MB R3T 2N2, Canada. Offers language and literacy (M Ed); second language education (M Ed); studies in curriculum, teaching and learning (M Ed). *Degree requirements:* For master's, thesis or alternative.

University of Maryland, Baltimore County, The Graduate School, College of Arts, Humanities and Social Sciences, Department of Education, Program in Teaching English to Speakers of Other Languages, Baltimore, MD 21250. Offers MA, Postbaccalaureate Certificate. *Program availability:* Part-time, evening/weekend, online learning. *Faculty:* 4 full-time (all women), 13 part-time/adjunct (9 women). *Students:* 20 full-time (11 women), 86 part-time (77 women); includes 30 minority (10 Black or African American, non-Hispanic/Latino; 13 Asian, non-Hispanic/Latino; 5 Hispanic/Latino; 1 Native Hawaiian or other Pacific Islander, non-Hispanic/Latino; 1 Two or more races, non-Hispanic/Latino), 2 international. Average age 36. 58 applicants, 79% accepted, 46 enrolled. In 2016, 20 master's, 26 other advanced degrees awarded. *Degree requirements:* For master's, thesis optional; for Postbaccalaureate Certificate, internship. *Entrance requirements:* For master's, GRE (minimum score 500 verbal, 150 on the new version, or 297 composite), 3 letters of reference, statement of purpose. Additional exam requirements/recommendations for international students: Required—TOEFL (minimum score 550 paper-based; 80 iBT). *Application deadline:* For fall admission, 8/1 priority date for domestic students, 4/1 priority date for international students; for spring admission, 1/1 priority date for domestic students, 11/1 priority date for international students. Applications are processed on a rolling basis. Application fee: $50. Electronic applications accepted. *Expenses:* Tuition, state resident: full-time $13,294. Tuition, nonresident: full-time $20,286. *Financial support:* In 2016–17, 34 students received support, including 1 research assistantship with full tuition reimbursement available (averaging $13,000 per year); career-related internships or fieldwork, Federal Work-Study, scholarships/grants, and unspecified assistantships also available. *Faculty research:* Adult education, bilingual language learning, online instruction, English grammar, cross-culture communication, ESL teacher professional identity. *Unit head:* Doaa Rashed, Director, 410-455-6773, E-mail: doaa1@umbc.edu. *Application contact:* Keneisha Murrell, Graduate Assistant, 410-455-3061, E-mail: esol@umbc.edu.
Website: http://www.umbc.edu/education/

University of Maryland, College Park, Academic Affairs, College of Education, Department of Teaching, Learning, Policy and Leadership, College Park, MD 20742. Offers reading (M Ed, MA, PhD, CAGS); secondary education (M Ed, MA, Ed D, PhD, CAGS); teaching English to speakers of other languages (M Ed). *Accreditation:* NCATE. *Program availability:* Part-time, evening/weekend, online learning. *Degree requirements:* For master's, comprehensive exam, seminar paper; for doctorate, comprehensive exam, thesis/dissertation, published paper, oral exam. *Entrance requirements:* For master's, GRE General Test or MAT, minimum GPA of 3.0, 3 letters of recommendation; for doctorate, GRE General Test or MAT, minimum undergraduate GPA of 3.0, graduate 3.5; 3 letters of recommendation. Electronic applications accepted. *Faculty research:* Teacher preparation, curriculum study, in-service education.

University of Massachusetts Amherst, Graduate School, College of Education, Program in Education, Amherst, MA 01003. Offers bilingual, English as a second language, and multicultural education (M Ed, Ed S); child study and early education (M Ed); children, families and schools (Ed D, Ed S); early childhood and elementary teacher education (M Ed); educational leadership (M Ed); educational policy and leadership (Ed D); higher education (M Ed); international education (M Ed); language, literacy and culture (Ed D); learning, media and technology (M Ed, Ed S); mathematics, science, and learning technologies (Ed D); reading and writing (M Ed); research, educational measurement and psychometrics (Ed D); school counselor education (M Ed, Ed S); school psychology (Ed S); science education (Ed S); secondary teacher education (M Ed); social justice education (M Ed, Ed D, Ed S); special education (M Ed, Ed D, Ed S); teacher education and school improvement (Ed D, Ed S). *Accreditation:* NCATE. *Program availability:* Part-time, online learning. Terminal master's awarded for partial completion of doctoral program. *Degree requirements:* For doctorate, comprehensive exam, thesis/dissertation. *Entrance requirements:* Additional exam requirements/recommendations for international students: Required—TOEFL (minimum score 550 paper-based; 80 iBT), IELTS (minimum score 6.5). Electronic applications accepted.

University of Massachusetts Dartmouth, Graduate School, College of Arts and Sciences, School of Education, Department of STEM Education and Teacher Development, North Dartmouth, MA 02747-2300. Offers education ESL preK-12 (Postbaccalaureate Certificate); mathematics education (PhD); middle school education (MAT); secondary school education (Postbaccalaureate Certificate); teaching secondary school education (MAT). *Program availability:* Part-time. *Faculty:* 9 full-time (6 women), 6 part-time/adjunct (3 women). *Students:* 25 full-time (12 women), 87 part-time (55 women); includes 15 minority (3 Black or African American, non-Hispanic/Latino; 2 Asian, non-Hispanic/Latino; 7 Hispanic/Latino; 3 Two or more races, non-Hispanic/Latino), 3 international. Average age 32. 53 applicants, 91% accepted, 38 enrolled. In 2016, 67 master's awarded. *Degree requirements:* For doctorate, thesis/dissertation. *Entrance requirements:* For master's, Massachusetts Tests for Educator Licensure (MTEL) Communication and Literacy Test and Subject Matter Test, statement of purpose (minimum of 300 words), resume, 2 letters of recommendation, official transcripts; for doctorate, GRE, statement of purpose (minimum of 300 words), resume, official transcripts, 3 letters of recommendation; for Postbaccalaureate Certificate, statement of purpose (minimum of 300 words), resume, 2 letters of recommendation, official transcripts. Additional exam requirements/recommendations for international students: Required—TOEFL (minimum score 533 paper-based; 72 iBT). *Application deadline:* For fall admission, 2/15 priority date for domestic students, 1/15 priority date for international students; for spring admission, 12/15 priority date for domestic students, 11/15 priority date for international students. Application fee: $60. Electronic applications accepted. *Expenses:* Tuition, state resident: full-time $14,994; part-time $624.75 per credit. Tuition, nonresident: full-time $27,068; part-time $1127.83 per credit. *Required fees:* $405; $25.88 per credit. Tuition and fees vary according to course load and reciprocity agreements. *Financial support:* In 2016–17, 3 fellowships (averaging $6,250 per year), 3 research assistantships (averaging $5,027 per year), 2 teaching assistantships (averaging $8,000 per year) were awarded; institutionally sponsored loans, scholarships/grants, unspecified assistantships, and instructional assistants, Fulbright scholarships also available. Financial award application deadline: 3/1; financial award applicants required to submit FAFSA. *Faculty research:* Reading/special education, education reform, English education, literacy, language arts K-12. *Total annual research expenditures:* $1.3 million. *Unit head:* Traci Almeida, Graduate Program Director, 508-999-8098, Fax: 508-910-8183, E-mail: talmeida@umassd.edu. *Application contact:* Steven Briggs, Director of Marketing and Recruitment for Graduate Studies, 508-999-8604, Fax: 508-999-8183, E-mail: graduate@umassd.edu.
Website: http://www.umassd.edu/cas/schoolofeducation/departments/stemeducationandteacherdevelopment/

University of Memphis, Graduate School, College of Arts and Sciences, Department of English, Memphis, TN 38152. Offers African-American literature (Graduate Certificate); applied linguistics (PhD); composition studies (PhD); creative writing (MFA); English as a second language (MA); linguistics (MA); literary and cultural studies (PhD), including African-American literature; literature (MA); professional writing (MA, PhD); teaching English as a second/foreign language (Graduate Certificate). *Program availability:* Part-time, evening/weekend, 100% online. *Faculty:* 31 full-time (14 women), 1 (woman) part-time/adjunct. *Students:* 86 full-time (44 women), 78 part-time (51 women); includes 36 minority (19 Black or African American, non-Hispanic/Latino; 3 Asian, non-Hispanic/Latino; 10 Hispanic/Latino; 4 Two or more races, non-Hispanic/Latino), 32 international. Average age 35. 68 applicants, 87% accepted, 33 enrolled. In 2016, 39 master's, 17 doctorates, 16 other advanced degrees awarded. Terminal master's awarded for partial completion of doctoral program. *Degree requirements:* For master's, one foreign language, comprehensive exam, thesis optional; for doctorate, 2 foreign languages, comprehensive exam, thesis/dissertation, qualifying exam. *Entrance requirements:* For master's, GRE, minimum undergraduate GPA of 3.0, statement of purpose, two letters of recommendation; for doctorate, GRE, minimum undergraduate and graduate GPA of 3.25, statement of purpose, writing sample, three letters of recommendation. Additional exam requirements/recommendations for international students: Required—TOEFL. *Application deadline:* For fall admission, 1/15 for domestic students; for spring admission, 10/15 for domestic students. Applications are processed on a rolling basis. Application fee: $35 ($60 for international students). Electronic applications accepted. *Expenses:* $5,231.50 per semester full-time in-state, $9,623.50 full-time out-of-state. *Financial support:* In 2016–17, 123 students received support, including 11 research assistantships with full tuition reimbursements available (averaging $17,064 per year), 25 teaching assistantships with full tuition reimbursements available (averaging $17,340 per year); Federal Work-Study, scholarships/grants, and unspecified assistantships also available. Financial award application deadline: 2/1; financial award applicants required to submit FAFSA. *Faculty research:* Applied linguistics, British and American literature, professional writing, composition studies. *Unit head:* Dr. Joshua Phillips, Chair, 901-678-2651, Fax: 901-678-2226, E-mail: jsphllps@memphis.edu. *Application contact:* Dr. Jeffrey Scraba, Coordinator of Graduate Studies, 901-678-4768, Fax: 901-678-2226, E-mail: jscraba@memphis.edu.
Website: http://www.memphis.edu/english

University of Minnesota, Twin Cities Campus, Graduate School, College of Education and Human Development, Department of Curriculum and Instruction, Minneapolis, MN 55455-0213. Offers art education (M Ed, MA, PhD); curriculum and instruction (M Ed, MA, PhD); elementary education (MA, PhD); English education (PhD); language and immersion education (Certificate); learning technologies (MA, PhD); literacy education (MA, PhD); second language education (MA, PhD); social studies education (MA, PhD); STEM education (MA, PhD); teaching (M Ed), including mathematics, science, social studies, teaching; teaching English to speakers of other languages (MA); technology enhanced learning (Certificate). *Faculty:* 37 full-time (20 women). *Students:* 411 full-time (288 women), 317 part-time (223 women); includes 153 minority (37 Black or African American, non-Hispanic/Latino; 7 American Indian or Alaska Native, non-Hispanic/Latino; 31 Asian, non-Hispanic/Latino; 48 Hispanic/Latino; 1 Native Hawaiian or other Pacific Islander, non-Hispanic/Latino; 29 Two or more races, non-Hispanic/Latino), 53 international. Average age 32. 672 applicants, 66% accepted, 400 enrolled. In 2016, 645 master's, 33 doctorates, 27 other advanced degrees awarded. Application fee: $75 ($95 for international students). *Financial support:* In 2016–17, 13 fellowships, 36 research assistantships with full tuition reimbursements (averaging $8,454 per year), 61 teaching assistantships with full tuition reimbursements (averaging $11,406 per year) were awarded. *Faculty research:* Teaching and learning; influence of cultural, linguistic, social, political, and technological factors on teaching, learning and educational research; relationship between educational practice and a democratic and just society; urban education; immigrant education, racial justice and education. *Total annual research expenditures:* $684,005. *Unit head:* Dr. Cynthia Lewis, Chair, 612-625-6313, E-mail: lewis@umn.edu. *Application contact:* Dr. Gillian Roehrig, Director of Graduate Studies, 612-625-0561, E-mail: roehr013@umn.edu.
Website: http://www.cehd.umn.edu/ci

University of Minnesota, Twin Cities Campus, Graduate School, College of Liberal Arts, Institute of Linguistics, English as a Second Language, and Slavic Languages and Literatures (ILES), English as a Second Language Program, Minneapolis, MN 55455-0213. Offers MA. *Degree requirements:* For master's, one foreign language, comprehensive exam, thesis. *Entrance requirements:* For master's, GRE, 3 letters of recommendation. Additional exam requirements/recommendations for international students: Required—TOEFL (minimum score 600 paper-based). Electronic applications accepted. *Faculty research:* Second language acquisitions, communication strategies, English for specific purposes, literacy, speech act, proymatics in general, language assessment, discourse analysis, research methods.

University of Missouri–St. Louis, College of Education, Department of Educator Preparation, Innovation and Research, St. Louis, MO 63121. Offers elementary education (M Ed), including early childhood, general, reading; secondary education (M Ed), including curriculum and instruction, general, middle level education, reading, teaching English to speakers of other languages (TESOL); special education (M Ed), including autism and developmental disabilities, early childhood special education. *Program availability:* Part-time, evening/weekend. *Faculty:* 26 full-time (14 women), 22 part-time/adjunct (14 women). *Students:* 151 full-time (127 women), 728 part-time (564 women); includes 222 minority (165 Black or African American, non-Hispanic/Latino; 1 American Indian or Alaska Native, non-Hispanic/Latino; 16 Asian, non-Hispanic/Latino; 31 Hispanic/Latino; 1 Native Hawaiian or other Pacific Islander, non-Hispanic/Latino; 8 Two or more races, non-Hispanic/Latino), 6 international. Average age 29. 363 applicants, 84% accepted, 211 enrolled. *Degree requirements:* For master's, comprehensive exam. *Entrance requirements:* Additional exam requirements/recommendations for international students: Recommended—TOEFL (minimum score 550 paper-based; 79 iBT), IELTS (minimum score 6.5). *Application deadline:* For fall

admission, 7/1 priority date for domestic and international students; for spring admission, 12/1 priority date for domestic and international students. Application fee: $50 ($40 for international students). Electronic applications accepted. *Financial support:* Application deadline: 4/1; applicants required to submit FAFSA. *Unit head:* Dr. Gayle Wilkinson, Chair, 314-516-5791. *Application contact:* 314-516-5458, Fax: 314-516-6996, E-mail: gadadm@umsl.edu.
Website: https://coe.umsl.edu/dept/epir.html

University of Nebraska at Kearney, College of Education, Department of Teacher Education, Kearney, NE 68849-0001. Offers curriculum and instruction (MA Ed), including early childhood education, elementary education, English as a second language, instructional effectiveness, reading/special education, secondary education; instructional technology (MS Ed), including information technology, instructional technology, school librarian; reading PK-12 (MA Ed); special education (MA Ed), including advanced practitioner: assistive technology specialist, advanced practitioner: behavioral interventionist, advanced practitioner: inclusive collaboration specialist, gifted, teacher education. *Program availability:* Part-time, evening/weekend, online only, 100% online. *Faculty:* 18 full-time (13 women). *Students:* 21 full-time (15 women), 296 part-time (240 women); includes 21 minority (3 Black or African American, non-Hispanic/Latino; 1 Asian, non-Hispanic/Latino; 14 Hispanic/Latino; 1 Native Hawaiian or other Pacific Islander, non-Hispanic/Latino; 2 Two or more races, non-Hispanic/Latino), 1 international. Average age 32. 81 applicants, 100% accepted, 61 enrolled. In 2016, 129 master's awarded. *Degree requirements:* For master's, comprehensive exam, thesis optional. *Entrance requirements:* For master's, portfolio or GRE. Additional exam requirements/recommendations for international students: Recommended—TOEFL (minimum score 550 paper-based; 79 iBT), IELTS (minimum score 6.5). *Application deadline:* For fall admission, 6/15 for domestic students, 5/15 for international students; for spring admission, 10/15 for domestic and international students; for summer admission, 3/15 for domestic and international students. Application fee: $45. Electronic applications accepted. *Expenses:* $285 per credit hour resident tuition, $415 per credit hour non-resident tuition (online). *Financial support:* In 2016–17, 6 students received support, including 6 research assistantships with full tuition reimbursements available (averaging $10,500 per year); career-related internships or fieldwork, scholarships/grants, health care benefits, and unspecified assistantships also available. Support available to part-time students. Financial award application deadline: 2/28; financial award applicants required to submit FAFSA. *Unit head:* Sarah Bartling, Administrative Assistant, 308-865-8513, E-mail: bartlingseg@unk.edu. *Application contact:* Linda Johnson, Director, Graduate Admissions and Programs, 308-865-8841, Fax: 308-865-8837, E-mail: johnsonli@unk.edu.
Website: http://www.unk.edu/academics/ted/index.php

University of Nebraska at Omaha, Graduate Studies, College of Arts and Sciences, Department of English, Omaha, NE 68182. Offers advanced writing (Certificate); English (MA); teaching English to speakers of other languages (Certificate); technical communication (Certificate). *Program availability:* Part-time, evening/weekend. *Faculty:* 10 full-time (6 women). *Students:* 9 full-time (7 women), 43 part-time (24 women); includes 1 minority (Two or more races, non-Hispanic/Latino), 3 international. Average age 32. 39 applicants, 46% accepted, 14 enrolled. In 2016, 21 master's, 12 other advanced degrees awarded. *Degree requirements:* For master's, comprehensive exam, thesis (for some programs). *Entrance requirements:* For master's, GRE or MAT, minimum GPA of 3.0, transcripts, 3 letters of recommendation, statement of purpose, writing sample; for Certificate, minimum GPA of 3.0, transcripts, statement of purpose. Additional exam requirements/recommendations for international students: Required—TOEFL, IELTS, PTE. *Application deadline:* Applications are processed on a rolling basis. Application fee: $45. Electronic applications accepted. *Financial support:* In 2016–17, 15 students received support, including 15 teaching assistantships with tuition reimbursements available; fellowships, research assistantships, Federal Work-Study, institutionally sponsored loans, scholarships/grants, health care benefits, tuition waivers (partial), and unspecified assistantships also available. Support available to part-time students. Financial award application deadline: 3/1; financial award applicants required to submit FAFSA. *Unit head:* Dr. Tracy Bridgeford, Chairperson, 402-554-2341, E-mail: graduate@unomaha.edu. *Application contact:* Dr. Ramon Guerra, Graduate Program Chair, 402-554-2341, E-mail: graduate@unomaha.edu.

University of Nevada, Las Vegas, Graduate College, College of Education, Department of Educational and Clinical Studies, Las Vegas, NV 89154-3066. Offers addiction studies (Advanced Certificate); counselor education (M Ed, MS), including clinical mental health (MS), school counseling (M Ed); early childhood education (M Ed); early childhood special education (Certificate), including infancy, preschool; English language learning (M Ed); mental health counseling (Advanced Certificate); special education (M Ed, PhD); PhD/JD. *Program availability:* Part-time, evening/weekend. *Faculty:* 17 full-time (8 women), 28 part-time/adjunct (20 women). *Students:* 269 full-time (219 women), 174 part-time (138 women); includes 181 minority (51 Black or African American, non-Hispanic/Latino; 2 American Indian or Alaska Native, non-Hispanic/Latino; 15 Asian, non-Hispanic/Latino; 81 Hispanic/Latino; 3 Native Hawaiian or other Pacific Islander, non-Hispanic/Latino; 29 Two or more races, non-Hispanic/Latino), 23 international. Average age 34. 256 applicants, 72% accepted, 145 enrolled. In 2016, 178 master's, 3 doctorates awarded. *Degree requirements:* For master's, comprehensive exam (for some programs); for doctorate, comprehensive exam, thesis/dissertation; for other advanced degree, final project. *Entrance requirements:* For master's, bachelor's degree; letter of recommendation; statement of purpose; for doctorate, GRE General Test, statement of purpose; writing sample; 3 letters of recommendation. Additional exam requirements/recommendations for international students: Required—TOEFL (minimum score 550 paper-based; 80 iBT), IELTS (minimum score 7). *Application deadline:* For fall admission, 7/15 for domestic students, 5/1 for international students; for spring admission, 11/15 for domestic students, 10/1 for international students; for summer admission, 4/15 for domestic students. Application fee: $60 ($95 for international students). Electronic applications accepted. *Expenses:* $269.25 per credit, $792 per 3-credit course; $9,634 per year resident; $23,274 per year non-resident; $7,094 fees non-resident (7 credits or more); $1,307 annual health insurance fee. *Financial support:* In 2016–17, 12 research assistantships with partial tuition reimbursements (averaging $12,569 per year), 27 teaching assistantships with partial tuition reimbursements (averaging $13,759 per year) were awarded; institutionally sponsored loans, scholarships/grants, health care benefits, and unspecified assistantships also available. Financial award application deadline: 3/15. *Faculty research:* Multicultural issues in counseling, academic interventions for students with disabilities, establishment of pro-social skills in young children with severe disabilities, inclusive strategies for students with disabilities, language and literacy for English language learners. *Total annual research expenditures:* $768,906. *Unit head:* Dr. Monica Brown, Interim Department Chair/Professor, 702-895-3167, Fax: 702-895-3205, E-mail: monica.brown@unlv.edu. *Application contact:* Dr. Cori More, Graduate Coordinator, 702-895-3271, Fax: 702-895-3205, E-mail: cori.more@unlv.edu.
Website: http://education.unlv.edu/ecs/

University of Nevada, Reno, Graduate School, College of Education, Department of Educational Specialties, Program in Teaching English to Speakers of Other Languages, Reno, NV 89557. Offers MA. Terminal master's awarded for partial completion of doctoral program. *Degree requirements:* For master's, thesis optional. *Entrance requirements:* For master's, minimum GPA of 2.75. Additional exam requirements/recommendations for international students: Required—TOEFL (minimum score 500 paper-based; 61 iBT), IELTS (minimum score 6). Electronic applications accepted. *Faculty research:* Bilingualism, multicultural education.

University of New Mexico, Graduate Studies, College of Education, Program in Language, Literacy and Sociocultural Studies, Albuquerque, NM 87131. Offers American Indian education (MA); bilingual education (MA, PhD); educational linguistics (PhD); educational thought and sociocultural studies (MA, PhD); literacy/language arts (MA, PhD); social studies (MA); TESOL (MA, PhD). *Faculty:* 17 full-time (10 women), 4 part-time/adjunct (3 women). *Students:* 57 full-time (38 women), 129 part-time (105 women); includes 102 minority (8 Black or African American, non-Hispanic/Latino; 16 American Indian or Alaska Native, non-Hispanic/Latino; 6 Asian, non-Hispanic/Latino; 67 Hispanic/Latino; 5 Two or more races, non-Hispanic/Latino), 32 international. Average age 39. 50 applicants, 60% accepted, 23 enrolled. In 2016, 36 master's, 4 doctorates awarded. *Degree requirements:* For master's, comprehensive exam, thesis optional; for doctorate, comprehensive exam, thesis/dissertation, research skills. *Entrance requirements:* For master's, letter of intent, 3 letters of recommendation, resume, BA/BS, department demographic form, transcripts; for doctorate, writing sample, letter of intent, 3 letters of recommendation, resume, BA/BS, MA, department demographic form, transcripts. Additional exam requirements/recommendations for international students: Required—TOEFL. *Application deadline:* For fall admission, 12/1 for domestic and international students; for spring admission, 9/15 for domestic and international students. Application fee: $50. Electronic applications accepted. *Financial support:* Fellowships, research assistantships, teaching assistantships with tuition reimbursements, career-related internships or fieldwork, institutionally sponsored loans, scholarships/grants, and unspecified assistantships available. Support available to part-time students. Financial award application deadline: 3/1; financial award applicants required to submit FAFSA. *Faculty research:* School reform, professional development, history of education, Native American education, politics of education, feminism and issues of sexual identity, critical race theory, bilingualism, literacy reading, adolescent literature, second language acquisition, critical theory and schooling, indigenous languages. *Unit head:* Dr. Lois M. Meyer, Chair, 505-277-7244, Fax: 505-277-8362, E-mail: lsmeyer@unm.edu. *Application contact:* Debra Schaffer, Administrative Assistant, 505-277-0437, Fax: 505-277-8362, E-mail: schaffer@unm.edu.
Website: http://coe.unm.edu/departments-programs/llss/index.html

The University of North Carolina at Chapel Hill, Graduate School, School of Education, Program in Secondary Education, Chapel Hill, NC 27599. Offers English (Grades 9-12) (MAT); English as a second language (MAT); French (Grades K-12) (MAT); German (Grades K-12) (MAT); Japanese (Grades K-12) (MAT); Latin (Grades 9-12) (MAT); mathematics (Grades 9-12) (MAT); music (Grades K-12) (MAT); science (Grades 9-12) (MAT); social studies (Grades 9-12) (MAT); Spanish (Grades K-12) (MAT). *Accreditation:* NCATE. *Degree requirements:* For master's, comprehensive exam. *Entrance requirements:* For master's, GRE General Test, minimum GPA of 3.0 during last 2 years of undergraduate course work. Additional exam requirements/recommendations for international students: Required—TOEFL (minimum score 550 paper-based). Electronic applications accepted.

The University of North Carolina at Charlotte, Cato College of Education, Department of Middle, Secondary and K-12 Education, Charlotte, NC 28223-0001. Offers middle grades and secondary education (M Ed); teaching English as a second language (M Ed, Graduate Certificate). *Program availability:* Part-time. *Faculty:* 17 full-time (9 women), 6 part-time/adjunct (5 women). *Students:* 6 full-time (5 women), 62 part-time (56 women); includes 9 minority (8 Black or African American, non-Hispanic/Latino; 1 Hispanic/Latino), 1 international. Average age 32. 32 applicants, 97% accepted, 28 enrolled. In 2016, 12 master's awarded. *Degree requirements:* For master's, thesis, comprehensive portfolio, or research project. *Entrance requirements:* For master's, GRE or MAT, bachelor's degree from accredited college or university; minimum GPA of 3.0 in undergraduate work; North Carolina Class A teaching license in appropriate middle grades or secondary education field; minimum of two years' teaching experience; written narrative providing statement of purpose for master's degree study; letters of recommendation; for Graduate Certificate, bachelor's degree from accredited institution; minimum undergraduate GPA of 2.5 overall or 3.0 in senior year, or 15 hours taken in the last 5 years; satisfactory recommendations from three persons knowledgeable of applicant's interactions with children or adolescents; statement of purpose. Additional exam requirements/recommendations for international students: Required—TOEFL (minimum score 523 paper-based, 70 iBT) or IELTS (6.5). *Application deadline:* For fall admission, 3/1 priority date for domestic and international students; for spring admission, 10/1 priority date for domestic and international students; for summer admission, 4/1 priority date for domestic and international students. Applications are processed on a rolling basis. Application fee: $75. Electronic applications accepted. *Expenses:* Tuition, state resident: full-time $4252. Tuition, nonresident: full-time $17,423. *Required fees:* $3026. Tuition and fees vary according to course load and program. *Financial support:* In 2016–17, 5 students received support, including 1 fellowship (averaging $32,786 per year), 4 research assistantships (averaging $14,309 per year); career-related internships or fieldwork, institutionally sponsored loans, scholarships/grants, and unspecified assistantships also available. Support available to part-time students. Financial award application deadline: 3/1; financial award applicants required to submit FAFSA. *Total annual research expenditures:* $58,472. *Unit head:* Scott Kissau, Chair, 704-687-8875, E-mail: spkissau@uncc.edu. *Application contact:* Kathy B. Giddings, Director of Graduate Admissions, 704-687-5503, Fax: 704-687-1668, E-mail: gradadm@uncc.edu.
Website: http://mdsk.uncc.edu/

The University of North Carolina at Charlotte, Cato College of Education, Interdisciplinary Education Programs, Charlotte, NC 28223-0001. Offers art education (Graduate Certificate); child and family development: early childhood education (MAT); curriculum and instruction (PhD); elementary education (MAT); foreign language education (MAT); middle grades education (MAT); secondary education (MAT); special education (MAT); teaching (Graduate Certificate); teaching English as a second language (MAT); theatre education (Graduate Certificate). *Program availability:* Part-time, 100% online, blended/hybrid learning. *Students:* 78 full-time (59 women), 619 part-time (484 women); includes 255 minority (186 Black or African American, non-Hispanic/Latino; 1 American Indian or Alaska Native, non-Hispanic/Latino; 16 Asian, non-Hispanic/Latino; 37 Hispanic/Latino; 15 Two or more races, non-Hispanic/Latino), 10 international. Average age 33. 380 applicants, 92% accepted, 264 enrolled. In 2016, 93 master's, 8 doctorates, 176 other advanced degrees awarded. *Degree requirements:* For master's, thesis or alternative, research project/portfolio. *Entrance requirements:* For master's, GRE or MAT, bachelor's degree, or its U.S. equivalent, from regionally-accredited college or university; minimum overall GPA of 3.0 on all previous work beyond high school; statement of purpose (essay); at least three recommendation forms; for doctorate, GRE or MAT, bachelor's degree (or its U.S. equivalent) from regionally-accredited college or university; minimum overall GPA of 3.5 in master's degree program; for Graduate Certificate, bachelor's degree from regionally-accredited university; minimum GPA of 2.75 on all post-secondary work attempted; transcripts; personal statement outlining why the applicant seeks admission to the program. Additional exam requirements/recommendations for international students: Required—

TOEFL (minimum score 523 paper-based, 70 iBT) or IELTS (6.5). *Application deadline:* For fall admission, 3/1 priority date for domestic and international students; for spring admission, 10/1 priority date for domestic and international students; for summer admission, 4/1 priority date for domestic and international students. Applications are processed on a rolling basis. Application fee: $75. Electronic applications accepted. *Expenses:* Tuition, state resident: full-time $4252. Tuition, nonresident: full-time $17,423. *Required fees:* $3026. Tuition and fees vary according to course load and program. *Financial support:* Career-related internships or fieldwork, institutionally sponsored loans, scholarships/grants, and unspecified assistantships available. Support available to part-time students. Financial award application deadline: 3/1; financial award applicants required to submit FAFSA. *Unit head:* Dr. Ellen McIntyre, Dean, 704-687-8722, E-mail: ellen.mcintyre@uncc.edu. *Application contact:* Kathy B. Giddings, Director of Graduate Admissions, 704-687-5503, Fax: 704-687-1668, E-mail: gradadm@uncc.edu.
Website: http://education.uncc.edu/academic-programs

The University of North Carolina at Greensboro, Graduate School, School of Education, Department of Teacher Education and Higher Education, Greensboro, NC 27412-5001. Offers college teaching and adult learning (Certificate); curriculum and instruction (M Ed), including chemistry education, elementary education, English as a second language, French education, instructional technology, mathematics education, middle grades education, reading education, science education, social studies education, Spanish education; curriculum and teaching (PhD), including higher education, teacher education and development; English as a second language (Certificate); higher education (M Ed); supervision (M Ed). *Accreditation:* NCATE. *Program availability:* Part-time. *Degree requirements:* For doctorate, thesis/dissertation. *Entrance requirements:* For master's and doctorate, GRE General Test. Additional exam requirements/recommendations for international students: Required—TOEFL. Electronic applications accepted. *Faculty research:* Community college literacy program, middle school mathematics/computer mathematics.

The University of North Carolina Wilmington, Watson College of Education, Department of Instructional Technology, Foundations and Secondary Education, Wilmington, NC 28403-3297. Offers academically or intellectually gifted (M Ed); English as a second language (M Ed, MAT); instructional technology (MS); physical education and health (M Ed, MAT); secondary education (M Ed, MAT); Spanish (MAT); Spanish education (MASS). *Program availability:* Part-time. *Faculty:* 17 full-time (11 women). *Students:* 36 full-time (22 women), 62 part-time (49 women); includes 17 minority (12 Black or African American, non-Hispanic/Latino; 3 Hispanic/Latino; 2 Two or more races, non-Hispanic/Latino), 5 international. Average age 34. 89 applicants, 89% accepted, 59 enrolled. In 2016, 36 master's awarded. *Degree requirements:* For master's, comprehensive exam (for some programs), thesis (for some programs), thesis or research project. *Entrance requirements:* For master's, GRE or MAT, statement of interest, 3 letters of recommendation, minimum GPA of 3.0 in undergraduate work. Additional exam requirements/recommendations for international students: Required—TOEFL (minimum score 79 iBT), IELTS (minimum score 6.5). *Application deadline:* For fall admission, 5/15 for domestic students; for spring admission, 10/15 for domestic students; for summer admission, 3/15 for domestic students. Applications are processed on a rolling basis. Application fee: $60. Electronic applications accepted. *Expenses:* Contact institution. *Financial support:* Scholarships/grants and unspecified assistantships available. Financial award application deadline: 3/15; financial award applicants required to submit FAFSA. *Unit head:* Dr. Donyell Roseboro, Chair, 910-962-2289, Fax: 910-962-3609, E-mail: roseborod@uncw.edu. *Application contact:* Dr. Mahnaz Moallem, Graduate Coordinator, 910-962-4183, E-mail: moallemm@uncw.edu.
Website: http://www.uncw.edu/ed/itfse/

University of Northern Colorado, Graduate School, College of Education and Behavioral Sciences, School of Teacher Education, Greeley, CO 80639. Offers curriculum studies (MAT); educational studies (Ed D); elementary education (MAT); English education (MAT); literacy (MA); multilingual education (MA), including TESOL, world languages; teaching diverse learners (MA). *Accreditation:* NCATE. *Program availability:* Part-time, evening/weekend. *Degree requirements:* For master's, comprehensive exam, thesis or alternative; for doctorate, comprehensive exam, thesis/dissertation. *Entrance requirements:* For master's and doctorate, GRE General Test, 3 letters of recommendation. *Application deadline:* Applications are processed on a rolling basis. Application fee: $50 ($60 for international students). Electronic applications accepted. *Financial support:* Fellowships, research assistantships, teaching assistantships, and unspecified assistantships available. Financial award application deadline: 3/1; financial award applicants required to submit FAFSA. *Unit head:* Dr. Alexander Sidorkin, Director, 970-351-2908, Fax: 970-351-1877. *Application contact:* Linda Sisson, Graduate Student Admission Coordinator, 970-351-1807, Fax: 970-351-2371, E-mail: linda.sisson@unco.edu.
Website: http://www.unco.edu/cebs/teachered/

University of Northern Iowa, Graduate College, College of Humanities, Arts and Sciences, Department of Languages and Literatures, MA Program in Teaching English to Speakers of Other Languages, Cedar Falls, IA 50614. Offers MA. *Degree requirements:* For master's, comprehensive exam, thesis or research paper.

University of North Florida, College of Education and Human Services, Department of Childhood Education, Literacy, and TESOL, Jacksonville, FL 32224. Offers literacy (M Ed); professional education (M Ed); TESOL (M Ed). *Accreditation:* NCATE. *Program availability:* Part-time, evening/weekend. *Faculty:* 10 full-time (8 women). *Students:* 9 full-time (7 women), 27 part-time (all women); includes 14 minority (7 Black or African American, non-Hispanic/Latino; 2 Asian, non-Hispanic/Latino; 2 Hispanic/Latino; 3 Two or more races, non-Hispanic/Latino), 2 international. Average age 31. 34 applicants, 50% accepted, 12 enrolled. In 2016, 22 master's awarded. *Entrance requirements:* For master's, GRE General Test, minimum GPA of 3.0 in last 60 hours, 3 letters of recommendation, interview. Additional exam requirements/recommendations for international students: Required—TOEFL (minimum score 500 paper-based). *Application deadline:* For fall admission, 8/1 priority date for domestic students, 5/1 for international students; for spring admission, 12/1 priority date for domestic students, 10/1 for international students; for summer admission, 3/15 priority date for domestic students, 2/1 for international students. Application fee: $30. Electronic applications accepted. Tuition and fees vary according to course load, campus/location and program. *Financial support:* In 2016–17, 3 students received support. Research assistantships, Federal Work-Study, tuition waivers (partial), and unspecified assistantships available. Support available to part-time students. Financial award application deadline: 4/1; financial award applicants required to submit FAFSA. *Faculty research:* Social context of and processes in learning, inter-disciplinary instruction, cross-cultural conflict resolution, the Vygotskian perspective on literacy diagnosis and instruction, performance poetry and teaching the language arts through drama. *Total annual research expenditures:* $2,531. *Unit head:* Dr. Paul Parkison, Chair, 904-620-5352, Fax: 904-620-1025, E-mail: n01230143@unf.edu. *Application contact:* Dr. Amanda Pascale, Director, The Graduate School, 904-620-1360, Fax: 904-620-1362, E-mail: graduateschool@unf.edu.
Website: http://www.unf.edu/coehs/celt/

University of North Texas, Robert B. Toulouse School of Graduate Studies, Denton, TX 76203-5459. Offers accounting (MS); applied anthropology (MA, MS); applied behavior analysis (Certificate); applied geography (MA); applied technology and performance improvement (M Ed, MS); art education (MA); art history (MA); art museum education (Certificate); arts leadership (Certificate); audiology (Au D); behavior analysis (MS); behavioral science (PhD); biochemistry and molecular biology (MS); biology (MA, MS); biomedical engineering (MS); business analysis (MS); chemistry (MS); clinical health psychology (PhD); communication studies (MA, MS); computer engineering (MS); computer science (MS); counseling (M Ed, MS), including clinical mental health counseling (MS), college and university counseling, elementary school counseling, secondary school counseling; creative writing (MA); criminal justice (MS); curriculum and instruction (M Ed); decision sciences (MBA); design (MA, MFA), including fashion design (MFA), innovation studies, interior design (MFA); early childhood studies (MS); economics (MS); educational leadership (M Ed, Ed D); educational psychology (MS, PhD), including family studies (MS), gifted and talented (MS), human development (MS), learning and cognition (MS), research, measurement and evaluation (MS); electrical engineering (MS); emergency management (MPA); engineering technology (MS); English (MA); English as a second language (MA); environmental science (MS); finance (MBA, MS); financial management (MPA); French (MA); health services management (MBA); higher education (M Ed, Ed D); history (MA, MS); hospitality management (MS); human resources management (MPA); information science (MS); information systems (PhD); information technologies (MBA); interdisciplinary studies (MA, MS); international studies (MA); international sustainable tourism (MS); jazz studies (MM); journalism (MA, MJ, Graduate Certificate), including interactive and virtual digital communication (Graduate Certificate), narrative journalism (Graduate Certificate), public relations (Graduate Certificate); kinesiology (MS); linguistics (MA); local government management (MPA); logistics (PhD); logistics and supply chain management (MBA); long-term care, senior housing, and aging services (MA); management (PhD); marketing (MBA); mathematics (MA, MS); mechanical and energy engineering (MS, PhD); music (MA), including ethnomusicology, music theory, musicology, performance; music composition (PhD); music education (MM Ed, PhD); nonprofit management (MPA); operations and supply chain management (MBA); performance (MM, DMA); philosophy (MA); political science (MA); professional and technical communication (MA); radio, television and film (MA, MFA); rehabilitation counseling (Certificate); sociology (MA); Spanish (MA); special education (M Ed); speech-language pathology (MA); strategic management (MBA); studio art (MFA); teaching (M Ed); MBA/MS. *Program availability:* Part-time, evening/weekend, online learning. Terminal master's awarded for partial completion of doctoral program. *Degree requirements:* For master's, variable foreign language requirement, comprehensive exam (for some programs), thesis (for some programs); for doctorate, variable foreign language requirement, comprehensive exam (for some programs), thesis/dissertation; for other advanced degree, variable foreign language requirement, comprehensive exam (for some programs). *Entrance requirements:* For master's and doctorate, GRE, GMAT. Additional exam requirements/recommendations for international students: Required—TOEFL (minimum score 550 paper-based; 79 iBT). Electronic applications accepted.

University of Pennsylvania, Graduate School of Education, Division of Educational Linguistics, Program in Teaching English to Speakers of Other Languages, Philadelphia, PA 19104. Offers MS Ed. *Program availability:* Part-time, online learning. *Students:* 119 full-time (107 women), 18 part-time (11 women); includes 7 minority (1 Black or African American, non-Hispanic/Latino; 3 Asian, non-Hispanic/Latino; 3 Hispanic/Latino), 114 international. Average age 25. 348 applicants, 39% accepted, 76 enrolled. In 2016, 69 degrees awarded. *Expenses: Tuition:* Full-time $31,068; part-time $5762 per course. *Required fees:* $3200; $336 per course. Full-time tuition and fees vary according to degree level, program and student level. Part-time tuition and fees vary according to course load, degree level and program.

University of Phoenix–Online Campus, College of Education, Phoenix, AZ 85034-7209. Offers administration and supervision (MAEd, Certificate); adult education and training (MAEd); curriculum and instruction (MAEd), including computer education, curriculum and instruction, English as a second language, language arts, mathematics, reading; early childhood education (MAEd); educational studies (MAEd); elementary teacher education (MAEd), including early childhood, elementary teacher education, high school middle level, middle level; principal licensure (Certificate); secondary teacher education (MAEd); special education (MAEd, Certificate); teacher education (MAEd), including middle level generalist; teacher education middle level mathematics (MAEd), including middle level mathematics; teacher education middle level science (MAEd), including middle level science; teacher education secondary mathematics (MAEd); teacher education secondary science (MAEd); teacher leadership (MAEd); teachers of English learners (Certificate); transition to teaching (Certificate), including elementary education, secondary education. *Program availability:* Evening/weekend, online learning. *Entrance requirements:* Additional exam requirements/recommendations for international students: Required—TOEFL, TOEIC (Test of English as an International Communication), Berlitz Online English Proficiency Exam, PTE, or IELTS. Electronic applications accepted. *Expenses:* Contact institution.

University of Phoenix–San Diego Campus, College of Education, San Diego, CA 92123. Offers curriculum and instruction (MA Ed), including computer education, curriculum and instruction, English as a second language; elementary teacher education (MA Ed); secondary teacher education (MA Ed). *Program availability:* Evening/weekend. *Degree requirements:* For master's, thesis (for some programs). *Entrance requirements:* For master's, 3 years of work experience, minimum undergraduate GPA of 3.0. Additional exam requirements/recommendations for international students: Required—TOEFL (minimum score 550 paper-based; 79 iBT). Electronic applications accepted.

University of Phoenix–Southern California Campus, College of Education, Costa Mesa, CA 92626. Offers administration and supervision (MA Ed, Certificate); adult education and training (MA Ed); educational studies (MA Ed); elementary teacher education (MA Ed); secondary teacher education (MA Ed); teacher leadership (MA Ed); teachers of English learners (Certificate). *Program availability:* Evening/weekend, online learning. *Entrance requirements:* Additional exam requirements/recommendations for international students: Required—TOEFL, TOEIC (Test of English as an International Communication), Berlitz Online English Proficiency Exam, PTE, or IELTS. Electronic applications accepted. *Expenses:* Contact institution.

University of Phoenix–Washington D.C. Campus, College of Education, Washington, DC 20001. Offers administration and supervision (MA Ed); adult education and training (MA Ed); computer education (MA Ed); curriculum and instruction (MA Ed, Ed D); early childhood education (MA Ed); education (Ed S); educational leadership (Ed D); educational technology (Ed D); elementary teacher education (MA Ed); English and language arts education (MA Ed); English as a second language (MA Ed); higher education administration (PhD); mathematics education (MA Ed); secondary teacher education (MA Ed); special education (MA Ed); teacher leadership (MA Ed).

University of Pittsburgh, Dietrich School of Arts and Sciences, Program in Hispanic Linguistics, Pittsburgh, PA 15260. Offers Hispanic linguistics (MA); TESOL (PhD). *Faculty:* 6 full-time (2 women). *Students:* 6 full-time (5 women), 1 (woman) part-time; includes 1 minority (Hispanic/Latino), 4 international. Average age 27. In 2016, 1 master's awarded. Terminal master's awarded for partial completion of doctoral program. *Degree requirements:* For master's, one foreign language, thesis optional; for doctorate, 2 foreign languages, comprehensive exam, thesis/dissertation. *Entrance*

requirements: For master's and doctorate, GRE General Test, proficiency in Spanish. Additional exam requirements/recommendations for international students: Required—TOEFL (minimum score 600 paper-based; 100 iBT). *Application deadline:* For fall admission, 12/15 priority date for domestic and international students. Application fee: $50. Electronic applications accepted. Tuition and fees vary according to program. *Financial support:* In 2016–17, 6 students received support, including 5 fellowships with full tuition reimbursements available (averaging $17,800 per year), 1 teaching assistantship with full tuition reimbursement available (averaging $17,100 per year). Financial award application deadline: 12/15; financial award applicants required to submit FAFSA. *Faculty research:* Hispanic linguistics, second language acquisition, phonetics, prosody, language variation and change. *Unit head:* Dr. Shelome Gooden, Chair, 412-624-5922, Fax: 412-624-5520, E-mail: sgooden@pitt.edu. *Application contact:* Margaret Bupp, Graduate Student Services Administrator, 412-624-6568, Fax: 412-624-6338, E-mail: maggiebupp@pitt.edu.
Website: http://www.linguistics.pitt.edu

University of Pittsburgh, Dietrich School of Arts and Sciences, TESOL Certificate Program, Pittsburgh, PA 15260. Offers Certificate. *Faculty:* 7 full-time (3 women). *Students:* 4 full-time (1 woman), 5 part-time (all women); includes 1 minority (Asian, non-Hispanic/Latino), 1 international. Average age 32. *Entrance requirements:* Additional exam requirements/recommendations for international students: Required—TOEFL (minimum score 600 paper-based; 100 iBT), IELTS (minimum score 7.5). *Application deadline:* For spring admission, 3/15 for domestic and international students. Application fee: $50. Tuition and fees vary according to program. *Faculty research:* Second language acquisition, applied linguistics, sociolinguistics, second language pedagogy. *Unit head:* Dr. Shelome Gooden, Chair, 412-624-5922, Fax: 412-624-5520, E-mail: sgooden@pitt.edu. *Application contact:* Dr. Dawn McCormick, Senior Lecturer/Associate Director, 412-624-5902, Fax: 412-624-6130, E-mail: mccormic@pitt.edu.
Website: http://www.linguistics.pitt.edu/tesol/

University of Portland, School of Education, Portland, OR 97203-5798. Offers education (MA, MAT); educational leadership (M Ed); English for speakers of other languages (M Ed); initial administrator licensure (M Ed); neuroeducation (M Ed, Ed D); organizational leadership and development (Ed D); reading (M Ed); school leadership and development (Ed D); special education (M Ed). M Ed also available through the Graduate Outreach Program for teachers residing in the Oregon and Washington state areas. *Accreditation:* NCATE. *Program availability:* Part-time, evening/weekend. *Entrance requirements:* For master's, minimum GPA of 3.0, teaching certificate, letters of recommendation, resume, statement of goals, official transcripts. Additional exam requirements/recommendations for international students: Required—TOEFL (minimum score 550 paper-based; 80 iBT), IELTS (minimum score 7). *Faculty research:* Multicultural education, supervision/leadership.

University of Puerto Rico, Río Piedras Campus, College of Education, Program in Teaching English as a Second Language, San Juan, PR 00931-3300. Offers M Ed. *Program availability:* Part-time. *Degree requirements:* For master's, thesis. *Entrance requirements:* For master's, PAEG or GRE, minimum GPA of 3.0, letter of recommendation. *Faculty research:* Second language acquisition, bilingual education.

University of St. Francis, College of Education, Joliet, IL 60435-6169. Offers educational leadership (MS, Ed D); elementary education (M Ed); reading (MS); secondary education (M Ed), including English education, math education, science education, social studies education, visual arts education; special education (M Ed); teaching and learning (MS); TESOL (Certificate). *Accreditation:* NCATE. *Program availability:* Part-time, evening/weekend, 100% online, blended/hybrid learning. *Faculty:* 11 full-time (8 women), 60 part-time/adjunct (42 women). *Students:* 34 full-time (26 women), 420 part-time (318 women); includes 92 minority (51 Black or African American, non-Hispanic/Latino; 5 Asian, non-Hispanic/Latino; 31 Hispanic/Latino; 5 Two or more races, non-Hispanic/Latino), 4 international. Average age 36. 242 applicants, 48% accepted, 96 enrolled. In 2016, 229 master's, 44 doctorates, 10 other advanced degrees awarded. *Degree requirements:* For master's, comprehensive exam; for doctorate, thesis/dissertation. *Entrance requirements:* Additional exam requirements/recommendations for international students: Required—TOEFL (minimum score 550 paper-based; 79 iBT), IELTS (minimum score 6). *Application deadline:* Applications are processed on a rolling basis. Application fee: $30. Electronic applications accepted. Application fee is waived when completed online. *Expenses:* Contact institution. *Financial support:* In 2016–17, 48 students received support. Career-related internships or fieldwork and unspecified assistantships available. Support available to part-time students. Financial award applicants required to submit FAFSA. *Unit head:* Dr. John Gambro, Dean, 815-740-3829, Fax: 815-740-2264, E-mail: jgambro@stfrancis.edu. *Application contact:* Sandra Sloka, Director of Admissions for Graduate and Degree Completion Programs, 800-735-7500, Fax: 815-740-3431, E-mail: ssloka@stfrancis.edu.
Website: http://www.stfrancis.edu/academics/college-of-education/

University of St. Thomas, School of Education and Human Services, Houston, TX 77006-4696. Offers all level education (M Ed); bilingual/dual language (M Ed); Catholic school teaching (M Ed); Catholic/private school leadership (M Ed); counselor education (M Ed); curriculum and instruction (M Ed); education (Ed D); educational leadership (M Ed); elementary teaching (M Ed); English as a second language (M Ed); exceptionality/educational diagnostician (M Ed); exceptionality/special education (M Ed); generalist (M Ed); reading (M Ed); secondary teaching (M Ed); teaching (MAT). *Accreditation:* TEAC. *Program availability:* Part-time, evening/weekend, online learning. *Faculty:* 44 full-time (29 women), 31 part-time/adjunct (17 women). *Students:* 65 full-time (61 women), 719 part-time (645 women); includes 515 minority (169 Black or African American, non-Hispanic/Latino; 25 Asian, non-Hispanic/Latino; 315 Hispanic/Latino; 2 Native Hawaiian or other Pacific Islander, non-Hispanic/Latino; 4 Two or more races, non-Hispanic/Latino), 24 international. Average age 36. 297 applicants, 92% accepted, 211 enrolled. In 2016, 403 master's awarded. *Degree requirements:* For master's, thesis, field experience. *Entrance requirements:* For master's, GRE or MAT if GPA is below 3.0, bachelor's degree; minimum GPA of 2.75 in bachelor's degree or last 60 credit hours; official transcripts from all institutions; goal statement of 250-300 words; 1 reference. Additional exam requirements/recommendations for international students: Required—TOEFL (minimum score 94 iBT), IELTS (minimum score 7), PTE (minimum score 53). *Application deadline:* Applications are processed on a rolling basis. Application fee: $35. Electronic applications accepted. *Expenses:* Contact institution. *Financial support:* In 2016–17, 52 students received support. Federal Work-Study, scholarships/grants, and state work-study, institutional employment available. Support available to part-time students. Financial award application deadline: 4/15; financial award applicants required to submit FAFSA. *Faculty research:* Leadership, diversity, personality traits, second language acquisition. *Unit head:* Dr. Robert LeBlanc, Dean, 713-525-3540, Fax: 713-525-3871, E-mail: education@stthom.edu. *Application contact:* Rita Paredes, Administrative Assistant, 713-525-3442, Fax: 713-525-3871, E-mail: rparede@stthom.edu.
Website: http://www.stthom.edu/Academics/School_of_Education_and_Human_Services/Index.aqf

University of San Diego, School of Leadership and Education Sciences, Department of Learning and Teaching, San Diego, CA 92110-2492. Offers inclusive learning (M Ed); literacy and digital learning (M Ed); school leadership (M Ed); special education with deaf and hard of hearing (M Ed); STEAM (science, technology, engineering, arts, and mathematics) (M Ed); teaching (MAT); TESOL, literacy and culture (M Ed). *Program availability:* Part-time, evening/weekend. *Faculty:* 9 full-time (7 women), 29 part-time/adjunct (19 women). *Students:* 161 full-time (126 women), 188 part-time (153 women); includes 127 minority (4 Black or African American, non-Hispanic/Latino; 24 Asian, non-Hispanic/Latino; 86 Hispanic/Latino; 1 Native Hawaiian or other Pacific Islander, non-Hispanic/Latino; 12 Two or more races, non-Hispanic/Latino), 20 international. Average age 33. 383 applicants, 83% accepted, 194 enrolled. In 2016, 114 master's awarded. *Degree requirements:* For master's, thesis (for some programs), international experience. *Entrance requirements:* For master's, California Basic Educational Skills Test, California Subject Examination for Teachers, minimum GPA of 2.75. Additional exam requirements/recommendations for international students: Required—TOEFL (minimum score 580 paper-based; 83 iBT), TWE. *Application deadline:* Applications are processed on a rolling basis. Application fee: $45. Electronic applications accepted. *Financial support:* In 2016–17, 46 students received support. Career-related internships or fieldwork, Federal Work-Study, institutionally sponsored loans, and stipends available. Financial award application deadline: 4/1; financial award applicants required to submit FAFSA. *Faculty research:* Action research methodology, cultural studies, instructional theories and practices, second language acquisition, school reform. *Unit head:* Dr. Maya Kalyanpur, Chair, 619-260-7655, E-mail: mkalyanpur@sandiego.edu. *Application contact:* Monica Mahon, Associate Director of Graduate Admissions, 619-260-4524, Fax: 619-260-4158, E-mail: grads@sandiego.edu.
Website: http://www.sandiego.edu/soles/departments/learning-and-teaching/

University of South Africa, College of Human Sciences, Pretoria, South Africa. Offers adult education (M Ed); African languages (MA, PhD); African politics (MA, PhD); Afrikaans (MA, PhD); ancient history (MA, PhD); ancient Near Eastern studies (MA, PhD); anthropology (MA, PhD); applied linguistics (MA); Arabic (MA, PhD); archaeology (MA); art history (MA); Biblical archaeology (MA); Biblical studies (M Th, D Th, PhD); Christian spirituality (M Th, D Th); church history (M Th, D Th); classical studies (MA, PhD); clinical psychology (MA); communication (MA, PhD); comparative education (M Ed, Ed D); consulting psychology (D Admin, D Com, PhD); curriculum studies (M Ed, Ed D); development studies (M Admin, MA, D Admin, PhD); didactics (M Ed, Ed D); education (M Tech); education management (M Ed, Ed D); educational psychology (M Ed); English (MA); environmental education (M Ed); French (MA, PhD); German (MA, PhD); Greek (MA); guidance and counseling (M Ed); health studies (MA, PhD), including health sciences education (MA), health services management (MA), medical and surgical nursing science (critical care general) (MA), midwifery and neonatal nursing science (MA), trauma and emergency care (MA); history (MA, PhD); history of education (Ed D); inclusive education (M Ed, Ed D); information and communications technology policy and regulation (MA); information science (MA, MIS, PhD); international politics (MA, PhD); Islamic studies (MA, PhD); Italian (MA, PhD); Judaica (MA, PhD); linguistics (MA, PhD); mathematical education (M Ed); mathematics education (MA); missiology (M Th, D Th); modern Hebrew (MA, PhD); musicology (MA, MMus, D Mus, PhD); natural science education (M Ed); New Testament (M Th, D Th); Old Testament (D Th); pastoral therapy (M Th, D Th); philosophy (MA); philosophy of education (M Ed, Ed D); politics (MA, PhD); Portuguese (MA, PhD); practical theology (M Th, D Th); psychology (MA, MS, PhD); psychology of education (M Ed, Ed D); public health (MA); religious studies (MA, D Th, PhD); Romance languages (MA); Russian (MA, PhD); Semitic languages (MA, PhD); social behavior studies in HIV/AIDS (MA); social science (mental health) (MA); social science in development studies (MA); social science in psychology (MA); social science in social work (MA); social science in sociology (MA); social work (MSW, DSW, PhD); socio-education (M Ed, Ed D); sociolinguistics (MA); sociology (MA, PhD); Spanish (MA, PhD); systematic theology (M Th, D Th); TESOL (teaching English to speakers of other languages) (MA); theological ethics (M Th, D Th); theory of literature (MA, PhD); urban ministries (D Th); urban ministry (M Th).

University of South Carolina, The Graduate School, College of Arts and Sciences, Linguistics Program, Columbia, SC 29208. Offers linguistics (MA, PhD); teaching English to speakers of other languages (Certificate). *Program availability:* Part-time. Terminal master's awarded for partial completion of doctoral program. *Degree requirements:* For master's, one foreign language, comprehensive exam, thesis optional; for doctorate, 3 foreign languages, comprehensive exam, thesis/dissertation. *Entrance requirements:* For master's and Certificate, GRE General Test, minimum GPA of 3.0; for doctorate, GRE General Test, minimum GPA of 3.5. Additional exam requirements/recommendations for international students: Required—TOEFL. Electronic applications accepted. *Faculty research:* Second language acquisition, sociolinguistics, syntax, historical linguistics and phonology.

University of Southern California, Graduate School, Rossier School of Education, Master's Programs in Education, Los Angeles, CA 90089-4038. Offers educational counseling (ME); marriage, family and child counseling (MMFT); postsecondary administration and student affairs [PASA] (ME); school counseling (ME); teaching (online) (MAT); teaching and teaching credential (MAT); teaching English to speakers of other languages (MAT). *Program availability:* Part-time, evening/weekend, online learning. *Degree requirements:* For master's, thesis optional. *Entrance requirements:* For master's, GRE (for all programs except MAT). Additional exam requirements/recommendations for international students: Required—TOEFL (minimum score 100 iBT). Electronic applications accepted. *Faculty research:* College access and equity, preparing teachers for culturally diverse populations, sociocultural basis of learning as mediated by instruction with focus on reading and literacy in English learners, social and political aspects of teaching and learning English, school counselor development and training.

University of Southern Indiana, Graduate Studies, College of Liberal Arts, Program in Second Language Acquisition, Policy, and Culture, Evansville, IN 47712-3590. Offers MA. *Program availability:* Part-time. *Students:* 16 full-time (11 women), 2 part-time (both women); includes 4 minority (1 Black or African American, non-Hispanic/Latino; 1 American Indian or Alaska Native, non-Hispanic/Latino; 1 Asian, non-Hispanic/Latino; 1 Hispanic/Latino), 4 international. Average age 38. *Entrance requirements:* For master's, minimum GPA of 3.0, letter of intent, 3 letters of recommendation. Additional exam requirements/recommendations for international students: Required—TOEFL (minimum score 550 paper-based; 79 iBT), IELTS (minimum score 6). *Expenses:* Tuition, state resident: full-time $8497. Tuition, nonresident: full-time $16,691. *Required fees:* $500. *Financial support:* In 2016–17, 3 students received support. Federal Work-Study, scholarships/grants, tuition waivers (full and partial), and unspecified assistantships available. Financial award application deadline: 3/1; financial award applicants required to submit FAFSA. *Unit head:* Dr. Silvia Rode, Chair, 812-465-7026, E-mail: sarode@usi.edu. *Application contact:* Dr. Mayola Rowser, Director, Graduate Studies, 812-465-7015, E-mail: mrowser@usi.edu.
Website: http://www.usi.edu/liberal-arts/ma-language/

University of Southern Maine, College of Management and Human Service, School of Education and Human Development, Program in Literacy Education, Portland, ME 04103. Offers applied literacy (MS Ed); English as a second language (MS Ed, CAS, CGS); literacy education (MS Ed, CAS, CGS). *Accreditation:* TEAC. *Program availability:* Part-time, evening/weekend. *Degree requirements:* For master's, comprehensive exam, thesis or alternative; for other advanced degree, thesis or alternative. *Entrance requirements:* For master's, teacher certification; for other advanced degree, master's degree. Additional exam requirements/recommendations for international students: Required—TOEFL (minimum score 550 paper-based; 79 iBT). Electronic applications accepted. *Faculty research:* Teacher research in literacy, multiliteracies, learning to teach culturally and linguistically diverse students, motivation to read.

University of South Florida, College of Arts and Sciences, Department of World Languages, Tampa, FL 33620-9951. Offers French (MA); linguistics (MA); linguistics and applied linguistics studies (PhD); linguistics: English as a second language (MA); Spanish (MA). *Program availability:* Part-time, evening/weekend. *Faculty:* 20 full-time (16 women). *Students:* 38 full-time (28 women), 18 part-time (16 women); includes 19 minority (3 Black or African American, non-Hispanic/Latino; 1 Asian, non-Hispanic/Latino; 14 Hispanic/Latino; 1 Two or more races, non-Hispanic/Latino), 9 international. Average age 34. 36 applicants, 58% accepted, 13 enrolled. In 2016, 26 master's awarded. *Degree requirements:* For master's, one foreign language, comprehensive exam, thesis optional; for doctorate, one foreign language, comprehensive exam, thesis/dissertation. *Entrance requirements:* For master's, GRE General Test, minimum undergraduate GPA of 3.0 and 2-3 letters of recommendation; two-page statement of purpose written in Spanish (for Spanish program); oral interview (for Spanish and French programs); writing sample (for French program); for doctorate, GRE General Test, minimum GPA of 3.5 or international equivalent; master's degree or equivalent academic level; statement of purpose; current curriculum vitae; three letters of recommendation; personal interview with faculty; evidence of research experience or scholarly promise. Additional exam requirements/recommendations for international students: Required—TOEFL (minimum score 600 paper-based; 80 iBT) or IELTS (minimum score 6.5) for MA; TOEFL (minimum score 550 paper-based; 80 iBT) or IELTS (minimum score 6.5) for PhD. *Application deadline:* For fall admission, 1/15 for domestic and international students; for spring admission, 10/15 for domestic students, 9/15 for international students. Application fee: $30. Electronic applications accepted. *Expenses:* Tuition, state resident: full-time $7766; part-time $431.43 per credit hour. Tuition, nonresident: full-time $15,789; part-time $877.17 per credit hour. *Required fees:* $37 per term. *Financial support:* In 2016–17, 4 students received support, including 43 teaching assistantships with tuition reimbursements available (averaging $10,152 per year); tuition waivers (partial) and unspecified assistantships also available. Financial award application deadline: 6/30. *Faculty research:* Second language acquisition, instructional technology, foreign language education, English for speakers of other languages, distance learning. *Total annual research expenditures:* $104,720. *Unit head:* Dr. Stephan Schindler, Chair and Professor, 813-974-2548, Fax: 813-905-9937, E-mail: skschindler@usf.edu. *Application contact:* Patricia Garcia, Academic Program Specialist, 813-974-2548, Fax: 813-905-9937, E-mail: pgarcia@usf.edu.
Website: http://languages.usf.edu/

University of South Florida, Innovative Education, Tampa, FL 33620-9951. Offers adult, career and higher education (Graduate Certificate), including college teaching, leadership in developing human resources, leadership in higher education; Africana studies (Graduate Certificate), including diasporas and health disparities, genocide and human rights; aging studies (Graduate Certificate), including gerontology; art research (Graduate Certificate), including museum studies; business foundations (Graduate Certificate); chemical and biomedical engineering (Graduate Certificate), including materials science and engineering, water, health and sustainability; child and family studies (Graduate Certificate), including positive behavior support; civil and industrial engineering (Graduate Certificate), including transportation systems analysis; community and family health (Graduate Certificate), including maternal and child health, social marketing and public health, violence and injury: prevention and intervention, women's health; criminology (Graduate Certificate), including criminal justice administration; educational measurement and research (Graduate Certificate), including evaluation; English (Graduate Certificate), including comparative literary studies, creative writing, professional and technical communication; entrepreneurship (Graduate Certificate); environmental health (Graduate Certificate), including safety management; epidemiology and biostatistics (Graduate Certificate), including applied biostatistics, biostatistics, concepts and tools of epidemiology, epidemiology, epidemiology of infectious diseases; geography, environment and planning (Graduate Certificate), including community development, environmental policy and management, geographical information systems; geology (Graduate Certificate), including hydrogeology; global health (Graduate Certificate), including disaster management, global health and Latin American and Caribbean studies, global health practice, humanitarian assistance, infection control; government and international affairs (Graduate Certificate), including Cuban studies, globalization studies; health policy and management (Graduate Certificate), including health management and leadership, public health policy and programs; hearing specialist: early intervention (Graduate Certificate); industrial and management systems engineering (Graduate Certificate), including systems engineering, technology management; information studies (Graduate Certificate), including school library media specialist; information systems/decision sciences (Graduate Certificate), including analytics and business intelligence; instructional technology (Graduate Certificate), including distance education, Florida digital/virtual educator, instructional design, multimedia design, Web design; internal medicine, bioethics and medical humanities (Graduate Certificate), including biomedical ethics; Latin American and Caribbean studies (Graduate Certificate); mass communications (Graduate Certificate), including multimedia journalism; mathematics and statistics (Graduate Certificate), including mathematics; medicine (Graduate Certificate), including aging and neuroscience, bioinformatics, biotechnology, brain fitness and memory management, clinical investigation, health informatics, health sciences, integrative weight management, intellectual property, medicine and gender, metabolic and nutritional medicine, metabolic cardiology, pharmacy sciences; national and competitive intelligence (Graduate Certificate); psychological and social foundations (Graduate Certificate), including career counseling, college teaching, diversity in education, mental health counseling, school counseling; public affairs (Graduate Certificate), including nonprofit management, public management, research administration; public health (Graduate Certificate), including environmental health, health equity, public health generalist, translational research in adolescent behavioral health; public health practices (Graduate Certificate), including planning for healthy communities; rehabilitation and mental health counseling (Graduate Certificate), including integrative mental health care, marriage and family therapy, rehabilitation technology; secondary education (Graduate Certificate), including ESOL, foreign language education: culture and content, foreign language education: professional; social work (Graduate Certificate), including geriatric social work/clinical gerontology; special education (Graduate Certificate), including autism spectrum disorder, disabilities education: severe/profound; world languages (Graduate Certificate), including teaching English as a second language (TESL) or foreign language. *Expenses:* Tuition, state resident: full-time $7766; part-time $431.43 per credit hour. Tuition, nonresident: full-time $15,789; part-time $877.17 per credit hour. *Required fees:* $37 per term. *Unit head:* Kathy Barnes, Interdisciplinary Programs Coordinator, 813-974-8031, Fax: 813-974-7061, E-mail: barnesk@usf.edu. *Application contact:* Karen Tylinski, Metro Initiatives, 813-974-9943, Fax: 813-974-7061, E-mail: ktylinsk@usf.edu.
Website: http://www.usf.edu/innovative-education/

The University of Tennessee, Graduate School, College of Education, Health and Human Sciences, Program in Education, Knoxville, TN 37996. Offers art education (MS); counseling education (PhD); cultural studies in education (PhD); curriculum (MS, Ed S); curriculum, educational research and evaluation (Ed D, PhD); early childhood education (PhD); early childhood special education (MS); education of deaf and hard of hearing (MS); educational administration and policy studies (Ed D, PhD); educational administration and supervision (Ed S); educational psychology (Ed D, PhD); elementary education (MS, Ed S); elementary teaching (MS); English education (MS, Ed S); exercise science (PhD); foreign language/ESL education (MS, Ed S); instructional technology (MS, Ed D, PhD, Ed S); literacy, language and ESL education (PhD); literacy, language education, and ESL education (Ed D); mathematics education (MS, Ed S); modified and comprehensive special education (MS); reading education (MS, Ed S); school counseling (Ed S); school psychology (PhD, Ed S); science education (MS, Ed S); secondary teaching (MS); social foundations (MS); social science education (MS, Ed S); socio-cultural foundations of sports and education (PhD); special education (Ed S); teacher education (Ed D, PhD). *Accreditation:* NCATE. *Program availability:* Part-time, evening/weekend. *Degree requirements:* For master's and Ed S, thesis optional; for doctorate, variable foreign language requirement, thesis/dissertation. *Entrance requirements:* For master's, minimum GPA of 2.7; for doctorate and Ed S, GRE General Test, minimum GPA of 2.7. Additional exam requirements/recommendations for international students: Required—TOEFL. Electronic applications accepted.

The University of Texas at Arlington, Graduate School, College of Liberal Arts, Department of Linguistics and TESOL, Program in Teaching English to Speakers of Other Languages, Arlington, TX 76019. Offers MA. *Accreditation:* NCATE. *Program availability:* Part-time, evening/weekend. *Degree requirements:* For master's, comprehensive exam (for some programs), thesis optional. *Entrance requirements:* For master's, GRE General Test, minimum undergraduate GPA of 3.0, 6 credits of undergraduate foundation courses, the equivalent of 2 years of university level foreign language study. Additional exam requirements/recommendations for international students: Required—TOEFL (minimum score 550 paper-based). *Application deadline:* For fall admission, 6/1 priority date for domestic students. Applications are processed on a rolling basis. Application fee: $35 ($50 for international students). Electronic applications accepted. *Unit head:* Dr. Laurel Stvan, Chair, 817-272-3133, Fax: 817-272-2731, E-mail: stvan@uta.edu. *Application contact:* Dr. Laurel Stvan, Graduate Advisor, 817-272-3133, Fax: 817-272-2731, E-mail: stvan@uta.edu.

The University of Texas at El Paso, Graduate School, College of Liberal Arts, Department of Languages and Linguistics, El Paso, TX 79968-0001. Offers linguistics (MA); Spanish (MA); teaching English to speakers of other languages (Certificate). *Program availability:* Part-time, evening/weekend. *Degree requirements:* For master's, thesis optional. *Entrance requirements:* For master's, GRE General Test, departmental exam, minimum GPA of 3.0, letters of recommendation. Additional exam requirements/recommendations for international students: Required—TOEFL; Recommended—IELTS. Electronic applications accepted.

The University of Texas at San Antonio, College of Education and Human Development, Department of Bicultural and Bilingual Studies, San Antonio, TX 78249-0617. Offers bicultural and bilingual studies (MA), including bicultural and bilingual education, bicultural studies; culture, literacy, and language (PhD); teaching English as a second language (MA). *Program availability:* Part-time, evening/weekend. *Faculty:* 19 full-time (13 women), 2 part-time/adjunct (1 woman). *Students:* 32 full-time (21 women), 109 part-time (86 women); includes 80 minority (3 Black or African American, non-Hispanic/Latino; 4 Asian, non-Hispanic/Latino; 72 Hispanic/Latino; 1 Two or more races, non-Hispanic/Latino), 11 international. Average age 37. 70 applicants, 77% accepted, 36 enrolled. In 2016, 28 master's, 10 doctorates awarded. *Degree requirements:* For master's, one foreign language, comprehensive exam, thesis optional; for doctorate, one foreign language, comprehensive exam, thesis/dissertation. *Entrance requirements:* For master's, bachelor's degree with 18 credit hours in field of study or in another appropriate field of study; for doctorate, GRE General Test, resume or curriculum vitae, 3 letters of recommendation, statement of purpose, master's degree. Additional exam requirements/recommendations for international students: Required—TOEFL (minimum score 550 paper-based; 79 iBT), IELTS (minimum score 6.5). *Application deadline:* For fall admission, 7/1 for domestic students, 4/1 for international students; for spring admission, 11/1 for domestic students, 9/1 for international students. Applications are processed on a rolling basis. Application fee: $45 ($80 for international students). Electronic applications accepted. *Expenses:* Contact institution. *Financial support:* In 2016–17, 18 students received support, including 18 fellowships (averaging $28,000 per year), 2 research assistantships (averaging $12,468 per year), 16 teaching assistantships (averaging $11,000 per year); scholarships/grants and unspecified assistantships also available. Financial award application deadline: 4/15. *Faculty research:* Bilingual and ESL teacher preparation; transnational communities; applied linguistics; cultural studies; bilingualism, biliteracy and second language acquisition. *Total annual research expenditures:* $300,234. *Unit head:* Dr. Belinda Flores, Chair, 210-458-5570, Fax: 210-458-5962, E-mail: belinda.flores@utsa.edu. *Application contact:* Rahnuma Islam, Student Development Specialist, 210-458-6619, Fax: 210-458-5576, E-mail: rahnuma.islam@utsa.edu.
Website: http://education.utsa.edu/bicultural-bilingual_studies

The University of Texas at San Antonio, College of Education and Human Development, Department of Educational Psychology, San Antonio, TX 78207. Offers applied behavioral analysis (Certificate); digital learning design (Certificate); language acquisition and bilingual psychoeducational assessment (Certificate); school psychology (MA). *Program availability:* Part-time. *Faculty:* 11 full-time (6 women), 1 (woman) part-time/adjunct. *Students:* 38 full-time (31 women), 29 part-time (25 women); includes 43 minority (4 Black or African American, non-Hispanic/Latino; 1 Asian, non-Hispanic/Latino; 35 Hispanic/Latino; 3 Two or more races, non-Hispanic/Latino). Average age 28. 23 applicants, 78% accepted, 13 enrolled. In 2016, 16 master's, 16 other advanced degrees awarded. *Degree requirements:* For master's, comprehensive exam, thesis (for some programs). *Entrance requirements:* For master's, GRE, bachelor's degree with 18 credit hours in field of study or in another appropriate field of study, two letters of recommendation, statement of purpose; for Certificate, 18 hours in psychology, sociology, education, or anything related (for applied behavioral analysis); minimum GPA of 2.7 in last 30 hours (for language acquisition and bilingual psychoeducational assessment). Additional exam requirements/recommendations for international students: Required—TOEFL (minimum score 550 paper-based; 79 iBT), IELTS (minimum score 6.5). *Application deadline:* For fall admission, 7/1 for domestic students, 4/1 for international students; for spring admission, 11/1 for domestic students, 9/1 for international students; for summer admission, 3/1 for international students. Applications are processed on a rolling basis. Application fee: $45 ($80 for international students). Electronic applications accepted. *Financial support:* In 2016–17, 9 research assistantships (averaging $2,829 per year) were awarded. Financial award application deadline: 3/5; financial award applicants required to submit FAFSA. *Faculty research:* Teacher consultation and culturally responsive school psychology practices, youth

mentoring, cross-age peer mentoring, adolescent connectedness, pair counseling. *Total annual research expenditures:* $91,630. *Unit head:* Dr. Jeremy Sullivan, Department Chair, 210-458-2378, Fax: 210-458-2019, E-mail: jeremy.sullivan@utsa.edu. *Application contact:* Dr. John Pruiett, Development Specialist, 210-458-2721, Fax: 210-458-2019, E-mail: johnny.pruiett@utsa.edu.
Website: http://education.utsa.edu/educational_psychology

The University of Texas of the Permian Basin, Office of Graduate Studies, School of Education, Program in Bilingual/English as a Second Language Education, Odessa, TX 79762-0001. Offers MA. *Degree requirements:* For master's, comprehensive exam (for some programs), thesis (for some programs). *Entrance requirements:* For master's, GRE General Test. Additional exam requirements/recommendations for international students: Required—TOEFL (minimum score 550 paper-based).

The University of Texas Rio Grande Valley, College of Liberal Arts, Department of Writing and Language Studies, Program in English as a Second Language, Edinburg, TX 78539. Offers MA. *Program availability:* Part-time, evening/weekend. *Degree requirements:* For master's, comprehensive exam, thesis optional. *Entrance requirements:* For master's, GRE General Test, minimum GPA of 3.0. Tuition and fees vary according to course load and program. *Faculty research:* Oral versus literary culture discourse analysis, language shift among Hispanics.

University of the Southwest, Graduate Programs, Hobbs, NM 88240-9129. Offers business administration (MBA); curriculum and instruction (MSE); curriculum and instruction: bilingual (MSE); curriculum and instruction: TESOL (MSE); early childhood education (MSE); educational administration (MSE); mental health counseling (MSE); school counseling (MSE); special education (MSE); sports management (MBA). *Program availability:* Part-time, evening/weekend, online learning. *Degree requirements:* For master's, comprehensive exam, thesis (for some programs). *Entrance requirements:* Additional exam requirements/recommendations for international students: Recommended—TOEFL. Electronic applications accepted.

The University of Toledo, College of Graduate Studies, College of Languages, Literature and Social Sciences, Department of English Language and Literature, Toledo, OH 43606-3390. Offers English as a second language (MA); teaching of writing (Certificate). *Program availability:* Part-time. *Degree requirements:* For master's, thesis. *Entrance requirements:* For master's, GRE if GPA is less than 3.0, minimum cumulative point-hour ratio of 2.7 for all previous academic work, three letters of recommendation, transcripts from all prior institutions attended, critical essay; for Certificate, statement of purpose, transcripts from all prior institutions attended, 2 letters of recommendation. Additional exam requirements/recommendations for international students: Required—TOEFL (minimum score 550 paper-based; 80 iBT). Electronic applications accepted. *Faculty research:* Literary criticism, linguistics, creative writing, folklore and cultural studies.

The University of Toledo, College of Graduate Studies, Judith Herb College of Education, Department of Curriculum and Instruction, Toledo, OH 43606-3390. Offers art education (ME); career and technical education (ME, Ed S); curriculum and instruction (ME, PhD, Ed S); early childhood education (Ed S); education and anthropology (MAE); education and biology (MES); education and chemistry (MES); education and classics (MAE); education and economics (MAE); education and English (MAE); education and French (MAE); education and geology (MES); education and German (MAE); education and history (MAE); education and mathematics (MAE, MES); education and physics (MES); education and political science (MAE); education and sociology (MAE); education and Spanish (MAE); educational media (PhD); educational technology (ME); educational technology: virtual educator (Certificate); elementary education (PhD); English as a second language (MAE); gifted and talented education (PhD); middle childhood education (ME); secondary education (ME, PhD); special education (PhD). *Accreditation:* NCATE. *Program availability:* Part-time, evening/weekend. *Degree requirements:* For master's, comprehensive exam, thesis or alternative; for doctorate, comprehensive exam, thesis/dissertation; for other advanced degree, thesis optional. *Entrance requirements:* For master's, doctorate, and other advanced degree, minimum cumulative GPA of 2.7 for all previous academic work, letters of recommendation. Additional exam requirements/recommendations for international students: Required—TOEFL (minimum score 550 paper-based; 80 iBT). Electronic applications accepted.

University of Washington, Graduate School, College of Arts and Sciences, Department of English, Seattle, WA 98195. Offers creative writing (MFA); English as a second language (MAT); English literature and language (MA, MAT, PhD). *Program availability:* Part-time. Terminal master's awarded for partial completion of doctoral program. *Degree requirements:* For master's, one foreign language, thesis (for some programs); for doctorate, one foreign language, thesis/dissertation. *Entrance requirements:* For master's, GRE General Test, GRE Subject Test (MA and MAT in English), minimum GPA of 3.0; for doctorate, GRE General Test, GRE Subject Test. Additional exam requirements/recommendations for international students: Required—TOEFL. Electronic applications accepted. *Faculty research:* English and American literature, critical theory, creative writing, language theory.

University of Wisconsin–Milwaukee, Graduate School, College of Letters and Science, Department of Linguistics, Milwaukee, WI 53201-0413. Offers linguistics (MA, PhD), including teaching English to speakers of other languages (MA); teaching English to speakers of other languages, adult- and university-level (Graduate Certificate). *Students:* 19 full-time (10 women), 6 part-time (5 women), 15 international. Average age 34. 75 applicants, 36% accepted, 10 enrolled. In 2016, 6 master's, 4 doctorates, 4 other advanced degrees awarded. *Unit head:* Hamid Ouali, Department Chair, 414-229-1113, E-mail: ouali@uwm.edu. *Application contact:* General Information Contact, 414-229-4982, Fax: 414-229-6967, E-mail: gradschool@uwm.edu.
Website: http://www4.uwm.edu/letsci/linguistics/

University of Wisconsin–River Falls, Outreach and Graduate Studies, College of Arts and Science, Program in Teaching English to Speakers of Other Languages, River Falls, WI 54022. Offers MA.

Upper Iowa University, Master of Education Program, Fayette, IA 52142-1857. Offers early childhood (M Ed); English as a second language (M Ed); higher education (M Ed); instructional strategist (M Ed); reading (M Ed); teacher leadership (M Ed).

Utah Valley University, Program in Education, Orem, UT 84058-5999. Offers educational technology (M Ed); elementary mathematics (M Ed); elementary STEM (M Ed); English as a second language (M Ed); reading (M Ed); teachers as leaders (M Ed). *Accreditation:* TEAC. *Program availability:* Part-time. *Degree requirements:* For master's, project. *Entrance requirements:* For master's, GRE, 3 letters of recommendation, interview, essay. Additional exam requirements/recommendations for international students: Required—TOEFL (minimum score 83 iBT). Electronic applications accepted. *Expenses:* Contact institution.

Valley City State University, Online Master of Education Program, Valley City, ND 58072. Offers elementary education (M Ed); English education (M Ed); library and information technologies (M Ed); teaching (MAT); teaching and technology (M Ed); teaching English language learners (M Ed); technology education (M Ed). *Accreditation:* NCATE. *Program availability:* Part-time, evening/weekend, online only, 100% online. *Faculty:* 21 full-time (12 women), 15 part-time/adjunct (11 women). *Students:* 4 full-time (3 women), 133 part-time (92 women); includes 9 minority (1 American Indian or Alaska Native, non-Hispanic/Latino; 4 Hispanic/Latino; 4 Two or more races, non-Hispanic/Latino), 1 international. Average age 34. 35 applicants, 91% accepted, 28 enrolled. In 2016, 45 master's awarded. *Degree requirements:* For master's, action research report, comprehensive portfolio. *Entrance requirements:* For master's, GRE, MAT, PRAXIS II or National Teaching Board for Professional Standards (if GPA is less than 3.0). Additional exam requirements/recommendations for international students: Required—TOEFL (minimum score 525 paper-based; 71 iBT); Recommended—IELTS (minimum score 5.5). *Application deadline:* For fall admission, 7/21 priority date for domestic and international students; for spring admission, 12/8 priority date for domestic and international students; for summer admission, 5/5 priority date for domestic and international students. Applications are processed on a rolling basis. Application fee: $35. Electronic applications accepted. *Expenses:* $373 per credit. *Financial support:* In 2016–17, 23 students received support. Scholarships/grants, tuition waivers (full and partial), and unspecified assistantships available. Financial award application deadline: 6/14; financial award applicants required to submit FAFSA. *Faculty research:* Universal accessibility, instructional design and technology, gender communication, STEM education in K-12. *Unit head:* Dr. Gary Thompson, Dean, 701-845-7197, E-mail: gary.thompson@vcsu.edu. *Application contact:* Misty Lindgren, Graduate Studies, 701-845-7303, Fax: 701-845-7190, E-mail: misty.lindgren@vcsu.edu.
Website: http://www.vcsu.edu/graduate

Valparaiso University, Graduate School and Continuing Education, Program in English Studies, Valparaiso, IN 46383. Offers English studies and communication (MA); teaching of English to speakers of other languages (MA); JD/MA. *Program availability:* Part-time, evening/weekend. *Entrance requirements:* For master's, minimum GPA of 3.0. Additional exam requirements/recommendations for international students: Required—TOEFL (minimum score 550 paper-based; 80 iBT), IELTS (minimum score 6). Electronic applications accepted. *Expenses: Tuition:* Full-time $11,070; part-time $615 per credit hour. *Required fees:* $116 per semester. Tuition and fees vary according to course load, degree level and program.

Valparaiso University, Graduate School and Continuing Education, TESOL Program, Valparaiso, IN 46383. Offers MA, Certificate. *Program availability:* Part-time, evening/weekend. *Entrance requirements:* For master's, minimum GPA of 3.0. Additional exam requirements/recommendations for international students: Required—TOEFL (minimum score 550 paper-based; 80 iBT), IELTS (minimum score 6). Electronic applications accepted. *Expenses: Tuition:* Full-time $11,070; part-time $615 per credit hour. *Required fees:* $116 per semester. Tuition and fees vary according to course load, degree level and program.

Virginia International University, School of Education, Fairfax, VA 22030. Offers applied linguistics (MS); education (M Ed); teaching English to speakers of other languages (MA). *Program availability:* Part-time, online learning. *Entrance requirements:* For master's, bachelor's degree. Additional exam requirements/recommendations for international students: Required—TOEFL (minimum score 550 paper-based; 80 iBT), IELTS (minimum score 6). Electronic applications accepted.

Walden University, Graduate Programs, Richard W. Riley College of Education and Leadership, Minneapolis, MN 55401. Offers adult education (Post-Master's Certificate); adult learning (Graduate Certificate); college teaching and learning (Graduate Certificate); community college leadership (Ed D); curriculum, instruction and assessment (Ed D, Ed S, Graduate Certificate); developmental education (Graduate Certificate); early childhood administration, management, and leadership (Graduate Certificate); early childhood education (Ed D, Ed S); early childhood public policy and advocacy (Graduate Certificate); early childhood studies (MS), including administration, management and leadership, early childhood public policy and advocacy, teaching adults in the early childhood field, teaching and diversity in early childhood education; education (MS, PhD), including adolescent literacy and learning (MS), curriculum, instruction, and assessment (grades K-12) (MS), curriculum, instruction, assessment, and evaluation (PhD), early childhood leadership and advocacy (PhD), early childhood special education (PhD), educational leadership (MS), educational leadership and administration (principal preparation) (MS), educational technology and design (PhD), elementary reading and literacy (PreK-6) (MS), elementary reading and mathematics (grades K-6) (MS), global and comparative education (PhD), higher education leadership management and policy (PhD), integrating technology in the classroom (grades K-12) (MS), learning, instruction and innovation (PhD), mathematics (grades 5-8) (MS), mathematics (grades K-6) (MS), mathematics and science (grades K-8) (MS), organizational research, assessment, and evaluation (PhD), reading and literacy with a reading K-12 endorsement (MS), reading literacy assessment and evaluation (PhD), science (grades K-8) (MS), special education (non-licensure) (grades K-12) (MS), teacher leadership (grades K-12) (MS), teaching English language learners (grades K-12) (MS); educational administration and leadership (Ed D); educational leadership and administration (principal preparation) (Ed S); educational technology (Ed D, Ed S, Post Master's Certificate); elementary reading and literacy (Graduate Certificate); engaging culturally diverse learners (Graduate Certificate); enrollment management and institutional marketing (Graduate Certificate); higher education (MS), including adult learning, college teaching and learning, enrollment management and institutional marketing, global higher education, leadership for student success, online and distance learning; higher education and adult learning (Ed D); higher education leadership and management (Ed D); higher education leadership for student success (Graduate Certificate); instructional design and technology (MS, Postbaccalaureate Certificate), including general program (MS), online learning (MS), training and performance improvement (MS); integrating technology in the classroom (Graduate Certificate); mathematics 5-8 (Graduate Certificate); mathematics K-6 (Graduate Certificate); online teaching for adult educators (Graduate Certificate); reading, literacy, and assessment (Ed D, Ed S); science K-8 (Graduate Certificate); special education (Ed D, Ed S, Graduate Certificate); special education (K-age 21) (MAT); teacher leadership (Graduate Certificate); teaching adults English as a second language (Graduate Certificate); teaching adults in the early childhood field (Graduate Certificate); teaching and diversity in early childhood education (Graduate Certificate); teaching English language learners (grades K-12) (Graduate Certificate); teaching K-12 students online (Graduate Certificate). *Accreditation:* NCATE. *Program availability:* Part-time, evening/weekend, online only, 100% online. *Degree requirements:* For doctorate, thesis/dissertation (for some programs), residency; for other advanced degree, residency (for some programs). *Entrance requirements:* For master's, bachelor's degree or higher; minimum GPA of 2.5; official transcripts; goal statement (for some programs); access to computer and Internet; for doctorate, master's degree or higher; three years of related professional or academic experience (preferred); minimum GPA of 3.0; goal statement and current resume (for select programs); official transcripts; access to computer and Internet; for other advanced degree, relevant work experience; access to computer and Internet. Additional exam requirements/recommendations for international students: Required—TOEFL (minimum score 550 paper-based, 79 iBT), IELTS (minimum score 6.5), Michigan English Language Assessment Battery (minimum score 82), or PTE (minimum score 53). Electronic applications accepted.

English as a Second Language

Washington State University, College of Education, Department of Teaching and Learning, Pullman, WA 99164-2132. Offers cultural studies and social thought in education (PhD); curriculum and instruction (Ed M, MA); English language learners (Ed M, MA); language, literacy and technology (PhD); literacy education (Ed M, MA); mathematics education (PhD); special education (Ed M, MA, PhD); teacher leadership (Ed D); teaching (MIT), including elementary education, secondary education. Programs offered at the Pullman, Spokane, Tri-cities, Vancouver and Global (online) campuses. *Program availability:* Part-time, online learning. *Degree requirements:* For master's, comprehensive exam, thesis, oral or written exam; for doctorate, comprehensive exam, thesis/dissertation, oral and written exam. *Entrance requirements:* For master's, GRE General Test, minimum GPA of 3.0, 3 letters of recommendation, letter of intent, transcripts, resume/curriculum vitae; for doctorate, GRE General Test, minimum GPA of 3.0, 3 letters of recommendation, letter of intent, transcripts, writing sample, resume/ curriculum vitae. Additional exam requirements/recommendations for international students: Required—TOEFL (minimum score 550 paper-based; 80 iBT). Electronic applications accepted. *Faculty research:* Intersection of gender, youth cultures and schooling; examination of ideology of power in children's literature; early childhood special education; analyzing pre-service and in-service teacher development; second language acquisition.

Wayland Baptist University, Graduate Programs, Program in Education, Plainview, TX 79072-6998. Offers education administration (M Ed); education diagnostics (M Ed); education literacy (M Ed); elementary certification (M Ed); English (M Ed); English as a second language (M Ed); higher education administration (M Ed); human resources (M Ed); instructional leadership (M Ed); instructional technology (M Ed); leadership training and development (M Ed); science education (M Ed); secondary certification (M Ed); social studies (M Ed); special education (M Ed); sports administration and management (M Ed). *Program availability:* Part-time, evening/weekend, online learning. *Degree requirements:* For master's, comprehensive exam, capstone course. *Entrance requirements:* For master's, GRE, GMAT or MAT. Additional exam requirements/ recommendations for international students: Required—TOEFL (minimum score 500 paper-based; 61 iBT). Electronic applications accepted.

Wayne State College, School of Education and Counseling, Department of Educational Foundations and Leadership, Program in Curriculum and Instruction, Wayne, NE 68787. Offers alternative education (MSE); business and information technology education (MSE); communication arts education (MSE); early childhood education (MSE); elementary education (MSE); English as a second language (MSE); English education (MSE); family and consumer sciences education (MSE); industrial technology and vocational education (MSE); learning communities (MSE); mathematics education (MSE); music education (MSE); science education (MSE); social science education (MSE). *Accreditation:* NCATE. *Program availability:* Part-time, evening/weekend. *Degree requirements:* For master's, comprehensive exam, thesis optional. *Entrance requirements:* For master's, GRE General Test. Additional exam requirements/ recommendations for international students: Required—TOEFL (minimum score 550 paper-based).

Wayne State University, College of Education, Division of Teacher Education, Detroit, MI 48202. Offers art education (M Ed); bilingual/bicultural education (M Ed, Certificate); career and technical education (M Ed); curriculum and instruction (Ed D, PhD, Ed S), including art education (Ed D, PhD), bilingual education (Ed D, Ed S), career and technical education (MAT, Ed D, PhD, Ed S), early childhood education (MAT, Ed D, PhD, Ed S), elementary education, English as a second language (MAT, Ed D, Ed S), English education (MAT, Ed D, PhD, Ed S), foreign language education (MAT, Ed D, PhD), K-12 curriculum, mathematics education (MAT, Ed D, PhD, Ed S), science education (MAT, Ed D, PhD, Ed S), secondary education, social studies education (MAT, Ed D, PhD, Ed S); early childhood education (M Ed); elementary education (M Ed, MAT), including bilingual/bicultural education (MAT), early childhood education (MAT, Ed D, PhD, Ed S), English as a second language (MAT, Ed D, Ed S), general elementary education (MAT), mathematics education (MAT, Ed D, PhD, Ed S), science education (MAT, Ed D, PhD, Ed S), social studies education (MAT, Ed D, PhD, Ed S); English as a second language (Certificate); English education (M Ed); foreign language education (M Ed); mathematics education (M Ed); reading (M Ed, Ed S); reading, language and literature (Ed D); science education (M Ed); secondary education (MAT), including art education (K-12), bilingual/bicultural education, career and technical education (MAT, Ed D, PhD, Ed S), English as a second language (MAT, Ed D, Ed S), English education (MAT, Ed D, PhD, Ed S), foreign language education (MAT, Ed D, PhD), kinesiology, mathematics education (MAT, Ed D, PhD, Ed S); social studies education (M Ed); special education (M Ed, MAT, Ed D, PhD, Ed S), including autism spectrum disorders (MAT), cognitive development (MAT), emotional impairment (MAT), learning disabilities (MAT). *Program availability:* Part-time, blended/hybrid learning. *Faculty:* 29. *Students:* 106 full-time (73 women), 351 part-time (276 women); includes 115 minority (76 Black or African American, non-Hispanic/Latino; 10 Asian, non-Hispanic/Latino; 20 Hispanic/Latino; 1 Native Hawaiian or other Pacific Islander, non-Hispanic/Latino; 8 Two or more races, non-Hispanic/Latino), 12 international. Average age 37. 242 applicants, 37% accepted, 72 enrolled. In 2016, 178 master's, 19 doctorates, 17 other advanced degrees awarded. *Degree requirements:* For master's, essay or project (for some M Ed programs), professional field experience (for MAT programs); for doctorate, thesis/dissertation. *Entrance requirements:* For master's, Michigan Test for Teacher Certification, verification of participation in group work with children, Michigan State Police criminal background check; for doctorate, minimum undergraduate GPA of 3.0, graduate 3.5; interview; curriculum vitae; references. Additional exam requirements/recommendations for international students: Required—TOEFL (minimum score 550 paper-based; 79 iBT), TWE (minimum score 5.5), Michigan English Language Assessment Battery (minimum score 85); Recommended—IELTS (minimum score 6.5). *Application deadline:* For fall admission, 6/1 priority date for domestic students, 5/1 priority date for international students; for winter admission, 10/1 priority date for domestic students, 9/1 priority date for international students; for spring admission, 2/1 priority date for domestic students, 1/1 priority date for international students. Applications are processed on a rolling basis. Application fee: $50. Electronic applications accepted. *Expenses:* $16,503 per year resident tuition and fees, $33,697 per year non-resident tuition and fees. *Financial support:* In 2016–17, 101 students received support, including 3 fellowships (averaging $11,409 per year); research assistantships with tuition reimbursements available, Federal Work-Study, scholarships/ grants, and unspecified assistantships also available. Support available to part-time students. Financial award applicants required to submit FAFSA. *Faculty research:* Improving students' skill achievement in mathematics, improving elementary children's understanding of informational text, teachers' use of their pedagogical and mathematical knowledge in the interactive work of teaching, the intersection of identity construction in teaching and learning, identifying effective methods of literacy instruction and assessments for bilingual students in elementary language arts classrooms. *Unit head:* Dr. Kathleen Crawford-McKinney, Assistant Dean, 313-577-0122. *Application contact:* Janice Green, Assistant Dean, 313-577-1605, E-mail: jwgreen@wayne.edu.
Website: http://coe.wayne.edu/ted/index.php

Webster University, School of Education, Department of Multidisciplinary Studies, St. Louis, MO 63119-3194. Offers applied educational psychology (MA, Ed S); communication arts (MA); early childhood education (MA, MAT); education and innovation (MA); educational technology (MET); elementary education (MAT); mathematics for educators (MA); middle school education (MAT); multidisciplinary studies (MAT); multimodal literacy for global impact (MA); reading (MA); secondary school education (MAT); special education (MA, MAT); teaching English as a second language (MA); transformative learning in the global community (Ed S). *Program availability:* Part-time. *Entrance requirements:* For master's, minimum GPA of 2.5. Additional exam requirements/recommendations for international students: Required—TOEFL. *Application deadline:* Applications are processed on a rolling basis. Application fee: $35 ($50 for international students). *Expenses: Tuition:* Full-time $21,900; part-time $730 per credit hour. Tuition and fees vary according to campus/location and program. *Financial support:* Federal Work-Study available. Support available to part-time students. Financial award application deadline: 4/1; financial award applicants required to submit FAFSA. *Unit head:* Dr. Deborah Stiles, Chair, 314-968-7056, Fax: 314-968-7118, E-mail: stilesda@webster.edu.

West Chester University of Pennsylvania, College of Arts and Humanities, Program in Teaching English as a Second Language, West Chester, PA 19383. Offers MA, Certificate. *Program availability:* Part-time, evening/weekend. *Students:* 8 full-time (6 women), 15 part-time (13 women); includes 3 minority (1 Black or African American, non-Hispanic/Latino; 1 Asian, non-Hispanic/Latino; 1 Hispanic/Latino), 2 international. Average age 33. 15 applicants, 87% accepted, 7 enrolled. In 2016, 9 master's awarded. *Degree requirements:* For master's, comprehensive exam, capstone review and teaching philosophy. *Entrance requirements:* For master's, minimum GPA of 2.8, two letters of recommendation, prior introduction to linguistics coursework, goals statement, experience in learning a second language (recommended); for Certificate, prior PA teaching certification. Additional exam requirements/recommendations for international students: Required—TOEFL or IELTS. *Application deadline:* For fall admission, 5/15 for international students; for spring admission, 10/15 for international students. Applications are processed on a rolling basis. Application fee: $50. Electronic applications accepted. *Expenses:* Tuition, state resident: full-time $8694; part-time $483 per credit. Tuition, nonresident: full-time $13,050; part-time $725 per credit. *Required fees:* $2399; $119.05 per credit. Tuition and fees vary according to campus/location and program. *Financial support:* Scholarships/grants and unspecified assistantships available. Financial award application deadline: 2/15; financial award applicants required to submit FAFSA. *Faculty research:* Second language acquisition, language teaching methods, discourse analysis, computer-assisted language learning, language teacher development. *Unit head:* Dr. Esther Smidt, Director of TESOL Program, 610-738-0410, E-mail: csmidt@wcupa.edu. *Application contact:* Office of Graduate Studies and Extended Education, 610-436-2943, Fax: 610-436-2763, E-mail: gradstudy@ wcupa.edu.
Website: http://www.wcupa.edu/_admissions/sch_dgr/tesl.aspx

Western Carolina University, Graduate School, College of Arts and Sciences, Department of English, Cullowhee, NC 28723. Offers teaching English as a second language or foreign language (MA). *Program availability:* Part-time, evening/weekend. *Degree requirements:* For master's, one foreign language, comprehensive exam, thesis (for some programs). *Entrance requirements:* For master's, GRE General Test, appropriate undergraduate degree, writing sample, 3 letters of recommendation. Additional exam requirements/recommendations for international students: Required—TOEFL (minimum score 550 paper-based; 79 iBT). *Expenses:* Tuition, state resident: full-time $2174. Tuition, nonresident: full-time $7377. *Required fees:* $1442. Part-time tuition and fees vary according to course load. *Faculty research:* Teaching English to speakers of other languages (TESOL), language assessment, applied linguistics, poetry, folk and fairy tales, post World War II British literature, Appalachian and southern literature.

Western Illinois University, School of Graduate Studies, College of Education and Human Services, Department of Educational Studies, Program in Educational and Interdisciplinary Studies, Macomb, IL 61455-1390. Offers educational and interdisciplinary studies (MS Ed); teaching English to speakers of other languages (Certificate). *Accreditation:* NCATE. *Program availability:* Part-time. *Students:* 4 full-time (all women), 23 part-time (19 women); includes 6 minority (1 Asian, non-Hispanic/Latino; 3 Hispanic/Latino; 2 Two or more races, non-Hispanic/Latino), 1 international. Average age 31. 7 applicants, 100% accepted, 3 enrolled. In 2016, 7 master's, 3 Certificates awarded. *Degree requirements:* For master's, thesis or alternative. *Entrance requirements:* For master's, minimum GPA of 2.75, interview. Additional exam requirements/recommendations for international students: Required—TOEFL (minimum score 550 paper-based; 80 iBT). *Application deadline:* Applications are processed on a rolling basis. Application fee: $30. Electronic applications accepted. *Financial support:* In 2016–17, 5 students received support, including 1 research assistantship with full tuition reimbursement available (averaging $7,544 per year); unspecified assistantships also available. Financial award applicants required to submit FAFSA. *Unit head:* Dr. Greg Montalvo, Interim Chairperson, 309-298-1183. *Application contact:* Dr. Nancy Parsons, Associate Provost and Director of Graduate Studies, 309-298-1806, Fax: 309-298-2345, E-mail: grad-office@wiu.edu.
Website: http://www.wiu.edu/coehs/es/programs/eis/eis.php

Western Kentucky University, Graduate Studies, Potter College of Arts and Letters, Department of English, Bowling Green, KY 42101. Offers education (MA); English (MA Ed); literature (MA), including American literature, British literature, literary theory, women writers, world literature; teaching English as a second language (MA); writing (MA). *Program availability:* Part-time, evening/weekend. *Degree requirements:* For master's, comprehensive exam, thesis optional, final exam. *Entrance requirements:* For master's, GRE General Test, minimum GPA of 2.75. Additional exam requirements/ recommendations for international students: Required—TOEFL (minimum score 555 paper-based; 79 iBT). *Faculty research:* Improving writing, linking teacher knowledge and performance, Victorian women writers, Kentucky women writers, Kentucky poets.

Western New Mexico University, Graduate Division, School of Education, Silver City, NM 88062-0680. Offers bilingual education (MAT); educational leadership (MA); elementary education (MAT); reading (MAT); secondary education (MAT); special education (MAT); TESOL (teaching English to speakers of other languages) (MAT). *Accreditation:* NCATE. *Program availability:* Part-time, online learning. *Degree requirements:* For master's, comprehensive exam. *Entrance requirements:* For master's, minimum GPA of 3.0 in last 64 hours of undergraduate study. Additional exam requirements/recommendations for international students: Required—TOEFL (minimum score 550 paper-based; 79 iBT). Electronic applications accepted. *Faculty research:* International education, electronic reading assessment, developing STEM teachers.

West Virginia University, Eberly College of Arts and Sciences, Department of World Languages, Literatures and Linguistics, Morgantown, WV 26506. Offers French (MA); linguistics (MA); Spanish (MA); teaching English to speakers of other languages (MA). *Program availability:* Part-time. *Degree requirements:* For master's, one foreign language, comprehensive exam (for some programs), thesis optional. *Entrance requirements:* For master's, minimum GPA of 3.0. Electronic applications accepted. *Faculty research:* French, German, and Spanish literature; foreign language pedagogy; English as a second language; cultural studies; linguistics.

Wheaton College, Graduate School, Department of Intercultural Studies, Wheaton, IL 60187-5593. Offers intercultural studies (MA); intercultural studies/teaching English as a

second language (MA); missions (MA); teaching English as a second language (Certificate). *Program availability:* Part-time. *Faculty:* 5 full-time (2 women), 2 part-time/adjunct (both women). *Students:* 25 full-time (20 women), 15 part-time (9 women); includes 8 minority (1 Black or African American, non-Hispanic/Latino; 6 Asian, non-Hispanic/Latino; 1 Hispanic/Latino), 8 international. Average age 32. 35 applicants, 94% accepted, 20 enrolled. In 2016, 23 master's awarded. *Degree requirements:* For master's, thesis or alternative. *Entrance requirements:* For master's, GRE General Test, MAT. Additional exam requirements/recommendations for international students: Required—TOEFL (minimum score 550 paper-based; 80 iBT), IELTS (minimum score 6.5), TOEFL (minimum score 600 paper-based; 90 iBT) or IELTS (minimum score 7.5) for MA in TESOL. *Application deadline:* For fall admission, 5/1 for domestic students, 1/1 for international students; for spring admission, 11/1 for domestic students. Applications are processed on a rolling basis. Application fee: $30. Electronic applications accepted. *Expenses: Tuition:* Full-time $19,080; part-time $795 per credit hour. Tuition and fees vary according to degree level and program. *Financial support:* Career-related internships or fieldwork, scholarships/grants, and unspecified assistantships available. Financial award application deadline: 3/1; financial award applicants required to submit FAFSA. *Unit head:* Dr. Robert Gallagher, Chair, 630-752-5948, E-mail: intercultural.studies@wheaton.edu. *Application contact:* Dusty Di Santo, Director of Graduate Admissions, 630-752-5195, Fax: 630-752-5047, E-mail: graduate.admissions@wheaton.edu.
Website: http://www.wheaton.edu/academics/departments/intr

Wilkes University, College of Graduate and Professional Studies, School of Education, Wilkes-Barre, PA 18766-0002. Offers 21st century teaching and learning (MS Ed); art and science of teaching (MS Ed); classroom technology (MS Ed); early childhood literacy (MS Ed); educational development and strategies (MS Ed); educational leadership (MS Ed, Ed D); effective teaching (MS Ed); instructional media (MS Ed); instructional technology (MS Ed); international school leadership (MS Ed); international teaching and learning (MS Ed); middle level education (MS Ed); online teaching (MS Ed); reading (MS Ed); school business leadership (MS Ed); special education (MS Ed); teaching English to speakers of other languages (MS Ed). *Program availability:* Part-time, evening/weekend, 100% online, blended/hybrid learning. *Students:* 87 full-time (70 women), 1,496 part-time (1,111 women); includes 77 minority (11 Black or African American, non-Hispanic/Latino; 2 American Indian or Alaska Native, non-Hispanic/Latino; 12 Asian, non-Hispanic/Latino; 28 Hispanic/Latino; 3 Native Hawaiian or other Pacific Islander, non-Hispanic/Latino; 21 Two or more races, non-Hispanic/Latino). Average age 33. In 2016, 524 master's, 21 doctorates awarded. *Entrance requirements:* Additional exam requirements/recommendations for international students: Required—TOEFL (minimum score 550 paper-based; 79 iBT). *Application deadline:* Applications are processed on a rolling basis. Application fee: $45. Electronic applications accepted. *Expenses:* Contact institution. *Financial support:* Unspecified assistantships available. Financial award application deadline: 3/1; financial award applicants required to submit FAFSA. *Unit head:* Dr. Rhonda Rabbitt, Dean, 570-408-4680, Fax: 570-408-7872, E-mail: rhonda.rabbitt@wilkes.edu. *Application contact:* Director of Graduate Education, 570-408-4234, Fax: 570-408-7846.
Website: http://www.wilkes.edu/academics/graduate-programs/masters-programs/graduate-education/index.aspx

Wilmington University, College of Education, New Castle, DE 19720-6491. Offers applied technology in education (M Ed); career and technical education (M Ed); educational leadership (Ed D); elementary and secondary school counseling (M Ed); elementary studies (M Ed); ESOL literacy (M Ed); higher education leadership (Ed D); instruction: gifted and talented (M Ed); instruction: teacher of reading (M Ed); instruction: teaching and learning (M Ed); organizational leadership (Ed D); school leadership (M Ed); secondary education (MAT); special education (M Ed). *Accreditation:* NCATE. *Program availability:* Part-time, evening/weekend. *Faculty:* 19 full-time (11 women), 178 part-time/adjunct (99 women). *Students:* 248 full-time (176 women), 999 part-time (738 women); includes 244 minority (193 Black or African American, non-Hispanic/Latino; 17 American Indian or Alaska Native, non-Hispanic/Latino; 9 Asian, non-Hispanic/Latino; 19 Hispanic/Latino; 2 Native Hawaiian or other Pacific Islander, non-Hispanic/Latino; 4 Two or more races, non-Hispanic/Latino), 7 international. Average age 34. 672 applicants, 96% accepted, 348 enrolled. In 2016, 529 master's, 87 doctorates awarded. *Entrance requirements:* For master's, 2 letters of recommendation, interview. Additional exam requirements/recommendations for international students: Required—TOEFL (minimum score 500 paper-based). *Application deadline:* For fall admission, 4/30 for domestic students. Applications are processed on a rolling basis. Application fee: $35. Electronic applications accepted. *Expenses: Tuition:* Full-time $8388; part-time $466 per credit. *Required fees:* $25 per semester. Tuition and fees vary according to degree level. *Financial support:* Applicants required to submit FAFSA. *Unit head:* Dr. John C. Gray, Dean. *Application contact:* Laura Morris, Director of Admissions, 877-967-5464, E-mail: infocenter@wilmu.edu.
Website: http://www.wilmu.edu/education/

Worcester State University, Graduate Studies, Department of Education, Program in English as a Second Language, Worcester, MA 01602-2597. Offers M Ed, Postbaccalaureate Certificate. *Program availability:* Part-time, evening/weekend. *Faculty:* 13 full-time (12 women), 16 part-time/adjunct (7 women). *Students:* 4 full-time (2 women), 6 part-time (5 women); includes 1 minority (Hispanic/Latino). Average age 38. 14 applicants, 71% accepted, 4 enrolled. In 2016, 1 other advanced degree awarded. *Degree requirements:* For master's, one foreign language. *Entrance requirements:* For master's, GRE or MAT, bachelor's degree from accredited institution with minimum cumulative GPA of 2.75, current teaching license in ESL at initial or professional level, essay, official transcripts, two letters of recommendation. Additional exam requirements/recommendations for international students: Required—TOEFL (minimum score 550 paper-based; 79 iBT). *Application deadline:* For fall admission, 6/15 for domestic and international students; for spring admission, 11/1 for domestic and international students; for summer admission, 4/1 for domestic and international students. Applications are processed on a rolling basis. Application fee: $50. Electronic applications accepted. *Expenses:* Tuition, state resident: part-time $150 per credit. Tuition, nonresident: part-time $150 per credit. *Financial support:* Career-related internships or fieldwork, scholarships/grants, and unspecified assistantships available. *Unit head:* Dr. Margarita Perez, Coordinator, 508-929-8609, E-mail: mperez@worcester.edu. *Application contact:* Sara Grady, Associate Dean of Graduate Studies and Professional Development, 508-929-8787, Fax: 508-929-8100, E-mail: sara.grady@worcester.edu.

Multilingual and Multicultural Education

Alliant International University–San Francisco, Shirley M. Hufstedler School of Education, Teacher Education Programs, San Francisco, CA 94133. Offers auditory oral education (Certificate); CLAD (Certificate); education specialist: mild/moderate disabilities (Credential); preliminary multiple subject (Credential); preliminary single subject (Credential); professional clear multiple subject (Credential); professional clear single subject (Credential); special education (MA); teaching (MA); TESOL (Certificate). *Program availability:* Part-time, evening/weekend. *Degree requirements:* For master's, thesis. *Entrance requirements:* For degree, California Basic Educational Skills Test, minimum GPA of 2.5. Additional exam requirements/recommendations for international students: Required—TOEFL (minimum score 550 paper-based), TWE (minimum score 5). Electronic applications accepted. *Faculty research:* Curriculum development, first year teachers, cross-cultural issues in teaching, biliteracy.

American College of Education, Graduate Programs, Indianapolis, IN 46204. Offers curriculum and instruction (M Ed), including bilingual, ESL; educational leadership (M Ed); educational technology (M Ed).

American University, School of Education, Program in Bilingual Education, Washington, DC 20016-8001. Offers MA, Certificate. *Students:* 2 part-time (both women); both minorities (both Black or African American, non-Hispanic/Latino). Average age 26. 5 applicants, 80% accepted, 2 enrolled. In 2016, 2 master's awarded. *Degree requirements:* For master's, comprehensive exam. *Entrance requirements:* For master's, GRE General Test, minimum GPA of 3.0, 2 recommendations, statement of purpose, transcripts, resume; for Certificate, bachelor's degree, statement of purpose, transcripts, 2 letters of recommendation, resume. Additional exam requirements/recommendations for international students: Required—TOEFL (minimum score 600 paper-based; 100 iBT), IELTS (minimum score 7), PTE (minimum score 68). *Application deadline:* For fall admission, 2/1 priority date for domestic students; for spring admission, 11/1 priority date for domestic students. Applications are processed on a rolling basis. Application fee: $55. Electronic applications accepted. *Expenses:* $1,579 per credit tuition; $690 mandatory fees. *Financial support:* Institutionally sponsored loans, scholarships/grants, and unspecified assistantships available. Financial award application deadline: 2/1. *Unit head:* Julie Sara M. Boyd, Director, Teacher Education Programs, 202-885-3727, E-mail: jboyd@american.edu. *Application contact:* Kathleen Clowery, Director, Graduate Admissions, 202-885-3620, Fax: 202-885-1344, E-mail: clowery@american.edu.

Azusa Pacific University, School of Education, Department of Foundations and Transdisciplinary Studies, Program in Curriculum and Instruction in Multicultural Contexts, Azusa, CA 91702-7000. Offers MA Ed. *Accreditation:* NCATE. *Program availability:* Part-time, evening/weekend. *Degree requirements:* For master's, core exams, oral presentation. *Entrance requirements:* For master's, 12 units of course work in education, minimum GPA of 3.0. *Faculty research:* Diversity in teacher education programs, teacher morale, student perception of school, case study instruction.

Bank Street College of Education, Graduate School, Program in Bilingual Education, New York, NY 10025. Offers bilingual childhood special education (Ed M); bilingual early childhood general education (MS Ed); bilingual early childhood special and general education (MS Ed); bilingual early childhood special education (Ed M, MS Ed); bilingual elementary/childhood general education (MS Ed); bilingual elementary/childhood special and general education (MS Ed); bilingual elementary/childhood special education (MS Ed). *Degree requirements:* For master's, thesis. *Entrance requirements:* For master's, interview, fluency in Spanish and English, essays. Additional exam requirements/recommendations for international students: Required—TOEFL (minimum score 600 paper-based; 100 iBT), IELTS (minimum score 7). Electronic applications accepted. *Faculty research:* Dual language education, language immersion, bilingual education in the urban classroom, community and school partnerships.

Belhaven University, School of Education, Jackson, MS 39202-1789. Offers educational technology (M Ed); elementary education (M Ed, MAT); reading literacy (M Ed); secondary education (M Ed, MAT). *Program availability:* Part-time, evening/weekend, 100% online, blended/hybrid learning. *Faculty:* 36 full-time (27 women), 9 part-time/adjunct (6 women). *Students:* 319 full-time (270 women), 403 part-time (318 women); includes 502 minority (486 Black or African American, non-Hispanic/Latino; 2 Asian, non-Hispanic/Latino; 3 Hispanic/Latino; 11 Two or more races, non-Hispanic/Latino). Average age 35. In 2016, 78 master's awarded. *Degree requirements:* For master's, comprehensive exam, portfolio. *Entrance requirements:* For master's, PRAXIS I and II, minimum GPA of 2.8. *Application deadline:* Applications are processed on a rolling basis. Application fee: $25. Electronic applications accepted. *Expenses:* $495 per credit hour plus $75 technology fee per course. *Financial support:* Applicants required to submit FAFSA. *Unit head:* Dr. David Hand, Dean, 601-965-7020, E-mail: dhand@belhaven.edu. *Application contact:* Sean Kirnan, Assistant Vice President for Adult and Graduate Enrollment and Student Services, 601-968-8727, Fax: 601-968-5953, E-mail: gradadmission@belhaven.edu.
Website: http://graduateed.belhaven.edu

Boise State University, College of Education, Department of Literacy, Language and Culture, Boise, ID 83725-1725. Offers bilingual education (M Ed); English as a new language (M Ed); literacy (MA). *Accreditation:* NCATE. *Program availability:* Part-time, evening/weekend. *Faculty:* 11 full-time (6 women). *Students:* 10 full-time (9 women), 53 part-time (46 women); includes 9 minority (1 Black or African American, non-Hispanic/Latino; 2 Asian, non-Hispanic/Latino; 5 Hispanic/Latino; 1 Native Hawaiian or other Pacific Islander, non-Hispanic/Latino), 6 international. Average age 36. 20 applicants, 75% accepted, 12 enrolled. In 2016, 26 master's awarded. *Degree requirements:* For master's, thesis optional. *Entrance requirements:* For master's, minimum GPA of 3.0. Additional exam requirements/recommendations for international students: Required—TOEFL (minimum score 550 paper-based; 80 iBT), IELTS (minimum score 6). Application fee: $65 ($95 for international students). Electronic applications accepted. *Expenses:* Tuition, state resident: full-time $6058; part-time $358 per credit hour. Tuition, nonresident: full-time $20,108; part-time $608 per credit hour. *Required fees:* $2108. Tuition and fees vary according to program. *Financial support:* In 2016–17, 4 students received support. Scholarships/grants and unspecified assistantships available. Financial award applicants required to submit FAFSA. *Unit head:* Dr. Maggie Chase, Department Chair, 208-426-3206, E-mail: maggiechase@boisestate.edu. *Application contact:* Dr. Arturo Rodriguez, Program Coordinator, 208-426-2243, E-mail: arturorodriguez@boisestate.edu.
Website: http://education.boisestate.edu/literacy/graduate/

Multilingual and Multicultural Education

Brooklyn College of the City University of New York, School of Education, Program in Childhood Education, Brooklyn, NY 11210-2889. Offers bilingual education (MS Ed); liberal arts (MS Ed); mathematics (MS Ed); science and environmental education (MS Ed). *Program availability:* Part-time, evening/weekend. *Entrance requirements:* For master's, LAST, interview, previous course work in education, writing sample, resume, 2 letters of recommendation. Additional exam requirements/recommendations for international students: Required—TOEFL (minimum score 500 paper-based; 61 iBT). Electronic applications accepted. *Faculty research:* Emotional intelligence, multiculturalism, arts immersion, the Holocaust.

Brown University, Graduate School, Department of Portuguese and Brazilian Studies, Providence, RI 02912. Offers Brazilian studies (AM); English as a second language and cross-cultural studies (AM); Portuguese and Brazilian studies (AM, PhD); Portuguese bilingual education and cross-cultural studies (AM). *Degree requirements:* For doctorate, thesis/dissertation.

Buffalo State College, State University of New York, The Graduate School, Faculty of Applied Science and Education, Department of Exceptional Education, Program in Teaching Bilingual Exceptional Individuals, Buffalo, NY 14222-1095. Offers MS Ed. *Accreditation:* NCATE. *Program availability:* Part-time, evening/weekend. *Degree requirements:* For master's, project. *Entrance requirements:* For master's, minimum GPA of 2.5. Additional exam requirements/recommendations for international students: Required—TOEFL (minimum score 550 paper-based).

California State University, Fullerton, Graduate Studies, College of Education, Department of Elementary and Bilingual Education, Fullerton, CA 92834-9480. Offers bilingual/bicultural education (MS); educational technology (MS); elementary curriculum and instruction (MS). *Accreditation:* NCATE. *Program availability:* Part-time. *Degree requirements:* For master's, comprehensive exam, project or thesis. *Entrance requirements:* For master's, minimum GPA of 2.5, teaching certificate. Application fee: $55. *Expenses:* Tuition, state resident: full-time $3369; part-time $1953 per unit. Tuition, nonresident: full-time $3915; part-time $2499 per unit. Tuition and fees vary according to course load, degree level and program. *Financial support:* Career-related internships or fieldwork, Federal Work-Study, institutionally sponsored loans, and scholarships/grants available. Support available to part-time students. Financial award application deadline: 3/1; financial award applicants required to submit FAFSA. *Faculty research:* Teacher training and tracking, model for improvement of teaching. *Unit head:* Lisa Kirtman, Chair, 657-278-4731. *Application contact:* Admissions/Applications, 657-278-2371.
Website: http://ed.fullerton.edu/EDEL/

California State University, Northridge, Graduate Studies, Michael D. Eisner College of Education, Department of Elementary Education, Northridge, CA 91330. Offers curriculum and instruction (MA); language and literacy (MA); multilingual/multicultural education (MA). *Accreditation:* NCATE. *Program availability:* Part-time, evening/weekend. *Faculty:* 12 full-time (4 women), 17 part-time/adjunct (7 women). *Students:* 37 part-time (33 women); includes 21 minority (1 Asian, non-Hispanic/Latino; 17 Hispanic/Latino; 3 Two or more races, non-Hispanic/Latino). Average age 29. 44 applicants, 55% accepted, 20 enrolled. *Degree requirements:* For master's, comprehensive exam. *Entrance requirements:* For master's, GRE General Test or minimum GPA of 3.0. Additional exam requirements/recommendations for international students: Required—TOEFL. *Application deadline:* For fall admission, 11/30 for domestic students. Application fee: $55. *Expenses:* Tuition, state resident: full-time $4152. *Financial support:* Federal Work-Study available. Financial award application deadline: 3/1. *Unit head:* Dr. Joyce Burstein, Chair, 818-677-2621.
Website: http://www.csun.edu/eisner-education/elementary-education

California State University, Sacramento, Office of Graduate Studies, College of Education, Graduate and Professional Studies in Education, Sacramento, CA 95819. Offers child development (MA); counseling (MS); curriculum and instruction (MA); education (Ed D); education leadership and policy studies (MA), including higher education, PreK-12; educational technology (MA); gender equity (MA); language and literacy (MA); multicultural education (MA); school psychology (MA); special education (MA); workforce development advocacy (MA). *Program availability:* Part-time. *Students:* 446 full-time (335 women), 125 part-time (97 women); includes 298 minority (39 Black or African American, non-Hispanic/Latino; 3 American Indian or Alaska Native, non-Hispanic/Latino; 97 Asian, non-Hispanic/Latino; 153 Hispanic/Latino; 6 Native Hawaiian or other Pacific Islander, non-Hispanic/Latino). Average age 32. 540 applicants, 76% accepted, 250 enrolled. In 2016, 107 master's, 7 doctorates awarded. *Degree requirements:* For master's, thesis or project; writing proficiency exam. *Entrance requirements:* For master's, minimum GPA of 2.5, 3.0 in last 60 units. Additional exam requirements/recommendations for international students: Required—TOEFL (minimum score 550 paper-based; 80 iBT). *Application deadline:* For fall admission, 2/15 for domestic students, 1/15 for international students. Applications are processed on a rolling basis. Application fee: $55. Electronic applications accepted. *Expenses:* $4,302 full-time tuition and fees per semester, $2,796 part-time. *Financial support:* Career-related internships or fieldwork and Federal Work-Study available. Support available to part-time students. Financial award application deadline: 3/1; financial award applicants required to submit FAFSA. *Unit head:* Dr. Susan Heredia, Chair, 916-278-5942, E-mail: coe@csus.edu. *Application contact:* Jose Martinez, Graduate Admissions Supervisor, 916-278-7871, E-mail: martinj@skymail.csus.edu.
Website: http://www.csus.edu/coe/academics/graduate/index.html

California State University, Stanislaus, College of Education, Program in Education (MA), Turlock, CA 95382. Offers curriculum and instruction (MA), including education technology, elementary education, multilingual education, physical education, reading, secondary education, special education; school administration (MA); school counseling (MA). *Program availability:* Part-time, evening/weekend. *Degree requirements:* For master's, comprehensive exam (for some programs), thesis (for some programs). *Entrance requirements:* For master's, MAT, GRE, or CBEST (varies by concentration), 3 letters of recommendation, personal statement. Additional exam requirements/recommendations for international students: Required—TOEFL (minimum score 550 paper-based). Electronic applications accepted. *Faculty research:* Children's perspectives on historical events, method elementary schools dual language education, K-12 reading programs.

Chicago State University, School of Graduate and Professional Studies, College of Education, Department of Special Education, Early Childhood Education and Bilingual Education, Program in Bilingual Education, Chicago, IL 60628. Offers M Ed. *Accreditation:* NCATE. *Degree requirements:* For master's, comprehensive exam, thesis optional. *Entrance requirements:* For master's, minimum GPA of 2.75.

City College of the City University of New York, Graduate School, School of Education, Department of Teaching, Learning and Culture, Program in Bilingual Education, New York, NY 10031-9198. Offers MS. *Accreditation:* NCATE. *Program availability:* Part-time. *Degree requirements:* For master's, thesis. *Entrance requirements:* For master's, Liberal Arts and Sciences Test (LAST), Content Specialty Test (CST). Additional exam requirements/recommendations for international students: Required—TOEFL. Tuition and fees vary according to course load, degree level and program.

The College at Brockport, State University of New York, School of Education, Health, and Human Services, Department of Education and Human Development, Program in Bilingual Education, Brockport, NY 14420-2997. Offers MS Ed, AGC. *Accreditation:* NCATE. *Program availability:* Part-time. *Students:* 6 part-time (5 women); includes 2 minority (both Hispanic/Latino). 2 applicants, 50% accepted, 1 enrolled. In 2016, 2 master's, 5 AGCs awarded. *Degree requirements:* For master's, thesis or alternative. *Entrance requirements:* For master's, minimum GPA of 3.0, letters of recommendation, statement of objectives, demonstrated proficiency in Spanish at the advanced level, appropriate provisional or initial teaching certificate; for AGC, minimum GPA of 3.0, appropriate New York state teaching certification, demonstrated proficiency in Spanish at the advanced level. Additional exam requirements/recommendations for international students: Required—TOEFL (minimum score 550 paper-based; 79 iBT), IELTS (minimum score 6.5). *Application deadline:* For fall admission, 3/15 priority date for domestic and international students; for spring admission, 10/15 priority date for domestic and international students. Application fee: $80. Electronic applications accepted. *Expenses:* Contact institution. *Financial support:* Federal Work-Study, scholarships/grants, and unspecified assistantships available. Support available to part-time students. Financial award application deadline: 3/15; financial award applicants required to submit FAFSA. *Unit head:* Dr. Sue Robb, Chairperson, 585-395-5935, Fax: 585-395-2172, E-mail: srobb@brockport.edu. *Application contact:* Anne Walton, Coordinator of Certification and Graduate Advisement, 585-395-2326, Fax: 585-395-2172, E-mail: awalton@brockport.edu.
Website: http://www.brockport.edu/ehd

College of Mount Saint Vincent, School of Professional and Graduate Studies, Department of Teacher Education, Riverdale, NY 10471-1093. Offers instructional technology and global perspectives (Certificate); middle level education (Certificate); multicultural studies (Certificate); teaching English to speakers of other languages (MS Ed); urban and multicultural education (MS Ed). *Accreditation:* TEAC. *Program availability:* Part-time. *Degree requirements:* For master's, comprehensive exam. *Entrance requirements:* For master's, interview, New York teaching certificate. Additional exam requirements/recommendations for international students: Required—TOEFL.

The College of New Rochelle, Graduate School, Division of Education, Program in Multilingual/Multicultural Education, New Rochelle, NY 10805-2308. Offers bilingual education (Certificate); multilingual/multicultural education (Certificate); teaching English to speakers of other languages (MS Ed, Certificate). *Program availability:* Part-time, evening/weekend. *Degree requirements:* For master's, student teaching or practicum. *Entrance requirements:* For master's, interview, minimum GPA of 3.0 in field, 2.7 overall.

Columbia International University, Columbia Graduate School, Columbia, SC 29230-3122. Offers Bible teaching (MABT); counseling (MACN); early childhood and elementary education (MAT); educational administration (M Ed); educational leadership (PhD); instruction and learning (M Ed); teaching English as a foreign language (Certificate); teaching English as a foreign language and intercultural studies (MATF). *Program availability:* Part-time, evening/weekend, online learning. *Degree requirements:* For master's, internships, professional project. *Entrance requirements:* For master's, MAT; GRE (for some programs), minimum GPA of 2.7. Additional exam requirements/recommendations for international students: Required—TOEFL. Electronic applications accepted.

Dallas Baptist University, Dorothy M. Bush College of Education, Program in Bilingual Education, Dallas, TX 75211-9299. Offers dual language (M Ed); English as a second language/multilingual (M Ed). *Program availability:* Part-time, evening/weekend. *Application deadline:* Applications are processed on a rolling basis. Application fee: $25. Electronic applications accepted. Application fee is waived when completed online. *Expenses: Tuition:* Full-time $15,408; part-time $856 per credit hour. *Required fees:* $400 per semester. Tuition and fees vary according to course load and degree level. *Unit head:* Dr. Carolyn Spain, Director, 214-333-5413, E-mail: carolyns@dbu.edu. *Application contact:* Bobby Soto, Director of Admissions, 214-333-5242, E-mail: graduate@dbu.edu.
Website: http://www3.dbu.edu/graduate/bilingual_education.asp

Dallas Baptist University, Dorothy M. Bush College of Education, Program in Reading and English as a Second Language, Dallas, TX 75211-9299. Offers bilingual education (M Ed); English as a second language (M Ed); master reading teacher (M Ed); reading specialist (M Ed). *Program availability:* Part-time, evening/weekend. *Application deadline:* Applications are processed on a rolling basis. Application fee: $25. Electronic applications accepted. Application fee is waived when completed online. *Expenses: Tuition:* Full-time $15,408; part-time $856 per credit hour. *Required fees:* $400 per semester. Tuition and fees vary according to course load and degree level. *Unit head:* Dr. Carolyn Spain, Director, 214-333-5200, E-mail: carolyns@dbu.edu. *Application contact:* Bobby Soto, Director of Admissions, 214-333-5242, E-mail: graduate@dbu.edu.
Website: http://www3.dbu.edu/graduate/english_reading.asp

DePaul University, College of Education, Chicago, IL 60614. Offers bilingual bicultural education (M Ed, MA); counseling (M Ed, MA), including clinical mental health counseling, college student development, school counseling; curriculum studies (M Ed, MA, Ed D); early childhood education (M Ed, MA, Ed D); educating adults (MA); educational leadership (M Ed, MA, Ed D), including administration and supervision (M Ed, MA), principal preparation (M Ed, MA); elementary education (MA); mathematics education (MA); mathematics for teaching (MS); middle school mathematics education (MS); reading specialist (M Ed, MA); secondary education (M Ed); social and cultural foundations in education (MA); special education (M Ed, MA); world languages education (M Ed, MA). *Program availability:* Part-time, evening/weekend, online learning. *Degree requirements:* For doctorate, thesis/dissertation. Electronic applications accepted.

Eastern New Mexico University, Graduate School, College of Education and Technology, Department of Curriculum and Instruction, Portales, NM 88130. Offers bilingual education (M Ed); educational technology (M Ed); elementary education (M Ed); English as a second language (M Ed); pedagogy and learning (M Ed); professional technical education (M Ed); reading/literacy (M Ed). *Program availability:* Part-time, online learning. *Degree requirements:* For master's, comprehensive exam, thesis optional. *Entrance requirements:* For master's, minimum GPA of 3.0, photocopy of teaching license, writing assessment, letter of recommendation. Additional exam requirements/recommendations for international students: Required—TOEFL (minimum score 550 paper-based; 79 iBT), IELTS (minimum score 6). Electronic applications accepted.

Eastern University, Loeb School of Education, St. Davids, PA 19087-3696. Offers ESL program specialist (K-12) (Certificate); general supervisor (PreK-12) (Certificate); health and physical education (K-12) (Certificate); middle level (4-8) (Certificate); multicultural education (M Ed); organizational leadership with education (PhD); Pre K-4 (Certificate); Pre K-4 with special education (Certificate); reading (M Ed); reading specialist (K-12) (Certificate); reading supervisor (K-12) (Certificate); school health supervisor (Certificate); school nurse (K-12) (Certificate); secondary biology education (7-12) (Certificate); secondary chemistry education (7-12) (Certificate); secondary

communication education (7-12) (Certificate); secondary education (7-12) (Certificate); secondary English education (7-12) (Certificate); secondary math education (7-12) (Certificate); secondary social studies education (7-12) (Certificate); special education (M Ed); special education (7-12) (Certificate); special education (Pre K-8) (Certificate); special education supervisor (N-12) (Certificate); TESOL (M Ed); world language (Certificate), including French, Spanish. *Program availability:* Part-time, evening/ weekend, online learning. *Students:* 41 full-time (32 women), 89 part-time (68 women); includes 54 minority (38 Black or African American, non-Hispanic/Latino; 3 Asian, non-Hispanic/Latino; 11 Hispanic/Latino; 2 Two or more races, non-Hispanic/Latino), 2 international. Average age 37. In 2016, 64 master's awarded. *Entrance requirements:* Additional exam requirements/recommendations for international students: Required—TOEFL. *Application deadline:* Applications are processed on a rolling basis. Application fee: $35. Electronic applications accepted. Application fee is waived when completed online. *Expenses:* $690 per credit. *Unit head:* Michael Dziedziak, Executive Director of Enrollment, 800-452-0996, E-mail: gpsadmissions@eastern.edu.
Website: http://www.eastern.edu/academics/programs/loeb-school-education-0

Fairfield University, Graduate School of Education and Allied Professions, Fairfield, CT 06824. Offers applied behavior analysis (ATC); applied psychology (MA); clinical mental health counseling (MA, CAS); educational technology (MA); elementary education (MA, CAS); family studies (MA); integration of spirituality and religion in counseling (ATC); marriage and family therapy (MA); reading and language development (Sixth Year Certificate); school counseling (MA, CAS); school psychology (MA, CAS); school-based marriage and family therapy (ATC); secondary education (MA); special education (MA, CAS); substance abuse counseling (ATC); teaching (Certificate); teaching and foundations (MA, CAS); TESOL, world languages, and bilingual education (MA, CAS). *Accreditation:* NCATE. *Program availability:* Part-time, evening/weekend. *Faculty:* 19 full-time (15 women), 38 part-time/adjunct (26 women). *Students:* 153 full-time (132 women), 302 part-time (252 women); includes 97 minority (24 Black or African American, non-Hispanic/Latino; 12 Asian, non-Hispanic/Latino; 55 Hispanic/Latino; 6 Two or more races, non-Hispanic/Latino), 6 international. Average age 32. 283 applicants, 61% accepted, 97 enrolled. In 2016, 130 master's awarded. *Degree requirements:* For master's, comprehensive exam. *Entrance requirements:* For master's, minimum GPA of 3.0, 2 recommendations, resume. Additional exam requirements/recommendations for international students: Required—TOEFL (minimum score 550 paper-based; 84 iBT) or IELTS (minimum score 7.5). *Application deadline:* For fall admission, 2/15 for international students; for spring admission, 10/1 for international students. Application fee: $60. Electronic applications accepted. *Expenses:* $725 per credit hour. *Financial support:* In 2016–17, 42 students received support. Career-related internships or fieldwork and unspecified assistantships available. Support available to part-time students. Financial award applicants required to submit FAFSA. *Faculty research:* Reading and literacy, writing, social justice and inequality in education, addictions and mental health issues, therapeutic relationships and clinical supervision. *Unit head:* Dr. Robert D. Hannafin, Dean, 203-254-4250, Fax: 203-254-4241, E-mail: rhannafin@fairfield.edu. *Application contact:* Marianne Gumpper, Director of Graduate Admission, 203-254-4184, Fax: 203-254-4073, E-mail: gradadmis@ fairfield.edu.
Website: http://www.fairfield.edu/gseap

Fairleigh Dickinson University, Metropolitan Campus, University College: Arts, Sciences, and Professional Studies, Peter Sammartino School of Education, Program in Multilingual Education, Teaneck, NJ 07666-1914. Offers MA. *Accreditation:* TEAC.

Florida Atlantic University, College of Education, Department of Curriculum, Culture, and Educational Inquiry, Boca Raton, FL 33431-0991. Offers curriculum and instruction (M Ed, PhD, Ed S); early childhood education (M Ed); multicultural education (M Ed); TESOL and bilingual education (MA). *Program availability:* Part-time, evening/weekend. *Faculty:* 12 full-time (9 women), 1 (woman) part-time/adjunct. *Students:* 31 full-time (27 women), 93 part-time (68 women); includes 37 minority (17 Black or African American, non-Hispanic/Latino; 4 Asian, non-Hispanic/Latino; 15 Hispanic/Latino; 1 Two or more races, non-Hispanic/Latino), 2 international. Average age 35. 65 applicants, 60% accepted, 25 enrolled. In 2016, 17 master's, 18 doctorates, 3 other advanced degrees awarded. *Entrance requirements:* Additional exam requirements/recommendations for international students: Required—TOEFL (minimum score 500 paper-based; 61 iBT), IELTS (minimum score 6). *Application deadline:* For fall admission, 7/1 for domestic students, 2/15 for international students; for spring admission, 11/1 for domestic students, 7/15 for international students. Application fee: $30. *Expenses:* Tuition, state resident: full-time $7392; part-time $369.82 per credit hour. Tuition, nonresident: full-time $19,432; part-time $1024.81 per credit hour. *Faculty research:* Multicultural education, early intervention strategies, family literacy, religious diversity in schools, early childhood curriculum. *Unit head:* Dr. Dilys Schoorman, Chair, 561-297-3965, E-mail: dschoorm@fau.edu. *Application contact:* Dr. Eliah Watlington, Associate Dean, 561-296-8520, Fax: 261-297-2991, E-mail: ewatling@fau.edu.
Website: http://www.coe.fau.edu/academicdepartments/ccei/

Florida Atlantic University, College of Education, Department of Teaching and Learning, Boca Raton, FL 33431-0991. Offers curriculum and instruction (M Ed), including art, biology, chemistry, English, French, German, mathematics, music, physics, Pre-K and primary education, reading, social sciences, Spanish; elementary education (M Ed); environmental education (M Ed); reading education (M Ed); social foundations of education (M Ed), including educational psychology, educational technology, multilingual education. *Accreditation:* NCATE. *Program availability:* Part-time, evening/weekend. *Faculty:* 15 full-time (12 women), 2 part-time/adjunct (1 woman). *Students:* 25 full-time (20 women), 41 part-time (37 women); includes 18 minority (9 Black or African American, non-Hispanic/Latino; 2 Asian, non-Hispanic/ Latino; 7 Hispanic/Latino), 7 international. Average age 32. 54 applicants, 59% accepted, 18 enrolled. In 2016, 36 master's awarded. *Entrance requirements:* For master's, GRE General Test, minimum GPA of 3.0 in last 2 years of undergraduate course work. Additional exam requirements/recommendations for international students: Required—TOEFL (minimum score 500 paper-based; 61 iBT), IELTS (minimum score 6). *Application deadline:* For fall admission, 7/1 for domestic students, 2/15 for international students; for spring admission, 11/1 for domestic students, 7/15 for international students. Applications are processed on a rolling basis. Application fee: $30. *Expenses:* Tuition, state resident: full-time $7392; part-time $369.82 per credit hour. Tuition, nonresident: full-time $19,432; part-time $1024.81 per credit hour. *Financial support:* Fellowships with partial tuition reimbursements, research assistantships with partial tuition reimbursements, teaching assistantships with partial tuition reimbursements, career-related internships or fieldwork, scholarships/grants, and unspecified assistantships available. *Faculty research:* Technology, teaching English to speakers of other languages, math teaching, electronic portfolio assessment, global perspectives through social studies. *Unit head:* Dr. Barbara Ridener, Chairperson, 561-297-3588, E-mail: bridener@fau.edu. *Application contact:* Dr. Eliah Watlington, Associate Dean, 561-296-8520, Fax: 261-297-2991, E-mail: ewatling@fau.edu.
Website: http://www.coe.fau.edu/academicdepartments/tl/

Florida International University, College of Arts, Sciences, and Education, Department of Leadership and Professional Studies, Miami, FL 33199. Offers adult education and human resource development (MS, Ed D); counseling (MS), including rehabilitation counseling, school counseling; counselor education (MS), including clinical mental health counseling; educational administration and supervision (Ed D); educational leadership (MS, Certificate, Ed S); higher education (Ed D); higher education administration (MS); international and comparative education (MS); recreation and sport management (MS), including recreation and sport management, recreational therapy; school psychology (Ed S); urban education (MS), including instruction in urban settings, learning technologies, multicultural/bilingual, multicultural/TESOL, urban education. *Program availability:* Part-time, evening/weekend. *Faculty:* 27 full-time (19 women), 38 part-time/adjunct (25 women). *Students:* 253 full-time (191 women), 306 part-time (241 women); includes 444 minority (129 Black or African American, non-Hispanic/Latino; 3 Asian, non-Hispanic/Latino; 304 Hispanic/Latino; 8 Two or more races, non-Hispanic/Latino), 18 international. Average age 31. 366 applicants, 60% accepted, 115 enrolled. In 2016, 193 master's, 8 doctorates awarded. *Degree requirements:* For doctorate, thesis/dissertation. *Entrance requirements:* For master's, minimum GPA of 3.0; for doctorate and other advanced degree, GRE General Test. Additional exam requirements/recommendations for international students: Required—TOEFL (minimum score 550 paper-based; 80 iBT), IELTS (minimum score 6.3). *Application deadline:* For fall admission, 6/1 priority date for domestic students, 4/1 for international students; for winter admission, 10/1 priority date for domestic students, 9/1 for international students; for spring admission, 3/1 priority date for domestic students, 2/ 1 for international students. Applications are processed on a rolling basis. Application fee: $30. Electronic applications accepted. *Expenses:* Tuition, state resident: full-time $8912; part-time $446 per credit hour. Tuition, nonresident: full-time $21,393; part-time $992 per credit hour. *Required fees:* $2185; $195 per semester. Tuition and fees vary according to program. *Financial support:* Fellowships, research assistantships with tuition reimbursements, teaching assistantships with tuition reimbursements, Federal Work-Study, and tuition waivers (full and partial) available. Support available to part-time students. Financial award applicants required to submit FAFSA. *Unit head:* Dr. Benjamin Baez, Chair, 305-348-3214, Fax: 305-348-1515, E-mail: benjamin.baez@fiu.edu. *Application contact:* Nanett Rojas, Assistant Director, Graduate Admissions, 305-348-7464, Fax: 305-348-7441, E-mail: gradadm@fiu.edu.
Website: http://education.fiu.edu

Gallaudet University, The Graduate School, Washington, DC 20002-3625. Offers American Sign Language/English bilingual early childhood deaf education: birth to 5 (Certificate); audiology (Au D); clinical psychology (PhD); deaf and hard of hearing infants, toddlers, and their families (Certificate); deaf education (MA, Ed S); deaf history (Certificate); deaf studies (Certificate); educating deaf students with disabilities (Certificate); education: teacher preparation (MA), including deaf education, early childhood education and deaf education, elementary education and deaf education, secondary education and deaf education; educational neuroscience (PhD); hearing, speech and language sciences (MS, PhD); international development (MA); interpretation (MA, PhD), including combined interpreting practice and research (MA), interpreting research (MA); linguistics (MA, PhD); mental health counseling (MA); peer mentoring (Certificate); public administration (MPA); school counseling (MA); school psychology (Psy S); sign language teaching (MA); social work (MSW); speech-language pathology (MS). *Program availability:* Part-time. *Students:* 297 full-time (231 women), 129 part-time (97 women); includes 105 minority (35 Black or African American, non-Hispanic/Latino; 20 Asian, non-Hispanic/Latino; 39 Hispanic/Latino; 11 Two or more races, non-Hispanic/Latino), 22 international. Average age 30. 471 applicants, 52% accepted, 147 enrolled. In 2016, 138 master's, 25 doctorates, 14 other advanced degrees awarded. Terminal master's awarded for partial completion of doctoral program. *Degree requirements:* For master's, comprehensive exam (for some programs), thesis optional; for doctorate, comprehensive exam, thesis/dissertation. *Entrance requirements:* For master's and doctorate, GRE General Test or MAT, letters of recommendation, interviews, goals statement, American Sign Language proficiency interview, written English competency. Additional exam requirements/recommendations for international students: Required—TOEFL. *Application deadline:* For fall admission, 2/ 15 for domestic students. Applications are processed on a rolling basis. Application fee: $75. Electronic applications accepted. *Expenses:* Tuition: Full-time $17,100; part-time $950 per credit hour. *Required fees:* $3725; $276 per semester. *Financial support:* Fellowships, research assistantships, teaching assistantships, career-related internships or fieldwork, Federal Work-Study, scholarships/grants, tuition waivers (partial), and unspecified assistantships available. Support available to part-time students. Financial award application deadline: 7/1; financial award applicants required to submit FAFSA. *Faculty research:* Signing math dictionaries, telecommunications access, cancer genetics, linguistics, visual language and visual learning, integrated quantum materials, deaf legal discourse, advance recruitment and retention in geosciences. *Unit head:* Dr. Gaurav Mathur, Dean, Graduate School and Continuing Studies, 202-250-2380, Fax: 202-651-5027, E-mail: gaurav.mathur@gallaudet.edu. *Application contact:* Wednesday Luria, Coordinator of Prospective Graduate Student Services, 202-651-5400, Fax: 202-651-5295, E-mail: graduate.school@gallaudet.edu.

George Mason University, College of Education and Human Development, Programs in Curriculum and Instruction, Fairfax, VA 22030. Offers advanced international baccalaureate (M Ed); assistive technology (M Ed); designing digital learning in schools (M Ed); early childhood education (M Ed); early childhood education for diverse learners (M Ed); elementary education (M Ed); English as a second language (M Ed); gifted child education (M Ed); history (M Ed); literacy (M Ed), including PK-12 classroom teachers, reading specialist; literacy leadership for diverse schools (M Ed), including K-12 reading; physical education (M Ed); science K-12 (M Ed); secondary education (M Ed), including biology, chemistry, earth science, English, history/social science, math, physics; special education (M Ed); teacher leadership (M Ed); teaching culturally, linguistically diverse and exceptional learners (M Ed); transformative teaching (M Ed). *Faculty:* 41 full-time (35 women), 53 part-time/adjunct (46 women). *Students:* 155 full-time (127 women), 821 part-time (697 women); includes 267 minority (82 Black or African American, non-Hispanic/Latino; 5 American Indian or Alaska Native, non-Hispanic/Latino; 75 Asian, non-Hispanic/Latino; 88 Hispanic/Latino; 1 Native Hawaiian or other Pacific Islander, non-Hispanic/Latino; 16 Two or more races, non-Hispanic/Latino), 19 international. Average age 33. 513 applicants, 90% accepted, 352 enrolled. In 2016, 347 master's awarded. *Degree requirements:* For master's, comprehensive exam, thesis (for some programs). *Entrance requirements:* For master's, PRAXIS Core (for some programs), minimum GPA of 3.0 in last 60 hours, licensed as teacher or educational administrator, official transcripts, goals statement, 3 recommendation letters, interview or writing sample (depending on program), up to 3 years' teaching experience (depending on program). Additional exam requirements/recommendations for international students: Required—TOEFL (minimum score 575 paper-based; 88 iBT), IELTS (minimum score 6.5), PTE (minimum score 59). *Application deadline:* For spring admission, 11/1 priority date for domestic and international students. Application fee: $75 ($80 for international students). Electronic applications accepted. *Expenses:* Tuition, state resident: full-time $10,628; part-time $443 per credit. Tuition, nonresident: full-time $29,306; part-time $1221 per credit. *Required fees:* $3096; $129 per credit. Tuition and fees vary according to program. *Financial support:* In 2016–17, 1 student received support, including 1 teaching assistantship (averaging $4,060 per year); career-related internships or fieldwork, Federal Work-Study, scholarships/grants, unspecified assistantships, and health care benefits (for full-time research or teaching assistantship recipients) also

available. Support available to part-time students. Financial award application deadline: 3/1; financial award applicants required to submit FAFSA. *Faculty research:* Achievement gaps and superintendent decisions, constructivist view of classroom teaching, cost of cheating, creating a critical literacy milieu in kindergarten. *Unit head:* Rebecca Fox, Professor and Academic Program Coordinator, 703-993-4123, E-mail: rfox@gmu.edu.
Website: http://gse.gmu.edu/programs/gsemasters

The George Washington University, Graduate School of Education and Human Development, Department of Counseling and Human Development, Washington, DC 20052. Offers clinical mental health counseling (MA); counseling (PhD, Ed S); counseling culturally and linguistically diverse persons (MA Ed/HD, Certificate); forensic rehabilitation counseling (Graduate Certificate); job development and placement (Graduate Certificate); rehabilitation counseling (MA Ed/HD), including autism spectrum disorder, substance abuse and psychiatric disabilities, traumatic brain injury; school counseling (MA Ed, Graduate Certificate). *Accreditation:* ACA (one or more programs are accredited). *Program availability:* Part-time, evening/weekend. *Faculty:* 13 full-time (7 women). *Students:* 103 full-time (79 women), 80 part-time (67 women); includes 66 minority (32 Black or African American, non-Hispanic/Latino; 2 American Indian or Alaska Native, non-Hispanic/Latino; 14 Asian, non-Hispanic/Latino; 16 Hispanic/Latino; 2 Two or more races, non-Hispanic/Latino), 13 international. Average age 31. 321 applicants, 54% accepted, 68 enrolled. In 2016, 54 master's, 9 doctorates, 8 other advanced degrees awarded. *Degree requirements:* For master's and other advanced degree, comprehensive exam; for doctorate, comprehensive exam, thesis/dissertation. *Entrance requirements:* For master's, GRE General Test or MAT, minimum GPA of 2.75; for doctorate, GRE General Test or MAT, interview, minimum GPA of 3.3; for other advanced degree, GRE General Test or MAT, minimum GPA of 3.3. *Application deadline:* For fall admission, 1/15 priority date for domestic students; for spring admission, 10/1 for domestic students. Applications are processed on a rolling basis. Application fee: $75. *Financial support:* In 2016–17, 58 students received support. Fellowships with tuition reimbursements available, research assistantships, teaching assistantships with tuition reimbursements available, career-related internships or fieldwork, Federal Work-Study, and tuition waivers (full and partial) available. Financial award application deadline: 1/15. *Faculty research:* Multiculturalism and counseling, models of adult development. *Unit head:* Dr. Kenneth C. Hergenrather, Chair, 202-994-6856, E-mail: hergenkc@gwu.edu. *Application contact:* Sarah Lang, Director of Graduate Admissions, 202-994-1447, Fax: 202-994-7207, E-mail: slang@gwu.edu.

The George Washington University, Graduate School of Education and Human Development, Department of Special Education and Disability Studies, Program in Bilingual Special Education, Washington, DC 20052. Offers MA Ed, Certificate. *Students:* 1 (woman) part-time. Average age 42. In 2016, 3 master's awarded. *Unit head:* Michael Feuer, Dean, 202-994-6161, E-mail: mjfeuer@gwu.edu. *Application contact:* Sarah Lang, Director of Graduate Admissions, 202-994-1447, Fax: 202-994-7207, E-mail: slang@gwu.edu.

The George Washington University, Graduate School of Education and Human Development, Department of Special Education and Disability Studies, Program in Special Education for Culturally and Linguistically Diverse Persons, Washington, DC 20052. Offers MA Ed/HD, Certificate. *Students:* 5 full-time (all women), 54 part-time (49 women); includes 31 minority (19 Black or African American, non-Hispanic/Latino; 6 Asian, non-Hispanic/Latino; 5 Hispanic/Latino; 1 Two or more races, non-Hispanic/Latino), 5 international. Average age 35. 77 applicants, 81% accepted, 42 enrolled. In 2016, 3 master's, 28 Certificates awarded.

Georgia Southern University, Jack N. Averitt College of Graduate Studies, College of Education, Department of Curriculum, Foundations, and Reading, Program in Curriculum Studies, Statesboro, GA 30460. Offers curriculum studies (Ed D), including cultural curriculum, instructional improvement, multicultural studies, teaching and learning. *Program availability:* Part-time. *Students:* 21 full-time (19 women), 131 part-time (99 women); includes 43 minority (35 Black or African American, non-Hispanic/Latino; 5 Hispanic/Latino; 3 Two or more races, non-Hispanic/Latino), 3 international. Average age 41. In 2016, 16 doctorates awarded. *Degree requirements:* For doctorate, comprehensive exam, thesis/dissertation, exams. *Entrance requirements:* For doctorate, GRE or MAT, letters of reference, minimum GPA of 3.5, writing sample. Additional exam requirements/recommendations for international students: Required—TOEFL (minimum score 550 paper-based; 80 iBT), IELTS (minimum score 6). *Application deadline:* For summer admission, 1/30 for domestic students. Application fee: $50. Electronic applications accepted. *Expenses:* Tuition, state resident: full-time $7236; part-time $277 per semester hour. Tuition, nonresident: full-time $27,118; part-time $1105 per semester hour. *Required fees:* $2092. *Financial support:* In 2016–17, 8 students received support. Research assistantships with partial tuition reimbursements available, career-related internships or fieldwork, Federal Work-Study, scholarships/grants, and unspecified assistantships available. Financial award application deadline: 4/15; financial award applicants required to submit FAFSA. *Faculty research:* Curriculum theory, cultural studies, narrative research, postmodern theory, critical race theory, international education, feminism, media literacy, documentary studies, post human condition, social and cultural foundations of education, democracy and education. *Unit head:* Dr. Daniel Chapman, Program Coordinator, 912-478-5715, E-mail: dechapman@georgiasouthern.edu. *Application contact:* Lydia Cross, Coordinator for Graduate Student Recruitment, 912-478-8664, E-mail: lcross@georgiasouthern.edu.
Website: http://coe.georgiasouthern.edu/cs/

Graduate Institute of Applied Linguistics, Graduate Programs, Dallas, TX 75236. Offers applied linguistics (MA, Certificate); language development (MA). *Program availability:* Part-time. *Degree requirements:* For master's, one foreign language, comprehensive exam (for some programs), thesis (for some programs). *Entrance requirements:* For master's, GRE. Additional exam requirements/recommendations for international students: Required—TOEFL (minimum score 577 paper-based; 90 iBT). Electronic applications accepted. *Faculty research:* Minority languages, endangered languages, language documentation.

Heritage University, Graduate Programs in Education, Program in Professional Studies, Toppenish, WA 98948-9599. Offers bilingual education/ESL (M Ed); biology (M Ed); English and literature (M Ed); reading/literacy (M Ed); special education (M Ed). *Program availability:* Part-time, evening/weekend. *Degree requirements:* For master's, comprehensive exam (for some programs), thesis (for some programs).

Hofstra University, School of Education, Programs in Teacher Education, Hempstead, NY 11549. Offers bilingual education (MA, Advanced Certificate); bilingual extension (Advanced Certificate), including education/speech language pathology; business education (MS Ed); early childhood and childhood education (MS Ed); early childhood education (MA, MS Ed); education technology (Advanced Certificate); elementary education (MA, MS Ed), including science, technology, engineering, and mathematics (STEM) (MA); English education (MS Ed); family and consumer science (MS Ed); fine arts and music education (Advanced Certificate); fine arts education (MS Ed); foreign language and TESOL (MS Ed); foreign language education (MS Ed), including French, German, Russian, Spanish; learning and teaching (Ed D), including applied linguistics, art education, arts and humanities, early childhood education, English education, human development, math education, math, science, and technology, multicultural education, physical education, science education, social studies education, special education; mathematics education (MA, MS Ed); middle school extension (Advanced Certificate), including grades 5-6, grades 7-9; music education (MA, MS Ed); science education (MA, MS Ed), including biology, chemistry, earth science, geology, physics; secondary education (Advanced Certificate); social studies education (MA, MS Ed); teaching languages other than English and TESOL (MS Ed); TESOL (MS Ed, Advanced Certificate). *Program availability:* Part-time, evening/weekend, blended/hybrid learning. *Students:* 139 full-time (97 women), 145 part-time (106 women); includes 60 minority (15 Black or African American, non-Hispanic/Latino; 1 American Indian or Alaska Native, non-Hispanic/Latino; 12 Asian, non-Hispanic/Latino; 31 Hispanic/Latino; 1 Two or more races, non-Hispanic/Latino), 21 international. Average age 29. 255 applicants, 86% accepted, 122 enrolled. In 2016, 101 master's, 4 doctorates, 43 other advanced degrees awarded. *Degree requirements:* For master's, comprehensive exam, thesis (for some programs), exit project, student teaching, fieldwork, electronic portfolio, curriculum project, minimum GPA of 3.0; for doctorate, thesis/dissertation; for Advanced Certificate, 3 foreign languages, comprehensive exam (for some programs), thesis project. *Entrance requirements:* For master's, GRE, MAT, 2 letters of recommendation, portfolio, teacher certification (MA), interview, essay; for doctorate, GMAT, GRE, LSAT, or MAT; for Advanced Certificate, 2 letters of recommendation, essay, interview and/or portfolio, teaching certificate. Additional exam requirements/recommendations for international students: Required—TOEFL (minimum score 550 paper-based; 80 iBT). *Application deadline:* Applications are processed on a rolling basis. Application fee: $75. Electronic applications accepted. *Expenses: Tuition:* Full-time $1240. *Required fees:* $970. Tuition and fees vary according to program. *Financial support:* In 2016–17, 149 students received support, including 58 fellowships with full and partial tuition reimbursements available (averaging $5,309 per year), 5 research assistantships with full and partial tuition reimbursements available (averaging $7,073 per year); career-related internships or fieldwork, Federal Work-Study, institutionally sponsored loans, scholarships/grants, traineeships, tuition waivers (full and partial), and unspecified assistantships also available. Support available to part-time students. Financial award applicants required to submit FAFSA. *Faculty research:* Educational interventions that foster critical-thinking skills; teachers' attitudes about professional development; threats to teacher quality. *Unit head:* Dr. Eustace Thompson, Chairperson, 516-463-5749, Fax: 516-463-6275, E-mail: eustace.g.thompson@hofstra.edu. *Application contact:* Sunil Samuel, Assistant Vice President of Admissions, 516-463-4723, Fax: 516-463-4664, E-mail: graduateadmission@hofstra.edu.
Website: http://www.hofstra.edu/education/

Howard University, School of Communications, Department of Communication and Culture, Washington, DC 20059-0002. Offers intercultural communication (MA, PhD); organizational communication (MA, PhD). Offered through the Graduate School of Arts and Sciences. *Program availability:* Part-time. Terminal master's awarded for partial completion of doctoral program. *Degree requirements:* For master's, comprehensive exam or thesis; for doctorate, one foreign language, comprehensive exam, thesis/dissertation. *Entrance requirements:* For master's, English proficiency exam, GRE General Test, minimum GPA of 3.0; for doctorate, English proficiency exam, GRE General Test, master's degree in related field, minimum GPA of 3.5. Additional exam requirements/recommendations for international students: Required—TOEFL. *Faculty research:* Media effects, black discourse, development communication, African-American organizations.

Hunter College of the City University of New York, Graduate School, School of Education, Department of Curriculum and Teaching, Program in Bilingual Education, New York, NY 10065-5085. Offers MS. *Accreditation:* NCATE. *Degree requirements:* For master's, one foreign language, thesis, research seminar, student teaching experience or practicum, New York State Teacher Certification Exams. *Entrance requirements:* For master's, interview, minimum GPA of 2.8, writing sample in English and Spanish. Additional exam requirements/recommendations for international students: Required—TOEFL, TWE. *Application deadline:* For fall admission, 4/1 for domestic students, 2/1 for international students; for spring admission, 11/1 for domestic students, 9/1 for international students. Applications are processed on a rolling basis. *Financial support:* Federal Work-Study, scholarships/grants, and tuition waivers (partial) available. Support available to part-time students. *Faculty research:* Teacher effectiveness, language development, Spanish language and linguistics and multicultural education. *Unit head:* Prof. Anne Ebe, Coordinator, 212-772-4693, E-mail: aebe@hunter.cuny.edu. *Application contact:* Milena Solo, Director for Graduate Admissions, 212-772-4482, E-mail: admissions@hunter.cuny.edu.

Immaculata University, College of Graduate Studies, Program in Cultural and Linguistic Diversity, Immaculata, PA 19345. Offers bilingual studies (MA); TESOL (MA). *Program availability:* Part-time, evening/weekend. *Degree requirements:* For master's, one foreign language, comprehensive exam, thesis optional, professional experience. *Entrance requirements:* For master's, GRE or MAT, proficiency in Spanish or Asian language, minimum GPA of 3.0. Additional exam requirements/recommendations for international students: Required—TOEFL, IELTS. Electronic applications accepted. *Faculty research:* Cognitive learning, Caribbean literature and culture, English as a second language, teaching English to speakers of other languages.

Indiana State University, College of Graduate and Professional Studies, College of Arts and Sciences, Department of Languages, Literatures, and Linguistics, Terre Haute, IN 47809. Offers applied linguistics/teaching English as a second language (MA); language education (PhD); Spanish/teaching english as a second language (MA); TESL/TEFL (CAS). *Degree requirements:* For master's, comprehensive exam. Electronic applications accepted.

Indiana University Bloomington, University Graduate School, College of Arts and Sciences, Department of Second Language Studies, Bloomington, IN 47405-7000. Offers second language studies (MA, PhD); TESOL and applied linguistics (MA). *Faculty:* 10 full-time (4 women). *Students:* 40 full-time (25 women), 1 (woman) part-time; includes 4 minority (2 Asian, non-Hispanic/Latino; 1 Hispanic/Latino; 1 Two or more races, non-Hispanic/Latino), 14 international. Average age 33. 64 applicants, 52% accepted, 12 enrolled. In 2016, 11 master's, 1 doctorate awarded. *Entrance requirements:* Additional exam requirements/recommendations for international students: Required—TOEFL (minimum score 100 iBT). *Application deadline:* For fall admission, 1/15 for domestic students, 12/1 for international students. Application fee: $55 ($65 for international students). Electronic applications accepted. *Financial support:* Fellowships with tuition reimbursements, research assistantships, teaching assistantships with tuition reimbursements, health care benefits, and unspecified assistantships available. *Unit head:* Laurent Dekydtspotter, Chair, 812-855-7951, E-mail: ldekydts@indiana.edu. *Application contact:* Mandy Stewart, Graduate Secretary, 812-855-7951, E-mail: dsls@indiana.edu.
Website: http://dsls.indiana.edu

James Madison University, The Graduate School, College of Education, Program in Education, Harrisonburg, VA 22807. Offers early childhood education (preK-3) (MAT); educational leadership (M Ed); educational technology (M Ed); elementary education (MAT); equity and cultural diversity (M Ed); inclusive early childhood education (MAT); K-8 mathematics specialist (M Ed); middle education (MAT); reading education (M Ed); secondary education (MAT); Spanish language and culture for educators (M Ed);

TESOL (MAT). *Accreditation:* NCATE. *Program availability:* Part-time, evening/weekend. *Faculty:* 21 full-time (12 women), 5 part-time/adjunct (2 women). *Students:* 249 full-time (220 women), 123 part-time (86 women); includes 43 minority (7 Black or African American, non-Hispanic/Latino; 7 Asian, non-Hispanic/Latino; 17 Hispanic/Latino; 12 Two or more races, non-Hispanic/Latino), 2 international. Average age 30. 355 applicants, 98% accepted, 312 enrolled. In 2016, 247 master's awarded. Application fee: $55. Electronic applications accepted. *Financial support:* In 2016–17, 16 students received support. Career-related internships or fieldwork, Federal Work-Study, and 22 assistantships (averaging $7911) available. Financial award application deadline: 3/1; financial award applicants required to submit FAFSA. *Unit head:* Dr. Phillip M. Wishon, Dean, 540-568-6572, E-mail: wishonpm@jmu.edu. *Application contact:* Lynette D. Michael, Director of Graduate Admissions, 540-568-6131 Ext. 6395, Fax: 540-568-7860, E-mail: michaeld@jmu.edu.
Website: http://www.jmu.edu/coe/index.shtml

Kean University, College of Education, Program in Instruction and Curriculum, Union, NJ 07083. Offers bilingual/bicultural education (MA); teaching English as a second language (MA). *Accreditation:* NCATE. *Program availability:* Part-time. *Faculty:* 15 full-time (9 women). *Students:* 3 full-time (all women), 25 part-time (19 women); includes 21 minority (1 Black or African American, non-Hispanic/Latino; 20 Hispanic/Latino), 2 international. Average age 37. 21 applicants, 52% accepted, 10 enrolled. In 2016, 25 master's awarded. *Degree requirements:* For master's, comprehensive exam (for some programs), thesis optional, two-semester advanced seminar. *Entrance requirements:* For master's, GRE General Test or MAT; PRAXIS (for some programs), minimum GPA of 3.0, personal statement, professional resume/curriculum vitae, commitment to working with children, certification (for some programs), two letters of recommendation. Additional exam requirements/recommendations for international students: Required—TOEFL (minimum score 550 paper-based; 79 iBT), IELTS (minimum score 6.5). *Application deadline:* For fall admission, 6/1 for domestic and international students; for spring admission, 12/1 for domestic and international students. Applications are processed on a rolling basis. Application fee: $75. Electronic applications accepted. *Expenses:* Tuition, state resident: full-time $13,156; part-time $640 per credit. Tuition, nonresident: full-time $17,831; part-time $785 per credit. *Required fees:* $3316; $151 per credit. Tuition and fees vary according to course level, course load, degree level and program. *Financial support:* Scholarships/grants and unspecified assistantships available. Financial award applicants required to submit FAFSA. *Unit head:* Dr. Gail Verdi, Program Coordinator, 908-737-3908, E-mail: gverdi@kean.edu. *Application contact:* Brittany Gerstenhaber, Admissions Counselor, 908-737-7100, E-mail: grad-adm@kean.edu.
Website: http://grad.kean.edu/masters-programs/bilingualbicultural-education-instruction-and-curriculum

Langston University, School of Education and Behavioral Sciences, Langston, OK 73050. Offers bilingual/multicultural (M Ed); elementary education (M Ed); English as a second language (M Ed); rehabilitation counseling (M Sc); urban education (M Ed). *Accreditation:* CORE; NCATE (one or more programs are accredited). *Program availability:* Part-time. *Degree requirements:* For master's, comprehensive exam, thesis optional. *Entrance requirements:* For master's, GRE, writing skills test, minimum GPA of 2.5, 3 letters of recommendation. Additional exam requirements/recommendations for international students: Required—TOEFL, TWE. *Faculty research:* Bilingual/multicultural education, financing post-secondary education.

La Salle University, School of Arts and Sciences, Hispanic Institute, Philadelphia, PA 19141-1199. Offers bilingual/bicultural studies (MA); ESL program specialist (Certificate); interpretation: English/Spanish-Spanish/English (Certificate); teaching English to speakers of other languages (MA); translation and interpretation (MA); translation: English/Spanish-Spanish/English (Certificate). *Program availability:* Part-time, evening/weekend. *Faculty:* 2 full-time (1 woman), 6 part-time/adjunct (3 women). *Students:* 1 (woman) full-time, 26 part-time (18 women); includes 15 minority (5 Black or African American, non-Hispanic/Latino; 10 Hispanic/Latino), 1 international. Average age 37. 17 applicants, 76% accepted, 7 enrolled. In 2016, 7 master's, 4 other advanced degrees awarded. *Degree requirements:* For master's, one foreign language, project or thesis. *Entrance requirements:* For master's, GRE, MAT, or GMAT, professional resume; two letters of recommendation; for Certificate, GRE, MAT, or GMAT, professional resume; two letters of recommendation; evidence of an advanced level in Spanish. Additional exam requirements/recommendations for international students: Required—TOEFL. *Application deadline:* For fall admission, 8/15 priority date for domestic students, 7/15 for international students; for spring admission, 12/15 priority date for domestic students, 11/15 for international students; for summer admission, 4/15 priority date for domestic students, 3/15 for international students. Applications are processed on a rolling basis. Application fee: $35. Electronic applications accepted. Application fee is waived when completed online. *Expenses:* Contact institution. *Financial support:* In 2016–17, 3 students received support. Scholarships/grants available. Support available to part-time students. Financial award application deadline: 8/31; financial award applicants required to submit FAFSA. *Faculty research:* Puerto Rican literature, cross-cultural communication, English as a second language methodology, Spanish language. *Unit head:* Guadalupe Da Costa Montesinos, Director, 215-951-1209, Fax: 215-991-3506, E-mail: montesin@lasalle.edu. *Application contact:* Elizabeth Heenan, Director, Graduate and Adult Enrollment, 215-951-1100, Fax: 215-951-1462, E-mail: heenan@lasalle.edu.
Website: http://www.lasalle.edu/hispanic-institute/

La Salle University, School of Arts and Sciences, Program in Education, Philadelphia, PA 19141-1199. Offers autism spectrum disorders (MA, Certificate); bilingual/bicultural studies (MA); classroom management (MA); dual early childhood and special education (MA); dual middle-level science and math and special education (MA); education (MA); English (MA); English as a second language (Certificate); history (MA); instructional coach (Certificate), instructional leadership (MA); reading specialist (MA, Certificate); secondary education (MA); special education (MA, Certificate). *Program availability:* Part-time, evening/weekend. *Faculty:* 5 full-time (4 women), 12 part-time/adjunct (8 women). *Students:* 10 full-time (all women), 98 part-time (74 women); includes 28 minority (13 Black or African American, non-Hispanic/Latino; 1 American Indian or Alaska Native, non-Hispanic/Latino; 1 Asian, non-Hispanic/Latino; 10 Hispanic/Latino; 3 Two or more races, non-Hispanic/Latino). Average age 34. 128 applicants, 84% accepted, 69 enrolled. In 2016, 53 master's awarded. *Degree requirements:* For master's, comprehensive exam. *Entrance requirements:* For master's, MAT or GRE, 2 letters of recommendation; for Certificate, GMAT or GRE, 2 letters of recommendation. Additional exam requirements/recommendations for international students: Required—TOEFL. *Application deadline:* For fall admission, 8/15 priority date for domestic students, 7/15 for international students; for spring admission, 12/15 priority date for domestic students, 11/15 for international students; for summer admission, 4/15 priority date for domestic students, 3/15 for international students. Applications are processed on a rolling basis. Application fee: $35. Electronic applications accepted. Application fee is waived when completed online. *Expenses:* Contact institution. *Financial support:* In 2016–17, 27 students received support. Scholarships/grants available. Support available to part-time students. Financial award application deadline: 8/31; financial award applicants required to submit FAFSA. *Unit head:* Dr. Greer Richardson, Director, 215-951-1806, Fax: 215-951-1843, E-mail: graded@lasalle.edu. *Application contact:* Elizabeth Heenan, Director, Graduate and Adult Enrollment, 215-951-1100, Fax: 215-951-1462, E-mail: heenan@lasalle.edu.
Website: http://www.lasalle.edu/grad-education-programs/

Lehman College of the City University of New York, School of Education, Department of Specialized Services in Education, Bronx, NY 10468-1589. Offers guidance and counseling (MS Ed); reading teacher (MS Ed); teachers of special education (MS Ed), including bilingual special education, early special education, emotional handicaps, learning disabilities, mental retardation. *Program availability:* Part-time, evening/weekend. *Faculty research:* Battered women, whole language classrooms, parent education, mainstreaming.

Lehman College of the City University of New York, School of Education, Department of Specialized Services in Education, Teachers of Special Education Program, Option in Bilingual Special Education, Bronx, NY 10468-1589. Offers MS Ed. *Accreditation:* NCATE. *Entrance requirements:* For master's, minimum GPA of 3.0.

Long Island University–Hudson, Graduate School, Purchase, NY 10577. Offers autism (Advanced Certificate); childhood education (MS Ed); early childhood education (MS Ed); educational leadership (MS Ed); finance (MBA); health administration (MPA); healthcare sector management (MBA); literacy (MS Ed); management (MBA); marriage and family therapy (MS); mental health counseling (MS), including credentialed alcoholism and substance abuse counselor; middle childhood and adolescence education (MS Ed); pharmaceutics (MS), including cosmetic science, industrial pharmacy; public administration (MPA); school counseling (MS Ed, Advanced Certificate); school psychology (MS Ed); special education (MS Ed); TESOL (all grades) (Advanced Certificate); TESOL and bilingual education (MS Ed); the business of pharmaceutics and biotechnology (MBA). *Program availability:* Part-time, evening/weekend, online learning. *Faculty:* 7 full-time (5 women), 42 part-time/adjunct (25 women). *Students:* 55 full-time (41 women), 158 part-time (123 women); includes 40 minority (8 Black or African American, non-Hispanic/Latino; 1 Asian, non-Hispanic/Latino; 31 Hispanic/Latino). Average age 35. *Entrance requirements:* Additional exam requirements/recommendations for international students: Required—TOEFL (minimum score 550 paper-based; 79 iBT). *Application deadline:* Applications are processed on a rolling basis. Application fee: $50. Electronic applications accepted. *Expenses:* Contact institution. *Unit head:* Dr. Sylvia Blake, Dean and Chief Operating Officer, 914-831-2700, E-mail: westchester@liu.edu. *Application contact:* Cindy Pagnotta, Director of Marketing and Enrollment, 914-831-2701, Fax: 914-251-5959, E-mail: cindy.pagnotta@liu.edu.

Long Island University–LIU Brooklyn, School of Education, Brooklyn, NY 11201-8423. Offers adolescence urban education (MS Ed); applied behavior analysis (Advanced Certificate); bilingual education (Advanced Certificate); bilingual school counselor (MS Ed, Advanced Certificate); childhood urban education (MS Ed); childhood/early childhood urban education (MS Ed); early childhood urban education (MS Ed, Advanced Certificate); educational leadership (Advanced Certificate); marriage and family therapy (MS, Advanced Certificate); mental health counseling (MS, Advanced Certificate); school building district leader (Advanced Certificate); school counselor (MS Ed, Advanced Certificate); school psychologist (MS Ed); teaching urban children/adolescents with disabilities (MS Ed); TESOL (MS Ed). *Accreditation:* TEAC. *Program availability:* Part-time, evening/weekend. *Faculty:* 23 full-time (17 women), 44 part-time/adjunct (32 women). *Students:* 161 full-time (144 women), 594 part-time (461 women); includes 493 minority (229 Black or African American, non-Hispanic/Latino; 1 American Indian or Alaska Native, non-Hispanic/Latino; 30 Asian, non-Hispanic/Latino; 218 Hispanic/Latino; 2 Native Hawaiian or other Pacific Islander, non-Hispanic/Latino; 13 Two or more races, non-Hispanic/Latino), 9 international. 513 applicants, 73% accepted, 272 enrolled. In 2016, 262 master's, 18 other advanced degrees awarded. *Degree requirements:* For master's, thesis optional, electronic portfolio. *Entrance requirements:* For master's, GRE (for MS Ed). Additional exam requirements/recommendations for international students: Required—TOEFL (minimum score 527 paper-based; 75 iBT). *Application deadline:* Applications are processed on a rolling basis. Application fee: $50. Electronic applications accepted. *Expenses: Tuition:* Full-time $28,272; part-time $1178 per credit. *Required fees:* $451 per term. Tuition and fees vary according to degree level, program and student level. *Financial support:* In 2016–17, 81 students received support. Career-related internships or fieldwork, Federal Work-Study, institutionally sponsored loans, scholarships/grants, and unspecified assistantships available. Support available to part-time students. Financial award application deadline: 2/15; financial award applicants required to submit FAFSA. *Faculty research:* Technology in education, teaching civics and sustainability, biliteracy and dual language instruction, diversity in organizations and leadership, counseling diverse couples and families. *Unit head:* Dr. Amy Ginsberg, Dean, 718-246-6308, E-mail: amy.ginsberg@liu.edu. *Application contact:* Gabrielle Gannon, Director of Graduate Admissions, 718-488-1011, Fax: 718-780-6110, E-mail: bkln-admissions@liu.edu.
Website: http://www.liu.edu/Brooklyn/Academics/School-of-Education

Loyola Marymount University, School of Education, Department of Elementary and Secondary Education, Program in Bilingual Elementary Education, Los Angeles, CA 90045-2659. Offers MA. *Program availability:* Part-time, evening/weekend. *Students:* 28 full-time (27 women), 3 part-time (all women); includes 17 minority (1 Asian, non-Hispanic/Latino; 16 Hispanic/Latino), 12 international. Average age 26. 22 applicants, 82% accepted, 17 enrolled. In 2016, 12 master's awarded. *Entrance requirements:* For master's, CBEST, CSET, CSET LOTE Test 3, RICA, 3 letters of recommendation. Additional exam requirements/recommendations for international students: Required—TOEFL (minimum score 600 paper-based; 100 iBT). *Application deadline:* For fall admission, 6/15 for domestic students; for spring admission, 11/15 for domestic students. Application fee: $50. Electronic applications accepted. *Financial support:* In 2016–17, 25 students received support. Scholarships/grants and unspecified assistantships available. Support available to part-time students. Financial award application deadline: 6/30; financial award applicants required to submit FAFSA. *Unit head:* Dr. Liza Mastrippolito, Program Director, 310-568-6697, E-mail: smastrip@lmu.edu. *Application contact:* Chake H. Kouyoumjian, Associate Dean of Graduate Studies, 310-338-2721, Fax: 310-338-6086, E-mail: ckouyoum@lmu.edu.
Website: http://soe.lmu.edu/academics/bilingualeducation/

Loyola Marymount University, School of Education, Department of Elementary and Secondary Education, Program in Bilingual Secondary Education, Los Angeles, CA 90064. Offers MA. *Program availability:* Part-time, evening/weekend. *Students:* 10 full-time (7 women), 4 part-time (3 women); includes 11 minority (4 Asian, non-Hispanic/Latino; 7 Hispanic/Latino), 1 international. Average age 28. 8 applicants, 88% accepted, 4 enrolled. *Entrance requirements:* For master's, CBEST, CSET, CEST LOTE Test 3, RICA, 3 letters of recommendation. Additional exam requirements/recommendations for international students: Required—TOEFL (minimum score 600 paper-based; 100 iBT). *Application deadline:* For fall admission, 6/15 for domestic students; for spring admission, 11/15 for domestic students. Application fee: $50. Electronic applications accepted. *Financial support:* In 2016–17, 9 students received support. Scholarships/grants and unspecified assistantships available. Support available to part-time students. Financial award application deadline: 6/30; financial award applicants required to submit FAFSA. *Unit head:* Dr. Liza Mastrippolito, Program Director, 310-568-6697, E-mail: smastrip@lmu.edu. *Application contact:* Chake H. Kouyoumjian, Associate Dean of

Graduate Studies, 310-338-2721, E-mail: ckouyoum@lmu.edu.
Website: http://soe.lmu.edu/academics/bilingualeducation/

Manhattan College, Graduate Programs, School of Education and Health, Program in Special Education, Riverdale, NY 10471. Offers adolescence education students with disabilities generalist extension in English or math or social studies - grades 7-12 (MS Ed); bilingual education (Advanced Certificate); dual childhood/students with disabilities - grades 1-6 (MS Ed); students with disabilities - grades 1-6 (MS Ed). *Program availability:* Part-time, evening/weekend. *Faculty:* 3 full-time (all women), 11 part-time/adjunct (7 women). *Students:* 62 full-time (59 women), 4 part-time (all women). Average age 24. 34 applicants, 79% accepted, 24 enrolled. In 2016, 32 master's awarded. *Degree requirements:* For master's, thesis, internship (if not certified). *Entrance requirements:* For master's, GRE, minimum GPA of 3.0. Additional exam requirements/recommendations for international students: Required—TOEFL (minimum score 550 paper-based; 80 iBT), IELTS (minimum score 6). *Application deadline:* For fall admission, 8/10 priority date for domestic students; for spring admission, 1/7 priority date for domestic students. Applications are processed on a rolling basis. Application fee: $75. Electronic applications accepted. Application fee is waived when completed online. *Expenses:* $900 per credit, $105 registration fee, $175 information service fee. *Financial support:* In 2016–17, 52 students received support. Federal Work-Study, scholarships/grants, and unspecified assistantships available. Financial award application deadline: 2/1; financial award applicants required to submit FAFSA. *Unit head:* Dr. Elizabeth Mary Kosky, Director of Childhood and Adolescent Special Education Programs, 718-862-7969, Fax: 718-862-7816, E-mail: elizabeth.kosky@manhattan.edu. *Application contact:* William Bisset, Information Contact, 718-862-8000, E-mail: william.bisset@manhattan.edu.

Molloy College, Graduate Education Program, Rockville Centre, NY 11571-5002. Offers adolescent education in biology (MS Ed); adolescent special education (Advanced Certificate); bilingual extension (Advanced Certificate); childhood education (MS Ed); childhood special education (Advanced Certificate); early childhood education (MS Ed); educational technology (MS Ed); English (MS Ed); mathematics (MS Ed); social studies (MS Ed); Spanish (MS Ed); special education on both childhood and adolescent levels (MS Ed); teaching English to speakers of other languages (TESOL) in grades Pre-K to 12 (MS Ed); TESOL (Advanced Certificate). *Accreditation:* NCATE. *Program availability:* Part-time, evening/weekend. *Faculty:* 17 full-time (16 women), 23 part-time/adjunct (19 women). *Students:* 95 full-time (75 women), 221 part-time (177 women); includes 59 minority (14 Black or African American, non-Hispanic/Latino; 6 Asian, non-Hispanic/Latino; 38 Hispanic/Latino; 1 Two or more races, non-Hispanic/Latino), 1 international. Average age 42. 214 applicants, 66% accepted, 125 enrolled. In 2016, 95 master's, 4 Advanced Certificates awarded. *Entrance requirements:* Additional exam requirements/recommendations for international students: Required—TOEFL (minimum score 550 paper-based; 79 iBT). *Application deadline:* Applications are processed on a rolling basis. Application fee: $60. Electronic applications accepted. *Expenses: Tuition:* Full-time $19,170; part-time $1065 per credit. *Required fees:* $950; $790 per credit. Tuition and fees vary according to course load. *Financial support:* Applicants required to submit FAFSA. *Faculty research:* ESL - general education teacher collaboration; special education; school desegregation; American intellectual and social history; families and schools. *Unit head:* Joanne O'Brien, Associate Dean/Director, 516-323-3116, E-mail: jobrien@molloy.edu. *Application contact:* Jaclyn Machowicz, Assistant Director for Admissions, 516-323-4010, E-mail: jmachowicz@molloy.edu.

Mount St. Joseph University, Graduate Education Program, Cincinnati, OH 45233-1670. Offers adolescent to young adult education (MA); dyslexia (Certificate); inclusive early childhood education (MA); middle childhood education (MA); multicultural special education (MA); reading science (MA). *Accreditation:* TEAC. *Program availability:* Part-time, evening/weekend, online learning. *Faculty:* 7 full-time (5 women), 12 part-time/adjunct (10 women). *Students:* 44 full-time (33 women), 112 part-time (104 women); includes 16 minority (15 Black or African American, non-Hispanic/Latino; 1 Two or more races, non-Hispanic/Latino). Average age 34. In 2016, 60 master's awarded. *Degree requirements:* For master's, comprehensive exam, thesis, research project, student teaching, clinical and field-based experiences. *Entrance requirements:* For master's, GRE (if GPA is below 3.0), letter of intent, 2 referrals, background check, interview, resume, minimum undergraduate GPA of 3.0. Additional exam requirements/recommendations for international students: Required—TOEFL (minimum score 560 paper-based; 83 iBT). *Application deadline:* Applications are processed on a rolling basis. Application fee: $50. Electronic applications accepted. *Expenses:* $580 per credit hour. *Financial support:* Applicants required to submit FAFSA. *Faculty research:* Foreign and second language learning problems/reading disabilities, multicultural/bilingual special education, science education, pedagogical content knowledge, early childhood, response to intervention. *Unit head:* Dr. Laura Saylor, Dean, 513-244-3263, E-mail: laura.saylor@msj.edu. *Application contact:* Mary Brigham, Assistant Director of Graduate Recruitment, 513-244-4233, Fax: 513-244-4629, E-mail: mary.brigham@msj.edu.
Website: http://www.msj.edu/academics/graduate-programs/master-of-arts-initial-teacher-licensure-programs/

New Jersey City University, Debra Cannon Partridge Wolfe College of Education, Department of Multicultural Education, Jersey City, NJ 07305-1597. Offers bilingual/bicultural education (MA); English as a second language (MA). *Program availability:* Part-time, evening/weekend. *Entrance requirements:* For master's, GRE General Test or MAT. Additional exam requirements/recommendations for international students: Required—TOEFL.

New Mexico State University, College of Education, Department of Curriculum and Instruction, Las Cruces, NM 88003. Offers bilingual education (MA); curriculum and instruction (Ed D); early childhood education (MA); educational diagnostics (Ed S); language, literacy and culture (MA); learning design and technologies (MA); teaching (MAT), including Spanish; teaching English to speakers of other languages (MA). *Accreditation:* NCATE. *Program availability:* Part-time, evening/weekend, 100% online. *Faculty:* 23 full-time (17 women), 7 part-time/adjunct (5 women). *Students:* 114 full-time (81 women), 219 part-time (159 women); includes 190 minority (16 Black or African American, non-Hispanic/Latino; 2 American Indian or Alaska Native, non-Hispanic/Latino; 5 Asian, non-Hispanic/Latino; 160 Hispanic/Latino; 7 Two or more races, non-Hispanic/Latino), 33 international. Average age 37. 126 applicants, 75% accepted, 65 enrolled. In 2016, 92 master's, 19 doctorates awarded. *Degree requirements:* For master's, comprehensive exam, thesis optional; for doctorate, comprehensive exam, thesis/dissertation. *Entrance requirements:* For master's, minimum cumulative GPA of 3.0; for doctorate, portfolio, minimum cumulative GPA of 3.0. Additional exam requirements/recommendations for international students: Required—TOEFL (minimum score 550 paper-based; 79 iBT), IELTS (minimum score 6.5). *Application deadline:* For fall admission, 12/15 priority date for domestic and international students; for spring admission, 11/1 for domestic students. Applications are processed on a rolling basis. Application fee: $40 ($50 for international students). Electronic applications accepted. *Expenses:* Tuition, state resident: full-time $4086. Tuition, nonresident: full-time $14,254. *Required fees:* $853. Tuition and fees vary according to course load. *Financial support:* In 2016–17, 102 students received support, including 2 fellowships (averaging $4,076 per year), 2 research assistantships (averaging $18,070 per year), 16 teaching assistantships (averaging $16,454 per year); career-related internships or fieldwork, Federal Work-Study, scholarships/grants, traineeships, health care benefits, and unspecified assistantships also available. Support available to part-time students. Financial award application deadline: 3/1. *Faculty research:* STEM education, bilingual and English as a second language education, critical pedagogy/multicultural education, learning design and technology, early childhood education. *Total annual research expenditures:* $29,926. *Unit head:* Dr. David Rutledge, Department Head, 575-646-5411, Fax: 575-646-5436, E-mail: rutledge@nmsu.edu. *Application contact:* Dr. David Rutledge, Associate Department Head for Graduate Programs, 575-646-5411, Fax: 575-646-5436, E-mail: rutledge@nmsu.edu.
Website: http://ci.education.nmsu.edu

New Mexico State University, College of Education, Department of Special Education and Communication Disorders, Las Cruces, NM 88003. Offers communication disorders (MA); curriculum and instruction (Ed S), including special education (MA, Ed S), special education/deaf-hard of hearing (MA, Ed S); education (MA), including autism spectrum disorders, special education (MA, Ed S), special education/deaf-hard of hearing (MA, Ed S), speech-language pathology; special education (Ed D, PhD), including bilingual/multicultural special education. *Accreditation:* ASHA (one or more programs are accredited); NCATE. *Program availability:* Part-time, evening/weekend, online learning. *Faculty:* 15 full-time (12 women), 4 part-time/adjunct (3 women). *Students:* 59 full-time (49 women), 64 part-time (52 women); includes 68 minority (3 Black or African American, non-Hispanic/Latino; 2 American Indian or Alaska Native, non-Hispanic/Latino; 2 Asian, non-Hispanic/Latino; 59 Hispanic/Latino; 2 Two or more races, non-Hispanic/Latino), 7 international. Average age 33. 175 applicants, 19% accepted, 29 enrolled. In 2016, 43 master's, 1 doctorate, 1 other advanced degree awarded. *Degree requirements:* For master's, comprehensive exam, thesis optional; for doctorate, comprehensive exam, thesis/dissertation. *Entrance requirements:* For master's, GRE General Test or MAT. Additional exam requirements/recommendations for international students: Required—TOEFL (minimum score 550 paper-based; 79 iBT), IELTS (minimum score 6.5). *Application deadline:* For fall admission, 2/1 priority date for domestic students. Applications are processed on a rolling basis. Application fee: $40 ($50 for international students). Electronic applications accepted. *Expenses:* Tuition, state resident: full-time $4086. Tuition, nonresident: full-time $14,254. *Required fees:* $853. Tuition and fees vary according to course load. *Financial support:* In 2016–17, 47 students received support, including 2 research assistantships (averaging $12,723 per year), 15 teaching assistantships (averaging $9,700 per year); career-related internships or fieldwork, Federal Work-Study, scholarships/grants, traineeships, health care benefits, and unspecified assistantships also available. Support available to part-time students. Financial award application deadline: 3/1. *Faculty research:* Multicultural special education, multicultural communication disorders, mild disability, multicultural assessment, deaf education, early childhood, bilingual special education. *Total annual research expenditures:* $156,279. *Unit head:* Dr. Bob Wood, Interim Department Head, 575-646-5972, Fax: 575-646-7712, E-mail: bobwood@nmsu.edu. *Application contact:* Dr. Karen Potter, Director, Special Education Program, 575-646-2402, Fax: 575-646-7712, E-mail: potterk@nmsu.edu.
Website: http://spedcd.education.nmsu.edu

New York University, Steinhardt School of Culture, Education, and Human Development, Department of Humanities and Social Sciences in the Professions, Program in Sociology of Education, New York, NY 10003. Offers education policy (MA); social and cultural studies of education (MA); sociology of education (PhD). *Program availability:* Part-time. *Degree requirements:* For master's, thesis (for some programs); for doctorate, thesis/dissertation. *Entrance requirements:* For master's, letters of recommendation; for doctorate, GRE General Test, interview. Additional exam requirements/recommendations for international students: Required—TOEFL (minimum score 100 iBT). Electronic applications accepted. *Faculty research:* Legal and institutional environments of schools; social inequality; high school reform and achievement; urban schooling, economics and education, educational policy.

New York University, Steinhardt School of Culture, Education, and Human Development, Department of Teaching and Learning, Program in Multilingual/Multicultural Studies, New York, NY 10003. Offers bilingual education (MA, PhD, Advanced Certificate); foreign language education (MA); teaching English to speakers of other languages (MA, PhD); teaching foreign languages, 7-12 (MA), including Chinese, French, Italian, Japanese, Spanish; teaching French as a foreign language (MA), including teaching English to speakers of other languages; teaching Spanish as a foreign language (MA), including teaching English to speakers of other languages. *Accreditation:* TEAC. *Program availability:* Part-time, evening/weekend. *Degree requirements:* For master's, thesis (for some programs); for doctorate, thesis/dissertation. *Entrance requirements:* For doctorate, GRE General Test, interview; for Advanced Certificate, master's degree. Additional exam requirements/recommendations for international students: Required—TOEFL (minimum score 100 iBT). Electronic applications accepted. *Faculty research:* Second language acquisition, cross-cultural communication, technology-enhanced language learning, language variation, action learning.

Northeastern Illinois University, College of Graduate Studies and Research, College of Education, MAT Program in Bicultural/Bilingual Education, Chicago, IL 60625-4699. Offers MAT. *Degree requirements:* For master's, research paper. *Entrance requirements:* For master's, GRE, Illinois Basic Skills Test, bachelor's degree, minimum undergraduate GPA of 2.75.

Northeastern Illinois University, College of Graduate Studies and Research, College of Education, Program in Bilingual/Bicultural Education, Chicago, IL 60625-4699. Offers MAT, MSI. *Entrance requirements:* For master's, GRE, minimum GPA of 2.75. Additional exam requirements/recommendations for international students: Required—TOEFL (minimum score 550 paper-based; 79 iBT). Electronic applications accepted. *Faculty research:* Bilingual teacher preparation, linguistics and phonetics, Middle Eastern languages and cultures, TOEFL.

Northern Arizona University, Graduate College, College of Education, Department of Educational Specialties, Flagstaff, AZ 86011. Offers autism spectrum disorders (Certificate); bilingual/multicultural education (M Ed), including bilingual education, ESL education; career and technical education (M Ed, Certificate); culturally and linguistically diverse special education (Certificate); early childhood special education (M Ed); educational technology (M Ed, Certificate); English as a second language (Certificate); mild/moderate disabilities (M Ed); positive behavior support (Certificate); special education (M Ed). *Degree requirements:* For master's, comprehensive exam (for some programs), thesis (for some programs). *Entrance requirements:* For master's, minimum GPA of 3.0. Additional exam requirements/recommendations for international students: Required—TOEFL (minimum score 550 paper-based; 80 iBT), IELTS (minimum score 7). Electronic applications accepted. *Expenses:* Tuition, state resident: full-time $8971; part-time $444 per credit hour. Tuition, nonresident: full-time $20,958; part-time $1164 per credit hour. *Required fees:* $1018; $644 per credit hour. Tuition and fees vary according to course load, campus/location and program.

Queens College of the City University of New York, Arts and Humanities Division, Department of Linguistics and Communication Disorders, Queens, NY 11367-1597.

Offers applied linguistics (MA); English language teaching (Advanced Certificate); speech-language pathology (MA); teaching English to speakers of other languages (MS Ed); TESOL (MS Ed); TESOL and bilingual education (MS Ed). *Accreditation:* ASHA. *Program availability:* Part-time. *Faculty:* 22 full-time (16 women), 19 part-time/adjunct (13 women). *Students:* 44 full-time (42 women), 123 part-time (107 women); includes 64 minority (11 Black or African American, non-Hispanic/Latino; 20 Asian, non-Hispanic/Latino; 31 Hispanic/Latino; 2 Two or more races, non-Hispanic/Latino), 4 international. Average age 28. 390 applicants, 25% accepted, 81 enrolled. In 2016, 71 master's, 30 other advanced degrees awarded. *Entrance requirements:* For master's, minimum GPA of 3.0. Additional exam requirements/recommendations for international students: Required—TOEFL, IELTS. *Application deadline:* For fall admission, 4/1 for domestic students. Applications are processed on a rolling basis. Application fee: $125. Electronic applications accepted. *Expenses:* Tuition, state resident: full-time $5065; part-time $425 per credit. Tuition, nonresident: part-time $780 per credit. *Required fees:* $522; $397 per credit. Part-time tuition and fees vary according to course load and program. *Financial support:* Career-related internships or fieldwork available. Financial award application deadline: 4/1; financial award applicants required to submit FAFSA. *Unit head:* Dr. Robert Vago, Chairperson, 718-997-2875, E-mail: robert.vago@qc.cuny.edu.

Queens College of the City University of New York, Division of Education, Department of Elementary and Early Childhood Education, Queens, NY 11367-1597. Offers bilingual education (MS Ed); child development psychology (AC); childhood education (MAT, MS Ed); childhood education and special education (MAT); childhood education-bilingual education (MAT, MS Ed, AC); children's literacy (AC); early childhood education (MAT); early childhood education birth-2 (MS Ed, AC); elementary education (MS Ed); literacy birth-grade 6 (AC); literacy technology birth-grade 6 (MS Ed); social studies education grades 1-6 (AC). *Program availability:* Part-time, evening/weekend. *Faculty:* 25 full-time (19 women), 33 part-time/adjunct (28 women). *Students:* 134 full-time (119 women), 374 part-time (349 women); includes 251 minority (55 Black or African American, non-Hispanic/Latino; 1 American Indian or Alaska Native, non-Hispanic/Latino; 82 Asian, non-Hispanic/Latino; 103 Hispanic/Latino; 10 Two or more races, non-Hispanic/Latino), 12 international. Average age 29. 364 applicants, 72% accepted, 224 enrolled. In 2016, 184 master's, 62 other advanced degrees awarded. *Degree requirements:* For master's, research project. *Entrance requirements:* For master's, minimum GPA of 3.0. Additional exam requirements/recommendations for international students: Required—TOEFL, IELTS. *Application deadline:* For fall admission, 4/1 for domestic students. Applications are processed on a rolling basis. Application fee: $125. Electronic applications accepted. *Expenses:* Tuition, state resident: full-time $5065; part-time $425 per credit. Tuition, nonresident: part-time $780 per credit. *Required fees:* $522; $397 per credit. Part-time tuition and fees vary according to course load and program. *Financial support:* Career-related internships or fieldwork available. Financial award application deadline: 4/1; financial award applicants required to submit FAFSA. *Unit head:* Dr. Mary Bushnell Greiner, Chairperson, 718-997-5328, E-mail: mary.greiner@qc.cuny.edu.

Quincy University, Master of Science in Education Programs, Quincy, IL 62301-2699. Offers curriculum and instruction (MS Ed), including bilingual/English as a second language; leadership (MS Ed); reading education (MS Ed); special education (MS Ed); teacher leader (MS Ed). *Program availability:* Part-time, evening/weekend, online learning. *Degree requirements:* For master's, comprehensive exam (for some programs), thesis optional. *Entrance requirements:* For master's, MAT or GRE. Additional exam requirements/recommendations for international students: Required—TOEFL (minimum score 550 paper-based; 79 iBT). Electronic applications accepted. Application fee is waived when completed online.

Rowan University, Graduate School, College of Education, Department of Interdisciplinary and Inclusive Education, Glassboro, NJ 08028-1701. Offers autism spectrum disorders (CGS); bilingual/bicultural education (CGS); educational technology (CGS); elementary education (MST); learning disabilities (MA, CGS); music education (MA); science teaching (MST); secondary education (MST); special education (MA, CGS); teacher leadership (M Ed); teacher of students with disabilities (Postbaccalaureate Certificate); teaching and learning (CGS); teaching STEM (MA). *Accreditation:* NCATE. *Program availability:* Part-time, evening/weekend. *Degree requirements:* For master's, comprehensive exam, thesis. *Entrance requirements:* For master's, GRE General Test, PRAXIS I, PRAXIS II, interview, minimum GPA of 2.8. Additional exam requirements/recommendations for international students: Required—TOEFL. Electronic applications accepted.

Rutgers University–New Brunswick, Graduate School-New Brunswick, Program in Spanish, Piscataway, NJ 08854-8097. Offers bilingualism and second language acquisition (MA, PhD); Spanish (MA, MAT, PhD); Spanish literature (MA, PhD); translation (MA). *Program availability:* Part-time. *Degree requirements:* For master's, comprehensive exam (for some programs), thesis (for some programs); for doctorate, 2 foreign languages, comprehensive exam, thesis/dissertation. *Entrance requirements:* For master's and doctorate, GRE General Test. Additional exam requirements/recommendations for international students: Required—TOEFL. Electronic applications accepted. *Faculty research:* Hispanic literature, Luso-Brazilian literature, Spanish linguistics, Spanish translation.

St. John's University, The School of Education, Department of Counselor Education, Program in School Counseling with Bilingual Extension, Queens, NY 11439. Offers MS Ed. *Program availability:* Part-time, evening/weekend. *Degree requirements:* For master's, comprehensive exam. *Entrance requirements:* For master's, GRE, New York State Bilingual Assessment (BEA), bachelor's degree from an accredited college or university, minimum GPA of 3.0, 2 letters of recommendation, interview, minimum of 18 credits in behavioral or social science. Additional exam requirements/recommendations for international students: Required—TOEFL (minimum score 600 paper-based; 100 iBT), IELTS (minimum score 7). Electronic applications accepted. *Faculty research:* Cross-cultural comparisons of predictors of active coping.

St. John's University, The School of Education, Department of Education Specialties, Program in Teaching English to Speakers of Other Languages and Bilingual Education, Queens, NY 11439. Offers MS Ed, Adv C. *Program availability:* Part-time, evening/weekend, online learning. *Degree requirements:* For master's, comprehensive exam, fieldwork. *Entrance requirements:* For master's, minimum GPA of 3.0, eligibility for teacher certification, 2 letters of recommendation, bachelor's degree; for Adv C, New York State initial teaching certification or eligibility. Additional exam requirements/recommendations for international students: Required—TOEFL (minimum score 600 paper-based; 100 iBT), IELTS (minimum score 7). Electronic applications accepted. *Faculty research:* Second language learning and academic achievement, heritage language education, assessing the progress of English language learners toward English acquisition, dual language acquisition, study of English Creoles and dialects of other Englishes.

Saint Mary's University of Minnesota, Schools of Graduate and Professional Programs, Graduate School of Education, Education Program, Winona, MN 55987-1399. Offers culturally responsive teaching (Certificate); education (MA); gifted inclusive education (Certificate). Tuition and fees vary according to degree level and program. *Unit head:* Lynn Albee, Director, 612-728-5179, Fax: 612-728-5128, E-mail: lalbee@smumn.edu. *Application contact:* James Callinan, Director of Admissions for Graduate and Professional Programs, 612-728-5185, Fax: 612-728-5121, E-mail: jcallina@smumn.edu.
Website: http://www.smumn.edu/graduate-home/areas-of-study/graduate-school-of-education/ma-in-education

San Diego State University, Graduate and Research Affairs, College of Education, Department of Policy Studies in Language and Cross Cultural Education, San Diego, CA 92182. Offers multi-cultural emphasis (PhD); policy studies in language and cross cultural education (MA). *Accreditation:* NCATE. *Entrance requirements:* For master's, GRE General Test, letters of reference; for doctorate, GRE General Test, 3 letters of reference, resumé. Additional exam requirements/recommendations for international students: Required—TOEFL. Electronic applications accepted.

Southern Connecticut State University, School of Graduate Studies, School of Arts and Sciences, Department of World Languages and Literatures, New Haven, CT 06515-1355. Offers multicultural-bilingual education/teaching English to speakers of other languages (MS); romance languages (MA). *Program availability:* Part-time, evening/weekend. *Faculty:* 8 full-time (6 women). *Students:* 10 full-time (8 women), 41 part-time (36 women); includes 16 minority (2 Black or African American, non-Hispanic/Latino; 1 Asian, non-Hispanic/Latino; 13 Hispanic/Latino), 2 international. Average age 36. 41 applicants, 51% accepted, 15 enrolled. In 2016, 18 master's awarded. *Degree requirements:* For master's, one foreign language, thesis or alternative. *Entrance requirements:* For master's, interview, minimum undergraduate GPA of 2.7. *Application deadline:* For fall admission, 7/15 priority date for domestic students. Applications are processed on a rolling basis. Application fee: $50. Electronic applications accepted. *Expenses:* Tuition, state resident: full-time $6497; part-time $519 per credit hour. Tuition, nonresident: full-time $18,102; part-time $535 per credit hour. *Required fees:* $4722; $55 per semester. Tuition and fees vary according to program. *Financial support:* Career-related internships or fieldwork, scholarships/grants, and unspecified assistantships available. Financial award application deadline: 4/15; financial award applicants required to submit FAFSA. *Unit head:* Dr. Resha Cardone, Chairperson, 203-392-7170, Fax: 203-392-6136, E-mail: cardoner1@southernct.edu. *Application contact:* Lisa Galvin, Director of Graduate Admissions, 203-392-5240, Fax: 203-392-5235, E-mail: galvinl1@southernct.edu.
Website: http://www.southernct.edu/academics/schools/arts/departments/world-languages/

Southern Methodist University, Annette Caldwell Simmons School of Education and Human Development, Department of Teaching and Learning, Dallas, TX 75275. Offers bilingual/ESL education (MBE); education (M Ed, PhD); gifted education (MBE); reading and writing (M Ed); special education (M Ed). *Program availability:* Part-time, evening/weekend. Terminal master's awarded for partial completion of doctoral program. *Degree requirements:* For master's, comprehensive exam, minimum GPA of 3.0; for doctorate, thesis/dissertation, qualifying exams, major area paper, evidence of teaching competency, dissemination of research (e.g., conference presentation), professional portfolio. *Entrance requirements:* For master's, minimum GPA of 3.0 or GRE, 3 letters of recommendation; for doctorate, GRE, minimum GPA of 3.3, 3 years of full-time teaching, 3 letters of recommendation, interview. Additional exam requirements/recommendations for international students: Required—TOEFL. Electronic applications accepted. *Faculty research:* Reading intervention, mathematics intervention, bilingual education, new literacies.

State University of New York at New Paltz, Graduate School, School of Education, Department of Educational Studies, Program in Humanistic/Multicultural Education, New Paltz, NY 12561. Offers humanistic/multicultural education (MPS); multicultural education (AC). *Accreditation:* NCATE. *Program availability:* Part-time, evening/weekend. *Students:* 8 full-time (all women), 26 part-time (21 women); includes 12 minority (4 Black or African American, non-Hispanic/Latino; 8 Hispanic/Latino). 11 applicants, 82% accepted, 8 enrolled. In 2016, 13 master's awarded. *Entrance requirements:* For master's, minimum GPA of 3.0. Additional exam requirements/recommendations for international students: Required—TOEFL (minimum score 550 paper-based; 80 iBT), IELTS (minimum score 6.5). *Application deadline:* For fall admission, 4/15 priority date for domestic students, 4/15 for international students; for spring admission, 10/15 for domestic and international students. Application fee: $50. Electronic applications accepted. *Financial support:* Application deadline: 8/1. *Unit head:* Dr. Nancy Schniedewind, Coordinator, 845-257-2827, E-mail: schniedn@newpaltz.edu. *Application contact:* Vika Shock, Director of Graduate Admissions, 845-257-3286, E-mail: gradschool@newpaltz.edu.
Website: http://www.newpaltz.edu/edstudies/humanistic.html

State University of New York College at Geneseo, Graduate Studies, School of Education, Program in Childhood Multicultural Education, Geneseo, NY 14454-1401. Offers MS Ed. *Program availability:* Part-time, evening/weekend. *Faculty:* 1 (woman) full-time. *Students:* 1 part-time (0 women); minority (Hispanic/Latino). Average age 27. 2 applicants. In 2016, 1 master's awarded. *Degree requirements:* For master's, culminating experience; thesis or research project. *Entrance requirements:* For master's, initial certification to teach in New York state. Additional exam requirements/recommendations for international students: Required—TOEFL, IELTS, PTE. *Application deadline:* For fall admission, 4/1 priority date for domestic students; for spring admission, 11/1 priority date for domestic students. Applications are processed on a rolling basis. Application fee: $50. Electronic applications accepted. *Expenses:* Tuition, state resident: full-time $10,870; part-time $453 per credit. Tuition, nonresident: full-time $22,210; part-time $925 per credit. *Required fees:* $865; $35.85 per credit hour. *Financial support:* In 2016–17, 1 fellowship with partial tuition reimbursement (averaging $10,000 per year) was awarded; scholarships/grants, health care benefits, tuition waivers (full), and unspecified assistantships also available. Support available to part-time students. Financial award application deadline: 4/1; financial award applicants required to submit FAFSA. *Unit head:* Dr. Anjoo Sikka, Dean of the School of Education, 585-245-5151, Fax: 585-245-5220, E-mail: sikka@geneseo.edu. *Application contact:* Michael R. George, Graduate Enrollment Coordinator, 585-245-5040, Fax: 585-245-5550, E-mail: georgem@geneseo.edu.

Sul Ross State University, Rio Grande College of Sul Ross State University, Alpine, TX 79832. Offers business administration (MBA); teacher education (M Ed), including bilingual education, counseling, educational diagnostics, elementary education, general education, reading, school administration, secondary education. *Program availability:* Part-time, evening/weekend, online learning. *Degree requirements:* For master's, comprehensive exam, thesis optional, minimum GPA of 3.0. *Entrance requirements:* For master's, GMAT or GRE General Test, minimum GPA of 2.5 in last 60 hours of undergraduate work. Additional exam requirements/recommendations for international students: Required—TOEFL.

Teachers College, Columbia University, Department of Arts and Humanities, New York, NY 10027. Offers applied linguistics (MA, Ed D); art and art education (Ed M, MA, Ed D, Ed DCT); arts administration (MA); bilingual and bicultural education (MA); global competence (Certificate); history and education (Ed D, PhD); music and music education (Ed DCT); philosophy and education (MA, Ed D, PhD); social studies education (Ed M, PhD); teaching English to speakers of other languages (Ed M); teaching of English and English education (Ed M, MA, Ed D, PhD), including English

education (Ed M, Ed D, PhD), teaching of English (MA); teaching of social studies (MA); TESOL (MA, Ed D). *Program availability:* Part-time, evening/weekend. *Students:* 429 full-time (329 women), 467 part-time (332 women); includes 268 minority (62 Black or African American, non-Hispanic/Latino; 1 American Indian or Alaska Native, non-Hispanic/Latino; 108 Asian, non-Hispanic/Latino; 76 Hispanic/Latino; 21 Two or more races, non-Hispanic/Latino), 212 international. 1,068 applicants, 53% accepted, 272 enrolled. Terminal master's awarded for partial completion of doctoral program. *Expenses: Tuition:* Full-time $36,288; part-time $1512 per credit. *Required fees:* $438 per semester. One-time fee: $510 full-time. Full-time tuition and fees vary according to course load. *Financial support:* Fellowships, research assistantships, teaching assistantships, career-related internships or fieldwork, Federal Work-Study, institutionally sponsored loans, tuition waivers (full and partial), and unspecified assistantships available. Support available to part-time students. *Unit head:* Prof. William Gaudelli, Department Chair, 212-678-3150, E-mail: wg74@columbia.edu. *Application contact:* David Estrella, Director of Admissions, 212-678-3305, Fax: 212-678-4171, E-mail: estrella@tc.columbia.edu.
Website: http://www.tc.edu/a%26h/

Texas A&M University, College of Education and Human Development, Department of Educational Psychology, College Station, TX 77843. Offers bilingual education (M Ed, MS); counseling psychology (PhD); educational psychology (M Ed, MS, PhD); educational technology (M Ed); school psychology (PhD); special education (M Ed, MS). *Accreditation:* APA (one or more programs are accredited). *Program availability:* Part-time, evening/weekend, blended/hybrid learning. *Faculty:* 42. *Students:* 172 full-time (139 women), 281 part-time (233 women); includes 144 minority (27 Black or African American, non-Hispanic/Latino; 1 American Indian or Alaska Native, non-Hispanic/Latino; 19 Asian, non-Hispanic/Latino; 86 Hispanic/Latino; 1 Native Hawaiian or other Pacific Islander, non-Hispanic/Latino; 10 Two or more races, non-Hispanic/Latino), 48 international. Average age 33. 181 applicants, 44% accepted, 45 enrolled. In 2016, 99 master's, 27 doctorates awarded. *Degree requirements:* For master's, thesis optional; for doctorate, thesis/dissertation. *Entrance requirements:* For master's and doctorate, GRE General Test. Additional exam requirements/recommendations for international students: Required—TOEFL (minimum score 550 paper-based; 80 iBT), IELTS (minimum score 6), PTE (minimum score 53). *Application deadline:* For fall admission, 12/1 for domestic students; for spring admission, 10/15 for domestic students. Application fee: $50 ($90 for international students). Electronic applications accepted. *Expenses:* Contact institution. *Financial support:* In 2016–17, 231 students received support, including 8 fellowships with tuition reimbursements available (averaging $9,919 per year), 98 research assistantships with tuition reimbursements available (averaging $6,004 per year), 13 teaching assistantships with tuition reimbursements available (averaging $9,368 per year); career-related internships or fieldwork, institutionally sponsored loans, scholarships/grants, traineeships, health care benefits, tuition waivers (full and partial), and unspecified assistantships also available. Support available to part-time students. Financial award application deadline: 3/15; financial award applicants required to submit FAFSA. *Unit head:* Dr. Victor Willson, Department Head, 979-845-1394, E-mail: v-willson@tamu.edu. *Application contact:* Kristie Stramaski, Senior Academic Advisor, 979-845-1833, E-mail: epsyadvisor@tamu.edu.
Website: http://epsy.tamu.edu

Texas A&M University–Kingsville, College of Graduate Studies, College of Education and Human Performance, Department of Teacher and Bilingual Education, Program in Bilingual Education, Kingsville, TX 78363. Offers M Ed, Ed D. *Degree requirements:* For master's, comprehensive exam. *Entrance requirements:* For master's, GRE General Test, MAT, minimum GPA of 3.0.

Texas A&M University–San Antonio, Department of Curriculum and Kinesiology, San Antonio, TX 78224. Offers bilingual education (MA); early childhood education (M Ed); kinesiology (MS); reading (MS); special education (M Ed), including educational diagnostician, instructional specialist. *Program availability:* Part-time, evening/weekend. *Degree requirements:* For master's, comprehensive exam, thesis or alternative. *Entrance requirements:* For master's, MAT. Additional exam requirements/recommendations for international students: Required—TOEFL (minimum score 550 paper-based; 80 iBT), IELTS (minimum score 6). Electronic applications accepted.

Texas Southern University, College of Education, Area of Curriculum and Instruction, Houston, TX 77004-4584. Offers bilingual education (M Ed); curriculum and instruction (Ed D); secondary education (M Ed). *Program availability:* Part-time, evening/weekend. *Degree requirements:* For master's, comprehensive exam; for doctorate, comprehensive exam, thesis/dissertation. *Entrance requirements:* For master's, GRE General Test, minimum GPA of 2.5; for doctorate, GRE General Test or MAT, master's degree, minimum B+ average. Additional exam requirements/recommendations for international students: Required—TOEFL. Electronic applications accepted.

Texas State University, The Graduate College, College of Education, Program in Elementary Education - Bilingual/Bicultural, San Marcos, TX 78666. Offers M Ed, MA. *Program availability:* Part-time. *Faculty:* 5 full-time (all women), 2 part-time/adjunct (both women). *Students:* 3 full-time (all women), 9 part-time (all women); includes 9 minority (all Hispanic/Latino), 2 international. Average age 33. 6 applicants, 67% accepted, 2 enrolled. In 2016, 4 master's awarded. *Degree requirements:* For master's, comprehensive exam, thesis (for some programs). *Entrance requirements:* For master's, GRE (preferred), baccalaureate degree from regionally-accredited institution with minimum GPA of 2.75 in last 60 hours of course work; meeting with bilingual coordinator to ensure proficiency in written and spoken Spanish. Additional exam requirements/recommendations for international students: Required—TOEFL (minimum score 550 paper-based; 78 iBT), IELTS (minimum score 6.5). *Application deadline:* For fall admission, 2/15 priority date for domestic and international students; for spring admission, 10/15 for domestic students, 10/1 for international students; for summer admission, 4/15 for domestic students, 3/15 for international students. Applications are processed on a rolling basis. Application fee: $40 ($90 for international students). Electronic applications accepted. *Expenses:* $4,851 per semester. *Financial support:* In 2016–17, 10 students received support. Research assistantships, teaching assistantships, career-related internships or fieldwork, Federal Work-Study, institutionally sponsored loans, scholarships/grants, and unspecified assistantships available. Support available to part-time students. Financial award application deadline: 3/1; financial award applicants required to submit FAFSA. *Unit head:* Dr. Mary Esther Huerta, Graduate Advisor, 512-245-3099, Fax: 512-245-7911, E-mail: mh75@txstate.edu. *Application contact:* Dr. Andrea Golato, Dean of Graduate School, 512-245-2581, Fax: 512-245-8365, E-mail: gradcollege@txstate.edu.
Website: http://www.education.txstate.edu/ci/degrees-programs/graduate/elementary-education.html

Texas Tech University, Graduate School, College of Education, Department of Curriculum and Instruction, Lubbock, TX 79409-1071. Offers bilingual education (M Ed); curriculum and instruction (M Ed); elementary education (M Ed); language/literacy education (M Ed); multidisciplinary science (MS); secondary education (M Ed). *Accreditation:* NCATE. *Program availability:* Part-time, evening/weekend, online learning. *Faculty:* 24 full-time (17 women), 1 part-time/adjunct (0 women). *Students:* 65 full-time (52 women), 237 part-time (191 women); includes 97 minority (30 Black or African American, non-Hispanic/Latino; 1 American Indian or Alaska Native, non-Hispanic/Latino; 10 Asian, non-Hispanic/Latino; 47 Hispanic/Latino; 9 Two or more races, non-Hispanic/Latino), 41 international. Average age 39. 181 applicants, 54% accepted, 78 enrolled. In 2016, 20 master's, 28 doctorates awarded. Terminal master's awarded for partial completion of doctoral program. *Degree requirements:* For master's, comprehensive exam (for some programs), thesis optional; for doctorate, comprehensive exam, thesis/dissertation. *Entrance requirements:* For master's, bachelor's degree; resume; letter of intent; academic writing sample; 2 letters of recommendation; for doctorate, GRE, master's degree; resume; letter of intent; academic writing sample; 3 letters of recommendation. Additional exam requirements/recommendations for international students: Required—TOEFL (minimum score 550 paper-based; 79 iBT). *Application deadline:* For fall admission, 6/1 priority date for domestic students, 1/15 priority date for international students; for spring admission, 9/1 priority date for domestic students, 6/15 priority date for international students. Applications are processed on a rolling basis. Application fee: $75. Electronic applications accepted. *Expenses:* $285 per credit hour full-time resident tuition, $693 per credit hour full-time non-resident tuition; $50.50 per credit hour fee plus $608 per term fee. *Financial support:* In 2016–17, 110 students received support, including 110 fellowships (averaging $3,132 per year); research assistantships, Federal Work-Study, institutionally sponsored loans, scholarships/grants, health care benefits, and unspecified assistantships also available. Support available to part-time students. Financial award application deadline: 2/1; financial award applicants required to submit FAFSA. *Faculty research:* Teacher education, curriculum studies, bilingual education, science and math education, language and literacy education. *Total annual research expenditures:* $120,552. *Unit head:* Dr. Jian Wang, Department Chair, Curriculum and Instruction, 806-834-5165, Fax: 806-742-2179, E-mail: jian.wang@ttu.edu. *Application contact:* Brianna Sanchez, Coordinator, 806-834-2353, Fax: 806-742-2179, E-mail: brianna.sanchez@ttu.edu.
Website: http://www.educ.ttu.edu

University at Buffalo, the State University of New York, Graduate School, Graduate School of Education, Department of Learning and Instruction, Buffalo, NY 14260. Offers biology education (Ed M, Certificate); chemistry education (Ed M, Certificate); childhood education (Ed M); childhood education with bilingual extension (Ed M); college teaching (Advanced Certificate); curriculum, instruction and the science of learning (PhD); early childhood education (Ed M); early childhood education with bilingual extension (Ed M); earth science education (Ed M, Certificate); education and technology (Ed M); education studies (Ed M); educational technology and new literacies (Certificate); educational technology and new literacies (Advanced Certificate); elementary education (Ed D); English education (Ed M, Certificate); English education studies (Ed M); English for speakers of other languages (Ed M); foreign and second language education (PhD); French education (Ed M, Certificate); German education (Ed M, Certificate); gifted education (Certificate); Latin education (Ed M, Certificate); literacy education studies (Ed M); literacy specialist (Ed M); literacy teaching and learning (Certificate); mathematics education (Ed M, Certificate); music education (Ed M, Certificate); music education studies (Ed M); music learning theory (Advanced Certificate); online education (Advanced Certificate); physics education (Ed M, Certificate); science and the public (Ed M); social studies education (Ed M, Certificate); Spanish education (Ed M, Certificate); special education (PhD); teaching English to speakers of other languages (Ed M). *Program availability:* Part-time, evening/weekend, 100% online. *Faculty:* 28 full-time (21 women), 67 part-time/adjunct (49 women). *Students:* 198 full-time (153 women), 312 part-time (220 women); includes 48 minority (28 Black or African American, non-Hispanic/Latino; 4 American Indian or Alaska Native, non-Hispanic/Latino; 15 Asian, non-Hispanic/Latino; 1 Hispanic/Latino), 66 international. Average age 33. 336 applicants, 86% accepted, 178 enrolled. In 2016, 137 master's, 24 doctorates, 25 other advanced degrees awarded. *Degree requirements:* For master's, comprehensive exam; for doctorate, thesis/dissertation, research analysis exam, research experience. *Entrance requirements:* For master's, letters of reference; for doctorate, GRE General Test or MAT, interview, writing sample, letters of recommendation. Additional exam requirements/recommendations for international students: Required—TOEFL (minimum score 600 paper-based; 96 iBT). *Application deadline:* For fall admission, 2/1 priority date for domestic and international students; for spring admission, 11/15 priority date for domestic students, 10/1 for international students. Applications are processed on a rolling basis. Application fee: $50. Electronic applications accepted. *Financial support:* In 2016–17, 44 fellowships (averaging $4,010 per year), 39 research assistantships with tuition reimbursements (averaging $9,897 per year) were awarded; teaching assistantships, career-related internships or fieldwork, Federal Work-Study, institutionally sponsored loans, scholarships/grants, tuition waivers (full and partial), and unspecified assistantships also available. Financial award application deadline: 2/28; financial award applicants required to submit FAFSA. *Faculty research:* Science assessment, foreign language teaching and learning, early learning, new literacies, gender and education. *Total annual research expenditures:* $534,880. *Unit head:* Dr. Deborah Moore-Russo, Chair, 716-645-4069, Fax: 716-645-3161, E-mail: dam29@buffalo.edu. *Application contact:* Luann Zak, Admissions Assistant, 716-645-2110, Fax: 716-645-7937, E-mail: luannzak@buffalo.edu.
Website: http://gse.buffalo.edu/lai

University of Alaska Fairbanks, College of Liberal Arts, Department of Cross-Cultural Studies, Fairbanks, AK 99775-6300. Offers MA. *Program availability:* Part-time. *Faculty:* 4 full-time (2 women). *Students:* 1 (woman) full-time, 4 part-time (all women); includes 6 minority (3 American Indian or Alaska Native, non-Hispanic/Latino; 2 Hispanic/Latino; 1 Native Hawaiian or other Pacific Islander, non-Hispanic/Latino). Average age 44. 1 applicant, 100% accepted, 1 enrolled. *Degree requirements:* For master's, comprehensive exam, project, oral defense of project. *Entrance requirements:* For master's, bachelor's degree from accredited institution with minimum cumulative undergraduate and major GPA of 3.0. Additional exam requirements/recommendations for international students: Required—TOEFL (minimum score 550 paper-based; 79 iBT), IELTS (minimum score 8.5). *Application deadline:* For fall admission, 6/1 for domestic students, 3/1 for international students; for spring admission, 10/15 for domestic students, 9/1 for international students. Applications are processed on a rolling basis. Application fee: $60. Electronic applications accepted. *Expenses:* Tuition, state resident: full-time $7992; part-time $444 per credit. Tuition, nonresident: full-time $16,326; part-time $907 per credit. *Required fees:* $39 per credit. $322 per semester. Tuition and fees vary according to course level, course load, campus/location, program and reciprocity agreements. *Financial support:* Fellowships with full tuition reimbursements, research assistantships with full tuition reimbursements, teaching assistantships with full tuition reimbursements, Federal Work-Study, scholarships/grants, health care benefits, and unspecified assistantships available. Support available to part-time students. Financial award application deadline: 7/1; financial award applicants required to submit FAFSA. *Faculty research:* Alaska native literature, oral traditions, history, law and policy, cultures, art; Native American religion and philosophy. *Total annual research expenditures:* $10,000. *Unit head:* Lawrence Kaplan, Acting Director of the Center for Cross-Cultural Studies, 907-474-1902, Fax: 907-474-1957, E-mail: fycxcs@uaf.edu. *Application contact:* Mary Kreta, Director of Admissions, 907-474-7500, Fax: 907-474-7097, E-mail: admissions@uaf.edu.
Website: http://www.uaf.edu/cxcs

University of Alaska Fairbanks, College of Liberal Arts, Program in Linguistics, Fairbanks, AK 99775-6280. Offers applied linguistics (MA), including language documentation, second language acquisition teacher education. *Program availability:* Part-time. *Faculty:* 2 full-time (both women). *Students:* 5 full-time (3 women), 21 part-time (17 women); includes 7 minority (all American Indian or Alaska Native, non-Hispanic/Latino), 1 international. Average age 37. 6 applicants, 83% accepted, 4 enrolled. In 2016, 12 master's awarded. *Degree requirements:* For master's, one foreign language, comprehensive exam, oral defense of project or thesis. *Entrance requirements:* For master's, bachelor's degree from accredited institution with minimum cumulative undergraduate and major GPA of 3.0. Additional exam requirements/recommendations for international students: Required—TOEFL (minimum score 550 paper-based; 79 iBT), IELTS (minimum score 6.5). *Application deadline:* For fall admission, 6/1 for domestic students, 3/1 for international students; for spring admission, 10/15 for domestic students, 9/1 for international students. Applications are processed on a rolling basis. Application fee: $60. Electronic applications accepted. *Expenses:* Tuition, state resident: full-time $7992; part-time $444 per credit. Tuition, nonresident: full-time $16,326; part-time $907 per credit. *Required fees:* $39 per credit. $322 per semester. Tuition and fees vary according to course level, course load, campus/location, program and reciprocity agreements. *Financial support:* In 2016–17, 3 teaching assistantships with full tuition reimbursements (averaging $5,908 per year) were awarded; fellowships with full tuition reimbursements, research assistantships with full tuition reimbursements, career-related internships or fieldwork, Federal Work-Study, scholarships/grants, health care benefits, and unspecified assistantships also available. Support available to part-time students. Financial award application deadline: 7/1; financial award applicants required to submit FAFSA. *Faculty research:* Second language acquisition/teaching, Inupiaq, Athabaskan languages, language maintenance and shift, phonology, morphology. *Total annual research expenditures:* $23,000. *Unit head:* Dr. Siri Tuttle, Program Head, 907-474-7876, Fax: 907-474-6586, E-mail: fyling@uaf.edu. *Application contact:* Mary Kreta, Director of Admissions, 907-474-7500, Fax: 907-474-7097, E-mail: admissions@uaf.edu.
Website: http://www.uaf.edu/linguist/

University of Alberta, Faculty of Graduate Studies and Research, Facultè Saint Jean, Edmonton, AB T6G 2E1, Canada. Offers M Ed. *Program availability:* Part-time, evening/weekend, online learning. *Degree requirements:* For master's, thesis (for some programs). *Entrance requirements:* For master's, proficiency in French, 2 years of teaching experience. *Faculty research:* First and second language acquisition, first and second language learning through subject matter, cultural transmission.

University of Calgary, Faculty of Graduate Studies, Werklund School of Education, Graduate Division of Educational Research, Calgary, AB T2N 1N4, Canada. Offers adult learning (M Ed, MA, Ed D, PhD); curriculum and learning (M Ed, MA, Ed D, PhD); educational leadership (M Ed, MA, Ed D, PhD); languages and diversity (M Ed, MA, Ed D, PhD); learning sciences (M Ed, MA, Ed D, PhD). Ed D in educational leadership offered via distance delivery. *Program availability:* Part-time, evening/weekend, online learning. *Degree requirements:* For master's, thesis (for some programs); for doctorate, thesis/dissertation, candidacy exam. *Entrance requirements:* For master's, minimum GPA of 3.0, 3 letters of reference; for doctorate, minimum GPA of 3.5, 3 letters of reference. Additional exam requirements/recommendations for international students: Required—TOEFL, IELTS. Electronic applications accepted. *Faculty research:* Curriculum, leadership, technology, contexts, gifted, second language teaching, work place and adult learning.

University of California, Riverside, Graduate Division, Graduate School of Education, Riverside, CA 92521-0102. Offers autism (M Ed); diversity and equity (M Ed); education specialist (Credential); education, society, and culture (MA, PhD); educational psychology (MA, PhD); general education (M Ed); higher education administration and policy (M Ed, PhD); multiple subject (Credential); reading (M Ed); school psychology (PhD); single subject (Credential); special education (M Ed, MA, PhD); TESOL (M Ed). Terminal master's awarded for partial completion of doctoral program. *Degree requirements:* For master's, thesis optional, comprehensive exams or thesis (MA), case study or analytical report (M Ed); for doctorate, thesis/dissertation, written and oral qualifying exams, college teaching practicum. *Entrance requirements:* For master's, GRE General Test (for MA); CBEST and CSET (for M Ed in general education only), UCR Extension TESOL certificate (for M Ed with TESOL emphasis only); for doctorate, GRE General Test, writing sample; for Credential, CBEST, CSET. Additional exam requirements/recommendations for international students: Required—TOEFL (minimum score 550 paper-based; 80 iBT), IELTS (minimum score 7). Electronic applications accepted. *Expenses:* Tuition, state resident: full-time $16,666. Tuition, nonresident: full-time $31,768. *Required fees:* $11,055.54 per quarter. $3685.18 per quarter. Tuition and fees vary according to campus/location and program. *Faculty research:* Responsiveness to intervention, faculty core, response to intervention of English language learners, advanced modeling techniques, study on social capital, trust, and motivation.

University of California, San Diego, Graduate Division, Program in Education Studies, La Jolla, CA 92093. Offers education (M Ed, PhD); educational leadership (Ed D); teaching and learning (MA, Ed D), including bilingual education (MA), curriculum design (MA). Ed D offered jointly with California State University, San Marcos. *Students:* 89 full-time (59 women), 52 part-time (38 women). 228 applicants, 52% accepted, 74 enrolled. In 2016, 68 master's, 6 doctorates awarded. *Degree requirements:* For master's, thesis (for some programs), student teaching; for doctorate, comprehensive exam, thesis/dissertation. *Entrance requirements:* For master's, GRE General Test; CBEST and appropriate CSET exam (for select tracks), current teaching or educational assignment (for select tracks); for doctorate, GRE General Test, current teaching or educational assignment (for select tracks). Additional exam requirements/recommendations for international students: Required—TOEFL (minimum score 550 paper-based; 80 iBT), IELTS (minimum score 7). *Application deadline:* For fall admission, 12/1 for domestic students. Application fee: $105 ($125 for international students). Electronic applications accepted. *Expenses:* Tuition, state resident: full-time $11,220. Tuition, nonresident: full-time $26,322. *Required fees:* $1864. *Financial support:* Fellowships, career-related internships or fieldwork, and scholarships/grants available. Financial award applicants required to submit FAFSA. *Faculty research:* Language, culture and literacy development of deaf/hard of hearing children; equity issues in education; educational reform; evaluation, assessment, and research methodologies; distributed learning. *Unit head:* Alan J. Daly, Chair, 858-822-6472, E-mail: ajdaly@ucsd.edu. *Application contact:* Giselle Van Luit, Graduate Coordinator, 858-534-2958, E-mail: edsinfo@ucsd.edu.

University of Colorado Boulder, Graduate School, School of Education, Division of Social Multicultural and Bilingual Foundations, Boulder, CO 80309. Offers educational equity and cultural diversity (PhD); multicultural education (MA). *Accreditation:* NCATE. *Students:* 24 full-time (23 women), 129 part-time (115 women); includes 57 minority (1 Black or African American, non-Hispanic/Latino; 1 American Indian or Alaska Native, non-Hispanic/Latino; 3 Asian, non-Hispanic/Latino; 50 Hispanic/Latino; 2 Two or more races, non-Hispanic/Latino), 3 international. Average age 36. 93 applicants, 73% accepted, 7 enrolled. In 2016, 56 master's, 3 doctorates awarded. Terminal master's awarded for partial completion of doctoral program. *Degree requirements:* For master's, comprehensive exam, thesis or alternative; for doctorate, one foreign language, comprehensive exam, thesis/dissertation. *Entrance requirements:* For master's, GRE General Test or MAT, minimum undergraduate GPA of 2.75; for doctorate, GRE General Test. *Application deadline:* For fall admission, 2/1 for domestic students, 12/1 for international students; for spring admission, 9/1 for domestic and international students. Application fee: $60 ($80 for international students). Electronic applications accepted. Application fee is waived when completed online. *Financial support:* In 2016–17, 123 students received support, including 16 fellowships (averaging $3,971 per year), 12 research assistantships with full and partial tuition reimbursements available (averaging $39,446 per year), 4 teaching assistantships with full and partial tuition reimbursements available (averaging $18,342 per year); institutionally sponsored loans, scholarships/grants, health care benefits, and unspecified assistantships also available. Financial award applicants required to submit FAFSA. *Faculty research:* Bilingual education, inclusion. *Application contact:* E-mail: edadvise@colorado.edu.
Website: http://www.colorado.edu/education/

University of Colorado Denver, School of Education and Human Development, Teacher Education Programs, Denver, CO 80217. Offers elementary linguistically diverse education (MA); elementary math and science education (MA); elementary math education (MA); elementary reading and writing (MA); elementary science education (MA); secondary English education (MA); secondary linguistically diverse education (MA); secondary math education (MA); secondary reading and writing (MA); secondary science education (MA); special education (MA). *Accreditation:* NCATE. *Program availability:* Part-time, evening/weekend. *Students:* 142 full-time (117 women), 184 part-time (159 women); includes 56 minority (6 Black or African American, non-Hispanic/Latino; 1 American Indian or Alaska Native, non-Hispanic/Latino; 4 Asian, non-Hispanic/Latino; 38 Hispanic/Latino; 1 Native Hawaiian or other Pacific Islander, non-Hispanic/Latino; 6 Two or more races, non-Hispanic/Latino), 1 international. Average age 30. 18 applicants, 67% accepted, 9 enrolled. In 2016, 134 master's awarded. *Degree requirements:* For master's, comprehensive exam. *Entrance requirements:* For master's, GRE or MAT (for those with GPA below 2.75), transcripts, resume, letters of recommendation. Additional exam requirements/recommendations for international students: Required—TOEFL (minimum score 537 paper-based; 75 iBT); Recommended—IELTS (minimum score 6.5). *Application deadline:* For fall admission, 4/15 for domestic students, 4/1 for international students; for spring admission, 9/15 for domestic students, 9/1 for international students; for summer admission, 2/15 for domestic students, 2/1 for international students. Applications are processed on a rolling basis. Application fee: $50 ($75 for international students). Electronic applications accepted. *Expenses:* Contact institution. *Financial support:* In 2016–17, 26 students received support. Fellowships, research assistantships, teaching assistantships, Federal Work-Study, institutionally sponsored loans, scholarships/grants, and traineeships available. Financial award application deadline: 4/1; financial award applicants required to submit FAFSA. *Faculty research:* Linguistically diverse education/ESL, elementary reading and writing, elementary teacher education, secondary teacher education, special education. *Unit head:* Cindy Gutierrez, Director, 303-315-4982, E-mail: cindy.gutierrez@ucdenver.edu. *Application contact:* 303-315-6300, E-mail: education@ucdenver.edu.
Website: http://www.ucdenver.edu/academics/colleges/SchoolOfEducation/Academics/MASTERS/Pages/default.aspx

University of Connecticut, Graduate School, Neag School of Education, Department of Curriculum and Instruction, Program in Bilingual and Bicultural Education, Storrs, CT 06269. Offers MA, PhD. *Accreditation:* NCATE. Terminal master's awarded for partial completion of doctoral program. *Degree requirements:* For master's, comprehensive exam; for doctorate, thesis/dissertation. *Entrance requirements:* For doctorate, GRE General Test. Additional exam requirements/recommendations for international students: Required—TOEFL (minimum score 550 paper-based). Electronic applications accepted.

University of Delaware, College of Education and Human Development, School of Education, Newark, DE 19716. Offers education (PhD); educational leadership (Ed D); higher education (M Ed); instruction (MI); reading (M Ed); school leadership (M Ed); school psychology (MA, Ed S); teaching English as a second language (TESL) (MA). *Accreditation:* NCATE. *Program availability:* Part-time, evening/weekend. Terminal master's awarded for partial completion of doctoral program. *Degree requirements:* For master's, comprehensive exam (for some programs), thesis (for some programs); for doctorate, comprehensive exam (for some programs), thesis/dissertation. *Entrance requirements:* For master's and doctorate, GRE, 3 letters of recommendation. Additional exam requirements/recommendations for international students: Required—TOEFL (minimum score 600 paper-based). Electronic applications accepted. *Faculty research:* Teacher education; curriculum theory and development; community based education models, educational leadership.

The University of Findlay, Office of Graduate Admissions, Findlay, OH 45840-3653. Offers applied security and analytics (MSAS); athletic training (MAT); business (MBA), including certified management accountant, certified public accountant, health care management, hospitality management; education (MA Ed, Ed D), including children's literature (MA Ed), curriculum and teaching (MA Ed), education (MA Ed), educational administration (MA Ed), human resource development (MA Ed), reading (MA Ed), science education (MA Ed), superintendent (Ed D), teaching (Ed D), technology (MA Ed); environmental, safety and health management (MSEM); health informatics (MS); occupational therapy (MOT); pharmacy (Pharm D); physical therapy (DPT); physician assistant (MPA); rhetoric and writing (MA); teaching English to speakers of other languages (TESOL) and bilingual education (MA). *Program availability:* Part-time, evening/weekend, 100% online, blended/hybrid learning. *Faculty:* 114 full-time (63 women), 44 part-time/adjunct (18 women). *Students:* 751 full-time (452 women), 573 part-time (323 women); includes 164 minority (82 Black or African American, non-Hispanic/Latino; 1 American Indian or Alaska Native, non-Hispanic/Latino; 27 Asian, non-Hispanic/Latino; 37 Hispanic/Latino; 17 Two or more races, non-Hispanic/Latino), 280 international. Average age 28. 661 applicants, 52% accepted, 288 enrolled. In 2016, 366 master's, 137 doctorates awarded. *Degree requirements:* For master's, comprehensive exam (for some programs), thesis, cumulative project, capstone project; for doctorate, thesis/dissertation. *Entrance requirements:* For master's, GRE (for some programs), bachelor's degree from accredited institution, minimum undergraduate GPA of 3.0 in last 64 hours of course work; for doctorate, MAT, minimum cumulative GPA of 3.0, master's degree. Additional exam requirements/recommendations for international students: Recommended—TOEFL (minimum score 79 iBT), IELTS (minimum score 7). *Application deadline:* For fall admission, 6/15 for international students; for spring admission, 12/1 for international students; for summer admission, 4/1 for international students. Applications are processed on a rolling basis. Electronic applications accepted. *Expenses:* Contact institution. *Financial support:* In 2016–17, 139 students received support, including 15 research assistantships with partial tuition reimbursements available (averaging $7,200 per year), 25 teaching assistantships with partial tuition reimbursements available (averaging $7,200 per year); Federal Work-Study, institutionally sponsored loans, and unspecified assistantships also available. Financial award application deadline: 4/1; financial award applicants required to submit FAFSA. *Unit head:* Christopher M. Harris, Director of Admissions, 419-434-4347, E-mail: harrisc1@findlay.edu. *Application contact:* Madeline Fauser Brennan, Graduate Admissions Counselor, 419-434-4636, Fax: 419-434-4898, E-mail: fauserbrennan@

findlay.edu.
Website: http://www.findlay.edu/admissions/graduate/Pages/default.aspx

University of Houston–Clear Lake, School of Education, Program in Foundations and Professional Studies, Houston, TX 77058-1002. Offers counseling (MS); instructional technology (MS); multicultural studies (MS). *Program availability:* Part-time, evening/weekend. *Degree requirements:* For master's, thesis optional. *Entrance requirements:* For master's, GRE or minimum GPA of 3.0 in last 60 hours. Additional exam requirements/recommendations for international students: Required—TOEFL (minimum score 550 paper-based). Electronic applications accepted.

University of Maryland, Baltimore County, The Graduate School, College of Arts, Humanities and Social Sciences, Department of Modern Languages and Linguistics, Program in Intercultural Communication, Baltimore, MD 21250. Offers MA. *Program availability:* Part-time, evening/weekend. *Faculty:* 16 full-time (9 women). *Students:* 12 full-time (5 women), 2 part-time (both women); includes 2 minority (1 Black or African American, non-Hispanic/Latino; 1 Hispanic/Latino), 6 international. Average age 27. 15 applicants, 80% accepted, 8 enrolled. In 2016, 8 master's awarded. *Degree requirements:* For master's, one foreign language, comprehensive exam (for some programs), thesis (for some programs). *Entrance requirements:* For master's, GRE General Test, minimum GPA of 3.0, 3 letters of recommendation, self-evaluation and statement of support, resume, writing sample in modern language. Additional exam requirements/recommendations for international students: Required—TOEFL (minimum score 550 paper-based, 80 iBT) or IELTS. *Application deadline:* For fall admission, 1/31 for domestic and international students. Application fee: $50. Electronic applications accepted. *Expenses:* Tuition, state resident: full-time $13,294. Tuition, nonresident: full-time $20,286. *Financial support:* In 2016–17, 7 students received support, including 5 teaching assistantships with full tuition reimbursements available (averaging $12,560 per year); Federal Work-Study, scholarships/grants, health care benefits, and tuition waivers (full) also available. Financial award application deadline: 1/31; financial award applicants required to submit FAFSA. *Faculty research:* Comparative television research-cross-cultural; cultural studies; social developments in Latin America; intercultural communication; French civilization and cultural studies; language, gender and sexuality; sociolinguistics; African linguistics; immigrants in U.S. and Latin American societies. *Unit head:* Dr. Edward Larkey, Interim Director, 410-455-2104, Fax: 410-455-1025, E-mail: larkey@umbc.edu.
Website: http://www.umbc.edu/mll/incc/

University of Maryland, Baltimore County, The Graduate School, College of Arts, Humanities and Social Sciences, Program in Language, Literacy, and Culture, Baltimore, MD 21250. Offers PhD. *Program availability:* Part-time, evening/weekend. *Faculty:* 4 full-time (2 women), 1 (woman) part-time/adjunct. *Students:* 21 full-time (14 women), 35 part-time (26 women); includes 22 minority (15 Black or African American, non-Hispanic/Latino; 4 Asian, non-Hispanic/Latino; 3 Two or more races, non-Hispanic/Latino), 6 international. Average age 40. 35 applicants, 46% accepted, 13 enrolled. In 2016, 5 doctorates awarded. *Degree requirements:* For doctorate, comprehensive exam, thesis/dissertation. *Entrance requirements:* For doctorate, research writing sample; resume or curriculum vitae; master's degree. Additional exam requirements/recommendations for international students: Required—TOEFL (minimum score 80 iBT). *Application deadline:* For fall admission, 12/1 for domestic and international students. Application fee: $50. Electronic applications accepted. *Expenses:* Tuition, state resident: full-time $13,294. Tuition, nonresident: full-time $20,286. *Financial support:* In 2016–17, 11 research assistantships with full and partial tuition reimbursements, 3 teaching assistantships with full and partial tuition reimbursements were awarded; health care benefits, tuition waivers (full and partial), and unspecified assistantships also available. Support available to part-time students. Financial award application deadline: 12/1. *Faculty research:* Educational equity, identity, intercultural communication, technology and communication, workplace diversity. *Unit head:* Dr. Cedric Herring, Director, 410-455-2313, Fax: 410-455-8947, E-mail: cherring@umbc.edu. *Application contact:* Liz Steenrod, Program Management Specialist, 410-455-2376, Fax: 410-455-8947, E-mail: llc@umbc.edu.
Website: http://llc.umbc.edu

University of Massachusetts Amherst, Graduate School, College of Education, Program in Education, Amherst, MA 01003. Offers bilingual, English as a second language, and multicultural education (M Ed, Ed S); child study and early education (M Ed); children, families and schools (Ed D, Ed S); early childhood and elementary teacher education (M Ed); educational leadership (M Ed); educational policy and leadership (Ed D); higher education (M Ed); international education (M Ed); language, literacy and culture (Ed D); learning, media and technology (M Ed, Ed S); mathematics, science, and learning technologies (Ed D); reading and writing (M Ed); research, educational measurement and psychometrics (Ed D); school counselor education (M Ed, Ed S); school psychology (Ed S); science education (Ed S); secondary teacher education (M Ed); social justice education (M Ed, Ed D, Ed S); special education (M Ed, Ed D, Ed S); teacher education and school improvement (Ed D, Ed S). *Accreditation:* NCATE. *Program availability:* Part-time, online learning. Terminal master's awarded for partial completion of doctoral program. *Degree requirements:* For doctorate, comprehensive exam, thesis/dissertation. *Entrance requirements:* Additional exam requirements/recommendations for international students: Required—TOEFL (minimum score 550 paper-based; 80 iBT), IELTS (minimum score 6.5). Electronic applications accepted.

University of Miami, Graduate School, School of Education and Human Development, Department of Teaching and Learning, Program in Teaching and Learning, Coral Gables, FL 33124. Offers language and literacy learning in multilingual settings (PhD); science, technology, engineering and mathematics (PhD); special education (PhD). *Faculty:* 14 full-time (10 women), 9 part-time/adjunct (all women). *Students:* 21 full-time (16 women); includes 6 minority (2 Black or African American, non-Hispanic/Latino; 3 Hispanic/Latino; 1 Two or more races, non-Hispanic/Latino), 7 international. Average age 33. 20 applicants, 30% accepted, 4 enrolled. In 2016, 1 doctorate awarded. *Degree requirements:* For doctorate, thesis/dissertation, qualifying exam, electronic portfolio. *Entrance requirements:* For doctorate, GRE General Test. Additional exam requirements/recommendations for international students: Required—TOEFL (minimum score 550 paper-based; 80 iBT); Recommended—IELTS (minimum score 6.5). *Application deadline:* For fall admission, 2/15 for domestic students, 10/1 for international students. Application fee: $65. Electronic applications accepted. *Financial support:* Fellowships, research assistantships, teaching assistantships, health care benefits, tuition waivers (full and partial), and unspecified assistantships available. Financial award application deadline: 3/1; financial award applicants required to submit FAFSA. *Faculty research:* Teacher education, multicultural education, special education, second language acquisition, math and science education. *Unit head:* Dr. Luciana de Oliveira, Department Chairperson/Associate Professor, 305-284-4961, Fax: 305-284-6998, E-mail: ludeoliveira@miami.edu. *Application contact:* Lois Heffernan, Graduate Admission Coordinator, 305-284-2167, Fax: 305-284-9395, E-mail: lheffernan@miami.edu.
Website: http://www.education.miami.edu

University of Minnesota, Twin Cities Campus, Graduate School, College of Education and Human Development, Department of Curriculum and Instruction, Minneapolis, MN 55455-0213. Offers art education (M Ed, MA, PhD); curriculum and instruction (M Ed, MA, PhD); elementary education (MA, PhD); English education (PhD); language and immersion education (Certificate); learning technologies (MA, PhD); literacy education (MA, PhD); second language education (MA, PhD); social studies education (MA, PhD); STEM education (MA, PhD); teaching (M Ed), including mathematics, science, social studies, teaching; teaching English to speakers of other languages (MA); technology enhanced learning (Certificate). *Faculty:* 37 full-time (20 women). *Students:* 411 full-time (288 women), 317 part-time (223 women); includes 153 minority (37 Black or African American, non-Hispanic/Latino; 7 American Indian or Alaska Native, non-Hispanic/Latino; 31 Asian, non-Hispanic/Latino; 48 Hispanic/Latino; 1 Native Hawaiian or other Pacific Islander, non-Hispanic/Latino; 29 Two or more races, non-Hispanic/Latino), 53 international. Average age 32. 672 applicants, 66% accepted, 400 enrolled. In 2016, 645 master's, 33 doctorates, 27 other advanced degrees awarded. Application fee: $75 ($95 for international students). *Financial support:* In 2016–17, 13 fellowships, 36 research assistantships with full tuition reimbursements (averaging $8,454 per year), 61 teaching assistantships with full tuition reimbursements (averaging $11,406 per year) were awarded. *Faculty research:* Teaching and learning; influence of cultural, linguistic, social, political, and technological factors on teaching, learning and educational research; relationship between educational practice and a democratic and just society; urban education; immigrant education, racial justice and education. *Total annual research expenditures:* $684,005. *Unit head:* Dr. Cynthia Lewis, Chair, 612-625-6313, E-mail: lewis@umn.edu. *Application contact:* Dr. Gillian Roehrig, Director of Graduate Studies, 612-625-0561, E-mail: roehr013@umn.edu.
Website: http://www.cehd.umn.edu/ci

University of New Mexico, Graduate Studies, College of Education, Program in Language, Literacy and Sociocultural Studies, Albuquerque, NM 87131. Offers American Indian education (MA); bilingual education (MA, PhD); educational linguistics (PhD); educational thought and sociocultural studies (MA, PhD); literacy/language arts (MA, PhD); social studies (MA); TESOL (MA, PhD). *Faculty:* 17 full-time (10 women), 4 part-time/adjunct (3 women). *Students:* 57 full-time (38 women), 129 part-time (105 women); includes 102 minority (8 Black or African American, non-Hispanic/Latino; 16 American Indian or Alaska Native, non-Hispanic/Latino; 6 Asian, non-Hispanic/Latino; 67 Hispanic/Latino; 5 Two or more races, non-Hispanic/Latino), 32 international. Average age 39. 50 applicants, 60% accepted, 23 enrolled. In 2016, 36 master's, 4 doctorates awarded. *Degree requirements:* For master's, comprehensive exam, thesis optional; for doctorate, comprehensive exam, thesis/dissertation, research skills. *Entrance requirements:* For master's, letter of intent, 3 letters of recommendation, resume, BA/BS, department demographic form, transcripts; for doctorate, writing sample, letter of intent, 3 letters of recommendation, resume, BA/BS, MA, department demographic form, transcripts. Additional exam requirements/recommendations for international students: Required—TOEFL. *Application deadline:* For fall admission, 12/1 for domestic and international students; for spring admission, 9/15 for domestic and international students. Application fee: $50. Electronic applications accepted. *Financial support:* Fellowships, research assistantships, teaching assistantships with tuition reimbursements, career-related internships or fieldwork, institutionally sponsored loans, scholarships/grants, and unspecified assistantships available. Support available to part-time students. Financial award application deadline: 3/1; financial award applicants required to submit FAFSA. *Faculty research:* School reform, professional development, history of education, Native American education, politics of education, feminism and issues of sexual identity, critical race theory, bilingualism, literacy reading, adolescent literature, second language acquisition, critical theory and schooling, indigenous languages. *Unit head:* Dr. Lois M. Meyer, Chair, 505-277-7244, Fax: 505-277-8362, E-mail: lsmeyer@unm.edu. *Application contact:* Debra Schaffer, Administrative Assistant, 505-277-0437, Fax: 505-277-8362, E-mail: schaffer@unm.edu.
Website: http://coe.unm.edu/departments-programs/llss/index.html

University of New Mexico, Graduate Studies, College of Education, Program in Multicultural Teacher and Childhood Education, Albuquerque, NM 87131-2039. Offers Ed D, PhD. *Accreditation:* NCATE. *Program availability:* Part-time. *Faculty:* 1 (woman) full-time. *Students:* 4 full-time (3 women), 9 part-time (6 women); includes 6 minority (5 Hispanic/Latino; 1 Two or more races, non-Hispanic/Latino). Average age 48. 1 applicant. In 2016, 1 doctorate awarded. *Degree requirements:* For doctorate, comprehensive exam, thesis/dissertation. *Entrance requirements:* For doctorate, GRE, master's degree, minimum GPA of 3.0, 3 years of teaching experience, 3-5 letters of reference, letter of intent, professional writing sample. Additional exam requirements/recommendations for international students: Required—TOEFL (minimum score 550 paper-based). *Application deadline:* For fall admission, 1/15 priority date for domestic students, 1/15 for international students; for spring admission, 10/30 for domestic and international students. Application fee: $50. Electronic applications accepted. *Financial support:* Fellowships, research assistantships, teaching assistantships with partial tuition reimbursements, scholarships/grants, and unspecified assistantships available. Financial award application deadline: 3/1; financial award applicants required to submit FAFSA. *Faculty research:* Teacher education, clinical preparation, reflective practice, science education, mathematics education, social justice, technology education, media literacy. *Unit head:* Dr. Cheryl Torrez, Department Chair, 505-277-9611, Fax: 505-277-0455, E-mail: ted@unm.edu. *Application contact:* Robert Romero, Program Coordinator, 505-277-0513, Fax: 505-277-0455, E-mail: ted@unm.edu.
Website: https://coe.unm.edu/departments-programs/ifce/ecme/

The University of North Carolina at Greensboro, Graduate School, School of Education, Department of Educational Leadership and Cultural Foundations, Greensboro, NC 27412-5001. Offers curriculum and teaching (PhD), including cultural studies; educational leadership (Ed D, Ed S); school administration (MSA). *Accreditation:* NCATE. *Degree requirements:* For doctorate, thesis/dissertation. *Entrance requirements:* For master's, doctorate, and Ed S, GRE General Test. Additional exam requirements/recommendations for international students: Required—TOEFL. Electronic applications accepted.

University of Northern Colorado, Graduate School, College of Education and Behavioral Sciences, School of Teacher Education, Greeley, CO 80639. Offers curriculum studies (MAT); educational studies (Ed D); elementary education (MAT); English education (MAT); literacy (MA); multilingual education (MA), including TESOL, world languages; teaching diverse learners (MA). *Accreditation:* NCATE. *Program availability:* Part-time, evening/weekend. *Degree requirements:* For master's, comprehensive exam, thesis or alternative; for doctorate, comprehensive exam, thesis/dissertation. *Entrance requirements:* For master's and doctorate, GRE General Test, 3 letters of recommendation. *Application deadline:* Applications are processed on a rolling basis. Application fee: $50 ($60 for international students). Electronic applications accepted. *Financial support:* Fellowships, research assistantships, teaching assistantships, and unspecified assistantships available. Financial award application deadline: 3/1; financial award applicants required to submit FAFSA. *Unit head:* Dr. Alexander Sidorkin, Director, 970-351-2908, Fax: 970-351-1877. *Application contact:* Linda Sisson, Graduate Student Admission Coordinator, 970-351-1807, Fax: 970-351-2371, E-mail: linda.sisson@unco.edu.
Website: http://www.unco.edu/cebs/teachered/

University of Pennsylvania, Graduate School of Education, Division of Educational Linguistics, Program in Intercultural Communication, Philadelphia, PA 19104. Offers MS Ed. *Program availability:* Part-time. *Students:* 23 full-time (21 women), 8 part-time (6 women); includes 4 minority (2 Asian, non-Hispanic/Latino; 2 Two or more races, non-Hispanic/Latino), 18 international. Average age 25. 110 applicants, 46% accepted, 20 enrolled. In 2016, 22 master's awarded. *Expenses: Tuition:* Full-time $31,068; part-time $5762 per course. *Required fees:* $3200; $336 per course. Full-time tuition and fees vary according to degree level, program and student level. Part-time tuition and fees vary according to course load, degree level and program.

University of St. Thomas, School of Education and Human Services, Houston, TX 77006-4696. Offers all level education (M Ed); bilingual/dual language (M Ed); Catholic school teaching (M Ed); Catholic/private school leadership (M Ed); counselor education (M Ed); curriculum and instruction (M Ed); education (Ed D); educational leadership (M Ed); elementary teaching (M Ed); English as a second language (M Ed); exceptionality/educational diagnostician (M Ed); exceptionality/special education (M Ed); generalist (M Ed); reading (M Ed); secondary teaching (M Ed); teaching (MAT). *Accreditation:* TEAC. *Program availability:* Part-time, evening/weekend, online learning. *Faculty:* 44 full-time (29 women), 31 part-time/adjunct (17 women). *Students:* 65 full-time (61 women), 719 part-time (645 women); includes 515 minority (169 Black or African American, non-Hispanic/Latino; 25 Asian, non-Hispanic/Latino; 315 Hispanic/Latino; 2 Native Hawaiian or other Pacific Islander, non-Hispanic/Latino; 4 Two or more races, non-Hispanic/Latino), 24 international. Average age 36. 297 applicants, 92% accepted, 211 enrolled. In 2016, 403 master's awarded. *Degree requirements:* For master's, thesis, field experience. *Entrance requirements:* For master's, GRE or MAT if GPA is below 3.0, bachelor's degree; minimum GPA of 2.75 in bachelor's degree or last 60 credit hours; official transcripts from all institutions; goal statement of 250-300 words; 1 reference. Additional exam requirements/recommendations for International students: Required—TOEFL (minimum score 94 iBT), IELTS (minimum score 7), PTE (minimum score 53). *Application deadline:* Applications are processed on a rolling basis. Application fee: $35. Electronic applications accepted. *Expenses:* Contact institution. *Financial support:* In 2016–17, 52 students received support. Federal Work-Study, scholarships/grants, and state work-study, institutional employment available. Support available to part-time students. Financial award application deadline: 4/15; financial award applicants required to submit FAFSA. *Faculty research:* Leadership, diversity, personality traits, second language acquisition. *Unit head:* Dr. Robert LeBlanc, Dean, 713-525-3540, Fax: 713-525-3871, E-mail: education@stthom.edu. *Application contact:* Rita Paredes, Administrative Assistant, 713-525-3442, Fax: 713-525-3871, E-mail: rparede@stthom.edu.
Website: http://www.stthom.edu/Academics/School_of_Education_and_Human_Services/Index.aqf

University of San Francisco, School of Education, Department of International and Multicultural Education, San Francisco, CA 94117-1080. Offers MA, Ed D. *Program availability:* Part-time, evening/weekend. *Faculty:* 11 full-time (9 women), 8 part-time/adjunct (6 women). *Students:* 128 full-time (112 women), 73 part-time (56 women); includes 86 minority (14 Black or African American, non-Hispanic/Latino; 21 Asian, non-Hispanic/Latino; 39 Hispanic/Latino; 1 Native Hawaiian or other Pacific Islander, non-Hispanic/Latino; 11 Two or more races, non-Hispanic/Latino), 40 international. Average age 34. 169 applicants, 96% accepted, 58 enrolled. In 2016, 57 master's, 12 doctorates awarded. *Degree requirements:* For doctorate, thesis/dissertation. *Entrance requirements:* Additional exam requirements/recommendations for international students: Required—TOEFL, IELTS, PTE. *Application deadline:* For fall admission, 3/1 priority date for domestic students, 3/1 for international students; for spring admission, 10/15 priority date for domestic and international students. Applications are processed on a rolling basis. Application fee: $55 ($65 for international students). Electronic applications accepted. *Expenses: Tuition:* Full-time $23,310; part-time $1295 per credit. Tuition and fees vary according to course load, degree level, campus/location and program. *Financial support:* In 2016–17, 41 students received support. Fellowships, research assistantships, and teaching assistantships available. Financial award application deadline: 3/2; financial award applicants required to submit FAFSA. *Unit head:* Dr. Emma Fuentes, Chair, 415-422-6878. *Application contact:* Peter Cole, Admission Coordinator, 415-422-5467, E-mail: schoolofeducation@usfca.edu.

University of Southern California, Graduate School, Rossier School of Education, Doctor of Education Programs, Los Angeles, CA 90089. Offers educational psychology (Ed D); higher education administration (Ed D); K-12 leadership in urban school settings (Ed D); teacher education in multicultural societies (Ed D). *Program availability:* Part-time, evening/weekend. *Degree requirements:* For doctorate, thesis/dissertation. *Entrance requirements:* For doctorate, GRE. Additional exam requirements/recommendations for international students: Required—TOEFL (minimum score 100 iBT). Electronic applications accepted. *Faculty research:* Data-driven decision-making in K-12 schools and districts; examination of college and university leadership and management in U. S. and Asia; studies in facilitating student learning; organizational change and the role of leaders; leadership, diversity, learning and accountability.

The University of Tennessee, Graduate School, College of Education, Health and Human Sciences, Program in Education, Knoxville, TN 37996. Offers art education (MS); counseling education (PhD), cultural studies in education (PhD); curriculum (MS, Ed S); curriculum, educational research and evaluation (Ed D, PhD); early childhood education (PhD); early childhood special education (MS); education of deaf and hard of hearing (MS); educational administration and policy studies (Ed D, PhD); educational administration and supervision (Ed S); educational psychology (Ed D, PhD); elementary education (MS, Ed S); elementary teaching (MS); English education (MS, Ed S); exercise science (PhD); foreign language/ESL education (MS, Ed S); instructional technology (MS, Ed D, PhD, Ed S); literacy, language and ESL education (PhD); literacy, language education, and ESL education (Ed D); mathematics education (MS, Ed S); modified and comprehensive special education (MS); reading education (MS, Ed S); school counseling (Ed S); school psychology (PhD, Ed S); science education (MS, Ed S); secondary teaching (MS); social foundations (MS); social science education (MS, Ed S); socio-cultural foundations of sports and education (PhD); special education (Ed S); teacher education (Ed D, PhD). *Accreditation:* NCATE. *Program availability:* Part-time, evening/weekend. *Degree requirements:* For master's and Ed S, thesis optional; for doctorate, variable foreign language requirement, thesis/dissertation. *Entrance requirements:* For master's, minimum GPA of 2.7; for doctorate and Ed S, GRE General Test, minimum GPA of 2.7. Additional exam requirements/recommendations for international students: Required—TOEFL. Electronic applications accepted.

The University of Texas at Austin, Graduate School, College of Education, Department of Curriculum and Instruction, Austin, TX 78712-1111. Offers bilingual/bicultural education (M Ed, MA, PhD); cultural studies in education (M Ed, MA, PhD); early childhood education (M Ed, MA, PhD); language and literacy studies (M Ed, PhD); learning technologies (M Ed, MA, PhD); physical education (M Ed, MA, PhD). Terminal master's awarded for partial completion of doctoral program. *Degree requirements:* For doctorate, thesis/dissertation. *Entrance requirements:* For master's and doctorate, GRE General Test. Electronic applications accepted.

The University of Texas at Austin, Graduate School, College of Education, Department of Special Education, Austin, TX 78712-1111. Offers autism and developmental disabilities (Ed D, PhD); autism and developmental disability (M Ed, MA); early childhood special education (M Ed, MA, Ed D, PhD); learning disabilities (Ed D, PhD); learning disabilities/behavior disorders (M Ed, MA); multicultural special education (M Ed, MA, Ed D, PhD); rehabilitation counselor (M Ed); rehabilitation counselor education (Ed D, PhD); special education administration (Ed D, PhD). *Accreditation:* CORE. *Program availability:* Part-time, evening/weekend, online learning. *Degree requirements:* For master's, thesis or alternative; for doctorate, thesis/dissertation. *Entrance requirements:* For master's and doctorate, GRE General Test. *Faculty research:* Anchored instruction, reading disabilities, multicultural/bilingual.

The University of Texas at El Paso, Graduate School, College of Liberal Arts, Department of English, El Paso, TX 79968-0001. Offers bilingual professional writing (Certificate); English and American literature (MA); rhetoric and composition (PhD); rhetoric and writing studies (MA); teaching English (MAT). *Program availability:* Part-time, evening/weekend. *Degree requirements:* For master's, thesis optional. *Entrance requirements:* For master's, GRE General Test, minimum GPA of 3.0. Additional exam requirements/recommendations for international students: Required—TOEFL. Electronic applications accepted. *Faculty research:* Literature, creative writing, literary theory.

The University of Texas at San Antonio, College of Education and Human Development, Department of Bicultural and Bilingual Studies, San Antonio, TX 78249-0617. Offers bicultural and bilingual studies (MA), including bicultural and bilingual education, bicultural studies; culture, literacy, and language (PhD); teaching English as a second language (MA). *Program availability:* Part-time, evening/weekend. *Faculty:* 19 full-time (13 women), 2 part-time/adjunct (1 woman). *Students:* 32 full-time (21 women), 109 part-time (86 women); includes 80 minority (3 Black or African American, non-Hispanic/Latino; 4 Asian, non-Hispanic/Latino; 72 Hispanic/Latino; 1 Two or more races, non-Hispanic/Latino), 11 international. Average age 37. 70 applicants, 77% accepted, 36 enrolled. In 2016, 28 master's, 10 doctorates awarded. *Degree requirements:* For master's, one foreign language, comprehensive exam, thesis optional; for doctorate, one foreign language, comprehensive exam, thesis/dissertation. *Entrance requirements:* For master's, bachelor's degree with 18 credit hours in field of study or in another appropriate field of study; for doctorate, GRE General Test, resume or curriculum vitae, 3 letters of recommendation, statement of purpose, master's degree. Additional exam requirements/recommendations for international students: Required—TOEFL (minimum score 550 paper-based; 79 iBT), IELTS (minimum score 6.5). *Application deadline:* For fall admission, 7/1 for domestic students, 4/1 for international students; for spring admission, 11/1 for domestic students, 9/1 for international students. Applications are processed on a rolling basis. Application fee: $45 ($80 for international students). Electronic applications accepted. *Expenses:* Contact institution. *Financial support:* In 2016–17, 18 students received support, including 18 fellowships (averaging $28,000 per year), 2 research assistantships (averaging $12,468 per year), 16 teaching assistantships (averaging $11,000 per year); scholarships/grants and unspecified assistantships also available. Financial award application deadline: 4/15. *Faculty research:* Bilingual and ESL teacher preparation; transnational communities; applied linguistics; cultural studies; bilingualism, biliteracy and second language acquisition. *Total annual research expenditures:* $300,234. *Unit head:* Dr. Belinda Flores, Chair, 210-458-5570, Fax: 210-458-5962, E-mail: belinda.flores@utsa.edu. *Application contact:* Rahnuma Islam, Student Development Specialist, 210-458-6619, Fax: 210-458-5576, E-mail: rahnuma.islam@utsa.edu.
Website: http://education.utsa.edu/bicultural-bilingual_studies

The University of Texas Rio Grande Valley, College of Education and P-16 Integration, Department of Bilingual and Literacy Studies, Edinburg, TX 78539. Offers bilingual education (M Ed); reading and literacy (M Ed). Tuition and fees vary according to course load and program.

University of the Southwest, Graduate Programs, Hobbs, NM 88240-9129. Offers business administration (MBA); curriculum and instruction (MSE); curriculum and instruction: bilingual (MSE); curriculum and instruction: TESOL (MSE); early childhood education (MSE); educational administration (MSE); mental health counseling (MSE); school counseling (MSE); special education (MSE); sports management (MBA). *Program availability:* Part-time, evening/weekend, online learning. *Degree requirements:* For master's, comprehensive exam, thesis (for some programs). *Entrance requirements:* Additional exam requirements/recommendations for international students: Recommended—TOEFL. Electronic applications accepted.

University of Washington, Graduate School, College of Education, Seattle, WA 98195. Offers curriculum and instruction (M Ed, Ed D, PhD), including educational technology, general curriculum (Ed D, PhD), language, literacy, and culture, mathematics education, multicultural education, reading and language arts education (Ed D), science education, social studies education, teaching and curriculum (M Ed); educational leadership and policy studies (M Ed, Ed D, PhD), including administration (Ed D), educational policy, organization, and leadership (M Ed, PhD), higher education, leadership for learning (Ed D), social and cultural foundations of education (M Ed, PhD); educational psychology (M Ed, PhD), including educational psychology (PhD), human development and cognition (M Ed), learning sciences, measurement, statistics and research design (M Ed), school psychology (M Ed); instructional leadership (M Ed); intercollegiate athletic leadership (M Ed); special education (M Ed, Ed D, PhD), including early childhood special education (M Ed), emotional and behavioral disabilities (M Ed), learning disabilities (M Ed), low-incidence disabilities (M Ed), severe disabilities (M Ed), special education (Ed D, PhD); teacher education (MIT). *Accreditation:* APA. *Program availability:* Part-time, evening/weekend. *Degree requirements:* For master's, thesis optional; for doctorate, thesis/dissertation. *Entrance requirements:* For master's and doctorate, GRE General Test, minimum GPA of 3.0. Additional exam requirements/recommendations for international students: Required—TOEFL. Electronic applications accepted. *Faculty research:* School restructuring/effective schools, special education interventions, literacy and writing, technology, school partnerships, teacher preparation.

University of Wisconsin–Milwaukee, Graduate School, School of Education, Department of Exceptional Education, Milwaukee, WI 53201-0413. Offers autism spectrum disorders (Graduate Certificate); exceptional education (MS); transition for students with disabilities (Graduate Certificate); urban education (PhD), including adult, continuing and higher education leadership, art education, curriculum and instruction, exceptional education, mathematics education, multicultural studies, social foundations of education. *Program availability:* Part-time. *Students:* 50 full-time (41 women), 66 part-time (51 women); includes 42 minority (24 Black or African American, non-Hispanic/Latino; 6 Asian, non-Hispanic/Latino; 1 Hispanic/Latino; 11 Two or more races, non-Hispanic/Latino), 4 international. Average age 39. 55 applicants, 51% accepted, 22 enrolled. In 2016, 14 master's, 10 doctorates, 3 other advanced degrees awarded. *Degree requirements:* For master's, thesis. *Entrance requirements:* Additional exam requirements/recommendations for international students: Required—TOEFL (minimum score 550 paper-based; 79 iBT), IELTS (minimum score 6.5). *Application deadline:* For fall admission, 1/1 priority date for domestic students; for spring admission, 9/1 for domestic students. Applications are processed on a rolling basis. Application fee: $56 ($96 for international students). Electronic applications accepted. *Financial support:*

Fellowships, research assistantships, teaching assistantships, career-related internships or fieldwork, health care benefits, and unspecified assistantships available. Support available to part-time students. Financial award application deadline: 4/15; financial award applicants required to submit FAFSA. *Faculty research:* Emotional disturbance, hearing impairment, learning disabilities, mental retardation. *Application contact:* General Information Contact, 414-229-4721, E-mail: soeinfo@uwm.edu.
Website: http://uwm.edu/education/academics/exceptional-edu-department/

Utah State University, School of Graduate Studies, College of Humanities, Arts and Social Sciences, Department of Languages, Philosophy, and Speech Communication, Logan, UT 84322. Offers second language teaching (MSLT). *Entrance requirements:* For master's, GRE General Test or MAT, minimum GPA of 3.0. Additional exam requirements/recommendations for international students: Required—TOEFL.

Vanderbilt University, Peabody College, Department of Teaching and Learning, Nashville, TN 37240-1001. Offers elementary education (M Ed); English language learners (M Ed); learning and design (M Ed); learning, diversity, and urban studies (M Ed); reading education (M Ed); secondary education (M Ed). *Accreditation:* NCATE. *Program availability:* Part-time. *Faculty:* 44 full-time (34 women), 26 part-time/adjunct (21 women). *Students:* 120 full-time (106 women), 26 part-time (18 women); includes 22 minority (9 Black or African American, non-Hispanic/Latino; 6 Asian, non-Hispanic/Latino; 6 Hispanic/Latino; 1 Two or more races, non-Hispanic/Latino), 44 international. Average age 24. 328 applicants, 73% accepted, 76 enrolled. In 2016, 110 master's awarded. *Degree requirements:* For master's, comprehensive exam, thesis optional. *Entrance requirements:* For master's, GRE General Test, MAT. Additional exam requirements/recommendations for international students: Required—TOEFL (minimum score 550 paper-based; 80 iBT). *Application deadline:* For fall admission, 12/31 priority date for domestic and international students; for spring admission, 11/1 priority date for domestic and international students. Applications are processed on a rolling basis. Application fee: $0. Electronic applications accepted. *Expenses: Tuition:* Part-time $1854 per credit hour. *Financial support:* Fellowships with partial tuition reimbursements, research assistantships with partial tuition reimbursements, teaching assistantships with partial tuition reimbursements, Federal Work-Study, institutionally sponsored loans, scholarships/grants, tuition waivers (partial), and unspecified assistantships available. Support available to part-time students. Financial award application deadline: 1/15; financial award applicants required to submit FAFSA. *Faculty research:* Children's learning and development in core conceptual domains (STEM, English language arts, social studies); classroom discourse structures that teachers can learn and use to support students' learning and development K-6; intervention and design-based research on educational improvement at classroom, school, and district levels; design-based and learning sciences research on relations between learning in schools and other settings. *Unit head:* Dr. Rogers Hall, Chair, 615-322-8100, Fax: 615-322-8999, E-mail: rogers.hall@vanderbilt.edu. *Application contact:* Angela Saylor, Educational Coordinator, 615-322-8092, Fax: 615-322-8999, E-mail: angela.saylor@vanderbilt.edu.

Vanderbilt University, Program in Learning, Teaching and Diversity, Nashville, TN 37240-1001. Offers PhD. *Faculty:* 24 full-time (15 women). *Students:* 44 full-time (33 women), 1 part-time (0 women); includes 11 minority (2 Black or African American, non-Hispanic/Latino; 4 Asian, non-Hispanic/Latino; 1 Hispanic/Latino; 4 Two or more races, non-Hispanic/Latino), 2 international. Average age 32. 144 applicants, 6% accepted, 9 enrolled. In 2016, 4 degrees awarded. *Degree requirements:* For doctorate, comprehensive exam, thesis/dissertation, qualifying examinations. *Entrance requirements:* For doctorate, GRE General Test. Additional exam requirements/recommendations for international students: Required—TOEFL (minimum score 570 paper-based; 88 iBT). *Application deadline:* For fall admission, 12/1 for domestic and international students. Application fee: $0. Electronic applications accepted. *Expenses:* Contact institution. *Financial support:* Fellowships with partial tuition reimbursements, research assistantships with full tuition reimbursements, teaching assistantships with full tuition reimbursements, Federal Work-Study, institutionally sponsored loans, scholarships/grants, traineeships, and health care benefits available. Financial award application deadline: 1/15; financial award applicants required to submit CSS PROFILE or FAFSA. *Faculty research:* New pedagogies for math, science, and language; the support of English language learners; the uses of new technology and media in the classroom; middle school mathematics and the institutional setting of teaching. *Unit head:* Dr. Melissa Gresalfi, Director of Graduate Studies, 615-322-8227, Fax: 615-322-8014, E-mail: melissa.gresalfi@vanderbilt.edu. *Application contact:* Angela Saylor, Educational Coordinator, 615-322-8092, Fax: 615-322-8014, E-mail: angela.saylor@vanderbilt.edu.
Website: http://peabody.vanderbilt.edu/departments/tl/index.php

Walden University, Graduate Programs, Richard W. Riley College of Education and Leadership, Minneapolis, MN 55401. Offers adult education (Post-Master's Certificate); adult learning (Graduate Certificate); college teaching and learning (Graduate Certificate); community college leadership (Ed D); curriculum, instruction and assessment (Ed D, Ed S, Graduate Certificate); developmental education (Graduate Certificate); early childhood administration, management, and leadership (Graduate Certificate); early childhood education (Ed D, Ed S); early childhood public policy and advocacy (Graduate Certificate); early childhood studies (MS), including administration, management and leadership, early childhood public policy and advocacy, teaching adults in the early childhood field, teaching and diversity in early childhood education; education (MS, PhD), including adolescent literacy and learning (MS), curriculum, instruction, and assessment (grades K-12) (MS), curriculum, instruction, assessment, and evaluation (PhD), early childhood leadership and advocacy (PhD), early childhood special education (PhD), educational leadership (MS), educational leadership and administration (principal preparation) (MS), educational technology and design (PhD), elementary reading and literacy (PreK-6) (MS), elementary reading and mathematics (grades K-6) (MS), global and comparative education (PhD), higher education leadership management and policy (PhD), integrating technology in the classroom (grades K-12) (MS), learning, instruction and innovation (PhD), mathematics (grades 5-8) (MS), mathematics (grades K-6) (MS), mathematics and science (grades K-8) (MS), organizational research, assessment, and evaluation (PhD), reading and literacy with a reading K-12 endorsement (MS), reading literacy assessment and evaluation (PhD), science (grades K-8) (MS), special education (non-licensure) (grades K-12) (MS), teacher leadership (grades K-12) (MS), teaching English language learners (grades K-12) (MS); educational administration and leadership (Ed D); educational leadership and administration (principal preparation) (Ed S); educational technology (Ed D, Ed S, Post Master's Certificate); elementary reading and literacy (Graduate Certificate); engaging culturally diverse learners (Graduate Certificate); enrollment management and institutional marketing (Graduate Certificate); higher education (MS), including adult learning, college teaching and learning, enrollment management and institutional marketing, global higher education, leadership for student success, online and distance learning; higher education and adult learning (Ed D); higher education leadership and management (Ed D); higher education leadership for student success (Graduate Certificate); instructional design and technology (MS, Postbaccalaureate Certificate), including general program (MS), online learning (MS), training and performance improvement (MS); integrating technology in the classroom (Graduate Certificate); mathematics 5-8 (Graduate Certificate); mathematics K-6 (Graduate Certificate); online teaching for adult educators (Graduate Certificate); reading, literacy, and assessment (Ed D, Ed S); science K-8 (Graduate Certificate); special education (Ed D, Ed S, Graduate Certificate); special education (K-age 21) (MAT); teacher leadership (Graduate Certificate); teaching adults English as a second language (Graduate Certificate); teaching adults in the early childhood field (Graduate Certificate); teaching and diversity in early childhood education (Graduate Certificate); teaching English language learners (grades K-12) (Graduate Certificate); teaching K-12 students online (Graduate Certificate). *Accreditation:* NCATE. *Program availability:* Part-time, evening/weekend, online only, 100% online. *Degree requirements:* For doctorate, thesis/dissertation (for some programs), residency; for other advanced degree, residency (for some programs). *Entrance requirements:* For master's, bachelor's degree or higher; minimum GPA of 2.5; official transcripts; goal statement (for some programs); access to computer and Internet; for doctorate, master's degree or higher; three years of related professional or academic experience (preferred); minimum GPA of 3.0; goal statement and current resume (for select programs); official transcripts; access to computer and Internet; for other advanced degree, relevant work experience; access to computer and Internet. Additional exam requirements/recommendations for international students: Required—TOEFL (minimum score 550 paper-based, 79 iBT), IELTS (minimum score 6.5), Michigan English Language Assessment Battery (minimum score 82), or PTE (minimum score 53). Electronic applications accepted.

Wayne State University, College of Education, Division of Teacher Education, Detroit, MI 48202. Offers art education (M Ed); bilingual/bicultural education (M Ed, Certificate); career and technical education (M Ed); curriculum and instruction (Ed D, PhD, Ed S), including art education (Ed D, PhD), bilingual education (Ed D, Ed S), career and technical education (MAT, Ed D, PhD, Ed S), early childhood education (MAT, Ed D, PhD, Ed S), elementary education, English as a second language (MAT, Ed D, Ed S), English education (MAT, Ed D, PhD, Ed S), foreign language education (MAT, Ed D, PhD), K-12 curriculum, mathematics education (MAT, Ed D, PhD, Ed S), science education (MAT, Ed D, PhD, Ed S), secondary education, social studies education (MAT, Ed D, PhD, Ed S); early childhood education (M Ed); elementary education (M Ed, MAT), including bilingual/bicultural education (MAT), early childhood education (MAT, Ed D, PhD, Ed S), English as a second language (MAT, Ed D, Ed S), general elementary education (MAT), mathematics education (MAT, Ed D, PhD, Ed S), science education (MAT, Ed D, PhD, Ed S), social studies education (MAT, Ed D, PhD, Ed S); English as a second language (Certificate); English education (M Ed); foreign language education (M Ed); mathematics education (M Ed); reading (M Ed, Ed S); reading, language and literature (Ed D); science education (M Ed); secondary education (MAT), including art education (K-12), bilingual/bicultural education, career and technical education (MAT, Ed D, PhD, Ed S), English as a second language (MAT, Ed D, Ed S), English education (MAT, Ed D, PhD, Ed S), foreign language education (MAT, Ed D, PhD), kinesiology, mathematics education (MAT, Ed D, PhD, Ed S); social studies education (M Ed); special education (M Ed, MAT, Ed D, PhD, Ed S), including autism spectrum disorders (MAT), cognitive development (MAT), emotional impairment (MAT), learning disabilities (MAT). *Program availability:* Part-time, blended/hybrid learning. *Faculty:* 29. *Students:* 106 full-time (73 women), 351 part-time (276 women); includes 115 minority (76 Black or African American, non-Hispanic/Latino; 10 Asian, non-Hispanic/Latino; 20 Hispanic/Latino; 1 Native Hawaiian or other Pacific Islander, non-Hispanic/Latino; 8 Two or more races, non-Hispanic/Latino), 12 international. Average age 37. 242 applicants, 37% accepted, 72 enrolled. In 2016, 178 master's, 19 doctorates, 17 other advanced degrees awarded. *Degree requirements:* For master's, essay or project (for some M Ed programs), professional field experience (for MAT programs); for doctorate, thesis/dissertation. *Entrance requirements:* For master's, Michigan Test for Teacher Certification, verification of participation in group work with children, Michigan State Police criminal background check; for doctorate, minimum undergraduate GPA of 3.0, graduate 3.5; interview; curriculum vitae; references. Additional exam requirements/recommendations for international students: Required—TOEFL (minimum score 550 paper-based; 79 iBT), TWE (minimum score 5.5), Michigan English Language Assessment Battery (minimum score 85); Recommended—IELTS (minimum score 6.5). *Application deadline:* For fall admission, 6/1 priority date for domestic students, 5/1 priority date for international students; for winter admission, 10/1 priority date for domestic students, 9/1 priority date for international students; for spring admission, 2/1 priority date for domestic students, 1/1 priority date for international students. Applications are processed on a rolling basis. Application fee: $50. Electronic applications accepted. *Expenses:* $16,503 per year resident tuition and fees, $33,697 per year non-resident tuition and fees. *Financial support:* In 2016–17, 101 students received support, including 3 fellowships (averaging $11,409 per year); research assistantships with tuition reimbursements available, Federal Work-Study, scholarships/grants, and unspecified assistantships also available. Support available to part-time students. Financial award applicants required to submit FAFSA. *Faculty research:* Improving students' skill achievement in mathematics, improving elementary children's understanding of informational text, teachers' use of their pedagogical and mathematical knowledge in the interactive work of teaching, the intersection of identity construction in teaching and learning, identifying effective methods of literacy instruction and assessments for bilingual students in elementary language arts classrooms. *Unit head:* Dr. Kathleen Crawford-McKinney, Assistant Dean, 313-577-0122. *Application contact:* Janice Green, Assistant Dean, 313-577-1605, E-mail: jwgreen@wayne.edu.
Website: http://coe.wayne.edu/ted/index.php

Western New Mexico University, Graduate Division, School of Education, Silver City, NM 88062-0680. Offers bilingual education (MAT); educational leadership (MA); elementary education (MAT); reading (MAT); secondary education (MAT); special education (MAT); TESOL (teaching English to speakers of other languages) (MAT). *Accreditation:* NCATE. *Program availability:* Part-time, online learning. *Degree requirements:* For master's, comprehensive exam. *Entrance requirements:* For master's, minimum GPA of 3.0 in last 64 hours of undergraduate study. Additional exam requirements/recommendations for international students: Required—TOEFL (minimum score 550 paper-based; 79 iBT). Electronic applications accepted. *Faculty research:* International education, electronic reading assessment, developing STEM teachers.

Western Oregon University, Graduate Programs, College of Education, Division of Teacher Education, Program in Secondary Education, Monmouth, OR 97361. Offers bilingual education (MS Ed); health (MS Ed); humanities (MAT, MS Ed); initial licensure (MAT); mathematics (MAT, MS Ed); science (MAT, MS Ed); social science (MAT, MS Ed). *Accreditation:* NCATE. *Program availability:* Part-time, evening/weekend. *Degree requirements:* For master's, thesis optional, written exam. *Entrance requirements:* For master's, minimum GPA of 3.0, teaching license. Additional exam requirements/recommendations for international students: Required—TOEFL (minimum score 550 paper-based; 79 iBT), IELTS (minimum score 6.5). *Faculty research:* Literacy, science in primary grades, geography education, retention, teacher burnout.

Xavier University, College of Social Sciences, Health and Education, School of Education, Department of Childhood Education and Literacy, Cincinnati, OH 45207. Offers children's multicultural literature (M Ed); elementary education (M Ed); Montessori education (M Ed); reading (M Ed). *Program availability:* Part-time. *Degree requirements:* For master's, comprehensive exam, thesis, 30 semester hours. *Entrance requirements:* For master's, GRE, MAT, official transcript; 3 letters of recommendation (for Montessori education); resume; statement of purpose. Additional exam requirements/recommendations for international students: Required—TOEFL (minimum score 550 paper-based; 79 iBT). Electronic applications accepted. Application fee is waived when completed online. *Expenses:* Contact institution. *Faculty research:* Multicultural literacy/fluency, early literacy development, writing/creative and across curriculum, assessment of reading abilities.

Special Education

Acacia University, American Graduate School of Education, Tempe, AZ 85284. Offers educational administration (M Ed); elementary education (MA); English as a second language (M Ed); secondary education (MA); special education (M Ed).

Acadia University, Faculty of Professional Studies, School of Education, Program in Inclusive Education, Wolfville, NS B4P 2R6, Canada. Offers M Ed. *Program availability:* Part-time. *Degree requirements:* For master's, thesis optional. *Entrance requirements:* For master's, bachelor's degree in education, minimum B average in undergraduate course work, course work in special education. Additional exam requirements/recommendations for international students: Required—TOEFL (minimum score 580 paper-based; 93 iBT), IELTS (minimum score 6.5). *Faculty research:* Technology and human interaction, inclusive education and community, accommodating diversity, program evaluation.

Adams State University, The Graduate School, Department of Teacher Education, Program in Special Education, Alamosa, CO 81101. Offers MA. *Program availability:* Part-time, online learning. *Degree requirements:* For master's, practicum, qualifying exam. *Entrance requirements:* For master's, GRE General Test or MAT, minimum undergraduate GPA of 3.0.

Adelphi University, Ruth S. Ammon School of Education, Program in Special Education, Garden City, NY 11530-0701. Offers MS, Certificate. *Program availability:* Part-time, evening/weekend. *Students:* 28 full-time (26 women), 39 part-time (34 women); includes 19 minority (6 Black or African American, non-Hispanic/Latino; 2 Asian, non-Hispanic/Latino; 10 Hispanic/Latino; 1 Native Hawaiian or other Pacific Islander, non-Hispanic/Latino), 3 international. Average age 29. 75 applicants, 61% accepted, 24 enrolled. In 2016, 40 master's, 25 other advanced degrees awarded. *Entrance requirements:* For master's, 2 letters of recommendation, resume detailing paid/volunteer experience and organizational membership. Additional exam requirements/recommendations for international students: Required—TOEFL (minimum score 550 paper-based; 80 iBT), IELTS (minimum score 6.5). *Application deadline:* For fall admission, 4/1 for international students; for spring admission, 11/1 for international students. Application fee: $50. Electronic applications accepted. *Expenses:* Contact institution. *Financial support:* Research assistantships with partial tuition reimbursements, teaching assistantships, career-related internships or fieldwork, institutionally sponsored loans, scholarships/grants, traineeships, and unspecified assistantships available. Support available to part-time students. Financial award application deadline: 2/15; financial award applicants required to submit FAFSA. *Unit head:* Dr. Anne Mungai, Director, 516-877-4096, E-mail: mungai@adelphi.edu. *Application contact:* Christine Murphy, Director of Admissions, 516-877-3050, Fax: 516-877-3039, E-mail: graduateadmissions@adelphi.edu.

Alabama Agricultural and Mechanical University, School of Graduate Studies, College of Education, Humanities, and Behavioral Sciences, Department of Reading, Elementary, Early Childhood and Special Education, Huntsville, AL 35811. Offers early childhood education (MS Ed, Ed S); elementary education (MS Ed, Ed S); reading/literacy (PhD); special education collaborative teacher training (MS Ed, Ed S). *Accreditation:* NCATE. *Program availability:* Evening/weekend. *Degree requirements:* For master's, comprehensive exam; for Ed S, thesis. *Entrance requirements:* For master's, GRE General Test. Additional exam requirements/recommendations for international students: Required—TOEFL (minimum score 500 paper-based; 61 iBT). *Application deadline:* For fall admission, 5/1 for domestic students. Applications are processed on a rolling basis. Application fee: $25. Electronic applications accepted. *Expenses:* Tuition, nonresident: part-time $826 per credit hour. Full-time tuition and fees vary according to course load and program. *Financial support:* Research assistantships with tuition reimbursements and career-related internships or fieldwork available. Financial award application deadline: 4/1. *Faculty research:* Multicultural education, learning styles, diagnostic-prescriptive instruction. *Unit head:* Dr. Derrick Davis, Interim Chair, 256-372-4047.

Alabama State University, College of Education, Department of Curriculum and Instruction, Montgomery, AL 36101-0271. Offers early childhood education (M Ed, Ed S); elementary education (M Ed, Ed S); secondary education (M Ed, Ed S), including biology education, English language arts education (M Ed), history education, math education, music education (M Ed), reading education (M Ed), social science education; special education (M Ed). *Program availability:* Part-time. *Faculty:* 7 full-time (4 women), 7 part-time/adjunct (4 women). *Students:* 37 full-time (30 women), 82 part-time (69 women); includes 117 minority (115 Black or African American, non-Hispanic/Latino; 2 Two or more races, non-Hispanic/Latino). Average age 33. 65 applicants, 55% accepted, 22 enrolled. In 2016, 25 master's, 5 Ed Ss awarded. *Degree requirements:* For master's, comprehensive exam, thesis optional; for Ed S, comprehensive exam, thesis. *Entrance requirements:* For master's, GRE General Test, MAT, writing competency test; for Ed S, writing competency test, GRE, MAT. Additional exam requirements/recommendations for international students: Required—TOEFL (minimum score 500 paper-based). *Application deadline:* For fall admission, 4/15 for domestic and international students; for spring admission, 11/15 for domestic and international students; for summer admission, 3/15 for domestic and international students. Applications are processed on a rolling basis. Application fee: $25. Electronic applications accepted. *Expenses:* Tuition, state resident: full-time $3087; part-time $2744 per credit. Tuition, nonresident: full-time $6174; part-time $5488 per credit. *Required fees:* $2284; $1142 per credit. $571 per semester. Tuition and fees vary according to class time, course level, course load, degree level, program and student level. *Financial support:* Research assistantships available. Financial award application deadline: 6/30; financial award applicants required to submit FAFSA. *Unit head:* Dr. Joyce Johnson, Acting Chairperson, 334-229-4485, Fax: 334-229-5603, E-mail: jjohnson@alasu.edu. *Application contact:* Dr. William Person, Dean of Graduate Studies, 334-229-4274, Fax: 334-229-4928, E-mail: wperson@alasu.edu.
Website: http://www.alasu.edu/academics/colleges—departments/college-of-education/curriculum—instruction/index.aspx

Albany State University, College of Education, Albany, GA 31705-2717. Offers early childhood education (M Ed); educational leadership (Ed S); health and physical education (M Ed); middle grades education (M Ed); school counseling (M Ed); special education (M Ed). *Accreditation:* NCATE. *Program availability:* Part-time, evening/weekend, online learning. *Degree requirements:* For master's, comprehensive exam, internship, GACE Content Exam. *Entrance requirements:* For master's, GRE or MAT. *Application deadline:* For fall admission, 6/1 for domestic students, 5/1 for international students; for spring admission, 11/1 for domestic students, 10/1 for international students. Applications are processed on a rolling basis. Application fee: $20. Electronic applications accepted. *Financial support:* Scholarships/grants available. Financial award application deadline: 4/15; financial award applicants required to submit FAFSA. *Faculty research:* GACE preparation, STEM (science, technology, engineering, and mathematics), technology education, special education, professional teacher development, health implications liberation philosophy, NET-Q, learning community, disabled or at-risk students. *Unit head:* Dr. Rhonda C. Porter, Interim Dean, 229-430-1718, Fax: 229-430-4993. *Application contact:* Jeffrey Pierce, II, Graduate Admissions Counselor, 229-430-4646, Fax: 229-430-4105, E-mail: jeffrey.pierce@asurams.edu.
Website: https://www.asurams.edu/Academics/collegeofeducation/

Albright College, Graduate Division, Reading, PA 19612-5234. Offers early childhood education (MS); elementary education (MS); English as a second language (MA); general education (MA); special education (MS). *Program availability:* Part-time, evening/weekend. *Degree requirements:* For master's, thesis. *Entrance requirements:* For master's, GRE General Test or MAT, minimum undergraduate GPA of 3.0, 2 letters of recommendation, interview. Additional exam requirements/recommendations for international students: Recommended—TOEFL (minimum score 525 paper-based). Electronic applications accepted.

Alcorn State University, School of Graduate Studies, School of Psychology and Education, Lorman, MS 39096-7500. Offers agricultural education (MS Ed); elementary education (MS Ed, Ed S); guidance and counseling (MS Ed); industrial education (MS Ed); secondary education (MS Ed), including health and physical education; special education (MS Ed). *Accreditation:* NCATE. *Degree requirements:* For master's, thesis optional.

Alliant International University–San Francisco, Shirley M. Hufstedler School of Education, Teacher Education Programs, San Francisco, CA 94133. Offers auditory oral education (Certificate); CLAD (Certificate); education specialist: mild/moderate disabilities (Credential); preliminary multiple subject (Credential); preliminary single subject (Credential); professional clear multiple subject (Credential); professional clear single subject (Credential); special education (MA); teaching (MA); TESOL (Certificate). *Program availability:* Part-time, evening/weekend. *Degree requirements:* For master's, thesis. *Entrance requirements:* For degree, California Basic Educational Skills Test, minimum GPA of 2.5. Additional exam requirements/recommendations for international students: Required—TOEFL (minimum score 550 paper-based), TWE (minimum score 5). Electronic applications accepted. *Faculty research:* Curriculum development, first year teachers, cross-cultural issues in teaching, biliteracy.

Alverno College, School of Education, Milwaukee, WI 53234-3922. Offers adaptive education (MA); administrative leadership (MA); adult education and organizational development (MA); adult educational and instructional design (MA); adult educational and instructional technology (MA); global connections in the humanities (MA); instructional leadership (MA); instructional technology for K-12 settings (MA); professional development (MA); reading education (MA); reading education with adaptive education (MA); science education (MA); special education (MA); teaching in alternative schools (MA). *Accreditation:* NCATE. *Program availability:* Part-time, evening/weekend. *Faculty:* 4 full-time (3 women), 23 part-time/adjunct (17 women). *Students:* 58 full-time (57 women), 62 part-time (54 women); includes 32 minority (22 Black or African American, non-Hispanic/Latino; 2 Asian, non-Hispanic/Latino; 8 Hispanic/Latino), 1 international. Average age 39. 77 applicants, 99% accepted, 61 enrolled. In 2016, 85 master's awarded. *Degree requirements:* For master's, presentation/defense of proposal, conference presentation of inquiry projects. *Entrance requirements:* For master's, bachelor's degree in related field, communication samples from work setting, 3 letters of recommendation. Additional exam requirements/recommendations for international students: Required—TOEFL. *Application deadline:* For fall admission, 7/15 priority date for domestic and international students; for spring admission, 12/15 priority date for domestic and international students. Applications are processed on a rolling basis. Application fee: $0. Electronic applications accepted. *Expenses:* Contact institution. *Financial support:* In 2016–17, 17 students received support. Federal Work-Study and scholarships/grants available. Support available to part-time students. Financial award applicants required to submit FAFSA. *Faculty research:* Student self-assessment, self-reflection, integration of curriculum, identifying needs of students in strategic situations and designing appropriate classroom strategies. *Unit head:* Dr. Desiree Pointer Mace, Associate Dean, Graduate Program, 414-382-6345, Fax: 414-382-6332, E-mail: desiree.pointer-mace@alverno.edu. *Application contact:* Katie Kipp, Graduate Admissions Counselor, 414-382-6045, Fax: 414-382-6354, E-mail: katie.kipp@alverno.edu.

American International College, School of Education, Springfield, MA 01109-3189. Offers early childhood education (M Ed, CAGS); elementary education (M Ed, CAGS); middle education/secondary education (M Ed, CAGS); moderate disabilities (M Ed, CAGS); reading specialist (M Ed, CAGS); school adjustment counseling (MAEP, CAGS); school guidance counseling (MAEP, CAGS); school leadership (M Ed, CAGS). *Program availability:* Evening/weekend. *Faculty:* 1 (woman) full-time, 90 part-time/adjunct (63 women). *Students:* 1,194 full-time (970 women), 118 part-time (83 women); includes 108 minority (15 Black or African American, non-Hispanic/Latino; 4 American Indian or Alaska Native, non-Hispanic/Latino; 12 Asian, non-Hispanic/Latino; 55 Hispanic/Latino; 2 Native Hawaiian or other Pacific Islander, non-Hispanic/Latino; 20 Two or more races, non-Hispanic/Latino). Average age 34. 517 applicants, 417 enrolled. In 2016, 879 master's, 194 CAGSs awarded. Terminal master's awarded for partial completion of doctoral program. *Degree requirements:* For master's, comprehensive exam (for some programs), thesis (for some programs), practicum/culminating experience; for CAGS, practicum/culminating experience. *Entrance requirements:* For master's, Communication and Literacy portion of the Massachusetts Tests for Education Licensure, graduate of accredited four-year college with minimum B- average in undergraduate course work; for CAGS, M Ed or master's degree in field related to licensure from accredited institution. *Application deadline:* Applications are processed on a rolling basis. Application fee: $50. Electronic applications accepted. *Expenses:* $439 per credit. *Financial support:* Applicants required to submit FAFSA. *Unit head:* Sylvia Mason, Dean, 413-205-1743, Fax: 413-205-3943, E-mail: sylvia.mason@aic.edu. *Application contact:* Kerry Barnes, Dean of Graduate Admissions, 413-205-3703, Fax:

413-205-3051, E-mail: kerry.barnes@aic.edu.
Website: http://www.aic.edu/school-of-education/

American Public University System, AMU/APU Graduate Programs, Charles Town, WV 25414. Offers accounting (MBA, MS); applied business analytics (MBA, MS); criminal justice (MA), including business administration, emergency and disaster management, general (MA, MS); educational leadership (M Ed); emergency and disaster management (MA); entrepreneurship (MBA); environmental policy and management (MS), including environmental planning, environmental sustainability, fish and wildlife management, general (MA, MS), global environmental management; finance (MBA); general (MBA); government contracting and acquisition (MBA); health care administration (MBA); health information management (MS); history (MA), including American history, ancient and classical history, European history, global history, public history; homeland security (MA), including business administration, counterterrorism studies, criminal justice, cyber, emergency management and public health, intelligence studies, transportation security; homeland security resource allocation (MBA); humanities (MA); information technology (MS), including digital forensics, enterprise software development, information assurance and security, IT project management; information technology management (MBA); intelligence studies (MA), including criminal intelligence, cyber, general (MA, MS), homeland security, intelligence analysis, intelligence collection, intelligence management, intelligence operations, terrorism studies; international relations and conflict resolution (MA), including comparative and security issues, conflict resolution, international and transnational security issues, peacekeeping; legal studies (MA); management (MA), including strategic consulting; marketing (MBA); military history (MA), including American military history, American Revolution, civil war, war since 1945, World War II; military studies (MA), including joint warfare, strategic leadership; national security studies (MA), including cyber, general (MA, MS), homeland security, regional security studies, security and intelligence analysis, terrorism studies; nonprofit management (MBA); political science (MA), including American politics and government, comparative government and development, general (MA, MS), international relations, public policy; psychology (MA); public administration (MPA), including disaster management, environmental policy, health policy, human resources, national security, organizational management, security management; public health (MPH); reverse logistics management (MA); security management (MA); space studies (MS), including aerospace science, general (MA, MS), planetary science; sports and health sciences (MS); sports management (MBA); teaching (M Ed), including autism spectrum disorder, curriculum and instruction for elementary teachers, elementary reading, English language learners, instructional leadership, online learning, special education, STEAM (STEM plus the arts); transportation and logistics management (MA). *Program availability:* Part-time, evening/weekend, online only, 100% online. *Faculty:* 401 full-time (228 women), 1,678 part-time/adjunct (781 women). *Students:* 378 full-time (184 women), 8,455 part-time (3,484 women); includes 2,972 minority (1,552 Black or African American, non-Hispanic/Latino; 52 American Indian or Alaska Native, non-Hispanic/Latino; 211 Asian, non-Hispanic/Latino; 791 Hispanic/Latino; 70 Native Hawaiian or other Pacific Islander, non-Hispanic/Latino; 296 Two or more races, non-Hispanic/Latino), 109 international. Average age 37. In 2016, 3,185 master's awarded. *Degree requirements:* For master's, comprehensive exam or practicum. *Entrance requirements:* For master's, official transcript showing earned bachelor's degree from institution accredited by recognized accrediting body. Additional exam requirements/recommendations for international students: Required—TOEFL (minimum score 550 paper-based), IELTS (minimum score 6.5). *Application deadline:* Applications are processed on a rolling basis. Application fee: $0. Electronic applications accepted. *Expenses: Tuition:* Part-time $350 per credit hour. *Required fees:* $50 per course. *Financial support:* Scholarships/grants available. Financial award applicants required to submit FAFSA. *Unit head:* Dr. Karan Powell, President, 877-468-6268, Fax: 304-724-3780. *Application contact:* Terry Grant, Vice President of Enrollment Management, 877-468-6268, Fax: 304-724-3780, E-mail: info@apus.edu.
Website: http://www.apus.edu

American University, School of Education, Program in Special Education: Learning Disabilities, Washington, DC 20016-8001. Offers MA. *Program availability:* Part-time, evening/weekend. *Students:* 20 full-time (19 women), 10 part-time (8 women); includes 9 minority (7 Black or African American, non-Hispanic/Latino; 1 Asian, non-Hispanic/Latino; 1 Hispanic/Latino), 2 international. Average age 28. 27 applicants, 100% accepted, 15 enrolled. In 2016, 19 master's awarded. *Degree requirements:* For master's, comprehensive exam. *Entrance requirements:* For master's, GRE General Test, PRAXIS I, minimum GPA of 3.0, 2 recommendations, statement of purpose, transcripts, resume. Additional exam requirements/recommendations for international students: Required—TOEFL (minimum score 100 iBT), IELTS (minimum score 7), PTE (minimum score 68). *Application deadline:* For fall admission, 2/1 priority date for domestic students; for spring admission, 11/1 for domestic students. Applications are processed on a rolling basis. Application fee: $55. Electronic applications accepted. *Expenses:* $1,579 per credit tuition; $690 mandatory fees. *Financial support:* Institutionally sponsored loans available. Financial award application deadline: 2/1; financial award applicants required to submit FAFSA. *Unit head:* Sarah Irvine Belson, Director, Master's in Special Education, 202-885-3714, E-mail: sirvine@american.edu. *Application contact:* Kathleen Clowery, Associate Director, Graduate Enrollment Management, 202-885-3620, Fax: 202-885-1344, E-mail: clowery@american.edu.
Website: http://www.american.edu/cas/seth/special/index.cfm

American University of Puerto Rico, Program in Education, Bayamon, PR 00960-2037. Offers art education (M Ed); elementary education 4-6 (M Ed); elementary education K-3 (M Ed); general science education (M Ed); physical education (M Ed); special education (M Ed). *Program availability:* Part-time, evening/weekend. *Faculty:* 17 part-time/adjunct (7 women). *Students:* 22 full-time (18 women), 54 part-time (42 women); all minorities (all Hispanic/Latino). Average age 33. 22 applicants, 86% accepted, 19 enrolled. In 2016, 53 master's awarded. *Entrance requirements:* For master's, EXADEP, GRE, or MAT, 2 letters of recommendation, minimum GPA of 2.5. *Application deadline:* For fall admission, 8/1 for domestic students; for winter admission, 10/18 for domestic students; for spring admission, 3/15 for domestic students. Applications are processed on a rolling basis. Application fee: $25. *Financial support:* In 2016–17, 79 students received support, including 76 fellowships (averaging $400 per year), 55 teaching assistantships (averaging $1,741 per year). Financial award applicants required to submit FAFSA. *Unit head:* Prof. Bolivar Ramirez-Carlo, III, Dean of Faculty, 787-620-2040 Ext. 2010, Fax: 787-620-2958, E-mail: bramirez@aupr.edu. *Application contact:* Keren I. Llanos-Figueroa, Information Contact, 787-620-2040 Ext. 2021, Fax: 787-785-7377, E-mail: oficnaadmisiones@aupr.edu.

Andrews University, School of Graduate Studies, School of Education, Department of Graduate Psychology and Counseling, Program in Special Education, Berrien Springs, MI 49104. Offers MS. *Students:* 3 part-time (all women); includes 1 minority (Black or African American, non-Hispanic/Latino). Average age 37. In 2016, 1 master's awarded. *Entrance requirements:* Additional exam requirements/recommendations for international students: Required—TOEFL (minimum score 550 paper-based). Application fee: $40. *Unit head:* Dr. Nona Elmendorf-Steele, Dean, 269-471-6468. *Application contact:* Justina Clayburn, Supervisor of Graduate Admission, 800-253-2874, Fax: 269-471-6321, E-mail: graduate@andrews.edu.

Antioch University Midwest, Graduate Programs, School of Education, Yellow Springs, OH 45387-1609. Offers conflict management (M Ed); dyslexia (M Ed); early childhood education (M Ed); educational leadership (M Ed); intervention specialist, mild to moderate (M Ed); middle childhood education (M Ed); trauma informed education (M Ed). *Accreditation:* NCATE. *Program availability:* Part-time, evening/weekend. *Degree requirements:* For master's, thesis or alternative. *Entrance requirements:* For master's, resume, goal statement, interview. *Application deadline:* For fall admission, 9/7 for domestic students; for winter admission, 12/10 for domestic students; for spring admission, 3/10 for domestic students. Applications are processed on a rolling basis. Application fee: $50. Electronic applications accepted. *Expenses:* $675 per credit hour. *Financial support:* Federal Work-Study available. Financial award applicants required to submit FAFSA. *Unit head:* Dr. Marian Glancy, Director, 937-769-1880, Fax: 937-769-1805, E-mail: mglancy@antioch.edu. *Application contact:* Deena Kent-Hummel, Director of Admissions, 937-769-1823, Fax: 937-769-1804, E-mail: dkent@antioch.edu.
Website: https://www.antioch.edu/midwest/degrees-programs/education-degree/

Antioch University New England, Graduate School, Department of Applied Psychology, Program in Autism Spectrum Disorders, Keene, NH 03431-3552. Offers applied behavior analysis (Certificate); applied behavior analysis internship (Certificate); autism spectrum disorders (Certificate). *Entrance requirements:* Additional exam requirements/recommendations for international students: Required—TOEFL (minimum score 550 paper-based).

Antioch University New England, Graduate School, Department of Education, Experienced Educators Program, Keene, NH 03431-3552. Offers foundations of education (M Ed), including applied behavioral analysis, autism spectrum disorders, educating for sustainability, next-generation learning using technology, problem-based learning using critical skills, teacher leadership; principal certification (PMC). *Degree requirements:* For master's, thesis, practicum. *Entrance requirements:* For master's, previous course work and work experience in education. Additional exam requirements/recommendations for international students: Required—TOEFL (minimum score 550 paper-based). Electronic applications accepted. *Expenses:* Contact institution. *Faculty research:* Classroom action research, school restructuring, problem-based learning, brain-based learning.

Antioch University New England, Graduate School, Department of Education, Integrated Learning Program, Keene, NH 03431-3552. Offers early childhood education (M Ed); elementary education (M Ed), including arts and humanities, science and environmental education; special education (M Ed). *Degree requirements:* For master's, internship. *Entrance requirements:* For master's, previous course work or work experience in education. Additional exam requirements/recommendations for international students: Required—TOEFL (minimum score 550 paper-based). Electronic applications accepted. *Expenses:* Contact institution. *Faculty research:* Problem-based learning, place-based education, mathematics education, democratic classrooms, art education.

Appalachian State University, Cratis D. Williams Graduate School, Department of Reading Education and Special Education, Boone, NC 28608. Offers reading education (MA); special education (MA). *Accreditation:* ASHA. *Program availability:* Part-time, evening/weekend, online learning. *Degree requirements:* For master's, comprehensive exam, thesis optional. *Entrance requirements:* For master's, GRE General Test or MAT, 3 letters of recommendation. Additional exam requirements/recommendations for international students: Required—TOEFL (minimum score 570 paper-based; 79 iBT), IELTS (minimum score 6.5). *Application deadline:* For fall admission, 3/15 priority date for domestic students, 2/1 for international students; for spring admission, 11/1 for domestic students, 7/1 for international students. Applications are processed on a rolling basis. Application fee: $55. Electronic applications accepted. *Expenses:* Tuition, state resident: full-time $4744. Tuition, nonresident: full-time $17,913. Full-time tuition and fees vary according to program. *Financial support:* Research assistantships, Federal Work-Study, scholarships/grants, and unspecified assistantships available. Financial award application deadline: 4/1; financial award applicants required to submit FAFSA. *Faculty research:* Special education, language arts, reading. *Unit head:* Dr. Monica Lambert, Chairperson, 828-262-7173, Fax: 828-262-6767, E-mail: lambertma@appstate.edu. *Application contact:* Dr. David Koppenhaver, Program Director, E-mail: koppenhaverd@appstate.edu.
Website: https://rese.appstate.edu/

Arcadia University, College of Arts and Sciences, Department of Psychology, Glenside, PA 19038-3295. Offers applied behavior analysis (MAC); autism (MAC); child/family therapy (MAC); community public health (MAC); counseling/international peace and conflict resolution dual degree (MAC); mental health counseling (MAC); trauma (MAC). *Program availability:* Part-time. *Faculty:* 14 full-time (9 women), 10 part-time/adjunct (9 women). *Students:* 33 full-time (27 women), 39 part-time (30 women); includes 22 minority (13 Black or African American, non-Hispanic/Latino; 2 Asian, non-Hispanic/Latino; 1 Hispanic/Latino; 6 Two or more races, non-Hispanic/Latino), 1 international. Average age 30. 61 applicants, 64% accepted, 24 enrolled. In 2016, 41 master's awarded. *Degree requirements:* For master's, practicum. *Entrance requirements:* For master's, GRE General Test or MAT. *Application deadline:* For fall admission, 1/15 for domestic students; for spring admission, 9/15 for domestic students. Applications are processed on a rolling basis. Application fee: $50. *Expenses:* Contact institution. *Financial support:* Research assistantships, career-related internships or fieldwork, and unspecified assistantships available. Support available to part-time students. Financial award application deadline: 8/15. *Unit head:* Dr. Steven Robbins, Chair, 215-572-2987. *Application contact:* 215-572-2925, Fax: 215-572-2126, E-mail: grad@arcadia.edu.

Arcadia University, School of Education, Glenside, PA 19038-3295. Offers art education (M Ed); computer education (CAS); curriculum (CAS); curriculum studies (M Ed); early childhood education (M Ed), including individualized, master teacher, research in child development; educational leadership (M Ed, Ed D, CAS); elementary education (M Ed); English education (MA Ed); environmental education (MA Ed); instructional technology (M Ed); language arts (M Ed); library science (M Ed); mathematics education (M Ed, MA Ed); music education (MA Ed); psychology (MA Ed); reading (M Ed, CAS); science education (M Ed, CAS); secondary education (M Ed, CAS); special education (M Ed, Ed D, CAS); theater arts (MA Ed); written communication (MA Ed). *Accreditation:* NASAD. *Program availability:* Part-time, evening/weekend, online learning. *Faculty:* 19 full-time (13 women), 3 part-time/adjunct (all women). *Students:* 22 full-time (16 women), 356 part-time (284 women); includes 84 minority (55 Black or African American, non-Hispanic/Latino; 2 American Indian or Alaska Native, non-Hispanic/Latino; 13 Asian, non-Hispanic/Latino; 11 Hispanic/Latino; 3 Two or more races, non-Hispanic/Latino), 4 international. Average age 34. 145 applicants, 73% accepted, 80 enrolled. In 2016, 95 master's, 11 doctorates awarded. *Application deadline:* Applications are processed on a rolling basis. Application fee: $50. Electronic applications accepted. *Expenses:* Contact institution. *Financial support:* Career-related internships or fieldwork, tuition waivers (partial), and unspecified assistantships available. *Unit head:* John T Groves, Interim Dean of the School of Education, 215-572-2940. *Application contact:* 215-572-2925, Fax: 215-572-2126, E-mail: grad@arcadia.edu.

Arizona State University at the Tempe campus, Mary Lou Fulton Teachers College, Program in Special Education, Phoenix, AZ 85069. Offers autism spectrum disorder (Graduate Certificate); special education (M Ed). *Program availability:* Online learning. *Degree requirements:* For master's, thesis or alternative, applied project, student teaching, interactive Program of Study (iPOS) submitted before completing 50 percent of required credit hours. *Entrance requirements:* For master's, Arizona Educator Proficiency Assessments (AEPA), minimum GPA of 3.0 or equivalent in last 2 years of work leading to bachelor's degree, 3 letters of recommendation, personal statement, resume, IVP fingerprint clearance card (for those seeking Arizona certification). Additional exam requirements/recommendations for international students: Required—TOEFL, IELTS, or PTE. Electronic applications accepted.

Arkansas State University, Graduate School, College of Education and Behavioral Science, Department of Psychology and Counseling, State University, AR 72467. Offers clinical mental health counseling (Graduate Certificate); college student personnel services (MS); dyslexia therapy (Graduate Certificate); psychological science (MS); psychology and counseling (Ed S); rehabilitation counseling (MRC); school counseling (MSE); student affairs (Graduate Certificate). *Accreditation:* ACA (one or more programs are accredited); CORE (one or more programs are accredited); NCATE. *Program availability:* Part-time. *Degree requirements:* For master's and other advanced degree, comprehensive exam, thesis or alternative. *Entrance requirements:* For master's, GRE General Test or MAT (for MSE), appropriate bachelor's degree, interview, letters of reference, official transcripts, immunization records, written statement, 2-3 page autobiography; for other advanced degree, GRE General Test, interview, master's degree, letters of reference, official transcript, personal statement, immunization records. Additional exam requirements/recommendations for international students: Required—TOEFL (minimum score 550 paper-based; 79 iBT), IELTS (minimum score 6), PTE (minimum score 56). Electronic applications accepted.

Arkansas State University, Graduate School, College of Education and Behavioral Science, School of Teacher Education and Leadership, State University, AR 72467. Offers community college administration (SCCT); curriculum and instruction (MSE); early childhood education (MSE); early childhood services (MS); educational leadership (MSE, Ed D, Ed S); educational theory and practice (MSE); middle level education (MAT, MSE); reading (MSE, Ed S); special education - gifted, talented, and creative (MSE); special education - instructional specialist grades 4-12 (MSE); special education - instructional specialist grades P-4 (MSE); special education, K-12 (MSE). *Accreditation:* NCATE. *Program availability:* Part-time, online learning. *Degree requirements:* For master's, comprehensive exam, thesis or alternative; for doctorate, comprehensive exam, thesis/dissertation; for other advanced degree, comprehensive exam. *Entrance requirements:* For master's, GRE General Test or MAT, appropriate bachelor's degree, official transcripts, immunization records, letters of reference, interview; for doctorate, GRE General Test or MAT, interview, master's degree, letters of reference, official transcript, personal statement, writing sample, immunization records; for other advanced degree, GRE General Test or MAT, interview, master's degree, official transcript, immunization records, letters of reference, 3 years of teaching experience, teaching license. Additional exam requirements/recommendations for international students: Required—TOEFL (minimum score 550 paper-based; 79 iBT), IELTS (minimum score 6), PTE (minimum score 56). Electronic applications accepted.

Arkansas State University, Graduate School, College of Nursing and Health Professions, Department of Communication Disorders, State University, AR 72467. Offers communication disorders (MCD); dyslexia therapy (Graduate Certificate). *Accreditation:* ASHA. *Program availability:* Part-time. *Degree requirements:* For master's, comprehensive exam, thesis or alternative. *Entrance requirements:* For master's, GRE General Test, appropriate bachelor's degree, letters of recommendation, official transcripts, immunization records. Additional exam requirements/recommendations for international students: Required—TOEFL (minimum score 550 paper-based; 79 iBT), IELTS (minimum score 6), PTE (minimum score 56). Electronic applications accepted. *Expenses:* Contact institution.

Armstrong State University, School of Graduate Studies, Department of Childhood and Exceptional Student Education, Savannah, GA 31419-1997. Offers early childhood education (M Ed, MAT); reading (Certificate); special education (M Ed, MAT); special education transition specialist (Certificate). *Accreditation:* NCATE. *Program availability:* Part-time, evening/weekend. *Faculty:* 14 full-time (12 women), 1 (woman) part-time/adjunct. *Students:* 10 full-time (9 women), 199 part-time (177 women); includes 67 minority (55 Black or African American, non-Hispanic/Latino; 1 Asian, non-Hispanic/Latino; 5 Hispanic/Latino; 6 Two or more races, non-Hispanic/Latino). Average age 34. 131 applicants, 42% accepted, 45 enrolled. In 2016, 72 master's, 24 other advanced degrees awarded. *Degree requirements:* For master's, portfolio. *Entrance requirements:* For master's, MAT, Georgia Assessment for the Certification of Educators. Additional exam requirements/recommendations for international students: Required—TOEFL (minimum score 523 paper-based; 70 iBT). *Application deadline:* For fall admission, 7/1 priority date for domestic students, 5/1 priority date for international students; for spring admission, 11/15 priority date for domestic students, 9/15 priority date for international students; for summer admission, 4/15 priority date for domestic students, 9/15 for international students. Applications are processed on a rolling basis. Application fee: $30. Electronic applications accepted. *Expenses:* Tuition, state resident: full-time $1781; part-time $161.93 per credit hour. Tuition, nonresident: full-time $6482; part-time $589.27 per credit hour. *Required fees:* $1224 per unit. $612 per semester. Tuition and fees vary according to course load, campus/location and program. *Financial support:* In 2016–17, research assistantships with full tuition reimbursements (averaging $5,000 per year) were awarded; career-related internships or fieldwork, Federal Work-Study, and scholarships/grants also available. Support available to part-time students. Financial award application deadline: 3/15; financial award applicants required to submit FAFSA. *Faculty research:* Literacy, instructional design, poetry, working with local schools. *Unit head:* Dr. John Hobe, Department Head, 912-344-2619, Fax: 912-344-3443, E-mail: john.hobe@armstrong.edu. *Application contact:* McKenzie Peterman, Assistant Director of Graduate Admissions, 912-344-2503, Fax: 912-344-3417, E-mail: graduate@armstrong.edu.
Website: https://www.armstrong.edu/academic-departments/education-ceed

Asbury University, School of Graduate and Professional Studies, Wilmore, KY 40390-1198. Offers biology: alternative certificate (MA Ed); chemistry: alternative certificate (MA Ed); English (MA Ed); English as a second language (MA Ed); ESL (MA Ed); French (MA Ed); Latin: alternative certificate (MA Ed); mathematics: alternative certificate (MA Ed); reading/writing endorsement (MA Ed); social studies (MA Ed); social work (MSW), including child and family services; Spanish (MA Ed); special education (MA Ed); special education: alternative certificate (MA Ed); teacher as leader endorsement (MA Ed). *Accreditation:* NCATE. *Program availability:* Part-time. *Degree requirements:* For master's, action research project, portfolio. *Entrance requirements:* For master's, PRAXIS/NTE, minimum GPA of 2.75, letters of recommendation. Additional exam requirements/recommendations for international students: Required—TOEFL (minimum score 550 paper-based). Electronic applications accepted.

Ashland University, Dwight Schar College of Education, Department of Inclusive Services and Exceptional Learners, Ashland, OH 44805-3702. Offers intervention specialist, mild/moderate (M Ed); intervention specialist, moderate/intensive (M Ed); talented and gifted (M Ed). *Program availability:* Part-time, evening/weekend. *Degree requirements:* For master's, thesis or alternative, internship, practicum, inquiry seminar. *Entrance requirements:* Additional exam requirements/recommendations for international students: Required—TOEFL. *Application deadline:* For fall admission, 8/15 for domestic students; for spring admission, 1/15 for domestic students. Applications are processed on a rolling basis. Application fee: $30. Electronic applications accepted. *Financial support:* Teaching assistantships with partial tuition reimbursements and scholarships/grants available. Financial award application deadline: 4/15. *Unit head:* Dr. Allison Dickey, Chair, 419-289-5376, Fax: 419-207-4949, E-mail: adickey@ashland.edu. *Application contact:* Dr. Linda Billman, Associate Dean, 419-289-5369, Fax: 419-289-5331, E-mail: lbillman@ashland.edu.

Assumption College, Special Education Program, Worcester, MA 01609-1296. Offers positive behavior support (CAGS); special education (MA). *Program availability:* Part-time, evening/weekend. *Faculty:* 2 full-time (both women), 3 part-time/adjunct (2 women). *Students:* 3 full-time (all women), 25 part-time (22 women); includes 1 minority (Hispanic/Latino). Average age 27. 17 applicants, 82% accepted, 11 enrolled. In 2016, 18 master's, 12 other advanced degrees awarded. *Degree requirements:* For master's, comprehensive exam, internship, practicum. *Entrance requirements:* For master's, bachelor's degree with minimum GPA of 3.0, 3 letters of recommendation, official transcripts, personal statement, current resume, teacher certification documents (if certified or licensed); for CAGS, MA or M Ed, minimum one year of full-time employment in educational setting, 3 letters of recommendation, official transcripts, personal statement, current resume, interview. Additional exam requirements/recommendations for international students: Required—TOEFL (minimum score 540 paper-based; 76 iBT), IELTS (minimum score 6). *Application deadline:* Applications are processed on a rolling basis. Application fee: $30. Electronic applications accepted. *Expenses:* *Tuition:* Full-time $11,610; part-time $645 per credit. *Required fees:* $70 per term. Tuition and fees vary according to course load and program. *Financial support:* In 2016–17, 5 students received support. Tuition waivers (full and partial), unspecified assistantships, and institutional discounts available. Financial award applicants required to submit FAFSA. *Unit head:* Dr. Nanho Vander Hart, Director, 508-767-7380, Fax: 508-767-7263, E-mail: nvanderh@assumption.edu. *Application contact:* Karen Stoyanoff, Director of Recruitment for Graduate Enrollment, 508-767-7442, Fax: 508-799-4915, E-mail: graduate@assumption.edu.
Website: http://graduate.assumption.edu/special-education/graduate-programs

Auburn University, Graduate School, College of Education, Department of Special Education, Rehabilitation, Counseling and School Psychology, Auburn University, AL 36849. Offers M Ed, MS, PhD. *Accreditation:* CORE; NCATE. *Program availability:* Part-time. *Faculty:* 20 full-time (15 women), 2 part-time/adjunct (1 woman). *Students:* 157 full-time (131 women), 73 part-time (58 women); includes 62 minority (48 Black or African American, non-Hispanic/Latino; 2 Asian, non-Hispanic/Latino; 8 Hispanic/Latino; 1 Native Hawaiian or other Pacific Islander, non-Hispanic/Latino; 3 Two or more races, non-Hispanic/Latino), 3 international. Average age 30. 206 applicants, 38% accepted, 62 enrolled. In 2016, 53 master's, 12 doctorates awarded. *Degree requirements:* For master's, thesis (for some programs); for doctorate, thesis/dissertation. *Entrance requirements:* For master's, GRE General Test; for doctorate, GRE General Test, interview. *Application deadline:* Applications are processed on a rolling basis. Application fee: $50 ($60 for international students). Electronic applications accepted. *Expenses:* Tuition, state resident: full-time $9072; part-time $504 per credit hour. Tuition, nonresident: full-time $27,216; part-time $1512 per credit hour. *Required fees:* $812 per semester. Tuition and fees vary according to degree level and program. *Financial support:* Research assistantships, teaching assistantships, and Federal Work-Study available. Support available to part-time students. Financial award application deadline: 3/15; financial award applicants required to submit FAFSA. *Faculty research:* Emotional conflict/behavior disorders, gifted and talented, learning disabilities, mental retardation, multi-handicapped. *Unit head:* Dr. Jamie Carney, Head, 334-844-7676. *Application contact:* Dr. George Flowers, Dean of the Graduate School, 334-844-2125.

Auburn University at Montgomery, College of Education, Department of Counselor, Leadership, and Special Education, Montgomery, AL 36124-4023. Offers counselor education (M Ed, Ed S), including clinical mental health counseling, school counseling; early childhood special education (M Ed); instructional leadership (M Ed, Ed S); special education/collaborative teacher (M Ed, Ed S). *Accreditation:* ACA; NCATE. *Program availability:* Part-time, evening/weekend. *Faculty:* 9 full-time (7 women), 3 part-time/adjunct (all women). *Students:* 7 full-time (5 women), 28 part-time (all women); includes 11 minority (10 Black or African American, non-Hispanic/Latino; 1 Asian, non-Hispanic/Latino). Average age 35. In 2016, 35 master's, 9 Ed Ss awarded. *Degree requirements:* For master's and Ed S, comprehensive exam. *Entrance requirements:* For master's, GRE General Test or MAT, certification, BS in teaching; for Ed S, GRE General Test or MAT, certification. Additional exam requirements/recommendations for international students: Recommended—TOEFL (minimum score 500 paper-based; 61 iBT), IELTS (minimum score 5.5), TSE (minimum score 44). *Application deadline:* Applications are processed on a rolling basis. Electronic applications accepted. *Expenses:* Tuition, state resident: full-time $6462; part-time $359 per credit hour. Tuition, nonresident: full-time $14,526; part-time $807 per credit hour. *Required fees:* $554. *Financial support:* Career-related internships or fieldwork and scholarships/grants available. Support available to part-time students. Financial award application deadline: 3/1; financial award applicants required to submit FAFSA. *Unit head:* Dr. Samuel Flynt, Head, 334-244-3835, Fax: 334-244-3101, E-mail: sflynt@aum.edu. *Application contact:* Dr. Rhonda Morton, Associate Dean/Graduate Coordinator, 334-244-3287, Fax: 334-244-3978, E-mail: rmorton@aum.edu.
Website: http://education.aum.edu/academic-departments/counselor-leadership-and-special-education

Augustana University, MA in Education Program, Sioux Falls, SD 57197. Offers instructional strategies (MA); reading (MA); special populations (MA); STEM (MA); technology (MA). *Accreditation:* NCATE. *Program availability:* Part-time, evening/weekend, online only, 100% online. *Degree requirements:* For master's, thesis. *Entrance requirements:* For master's, appropriate bachelor's degree, minimum GPA of 3.0, teaching certificate. Additional exam requirements/recommendations for international students: Required—TOEFL (minimum score 550 paper-based). *Application deadline:* For fall admission, 8/1 for domestic and international students; for spring admission, 11/1 for domestic and international students; for summer admission, 4/1 for domestic and international students. Applications are processed on a rolling basis. Application fee: $50. Electronic applications accepted. *Expenses:* Contact institution. *Financial support:* Application deadline: 3/1; applicants required to submit FAFSA. *Unit head:* Dr. Laurie Daily, Chair, 605-274-5211, E-mail: laurie.daily@augie.edu. *Application contact:* Jody Nitz, Graduate Coordinator, 605-274-4043, Fax: 605-274-4450, E-mail: graduate@augie.edu.
Website: http://www.augie.edu/master-arts-education

Augusta University, The Graduate School, College of Education, Program in Curriculum and Instruction, Augusta, GA 30912. Offers curriculum and instruction (Ed S); elementary education (MAT); foreign language education (MAT); instruction (M Ed); middle grades education (MAT); music education (MAT); secondary education (MAT); special education (MAT). *Degree requirements:* For master's, thesis, portfolio.

Entrance requirements: For master's, GRE, MAT, minimum GPA of 2.5. Application fee: $20. *Financial support:* Career-related internships or fieldwork, Federal Work-Study, institutionally sponsored loans, and unspecified assistantships available. Support available to part-time students. Financial award application deadline: 4/15; financial award applicants required to submit FAFSA. *Unit head:* Dr. Gordon Eisenman, Director, 706-737-1496, Fax: 706-667-4706, E-mail: geisenman@augusta.edu. *Application contact:* Dr. Gordon Eisenman, Director, 706-737-1496, Fax: 706-667-4706, E-mail: geisenman@augusta.edu.

Aurora University, School of Education and Human Performance, Aurora, IL 60506-4892. Offers bilingual-ESL education (MA); educational leadership (MA); educational technology (MA); leadership in administration (Ed D); leadership in adult learning and higher education (Ed D); leadership in curriculum and instruction (Ed D); reading instruction (MA); special education (MA). *Accreditation:* NCATE. *Program availability:* Part-time, evening/weekend. *Faculty:* 22 full-time (12 women), 46 part-time/adjunct (27 women). *Students:* 36 full-time (30 women), 559 part-time (372 women); includes 68 minority (27 Black or African American, non-Hispanic/Latino; 1 American Indian or Alaska Native, non-Hispanic/Latino; 6 Asian, non-Hispanic/Latino; 29 Hispanic/Latino; 2 Native Hawaiian or other Pacific Islander, non-Hispanic/Latino; 3 Two or more races, non-Hispanic/Latino). Average age 37. 126 applicants, 98% accepted, 72 enrolled. In 2016, 178 master's, 27 doctorates awarded. *Degree requirements:* For master's, student teaching; for doctorate, comprehensive exam, thesis/dissertation. *Entrance requirements:* For master's, 2 years of teaching experience, valid teaching certificate; for doctorate, appropriate master's degree, two references, curriculum vitae, personal statement, professional project, reflective essay. Additional exam requirements/recommendations for international students: Required—TOEFL (minimum score 550 paper-based; 79 iBT). *Application deadline:* For fall admission, 6/1 for international students; for spring admission, 10/1 for international students. Applications are processed on a rolling basis. Application fee: $0. Electronic applications accepted. *Expenses:* Contact institution. *Financial support:* In 2016–17, 10 students received support. Federal Work-Study, scholarships/grants, and unspecified assistantships available. Support available to part-time students. Financial award applicants required to submit FAFSA. *Unit head:* Dr. Jen Buckley, Executive Director of the School of Education and Human Performance, 630-844-1542, Fax: 630-844-6155, E-mail: jbuckley@aurora.edu. *Application contact:* Elizabeth Botica, Graduate Education Recruiter, 630-947-8918, E-mail: ebotica@aurora.edu.
Website: http://aurora.edu/education

Austin Peay State University, College of Graduate Studies, College of Education, Department of Teaching and Learning, Clarksville, TN 37044. Offers elementary education K-6 (MAT); reading (MA Ed); secondary education 7-12 (MAT); special education K-12 (MAT). *Program availability:* Part-time, evening/weekend, online learning. *Faculty:* 12 full-time (8 women), 1 (woman) part-time/adjunct. *Students:* 62 full-time (39 women), 79 part-time (72 women); includes 31 minority (16 Black or African American, non-Hispanic/Latino; 1 Asian, non-Hispanic/Latino; 8 Hispanic/Latino; 6 Two or more races, non-Hispanic/Latino), 2 international. Average age 33. 60 applicants, 80% accepted, 33 enrolled. In 2016, 53 master's awarded. *Degree requirements:* For master's, comprehensive exam, thesis optional. *Entrance requirements:* For master's, GRE General Test, minimum undergraduate GPA of 2.75. Additional exam requirements/recommendations for international students: Required—TOEFL (minimum score 500 paper-based). *Application deadline:* For fall admission, 8/9 priority date for domestic students. Applications are processed on a rolling basis. Application fee: $45 ($50 for international students). Electronic applications accepted. *Expenses:* Tuition, state resident: full-time $8300; part-time $415 per credit hour. Tuition, nonresident: full-time $22,280; part-time $1114 per credit hour. *Required fees:* $1473; $73.65 per credit hour. *Financial support:* Research assistantships, career-related internships or fieldwork, Federal Work-Study, institutionally sponsored loans, scholarships/grants, and unspecified assistantships available. Support available to part-time students. Financial award application deadline: 4/1; financial award applicants required to submit FAFSA. *Unit head:* Dr. Benita Bruster, Interim Chair, 931-221-6491, Fax: 931-221-1292, E-mail: brusterb@apsu.edu. *Application contact:* Brad Averitt, Coordinator of Graduate Admissions, 800-859-4723, Fax: 931-221-7641, E-mail: gradadmissions@apsu.edu.

Averett University, Master in Education Program, Danville, VA 24541-3692. Offers administration and supervision (M Ed); curriculum and instruction (M Ed); special education with endorsement (M Ed); special education with licensure (M Ed). Program offered on Danville Campus only. *Program availability:* Part-time, online only, 100% online. *Faculty:* 1 full-time (0 women), 15 part-time/adjunct (12 women). *Students:* 26 full-time (22 women), 98 part-time (73 women); includes 39 minority (34 Black or African American, non-Hispanic/Latino; 3 American Indian or Alaska Native, non-Hispanic/Latino; 2 Hispanic/Latino). Average age 36. 109 applicants, 54% accepted, 56 enrolled. In 2016, 19 master's awarded. *Degree requirements:* For master's, 30-credit core curriculum, minimum GPA of 3.0 throughout program, completion of degree requirements within six years from start of program. *Entrance requirements:* For master's, PRAXIS I, GRE, or MAT; writing proficiency test, minimum cumulative GPA of 3.0 over the last 60 hours of undergraduate study toward a baccalaureate degree, three letters of recommendation, Virginia teaching license (or eligibility). Additional exam requirements/recommendations for international students: Required—TOEFL (minimum score 600 paper-based; 100 iBT). *Application deadline:* Applications are processed on a rolling basis. Electronic applications accepted. *Expenses:* $9,600. *Financial support:* Application deadline: 3/1; applicants required to submit FAFSA. *Faculty research:* Digital story telling for instruction and assessment; online collaborative tools; digital field trips with Google Earth; teacher preparation in special education in Kenya, Malawi, Zambia, and Zimbabwe; self-efficacy of regular education teachers regarding inclusion of special education students in their classrooms. *Total annual research expenditures:* $5,000. *Unit head:* Dr. Sue Davis, Education Chair, 434-791-5741, Fax: 434-791-5020, E-mail: suedavis@averett.edu.
Website: http://gps.averett.edu/online/education/

Azusa Pacific University, School of Education, Department of Special Education, Program in Special Education, Azusa, CA 91702-7000. Offers MA Ed. *Accreditation:* NCATE. *Program availability:* Part-time, evening/weekend. *Degree requirements:* For master's, core exams, oral presentations. *Entrance requirements:* For master's, 12 units of course work in education, minimum GPA of 3.0.

Azusa Pacific University, School of Education, Department of Special Education, Program in Special Education and Educational Technology, Azusa, CA 91702-7000. Offers M Ed.

Baldwin Wallace University, Graduate Programs, School of Education, Specialization in Mild/Moderate Educational Needs, Berea, OH 44017-2088. Offers MA Ed. *Accreditation:* NCATE. *Program availability:* Part-time, evening/weekend, 100% online. *Students:* 39 full-time (35 women), 23 part-time (16 women); includes 7 minority (3 Black or African American, non-Hispanic/Latino; 2 Hispanic/Latino; 2 Two or more races, non-Hispanic/Latino). Average age 34. 18 applicants, 28% accepted, 5 enrolled. In 2016, 14 master's awarded. *Degree requirements:* For master's, comprehensive exam, capstone practicum. *Entrance requirements:* For master's, bachelor's degree in field, MAT or minimum GPA of 3.0. Additional exam requirements/recommendations for international students: Required—TOEFL (minimum score 550 paper-based; 79 iBT). *Application deadline:* For fall admission, 8/15 priority date for domestic students; for spring admission, 12/15 priority date for domestic students. Applications are processed on a rolling basis. Application fee: $25. Electronic applications accepted. Application fee is waived when completed online. *Expenses:* $721 per credit hour. *Financial support:* Career-related internships or fieldwork available. Financial award applicants required to submit FAFSA. *Faculty research:* Adult adjustment of individuals formerly identified as having mild/moderate special education needs, professional development of special educators, teacher beliefs and special education, classroom assessment practices. *Unit head:* Dr. Debra Janus, Coordinator, 440-826-8177, Fax: 440-826-3779, E-mail: djanas@bw.edu. *Application contact:* Winifred W. Gerhardt, Director of Transfer, Adult and Graduate Admission, 440-826-2222, Fax: 440-826-3830, E-mail: admission@bw.edu.
Website: http://www.bw.edu/academics/master-of-arts-in-education/maed-mild-moderate/

Ball State University, Graduate School, Teachers College, Department of Educational Studies, Muncie, IN 47306. Offers adult education (MA, Ed D, Certificate), including adult and community education (MA), adult, higher and community education (Ed D); college and university teaching (Certificate); community college leadership (Certificate); community education (Certificate); computer education (Certificate); curriculum and educational technology (MA); diversity studies (Certificate); educational studies (PhD), including educational studies; executive development for public service (MA); middle-level education (Certificate); qualitative research in education (Certificate); secondary education (MA); student affairs administration in higher education (MA), including student affairs administration in higher education. *Accreditation:* NCATE. *Program availability:* Part-time, 100% online, blended/hybrid learning. *Degree requirements:* For doctorate, thesis/dissertation. *Entrance requirements:* For master's, minimum baccalaureate GPA of 2.75 or 3.0 in latter half of baccalauareate; for doctorate, minimum graduate GPA of 3.2. Additional exam requirements/recommendations for international students: Required—TOEFL (minimum score 550 paper-based; 79 iBT), IELTS (minimum score 6.5). Electronic applications accepted.

Ball State University, Graduate School, Teachers College, Department of Special Education, Program in Applied Behavior Analysis, Muncie, IN 47306. Offers applied behavior analysis (MA), including autism. *Program availability:* Part-time, online only, 100% online. *Entrance requirements:* For master's, minimum baccalaureate GPA of 2.75 or 3.0 in latter half of baccalauareate. Additional exam requirements/recommendations for international students: Required—TOEFL (minimum score 550 paper-based; 79 iBT), IELTS (minimum score 6.5). Electronic applications accepted.

Ball State University, Graduate School, Teachers College, Department of Special Education, Program in Special Education, Muncie, IN 47306. Offers special education (MA, Ed D). *Program availability:* Part-time, 100% online, blended/hybrid learning. *Degree requirements:* For doctorate, thesis/dissertation. *Entrance requirements:* For master's, minimum baccalaureate GPA of 2.75 or 3.0 in latter half of baccalauareate; for doctorate, GRE General Test, minimum graduate GPA of 3.2. Additional exam requirements/recommendations for international students: Required—TOEFL (minimum score 550 paper-based; 79 iBT), IELTS (minimum score 6.5). Electronic applications accepted.

Bank Street College of Education, Graduate School, Program in Infant and Family Development and Early Intervention, New York, NY 10025. Offers infant and family development (MS Ed); infant and family early childhood special and general education (MS Ed); infant and family/early childhood special education (Ed M). *Degree requirements:* For master's, thesis. *Entrance requirements:* For master's, interview, essays. Additional exam requirements/recommendations for international students: Required—TOEFL (minimum score 600 paper-based; 100 iBT), IELTS (minimum score 7). Electronic applications accepted. *Faculty research:* Early intervention, early attachment practice in infant and toddler childcare, parenting skills in adolescents.

Bank Street College of Education, Graduate School, Program in Special Education, New York, NY 10025. Offers early childhood special and general education (MS Ed); early childhood special education (Ed M, MS Ed); elementary/childhood special and general education (MS Ed); elementary/childhood special education (MS Ed); elementary/childhood special education certification (Ed M). *Degree requirements:* For master's, thesis. *Entrance requirements:* For master's, interview, essays. Additional exam requirements/recommendations for international students: Required—TOEFL (minimum score 600 paper-based; 100 iBT), IELTS (minimum score 7). Electronic applications accepted. *Faculty research:* Teaching students with disabilities, inclusion, observation and assessment, early intervention, neurodevelopmental assessment, equity and social justice in education.

Barry University, School of Education, Program in Education for Teachers of Students with Hearing Impairments, Miami Shores, FL 33161-6695. Offers MS.

Barry University, School of Education, Program in Exceptional Student Education, Miami Shores, FL 33161-6695. Offers MS, Ed S. *Program availability:* Part-time, evening/weekend. *Degree requirements:* For master's, comprehensive exam; for Ed S, practicum. *Entrance requirements:* For master's, GRE General Test or MAT, minimum GPA of 3.0; for Ed S, GRE General Test, minimum GPA of 3.0. Electronic applications accepted.

Barry University, School of Education, Program in Leadership and Education, Miami Shores, FL 33161-6695. Offers educational technology (PhD); exceptional student education (PhD); higher education administration (PhD); human resource development (PhD); leadership (PhD). *Program availability:* Part-time, evening/weekend. *Degree requirements:* For doctorate, thesis/dissertation. *Entrance requirements:* For doctorate, GRE General Test, minimum GPA of 3.25. Electronic applications accepted.

Bayamón Central University, Graduate Programs, Program in Education, Bayamón, PR 00960-1725. Offers administration and supervision (MA Ed); commercial education (MA Ed); elementary education (K–3) (MA Ed); family counseling (Graduate Certificate); guidance and counseling (MA Ed); pre-elementary teacher (MA Ed); rehabilitation counseling (MA Ed); special education (MA Ed), including attention deficit disorder, education of the autistic, learning disabilities. *Program availability:* Part-time, evening/weekend. *Degree requirements:* For master's, comprehensive exam. *Entrance requirements:* For master's, EXADEP, bachelor's degree in education or related field.

Baylor University, Graduate School, School of Education, Department of Educational Psychology, Waco, TX 76798. Offers applied behavior analysis (MS Ed); educational psychology (MA, MS Ed, PhD); exceptionalities (PhD); gifted and talented studies (MS Ed); learning and development (PhD); measurement (PhD); quantitative methods (MA); school psychology (Ed S). *Accreditation:* NCATE. *Faculty:* 11 full-time (6 women). *Students:* 48 full-time (42 women), 17 part-time (15 women); includes 15 minority (4 Black or African American, non-Hispanic/Latino; 2 Asian, non-Hispanic/Latino; 8 Hispanic/Latino; 1 Two or more races, non-Hispanic/Latino), 2 international. Average age 29. 90 applicants, 33% accepted, 30 enrolled. In 2016, 13 master's, 4 doctorates, 7 other advanced degrees awarded. Terminal master's awarded for partial completion of doctoral program. *Degree requirements:* For master's, thesis optional; for doctorate, comprehensive exam, thesis/dissertation; for Ed S, comprehensive exam, thesis or alternative. *Entrance requirements:* For master's, GRE, minimum GPA of 3.0; for doctorate, GRE General Test, master's degree; for Ed S, GRE General Test. Additional

exam requirements/recommendations for international students: Required—TOEFL (minimum score 550 paper-based; 80 iBT), IELTS (minimum score 6.5). *Application deadline:* For fall admission, 2/1 priority date for domestic and international students. Application fee: $80. Electronic applications accepted. *Expenses: Tuition:* Full-time $28,494; part-time $1583 per credit hour. *Required fees:* $167 per credit hour. Tuition and fees vary according to course load and program. *Financial support:* In 2016–17, 42 students received support, including 20 fellowships with full and partial tuition reimbursements available, 22 research assistantships with full and partial tuition reimbursements available; career-related internships or fieldwork, Federal Work-Study, institutionally sponsored loans, scholarships/grants, health care benefits, tuition waivers (full and partial), unspecified assistantships, and stipends also available. Financial award application deadline: 2/1; financial award applicants required to submit FAFSA. *Faculty research:* Individual differences, quantitative methods, gifted and talented, special education, school psychology, autism, applied behavior analysis, learning, human development. *Total annual research expenditures:* $300,000. *Unit head:* Dr. Terrill F. Saxon, Professor and Chairman, 254-710-6101, E-mail: terrill_saxon@baylor.edu. *Application contact:* Heather Tindle, Office Manager, 254-710-3112, E-mail: heather_tindle@baylor.edu.
Website: http://www.baylor.edu/soe/EDP/

Bay Path University, Program in Clinical Mental Health Counseling, Longmeadow, MA 01106-2292. Offers clinical mental health counseling (MS), including alcohol and drug abuse counseling, early intervention. Program also offered in Sturbridge and Burlington, MA. *Program availability:* Part-time, blended/hybrid learning. *Students:* 85 full-time (78 women), 83 part-time (76 women); includes 43 minority (19 Black or African American, non-Hispanic/Latino; 1 Asian, non-Hispanic/Latino; 17 Hispanic/Latino; 6 Two or more races, non-Hispanic/Latino), 16 international. Average age 31. 75 applicants, 72% accepted, 40 enrolled. In 2016, 21 master's awarded. *Degree requirements:* For master's, 48 course credits plus 12 credit practicum, internship. *Application deadline:* Applications are processed on a rolling basis. Application fee: $45. Electronic applications accepted. Application fee is waived when completed online. *Expenses:* $21,465. *Financial support:* Unspecified assistantships available. Financial award applicants required to submit FAFSA. *Unit head:* Dr. Mark Benander, Director, 413-565-1332, E-mail: mbenander@baypath.edu. *Application contact:* Diane Ranaldi, Dean of Graduate Admissions, 413-565-1332, Fax: 413-565-1250, E-mail: dranaldi@baypath.edu.
Website: http://graduate.baypath.edu/graduate-programs/programs-on-campus/ms-programs/clinical-mental-health

Bay Path University, Program in Education, Longmeadow, MA 01106-2292. Offers MS Ed/Ed S. *Program availability:* Part-time, 100% online. *Students:* 37 full-time (33 women), 124 part-time (104 women); includes 15 minority (6 Black or African American, non-Hispanic/Latino; 1 Asian, non-Hispanic/Latino; 6 Hispanic/Latino; 1 Native Hawaiian or other Pacific Islander, non-Hispanic/Latino; 1 Two or more races, non-Hispanic/Latino). Average age 33. 65 applicants, 68% accepted, 36 enrolled. *Application deadline:* Applications are processed on a rolling basis. Application fee: $45. Electronic applications accepted. Application fee is waived when completed online. *Expenses:* $13,365. *Financial support:* Unspecified assistantships available. Financial award applicants required to submit FAFSA. *Unit head:* Dr. Karen DeAngelis, Program Coordinator, E-mail: kdeangelis@baypath.edu. *Application contact:* Diane Ranaldi, Dean of Graduate Admissions, 413-565-1332, Fax: 413-565-1250, E-mail: dranaldi@baypath.edu.
Website: http://graduate.baypath.edu/Graduate-Programs/Programs-On-Campus/MS-Programs/Education-Special-Education

Bellarmine University, Annsley Frazier Thornton School of Education, Louisville, KY 40205. Offers education and district leadership (Ed D); education and social change (PhD); elementary education (MA Ed, MAT); leadership in higher education (PhD); learning and behavior disorders (MA Ed, MAT); middle grades education (MA Ed, MAT); principalship (Ed S); reading and writing (MA Ed); secondary education (MAT); teacher leadership (MA Ed). *Accreditation:* NCATE. *Program availability:* Part-time, evening/weekend. *Faculty:* 15 full-time (7 women), 44 part-time/adjunct (36 women). *Students:* 39 full-time (28 women), 211 part-time (164 women); includes 46 minority (35 Black or African American, non-Hispanic/Latino; 3 Asian, non-Hispanic/Latino; 5 Hispanic/Latino; 3 Two or more races, non-Hispanic/Latino). Average age 34. In 2016, 66 master's, 3 doctorates, 43 other advanced degrees awarded. *Degree requirements:* For master's, thesis (for some programs); for doctorate, thesis/dissertation. *Entrance requirements:* For master's, GRE, baccalaureate degree from accredited institution; minimum cumulative GPA of 2.75; recommendations from employers, supervisors, or professors attesting to applicant's potential as graduate student; statement of intent to pursue graduate degree; for doctorate, GRE, minimum GPA of 3.5 in all graduate coursework; baccalaureate and master's degrees in education or fields directly relevant to education; three letters of recommendation; two essays (no more than 1,000 words each); interview. Additional exam requirements/recommendations for international students: Required—TOEFL (minimum score 550 paper-based, 68 iBT), IELTS (minimum score 6), or Michigan English Language Assessment Battery. *Application deadline:* For fall admission, 8/1 priority date for domestic and international students; for spring admission, 12/1 priority date for domestic and international students; for summer admission, 4/10 priority date for domestic and international students. Applications are processed on a rolling basis. Application fee: $40. Electronic applications accepted. Tuition and fees vary according to program. *Financial support:* Scholarships/grants available. Financial award applicants required to submit FAFSA. *Faculty research:* Literacy, service-learning, dispositions, educational technology, special education. *Unit head:* Dr. Robert Cooter, Dean, 502-272-8191, Fax: 502-272-8189, E-mail: rcooter@bellarmine.edu. *Application contact:* Sarah Shumway Schuble, Senior Graduate Recruiter, 502-272-8271, Fax: 502-272-8002, E-mail: sshumway@bellarmine.edu.
Website: http://www.bellarmine.edu/education/graduate

Bemidji State University, School of Graduate Studies, Bemidji, MN 56601. Offers biology (MS); education (MS); English (MA, MS); environmental studies (MS); mathematics (MS); mathematics (elementary and middle level education) (MS); special education (M Sp Ed). *Program availability:* Part-time, online learning. *Degree requirements:* For master's, comprehensive exam, thesis (for some programs). *Entrance requirements:* For master's, GRE; GMAT, letters of recommendation, letters of interest. Additional exam requirements/recommendations for international students: Required—TOEFL (minimum score 550 paper-based; 80 iBT). Electronic applications accepted. *Expenses:* Contact institution. *Faculty research:* Human performance, sport, and health: physical education teacher education, continuum models, spiritual health, intellectual health, resiliency, health priorities; psychology: health psychology, college student drinking behavior, micro-aggressions, infant cognition, false memories, leadership assessment; biology: structure and dynamics of forest communities, aquatic and riverine ecology, interaction between animal populations and aquatic environments, cellular motility.

Benedictine University, Graduate Programs, Program in Education, Lisle, IL 60532. Offers curriculum and instruction and collaborative teaching (M Ed); elementary education (MA Ed); leadership and administration (M Ed); reading and literacy (M Ed); secondary education (MA Ed); special education (MA Ed). *Program availability:* Part-time, evening/weekend. *Students:* 17 full-time (16 women), 30 part-time (26 women); includes 2 minority (both Black or African American, non-Hispanic/Latino). 21 applicants, 62% accepted, 8 enrolled. In 2016, 68 master's awarded. *Degree requirements:* For master's, comprehensive exam, thesis (for some programs). *Entrance requirements:* For master's, GRE or MAT. Additional exam requirements/recommendations for international students: Required—TOEFL (minimum score 550 paper-based). *Application deadline:* For fall admission, 9/1 for domestic students; for winter admission, 12/1 for domestic students; for spring admission, 2/15 for domestic students. Applications are processed on a rolling basis. Application fee: $40. Electronic applications accepted. *Expenses:* Contact institution. *Financial support:* Career-related internships or fieldwork and health care benefits available. Support available to part-time students. *Unit head:* MeShelda Jackson, Director, 630-829-6282, E-mail: mjackson@ben.edu. *Application contact:* Kari Gibbons, Associate Vice President, Enrollment Center, 630-829-6200, Fax: 630-829-6584, E-mail: kgibbons@ben.edu.

Bethel University, Graduate School, St. Paul, MN 55112-6999. Offers business administration (MBA); classroom management (Certificate); counseling (MA); international baccalaureate teaching and learning (Certificate); K-12 education (MA); leadership (Ed D); leadership foundations (Certificate); nurse educator (MS, Certificate); nurse-midwifery (MS); physician assistant (MS); special education (MA); strategic leadership (MA); teaching (MA). *Program availability:* Part-time, evening/weekend, 100% online, blended/hybrid learning. *Faculty:* 19 full-time (15 women), 57 part-time/adjunct (37 women). *Students:* 674 full-time (466 women), 378 part-time (256 women); includes 188 minority (94 Black or African American, non-Hispanic/Latino; 3 American Indian or Alaska Native, non-Hispanic/Latino; 43 Asian, non-Hispanic/Latino; 31 Hispanic/Latino; 1 Native Hawaiian or other Pacific Islander, non-Hispanic/Latino; 16 Two or more races, non-Hispanic/Latino), 33 international. *Degree requirements:* For master's, comprehensive exam (for some programs), thesis (for some programs); for doctorate, comprehensive exam, thesis/dissertation. *Entrance requirements:* Additional exam requirements/recommendations for international students: Required—TOEFL (minimum score 550 paper-based, 80 iBT) or IELTS. *Application deadline:* Applications are processed on a rolling basis. Application fee: $0. Electronic applications accepted. *Expenses:* Contact institution. *Financial support:* Teaching assistantships, career-related internships or fieldwork, and scholarships/grants available. Support available to part-time students. Financial award applicants required to submit FAFSA. *Unit head:* Dick Crombie, Vice-President/Dean, 651-635-8000, Fax: 651-635-8004, E-mail: gs@bethel.edu. *Application contact:* Director of Admissions, 651-635-8000, Fax: 651-635-8004, E-mail: gs@bethel.edu.
Website: https://www.bethel.edu/graduate/

Binghamton University, State University of New York, Graduate School, Graduate School of Education, Program in Special Education, Binghamton, NY 13902-6000. Offers MS Ed. *Accreditation:* TEAC. *Program availability:* Part-time, evening/weekend. *Students:* 28 full-time (26 women), 24 part-time (16 women); includes 3 minority (1 Black or African American, non-Hispanic/Latino; 1 Asian, non-Hispanic/Latino; 1 Two or more races, non-Hispanic/Latino). Average age 25. 30 applicants, 83% accepted, 19 enrolled. In 2016, 28 master's awarded. *Degree requirements:* For master's, portfolio. *Entrance requirements:* For master's, GRE General Test, teaching certification. Additional exam requirements/recommendations for international students: Required—TOEFL (minimum score 550 paper-based; 80 iBT). *Application deadline:* For fall admission, 2/1 priority date for domestic and international students; for spring admission, 10/15 priority date for domestic and international students. Application fee: $75. Electronic applications accepted. *Financial support:* In 2016–17, 2 students received support, including 1 fellowship with full tuition reimbursement available (averaging $4,500 per year); career-related internships or fieldwork, Federal Work-Study, institutionally sponsored loans, and unspecified assistantships also available. Support available to part-time students. Financial award applicants required to submit FAFSA. *Unit head:* Dr. Susan Strehle, Dean, 607-777-7329, E-mail: sstrehle@binghamton.edu. *Application contact:* Ben Balkaya, Assistant Dean and Director, 607-777-2151, Fax: 607-777-2501, E-mail: balkaya@binghamton.edu.

Biola University, School of Education, La Mirada, CA 90639-0001. Offers curriculum and instruction (Certificate); early childhood (MA Ed, MAT); multiple subject (MAT); single subject (MAT); special education (MA Ed, MAT, Certificate). *Program availability:* Part-time, evening/weekend, online learning. *Entrance requirements:* For master's, CBEST, CSET, GRE (waived if cumulative GPA is 3.5 or above or if CBEST and all CSET subtests are passed). Additional exam requirements/recommendations for international students: Required—TOEFL (minimum score 100 iBT). Electronic applications accepted. *Faculty research:* Early childhood education, elementary education, special education, curriculum development, teacher preparation.

Bloomsburg University of Pennsylvania, School of Graduate Studies, College of Education, Department of Exceptionality Programs, Program in Special Education, Bloomsburg, PA 17815-1301. Offers M Ed, MS, Certificate. *Accreditation:* NCATE. *Faculty:* 9 full-time (6 women), 3 part-time/adjunct (all women). *Students:* 17 full-time (12 women), 29 part-time (24 women); includes 4 minority (2 Black or African American, non-Hispanic/Latino; 1 Asian, non-Hispanic/Latino; 1 Two or more races, non-Hispanic/Latino). Average age 29. 19 applicants, 58% accepted, 10 enrolled. In 2016, 9 master's awarded. *Degree requirements:* For master's, thesis, minimum QPA of 3.0, practicum. *Entrance requirements:* For master's, teaching certificate, minimum QPA of 2.8, letter of intent, 2 letters of recommendation, interview, professional liability insurance, recent TB screening. Additional exam requirements/recommendations for international students: Required—TOEFL (minimum score 550 paper-based), IELTS. *Application deadline:* Applications are processed on a rolling basis. Application fee: $35 ($60 for international students). Electronic applications accepted. *Expenses:* Tuition, state resident: full-time $9660; part-time $483 per credit. Tuition, nonresident: full-time $14,500; part-time $725 per credit. *Required fees:* $2410; $107 per credit. $75 per term. Tuition and fees vary according to course load, degree level and program. *Financial support:* Federal Work-Study and unspecified assistantships available. Financial award applicants required to submit FAFSA. *Unit head:* Dr. Robin Drogan, Exceptionalities Program Coordinator, 570-389-4877, Fax: 570-389-3980, E-mail: rdrogan@bloomu.edu. *Application contact:* Jennifer Kessler, Administrative Assistant, 570-389-4015, Fax: 570-389-3054, E-mail: jkessler@bloomu.edu.
Website: http://www.bloomu.edu/gradschool/special-education

Bluffton University, Programs in Education, Bluffton, OH 45817. Offers faith-based education (MA Ed); intervention specialist (MA Ed); leadership (MA Ed); reading (MA Ed). *Accreditation:* NCATE. *Program availability:* Part-time. *Faculty:* 6 full-time (3 women), 1 part-time/adjunct (0 women). *Students:* 9 full-time (all women), 10 part-time (9 women); includes 1 minority (Black or African American, non-Hispanic/Latino). Average age 34. 14 applicants, 50% accepted, 6 enrolled. In 2016, 1 master's awarded. *Degree requirements:* For master's, action research project, public presentation. *Entrance requirements:* For master's, PHAXIS I, bachelor's degree, minimum GPA of 3.0. Additional exam requirements/recommendations for international students: Required—TOEFL. *Application deadline:* For fall admission, 8/15 priority date for domestic students, 6/15 priority date for international students; for spring admission, 12/15 priority date for domestic students, 9/15 priority date for international students. Applications are processed on a rolling basis. Application fee: $25. Electronic

applications accepted. Application fee is waived when completed online. *Expenses:* $453 per credit. *Financial support:* Health care benefits available. Support available to part-time students. Financial award application deadline: 9/15; financial award applicants required to submit FAFSA. *Faculty research:* Mentoring. *Unit head:* Dr. Gayle M. Trollinger, Director of Graduate Programs in Education, 419-358-3341, E-mail: trollingerg@bluffton.edu. *Application contact:* Nancey Schortgen, Program Representative, 419-358-3202, Fax: 419-358-3399, E-mail: schortgenn@bluffton.edu.
Website: http://www.bluffton.edu/grad/

Bob Jones University, Graduate Programs, Greenville, SC 29614. Offers accountancy (MS); Bible (MA); Bible translation (MA); Biblical studies (Certificate); broadcast management (MS); business administration (MBA); church history (MA, PhD); church ministries (MA); church music (MM); cinema and video production (MA); counseling (MS); curriculum and instruction (Ed D); divinity (M Div); dramatic production (MA); educational leadership (MS, Ed D, Ed S); elementary education (M Ed, MAT); English (M Ed, MA, MAT); fine arts (MA); graphic design (MA); history (M Ed, MA); illustration (MA); interpretative speech (MA); mathematics (M Ed, MAT); medical missions (Certificate); ministry (MM, D Min); multi-categorical special education (M Ed, MAT); music (M Ed); New Testament interpretation (PhD); Old Testament interpretation (PhD); orchestral instrument performance (MM); organ performance (MM); pastoral studies (MA); personnel services (MS, Ed S); piano pedagogy (MM); piano performance (MM); platform arts (MA); radio and television broadcasting (MS); rhetoric and public address (MA); secondary education (M Ed); studio art (MA); teaching Bible (MA); theology (MA, PhD); voice performance (MM); youth ministries (MA); M Div/MM.

Boise State University, College of Education, Department of Early and Special Education, Boise, ID 83725-1725. Offers early and special education (M Ed). *Accreditation:* NCATE. *Program availability:* Part-time. *Faculty:* 14. *Students:* 29 full-time (27 women), 13 part-time (10 women); includes 4 minority (2 Asian, non-Hispanic/Latino; 1 Hispanic/Latino; 1 Native Hawaiian or other Pacific Islander, non-Hispanic/Latino). Average age 38. 18 applicants, 33% accepted, 3 enrolled. In 2016, 10 master's awarded. *Degree requirements:* For master's, thesis optional. *Entrance requirements:* For master's, minimum GPA of 3.0. Additional exam requirements/recommendations for international students: Required—TOEFL (minimum score 587 paper-based; 95 iBT), IELTS (minimum score 6.5). *Application deadline:* For fall admission, 3/31 for domestic and international students. Application fee: $65 ($95 for international students). Electronic applications accepted. *Expenses:* Tuition, state resident: full-time $6058; part-time $358 per credit hour. Tuition, nonresident: full-time $20,108; part-time $608 per credit hour. *Required fees:* $2108. Tuition and fees vary according to program. *Financial support:* In 2016–17, 4 students received support. Scholarships/grants and unspecified assistantships available. Financial award application deadline: 3/31; financial award applicants required to submit FAFSA. *Unit head:* Dr. Deb Carter, Department Chair, 208-426-2804, E-mail: debcarter@boisestate.edu. *Application contact:* Dr. Carrie Semmelroth, Graduate Coordinator, 208-426-2818, E-mail: carriesemmelroth@boisestate.edu.
Website: http://education.boisestate.edu/spedecs/

Boston College, Lynch School of Education, Program in Special Needs: Moderate Disabilities, Chestnut Hill, MA 02467-3800. Offers M Ed, CAES. *Accreditation:* TEAC. *Program availability:* Part-time, evening/weekend. *Faculty:* 4 full-time (1 woman). *Students:* 17 full-time (all women), 15 part-time (13 women); includes 6 minority (1 Black or African American, non-Hispanic/Latino; 3 Asian, non-Hispanic/Latino; 1 Hispanic/Latino; 1 Two or more races, non-Hispanic/Latino). Average age 23. 13 applicants, 62% accepted, 1 enrolled. In 2016, 35 master's awarded. *Degree requirements:* For master's and CAES, comprehensive exam. *Entrance requirements:* For master's, GRE General Test or MAT, general licensure at the elementary or secondary level; for CAES, GRE General Test or MAT. Additional exam requirements/recommendations for international students: Required—TOEFL (minimum score 100 iBT). *Application deadline:* For fall admission, 12/1 priority date for domestic and international students; for spring admission, 11/1 priority date for domestic and international students. Application fee: $65. Electronic applications accepted. Tuition and fees vary according to program. *Financial support:* Fellowships with tuition reimbursements, research assistantships with tuition reimbursements, teaching assistantships with tuition reimbursements, Federal Work-Study, scholarships/grants, and tuition waivers available. Financial award applicants required to submit FAFSA. *Unit head:* Dr. Susan Bruce, Chairperson, 617-552-4214, Fax: 617-552-0398. *Application contact:* Kimberly Rose, Graduate Admission Assistant, 617-552-4214, Fax: 617-552-0398, E-mail: roseki@bc.edu.

Boston College, Lynch School of Education, Program in Special Needs: Severe Disabilities, Chestnut Hill, MA 02467-3800. Offers M Ed, CAES. *Accreditation:* TEAC. *Program availability:* Part-time, evening/weekend. *Faculty:* 2 full-time (both women). *Students:* 6 full-time (5 women), 16 part-time (13 women); includes 2 minority (1 Asian, non-Hispanic/Latino; 1 Hispanic/Latino), 1 international. Average age 24. 14 applicants, 79% accepted, 7 enrolled. In 2016, 15 master's awarded. *Degree requirements:* For master's, comprehensive exam. *Entrance requirements:* For master's, GRE General Test or MAT. Additional exam requirements/recommendations for international students: Required—TOEFL (minimum score 100 iBT). *Application deadline:* For fall admission, 12/1 priority date for domestic and international students; for spring admission, 11/1 priority date for domestic and international students. Application fee: $65. Electronic applications accepted. Tuition and fees vary according to program. *Financial support:* Fellowships with tuition reimbursements, research assistantships with tuition reimbursements, teaching assistantships with tuition reimbursements, Federal Work-Study, scholarships/grants, and tuition waivers (full and partial) available. Financial award applicants required to submit FAFSA. *Unit head:* Dr. Susan Bruce, Chairperson, 617-552-4214, Fax: 617-552-0398. *Application contact:* Kimberly Rose, Graduate Admission Assistant, 617-552-4214, Fax: 617-552-0398, E-mail: roseki@bc.edu.

Bowie State University, Graduate Programs, Program in Special Education, Bowie, MD 20715-9465. Offers M Ed. *Accreditation:* NCATE. *Program availability:* Part-time, evening/weekend. *Degree requirements:* For master's, comprehensive exam, thesis optional, research paper. *Entrance requirements:* For master's, teaching experience, 3 professional letters of recommendation. Electronic applications accepted.

Bowling Green State University, Graduate College, College of Education and Human Development, School of Intervention Services, Program in Special Education, Bowling Green, OH 43403. Offers assistive technology (M Ed); autism spectrum disorders (M Ed); general special education (M Ed); intervention specialist: mild/moderate disabilities (M Ed); intervention specialist: moderate/intensive disabilities (M Ed); secondary transition/transition-to-work (M Ed). *Accreditation:* NCATE. *Program availability:* Part-time. *Degree requirements:* For master's, thesis or alternative. *Entrance requirements:* For master's, GRE General Test. Additional exam requirements/recommendations for international students: Required—TOEFL. *Application deadline:* For fall admission, 3/1 priority date for domestic students. Applications are processed on a rolling basis. Application fee: $30. Electronic applications accepted. *Financial support:* Research assistantships with full tuition reimbursements, teaching assistantships with full tuition reimbursements, Federal Work-Study, and unspecified assistantships available. Financial award applicants required to submit FAFSA. *Faculty research:* Reading and special populations, deafness, early childhood, gifted and talented, behavior disorders. *Unit head:* William Morrison, Director, 419-372-7281, E-mail: fmorris@bgsu.edu. *Application contact:* William Morrison, Director, 419-372-7281, E-mail: fmorris@bgsu.edu.

Brandman University, School of Education, Irvine, CA 92618. Offers education (MA); elementary education (MAT); organizational leadership (Ed D); school counseling (MA); secondary education (MAT); special education (MA). *Expenses:* *Tuition:* Full-time $14,880; part-time $620 per credit hour. Tuition and fees vary according to degree level and program. *Unit head:* Dr. Christine G. Zeppos, Dean, 949-341-9948, E-mail: zeppos@brandman.edu.
Website: http://www.brandman.edu/education/

Brandon University, Faculty of Education, Brandon, MB R7A 6A9, Canada. Offers curriculum and instruction (M Ed, Diploma); educational administration (M Ed, Diploma); guidance and counseling (M Ed, Diploma); special education (M Ed, Diploma). *Degree requirements:* For master's, thesis. *Entrance requirements:* For master's, minimum GPA of 3.0, teaching certificate or equivalent. Additional exam requirements/recommendations for international students: Required—TOEFL. *Faculty research:* Comparative education, environmental studies, parent/school council.

Brenau University, Sydney O. Smith Graduate School, College of Education, Gainesville, GA 30501. Offers early childhood (Ed S); early childhood education (M Ed, MAT); middle grades (Ed S); middle grades education (M Ed, MAT); secondary education (MAT); special education (M Ed, MAT). *Accreditation:* NCATE. *Program availability:* Part-time, evening/weekend, online learning. *Degree requirements:* For master's, thesis optional, comprehensive exam or applied research project, effective portfolio; for Ed S, thesis, applied research project. *Entrance requirements:* For master's, GRE, MAT, interview, minimum GPA of 3.0, 3 references, writing samples; for Ed S, GRE, MAT, master's degree, minimum GPA of 3.0, writing sample, letters of reference. Additional exam requirements/recommendations for international students: Required—TOEFL (minimum score 500 paper-based; 61 iBT); Recommended—IELTS (minimum score 5). Electronic applications accepted. *Expenses:* Contact institution.

Bridgewater State University, College of Graduate Studies, College of Education and Allied Studies, Department of Special Education, Bridgewater, MA 02325. Offers M Ed. *Accreditation:* NCATE. *Program availability:* Part-time, evening/weekend. *Entrance requirements:* For master's, GRE General Test or Massachusetts Test for Educator Licensure.

Brigham Young University, Graduate Studies, David O. McKay School of Education, Department of Counseling Psychology and Special Education, Provo, UT 84602. Offers counseling psychology (PhD); school psychology (Ed S); special education (MS). *Program availability:* Part-time, evening/weekend. *Faculty:* 13 full-time (3 women), 9 part-time/adjunct (3 women). *Students:* 66 full-time (45 women), 15 part-time (14 women); includes 8 minority (1 Black or African American, non-Hispanic/Latino; 2 American Indian or Alaska Native, non-Hispanic/Latino; 4 Hispanic/Latino; 1 Native Hawaiian or other Pacific Islander, non-Hispanic/Latino), 4 international. Average age 29. 73 applicants, 42% accepted, 27 enrolled. In 2016, 2 master's, 7 doctorates, 12 other advanced degrees awarded. *Degree requirements:* For master's and Ed S, comprehensive exam, thesis; for doctorate, comprehensive exam, thesis/dissertation. *Entrance requirements:* For master's, GRE General Test or MAT, minimum cumulative GPA of 3.0 in undergraduate coursework; for doctorate and Ed S, GRE General Test, minimum cumulative GPA of 3.0 in undergraduate coursework. Additional exam requirements/recommendations for international students: Required—TOEFL (minimum score 580 paper-based; 85 iBT), IELTS (minimum score 7). *Application deadline:* For fall admission, 1/15 for domestic and international students. Application fee: $50. Electronic applications accepted. *Expenses:* Contact institution. *Financial support:* In 2016–17, 51 students received support, including 51 research assistantships (averaging $9,000 per year); institutionally sponsored loans and tuition waivers (partial) also available. Financial award application deadline: 3/31. *Faculty research:* Autism, religious and spiritual values in counseling, school-based crisis intervention, behavior interventions in MTSS framework, counseling and psychotherapy process and outcomes. *Unit head:* Dr. Lane Fischer, Department Chair, 801-422-3857, E-mail: lane_fischer@byu.edu. *Application contact:* Diane E. Hancock, Executive Secretary, 801-422-3859, E-mail: diane_hancock@byu.edu.
Website: http://education.byu.edu/cpse/

Brooklyn College of the City University of New York, School of Education, Program in Special Education, Brooklyn, NY 11210-2889. Offers autism spectrum disorders (AC); teacher of students with disabilities (MS Ed), including adolescence education, childhood education, early childhood education. *Program availability:* Part-time. *Entrance requirements:* For master's, LAST, interview; previous course work in education and psychology; minimum GPA of 3.0 in education, 2.8 overall; resume, 2 letters of recommendation; essay. Additional exam requirements/recommendations for international students: Required—TOEFL (minimum score 500 paper-based; 61 iBT). Electronic applications accepted. *Faculty research:* School reform, conflict resolution, curriculum for inclusive settings, urban issues in special education.

Buffalo State College, State University of New York, The Graduate School, Faculty of Applied Science and Education, Department of Exceptional Education, Programs in Special Education, Buffalo, NY 14222-1095. Offers special education (MS Ed); special education: adolescents (MS Ed); special education: childhood (MS Ed); special education: early childhood (MS Ed). *Accreditation:* NCATE. *Program availability:* Part-time, evening/weekend. *Degree requirements:* For master's, thesis or project. *Entrance requirements:* For master's, minimum GPA of 2.5. Additional exam requirements/recommendations for international students: Required—TOEFL (minimum score 550 paper-based).

Butler University, College of Education, Indianapolis, IN 46208-3485. Offers alternative special education licensure (Certificate); educational administration (MS); effective teaching and leadership (MS); international baccalaureate teaching and learning (Certificate); licensed mental health counselor (Certificate); school counseling (MS); teachers of the visually impaired (Certificate). *Accreditation:* ACA; NCATE. *Program availability:* Part-time. *Faculty:* 13 full-time (10 women), 5 part-time/adjunct (4 women). *Students:* 9 full-time (7 women), 119 part-time (85 women); includes 14 minority (10 Black or African American, non-Hispanic/Latino; 1 Asian, non-Hispanic/Latino; 2 Hispanic/Latino; 1 Two or more races, non-Hispanic/Latino). Average age 32. 79 applicants, 76% accepted, 63 enrolled. In 2016, 42 master's, 30 other advanced degrees awarded. *Entrance requirements:* For master's, GRE (minimum score 291) or MAT (minimum score 396) unless undergraduate GPA is a 3.0 or higher, two letters of recommendation, transcripts, interview, professional resume. Additional exam requirements/recommendations for international students: Required—TOEFL (minimum score 550 paper-based; 79 iBT), IELTS (minimum score 6). *Application deadline:* For fall admission, 2/1 for domestic and international students; for spring admission, 11/1 for domestic and international students; for summer admission, 4/1 for domestic and international students. Applications are processed on a rolling basis. Application fee: $0. Electronic applications accepted. *Expenses:* Contact institution. *Financial support:* In 2016–17, 60 students received support. Scholarships/grants and unspecified assistantships available. Financial award application deadline: 7/15; financial award applicants required to submit FAFSA. *Faculty research:* Principals role in school improvement, leadership and school climate, retention of teachers in special education,

the neuro-diversity brain, school counseling intervention. *Unit head:* Dr. Ena Shelley, Dean, 317-940-9752, Fax: 317-940-6481. *Application contact:* Diane Dubord, Graduate Student Services Specialist, 317-940-8100, Fax: 317-940-8250, E-mail: ddubord@butler.edu.
Website: https://www.butler.edu/coe/graduate-programs

Caldwell University, Graduate Studies, Division of Education, Caldwell, NJ 07006-6195. Offers curriculum and instruction (MA); education (Ed D, Postbaccalaureate Certificate); educational administration (MA); learning disabilities teacher-consultant (Post-Master's Certificate); literacy instruction (MA); principal (Post-Master's Certificate); reading specialist (Post-Master's Certificate); special education (MA), including special education, teaching of students with disabilities, teaching of students with disabilities and learning disabilities teacher-consultant; superintendent (Post-Master's Certificate); supervisor (Post-Master's Certificate). *Program availability:* Part-time, evening/weekend. *Degree requirements:* For master's, comprehensive exam (for some programs). *Entrance requirements:* For master's, PRAXIS, 3 years of work experience, prior teaching certification. Additional exam requirements/recommendations for international students: Required—TOEFL (minimum score 580 paper-based). Electronic applications accepted. *Faculty research:* Curriculum and instruction, secondary education, special education, education and technology.

California Baptist University, Program in Education, Riverside, CA 92504-3206. Offers educational leadership (MS); educational leadership for faith-based institutions (MS); educational leadership for public institutions (MS); educational technology (MS); instructional computer applications (MS); international education (MS); leadership and adult learning (MS); leadership and organizational studies (MS); online teaching and learning (MS); reading (MS); science education (MA); special education in mild/moderate disabilities (MS); special education in moderate/severe disabilities (MS); teacher leadership (MS); teaching (MS); teaching and learning (MS). *Program availability:* Part-time, evening/weekend, 100% online, blended/hybrid learning. *Faculty:* 20 full-time (8 women), 11 part-time/adjunct (7 women). *Students:* 191 full-time (148 women), 234 part-time (178 women); includes 194 minority (23 Black or African American, non-Hispanic/Latino; 5 American Indian or Alaska Native, non-Hispanic/Latino; 15 Asian, non-Hispanic/Latino; 131 Hispanic/Latino; 4 Native Hawaiian or other Pacific Islander, non-Hispanic/Latino; 16 Two or more races, non-Hispanic/Latino), 2 international. Average age 31. 277 applicants, 61% accepted, 150 enrolled. In 2016, 280 master's awarded. *Degree requirements:* For master's, comprehensive exam, project, or thesis. *Entrance requirements:* For master's, minimum undergraduate GPA of 2.75; 500-word essay; three letters of recommendation; two prerequisite courses completed with minimum C grade. Additional exam requirements/recommendations for international students: Required—TOEFL (minimum score 80 iBT). *Application deadline:* For fall admission, 8/1 priority date for domestic students, 7/1 for international students; for spring admission, 12/1 priority date for domestic students, 11/1 for international students. Applications are processed on a rolling basis. Application fee: $45. Electronic applications accepted. *Expenses:* Contact institution. *Financial support:* In 2016–17, 162 students received support. Federal Work-Study and scholarships/grants available. Financial award applicants required to submit CSS PROFILE or FAFSA. *Faculty research:* Leadership development, complexity theory, faith and learning, special education, social and philosophical contexts of education. *Unit head:* Dr. John Shoup, Dean, School of Education, 951-343-4516, E-mail: jshoup@calbaptist.edu.
Website: http://www.calbaptist.edu/mastersined/

California Lutheran University, Graduate Studies, Graduate School of Education, Thousand Oaks, CA 91360-2787. Offers counseling and guidance (MS), including college student personnel, counseling and guidance; educational leadership (MA, Ed D), including educational leadership (K-12) (Ed D), higher education leadership (Ed D); special education (MS); teacher leadership (M Ed); teaching (M Ed). *Accreditation:* NCATE. *Program availability:* Part-time, evening/weekend. *Faculty:* 23 full-time (17 women), 39 part-time/adjunct (26 women). *Students:* 518 full-time (411 women), 79 part-time (67 women); includes 252 minority (12 Black or African American, non-Hispanic/Latino; 3 American Indian or Alaska Native, non-Hispanic/Latino; 17 Asian, non-Hispanic/Latino; 108 Hispanic/Latino; 1 Native Hawaiian or other Pacific Islander, non-Hispanic/Latino; 111 Two or more races, non-Hispanic/Latino), 14 international. Average age 35. 319 applicants, 74% accepted, 192 enrolled. In 2016, 93 master's, 13 doctorates awarded. *Degree requirements:* For master's, comprehensive exam or thesis; for doctorate, thesis/dissertation. *Entrance requirements:* For master's, GRE General Test, interview, minimum GPA of 3.0. *Application deadline:* For fall admission, 7/1 priority date for domestic students; for spring admission, 11/1 priority date for domestic students; for summer admission, 4/1 priority date for domestic students. Applications are processed on a rolling basis. Application fee: $50. Electronic applications accepted. *Unit head:* Dr. Michael Hillis, Dean, 805-493-3421. *Application contact:* 805-493-3325, Fax: 805-493-3861, E-mail: clugrad@callutheran.edu.

California State University, Bakersfield, Division of Graduate Studies, School of Social Sciences and Education, Program in Special Education, Bakersfield, CA 93311. Offers MA. *Accreditation:* NCATE. *Degree requirements:* For master's, thesis or alternative, project or culminating exam. *Entrance requirements:* For master's, 3 letters of recommendation, minimum GPA of 2.67, interview. *Application deadline:* Applications are processed on a rolling basis. Application fee: $55. *Expenses:* Tuition, state resident: full-time $2246; part-time $1302 per semester. *Unit head:* Dr. Yeunjoo Lee, Graduate Coordinator, 661-654-3055, Fax: 661-654-2479, E-mail: ylee@csub.edu. *Application contact:* Julia Bavier, Admissions Advisor, 661-654-2479, E-mail: jbavier@csub.edu.
Website: https://www.csub.edu/specialed/index.html

California State University, Chico, Office of Graduate Studies, College of Communication and Education, School of Education, Chico, CA 95929-0722. Offers curriculum and instruction (MA); teaching English learners and special education advising patterns (MA), including special education, teaching English learners. *Program availability:* Part-time. *Faculty:* 26 full-time (20 women), 48 part-time/adjunct (35 women). *Students:* 45 full-time (33 women), 30 part-time (23 women); includes 26 minority (1 Black or African American, non-Hispanic/Latino; 4 Asian, non-Hispanic/Latino; 16 Hispanic/Latino; 1 Native Hawaiian or other Pacific Islander, non-Hispanic/Latino; 4 Two or more races, non-Hispanic/Latino). 29 applicants, 69% accepted, 16 enrolled. In 2016, 69 master's awarded. *Degree requirements:* For master's, thesis or project and comprehensive exam. *Entrance requirements:* For master's, writing assessment, two letters of recommendation, statement of purpose. Additional exam requirements/recommendations for international students: Required—TOEFL (minimum score 550 paper-based; 80 iBT), IELTS (minimum score 6.5), PTE (minimum score 59). *Application deadline:* For fall admission, 3/1 priority date for domestic students, 3/1 for international students; for spring admission, 9/15 priority date for domestic students, 9/15 for international students. Application fee: $55. Electronic applications accepted. *Financial support:* Fellowships, career-related internships or fieldwork, scholarships/grants, and stipends available. Financial award application deadline: 3/1; financial award applicants required to submit FAFSA. *Unit head:* Dr. Deborah Summers, Director, 530-898-6421, Fax: 530-898-6177, E-mail: educ@csuchico.edu. *Application contact:* Judy L. Morris, Graduate Admission Coordinator, 530-898-5416, Fax: 530-898-3342, E-mail: jlmorris@csuchico.edu.
Website: http://www.csuchico.edu/soe/

California State University, Dominguez Hills, College of Education, Division of Teacher Education, Program in Special Education, Carson, CA 90747-0001. Offers early childhood special education (MA); mild/moderate disabilities (MA); moderate/severe disabilities (MA). *Program availability:* Part-time, evening/weekend. *Degree requirements:* For master's, comprehensive exam, thesis or alternative. *Entrance requirements:* For master's, minimum GPA of 2.75 in last 60 units, 3 letters of recommendation. Additional exam requirements/recommendations for international students: Required—TOEFL.

California State University, East Bay, Office of Graduate Studies, College of Education and Allied Studies, Department of Educational Psychology, Special Education Program, Hayward, CA 94542-3000. Offers mild-moderate disabilities (MS); moderate-severe disabilities (MS). *Accreditation:* NCATE. *Students:* 19 full-time (16 women), 16 part-time (all women); includes 10 minority (1 Black or African American, non-Hispanic/Latino; 4 Asian, non-Hispanic/Latino; 5 Hispanic/Latino). Average age 32. 25 applicants, 84% accepted, 5 enrolled. In 2016, 5 master's awarded. *Degree requirements:* For master's, project or thesis. *Entrance requirements:* For master's, GRE or MAT, interview, minimum GPA of 2.5 during previous 2 years of course work. Additional exam requirements/recommendations for international students: Required—TOEFL (minimum score 550 paper-based). *Application deadline:* For fall admission, 6/30 for domestic and international students. Application fee: $55. Electronic applications accepted. *Financial support:* Career-related internships or fieldwork, Federal Work-Study, and institutionally sponsored loans available. Support available to part-time students. Financial award application deadline: 3/2; financial award applicants required to submit FAFSA. *Unit head:* Dr. Jack Davis, Chair, Educational Psychology, 510-885-3052, E-mail: jack.davis@csueastbay.edu. *Application contact:* Prof. Linda Smetana, Graduate Coordinator, 510-885-4489, Fax: 510-885-4642, E-mail: linda.smetana@csueastbay.edu.
Website: http://www20.csueastbay.edu/ceas/departments/epsy/

California State University, Fresno, Division of Research and Graduate Studies, Kremen School of Education and Human Development, Department of Literacy, Early, Bilingual, and Special Education, Fresno, CA 93740-8027. Offers education (MA), including early childhood education, reading/language arts; special education (MA). *Accreditation:* NCATE. *Program availability:* Part-time, evening/weekend. *Degree requirements:* For master's, thesis or alternative. *Entrance requirements:* For master's, GRE General Test, MAT, minimum GPA of 2.75. Additional exam requirements/recommendations for international students: Required—TOEFL. *Application deadline:* For fall admission, 5/1 for domestic and international students; for spring admission, 10/1 for domestic and international students. Applications are processed on a rolling basis. Application fee: $55. Electronic applications accepted. *Financial support:* Career-related internships or fieldwork, Federal Work-Study, scholarships/grants, and research awards available. Support available to part-time students. Financial award application deadline: 3/1; financial award applicants required to submit FAFSA. *Faculty research:* Reading recovery, monitoring/tutoring programs, character and academics, professional ethics, low-performing partnership schools. *Unit head:* Dr. Laura Alamillo, Chair, 559-278-0250, Fax: 559-278-0107. *Application contact:* Dr. Monica Billen, Coordinator, Early Childhood Education, 559-278-0267, E-mail: mbillen@csufresno.edu.
Website: http://www.fresnostate.edu/kremen/departments/lebse.html

California State University, Fullerton, Graduate Studies, College of Education, Department of Special Education, Fullerton, CA 92834-9480. Offers MS. *Accreditation:* NCATE. *Program availability:* Part-time. *Degree requirements:* For master's, comprehensive exam, project or thesis. *Entrance requirements:* For master's, minimum GPA of 2.75. Application fee: $55. *Expenses:* Tuition, state resident: full-time $3369; part-time $1953 per unit. Tuition, nonresident: full-time $3915; part-time $2499 per unit. Tuition and fees vary according to course load, degree level and program. *Financial support:* Career-related internships or fieldwork, Federal Work-Study, institutionally sponsored loans, and scholarships/grants available. Support available to part-time students. Financial award application deadline: 3/1; financial award applicants required to submit FAFSA. *Unit head:* Dr. Melinda Pierson, Chair, 657-278-4711. *Application contact:* Admissions/Applications, 657-278-2371.

California State University, Long Beach, Graduate Studies, College of Education, Department of Advanced Studies in Education and Counseling, Long Beach, CA 90840. Offers counseling (MS), including marriage and family therapy, school counseling, student development in higher education; education (MA, Ed D); educational administration (MA, Ed D); educational psychology (MA); special education (MS). *Program availability:* Part-time, evening/weekend. *Entrance requirements:* For master's, GRE General Test, minimum GPA of 2.75. *Application deadline:* For fall admission, 3/1 for domestic students. Applications are processed on a rolling basis. Application fee: $55. Electronic applications accepted. *Financial support:* Federal Work-Study, institutionally sponsored loans, and scholarships/grants available. Financial award application deadline: 3/2. *Unit head:* Dr. Hiromi Masunaga, Chair, 562-985-4517, E-mail: asec@csulb.edu.

California State University, Los Angeles, Graduate Studies, Charter College of Education, Division of Special Education and Counseling, Los Angeles, CA 90032-8530. Offers counseling (MS), including applied behavior analysis, community college counseling, rehabilitation counseling, school counseling, school psychology; special education (MA, PhD). *Accreditation:* ACA. *Program availability:* Part-time, evening/weekend. *Entrance requirements:* For master's, minimum GPA of 2.75 in last 90 units of course work, teaching certificate. Additional exam requirements/recommendations for international students: Required—TOEFL (minimum score 500 paper-based). Electronic applications accepted.

California State University, Northridge, Graduate Studies, Michael D. Eisner College of Education, Department of Special Education, Northridge, CA 91330. Offers early childhood special education (MA); education of the deaf and hard of hearing (MA); educational therapy (MA); mild/moderate disabilities (MA); moderate/severe disabilities (MA). *Accreditation:* NCATE. *Faculty:* 14 full-time (1 woman), 22 part-time/adjunct (7 women). *Students:* 24 full-time (21 women), 77 part-time (66 women); includes 45 minority (4 Black or African American, non-Hispanic/Latino; 4 Asian, non-Hispanic/Latino; 35 Hispanic/Latino; 2 Two or more races, non-Hispanic/Latino), 7 international. Average age 35. 76 applicants, 61% accepted, 27 enrolled. *Entrance requirements:* For master's, GRE General Test (if cumulative undergraduate GPA less than 3.0). Additional exam requirements/recommendations for international students: Required—TOEFL. *Application deadline:* For fall admission, 11/30 for domestic students. Application fee: $55. *Expenses:* Tuition, state resident: full-time $4152. *Financial support:* Application deadline: 3/1. *Faculty research:* Teacher training, classroom aide training. *Unit head:* Dr. Kathryn Peckham-Hardin, Chair, 818-677-2596. *Application contact:* Dr. Ellen Schneiderman, Graduate Studies Coordinator, 818-677-2649.
Website: http://www.csun.edu/eisner-education/special-education

California State University, Sacramento, Office of Graduate Studies, College of Education, Graduate and Professional Studies in Education, Sacramento, CA 95819. Offers child development (MA); counseling (MS); curriculum and instruction (MA); education (Ed D); education leadership and policy studies (MA), including higher education, PreK-12; educational technology (MA); gender equity (MA); language and literacy (MA); multicultural education (MA); school psychology (MA); special education

(MA); workforce development advocacy (MA). *Program availability:* Part-time. *Students:* 446 full-time (335 women), 125 part-time (97 women); includes 298 minority (39 Black or African American, non-Hispanic/Latino; 3 American Indian or Alaska Native, non-Hispanic/Latino; 97 Asian, non-Hispanic/Latino; 153 Hispanic/Latino; 6 Native Hawaiian or other Pacific Islander, non-Hispanic/Latino). Average age 32. 540 applicants, 76% accepted, 250 enrolled. In 2016, 107 master's, 7 doctorates awarded. *Degree requirements:* For master's, thesis or project; writing proficiency exam. *Entrance requirements:* For master's, minimum GPA of 2.5, 3.0 in last 60 units. Additional exam requirements/recommendations for international students: Required—TOEFL (minimum score 550 paper-based; 80 iBT). *Application deadline:* For fall admission, 2/15 for domestic students, 1/15 for international students. Applications are processed on a rolling basis. Application fee: $55. Electronic applications accepted. *Expenses:* $4,302 full-time tuition and fees per semester, $2,796 part-time. *Financial support:* Career-related internships or fieldwork and Federal Work-Study available. Support available to part-time students. Financial award application deadline: 3/1; financial award applicants required to submit FAFSA. *Unit head:* Dr. Susan Heredia, Chair, 916-278-5942, E-mail: coe@csus.edu. *Application contact:* Jose Martinez, Graduate Admissions Supervisor, 916-278-7871, E-mail: martinj@skymail.csus.edu.
Website: http://www.csus.edu/coe/academics/graduate/index.html

California State University, San Marcos, College of Education, Health and Human Services, School of Education, San Marcos, CA 92096-0001. Offers educational administration (MA); educational leadership (Ed D); general education (MA); literacy education (MA); special education (MA). *Accreditation:* NCATE (one or more programs are accredited). *Program availability:* Part-time, evening/weekend. *Degree requirements:* For master's, thesis. *Entrance requirements:* For master's, minimum GPA of 3.0, teaching credentials, 1 year of teaching experience. *Expenses:* Tuition, state resident: full-time $6738. Tuition, nonresident: full-time $13,434. *Required fees:* $1906. Tuition and fees vary according to campus/location and program. *Faculty research:* Multicultural literature, art as knowledge, poetry and second language acquisition, restructuring K–12 education and improving the training of K–8 science teachers.

California State University, Stanislaus, College of Education, Program in Education (MA), Turlock, CA 95382. Offers curriculum and instruction (MA), including education technology, elementary education, multilingual education, physical education, reading, secondary education, special education; school administration (MA); school counseling (MA). *Program availability:* Part-time, evening/weekend. *Degree requirements:* For master's, comprehensive exam (for some programs), thesis (for some programs). *Entrance requirements:* For master's, MAT, GRE, or CBEST (varies by concentration), 3 letters of recommendation, personal statement. Additional exam requirements/recommendations for international students: Required—TOEFL (minimum score 550 paper-based). Electronic applications accepted. *Faculty research:* Children's perspectives on historical events, method elementary schools dual language education, K-12 reading programs.

California University of Pennsylvania, School of Graduate Studies and Research, College of Education and Human Services, Department of Special Education, California, PA 15419-1394. Offers mentally and/or physically handicapped education (M Ed). *Accreditation:* NCATE. *Program availability:* Part-time, evening/weekend. *Degree requirements:* For master's, comprehensive exam, thesis optional. *Entrance requirements:* For master's, MAT, PRAXIS. Additional exam requirements/recommendations for international students: Required—TOEFL (minimum score 550 paper-based; 80 iBT). Electronic applications accepted. *Expenses:* Tuition, state resident: full-time $11,592; part-time $483 per credit. Tuition, nonresident: full-time $17,400; part-time $725 per credit. *Required fees:* $3916. Tuition and fees vary according to course load, degree level, campus/location and reciprocity agreements. *Faculty research:* Case-based instruction, electronic performance support tools, students with disabilities, teacher preparation, No Child Left Behind.

Cambridge College, School of Education, Cambridge, MA 02138-5304. Offers autism specialist (M Ed); autism/behavior analyst (M Ed); behavior analyst (Post-Master's Certificate); behavioral management (M Ed); early childhood teacher (M Ed); education specialist in curriculum and instruction (CAGS); educational leadership (Ed D); elementary teacher (M Ed); English as a second language (M Ed, Certificate); general science (M Ed); health education (Post-Master's Certificate); health/family and consumer sciences (M Ed); history (M Ed); individualized (M Ed); information technology literacy (M Ed); instructional technology (M Ed); interdisciplinary studies (M Ed); library teacher (M Ed); literacy education (M Ed); mathematics (M Ed); mathematics specialist (Certificate); middle school mathematics and science (M Ed); school administration (M Ed, CAGS); school guidance counselor (M Ed); school nurse education (M Ed); school social worker/school adjustment counselor (M Ed); special education administrator (CAGS); special education/moderate disabilities (M Ed); teaching skills and methodologies (M Ed). *Program availability:* Part-time, evening/weekend, online learning. *Degree requirements:* For master's, thesis, internship/practicum (licensure program only); for doctorate, thesis/dissertation; for other advanced degree, thesis. *Entrance requirements:* For master's, interview, resume, documentation of licensure, 2 professional references; for doctorate, official transcripts, interview, resume, documentation of licensure (if any), written personal statement/essay, portfolio of scholarly and professional work, qualifying assessment, 2 professional references, health insurance, immunizations form; for other advanced degree, official transcripts, interview, resume, documentation of licensure (if any), written personal statement/essay, 2 professional references, health insurance, immunizations form. Additional exam requirements/recommendations for international students: Required—TOEFL (minimum score 550 paper-based; 79 iBT), Michigan English Language Assessment Battery (minimum score 85); Recommended—IELTS (minimum score 6). Electronic applications accepted. *Expenses:* Contact institution. *Faculty research:* Adult education, accelerated learning, mathematics education, brain compatible learning, special education and law.

Campbellsville University, School of Education, Campbellsville, KY 42718-2799. Offers special education (MASE). *Accreditation:* NCATE. *Program availability:* Part-time, evening/weekend, 100% online, blended/hybrid learning. *Faculty:* 13 full-time (11 women), 12 part-time/adjunct (7 women). *Students:* 36 full-time (29 women), 163 part-time (128 women); includes 16 minority (14 Black or African American, non-Hispanic/Latino; 1 Hispanic/Latino; 1 Two or more races, non-Hispanic/Latino). Average age 35. 173 applicants, 58% accepted, 87 enrolled. In 2016, 58 master's awarded. *Degree requirements:* For master's, thesis, research paper. *Entrance requirements:* For master's, GRE or PRAXIS, minimum undergraduate GPA of 2.75, teaching certificate, professional growth plan, letters of recommendation, interview. Additional exam requirements/recommendations for international students: Recommended—TOEFL (minimum score 550 paper-based; 79 iBT), IELTS (minimum score 6). *Application deadline:* Applications are processed on a rolling basis. Application fee: $25. Electronic applications accepted. Application fee is waived when completed online. *Expenses:* $399 per credit hour. *Financial support:* Applicants required to submit FAFSA. *Faculty research:* Professional development, curriculum development, school governance, assessment, special education. *Unit head:* Dr. Beverly Ennis, Dean, 270-789-5344, Fax: 270-789-5206, E-mail: bcennis@campbellsville.edu. *Application contact:* Monica Bamwine, Assistant Director of Graduate Admissions, 270-789-5221, Fax: 270-789-5071, E-mail: mkbamwine@campbellsville.edu.

Canisius College, Graduate Division, School of Education and Human Services, Department of Graduate Education and Leadership, Buffalo, NY 14208-1098. Offers business and marketing education (MS Ed); college student personnel (MS Ed); deaf education (MS Ed); deaf/adolescent education, grades 7-12 (MS Ed); deaf/childhood education, grades 1-6 (MS Ed); differentiated instruction (MS Ed); education administration (MS); educational administration (MS Ed); educational technologies (Certificate); gifted education extension (Certificate); literacy (MS Ed); reading (Certificate); school building leadership (MS Ed, Certificate); school district leadership (Certificate); teacher leader (Certificate); TESOL (MS Ed). *Accreditation:* NCATE. *Program availability:* Part-time, evening/weekend, 100% online, blended/hybrid learning. *Faculty:* 5 full-time (all women), 23 part-time/adjunct (16 women). *Students:* 95 full-time (78 women), 223 part-time (177 women); includes 31 minority (15 Black or African American, non-Hispanic/Latino; 2 American Indian or Alaska Native, non-Hispanic/Latino; 4 Asian, non-Hispanic/Latino; 9 Hispanic/Latino; 1 Two or more races, non-Hispanic/Latino), 1 international. Average age 30. 162 applicants, 89% accepted, 135 enrolled. In 2016, 135 master's, 39 other advanced degrees awarded. *Entrance requirements:* For master's, GRE (if cumulative GPA less than 2.7), transcripts, two letters of recommendation. Additional exam requirements/recommendations for international students: Required—TOEFL (minimum score 550 paper-based, 79 iBT), IELTS (minimum score 6.5), or CAEL (minimum score 70). *Application deadline:* Applications are processed on a rolling basis. Application fee: $25. Electronic applications accepted. Application fee is waived when completed online. *Expenses: Tuition:* Full-time $14,742. *Required fees:* $724. *Financial support:* Career-related internships or fieldwork, Federal Work-Study, scholarships/grants, tuition waivers (partial), and unspecified assistantships available. Support available to part-time students. Financial award application deadline: 4/30; financial award applicants required to submit FAFSA. *Faculty research:* Asperger's disease, autism, private higher education, reading strategies. *Unit head:* Dr. Rosemary K. Murray, Chair/Associate Professor of Graduate Education and Leadership, 716-888-3723, E-mail: murray1@canisius.edu. *Application contact:* Kathleen B. Davis, Vice President of Enrollment Management, 716-888-2500, Fax: 716-888-3195, E-mail: daviskb@canisius.edu.
Website: http://www.canisius.edu/graduate/

Canisius College, Graduate Division, School of Education and Human Services, Department of Teacher Education, Buffalo, NY 14208-1098. Offers adolescence education (MS Ed); childhood education (MS Ed); general education (MS Ed); special education (MS), including adolescence special education, advanced special education, childhood education grade 1-6, childhood special education. *Program availability:* Part-time, evening/weekend, 100% online, blended/hybrid learning. *Faculty:* 10 full-time (9 women), 7 part-time/adjunct (all women). *Students:* 46 full-time (33 women), 22 part-time (17 women); includes 7 minority (4 Black or African American, non-Hispanic/Latino; 1 American Indian or Alaska Native, non-Hispanic/Latino; 1 Hispanic/Latino; 1 Two or more races, non-Hispanic/Latino), 3 international. Average age 27. 74 applicants, 74% accepted, 43 enrolled. In 2016, 57 master's awarded. *Degree requirements:* For master's, research project or thesis, project internship. *Entrance requirements:* For master's, GRE (if cumulative GPA less than 2.7), transcripts, letters of recommendation. Additional exam requirements/recommendations for international students: Required—TOEFL (minimum score 550 paper-based, 79 iBT), IELTS (minimum score 6.5), or CAEL (minimum score 70). *Application deadline:* Applications are processed on a rolling basis. Application fee: $25. Electronic applications accepted. Application fee is waived when completed online. *Expenses: Tuition:* Full-time $14,742. *Required fees:* $724. *Financial support:* Career-related internships or fieldwork, Federal Work-Study, scholarships/grants, tuition waivers (partial), and unspecified assistantships available. Support available to part-time students. Financial award application deadline: 4/30; financial award applicants required to submit FAFSA. *Unit head:* Dr. Julie Henry, Chair/Professor, 716-888-3729, E-mail: henry1@canisius.edu. *Application contact:* Kathleen B. Davis, Director of Graduate Admissions, 716-888-2500, Fax: 716-888-3195, E-mail: daviskb@canisius.edu.
Website: http://www.canisius.edu/academics/graduate/

Capella University, School of Education, Doctoral Programs in Education, Minneapolis, MN 55402. Offers curriculum and instruction (PhD); educational leadership and management (Ed D); instructional design for online learning (PhD); K-12 studies in education (PhD); leadership for higher education (PhD); leadership in educational administration (PhD); postsecondary and adult education (PhD); professional studies in education (PhD); reading and literacy (Ed D); special education leadership (PhD); training and performance improvement (PhD).

Capella University, School of Education, Master's Programs in Education, Minneapolis, MN 55402. Offers adult education (MS); curriculum and instruction (MS); early childhood education (MS); enrollment management (MS); higher education leadership and management (MS); instructional design for online learning (MS); integrative studies (MS); K-12 studies in education (MS); leadership in educational administration (MS); reading and literacy (MS); special education teaching (MS).

Cardinal Stritch University, College of Education and Leadership, Department of Special Education, Milwaukee, WI 53217-3985. Offers special education (PhD); urban special education (MA). *Accreditation:* NCATE. *Program availability:* Part-time, evening/weekend. *Degree requirements:* For master's, comprehensive exam, thesis, practica. *Entrance requirements:* For master's, 2 letters of recommendation, minimum GPA of 2.75. *Application deadline:* For fall admission, 7/15 priority date for domestic students; for spring admission, 12/15 priority date for domestic students. Applications are processed on a rolling basis. Application fee: $25. *Expenses: Tuition:* Full-time $11,890; part-time $765 per credit hour. Tuition and fees vary according to class time, course load, degree level, program and student's religious affiliation. *Financial support:* Research assistantships with partial tuition reimbursements, Federal Work-Study, and scholarships/grants available. Financial award applicants required to submit FAFSA. *Unit head:* Dr. Robert King, Chair, 414-410-4362. *Application contact:* 800-347-8822 Ext. 4042, E-mail: gradadm@stritch.edu.

Caribbean University, Graduate School, Bayamón, PR 00960-0493. Offers administration and supervision (MA Ed); criminal justice (MA); curriculum and instruction (MA Ed, PhD), including elementary education (MA Ed), English education (MA Ed), history education (MA Ed), mathematics education (MA Ed), primary education (MA Ed), science education (MA Ed), Spanish education (MA Ed); educational technology in instructional systems (MA Ed); gerontology (MSN); human resources (MBA); museology, archiving and art history (MA Ed); neonatal pediatrics (MSN); physical education (MA Ed); special education (MA Ed). *Entrance requirements:* For master's, interview, minimum GPA of 2.5.

Carlos Albizu University, Miami Campus, Graduate Programs, Miami, FL 33172-2209. Offers clinical psychology (PhD, Psy D); entrepreneurship (MBA); exceptional student education (MS); human services (PhD); industrial/organizational psychology (MS); marriage and family therapy (MS); mental health counseling (MS); nonprofit management (MBA); organizational management (MBA); psychology (MS); school counseling (MS); speech and language pathology (MS); teaching English for speakers of other languages (MS). *Accreditation:* APA. *Program availability:* Part-time, evening/

weekend, 100% online. *Faculty:* 28 full-time (22 women), 31 part-time/adjunct (19 women). *Students:* 475 full-time (396 women), 191 part-time (161 women); includes 560 minority (56 Black or African American, non-Hispanic/Latino; 1 American Indian or Alaska Native, non-Hispanic/Latino; 4 Asian, non-Hispanic/Latino; 494 Hispanic/Latino; 5 Two or more races, non-Hispanic/Latino), 15 international. Average age 34. 335 applicants, 46% accepted, 122 enrolled. In 2016, 143 master's, 48 doctorates awarded. Terminal master's awarded for partial completion of doctoral program. *Degree requirements:* For master's, comprehensive exam, integrative project (for MBA); research project (for exceptional student education, teaching English as a second language); for doctorate, comprehensive exam, thesis/dissertation, internship, project. *Entrance requirements:* For master's, 3 letters of recommendation, interview, minimum GPA of 3.0, resume, statement of purpose, official transcripts; for doctorate, 3 letters of recommendation, minimum GPA of 3.0, resume, interview, statement of purpose, official transcripts. Additional exam requirements/recommendations for international students: Required—Michigan Test of English Language Proficiency. *Application deadline:* For fall admission, 4/1 priority date for domestic students, 5/1 priority date for international students; for spring admission, 11/1 priority date for domestic students, 9/1 priority date for international students. Applications are processed on a rolling basis. Application fee: $50. Electronic applications accepted. *Expenses:* Contact institution. *Financial support:* In 2016–17, 131 students received support. Federal Work-Study, scholarships/grants, unspecified assistantships, and tuition discounts available. Financial award application deadline: 6/1; financial award applicants required to submit FAFSA. *Faculty research:* Psychotherapy, forensic psychology, neuropsychology, marketing strategy, entrepreneurship, special education, speech-language pathology. *Unit head:* Dr. Etiony Aldarondo, Provost, 305-593-1223 Ext. 3138, Fax: 305-592-7930, E-mail: ealdarondo@albizu.edu. *Application contact:* Sonia Feliciano, Institutional Director of Student Recruitment, 305-593-1223 Ext. 3108, Fax: 305-477-8983, E-mail: sfeliciano@albizu.edu.

Carlow University, College of Learning and Innovation, Program in Education, Pittsburgh, PA 15213-3165. Offers early childhood education (M Ed); special education (M Ed), including early childhood. *Program availability:* Part-time, evening/weekend, 100% online, blended/hybrid learning. *Students:* 47 full-time (43 women), 19 part-time (18 women); includes 10 minority (7 Black or African American, non-Hispanic/Latino; 3 Two or more races, non-Hispanic/Latino). Average age 31. 27 applicants, 81% accepted, 19 enrolled. In 2016, 14 master's awarded. *Entrance requirements:* For master's, personal essay; resume or curriculum vitae; two recommendations; official transcripts; interview; minimum undergraduate GPA of 3.0. Additional exam requirements/recommendations for international students: Required—TOEFL (minimum score 550 paper-based). *Application deadline:* Applications are processed on a rolling basis. Electronic applications accepted. *Expenses: Tuition:* Full-time $11,855; part-time $801 per credit. *Required fees:* $182; $13 per credit. Tuition and fees vary according to course load, degree level and program. *Financial support:* Application deadline: 4/1; applicants required to submit FAFSA. *Unit head:* Dr. Judith Toure, Chair, Department of Education, 412-578-6215, Fax: 412-578-8816, E-mail: jltoure@carlow.edu.
Website: http://www.carlow.edu/education.aspx

Castleton University, Division of Graduate Studies, Department of Education, Program in Special Education, Castleton, VT 05735. Offers MA Ed, CAGS. *Program availability:* Part-time, evening/weekend. *Degree requirements:* For master's, thesis or alternative; for CAGS, publishable paper. *Entrance requirements:* For master's, GRE General Test, MAT, interview, minimum undergraduate GPA of 3.0; for CAGS, educational research, master's degree, minimum undergraduate GPA of 3.0.

The Catholic University of America, School of Arts and Sciences, Department of Education, Washington, DC 20064. Offers Catholic school leadership (MA); education (Certificate); secondary education (MA); special education (MA), including early childhood, non-categorical. *Accreditation:* NCATE. *Program availability:* Part-time. *Faculty:* 8 full-time (7 women), 2 part-time/adjunct (both women). *Students:* 7 full-time (6 women), 21 part-time (13 women); includes 5 minority (2 Black or African American, non-Hispanic/Latino; 3 Hispanic/Latino), 3 international. Average age 38. 22 applicants, 45% accepted, 3 enrolled. In 2016, 14 master's awarded. *Degree requirements:* For master's, comprehensive exam, thesis or alternative; for Certificate, action research project. *Entrance requirements:* For master's, GRE General Test or MAT, statement of purpose, official copies of academic transcripts, three letters of recommendation, interview; for Certificate, PRAXIS I, statement of purpose, official copies of academic transcripts, three letters of recommendation, interview. Additional exam requirements/recommendations for international students: Required—TOEFL (minimum score 550 paper-based; 80 iBT). *Application deadline:* For fall admission, 7/15 priority date for domestic students, 7/1 for international students; for spring admission, 11/15 priority date for domestic students, 11/1 for international students. Applications are processed on a rolling basis. Application fee: $55. Electronic applications accepted. *Expenses:* $42,850 per year; $1,170 per credit; $200 per semester part-time fees. *Financial support:* Fellowships, research assistantships, teaching assistantships, Federal Work-Study, scholarships/grants, tuition waivers (full and partial), and unspecified assistantships available. Financial award application deadline: 2/1; financial award applicants required to submit FAFSA. *Faculty research:* Special education, early childhood education, educational psychology, Catholic school administration, leadership and policy studies, counseling, curriculum and instruction. *Total annual research expenditures:* $54,518. *Unit head:* Dr. John Convey, Chair, 202-319-5810, Fax: 202-319-5815, E-mail: convey@cua.edu. *Application contact:* Director of Graduate Admissions, 202-319-5057, Fax: 202-319-6533, E-mail: cua-admissions@cua.edu.
Website: http://education.cua.edu/

Centenary University, Program in Education, Hackettstown, NJ 07840-2100. Offers education practice (M Ed); educational leadership (MA, Ed D); instructional leadership (MA); reading (M Ed); special education (MA). *Accreditation:* TEAC. *Program availability:* Part-time, evening/weekend, online learning. *Degree requirements:* For master's, thesis. *Entrance requirements:* For master's, interview, minimum undergraduate GPA of 2.8.

Central Connecticut State University, School of Graduate Studies, School of Education and Professional Studies, Department of Special Education and Interventions, New Britain, CT 06050-4010. Offers MS, Certificate. *Program availability:* Part-time, evening/weekend. *Faculty:* 7 full-time (4 women), 11 part-time/adjunct (7 women). *Students:* 33 full-time (27 women), 123 part-time (98 women); includes 18 minority (6 Black or African American, non-Hispanic/Latino; 1 Asian, non-Hispanic/Latino; 9 Hispanic/Latino; 2 Two or more races, non-Hispanic/Latino). Average age 29. 74 applicants, 77% accepted, 43 enrolled. In 2016, 54 master's, 12 other advanced degrees awarded. *Degree requirements:* For master's, thesis or alternative; for Certificate, qualifying exam. *Entrance requirements:* For master's, minimum undergraduate GPA of 2.7, teacher certification. Additional exam requirements/recommendations for international students: Required—TOEFL (minimum score 550 paper-based; 79 iBT). *Application deadline:* For fall admission, 6/1 for domestic students, 5/1 for international students; for spring admission, 11/1 for domestic and international students. Applications are processed on a rolling basis. Application fee: $50. Electronic applications accepted. *Expenses: Tuition, area resident:* Full-time $6497; part-time $606 per credit. Tuition, state resident: full-time $9748; part-time $622 per credit. Tuition, nonresident: full-time $18,102; part-time $622 per credit. *Required fees:* $4459; $246 per credit. *Financial support:* In 2016–17, 3 students received support. Career-related internships or fieldwork, Federal Work-Study, scholarships/grants, and unspecified assistantships available. Support available to part-time students. Financial award application deadline: 3/1; financial award applicants required to submit FAFSA. *Faculty research:* Learning disabilities and language development, consulting teacher practice, occupational and special education, teaching emotionally disturbed students. *Unit head:* Dr. Joan Nicoll-Senft, Chair, 860-832-2400, E-mail: nicoll-senftj@ccsu.edu. *Application contact:* Patricia Gardner, Associate Director of Graduate Studies, 860-832-2350, Fax: 860-832-2362.
Website: http://www.ccsu.edu/sped/

Central Michigan University, College of Graduate Studies, College of Education and Human Services, Department of Counseling and Special Education, Program in Special Education, Mount Pleasant, MI 48859. Offers autism (Graduate Certificate); special education (MA), including the master teacher. *Accreditation:* TEAC. *Program availability:* Part-time. *Degree requirements:* For master's, comprehensive exam (for some programs), thesis or alternative. *Entrance requirements:* For master's, Michigan elementary or secondary provisional, permanent, or life certificate or special education endorsement. Electronic applications accepted. *Faculty research:* Mainstreaming, learning disabled, attention and organization disorders.

Central Washington University, Graduate Studies and Research, College of Education and Professional Studies, Department of Language, Literacy and Special Education, Program in Special Education, Ellensburg, WA 98926. Offers M Ed. *Program availability:* Part-time. *Degree requirements:* For master's, thesis or alternative. *Entrance requirements:* For master's, minimum GPA of 3.0. Additional exam requirements/recommendations for international students: Required—TOEFL (minimum score 550 paper-based; 79 iBT), IELTS (minimum score 6.5).

Chaminade University of Honolulu, Office of Professional and Continuing Education, Program in Education, Honolulu, HI 96816-1578. Offers child development (M Ed); early childhood education (MAT); educational leadership (M Ed); elementary education (MAT); instructional leadership (M Ed); Montessori (M Ed); secondary education (MAT); special education (MAT). *Program availability:* Part-time, evening/weekend, 100% online, blended/hybrid learning. *Faculty:* 7 full-time (4 women), 8 part-time/adjunct (6 women). *Students:* 98 full-time (80 women), 82 part-time (62 women); includes 110 minority (6 Black or African American, non-Hispanic/Latino; 2 American Indian or Alaska Native, non-Hispanic/Latino; 51 Asian, non-Hispanic/Latino; 9 Hispanic/Latino; 41 Native Hawaiian or other Pacific Islander, non-Hispanic/Latino; 1 Two or more races, non-Hispanic/Latino), 1 international. Average age 35. 38 applicants, 100% accepted, 29 enrolled. In 2016, 79 master's awarded. *Degree requirements:* For master's, thesis or alternative. *Entrance requirements:* For master's, PRAXIS (for MAT), minimum GPA of 2.75 (for M Ed), 3.0 (for MAT); 2 letters of recommendation, resume, writing sample (for MAT). Additional exam requirements/recommendations for international students: Required—TOEFL (minimum score 550 paper-based; 79 iBT). *Application deadline:* Applications are processed on a rolling basis. Application fee: $40. Electronic applications accepted. *Expenses:* $740 per credit hour plus $93 fee per online course. *Financial support:* Applicants required to submit FAFSA. *Unit head:* Dr. Dale Fryxell, Interim Dean, 808-739-4684, Fax: 808-739-4607, E-mail: edu-advising@chaminade.edu. *Application contact:* 808-735-4755, E-mail: gradserv@chaminade.edu.
Website: http://www.chaminade.edu/education

Chapman University, College of Educational Studies, Orange, CA 92866. Offers counseling (MA), including school counseling (MA, Credential); education (PhD), including cultural and curricular studies, disability studies, leadership studies, school psychology (PhD, Credential); educational psychology (MA); leadership development (MA); multiple subjects (Credential), including Spanish/English bilingual; pupil personnel services (Credential), including school counseling (MA, Credential), school psychology (PhD, Credential); school psychology (Ed S); single subject (Credential); special education (MA, Credential), including mild/moderate (Credential), moderate/severe (Credential); teaching (MA), including elementary education, secondary education, secondary music education. *Accreditation:* TEAC. *Program availability:* Part-time, evening/weekend. *Faculty:* 29 full-time (14 women), 36 part-time/adjunct (28 women). *Students:* 186 full-time (148 women), 186 part-time (134 women); includes 144 minority (9 Black or African American, non-Hispanic/Latino; 39 Asian, non-Hispanic/Latino; 78 Hispanic/Latino; 2 Native Hawaiian or other Pacific Islander, non-Hispanic/Latino; 16 Two or more races, non-Hispanic/Latino), 8 international. Average age 29. 143 applicants, 63% accepted, 64 enrolled. In 2016, 111 master's, 24 doctorates awarded. *Degree requirements:* For doctorate, thesis/dissertation. *Entrance requirements:* Additional exam requirements/recommendations for international students: Required—TOEFL (minimum score 550 paper-based, 80 iBT), IELTS (6.5), PTE Academic (53), or CAE. *Application deadline:* Applications are processed on a rolling basis. Application fee: $60. Electronic applications accepted. *Expenses:* Contact institution. *Financial support:* Fellowships and scholarships/grants available. Financial award application deadline: 3/2; financial award applicants required to submit FAFSA. *Unit head:* Dr. Margaret Grogan, Dean, 714-516-5968, E-mail: grogan@chapman.edu. *Application contact:* Sara Simon, Graduate Admission Counselor, 714-997-6770, E-mail: simon@chapman.edu.
Website: http://www.chapman.edu/CES/

Chatham University, Program in Education, Pittsburgh, PA 15232-2826. Offers early childhood education (MAT); elementary education (MAT); environmental education (K-12) (MAT); secondary art (MAT); secondary biology education (MAT); secondary chemistry education (MAT); secondary English education (MAT); secondary math education (MAT); secondary physics education (MAT); secondary social studies education (MAT); special education (MAT). *Degree requirements:* For master's, thesis, teaching experience. *Entrance requirements:* For master's, minimum GPA of 3.0, sample of written work, recommendation letters. Additional exam requirements/recommendations for international students: Required—TOEFL (minimum score 600 paper-based; 100 iBT), IELTS (minimum score 7), TWE. Electronic applications accepted. Application fee is waived when completed online. *Expenses: Tuition:* Full-time $16,254; part-time $903 per credit hour. *Required fees:* $468; $26 per credit hour. *Faculty research:* Gifted education, environmental education, technology in education, writing as learning, class size and achievement.

Chestnut Hill College, School of Graduate Studies, Department of Education, Program in Early Education, Philadelphia, PA 19118-2693. Offers early education (M Ed), including Montessori certificate preparation, preK-4 education, preK-4 education and special education preK-8. *Program availability:* Part-time, evening/weekend. *Degree requirements:* For master's, thesis optional. *Entrance requirements:* For master's, PRAXIS I or proof of teaching certification, writing sample, letters of recommendation, 6 graduate credits with minimum B grade or minimum undergraduate GPA of 3.0. Additional exam requirements/recommendations for international students: Required—TOEFL (minimum score 500 paper-based), IELTS (minimum score 6.0), or TWE (minimum score 22). Electronic applications accepted. *Expenses:* Contact institution. *Faculty research:* Gender issues, early childhood education standardized testing.

Chestnut Hill College, School of Graduate Studies, Department of Education, Program in Reading, Philadelphia, PA 19118-2693. Offers reading specialist (M Ed), including K-

12, special education 7-12, special education PreK-8. *Program availability:* Part-time, evening/weekend. *Degree requirements:* For master's, thesis optional. *Entrance requirements:* Additional exam requirements/recommendations for international students: Required—TOEFL (minimum score 500 paper-based) or IELTS (minimum score 6). Electronic applications accepted. *Expenses:* Contact institution. *Faculty research:* Inclusive education, cultural issues in education.

Chestnut Hill College, School of Graduate Studies, Department of Education, Program in Special Education, Philadelphia, PA 19118-2693. Offers special education (M Ed), including 7-12, PreK-8. *Program availability:* Part-time, evening/weekend. *Degree requirements:* For master's, thesis optional. *Entrance requirements:* For master's, PRAXIS I or proof of teaching certification, letters of recommendation, writing sample, 6 graduate credits with minimum B grade if undergraduate GPA less than 3.0. Additional exam requirements/recommendations for international students: Required—TOEFL (minimum score 500 paper-based), IELTS (minimum score 6), or TWE (minimum score 22). Electronic applications accepted. *Expenses:* Contact institution. *Faculty research:* Inclusive education, cultural issues in education.

Chestnut Hill College, School of Graduate Studies, Division of Psychology, Program in Clinical and Counseling Psychology, Philadelphia, PA 19118-2693. Offers clinical and counseling psychology (MS, CAS), including child and adolescent therapy, child and adolescent therapy with autism spectrum disorders, co-occurring disorders, couple and family therapy, diverse and underserved communities, generalist (MS), trauma studies. *Program availability:* Part-time, evening/weekend. *Degree requirements:* For master's, thesis optional, practica. *Entrance requirements:* For master's, GRE General Test, writing sample, letters of recommendation. Additional exam requirements/ recommendations for international students: Required—TOEFL (minimum score 500 paper-based), IELTS (minimum score 6.0), or TWE (minimum score 22). Electronic applications accepted. *Expenses:* Contact institution. *Faculty research:* Play therapy, eating disorders, addictions, group psychology and group therapy, health psychology.

Cheyney University of Pennsylvania, Graduate Programs, Program in Special Education, Cheyney, PA 19319. Offers M Ed. *Program availability:* Part-time, evening/ weekend. *Degree requirements:* For master's, thesis. *Entrance requirements:* For master's, GRE General Test, MAT, minimum GPA of 2.75. Electronic applications accepted.

Chicago State University, School of Graduate and Professional Studies, College of Education, Department of Special Education, Early Childhood Education and Bilingual Education, Program in Special Education, Chicago, IL 60628. Offers M Ed. *Accreditation:* NCATE. *Degree requirements:* For master's, thesis optional. *Entrance requirements:* For master's, minimum GPA of 2.75. *Faculty research:* Assistive technology, teacher efficiency.

City College of the City University of New York, Graduate School, School of Education, Department of Leadership and Special Education, New York, NY 10031-9198. Offers educational leadership (MS, AC); teacher of students with disabilities in adolescent education (MS Ed); teacher of students with disabilities in childhood education (MS Ed). *Degree requirements:* For master's, thesis, research paper. *Entrance requirements:* For master's, Liberal Arts and Sciences Test (LAST), Content Specialty Test (CST), interview; minimum GPA of 3.0 in major, 2.5 overall. Additional exam requirements/recommendations for international students: Required—TOEFL. Tuition and fees vary according to course load, degree level and program. *Faculty research:* Dynamics of organizational change, impact of laws on educational policy, leadership development in schools.

City University of Seattle, Graduate Division, Albright School of Education, Seattle, WA 98121. Offers administrator certification (Certificate); curriculum and instruction (M Ed); elementary education (MIT); guidance and counseling (M Ed); leadership (M Ed); reading and literacy (M Ed); school counseling (M Ed); special education (MIT); superintendent certification (Certificate). *Program availability:* Part-time, evening/ weekend, online learning. *Degree requirements:* For master's, comprehensive exam (for some programs), thesis (for some programs). *Entrance requirements:* For master's, baccalaureate degree or equivalent from an accredited or otherwise recognized institution. Additional exam requirements/recommendations for international students: Required—TOEFL (minimum score 567 paper-based; 87 iBT); Recommended—IELTS. Electronic applications accepted. *Expenses:* Contact institution.

Claremont Graduate University, Graduate Programs, School of Educational Studies, Claremont, CA 91711-6160. Offers Africana education (Certificate); education and policy (MA, PhD); higher education/student affairs (MA, PhD); human development (MA, PhD); public school administration (MA, PhD); quantitative evaluation (MA, PhD); special education (MA, PhD); teacher education (MA); teaching and learning (MA, PhD); urban leadership (PhD); MBA/PhD. PhD program offered jointly with San Diego State University. *Program availability:* Part-time. *Faculty:* 14 full-time (9 women), 1 part-time/ adjunct (0 women). *Students:* 195 full-time (143 women), 196 part-time (137 women); includes 217 minority (43 Black or African American, non-Hispanic/Latino; 4 American Indian or Alaska Native, non-Hispanic/Latino; 32 Asian, non-Hispanic/Latino; 117 Hispanic/Latino; 2 Native Hawaiian or other Pacific Islander, non-Hispanic/Latino; 19 Two or more races, non-Hispanic/Latino), 14 international. Average age 38. In 2016, 48 master's, 39 doctorates, 7 other advanced degrees awarded. Terminal master's awarded for partial completion of doctoral program. *Entrance requirements:* For master's and doctorate, GRE General Test. Additional exam requirements/ recommendations for international students: Required—TOEFL (minimum score 75 iBT). *Application deadline:* For fall admission, 3/1 priority date for domestic and international students. Applications are processed on a rolling basis. Application fee: $80. Electronic applications accepted. *Expenses: Tuition:* Full-time $44,328; part-time $1847 per unit. *Required fees:* $600; $300 per semester. Tuition and fees vary according to course load and program. *Financial support:* Fellowships, research assistantships, Federal Work-Study, institutionally sponsored loans, and scholarships/ grants available. Support available to part-time students. Financial award application deadline: 2/15; financial award applicants required to submit FAFSA. *Faculty research:* Education administration, K-12 and higher education, multicultural education, education policy, diversity in higher education, faculty issues. *Unit head:* Allen Omoto, Dean, 909-607-3786, E-mail: allen.omoto@cgu.edu. *Application contact:* Rachel Camacho, Senior Assistant Director of Admission, 909-607-9418, E-mail: camacho@cgu.edu.
Website: https://www.cgu.edu/school/school-of-educational-studies/

Clarion University of Pennsylvania, Office of Transfer, Adult and Graduate Admissions, Master of Education Program, Clarion, PA 16214. Offers curriculum and instruction (M Ed); early childhood (M Ed); math education (M Ed); reading (M Ed); science education (M Ed); special education (M Ed); technology (M Ed). *Accreditation:* NCATE. *Program availability:* Part-time, evening/weekend, 100% online, blended/hybrid learning. *Faculty:* 12 full-time (8 women), 5 part-time/adjunct (all women). *Students:* 17 full-time (15 women), 97 part-time (78 women); includes 1 minority (Two or more races, non-Hispanic/Latino). Average age 29. 76 applicants, 99% accepted, 48 enrolled. In 2016, 34 master's awarded. *Degree requirements:* For master's, comprehensive exam, thesis, or portfolio. *Entrance requirements:* For master's, minimum QPA of 3.0. Additional exam requirements/recommendations for international students: Required—TOEFL (minimum score 550 paper-based; 80 iBT), IELTS (minimum score 7). *Application deadline:* For fall admission, 8/1 for domestic students, 4/15 for international students; for spring admission, 8/1 for domestic students, 9/15 for international students. Applications are processed on a rolling basis. Application fee: $40. Electronic applications accepted. *Expenses:* $632.35 per credit. *Financial support:* Career-related internships or fieldwork, Federal Work-Study, scholarships/grants, and unspecified assistantships available. Support available to part-time students. Financial award application deadline: 3/1; financial award applicants required to submit FAFSA. *Unit head:* Dr. John McCullough, Chair, Department of Education, 814-393-2104, Fax: 814-393-2446, E-mail: gradstudies@clarion.edu. *Application contact:* Dana Bearer, Associate Director for Transfer, Adult, and Graduate Programs, 814-393-2337, Fax: 814-393-2722, E-mail: gradstudies@clarion.edu.

Clarion University of Pennsylvania, Office of Transfer, Adult and Graduate Admissions, On-Campus Master's Programs, Clarion, PA 16214. Offers special education (MS); speech language pathology (MS). *Accreditation:* ASHA. *Program availability:* Part-time. *Faculty:* 13 full-time (11 women), 10 part-time/adjunct (all women). *Students:* 94 full-time (89 women), 25 part-time (24 women); includes 7 minority (2 Hispanic/Latino; 5 Two or more races, non-Hispanic/Latino). Average age 23. 264 applicants, 41% accepted, 54 enrolled. In 2016, 70 master's awarded. *Degree requirements:* For master's, comprehensive exam (for some programs), thesis or alternative. *Entrance requirements:* For master's, GRE, minimum QPA of 3.0, interview. Additional exam requirements/recommendations for international students: Required—TOEFL (minimum score 600 paper-based; 89 iBT), IELTS (minimum score 7.5). *Application deadline:* For fall admission, 1/31 for domestic and international students. Applications are processed on a rolling basis. Application fee: $40. Electronic applications accepted. *Expenses:* $632.35 per credit (for MS in special education), $722.95 per credit (for MS in speech pathology). *Financial support:* Career-related internships or fieldwork, Federal Work-Study, scholarships/grants, and unspecified assistantships available. Support available to part-time students. Financial award application deadline: 3/1; financial award applicants required to submit FAFSA. *Unit head:* 814-393-2581, Fax: 814-393-2206. *Application contact:* Dana Bearer, Associate Director, Transfer, Adult, and Graduate Programs, 814-393-2337, Fax: 814-393-2722, E-mail: gradstudies@clarion.edu.
Website: http://www.clarion.edu/admissions/graduate/index.html

Clark Atlanta University, School of Education, Department of Curriculum, Atlanta, GA 30314. Offers special education general curriculum (MA); teaching math and science (MAT). *Program availability:* Part-time. *Faculty:* 2 full-time (both women), 1 part-time/ adjunct (0 women). *Students:* 6 full-time (1 woman), 2 part-time (1 woman); includes 6 minority (all Black or African American, non-Hispanic/Latino), 1 international. Average age 34. 17 applicants, 76% accepted, 2 enrolled. In 2016, 2 master's awarded. *Degree requirements:* For master's, one foreign language, comprehensive exam. *Entrance requirements:* For master's, GRE General Test, minimum undergraduate GPA of 2.6. Additional exam requirements/recommendations for international students: Required—TOEFL (minimum score 500 paper-based; 61 iBT). *Application deadline:* For fall admission, 4/1 for domestic and international students; for spring admission, 11/1 for domestic and international students. Applications are processed on a rolling basis. Application fee: $40 ($55 for international students). *Expenses: Tuition:* Full-time $15,498; part-time $861 per credit hour. *Required fees:* $1326; $1326 per credit hour. Tuition and fees vary according to course load. *Financial support:* Career-related internships or fieldwork, Federal Work-Study, scholarships/grants, and unspecified assistantships available. Support available to part-time students. Financial award application deadline: 4/30; financial award applicants required to submit FAFSA. *Unit head:* Dr. James Young, Chairperson, 404-880-6079, E-mail: jyoung@cau.edu. *Application contact:* Graduate Program Admissions, 404-880-8483, E-mail: graduateadmissions@cau.edu.
Website: http://www.cau.edu/school-of-education/Dept-of-Curriculum-and-Instruction/ index.html

Clemson University, Graduate School, College of Education, Department of Education and Human Development, Program in Special Education, Clemson, SC 29634. Offers M Ed, MAT, PhD. *Accreditation:* NCATE. *Program availability:* Part-time. *Faculty:* 9 full-time (6 women). *Students:* 16 full-time (13 women), 1 (woman) part-time; includes 3 minority (2 Black or African American, non-Hispanic/Latino; 1 Two or more races, non-Hispanic/Latino), 2 international. Average age 33. 6 applicants, 50% accepted, 3 enrolled. In 2016, 10 master's awarded. *Degree requirements:* For master's, comprehensive exam, student teaching; for doctorate, comprehensive exam, thesis/ dissertation. *Entrance requirements:* For master's, GRE General Test, unofficial transcripts, teaching certificate, letters of recommendation, personal statement, resume; for doctorate, GRE General Test, unofficial transcripts, teaching/administration certificate, two letters of recommendation, personal statement, resume, minimum of two years teaching experience, master's degree with minimum GPA of 3.5. Additional exam requirements/recommendations for international students: Required—TOEFL (minimum score 80 iBT), IELTS (minimum score 7). *Application deadline:* For fall admission, 3/1 priority date for domestic and international students; for spring admission, 10/1 priority date for domestic and international students; for summer admission, 4/1 priority date for domestic and international students. Applications are processed on a rolling basis. Application fee: $80 ($90 for international students). Electronic applications accepted. *Expenses:* $4,264 per semester full-time resident, $8,485 per semester full-time non-resident, $471 per credit hour part-time resident, $942 per credit hour part-time non-resident. *Financial support:* In 2016–17, 8 students received support, including 5 fellowships with partial tuition reimbursements available (averaging $7,667 per year), 3 teaching assistantships with partial tuition reimbursements available (averaging $20,333 per year). Financial award application deadline: 3/1. *Faculty research:* Gifted students with learning disabilities and/or ADHD, instructional interventions in reading for individuals with learning disabilities, legal and policy issues in special education, response to intervention, behavior management. *Unit head:* Dr. Janie Hodge, MAT and M Ed Program Coordinator, 864-656-1613, E-mail: hodge@clemson.edu. *Application contact:* Dr. Joseph Ryan, PhD Program Coordinator, 864-656-1531, E-mail: jbryan@ clemson.edu.
Website: http://www.clemson.edu/education/departments/education-human-development/academics/index.html

Cleveland State University, College of Graduate Studies, College of Education and Human Services, Department of Curriculum and Foundations, Cleveland, OH 44115. Offers art education (M Ed); early childhood education (M Ed); foreign language education (M Ed); middle childhood mathematics and science education (M Ed); special education (M Ed), including mild/moderate disabilities, moderate/intensive disabilities; teaching English to speakers of other languages (M Ed). *Program availability:* Part-time, evening/weekend. *Faculty:* 19 full-time (14 women), 32 part-time/adjunct (27 women). *Students:* 86 full-time (65 women), 369 part-time (301 women); includes 119 minority (89 Black or African American, non-Hispanic/Latino; 1 American Indian or Alaska Native, non-Hispanic/Latino; 2 Asian, non-Hispanic/Latino; 16 Hispanic/Latino; 11 Two or more races, non-Hispanic/Latino), 35 international. Average age 34. 177 applicants, 55% accepted, 68 enrolled. In 2016, 179 master's awarded. *Degree requirements:* For master's, comprehensive exam (for some programs), thesis or alternative. *Entrance requirements:* For master's, GRE General Test or MAT, minimum GPA of 2.75. Additional exam requirements/recommendations for international students: Required—

TOEFL (minimum score 550 paper-based; 78 iBT), IELTS (minimum score 6). *Application deadline:* For fall admission, 7/1 priority date for domestic students, 5/15 for international students; for spring admission, 11/15 for domestic students, 11/1 for international students; for summer admission, 4/1 for domestic students, 3/15 for international students. Applications are processed on a rolling basis. Application fee: $30. *Expenses:* Tuition, state resident: full-time $9565. Tuition, nonresident: full-time $17,980. Tuition and fees vary according to program. *Financial support:* In 2016–17, 13 research assistantships with full tuition reimbursements (averaging $15,845 per year) were awarded; tuition waivers (partial) and unspecified assistantships also available. Financial award application deadline: 2/15; financial award applicants required to submit FAFSA. *Faculty research:* Early childhood education, literacy education, special education: mild/moderate, moderate/intensive, early childhood intervention specialist), teaching English to speakers of other languages (TESOL). *Total annual research expenditures:* $275,907. *Unit head:* Dr. Tachelle I. Banks, Chairperson, 216-687-4608, Fax: 216-687-5379, E-mail: t.i.banks@csuohio.edu. *Application contact:* Michael Almony, Senior Student Services Specialist, 216-875-9929, Fax: 216-687-5491, E-mail: m.almony@csuohio.edu.
Website: http://www.csuohio.edu/cehs/te/te

Coastal Carolina University, Spadoni College of Education, Conway, SC 29528-6054. Offers education (MAT); educational leadership (M Ed, Ed S); English for speakers of other languages (Certificate); instructional technology (M Ed, Ed S); learning and teaching (M Ed); online teaching and training (Certificate); special education (M Ed). *Accreditation:* NCATE. *Program availability:* Part-time, evening/weekend. *Faculty:* 16 full-time (8 women), 12 part-time/adjunct (7 women). *Students:* 74 full-time (48 women), 340 part-time (271 women); includes 78 minority (70 Black or African American, non-Hispanic/Latino; 1 American Indian or Alaska Native, non-Hispanic/Latino; 2 Asian, non-Hispanic/Latino; 4 Hispanic/Latino; 1 Two or more races, non-Hispanic/Latino), 2 international. Average age 33. 298 applicants, 93% accepted, 213 enrolled. In 2016, 167 master's, 8 other advanced degrees awarded. *Degree requirements:* For master's and other advanced degree, comprehensive exam. *Entrance requirements:* For master's, GRE, GMAT, 2 letters of recommendation, evidence of teacher certification, official transcripts; for other advanced degree, official transcripts, minimum of 3 years' teaching experience, statement of interest in the program, 3 letters of reference, master's degree in educational leadership or related field with minimum overall GPA of 3.0. Additional exam requirements/recommendations for international students: Required—TOEFL (minimum score 550 paper-based; 79 iBT), IELTS (minimum score 6.5). *Application deadline:* For fall admission, 7/1 priority date for domestic and international students; for spring admission, 11/1 priority date for domestic and international students; for summer admission, 3/1 priority date for domestic and international students. Applications are processed on a rolling basis. Application fee: $45. Electronic applications accepted. *Expenses:* Tuition, state resident: full-time $9990; part-time $555 per credit hour. Tuition, nonresident: full-time $18,108; part-time $1006 per credit hour. *Required fees:* $90; $5 per credit hour. *Financial support:* Fellowships, research assistantships, and unspecified assistantships available. Support available to part-time students. Financial award application deadline: 3/1; financial award applicants required to submit FAFSA. *Unit head:* Dr. Edward Jadallah, Dean, 843-349-2773, Fax: 843-349-2106, E-mail: ejadalla@coastal.edu. *Application contact:* Dr. James O. Luken, Associate Provost/Vice-Dean of the Coastal Environment, 843-349-2235, Fax: 843-349-6444, E-mail: joluken@coastal.edu.
Website: http://www.coastal.edu/education/

College of Charleston, Graduate School, School of Education, Health, and Human Performance, Department of Foundations, Secondary, and Special Education, Program in Special Education, Charleston, SC 29424-0001. Offers MAT. *Program availability:* Part-time, evening/weekend. *Entrance requirements:* For master's, GRE, minimum GPA of 2.5, 2 letters of recommendation. Additional exam requirements/recommendations for international students: Required—TOEFL (minimum score 81 iBT). *Application deadline:* For fall admission, 4/1 for domestic students; for spring admission, 11/1 for domestic students. Application fee: $45. Electronic applications accepted. *Financial support:* Fellowships, scholarships/grants, and unspecified assistantships available. *Unit head:* Dr. Angela Cozart, Director, 843-953-6353, Fax: 843-953-5407, E-mail: cozarta@cofc.edu. *Application contact:* Susan Hallatt, Director of Graduate Admissions, 843-953-5614, Fax: 843-953-1434, E-mail: hallatts@cofc.edu.
Website: http://teachered.cofc.edu/grad-progs/edsp.php

The College of New Jersey, Office of Graduate and Advancing Education, School of Education, Department of Special Education, Language and Literacy, Program in Special Education, Ewing, NJ 08628. Offers M Ed, MAT. *Accreditation:* NCATE. *Program availability:* Part-time. *Degree requirements:* For master's, comprehensive exam. *Entrance requirements:* For master's, GRE General Test, minimum GPA of 3.0 in field or 2.75 overall. Additional exam requirements/recommendations for international students: Required—TOEFL. Electronic applications accepted.

The College of New Jersey, Office of Graduate and Advancing Education, School of Education, Department of Special Education, Language and Literacy, Program in Special Education with Learning Disabilities, Ewing, NJ 08628. Offers Certificate. *Accreditation:* NCATE. *Program availability:* Part-time. *Entrance requirements:* Additional exam requirements/recommendations for international students: Required—TOEFL. Electronic applications accepted.

The College of New Rochelle, Graduate School, Division of Education, Program in Special Education, New Rochelle, NY 10805-2308. Offers MS Ed. *Program availability:* Part-time. *Degree requirements:* For master's, practicum. *Entrance requirements:* For master's, interview, minimum GPA of 3.0 in field, 2.7 overall.

College of St. Joseph, Graduate Programs, Division of Education, Program in Special Education, Rutland, VT 05701-3899. Offers M Ed. *Program availability:* Part-time, evening/weekend. *Degree requirements:* For master's, comprehensive exam. *Entrance requirements:* For master's, PRAXIS I (for initial licensure), official college transcripts; 2 letters of reference, minimum GPA of 3.0 (initial licensure) or 2.7 (nonlicensure); interview. Additional exam requirements/recommendations for international students: Required—TOEFL (minimum score 550 paper-based). *Application deadline:* Applications are processed on a rolling basis. Application fee: $35. Electronic applications accepted. *Expenses: Tuition:* Full-time $13,800; part-time $560 per credit. *Required fees:* $75 per semester. Full-time tuition and fees vary according to course load. *Financial support:* Career-related internships or fieldwork, Federal Work-Study, and unspecified assistantships available. Support available to part-time students. Financial award application deadline: 3/1. *Faculty research:* Co-teaching, Response to Intervention (RTI). *Unit head:* Dr. Maria Bove, Chair, 802-773-5900 Ext. 3243, Fax: 802-776-5258, E-mail: mbove@csj.edu. *Application contact:* Alan Young, Director of Admissions, 802-773-5900 Ext. 3227, Fax: 802-776-5310, E-mail: alanyoung@csj.edu.

The College of Saint Rose, Graduate Studies, Thelma P. Lally School of Education, Programs in Special Education, Albany, NY 12203-1419. Offers adolescence education and special education (MS Ed); childhood education and special education (MS Ed); childhood special education (MS Ed); early childhood special education (MS Ed); special education (Certificate); special education professional (MS Ed). *Accreditation:* NCATE. *Students:* 11 full-time (9 women), 19 part-time (17 women), 2 international. Average age 28. 17 applicants, 76% accepted, 7 enrolled. In 2016, 19 master's, 4 Certificates awarded. *Degree requirements:* For master's, comprehensive exam (for some programs), thesis or alternative, research project. *Entrance requirements:* For master's, minimum undergraduate GPA of 3.0. Additional exam requirements/recommendations for international students: Required—TOEFL (minimum score 550 paper-based; 80 iBT), IELTS (minimum score 6), PTE (minimum score 56). *Application deadline:* For fall admission, 4/1 priority date for domestic and international students; for spring admission, 10/15 priority date for domestic and international students; for summer admission, 3/15 priority date for domestic and international students. Applications are processed on a rolling basis. Application fee: $40. Electronic applications accepted. *Expenses: Tuition:* Full-time $14,382; part-time $799 per credit. *Required fees:* $814; $32 per credit. $88 per semester. Tuition and fees vary according to course load. *Financial support:* Career-related internships or fieldwork, scholarships/grants, tuition waivers (partial), and unspecified assistantships available. Support available to part-time students. Financial award application deadline: 4/15. *Unit head:* Susan DeLuke, Chair, 518-454-5194, E-mail: delukes@strose.edu. *Application contact:* Cris Murray, Assistant Vice President for Graduate Recruitment and Enrollment, 518-485-3390, E-mail: grad@strose.edu.
Website: https://www.strose.edu/special-education/

The College of Saint Rose, Graduate Studies, Thelma P. Lally School of Education, Teacher Education Programs, Albany, NY 12203-1419. Offers adolescence education (MS Ed, Advanced Certificate); adolescence education/special education (Advanced Certificate); childhood education (MS Ed); curriculum and instruction (MS Ed); early childhood education (MS Ed). *Students:* 72 full-time (59 women), 32 part-time (26 women); includes 6 minority (4 Black or African American, non-Hispanic/Latino; 2 Hispanic/Latino), 2 international. Average age 28. 60 applicants, 78% accepted, 25 enrolled. In 2016, 37 master's awarded. *Entrance requirements:* For master's, minimum undergraduate GPA of 3.0. Additional exam requirements/recommendations for international students: Required—TOEFL (minimum score 550 paper-based; 80 iBT), IELTS (minimum score 6), PTE (minimum score 56). *Application deadline:* For fall admission, 4/1 priority date for domestic and international students; for spring admission, 10/15 priority date for domestic and international students; for summer admission, 3/15 priority date for domestic and international students. Applications are processed on a rolling basis. Application fee: $40. Electronic applications accepted. *Expenses: Tuition:* Full-time $14,382; part-time $799 per credit. *Required fees:* $814; $32 per credit. $88 per semester. Tuition and fees vary according to course load. *Financial support:* Career-related internships or fieldwork, scholarships/grants, tuition waivers (partial), and unspecified assistantships available. Support available to part-time students. Financial award application deadline: 4/15. *Unit head:* Dr. Drey Martone, Chair, 518-454-5262, E-mail: martoned@strose.edu. *Application contact:* Cris Murray, Assistant Vice President for Graduate Recruitment and Enrollment, 518-485-3390, Fax: 518-458-5479, E-mail: grad@strose.edu.
Website: https://www.strose.edu/academics/schools/school-of-education/

College of Staten Island of the City University of New York, Graduate Programs, Division of Humanities and Social Sciences, Program in Autism Spectrum Disorders, Staten Island, NY 10314-6600. Offers Advanced Certificate. *Program availability:* Part-time, evening/weekend. *Faculty:* 1 full-time, 1 part-time/adjunct. *Students:* 6 part-time. Average age 34. 8 applicants, 75% accepted, 4 enrolled. In 2016, 3 Advanced Certificates awarded. *Degree requirements:* For Advanced Certificate, 12 credits. *Entrance requirements:* For degree, bachelor's degree with minimum GPA of 3.0, 2 letters of recommendation, résumé. Additional exam requirements/recommendations for international students: Required—TOEFL (minimum score 550 paper-based; 79 iBT), IELTS (minimum score 6.5). *Application deadline:* For fall admission, 5/16 priority date for domestic and international students; for spring admission, 11/25 priority date for domestic and international students. Applications are processed on a rolling basis. Application fee: $125. Electronic applications accepted. *Expenses:* Tuition, state resident: full-time $10,130; part-time $425 per credit. Tuition, nonresident: full-time $18,720; part-time $780 per credit. *Required fees:* $181.10 per semester. Tuition and fees vary according to program. *Faculty research:* Autism spectrum disorder, nonverbal communication, applied behavior analysis, computer-mediated interventions. *Unit head:* Dr. Kristen Gillespie-Lynch, Graduate Program Coordinator, 718-982-4121, Fax: 718-982-4114, E-mail: kristen.gillespie@csi.cuny.edu. *Application contact:* Sasha Spence, Associate Director for Graduate Admissions, 718-982-2019, Fax: 718-982-2500, E-mail: sasha.spence@csi.cuny.edu.
Website: http://www.csi.cuny.edu/catalog/graduate/autism-spectrum-disorders-advanced-certificate.htm

College of Staten Island of the City University of New York, Graduate Programs, School of Education, Program in Special Education, Staten Island, NY 10314-6600. Offers MS Ed. *Program availability:* Part-time, evening/weekend. *Faculty:* 3 full-time, 14 part-time/adjunct. *Students:* 7 full-time, 131 part-time. Average age 28. 63 applicants, 71% accepted, 32 enrolled. In 2016, 56 master's awarded. *Degree requirements:* For master's, comprehensive exam, fieldwork; ten three-credit required courses and one elective for a total of 11 courses (33 credits) or 14 three-credit required courses and a three- to six-credit, field-based requirement for a total of 45-48 credits; research project. *Entrance requirements:* For master's, GRE General Test or an approved equivalent examination, BA/BS or 36 approved credits with minimum GPA of 3.0, 2 letters of recommendation, 1-2 page statement of experience. Additional exam requirements/recommendations for international students: Required—TOEFL (minimum score 550 paper-based; 79 iBT), IELTS (minimum score 6.5). *Application deadline:* For fall admission, 4/25 for domestic and international students; for spring admission, 11/25 for domestic and international students. Applications are processed on a rolling basis. Application fee: $125. Electronic applications accepted. *Expenses:* Tuition, state resident: full-time $10,130; part-time $425 per credit. Tuition, nonresident: full-time $18,720; part-time $780 per credit. *Required fees:* $181.10 per semester. Tuition and fees vary according to program. *Faculty research:* Disabilities studies, social justice, arts-based research on disabilities, assessment of students with disabilities, technological pedagogical and content knowledge (TPACK) in special education teachers, juvenile justice. *Unit head:* Dr. Nelly Tournaki, Graduate Faculty Advisor, 718-982-3728, E-mail: nelly.tournaki@csi.cuny.edu. *Application contact:* Sasha Spence, Associate Director for Graduate Admissions, 718-982-2019, Fax: 718-982-2500, E-mail: sasha.spence@csi.cuny.edu.
Website: http://www.csi.cuny.edu/catalog/graduate/graduate-programs-in-education.htm#o2611

The College of William and Mary, School of Education, Program in Curriculum and Instruction, Williamsburg, VA 23187-8795. Offers elementary education (MA Ed); gifted education (MA Ed); literacy leadership (MA Ed); math specialist (MA Ed); secondary education (MA Ed), including English, foreign language, math, science, social studies; special education (MA Ed). *Accreditation:* NCATE. *Program availability:* Part-time. *Faculty:* 30 full-time (21 women), 48 part-time/adjunct (38 women). *Students:* 60 full-time (47 women), 14 part-time (all women); includes 13 minority (1 Black or African American, non-Hispanic/Latino; 1 American Indian or Alaska Native, non-Hispanic/Latino; 2 Asian, non-Hispanic/Latino; 7 Hispanic/Latino; 2 Two or more races, non-Hispanic/Latino). Average age 26. 134 applicants, 79% accepted, 66 enrolled. In 2016, 77 master's awarded. *Degree requirements:* For master's, project. *Entrance requirements:* For master's, GRE, MAT, PRAXIS Core Academic Skills for Educators,

minimum GPA of 2.5. Additional exam requirements/recommendations for international students: Required—TOEFL (minimum score 100 iBT), IELTS (minimum score 7). *Application deadline:* For fall admission, 1/15 for domestic and international students; for spring admission, 10/1 for domestic and international students. Application fee: $50. Electronic applications accepted. *Expenses:* $14,258 per year in-state full-time, $275 per credit in-state part-time; $30,500 per year out-of-state full-time, $1,200 per credit out-of-state part-time. *Financial support:* In 2016–17, 30 students received support, including 3 research assistantships (averaging $14,259 per year); scholarships/grants and unspecified assistantships also available. Financial award application deadline: 1/15; financial award applicants required to submit FAFSA. *Faculty research:* Educational technology, professional development and evaluation, inclusive education, rural education, education policy. *Unit head:* Dr. Jeremy D. Stoddard, Department Chair, 757-221-2348, E-mail: jdstod@wm.edu. *Application contact:* Dorothy Smith Osborne, Assistant Dean for Academic Programs and Student Services, 757-221-2317, E-mail: dsosbo@wm.edu.
Website: http://education.wm.edu

Colorado Christian University, Program in Curriculum and Instruction, Lakewood, CO 80226. Offers corporate education (MACI); early childhood educator (MACI); elementary educator (MACI); instructional technology (MACI); master educator (MACI); online course developer (MACI); online teaching and learning (MACI); special education generalist (MACI). *Program availability:* Part-time, evening/weekend. *Degree requirements:* For master's, thesis optional, practicum. *Entrance requirements:* For master's, interviews, letters of recommendation. Additional exam requirements/recommendations for international students: Required—TOEFL. Electronic applications accepted. *Expenses:* Contact institution.

Colorado Mesa University, Center for Teacher Education, Grand Junction, CO 81501-3122. Offers educational leadership (MAEd); English for speakers of other languages (MAEd); exceptional learner/special education (MAEd); teacher education (Graduate Certificate); teacher leader (MAEd). *Accreditation:* NCATE. *Program availability:* Part-time. *Faculty:* 6 full-time (5 women), 12 part-time/adjunct (6 women). *Students:* 18 full-time (13 women), 35 part-time (28 women); includes 4 minority (1 American Indian or Alaska Native, non-Hispanic/Latino; 3 Hispanic/Latino), 1 international. Average age 34. 28 applicants, 25% accepted, 6 enrolled. In 2016, 26 master's, 36 other advanced degrees awarded. *Degree requirements:* For master's, comprehensive exam (for some programs), capstone presentation. *Entrance requirements:* For master's, 3 professional letters of recommendation, Colorado teaching license, minimum baccalaureate GPA of 3.0; for Graduate Certificate, minimum baccalaureate GPA of 3.0. Additional exam requirements/recommendations for international students: Required—TOEFL (minimum score 550 paper-based). *Application deadline:* For fall admission, 6/1 priority date for domestic and international students; for spring admission, 11/1 priority date for domestic and international students; for summer admission, 3/1 priority date for domestic and international students. Applications are processed on a rolling basis. Application fee: $50. Electronic applications accepted. *Expenses:* $406.43 per credit hour resident tuition and fees, $1,092.43 per credit hour non-resident tuition and fees. *Financial support:* In 2016–17, 2 students received support. Scholarships/grants available. Financial award applicants required to submit FAFSA. *Faculty research:* K-8 STEM instruction, special education inclusion, elementary math literacy, secondary literacy, elementary/early childhood education literacy. *Unit head:* Dr. Blake Bickham, Department Head, 970-248-1729, E-mail: bbickham@coloradomesa.edu. *Application contact:* Mary Kienietz, Administrative Assistant, 970-248-1786, E-mail: mkieniet@coloradomesa.edu.
Website: http://coloradomesa.edu/teachered/index.html

Colorado State University–Pueblo, College of Education, Engineering and Professional Studies, Education Program, Pueblo, CO 81001-4901. Offers art education (M Ed); foreign language education (M Ed); health and physical education (M Ed); instructional technology (M Ed); linguistically diverse education (M Ed); music education (M Ed); special education (M Ed). *Accreditation:* TEAC. *Program availability:* Part-time. *Degree requirements:* For master's, portfolio. *Entrance requirements:* For master's, 3 recommendations, teaching license. Additional exam requirements/recommendations for international students: Required—TOEFL (minimum score 500 paper-based). Electronic applications accepted. *Faculty research:* Portfolio assessment, math education, science education.

Columbus State University, Graduate Studies, College of Education and Health Professions, Department of Teacher Education, Columbus, GA 31907-5645. Offers curriculum and instruction in accomplished teaching (M Ed); early childhood education (M Ed, MAT, Ed S); middle grades education (M Ed, MAT, Ed S); secondary education (M Ed, MAT, Ed S), including biology (MAT), chemistry (MAT), earth and space science (MAT), English/language arts, general science (M Ed), history (MAT), mathematics, science (Ed S), social science (M Ed, Ed S); special education (M Ed, MAT, Ed S), including general curriculum (M Ed, MAT); teacher leadership (M Ed). *Accreditation:* NCATE. *Program availability:* Part-time, evening/weekend, 100% online, blended/hybrid learning. *Faculty:* 20 full-time (13 women), 19 part-time/adjunct (16 women). *Students:* 92 full-time (66 women), 212 part-time (179 women); includes 113 minority (104 Black or African American, non-Hispanic/Latino; 1 American Indian or Alaska Native, non-Hispanic/Latino; 2 Asian, non-Hispanic/Latino; 4 Hispanic/Latino; 2 Two or more races, non-Hispanic/Latino), 5 international. Average age 34. 209 applicants, 56% accepted, 79 enrolled. In 2016, 111 master's, 18 other advanced degrees awarded. *Degree requirements:* For Ed S, thesis or alternative. *Entrance requirements:* For master's, GRE General Test, minimum undergraduate GPA of 2.75; for Ed S, GRE General Test, minimum undergraduate GPA of 2.75, graduate 3.0. Additional exam requirements/recommendations for international students: Required—TOEFL (minimum score 550 paper-based; 79 iBT). *Application deadline:* For fall admission, 6/30 for domestic students, 5/1 for international students; for spring admission, 11/1 for domestic and international students; for summer admission, 3/1 for domestic and international students. Applications are processed on a rolling basis. Application fee: $50. Electronic applications accepted. *Expenses:* Tuition, state resident: full-time $4804; part-time $2412 per semester hour. Tuition, nonresident: full-time $19,218; part-time $9612 per semester hour. *Required fees:* $1850; $1850 per semester hour. Tuition and fees vary according to program. *Financial support:* In 2016–17, 60 students received support, including 12 research assistantships with partial tuition reimbursements available (averaging $3,000 per year); career-related internships or fieldwork, Federal Work-Study, institutionally sponsored loans, scholarships/grants, tuition waivers (partial), and unspecified assistantships also available. Support available to part-time students. Financial award application deadline: 5/1; financial award applicants required to submit FAFSA. *Unit head:* Dr. Jan Burcham, Department Chair, 706-507-8519, Fax: 706-568-3134, E-mail: burcham_jan@columbusstate.edu. *Application contact:* Kristin Williams, Director of International and Graduate Recruitment, 706-507-8848, Fax: 706-568-5091, E-mail: williams_kristin@columbusstate.edu.
Website: http://te.columbusstate.edu/

Concordia College–New York, Program in Childhood Special Education, Bronxville, NY 10708-1998. Offers MS Ed.

Concordia University, College of Education, Portland, OR 97211-6099. Offers career and technical education (M Ed); curriculum and instruction (M Ed), including adolescent literacy, career and technical education, e-learning/technology education, early childhood education, English for speakers of other languages, English language development, environmental education, mathematics, methods and curriculum, reading, science, teacher leadership, the inclusive classroom; early childhood (MAT); education leadership (Ed D); educational administration (M Ed); elementary education (MAT); secondary education (MAT); special education (M Ed); teacher leadership (Ed D). *Program availability:* Part-time, online learning. *Degree requirements:* For master's, comprehensive exam, work samples/portfolio. *Entrance requirements:* For master's, California Basic Educational Skills Test or PRAXIS I, minimum undergraduate GPA of 2.8, graduate 3.0; 2 letters of recommendation. Additional exam requirements/recommendations for international students: Required—TOEFL (minimum score 525 paper-based). Electronic applications accepted. *Faculty research:* Learner-centered classroom, brain-based learning, future of online learning.

Concordia University, St. Paul, College of Education, St. Paul, MN 55104-5494. Offers classroom instruction (MA Ed), including K-12 reading; differentiated instruction (MA Ed); education (Ed D); educational leadership (MA Ed); educational technology (MA Ed); K-12 principal licensure (Ed S); special education (MA Ed, Certificate), including autism spectrum disorder (MA Ed), emotional and behavioral disorders (MA Ed), learning disabilities (MA Ed); superintendent (Ed S); teaching (MAT). *Accreditation:* NCATE. *Program availability:* Part-time, evening/weekend, 100% online, blended/hybrid learning. *Faculty:* 9 full-time (5 women), 88 part-time/adjunct (52 women). *Students:* 994 full-time (745 women), 40 part-time (34 women); includes 118 minority (40 Black or African American, non-Hispanic/Latino; 7 American Indian or Alaska Native, non-Hispanic/Latino; 33 Asian, non-Hispanic/Latino; 20 Hispanic/Latino; 18 Two or more races, non-Hispanic/Latino), 15 international. Average age 34. 549 applicants, 82% accepted, 372 enrolled. In 2016, 399 master's, 108 other advanced degrees awarded. *Degree requirements:* For master's, thesis (for some programs); for doctorate, thesis/dissertation, capstone projects; for other advanced degree, e-folio review of competencies. *Entrance requirements:* For master's, official transcripts from regionally-accredited institution stating the conferral of a bachelor's degree with minimum cumulative GPA of 3.0; personal statement; professional resume; practitioner in field through work or volunteerism; resume; for doctorate, minimum master's or specialist degree GPA of 3.25; transcript; writing sample; three letters of recommendation; current resume; on-campus interview; for other advanced degree, at least three years of teaching experience; master's degree; valid MN teaching license; writing sample; two letters of recommendation; resume. Additional exam requirements/recommendations for international students: Recommended—TOEFL (minimum score 547 paper-based; 78 iBT), IELTS (minimum score 6). *Application deadline:* For fall admission, 8/1 for domestic and international students; for spring admission, 12/1 for domestic and international students; for summer admission, 5/1 for domestic and international students. Applications are processed on a rolling basis. Application fee: $50. Electronic applications accepted. *Expenses:* Contact institution. *Financial support:* In 2016–17, 112 students received support. Scholarships/grants and unspecified assistantships available. Financial award applicants required to submit FAFSA. *Faculty research:* Differentiated instruction in K-12 educational settings; educational leadership; effective online pedagogy in higher education; equine-assisted learning; faculty development in higher education. *Unit head:* Lonn Maly, Dean, 651-641-8203, E-mail: maly@csp.edu. *Application contact:* Kimberly Craig, Associate Vice President, Cohort Enrollment Management, 651-603-6223, Fax: 651-603-6320, E-mail: craig@csp.edu.

Concordia University Wisconsin, Graduate Programs, Department of Education, Mequon, WI 53097-2402. Offers art education (MS Ed); early childhood (MS Ed); educational administration (MS Ed); environmental education (MS Ed); family studies (MS Ed); literacy (MS Ed); school counseling (MS Ed); special education (MS Ed). *Program availability:* Part-time, evening/weekend, online learning. *Degree requirements:* For master's, comprehensive exam, thesis or alternative. *Entrance requirements:* For master's, minimum GPA of 3.0, teaching license. Additional exam requirements/recommendations for international students: Required—TOEFL. Application fee: $35. *Financial support:* Career-related internships or fieldwork and tuition waivers (partial) available. Financial award application deadline: 8/1. *Faculty research:* Motivation, developmental learning, learning styles. *Unit head:* Dr. James Juergensen, Director, 262-243-4214, E-mail: james.juergensen@cuw.edu. *Application contact:* Graduate Admissions, 262-243-4248, Fax: 262-243-4428.

Concord University, Graduate Studies, Athens, WV 24712-1000. Offers educational leadership and supervision (M Ed); health promotion (MA); reading specialist (M Ed); social work (MSW); special education (M Ed); teaching (MAT). *Program availability:* Part-time, evening/weekend, online learning. *Faculty:* 16 full-time (10 women), 7 part-time/adjunct (4 women). *Students:* 129 full-time (105 women), 220 part-time (169 women); includes 28 minority (26 Black or African American, non-Hispanic/Latino; 1 American Indian or Alaska Native, non-Hispanic/Latino; 1 Hispanic/Latino), 2 international. *Degree requirements:* For master's, thesis (for some programs). *Entrance requirements:* For master's, GRE or MAT, baccalaureate degree with minimum GPA of 2.5 from regionally-accredited institution; teaching license; 2 letters of recommendation; completed disposition assessment form. *Application deadline:* Applications are processed on a rolling basis. Application fee: $30. Electronic applications accepted. *Expenses:* Tuition, state resident: full-time $3800; part-time $2539 per semester. Tuition, nonresident: full-time $6627; part-time $4416 per semester. Tuition and fees vary according to course load. *Financial support:* Tuition waivers and unspecified assistantships available. Financial award applicants required to submit FAFSA. *Unit head:* Dr. Cheryl Barnes, Director, 304-384-6306, E-mail: cbarnes@concord.edu. *Application contact:* Debra Moore, Special Events Assistant, 304-384-5113, E-mail: dlm@concord.edu.
Website: http://www.concord.edu/graduate

Converse College, School of Education and Graduate Studies, Program in Special Education, Spartanburg, SC 29302. Offers intellectual disabilities (MAT); learning disabilities (MAT); special education (M Ed). *Program availability:* Part-time. *Degree requirements:* For master's, capstone paper. *Entrance requirements:* For master's, NTE or PRAXIS II (M Ed), minimum GPA of 2.75, 2 recommendations. *Application deadline:* For fall admission, 8/1 for domestic and international students; for winter admission, 11/15 for domestic and international students; for spring admission, 1/15 for domestic and international students. Applications are processed on a rolling basis. Application fee: $40. Electronic applications accepted. *Expenses:* *Tuition:* Full-time $3600; part-time $400 per credit hour. *Required fees:* $70 per term. *Financial support:* Available to part-time students. Applicants required to submit FAFSA. *Application contact:* 864-596-9404, E-mail: graduate@converse.edu.

Coppin State University, Division of Graduate Studies, Division of Education, Department of Special Education, Baltimore, MD 21216-3698. Offers M Ed. *Program availability:* Part-time, evening/weekend. *Degree requirements:* For master's, exit portfolio. *Entrance requirements:* For master's, PRAXIS I, minimum GPA of 3.0, interview, writing sample, resume, references. *Faculty research:* Survey of colleges and universities in Maryland with programs for the learning disabled.

Curry College, Graduate Studies, Program in Education, Milton, MA 02186-9984. Offers elementary education (M Ed); foundations (non-license) (M Ed); reading (M Ed, Certificate); special education (M Ed). *Program availability:* Part-time, evening/weekend.

Degree requirements: For master's, project or thesis. *Entrance requirements:* For master's, interview, recommendations, resume, written statement. Additional exam requirements/recommendations for international students: Required—TOEFL (minimum score 550 paper-based; 80 iBT). *Expenses:* Contact institution. *Faculty research:* Classroom trauma, therapeutic writing, inclusionary practices.

Daemen College, Education Department, Amherst, NY 14226-3592. Offers adolescence education (MS); childhood education (MS); childhood special education (MS); childhood special-alternative certification (MS); early childhood special-alternative certification (MS). *Accreditation:* TEAC. *Program availability:* Part-time. *Degree requirements:* For master's, thesis optional, research thesis in lieu of comprehensive exam; completion of degree within 5 years. *Entrance requirements:* For master's, 2 letters of recommendation (professional and character), proof of initial certificate of license for professional programs, resume. Additional exam requirements/ recommendations for international students: Required—TOEFL (minimum score 500 paper-based; 63 iBT), IELTS (minimum score 5.5). Electronic applications accepted. *Faculty research:* Transition for students with disabilities, early childhood special education, traumatic brain injury (TBI), reading assessment.

Dallas Baptist University, Dorothy M. Bush College of Education, Program in Curriculum and Instruction, Dallas, TX 75211-9299. Offers Christian school administration (M Ed); distance learning (M Ed); English as a second language (M Ed); instructional technology (M Ed); professional life coaching (M Ed); special education (M Ed); supervision (M Ed). *Program availability:* Part-time, evening/weekend, 100% online, blended/hybrid learning. *Application deadline:* Applications are processed on a rolling basis. Application fee: $25. Electronic applications accepted. Application fee is waived when completed online. *Expenses: Tuition:* Full-time $15,408; part-time $856 per credit hour. *Required fees:* $400 per semester. Tuition and fees vary according to course load and degree level. *Unit head:* Dr. Deborah H. Tribble, Director, 214-333-5201, E-mail: debbiet@dbu.edu. *Application contact:* Bobby Soto, Director of Admissions, 214-333-5242, E-mail: graduate@dbu.edu.
Website: http://www3.dbu.edu/graduate/curriculum_instruction.asp

Dallas Baptist University, Dorothy M. Bush College of Education, Program in Special Education, Dallas, TX 75211-9299. Offers diagnostician (M Ed). *Program availability:* Part-time, evening/weekend. *Application deadline:* Applications are processed on a rolling basis. Application fee: $25. Electronic applications accepted. Application fee is waived when completed online. *Expenses: Tuition:* Full-time $15,408; part-time $856 per credit hour. *Required fees:* $400 per semester. Tuition and fees vary according to course load and degree level. *Unit head:* Dr. Mary Beth Sanders, Director, 214-333-5413, E-mail: marys@dbu.edu. *Application contact:* Bobby Soto, Director of Admissions, 214-333-5242, E-mail: graduate@dbu.edu.
Website: http://www3.dbu.edu/graduate/special_education.asp

Delaware State University, Graduate Programs, College of Education, Health and Public Policy, Program in Special Education, Dover, DE 19901-2277. Offers MA. *Program availability:* Part-time, evening/weekend. *Degree requirements:* For master's, comprehensive exam, thesis optional. *Entrance requirements:* For master's, GRE General Test, minimum GPA of 3.0 in field, 2.75 overall. Additional exam requirements/ recommendations for international students: Required—TOEFL (minimum score 550 paper-based). Electronic applications accepted. *Faculty research:* Curriculum and instruction, distributive education.

Delta State University, Graduate Programs, College of Education, Division of Teacher Education, Leadership, and Research, Program in Special Education, Cleveland, MS 38733-0001. Offers M Ed. *Accreditation:* NCATE. *Program availability:* Part-time, evening/weekend. *Degree requirements:* For master's, thesis optional, practicum.

DePaul University, College of Education, Chicago, IL 60614. Offers bilingual bicultural education (M Ed, MA); counseling (M Ed, MA), including clinical mental health counseling, college student development, school counseling; curriculum studies (M Ed, MA, Ed D); early childhood education (M Ed, MA, Ed D); educating adults (MA); educational leadership (M Ed, MA, Ed D), including administration and supervision (M Ed, MA), principal preparation (M Ed, MA); elementary education (MA); mathematics education (MA); mathematics for teaching (MS); middle school mathematics education (MS); reading specialist (M Ed, MA); secondary education (M Ed); social and cultural foundations in education (MA); special education (M Ed, MA); world languages education (M Ed, MA). *Program availability:* Part-time, evening/weekend, online learning. *Degree requirements:* For doctorate, thesis/dissertation. Electronic applications accepted.

DeSales University, Division of Liberal Arts and Social Sciences, Center Valley, PA 18034-9568. Offers criminal justice (MCJ); digital forensics (MCJ, Postbaccalaureate Certificate); education (M Ed), including instructional technology, secondary education, special education, teaching English to speakers of other languages; investigative forensics (MCJ, Postbaccalaureate Certificate). *Program availability:* Part-time, 100% online, blended/hybrid learning. *Faculty:* 5 full-time (3 women), 20 part-time/adjunct (13 women). *Students:* 55 full-time (36 women), 100 part-time (64 women); includes 25 minority (5 Black or African American, non-Hispanic/Latino; 14 Hispanic/Latino; 6 Two or more races, non-Hispanic/Latino). Average age 33. 145 applicants, 80% accepted, 103 enrolled. In 2016, 36 master's awarded. *Entrance requirements:* For master's, bachelor's degree from accredited institution, minimum undergraduate GPA of 3.0, personal statement showing potential of graduate work, three letters of recommendation, professional goal statement. Additional exam requirements/ recommendations for international students: Required—TOEFL. *Application deadline:* Applications are processed on a rolling basis. Application fee: $50. Electronic applications accepted. *Expenses: Tuition:* Part-time $815 per credit hour. Tuition and fees vary according to degree level and program. *Financial support:* Applicants required to submit FAFSA. *Unit head:* Dr. Brain Kane, Division Head of Liberal Arts and Social Studies, 610-282-1100 Ext. 1274, E-mail: brian.kane@desales.edu. *Application contact:* Julia Ferraro, Director of Graduate Admissions, 610-282-1100 Ext. 1700, E-mail: gradadmissions@desales.edu.

Dominican College, Division of Teacher Education, Orangeburg, NY 10962-1210. Offers education/teaching of individuals with multiple disabilities (MS Ed). *Program availability:* Part-time, evening/weekend, online learning. *Faculty:* 6 full-time (4 women), 4 part-time/adjunct (all women). *Students:* 3 full-time (all women), 53 part-time (41 women); includes 13 minority (3 Black or African American, non-Hispanic/Latino; 10 Hispanic/Latino). In 2016, 28 master's awarded. *Degree requirements:* For master's, comprehensive exam (for some programs), thesis. *Entrance requirements:* For master's, 3 letters of recommendation (written by former or current work supervisors or instructors), interview. Additional exam requirements/recommendations for international students: Required—TOEFL (minimum score 90 iBT) *Application deadline:* Applications are processed on a rolling basis. *Expenses: Tuition:* Part-time $900 per credit. One-time fee: $200 full-time. *Financial support:* Application deadline: 2/1; applicants required to submit FAFSA. *Unit head:* Dr. Mike Kelly, Director, 845-848-4090, Fax: 845-359-7802, E-mail: mike.kelly@dc.edu. *Application contact:* Christina Lifshey, Assistant Director of Graduate Admissions, 845-848-7908 Ext. 15, Fax: 845-365-3150, E-mail: admissions@dc.edu.

Dominican University, School of Education, River Forest, IL 60305-1099. Offers early childhood education (MS); education (MAT); elementary education (MA Ed); English as a second language (MA Ed); reading (MA Ed); special education (MS). *Accreditation:* NCATE. *Program availability:* Part-time, evening/weekend, 100% online, blended/hybrid learning. *Faculty:* 12 full-time (8 women), 64 part-time/adjunct (57 women). *Students:* 13 full-time (all women), 500 part-time (385 women); includes 88 minority (40 Black or African American, non-Hispanic/Latino; 3 American Indian or Alaska Native, non-Hispanic/Latino; 18 Asian, non-Hispanic/Latino; 11 Hispanic/Latino; 2 Native Hawaiian or other Pacific Islander, non-Hispanic/Latino; 14 Two or more races, non-Hispanic/ Latino), 1 international. Average age 32. 162 applicants, 96% accepted, 104 enrolled. In 2016, 200 master's awarded. *Entrance requirements:* For master's, Illinois Test of Basic Skills. Additional exam requirements/recommendations for international students: Required—TOEFL (minimum score 550 paper-based; 79 iBT). *Application deadline:* Applications are processed on a rolling basis. Application fee: $25. *Expenses:* $550 per credit hour. *Financial support:* Career-related internships or fieldwork, scholarships/ grants, tuition waivers (partial), and unspecified assistantships available. Support available to part-time students. Financial award application deadline: 8/15; financial award applicants required to submit FAFSA. *Faculty research:* Governance of private education institutions, reading and language arts, inclusion, organizational planning, leadership and vision. *Unit head:* Dr. Colleen Reardon, Interim Executive Director, School of Education, 708-524-6643, Fax: 708-524-6665, E-mail: creardon@dom.edu. *Application contact:* Keven Hansen, Coordinator of Recruitment and Admissions, 708-524-6921, Fax: 708-524-6665, E-mail: educate@dom.edu.
Website: http://educate.dom.edu/

Dominican University of California, School of Education and Counseling Psychology, Program in Education plus Dual Teacher Preparation Programs, San Rafael, CA 94901-2298. Offers multiple subject (MS); single subject (MS). *Program availability:* Part-time, evening/weekend. *Degree requirements:* For master's, thesis. *Entrance requirements:* Additional exam requirements/recommendations for international students: Required—TOEFL (minimum score 550 paper-based; 80 iBT), IELTS (minimum score 6.5). Electronic applications accepted. Application fee is waived when completed online. *Expenses:* Contact institution.

Drew University, Caspersen School of Graduate Studies, Madison, NJ 07940-1493. Offers conflict resolution and leadership (Certificate), including community leadership, moderation, peace building; history and culture (MA, PhD), including American history, book history, British history, European history, Holocaust and genocide (M Litt, MA, D Litt, PhD), intellectual history, Irish history, print culture, public history; K-12 education (MAT), including art, biology, chemistry, elementary education, English, French, Italian, math, secondary education, special education, teacher of students with disabilities; liberal studies (M Litt, D Litt), including history, Holocaust and genocide (M Litt, MA, D Litt, PhD), Irish/Irish-American studies, literature (M Litt, MMH, D Litt, DMH, CMH), religion, spirituality, teaching in the two-year college, writing; medical humanities (MMH, DMH, CMH), including arts, health, healthcare, literature (M Litt, MMH, D Litt, DMH, CMH), scientific research; poetry (MFA). *Program availability:* Part-time, evening/ weekend. *Faculty:* 4 full-time (2 women), 31 part-time/adjunct (16 women). *Students:* 62 full-time (41 women), 199 part-time (130 women); includes 38 minority (17 Black or African American, non-Hispanic/Latino; 3 Asian, non-Hispanic/Latino; 17 Hispanic/ Latino; 1 Two or more races, non-Hispanic/Latino), 3 international. Average age 27. 93 applicants, 81% accepted, 46 enrolled. In 2016, 39 master's, 27 doctorates, 26 other advanced degrees awarded. Terminal master's awarded for partial completion of doctoral program. *Degree requirements:* For master's and other advanced degree, thesis (for some programs); for doctorate, one foreign language, comprehensive exam (for some programs), thesis/dissertation. *Entrance requirements:* For master's, PRAXIS Core and Subject Area tests (for MAT), resume, transcripts, writing sample, personal statement, letters of recommendation; for doctorate, GRE (PhD in history and culture), resume, transcripts, writing sample, personal statement, letters of recommendation. Additional exam requirements/recommendations for international students: Required—TOEFL (minimum score 587 paper-based; 94 iBT), IELTS (minimum score 7), TWE (minimum score 4). *Application deadline:* For fall admission, 8/1 for domestic students, 6/1 for international students; for spring admission, 12/1 for domestic students, 10/1 for international students. Applications are processed on a rolling basis. Application fee: $35. Electronic applications accepted. Tuition and fees vary according to program. *Financial support:* Fellowships, research assistantships, teaching assistantships, career-related internships or fieldwork, Federal Work-Study, scholarships/grants, and unspecified assistantships available. Support available to part-time students. Financial award applicants required to submit FAFSA. *Application contact:* Leanne Horinko, Director of Caspersen Admissions, 973-408-3280, E-mail: gradm@drew.edu.
Website: http://www.drew.edu/caspersen

Drexel University, Goodwin College of Professional Studies, School of Education, Philadelphia, PA 19104-2875. Offers applied behavior analysis (MS); creativity and innovation (MS); education improvement and transformation (MS); educational administration (MS); educational leadership and management (Ed D); educational leadership development and learning technologies (PhD); global and international education (MS); higher education (MS); human resources development (MS); learning technologies (MS); mathematics, learning and teaching (MS); special education (MS); teaching, learning and curriculum (MS). *Program availability:* Part-time, evening/ weekend, online learning. *Degree requirements:* For doctorate, thesis/dissertation. *Entrance requirements:* For doctorate, GRE or GMAT. Additional exam requirements/ recommendations for international students: Required—TOEFL, IELTS. Electronic applications accepted. Application fee is waived when completed online. *Expenses:* Contact institution. *Faculty research:* Leadership development, mathematics education, literacy, autism, educational technology.

See Display on page 660 and Close-Up on page 727.

Drury University, Master in Education Program, Springfield, MO 5802. Offers curriculum and instruction (M Ed), including elementary, middle school, secondary; gifted education (M Ed); instructional leadership (M Ed); instructional technology (M Ed); integrated learning (M Ed); online teaching (M Ed); special education (M Ed); special reading (M Ed). *Accreditation:* NCATE. *Program availability:* Part-time, evening/ weekend, 100% online, blended/hybrid learning. *Students:* 146 full-time (111 women); includes 6 minority (1 Asian, non-Hispanic/Latino; 3 Hispanic/Latino; 2 Two or more races, non-Hispanic/Latino), 1 international. Average age 34. 42 applicants, 74% accepted. In 2016, 74 master's awarded. *Entrance requirements:* For master's, GRE, bachelor's degree with minimum GPA of 2.75. Additional exam requirements/ recommendations for international students: Recommended—TOEFL (minimum score 80 iBT), IELTS (minimum score 6.5). *Application deadline:* For fall admission, 8/4 priority date for domestic and international students; for spring admission, 1/5 priority date for domestic and international students; for summer admission, 5/26 priority date for domestic and international students. Applications are processed on a rolling basis. Application fee: $25 ($50 for international students). Electronic applications accepted. *Expenses:* $352 tuition per credit hour; $7 per credit hour technology fee; $100 graduation fee; $59 portfolio fee (one-time). *Financial support:* In 2016–17, 20 students received support. Career-related internships or fieldwork, scholarships/grants, tuition waivers (partial), and unspecified assistantships available. Financial award application

deadline: 6/30; financial award applicants required to submit FAFSA. *Faculty research:* Gifted students, instructional technology, autism, diversity and social justice. *Unit head:* Dr. Asikaa Cosgrove, Director, Master in Education, 417-873-7806, E-mail: acosgrov@drury.edu.
Website: http://www.drury.edu/education-masters

Duquesne University, School of Education, Department of Counseling, Psychology, and Special Education, Program in Special Education, Pittsburgh, PA 15282-0001. Offers cognitive, behavior, physical/health disabilities (MS Ed); community and special education support (MS Ed); special education (PhD); special education 7-12 (MS Ed); special education PreK-8 (MS Ed). *Program availability:* Part-time, evening/weekend. *Faculty:* 7 full-time (6 women). *Students:* 22 full-time (13 women); includes 3 minority (1 Hispanic/Latino; 2 Two or more races, non-Hispanic/Latino), 12 international. Average age 30. 29 applicants, 55% accepted, 13 enrolled. In 2016, 9 master's awarded. *Degree requirements:* For master's, thesis optional. *Entrance requirements:* For master's, bachelor's degree. Additional exam requirements/recommendations for international students: Required—TOEFL (minimum score 550 paper-based), IELTS (minimum score 7). *Application deadline:* For fall admission, 9/1 for domestic students; for spring admission, 1/1 for domestic students. Applications are processed on a rolling basis. Application fee: $0. Electronic applications accepted. *Expenses: Tuition:* Full-time $22,212; part-time $1234 per credit. Tuition and fees vary according to program. *Financial support:* In 2016–17, 1 research assistantship was awarded. Support available to part-time students. *Unit head:* Dr. Morgan Chitiyo, Associate Professor, 412-396-4036, Fax: 412-396-1340, E-mail: chitiyom@duq.edu. *Application contact:* Michael Dolinger, Director of Student and Academic Services, 412-396-6647, Fax: 412-396-5585, E-mail: dolingerm@duq.edu.

D'Youville College, Department of Education, Buffalo, NY 14201-1084. Offers educational leadership (Ed D); elementary education (MS Ed); secondary education (MS Ed); special education (MS Ed). *Program availability:* Part-time, evening/weekend. *Degree requirements:* For master's, one foreign language, comprehensive exam, project or thesis. *Entrance requirements:* For master's, GRE (if GPA less than 2.75), minimum GPA of 3.0. Additional exam requirements/recommendations for international students: Required—TOEFL (minimum score 500 paper-based). Electronic applications accepted. *Faculty research:* Developmental disabilities, multiculturalism, early childhood education.

East Carolina University, Graduate School, College of Education, Department of Elementary and Middle Grades Education, Greenville, NC 27858-4353. Offers elementary education (MA Ed, MAT); English education (MAT); family and consumer science (MAT); health education (MAT); Hispanic studies (MAT); history education (MAT); middle grades education (MA Ed, MAT); music education (MAT); science education (MAT); special education (MAT), including general curriculum; vocational education (MAT). *Accreditation:* NCATE. *Program availability:* Part-time, evening/weekend, online learning. *Students:* 5 full-time (4 women), 18 part-time (16 women); includes 4 minority (3 Black or African American, non-Hispanic/Latino; 1 Hispanic/Latino). Average age 31. 19 applicants, 95% accepted, 13 enrolled. In 2016, 8 master's awarded. *Degree requirements:* For master's, comprehensive exam, thesis optional. *Entrance requirements:* For master's, GRE or MAT, minimum GPA of 2.5, bachelor's degree in related field, teaching license (MA Ed). Additional exam requirements/recommendations for international students: Required—TOEFL. *Application deadline:* For fall admission, 6/1 priority date for domestic students. Applications are processed on a rolling basis. Application fee: $70. *Financial support:* Federal Work-Study available. Support available to part-time students. Financial award application deadline: 6/1. *Unit head:* Dr. Ann Bullock, Chair, 252-328-1126, E-mail: bullockv@ecu.edu. *Application contact:* Dean of Graduate School, 252-328-6012, Fax: 252-328-6071, E-mail: gradschool@ecu.edu.
Website: http://www.ecu.edu/cs-educ/elmid/index.cfm

East Carolina University, Graduate School, College of Education, Department of Special Education, Foundations, and Research, Greenville, NC 27858-4353. Offers assistive technology (Certificate); autism (Certificate); behavior specialist (Certificate); deaf-blindness (Certificate); special education (MA Ed). *Program availability:* Part-time, online learning. *Degree requirements:* For master's, comprehensive exam, thesis optional. *Entrance requirements:* For master's, GRE General Test or MAT, interview, bachelor's degree in related field, minimum GPA of 2.5, teaching license. Additional exam requirements/recommendations for international students: Required—TOEFL. *Application deadline:* For fall admission, 6/1 priority date for domestic students. Applications are processed on a rolling basis. Application fee: $50. *Financial support:* Research assistantships, teaching assistantships, and Federal Work-Study available. Support available to part-time students. Financial award application deadline: 6/1; financial award applicants required to submit FAFSA. *Unit head:* Dr. Guili Zhang, Interim Chair, 252-328-4989, E-mail: zhangg@ecu.edu. *Application contact:* Dean of Graduate School, 252-328-6012, Fax: 252-328-6071, E-mail: gradschool@ecu.edu.
Website: http://www.ecu.edu/cs-educ/sefr/index.cfm

Eastern Illinois University, Graduate School, College of Education and Professional Studies, Department of Special Education, Charleston, IL 61920. Offers MS Ed. *Accreditation:* NCATE. *Program availability:* Part-time, evening/weekend. *Degree requirements:* For master's, comprehensive exam (for some programs), thesis (for some programs). *Entrance requirements:* For master's, GMAT or GRE. Additional exam requirements/recommendations for international students: Required—TOEFL (minimum score 500 paper-based; 61 iBT), IELTS (minimum score 6). Electronic applications accepted.

Eastern Kentucky University, The Graduate School, College of Education, Department of Special Education, Richmond, KY 40475-3102. Offers communication disorders (MA Ed). *Accreditation:* NCATE. *Program availability:* Part-time. *Degree requirements:* For master's, comprehensive exam. *Entrance requirements:* For master's, GRE General Test, MAT, minimum GPA of 2.5. *Faculty research:* Personnel needs in communication disorders, education needs of people who stutter, attention of special ed teacher.

Eastern Michigan University, Graduate School, College of Education, Department of Special Education, Program in Autism Spectrum Disorders, Ypsilanti, MI 48197. Offers MA. *Students:* 2 full-time (both women), 18 part-time (16 women); includes 1 minority (Black or African American, non-Hispanic/Latino), 1 international. Average age 34. 7 applicants, 71% accepted, 4 enrolled. In 2016, 11 master's awarded. Application fee: $45. *Application contact:* Dr. Sally Burton-Hoyle, Program Coordinator, 734-487-3300, Fax: 734-487-2473, E-mail: sburtonh@emich.edu.

Eastern Michigan University, Graduate School, College of Education, Department of Special Education, Program in Cognitive Impairment, Ypsilanti, MI 48197. Offers M Ed. *Students:* 14 full-time (11 women), 24 part-time (17 women); includes 3 minority (all Black or African American, non-Hispanic/Latino). Average age 36. 10 applicants, 80% accepted, 6 enrolled. In 2016, 7 master's awarded. Application fee: $45. *Application contact:* Dr. Jacquelyn McGinnis, Advisor, 734-487-3300, Fax: 734-487-2473, E-mail: jmcginnis@emich.edu.

Eastern Michigan University, Graduate School, College of Education, Department of Special Education, Program in Emotional Impairment, Ypsilanti, MI 48197. Offers M Ed. *Students:* 4 full-time (3 women), 10 part-time (7 women); includes 3 minority (2 Black or African American, non-Hispanic/Latino; 1 Hispanic/Latino), 1 international. Average age 35. 3 applicants, 100% accepted, 3 enrolled. In 2016, 4 master's awarded. Application fee: $45. *Application contact:* Dr. Janet Fisher, Department Head, 734-487-3300, Fax: 734-487-2473, E-mail: jfisher3@emich.edu.

Eastern Michigan University, Graduate School, College of Education, Department of Special Education, Program in Learning Disabilities, Ypsilanti, MI 48197. Offers MA. *Students:* 2 full-time (both women), 24 part-time (21 women); includes 1 minority (Black or African American, non-Hispanic/Latino). Average age 36. 9 applicants, 67% accepted, 3 enrolled. In 2016, 2 master's awarded. Application fee: $45. *Application contact:* Dr. Loreena Parks, Coordinator, 734-487-2769, Fax: 734-487-2473, E-mail: lparks1@emich.edu.

Eastern Michigan University, Graduate School, College of Education, Department of Special Education, Program in Physical/Other Health Impairment, Ypsilanti, MI 48197. Offers M Ed. *Students:* 1 (woman) full-time, 5 part-time (all women). Average age 36. 3 applicants, 100% accepted, 3 enrolled. In 2016, 1 master's awarded. Application fee: $45. *Application contact:* Dr. Jacquelyn McGinnis, Advisor, 734-487-3300, Fax: 734-487-2473, E-mail: jmcginnis@emich.edu.

Eastern Michigan University, Graduate School, College of Education, Department of Special Education, Program in Visual Impairment, Ypsilanti, MI 48197. Offers M Ed. Application fee: $45. *Application contact:* Dr. Alicia Li, Advisor, 734-487-3300, Fax: 734-487-2473, E-mail: tli@emich.edu.

Eastern Michigan University, Graduate School, College of Education, Department of Special Education, Programs in Special Education, Ypsilanti, MI 48197. Offers administration and supervision (SPA); curriculum development (SPA); special education (MA). *Accreditation:* NCATE. *Program availability:* Part-time, evening/weekend, online learning. *Students:* 4 full-time (3 women), 23 part-time (20 women); includes 4 minority (2 Black or African American, non-Hispanic/Latino; 1 Asian, non-Hispanic/Latino; 1 Hispanic/Latino), 3 international. Average age 40. 13 applicants, 85% accepted, 7 enrolled. In 2016, 1 master's, 5 other advanced degrees awarded. *Entrance requirements:* For master's, GRE General Test. Additional exam requirements/recommendations for international students: Required—TOEFL. *Application deadline:* Applications are processed on a rolling basis. Application fee: $45. *Financial support:* Fellowships, research assistantships with full tuition reimbursements, teaching assistantships with full tuition reimbursements, career-related internships or fieldwork, Federal Work-Study, institutionally sponsored loans, scholarships/grants, tuition waivers (partial), and unspecified assistantships available. Support available to part-time students. Financial award applicants required to submit FAFSA. *Application contact:* Dr. Derrick Fries, Advisor, 734-487-3300, Fax: 734-487-2473, E-mail: dfries@emich.edu.

Eastern Michigan University, Graduate School, College of Education, Department of Teacher Education, Program in Urban/Diversity Education, Ypsilanti, MI 48197. Offers MA. *Students:* 1 (woman) part-time; minority (Asian, non-Hispanic/Latino). Average age 26. In 2016, 1 master's awarded. Application fee: $45. *Application contact:* Dr. Patricia Williams-Boyd, Advisor, 734-487-3260, Fax: 734-487-2101, E-mail: pwilliams1@emich.edu.

Eastern Nazarene College, Adult and Graduate Studies, Division of Teacher Education, Quincy, MA 02170. Offers administration (M Ed); early childhood education (M Ed, Certificate); elementary education (M Ed, Certificate); English as a second language (Certificate); instructional enrichment and development (Certificate); middle school education (M Ed, Certificate); moderate special needs education (Certificate); principal (Certificate); program development and supervision (Certificate); secondary education (M Ed, Certificate); special education administrator (Certificate); special needs (M Ed); supervisor (Certificate); teacher of reading (M Ed, Certificate). M Ed also available through weekend program for administration, special needs, and teacher of reading only. *Program availability:* Part-time, evening/weekend. *Entrance requirements:* Additional exam requirements/recommendations for international students: Required—TOEFL (minimum score 550 paper-based).

Eastern New Mexico University, Graduate School, College of Education and Technology, Department of Educational Studies, Program in Special Education, Portales, NM 88130. Offers early childhood special education (M Sp Ed); general (M Sp Ed). *Program availability:* Part-time. *Degree requirements:* For master's, comprehensive exam, thesis optional. *Entrance requirements:* For master's, minimum GPA of 3.0, letter of recommendation, photocopy of teaching license or confirmation of entrance into alternative licensure program, writing assessment, 2 letters of application, special education license or minimum 30 hours of undergraduate course work. Additional exam requirements/recommendations for international students: Required—TOEFL (minimum score 550 paper-based; 79 iBT), IELTS (minimum score 6). Electronic applications accepted.

Eastern University, Loeb School of Education, St. Davids, PA 19087-3696. Offers ESL program specialist (K-12) (Certificate); general supervisor (PreK-12) (Certificate); health and physical education (K-12) (Certificate); middle level (4-8) (Certificate); multicultural education (M Ed); organizational leadership with education (PhD); Pre K-4 (Certificate); Pre K-4 with special education (Certificate); reading (M Ed); reading specialist (K-12) (Certificate); reading supervisor (K-12) (Certificate); school health supervisor (Certificate); school nurse (K-12) (Certificate); secondary biology education (7-12) (Certificate); secondary chemistry education (7-12) (Certificate); secondary communication education (7-12) (Certificate); secondary education (7-12) (Certificate); secondary English education (7-12) (Certificate); secondary math education (7-12) (Certificate); secondary social studies education (7-12) (Certificate); special education (M Ed); special education (7-12) (Certificate); special education (Pre K-8) (Certificate); special education supervisor (N-12) (Certificate); TESOL (M Ed); world language (Certificate), including French, Spanish. *Program availability:* Part-time, evening/weekend, online learning. *Students:* 41 full-time (32 women), 89 part-time (68 women); includes 54 minority (38 Black or African American, non-Hispanic/Latino; 3 Asian, non-Hispanic/Latino; 11 Hispanic/Latino; 2 Two or more races, non-Hispanic/Latino), 2 international. Average age 37. In 2016, 64 master's awarded. *Entrance requirements:* Additional exam requirements/recommendations for international students: Required—TOEFL. *Application deadline:* Applications are processed on a rolling basis. Application fee: $35. Electronic applications accepted. Application fee is waived when completed online. *Expenses:* $690 per credit. *Unit head:* Michael Dziedziak, Executive Director of Enrollment, 800-452-0996, E-mail: gpsadmissions@eastern.edu.
Website: http://www.eastern.edu/academics/programs/loeb-school-education-0

East Stroudsburg University of Pennsylvania, Graduate and Extended Studies, College of Education, Department of Special Education and Rehabilitation, East Stroudsburg, PA 18301-2999. Offers special education (M Ed). *Program availability:* Part-time, evening/weekend, online learning. *Students:* 4 full-time (3 women), 42 part-time (34 women); includes 2 minority (1 Black or African American, non-Hispanic/Latino; 1 Hispanic/Latino). *Degree requirements:* For master's, comprehensive exam. *Entrance requirements:* For master's, PRAXIS/teacher certification, letter of recommendation, Pennsylvania Department of Education requirements. Additional exam requirements/recommendations for international students: Recommended—TOEFL (minimum score 560 paper-based; 83 iBT), IELTS. *Application deadline:* For fall admission, 7/31 priority date for domestic students, 6/30 priority date for international students; for spring admission, 11/30 for domestic students, 10/31 for international students. Applications are processed on a rolling basis. Application fee: $50. Electronic applications accepted. *Expenses:* Tuition, state resident: full-time $8694; part-time $5796 per year. Tuition, nonresident: full-time $13,050; part-time $8700 per year. *Required fees:* $2550; $1690 per unit. $845 per semester. Tuition and fees vary according to course load, campus/location and program. *Financial support:* Research assistantships with tuition reimbursements, career-related internships or fieldwork, Federal Work-Study, and unspecified assistantships available. Support available to part-time students. Financial award application deadline: 3/1; financial award applicants required to submit FAFSA. *Unit head:* Dr. Gina Scala, Chair, 570-422-3781, Fax: 570-422-3506, E-mail: gscala@esu.edu. *Application contact:* Kevin Quintero, Associate Director, Graduate and Extended Studies, 570-422-3890, Fax: 570-422-2711, E-mail: kquintero@esu.edu.

East Tennessee State University, School of Graduate Studies, College of Education, Department of Teaching and Learning, Johnson City, TN 37614. Offers early childhood education (MA, PhD); early childhood education emergent inquiry (Post-Master's Certificate); special education (M Ed), including advanced practitioner, early childhood special education, special education. *Program availability:* Part-time. *Degree requirements:* For master's, thesis (for some programs), practicum, residency, or thesis; for doctorate, comprehensive exam, thesis/dissertation, apprenticeship. *Entrance requirements:* For master's, PRAXIS I or Tennessee teaching license (for special education only), minimum GPA of 3.0 (or complete probationary period with no grade lower than B for first 9 graduate hours for early childhood education); for doctorate, GRE General Test, professional resume; master's degree in early childhood or related field; interview; four letters of recommendation; for Post-Master's Certificate, bachelor's or master's degree in early childhood or related field; two years of experience working with young children (preferred). Additional exam requirements/recommendations for international students: Required—TOEFL (minimum score 550 paper-based; 79 iBT). *Faculty research:* Teaching students with significant disabilities, problem solving in toddlers, children and their development and learning, connecting classroom environment to student engagement in PreK-3, bilingual education in Ecuador, positive discipline/behavior support programs, early childhood relationships, international and comparative special education.

Edgewood College, Program in Education, Madison, WI 53711-1997. Offers adult learning (MA Ed); director of special education and pupil services (Certificate); education (MA Ed); teaching and learning (MA Ed). *Accreditation:* NCATE (one or more programs are accredited). *Program availability:* Part-time, evening/weekend. *Faculty:* 13 full-time (9 women), 15 part-time/adjunct (10 women). *Students:* 137 full-time (91 women), 215 part-time (150 women); includes 51 minority (23 Black or African American, non-Hispanic/Latino; 3 American Indian or Alaska Native, non-Hispanic/Latino; 5 Asian, non-Hispanic/Latino; 17 Hispanic/Latino; 3 Two or more races, non-Hispanic/Latino), 18 international. Average age 37. In 2016, 74 master's, 18 doctorates awarded. *Degree requirements:* For master's, practicum, research project; for doctorate, comprehensive exam, thesis/dissertation. *Entrance requirements:* For master's, minimum GPA of 2.75, 2 letters of recommendation, personal statement; for doctorate, resume, letter of intent, 2 letters of recommendation, interview, writing sample. Additional exam requirements/recommendations for international students: Required—TOEFL (minimum score 525 paper-based; 72 iBT). *Application deadline:* For fall admission, 8/15 for domestic students, 5/1 for international students; for spring admission, 1/8 for domestic students, 11/1 for international students. Applications are processed on a rolling basis. Application fee: $30. Electronic applications accepted. *Expenses: Tuition:* Part-time $898 per credit. Tuition and fees vary according to course load. *Financial support:* Applicants required to submit FAFSA. *Faculty research:* Urban high schools, transgender students, literacy pedagogy, funds of knowledge, English language learners. *Unit head:* Dr. Timothy D. Slekar, Dean, E-mail: tslekar@edgewood.edu. *Application contact:* Joann Eastman, Admissions Counselor, 608-663-3250, Fax: 608-663-2214, E-mail: gps@edgewood.edu.
Website: https://www.edgewood.edu/academics/schools/school-of-education

Edinboro University of Pennsylvania, Department of Counseling, School Psychology and Special Education, Edinboro, PA 16444. Offers counseling (MA), including art therapy, clinical mental health counseling, college counseling, rehabilitation counseling, school counseling; educational psychology (M Ed); school psychology (Ed S); special education (M Ed), including autism, behavior management. *Accreditation:* ACA. *Program availability:* Part-time, evening/weekend. *Degree requirements:* For master's, thesis or alternative, competency exam; for Ed S, thesis or alternative. *Entrance requirements:* For master's and Ed S, GRE or MAT, minimum QPA of 2.5. Electronic applications accepted.

Elmhurst College, Graduate Programs, Program in Early Childhood Special Education, Elmhurst, IL 60126-3296. Offers M Ed. *Program availability:* Part-time, evening/weekend. *Faculty:* 2 full-time (both women), 3 part-time/adjunct (all women). *Students:* 7 full-time (all women), 19 part-time (all women); includes 6 minority (1 Black or African American, non-Hispanic/Latino; 1 Asian, non-Hispanic/Latino; 3 Hispanic/Latino; 1 Two or more races, non-Hispanic/Latino). Average age 29. 19 applicants, 68% accepted, 11 enrolled. In 2016, 12 master's awarded. *Entrance requirements:* For master's, 3 recommendations, resume, statement of purpose. Additional exam requirements/recommendations for international students: Required—TOEFL (minimum score 550 paper-based; 79 iBT). *Application deadline:* Applications are processed on a rolling basis. Application fee: $0. Electronic applications accepted. *Expenses:* $650 per semester hour. *Financial support:* In 2016–17, 17 students received support. Scholarships/grants available. Support available to part-time students. Financial award application deadline: 3/1; financial award applicants required to submit FAFSA. *Unit head:* Dr. Therese Wehman. *Application contact:* Timothy J. Panfil, Director of Enrollment Management, School for Professional Studies, 630-617-3300 Ext. 3256, Fax: 630-617-6471, E-mail: panfilt@elmhurst.edu.
Website: http://www.elmhurst.edu/ecse

Elmhurst College, Graduate Programs, Program in Special Education, Elmhurst, IL 60126-3296. Offers MS Ed. *Program availability:* Part-time, evening/weekend. *Faculty:* 4 full-time (all women), 1 (woman) part-time/adjunct. *Students:* 5 part-time (all women). Average age 29. 7 applicants, 43% accepted, 3 enrolled. *Entrance requirements:* For master's, 3 recommendations, resume, statement of purpose. Additional exam requirements/recommendations for international students: Required—TOEFL (minimum score 550 paper-based; 79 iBT). *Application deadline:* Applications are processed on a rolling basis. Application fee: $0. Electronic applications accepted. *Expenses:* $450 per semester hour. *Financial support:* In 2016–17, 3 students received support. Scholarships/grants available. Support available to part-time students. Financial award application deadline: 3/1; financial award applicants required to submit FAFSA. *Application contact:* Timothy J. Panfil, Director of Enrollment Management, School for Professional Studies, 630-617-3300 Ext. 3256, Fax: 630-617-6471, E-mail: panfilt@elmhurst.edu.
Website: http://www.elmhurst.edu/admission/graduate/se

Elms College, Division of Education, Chicopee, MA 01013-2839. Offers early childhood education (MAT); education (M Ed, CAGS); elementary education (MAT); English as a second language (MAT); reading (MAT); secondary education (MAT), including biology education, English education, Spanish education; special education (MAT). *Program availability:* Part-time, evening/weekend. *Faculty:* 5 full-time (all women), 7 part-time/adjunct (6 women). *Students:* 6 full-time (all women), 136 part-time (111 women); includes 6 minority (1 Asian, non-Hispanic/Latino; 5 Hispanic/Latino). Average age 33. 27 applicants, 89% accepted, 20 enrolled. In 2016, 47 master's, 3 other advanced degrees awarded. *Degree requirements:* For master's, thesis (for some programs). *Entrance requirements:* For master's, Massachusetts Educators Certification Test, minimum GPA of 3.0; for CAGS, master's degree in education. Additional exam requirements/recommendations for international students: Required—TOEFL. *Application deadline:* For fall admission, 7/1 priority date for domestic students; for spring admission, 11/1 priority date for domestic students. Applications are processed on a rolling basis. Application fee: $30. *Expenses: Tuition:* Full-time $13,392. *Required fees:* $200. *Financial support:* In 2016–17, 2 teaching assistantships with partial tuition reimbursements were awarded; tuition waivers (partial) also available. Support available to part-time students. Financial award applicants required to submit FAFSA. *Unit head:* Dr. Mary Janeczek, Chair, Division of Education, 413-594-2761, Fax: 413-592-4871, E-mail: janeczeke@elms.edu. *Application contact:* Dr. Elizabeth Teahan Hukowicz, Dean, School of Graduate and Professional Studies, 413-265-2360, Fax: 413-265-2459, E-mail: hukowicze@elms.edu.

Elon University, Program in Education, Elon, NC 27244-2010. Offers elementary education (M Ed); gifted education (M Ed); special education (M Ed). *Accreditation:* NCATE. *Program availability:* Part-time. *Faculty:* 9 full-time (7 women), 2 part-time/adjunct (both women). *Students:* 17 part-time (all women); includes 7 minority (3 Black or African American, non-Hispanic/Latino; 1 American Indian or Alaska Native, non-Hispanic/Latino; 2 Hispanic/Latino; 1 Two or more races, non-Hispanic/Latino). Average age 33. 24 applicants, 50% accepted, 8 enrolled. In 2016, 24 master's awarded. *Entrance requirements:* For master's, GRE, MAT. Additional exam requirements/recommendations for international students: Required—TOEFL (minimum score 550 paper-based; 79 iBT). *Application deadline:* For fall admission, 5/1 for domestic students. Applications are processed on a rolling basis. Application fee: $50. Electronic applications accepted. *Financial support:* Federal Work-Study and scholarships/grants available. Support available to part-time students. Financial award application deadline: 6/1; financial award applicants required to submit FAFSA. *Faculty research:* Teaching reading to low-achieving second and third graders, pre- and post-student teaching attitudes, children's writing, whole language methodology, critical creative thinking. *Unit head:* Dr. Ann Bullock, Dean of the School of Education/Professor, 336-278-5900, E-mail: abullock9@elon.edu. *Application contact:* Art Fadde, Director of Graduate Admissions, 800-334-8448 Ext. 3, Fax: 336-278-7699, E-mail: afadde@elon.edu.
Website: http://www.elon.edu/med

Emporia State University, Program in Special Education, Emporia, KS 66801-5415. Offers behavior disorders (MS); gifted, talented, and creative (MS); interrelated special education (MS). *Accreditation:* NCATE. *Program availability:* Part-time. *Faculty:* 29 full-time (21 women), 3 part-time/adjunct (2 women). *Students:* 5 full-time (all women), 158 part-time (119 women); includes 6 minority (1 Asian, non-Hispanic/Latino; 4 Hispanic/Latino; 1 Two or more races, non-Hispanic/Latino). 35 applicants, 100% accepted, 23 enrolled. In 2016, 40 master's awarded. *Degree requirements:* For master's, comprehensive exam or thesis, practicum. *Entrance requirements:* For master's, GRE General Test or MAT, essay exam, appropriate bachelor's degree, teacher certification, letters of recommendation. Additional exam requirements/recommendations for international students: Required—TOEFL (minimum score 520 paper-based; 68 iBT). *Application deadline:* For fall admission, 8/15 priority date for domestic students. Applications are processed on a rolling basis. Application fee: $30 ($75 for international students). Electronic applications accepted. *Expenses:* Tuition, state resident: full-time $5922; part-time $246.75 per credit hour. Tuition, nonresident: full-time $18,414; part-time $767.25 per credit hour. *Required fees:* $1884; $78.50 per credit hour. *Financial support:* In 2016–17, 1 teaching assistantship with full tuition reimbursement (averaging $7,335 per year) was awarded; Federal Work-Study, institutionally sponsored loans, health care benefits, and unspecified assistantships also available. Financial award application deadline: 3/15; financial award applicants required to submit FAFSA. *Unit head:* Dr. Matt Siemears, Chair, 620-341-6057, E-mail: msiemear@emporia.edu. *Application contact:* Mary Sewell, Admissions Coordinator, 800-950-GRAD, Fax: 620-341-5909, E-mail: msewell@emporia.edu.
Website: http://www.emporia.edu/elecse/sped/

Endicott College, Van Loan School of Graduate and Professional Studies, Program in Autism and Applied Behavior Analysis, Beverly, MA 01915-2096. Offers M Ed, PhD. *Program availability:* Part-time, evening/weekend, 100% online, blended/hybrid learning. *Faculty:* 4 full-time (2 women), 22 part-time/adjunct (19 women). *Students:* 17 full-time (15 women), 126 part-time (112 women); includes 24 minority (5 Black or African American, non-Hispanic/Latino; 4 Asian, non-Hispanic/Latino; 15 Hispanic/Latino). Average age 31. 55 applicants, 96% accepted, 43 enrolled. In 2016, 37 master's awarded. *Degree requirements:* For master's, thesis; for doctorate, thesis/dissertation, qualifying examination. *Entrance requirements:* For master's, MAT or GRE, undergraduate transcript, two recommendations, personal statement. Additional exam requirements/recommendations for international students: Required—TOEFL. *Application deadline:* Applications are processed on a rolling basis. Application fee: $50. Electronic applications accepted. *Expenses:* Contact institution. *Financial support:* Applicants required to submit FAFSA. *Faculty research:* ABA intervention for autism, behavioral assessment, evidence-based treatments. *Unit head:* Dr. Mary Jane Weiss, Director of Autism and Applied Behavior Analysis, 978-232-2199, E-mail: mweiss@endicott.edu. *Application contact:* Ian Menchini, Director, Graduate Enrollment and Advising, 978-232-5292, Fax: 978-232-3000, E-mail: imenchin@endicott.edu.
Website: http://www.endicott.edu/VanLoan/Institute-Behavioral-Studies/Degree-Programs/Master-Ed-Autism-ABA.aspx

Endicott College, Van Loan School of Graduate and Professional Studies, Program in Special Needs and Applied Behavior Analysis, Beverly, MA 01915-2096. Offers M Ed. *Program availability:* Part-time, evening/weekend, 100% online, blended/hybrid learning. *Faculty:* 6 full-time (3 women), 34 part-time/adjunct (28 women). *Students:* 52 full-time (46 women), 103 part-time (86 women); includes 8 minority (2 Black or African American, non-Hispanic/Latino; 1 Asian, non-Hispanic/Latino; 3 Hispanic/Latino; 2 Two or more races, non-Hispanic/Latino). Average age 29. 18 applicants, 100% accepted, 15 enrolled. In 2016, 62 master's awarded. *Degree requirements:* For master's, comprehensive exam, thesis, practicum. *Entrance requirements:* For master's, MAT or GRE, Massachusetts teaching certificate, letters of recommendation, undergraduate transcript, essay. Additional exam requirements/recommendations for international students: Required—TOEFL. *Application deadline:* Applications are processed on a rolling basis. Application fee: $50. Electronic applications accepted. *Expenses:* Contact institution. *Financial support:* Career-related internships or fieldwork, Federal Work-Study, and institutionally sponsored loans available. Financial award applicants required to submit FAFSA. *Faculty research:* Evidence-based treatments, developmental disabilities, challenging behaviors, staff training/management, behavioral assessments. *Unit head:* Allyson Penaloza, Assistant Director and Recruiter, 978-816-7642, Fax: 978-232-3000, E-mail: apenaloz@endicott.edu. *Application contact:* Ian Menchini, Director, Graduate Enrollment and Advising, 978-232-5292, E-mail: imenchin@endicott.edu.

Website: http://www.endicott.edu/VanLoan/Institute-Behavioral-Studies/Degree-Programs/Special-Needs-App-Behav-Analysis.aspx

Fairfield University, Graduate School of Education and Allied Professions, Fairfield, CT 06824. Offers applied behavior analysis (ATC); applied psychology (MA); clinical mental health counseling (MA, CAS); educational technology (MA); elementary education (MA, CAS); family studies (MA); integration of spirituality and religion in counseling (ATC); marriage and family therapy (MA); reading and language development (Sixth Year Certificate); school counseling (MA, CAS); school psychology (MA, CAS); school-based marriage and family therapy (ATC); secondary education (MA); special education (MA, CAS); substance abuse counseling (ATC); teaching (Certificate); teaching and foundations (MA, CAS); TESOL, world languages, and bilingual education (MA, CAS). *Accreditation:* NCATE. *Program availability:* Part-time, evening/weekend. *Faculty:* 19 full-time (15 women), 38 part-time/adjunct (26 women). *Students:* 153 full-time (132 women), 302 part-time (252 women); includes 97 minority (24 Black or African American, non-Hispanic/Latino; 12 Asian, non-Hispanic/Latino; 55 Hispanic/Latino; 6 Two or more races, non-Hispanic/Latino), 6 international. Average age 32. 283 applicants, 61% accepted, 97 enrolled. In 2016, 130 master's awarded. *Degree requirements:* For master's, comprehensive exam. *Entrance requirements:* For master's, minimum GPA of 3.0, 2 recommendations, resume. Additional exam requirements/recommendations for international students: Required—TOEFL (minimum score 550 paper-based; 84 iBT) or IELTS (minimum score 7.5). *Application deadline:* For fall admission, 2/15 for international students; for spring admission, 10/1 for international students. Application fee: $60. Electronic applications accepted. *Expenses:* $725 per credit hour. *Financial support:* In 2016–17, 42 students received support. Career-related internships or fieldwork and unspecified assistantships available. Support available to part-time students. Financial award applicants required to submit FAFSA. *Faculty research:* Reading and literacy, writing, social justice and inequality in education, addictions and mental health issues, therapeutic relationships and clinical supervision. *Unit head:* Dr. Robert D. Hannafin, Dean, 203-254-4250, Fax: 203-254-4241, E-mail: rhannafin@fairfield.edu. *Application contact:* Marianne Gumpper, Director of Graduate Admission, 203-254-4184, Fax: 203-254-4073, E-mail: gradadmis@fairfield.edu.
Website: http://www.fairfield.edu/gseap

Fairleigh Dickinson University, Metropolitan Campus, University College: Arts, Sciences, and Professional Studies, Peter Sammartino School of Education, Program in Learning Disabilities, Teaneck, NJ 07666-1914. Offers MA. *Accreditation:* TEAC.

Fairmont State University, Programs in Education, Fairmont, WV 26554. Offers digital media, new literacies and learning (M Ed); education (MAT); exercise science, fitness and wellness (M Ed); professional studies (M Ed); reading (M Ed); special education (M Ed). *Accreditation:* NCATE. *Program availability:* Part-time, evening/weekend, 100% online. *Faculty:* 18 full-time (11 women), 5 part-time/adjunct (3 women). *Students:* 62 full-time (52 women), 102 part-time (82 women); includes 6 minority (2 Black or African American, non-Hispanic/Latino; 1 American Indian or Alaska Native, non-Hispanic/Latino; 1 Hispanic/Latino; 2 Two or more races, non-Hispanic/Latino). Average age 33. 68 applicants, 84% accepted, 47 enrolled. In 2016, 44 degrees awarded. *Entrance requirements:* For master's, GRE. Additional exam requirements/recommendations for international students: Required—TOEFL (minimum score 80 iBT), IELTS (minimum score 6.5). *Application deadline:* For fall admission, 5/1 for domestic and international students. Applications are processed on a rolling basis. Application fee: $40. Electronic applications accepted. *Expenses:* Tuition, state resident: full-time $7504; part-time $405 per credit hour. Tuition, nonresident: full-time $16,060; part-time $880 per credit hour. Part-time tuition and fees vary according to course load. *Financial support:* In 2016–17, 20 students received support. Research assistantships, teaching assistantships, scholarships/grants, and unspecified assistantships available. Financial award applicants required to submit FAFSA. *Unit head:* Dr. Carolyn Crislip-Tacy, Interim Dean, School of Education, 304-367-4143, Fax: 304-367-4599, E-mail: carolyn.crislip-tacy@fairmontstate.edu. *Application contact:* Jack Kirby, Director of Graduate Studies, 304-367-4101, E-mail: jack.kirby@fairmontstate.edu.
Website: http://www.fairmontstate.edu/graduatestudies/

Ferris State University, College of Education and Human Services, School of Education, Big Rapids, MI 49307. Offers curriculum and instruction (M Ed), including special education, subject area; educational leadership (MS); instructor (MSCTE); post-secondary administration (MSCTE); training and development (MSCTE). *Program availability:* Part-time, evening/weekend, blended/hybrid learning. *Faculty:* 7 full-time (4 women), 9 part-time/adjunct (6 women). *Students:* 3 full-time (1 woman), 62 part-time (34 women); includes 8 minority (3 Black or African American, non-Hispanic/Latino; 1 Hispanic/Latino; 4 Two or more races, non-Hispanic/Latino), 9 international. Average age 37. 24 applicants, 71% accepted, 10 enrolled. In 2016, 36 master's awarded. *Degree requirements:* For master's, thesis, research paper or project. *Entrance requirements:* For master's, minimum undergraduate GPA of 3.0. Additional exam requirements/recommendations for international students: Required—TOEFL (minimum score 500 paper-based, 79 iBT) or IELTS. *Application deadline:* For fall admission, 7/1 priority date for domestic and international students; for spring admission, 11/1 priority date for domestic and international students; for summer admission, 3/1 priority date for domestic and international students. Applications are processed on a rolling basis. Application fee: $30. Electronic applications accepted. Application fee is waived when completed online. Tuition and fees vary according to degree level and program. *Financial support:* Career-related internships or fieldwork and scholarships/grants available. Support available to part-time students. Financial award applicants required to submit FAFSA. *Faculty research:* Suicide prevention, reading, women in education, special needs, administration. *Unit head:* Arrick L. Jackson, Dean, 231-591-2702, Fax: 231-591-2043, E-mail: arrickJackson@ferris.edu. *Application contact:* Liza Ing, Graduate Program Coordinator, 231-591-5362, Fax: 231-591-2043, E-mail: lizaIng@ferris.edu.
Website: http://www.ferris.edu/education/education/

Fitchburg State University, Division of Graduate and Continuing Education, Program in Special Education, Fitchburg, MA 01420-2697. Offers guided studies (M Ed); reading specialist (M Ed); teaching students with moderate disabilities (M Ed); teaching students with severe disabilities (M Ed). *Accreditation:* NCATE. *Program availability:* Part-time, evening/weekend. *Degree requirements:* For master's, internship. *Entrance requirements:* Additional exam requirements/recommendations for international students: Required—TOEFL (minimum score 550 paper-based; 79 iBT). Electronic applications accepted. *Expenses:* Tuition, state resident: full-time $2871; part-time $1914 per year. Tuition, nonresident: full-time $2871; part-time $1914 per year. *Required fees:* $3828. Tuition and fees vary according to program.

Florida Atlantic University, College of Education, Department of Exceptional Student Education, Boca Raton, FL 33431-0991. Offers M Ed, Ed D. *Accreditation:* NCATE. *Program availability:* Part-time, evening/weekend. *Faculty:* 13 full-time (6 women). *Students:* 18 full-time (17 women), 44 part-time (39 women); includes 21 minority (8 Black or African American, non-Hispanic/Latino; 2 Asian, non-Hispanic/Latino; 9 Hispanic/Latino; 2 Two or more races, non-Hispanic/Latino). Average age 33. 58 applicants, 53% accepted, 21 enrolled. In 2016, 11 master's, 1 doctorate awarded. *Degree requirements:* For master's, thesis optional, internship; for doctorate, comprehensive exam, thesis/dissertation, internship. *Entrance requirements:* For master's, GRE General Test, minimum GPA of 3.0 during previous 2 years; for doctorate, GRE General Test, 3 years of teaching experience, interview. Additional exam requirements/recommendations for international students: Required—TOEFL (minimum score 500 paper-based; 61 iBT), IELTS (minimum score 6). *Application deadline:* For fall admission, 7/1 for domestic students, 2/15 for international students; for spring admission, 11/1 for domestic students, 7/15 for international students. Applications are processed on a rolling basis. Application fee: $30. Electronic applications accepted. *Expenses:* Tuition, state resident: full-time $7392; part-time $369.82 per credit hour. Tuition, nonresident: full-time $19,432; part-time $1024.81 per credit hour. *Financial support:* Fellowships with tuition reimbursements, research assistantships with tuition reimbursements, teaching assistantships with partial tuition reimbursements, career-related internships or fieldwork, Federal Work-Study, scholarships/grants, tuition waivers (partial), and unspecified assistantships available. Support available to part-time students. Financial award applicants required to submit FAFSA. *Faculty research:* Instructional design, assessment, educational reform, behavioral research, social integration. *Unit head:* Ellen Ismalom, 561-297-3284, E-mail: eismalon@fau.edu.
Website: http://www.coe.fau.edu/academicdepartments/ese/

Florida Gulf Coast University, College of Education, Program in Special Education, Fort Myers, FL 33965-6565. Offers behavior disorders (M Ed); mental retardation (M Ed); specific learning disabilities (M Ed); varying exceptionalities (M Ed). *Program availability:* Part-time, evening/weekend. *Faculty:* 26 full-time (18 women), 44 part-time/adjunct (32 women). *Students:* 7 part-time (all women); includes 3 minority (2 Hispanic/Latino; 1 Two or more races, non-Hispanic/Latino). Average age 32. 7 applicants, 86% accepted, 1 enrolled. In 2016, 3 master's awarded. *Degree requirements:* For master's, thesis or alternative. *Entrance requirements:* For master's, GRE General Test, MAT, minimum GPA of 3.0. Additional exam requirements/recommendations for international students: Required—TOEFL (minimum score 550 paper-based). *Application deadline:* For fall admission, 7/1 priority date for domestic students; for spring admission, 10/15 for domestic students. Applications are processed on a rolling basis. Application fee: $30. Electronic applications accepted. *Expenses:* Tuition, state resident: full-time $6721. Tuition, nonresident: full-time $28,170. *Required fees:* $1987. Tuition and fees vary according to course load and degree level. *Financial support:* In 2016–17, 2 students received support. Application deadline: 3/1; applicants required to submit FAFSA. *Faculty research:* Inclusion, interacting with families, alternative certification. *Unit head:* Dr. Carolynne Gischel, Department Chair, 239-590-7795, Fax: 239-590-7801, E-mail: cgischel@fgcu.edu. *Application contact:* Gil Medina, Executive Secretary, 239-590-7776, Fax: 239-590-7801, E-mail: gmedina@fgcu.edu.

Florida International University, College of Arts, Sciences, and Education, Department of Teaching and Learning, Miami, FL 33199. Offers art education (MA, MS); curriculum and instruction (MS, Ed D, PhD, Ed S), including curriculum development (MS), elementary education (MS), English education (MS), learning technologies (MS), mathematics education (MS), modern language education (MS), physical education (MS), science education (MS), social studies education (MS), special education (MS); early childhood education (MS); exceptional student education (Ed D); foreign language education (MS), including foreign language education, teaching English to speakers of other languages (TESOL); international/intercultural education (MS); language, literacy and culture (PhD); mathematics, science, and learning technologies (PhD); physical education (MS), including sport and fitness; reading education (MS). *Program availability:* Part-time, evening/weekend. *Faculty:* 34 full-time (23 women), 64 part-time/adjunct (48 women). *Students:* 182 full-time (154 women), 231 part-time (190 women); includes 323 minority (69 Black or African American, non-Hispanic/Latino; 10 Asian, non-Hispanic/Latino; 237 Hispanic/Latino; 7 Two or more races, non-Hispanic/Latino), 19 international. Average age 34. 282 applicants, 58% accepted, 113 enrolled. In 2016, 184 master's, 12 doctorates awarded. *Degree requirements:* For doctorate, comprehensive exam, thesis/dissertation. *Entrance requirements:* For master's, GRE General Test, Florida General Knowledge Test or Florida College Level Academic Skills Test; for doctorate and Ed S, GRE General Test. Additional exam requirements/recommendations for international students: Required—TOEFL (minimum score 550 paper-based; 80 iBT), IELTS (minimum score 6.3). *Application deadline:* For fall admission, 6/1 priority date for domestic students, 4/1 for international students; for winter admission, 10/1 priority date for domestic students, 9/1 for international students; for spring admission, 3/1 priority date for domestic students, 2/1 for international students. Applications are processed on a rolling basis. Application fee: $30. Electronic applications accepted. *Expenses:* Tuition, state resident: full-time $8912; part-time $446 per credit hour. Tuition, nonresident: full-time $21,393; part-time $992 per credit hour. *Required fees:* $2185; $195 per semester. Tuition and fees vary according to program. *Financial support:* Research assistantships with tuition reimbursements and teaching assistantships with tuition reimbursements available. *Unit head:* Dr. Lynn Miller, Chair, 305-348-2005, Fax: 305-348-2086, E-mail: lynne.miller@fiu.edu. *Application contact:* Nanett Rojas, Assistant Director, Graduate Admissions, 305-348-7464, Fax: 305-348-7441, E-mail: gradadm@fiu.edu.
Website: http://education.fiu.edu

Florida Memorial University, School of Education, Miami-Dade, FL 33054. Offers elementary education (MS); exceptional student education (MS); reading (MS). *Degree requirements:* For master's, comprehensive exam or thesis, field and clinical experiences, exit exam. *Entrance requirements:* For master's, GRE, CLAST, PRAXIS I, baccalaureate or graduate degree with minimum GPA of 3.0 in last 60 hours, 3 recommendations. Additional exam requirements/recommendations for international students: Recommended—TOEFL.

Florida State University, The Graduate School, College of Education, Program in Curriculum and Instruction, Tallahassee, FL 32306. Offers curriculum and instruction (MS, PhD, Ed S), including early childhood education, elementary education, English education, English teaching (MS), exceptional student education (MS), foreign and second language education, foreign and second language teaching (MS), mathematics education, mathematics teaching (MS), reading education and language arts, science education, social science education, social science teaching (MS), special education, special education studies (MS), visual disabilities (MS, Ed S). *Program availability:* Part-time, evening/weekend. Terminal master's awarded for partial completion of doctoral program. *Degree requirements:* For master's and Ed S, comprehensive exam, thesis optional; for doctorate, comprehensive exam, thesis/dissertation, diagnostic exam, preliminary exam, prospectus defense, dissertation defense. *Entrance requirements:* For master's, doctorate, and Ed S, GRE General Test, minimum upper-division GPA of 3.0. Additional exam requirements/recommendations for international students: Required—TOEFL (minimum score 550 paper-based, 80 iBT), IELTS (minimum score 6.5), Michigan English Language Assessment Battery (minimum score 77), or PTE (minimum score 55). Application fee: $30. Electronic applications accepted. *Expenses:* Tuition, state resident: full-time $7263; part-time $403.51 per credit hour. Tuition, nonresident: full-time $18,087; part-time $1004.85 per credit hour. *Required fees:* $1365; $75.81 per credit hour. $20 per semester. Tuition and fees vary according to campus/location. *Financial support:* Fellowships, research assistantships, teaching assistantships, scholarships/grants, tuition waivers (full and partial), and unspecified assistantships available. Financial award application deadline: 1/15; financial award

applicants required to submit FAFSA. *Faculty research:* Identifying effective intervention strategies to improve reading skills; improving literacy teaching and learning through technology; understanding of student sense making, problem solving, the history and structure of STEM disciplines, and teacher education to support the development of ambitious instruction that supports the STEM learning of all students; examining practices of international education; identifying ways to support the professional development of teachers. *Unit head:* Dr. Sherry Southerland, Professor/Department Chair, 850-644-4880, Fax: 850-644-7736, E-mail: ssoutherland@admin.fsu.edu. *Application contact:* Libbie Crowley, Academic Support Specialist, 850-644-2122, Fax: 850-644-7736, E-mail: ecrowley@fsu.edu.
Website: http://education.fsu.edu/degrees-and-programs/graduate-programs

Fontbonne University, Graduate Programs, St. Louis, MO 63105-3098. Offers accounting (MBA, MS); art (MA); art (K-12) (MAT); business (MBA); computer science (MS); deaf education (MA); early intervention in deaf education (MA); education (MA), including autism spectrum disorders, curriculum and instruction, diverse learners, early childhood education, reading, special education; elementary education (MAT); family and consumer sciences (MA), including multidisciplinary health communication studies; fine arts (MFA); instructional design and technology (MS); management and leadership (MM); middle school education (MAT); secondary education (MAT); special education (MAT); speech-language pathology (MS); supply chain management (MS); theatre (MA). *Program availability:* Part-time, evening/weekend, online learning. *Faculty:* 32 full-time (24 women), 43 part-time/adjunct (26 women). *Students:* 456 full-time (313 women), 102 part-time (77 women); includes 138 minority (118 Black or African American, non-Hispanic/Latino; 1 American Indian or Alaska Native, non-Hispanic/Latino; 7 Asian, non-Hispanic/Latino; 9 Hispanic/Latino; 3 Two or more races, non-Hispanic/Latino), 37 international. *Degree requirements:* For master's, comprehensive exam (for some programs), thesis (for some programs). *Entrance requirements:* Additional exam requirements/recommendations for international students: Required—TOEFL (minimum score 500 paper-based; 65 iBT). *Application deadline:* For fall admission, 8/1 for international students; for spring admission, 12/1 for international students. Applications are processed on a rolling basis. Application fee: $25 ($30 for international students). Electronic applications accepted. *Expenses: Tuition:* Full-time $8436; part-time $703 per credit hour. *Required fees:* $18 per credit hour. Tuition and fees vary according to course load. *Financial support:* Teaching assistantships with partial tuition reimbursements and scholarships/grants available. Support available to part-time students. Financial award application deadline: 4/1; financial award applicants required to submit FAFSA. *Unit head:* Dr. Carey Adams, Vice President for Academic Affairs, 314-719-3609, E-mail: cadams@fontbonne.edu. *Application contact:* Lauryn Filip, Coordinator, Graduate Admission and Professional Studies, 314-889-4650, E-mail: admissions@fontbonne.edu.
Website: https://www.fontbonne.edu/academics/graduate-programs/

Fordham University, Graduate School of Education, Division of Curriculum and Teaching, New York, NY 10023. Offers curriculum and teaching (MSE); early childhood education (MSE); elementary education (MST); special education (MSE, Adv C); teaching English as a second language (MSE). *Accreditation:* NCATE. *Program availability:* Part-time, evening/weekend. *Degree requirements:* For Adv C, thesis. *Entrance requirements:* Additional exam requirements/recommendations for international students: Required—TOEFL (minimum score 577 paper-based; 90 iBT), IELTS (minimum score 7). Electronic applications accepted.

Fort Hays State University, Graduate School, College of Education, Department of Special Education, Hays, KS 67601-4099. Offers MS. *Accreditation:* NCATE. *Degree requirements:* For master's, comprehensive exam, thesis optional. *Entrance requirements:* Additional exam requirements/recommendations for international students: Required—TOEFL (minimum score 550 paper-based). Electronic applications accepted. *Faculty research:* Severe behavior disorders, early childhood language, multicultural speech.

Framingham State University, Continuing Education, Program in Special Education, Framingham, MA 01701-9101. Offers M Ed. *Program availability:* Part-time, evening/weekend. *Entrance requirements:* For master's, MAT, interview.

Francis Marion University, Graduate Programs, School of Education, Florence, SC 29502-0547. Offers learning disabilities (M Ed, MAT). *Accreditation:* NCATE. *Program availability:* Part-time. *Degree requirements:* For master's, comprehensive exam (for some programs), thesis (for some programs), supervised internship (for MAT). *Entrance requirements:* For master's, GRE General Test, MAT, NTE, or PRAXIS II, official transcripts; two letters of recommendation. Additional exam requirements/recommendations for international students: Required—TOEFL (minimum score 550 paper-based; 79 iBT). *Expenses:* Tuition, state resident: full-time $10,100; part-time $505 per credit hour. Tuition, nonresident: full-time $20,196; part-time $1009.80 per credit hour. *Required fees:* $14.80 per credit hour. $73 per semester. Tuition and fees vary according to course load and program. *Faculty research:* Identification and alternate assessment of at risk students.

Franklin Pierce University, Graduate and Professional Studies, Rindge, NH 03461-0060. Offers curriculum and instruction (M Ed); elementary education (MS Ed); emerging network technologies (Graduate Certificate); energy and sustainability studies (MBA, Graduate Certificate); health administration (MBA, Graduate Certificate); human resource management (MBA, Graduate Certificate); information technology (MBA); leadership (MBA); nursing education (MS); nursing leadership (MS); physical therapy (DPT); physician assistant studies (MPAS); special education (M Ed); sports management (MBA). *Accreditation:* APTA. *Program availability:* Part-time, 100% online, blended/hybrid learning. *Faculty:* 47 full-time (36 women), 165 part-time/adjunct (108 women). *Students:* 380 full-time (226 women), 245 part-time (158 women); includes 52 minority (13 Black or African American, non-Hispanic/Latino; 2 American Indian or Alaska Native, non-Hispanic/Latino; 14 Asian, non-Hispanic/Latino; 22 Hispanic/Latino; 1 Native Hawaiian or other Pacific Islander, non-Hispanic/Latino), 13 international. Average age 29. 1,995 applicants, 28% accepted, 267 enrolled. In 2016, 120 master's, 86 doctorates awarded. *Degree requirements:* For master's, concentrated original research projects; student teaching; fieldwork and/or internship; leadership project; PRAXIS I and II (for M Ed); for doctorate, concentrated original research projects, clinical fieldwork and/or internship, leadership project. *Entrance requirements:* For master's, minimum GPA of 2.5, 3 letters of recommendation; competencies in accounting, economics, statistics, and computer skills through life experience or undergraduate coursework (for MBA); certification/e-portfolio, minimum C grade in all education courses (for M Ed); license to practice as RN (for MS); for doctorate, GRE, 80 hours of observation/work in PT settings; completion of anatomy, chemistry, physics, and statistics; minimum GPA of 3.0. Additional exam requirements/recommendations for international students: Required—TOEFL (minimum score 550 paper-based; 61 iBT). *Application deadline:* Applications are processed on a rolling basis. Application fee: $0. Electronic applications accepted. *Expenses: Tuition:* Full-time $15,960; part-time $665 per credit hour. Tuition and fees vary according to program. *Financial support:* Teaching assistantships with tuition reimbursements, career-related internships or fieldwork, and unspecified assistantships available. Support available to part-time students. Financial award applicants required to submit FAFSA. *Faculty research:* Evidence-based practice in sports physical therapy, human resource management in economic crisis, leadership in nursing, innovation in sports facility management, differentiated learning and understanding by design. *Unit head:* Dr. Maria Altobello, Dean, 603-647-3509, Fax: 603-229-4580, E-mail: altobellom@franklinpierce.edu. *Application contact:* Graduate Studies, 800-325-1090, Fax: 603-626-4815, E-mail: cgps@franklinpierce.edu.
Website: http://www.franklinpierce.edu/academics/gradstudies/index.htm

Freed-Hardeman University, Program in Education, Henderson, TN 38340-2399. Offers curriculum and instruction (M Ed); school counseling (M Ed), including administration and supervision, special education; school leadership (Ed S). *Accreditation:* NCATE. *Program availability:* Part-time, evening/weekend. *Degree requirements:* For master's, comprehensive exam, thesis optional; for Ed S, thesis. *Entrance requirements:* For master's, GRE General Test or NTE; for Ed S, 3 years of teaching experience. Additional exam requirements/recommendations for international students: Required—TOEFL (minimum score 500 paper-based).

Fresno Pacific University, Graduate Programs, School of Education, Division of Special Education, Fresno, CA 93702-4709. Offers MA. *Program availability:* Part-time, evening/weekend. *Degree requirements:* For master's, thesis or alternative. *Entrance requirements:* Additional exam requirements/recommendations for international students: Required—TOEFL (minimum score 550 paper-based).

Frostburg State University, Graduate School, College of Education, Department of Educational Professions, Program in Special Education, Frostburg, MD 21532-1099. Offers M Ed. *Accreditation:* NCATE. *Program availability:* Part-time, evening/weekend. *Degree requirements:* For master's, thesis or alternative, PRAXIS II (special education section). *Entrance requirements:* For master's, teaching certificate. Additional exam requirements/recommendations for international students: Required—TOEFL. Electronic applications accepted.

Furman University, Graduate Division, Department of Education, Greenville, SC 29613. Offers curriculum and instruction (MA); early childhood education (MA); educational leadership (Ed S); English as a second language (MA); literacy (MA); school leadership (MA); special education (MA). *Accreditation:* NCATE. *Program availability:* Part-time, online learning. *Degree requirements:* For master's, comprehensive exam (for some programs), thesis or alternative. *Entrance requirements:* For master's, PRAXIS II. *Faculty research:* Literacy, pedagogy and practice, social justice, advanced leadership, achievement in high poverty schools.

Gallaudet University, The Graduate School, Washington, DC 20002-3625. Offers American Sign Language/English bilingual early childhood deaf education: birth to 5 (Certificate); audiology (Au D); clinical psychology (PhD); deaf and hard of hearing infants, toddlers, and their families (Certificate); deaf education (MA, Ed S); deaf history (Certificate); deaf studies (Certificate); educating deaf students with disabilities (Certificate); education: teacher preparation (MA), including deaf education, early childhood education and deaf education, elementary education and deaf education, secondary education and deaf education; educational neuroscience (PhD); hearing, speech and language sciences (MS, PhD); international development (MA); interpretation (MA, PhD), including combined interpreting practice and research (MA), interpreting research (MA); linguistics (MA, PhD); mental health counseling (MA); peer mentoring (Certificate); public administration (MPA); school counseling (MA); school psychology (Psy S); sign language teaching (MA); social work (MSW); speech-language pathology (MS). *Program availability:* Part-time. *Students:* 297 full-time (231 women), 129 part-time (97 women); includes 105 minority (35 Black or African American, non-Hispanic/Latino; 20 Asian, non-Hispanic/Latino; 39 Hispanic/Latino; 11 Two or more races, non-Hispanic/Latino), 22 international. Average age 30. 471 applicants, 52% accepted, 147 enrolled. In 2016, 138 master's, 25 doctorates, 14 other advanced degrees awarded. Terminal master's awarded for partial completion of doctoral program. *Degree requirements:* For master's, comprehensive exam (for some programs), thesis optional; for doctorate, comprehensive exam, thesis/dissertation. *Entrance requirements:* For master's and doctorate, GRE General Test or MAT, letters of recommendation, interviews, goals statement, American Sign Language proficiency interview, written English competency. Additional exam requirements/recommendations for international students: Required—TOEFL. *Application deadline:* For fall admission, 2/15 for domestic students. Applications are processed on a rolling basis. Application fee: $75. Electronic applications accepted. *Expenses: Tuition:* Full-time $17,100; part-time $950 per credit hour. *Required fees:* $3725; $276 per semester. *Financial support:* Fellowships, research assistantships, teaching assistantships, career-related internships or fieldwork, Federal Work-Study, scholarships/grants, tuition waivers (partial), and unspecified assistantships available. Support available to part-time students. Financial award application deadline: 7/1; financial award applicants required to submit FAFSA. *Faculty research:* Signing math dictionaries, telecommunications access, cancer genetics, linguistics, visual language and visual learning, integrated quantum materials, deaf legal discourse, advance recruitment and retention in geosciences. *Unit head:* Dr. Gaurav Mathur, Dean, Graduate School and Continuing Studies, 202-250-2380, Fax: 202-651-5027, E-mail: gaurav.mathur@gallaudet.edu. *Application contact:* Wednesday Luria, Coordinator of Prospective Graduate Student Services, 202-651-5400, Fax: 202-651-5295, E-mail: graduate.school@gallaudet.edu.

George Fox University, College of Education, Graduate Teaching and Leading Program, Newberg, OR 97132-2697. Offers administrative leadership (Ed S); continuing administrator license (Certificate); educational leadership (M Ed); educational technology (M Ed); English for speakers of other languages (M Ed); ESOL (Certificate); initial administrator license (Certificate); reading (M Ed, Certificate); special education (M Ed); teaching (MAT). *Accreditation:* NCATE. *Program availability:* Part-time, evening/weekend, online learning. *Degree requirements:* For master's, thesis (for some programs). *Entrance requirements:* For master's, minimum undergraduate GPA of 3.0 during previous 2 years of course work, resume, 3 professional recommendations on university forms, official transcripts. Additional exam requirements/recommendations for international students: Required—TOEFL (minimum score 577 paper-based; 90 iBT). Electronic applications accepted. *Expenses:* Contact institution.

George Mason University, College of Education and Human Development, Program in Special Education, Fairfax, VA 22030. Offers M Ed, PhD, Certificate. *Faculty:* 19 full-time (16 women), 37 part-time/adjunct (31 women). *Students:* 93 full-time (81 women), 438 part-time (366 women); includes 144 minority (57 Black or African American, non-Hispanic/Latino; 2 American Indian or Alaska Native, non-Hispanic/Latino; 36 Asian, non-Hispanic/Latino; 38 Hispanic/Latino; 11 Two or more races, non-Hispanic/Latino), 8 international. Average age 34. 240 applicants, 95% accepted, 163 enrolled. In 2016, 189 master's awarded. *Degree requirements:* For master's, professional portfolio. *Entrance requirements:* For master's, bachelor's degree from regionally-accredited institution with minimum GPA of 3.0 cumulative or in last 60 credits of undergraduate study (or PRAXIS I, SAT, ACT or VCLA); 2 official transcripts; 3 letters of recommendation. Additional exam requirements/recommendations for international students: Required—TOEFL (minimum score 575 paper-based; 88 iBT), IELTS (minimum score 6.5), PTE (minimum score 59). *Application deadline:* For spring admission, 11/1 priority date for domestic and international students. Application fee: $75 ($80 for international students). Electronic applications accepted. *Expenses:* Tuition, state resident: full-time $10,628; part-time $443 per credit. Tuition, nonresident: full-time $29,306; part-time $1221 per credit. *Required fees:* $3096; $129 per credit. Tuition and fees vary according to program. *Financial support:* In 2016–17, 3 students received support, including 3

research assistantships (averaging $9,150 per year); career-related internships or fieldwork, Federal Work-Study, and scholarships/grants also available. Financial award application deadline: 3/1; financial award applicants required to submit FAFSA. *Faculty research:* Adapted captions through interactive video, DEVISE Project (multi-sensory virtual learning environment), KIHd System Project (teachers utilizing Kellar Institute handheld data system and Literary Online). *Unit head:* Pam Baker, Director, 703-993-1787, Fax: 703-993-3681, E-mail: pbaker5@gmu.edu. *Application contact:* Jancy Templeton, Advisor, 703-993-2387, Fax: 703-993-3681, E-mail: jtemple1@gmu.edu.
Website: http://gse.gmu.edu/programs/sped/

George Mason University, College of Education and Human Development, Programs in Curriculum and Instruction, Fairfax, VA 22030. Offers advanced international baccalaureate (M Ed); assistive technology (M Ed); designing digital learning in schools (M Ed); early childhood education (M Ed); early childhood education for diverse learners (M Ed); elementary education (M Ed); English as a second language (M Ed); gifted child education (M Ed); history (M Ed); literacy (M Ed), including PK-12 classroom teachers, reading specialist; literacy leadership for diverse schools (M Ed), including K-12 reading; physical education (M Ed); science K-12 (M Ed); secondary education (M Ed), including biology, chemistry, earth science, English, history/social science, math, physics; special education (M Ed); teacher leadership (M Ed); teaching culturally, linguistically diverse and exceptional learners (M Ed); transformative teaching (M Ed). *Faculty:* 41 full-time (35 women), 53 part-time/adjunct (46 women). *Students:* 155 full-time (127 women), 821 part-time (697 women); includes 267 minority (82 Black or African American, non-Hispanic/Latino; 5 American Indian or Alaska Native, non-Hispanic/Latino; 75 Asian, non-Hispanic/Latino; 88 Hispanic/Latino; 1 Native Hawaiian or other Pacific Islander, non-Hispanic/Latino; 16 Two or more races, non-Hispanic/Latino), 19 international. Average age 33. 513 applicants, 90% accepted, 352 enrolled. In 2016, 347 master's awarded. *Degree requirements:* For master's, comprehensive exam, thesis (for some programs). *Entrance requirements:* For master's, PRAXIS Core (for some programs), minimum GPA of 3.0 in last 60 hours, licensed as teacher or educational administrator, official transcripts, goals statement, 3 recommendation letters, interview or writing sample (depending on program), up to 3 years' teaching experience (depending on program). Additional exam requirements/recommendations for international students: Required—TOEFL (minimum score 575 paper-based; 88 iBT), IELTS (minimum score 6.5), PTE (minimum score 59). *Application deadline:* For spring admission, 11/1 priority date for domestic and international students. Application fee: $75 ($80 for international students). Electronic applications accepted. *Expenses:* Tuition, state resident: full-time $10,628; part-time $443 per credit. Tuition, nonresident: full-time $29,306; part-time $1221 per credit. *Required fees:* $3096; $129 per credit. Tuition and fees vary according to program. *Financial support:* In 2016–17, 1 student received support, including 1 teaching assistantship (averaging $4,060 per year); career-related internships or fieldwork, Federal Work-Study, scholarships/grants, unspecified assistantships, and health care benefits (for full-time research or teaching assistantship recipients) also available. Support available to part-time students. Financial award application deadline: 3/1; financial award applicants required to submit FAFSA. *Faculty research:* Achievement gaps and superintendent decisions, constructivist view of classroom teaching, cost of cheating, creating a critical literacy milieu in kindergarten. *Unit head:* Rebecca Fox, Professor and Academic Program Coordinator, 703-993-4123, E-mail: rfox@gmu.edu.
Website: http://gse.gmu.edu/programs/gsemasters

Georgetown College, Department of Education, Georgetown, KY 40324-1696. Offers reading and writing (MA Ed); special education (MA Ed); teaching (MA Ed). *Accreditation:* NCATE. *Program availability:* Part-time. *Degree requirements:* For master's, portfolio. *Entrance requirements:* For master's, teaching certificate, minimum GPA of 2.7 or GRE General Test.

The George Washington University, Graduate School of Education and Human Development, Department of Counseling and Human Development, Washington, DC 20052. Offers clinical mental health counseling (MA); counseling (PhD, Ed S); counseling culturally and linguistically diverse persons (MA Ed/HD, Certificate); forensic rehabilitation counseling (Graduate Certificate); job development and placement (Graduate Certificate); rehabilitation counseling (MA Ed/HD), including autism spectrum disorder, substance abuse and psychiatric disabilities, traumatic brain injury; school counseling (MA Ed, Graduate Certificate). *Accreditation:* ACA (one or more programs are accredited). *Program availability:* Part-time, evening/weekend. *Faculty:* 13 full-time (7 women). *Students:* 103 full-time (79 women), 80 part-time (67 women); includes 66 minority (32 Black or African American, non-Hispanic/Latino; 2 American Indian or Alaska Native, non-Hispanic/Latino; 14 Asian, non-Hispanic/Latino; 16 Hispanic/Latino; 2 Two or more races, non-Hispanic/Latino), 13 international. Average age 31. 321 applicants, 54% accepted, 68 enrolled. In 2016, 54 master's, 9 doctorates, 8 other advanced degrees awarded. *Degree requirements:* For master's and other advanced degree, comprehensive exam; for doctorate, comprehensive exam, thesis/dissertation. *Entrance requirements:* For master's, GRE General Test or MAT, minimum GPA of 2.75; for doctorate, GRE General Test or MAT, interview, minimum GPA of 3.3; for other advanced degree, GRE General Test or MAT, minimum GPA of 3.3. *Application deadline:* For fall admission, 1/15 priority date for domestic students; for spring admission, 10/1 for domestic students. Applications are processed on a rolling basis. Application fee: $75. *Financial support:* In 2016–17, 58 students received support. Fellowships with tuition reimbursements available, research assistantships, teaching assistantships with tuition reimbursements available, career-related internships or fieldwork, Federal Work-Study, and tuition waivers (full and partial) available. Financial award application deadline: 1/15. *Faculty research:* Multiculturalism and counseling, models of adult development. *Unit head:* Dr. Kenneth C. Hergenrather, Chair, 202-994-6856, E-mail: hergenkc@gwu.edu. *Application contact:* Sarah Lang, Director of Graduate Admissions, 202-994-1447, Fax: 202-994-7207, E-mail: slang@gwu.edu.

The George Washington University, Graduate School of Education and Human Development, Department of Special Education and Disability Studies, Program in Bilingual Special Education, Washington, DC 20052. Offers MA Ed, Certificate. *Students:* 1 (woman) part-time. Average age 42. In 2016, 3 master's awarded. *Unit head:* Michael Feuer, Dean, 202-994-6161, E-mail: mjfeuer@gwu.edu. *Application contact:* Sarah Lang, Director of Graduate Admissions, 202-994-1447, Fax: 202-994-7207, E-mail: slang@gwu.edu.

The George Washington University, Graduate School of Education and Human Development, Department of Special Education and Disability Studies, Program in Early Childhood Special Education, Washington, DC 20052. Offers infant special education (MA Ed/HD). *Accreditation:* NCATE. *Students:* 13 full-time (all women), 11 part-time (all women); includes 6 minority (3 Black or African American, non-Hispanic/Latino; 1 Hispanic/Latino; 2 Two or more races, non-Hispanic/Latino), 7 international. Average age 32. 30 applicants, 87% accepted, 12 enrolled. In 2016, 12 master's awarded. *Degree requirements:* For master's, comprehensive exam. *Entrance requirements:* For master's, GRE General Test or MAT, minimum GPA of 2.75. *Application deadline:* For fall admission, 1/15 priority date for domestic students; for spring admission, 10/1 for domestic students. Applications are processed on a rolling basis. Application fee: $75. *Financial support:* In 2016–17, 19 students received support. Fellowships, career-related internships or fieldwork, Federal Work-Study, and tuition waivers (full) available. Financial award application deadline: 1/15; financial award applicants required to submit FAFSA. *Faculty research:* Computer-assisted instruction and learning, disabled learner assessment of preschool, handicapped children. *Unit head:* Dr. Marian H. Jarrett, Faculty Coordinator, 202-994-1509, E-mail: mjarrett@gwu.edu. *Application contact:* Sarah Lang, Director of Graduate Admissions, 202-994-1447, Fax: 202-994-7207, E-mail: slang@gwu.edu.

The George Washington University, Graduate School of Education and Human Development, Department of Special Education and Disability Studies, Program in Secondary Special Education and Transition Services, Washington, DC 20052. Offers adolescents with emotional and behavioral disabilities (MA Ed/HD); adolescents with learning disabilities (MA Ed/HD); brain injury special education (MA Ed/HD); brain injury specialist (MA Ed/HD); interdisciplinary transition services (MA Ed/HD). *Unit head:* Michael Feuer, Dean, 202-994-6161, E-mail: mjfeuer@gwu.edu. *Application contact:* Sarah Lang, Director of Graduate Admissions, 202-994-1447, Fax: 202-994-7207, E-mail: slang@gwu.edu.
Website: http://gsehd.gwu.edu/

The George Washington University, Graduate School of Education and Human Development, Department of Special Education and Disability Studies, Program in Special Education, Washington, DC 20052. Offers Ed D, Ed S. *Accreditation:* NCATE. *Students:* 8 full-time (all women), 56 part-time (48 women); includes 27 minority (14 Black or African American, non-Hispanic/Latino; 3 Asian, non-Hispanic/Latino; 8 Hispanic/Latino; 2 Two or more races, non-Hispanic/Latino), 4 international. Average age 40. 26 applicants, 65% accepted, 9 enrolled. In 2016, 5 doctorates, 9 other advanced degrees awarded. *Degree requirements:* For doctorate, comprehensive exam, thesis/dissertation; for Ed S, comprehensive exam. *Entrance requirements:* For doctorate and Ed S, GRE General Test or MAT, interview, minimum GPA of 3.3. *Application deadline:* For fall admission, 1/15 priority date for domestic students; for spring admission, 10/1 for domestic students. Applications are processed on a rolling basis. Application fee: $75. *Financial support:* In 2016–17, 46 students received support. Fellowships, research assistantships, career-related internships or fieldwork, Federal Work-Study, and tuition waivers (partial) available. Financial award application deadline: 1/15; financial award applicants required to submit FAFSA. *Unit head:* Dr. Carol Kochhar, Faculty Coordinator, 202-994-6170, E-mail: kochhar@gwu.edu. *Application contact:* Sarah Lang, Director of Graduate Admissions, 202-994-1447, Fax: 202-994-7207, E-mail: slang@gwu.edu.

The George Washington University, Graduate School of Education and Human Development, Department of Special Education and Disability Studies, Program in Special Education for Children with Emotional and Behavioral Disabilities, Washington, DC 20052. Offers MA Ed/HD. *Accreditation:* NCATE. *Students:* 11 full-time (all women), 1 (woman) part-time; includes 6 minority (4 Black or African American, non-Hispanic/Latino; 1 Asian, non-Hispanic/Latino; 1 Hispanic/Latino), 2 international. Average age 28. 26 applicants, 69% accepted, 11 enrolled. In 2016, 15 master's awarded. *Degree requirements:* For master's, comprehensive exam. *Entrance requirements:* For master's, PRAXIS, interview, minimum GPA of 2.75, two recommendations. *Application deadline:* For fall admission, 1/15 priority date for domestic students. Applications are processed on a rolling basis. Application fee: $75. *Financial support:* Fellowships, career-related internships or fieldwork, and Federal Work-Study available. Financial award application deadline: 1/15; financial award applicants required to submit FAFSA. *Faculty research:* Action research on the act of teaching emotionally disturbed students, teacher training. *Unit head:* Elisabeth Rice, Program Coordinator, 202-994-1535, E-mail: ehess@gwu.edu. *Application contact:* Sarah Lang, Director of Admission, 202-994-1447, Fax: 202-994-7207, E-mail: slang@gwu.edu.

The George Washington University, Graduate School of Education and Human Development, Department of Special Education and Disability Studies, Program in Special Education for Culturally and Linguistically Diverse Persons, Washington, DC 20052. Offers MA Ed/HD, Certificate. *Students:* 5 full-time (all women), 54 part-time (49 women); includes 31 minority (19 Black or African American, non-Hispanic/Latino; 6 Asian, non-Hispanic/Latino; 5 Hispanic/Latino; 1 Two or more races, non-Hispanic/Latino), 5 international. Average age 35. 77 applicants, 81% accepted, 42 enrolled. In 2016, 3 master's, 28 Certificates awarded.

The George Washington University, Graduate School of Education and Human Development, Department of Special Education and Disability Studies, Program in Transition Special Education, Washington, DC 20052. Offers Teaching Certificate. *Accreditation:* NCATE. *Program availability:* Evening/weekend. *Students:* 1 full-time (0 women), 7 part-time (6 women); includes 2 minority (1 Black or African American, non-Hispanic/Latino; 1 Hispanic/Latino). Average age 37. 7 applicants, 71% accepted, 5 enrolled. In 2016, 3 Teaching Certificates awarded. *Degree requirements:* For Teaching Certificate, comprehensive exam. *Entrance requirements:* For degree, GRE General Test or MAT, interview, minimum GPA of 2.75. *Application deadline:* For fall admission, 1/15 priority date for domestic students; for spring admission, 10/1 for domestic students. Applications are processed on a rolling basis. Application fee: $75. *Financial support:* Fellowships, research assistantships, career-related internships or fieldwork, Federal Work-Study, tuition waivers (full and partial), and stipends available. Financial award application deadline: 1/15. *Faculty research:* Computer applications for transition, transition follow-up research, curriculum-based vocational assessment, traumatic brain injury. *Unit head:* Dr. Lynda West, Coordinator, 202-994-1533, E-mail: lwest@gwu.edu. *Application contact:* Sarah Lang, Director of Graduate Admissions, 202-994-1447, Fax: 202-994-7207, E-mail: slang@gwu.edu.

Georgia College & State University, Graduate School, The John H. Lounsbury College of Education, Program in Special Education, Milledgeville, GA 31061. Offers M Ed, MAT, Ed S. *Accreditation:* NCATE. *Program availability:* Part-time, evening/weekend. *Students:* 22 full-time (19 women), 16 part-time (all women); includes 17 minority (16 Black or African American, non-Hispanic/Latino; 1 Two or more races, non-Hispanic/Latino). Average age 37. 2 applicants, 100% accepted. In 2016, 25 master's, 15 other advanced degrees awarded. *Degree requirements:* For master's, comprehensive exam, complete program within 6 years, minimum GPA of 3.0; for Ed S, comprehensive exam, complete program within 4 years, minimum GPA of 3.0. *Entrance requirements:* For master's, on-site writing assessment, GRE General Test taken within six years (minimum scores 1,000 verbal and quantitative combined if taken before August 1, 2011; 305 if taken on or after August 1, 2011), or MAT, 2 professional recommendations, transcript, immunization verification; for Ed S, on-site writing assessment, GRE General Test taken within six years (minimum scores 1,000 verbal and quantitative combined if taken before August 1, 2011, 305 if taken on or after August 1, 2011), or MAT (minimum score 400), 2 years of teaching experience, minimum GPA of 3.25, master's degree, 2 professional recommendations, level 5 certificate eligibility, transcript, degree in special education or completion of state-approved training/prep program in special education. *Application deadline:* For fall admission, 7/1 priority date for domestic students; for spring admission, 11/1 priority date for domestic students; for summer admission, 4/1 priority date for domestic students. Applications are processed on a rolling basis. Electronic applications accepted. *Expenses:* $288 per credit hour in-state tuition; $1,027 per credit hour out-of-state; fees vary by hours enrolled. *Financial support:* Application deadline: 3/1; applicants required to submit FAFSA. *Unit head:* Dr. Joseph Peters, Dean, College of Education, 478-445-2518, Fax: 478-445-6582, E-mail:

joseph.peters@gcsu.edu. *Application contact:* Shanda Brand, Graduate Admissions Advisor, 478-445-1383, E-mail: shanda.brand@gcsu.edu.

Georgian Court University, School of Education, Lakewood, NJ 08701-2697. Offers administration and leadership (MA); autism spectrum disorders (Certificate); education (MA); instructional technology (Certificate). *Accreditation:* TEAC. *Program availability:* Part-time, evening/weekend. *Faculty:* 14 full-time (8 women), 31 part-time/adjunct (18 women). *Students:* 66 full-time (55 women), 376 part-time (312 women); includes 92 minority (44 Black or African American, non-Hispanic/Latino; 1 American Indian or Alaska Native, non-Hispanic/Latino; 8 Asian, non-Hispanic/Latino; 34 Hispanic/Latino; 5 Two or more races, non-Hispanic/Latino). Average age 34. 409 applicants, 62% accepted, 174 enrolled. In 2016, 95 master's, 1 other advanced degree awarded. *Degree requirements:* For master's, comprehensive exam (for some programs), thesis (for some programs). *Entrance requirements:* For master's, GRE, GMAT or NTE/PRAXIS, 3 letters of recommendation. Additional exam requirements/recommendations for international students: Required—TOEFL (minimum score 550 paper-based). *Application deadline:* For fall admission, 8/15 priority date for domestic students, 5/1 for international students; for spring admission, 1/15 priority date for domestic students, 10/1 for international students. Applications are processed on a rolling basis. Application fee: $40. Electronic applications accepted. *Expenses: Tuition:* Full-time $15,079; part-time $839 per credit. *Required fees:* $968; $496 per credit. Tuition and fees vary according to campus/location and program. *Financial support:* Scholarships/grants, health care benefits, and unspecified assistantships available. Financial award application deadline: 4/15; financial award applicants required to submit FAFSA. *Unit head:* Dr. Lynn DeCapua, Dean, 732-987-2729, E-mail: ldecapua@georgian.edu. *Application contact:* Patrick Givens, Director of Graduate and Professional Studies Admissions, 732-987-2736, Fax: 732-987-2000, E-mail: gps@georgian.edu.
Website: http://georgian.edu/academics/school-of-education/

Georgia Southern University, Jack N. Averitt College of Graduate Studies, College of Education, Department of Teaching and Learning, Program in Special Education, Statesboro, GA 30460. Offers M Ed, MAT, Ed S. *Accreditation:* NCATE. *Program availability:* Part-time, evening/weekend. *Students:* 33 full-time (29 women), 58 part-time (53 women); includes 15 minority (11 Black or African American, non-Hispanic/Latino; 2 Hispanic/Latino; 2 Two or more races, non-Hispanic/Latino), 1 international. Average age 33. 6 applicants, 83% accepted, 2 enrolled. In 2016, 28 master's, 5 other advanced degrees awarded. *Degree requirements:* For master's, portfolio, transition point assessments, exit assessment. *Entrance requirements:* For master's, GRE General Test or MAT; GACE Basic Skills and Content Assessments (for MAT), minimum cumulative GPA of 2.5. Additional exam requirements/recommendations for international students: Required—TOEFL (minimum score 550 paper-based; 80 iBT), IELTS (minimum score 6). *Application deadline:* For fall admission, 3/15 priority date for domestic and international students; for spring admission, 10/1 priority date for domestic students, 10/1 for international students; for summer admission, 3/1 for domestic and international students. Applications are processed on a rolling basis. Application fee: $50. Electronic applications accepted. *Expenses:* Tuition, state resident: full-time $7236; part-time $277 per semester hour. Tuition, nonresident: full-time $27,118; part-time $1105 per semester hour. *Required fees:* $2092. *Financial support:* In 2016–17, 24 students received support, including 4 fellowships with full tuition reimbursements available (averaging $7,750 per year); career-related internships or fieldwork, Federal Work-Study, scholarships/grants, tuition waivers (full), and unspecified assistantships also available. Support available to part-time students. Financial award application deadline: 4/15; financial award applicants required to submit FAFSA. *Faculty research:* Learning disorders, behavior disorders, education of the mentally retarded. *Unit head:* Dr. Eric Landers, Department Chair, 912-478-5203, Fax: 912-478-0026, E-mail: ericlanders@georgiasouthern.edu. *Application contact:* Lydia Cross, Coordinator for Graduate Academic Services Center, 912-478-8664, E-mail: lcross@georgiasouthern.edu.

Georgia Southwestern State University, School of Education, Americus, GA 31709-4693. Offers early childhood education (M Ed, Ed S); middle grades education (Ed S); middle grades language arts (M Ed); middle grades mathematics (M Ed); special education (M Ed). *Accreditation:* NCATE. *Faculty:* 13 full-time (8 women), 7 part-time/adjunct (6 women). *Students:* 209 full-time (199 women), 6 part-time (all women); includes 52 minority (45 Black or African American, non-Hispanic/Latino; 6 Hispanic/Latino; 1 Two or more races, non-Hispanic/Latino). Average age 33. In 2016, 57 master's awarded. *Degree requirements:* For master's, minimum cumulative GPA of 3.0; for Ed S, minimum GPA of 3.25 in all courses with no grade less than a B; degree must be completed within 7 calendar years from date of initial enrollment in graduate work. *Entrance requirements:* For master's, undergraduate degree from accredited institution; professional Georgia Teaching Certificate or eligibility; minimum undergraduate GPA of 2.75 as reported on official final transcripts from all accredited institutions attended; 2 confidential Administrative Recommendation Forms; for Ed S, master's degree from accredited college or university; professional Georgia Teaching Certificate or eligibility; minimum graduate GPA of 3.0 as reported on official final graduate transcripts from all accredited institutions attended; 2 confidential Administrative Recommendation Forms. *Application deadline:* For summer admission, 4/15 for domestic students. Application fee: $25. Electronic applications accepted. *Expenses:* $257 per credit hour for online program courses, plus fees, which vary according to enrolled credit hours. *Financial support:* Application deadline: 6/1; applicants required to submit FAFSA. *Unit head:* Dr. Rachel Abbott, Dean, 229-931-2145. *Application contact:* Whitney Ford, Admissions Specialist, Office of Graduate Admissions, 800-338-0082, Fax: 229-931-2983.
Website: https://gsw.edu/Academics/Schools-and-Departments/School-of-Education/index

Georgia State University, College of Education and Human Development, Department of Educational Psychology, Special Education, and Communication Disorders, Program in Behavior and Learning Disabilities, Atlanta, GA 30302-3083. Offers M Ed. *Accreditation:* NCATE. *Program availability:* Part-time, evening/weekend. *Degree requirements:* For master's, comprehensive exam, minimum grade of B in each course in the teaching field/major. *Entrance requirements:* For master's, GRE (minimum scores at or above the 50th percentile), GACE Basics Skills Assessment, two official transcripts, minimum GPA of 3.0, certification in special education/T4 certificate, written statement of goals, resume, two letters of recommendation. Additional exam requirements/recommendations for international students: Required—TOEFL (minimum score 550 paper-based; 79 iBT) or IELTS (minimum score 6.5). *Application deadline:* For fall admission, 6/1 for domestic and international students; for winter admission, 11/1 for domestic and international students; for spring admission, 5/1 for domestic and international students. Application fee: $50. Electronic applications accepted. *Expenses:* Tuition, state resident: full-time $6876; part-time $382 per credit hour. Tuition, nonresident: full-time $22,374; part-time $1243 per credit hour. *Required fees:* $2128; $1064 per term. Part-time tuition and fees vary according to course load and program. *Financial support:* In 2016–17, fellowships with full tuition reimbursements (averaging $30,000 per year), research assistantships with full tuition reimbursements (averaging $2,000 per year) were awarded; teaching assistantships with full tuition reimbursements, scholarships/grants, health care benefits, and unspecified assistantships also available. *Faculty research:* Academic and behavioral supports for students with emotional/behavior disorders; academic interventions for learning disabilities; cultural, socioeconomic, and linguistic diversity; language and literacy development, disorders, and instruction, positive behavior supports. *Unit head:* Dr. Kristine Jolivette, Associate Professor, 404-413-8040, Fax: 404-413-8043, E-mail: kjolivette@gsu.edu. *Application contact:* Sandy Vaughn, Senior Administrative Coordinator, 404-413-8318, Fax: 404-413-8043, E-mail: svaughn@gsu.edu.
Website: http://esc.education.gsu.edu/academics-and-admissions/special-education/behavior-learning-disabilities-bld/

Georgia State University, College of Education and Human Development, Department of Educational Psychology, Special Education, and Communication Disorders, Program in Communication Disorders, Atlanta, GA 30302-3083. Offers M Ed. *Accreditation:* ASHA; NCATE. *Entrance requirements:* For master's, GRE, minimum undergraduate GPA of 3.0. Additional exam requirements/recommendations for international students: Required—TOEFL (minimum score 550 paper-based; 79 iBT), IELTS (minimum score 6.5). *Application deadline:* For fall admission, 1/15 for domestic and international students. Application fee: $50. Electronic applications accepted. *Expenses:* Tuition, state resident: full-time $6876; part-time $382 per credit hour. Tuition, nonresident: full-time $22,374; part-time $1243 per credit hour. *Required fees:* $2128; $1064 per term. Part-time tuition and fees vary according to course load and program. *Faculty research:* Dialect, aphasia, motor speech disorders, child language development, high risk populations. *Unit head:* Dr. Jacqueline Sue Laures-Gore, Program Coordinator, 404-413-8299, E-mail: jlaures@gsu.edu. *Application contact:* Sandy Vaughn, Senior Administrative Coordinator, 404-413-8318, Fax: 404-413-8043, E-mail: svaughn@gsu.edu.
Website: http://esc.education.gsu.edu/academics-and-admissions/communication-sciences-and-disorders/

Georgia State University, College of Education and Human Development, Department of Educational Psychology, Special Education, and Communication Disorders, Program in Education of Students with Exceptionalities, Atlanta, GA 30302-3083. Offers autism spectrum disorders (PhD); behavior disorders (PhD); communication disorders (PhD); early childhood special education (PhD); learning disabilities (PhD); mental retardation (PhD); orthopedic impairments (PhD); sensory impairments (PhD). *Accreditation:* NCATE. *Program availability:* Part-time, evening/weekend. *Degree requirements:* For doctorate, comprehensive exam, thesis/dissertation. *Entrance requirements:* Additional exam requirements/recommendations for international students: Required—TOEFL (minimum score 550 paper-based; 79 iBT) or IELTS (minimum score 6.5). *Application deadline:* For fall admission, 6/1 for domestic and international students; for winter admission, 11/1 for domestic and international students; for spring admission, 5/1 for domestic and international students. Application fee: $50. Electronic applications accepted. *Expenses:* Tuition, state resident: full-time $6876; part-time $382 per credit hour. Tuition, nonresident: full-time $22,374; part-time $1243 per credit hour. *Required fees:* $2128; $1064 per term. Part-time tuition and fees vary according to course load and program. *Financial support:* In 2016–17, fellowships with full tuition reimbursements (averaging $28,000 per year), research assistantships with full tuition reimbursements (averaging $2,000 per year) were awarded; scholarships/grants, health care benefits, and unspecified assistantships also available. *Faculty research:* Academic and behavioral supports for students with emotional/behavior disorders; academic interventions for learning disabilities; cultural, socioeconomic, and linguistic diversity; language and literacy development, disorders, and instruction. *Unit head:* Dr. Kristine Jolivette, Associate Professor, 404-413-8040, Fax: 404-413-8043, E-mail: kjolivette@gsu.edu. *Application contact:* Sandy Vaughn, Senior Administrative Coordinator, 404-413-8318, Fax: 404-413-8043, E-mail: svaughn@gsu.edu.
Website: http://esc.education.gsu.edu/academics-and-admissions/special-education/education-of-students-with-exceptionalities-ph-d/

Georgia State University, College of Education and Human Development, Department of Educational Psychology, Special Education, and Communication Disorders, Program in Multiple and Severe Disabilities, Atlanta, GA 30302-3083. Offers early childhood special education (M Ed); special education adapted curriculum (intellectual disabilities) (M Ed); special education deaf education (M Ed); special education general and adapted curriculum (autism spectrum disorders) (M Ed); special education physical and health disabilities (orthopedic impairments) (M Ed). *Accreditation:* NCATE. *Program availability:* Part-time. *Degree requirements:* For master's, variable foreign language requirement, comprehensive exam, thesis (for some programs). *Entrance requirements:* For master's, GRE. Additional exam requirements/recommendations for international students: Required—TOEFL (minimum score 550 paper-based; 79 iBT) or IELTS (minimum score 6.5). *Application deadline:* For fall admission, 6/1 for domestic and international students; for winter admission, 11/1 for domestic and international students; for spring admission, 5/1 for domestic and international students. Application fee: $50. Electronic applications accepted. *Expenses:* Tuition, state resident: full-time $6876; part-time $382 per credit hour. Tuition, nonresident: full-time $22,374; part-time $1243 per credit hour. *Required fees:* $2128; $1064 per term. Part-time tuition and fees vary according to course load and program. *Financial support:* In 2016–17, fellowships with full tuition reimbursements (averaging $25,000 per year), research assistantships with full tuition reimbursements (averaging $2,000 per year) were awarded; teaching assistantships with full tuition reimbursements, scholarships/grants, health care benefits, and unspecified assistantships also available. *Faculty research:* Literacy, language, behavioral supports. *Unit head:* Dr. Kathryn Wolff Heller, Professor, 404-413-8040, E-mail: kheller@gsu.edu. *Application contact:* Sandy Vaughn, Senior Administrative Coordinator, 404-413-8318, Fax: 404-413-8043, E-mail: svaughn@gsu.edu.

Gonzaga University, School of Education, Spokane, WA 99258. Offers clinical mental health counseling (MA); elementary education (MIT); leadership and administration (MA); marriage and family counseling (MA); school counseling (MA); secondary education (MIT); special education (M Ed, MIT); sport and athletic administration (MA). *Accreditation:* NCATE. *Program availability:* Part-time, evening/weekend, 100% online. *Faculty:* 22 full-time (17 women), 38 part-time/adjunct (22 women). *Students:* 104 full-time (73 women), 275 part-time (184 women); includes 31 minority (5 Black or African American, non-Hispanic/Latino; 1 American Indian or Alaska Native, non-Hispanic/Latino; 3 Asian, non-Hispanic/Latino; 18 Hispanic/Latino; 4 Two or more races, non-Hispanic/Latino), 163 international. Average age 32. 419 applicants, 67% accepted, 165 enrolled. In 2016, 39 master's awarded. *Degree requirements:* For master's, comprehensive exam. *Entrance requirements:* For master's, GRE, MAT, and/or Washington Educators Skills Test-Basic (WEST-B), official transcripts from all colleges or universities attended, interview, two letters of recommendation, resume, essay, minimum GPA of 3.0. Additional exam requirements/recommendations for international students: Required—TOEFL (minimum score 580 paper-based, 88 iBT) or IELTS (minimum score 6.5). *Application deadline:* Applications are processed on a rolling basis. Application fee: $50. Electronic applications accepted. *Expenses:* Contact institution. *Financial support:* In 2016–17, 28 students received support. Scholarships/grants and tuition waivers available. Support available to part-time students. Financial award applicants required to submit FAFSA. *Unit head:* Dr. Vincent Alfonso, Dean, 509-313-3594, Fax: 509-313-5821, E-mail: alfonso@gonzaga.edu. *Application contact:* Luke Cairney, Graduate Admissions Program Specialist, 509-313-3821, E-mail: cairney@gonzaga.edu.
Website: http://www.gonzaga.edu/Academics/Colleges-and-Schools/School-of-Education

Special Education

Gordon College, Graduate Education Program, Wenham, MA 01984-1899. Offers early childhood (M Ed, Ed S); educational leadership (M Ed, Ed S); elementary education (M Ed); English as a second language (M Ed, Ed S); math specialist (M Ed); mathematics specialist (Ed S); middle school education (M Ed); moderate disabilities (M Ed); Montessori education (M Ed); reading (M Ed, Ed S); secondary education (M Ed). *Program availability:* Part-time, evening/weekend. *Faculty:* 17 full-time (9 women), 41 part-time/adjunct (34 women). *Students:* 81 full-time (61 women), 109 part-time (87 women); includes 28 minority (2 Black or African American, non-Hispanic/Latino; 11 Asian, non-Hispanic/Latino; 13 Hispanic/Latino; 2 Two or more races, non-Hispanic/Latino), 12 international. Average age 34. 190 applicants, 100% accepted, 141 enrolled. In 2016, 110 master's, 16 Ed Ss awarded. *Degree requirements:* For master's, action research or clinical experience (for most programs); for Ed S, action research or clinical experience (for some programs). *Entrance requirements:* For master's, minimum undergraduate GPA of 3.0; 2 official undergraduate transcripts; professional resume; 3 recommendation letters (one professional reference, one academic reference, one personal reference); 500-700 word statement of purpose; for Ed S, minimum master's GPA of 3.3; 2 official transcripts from undergraduate and graduate schools; professional resume; 3 recommendation letters (one professional reference, one academic reference, one personal reference); 500-700 word statement of purpose. Additional exam requirements/recommendations for international students: Required—TOEFL (minimum score 550 paper-based, 80 iBT) or IELTS (minimum score 6.5). *Application deadline:* Applications are processed on a rolling basis. Application fee: $75. *Expenses:* $325 per credit tuition, $75 per term fee. *Financial support:* Applicants required to submit FAFSA. *Faculty research:* Reading, early childhood development, English language learners, universal design for learning. *Unit head:* Dr. Janet Arndt, Director of Graduate Studies, 978-867-4355, Fax: 978-867-4663. *Application contact:* Julie Lenocker, Program Administrator, 978-867-4322, Fax: 978-867-4663, E-mail: graduate-education@gordon.edu.
Website: http://www.gordon.edu/graduate

Goucher College, Graduate Programs in Education, Baltimore, MD 21204-2794. Offers at-risk and diverse learners (M Ed, Certificate); athletic program leadership and administration (M Ed, Certificate); elementary and special education (MAT); elementary education (MAT); literacy strategies for content learning (M Ed, Certificate); middle school (M Ed, Certificate); Montessori studies (M Ed); reading instruction (M Ed, Certificate); school improvement leadership (M Ed, Certificate); school mediation (M Ed, Certificate); secondary and special education (MAT); secondary education (MAT); special education (MAT), including elementary education, secondary education; special education for certified teachers (M Ed, Certificate); teacher as leader in technology (M Ed, Certificate). *Program availability:* Part-time, evening/weekend. *Faculty:* 3 full-time (all women), 52 part-time/adjunct (40 women). *Students:* 29 full-time (20 women), 285 part-time (217 women); includes 54 minority (41 Black or African American, non-Hispanic/Latino; 3 Asian, non-Hispanic/Latino; 7 Hispanic/Latino; 3 Two or more races, non-Hispanic/Latino), 1 international. Average age 34. 85 applicants, 100% accepted, 61 enrolled. In 2016, 207 master's awarded. *Degree requirements:* For master's, thesis (M Ed), final presentation (MAT). *Entrance requirements:* For master's, minimum GPA of 3.0. Additional exam requirements/recommendations for international students: Required—TOEFL (minimum score 560 paper-based). *Application deadline:* For fall admission, 9/1 for domestic students; for spring admission, 1/15 for domestic students. Applications are processed on a rolling basis. Application fee: $75. Electronic applications accepted. *Expenses:* Contact institution. *Financial support:* Career-related internships or fieldwork and unspecified assistantships available. Support available to part-time students. Financial award application deadline: 4/15; financial award applicants required to submit FAFSA. *Faculty research:* Urban education, middle school, school improvement, teacher education, at-risk student achievement. *Unit head:* Dr. Phyllis Sunshine, Assistant Provost, 410-337-6047, Fax: 410-337-6394, E-mail: psunshin@goucher.edu. *Application contact:* Shelby Hillers, Admissions Coordinator, 410-337-6200, Fax: 410-337-6085, E-mail: shelby.hillers@goucher.edu.
Website: http://www.goucher.edu/graduate-programs/graduate-programs-in-education

Governors State University, College of Education, Program in Multi-Categorical Special Education, University Park, IL 60484. Offers MA. *Accreditation:* NCATE. *Program availability:* Part-time. *Faculty:* 47 full-time (31 women), 49 part-time/adjunct (39 women). *Students:* 12 full-time (11 women), 31 part-time (21 women); includes 20 minority (16 Black or African American, non-Hispanic/Latino; 3 Hispanic/Latino; 1 Two or more races, non-Hispanic/Latino). Average age 36. 38 applicants, 68% accepted, 19 enrolled. In 2016, 12 master's awarded. *Entrance requirements:* Additional exam requirements/recommendations for international students: Required—TOEFL (minimum score 550 paper-based; 80 iBT), IELTS. *Application deadline:* For fall admission, 4/1 for domestic students. Application fee: $50. Electronic applications accepted. *Expenses:* $307 per credit hour; $38 per term or $76 per credit hour fees. *Financial support:* Application deadline: 5/1; applicants required to submit FAFSA. *Unit head:* Timothy Harrington, Chair, Division of Education, 708-534-4361, E-mail: tharrington2@govst.edu. *Application contact:* Yakeea Daniels, Assistant Vice President for Enrollment Services/Director of Admission, 708-534-4510, E-mail: ydaniels@govst.edu.

Graceland University, Gleazer School of Education, Independence, MO 64050. Offers curriculum and instruction (M Ed); differentiated instruction (M Ed); instructional leadership (M Ed); literacy and instruction (M Ed); management in the inclusive classroom (M Ed); special education (M Ed); technology integration (M Ed). *Accreditation:* NCATE. *Program availability:* Part-time, evening/weekend, online learning. *Faculty:* 2 full-time (both women), 9 part-time/adjunct (5 women). *Students:* 115 full-time (96 women), 20 part-time (17 women); includes 10 minority (5 Black or African American, non-Hispanic/Latino; 1 Asian, non-Hispanic/Latino; 1 Hispanic/Latino; 1 Native Hawaiian or other Pacific Islander, non-Hispanic/Latino; 2 Two or more races, non-Hispanic/Latino), 2 international. 155 applicants, 61% accepted, 85 enrolled. In 2016, 61 master's awarded. *Degree requirements:* For master's, action research project. *Entrance requirements:* For master's, minimum GPA of 3.0, teaching certificate, current teaching contract. Additional exam requirements/recommendations for international students: Required—TOEFL. *Application deadline:* For fall admission, 10/1 for domestic students; for winter admission, 11/15 for domestic students; for spring admission, 2/15 priority date for domestic students; for summer admission, 6/1 for domestic students. Applications are processed on a rolling basis. Application fee: $50. Electronic applications accepted. *Expenses:* Contact institution. *Financial support:* Institutionally sponsored loans and scholarships/grants available. Financial award application deadline: 12/15; financial award applicants required to submit FAFSA. *Faculty research:* Literacy, technology, faculty mentoring, adult literacy, e-learning, online teaching. *Unit head:* Dr. Lee Bash, Interim Dean, 641-784-5072, E-mail: bash@graceland.edu. *Application contact:* Jeanette Calipetro, Admissions Representative, 816-423-4716, Fax: 816-833-2990, E-mail: jcali1@graceland.edu.
Website: http://www.graceland.edu/education

Grambling State University, School of Graduate Studies and Research, College of Education, Department of Curriculum and Instruction, Grambling, LA 71245. Offers curriculum and instruction (MS); special education (M Ed). *Program availability:* Part-time. *Degree requirements:* For master's, comprehensive exam, thesis (for some programs). *Entrance requirements:* Additional exam requirements/recommendations for international students: Required—TOEFL (minimum score 500 paper-based; 62 iBT).

Grand Canyon University, College of Education, Phoenix, AZ 85017-1097. Offers autism spectrum disorders (MA); curriculum and instruction (MA); early childhood education (M Ed); educational administration (M Ed); educational leadership (M Ed); elementary education (M Ed); gifted education (MA); instructional technology (MS); K-12 leadership (Ed S); reading (MA); secondary education (M Ed); secondary humanities education (M Ed); secondary STEM education (M Ed); special education (M Ed); teaching and learning (Ed D); teaching English to speakers of other languages (MA). *Program availability:* Part-time, evening/weekend, online learning. *Degree requirements:* For master's, publishable research paper (M Ed), e-portfolio. *Entrance requirements:* For master's, undergraduate degree from accredited, GCU-approved college, university, or program with minimum GPA 2.8. Additional exam requirements/recommendations for international students: Required—TOEFL (minimum score 550 paper-based; 79 iBT), IELTS (minimum score 6). *Application deadline:* For fall admission, 8/21 for domestic students, 7/2 for international students; for spring admission, 12/24 for domestic students, 11/1 for international students. Applications are processed on a rolling basis. Application fee: $100. Electronic applications accepted. *Financial support:* Federal Work-Study available. Support available to part-time students. Financial award applicants required to submit FAFSA. *Unit head:* Dr. Kimberly L. LaPrade, Dean, 602-639-6360, E-mail: kimberly.laprade@gcu.edu. *Application contact:* Dr. Kimberly L. LaPrade, Dean, 602-639-6360, E-mail: kimberly.laprade@gcu.edu.
Website: https://www.gcu.edu/college-of-education.php

Grand Valley State University, College of Education, Program in Special Education, Allendale, MI 49401-9403. Offers cognitive impairment (M Ed); early childhood developmental delay (M Ed); emotional impairment (M Ed); learning disabilities (M Ed); special education (M Ed). *Accreditation:* NCATE. *Program availability:* Part-time, evening/weekend. *Students:* 2 full-time (1 woman), 71 part-time (57 women); includes 3 minority (1 Hispanic/Latino; 2 Two or more races, non-Hispanic/Latino), 2 international. Average age 33. 9 applicants, 89% accepted, 2 enrolled. In 2016, 33 master's awarded. *Degree requirements:* For master's, project or thesis. *Entrance requirements:* For master's, GRE General Test or minimum GPA of 3.0, last 60 credits from regionally-accredited college/university, 3 letters of recommendation. Additional exam requirements/recommendations for international students: Required—TOEFL. *Application deadline:* Applications are processed on a rolling basis. Application fee: $30. Electronic applications accepted. *Expenses:* $628 per credit hour. *Financial support:* In 2016–17, 15 students received support. Career-related internships or fieldwork, Federal Work-Study, scholarships/grants, and unspecified assistantships available. *Faculty research:* Evaluation of special education program effects, adaptive behavior assessment, language development, writing disorders, comparative effects of presentation methods. *Unit head:* Dr. Amy Schelling, Director, 616-331-6243, Fax: 616-331-6294, E-mail: schellia@gvsu.edu. *Application contact:* Thomas Owens, Director, Student Information and Services Center, 616-331-6282, Fax: 616-331-6217, E-mail: owenst@gvsu.edu.

Greensboro College, Program in Education, Greensboro, NC 27401-1875. Offers elementary education (M Ed); special education (M Ed). *Program availability:* Part-time, evening/weekend. *Degree requirements:* For master's, thesis. *Entrance requirements:* For master's, GRE, teacher license, 2 years of teaching experience, 2 letters of recommendation. Additional exam requirements/recommendations for international students: Required—TOEFL (minimum score 550 paper-based). Electronic applications accepted.

Gwynedd Mercy University, School of Education, Gwynedd Valley, PA 19437-0901. Offers educational administration (MS); master teacher (MS); school counseling (MS); special education (MS). *Program availability:* Part-time, evening/weekend, 100% online. *Faculty:* 8 full-time (5 women), 38 part-time/adjunct (24 women). *Students:* 466 full-time (355 women); includes 93 minority (66 Black or African American, non-Hispanic/Latino; 12 Asian, non-Hispanic/Latino; 15 Hispanic/Latino). Average age 36. 127 applicants, 18% accepted, 9 enrolled. In 2016, 86 master's awarded. *Degree requirements:* For master's, thesis, internship, practicum. *Entrance requirements:* For master's, GRE or MAT; PRAXIS I, minimum GPA of 3.0. *Application deadline:* Applications are processed on a rolling basis. *Expenses: Tuition:* Full-time $14,400; part-time $800 per credit hour. One-time fee: $165. Tuition and fees vary according to degree level and program. *Financial support:* In 2016–17, 2 research assistantships were awarded; career-related internships or fieldwork, Federal Work-Study, institutionally sponsored loans, tuition waivers (full and partial), and unspecified assistantships also available. Financial award applicants required to submit FAFSA. *Faculty research:* Learning and the brain, reading literacy, ethics and moral judgment, leadership, teaching and multicultural education. *Unit head:* Dr. Heather Pfleger, Dean, 215-646-7300 Ext. 21581, E-mail: pfleger.h@gmercyu.edu. *Application contact:* Graduate Program Coordinator, 877-499-6333, E-mail: graduate@gmercyu.edu.
Website: https://www.gmercyu.edu/academics/graduate-education-programs

Harding University, Cannon-Clary College of Education, Searcy, AR 72149-0001. Offers advanced studies in teaching and learning (M Ed); art (MSE); behavioral science (MSE); counseling (MS, Ed S); early childhood special education (M Ed, MSE); education (MSE); educational leadership (M Ed, Ed S); elementary education (M Ed); English (MSE); French (MSE); history/social science (MSE); kinesiology (MSE); math (MSE); reading (M Ed); secondary education (M Ed); Spanish (MSE); teaching (MAT); teaching English as a second language (MSE). *Accreditation:* NCATE. *Program availability:* Part-time, evening/weekend. *Faculty:* 22 full-time (9 women), 51 part-time/adjunct (37 women). *Students:* 130 full-time (94 women), 321 part-time (234 women); includes 83 minority (50 Black or African American, non-Hispanic/Latino; 4 American Indian or Alaska Native, non-Hispanic/Latino; 6 Asian, non-Hispanic/Latino; 13 Hispanic/Latino; 10 Two or more races, non-Hispanic/Latino), 11 international. Average age 35. 125 applicants, 88% accepted, 110 enrolled. In 2016, 124 master's, 27 other advanced degrees awarded. *Degree requirements:* For master's, comprehensive exam (for some programs), thesis optional, portfolio(s); for Ed S, comprehensive exam, portfolio, project. *Entrance requirements:* For master's, GRE, MAT, PRAXIS; for Ed S, MAT or GRE. Additional exam requirements/recommendations for international students: Required—TOEFL (minimum score 550 paper-based; 79 iBT). *Application deadline:* For fall admission, 8/1 for domestic and international students; for spring admission, 1/1 for domestic and international students. Applications are processed on a rolling basis. Application fee: $35. Tuition and fees vary according to degree level and program. *Financial support:* In 2016–17, 31 students received support. Unspecified assistantships available. *Faculty research:* Reading, comprehension, school violence, educational technology, behavior, college choice, differentiated instruction, brain-based teaching. *Unit head:* Dr. Clara Carroll, Chair, 501-279-4501, Fax: 501-279-4083, E-mail: ccarroll@harding.edu. *Application contact:* Information Contact, 501-279-4315, E-mail: gradstudiesedu@harding.edu.
Website: http://www.harding.edu/education

Hebrew College, Shoolman Graduate School of Jewish Education, Newton Centre, MA 02459. Offers early childhood Jewish education (Certificate); Jewish day school education (Certificate); Jewish education (MJ Ed); Jewish family education (Certificate); Jewish special education (Certificate); Jewish youth education, informal education and camping (Certificate). *Program availability:* Part-time, evening/weekend, online learning. *Degree requirements:* For master's, one foreign language. *Entrance requirements:* For master's, GRE, interview. Additional exam requirements/recommendations for international students: Required—TOEFL.

Henderson State University, Graduate Studies, Teachers College, Department of Advanced Instructional Studies, Arkadelphia, AR 71999-0001. Offers developmental therapy (MSE); dyslexia therapy (Graduate Certificate); education (MAT); educational technology leadership (Graduate Certificate); English as a second language (MSE, Graduate Certificate); instructional facilitator (MSE, Graduate Certificate); middle level education (MAT); special education (K-12) (MAT, MSE); special education/early childhood (MAT). *Accreditation:* NCATE. *Program availability:* Part-time. *Faculty:* 12 full-time (9 women), 5 part-time/adjunct (4 women). *Students:* 13 full-time (8 women), 79 part-time (66 women); includes 14 minority (8 Black or African American, non-Hispanic/Latino; 2 American Indian or Alaska Native, non-Hispanic/Latino; 2 Hispanic/Latino; 2 Two or more races, non-Hispanic/Latino). Average age 33. 21 applicants, 100% accepted, 21 enrolled. In 2016, 29 master's awarded. *Entrance requirements:* For master's, GRE General Test or MAT, minimum GPA of 2.7, teacher certification. Additional exam requirements/recommendations for international students: Required—TOEFL (minimum score 600 paper-based); Recommended—IELTS (minimum score 6.5). *Application deadline:* For fall admission, 8/1 priority date for domestic students, 6/30 priority date for international students; for spring admission, 1/1 priority date for domestic students, 11/30 priority date for international students. Applications are processed on a rolling basis. Application fee: $25 ($75 for international students). *Expenses:* Tuition, state resident: full-time $6288; part-time $3144 per credit hour. Tuition, nonresident: full-time $12,888; part-time $6444 per credit hour. *Required fees:* $1429; $1024 per credit hour. Tuition and fees vary according to course load and student level. *Financial support:* In 2016–17, 1 teaching assistantship with partial tuition reimbursement (averaging $4,000 per year) was awarded; scholarships/grants and unspecified assistantships also available. Financial award application deadline: 4/15; financial award applicants required to submit FAFSA. *Unit head:* Dr. Gary Smithey, Coordinator, 870-230-5361, Fax: 870-230-5455, E-mail: smitheg@hsu.edu. *Application contact:* Dr. Ken Taylor, Graduate Dean, 870-230-5126, Fax: 870-230-5479, E-mail: taylorke@hsu.edu.
Website: http://www.hsu.edu/Academics/TeachersCollege/AIS/index.html

Heritage University, Graduate Programs in Education, Program in Professional Studies, Toppenish, WA 98948-9599. Offers bilingual education/ESL (M Ed); biology (M Ed); English and literature (M Ed); reading/literacy (M Ed); special education (M Ed). *Program availability:* Part-time, evening/weekend. *Degree requirements:* For master's, comprehensive exam (for some programs), thesis (for some programs).

High Point University, Norcross Graduate School, High Point, NC 27268. Offers business administration (MBA); educational leadership (M Ed); elementary education (M Ed); history (MA); nonprofit management (MA); secondary math (M Ed); special education (M Ed); strategic communication (MA); teaching elementary education k-6 (MAT); teaching secondary mathematics 9-12 (MAT). *Accreditation:* NCATE. *Program availability:* Part-time, evening/weekend. *Degree requirements:* For master's, comprehensive exam (for some programs), thesis (for some programs). *Entrance requirements:* For master's, GMAT (MBA), GRE, MAT, minimum GPA of 3.0. Additional exam requirements/recommendations for international students: Required—TOEFL (minimum score 550 paper-based). Electronic applications accepted.

Hofstra University, School of Education, Programs in Teacher Education, Hempstead, NY 11549. Offers bilingual education (MA, Advanced Certificate); bilingual extension (Advanced Certificate), including education/speech language pathology; business education (MS Ed); early childhood and childhood education (MS Ed); early childhood education (MA, MS Ed); education technology (Advanced Certificate); elementary education (MA, MS Ed), including science, technology, engineering, and mathematics (STEM) (MA); English education (MS Ed); family and consumer science (MS Ed); fine arts and music education (Advanced Certificate); fine arts education (MS Ed); foreign language and TESOL (MS Ed); foreign language education (MS Ed), including French, German, Russian, Spanish; learning and teaching (Ed D), including applied linguistics, art education, arts and humanities, early childhood education, English education, human development, math education, math, science, and technology, multicultural education, physical education, science education, social studies education, special education; mathematics education (MA, MS Ed); middle school extension (Advanced Certificate), including grades 5-6, grades 7-9; music education (MA, MS Ed); science education (MA, MS Ed), including biology, chemistry, earth science, geology, physics; secondary education (Advanced Certificate); social studies education (MA, MS Ed); teaching languages other than English and TESOL (MS Ed); TESOL (MS Ed, Advanced Certificate). *Program availability:* Part-time, evening/weekend, blended/hybrid learning. *Students:* 139 full-time (97 women), 145 part-time (106 women); includes 60 minority (15 Black or African American, non-Hispanic/Latino; 1 American Indian or Alaska Native, non-Hispanic/Latino; 12 Asian, non-Hispanic/Latino; 31 Hispanic/Latino; 1 Two or more races, non-Hispanic/Latino), 21 international. Average age 29. 255 applicants, 86% accepted, 122 enrolled. In 2016, 101 master's, 4 doctorates, 43 other advanced degrees awarded. *Degree requirements:* For master's, comprehensive exam, thesis (for some programs), exit project, student teaching, fieldwork, electronic portfolio, curriculum project, minimum GPA of 3.0; for doctorate, thesis/dissertation; for Advanced Certificate, 3 foreign languages, comprehensive exam (for some programs), thesis project. *Entrance requirements:* For master's, GRE, MAT, 2 letters of recommendation, portfolio, teacher certification (MA), interview, essay; for doctorate, GMAT, GRE, LSAT, or MAT; for Advanced Certificate, 2 letters of recommendation, essay, interview and/or portfolio, teaching certificate. Additional exam requirements/recommendations for international students: Required—TOEFL (minimum score 550 paper-based; 80 iBT). *Application deadline:* Applications are processed on a rolling basis. Application fee: $75. Electronic applications accepted. *Expenses: Tuition:* Full-time $1240. *Required fees:* $970. Tuition and fees vary according to program. *Financial support:* In 2016–17, 149 students received support, including 58 fellowships with full and partial tuition reimbursements available (averaging $5,309 per year), 5 research assistantships with full and partial tuition reimbursements available (averaging $7,073 per year); career-related internships or fieldwork, Federal Work-Study, institutionally sponsored loans, scholarships/grants, traineeships, tuition waivers (full and partial), and unspecified assistantships also available. Support available to part-time students. Financial award applicants required to submit FAFSA. *Faculty research:* Educational interventions that foster critical-thinking skills; teachers' attitudes about professional development; threats to teacher quality. *Unit head:* Dr. Eustace Thompson, Chairperson, 516-463-5749, Fax: 516-463-6275, E-mail: eustace.g.thompson@hofstra.edu. *Application contact:* Sunil Samuel, Assistant Vice President of Admissions, 516-463-4723, Fax: 516-463-4664, E-mail: graduateadmission@hofstra.edu.
Website: http://www.hofstra.edu/education/

Hofstra University, School of Education, Specialized Programs in Education, Hempstead, NY 11549. Offers applied behavior analysis (Advanced Certificate); early childhood special education (MS Ed, Advanced Certificate); educational and policy leadership (Ed D); educational leadership (Advanced Certificate), including school building leader/school district business leader; educational leadership and policy studies (MS Ed), including K-12; gifted education (Advanced Certificate), including school building leader/school district business leader; health education PK-12 teaching certification (MS); inclusive early childhood special education (MS Ed); inclusive elementary special education (MS Ed); inclusive secondary special education (MS Ed); literacy studies (MS Ed, Ed D, PhD, Advanced Certificate), including birth-grade 6 (MS Ed, Advanced Certificate), birth-grade 6 and special education (birth-grade2) (MS Ed), grades 5-12 (MS Ed, Advanced Certificate); physical education (MS); secondary education generalist (MS Ed), including students with disabilities 7-12; special education (MS Ed, Advanced Certificate); special education assessment and diagnosis (Advanced Certificate); special education generalist (MS Ed), including extension in secondary education; sport science (MS), including strength and conditioning; teaching students with severe or multiple disabilities (Advanced Certificate). *Program availability:* Part-time, evening/weekend, 100% online, blended/hybrid learning. *Students:* 149 full-time (115 women), 258 part-time (187 women); includes 97 minority (50 Black or African American, non-Hispanic/Latino; 1 American Indian or Alaska Native, non-Hispanic/Latino; 11 Asian, non-Hispanic/Latino; 34 Hispanic/Latino; 1 Native Hawaiian or other Pacific Islander, non-Hispanic/Latino), 5 international. Average age 32. 250 applicants, 88% accepted, 146 enrolled. In 2016, 85 master's, 13 doctorates, 35 other advanced degrees awarded. *Degree requirements:* For master's, one foreign language, comprehensive exam (for some programs), thesis (for some programs), electronic portfolio, capstone course, internship, practicum, student teaching, seminars, minimum GPA of 3.0; for doctorate, one foreign language, comprehensive exam, thesis/dissertation, qualifying hearing. *Entrance requirements:* For master's, GRE, interview, letters of recommendation, portfolio, essay, certification; for doctorate, GRE or MAT, interview, resume, essay, master's degree, 3 letters of recommendation, writing sample; for Advanced Certificate, GRE, interview, letters of recommendation, essay, professional experience, resume, master's degree. Additional exam requirements/recommendations for international students: Required—TOEFL (minimum score 550 paper-based; 80 iBT). *Application deadline:* Applications are processed on a rolling basis. Application fee: $75. Electronic applications accepted. *Expenses: Tuition:* Full-time $1240. *Required fees:* $970. Tuition and fees vary according to program. *Financial support:* In 2016–17, 244 students received support, including 117 fellowships with full and partial tuition reimbursements available (averaging $3,705 per year), 12 research assistantships with full and partial tuition reimbursements available (averaging $6,490 per year); career-related internships or fieldwork, Federal Work-Study, institutionally sponsored loans, scholarships/grants, traineeships, tuition waivers (full and partial), and unspecified assistantships also available. Support available to part-time students. Financial award applicants required to submit FAFSA. *Faculty research:* Collaborative teaching and learning; language and culture; new media literacies; applied behavior analysis; K-12 leadership development. *Unit head:* Dr. Elfreda Blue, Chairperson, 516-463-5762, Fax: 516-463-6184, E-mail: elfreda.blue@hofstra.edu. *Application contact:* Sunil Samuel, Assistant Vice President of Admissions, 516-463-4723, Fax: 516-463-4664, E-mail: graduateadmission@hofstra.edu.
Website: http://www.hofstra.edu/education/

Holy Family University, Graduate and Professional Programs, School of Education, Master of Education Programs, Philadelphia, PA 19114. Offers early elementary education (PreK-Grade 4) (M Ed); education leadership (M Ed); general education (M Ed); reading specialist (M Ed); special education (M Ed); TESOL and literacy (M Ed). *Program availability:* Part-time. *Students:* 202 full-time, 58 part-time. 209 applicants, 77% accepted, 140 enrolled. In 2016, 123 master's awarded. *Degree requirements:* For master's, thesis optional. *Application deadline:* Applications are processed on a rolling basis. Application fee: $25. Electronic applications accepted. *Expenses: Tuition:* Part-time $751 per hour. *Required fees:* $140 per semester. One-time fee: $165 part-time. Part-time tuition and fees vary according to degree level and program. *Unit head:* Dr. Kevin Zook, Dean, 267-341-3246, Fax: 215-824-2438, E-mail: kzook@holyfamily.edu. *Application contact:* Donald Reimold, Director of Graduate Admissions, 267-341-5001, Fax: 215-637-1478, E-mail: dreimold@holyfamily.edu.

Holy Names University, Graduate Division, Department of Education, Oakland, CA 94619-1699. Offers educational therapy (Certificate); mild/moderate disabilities (Ed S); multiple subject teaching (Credential); single subject teaching (Credential); urban education: educational therapy (M Ed); urban education: K-12 education (M Ed); urban education: special education (M Ed). *Program availability:* Part-time. *Students:* 18 full-time (11 women), 111 part-time (79 women); includes 74 minority (37 Black or African American, non-Hispanic/Latino; 1 American Indian or Alaska Native, non-Hispanic/Latino; 10 Asian, non-Hispanic/Latino; 24 Hispanic/Latino; 1 Native Hawaiian or other Pacific Islander, non-Hispanic/Latino; 1 Two or more races, non-Hispanic/Latino), 3 international. Average age 35. 62 applicants, 81% accepted, 39 enrolled. In 2016, 11 master's, 33 Certificates awarded. *Degree requirements:* For master's, comprehensive exam, research paper, thesis or project. *Entrance requirements:* For master's, minimum undergraduate GPA of 2.6 overall, 3.0 in major; personal statement; two recommendations; interview. Additional exam requirements/recommendations for international students: Required—TOEFL (minimum score 550 paper-based; 79 iBT). *Application deadline:* For fall admission, 8/1 priority date for domestic students, 7/15 for international students; for spring admission, 12/1 priority date for domestic students, 12/1 for international students; for summer admission, 5/1 priority date for domestic students, 5/1 for international students. Applications are processed on a rolling basis. Application fee: $65. Electronic applications accepted. Application fee is waived when completed online. *Expenses: Tuition:* Full-time $17,532; part-time $974 per credit hour. *Required fees:* $500; $250 per credit hour. *Financial support:* Career-related internships or fieldwork, Federal Work-Study, scholarships/grants, and unspecified assistantships available. Support available to part-time students. Financial award application deadline: 3/2; financial award applicants required to submit FAFSA. *Faculty research:* Cognitive development, language development, learning handicaps. *Unit head:* Dr. Kimberly Mayfield, Chair, 510-436-1396, Fax: 510-436-1325, E-mail: mayfield@hnu.edu. *Application contact:* Graduate Admission, 800-430-1321, Fax: 510-436-1325, E-mail: graduateadmissions@hnu.edu.
Website: http://www.hnu.edu/academics/graduatePrograms/education.html

Hood College, Graduate School, Department of Education, Frederick, MD 21701-8575. Offers curriculum and instruction (MS), including elementary education, elementary science and mathematics education, secondary education, special education; educational leadership (MS); reading specialization (MS); STEM education (Certificate). *Accreditation:* NCATE. *Program availability:* Part-time-only, evening/weekend. *Faculty:* 3 full-time, 37 part-time/adjunct. *Students:* 1 (woman) full-time, 357 part-time (283 women); includes 71 minority (41 Black or African American, non-Hispanic/Latino; 6 Asian, non-Hispanic/Latino; 15 Hispanic/Latino; 9 Two or more races, non-Hispanic/Latino). Average age 33. 96 applicants, 95% accepted, 83 enrolled. In 2016, 47 master's awarded. *Degree requirements:* For master's, action research project, portfolio (for reading specialization); for Certificate, STEM capstone activity. *Entrance requirements:* For master's, minimum GPA of 2.75, teaching certification, writing sample during interview, letter of recommendation from principal (for educational leadership program only). Additional exam requirements/recommendations for international students: Required—TOEFL (minimum score 575 paper-based; 89 iBT), IELTS (minimum score 6.5). *Application deadline:* For fall admission, 8/15 priority date for domestic students, 8/5 for international students; for spring admission, 12/1 priority date for domestic students, 12/1 for international students; for summer admission, 5/1 priority date for

domestic students, 4/15 for international students. Applications are processed on a rolling basis. Application fee: $35. Electronic applications accepted. *Expenses:* $450 per credit; $105 comprehensive fee per semester. *Financial support:* Tuition waivers (partial) and unspecified assistantships available. Financial award applicants required to submit FAFSA. *Faculty research:* Leadership, action research, brain research, learning styles. *Unit head:* April Boulton, Interim Dean of the Graduate School, E-mail: gofurther@hood.edu. *Application contact:* Jan Marcus, Assistant Director of Graduate Admissions, 301-696-3600, E-mail: gofurther@hood.edu.
Website: http://www.hood.edu/academics/education/index.html

Howard University, School of Education, Department of Curriculum and Instruction, Program in Special Education, Washington, DC 20059-0002. Offers M Ed. *Accreditation:* NCATE. *Program availability:* Part-time. *Degree requirements:* For master's, comprehensive exam, thesis (for some programs), expository writing exam, internships, practicum. *Entrance requirements:* For master's, minimum GPA of 2.7. Additional exam requirements/recommendations for international students: Required—TOEFL (minimum score 550 paper-based; 79 iBT). Electronic applications accepted.

Hunter College of the City University of New York, Graduate School, School of Education, Department of Special Education, New York, NY 10065-5085. Offers blind and visually impaired (MS Ed); severe/multiple disabilities (MS Ed). *Accreditation:* NCATE. *Students:* 57 full-time (47 women), 832 part-time (688 women); includes 357 minority (159 Black or African American, non-Hispanic/Latino; 1 American Indian or Alaska Native, non-Hispanic/Latino; 63 Asian, non-Hispanic/Latino; 134 Hispanic/Latino), 14 international. Average age 29. 504 applicants, 84% accepted, 311 enrolled. In 2016, 322 master's awarded. *Degree requirements:* For master's, comprehensive exam, thesis, student teaching practica, clinical teaching lab courses, New York State Teacher Certification Exams. *Entrance requirements:* For master's, minimum GPA of 2.8. Additional exam requirements/recommendations for international students: Required—TOEFL, TWE. *Application deadline:* For fall admission, 4/1 for domestic students, 2/1 for international students; for spring admission, 11/1 for domestic students, 9/1 for international students. Applications are processed on a rolling basis. *Financial support:* Career-related internships or fieldwork, Federal Work-Study, institutionally sponsored loans, and tuition waivers (partial) available. Support available to part-time students. *Faculty research:* Mathematics learning disabilities; street behavior; assessment; bilingual special education; families, diversity, and disabilities. *Unit head:* Prof. David Connor, Chairperson, 212-772-4700, E-mail: dconnor@hunter.cuny.edu. *Application contact:* Milena Solo, Director for Graduate Admissions, 212-772-4480, E-mail: admissions@hunter.cuny.edu.

Idaho State University, Office of Graduate Studies, College of Education, Department of School Psychology, Literacy, and Special Education, Pocatello, ID 83209-8059. Offers deaf education (M Ed); human exceptionality (M Ed); literacy (M Ed); school psychology (Ed S); special education (Ed S). *Program availability:* Part-time. *Degree requirements:* For master's, comprehensive exam, thesis (for some programs), oral thesis defense or written comprehensive exam and oral exam; for Ed S, comprehensive exam, thesis (for some programs), oral exam, specialist paper or portfolio. *Entrance requirements:* For master's, GRE or MAT, minimum undergraduate GPA of 3.0, bachelor's degree, professional experience in an educational context; for Ed S, GRE or MAT, master's degree in related field. Additional exam requirements/recommendations for international students: Required—TOEFL (minimum score 550 paper-based; 80 iBT). Electronic applications accepted. *Faculty research:* Literacy, school psychology, special education.

Idaho State University, Office of Graduate Studies, Kasiska College of Health Professions, Department of Communication Sciences and Disorders and Education of the Deaf, Pocatello, ID 83209-8116. Offers audiology (MS, Au D); communication sciences and disorders (Postbaccalaureate Certificate); communication sciences and disorders and education of the deaf (Certificate); deaf education (MS); speech language pathology (MS). *Accreditation:* ASHA (one or more programs are accredited). *Program availability:* Part-time. *Degree requirements:* For master's, thesis optional, written and oral comprehensive exams; for doctorate, comprehensive exam, thesis/dissertation optional, externship, 1 year full time clinical practicum, 3rd year spent in Boise. *Entrance requirements:* For master's, GRE General Test, minimum GPA of 3.0, 3 letters of recommendation; for doctorate, GRE General Test (at least 2 scores minimum 40th percentile), minimum GPA of 3.0, 3 letters of recommendation, bachelor's degree. Additional exam requirements/recommendations for international students: Required—TOEFL (minimum score 600 paper-based; 80 iBT). Electronic applications accepted. *Faculty research:* Neurogenic disorders, central auditory processing disorders, vestibular disorders, cochlear implants, language disorders, professional burnout, swallowing disorders.

Illinois State University, Graduate School, College of Education, Department of Special Education, Normal, IL 61790-2200. Offers MS, MS Ed, Ed D, Certificate. *Accreditation:* NCATE. *Degree requirements:* For doctorate, thesis/dissertation, 2 terms of residency. *Entrance requirements:* For master's, GRE General Test, minimum GPA of 3.0 in last 60 hours; for doctorate, GRE General Test. *Faculty research:* Center for adult learning leadership, promoting a learning community, autism spectrum professional development and technical assistance project, preparing qualified personnel to provide early intervention for children who are deaf.

Immaculata University, College of Graduate Studies, Program in Educational Leadership, Immaculata, PA 19345. Offers educational leadership (MA, Ed D); principal (Certificate); secondary education (Certificate); supervisor of special education (Certificate). *Program availability:* Part-time, evening/weekend. *Degree requirements:* For master's, comprehensive exam, thesis optional; for doctorate, comprehensive exam, thesis/dissertation. *Entrance requirements:* For master's, GRE or MAT, minimum GPA of 3.0; for doctorate, GRE General Test or MAT, minimum GPA of 3.5. Additional exam requirements/recommendations for international students: Required—TOEFL. Electronic applications accepted. *Faculty research:* Cooperative learning, school-based management, whole language, performance assessment.

Indiana University Bloomington, School of Education, Department of Curriculum and Instruction, Bloomington, IN 47405-7000. Offers art education (MS, Ed D, PhD); curriculum studies (Ed D, PhD); elementary education (MS, Ed D, PhD, Ed S); mathematics education (MS, Ed D, PhD); science education (MS, Ed D, PhD); secondary education (MS, Ed D, PhD); social studies education (MS, PhD); special education (PhD, Ed S). *Accreditation:* NCATE. *Program availability:* Part-time, evening/weekend. Terminal master's awarded for partial completion of doctoral program. *Degree requirements:* For doctorate, thesis/dissertation; for Ed S, comprehensive exam or project. *Entrance requirements:* For master's, doctorate, and Ed S, GRE General Test. Electronic applications accepted.

Indiana University of Pennsylvania, School of Graduate Studies and Research, College of Education and Educational Technology, Department of Communication Disorders, Special Education, and Disability Services, Program in Special Education, Indiana, PA 15705. Offers M Ed. *Accreditation:* NCATE. *Program availability:* Part-time. *Faculty:* 9 full-time (7 women), 3 part-time/adjunct (2 women). *Students:* 4 full-time (all women), 20 part-time (19 women). Average age 31. 28 applicants, 68% accepted, 15 enrolled. In 2016, 8 master's awarded. *Degree requirements:* For master's, comprehensive exam, thesis optional. *Entrance requirements:* For master's, 2 letters of recommendation. Additional exam requirements/recommendations for international students: Required—TOEFL (minimum score 540 paper-based). *Application deadline:* For fall admission, 3/1 for domestic students; for spring admission, 7/1 for domestic students. Applications are processed on a rolling basis. Application fee: $50. Electronic applications accepted. *Expenses:* Tuition, state resident: full-time $8694; part-time $483 per credit. Tuition, nonresident: full-time $13,050; part-time $725 per credit. *Required fees:* $157 per credit. $50 per term. Tuition and fees vary according to course load and program. *Financial support:* In 2016–17, 2 research assistantships with tuition reimbursements (averaging $5,440 per year) were awarded; career-related internships or fieldwork, Federal Work-Study, scholarships/grants, and unspecified assistantships also available. Support available to part-time students. Financial award application deadline: 4/15; financial award applicants required to submit FAFSA. *Unit head:* Dr. Alexandria Kappel, Graduate Coordinator, 724-357-2454, E-mail: alexandria.kappel@iup.edu.
Website: http://www.iup.edu/grad/edex/default.aspx

Indiana University–Purdue University Fort Wayne, College of Education and Public Policy, Department of Professional Studies, Fort Wayne, IN 46805-1499. Offers couple and family counseling (MS Ed); educational leadership (MS Ed); school counseling (MS Ed); special education (MS Ed, Certificate). *Program availability:* Part-time. *Degree requirements:* For master's, comprehensive exam, practicum, internship, portfolio. *Entrance requirements:* For master's, minimum GPA of 2.5, three professional letters of recommendation. Additional exam requirements/recommendations for international students: Required—TOEFL (minimum score 550 paper-based; 79 iBT). *Faculty research:* Learning opportunities with deafness and the hearing impaired, adolescent emotion, student evaluation of teaching.

Indiana University–Purdue University Indianapolis, School of Education, Indianapolis, IN 46202-5155. Offers curriculum and instruction (MS); early childhood (MS); educational leadership (MS, Certificate); English as a second language (Certificate); kindergarten (Certificate); language education (MS); reading (Certificate); school counseling (MS); special education (MS, Certificate). *Program availability:* Part-time, evening/weekend. *Faculty:* 35 full-time (27 women), 56 part-time/adjunct (42 women). *Students:* 125 full-time (86 women), 181 part-time (139 women); includes 106 minority (78 Black or African American, non-Hispanic/Latino; 9 Asian, non-Hispanic/Latino; 12 Hispanic/Latino; 7 Two or more races, non-Hispanic/Latino), 3 international. Average age 32. 73 applicants, 93% accepted, 68 enrolled. In 2016, 73 master's awarded. Terminal master's awarded for partial completion of doctoral program. *Degree requirements:* For master's, thesis optional. *Entrance requirements:* For master's, GRE General Test, minimum GPA of 2.5; for Certificate, official transcripts. Additional exam requirements/recommendations for international students: Required—TOEFL (minimum score 60 iBT), IELTS (minimum score 5.5). *Application deadline:* For fall admission, 5/1 for domestic students; for spring admission, 11/1 for domestic students. Application fee: $60 ($65 for international students). Electronic applications accepted. *Expenses:* $1,262 tuition, $213 general fee. *Financial support:* Applicants required to submit FAFSA. *Faculty research:* Educational policies and school leaders' responses to these; issues of intersectionality in the experiences of African American lesbian, gay, and bisexual students attending historically black colleges and universities and those who belong to black Greek-letter organizations; students' experiential knowledge and their evolving disciplinary-specific literacy and understanding; innovative program development; urban ESL teacher preparation; target-based instructional coaching. *Total annual research expenditures:* $2.1 million. *Unit head:* Dr. Robin Hughes, Executive Associate Dean, 317-274-6817, E-mail: roblhugh@iupui.edu. *Application contact:* Ky Shaw, Graduate Admissions Coordinator, 317-278-6778, E-mail: kycshaw@iupui.edu.
Website: http://education.iupui.edu/

Indiana University South Bend, School of Education, South Bend, IN 46634-7111. Offers addiction counseling (MS Ed); alcohol and drug counseling (Graduate Certificate); clinical mental health counseling (MS Ed); educational leadership (MS Ed); elementary education (MS Ed); marriage, couple, and family counseling (MS Ed); school counseling (MS Ed); secondary education (MS Ed); special education (MAT, MS Ed), including intense intervention (MS Ed), mild intervention (MS Ed). *Accreditation:* NCATE. *Program availability:* Part-time, evening/weekend. *Faculty:* 21 full-time (11 women), 9 part-time/adjunct (3 women). *Students:* 26 full-time (19 women), 104 part-time (80 women); includes 22 minority (13 Black or African American, non-Hispanic/Latino; 5 Hispanic/Latino; 4 Two or more races, non-Hispanic/Latino). Average age 35. 51 applicants, 69% accepted, 22 enrolled. In 2016, 31 master's, 2 other advanced degrees awarded. *Degree requirements:* For master's, thesis or alternative, exit project. *Entrance requirements:* For master's, letters of recommendation, GRE or minimum GPA of 3.0. Additional exam requirements/recommendations for international students: Required—TOEFL. *Application deadline:* For fall admission, 7/1 for domestic students; for spring admission, 11/1 for domestic students. Applications are processed on a rolling basis. Application fee: $40 ($60 for international students). Electronic applications accepted. *Expenses:* $276.98 per credit hour in-state; $652.54 per credit hour out-of-state. *Financial support:* Career-related internships or fieldwork available. Support available to part-time students. Financial award application deadline: 3/1; financial award applicants required to submit FAFSA. *Faculty research:* Professional dispositions, early childhood literacy, online learning, program assessments, problem-based learning. *Unit head:* Dr. Marvin Lynn, Dean, 574-520-4339, E-mail: lynnm@iusb.edu. *Application contact:* Yvonne Walker, Student Services Representative, 574-520-4185, E-mail: ydwalker@iusb.edu.
Website: https://www.iusb.edu/education/index.php

Inter American University of Puerto Rico, Barranquitas Campus, Program in Education, Barranquitas, PR 00794. Offers curriculum and teaching (M Ed), including biology education, English as a second language, history education, mathematics education, Spanish; educational leadership and management (MA); elementary education (M Ed); information and library service technology (M Ed); special education (MA). *Accreditation:* TEAC. *Degree requirements:* For master's, comprehensive exam, thesis optional. *Entrance requirements:* For master's, EXADEP, letter of recommendation. Electronic applications accepted.

Inter American University of Puerto Rico, Fajardo Campus, Graduate Programs, Fajardo, PR 00738-7003. Offers computer science (MS); educational management and leadership (MA Ed); elementary education (MA Ed); general business (MBA); management information systems (MBA); marketing (MBA); special education (MA Ed).

Inter American University of Puerto Rico, Metropolitan Campus, Graduate Programs, Program in Special Education, San Juan, PR 00919-1293. Offers MA. *Degree requirements:* For master's, comprehensive exam. *Entrance requirements:* For master's, GRE or EXADEP, interview. Electronic applications accepted.

Inter American University of Puerto Rico, San Germán Campus, Graduate Studies Center, Program in Special Education, San Germán, PR 00683-5008. Offers MA. *Accreditation:* TEAC. *Program availability:* Part-time, evening/weekend. *Degree requirements:* For master's, comprehensive exam. *Entrance requirements:* For master's, GRE General Test or EXADEP, minimum GPA of 3.0.

Iona College, School of Arts and Science, Department of Education, New Rochelle, NY 10801-1890. Offers adolescence education: biology (MS Ed, MST); adolescence education: English (MS Ed); adolescence education: mathematics (MST); adolescence education: social studies (MS Ed, MST); adolescence education: Spanish (MS Ed); adolescence special education 5-12 (MST); childhood and special education (MST); early childhood and childhood (MST); educational leadership (MS Ed). *Accreditation:* NCATE. *Program availability:* Part-time, evening/weekend. *Faculty:* 7 full-time (6 women), 4 part-time/adjunct (2 women). *Students:* 27 full-time (19 women), 27 part-time (18 women); includes 18 minority (4 Black or African American, non-Hispanic/Latino; 1 Asian, non-Hispanic/Latino; 12 Hispanic/Latino; 1 Two or more races, non-Hispanic/Latino). Average age 26. 6 applicants, 67% accepted, 3 enrolled. In 2016, 25 master's awarded. *Degree requirements:* For master's, thesis or alternative. *Entrance requirements:* For master's, minimum GPA of 3.0, NY State teaching certificate and bachelor's degree (for MS Ed). Additional exam requirements/recommendations for international students: Required—TOEFL (minimum score 550 paper-based; 80 iBT), IELTS (minimum score 6.5). *Application deadline:* For fall admission, 8/1 priority date for domestic students, 5/1 priority date for international students; for spring admission, 1/1 priority date for domestic students, 9/1 priority date for international students. Applications are processed on a rolling basis. Application fee: $50. Electronic applications accepted. *Expenses: Tuition:* Full-time $19,692; part-time $1094 per credit. *Required fees:* $245 per term. Tuition and fees vary according to program. *Financial support:* In 2016–17, 3 students received support. Unspecified assistantships available. Support available to part-time students. Financial award application deadline: 4/15; financial award applicants required to submit FAFSA. *Faculty research:* Engaging teacher educators in scientific process, cross-national comparisons of mathematics teaching, questioning strategies in the classroom, research methods, literacy development. *Unit head:* Margaret Smith, PhD, Chair, 914-633-2210, Fax: 914-633-2608, E-mail: msmith@iona.edu. *Application contact:* Richard McMahon, Coordinator, Graduate School of Education, 914-633-2552, E-mail: rmcmahon@iona.edu.
Website: http://www.iona.edu/Academics/School-of-Arts-Science/Departments/Education/Graduate-Programs.aspx

Iowa State University of Science and Technology, Department of Education, Ames, IA 50011. Offers curriculum and instructional technology (M Ed, MS, PhD); elementary education (M Ed, MS); historical, philosophical, and comparative studies in education (M Ed, MS); special education (M Ed, MS, PhD). *Degree requirements:* For master's, thesis or alternative; for doctorate, thesis/dissertation. *Entrance requirements:* For master's and doctorate, GRE General Test. Additional exam requirements/recommendations for international students: Required—TOEFL (minimum score 560 paper-based; 83 iBT), IELTS (minimum score 6.5). *Application deadline:* For fall admission, 1/1 priority date for domestic and international students; for spring admission, 9/1 for domestic and international students. Application fee: $60 ($90 for international students). Electronic applications accepted. *Application contact:* Robyn Goldy, Application Contact, 515-294-1241, Fax: 515-294-4942, E-mail: rgoldy@iastate.edu.
Website: http://www.ci.hs.iastate.edu

Jackson State University, Graduate School, College of Education and Human Development, Department of Special Education, Jackson, MS 39217. Offers special education (MS Ed, Ed S). *Accreditation:* NCATE. *Program availability:* Part-time, evening/weekend, online only, 100% online, blended/hybrid learning. *Faculty:* 4 full-time (3 women), 2 part-time/adjunct (1 woman). *Students:* 3 part-time (all women); includes 2 minority (both Black or African American, non-Hispanic/Latino), 1 international. Average age 47. 130 applicants, 52% accepted, 47 enrolled. In 2016, 2 master's awarded. *Degree requirements:* For master's, comprehensive exam, thesis or alternative. *Entrance requirements:* For master's, GRE General Test. Additional exam requirements/recommendations for international students: Required—TOEFL (minimum score 520 paper-based; 67 iBT). *Application deadline:* For fall admission, 3/1 priority date for domestic students, 3/1 for international students; for spring admission, 10/1 for domestic and international students. Applications are processed on a rolling basis. Application fee: $25. Electronic applications accepted. *Expenses:* Contact institution. *Financial support:* Career-related internships or fieldwork, Federal Work-Study, scholarships/grants, and unspecified assistantships available. Support available to part-time students. Financial award application deadline: 3/1; financial award applicants required to submit FAFSA. *Unit head:* Dr. Gwendolyn Williams, Chair, 601-979-2370, Fax: 601-979-7048, E-mail: gwendolyn.j.williams@jsums.edu. *Application contact:* Dr. Gwendolyn Williams, Chair, 601-979-2370, Fax: 601-979-7048, E-mail: gwendolyn.j.williams@jsums.edu.

Jacksonville State University, College of Graduate Studies and Continuing Education, College of Education and Professional Studies, Program in Special Education, Jacksonville, AL 36265-1602. Offers MS Ed. *Accreditation:* NCATE. *Faculty:* 11 full-time (9 women), 1 (woman) part-time/adjunct. *Students:* 24 full-time (22 women), 22 part-time (19 women); includes 4 minority (all Black or African American, non-Hispanic/Latino). Average age 33. 24 applicants, 63% accepted, 11 enrolled. In 2016, 14 master's awarded. *Degree requirements:* For master's, comprehensive exam, thesis (for some programs). *Entrance requirements:* For master's, GRE General Test or MAT. Additional exam requirements/recommendations for international students: Required—TOEFL (minimum score 500 paper-based; 61 iBT). *Application deadline:* Applications are processed on a rolling basis. Application fee: $35. Electronic applications accepted. *Financial support:* In 2016–17, 5 students received support. Available to part-time students. Application deadline: 4/1; applicants required to submit FAFSA. *Unit head:* Dr. Janet Bavonese, Head, 256-782-8340, E-mail: jbavonese@jsu.edu. *Application contact:* Dr. Jean Pugliese, Associate Dean, 256-782-8278, Fax: 256-782-5321, E-mail: pugliese@jsu.edu.

James Madison University, The Graduate School, College of Education, Program in Special Education, Harrisonburg, VA 22807. Offers adapted curriculum (MAT); autism (M Ed); behavior specialist (M Ed); early childhood special education (MAT); general curriculum K-12 special education (MAT); gifted education (M Ed); inclusive early childhood special education (MAT); instructional specialist (M Ed); K-12 special education (MAT); visual impairments (MAT). *Accreditation:* NCATE. *Program availability:* Part-time. *Students:* 31 full-time (30 women), 7 part-time (3 women); includes 2 minority (1 Hispanic/Latino; 1 Two or more races, non-Hispanic/Latino). Average age 30. In 2016, 67 master's awarded. Application fee: $55. Electronic applications accepted. *Financial support:* In 2016–17, 6 students received support, including 1 fellowship; Federal Work-Study and 6 assistantships (averaging $7911) also available. Financial award application deadline: 3/1; financial award applicants required to submit FAFSA. *Unit head:* Dr. David A. Slykhuis, Interim Department Head, 540-568-4314, E-mail: slykhuda@jmu.edu. *Application contact:* Lynette D. Michael, Director of Graduate Admissions, 540-568-6131 Ext. 6395, Fax: 540-568-7860, E-mail: michaeld@jmu.edu.
Website: http://www.jmu.edu/coe/efex/index.shtml

Johns Hopkins University, School of Education, Certificate Programs in Education, Baltimore, MD 21218. Offers advanced methods for differentiated instruction and inclusive education (Graduate Certificate); applied behavior analysis (Post-Master's Certificate); clinical mental health counseling (Post-Master's Certificate); counseling (Advanced Certificate); data-based decision making and organizational improvement (Graduate Certificate); early intervention/preschool special education specialist (Graduate Certificate); education of students with autism and other pervasive developmental disorders (Graduate Certificate); educational leadership for independent schools (Graduate Certificate); evidence-based teaching in the health professions (Post-Master's Certificate); gifted education (Graduate Certificate); leadership in technology integration (Graduate Certificate); mind, brain and teaching (Graduate Certificate); school administration and supervision (Graduate Certificate); urban education (Graduate Certificate). *Program availability:* Part-time-only, evening/weekend, 100% online, blended/hybrid learning. *Students:* 5 full-time (all women), 194 part-time (164 women); includes 46 minority (29 Black or African American, non-Hispanic/Latino; 2 American Indian or Alaska Native, non-Hispanic/Latino; 3 Asian, non-Hispanic/Latino; 8 Hispanic/Latino; 4 Two or more races, non-Hispanic/Latino), 7 international. Average age 37. 240 applicants, 75% accepted, 143 enrolled. In 2016, 167 Advanced Certificates awarded. *Entrance requirements:* For degree, minimum of bachelor's degree from regionally- or nationally-accredited institution (master's degree for some programs); minimum GPA of 3.0 in all previous programs of study; official transcripts from all post-secondary institutions attended; essay; curriculum vitae/resume; two letters of recommendation; dispositions survey. *Application deadline:* For fall admission, 4/1 priority date for domestic students; for spring admission, 10/1 priority date for domestic students; for summer admission, 2/1 priority date for domestic students. Applications are processed on a rolling basis. Application fee: $80. Electronic applications accepted. *Expenses:* Contact institution. *Financial support:* Application deadline: 4/1; applicants required to submit FAFSA. *Unit head:* Dr. Christopher C. Morphew, Dean. *Application contact:* Elisabeth Woodward, Director of Admissions, 410-516-9796, Fax: 410-516-9817, E-mail: soe.info@jhu.edu.
Website: http://education.jhu.edu

Johns Hopkins University, School of Education, Master's Programs in Education, Baltimore, MD 21218. Offers counseling (MS), including clinical mental health counseling, school counseling; education (MS), including educational studies, gifted education, reading, school administration and supervision, technology for educators; elementary education (MAT); health professions (M Ed); intelligence analysis (MS); organizational leadership (MS); secondary education (MAT), including biology, chemistry, earth/space science, English, physics, social studies; special education (MS), including early childhood special education, general special education studies, mild to moderate disabilities, severe disabilities. *Program availability:* Part-time, evening/weekend, 100% online, blended/hybrid learning. *Students:* 345 full-time (265 women), 1,601 part-time (1,245 women); includes 837 minority (392 Black or African American, non-Hispanic/Latino; 7 American Indian or Alaska Native, non-Hispanic/Latino; 141 Asian, non-Hispanic/Latino; 207 Hispanic/Latino; 7 Native Hawaiian or other Pacific Islander, non-Hispanic/Latino; 83 Two or more races, non-Hispanic/Latino), 55 international. Average age 27. 1,352 applicants, 76% accepted, 819 enrolled. In 2016, 642 master's awarded. *Degree requirements:* For master's, comprehensive exam (for some programs), portfolio, capstone project and/or internship; PRAXIS II (subject area assessments) for initial teacher preparation programs that lead to licensure. *Entrance requirements:* For master's, GRE (for full-time programs only); PRAXIS I/core or state-approved alternative (for initial teacher preparation programs that lead to licensure), minimum of bachelor's degree from regionally- or nationally-accredited institution; minimum GPA of 3.0 in all previous programs of study; official transcripts from all post-secondary institutions attended; essay; curriculum vitae/resume; letters of recommendation (3 for full-time programs, 2 for part-time programs); dispositions survey. Additional exam requirements/recommendations for international students: Required—TOEFL (minimum score 600 paper-based; 100 iBT), IELTS (minimum score 7). *Application deadline:* For fall admission, 4/1 priority date for domestic students, 4/1 for international students; for spring admission, 10/1 priority date for domestic students, 10/1 for international students; for summer admission, 2/1 priority date for domestic students, 2/1 for international students. Applications are processed on a rolling basis. Application fee: $80. Electronic applications accepted. *Expenses:* Contact institution. *Financial support:* Application deadline: 4/1; applicants required to submit FAFSA. *Unit head:* Dr. Christopher C. Morphew, Dean. *Application contact:* Elisabeth Woodward, Director of Admissions, 410-516-9796, Fax: 410-516-9817, E-mail: soe.info@jhu.edu.
Website: http://education.jhu.edu

Johnson & Wales University, Graduate Studies, MAT Program in Teacher Education, Providence, RI 02903-3703. Offers business education and secondary special education (MAT); culinary arts education (MAT); elementary education and elementary special education (MAT); elementary education and elementary/secondary special education (MAT); elementary education and secondary special education (MAT); food service education (MAT). *Program availability:* Part-time, evening/weekend. *Entrance requirements:* For master's, MAT, minimum GPA of 2.75. Additional exam requirements/recommendations for international students: Required—TOEFL (minimum score 550 paper-based) or IELTS (recommended). *Faculty research:* Secondary education, student teaching, educational reform, evaluation procedures.

Johnson State College, Program in Education, Johnson, VT 05656. Offers applied behavior analysis (MA Ed); curriculum and instruction (MA Ed); foundations of education (MA Ed); special education (MA Ed). *Program availability:* Part-time. *Degree requirements:* For master's, thesis or alternative, exit interview. *Entrance requirements:* For master's, interview. Additional exam requirements/recommendations for international students: Required—TOEFL. *Application deadline:* For fall admission, 5/1 for domestic students, 2/1 for international students. Applications are processed on a rolling basis. Electronic applications accepted. *Expenses:* Tuition, state resident: part-time $555 per credit. Tuition, nonresident: part-time $800 per credit. *Financial support:* Scholarships/grants and unspecified assistantships available. Financial award application deadline: 3/1; financial award applicants required to submit FAFSA. *Unit head:* Dr. Kathleen Brinegar, Chair, Department of Education, 802-635-1472, Fax: 802-635-1465, E-mail: kathleen.brinegar@jsc.edu. *Application contact:* Catherine H. Higley, Administrative Assistant, 800-635-2356 Ext. 1244, Fax: 802-635-1248, E-mail: catherine.higley@jsc.edu.
Website: http://www.jsc.edu/academics/education/majors-and-minors/master of arts in education/

Kansas State University, Graduate School, College of Education, Department of Special Education, Counseling and Student Affairs, Manhattan, KS 66506. Offers academic advising (MS, Certificate); counseling and student development (MS), including college student development, school counseling; special education (MS, Ed D); special education, counseling, and student affairs (PhD). *Accreditation:* ACA; NCATE. *Program availability:* Part-time, online learning. *Faculty:* 16 full-time (11 women), 11 part-time/adjunct (5 women). *Students:* 108 full-time (63 women), 252 part-time (193 women); includes 83 minority (33 Black or African American, non-Hispanic/Latino; 4 American Indian or Alaska Native, non-Hispanic/Latino; 7 Asian, non-Hispanic/Latino; 28 Hispanic/Latino; 2 Native Hawaiian or other Pacific Islander, non-Hispanic/Latino; 9 Two or more races, non-Hispanic/Latino), 6 international. Average age 33. 189 applicants, 82% accepted, 96 enrolled. In 2016, 134 master's, 4 doctorates, 70 other advanced degrees awarded. *Degree requirements:* For master's, comprehensive exam; for doctorate, comprehensive exam, thesis/dissertation. *Entrance requirements:* For master's, minimum undergraduate GPA of 3.0; for doctorate, GRE General Test, minimum GPA of 3.0 in last 60 hours. Additional exam requirements/recommendations

for international students: Required—TOEFL. *Application deadline:* For fall admission, 2/1 for domestic students, 1/1 priority date for international students; for spring admission, 8/1 for domestic students, 8/1 priority date for international students; for summer admission, 12/1 priority date for international students. Applications are processed on a rolling basis. Application fee: $50 ($75 for international students). Electronic applications accepted. *Expenses:* Tuition, state resident: full-time $9670. Tuition, nonresident: full-time $21,828. *Required fees:* $862. *Financial support:* In 2016–17, 3 teaching assistantships (averaging $14,727 per year) were awarded; career-related internships or fieldwork, institutionally sponsored loans, and scholarships/grants also available. Financial award application deadline: 3/1; financial award applicants required to submit FAFSA. *Faculty research:* Counseling supervision, academic advising, career development, student development, universal design for learning, autism, learning disabilities. *Total annual research expenditures:* $17,900. *Unit head:* Dr. Kenneth Hughey, Head, 785-532-5541, Fax: 785-532-7304, E-mail: khughey@ksu.edu. *Application contact:* Cassandra Llewelyn, Application Contact, 785-532-5541, Fax: 785-532-7304, E-mail: cjwalker@ksu.edu.
Website: http://www.coe.k-state.edu/departments/secsa/

Kaplan University, Davenport Campus, School of Teacher Education, Davenport, IA 52807. Offers education (M Ed); secondary education (M Ed); teaching and learning (MA); teaching literacy and language: grades 6-12 (MA); teaching literacy and language: grades K-6 (MA); teaching mathematics: grades 6-8 (MA); teaching mathematics: grades 9-12 (MA); teaching mathematics: grades K-5 (MA); teaching science: grades 6-12 (MA); teaching science: grades K-6 (MA); teaching students with special needs (MA); teaching with technology (MA). *Program availability:* Part-time, evening/weekend, online learning. *Entrance requirements:* Additional exam requirements/recommendations for international students: Required—TOEFL (minimum score 550 paper-based; 80 iBT).

Kean University, College of Education, Program in Special Education, Union, NJ 07083. Offers autism and developmental disabilities (MA); learning and behavioral disabilities (MA). *Accreditation:* NCATE. *Program availability:* Part-time. *Faculty:* 12 full-time (11 women). *Students:* 7 full-time (all women), 77 part-time (61 women); includes 23 minority (6 Black or African American, non-Hispanic/Latino; 2 Asian, non-Hispanic/Latino; 14 Hispanic/Latino; 1 Two or more races, non-Hispanic/Latino). Average age 33. 87 applicants, 62% accepted, 52 enrolled. In 2016, 45 master's awarded. *Degree requirements:* For master's, comprehensive exam, thesis, portfolio, two semesters of advanced seminar. *Entrance requirements:* For master's, GRE General Test or MAT, minimum GPA of 3.0, New Jersey Standard Instructional Certificate or Certificate of Eligibility with Advanced Standing, 2 letters of recommendation, transcripts. Additional exam requirements/recommendations for international students: Required—TOEFL (minimum score 550 paper-based; 79 iBT), IELTS (minimum score 6.5). *Application deadline:* For fall admission, 6/1 for domestic and international students; for spring admission, 12/1 for domestic and international students. Applications are processed on a rolling basis. Application fee: $75. Electronic applications accepted. *Expenses:* Tuition, state resident: full-time $13,156; part-time $640 per credit. Tuition, nonresident: full-time $17,831; part-time $785 per credit. *Required fees:* $3316; $151 per credit. Tuition and fees vary according to course level, course load, degree level and program. *Financial support:* Scholarships/grants and unspecified assistantships available. Financial award applicants required to submit FAFSA. *Unit head:* Dr. Beverly Kling, Program Coordinator, 908-737-3845, E-mail: bkling@kean.edu. *Application contact:* Brittany Gerstenhaber, Admissions Counselor, 908-737-7100, E-mail: grad-adm@kean.edu.
Website: http://grad.kean.edu/masters-programs/special-education-autism-and-developmental-disabilities

Keene State College, School of Professional and Graduate Studies, Keene, NH 03435. Offers curriculum and instruction (M Ed); education leadership (PMC); educational leadership (M Ed); safety and occupational health applied science (MS); school counselor (M Ed, PMC); special education (M Ed). *Accreditation:* NCATE. *Program availability:* Part-time, evening/weekend. *Faculty:* 9 full-time (4 women), 8 part-time/adjunct (3 women). *Students:* 24 full-time (17 women), 66 part-time (38 women); includes 3 minority (1 Black or African American, non-Hispanic/Latino; 1 Hispanic/Latino; 1 Two or more races, non-Hispanic/Latino), 1 international. Average age 33. 24 applicants, 100% accepted, 24 enrolled. In 2016, 26 master's, 1 other advanced degree awarded. *Degree requirements:* For master's, thesis (for some programs). *Entrance requirements:* For master's, PRAXIS I, 3 references; official transcripts; minimum GPA of 2.5; interview; essay; teacher/educator certificate; work/internship experience. Additional exam requirements/recommendations for international students: Required—TOEFL (minimum score 550 paper-based; 61 iBT). *Application deadline:* For fall admission, 4/1 for domestic and international students; for spring admission, 11/1 for domestic and international students; for summer admission, 3/1 for domestic and international students. Applications are processed on a rolling basis. Application fee: $50. Electronic applications accepted. *Expenses:* Tuition, state resident: full-time $9180; part-time $510 per credit. Tuition, nonresident: full-time $10,080; part-time $560 per credit. *Required fees:* $1908; $106 per credit. Tuition and fees vary according to course load. *Financial support:* In 2016–17, 27 students received support. Career-related internships or fieldwork, Federal Work-Study, institutionally sponsored loans, scholarships/grants, and unspecified assistantships available. Support available to part-time students. Financial award application deadline: 3/1; financial award applicants required to submit FAFSA. *Unit head:* Dr. Karrie Kalich, Dean of Professional and Graduate Studies, 603-358-2885, E-mail: kkalich@keene.edu. *Application contact:* Peter Tandy, Assistant Director for Graduate Studies, 603-358-2332, E-mail: kscgraduatestudies@keene.edu.
Website: http://www.keene.edu/academics/graduate/

Kennesaw State University, Leland and Clarice C. Bagwell College of Education, Program in Graduate Education, Kennesaw, GA 30144. Offers educational leadership (M Ed); educational leadership technology (M Ed); elementary and early childhood education (M Ed); instructional technology (M Ed); middle grades education (M Ed); reading (M Ed); secondary education (M Ed); special education (M Ed); teaching English to speakers of other languages (M Ed). *Accreditation:* NCATE. *Program availability:* Part-time. *Degree requirements:* For master's, thesis or alternative. *Entrance requirements:* For master's, GRE General Test, T-4 state certification, minimum GPA of 2.75. Additional exam requirements/recommendations for international students: Required—TOEFL (minimum score 550 paper-based; 80 iBT), IELTS (minimum score 6.5). Electronic applications accepted.

Kennesaw State University, Leland and Clarice C. Bagwell College of Education, Program in Teaching, Kennesaw, GA 30144. Offers art education (MAT); biology (MAT); chemistry (MAT); foreign language education (Chinese and Spanish) (MAT); physics (MAT); secondary English (MAT); secondary mathematics (MAT); special education (MAT); teaching English to speakers of other languages (MAT). *Program availability:* Part-time, evening/weekend. *Entrance requirements:* For master's, GRE, GACE I (state certificate exam), minimum GPA of 2.75, 2 recommendations, resume. Additional exam requirements/recommendations for international students: Required—TOEFL (minimum score 550 paper-based; 80 iBT), IELTS (minimum score 6.5). Electronic applications accepted.

Kent State University, College of Education, Health and Human Services, School of Lifespan Development and Educational Sciences, Program in Special Education, Kent, OH 44242-0001. Offers deaf education (M Ed); early childhood education (M Ed); educational interpreter K-12 (M Ed); general special education (M Ed); mild/moderate intervention (M Ed); special education (PhD, Ed S); transition to work (M Ed). *Accreditation:* NCATE. *Degree requirements:* For doctorate, comprehensive exam, thesis/dissertation. *Entrance requirements:* For master's, minimum undergraduate GPA of 2.75, moral character form, 2 letters of reference, goals statement; for doctorate and Ed S, GRE General Test, goals statement, 2 letters of reference, interview, resume. Additional exam requirements/recommendations for international students: Required—TOEFL (minimum score 550 paper-based; 80 iBT). Electronic applications accepted. *Expenses:* Tuition, state resident: full-time $10,864; part-time $495 per credit hour. Tuition, nonresident: full-time $18,380; part-time $837 per credit hour. *Faculty research:* Social/emotional needs of gifted, inclusion transition services, early intervention/ecobehavioral assessments, applied behavioral analysis.

Kentucky State University, College of Professional Studies, Frankfort, KY 40601. Offers nursing (DNP); public administration (MPA), including human resource management; special education (MA). *Program availability:* Part-time, evening/weekend, 100% online, blended/hybrid learning. *Faculty:* 6 full-time (3 women), 7 part-time/adjunct (6 women). *Students:* 32 full-time (22 women), 37 part-time (30 women); includes 48 minority (47 Black or African American, non-Hispanic/Latino; 1 Asian, non-Hispanic/Latino). Average age 34. 42 applicants, 79% accepted, 24 enrolled. In 2016, 19 master's awarded. *Degree requirements:* For master's, comprehensive exam, thesis optional; for doctorate, comprehensive exam, thesis/dissertation optional, 180 clinical hours. *Entrance requirements:* For master's, GMAT, GRE, transcript, essay, letters of recommendation; for doctorate, RN license; resume; graduate research and statistics courses (strongly recommended). Additional exam requirements/recommendations for international students: Required—TOEFL (minimum score 525 paper-based). *Application deadline:* For fall admission, 7/1 for domestic students, 4/1 for international students; for spring admission, 11/15 for domestic students, 8/15 for international students; for summer admission, 5/1 for domestic students, 2/1 for international students. Applications are processed on a rolling basis. Application fee: $30 ($100 for international students). Electronic applications accepted. *Expenses:* Tuition, state resident: full-time $7524; part-time $418 per credit hour. Tuition, nonresident: full-time $11,322; part-time $629 per credit hour. Tuition and fees vary according to course load. *Financial support:* In 2016–17, 57 students received support, including 3 research assistantships (averaging $10,083 per year); scholarships/grants, tuition waivers (partial), and unspecified assistantships also available. Financial award application deadline: 4/15; financial award applicants required to submit FAFSA. *Faculty research:* Risk assessment and failure modeling for the public sector implication of property rights on economic development, the social stability of communities, civil peace of nations. *Total annual research expenditures:* $129,604. *Unit head:* Dr. Candice L. Jackson, Vice President of Academic Affairs, 502-597-6442, E-mail: candice.jackson@kysu.edu. *Application contact:* Dr. James Obielodan, Director of Graduate Studies, 502-597-4723, E-mail: james.obielodan@kysu.edu.
Website: http://kysu.edu/academics/college-of-professional-studies/

Lamar University, College of Graduate Studies, College of Education and Human Development, Department of Counseling and Special Populations, Beaumont, TX 77710. Offers clinical mental health counseling (M Ed); school counseling (M Ed); special education (M Ed), including special education. *Accreditation:* ACA. *Faculty:* 6 full-time (3 women), 29 part-time/adjunct (11 women). *Students:* 16 full-time (9 women), 1,586 part-time (1,424 women); includes 758 minority (373 Black or African American, non-Hispanic/Latino; 6 American Indian or Alaska Native, non-Hispanic/Latino; 20 Asian, non-Hispanic/Latino; 337 Hispanic/Latino; 2 Native Hawaiian or other Pacific Islander, non-Hispanic/Latino; 20 Two or more races, non-Hispanic/Latino), 5 international. Average age 37. 840 applicants, 96% accepted, 393 enrolled. In 2016, 703 master's awarded. *Entrance requirements:* Additional exam requirements/recommendations for international students: Required—TOEFL (minimum score 550 paper-based; 79 iBT), IELTS (minimum score 6.5). *Application deadline:* For fall admission, 8/10 for domestic students, 7/1 for international students; for spring admission, 1/5 for domestic students, 12/1 for international students. Applications are processed on a rolling basis. Application fee: $25 ($50 for international students). Electronic applications accepted. *Expenses:* $8,134 in-state full-time, $5,574 in-state part-time; $15,604 out-of-state full-time, $10,554 out-of-state part-time per year. *Financial support:* Applicants required to submit FAFSA. *Unit head:* Dr. Rebecca Weinbaum, Interim Chair, 409-880-8978, Fax: 409-880-2263. *Application contact:* Deidre Mayer, Interim Director, Admissions and Academic Services, 409-880-8888, Fax: 409-880-7419, E-mail: gradmissions@lamar.edu.
Website: http://education.lamar.edu/counseling-and-special-populations

Lamar University, College of Graduate Studies, College of Fine Arts and Communication, Department of Deaf Studies and Deaf Education, Beaumont, TX 77710. Offers MS, Ed D. *Accreditation:* ASHA. *Program availability:* Part-time, evening/weekend. *Faculty:* 3 full-time (all women), 2 part-time/adjunct (1 woman). *Students:* 15 full-time (9 women), 16 part-time (10 women); includes 6 minority (3 Black or African American, non-Hispanic/Latino; 1 Hispanic/Latino; 2 Two or more races, non-Hispanic/Latino), 8 international. Average age 40. 13 applicants, 92% accepted, 9 enrolled. In 2016, 4 master's awarded. *Degree requirements:* For master's, thesis optional; for doctorate, thesis/dissertation. *Entrance requirements:* For master's, GRE General Test, performance IQ score of 115 (for deaf students), minimum GPA of 2.5; for doctorate, GRE General Test, performance IQ score of 115 (for deaf students). Additional exam requirements/recommendations for international students: Required—TOEFL (minimum score 550 paper-based; 79 iBT), IELTS (minimum score 6.5). *Application deadline:* For fall admission, 8/10 for domestic students, 7/1 for international students; for spring admission, 1/5 for domestic students, 12/1 for international students. Applications are processed on a rolling basis. Application fee: $25 ($50 for international students). Electronic applications accepted. *Expenses:* $8,134 in-state full-time, $5,574 in-state part-time; $15,604 out-of-state full-time, $10,554 out-of-state part-time per year. *Financial support:* Fellowships and research assistantships available. Financial award application deadline: 4/1; financial award applicants required to submit FAFSA. *Faculty research:* Multicultural and deaf teacher training, central auditory processing, voice sign language. *Unit head:* Dr. Diane Clark, Chair, 409-880-8170, Fax: 409-880-2265. *Application contact:* Deidre Mayer, Interim Director, Admissions and Academic Services, 409-880-8888, Fax: 409-880-7419, E-mail: gradmissions@lamar.edu.
Website: http://fineartscomm.lamar.edu/deaf-studies-deaf-education

Lancaster Bible College, Graduate School, Lancaster, PA 17601-5036. Offers adult ministries (MA); Bible (MA); children and family ministry (MA); church planting (MA); consulting resource teacher (M Ed); elementary school counseling (M Ed); leadership (PhD); leadership studies (MA); marriage and family counseling (MA); mental health counseling (MA); pastoral studies (MA); secondary school counseling (M Ed); sports ministry (MA); student ministry (MA); town and country ministry (MA). *Program availability:* Part-time, evening/weekend. *Degree requirements:* For master's, comprehensive exam (for some programs), thesis (for some programs). *Entrance requirements:* For master's, bachelor's degree with a minimum of 30 credits of course work in Bible, minimum undergraduate GPA of 3.0, interview. Additional exam requirements/recommendations for international students: Required—TOEFL.

La Salle University, School of Arts and Sciences, Program in Education, Philadelphia, PA 19141-1199. Offers autism spectrum disorders (MA, Certificate); bilingual/bicultural studies (MA); classroom management (MA); dual early childhood and special education (MA); dual middle-level science and math and special education (MA); education (MA); English (MA); English as a second language (Certificate); history (MA); instructional coach (Certificate); instructional leadership (MA); reading specialist (MA, Certificate); secondary education (MA); special education (MA, Certificate). *Program availability:* Part-time, evening/weekend. *Faculty:* 5 full-time (4 women), 12 part-time/adjunct (8 women). *Students:* 10 full-time (all women), 98 part-time (74 women); includes 28 minority (13 Black or African American, non-Hispanic/Latino; 1 American Indian or Alaska Native, non-Hispanic/Latino; 1 Asian, non-Hispanic/Latino; 10 Hispanic/Latino; 3 Two or more races, non-Hispanic/Latino). Average age 34. 128 applicants, 84% accepted, 69 enrolled. In 2016, 53 master's awarded. *Degree requirements:* For master's, comprehensive exam. *Entrance requirements:* For master's, MAT or GRE, 2 letters of recommendation; for Certificate, GMAT or GRE, 2 letters of recommendation. Additional exam requirements/recommendations for international students: Required—TOEFL. *Application deadline:* For fall admission, 8/15 priority date for domestic students, 7/15 for international students; for spring admission, 12/15 priority date for domestic students, 11/15 for international students; for summer admission, 4/15 priority date for domestic students, 3/15 for international students. Applications are processed on a rolling basis. Application fee: $35. Electronic applications accepted. Application fee is waived when completed online. *Expenses:* Contact institution. *Financial support:* In 2016–17, 27 students received support. Scholarships/grants available. Support available to part-time students. Financial award application deadline: 8/31; financial award applicants required to submit FAFSA. *Unit head:* Dr. Greer Richardson, Director, 215-951-1806, Fax: 215-951-1843, E-mail: graded@lasalle.edu. *Application contact:* Elizabeth Heenan, Director, Graduate and Adult Enrollment, 215-951-1100, Fax: 215-951-1462, E-mail: heenan@lasalle.edu.
Website: http://www.lasalle.edu/grad-education-programs/

Lasell College, Graduate and Professional Studies in Education, Newton, MA 02466. Offers elementary education (M Ed); special education (M Ed), including moderate disabilities. *Program availability:* Part-time-only, evening/weekend, blended/hybrid learning. *Faculty:* 3 full-time (all women), 6 part-time/adjunct (5 women). *Students:* 4 full-time (3 women), 45 part-time (40 women); includes 2 minority (1 Hispanic/Latino; 1 Two or more races, non-Hispanic/Latino). Average age 28. 31 applicants, 58% accepted, 9 enrolled. In 2016, 12 master's awarded. *Degree requirements:* For master's, minimum GPA of 3.0; practicum. *Entrance requirements:* For master's, Massachusetts Tests for Educator Licensure (MTEL) Curriculum and Literacy foundations of reading and writing subtest, one-page personal statement, 2 letters of recommendation, resume, bachelor's degree transcript. Additional exam requirements/recommendations for international students: Required—TOEFL (minimum score 550 paper-based, 79 iBT) or IELTS (minimum score 6). *Application deadline:* For fall admission, 8/31 priority date for domestic students, 6/30 priority date for international students; for spring admission, 12/31 priority date for domestic students, 10/31 priority date for international students. Applications are processed on a rolling basis. Electronic applications accepted. *Expenses:* $600 per credit. *Financial support:* In 2016–17, 13 students received support. Federal Work-Study, scholarships/grants, and tuition discounts available. Support available to part-time students. Financial award application deadline: 8/31; financial award applicants required to submit FAFSA. *Faculty research:* Inclusion, English language learners, literacy, and urban education; teacher inquiry; universal design for learning, deaf-blindness, and visual impairments; social and emotional learning; educational law, applied behavior analysis, and classroom management. *Unit head:* Dr. Joan Dolamore, Dean of Graduate and Professional Studies, 617-243-2485, Fax: 617-243-2450, E-mail: gradinfo@lasell.edu. *Application contact:* Adrienne Franciosi, Director of Graduate Enrollment, 617-243-2214, Fax: 617-243-2450, E-mail: gradinfo@lasell.edu.
Website: http://www.lasell.edu/academics/graduate-and-professional-studies/programs-of-study/master-of-education.html

Lee University, Program in Education, Cleveland, TN 37320-3450. Offers art (MAT); curriculum and instruction (M Ed, Ed S); early childhood (MAT); educational leadership (M Ed, Ed S); elementary education (MAT); English and math (MAT); English and science (MAT); English and social studies (MAT); higher education administration (MS); history (MAT); history and economics (MAT); math and science (MAT); math and social studies (MAT); middle grades (MAT); science and social studies (MASW); secondary education (MAT); Spanish (MAT); special education (M Ed, MAT); TESOL (MAT). *Accreditation:* NCATE. *Program availability:* Part-time. *Faculty:* 13 full-time (6 women), 9 part-time/adjunct (4 women). *Students:* 35 full-time (27 women), 50 part-time (32 women); includes 12 minority (5 Black or African American, non-Hispanic/Latino; 5 Hispanic/Latino; 2 Two or more races, non-Hispanic/Latino), 4 international. Average age 30. 43 applicants, 79% accepted, 28 enrolled. In 2016, 42 master's, 6 other advanced degrees awarded. *Degree requirements:* For master's, variable foreign language requirement, thesis optional, internship. *Entrance requirements:* For master's, MAT or GRE General Test, minimum undergraduate GPA of 2.75, 3 letters of recommendation, interview, writing sample, official transcripts, background check; for Ed S, minimum undergraduate and master's GPA of 2.75, official transcripts for undergraduate and master's degrees. Additional exam requirements/recommendations for international students: Required—TOEFL (minimum score 61 iBT). *Application deadline:* For fall admission, 6/1 priority date for domestic and international students; for spring admission, 11/1 priority date for domestic and international students; for summer admission, 4/1 priority date for domestic and international students. Applications are processed on a rolling basis. Application fee: $25. Electronic applications accepted. *Expenses: Tuition:* Full-time $11,367; part-time $632 per credit hour. *Required fees:* $35 per term. One-time fee: $25. Tuition and fees vary according to program. *Financial support:* In 2016–17, 42 students received support. Career-related internships or fieldwork, Federal Work-Study, institutionally sponsored loans, scholarships/grants, and unspecified assistantships available. Financial award application deadline: 3/1; financial award applicants required to submit FAFSA. *Unit head:* Dr. William Kamm, Director, 423-614-8544, E-mail: wkamm@leeuniversity.edu. *Application contact:* Crystal Keeter, Graduate Education Secretary, 423-614-8544, E-mail: ckeeter@leeuniversity.edu.
Website: http://www.leeuniversity.edu/academics/graduate/education

Lehigh University, College of Education, Program in Special Education, Bethlehem, PA 18015. Offers M Ed, PhD. *Program availability:* Part-time. *Faculty:* 4 full-time (all women), 5 part-time/adjunct (all women). *Students:* 10 full-time (all women), 44 part-time (36 women); includes 4 minority (1 Black or African American, non-Hispanic/Latino; 1 Asian, non-Hispanic/Latino; 1 Hispanic/Latino; 1 Two or more races, non-Hispanic/Latino), 2 international. Average age 30. 40 applicants, 63% accepted, 12 enrolled. In 2016, 16 master's, 1 doctorate awarded. *Degree requirements:* For doctorate, comprehensive exam, thesis/dissertation. *Entrance requirements:* For master's, minimum GPA of 3.0, 2 academic letters of recommendation, essay, transcripts; for doctorate, GRE General Test, minimum GPA of 3.0, 2 academic letters of recommendation, essay, transcripts. Additional exam requirements/recommendations for international students: Required—TOEFL (minimum score 600 paper-based; 93 iBT). *Application deadline:* For fall admission, 1/15 for domestic and international students. Applications are processed on a rolling basis. Application fee: $65. Electronic applications accepted. *Expenses:* $565 per credit. *Financial support:* In 2016–17, 2 research assistantships (averaging $4,200 per year) were awarded; fellowships and unspecified assistantships also available. Financial award application deadline: 1/31. *Faculty research:* Special education, autism spectrum disorder, emotional and behavioral disorders, positive behavior support, early childhood special education. *Unit head:* Dr. Linda Bambara, Director, 610-758-3271, Fax: 610-758-6223, E-mail: lmb1@lehigh.edu. *Application contact:* Donna Toothman, Coordinator, 610-758-3230, Fax: 610-758-3243, E-mail: djt2@lehigh.edu.
Website: http://ed.lehigh.edu/academics/degrees

Lehman College of the City University of New York, School of Education, Department of Specialized Services in Education, Bronx, NY 10468-1589. Offers guidance and counseling (MS Ed); reading teacher (MS Ed); teachers of special education (MS Ed), including bilingual special education, early special education, emotional handicaps, learning disabilities, mental retardation. *Program availability:* Part-time, evening/weekend. *Faculty research:* Battered women, whole language classrooms, parent education, mainstreaming.

Lehman College of the City University of New York, School of Education, Department of Specialized Services in Education, Teachers of Special Education Program, Option in Bilingual Special Education, Bronx, NY 10468-1589. Offers MS Ed. *Accreditation:* NCATE. *Entrance requirements:* For master's, minimum GPA of 3.0.

Lehman College of the City University of New York, School of Education, Department of Specialized Services in Education, Teachers of Special Education Program, Option in Early Special Education, Bronx, NY 10468-1589. Offers MS Ed. *Accreditation:* NCATE. *Entrance requirements:* For master's, minimum GPA of 3.0.

Lehman College of the City University of New York, School of Education, Department of Specialized Services in Education, Teachers of Special Education Program, Option in Emotional Handicaps, Bronx, NY 10468-1589. Offers MS Ed. *Accreditation:* NCATE. *Program availability:* Part-time, evening/weekend. *Entrance requirements:* For master's, minimum GPA of 2.7. *Faculty research:* Behavioral disorders, self-evaluation, applied behavior analysis.

Lehman College of the City University of New York, School of Education, Department of Specialized Services in Education, Teachers of Special Education Program, Option in Learning Disabilities, Bronx, NY 10468-1589. Offers MS Ed. *Accreditation:* NCATE. *Program availability:* Part-time, evening/weekend. *Entrance requirements:* For master's, interview, minimum GPA of 2.7. *Faculty research:* Emergent literacy, language-based classrooms, primary and secondary social contexts of language and literacy, innovative in-service education models, adult literacy.

Lehman College of the City University of New York, School of Education, Department of Specialized Services in Education, Teachers of Special Education Program, Option in Mental Retardation, Bronx, NY 10468-1589. Offers MS Ed. *Accreditation:* NCATE. *Program availability:* Part-time, evening/weekend. *Entrance requirements:* For master's, minimum GPA of 2.7. *Faculty research:* Conductive education, homeless infants and their families, infant stimulation, hospitalizing infants with AIDS, legislation PL99-457.

Le Moyne College, Department of Education, Syracuse, NY 13214. Offers adolescent education (MS Ed, MST); adolescent education/special education (MS Ed, MST); adolescent English (MST), including grades 7-12; adolescent English/special education (MST), including grades 7-12; adolescent foreign language (MST), including grades 7-12; adolescent history (MST), including grades 7-12; childhood education (MS Ed); childhood education/special education (MS Ed); elementary education (MS Ed); general education (MS Ed); inclusive childhood education (MST); literacy education (MS Ed), including birth to grade 6, grades 5-12; school building leader (MS Ed); school building leadership (CAS); school district business leader (MS Ed, CAS); school district leader (MS Ed); school district leadership (CAS); secondary education (MS Ed); special education (MS Ed); teaching English to speakers of other languages (MS Ed); urban studies (MS Ed). *Accreditation:* TEAC. *Program availability:* Part-time, evening/weekend. *Faculty:* 8 full-time (5 women), 20 part-time/adjunct (12 women). *Students:* 66 full-time (40 women), 155 part-time (117 women); includes 13 minority (4 Black or African American, non-Hispanic/Latino; 2 American Indian or Alaska Native, non-Hispanic/Latino; 2 Asian, non-Hispanic/Latino; 5 Hispanic/Latino), 3 international. Average age 30. 74 applicants, 99% accepted, 66 enrolled. In 2016, 81 master's, 53 CASs awarded. *Degree requirements:* For master's, thesis. *Entrance requirements:* For master's, bachelor's degree with minimum undergraduate GPA of 3.0, 2 letters of recommendation, transcripts. Additional exam requirements/recommendations for international students: Required—TOEFL (minimum score 550 paper-based; 79 iBT); Recommended—IELTS (minimum score 6.5). *Application deadline:* For fall admission, 4/1 priority date for domestic and international students; for spring admission, 10/1 priority date for domestic and international students; for summer admission, 3/1 priority date for domestic and international students. Applications are processed on a rolling basis. Application fee: $50. Electronic applications accepted. *Expenses:* $700 per credit hour. *Financial support:* In 2016–17, 21 students received support. Career-related internships or fieldwork, scholarships/grants, and health care benefits available. Support available to part-time students. Financial award applicants required to submit FAFSA. *Faculty research:* Minority teachers, special education, multiculturalism, literacy, technology, media literacy learning, autism, school district organization, service-learning, higher level problem solving, teacher leadership. *Unit head:* Dr. Stephen C. Fleury, Chair, Department of Education, 315-445-4376, Fax: 315-445-4744, E-mail: fleurysc@lemoyne.edu. *Application contact:* Kristen P. Richards, Senior Director of Enrollment Management, 315-445-5444, Fax: 315-445-6092, E-mail: trapaskp@lemoyne.edu.
Website: http://www.lemoyne.edu/education

Lesley University, Graduate School of Education, Cambridge, MA 02138-2790. Offers arts, community, and education (M Ed); autism studies (Certificate); curriculum and instruction (M Ed, CAGS); early childhood education (M Ed); ecological teaching and learning (MS); educational studies (PhD), including adult learning, educational leadership, individually designed; elementary education (M Ed); emergent technologies for educators (Certificate); ESLArts: language learning through the arts (M Ed); high school education (M Ed); individually designed (M Ed); integrated teaching through the arts (M Ed); literacy for K-8 classroom teachers (M Ed); mathematics education (M Ed); middle school education (M Ed); moderate disabilities (M Ed); online learning (Certificate); reading (CAGS); science in education (M Ed); severe disabilities (M Ed); special needs (CAGS); specialist teacher of reading (M Ed); teacher of visual art (M Ed); technology in education (M Ed, CAGS). *Accreditation:* TEAC. *Program availability:* Part-time, evening/weekend, online learning. *Degree requirements:* For master's, practicum; for doctorate, thesis/dissertation. *Entrance requirements:* For master's, Massachusetts Tests for Educator Licensure (MTEL), transcripts, statement of purpose, recommendations; interview (for special education); for doctorate, GRE General Test, transcripts, statement of purpose, recommendations, interview, master's degree, resume; for other advanced degree, interview, master's degree. Additional exam requirements/recommendations for international students: Required—TOEFL (minimum score 550 paper-based; 80 iBT). Electronic applications accepted. *Faculty research:* Assessment in literacy, mathematics and science; autism spectrum disorders; instructional technology and online learning; multicultural education and English language learners.

Lewis & Clark College, Graduate School of Education and Counseling, Department of Teacher Education, Program in Special Education, Portland, OR 97219-7899. Offers M Ed. *Accreditation:* NCATE. *Program availability:* Part-time, evening/weekend. *Entrance requirements:* For master's, minimum GPA of 2.75. Additional exam requirements/recommendations for international students: Required—TOEFL (minimum score 575 paper-based). *Application deadline:* Applications are processed on a rolling basis. Application fee: $50. Electronic applications accepted. *Financial support:* Career-related internships or fieldwork, Federal Work-Study, institutionally sponsored loans, scholarships/grants, health care benefits, and tuition waivers (partial) available. Support available to part-time students. Financial award application deadline: 3/1; financial award applicants required to submit FAFSA. *Unit head:* Kimberly Campbell, Director, 503-768-6128, E-mail: kimberly@lclark.edu. *Application contact:* Becky Haas, Director of Admissions, 503-768-6200, Fax: 503-768-6205, E-mail: gseadmit@lclark.edu.
Website: http://graduate.lclark.edu/departments/teacher_education/current_teachers/masters_special_education/

Lewis University, College of Education, Program in Special Education, Romeoville, IL 60446. Offers MA. *Students:* 25 part-time (17 women); includes 1 minority (Black or African American, non-Hispanic/Latino), 1 international. Average age 30. *Degree requirements:* For master's, departmental qualifying exam. *Entrance requirements:* For master's, writing exam, minimum GPA of 2.75, 2 letters of recommendation, interview. Additional exam requirements/recommendations for international students: Required—TOEFL (minimum score 550 paper-based; 80 iBT). *Application deadline:* For fall admission, 5/1 priority date for international students; for spring admission, 11/15 priority date for international students. Applications are processed on a rolling basis. Application fee: $40. Electronic applications accepted. *Expenses: Tuition:* Full-time $13,860; part-time $770 per credit hour. *Required fees:* $75 per semester. Tuition and fees vary according to degree level and program. *Financial support:* Federal Work-Study, scholarships/grants, and unspecified assistantships available. Financial award application deadline: 5/1; financial award applicants required to submit FAFSA. *Unit head:* Dr. Christy Roberts, Director, 815-838-0500 Ext. 5317, E-mail: robertch@lewisu.edu. *Application contact:* Linda Campbell, Graduate Admission Counselor, 815-838-5704, E-mail: campbeli@lewisu.edu.

Lincoln University, Graduate Programs, Philadelphia, PA 19104. Offers counseling (MSC); early childhood education (M Ed), including PreK-4; early childhood education and special education (M Ed); educational leadership (M Ed), including principal certification; finance (MSB); human resources management (MSB); human services (MAHS). *Program availability:* Part-time, evening/weekend. *Faculty:* 11 full-time (5 women), 45 part-time/adjunct (24 women). *Students:* 191 full-time (131 women), 77 part-time (60 women); includes 245 minority (236 Black or African American, non-Hispanic/Latino; 1 American Indian or Alaska Native, non-Hispanic/Latino; 7 Hispanic/Latino; 1 Two or more races, non-Hispanic/Latino), 4 international. Average age 34. 221 applicants, 58% accepted, 55 enrolled. In 2016, 97 master's awarded. *Degree requirements:* For master's, thesis or alternative. *Entrance requirements:* For master's, official academic transcript from accredited institution presenting conferred bachelor's degree. *Application deadline:* For fall admission, 6/1 priority date for domestic and international students. Applications are processed on a rolling basis. Application fee: $50. Electronic applications accepted. *Expenses:* Tuition, state resident: full-time $12,264; part-time $511 per credit hour. Tuition, nonresident: full-time $21,264; part-time $886 per credit hour. *Required fees:* $1344; $56 per credit hour. Tuition and fees vary according to course load. *Financial support:* In 2016–17, 9 students received support. Scholarships/grants available. Financial award application deadline: 8/1; financial award applicants required to submit FAFSA. *Unit head:* Dr. Patricia Joseph, Dean, College of Professional, Graduate and Extended Studies, 484-365-7659, E-mail: joseph@lincoln.edu. *Application contact:* Jernice Lea, Director of Graduate Admissions, 215-590-8231, Fax: 215-387-3859, E-mail: jlea@lincoln.edu.
Website: http://www.lincoln.edu/academics/graduate-programs

Lipscomb University, College of Education, Nashville, TN 37204-3951. Offers applied behavior analysis (MS, Certificate); educational leadership (M Ed, Ed S); English language learning (M Ed, Ed S); instructional coaching (M Ed, Certificate, Ed S); instructional practice (M Ed); learning organizations and strategic change (Ed D); literacy coaching (Certificate); reading specialty (M Ed, Ed S); special education (M Ed); teaching, learning, and leading (M Ed); technology integration (M Ed, Ed S); technology integration specialist (Certificate). *Accreditation:* NCATE. *Program availability:* Part-time, evening/weekend, 100% online. *Faculty:* 21 full-time (15 women), 38 part-time/adjunct (26 women). *Students:* 111 full-time (80 women), 345 part-time (292 women); includes 104 minority (70 Black or African American, non-Hispanic/Latino; 1 American Indian or Alaska Native, non-Hispanic/Latino; 3 Asian, non-Hispanic/Latino; 20 Hispanic/Latino; 10 Two or more races, non-Hispanic/Latino), 1 international. Average age 33. In 2016, 201 master's, 36 doctorates, 86 other advanced degrees awarded. *Degree requirements:* For master's, comprehensive exam, portfolio, research project and presentation; for doctorate, practical capstone project in experiential setting. *Entrance requirements:* For master's, MAT (minimum score 31) or GRE General Test (minimum score 294), 2 reference letters, goals statement, writing sample, interview; for doctorate, MAT or GRE General Test, 3 reference letters, artifact of demonstrated academic excellence, written personal statements, interview. Additional exam requirements/recommendations for international students: Required—TOEFL (minimum score 570 paper-based; 80 iBT). *Application deadline:* For fall admission, 8/29 priority date for domestic students; for spring admission, 1/15 priority date for domestic students. Applications are processed on a rolling basis. Application fee: $50 ($75 for international students). Electronic applications accepted. *Expenses:* $934 per hour; $570 per hour (Teach for America). *Financial support:* Scholarships/grants, unspecified assistantships, and partnerships with local school districts available. Financial award applicants required to submit FAFSA. *Faculty research:* Facilitative learning styles, leadership, student assessment, interactive multimedia inclusion, learning organizations and strategic change. *Unit head:* Dr. Deborah Boyd, Director of Graduate Studies, 615-966-6263, E-mail: deborah.boyd@lipscomb.edu. *Application contact:* Amanda Logsdon, Director of Enrollment and Outreach, 615-966-7199, E-mail: amanda.logsdon@lipscomb.edu.
Website: http://www.lipscomb.edu/education/graduate-programs

London Metropolitan University, Graduate Programs, London, United Kingdom. Offers applied psychology (M Sc); architecture (MA); biomedical science (M Sc); blood science (M Sc); cancer pharmacology (M Sc); computer networking and cyber security (M Sc); computing and information systems (M Sc); conference interpreting (MA); counter-terrorism studies (M Sc); creative, digital and professional writing (MA); crime, violence and prevention (M Sc); criminology (M Sc); curating contemporary art (MA); data analytics (M Sc); digital media (MA); early childhood studies (MA); education (MA, Ed D); financial services law, regulation and compliance (LL M); food science (M Sc); forensic psychology (M Sc); health and social care management and policy (M Sc); human nutrition (M Sc); human resource management (MA); human rights and international conflict (MA); information technology (M Sc); intelligence and security studies (M Sc); international oil, gas and energy law (LL M); international relations (MA); interpreting (MA); learning and teaching in higher education (MA); legal practice (LL M); media and entertainment law (LL M); organizational and consumer psychology (M Sc); psychological therapy (M Sc); psychology of mental health (M Sc); public health (M Sc); public policy and management (MPA); security studies (M Sc); social work (M Sc); spatial planning and urban design (MA); sports therapy (M Sc); supporting older children and young people with dyslexia (MA); teaching languages (MA), including Arabic, English; translation (MA); woman and child abuse (MA).

Long Island University–Brentwood Campus, Graduate Programs, Brentwood, NY 11717. Offers childhood education (grades 1-6) (MS), including grades 1-6; childhood education/literacy (grades 1-6) (MS); childhood education/special education (grades 1-6) (MS); clinical mental health counseling (MS, Advanced Certificate); early childhood education (B-2) (MS); literacy (B-6) (MS Ed); school counselor (MS); special education (grades 1-6) (MS Ed); students with disabilities generalist (grades 7-12) (Advanced Certificate). *Program availability:* Part-time. *Faculty:* 54 part-time/adjunct (30 women). *Students:* 98 full-time (80 women), 57 part-time (47 women); includes 28 minority (7 Black or African American, non-Hispanic/Latino; 1 Asian, non-Hispanic/Latino; 20 Hispanic/Latino). 85 applicants, 89% accepted, 43 enrolled. In 2016, 99 master's, 11 other advanced degrees awarded. *Degree requirements:* For master's, comprehensive exam (for some programs), thesis optional. *Entrance requirements:* For master's and Advanced Certificate, GRE. Additional exam requirements/recommendations for international students: Required—TOEFL or IELTS. *Application deadline:* Applications are processed on a rolling basis. Application fee: $50. Electronic applications accepted. Application fee is waived when completed online. *Expenses: Tuition:* Full-time $28,272; part-time $1178 per credit. *Required fees:* $451 per term. *Financial support:* Scholarships/grants and unspecified assistantships available. Support available to part-time students. Financial award applicants required to submit FAFSA. *Unit head:* Donna Di Donato, Dean and Chief Operating Officer, 631-287-8010, Fax: 631-287-8575, E-mail: donna.didonato@liu.edu. *Application contact:* Scott Aug, Associate Director of Enrollment Management, 631-287-8500, Fax: 631-287-8575, E-mail: scott.aug@liu.edu.
Website: http://liu.edu/brentwood

Long Island University–Hudson, Graduate School, Purchase, NY 10577. Offers autism (Advanced Certificate); childhood education (MS Ed); early childhood education (MS Ed); educational leadership (MS Ed); finance (MBA); health administration (MPA); healthcare sector management (MBA); literacy (MS Ed); management (MBA); marriage and family therapy (MS); mental health counseling (MS), including credentialed alcoholism and substance abuse counselor; middle childhood and adolescence education (MS Ed); pharmaceutics (MS), including cosmetic science, industrial pharmacy; public administration (MPA); school counseling (MS Ed, Advanced Certificate); school psychology (MS Ed); special education (MS Ed); TESOL (all grades) (Advanced Certificate); TESOL and bilingual education (MS Ed); the business of pharmaceutics and biotechnology (MBA). *Program availability:* Part-time, evening/weekend, online learning. *Faculty:* 7 full-time (5 women), 42 part-time/adjunct (25 women). *Students:* 55 full-time (41 women), 158 part-time (123 women); includes 40 minority (8 Black or African American, non-Hispanic/Latino; 1 Asian, non-Hispanic/Latino; 31 Hispanic/Latino). Average age 35. *Entrance requirements:* Additional exam requirements/recommendations for international students: Required—TOEFL (minimum score 550 paper-based; 79 iBT). *Application deadline:* Applications are processed on a rolling basis. Application fee: $50. Electronic applications accepted. *Expenses:* Contact institution. *Unit head:* Dr. Sylvia Blake, Dean and Chief Operating Officer, 914-831-2700, E-mail: westchester@liu.edu. *Application contact:* Cindy Pagnotta, Director of Marketing and Enrollment, 914-831-2701, Fax: 914-251-5959, E-mail: cindy.pagnotta@liu.edu.

Long Island University–LIU Brooklyn, School of Education, Brooklyn, NY 11201-8423. Offers adolescence urban education (MS Ed); applied behavior analysis (Advanced Certificate); bilingual education (Advanced Certificate); bilingual school counselor (MS Ed, Advanced Certificate); childhood urban education (MS Ed); childhood/early childhood urban education (MS Ed); early childhood urban education (MS Ed, Advanced Certificate); educational leadership (Advanced Certificate); marriage and family therapy (MS, Advanced Certificate); mental health counseling (MS, Advanced Certificate); school building district leader (Advanced Certificate); school counselor (MS Ed, Advanced Certificate); school psychologist (MS Ed); teaching urban children/adolescents with disabilities (MS Ed); TESOL (MS Ed). *Accreditation:* TEAC. *Program availability:* Part-time, evening/weekend. *Faculty:* 23 full-time (17 women), 44 part-time/adjunct (32 women). *Students:* 161 full-time (144 women), 594 part-time (461 women); includes 493 minority (229 Black or African American, non-Hispanic/Latino; 1 American Indian or Alaska Native, non-Hispanic/Latino; 30 Asian, non-Hispanic/Latino; 218 Hispanic/Latino; 2 Native Hawaiian or other Pacific Islander, non-Hispanic/Latino; 13 Two or more races, non-Hispanic/Latino), 9 international. 513 applicants, 73% accepted, 272 enrolled. In 2016, 262 master's, 18 other advanced degrees awarded. *Degree requirements:* For master's, thesis optional, electronic portfolio. *Entrance requirements:* For master's, GRE (for MS Ed). Additional exam requirements/recommendations for international students: Required—TOEFL (minimum score 527 paper-based; 75 iBT). *Application deadline:* Applications are processed on a rolling basis. Application fee: $50. Electronic applications accepted. *Expenses: Tuition:* Full-time $28,272; part-time $1178 per credit. *Required fees:* $451 per term. Tuition and fees vary according to degree level, program and student level. *Financial support:* In 2016–17, 81 students received support. Career-related internships or fieldwork, Federal Work-Study, institutionally sponsored loans, scholarships/grants, and unspecified assistantships available. Support available to part-time students. Financial award application deadline: 2/15; financial award applicants required to submit FAFSA. *Faculty research:* Technology in education, teaching civics and sustainability, biliteracy and dual language instruction, diversity in organizations and leadership, counseling diverse couples and families. *Unit head:* Dr. Amy Ginsberg, Dean, 718-246-6308, E-mail: amy.ginsberg@liu.edu. *Application contact:* Gabrielle Gannon, Director of Graduate Admissions, 718-488-1011, Fax: 718-780-6110, E-mail: bkln-admissions@liu.edu.
Website: http://www.liu.edu/Brooklyn/Academics/School-of-Education

Long Island University–LIU Post, College of Education, Information and Technology, Brookville, NY 11548-1300. Offers adolescence education (MS); adolescence education 7-12 (MS); archives and records management (AC); art education (MS); childhood education (MS); childhood teaching literacy B-6 (MS); childhood/special education (MS); clinical mental health counseling (MS, AC); early childhood education (MS); early childhood education/childhood education (MS); educational leadership (AC); educational technology (MS); information studies (PhD); interdisciplinary educational studies (Ed D); middle childhood education (MS); music education (MS); school counselor (MS); special education (MS Ed); speech-language pathology (MA); students with disabilities, 7-12 generalist (AC); TESOL (MA). *Accreditation:* TEAC. *Program availability:* Part-time, 100% online, blended/hybrid learning. *Faculty:* 55 full-time (35 women), 104 part-time/adjunct (57 women). *Students:* 464 full-time (390 women), 740 part-time (580 women); includes 265 minority (99 Black or African American, non-Hispanic/Latino; 45 Asian, non-Hispanic/Latino; 113 Hispanic/Latino; 1 Native Hawaiian or other Pacific Islander, non-Hispanic/Latino; 7 Two or more races, non-Hispanic/Latino), 33 international. 928 applicants, 76% accepted, 406 enrolled. In 2016, 334 master's, 10 doctorates, 137 other advanced degrees awarded. Terminal master's awarded for partial completion of doctoral program. *Degree requirements:* For master's, variable foreign language requirement, comprehensive exam (for some programs), thesis optional; for doctorate, comprehensive exam, thesis/dissertation. *Entrance requirements:* For master's and AC, GRE. Additional exam requirements/recommendations for international students: Required—PTE, TOEFL (minimum score 550 paper-based, 75 iBT) or IELTS. *Application deadline:* Applications are processed on a rolling basis. Application fee: $50. Electronic applications accepted. *Expenses: Tuition:* Full-time $28,272; part-time $1178 per credit. *Required fees:* $451 per term. Tuition and fees vary according to degree level and program. *Financial support:* Career-related internships or fieldwork, Federal Work-Study, institutionally sponsored loans, scholarships/grants, tuition waivers (partial), and unspecified assistantships available. Support available to part-time students. Financial award application deadline: 2/15; financial award applicants required to submit FAFSA. *Faculty research:* English language learners, early childhood literacy development through play, sleep, social justice through education, using a structured protocol for discussing bad news. *Total annual research expenditures:* $575,000. *Unit head:* Dr. Albert Inserra, Dean, 516-299-2210, E-mail: albert.inserra@liu.edu. *Application contact:* Carol Zerah, Director of Graduate Admissions, 516-299-2900, Fax: 516-299-2137, E-mail: post-enroll@liu.edu. Website: http://liu.edu/CWPost/Academics/College-of-Education-Information-and-Technology

Long Island University–Riverhead, Graduate Programs, Riverhead, NY 11901. Offers childhood education (MS), including grades 1-6; homeland security management (MS); literacy education (MS); teaching students with disabilities (MS), including grades 1-6, grades 7-12; TESOL (Advanced Certificate). *Accreditation:* TEAC. *Program availability:* Part-time. *Degree requirements:* For master's, thesis (for some programs); for Advanced Certificate, comprehensive exam (for some programs). *Entrance requirements:* Additional exam requirements/recommendations for international students: Required—TOEFL (minimum score 550 paper-based; 79 iBT), IELTS (minimum score 6). *Application deadline:* Applications are processed on a rolling basis. Application fee: $50. Electronic applications accepted. *Expenses:* Contact institution. *Financial support:* Institutionally sponsored loans, scholarships/grants, tuition waivers (partial), and unspecified assistantships available. Support available to part-time students. Financial award application deadline: 2/15; financial award applicants required to submit FAFSA. *Unit head:* Donna Di Donato, Dean and Chief Operating Officer, LIU Brentwood and LIU Riverhead, 631-287-8010, Fax: 631-287-8575, E-mail: donna.didonato@liu.edu. *Application contact:* Christina Seifert, Director of Admission, LIU Brentwood and LIU Riverhead, 631-287-8505, Fax: 631-287-8253, E-mail: christina.seifert@liu.edu.

Longwood University, College of Graduate and Professional Studies, College of Education and Human Services, Farmville, VA 23909. Offers education (MS), including algebra and middle school mathematics, counselor education, elementary and middle school mathematics, elementary education, elementary education initial licensure, health and physical education, special education general curriculum, special education initial licensure; reading, literacy and learning (M Ed); school librarianship (M Ed); social work and communication sciences and disorders (MS), including communication sciences and disorders. *Accreditation:* NCATE. *Program availability:* Part-time, evening/weekend. *Degree requirements:* For master's, comprehensive exam (for some programs), thesis optional, professional portfolio, internship, clinical experience, or practicum. *Entrance requirements:* For master's, PRAXIS I (for initial teaching licensure programs); GRE (for some programs), bachelor's degree from regionally-accredited institution, 2 recommendations (3 for some programs), minimum 500-word personal essay, official transcripts, minimum GPA of 2.75, valid teaching license (for some programs). Additional exam requirements/recommendations for international students: Required—TOEFL (minimum score 570 paper-based), IELTS (minimum score 6.5). Electronic applications accepted. *Expenses:* Contact institution.

Loras College, Graduate Division, Program in Education with an Emphasis in Special Education, Dubuque, IA 52004-0178. Offers instructional strategist I K-6 and 7-12 (MA). *Program availability:* Part-time, evening/weekend. *Degree requirements:* For master's, comprehensive exam, thesis optional. *Entrance requirements:* For master's, minimum cumulative undergraduate GPA of 3.0.

Loyola Marymount University, School of Education, Department of Elementary and Secondary Education, Program in Special Education, Los Angeles, CA 90045-2659. Offers MA. *Program availability:* Part-time, evening/weekend. *Students:* 47 full-time (41 women), 1 (woman) part-time; includes 36 minority (7 Black or African American, non-Hispanic/Latino; 26 Hispanic/Latino; 3 Two or more races, non-Hispanic/Latino), 1 international. Average age 29. 32 applicants, 88% accepted, 27 enrolled. In 2016, 84 master's awarded. *Entrance requirements:* For master's, CBEST, CSET, RICA, 3 letters of recommendation. Additional exam requirements/recommendations for international students: Required—TOEFL (minimum score 600 paper-based; 100 iBT). *Application deadline:* For fall admission, 6/15 for domestic students. Application fee: $50. Electronic applications accepted. *Financial support:* In 2016–17, 24 students received support. Scholarships/grants and unspecified assistantships available. Support available to part-time students. Financial award application deadline: 6/30; financial award applicants required to submit FAFSA. *Unit head:* Dr. Edmundo Litton, Acting Program Director, 310-338-1859, E-mail: elitton@lmu.edu. *Application contact:* Chake H. Kouyoumjian, Associate Dean of Graduate Studies, 310-338-2721, E-mail: ckouyoum@lmu.edu. Website: http://soe.lmu.edu/academics/specialeducation/

Loyola University Chicago, School of Education, Program in Teaching and Learning, Chicago, IL 60660. Offers elementary education (M Ed); English language teaching and learning (M Ed); secondary education (M Ed). *Accreditation:* NCATE. *Faculty:* 22 full-time (16 women), 38 part-time/adjunct (30 women). *Students:* 31 full-time (25 women), 20 part-time (15 women); includes 6 minority (5 Hispanic/Latino; 1 Two or more races, non-Hispanic/Latino), 3 international. Average age 27. 113 applicants, 52% accepted, 37 enrolled. In 2016, 35 master's awarded. *Degree requirements:* For master's, comprehensive exam. *Entrance requirements:* For master's, Illinois Basic Skills Test, 3 letters of recommendation, minimum GPA of 3.0, resume. Additional exam requirements/recommendations for international students: Required—TOEFL (minimum score 550 paper-based; 79 iBT). *Application deadline:* For fall admission, 7/1 for domestic and international students; for spring admission, 11/1 priority date for domestic and international students; for summer admission, 3/1 priority date for domestic and international students. Applications are processed on a rolling basis. Application fee: $50. Electronic applications accepted. Application fee is waived when completed online. *Expenses:* $949 per hour; $2,847 per course; $8,541-$11,388 per semester plus fees $432 per semester and $225 the first semester. *Financial support:* In 2016–17, 19 students received support, including 19 fellowships with partial tuition reimbursements available; institutionally sponsored loans, scholarships/grants, and unspecified assistantships also available. Support available to part-time students. Financial award application deadline: 2/1; financial award applicants required to submit FAFSA. *Faculty research:* Positive behavior support, school reform, school improvement. *Unit head:* Dr. David Ensminger, Program Chair, 312-915-7257, E-mail: densmin@luc.edu. *Application contact:* Thomas Ott, Information Contact, 312-915-8907, E-mail: tott@luc.edu.

Lynchburg College, Graduate Studies, M Ed Program in Special Education, Lynchburg, VA 24501-3199. Offers M Ed. *Program availability:* Part-time, evening/weekend. *Students:* 3 full-time (all women), 30 part-time (26 women); includes 6 minority (4 Black or African American, non-Hispanic/Latino; 1 American Indian or Alaska Native, non-Hispanic/Latino; 1 Hispanic/Latino), 2 international. In 2016, 18 master's awarded. *Degree requirements:* For master's, comprehensive exam. *Entrance requirements:* For master's, GRE, minimum GPA of 3.0 (preferred), official transcripts (bachelor's, others as relevant), three letters of recommendation, career goals statement. Additional exam requirements/recommendations for international students: Required—TOEFL (minimum score 550 paper-based; 79 iBT), IELTS (minimum score 6.5). *Application deadline:* For fall admission, 7/31 for domestic students, 6/1 for international students; for spring admission, 11/30 for domestic students, 10/15 for international students. Applications are processed on a rolling basis. Application fee: $30. Electronic applications accepted. Application fee is waived when completed online. *Expenses:* Contact institution. *Financial support:* Federal Work-Study, scholarships/grants, health care benefits, and unspecified assistantships available. Support available to part-time students. Financial award application deadline: 7/31; financial award applicants required to submit FAFSA. *Unit head:* Dr. Gena Barnhill, Associate Professor/Director of M Ed in Special Education, 434-544-8771, E-mail: barnhill@lynchburg.edu. Website: http://www.lynchburg.edu/graduate/master-of-education-in-special-education/

Lyndon State College, Graduate Programs in Education, Department of Education, Lyndonville, VT 05851-0919. Offers curriculum and instruction (M Ed); reading specialist (M Ed); special education (M Ed); teaching and counseling (M Ed). *Program availability:* Part-time, evening/weekend. *Degree requirements:* For master's, exam or major field project. *Entrance requirements:* Additional exam requirements/recommendations for international students: Recommended—TOEFL (minimum score 500 paper-based).

Lynn University, Donald E. and Helen L. Ross College of Education, Boca Raton, FL 33431-5598. Offers educational leadership (M Ed, Ed D), including K-12 (Ed D); exceptional student education (M Ed), including school administration K-12. *Program availability:* Part-time, evening/weekend, online learning. *Faculty:* 5 full-time (4 women), 8 part-time/adjunct (all women). *Students:* 85 full-time (63 women), 10 part-time (6 women); includes 27 minority (19 Black or African American, non-Hispanic/Latino; 7 Hispanic/Latino; 1 Two or more races, non-Hispanic/Latino), 4 international. Average age 36. 17 applicants, 94% accepted, 11 enrolled. In 2016, 24 master's, 22 doctorates awarded. *Degree requirements:* For master's, comprehensive exam, thesis (for some programs); for doctorate, thesis/dissertation, mid-program review. *Entrance requirements:* For master's, bachelor's degree from accredited institution, letter of recommendation, statement of professional goals, official transcripts; for doctorate, master's degree from accredited institution, resume, 2 letters of recommendation, professional practice statement, official transcripts. Additional exam requirements/recommendations for international students: Required—TOEFL (minimum score 550 paper-based; 80 iBT), IELTS (minimum score 6.5). *Application deadline:* For fall admission, 8/18 for domestic students, 8/4 for international students; for spring admission, 12/15 for domestic students, 12/1 for international students; for summer admission, 4/17 for domestic students, 4/3 for international students. Applications are processed on a rolling basis. Application fee: $45. Electronic applications accepted. *Expenses:* $850 per credit hour, $44,200 per year tuition and fees (for Ed D); $725 per credit hour, $29,000 per year tuition and fees (for master's). *Financial support:* In 2016–17, 74 students received support. Career-related internships or fieldwork, Federal Work-Study, scholarships/grants, tuition waivers (partial), and unspecified assistantships available. Support available to part-time students. Financial award application deadline: 3/1; financial award applicants required to submit FAFSA. *Unit head:* Dr. Kathleen Weigel, Dean, College of Education, 561-237-7441, E-mail: kweigel@lynn.edu. *Application contact:* Steven Pruitt, Director of Graduate and Undergraduate Evening Admission, 561-237-7834, Fax: 561-237-7100, E-mail: spruitt@lynn.edu. Website: http://www.lynn.edu/academics/colleges/education

Madonna University, Programs in Education, Livonia, MI 48150-1173. Offers Catholic school leadership (MSA); educational leadership (MSA); learning disabilities (MAT); literacy education (MAT); teaching and learning (MAT). *Accreditation:* NCATE. *Program availability:* Part-time, evening/weekend. *Degree requirements:* For master's, thesis or alternative. Electronic applications accepted.

Malone University, Graduate Program in Education, Canton, OH 44709. Offers curriculum and instruction (MA); curriculum, instruction, and professional development (MA); educational leadership (principal license) (MA); intervention specialist (MA). *Accreditation:* NCATE. *Program availability:* Part-time, evening/weekend. *Degree requirements:* For master's, research project. *Entrance requirements:* For master's, minimum GPA of 3.0, teaching license. Additional exam requirements/recommendations for international students: Required—TOEFL (minimum score 550 paper-based; 79 iBT). *Faculty research:* Educational leadership styles: Jesus as master teacher, assessment accommodations for English language learners, preparing culturally proficient teachers, using naturally occurring text in the classroom to meet the syntactic needs of students with learning disabilities, using tablet instructional technology to meet the needs of students with disabilities.

Manhattan College, Graduate Programs, School of Education and Health, Program in Special Education, Riverdale, NY 10471. Offers adolescence education students with disabilities generalist extension in English or math or social studies - grades 7-12 (MS Ed); bilingual education (Advanced Certificate); dual childhood/students with disabilities - grades 1-6 (MS Ed); students with disabilities - grades 1-6 (MS Ed). *Program availability:* Part-time, evening/weekend. *Faculty:* 3 full-time (all women), 11 part-time/adjunct (7 women). *Students:* 62 full-time (59 women), 4 part-time (all women). Average age 24. 34 applicants, 79% accepted, 24 enrolled. In 2016, 32 master's awarded. *Degree requirements:* For master's, thesis, internship (if not certified). *Entrance requirements:* For master's, GRE, minimum GPA of 3.0. Additional exam requirements/recommendations for international students: Required—TOEFL (minimum score 550 paper-based; 80 iBT), IELTS (minimum score 6). *Application deadline:* For fall admission, 8/10 priority date for domestic students; for spring admission, 1/7 priority date for domestic students. Applications are processed on a rolling basis. Application fee: $75. Electronic applications accepted. Application fee is waived when completed online. *Expenses:* $900 per credit, $105 registration fee, $175 information service fee. *Financial support:* In 2016–17, 52 students received support. Federal Work-Study, scholarships/grants, and unspecified assistantships available. Financial award application deadline: 2/1; financial award applicants required to submit FAFSA. *Unit head:* Dr. Elizabeth Mary Kosky, Director of Childhood and Adolescent Special Education Programs, 718-862-7969, Fax: 718-862-7816, E-mail: elizabeth.kosky@manhattan.edu. *Application contact:* William Bisset, Information Contact, 718-862-8000, E-mail: william.bisset@manhattan.edu.

Manhattanville College, School of Education, Jump Start Program, Purchase, NY 10577-2132. Offers childhood and special education (MPS); education (Advanced Certificate); secondary subject areas and special education (MPS); TESOL (MPS). *Program availability:* Part-time, evening/weekend. *Students:* 26 applicants, 46% accepted, 7 enrolled. In 2016, 17 master's awarded. *Degree requirements:* For master's, comprehensive exam (for some programs), thesis (for some programs), student teaching, research seminars, portfolios, internships, writing assessment; for Advanced Certificate, comprehensive exam (for some programs). *Entrance requirements:* For master's, GRE or MAT, minimum undergraduate GPA of 3.0, 2 letters of recommendation, interview. Additional exam requirements/recommendations for

international students: Required—TOEFL (minimum score 85 iBT); Recommended—IELTS. *Application deadline:* For fall admission, 7/1 priority date for domestic and international students; for spring admission, 11/1 priority date for domestic and international students; for summer admission, 4/1 priority date for domestic and international students. Applications are processed on a rolling basis. Application fee: $75. Electronic applications accepted. *Expenses: Tuition:* Full-time $16,470; part-time $915 per credit. *Required fees:* $60 per semester. Part-time tuition and fees vary according to course load and program. *Financial support:* Teaching assistantships, career-related internships or fieldwork, Federal Work-Study, institutionally sponsored loans, scholarships/grants, and unspecified assistantships available. Financial award applicants required to submit FAFSA. *Unit head:* Robert Cooper, Program Director, 914-323-5368, E-mail: robert.cooper@mville.edu. *Application contact:* Jeanine Pardey-Levine, Director of Graduate Enrollment Management, 914-323-3208, Fax: 914-694-1732, E-mail: edschool@mville.edu.
Website: http://www.mville.edu/programs/jump-start

Manhattanville College, School of Education, Program in Early Childhood Education, Purchase, NY 10577-2132. Offers childhood education (grades 1-6) (MAT); early childhood and special education (birth-grade 2) (MPS); early childhood education (birth-grade 2) (MAT); special education (birth-grade 2) (MPS); special education (birth-grade 6) (MPS). *Program availability:* Part-time, evening/weekend. *Students:* 22 applicants, 64% accepted, 10 enrolled. In 2016, 10 master's awarded. *Degree requirements:* For master's, comprehensive exam (for some programs), thesis (for some programs), student teaching, research seminars, portfolios, internships, writing assessment. *Entrance requirements:* For master's, GRE or MAT, minimum undergraduate GPA of 3.0, 2 letters of recommendation. Additional exam requirements/recommendations for international students: Required—TOEFL (minimum score 85 iBT); Recommended—IELTS. *Application deadline:* For fall admission, 7/1 priority date for domestic and international students; for spring admission, 11/1 priority date for domestic and international students; for summer admission, 4/1 priority date for domestic and international students. Applications are processed on a rolling basis. Application fee: $75. Electronic applications accepted. *Expenses: Tuition:* Full-time $16,470; part-time $915 per credit. *Required fees:* $60 per semester. Part-time tuition and fees vary according to course load and program. *Financial support:* Teaching assistantships, career-related internships or fieldwork, Federal Work-Study, institutionally sponsored loans, scholarships/grants, and unspecified assistantships available. Financial award applicants required to submit FAFSA. *Faculty research:* Technology support for emergent literacies and storytelling in preschool; technology, teacher and reader identities in preservice teacher education; student teacher and mentor relationship; curriculum history and historiography of John Dewey and the Dewey School. *Unit head:* Dr. Patricia Vardin, Chairperson, Department of Early Childhood, 914-798-2714, Fax: 914-694-2386, E-mail: patricia.vardin@mville.edu. *Application contact:* Jeanine Pardey-Levine, Director of Graduate Enrollment Management, 914-323-3208, Fax: 914-694-1732, E-mail: edschool@mville.edu.
Website: http://www.mville.edu/programs/early-childhood-education

Manhattanville College, School of Education, Program in Middle Childhood/Adolescence Education (Grades 5-12), Purchase, NY 10577-2132. Offers biology (MAT); biology and special education (MPS); chemistry (MAT); chemistry and special education (MPS); English (MAT); English and special education (MPS); literacy and special education (MPS); literacy specialist (MPS); math and special education (MPS); mathematics (MAT); physics (MAT); social studies (MAT); social studies and special education (MPS); special education generalist (MPS); teaching languages other than English (MAT), including French, Italian, Latin, Spanish. *Program availability:* Part-time, evening/weekend. *Students:* 28 applicants, 86% accepted, 21 enrolled. In 2016, 23 master's awarded. *Degree requirements:* For master's, comprehensive exam (for some programs), thesis (for some programs), student teaching, research seminars, portfolios, internships, writing assessment. *Entrance requirements:* For master's, GRE or MAT, minimum undergraduate GPA of 3.0, 2 letters of recommendation. Additional exam requirements/recommendations for international students: Required—TOEFL (minimum score 85 iBT); Recommended—IELTS. *Application deadline:* For fall admission, 7/1 priority date for domestic and international students; for spring admission, 11/1 priority date for domestic and international students; for summer admission, 4/1 priority date for domestic and international students. Applications are processed on a rolling basis. Application fee: $75. Electronic applications accepted. *Expenses: Tuition:* Full-time $16,470; part-time $915 per credit. *Required fees:* $60 per semester. Part-time tuition and fees vary according to course load and program. *Financial support:* Teaching assistantships, career-related internships or fieldwork, Federal Work-Study, institutionally sponsored loans, scholarships/grants, and unspecified assistantships available. Financial award applicants required to submit FAFSA. *Unit head:* Victoria Fantozzi, Chairperson, Department of Curriculum and Instruction, 914-323-7138, E-mail: victoria.fantozzi@mville.edu. *Application contact:* Jeanine Pardey-Levine, Director of Graduate Enrollment Management, 914-323-3208, Fax: 914-694-1732, E-mail: edschool@mville.edu.
Website: http://www.mville.edu/programs#/search/19

Manhattanville College, School of Education, Program in Special Education, Purchase, NY 10577-2132. Offers childhood education (MPS); early childhood education (MPS); secondary education (MPS). *Program availability:* Part-time, evening/weekend. *Students:* 45 applicants, 69% accepted, 28 enrolled. In 2016, 26 master's, 1 Advanced Certificate awarded. *Degree requirements:* For master's, comprehensive exam (for some programs), thesis (for some programs), student teaching, research seminars, portfolios, internships, writing assessment; for Advanced Certificate, comprehensive exam (for some programs). *Entrance requirements:* For master's, GRE or MAT, minimum undergraduate GPA of 3.0, 2 letters of recommendation. Additional exam requirements/recommendations for international students: Required—TOEFL (minimum score 85 iBT); Recommended—IELTS. *Application deadline:* For fall admission, 7/1 priority date for domestic and international students; for spring admission, 11/1 priority date for domestic and international students; for summer admission, 4/1 priority date for domestic and international students. Applications are processed on a rolling basis. Application fee: $75. Electronic applications accepted. *Expenses: Tuition:* Full-time $16,470; part-time $915 per credit. *Required fees:* $60 per semester. Part-time tuition and fees vary according to course load and program. *Financial support:* Teaching assistantships, career-related internships or fieldwork, Federal Work-Study, institutionally sponsored loans, scholarships/grants, and unspecified assistantships available. Financial award applicants required to submit FAFSA. *Faculty research:* Aspects of verbal behavior and communication skills in autistic children, PBIS systems and their implementation, effective instructional practices for students with E/BDs, effective pedagogical practices that improve student behavioral and academic performance, increasing communication skills of young non-vocal children with autism. *Unit head:* Vance Austin, Chairperson, Department of Special Education, 914-323-7262, E-mail: vance.austin@mville.edu. *Application contact:* Jeanine Pardey-Levine, Director of Admissions, 914-323-3208, Fax: 914-694-1732, E-mail: edschool@mville.edu.
Website: http://www.mville.edu/programs/special-education

Mansfield University of Pennsylvania, Graduate Studies, Department of Education and Special Education, Mansfield, PA 16933. Offers elementary education (M Ed); secondary education (MS); special education (M Ed). *Accreditation:* NCATE (one or more programs are accredited). *Program availability:* Part-time, evening/weekend, online learning. *Degree requirements:* For master's, comprehensive exam, thesis optional. *Entrance requirements:* For master's, minimum GPA of 3.0. Additional exam requirements/recommendations for international students: Required—TOEFL (minimum score 550 paper-based). Electronic applications accepted.

Marian University, School of Education, Fond du Lac, WI 54935-4699. Offers curriculum and instruction leadership (PhD); educational administration (PhD); educational leadership (MAE); educational technology (MAE); leadership studies (PhD); special education (MAE); teacher education (MAE). *Accreditation:* NCATE. *Program availability:* Part-time, evening/weekend, online learning. *Faculty:* 11 full-time (7 women), 14 part-time/adjunct (8 women). *Students:* 13 full-time (9 women), 179 part-time (113 women); includes 16 minority (6 Black or African American, non-Hispanic/Latino; 3 American Indian or Alaska Native, non-Hispanic/Latino; 2 Asian, non-Hispanic/Latino; 3 Hispanic/Latino; 2 Two or more races, non-Hispanic/Latino). Average age 39. In 2016, 72 master's, 8 doctorates awarded. *Degree requirements:* For master's, exam, field-based experience project, portfolio; for doctorate, comprehensive exam, thesis/dissertation, field-based experience. *Entrance requirements:* For master's, minimum GPA of 3.0, BA in education or related field, teaching license; for doctorate, GRE, MAT, resume, 2 writing samples, interview. Additional exam requirements/recommendations for international students: Required—TOEFL (minimum score 525 paper-based; 70 iBT). *Application deadline:* Applications are processed on a rolling basis. Application fee: $50. *Expenses: Tuition:* Full-time $5130; part-time $570 per credit hour. *Financial support:* In 2016–17, 3 students received support. Federal Work-Study available. Support available to part-time students. Financial award application deadline: 3/1; financial award applicants required to submit FAFSA. *Faculty research:* At-risk youth, multicultural issues, values in education, teaching/learning strategies. *Unit head:* Dr. Kelly Chaney, Dean, 920-923-8610, Fax: 920-923-7663, E-mail: kachaney01@marianuniversity.edu.
Website: https://www.marianuniversity.edu/academic-programs/graduate-studies/

Marshall University, Academic Affairs Division, College of Education and Professional Development, Program in Special Education, Huntington, WV 25755. Offers MA. *Accreditation:* NCATE. *Program availability:* Part-time, evening/weekend. *Degree requirements:* For master's, thesis optional, comprehensive or oral assessment, research project. *Entrance requirements:* For master's, GRE General Test or MAT, minimum GPA of 3.0. *Faculty research:* Teaching the severely handicapped, career/vocational education, education of the gifted.

Martin Luther College, Graduate Studies, New Ulm, MN 56073. Offers early childhood director (MS Ed Admin); educational technology (MS Ed); instruction (MS Ed); leadership (MS Ed); principal (MS Ed Admin); special education (MS Ed). *Program availability:* Part-time, evening/weekend. *Faculty:* 9 full-time (1 woman), 21 part-time/adjunct (10 women). *Students:* 1 (woman) full-time, 77 part-time (30 women); includes 2 minority (1 Asian, non-Hispanic/Latino; 1 Two or more races, non-Hispanic/Latino), 4 international. Average age 37. 6 applicants, 100% accepted, 6 enrolled. In 2016, 15 master's awarded. *Degree requirements:* For master's, capstone project or comprehensive exam. *Entrance requirements:* For master's, undergraduate degree in education from an accredited college or university, minimum undergraduate GPA of 3.0. Additional exam requirements/recommendations for international students: Required—TOEFL (minimum score 550 paper-based; 80 iBT); Recommended—IELTS (minimum score 6.5). *Application deadline:* Applications are processed on a rolling basis. Application fee: $35. Electronic applications accepted. *Expenses:* $11,220 tuition, $140 graduation fee. *Financial support:* In 2016–17, 2 students received support. Scholarships/grants available. Financial award application deadline: 9/1. *Faculty research:* Principal effectiveness, principal support, cognitive load in math instruction, reading strategies in multigrade classrooms, mentor provided professional development for new teachers. *Unit head:* John E. Meyer, Director of Graduate Studies, 507-354-8221 Ext. 398, E-mail: meyerjd@mlc-wels.edu.
Website: https://mlc-wels.edu/graduate-studies/

Marymount University, School of Education and Human Services, Program in Education, Arlington, VA 22207-4299. Offers elementary education (M Ed); English as a second language (M Ed); professional studies (M Ed); secondary education (M Ed); special education: general curriculum (M Ed). *Accreditation:* NCATE. *Program availability:* Part-time, evening/weekend. *Faculty:* 28 full-time (all women), 8 part-time/adjunct (5 women). *Students:* 42 full-time (33 women), 94 part-time (72 women); includes 25 minority (6 Black or African American, non-Hispanic/Latino; 6 Asian, non-Hispanic/Latino; 8 Hispanic/Latino; 5 Two or more races, non-Hispanic/Latino), 12 international. Average age 32. 32 applicants, 100% accepted, 24 enrolled. In 2016, 79 master's awarded. *Degree requirements:* For master's, thesis or alternative, capstone/internship. *Entrance requirements:* For master's, GRE or MAT and PRAXIS I or SAT/ACT and Virginia Communication and Literacy Assessment (VCLA), 2 letters of recommendation, resume, interview, minimum undergraduate GPA of 2.75 or 3.25 in the last 60 hours. Additional exam requirements/recommendations for international students: Required—TOEFL (minimum score 600 paper-based; 96 iBT), IELTS (minimum score 6.5). *Application deadline:* Applications are processed on a rolling basis. Application fee: $40. Electronic applications accepted. *Expenses:* $690 per credit hour. *Financial support:* In 2016–17, 6 students received support, including 2 teaching assistantships with tuition reimbursements available; career-related internships or fieldwork, Federal Work-Study, scholarships/grants, and unspecified assistantships also available. Support available to part-time students. Financial award applicants required to submit FAFSA. *Unit head:* Dr. Lisa Turissini, Chair, Education, 703-526-1668, Fax: 703-284-1631, E-mail: lisa.turissini@marymount.edu. *Application contact:* Francesca Reed, Director, Graduate Admissions, 703-284-5901, Fax: 703-527-3815, E-mail: grad.admissions@marymount.edu.
Website: http://www.marymount.edu/Academics/School-of-Education-Human-Services/Graduate-Programs/Education-(M-Ed-)

Marywood University, Academic Affairs, Reap College of Education and Human Development, Department of Education, Program in Special Education, Scranton, PA 18509-1598. Offers MS. *Accreditation:* NCATE. *Program availability:* Part-time. Electronic applications accepted.

Marywood University, Academic Affairs, Reap College of Education and Human Development, Department of Education, Program in Special Education Administration and Supervision, Scranton, PA 18509-1598. Offers MS. *Accreditation:* NCATE. *Program availability:* Part-time. Electronic applications accepted.

Massachusetts College of Liberal Arts, Graduate Programs, North Adams, MA 01247-4100. Offers business (MBA); educational administration (M Ed); educational leadership (CAGS); instruction and curriculum (M Ed); instructional technology (M Ed); physical education and health (M Ed); reading (M Ed); special education (M Ed). *Program availability:* Part-time, evening/weekend. *Degree requirements:* For master's, thesis. *Entrance requirements:* For master's, writing sample.

McDaniel College, Graduate and Professional Studies, Program in Deaf Education, Westminster, MD 21157-4390. Offers MS. *Accreditation:* NCATE. *Program availability:* Part-time. *Faculty:* 3 full-time (1 woman), 2 part-time/adjunct (both women). *Students:* 7 full-time (5 women), 15 part-time (11 women); includes 2 minority (1 Hispanic/Latino; 1 Two or more races, non-Hispanic/Latino), 2 international. Average age 31. 11

applicants, 73% accepted. In 2016, 17 master's awarded. *Degree requirements:* For master's, comprehensive exam, thesis optional. *Entrance requirements:* For master's, American Sign Language Proficiency Interview (ASLPI); English Proficiency Essay (EPE). Additional exam requirements/recommendations for international students: Required—TOEFL (minimum score 79 iBT), IELTS (minimum score 6). *Application deadline:* For fall admission, 6/1 priority date for domestic students; for spring admission, 11/1 priority date for domestic students; for summer admission, 3/1 priority date for domestic students. Applications are processed on a rolling basis. Application fee: $75. Electronic applications accepted. *Expenses: Tuition:* Full-time $8370; part-time $465 per credit. *Required fees:* $75 per semester. Tuition and fees vary according to course load, program and reciprocity agreements. *Financial support:* Career-related internships or fieldwork, institutionally sponsored loans, and scholarships/grants available. Financial award application deadline: 3/1; financial award applicants required to submit FAFSA. *Faculty research:* Mainstreaming of multi-handicapped children. *Unit head:* Fax: 410-857-2516, E-mail: gradadms@mcdaniel.edu. *Application contact:* Anna Collins, Program Assistant, 410-857-2506, Fax: 410-857-2515, E-mail: deafedoffice@mcdaniel.edu.

McDaniel College, Graduate and Professional Studies, Program in Human Services Management, Westminster, MD 21157-4390. Offers MS. *Accreditation:* NCATE. *Program availability:* Evening/weekend. *Faculty:* 1 full-time (0 women), 2 part-time/adjunct (1 woman). *Students:* 18 full-time (14 women); includes 4 minority (3 Black or African American, non-Hispanic/Latino; 1 Asian, non-Hispanic/Latino). Average age 26. 4 applicants, 75% accepted. In 2016, 7 master's awarded. *Degree requirements:* For master's, internship. *Entrance requirements:* For master's, 3 recommendations; successful employment interview with Target Community and Educational Services, Inc. Additional exam requirements/recommendations for international students: Required—TOEFL (minimum score 79 iBT), IELTS (minimum score 6). *Application deadline:* Applications are processed on a rolling basis. Application fee: $75. Electronic applications accepted. *Expenses: Tuition:* Full-time $8370; part-time $465 per credit. *Required fees:* $75 per semester. Tuition and fees vary according to course load, program and reciprocity agreements. *Financial support:* Application deadline: 3/1; applicants required to submit FAFSA. *Unit head:* E-mail: gradadms@mcdaniel.edu. *Application contact:* Crystal L. Perry, Assistant Director, Graduate Enrollment Management, 410-857-2516, Fax: 410-857-2515, E-mail: cperry@mcdaniel.edu.

McDaniel College, Graduate and Professional Studies, Program in Special Education, Westminster, MD 21157-4390. Offers MS. *Accreditation:* NCATE. *Program availability:* Part-time, evening/weekend. *Faculty:* 2 full-time (1 woman), 4 part-time/adjunct (2 women). *Students:* 4 full-time (3 women), 28 part-time (25 women); includes 1 minority (Two or more races, non-Hispanic/Latino), 1 international. Average age 32. 5 applicants, 80% accepted. In 2016, 7 master's awarded. *Degree requirements:* For master's, comprehensive exam, thesis optional. *Entrance requirements:* For master's, PRAXIS, 3 recommendations. Additional exam requirements/recommendations for international students: Required—TOEFL (minimum score 79 iBT), IELTS (minimum score 6). *Application deadline:* For fall admission, 6/1 priority date for domestic students; for spring admission, 11/1 priority date for domestic students; for summer admission, 3/1 priority date for domestic students. Applications are processed on a rolling basis. Application fee: $75. Electronic applications accepted. *Expenses: Tuition:* Full-time $8370; part-time $465 per credit. *Required fees:* $75 per semester. Tuition and fees vary according to course load, program and reciprocity agreements. *Financial support:* Application deadline: 3/1; applicants required to submit FAFSA. *Unit head:* E-mail: gradadms@mcdaniel.edu. *Application contact:* Crystal L. Perry, Assistant Director, Graduate Enrollment Management, 410-857-2516, Fax: 410-857-2515, E-mail: cperry@mcdaniel.edu.

McKendree University, Graduate Programs, Programs in Education, Lebanon, IL 62254-1299. Offers curriculum design and instruction (Ed D, Ed S); educational administration and leadership (MA Ed); educational studies (MA Ed); higher education administrative services (MA Ed); music education (MA Ed); reading (MA Ed); special education (MA Ed); teacher leadership (MA Ed); teaching certification (MA Ed). *Accreditation:* NCATE. *Program availability:* Part-time, evening/weekend, online learning. *Entrance requirements:* For master's, official transcripts from all institutions previously attended, minimum GPA of 3.0, resume, references; for doctorate, GRE (within the past 5 years), master's degree in education and Ed S, or the equivalent, from regionally-accredited institution; official transcripts from all institutions previously attended; curriculum vitae/resume; essay/personal statement; two years of teaching/professional experience; for Ed S, GRE (within the past 5 years), master's degree in education from regionally-accredited institution of higher education; official transcripts from all institutions previously attended; curriculum vitae/resume; essay/personal statement; two years of teaching/professional experience. Additional exam requirements/recommendations for international students: Required—TOEFL. Electronic applications accepted.

McNeese State University, Doré School of Graduate Studies, Burton College of Education, Office of Graduate Education Programs, Program in Special Education, Lake Charles, LA 70609. Offers advanced professional (M Ed); autism (M Ed); educational diagnostician (M Ed). *Entrance requirements:* For master's, GRE, teaching certificate.

McNeese State University, Doré School of Graduate Studies, Burton College of Education, Office of Graduate Education Programs, Program in Special Education - Mild/Moderate Grades 1-12, Lake Charles, LA 70609. Offers MAT. *Entrance requirements:* For master's, GRE, PRAXIS, 2 letters of recommendation; autobiography.

McNeese State University, Doré School of Graduate Studies, Burton College of Education, Office of Student Teaching and Professional Education Services, Program in Special Education Intervention Birth-5, Lake Charles, LA 70609. Offers Postbaccalaureate Certificate. *Entrance requirements:* For degree, PRAXIS, 2 letters of recommendation, autobiography.

McNeese State University, Doré School of Graduate Studies, Burton College of Education, Office of Student Teaching and Professional Education Services, Program in Special Education, Mild/Moderate for Elementary Education Grades 1-5, Lake Charles, LA 70609. Offers Postbaccalaureate Certificate. *Entrance requirements:* For degree, PRAXIS, 2 letters of recommendation, autobiography.

McNeese State University, Doré School of Graduate Studies, Burton College of Education, Office of Student Teaching and Professional Education Services, Program in Special Education, Mild/Moderate for Secondary Education Grades 6-12, Lake Charles, LA 70609. Offers Postbaccalaureate Certificate. *Entrance requirements:* For degree, PRAXIS, 2 letters of recommendation, autobiography.

Medaille College, Program in Education, Buffalo, NY 14214-2695. Offers adolescent education (MS Ed); curriculum and instruction (MS Ed); education preparation (MS Ed); literacy (MS Ed); special education (MS). *Accreditation:* TEAC. *Program availability:* Part-time, evening/weekend. *Degree requirements:* For master's, comprehensive exam (for some programs), thesis or alternative. *Entrance requirements:* For master's, minimum undergraduate GPA of 2.7. Additional exam requirements/recommendations for international students: Required—TOEFL (minimum score 550 paper-based). Electronic applications accepted. *Faculty research:* Curriculum planning, truancy, tracking minority students, curriculum design, mentoring students.

Mercyhurst University, Graduate Studies, Program in Special Education, Erie, PA 16546. Offers applied behavior analysis (MS); autism (MS); generalist (MS); higher education leadership and disabilities (MS). *Program availability:* Part-time, evening/weekend. *Degree requirements:* For master's, thesis optional. *Entrance requirements:* For master's, GRE or PRAXIS I, interview, resume, essay, three professional references, transcripts. Additional exam requirements/recommendations for international students: Required—TOEFL. Electronic applications accepted. *Faculty research:* College-age learning disabled program, teacher preparation/collaboration, applied behavior analysis, special education policy issues.

Meredith College, School of Education, Health and Human Sciences, Raleigh, NC 27607-5298. Offers academically and intellectually gifted (M Ed); curriculum instruction specialist (M Ed); elementary education (M Ed, MAT); English as a second language (M Ed, MAT); health and physical education (MAT); nutrition, health and human performance (MS, Postbaccalaureate Certificate), including dietetic internship (Postbaccalaureate Certificate), nutrition (MS); reading (M Ed); special education (MAT). *Accreditation:* NCATE. *Program availability:* Part-time, evening/weekend. *Degree requirements:* For master's, thesis optional. *Entrance requirements:* For master's, GRE General Test or MAT, minimum GPA of 2.5, teaching license, recommendations. Additional exam requirements/recommendations for international students: Required—TOEFL. Electronic applications accepted. *Expenses:* Contact institution.

Merrimack College, School of Education and Social Policy, North Andover, MA 01845-5800. Offers community engagement (M Ed), including community organizations, higher education, K-12 education; criminology and criminal justice (MS); curriculum and instruction (M Ed); early childhood education (M Ed); educational leadership (CAGS), including instructional leadership; elementary education (M Ed); English as a second language (PreK-6) (M Ed); high school education (M Ed); higher education (M Ed), including leadership and organizational development, student affairs; middle school education (M Ed); moderate disabilities (PreK-8) (M Ed); school counseling (M Ed). *Program availability:* Part-time, evening/weekend, 100% online courses with immersion events and in-classroom practicum close to home. *Faculty:* 17 full-time, 34 part-time/adjunct. *Students:* 204 full-time (172 women), 83 part-time (67 women); includes 32 minority (4 Black or African American, non-Hispanic/Latino; 2 Asian, non-Hispanic/Latino; 23 Hispanic/Latino; 3 Two or more races, non-Hispanic/Latino), 1 international. Average age 27. 261 applicants, 89% accepted, 200 enrolled. In 2016, 153 master's, 2 other advanced degrees awarded. *Degree requirements:* For master's, practicum, portfolio, and state test (for licensure track); capstone (for higher education, curriculum and instruction, and community engagement tracks). *Entrance requirements:* For master's, Massachusetts Teacher Education Licensure (MTEL), official transcripts from other colleges, resume, personal statement, 2 letters of recommendation. Additional exam requirements/recommendations for international students: Required—TOEFL (minimum score 84 iBT), IELTS (minimum score 6.5), PTE (minimum score 56). *Application deadline:* For fall admission, 8/14 for domestic students, 7/14 for international students; for spring admission, 1/10 for domestic students, 12/10 for international students; for summer admission, 5/10 for domestic students, 4/10 for international students. Applications are processed on a rolling basis. Application fee: $0. Electronic applications accepted. *Expenses:* Contact institution. *Financial support:* Fellowships with full tuition reimbursements, career-related internships or fieldwork, scholarships/grants, and health care benefits available. Support available to part-time students. Financial award application deadline: 5/1; financial award applicants required to submit FAFSA. *Faculty research:* Feminist praxis in higher education, transgender student agency and belonging, campus sexual violence prevention, the scholarship of engagement; community engagement; service learning; diversity education; community-university partnerships, college going behaviors and indicators of success for inner city youth, strategies to increase students pursuit and success in STEM higher education, effective workforce development for displaced or under employed individuals, police reform, e.g. surveillance. *Application contact:* Alyssa Frey, Graduate Admissions Counselor, 978-837-3563, E-mail: freya@merrimack.edu.
Website: http://www.merrimack.edu/academics/graduate/education/

Messiah College, Program in Education, Mechanicsburg, PA 17055. Offers curriculum and instruction (M Ed); special education (M Ed); teaching English to speakers of other languages (M Ed). *Program availability:* Part-time, online learning. Electronic applications accepted. *Faculty research:* Socio-cultural perspectives on education, TESOL, autism, special education.

Metropolitan College of New York, Program in Childhood/Special Education, New York, NY 10006. Offers dual childhood 1-6 special education (MS). *Accreditation:* NCATE. *Students:* 21 full-time (19 women), 1 (woman) part-time; includes 15 minority (13 Black or African American, non-Hispanic/Latino; 2 Hispanic/Latino), 1 international. Average age 32. In 2016, 21 master's awarded. *Entrance requirements:* For master's, GRE or MAT, minimum GPA of 3.0, 2 letters of reference, interview, resume. Additional exam requirements/recommendations for international students: Required—TOEFL (minimum score 550 paper-based; 80 iBT), IELTS (minimum score 6.5). *Application deadline:* Applications are processed on a rolling basis. Application fee: $45. Electronic applications accepted. *Expenses:* Contact institution. *Financial support:* Career-related internships or fieldwork, Federal Work-Study, institutionally sponsored loans, and scholarships/grants available. Financial award application deadline: 8/15; financial award applicants required to submit FAFSA. *Faculty research:* Classroom management, learner autonomy, teacher research, math and gender, intelligence. *Unit head:* Dr. Patrick Ianniello, Director, 212-343-1234 Ext. 2424, E-mail: pianniello@metropolitan.edu. *Application contact:* Sylvia Cameron, Graduate Admissions Coordinator, 212-343-1234 Ext. 2704, Fax: 212-343-7900, E-mail: scameron@mcny.edu.
Website: http://www.mcny.edu/human_serv/msedc.php

Metropolitan State University of Denver, School of Education, Denver, CO 80204. Offers elementary education (MAT); special education (MAT). *Faculty:* 20 full-time (16 women), 1 part-time/adjunct (0 women). *Students:* 115 full-time (90 women), 14 part-time (11 women); includes 23 minority (7 Black or African American, non-Hispanic/Latino; 2 American Indian or Alaska Native, non-Hispanic/Latino; 1 Asian, non-Hispanic/Latino; 9 Hispanic/Latino; 4 Two or more races, non-Hispanic/Latino). Average age 32. In 2016, 59 master's awarded. *Application deadline:* For fall admission, 2/1 for domestic and international students; for spring admission, 10/1 for domestic and international students; for summer admission, 2/1 for domestic and international students. Application fee: $50. *Expenses:* $6,429.60 for full-time residents, $8,881.20 for full-time non-residents; $357.20 per credit hour for part-time residents, $493.40 per credit hour for part-time non-residents. *Unit head:* Kathy Heyl, Interim Dean, 303-556-2978, E-mail: heyl@msudenver.edu. *Application contact:* Ellen Sunbury, Graduate Admissions Coordinator, 303-556-6228, E-mail: esunbury@msudenver.edu.
Website: http://www.msudenver.edu/scops/

Michigan State University, The Graduate School, College of Education, Department of Counseling, Educational Psychology and Special Education, East Lansing, MI 48824. Offers counseling (MA); educational psychology and educational technology (PhD); educational technology (MA); measurement and quantitative methods (PhD); rehabilitation counseling (MA); rehabilitation counselor education (PhD); school psychology (MA, PhD, Ed S); special education (MA, PhD). *Accreditation:* APA (one or more programs are accredited); CORE (one or more programs are accredited). *Program availability:* Part-time. *Entrance requirements:* Additional exam requirements/recommendations for international students: Required—TOEFL. Electronic applications accepted.

Middle Tennessee State University, College of Graduate Studies, College of Education, Department of Elementary and Special Education, Major in Special Education, Murfreesboro, TN 37132. Offers M Ed. *Accreditation:* NCATE. *Program availability:* Part-time, evening/weekend, online learning. *Degree requirements:* For master's, comprehensive exam. *Entrance requirements:* For master's, GRE, MAT or PRAXIS. Additional exam requirements/recommendations for international students: Required—TOEFL (minimum score 525 paper-based; 71 iBT) or IELTS (minimum score 6). Electronic applications accepted.

Midwestern State University, Billie Doris McAda Graduate School, West College of Education, Program in Special Education, Wichita Falls, TX 76308. Offers M Ed. *Program availability:* Part-time, evening/weekend. *Degree requirements:* For master's, comprehensive exam. *Entrance requirements:* For master's, GRE General Test, MAT, or GMAT, Texas teacher certificate or equivalent minimum GPA of 3.0 in previous education courses. Additional exam requirements/recommendations for international students: Required—TOEFL (minimum score 550 paper-based). Electronic applications accepted. *Faculty research:* Fragile-X syndrome, phenylketonuria and other causes of handicapping conditions, autism, social development of students with disabilities.

Millersville University of Pennsylvania, College of Graduate Studies and Adult Learning, College of Education and Human Services, Department of Educational Foundations, Program in Special Education, Millersville, PA 17551-0302. Offers M Ed. *Accreditation:* NCATE. *Program availability:* Part-time, online only, 100% online. *Faculty:* 20 full-time (13 women), 2 part-time/adjunct (both women). *Students:* 1 (woman) full-time, 11 part-time (all women). Average age 31. 1 applicant, 100% accepted, 1 enrolled. In 2016, 3 master's awarded. *Degree requirements:* For master's, comprehensive exam, thesis (for some programs), clinical practicum. *Entrance requirements:* For master's, GRE or MAT, teaching certificate; interview; 3 current professional letters of recommendation. Additional exam requirements/recommendations for international students: Required—TOEFL (minimum score 600 paper-based), IELTS (minimum score 6). *Application deadline:* Applications are processed on a rolling basis. Application fee: $40. Electronic applications accepted. *Expenses:* $483 per credit resident tuition; $566 per credit non-resident tuition. *Financial support:* Unspecified assistantships available. Financial award application deadline: 3/15; financial award applicants required to submit FAFSA. *Unit head:* Dr. Ellen Long, Coordinator, 717-871-7328, E-mail: ellen.long@millersville.edu. *Application contact:* Dr. Victor S. DeSantis, Dean of College of Graduate Studies and Adult Learning/Associate Provost for Civic and Community Engagement, 717-871-7619, Fax: 717-871-7954, E-mail: victor.desantis@millersville.edu.
Website: https://www.millersville.edu/edfoundations/m_ed_sped.php

Millersville University of Pennsylvania, College of Graduate Studies and Adult Learning, College of Education and Human Services, Department of Educational Foundations, Program in Special Education: 7-12 Option, Millersville, PA 17551-0302. Offers M Ed. *Program availability:* Part-time, online only, 100% online. *Faculty:* 20 full-time (13 women), 2 part-time/adjunct (both women). *Students:* 2 part-time (both women). Average age 33. 2 applicants, 100% accepted, 2 enrolled. *Degree requirements:* For master's, thesis (for some programs), practicum field experience. *Entrance requirements:* For master's, GRE or MAT, teaching certificate; interview; 3 current professional letters of recommendation. Additional exam requirements/recommendations for international students: Required—TOEFL (minimum score 600 paper-based), IELTS (minimum score 6). *Application deadline:* Applications are processed on a rolling basis. Application fee: $40. Electronic applications accepted. *Expenses:* $483 per credit resident tuition; $566 per credit non-resident tuition. *Financial support:* Unspecified assistantships available. Financial award application deadline: 3/15; financial award applicants required to submit FAFSA. *Unit head:* Dr. Ellen Long, Coordinator, 717-871-7328, E-mail: ellen.long@millersville.edu. *Application contact:* Dr. Victor S. DeSantis, Dean of College of Graduate Studies and Adult Learning/Associate Provost for Civic and Community Engagement, 717-871-7619, Fax: 717-871-7954, E-mail: victor.desantis@millersville.edu.
Website: https://www.millersville.edu/edfoundations/m_ed_sped.php

Millersville University of Pennsylvania, College of Graduate Studies and Adult Learning, College of Education and Human Services, Department of Educational Foundations, Program in Special Education: PreK-8 Option, Millersville, PA 17551-0302. Offers M Ed. *Program availability:* Part-time, online only, 100% online. *Faculty:* 20 full-time (13 women), 2 part-time/adjunct (both women). *Students:* 1 full-time (0 women), 5 part-time (4 women). Average age 28. 2 applicants, 100% accepted, 1 enrolled. In 2016, 2 master's awarded. *Degree requirements:* For master's, thesis (for some programs), practicum field experience. *Entrance requirements:* For master's, GRE or MAT, teaching certificate; interview; 3 current professional letters of recommendation. Additional exam requirements/recommendations for international students: Required—TOEFL (minimum score 600 paper-based), IELTS (minimum score 6). *Application deadline:* Applications are processed on a rolling basis. Application fee: $40. Electronic applications accepted. *Expenses:* $483 per credit resident tuition; $566 per credit non-resident tuition. *Financial support:* Unspecified assistantships available. Financial award application deadline: 3/15; financial award applicants required to submit FAFSA. *Unit head:* Dr. Ellen Long, Coordinator, 717-871-7328, Fax: 717-871-2376, E-mail: ellen.long@millersville.edu. *Application contact:* Dr. Victor S. DeSantis, Dean of College of Graduate Studies and Adult Learning/Associate Provost for Civic and Community Engagement, 717-871-7619, Fax: 717-871-7954, E-mail: victor.desantis@millersville.edu.
Website: https://www.millersville.edu/edfoundations/m_ed_sped.php

Milligan College, Area of Education, Milligan College, TN 37682. Offers combined preK-3/K-5 education (M Ed); educational leadership (Ed D, Ed S); K-5 education (M Ed); middle grades education (M Ed); preK-3 education (M Ed); preK-3 special education (M Ed); secondary education (M Ed). *Accreditation:* NCATE. *Program availability:* Part-time. *Faculty:* 5 full-time (3 women), 3 part-time/adjunct (1 woman). *Students:* 26 full-time (19 women), 20 part-time (10 women); includes 2 minority (1 Black or African American, non-Hispanic/Latino; 1 Hispanic/Latino), 2 international. Average age 28. 16 applicants, 81% accepted, 11 enrolled. In 2016, 19 master's awarded. *Degree requirements:* For master's, thesis, portfolio, research project; for doctorate, thesis/dissertation, portfolio, research project. *Entrance requirements:* For master's, MAT, GRE General Test, ACT, SAT, or PRAXIS, undergraduate degree and supporting transcripts, professional recommendations, interview; for doctorate, MAT or GRE, master's degree and supporting transcripts, demonstrated scholastic ability, recognized leadership role within education, professional recommendations, essay/personal statement, portfolio (professional development plan, evidence of ability, knowledge and qualities), interview. Additional exam requirements/recommendations for international students: Required—TOEFL (minimum score 550 paper-based, 79 iBT) or IELTS (6.5). *Application deadline:* For fall admission, 8/1 priority date for domestic students, 6/1 for international students; for spring admission, 11/15 priority date for domestic students, 12/1 for international students; for summer admission, 4/1 for domestic students. Applications are processed on a rolling basis. Application fee: $30. Electronic applications accepted. *Expenses:* $360 per hour tuition (for M Ed); $475 per hour tuition (for Ed D and Ed S); $325 per semester tech/activity fees. *Financial support:* Scholarships/grants available. Financial award application deadline: 12/1; financial award applicants required to submit FAFSA. *Faculty research:* Assessment; school mental health; literacy; technology; educator preparation. *Unit head:* Dr. Angela Hilton-Prillhart, Area Chair of Education, 423-461-8769, Fax: 423-461-3103, E-mail: anhilton-prillhart@milligan.edu. *Application contact:* Melissa Dillow, Graduate Admissions Recruiter, Education, 423-461-8306, Fax: 423-461-8982, E-mail: msdillow@milligan.edu.
Website: http://www.Milligan.edu/GPS

Minnesota State University Mankato, College of Graduate Studies and Research, College of Education, Department of Special Education, Mankato, MN 56001. Offers emotional and behavioral disorders (MS, Certificate); learning disabilities (MS, Certificate). *Accreditation:* NCATE. *Program availability:* Part-time, online learning. *Students:* 32 full-time (29 women), 75 part-time (50 women). *Degree requirements:* For master's, comprehensive exam, thesis or alternative. *Entrance requirements:* For master's, Council for Exceptional Children pre-program assessment, minimum GPA of 3.2 during previous 2 years. Additional exam requirements/recommendations for international students: Required—TOEFL. *Application deadline:* For fall admission, 7/1 for domestic students; for spring admission, 11/20 for domestic students; for summer admission, 4/20 for domestic students. Applications are processed on a rolling basis. Application fee: $40. Electronic applications accepted. *Financial support:* Research assistantships, teaching assistantships with full tuition reimbursements, career-related internships or fieldwork, Federal Work-Study, and institutionally sponsored loans available. Support available to part-time students. Financial award application deadline: 3/15; financial award applicants required to submit FAFSA. *Unit head:* Dr. Alexandra Panahon, Chair, 507-389-2908, E-mail: alexandra.panahon@mnsu.edu.
Website: http://ed.mnsu.edu/sped/

Minnesota State University Moorhead, Graduate Studies, College of Education and Human Services, Moorhead, MN 56563. Offers counseling and student affairs (MS); curriculum and instruction (MS); educational leadership (MS, Ed S); special education (MS); speech-language pathology (MS). *Accreditation:* NCATE. *Program availability:* Part-time, 100% online, blended/hybrid learning. *Students:* 133 full-time (116 women), 363 part-time (274 women). Average age 32. 273 applicants, 49% accepted. In 2016, 114 master's awarded. *Degree requirements:* For master's, comprehensive exam (for some programs), thesis. *Entrance requirements:* For master's, GRE, essay, letter of intent, letters of reference, teaching license, teaching verification. Additional exam requirements/recommendations for international students: Required—TOEFL (minimum score 550 paper-based). *Application deadline:* For fall admission, 4/15 priority date for domestic students; for spring admission, 11/1 priority date for domestic students. Applications are processed on a rolling basis. Application fee: $20. Electronic applications accepted. *Expenses:* Tuition, state resident: full-time $9000; part-time $4500 per credit. Tuition, nonresident: full-time $18,000; part-time $9000 per credit. *Required fees:* $942; $39.25 per credit. One-time fee: $90 full-time. Full-time tuition and fees vary according to course load, degree level, program and reciprocity agreements. *Financial support:* Federal Work-Study and unspecified assistantships available. Financial award application deadline: 10/1; financial award applicants required to submit FAFSA. *Unit head:* Dr. Ok-Hee Lee, Dean, 218-477-2095, E-mail: okheelee@mnstate.edu. *Application contact:* Karla Wenger, Office Manager, 218-477-2344, Fax: 218-477-2482, E-mail: wengerk@mnstate.edu.
Website: http://www.mnstate.edu/cehs/

Minot State University, Graduate School, Program in Special Education, Minot, ND 58707-0002. Offers deaf/hard of hearing education (MS); specific learning disabilities (MS). *Accreditation:* NCATE. *Degree requirements:* For master's, comprehensive exam (for some programs), thesis (for some programs). *Entrance requirements:* For master's, minimum GPA of 2.75, bachelor's degree in education or related field, teacher licensure (for some concentrations). Additional exam requirements/recommendations for international students: Required—TOEFL (minimum score 79 iBT), IELTS (minimum score 6).

Misericordia University, College of Health Sciences and Education, Program in Education, Dallas, PA 18612-1098. Offers instructional technology (MS); reading specialist (MS); special education (MS). *Program availability:* Part-time, evening/weekend. *Entrance requirements:* For master's, minimum undergraduate GPA of 3.0. Additional exam requirements/recommendations for international students: Required—TOEFL. Electronic applications accepted.

Mississippi College, Graduate School, School of Education, Department of Teacher Education and Leadership, Clinton, MS 39058. Offers art (M Ed); biological science (M Ed); business education (M Ed); computer science (M Ed); dyslexia therapy (M Ed); educational leadership (M Ed, Ed D, Ed S); elementary education (M Ed, Ed S); English (M Ed); higher education administration (MS); mathematics (M Ed); secondary education (M Ed); social studies (history) (M Ed); teaching arts (M Ed). *Program availability:* Part-time, online learning. *Degree requirements:* For master's, comprehensive exam, thesis optional. *Entrance requirements:* For master's, NTE. Additional exam requirements/recommendations for international students: Recommended—TOEFL, IELTS. Electronic applications accepted.

Mississippi State University, College of Education, Department of Curriculum, Instruction and Special Education, Mississippi State, MS 39762. Offers early childhood education (PhD); elementary education (MS, PhD, Ed S), including early childhood education (MS), general elementary education (MS), middle level education (MS); general curriculum and instruction (PhD); middle level (MAT); reading education (PhD); secondary education (MAT, MS, PhD, Ed S); special education (MAT, MS, PhD, Ed S). *Accreditation:* NCATE. *Program availability:* Part-time, evening/weekend. *Faculty:* 21 full-time (16 women), 1 (woman) part-time/adjunct. *Students:* 39 full-time (26 women), 168 part-time (128 women); includes 49 minority (43 Black or African American, non-Hispanic/Latino; 2 American Indian or Alaska Native, non-Hispanic/Latino; 1 Hispanic/Latino; 1 Native Hawaiian or other Pacific Islander, non-Hispanic/Latino; 2 Two or more races, non-Hispanic/Latino), 4 international. Average age 33. 98 applicants, 56% accepted, 47 enrolled. In 2016, 69 master's, 6 doctorates, 10 other advanced degrees awarded. *Degree requirements:* For master's, comprehensive exam; for doctorate, thesis/dissertation; for Ed S, comprehensive exam, thesis or alternative. *Entrance requirements:* For master's, GRE, minimum GPA of 2.75 in junior and senior year, eligibility for initial teacher certification; for doctorate, GRE, minimum GPA of 3.4 on previous graduate work; for Ed S, GRE, minimum GPA of 3.2 on master's degree. Additional exam requirements/recommendations for international students: Required—TOEFL (minimum score 550 paper-based; 79 iBT); Recommended—IELTS (minimum score 6.5). *Application deadline:* For fall admission, 3/1 priority date for domestic students, 5/1 for international students; for spring admission, 9/1 priority date for domestic students, 9/1 for international students. Applications are processed on a rolling basis. Application fee: $60. Electronic applications accepted. *Expenses:* Tuition, state resident: full-time $7670; part-time $852.50 per credit hour. Tuition, nonresident: full-time $20,790; part-time $2310.50 per credit hour. Part-time tuition and fees vary according to course load. *Financial support:* In 2016–17, 8 research assistantships with partial tuition reimbursements (averaging $11,381 per year) were awarded; Federal

Work-Study, institutionally sponsored loans, scholarships/grants, and unspecified assistantships also available. Financial award application deadline: 4/1; financial award applicants required to submit FAFSA. *Faculty research:* Early childhood education, reading, rural schools, multicultural education, use of technology in instruction. *Unit head:* Dr. Janice Nicholson, Interim Department Head, 662-325-3704, Fax: 662-325-7857, E-mail: jin4@msstate.edu. *Application contact:* Linda Bonner, Senior Admissions Assistant, 662-325-3363, E-mail: lbonner@grad.msstate.edu.
Website: http://www.cise.msstate.edu/

Missouri State University, Graduate College, College of Education, Department of Counseling, Leadership, and Special Education, Program in Special Education, Springfield, MO 65897. Offers alternative certification (MS Ed); autism spectrum disorder (MS Ed); blindness and low vision (MS Ed); orientation and mobility (MS Ed). *Program availability:* Part-time, evening/weekend, 100% online, blended/hybrid learning. *Students:* 10 full-time (9 women), 83 part-time (68 women); includes 5 minority (2 Black or African American, non-Hispanic/Latino; 3 Hispanic/Latino), 5 international. Average age 35. 31 applicants, 52% accepted, 13 enrolled. In 2016, 19 master's awarded. *Degree requirements:* For master's, comprehensive exam, thesis or alternative. *Entrance requirements:* For master's, GRE or minimum GPA of 3.0, teaching certificate. Additional exam requirements/recommendations for international students: Required—TOEFL (minimum score 550 paper-based; 79 iBT), IELTS (minimum score 6). *Application deadline:* For fall admission, 7/20 priority date for domestic students, 5/1 for international students; for spring admission, 12/20 priority date for domestic students, 9/1 for international students; for summer admission, 5/20 priority date for domestic students. Applications are processed on a rolling basis. Application fee: $35 ($50 for international students). Electronic applications accepted. *Expenses:* Tuition, state resident: full-time $5830. Tuition, nonresident: full-time $10,708. *Required fees:* $1130. Tuition and fees vary according to class time, course level, course load and program. *Financial support:* Federal Work-Study, institutionally sponsored loans, scholarships/grants, and unspecified assistantships available. Financial award application deadline: 3/31; financial award applicants required to submit FAFSA. *Unit head:* Dr. James Satterfield, Department Head, 417-836-5392, Fax: 417-836-4918, E-mail: spe@missouristate.edu. *Application contact:* Michael Edwards, Coordinator of Graduate Admissions, 417-836-5300, Fax: 417-836-6200, E-mail: michaeledwards@missouristate.edu.
Website: http://education.missouristate.edu/sped/

Missouri Western State University, Program in Assessment, St. Joseph, MO 64507-2294. Offers autism spectrum disorders (MAS, Graduate Certificate); TESOL (MAS, Graduate Certificate); writing (MAS). *Program availability:* Part-time. *Students:* 1 (woman) full-time, 33 part-time (25 women). Average age 37. 9 applicants, 100% accepted, 5 enrolled. In 2016, 6 master's, 1 other advanced degree awarded. *Entrance requirements:* For master's, minimum GPA of 2.75. Additional exam requirements/recommendations for international students: Recommended—TOEFL (minimum score 79 iBT), IELTS (minimum score 6). *Application deadline:* For fall admission, 7/15 for domestic and international students; for spring admission, 10/1 for domestic and international students; for summer admission, 3/15 for domestic students. Applications are processed on a rolling basis. Application fee: $50. Electronic applications accepted. *Expenses:* Tuition, state resident: full-time $6548; part-time $327.39 per credit hour. Tuition, nonresident: full-time $11,848; part-time $592.39 per credit hour. *Required fees:* $542; $99 per credit hour. $176 per semester. One-time fee: $50. Tuition and fees vary according to course load and program. *Financial support:* Scholarships/grants and unspecified assistantships available. Support available to part-time students. *Unit head:* Dr. Susan Bashinski, Director of Graduate Programs in Education, 816-271-5629, E-mail: sbashinski@missouriwestern.edu. *Application contact:* Dr. Benjamin D. Caldwell, Dean of the Graduate School, 816-271-4394, Fax: 816-271-4525, E-mail: graduate@missouriwestern.edu.
Website: https://www.missouriwestern.edu/masa/

Molloy College, Graduate Education Program, Rockville Centre, NY 11571-5002. Offers adolescent education in biology (MS Ed); adolescent special education (Advanced Certificate); bilingual extension (Advanced Certificate); childhood education (MS Ed); childhood special education (Advanced Certificate); early childhood education (MS Ed); educational technology (MS Ed); English (MS Ed); mathematics (MS Ed); social studies (MS Ed); Spanish (MS Ed); special education on both childhood and adolescent levels (MS Ed); teaching English to speakers of other languages (TESOL) in grades Pre-K to 12 (MS Ed); TESOL (Advanced Certificate). *Accreditation:* NCATE. *Program availability:* Part-time, evening/weekend. *Faculty:* 17 full-time (16 women), 23 part-time/adjunct (19 women). *Students:* 95 full-time (75 women), 221 part-time (177 women); includes 59 minority (14 Black or African American, non-Hispanic/Latino; 6 Asian, non-Hispanic/Latino; 38 Hispanic/Latino; 1 Two or more races, non-Hispanic/Latino), 1 international. Average age 42. 214 applicants, 66% accepted, 125 enrolled. In 2016, 95 master's, 4 Advanced Certificates awarded. *Entrance requirements:* Additional exam requirements/recommendations for international students: Required—TOEFL (minimum score 550 paper-based; 79 iBT). *Application deadline:* Applications are processed on a rolling basis. Application fee: $60. Electronic applications accepted. *Expenses: Tuition:* Full-time $19,170; part-time $1065 per credit. *Required fees:* $950; $790 per credit. Tuition and fees vary according to course load. *Financial support:* Applicants required to submit FAFSA. *Faculty research:* ESL - general education teacher collaboration; special education; school desegregation; American intellectual and social history; families and schools. *Unit head:* Joanne O'Brien, Associate Dean/Director, 516-323-3116, E-mail: jobrien@molloy.edu. *Application contact:* Jaclyn Machowicz, Assistant Director for Admissions, 516-323-4010, E-mail: jmachowicz@molloy.edu.

Monmouth University, Graduate Studies, School of Education, West Long Branch, NJ 07764-1898. Offers applied behavior analysis (Certificate); autism (Certificate); director of school counseling services (Post-Master's Certificate); early childhood (M Ed); educational leadership (Ed D); elementary education (MAT), including elementary level, secondary level; English as a second language (M Ed); learning disabilities teacher-consultant (Post-Master's Certificate); literacy (MS Ed); school counseling (MS Ed); special education (MS Ed), including autism, learning disabilities teacher-consultant, teacher of students with disabilities, teaching in inclusive settings; speech-language pathology (MS Ed); student affairs and college counseling (MS Ed); supervisor (Post-Master's Certificate); teaching English to speakers of other languages (Certificate). *Accreditation:* NCATE. *Program availability:* Part-time, evening/weekend, 100% online, blended/hybrid learning. *Faculty:* 23 full-time (19 women), 33 part-time/adjunct (25 women). *Students:* 191 full-time (172 women), 141 part-time (122 women); includes 56 minority (10 Black or African American, non-Hispanic/Latino; 9 Asian, non-Hispanic/Latino; 31 Hispanic/Latino; 6 Two or more races, non-Hispanic/Latino). Average age 26. 423 applicants, 53% accepted, 139 enrolled. In 2016, 148 master's, 4 other advanced degrees awarded. *Entrance requirements:* For master's, GRE taken within last 5 years (for MS Ed in speech-language pathology); SAT (minimum combined score of 1660 in 3 sections), ACT (23), GRE (minimum score of 4.0 on analytical writing section and minimum combined score of 310 on quantitative and verbal sections), or passing scores on 3 parts of Core Academic Skills Educators, minimum GPA of 3.0 in major; 2 letters of recommendation (for some programs); resume, personal statement or essay (depending on program). Additional exam requirements/recommendations for international students: Required—TOEFL (minimum score 550 paper-based; 79 iBT), IELTS (minimum score 6), Michigan English Language Assessment Battery (minimum score 77) or Certificate of Advanced English (minimum score B2). *Application deadline:* For fall admission, 7/15 priority date for domestic students, 7/1 for international students; for spring admission, 12/1 priority date for domestic students, 11/1 for international students; for summer admission, 5/1 for domestic students. Applications are processed on a rolling basis. Application fee: $50. Electronic applications accepted. *Expenses: Tuition, area resident:* Full-time $19,764; part-time $1098 per credit hour. *Required fees:* $175 per semester. Tuition and fees vary according to program. *Financial support:* In 2016–17, 349 students received support, including 305 fellowships (averaging $3,558 per year), 48 teaching assistantships (averaging $9,619 per year); research assistantships, institutionally sponsored loans, scholarships/grants, and unspecified assistantships also available. Support available to part-time students. Financial award application deadline: 2/1; financial award applicants required to submit FAFSA. *Faculty research:* Multicultural literacy, science and mathematics teaching strategies, teacher as reflective practitioner, children with disabilities. *Unit head:* Dr. John E. Henning, Dean, 732-263-5513, Fax: 732-263-5277. *Application contact:* Laurie Kuhn, Associate Director of Graduate Admission, 732-571-3452, Fax: 732-263-5123, E-mail: gradadm@monmouth.edu.
Website: http://www.monmouth.edu/academics/schools/education/default.asp

Montana State University Billings, College of Education, Department of Educational Theory and Practice, Program in Special Education, Billings, MT 59101. Offers advanced studies (MS Sp Ed); applied behavior analysis (MS Sp Ed); generalist (MS Sp Ed). *Accreditation:* NCATE. *Program availability:* Part-time. *Faculty:* 2 full-time (both women). *Students:* 42. *Degree requirements:* For master's, thesis or professional paper and/or field experience. *Entrance requirements:* For master's, GRE General Test or MAT, minimum GPA of 3.0. Additional exam requirements/recommendations for international students: Required—TOEFL (minimum score 79 iBT), IELTS (minimum score 6.5). *Application deadline:* Applications are processed on a rolling basis. Application fee: $40. Electronic applications accepted. *Expenses:* Tuition, state resident: full-time $5265; part-time $3436 per year. Tuition, nonresident: full-time $14,030; part-time $9280 per year. *International tuition:* $19,295 full-time. Tuition and fees vary according to degree level, campus/location and program. *Financial support:* Research assistantships with partial tuition reimbursements, teaching assistantships with partial tuition reimbursements, career-related internships or fieldwork, Federal Work-Study, institutionally sponsored loans, scholarships/grants, tuition waivers (partial), and unspecified assistantships available. Support available to part-time students. Financial award application deadline: 5/1; financial award applicants required to submit FAFSA. *Unit head:* Dr. Ken Miller, Chair, 406-657-2034, E-mail: kmiller@msubillings.edu. *Application contact:* David M. Sullivan, Graduate Studies Counselor, 406-657-2053, Fax: 406-657-2299, E-mail: dsullivan@msubillings.edu.

Montclair State University, The Graduate School, College of Education and Human Services, Program in Inclusive Early Childhood Education, Montclair, NJ 07043-1624. Offers M Ed. *Degree requirements:* For master's, comprehensive exam, thesis or alternative. *Entrance requirements:* For master's, GRE General Test, interview, 2 letters of recommendation. Additional exam requirements/recommendations for international students: Required—TOEFL (minimum score 83 iBT), IELTS (minimum score 6.5). Electronic applications accepted. *Expenses:* Tuition, state resident: part-time $553 per credit. Tuition, nonresident: part-time $854 per credit. *Required fees:* $91 per credit. Tuition and fees vary according to program.

Morehead State University, Graduate Programs, College of Education, Department of Curriculum and Instruction, Morehead, KY 40351. Offers curriculum and instruction (Ed S); elementary education (MA Ed), including elementary education, international education, middle school education, reading; secondary education (MA Ed); special education (MA Ed); teaching (MAT). *Program availability:* Part-time, evening/weekend. *Degree requirements:* For master's, comprehensive exam, thesis optional; for Ed S, thesis, oral exam. *Entrance requirements:* For master's, GRE General Test, minimum GPA of 2.75, teaching certificate; for Ed S, GRE General Test, interview, master's degree, minimum GPA of 3.5, work experience. Additional exam requirements/recommendations for international students: Required—TOEFL (minimum score 500 paper-based). Electronic applications accepted. *Faculty research:* Communicative competence of learning-disabled students, teaching social studies in elementary schools, ungraded primary school organization, study skills.

Morehead State University, Graduate Programs, College of Education, Department of Early Childhood, Elementary and Special Education, Morehead, KY 40351. Offers learning and behavioral disorders P-12 (MAT); moderate and severe disabilities P-12 (MAT). *Program availability:* Part-time, evening/weekend. *Degree requirements:* For master's, thesis. *Entrance requirements:* For master's, GRE or PRAXIS II content exam, minimum overall undergraduate GPA of 2.5. Additional exam requirements/recommendations for international students: Required—TOEFL (minimum score 500 paper-based). Electronic applications accepted.

Morehead State University, Graduate Programs, College of Education, Department of Foundational and Graduate Studies in Education, Morehead, KY 40351. Offers adult and higher education (MA, Ed S); certified professional counselor (Ed S); counseling P-12 (MA); curriculum and instruction (Ed S); educational technology (MA Ed); instructional leadership (Ed S); school administration (MA); school counseling (Ed S); teacher leader business and marketing content (MA Ed); teacher leader business and marketing technology (MA Ed); teacher leader educational technology (MA Ed); teacher leader English (MA Ed); teacher leader gifted education (MA Ed); teacher leader IECE certification (MA Ed); teacher leader interdisciplinary education P-5 (MA Ed); teacher leader middle grades (MA Ed); teacher leader non IECE certification (MA Ed); teacher leader reading/writing - non-certification (MA Ed); teacher leader reading/writing certification (MA Ed); teacher leader school communication - certification (MA Ed); teacher leader school communication - non-certification (MA Ed); teacher leader social studies (MA Ed); teacher leader special education (MA Ed). *Accreditation:* NCATE. *Program availability:* Part-time, evening/weekend. *Degree requirements:* For master's, thesis optional, oral and/or written comprehensive exams; for Ed S, thesis, oral exam. *Entrance requirements:* For master's, GRE General Test, minimum overall undergraduate GPA of 2.5; for Ed S, GRE General Test, interview, master's degree, minimum GPA of 3.5, work experience. Additional exam requirements/recommendations for international students: Required—TOEFL (minimum score 500 paper-based). Electronic applications accepted. *Faculty research:* Character education, school accountability, computer applications for school administrators.

Morningside College, Graduate Division, Sharon Walker School of Education, Sioux City, IA 51106. Offers professional educator (MAT); special education (MAT), including instructional strategist: mild/moderate (7-12), instructional strategist: mild/moderate (K-6), K-12 instructional strategist: behavior disorders/learning disabilities, K-12 instructional strategist: mental disabilities. *Program availability:* Part-time, evening/weekend, online only, 100% online. *Faculty:* 4 full-time (1 woman), 108 part-time/adjunct (80 women). *Students:* 23 full-time (20 women), 1,468 part-time (1,191 women); includes 51 minority (5 Black or African American, non-Hispanic/Latino; 4 American Indian or Alaska Native, non-Hispanic/Latino; 9 Asian, non-Hispanic/Latino; 27 Hispanic/Latino; 1 Native Hawaiian or other Pacific Islander, non-Hispanic/Latino; 5 Two or more races, non-Hispanic/Latino), 1 international. Average age 35. In 2016, 316 master's awarded. *Entrance requirements:* For master's, MAT, writing sample. *Application deadline:* Applications are processed on a rolling basis. Application fee: $15. Electronic applications accepted. Application fee is waived when completed online. *Expenses:* $240 per credit hour. *Financial support:* Institutionally sponsored loans and tuition waivers (partial) available. Support available to part-time students. *Unit head:* Barbara Chambers, Director, 712-274-5465, Fax: 712-274-5488, E-mail: chambersb@morningside.edu. *Application contact:* Tracy Sursely, Student Records Enrollment Coordinator, 712-274-5576, Fax: 712-274-5101, E-mail: surselyt@morningside.edu.

Mount Mercy University, Program in Education, Cedar Rapids, IA 52402-4797. Offers reading (MA Ed); special education (MA Ed); teacher leadership (MA Ed). *Entrance requirements:* For master's, minimum cumulative GPA of 3.0, 2 letters of recommendation, resume, valid teaching license. Additional exam requirements/recommendations for international students: Required—TOEFL (minimum score 570 paper-based; 88 iBT). Electronic applications accepted.

Mount St. Joseph University, Graduate Education Program, Cincinnati, OH 45233-1670. Offers adolescent to young adult education (MA); dyslexia (Certificate); inclusive early childhood education (MA); middle childhood education (MA); multicultural special education (MA); reading science (MA). *Accreditation:* TEAC. *Program availability:* Part-time, evening/weekend, online learning. *Faculty:* 7 full-time (5 women), 12 part-time/adjunct (10 women). *Students:* 44 full-time (33 women), 112 part-time (104 women); includes 16 minority (15 Black or African American, non-Hispanic/Latino; 1 Two or more races, non-Hispanic/Latino). Average age 34. In 2016, 60 master's awarded. *Degree requirements:* For master's, comprehensive exam, thesis, research project, student teaching, clinical and field-based experiences. *Entrance requirements:* For master's, GRE (if GPA is below 3.0), letter of intent, 2 referrals, background check, interview, resume, minimum undergraduate GPA of 3.0. Additional exam requirements/recommendations for international students: Required—TOEFL (minimum score 560 paper-based; 83 iBT). *Application deadline:* Applications are processed on a rolling basis. Application fee: $50. Electronic applications accepted. *Expenses:* $580 per credit hour. *Financial support:* Applicants required to submit FAFSA. *Faculty research:* Foreign and second language learning problems/reading disabilities, multicultural/bilingual special education, science education, pedagogical content knowledge, early childhood, response to intervention. *Unit head:* Dr. Laura Saylor, Dean, 513-244-3263, E-mail: laura.saylor@msj.edu. *Application contact:* Mary Brigham, Assistant Director of Graduate Recruitment, 513-244-4233, Fax: 513-244-4629, E-mail: mary.brigham@msj.edu.
Website: http://www.msj.edu/academics/graduate-programs/master-of-arts-initial-teacher-licensure-programs/

Mount Saint Mary College, Division of Education, Newburgh, NY 12550-3494. Offers adolescence and special education (MS Ed); childhood education (MS Ed); literacy education (MS Ed); middle school (7-9) (MS Ed). *Accreditation:* NCATE. *Program availability:* Part-time, evening/weekend. *Faculty:* 12 full-time (10 women), 3 part-time/adjunct (all women). *Students:* 27 full-time (19 women), 78 part-time (59 women); includes 12 minority (1 Black or African American, non-Hispanic/Latino; 1 Asian, non-Hispanic/Latino; 7 Hispanic/Latino; 3 Two or more races, non-Hispanic/Latino). Average age 28. 30 applicants, 100% accepted, 16 enrolled. In 2016, 62 master's awarded. *Entrance requirements:* Additional exam requirements/recommendations for international students: Required—TOEFL (minimum score 80 iBT). *Application deadline:* Applications are processed on a rolling basis. Application fee: $45. Electronic applications accepted. Application fee is waived when completed online. *Expenses:* Tuition: Full-time $13,914; part-time $773 per credit. *Required fees:* $82 per semester. *Financial support:* In 2016–17, 18 students received support. Unspecified assistantships available. Financial award application deadline: 4/15; financial award applicants required to submit FAFSA. *Faculty research:* Learning and teaching styles, computers in special education, language development. *Unit head:* Dr. Monica Merritt, Graduate Coordinator, 845-569-3430, Fax: 845-569-3535, E-mail: monica.merritt@msmc.edu. *Application contact:* Lisa Gallina, Director of Admissions for Graduate Programs and Adult Degree Completion, 845-569-3166, Fax: 845-569-3450, E-mail: lisa.gallina@msmc.edu.
Website: http://www.msmc.edu/Academics/Graduate_Programs/Master_of_Science_in_Education

Mount Saint Vincent University, Graduate Programs, Faculty of Education, Program in Educational Psychology, Halifax, NS B3M 2J6, Canada. Offers education of the blind or visually impaired (M Ed, MA Ed); education of the deaf or hard of hearing (M Ed, MA Ed); educational psychology (MA-R); human relations (M Ed, MA Ed). *Program availability:* Part-time, evening/weekend, online learning. *Degree requirements:* For master's, thesis (for some programs). *Entrance requirements:* For master's, bachelor's degree in related field, 1 year of teaching experience. Electronic applications accepted. *Faculty research:* Personality measurement, values reasoning, aggression and sexuality, power and control, quantitative and qualitative research methodologies.

Murray State University, College of Education, Department of Adolescent, Career and Special Education, Program in Special Education, Murray, KY 42071. Offers advanced learning behavior disorders (MA Ed); learning disabilities (MA Ed); moderate/severe disorders (MA Ed). *Accreditation:* NCATE. *Program availability:* Part-time, evening/weekend. *Degree requirements:* For master's, thesis optional, portfolio. *Entrance requirements:* For master's, GRE General Test or MAT, teacher certification. Additional exam requirements/recommendations for international students: Required—TOEFL. *Faculty research:* Attention Deficit Hyperactivity Disorder, assistive technology.

National Louis University, National College of Education, Chicago, IL 60603. Offers administration and supervision (M Ed, Ed D, CAS, Ed S); curriculum and instruction (M Ed, MS Ed, CAS); early childhood administration (M Ed, CAS); early childhood education (M Ed, MAT, MS Ed, CAS); education (Ed D); educational psychology/human learning and development (M Ed, MS Ed, CAS, Ed S); elementary education (MAT); interdisciplinary curriculum and instruction (M Ed); mathematics education (M Ed, MS Ed, CAS); middle grades education (MAT); reading and language (M Ed, MS Ed, CAS); school psychology (M Ed, Ed S); science education (M Ed, MS Ed, CAS); secondary education (MAT); special education (M Ed, MAT, CAS); technology in education (M Ed, CAS). *Accreditation:* NCATE. *Program availability:* Part-time, evening/weekend. *Degree requirements:* For doctorate, comprehensive exam, thesis/dissertation. *Entrance requirements:* For master's, MAT or GRE, minimum GPA of 3.0; for doctorate, GRE General Test, minimum GPA of 3.25, interview, resume, writing sample, 4 recommendations. Additional exam requirements/recommendations for international students: Required—TOEFL (minimum score 550 paper-based; 79 iBT).

National University College, Graduate Programs, Bayamón, PR 00960. Offers digital marketing (MBA); general business (MBA); special education (M Ed).

Neumann University, Graduate Program in Education, Aston, PA 19014-1298. Offers education (MS), including administrative (principal K-12), autism, early elementary education, secondary education, special education. *Program availability:* Part-time, evening/weekend, 100% online, blended/hybrid learning. *Faculty:* 6 full-time (5 women), 18 part-time/adjunct (7 women). *Students:* 80 full-time (64 women), 108 part-time (91 women); includes 40 minority (30 Black or African American, non-Hispanic/Latino; 6 Hispanic/Latino; 4 Two or more races, non-Hispanic/Latino), 1 international. Average age 34. 152 applicants, 67% accepted, 82 enrolled. In 2016, 42 master's awarded. *Entrance requirements:* For master's, official transcripts from all institutions attended, letter of intent, three professional references, copy of any teaching certifications. Additional exam requirements/recommendations for international students: Required—TOEFL (minimum score 70 iBT). *Application deadline:* Applications are processed on a rolling basis. Application fee: $0. Electronic applications accepted. *Expenses:* $700 per credit on-campus tuition; $480 per credit online or off-campus tuition; additional $320 for student teaching course. *Financial support:* Scholarships/grants and health care benefits available. Support available to part-time students. Financial award application deadline: 3/15; financial award applicants required to submit FAFSA. *Unit head:* Dr. Stephanie Smith-Budhai, Director of Graduate Education, 610-358-4249, E-mail: budhais@neumann.edu. *Application contact:* Dr. Erika Davis, Director of Adult and Graduate Admissions, 800-9-NEUMANN Ext. 5208, Fax: 610-361-2548, E-mail: GradAdultAdmiss@neumann.edu.
Website: https://www.neumann.edu/academics/grad/education/index.asp

New England College, Program in Education, Henniker, NH 03242-3293. Offers higher education administration (MS, Ed D); K-12 leadership (Ed D); literacy and language arts (M Ed); meeting the needs of all learners/special education (M Ed); teacher leadership/school reform (M Ed). *Program availability:* Part-time, evening/weekend.

New Jersey City University, Debra Cannon Partridge Wolfe College of Education, Department of Special Education, Jersey City, NJ 07305-1597. Offers MA. *Accreditation:* TEAC. *Program availability:* Part-time, evening/weekend. *Entrance requirements:* Additional exam requirements/recommendations for international students: Required—TOEFL (minimum score 79 iBT). *Faculty research:* Mainstreaming the handicapped child and the autistic child.

New Mexico Highlands University, Graduate Studies, School of Education, Las Vegas, NM 87701. Offers curriculum and instruction (MA); educational leadership (MA); professional counseling (MA); special education (MA). *Accreditation:* NCATE. *Program availability:* Part-time. *Degree requirements:* For master's, comprehensive exam, thesis or alternative. *Entrance requirements:* For master's, minimum undergraduate GPA of 3.0. Additional exam requirements/recommendations for international students: Required—TOEFL (minimum score 540 paper-based). *Faculty research:* Middle school curriculum, integrated computer applications for pre-service classroom teachers, adolescent literacy, narrative cognitive modes in New Mexico multicultural setting, math and math education.

New Mexico State University, College of Education, Department of Special Education and Communication Disorders, Las Cruces, NM 88003. Offers communication disorders (MA); curriculum and instruction (Ed S), including special education (MA, Ed S), special education/deaf-hard of hearing (MA, Ed S); education (MA), including autism spectrum disorders, special education (MA, Ed S), special education/deaf-hard of hearing (MA, Ed S), speech-language pathology; special education (Ed D, PhD), including bilingual/multicultural special education. *Accreditation:* ASHA (one or more programs are accredited); NCATE. *Program availability:* Part-time, evening/weekend, online learning. *Faculty:* 15 full-time (12 women), 4 part-time/adjunct (3 women). *Students:* 59 full-time (49 women), 64 part-time (52 women); includes 68 minority (3 Black or African American, non-Hispanic/Latino; 2 American Indian or Alaska Native, non-Hispanic/Latino; 2 Asian, non-Hispanic/Latino; 59 Hispanic/Latino; 2 Two or more races, non-Hispanic/Latino), 7 international. Average age 33. 175 applicants, 19% accepted, 29 enrolled. In 2016, 43 master's, 1 doctorate, 1 other advanced degree awarded. *Degree requirements:* For master's, comprehensive exam, thesis optional; for doctorate, comprehensive exam, thesis/dissertation. *Entrance requirements:* For master's, GRE General Test or MAT. Additional exam requirements/recommendations for international students: Required—TOEFL (minimum score 550 paper-based; 79 iBT), IELTS (minimum score 6.5). *Application deadline:* For fall admission, 2/1 priority date for domestic students. Applications are processed on a rolling basis. Application fee: $40 ($50 for international students). Electronic applications accepted. *Expenses:* Tuition, state resident: full-time $4086. Tuition, nonresident: full-time $14,254. *Required fees:* $853. Tuition and fees vary according to course load. *Financial support:* In 2016–17, 47 students received support, including 2 research assistantships (averaging $12,723 per year), 15 teaching assistantships (averaging $9,700 per year); career-related internships or fieldwork, Federal Work-Study, scholarships/grants, traineeships, health care benefits, and unspecified assistantships also available. Support available to part-time students. Financial award application deadline: 3/1. *Faculty research:* Multicultural special education, multicultural communication disorders, mild disability, multicultural assessment, deaf education, early childhood, bilingual special education. *Total annual research expenditures:* $156,279. *Unit head:* Dr. Bob Wood, Interim Department Head, 575-646-5972, Fax: 575-646-7712, E-mail: bobwood@nmsu.edu. *Application contact:* Dr. Karen Potter, Director, Special Education Program, 575-646-2402, Fax: 575-646-7712, E-mail: potterk@nmsu.edu.
Website: http://spedcd.education.nmsu.edu

New York University, Steinhardt School of Culture, Education, and Human Development, Department of Teaching and Learning, Program in Early Childhood and Childhood Education, New York, NY 10003. Offers childhood education (MA); early childhood education (MA); early childhood education/early childhood special education (MA). *Accreditation:* TEAC. *Program availability:* Part-time. *Degree requirements:* For master's, thesis (for some programs). *Entrance requirements:* Additional exam requirements/recommendations for international students: Required—TOEFL (minimum score 100 iBT). Electronic applications accepted. *Faculty research:* Teacher evaluation and beliefs about teaching, early literacy development, language arts, child development and education, cultural differences.

New York University, Steinhardt School of Culture, Education, and Human Development, Department of Teaching and Learning, Program in Special Education, New York, NY 10012-1019. Offers childhood (MA); early childhood (MA). *Accreditation:* TEAC. *Program availability:* Part-time. *Degree requirements:* For master's, thesis (for some programs). *Entrance requirements:* Additional exam requirements/recommendations for international students: Required—TOEFL (minimum score 100 iBT). Electronic applications accepted. *Faculty research:* Special education referrals, attention deficit disorders in children, mainstreaming, curriculum-based assessment and program implementation, special education policy.

Niagara University, Graduate Division of Education, Concentration in Teacher Education, Niagara University, NY 14109. Offers early childhood and childhood education (MS Ed, Certificate); early childhood special education (MS); middle and adolescence education (MS Ed); special education (MS Ed), including 1-6, 7-12; special education (grades 1-12) (Certificate); teaching English to speakers of other languages (MS Ed, Certificate). *Accreditation:* NCATE. *Students:* 101 full-time (83 women), 123 part-time (101 women); includes 14 minority (6 Black or African American, non-Hispanic/Latino; 1 American Indian or Alaska Native, non-Hispanic/Latino; 6 Hispanic/Latino; 1 Two or more races, non-Hispanic/Latino), 28 international. Average age 28. In 2016, 86 master's, 18 other advanced degrees awarded. *Entrance requirements:* For master's, GRE General Test or Academic Literacy Skills Test (ALST). Additional exam requirements/recommendations for international students: Required—TOEFL (minimum score 550 paper-based; 79 iBT), IELTS (minimum score 6). *Application deadline:* For fall admission, 8/1 for domestic students. Applications are processed on a rolling basis.

Application fee: $30. *Expenses:* Contact institution. *Financial support:* Research assistantships with tuition reimbursements, teaching assistantships with tuition reimbursements, career-related internships or fieldwork, Federal Work-Study, scholarships/grants, and unspecified assistantships available. Financial award application deadline: 4/15; financial award applicants required to submit FAFSA. *Unit head:* Dr. Chandra Foote, Dean, College of Education, 716-286-8549, E-mail: cjf@niagara.edu. *Application contact:* Evan Pierce, Associate Director, Graduate Studies, 716-286-8327, E-mail: epierce@niagara.edu.
Website: http://www.niagara.edu/teacher-education

Norfolk State University, School of Graduate Studies, School of Education, Department of Special Education, Norfolk, VA 23504. Offers severe disabilities (MA). *Accreditation:* NCATE. *Program availability:* Part-time. *Degree requirements:* For master's, thesis or alternative. *Entrance requirements:* For master's, minimum GPA of 3.0 in major, 2.5 overall.

North Carolina Central University, School of Education, Special Education Program, Durham, NC 27707-3129. Offers M Ed. *Accreditation:* NCATE. *Program availability:* Part-time, evening/weekend. *Degree requirements:* For master's, comprehensive exam, thesis or alternative. *Entrance requirements:* For master's, GRE, minimum GPA of 3.0 in major, 2.5 overall. Additional exam requirements/recommendations for international students: Required—TOEFL.

North Carolina State University, Graduate School, College of Education, Department of Curriculum and Instruction, Program in Special Education, Raleigh, NC 27695. Offers M Ed, MS. *Accreditation:* NCATE. *Degree requirements:* For master's, thesis optional. *Entrance requirements:* For master's, GRE General Test and MAT, minimum GPA of 3.0 in major. Electronic applications accepted. *Faculty research:* Nature of disabilities, intervention research.

Northeastern Illinois University, College of Graduate Studies and Research, College of Education, Program in Learning Behavior Specialist I, Chicago, IL 60625-4699. Offers MA. *Degree requirements:* For master's, internship. *Entrance requirements:* For master's, bachelor's degree, minimum GPA of 2.75, two professional letters of recommendation. Electronic applications accepted.

Northeastern Illinois University, College of Graduate Studies and Research, College of Education, Program in Learning Behavior Specialist II, Chicago, IL 60625-4699. Offers MS. *Entrance requirements:* For master's, Illinois Test of Basic Skills (or equivalent), bachelor's degree; minimum GPA of 2.75 undergraduate, 3.0 graduate; writing sample; interview. Electronic applications accepted.

Northeastern State University, College of Education, Department of Curriculum and Instruction, Program in Special Education-Autism Spectrum Disorders, Tahlequah, OK 74464-2399. Offers M Ed. *Program availability:* Part-time. *Faculty:* 13 full-time (10 women). *Students:* 6 full-time (5 women), 26 part-time (25 women); includes 13 minority (1 Black or African American, non-Hispanic/Latino; 6 American Indian or Alaska Native, non-Hispanic/Latino; 1 Asian, non-Hispanic/Latino; 1 Hispanic/Latino; 4 Two or more races, non-Hispanic/Latino). Average age 39. *Degree requirements:* For master's, thesis. *Entrance requirements:* For master's, MAT or GRE. Additional exam requirements/recommendations for international students: Required—TOEFL. *Application deadline:* For fall admission, 6/1 priority date for domestic students. Applications are processed on a rolling basis. Application fee: $0 ($25 for international students). Electronic applications accepted. *Expenses:* Tuition, state resident: full-time $2816; part-time $216.60 per credit hour. Tuition, nonresident: full-time $6365; part-time $489.60 per credit hour. *Required fees:* $37.40 per credit hour. *Financial support:* Teaching assistantships available. Financial award application deadline: 3/1. *Unit head:* Jarilyn Haney, Program Chair, 918-449-3786, E-mail: haneyjw@nsuok.edu. *Application contact:* Josh McCollum, Graduate Coordinator, 918-444-2093, E-mail: mccolluj@nsuok.edu.

Northeastern University, College of Professional Studies, Boston, MA 02115-5096. Offers applied nutrition (MS); college athletics administration (MSL); commerce and economic development (MS); corporate and organizational communication (MS); criminal justice (MS); digital media (MPS); elearning and instructional design (M Ed); elementary education (MAT); geographic information technology (MPS); global studies and international relations (MS); higher education administration (M Ed); homeland security (MA); human services (MS); informatics (MPS); leadership (MS); learning analytics (M Ed); learning and instruction (M Ed); nonprofit management (MS); professional sports administration (MSL); project management (MS); regulatory affairs for drugs, biologics, and medical devices (MS); respiratory care leadership (MS); special education (M Ed); technical communication (MS). *Program availability:* Part-time, evening/weekend, 100% online, blended/hybrid learning. *Faculty:* 82 full-time (51 women), 853 part-time/adjunct (366 women). *Students:* 4,947 part-time (3,076 women). In 2016, 1,456 master's awarded. *Application deadline:* Applications are processed on a rolling basis. Application fee: $0. Electronic applications accepted. *Expenses:* Contact institution. *Financial support:* Applicants required to submit FAFSA. *Unit head:* Dr. Mary Loeffelholz, Interim Dean of the College of Professional Studies.
Website: http://www.cps.neu.edu/

Northern Arizona University, Graduate College, College of Education, Department of Educational Specialties, Flagstaff, AZ 86011. Offers autism spectrum disorders (Certificate); bilingual/multicultural education (M Ed), including bilingual education, ESL education; career and technical education (M Ed, Certificate); culturally and linguistically diverse special education (Certificate); early childhood special education (M Ed); educational technology (M Ed, Certificate); English as a second language (Certificate); mild/moderate disabilities (M Ed); positive behavior support (Certificate); special education (M Ed). *Degree requirements:* For master's, comprehensive exam (for some programs), thesis (for some programs). *Entrance requirements:* For master's, minimum GPA of 3.0. Additional exam requirements/recommendations for international students: Required—TOEFL (minimum score 550 paper-based; 80 iBT), IELTS (minimum score 7). Electronic applications accepted. *Expenses:* Tuition, state resident: full-time $8971; part-time $444 per credit hour. Tuition, nonresident: full-time $20,958; part-time $1164 per credit hour. *Required fees:* $1018; $644 per credit hour. Tuition and fees vary according to course load, campus/location and program.

Northern Illinois University, Graduate School, College of Education, Department of Special and Early Education, De Kalb, IL 60115-2854. Offers curriculum and instruction (MS Ed, Ed D), including curriculum leadership (Ed D), elementary education (Ed D), secondary education (Ed D); early childhood education (MS Ed); elementary education (MS Ed); special education (MS Ed). *Program availability:* Part-time, evening/weekend. *Faculty:* 22 full-time (14 women), 2 part-time/adjunct (both women). *Students:* 42 full-time (34 women), 85 part-time (68 women); includes 16 minority (4 Black or African American, non-Hispanic/Latino; 3 Asian, non-Hispanic/Latino; 6 Hispanic/Latino; 3 Two or more races, non-Hispanic/Latino), 6 international. Average age 33. 70 applicants, 73% accepted, 30 enrolled. In 2016, 19 master's, 1 doctorate awarded. *Degree requirements:* For master's, comprehensive exam, thesis optional; for doctorate, thesis/dissertation, candidacy exam, dissertation defense. *Entrance requirements:* For master's, GRE General Test or MAT, minimum undergraduate GPA of 2.75; for doctorate, GRE General Test or MAT, minimum undergraduate GPA of 2.75, graduate 3.2. Additional exam requirements/recommendations for international students: Required—TOEFL (minimum score 550 paper-based). *Application deadline:* For fall admission, 6/1 for domestic students, 5/1 for international students; for spring admission, 11/1 for domestic students, 10/1 for international students. Applications are processed on a rolling basis. Application fee: $40. Electronic applications accepted. *Financial support:* In 2016–17, 14 research assistantships with full tuition reimbursements were awarded; fellowships with full tuition reimbursements, teaching assistantships with full tuition reimbursements, career-related internships or fieldwork, Federal Work-Study, scholarships/grants, tuition waivers (full), and unspecified assistantships also available. Support available to part-time students. Financial award applicants required to submit FAFSA. *Faculty research:* Teacher certification, stress reduction during student teaching, teaching history, portfolios in student teaching. *Unit head:* Gregory Conderman, Chair, 815-753-1619, E-mail: seed@niu.edu. *Application contact:* Gail Myers, Clerk, Graduate Advising, 815-753-0381, E-mail: gmyers@niu.edu.
Website: http://www.cedu.niu.edu/seed/

Northern Kentucky University, Office of Graduate Programs, College of Education and Human Services, Program in Teaching, Highland Heights, KY 41099. Offers education (Certificate); special education (Certificate); teaching (MAT). *Degree requirements:* For master's, comprehensive exam, thesis optional. *Entrance requirements:* For master's, GRE. Additional exam requirements/recommendations for international students: Required—TOEFL (minimum score 79 iBT); Recommended—IELTS (minimum score 6.5). Electronic applications accepted. *Faculty research:* Teacher education, classroom management.

Northern Michigan University, Office of Graduate Education and Research, College of Health Sciences and Professional Studies, School of Education, Leadership and Public Service, Marquette, MI 49855-5301. Offers administration and supervision (MAE); elementary education (MAE); higher education in student affairs (MA); instruction (MAE); learning disabilities (MAE); public administration (MPA), including criminal justice administration, human resource administration, public administration, public management, state and local government; reading education (MAE), including reading, reading specialist; science education (MS); secondary education (MAE). *Accreditation:* TEAC. *Program availability:* Part-time, online learning. *Degree requirements:* For master's, thesis (for some programs). *Entrance requirements:* For master's, minimum GPA of 3.0. Additional exam requirements/recommendations for international students: Required—TOEFL (minimum score 550 paper-based; 79 iBT), IELTS (minimum score 6.5). Electronic applications accepted.

Northwestern State University of Louisiana, Graduate Studies and Research, College of Education and Human Development, Program in Special Education, Natchitoches, LA 71497. Offers M Ed, MAT. *Degree requirements:* For master's, comprehensive exam, thesis (for some programs). *Entrance requirements:* For master's, GRE General Test. Additional exam requirements/recommendations for international students: Required—TOEFL. Electronic applications accepted.

Northwestern State University of Louisiana, Graduate Studies and Research, College of Education and Human Development, Programs in Educational Leadership and Instruction, Natchitoches, LA 71497. Offers counseling (Ed S); educational leadership (M Ed, Ed S); educational technology (Ed S); elementary teaching (Ed S); reading (Ed S); secondary teaching (Ed S); special education (Ed S). *Accreditation:* NASAD. *Degree requirements:* For master's, comprehensive exam, thesis (for some programs). *Entrance requirements:* For master's and Ed S, GRE General Test. Additional exam requirements/recommendations for international students: Required—TOEFL. Electronic applications accepted.

Northwest Missouri State University, Graduate School, School of Education, Maryville, MO 64468-6001. Offers early childhood education (MS Ed); education leadership (MS Ed), including elementary, K-12, secondary; educational leadership (Ed S), including elementary school principalship, secondary school principalship, superintendency; educational leadership and policy analysis (Ed D); elementary education (MS Ed); elementary mathematics (MS Ed); higher education leadership (MS); middle school education (MS Ed); reading (MS Ed); special education (MS Ed); teacher leadership (MS Ed); teaching English language learners (MS Ed). *Accreditation:* NCATE. *Program availability:* Part-time. *Students:* 15 full-time (11 women), 150 part-time (103 women). In 2016, 46 master's awarded. *Degree requirements:* For master's, comprehensive exam; for Ed S, comprehensive exam, thesis. *Entrance requirements:* For master's, GRE General Test, writing sample; for Ed S, minimum graduate GPA of 3.25. Additional exam requirements/recommendations for international students: Required—TOEFL (minimum score 550 paper-based). *Application deadline:* For fall admission, 7/1 for domestic and international students; for spring admission, 11/15 for domestic and international students. Applications are processed on a rolling basis. Application fee: $0 ($50 for international students). Electronic applications accepted. *Expenses:* Tuition, state resident: full-time $3447; part-time $383 per credit hour. Tuition, nonresident: full-time $5724; part-time $636 per credit hour. *Required fees:* $130 per credit hour. *Financial support:* Research assistantships with full tuition reimbursements, teaching assistantships with full tuition reimbursements, and unspecified assistantships available. Financial award application deadline: 4/1; financial award applicants required to submit FAFSA. *Faculty research:* Great books of educational administration. *Unit head:* Dr. Tim Wall, Dean, 660-562-1179, E-mail: timwall@nwmissouri.edu.
Website: http://www.nwmissouri.edu/academics/ed/

Northwest Nazarene University, Graduate Education Program, Nampa, ID 83686-5897. Offers curriculum and instruction (M Ed); educational leadership (M Ed, Ed D, PhD, Ed S), including building administrator (M Ed, Ed S), director of special education (Ed S), leadership and organizational development (Ed S), superintendent (Ed S). *Accreditation:* ACA (one or more programs are accredited); NCATE. *Program availability:* Part-time, online only, 100% online, 2-week face-to-face residency (for doctoral programs). *Faculty:* 4 full-time (3 women), 17 part-time/adjunct (6 women). *Students:* 112 full-time (72 women), 73 part-time (36 women); includes 19 minority (3 Black or African American, non-Hispanic/Latino; 2 Asian, non-Hispanic/Latino; 6 Hispanic/Latino; 1 Native Hawaiian or other Pacific Islander, non-Hispanic/Latino; 7 Two or more races, non-Hispanic/Latino), 5 international. Average age 39. 96 applicants, 72% accepted, 67 enrolled. In 2016, 59 master's, 13 doctorates, 33 other advanced degrees awarded. *Degree requirements:* For master's, comprehensive exam (for some programs), action research project; for doctorate, thesis/dissertation; for Ed S, comprehensive exam, research project. *Entrance requirements:* For master's, minimum undergraduate GPA of 3.0 overall or during final 30 semester credits, undergraduate degree, valid teaching certificate; for doctorate, Ed S or equivalent, minimum GPA of 3.5; for Ed S, undergraduate degree, valid teaching certificate. Additional exam requirements/recommendations for international students: Recommended—TOEFL. *Application deadline:* Applications are processed on a rolling basis. Application fee: $50. Electronic applications accepted. *Expenses:* Contact institution. *Financial support:* In 2016–17, research assistantships (averaging $5,000 per year) were awarded. Financial award application deadline: 1/15; financial award applicants required to submit FAFSA. *Faculty research:* Action research, cooperative learning, accountability, institutional accreditation. *Unit head:* Dr. Heidi Curtis, Chair, 208-467-8250, E-mail: hlcurtis@nnu.edu. *Application contact:* Charlene Brown, Admissions Counselor, 208-467-8492,

Fax: 208-467-8384, E-mail: gradeducationinfo@nnu.edu.
Website: http://www.nnu.edu/graded/

Notre Dame College, Graduate Programs, South Euclid, OH 44121-4293. Offers mild/moderate needs (M Ed); reading (M Ed); security policy studies (MA, Graduate Certificate); technology (M Ed). *Program availability:* Part-time, evening/weekend. *Degree requirements:* For master's, thesis. *Entrance requirements:* For master's, GRE General Test, MAT, minimum undergraduate GPA of 2.75, valid teaching certificate, bachelor's degree in an education-related field from accredited college or university, official transcripts of most recent college work. *Faculty research:* Cognitive psychology, teaching critical thinking in the classroom.

Notre Dame de Namur University, Division of Academic Affairs, School of Education and Leadership, Program in Special Education, Belmont, CA 94002-1908. Offers MA. *Program availability:* Part-time, evening/weekend. *Degree requirements:* For master's, thesis optional, capstone course. *Entrance requirements:* For master's, interview, minimum GPA of 2.5. Additional exam requirements/recommendations for international students: Required—TOEFL (minimum score 550 paper-based; 79 iBT). Electronic applications accepted.

Nyack College, School of Education, Nyack, NY 10960. Offers childhood education (MS); childhood special education (MS); inclusive education (MA); TESOL (MAT, MS). *Program availability:* Part-time, 100% online, blended/hybrid learning. *Students:* 21 full-time (20 women), 36 part-time (31 women); includes 34 minority (7 Black or African American, non-Hispanic/Latino; 3 Asian, non-Hispanic/Latino; 22 Hispanic/Latino; 1 Native Hawaiian or other Pacific Islander, non-Hispanic/Latino; 1 Two or more races, non-Hispanic/Latino), 5 international. Average age 33. In 2016, 23 master's awarded. *Degree requirements:* For master's, comprehensive exam, clinical experience. *Entrance requirements:* For master's, GRE, transcripts, autobiography and statement on reasons for pursuing graduate study in education, recommendations, 6 credits of language, evidence of computer literacy, introductory course in psychology. Additional exam requirements/recommendations for international students: Required—TOEFL (minimum score 550 paper-based; 80 iBT), GRE. *Application deadline:* For fall admission, 8/4 for domestic students, 7/4 for international students; for spring admission, 12/15 for domestic students, 11/15 for international students; for summer admission, 4/7 for domestic students, 3/7 for international students. Applications are processed on a rolling basis. Application fee: $30. Electronic applications accepted. *Expenses:* $700 per credit. *Financial support:* Scholarships/grants available. Financial award applicants required to submit FAFSA. *Unit head:* Dr. JoAnn Looney, Dean, 845-675-4538, Fax: 845-358-0874. *Application contact:* Joseph Kim, Admissions Associate, 845-675-4400 Ext. 5708, Fax: 845-348-3912, E-mail: admissions.grad@nyack.edu.
Website: http://www.nyack.edu/edu

Oakland University, Graduate Study and Lifelong Learning, School of Education and Human Services, Department of Human Development and Child Studies, Program in Special Education, Rochester, MI 48309-4401. Offers applied behavior analysis (Graduate Certificate); autism spectrum disorder (Graduate Certificate); emotional impairment (Graduate Certificate); special education (M Ed), including applied behavior analysis, autism spectrum disorder, emotional impairment, specific learning disabilities; specific learning disabilities (Graduate Certificate). *Accreditation:* TEAC. *Entrance requirements:* For master's, minimum GPA of 3.0, interview. Additional exam requirements/recommendations for international students: Required—TOEFL (minimum score 550 paper-based). Electronic applications accepted.

The Ohio State University, Graduate School, College of Arts and Sciences, Division of Social and Behavioral Sciences, Department of Psychology, Columbus, OH 43210. Offers behavioral neuroscience (PhD); clinical psychology (PhD); cognitive psychology (PhD); developmental psychology (PhD); intellectual and developmental disabilities psychology (PhD); quantitative psychology (PhD); social psychology (PhD). *Accreditation:* APA. *Faculty:* 57. *Students:* 156 full-time (95 women); includes 23 minority (6 Black or African American, non-Hispanic/Latino; 9 Asian, non-Hispanic/Latino; 8 Hispanic/Latino), 26 international. Average age 26. In 2016, 26 doctorates awarded. *Degree requirements:* For doctorate, thesis/dissertation. *Entrance requirements:* For doctorate, GRE General Test. Additional exam requirements/recommendations for international students: Required—TOEFL (minimum score 600 paper-based; 100 iBT); Recommended—IELTS (minimum score 8). *Application deadline:* For fall admission, 12/1 for domestic and international students. Applications are processed on a rolling basis. Application fee: $60 ($70 for international students). Electronic applications accepted. *Financial support:* Fellowships with tuition reimbursements, research assistantships with tuition reimbursements, and teaching assistantships with tuition reimbursements available. *Unit head:* Dr. John Bruno, Chair, 614-292-3038, E-mail: bruno.1@osu.edu. *Application contact:* Graduate and Professional Admissions, 614-292-9444, Fax: 614-292-3895, E-mail: gpadmissions@osu.edu.
Website: http://www.psy.ohio-state.edu/

Ohio University, Graduate College, Gladys W. and David H. Patton College of Education and Human Services, Department of Teacher Education, Athens, OH 45701-2979. Offers adolescent to young adult education (M Ed); curriculum and instruction (M Ed, PhD); early childhood/special education (M Ed); intervention specialist/mild-moderate needs (M Ed); intervention specialist/moderate-intensive needs (M Ed); middle childhood education (M Ed); reading education (M Ed). *Program availability:* Part-time, evening/weekend. *Degree requirements:* For master's, thesis or alternative; for doctorate, comprehensive exam, thesis/dissertation. *Entrance requirements:* For master's, GRE General Test or MAT (if GPA is below 2.9); for doctorate, GRE General Test, minimum GPA of 3.4, work experience. Additional exam requirements/recommendations for international students: Required—TOEFL (minimum score 550 paper-based; 80 iBT) or IELTS (minimum score 6.5). *Application deadline:* For fall admission, 5/1 priority date for domestic students, 4/1 priority date for international students; for winter admission, 11/1 priority date for domestic students, 10/1 priority date for international students; for spring admission, 2/15 priority date for domestic students, 1/1 priority date for international students. Applications are processed on a rolling basis. Application fee: $50 ($55 for international students). Electronic applications accepted. *Financial support:* Research assistantships with full tuition reimbursements, teaching assistantships with full tuition reimbursements, Federal Work-Study, institutionally sponsored loans, tuition waivers (partial), and unspecified assistantships available. Financial award application deadline: 3/1. *Faculty research:* Cognition literacy, character education, teacher's education reform, disabilities. *Unit head:* Dr. John Henning, Chair, 740-597-1830, Fax: 740-593-0477, E-mail: henningj@ohio.edu. *Application contact:* Floyd J. Doney, Director of Student Affairs, 740-593-4400, Fax: 740-593-9310, E-mail: doney@ohio.edu.
Website: http://www.cehs.ohio.edu/academics/te/index.htm

Old Dominion University, Darden College of Education, Program in Special Education, Norfolk, VA 23529. Offers adapted curriculum K-12 (MS Ed); early childhood special education (MS Ed); general curriculum K-12 (MS Ed); special education (PhD). *Accreditation:* NCATE. *Program availability:* Part-time, evening/weekend, 100% online, blended/hybrid learning. *Faculty:* 12 full-time (9 women), 13 part-time/adjunct (9 women). *Students:* 42 full-time (38 women), 65 part-time (56 women); includes 25 minority (18 Black or African American, non-Hispanic/Latino; 3 Asian, non-Hispanic/Latino; 1 Hispanic/Latino; 3 Two or more races, non-Hispanic/Latino), 7 international. Average age 34. 78 applicants, 85% accepted, 61 enrolled. In 2016, 24 master's awarded. *Degree requirements:* For master's, comprehensive exam, thesis or alternative; for doctorate, comprehensive exam, thesis/dissertation. *Entrance requirements:* For master's, GRE General Test or MAT, PRAXIS Core Academic Skills for Educator Tests, minimum GPA of 2.8; for doctorate, GRE. Additional exam requirements/recommendations for international students: Recommended—TOEFL (minimum score 550 paper-based). *Application deadline:* For fall admission, 6/1 priority date for domestic and international students; for winter admission, 11/1 priority date for domestic and international students; for spring admission, 3/1 priority date for domestic and international students. Applications are processed on a rolling basis. Application fee: $50. Electronic applications accepted. *Expenses:* Contact institution. *Financial support:* In 2016–17, 70 students received support, including 1 teaching assistantship with full tuition reimbursement available (averaging $15,000 per year); fellowships, research assistantships with tuition reimbursements available, scholarships/grants, and unspecified assistantships also available. Support available to part-time students. Financial award application deadline: 2/15; financial award applicants required to submit FAFSA. *Faculty research:* Inclusion, autism spectrum disorder, functional behavioral assessment, infant, preschool, and school-age children and youth with disabilities, distance learning. *Total annual research expenditures:* $3.6 million. *Unit head:* Dr. Sabra Gear, Graduate Program Director, 757-683-4383, Fax: 757-683-4129, E-mail: sgear@odu.edu. *Application contact:* William Heffelfinger, Director of Graduate Admissions, 757-683-5554, Fax: 757-683-3255, E-mail: gradadmit@odu.edu.
Website: https://www.odu.edu/cdse/academics/sped

Ottawa University, Graduate Studies-Arizona, Program in Education, Ottawa, KS 66067-3399. Offers community college counseling (MA); curriculum and instruction (MA); early childhood (MA); education intervention (MA); education leadership (MA); education technology (MA); Montessori early childhood education (MA); Montessori elementary education (MA); professional development (MA); school guidance counseling (MA); special education - cross categorical (MA). Programs offered in Mesa, Phoenix, Tempe and West Valley, AZ. *Accreditation:* NCATE. *Program availability:* Part-time. *Degree requirements:* For master's, thesis or alternative. *Entrance requirements:* For master's, minimum undergraduate GPA of 3.0, copy of current state certification or teaching license. Additional exam requirements/recommendations for international students: Required—TOEFL (minimum score 550 paper-based). Electronic applications accepted. *Expenses:* Contact institution.

Pace University, School of Education, New York, NY 10038. Offers adolescent education (MST), including biology, business education, chemistry, earth science, English, foreign languages, mathematics, physics, social studies, visual arts; childhood education (MST); early childhood development, learning and intervention (MST); educational technology studies (MS); inclusive adolescent education (MST), including biology, business education, chemistry, earth science, English, foreign languages, mathematics, physics, social studies, visual arts; integrated instruction for educational technology (Certificate); integrated instruction for literacy and technology (Certificate); literacy (MS Ed); special education (MS Ed). *Accreditation:* NCATE. *Program availability:* Part-time, evening/weekend, blended/hybrid learning. *Faculty:* 19 full-time (13 women), 86 part-time/adjunct (49 women). *Students:* 115 full-time (97 women), 543 part-time (381 women); includes 280 minority (137 Black or African American, non-Hispanic/Latino; 1 American Indian or Alaska Native, non-Hispanic/Latino; 40 Asian, non-Hispanic/Latino; 87 Hispanic/Latino; 15 Two or more races, non-Hispanic/Latino), 13 international. Average age 30. 181 applicants, 78% accepted, 72 enrolled. In 2016, 193 master's, 9 other advanced degrees awarded. *Degree requirements:* For master's, certification exams. *Entrance requirements:* For master's, GRE, interview, teaching certificate (except for MST). Additional exam requirements/recommendations for international students: Required—TOEFL (minimum score 88 iBT), IELTS or PTE. *Application deadline:* For fall admission, 8/1 priority date for domestic students, 6/1 for international students; for spring admission, 12/1 priority date for domestic students, 10/1 for international students. Applications are processed on a rolling basis. Application fee: $70. Electronic applications accepted. *Expenses:* Contact institution. *Financial support:* In 2016–17, 17 students received support, including 17 research assistantships with partial tuition reimbursements available (averaging $6,020 per year); career-related internships or fieldwork and Federal Work-Study also available. Financial award application deadline: 9/1; financial award applicants required to submit FAFSA. *Faculty research:* STEM education, TESOL, teacher education, special education, language and literary development. *Total annual research expenditures:* $290,153. *Unit head:* Dr. Xiao-Lei Wang, Dean, School of Education, 914-773-3876, E-mail: xwang@pace.edu. *Application contact:* Susan Ford-Goldschein, Director of Graduate Admissions, 212-346-1531, Fax: 212-346-1585, E-mail: graduateadmission@pace.edu.
Website: http://www.pace.edu/school-of-education

Pacific Oaks College, Graduate School, Program in Education, Pasadena, CA 91103. Offers preliminary education specialist (MA); preliminary multiple subject (MA). *Program availability:* Online learning. *Degree requirements:* For master's, practicum. *Entrance requirements:* For master's, bachelor's degree from accredited college or university.

Pacific University, College of Education, Forest Grove, OR 97116-1797. Offers early childhood education (MAT); education (MAE); elementary education (MAT); ESOL (MAT); high school education (MAT); middle school education (MAT); special education (MAT); speech-language pathology (MS); STEM education (MAT); talented and gifted (M Ed); visual function in learning (M Ed). *Accreditation:* NCATE. *Program availability:* Part-time, evening/weekend. *Degree requirements:* For master's, research project. *Entrance requirements:* For master's, California Basic Educational Skills Test, PRAXIS II, minimum undergraduate GPA of 2.75, 3.0 graduate. Additional exam requirements/recommendations for international students: Required—TOEFL. Electronic applications accepted. *Expenses:* Contact institution. *Faculty research:* Defining a culturally competent classroom, technology in the k-12 classroom, Socratic seminars, social studies education.

Penn State University Park, Graduate School, College of Education, Department of Educational Psychology, Counseling, and Special Education, University Park, PA 16802. Offers counselor education (M Ed, D Ed, PhD, Certificate); educational psychology (MS, PhD, Certificate); school psychology (M Ed, MS, PhD, Certificate); special education (M Ed, MS, PhD, Certificate). *Unit head:* Dr. David H. Monk, Dean, 814-865-2523, Fax: 814-865-0555. *Application contact:* Lori Hawn, Director, Graduate Student Services, 814-865-1795, Fax: 814-863-4627, E-mail: l-gswww@lists.psu.edu.
Website: http://ed.psu.edu/epcse

Piedmont College, School of Education, Demorest, GA 30535. Offers art education (MAT); curriculum and instruction (Ed S); early childhood education (MA, MAT); instructional technology (MAT); middle grades education (MA, MAT); music education (MAT); secondary education (MA, MAT); special education (MA, MAT). *Program availability:* Part-time, evening/weekend. *Students:* 290 full-time (217 women), 614 part-time (508 women); includes 131 minority (97 Black or African American, non-Hispanic/Latino; 4 American Indian or Alaska Native, non-Hispanic/Latino; 5 Asian, non-Hispanic/Latino; 11 Hispanic/Latino; 6 Native Hawaiian or other Pacific Islander, non-Hispanic/Latino; 8 Two or more races, non-Hispanic/Latino), 6 international. Average age 37. 257 applicants, 64% accepted, 160 enrolled. In 2016, 288 master's, 243 other advanced degrees awarded. *Degree requirements:* For master's, thesis, field experience in the classroom teaching. *Entrance requirements:* For master's, GRE General Test, MAT, minimum undergraduate GPA of 2.5; for Ed S, minimum graduate GPA of 3.5, valid teaching certificate. Additional exam requirements/recommendations for international students: Required—TOEFL (minimum score 550 paper-based). *Application deadline:* For fall admission, 7/15 for domestic students; for spring admission, 12/1 for domestic students. Applications are processed on a rolling basis. Electronic applications accepted. *Expenses: Tuition:* Full-time $8910. *Financial support:* Career-related internships or fieldwork, Federal Work-Study, and unspecified assistantships available. Support available to part-time students. Financial award applicants required to submit FAFSA. *Unit head:* Dr. Don Gnecco, Dean, 706-778-3000 Ext. 1201, Fax: 706-776-9608, E-mail: dgnecco@piedmont.edu. *Application contact:* Kathleen Anderson, Director of Graduate Enrollment Management, 706-778-8500 Ext. 1181, Fax: 706-778-0150, E-mail: kanderson@piedmont.edu.

Pittsburg State University, Graduate School, College of Education, Department of Teaching and Leadership, Advanced Studies in Leadership Program, Pittsburg, KS 66762. Offers advanced studies in leadership (Ed S), including general school administration, special education. *Program availability:* Part-time, online only, 100% online. *Students:* 16. In 2016, 11 Ed Ss awarded. *Degree requirements:* For Ed S, thesis optional. *Entrance requirements:* Additional exam requirements/recommendations for international students: Required—TOEFL (minimum score 520 paper-based; 68 iBT), IELTS (minimum score 6), PTE (minimum score 47). *Application deadline:* For fall admission, 6/1 for international students; for spring admission, 10/15 for international students; for summer admission, 4/1 for international students. Applications are processed on a rolling basis. Application fee: $35 ($65 for international students). Electronic applications accepted. *Expenses:* Contact institution. *Financial support:* Application deadline: 2/1; applicants required to submit FAFSA. *Unit head:* Dr. Brenda Roberts, Program Coordinator, 620-235-4498, Fax: 620-235-4520, E-mail: broberts@pittstate.edu. *Application contact:* Lisa Allen, Assistant Director of Graduate and Continuing Studies, 620-235-4218, Fax: 620-235-4219, E-mail: lallen@pittstate.edu.

Pittsburg State University, Graduate School, College of Education, Department of Teaching and Leadership, Program in Special Education, Pittsburg, KS 66762. Offers MAT, MS. *Accreditation:* NCATE. *Program availability:* Part-time, online only, 100% online. *Students:* 102. In 2016, 32 master's awarded. Terminal master's awarded for partial completion of doctoral program. *Degree requirements:* For master's, thesis or alternative. *Entrance requirements:* For master's, PPST. Additional exam requirements/recommendations for international students: Required—TOEFL (minimum score 520 paper-based; 68 iBT), IELTS (minimum score 6), PTE (minimum score 47). *Application deadline:* For fall admission, 7/15 for domestic students, 6/1 for international students; for spring admission, 12/15 for domestic students, 10/15 for international students; for summer admission, 5/15 for domestic students, 4/1 for international students. Applications are processed on a rolling basis. Application fee: $35 ($60 for international students). Electronic applications accepted. *Expenses:* Contact institution. *Financial support:* In 2016–17, teaching assistantships (averaging $5,000 per year) were awarded; career-related internships or fieldwork, Federal Work-Study, and unspecified assistantships also available. Financial award application deadline: 2/1; financial award applicants required to submit FAFSA. *Unit head:* Dr. Brian Sims, Program Coordinator, 620-235-6090, Fax: 620-235-4498, E-mail: bsims@pittstate.edu. *Application contact:* Lisa Allen, Assistant Director of Graduate and Continuing Studies, 620-235-4218, Fax: 620-235-4219, E-mail: lallen@pittstate.edu.

Plymouth State University, College of Graduate Studies, Graduate Studies in Education, Program in Secondary Education, Plymouth, NH 03264-1595. Offers curriculum and instruction (M Ed); language education (M Ed); library media (M Ed); physical education (M Ed); social studies education (M Ed); special education (M Ed). *Program availability:* Part-time, evening/weekend. *Entrance requirements:* For master's, MAT.

Point Loma Nazarene University, School of Education, Program in Special Education, San Diego, CA 92106-2899. Offers MA. *Program availability:* Part-time, evening/weekend. *Students:* 13 full-time (10 women), 45 part-time (39 women); includes 21 minority (3 Asian, non-Hispanic/Latino; 14 Hispanic/Latino; 1 Native Hawaiian or other Pacific Islander, non-Hispanic/Latino; 3 Two or more races, non-Hispanic/Latino). Average age 35. 11 applicants, 82% accepted, 7 enrolled. In 2016, 21 master's awarded. *Entrance requirements:* For master's, letters of recommendation, essay, interview. Additional exam requirements/recommendations for international students: Required—TOEFL. *Application deadline:* For fall admission, 8/4 priority date for domestic students; for spring admission, 12/8 priority date for domestic students; for summer admission, 4/13 priority date for domestic students. Applications are processed on a rolling basis. Application fee: $50. Electronic applications accepted. *Expenses:* $610 per credit (for San Diego campus), $595 per credit (for Bakersfield campus). *Financial support:* Career-related internships or fieldwork and scholarships/grants available. Support available to part-time students. Financial award applicants required to submit FAFSA. *Faculty research:* Co-teaching, inclusion, teacher preparation, intern teacher support. *Unit head:* Dr. Shirlee Gibbs, Special Education Coordinator, 619-849-2852, E-mail: shirleegibbs@pointloma.edu. *Application contact:* Claire Buckley, Director of Graduate Admission, 866-692-4723, E-mail: gradinfo@pointloma.edu.
Website: http://gps.pointloma.edu/education

Point Park University, School of Arts and Sciences, Department of Education, Pittsburgh, PA 15222-1984. Offers curriculum and instruction (MA); educational administration (MA); special education (M Ed); teaching and leadership (M Ed). *Program availability:* Part-time, evening/weekend. *Degree requirements:* For master's, comprehensive exam (for some programs), thesis or alternative. *Entrance requirements:* For master's, minimum GPA of 3.0, resume, 2 letters of recommendation. Additional exam requirements/recommendations for international students: Required—TOEFL. Electronic applications accepted.

Prescott College, Graduate Programs, Program in Education, Prescott, AZ 86301. Offers early childhood education (MA); early childhood special education (MA); education (MA); elementary education (MA); environmental education leadership and administration (MA); equine-assisted learning (MA); school guidance counseling (MA); secondary education (MA); special education: learning disabilities (MA); special education: mental retardation (MA); special education: serious emotional disabilities (MA); student-directed independent study (MA); sustainability education (PhD). *Program availability:* Part-time, online learning. *Faculty:* 3 full-time (all women). *Students:* 9 full-time (8 women), 30 part-time (20 women); includes 11 minority (3 Black or African American, non-Hispanic/Latino; 2 American Indian or Alaska Native, non-Hispanic/Latino; 6 Hispanic/Latino). Average age 36. 66 applicants, 82% accepted, 32 enrolled. In 2016, 12 master's, 8 doctorates awarded. *Degree requirements:* For master's, thesis, fieldwork or internship, practicum; for doctorate, thesis/dissertation. *Entrance requirements:* For master's, 2 letters of recommendation, resume; for doctorate, 3 letters of recommendation, resume, official transcripts, personal statement, program proposal. Additional exam requirements/recommendations for international students: Required—TOEFL (minimum score 500 paper-based). *Application deadline:* For fall admission, 4/15 priority date for domestic and international students; for spring admission, 9/15 priority date for domestic and international students. Applications are processed on a rolling basis. Application fee: $40. Electronic applications accepted. *Expenses: Tuition:* Full-time $19,680. One-time fee: $260 part-time. *Financial support:* Fellowships, research assistantships, teaching assistantships, career-related internships or fieldwork, Federal Work-Study, institutionally sponsored loans, scholarships/grants, traineeships, health care benefits, tuition waivers, and unspecified assistantships available. Support available to part-time students. Financial award applicants required to submit FAFSA. *Unit head:* Bob Ellis, 928-350-2217, E-mail: bellis@prescott.edu. *Application contact:* Melanie Lefever, Assistant Director, Limited-residency Programs, 928-350-2106, Fax: 928-776-5242, E-mail: mlefever@prescott.edu.

Providence College, Program in Special Education, Providence, RI 02918. Offers special education (M Ed), including elementary teaching, secondary teaching. *Program availability:* Part-time, evening/weekend. *Faculty:* 6 full-time (4 women), 33 part-time/adjunct (21 women). *Students:* 3 full-time (2 women), 25 part-time (22 women); includes 2 minority (1 Asian, non-Hispanic/Latino; 1 Hispanic/Latino). Average age 28. 13 applicants, 100% accepted, 12 enrolled. In 2016, 14 master's awarded. *Degree requirements:* For master's, comprehensive exam, portfolio. *Entrance requirements:* Additional exam requirements/recommendations for international students: Required—TOEFL (minimum score 577 paper-based; 90 iBT). *Application deadline:* For fall admission, 7/15 priority date for domestic and international students; for spring admission, 11/15 priority date for domestic and international students; for summer admission, 3/15 priority date for domestic students, 3/15 for international students. Application fee: $55. *Expenses: Tuition:* Part-time $1260 per course. One-time fee: $265. Tuition and fees vary according to course load and program. *Financial support:* Career-related internships or fieldwork, institutionally sponsored loans, and unspecified assistantships available. Support available to part-time students. Financial award application deadline: 8/1; financial award applicants required to submit FAFSA.
Website: http://www.providence.edu/professional-studies/graduate-degrees

Purdue University, Graduate School, College of Education, Department of Educational Studies, West Lafayette, IN 47907. Offers administration (MS Ed, PhD, Ed S); counseling and development (MS Ed, PhD); education of the gifted (MS Ed); educational psychology (MS Ed, PhD); foundations of education (MS Ed, PhD); higher education administration (MS Ed, PhD); special education (MS Ed, PhD). *Accreditation:* ACA (one or more programs are accredited); NCATE (one or more programs are accredited). *Program availability:* Part-time, evening/weekend. *Faculty:* 29 full-time (22 women), 1 part-time/adjunct (0 women). *Students:* 78 full-time (60 women), 226 part-time (162 women); includes 45 minority (16 Black or African American, non-Hispanic/Latino; 8 Asian, non-Hispanic/Latino; 15 Hispanic/Latino; 6 Two or more races, non-Hispanic/Latino), 45 international. Average age 32. 214 applicants, 53% accepted, 70 enrolled. In 2016, 38 master's, 20 doctorates, 4 other advanced degrees awarded. *Degree requirements:* For master's, thesis optional; for doctorate, thesis/dissertation, oral and written exams; for Ed S, oral presentation, project. *Entrance requirements:* For master's, GRE General Test (except for special education if undergraduate GPA is higher than a 3.0), minimum undergraduate GPA of 3.0; for doctorate and Ed S, GRE General Test (minimum combined score of 1000, 300 for new scoring), minimum undergraduate GPA of 3.0. Additional exam requirements/recommendations for international students: Required—TOEFL (minimum score 550 paper-based; 77 iBT), TWE (minimum score 5). *Application deadline:* Applications are processed on a rolling basis. Application fee: $60 ($75 for international students). Electronic applications accepted. *Financial support:* Fellowships with full tuition reimbursements, research assistantships with full tuition reimbursements, teaching assistantships with full tuition reimbursements, career-related internships or fieldwork, and tuition waivers (full) available. Support available to part-time students. Financial award application deadline: 3/1; financial award applicants required to submit FAFSA. *Faculty research:* Motivation, learning disabilities, school learning, group processes, cognitive development. *Unit head:* F. Richard Olenchak, Head, 765-494-9170, E-mail: olenchak@purdue.edu. *Application contact:* Heather Brinkman, Graduate Contact, 765-494-2345, Fax: 765-494-5832, E-mail: hbrinkma@purdue.edu.
Website: http://www.edst.purdue.edu/

Purdue University Northwest, Graduate Studies Office, School of Education, Program in Special Education, Hammond, IN 46323-2094. Offers MS Ed.

Queens College of the City University of New York, Division of Education, Department of Educational and Community Programs, Queens, NY 11367-1597. Offers bilingual pupil personnel (AC); counselor education (MS Ed); mental health counseling (MS); school building leader (AC); school district leader (AC); school psychologist (MS Ed); special education-childhood education (AC); special education-early childhood (MS Ed); teacher of special education 1-6 (MS Ed); teacher of special education birth-2 (MS Ed); teaching students with disabilities, grades 7-12 (MS Ed, AC). *Program availability:* Part-time. *Faculty:* 20 full-time (14 women), 50 part-time/adjunct (26 women). *Students:* 101 full-time (85 women), 459 part-time (383 women); includes 230 minority (44 Black or African American, non-Hispanic/Latino; 3 American Indian or Alaska Native, non-Hispanic/Latino; 46 Asian, non-Hispanic/Latino; 128 Hispanic/Latino; 1 Native Hawaiian or other Pacific Islander, non-Hispanic/Latino; 8 Two or more races, non-Hispanic/Latino), 3 international. Average age 28. 515 applicants, 57% accepted, 230 enrolled. In 2016, 158 master's, 68 other advanced degrees awarded. *Degree requirements:* For master's, research project; for AC, internship. *Entrance requirements:* For master's, minimum GPA of 3.0. Additional exam requirements/recommendations for international students: Required—TOEFL, IELTS. *Application deadline:* For fall admission, 3/1 for domestic students. Applications are processed on a rolling basis. Application fee: $125. Electronic applications accepted. *Expenses:* Tuition, state resident: full-time $5065; part-time $425 per credit. Tuition, nonresident: part-time $780 per credit. *Required fees:* $522; $397 per credit. Part-time tuition and fees vary according to course load and program. *Financial support:* Career-related internships or fieldwork available. Financial award application deadline: 4/1; financial award applicants required to submit FAFSA. *Unit head:* Dr. Lynn Howell, Chairperson, 718-997-5250, E-mail: lynn.howell@qc.cuny.edu.

Queens College of the City University of New York, Division of Education, Department of Elementary and Early Childhood Education, Queens, NY 11367-1597. Offers bilingual education (MS Ed); child development psychology (AC); childhood education (MAT, MS Ed); childhood education and special education (MAT); childhood education-bilingual education (MAT, MS Ed, AC); children's literacy (AC); early childhood education (MAT); early childhood education birth-2 (MS Ed, AC); elementary education (MS Ed); literacy birth-grade 6 (AC); literacy technology birth-grade 6 (MS Ed); social studies education grades 1-6 (AC). *Program availability:* Part-time, evening/weekend. *Faculty:* 25 full-time (19 women), 33 part-time/adjunct (28 women). *Students:* 134 full-time (119 women), 374 part-time (349 women); includes 251 minority (55 Black or African American, non-Hispanic/Latino; 1 American Indian or Alaska Native, non-Hispanic/Latino; 82 Asian, non-Hispanic/Latino; 103 Hispanic/Latino; 10 Two or more races, non-Hispanic/Latino), 12 international. Average age 29. 364 applicants, 72% accepted, 224 enrolled. In 2016, 184 master's, 62 other advanced degrees awarded. *Degree requirements:* For master's, research project. *Entrance requirements:* For master's, minimum GPA of 3.0. Additional exam requirements/recommendations for international students: Required—TOEFL, IELTS. *Application deadline:* For fall admission, 4/1 for domestic students. Applications are processed on a rolling basis.

Application fee: $125. Electronic applications accepted. *Expenses:* Tuition, state resident: full-time $5065; part-time $425 per credit. Tuition, nonresident: part-time $780 per credit. *Required fees:* $522; $397 per credit. Part-time tuition and fees vary according to course load and program. *Financial support:* Career-related internships or fieldwork available. Financial award application deadline: 4/1; financial award applicants required to submit FAFSA. *Unit head:* Dr. Mary Bushnell Greiner, Chairperson, 718-997-5328, E-mail: mary.greiner@qc.cuny.edu.

Quincy University, Master of Science in Education Programs, Quincy, IL 62301-2699. Offers curriculum and instruction (MS Ed), including bilingual/English as a second language; leadership (MS Ed); reading education (MS Ed); special education (MS Ed); teacher leader (MS Ed). *Program availability:* Part-time, evening/weekend, online learning. *Degree requirements:* For master's, comprehensive exam (for some programs), thesis optional. *Entrance requirements:* For master's, MAT or GRE. Additional exam requirements/recommendations for international students: Required—TOEFL (minimum score 550 paper-based; 79 iBT). Electronic applications accepted. Application fee is waived when completed online.

Radford University, College of Graduate Studies and Research, Program in Special Education, Radford, VA 24142. Offers MS, Certificate. *Accreditation:* NCATE. *Program availability:* Part-time, evening/weekend. *Faculty:* 12 full-time (10 women), 4 part-time/adjunct (all women). *Students:* 36 full-time (31 women), 41 part-time (38 women); includes 8 minority (5 Black or African American, non-Hispanic/Latino; 3 Hispanic/Latino). Average age 30. 30 applicants, 97% accepted, 28 enrolled. In 2016, 39 master's awarded. *Degree requirements:* For master's, comprehensive exam. *Entrance requirements:* For master's, minimum GPA of 2.75, 3 letters of reference, resume, personal essay, official transcripts. Additional exam requirements/recommendations for international students: Required—TOEFL (minimum score 550 paper-based; 79 iBT), IELTS (minimum score 6.5). *Application deadline:* For fall admission, 2/15 for domestic students, 12/1 for international students; for spring admission, 7/1 for international students. Applications are processed on a rolling basis. Application fee: $50. Electronic applications accepted. *Expenses:* Tuition, state resident: full-time $7868; part-time $328 per credit hour. Tuition, nonresident: full-time $16,394; part-time $683 per credit hour. *Required fees:* $3090; $130 per credit hour. Tuition and fees vary according to course load and program. *Financial support:* In 2016–17, 17 students received support. Career-related internships or fieldwork, scholarships/grants, and unspecified assistantships available. Support available to part-time students. Financial award application deadline: 3/1; financial award applicants required to submit FAFSA. *Unit head:* Dr. Brenda-Jean Tyler, Coordinator, 540-831-6425, E-mail: ruspecialed@radford.edu.
Website: http://www.radford.edu/content/cehd/home/teacher-ed/programs/special-educationms.html

Ramapo College of New Jersey, Master of Arts in Special Education Program, Mahwah, NJ 07430-1680. Offers MA. *Program availability:* Part-time. *Faculty:* 1 (woman) full-time, 3 part-time/adjunct (2 women). *Students:* 39 part-time (34 women); includes 4 minority (all Hispanic/Latino). Average age 27. 35 applicants, 74% accepted, 21 enrolled. In 2016, 23 master's awarded. *Degree requirements:* For master's, thesis, field internship, applied capstone research component. *Entrance requirements:* For master's, official transcript of baccalaureate degree from accredited institution with minimum recommended GPA of 3.0; personal statement; 2 letters of recommendation; resume; state-issued teaching certificate. Additional exam requirements/recommendations for international students: Required—TOEFL (minimum score 550 paper-based; 79 iBT); Recommended—IELTS (minimum score 6). *Application deadline:* For fall admission, 5/1 for domestic and international students. Applications are processed on a rolling basis. Application fee: $60. Electronic applications accepted. *Expenses:* $606.05 per credit tuition, $130.45 per credit fees. *Financial support:* Career-related internships or fieldwork available. Financial award application deadline: 3/1; financial award applicants required to submit FAFSA. *Faculty research:* Differentiated instruction, inclusion, charter schools, technology integration in content areas, infusing literacy strategies in education. *Unit head:* Dr. Julie Norflus-Good, Director, 201-684-7246, E-mail: jgood@ramapo.edu. *Application contact:* M. Joyce Wilson, Secretarial Assistant, 201-684-7721, Fax: 201-684-6699, E-mail: jwilson@ramapo.edu.
Website: http://www.ramapo.edu/mase/

Randolph College, Programs in Education, Lynchburg, VA 24503. Offers curriculum and instruction (MAT); special education-learning disabilities (M Ed, MAT). *Accreditation:* TEAC. *Entrance requirements:* For master's, minimum GPA of 3.0 in prerequisite education coursework, 2.7 in major or field of interest (MAT); teaching license (M Ed); 2 recommendations; interview.

Regent University, Graduate School, School of Education, Virginia Beach, VA 23464-9800. Offers adult education (Ed D, PhD, Ed S); advanced educational leadership (Ed D, PhD, Ed S); career switcher (M Ed); character education (Ed D, PhD, Ed S); Christian education leadership (Ed D, PhD, Ed S); Christian school administration (M Ed); curriculum and instruction (M Ed), including adult education, Christian school, gifted and talented education, STEM education, teacher leader; educational leadership (M Ed); educational psychology (Ed D, PhD, Ed S); educational technology and online learning (Ed D, PhD, Ed S); elementary education (M Ed); exceptional education executive leadership (Ed D, PhD, Ed S); higher education (Ed D, PhD, Ed S); higher education leadership and management (Ed D, PhD, Ed S); individualized degree plan (M Ed); K-12 school leadership (Ed D, PhD, Ed S); K-12 special education (M Ed); K-8 leadership in mathematics education (M Ed); leadership in mathematics education (Ed S); reading specialist (M Ed); special education (Ed D, PhD, Ed S); student affairs (M Ed); TESOL (M Ed), including adult education - collegiate, K-12. *Accreditation:* TEAC. *Program availability:* Part-time, evening/weekend, 100% online, blended/hybrid learning. *Faculty:* 22 full-time (10 women), 42 part-time/adjunct (31 women). *Students:* 89 full-time (62 women), 1,035 part-time (823 women); includes 466 minority (381 Black or African American, non-Hispanic/Latino; 3 American Indian or Alaska Native, non-Hispanic/Latino; 19 Asian, non-Hispanic/Latino; 50 Hispanic/Latino; 13 Two or more races, non-Hispanic/Latino), 11 international. Average age 39. 976 applicants, 59% accepted, 449 enrolled. In 2016, 241 master's, 22 doctorates, 4 other advanced degrees awarded. *Degree requirements:* For master's, thesis or alternative; for doctorate, comprehensive exam, thesis/dissertation. *Entrance requirements:* For master's, Virginia Communication and Literacy Assessment (VCLA), PRAXIS, college transcripts, writing sample, interview; for doctorate, GRE, writing sample, resume, transcripts, interview. Additional exam requirements/recommendations for international students: Required—TOEFL (minimum score 577 paper-based). *Application deadline:* For fall admission, 4/1 priority date for domestic students; for spring admission, 10/15 priority date for domestic students. Applications are processed on a rolling basis. Application fee: $50. Electronic applications accepted. *Expenses:* Contact institution. *Financial support:* In 2016–17, 622 students received support, including 1 fellowship (averaging $5,000 per year); career-related internships or fieldwork, scholarships/grants, and unspecified assistantships also available. Support available to part-time students. *Faculty research:* Christian school administration, curriculum and instruction, educational technology and online learning, higher education, special education. *Unit head:* Dr. Donald Finn, Dean, 757-352-4278, Fax: 757-352-4318, E-mail: dfinn@regent.edu. *Application contact:* Heidi Cece, Assistant Vice President of Enrollment Management, 800-373-5504, Fax: 757-352-4381, E-mail: admissions@regent.edu.
Website: http://www.regent.edu/soe/

Regis College, Department of Education, Weston, MA 02493. Offers elementary teacher (MAT); higher education leadership (Ed D); reading (MAT); special education (MAT). *Program availability:* Part-time, evening/weekend, blended/hybrid learning. *Degree requirements:* For master's, thesis. *Entrance requirements:* For master's, GRE or MAT. Additional exam requirements/recommendations for international students: Required—TOEFL; Recommended—IELTS. *Application deadline:* Applications are processed on a rolling basis. Application fee: $50. Electronic applications accepted. *Financial support:* Federal Work-Study, scholarships/grants, and unspecified assistantships available. Financial award applicants required to submit FAFSA. *Unit head:* Dr. Priscilla Boerger, Department Chair/Graduate Program Director, 781-768-7422, E-mail: priscilla.boerger@regiscollege.edu.

Regis University, College of Contemporary Liberal Studies, Denver, CO 80221-1099. Offers creative writing (MFA); criminology (M Sc); curriculum, instruction and assessment (M Ed); education - teacher leadership (M Ed); educational leadership (M Ed); elementary education (M Ed); literacy (Certificate); reading (M Ed); secondary education (M Ed); special education (M Ed); teacher academic leadership (Certificate); teacher leadership (MA); teacher/educational leadership (M Ed); teaching the linguistically diverse (M Ed). *Program availability:* Part-time, evening/weekend, 100% online, blended/hybrid learning. *Faculty:* 18 full-time (12 women), 42 part-time/adjunct (26 women). *Students:* 302 full-time (234 women), 270 part-time (218 women); includes 148 minority (33 Black or African American, non-Hispanic/Latino; 3 American Indian or Alaska Native, non-Hispanic/Latino; 13 Asian, non-Hispanic/Latino; 83 Hispanic/Latino; 16 Two or more races, non-Hispanic/Latino), 3 international. Average age 36. 431 applicants, 90% accepted, 110 enrolled. In 2016, 308 master's awarded. *Degree requirements:* For master's, thesis (for some programs). *Entrance requirements:* For master's, official transcript reflecting baccalaureate degree awarded from regionally-accredited college or university, work experience, resume, letters of recommendation. Additional exam requirements/recommendations for international students: Required—TOEFL (minimum score 550 paper-based; 82 iBT). *Application deadline:* For fall admission, 8/15 priority date for domestic students, 7/13 for international students; for winter admission, 10/10 priority date for domestic students, 9/8 for international students; for spring admission, 1/10 priority date for domestic students, 11/17 for international students; for summer admission, 5/1 priority date for domestic students. Applications are processed on a rolling basis. Application fee: $75. Electronic applications accepted. *Expenses:* $485 per credit hour. *Financial support:* Scholarships/grants available. Financial award application deadline: 4/15; financial award applicants required to submit FAFSA. *Unit head:* Dr. Elisa Robyn, Academic Dean. *Application contact:* Cate Clark, Director of Admissions, 303-458-4900, Fax: 303-964-5534, E-mail: ruadmissions@regis.edu.
Website: http://www.regis.edu/CCLS.aspx

Rhode Island College, School of Graduate Studies, Feinstein School of Education and Human Development, Department of Special Education, Providence, RI 02908-1991. Offers autism education (CGS); severe intellectual disabilities (CGS); special education (M Ed). *Accreditation:* NCATE. *Program availability:* Part-time, evening/weekend. *Faculty:* 3 full-time (2 women), 7 part-time/adjunct (all women). *Students:* 50 part-time (48 women); includes 4 minority (1 Black or African American, non-Hispanic/Latino; 1 Asian, non-Hispanic/Latino; 2 Hispanic/Latino). Average age 32. In 2016, 20 master's, 2 CGSs awarded. *Degree requirements:* For master's, comprehensive assessment/assignment. *Entrance requirements:* For master's, GRE General Test or MAT, undergraduate transcripts; minimum undergraduate GPA of 3.0; 3 letters of recommendation; for CGS, GRE or MAT, master's degree or equivalent, teaching certificate, 3 letters of recommendation, interview. Additional exam requirements/recommendations for international students: Recommended—TOEFL (minimum score 550 paper-based; 79 iBT). *Application deadline:* For fall admission, 3/1 for domestic students; for spring admission, 11/1 for domestic students. Applications are processed on a rolling basis. Application fee: $50. Electronic applications accepted. *Expenses:* Tuition, state resident: full-time $8928; part-time $372 per credit. Tuition, nonresident: full-time $17,376; part-time $724 per credit. *Required fees:* $604; $22 per credit. One-time fee: $74. *Financial support:* Teaching assistantships with full tuition reimbursements, career-related internships or fieldwork, Federal Work-Study, scholarships/grants, health care benefits, and unspecified assistantships available. Support available to part-time students. Financial award application deadline: 5/15; financial award applicants required to submit FAFSA. *Unit head:* Dr. Ying Hui-Michael, Chair, 401-456-8763, E-mail: yhui@ric.edu. *Application contact:* Graduate Studies, 401-456-8700.
Website: http://www.ric.edu/specialEducation/

Rider University, Department of Graduate Education, Leadership and Counseling, Program in Special Education, Lawrenceville, NJ 08648-3001. Offers alternative route in special education (Certificate); special education (MA); teacher of students with disabilities (Certificate); teacher of the handicapped (Certificate). *Program availability:* Part-time, evening/weekend. *Degree requirements:* For master's, comprehensive exam. *Entrance requirements:* For master's, letters of reference, resume, NJ teaching license, interview. Additional exam requirements/recommendations for international students: Required—TOEFL (minimum score 550 paper-based). Electronic applications accepted. *Faculty research:* Collaboration/inclusive, practice, service learning, transition.

Rivier University, School of Graduate Studies, Department of Education, Nashua, NH 03060. Offers curriculum and instruction (M Ed); early childhood education (M Ed); educational administration (M Ed); educational studies (M Ed); elementary education (M Ed); elementary education and general special education (M Ed); emotional and behavioral disorders (M Ed); general social education (M Ed); leadership and learning (Ed D, CAGS); learning disabilities (M Ed); learning disabilities and reading (M Ed); mental health counseling (MA); reading (M Ed); school counseling (M Ed). *Program availability:* Part-time, evening/weekend. *Degree requirements:* For master's, comprehensive exam (for some programs), internships. *Entrance requirements:* For master's, GRE General Test or MAT.

Robert Morris University, School of Education and Social Sciences, Moon Township, PA 15108-1189. Offers business education (MS); counseling psychology (MS); education (Postbaccalaureate Certificate); higher education (MS); instructional leadership (MS), including education; instructional management and leadership (PhD); literacy (MS); special education (MS). *Accreditation:* TEAC. *Program availability:* Part-time, evening/weekend, online learning. *Faculty:* 17 full-time (9 women), 4 part-time/adjunct (3 women). *Students:* 154 part-time (104 women); includes 18 minority (11 Black or African American, non-Hispanic/Latino; 2 Hispanic/Latino; 5 Two or more races, non-Hispanic/Latino), 1 international. Average age 26. 69 applicants, 26% accepted, 18 enrolled. In 2016, 40 master's, 15 doctorates awarded. *Degree requirements:* For doctorate, thesis/dissertation. *Entrance requirements:* Additional exam requirements/recommendations for international students: Required—TOEFL (minimum score 550 paper-based; 79 iBT). *Application deadline:* For fall admission, 7/1 priority date for domestic and international students; for spring admission, 11/1 priority date for domestic and international students. Applications are processed on a rolling basis. Application fee: $35. Electronic applications accepted. *Expenses:* $840 per credit (for master's

degree). *Unit head:* Dr. Mary Ann Rafoth, Dean, 412-397-6020, Fax: 412-397-6044, E-mail: rafoth@rmu.edu.
Website: http://www.rmu.edu/web/cms/schools/sess/

Roberts Wesleyan College, Graduate Teacher Education Programs, Rochester, NY 14624-1997. Offers adolescence and special education (M Ed); childhood and special education (M Ed); literacy education (M Ed); special education (M Ed). *Program availability:* Part-time, evening/weekend. *Degree requirements:* For master's, thesis. Electronic applications accepted.

Rochester Institute of Technology, Graduate Enrollment Services, National Technical Institute for the Deaf, Research and Teacher Education Department, MS Program in Secondary Education for the Deaf and Hard of Hearing, Rochester, NY 14623. Offers MS. *Program availability:* Part-time, evening/weekend, blended/hybrid learning. *Students:* 28 full-time (21 women), 2 part-time (both women); includes 7 minority (1 Black or African American, non-Hispanic/Latino; 4 Hispanic/Latino; 2 Two or more races, non-Hispanic/Latino), 6 international. Average age 28. 44 applicants, 43% accepted, 17 enrolled. In 2016, 20 master's awarded. *Degree requirements:* For master's, comprehensive exam, student teaching and observations. *Entrance requirements:* For master's, GRE, minimum cumulative GPA of 3.0. *Application deadline:* For fall admission, 6/1 priority date for domestic and international students. Applications are processed on a rolling basis. Electronic applications accepted. *Expenses:* $17,390. *Financial support:* Fellowships with partial tuition reimbursements, research assistantships with partial tuition reimbursements, teaching assistantships with partial tuition reimbursements, career-related internships or fieldwork, scholarships/grants, and unspecified assistantships available. Support available to part-time students. Financial award applicants required to submit FAFSA. *Faculty research:* Effective use of technology and online learning in teaching deaf students; strategies for inclusive instruction/deaf students with other disabilities; effective literacy instruction strategies for DHH readers; single case experimental design methods; STEM language, literacy and learning; deaf studies; international deaf education; stereotype threat effects on mathematical performance. *Unit head:* Dr. Gerald C. Bateman, Director, 585-475-6480, E-mail: gcbnmp@rit.edu. *Application contact:* Diane Ellison, Assistant Vice President, Graduate Enrollment Services, 585-475-2229, Fax: 585-475-7164, E-mail: gradinfo@rit.edu.
Website: http://www.ntid.rit.edu/msse/

Rockford University, Graduate Studies, Department of Education, Program in Special Education, Rockford, IL 61108-2393. Offers MAT. *Program availability:* Part-time, evening/weekend. *Degree requirements:* For master's, thesis optional. *Entrance requirements:* For master's, GRE General Test, 3 letters of recommendation. Additional exam requirements/recommendations for international students: Required—TOEFL (minimum score 550 paper-based; 79 iBT). *Application deadline:* Applications are processed on a rolling basis. Application fee: $50. Electronic applications accepted. *Expenses: Tuition:* Part-time $710 per credit. *Required fees:* $50 per semester. *Financial support:* Scholarships/grants and unspecified assistantships available. Support available to part-time students. Financial award application deadline: 3/1; financial award applicants required to submit FAFSA. *Application contact:* Michele Mehren, Assistant Director, Office of Graduate Studies, 815-226-4040, Fax: 815-394-3706, E-mail: mmehren@rockford.edu.
Website: https://www.rockford.edu/admission/graduate/mat/

Roosevelt University, Graduate Division, College of Education, Program in Special Education, Chicago, IL 60605. Offers MA. *Students:* 2 full-time (0 women), 1 (woman) part-time. Average age 28. 6 applicants, 83% accepted, 1 enrolled. In 2016, 7 master's awarded. *Expenses: Tuition, area resident:* Full-time $19,566; part-time $880 per credit hour. *Required fees:* $175 per semester. One-time fee: $200. Part-time tuition and fees vary according to course load, degree level and program. *Unit head:* Lilibeth Castillo, Director, 312-853-4789. *Application contact:* Angela Ryan, Director of Graduate Enrollment, 312-341-2420, Fax: 312-281-3356, E-mail: aryan@roosevelt.edu.
Website: https://www.roosevelt.edu/academics/programs/masters-in-special-education-ma

Rowan University, Graduate School, College of Education, Department of Interdisciplinary and Inclusive Education, Autism Spectrum Disorders Certificate of Graduate Study Program, Glassboro, NJ 08028-1701. Offers CGS. Electronic applications accepted.

Rowan University, Graduate School, College of Education, Department of Interdisciplinary and Inclusive Education, Program in Learning Disabilities, Glassboro, NJ 08028-1701. Offers MA. *Accreditation:* NCATE. *Program availability:* Part-time, evening/weekend. *Degree requirements:* For master's, comprehensive exam, thesis. *Entrance requirements:* For master's, GRE General Test, minimum GPA of 2.8, 1 year of teaching experience. Additional exam requirements/recommendations for international students: Required—TOEFL. Electronic applications accepted.

Rowan University, Graduate School, College of Education, Department of Interdisciplinary and Inclusive Education, Program in Special Education, Glassboro, NJ 08028-1701. Offers MA, CGS. *Accreditation:* NCATE. *Program availability:* Part-time, evening/weekend. *Degree requirements:* For master's, comprehensive exam, thesis. *Entrance requirements:* For master's, GRE General Test, minimum GPA of 2.8. Additional exam requirements/recommendations for international students: Required—TOEFL. Electronic applications accepted.

Rowan University, Graduate School, College of Education, Department of Interdisciplinary and Inclusive Education, Teacher of Students with Disabilities Post-Baccalaureate Certification Program, Glassboro, NJ 08028-1701. Offers Postbaccalaureate Certificate. *Program availability:* Part-time, online learning. *Entrance requirements:* For degree, official transcripts from all colleges attended; current professional resume; two letters of recommendation; minimum cumulative undergraduate GPA of 2.75; essay; BA or BS. Electronic applications accepted.

Rutgers University–New Brunswick, Graduate School of Education, Department of Educational Psychology, Program in Special Education, Piscataway, NJ 08854-8097. Offers Ed M, Ed D. *Program availability:* Part-time, evening/weekend. *Degree requirements:* For doctorate, thesis/dissertation, residency. *Entrance requirements:* For master's, GRE General Test, 3 letters of recommendation; for doctorate, GRE General Test, 3 letters of recommendation, master's degree. Additional exam requirements/recommendations for international students: Required—TOEFL (minimum score 550 paper-based; 83 iBT). Electronic applications accepted. *Faculty research:* Pre- and in-service teacher education, teacher development, inclusion, early identification and intervention of reading disabilities, special education law and social policy.

Sage Graduate School, Esteves School of Education, Program in Childhood Special Education, Troy, NY 12180-4115. Offers MS Ed. *Accreditation:* NCATE. *Program availability:* Part-time, evening/weekend. *Faculty:* 17 full-time (13 women), 18 part-time/adjunct (12 women). *Students:* 1 (woman) full-time. Average age 22. 3 applicants, 67% accepted, 1 enrolled. In 2016, 1 master's awarded. *Degree requirements:* For master's, thesis optional. *Entrance requirements:* For master's, bachelor's degree in a liberal arts or sciences area or the equivalent. Additional exam requirements/recommendations for international students: Required—TOEFL (minimum score 550 paper-based). *Application deadline:* Applications are processed on a rolling basis. Application fee: $40. Electronic applications accepted. *Expenses: Tuition:* Full-time $12,240; part-time $680 per credit hour. Tuition and fees vary according to degree level and program. *Financial support:* Fellowships, research assistantships, Federal Work-Study, scholarships/grants, and unspecified assistantships available. Support available to part-time students. Financial award application deadline: 3/1; financial award applicants required to submit FAFSA. *Faculty research:* Effective behavioral strategies for classroom instruction. *Unit head:* Dr. John Pelizza, Interim Dean, Esteves School of Education, 518-244-2051, Fax: 518-244-2334, E-mail: pelizj@sage.edu. *Application contact:* Tracey McLeod, Chair and Assistant Professor, 518-244-3132, Fax: 518-244-2334, E-mail: mcleot@sage.edu.

Sage Graduate School, Esteves School of Education, Program in Literacy/Childhood Special Education, Troy, NY 12180-4115. Offers MS Ed. *Accreditation:* NCATE. *Program availability:* Part-time, evening/weekend. *Faculty:* 4 full-time (all women), 4 part-time/adjunct (2 women). *Students:* 8 full-time (all women), 5 part-time (all women). Average age 26. 4 applicants, 25% accepted. In 2016, 10 master's awarded. *Entrance requirements:* For master's, current teacher certification, interview with appropriate advisor, assessment of writing. Additional exam requirements/recommendations for international students: Required—TOEFL (minimum score 550 paper-based). *Application deadline:* Applications are processed on a rolling basis. Application fee: $40. Electronic applications accepted. *Expenses: Tuition:* Full-time $12,240; part-time $680 per credit hour. Tuition and fees vary according to degree level and program. *Financial support:* Fellowships, research assistantships, Federal Work-Study, scholarships/grants, and unspecified assistantships available. Support available to part-time students. Financial award application deadline: 3/1; financial award applicants required to submit FAFSA. *Faculty research:* Commonalities in the roles of reading specialists and resource/consultant teachers. *Unit head:* Dr. John Pelizza, Interim Dean, Esteves School of Education, 518-244-2051, Fax: 518-244-2334, E-mail: pelizj@sage.edu. *Application contact:* Dr. Kathleen Gormley, Chair and Professor of Education, 518-244-2403, Fax: 518-244-2334, E-mail: gormlk@sage.edu.

Sage Graduate School, Esteves School of Education, Program in Special Education, Troy, NY 12180-4115. Offers MS Ed. *Program availability:* Part-time, evening/weekend. *Faculty:* 4 full-time (all women), 4 part-time/adjunct (2 women). *Students:* 14 full-time (12 women), 2 part-time (1 woman). Average age 26. 15 applicants, 20% accepted, 2 enrolled. In 2016, 6 master's awarded. *Entrance requirements:* For master's, interview with advisor, assessment of writing skills, New York state initial certification in childhood education or closely-related field. Additional exam requirements/recommendations for international students: Required—TOEFL (minimum score 550 paper-based). *Application deadline:* Applications are processed on a rolling basis. Application fee: $40. Electronic applications accepted. *Expenses: Tuition:* Full-time $12,240; part-time $680 per credit hour. Tuition and fees vary according to degree level and program. *Financial support:* Fellowships, research assistantships, Federal Work-Study, scholarships/grants, tuition waivers (partial), and unspecified assistantships available. Support available to part-time students. Financial award application deadline: 3/1; financial award applicants required to submit FAFSA. *Unit head:* Dr. John Pelizza, Interim Dean, Esteves School of Education, 518-244-2051, Fax: 518-244-2334, E-mail: pelizj@sage.edu. *Application contact:* Tracey McLeod, Assistant Professor, 518-244-3132, Fax: 518-244-2334, E-mail: mcleot@sage.edu.

Saginaw Valley State University, College of Education, Program in Special Education, University Center, MI 48710. Offers MAT. *Program availability:* Part-time, evening/weekend. *Students:* 4 full-time (3 women), 64 part-time (54 women); includes 6 minority (2 Black or African American, non-Hispanic/Latino; 1 Asian, non-Hispanic/Latino; 2 Hispanic/Latino; 1 Two or more races, non-Hispanic/Latino). Average age 34. 24 applicants, 88% accepted, 9 enrolled. In 2016, 31 master's awarded. *Degree requirements:* For master's, capstone course and practicum or thesis. *Entrance requirements:* For master's, minimum GPA of 3.0, teacher certification. Additional exam requirements/recommendations for international students: Required—TOEFL (minimum score 550 paper-based; 79 iBT). *Application deadline:* For fall admission, 7/15 for international students; for winter admission, 11/15 for international students; for spring admission, 4/15 for international students. Applications are processed on a rolling basis. Application fee: $30 ($90 for international students). Electronic applications accepted. *Expenses:* Tuition, state resident: full-time $9652; part-time $536 per credit hour. Tuition, nonresident: full-time $12,259; part-time $1022 per credit hour. *Required fees:* $263; $14.60 per credit hour. Tuition and fees vary according to degree level. *Financial support:* Federal Work-Study and scholarships/grants available. Support available to part-time students. Financial award applicants required to submit FAFSA. *Unit head:* Dr. Dottie Millar, Professor, Teacher Education, 989-964-4958, Fax: 989-964-4563, E-mail: coeconnect@svsu.edu. *Application contact:* Jenna Briggs, Director, Graduate and International Admissions, 989-964-6096, Fax: 989-964-2788, E-mail: gradadm@svsu.edu.

St. Ambrose University, College of Education and Health Sciences, Program in Education, Davenport, IA 52803-2898. Offers special education (M Ed); teaching (M Ed). *Accreditation:* TEAC. *Program availability:* Part-time, evening/weekend, online learning. *Degree requirements:* For master's, comprehensive exam. *Entrance requirements:* For master's, GRE General Test or MAT, minimum GPA of 2.75. Additional exam requirements/recommendations for international students: Required—TOEFL. Electronic applications accepted. *Faculty research:* Disabilities and postsecondary career avenues, self-determination.

St. Bonaventure University, School of Graduate Studies, School of Education, Differentiated Instruction Program, St. Bonaventure, NY 14778-2284. Offers gifted education (MS Ed, Adv C); gifted education and students with disabilities (MS Ed). *Program availability:* Part-time, evening/weekend. *Faculty:* 3 full-time (all women), 1 (woman) part-time/adjunct. *Students:* 20 full-time (17 women), 17 part-time (16 women); includes 1 minority (Two or more races, non-Hispanic/Latino). Average age 25. 7 applicants, 100% accepted, 6 enrolled. In 2016, 16 master's awarded. *Degree requirements:* For master's, comprehensive exam, internship, portfolio; for Adv C, practicum, portfolio. *Entrance requirements:* For master's, GRE or MAT, disabilities or special education teaching certification (or letter of eligibility); interview; transcripts from all colleges previously attended; 2 letters of recommendation; writing sample; for Adv C, teaching certification (or letter of eligibility); interview; transcripts from all colleges previously attended; 2 references; master's degree; writing sample. Additional exam requirements/recommendations for international students: Required—TOEFL (minimum score 550 paper-based; 79 iBT). *Application deadline:* For fall admission, 6/15 priority date for domestic students, 2/1 priority date for international students; for spring admission, 11/15 priority date for domestic students, 7/1 priority date for international students. Applications are processed on a rolling basis. Application fee: $0. Electronic applications accepted. *Expenses:* $733 per credit, $100 graduation fee. *Financial support:* Federal Work-Study, scholarships/grants, health care benefits, and unspecified assistantships available. Support available to part-time students. Financial award application deadline: 4/15; financial award applicants required to submit FAFSA. *Faculty research:* Disproportionality in special education, gifted education, teacher education and curriculum, specializing in authentic and responsive pedagogy for diverse learners. *Unit head:* Dr. Rene' Hauser, Director, 716-375-4078, Fax: 716-375-2360, E-mail: rhauser@sbu.edu. *Application contact:* Bruce Campbell, Director of Graduate Admissions, 716-375-2429, Fax: 716-375-4015, E-mail: gradsch@sbu.edu.

Website: http://www.sbu.edu/academics/schools/education/graduate-degrees-certificates/msed-in-differentiated-instruction-gifted

St. Cloud State University, School of Graduate Studies, School of Education, Department of Special Education, St. Cloud, MN 56301-4498. Offers developmental/ cognitive disabilities (MS); emotional/behavioral disorders (MS); gifted and talented (MS); learning disabilities (MS); special education (MS). *Accreditation:* NCATE. *Degree requirements:* For master's, thesis or alternative. *Entrance requirements:* For master's, GRE General Test, minimum GPA of 2.75. Additional exam requirements/ recommendations for international students: Required—Michigan English Language Assessment Battery; Recommended—TOEFL (minimum score 550 paper-based), IELTS (minimum score 6.5). Electronic applications accepted.

St. John Fisher College, Ralph C. Wilson Jr. School of Education, Program in Adolescence Education and Special Education, Rochester, NY 14618-3597. Offers adolescence education: biology with special education (MS Ed); adolescence education: chemistry with special education (MS Ed); adolescence education: English with special education (MS Ed); adolescence education: French with special education (MS Ed); adolescence education: math with special education (MS Ed); adolescence education: physics with special education (MS Ed); adolescence education: social studies with special education (MS Ed); adolescence education: Spanish with special education (MS Ed). *Program availability:* Part-time, evening/weekend. *Faculty:* 7 full-time (6 women), 5 part-time/adjunct (all women). *Students:* 15 full-time (6 women), 9 part-time (6 women); includes 3 minority (2 Black or African American, non-Hispanic/Latino; 1 Hispanic/Latino). Average age 28. 16 applicants, 56% accepted, 6 enrolled. In 2016, 8 master's awarded. *Degree requirements:* For master's, field experiences, student teaching, LAST. *Entrance requirements:* For master's, 2 letters of recommendation, personal statement, current resume. Additional exam requirements/recommendations for international students: Required—TOEFL (minimum score 575 paper-based; 80 iBT). *Application deadline:* Applications are processed on a rolling basis. Application fee: $30. Electronic applications accepted. *Expenses:* $885 per credit hour. *Financial support:* Scholarships/grants available. Financial award applicants required to submit FAFSA. *Faculty research:* Arts and humanities, urban schools, constructivist learning, at-risk students, mentoring. *Unit head:* Dr. Susan Hildenbrand, Program Director, 585-385-7297, E-mail: shildenbrand@sjfc.edu. *Application contact:* Michelle Gosier, Associate Director of Transfer and Graduate Admissions, 585-385-8064, E-mail: mgosier@sjfc.edu.

St. John Fisher College, Ralph C. Wilson Jr. School of Education, Program in Childhood Education/Special Education, Rochester, NY 14618-3597. Offers childhood education (MS); childhood education/special education (Certificate). *Program availability:* Part-time, evening/weekend. *Faculty:* 8 full-time (6 women), 4 part-time/ adjunct (all women). *Students:* 19 full-time (16 women), 10 part-time (9 women); includes 2 minority (1 Black or African American, non-Hispanic/Latino; 1 Two or more races, non-Hispanic/Latino). Average age 27. 30 applicants, 67% accepted, 15 enrolled. In 2016, 17 master's awarded. *Degree requirements:* For master's, field experience, student teaching, LAST. *Entrance requirements:* For master's, 2 letters of recommendation, personal statement, current resume. Additional exam requirements/ recommendations for international students: Required—TOEFL (minimum score 575 paper-based; 80 iBT). *Application deadline:* Applications are processed on a rolling basis. Application fee: $30. Electronic applications accepted. *Expenses:* $885 per credit hour. *Financial support:* Scholarships/grants available. Financial award applicants required to submit FAFSA. *Faculty research:* Professional development, science assessment, multi-cultural, educational technology. *Unit head:* Dr. Susan Hildenbrand, Program Director, 585-385-7297, E-mail: shildenbrand@sjfc.edu. *Application contact:* Michelle Gosier, Associate Director of Transfer and Graduate Admissions, 585-385-8064, E-mail: mgosier@sjfc.edu.
Website: https://www.sjfc.edu/graduate-programs/ms-in-childhood-educationspecial-education/

St. John's University, The School of Education, Department of Education Specialties, Literacy Program, Queens, NY 11439. Offers literacy (PhD); teaching literacy (Adv C); teaching literacy 5-12 (MS Ed); teaching literacy B-12 (MS Ed); teaching literacy B-6 (MS Ed); teaching literacy B-6 and children with disabilities (MS Ed). *Program availability:* Part-time, evening/weekend. *Degree requirements:* For master's, comprehensive exam; for doctorate, thesis/dissertation, residency; for Adv C, 50-hour practicum, content specialty test in literacy. *Entrance requirements:* For master's, minimum GPA of 3.0, transcript, personal statement; for doctorate, MAT, GRE General Test (analytical), statement of goals, official transcripts showing conferral of degree, minimum GPA of 3.2, 2 letters of recommendation, resume, evidence of teaching experience, interview; for Adv C, master's degree, initial teaching certification, minimum GPA of 3.0. Additional exam requirements/recommendations for international students: Required—TOEFL (minimum score 600 paper-based; 100 iBT), IELTS (minimum score 7). Electronic applications accepted. *Faculty research:* Higher order reading comprehension development and instruction, children's literature theory and children's reading interests, critical comprehension development, early writing development at the primary level, self-efficacy with textbook formats, out of school time program effects for at-risk students, teacher training effects for low performing parochial school students.

St. John's University, The School of Education, Department of Education Specialties, Program in Teaching Children with Disabilities in Childhood Education, Queens, NY 11439. Offers MS Ed, Adv C. *Program availability:* Part-time, evening/weekend, online learning. *Degree requirements:* For master's, comprehensive exam. *Entrance requirements:* For master's, bachelor's degree from accredited college or university, minimum GPA of 3.0, 2 letters of recommendation. Additional exam requirements/ recommendations for international students: Required—TOEFL (minimum score 600 paper-based; 100 iBT), IELTS (minimum score 7). Electronic applications accepted. *Faculty research:* Demographics in special education, literacy skill development in special populations, effects of distance learning in teacher training programs.

St. Joseph's College, Long Island Campus, Programs in Education, Field in Special Education, Patchogue, NY 11772-2399. Offers MA. *Expenses: Tuition:* Full-time $16,182; part-time $899 per credit. *Required fees:* $440.

St. Joseph's College, Long Island Campus, Programs in Education, Field of Infant/ Toddler Early Childhood Special Education, Patchogue, NY 11772-2399. Offers MA. *Program availability:* Part-time, evening/weekend. *Degree requirements:* For master's, thesis, full-time practicum experience. *Entrance requirements:* For master's, 1 course in child development, 2 courses in special education, minimum undergraduate GPA of 3.0, New York state teaching certificate, writing sample, resume, 2 letters of recommendation, interview. Additional exam requirements/recommendations for international students: Recommended—TOEFL (minimum score 550 paper-based; 79 iBT), IELTS (minimum score 7). Electronic applications accepted. *Expenses: Tuition:* Full-time $16,182; part-time $899 per credit. *Required fees:* $440.

St. Joseph's College, New York, Programs in Education, Field of Special Education, Brooklyn, NY 11205-3688. Offers severe and multiple disabilities (MA). *Program availability:* Part-time, evening/weekend. *Faculty:* 2 part-time/adjunct (both women). *Students:* 17 part-time (12 women); includes 3 minority (1 Black or African American, non-Hispanic/Latino; 2 Hispanic/Latino). Average age 23. 20 applicants, 65% accepted, 9 enrolled. In 2016, 7 master's awarded. *Entrance requirements:* For master's, GRE, PRAXIS or MAT, official transcripts, two letters of recommendation, resume, copy of teaching certification. Additional exam requirements/recommendations for international students: Required—TOEFL (minimum score 80 iBT). *Application deadline:* Applications are processed on a rolling basis. Application fee: $25. Electronic applications accepted. *Expenses:* Contact institution. *Financial support:* In 2016–17, 14 students received support. *Unit head:* Sr. Nancy Gilchriest, Professor/Department Chair, 631-687-1472, E-mail: ngilchriest@sjcny.edu.
Website: http://www.sjcny.edu

Saint Joseph's University, College of Arts and Sciences, Graduate Programs in Education, Philadelphia, PA 19131-1395. Offers curriculum supervisor (Certificate); educational leadership (MS, Ed D); elementary education (MS, Certificate); elementary/ middle school education (Certificate); instructional technology (MS, Certificate); organizational development and leadership (MS); principal (Certificate); professional education (MS); reading specialist (MS, Certificate); reading supervisor (Certificate); secondary education (MS, Certificate); special education (MS); special education 7-12 (Certificate); special education PK-8 (Certificate); superintendent's letter of eligibility (Certificate); supervisor of special education (Certificate); teacher of the deaf and hard of hearing (Certificate). *Program availability:* Part-time, evening/weekend, blended/hybrid learning. *Faculty:* 26 full-time (21 women), 74 part-time/adjunct (45 women). *Students:* 107 full-time (88 women), 826 part-time (622 women); includes 170 minority (115 Black or African American, non-Hispanic/Latino; 2 American Indian or Alaska Native, non-Hispanic/Latino; 11 Asian, non-Hispanic/Latino; 31 Hispanic/Latino; 1 Native Hawaiian or other Pacific Islander, non-Hispanic/Latino; 10 Two or more races, non-Hispanic/ Latino), 18 international. Average age 33. 338 applicants, 76% accepted, 173 enrolled. In 2016, 419 master's, 16 doctorates, 24 other advanced degrees awarded. *Degree requirements:* For master's, thesis or alternative; for doctorate, comprehensive exam, thesis/dissertation. *Entrance requirements:* For master's, 2 letters of recommendation, minimum GPA of 3.0, official transcripts, personal statement; for doctorate, GRE, master's degree from accredited institution, minimum graduate GPA of 3.5, computer competence, interview with program director. Additional exam requirements/ recommendations for international students: Required—TOEFL (minimum score 550 paper-based; 80 iBT), IELTS (minimum score 6.5), PTE (minimum score 60). *Application deadline:* For fall admission, 7/15 for international students; for spring admission, 11/1 for international students. Applications are processed on a rolling basis. Application fee: $35. Electronic applications accepted. *Expenses:* $750 per credit, $100 education fee, $360 online organization development and leadership residency fee. *Financial support:* In 2016–17, 25 students received support. Unspecified assistantships available. Financial award application deadline: 5/1; financial award applicants required to submit FAFSA. *Faculty research:* Factors predicting early mathematics skills for low income children, early child care and development, preschool quality, parent communication and home-school collaboration issues, education of terminally ill children, preparing literacy teachers for urban schools. *Total annual research expenditures:* $18,118. *Unit head:* Dr. John Vacca, Associate Dean, Education, 610-660-3131, E-mail: gradcas@sju.edu. *Application contact:* Graduate Admissions, College of Arts and Sciences, 610-660-3131, E-mail: gradcas@sju.edu.
Website: http://sju.edu/int/academics/cas/grad/education/index.html

Saint Louis University, Graduate Education, College of Education and Public Service, Department of Educational Studies, St. Louis, MO 63103. Offers curriculum and instruction (MA, Ed D, PhD); educational foundations (MA, Ed D, PhD); special education (MA); teaching (MAT). *Accreditation:* NCATE. *Program availability:* Part-time. *Degree requirements:* For master's, comprehensive exam; for doctorate, comprehensive exam, thesis/dissertation, preliminary oral and written exams. *Entrance requirements:* For master's, GRE General Test or MAT, letters of recommendation, resume; for doctorate, GRE General Test, letters of recommendation, resumé, goal statement, transcripts. Additional exam requirements/recommendations for international students: Required—TOEFL (minimum score 525 paper-based). Electronic applications accepted. *Faculty research:* Teacher preparation, multicultural issues, children with special needs, qualitative research in education, inclusion.

Saint Mary's College of California, Kalmanovitz School of Education, Program in Special Education, Moraga, CA 94575. Offers M Ed. *Program availability:* Part-time. *Degree requirements:* For master's, thesis or project. *Entrance requirements:* For master's, writing proficiency exam, interview, minimum GPA of 3.0, teaching experience. *Faculty research:* Consultation model, impact of gifted model on special education.

Saint Mary's University of Minnesota, Schools of Graduate and Professional Programs, Graduate School of Education, Educational Administration Program, Winona, MN 55987-1399. Offers educational administration (Certificate, Ed S), including director of special education, K-12 principal, superintendent. Tuition and fees vary according to degree level and program. *Unit head:* Dr. William Bjorum, Director, 612-728-5126, Fax: 612-728-5121, E-mail: wbjorum@smumn.edu. *Application contact:* James Callinan, Director of Admissions for Graduate and Professional Programs, 612-728-5185, Fax: 612-728-5121, E-mail: jcallina@smumn.edu.

Saint Mary's University of Minnesota, Schools of Graduate and Professional Programs, Graduate School of Education, Special Education Program, Winona, MN 55987-1399. Offers behavioral disorders (Certificate); learning disabilities (Certificate); special education (MA). *Program availability:* Part-time, evening/weekend, online learning. Tuition and fees vary according to degree level and program. *Unit head:* Dr. Judith Nagel Lam, Director, 612-238-4565, E-mail: jnagel@smumn.edu. *Application contact:* James Callinan, Director of Admission, 612-728-5185, Fax: 612-728-5121, E-mail: jcallina@smumn.edu.
Website: http://www.smumn.edu/graduate-home/areas-of-study/graduate-school-of-education/ma-in-special-education

Saint Michael's College, Graduate Programs, Program in Education, Colchester, VT 05439. Offers arts in education (CAGS); literacy (M Ed); school leadership (CAGS); special education (M Ed). *Program availability:* Part-time, evening/weekend. *Students:* 5 full-time (4 women), 239 part-time (199 women); includes 9 minority (2 Black or African American, non-Hispanic/Latino; 1 American Indian or Alaska Native, non-Hispanic/ Latino; 1 Asian, non-Hispanic/Latino; 4 Hispanic/Latino; 1 Two or more races, non-Hispanic/Latino), 1 international. Average age 36. In 2016, 31 master's awarded. *Degree requirements:* For master's, thesis. *Entrance requirements:* For master's, minimum GPA of 3.0, official transcripts, essay, interview. *Application deadline:* Applications are processed on a rolling basis. Application fee: $50. Electronic applications accepted. *Expenses: Tuition:* Full-time $10,620; part-time $590 per credit. Part-time tuition and fees vary according to course load and program. *Financial support:* Fellowships with partial tuition reimbursements and scholarships/grants available. Support available to part-time students. Financial award applicants required to submit FAFSA. *Faculty research:* Integrative curriculum, moral and spiritual dimensions of education, learning styles, multiple intelligences, integrating technology into the curriculum. *Unit head:* Jonathan Silverman, Department Chair, 802-654-2306, Fax: 802-654-2664, E-mail: jsilverman@smcvt.edu. *Application contact:* Lindsay A. Damici, Marketing Communications Manager, 802-654-2556, Fax: 802-654-2732.
Website: http://www.smcvt.edu/graduate-programs/academic-programs/education.aspx

Saint Peter's University, Graduate Programs in Education, Program in Special Education, Jersey City, NJ 07306-5997. Offers literacy (MA Ed). *Program availability:* Part-time, evening/weekend. *Degree requirements:* For master's, comprehensive exam. *Entrance requirements:* For master's, GRE or MAT. Additional exam requirements/recommendations for international students: Required—TOEFL. Electronic applications accepted.

St. Thomas Aquinas College, Division of Teacher Education, Sparkill, NY 10976. Offers adolescence education (MST); childhood and special education (MST); childhood education (MST); educational leadership (MS Ed); reading (MS Ed, PMC); special education (MS Ed, PMC); teaching (MS Ed), including elementary education, middle school education, secondary education. *Accreditation:* NCATE. *Program availability:* Part-time, evening/weekend. *Degree requirements:* For master's, comprehensive exam, comprehensive professional portfolio; for PMC, action research project. *Entrance requirements:* For master's, New York State Qualifying Exam, GRE General Test or minimum GPA of 3.0, teaching certificate; for PMC, GRE General Test or minimum GPA of 3.0. Electronic applications accepted. *Faculty research:* Computer applications in education, adolescent special education students, literacy development, inclusive practices for special education students.

St. Thomas University, School of Leadership Studies, Institute for Education, Miami Gardens, FL 33054-6459. Offers earth/space science (Certificate); educational administration (MS, Certificate); educational leadership (Ed D); elementary education (MS); ESOL (Certificate); gifted education (Certificate); instructional technology (MS, Certificate); professional/studies (Certificate); reading (MS, Certificate); special education (MS). *Program availability:* Part-time, evening/weekend. *Degree requirements:* For master's, comprehensive exam; for doctorate, comprehensive exam, thesis/dissertation. *Entrance requirements:* For master's, interview, minimum GPA of 3.0 or GRE; for doctorate, GRE or MAT. Additional exam requirements/recommendations for international students: Required—TOEFL (minimum score 550 paper-based; 79 iBT). Electronic applications accepted.

Saint Vincent College, Program in Education, Latrobe, PA 15650-2690. Offers curriculum and instruction (MS); instructional design and technology (MS); school administration and supervision (MS); special education (MS). *Program availability:* Part-time, evening/weekend. *Degree requirements:* For master's, comprehensive exam. *Entrance requirements:* For master's, GRE (if undergraduate GPA less than 3.0). Additional exam requirements/recommendations for international students: Required—TOEFL (minimum score 550 paper-based). *Faculty research:* Assessment and instructional technology.

Saint Xavier University, Graduate Studies, School of Education, Chicago, IL 60655-3105. Offers counseling (MA); curriculum and instruction (MA); early childhood education (MA); educational administration (MA); elementary education (MA); individualized studies (MA), including educational technology, English as a second language (ESL), ISTEM (integrative science, technology, engineering, and math), science education; music education (MA); reading (MA); secondary education (MA); Spanish education (MA); special education (MA); teaching and leadership (MA). *Accreditation:* NCATE. *Program availability:* Part-time, evening/weekend. *Degree requirements:* For master's, thesis or project. *Entrance requirements:* For master's, minimum GPA of 3.0. *Expenses:* Contact institution.

Salem College, Department of Education, Winston-Salem, NC 27101. Offers art education (MAT); elementary education (M Ed, MAT); language and literacy (M Ed); middle school education (MAT); school counseling (M Ed); second language studies (MAT); secondary education (MAT); special education (M Ed, MAT). *Accreditation:* NCATE. *Program availability:* Part-time, evening/weekend, online learning. *Degree requirements:* For master's, practicum (MAT), project (M Ed), oral and written comprehensive exams. *Entrance requirements:* For master's, minimum GPA of 2.5. *Faculty research:* Content area reading strategies, literacy development, brain compatible instruction.

Salem State University, School of Graduate Studies, Program in Special Education, Salem, MA 01970-5353. Offers M Ed. *Accreditation:* NCATE. *Program availability:* Part-time, evening/weekend. *Entrance requirements:* For master's, GRE, MAT. Additional exam requirements/recommendations for international students: Required—TOEFL (minimum score 550 paper-based; 80 iBT) or IELTS (minimum score 5.5).

Salus University, College of Education and Rehabilitation, Elkins Park, PA 19027-1598. Offers education of children and youth with visual and multiple impairments (M Ed, Certificate); low vision rehabilitation (MS, Certificate); orientation and mobility therapy (MS, Certificate); vision rehabilitation therapy (MS, Certificate); OD/MS. *Program availability:* Part-time, online learning. *Entrance requirements:* For master's, GRE or MAT, letters of reference (3), interviews (2). Additional exam requirements/recommendations for international students: Required—TOEFL, TWE. *Expenses:* Contact institution. *Faculty research:* Knowledge utilization, technology transfer.

Samford University, Orlean Beeson School of Education, Birmingham, AL 35229. Offers education (Ed D, Certificate); educational leadership: policy, organizations, leadership (MSE); elementary education (MS Ed); gifted certification (MSE); instructional design and technology (MSE); instructional leadership (MSE, Ed S); K-12 collaborative special education (MSE); teacher leader (Ed S). *Accreditation:* NCATE. *Program availability:* Part-time, evening/weekend, 100% online, blended/hybrid learning. *Faculty:* 15 full-time (9 women), 17 part-time/adjunct (12 women). *Students:* 219 full-time (161 women), 86 part-time (55 women); includes 97 minority (86 Black or African American, non-Hispanic/Latino; 5 American Indian or Alaska Native, non-Hispanic/Latino; 1 Asian, non-Hispanic/Latino; 1 Hispanic/Latino; 4 Two or more races, non-Hispanic/Latino), 2 international. Average age 38. 244 applicants, 52% accepted, 112 enrolled. In 2016, 84 master's, 22 doctorates, 12 Certificates awarded. *Degree requirements:* For master's, comprehensive exam (for some programs); for doctorate, comprehensive exam, thesis/dissertation; for other advanced degree, comprehensive exam. *Entrance requirements:* For master's, GRE or MAT; Alabama Educator Certification Testing Program (AECTP), transcripts, essays, recommendations; for doctorate, professional resume, recommendations, transcripts, interview, essays; for other advanced degree, recommendations, transcripts. Additional exam requirements/recommendations for international students: Required—TOEFL (minimum score 90 iBT), IELTS (minimum score 6.5). *Application deadline:* For fall admission, 7/15 for domestic students, 7/1 for international students; for spring admission, 11/15 for domestic and international students; for summer admission, 4/15 for domestic and international students. Application fee: $35. Electronic applications accepted. *Expenses: Tuition:* Full-time $18,530; part-time $789 per credit hour. *Required fees:* $610. Tuition and fees vary according to course load, degree level, program and student level. *Financial support:* In 2016–17, 246 students received support. Scholarships/grants available. Financial award application deadline: 3/1; financial award applicants required to submit FAFSA. *Faculty research:* Standards-based grading in K-12 schools, effective school principal leadership, effective educational leadership preparation programs, teacher/administrator shortages and job retention, instructional strategies to maximize student learning. *Total annual research expenditures:* $254,360. *Unit head:* Dr. Jean Box, Dean, 205-726-2565, Fax: 205-726-4233, E-mail: jabox@samford.edu. *Application contact:* Brooke Karr, Graduate Admissions Coordinator, 205-729-2783, Fax: 205-726-4233, E-mail: kbgilrea@samford.edu.
Website: http://www.samford.edu/education/

Sam Houston State University, College of Education, Department of Language, Literacy, and Special Populations, Huntsville, TX 77341. Offers international literacy (M Ed); reading (M Ed); special education (M Ed, MA), including low incidence disabilities and autism. *Program availability:* Part-time, evening/weekend, online learning. *Degree requirements:* For master's, comprehensive exam (for some programs), thesis optional, comprehensive portfolio; for doctorate, comprehensive exam, thesis/dissertation. *Entrance requirements:* For master's, GRE General Test, MAT, writing sample, recommendations; for doctorate, GRE General Test, MAT, master's degree, personal statement, recommendations. Additional exam requirements/recommendations for international students: Required—TOEFL (minimum score 550 paper-based; 79 iBT), IELTS (minimum score 6.5). Electronic applications accepted.

San Diego State University, Graduate and Research Affairs, College of Education, Department of Administration, Rehabilitation and Post-Secondary Education, San Diego, CA 92182. Offers educational leadership in post-secondary education (MA); rehabilitation counseling (MS), including deafness. *Program availability:* Evening/weekend, online learning. *Degree requirements:* For master's, comprehensive exam (for some programs), thesis (for some programs). *Entrance requirements:* For master's, GRE General Test, letters of reference. Additional exam requirements/recommendations for international students: Required—TOEFL. Electronic applications accepted. *Faculty research:* Rehabilitation in cultural diversity, distance learning technology.

San Diego State University, Graduate and Research Affairs, College of Education, Department of Special Education, San Diego, CA 92182. Offers MA. *Accreditation:* NCATE. *Program availability:* Evening/weekend. *Entrance requirements:* For master's, GRE General Test, letters of reference. Additional exam requirements/recommendations for international students: Required—TOEFL. Electronic applications accepted.

San Francisco State University, Division of Graduate Studies, College of Education, Department of Special Education and Communicative Disorders, Program in Orientation and Mobility, San Francisco, CA 94132-1722. Offers orientation and mobility (Credential); special education (MA), including orientation and mobility. *Expenses:* Tuition, state resident: full-time $6738. Tuition, nonresident: full-time $15,666. *Required fees:* $1012. Tuition and fees vary according to degree level and program. *Unit head:* Dr. Sandra Rosen, Program Coordinator, 415-338-1245, Fax: 415-338-0566, E-mail: mobility@sfsu.edu. *Application contact:* Anna Kozubek, Office Coordinator, 415-338-2501, Fax: 415-338-0566, E-mail: annak@sfsu.edu.
Website: http://online.sfsu.edu/~mobility/

Seattle University, College of Education, Program in Special Education, Seattle, WA 98122-1090. Offers M Ed, MA, Certificate. *Faculty:* 1 (woman) full-time, 5 part-time/adjunct (2 women). *Students:* 1 (woman) full-time, 6 part-time (3 women); includes 2 minority (both Two or more races, non-Hispanic/Latino), 1 international. Average age 38. 6 applicants, 100% accepted, 4 enrolled. In 2016, 3 master's awarded. *Entrance requirements:* For master's, GRE, MAT or minimum GPA of 3.0, 1 year of K-12 teaching experience; for Certificate, master's degree, minimum GPA of 3.0, 1 year of K-12 teaching experience. *Application deadline:* For fall admission, 8/20 priority date for domestic students; for winter admission, 11/20 priority date for domestic students; for spring admission, 2/20 priority date for domestic students. *Financial support:* In 2016–17, 4 students received support. *Unit head:* Dr. Katherine Schlick Noe, Director, 206-296-5768, E-mail: kschlnoe@seattleu.edu. *Application contact:* Janet Shandley, Associate Dean of Graduate Admissions, 206-296-5900, Fax: 206-298-5656, E-mail: grad_admissions@seattleu.edu.
Website: https://www.seattleu.edu/education/specialed/

Seton Hall University, College of Education and Human Services, Department of Educational Studies, South Orange, NJ 07079-2697. Offers instructional design and technology (MA); special education (MA). *Program availability:* Part-time, evening/weekend, blended/hybrid learning. *Faculty:* 6 full-time (3 women), 13 part-time/adjunct (8 women). *Students:* 6 full-time (4 women), 50 part-time (43 women); includes 6 minority (2 Asian, non-Hispanic/Latino; 4 Hispanic/Latino). Average age 32. 39 applicants, 90% accepted, 27 enrolled. In 2016, 13 master's awarded. *Degree requirements:* For master's, comprehensive exam, capstone project. *Entrance requirements:* For master's, GRE or MAT, PRAXIS (for certification candidates), minimum GPA of 2.75. *Application deadline:* For fall admission, 5/1 for domestic students; for spring admission, 10/1 for domestic students. Applications are processed on a rolling basis. Application fee: $75. Electronic applications accepted. *Expenses:* $1,212 per credit. *Financial support:* In 2016–17, 3 research assistantships with full tuition reimbursements (averaging $4,000 per year) were awarded; fellowships, career-related internships or fieldwork, institutionally sponsored loans, and unspecified assistantships also available. Financial award application deadline: 2/1; financial award applicants required to submit FAFSA. *Faculty research:* Special education, applied behavioral analysis, educational technology. *Unit head:* Dr. Daniel Katz, Chair, 973-275-2724, E-mail: daniel.katz@shu.edu.
Website: http://www.shu.edu/academics/education/graduate-studies.cfm

Seton Hill University, Program in Special Education, Greensburg, PA 15601. Offers MA. *Program availability:* Part-time, evening/weekend, online learning. *Entrance requirements:* For master's, 3 letters of recommendation, copy of teacher's certification, transcripts, resume, letter of intent. Additional exam requirements/recommendations for international students: Required—TOEFL (minimum score 600 paper-based; 100 iBT), IELTS (minimum score 6.5). Electronic applications accepted.

Shenandoah University, School of Education and Human Development, Winchester, VA 22601-5195. Offers administrative leadership (D Ed); educational administration (MSE); emphasis in teaching (MSE); health and physical education (Certificate); individual focus (MSE); literacy education (MS); middle school teacher education (Certificate); organizational leadership (MS, D Prof); secondary school teacher education (Certificate); special education (MSE). *Accreditation:* TEAC. *Program availability:* Part-time, evening/weekend. *Faculty:* 9 full-time (7 women), 43 part-time/adjunct (33 women). *Students:* 31 full-time (25 women), 236 part-time (160 women); includes 39 minority (19 Black or African American, non-Hispanic/Latino; 1 American Indian or Alaska Native, non-Hispanic/Latino; 10 Asian, non-Hispanic/Latino; 7 Hispanic/Latino; 1 Native Hawaiian or other Pacific Islander, non-Hispanic/Latino; 1 Two or more races, non-Hispanic/Latino), 4 international. Average age 37. 90 applicants, 97% accepted, 56 enrolled. In 2016, 113 master's, 13 doctorates, 38 other advanced degrees awarded. *Degree requirements:* For master's, comprehensive exam (for some programs), thesis (for some programs); for doctorate, comprehensive exam, thesis/dissertation. *Entrance requirements:* For degree, PRAXIS Academic Core, SAT/ACT, PRAXIS Academic Core Math, or VCLA, three letters of recommendation, writing sample, undergraduate degree. Additional exam requirements/recommendations for international students: Required—TOEFL (minimum score 550 paper-based; 79 iBT), IELTS (minimum score 6.5). *Application deadline:* For fall admission, 5/1 priority date for domestic students, 5/1 for international students; for spring admission, 10/15 priority date for domestic students, 10/15 for international students; for summer admission, 3/15

priority date for domestic students, 3/15 for international students. Application fee: $30. Electronic applications accepted. *Expenses:* Contact institution. *Financial support:* In 2016–17, 18 students received support. Scholarships/grants and unspecified assistantships available. Financial award applicants required to submit FAFSA. *Faculty research:* Exploring helplessness and anxiety in learning statistics, facilitating effective classroom group work, expert-novice dynamics in teaching, K-12 policy implementation and change, adult education, family-school-community relations, mentoring of first-year school principals. *Total annual research expenditures:* $2,000. *Unit head:* Dennis William Kellison, PhD, Director, 540-535-7324, Fax: 540-665-4726, E-mail: dkelliso@su.edu. *Application contact:* Andrew Woodall, Executive Director of Recruitment and Admissions, 540-665-4581, Fax: 540-665-4627, E-mail: admit@su.edu.
Website: http://www.su.edu/education/

Shippensburg University of Pennsylvania, School of Graduate Studies, College of Education and Human Services, Department of Educational Leadership and Special Education, Shippensburg, PA 17257-2299. Offers educational leadership (M Ed, Ed D); special education (M Ed), including behavior disorders, comprehensive, learning disabilities, mental retardation/developmental disabilities. *Accreditation:* NCATE. *Program availability:* Part-time, evening/weekend, blended/hybrid learning. *Faculty:* 7 full-time (1 woman), 6 part-time/adjunct (all women). *Students:* 14 full-time (9 women), 89 part-time (47 women); includes 5 minority (3 Black or African American, non-Hispanic/Latino; 2 Two or more races, non-Hispanic/Latino), 11 international. Average age 34. 118 applicants, 69% accepted, 68 enrolled. In 2016, 40 master's awarded. *Degree requirements:* For master's, candidacy, thesis, or practicum; for doctorate, comprehensive exam, thesis/dissertation, candidacy exam; 24 credits (six 4-credit residencies) of field-based courses leading to the superintendent's letter of eligibility. *Entrance requirements:* For master's, GRE or MAT (if GPA is less than 2.75), 2 years of successful teaching experience; for doctorate, resume; three letters of recommendation; 500-1000 word goals statement; teaching certifications and endorsements currently held; experience as public school administrator or supervisor that requires an administrative/supervisory certificate. Additional exam requirements/recommendations for international students: Required—TOEFL (minimum score 550 paper-based, 68 iBT) or IELTS (minimum score 6). *Application deadline:* For fall admission, 2/1 for domestic students, 4/30 for international students; for spring admission, 7/1 for domestic students, 9/30 for international students. Applications are processed on a rolling basis. Application fee: $45. Electronic applications accepted. *Expenses:* Tuition, state resident: part-time $483 per credit. Tuition, nonresident: part-time $725 per credit. *Required fees:* $141 per credit. *Financial support:* In 2016–17, 4 students received support. Career-related internships or fieldwork, scholarships/grants, unspecified assistantships, and resident hall director and student payroll positions available. Support available to part-time students. Financial award application deadline: 3/1; financial award applicants required to submit FAFSA. *Unit head:* Dr. Thomas C. Gibbon, Interim Departmental Chair, 717-477-1498, Fax: 717-477-4036, E-mail: tcgibb@ship.edu. *Application contact:* Megan N. Luft, Assistant Dean of Graduate Admissions, 717-477-1231, Fax: 717-477-4016, E-mail: mnluft@ship.edu.
Website: http://www.ship.edu/else/

Siena Heights University, Graduate College, Adrian, MI 49221-1796. Offers clinical mental health counseling (MA); educational leadership (Specialist); leadership (MA), including health care leadership, organizational leadership; teacher education (MA), including early childhood education, early childhood education: Montessori, education leadership: principal, elementary education: reading K-12, leadership: higher education, secondary education: reading K-12, special education: cognitive impairment, special education: learning disabilities. *Program availability:* Part-time, evening/weekend. *Degree requirements:* For master's, thesis, presentation. *Entrance requirements:* For master's, minimum GPA of 3.0, current resume, essay, all post-secondary transcripts, 3 letters of reference, conviction disclosure form; copy of teaching certificate (for some education programs); for Specialist, master's degree, minimum GPA of 3.0, current resume, essay, all post-secondary transcripts, 3 letters of reference, conviction disclosure form; copy of teaching certificate (for some education programs). Electronic applications accepted.

Simmons College, School of Social Work, Boston, MA 02115. Offers behavior analysis (MS, PhD, Ed S); education (MS Ed); social work (MSW, PhD); special education (MS Ed), including moderate and severe disabilities; teaching (MAT), including elementary education; MSW/MBA. *Accreditation:* CSWE (one or more programs are accredited). *Program availability:* Part-time, 100% online. *Faculty:* 37 full-time (28 women), 62 part-time/adjunct (44 women). *Students:* 797 full-time (705 women), 951 part-time (829 women); includes 420 minority (200 Black or African American, non-Hispanic/Latino; 5 American Indian or Alaska Native, non-Hispanic/Latino; 46 Asian, non-Hispanic/Latino; 122 Hispanic/Latino; 4 Native Hawaiian or other Pacific Islander, non-Hispanic/Latino; 43 Two or more races, non-Hispanic/Latino), 13 international. Average age 31. 1,356 applicants, 78% accepted, 592 enrolled. In 2016, 342 master's, 2 doctorates, 1 other advanced degree awarded. Terminal master's awarded for partial completion of doctoral program. *Degree requirements:* For master's, thesis (for some programs); for doctorate, comprehensive exam (for some programs), thesis/dissertation (for some programs). *Entrance requirements:* For master's, GRE, MAT, Massachusetts Tests for Education Licensure (for different programs); for doctorate, GRE, BCBA Analyst Exam. Additional exam requirements/recommendations for international students: Required—TOEFL (minimum score 600 paper-based; 100 iBT). *Application deadline:* For fall admission, 8/1 for domestic students; for spring admission, 12/15 for domestic students; for summer admission, 5/1 for domestic students. Applications are processed on a rolling basis. Application fee: $35. Electronic applications accepted. *Expenses:* $1,010 per credit; $52 activity fee per semester. *Financial support:* In 2016–17, 12 fellowships with partial tuition reimbursements were awarded; scholarships/grants and unspecified assistantships also available. Support available to part-time students. *Unit head:* Dr. Cheryl Parks, Dean, 617-521-3293, E-mail: cheryl.parks@simmons.edu. *Application contact:* Carlos D. Frontado, Director of Admissions, 617-521-3920, Fax: 617-521-3980, E-mail: ssw@simmons.edu.
Website: http://www.simmons.edu/ssw/

Slippery Rock University of Pennsylvania, Graduate Studies (Recruitment), College of Education, Department of Special Education, Slippery Rock, PA 16057-1383. Offers autism (M Ed); master teacher (M Ed), including birth to grade 8, grades 7 to 12; special education (Ed D); supervision (M Ed); technology for online instruction (M Ed). *Accreditation:* NCATE. *Program availability:* Part-time, evening/weekend, 100% online. *Faculty:* 13 full-time (7 women). *Students:* 42 full-time (36 women), 278 part-time (230 women); includes 7 minority (3 Black or African American, non-Hispanic/Latino; 1 Asian, non-Hispanic/Latino; 2 Hispanic/Latino; 1 Two or more races, non-Hispanic/Latino). Average age 32. 231 applicants, 77% accepted, 100 enrolled. In 2016, 134 master's awarded. *Degree requirements:* For master's, thesis optional. *Entrance requirements:* For master's, minimum GPA of 3.0, official transcripts, teaching certification. Additional exam requirements/recommendations for international students: Required—TOEFL (minimum score 550 paper-based; 80 iBT). *Application deadline:* For fall admission, 3/1 priority date for domestic students, 5/1 priority date for international students; for spring admission, 10/1 priority date for domestic students, 9/1 priority date for international students. Applications are processed on a rolling basis. Application fee: $25 ($30 for international students). Electronic applications accepted. *Expenses:* $646.50 per credit in-state, $936.80 per credit out-of-state; $581.45 per online credit in-state, $648.65 per online credit out-of-state. *Financial support:* In 2016–17, 14 students received support. Career-related internships or fieldwork, Federal Work-Study, institutionally sponsored loans, scholarships/grants, tuition waivers (partial), and unspecified assistantships available. Support available to part-time students. Financial award application deadline: 5/1; financial award applicants required to submit FAFSA. *Unit head:* Dr. Rachel Barger-Anderson, Graduate Coordinator, 724-738-2873, Fax: 724-738-4395, E-mail: rachel.barger-ander@sru.edu. *Application contact:* Brandi Weber-Mortimer, Director of Graduate Admissions, 724-738-2051, Fax: 724-738-2146, E-mail: graduate.admissions@sru.edu.
Website: http://www.sru.edu/academics/colleges-and-departments/coe/departments/special-education/graduate-programs

Sonoma State University, School of Education, Rohnert Park, CA 94928-3609. Offers administrative services (Credential); curriculum, teaching, and learning (MA); early childhood education (MA); education specialist (Credential); educational leadership (MA); multiple subject (Credential); reading and literacy (MA, Credential); single subject (Credential); special education (MA). *Accreditation:* NCATE. *Program availability:* Part-time, evening/weekend. *Degree requirements:* For master's, thesis or alternative. *Entrance requirements:* For master's, minimum GPA of 2.5. Additional exam requirements/recommendations for international students: Required—TOEFL (minimum score 500 paper-based). Application fee: $55. *Expenses:* Tuition, state resident: full-time $6738; part-time $3906 per unit. *Required fees:* $1916; $1916 per year. Tuition and fees vary according to course load, degree level and program. *Financial support:* Fellowships, research assistantships, career-related internships or fieldwork, and Federal Work-Study available. Support available to part-time students. Financial award application deadline: 3/2; financial award applicants required to submit FAFSA. *Unit head:* Dr. Carlos Ayala, Dean, 707-664-4412, E-mail: carlos.ayala@sonoma.edu. *Application contact:* Dr. Jennifer Mahdavi, Coordinator of Graduate Studies, 707-664-3311, E-mail: jennifer.mahdavi@sonoma.edu.
Website: http://www.sonoma.edu/education/

South Carolina State University, College of Graduate and Professional Studies, Department of Education, Orangeburg, SC 29117-0001. Offers early childhood education (MAT); education (M Ed); elementary education (M Ed, MAT); English (MAT); general science/biology (MAT); mathematics (MAT); secondary education (M Ed), including biology education, business education, counselor education, English education, home economics education, industrial education, mathematics education, science education, social studies education; special education (M Ed), including emotionally handicapped, learning disabilities, mentally handicapped. *Accreditation:* NCATE. *Program availability:* Part-time, evening/weekend. *Faculty:* 12 full-time (8 women), 3 part-time/adjunct (1 woman). *Students:* 28 full-time (20 women), 20 part-time (17 women); includes 45 minority (44 Black or African American, non-Hispanic/Latino; 1 Two or more races, non-Hispanic/Latino). Average age 31. 22 applicants, 100% accepted, 16 enrolled. In 2016, 9 master's awarded. *Degree requirements:* For master's, thesis optional, departmental qualifying exam. *Entrance requirements:* For master's, GRE General Test, NTE, interview, teaching certificate. *Application deadline:* For fall admission, 6/15 priority date for domestic students, 6/15 for international students; for spring admission, 11/1 for domestic and international students. Application fee: $25. Electronic applications accepted. *Expenses:* Tuition, state resident: full-time $8938; part-time $579 per credit hour. Tuition, nonresident: full-time $19,018; part-time $1139 per credit hour. *Required fees:* $1482; $82 per credit hour. *Financial support:* Fellowships, career-related internships or fieldwork, Federal Work-Study, and scholarships/grants available. Financial award application deadline: 6/1. *Unit head:* Dr. Charlie Spell, Interim Chair, Department of Education, 803-536-8963, Fax: 803-516-4568, E-mail: cspell@scsu.edu. *Application contact:* Curtis Foskey, Coordinator of Graduate Studies, 803-536-8419, Fax: 803-536-8812, E-mail: cfoskey@scsu.edu.

Southeastern Louisiana University, College of Education, Department of Teaching and Learning, Hammond, LA 70402. Offers curriculum and instruction (M Ed); elementary education (MAT); special education (M Ed); special education: early interventionist (MAT). *Accreditation:* NCATE. *Program availability:* Part-time, evening/weekend. *Faculty:* 14 full-time (all women), 2 part-time/adjunct (1 woman). *Students:* 8 full-time (all women), 48 part-time (46 women); includes 7 minority (6 Black or African American, non-Hispanic/Latino; 1 Hispanic/Latino). Average age 32. 79 applicants, 49% accepted, 21 enrolled. In 2016, 34 master's awarded. *Degree requirements:* For master's, comprehensive exam (for some programs), thesis (for some programs), action research project, oral defense of research project, portfolio, teaching certificate, minimum cumulative GPA of 3.0. *Entrance requirements:* For master's, GRE (verbal and quantitative), PRAXIS (for MAT). Additional exam requirements/recommendations for international students: Required—TOEFL (minimum score 500 paper-based; 61 iBT). *Application deadline:* For fall admission, 7/15 priority date for domestic students, 6/1 priority date for international students; for spring admission, 12/1 priority date for domestic students, 10/1 priority date for international students. Applications are processed on a rolling basis. Application fee: $20 ($30 for international students). Electronic applications accepted. *Expenses:* Tuition, state resident: full-time $6540; part-time $465 per credit hour. Tuition, nonresident: full-time $19,017; part-time $1158 per credit hour. *Required fees:* $1829. *Financial support:* In 2016–17, 13 students received support. Research assistantships, career-related internships or fieldwork, Federal Work-Study, institutionally sponsored loans, scholarships/grants, and unspecified assistantships available. Support available to part-time students. Financial award application deadline: 5/1; financial award applicants required to submit FAFSA. *Faculty research:* Teacher in services, STEM, educational technology, pre-service teacher education. *Unit head:* Dr. Colleen Klein-Ezell, Department Head, 985-549-2221, Fax: 985-549-5009, E-mail: colleen.klein-ezell@southeastern.edu. *Application contact:* Amanda Harper, Graduate Admissions Analyst, 985-549-5620, Fax: 985-549-5632, E-mail: admissions@southeastern.edu.
Website: http://www.southeastern.edu/acad_research/depts/teach_lrn/index.html

Southeast Missouri State University, School of Graduate Studies, Department of Elementary, Early and Special Education, Program in Exceptional Child Education, Cape Girardeau, MO 63701-4799. Offers MA. *Accreditation:* NCATE. *Program availability:* Part-time, evening/weekend, 100% online. *Faculty:* 10 full-time (all women), 5 part-time/adjunct (4 women). *Students:* 7 full-time (all women), 40 part-time (38 women); includes 2 minority (1 Black or African American, non-Hispanic/Latino; 1 Hispanic/Latino). Average age 31. 14 applicants, 100% accepted, 14 enrolled. In 2016, 12 master's awarded. *Degree requirements:* For master's, action research project and presentation. *Entrance requirements:* For master's, state licensure exam or GRE, minimum GPA of 2.75; teaching certificate. Additional exam requirements/recommendations for international students: Required—TOEFL (minimum score 95 iBT), IELTS (minimum score 7), PTE. *Application deadline:* For fall admission, 8/1 for domestic students, 6/1 for international students; for spring admission, 11/21 for domestic students, 10/1 for international students; for summer admission, 5/15 for domestic students. Applications are processed on a rolling basis. Application fee: $30 ($40 for international students). Electronic applications accepted. *Expenses:* Tuition, state resident: full-time $3130; part-time $260.80 per credit hour. Tuition, nonresident: full-time $5842; part-time $486.80 per credit hour. *Required fees:* $33.70 per credit hour. *Financial support:* In 2016–17, 1 student received support. Career-related internships or

fieldwork, Federal Work-Study, scholarships/grants, traineeships, tuition waivers (full), and unspecified assistantships available. Financial award application deadline: 6/30; financial award applicants required to submit FAFSA. *Faculty research:* Instructional technology, field and clinical experiences, student professional dispositions, autism spectrum disorder, applied behavior analysis. *Unit head:* Dr. Julie Ray, Department of Elementary, Early, and Special Education Chair/Professor, 573-651-2444, E-mail: jaray@semo.edu. *Application contact:* Dr. Sharon Gunn, Associate Professor, 573-651-2122, E-mail: sgunn@semo.edu.
Website: http://www.semo.edu/eese/

Southern Connecticut State University, School of Graduate Studies, School of Education, Program in Special Education, New Haven, CT 06515-1355. Offers MS Ed. *Program availability:* Part-time, evening/weekend. *Faculty:* 9 full-time (7 women), 9 part-time/adjunct (8 women). *Students:* 42 full-time (32 women), 114 part-time (85 women); includes 11 minority (3 Black or African American, non-Hispanic/Latino; 1 Asian, non-Hispanic/Latino; 6 Hispanic/Latino; 1 Two or more races, non-Hispanic/Latino), 1 international. Average age 30. 240 applicants, 28% accepted, 35 enrolled. In 2016, 78 master's awarded. *Degree requirements:* For master's, thesis or alternative. *Entrance requirements:* For master's, interview. *Application deadline:* For fall admission, 7/15 for domestic students. Applications are processed on a rolling basis. Application fee: $50. Electronic applications accepted. *Expenses:* Tuition, state resident: full-time $6497; part-time $519 per credit hour. Tuition, nonresident: full-time $18,102; part-time $535 per credit hour. *Required fees:* $4722; $55 per semester. Tuition and fees vary according to program. *Financial support:* Career-related internships or fieldwork, scholarships/grants, and unspecified assistantships available. Financial award application deadline: 4/15; financial award applicants required to submit FAFSA. *Unit head:* Dr. Ron Tamura, Chairperson, 203-392-6426, Fax: 203-392-5927, E-mail: tamurar1@southernct.edu. *Application contact:* Lisa Galvin, Director of Graduate Admissions, 203-392-5240, Fax: 203-392-5235, E-mail: galvinl1@southernct.edu.

Southern Illinois University Carbondale, Graduate School, College of Education and Human Services, Department of Educational Psychology and Special Education, Program in Special Education, Carbondale, IL 62901-4701. Offers special education (MS Ed, PhD), including behavior (MS Ed), curriculum (MS Ed), early childhood special education (MS Ed), special education supervision (MS Ed). *Accreditation:* NCATE. *Program availability:* Part-time. *Degree requirements:* For master's, thesis. *Entrance requirements:* For master's, GRE General Test, minimum GPA of 2.7. Additional exam requirements/recommendations for international students: Required—TOEFL. *Faculty research:* Applied and action research; scientific methods used to evaluate effectiveness of products and programs for the handicapped; scientific methods used to develop generalizations about instructional, motivational, and learning processes of the handicapped.

Southern Illinois University Edwardsville, Graduate School, School of Education, Health, and Human Behavior, Department of Special Education and Communication Disorders, Program in Special Education, Edwardsville, IL 62026. Offers MS Ed, Post-Master's Certificate. *Program availability:* Part-time, evening/weekend. *Degree requirements:* For master's, thesis or alternative, final project. *Entrance requirements:* Additional exam requirements/recommendations for international students: Required—TOEFL (minimum score 550 paper-based; 79 iBT), IELTS (minimum score 6.5). Electronic applications accepted.

Southern Methodist University, Annette Caldwell Simmons School of Education and Human Development, Department of Teaching and Learning, Dallas, TX 75275. Offers bilingual/ESL education (MBE); education (M Ed, PhD); gifted education (MBE); reading and writing (M Ed); special education (M Ed). *Program availability:* Part-time, evening/weekend. Terminal master's awarded for partial completion of doctoral program. *Degree requirements:* For master's, comprehensive exam, minimum GPA of 3.0; for doctorate, thesis/dissertation, qualifying exams, major area paper, evidence of teaching competency, dissemination of research (e.g., conference presentation), professional portfolio. *Entrance requirements:* For master's, minimum GPA of 3.0 or GRE, 3 letters of recommendation; for doctorate, GRE, minimum GPA of 3.3, 3 years of full-time teaching, 3 letters of recommendation, interview. Additional exam requirements/recommendations for international students: Required—TOEFL. Electronic applications accepted. *Faculty research:* Reading intervention, mathematics intervention, bilingual education, new literacies.

Southern New Hampshire University, School of Education, Manchester, NH 03106-1045. Offers business education (M Ed); child development (M Ed); curriculum and instruction (M Ed), including education leadership, reading, special education, technology integration; education (M Ed); educational leadership (M Ed, Ed D); educational studies (M Ed); elementary education (M Ed); English (MAT); English for speakers of other languages (M Ed); reading and writing specialist (M Ed); school business administration (Certificate); secondary education (M Ed); special education (M Ed); technology integration specialist (M Ed). *Program availability:* Part-time, evening/weekend, online learning. *Degree requirements:* For master's, comprehensive exam (for some programs), thesis or alternative. *Entrance requirements:* For master's, PRAXIS I, minimum GPA of 2.75. Additional exam requirements/recommendations for international students: Required—TOEFL (minimum score 550 paper-based). Electronic applications accepted. *Expenses:* Contact institution.

Southern Oregon University, Graduate Studies, School of Education, Ashland, OR 97520. Offers elementary education (MA Ed, MS Ed), including classroom teacher, early childhood, handicapped learner, reading, supervision; secondary education (MA Ed, MS Ed), including classroom teacher, handicapped learner, reading, supervision; teaching (MAT). *Program availability:* Online learning. *Faculty:* 15 full-time (10 women), 27 part-time/adjunct (21 women). *Students:* 116 full-time (82 women), 86 part-time (68 women); includes 22 minority (1 American Indian or Alaska Native, non-Hispanic/Latino; 4 Asian, non-Hispanic/Latino; 8 Hispanic/Latino; 9 Two or more races, non-Hispanic/Latino). Average age 34. 81 applicants, 80% accepted, 49 enrolled. In 2016, 107 master's awarded. *Degree requirements:* For master's, thesis optional. *Entrance requirements:* For master's, GRE General Test, minimum cumulative GPA of 3.0 in the last 90 quarter credits (60 semester credits) of undergraduate coursework. Additional exam requirements/recommendations for international students: Required—TOEFL (minimum score 540 paper-based; 76 iBT), IELTS (minimum score 6), ELPT (minimum score 964) or ELS (minimum score 112). *Application deadline:* For fall admission, 7/31 priority date for domestic and international students; for winter admission, 11/15 priority date for domestic and international students; for spring admission, 1/7 priority date for domestic and international students. Applications are processed on a rolling basis. Application fee: $60. Electronic applications accepted. *Expenses:* Tuition, state resident: full-time $10,719; part-time $397 per credit. Tuition, nonresident: full-time $13,419; part-time $497 per credit. *Required fees:* $540. *Financial support:* In 2016–17, 2 students received support. Career-related internships or fieldwork, institutionally sponsored loans, scholarships/grants, and unspecified assistantships available. *Unit head:* Dr. Gerry McCain, Graduate Program Coordinator, 541-552-6934, E-mail: mccaing@sou.edu. *Application contact:* Kelly Moutsatson, Director of Admissions, 541-552-6411, Fax: 541-552-8403, E-mail: admissions@sou.edu.
Website: http://www.sou.edu/education/

Southern University and Agricultural and Mechanical College, Graduate School and College of Education, Department of Special Education, Baton Rouge, LA 70813. Offers M Ed, PhD. *Accreditation:* NCATE. *Program availability:* Part-time, evening/weekend. *Degree requirements:* For master's, comprehensive exam, thesis optional; for doctorate, thesis/dissertation, comprehensive qualifying exam, oral defense of dissertation. *Entrance requirements:* For master's, GMAT or GRE General Test, PRAXIS; for doctorate, GRE General Test, PRAXIS, letters of recommendation, 2 years experience (individuals with disabilities). Additional exam requirements/recommendations for international students: Required—TOEFL. *Faculty research:* Classroom discipline/management, minority students in gifted/special education, learning styles/brain hemisphericity, school violence and prevention, certifications for special education teachers.

Southwestern College, Education Programs, Winfield, KS 67156-2499. Offers curriculum and instruction (M Ed); early childhood education (M Ed); educational leadership (Ed D); special education (M Ed), including adaptive, functional; teaching (MA). *Accreditation:* NCATE. *Program availability:* Part-time, evening/weekend, 100% online, blended/hybrid learning. *Faculty:* 7 full-time (5 women), 15 part-time/adjunct (12 women). *Students:* 27 full-time (18 women), 102 part-time (77 women); includes 17 minority (8 Black or African American, non-Hispanic/Latino; 1 American Indian or Alaska Native, non-Hispanic/Latino; 1 Asian, non-Hispanic/Latino; 6 Hispanic/Latino; 1 Native Hawaiian or other Pacific Islander, non-Hispanic/Latino), 32 international. Average age 38. 36 applicants, 64% accepted, 16 enrolled. In 2016, 71 master's, 10 doctorates awarded. *Degree requirements:* For master's, practicum, portfolio; for doctorate, thesis/dissertation, professional portfolio. *Entrance requirements:* For master's, baccalaureate degree, minimum GPA of 3.0, valid teaching certificate (for special education); for doctorate, GRE if no master's degree, baccalaureate degree with minimum GPA of 3.25 and current teaching experience, or master's degree with minimum GPA of 3.5. Additional exam requirements/recommendations for international students: Required—TOEFL (minimum score 550 paper-based; 80 iBT). *Application deadline:* Applications are processed on a rolling basis. Application fee: $40. Electronic applications accepted. *Expenses:* $550 per credit; $485 per credit (online); $580 per credit (doctorate program). *Financial support:* In 2016–17, 8 students received support. Scholarships/grants available. Financial award applicants required to submit FAFSA. *Unit head:* Dana Thomson, Director of Education Operations, 800-846-1543 Ext. 6253, Fax: 620-229-6253, E-mail: dana.thomson@sckans.edu. *Application contact:* Dennis Russell, Director of Admissions and Student Services, 888-684-5335 Ext. 3372, Fax: 888-684-5218, E-mail: dennis.russell@sckans.edu.
Website: http://www.sckans.edu/graduate/education-med/

Southwestern Oklahoma State University, College of Professional and Graduate Studies, School of Behavioral Sciences and Education, Specialization in Special Education, Weatherford, OK 73096-3098. Offers M Ed. M Ed distance learning degree program offered to Oklahoma residents only. *Accreditation:* NCATE. *Program availability:* Part-time, evening/weekend. *Degree requirements:* For master's, exam. *Entrance requirements:* For master's, GRE General Test or minimum undergraduate GPA of 3.0. Additional exam requirements/recommendations for international students: Required—TOEFL.

Southwest Minnesota State University, Department of Education, Marshall, MN 56258. Offers ESL (MS); math (MS); reading (MS); special education (MS), including developmental disabilities, early childhood education, emotional behavioral disorders, learning disabilities; teaching, learning and leadership (MS). *Program availability:* Part-time, evening/weekend, online learning. *Entrance requirements:* Additional exam requirements/recommendations for international students: Required—TOEFL or IELTS; Recommended—TOEFL (minimum score 550 paper-based; 80 iBT), IELTS.

Spalding University, Graduate Studies, College of Education, Programs in Education, Louisville, KY 40203-2188. Offers art teacher education (MAT); business teacher education (MAT); elementary school education (MAT); foreign language (MAT); high school education (MAT); middle school education (MAT); secondary education (MAT); special education (learning and behavioral disorders) (MAT); student guidance counselor (MA); teacher leader (M Ed). *Accreditation:* NCATE. *Program availability:* Part-time, evening/weekend. *Faculty:* 39 full-time (26 women), 13 part-time/adjunct (4 women). *Students:* 97 full-time (76 women), 31 part-time (23 women); includes 39 minority (33 Black or African American, non-Hispanic/Latino; 1 Asian, non-Hispanic/Latino; 3 Hispanic/Latino; 2 Two or more races, non-Hispanic/Latino). Average age 35. 62 applicants, 55% accepted, 33 enrolled. In 2016, 49 master's awarded. *Entrance requirements:* For master's, GRE General Test or MAT, interview, letters of recommendation, resume. Additional exam requirements/recommendations for international students: Required—TOEFL (minimum score 535 paper-based). *Application deadline:* Applications are processed on a rolling basis. Application fee: $30. Electronic applications accepted. *Expenses:* *Tuition:* Full-time $15,300. *Financial support:* Scholarships/grants, traineeships, and unspecified assistantships available. Financial award applicants required to submit FAFSA. *Faculty research:* Instructional technology, achievement gap, classroom management, assessment. *Unit head:* Dr. Chris Walsh, Associate Dean, 502-873-4272, Fax: 502-585-7123, E-mail: cwalsh@spalding.edu. *Application contact:* Valerie Anderson, Administrative Assistant, 502-873-4260, E-mail: vanderson@spalding.edu.

Spring Arbor University, School of Education, Spring Arbor, MI 49283-9799. Offers education (MAE); reading (MAR); special education (MSE). *Accreditation:* TEAC. *Program availability:* Part-time, evening/weekend, online learning. *Degree requirements:* For master's, thesis. *Entrance requirements:* For master's, official transcripts from all institutions attended, including evidence of an earned bachelor's degree from regionally-accredited college or university with minimum cumulative GPA of 3.0 for the last two years of the bachelor's degree; two professional letters of recommendation. Additional exam requirements/recommendations for international students: Required—TOEFL (minimum score 600 paper-based). Electronic applications accepted.

Springfield College, Graduate Programs, Programs in Education, Springfield, MA 01109-3797. Offers educational studies (M Ed); school guidance counseling (M Ed); secondary education (M Ed); special education (M Ed). *Program availability:* Part-time, evening/weekend. *Entrance requirements:* Additional exam requirements/recommendations for international students: Required—TOEFL (minimum score 550 paper-based); Recommended—IELTS (minimum score 6). Electronic applications accepted. *Expenses:* *Tuition:* Full-time $29,640; part-time $988 per credit. *Required fees:* $195.

State University of New York at New Paltz, Graduate School, School of Education, Department of Educational Studies, Program in Special Education, New Paltz, NY 12561. Offers adolescence special education (7-12) (MS Ed); adolescence special education and literacy (MS Ed); childhood special education (1-6) (MS Ed); childhood special education and literacy (MS Ed); early childhood special education (B-2) (MS Ed). *Accreditation:* NCATE. *Program availability:* Part-time, evening/weekend. *Students:* 25 full-time (19 women), 39 part-time (29 women); includes 9 minority (2 Asian, non-Hispanic/Latino; 7 Hispanic/Latino). 13 applicants, 85% accepted, 10 enrolled. In 2016, 36 master's awarded. *Entrance requirements:* For master's, minimum GPA of 3.0 (3.2 for special education and literacy programs), New York state teaching certificate. Additional exam requirements/recommendations for international students: Required—

TOEFL (minimum score 550 paper-based; 80 iBT), IELTS (minimum score 6.5). *Application deadline:* For fall admission, 3/15 priority date for domestic students, 3/15 for international students; for spring admission, 11/1 for domestic and international students. Application fee: $50. Electronic applications accepted. *Financial support:* Application deadline: 8/1. *Unit head:* Dr. Jane Sileo, Coordinator, 845-257-2835, E-mail: sileoj@newpaltz.edu. *Application contact:* Vika Shock, Director of Graduate Admissions, 845-257-3286, E-mail: gradschool@newpaltz.edu.
Website: http://www.newpaltz.edu/schoolofed/department-of-teaching—learning/special_ed.html

State University of New York at New Paltz, Graduate School, School of Education, Department of Elementary Education, New Paltz, NY 12561. Offers childhood education 1-6 (MS Ed, MST), including childhood education 1-6 (MST), early childhood B-2 (MS Ed), mathematics, science and technology (MS Ed), reading/literacy (MS Ed); literacy education 5-12 (MS Ed); literacy education and childhood special education (MS Ed); literacy education B-6 (MS Ed). *Accreditation:* NCATE. *Program availability:* Part-time, evening/weekend. *Students:* 32 full-time (29 women), 100 part-time (91 women); includes 22 minority (5 Black or African American, non-Hispanic/Latino; 1 American Indian or Alaska Native, non-Hispanic/Latino; 2 Asian, non-Hispanic/Latino; 10 Hispanic/Latino; 4 Two or more races, non-Hispanic/Latino). 30 applicants, 73% accepted, 14 enrolled. In 2016, 70 master's awarded. *Degree requirements:* For master's, comprehensive exam (for some programs), portfolio. *Entrance requirements:* For master's, GRE or MAT (for MST), minimum GPA of 3.0 (3.2 for literacy and special education), New York state teaching certificate (for MS Ed). Additional exam requirements/recommendations for international students: Required—TOEFL (minimum score 550 paper-based; 80 iBT), IELTS (minimum score 6.5). *Application deadline:* For fall admission, 4/1 for domestic and international students; for spring admission, 11/1 priority date for domestic and international students; for summer admission, 4/15 priority date for domestic and international students. Applications are processed on a rolling basis. Application fee: $50. Electronic applications accepted. *Financial support:* Application deadline: 8/1. *Faculty research:* Multi-sensory teaching methods, volunteer tutoring programs for struggling readers, school readiness and transition, math/science/technology, university-school partnerships. *Unit head:* Dr. Aaron Isabelle, Chair, 845-257-2837, E-mail: isabella@newpaltz.edu. *Application contact:* Vika Shock, Assistant Director of Graduate Admissions, 845-257-3285, Fax: 845-257-3284, E-mail: gradschool@newpaltz.edu.
Website: http://www.newpaltz.edu/elementaryed/

State University of New York at Oswego, Graduate Studies, School of Education, Department of Curriculum and Instruction, Oswego, NY 13126. Offers adolescence education (MST); art education (MAT); childhood education (MST); curriculum and instruction (MS Ed); literacy education (MS Ed); special education (MS Ed). *Program availability:* Part-time, evening/weekend. *Degree requirements:* For master's, comprehensive exam (for some programs), thesis optional. *Entrance requirements:* For master's, GRE General Test, minimum GPA of 2.7, provisional teaching certificate. Additional exam requirements/recommendations for international students: Required—TOEFL (minimum score 560 paper-based). *Faculty research:* Classroom applications for microcomputers; classroom questioning, wait-time, and achievement; values clarification and academic achievement.

State University of New York at Plattsburgh, School of Education, Health, and Human Services, Program in Teacher Education: Special Education, Plattsburgh, NY 12901-2681. Offers birth to grade 2 (MS Ed); birth to grade 6 (MS Ed); grades 1 to 6 (MS Ed); grades 7 to 12 (MS Ed). *Accreditation:* TEAC. *Program availability:* Part-time, evening/weekend. *Entrance requirements:* For master's, minimum GPA of 2.75. Additional exam requirements/recommendations for international students: Required—TOEFL. *Faculty research:* Inclusion behavior management technology, applied behavior analysis.

State University of New York College at Cortland, Graduate Studies, School of Education, Programs in Teaching Students with Disabilities, Cortland, NY 13045. Offers MS Ed. *Accreditation:* NCATE. *Program availability:* Part-time, evening/weekend. *Degree requirements:* For master's, one foreign language, comprehensive exam, thesis (for some programs). *Entrance requirements:* For master's, provisional certification. Additional exam requirements/recommendations for international students: Required—TOEFL.

State University of New York College at Oneonta, Graduate Programs, Division of Education, Department of Educational Psychology, Counseling and Special Education, Oneonta, NY 13820-4015. Offers school counselor K-12 (MS Ed, CAS); special education (MS Ed). *Accreditation:* NCATE. *Program availability:* Part-time, evening/weekend. *Degree requirements:* For master's, comprehensive exam. *Entrance requirements:* For master's, GRE General Test. *Application deadline:* For fall admission, 3/1 for domestic students. Application fee: $50. *Unit head:* Dr. Dawn Hamlin, Chair, 607-436-3526, Fax: 607-436-3799, E-mail: dawn.hamlin@oneonta.edu. *Application contact:* Patrick J. Mente, Director of Graduate Studies, 607-436-2523, Fax: 607-436-3084, E-mail: gradstudies@oneonta.edu.
Website: http://www.oneonta.edu/academics/ed/edpsych/

State University of New York College at Potsdam, School of Education and Professional Studies, Program in Special Education, Potsdam, NY 13676. Offers adolescence (grades 7-12) (MS Ed); childhood (grades 1-6) (MS Ed); early childhood (birth-grade 2) (MS Ed). *Accreditation:* NCATE. *Program availability:* Part-time. *Degree requirements:* For master's, culminating experience. *Entrance requirements:* For master's, minimum GPA of 3.0 in last 60 hours of course work. Additional exam requirements/recommendations for international students: Required—TOEFL (minimum score 550 paper-based; 80 iBT), IELTS (minimum score 6). Electronic applications accepted.

Stephen F. Austin State University, Graduate School, College of Education, Department of Human Services, Nacogdoches, TX 75962. Offers counseling (MA); school psychology (MA); special education (M Ed); speech pathology (MS). *Accreditation:* ACA (one or more programs are accredited); ASHA (one or more programs are accredited); CORE; NCATE. *Degree requirements:* For master's, comprehensive exam, thesis (for some programs). *Entrance requirements:* For master's, GRE General Test, minimum GPA of 2.8. Additional exam requirements/recommendations for international students: Required—TOEFL.

Syracuse University, School of Education, MS Program in Early Childhood Special Education, Syracuse, NY 13244. Offers MS. *Program availability:* Part-time. *Entrance requirements:* For master's, GRE, baccalaureate degree from regionally-accredited college/university, strong teacher and/or employer recommendations, personal statement, experience working with children. Additional exam requirements/recommendations for international students: Required—TOEFL (minimum score 100 iBT). *Application deadline:* For fall admission, 1/15 priority date for domestic and international students; for spring admission, 10/15 priority date for domestic and international students; for summer admission, 1/15 priority date for domestic and international students. Applications are processed on a rolling basis. Application fee: $75. Electronic applications accepted. *Expenses: Tuition:* Full-time $25,974; part-time $1443 per credit hour. *Required fees:* $802; $50 per course. Tuition and fees vary according to course load and program. *Financial support:* Fellowships with full tuition reimbursements, research assistantships, teaching assistantships with tuition reimbursements, career-related internships or fieldwork, and scholarships/grants available. Financial award application deadline: 1/15; financial award applicants required to submit FAFSA. *Faculty research:* Teaching children with diverse backgrounds and abilities, home-based itinerant teaching, early childhood special education, general preschool teaching, teacher consulting. *Unit head:* Dr. Gail Ensher, Program Coordinator, 315-443-9650, E-mail: glensher@syr.edu. *Application contact:* Speranza Migliore, Graduate Admissions Recruiter, 315-443-2505, E-mail: gradrcrt@syr.edu.
Website: http://soe.syr.edu/academic/teaching_and_leadership/graduate/masters/early_childhood_special_education/default.aspx

Syracuse University, School of Education, MS Program in Inclusive Special Education (Grades 1-6), Syracuse, NY 13244. Offers MS. *Program availability:* Part-time. In 2016, 6 master's awarded. *Degree requirements:* For master's, thesis or alternative. *Entrance requirements:* For master's, GRE, baccalaureate degree from regionally-accredited college/university, initial New York State certification in childhood education, three letters of recommendation, personal statement, transcripts. Additional exam requirements/recommendations for international students: Required—TOEFL (minimum score 100 iBT). *Application deadline:* For fall admission, 1/15 priority date for domestic and international students; for spring admission, 10/15 priority date for domestic and international students. Applications are processed on a rolling basis. Application fee: $75. Electronic applications accepted. *Expenses: Tuition:* Full-time $25,974; part-time $1443 per credit hour. *Required fees:* $802; $50 per course. Tuition and fees vary according to course load and program. *Financial support:* Fellowships with full tuition reimbursements, research assistantships, teaching assistantships with tuition reimbursements, career-related internships or fieldwork, and scholarships/grants available. Financial award application deadline: 1/15; financial award applicants required to submit FAFSA. *Faculty research:* Creating safe and peaceful schools, adapting instruction for diverse student needs, early intervention for children's reading problems, teaching children with autism, augmentative and alternative communication in inclusive classrooms. *Unit head:* Dr. Christine Ashby, Assistant Professor/Inclusive Master's Program Coordinator, 315-443-8689, E-mail: ceashby@syr.edu. *Application contact:* Speranza Migliore, Graduate Admissions Recruiter, 315-443-2505, E-mail: gradrcrt@syr.edu.
Website: http://soe.syr.edu/academic/teaching_and_leadership/graduate/masters/inclusive_special_education_grades_1_6/default.aspx

Syracuse University, School of Education, MS Program in Inclusive Special Education (Grades 7-12), Syracuse, NY 13244. Offers MS. *Program availability:* Part-time. *Students:* Average age 29. In 2016, 2 master's awarded. *Degree requirements:* For master's, thesis or alternative. *Entrance requirements:* For master's, GRE, baccalaureate degree from regionally-accredited college/university, recommendation letters, personal statement, experience working with youth. Additional exam requirements/recommendations for international students: Required—TOEFL (minimum score 100 iBT). *Application deadline:* For fall admission, 1/15 priority date for domestic and international students; for spring admission, 10/15 priority date for domestic and international students. Applications are processed on a rolling basis. Application fee: $75. Electronic applications accepted. *Expenses: Tuition:* Full-time $25,974; part-time $1443 per credit hour. *Required fees:* $802; $50 per course. Tuition and fees vary according to course load and program. *Financial support:* Fellowships with full tuition reimbursements, research assistantships, teaching assistantships with tuition reimbursements, career-related internships or fieldwork, and scholarships/grants available. Financial award application deadline: 1/15; financial award applicants required to submit FAFSA. *Faculty research:* Students with disabilities, inclusive education and disability studies, extensive placements in schools, adapting instruction for diverse student needs, assistive technologies. *Unit head:* Dr. Christine Ashby, Assistant Professor, 315-443-8689, E-mail: ceashby@syr.edu. *Application contact:* Speranza Migliore, Graduate Admissions Recruiter, 315-443-2505, E-mail: gradrcrt@syr.edu.
Website: http://soe.syr.edu/academic/teaching_and_leadership/graduate/masters/inclusive_special_education_grades_7_12/default.aspx

Syracuse University, School of Education, MS Program in Inclusive Special Education: Severe/Multiple Disabilities, Syracuse, NY 13244. Offers MS. *Program availability:* Part-time. *Students:* Average age 27. *Entrance requirements:* For master's, GRE, baccalaureate degree from regionally-accredited college/university, New York State initial certification in students with disabilities, strong professor and/or employer recommendations, personal statement, interview. Additional exam requirements/recommendations for international students: Required—TOEFL (minimum score 100 iBT). *Application deadline:* For fall admission, 1/15 priority date for domestic and international students; for spring admission, 10/15 priority date for domestic and international students. Applications are processed on a rolling basis. Application fee: $75. Electronic applications accepted. *Expenses: Tuition:* Full-time $25,974; part-time $1443 per credit hour. *Required fees:* $802; $50 per course. Tuition and fees vary according to course load and program. *Financial support:* Fellowships with full tuition reimbursements, research assistantships, teaching assistantships with tuition reimbursements, career-related internships or fieldwork, and scholarships/grants available. Financial award application deadline: 1/15. *Faculty research:* Teaching children and adolescents with autism, augmentation of communication in the inclusive classroom, families of students with disabilities, positive approaches to challenging behaviors, creating safe and peaceful schools. *Unit head:* Dr. Gail Ensher, Program Coordinator, 315-443-9650, E-mail: glensher@syr.edu. *Application contact:* Speranza Migliore, Graduate Admissions Recruiter, 315-443-2505, E-mail: gradrcrt@syr.edu.
Website: http://soe.syr.edu/academic/teaching_and_leadership/graduate/masters/inclusive_special_education_grades_1_6/admissions.aspx

Syracuse University, School of Education, PhD Program in Special Education, Syracuse, NY 13244. Offers PhD. *Program availability:* Part-time. *Degree requirements:* For doctorate, comprehensive exam, thesis/dissertation. *Entrance requirements:* For doctorate, GRE General Test, master's degree, interview, writing sample, disability experience (preferred), three letters of recommendation. Additional exam requirements/recommendations for international students: Required—TOEFL (minimum score 100 iBT). *Application deadline:* For fall admission, 10/15 priority date for domestic and international students. Applications are processed on a rolling basis. Application fee: $75. Electronic applications accepted. *Expenses: Tuition:* Full-time $25,974; part-time $1443 per credit hour. *Required fees:* $802; $50 per course. Tuition and fees vary according to course load and program. *Financial support:* Fellowships with full tuition reimbursements, research assistantships with tuition reimbursements, teaching assistantships with tuition reimbursements, career-related internships or fieldwork, and institutionally sponsored loans available. Support available to part-time students. Financial award application deadline: 1/15. *Faculty research:* Curriculum development and field-based projects, psychoeducational evaluation and planning, perspectives on learning disabilities, teaching children and adolescents with autism, positive approaches to challenging behavior. *Unit head:* Dr. Beth Ferri, Program Director, 315-443-1465, E-mail: baferri@syr.edu. *Application contact:* Speranza Migliore, Graduate Admissions Recruiter, 315-443-2505, E-mail: gradrcrt@syr.edu.
Website: http://soe.syr.edu/academic/teaching_and_leadership/graduate/PhD/special_education/default.aspx

Tarleton State University, College of Graduate Studies, College of Education, Department of Curriculum and Instruction, Stephenville, TX 76402. Offers educational diagnostician (M Ed); elementary education (M Ed); instructional design and technology (M Ed); instructional leadership (M Ed); professional reading specialist (M Ed); secondary education (M Ed); special education (M Ed); technology applications (M Ed); technology director (M Ed). *Program availability:* Part-time, evening/weekend. *Faculty:* 9 full-time (7 women), 6 part-time/adjunct (4 women). *Students:* 17 full-time (0 women), 104 part-time (101 women); includes 28 minority (5 Black or African American, non-Hispanic/Latino; 1 American Indian or Alaska Native, non-Hispanic/Latino; 19 Hispanic/Latino; 3 Two or more races, non-Hispanic/Latino). 62 applicants, 94% accepted, 35 enrolled. In 2016, 34 master's awarded. *Degree requirements:* For master's, comprehensive exam. *Entrance requirements:* For master's, GRE General Test, minimum GPA of 3.0. Additional exam requirements/recommendations for international students: Required—TOEFL (minimum score 550 paper-based; 80 iBT). *Application deadline:* For fall admission, 8/15 priority date for domestic students; for spring admission, 1/7 for domestic students. Applications are processed on a rolling basis. Application fee: $45 ($145 for international students). Electronic applications accepted. *Expenses:* $3,672 tuition; $2,437 fees. *Financial support:* Research assistantships, teaching assistantships, career-related internships or fieldwork, Federal Work-Study, and institutionally sponsored loans available. Support available to part-time students. Financial award application deadline: 5/1; financial award applicants required to submit FAFSA. *Unit head:* Dr. Jordan Barkley, Department Head, 254-968-9089, E-mail: jbarkley@tarleton.edu. *Application contact:* Information Contact, 254-968-9104, Fax: 254-968-9670, E-mail: gradoffice@tarleton.edu.
Website: http://www.tarleton.edu/cimasters/

Teachers College, Columbia University, Department of Curriculum and Teaching, New York, NY 10027-6696. Offers curriculum and teaching (Ed M, MA, Ed D); curriculum and teaching: elementary education (MA); curriculum and teaching: secondary education (MA); early childhood education (MA, Ed D); early childhood education: special education (MA); elementary education-gifted extension (MA); elementary inclusive education (MA); gifted education (MA); literacy specialist (MA); secondary inclusive education (MA); special inclusive elementary education (MA). *Program availability:* Part-time, evening/weekend. *Students:* 236 full-time (219 women), 198 part-time (176 women); includes 160 minority (53 Black or African American, non-Hispanic/Latino; 1 American Indian or Alaska Native, non-Hispanic/Latino; 43 Asian, non-Hispanic/Latino; 41 Hispanic/Latino; 22 Two or more races, non-Hispanic/Latino), 38 international. 399 applicants, 66% accepted, 104 enrolled. Terminal master's awarded for partial completion of doctoral program. *Degree requirements:* For doctorate, thesis/dissertation. *Expenses: Tuition:* Full-time $36,288; part-time $1512 per credit. *Required fees:* $438 per semester. One-time fee: $510 full-time. Full-time tuition and fees vary according to course load. *Unit head:* Prof. Nancy Lesko, Chair, 212-678-3264, E-mail: lesko@tc.columbia.edu. *Application contact:* David Estrella, Director of Admission, 212-678-3305, Fax: 212-678-4171, E-mail: estrella@tc.columbia.edu.

Teachers College, Columbia University, Department of Health and Behavior Studies, New York, NY 10027-6696. Offers applied behavior analysis (MA, PhD); applied educational psychology: school psychology (Ed M, PhD); behavioral nutrition (PhD), including nutrition (Ed D, PhD); community health education (MS); community nutrition education (Ed M), including community nutrition education; education of deaf and hard of hearing (MA, PhD); health education (MA, Ed D); hearing impairment (Ed D); intellectual disability/autism (MA, Ed D, PhD); nursing education (Ed D, Advanced Certificate); nutrition and education (MS); nutrition and exercise physiology (MS); nutrition and public health (MS); nutrition education (Ed D), including nutrition (Ed D, PhD); physical disabilities (Ed D); reading specialist (MA); severe or multiple disabilities (MA); special education (Ed M, MA, Ed D); teaching of sign language (MA). *Program availability:* Part-time, evening/weekend. *Students:* 282 full-time (262 women), 262 part-time (222 women); includes 180 minority (54 Black or African American, non-Hispanic/Latino; 1 American Indian or Alaska Native, non-Hispanic/Latino; 56 Asian, non-Hispanic/Latino; 56 Hispanic/Latino; 1 Native Hawaiian or other Pacific Islander, non-Hispanic/Latino; 12 Two or more races, non-Hispanic/Latino), 55 international. 503 applicants, 57% accepted, 146 enrolled. Terminal master's awarded for partial completion of doctoral program. *Expenses: Tuition:* Full-time $36,288; part-time $1512 per credit. *Required fees:* $438 per semester. One-time fee: $510 full-time. Full-time tuition and fees vary according to course load. *Unit head:* Prof. Stephen T. Peverly, Chair, 212-678-3964, Fax: 212-678-8259, E-mail: stp4@columbia.edu. *Application contact:* David Estrella, Director of Admission, 212-678-3305, E-mail: estrella@tc.columbia.edu.
Website: http://www.tc.columbia.edu/health-and-behavior-studies/

Tennessee State University, The School of Graduate Studies and Research, College of Education, Department of Teaching and Learning, Nashville, TN 37209-1561. Offers curriculum and instruction (M Ed, Ed D); elementary education (M Ed); special education (M Ed). *Accreditation:* NCATE. *Degree requirements:* For doctorate, thesis/dissertation. *Entrance requirements:* For master's, GRE General Test, GRE Subject Test, or MAT, minimum GPA of 2.5; for doctorate, GRE General Test, GRE Subject Test, or MAT, minimum GPA of 3.25. Electronic applications accepted. *Faculty research:* Multicultural education, teacher education reform, whole language, interactive video teaching, English as a second language.

Tennessee Technological University, College of Graduate Studies, College of Education, Department of Curriculum and Instruction, Program in Special Education, Cookeville, TN 38505. Offers MA, Ed S. *Accreditation:* NCATE. *Program availability:* Part-time. *Faculty:* 6 full-time (3 women). *Students:* 2 full-time (1 woman), 12 part-time (10 women); includes 1 minority (Black or African American, non-Hispanic/Latino). Average age 27. 8 applicants, 75% accepted, 4 enrolled. In 2016, 7 master's awarded. *Degree requirements:* For master's and Ed S, comprehensive exam, thesis or alternative. *Entrance requirements:* For master's and Ed S, MAT or GRE. Additional exam requirements/recommendations for international students: Required—TOEFL (minimum score 527 paper-based; 71 iBT), IELTS (minimum score 5.5), PTE (minimum score 48), or TOEIC (Test of English as an International Communication). *Application deadline:* For fall admission, 8/1 for domestic students, 5/1 for international students; for spring admission, 12/1 for domestic students, 10/1 for international students; for summer admission, 5/1 for domestic students, 2/1 for international students. Applications are processed on a rolling basis. Application fee: $35 ($40 for international students). Electronic applications accepted. *Expenses:* Tuition, state resident: full-time $9375; part-time $534 per credit hour. Tuition, nonresident: full-time $22,443; part-time $1260 per credit hour. *Financial support:* Fellowships, research assistantships, teaching assistantships, and career-related internships or fieldwork available. Financial award application deadline: 4/1. *Unit head:* Dr. Jeremy Wendt, Interim Chairperson, 931-372-3181, Fax: 931-372-6270, E-mail: jwendt@tntech.edu. *Application contact:* Shelia K. Kendrick, Coordinator of Graduate Studies, 931-372-3808, Fax: 931-372-3497, E-mail: skendrick@tntech.edu.

Texas A&M International University, Office of Graduate Studies and Research, College of Education, Department of Professional Programs, Laredo, TX 78041-1900. Offers educational administration (MS Ed); generic special education (MS Ed); school counseling (MS). *Entrance requirements:* Additional exam requirements/recommendations for international students: Required—TOEFL (minimum score 550 paper-based; 79 iBT).

Texas A&M University, College of Education and Human Development, Department of Educational Psychology, College Station, TX 77843. Offers bilingual education (M Ed, MS); counseling psychology (PhD); educational psychology (M Ed, MS, PhD); educational technology (M Ed); school psychology (PhD); special education (M Ed, MS). *Accreditation:* APA (one or more programs are accredited). *Program availability:* Part-time, evening/weekend, blended/hybrid learning. *Faculty:* 42. *Students:* 172 full-time (139 women), 281 part-time (233 women); includes 144 minority (27 Black or African American, non-Hispanic/Latino; 1 American Indian or Alaska Native, non-Hispanic/Latino; 19 Asian, non-Hispanic/Latino; 86 Hispanic/Latino; 1 Native Hawaiian or other Pacific Islander, non-Hispanic/Latino; 10 Two or more races, non-Hispanic/Latino), 48 international. Average age 33. 181 applicants, 44% accepted, 45 enrolled. In 2016, 99 master's, 27 doctorates awarded. *Degree requirements:* For master's, thesis optional; for doctorate, thesis/dissertation. *Entrance requirements:* For master's and doctorate, GRE General Test. Additional exam requirements/recommendations for international students: Required—TOEFL (minimum score 550 paper-based; 80 iBT), IELTS (minimum score 6), PTE (minimum score 53). *Application deadline:* For fall admission, 12/1 for domestic students; for spring admission, 10/15 for domestic students. Application fee: $50 ($90 for international students). Electronic applications accepted. *Expenses:* Contact institution. *Financial support:* In 2016–17, 231 students received support, including 8 fellowships with tuition reimbursements available (averaging $9,919 per year), 98 research assistantships with tuition reimbursements available (averaging $6,004 per year), 13 teaching assistantships with tuition reimbursements available (averaging $9,368 per year); career-related internships or fieldwork, institutionally sponsored loans, scholarships/grants, traineeships, health care benefits, tuition waivers (full and partial), and unspecified assistantships also available. Support available to part-time students. Financial award application deadline: 3/15; financial award applicants required to submit FAFSA. *Unit head:* Dr. Victor Willson, Department Head, 979-845-1394, E-mail: v-willson@tamu.edu. *Application contact:* Kristie Stramaski, Senior Academic Advisor, 979-845-1833, E-mail: epsyadvisor@tamu.edu.
Website: http://epsy.tamu.edu

Texas A&M University–Commerce, College of Education and Human Services, Commerce, TX 75429-3011. Offers counseling (MS); curriculum and instruction (M Ed, MS); early childhood education (M Ed, MS); educational administration (M Ed, Ed D); educational psychology (PhD); educational technology leadership (MS); educational technology library science (MS); health, kinesiology and sports studies (MS); higher education (MS, Ed D); organization, learning, and technology (MS); psychology (MS); reading (M Ed, MS); school psychology (SSP); secondary education (M Ed, MS); social work (MSW); special education (M Ed); supervision, curriculum and instruction-elementary education (Ed D). *Program availability:* Part-time, 100% online, blended/hybrid learning. *Faculty:* 88 full-time (52 women), 31 part-time/adjunct (24 women). *Students:* 341 full-time (276 women), 1,495 part-time (1,156 women); includes 762 minority (429 Black or African American, non-Hispanic/Latino; 4 American Indian or Alaska Native, non-Hispanic/Latino; 27 Asian, non-Hispanic/Latino; 247 Hispanic/Latino; 1 Native Hawaiian or other Pacific Islander, non-Hispanic/Latino; 54 Two or more races, non-Hispanic/Latino), 18 international. Average age 37. 1,070 applicants, 54% accepted, 452 enrolled. In 2016, 579 master's, 31 doctorates awarded. *Degree requirements:* For master's, one foreign language, comprehensive exam, thesis optional, departmental qualifying exams (for some programs); for doctorate, comprehensive exam, thesis/dissertation, departmental qualifying exam; for SSP, comprehensive exam, thesis optional. *Entrance requirements:* For master's and doctorate, GRE General Test. Additional exam requirements/recommendations for international students: Required—TOEFL (minimum score 550 paper-based; 79 iBT), IELTS (minimum score 6). *Application deadline:* For fall admission, 6/1 priority date for international students; for spring admission, 10/15 priority date for international students; for summer admission, 3/15 priority date for international students. Applications are processed on a rolling basis. Application fee: $50. Electronic applications accepted. *Expenses:* $2,254 resident; $4,744 non-resident. *Financial support:* In 2016–17, 301 students received support, including 39 research assistantships with partial tuition reimbursements available (averaging $9,000 per year), 17 teaching assistantships with partial tuition reimbursements available (averaging $9,000 per year); career-related internships or fieldwork, Federal Work-Study, institutionally sponsored loans, scholarships/grants, health care benefits, and unspecified assistantships also available. Financial award application deadline: 5/1; financial award applicants required to submit FAFSA. *Faculty research:* Cognitive and bilingual education, positive behavioral intervention, literacy, math readiness. *Total annual research expenditures:* $470,963. *Unit head:* Dr. Timothy Letzring, Dean, 903-886-5181, Fax: 903-886-5905, E-mail: tim.letzring@tamuc.edu. *Application contact:* Jennifer Faunce, Graduate Recruiter, 903-886-5030, Fax: 903-886-5905, E-mail: jennifer.faunce@tamuc.edu.
Website: http://www.tamuc.edu/academics/graduateSchool/programs/education/default.aspx

Texas A&M University–Corpus Christi, College of Graduate Studies, College of Education, Program in Special Education, Corpus Christi, TX 78412-5503. Offers MS. *Program availability:* Part-time, evening/weekend. *Students:* 1 (woman) full-time, 28 part-time (all women); includes 11 minority (2 Black or African American, non-Hispanic/Latino; 9 Hispanic/Latino). Average age 37. 9 applicants, 67% accepted, 6 enrolled. In 2016, 2 master's awarded. *Degree requirements:* For master's, comprehensive exam. *Entrance requirements:* For master's, minimum GPA of 3.0 in last 60 hours; essay (approximately 300-400 words in length). Additional exam requirements/recommendations for international students: Required—TOEFL (minimum score 550 paper-based; 79 iBT), IELTS (minimum score 6.5). *Application deadline:* For fall admission, 7/15 priority date for domestic students, 5/1 priority date for international students; for spring admission, 11/15 priority date for domestic students, 9/1 priority date for international students; for summer admission, 4/15 priority date for domestic students, 2/1 priority date for international students. Applications are processed on a rolling basis. Application fee: $50 ($70 for international students). Electronic applications accepted. *Financial support:* In 2016–17, 5 students received support. Research assistantships, teaching assistantships, career-related internships or fieldwork, Federal Work-Study, institutionally sponsored loans, scholarships/grants, health care benefits, and unspecified assistantships available. Support available to part-time students. Financial award application deadline: 3/15. *Unit head:* Dr. Karen McCaleb, Chair, 361-825-2449, E-mail: karen.mccaleb@tamucc.edu. *Application contact:* Graduate Admissions Coordinator, 361-825-2177, Fax: 361-825-2755, E-mail: gradweb@tamucc.edu.
Website: http://gradschool.tamucc.edu/degrees/education/special_ed.html

Texas A&M University–Kingsville, College of Graduate Studies, College of Education and Human Performance, Department of Teacher and Bilingual Education, Program in Special Education, Kingsville, TX 78363. Offers M Ed. *Program availability:* Part-time, evening/weekend. *Degree requirements:* For master's, variable foreign language requirement, comprehensive exam, thesis (for some programs). *Entrance requirements:* For master's, GRE, MAT, GMAT. Additional exam requirements/recommendations for international students: Required—TOEFL (minimum score 550 paper-based; 79 iBT). Electronic applications accepted.

Special Education

Texas A&M University–San Antonio, Department of Curriculum and Kinesiology, San Antonio, TX 78224. Offers bilingual education (MA); early childhood education (M Ed); kinesiology (MS); reading (MS); special education (M Ed), including educational diagnostician, instructional specialist. *Program availability:* Part-time, evening/weekend. *Degree requirements:* For master's, comprehensive exam, thesis or alternative. *Entrance requirements:* For master's, MAT. Additional exam requirements/ recommendations for international students: Required—TOEFL (minimum score 550 paper-based; 80 iBT), IELTS (minimum score 6). Electronic applications accepted.

Texas A&M University–Texarkana, Graduate Studies and Research, College of Education and Liberal Arts, Texarkana, TX 75505-5518. Offers adult education (MS); curriculum and instruction (M Ed); education (MS); educational administration (M Ed); English (MA); instructional technology (MS); interdisciplinary studies (MA, MS); special education (MS). *Program availability:* Part-time, evening/weekend. *Degree requirements:* For master's, comprehensive exam (for some programs), thesis optional. *Entrance requirements:* For master's, minimum GPA of 2.5 on last 60 hours of bachelor's degree. Additional exam requirements/recommendations for international students: Required—TOEFL. Electronic applications accepted.

Texas Christian University, College of Education, Master's Programs in Education, Fort Worth, TX 76129. Offers counseling (M Ed); curriculum and instruction (M Ed), including curriculum studies, language and literacy, math education, science education; educational leadership (M Ed); special education (M Ed). *Program availability:* Part-time, evening/weekend. *Faculty:* 29 full-time (21 women), 8 part-time/adjunct (5 women). *Students:* 112 full-time (95 women), 12 part-time (11 women); includes 39 minority (6 Black or African American, non-Hispanic/Latino; 2 Asian, non-Hispanic/Latino; 27 Hispanic/Latino; 1 Native Hawaiian or other Pacific Islander, non-Hispanic/Latino; 3 Two or more races, non-Hispanic/Latino), 2 international. Average age 29. 107 applicants, 78% accepted, 66 enrolled. In 2016, 54 master's awarded. *Degree requirements:* For master's, comprehensive exam (for some programs), thesis (for some programs). *Entrance requirements:* For master's, GRE General Test. Additional exam requirements/ recommendations for international students: Required—TOEFL (minimum score 550 paper-based; 80 iBT). *Application deadline:* For fall admission, 3/1 for domestic and international students; for spring admission, 11/16 for domestic and international students; for summer admission, 3/1 for domestic and international students. Application fee: $60. Electronic applications accepted. *Expenses: Tuition:* Full-time $26,640; part-time $1480 per credit hour. *Required fees:* $48. Tuition and fees vary according to program. *Financial support:* In 2016–17, 104 students received support, including 4 research assistantships with full tuition reimbursements available (averaging $15,000 per year), 31 teaching assistantships with full tuition reimbursements available (averaging $15,000 per year); career-related internships or fieldwork, scholarships/ grants, and unspecified assistantships also available. Support available to part-time students. Financial award application deadline: 3/1; financial award applicants required to submit FAFSA. *Unit head:* Dr. Jan Lacina, Associate Dean, 817-257-6786, Fax: 817-257-7466, E-mail: j.lacina@tcu.edu. *Application contact:* Lori Kimball, Administrative Program Specialist, 817-257-7661, Fax: 817-257-7466, E-mail: l.kimball@tcu.edu.
Website: http://coe.tcu.edu/graduate-overview/

Texas State University, The Graduate College, College of Education, Program in Special Education, San Marcos, TX 78666. Offers M Ed. *Program availability:* Part-time. *Faculty:* 10 full-time (8 women), 3 part-time/adjunct (all women). *Students:* 23 full-time (20 women), 12 part-time (9 women); includes 12 minority (1 Black or African American, non-Hispanic/Latino; 1 Asian, non-Hispanic/Latino; 10 Hispanic/Latino), 2 international. Average age 32. 48 applicants, 63% accepted, 10 enrolled. In 2016, 24 master's awarded. *Degree requirements:* For master's, comprehensive exam. *Entrance requirements:* For master's, GRE General Test (minimum preferred score of 300 [151 verbal, 149 quantitative]), baccalaureate degree from regionally-accredited institution with minimum GPA of 2.75 in last 60 hours of course work, statement of purpose, resume (include license, certificates, teaching experience), 2 letters of recommendation from those familiar with professional work (at least one supervisor). Additional exam requirements/recommendations for international students: Required—TOEFL (minimum score 550 paper-based; 78 iBT), IELTS (minimum score 6.5). *Application deadline:* For fall admission, 6/15 priority date for domestic students, 6/1 priority date for international students; for spring admission, 10/15 priority date for domestic students, 10/1 for international students; for summer admission, 4/15 for domestic students, 3/15 for international students. Applications are processed on a rolling basis. Application fee: $40 ($90 for international students). Electronic applications accepted. *Expenses:* $4,851 per semester. *Financial support:* In 2016–17, 19 students received support, including 6 research assistantships (averaging $12,280 per year); fellowships, teaching assistantships, career-related internships or fieldwork, Federal Work-Study, institutionally sponsored loans, and scholarships/grants also available. Support available to part-time students. Financial award application deadline: 3/1; financial award applicants required to submit FAFSA. *Unit head:* Dr. Brenda Scheuermann, Graduate Adviser, 512-245-2157, Fax: 512-245-7911, E-mail: bs10@txstate.edu. *Application contact:* Dr. Andrea Golato, Dean of Graduate School, 512-245-2581, Fax: 512-245-8365, E-mail: gradcollege@txstate.edu.
Website: http://www.education.txstate.edu/ci/degrees-certifications/graduate/special-education.html

Texas Tech University, Graduate School, College of Education, Department of Educational Psychology and Leadership, Lubbock, TX 79409-1071. Offers counselor education (M Ed, PhD); distance education (M Ed); educational leadership (M Ed, Ed D, PhD); educational psychology (M Ed, PhD); higher education (M Ed, Ed D); higher education research (PhD); instructional technology (M Ed, Ed D); special education (M Ed, Ed D, PhD). *Accreditation:* ACA; NCATE. *Program availability:* Part-time, evening/weekend. *Faculty:* 59 full-time (29 women), 3 part-time/adjunct (all women). *Students:* 300 full-time (218 women), 656 part-time (482 women); includes 320 minority (87 Black or African American, non-Hispanic/Latino; 5 American Indian or Alaska Native, non-Hispanic/Latino; 5 Asian, non-Hispanic/Latino; 200 Hispanic/Latino; 23 Two or more races, non-Hispanic/Latino), 51 international. Average age 36. 668 applicants, 56% accepted, 285 enrolled. In 2016, 171 master's, 47 doctorates awarded. Terminal master's awarded for partial completion of doctoral program. *Degree requirements:* For master's, comprehensive exam, thesis optional; for doctorate, comprehensive exam, thesis/dissertation. *Entrance requirements:* For master's, GRE (for some programs); for doctorate, GRE. Additional exam requirements/recommendations for international students: Required—TOEFL (minimum score 550 paper-based; 79 iBT). *Application deadline:* For fall admission, 6/1 priority date for domestic students, 1/15 priority date for international students; for spring admission, 9/1 priority date for domestic students, 6/15 priority date for international students. Applications are processed on a rolling basis. Application fee: $75. Electronic applications accepted. *Expenses:* $285 per credit hour full-time resident tuition, $693 per credit hour full-time non-resident tuition; $50.50 per credit hour fee plus $608 per term fee. *Financial support:* In 2016–17, 384 students received support, including 384 fellowships (averaging $3,632 per year); scholarships/ grants and unspecified assistantships also available. Support available to part-time students. Financial award application deadline: 1/3; financial award applicants required to submit FAFSA. *Faculty research:* Cognitive, motivational, and developmental processes in learning; counseling education; instructional technology; generic special education and sensory impairment; community college administration; K-12 school administration. *Total annual research expenditures:* $1,371. *Unit head:* Dr. Hansel Burley, Chair, 806-834-5135, Fax: 806-742-2179, E-mail: hansel.burley@ttu.edu. *Application contact:* Pam Smith, Admissions Advisor, 806-834-2969, Fax: 806-742-2179, E-mail: pam.smith@ttu.edu.
Website: http://www.educ.ttu.edu/

Texas Woman's University, Graduate School, College of Professional Education, Department of Teacher Education, Denton, TX 76204-5769. Offers educational administration (M Ed, MA); special education (M Ed, MA, PhD), including educational diagnostician (M Ed, MA), intervention specialist (M Ed); teaching, learning, and curriculum (M Ed, MA). *Program availability:* Part-time. *Students:* 15 full-time (13 women), 98 part-time (85 women); includes 36 minority (13 Black or African American, non-Hispanic/Latino; 3 American Indian or Alaska Native, non-Hispanic/Latino; 3 Asian, non-Hispanic/Latino; 16 Hispanic/Latino; 1 Two or more races, non-Hispanic/Latino). Average age 38. In 2016, 111 master's, 1 doctorate awarded. Terminal master's awarded for partial completion of doctoral program. *Degree requirements:* For master's, comprehensive exam, thesis, professional paper (M Ed); for doctorate, comprehensive exam, thesis/dissertation. *Entrance requirements:* For master's, minimum GPA of 3.0 on last 60 undergraduate hours, 2 letters of reference, resume, copy of certifications, teacher service record, statement of intent; for doctorate, GRE General Test, minimum GPA of 3.0, 3 letters of reference, resume, copy of certifications, teacher service record, statement of intent. Additional exam requirements/recommendations for international students: Required—TOEFL (minimum score 550 paper-based; 79 iBT). *Application deadline:* For fall admission, 7/1 priority date for domestic students, 3/1 for international students; for spring admission, 11/1 priority date for domestic students, 7/1 for international students. Applications are processed on a rolling basis. Application fee: $50 ($75 for international students). Electronic applications accepted. *Expenses:* Tuition, state resident: full-time $9046; part-time $251 per credit hour. Tuition, nonresident: full-time $22,922; part-time $614 per credit hour. *International tuition:* $23,046 full-time. *Required fees:* $2690; $1285 per credit hour. One-time fee: $50. Tuition and fees vary according to course level, course load, program and reciprocity agreements. *Financial support:* Research assistantships, career-related internships or fieldwork, Federal Work-Study, institutionally sponsored loans, scholarships/grants, traineeships, health care benefits, and unspecified assistantships available. Support available to part-time students. Financial award application deadline: 3/1; financial award applicants required to submit FAFSA. *Faculty research:* Language and literacy, classroom management, learning disabilities, staff and professional development, leadership preparation practice. *Unit head:* Dr. Jane Pemberton, Chair, 940-898-2273, Fax: 940-898-2270, E-mail: teachereducation@twu.edu. *Application contact:* Dr. Samuel Wheeler, Assistant Director of Admissions, 940-898-3188, Fax: 940-898-3081, E-mail: wheelersr@twu.edu.
Website: http://www.twu.edu/teacher-education/

Touro College, Graduate School of Education, New York, NY 10010. Offers education and special education (MS); education biology (MS); instructional technology (MS); mathematics education (MS); school leadership (MS); teaching English to speakers of other languages (MS); teaching literacy (MS). *Accreditation:* TEAC. *Program availability:* Part-time, evening/weekend, online learning. *Faculty:* 52 full-time (34 women), 199 part-time/adjunct (136 women). *Students:* 578 full-time (483 women), 1,932 part-time (1,626 women); includes 749 minority (318 Black or African American, non-Hispanic/Latino; 5 American Indian or Alaska Native, non-Hispanic/Latino; 108 Asian, non-Hispanic/Latino; 288 Hispanic/Latino; 2 Native Hawaiian or other Pacific Islander, non-Hispanic/Latino; 28 Two or more races, non-Hispanic/Latino), 17 international. Average age 32. 1,422 applicants, 50% accepted, 675 enrolled. In 2016, 6 master's awarded. *Entrance requirements:* Additional exam requirements/recommendations for international students: Required—TOEFL (minimum score 83 iBT), IELTS (minimum score 6.5). *Application deadline:* For fall admission, 8/26 for domestic students, 7/15 for international students; for spring admission, 12/31 for domestic students, 12/15 for international students. Applications are processed on a rolling basis. Application fee: $50. *Financial support:* Federal Work-Study available. Financial award applicants required to submit FAFSA. *Faculty research:* Equity assistance, language development, scholarly communications, Latin American studies and cultural sensitivity, behavior management techniques and strategies in special education. *Unit head:* Dr. Arnold Spinner, Dean, 212-463-0400 Ext. 5561, Fax: 212-462-4889, E-mail: aspinner@touro.edu. *Application contact:* Luna Feliciano, Admissions, 212-463-0400.

Towson University, Program in Autism Studies, Towson, MD 21252-0001. Offers Postbaccalaureate Certificate. *Students:* 8 full-time (all women), 48 part-time (41 women); includes 6 minority (4 Black or African American, non-Hispanic/Latino; 2 Hispanic/Latino). *Entrance requirements:* For degree, bachelor's degree with minimum GPA of 3.0, 30 hours of human service activity as part of field experience, volunteer or paid work in the last five years. *Application deadline:* Applications are processed on a rolling basis. Application fee: $45. Electronic applications accepted. *Expenses:* Tuition, state resident: full-time $7580; part-time $379 per unit. Tuition, nonresident: full-time $15,700; part-time $785 per unit. *Required fees:* $2480. *Unit head:* Dr. Connie Anderson, Graduate Program Director, 410-704-4640, E-mail: connieanderson@towson.edu. *Application contact:* Coverley Beidleman, Assistant Director of Graduate Admissions, 410-704-2113, Fax: 410-704-3030, E-mail: grads@towson.edu.
Website: http://www.towson.edu/chp/departments/interprofessional/grad/autismpbc/

Towson University, Program in Special Education, Towson, MD 21252-0001. Offers M Ed. *Accreditation:* NCATE. *Program availability:* Part-time, evening/weekend. *Students:* 2 full-time (both women), 133 part-time (121 women); includes 19 minority (7 Black or African American, non-Hispanic/Latino; 1 American Indian or Alaska Native, non-Hispanic/Latino; 1 Asian, non-Hispanic/Latino; 8 Hispanic/Latino; 2 Two or more races, non-Hispanic/Latino). *Degree requirements:* For master's, thesis optional. *Entrance requirements:* For master's, letter of recommendation, bachelor's degree, professional teacher certification, minimum GPA of 3.0. *Application deadline:* For fall admission, 2/15 for domestic and international students; for spring admission, 10/15 for domestic and international students. Applications are processed on a rolling basis. Application fee: $45. Electronic applications accepted. *Expenses:* Tuition, state resident: full-time $7580; part-time $379 per unit. Tuition, nonresident: full-time $15,700; part-time $785 per unit. *Required fees:* $2480. *Unit head:* Dr. Andrea Parrish, Graduate Program Director, 410-704-3835, E-mail: aparrish@towson.edu. *Application contact:* Coverley Beidleman, Assistant Director of Graduate Admissions, 410-704-2113, Fax: 410-704-3030, E-mail: grads@towson.edu.
Website: http://www.towson.edu/coe/departments/specialed/gradspecialed/

Trevecca Nazarene University, Graduate Education Program, Nashville, TN 37210-2877. Offers accountability and instructional leadership (Ed S); curriculum and instruction for Christian school educators (M Ed); curriculum and instruction K-12 (M Ed); educational leadership (M Ed); English second language (M Ed); library and information science (MLI Sc); special education: visual impairments (M Ed); teaching (MAT), including teaching 6-12, teaching K-5. *Accreditation:* NCATE. *Program availability:* Part-time, evening/weekend, online learning. *Faculty:* 5 full-time (3 women), 18 part-time/adjunct (12 women). *Students:* 80 full-time (64 women), 16 part-time (13 women); includes 19 minority (17 Black or African American, non-Hispanic/Latino; 2 Hispanic/Latino). Average age 35. In 2016, 68 master's, 7 other advanced degrees

awarded. *Degree requirements:* For master's, comprehensive exam, exit assessment/e-portfolio. *Entrance requirements:* For master's, GRE (minimum score of 290) or MAT (minimum score of 378); PRAXIS (for MAT), minimum GPA of 3.0, official transcript from regionally-accredited institution, at least 3 years' successful teaching experience (for M Ed in educational leadership major). Additional exam requirements/recommendations for international students: Required—TOEFL (minimum score 550 paper-based). *Application deadline:* Applications are processed on a rolling basis. Electronic applications accepted. *Expenses:* Contact institution. *Financial support:* Applicants required to submit FAFSA. *Unit head:* Dr. Suzie Harris, Dean, School of Education/ Director of Graduate Education Programs, 615-248-1201, Fax: 615-248-1597, E-mail: admissions_ged@trevecca.edu. *Application contact:* 844-TNU-GRAD, E-mail: sgcsadmissions@trevecca.edu.
Website: http://www.trevecca.edu/soe

Trinity Baptist College, Graduate Programs, Jacksonville, FL 32221. Offers educational leadership (M Ed); special education (M Ed). *Program availability:* Online learning. *Entrance requirements:* For master's, GRE (for M Ed), 2 letters of recommendation; minimum GPA of 2.5 (for M Min), 3.0 (for M Ed); computer proficiency.

Trinity Christian College, Program in Special Education, Palos Heights, IL 60463-0929. Offers MA. *Program availability:* Evening/weekend. *Degree requirements:* For master's, project. *Entrance requirements:* For master's, valid teaching license, official transcripts, two letters of recommendation. Electronic applications accepted.

Trinity Washington University, School of Education, Washington, DC 20017-1094. Offers clinical mental health counseling (MA); early childhood education (MAT); educating for change (M Ed); educational administration (MSA); elementary education (MAT); reading (M Ed); school counseling (MA); secondary education (MAT), including English, social studies; special education (MAT). *Accreditation:* NCATE. *Program availability:* Part-time, evening/weekend. *Degree requirements:* For master's, thesis (for some programs), capstone project(s). *Entrance requirements:* For master's, PRAXIS I, minimum GPA of 2.8. Additional exam requirements/recommendations for international students: Required—TOEFL (minimum score 550 paper-based). *Faculty research:* Technology, literacy, special education, organizations, inclusion models.

Tusculum College, Graduate and Professional Studies, Program in Curriculum and Instruction, Greeneville, TN 37743-9997. Offers mathematics education (MA Ed); special education (MA Ed). *Program availability:* Evening/weekend. *Degree requirements:* For master's, thesis or alternative. *Entrance requirements:* For master's, NTE, PRAXIS II, GRE, MAT, 3 years of work experience, minimum GPA of 3.0, bachelor's degree. Additional exam requirements/recommendations for international students: Required—TOEFL (minimum score 540 paper-based; 73 iBT). *Application deadline:* Applications are processed on a rolling basis. Application fee: $0. *Expenses: Tuition:* Full-time $7497; part-time $357 per credit hour. *Unit head:* Dr. Tricia Hunsader, Dean, School of Education, 423-636-7300 Ext. 5693, E-mail: thunsader@tusculum.edu. *Application contact:* Lindsey Seal, Director of Enrollment, 423-636-7300 Ext. 5006, E-mail: lseal@tusculum.edu.
Website: http://home.tusculum.edu/gps/graduate-degrees/master-arts-education-curriculum-instruction/

Union College, Graduate Programs, Department of Education, Program in Special Education, Barbourville, KY 40906-1499. Offers MA. *Degree requirements:* For master's, thesis optional. *Entrance requirements:* For master's, GRE General Test, NTE.

Universidad del Este, Graduate School, Carolina, PR 00984. Offers accounting (MBA); adult education (M Ed); agribusiness (MBA); criminal justice and criminology (MA); curriculum and instruction - early education (M Ed); curriculum and instruction - elementary (M Ed); curriculum and instruction - English (M Ed); curriculum and instruction - Spanish (M Ed); human resources (MBA); information security management (MBA); information technology and Web business development (MBA); management (MBA); public policy (MPA); social work (MA), including clinical social work; special education (M Ed); strategic leadership (MBA).

Universidad del Turabo, Graduate Programs, Programs in Education, Program in Special Education, Gurabo, PR 00778-3030. Offers M Ed. *Program availability:* Part-time, evening/weekend. *Students:* 37 full-time (31 women), 24 part-time (20 women); all minorities (all Hispanic/Latino). Average age 34. 41 applicants, 61% accepted, 22 enrolled. In 2016, 16 master's awarded. *Entrance requirements:* For master's, GRE, EXADEP, GMAT, interview, official transcript, essay, recommendation letters. *Application deadline:* For fall admission, 8/5 for domestic students. Applications are processed on a rolling basis. Application fee: $25. Electronic applications accepted. *Financial support:* Institutionally sponsored loans available. Financial award applicants required to submit FAFSA. *Unit head:* Israel Rodríguez, Dean, 787-743-7979. *Application contact:* Diriee Rodríguez, Admissions Director, 787-743-7979 Ext. 4453, E-mail: admisiones-ut@suagm.edu.
Website: http://ut.suagm.edu/es/educacion

Universidad Iberoamericana, Graduate School, Santo Domingo D.N., Dominican Republic. Offers business administration (MBA, PMBA); constitutional law (LL M); dentistry (DMD); educational management (MA); integrated marketing communication (MA); psychopedagogical intervention (M Ed); real estate law (LL M); strategic management of human talent (MM).

Universidad Metropolitana, School of Education, Program in Special Education, San Juan, PR 00928-1150. Offers M Ed. *Degree requirements:* For master's, thesis or alternative. Electronic applications accepted.

Université de Sherbrooke, Faculty of Education, Program in Special Education, Sherbrooke, QC J1K 2R1, Canada. Offers M Ed, Diploma. *Program availability:* Part-time, evening/weekend. *Degree requirements:* For master's, thesis.

University at Albany, State University of New York, School of Education, Division of Special Education, Albany, NY 12222-0001. Offers MS. *Entrance requirements:* Additional exam requirements/recommendations for international students: Required—TOEFL (minimum score 550 paper-based). *Application deadline:* For fall admission, 3/1 for domestic students, 5/1 for international students. Applications are processed on a rolling basis. Application fee: $75. Electronic applications accepted. *Expenses:* Tuition, state resident: full-time $10,870; part-time $453 per credit hour. Tuition, nonresident: full-time $22,210; part-time $925 per credit hour. *International tuition:* $21,550 full-time. *Required fees:* $1864; $96 per credit hour. *Financial support:* Fellowships and career-related internships or fieldwork available. *Unit head:* Bruce Saddler, Program Director, 516-442-5062, E-mail: bsaddler@albany.edu.
Website: http://www.albany.edu/special_education/

University at Buffalo, the State University of New York, Graduate School, Graduate School of Education, Department of Learning and Instruction, Buffalo, NY 14260. Offers biology education (Ed M, Certificate); chemistry education (Ed M, Certificate); childhood education (Ed M); childhood education with bilingual extension (Ed M); college teaching (Advanced Certificate); curriculum, instruction and the science of learning (PhD); early childhood education (Ed M); early childhood education with bilingual extension (Ed M); earth science education (Ed M, Certificate); education and technology (Ed M); education studies (Ed M); educational technology and new literacies (Certificate); educational technology and new literacies (Advanced Certificate); elementary education (Ed D); English education (Ed M, Certificate); English education studies (Ed M); English for speakers of other languages (Ed M); foreign and second language education (PhD); French education (Ed M, Certificate); German education (Ed M, Certificate); gifted education (Certificate); Latin education (Ed M, Certificate); literacy education studies (Ed M); literacy specialist (Ed M); literacy teaching and learning (Certificate); mathematics education (Ed M, Certificate); music education (Ed M, Certificate); music education studies (Ed M); music learning theory (Advanced Certificate); online education (Advanced Certificate); physics education (Ed M, Certificate); science and the public (Ed M); social studies education (Ed M, Certificate); Spanish education (Ed M, Certificate); special education (PhD); teaching English to speakers of other languages (Ed M). *Program availability:* Part-time, evening/weekend, 100% online. *Faculty:* 28 full-time (21 women), 67 part-time/adjunct (49 women). *Students:* 198 full-time (153 women), 312 part-time (220 women); includes 48 minority (28 Black or African American, non-Hispanic/Latino; 4 American Indian or Alaska Native, non-Hispanic/ Latino; 15 Asian, non-Hispanic/Latino; 1 Hispanic/Latino), 66 international. Average age 33. 336 applicants, 86% accepted, 178 enrolled. In 2016, 137 master's, 24 doctorates, 25 other advanced degrees awarded. *Degree requirements:* For master's, comprehensive exam; for doctorate, thesis/dissertation, research analysis exam, research experience. *Entrance requirements:* For master's, letters of reference; for doctorate, GRE General Test or MAT, interview, writing sample, letters of recommendation. Additional exam requirements/recommendations for international students: Required—TOEFL (minimum score 600 paper-based; 96 iBT). *Application deadline:* For fall admission, 2/1 priority date for domestic and international students; for spring admission, 11/15 priority date for domestic students, 10/1 for international students. Applications are processed on a rolling basis. Application fee: $50. Electronic applications accepted. *Financial support:* In 2016–17, 44 fellowships (averaging $4,010 per year), 39 research assistantships with tuition reimbursements (averaging $9,897 per year) were awarded; teaching assistantships, career-related internships or fieldwork, Federal Work-Study, institutionally sponsored loans, scholarships/grants, tuition waivers (full and partial), and unspecified assistantships also available. Financial award application deadline: 2/28; financial award applicants required to submit FAFSA. *Faculty research:* Science assessment, foreign language teaching and learning, early learning, new literacies, gender and education. *Total annual research expenditures:* $534,880. *Unit head:* Dr. Deborah Moore-Russo, Chair, 716-645-4069, Fax: 716-645-3161, E-mail: dam29@buffalo.edu. *Application contact:* Luann Zak, Admissions Assistant, 716-645-2110, Fax: 716-645-7937, E-mail: luannzak@buffalo.edu.
Website: http://gse.buffalo.edu/lai

The University of Akron, Graduate School, College of Education, Department of Curricular and Instructional Studies, Program in Special Education, Akron, OH 44325. Offers MA. *Accreditation:* NCATE. *Students:* 25 full-time (14 women), 25 part-time (20 women); includes 5 minority (all Black or African American, non-Hispanic/Latino), 7 international. Average age 31. 21 applicants, 71% accepted, 15 enrolled. In 2016, 26 master's awarded. *Degree requirements:* For master's, comprehensive exam. *Entrance requirements:* For master's, valid teaching license. Additional exam requirements/ recommendations for international students: Required—TOEFL (minimum score 550 paper-based; 79 iBT), IELTS (minimum score 6.5). *Application deadline:* Applications are processed on a rolling basis. Application fee: $45 ($70 for international students). Electronic applications accepted. *Expenses:* Tuition, state resident: full-time $8618; part-time $359 per credit hour. Tuition, nonresident: full-time $17,149; part-time $715 per credit hour. *Required fees:* $1652. *Unit head:* Dr. Susan Clark, Interim Chair, 330-972-7780, E-mail: sclark1@uakron.edu. *Application contact:* Kelly Chaff, College Program Specialist, 330-972-7028, E-mail: klchaff@uakron.edu.

The University of Alabama, Graduate School, College of Education, Department of Special Education and Multiple Abilities, Tuscaloosa, AL 35487. Offers collaborative special education (M Ed, Ed S); early intervention (M Ed, Ed S); gifted and talented education (M Ed, Ed S); multiple abilities (M Ed); special education (Ed D, PhD). *Program availability:* Part-time, evening/weekend. *Faculty:* 12 full-time (8 women). *Students:* 26 full-time (24 women), 34 part-time (33 women); includes 8 minority (5 Black or African American, non-Hispanic/Latino; 1 American Indian or Alaska Native, non-Hispanic/Latino; 1 Asian, non-Hispanic/Latino; 1 Hispanic/Latino). Average age 33. 50 applicants, 54% accepted, 24 enrolled. In 2016, 34 master's, 1 doctorate, 1 other advanced degree awarded. Terminal master's awarded for partial completion of doctoral program. *Degree requirements:* For master's, comprehensive exam, thesis optional; for doctorate, one foreign language, comprehensive exam, thesis/dissertation. *Entrance requirements:* For master's, GRE, minimum undergraduate GPA of 3.0, teaching certificate, 3 letters of recommendation; for doctorate, GRE, 3 years of teaching experience, minimum undergraduate GPA of 3.25. Additional exam requirements/ recommendations for international students: Required—TOEFL. *Application deadline:* Applications are processed on a rolling basis. Application fee: $50 ($60 for international students). Electronic applications accepted. *Expenses:* Tuition, state resident: full-time $10,470. Tuition, nonresident: full-time $26,950. *Financial support:* In 2016–17, 10 students received support, including 5 research assistantships with tuition reimbursements available (averaging $9,000 per year), 5 teaching assistantships with tuition reimbursements available (averaging $9,000 per year); health care benefits and unspecified assistantships also available. Financial award application deadline: 7/1; financial award applicants required to submit FAFSA. *Faculty research:* Gifted education, mild disabilities, early intervention, severe disabilities, behavior disorders. *Unit head:* Dr. Robert Alexander McWilliam, Professor and Department Head, 205-348-6527, Fax: 205-348-6782, E-mail: ramcwilliam@ua.edu. *Application contact:* Bernice Ofori-Parku, Office Associate II, 205-348-6093, Fax: 205-348-6782, E-mail: bsoforiparku@ua.edu.
Website: http://education.ua.edu/departments/spema/

The University of Alabama at Birmingham, School of Education, Program in Special Education, Birmingham, AL 35294. Offers MA Ed. *Accreditation:* NCATE. *Degree requirements:* For master's, thesis optional. *Entrance requirements:* For master's, GRE General Test or NTE, minimum GPA of 3.0. Electronic applications accepted. Full time tuition and fees vary according to course load and program.

The University of Alabama in Huntsville, School of Graduate Studies, College of Education, Huntsville, AL 35899. Offers autism spectrum disorders (M Ed, Graduate Certificate); biology (MAT); chemistry (MAT); differentiated instruction in elementary education (M Ed); English language arts (MAT); English speakers of other languages (M Ed, MAT); history (MAT); mathematics (MAT); physics (MAT); reading education (M Ed); secondary education (M Ed). *Expenses:* Tuition, state resident: full-time $9834; part-time $600 per credit hour. Tuition, nonresident: full-time $21,830; part-time $1325 per credit hour.

University of Alaska Anchorage, College of Education, Program in Special Education, Anchorage, AK 99508. Offers early childhood special education (M Ed); special education (M Ed, Certificate). *Program availability:* Part-time. *Degree requirements:* For master's, comprehensive exam (for some programs), thesis or alternative. *Entrance requirements:* For master's, GRE or MAT, interview, minimum GPA of 2.75. Additional exam requirements/recommendations for international students: Required—TOEFL (minimum score 550 paper-based). *Faculty research:* Mild disabilities, substance abuse issues for educators, partnerships to improve at-risk youth, analysis of planning models for teachers in special education.

University of Alaska Fairbanks, School of Education, Program in Education, Fairbanks, AK 99775. Offers special education (M Ed). *Program availability:* 100% online, blended/hybrid learning. *Faculty:* 16 full-time (11 women), 2 part-time/adjunct (1 woman). *Students:* 35 full-time (22 women), 80 part-time (66 women); includes 10 minority (5 American Indian or Alaska Native, non-Hispanic/Latino; 3 Hispanic/Latino; 2 Two or more races, non-Hispanic/Latino), 2 international. Average age 36. 30 applicants, 67% accepted, 17 enrolled. In 2016, 27 master's awarded. *Degree requirements:* For master's, comprehensive exam, oral defense of project or thesis. *Entrance requirements:* For master's, GRE General Test, PRAXIS I, PRAXIS II, bachelor's degree from accredited institution with minimum cumulative undergraduate and major GPA of 3.0, writing sample, evidence of technology competence, criminal background check. Additional exam requirements/recommendations for international students: Required—TOEFL (minimum score 550 paper-based; 79 iBT), IELTS (minimum score 6.5). *Application deadline:* For fall admission, 2/15 for domestic and international students; for spring admission, 10/15 for domestic students, 8/1 for international students. Applications are processed on a rolling basis. Application fee: $60. Electronic applications accepted. *Expenses:* Tuition, state resident: full-time $7992; part-time $444 per credit. Tuition, nonresident: full-time $16,326; part-time $907 per credit. *Required fees:* $39 per credit. $322 per semester. Tuition and fees vary according to course level, course load, campus/location, program and reciprocity agreements. *Financial support:* In 2016–17, 1 teaching assistantship with full tuition reimbursement (averaging $5,251 per year) was awarded; fellowships with full tuition reimbursements, research assistantships with full tuition reimbursements, career-related internships or fieldwork, Federal Work-Study, scholarships/grants, health care benefits, and unspecified assistantships also available. Support available to part-time students. Financial award application deadline: 6/1; financial award applicants required to submit FAFSA. *Total annual research expenditures:* $203,000. *Unit head:* Steve Atwater, Interim Dean, 907-474-7341, Fax: 907-474-5451, E-mail: uaf-soe-school@alaska.edu. *Application contact:* Mary Kreta, Director of Admissions, 907-474-7500, Fax: 907-474-7097, E-mail: admissions@uaf.edu.
Website: https://sites.google.com/a/alaska.edu/uaf-soe-graduate/

University of Alaska Southeast, Graduate Programs, Program in Education, Juneau, AK 99801. Offers educational leadership (M Ed); elementary education (MAT); learning design and technology (M Ed); mathematics education (M Ed); reading specialist (M Ed); secondary education (MAT); special education (M Ed, MAT). *Accreditation:* NCATE. *Program availability:* Part-time, evening/weekend, online learning. *Degree requirements:* For master's, comprehensive exam or project, portfolio. *Entrance requirements:* For master's, PRAXIS, minimum GPA of 3.0, writing sample, letters of recommendation. *Application deadline:* For fall admission, 3/8 for domestic students. Applications are processed on a rolling basis. Application fee: $60. Electronic applications accepted. *Expenses:* Tuition, state resident: part-time $466 per credit. Tuition, nonresident: part-time $979 per credit. *Required fees:* $19 per credit. Part-time tuition and fees vary according to course level, campus/location and reciprocity agreements. *Financial support:* Federal Work-Study, scholarships/grants, and tuition waivers (full and partial) available. Support available to part-time students. Financial award applicants required to submit FAFSA. *Faculty research:* Applied classroom research, culturally responsive practices, action research, teaching effectiveness. *Unit head:* Dr. Larry Harris, Dean, 907-796-6551, Fax: 907-796-6550, E-mail: larry.harris@uas.alaska.edu. *Application contact:* Susan A. Stuck, Administrative Assistant, 866-465-6424, Fax: 866-465-5159, E-mail: jnsas@uas.alaska.edu.

University of Alberta, Faculty of Graduate Studies and Research, Department of Educational Psychology, Edmonton, AB T6G 2E1, Canada. Offers counseling psychology (M Ed, PhD); educational psychology (M Ed, PhD); instructional technology (M Ed); school counseling (M Ed); school psychology (M Ed, PhD); special education (M Ed, PhD); special education-deafness studies (M Ed); teaching English as a second language (M Ed). *Program availability:* Part-time. *Degree requirements:* For master's, thesis optional; for doctorate, comprehensive exam, thesis/dissertation. *Entrance requirements:* For master's and doctorate, minimum GPA of 3.0. Additional exam requirements/recommendations for international students: Required—TOEFL. *Faculty research:* Human learning, development and assessment.

The University of Arizona, College of Education, Department of Disability and Psychoeducational Studies, Program in Special Education, Tucson, AZ 85721. Offers cross-categorical special education (MA); deaf and hard of hearing (MA); learning disabilities (MA); severe and multiple disabilities (MA); special education (PhD); visual impairment (MA). *Program availability:* Part-time. *Entrance requirements:* Additional exam requirements/recommendations for international students: Required—TOEFL (minimum score 550 paper-based; 79 iBT). Electronic applications accepted.

University of Arkansas, Graduate School, College of Education and Health Professions, Department of Curriculum and Instruction, Program in Special Education, Fayetteville, AR 72701. Offers M Ed, MAT. *Accreditation:* NCATE. *Program availability:* Part-time, evening/weekend, online learning. In 2016, 12 master's awarded. *Entrance requirements:* For master's, GRE General Test or MAT. *Application deadline:* For fall admission, 4/1 for international students; for spring admission, 10/1 for international students. Applications are processed on a rolling basis. Application fee: $40 ($50 for international students). Electronic applications accepted. *Financial support:* Fellowships, research assistantships, teaching assistantships, career-related internships or fieldwork, and Federal Work-Study available. Support available to part-time students. Financial award application deadline: 4/1; financial award applicants required to submit FAFSA. *Unit head:* Dr. Michael Daugherty, Unit Head, 479-575-4209, E-mail: mkd03@uark.edu. *Application contact:* Dr. Peggy Schaefer-Whitby, Graduate Coordinator, 479-575-3302, Fax: 479-575-6676, E-mail: pschaefe@uark.edu.
Website: http://cied.uark.edu/

University of Arkansas at Little Rock, Graduate School, College of Education and Health Professions, Department of Counseling, Adult and Rehabilitation Education, Little Rock, AR 72204-1099. Offers adult education (M Ed); counselor education (M Ed); rehabilitation counseling (MA, Graduate Certificate); rehabilitation for the blind: orientation and mobility (MA). *Accreditation:* CORE; NCATE. *Program availability:* Part-time. *Entrance requirements:* For master's, interview, minimum GPA of 2.75. *Faculty research:* Low vision, orientation and mobility instruction.

University of Arkansas at Little Rock, Graduate School, College of Education and Health Professions, Department of Teacher Education, Program in Special Education, Little Rock, AR 72204-1099. Offers M Ed. *Accreditation:* NCATE. *Program availability:* Part-time, evening/weekend. *Degree requirements:* For master's, comprehensive exam, portfolio or thesis. *Entrance requirements:* For master's, interview, minimum GPA of 2.75, GRE General Test or teaching certificate.

The University of British Columbia, Faculty of Education, Department of Educational and Counseling Psychology, and Special Education, Vancouver, BC V6T 1Z4, Canada. Offers counseling psychology (M Ed, MA, PhD); guidance studies (Diploma); human development, learning and culture (M Ed, MA, PhD); measurement, evaluation, and research methodology (M Ed, MA, PhD); school psychology (M Ed, MA, PhD); special education (M Ed, MA, PhD, Diploma). *Program availability:* Part-time. *Degree requirements:* For master's, thesis (for some programs); for doctorate, comprehensive exam, thesis/dissertation. *Entrance requirements:* For master's, GRE General Test (counseling psychology MA); for doctorate, GRE General Test. Additional exam requirements/recommendations for international students: Required—TOEFL. Application fee: $102 Canadian dollars ($165 Canadian dollars for international students). Electronic applications accepted. *Expenses:* $6,865 per year tuition, $10,938 per year international (for MA, M Ed); $4,802 per year tuition, $8,436 per year international (for PhD). *Financial support:* Fellowships, research assistantships, teaching assistantships, career-related internships or fieldwork, Federal Work-Study, institutionally sponsored loans, scholarships/grants, health care benefits, tuition waivers (full and partial), and unspecified assistantships available. *Faculty research:* Women, family, social problems, career transition, stress and coping problems. *Application contact:* Karen Yan, Graduate Program Assistant, 604-822-6371, Fax: 604-822-3302, E-mail: karen.yan@ubc.ca.
Website: http://ecps.educ.ubc.ca/

University of California, Berkeley, Graduate Division, School of Education, Program in Special Education, Berkeley, CA 94720-1500. Offers PhD. Program held jointly with San Francisco State University. *Students:* 20 full-time (17 women); includes 3 minority (2 Asian, non-Hispanic/Latino; 1 Hispanic/Latino), 2 international. Average age 34. 21 applicants, 3 enrolled. In 2016, 2 doctorates awarded. *Degree requirements:* For doctorate, thesis/dissertation, oral qualifying exam. *Entrance requirements:* For doctorate, GRE General Test, minimum undergraduate GPA of 3.0 during last 2 years, 3 letters of recommendation. *Application deadline:* For fall admission, 12/16 for domestic students. Application fee: $105 ($125 for international students). Electronic applications accepted. *Financial support:* Fellowships, research assistantships, teaching assistantships, institutionally sponsored loans, health care benefits, and unspecified assistantships available. *Application contact:* Caron Williams, Program Assistant, 510-643-6871, E-mail: spedinfo@berkeley.edu.
Website: https://gse.berkeley.edu/cognition-development/joint-special-ed

University of California, Berkeley, Graduate Division, School of Education, Programs in Education, Berkeley, CA 94720-1500. Offers development in mathematics and science (MA); education in mathematics, science, and technology (MA, PhD); human development and education (MA, PhD); leadership education (MA); special education (PhD); teacher education (MA); MA/Credential; PhD/Credential; PhD/MA. *Students:* 286 full-time (207 women); includes 133 minority (31 Black or African American, non-Hispanic/Latino; 2 American Indian or Alaska Native, non-Hispanic/Latino; 44 Asian, non-Hispanic/Latino; 56 Hispanic/Latino), 29 international. Average age 33. 643 applicants, 84 enrolled. In 2016, 105 master's, 31 doctorates awarded. Terminal master's awarded for partial completion of doctoral program. *Degree requirements:* For master's, exam or thesis; for doctorate, thesis/dissertation, oral qualifying exam. *Entrance requirements:* For master's and doctorate, GRE General Test, minimum GPA of 3.0 during last 2 years of undergraduate course work. *Application deadline:* For fall admission, 12/16 for domestic students. Application fee: $105 ($125 for international students). Electronic applications accepted. *Financial support:* Fellowships, research assistantships, teaching assistantships, institutionally sponsored loans, health care benefits, and unspecified assistantships available. *Faculty research:* Human development, social and moral educational psychology, developmental teacher preparation. *Unit head:* Prof. Prudence L. Carter, Dean, 510-642-3726, E-mail: gsedeansoffice@lists.berkeley.edu.
Website: https://gse.berkeley.edu

University of California, Los Angeles, Graduate Division, Graduate School of Education and Information Studies, Program in Special Education, Los Angeles, CA 90095. Offers PhD. Program offered jointly with California State University, Los Angeles. *Degree requirements:* For doctorate, thesis/dissertation, oral and written qualifying exams. *Entrance requirements:* For doctorate, GRE General Test, minimum undergraduate GPA of 3.0. Additional exam requirements/recommendations for international students: Required—TOEFL (minimum score 560 paper-based; 87 iBT). Electronic applications accepted.

University of California, Riverside, Graduate Division, Graduate School of Education, Riverside, CA 92521-0102. Offers autism (M Ed); diversity and equity (M Ed); education specialist (Credential); education, society, and culture (MA, PhD); educational psychology (MA, PhD); general education (M Ed); higher education administration and policy (M Ed, PhD); multiple subject (Credential); reading (M Ed); school psychology (PhD); single subject (Credential); special education (M Ed, MA, PhD); TESOL (M Ed). Terminal master's awarded for partial completion of doctoral program. *Degree requirements:* For master's, thesis optional, comprehensive exams or thesis (MA), case study or analytical report (M Ed); for doctorate, thesis/dissertation, written and oral qualifying exams, college teaching practicum. *Entrance requirements:* For master's, GRE General Test (for MA); CBEST and CSET (for M Ed in general education only), UCR Extension TESOL certificate (for M Ed with TESOL emphasis only); for doctorate, GRE General Test, writing sample; for Credential, CBEST, CSET. Additional exam requirements/recommendations for international students: Required—TOEFL (minimum score 550 paper-based; 80 iBT), IELTS (minimum score 7). Electronic applications accepted. *Expenses:* Tuition, state resident: full-time $16,666. Tuition, nonresident: full-time $31,768. *Required fees:* $11,055.54 per quarter. $3685.18 per quarter. Tuition and fees vary according to campus/location and program. *Faculty research:* Responsiveness to intervention, faculty core, response to intervention of English language learners, advanced modeling techniques, study on social capital, trust, and motivation.

University of Central Arkansas, Graduate School, College of Education, Department of Early Childhood and Special Education, Program in Special Education, Conway, AR 72035-0001. Offers collaborative instructional specialist (ages 0-8) (MSE); collaborative instructional specialist (grades 4-12) (MSE); special education instructional specialist grades 4-12 (Graduate Certificate); special education instructional specialist P-4 (Graduate Certificate). *Accreditation:* NCATE. *Program availability:* Part-time, evening/weekend, online learning. *Degree requirements:* For master's, comprehensive exam, thesis optional. *Entrance requirements:* For master's, GRE General Test, minimum GPA of 2.7. Additional exam requirements/recommendations for international students: Required—TOEFL (minimum score 550 paper-based; 80 iBT).

University of Central Arkansas, Graduate School, College of Education, Department of Leadership Studies, Conway, AR 72035-0001. Offers college student personnel (MS); district-level administration (PMC); educational leadership - district level (Ed S); instructional technology (MS); library media and information technology (MS); school counseling (MS); school leadership (MS); school-based leadership adult education program administration (PMC); school-based leadership building administration (PMC); school-based leadership curriculum administration (PMC); school-based leadership gifted and talented program administration (PMC); school-based leadership special education program administration (PMC). *Accreditation:* NCATE. *Program availability:* Part-time, evening/weekend, online learning. *Degree requirements:* For master's and other advanced degree, comprehensive exam. *Entrance requirements:* For master's, GRE. Additional exam requirements/recommendations for international students: Required—TOEFL (minimum score 80 iBT). Electronic applications accepted. *Expenses:* Contact institution.

University of Central Florida, College of Education and Human Performance, Department of Child, Family and Community Sciences, Program in Exceptional Student Education, Orlando, FL 32816. Offers autism spectrum disorders (Certificate); exceptional student education (M Ed); exceptional student education K-12 (MA); intervention specialist (Certificate); pre-kindergarten disabilities (Certificate); severe or profound disabilities (Certificate); special education (Certificate). *Accreditation:* NCATE. *Program availability:* Part-time, evening/weekend. *Students:* 22 full-time (19 women), 162 part-time (142 women); includes 64 minority (22 Black or African American, non-Hispanic/Latino; 1 American Indian or Alaska Native, non-Hispanic/Latino; 2 Asian, non-Hispanic/Latino; 39 Hispanic/Latino). Average age 35. 100 applicants, 82% accepted, 55 enrolled. In 2016, 41 master's, 64 other advanced degrees awarded. *Degree requirements:* For master's, comprehensive exam, thesis or alternative. *Entrance requirements:* For master's, GRE General Test. Additional exam requirements/recommendations for international students: Required—TOEFL. *Application deadline:* For fall admission, 7/15 for domestic students; for spring admission, 11/15 for domestic students. Application fee: $30. Electronic applications accepted. *Expenses:* Tuition, state resident: part-time $288.16 per credit hour. Tuition, nonresident: part-time $1071.31 per credit hour. *Financial support:* Career-related internships or fieldwork, Federal Work-Study, institutionally sponsored loans, and unspecified assistantships available. Financial award application deadline: 3/1; financial award applicants required to submit FAFSA. *Unit head:* Dr. Matthew Marino, Program Coordinator, 407-823-1227, E-mail: matthew.marino@ucf.edu. *Application contact:* Assistant Director, Graduate Admissions, 407-823-2766, Fax: 407-823-6442, E-mail: gradadmissions@ucf.edu.
Website: http://education.ucf.edu/exed/

University of Central Florida, College of Education and Human Performance, Education Doctoral Programs, Orlando, FL 32816. Offers communication sciences and disorders (PhD); curriculum and instruction (Ed D); early childhood education (PhD); educational leadership (Ed D); elementary education (PhD); exceptional education (PhD); exercise physiology (PhD); higher education (PhD); instructional technology (PhD); mathematics education (PhD); methodology, measurement and analysis (PhD); reading education (PhD); science education (PhD); social science education (PhD); TESOL (PhD). *Students:* 127 full-time (91 women), 43 part-time (29 women); includes 33 minority (17 Black or African American, non-Hispanic/Latino; 5 Asian, non-Hispanic/Latino; 7 Hispanic/Latino; 4 Two or more races, non-Hispanic/Latino), 26 international. Average age 37. 163 applicants, 40% accepted, 52 enrolled. In 2016, 57 doctorates awarded. Application fee: $30. Electronic applications accepted. *Expenses:* Tuition, state resident: part-time $288.16 per credit hour. Tuition, nonresident: part-time $1071.31 per credit hour. *Financial support:* In 2016–17, 78 students received support, including 41 fellowships with partial tuition reimbursements available (averaging $5,916 per year), 44 research assistantships with partial tuition reimbursements available (averaging $7,637 per year), 48 teaching assistantships with partial tuition reimbursements available (averaging $9,633 per year). Financial award application deadline: 3/1; financial award applicants required to submit FAFSA. *Unit head:* Dr. Edward Robinson, Director of Doctoral Programs, 407-823-6106, E-mail: edward.robinson@ucf.edu. *Application contact:* Assistant Director, Graduate Admissions, 407-823-2766, Fax: 407-823-6442, E-mail: gradadmissions@ucf.edu.
Website: http://education.ucf.edu/programs.cfm?pid=g&cat=2

University of Central Missouri, The Graduate School, Warrensburg, MO 64093. Offers accountancy (MA); accounting (MBA); applied mathematics (MS); aviation safety (MA); biology (MS); business administration (MBA); career and technical education leadership (MS); college student personnel administration (MS); communication (MA); computer science (MS); counseling (MS); criminal justice (MS); educational leadership (Ed D); educational technology (MS); elementary and early childhood education (MSE); English (MA); environmental studies (MA); finance (MBA); history (MA); human services/educational technology (Ed S); human services/learning resources (Ed S); human services/professional counseling (Ed S); industrial hygiene (MS); industrial management (MS); information systems (MBA); information technology (MS); kinesiology (MS); library science and information services (MS); literacy education (MSE); marketing (MBA); mathematics (MS); music (MA); occupational safety management (MS); psychology (MS); rural family nursing (MS); school administration (MSE); social gerontology (MS); sociology (MA); special education (MSE); speech language pathology (MS); superintendency (Ed S); teaching (MAT); teaching English as a second language (MA); technology (MS); technology management (PhD); theatre (MA). *Program availability:* Part-time, 100% online, blended/hybrid learning. *Degree requirements:* For master's and Ed S, comprehensive exam (for some programs), thesis (for some programs). *Entrance requirements:* Additional exam requirements/recommendations for international students: Required—TOEFL (minimum score 550 paper-based; 79 iBT). Electronic applications accepted.

University of Central Oklahoma, The Jackson College of Graduate Studies, College of Education and Professional Studies, Department of Advanced Professional and Special Services, Edmond, OK 73034-5209. Offers educational leadership (M Ed); library media education (M Ed); reading (M Ed); school counseling (M Ed); special education (M Ed), including mild/moderate disabilities, severe-profound/multiple disabilities, special education; speech-language pathology (MS). *Accreditation:* ASHA. *Program availability:* Part-time. *Degree requirements:* For master's, comprehensive exam (for some programs), thesis (for some programs). *Entrance requirements:* For master's, GRE. Additional exam requirements/recommendations for international students: Required—TOEFL (minimum score 550 paper-based; 79 iBT), IELTS (minimum score 6.5). Electronic applications accepted. *Faculty research:* Intellectual freedom, fair use copyright, technology integration, young adult literature, distance learning.

University of Cincinnati, Graduate School, College of Education, Criminal Justice, and Human Services, Division of Teacher Education, Program in Special Education, Cincinnati, OH 45221. Offers M Ed, Ed D. *Accreditation:* NCATE. *Program availability:* Part-time. *Degree requirements:* For master's, thesis or alternative; for doctorate, thesis/dissertation. *Entrance requirements:* For master's, GRE General Test; for doctorate, GRE General Test, GRE Subject Test. Additional exam requirements/recommendations for international students: Required—TOEFL (minimum score 550 paper-based), TWE (minimum score 4.5), OEPT. Electronic applications accepted. *Expenses: Tuition, area resident:* Full-time $12,790; part-time $389 per credit hour. Tuition, state resident: full-time $13,290; part-time $419 per credit hour. Tuition, nonresident: full-time $24,532; part-time $976 per credit hour. *International tuition:* $24,832 full-time. *Required fees:* $3958; $140 per credit hour. Tuition and fees vary according to course load, degree level, program and reciprocity agreements.

University of Colorado Colorado Springs, College of Education, Colorado Springs, CO 80918. Offers counseling and human services (MA); curriculum and instruction (MA); educational leadership (MA); educational leadership, research and policy (PhD); special education (MA); teaching English to speakers of other languages (MA). *Accreditation:* ACA; NCATE. *Program availability:* Part-time, evening/weekend, 100% online, blended/hybrid learning. *Faculty:* 26 full-time (18 women), 33 part-time/adjunct (21 women). *Students:* 136 full-time (94 women), 264 part-time (177 women); includes 99 minority (17 Black or African American, non-Hispanic/Latino; 1 American Indian or Alaska Native, non-Hispanic/Latino; 8 Asian, non-Hispanic/Latino; 55 Hispanic/Latino; 18 Two or more races, non-Hispanic/Latino), 9 international. Average age 35. 152 applicants, 89% accepted, 88 enrolled. In 2016, 161 master's, 11 doctorates awarded. *Degree requirements:* For master's, comprehensive exam, thesis or alternative, microcomputer proficiency; for doctorate, comprehensive exam, thesis/dissertation, research lab. *Entrance requirements:* For master's and doctorate, GRE General Test. Additional exam requirements/recommendations for international students: Recommended—TOEFL (minimum score 550 paper-based; 80 iBT), IELTS (minimum score 6). *Application deadline:* For fall admission, 2/1 priority date for domestic students, 2/1 for international students; for spring admission, 10/15 for domestic students, 10/1 for international students. Applications are processed on a rolling basis. Application fee: $60 ($100 for international students). Electronic applications accepted. *Expenses:* Contact institution. *Financial support:* In 2016–17, 108 students received support. Career-related internships or fieldwork, Federal Work-Study, scholarships/grants, and unspecified assistantships available. Support available to part-time students. Financial award application deadline: 3/1; financial award applicants required to submit FAFSA. *Faculty research:* Linguistically diverse education (LDE), educational policy, evidence-based reading and writing instruction, relational and social aggression, positive behavior supports, inclusive schooling, K-12 education policy. *Total annual research expenditures:* $272,136. *Unit head:* Dr. Valerie Martin Conley, Dean, 719-255-4133, E-mail: vmconley@uccs.edu. *Application contact:* The College of Education Student Resource Office, 719-255-4996, E-mail: education@uccs.edu.
Website: http://www.uccs.edu/coe

University of Colorado Denver, School of Education and Human Development, Early Childhood Education Program, Denver, CO 80217. Offers early childhood education (MA); special education (MA). *Accreditation:* NCATE. *Program availability:* Part-time, evening/weekend, online learning. *Students:* 56 full-time (55 women), 33 part-time (29 women); includes 16 minority (4 Black or African American, non-Hispanic/Latino; 1 Asian, non-Hispanic/Latino; 7 Hispanic/Latino; 4 Two or more races, non-Hispanic/Latino), 4 international. Average age 34. 26 applicants, 65% accepted, 12 enrolled. In 2016, 38 master's awarded. *Degree requirements:* For master's, comprehensive exam, fieldwork, practica, 40 credit hours. *Entrance requirements:* For master's, GRE or MAT (if GPA is below 2.75), minimum GPA of 2.75, resume, three letters of recommendation, documented experience with young children, transcripts from all previous colleges/universities attended. Additional exam requirements/recommendations for international students: Required—TOEFL (minimum score 537 paper-based; 75 iBT); Recommended—IELTS (minimum score 6.5). *Application deadline:* For fall admission, 4/15 for domestic students, 4/1 for international students; for spring admission, 9/15 for domestic students, 9/1 for international students; for summer admission, 2/15 for domestic and international students. Application fee: $50 ($75 for international students). Electronic applications accepted. *Expenses:* Contact institution. *Financial support:* In 2016–17, 43 students received support. Research assistantships, teaching assistantships, Federal Work-Study, institutionally sponsored loans, scholarships/grants, and traineeships available. Financial award application deadline: 4/1; financial award applicants required to submit FAFSA. *Faculty research:* Early childhood growth and development, faculty development, adult learning, gender and equity issues, research methodology. *Unit head:* Lori Ryan, Professor, 303-315-2578, E-mail: lori.ryan@ucdenver.edu. *Application contact:* 303-315-6351, E-mail: education@ucdenver.edu.
Website: http://www.ucdenver.edu/academics/colleges/SchoolOfEducation/Academics/MASTERS/ECE/Pages/EarlyChildhoodEducation.aspx

University of Colorado Denver, School of Education and Human Development, Program in Educational Leadership and Innovation, Denver, CO 80217. Offers educational studies and research (PhD), including administrative leadership and policy, early childhood special education, math education, research, assessment and evaluation, science education, urban ecologies. *Program availability:* Part-time, evening/weekend. *Students:* 30 full-time (25 women), 14 part-time (11 women); includes 16 minority (7 Black or African American, non-Hispanic/Latino; 1 American Indian or Alaska Native, non-Hispanic/Latino; 1 Asian, non-Hispanic/Latino; 6 Hispanic/Latino; 1 Two or more races, non-Hispanic/Latino), 5 international. Average age 40. 21 applicants, 67% accepted, 8 enrolled. In 2016, 3 doctorates awarded. *Degree requirements:* For doctorate, comprehensive exam, thesis/dissertation, 75 credit hours (for PhD). *Entrance requirements:* For doctorate, GRE or equivalent, resume or curriculum vitae, letters of recommendation, master's degree or equivalent, completion of basic or advanced statistics course with minimum B grade. Additional exam requirements/recommendations for international students: Required—TOEFL (minimum score 537 paper-based; 75 iBT); Recommended—IELTS (minimum score 6.5). *Application deadline:* For fall admission, 12/1 priority date for domestic students, 11/1 priority date for international students. Applications are processed on a rolling basis. Application fee: $50 ($75 for international students). Electronic applications accepted. *Expenses:* Contact institution. *Financial support:* In 2016–17, 45 students received support. Fellowships, research assistantships, teaching assistantships, Federal Work-Study, institutionally sponsored loans, scholarships/grants, and traineeships available. Financial award application deadline: 4/1; financial award applicants required to submit FAFSA. *Faculty research:* Administrative leadership and policy studies, early childhood education, research in diversity, paraprofessionals in education, urban schools lab. *Unit head:* 303-315-6300, E-mail: education@ucdenver.edu. *Application contact:* 303-315-6300, E-mail: education@ucdenver.edu.
Website: http://www.ucdenver.edu/academics/colleges/SchoolOfEducation/Academics/Doctorate/Pages/PhD%20in%20Education%20and%20Human%20Development.aspx

University of Colorado Denver, School of Education and Human Development, Teacher Education Programs, Denver, CO 80217. Offers elementary linguistically diverse education (MA); elementary math and science education (MA); elementary math education (MA); elementary reading and writing (MA); elementary science education (MA); secondary English education (MA); secondary linguistically diverse education (MA); secondary math education (MA); secondary reading and writing (MA); secondary science education (MA); special education (MA). *Accreditation:* NCATE. *Program availability:* Part-time, evening/weekend. *Students:* 142 full-time (117 women), 184 part-time (159 women); includes 56 minority (6 Black or African American, non-Hispanic/Latino; 1 American Indian or Alaska Native, non-Hispanic/Latino; 4 Asian, non-Hispanic/Latino; 38 Hispanic/Latino; 1 Native Hawaiian or other Pacific Islander, non-Hispanic/Latino; 6 Two or more races, non-Hispanic/Latino), 1 international. Average age 30. 18 applicants, 67% accepted, 9 enrolled. In 2016, 134 master's awarded. *Degree requirements:* For master's, comprehensive exam. *Entrance requirements:* For master's, GRE or MAT (for those with GPA below 2.75), transcripts, resume, letters of recommendation. Additional exam requirements/recommendations for international students: Required—TOEFL (minimum score 537 paper-based; 75 iBT); Recommended—IELTS (minimum score 6.5). *Application deadline:* For fall admission, 4/15 for domestic students, 4/1 for international students; for spring admission, 9/15 for domestic students, 9/1 for international students; for summer admission, 2/15 for domestic students, 2/1 for international students. Applications are processed on a rolling basis. Application fee: $50 ($75 for international students). Electronic applications accepted. *Expenses:* Contact institution. *Financial support:* In 2016–17, 26 students received support. Fellowships, research assistantships, teaching assistantships, Federal Work-Study, institutionally sponsored loans, scholarships/grants, and traineeships available. Financial award application deadline: 4/1; financial award applicants required

to submit FAFSA. *Faculty research:* Linguistically diverse education/ESL, elementary reading and writing, elementary teacher education, secondary teacher education, special education. *Unit head:* Cindy Gutierrez, Director, 303-315-4982, E-mail: cindy.gutierrez@ucdenver.edu. *Application contact:* 303-315-6300, E-mail: education@ucdenver.edu.
Website: http://www.ucdenver.edu/academics/colleges/SchoolOfEducation/Academics/MASTERS/Pages/default.aspx

University of Denver, Morgridge College of Education, Denver, CO 80208. Offers child, family and school psychology (MA, PhD, Ed S); counseling psychology (MA, PhD); curriculum and instruction (MA, Ed D, PhD); curriculum instruction and teaching (Certificate); early childhood special education (MA, Certificate); educational leadership and policy studies (MA, Ed D, PhD, Certificate); higher education (Ed D, PhD); library and information science (MLIS); research methods and statistics (MA, PhD). *Accreditation:* ALA; APA (one or more programs are accredited). *Program availability:* Part-time, evening/weekend, online learning. *Faculty:* 39 full-time (29 women), 60 part-time/adjunct (42 women). *Students:* 498 full-time (392 women), 362 part-time (282 women); includes 223 minority (63 Black or African American, non-Hispanic/Latino; 6 American Indian or Alaska Native, non-Hispanic/Latino; 20 Asian, non-Hispanic/Latino; 102 Hispanic/Latino; 1 Native Hawaiian or other Pacific Islander, non-Hispanic/Latino; 31 Two or more races, non-Hispanic/Latino), 40 international. Average age 32. 1,027 applicants, 69% accepted, 386 enrolled. In 2016, 252 master's, 36 doctorates, 141 other advanced degrees awarded. Terminal master's awarded for partial completion of doctoral program. *Degree requirements:* For master's, comprehensive exam; for doctorate, 2 foreign languages, comprehensive exam, thesis/dissertation. *Entrance requirements:* For master's and doctorate, GRE General Test or GMAT. Additional exam requirements/recommendations for international students: Required—TOEFL (minimum score 550 paper-based; 80 iBT). *Application deadline:* Applications are processed on a rolling basis. Application fee: $65. Electronic applications accepted. *Expenses:* $29,022 per year full-time. *Financial support:* In 2016–17, 697 students received support, including 37 research assistantships with tuition reimbursements available (averaging $11,209 per year), 66 teaching assistantships with tuition reimbursements available (averaging $3,742 per year); career-related internships or fieldwork, Federal Work-Study, institutionally sponsored loans, scholarships/grants, and unspecified assistantships also available. Support available to part-time students. Financial award application deadline: 2/15; financial award applicants required to submit FAFSA. *Faculty research:* Early childhood education, access and equity, educational leadership, family and school partnerships, neurodevelopmental disorders. *Total annual research expenditures:* $3.3 million. *Unit head:* Dr. Karen Riley, Dean, 303-871-3665, Fax: 303-871-4456, E-mail: karen.riley@du.edu. *Application contact:* Jodi Dye, Director of Admissions, 303-871-2510, Fax: 303-871-4456, E-mail: jodi.dye@du.edu.
Website: http://morgridge.du.edu

University of Detroit Mercy, College of Liberal Arts and Education, Detroit, MI 48221. Offers addiction counseling (MA); addiction studies (Certificate); clinical mental health counseling (MA); clinical psychology (MA, PhD); computer and information systems (MS); criminal justice (MA); curriculum and instruction (MA); economics (MA); educational administration (MA); financial economics (MA); industrial/organizational psychology (MA); information assurance (MS); intelligence analysis (MA); liberal studies (MALS); religious studies (MA); school counseling (MA, Certificate); school psychology (Spec); security administration (MS); special education: emotionally impaired/behaviorally disordered (MA); special education: learning disabilities (MA). *Program availability:* Part-time, evening/weekend. *Degree requirements:* For doctorate, departmental qualifying exam. *Faculty research:* Psychology of aging, history of technology, Renaissance humanism, U.S. and Japanese economic relations.

University of Florida, Graduate School, College of Education, School of Special Education, School Psychology and Early Childhood Studies, Gainesville, FL 32611. Offers early childhood education (M Ed, MAE); school psychology (M Ed, MAE, Ed D, PhD, Ed S); special education (M Ed, MAE, Ed D, PhD, Ed S). *Accreditation:* NCATE. *Program availability:* Part-time, evening/weekend, online learning. *Degree requirements:* For master's, comprehensive exam (for some programs), thesis (MAE); for doctorate, comprehensive exam, thesis/dissertation. *Entrance requirements:* For master's and doctorate, GRE General Test, minimum GPA of 3.0; for Ed S, GRE General Test. Additional exam requirements/recommendations for international students: Required—TOEFL (minimum score 550 paper-based; 80 iBT), IELTS (minimum score 6). Electronic applications accepted. *Faculty research:* Teacher quality/teacher education, early childhood, autism, academic and behavioral assessment and interventions.

University of Georgia, College of Education, Department of Communication Sciences and Special Education, Athens, GA 30602. Offers communication science and disorders (M Ed, MA, PhD, Ed S); special education (Ed D). *Accreditation:* ASHA (one or more programs are accredited). Terminal master's awarded for partial completion of doctoral program. *Degree requirements:* For master's, comprehensive exam (for some programs), thesis (for some programs); for doctorate, thesis/dissertation. *Entrance requirements:* For master's, doctorate, and Ed S, GRE General Test. Additional exam requirements/recommendations for international students: Required—TOEFL. *Application deadline:* For fall admission, 7/1 priority date for domestic students; for spring admission, 11/15 for domestic students. Application fee: $50. Electronic applications accepted. *Financial support:* Fellowships, research assistantships, teaching assistantships, and unspecified assistantships available. *Unit head:* Dr. Albert De Chicchis, Interim Head, 706-542-4582, Fax: 706-542-5348. *Application contact:* Kevin Ayers, Graduate Coordinator, 706-542-4617, E-mail: kayres@uga.edu.
Website: http://www.coe.uga.edu/csse/

University of Guam, Office of Graduate Studies, School of Education, Program in Special Education, Mangilao, GU 96923. Offers M Ed. *Degree requirements:* For master's, comprehensive oral and written exams, special project or thesis. *Entrance requirements:* For master's, GRE General Test. Additional exam requirements/recommendations for international students: Required—TOEFL. *Faculty research:* Mainstreaming, multiculturalism.

University of Hawaii at Manoa, Graduate Division, College of Education, Department of Special Education, Honolulu, HI 96822. Offers M Ed. *Accreditation:* NCATE. *Program availability:* Part-time. *Degree requirements:* For master's, thesis optional. *Entrance requirements:* For master's, GRE General Test, interview, minimum GPA of 3.0. Additional exam requirements/recommendations for international students: Required—TOEFL (minimum score 580 paper-based; 92 iBT), IELTS (minimum score 5). *Faculty research:* Mild/moderate/severe disabilities, early childhood interventions, inclusion, transition.

University of Hawaii at Manoa, Graduate Division, College of Education, PhD in Education Program, Honolulu, HI 96822. Offers curriculum and instruction (PhD); educational administration (PhD); educational foundations (PhD); educational policy studies (PhD); educational psychology (PhD); exceptionalities (PhD); kinesiology (PhD); learning design and technology (PhD). *Program availability:* Part-time, evening/weekend. *Degree requirements:* For doctorate, thesis/dissertation. *Entrance requirements:* For doctorate, GRE General Test, sample of written work. Additional exam requirements/recommendations for international students: Required—TOEFL (minimum score 600 paper-based; 100 iBT), IELTS (minimum score 7).

University of Houston, College of Education, Department of Educational Psychology, Houston, TX 77204. Offers administration and supervision - higher education (M Ed); counseling (M Ed); counseling psychology (PhD); educational psychology (M Ed); school psychology (PhD); school psychology and individual differences (PhD); special education (M Ed). *Accreditation:* NCATE. *Program availability:* Part-time, evening/weekend, online learning. *Degree requirements:* For master's, comprehensive exam or thesis; for doctorate, comprehensive exam, thesis/dissertation. *Entrance requirements:* For master's, GRE, transcripts, 3 letters of recommendation, curriculum vita, goal statement; for doctorate, GRE, transcripts, 3 letters of recommendation, curriculum vita, goal statement, writing sample, interview. Additional exam requirements/recommendations for international students: Required—TOEFL (minimum score 550 paper-based; 79 iBT), IELTS (minimum score 6.5). Electronic applications accepted. *Faculty research:* Evidence-based assessment and intervention, multicultural issues in psychology, social and cultural context of learning, systemic barriers to college, motivational aspects of self-regulated learning.

University of Houston–Victoria, School of Education, Health Professions and Human Development, Victoria, TX 77901-4450. Offers administration and supervision (M Ed); adult and higher education (M Ed); counselor education (M Ed); curriculum and instruction (M Ed); educational technology (M Ed); special education (M Ed). *Program availability:* Part-time, evening/weekend, online learning. *Degree requirements:* For master's, comprehensive exam, project or thesis. *Entrance requirements:* For master's, GRE General Test. Additional exam requirements/recommendations for international students: Required—TOEFL. Electronic applications accepted. *Faculty research:* Reading and language arts education, evaluation and diagnosis of special children's abilities.

University of Idaho, College of Graduate Studies, College of Education, Department of Curriculum and Instruction, Moscow, ID 83844. Offers career and technology education (M Ed); curriculum and instruction (M Ed, Ed S); special education (M Ed). *Faculty:* 25 full-time, 2 part-time/adjunct. *Students:* 21 full-time (16 women), 35 part-time (29 women). Average age 37. In 2016, 17 master's awarded. *Entrance requirements:* For master's, minimum GPA of 3.0. Additional exam requirements/recommendations for international students: Required—TOEFL. *Application deadline:* For fall admission, 8/1 for domestic students; for spring admission, 12/15 for domestic students. Applications are processed on a rolling basis. Application fee: $60. Electronic applications accepted. *Expenses:* Tuition, state resident: full-time $6460; part-time $414 per credit hour. Tuition, nonresident: full-time $21,268; part-time $1237 per credit hour. *Required fees:* $2070; $60 per credit hour. Full-time tuition and fees vary according to course load and reciprocity agreements. *Financial support:* Research assistantships and teaching assistantships available. Financial award applicants required to submit FAFSA. *Unit head:* Dr. Allen Kitchel, Interim Chair, 208-885-6587, E-mail: teached@uidaho.edu. *Application contact:* Sean Scoggin, Graduate Recruitment Coordinator, 208-885-4001, Fax: 208-885-4406, E-mail: graduateadmissions@uidaho.edu.
Website: http://www.uidaho.edu/ed/ci

University of Idaho, College of Graduate Studies, College of Education, Department of Leadership and Counseling, Boise, ID 83702. Offers adult/organizational learning and leadership (MS, Ed S); educational leadership (M Ed, Ed S); rehabilitation counseling and human services (M Ed, MS); school counseling (M Ed, MS); special education (M Ed). *Faculty:* 14 full-time, 7 part-time/adjunct. *Students:* 37 full-time (26 women), 154 part-time (84 women). Average age 39. In 2016, 75 master's, 21 other advanced degrees awarded. *Entrance requirements:* For master's, minimum GPA of 3.0. Additional exam requirements/recommendations for international students: Required—TOEFL. *Application deadline:* Applications are processed on a rolling basis. Application fee: $60. Electronic applications accepted. *Expenses:* Tuition, state resident: full-time $6460; part-time $414 per credit hour. Tuition, nonresident: full-time $21,268; part-time $1237 per credit hour. *Required fees:* $2070; $60 per credit hour. Full-time tuition and fees vary according to course load and reciprocity agreements. *Financial support:* Applicants required to submit FAFSA. *Unit head:* Dr. Kathy Canfield-Davis, Chair, 208-364-4047, E-mail: lead@uidaho.edu. *Application contact:* Sean Scoggin, Graduate Recruitment Coordinator, 208-885-4723, Fax: 208-885-4406, E-mail: graduateadmissions@uidaho.edu.
Website: https://www.uidaho.edu/ed/lc

University of Illinois at Chicago, College of Education, Department of Special Education, Chicago, IL 60607-7128. Offers M Ed, PhD. *Program availability:* Part-time. Terminal master's awarded for partial completion of doctoral program. *Degree requirements:* For doctorate, thesis/dissertation. *Entrance requirements:* For master's, minimum GPA of 2.75; for doctorate, GRE General Test, minimum GPA of 2.75. Additional exam requirements/recommendations for international students: Required—TOEFL. Electronic applications accepted. *Faculty research:* Teaching and learning for special learners, individual differences.

University of Illinois at Urbana–Champaign, Graduate College, College of Education, Department of Special Education, Champaign, IL 61820. Offers Ed M, MS, Ed D, PhD, CAS. *Program availability:* Part-time, online learning.

The University of Iowa, Graduate College, College of Education, Department of Teaching and Learning, Program in Special Education, Iowa City, IA 52242-1316. Offers MA, PhD. *Degree requirements:* For master's, thesis optional, exam; for doctorate, comprehensive exam, thesis/dissertation. *Entrance requirements:* For master's and doctorate, GRE General Test, minimum GPA of 3.0. Additional exam requirements/recommendations for international students: Required—TOEFL (minimum score 550 paper-based; 81 iBT). Electronic applications accepted.

The University of Kansas, Graduate Studies, School of Education, Department of Special Education, Lawrence, KS 66045. Offers autism spectrum disorder (MS Ed, Certificate); early childhood unified (MS Ed); high incidence disabilities (MS Ed); leadership in special and inclusive education (Certificate); low incidence disabilities (MS Ed); secondary special education and transition (MS Ed); special education (PhD). *Accreditation:* NCATE. *Program availability:* Part-time, online learning. *Students:* 91 full-time (82 women), 293 part-time (255 women); includes 50 minority (19 Black or African American, non-Hispanic/Latino; 4 American Indian or Alaska Native, non-Hispanic/Latino; 6 Asian, non-Hispanic/Latino; 7 Hispanic/Latino; 14 Two or more races, non-Hispanic/Latino), 28 international. Average age 33. 759 applicants, 27% accepted, 166 enrolled. In 2016, 51 master's, 3 doctorates awarded. *Median time to degree:* Of those who began their doctoral program in fall 2008, 90% received their degree in 8 years or less. *Entrance requirements:* For master's, minimum GPA of 3.0, official transcripts, 3 letters of reference, professional resume; for doctorate, GRE General Test, official transcripts, 3 letters of reference, professional resume, professional writing sample. Additional exam requirements/recommendations for international students: Required—TOEFL or IELTS. Application fee: $65 ($85 for international students). Electronic applications accepted. *Financial support:* Fellowships, research assistantships, teaching assistantships, Federal Work-Study, scholarships/grants, and unspecified assistantships available. Support available to part-time students. Financial award application deadline: 2/21; financial award applicants required to submit FAFSA. *Faculty research:* Autism spectrum disorders, learning disabilities research, leadership development, qualitative research and evaluation. *Unit head:* Elizabeth B. Kozleski, Chair, 785-864-0556, E-mail: elizabeth.kozleski@ku.edu. *Application contact:* Graduate

Admission Contact, 785-864-4342, E-mail: specialeduadm@ku.edu.
Website: http://specialedu.ku.edu/

University of Kentucky, Graduate School, College of Education, Program in Special Education, Lexington, KY 40506-0032. Offers early childhood (MS Ed); rehabilitation counseling (MRC, PhD); special education (MS Ed, PhD). *Accreditation:* CORE; NCATE. Terminal master's awarded for partial completion of doctoral program. *Degree requirements:* For master's, comprehensive exam, thesis optional; for doctorate, comprehensive exam, thesis/dissertation. *Entrance requirements:* For master's, GRE General Test, minimum undergraduate GPA of 2.75; for doctorate, GRE General Test, minimum graduate GPA of 3.0. Additional exam requirements/recommendations for international students: Required—TOEFL (minimum score 550 paper-based). Electronic applications accepted. *Faculty research:* Applied behavior analysis applications in special education, single subject research design in classroom settings, transition research across life span, rural special education personnel.

University of La Verne, LaFetra College of Education, Program in Special Education, La Verne, CA 91750-4443. Offers mild/moderate education specialist (Credential); special education studies (MS). *Students:* 19 full-time (16 women), 57 part-time (43 women); includes 37 minority (3 Black or African American, non-Hispanic/Latino; 2 Asian, non-Hispanic/Latino; 32 Hispanic/Latino). Average age 34. *Entrance requirements:* For master's, bachelor's degree, minimum undergraduate GPA of 3.0. Application fee: $50. *Expenses:* Contact institution. *Financial support:* Scholarships/grants and traineeships available. *Unit head:* Dr. Patricia Taylor, Program Chairperson, 909-448-4637, E-mail: ptaylor@laverne.edu. *Application contact:* Kristen Ahn, Assistant Director of Graduate Admissions, 909-448-4480, Fax: 909-971-2295, E-mail: sahn@laverne.edu.
Website: http://laverne.edu/education/

University of La Verne, Regional and Online Campuses, Graduate Credential Program in Education, California Statewide Campus, La Verne, CA 91750-4443. Offers administration services (preliminary) (Credential); education specialist: mild/moderate (Credential); English (Certificate); multiple subject teaching (Credential); pupil personnel services: school counseling (Credential); single subject teaching (Credential); special education (MS); special emphasis (M Ed). *Accreditation:* NCATE. *Program availability:* Part-time. *Entrance requirements:* For degree, California Basic Educational Skills Test, minimum undergraduate GPA of 2.75, 3 letters of recommendation, interview. *Expenses:* Contact institution.

University of La Verne, Regional and Online Campuses, Graduate Programs, Kern County Campus, Bakersfield, CA 93301. Offers business administration for experienced professionals (MBA-EP); education (special emphasis) (M Ed); educational counseling (MS); educational leadership (M Ed); health administration (MHA); leadership and management (MS); mild/moderate education specialist (Credential); multiple subject (elementary) (Credential); organizational leadership (Ed D); preliminary administrative services (Credential); single subject (secondary) (Credential); special education studies (MS). *Program availability:* Part-time, evening/weekend. *Expenses:* Contact institution.

University of La Verne, Regional and Online Campuses, Master's Programs in Education, California Statewide Campus, La Verne, CA 91750-4443. Offers administration services (preliminary) (Credential); education specialist: mild/moderate (Credential); educational counseling (MS); educational leadership (M Ed); multiple subject teaching (Credential); pupil personnel services: school counseling (Credential); single subject teaching (Credential); special education studies (MS); special emphasis (M Ed). *Accreditation:* NCATE. *Entrance requirements:* For master's, California Basic Educational Skills Test, 3 letters of recommendation, teaching credential. *Expenses:* Contact institution.

University of Louisiana at Monroe, Graduate School, College of Arts, Education, and Sciences, School of Education, Program in Curriculum and Instruction, Monroe, LA 71209-0001. Offers art education (M Ed); biology education (M Ed); chemistry education (M Ed); curriculum and instruction (Ed D); early childhood education (M Ed); earth science education (M Ed); educational leadership (M Ed); elementary education (1-5) (M Ed); English as a second language (M Ed); English education (M Ed); family and consumer education (M Ed); French education (M Ed); history education (M Ed); math education (M Ed); middle school education (M Ed); music education (M Ed); reading education (K-12) (M Ed); Spanish education (M Ed); special education - academically gifted (M Ed); special education - early intervention (M Ed); special education - educational diagnostician (M Ed); special education - mild/moderate disabilities (M Ed); speech education (M Ed). *Accreditation:* NCATE. *Faculty:* 8 full-time (4 women), 4 part-time/adjunct (3 women). *Students:* 13 full-time (11 women), 80 part-time (65 women); includes 25 minority (19 Black or African American, non-Hispanic/Latino; 1 Asian, non-Hispanic/Latino; 3 Hispanic/Latino; 2 Two or more races, non-Hispanic/Latino). Average age 37. 118 applicants, 30% accepted, 16 enrolled. In 2016, 23 master's, 4 doctorates awarded. *Degree requirements:* For master's, comprehensive exam (for some programs), thesis; for doctorate, thesis/dissertation, internships. *Entrance requirements:* For master's, GRE General Test; for doctorate, GRE General Test, minimum undergraduate GPA of 2.75, graduate 3.25. Additional exam requirements/recommendations for international students: Required—TOEFL (minimum score 500 paper-based; 61 iBT). *Application deadline:* For fall admission, 8/24 priority date for domestic students, 7/1 for international students; for winter admission, 12/14 priority date for domestic students; for spring admission, 1/19 for domestic students, 11/1 for international students. Applications are processed on a rolling basis. Application fee: $20 ($30 for international students). Electronic applications accepted. *Expenses:* Tuition, state resident: full-time $6489. Tuition, nonresident: full-time $18,589. *Required fees:* $8984. Tuition and fees vary according to course level, course load, degree level and program. *Financial support:* Research assistantships, career-related internships or fieldwork, Federal Work-Study, and unspecified assistantships available. Financial award application deadline: 4/1; financial award applicants required to submit FAFSA. *Unit head:* Dr. Dorothy Schween, Director, 318-342-1268, Fax: 318-342-3131, E-mail: schween@ulm.edu.

University of Louisiana at Monroe, Graduate School, College of Arts, Education, and Sciences, School of Education, Program in Special Education, Monroe, LA 71209-0001. Offers MAT. *Accreditation:* NCATE. *Program availability:* Part-time, evening/weekend. *Faculty:* 8 full-time (4 women), 4 part-time/adjunct (3 women). *Students:* 7 full-time (all women), 23 part-time (16 women); includes 4 minority (3 Black or African American, non-Hispanic/Latino; 1 Hispanic/Latino). Average age 34. 54 applicants, 43% accepted, 8 enrolled. In 2016, 12 master's awarded. *Entrance requirements:* For master's, GRE General Test, minimum GPA of 2.5. Additional exam requirements/recommendations for international students: Required—TOEFL (minimum score 500 paper-based; 61 iBT). *Application deadline:* For fall admission, 8/22 priority date for domestic students, 7/1 for international students; for winter admission, 12/12 priority date for domestic students; for spring admission, 1/17 for domestic students, 11/1 for international students. Applications are processed on a rolling basis. Application fee: $20 ($30 for international students). Electronic applications accepted. *Expenses:* Tuition, state resident: full-time $6489. Tuition, nonresident: full-time $18,589. *Required fees:* $8984. Tuition and fees vary according to course level, course load, degree level and program. *Financial support:* Research assistantships, career-related internships or fieldwork, Federal Work-Study, and unspecified assistantships available. Financial award application deadline: 4/1; financial award applicants required to submit FAFSA. *Unit head:* Dr. Dorothy Schween, Director, 318-342-1268, E-mail: schween@ulm.edu.

University of Louisville, Graduate School, College of Education and Human Development, Department of Teaching and Learning, Louisville, KY 40292-0001. Offers art education (MAT); autism and applied behavior analysis (Certificate); curriculum and instruction (PhD); early elementary education (MAT); exercise physiology (MS); health and physical education (MAT); health professions education (Certificate); higher education (MA); human resources and organization development (MS); instructional technology (M Ed); interdisciplinary early childhood education (MAT); middle school education (MAT); music education (MAT); secondary education (MAT); special education (MAT); sport administration (MS); teacher leadership (M Ed). *Program availability:* Part-time, evening/weekend. *Students:* 116 full-time (68 women), 158 part-time (112 women); includes 46 minority (24 Black or African American, non-Hispanic/Latino; 8 Asian, non-Hispanic/Latino; 5 Hispanic/Latino; 9 Two or more races, non-Hispanic/Latino), 6 international. Average age 30. 114 applicants, 71% accepted, 57 enrolled. In 2016, 59 master's, 3 doctorates awarded. *Application deadline:* For spring admission, 1/1 priority date for international students. Application fee: $60. *Expenses:* Tuition, state resident: full-time $12,246; part-time $681 per credit hour. Tuition, nonresident: full-time $25,486; part-time $1417 per credit hour. *Required fees:* $196. Tuition and fees vary according to program and reciprocity agreements. *Financial support:* Application deadline: 6/1; applicants required to submit FAFSA. *Faculty research:* STEM teaching and learning; content literacy for English language learners; social justice in teacher education; adolescent literacy; mathematics teacher development. *Total annual research expenditures:* $1.7 million. *Unit head:* Dr. Ann E. Larson, Dean, College of Education and Human Development, 502-852-6411, Fax: 502-852-1464, E-mail: ann@louisville.edu. *Application contact:* Betty Hampton, Director of Graduate Student Services, 502-852-5597, Fax: 502-852-1465, E-mail: edadvise@louisville.edu.
Website: http://louisville.edu/delphi

University of Maine, Graduate School, College of Education and Human Development, School of Learning and Teaching, Orono, ME 04469. Offers counselor education (M Ed, MA, MS, CAS); early childhood teacher (CGS); education (PhD), including counselor education, literacy education, prevention and intervention studies; elementary education (M Ed, CAS); individualized education (M Ed); literacy education (CAS); response to intervention for behavior (CGS); secondary education (M Ed, CAS); social studies education (M Ed); special education (M Ed, CAS). *Program availability:* Part-time. *Students:* 89 full-time (82 women), 184 part-time (162 women); includes 13 minority (8 American Indian or Alaska Native, non-Hispanic/Latino; 3 Hispanic/Latino; 1 Native Hawaiian or other Pacific Islander, non-Hispanic/Latino; 1 Two or more races, non-Hispanic/Latino), 4 international. Average age 37. 132 applicants, 97% accepted, 100 enrolled. In 2016, 50 master's, 3 doctorates, 19 other advanced degrees awarded. *Degree requirements:* For master's, thesis (for some programs); for doctorate, comprehensive exam, thesis/dissertation. *Entrance requirements:* For master's, GRE General Test, MAT. Additional exam requirements/recommendations for international students: Required—TOEFL. *Application deadline:* For fall admission, 2/1 priority date for domestic students. Applications are processed on a rolling basis. Application fee: $65. Electronic applications accepted. *Expenses:* Tuition, state resident: full-time $7524; part-time $2508 per credit. Tuition, nonresident: full-time $24,498; part-time $8166 per credit. *Required fees:* $1148; $571 per credit. *Financial support:* In 2016–17, 20 students received support, including 12 teaching assistantships (averaging $14,600 per year); Federal Work-Study, scholarships/grants, and unspecified assistantships also available. Financial award application deadline: 3/1. *Unit head:* Dr. Jim Artesani, Associate Dean of Accreditation and Graduate Affairs, 207-581-4061. *Application contact:* Scott G. Delcourt, Assistant Vice President for Graduate Studies and Senior Associate Dean, 207-581-3291, Fax: 207-581-3232, E-mail: graduate@maine.edu.
Website: http://umaine.edu/edhd/

University of Manitoba, Faculty of Graduate Studies, Faculty of Education, Department of Educational Administration, Foundations and Psychology, Winnipeg, MB R3T 2N2, Canada. Offers adult and post-secondary education (M Ed); educational administration (M Ed); guidance and counseling (M Ed); inclusive special education (M Ed); social foundations of education (M Ed). *Degree requirements:* For master's, thesis or alternative.

University of Mary, Liffrig Family School of Education and Behavioral Sciences, Department of Education, Bismarck, ND 58504-9652. Offers curriculum, instruction and assessment (M Ed); education (Ed D); elementary administration (M Ed); reading (M Ed); secondary administration (M Ed); special education strategist (M Ed). *Program availability:* Part-time. *Degree requirements:* For master's, portfolio or thesis. *Entrance requirements:* For master's, interview, letters of reference, minimum GPA of 2.5. Additional exam requirements/recommendations for international students: Required—TOEFL (minimum score 500 paper-based; 71 iBT). Electronic applications accepted.

University of Maryland Eastern Shore, Graduate Programs, Department of Education, Program in Special Education, Princess Anne, MD 21853-1299. Offers M Ed. *Accreditation:* NCATE. *Degree requirements:* For master's, comprehensive exam, seminar paper, internship. *Entrance requirements:* For master's, PRAXIS I, interview, minimum GPA of 3.0. Additional exam requirements/recommendations for international students: Required—TOEFL (minimum score 80 iBT). Electronic applications accepted.

University of Massachusetts Amherst, Graduate School, College of Education, Program in Education, Amherst, MA 01003. Offers bilingual, English as a second language, and multicultural education (M Ed, Ed S); child study and early education (M Ed); children, families and schools (Ed D, Ed S); early childhood and elementary teacher education (M Ed); educational leadership (M Ed); educational policy and leadership (Ed D); higher education (M Ed); international education (M Ed); language, literacy and culture (Ed D); learning, media and technology (M Ed, Ed S); mathematics, science, and learning technologies (Ed D); reading and writing (M Ed); research, educational measurement and psychometrics (Ed D); school counselor education (M Ed, Ed S); school psychology (Ed S); science education (Ed S), secondary teacher education (M Ed); social justice education (M Ed, Ed D, Ed S); special education (M Ed, Ed D, Ed S); teacher education and school improvement (Ed D, Ed S). *Accreditation:* NCATE. *Program availability:* Part-time, online learning. Terminal master's awarded for partial completion of doctoral program. *Degree requirements:* For doctorate, comprehensive exam, thesis/dissertation. *Entrance requirements:* Additional exam requirements/recommendations for international students: Required—TOEFL (minimum score 550 paper-based; 80 iBT), IELTS (minimum score 6.5). Electronic applications accepted.

University of Massachusetts Boston, College of Education and Human Development, Program in Special Education, Boston, MA 02125-3393. Offers M Ed. *Program availability:* Part-time, evening/weekend. *Students:* 6 full-time (5 women), 38 part-time (29 women); includes 6 minority (1 Black or African American, non-Hispanic/Latino; 5 Hispanic/Latino), 1 international. Average age 29. 20 applicants, 70% accepted, 12 enrolled. In 2016, 35 master's awarded. *Degree requirements:* For master's, comprehensive exam, practicum. *Entrance requirements:* For master's, GRE General Test or MAT, minimum GPA of 2.75. *Application deadline:* For fall admission, 3/1 for domestic students; for spring admission, 11/1 for domestic students. *Expenses:* Tuition, state resident: full-time $16,863. Tuition, nonresident: full-time $32,913. *Required fees:* $177. *Financial support:* Research assistantships with full tuition reimbursements, teaching assistantships with full tuition reimbursements, career-related internships or fieldwork, Federal Work-Study, and unspecified assistantships available. Support available to part-time students. Financial award application deadline: 3/1; financial award applicants required to submit FAFSA. *Faculty research:* Inclusionary learning, cross-cultural special needs, special education restructuring. *Unit head:* Dr. Elizabeth Glenn Mitchell, Director, 617-287-7620, E-mail: glen.mitchell@umb.edu. *Application contact:* Peggy Roldan Patel, Graduate Admissions Coordinator, 617-287-6400, Fax: 617-287-6236, E-mail: bos.gadm@dpc.umassp.edu.

University of Massachusetts Dartmouth, Graduate School, College of Arts and Sciences, Department of Psychology, North Dartmouth, MA 02747-2300. Offers applied behavioral analysis (MA, Post-Master's Certificate); autism studies (Graduate Certificate); clinical psychology (MA); research psychology (MA). *Program availability:* Part-time, 100% online, blended/hybrid learning. *Faculty:* 19 full-time (12 women), 7 part-time/adjunct (3 women). *Students:* 34 full-time (27 women), 50 part-time (39 women); includes 17 minority (3 Black or African American, non-Hispanic/Latino; 1 Asian, non-Hispanic/Latino; 8 Hispanic/Latino; 5 Two or more races, non-Hispanic/Latino). Average age 29. 99 applicants, 57% accepted, 32 enrolled. In 2016, 25 master's, 2 other advanced degrees awarded. *Degree requirements:* For master's, thesis or comprehensive exam (for clinical psychology); thesis (for research psychology). *Entrance requirements:* For master's, GRE (for research psychology), statement of purpose (minimum of 300 words), resume, 3 letters of recommendation, official transcripts; for other advanced degree, statement of purpose (minimum of 300 words), resume, 3 letters of recommendation, official transcripts. Additional exam requirements/recommendations for international students: Required—TOEFL (minimum score 533 paper-based; 72 iBT). *Application deadline:* For fall admission, 3/1 priority date for domestic students, 2/1 priority date for international students; for spring admission, 12/20 priority date for domestic students, 11/20 priority date for international students. Application fee: $60. Electronic applications accepted. *Expenses:* Tuition, state resident: full-time $14,994; part-time $624.75 per credit. Tuition, nonresident: full-time $27,068; part-time $1127.83 per credit. *Required fees:* $405; $25.88 per credit. Tuition and fees vary according to course load and reciprocity agreements. *Financial support:* In 2016–17, 2 fellowships (averaging $7,000 per year) were awarded; institutionally sponsored loans, scholarships/grants, and unspecified assistantships also available. Support available to part-time students. Financial award application deadline: 3/1; financial award applicants required to submit FAFSA. *Faculty research:* Behavioral medicine, learning, social and developmental psychology, child neuropsychology, clinical research, counseling, psychotherapy, nonverbal communication, emotion, cognition, problem solving. *Total annual research expenditures:* $500,000. *Unit head:* Mahzad Hojjat, Graduate Program Director, Research Psychology, 508-999-8951, E-mail: mhojjat@umassd.edu. *Application contact:* Steven Briggs, Director of Marketing and Recruitment for Graduate Studies, 508-999-8604, Fax: 508-999-8183, E-mail: graduate@umassd.edu.
Website: http://www.umassd.edu/cas/psychology/graduateprograms

University of Memphis, Graduate School, College of Education, Department of Instruction and Curriculum Leadership, Memphis, TN 38152. Offers advanced studies in teaching and learning (M Ed); applied behavior analysis (Graduate Certificate); autism studies (Graduate Certificate); early childhood education (MAT, MS, Ed D); elementary education (MAT); instruction and curriculum (MS, Ed D); instruction design and technology (MS, Ed D); instructional design and technology (Graduate Certificate); literacy, leadership, and coaching (Graduate Certificate); reading (MS, Ed D); school library information specialist (Graduate Certificate); secondary education (MAT); special education (MAT, MS, Ed D); STEM teacher leadership (Graduate Certificate); urban education (Graduate Certificate). *Accreditation:* NCATE (one or more programs are accredited). *Program availability:* Part-time. *Faculty:* 24 full-time (14 women), 17 part-time/adjunct (12 women). *Students:* 66 full-time (52 women), 315 part-time (243 women); includes 163 minority (132 Black or African American, non-Hispanic/Latino; 1 American Indian or Alaska Native, non-Hispanic/Latino; 6 Asian, non-Hispanic/Latino; 13 Hispanic/Latino; 1 Native Hawaiian or other Pacific Islander, non-Hispanic/Latino; 10 Two or more races, non-Hispanic/Latino), 4 international. Average age 35. 215 applicants, 78% accepted, 120 enrolled. In 2016, 111 master's, 21 doctorates, 8 other advanced degrees awarded. Terminal master's awarded for partial completion of doctoral program. *Degree requirements:* For master's, comprehensive exam, thesis or alternative; for doctorate, comprehensive exam, thesis/dissertation. *Entrance requirements:* For master's, GRE General Test, PRAXIS, minimum GPA of 2.5, letters of reference; for doctorate, GRE General Test, GRE Subject Test, 2 years of teaching experience, letters of reference, statement of purpose, interview. Additional exam requirements/recommendations for international students: Required—TOEFL (minimum score 550 paper-based; 79 iBT). *Application deadline:* For fall admission, 4/1 priority date for domestic students; for spring admission, 10/1 priority date for domestic students; for summer admission, 2/1 priority date for domestic students. Applications are processed on a rolling basis. Application fee: $35 ($60 for international students). Electronic applications accepted. *Expenses:* $5,231.50 per semester full-time in-state, $9,623.50 full-time out-of-state. *Financial support:* In 2016–17, 2 research assistantships with full tuition reimbursements (averaging $10,000 per year), 3 teaching assistantships with full tuition reimbursements (averaging $10,666 per year) were awarded; career-related internships or fieldwork, Federal Work-Study, institutionally sponsored loans, scholarships/grants, traineeships, and unspecified assistantships also available. Support available to part-time students. Financial award application deadline: 2/1; financial award applicants required to submit FAFSA. *Faculty research:* Effective urban teachers, preparation and retention of urban teachers, technology utilization in schools, field-based teacher preparation programs, effective use of online instruction. *Unit head:* Dr. Angiline Powell, Interim Chair, 901-678-3310, E-mail: apowell3@memphis.edu. *Application contact:* Dr. James Meindl, Coordinator of Graduate Studies, 901-678-3310, E-mail: jnmeindl@memphis.edu.
Website: http://www.memphis.edu/icl/

University of Miami, Graduate School, School of Education and Human Development, Department of Teaching and Learning, Program in Early Childhood Special Education, Coral Gables, FL 33124. Offers MS Ed, Ed S. *Program availability:* Part-time, evening/weekend. *Faculty:* 4 full-time (3 women), 6 part-time/adjunct (all women). *Students:* 14 part-time (13 women); all minorities (4 Black or African American, non-Hispanic/Latino; 1 American Indian or Alaska Native, non-Hispanic/Latino; 9 Hispanic/Latino). Average age 33. *Degree requirements:* For master's, electronic portfolio. *Entrance requirements:* For master's, GRE General Test. Additional exam requirements/recommendations for international students: Required—TOEFL (minimum score 550 paper-based; 80 iBT); Recommended—IELTS (minimum score 6.5). *Application deadline:* For fall admission, 6/30 for domestic students. Application fee: $65. Electronic applications accepted. *Financial support:* Scholarships/grants available. Financial award application deadline: 3/1; financial award applicants required to submit FAFSA. *Unit head:* Dr. Elizabeth Harry, Professor, 305-284-4961, Fax: 305-284-6998, E-mail: bharry@miami.edu. *Application contact:* Lois Heffernan, Graduate Admissions Coordinator, 305-284-2167, E-mail: lheffernan@miami.edu.
Website: http://www.education.miami.edu

University of Miami, Graduate School, School of Education and Human Development, Department of Teaching and Learning, Program in Teaching and Learning, Coral Gables, FL 33124. Offers language and literacy learning in multilingual settings (PhD); science, technology, engineering and mathematics (PhD); special education (PhD). *Faculty:* 14 full-time (10 women), 9 part-time/adjunct (all women). *Students:* 21 full-time (16 women); includes 6 minority (2 Black or African American, non-Hispanic/Latino; 3 Hispanic/Latino; 1 Two or more races, non-Hispanic/Latino), 7 international. Average age 33. 20 applicants, 30% accepted, 4 enrolled. In 2016, 1 doctorate awarded. *Degree requirements:* For doctorate, thesis/dissertation, qualifying exam, electronic portfolio. *Entrance requirements:* For doctorate, GRE General Test. Additional exam requirements/recommendations for international students: Required—TOEFL (minimum score 550 paper-based; 80 iBT); Recommended—IELTS (minimum score 6.5). *Application deadline:* For fall admission, 2/15 for domestic students, 10/1 for international students. Application fee: $65. Electronic applications accepted. *Financial support:* Fellowships, research assistantships, teaching assistantships, health care benefits, tuition waivers (full and partial), and unspecified assistantships available. Financial award application deadline: 3/1; financial award applicants required to submit FAFSA. *Faculty research:* Teacher education, multicultural education, special education, second language acquisition, math and science education. *Unit head:* Dr. Luciana de Oliveira, Department Chairperson/Associate Professor, 305-284-4961, Fax: 305-284-6998, E-mail: ludeoliveira@miami.edu. *Application contact:* Lois Heffernan, Graduate Admission Coordinator, 305-284-2167, Fax: 305-284-9395, E-mail: lheffernan@miami.edu.
Website: http://www.education.miami.edu

University of Michigan–Dearborn, College of Education, Health, and Human Services, Master of Education Program in Special Education, Dearborn, MI 48126. Offers M Ed. *Accreditation:* TEAC. *Program availability:* Part-time, evening/weekend, 100% online. *Faculty:* 2 full-time (1 woman), 4 part-time/adjunct (3 women). *Students:* 20 part-time (18 women); includes 1 minority (Hispanic/Latino). Average age 35. 4 applicants, 100% accepted, 2 enrolled. In 2016, 14 master's awarded. *Entrance requirements:* For master's, minimum GPA of 3.0; statement of purpose; 3 letters of recommendation. Additional exam requirements/recommendations for international students: Required—TOEFL (minimum score 560 paper-based; 84 iBT), IELTS (minimum score 6.5). *Application deadline:* For fall admission, 8/1 priority date for domestic students, 5/1 priority date for international students; for winter admission, 12/1 priority date for domestic students, 9/1 priority date for international students; for spring admission, 4/1 priority date for domestic students, 1/1 priority date for international students. Applications are processed on a rolling basis. Application fee: $60. Electronic applications accepted. *Expenses:* Contact institution. *Financial support:* In 2016–17, 1 student received support. Career-related internships or fieldwork and scholarships/grants available. Financial award application deadline: 3/1; financial award applicants required to submit FAFSA. *Faculty research:* Education policy, literacy, pedagogy and interventions, technology and teacher education. *Unit head:* Dr. Stein Brunvand, Director, Master's Programs, 313-583-6415, E-mail: sbrunvan@umich.edu. *Application contact:* Elizabeth Morden, Graduate Programs Assistant, 313-593-5090, E-mail: emorden@umich.edu.
Website: http://umdearborn.edu/cehhs/cehhs_medsped/

University of Minnesota, Twin Cities Campus, Graduate School, College of Education and Human Development, Department of Educational Psychology, Program in Special Education, Minneapolis, MN 55455-0213. Offers M Ed, MA, PhD. *Students:* 103 full-time (80 women), 23 part-time (21 women); includes 20 minority (3 Black or African American, non-Hispanic/Latino; 10 Asian, non-Hispanic/Latino; 5 Hispanic/Latino; 2 Two or more races, non-Hispanic/Latino), 6 international. Average age 29. 115 applicants, 58% accepted, 59 enrolled. In 2016, 102 master's, 11 doctorates awarded. Application fee: $75 ($95 for international students). *Unit head:* Dr. Geoffrey Maruyama, Chair, 612-625-5861, Fax: 612-624-8241, E-mail: geoff@umn.edu. *Application contact:* Dr. Ernest Davenport, Director of Graduate Studies, 612-624-1040, E-mail: lqr6576@umn.edu.
Website: http://www.cehd.umn.edu/EdPsych/Programs/SpecialEd/

University of Missouri, Office of Research and Graduate Studies, College of Education, Department of Special Education, Columbia, MO 65211. Offers administration and supervision of special education (PhD); behavior disorders (M Ed, PhD); curriculum development of exceptional students (M Ed, PhD); early childhood special education (M Ed, PhD); general special education (M Ed, MA, PhD); learning and instruction (M Ed); learning disabilities (M Ed, PhD); mental retardation (M Ed, PhD). *Accreditation:* TEAC. *Program availability:* Part-time, evening/weekend, online learning. *Faculty:* 13 full-time (11 women). *Students:* 22 full-time (20 women), 36 part-time (32 women). *Degree requirements:* For master's, comprehensive exam, thesis or alternative; for doctorate, comprehensive exam, thesis/dissertation. *Entrance requirements:* For master's and doctorate, GRE General Test, letters of recommendation. Additional exam requirements/recommendations for international students: Required—TOEFL (minimum score 500 paper-based; 61 iBT). *Application deadline:* For fall admission, 1/15 priority date for domestic and international students; for winter admission, 11/1 priority date for domestic and international students; for spring admission, 4/1 priority date for domestic and international students. Application fee: $75 ($90 for international students). Electronic applications accepted. *Expenses:* Tuition, state resident: full-time $6347; part-time $352.60 per credit hour. Tuition, nonresident: full-time $17,379; part-time $965.50 per credit hour. *Required fees:* $1035. Tuition and fees vary according to course load, campus/location and program. *Financial support:* Fellowships with tuition reimbursements, research assistantships with tuition reimbursements, teaching assistantships with tuition reimbursements, career-related internships or fieldwork, scholarships/grants, health care benefits, and unspecified assistantships available.
Website: http://education.missouri.edu/SPED/

University of Missouri–Kansas City, School of Education, Kansas City, MO 64110-2499. Offers administration (Ed D); counseling and guidance (MA, Ed S), including mental health counseling (Ed S), school counseling (Ed S); counseling psychology (PhD); curriculum and instruction (MA, Ed S), including language and literacy (Ed S); education (PhD), including higher education administration, PK-12 education administration; educational administration (MA, Ed S), including advanced principal (Ed S), beginning principal (Ed S), district-level administration (Ed S); reading education (MA); special education (MA). PhD in education offered through the School of Graduate Studies. *Accreditation:* NCATE. *Program availability:* Part-time, evening/weekend. *Faculty:* 33 full-time (26 women), 51 part-time/adjunct (39 women). *Students:* 136 full-time (103 women), 275 part-time (194 women); includes 110 minority (71 Black or African American, non-Hispanic/Latino; 3 American Indian or Alaska Native, non-Hispanic/Latino; 8 Asian, non-Hispanic/Latino; 22 Hispanic/Latino; 6 Two or more races, non-Hispanic/Latino), 20 international. Average age 32. 324 applicants, 45% accepted, 108 enrolled. In 2016, 152 master's, 13 doctorates, 50 other advanced degrees awarded. *Degree requirements:* For doctorate, thesis/dissertation, internship, practicum. *Entrance requirements:* For master's, GRE, minimum GPA of 2.75, 2 letters of reference, written statement of purpose; for doctorate, GRE, minimum GPA of 3.0; for Ed S, minimum GPA of 3.0. Additional exam requirements/recommendations for international students: Required—TOEFL (minimum score 550 paper-based; 80 iBT).

Application deadline: For fall admission, 4/1 priority date for domestic and international students; for spring admission, 11/1 priority date for domestic and international students. Applications are processed on a rolling basis. Application fee: $45 ($50 for international students). *Financial support:* In 2016–17, 12 research assistantships with partial tuition reimbursements (averaging $12,476 per year) were awarded; career-related internships or fieldwork, Federal Work-Study, institutionally sponsored loans, and tuition waivers (full and partial) also available. Support available to part-time students. Financial award application deadline: 3/1; financial award applicants required to submit FAFSA. *Faculty research:* Urban education, inquiry-based field study, theories of counseling and psychotherapy, school literacy, educational technology. *Unit head:* Justin Perry, Dean, 816-235-5663, Fax: 816-235-5270, E-mail: education@umkc.edu.
Website: http://education.umkc.edu

University of Missouri–St. Louis, College of Education, Department of Educator Preparation, Innovation and Research, St. Louis, MO 63121. Offers elementary education (M Ed), including early childhood, general, reading; secondary education (M Ed), including curriculum and instruction, general, middle level education, reading, teaching English to speakers of other languages (TESOL); special education (M Ed), including autism and developmental disabilities, early childhood special education. *Program availability:* Part-time, evening/weekend. *Faculty:* 26 full-time (14 women), 22 part-time/adjunct (14 women). *Students:* 151 full-time (127 women), 728 part-time (564 women); includes 222 minority (165 Black or African American, non-Hispanic/Latino; 1 American Indian or Alaska Native, non-Hispanic/Latino; 16 Asian, non-Hispanic/Latino; 31 Hispanic/Latino; 1 Native Hawaiian or other Pacific Islander, non-Hispanic/Latino; 8 Two or more races, non-Hispanic/Latino), 6 international. Average age 29. 363 applicants, 84% accepted, 211 enrolled. *Degree requirements:* For master's, comprehensive exam. *Entrance requirements:* Additional exam requirements/recommendations for international students: Recommended—TOEFL (minimum score 550 paper-based; 79 iBT), IELTS (minimum score 6.5). *Application deadline:* For fall admission, 7/1 priority date for domestic and international students; for spring admission, 12/1 priority date for domestic and international students. Application fee: $50 ($40 for international students). Electronic applications accepted. *Financial support:* Application deadline: 4/1; applicants required to submit FAFSA. *Unit head:* Dr. Gayle Wilkinson, Chair, 314-516-5791. *Application contact:* 314-516-5458, Fax: 314-516-6996, E-mail: gadadm@umsl.edu.
Website: https://coe.umsl.edu/dept/epir.html

University of Nebraska at Kearney, College of Education, Department of Educational Administration, Kearney, NE 68849-0001. Offers curriculum supervisor of academic area (MA Ed); school principalship 7-12 (MA Ed); school principalship PK-8 (MA Ed); school superintendent (Ed S); supervisor of special education (MA Ed). *Accreditation:* NCATE. *Program availability:* Part-time, evening/weekend, online only, 100% online. *Faculty:* 4 full-time (1 woman). *Students:* 4 full-time (2 women), 131 part-time (59 women); includes 5 minority (all Hispanic/Latino). Average age 35. 18 applicants, 94% accepted, 9 enrolled. In 2016, 40 master's, 7 Ed Ss awarded. *Degree requirements:* For master's and Ed S, comprehensive exam, thesis optional. *Entrance requirements:* For master's, letters of recommendation, resume, letter of interest; for Ed S, letters of recommendation, resume, essay. Additional exam requirements/recommendations for international students: Recommended—TOEFL (minimum score 550 paper-based; 79 iBT), IELTS (minimum score 6.5). *Application deadline:* For fall admission, 6/15 for domestic and international students; for spring admission, 10/15 for domestic and international students; for summer admission, 3/15 for domestic and international students. Application fee: $45. Electronic applications accepted. *Expenses:* Tuition, state resident: full-time $4064; part-time $225.75 per credit hour. Tuition, nonresident: full-time $8915; part-time $495.25 per credit hour. *Required fees:* $772; $23 per credit hour. Part-time tuition and fees vary according to course load, campus/location, program and reciprocity agreements. *Financial support:* In 2016–17, 2 students received support, including 2 research assistantships with full tuition reimbursements available (averaging $10,500 per year); career-related internships or fieldwork, scholarships/grants, health care benefits, and unspecified assistantships also available. Support available to part-time students. Financial award application deadline: 2/28; financial award applicants required to submit FAFSA. *Faculty research:* Leadership and organizational behavior. *Unit head:* Dr. Richard Meyer, Chair, Educational Administration, 308-865-8512, E-mail: meyerdc@unk.edu. *Application contact:* Linda Johnson, Director, Graduate Admissions and Programs, 308-865-8841, Fax: 308-865-8837, E-mail: johnsonli@unk.edu.
Website: http://www.unk.edu/academics/edad/

University of Nebraska at Kearney, College of Education, Department of Teacher Education, Kearney, NE 68849-0001. Offers curriculum and instruction (MA Ed), including early childhood education, elementary education, English as a second language, instructional effectiveness, reading/special education, secondary education; instructional technology (MS Ed), including information technology, instructional technology, school librarian; reading PK-12 (MA Ed); special education (MA Ed), including advanced practitioner: assistive technology specialist, advanced practitioner: behavioral interventionist, advanced practitioner: inclusive collaboration specialist, gifted, teacher education. *Program availability:* Part-time, evening/weekend, online only, 100% online. *Faculty:* 18 full-time (13 women). *Students:* 21 full-time (15 women), 296 part-time (240 women); includes 21 minority (3 Black or African American, non-Hispanic/Latino; 1 Asian, non-Hispanic/Latino; 14 Hispanic/Latino; 1 Native Hawaiian or other Pacific Islander, non-Hispanic/Latino; 2 Two or more races, non-Hispanic/Latino), 1 international. Average age 32. 81 applicants, 100% accepted, 61 enrolled. In 2016, 129 master's awarded. *Degree requirements:* For master's, comprehensive exam, thesis optional. *Entrance requirements:* For master's, portfolio or GRE. Additional exam requirements/recommendations for international students: Recommended—TOEFL (minimum score 550 paper-based; 79 iBT), IELTS (minimum score 6.5). *Application deadline:* For fall admission, 6/15 for domestic students, 5/15 for international students; for spring admission, 10/15 for domestic and international students; for summer admission, 3/15 for domestic and international students. Application fee: $45. Electronic applications accepted. *Expenses:* $285 per credit hour resident tuition, $415 per credit hour non-resident tuition (online). *Financial support:* In 2016–17, 6 students received support, including 6 research assistantships with full tuition reimbursements available (averaging $10,500 per year); career-related internships or fieldwork, scholarships/grants, health care benefits, and unspecified assistantships also available. Support available to part-time students. Financial award application deadline: 2/28; financial award applicants required to submit FAFSA. *Unit head:* Sarah Bartling, Administrative Assistant, 308-865-8513, E-mail: bartlingseg@unk.edu. *Application contact:* Linda Johnson, Director, Graduate Admissions and Programs, 308-865-8841, Fax: 308-865-8837, E-mail: johnsonli@unk.edu.
Website: http://www.unk.edu/academics/ted/index.php

University of Nebraska at Kearney, College of Education, Kinesiology and Sport Sciences Department, Kearney, NE 68849-0001. Offers general physical education (MA Ed), including recreation and leisure, sports administration; physical education exercise science (MA Ed); physical education master teacher (MA Ed), including pedagogy, special populations. *Program availability:* Part-time, evening/weekend, 100% online. *Faculty:* 17 full-time (5 women). *Students:* 4 full-time (2 women), 39 part-time (16 women); includes 3 minority (2 Black or African American, non-Hispanic/Latino; 1 Hispanic/Latino). Average age 28. 20 applicants, 100% accepted, 14 enrolled. In 2016, 25 master's awarded. *Degree requirements:* For master's, comprehensive exam, thesis optional. *Entrance requirements:* For master's, GRE General Test (for some programs), personal statement. Additional exam requirements/recommendations for international students: Recommended—TOEFL (minimum score 550 paper-based; 79 iBT), IELTS (minimum score 6.5). *Application deadline:* For fall admission, 6/15 for domestic and international students; for spring admission, 10/15 for domestic and international students; for summer admission, 3/15 for domestic and international students. Application fee: $45. Electronic applications accepted. *Expenses:* Tuition, state resident: full-time $4064; part-time $225.75 per credit hour. Tuition, nonresident: full-time $8915; part-time $495.25 per credit hour. *Required fees:* $772; $23 per credit hour. Part-time tuition and fees vary according to course load, campus/location, program and reciprocity agreements. *Financial support:* In 2016–17, 9 students received support, including 3 research assistantships with full tuition reimbursements available (averaging $10,500 per year), 6 teaching assistantships with full tuition reimbursements available (averaging $10,500 per year); career-related internships or fieldwork, scholarships/grants, health care benefits, and unspecified assistantships also available. Support available to part-time students. Financial award application deadline: 2/28; financial award applicants required to submit FAFSA. *Faculty research:* Ergonomic aids, nutrition, motor development, sports pedagogy, applied behavior analysis, physical activity and wellness, athletic training, therapeutic interventions, exercise physiology, endocrinology and metabolism. *Unit head:* Dr. Nita Unruh, Chair, 308-865-8335, E-mail: unruhnc@unk.edu. *Application contact:* Linda Johnson, Director, Graduate Admissions and Programs, 308-865-8841, Fax: 308-865-8837, E-mail: johnsonli@unk.edu.
Website: http://www.unk.edu/academics/hperls/index.php

University of Nebraska at Omaha, Graduate Studies, College of Education, Department of Special Education and Communication Disorders, Omaha, NE 68182. Offers special education (MS); speech-language pathology (MS). *Accreditation:* ASHA; NCATE. *Program availability:* Part-time, evening/weekend. *Faculty:* 9 full-time (8 women). *Students:* 21 full-time (20 women), 71 part-time (63 women); includes 6 minority (2 Asian, non-Hispanic/Latino; 2 Hispanic/Latino; 2 Two or more races, non-Hispanic/Latino). Average age 29. 95 applicants, 34% accepted, 24 enrolled. In 2016, 42 master's awarded. *Degree requirements:* For master's, comprehensive exam, thesis (for some programs). *Entrance requirements:* For master's, minimum GPA of 3.0, statement of purpose, 2 letters of recommendation, copy of teaching certificate. Additional exam requirements/recommendations for international students: Required—TOEFL, IELTS, PTE. *Application deadline:* For fall admission, 2/1 for domestic and international students; for spring admission, 11/1 for domestic and international students; for summer admission, 4/1 for domestic and international students. Applications are processed on a rolling basis. Application fee: $45. Electronic applications accepted. *Financial support:* In 2016–17, 5 students received support, including 4 research assistantships with tuition reimbursements available, 1 teaching assistantship with tuition reimbursement available; fellowships, career-related internships or fieldwork, Federal Work-Study, institutionally sponsored loans, scholarships/grants, health care benefits, tuition waivers (partial), and unspecified assistantships also available. Support available to part-time students. Financial award application deadline: 3/1; financial award applicants required to submit FAFSA. *Unit head:* Dr. Kristine Swain, Chairperson, 402-554-2341, E-mail: graduate@unomaha.edu. *Application contact:* Dr. Philip Nordness, Graduate Program Chair, 402-554-2341, E-mail: graduate@unomaha.edu.

University of Nebraska–Lincoln, Graduate College, College of Education and Human Sciences, Department of Special Education and Communication Disorders, Program in Special Education, Lincoln, NE 68588. Offers M Ed, MA, Ed S. *Accreditation:* NCATE; TEAC. *Degree requirements:* For master's, thesis optional. *Entrance requirements:* For master's, GRE. Additional exam requirements/recommendations for international students: Required—TOEFL (minimum score 500 paper-based). Electronic applications accepted.

University of Nebraska–Lincoln, Graduate College, College of Education and Human Sciences, Department of Teaching, Learning and Teacher Education, Lincoln, NE 68588. Offers adult and continuing education (MA); educational studies (Ed D, PhD), including special education (Ed D); teaching, learning and teacher education (M Ed, MA, MST, Ed D, PhD); vocational and adult education (M Ed, MA). *Accreditation:* NCATE. *Degree requirements:* For master's, thesis optional. *Entrance requirements:* Additional exam requirements/recommendations for international students: Required—TOEFL (minimum score 550 paper-based). Electronic applications accepted. *Faculty research:* Teacher education, instructional leadership, literacy education, technology, improvement of school curriculum.

University of Nevada, Las Vegas, Graduate College, College of Education, Department of Educational and Clinical Studies, Las Vegas, NV 89154-3066. Offers addiction studies (Advanced Certificate); counselor education (M Ed, MS), including clinical mental health (MS), school counseling (M Ed); early childhood education (M Ed); early childhood special education (Certificate), including infancy, preschool; English language learning (M Ed); mental health counseling (Advanced Certificate); special education (M Ed, PhD); PhD/JD. *Program availability:* Part-time, evening/weekend. *Faculty:* 17 full-time (8 women), 28 part-time/adjunct (20 women). *Students:* 269 full-time (219 women), 174 part-time (138 women); includes 181 minority (51 Black or African American, non-Hispanic/Latino; 2 American Indian or Alaska Native, non-Hispanic/Latino; 15 Asian, non-Hispanic/Latino; 81 Hispanic/Latino; 3 Native Hawaiian or other Pacific Islander, non-Hispanic/Latino; 29 Two or more races, non-Hispanic/Latino), 23 international. Average age 34. 256 applicants, 72% accepted, 145 enrolled. In 2016, 178 master's, 3 doctorates awarded. *Degree requirements:* For master's, comprehensive exam (for some programs); for doctorate, comprehensive exam, thesis/dissertation; for other advanced degree, final project. *Entrance requirements:* For master's, bachelor's degree; letter of recommendation; statement of purpose; for doctorate, GRE General Test, statement of purpose; writing sample; 3 letters of recommendation. Additional exam requirements/recommendations for international students: Required—TOEFL (minimum score 550 paper-based; 80 iBT), IELTS (minimum score 7). *Application deadline:* For fall admission, 7/15 for domestic students, 5/1 for international students; for spring admission, 11/15 for domestic students, 10/1 for international students; for summer admission, 4/15 for domestic students. Application fee: $60 ($95 for international students). Electronic applications accepted. *Expenses:* $269.25 per credit, $792 per 3-credit course; $9,634 per year resident; $23,274 per year non-resident; $7,094 fees non-resident (7 credits or more); $1,307 annual health insurance fee. *Financial support:* In 2016–17, 12 research assistantships with partial tuition reimbursements (averaging $12,569 per year), 27 teaching assistantships with partial tuition reimbursements (averaging $13,759 per year) were awarded; institutionally sponsored loans, scholarships/grants, health care benefits, and unspecified assistantships also available. Financial award application deadline: 3/15. *Faculty research:* Multicultural issues in counseling, academic interventions for students with disabilities, establishment of pro-social skills in young children with severe disabilities, inclusive strategies for students with disabilities, language and literacy for English language learners. *Total annual research expenditures:* $768,906. *Unit head:* Dr. Monica Brown, Interim Department Chair/Professor, 702-895-3167, Fax: 702-895-3205, E-mail: monica.brown@unlv.edu. *Application contact:* Dr. Cori More, Graduate

Coordinator, 702-895-3271, Fax: 702-895-3205, E-mail: cori.more@unlv.edu.
Website: http://education.unlv.edu/ecs/

University of Nevada, Reno, Graduate School, College of Education, Department of Curriculum, Teaching and Learning, Reno, NV 89557. Offers curriculum and instruction (PhD); curriculum, teaching and learning (Ed D, PhD); elementary education (M Ed, MA, MS); secondary education (M Ed, MA, MS); special education and disability studies (PhD). *Degree requirements:* For master's, thesis optional; for doctorate, thesis/dissertation. *Entrance requirements:* For master's, GRE General Test, minimum GPA of 2.75; for doctorate, GRE General Test, minimum GPA of 3.0. Additional exam requirements/recommendations for international students: Required—TOEFL (minimum score 500 paper-based; 61 iBT), IELTS (minimum score 6). Electronic applications accepted. *Faculty research:* Education, curricula, pedagogy.

University of Nevada, Reno, Graduate School, College of Education, Department of Educational Specialties, Program in Special Education, Reno, NV 89557. Offers M Ed, MA, MS, Ed D, PhD. Terminal master's awarded for partial completion of doctoral program. *Degree requirements:* For master's, thesis optional; for doctorate, thesis/dissertation. *Entrance requirements:* For master's, minimum GPA of 2.75; for doctorate, GRE General Test, minimum GPA of 3.0. Additional exam requirements/recommendations for international students: Required—TOEFL (minimum score 500 paper-based; 61 iBT), IELTS (minimum score 6). Electronic applications accepted. *Faculty research:* Learning disabilities, equity and diversity in educational settings.

University of New Hampshire, Graduate School, College of Liberal Arts, Department of Education, Program in Early Childhood Education, Durham, NH 03824. Offers early childhood eduaction: special needs (M Ed); early childhood education (M Ed). *Program availability:* Part-time. *Degree requirements:* For master's, thesis or alternative. *Entrance requirements:* For master's, GRE General Test. Additional exam requirements/recommendations for international students: Required—TOEFL (minimum score 550 paper-based; 80 iBT). *Application deadline:* For fall admission, 2/1 priority date for domestic students, 2/1 for international students; for spring admission, 12/1 for domestic students. Applications are processed on a rolling basis. Application fee: $65. Electronic applications accepted. *Financial support:* Fellowships, research assistantships, teaching assistantships, career-related internships or fieldwork, Federal Work-Study, scholarships/grants, and tuition waivers (full and partial) available. Support available to part-time students. Financial award application deadline: 2/15. *Faculty research:* Young children with special needs. *Unit head:* Dr. Leslie Couse, Chair, 603-862-0638, E-mail: education.department@unh.edu. *Application contact:* Lisa Wilder, Administrative Assistant, 603-862-2381, E-mail: education.department@unh.edu.
Website: http://cola.unh.edu/education

University of New Mexico, Graduate Studies, College of Education, Program in Intensive Social, Language and Behavioral Needs, Albuquerque, NM 87131-2039. Offers Graduate Certificate. *Program availability:* Part-time, evening/weekend. *Faculty:* 2 full-time (both women). *Students:* 6 part-time (all women). Average age 44. 5 applicants, 80% accepted, 3 enrolled. In 2016, 1 Graduate Certificate awarded. *Entrance requirements:* Additional exam requirements/recommendations for international students: Required—TOEFL (minimum score 550 paper-based). *Application deadline:* For fall admission, 3/31 priority date for domestic students, 3/1 for international students; for spring admission, 9/30 priority date for domestic students, 8/1 for international students. Applications are processed on a rolling basis. Application fee: $50. Electronic applications accepted. *Financial support:* Fellowships available. Financial award application deadline: 3/1; financial award applicants required to submit FAFSA. *Unit head:* Prof. Ruth Luckasson, Chair, 505-266-6510, Fax: 505-277-6929, E-mail: ruthl@unm.edu. *Application contact:* Jo Sanchez, Information Contact, 505-277-5018, Fax: 505-277-8679, E-mail: jsanchez@unm.edu.
Website: http://coe.unm.edu

University of New Mexico, Graduate Studies, College of Education, Program in Special Education, Albuquerque, NM 87131. Offers learning and behavioral exceptionalities (MA); mental retardation and severe disabilities (MA); special education (Ed D, PhD, Ed S). *Accreditation:* NCATE. *Program availability:* Part-time, evening/weekend. *Faculty:* 6 full-time (5 women), 2 part-time/adjunct (1 woman). *Students:* 42 full-time (35 women), 58 part-time (48 women); includes 38 minority (2 Black or African American, non-Hispanic/Latino; 2 Asian, non-Hispanic/Latino; 33 Hispanic/Latino; 1 Two or more races, non-Hispanic/Latino), 9 international. Average age 36. 36 applicants, 78% accepted, 24 enrolled. In 2016, 37 master's, 6 doctorates, 4 other advanced degrees awarded. *Degree requirements:* For master's, comprehensive exam, thesis optional; for doctorate, comprehensive exam, thesis/dissertation, screening, proposal hearing. *Entrance requirements:* For master's, minimum GPA of 3.2; for doctorate, minimum GPA of 3.2, 2 years of relevant experience; for Ed S, special education degree, 2 years of teaching experience with people with disabilities, writing sample, minimum GPA of 3.2. *Application deadline:* For fall admission, 3/31 priority date for domestic students; for spring admission, 9/30 priority date for domestic students. Applications are processed on a rolling basis. Application fee: $50. Electronic applications accepted. *Financial support:* Fellowships, research assistantships with tuition reimbursements, teaching assistantships with tuition reimbursements, career-related internships or fieldwork, Federal Work-Study, scholarships/grants, traineeships, health care benefits, unspecified assistantships, and stipends available. Support available to part-time students. Financial award application deadline: 3/1; financial award applicants required to submit FAFSA. *Faculty research:* Mathematics instruction, bilingual special education, inclusive education, autism, reading instruction for students with cognitive disabilities, alternative assessment, human rights and disability, applied behavior analysis, bilingualism, language and literacy, mathematics, science instruction, special education. *Unit head:* Prof. Ruth Luckasson, Chair, 505-277-6510, Fax: 505-277-6929, E-mail: luckasson@unm.edu. *Application contact:* Della Gallegos, Information Contact, 505-277-5018, Fax: 505-277-8679, E-mail: dgalle06@unm.edu.
Website: http://coe.unm.edu/departments-programs/es/special-education-program/index.html

University of New Orleans, Graduate School, College of Education and Human Development, Department of Special Education and Habilitative Services, New Orleans, LA 70148. Offers M Ed, PhD. *Accreditation:* NCATE. *Program availability:* Evening/weekend. *Degree requirements:* For doctorate, variable foreign language requirement, thesis/dissertation. *Entrance requirements:* For master's, GRE General Test; for doctorate, GRE General Test, GRE Subject Test. Additional exam requirements/recommendations for international students: Required—TOEFL (minimum score 550 paper-based; 79 iBT). Electronic applications accepted. *Faculty research:* Inclusion, transition, early childhood, mild/moderate, severe/profound.

University of North Alabama, College of Education, Department of Elementary Education, Collaborative Teacher Special Education Program, Florence, AL 35632-0001. Offers MA Ed. *Accreditation:* NCATE. *Program availability:* Part-time. *Faculty:* 5 full-time (all women), 1 part-time/adjunct (0 women). *Students:* 12 part-time (10 women). Average age 35. 5 applicants, 80% accepted, 4 enrolled. In 2016, 6 master's awarded. *Degree requirements:* For master's, comprehensive exam. *Entrance requirements:* For master's, GRE, MAT, or NTE, minimum GPA of 2.5, Alabama Class B Certificate or equivalent, teaching experience. Additional exam requirements/recommendations for international students: Required—TOEFL (minimum score 79 iBT), IELTS (minimum score 6), PTE (minimum score 54). *Application deadline:* Applications are processed on a rolling basis. Application fee: $50 ($100 for international students). Electronic applications accepted. *Expenses:* Tuition, state resident: full-time $2799; part-time $1866 per semester. Tuition, nonresident: full-time $5598; part-time $3732 per semester. *Required fees:* $915; $642 per semester. Tuition and fees vary according to course load. *Financial support:* Scholarships/grants available. Financial award application deadline: 2/1; financial award applicants required to submit FAFSA. *Unit head:* Dr. Donna Lefort, Dean, College of Education and Human Sciences, 256-765-4252, E-mail: dpjacobs@una.edu. *Application contact:* Hillary N. Coats, Graduate Admissions Coordinator, 256-765-4447, E-mail: graduate@una.edu.

University of North Alabama, College of Education, Department of Secondary Education, Program in Secondary Education, Florence, AL 35632-0001. Offers secondary education (MA Ed); special education (MA Ed). *Accreditation:* NCATE. *Program availability:* Part-time, 100% online, blended/hybrid learning. *Faculty:* 14 full-time (5 women), 8 part-time/adjunct (6 women). *Students:* 47 full-time (25 women), 33 part-time (26 women); includes 12 minority (5 Black or African American, non-Hispanic/Latino; 3 American Indian or Alaska Native, non-Hispanic/Latino; 3 Hispanic/Latino; 1 Two or more races, non-Hispanic/Latino), 3 international. Average age 29. 46 applicants, 67% accepted, 25 enrolled. In 2016, 21 master's awarded. *Degree requirements:* For master's, comprehensive exam. *Entrance requirements:* For master's, GRE, MAT, or NTE, minimum GPA of 2.5, Alabama Class B Certificate or equivalent, teaching experience. Additional exam requirements/recommendations for international students: Required—TOEFL (minimum score 79 iBT), IELTS (minimum score 6), PTE (minimum score 54). *Application deadline:* Applications are processed on a rolling basis. Application fee: $50 ($100 for international students). Electronic applications accepted. *Expenses:* Tuition, state resident: full-time $2799; part-time $1866 per semester. Tuition, nonresident: full-time $5598; part-time $3732 per semester. *Required fees:* $915; $642 per semester. Tuition and fees vary according to course load. *Financial support:* In 2016–17, 9 students received support. Scholarships/grants and unspecified assistantships available. Financial award application deadline: 2/1; financial award applicants required to submit FAFSA. *Unit head:* Dr. Leah Whitten, Interim Chair, 256-765-4575, E-mail: lswhitten@una.edu. *Application contact:* Hillary N. Coats, Graduate Admissions Coordinator, 256-765-4447, E-mail: graduate@una.edu.
Website: https://www.una.edu/education/departments/secondary-education.html

The University of North Carolina at Charlotte, Cato College of Education, Department of Special Education and Child Development, Charlotte, NC 28223-0001. Offers academically or intellectually gifted (Graduate Certificate); autism spectrum disorders (Graduate Certificate); child and family development: birth through kindergarten (Graduate Certificate); child and family studies: early education (M Ed); special education (M Ed, PhD, Graduate Certificate), including academically or intellectually gifted (M Ed). *Program availability:* Part-time, 100% online, blended/hybrid learning. *Faculty:* 25 full-time (18 women), 8 part-time/adjunct (6 women). *Students:* 21 full-time (17 women), 106 part-time (101 women); includes 11 minority (8 Black or African American, non-Hispanic/Latino; 1 Hispanic/Latino; 2 Two or more races, non-Hispanic/Latino), 4 international. Average age 34. 83 applicants, 95% accepted, 66 enrolled. In 2016, 6 master's, 7 doctorates, 42 other advanced degrees awarded. *Degree requirements:* For master's, thesis or alternative, research project; for doctorate, thesis/dissertation, portfolio; for Graduate Certificate, internship. *Entrance requirements:* For master's, GRE or MAT, personal statement, letters of recommendation; for doctorate, GRE or MAT, 2 official transcripts of all academic work attempted since high school indicating minimum GPA of 3.5 in graduate degree program; at least 3 references of someone who knows applicant's current work and/or academic achievements in previous degree work; two-page essay; current resume or curriculum vitae; writing sample; documentation of teaching; for Graduate Certificate, undergraduate degree from regionally-accredited four-year institution; minimum cumulative undergraduate GPA of 3.0; three recommendations from persons knowledgeable of applicant's interaction with children and families; statement of purpose; clear criminal background check. Additional exam requirements/recommendations for international students: Required—TOEFL (minimum score 523 paper-based, 70 iBT) or IELTS (6.5). *Application deadline:* For fall admission, 12/1 for domestic and international students; for spring admission, 10/1 priority date for domestic and international students; for summer admission, 4/1 priority date for domestic and international students. Applications are processed on a rolling basis. Application fee: $75. Electronic applications accepted. *Expenses:* Tuition, state resident: full-time $4252. Tuition, nonresident: full-time $17,423. *Required fees:* $3026. Tuition and fees vary according to course load and program. *Financial support:* In 2016–17, 11 students received support, including 10 research assistantships (averaging $9,195 per year), 1 teaching assistantship (averaging $16,848 per year); career-related internships or fieldwork, institutionally sponsored loans, scholarships/grants, and unspecified assistantships also available. Support available to part-time students. Financial award application deadline: 3/1; financial award applicants required to submit FAFSA. *Total annual research expenditures:* $4 million. *Unit head:* Dr. Belva Collins, Chair, 704-687-8828, E-mail: belva.collins@uncc.edu. *Application contact:* Kathy B. Giddings, Director of Graduate Admissions, 704-687-5503, Fax: 704-687-1668, E-mail: gradadm@uncc.edu.
Website: http://spcd.uncc.edu/

The University of North Carolina at Charlotte, Cato College of Education, Interdisciplinary Education Programs, Charlotte, NC 28223-0001. Offers art education (Graduate Certificate); child and family development: early childhood education (MAT); curriculum and instruction (PhD); elementary education (MAT); foreign language education (MAT); middle grades education (MAT); secondary education (MAT); special education (MAT); teaching (Graduate Certificate); teaching English as a second language (MAT); theatre education (Graduate Certificate). *Program availability:* Part-time, 100% online, blended/hybrid learning. *Students:* 78 full-time (59 women), 619 part-time (484 women); includes 255 minority (186 Black or African American, non-Hispanic/Latino; 1 American Indian or Alaska Native, non-Hispanic/Latino; 16 Asian, non-Hispanic/Latino; 37 Hispanic/Latino; 15 Two or more races, non-Hispanic/Latino), 10 international. Average age 33. 380 applicants, 92% accepted, 264 enrolled. In 2016, 93 master's, 8 doctorates, 176 other advanced degrees awarded. *Degree requirements:* For master's, thesis or alternative, research project/portfolio. *Entrance requirements:* For master's, GRE or MAT, bachelor's degree, or its U.S. equivalent, from regionally-accredited college or university; minimum overall GPA of 3.0 on all previous work beyond high school; statement of purpose (essay); at least three recommendation forms; for doctorate, GRE or MAT, bachelor's degree (or its U.S. equivalent) from regionally-accredited college or university; minimum overall GPA of 3.5 in master's degree program; for Graduate Certificate, bachelor's degree from regionally-accredited university; minimum GPA of 2.75 on all post-secondary work attempted; transcripts; personal statement outlining why the applicant seeks admission to the program. Additional exam requirements/recommendations for international students: Required—TOEFL (minimum score 523 paper-based, 70 iBT) or IELTS (6.5). *Application deadline:* For fall admission, 3/1 priority date for domestic and international students; for spring admission, 10/1 priority date for domestic and international students; for summer admission, 4/1 priority date for domestic and international students. Applications are processed on a rolling basis. Application fee: $75. Electronic applications accepted. *Expenses:* Tuition, state resident: full-time $4252. Tuition, nonresident: full-time

$17,423. *Required fees:* $3026. Tuition and fees vary according to course load and program. *Financial support:* Career-related internships or fieldwork, institutionally sponsored loans, scholarships/grants, and unspecified assistantships available. Support available to part-time students. Financial award application deadline: 3/1; financial award applicants required to submit FAFSA. *Unit head:* Dr. Ellen McIntyre, Dean, 704-687-8722, E-mail: ellen.mcintyre@uncc.edu. *Application contact:* Kathy B. Giddings, Director of Graduate Admissions, 704-687-5503, Fax: 704-687-1668, E-mail: gradadm@uncc.edu.
Website: http://education.uncc.edu/academic-programs

The University of North Carolina at Greensboro, Graduate School, School of Education, Department of Specialized Education Services, Greensboro, NC 27412-5001. Offers cross-categorical special education (M Ed); interdisciplinary studies in special education (M Ed); leadership early care and education (Certificate); special education (M Ed, PhD). *Degree requirements:* For master's, thesis or alternative. *Entrance requirements:* For master's, GRE General Test. Additional exam requirements/recommendations for international students: Required—TOEFL. Electronic applications accepted.

The University of North Carolina Wilmington, Watson College of Education, Department of Early Childhood, Elementary, Middle, Literacy and Special Education, Wilmington, NC 28403-3297. Offers educational leadership, policy, and advocacy (M Ed); elementary education (M Ed, MAT); language and literacy (M Ed); middle grades education (M Ed, MAT). *Accreditation:* NCATE. *Program availability:* Part-time. *Faculty:* 26 full-time (19 women). *Students:* 121 full-time (89 women), 139 part-time (135 women); includes 70 minority (47 Black or African American, non-Hispanic/Latino; 1 Asian, non-Hispanic/Latino; 14 Hispanic/Latino; 8 Two or more races, non-Hispanic/Latino). Average age 34. 109 applicants, 78% accepted, 65 enrolled. In 2016, 83 master's awarded. *Degree requirements:* For master's, comprehensive exam, capstone experience. *Entrance requirements:* For master's, GRE General Test, MAT, minimum GPA of 3.0 in undergraduate work, 3 letters of recommendations, NC Class A teacher license in related field, statement of interest. *Application deadline:* For fall admission, 5/15 for domestic students; for spring admission, 10/15 for domestic students; for summer admission, 3/15 for domestic students. Applications are processed on a rolling basis. Application fee: $60. Electronic applications accepted. *Expenses:* Contact institution. *Financial support:* Scholarships/grants and unspecified assistantships available. Support available to part-time students. Financial award application deadline: 3/15; financial award applicants required to submit FAFSA. *Unit head:* Dr. Kathy Fox, Chair, 910-962-3240, Fax: 910-962-3988, E-mail: foxk@uncw.edu. *Application contact:* Dr. Elizabeth Crawford, Graduate Program Coordinator, 910-962-2916, Fax: 910-962-3988, E-mail: crawforde@uncw.edu.
Website: http://www.uncw.edu/ed/eemls/index.html

University of North Dakota, Graduate School, College of Education and Human Development, Program in Special Education, Grand Forks, ND 58202. Offers M Ed, MS. *Accreditation:* NCATE. *Program availability:* Part-time, online learning. *Degree requirements:* For master's, comprehensive exam, thesis or alternative. *Entrance requirements:* For master's, minimum GPA of 3.0. Additional exam requirements/recommendations for international students: Required—TOEFL (minimum score 550 paper-based; 79 iBT), IELTS (minimum score 6.5). *Application deadline:* For fall admission, 6/1 for domestic and international students; for spring admission, 11/1 for domestic and international students. Application fee: $35. Electronic applications accepted. *Financial support:* Fellowships with full and partial tuition reimbursements, research assistantships with full and partial tuition reimbursements, teaching assistantships with full and partial tuition reimbursements, career-related internships or fieldwork, Federal Work-Study, institutionally sponsored loans, scholarships/grants, health care benefits, tuition waivers (full and partial), and unspecified assistantships available. Support available to part-time students. Financial award application deadline: 3/15; financial award applicants required to submit FAFSA. *Faculty research:* Visual, emotional, and mental disabilities; early childhood. *Unit head:* Dr. Lynne Chalmers, Director, 701-777-3187, Fax: 701-777-4393, E-mail: lynne.chalmers@mail.und.nodak.edu. *Application contact:* Staci Wells, Admissions Specialist, 701-777-0748, Fax: 701-777-3619, E-mail: staci.wells@gradschool.und.edu.
Website: http://www.und.nodak.edu/dept/tl/specialed/

University of Northern Colorado, Graduate School, College of Education and Behavioral Sciences, School of Special Education, Greeley, CO 80639. Offers deaf/hard of hearing (MA); early childhood special education (MA); gifted and talented (MA); special education (MA, PhD); visual impairment (MA). *Program availability:* Part-time, evening/weekend, online learning. *Degree requirements:* For master's, comprehensive exam, thesis or alternative; for doctorate, comprehensive exam, thesis/dissertation. *Entrance requirements:* For master's, letters of recommendation, interview; for doctorate, GRE General Test, resume. *Application deadline:* Applications are processed on a rolling basis. Application fee: $50 ($60 for international students). Electronic applications accepted. *Financial support:* Fellowships, research assistantships, teaching assistantships, and unspecified assistantships available. Financial award application deadline: 3/1; financial award applicants required to submit FAFSA. *Unit head:* Dr. Harvey Rude, Director, 970-351-2691, Fax: 970-351-1061. *Application contact:* Linda Sisson, Graduate Student Admission Coordinator, 970-351-1807, Fax: 970-351-2371, E-mail: linda.sisson@unco.edu.
Website: http://www.unco.edu/cebs/sped/

University of Northern Colorado, Graduate School, College of Education and Behavioral Sciences, School of Teacher Education, Program in Teaching Diverse Learners, Greeley, CO 80639. Offers MA. *Program availability:* Online learning. *Unit head:* Dr. Rosann Englebretson, Coordinator, 719-232-0582, E-mail: rosann.englebretson@unco.edu. *Application contact:* Linda Sisson, Graduate Student Admission Coordinator, 970-351-1807, Fax: 970-351-2371, E-mail: linda.sisson@unco.edu.

University of Northern Iowa, Graduate College, College of Education, Department of Special Education, MAE Program in Special Education, Cedar Falls, IA 50614. Offers career/vocational programming and transition (MAE); consultant (MAE); field specialization (MAE).

University of North Florida, College of Education and Human Services, Department of Exceptional, Deaf, and Interpreter Education, Jacksonville, FL 32224. Offers American Sign Language (MS); American Sign Language/English interpreting (M Ed); applied behavior analysis (M Ed); autism (M Ed); deaf education (M Ed); disability services (M Ed); exceptional student education (M Ed). *Accreditation:* NCATE. *Program availability:* Part-time, evening/weekend. *Faculty:* 11 full-time (9 women), 6 part-time/adjunct (all women). *Students:* 32 full-time (29 women), 50 part-time (40 women); includes 14 minority (5 Black or African American, non-Hispanic/Latino; 2 Asian, non-Hispanic/Latino; 5 Hispanic/Latino; 2 Two or more races, non-Hispanic/Latino), 4 international. Average age 33. 28 applicants, 46% accepted, 7 enrolled. In 2016, 42 master's awarded. *Entrance requirements:* For master's, GRE General Test, minimum GPA of 3.0 in last 60 hours, interview, 3 letters of recommendation. Additional exam requirements/recommendations for international students: Required—TOEFL (minimum score 500 paper-based). *Application deadline:* For fall admission, 3/31 priority date for domestic students, 5/1 for international students; for spring admission, 12/1 priority date for domestic students, 10/1 for international students; for summer admission, 3/31 priority date for domestic students, 2/1 for international students. Application fee: $30. Electronic applications accepted. Tuition and fees vary according to course load, campus/location and program. *Financial support:* In 2016–17, 7 students received support, including 2 research assistantships (averaging $2,639 per year); teaching assistantships, career-related internships or fieldwork, Federal Work-Study, scholarships/grants, tuition waivers (partial), and unspecified assistantships also available. Support available to part-time students. Financial award application deadline: 4/1; financial award applicants required to submit FAFSA. *Faculty research:* Transportation, energy, communications, healthcare, nano-science and engineering, unmanned aircraft systems, biomedical applications. *Total annual research expenditures:* $706,370. *Unit head:* Dr. Janice Seabrooks-Blackmore, Chair, 904-620-2930, Fax: 904-620-3895, E-mail: janice.seabrooks-blackmore@unf.edu. *Application contact:* Dr. Amanda Pascale, Director, The Graduate School, 904-620-1360, Fax: 904-620-1362, E-mail: graduateschool@unf.edu.
Website: http://www.unf.edu/coehs/edie/

University of North Texas, Robert B. Toulouse School of Graduate Studies, Denton, TX 76203-5459. Offers accounting (MS); applied anthropology (MA, MS); applied behavior analysis (Certificate); applied geography (MA); applied technology and performance improvement (M Ed, MS); art education (MA); art history (MA); art museum education (Certificate); arts leadership (Certificate); audiology (Au D); behavior analysis (MS); behavioral science (PhD); biochemistry and molecular biology (MS); biology (MA, MS); biomedical engineering (MS); business analysis (MS); chemistry (MS); clinical health psychology (PhD); communication studies (MA, MS); computer engineering (MS); computer science (MS); counseling (M Ed, MS), including clinical mental health counseling (MS), college and university counseling, elementary school counseling, secondary school counseling; creative writing (MA); criminal justice (MS); curriculum and instruction (M Ed); decision sciences (MBA); design (MA, MFA), including fashion design (MFA), innovation studies, interior design (MFA); early childhood studies (MS); economics (MS); educational leadership (M Ed, Ed D); educational psychology (MS, PhD), including family studies (MS), gifted and talented (MS), human development (MS), learning and cognition (MS), research, measurement and evaluation (MS); electrical engineering (MS); emergency management (MPA); engineering technology (MS); English (MA); English as a second language (MA); environmental science (MS); finance (MBA, MS); financial management (MPA); French (MA); health services management (MBA); higher education (M Ed, Ed D); history (MA, MS); hospitality management (MS); human resources management (MPA); information science (MS); information systems (PhD); information technologies (MBA); interdisciplinary studies (MA, MS); international studies (MA); international sustainable tourism (MS); jazz studies (MM); journalism (MA, MJ, Graduate Certificate), including interactive and virtual digital communication (Graduate Certificate), narrative journalism (Graduate Certificate), public relations (Graduate Certificate); kinesiology (MS); linguistics (MA); local government management (MPA); logistics (PhD); logistics and supply chain management (MBA); long-term care, senior housing, and aging services (MA); management (PhD); marketing (MBA); mathematics (MA, MS); mechanical and energy engineering (MS, PhD); music (MA), including ethnomusicology, music theory, musicology, performance; music composition (PhD); music education (MM Ed, PhD); nonprofit management (MPA); operations and supply chain management (MBA); performance (MM, DMA); philosophy (MA); political science (MA); professional and technical communication (MA); radio, television and film (MA, MFA); rehabilitation counseling (Certificate); sociology (MA); Spanish (MA); special education (M Ed); speech-language pathology (MA); strategic management (MBA); studio art (MFA); teaching (M Ed); MBA/MS. *Program availability:* Part-time, evening/weekend, online learning. Terminal master's awarded for partial completion of doctoral program. *Degree requirements:* For master's, variable foreign language requirement, comprehensive exam (for some programs), thesis (for some programs); for doctorate, variable foreign language requirement, comprehensive exam (for some programs), thesis/dissertation; for other advanced degree, variable foreign language requirement, comprehensive exam (for some programs). *Entrance requirements:* For master's and doctorate, GRE, GMAT. Additional exam requirements/recommendations for international students: Required—TOEFL (minimum score 550 paper-based; 79 iBT). Electronic applications accepted.

University of Oklahoma, Jeannine Rainbolt College of Education, Department of Educational Psychology, Norman, OK 73019. Offers counseling psychology (PhD); instructional psychology and technology (M Ed, PhD), including 21st century teaching and learning (M Ed), educational psychology (M Ed), instructional design and technology (M Ed), instructional psychology and technology (PhD), integrating technology in teaching (M Ed); professional counseling (M Ed), including professional counseling; special education (M Ed, PhD), including applied behavior analysis (M Ed), higher education and community support (PhD), higher education professor (PhD), school instructional leaders (PhD), secondary transition (M Ed). *Accreditation:* NCATE. *Program availability:* Part-time, 100% online, blended/hybrid learning. *Faculty:* 24 full-time (17 women), 1 (woman) part-time/adjunct. *Students:* 80 full-time (61 women), 102 part-time (84 women); includes 55 minority (13 Black or African American, non-Hispanic/Latino; 8 American Indian or Alaska Native, non-Hispanic/Latino; 4 Asian, non-Hispanic/Latino; 14 Hispanic/Latino; 16 Two or more races, non-Hispanic/Latino), 18 international. Average age 34. 171 applicants, 46% accepted, 54 enrolled. In 2016, 48 master's, 12 doctorates awarded. Terminal master's awarded for partial completion of doctoral program. *Degree requirements:* For master's, comprehensive exam (for some programs), thesis (for some programs); for doctorate, comprehensive exam (for some programs), thesis/dissertation. *Entrance requirements:* For doctorate, GRE. Additional exam requirements/recommendations for international students: Required—TOEFL (minimum score 79 iBT) or IELTS (minimum score 6.5). Application fee: $50 ($100 for international students). Electronic applications accepted. *Expenses:* Tuition, state resident: full-time $4886; part-time $203.60 per credit hour. Tuition, nonresident: full-time $18,989; part-time $791.20 per credit hour. *Required fees:* $3283; $126.25 per credit hour. $126.50 per semester. *Financial support:* In 2016–17, 116 students received support, including 7 research assistantships with full and partial tuition reimbursements available (averaging $12,038 per year), 5 teaching assistantships with full and partial tuition reimbursements available (averaging $12,695 per year); fellowships with full and partial tuition reimbursements available, scholarships/grants, health care benefits, and unspecified assistantships also available. Financial award application deadline: 6/1; financial award applicants required to submit FAFSA. *Faculty research:* Clinical expertise and social justice commitments; scaffolding higher order and critical thinking; evidence=based reading and writing strategies for students with disabilities; technology integration by preservice teachers; achievement motivation. *Total annual research expenditures:* $294,737. *Unit head:* Dr. Nancy E. Marchand-Martella, Chair, Department of Educational Psychology, 405-325-0624, Fax: 405-325-6655, E-mail: nmarchand-martella@ou.edu. *Application contact:* Anna Steele, Graduate Programs Specialist, 405-325-4525, Fax: 405-325-7390, E-mail: jrcoe_gps@ou.edu.
Website: http://www.ou.edu/content/education/edpy/

University of Oklahoma Health Sciences Center, Graduate College, College of Allied Health, Department of Communication Sciences and Disorders, Oklahoma City, OK 73190. Offers audiology (MS, Au D, PhD); communication sciences and disorders (Certificate), including reading, speech-language pathology; education of the deaf (MS);

speech-language pathology (MS, PhD). *Accreditation:* ASHA (one or more programs are accredited). *Program availability:* Part-time. Terminal master's awarded for partial completion of doctoral program. *Degree requirements:* For master's, comprehensive exam, thesis optional; for doctorate, one foreign language, comprehensive exam, thesis/dissertation. *Entrance requirements:* For master's and doctorate, GRE General Test, 3 letters of recommendation. Additional exam requirements/recommendations for international students: Required—TOEFL (minimum score 550 paper-based). *Faculty research:* Event-related potentials, cleft palate, fluency disorders, language disorders, hearing and speech science.

University of Phoenix–Bay Area Campus, College of Education, San Jose, CA 95134-1805. Offers administration and supervision (MA Ed); adult education and training (MA Ed); early childhood education (MA Ed); education (Ed S); educational leadership (Ed D); elementary teacher education (MA Ed); higher education administration (PhD); secondary teacher education (MA Ed); special education (MA Ed); teacher leadership (MA Ed). *Program availability:* Evening/weekend, online learning. *Degree requirements:* For master's, thesis (for some programs). *Entrance requirements:* For master's, minimum undergraduate GPA of 2.5, 3 years of work experience. Additional exam requirements/recommendations for international students: Required—TOEFL (minimum score 550 paper-based; 79 iBT). Electronic applications accepted.

University of Phoenix–Hawaii Campus, College of Education, Honolulu, HI 96813-3800. Offers administration and supervision (MA Ed); curriculum and instruction (MA Ed); elementary education (MA Ed); secondary education (MA Ed); special education (MA Ed); teacher education for elementary licensure (MA Ed). *Program availability:* Evening/weekend. *Degree requirements:* For master's, thesis (for some programs). *Entrance requirements:* For master's, minimum undergraduate GPA of 2.5, 3 years of work experience. Additional exam requirements/recommendations for international students: Required—TOEFL (minimum score 550 paper-based; 79 iBT). Electronic applications accepted.

University of Phoenix–Online Campus, College of Education, Phoenix, AZ 85034-7209. Offers administration and supervision (MAEd, Certificate); adult education and training (MAEd); curriculum and instruction (MAEd), including computer education, curriculum and instruction, English as a second language, language arts, mathematics, reading; early childhood education (MAEd); educational studies (MAEd); elementary teacher education (MAEd), including early childhood, elementary teacher education, high school middle level, middle level; principal licensure (Certificate); secondary teacher education (MAEd); special education (MAEd, Certificate); teacher education (MAEd), including middle level generalist; teacher education middle level mathematics (MAEd), including middle level mathematics; teacher education middle level science (MAEd), including middle level science; teacher education secondary mathematics (MAEd); teacher education secondary science (MAEd); teacher leadership (MAEd); teachers of English learners (Certificate); transition to teaching (Certificate), including elementary education, secondary education. *Program availability:* Evening/weekend, online learning. *Entrance requirements:* Additional exam requirements/recommendations for international students: Required—TOEFL, TOEIC (Test of English as an International Communication), Berlitz Online English Proficiency Exam, PTE, or IELTS. Electronic applications accepted. *Expenses:* Contact institution.

University of Phoenix–Phoenix Campus, College of Education, Tempe, AZ 85282-2371. Offers administration and supervision (MA Ed); adult education and training (MA Ed); curriculum and instruction reading (MA Ed); early childhood education (MA Ed); education studies (MA Ed); elementary teacher education (MA Ed); secondary teacher education (MA Ed); special education (MA Ed); teacher leadership (MA Ed). *Program availability:* Evening/weekend, online learning. *Entrance requirements:* Additional exam requirements/recommendations for international students: Required—TOEFL, TOEIC (Test of English as an International Communication), Berlitz Online English Proficiency Exam, PTE, or IELTS. Electronic applications accepted. *Expenses:* Contact institution.

University of Phoenix–Southern Arizona Campus, College of Education, Tucson, AZ 85711. Offers administration and supervision (MA Ed); adult education and training (MA Ed); curriculum instruction (MA Ed); educational counseling (MA Ed); elementary teacher education (MA Ed); school counseling (MSC); secondary teacher education (MA Ed); special education (MA Ed, Certificate). *Program availability:* Evening/weekend. *Degree requirements:* For master's, thesis (for some programs). *Entrance requirements:* For master's, minimum undergraduate GPA of 2.5, 3 years of work experience. Additional exam requirements/recommendations for international students: Required—TOEFL (minimum score 550 paper-based; 79 iBT). Electronic applications accepted.

University of Phoenix–Utah Campus, College of Education, Salt Lake City, UT 84123-4642. Offers administration and supervision (MA Ed); curriculum and instruction (MA Ed); elementary teacher education (MA Ed); school counseling (MSC); secondary teacher education (MA Ed); special education (MA Ed). *Program availability:* Evening/weekend. *Degree requirements:* For master's, thesis (for some programs). *Entrance requirements:* For master's, minimum undergraduate GPA of 2.5, 3 years work experience. Additional exam requirements/recommendations for international students: Required—TOEFL (minimum score 550 paper-based; 79 iBT). Electronic applications accepted.

University of Phoenix–Washington D.C. Campus, College of Education, Washington, DC 20001. Offers administration and supervision (MA Ed); adult education and training (MA Ed); computer education (MA Ed); curriculum and instruction (MA Ed, Ed D); early childhood education (MA Ed); education (Ed S); educational leadership (Ed D); educational technology (Ed D); elementary teacher education (MA Ed); English and language arts education (MA Ed); English as a second language (MA Ed); higher education administration (PhD); mathematics education (MA Ed); secondary teacher education (MA Ed); special education (MA Ed); teacher leadership (MA Ed).

University of Pittsburgh, School of Education, Department of Instruction and Learning, Program in Special Education, Pittsburgh, PA 15260. Offers applied behavior analysis (M Ed); early intervention (M Ed, PhD); general special education (M Ed, Ed D); special education teacher preparation (M Ed); vision studies (M Ed, PhD). *Program availability:* Part-time, evening/weekend. *Degree requirements:* For master's, thesis; for doctorate, thesis/dissertation. *Entrance requirements:* For master's, PRAXIS I; for doctorate, GRE General Test. Additional exam requirements/recommendations for international students: Required—TOEFL. Tuition and fees vary according to program.

University of Portland, School of Education, Portland, OR 97203-5798. Offers education (MA, MAT); educational leadership (M Ed); English for speakers of other languages (M Ed); initial administrator licensure (M Ed); neuroeducation (M Ed, Ed D); organizational leadership and development (Ed D); reading (M Ed); school leadership and development (Ed D); special education (M Ed). M Ed also available through the Graduate Outreach Program for teachers residing in the Oregon and Washington state areas. *Accreditation:* NCATE. *Program availability:* Part-time, evening/weekend. *Entrance requirements:* For master's, minimum GPA of 3.0, teaching certificate, letters of recommendation, resume, statement of goals, official transcripts. Additional exam requirements/recommendations for international students: Required—TOEFL (minimum score 550 paper-based; 80 iBT), IELTS (minimum score 7). *Faculty research:* Multicultural education, supervision/leadership.

University of Puerto Rico, Medical Sciences Campus, Graduate School of Public Health, Department of Human Development, Program in Developmental Disabilities-Early Intervention, San Juan, PR 00936-5067. Offers Certificate. *Program availability:* Part-time, evening/weekend.

University of Puerto Rico, Río Piedras Campus, College of Education, Program in Special and Differentiated Education, San Juan, PR 00931-3300. Offers M Ed. *Degree requirements:* For master's, thesis. *Entrance requirements:* For master's, GRE or PAEG, interview, minimum GPA of 3.0, letter of recommendation.

University of Rhode Island, Graduate School, Alan Shawn Feinstein College of Education and Professional Studies, School of Education, Kingston, RI 02881. Offers education (PhD); reading (MA); special education (MA). *Accreditation:* NCATE. *Program availability:* Part-time, evening/weekend. *Faculty:* 18 full-time (13 women). *Students:* 65 full-time (51 women), 147 part-time (108 women); includes 27 minority (7 Black or African American, non-Hispanic/Latino; 6 American Indian or Alaska Native, non-Hispanic/Latino; 7 Asian, non-Hispanic/Latino; 6 Hispanic/Latino; 1 Two or more races, non-Hispanic/Latino), 10 international. In 2016, 26 master's, 7 doctorates awarded. *Degree requirements:* For master's, comprehensive exam (for some programs), thesis optional; for doctorate, comprehensive exam, thesis/dissertation. *Entrance requirements:* For master's, 2 letters of recommendation; interview (for special education applicants); for doctorate, GRE, 3 letters of recommendation, resume. Additional exam requirements/recommendations for international students: Required—TOEFL. *Application deadline:* For fall admission, 1/15 for domestic students, 1/31 for international students; for spring admission, 11/15 for domestic students; for summer admission, 4/15 for domestic students. Application fee: $65. Electronic applications accepted. *Expenses:* Tuition, state resident: full-time $11,796; part-time $655 per credit. Tuition, nonresident: full-time $24,206; part-time $1345 per credit. *Required fees:* $1546; $44 per credit. One-time fee: $155 full-time; $35 part-time. *Financial support:* In 2016–17, 1 research assistantship with tuition reimbursement (averaging $8,592 per year), 4 teaching assistantships with tuition reimbursements (averaging $15,036 per year) were awarded. Financial award application deadline: 1/31; financial award applicants required to submit FAFSA. *Unit head:* Dr. David Byrd, Director, School of Education, 401-874-5484, Fax: 401-874-5471, E-mail: dbyrd@uri.edu. *Application contact:* Graduate Admissions, 401-874-2872, E-mail: gradadm@etal.uri.edu.
Website: http://www.uri.edu/hss/education/

University of Rio Grande, Graduate School, Rio Grande, OH 45674. Offers athletic coaching leadership (M Ed); educational leadership (M Ed); integrated arts (M Ed); intervention specialist in early childhood (M Ed); intervention specialist in mild/moderate (M Ed). *Accreditation:* NCATE. *Program availability:* Part-time. *Degree requirements:* For master's, final research project, portfolio. *Entrance requirements:* For master's, minimum GPA of 2.7 in major, 2.5 overall. Additional exam requirements/recommendations for international students: Required—TOEFL. *Application deadline:* Applications are processed on a rolling basis. Application fee: $20. *Financial support:* Career-related internships or fieldwork available. Support available to part-time students. Financial award application deadline: 7/1; financial award applicants required to submit FAFSA. *Faculty research:* Interagency collaboration, reading and mathematics, learning styles, college access, literacy. *Unit head:* Dr. Greg Miller, Director, 740-245-7030, E-mail: gmiller@rio.edu. *Application contact:* Nancy Downs, Secretary, 740-245-7328, Fax: 740-245-7175, E-mail: ndowns@rio.edu.

University of St. Francis, College of Education, Joliet, IL 60435-6169. Offers educational leadership (MS, Ed D); elementary education (M Ed); reading (MS); secondary education (M Ed), including English education, math education, science education, social studies education, visual arts education; special education (M Ed); teaching and learning (MS); TESOL (Certificate). *Accreditation:* NCATE. *Program availability:* Part-time, evening/weekend, 100% online, blended/hybrid learning. *Faculty:* 11 full-time (8 women), 60 part-time/adjunct (42 women). *Students:* 34 full-time (26 women), 420 part-time (318 women); includes 92 minority (51 Black or African American, non-Hispanic/Latino; 5 Asian, non-Hispanic/Latino; 31 Hispanic/Latino; 5 Two or more races, non-Hispanic/Latino), 4 international. Average age 36. 242 applicants, 48% accepted, 96 enrolled. In 2016, 229 master's, 44 doctorates, 10 other advanced degrees awarded. *Degree requirements:* For master's, comprehensive exam; for doctorate, thesis/dissertation. *Entrance requirements:* Additional exam requirements/recommendations for international students: Required—TOEFL (minimum score 550 paper-based; 79 iBT), IELTS (minimum score 6). *Application deadline:* Applications are processed on a rolling basis. Application fee: $30. Electronic applications accepted. Application fee is waived when completed online. *Expenses:* Contact institution. *Financial support:* In 2016–17, 48 students received support. Career-related internships or fieldwork and unspecified assistantships available. Support available to part-time students. Financial award applicants required to submit FAFSA. *Unit head:* Dr. John Gambro, Dean, 815-740-3829, Fax: 815-740-2264, E-mail: jgambro@stfrancis.edu. *Application contact:* Sandra Sloka, Director of Admissions for Graduate and Degree Completion Programs, 800-735-7500, Fax: 815-740-3431, E-mail: ssloka@stfrancis.edu.
Website: http://www.stfrancis.edu/academics/college-of-education/

University of Saint Francis, Graduate School, Department of Education, Fort Wayne, IN 46808-3994. Offers education (MAT); secondary education (MAT); special education (MS Ed), including intense intervention, mild intervention. *Accreditation:* NCATE. *Program availability:* Part-time, evening/weekend, online only, 100% online. *Faculty:* 1 (woman) full-time, 4 part-time/adjunct (2 women). *Students:* 4 full-time (3 women), 16 part-time (8 women); includes 2 minority (both Black or African American, non-Hispanic/Latino). Average age 29. 5 applicants, 100% accepted, 4 enrolled. In 2016, 2 master's awarded. *Degree requirements:* For master's, comprehensive exam. *Entrance requirements:* For master's, GRE (minimum composite score of 280 verbal and quantitative subtests) or MAT (minimum score of 389) if undergraduate GPA is below a 2.8 or prior graduate level GPA is below 3.0; GRE, ACT, SAT, or CASA exam if no license, minimum undergraduate GPA of 2.8; resume (if GPA is below 3.0); standard teaching license and/or bachelor's degree from regionally-accredited institution; background check; two professional recommendations. Additional exam requirements/recommendations for international students: Required—TOEFL (minimum score 550 paper-based) or IELTS (minimum score 6.5). *Application deadline:* Applications are processed on a rolling basis. Application fee: $0. Electronic applications accepted. *Expenses:* $475 per credit hour. *Financial support:* Federal Work-Study, scholarships/grants, and unspecified assistantships available. Financial award application deadline: 3/10; financial award applicants required to submit FAFSA. *Unit head:* Mary Riepenhoff, Assistant Professor/Department Chair, 260-399-7700 Ext. 8409, Fax: 260-399-8170, E-mail: mriepenhoff@sf.edu. *Application contact:* Kyle Richardson, Enrollment Specialist, 260-399-7700 Ext. 6310, Fax: 260-399-8152, E-mail: krichardson@sf.edu.
Website: http://education.sf.edu/

University of Saint Joseph, Department of Special Education, West Hartford, CT 06117-2700. Offers autism and applied behavior analysis (MS); special education (MA). *Program availability:* Part-time, evening/weekend. *Degree requirements:* For master's, thesis. Electronic applications accepted. Application fee is waived when completed online. *Expenses: Tuition:* Full-time $14,580; part-time $729 per credit hour. *Required* *fees:* $920; $46 per credit hour. Tuition and fees vary according to course load, degree level and program.

University of Saint Mary, Graduate Programs, Program in Special Education, Leavenworth, KS 66048-5082. Offers MA. *Program availability:* Part-time, evening/weekend. *Students:* 3 full-time (all women), 1 (woman) part-time. Average age 40. In 2016, 5 master's awarded. *Entrance requirements:* For master's, bachelor's degree, minimum undergraduate GPA of 2.75, two letters of recommendation, teaching certification. Application fee: $25. Electronic applications accepted. *Expenses:* $395 per hour. *Unit head:* Dr. Gwen Landever, Chair, 913-758-6159, E-mail: gwen.landever@stmary.edu.
Website: http://www.stmary.edu/success/Grad-Program/Master-of-Arts-Special-Education.aspx

University of St. Thomas, Graduate Studies, College of Education, Leadership and Counseling, Department of Special Education, St. Paul, MN 55105-1096. Offers MA, Certificate, Ed S. *Accreditation:* NCATE. *Program availability:* Part-time-only, evening/weekend, online only, 100% online, blended/hybrid learning. *Degree requirements:* For master's, thesis; for other advanced degree, professional portfolio. *Entrance requirements:* For master's, minimum GPA of 3.0 or MAT; for other advanced degree, MAT or minimum GPA of 2.75. Additional exam requirements/recommendations for international students: Required—TOEFL (minimum score 550 paper-based; 80 iBT). *Application deadline:* For fall admission, 7/15 priority date for domestic and international students; for spring admission, 12/9 priority date for domestic and international students; for summer admission, 4/3 priority date for domestic and international students. Applications are processed on a rolling basis. Electronic applications accepted. *Expenses:* Contact institution. *Financial support:* Fellowships, research assistantships, institutionally sponsored loans, and scholarships/grants available. Support available to part-time students. Financial award application deadline: 8/1; financial award applicants required to submit FAFSA. *Faculty research:* Reading and math fluency, inclusion curriculum for developmental disorders, parent involvement in positive behavior supports, children's friendships, preschool inclusion. *Unit head:* Dr. Terri L. Vandercook, Chair, 651-962-4389, Fax: 651-962-4169, E-mail: tlvandercook@stthomas.edu.

University of St. Thomas, School of Education and Human Services, Houston, TX 77006-4696. Offers all level education (M Ed); bilingual/dual language (M Ed); Catholic school teaching (M Ed); Catholic/private school leadership (M Ed); counselor education (M Ed); curriculum and instruction (M Ed); education (Ed D); educational leadership (M Ed); elementary teaching (M Ed); English as a second language (M Ed); exceptionality/educational diagnostician (M Ed); exceptionality/special education (M Ed); generalist (M Ed); reading (M Ed); secondary teaching (M Ed); teaching (MAT). *Accreditation:* TEAC. *Program availability:* Part-time, evening/weekend, online learning. *Faculty:* 44 full-time (29 women), 31 part-time/adjunct (17 women). *Students:* 65 full-time (61 women), 719 part-time (645 women); includes 515 minority (169 Black or African American, non-Hispanic/Latino; 25 Asian, non-Hispanic/Latino; 315 Hispanic/Latino; 2 Native Hawaiian or other Pacific Islander, non-Hispanic/Latino; 4 Two or more races, non-Hispanic/Latino), 24 international. Average age 36. 297 applicants, 92% accepted, 211 enrolled. In 2016, 403 master's awarded. *Degree requirements:* For master's, thesis, field experience. *Entrance requirements:* For master's, GRE or MAT if GPA is below 3.0, bachelor's degree; minimum GPA of 2.75 in bachelor's degree or last 60 credit hours; official transcripts from all institutions; goal statement of 250-300 words; 1 reference. Additional exam requirements/recommendations for international students: Required—TOEFL (minimum score 94 iBT), IELTS (minimum score 7), PTE (minimum score 53). *Application deadline:* Applications are processed on a rolling basis. Application fee: $35. Electronic applications accepted. *Expenses:* Contact institution. *Financial support:* In 2016–17, 52 students received support. Federal Work-Study, scholarships/grants, and state work-study, institutional employment available. Support available to part-time students. Financial award application deadline: 4/15; financial award applicants required to submit FAFSA. *Faculty research:* Leadership, diversity, personality traits, second language acquisition. *Unit head:* Dr. Robert LeBlanc, Dean, 713-525-3540, Fax: 713-525-3871, E-mail: education@stthom.edu. *Application contact:* Rita Paredes, Administrative Assistant, 713-525-3442, Fax: 713-525-3871, E-mail: rparede@stthom.edu.
Website: http://www.stthom.edu/Academics/School_of_Education_and_Human_Services/Index.aqf

University of San Diego, School of Leadership and Education Sciences, Department of Learning and Teaching, San Diego, CA 92110-2492. Offers inclusive learning (M Ed); literacy and digital learning (M Ed); school leadership (M Ed); special education with deaf and hard of hearing (M Ed); STEAM (science, technology, engineering, arts, and mathematics) (M Ed); teaching (MAT); TESOL, literacy and culture (M Ed). *Program availability:* Part-time, evening/weekend. *Faculty:* 9 full-time (7 women), 29 part-time/adjunct (19 women). *Students:* 161 full-time (126 women), 188 part-time (153 women); includes 127 minority (4 Black or African American, non-Hispanic/Latino; 24 Asian, non-Hispanic/Latino; 86 Hispanic/Latino; 1 Native Hawaiian or other Pacific Islander, non-Hispanic/Latino; 12 Two or more races, non-Hispanic/Latino), 20 international. Average age 33. 383 applicants, 83% accepted, 194 enrolled. In 2016, 114 master's awarded. *Degree requirements:* For master's, thesis (for some programs), international experience. *Entrance requirements:* For master's, California Basic Educational Skills Test, California Subject Examination for Teachers, minimum GPA of 2.75. Additional exam requirements/recommendations for international students: Required—TOEFL (minimum score 580 paper-based; 83 iBT), TWE. *Application deadline:* Applications are processed on a rolling basis. Application fee: $45. Electronic applications accepted. *Financial support:* In 2016–17, 46 students received support. Career-related internships or fieldwork, Federal Work-Study, institutionally sponsored loans, and stipends available. Financial award application deadline: 4/1; financial award applicants required to submit FAFSA. *Faculty research:* Action research methodology, cultural studies, instructional theories and practices, second language acquisition, school reform. *Unit head:* Dr. Maya Kalyanpur, Chair, 619-260-7655, E-mail: mkalyanpur@sandiego.edu. *Application contact:* Monica Mahon, Associate Director of Graduate Admissions, 619-260-4524, Fax: 619-260-4158, E-mail: grads@sandiego.edu.
Website: http://www.sandiego.edu/soles/departments/learning-and-teaching/

University of San Francisco, School of Education, Department of Learning and Instruction, San Francisco, CA 94117-1080. Offers digital technologies for teaching and learning (MA); learning and instruction (MA, Ed D); special education (MA, Ed D); teaching reading (MA). *Program availability:* Part-time, evening/weekend. *Faculty:* 9 full-time (5 women), 2 part-time/adjunct (both women). *Students:* 79 full-time (61 women), 30 part-time (23 women); includes 41 minority (12 Black or African American, non-Hispanic/Latino; 12 Asian, non-Hispanic/Latino; 14 Hispanic/Latino; 3 Two or more races, non-Hispanic/Latino), 7 international. Average age 37. 64 applicants, 94% accepted, 41 enrolled. In 2016, 20 master's, 8 doctorates awarded. *Degree requirements:* For doctorate, thesis/dissertation. *Entrance requirements:* Additional exam requirements/recommendations for international students: Required—TOEFL, IELTS, PTE. *Application deadline:* For fall admission, 3/1 priority date for domestic and international students; for spring admission, 11/1 priority date for domestic and international students. Applications are processed on a rolling basis. Application fee: $55 ($65 for international students). Electronic applications accepted. *Expenses:* *Tuition:* Full-time $23,310; part-time $1295 per credit. Tuition and fees vary according to course load, degree level, campus/location and program. *Financial support:* In 2016–17, 13 students received support. Fellowships, research assistantships, and teaching assistantships available. Financial award application deadline: 3/2; financial award applicants required to submit FAFSA. *Unit head:* Dr. Kevin Oh, Chair, 415-422-2099. *Application contact:* Amy Fogliani, Admission Coordinator, 415-422-5467, E-mail: schoolofeducation@usfca.edu.

University of Saskatchewan, College of Graduate Studies and Research, College of Education, Department of Educational Psychology and Special Education, Saskatoon, SK S7N 5A2, Canada. Offers M Ed, PhD, Diploma. *Degree requirements:* For master's, thesis (for some programs); for doctorate, comprehensive exam (for some programs), thesis/dissertation. *Entrance requirements:* Additional exam requirements/recommendations for international students: Required—TOEFL (minimum score 80 iBT); Recommended—IELTS (minimum score 6.5). Electronic applications accepted.

The University of Scranton, Panuska College of Professional Studies, Department of Education, Program in Special Education, Scranton, PA 18510. Offers MS. *Program availability:* Part-time. *Degree requirements:* For master's, comprehensive exam (for some programs), thesis (for some programs), capstone experience. *Entrance requirements:* For master's, GRE General Test accepted but not required, minimum GPA of 3.0, three letters of reference. Additional exam requirements/recommendations for international students: Required—TOEFL (minimum score 500 paper-based; 80 iBT), IELTS (minimum score 6.5). Electronic applications accepted. Application fee is waived when completed online.

University of South Alabama, College of Education and Professional Studies, Department of Leadership and Teacher Education, Mobile, AL 36688. Offers art education (M Ed); early childhood education (M Ed); educational leadership (M Ed, Ed D); elementary education (M Ed); reading education (M Ed); science education (M Ed); secondary education (M Ed); special education (M Ed). *Accreditation:* NCATE. *Program availability:* Part-time, 100% online, blended/hybrid learning. *Faculty:* 16 full-time (12 women), 6 part-time/adjunct (3 women). *Students:* 198 full-time (150 women), 77 part-time (58 women); includes 77 minority (61 Black or African American, non-Hispanic/Latino; 2 American Indian or Alaska Native, non-Hispanic/Latino; 2 Asian, non-Hispanic/Latino; 7 Hispanic/Latino; 1 Native Hawaiian or other Pacific Islander, non-Hispanic/Latino; 4 Two or more races, non-Hispanic/Latino). Average age 34. 153 applicants, 53% accepted, 69 enrolled. In 2016, 80 master's, 1 doctorate awarded. *Degree requirements:* For master's, comprehensive exam, thesis (for some programs); for doctorate, comprehensive exam, thesis/dissertation. *Entrance requirements:* For master's, GRE General Test or MAT, minimum GPA of 3.0; for doctorate, GRE, minimum graduate GPA of 3.25, 3 years of experience in field, 3 letters of recommendation, interview, official transcripts. Additional exam requirements/recommendations for international students: Required—TOEFL. *Application deadline:* For fall admission, 7/15 for domestic students; for spring admission, 11/15 for domestic students; for summer admission, 4/15 for domestic students. Applications are processed on a rolling basis. Application fee: $35. Electronic applications accepted. *Expenses:* Tuition, state resident: full-time $9768; part-time $407 per credit hour. Tuition, nonresident: full-time $19,536; part-time $814 per credit hour. *Financial support:* Fellowships, research assistantships, teaching assistantships, career-related internships or fieldwork, Federal Work-Study, institutionally sponsored loans, scholarships/grants, and unspecified assistantships available. Support available to part-time students. Financial award application deadline: 5/31; financial award applicants required to submit FAFSA. *Unit head:* Dr. Susan Santoli, Department Chair, 251-380-2836, Fax: 251-380-2758, E-mail: ssantoli@southalabama.edu. *Application contact:* Dr. Susan Santoli, Director of Graduate Studies, 251-380-2836, Fax: 251-380-2758, E-mail: ssantoli@southalabama.edu.
Website: http://www.southalabama.edu/colleges/coe/lte/index.html

University of South Carolina, The Graduate School, College of Education, Department of Educational Studies, Program in Special Education, Columbia, SC 29208. Offers M Ed, MAT, PhD. *Accreditation:* NCATE. *Program availability:* Part-time. *Degree requirements:* For master's, comprehensive exam; for doctorate, one foreign language, comprehensive exam, thesis/dissertation. *Entrance requirements:* For master's, GRE General Test, MAT, interview, sample of written work; for doctorate, GRE General Test or MAT, interview, sample of written work. *Faculty research:* Strategy training, transition, technology, rural special education, behavior management.

University of South Carolina Upstate, Graduate Programs, Spartanburg, SC 29303-4999. Offers early childhood education (M Ed); elementary education (M Ed); informatics (MS); special education: visual impairment (M Ed). *Accreditation:* NCATE. *Program availability:* Part-time, evening/weekend. *Degree requirements:* For master's, professional portfolio. *Entrance requirements:* For master's, GRE General Test or MAT, interview, minimum undergraduate GPA of 2.5, teaching certificate, 2 letters of recommendation. *Faculty research:* Promoting university diversity awareness, rough and tumble play, social justice education, American Indian literatures and cultures, diversity and multicultural education, science teaching strategy.

The University of South Dakota, Graduate School, School of Education, Division of Curriculum and Instruction, Program in Special Education, Vermillion, SD 57069. Offers special education (MA), including advanced specialist in disabilities, early childhood special education, multicategorical special education K-12. *Accreditation:* NCATE. *Program availability:* Part-time, online learning. *Degree requirements:* For master's, comprehensive exam, thesis or alternative. *Entrance requirements:* For master's, GRE General Test, MAT, minimum GPA of 2.7. Additional exam requirements/recommendations for international students: Required—TOEFL (minimum score 550 paper-based; 79 iBT). Electronic applications accepted.

The University of South Dakota, Graduate School, School of Education, Division of Educational Administration, Vermillion, SD 57069. Offers educational administration (MA, Ed D, Ed S), including adult and higher education (MA, Ed D), curriculum director, director of special education (Ed D, Ed S), preK-12 principal, school district superintendent. *Accreditation:* NCATE. *Program availability:* Part-time, evening/weekend, 100% online, blended/hybrid learning. *Degree requirements:* For master's and Ed S, comprehensive exam, thesis or alternative; for doctorate, comprehensive exam, thesis/dissertation. *Entrance requirements:* For master's and doctorate, GRE General Test, MAT, minimum GPA of 2.7. Additional exam requirements/recommendations for international students: Required—TOEFL (minimum score 550 paper-based; 79 iBT). Electronic applications accepted.

University of Southern Maine, College of Management and Human Service, School of Education and Human Development, Program in Special Education, Portland, ME 04103. Offers gifted and talented education (CGS); special education (MS); teaching all students (CGS); youth with moderate to severe disabilities (CGS). *Accreditation:* TEAC. *Program availability:* Part-time, evening/weekend. *Degree requirements:* For master's, thesis or alternative, portfolio. *Entrance requirements:* For master's, proof of teacher certification. Additional exam requirements/recommendations for international students: Required—TOEFL (minimum score 550 paper-based; 79 iBT). Electronic applications accepted. *Faculty research:* Special education, gifted and talented education, diversity education, positive behavioral interventions and supports.

University of Southern Mississippi, Graduate School, College of Education and Psychology, Department of Curriculum, Instruction and Special Education, Hattiesburg, MS 39406. Offers elementary education (M Ed, PhD); instructional technology (MS); instructional technology and design (PhD); secondary education (MAT); special education (M Ed, PhD). *Program availability:* Part-time, online learning. *Degree requirements:* For master's, comprehensive exam, thesis (for some programs); for doctorate, comprehensive exam, thesis/dissertation. *Entrance requirements:* For master's, GRE General Test, MAT, minimum GPA of 3.0; for doctorate, GRE General Test, minimum GPA of 3.5. Additional exam requirements/recommendations for international students: Required—TOEFL, IELTS. *Application deadline:* For fall admission, 3/1 priority date for domestic students, 3/1 for international students; for spring admission, 1/10 priority date for domestic and international students. Applications are processed on a rolling basis. Application fee: $60. *Expenses: Tuition, area resident:* Full-time $15,708; part-time $437 per credit hour. *Financial support:* Research assistantships with tuition reimbursements, teaching assistantships with full tuition reimbursements, Federal Work-Study, institutionally sponsored loans, scholarships/grants, health care benefits, tuition waivers (partial), and unspecified assistantships available. Financial award application deadline: 3/15; financial award applicants required to submit FAFSA. *Faculty research:* Mathematical problem solving, integrative curriculum, writing process, teacher education models. *Unit head:* Dr. Mary Ariail, Chair, 601-266-5247, Fax: 601-266-4548.
Website: https://www.usm.edu/elementary-special-technology-education

University of South Florida, Innovative Education, Tampa, FL 33620-9951. Offers adult, career and higher education (Graduate Certificate), including college teaching, leadership in developing human resources, leadership in higher education; Africana studies (Graduate Certificate), including diasporas and health disparities, genocide and human rights; aging studies (Graduate Certificate), including gerontology; art research (Graduate Certificate), including museum studies; business foundations (Graduate Certificate); chemical and biomedical engineering (Graduate Certificate), including materials science and engineering, water, health and sustainability; child and family studies (Graduate Certificate), including positive behavior support; civil and industrial engineering (Graduate Certificate), including transportation systems analysis; community and family health (Graduate Certificate), including maternal and child health, social marketing and public health, violence and injury: prevention and intervention, women's health; criminology (Graduate Certificate), including criminal justice administration; educational measurement and research (Graduate Certificate), including evaluation; English (Graduate Certificate), including comparative literary studies, creative writing, professional and technical communication; entrepreneurship (Graduate Certificate); environmental health (Graduate Certificate), including safety management; epidemiology and biostatistics (Graduate Certificate), including applied biostatistics, biostatistics, concepts and tools of epidemiology, epidemiology, epidemiology of infectious diseases; geography, environment and planning (Graduate Certificate), including community development, environmental policy and management, geographical information systems; geology (Graduate Certificate), including hydrogeology; global health (Graduate Certificate), including disaster management, global health and Latin American and Caribbean studies, global health practice, humanitarian assistance, infection control; government and international affairs (Graduate Certificate), including Cuban studies, globalization studies; health policy and management (Graduate Certificate), including health management and leadership, public health policy and programs; hearing specialist: early intervention (Graduate Certificate); industrial and management systems engineering (Graduate Certificate), including systems engineering, technology management; information studies (Graduate Certificate), including school library media specialist; information systems/decision sciences (Graduate Certificate), including analytics and business intelligence; instructional technology (Graduate Certificate), including distance education, Florida digital/virtual educator, instructional design, multimedia design, Web design; internal medicine, bioethics and medical humanities (Graduate Certificate), including biomedical ethics; Latin American and Caribbean studies (Graduate Certificate); mass communications (Graduate Certificate), including multimedia journalism; mathematics and statistics (Graduate Certificate), including mathematics; medicine (Graduate Certificate), including aging and neuroscience, bioinformatics, biotechnology, brain fitness and memory management, clinical investigation, health informatics, health sciences, integrative weight management, intellectual property, medicine and gender, metabolic and nutritional medicine, metabolic cardiology, pharmacy sciences; national and competitive intelligence (Graduate Certificate); psychological and social foundations (Graduate Certificate), including career counseling, college teaching, diversity in education, mental health counseling, school counseling; public affairs (Graduate Certificate), including nonprofit management, public management, research administration; public health (Graduate Certificate), including environmental health, health equity, public health generalist, translational research in adolescent behavioral health; public health practices (Graduate Certificate), including planning for healthy communities; rehabilitation and mental health counseling (Graduate Certificate), including integrative mental health care, marriage and family therapy, rehabilitation technology; secondary education (Graduate Certificate), including ESOL, foreign language education: culture and content, foreign language education: professional; social work (Graduate Certificate), including geriatric social work/clinical gerontology; special education (Graduate Certificate), including autism spectrum disorder, disabilities education: severe/profound; world languages (Graduate Certificate), including teaching English as a second language (TESL) or foreign language. *Expenses:* Tuition, state resident: full-time $7766; part-time $431.43 per credit hour. Tuition, nonresident: full-time $15,789; part-time $877.17 per credit hour. *Required fees:* $37 per term. *Unit head:* Kathy Barnes, Interdisciplinary Programs Coordinator, 813-974-8031, Fax: 813-974-7061, E-mail: barnesk@usf.edu. *Application contact:* Karen Tylinski, Metro Initiatives, 813-974-9943, Fax: 813-974-7061, E-mail: ktylinsk@usf.edu.
Website: http://www.usf.edu/innovative-education/

The University of Tennessee, Graduate School, College of Education, Health and Human Sciences, Program in Education, Knoxville, TN 37996. Offers art education (MS); counseling education (PhD); cultural studies in education (PhD); curriculum (MS, Ed S); curriculum, educational research and evaluation (Ed D, PhD); early childhood education (PhD); early childhood special education (MS); education of deaf and hard of hearing (MS); educational administration and policy studies (Ed D, PhD); educational administration and supervision (Ed S); educational psychology (Ed D, PhD); elementary education (MS, Ed S); elementary teaching (MS); English education (MS, Ed S); exercise science (PhD); foreign language/ESL education (MS, Ed S); instructional technology (MS, Ed D, PhD, Ed S); literacy, language and ESL education (PhD); literacy, language education, and ESL education (Ed D); mathematics education (MS, Ed S); modified and comprehensive special education (MS); reading education (MS, Ed S); school counseling (Ed S); school psychology (PhD, Ed S); science education (MS, Ed S); secondary teaching (MS); social foundations (MS); social science education (MS, Ed S); socio-cultural foundations of sports and education (PhD); special education (Ed S); teacher education (Ed D, PhD). *Accreditation:* NCATE. *Program availability:* Part-time, evening/weekend. *Degree requirements:* For master's and Ed S, thesis optional; for doctorate, variable foreign language requirement, thesis/dissertation. *Entrance requirements:* For master's, minimum GPA of 2.7; for doctorate and Ed S, GRE General Test, minimum GPA of 2.7. Additional exam requirements/recommendations for international students: Required—TOEFL. Electronic applications accepted.

The University of Tennessee at Chattanooga, School of Education, Chattanooga, TN 37403. Offers counseling (M Ed), including community counseling, school counseling; education (M Ed, Post-Master's Certificate), including elementary education (M Ed), school leadership, secondary education (M Ed), special education (M Ed); educational specialist (Ed S), including educational technology, school psychology; learning and leadership (Ed D), including educational leadership. *Accreditation:* ACA; NCATE. *Program availability:* Part-time. *Faculty:* 13 full-time (8 women), 2 part-time/adjunct (both women). *Students:* 50 full-time (32 women), 157 part-time (107 women); includes 42 minority (28 Black or African American, non-Hispanic/Latino; 4 Asian, non-Hispanic/Latino; 2 Hispanic/Latino; 8 Two or more races, non-Hispanic/Latino), 1 international. Average age 36. 169 applicants, 76% accepted, 49 enrolled. In 2016, 77 master's, 5 other advanced degrees awarded. *Degree requirements:* For master's, comprehensive exam, thesis optional, culminating experience; for doctorate, comprehensive exam, thesis/dissertation; for other advanced degree, internship. *Entrance requirements:* For master's, GRE General Test, PPST 1, teaching certificate; for doctorate, GRE General Test, master's degree, two years of practical work experience in organizational environment; for other advanced degree, GRE General Test, letters of reference. Additional exam requirements/recommendations for international students: Required—TOEFL (minimum score 550 paper-based; 79 iBT), IELTS (minimum score 6). *Application deadline:* For fall admission, 6/15 for domestic students, 7/1 for international students; for spring admission, 11/1 for domestic and international students. Applications are processed on a rolling basis. Application fee: $35 ($40 for international students). Electronic applications accepted. *Expenses:* $9,876 full-time in-state; $25,994 full-time out-of-state; $450 per credit part-time in-state; $1,345 per credit part-time out-of-state. *Financial support:* In 2016–17, 18 research assistantships, 5 teaching assistantships were awarded; career-related internships or fieldwork, institutionally sponsored loans, scholarships/grants, and unspecified assistantships also available. Support available to part-time students. Financial award application deadline: 7/1; financial award applicants required to submit FAFSA. *Faculty research:* School counseling, community counseling, elementary and secondary education, school leadership and administration. *Total annual research expenditures:* $247,231. *Unit head:* Dr. Renee Murley, Director, 423-425-4684, Fax: 423-425-5380, E-mail: renee-murley@utc.edu. *Application contact:* Dr. Joanne Romagni, Dean of the Graduate School, 423-425-4478, Fax: 423-425-5223, E-mail: joanne-romagni@utc.edu.
Website: http://www.utc.edu/school-education/abouttheschool/gradprograms.php

The University of Tennessee at Martin, Graduate Programs, College of Education, Health and Behavioral Sciences, Program in Teaching, Martin, TN 38238. Offers curriculum and instruction (MS Ed), including 7-12, K-6; initial licensure (MS Ed), including elementary education, secondary education; initial licensure K-12 (MS Ed), including physical education, special education; interdisciplinary (MS Ed). *Students:* 21 full-time (14 women), 125 part-time (87 women); includes 22 minority (18 Black or African American, non-Hispanic/Latino; 3 Hispanic/Latino; 1 Two or more races, non-Hispanic/Latino). 115 applicants, 81% accepted, 51 enrolled. In 2016, 26 master's awarded. *Expenses:* Tuition, state resident: full-time $8254; part-time $459 per credit hour. Tuition, nonresident: full-time $22,198; part-time $1234 per credit hour. *Required fees:* $79 per credit hour. Part-time tuition and fees vary according to course load and campus/location. *Faculty research:* Special education, science/math/technology, school reform, reading. *Unit head:* Cynthia West, Dean, 731-881-7125, Fax: 731-881-7975, E-mail: cwest@utm.edu. *Application contact:* Jolene L. Cunningham, Student Services Specialist, 731-881-7012, Fax: 731-881-7499, E-mail: jcunningham@utm.edu.

The University of Texas at Austin, Graduate School, College of Education, Department of Special Education, Austin, TX 78712-1111. Offers autism and developmental disabilities (Ed D, PhD); autism and developmental disability (M Ed, MA); early childhood special education (M Ed, MA, Ed D, PhD); learning disabilities (Ed D, PhD); learning disabilities/behavior disorders (M Ed, MA); multicultural special education (M Ed, MA, Ed D, PhD); rehabilitation counselor (M Ed); rehabilitation counselor education (Ed D, PhD); special education administration (Ed D, PhD). *Accreditation:* CORE. *Program availability:* Part-time, evening/weekend, online learning. *Degree requirements:* For master's, thesis or alternative; for doctorate, thesis/dissertation. *Entrance requirements:* For master's and doctorate, GRE General Test. *Faculty research:* Anchored instruction, reading disabilities, multicultural/bilingual.

The University of Texas at El Paso, Graduate School, College of Education, Department of Educational Psychology and Special Services, El Paso, TX 79968-0001. Offers educational diagnostics (M Ed); guidance and counseling (M Ed); special education (M Ed). *Program availability:* Part-time, evening/weekend. *Degree requirements:* For master's, thesis optional. *Entrance requirements:* For master's, minimum GPA of 3.0. Additional exam requirements/recommendations for international students: Required—TOEFL. Electronic applications accepted.

The University of Texas at San Antonio, College of Education and Human Development, Department of Interdisciplinary Learning and Teaching, San Antonio, TX 78249-0617. Offers education (MA), including curriculum and instruction, early childhood and elementary education, instructional technology, reading and literacy, special education; interdisciplinary learning and teaching (PhD). *Program availability:* Part-time, evening/weekend. *Faculty:* 25 full-time (18 women), 4 part-time/adjunct (2 women). *Students:* 70 full-time (53 women), 256 part-time (222 women); includes 185 minority (22 Black or African American, non-Hispanic/Latino; 10 Asian, non-Hispanic/Latino; 148 Hispanic/Latino; 1 Native Hawaiian or other Pacific Islander, non-Hispanic/Latino; 4 Two or more races, non-Hispanic/Latino), 4 international. Average age 34. 145 applicants, 88% accepted, 100 enrolled. In 2016, 90 master's, 4 doctorates awarded. *Degree requirements:* For master's, comprehensive exam, thesis optional, 36 hours of course work without thesis (33 with thesis); for doctorate, comprehensive exam, thesis/dissertation, minimum of 60 semester credit hours. *Entrance requirements:* For master's, bachelor's degree with minimum GPA of 3.0 in last 60 hours of coursework; 18 hours of undergraduate coursework in education or related field; for doctorate, GRE, transcripts from all colleges and universities attended, professional vitae demonstrating experience in work environment where education was primary professional emphasis, 3 letters of recommendation, statement of purpose, minimum GPA of 3.5. Additional exam requirements/recommendations for international students: Required—TOEFL (minimum score 550 paper-based; 79 iBT), IELTS (minimum score 6.5). *Application deadline:* For fall admission, 7/1 for domestic students, 4/1 for international students; for spring admission, 11/1 for domestic students, 9/1 for international students. Applications are processed on a rolling basis. Application fee: $45 ($80 for international students). Electronic applications accepted. *Financial support:* Career-related internships or fieldwork, Federal Work-Study, and scholarships/grants available. Support available to part-time students. *Faculty research:* Explorations of science, learning and teaching, family involvement in early childhood, culturally-responsive literacy instruction in diverse settings, STEM education, autism spectrum disorder. *Total annual research expenditures:* $766,662. *Unit head:* Dr. Maria R. Cortez, Department Chair, 210-458-4413, Fax: 210-458-7281, E-mail: mari.cortez@utsa.edu. *Application contact:* Elizabeth Narvaes, Student Development Specialist, 210-458-7443, Fax: 210-458-7281, E-mail:

elizabeth.narvaez@utsa.edu.
Website: http://education.utsa.edu/interdisciplinary_learning_and_teaching/

The University of Texas at Tyler, College of Education and Psychology, School of Education, Tyler, TX 75799-0001. Offers early childhood education (M Ed, MA); reading (M Ed, MA); special education (M Ed, MA). *Program availability:* Part-time, evening/weekend. *Degree requirements:* For master's, comprehensive exam, thesis (for some programs), research project. *Entrance requirements:* For master's, GRE General Test. Additional exam requirements/recommendations for international students: Required—TOEFL. Electronic applications accepted. *Faculty research:* Improving quality in childcare settings, play and creativity, teacher interactions, effects of modeling on early childhood teachers, biofeedback, literacy instruction.

The University of Texas Health Science Center at San Antonio, School of Medicine, San Antonio, TX 78229-3900. Offers deaf education and hearing (MS); medicine (MD); MPH/MD. *Accreditation:* LCME/AMA. *Degree requirements:* For master's, comprehensive exam, practicum assignments. *Entrance requirements:* For master's, minimum GPA of 3.0, interview, 3 professional letters of recommendation; for doctorate, MCAT. Electronic applications accepted. *Expenses:* Contact institution. *Faculty research:* Geriatrics, diabetes, cancer, AIDS, obesity.

The University of Texas of the Permian Basin, Office of Graduate Studies, School of Education, Program in Special Education, Odessa, TX 79762-0001. Offers MA. *Degree requirements:* For master's, comprehensive exam (for some programs), thesis (for some programs). *Entrance requirements:* For master's, GRE General Test. Additional exam requirements/recommendations for international students: Required—TOEFL (minimum score 550 paper-based).

The University of Texas Rio Grande Valley, College of Education and P-16 Integration, Department of Human Development and School Services, Edinburg, TX 78539. Offers early childhood education (M Ed); early childhood special education (M Ed); educational diagnostician (M Ed); school psychology (MA). *Program availability:* Part-time, evening/weekend. *Degree requirements:* For master's, comprehensive exam (for some programs), thesis (for some programs). *Entrance requirements:* For master's, GRE General Test, interview. Tuition and fees vary according to course load and program. *Faculty research:* Reading instruction, assessment practice, behavior interventions consultation, mental retardation.

University of the Cumberlands, Graduate Programs in Education, Williamsburg, KY 40769-1372. Offers all grades (P-12) (M Ed); business and marketing (MA Ed, MAT); counselor education and supervision (Ed D); director of pupil personnel (Certificate); director of special education (Certificate); educational administration and supervision (Ed S); educational leadership (Ed D); elementary education (MA Ed, MAT); instructional leadership - principalship (MA Ed); instructional leadership - school principal (Certificate); middle school education (MA Ed, MAT); reading and writing (MA Ed); school counseling (MA Ed); school superintendent (Certificate); secondary education (MA Ed, MAT); special education (MAT); supervisor of instruction (Certificate); teacher leader (MA Ed). *Program availability:* Part-time, evening/weekend, online learning. *Degree requirements:* For master's, comprehensive exam. Electronic applications accepted.

University of the Pacific, Gladys L. Benerd School of Education, Department of Curriculum and Instruction, Stockton, CA 95211-0197. Offers curriculum and instruction (MA); special education (MA). *Accreditation:* NCATE. *Faculty:* 9 full-time (6 women), 32 part-time/adjunct (25 women). *Students:* 6 full-time (all women), 18 part-time (12 women); includes 11 minority (1 Asian, non-Hispanic/Latino; 9 Hispanic/Latino; 1 Two or more races, non-Hispanic/Latino), 1 international. Average age 33. *Degree requirements:* For master's, thesis (for some programs). *Entrance requirements:* For master's, GRE General Test. Additional exam requirements/recommendations for international students: Required—TOEFL. *Application deadline:* For fall admission, 3/1 priority date for domestic students; for spring admission, 10/1 priority date for domestic students. Applications are processed on a rolling basis. Application fee: $75. *Financial support:* Teaching assistantships available. Financial award application deadline: 3/1; financial award applicants required to submit FAFSA. *Unit head:* Dr. Marilyn Draheim, Chairperson, 209-946-2558, E-mail: mdraheim@pacific.edu. *Application contact:* Office of Graduate Admissions, 209-946-2344.

University of the Southwest, Graduate Programs, Hobbs, NM 88240-9129. Offers business administration (MBA); curriculum and instruction (MSE); curriculum and instruction: bilingual (MSE); curriculum and instruction: TESOL (MSE); early childhood education (MSE); educational administration (MSE); mental health counseling (MSE); school counseling (MSE); special education (MSE); sports management (MBA). *Program availability:* Part-time, evening/weekend, online learning. *Degree requirements:* For master's, comprehensive exam, thesis (for some programs). *Entrance requirements:* Additional exam requirements/recommendations for international students: Recommended—TOEFL. Electronic applications accepted.

The University of Toledo, College of Graduate Studies, Judith Herb College of Education, Department of Curriculum and Instruction, Toledo, OH 43606-3390. Offers art education (ME); career and technical education (ME, Ed S); curriculum and instruction (ME, PhD, Ed S); early childhood education (Ed S); education and anthropology (MAE); education and biology (MES); education and chemistry (MES); education and classics (MAE); education and economics (MAE); education and English (MAE); education and French (MAE); education and geology (MES); education and German (MAE); education and history (MAE); education and mathematics (MAE, MES); education and physics (MES); education and political science (MAE); education and sociology (MAE); education and Spanish (MAE); educational media (PhD); educational technology (ME); educational technology: virtual educator (Certificate); elementary education (PhD); English as a second language (MAE); gifted and talented education (PhD); middle childhood education (ME); secondary education (ME, PhD); special education (PhD). *Accreditation:* NCATE. *Program availability:* Part-time, evening/weekend. *Degree requirements:* For master's, comprehensive exam, thesis or alternative; for doctorate, comprehensive exam, thesis/dissertation; for other advanced degree, thesis optional. *Entrance requirements:* For master's, doctorate, and other advanced degree, minimum cumulative GPA of 2.7 for all previous academic work, letters of recommendation. Additional exam requirements/recommendations for international students: Required—TOEFL (minimum score 550 paper-based; 80 iBT). Electronic applications accepted.

The University of Toledo, College of Graduate Studies, Judith Herb College of Education, Department of Early Childhood, Physical and Special Education, Toledo, OH 43606-3390. Offers early childhood education (ME); physical education (ME); special education (ME). *Program availability:* Part-time. *Degree requirements:* For master's, thesis. *Entrance requirements:* For master's, minimum cumulative GPA of 2.7 for all previous academic work, letters of recommendation. Additional exam requirements/recommendations for international students: Required—TOEFL (minimum score 550 paper-based; 80 iBT). Electronic applications accepted.

University of Utah, Graduate School, College of Education, Department of Special Education, Salt Lake City, UT 84112. Offers deaf and hard of hearing (M Ed); deaf/blind (M Ed, MS); early childhood deaf and hard of hearing (MS); early childhood special education (M Ed, MS, PhD); early childhood vision impairments (M Ed); mild/moderate disabilities (M Ed, MS, PhD); severe disabilities (M Ed, MS, PhD); visual impairment (M Ed, MS). *Program availability:* Part-time, evening/weekend, 100% online, blended/hybrid learning. *Faculty:* 14 full-time (11 women), 26 part-time/adjunct (19 women). *Students:* 52 full-time (45 women), 20 part-time (15 women); includes 6 minority (2 Asian, non-Hispanic/Latino; 3 Hispanic/Latino; 1 Two or more races, non-Hispanic/Latino). Average age 34. 30 applicants, 97% accepted, 28 enrolled. In 2016, 17 master's, 2 doctorates awarded. Terminal master's awarded for partial completion of doctoral program. *Degree requirements:* For master's, comprehensive exam, thesis (for some programs), qualifying exam; for doctorate, thesis/dissertation, qualifying exam. *Entrance requirements:* For master's, GRE, minimum GPA of 3.0; for doctorate, GRE General Test, minimum GPA of 3.5. Additional exam requirements/recommendations for international students: Required—TOEFL (minimum score 600 paper-based; 100 iBT); Recommended—IELTS (minimum score 7). *Application deadline:* For fall admission, 3/1 for domestic and international students; for spring admission, 11/1 for domestic and international students; for summer admission, 5/16 for domestic and international students. Application fee: $55 ($65 for international students). Electronic applications accepted. *Expenses:* $4,270 per semester. *Financial support:* In 2016–17, 22 students received support, including 33 fellowships with partial tuition reimbursements available (averaging $4,350 per year), 3 teaching assistantships with tuition reimbursements available (averaging $10,000 per year); career-related internships or fieldwork and health care benefits also available. Support available to part-time students. Financial award application deadline: 3/1; financial award applicants required to submit FAFSA. *Faculty research:* Inclusive education, positive behavior support, reading, instruction and intervention strategies. *Total annual research expenditures:* $139,750. *Unit head:* Dr. Robert E. O'Neill, Chair, 801-581-8121, Fax: 801-585-6476, E-mail: rob.oneill@utah.edu. *Application contact:* Patty Davis, Academic Advisor, 801-581-4764, Fax: 801-585-6476, E-mail: patty.davis@utah.edu.
Website: http://special-ed.utah.edu/

University of Vermont, Graduate College, College of Education and Social Services, Program in Special Education, Burlington, VT 05405. Offers M Ed. *Accreditation:* NCATE. *Degree requirements:* For master's, thesis or alternative. *Entrance requirements:* For master's, license (or eligible for licensure). Additional exam requirements/recommendations for international students: Required—TOEFL (minimum score 550 paper-based; 80 iBT). Electronic applications accepted. *Expenses:* Tuition, state resident: full-time $5814. Tuition, nonresident: full-time $14,670.

University of Victoria, Faculty of Graduate Studies, Faculty of Education, Department of Educational Psychology and Leadership Studies, Victoria, BC V8W 2Y2, Canada. Offers aboriginal communities counseling (M Ed); counseling (M Ed, MA); educational psychology (M Ed, MA, PhD), including counseling psychology (M Ed, MA), leadership studies (PhD), learning and development (MA, PhD), measurement and evaluation, special education (M Ed, MA); leadership studies (M Ed, MA). *Program availability:* Part-time. *Degree requirements:* For master's, thesis (for some programs), comprehensive exam (M Ed); for doctorate, comprehensive exam, thesis/dissertation, candidacy exam. *Entrance requirements:* For master's, 2 years of work experience in a relevant field; for doctorate, GRE, 2 years of work experience in a relevant field, minimum B average. Additional exam requirements/recommendations for international students: Required—TOEFL (minimum score 575 paper-based), IELTS (minimum score 7). *Faculty research:* Learning and development (child, adolescent and adult), special education and exceptional children.

University of Virginia, Curry School of Education, Department of Curriculum, Instruction, and Special Education, Program in Special Education, Charlottesville, VA 22903. Offers M Ed, Ed D, Ed S. *Accreditation:* TEAC. *Students:* 2. In 2016, 13 master's awarded. *Entrance requirements:* For master's, doctorate, and Ed S, GRE General Test, 2 letters of recommendation. Additional exam requirements/recommendations for international students: Required—TOEFL (minimum score 600 paper-based; 90 iBT), IELTS (minimum score 7). *Application deadline:* Applications are processed on a rolling basis. Application fee: $60. Electronic applications accepted. *Expenses:* Tuition, state resident: full-time $15,026; part-time $834 per credit hour. Tuition, nonresident: full-time $25,168; part-time $1378 per credit hour. *Required fees:* $2654. *Financial support:* Applicants required to submit FAFSA. *Unit head:* William Therrien, Program Area Director, 434-246-2962, E-mail: wjt2c@virginia.edu. *Application contact:* Eric Molnar, Assistant Director, Admissions and Enrollment Reporting, 434-243-2085, E-mail: eric.molnar@virginia.edu.
Website: http://curry.virginia.edu/academics/areas-of-study/special-education

University of Virginia, Curry School of Education, Program in Education, Charlottesville, VA 22903. Offers administration and supervision (PhD); applied developmental science (PhD); counselor education (PhD); curriculum and instruction (PhD); early childhood special education (MT); education evaluation (PhD); educational psychology (PhD); educational research (PhD); elementary education (MT); English education (MT, PhD); foreign language education (MT); higher education (PhD); instructional technology (PhD); kinesiology (MT, PhD); math education (PhD); reading education (PhD); research, statistics and evaluation (PhD); school psychology (PhD); science education (PhD); social studies education (MT, PhD); special education (PhD); world languages education (MT). *Students:* 452 full-time (357 women), 18 part-time (13 women); includes 100 minority (28 Black or African American, non-Hispanic/Latino; 39 Asian, non-Hispanic/Latino; 18 Hispanic/Latino; 15 Two or more races, non-Hispanic/Latino), 14 international. Average age 25. 309 applicants, 51% accepted, 87 enrolled. In 2016, 144 master's, 31 doctorates awarded. *Degree requirements:* For master's, comprehensive exam (for some programs), field project; for doctorate, comprehensive exam, thesis/dissertation. *Entrance requirements:* For doctorate, GRE General Test. Additional exam requirements/recommendations for international students: Required—TOEFL (minimum score 600 paper-based; 90 iBT), IELTS (minimum score 7). *Application deadline:* Applications are processed on a rolling basis. Application fee: $60. Electronic applications accepted. *Expenses:* Tuition, state resident: full-time $15,026; part-time $834 per credit hour. Tuition, nonresident: full-time $25,168; part-time $1378 per credit hour. *Required fees:* $2654. *Financial support:* Fellowships, research assistantships, and teaching assistantships available. Financial award application deadline: 1/5; financial award applicants required to submit FAFSA. *Unit head:* Robert C. Pianta, Dean, 434-924-3334, E-mail: pianta@virginia.edu. *Application contact:* Eric Molnar, Assistant Director, Admissions and Enrollment Reporting, 434-243-2085, E-mail: eric.molnar@virginia.edu.
Website: http://curry.virginia.edu/teacher-education

University of Washington, Graduate School, College of Education, Program in Special Education, Seattle, WA 98195. Offers early childhood special education (M Ed); emotional and behavioral disabilities (M Ed); learning disabilities (M Ed); low-incidence disabilities (M Ed); severe disabilities (M Ed); special education (Ed D, PhD). *Degree requirements:* For master's, thesis optional; for doctorate, thesis/dissertation. *Entrance requirements:* For master's and doctorate, GRE General Test, minimum GPA of 3.0. Additional exam requirements/recommendations for international students: Required—TOEFL.

University of Washington, Tacoma, Graduate Programs, Program in Education, Tacoma, WA 98402-3100. Offers education (M Ed); educational administration (principal or program administrator certification) (M Ed); elementary education teacher certification (M Ed); elementary education/special education teacher certification (M Ed); secondary science or math teacher certification (M Ed). *Program availability:* Part-time, evening/weekend. *Degree requirements:* For master's, culminating project. *Entrance requirements:* For master's, WEST-B, WEST-E (teacher certification programs only), official sealed transcript from every college/university attended, personal goal statement, letters of recommendation, copy of valid teaching certificate. Additional exam requirements/recommendations for international students: Required—TOEFL (minimum score 580 paper-based; 92 iBT). Electronic applications accepted. *Faculty research:* Global learning communities for English/Chinese languages, evaluation of mathematics and reading intervention programs, response to intervention, school-wide behavioral and emotional support, mathematics education and culturally responsive mathematics education.

The University of West Alabama, School of Graduate Studies, College of Education, Departments of Instructional Leadership and Support/Curriculum and Instruction, Program in Special Education, Livingston, AL 35470. Offers collaborative special education 6-12 (Ed S); collaborative special education K-6 (Ed S); special education collaborative teacher 6-12 (M Ed); special education collaborative teacher K-6 (M Ed). *Accreditation:* NCATE. *Program availability:* Part-time, evening/weekend, 100% online. *Faculty:* 8 full-time (all women), 27 part-time/adjunct (19 women). *Students:* 191 (160 women); includes 55 minority (50 Black or African American, non-Hispanic/Latino; 1 American Indian or Alaska Native, non-Hispanic/Latino; 4 Two or more races, non-Hispanic/Latino). Average age 35. 81 applicants, 86% accepted, 52 enrolled. In 2016, 30 master's, 10 Ed Ss awarded. *Degree requirements:* For master's, comprehensive exam, thesis optional; for Ed S, comprehensive exam. *Entrance requirements:* For master's, GRE General Test, MAT, minimum GPA of 2.75. Additional exam requirements/recommendations for international students: Required—TOEFL (minimum score 500 paper-based; 61 iBT). *Application deadline:* Applications are processed on a rolling basis. Application fee: $40. Electronic applications accepted. *Expenses:* Tuition, state resident: part-time $355 per credit hour. Tuition, nonresident: part-time $710 per credit hour. *Required fees:* $130 per semester. *Financial support:* Teaching assistantships, Federal Work-Study, scholarships/grants, and unspecified assistantships available. Support available to part-time students. Financial award application deadline: 3/1; financial award applicants required to submit FAFSA. *Unit head:* Dr. Jodie Winship, Chair of Curriculum and Instruction, 205-652-5415, Fax: 205-652-3706, E-mail: jwinship@uwa.edu. *Application contact:* Dr. B. J. Kimbrough, Dean of Graduate Studies, 205-652-3647, Fax: 205-652-3706, E-mail: bkimbrough@uwa.edu.
Website: http://www.uwa.edu/medspecialeducation612.aspx

The University of Western Ontario, Faculty of Graduate Studies, Social Sciences Division, Faculty of Education, Program in Educational Studies, London, ON N6A 5B8, Canada. Offers curriculum studies (M Ed); educational policy studies (M Ed); educational psychology/special education (M Ed). *Program availability:* Part-time. *Faculty research:* Reflective practice, gender and schooling, feminist pedagogy, narrative inquiry, second language, multiculturalism in Canada, education and law.

University of West Florida, College of Education and Professional Studies, Department of Teacher Education and Educational Leadership, Program in Exceptional Student Education, Pensacola, FL 32514-5750. Offers applied behavior analysis (MA); special and alternative education (MA). *Accreditation:* NCATE. *Program availability:* Part-time, evening/weekend, online learning. *Entrance requirements:* For master's, GRE (minimum score 450 verbal) or MAT (minimum score 396) if bachelor's GPA less than 3.0, state teaching certification; letter of intent; two professional references. Additional exam requirements/recommendations for international students: Required—TOEFL (minimum score 550 paper-based). *Application deadline:* For fall admission, 6/1 for domestic and international students; for spring admission, 10/1 for domestic and international students. Applications are processed on a rolling basis. Application fee: $30. *Expenses:* Tuition, state resident: full-time $5316.12. Tuition, nonresident: full-time $11,308. *Required fees:* $583.92. Tuition and fees vary according to course load and program. *Financial support:* Unspecified assistantships available. Financial award application deadline: 4/15; financial award applicants required to submit FAFSA. *Faculty research:* Memory, semantic structure, remedial programming. *Unit head:* Dr. William H. Evans, Acting Director, 850-474-2892, Fax: 850-474-2844, E-mail: wevans@uwf.edu. *Application contact:* Terry McCray, Assistant Director of Graduate Admissions, 850-473-7718, Fax: 850-473-7714, E-mail: gradadmissions@uwf.edu.

University of West Georgia, College of Education, Carrollton, GA 30118. Offers business education (M Ed); early childhood education (M Ed, Ed S); educational leadership (M Ed, Ed S); media (M Ed, Ed S); professional counseling (M Ed, Ed S); professional counseling and supervision (Ed D); reading instruction (M Ed); school improvement (Ed D); secondary education (M Ed); special education (M Ed, Ed S), including teaching (M Ed); speech language pathology (M Ed); teaching (MAT). *Accreditation:* NCATE. *Program availability:* Part-time, evening/weekend, 100% online, blended/hybrid learning. *Faculty:* 46 full-time (31 women). *Students:* 321 full-time (266 women), 1,007 part-time (813 women); includes 456 minority (389 Black or African American, non-Hispanic/Latino; 1 American Indian or Alaska Native, non-Hispanic/Latino; 13 Asian, non-Hispanic/Latino; 43 Hispanic/Latino; 10 Two or more races, non-Hispanic/Latino), 12 international. Average age 33. 541 applicants, 79% accepted, 305 enrolled. In 2016, 286 master's, 20 doctorates, 156 other advanced degrees awarded. *Entrance requirements:* Additional exam requirements/recommendations for international students: Required—TOEFL (minimum score 523 paper-based; 69 iBT); Recommended—IELTS (minimum score 6.5). *Application deadline:* For fall admission, 7/21 for domestic students, 6/1 for international students; for spring admission, 11/30 for domestic students, 10/15 for international students; for summer admission, 4/15 for domestic students, 3/30 for international students. Applications are processed on a rolling basis. Application fee: $40. Electronic applications accepted. *Expenses:* Tuition, state resident: full-time $5316; part-time $222 per semester hour. Tuition, nonresident: full-time $20,658; part-time $861 per semester hour. *Required fees:* $1962. Tuition and fees vary according to course load, degree level and program. *Financial support:* Fellowships, research assistantships, teaching assistantships, career-related internships or fieldwork, Federal Work-Study, institutionally sponsored loans, scholarships/grants, and unspecified assistantships available. Support available to part-time students. Financial award application deadline: 4/1; financial award applicants required to submit FAFSA. *Unit head:* Dr. Diane Hoff, Dean, College of Education, 678-839-6570, Fax: 678-839-6098, E-mail: dhoff@westga.edu. *Application contact:* Dr. Toby Ziglar, Assistant Dean of the Graduate School, 678-839-1394, Fax: 678-839-1395, E-mail: graduate@westga.edu.
Website: http://www.westga.edu/education/

University of Wisconsin–Eau Claire, College of Education and Human Sciences, Program in Special Education, Eau Claire, WI 54702-4004. Offers MSE. *Program availability:* Part-time. *Degree requirements:* For master's, comprehensive exam, thesis, research paper, or written exam; oral exam. *Entrance requirements:* For master's, minimum GPA of 2.75. Additional exam requirements/recommendations for international students: Required—TOEFL (minimum score 79 iBT).

University of Wisconsin–La Crosse, School of Education, La Crosse, WI 54601-3742. Offers English language arts elementary (Graduate Certificate); professional development (ME-PD); reading (MS Ed); special education (MS Ed). *Program availability:* Part-time, evening/weekend. *Faculty:* 5 full-time (3 women), 25 part-time/adjunct (17 women). *Students:* 85 part-time (74 women); includes 2 minority (1 Asian, non-Hispanic/Latino; 1 Hispanic/Latino). Average age 27. 32 applicants, 100% accepted, 23 enrolled. In 2016, 25 master's, 5 other advanced degrees awarded. *Entrance requirements:* For master's, GRE. Additional exam requirements/recommendations for international students: Required—TOEFL (minimum score 550 paper-based; 79 iBT). *Application deadline:* Applications are processed on a rolling basis. Electronic applications accepted. *Financial support:* Research assistantships, Federal Work-Study, scholarships/grants, health care benefits, and tuition waivers (partial) available. Support available to part-time students. Financial award application deadline: 3/15; financial award applicants required to submit FAFSA. *Unit head:* Marcie Wycoff-Horn, Dean, School of Education, 608-785-6786, E-mail: mwycoff-horn@uwlax.edu. *Application contact:* Brandon Schaller, Senior Graduate Student Status Examiner, 608-785-8941, E-mail: admissions@uwlax.edu.
Website: https://www.uwlax.edu/soe/

University of Wisconsin–Madison, Graduate School, School of Education, Department of Rehabilitation Psychology and Special Education, Program in Special Education, Madison, WI 53706-1380. Offers MA, MS, PhD. *Degree requirements:* For doctorate, thesis/dissertation. Electronic applications accepted.

University of Wisconsin–Milwaukee, Graduate School, School of Education, Department of Exceptional Education, Milwaukee, WI 53201-0413. Offers autism spectrum disorders (Graduate Certificate); exceptional education (MS); transition for students with disabilities (Graduate Certificate); urban education (PhD), including adult, continuing and higher education leadership, art education, curriculum and instruction, exceptional education, mathematics education, multicultural studies, social foundations of education. *Program availability:* Part-time. *Students:* 50 full-time (41 women), 66 part-time (51 women); includes 42 minority (24 Black or African American, non-Hispanic/Latino; 6 Asian, non-Hispanic/Latino; 1 Hispanic/Latino; 11 Two or more races, non-Hispanic/Latino), 4 international. Average age 39. 55 applicants, 51% accepted, 22 enrolled. In 2016, 14 master's, 10 doctorates, 3 other advanced degrees awarded. *Degree requirements:* For master's, thesis. *Entrance requirements:* Additional exam requirements/recommendations for international students: Required—TOEFL (minimum score 550 paper-based; 79 iBT), IELTS (minimum score 6.5). *Application deadline:* For fall admission, 1/1 priority date for domestic students; for spring admission, 9/1 for domestic students. Applications are processed on a rolling basis. Application fee: $56 ($96 for international students). Electronic applications accepted. *Financial support:* Fellowships, research assistantships, teaching assistantships, career-related internships or fieldwork, health care benefits, and unspecified assistantships available. Support available to part-time students. Financial award application deadline: 4/15; financial award applicants required to submit FAFSA. *Faculty research:* Emotional disturbance, hearing impairment, learning disabilities, mental retardation. *Application contact:* General Information Contact, 414-229-4721, E-mail: soeinfo@uwm.edu.
Website: http://uwm.edu/education/academics/exceptional-edu-department/

University of Wisconsin–Oshkosh, Graduate Studies, College of Education and Human Services, Department of Special Education, Oshkosh, WI 54901. Offers cross-categorical (MSE); early childhood: exceptional education needs (MSE); non-licensure (MSE). *Program availability:* Part-time, evening/weekend. *Degree requirements:* For master's, comprehensive exam (for some programs), thesis or alternative, field report. *Entrance requirements:* For master's, interview, minimum GPA of 3.0, teaching license, letters of recommendation. Additional exam requirements/recommendations for international students: Required—TOEFL (minimum score 550 paper-based; 79 iBT). Electronic applications accepted. *Faculty research:* Private agency contributions to the disabled, graduation requirements for exceptional education needs students, direct instruction in spelling for learning disabled, effects of behavioral parent training, secondary education programming issues.

University of Wisconsin–Stevens Point, College of Professional Studies, School of Education, Program in Education—General/Special, Stevens Point, WI 54481-3897. Offers MSE. *Program availability:* Part-time. *Degree requirements:* For master's, comprehensive exam, thesis or alternative. *Entrance requirements:* For master's, minimum undergraduate GPA of 3.0, 2 years teaching experience, letters of recommendation, teacher certification. *Faculty research:* Curriculum and instruction, early childhood special education, standards-based education.

University of Wisconsin–Superior, Graduate Division, Department of Teacher Education, Program in Special Education, Superior, WI 54880-4500. Offers emotional/behavior disabilities (MSE); learning disabilities (MSE). *Program availability:* Part-time, evening/weekend, online learning. *Degree requirements:* For master's, research project. *Entrance requirements:* For master's, minimum GPA of 2.75, teaching certificate. Electronic applications accepted.

University of Wisconsin–Whitewater, School of Graduate Studies, College of Education and Professional Studies, Department of Special Education, Whitewater, WI 53190-1790. Offers cross categorical licensure (MSE); professional development (MSE); special education (Postbaccalaureate Certificate). *Accreditation:* NCATE. *Program availability:* Part-time, evening/weekend, online learning. *Degree requirements:* For master's, thesis or alternative. *Entrance requirements:* Additional exam requirements/recommendations for international students: Required—TOEFL (minimum score 550 paper-based; 80 iBT), IELTS (minimum score 6). Electronic applications accepted.

University of Wyoming, College of Education, Program in Special Education, Laramie, WY 82071. Offers MA, PhD, Ed S. *Degree requirements:* For master's, comprehensive exam, thesis. *Entrance requirements:* For master's, GRE, 2 years teaching experience, 3 letters of recommendation, writing sample. *Faculty research:* Self-determination; transition; digital learning; severe disabilities; response to intervention.

Ursuline College, School of Graduate Studies, Master Apprenticeship Program, Pepper Pike, OH 44124-4398. Offers adolescent to young adult education (MA); early childhood education (MA); middle childhood education (MA); special education (MA). *Accreditation:* NCATE. *Degree requirements:* For master's, comprehensive exam. *Entrance requirements:* For master's, minimum undergraduate GPA of 3.0. Additional exam requirements/recommendations for international students: Required—TOEFL (minimum score 500 paper-based). *Application deadline:* For fall admission, 8/1 priority date for domestic students. Applications are processed on a rolling basis. Application fee: $25. Electronic applications accepted. *Expenses:* Contact institution. *Financial support:* Application deadline: 3/1; applicants required to submit FAFSA. *Unit head:* Dr. Mary Jo Cherry, Director, 440-646-8147, Fax: 440-646-8328, E-mail: mcherry@ursuline.edu. *Application contact:* Stephanie Pratt McRoberts, Graduate Admission Coordinator, 440-646-8119, Fax: 440-684-6138, E-mail: graduateadmissions@ursuline.edu.
Website: http://www.ursuline.edu/Academics/Graduate_Professional/Masters_Programs/MAP/index.html

Utah State University, School of Graduate Studies, Emma Eccles Jones College of Education and Human Services, Department of Special Education and Rehabilitation, Logan, UT 84322. Offers disability disciplines (PhD); rehabilitation counselor education (MRC); special education (M Ed, MS, Ed S). *Program availability:* Part-time, online learning. *Degree requirements:* For master's, thesis (for some programs), internships (for some programs); for doctorate, comprehensive exam, thesis/dissertation. *Entrance requirements:* For master's and doctorate, GRE General Test, minimum GPA of 3.0. Additional exam requirements/recommendations for international students: Required—TOEFL (minimum score 550 paper-based). Electronic applications accepted. *Faculty research:* Applied behavior analysis, effective instructional practices, early childhood teacher training research, distance education, multicultural rehabilitation.

Valdosta State University, Department of Early Childhood and Special Education, Valdosta, GA 31698. Offers early childhood (M Ed); special education (M Ed, MAT, Ed S). *Accreditation:* ASHA (one or more programs are accredited); NCATE. *Program availability:* Part-time, evening/weekend, blended/hybrid learning. *Degree requirements:* For master's, thesis (for some programs), comprehensive written and/or oral exams; for Ed S, thesis. *Entrance requirements:* For master's, GRE General Test or MAT, minimum GPA of 2.75; for Ed S, GRE General Test or MAT, minimum GPA of 3.0. Additional exam requirements/recommendations for international students: Required—TOEFL (minimum score 523 paper-based); Recommended—IELTS. Electronic applications accepted. *Expenses:* Contact institution.

Vanderbilt University, Peabody College, Department of Special Education, Nashville, TN 37240-1001. Offers M Ed. *Accreditation:* NCATE. *Program availability:* Part-time. *Faculty:* 26 full-time (18 women), 10 part-time/adjunct (8 women). *Students:* 94 full-time (88 women), 5 part-time (all women); includes 13 minority (2 Black or African American, non-Hispanic/Latino; 3 Asian, non-Hispanic/Latino; 3 Hispanic/Latino; 5 Two or more races, non-Hispanic/Latino), 3 international. Average age 24. 111 applicants, 69% accepted, 51 enrolled. In 2016, 49 master's awarded. *Degree requirements:* For master's, comprehensive exam, thesis optional. *Entrance requirements:* For master's, GRE General Test. Additional exam requirements/recommendations for international students: Required—TOEFL (minimum score 550 paper-based; 80 iBT). *Application deadline:* For fall admission, 12/31 priority date for domestic and international students; for spring admission, 11/1 priority date for domestic and international students. Applications are processed on a rolling basis. Application fee: $0. Electronic applications accepted. *Expenses: Tuition:* Part-time $1854 per credit hour. *Financial support:* Fellowships with partial tuition reimbursements, research assistantships with partial tuition reimbursements, teaching assistantships with partial tuition reimbursements, Federal Work-Study, institutionally sponsored loans, scholarships/grants, traineeships, health care benefits, tuition waivers (partial), and unspecified assistantships available. Support available to part-time students. Financial award application deadline: 1/15; financial award applicants required to submit CSS PROFILE or FAFSA. *Faculty research:* Early language and social skills development, learning and behavior disorders, autism and developmental/intellectual disabilities, low vision and blindness, giftedness and diversity. *Unit head:* Dr. Joseph Wehby, Chair, 615-322-8150, Fax: 615-343-1570, E-mail: joseph.wehby@vanderbilt.edu. *Application contact:* Alfred Brady, Admissions Coordinator, 615-322-8195, Fax: 615-343-1570, E-mail: alfred.l.brady@vanderbilt.edu.

Vanderbilt University, PhD Program in Special Education, Nashville, TN 37240-1001. Offers PhD. *Faculty:* 21 full-time (13 women). *Students:* 45 full-time (41 women); includes 7 minority (2 Asian, non-Hispanic/Latino; 2 Hispanic/Latino; 3 Two or more races, non-Hispanic/Latino), 1 international. Average age 31. 84 applicants, 20% accepted, 15 enrolled. In 2016, 8 doctorates awarded. *Degree requirements:* For doctorate, thesis/dissertation, qualifying examinations. *Entrance requirements:* For doctorate, GRE. Additional exam requirements/recommendations for international students: Required—TOEFL (minimum score 570 paper-based; 88 iBT). *Application deadline:* For fall admission, 12/1 for domestic and international students. Application fee: $0. Electronic applications accepted. *Expenses:* Contact institution. *Financial support:* Fellowships with full tuition reimbursements, research assistantships with full tuition reimbursements, teaching assistantships with full tuition reimbursements, Federal Work-Study, institutionally sponsored loans, traineeships, and health care benefits available. Financial award application deadline: 1/15; financial award applicants required to submit CSS PROFILE or FAFSA. *Faculty research:* Early language and social skills development, learning and behavior disorders, autism and developmental/intellectual disabilities, low vision and blindness, giftedness and diversity. *Unit head:* Dr. Joseph Wehby, Chair, 615-322-8150, Fax: 615-343-1570, E-mail: joseph.wehby@vanderbilt.edu. *Application contact:* Dr. Robert Hodapp, Director of Graduate Studies, 615-322-8150, Fax: 615-343-1570, E-mail: robert.hodapp@vanderbilt.edu.

Vanderbilt University, School of Medicine, Department of Hearing and Speech Sciences, Nashville, TN 37240-1001. Offers audiology (Au D, PhD); deaf education (MED); speech-language pathology (MS). *Accreditation:* ASHA. *Faculty:* 22 full-time (7 women). *Students:* 29 full-time (22 women), 2 part-time (1 woman); includes 4 minority (1 Black or African American, non-Hispanic/Latino; 1 Asian, non-Hispanic/Latino; 1 Hispanic/Latino; 1 Two or more races, non-Hispanic/Latino), 5 international. Average age 28. 27 applicants, 33% accepted, 7 enrolled. In 2016, 3 doctorates awarded. *Degree requirements:* For master's, thesis optional; for doctorate, thesis/dissertation, final and qualifying exams. *Entrance requirements:* For master's and doctorate, GRE General Test. Additional exam requirements/recommendations for international students: Required—TOEFL. *Application deadline:* For fall admission, 1/15 for domestic and international students. Application fee: $0. Electronic applications accepted. *Expenses: Tuition:* Part-time $1854 per credit hour. *Financial support:* Fellowships with full tuition reimbursements, research assistantships with full tuition reimbursements, career-related internships or fieldwork, institutionally sponsored loans, traineeships, and tuition waivers (full and partial) available. Financial award application deadline: 1/15; financial award applicants required to submit FAFSA. *Faculty research:* Child language. *Total annual research expenditures:* $3.6 million. *Unit head:* Dr. Anne Marie Tharpe, Chair, 615-936-5103, Fax: 615-936-5014, E-mail: anne.m.tharpe@vanderbilt.edu. *Application contact:* Todd Ricketts, Director of Graduate Studies, 615-936-5103, Fax: 615-936-6914, E-mail: todd.a.ricketts@vanderbilt.edu.
Website: http://www.vanderbiltbillwilkersoncenter.com

Virginia Commonwealth University, Graduate School, School of Education, Doctoral Program in Education, Richmond, VA 23284-9005. Offers art education (PhD); counselor education and supervision (PhD); curriculum, culture and change (PhD); educational leadership (PhD); educational psychology (PhD); leadership (Ed D); research and evaluation (PhD); special education and disability leadership (PhD); sport leadership (PhD); urban services leadership (PhD). *Accreditation:* NCATE. *Program availability:* Part-time. *Degree requirements:* For doctorate, thesis/dissertation. *Entrance requirements:* For doctorate, GRE (for PhD), MAT (for Ed D), interview, master's degree, writing sample. Additional exam requirements/recommendations for international students: Required—TOEFL (minimum score 600 paper-based; 100 iBT). *Application deadline:* For fall admission, 2/15 for domestic students. Application fee: $50. Electronic applications accepted. *Financial support:* Fellowships, research assistantships, career-related internships or fieldwork, Federal Work-Study, and institutionally sponsored loans available. Financial award application deadline: 3/1; financial award applicants required to submit FAFSA. *Unit head:* Dr. Kathleen Cauley, Interim Director, 804-827-2657, E-mail: kmcauley@vcu.edu. *Application contact:* Dr. Colleen A. Thoma, Administrative Assistant, 804-827-2651, E-mail: cathoma@vcu.edu.
Website: http://www.soe.vcu.edu/programs/doctoral-programs/

Virginia Commonwealth University, Graduate School, School of Education, Program in Special Education, Richmond, VA 23284-9005. Offers early childhood (M Ed); general education (M Ed); severe disabilities (M Ed). *Accreditation:* NCATE. *Degree requirements:* For master's, comprehensive exam. *Entrance requirements:* For master's, GRE General Test or MAT. Additional exam requirements/recommendations for international students: Required—TOEFL (minimum score 600 paper-based; 100 iBT). *Application deadline:* For fall admission, 3/15 for domestic students; for spring admission, 11/1 for domestic students. Applications are processed on a rolling basis. Application fee: $50. Electronic applications accepted. *Financial support:* Tuition waivers (partial) available. Financial award application deadline: 3/1; financial award applicants required to submit FAFSA. *Unit head:* Dr. Evelyn Reed, Department Chair, 804-827-2653, E-mail: mereed@vcu.edu. *Application contact:* Dr. Mary Ellen Huennekens, Graduate Studies Specialist, 804-827-2663, E-mail: huennekensme@vcu.edu.
Website: http://www.soe.vcu.edu/departments/sedp/programs.html

Viterbo University, Graduate Programs in Education, La Crosse, WI 54601-4797. Offers cross-categorical special education (Certificate); director of instruction (Certificate); director of special education and pupil services (Certificate); early childhood (Certificate); education (MAE); literacy coaching (Certificate); PreK-12 principal/supervisor of special education (Certificate); principal (Certificate); reading specialist endorsement (Certificate); reading teacher (Certificate); reading teacher 5-12 endorsement (Certificate); reading teacher K-8 endorsement (Certificate); superintendent (Certificate); talented and gifted endorsement (Certificate); Wisconsin school business administrator (Certificate). Weekend courses available in summer. *Accreditation:* NCATE. *Program availability:* Part-time, evening/weekend. *Degree requirements:* For master's, comprehensive exam, thesis, 30 credits of course work. *Entrance requirements:* For master's, BS, transcripts, teaching license, written narrative. Electronic applications accepted. *Expenses:* Contact institution.

Wagner College, Division of Graduate Studies, Education Department, Program in Childhood Education/Students with Disabilities, Staten Island, NY 10301-4495. Offers MS Ed. *Program availability:* Part-time, evening/weekend. *Degree requirements:* For master's, thesis (for some programs), passage of New York State certification exams before student teaching. *Entrance requirements:* For master's, minimum GPA of 3.0, interview, recommendations. Additional exam requirements/recommendations for international students: Required—TOEFL. Electronic applications accepted. Tuition and fees vary according to degree level.

Wagner College, Division of Graduate Studies, Education Department, Program in Early Childhood Education/Students with Disabilities (Birth-Grade 2), Staten Island, NY 10301-4495. Offers MS Ed. *Program availability:* Part-time, evening/weekend. *Degree requirements:* For master's, thesis. *Entrance requirements:* For master's, minimum GPA of 3.0, valid initial NY State Certificate or equivalent, interview, recommendations. Electronic applications accepted. Tuition and fees vary according to degree level.

Wagner College, Division of Graduate Studies, Education Department, Program in Secondary Education/Students with Disabilities, Staten Island, NY 10301-4495. Offers secondary education 7-12 (MS Ed), including language arts, languages other than English, mathematics and technology, science and technology, social studies. *Program availability:* Part-time, evening/weekend. *Degree requirements:* For master's, thesis (for some programs), completion of state certification exams before student teaching. *Entrance requirements:* For master's, minimum GPA of 3.0, interview, recommendations. Electronic applications accepted. Tuition and fees vary according to degree level.

Walden University, Graduate Programs, Richard W. Riley College of Education and Leadership, Minneapolis, MN 55401. Offers adult education (Post-Master's Certificate); adult learning (Graduate Certificate); college teaching and learning (Graduate Certificate); community college leadership (Ed D); curriculum, instruction and assessment (Ed D, Ed S, Graduate Certificate); developmental education (Graduate Certificate); early childhood administration, management, and leadership (Graduate Certificate); early childhood education (Ed D, Ed S); early childhood public policy and advocacy (Graduate Certificate); early childhood studies (MS), including administration, management and leadership, early childhood public policy and advocacy, teaching adults in the early childhood field, teaching and diversity in early childhood education; education (MS, PhD), including adolescent literacy and learning (MS), curriculum, instruction, and assessment (grades K-12) (MS), curriculum, instruction, assessment, and evaluation (PhD), early childhood leadership and advocacy (PhD), early childhood special education (PhD), educational leadership (MS), educational leadership and administration (principal preparation) (MS), educational technology and design (PhD), elementary reading and literacy (PreK-6) (MS), elementary reading and mathematics (grades K-6) (MS), global and comparative education (PhD), higher education leadership management and policy (PhD), integrating technology in the classroom (grades K-12) (MS), learning, instruction and innovation (PhD), mathematics (grades 5-8) (MS), mathematics (grades K-6) (MS), mathematics and science (grades K-8) (MS), organizational research, assessment, and evaluation (PhD), reading and literacy with a reading K-12 endorsement (MS), reading literacy assessment and evaluation (PhD), science (grades K-8) (MS), special education (non-licensure) (grades K-12) (MS), teacher leadership (grades K-12) (MS), teaching English language learners (grades K-12) (MS); educational administration and leadership (Ed D); educational leadership and administration (principal preparation) (Ed S); educational technology (Ed D, Ed S, Post Master's Certificate); elementary reading and literacy (Graduate Certificate); engaging culturally diverse learners (Graduate Certificate); enrollment management and institutional marketing (Graduate Certificate); higher education (MS), including adult learning, college teaching and learning, enrollment management and institutional marketing, global higher education, leadership for student success, online and distance learning; higher education and adult learning (Ed D); higher education leadership and management (Ed D); higher education leadership for student success (Graduate Certificate); instructional design and technology (MS, Postbaccalaureate Certificate), including general program (MS), online learning (MS), training and performance improvement (MS); integrating technology in the classroom (Graduate Certificate); mathematics 5-8 (Graduate Certificate); mathematics K-6 (Graduate Certificate); online teaching for adult educators (Graduate Certificate); reading, literacy, and assessment (Ed D, Ed S); science K-8 (Graduate Certificate); special education (Ed D, Ed S, Graduate Certificate); special education (K-age 21) (MAT); teacher leadership (Graduate Certificate); teaching adults English as a second language (Graduate Certificate); teaching adults in the early childhood field (Graduate Certificate); teaching and diversity in early childhood education (Graduate Certificate); teaching English language learners (grades K-12) (Graduate Certificate); teaching K-12 students online (Graduate Certificate). *Accreditation:* NCATE. *Program availability:* Part-time, evening/weekend, online only, 100% online. *Degree requirements:* For doctorate, thesis/dissertation (for some programs), residency; for other advanced degree, residency (for some programs). *Entrance requirements:* For master's, bachelor's degree or higher; minimum GPA of 2.5; official transcripts; goal statement (for some programs); access to computer and Internet; for doctorate, master's degree or higher; three years of related professional or academic experience (preferred); minimum GPA of 3.0; goal statement and current resume (for select programs); official transcripts; access to computer and

Internet; for other advanced degree, relevant work experience; access to computer and Internet. Additional exam requirements/recommendations for international students: Required—TOEFL (minimum score 550 paper-based, 79 iBT), IELTS (minimum score 6.5), Michigan English Language Assessment Battery (minimum score 82), or PTE (minimum score 53). Electronic applications accepted.

Walla Walla University, Graduate Studies, School of Education and Psychology, College Place, WA 99324. Offers curriculum and instruction (M Ed, MA, MAT); educational leadership (M Ed, MA, MAT); literacy instruction (M Ed, MA, MAT); students at risk (M Ed, MA, MAT); teaching (MAT). *Program availability:* Part-time. *Entrance requirements:* For master's, GRE General Test, minimum GPA of 2.75. Additional exam requirements/recommendations for international students: Required—TOEFL (minimum score 550 paper-based; 79 iBT). *Application deadline:* For fall admission, 4/1 priority date for domestic students. Applications are processed on a rolling basis. Application fee: $50. Electronic applications accepted. *Expenses: Tuition:* Part-time $592 per quarter hour. *Financial support:* Research assistantships, teaching assistantships, Federal Work-Study, and tuition waivers (partial) available. Support available to part-time students. Financial award application deadline: 4/30; financial award applicants required to submit FAFSA. *Faculty research:* Admissions/retention, instructional psychology, moral development, teaching of reading. *Unit head:* Denise Dunzweiler, Dean, 509-527-2212, Fax: 509-527-2248, E-mail: denise.dunzweiler@wallawalla.edu. *Application contact:* Dr. Joe G. Galusha, Dean of Graduate Studies, 509-527-2421, Fax: 509-527-2237, E-mail: joe.galusha@wallawalla.edu.
Website: https://wallawalla.edu/academics/areas-of-study/undergraduate-programs/education-and-psychology/

Washburn University, College of Arts and Sciences, Department of Education, Topeka, KS 66621. Offers curriculum and instruction (M Ed); educational leadership (M Ed); reading (M Ed); special education (M Ed). *Accreditation:* NCATE. *Program availability:* Part-time. *Degree requirements:* For master's, comprehensive exam, thesis or alternative, portfolio, comprehensive paper, or action research project. *Entrance requirements:* For master's, department exam, GRE General Test, or MAT, minimum GPA of 3.0 in graduate coursework or last 60 hours of undergraduate coursework. Additional exam requirements/recommendations for international students: Required—TOEFL (minimum score 80 iBT). *Faculty research:* Reading/literature/literacy, foundations, special education, diversity, teaching and technology.

Washington State University, College of Education, Department of Teaching and Learning, Pullman, WA 99164-2132. Offers cultural studies and social thought in education (PhD); curriculum and instruction (Ed M, MA); English language learners (Ed M, MA); language, literacy and technology (PhD); literacy education (Ed M, MA); mathematics education (PhD); special education (Ed M, MA, PhD); teacher leadership (Ed D); teaching (MIT), including elementary education, secondary education. Programs offered at the Pullman, Spokane, Tri-cities, Vancouver and Global (online) campuses. *Program availability:* Part-time, online learning. *Degree requirements:* For master's, comprehensive exam, thesis, oral or written exam; for doctorate, comprehensive exam, thesis/dissertation, oral and written exam. *Entrance requirements:* For master's, GRE General Test, minimum GPA of 3.0, 3 letters of recommendation, letter of intent, transcripts, resume/curriculum vitae; for doctorate, GRE General Test, minimum GPA of 3.0, 3 letters of recommendation, letter of intent, transcripts, writing sample, resume/curriculum vitae. Additional exam requirements/recommendations for international students: Required—TOEFL (minimum score 550 paper-based; 80 iBT). Electronic applications accepted. *Faculty research:* Intersection of gender, youth cultures and schooling; examination of ideology of power in children's literature; early childhood special education; analyzing pre-service and in-service teacher development; second language acquisition.

Washington University in St. Louis, School of Medicine, Program in Audiology and Communication Sciences, St. Louis, MO 63110. Offers audiology (Au D); deaf education (MS); speech and hearing sciences (PhD). *Accreditation:* ASHA (one or more programs are accredited). *Faculty:* 22 full-time (12 women), 18 part-time/adjunct (12 women). *Students:* 72 full-time (67 women). Average age 24. 101 applicants, 32% accepted, 22 enrolled. In 2016, 8 master's, 14 doctorates awarded. *Degree requirements:* For master's, comprehensive exam, thesis, independent study project, oral exam; for doctorate, comprehensive exam, thesis/dissertation, capstone project. *Entrance requirements:* For master's and doctorate, GRE General Test, minimum B average in previous college/university coursework (recommended). Additional exam requirements/recommendations for international students: Required—TOEFL (minimum score 100 iBT). *Application deadline:* For fall admission, 2/15 for domestic and international students. Application fee: $60 ($80 for international students). Electronic applications accepted. *Expenses:* Contact institution. *Financial support:* In 2016–17, 72 students received support, including 72 fellowships with full and partial tuition reimbursements available (averaging $16,104 per year), 6 teaching assistantships with partial tuition reimbursements available (averaging $1,000 per year); career-related internships or fieldwork, Federal Work-Study, institutionally sponsored loans, scholarships/grants, traineeships, health care benefits, tuition waivers (partial), and unspecified assistantships also available. Financial award application deadline: 2/15; financial award applicants required to submit FAFSA. *Faculty research:* Audiology, deaf education, speech and hearing sciences, sensory neuroscience. *Unit head:* Dr. William W. Clark, Program Director, 314-747-0104, Fax: 314-747-0105. *Application contact:* Beth Elliott, Director, Finance and Student/Academic Affairs, 314-747-0104, Fax: 314-747-0105, E-mail: elliottb@wustl.edu.
Website: http://pacs.wustl.edu/

Wayland Baptist University, Graduate Programs, Program in Education, Plainview, TX 79072-6998. Offers education administration (M Ed); education diagnostics (M Ed); education literacy (M Ed); elementary certification (M Ed); English (M Ed); English as a second language (M Ed); higher education administration (M Ed); human resources (M Ed); instructional leadership (M Ed); instructional technology (M Ed); leadership training and development (M Ed); science education (M Ed); secondary certification (M Ed); social studies (M Ed); special education (M Ed); sports administration and management (M Ed). *Program availability:* Part-time, evening/weekend, online learning. *Degree requirements:* For master's, comprehensive exam, capstone course. *Entrance requirements:* For master's, GRE, GMAT or MAT. Additional exam requirements/recommendations for international students: Required—TOEFL (minimum score 500 paper-based; 61 iBT). Electronic applications accepted.

Waynesburg University, Graduate and Professional Studies, Canonsburg, PA 15370. Offers business (MBA), including energy management, finance, health systems, human resources, leadership, market development; counseling (MA), including addictions counseling, clinical mental health; counselor education and supervision (PhD); criminal investigation (MA); education (M Ed), including autism, curriculum and instruction, educational leadership, online teaching; nursing (MSN), including administration, education, informatics; nursing practice (DNP); special education (M Ed); technology (M Ed); MSN/MBA. *Accreditation:* AACN. *Program availability:* Part-time, evening/weekend. *Degree requirements:* For doctorate, thesis/dissertation. *Entrance requirements:* Additional exam requirements/recommendations for international students: Required—TOEFL. Electronic applications accepted.

Wayne State College, School of Education and Counseling, Department of Counseling and Special Education, Program in Special Education, Wayne, NE 68787. Offers MSE. *Accreditation:* NCATE. *Program availability:* Part-time, evening/weekend. *Degree requirements:* For master's, comprehensive exam, thesis. *Entrance requirements:* For master's, GRE General Test, minimum GPA of 3.0. Additional exam requirements/recommendations for international students: Required—TOEFL (minimum score 550 paper-based). Electronic applications accepted.

Wayne State University, College of Education, Division of Teacher Education, Detroit, MI 48202. Offers art education (M Ed); bilingual/bicultural education (M Ed, Certificate); career and technical education (M Ed); curriculum and instruction (Ed D, PhD, Ed S), including art education (Ed D, PhD), bilingual education (Ed D, Ed S), career and technical education (MAT, Ed D, PhD, Ed S), early childhood education (MAT, Ed D, PhD, Ed S), elementary education, English as a second language (MAT, Ed D, Ed S), English education (MAT, Ed D, PhD, Ed S), foreign language education (MAT, Ed D, PhD), K-12 curriculum, mathematics education (MAT, Ed D, PhD, Ed S), science education (MAT, Ed D, PhD, Ed S), secondary education, social studies education (MAT, Ed D, PhD, Ed S); early childhood education (M Ed); elementary education (M Ed, MAT), including bilingual/bicultural education (MAT), early childhood education (MAT, Ed D, PhD, Ed S), English as a second language (MAT, Ed D, Ed S), general elementary education (MAT), mathematics education (MAT, Ed D, PhD, Ed S), science education (MAT, Ed D, PhD, Ed S), social studies education (MAT, Ed D, PhD, Ed S); English as a second language (Certificate); English education (M Ed); foreign language education (M Ed); mathematics education (M Ed); reading (M Ed, Ed S); reading, language and literature (Ed D); science education (M Ed); secondary education (MAT), including art education (K-12), bilingual/bicultural education, career and technical education (MAT, Ed D, PhD, Ed S), English as a second language (MAT, Ed D, Ed S), English education (MAT, Ed D, PhD, Ed S), foreign language education (MAT, Ed D, PhD), kinesiology, mathematics education (MAT, Ed D, PhD, Ed S); social studies education (M Ed); special education (M Ed, MAT, Ed D, PhD, Ed S), including autism spectrum disorders (MAT), cognitive development (MAT), emotional impairment (MAT), learning disabilities (MAT). *Program availability:* Part-time, blended/hybrid learning. *Faculty:* 29. *Students:* 106 full-time (73 women), 351 part-time (276 women); includes 115 minority (76 Black or African American, non-Hispanic/Latino; 10 Asian, non-Hispanic/Latino; 20 Hispanic/Latino; 1 Native Hawaiian or other Pacific Islander, non-Hispanic/Latino; 8 Two or more races, non-Hispanic/Latino), 12 international. Average age 37. 242 applicants, 37% accepted, 72 enrolled. In 2016, 178 master's, 19 doctorates, 17 other advanced degrees awarded. *Degree requirements:* For master's, essay or project (for some M Ed programs), professional field experience (for MAT programs); for doctorate, thesis/dissertation. *Entrance requirements:* For master's, Michigan Test for Teacher Certification, verification of participation in group work with children, Michigan State Police criminal background check; for doctorate, minimum undergraduate GPA of 3.0, graduate 3.5; interview; curriculum vitae; references. Additional exam requirements/recommendations for international students: Required—TOEFL (minimum score 550 paper-based; 79 iBT), TWE (minimum score 5.5), Michigan English Language Assessment Battery (minimum score 85); Recommended—IELTS (minimum score 6.5). *Application deadline:* For fall admission, 6/1 priority date for domestic students, 5/1 priority date for international students; for winter admission, 10/1 priority date for domestic students, 9/1 priority date for international students; for spring admission, 2/1 priority date for domestic students, 1/1 priority date for international students. Applications are processed on a rolling basis. Application fee: $50. Electronic applications accepted. *Expenses:* $16,503 per year resident tuition and fees, $33,697 per year non-resident tuition and fees. *Financial support:* In 2016–17, 101 students received support, including 3 fellowships (averaging $11,409 per year); research assistantships with tuition reimbursements available, Federal Work-Study, scholarships/grants, and unspecified assistantships also available. Support available to part-time students. Financial award applicants required to submit FAFSA. *Faculty research:* Improving students' skill achievement in mathematics, improving elementary children's understanding of informational text, teachers' use of their pedagogical and mathematical knowledge in the interactive work of teaching, the intersection of identity construction in teaching and learning, identifying effective methods of literacy instruction and assessments for bilingual students in elementary language arts classrooms. *Unit head:* Dr. Kathleen Crawford-McKinney, Assistant Dean, 313-577-0122. *Application contact:* Janice Green, Assistant Dean, 313-577-1605, E-mail: jwgreen@wayne.edu.
Website: http://coe.wayne.edu/ted/index.php

Webster University, School of Education, Department of Multidisciplinary Studies, St. Louis, MO 63119-3194. Offers applied educational psychology (MA, Ed S); communication arts (MA); early childhood education (MA, MAT); education and innovation (MA); educational technology (MET); elementary education (MAT); mathematics for educators (MA); middle school education (MAT); multidisciplinary studies (MAT); multimodal literacy for global impact (MA); reading (MA); secondary school education (MAT); special education (MA, MAT); teaching English as a second language (MA); transformative learning in the global community (Ed S). *Program availability:* Part-time. *Entrance requirements:* For master's, minimum GPA of 2.5. Additional exam requirements/recommendations for international students: Required—TOEFL. *Application deadline:* Applications are processed on a rolling basis. Application fee: $35 ($50 for international students). *Expenses: Tuition:* Full-time $21,900; part-time $730 per credit hour. Tuition and fees vary according to campus/location and program. *Financial support:* Federal Work-Study available. Support available to part-time students. Financial award application deadline: 4/1; financial award applicants required to submit FAFSA. *Unit head:* Dr. Deborah Stiles, Chair, 314-968-7056, Fax: 314-968-7118, E-mail: stilesda@webster.edu.

West Chester University of Pennsylvania, College of Education and Social Work, Department of Special Education, West Chester, PA 19383. Offers autism (Certificate); special education (Teaching Certificate); special education (M Ed); universal design for learning and assistive technology (Certificate). *Accreditation:* NCATE. *Program availability:* Part-time, 100% online. *Faculty:* 8 full-time (7 women), 1 (woman) part-time/adjunct. *Students:* 13 full-time (10 women), 182 part-time (165 women); includes 14 minority (8 Black or African American, non-Hispanic/Latino; 1 Asian, non-Hispanic/Latino; 3 Hispanic/Latino; 2 Two or more races, non-Hispanic/Latino), 1 international. Average age 29. 84 applicants, 89% accepted, 60 enrolled. In 2016, 38 master's, 26 Certificates awarded. *Degree requirements:* For master's, minimum GPA of 3.0, action research; for other advanced degree, minimum GPA of 3.0; modified student teaching. *Entrance requirements:* For master's, GRE if GPA is below 3.0, two letters of recommendation; for other advanced degree, GRE if GPA is below 3.0. Additional exam requirements/recommendations for international students: Required—TOEFL or IELTS. *Application deadline:* For fall admission, 5/15 for international students; for spring admission, 10/15 for international students. Applications are processed on a rolling basis. Application fee: $50. Electronic applications accepted. *Expenses:* Tuition, state resident: full-time $8694; part-time $483 per credit. Tuition, nonresident: full-time $13,050; part-time $725 per credit. *Required fees:* $2399; $119.05 per credit. Tuition and fees vary according to campus/location and program. *Financial support:* Scholarships/grants and unspecified assistantships available. Financial award application deadline: 2/15; financial award applicants required to submit FAFSA. *Faculty research:* Instructional strategies for students with moderate to severe disabilities; family

involvement for families of students with disabilities; instructional strategies for students with autism; math instruction for students with learning disabilities; transitions for students with disabilities; behavior management for students with behavior disorders. *Unit head:* Dr. Corrine Murphy, Chair, 610-436-0040, Fax: 610-436-3102, E-mail: cmurphy@wcupa.edu. *Application contact:* Dr. S. Christy Hicks, Graduate Coordinator, 610-436-3067, E-mail: shicks@wcupa.edu.
Website: http://www.wcupa.edu/education-socialWork/specialEducation/

Western Connecticut State University, Division of Graduate Studies, School of Professional Studies, Department of Education and Educational Psychology, Special Education Option, Danbury, CT 06810-6885. Offers MS. *Program availability:* Part-time. *Degree requirements:* For master's, thesis or research project. *Entrance requirements:* For master's, minimum GPA of 2.8, teaching certificate. Additional exam requirements/recommendations for international students: Recommended—TOEFL (minimum score 550 paper-based; 79 iBT), IELTS (minimum score 6). *Faculty research:* Education and development of exceptional, gifted, talented, and disabled students in a regular (mainstream) classroom.

Western Governors University, Teachers College, Salt Lake City, UT 84107. Offers curriculum and instruction (MS); educational leadership (MS); educational studies (MA); educational studies (5-12) (MA), including mathematics; elementary education (K-8) (MAT, Postbaccalaureate Certificate); elementary education (PreK-8) (MAT); English language learning (K-12) (MA); instructional design (MAT); learning and technology (M Ed, MA); management and innovation (M Ed); mathematics (5-12) (MAT, Postbaccalaureate Certificate); mathematics (5-9) (MAT, Postbaccalaureate Certificate); mathematics education (5-12) (MA); mathematics education (5-9) (MA); mathematics education (K-6) (MA); measurement and evaluation (M Ed); science (5-12) (Postbaccalaureate Certificate); science (5-9) (MAT, Postbaccalaureate Certificate); science education (5-12) (MA), including biology, chemistry, geology, physics; science education (5-9) (MA); social science (5-12) (MAT, Postbaccalaureate Certificate); special education (MAT, MS). *Accreditation:* NCATE. *Program availability:* Evening/weekend, online learning. *Degree requirements:* For master's, capstone project. *Entrance requirements:* For master's and Postbaccalaureate Certificate, Readiness Assessment, transcripts. Additional exam requirements/recommendations for international students: Required—TOEFL (minimum score 450 paper-based; 80 iBT). Electronic applications accepted. *Expenses:* Contact institution.

Western Illinois University, School of Graduate Studies, College of Education and Human Services, Department of Curriculum and Instruction, Program in Special Education, Macomb, IL 61455-1390. Offers MS Ed. *Accreditation:* NCATE. *Program availability:* Part-time. *Students:* 1 (woman) full-time, 17 part-time (16 women); includes 1 minority (Black or African American, non-Hispanic/Latino). Average age 34. 4 applicants, 100% accepted, 3 enrolled. In 2016, 9 master's awarded. *Degree requirements:* For master's, comprehensive exam, thesis or alternative. *Entrance requirements:* For master's, teacher certification. Additional exam requirements/recommendations for international students: Required—TOEFL (minimum score 550 paper-based; 80 iBT). *Application deadline:* Applications are processed on a rolling basis. Application fee: $30. Electronic applications accepted. *Financial support:* Applicants required to submit FAFSA. *Unit head:* Dr. Barry Witten, Interim Chairperson, 309-298-1961. *Application contact:* Dr. Nancy Parsons, Associate Provost and Director of Graduate Studies, 309-298-1806, Fax: 309-298-2345, E-mail: grad-office@wiu.edu.
Website: http://www.wiu.edu/coehs/curriculum_and_instruction/prospective_students/spedgrad.php

Western Kentucky University, Graduate Studies, College of Education and Behavioral Sciences, School of Teacher Education, Bowling Green, KY 42101. Offers elementary education (MAE, Ed S); exceptional education: learning and behavioral disorders (MAE); exceptional education: moderate and severe disabilities (MAE); instructional design (MS); interdisciplinary early childhood education (MAE); library media education (MS); literacy education (MAE); middle grades education (MAE); secondary education (MAE, Ed S). *Program availability:* Part-time, evening/weekend, online learning. *Degree requirements:* For master's, comprehensive exam. *Entrance requirements:* For master's, GRE General Test. Additional exam requirements/recommendations for international students: Required—TOEFL (minimum score 555 paper-based; 79 iBT). *Faculty research:* Teacher preparation in moderate/severe disabilities.

Western Michigan University, Graduate College, College of Education and Human Development, Department of Special Education and Literacy Studies, Kalamazoo, MI 49008. Offers literacy studies (MA); special education (MA, Ed D), including clinical teacher (MA); teaching children with visual impairments (MA).

Western New Mexico University, Graduate Division, School of Education, Silver City, NM 88062-0680. Offers bilingual education (MAT); educational leadership (MA); elementary education (MAT); reading (MAT); secondary education (MAT); special education (MAT); TESOL (teaching English to speakers of other languages) (MAT). *Accreditation:* NCATE. *Program availability:* Part-time, online learning. *Degree requirements:* For master's, comprehensive exam. *Entrance requirements:* For master's, minimum GPA of 3.0 in last 64 hours of undergraduate study. Additional exam requirements/recommendations for international students: Required—TOEFL (minimum score 550 paper-based; 79 iBT). Electronic applications accepted. *Faculty research:* International education, electronic reading assessment, developing STEM teachers.

Western Oregon University, Graduate Programs, College of Education, Division of Special Education, Program in Deaf Education, Monmouth, OR 97361. Offers MS Ed. *Accreditation:* NCATE. *Program availability:* Part-time, evening/weekend. *Degree requirements:* For master's, thesis, portfolio. *Entrance requirements:* For master's, California Basic Educational Skills Test or PRAXIS, GRE General Test or MAT, interview, minimum GPA of 3.0, teaching license. Additional exam requirements/recommendations for international students: Required—TOEFL (minimum score 550 paper-based; 79 iBT), IELTS (minimum score 6.5). *Faculty research:* Effects of infant massage on the interactions between high-risk infants and their caregivers, work sample methodology.

Western Oregon University, Graduate Programs, College of Education, Division of Special Education, Special Education Program, Monmouth, OR 97361. Offers MS Ed. *Program availability:* Part-time, evening/weekend. *Degree requirements:* For master's, comprehensive exam (for some programs), thesis optional, oral exam, portfolio, written exam. *Entrance requirements:* For master's, California Basic Educational Skills Test or PRAXIS, GRE General Test or MAT, interview, minimum GPA of 3.0, teaching license. Additional exam requirements/recommendations for international students: Required—TOEFL (minimum score 550 paper-based; 79 iBT), IELTS (minimum score 6.5). *Faculty research:* Interpreter teacher training, hearing disabilities, mental retardation.

Westfield State University, College of Graduate and Continuing Education, Department of Education, Program in Special Education, Westfield, MA 01086. Offers moderate disabilities, 5-12 (M Ed); moderate disabilities, preK-8 (M Ed). *Accreditation:* NCATE. *Program availability:* Part-time, evening/weekend. *Students:* 2 full-time (0 women), 34 part-time (26 women); includes 1 minority (Black or African American, non-Hispanic/Latino). Average age 33. 6 applicants, 67% accepted, 4 enrolled. In 2016, 12 master's awarded. *Degree requirements:* For master's, comprehensive exam, practicum. *Entrance requirements:* For master's, GRE General Test or MAT, minimum undergraduate GPA of 2.8. Additional exam requirements/recommendations for international students: Recommended—TOEFL (minimum score 550 paper-based; 79 iBT). *Application deadline:* For fall admission, 6/30 for domestic students; for spring admission, 10/31 for domestic students; for summer admission, 3/31 for domestic students. Applications are processed on a rolling basis. Application fee: $50. *Expenses:* Tuition, state resident: part-time $318 per semester hour. Tuition, nonresident: part-time $318 per semester hour. *Required fees:* $75 per semester. Tuition and fees vary according to course load and program. *Financial support:* Unspecified assistantships and SOS scholarships for education majors only available. Financial award application deadline: 3/1; financial award applicants required to submit FAFSA. *Unit head:* Dr. Sandra Berkowitz, Chair, 413-572-5323. *Application contact:* Shelly Henrichon, Coordinator of DGCE Admissions, 413-572-8022, Fax: 413-572-5227, E-mail: mhenrichon@westfield.ma.edu.

Westminster College, Graduate School, Program in Special Education and Reading Specialist, New Wilmington, PA 16172-0001. Offers M Ed, Certificate. *Program availability:* Part-time, evening/weekend. *Degree requirements:* For master's, comprehensive exam, portfolio. *Entrance requirements:* For master's, minimum GPA of 3.0. *Application deadline:* For fall admission, 8/15 priority date for domestic students; for spring admission, 1/8 priority date for domestic students. Applications are processed on a rolling basis. Application fee: $35. *Expenses: Tuition:* Full-time $1362; part-time $454 per semester hour. One-time fee: $235.50 full-time. *Financial support:* Career-related internships or fieldwork and scholarships/grants available. *Unit head:* Dr. Amy Camardese, Co-Coordinator, 724-946-7183. *Application contact:* Dr. Darwin W. Huey, Graduate Education Director, 724-946-7186, Fax: 724-946-6158, E-mail: hueydw@westminster.edu.

West Virginia University, College of Education and Human Services, Department of Curriculum and Instruction/Literacy Studies, Morgantown, WV 26506. Offers curriculum and instruction (Ed D); elementary education (MA); reading (MA); secondary education (MA), including higher education curriculum and teaching, secondary education; special education (Ed D), including special education. *Accreditation:* NCATE. *Program availability:* Part-time, evening/weekend. *Degree requirements:* For doctorate, comprehensive exam, thesis/dissertation. *Entrance requirements:* For master's, minimum GPA of 2.75; for doctorate, GRE General Test or MAT, 3 letters of recommendation, curriculum vitae. Additional exam requirements/recommendations for international students: Required—TOEFL. *Faculty research:* Teacher education, curriculum development, educational technology, curriculum assessment.

West Virginia University, College of Education and Human Services, Department of Special Education, Morgantown, WV 26506. Offers autism spectrum disorder (5-adult) (MA); autism spectrum disorder (K-6) (MA); early intervention/early childhood special education (MA); gifted education (1-12) (MA); low vision (PreK-adult) (MA); multicategorical special education (5-adult) (MA); multicategorical special education (K-6) (MA); severe/multiple disabilities (K-adult) (MA); special education (MA, Ed D); vision impairments (PreK-adult) (MA). *Accreditation:* NCATE. *Program availability:* Part-time, evening/weekend, online learning. *Degree requirements:* For master's, thesis optional; for doctorate, comprehensive exam, thesis/dissertation. *Entrance requirements:* For master's, minimum GPA of 2.75 passing scores on PRAXIS PPST; for doctorate, GRE General Test or MAT. Additional exam requirements/recommendations for international students: Required—TOEFL.

Wheelock College, Graduate Programs, Division of Education, Boston, MA 02215. Offers early childhood education (MS); education leadership (MS); elementary education (MS); language, literacy, and reading (MS); teaching students with moderate disabilities (MS). *Accreditation:* NCATE. *Program availability:* Online learning. *Degree requirements:* For master's, comprehensive exam. *Entrance requirements:* Additional exam requirements/recommendations for international students: Required—TOEFL. Electronic applications accepted. *Faculty research:* Symbolic learning, emergent literacy, diversity inclusion, beginning reading language and culture, math education.

Whitworth University, School of Education, Graduate Studies in Education, Program in Special Education, Spokane, WA 99251-0001. Offers MAT. *Accreditation:* NCATE. *Program availability:* Part-time, evening/weekend. *Degree requirements:* For master's, comprehensive exam, internship, practicum, research project, or thesis. *Entrance requirements:* For master's, GRE General Test, MAT. Additional exam requirements/recommendations for international students: Required—TOEFL.

Wichita State University, Graduate School, College of Education, Department of Curriculum and Instruction, Wichita, KS 67260. Offers learning and instructional design (M Ed); special education (M Ed), including early childhood (M Ed, MAT), gifted, high incidence, low incidence; teaching (MAT), including early childhood (M Ed, MAT), middle level/secondary, transition to teaching. *Accreditation:* NCATE. *Program availability:* Part-time, evening/weekend, 100% online, blended/hybrid learning. *Entrance requirements:* For master's, MAT, minimum GPA of 2.75. *Unit head:* Dr. Kimberly McDowell, Department Head, 316-978-3322, E-mail: kim.mcdowell@wichita.edu. *Application contact:* Jordan Oleson, Admission Coordinator, 316-978-3095, Fax: 316-978-3253, E-mail: jordan.oleson@wichita.edu.

Widener University, School of Education, Hospitality, and Continuing Studies, Chester, PA 19013-5792. Offers adult education (M Ed); counseling in higher education (M Ed); counselor education (M Ed); early childhood education (M Ed); educational foundations (M Ed); educational leadership (M Ed); educational psychology (M Ed); elementary education (M Ed); English and language arts (M Ed); health education (M Ed); higher education leadership (Ed D); home and school visitor (M Ed); human sexuality (M Ed, PhD); mathematics education (M Ed); middle school education (M Ed); principalship (M Ed); reading and language arts (Ed D); reading education (M Ed); school administration (Ed D); science education (M Ed); social studies education (M Ed); special education (M Ed); technology education (M Ed). *Accreditation:* NCATE. *Program availability:* Part-time, evening/weekend. *Faculty:* 34 full-time (22 women), 37 part-time/adjunct (14 women). *Students:* 97 full-time (64 women), 201 part-time (143 women); includes 56 minority (44 Black or African American, non-Hispanic/Latino; 1 American Indian or Alaska Native, non-Hispanic/Latino; 2 Asian, non-Hispanic/Latino; 8 Hispanic/Latino; 1 Two or more races, non-Hispanic/Latino), 32 international. Average age 39. 139 applicants, 88% accepted. In 2016, 45 master's, 21 doctorates awarded. Terminal master's awarded for partial completion of doctoral program. *Degree requirements:* For doctorate, thesis/dissertation. *Entrance requirements:* For master's, minimum GPA of 2.5; for doctorate, GRE or MAT, minimum GPA of 2.0 (undergraduate), 3.5 (graduate). *Application deadline:* Applications are processed on a rolling basis. Application fee: $25 ($300 for international students). Electronic applications accepted. *Expenses:* Contact institution. *Financial support:* Career-related internships or fieldwork, tuition waivers (full and partial), and unspecified assistantships available. Support available to part-time students. Financial award application deadline: 5/1. *Faculty research:* Reading and cognition, adult education, technology education, educational leadership, special education. *Unit head:* Dr. Shawn Fitzgerald, Dean, 610-499-4294, Fax: 610-499-4623, E-mail: smfitzgerald@widener.edu. *Application contact:* Dr. Roberta Nolan, Director of Graduate Admissions, 610-499-4125, E-mail: rdnolan@widener.edu.
Website: http://www.widener.edu/academics/schools/eics

Wilkes University, College of Graduate and Professional Studies, School of Education, Wilkes-Barre, PA 18766-0002. Offers 21st century teaching and learning (MS Ed); art and science of teaching (MS Ed); classroom technology (MS Ed); early childhood literacy (MS Ed); educational development and strategies (MS Ed); educational leadership (MS Ed, Ed D); effective teaching (MS Ed); instructional media (MS Ed); instructional technology (MS Ed); international school leadership (MS Ed); international teaching and learning (MS Ed); middle level education (MS Ed); online teaching (MS Ed); reading (MS Ed); school business leadership (MS Ed); special education (MS Ed); teaching English to speakers of other languages (MS Ed). *Program availability:* Part-time, evening/weekend, 100% online, blended/hybrid learning. *Students:* 87 full-time (70 women), 1,496 part-time (1,111 women); includes 77 minority (11 Black or African American, non-Hispanic/Latino; 2 American Indian or Alaska Native, non-Hispanic/Latino; 12 Asian, non-Hispanic/Latino; 28 Hispanic/Latino; 3 Native Hawaiian or other Pacific Islander, non-Hispanic/Latino; 21 Two or more races, non-Hispanic/Latino). Average age 33. In 2016, 524 master's, 21 doctorates awarded. *Entrance requirements:* Additional exam requirements/recommendations for international students: Required—TOEFL (minimum score 550 paper-based; 79 iBT). *Application deadline:* Applications are processed on a rolling basis. Application fee: $45. Electronic applications accepted. *Expenses:* Contact institution. *Financial support:* Unspecified assistantships available. Financial award application deadline: 3/1; financial award applicants required to submit FAFSA. *Unit head:* Dr. Rhonda Rabbitt, Dean, 570-408-4680, Fax: 570-408-7872, E-mail: rhonda.rabbitt@wilkes.edu. *Application contact:* Director of Graduate Education, 570-408-4234, Fax: 570-408-7846.
Website: http://www.wilkes.edu/academics/graduate-programs/masters-programs/graduate-education/index.aspx

William Carey University, School of Education, Hattiesburg, MS 39401-5499. Offers art education (M Ed); art of teaching (M Ed); elementary education (M Ed, Ed S); English education (M Ed); gifted education (M Ed); history and social science (M Ed); mild/moderate disabilities (M Ed); secondary education (M Ed). *Accreditation:* NCATE. *Program availability:* Part-time. *Degree requirements:* For master's, comprehensive exam. *Entrance requirements:* For master's, GRE, MAT, minimum GPA of 2.5, Class A teacher's license. Additional exam requirements/recommendations for international students: Required—TOEFL (minimum score 550 paper-based).

William Paterson University of New Jersey, College of Education, Wayne, NJ 07470-8420. Offers curriculum and learning (M Ed); educational leadership (M Ed); elementary education (MAT); literacy (M Ed); professional counseling (M Ed); secondary education (MAT); special education (M Ed). *Accreditation:* NCATE. *Program availability:* Part-time, evening/weekend. *Faculty:* 36 full-time (25 women), 32 part-time/adjunct (27 women). *Students:* 74 full-time (51 women), 607 part-time (515 women); includes 194 minority (42 Black or African American, non-Hispanic/Latino; 21 Asian, non-Hispanic/Latino; 116 Hispanic/Latino; 15 Two or more races, non-Hispanic/Latino), 1 international. Average age 35. 390 applicants, 83% accepted, 263 enrolled. In 2016, 170 master's awarded. *Degree requirements:* For master's, comprehensive exam, thesis (for some programs), exit interview (for some programs); practicum/internship; minimum GPA of 3.0 (for some programs); exit portfolio (for some programs). *Entrance requirements:* For master's, GRE/MAT, minimum GPA of 2.75; teaching certificate; essay; interview; 2 letters of recommendation; personal statement. Additional exam requirements/recommendations for international students: Required—TOEFL (minimum score 550 paper-based; 79 iBT), IELTS (minimum score 6). *Application deadline:* For fall admission, 8/1 for domestic students, 4/1 for international students; for spring admission, 12/1 for domestic students, 11/1 for international students; for summer admission, 5/1 for domestic students, 2/1 for international students. Applications are processed on a rolling basis. Application fee: $50. Electronic applications accepted. *Expenses:* Tuition, state resident: full-time $12,480; part-time $611 per credit. Tuition, nonresident: full-time $20,263; part-time $992 per credit. *Required fees:* $1573; $77 per credit. Tuition and fees vary according to course load, degree level and program. *Financial support:* Career-related internships or fieldwork, Federal Work-Study, scholarships/grants, and unspecified assistantships available. Support available to part-time students. Financial award application deadline: 4/1; financial award applicants required to submit FAFSA. *Faculty research:* History of education, social media in classrooms and education, integrating environmental lessons into urban classrooms, minority student self-advocacy in higher education, factors affecting high school teacher retention. *Total annual research expenditures:* $289,197. *Unit head:* Dr. Candace Burns, Dean, 973-720-2137, Fax: 973-720-3467, E-mail: burnsc@wpunj.edu. *Application contact:* Liana Fornarotto, Director of Education Enrollment and Certification, 973-720-2206, Fax: 973-720-2989, E-mail: fornarottol@wpunj.edu.
Website: http://www.wpunj.edu/coe

Wilmington College, Department of Education, Wilmington, OH 45177. Offers reading (M Ed); special education (M Ed). *Accreditation:* TEAC. *Program availability:* Part-time. *Degree requirements:* For master's, comprehensive exam. *Entrance requirements:* For master's, GRE or MAT, minimum GPA of 3.0, 2 letters of recommendation. Additional exam requirements/recommendations for international students: Required—TOEFL. *Faculty research:* Reading instruction, special education practices, conflict resolution in the schools, models of higher education for teachers.

Wilmington University, College of Education, New Castle, DE 19720-6491. Offers applied technology in education (M Ed); career and technical education (M Ed); educational leadership (Ed D); elementary and secondary school counseling (M Ed); elementary studies (M Ed); ESOL literacy (M Ed); higher education leadership (Ed D); instruction: gifted and talented (M Ed); instruction: teacher of reading (M Ed); instruction: teaching and learning (M Ed); organizational leadership (Ed D); school leadership (M Ed); secondary education (MAT); special education (M Ed). *Accreditation:* NCATE. *Program availability:* Part-time, evening/weekend. *Faculty:* 19 full-time (11 women), 178 part-time/adjunct (99 women). *Students:* 248 full-time (176 women), 999 part-time (738 women); includes 244 minority (193 Black or African American, non-Hispanic/Latino; 17 American Indian or Alaska Native, non-Hispanic/Latino; 9 Asian, non-Hispanic/Latino; 19 Hispanic/Latino; 2 Native Hawaiian or other Pacific Islander, non-Hispanic/Latino; 4 Two or more races, non-Hispanic/Latino), 7 international. Average age 34. 672 applicants, 96% accepted, 348 enrolled. In 2016, 529 master's, 87 doctorates awarded. *Entrance requirements:* For master's, 2 letters of recommendation, interview. Additional exam requirements/recommendations for international students: Required—TOEFL (minimum score 500 paper-based). *Application deadline:* For fall admission, 4/30 for domestic students. Applications are processed on a rolling basis. Application fee: $35. Electronic applications accepted. *Expenses: Tuition:* Full-time $8388; part-time $466 per credit. *Required fees:* $25 per semester. Tuition and fees vary according to degree level. *Financial support:* Applicants required to submit FAFSA. *Unit head:* Dr. John C. Gray, Dean. *Application contact:* Laura Morris, Director of Admissions, 877-967-5464, E-mail: infocenter@wilmu.edu.
Website: http://www.wilmu.edu/education/

Winona State University, College of Education, Department of Special Education, Winona, MN 55987. Offers special education (MS), including developmental disabilities, learning disabilities. *Program availability:* Part-time, evening/weekend. *Degree requirements:* For master's, comprehensive exam, thesis.

Winston-Salem State University, MAT Program, Winston-Salem, NC 27110-0003. Offers middle grades education (MAT); special education (MAT). *Accreditation:* NCATE. *Program availability:* Part-time, evening/weekend, online learning. *Entrance requirements:* For master's, GRE, MAT, NC teacher licensure. Electronic applications accepted. *Faculty research:* Action research on issues in elementary classroom.

Winthrop University, College of Education, Program in Special Education, Rock Hill, SC 29733. Offers M Ed. *Accreditation:* NCATE. *Program availability:* Part-time. *Entrance requirements:* For master's, PRAXIS, South Carolina Class III Teaching Certificate, sample of written work. Additional exam requirements/recommendations for international students: Required—TOEFL (minimum score 550 paper-based; 79 iBT), IELTS (minimum score 6). Electronic applications accepted. *Expenses:* Tuition, state resident: full-time $14,312; part-time $599 per credit hour. Tuition, nonresident: full-time $27,570; part-time $1153 per credit hour.

Worcester State University, Graduate Studies, Department of Education, Program in Moderate Disabilities, Worcester, MA 01602-2597. Offers M Ed, Postbaccalaureate Certificate. *Program availability:* Part-time, evening/weekend. *Faculty:* 13 full-time (12 women), 16 part-time/adjunct (7 women). *Students:* 25 part-time (22 women); includes 1 minority (Hispanic/Latino). Average age 35. 37 applicants, 59% accepted, 14 enrolled. In 2016, 11 master's, 12 other advanced degrees awarded. *Degree requirements:* For master's, comprehensive exam (for some programs), thesis optional. *Entrance requirements:* For master's, GRE General Test or MAT, initial license as a Teacher of Students with Moderate Disabilities from the Commonwealth of Massachusetts; for Postbaccalaureate Certificate, MTEL (Communication and Literacy, Foundations of Reading, and General Curriculum), bachelor's degree with minimum GPA of 2.7. Additional exam requirements/recommendations for international students: Required—TOEFL (minimum score 550 paper-based; 79 iBT). *Application deadline:* For fall admission, 6/15 for domestic and international students; for spring admission, 11/1 for domestic and international students; for summer admission, 4/1 for domestic and international students. Applications are processed on a rolling basis. Application fee: $50. Electronic applications accepted. *Expenses:* Tuition, state resident: part-time $150 per credit. Tuition, nonresident: part-time $150 per credit. *Financial support:* Career-related internships or fieldwork, scholarships/grants, and unspecified assistantships available. Financial award application deadline: 3/1; financial award applicants required to submit FAFSA. *Unit head:* Dr. Sue Fan Foo, Coordinator, 508-929-8071, Fax: 508-929-8164, E-mail: sfoo@worcester.edu. *Application contact:* Sara Grady, Associate Dean for Graduate Studies and Professional Development, 508-929-8787, Fax: 508-929-8100, E-mail: sara.grady@worcester.edu.

Wright State University, Graduate School, College of Education and Human Services, Department of Teacher Education, Programs in Intervention Specialist, Dayton, OH 45435. Offers intervention specialist (M Ed). *Accreditation:* NCATE. *Degree requirements:* For master's, thesis (for some programs). *Entrance requirements:* For master's, GRE General Test, MAT. Additional exam requirements/recommendations for international students: Required—TOEFL. Application fee: $25. *Expenses:* Tuition, state resident: full-time $9952; part-time $622 per credit hour. Tuition, nonresident: full-time $16,960; part-time $1060 per credit hour. *Financial support:* Available to part-time students. Applicants required to submit FAFSA. *Unit head:* Dr. Patricia R. Renick, Program Advisor, 937-775-2677, Fax: 937-775-3308, E-mail: patricia.renick@wright.edu. *Application contact:* John Kimble, Associate Director of Graduate Admissions and Records, 937-775-2957, Fax: 937-775-2453, E-mail: john.kimble@wright.edu.

Xavier University, College of Social Sciences, Health and Education, School of Education, Department of Secondary and Special Education, Cincinnati, OH 45207. Offers secondary education (M Ed); special education (M Ed). *Entrance requirements:* Additional exam requirements/recommendations for international students: Required—TOEFL (minimum score 550 paper-based; 79 iBT). Application fee is waived when completed online. *Expenses:* Contact institution.

Youngstown State University, Graduate School, Beeghly College of Education, Department of Teacher Education, Program in Special Education, Youngstown, OH 44555-0001. Offers gifted and talented education (MS Ed); special education (MS Ed). *Accreditation:* NCATE. *Program availability:* Part-time, evening/weekend. *Degree requirements:* For master's, comprehensive exam. *Entrance requirements:* For master's, GRE, MAT, or teaching certificate; interview; minimum GPA of 2.7. Additional exam requirements/recommendations for international students: Required—TOEFL. *Faculty research:* Learning disabilities, learning styles, developing self-esteem and social skills of severe behaviorally handicapped students, inclusion.

Urban Education

Alvernia University, School of Graduate Studies, Program in Education, Reading, PA 19607-1799. Offers urban education (M Ed). *Program availability:* Part-time, evening/weekend. *Degree requirements:* For master's, thesis optional. *Entrance requirements:* For master's, GRE or MAT (alumni excluded). Electronic applications accepted.

Bakke Graduate University, Programs in Pastoral Ministry and Business, Dallas, TX 75243-7039. Offers business administration (MBA); church and ministry multiplication (D Min); global urban leadership (MA); leadership (D Min); ministry in complex contexts (D Min); social and civic entrepreneurship (MA); theology of work (D Min); theology reflection (D Min); transformational leadership (DTL); urban youth ministry (D Min). *Program availability:* Part-time, online learning. *Degree requirements:* For master's, thesis; for doctorate, thesis/dissertation. *Entrance requirements:* For master's, 2 years of ministry experience, BA in Biblical studies or theology; for doctorate, 3 years of ministry experience, M Div. Additional exam requirements/recommendations for international students: Required—TOEFL. Electronic applications accepted. *Faculty research:* Theological systems, church management, worship.

Brown University, Graduate School, Department of Education, Program in Urban Education Policy, Providence, RI 02912. Offers AM. *Entrance requirements:* For master's, GRE General Test, official transcripts, 3 letters of recommendation, personal statement. Additional exam requirements/recommendations for international students: Required—TOEFL. Electronic applications accepted. *Faculty research:* Mayoral control of school systems.

Cardinal Stritch University, College of Education and Leadership, Department of Education, Milwaukee, WI 53217-3985. Offers educational leadership (MS); higher education student affairs leadership (MS); leadership for the advancement of learning and service (Ed D, PhD); leadership for the advancement of learning and service in higher education (Ed D, PhD); teaching (MAT); urban education (MA). *Accreditation:* NCATE. *Program availability:* Evening/weekend. *Degree requirements:* For master's, comprehensive exam, thesis (for some programs), research project, faculty recommendation; for doctorate, thesis/dissertation, practica, field experience. *Entrance requirements:* For master's, 3 letters of recommendation, minimum GPA of 3.0; for doctorate, minimum GPA of 3.5 in master's coursework, 3 letters of recommendation. *Application deadline:* For fall admission, 7/15 priority date for domestic students; for spring admission, 12/15 priority date for domestic students. Applications are processed on a rolling basis. Application fee: $25. *Expenses: Tuition:* Full-time $11,890; part-time $765 per credit hour. Tuition and fees vary according to class time, course load, degree level, program and student's religious affiliation. *Financial support:* Fellowships, research assistantships with partial tuition reimbursements, career-related internships or fieldwork, Federal Work-Study, and scholarships/grants available. Financial award applicants required to submit FAFSA. *Unit head:* Dr. Nancy Blair, Chair, 414-410-4367. *Application contact:* 800-347-8822 Ext. 4042, E-mail: gradadm@stritch.edu.

Cheyney University of Pennsylvania, Graduate Programs, Program in Urban Education, Cheyney, PA 19319. Offers M Ed. *Program availability:* Part-time, evening/weekend. *Degree requirements:* For master's, thesis or alternative. Electronic applications accepted.

Claremont Graduate University, Graduate Programs, School of Educational Studies, Claremont, CA 91711-6160. Offers Africana education (Certificate); education and policy (MA, PhD); higher education/student affairs (MA, PhD); human development (MA, PhD); public school administration (MA, PhD); quantitative evaluation (MA, PhD); special education (MA, PhD); teacher education (MA); teaching and learning (MA, PhD); urban leadership (PhD); MBA/PhD. PhD program offered jointly with San Diego State University. *Program availability:* Part-time. *Faculty:* 14 full-time (9 women), 1 part-time/adjunct (0 women). *Students:* 195 full-time (143 women), 196 part-time (137 women); includes 217 minority (43 Black or African American, non-Hispanic/Latino; 4 American Indian or Alaska Native, non-Hispanic/Latino; 32 Asian, non-Hispanic/Latino; 117 Hispanic/Latino; 2 Native Hawaiian or other Pacific Islander, non-Hispanic/Latino; 19 Two or more races, non-Hispanic/Latino), 14 international. Average age 38. In 2016, 48 master's, 39 doctorates, 7 other advanced degrees awarded. Terminal master's awarded for partial completion of doctoral program. *Entrance requirements:* For master's and doctorate, GRE General Test. Additional exam requirements/recommendations for international students: Required—TOEFL (minimum score 75 iBT). *Application deadline:* For fall admission, 3/1 priority date for domestic and international students. Applications are processed on a rolling basis. Application fee: $80. Electronic applications accepted. *Expenses: Tuition:* Full-time $44,328; part-time $1847 per unit. *Required fees:* $600; $300 per semester. Tuition and fees vary according to course load and program. *Financial support:* Fellowships, research assistantships, Federal Work-Study, institutionally sponsored loans, and scholarships/grants available. Support available to part-time students. Financial award application deadline: 2/15; financial award applicants required to submit FAFSA. *Faculty research:* Education administration, K-12 and higher education, multicultural education, education policy, diversity in higher education, faculty issues. *Unit head:* Allen Omoto, Dean, 909-607-3786, E-mail: allen.omoto@cgu.edu. *Application contact:* Rachel Camacho, Senior Assistant Director of Admission, 909-607-9418, E-mail: camacho@cgu.edu.
Website: https://www.cgu.edu/school/school-of-educational-studies/

Cleveland State University, College of Graduate Studies, College of Education and Human Services, Program in Urban Education, Cleveland, OH 44115. Offers PhD. *Program availability:* Part-time. *Faculty:* 19 full-time (10 women), 12 part-time/adjunct (7 women). *Students:* 27 full-time (20 women), 60 part-time (40 women); includes 27 minority (20 Black or African American, non-Hispanic/Latino; 4 Hispanic/Latino; 3 Two or more races, non-Hispanic/Latino), 7 international. Average age 40. In 2016, 12 doctorates awarded. *Degree requirements:* For doctorate, one foreign language, comprehensive exam, thesis/dissertation. *Entrance requirements:* For doctorate, GRE General Test, minimum graduate GPA of 3.25. Additional exam requirements/recommendations for international students: Required—TOEFL (minimum score 550 paper-based; 78 iBT), IELTS (minimum score 6). *Application deadline:* For fall admission, 2/1 for domestic and international students. Application fee: $30. *Expenses:* Tuition, state resident: full-time $9565. Tuition, nonresident: full-time $17,980. Tuition and fees vary according to program. *Financial support:* In 2016–17, 16 students received support, including 12 research assistantships with tuition reimbursements available (averaging $10,325 per year), 4 teaching assistantships with tuition reimbursements available (averaging $10,325 per year); tuition waivers (full and partial) and tuition grants with hourly work assignments also available. Financial award application deadline: 4/30; financial award applicants required to submit FAFSA. *Faculty research:* Equity issues (race, ethnicity, and gender), education development consequences for special needs of urban populations, urban education programming, counseling the violent or aggressive adolescent. *Unit head:* Dr. Graham Stead, Director, 216-875-9869, Fax: 216-875-9697, E-mail: g.b.stead@csuohio.edu. *Application contact:* Rita M. Grabowski, Administrative Coordinator, 216-687-4697, Fax: 216-875-9697, E-mail: r.grabowski@csuohio.edu.
Website: http://www.csuohio.edu/cehs/doc/doc

College of Mount Saint Vincent, School of Professional and Graduate Studies, Department of Teacher Education, Riverdale, NY 10471-1093. Offers instructional technology and global perspectives (Certificate); middle level education (Certificate); multicultural studies (Certificate); teaching English to speakers of other languages (MS Ed); urban and multicultural education (MS Ed). *Accreditation:* TEAC. *Program availability:* Part-time. *Degree requirements:* For master's, comprehensive exam. *Entrance requirements:* For master's, interview, New York teaching certificate. Additional exam requirements/recommendations for international students: Required—TOEFL.

Eastern Michigan University, Graduate School, College of Education, Department of Teacher Education, Program in Urban/Diversity Education, Ypsilanti, MI 48197. Offers MA. *Students:* 1 (woman) part-time; minority (Asian, non-Hispanic/Latino). Average age 26. In 2016, 1 master's awarded. Application fee: $45. *Application contact:* Dr. Patricia Williams-Boyd, Advisor, 734-487-3260, Fax: 734-487-2101, E-mail: pwilliams1@emich.edu.

Eastern Michigan University, Graduate School, College of Education, Department of Teacher Education, Programs in Curriculum and Instruction, Ypsilanti, MI 48197. Offers advanced teaching and learning (MA); early literacy instruction (Graduate Certificate); instructional leadership (MA); learning, motivation and creativity (Graduate Certificate); literacy coaching (Graduate Certificate); online teaching (Certificate); secondary literacy instruction (Graduate Certificate); urban and diversity education (MA). *Students:* 1 (woman) full-time, 31 part-time (29 women); includes 6 minority (2 Black or African American, non-Hispanic/Latino; 2 Asian, non-Hispanic/Latino; 2 Two or more races, non-Hispanic/Latino), 1 international. Average age 33. 11 applicants, 73% accepted, 4 enrolled. In 2016, 8 master's, 1 other advanced degree awarded. Application fee: $45. *Application contact:* Dr. Virginia Harder, Graduate Coordinator/Advisor, 734-487-2729, Fax: 734-487-2101, E-mail: vharder1@emich.edu.

Florida International University, College of Arts, Sciences, and Education, Department of Leadership and Professional Studies, Miami, FL 33199. Offers adult education and human resource development (MS, Ed D); counseling (MS), including rehabilitation counseling, school counseling; counselor education (MS), including clinical mental health counseling; educational administration and supervision (Ed D); educational leadership (MS, Certificate, Ed S); higher education (Ed D); higher education administration (MS); international and comparative education (MS); recreation and sport management (MS), including recreation and sport management, recreational therapy; school psychology (Ed S); urban education (MS), including instruction in urban settings, learning technologies, multicultural/bilingual, multicultural/TESOL, urban education. *Program availability:* Part-time, evening/weekend. *Faculty:* 27 full-time (19 women), 38 part-time/adjunct (25 women). *Students:* 253 full-time (191 women), 306 part-time (241 women); includes 444 minority (129 Black or African American, non-Hispanic/Latino; 3 Asian, non-Hispanic/Latino; 304 Hispanic/Latino; 8 Two or more races, non-Hispanic/Latino), 18 international. Average age 31. 366 applicants, 60% accepted, 115 enrolled. In 2016, 193 master's, 8 doctorates awarded. *Degree requirements:* For doctorate, thesis/dissertation. *Entrance requirements:* For master's, minimum GPA of 3.0; for doctorate and other advanced degree, GRE General Test. Additional exam requirements/recommendations for international students: Required—TOEFL (minimum score 550 paper-based; 80 iBT), IELTS (minimum score 6.3). *Application deadline:* For fall admission, 6/1 priority date for domestic students, 4/1 for international students; for winter admission, 10/1 priority date for domestic students, 9/1 for international students; for spring admission, 3/1 priority date for domestic students, 2/1 for international students. Applications are processed on a rolling basis. Application fee: $30. Electronic applications accepted. *Expenses:* Tuition, state resident: full-time $8912; part-time $446 per credit hour. Tuition, nonresident: full-time $21,393; part-time $992 per credit hour. *Required fees:* $2185; $195 per semester. Tuition and fees vary according to program. *Financial support:* Fellowships, research assistantships with tuition reimbursements, teaching assistantships with tuition reimbursements, Federal Work-Study, and tuition waivers (full and partial) available. Support available to part-time students. Financial award applicants required to submit FAFSA. *Unit head:* Dr. Benjamin Baez, Chair, 305-348-3214, Fax: 305-348-1515, E-mail: benjamin.baez@fiu.edu. *Application contact:* Nanett Rojas, Assistant Director, Graduate Admissions, 305-348-7464, Fax: 305-348-7441, E-mail: gradadm@fiu.edu.
Website: http://education.fiu.edu

Georgia State University, College of Education and Human Development, Department of Early Childhood Education, Atlanta, GA 30302-3083. Offers early childhood and elementary education (PhD); early childhood education (M Ed, Ed S); mathematics education (M Ed); urban education (M Ed). *Accreditation:* NCATE. *Program availability:* Part-time, evening/weekend. *Faculty:* 27 full-time (22 women). *Students:* 68 full-time (60 women), 7 part-time (all women); includes 40 minority (33 Black or African American, non-Hispanic/Latino; 1 Asian, non-Hispanic/Latino; 4 Hispanic/Latino; 2 Two or more races, non-Hispanic/Latino), 3 international. Average age 32. 16 applicants, 44% accepted, 6 enrolled. In 2016, 35 master's, 4 doctorates awarded. *Degree requirements:* For master's, comprehensive exam (for some programs), thesis (for some programs); for doctorate, comprehensive exam, thesis/dissertation (for some programs); for Ed S, comprehensive exam (for some programs). *Entrance requirements:* For master's, GRE, undergraduate diploma; for doctorate and Ed S, GRE, master's degree. Additional exam requirements/recommendations for international students: Required—TOEFL (minimum score 550 paper-based; 79 iBT) or IELTS (minimum score 6.5). *Application deadline:* Applications are processed on a rolling basis. Application fee: $50. Electronic applications accepted. *Expenses:* Tuition, state resident: full-time $6876; part-time $382 per credit hour. Tuition, nonresident: full-time $22,374; part-time $1243 per credit hour. *Required fees:* $2128; $1064 per term. Part-time tuition and fees vary according to course load and program. *Financial support:* In 2016–17, fellowships with full tuition reimbursements (averaging $24,000 per year), research assistantships with tuition reimbursements (averaging $4,000 per year), teaching assistantships with full tuition reimbursements (averaging $2,000 per year) were awarded; career-related internships or fieldwork, Federal Work-Study, institutionally sponsored loans, scholarships/grants, traineeships, health care benefits, tuition waivers (partial), and unspecified assistantships also available. Support available to part-time students. Financial award applicants required to submit FAFSA. *Faculty research:* Teacher development; language arts/literacy education; mathematics education; intersection of science, urban, and multicultural education; diversity in education. *Unit head:* Dr. Barbara Meyers, Department Chair, 404-413-8021, Fax: 404-413-8023, E-mail: barbara@gsu.edu. *Application contact:* Elaine King Jones, Administrative Curriculum Specialist, 404-413-8234, Fax: 404-413-8023, E-mail: ekjones@gsu.edu.
Website: http://ecee.education.gsu.edu/

Georgia State University, College of Education and Human Development, Department of Educational Policy Studies, Program in Educational Leadership, Atlanta, GA 30302-3083. Offers educational leadership (M Ed, Ed D, Ed S); urban teacher leadership (M Ed). *Accreditation:* NCATE. *Program availability:* Part-time. *Degree requirements:* For master's, comprehensive exam, thesis or alternative, 36 semester hours; for doctorate, comprehensive exam, thesis/dissertation, 54 semester hours (for Ed D); 69 semester hours (for PhD); for Ed S, thesis, 30 semester hours of coursework. *Entrance requirements:* For master's, GRE; for doctorate and Ed S, GRE, MAT. Additional exam requirements/recommendations for international students: Required—TOEFL (minimum score 550 paper-based; 79 iBT) or IELTS (minimum score 6.5). *Application deadline:* For fall admission, 5/1 for domestic and international students; for winter admission, 2/1 for domestic students; for spring admission, 10/1 for domestic and international students. Applications are processed on a rolling basis. Application fee: $50. Electronic applications accepted. *Expenses:* Tuition, state resident: full-time $6876; part-time $382 per credit hour. Tuition, nonresident: full-time $22,374; part-time $1243 per credit hour. *Required fees:* $2128; $1064 per term. Part-time tuition and fees vary according to course load and program. *Financial support:* In 2016–17, research assistantships with full tuition reimbursements (averaging $6,000 per year) were awarded; fellowships, teaching assistantships with full tuition reimbursements, career-related internships or fieldwork, scholarships/grants, health care benefits, tuition waivers, and unspecified assistantships also available. Support available to part-time students. Financial award application deadline: 3/15. *Faculty research:* Practices with diverse populations, leadership and success, the cohort model of instruction, technology in the schools, instructional supervision and academic coaching. *Unit head:* Dr. Jami Berry, Clinical Assistant Professor, 404-413-8030, Fax: 404-413-8003, E-mail: jberry2@gsu.edu. *Application contact:* Aishah Cowan, Administrative Academic Specialist, 404-413-8273, Fax: 404-413-8033, E-mail: acowan@gsu.edu.
Website: http://eps.education.gsu.edu/programs-courses/educational-leadership/

The Graduate Center, City University of New York, Graduate Studies, Program in Urban Education, New York, NY 10016-4039. Offers PhD. *Entrance requirements:* For doctorate, GRE General Test. Additional exam requirements/recommendations for international students: Required—TOEFL. Electronic applications accepted.

Grand View University, Graduate Studies, Des Moines, IA 50316-1599. Offers athletic training (MS); clinical nurse leader (MSN, Post Master's Certificate); nursing education (MSN, Post Master's Certificate); organizational leadership (MS); sport management (MS); teacher leadership (M Ed); urban education (M Ed). *Program availability:* Part-time, evening/weekend. *Degree requirements:* For master's, completion of all required coursework in common core and selected track with minimum cumulative GPA of 3.0 and no more than two grades of C. *Entrance requirements:* For master's, GRE, GMAT, or essay, minimum undergraduate GPA of 3.0, professional resume, 3 letters of recommendation, interview. Additional exam requirements/recommendations for international students: Required—TOEFL (minimum score 550 paper-based). Electronic applications accepted.

Holy Names University, Graduate Division, Department of Education, Oakland, CA 94619-1699. Offers educational therapy (Certificate); mild/moderate disabilities (Ed S); multiple subject teaching (Credential); single subject teaching (Credential); urban education: educational therapy (M Ed); urban education: K-12 education (M Ed); urban education: special education (M Ed). *Program availability:* Part-time. *Students:* 18 full-time (11 women), 111 part-time (79 women); includes 74 minority (37 Black or African American, non-Hispanic/Latino; 1 American Indian or Alaska Native, non-Hispanic/Latino; 10 Asian, non-Hispanic/Latino; 24 Hispanic/Latino; 1 Native Hawaiian or other Pacific Islander, non-Hispanic/Latino; 1 Two or more races, non-Hispanic/Latino), 3 international. Average age 35. 62 applicants, 81% accepted, 39 enrolled. In 2016, 11 master's, 33 Certificates awarded. *Degree requirements:* For master's, comprehensive exam, research paper, thesis or project. *Entrance requirements:* For master's, minimum undergraduate GPA of 2.6 overall, 3.0 in major; personal statement; two recommendations; interview. Additional exam requirements/recommendations for international students: Required—TOEFL (minimum score 550 paper-based; 79 iBT). *Application deadline:* For fall admission, 8/1 priority date for domestic students, 7/15 for international students; for spring admission, 12/1 priority date for domestic students, 12/1 for international students; for summer admission, 5/1 priority date for domestic students, 5/1 for international students. Applications are processed on a rolling basis. Application fee: $65. Electronic applications accepted. Application fee is waived when completed online. *Expenses: Tuition:* Full-time $17,532; part-time $974 per credit hour. *Required fees:* $500; $250 per credit hour. *Financial support:* Career-related internships or fieldwork, Federal Work-Study, scholarships/grants, and unspecified assistantships available. Support available to part-time students. Financial award application deadline: 3/2; financial award applicants required to submit FAFSA. *Faculty research:* Cognitive development, language development, learning handicaps. *Unit head:* Dr. Kimberly Mayfield, Chair, 510-436-1396, Fax: 510-436-1325, E-mail: mayfield@hnu.edu. *Application contact:* Graduate Admission, 800-430-1321, Fax: 510-436-1325, E-mail: graduateadmissions@hnu.edu.
Website: http://www.hnu.edu/academics/graduatePrograms/education.html

Johns Hopkins University, School of Education, Certificate Programs in Education, Baltimore, MD 21218. Offers advanced methods for differentiated instruction and inclusive education (Graduate Certificate); applied behavior analysis (Post-Master's Certificate); clinical mental health counseling (Post-Master's Certificate); counseling (Advanced Certificate); data-based decision making and organizational improvement (Graduate Certificate); early intervention/preschool special education specialist (Graduate Certificate); education of students with autism and other pervasive developmental disorders (Graduate Certificate); educational leadership for independent schools (Graduate Certificate); evidence-based teaching in the health professions (Post-Master's Certificate); gifted education (Graduate Certificate); leadership in technology integration (Graduate Certificate); mind, brain and teaching (Graduate Certificate); school administration and supervision (Graduate Certificate); urban education (Graduate Certificate). *Program availability:* Part-time-only, evening/weekend, 100% online, blended/hybrid learning. *Students:* 5 full-time (all women), 194 part-time (164 women); includes 46 minority (29 Black or African American, non-Hispanic/Latino; 2 American Indian or Alaska Native, non-Hispanic/Latino; 3 Asian, non-Hispanic/Latino; 8 Hispanic/Latino; 4 Two or more races, non-Hispanic/Latino), 7 international. Average age 37. 240 applicants, 75% accepted, 143 enrolled. In 2016, 167 Advanced Certificates awarded. *Entrance requirements:* For degree, minimum of bachelor's degree from regionally- or nationally-accredited institution (master's degree for some programs); minimum GPA of 3.0 in all previous programs of study; official transcripts from all post-secondary institutions attended; essay; curriculum vitae/resume; two letters of recommendation; dispositions survey. *Application deadline:* For fall admission, 4/1 priority date for domestic students; for spring admission, 10/1 priority date for domestic students; for summer admission, 2/1 priority date for domestic students. Applications are processed on a rolling basis. Application fee: $80. Electronic applications accepted. *Expenses:* Contact institution. *Financial support:* Application deadline: 4/1; applicants required to submit FAFSA. *Unit head:* Dr. Christopher C. Morphew, Dean. *Application contact:* Elisabeth Woodward, Director of Admissions, 410-516-9796, Fax: 410-516-9817, E-mail: soe.info@jhu.edu.
Website: http://education.jhu.edu

Langston University, School of Education and Behavioral Sciences, Langston, OK 73050. Offers bilingual/multicultural (M Ed); elementary education (M Ed); English as a second language (M Ed); rehabilitation counseling (M Sc); urban education (M Ed). *Accreditation:* CORE; NCATE (one or more programs are accredited). *Program availability:* Part-time. *Degree requirements:* For master's, comprehensive exam, thesis optional. *Entrance requirements:* For master's, GRE, writing skills test, minimum GPA of 2.5, 3 letters of recommendation. Additional exam requirements/recommendations for international students: Required—TOEFL, TWE. *Faculty research:* Bilingual/multicultural education, financing post-secondary education.

Long Island University–LIU Brooklyn, School of Education, Brooklyn, NY 11201-8423. Offers adolescence urban education (MS Ed); applied behavior analysis (Advanced Certificate); bilingual education (Advanced Certificate); bilingual school counselor (MS Ed, Advanced Certificate); childhood urban education (MS Ed); childhood/early childhood urban education (MS Ed); early childhood urban education (MS Ed, Advanced Certificate); educational leadership (Advanced Certificate); marriage and family therapy (MS, Advanced Certificate); mental health counseling (MS, Advanced Certificate); school building district leader (Advanced Certificate); school counselor (MS Ed, Advanced Certificate); school psychologist (MS Ed); teaching urban children/adolescents with disabilities (MS Ed); TESOL (MS Ed). *Accreditation:* TEAC. *Program availability:* Part-time, evening/weekend. *Faculty:* 23 full-time (17 women), 44 part-time/adjunct (32 women). *Students:* 161 full-time (144 women), 594 part-time (461 women); includes 493 minority (229 Black or African American, non-Hispanic/Latino; 1 American Indian or Alaska Native, non-Hispanic/Latino; 30 Asian, non-Hispanic/Latino; 218 Hispanic/Latino; 2 Native Hawaiian or other Pacific Islander, non-Hispanic/Latino; 13 Two or more races, non-Hispanic/Latino), 9 international. 513 applicants, 73% accepted, 272 enrolled. In 2016, 262 master's, 18 other advanced degrees awarded. *Degree requirements:* For master's, thesis optional, electronic portfolio. *Entrance requirements:* For master's, GRE (for MS Ed). Additional exam requirements/recommendations for international students: Required—TOEFL (minimum score 527 paper-based; 75 iBT). *Application deadline:* Applications are processed on a rolling basis. Application fee: $50. Electronic applications accepted. *Expenses: Tuition:* Full-time $28,272; part-time $1178 per credit. *Required fees:* $451 per term. Tuition and fees vary according to degree level, program and student level. *Financial support:* In 2016–17, 81 students received support. Career-related internships or fieldwork, Federal Work-Study, institutionally sponsored loans, scholarships/grants, and unspecified assistantships available. Support available to part-time students. Financial award application deadline: 2/15; financial award applicants required to submit FAFSA. *Faculty research:* Technology in education, teaching civics and sustainability, biliteracy and dual language instruction, diversity in organizations and leadership, counseling diverse couples and families. *Unit head:* Dr. Amy Ginsberg, Dean, 718-246-6308, E-mail: amy.ginsberg@liu.edu. *Application contact:* Gabrielle Gannon, Director of Graduate Admissions, 718-488-1011, Fax: 718-780-6110, E-mail: bkln-admissions@liu.edu.
Website: http://www.liu.edu/Brooklyn/Academics/School-of-Education

Loyola Marymount University, School of Education, Department of Specialized Programs in Urban Education, Program in Urban Education, Los Angeles, CA 90045-2659. Offers MA. *Students:* 115 full-time (80 women), 7 part-time (5 women); includes 92 minority (16 Black or African American, non-Hispanic/Latino; 11 Asian, non-Hispanic/Latino; 58 Hispanic/Latino; 1 Native Hawaiian or other Pacific Islander, non-Hispanic/Latino; 6 Two or more races, non-Hispanic/Latino), 4 international. Average age 25. 120 applicants, 100% accepted, 111 enrolled. In 2016, 120 master's awarded. *Entrance requirements:* For master's, CBEST, CSET, letters of recommendation, statement of intent, interview, verification of employment as full-time teacher. Additional exam requirements/recommendations for international students: Required—TOEFL (minimum score 600 paper-based; 100 iBT). *Application deadline:* For fall admission, 6/15 for domestic students; for spring admission, 11/15 for domestic students. Application fee: $50. Electronic applications accepted. *Financial support:* In 2016–17, 116 students received support. Scholarships/grants and unspecified assistantships available. Support available to part-time students. Financial award application deadline: 6/30; financial award applicants required to submit FAFSA. *Unit head:* Dr. Edmundo Litton, Chair, 310-338-1859, E-mail: elitton@lmu.edu. *Application contact:* Chake H. Kouyoumjian, Associate Dean of Graduate Studies, 310-338-2721, E-mail: ckouyoum@lmu.edu.
Website: http://soe.lmu.edu/

Manhattanville College, School of Education, Jump Start Program, Purchase, NY 10577-2132. Offers childhood and special education (MPS); education (Advanced Certificate); secondary subject areas and special education (MPS); TESOL (MPS). *Program availability:* Part-time, evening/weekend. *Students:* 26 applicants, 46% accepted, 7 enrolled. In 2016, 17 master's awarded. *Degree requirements:* For master's, comprehensive exam (for some programs), thesis (for some programs), student teaching, research seminars, portfolios, internships, writing assessment; for Advanced Certificate, comprehensive exam (for some programs). *Entrance requirements:* For master's, GRE or MAT, minimum undergraduate GPA of 3.0, 2 letters of recommendation, interview. Additional exam requirements/recommendations for international students: Required—TOEFL (minimum score 85 iBT); Recommended—IELTS. *Application deadline:* For fall admission, 7/1 priority date for domestic and international students; for spring admission, 11/1 priority date for domestic and international students; for summer admission, 4/1 priority date for domestic and international students. Applications are processed on a rolling basis. Application fee: $75. Electronic applications accepted. *Expenses: Tuition:* Full-time $16,470; part-time $915 per credit. *Required fees:* $60 per semester. Part-time tuition and fees vary according to course load and program. *Financial support:* Teaching assistantships, career-related internships or fieldwork, Federal Work-Study, institutionally sponsored loans, scholarships/grants, and unspecified assistantships available. Financial award applicants required to submit FAFSA. *Unit head:* Robert Cooper, Program Director, 914-323-5368, E-mail: robert.cooper@mville.edu. *Application contact:* Jeanine Pardey-Levine, Director of Graduate Enrollment Management, 914-323-3208, Fax: 914-694-1732, E-mail: edschool@mville.edu.
Website: http://www.mville.edu/programs/jump-start

Marygrove College, Graduate Division, Griot Program, Detroit, MI 48221-2599. Offers M Ed. *Accreditation:* TEAC.

Morgan State University, School of Graduate Studies, School of Education and Urban Studies, Department of Advanced Studies, Leadership and Policy, Program in Educational Administration and Supervision, Baltimore, MD 21251. Offers urban educational leadership (Ed D). *Accreditation:* NCATE. *Program availability:* Part-time, evening/weekend. *Faculty research:* Multicultural education, cooperative learning, psychology of cognition.

New Jersey City University, Debra Cannon Partridge Wolfe College of Education, Department of Educational Leadership and Counseling, Jersey City, NJ 07305-1597. Offers counselor education (MA); educational administration and supervision (MA); urban education (MA). *Accreditation:* TEAC. *Program availability:* Part-time, evening/weekend. *Entrance requirements:* Additional exam requirements/recommendations for international students: Required—TOEFL (minimum score 79 iBT).

New Jersey City University, Debra Cannon Partridge Wolfe College of Education, Department of Modern Languages, Jersey City, NJ 07305-1597. Offers urban education world language (MA).

Norfolk State University, School of Graduate Studies, School of Education, Department of Secondary Education and School Leadership, Program in Urban Education/Administration, Norfolk, VA 23504. Offers teaching (MA). *Accreditation:* NCATE. *Program availability:* Part-time. *Entrance requirements:* For master's, GRE General Test, PRAXIS I, minimum GPA of 3.0 in major, 2.5 overall.

Northeastern Illinois University, College of Graduate Studies and Research, College of Education, Program in Inner City Studies, Chicago, IL 60625-4699. Offers MA. *Program availability:* Part-time, evening/weekend. *Degree requirements:* For master's, comprehensive exam, thesis or alternative. *Entrance requirements:* For master's, minimum GPA of 2.75. Additional exam requirements/recommendations for international students: Required—TOEFL (minimum score 550 paper-based; 79 iBT). Electronic applications accepted.

Providence College, Program in Urban Teaching, Providence, RI 02918. Offers M Ed. *Program availability:* Part-time, evening/weekend. *Faculty:* 6 full-time (4 women), 33 part-time/adjunct (21 women). *Students:* 9 full-time (7 women), 21 part-time (16 women); includes 7 minority (4 Black or African American, non-Hispanic/Latino; 1 Asian, non-Hispanic/Latino; 1 Hispanic/Latino; 1 Two or more races, non-Hispanic/Latino). Average age 31. 18 applicants, 100% accepted, 16 enrolled. In 2016, 7 master's awarded. *Entrance requirements:* Additional exam requirements/recommendations for international students: Required—TOEFL (minimum score 577 paper-based; 90 iBT). *Application deadline:* For fall admission, 7/15 priority date for domestic students, 7/15 for international students; for spring admission, 11/15 priority date for domestic students, 11/15 for international students; for summer admission, 3/15 priority date for domestic students, 3/15 for international students. Application fee: $55. *Expenses: Tuition:* Part-time $1260 per course. One-time fee: $265. Tuition and fees vary according to course load and program. *Financial support:* Career-related internships or fieldwork, institutionally sponsored loans, and unspecified assistantships available. Support

available to part-time students. Financial award application deadline: 8/1; financial award applicants required to submit FAFSA.
Website: http://www.providence.edu/professional-studies/graduate-degrees/Pages/master-education-urban-teaching.aspx

Teachers College, Columbia University, Department of Organization and Leadership, New York, NY 10027-6696. Offers adult education guided intensive study (Ed D); adult learning and leadership (Ed M, MA, Ed D); educational leadership (Ed D); higher and postsecondary education (MA, Ed D); leadership, policy and politics (Ed D); nurse executive (MA, Ed D), including administration studies (MA), professorial studies (MA); private school leadership (Ed M, MA); public school building leadership (Ed M, MA); social and organizational psychology (MA); urban education leaders (Ed D); MA/MBA. *Program availability:* Part-time, evening/weekend. *Students:* 310 full-time (214 women), 390 part-time (250 women); includes 276 minority (116 Black or African American, non-Hispanic/Latino; 3 American Indian or Alaska Native, non-Hispanic/Latino; 61 Asian, non-Hispanic/Latino; 79 Hispanic/Latino; 17 Two or more races, non-Hispanic/Latino), 93 international. 624 applicants, 57% accepted, 172 enrolled. *Degree requirements:* For doctorate, thesis/dissertation. *Expenses: Tuition:* Full-time $36,288; part-time $1512 per credit. *Required fees:* $438 per semester. One-time fee: $510 full-time. Full-time tuition and fees vary according to course load. *Unit head:* Prof. Anna Neumann, Chair, 212-678-3272, Fax: 212-678-3036, E-mail: neumann@tc.columbia.edu. *Application contact:* David Estrella, Director of Admission, 212-678-3305, E-mail: estrella@tc.columbia.edu.

Temple University, College of Education, Department of Teaching and Learning, Philadelphia, PA 19122-6096. Offers career and technical education (Ed M), including business, computing, and information technology, industrial education, marketing education; middle grades education (Ed M), including math and language arts, math and science, science and language arts; secondary education (Ed M), including English, math, social studies; teaching English to speakers of other languages (MS Ed); urban education (Ed M). *Program availability:* Part-time, evening/weekend. *Faculty:* 26 full-time (16 women), 74 part-time/adjunct (54 women). *Students:* 204 full-time (139 women), 320 part-time (201 women); includes 112 minority (66 Black or African American, non-Hispanic/Latino; 17 Asian, non-Hispanic/Latino; 18 Hispanic/Latino; 11 Two or more races, non-Hispanic/Latino), 18 international. 300 applicants, 55% accepted, 99 enrolled. In 2016, 93 master's awarded. Terminal master's awarded for partial completion of doctoral program. *Degree requirements:* For master's, thesis or alternative. *Entrance requirements:* Additional exam requirements/recommendations for international students: Required—TOEFL (minimum score 550 paper-based; 79 iBT). *Application deadline:* For fall admission, 4/1 for domestic students, 12/15 for international students; for spring admission, 10/1 for domestic students, 8/1 for international students. Application fee: $60. Electronic applications accepted. *Expenses:* Contact institution. *Financial support:* Fellowships, research assistantships, and teaching assistantships available. Financial award application deadline: 1/15; financial award applicants required to submit FAFSA. *Faculty research:* Workforce development, vocational education, technical education, industrial education, professional development, literacy, classroom management, school communities, curriculum development, instruction, applied linguistics, cross linguistic influence, bilingual education, oral proficiency, multilingualism. *Unit head:* Dr. Christine Woyshner, Chairperson, 215-204-6387, E-mail: christine.woyshner@temple.edu. *Application contact:* Sarah Stapleton, Assistant Director, Academic Operations, 215-204-8220, E-mail: sarah.stapleton@temple.edu.
Website: http://education.temple.edu/tl

University of Chicago, Graham School of Continuing Liberal and Professional Studies, Urban Teacher Education Program, Chicago, IL 60637. Offers MAT. *Students:* 34 full-time (24 women), 28 part-time (17 women); includes 31 minority (12 Black or African American, non-Hispanic/Latino; 6 Asian, non-Hispanic/Latino; 12 Hispanic/Latino; 1 Two or more races, non-Hispanic/Latino). Average age 29. 51 applicants, 92% accepted, 32 enrolled. *Degree requirements:* For master's, exams. *Entrance requirements:* For master's, ACT or TAP. *Application deadline:* For winter admission, 1/11 for domestic students. Application fee: $50. Electronic applications accepted. *Financial support:* Federal Work-Study and institutionally sponsored loans available. Financial award application deadline: 1/11; financial award applicants required to submit FAFSA. *Unit head:* Tanika Island, Director, Urban Education Institute, 773-702-2797. *Application contact:* Candis Jackson, Recruiter, E-mail: candis@uchicago.edu.
Website: http://utep.uchicago.edu/

University of Houston–Downtown, College of Public Service, Department of Urban Education, Houston, TX 77002. Offers curriculum and instruction (MAT); elementary and secondary education (MAT). *Program availability:* Part-time, evening/weekend, 100% online. *Faculty:* 6 full-time (2 women), 2 part-time/adjunct (both women). *Students:* 7 full-time (3 women), 47 part-time (42 women); includes 45 minority (18 Black or African American, non-Hispanic/Latino; 6 Asian, non-Hispanic/Latino; 21 Hispanic/Latino). Average age 34. 36 applicants, 89% accepted, 28 enrolled. In 2016, 11 master's awarded. *Degree requirements:* For master's, capstone course with completed project, position paper, grant proposal, empirical study, curriculum development/revision, or advanced technology project presented at annual Graduate Project Exhibition. *Entrance requirements:* For master's, GRE, personal statement, 3 recommendation forms. Additional exam requirements/recommendations for international students: Required—TOEFL (minimum score 550 paper-based; 80 iBT). *Application deadline:* For fall admission, 7/15 for domestic and international students; for spring admission, 11/15 for domestic and international students. Application fee: $35 ($60 for international students). Electronic applications accepted. *Expenses:* $305.50 in-state, per credit; $663.50 out-of-state, per credit. *Financial support:* Federal Work-Study and scholarships/grants available. Financial award application deadline: 4/1; financial award applicants required to submit FAFSA. *Unit head:* Dr. Ron Beebe, Department Chair, 713-221-0680, Fax: 713-226-5294, E-mail: beeber@uhd.edu. *Application contact:* Ceshia Love, Director of Graduate and International Admissions, 713-221-8093, Fax: 713-223-7408, E-mail: gradadmissions@uhd.edu.
Website: https://www.uhd.edu/academics/public-service/urban-education/Pages/default.aspx

University of Illinois at Chicago, College of Education, Department of Educational Policy Studies, Chicago, IL 60607-7128. Offers policy studies (M Ed); policy studies in urban education (PhD); urban education leadership (Ed D). *Faculty research:* Social foundations of education, educational organizations and leadership, education policy analysis, understanding and addressing educational problems in urban contexts.

University of Massachusetts Boston, College of Education and Human Development, Program in Urban Education, Leadership, and Policy Studies, Boston, MA 02125-3393. Offers Ed D, PhD. *Program availability:* Part-time, evening/weekend. *Degree requirements:* For doctorate, comprehensive exam, thesis/dissertation. *Entrance requirements:* For doctorate, GRE General Test or MAT, minimum GPA of 2.75. *Expenses:* Tuition, state resident: full-time $16,863. Tuition, nonresident: full-time $32,913. *Required fees:* $177. *Faculty research:* School reform, race and culture in schools, race and higher education, language, literacy and writing.

University of Memphis, Graduate School, College of Education, Department of Instruction and Curriculum Leadership, Memphis, TN 38152. Offers advanced studies in teaching and learning (M Ed); applied behavior analysis (Graduate Certificate); autism studies (Graduate Certificate); early childhood education (MAT, MS, Ed D); elementary education (MAT); instruction and curriculum (MS, Ed D); instruction design and technology (MS, Ed D); instructional design and technology (Graduate Certificate); literacy, leadership, and coaching (Graduate Certificate); reading (MS, Ed D); school library information specialist (Graduate Certificate); secondary education (MAT); special education (MAT, MS, Ed D); STEM teacher leadership (Graduate Certificate); urban education (Graduate Certificate). *Accreditation:* NCATE (one or more programs are accredited). *Program availability:* Part-time. *Faculty:* 24 full-time (14 women), 17 part-time/adjunct (12 women). *Students:* 66 full-time (52 women), 315 part-time (243 women); includes 163 minority (132 Black or African American, non-Hispanic/Latino; 1 American Indian or Alaska Native, non-Hispanic/Latino; 6 Asian, non-Hispanic/Latino; 13 Hispanic/Latino; 1 Native Hawaiian or other Pacific Islander, non-Hispanic/Latino; 10 Two or more races, non-Hispanic/Latino), 4 international. Average age 35. 215 applicants, 78% accepted, 120 enrolled. In 2016, 111 master's, 21 doctorates, 8 other advanced degrees awarded. Terminal master's awarded for partial completion of doctoral program. *Degree requirements:* For master's, comprehensive exam, thesis or alternative; for doctorate, comprehensive exam, thesis/dissertation. *Entrance requirements:* For master's, GRE General Test, PRAXIS, minimum GPA of 2.5, letters of reference; for doctorate, GRE General Test, GRE Subject Test, 2 years of teaching experience, letters of reference, statement of purpose, interview. Additional exam requirements/recommendations for international students: Required—TOEFL (minimum score 550 paper-based; 79 iBT). *Application deadline:* For fall admission, 4/1 priority date for domestic students; for spring admission, 10/1 priority date for domestic students; for summer admission, 2/1 priority date for domestic students. Applications are processed on a rolling basis. Application fee: $35 ($60 for international students). Electronic applications accepted. *Expenses:* $5,231.50 per semester full-time in-state, $9,623.50 full-time out-of-state. *Financial support:* In 2016–17, 2 research assistantships with full tuition reimbursements (averaging $10,000 per year), 3 teaching assistantships with full tuition reimbursements (averaging $10,666 per year) were awarded; career-related internships or fieldwork, Federal Work-Study, institutionally sponsored loans, scholarships/grants, traineeships, and unspecified assistantships also available. Support available to part-time students. Financial award application deadline: 2/1; financial award applicants required to submit FAFSA. *Faculty research:* Effective urban teachers, preparation and retention of urban teachers, technology utilization in schools, field-based teacher preparation programs, effective use of online instruction. *Unit head:* Dr. Angiline Powell, Interim Chair, 901-678-3310, E-mail: apowell3@memphis.edu. *Application contact:* Dr. James Meindl, Coordinator of Graduate Studies, 901-678-3310, E-mail: jnmeindl@memphis.edu.
Website: http://www.memphis.edu/icl/

University of Michigan–Dearborn, College of Education, Health, and Human Services, Doctoral Program in Education, Dearborn, MI 48126. Offers curriculum and practice (Ed D); educational leadership (Ed D); metropolitan education (Ed D). *Program availability:* Part-time, evening/weekend. *Faculty:* 27 full-time (19 women), 5 part-time/adjunct (0 women). *Students:* 2 full-time (both women), 21 part-time (15 women); includes 9 minority (7 Black or African American, non-Hispanic/Latino; 1 Asian, non-Hispanic/Latino; 1 Hispanic/Latino). Average age 43. 14 applicants, 64% accepted, 7 enrolled. In 2016, 3 doctorates awarded. *Degree requirements:* For doctorate, comprehensive exam, thesis/dissertation. *Entrance requirements:* For doctorate, GRE (taken within the last 5 years), master's degree with minimum GPA of 3.3, 3 letters of recommendation (1 from faculty), 3 years' professional and/or teaching experience. Additional exam requirements/recommendations for international students: Required—TOEFL (minimum score 560 paper-based; 84 iBT), IELTS (minimum score 6.5). *Application deadline:* For fall admission, 3/1 for domestic and international students. Application fee: $60. Electronic applications accepted. *Expenses:* Contact institution. *Financial support:* In 2016–17, 5 students received support. Scholarships/grants available. Financial award application deadline: 3/1; financial award applicants required to submit FAFSA. *Faculty research:* Educational leadership, English language learning, community-based education, urban education, educational technology. *Unit head:* Dr. Chris Burke, Director, 313-593-5319, E-mail: cjfburke@umich.edu. *Application contact:* Joann Otlewski, Program Assistant, 313-593-5090, E-mail: joanno@umich.edu.
Website: http://umdearborn.edu/cehhs/cehhs_edd/

University of Michigan–Dearborn, College of Education, Health, and Human Services, Master of Arts Program in Community Based Education, Dearborn, MI 48126. Offers MA. *Program availability:* Part-time, evening/weekend. *Faculty:* 6 full-time (4 women), 1 part-time/adjunct (0 women). *Students:* 4 part-time (3 women); includes 3 minority (2 Black or African American, non-Hispanic/Latino; 1 Two or more races, non-Hispanic/Latino). Average age 35. 6 applicants, 33% accepted, 2 enrolled. *Degree requirements:* For master's, essay. *Entrance requirements:* Additional exam requirements/recommendations for international students: Required—TOEFL (minimum score 560 paper-based; 84 iBT), IELTS (minimum score 6.5). *Application deadline:* For fall admission, 8/1 for domestic students, 5/1 for international students; for winter admission, 12/1 for domestic students, 9/1 for international students; for spring admission, 4/1 for domestic students, 1/1 for international students. Applications are processed on a rolling basis. Application fee: $60. Electronic applications accepted. *Expenses:* Contact institution. *Financial support:* Application deadline: 3/1; applicants required to submit FAFSA. *Faculty research:* Ecojustice education, multicultural education, place based education, urban education. *Unit head:* Dr. Chris Burke, Academic Advisor, 313-593-5319, E-mail: cjfburke@umich.edu. *Application contact:* Dr. Stein Brunvand, Director, Master's Programs, 313-583-6415, E-mail: sbrunvan@umich.edu.
Website: https://umdearborn.edu/cehhs/graduate-programs/areas-study/ma-community-based-education

University of Nebraska at Omaha, Graduate Studies, College of Education, Department of Teacher Education, Program in Secondary Education, Omaha, NE 68182. Offers instruction in urban schools (Certificate); secondary education (MS). *Accreditation:* NCATE. *Program availability:* Part-time, evening/weekend. *Faculty:* 8 full-time (all women). *Students:* 14 full-time (9 women), 61 part-time (45 women); includes 9 minority (3 Black or African American, non-Hispanic/Latino; 3 Asian, non-Hispanic/Latino; 2 Hispanic/Latino; 1 Two or more races, non-Hispanic/Latino), 1 international. Average age 34. 21 applicants, 71% accepted, 14 enrolled. In 2016, 22 master's awarded. *Degree requirements:* For master's, comprehensive exam, thesis (for some programs). *Entrance requirements:* For master's, minimum GPA of 3.0, transcripts. Additional exam requirements/recommendations for international students: Required—TOEFL, IELTS, PTE. *Application deadline:* For fall admission, 8/1 priority date for domestic and international students; for spring admission, 12/1 priority date for domestic and international students; for summer admission, 6/1 for domestic and international students. Applications are processed on a rolling basis. Application fee: $45. Electronic applications accepted. *Financial support:* In 2016–17, 2 students received support, including 2 research assistantships with tuition reimbursements available; fellowships, teaching assistantships with tuition reimbursements available, Federal Work-Study, institutionally sponsored loans, scholarships/grants, health care benefits, tuition waivers (full), and unspecified assistantships also available. Support available to part-time students. Financial award application deadline: 3/1. *Unit head:* Dr. Sarah Edwards, Chairperson, 402-554-2341, E-mail: graduate@unomaha.edu. *Application contact:* Dr.

Rebecca Pasco, Graduate Program Chair, 402-554-2341, E-mail: graduate@unomaha.edu.

University of Pennsylvania, Graduate School of Education, Teach for America Program, Philadelphia, PA 19104. Offers MS Ed. Program designed for Teach For America corps members teaching in Philadelphia public and charter schools. *Program availability:* Evening/weekend. *Students:* 35 full-time (27 women), 82 part-time (61 women); includes 58 minority (23 Black or African American, non-Hispanic/Latino; 11 Asian, non-Hispanic/Latino; 16 Hispanic/Latino; 8 Two or more races, non-Hispanic/Latino). Average age 25. 70 applicants, 96% accepted, 58 enrolled. In 2016, 55 master's awarded. *Degree requirements:* For master's, thesis. *Entrance requirements:* For master's, bachelor's degree; Teach for America placement. Additional exam requirements/recommendations for international students: Required—TOEFL, IELTS. *Application deadline:* Applications are processed on a rolling basis. Application fee: $75. Electronic applications accepted. *Expenses: Tuition:* Full-time $31,068; part-time $5762 per course. *Required fees:* $3200; $336 per course. Full-time tuition and fees vary according to degree level, program and student level. Part-time tuition and fees vary according to course load, degree level and program. *Unit head:* Mary DelSavio, Program Director, 215-746-4855, E-mail: mary1@upenn.edu.
Website: http://www.gse.upenn.edu/exec-ed/tfa

University of San Francisco, School of Education, Department of Teacher Education, San Francisco, CA 94117-1080. Offers digital media and learning (MA); teaching (MA); teaching reading (MA); teaching urban education and social justice (MA). *Program availability:* Part-time. *Faculty:* 6 full-time (2 women), 50 part-time/adjunct (33 women). *Students:* 212 full-time (154 women), 25 part-time (20 women); includes 106 minority (16 Black or African American, non-Hispanic/Latino; 30 Asian, non-Hispanic/Latino; 48 Hispanic/Latino; 2 Native Hawaiian or other Pacific Islander, non-Hispanic/Latino; 10 Two or more races, non-Hispanic/Latino), 1 international. Average age 29. 246 applicants, 95% accepted, 125 enrolled. In 2016, 127 master's awarded. *Entrance requirements:* Additional exam requirements/recommendations for international students: Required—TOEFL, IELTS, PTE. *Application deadline:* For fall admission, 3/1 priority date for domestic and international students; for spring admission, 10/15 priority date for domestic students, 10/1 for international students. Applications are processed on a rolling basis. Electronic applications accepted. *Expenses: Tuition:* Full-time $23,310; part-time $1295 per credit. Tuition and fees vary according to course load, degree level, campus/location and program. *Financial support:* In 2016–17, 25 students received support. Applicants required to submit FAFSA. *Unit head:* Dr. Noah Borrero, Chair, 415-422-6481. *Application contact:* Peter Cole, Admission Coordinator, 415-422-5467, E-mail: schoolofeducation@usfca.edu.
Website: https://www.usfca.edu/catalog/graduate/school-of-education/programs-teacher-education

University of Southern California, Graduate School, Rossier School of Education, Doctor of Education Programs, Los Angeles, CA 90089. Offers educational psychology (Ed D); higher education administration (Ed D); K-12 leadership in urban school settings (Ed D); teacher education in multicultural societies (Ed D). *Program availability:* Part-time, evening/weekend. *Degree requirements:* For doctorate, thesis/dissertation. *Entrance requirements:* For doctorate, GRE. Additional exam requirements/recommendations for international students: Required—TOEFL (minimum score 100 iBT). Electronic applications accepted. *Faculty research:* Data-driven decision-making in K-12 schools and districts; examination of college and university leadership and management in U. S. and Asia; studies in facilitating student learning; organizational change and the role of leaders; leadership, diversity, learning and accountability.

University of Wisconsin–Milwaukee, Graduate School, School of Education, Department of Curriculum and Instruction, Milwaukee, WI 53201-0413. Offers curriculum and instruction (MS), including cross-curricular focus, early childhood education, English education, mathematics education, middle childhood/early adolescence education, reading education, science education, urban social studies education. *Program availability:* Part-time. *Students:* 21 full-time (13 women), 44 part-time (42 women); includes 10 minority (1 Black or African American, non-Hispanic/Latino; 1 Asian, non-Hispanic/Latino; 2 Hispanic/Latino; 6 Two or more races, non-Hispanic/Latino), 2 international. Average age 33. 42 applicants, 71% accepted, 20 enrolled. In 2016, 45 master's awarded. *Degree requirements:* For master's, thesis or alternative. *Entrance requirements:* Additional exam requirements/recommendations for international students: Required—TOEFL (minimum score 550 paper-based; 79 iBT), IELTS (minimum score 6.5). *Application deadline:* For fall admission, 1/1 priority date for domestic students; for spring admission, 9/1 for domestic students. Applications are processed on a rolling basis. Application fee: $56 ($96 for international students). Electronic applications accepted. *Financial support:* In 2016–17, 1 fellowship was awarded; research assistantships, teaching assistantships, career-related internships or fieldwork, health care benefits, unspecified assistantships, and project assistantships also available. Support available to part-time students. Financial award application deadline: 4/15; financial award applicants required to submit FAFSA. *Application contact:* General Information Contact, 414-229-4721, E-mail: soeinfo@uwm.edu.
Website: http://uwm.edu/education/academics/curriculum-instruction-department/

University of Wisconsin–Milwaukee, Graduate School, School of Education, Department of Exceptional Education, Milwaukee, WI 53201-0413. Offers autism spectrum disorders (Graduate Certificate); exceptional education (MS); transition for students with disabilities (Graduate Certificate); urban education (PhD), including adult, continuing and higher education leadership, art education, curriculum and instruction, exceptional education, mathematics education, multicultural studies, social foundations of education. *Program availability:* Part-time. *Students:* 50 full-time (41 women), 66 part-time (51 women); includes 42 minority (24 Black or African American, non-Hispanic/Latino; 6 Asian, non-Hispanic/Latino; 1 Hispanic/Latino; 11 Two or more races, non-Hispanic/Latino), 4 international. Average age 39. 55 applicants, 51% accepted, 22 enrolled. In 2016, 14 master's, 10 doctorates, 3 other advanced degrees awarded. *Degree requirements:* For master's, thesis. *Entrance requirements:* Additional exam requirements/recommendations for international students: Required—TOEFL (minimum score 550 paper-based; 79 iBT), IELTS (minimum score 6.5). *Application deadline:* For fall admission, 1/1 priority date for domestic students; for spring admission, 9/1 for domestic students. Applications are processed on a rolling basis. Application fee: $56 ($96 for international students). Electronic applications accepted. *Financial support:* Fellowships, research assistantships, teaching assistantships, career-related internships or fieldwork, health care benefits, and unspecified assistantships available. Support available to part-time students. Financial award application deadline: 4/15; financial award applicants required to submit FAFSA. *Faculty research:* Emotional disturbance, hearing impairment, learning disabilities, mental retardation. *Application contact:* General Information Contact, 414-229-4721, E-mail: soeinfo@uwm.edu.
Website: http://uwm.edu/education/academics/exceptional-edu-department/

Vanderbilt University, Peabody College, Department of Teaching and Learning, Nashville, TN 37240-1001. Offers elementary education (M Ed); English language learners (M Ed); learning and design (M Ed); learning, diversity, and urban studies (M Ed); reading education (M Ed); secondary education (M Ed). *Accreditation:* NCATE. *Program availability:* Part-time. *Faculty:* 44 full-time (34 women), 26 part-time/adjunct (21 women). *Students:* 120 full-time (106 women), 26 part-time (18 women); includes 22 minority (9 Black or African American, non-Hispanic/Latino; 6 Asian, non-Hispanic/Latino; 6 Hispanic/Latino; 1 Two or more races, non-Hispanic/Latino), 44 international. Average age 24. 328 applicants, 73% accepted, 76 enrolled. In 2016, 110 master's awarded. *Degree requirements:* For master's, comprehensive exam, thesis optional. *Entrance requirements:* For master's, GRE General Test, MAT. Additional exam requirements/recommendations for international students: Required—TOEFL (minimum score 550 paper-based; 80 iBT). *Application deadline:* For fall admission, 12/31 priority date for domestic and international students; for spring admission, 11/1 priority date for domestic and international students. Applications are processed on a rolling basis. Application fee: $0. Electronic applications accepted. *Expenses: Tuition:* Part-time $1854 per credit hour. *Financial support:* Fellowships with partial tuition reimbursements, research assistantships with partial tuition reimbursements, teaching assistantships with partial tuition reimbursements, Federal Work-Study, institutionally sponsored loans, scholarships/grants, tuition waivers (partial), and unspecified assistantships available. Support available to part-time students. Financial award application deadline: 1/15; financial award applicants required to submit FAFSA. *Faculty research:* Children's learning and development in core conceptual domains (STEM, English language arts, social studies); classroom discourse structures that teachers can learn and use to support students' learning and development K-6; intervention and design-based research on educational improvement at classroom, school, and district levels; design-based and learning sciences research on relations between learning in schools and other settings. *Unit head:* Dr. Rogers Hall, Chair, 615-322-8100, Fax: 615-322-8999, E-mail: rogers.hall@vanderbilt.edu. *Application contact:* Angela Saylor, Educational Coordinator, 615-322-8092, Fax: 615-322-8999, E-mail: angela.saylor@vanderbilt.edu.

Virginia Commonwealth University, Graduate School, School of Education, Doctoral Program in Education, Richmond, VA 23284-9005. Offers art education (PhD); counselor education and supervision (PhD); curriculum, culture and change (PhD); educational leadership (PhD); educational psychology (PhD); leadership (Ed D); research and evaluation (PhD); special education and disability leadership (PhD); sport leadership (PhD); urban services leadership (PhD). *Accreditation:* NCATE. *Program availability:* Part-time. *Degree requirements:* For doctorate, thesis/dissertation. *Entrance requirements:* For doctorate, GRE (for PhD), MAT (for Ed D), interview, master's degree, writing sample. Additional exam requirements/recommendations for international students: Required—TOEFL (minimum score 600 paper-based; 100 iBT). *Application deadline:* For fall admission, 2/15 for domestic students. Application fee: $50. Electronic applications accepted. *Financial support:* Fellowships, research assistantships, career-related internships or fieldwork, Federal Work-Study, and institutionally sponsored loans available. Financial award application deadline: 3/1; financial award applicants required to submit FAFSA. *Unit head:* Dr. Kathleen Cauley, Interim Director, 804-827-2657, E-mail: kmcauley@vcu.edu. *Application contact:* Dr. Colleen A. Thoma, Administrative Assistant, 804-827-2651, E-mail: cathoma@vcu.edu.
Website: http://www.soe.vcu.edu/programs/doctoral-programs/

Section 26
Subject Areas

This section contains a directory of institutions offering graduate work in subject areas. Additional information about programs listed in the directory may be obtained by writing directly to the dean of a graduate school or chair of a department at the address given in the directory.

For programs offering related work, see also in this book *Administration, Instruction, and Theory; Business Administration and Management; Education; Instructional Levels; Leisure Studies and Recreation; Physical Education and Kinesiology;* and *Special Focus.* In the other guides in this series:

Graduate Programs in the Humanities, Arts & Social Sciences

See *Art and Art History; Family and Consumer Sciences; Language and Literature; Performing Arts; Psychology and Counseling (School Psychology); Public, Regional, and Industrial Affairs (Urban Studies); Religious Studies;* and *Social Sciences*

Graduate Programs in the Biological/Biomedical Sciences & Health-Related Medical Professions

See *Health-Related Professions*

Graduate Programs in the Physical Sciences, Mathematics, Agricultural Sciences, the Environment & Natural Resources

See *Mathematical Sciences*

Graduate Programs in Engineering & Applied Sciences

See *Computer Science and Information Technology*

CONTENTS

Program Directories

Featured School: Display and Close-Up

See:

Agricultural Education

Alcorn State University, School of Graduate Studies, School of Psychology and Education, Lorman, MS 39096-7500. Offers agricultural education (MS Ed); elementary education (MS Ed, Ed S); guidance and counseling (MS Ed); industrial education (MS Ed); secondary education (MS Ed), including health and physical education; special education (MS Ed). *Accreditation:* NCATE. *Degree requirements:* For master's, thesis optional.

Arkansas State University, Graduate School, College of Agriculture and Technology, State University, AR 72467. Offers agricultural education (SCCT); agriculture (MSA); vocational-technical administration (SCCT). *Program availability:* Part-time. *Degree requirements:* For master's, comprehensive exam, thesis or alternative; for SCCT, comprehensive exam. *Entrance requirements:* For master's, GRE General Test or MAT, appropriate bachelor's degree, official transcripts, immunization records; for SCCT, GRE General Test or MAT, interview, master's degree, official transcript, immunization records. Additional exam requirements/recommendations for international students: Required—TOEFL (minimum score 550 paper-based; 79 iBT), IELTS (minimum score 6), PTE (minimum score 56). Electronic applications accepted.

California Polytechnic State University, San Luis Obispo, College of Agriculture, Food and Environmental Sciences, Department of Agricultural Education and Communication, San Luis Obispo, CA 93407. Offers MAE. *Program availability:* Part-time. *Faculty:* 4 full-time (2 women), 1 (woman) part-time/adjunct. *Students:* 23 full-time (14 women), 2 part-time (0 women); includes 6 minority (4 Hispanic/Latino; 2 Two or more races, non-Hispanic/Latino). Average age 27. 16 applicants, 75% accepted, 9 enrolled. In 2016, 18 master's awarded. *Degree requirements:* For master's, comprehensive exam. *Entrance requirements:* For master's, GRE. Additional exam requirements/recommendations for international students: Required—TOEFL (minimum score 80 iBT). *Application deadline:* For fall admission, 4/1 for domestic and international students; for winter admission, 10/1 for domestic students, 6/30 for international students; for spring admission, 10/1 for domestic students. Applications are processed on a rolling basis. Application fee: $55. Electronic applications accepted. *Expenses:* Tuition, state resident: full-time $6738; part-time $3906 per year. Tuition, nonresident: full-time $15,666; part-time $8370 per year. *Required fees:* $3603; $3141 per unit. $1047 per term. *Financial support:* Teaching assistantships and unspecified assistantships available. Financial award application deadline: 3/2; financial award applicants required to submit FAFSA. *Faculty research:* Agricultural education with emphasis on public school teaching. *Unit head:* Dr. Robert Flores, Department Head, 805-756-2169, E-mail: rflores@calpoly.edu. *Application contact:* Dr. Ann De Lay, Graduate Coordinator, 805-756-7272, E-mail: adelay@calpoly.edu.
Website: http://aged.calpoly.edu/

California State University, Chico, Office of Graduate Studies, College of Agriculture, Chico, CA 95929-0722. Offers agricultural education (MS). *Degree requirements:* For master's, thesis or alternative, oral exam. *Entrance requirements:* For master's, GRE or MAT, 3 letters of recommendation, three departmental recommendation forms, statement of purpose. Additional exam requirements/recommendations for international students: Required—TOEFL (minimum score 550 paper-based; 80 iBT), IELTS (minimum score 6.5), PTE (minimum score 59).

Clemson University, Graduate School, College of Agriculture, Forestry and Life Sciences, Department of Agricultural Sciences, Program in Agricultural Education, Clemson, SC 29634. Offers M Ag Ed. *Accreditation:* NCATE. *Program availability:* Part-time. *Faculty:* 19 full-time (3 women). *Students:* 13 full-time (11 women), 10 part-time (6 women), 1 international. Average age 26. 14 applicants, 93% accepted, 10 enrolled. In 2016, 5 master's awarded. *Degree requirements:* For master's, comprehensive exam, thesis or alternative, research project. *Entrance requirements:* For master's, GRE General Test (minimum scores: 150 Verbal, 141 Quantitative, 3 Analytical Writing recommended), unofficial transcripts, letters of recommendation. Additional exam requirements/recommendations for international students: Required—TOEFL (minimum score 80 iBT), IELTS (minimum score 6.5). *Application deadline:* Applications are processed on a rolling basis. Application fee: $80 ($90 for international students). Electronic applications accepted. *Expenses:* $4,841 per semester full-time resident, $9,640 per semester full-time non-resident, $612 per credit hour part-time resident, $1,223 per credit hour part-time non-resident. *Financial support:* In 2016–17, 12 students received support, including 6 research assistantships with partial tuition reimbursements available (averaging $15,917 per year), 3 teaching assistantships with partial tuition reimbursements available (averaging $11,359 per year); career-related internships or fieldwork and unspecified assistantships also available. Financial award application deadline: 2/15. *Faculty research:* Adaptation and change, curriculum assessment and innovation, career development, adult and extension education, technology transfer. *Unit head:* Dr. YoungJo Han, Department Chair, 864-656-3250, Fax: 864-656-0338, E-mail: yhan@clemson.edu. *Application contact:* Dr. Dale Layfield, Graduate Program Coordinator, 864-656-5676, E-mail: dlayfie@clemson.edu.
Website: http://www.clemson.edu/graduate/academics/program-details.html?m_id-105

Cornell University, Graduate School, Graduate Fields of Agriculture and Life Sciences, Field of Education, Ithaca, NY 14853. Offers adult and extension education (MPS, MS, PhD); learning, teaching, and social policy (MPS, MS, PhD); mathematics 7-12 (MS). Terminal master's awarded for partial completion of doctoral program. *Degree requirements:* For master's, thesis (MS); for doctorate, comprehensive exam, thesis/dissertation. *Entrance requirements:* For master's and doctorate, GRE General Test, sample of written work (recommended), 2 letters of recommendation. Additional exam requirements/recommendations for international students: Required—TOEFL (minimum score 550 paper-based; 77 iBT). Electronic applications accepted. *Faculty research:* Moral development and professional ethics, public issues education and community development, socio/political issues in public education, teacher education and curriculum in agricultural science and mathematics, extension research.

Eastern Kentucky University, The Graduate School, College of Education, Department of Curriculum and Instruction, Program in Secondary and Higher Education, Richmond, KY 40475-3102. Offers secondary education (MA Ed), including agricultural education, art education, biological sciences education, business education, English education, geography education, history education, home economics education, industrial education, mathematical sciences education, physical education, school health education. *Accreditation:* NCATE. *Program availability:* Part-time. *Entrance requirements:* For master's, GRE General Test, minimum GPA of 2.5.

Iowa State University of Science and Technology, Department of Agricultural Education and Studies, Ames, IA 50011. Offers MS, PhD. *Entrance requirements:* For master's and doctorate, resume. Additional exam requirements/recommendations for international students: Required—TOEFL (minimum score 550 paper-based; 79 iBT), IELTS (minimum score 6.5). *Application deadline:* For fall admission, 3/15 priority date for domestic and international students; for spring admission, 10/15 priority date for domestic and international students. Application fee: $60 ($90 for international students). Electronic applications accepted. *Faculty research:* Agricultural extension education, teaching, learning processes, distance education, international education, adult education. *Application contact:* Wendy Ortmann, Application Contact, 515-294-5872, Fax: 515-294-0530, E-mail: agedsinfo@iastate.edu.
Website: http://www.ageds.iastate.edu/graduate.html

Ithaca College, School of Humanities and Sciences, Program in Agriculture Education, Ithaca, NY 14850. Offers MAT. Program offered in collaboration with Cornell University. *Program availability:* Part-time. *Faculty:* 26 full-time (12 women). *Students:* 4 full-time (all women); includes 1 minority (Hispanic/Latino). Average age 23. 5 applicants, 100% accepted, 4 enrolled. *Degree requirements:* For master's, thesis or alternative. *Entrance requirements:* Additional exam requirements/recommendations for international students: Required—TOEFL (minimum score 550 paper-based; 80 iBT). *Application deadline:* For fall admission, 2/15 for domestic and international students; for spring admission, 12/1 for domestic and international students. Applications are processed on a rolling basis. Application fee: $40. Electronic applications accepted. *Expenses:* Contact institution. *Financial support:* Research assistantships, career-related internships or fieldwork, Federal Work-Study, scholarships/grants, and unspecified assistantships available. Support available to part-time students. Financial award application deadline: 2/15; financial award applicants required to submit CSS PROFILE or FAFSA. *Unit head:* Peter Martin, Chair, 607-274-1076, E-mail: pmartin@ithaca.edu. *Application contact:* Nicole Eversley Bradwell, Director, Office of Admission, 607-274-3124, Fax: 607-274-1263, E-mail: admission@ithaca.edu.
Website: http://www.ithaca.edu/gradprograms/education/programs/aded

Kansas State University, Graduate School, College of Agriculture, Department of Communications and Agricultural Education, Manhattan, KS 66506. Offers agricultural education and communication (MS). *Program availability:* Part-time, online learning. *Faculty:* 12 full-time (10 women). *Students:* 7 full-time (6 women), 10 part-time (9 women); includes 1 minority (Two or more races, non-Hispanic/Latino), 1 international. Average age 29. 10 applicants, 60% accepted, 4 enrolled. In 2016, 6 master's awarded. *Degree requirements:* For master's, comprehensive exam, thesis or alternative. *Entrance requirements:* For master's, GRE if GPA on last 60 undergraduate credits is less than 3.0. *Application deadline:* For fall admission, 5/1 for domestic students, 1/1 for international students; for spring admission, 10/1 for domestic students, 8/1 for international students; for summer admission, 3/1 for domestic students, 12/1 for international students. Application fee: $50 ($75 for international students). Electronic applications accepted. *Expenses:* Tuition, state resident: full-time $9670. Tuition, nonresident: full-time $21,828. *Required fees:* $862. *Faculty research:* Curriculum development, instructional design, strategic communications, risk and crisis communications. *Total annual research expenditures:* $31,955. *Unit head:* Dr. Kristina M. Boone, Head, 785-532-5804, Fax: 785-532-5633, E-mail: kboone@ksu.edu. *Application contact:* Dr. Jason D. Ellis, Associate Professor, 785-532-5804, Fax: 785-532-5633, E-mail: jdellis@ksu.edu.
Website: http://www.communications.k-state.edu/

Louisiana State University and Agricultural & Mechanical College, Graduate School, College of Human Sciences and Education, School of Human Resource Education and Workforce Development, Baton Rouge, LA 70803. Offers agriculture and extension education and youth development (MS, PhD); career and technical education (MS, PhD); comprehensive vocational education (MS, PhD); extension and international education (MS, PhD); human resource and leadership development (MS, PhD); industrial education (MS); vocational agriculture education (MS, PhD); vocational business education (MS); vocational home economics education (MS). *Accreditation:* NCATE.

Mississippi State University, College of Agriculture and Life Sciences, School of Human Sciences, Mississippi State, MS 39762. Offers agriculture and extension education (MS, PhD), including agriculture and extension education (PhD), leadership (MS), teaching (MS); human development and family studies (MS, PhD). *Accreditation:* NCATE (one or more programs are accredited). *Program availability:* Part-time. *Faculty:* 23 full-time (13 women), 1 part-time/adjunct (0 women). *Students:* 35 full-time (25 women), 61 part-time (45 women); includes 19 minority (15 Black or African American, non-Hispanic/Latino; 2 Hispanic/Latino; 2 Two or more races, non-Hispanic/Latino), 5 international. Average age 35. 22 applicants, 73% accepted, 12 enrolled. In 2016, 8 master's, 4 doctorates awarded. *Degree requirements:* For master's, thesis optional, comprehensive oral or written exam. *Entrance requirements:* For master's, GRE, minimum GPA of 2.75 in last 4 semesters of course work; for doctorate, minimum GPA of 3.0 on prior graduate work. Additional exam requirements/recommendations for international students: Required—TOEFL (minimum score 477 paper-based; 53 iBT); Recommended—IELTS (minimum score 4.5). *Application deadline:* For fall admission, 7/1 for domestic students, 5/1 for international students; for spring admission, 11/1 for domestic students, 9/1 for international students. Applications are processed on a rolling basis. Application fee: $60. Electronic applications accepted. *Expenses:* Tuition, state resident: full-time $7670; part-time $852.50 per credit hour. Tuition, nonresident: full-time $20,790; part-time $2310.50 per credit hour. Part-time tuition and fees vary according to course load. *Financial support:* Federal Work-Study, institutionally sponsored loans, and unspecified assistantships available. Financial award application deadline: 4/1; financial award applicants required to submit FAFSA. *Faculty research:* Animal welfare, agro science, information technology, learning styles, problem solving. *Unit head:* Dr. Michael Newman, Director and Professor, 662-325-2950, E-mail: mnewman@humansci.msstate.edu. *Application contact:* Marina Hunt, Admissions and Enrollment Assistant, 662-325-5188, E-mail: mhunt@grad.msstate.edu.
Website: http://www.humansci.msstate.edu

Montana State University, The Graduate School, College of Agriculture, Division of Agricultural Education, Bozeman, MT 59717. Offers MS. *Program availability:* Part-time, online learning. *Degree requirements:* For master's, comprehensive exam. *Entrance requirements:* For master's, GRE General Test. Additional exam requirements/recommendations for international students: Required—TOEFL (minimum score 550 paper-based). Electronic applications accepted. *Faculty research:* Extension systems, youth leadership, agricultural, adult and youth education in agriculture, international agricultural education, enzymology of vitamins, coenzymes and metal ions, steroid metabolism, protein structure, impact of wolves on big game hunting demand, prescription drug price dispersion in heterogeneous markets, divorce risk and the labor force participation of women with and without children, the economics of terraces in the Peruvian Andes.

Murray State University, School of Agriculture, Murray, KY 42071. Offers agriculture (MS); agriculture education (MS). *Program availability:* Evening/weekend, online learning. *Degree requirements:* For master's, comprehensive exam, thesis (for some programs). *Entrance requirements:* Additional exam requirements/recommendations for international students: Required—TOEFL. *Faculty research:* Ultrasound in beef, corn and soybean research, tobacco research.

New Mexico State University, College of Agricultural, Consumer and Environmental Sciences, Department of Agricultural and Extension Education, Las Cruces, NM 88003. Offers MA. *Accreditation:* NCATE. *Program availability:* Part-time, evening/weekend, blended/hybrid learning. *Faculty:* 5 full-time (1 woman). *Students:* 12 full-time (10 women), 15 part-time (8 women); includes 6 minority (1 American Indian or Alaska Native, non-Hispanic/Latino; 4 Hispanic/Latino; 1 Two or more races, non-Hispanic/Latino). Average age 32. 16 applicants, 75% accepted, 8 enrolled. In 2016, 9 master's awarded. *Degree requirements:* For master's, comprehensive exam, thesis or creative component. *Entrance requirements:* For master's, 3 letters of recommendation. Additional exam requirements/recommendations for international students: Required—TOEFL (minimum score 550 paper-based; 79 iBT), IELTS (minimum score 6.5). *Application deadline:* For fall admission, 7/1 priority date for domestic and international students; for spring admission, 11/1 priority date for domestic and international students. Applications are processed on a rolling basis. Application fee: $40 ($50 for international students). Electronic applications accepted. *Expenses:* Tuition, state resident: full-time $4086. Tuition, nonresident: full-time $14,254. *Required fees:* $853. Tuition and fees vary according to course load. *Financial support:* In 2016–17, 12 students received support, including 4 teaching assistantships (averaging $16,964 per year); career-related internships or fieldwork, Federal Work-Study, scholarships/grants, traineeships, health care benefits, and unspecified assistantships also available. Support available to part-time students. Financial award application deadline: 3/1. *Faculty research:* Secondary agricultural education programs, teaching and learning, agricultural technology and safety, youth leadership development, agricultural development, youth development. *Total annual research expenditures:* $250,783. *Unit head:* Dr. Frank E. Hodnett, Department Head, 575-646-4511, Fax: 575-646-4082, E-mail: fhodnett@nmsu.edu. *Application contact:* Dr. Brenda S. Seevers, Graduate Program Coordinator, 575-646-4511, Fax: 575-646-4082, E-mail: bseevers@nmsu.edu.
Website: http://aces.nmsu.edu/academics/axed

North Carolina Agricultural and Technical State University, School of Graduate Studies, School of Agriculture and Environmental Sciences, Department of Agribusiness, Applied Economics, and Agriscience Education, Greensboro, NC 27411. Offers agricultural economics (MS); agricultural education (MS). *Accreditation:* NCATE. *Program availability:* Part-time, evening/weekend. *Degree requirements:* For master's, comprehensive exam, thesis or alternative, qualifying exam. *Entrance requirements:* For master's, GRE General Test, minimum GPA of 3.0. *Faculty research:* Aid for small farmers, agricultural technology resources, labor force mobility, agrology.

North Carolina State University, Graduate School, College of Agriculture and Life Sciences, Department of Agricultural and Extension Education, Program in Agricultural Education, Raleigh, NC 27695. Offers MAE, MS, Certificate. *Program availability:* Online learning. *Degree requirements:* For master's, thesis optional. *Entrance requirements:* For master's, GRE or MAT. Electronic applications accepted. *Faculty research:* Instructional methodology, distance education, leadership development, foundations, curriculum development.

North Dakota State University, College of Graduate and Interdisciplinary Studies, College of Human Development and Education, School of Education, Program in Agricultural Education, Fargo, ND 58102. Offers M Ed, MS. *Accreditation:* NCATE. *Program availability:* Part-time. *Degree requirements:* For master's, comprehensive exam, thesis or alternative. *Entrance requirements:* Additional exam requirements/recommendations for international students: Required—TOEFL (minimum score 525 paper-based; 71 iBT). *Faculty research:* Vocational and cooperative extension education, rural leadership, rural education, international extension.

Northwest Missouri State University, Graduate School, School of Agricultural Sciences, Maryville, MO 64468-6001. Offers agricultural economics (MBA); agricultural education (MS Ed); agriculture (MS); teaching: agriculture (MS Ed). *Program availability:* Part-time. *Students:* 4 full-time (1 woman), 8 part-time (3 women). In 2016, 3 master's awarded. *Degree requirements:* For master's, comprehensive exam, thesis (for some programs). *Entrance requirements:* For master's, GRE General Test, minimum undergraduate GPA of 2.5, writing sample. Additional exam requirements/recommendations for international students: Required—TOEFL (minimum score 550 paper-based). *Application deadline:* For fall admission, 7/1 for domestic and international students; for spring admission, 11/15 for domestic and international students. Applications are processed on a rolling basis. Application fee: $0 ($50 for international students). *Expenses:* Tuition, state resident: full-time $3447; part-time $383 per credit hour. Tuition, nonresident: full-time $5724; part-time $636 per credit hour. *Required fees:* $130 per credit hour. *Financial support:* Research assistantships with full tuition reimbursements, teaching assistantships with full tuition reimbursements, and unspecified assistantships available. Financial award application deadline: 4/1; financial award applicants required to submit FAFSA. *Unit head:* Rodney Barr, Director, 660-562-1620.
Website: http://www.nwmissouri.edu/ag/

The Ohio State University, Graduate School, College of Food, Agricultural, and Environmental Sciences, Department of Agricultural Communication, Education and Leadership, Program in Agricultural and Extension Education, Columbus, OH 43210. Offers MS. *Program availability:* Part-time, online learning. *Students:* 1 (woman) full-time, 11 part-time (10 women). Average age 30. In 2016, 1 master's awarded. *Entrance requirements:* For master's, GRE. Additional exam requirements/recommendations for international students: Required—TOEFL (minimum score 550 paper-based; 79 iBT), Michigan English Language Assessment Battery (minimum score 82); Recommended—IELTS (minimum score 7). *Application deadline:* For fall admission, 1/1 priority date for domestic students, 12/1 priority date for international students; for spring admission, 11/11 for domestic and international students, for summer admission, 3/1 for domestic and international students. Applications are processed on a rolling basis. Application fee: $60 ($70 for international students). Electronic applications accepted. *Financial support:* Institutionally sponsored loans available. Support available to part-time students. *Unit head:* Dr. Scott Scheer, Graduate Studies Chair, 614-292-6758, E-mail: scheer.9@osu.edu. *Application contact:* Graduate and Professional Admissions, 614-292-9444, Fax: 614-292-3895, E-mail: gpadmissions@osu.edu.
Website: http://acel.osu.edu/

Oklahoma State University, College of Agricultural Science and Natural Resources, Department of Agricultural Education, Communications and Leadership, Stillwater, OK 74078. Offers M Ag, MS, PhD. *Program availability:* Online learning. *Faculty:* 9 full-time (3 women), 5 part-time/adjunct (3 women). *Students:* 18 full-time (12 women), 41 part-time (31 women); includes 7 minority (1 Black or African American, non Hispanic/Latino; 1 American Indian or Alaska Native, non-Hispanic/Latino; 4 Hispanic/Latino; 1 Two or more races, non-Hispanic/Latino), 1 international. Average age 30. 27 applicants, 81% accepted, 17 enrolled. In 2016, 9 master's, 3 doctorates awarded. *Degree requirements:* For master's, thesis (for some programs), thesis or report; for doctorate, comprehensive exam, thesis/dissertation. *Entrance requirements:* For master's and doctorate, GRE or GMAT. Additional exam requirements/recommendations for international students: Required—TOEFL (minimum score 550 paper-based; 79 iBT). *Application deadline:* For fall admission, 3/1 priority date for international students; for spring admission, 8/1 priority date for international students. Applications are processed on a rolling basis. Application fee: $40 ($75 for international students). Electronic applications accepted. *Expenses:* Tuition, state resident: full-time $3775; part-time $209.70 per credit hour. Tuition, nonresident: full-time $14,851; part-time $825.05 per credit hour. *Required fees:* $2027; $112.60 per credit hour. Tuition and fees vary according to campus/location. *Financial support:* In 2016–17, 2 research assistantships (averaging $15,600 per year), 14 teaching assistantships (averaging $15,164 per year) were awarded; career-related internships or fieldwork, Federal Work-Study, scholarships/grants, health care benefits, tuition waivers (partial), and unspecified assistantships also available. Support available to part-time students. Financial award application deadline: 3/1; financial award applicants required to submit FAFSA. *Faculty research:* Teaching in and learning about agriculture, agriculture teacher evaluation, evaluation of information dissemination delivery methods, agricultural literacy curriculum model development, distance education delivery methods. *Unit head:* Dr. Robert Terry, Department Head, 405-744-8036, Fax: 405-744-5176, E-mail: rob.terry@okstate.edu.
Website: http://aged.okstate.edu/

Oregon State University, College of Agricultural Sciences, Program in Agricultural Education, Corvallis, OR 97331. Offers leadership and communication in agriculture (MS); teacher preparation (MS). *Program availability:* Part-time. *Students:* 10 full-time (8 women), 1 (woman) part-time; includes 2 minority (1 Hispanic/Latino; 1 Two or more races, non-Hispanic/Latino). Average age 24. 14 applicants, 79% accepted, 11 enrolled. In 2016, 9 master's awarded. *Entrance requirements:* Additional exam requirements/recommendations for international students: Required—TOEFL (minimum score 80 iBT), IELTS (minimum score 6.5). *Application deadline:* For fall admission, 8/1 for domestic students, 4/1 for international students; for winter admission, 12/1 for domestic students, 7/1 for international students; for spring admission, 2/1 for domestic students, 10/1 for international students; for summer admission, 5/1 for domestic students, 1/1 for international students. Application fee: $75 ($85 for international students). *Expenses:* Tuition, state resident: full-time $12,150; part-time $450 per credit. Tuition, nonresident: full-time $21,789; part-time $807 per credit. *Required fees:* $1651; $1507 per credit. One-time fee: $350. Tuition and fees vary according to course load, campus/location and program. *Unit head:* Prof. Barry Croom, Professor and Department Head, 541-737-1337.
Website: http://agsci.oregonstate.edu/ag-ed

Oregon State University, College of Education, Program in Education, Corvallis, OR 97331. Offers advanced science and mathematics education (Ed M); agricultural education (PhD); education (Ed D); free-choice learning (Ed M); language equity and educational policy (PhD); mathematics education (MS); pre-K-12 English to speakers of other languages (ESOL) (Ed M); science education (MS); science/mathematics education (PhD); social justice in education (Ed M). *Program availability:* Part-time, 100% online, blended/hybrid learning. *Faculty:* 9 full-time (8 women), 6 part-time/adjunct (2 women). *Students:* 14 full-time (8 women), 76 part-time (53 women); includes 25 minority (6 Black or African American, non-Hispanic/Latino; 2 American Indian or Alaska Native, non-Hispanic/Latino; 5 Asian, non-Hispanic/Latino; 10 Hispanic/Latino; 2 Two or more races, non-Hispanic/Latino), 3 international. Average age 38. 72 applicants, 69% accepted, 40 enrolled. In 2016, 14 master's, 21 doctorates awarded. Terminal master's awarded for partial completion of doctoral program. *Degree requirements:* For master's, variable foreign language requirement, thesis (for some programs); for doctorate, variable foreign language requirement, thesis/dissertation. *Entrance requirements:* Additional exam requirements/recommendations for international students: Required—TOEFL (minimum score 575 paper-based). Application fee: $75 ($85 for international students). *Expenses:* Tuition, state resident: full-time $12,150; part-time $450 per credit. Tuition, nonresident: full-time $21,789; part-time $807 per credit. *Required fees:* $1651; $1507 per credit. One-time fee: $350. Tuition and fees vary according to course load, campus/location and program. *Financial support:* Fellowships, research assistantships, teaching assistantships, career-related internships or fieldwork, Federal Work-Study, and institutionally sponsored loans available. Support available to part-time students. *Faculty research:* School administration, educational foundations, research methodology, education policy development, higher education administration. *Unit head:* Dr. Larry Flick, Dean. *Application contact:* E-mail: askcoed@oregonstate.edu.

Penn State University Park, Graduate School, College of Agricultural Sciences, Department of Agricultural Economics, Sociology, and Education, University Park, PA 16802. Offers agricultural and extension education (M Ed, MS, PhD, Certificate); agricultural, environmental and regional economics (MS, PhD); applied youth, family and community education (M Ed); community and economic development (MPS); rural sociology (MS, PhD). *Unit head:* Dr. Richard T. Roush, Dean, 814-865-2541, Fax: 814-865-3103. *Application contact:* Lori Hawn, Director, Graduate Student Services, 814-865-1795, Fax: 814-863-4627, E-mail: l-gswww@lists.psu.edu.
Website: http://aese.psu.edu/

Purdue University, Graduate School, College of Agriculture, Department of Youth Development and Agricultural Education, West Lafayette, IN 47907. Offers MA, PhD. *Faculty:* 11 full-time (5 women). *Students:* 17 full-time (14 women), 8 part-time (7 women); includes 6 minority (5 Black or African American, non-Hispanic/Latino; 1 Asian, non-Hispanic/Latino), 3 international. Average age 27. 16 applicants, 69% accepted, 8 enrolled. In 2016, 6 master's, 1 doctorate awarded. *Degree requirements:* For doctorate, comprehensive exam. *Entrance requirements:* For master's and doctorate, GRE General Test (minimum combined score of 1000), minimum undergraduate GPA of 3.0 or equivalent. Additional exam requirements/recommendations for international students: Required—TOEFL (minimum score 550 paper-based; 77 iBT), TWE with minimum score of 5 (recommended for MA, required for PhD). *Application deadline:* For fall admission, 3/15 priority date for domestic students, 3/1 for international students; for spring admission, 10/15 priority date for domestic students, 8/1 for international students; for summer admission, 3/15 for domestic students, 1/1 for international students. Applications are processed on a rolling basis. Application fee: $60 ($75 for international students). Electronic applications accepted. *Unit head:* Mark A. Russell, Head, 765-494-8423, E-mail: mrussell@purdue.edu. *Application contact:* Taylor Dunfee, Graduate Contact, 765-494-8439, E-mail: tdunfee@purdue.edu.
Website: https://ag.purdue.edu/ydae

Purdue University, Graduate School, College of Education, Department of Curriculum and Instruction, West Lafayette, IN 47907. Offers agricultural and extension education (MS, MS Ed, PhD, Ed S); art education (PhD); career and technical education (MS Ed, PhD, Ed S); curriculum studies (MS Ed, PhD, Ed S); educational technology (MS Ed, PhD, Ed S); elementary education (MS Ed); family and consumer sciences education (MS Ed, PhD, Ed S); foreign language education (MS Ed, PhD, Ed S); industrial technology (PhD, Ed S); language arts (MS Ed, PhD, Ed S); literacy (MS Ed, PhD, Ed S); mathematics education (MS, MS Ed, PhD, Ed S); science education (MS, MS Ed, PhD, Ed S); social studies education (MS Ed, PhD, Ed S). *Accreditation:* NCATE. *Program availability:* Part-time, evening/weekend. *Faculty:* 37 full-time (27 women), 1 (woman) part-time/adjunct. *Students:* 78 full-time (50 women), 286 part-time (195 women); includes 68 minority (25 Black or African American, non-Hispanic/Latino; 3 American Indian or Alaska Native, non-Hispanic/Latino; 10 Asian, non-Hispanic/Latino; 22 Hispanic/Latino; 1 Native Hawaiian or other Pacific Islander, non-Hispanic/Latino; 7

Two or more races, non-Hispanic/Latino), 44 international. Average age 36. 150 applicants, 79% accepted, 73 enrolled. In 2016, 107 master's, 20 doctorates, 2 other advanced degrees awarded. *Degree requirements:* For master's, thesis optional; for doctorate, thesis/dissertation, oral and written exams; for Ed S, oral presentation, project. *Entrance requirements:* For master's, GRE General Test (if undergraduate GPA is below 3.0), minimum undergraduate GPA of 3.0 or equivalent; for doctorate, GRE General Test (minimum combined verbal and quantitative score of 1000, 300 for new scoring), minimum undergraduate GPA of 3.0 or equivalent; master's degree with minimum GPA of 3.0 or equivalent; for Ed S, GRE General Test (minimum combined verbal and quantitative score of 1000, 300 for new scoring), minimum undergraduate GPA of 3.0 or equivalent; master's degree. Additional exam requirements/recommendations for international students: Required—TOEFL (minimum score 550 paper-based; 77 iBT). *Application deadline:* For fall admission, 12/15 for domestic students, 3/1 for international students; for spring admission, 9/15 for domestic students, 8/1 for international students. Application fee: $60 ($75 for international students). Electronic applications accepted. *Financial support:* Fellowships with full tuition reimbursements, research assistantships with full tuition reimbursements, teaching assistantships with full tuition reimbursements, career-related internships or fieldwork, and tuition waivers (full) available. Support available to part-time students. Financial award application deadline: 3/1; financial award applicants required to submit FAFSA. *Faculty research:* Literacy acquisition and development, teacher beliefs and knowledge, recruitment and retention of underrepresented students, economic education, literacy discourse. *Unit head:* Janet M. Alsup, Head, 765-494-9667, E-mail: alsupj@purdue.edu. *Application contact:* Heather Brinkman, Graduate Contact, 765-494-2345, E-mail: hbrinkma@purdue.edu.
Website: http://www.edci.purdue.edu/

Saint Leo University, Graduate Studies in Public Safety Administration, Saint Leo, FL 33574-6665. Offers criminal justice (MS), including corrections, criminal investigation, emergency and disaster management, forensic science, legal studies; emergency and disaster management (MS). *Program availability:* Part-time, evening/weekend, 100% online, blended/hybrid learning. *Faculty:* 7 full-time (2 women), 32 part-time/adjunct (8 women). *Students:* 3 full-time (1 woman), 667 part-time (446 women); includes 355 minority (275 Black or African American, non-Hispanic/Latino; 6 American Indian or Alaska Native, non-Hispanic/Latino; 4 Asian, non-Hispanic/Latino; 56 Hispanic/Latino; 3 Native Hawaiian or other Pacific Islander, non-Hispanic/Latino; 11 Two or more races, non-Hispanic/Latino). Average age 37. 361 applicants, 87% accepted, 177 enrolled. In 2016, 265 master's awarded. *Degree requirements:* For master's, comprehensive project. *Entrance requirements:* For master's, official transcripts, bachelor's degree from regionally-accredited university with minimum GPA of 3.0. Additional exam requirements/recommendations for international students: Required—TOEFL (minimum score 550 paper-based; 80 iBT). *Application deadline:* For fall admission, 7/1 priority date for domestic and international students; for spring admission, 11/1 priority date for domestic and international students. Applications are processed on a rolling basis. Application fee: $80. Electronic applications accepted. *Expenses:* $535 per semester hour (for MS in emergency/disaster management); $555 per semester hour (for MS in criminal justice). *Financial support:* In 2016–17, 14 students received support. Scholarships/grants and health care benefits available. Financial award application deadline: 3/1; financial award applicants required to submit FAFSA. *Unit head:* Dr. Robert Diemer, Director of Graduate Studies in Safety Administration, 352-588-8974, Fax: 352-588-8289, E-mail: graduatepublicsafety@saintleo.edu. *Application contact:* Jennifer Shelley, Senior Associate Director of Graduate Admissions, 800-707-8846, Fax: 352-588-7873, E-mail: grad.admissions@saintleo.edu.
Website: http://www.saintleo.edu/academics/graduate

South Dakota State University, Graduate School, College of Education and Human Sciences, Department of Teaching, Learning and Leadership, Brookings, SD 57007. Offers agricultural education (MS); curriculum and instruction (M Ed); educational administration (M Ed). *Program availability:* Part-time, evening/weekend, online learning. *Degree requirements:* For master's, portfolio, oral exam. *Entrance requirements:* For master's, minimum GPA of 2.75. Additional exam requirements/recommendations for international students: Required—TOEFL (minimum score 550 paper-based; 80 iBT). *Faculty research:* Inclusion school climate, K-12 reform and restructuring, rural development, ESL, leadership.

State University of New York at Oswego, Graduate Studies, School of Education, Department of Vocational Teacher Preparation, Oswego, NY 13126. Offers agriculture (MS Ed); business and marketing (MS Ed); family and consumer sciences (MS Ed); health careers (MS Ed); technical education (MS Ed); trade education (MS Ed). *Accreditation:* NCATE. *Program availability:* Part-time, evening/weekend. *Degree requirements:* For master's, comprehensive exam, thesis or alternative. *Entrance requirements:* Additional exam requirements/recommendations for international students: Required—TOEFL (minimum score 560 paper-based).

Stephen F. Austin State University, Graduate School, College of Forestry and Agriculture, Department of Agriculture, Nacogdoches, TX 75962. Offers MS. *Accreditation:* NCATE. *Degree requirements:* For master's, comprehensive exam, thesis (for some programs). *Entrance requirements:* For master's, GRE General Test, minimum GPA of 2.8 in last half of major, 2.5 overall. Additional exam requirements/recommendations for international students: Required—TOEFL (minimum score 550 paper-based). *Faculty research:* Asian vegetables, soil fertility, animal breeding, animal nutrition.

Tennessee State University, The School of Graduate Studies and Research, College of Agriculture, Human and Natural Sciences, Nashville, TN 37209-1561. Offers agricultural sciences (MS), including agribusiness, agricultural and extension education, animal science, plant and soil science; biological sciences (MS, PhD); biotechnology (PhD); chemistry (MS). *Program availability:* Part-time, evening/weekend. *Degree requirements:* For master's, thesis. *Entrance requirements:* For master's, GRE General Test, GRE Subject Test, MAT. *Faculty research:* Small farm economics, ornamental horticulture, beef cattle production, rural elderly.

Texas A&M University, College of Agriculture and Life Sciences, Department of Agricultural Leadership, Education and Communications, College Station, TX 77843. Offers agricultural development (M Agr); agricultural education (Ed D); agricultural leadership, education and communication (M Ed, MS, Ed D, PhD). *Program availability:* Part-time, blended/hybrid learning. *Faculty:* 23. *Students:* 51 full-time (36 women), 68 part-time (45 women); includes 21 minority (5 Black or African American, non-Hispanic/Latino; 1 American Indian or Alaska Native, non-Hispanic/Latino; 3 Asian, non-Hispanic/Latino; 12 Hispanic/Latino), 2 international. Average age 31. 32 applicants, 94% accepted, 17 enrolled. In 2016, 41 master's, 12 doctorates awarded. Terminal master's awarded for partial completion of doctoral program. *Degree requirements:* For master's, comprehensive exam, thesis (for some programs); for doctorate, comprehensive exam, thesis/dissertation. *Entrance requirements:* For master's, GRE General Test, letters of reference, curriculum vitae; for doctorate, GRE General Test, 3 years of professional experience, letters of reference, curriculum vitae. Additional exam requirements/recommendations for international students: Required—TOEFL (minimum score 550 paper-based; 80 iBT), IELTS (minimum score 6), PTE (minimum score 53). *Application deadline:* For fall admission, 3/15 priority date for domestic students; for spring admission, 10/15 for domestic students. Application fee: $50 ($90 for international students). Electronic applications accepted. *Expenses:* Contact institution. *Financial support:* In 2016–17, 70 students received support, including 3 fellowships with tuition reimbursements available (averaging $6,960 per year), 3 research assistantships with tuition reimbursements available (averaging $3,799 per year), 15 teaching assistantships with tuition reimbursements available (averaging $7,664 per year); career-related internships or fieldwork, institutionally sponsored loans, scholarships/grants, traineeships, health care benefits, tuition waivers (full and partial), and unspecified assistantships also available. Support available to part-time students. Financial award application deadline: 3/15; financial award applicants required to submit FAFSA. *Faculty research:* Planning and needs assessment, instructional design, delivery strategies, evaluation and accountability, distance education. *Unit head:* Dr. Jack Elliot, Department Head, 979-862-3003, E-mail: jelliot@tamu.edu. *Application contact:* Clarice Fulton, Graduate Program Coordinator, 979-862-7180, E-mail: cfulton@tamu.edu.
Website: http://alec.tamu.edu/

Texas State University, The Graduate College, College of Applied Arts, Program in Agricultural Education, San Marcos, TX 78666. Offers M Ed. *Program availability:* Part-time, evening/weekend. *Faculty:* 7 full-time (2 women). *Students:* 12 full-time (9 women), 5 part-time (3 women); includes 5 minority (1 Asian, non-Hispanic/Latino; 4 Hispanic/Latino). Average age 31. 14 applicants, 71% accepted, 4 enrolled. In 2016, 3 master's awarded. *Degree requirements:* For master's, comprehensive exam, thesis (for some programs). *Entrance requirements:* For master's, baccalaureate degree from regionally-accredited university in agriculture or closely-related field with minimum GPA of 2.75 in last 60 hours of course work; 3 letters of reference (2 from academia). Additional exam requirements/recommendations for international students: Required—TOEFL (minimum score 550 paper-based; 78 iBT). *Application deadline:* For fall admission, 6/15 for domestic students, 6/1 for international students; for spring admission, 10/15 for domestic students, 10/1 for international students; for summer admission, 4/15 for domestic students, 3/15 for international students. Applications are processed on a rolling basis. Application fee: $40 ($90 for international students). Electronic applications accepted. *Expenses:* $9,702 per year. *Financial support:* In 2016–17, 12 students received support, including 6 research assistantships (averaging $14,680 per year); teaching assistantships, career-related internships or fieldwork, Federal Work-Study, institutionally sponsored loans, and scholarships/grants also available. Support available to part-time students. Financial award application deadline: 4/1; financial award applicants required to submit FAFSA. *Faculty research:* Food safety and agroterrorism, sustainable agriculture, soil and water conservation. *Unit head:* Dr. Douglas Morrish, Graduate Advisor, 512-245-2130, E-mail: dm43@txstate.edu. *Application contact:* Dr. Andrea Golato, Dean of the Graduate College, 512-245-2581, Fax: 512-245-8365, E-mail: gradcollege@txstate.edu.
Website: http://ag.txstate.edu/

Texas Tech University, Graduate School, College of Agricultural Sciences and Natural Resources, Department of Agricultural Education and Communications, Lubbock, TX 79409-2131. Offers agricultural communications (MS); agricultural communications and education (PhD); agricultural education (MS, Ed D). *Program availability:* Part-time, evening/weekend, 100% online. *Faculty:* 13 full-time (7 women), 2 part-time/adjunct (0 women). *Students:* 40 full-time (29 women), 49 part-time (36 women); includes 10 minority (2 Black or African American, non-Hispanic/Latino; 6 Hispanic/Latino; 2 Two or more races, non-Hispanic/Latino), 8 international. Average age 30. 42 applicants, 69% accepted, 23 enrolled. In 2016, 14 master's, 5 doctorates awarded. Terminal master's awarded for partial completion of doctoral program. *Degree requirements:* For master's, variable foreign language requirement, comprehensive exam, thesis optional; for doctorate, variable foreign language requirement, comprehensive exam, thesis/dissertation, experience plan. *Entrance requirements:* For master's and doctorate, GRE. Additional exam requirements/recommendations for international students: Required—TOEFL (minimum score 550 paper-based; 79 iBT). *Application deadline:* For fall admission, 6/1 priority date for domestic students, 1/15 priority date for international students; for spring admission, 9/1 priority date for domestic students, 6/15 priority date for international students. Applications are processed on a rolling basis. Application fee: $75. Electronic applications accepted. *Expenses:* $325 per credit hour full-time resident tuition, $733 per credit hour full-time non-resident tuition; $53.75 per credit hour fee plus $608 per term fee. *Financial support:* In 2016–17, 57 students received support, including 47 fellowships (averaging $4,893 per year), 32 research assistantships (averaging $11,790 per year), 4 teaching assistantships (averaging $4,500 per year); institutionally sponsored loans and scholarships/grants also available. Financial award application deadline: 4/15; financial award applicants required to submit FAFSA. *Faculty research:* Sustainable agriculture, food safety, international development, use of technology in agriculture, improvement of teaching and pedagogy. *Total annual research expenditures:* $316,376. *Unit head:* Dr. Scott Burris, Professor and Interim Chair, 806-834-8689, Fax: 806-742-2880, E-mail: scott.burris@ttu.edu. *Application contact:* Dr. Courtney Meyers, Associate Professor and Graduate Coordinator, 806-834-4364, Fax: 806-742-2880, E-mail: courtney.meyers@ttu.edu.
Website: http://www.aged.ttu.edu

The University of Arizona, College of Agriculture and Life Sciences, Department of Agricultural Education, Tucson, AZ 85721. Offers MAE, MS, Graduate Certificate. *Degree requirements:* For master's, thesis. *Entrance requirements:* For master's, teaching/extension experience or equivalent, minimum GPA of 3.0, 2 letters of recommendation. Additional exam requirements/recommendations for international students: Required—TOEFL (minimum score 550 paper-based; 79 iBT). Electronic applications accepted. *Faculty research:* Career placement, learning styles, noise impact on learning, computer technology, vocational education.

University of Arkansas, Graduate School, Dale Bumpers College of Agricultural, Food and Life Sciences, Department of Agricultural and Extension Education, Fayetteville, AR 72701. Offers MS. *Accreditation:* NCATE. *Students:* 11 applicants, 100% accepted. In 2016, 8 master's awarded. *Application deadline:* For fall admission, 4/1 for international students; for spring admission, 10/1 for international students. Applications are processed on a rolling basis. Application fee: $40 ($50 for international students). Electronic applications accepted. *Financial support:* In 2016–17, 3 research assistantships, 4 teaching assistantships were awarded; fellowships, career-related internships or fieldwork, and Federal Work-Study also available. Support available to part-time students. Financial award application deadline: 4/1; financial award applicants required to submit FAFSA. *Unit head:* Dr. George Wardlow, Graduate Coordinator, 479-575-2035, E-mail: wardlow@uark.edu. *Application contact:* Dr. Donna Graham, Graduate Coordinator, 479-575-2039, E-mail: dgraham@uark.edu.
Website: http://aeed.uark.edu/

University of Connecticut, Graduate School, Neag School of Education, Department of Curriculum and Instruction, Storrs, CT 06269. Offers agriculture (MA), including agriculture education; agriculture education (PhD); bilingual and bicultural education (MA, PhD); elementary education (MA, PhD); English education (MA, PhD); history and social sciences education (MA, PhD); mathematics education (MA, PhD); music education (MA); reading education (MA, PhD); science education (MA, PhD); secondary education (MA, PhD); world languages education (MA, PhD). *Accreditation:* NCATE.

Terminal master's awarded for partial completion of doctoral program. *Degree requirements:* For master's, comprehensive exam, thesis or alternative; for doctorate, thesis/dissertation. *Entrance requirements:* For doctorate, GRE General Test. Additional exam requirements/recommendations for international students: Required—TOEFL (minimum score 550 paper-based). Electronic applications accepted.

University of Delaware, College of Agriculture and Natural Resources, Department of Food and Resource Economics, Agricultural Education Program, Newark, DE 19716. Offers MA.

University of Florida, Graduate School, College of Agricultural and Life Sciences, Department of Agricultural Education and Communication, Gainesville, FL 32611. Offers agricultural education and communication (MS, PhD); tropical conservation and development (MS, PhD). *Program availability:* Part-time, evening/weekend, online learning. *Degree requirements:* For master's, comprehensive exam (for some programs), thesis (for some programs); for doctorate, comprehensive exam, thesis/dissertation. *Entrance requirements:* For master's and doctorate, GRE General Test, minimum GPA of 3.0. Additional exam requirements/recommendations for international students: Required—TOEFL (minimum score 550 paper-based; 80 iBT), IELTS (minimum score 6). Electronic applications accepted. *Faculty research:* Teaching and learning in formal and non-formal settings, program evaluation and development, leadership development in agriculture and natural resources, public issues education in agriculture and natural resources.

University of Illinois at Urbana–Champaign, Graduate College, College of Agricultural, Consumer and Environmental Sciences, Agricultural Education Program, Champaign, IL 61820. Offers MS. *Program availability:* Part-time, online learning.

University of Missouri, Office of Research and Graduate Studies, College of Agriculture, Food and Natural Resources, Department of Agricultural Education, Columbia, MO 65211. Offers MS, PhD. *Accreditation:* TEAC. *Faculty:* 4 full-time (1 woman). *Students:* 14 full-time (10 women), 23 part-time (21 women). Average age 28. *Degree requirements:* For doctorate, comprehensive exam, thesis/dissertation. *Entrance requirements:* For master's, minimum GPA of 3.0 for last 60 hours of undergraduate coursework; for doctorate, GRE (preferred minimum score of 1000), minimum GPA of 3.5 on prior graduate course work; minimum of 3 years of full-time appropriate teaching or other professional experience; correspondence with one department faculty member in proposed area of concentration. Additional exam requirements/recommendations for international students: Required—TOEFL (minimum score 550 paper-based; 80 iBT). *Application deadline:* For fall admission, 7/15 for domestic students. Applications are processed on a rolling basis. Application fee: $65 ($90 for international students). Electronic applications accepted. *Expenses:* Tuition, state resident: full-time $6347; part-time $352.60 per credit hour. Tuition, nonresident: full-time $17,379; part-time $965.50 per credit hour. *Required fees:* $1035. Tuition and fees vary according to course load, campus/location and program. *Financial support:* Fellowships, research assistantships with tuition reimbursements, teaching assistantships with tuition reimbursements, Federal Work-Study, scholarships/grants, health care benefits, and unspecified assistantships available. *Faculty research:* Program and professional development, evaluation, teaching and learning theories and practices, educational methods, organization and administration, leadership and communication.
Website: http://dass.missouri.edu/aged/grad/

University of Missouri, Office of Research and Graduate Studies, College of Education, Department of Learning, Teaching and Curriculum, Columbia, MO 65211. Offers agricultural education (M Ed, PhD, Ed S); art education (M Ed, PhD, Ed S); business and office education (M Ed, PhD, Ed S); early childhood education (M Ed, PhD, Ed S); elementary education (M Ed, PhD, Ed S); English education (M Ed, PhD, Ed S); foreign language education (M Ed, PhD, Ed S); health education and promotion (M Ed, PhD); learning and instruction (M Ed); marketing education (M Ed, PhD, Ed S); mathematics education (M Ed, PhD, Ed S); music education (M Ed, PhD, Ed S); reading education (M Ed, PhD, Ed S); science education (M Ed, PhD, Ed S); social studies education (M Ed, PhD, Ed S); vocational education (M Ed, PhD, Ed S). *Program availability:* Part-time. *Faculty:* 30 full-time (18 women), 1 (woman) part-time/adjunct. *Students:* 157 full-time (124 women), 157 part-time (125 women). Terminal master's awarded for partial completion of doctoral program. *Degree requirements:* For doctorate, thesis/dissertation. *Entrance requirements:* For master's and Ed S, GRE General Test or MAT, minimum GPA of 3.0; for doctorate, GRE General Test, minimum GPA of 3.0. Additional exam requirements/recommendations for international students: Required—TOEFL (minimum score 600 paper-based; 100 iBT). *Application deadline:* For fall admission, 12/1 priority date for domestic and international students. Applications are processed on a rolling basis. Application fee: $75 ($90 for international students). Electronic applications accepted. *Expenses:* Tuition, state resident: full-time $6347; part-time $352.60 per credit hour. Tuition, nonresident: full-time $17,379; part-time $965.50 per credit hour. *Required fees:* $1035. Tuition and fees vary according to course load, campus/location and program. *Financial support:* Fellowships, research assistantships, teaching assistantships, institutionally sponsored loans, traineeships, health care benefits, and unspecified assistantships available. Support available to part-time students.
Website: http://education.missouri.edu/LTC/index.php

University of Nebraska–Lincoln, Graduate College, College of Agricultural Sciences and Natural Resources, Department of Agricultural Leadership, Education and Communication, Lincoln, NE 68588. Offers leadership development (MS); leadership education (MS); teaching and extension education (MS). *Accreditation:* TEAC. *Degree requirements:* For master's, thesis optional. *Entrance requirements:* For master's, resume. Additional exam requirements/recommendations for international students: Required—TOEFL (minimum score 550 paper-based). Electronic applications accepted. *Faculty research:* Teaching and instruction, extension education, leadership and human resource development, international agricultural education.

University of Puerto Rico, Mayagüez Campus, Graduate Studies, College of Agricultural Sciences, Department of Agricultural Education, Mayagüez, PR 00681-9000. Offers agricultural education (MS); agricultural extension (MS). *Accreditation:* NCATE. *Program availability:* Part-time. *Faculty:* 3 full-time (1 woman). *Students:* 1 (woman) full-time; minority (Hispanic/Latino). Average age 25. 2 applicants, 100% accepted, 1 enrolled. *Degree requirements:* For master's, comprehensive exam, thesis. *Entrance requirements:* For master's, BA in home economics; BS in agricultural education, agriculture, home economics, or equivalent. *Application deadline:* For fall admission, 2/15 for domestic and international students; for spring admission, 9/15 for domestic and international students. Applications are processed on a rolling basis. Application fee: $25. Electronic applications accepted. *Expenses: Tuition, area resident:* Full-time $2466. *International tuition:* $7166 full-time. *Required fees:* $210. Tuition and fees vary according to course level, campus/location, program and student level. *Financial support:* In 2016–17, 2 students received support, including 2 teaching assistantships with tuition reimbursements available (averaging $2,068 per year); unspecified assistantships also available. *Faculty research:* Curricular development and supervision, youth education, rural sociology. *Unit head:* David Padilla, PhD, Director, 787-832-4040 Ext. 3855, Fax: 787-265-3814, E-mail: david.padilla@upr.edu. *Application contact:* Nydia Sanchez, Secretary, 787-832-4040 Ext. 3120, Fax: 787-265-3814, E-mail: nydiaris.sanchez@upr.edu.
Website: http://educacion.cca.uprm.edu/

The University of Tennessee, Graduate School, College of Agricultural Sciences and Natural Resources, Department of Agricultural Economics, Knoxville, TN 37996. Offers agricultural education (MS); agricultural extension education (MS). *Accreditation:* NCATE. *Program availability:* Part-time, online learning. *Degree requirements:* For master's, thesis or alternative. *Entrance requirements:* For master's, minimum GPA of 2.7. Additional exam requirements/recommendations for international students: Required—TOEFL. Electronic applications accepted.

University of Wisconsin–River Falls, Outreach and Graduate Studies, College of Agriculture, Food, and Environmental Sciences, Department of Agricultural Education, River Falls, WI 54022. Offers MS. *Program availability:* Part-time. *Degree requirements:* For master's, comprehensive exam, thesis (for some programs). *Entrance requirements:* For master's, minimum GPA of 2.75. Additional exam requirements/recommendations for international students: Required—TOEFL (minimum score 500 paper-based; 65 iBT), IELTS (minimum score 5.5). Electronic applications accepted.

Utah State University, School of Graduate Studies, College of Agriculture, Department of Agricultural Systems Technology and Education, Logan, UT 84322. Offers agricultural systems technology (MS), including agricultural extension education, agricultural mechanization, international agricultural extension, secondary and postsecondary agricultural education; family and consumer sciences education (MS). *Program availability:* Part-time, online learning. *Degree requirements:* For master's, comprehensive exam (for some programs), thesis (for some programs). *Entrance requirements:* For master's, GRE General Test, MAT, BS in agricultural education, agricultural extension, or related agricultural or science discipline; minimum GPA of 3.0. Additional exam requirements/recommendations for international students: Required—TOEFL. *Faculty research:* Extension and adult education; structures and environment; low-input agriculture; farm safety, systems, and mechanizations.

West Virginia University, Davis College of Agriculture, Forestry and Consumer Sciences, Division of Resource Management and Sustainable Development, Program in Agricultural and Extension Education, Morgantown, WV 26506. Offers agricultural and extension education (MS, PhD); teaching vocational-agriculture (MS). *Accreditation:* NCATE. *Program availability:* Part-time. *Degree requirements:* For master's, thesis. *Entrance requirements:* For master's, GRE General Test, minimum GPA of 2.75. Additional exam requirements/recommendations for international students: Required—TOEFL. *Faculty research:* Program development in vocational agriculture, agricultural extension, supervised experience programs, leadership development.

Art Education

Academy of Art University, Graduate Programs, School of Art Education, San Francisco, CA 94105-3410. Offers MA, MAT. *Program availability:* Part-time, 100% online. *Faculty:* 2 full-time (both women), 10 part-time/adjunct (9 women). *Students:* 33 full-time (30 women), 20 part-time (17 women); includes 0 minority (2 Black or African American, non-Hispanic/Latino; 1 American Indian or Alaska Native, non-Hispanic/Latino; 2 Asian, non-Hispanic/Latino; 2 Hispanic/Latino; 1 Two or more races, non-Hispanic/Latino), 26 international. Average age 33. 30 applicants, 100% accepted, 15 enrolled. In 2016, 8 master's awarded. *Degree requirements:* For master's, final review. *Entrance requirements:* For master's, statement of intent; resume; portfolio/reel; official college transcripts. *Application deadline:* Applications are processed on a rolling basis. Application fee: $50. Electronic applications accepted. *Expenses: Tuition:* Part-time $982 per unit. *Financial support:* Career-related internships or fieldwork, Federal Work-Study, and scholarships/grants available. Financial award application deadline: 8/10; financial award applicants required to submit FAFSA. *Unit head:* 800-544-ARTS, E-mail: info@academyart.edu. *Application contact:* 800-544-ARTS, E-mail: info@academyart.edu.
Website: http://www.academyart.edu/art-education-school/index.html

Adelphi University, Ruth S. Ammon School of Education, Program in Art Education, Garden City, NY 11530-0701. Offers MA. *Program availability:* Part-time. *Students:* 1 (woman) full-time, 6 part-time (5 women); includes 28 minority (14 Asian, non-Hispanic/Latino; 14 Hispanic/Latino), 43 international. Average age 29. 15 applicants, 33% accepted, 2 enrolled. In 2016, 4 master's awarded. *Entrance requirements:* For master's, 2 letters of recommendation, visual arts portfolio, essay. Additional exam requirements/recommendations for international students: Required—TOEFL (minimum score 550 paper-based; 80 iBT), IELTS (minimum score 6.5). *Application deadline:* For fall admission, 4/1 for international students; for spring admission, 11/1 for international students. Application fee: $50. Electronic applications accepted. *Expenses:* Contact institution. *Financial support:* Research assistantships, teaching assistantships, career-related internships or fieldwork, institutionally sponsored loans, scholarships/grants, traineeships, and unspecified assistantships available. Support available to part-time students. Financial award application deadline: 2/15; financial award applicants required to submit FAFSA. *Unit head:* Courtney Lee Weida, Director, 516-877-4105, E-mail: cweida@adelphi.edu. *Application contact:* Christine Murphy, Director of Admissions, 516-877-3050, Fax: 516-877-3039, E-mail: graduateadmissions@adelphi.edu.

Alabama Agricultural and Mechanical University, School of Graduate Studies, College of Education, Humanities, and Behavioral Sciences, Department of Visual, Performing, and Communication Arts, Huntsville, AL 35811. Offers art education (MS); music education (M Ed). *Accreditation:* NCATE. *Program availability:* Part-time, evening/weekend. *Degree requirements:* For master's, comprehensive exam. *Entrance requirements:* For master's, GRE General Test. Additional exam requirements/recommendations for international students: Required—TOEFL (minimum score 500 paper-based; 61 iBT). *Application deadline:* For fall admission, 5/1 for domestic students. Applications are processed on a rolling basis. Application fee: $25. Electronic applications accepted. *Expenses:* Tuition, nonresident: part-time $826 per credit hour.

Art Education

Full-time tuition and fees vary according to course load and program. *Financial support:* Career-related internships or fieldwork and traineeships available. Financial award application deadline: 4/1. *Faculty research:* Jazz and black music, Alabama folk music. *Unit head:* Dr. Horace Carney, Chair, 256-372-5512.

American University of Puerto Rico, Program in Education, Bayamon, PR 00960-2037. Offers art education (M Ed); elementary education 4-6 (M Ed); elementary education K-3 (M Ed); general science education (M Ed); physical education (M Ed); special education (M Ed). *Program availability:* Part-time, evening/weekend. *Faculty:* 17 part-time/adjunct (7 women). *Students:* 22 full-time (18 women), 54 part-time (42 women); all minorities (all Hispanic/Latino). Average age 33. 22 applicants, 86% accepted, 19 enrolled. In 2016, 53 master's awarded. *Entrance requirements:* For master's, EXADEP, GRE, or MAT, 2 letters of recommendation, minimum GPA of 2.5. *Application deadline:* For fall admission, 8/1 for domestic students; for winter admission, 10/18 for domestic students; for spring admission, 3/15 for domestic students. Applications are processed on a rolling basis. Application fee: $25. *Financial support:* In 2016–17, 79 students received support, including 76 fellowships (averaging $400 per year), 55 teaching assistantships (averaging $1,741 per year). Financial award applicants required to submit FAFSA. *Unit head:* Prof. Bolivar Ramirez-Carlo, III, Dean of Faculty, 787-620-2040 Ext. 2010, Fax: 787-620-2958, E-mail: bramirez@aupr.edu. *Application contact:* Keren I. Llanos-Figueroa, Information Contact, 787-620-2040 Ext. 2021, Fax: 787-785-7377, E-mail: oficnaadmisiones@aupr.edu.

Arcadia University, School of Education, Glenside, PA 19038-3295. Offers art education (M Ed); computer education (CAS); curriculum (CAS); curriculum studies (M Ed); early childhood education (M Ed), including individualized, master teacher, research in child development; educational leadership (M Ed, Ed D, CAS); elementary education (M Ed); English education (MA Ed); environmental education (MA Ed); instructional technology (M Ed); language arts (M Ed); library science (M Ed); mathematics education (M Ed, MA Ed); music education (MA Ed); psychology (MA Ed); reading (M Ed, CAS); science education (M Ed, CAS); secondary education (M Ed, CAS); special education (M Ed, Ed D, CAS); theater arts (MA Ed); written communication (MA Ed). *Accreditation:* NASAD. *Program availability:* Part-time, evening/weekend, online learning. *Faculty:* 19 full-time (13 women), 3 part-time/adjunct (all women). *Students:* 22 full-time (16 women), 356 part-time (284 women); includes 84 minority (55 Black or African American, non-Hispanic/Latino; 2 American Indian or Alaska Native, non-Hispanic/Latino; 13 Asian, non-Hispanic/Latino; 11 Hispanic/Latino; 3 Two or more races, non-Hispanic/Latino), 4 international. Average age 34. 145 applicants, 73% accepted, 80 enrolled. In 2016, 95 master's, 11 doctorates awarded. *Application deadline:* Applications are processed on a rolling basis. Application fee: $50. Electronic applications accepted. *Expenses:* Contact institution. *Financial support:* Career-related internships or fieldwork, tuition waivers (partial), and unspecified assistantships available. *Unit head:* John T Groves, Interim Dean of the School of Education, 215-572-2940. *Application contact:* 215-572-2925, Fax: 215-572-2126, E-mail: grad@arcadia.edu.

Arizona State University at the Tempe campus, Herberger Institute for Design and the Arts, School of Art, Tempe, AZ 85287-1505. Offers art education (MA); art history (MA); ceramics (MFA); design, environment and the arts (PhD), including history, theory and criticism; drawing (MFA); fibers (MFA); intermedia (MFA); metals (MFA); museum studies (MFA); painting (MFA); printmaking (MFA); sculpture (MFA); wood (MFA); MFA/MA. Terminal master's awarded for partial completion of doctoral program. *Degree requirements:* For master's, thesis/exhibition (MFA, MA in art education); interactive Program of Study (iPOS) submitted before completing 50 percent of required credit hours; for doctorate, comprehensive exam, thesis/dissertation, interactive Program of Study (iPOS) submitted before completing 50 percent of required credit hours. *Entrance requirements:* For master's, GRE or MAT, minimum GPA of 3.0 or equivalent in last 2 years of work leading to bachelor's degree; for doctorate, GRE, master's degree in architecture, graphic design, industrial design, interior design, landscape architecture, or art history or equivalent standing; statement of purpose; 3 letters of recommendation; indication of potential faculty mentor; sample of written work. Additional exam requirements/recommendations for international students: Required—TOEFL, IELTS, or PTE. Electronic applications accepted.

Art Academy of Cincinnati, Program in Art Education, Cincinnati, OH 45202. Offers MAAE. Offered during summer only. *Accreditation:* NASAD. *Program availability:* Part-time. *Degree requirements:* For master's, thesis, portfolio/exhibit. *Entrance requirements:* For master's, 2 letters of recommendation, portfolio, artist statement, undergraduate transcript. Additional exam requirements/recommendations for international students: Required—TOEFL (minimum score 550 paper-based; 80 iBT). Electronic applications accepted.

Boise State University, College of Arts and Sciences, Department of Art, Boise, ID 83725. Offers art education (MA); visual arts (MFA). *Program availability:* Part-time. *Faculty:* 8. *Students:* 8 full-time (5 women), 4 part-time (2 women); includes 1 minority (Hispanic/Latino). Average age 38. 22 applicants, 23% accepted, 4 enrolled. In 2016, 5 master's awarded. *Degree requirements:* For master's, thesis optional. *Entrance requirements:* For master's, minimum GPA of 3.0, portfolio. Additional exam requirements/recommendations for international students: Required—TOEFL (minimum score 550 paper-based; 80 iBT), IELTS (minimum score 6). *Application deadline:* For fall admission, 1/15 priority date for domestic and international students. Application fee: $80 ($110 for international students). Electronic applications accepted. *Expenses:* Tuition, state resident: full-time $6058; part-time $358 per credit hour. Tuition, nonresident: full-time $20,108; part-time $608 per credit hour. *Required fees:* $2108. Tuition and fees vary according to program. *Financial support:* In 2016–17, 1 student received support, including 2 teaching assistantships (averaging $5,541 per year); scholarships/grants and unspecified assistantships also available. Financial award application deadline: 1/15; financial award applicants required to submit FAFSA. *Unit head:* Dr. Kathleen Keys, Department Chair, 208-426-1230, E-mail: kathleenkeys@boisestate.edu. *Application contact:* Chad Erpelding, Graduate Program Coordinator, 208-426-4081, E-mail: chaderpelding@boisestate.edu.
Website: http://art.boisestate.edu/gradprogram/

Boston University, College of Fine Arts, School of Visual Arts, Boston, MA 02226. Offers art education (MA); graphic design (MFA); painting (MFA); sculpture (MFA); studio teaching (MA). *Faculty:* 17 full-time, 4 part-time/adjunct. *Students:* 197 full-time (166 women), 3 part-time (all women); includes 24 minority (2 Black or African American, non-Hispanic/Latino; 9 Asian, non-Hispanic/Latino; 8 Hispanic/Latino; 5 Two or more races, non-Hispanic/Latino), 58 international. Average age 31. 257 applicants, 27% accepted, 21 enrolled. In 2016, 122 master's awarded. *Entrance requirements:* For master's, portfolio. Additional exam requirements/recommendations for international students: Required—TOEFL (minimum score 90 iBT), IELTS (minimum score 7). *Application deadline:* For fall admission, 2/1 for domestic and international students. Applications are processed on a rolling basis. Application fee: $80. *Expenses:* Contact institution. *Financial support:* In 2016–17, 36 students received support. Fellowships, teaching assistantships, scholarships/grants, and unspecified assistantships available. Financial award application deadline: 2/1. *Unit head:* Jeannette Guillemin, Interim Director, 617-353-3371. *Application contact:* Jessica Caccamo, Assistant Director, 617-353-3371, E-mail: visuarts@bu.edu.

Bowling Green State University, Graduate College, College of Arts and Sciences, School of Art, Bowling Green, OH 43403. Offers 2-D studio art (MA, MFA); 3-D studio art (MA, MFA); art education (MA); art history (MA); computer art (MA); design (MFA); digital arts (MFA); graphics (MFA). *Accreditation:* NASAD. *Program availability:* Part-time. *Degree requirements:* For master's, thesis or alternative, final exhibit (MFA). *Entrance requirements:* For master's, GRE General Test (MA), slide portfolio (15-20 slides). Additional exam requirements/recommendations for international students: Required—TOEFL. *Application deadline:* For fall admission, 2/15 for domestic students. Application fee: $30. Electronic applications accepted. *Financial support:* Research assistantships with full and partial tuition reimbursements, teaching assistantships with full and partial tuition reimbursements, career-related internships or fieldwork, institutionally sponsored loans, and unspecified assistantships available. Support available to part-time students. Financial award applicants required to submit FAFSA. *Faculty research:* Computer animation and virtual reality, Spanish still-life painting from 1600 to 1800, art and psychotherapy, Japanese wood-firing techniques in ceramics, non-toxic printmaking technologies. *Unit head:* Dr. Katerina Ruedi Ray, Director, 419-372-8575. *Application contact:* Marisa Cline, Graduate Coordinator, 419-372-2786, E-mail: mlcline@bgsu.edu.

Bridgewater State University, College of Graduate Studies, College of Humanities and Social Sciences, Department of Art, Bridgewater, MA 02325. Offers MAT. *Accreditation:* NASAD. *Program availability:* Part-time, evening/weekend. *Degree requirements:* For master's, comprehensive exam. *Entrance requirements:* For master's, GRE General Test.

Brigham Young University, Graduate Studies, College of Fine Arts and Communications, Department of Art, Provo, UT 84602-6414. Offers art education (MA); studio arts (MFA). Art education applications accepted biennially. *Accreditation:* NASAD. *Faculty:* 13 full-time (2 women). *Students:* 24 full-time (14 women); includes 4 minority (2 Asian, non-Hispanic/Latino; 1 Hispanic/Latino; 1 Native Hawaiian or other Pacific Islander, non-Hispanic/Latino). Average age 26. 16 applicants, 13% accepted, 2 enrolled. In 2016, 7 master's awarded. *Degree requirements:* For master's, one foreign language, comprehensive exam, thesis, selected project (for MFA); curriculum project (for art education). *Entrance requirements:* For master's, minimum GPA of 3.0 (for MFA, MA in art education), portfolio submitted on a flash drive (for MFA); writing samples (for MA). Additional exam requirements/recommendations for international students: Required—TOEFL (minimum score 580 paper-based; 85 iBT). *Application deadline:* For fall admission, 2/1 for domestic and international students. Application fee: $50. Electronic applications accepted. *Expenses: Tuition:* Full-time $66[illegible]; part-time $393 per credit. Tuition and fees vary according to course load, program and student's religious affiliation. *Financial support:* In 2016–17, 16 students received support. Teaching assistantships with partial tuition reimbursements available, scholarships/grants, and tuition waivers (partial) available. Financial award application deadline: 2/1. *Faculty research:* Methodology-standards-assessment, exploration of art making processes, new genre, installation, photography, theory and critical studies, art history. *Unit head:* Prof. Gary C. Barton, Chair, 801-422-4429, Fax: 801-422-0695, E-mail: garold_barton@byu.edu. *Application contact:* Sharon Lyn Heelis, Secretary, 801-422-4429, Fax: 801-422-0695, E-mail: sharon_heelis@byu.edu.
Website: http://art.byu.edu

Brooklyn College of the City University of New York, School of Education, Program in Early Childhood Education, Brooklyn, NY 11210-2889. Offers art teacher (K-12) (MA); birth-grade 2 (MS Ed). *Program availability:* Part-time, evening/weekend. *Entrance requirements:* For master's, LAST, bachelor's degree in early childhood education, resume, 2 letters of recommendation, essay. Additional exam requirements/recommendations for international students: Required—TOEFL (minimum score 500 paper-based; 61 iBT). Electronic applications accepted. *Faculty research:* Children's narrations, language acquisition, culture and education.

Buffalo State College, State University of New York, The Graduate School, Faculty of Arts and Humanities, Department of Art Education, Buffalo, NY 14222-1095. Offers MS Ed. *Accreditation:* NASAD; NCATE. *Program availability:* Part-time, evening/weekend. *Degree requirements:* For master's, thesis or alternative, project. *Entrance requirements:* For master's, New York teaching certificate, interview, minimum GPA of 3.0. Additional exam requirements/recommendations for international students: Required—TOEFL (minimum score 550 paper-based).

California State University, Long Beach, Graduate Studies, College of the Arts, Department of Art, Long Beach, CA 90840. Offers art education (MA); studio art (MFA). *Accreditation:* NASAD. *Program availability:* Part-time. *Degree requirements:* For master's, thesis (for some programs). *Entrance requirements:* For master's, minimum GPA of 3.0 in last 60 hours. *Application deadline:* For fall admission, 7/1 for domestic students; for spring admission, 12/1 for domestic students. Applications are processed on a rolling basis. Application fee: $55. Electronic applications accepted. *Financial support:* Federal Work-Study, institutionally sponsored loans, and scholarships/grants available. Financial award application deadline: 3/2. *Unit head:* Prof. David Hadlock, Chair, 562-985-7908, Fax: 562-985-1650, E-mail: dhadlock@csulb.edu. *Application contact:* Margaret Black, Graduate Advisor, 562-985-7910, Fax: 562-985-1650.

California State University, Los Angeles, Graduate Studies, College of Arts and Letters, Department of Art, Los Angeles, CA 90032-8530. Offers art (MA), including art education, art history, art therapy, ceramics, metals, and textiles, design (MA, MFA), painting, sculpture, and graphic arts, photography; fine arts (MFA), including crafts, design (MA, MFA), studio arts. *Accreditation:* NASAD (one or more programs are accredited). *Program availability:* Part-time, evening/weekend. *Degree requirements:* For master's, comprehensive exam, project or thesis. *Entrance requirements:* For master's, portfolio. Additional exam requirements/recommendations for international students: Required—TOEFL (minimum score 500 paper-based). Electronic applications accepted. *Faculty research:* The artist and the book, conceptual art, ceramic processes, computer graphics, architectural graphics.

California State University, Northridge, Graduate Studies, College of Arts, Media, and Communication, Department of Art, Northridge, CA 91330. Offers art education (MA); art history (MA); studio art (MA, MFA); visual communications (MA, MFA). *Accreditation:* NASAD. *Faculty:* 23 full-time (10 women), 75 part-time/adjunct (38 women). *Students:* 22 full-time (15 women), 5 part-time (2 women); includes 12 minority (1 Asian, non-Hispanic/Latino; 8 Hispanic/Latino; 3 Two or more races, non-Hispanic/Latino), 3 international. Average age 30. 51 applicants, 27% accepted, 12 enrolled. *Application deadline:* For fall admission, 11/30 for domestic students. Application fee: $55. *Expenses:* Tuition, state resident: full-time $4152. *Financial support:* Application deadline: 3/1. *Unit head:* Prof. Edward Alfano, Chair, 818-677-2242, E-mail: art.dept@csun.edu.
Website: http://www.csun.edu/art/

Carthage College, Division of Teacher Education, Kenosha, WI 53140. Offers classroom guidance and counseling (M Ed); creative arts (M Ed); gifted and talented children (M Ed); language arts (M Ed); modern language (M Ed); natural sciences (M Ed); reading (M Ed, Certificate); social sciences (M Ed); teacher leadership (M Ed). *Program availability:* Part-time, evening/weekend. *Degree requirements:* For master's, thesis optional. *Entrance requirements:* For master's, MAT, minimum B average, letters of reference.

Case Western Reserve University, School of Graduate Studies, Department of Art History and Art, Program in Art Education, Cleveland, OH 44106. Offers MA. Program offered jointly with The Cleveland Museum of Art. *Accreditation:* TEAC. *Program availability:* Part-time. *Faculty:* 9 full-time (8 women), 2 part-time/adjunct (1 woman). *Students:* 4 full-time (3 women), 2 part-time (both women); includes 1 minority (Two or more races, non-Hispanic/Latino), 1 international. Average age 26. 5 applicants, 60% accepted, 3 enrolled. In 2016, 3 master's awarded. *Degree requirements:* For master's, thesis, art exhibit. *Entrance requirements:* For master's, NTE, interview, portfolio, three letters of recommendation. Additional exam requirements/recommendations for international students: Required—TOEFL (minimum score 577 paper-based; 90 iBT); Recommended—IELTS (minimum score 7). *Application deadline:* For fall admission, 3/1 for domestic students; for spring admission, 11/1 for domestic students. Applications are processed on a rolling basis. Application fee: $50. Electronic applications accepted. *Expenses: Tuition:* Full-time $42,576; part-time $1774 per credit hour. *Required fees:* $34. Tuition and fees vary according to course load and program. *Faculty research:* Visual and aesthetic education, ethnographic arts, multiculturalism. *Unit head:* Tim Shuckerow, Director of Art Education and Art Studio, 216-368-2714, Fax: 216-368-2715, E-mail: tim.shuckerow@case.edu. *Application contact:* Dawn Rohm, Department Assistant, 216-368-2714, Fax: 216-368-4681, E-mail: dawn.rohm@case.edu.
Website: http://arthistory.case.edu/graduate/art-education/

Central Connecticut State University, School of Graduate Studies, College of Liberal Arts and Social Sciences, Department of Art, New Britain, CT 06050-4010. Offers art education (MS, Certificate). *Program availability:* Part-time, evening/weekend. *Faculty:* 5 full-time (1 woman), 1 (woman) part-time/adjunct. *Students:* 15 full-time (13 women), 23 part-time (14 women); includes 3 minority (1 Black or African American, non-Hispanic/Latino; 1 Asian, non-Hispanic/Latino; 1 Hispanic/Latino). Average age 34. 21 applicants, 62% accepted, 9 enrolled. In 2016, 3 master's, 4 other advanced degrees awarded. *Degree requirements:* For master's, thesis or alternative, exhibit or special project; for Certificate, qualifying exam. *Entrance requirements:* For master's, portfolio, essay. Additional exam requirements/recommendations for international students: Required—TOEFL (minimum score 550 paper-based; 79 iBT). *Application deadline:* For fall admission, 6/1 for domestic students, 5/1 for international students; for spring admission, 11/1 for domestic and international students. Applications are processed on a rolling basis. Application fee: $50. Electronic applications accepted. *Expenses: Tuition, area resident:* Full-time $6497; part-time $606 per credit. Tuition, state resident: full-time $9748; part-time $622 per credit. Tuition, nonresident: full-time $18,102; part-time $622 per credit. *Required fees:* $4459; $246 per credit. *Financial support:* In 2016–17, 2 students received support. Career-related internships or fieldwork, Federal Work-Study, scholarships/grants, and unspecified assistantships available. Support available to part-time students. Financial award application deadline: 3/1; financial award applicants required to submit FAFSA. *Faculty research:* Visual arts. *Unit head:* Prof. Rachel Siporin, Chair, 860-832-2620, E-mail: siporinr@ccsu.edu. *Application contact:* Patricia Gardner, Associate Director of Graduate Studies, 860-832-2350, Fax: 860-832-2362.
Website: http://www.ccsu.edu/art/

Chatham University, Program in Education, Pittsburgh, PA 15232-2826. Offers early childhood education (MAT); elementary education (MAT); environmental education (K-12) (MAT); secondary art (MAT); secondary biology education (MAT); secondary chemistry education (MAT); secondary English education (MAT); secondary math education (MAT); secondary physics education (MAT); secondary social studies education (MAT); special education (MAT). *Degree requirements:* For master's, thesis, teaching experience. *Entrance requirements:* For master's, minimum GPA of 3.0, sample of written work, recommendation letters. Additional exam requirements/recommendations for international students: Required—TOEFL (minimum score 600 paper-based; 100 iBT), IELTS (minimum score 7), TWE. Electronic applications accepted. Application fee is waived when completed online. *Expenses: Tuition:* Full-time $16,254; part-time $903 per credit hour. *Required fees:* $468; $26 per credit hour. *Faculty research:* Gifted education, environmental education, technology in education, writing as learning, class size and achievement.

Cleveland State University, College of Graduate Studies, College of Education and Human Services, Department of Curriculum and Foundations, Cleveland, OH 44115. Offers art education (M Ed); early childhood education (M Ed); foreign language education (M Ed); middle childhood mathematics and science education (M Ed); special education (M Ed), including mild/moderate disabilities, moderate/intensive disabilities; teaching English to speakers of other languages (M Ed). *Program availability:* Part-time, evening/weekend. *Faculty:* 19 full-time (14 women), 32 part-time/adjunct (27 women). *Students:* 86 full-time (65 women), 369 part-time (301 women); includes 119 minority (89 Black or African American, non-Hispanic/Latino; 1 American Indian or Alaska Native, non-Hispanic/Latino; 2 Asian, non-Hispanic/Latino; 16 Hispanic/Latino; 11 Two or more races, non-Hispanic/Latino), 35 international. Average age 34. 177 applicants, 55% accepted, 68 enrolled. In 2016, 179 master's awarded. *Degree requirements:* For master's, comprehensive exam (for some programs), thesis or alternative. *Entrance requirements:* For master's, GRE General Test or MAT, minimum GPA of 2.75. Additional exam requirements/recommendations for international students: Required—TOEFL (minimum score 550 paper-based; 78 iBT), IELTS (minimum score 6). *Application deadline:* For fall admission, 7/1 priority date for domestic students, 5/15 for international students; for spring admission, 11/15 for domestic students, 11/1 for international students; for summer admission, 4/1 for domestic students, 3/15 for international students. Applications are processed on a rolling basis. Application fee: $30. *Expenses:* Tuition, state resident: full-time $9565. Tuition, nonresident: full-time $17,980. Tuition and fees vary according to program. *Financial support:* In 2016–17, 13 research assistantships with full tuition reimbursements (averaging $15,845 per year) were awarded; tuition waivers (partial) and unspecified assistantships also available. Financial award application deadline: 2/15; financial award applicants required to submit FAFSA. *Faculty research:* Early childhood education, literacy education, special education: mild/moderate, moderate/intensive, early childhood intervention specialist), teaching English to speakers of other languages (TESOL). *Total annual research expenditures:* $275,907. *Unit head:* Dr. Tachelle I. Banks, Chairperson, 216-687-4608, Fax: 216-687-5379, E-mail: t.i.banks@csuohio.edu. *Application contact:* Michael Almony, Senior Student Services Specialist, 216-875-9929, Fax: 216-687-5491, E-mail: m.almony@csuohio.edu.
Website: http://www.csuohio.edu/cehs/te/te

The College of New Rochelle, Graduate School, Division of Education, Program in Art Education, New Rochelle, NY 10805-2308. Offers MS. *Program availability:* Part-time, evening/weekend. *Degree requirements:* For master's, thesis. *Entrance requirements:* For master's, interview, minimum GPA of 3.0 in field, 2.7 overall, portfolio. *Faculty research:* Developmental stages in art, assessment and evaluation, curriculum development, multicultural education, art museum education.

The Colorado College, Education Department, Program in Secondary Education, Colorado Springs, CO 80903-3294. Offers art teaching (K-12) (MAT); English teaching (MAT); foreign language teaching (MAT); mathematics teaching (MAT); music teaching (MAT); science teaching (MAT); social studies teaching (MAT). *Degree requirements:* For master's, thesis, internship. Electronic applications accepted.

Colorado State University–Pueblo, College of Education, Engineering and Professional Studies, Education Program, Pueblo, CO 81001-4901. Offers art education (M Ed); foreign language education (M Ed); health and physical education (M Ed); instructional technology (M Ed); linguistically diverse education (M Ed); music education (M Ed); special education (M Ed). *Accreditation:* TEAC. *Program availability:* Part-time. *Degree requirements:* For master's, portfolio. *Entrance requirements:* For master's, 3 recommendations, teaching license. Additional exam requirements/recommendations for international students: Required—TOEFL (minimum score 500 paper-based). Electronic applications accepted. *Faculty research:* Portfolio assessment, math education, science education.

Columbus State University, Graduate Studies, College of the Arts, Department of Art, Columbus, GA 31907-5645. Offers art education (M Ed, MAT). *Accreditation:* NASAD; NCATE. *Program availability:* Part-time, evening/weekend. *Faculty:* 1 full-time (0 women). *Students:* 1 full-time (0 women), 5 part-time (4 women); includes 3 minority (2 Black or African American, non-Hispanic/Latino; 1 Hispanic/Latino). Average age 29. 1 applicant, 100% accepted, 1 enrolled. In 2016, 2 master's awarded. *Degree requirements:* For master's, comprehensive exam, exhibit. *Entrance requirements:* For master's, portfolio, interview. Additional exam requirements/recommendations for international students: Required—TOEFL (minimum score 550 paper-based; 79 iBT). *Application deadline:* For fall admission, 6/30 for domestic students, 5/1 for international students; for spring admission, 11/1 for domestic and international students; for summer admission, 3/1 for domestic and international students. Applications are processed on a rolling basis. Application fee: $50. Electronic applications accepted. *Expenses:* Tuition, state resident: full-time $4804; part-time $2412 per semester hour. Tuition, nonresident: full-time $19,218; part-time $9612 per semester hour. *Required fees:* $1850; $1850 per semester hour. Tuition and fees vary according to program. *Financial support:* In 2016–17, 1 research assistantship was awarded; career-related internships or fieldwork, Federal Work-Study, institutionally sponsored loans, scholarships/grants, tuition waivers (partial), and unspecified assistantships also available. Support available to part-time students. Financial award application deadline: 5/1; financial award applicants required to submit FAFSA. *Unit head:* Prof. Joe Sanders, Department Chair, 706-507-8302, E-mail: sanders_joe@columbusstate.edu. *Application contact:* Kristin Williams, Director of International and Graduate Recruitment, 706-507-8848, Fax: 706-568-5091, E-mail: williams_kristin@columbusstate.edu.
Website: http://art.columbusstate.edu/

Concordia University, School of Graduate Studies, Faculty of Fine Arts, Department of Art Education, Montréal, QC H3G 1M8, Canada. Offers art education (MA, PhD), including art in education (MA). *Degree requirements:* For master's, thesis (for some programs), practicum; for doctorate, comprehensive exam, thesis/dissertation. *Entrance requirements:* For master's, teaching experience; for doctorate, teaching or related professional experience. *Faculty research:* Vernacular culture, museum education, psychotic art, adults and families.

Concordia University Wisconsin, Graduate Programs, Department of Education, Mequon, WI 53097-2402. Offers art education (MS Ed); early childhood (MS Ed); educational administration (MS Ed); environmental education (MS Ed); family studies (MS Ed); literacy (MS Ed); school counseling (MS Ed); special education (MS Ed). *Program availability:* Part-time, evening/weekend, online learning. *Degree requirements:* For master's, comprehensive exam, thesis or alternative. *Entrance requirements:* For master's, minimum GPA of 3.0, teaching license. Additional exam requirements/recommendations for international students: Required—TOEFL. Application fee: $35. *Financial support:* Career-related internships or fieldwork and tuition waivers (partial) available. Financial award application deadline: 8/1. *Faculty research:* Motivation, developmental learning, learning styles. *Unit head:* Dr. James Juergensen, Director, 262-243-4214, E-mail: james.juergensen@cuw.edu. *Application contact:* Graduate Admissions, 262-243-4248, Fax: 262-243-4428.

Converse College, School of Education and Graduate Studies, Program in Art Education, Spartanburg, SC 29302. Offers M Ed, MAT. *Accreditation:* NASAD. *Expenses: Tuition:* Full-time $3600; part-time $400 per credit hour. *Required fees:* $70 per term. *Unit head:* Susanne Gunter, Department Chair, 864-596-9126, E-mail: susanne.gunter@converse.edu. *Application contact:* 864-596-9404, E-mail: graduate@converse.edu.

Delaware State University, Graduate Programs, College of Education, Health and Public Policy, Program in Art Education, Dover, DE 19901-2277. Offers MA. *Entrance requirements:* Additional exam requirements/recommendations for international students: Required—TOEFL (minimum score 550 paper-based). Electronic applications accepted.

East Carolina University, Graduate School, College of Fine Arts and Communication, School of Art and Design, Greenville, NC 27858-4353. Offers art education (MA Ed); ceramics (MFA); graphic design (MFA); illustration (MFA); metal design (MFA); painting and drawing (MFA); photography (MFA); printmaking (MFA); sculpture (MFA); textile design (MFA); wood design (MFA). *Accreditation:* NASAD (one or more programs are accredited). *Program availability:* Part-time, evening/weekend. *Students:* 25 full-time (15 women), 17 part-time (12 women); includes 5 minority (2 Asian, non-Hispanic/Latino; 2 Hispanic/Latino; 1 Two or more races, non-Hispanic/Latino). Average age 33. 37 applicants, 62% accepted, 16 enrolled. In 2016, 17 master's awarded. *Degree requirements:* For master's, comprehensive exam, thesis (for some programs). *Entrance requirements:* For master's, GRE General Test or MAT, portfolio. Additional exam requirements/recommendations for international students: Required—TOEFL. *Application deadline:* For fall admission, 2/1 for domestic students; for spring admission, 10/1 for domestic students. Applications are processed on a rolling basis. Application fee: $50. *Financial support:* Research assistantships with partial tuition reimbursements, teaching assistantships with partial tuition reimbursements, and Federal Work-Study available. Support available to part-time students. Financial award application deadline: 6/1. *Unit head:* Michael H. Drought, Director, 252-328-6665, E-mail: droughtm@ecu.edu. *Application contact:* Dr. Linda H. Nelson, Information Contact, 252-328-1286, E-mail: nelsonlh@ecu.edu.
Website: http://www.ecu.edu/cs-cfac/soad/gradschool.cfm

Eastern Illinois University, Graduate School, College of Arts and Humanities, Department of Art, Charleston, IL 61920. Offers art (MA); art education (MA); community arts (MA). *Accreditation:* NASAD. *Program availability:* Part-time, evening/weekend, online learning. *Degree requirements:* For master's, comprehensive exam (for some programs), thesis (for some programs). *Entrance requirements:* For master's, GMAT or GRE. Additional exam requirements/recommendations for international students: Required—TOEFL (minimum score 500 paper-based; 61 iBT), IELTS (minimum score 6). Electronic applications accepted.

Eastern Kentucky University, The Graduate School, College of Education, Department of Curriculum and Instruction, Program in Secondary and Higher Education, Richmond, KY 40475-3102. Offers secondary education (MA Ed), including agricultural education, art education, biological sciences education, business education, English education, geography education, history education, home economics education, industrial education, mathematical sciences education, physical education, school health education. *Accreditation:* NCATE. *Program availability:* Part-time. *Entrance requirements:* For master's, GRE General Test, minimum GPA of 2.5.

Eastern Michigan University, Graduate School, College of Arts and Sciences, School of Art and Design, Program in Visual Art Education, Ypsilanti, MI 48197. Offers MA. *Program availability:* Part-time, evening/weekend, online learning. *Students:* 8 part-time (6 women). Average age 31. In 2016, 1 master's awarded. *Entrance requirements:* Additional exam requirements/recommendations for international students: Required—TOEFL. *Application deadline:* Applications are processed on a rolling basis. Application fee: $45. *Financial support:* Fellowships with tuition reimbursements, research assistantships with full tuition reimbursements, teaching assistantships with full tuition reimbursements, career-related internships or fieldwork, Federal Work-Study, institutionally sponsored loans, scholarships/grants, and unspecified assistantships available. Support available to part-time students. Financial award applicants required to submit FAFSA. *Application contact:* Michael Reedy, Graduate Coordinator, 734-487-1268, Fax: 734-487-2324, E-mail: mreedy@emich.edu.

Edinboro University of Pennsylvania, Department of Art, Edinboro, PA 16444. Offers art education (MA); fine arts (MFA), including ceramics (MA, MFA), metals/jewelry, painting (MA, MFA), printmaking (MA, MFA), sculpture (MA, MFA); studio art (MA), including ceramics (MA, MFA), jewelry/metals, painting (MA, MFA), printmaking (MA, MFA), sculpture (MA, MFA). *Accreditation:* NASAD. *Program availability:* Evening/weekend. *Degree requirements:* For master's, comprehensive exam, thesis or alternative, competency exam, exhibit, portfolio. *Entrance requirements:* For master's, GRE or MAT, interview, minimum QPA of 2.5, portfolio. Electronic applications accepted.

Ferris State University, Kendall College of Art and Design, Grand Rapids, MI 49503. Offers architecture (M Arch); art education (MAE); design (MA); drawing (MFA); painting (MFA); photography (MFA); printmaking (MFA); visual and critical studies (MA). *Program availability:* Part-time. *Faculty:* 15 full-time (10 women), 9 part-time/adjunct (2 women). *Students:* 40 full-time (33 women), 5 part-time (3 women); includes 9 minority (3 Black or African American, non-Hispanic/Latino; 3 Asian, non-Hispanic/Latino; 3 Hispanic/Latino), 6 international. Average age 30. 43 applicants, 53% accepted, 16 enrolled. In 2016, 16 master's awarded. *Degree requirements:* For master's, thesis, seminars. *Entrance requirements:* For master's, portfolio, 3 letters of recommendation, curriculum vitae, artist statement, letter of intent. Additional exam requirements/recommendations for international students: Required—TOEFL (minimum score 70 iBT). *Application deadline:* For fall admission, 2/1 priority date for domestic and international students; for spring admission, 11/1 priority date for domestic and international students. Applications are processed on a rolling basis. Application fee: $0. Electronic applications accepted. *Expenses:* $1,017 per credit hour plus $390 fees per year. *Financial support:* In 2016–17, 32 students received support, including 8 fellowships (averaging $16,781 per year); scholarships/grants and unspecified assistantships also available. Financial award application deadline: 2/1; financial award applicants required to submit FAFSA. *Unit head:* Leslie Bellavance, President, 616-451-2787. *Application contact:* Thomas Post, Graduate Recruitment Specialist, 616-451-2787, Fax: 616-831-9689, E-mail: thomaspost@ferris.edu.
Website: http://www.kcad.edu/

Fitchburg State University, Division of Graduate and Continuing Education, Program in Arts Education, Fitchburg, MA 01420-2697. Offers arts education (M Ed); fine arts director (Certificate). *Accreditation:* NCATE. *Program availability:* Part-time, evening/weekend. *Entrance requirements:* Additional exam requirements/recommendations for international students: Required—TOEFL (minimum score 550 paper-based; 79 iBT). Electronic applications accepted. *Expenses:* Tuition, state resident: full-time $2871; part-time $1914 per year. Tuition, nonresident: full-time $2871; part-time $1914 per year. *Required fees:* $3828. Tuition and fees vary according to program.

Florida Atlantic University, College of Education, Department of Teaching and Learning, Boca Raton, FL 33431-0991. Offers curriculum and instruction (M Ed), including art, biology, chemistry, English, French, German, mathematics, music, physics, Pre-K and primary education, reading, social sciences, Spanish; elementary education (M Ed); environmental education (M Ed); reading education (M Ed); social foundations of education (M Ed), including educational psychology, educational technology, multilingual education. *Accreditation:* NCATE. *Program availability:* Part-time, evening/weekend. *Faculty:* 15 full-time (12 women), 2 part-time/adjunct (1 woman). *Students:* 25 full-time (20 women), 41 part-time (37 women); includes 18 minority (9 Black or African American, non-Hispanic/Latino; 2 Asian, non-Hispanic/Latino; 7 Hispanic/Latino), 7 international. Average age 32. 54 applicants, 59% accepted, 18 enrolled. In 2016, 36 master's awarded. *Entrance requirements:* For master's, GRE General Test, minimum GPA of 3.0 in last 2 years of undergraduate course work. Additional exam requirements/recommendations for international students: Required—TOEFL (minimum score 500 paper-based; 61 iBT), IELTS (minimum score 6). *Application deadline:* For fall admission, 7/1 for domestic students, 2/15 for international students; for spring admission, 11/1 for domestic students, 7/15 for international students. Applications are processed on a rolling basis. Application fee: $30. *Expenses:* Tuition, state resident: full-time $7392; part-time $369.82 per credit hour. Tuition, nonresident: full-time $19,432; part-time $1024.81 per credit hour. *Financial support:* Fellowships with partial tuition reimbursements, research assistantships with partial tuition reimbursements, teaching assistantships with partial tuition reimbursements, career-related internships or fieldwork, scholarships/grants, and unspecified assistantships available. *Faculty research:* Technology, teaching English to speakers of other languages, math teaching, electronic portfolio assessment, global perspectives through social studies. *Unit head:* Dr. Barbara Ridener, Chairperson, 561-297-3588, E-mail: bridener@fau.edu. *Application contact:* Dr. Eliah Watlington, Associate Dean, 561-296-8520, Fax: 261-297-2991, E-mail: ewatling@fau.edu.
Website: http://www.coe.fau.edu/academicdepartments/tl/

Florida International University, College of Arts, Sciences, and Education, Department of Teaching and Learning, Miami, FL 33199. Offers art education (MA, MS); curriculum and instruction (MS, Ed D, PhD, Ed S), including curriculum development (MS), elementary education (MS), English education (MS), learning technologies (MS), mathematics education (MS), modern language education (MS), physical education (MS), science education (MS), social studies education (MS), special education (MS); early childhood education (MS); exceptional student education (Ed D); foreign language education (MS), including foreign language education, teaching English to speakers of other languages (TESOL); international/intercultural education (MS); language, literacy and culture (PhD); mathematics, science, and learning technologies (PhD); physical education (MS), including sport and fitness; reading education (MS). *Program availability:* Part-time, evening/weekend. *Faculty:* 34 full-time (23 women), 64 part-time/adjunct (48 women). *Students:* 182 full-time (154 women), 231 part-time (190 women); includes 323 minority (69 Black or African American, non-Hispanic/Latino; 10 Asian, non-Hispanic/Latino; 237 Hispanic/Latino; 7 Two or more races, non-Hispanic/Latino), 19 international. Average age 34. 282 applicants, 58% accepted, 113 enrolled. In 2016, 184 master's, 12 doctorates awarded. *Degree requirements:* For doctorate, comprehensive exam, thesis/dissertation. *Entrance requirements:* For master's, GRE General Test, Florida General Knowledge Test or Florida College Level Academic Skills Test; for doctorate and Ed S, GRE General Test. Additional exam requirements/recommendations for international students: Required—TOEFL (minimum score 550 paper-based; 80 iBT), IELTS (minimum score 6.3). *Application deadline:* For fall admission, 6/1 priority date for domestic students, 4/1 for international students; for winter admission, 10/1 priority date for domestic students, 9/1 for international students; for spring admission, 3/1 priority date for domestic students, 2/1 for international students. Applications are processed on a rolling basis. Application fee: $30. Electronic applications accepted. *Expenses:* Tuition, state resident: full-time $8912; part-time $446 per credit hour. Tuition, nonresident: full-time $21,393; part-time $992 per credit hour. *Required fees:* $2185; $195 per semester. Tuition and fees vary according to program. *Financial support:* Research assistantships with tuition reimbursements and teaching assistantships with tuition reimbursements available. *Unit head:* Dr. Lynn Miller, Chair, 305-348-2005, Fax: 305-348-2086, E-mail: lynne.miller@fiu.edu. *Application contact:* Nanett Rojas, Assistant Director, Graduate Admissions, 305-348-7464, Fax: 305-348-7441, E-mail: gradadm@fiu.edu.
Website: http://education.fiu.edu

Florida State University, The Graduate School, College of Fine Arts, Department of Art Education, Tallahassee, FL 32306. Offers MA, MS, Ed D, PhD. *Accreditation:* NASAD (one or more programs are accredited). *Program availability:* Part-time. *Faculty:* 9 full-time (6 women), 2 part-time/adjunct (both women). *Students:* 66 full-time (60 women), 14 part-time (10 women); includes 27 minority (6 Black or African American, non-Hispanic/Latino; 14 Asian, non-Hispanic/Latino; 7 Hispanic/Latino). Average age 31. 100 applicants, 49% accepted, 35 enrolled. In 2016, 21 master's, 3 doctorates awarded. *Degree requirements:* For master's, thesis (for some programs); for doctorate, thesis/dissertation. *Entrance requirements:* For master's, GRE, minimum GPA of 3.0 in last 2 years; for doctorate, GRE. Additional exam requirements/recommendations for international students: Required—TOEFL (minimum score 550 paper-based; 80 iBT). *Application deadline:* For fall admission, 1/15 priority date for domestic and international students; for spring admission, 10/1 priority date for domestic and international students. Application fee: $30. Electronic applications accepted. *Expenses:* Tuition, state resident: full-time $7263; part-time $403.51 per credit hour. Tuition, nonresident: full-time $18,087; part-time $1004.85 per credit hour. *Required fees:* $1365; $75.81 per credit hour. $20 per semester. Tuition and fees vary according to campus/location. *Financial support:* In 2016–17, 27 students received support, including 20 research assistantships with full tuition reimbursements available (averaging $3,800 per year), 7 teaching assistantships with full tuition reimbursements available (averaging $8,500 per year); fellowships, career-related internships or fieldwork, Federal Work-Study, and scholarships/grants also available. Financial award applicants required to submit FAFSA. *Faculty research:* Teaching and learning in art, museum education, art therapy, arts administration, discipline-based art education. *Total annual research expenditures:* $110,000. *Unit head:* Dr. David E. Gussak, Chairman, 850-665-5663, Fax: 850-644-5067, E-mail: dgussak@fsu.edu. *Application contact:* Susan Messersmith, Academic Support Assistant, 850-644-5473, Fax: 850-644-6067, E-mail: smessersmith@fsu.edu.
Website: http://www.fsu.edu/~are/

Fontbonne University, Graduate Programs, St. Louis, MO 63105-3098. Offers accounting (MBA, MS); art (MA); art (K-12) (MAT); business (MBA); computer science (MS); deaf education (MA); early intervention in deaf education (MA); education (MA), including autism spectrum disorders, curriculum and instruction, diverse learners, early childhood education, reading, special education; elementary education (MAT); family and consumer sciences (MA), including multidisciplinary health communication studies; fine arts (MFA); instructional design and technology (MS); management and leadership (MM); middle school education (MAT); secondary education (MAT); special education (MAT); speech-language pathology (MS); supply chain management (MS); theatre (MA). *Program availability:* Part-time, evening/weekend, online learning. *Faculty:* 32 full-time (24 women), 43 part-time/adjunct (26 women). *Students:* 456 full-time (313 women), 102 part-time (77 women); includes 138 minority (118 Black or African American, non-Hispanic/Latino; 1 American Indian or Alaska Native, non-Hispanic/Latino; 7 Asian, non-Hispanic/Latino; 9 Hispanic/Latino; 3 Two or more races, non-Hispanic/Latino), 37 international. *Degree requirements:* For master's, comprehensive exam (for some programs), thesis (for some programs). *Entrance requirements:* Additional exam requirements/recommendations for international students: Required—TOEFL (minimum score 500 paper-based; 65 iBT). *Application deadline:* For fall admission, 8/1 for international students; for spring admission, 12/1 for international students. Applications are processed on a rolling basis. Application fee: $25 ($30 for international students). Electronic applications accepted. *Expenses: Tuition:* Full-time $8436; part-time $703 per credit hour. *Required fees:* $18 per credit hour. Tuition and fees vary according to course load. *Financial support:* Teaching assistantships with partial tuition reimbursements and scholarships/grants available. Support available to part-time students. Financial award application deadline: 4/1; financial award applicants required to submit FAFSA. *Unit head:* Dr. Carey Adams, Vice President for Academic Affairs, 314-719-3609, E-mail: cadams@fontbonne.edu. *Application contact:* Lauryn Filip, Coordinator, Graduate Admission and Professional Studies, 314-889-4650, E-mail: admissions@fontbonne.edu.
Website: https://www.fontbonne.edu/academics/graduate-programs/

George Mason University, College of Visual and Performing Arts, Program in Art Education, Fairfax, VA 22030. Offers MAT. *Faculty:* 3 full-time (2 women), 2 part-time/adjunct (both women). *Students:* 1 (woman) full-time, 23 part-time (19 women); includes 9 minority (7 Asian, non-Hispanic/Latino; 1 Hispanic/Latino; 1 Two or more races, non-Hispanic/Latino). Average age 31. 6 applicants, 100% accepted, 3 enrolled. In 2016, 9 master's awarded. *Entrance requirements:* For master's, PRAXIS I or SAT equivalent, college transcript, expanded goals statement, 3 letters of recommendation, resume, portfolio, BFA or approved equivalent. Additional exam requirements/recommendations for international students: Required—TOEFL (minimum score 575 paper-based; 88 iBT), IELTS (minimum score 6.5), PTE (minimum score 59). *Application deadline:* For fall admission, 4/1 for domestic students. Application fee: $75 ($80 for international students). Electronic applications accepted. *Expenses:* Tuition, state resident: full-time $10,628; part-time $443 per credit. Tuition, nonresident: full-time $29,306; part-time $1221 per credit. *Required fees:* $3096; $129 per credit. Tuition and fees vary according to program. *Financial support:* Career-related internships or fieldwork, Federal Work-Study, and scholarships/grants available. Financial award application deadline: 3/1; financial award applicants required to submit FAFSA. *Unit head:* Mary Del Popolo, Program Director, 703-993-8562, Fax: 703-993-8798, E-mail: mdelpopo@gmu.edu. *Application contact:* Nikki Brugnoli-Whipkey, Administrative Assistant for Graduate Study, 703-993-5792, Fax: 703-993-8798, E-mail: nbrugnol@gmu.edu.
Website: http://arteducation.gmu.edu/

The George Washington University, Columbian College of Arts and Sciences, Corcoran School of the Arts and Design, Washington, DC 20007. Offers art and the book (MA); art education (MA, MAT); exhibition design (MA); interior design (MA); new media photojournalism (MA). *Accreditation:* NASAD. *Program availability:* Part-time. *Entrance requirements:* Additional exam requirements/recommendations for international students: Required—TOEFL (minimum score 95 iBT).

Georgia State University, College of Arts and Sciences, Ernest G. Welch School of Art and Design, Program in Art Education, Atlanta, GA 30302-3083. Offers MA Ed.

Accreditation: NASAD. *Program availability:* Part-time. *Degree requirements:* For master's, thesis. *Entrance requirements:* For master's, GRE. Additional exam requirements/recommendations for international students: Required—TOEFL. *Application deadline:* For fall admission, 4/15 for domestic and international students; for spring admission, 9/15 for domestic and international students. Application fee: $50. Electronic applications accepted. *Expenses:* Tuition, state resident: full-time $6876; part-time $382 per credit hour. Tuition, nonresident: full-time $22,374; part-time $1243 per credit hour. *Required fees:* $2128; $1064 per term. Part-time tuition and fees vary according to course load and program. *Financial support:* Tuition waivers (full) and unspecified assistantships available. Financial award application deadline: 4/15; financial award applicants required to submit FAFSA. *Faculty research:* Critical theories, museum education, instructional technology, multi-culture and interdisciplinary art education, Chinese art history. *Unit head:* Michael White, Director, Welch School of Art and Design, 404-413-5221, Fax: 404-413-5261, E-mail: mwhite@gsu.edu. *Application contact:* Hubert Stanley Anderson, Director of Graduate Studies, 404-413-5229, Fax: 404-413-5261, E-mail: artgrad@gsu.edu.
Website: http://artdesign.gsu.edu/graduate/admissions/masters-of-art-education/

Harding University, Cannon-Clary College of Education, Searcy, AR 72149-0001. Offers advanced studies in teaching and learning (M Ed); art (MSE); behavioral science (MSE); counseling (MS, Ed S); early childhood special education (M Ed, MSE); education (MSE); educational leadership (M Ed, Ed S); elementary education (M Ed); English (MSE); French (MSE); history/social science (MSE); kinesiology (MSE); math (MSE); reading (M Ed); secondary education (M Ed); Spanish (MSE); teaching (MAT); teaching English as a second language (MSE). *Accreditation:* NCATE. *Program availability:* Part-time, evening/weekend. *Faculty:* 22 full-time (9 women), 51 part-time/adjunct (37 women). *Students:* 130 full-time (94 women), 321 part-time (234 women); includes 83 minority (50 Black or African American, non-Hispanic/Latino; 4 American Indian or Alaska Native, non-Hispanic/Latino; 6 Asian, non-Hispanic/Latino; 13 Hispanic/Latino; 10 Two or more races, non-Hispanic/Latino), 11 international. Average age 35. 125 applicants, 88% accepted, 110 enrolled. In 2016, 124 master's, 27 other advanced degrees awarded. *Degree requirements:* For master's, comprehensive exam (for some programs), thesis optional, portfolio(s); for Ed S, comprehensive exam, portfolio, project. *Entrance requirements:* For master's, GRE, MAT, PRAXIS; for Ed S, MAT or GRE. Additional exam requirements/recommendations for international students: Required—TOEFL (minimum score 550 paper-based; 79 iBT). *Application deadline:* For fall admission, 8/1 for domestic and international students; for spring admission, 1/1 for domestic and international students. Applications are processed on a rolling basis. Application fee: $35. Tuition and fees vary according to degree level and program. *Financial support:* In 2016–17, 31 students received support. Unspecified assistantships available. *Faculty research:* Reading, comprehension, school violence, educational technology, behavior, college choice, differentiated instruction, brain-based teaching. *Unit head:* Dr. Clara Carroll, Chair, 501-279-4501, Fax: 501-279-4083, E-mail: ccarroll@harding.edu. *Application contact:* Information Contact, 501-279-4315, E-mail: gradstudiesedu@harding.edu.
Website: http://www.harding.edu/education

Harvard University, Harvard Graduate School of Education, Master's Programs in Education, Cambridge, MA 02138. Offers arts in education (Ed M); education policy and management (Ed M); higher education (Ed M); human development and psychology (Ed M); international education policy (Ed M); language and literacy (Ed M); learning and teaching (Ed M); mind, brain, and education (Ed M); prevention science and practice (Ed M); school leadership (Ed M); special studies (Ed M); teacher education (Ed M); technology, innovation, and education (Ed M). *Program availability:* Part-time. *Entrance requirements:* For master's, GRE General Test, statement of purpose, 3 letters of recommendation, resume, official transcripts. Additional exam requirements/recommendations for international students: Required—TOEFL (minimum score 613 paper-based; 104 iBT), TWE (minimum score 5). Electronic applications accepted. *Faculty research:* Learning and development, educational leadership and organizations, education policy analysis.

Hofstra University, School of Education, Programs in Teacher Education, Hempstead, NY 11549. Offers bilingual education (MA, Advanced Certificate); bilingual extension (Advanced Certificate), including education/speech language pathology; business education (MS Ed); early childhood and childhood education (MS Ed); early childhood education (MA, MS Ed); education technology (Advanced Certificate); elementary education (MA, MS Ed), including science, technology, engineering, and mathematics (STEM) (MA); English education (MS Ed); family and consumer science (MS Ed); fine arts and music education (Advanced Certificate); fine arts education (MS Ed); foreign language and TESOL (MS Ed); foreign language education (MS Ed), including French, German, Russian, Spanish; learning and teaching (Ed D), including applied linguistics, art education, arts and humanities, early childhood education, English education, human development, math education, math, science, and technology, multicultural education, physical education, science education, social studies education, special education; mathematics education (MA, MS Ed); middle school extension (Advanced Certificate), including grades 5-6, grades 7-9; music education (MA, MS Ed); science education (MA, MS Ed), including biology, chemistry, earth science, geology, physics; secondary education (Advanced Certificate); social studies education (MA, MS Ed); teaching languages other than English and TESOL (MS Ed); TESOL (MS Ed, Advanced Certificate). *Program availability:* Part-time, evening/weekend, blended/hybrid learning. *Students:* 139 full-time (97 women), 145 part-time (106 women); includes 60 minority (15 Black or African American, non-Hispanic/Latino; 1 American Indian or Alaska Native, non-Hispanic/Latino; 12 Asian, non-Hispanic/Latino; 31 Hispanic/Latino; 1 Two or more races, non-Hispanic/Latino), 21 international. Average age 29. 255 applicants, 86% accepted, 122 enrolled. In 2016, 101 master's, 4 doctorates, 43 other advanced degrees awarded. *Degree requirements:* For master's, comprehensive exam, thesis (for some programs), exit project, student teaching, fieldwork, electronic portfolio, curriculum project, minimum GPA of 3.0; for doctorate, thesis/dissertation; for Advanced Certificate, 3 foreign languages, comprehensive exam (for some programs), thesis project. *Entrance requirements:* For master's, GRE, MAT, 2 letters of recommendation, portfolio, teacher certification (MA), interview, essay; for doctorate, GMAT, GRE, LSAT, or MAT; for Advanced Certificate, 2 letters of recommendation, essay, interview and/or portfolio, teaching certificate. Additional exam requirements/recommendations for international students: Required—TOEFL (minimum score 550 paper-based; 80 iBT). *Application deadline:* Applications are processed on a rolling basis. Application fee: $75. Electronic applications accepted. *Expenses: Tuition:* Full-time $1240. *Required fees:* $970. Tuition and fees vary according to program. *Financial support:* In 2016–17, 149 students received support, including 58 fellowships with full and partial tuition reimbursements available (averaging $5,309 per year), 5 research assistantships with full and partial tuition reimbursements available (averaging $7,073 per year); career-related internships or fieldwork, Federal Work-Study, institutionally sponsored loans, scholarships/grants, traineeships, tuition waivers (full and partial), and unspecified assistantships also available. Support available to part-time students. Financial award applicants required to submit FAFSA. *Faculty research:* Educational interventions that foster critical-thinking skills; teachers' attitudes about professional development; threats to teacher quality. *Unit head:* Dr. Eustace Thompson, Chairperson, 516-463-5749, Fax: 516-463-6275, E-mail: eustace.g.thompson@hofstra.edu. *Application contact:* Sunil Samuel, Assistant Vice President of Admissions, 516-463-4723, Fax: 516-463-4664, E-mail: graduateadmission@hofstra.edu.
Website: http://www.hofstra.edu/education/

Indiana University Bloomington, School of Education, Department of Curriculum and Instruction, Bloomington, IN 47405-7000. Offers art education (MS, Ed D, PhD); curriculum studies (Ed D, PhD); elementary education (MS, Ed D, PhD, Ed S); mathematics education (MS, Ed D, PhD); science education (MS, Ed D, PhD); secondary education (MS, Ed D, PhD); social studies education (MS, PhD); special education (PhD, Ed S). *Accreditation:* NCATE. *Program availability:* Part-time, evening/weekend. Terminal master's awarded for partial completion of doctoral program. *Degree requirements:* For doctorate, thesis/dissertation; for Ed S, comprehensive exam or project. *Entrance requirements:* For master's, doctorate, and Ed S, GRE General Test. Electronic applications accepted.

James Madison University, The Graduate School, College of Visual and Performing Arts, School of Art, Design and Art History, Harrisonburg, VA 22802. Offers art education (MA); studio art (MA, MFA), including ceramics (MFA), drawing/painting (MFA), intermedia (MFA), metal/jewelry (MFA), photography (MFA), sculpture (MFA). *Accreditation:* NASAD. *Program availability:* Part-time. *Faculty:* 25 full-time (15 women). *Students:* 10 full-time (6 women), 1 (woman) part-time, 1 international. Average age 30. 18 applicants, 39% accepted, 6 enrolled. In 2016, 6 master's awarded. Application fee: $55. Electronic applications accepted. *Financial support:* In 2016–17, 10 students received support, including 3 teaching assistantships with full tuition reimbursements available (averaging $9,284 per year); Federal Work-Study and 7 assistantships (averaging $7911) also available. Financial award application deadline: 3/1; financial award applicants required to submit FAFSA. *Unit head:* Dr. Kathy A. Schwartz, Director of School of Art, Design and Art History, 540-568-6216, E-mail: schwarka@jmu.edu. *Application contact:* Lynette D. Michael, Director of Graduate Student Admissions, 540-568-6131 Ext. 6395, Fax: 540-568-7860, E-mail: michaeld@jmu.edu.
Website: http://www.jmu.edu/artandarthistory/

Kean University, College of Liberal Arts, Program in Fine Arts Education, Union, NJ 07083. Offers initial teaching certification (MA); studio (MA); supervision (MA). *Accreditation:* NASAD. *Program availability:* Part-time. *Faculty:* 6 full-time (4 women). *Students:* 11 full-time (8 women), 17 part-time (12 women); includes 8 minority (2 Black or African American, non-Hispanic/Latino; 6 Hispanic/Latino). Average age 33. 16 applicants, 50% accepted, 8 enrolled. In 2016, 11 master's awarded. *Degree requirements:* For master's, thesis (for some programs), exhibition, 3 years of teaching experience (for supervision), PRAXIS and fieldwork (for initial teaching certification). *Entrance requirements:* For master's, studio portfolio, proficiencies in academic writing, dialogue skills, minimum GPA of 3.0, interview, 2 letters of recommendation, official transcripts from all institutions attended. Additional exam requirements/recommendations for international students: Required—TOEFL (minimum score 550 paper-based; 79 iBT), IELTS (minimum score 6.5). *Application deadline:* For fall admission, 6/1 for domestic and international students; for spring admission, 12/1 for domestic and international students. Applications are processed on a rolling basis. Application fee: $75. Electronic applications accepted. *Expenses:* Tuition, state resident: full-time $13,156; part-time $640 per credit. Tuition, nonresident: full-time $17,831; part-time $785 per credit. *Required fees:* $3316; $151 per credit. Tuition and fees vary according to course level, course load, degree level and program. *Financial support:* Scholarships/grants and unspecified assistantships available. Financial award applicants required to submit FAFSA. *Unit head:* Dr. Joseph Amorino, Program Coordinator, 908-737-4403, Fax: 908-737-4377, E-mail: jamorino@kean.edu. *Application contact:* Amy Hadjusek, Program Assistant, 908-737-7100, E-mail: grad-adm@kean.edu.
Website: http://grad.kean.edu/masters-programs/initial-teaching-certification

Kennesaw State University, Leland and Clarice C. Bagwell College of Education, Program in Teaching, Kennesaw, GA 30144. Offers art education (MAT); biology (MAT); chemistry (MAT); foreign language education (Chinese and Spanish) (MAT); physics (MAT); secondary English (MAT); secondary mathematics (MAT); special education (MAT); teaching English to speakers of other languages (MAT). *Program availability:* Part-time, evening/weekend. *Entrance requirements:* For master's, GRE, GACE I (state certificate exam), minimum GPA of 2.75, 2 recommendations, resume. Additional exam requirements/recommendations for international students: Required—TOEFL (minimum score 550 paper-based; 80 iBT), IELTS (minimum score 6.5). Electronic applications accepted.

Kent State University, College of the Arts, School of Art, Kent, OH 44242-0001. Offers art education (MA); art history (MA); crafts (MA, MFA), including glass; fine arts (MA, MFA), including fashion (MA). *Accreditation:* NASAD (one or more programs are accredited). *Program availability:* Part-time, online learning. *Faculty:* 23 full-time (15 women). *Students:* 51 full-time (23 women), 167 part-time (120 women); includes 18 minority (8 Black or African American, non-Hispanic/Latino; 1 American Indian or Alaska Native, non-Hispanic/Latino; 1 Asian, non-Hispanic/Latino; 4 Hispanic/Latino; 1 Native Hawaiian or other Pacific Islander, non-Hispanic/Latino; 3 Two or more races, non-Hispanic/Latino), 25 international. Average age 31. 57 applicants, 53% accepted, 21 enrolled. In 2016, 30 master's awarded. *Degree requirements:* For master's, comprehensive exam, thesis (for some programs), 1 foreign language (for art history); final project (for crafts and fine arts). *Entrance requirements:* For master's, transcripts, goal statement, 3 letters of recommendation, curriculum vitae, portfolio. Additional exam requirements/recommendations for international students: Required—TOEFL (minimum score of 575 paper-based, 90 iBT), IELTS (minimum score of 7.0), Michigan English Language Assessment Battery (minimum score of 85), or PTE (minimum score of 68). *Application deadline:* For fall admission, 2/2 for domestic and international students; for spring admission, 10/15 for domestic and international students. Applications are processed on a rolling basis. Application fee: $45 ($70 for international students). Electronic applications accepted. *Expenses:* Tuition, state resident: full-time $10,864; part-time $495 per credit hour. Tuition, nonresident: full-time $18,380; part-time $837 per credit hour. *Financial support:* Career-related internships or fieldwork, scholarships/grants, and unspecified assistantships available. Financial award application deadline: 2/2. *Unit head:* Michael J. Loderstedt, Interim Director/Professor, Print Media and Photography, 330-672-2192, E-mail: mloderst@kent.edu. *Application contact:* Linda Hoeptner Poling, Graduate Coordinator and Associate Professor of Art Education, 330-672-7895, E-mail: lhoeptne@kent.edu.
Website: http://www.kent.edu/art

Kutztown University of Pennsylvania, College of Visual and Performing Arts, Program in Art Education, Kutztown, PA 19530-0730. Offers M Ed. *Accreditation:* NASAD; NCATE. *Program availability:* Part-time. *Faculty:* 8 full-time (7 women). *Students:* 9 full-time (7 women), 34 part-time (all women). Average age 32. 28 applicants, 86% accepted, 12 enrolled. In 2016, 26 master's awarded. *Degree requirements:* For master's, comprehensive exam, thesis optional. *Entrance requirements:* For master's, PRAXIS II, valid instructional I or II teaching certificate, or GRE, minimum undergraduate GPA of 3.0, 3 letters of recommendation. Additional exam requirements/recommendations for international students: Required—TOEFL (minimum score 550 paper-based, 79 iBT) or IELTS (minimum score 6.5). *Application deadline:* For fall admission, 8/1 for domestic and international students; for spring

admission, 12/1 for domestic and international students. Application fee: $35. Electronic applications accepted. *Expenses:* Tuition, state resident: full-time $4347; part-time $483 per credit. Tuition, nonresident: full-time $6525; part-time $725 per credit. *Required fees:* $88 per credit. One-time fee: $50 full-time. *Financial support:* Career-related internships or fieldwork, Federal Work-Study, scholarships/grants, and unspecified assistantships available. Financial award application deadline: 3/1; financial award applicants required to submit FAFSA. *Faculty research:* Teaching of art history, child development in art, aesthetics and criticism curriculum, multicultural education, assessment in art. *Unit head:* Dr. John White, Chairperson, 610-683-4520, Fax: 610-683-4502, E-mail: white@kutztown.edu.
Website: https://www.kutztown.edu/academics/graduate-programs/art-education.htm

Lake Forest College, Master of Arts in Teaching Program, Lake Forest, IL 60045. Offers elementary education (MAT); K-12 French (MAT); K-12 music (MAT); K-12 Spanish (MAT); K-12 visual art (MAT); secondary biology (MAT); secondary chemistry (MAT); secondary English (MAT); secondary history (MAT); secondary mathematics (MAT). *Degree requirements:* For master's, comprehensive exam, portfolio. *Entrance requirements:* For master's, GRE.

Lesley University, Graduate School of Education, Cambridge, MA 02138-2790. Offers arts, community, and education (M Ed); autism studies (Certificate); curriculum and instruction (M Ed, CAGS); early childhood education (M Ed); ecological teaching and learning (MS); educational studies (PhD), including adult learning, educational leadership, individually designed; elementary education (M Ed); emergent technologies for educators (Certificate); ESLArts: language learning through the arts (M Ed); high school education (M Ed); individually designed (M Ed); integrated teaching through the arts (M Ed); literacy for K-8 classroom teachers (M Ed); mathematics education (M Ed); middle school education (M Ed); moderate disabilities (M Ed); online learning (Certificate); reading (CAGS); science in education (M Ed); severe disabilities (M Ed); special needs (CAGS); specialist teacher of reading (M Ed); teacher of visual art (M Ed); technology in education (M Ed, CAGS). *Accreditation:* TEAC. *Program availability:* Part-time, evening/weekend, online learning. *Degree requirements:* For master's, practicum; for doctorate, thesis/dissertation. *Entrance requirements:* For master's, Massachusetts Tests for Educator Licensure (MTEL), transcripts, statement of purpose, recommendations; interview (for special education); for doctorate, GRE General Test, transcripts, statement of purpose, recommendations, interview, master's degree, resume; for other advanced degree, interview, master's degree. Additional exam requirements/recommendations for international students: Required—TOEFL (minimum score 550 paper-based; 80 iBT). Electronic applications accepted. *Faculty research:* Assessment in literacy, mathematics and science; autism spectrum disorders; instructional technology and online learning; multicultural education and English language learners.

Long Island University–LIU Post, College of Education, Information and Technology, Brookville, NY 11548-1300. Offers adolescence education (MS); adolescence education 7-12 (MS); archives and records management (AC); art education (MS); childhood education (MS); childhood teaching literacy B-6 (MS); childhood/special education (MS); clinical mental health counseling (MS, AC); early childhood education (MS); early childhood education/childhood education (MS); educational leadership (AC); educational technology (MS); information studies (PhD); interdisciplinary educational studies (Ed D); middle childhood education (MS); music education (MS); school counselor (MS); special education (MS Ed); speech-language pathology (MA); students with disabilities, 7-12 generalist (AC); TESOL (MA). *Accreditation:* TEAC. *Program availability:* Part-time, 100% online, blended/hybrid learning. *Faculty:* 55 full-time (35 women), 104 part-time/adjunct (57 women). *Students:* 464 full-time (390 women), 740 part-time (580 women); includes 265 minority (99 Black or African American, non-Hispanic/Latino; 45 Asian, non-Hispanic/Latino; 113 Hispanic/Latino; 1 Native Hawaiian or other Pacific Islander, non-Hispanic/Latino; 7 Two or more races, non-Hispanic/Latino), 33 international. 928 applicants, 76% accepted, 406 enrolled. In 2016, 334 master's, 10 doctorates, 137 other advanced degrees awarded. Terminal master's awarded for partial completion of doctoral program. *Degree requirements:* For master's, variable foreign language requirement, comprehensive exam (for some programs), thesis optional; for doctorate, comprehensive exam, thesis/dissertation. *Entrance requirements:* For master's and AC, GRE. Additional exam requirements/recommendations for international students: Required—PTE, TOEFL (minimum score 550 paper-based, 75 iBT) or IELTS. *Application deadline:* Applications are processed on a rolling basis. Application fee: $50. Electronic applications accepted. *Expenses: Tuition:* Full-time $28,272; part-time $1178 per credit. *Required fees:* $451 per term. Tuition and fees vary according to degree level and program. *Financial support:* Career-related internships or fieldwork, Federal Work-Study, institutionally sponsored loans, scholarships/grants, tuition waivers (partial), and unspecified assistantships available. Support available to part-time students. Financial award application deadline: 2/15; financial award applicants required to submit FAFSA. *Faculty research:* English language learners, early childhood literacy development through play, sleep, social justice through education, using a structured protocol for discussing bad news. *Total annual research expenditures:* $575,000. *Unit head:* Dr. Albert Inserra, Dean, 516-299-2210, E-mail: albert.inserra@liu.edu. *Application contact:* Carol Zerah, Director of Graduate Admissions, 516-299-2900, Fax: 516-299-2137, E-mail: post-enroll@liu.edu.
Website: http://liu.edu/CWPost/Academics/College-of-Education-Information-and-Technology

Manhattanville College, School of Education, Program in Visual Arts Education, Purchase, NY 10577-2132. Offers MAT. *Program availability:* Part-time, evening/weekend. *Students:* 5 applicants, 100% accepted, 4 enrolled. In 2016, 1 master's awarded. *Degree requirements:* For master's, comprehensive exam (for some programs), thesis (for some programs), student teaching, research seminars, portfolios, internships, writing assessment. *Entrance requirements:* For master's, GRE or MAT, minimum undergraduate GPA of 3.0, 2 letters of recommendation, art department portfolio review. Additional exam requirements/recommendations for international students: Required—TOEFL (minimum score 85 iBT); Recommended—IELTS. *Application deadline:* For fall admission, 7/1 priority date for domestic and international students; for spring admission, 11/1 priority date for domestic and international students; for summer admission, 4/1 priority date for domestic and international students. Applications are processed on a rolling basis. Application fee: $75. Electronic applications accepted. *Expenses: Tuition:* Full-time $16,470; part-time $915 per credit. *Required fees:* $60 per semester. Part-time tuition and fees vary according to course load and program. *Financial support:* Teaching assistantships, career-related internships or fieldwork, Federal Work-Study, institutionally sponsored loans, scholarships/grants, and unspecified assistantships available. Financial award applicants required to submit FAFSA. *Unit head:* Randy Williams, Program Director, 914-323-5331, E-mail: randy.williams@mville.edu. *Application contact:* Jeanine Pardey-Levine, Director of Graduate Enrollment Management, 914-323-3208, Fax: 914-694-1732, E-mail: edschool@mville.edu.
Website: http://www.mville.edu/programs/visual-art-education

Mansfield University of Pennsylvania, Graduate Studies, Department of Art, Mansfield, PA 16933. Offers art education (M Ed). *Program availability:* Part-time. *Degree requirements:* For master's, thesis optional. *Entrance requirements:* For master's, minimum GPA of 3.0, portfolio. Additional exam requirements/recommendations for international students: Required—TOEFL (minimum score 550 paper-based). Electronic applications accepted.

Maryland Institute College of Art, Graduate Studies, MA Program in Art Education, Baltimore, MD 21201. Offers MA. Program offered in summer only. *Accreditation:* NASAD. *Faculty:* 4 full-time (all women). *Students:* 20 full-time (17 women); includes 3 minority (1 Black or African American, non-Hispanic/Latino; 1 Asian, non-Hispanic/Latino; 1 Two or more races, non-Hispanic/Latino). Average age 26. 30 applicants, 50% accepted, 10 enrolled. In 2016, 10 master's awarded. *Degree requirements:* For master's, thesis, exhibition and documentation. *Entrance requirements:* For master's, portfolio, bachelor's degree in any field. Additional exam requirements/recommendations for international students: Required—TOEFL (minimum score 550 paper-based; 80 iBT), IELTS (minimum score 6.5). *Application deadline:* For fall admission, 1/15 priority date for domestic and international students; for spring admission, 4/1 for domestic students, 4/1 priority date for international students. Application fee: $75. Electronic applications accepted. *Expenses:* Contact institution. *Financial support:* In 2016–17, 10 students received support, including 10 fellowships with partial tuition reimbursements available (averaging $6,500 per year); teaching assistantships and scholarships/grants also available. Financial award application deadline: 1/15; financial award applicants required to submit FAFSA. *Unit head:* Dr. Stacey Salazar, Dean, 410-225-2267. *Application contact:* Chris D. Harring, Director of Graduate Admission, 410-225-2256, Fax: 410-225-5275, E-mail: graduate@mica.edu.
Website: http://www.mica.edu/Programs_of_Study/Graduate_Programs.html

Maryland Institute College of Art, Graduate Studies, MAT Program, Baltimore, MD 21201. Offers MAT. *Faculty:* 5 full-time (all women). *Students:* 36 full-time (23 women); includes 17 minority (3 Black or African American, non-Hispanic/Latino; 6 Asian, non-Hispanic/Latino; 5 Hispanic/Latino; 3 Two or more races, non-Hispanic/Latino). Average age 24. 65 applicants, 38% accepted, 18 enrolled. In 2016, 22 master's awarded. *Degree requirements:* For master's, thesis, student teaching, thesis exhibition, thesis writing. *Entrance requirements:* For master's, PRAXIS I, portfolio, writing samples. Additional exam requirements/recommendations for international students: Required—TOEFL (minimum score 550 paper-based; 80 iBT), IELTS (minimum score 6.5). *Application deadline:* For fall admission, 1/15 priority date for domestic and international students. Application fee: $75. Electronic applications accepted. *Expenses: Tuition:* Full-time $45,290; part-time $1510 per credit. *Required fees:* $1700. One-time fee: $335 full-time. Full-time tuition and fees vary according to course load. *Financial support:* In 2016–17, 36 fellowships (averaging $15,000 per year) were awarded; career-related internships or fieldwork, scholarships/grants, and traineeships also available. Financial award application deadline: 1/15. *Unit head:* Shyla Rao, Director, 410-225-2267. *Application contact:* Chris D. Harring, Director of Graduate Admission, 410-225-2256, Fax: 410-225-5275, E-mail: graduate@mica.edu.
Website: http://www.mica.edu/Programs_of_Study/Graduate_Programs/Teaching_(MAT).html

Marywood University, Academic Affairs, Insalaco College of Creative and Performing Arts, Art Department, Program in Art Education, Scranton, PA 18509-1598. Offers MA. *Accreditation:* NASAD; NCATE. Electronic applications accepted.

Massachusetts College of Art and Design, Graduate Programs, Program in Art Education, Boston, MA 02115-5882. Offers MAT, Postbaccalaureate Certificate. *Accreditation:* NASAD. *Faculty:* 5 full-time (3 women), 5 part-time/adjunct (3 women). *Students:* 13 full-time (10 women), 4 part-time (3 women); includes 2 minority (both Asian, non-Hispanic/Latino), 1 international. 26 applicants, 85% accepted, 9 enrolled. In 2016, 9 master's, 2 other advanced degrees awarded. *Entrance requirements:* For master's and Postbaccalaureate Certificate, portfolio, college transcripts, resume, statement of purpose, letters of reference, interview. Additional exam requirements/recommendations for international students: Required—TOEFL (minimum score 550 paper-based; 85 iBT); Recommended—IELTS (minimum score 6). *Application deadline:* For fall admission, 1/4 priority date for domestic and international students. Application fee: $90. Electronic applications accepted. *Expenses:* $780 per credit (for master's); $572 per credit (for Certificate). *Financial support:* In 2016–17, 8 students received support, including 1 research assistantship (averaging $2,160 per year), 2 teaching assistantships (averaging $2,160 per year); career-related internships or fieldwork, scholarships/grants, tuition waivers (partial), and 2 general assistantships also available. Support available to part-time students. Financial award application deadline: 1/4; financial award applicants required to submit FAFSA. *Faculty research:* Cognitive and developmental psychology, research methodologies and synthesis, embodied aesthetics, neuro-aesthetics and neuro-philosophy, interactive art. *Unit head:* Paul Paturzo, Dean of Graduate Studies, 617-879-7166, E-mail: pjpaturzo@massart.edu. *Application contact:* Lauren O'Neill, Assistant Director of Graduate Admissions, 617-879-7222, E-mail: gradadmissions@massart.edu.
Website: http://www.massart.edu/Admissions/Graduate_Programs.html

Memphis College of Art, Graduate Programs, Program in Art Education, Memphis, TN 38104-2764. Offers MA, MAT. *Program availability:* Part-time, evening/weekend. *Faculty:* 27 full-time (16 women), 25 part-time/adjunct (13 women). *Students:* 20 part-time (12 women); includes 9 minority (8 Black or African American, non-Hispanic/Latino; 1 Two or more races, non-Hispanic/Latino). Average age 35. 16 applicants, 88% accepted, 10 enrolled. In 2016, 3 master's awarded. *Degree requirements:* For master's, thesis, exhibition. *Entrance requirements:* For master's, portfolio, resume, interview, teaching philosophy. Additional exam requirements/recommendations for international students: Required—TOEFL (minimum score 525 paper-based). *Application deadline:* For fall admission, 3/1 for domestic and international students; for spring admission, 11/1 for domestic and international students. Applications are processed on a rolling basis. Application fee: $50. *Expenses:* Contact institution. *Financial support:* Scholarships/grants and teaching professional tuition discounts available. Financial award application deadline: 8/1; financial award applicants required to submit FAFSA. *Unit head:* Dr. Shannon Elliott, Director of Graduate Education, 901-272-5100, Fax: 901-272-5158, E-mail: selliott@mca.edu. *Application contact:* Katey Henriksen, Director of Admissions, 901-272-5151, Fax: 901-272-5158, E-mail: khenriksen@mca.edu.

Miami University, College of Creative Arts, Department of Art, Oxford, OH 45056. Offers art education (MA); studio art (MFA). *Accreditation:* NASAD (one or more programs are accredited). *Students:* 22 full-time (11 women), 2 part-time (1 woman); includes 6 minority (2 Black or African American, non-Hispanic/Latino; 2 Asian, non-Hispanic/Latino; 1 Hispanic/Latino; 1 Two or more races, non-Hispanic/Latino), 4 international. Average age 33. In 2016, 4 master's awarded. *Expenses:* Tuition, state resident: full-time $12,890; part-time $564 per credit hour. Tuition, nonresident: full-time $29,604; part-time $1260 per credit hour. *Required fees:* $638. Part-time tuition and fees vary according to course load and program. *Unit head:* Thomas Effler, Interim Chair, 513-529-2900, E-mail: art@miamioh.edu.
Website: http://www.MiamiOH.edu/art

Millersville University of Pennsylvania, College of Graduate Studies and Adult Learning, College of Arts, Humanities and Social Sciences, Department of Art and Design, Millersville, PA 17551-0302. Offers art education (M Ed). *Accreditation:* NASAD; NCATE. *Program availability:* Part-time. *Faculty:* 12 full-time (8 women). *Students:* 2 full-time (1 woman), 13 part-time (9 women); includes 2 minority (1 Asian, non-Hispanic/

Latino; 1 Hispanic/Latino). Average age 31. 5 applicants, 100% accepted, 3 enrolled. In 2016, 4 master's awarded. *Degree requirements:* For master's, comprehensive exam, thesis optional. *Entrance requirements:* For master's, teaching certificate (unless enrolled in post baccalaureate certificate at same time); portfolio (if not MU graduate). Additional exam requirements/recommendations for international students: Required—TOEFL (minimum score 600 paper-based), IELTS (minimum score 6). *Application deadline:* Applications are processed on a rolling basis. Application fee: $40. Electronic applications accepted. *Expenses:* $483 per credit resident tuition; $725 per credit non-resident tuition. *Financial support:* Unspecified assistantships available. Financial award application deadline: 3/15; financial award applicants required to submit FAFSA. *Faculty research:* Ceramics; representational painting; material investigations involving bronze casting, steel forming and fabrication, mold-making, wood working; art educator's professional learning, assessment in the arts, and postmodern; interactive design fundamentals, interdisciplinary design, interaction, visual storytelling and digital narrative forms and choice-based approaches to teaching art. *Unit head:* Deborah S. Sigel, Chair, 717-871-7249, Fax: 717-871-2004, E-mail: deborah.sigel@millersville.edu. *Application contact:* Dr. Victor S. DeSantis, Dean of College of Graduate Studies and Adult Learning/Associate Provost for Civic and Community Engagement, 717-871-7619, Fax: 717-871-7954, E-mail: victor.desantis@millersville.edu.
Website: http://www.millersville.edu/art/

Minnesota State University Mankato, College of Graduate Studies and Research, College of Arts and Humanities, Department of Art, Mankato, MN 56001. Offers art (MA); art education (MAT). *Accreditation:* NASAD (one or more programs are accredited). *Program availability:* Part-time. *Students:* 5 full-time (3 women), 7 part-time (3 women). *Degree requirements:* For master's, one foreign language, comprehensive exam, thesis or alternative. *Entrance requirements:* For master's, portfolio, three letters of reference. Additional exam requirements/recommendations for international students: Required—TOEFL. *Application deadline:* For fall admission, 3/15 priority date for domestic students. Applications are processed on a rolling basis. Application fee: $40. Electronic applications accepted. *Financial support:* Research assistantships, teaching assistantships with full tuition reimbursements, and unspecified assistantships available. Financial award application deadline: 3/15; financial award applicants required to submit FAFSA. *Unit head:* Brian Frink, Chairperson, 507-389-5213, E-mail: brian.frink@mnsu.edu.
Website: http://www.mnsu.edu/artdept/

Mississippi College, Graduate School, School of Education, Department of Teacher Education and Leadership, Clinton, MS 39058. Offers art (M Ed); biological science (M Ed); business education (M Ed); computer science (M Ed); dyslexia therapy (M Ed); educational leadership (M Ed, Ed D, Ed S); elementary education (M Ed, Ed S); English (M Ed); higher education administration (MS); mathematics (M Ed); secondary education (M Ed); social studies (history) (M Ed); teaching arts (M Ed). *Program availability:* Part-time, online learning. *Degree requirements:* For master's, comprehensive exam, thesis optional. *Entrance requirements:* For master's, NTE. Additional exam requirements/recommendations for international students: Recommended—TOEFL, IELTS. Electronic applications accepted.

Montclair State University, The Graduate School, College of Education and Human Services, MAT Program in Teaching, Montclair, NJ 07043-1624. Offers art (MAT); biology (MAT); chemistry (MAT); earth science (MAT); English (MAT); French (MAT); health and physical education (MAT); health education (MAT); mathematics (MAT); music (MAT); physical education (MAT); physical science (MAT); social studies (MAT); Spanish (MAT); teacher of English as a second language (MAT). *Degree requirements:* For master's, comprehensive exam, thesis or alternative. *Entrance requirements:* For master's, interview, 2 letters of recommendation. Additional exam requirements/recommendations for international students: Required—TOEFL (minimum score 83 iBT), IELTS (minimum score 6.5). Electronic applications accepted. *Expenses:* Tuition, state resident: part-time $553 per credit. Tuition, nonresident: part-time $854 per credit. *Required fees:* $91 per credit. Tuition and fees vary according to program.

Moore College of Art & Design, Program in Art Education, Philadelphia, PA 19103. Offers MA. *Program availability:* Part-time. *Degree requirements:* For master's, thesis, field practicum. *Entrance requirements:* For master's, minimum GPA of 3.0, on-site interview, portfolio, 3 letters of recommendation, resume.

Morehead State University, Graduate Programs, Caudill College of Arts, Humanities and Social Sciences, Department of Art and Design, Morehead, KY 40351. Offers art education (MA); graphic design (MA); studio art (MA). *Accreditation:* NASAD. *Program availability:* Part-time, evening/weekend. *Degree requirements:* For master's, comprehensive exam, thesis (for some programs), oral exam during exhibition. *Entrance requirements:* For master's, GRE General Test, minimum undergraduate GPA of 3.0 in major, 2.5 overall; portfolio; bachelor's degree in art. Additional exam requirements/recommendations for international students: Required—TOEFL (minimum score 500 paper-based). Electronic applications accepted. *Faculty research:* Computer art, painting, drawing, ceramics, photography.

Nazareth College of Rochester, Graduate Studies, Department of Art, Program in Art Education, Rochester, NY 14618. Offers MS Ed. *Accreditation:* TEAC. *Program availability:* Part-time. *Students:* 6 full-time (5 women), 7 part-time (6 women); includes 1 minority (Asian, non-Hispanic/Latino). Average age 26. 5 applicants, 80% accepted, 3 enrolled. *Entrance requirements:* For master's, GRE (for speech-language pathology); GRE or MAT (for education programs), minimum GPA of 3.0, portfolio review. Additional exam requirements/recommendations for international students: Required—TOEFL (minimum score 550 paper-based, 79 iBT) or IELTS (6.5). *Application deadline:* For fall admission, 4/1 for domestic students. Applications are processed on a rolling basis. Electronic applications accepted. *Expenses: Tuition:* Part-time $880 per credit hour. Part-time tuition and fees vary according to course load, degree level and program. *Financial support:* Unspecified assistantships available. Financial award application deadline: 3/1; financial award applicants required to submit FAFSA. *Unit head:* Samantha Nolte, Director, 585-389-2537, E-mail: snolte5@naz.edu. *Application contact:* Judith Baker, Director, Transfer and Graduate Admissions, 585-531-1154, Fax: 585-389-2826, E-mail: gradadmissions@naz.edu.

New Hampshire Institute of Art, Graduate Studies, Manchester, NH 03104. Offers art education (MA); creative writing (MFA); photography (MFA); teaching visual arts (MAT); visual arts (MFA); writing for stage and screen (MFA). *Accreditation:* NASAD. *Faculty:* 31 part-time/adjunct (14 women). *Students:* 59 full-time (42 women), 6 part-time (3 women); includes 2 minority (1 Asian, non-Hispanic/Latino; 1 Hispanic/Latino). Average age 43. 36 applicants, 58% accepted, 12 enrolled. In 2016, 2 master's awarded. *Degree requirements:* For master's, thesis, corresponding exhibition and artist talk. *Entrance requirements:* For master's, writing sample or visual art portfolio; curriculum vitae; transcripts; letters of recommendation. Additional exam requirements/recommendations for international students: Required—TOEFL (minimum score 530 paper-based; 71 iBT). *Application deadline:* For fall admission, 5/1 priority date for domestic students; for spring admission, 11/1 priority date for domestic students. Applications are processed on a rolling basis. Application fee: $75. Electronic applications accepted. *Expenses:* $9,745 tuition per semester/residency plus $745 residency fee. *Financial support:* In 2016–17, 2 teaching assistantships (averaging $1,200 per year) were awarded; scholarships/grants and unspecified assistantships also available. Support available to part-time students. Financial award application deadline: 6/1; financial award applicants required to submit FAFSA. *Faculty research:* Fine arts - visual arts, photography, creative writing, writing for stage and screen; art education. *Unit head:* Lucinda Bliss, Dean of Graduate Studies, 603-836 2522, E-mail: lucindabliss@nhia.edu. *Application contact:* Moriah Billups, Graduate Admissions Coordinator, 603-836 2588, E-mail: gradadmissions@nhia.edu.
Website: http://www.nhia.edu/graduate-studies

New Jersey City University, William J. Maxwell College of Arts and Sciences, Department of Art, Jersey City, NJ 07305-1597. Offers art (MFA); art education (MA); studio art (MFA). *Accreditation:* NASAD. *Program availability:* Part-time, evening/weekend. *Degree requirements:* For master's, thesis or alternative, exhibit. *Entrance requirements:* For master's, portfolio. Additional exam requirements/recommendations for international students: Required—TOEFL (minimum score 79 iBT).

New York University, Steinhardt School of Culture, Education, and Human Development, Department of Art and Art Professions, Program in Art Education, New York, NY 10003-5799. Offers art, education, and community practice (MA); teachers of art, all grades (MA); teaching art/social studies 7-12 (MA), including 5-6 extension. *Accreditation:* TEAC. *Program availability:* Part-time. *Degree requirements:* For master's, thesis (for some programs). *Entrance requirements:* For master's, portfolio. Additional exam requirements/recommendations for international students: Required—TOEFL (minimum score 100 iBT). Electronic applications accepted. *Faculty research:* Multicultural aesthetic inquiry, urban art education, feminism, equity and social justice.

New York University, Steinhardt School of Culture, Education, and Human Development, Department of Teaching and Learning, Program in Social Studies Education, New York, NY 10003. Offers teaching art/social studies 7-12 (MA), including 5-6 extension; teaching social studies 7-12 (MA). *Accreditation:* TEAC. *Program availability:* Part-time, evening/weekend. *Degree requirements:* For master's, thesis (for some programs). *Entrance requirements:* Additional exam requirements/recommendations for international students: Required—TOEFL (minimum score 100 iBT). Electronic applications accepted. *Faculty research:* Social studies education reform, ethnography and oral history, civic education, labor history and social studies curriculum, material culture.

The Ohio State University, Graduate School, College of Arts and Sciences, Division of Arts and Humanities, Department of Arts Administration, Education and Policy, Columbus, OH 43210. Offers art education (MA); arts administration, education and policy (PhD); arts policy and administration (MA). *Accreditation:* NASAD; NCATE. *Program availability:* Online learning. *Faculty:* 11. *Students:* 47 full-time (36 women), 13 part-time (11 women), 19 international. Average age 32. In 2016, 8 master's, 7 doctorates awarded. Terminal master's awarded for partial completion of doctoral program. *Degree requirements:* For master's, thesis; for doctorate, thesis/dissertation. *Entrance requirements:* For master's, GRE; for doctorate, GRE General Test. Additional exam requirements/recommendations for international students: Required—TOEFL (minimum score 600 paper-based; 100 iBT); Recommended—IELTS (minimum score 8). *Application deadline:* For fall admission, 11/30 priority date for domestic and international students; for winter admission, 12/1 for domestic students, 11/1 for international students; for spring admission, 11/30 priority date for domestic and international students. Applications are processed on a rolling basis. Application fee: $60 ($70 for international students). Electronic applications accepted. *Financial support:* Fellowships with tuition reimbursements, research assistantships with tuition reimbursements, teaching assistantships with tuition reimbursements, career-related internships or fieldwork, Federal Work-Study, institutionally sponsored loans, and unspecified assistantships available. Support available to part-time students. Financial award applicants required to submit FAFSA. *Unit head:* Dr. Karen Hutzel, Chair and Associate Professor, 614-292-9852, E-mail: hutzel.4@osu.edu. *Application contact:* Graduate Admissions, 614-292-9444, Fax: 614-292-3895, E-mail: gradadmissions@osu.edu.
Website: http://aaep.osu.edu/

Penn State University Park, Graduate School, College of Arts and Architecture, School of Visual Arts, University Park, PA 16802. Offers art (MFA); art education (MPS, MS, PhD, Certificate). *Unit head:* Dr. Barbara O. Korner, Dean, 814-865-2592, Fax: 814-865-2018. *Application contact:* Lori Hawn, Director, Graduate Student Services, 814-865-1795, Fax: 814-863-4627, E-mail: l-gswww@lists.psu.edu.
Website: http://sova.psu.edu/

Piedmont College, School of Education, Demorest, GA 30535. Offers art education (MAT); curriculum and instruction (Ed S); early childhood education (MA, MAT); instructional technology (MAT); middle grades education (MA, MAT); music education (MAT); secondary education (MA, MAT); special education (MA, MAT). *Program availability:* Part-time, evening/weekend. *Students:* 290 full-time (217 women), 614 part-time (508 women); includes 131 minority (97 Black or African American, non-Hispanic/Latino; 4 American Indian or Alaska Native, non-Hispanic/Latino; 5 Asian, non-Hispanic/Latino; 11 Hispanic/Latino; 6 Native Hawaiian or other Pacific Islander, non-Hispanic/Latino; 8 Two or more races, non-Hispanic/Latino), 6 international. Average age 37. 257 applicants, 64% accepted, 160 enrolled. In 2016, 288 master's, 243 other advanced degrees awarded. *Degree requirements:* For master's, thesis, field experience in the classroom teaching. *Entrance requirements:* For master's, GRE General Test, MAT, minimum undergraduate GPA of 2.5; for Ed S, minimum graduate GPA of 3.5, valid teaching certificate. Additional exam requirements/recommendations for international students: Required—TOEFL (minimum score 550 paper-based). *Application deadline:* For fall admission, 7/15 for domestic students; for spring admission, 12/1 for domestic students. Applications are processed on a rolling basis. Electronic applications accepted. *Expenses: Tuition:* Full-time $8910. *Financial support:* Career-related internships or fieldwork, Federal Work-Study, and unspecified assistantships available. Support available to part-time students. Financial award applicants required to submit FAFSA. *Unit head:* Dr. Don Gnecco, Dean, 706-778-3000 Ext. 1201, Fax: 706-776-9608, E-mail: dgnecco@piedmont.edu. *Application contact:* Kathleen Anderson, Director of Graduate Enrollment Management, 706-778-8500 Ext. 1181, Fax: 706-778-0150, E-mail: kanderson@piedmont.edu.

Plymouth State University, College of Graduate Studies, Graduate Studies in Education, Program in Teaching, Plymouth, NH 03264-1595. Offers art education (MAT); science education (MAT). *Program availability:* Evening/weekend. *Degree requirements:* For master's, internship or teaching experience.

Pratt Institute, School of Art, Program in Art and Design Education, Brooklyn, NY 11205-3899. Offers MS, Adv C. *Accreditation:* NASAD. *Program availability:* Part-time. *Faculty:* 4 full-time (all women), 3 part-time/adjunct (all women). *Students:* 10 full-time (7 women); includes 3 minority (1 Black or African American, non-Hispanic/Latino; 2 Hispanic/Latino). Average age 28. 20 applicants, 80% accepted, 4 enrolled. In 2016, 2 master's, 1 other advanced degree awarded. *Degree requirements:* For master's, thesis. *Entrance requirements:* For master's, portfolio. Additional exam requirements/recommendations for international students: Required—TOEFL (minimum score 600 paper-based; 100 iBT). *Application deadline:* For fall admission, 1/5 for domestic and international students; for spring admission, 10/1 for domestic and international students. Application fee: $50 ($90 for international students). Electronic applications

accepted. *Expenses:* $29,646 full-time tuition, $1,938 fees. *Financial support:* Career-related internships or fieldwork, Federal Work-Study, institutionally sponsored loans, scholarships/grants, health care benefits, and unspecified assistantships available. Support available to part-time students. Financial award application deadline: 2/1; financial award applicants required to submit FAFSA. *Unit head:* Heather Lewis, Chairperson, 718-636-3637, Fax: 718-636-3632, E-mail: hlewis@pratt.edu. *Application contact:* Natalie Capannelli, Director of Graduate Admissions, 718-636-3551, Fax: 718-399-4242, E-mail: ncapanne@pratt.edu.
Website: https://www.pratt.edu/academics/school-of-art/graduate-school-of-art/art-and-design-education-grad/

Purdue University, Graduate School, College of Education, Department of Curriculum and Instruction, West Lafayette, IN 47907. Offers agricultural and extension education (MS, MS Ed, PhD, Ed S); art education (PhD); career and technical education (MS Ed, PhD, Ed S); curriculum studies (MS Ed, PhD, Ed S); educational technology (MS Ed, PhD, Ed S); elementary education (MS Ed); family and consumer sciences education (MS Ed, PhD, Ed S); foreign language education (MS Ed, PhD, Ed S); industrial technology (PhD, Ed S); language arts (MS Ed, PhD, Ed S); literacy (MS Ed, PhD, Ed S); mathematics education (MS, MS Ed, PhD, Ed S); science education (MS, MS Ed, PhD, Ed S); social studies education (MS Ed, PhD, Ed S). *Accreditation:* NCATE. *Program availability:* Part-time, evening/weekend. *Faculty:* 37 full-time (27 women), 1 (woman) part-time/adjunct. *Students:* 78 full-time (50 women), 286 part-time (195 women); includes 68 minority (25 Black or African American, non-Hispanic/Latino; 3 American Indian or Alaska Native, non-Hispanic/Latino; 10 Asian, non-Hispanic/Latino; 22 Hispanic/Latino; 1 Native Hawaiian or other Pacific Islander, non-Hispanic/Latino; 7 Two or more races, non-Hispanic/Latino), 44 international. Average age 36. 150 applicants, 79% accepted, 73 enrolled. In 2016, 107 master's, 20 doctorates, 2 other advanced degrees awarded. *Degree requirements:* For master's, thesis optional; for doctorate, thesis/dissertation, oral and written exams; for Ed S, oral presentation, project. *Entrance requirements:* For master's, GRE General Test (if undergraduate GPA is below 3.0), minimum undergraduate GPA of 3.0 or equivalent; for doctorate, GRE General Test (minimum combined verbal and quantitative score of 1000, 300 for new scoring), minimum undergraduate GPA of 3.0 or equivalent; master's degree with minimum GPA of 3.0 or equivalent; for Ed S, GRE General Test (minimum combined verbal and quantitative score of 1000, 300 for new scoring), minimum undergraduate GPA of 3.0 or equivalent; master's degree. Additional exam requirements/recommendations for international students: Required—TOEFL (minimum score 550 paper-based; 77 iBT). *Application deadline:* For fall admission, 12/15 for domestic students, 3/1 for international students; for spring admission, 9/15 for domestic students, 8/1 for international students. Application fee: $60 ($75 for international students). Electronic applications accepted. *Financial support:* Fellowships with full tuition reimbursements, research assistantships with full tuition reimbursements, teaching assistantships with full tuition reimbursements, career-related internships or fieldwork, and tuition waivers (full) available. Support available to part-time students. Financial award application deadline: 3/1; financial award applicants required to submit FAFSA. *Faculty research:* Literacy acquisition and development, teacher beliefs and knowledge, recruitment and retention of underrepresented students, economic education, literacy discourse. *Unit head:* Janet M. Alsup, Head, 765-494-9667, E-mail: alsupj@purdue.edu. *Application contact:* Heather Brinkman, Graduate Contact, 765-494-2345, E-mail: hbrinkma@purdue.edu.
Website: http://www.edci.purdue.edu/

Purdue University, Graduate School, College of Liberal Arts, Department of Art and Design, West Lafayette, IN 47907. Offers art education (MA, PhD); industrial design (MFA); integrated studio arts (MFA); interior design (MFA); photography (MFA); visual communications design (MFA). *Accreditation:* NASAD; NAST. *Program availability:* Part-time. *Students:* 20 full-time (14 women), 1 part-time (0 women); includes 1 minority (Two or more races, non-Hispanic/Latino), 16 international. Average age 26. 97 applicants, 26% accepted, 10 enrolled. In 2016, 6 master's awarded. *Degree requirements:* For master's, terminal exhibit, project, or thesis. *Entrance requirements:* For master's, GRE General Test (for art education), minimum undergraduate GPA of 3.0 or equivalent; 9 undergraduate hours in an art or design history; BA in art (for MA in art education); for doctorate, GRE General Test (minimum scores 600 in verbal and 1000 total), master's degree in art education or art with teaching certification; 3 years of teaching experience at the K-12 level. Additional exam requirements/recommendations for international students: Required—TOEFL (minimum score 550 paper-based; 77 iBT). *Application deadline:* For fall admission, 2/1 for domestic students, 2/1 priority date for international students. Applications are processed on a rolling basis. Application fee: $60 ($75 for international students). Electronic applications accepted. *Financial support:* Teaching assistantships with tuition reimbursements and career-related internships or fieldwork available. Support available to part-time students. Financial award applicants required to submit FAFSA. *Faculty research:* Design, fine arts, photography, acting, directing, theatre technology. *Unit head:* Harry T. Bulow, Head of the Graduate Program, 765-494-3056, E-mail: hbulow@purdue.edu. *Application contact:* Sara J. Unser, Graduate Contact, 765-494-8662, E-mail: sunser@purdue.edu.
Website: https://www.cla.purdue.edu/vpa/ad/

Queens College of the City University of New York, Division of Education, Department of Secondary Education and Youth Services, Queens, NY 11367-1597. Offers adolescent biology (MAT); art (MS Ed); biology (MS Ed, AC); chemistry (MS Ed, AC); earth sciences (MS Ed, AC); English (MS Ed, AC); French (MS Ed); Italian (MS Ed, AC); literacy education (MS Ed); mathematics (MS Ed, AC); music (MS Ed, AC); physics (MS Ed, AC); social studies (MS Ed, AC); Spanish (MS Ed, AC). *Program availability:* Part-time, evening/weekend. *Faculty:* 22 full-time (14 women), 40 part-time/adjunct (26 women). *Students:* 31 full-time (21 women), 356 part-time (211 women); includes 164 minority (22 Black or African American, non-Hispanic/Latino; 54 Asian, non-Hispanic/Latino; 81 Hispanic/Latino; 7 Two or more races, non-Hispanic/Latino), 11 international. Average age 29. 236 applicants, 88% accepted, 121 enrolled. In 2016, 119 master's, 51 other advanced degrees awarded. *Degree requirements:* For master's, research project. *Entrance requirements:* For master's, minimum GPA of 3.0. Additional exam requirements/recommendations for international students: Required—TOEFL, IELTS. *Application deadline:* For fall admission, 4/1 for domestic students; for spring admission, 11/1 for domestic students. Applications are processed on a rolling basis. Application fee: $125. Electronic applications accepted. *Expenses:* Tuition, state resident: full-time $5065; part-time $425 per credit. Tuition, nonresident: part-time $780 per credit. *Required fees:* $522; $397 per credit. Part-time tuition and fees vary according to course load and program. *Financial support:* Career-related internships or fieldwork available. Financial award application deadline: 4/1; financial award applicants required to submit FAFSA. *Unit head:* Dr. Eleanor Armour-Thomas, Chairperson, 718-997-5150, E-mail: armourthomas@yahoo.com.

Rhode Island College, School of Graduate Studies, Faculty of Arts and Sciences, Department of Art, Providence, RI 02908-1991. Offers art education (MA, MAT); media studies (MA). *Accreditation:* NASAD (one or more programs are accredited). *Program availability:* Part-time, evening/weekend. *Faculty:* 6 full-time (3 women), 2 part-time/adjunct (1 woman). *Students:* 7 full-time (5 women), 5 part-time (4 women); includes 1 minority (Hispanic/Latino). Average age 33. In 2016, 4 master's awarded. *Degree requirements:* For master's, thesis. *Entrance requirements:* For master's, GRE General Test, portfolio (MA), 3 letters of recommendation, interview. Additional exam requirements/recommendations for international students: Recommended—TOEFL (minimum score 550 paper-based; 79 iBT). *Application deadline:* For fall admission, 3/1 for domestic students. Applications are processed on a rolling basis. Application fee: $50. Electronic applications accepted. *Expenses:* Tuition, state resident: full-time $8928; part-time $372 per credit. Tuition, nonresident: full-time $17,376; part-time $724 per credit. *Required fees:* $604; $22 per credit. One-time fee: $74. *Financial support:* In 2016–17, 2 teaching assistantships with full tuition reimbursements (averaging $1,500 per year) were awarded; career-related internships or fieldwork, Federal Work-Study, scholarships/grants, health care benefits, and unspecified assistantships also available. Support available to part-time students. Financial award application deadline: 5/15; financial award applicants required to submit FAFSA. *Unit head:* Prof. Richard Whitten, Chair, 401-456-9635. *Application contact:* Graduate Studies, 401-456-8700.
Website: http://www.ric.edu/art/index.php

Rhode Island School of Design, Graduate Studies, Department of Teaching and Learning in Art and Design, Providence, RI 02903-2784. Offers art education (MA, MAT). *Accreditation:* NASAD. *Faculty:* 11 full-time (3 women), 11 part-time/adjunct (6 women). *Students:* 22 full-time (21 women); includes 1 minority (Asian, non-Hispanic/Latino), 6 international. Average age 27. 42 applicants, 76% accepted, 21 enrolled. In 2016, 17 master's awarded. *Degree requirements:* For master's, thesis, exhibition. *Entrance requirements:* For master's, portfolio, statement of purpose, 3 letters of recommendation. Additional exam requirements/recommendations for international students: Required—TOEFL (minimum score 580 paper-based; 93 iBT). *Application deadline:* For fall admission, 2/1 for domestic and international students. Application fee: $60. Electronic applications accepted. *Expenses: Tuition:* Full-time $46,800. *Required fees:* $310. *Financial support:* Fellowships, research assistantships, teaching assistantships, Federal Work-Study, scholarships/grants, and unspecified assistantships available. Financial award application deadline: 2/15; financial award applicants required to submit FAFSA. *Unit head:* Paul Sproll, Department Head and Graduate Program Director, 401-454-6695, Fax: 401-454-6694, E-mail: psproll@risd.edu. *Application contact:* Molly Pettengil, Assistant Director for Graduate Recruitment, 401-454-6312, Fax: 401-454-6309, E-mail: mpetteng@risd.edu.
Website: http://www.risd.edu/academics/tlad/

Rochester Institute of Technology, Graduate Enrollment Services, College of Imaging Arts and Sciences, School of Art, MST Program in Visual Arts-All Grades, Rochester, NY 14623-5603. Offers MST. *Accreditation:* NASAD; TEAC. *Students:* 5 full-time (3 women). Average age 35. 15 applicants, 47% accepted, 5 enrolled. In 2016, 4 master's awarded. *Degree requirements:* For master's, practicum in student teaching. *Entrance requirements:* For master's, GRE, portfolio, minimum GPA of 3.0 (recommended). Additional exam requirements/recommendations for international students: Required—TOEFL (minimum score 550 paper-based; 79 iBT), IELTS (minimum score 6.5), PTE (minimum score 58). *Application deadline:* For fall admission, 2/15 priority date for domestic and international students. Applications are processed on a rolling basis. Application fee: $60. Electronic applications accepted. *Expenses:* $1,742 per credit hour. *Financial support:* In 2016–17, 4 students received support. Scholarships/grants and unspecified assistantships available. Financial award applicants required to submit FAFSA. *Faculty research:* Innovation and creativity in teaching and learning. *Unit head:* Lauren Ramich, Graduate Program Director, 585-475-2643, E-mail: larfaa@rit.edu. *Application contact:* Diane Ellison, Associate Vice President, Graduate Enrollment Services, 585-475-2229, Fax: 585-475-7164, E-mail: gradinfo@rit.edu.
Website: http://cias.rit.edu/schools/art/graduate-teaching-visual-arts

Rocky Mountain College of Art + Design, Program in Education, Leadership + Emerging Technologies, Lakewood, CO 80214. Offers MA. *Accreditation:* NASAD. *Program availability:* Online learning.

Saint Michael's College, Graduate Programs, Program in Education, Colchester, VT 05439. Offers arts in education (CAGS); literacy (M Ed); school leadership (CAGS); special education (M Ed). *Program availability:* Part-time, evening/weekend. *Students:* 5 full-time (4 women), 239 part-time (199 women); includes 9 minority (2 Black or African American, non-Hispanic/Latino; 1 American Indian or Alaska Native, non-Hispanic/Latino; 1 Asian, non-Hispanic/Latino; 4 Hispanic/Latino; 1 Two or more races, non-Hispanic/Latino), 1 international. Average age 36. In 2016, 31 master's awarded. *Degree requirements:* For master's, thesis. *Entrance requirements:* For master's, minimum GPA of 3.0, official transcripts, essay, interview. *Application deadline:* Applications are processed on a rolling basis. Application fee: $50. Electronic applications accepted. *Expenses: Tuition:* Full-time $10,620; part-time $590 per credit. Part-time tuition and fees vary according to course load and program. *Financial support:* Fellowships with partial tuition reimbursements and scholarships/grants available. Support available to part-time students. Financial award applicants required to submit FAFSA. *Faculty research:* Integrative curriculum, moral and spiritual dimensions of education, learning styles, multiple intelligences, integrating technology into the curriculum. *Unit head:* Jonathan Silverman, Department Chair, 802-654-2306, Fax: 802-654-2664, E-mail: jsilverman@smcvt.edu. *Application contact:* Lindsay A. Damici, Marketing Communications Manager, 802-654-2556, Fax: 802-654-2732.
Website: http://www.smcvt.edu/graduate-programs/academic-programs/education.aspx

Salem College, Department of Education, Winston-Salem, NC 27101. Offers art education (MAT); elementary education (M Ed, MAT); language and literacy (M Ed); middle school education (MAT); school counseling (M Ed); second language studies (MAT); secondary education (MAT); special education (M Ed, MAT). *Accreditation:* NCATE. *Program availability:* Part-time, evening/weekend, online learning. *Degree requirements:* For master's, practicum (MAT), project (M Ed), oral and written comprehensive exams. *Entrance requirements:* For master's, minimum GPA of 2.5. *Faculty research:* Content area reading strategies, literacy development, brain compatible instruction.

Salem State University, School of Graduate Studies, Program in Art, Salem, MA 01970-5353. Offers MAT. *Accreditation:* NASAD. *Program availability:* Part-time, evening/weekend. *Entrance requirements:* For master's, GRE or MAT. Additional exam requirements/recommendations for international students: Required—TOEFL (minimum score 550 paper-based; 80 iBT) or IELTS (minimum score 5.5).

School of the Art Institute of Chicago, Graduate Division, Program in Art Education and Art Teaching, Chicago, IL 60603-3103. Offers MAAE, MAT. *Accreditation:* NASAD. *Entrance requirements:* Additional exam requirements/recommendations for international students: Required—TOEFL (minimum score 600 paper-based; 100 iBT), IELTS (minimum score 7).

School of Visual Arts, Graduate Programs, Art Education Department, New York, NY 10010-3994. Offers MAT. *Program availability:* Part-time. *Degree requirements:* For master's, one foreign language, thesis, 60 credits, including all required courses; minimum cumulative GPA of 3.0; residency of two academic years. *Entrance requirements:* For master's, Liberal Arts and Sciences Test (strongly recommended), CD with 15 to 20 images (jpeg or tiff formats, and at least 600x500 pixels); 30 credits each in studio art and liberal arts and sciences; 12 credits in art history; coursework in language other than English; personal interview. Additional exam requirements/recommendations for international students: Required—TOEFL (minimum score 550 paper-based; 79 iBT). Electronic applications accepted. *Faculty research:* Teaching art to children in pre-kindergarten through grade 12.

School of Visual Arts, Graduate Programs, Program in Art Writing, New York, NY 10010. Offers MFA. *Degree requirements:* For master's, thesis, 60 credits, including all required courses; residency of two academic years. *Entrance requirements:* For master's, typed writing sample between 2,500 and 3,000 words in length; personal interviews. Additional exam requirements/recommendations for international students: Required—TOEFL (minimum score 550 paper-based; 79 iBT). Electronic applications accepted. *Faculty research:* Art, writing, criticism, editing, art history, philosophy.

Simon Fraser University, Office of Graduate Studies and Postdoctoral Fellows, Faculty of Education, Program in Arts Education, Burnaby, BC V5A 1S6, Canada. Offers M Ed, MA, Ed D, PhD. *Program availability:* Part-time, evening/weekend. *Degree requirements:* For master's, comprehensive exam (for some programs), thesis (for some programs); for doctorate, comprehensive exam (for some programs), thesis/dissertation (for some programs). *Entrance requirements:* For master's, minimum GPA of 3.0 (on scale of 4.33) or 3.33 based on last 60 credits of undergraduate courses; for doctorate, minimum GPA of 3.5 (on scale of 4.33). Additional exam requirements/recommendations for international students: Recommended—TOEFL (minimum score 580 paper-based; 93 iBT), IELTS (minimum score 7), TWE (minimum score 5). *Application deadline:* For fall admission, 1/31 for domestic and international students. Application fee: $90 ($125 for international students). *Financial support:* In 2016–17, fellowships (averaging $6,250 per year) were awarded; research assistantships, teaching assistantships, and scholarships/grants also available. *Faculty research:* Drama education, poetic and performative inquiry, the integration of the arts in education, art therapy, arts-based narrative and arts-informed research methodologies. *Unit head:* Dr. Shawn Bullock, Associate Dean, Graduate Studies in Education, 778-782-4102, Fax: 778-782-4320, E-mail: mesbit@sfu.ca. *Application contact:* Graduate Secretary, 778-782-3984, Fax: 778-782-4320, E-mail: educmast@sfu.ca.

Southern Connecticut State University, School of Graduate Studies, School of Arts and Sciences, Department of Art, New Haven, CT 06515-1355. Offers art education (MS). *Program availability:* Part-time, evening/weekend. *Faculty:* 1 full-time (0 women). *Students:* 5 part-time (4 women); includes 1 minority (Asian, non-Hispanic/Latino). Average age 36. 15 applicants, 33% accepted, 2 enrolled. In 2016, 8 master's awarded. *Degree requirements:* For master's, thesis or alternative. *Entrance requirements:* For master's, interview. *Application deadline:* For fall admission, 5/1 priority date for domestic students; for spring admission, 12/1 priority date for domestic students. Applications are processed on a rolling basis. Application fee: $50. Electronic applications accepted. *Expenses:* Tuition, state resident: full-time $6497; part-time $519 per credit hour. Tuition, nonresident: full-time $18,102; part-time $535 per credit hour. *Required fees:* $4722; $55 per semester. Tuition and fees vary according to program. *Financial support:* Career-related internships or fieldwork, scholarships/grants, and unspecified assistantships available. Financial award application deadline: 4/15; financial award applicants required to submit FAFSA. *Unit head:* Dr. David Levine, Chairperson, 203-392-6642, Fax: 203-392-6658, E-mail: levined1@southernct.edu. *Application contact:* Lisa Galvin, Director of Graduate Admissions, 203-392-5240, Fax: 203-392-5235, E-mail: galvinl1@southernct.edu.

Southwestern Oklahoma State University, College of Arts and Sciences, Department of Art, Weatherford, OK 73096-3098. Offers art education (M Ed). *Program availability:* Part-time. *Degree requirements:* For master's, exam. *Entrance requirements:* For master's, GRE General Test or minimum undergraduate GPA of 3.0. Additional exam requirements/recommendations for international students: Required—TOEFL.

Spalding University, Graduate Studies, College of Education, Programs in Education, Louisville, KY 40203-2188. Offers art teacher education (MAT); business teacher education (MAT); elementary school education (MAT); foreign language (MAT); high school education (MAT); middle school education (MAT); secondary education (MAT); special education (learning and behavioral disorders) (MAT); student guidance counselor (MA); teacher leader (M Ed). *Accreditation:* NCATE. *Program availability:* Part-time, evening/weekend. *Faculty:* 39 full-time (26 women), 13 part-time/adjunct (4 women). *Students:* 97 full-time (76 women), 31 part-time (23 women); includes 39 minority (33 Black or African American, non-Hispanic/Latino; 1 Asian, non-Hispanic/Latino; 3 Hispanic/Latino; 2 Two or more races, non-Hispanic/Latino). Average age 35. 62 applicants, 55% accepted, 33 enrolled. In 2016, 49 master's awarded. *Entrance requirements:* For master's, GRE General Test or MAT, interview, letters of recommendation, resume. Additional exam requirements/recommendations for international students: Required—TOEFL (minimum score 535 paper-based). *Application deadline:* Applications are processed on a rolling basis. Application fee: $30. Electronic applications accepted. *Expenses: Tuition:* Full-time $15,300. *Financial support:* Scholarships/grants, traineeships, and unspecified assistantships available. Financial award applicants required to submit FAFSA. *Faculty research:* Instructional technology, achievement gap, classroom management, assessment. *Unit head:* Dr. Chris Walsh, Associate Dean, 502-873-4272, Fax: 502-585-7123, E-mail: cwalsh@spalding.edu. *Application contact:* Valerie Anderson, Administrative Assistant, 502-873-4260, E-mail: vanderson@spalding.edu.

State University of New York at New Paltz, Graduate School, School of Fine and Performing Arts, Department of Art Education, New Paltz, NY 12561. Offers visual arts education (MS Ed). *Accreditation:* NASAD. *Program availability:* Part-time, evening/weekend. *Students:* 1 (woman) full-time, 6 part-time (all women). In 2016, 1 master's awarded. *Degree requirements:* For master's, thesis, portfolio. *Entrance requirements:* For master's, New York state art education teaching certificate, minimum GPA of 3.0, portfolio. Additional exam requirements/recommendations for international students: Required—TOEFL (minimum score 550 paper-based; 80 iBT), IELTS (minimum score 6.5). *Application deadline:* For fall admission, 4/15 for domestic and international students; for summer admission, 3/15 priority date for domestic and international students. Application fee: $50. Electronic applications accepted. *Financial support:* Application deadline: 8/1. *Unit head:* Prof. Beth Thomas, Director, 845-257-2641, E-mail: thomasb@newpaltz.edu. *Application contact:* Vika Shock, Director of Graduate Admissions, 845-257-3286, E-mail: gradschool@newpaltz.edu.
Website: http://www.newpaltz.edu/arted/

State University of New York at Oswego, Graduate Studies, School of Education, Department of Curriculum and Instruction, Oswego, NY 13126. Offers adolescence education (MST); art education (MAT); childhood education (MST); curriculum and instruction (MS Ed); literacy education (MS Ed); special education (MS Ed). *Program availability:* Part-time, evening/weekend. *Degree requirements:* For master's, comprehensive exam (for some programs), thesis optional. *Entrance requirements:* For master's, GRE General Test, minimum GPA of 2.7, provisional teaching certificate. Additional exam requirements/recommendations for international students: Required—TOEFL (minimum score 560 paper-based). *Faculty research:* Classroom applications for microcomputers; classroom questioning, wait-time, and achievement; values clarification and academic achievement.

Sul Ross State University, College of Arts and Sciences, Department of Fine Arts and Communication, Alpine, TX 79832. Offers art history (MA); studio art (MA), including art education. *Program availability:* Part-time. *Degree requirements:* For master's, oral or written exam. *Entrance requirements:* For master's, GRE General Test, minimum GPA of 2.5 in last 60 hours of undergraduate work. *Faculty research:* Ceramic sculpture, watercolor, wood sculpture, rock art.

Syracuse University, School of Education, MS Program in Art Education, Syracuse, NY 13244. Offers MS. *Program availability:* Part-time. *Degree requirements:* For master's, thesis or alternative. *Entrance requirements:* For master's, GRE, strong teacher and/or employer recommendations, portfolio review. Additional exam requirements/recommendations for international students: Required—TOEFL (minimum score 100 iBT). *Application deadline:* For fall admission, 1/15 for domestic and international students. Application fee: $75 ($0 for international students). Electronic applications accepted. *Expenses: Tuition:* Full-time $25,974; part-time $1443 per credit hour. *Required fees:* $802; $50 per course. Tuition and fees vary according to course load and program. *Financial support:* Fellowships with full tuition reimbursements, research assistantships, teaching assistantships with tuition reimbursements, career-related internships or fieldwork, and scholarships/grants available. Financial award application deadline: 1/15. *Faculty research:* Art educational practice, arts and design practices as a means for personal agency and social responsibility, developing art and design curricula for teaching and learning in multiple contexts, interdisciplinary research promoting creative leadership and entrepreneurship. *Unit head:* Dr. James Haywood Rolling, Jr., Director, 315-443-2355, E-mail: jrolling@syr.edu. *Application contact:* Speranza Migliore, Graduate Admissions Recruiter, 315-443-2505, E-mail: gradrcrt@syr.edu.
Website: http://soe.syr.edu/academic/teaching_and_leadership/graduate/masters/art_education/preparation/default.aspx

Teachers College, Columbia University, Department of Arts and Humanities, New York, NY 10027. Offers applied linguistics (MA, Ed D); art and art education (Ed M, MA, Ed D, Ed DCT); arts administration (MA); bilingual and bicultural education (MA); global competence (Certificate); history and education (Ed D, PhD); music and music education (Ed DCT); philosophy and education (MA, Ed D, PhD); social studies education (Ed M, PhD); teaching English to speakers of other languages (Ed M); teaching of English and English education (Ed M, MA, Ed D, PhD), including English education (Ed M, Ed D, PhD), teaching of English (MA); teaching of social studies (MA); TESOL (MA, Ed D). *Program availability:* Part-time, evening/weekend. *Students:* 429 full-time (329 women), 467 part-time (332 women); includes 268 minority (62 Black or African American, non-Hispanic/Latino; 1 American Indian or Alaska Native, non-Hispanic/Latino; 108 Asian, non-Hispanic/Latino; 76 Hispanic/Latino; 21 Two or more races, non-Hispanic/Latino), 212 international. 1,068 applicants, 53% accepted, 272 enrolled. Terminal master's awarded for partial completion of doctoral program. *Expenses: Tuition:* Full-time $36,288; part-time $1512 per credit. *Required fees:* $438 per semester. One-time fee: $510 full-time. Full-time tuition and fees vary according to course load. *Financial support:* Fellowships, research assistantships, teaching assistantships, career-related internships or fieldwork, Federal Work-Study, institutionally sponsored loans, tuition waivers (full and partial), and unspecified assistantships available. Support available to part-time students. *Unit head:* Prof. William Gaudelli, Department Chair, 212-678-3150, E-mail: wg74@columbia.edu. *Application contact:* David Estrella, Director of Admissions, 212-678-3305, Fax: 212-678-4171, E-mail: estrella@tc.columbia.edu.
Website: http://www.tc.edu/a%26h/

Temple University, Tyler School of Art, Department of Art Education and Community Arts Practices, Philadelphia, PA 19122-6096. Offers art education (Ed M). *Program availability:* Part-time, evening/weekend. *Faculty:* 7 full-time (5 women), 9 part-time/adjunct (6 women). *Students:* 7 full-time (6 women), 5 part-time (all women); includes 3 minority (all Hispanic/Latino). 8 applicants, 75% accepted, 5 enrolled. In 2016, 6 master's awarded. *Degree requirements:* For master's, paper, portfolio review. *Entrance requirements:* For master's, GRE or MAT, minimum GPA of 3.0, slide portfolio, 40 credits in studio art, 9 credits in art history, letters of recommendation, resume/curriculum vitae. Additional exam requirements/recommendations for international students: Required—TOEFL (minimum score 550 paper-based; 79 iBT), IELTS (minimum score 6.5). *Application deadline:* For fall admission, 1/15 for domestic and international students; for spring admission, 11/1 for domestic and international students. Applications are processed on a rolling basis. Application fee: $60. Electronic applications accepted. *Expenses:* Contact institution. *Financial support:* Research assistantships with full tuition reimbursements, teaching assistantships, and Federal Work-Study available. Support available to part-time students. Financial award application deadline: 1/15; financial award applicants required to submit FAFSA. *Unit head:* Dr. Lisa Kay, Chair, 215-777-9763, E-mail: lisakay@temple.edu. *Application contact:* Tamryn McDermott, Director of Admissions, 215-777-9090, E-mail: tylerart@temple.edu.

Texas Tech University, Graduate School, J.T. and Margaret Talkington College of Visual and Performing Arts, School of Art, Lubbock, TX 79409. Offers art (MFA); art education (MAE); art history (MA). *Accreditation:* NASAD (one or more programs are accredited). *Program availability:* Part-time, online learning. *Faculty:* 32 full-time (14 women), 8 part-time/adjunct (5 women). *Students:* 36 full-time (23 women), 26 part-time (19 women); includes 15 minority (1 Black or African American, non-Hispanic/Latino; 1 Asian, non-Hispanic/Latino; 11 Hispanic/Latino; 2 Two or more races, non-Hispanic/Latino), 4 international. Average age 35. 39 applicants, 62% accepted, 19 enrolled. In 2016, 19 master's awarded. *Degree requirements:* For master's, variable foreign language requirement, comprehensive exam, thesis (for some programs), exhibition (for MFA). *Entrance requirements:* For master's, GRE (for MA). Additional exam requirements/recommendations for international students: Required—TOEFL (minimum score 550 paper-based; 79 iBT), IELTS (minimum score 6.5). *Application deadline:* For fall admission, 6/1 priority date for domestic students, 1/15 priority date for international students; for spring admission, 9/1 priority date for domestic students, 6/15 priority date for international students. Applications are processed on a rolling basis. Application fee: $75. Electronic applications accepted. *Expenses:* $325 per credit hour full-time resident tuition, $733 per credit hour full-time non-resident tuition; $53.75 per credit hour fee plus $608 per term fee. *Financial support:* In 2016–17, 60 students received support, including 57 fellowships (averaging $2,318 per year), 56 teaching assistantships (averaging $9,357 per year); research assistantships, Federal Work-Study, institutionally sponsored loans, scholarships/grants, health care benefits, tuition waivers (partial), and unspecified assistantships also available. Financial award application deadline: 2/15; financial award applicants required to submit FAFSA. *Faculty research:* Modern and contemporary art; contemporary Chicano/a art; transformation of multidisciplinary approach to printmaking; figurative painting and an intense interest in space as metaphor for community; working-class, sexuality and race issues; letter press posters; conceptual three dimensional concepts. *Total annual research expenditures:* $11,986. *Unit head:* Prof. Lydia Thompson, Director and Professor, 806-742-3825 Ext. 255, E-mail: lydia.thompson@ttu.edu. *Application contact:* Linda Rumbelow, Academic Advisor, 806-742-3825 Ext. 222, E-mail: linda.rumbelow@ttu.edu.
Website: http://www.art.ttu.edu

Towson University, Program in Art Education, Towson, MD 21252-0001. Offers M Ed. *Accreditation:* NCATE. *Program availability:* Part-time, evening/weekend. *Students:* 20 part-time (16 women); includes 6 minority (2 Black or African American, non-Hispanic/

Latino; 1 Asian, non-Hispanic/Latino; 1 Hispanic/Latino; 2 Two or more races, non-Hispanic/Latino). *Degree requirements:* For master's, thesis optional. *Entrance requirements:* For master's, bachelor's degree and/or certification in art education, minimum GPA of 3.0, resume. *Application deadline:* Applications are processed on a rolling basis. Application fee: $45. Electronic applications accepted. *Expenses:* Tuition, state resident: full-time $7580; part-time $379 per unit. Tuition, nonresident: full-time $15,700; part-time $785 per unit. *Required fees:* $2480. *Financial support:* Application deadline: 4/1. *Unit head:* Dr. Ray Martens, Graduate Program Director, 410-704-3819, E-mail: rmartens@towson.edu. *Application contact:* Coverley Beidleman, Assistant Director of Graduate Admissions, 410-704-2113, Fax: 410-704-3030, E-mail: grads@towson.edu.
Website: http://www.towson.edu/cofac/departments/art/grad/education/

Towson University, Program in Arts Integration, Towson, MD 21252-0001. Offers Postbaccalaureate Certificate. Program offered jointly with Johns Hopkins University, University of Maryland, College Park and University of Maryland, Baltimore County. *Students:* 29 part-time (28 women). *Entrance requirements:* For degree, bachelor's degree, minimum GPA of 3.0 (based upon last 60 credits of study); teaching experience (preferred). *Application deadline:* Applications are processed on a rolling basis. Application fee: $45. Electronic applications accepted. *Expenses:* Tuition, state resident: full-time $7580; part-time $379 per unit. Tuition, nonresident: full-time $15,700; part-time $785 per unit. *Required fees:* $2480. *Unit head:* Prof. Susan Rotkovitz, Program Director, 410-704-3658, E-mail: srotkovitz@towson.edu. *Application contact:* Coverley Beidleman, Assistant Director of Graduate Admissions, 410-704-2113, Fax: 410-704-3030, E-mail: grads@towson.edu.
Website: http://www.towson.edu/cofac/departments/gradartsintegrationpbc/

Towson University, Program in Interdisciplinary Arts Infusion, Towson, MD 21252-0001. Offers MA. *Students:* 20 part-time (19 women); includes 6 minority (5 Black or African American, non-Hispanic/Latino; 1 Hispanic/Latino). *Application deadline:* For fall admission, 4/22 priority date for domestic students. *Expenses:* Tuition, state resident: full-time $7580; part-time $379 per unit. Tuition, nonresident: full-time $15,700; part-time $785 per unit. *Required fees:* $2480. *Unit head:* Dr. Kate Collins, Director, 410-704-5614, E-mail: maiai@towson.edu. *Application contact:* Coverley Beidleman, Assistant Director of Graduate Admissions, 410-704-2113, Fax: 410-704-3030, E-mail: grads@towson.edu.
Website: https://www.towson.edu/cofac/departments/gradartsinfusion/

Tufts University, Graduate School of Arts and Sciences, Department of Education, Medford, MA 02155. Offers art education (MAT); education (MA, MAT, MS, PhD), including educational studies (MA), elementary education (MAT), middle and secondary education (MAT), museum education (MA), secondary education (MA), STEM education (MS, PhD); school psychology (MA, Ed S). *Program availability:* Part-time. *Students:* 109 full-time (84 women), 15 part-time (12 women); includes 25 minority (7 Black or African American, non-Hispanic/Latino; 10 Asian, non-Hispanic/Latino; 7 Hispanic/Latino; 1 Two or more races, non-Hispanic/Latino), 7 international. Average age 27. 197 applicants, 57% accepted, 65 enrolled. In 2016, 55 master's, 14 other advanced degrees awarded. *Degree requirements:* For master's, thesis optional; for doctorate, thesis/dissertation. *Entrance requirements:* For master's and doctorate, GRE General Test. Additional exam requirements/recommendations for international students: Required—TOEFL (minimum score 550 paper-based; 80 iBT), IELTS (minimum score 6.5). *Application deadline:* For fall admission, 1/2 for domestic and international students; for spring admission, 10/15 for domestic and international students. Applications are processed on a rolling basis. Application fee: $85. Electronic applications accepted. *Expenses:* Contact institution. *Financial support:* Teaching assistantships, Federal Work-Study, scholarships/grants, and tuition waivers (full and partial) available. Support available to part-time students. Financial award application deadline: 1/2. *Unit head:* Dr. Sabina Vaught, Graduate Program Director. *Application contact:* Office of Graduate Admissions, 617-627-3395, E-mail: gradadmissions@tufts.edu.
Website: http://www.ase.tufts.edu/education/

Tufts University, School of the Museum of Fine Arts, Medford, MA 02155. Offers art education (MAT); studio art (MFA, Postbaccalaureate Certificate). *Accreditation:* NASAD (one or more programs are accredited). Terminal master's awarded for partial completion of doctoral program. *Degree requirements:* For master's, thesis (for some programs), exhibition thesis. *Entrance requirements:* For master's, BFA (preferred) or bachelor's degree or equivalent in related area; portfolio; for Postbaccalaureate Certificate, portfolio, BFA or equivalent. Additional exam requirements/recommendations for international students: Required—TOEFL (minimum score 550 paper-based). Electronic applications accepted. *Expenses: Tuition:* Full-time $49,892; part-time $1248 per credit hour. *Required fees:* $844. Full-time tuition and fees vary according to degree level, program and student level. Part-time tuition and fees vary according to course load. *Faculty research:* Public art commissions, National Endowment for the Arts grant recipients, international exhibitions.

The University of Akron, Graduate School, College of Education, Department of Curricular and Instructional Studies, Program in P-12 Multi-Age Education, Akron, OH 44325. Offers art education (MS); drama/theatre (MS). *Expenses:* Tuition, state resident: full-time $8618; part-time $359 per credit hour. Tuition, nonresident: full-time $17,149; part-time $715 per credit hour. *Required fees:* $1652. *Unit head:* Dr. Susan Clark, Interim Chair, 330-972-7780, E-mail: sclark1@uakron.edu. *Application contact:* Kelly Chaff, College Program Specialist, 330-972-7028, E-mail: klchaff@uakron.edu.

The University of Alabama at Birmingham, School of Education, Program in Arts Education, Birmingham, AL 35294. Offers MA Ed. *Accreditation:* NCATE. *Program availability:* Part-time. *Degree requirements:* For master's, thesis optional. *Entrance requirements:* For master's, MAT (minimum score 388 scaled, 35 raw) or GRE (minimum score 385). Electronic applications accepted. Full-time tuition and fees vary according to course load and program.

The University of Arizona, College of Fine Arts, School of Art, Program in Art Education, Tucson, AZ 85721. Offers MA. *Accreditation:* NASAD. *Degree requirements:* For master's, thesis. *Entrance requirements:* For master's, portfolio, resume, autobiography, 3 letters of reference, writing sample. Additional exam requirements/recommendations for international students: Required—TOEFL (minimum score 550 paper-based; 79 iBT). Electronic applications accepted. *Faculty research:* Artistic styles, visual perception, integration of arts into elementary curricula, aesthetics of the vanishing roadsides of America.

The University of Arizona, College of Fine Arts, School of Art, Program in Art History and Education, Tucson, AZ 85721. Offers PhD. *Degree requirements:* For doctorate, thesis/dissertation. *Entrance requirements:* Additional exam requirements/recommendations for international students: Required—TOEFL (minimum score 550 paper-based; 79 iBT). Electronic applications accepted.

University of Arkansas at Little Rock, Graduate School, College of Arts, Letters, and Sciences, Department of Art, Little Rock, AR 72204-1099. Offers art education (MA); art history (MA); studio art (MA). *Accreditation:* NASAD. *Program availability:* Part-time. *Degree requirements:* For master's, 4 foreign languages, oral exam, oral defense of thesis or exhibit. *Entrance requirements:* For master's, portfolio review or term paper evaluation, minimum GPA of 2.7.

The University of British Columbia, Faculty of Education, Department of Curriculum and Pedagogy, Vancouver, BC V6T 1Z4, Canada. Offers art education (M Ed, MA); curriculum studies (M Ed, MA, PhD); home economics education (M Ed, MA); mathematics education (M Ed, MA); media and technology studies education (M Ed, MA); music education (M Ed, MA); physical education (M Ed, MA); science education (M Ed, MA); social studies education (M Ed, MA). *Program availability:* Part-time, online learning. *Degree requirements:* For master's, thesis (MA); for doctorate, comprehensive exam, thesis/dissertation. *Entrance requirements:* Additional exam requirements/recommendations for international students: Required—TOEFL, IELTS. Application fee: $100 Canadian dollars ($162 Canadian dollars for international students). Electronic applications accepted. *Expenses:* $6,865 per year tuition and fees domestic, $10,938 per year international (for MA and M Ed); $4,802 per year tuition and fees, $8,436 per year international (for PhD). *Financial support:* Fellowships with partial tuition reimbursements, research assistantships with partial tuition reimbursements, teaching assistantships with partial tuition reimbursements, and tuition waivers (partial) available. *Faculty research:* School subjects, teaching and learning. *Application contact:* Alan Jay, Graduate Programs Assistant, 604-822-5367, Fax: 604-822-4714, E-mail: edcp.grad@ubc.ca.
Website: http://www.edcp.educ.ubc.ca/

University of Central Florida, College of Education and Human Performance, School of Teaching, Learning, and Leadership, Program in Teacher Education, Orlando, FL 32816. Offers art education (MAT); English language (MAT); mathematics education (MAT); middle school mathematics (MAT); middle school science (MAT); science education (MAT), including biology, chemistry, physics; social science education (MAT). *Accreditation:* NCATE. *Program availability:* Part-time, evening/weekend. *Students:* 16 full-time (11 women), 28 part-time (23 women); includes 16 minority (6 Black or African American, non-Hispanic/Latino; 1 Asian, non-Hispanic/Latino; 8 Hispanic/Latino; 1 Two or more races, non-Hispanic/Latino), 1 international. Average age 31. 1 applicant, 100% accepted. In 2016, 33 master's awarded. *Entrance requirements:* For master's, GRE General Test. Additional exam requirements/recommendations for international students: Required—TOEFL. *Application deadline:* For spring admission, 12/1 for domestic students; for summer admission, 4/15 for domestic students. Application fee: $30. Electronic applications accepted. *Expenses:* Tuition, state resident: part-time $288.16 per credit hour. Tuition, nonresident: part-time $1071.31 per credit hour. *Financial support:* Fellowships, research assistantships, teaching assistantships, career-related internships or fieldwork, Federal Work-Study, institutionally sponsored loans, tuition waivers (partial), and unspecified assistantships available. Financial award application deadline: 3/1; financial award applicants required to submit FAFSA. *Unit head:* Dr. Michael Hynes, Director, 407-823-2005, E-mail: mychael.hynes@ucf.edu. *Application contact:* Assistant Director, Graduate Admissions, 407-823-2766, Fax: 407-823-6442, E-mail: gradadmissions@ucf.edu.
Website: http://education.ucf.edu/programs.cfm?pid=g&cat=2

University of Cincinnati, Graduate School, College of Design, Architecture, Art, and Planning, School of Art, Program in Visual Arts Education, Cincinnati, OH 45221. Offers MA. *Accreditation:* NASAD; NCATE. *Entrance requirements:* For master's, MAT. Electronic applications accepted. *Expenses: Tuition, area resident:* Full-time $12,790; part-time $389 per credit hour. Tuition, state resident: full-time $13,290; part-time $419 per credit hour. Tuition, nonresident: full-time $24,532; part-time $976 per credit hour. *International tuition:* $24,832 full-time. *Required fees:* $3958; $140 per credit hour. Tuition and fees vary according to course load, degree level, program and reciprocity agreements.

University of Denver, University College, Denver, CO 80208. Offers arts and culture (MA, Certificate); communication management (MS, Certificate), including translation studies (Certificate), world history and culture (Certificate); environmental policy and management (MS); geographic information systems (MS); global affairs (MA, Certificate), including human capital in organizations (Certificate), philanthropic leadership (Certificate), project management (Certificate), strategic innovation and change (Certificate); healthcare leadership (MS); information communications and technology (MS); leadership and organizations (MS); professional creative writing (MA, Certificate), including emergency planning and response (Certificate), organizational security (Certificate); security management (MS, Certificate); strategic human resources (Certificate). *Program availability:* Part-time, evening/weekend, online learning. *Faculty:* 118 part-time/adjunct (62 women). *Students:* 59 full-time (22 women), 1,285 part-time (750 women); includes 316 minority (111 Black or African American, non-Hispanic/Latino; 8 American Indian or Alaska Native, non-Hispanic/Latino; 39 Asian, non-Hispanic/Latino; 123 Hispanic/Latino; 3 Native Hawaiian or other Pacific Islander, non-Hispanic/Latino; 32 Two or more races, non-Hispanic/Latino), 85 international. Average age 35. 703 applicants, 89% accepted, 390 enrolled. In 2016, 428 master's, 138 other advanced degrees awarded. *Degree requirements:* For master's, capstone project. *Entrance requirements:* For master's, transcripts, two letters of recommendation, personal statement, resume. Additional exam requirements/recommendations for international students: Required—TOEFL (minimum score 550 paper-based; 80 iBT). *Application deadline:* For fall admission, 6/21 priority date for domestic students, 5/1 priority date for international students; for winter admission, 9/14 priority date for domestic students, 9/19 priority date for international students; for spring admission, 1/11 priority date for domestic students, 12/12 priority date for international students; for summer admission, 3/29 priority date for domestic students, 3/6 priority date for international students. Applications are processed on a rolling basis. Application fee: $75. Electronic applications accepted. *Expenses:* $7,236 per year full-time. *Financial support:* In 2016–17, 27 students received support, including 1 teaching assistantship (averaging $1,489 per year). Financial award applicants required to submit FAFSA. *Unit head:* Dr. Michael McGuire, Dean, 303-871-3518, Fax: 303-871-3303, E-mail: mmcguire@du.edu. *Application contact:* Information Contact, 303-871-2291, E-mail: ucoladm@du.edu.
Website: http://universitycollege.du.edu/

University of Florida, Graduate School, College of The Arts, School of Art and Art History, Gainesville, FL 32611. Offers art (MA), including digital arts and sciences; art education (MA); art history (MA, PhD); museology (MA), including historic preservation. *Accreditation:* NASAD. *Program availability:* Online learning. *Degree requirements:* For master's, project or thesis (MFA); 1 foreign language (MA in art history); for doctorate, 2 foreign languages, comprehensive exam, thesis/dissertation. *Entrance requirements:* For master's, GRE General Test, portfolio (MFA), writing sample (MA), minimum GPA 3.0; for doctorate, GRE General Test, minimum GPA of 3.0. Additional exam requirements/recommendations for international students: Required—TOEFL (minimum score 550 paper-based; 80 iBT), IELTS (minimum score 6). Electronic applications accepted. *Faculty research:* Studio production, art historical studies of style context.

University of Illinois at Urbana–Champaign, Graduate College, College of Fine and Applied Arts, School of Art and Design, Program in Art Education, Champaign, IL 61820. Offers Ed M, MA, PhD. *Accreditation:* NASAD.

University of Indianapolis, Graduate Programs, School of Education, Indianapolis, IN 46227-3697. Offers art education (MAT); biology (MAT); chemistry (MAT); curriculum and instruction (MA); earth sciences (MAT); education (MA, MAT); educational leadership (MA); elementary education (MA); English (MAT); French (MAT); math (MAT); physical education (MAT); physics (MAT); secondary education (MA), including art education, education, English education, social studies education; social studies (MAT); Spanish (MAT). *Accreditation:* NCATE. *Program availability:* Part-time, evening/weekend. *Entrance requirements:* For master's, GRE Subject Test, PRAXIS I, minimum GPA of 2.5, 3 letters of recommendation, interview. Additional exam requirements/recommendations for international students: Required—TOEFL (minimum score 550 paper-based). *Faculty research:* Assessment of teacher education, perceptions of prospective teachers by parents.

The University of Iowa, Graduate College, College of Education, Department of Teaching and Learning, Program in Education, Iowa City, IA 52242-1316. Offers art education (MA); developmental reading (MA); elementary education (MA); English education (MA, MAT); foreign and second language education (MAT); foreign language education (MA); foreign language/ESL education (PhD); language, literacy and culture (PhD); mathematics education (MA, MAT, PhD); music education (MM, PhD); science education (MA); secondary education (MA); social studies (MA, PhD). *Degree requirements:* For master's, thesis optional, exam; for doctorate, comprehensive exam, thesis/dissertation. *Entrance requirements:* For master's and doctorate, GRE General Test, minimum GPA of 3.0. Additional exam requirements/recommendations for international students: Required—TOEFL (minimum score 550 paper-based; 81 iBT). Electronic applications accepted.

The University of Kansas, Graduate Studies, College of Liberal Arts and Sciences, Department of Visual Art, Program in Visual Art Education, Lawrence, KS 66045. Offers MA. *Program availability:* Part-time. *Students:* 3 full-time (all women), 2 part-time (both women). Average age 34. 2 applicants, 100% accepted, 2 enrolled. In 2016, 4 master's awarded. *Entrance requirements:* For master's, portfolio, 3 letters of recommendation, minimum GPA of 3.0. Additional exam requirements/recommendations for international students: Required—TOEFL (minimum score 570 paper-based) or IELTS (minimum score 6.5). *Application deadline:* For fall admission, 5/1 for domestic and international students; for spring admission, 12/1 for domestic and international students. Application fee: $65 ($85 for international students). Electronic applications accepted. *Financial support:* Teaching assistantships, Federal Work-Study, scholarships/grants, and unspecified assistantships available. *Faculty research:* Emphasizing a balance of studio, art history, and education courses. *Unit head:* Mary Anne Jordan, Chairperson, 785-864-2952, E-mail: majordan@ku.edu. *Application contact:* Lauren Chaney, Graduate Admissions Contact, 785-864-2306, E-mail: lkchaney@ku.edu.
Website: http://art.ku.edu/programs/visual_art_education/

University of Kentucky, Graduate School, College of Fine Arts, Program in Art Education, Lexington, KY 40506-0032. Offers MA. *Degree requirements:* For master's, comprehensive exam, thesis optional. *Entrance requirements:* For master's, GRE General Test, minimum undergraduate GPA of 2.75. Additional exam requirements/recommendations for international students: Required—TOEFL (minimum score 550 paper-based). Electronic applications accepted. *Faculty research:* Multicultural art education, women's issues in art education, lifelong learning in the arts, the artist-teacher, art teaching as a form of art, place and art, children's home art and creativity as a basis for school art instruction.

University of Louisiana at Monroe, Graduate School, College of Arts, Education, and Sciences, School of Education, Program in Curriculum and Instruction, Monroe, LA 71209-0001. Offers art education (M Ed); biology education (M Ed); chemistry education (M Ed); curriculum and instruction (Ed D); early childhood education (M Ed); earth science education (M Ed); educational leadership (M Ed); elementary education (1-5) (M Ed); English as a second language (M Ed); English education (M Ed); family and consumer education (M Ed); French education (M Ed); history education (M Ed); math education (M Ed); middle school education (M Ed); music education (M Ed); reading education (K-12) (M Ed); Spanish education (M Ed); special education - academically gifted (M Ed); special education - early intervention (M Ed); special education - educational diagnostician (M Ed); special education - mild/moderate disabilities (M Ed); speech education (M Ed). *Accreditation:* NCATE. *Faculty:* 8 full-time (4 women), 4 part-time/adjunct (3 women). *Students:* 13 full-time (11 women), 80 part-time (65 women); includes 25 minority (19 Black or African American, non-Hispanic/Latino; 1 Asian, non-Hispanic/Latino; 3 Hispanic/Latino; 2 Two or more races, non-Hispanic/Latino). Average age 37. 118 applicants, 30% accepted, 16 enrolled. In 2016, 23 master's, 4 doctorates awarded. *Degree requirements:* For master's, comprehensive exam (for some programs), thesis; for doctorate, thesis/dissertation, internships. *Entrance requirements:* For master's, GRE General Test; for doctorate, GRE General Test, minimum undergraduate GPA of 2.75, graduate 3.25. Additional exam requirements/recommendations for international students: Required—TOEFL (minimum score 500 paper-based; 61 iBT). *Application deadline:* For fall admission, 8/24 priority date for domestic students, 7/1 for international students; for winter admission, 12/14 priority date for domestic students; for spring admission, 1/19 for domestic students, 11/1 for international students. Applications are processed on a rolling basis. Application fee: $20 ($30 for international students). Electronic applications accepted. *Expenses:* Tuition, state resident: full-time $6489. Tuition, nonresident: full-time $18,589. *Required fees:* $8984. Tuition and fees vary according to course level, course load, degree level and program. *Financial support:* Research assistantships, career-related internships or fieldwork, Federal Work-Study, and unspecified assistantships available. Financial award application deadline: 4/1; financial award applicants required to submit FAFSA. *Unit head:* Dr. Dorothy Schween, Director, 318-342-1268, Fax: 318-342-3131, E-mail: schween@ulm.edu.

University of Louisville, Graduate School, College of Education and Human Development, Department of Teaching and Learning, Louisville, KY 40292-0001. Offers art education (MAT); autism and applied behavior analysis (Certificate); curriculum and instruction (PhD); early elementary education (MAT); exercise physiology (MS); health and physical education (MAT); health professions education (Certificate); higher education (MA); human resources and organization development (MS); instructional technology (M Ed); interdisciplinary early childhood education (MAT); middle school education (MAT); music education (MAT); secondary education (MAT); special education (MAT); sport administration (MS); teacher leadership (M Ed). *Program availability:* Part-time, evening/weekend. *Students:* 116 full-time (68 women), 158 part-time (112 women); includes 46 minority (24 Black or African American, non-Hispanic/Latino; 8 Asian, non-Hispanic/Latino; 5 Hispanic/Latino; 9 Two or more races, non-Hispanic/Latino), 6 international. Average age 30. 114 applicants, 71% accepted, 57 enrolled. In 2016, 59 master's, 3 doctorates awarded. *Application deadline:* For spring admission, 1/1 priority date for international students. Application fee: $60. *Expenses:* Tuition, state resident: full-time $12,246; part-time $681 per credit hour. Tuition, nonresident: full-time $25,486; part-time $1417 per credit hour. *Required fees:* $196. Tuition and fees vary according to program and reciprocity agreements. *Financial support:* Application deadline: 6/1; applicants required to submit FAFSA. *Faculty research:* STEM teaching and learning; content literacy for English language learners; social justice in teacher education; adolescent literacy; mathematics teacher development. *Total annual research expenditures:* $1.7 million. *Unit head:* Dr. Ann E. Larson, Dean, College of Education and Human Development, 502-852-6411, Fax: 502-852-1464, E-mail: ann@louisville.edu. *Application contact:* Betty Hampton, Director of Graduate Student Services, 502-852-5597, Fax: 502-852-1465, E-mail: edadvise@louisville.edu.
Website: http://louisville.edu/delphi

University of Maryland, Baltimore County, The Graduate School, College of Arts, Humanities and Social Sciences, Department of Education, Program in Teaching, Baltimore, MD 21250. Offers early childhood education (MAT); elementary education (MAT); teaching (MAT), including art, biology, chemistry, choral music, classical foreign language, dance, earth/space science, English, instrumental music, mathematics, modern foreign language, physical science, physics, social studies, theatre. *Program availability:* Part-time, evening/weekend. *Faculty:* 24 full-time (18 women), 25 part-time/adjunct (19 women). *Students:* 41 full-time (34 women), 27 part-time (18 women); includes 26 minority (6 Black or African American, non-Hispanic/Latino; 9 Asian, non-Hispanic/Latino; 7 Hispanic/Latino; 1 Native Hawaiian or other Pacific Islander, non-Hispanic/Latino; 3 Two or more races, non-Hispanic/Latino), 2 international. Average age 30. 54 applicants, 83% accepted, 35 enrolled. In 2016, 50 master's awarded. *Degree requirements:* For master's, comprehensive exam (for some programs), thesis (for some programs). *Entrance requirements:* For master's, PRAXIS Core Examination or GRE (minimum score of 1000), minimum GPA of 3.0. Additional exam requirements/recommendations for international students: Required—TOEFL. *Application deadline:* For fall admission, 6/1 for domestic and international students; for spring admission, 11/1 for domestic and international students. Applications are processed on a rolling basis. Application fee: $50. Electronic applications accepted. *Expenses:* Tuition, state resident: full-time $13,294. Tuition, nonresident: full-time $20,286. *Financial support:* In 2016–17, 8 students received support, including teaching assistantships with tuition reimbursements available (averaging $12,000 per year); career-related internships or fieldwork, Federal Work-Study, scholarships/grants, tuition waivers, and unspecified assistantships also available. Financial award application deadline: 3/15. *Faculty research:* STEM teacher education, culturally sensitive pedagogy, ESOL/bilingual education, early childhood education, language, literacy and culture. *Total annual research expenditures:* $100,000. *Unit head:* Dr. Susan M. Blunck, Graduate Program Director, 410-455-2869, Fax: 410-455-3986, E-mail: blunck@umbc.edu. *Application contact:* Cheryl Johnson, MAT Program Specialist, 410-455-3388, E-mail: blackwel@umbc.edu.
Website: http://www.umbc.edu/education/

University of Massachusetts Amherst, Graduate School, College of Humanities and Fine Arts, Department of Art, Amherst, MA 01003. Offers art (MA, MFA), including art education (MA), studio art (MFA). *Program availability:* Part-time. *Degree requirements:* For master's, comprehensive exam (for some programs), thesis (for some programs). *Entrance requirements:* For master's, portfolio. Additional exam requirements/recommendations for international students: Required—TOEFL (minimum score 550 paper-based; 80 iBT), IELTS (minimum score 6.5). Electronic applications accepted.

University of Massachusetts Dartmouth, Graduate School, College of Visual and Performing Arts, Department of Art Education, North Dartmouth, MA 02747-2300. Offers MAE. *Accreditation:* NASAD. *Program availability:* Part-time. *Faculty:* 3 full-time (all women), 2 part-time/adjunct (1 woman). *Students:* 4 full-time (3 women), 16 part-time (13 women). Average age 34. 5 applicants, 100% accepted, 3 enrolled. *Degree requirements:* For master's, written and visual thesis. *Entrance requirements:* For master's, Massachusetts Tests for Educator Licensure (MTEL) Communication and Literacy Test and Subject Matter Test, statement of purpose (minimum of 300 words), resume, 2 letters of recommendation, official transcripts, portfolio (20 images representing applicant's art work, process of thinking, implementation of concepts and studio production). Additional exam requirements/recommendations for international students: Required—TOEFL (minimum score 533 paper-based; 72 iBT). *Application deadline:* For fall admission, 8/1 priority date for domestic students, 7/1 priority date for international students; for spring admission, 10/15 priority date for domestic students, 9/15 priority date for international students. Application fee: $60. Electronic applications accepted. *Expenses:* Tuition, state resident: full-time $14,994; part-time $624.75 per credit. Tuition, nonresident: full-time $27,068; part-time $1127.83 per credit. *Required fees:* $405; $25.88 per credit. Tuition and fees vary according to course load and reciprocity agreements. *Financial support:* In 2016–17, 1 teaching assistantship (averaging $2,000 per year) was awarded; institutionally sponsored loans and scholarships/grants also available. Support available to part-time students. Financial award application deadline: 3/1; financial award applicants required to submit FAFSA. *Faculty research:* Creative art, in-service and pre-service teachers, museum partnership in education, authentic visual arts integration, studio and culture based research, arts based literacy, creativity development and assessment. *Unit head:* Cathy Smilan, Graduate Program Director, 508-910-6594, Fax: 508-999-8901, E-mail: csmilan@umassd.edu. *Application contact:* Steven Briggs, Director of Marketing and Recruitment for Graduate Studies, 508-999-8604, Fax: 508-999-8183, E-mail: graduate@umassd.edu.
Website: http://www.umassd.edu/cvpa/graduate/arteducation

University of Minnesota, Twin Cities Campus, Graduate School, College of Education and Human Development, Department of Curriculum and Instruction, Program in Teaching, Minneapolis, MN 55455-0213. Offers teaching (M Ed), including arts in education, elementary education, English education, mathematics, science, second language education, social studies. *Students:* 237 full-time (169 women), 171 part-time (112 women); includes 91 minority (23 Black or African American, non-Hispanic/Latino; 3 American Indian or Alaska Native, non-Hispanic/Latino; 19 Asian, non-Hispanic/Latino; 25 Hispanic/Latino; 21 Two or more races, non-Hispanic/Latino), 10 international. Average age 27. 421 applicants, 72% accepted, 275 enrolled. In 2016, 584 master's awarded. Application fee: $75 ($95 for international students). *Unit head:* Dr. Cynthia Lewis, Chair, 612-625-6313, Fax: 612-624-8277, E-mail: lewis@umn.edu. *Application contact:* Dr. Kendall King, Director of Graduate Studies, 612-625-3692, E-mail: roenr013@umn.edu.
Website: http://www.cehd.umn.edu/ci/

University of Missouri, Office of Research and Graduate Studies, College of Education, Department of Learning, Teaching and Curriculum, Columbia, MO 65211. Offers agricultural education (M Ed, PhD, Ed S); art education (M Ed, PhD, Ed S); business and office education (M Ed, PhD, Ed S); early childhood education (M Ed, PhD, Ed S); elementary education (M Ed, PhD, Ed S); English education (M Ed, PhD, Ed S); foreign language education (M Ed, PhD, Ed S); health education and promotion (M Ed, PhD); learning and instruction (M Ed); marketing education (M Ed, PhD, Ed S); mathematics education (M Ed, PhD, Ed S); music education (M Ed, PhD, Ed S); reading education (M Ed, PhD, Ed S); science education (M Ed, PhD, Ed S); social studies education (M Ed, PhD, Ed S); vocational education (M Ed, PhD, Ed S). *Program availability:* Part-time. *Faculty:* 30 full-time (18 women), 1 (woman) part-time/adjunct. *Students:* 157 full-time (124 women), 157 part-time (125 women). Terminal master's awarded for partial completion of doctoral program. *Degree requirements:* For doctorate, thesis/dissertation. *Entrance requirements:* For master's and Ed S, GRE General Test or MAT, minimum GPA of 3.0; for doctorate, GRE General Test, minimum GPA of 3.0. Additional exam requirements/recommendations for international students: Required—TOEFL (minimum score 600 paper-based; 100 iBT). *Application deadline:* For fall

admission, 12/1 priority date for domestic and international students. Applications are processed on a rolling basis. Application fee: $75 ($90 for international students). Electronic applications accepted. *Expenses:* Tuition, state resident: full-time $6347; part-time $352.60 per credit hour. Tuition, nonresident: full-time $17,379; part-time $965.50 per credit hour. *Required fees:* $1035. Tuition and fees vary according to course load, campus/location and program. *Financial support:* Fellowships, research assistantships, teaching assistantships, institutionally sponsored loans, traineeships, health care benefits, and unspecified assistantships available. Support available to part-time students.
Website: http://education.missouri.edu/LTC/index.php

University of Montana, Graduate School, College of Visual and Performing Arts, Creative Pulse: Master's in Integrated Arts and Education, Missoula, MT 59812-0002. Offers MA. *Degree requirements:* For master's, field project.

University of Nebraska at Kearney, College of Fine Arts and Humanities, Department of Art and Design, Kearney, NE 68849-0001. Offers art education (MA Ed), including classroom education, museum education. *Accreditation:* NCATE. *Program availability:* Part-time, evening/weekend, 100% online. *Faculty:* 7 full-time (2 women). *Students:* 2 full-time (both women), 70 part-time (59 women); includes 3 minority (1 Hispanic/Latino; 2 Two or more races, non-Hispanic/Latino). Average age 36. 15 applicants, 93% accepted, 12 enrolled. In 2016, 17 master's awarded. *Degree requirements:* For master's, comprehensive exam, thesis optional. *Entrance requirements:* For master's, two letters of recommendation, resume, statement of purpose, 24 undergraduate hours of art/art history/art education. Additional exam requirements/recommendations for international students: Recommended—TOEFL (minimum score 550 paper-based; 79 iBT), IELTS (minimum score 6.5). *Application deadline:* For fall admission, 6/15 for domestic and international students; for spring admission, 10/15 for domestic and international students; for summer admission, 3/15 for domestic and international students. Application fee: $45. Electronic applications accepted. *Expenses:* Tuition, state resident: full-time $4064; part-time $225.75 per credit hour. Tuition, nonresident: full-time $8915; part-time $495.25 per credit hour. *Required fees:* $772; $23 per credit hour. Part-time tuition and fees vary according to course load, campus/location, program and reciprocity agreements. *Financial support:* In 2016–17, 1 student received support, including 1 research assistantship with full tuition reimbursement available (averaging $10,500 per year); career-related internships or fieldwork, scholarships/grants, tuition waivers, and unspecified assistantships also available. Support available to part-time students. Financial award application deadline: 2/28; financial award applicants required to submit FAFSA. *Faculty research:* Fibers, art education, kiln design construction and low-fire glaze, relationship between environment and photography, digital arts, graphic design, three-dimensional design, atomic testing imagery. *Unit head:* Dr. Rick Schuessler, Department Chair, 308-865-8353, E-mail: schuesslerr@unk.edu. *Application contact:* Linda Johnson, Director, Graduate Admissions and Programs, 800-717-7881, Fax: 308-865-8837, E-mail: johnsonli@unk.edu.
Website: http://www.unk.edu/academics/art/

University of New Mexico, Graduate Studies, College of Education, Program in Art Education, Albuquerque, NM 87131-2039. Offers MA. *Accreditation:* NCATE. *Program availability:* Part-time, evening/weekend. *Faculty:* 8 full-time (5 women), 1 part-time/adjunct (0 women). *Students:* 12 full-time (10 women), 18 part-time (15 women); includes 9 minority (1 Black or African American, non-Hispanic/Latino; 1 American Indian or Alaska Native, non-Hispanic/Latino; 5 Hispanic/Latino; 2 Two or more races, non-Hispanic/Latino), 1 international. Average age 43. 9 applicants, 78% accepted, 6 enrolled. In 2016, 16 master's awarded. *Degree requirements:* For master's, comprehensive exam, thesis optional, participation in art exhibit. *Entrance requirements:* For master's, letter of intent, resume, 3 letters of recommendation, portfolio of 10 samples of art work. Additional exam requirements/recommendations for international students: Required—TOEFL. *Application deadline:* For fall admission, 3/30 for domestic and international students; for spring admission, 10/30 for domestic and international students. Application fee: $50. Electronic applications accepted. *Financial support:* Fellowships, research assistantships with full tuition reimbursements, teaching assistantships, Federal Work-Study, institutionally sponsored loans, scholarships/grants, and unspecified assistantships available. Financial award application deadline: 3/1; financial award applicants required to submit FAFSA. *Faculty research:* Studio in art education, visual culture, curricular issues regarding gender and sexual identity, archetypal thought in art education, teacher preparation. *Unit head:* Prof. Ruth Luckasson, Chair, 505-277-6510, Fax: 505-277-6929, E-mail: ruthl@unm.edu. *Application contact:* Katherine Vazquez, Information Contact, 505-277-4112, Fax: 505-277-0576, E-mail: arted@unm.edu.
Website: http://www.unm.edu/~arted

The University of North Carolina at Charlotte, Cato College of Education, Interdisciplinary Education Programs, Charlotte, NC 28223-0001. Offers art education (Graduate Certificate); child and family development: early childhood education (MAT); curriculum and instruction (PhD); elementary education (MAT); foreign language education (MAT); middle grades education (MAT); secondary education (MAT); special education (MAT); teaching (Graduate Certificate); teaching English as a second language (MAT); theatre education (Graduate Certificate). *Program availability:* Part-time, 100% online, blended/hybrid learning. *Students:* 78 full-time (59 women), 619 part-time (484 women); includes 255 minority (186 Black or African American, non-Hispanic/Latino; 1 American Indian or Alaska Native, non-Hispanic/Latino; 16 Asian, non-Hispanic/Latino; 37 Hispanic/Latino; 15 Two or more races, non-Hispanic/Latino), 10 international. Average age 33. 380 applicants, 92% accepted, 264 enrolled. In 2016, 93 master's, 8 doctorates, 176 other advanced degrees awarded. *Degree requirements:* For master's, thesis or alternative, research project/portfolio. *Entrance requirements:* For master's, GRE or MAT, bachelor's degree, or its U.S. equivalent, from regionally-accredited college or university; minimum overall GPA of 3.0 on all previous work beyond high school; statement of purpose (essay); at least three recommendation forms; for doctorate, GRE or MAT, bachelor's degree (or its U.S. equivalent) from regionally-accredited college or university; minimum overall GPA of 3.5 in master's degree program; for Graduate Certificate, bachelor's degree from regionally-accredited university; minimum GPA of 2.75 on all post-secondary work attempted; transcripts; personal statement outlining why the applicant seeks admission to the program. Additional exam requirements/recommendations for international students: Required—TOEFL (minimum score 523 paper-based, 70 iBT) or IELTS (6.5). *Application deadline:* For fall admission, 3/1 priority date for domestic and international students; for spring admission, 10/1 priority date for domestic and international students; for summer admission, 4/1 priority date for domestic and international students. Applications are processed on a rolling basis. Application fee: $75. Electronic applications accepted. *Expenses:* Tuition, state resident: full-time $4252. Tuition, nonresident: full-time $17,423. *Required fees:* $3026. Tuition and fees vary according to course load and program. *Financial support:* Career-related internships or fieldwork, institutionally sponsored loans, scholarships/grants, and unspecified assistantships available. Support available to part-time students. Financial award application deadline: 3/1; financial award applicants required to submit FAFSA. *Unit head:* Dr. Ellen McIntyre, Dean, 704-687-8722, E-mail: ellen.mcintyre@uncc.edu. *Application contact:* Kathy B. Giddings, Director of Graduate Admissions, 704-687-5503, Fax: 704-687-1668, E-mail: gradadm@uncc.edu.
Website: http://education.uncc.edu/academic-programs

The University of North Carolina at Pembroke, The Graduate School, Department of Art, Pembroke, NC 28372-1510. Offers art education (MA, MAT). *Program availability:* Part-time, evening/weekend. *Degree requirements:* For master's, comprehensive exam, capstone show. *Entrance requirements:* For master's, GRE or MAT, minimum GPA of 3.0 in major or 2.5 overall. Additional exam requirements/recommendations for international students: Required—TOEFL. *Expenses:* Contact institution.

University of Northern Colorado, Graduate School, College of Performing and Visual Arts, School of Art and Design, Greeley, CO 80639. Offers art education (MA); art history (MA); studio art (MA). *Accreditation:* NASAD. *Program availability:* Part-time. *Faculty:* 5 full-time (3 women). *Students:* 8 part-time (7 women). Average age 43. 10 applicants, 80% accepted. In 2016, 8 master's awarded. *Degree requirements:* For master's, comprehensive exam, thesis. *Entrance requirements:* For master's, GRE General Test, portfolio, 3 letters of recommendation, minimum undergraduate GPA of 3.0. *Application deadline:* Applications are processed on a rolling basis. Application fee: $50 ($60 for international students). Electronic applications accepted. *Financial support:* In 2016–17, 3 teaching assistantships (averaging $5,065 per year) were awarded; fellowships, research assistantships, and unspecified assistantships also available. Financial award application deadline: 3/1; financial award applicants required to submit FAFSA. *Unit head:* Dr. Dennis Morimoto, Director, 970-351-2143, Fax: 970-351-2299. *Application contact:* Linda Sisson, Graduate Student Admission Coordinator, 970-351-1807, Fax: 970-351-2371, E-mail: linda.sisson@unco.edu.
Website: http://arts.unco.edu/art/

University of Northern Iowa, Graduate College, College of Humanities, Arts and Sciences, Department of Art, Cedar Falls, IA 50614. Offers art education (MA). *Program availability:* Part-time, evening/weekend. *Degree requirements:* For master's, comprehensive exam (for some programs), thesis or alternative. *Entrance requirements:* For master's, minimum GPA of 3.0, portfolio. Additional exam requirements/recommendations for international students: Required—TOEFL (minimum score 500 paper-based; 61 iBT). Electronic applications accepted.

University of North Texas, Robert B. Toulouse School of Graduate Studies, Denton, TX 76203-5459. Offers accounting (MS); applied anthropology (MA, MS); applied behavior analysis (Certificate); applied geography (MA); applied technology and performance improvement (M Ed, MS); art education (MA); art history (MA); art museum education (Certificate); arts leadership (Certificate); audiology (Au D); behavior analysis (MS); behavioral science (PhD); biochemistry and molecular biology (MS); biology (MA, MS); biomedical engineering (MS); business analysis (MS); chemistry (MS); clinical health psychology (PhD); communication studies (MA, MS); computer engineering (MS); computer science (MS); counseling (M Ed, MS), including clinical mental health counseling (MS), college and university counseling, elementary school counseling, secondary school counseling; creative writing (MA); criminal justice (MS); curriculum and instruction (M Ed); decision sciences (MBA); design (MA, MFA), including fashion design (MFA), innovation studies, interior design (MFA); early childhood studies (MS); economics (MS); educational leadership (M Ed, Ed D); educational psychology (MS, PhD), including family studies (MS), gifted and talented (MS), human development (MS), learning and cognition (MS), research, measurement and evaluation (MS); electrical engineering (MS); emergency management (MPA); engineering technology (MS); English (MA); English as a second language (MA); environmental science (MS); finance (MBA, MS); financial management (MPA); French (MA); health services management (MBA); higher education (M Ed, Ed D); history (MA, MS); hospitality management (MS); human resources management (MPA); information science (MS); information systems (PhD); information technologies (MBA); interdisciplinary studies (MA, MS); international studies (MA); international sustainable tourism (MS); jazz studies (MM); journalism (MA, MJ, Graduate Certificate), including interactive and virtual digital communication (Graduate Certificate), narrative journalism (Graduate Certificate), public relations (Graduate Certificate); kinesiology (MS); linguistics (MA); local government management (MPA); logistics (PhD); logistics and supply chain management (MBA); long-term care, senior housing, and aging services (MA); management (PhD); marketing (MBA); mathematics (MA, MS); mechanical and energy engineering (MS, PhD); music (MA), including ethnomusicology, music theory, musicology, performance; music composition (PhD); music education (MM Ed, PhD); nonprofit management (MPA); operations and supply chain management (MBA); performance (MM, DMA); philosophy (MA); political science (MA); professional and technical communication (MA); radio, television and film (MA, MFA); rehabilitation counseling (Certificate); sociology (MA); Spanish (MA); special education (M Ed); speech-language pathology (MA); strategic management (MBA); studio art (MFA); teaching (M Ed); MBA/MS. *Program availability:* Part-time, evening/weekend, online learning. Terminal master's awarded for partial completion of doctoral program. *Degree requirements:* For master's, variable foreign language requirement, comprehensive exam (for some programs), thesis (for some programs); for doctorate, variable foreign language requirement, comprehensive exam (for some programs), thesis/dissertation; for other advanced degree, variable foreign language requirement, comprehensive exam (for some programs). *Entrance requirements:* For master's and doctorate, GRE, GMAT. Additional exam requirements/recommendations for international students: Required—TOEFL (minimum score 550 paper-based; 79 iBT). Electronic applications accepted.

University of Rio Grande, Graduate School, Rio Grande, OH 45674. Offers athletic coaching leadership (M Ed); educational leadership (M Ed); integrated arts (M Ed); intervention specialist in early childhood (M Ed); intervention specialist in mild/moderate (M Ed). *Accreditation:* NCATE. *Program availability:* Part-time. *Degree requirements:* For master's, final research project, portfolio. *Entrance requirements:* For master's, minimum GPA of 2.7 in major, 2.5 overall. Additional exam requirements/recommendations for international students: Required—TOEFL. *Application deadline:* Applications are processed on a rolling basis. Application fee: $20. *Financial support:* Career-related internships or fieldwork available. Support available to part-time students. Financial award application deadline: 7/1; financial award applicants required to submit FAFSA. *Faculty research:* Interagency collaboration, reading and mathematics, learning styles, college access, literacy. *Unit head:* Dr. Greg Miller, Director, 740-245-7030, E-mail: gmiller@rio.edu. *Application contact:* Nancy Downs, Secretary, 740-245-7328, Fax: 740-245-7175, E-mail: ndowns@rio.edu.

University of St. Francis, College of Education, Joliet, IL 60435-6169. Offers educational leadership (MS, Ed D); elementary education (M Ed); reading (MS); secondary education (M Ed), including English education, math education, science education, social studies education, visual arts education; special education (M Ed); teaching and learning (MS); TESOL (Certificate). *Accreditation:* NCATE. *Program availability:* Part-time, evening/weekend, 100% online, blended/hybrid learning. *Faculty:* 11 full-time (8 women), 60 part-time/adjunct (42 women). *Students:* 34 full-time (26 women), 420 part-time (318 women); includes 92 minority (51 Black or African American, non-Hispanic/Latino; 5 Asian, non-Hispanic/Latino; 31 Hispanic/Latino; 5 Two or more races, non-Hispanic/Latino), 4 international. Average age 36. 242 applicants, 48% accepted, 96 enrolled. In 2016, 229 master's, 44 doctorates, 10 other advanced degrees awarded. *Degree requirements:* For master's, comprehensive exam; for doctorate, thesis/dissertation. *Entrance requirements:* Additional exam requirements/

recommendations for international students: Required—TOEFL (minimum score 550 paper-based; 79 iBT), IELTS (minimum score 6). *Application deadline:* Applications are processed on a rolling basis. Application fee: $30. Electronic applications accepted. Application fee is waived when completed online. *Expenses:* Contact institution. *Financial support:* In 2016–17, 48 students received support. Career-related internships or fieldwork and unspecified assistantships available. Support available to part-time students. Financial award applicants required to submit FAFSA. *Unit head:* Dr. John Gambro, Dean, 815-740-3829, Fax: 815-740-2264, E-mail: jgambro@stfrancis.edu. *Application contact:* Sandra Sloka, Director of Admissions for Graduate and Degree Completion Programs, 800-735-7500, Fax: 815-740-3431, E-mail: ssloka@stfrancis.edu.
Website: http://www.stfrancis.edu/academics/college-of-education/

University of South Alabama, College of Education and Professional Studies, Department of Leadership and Teacher Education, Mobile, AL 36688. Offers art education (M Ed); early childhood education (M Ed); educational leadership (M Ed, Ed D); elementary education (M Ed); reading education (M Ed); science education (M Ed); secondary education (M Ed); special education (M Ed). *Accreditation:* NCATE. *Program availability:* Part-time, 100% online, blended/hybrid learning. *Faculty:* 16 full-time (12 women), 6 part-time/adjunct (3 women). *Students:* 198 full-time (150 women), 77 part-time (58 women); includes 77 minority (61 Black or African American, non-Hispanic/Latino; 2 American Indian or Alaska Native, non-Hispanic/Latino; 2 Asian, non-Hispanic/Latino; 7 Hispanic/Latino; 1 Native Hawaiian or other Pacific Islander, non-Hispanic/Latino; 4 Two or more races, non-Hispanic/Latino). Average age 34. 153 applicants, 53% accepted, 69 enrolled. In 2016, 80 master's, 1 doctorate awarded. *Degree requirements:* For master's, comprehensive exam, thesis (for some programs); for doctorate, comprehensive exam, thesis/dissertation. *Entrance requirements:* For master's, GRE General Test or MAT, minimum GPA of 3.0; for doctorate, GRE, minimum graduate GPA of 3.25, 3 years of experience in field, 3 letters of recommendation, interview, official transcripts. Additional exam requirements/recommendations for international students: Required—TOEFL. *Application deadline:* For fall admission, 7/15 for domestic students; for spring admission, 11/15 for domestic students; for summer admission, 4/15 for domestic students. Applications are processed on a rolling basis. Application fee: $35. Electronic applications accepted. *Expenses:* Tuition, state resident: full-time $9768; part-time $407 per credit hour. Tuition, nonresident: full-time $19,536; part-time $814 per credit hour. *Financial support:* Fellowships, research assistantships, teaching assistantships, career-related internships or fieldwork, Federal Work-Study, institutionally sponsored loans, scholarships/grants, and unspecified assistantships available. Support available to part-time students. Financial award application deadline: 5/31; financial award applicants required to submit FAFSA. *Unit head:* Dr. Susan Santoli, Department Chair, 251-380-2836, Fax: 251-380-2758, E-mail: ssantoli@southalabama.edu. *Application contact:* Dr. Susan Santoli, Director of Graduate Studies, 251-380-2836, Fax: 251-380-2758, E-mail: ssantoli@southalabama.edu.
Website: http://www.southalabama.edu/colleges/coe/lte/index.html

University of South Carolina, The Graduate School, College of Arts and Sciences, Department of Art, Program in Art Education, Columbia, SC 29208. Offers IMA, MA, MAT. IMA and MAT offered in cooperation with the College of Education. *Accreditation:* NCATE. *Degree requirements:* For master's, comprehensive exam, thesis (for some programs). *Entrance requirements:* For master's, GRE General Test or MAT, portfolio. Additional exam requirements/recommendations for international students: Required—TOEFL. Electronic applications accepted. *Faculty research:* Teaching art at the primary and secondary levels of education.

University of South Carolina, The Graduate School, College of Education, Department of Instruction and Teacher Education, Program in Secondary Education, Columbia, SC 29208. Offers art education (IMA, MAT); business education (IMA, MAT); English (MAT); foreign language (MAT); health education (MAT); mathematics (MAT); science (IMA, MAT); secondary (Ed D); secondary education (MT, PhD); social studies (MAT); theatre and speech (MAT). IMA and MT offered jointly with the subject areas. *Accreditation:* NCATE. *Degree requirements:* For master's, comprehensive exam, thesis (for some programs), foreign language (MA); for doctorate, one foreign language, comprehensive exam, thesis/dissertation. *Entrance requirements:* For master's, GRE General Test or MAT, teaching certificate (IMA, M Ed), interview; for doctorate, GRE General Test or MAT, interview. *Faculty research:* Middle school programs, professional development, school collaboration.

The University of South Dakota, Graduate School, College of Fine Arts, Department of Art, Vermillion, SD 57069. Offers art education (MFA); ceramics (MFA); graphic design (MFA); painting (MFA); photography (MFA); printmaking (MFA); sculpture (MFA). *Accreditation:* NASAD. *Degree requirements:* For master's, thesis or alternative. *Entrance requirements:* For master's, portfolio, minimum GPA of 2.7. Additional exam requirements/recommendations for international students: Required—TOEFL (minimum score 550 paper-based; 79 iBT). Electronic applications accepted.

The University of Tennessee, Graduate School, College of Education, Health and Human Sciences, Program in Education, Knoxville, TN 37996. Offers art education (MS); counseling education (PhD); cultural studies in education (PhD); curriculum (MS, Ed S); curriculum, educational research and evaluation (Ed D, PhD); early childhood education (PhD); early childhood special education (MS); education of deaf and hard of hearing (MS); educational administration and policy studies (Ed D, PhD); educational administration and supervision (Ed S); educational psychology (Ed D, PhD); elementary education (MS, Ed S); elementary teaching (MS); English education (MS, Ed S); exercise science (PhD); foreign language/ESL education (MS, Ed S); instructional technology (MS, Ed D, PhD, Ed S); literacy, language and ESL education (PhD); literacy, language education, and ESL education (Ed D); mathematics education (MS, Ed S); modified and comprehensive special education (MS); reading education (MS, Ed S); school counseling (Ed S); school psychology (PhD, Ed S); science education (MS, Ed S); secondary teaching (MS); social foundations (MS); social science education (MS, Ed S); socio-cultural foundations of sports and education (PhD); special education (Ed S); teacher education (Ed D, PhD). *Accreditation:* NCATE. *Program availability:* Part-time, evening/weekend. *Degree requirements:* For master's and Ed S, thesis optional; for doctorate, variable foreign language requirement, thesis/dissertation. *Entrance requirements:* For master's, minimum GPA of 2.7; for doctorate and Ed S, GRE General Test, minimum GPA of 2.7. Additional exam requirements/recommendations for international students: Required—TOEFL. Electronic applications accepted.

The University of Texas at Austin, Graduate School, College of Fine Arts, Department of Art and Art History, Program in Art Education, Austin, TX 78712-1111. Offers MA. *Accreditation:* NASAD. *Program availability:* Part-time. *Degree requirements:* For master's, thesis, oral and written exam. *Entrance requirements:* For master's, GRE General Test, 2 samples of written work, 10 slides of art work. Electronic applications accepted. *Faculty research:* Museum education; community-based, environmental, and multicultural art education; interdisciplinary art education, elementary and secondary art education.

The University of Texas at El Paso, Graduate School, College of Liberal Arts, Department of Art, El Paso, TX 79968-0001. Offers art education (MA); studio art (MA). *Program availability:* Part-time, evening/weekend. *Degree requirements:* For master's, thesis optional. *Entrance requirements:* For master's, minimum GPA of 3.0, digital portfolio, letters of recommendation. Additional exam requirements/recommendations for international students: Required—TOEFL; Recommended—IELTS. Electronic applications accepted.

The University of the Arts, College of Art, Media and Design, Department of Art Education, Philadelphia, PA 19102-4944. Offers art education (MA); visual arts (MAT). *Accreditation:* NASAD (one or more programs are accredited). *Program availability:* Part-time. *Degree requirements:* For master's, student teaching (MAT); thesis (MA). *Entrance requirements:* For master's, portfolio, official transcripts from each undergraduate or graduate school attended, three letters of recommendation, one- to two-page statement of professional plans and goals, personal interview, writing sample. Additional exam requirements/recommendations for international students: Required—TOEFL (minimum score 580 paper-based, 92 iBT) or IELTS (minimum score 6.5). *Faculty research:* Using technology and visual arts concepts to develop critical and creative thinking skills.

The University of Toledo, College of Graduate Studies, Judith Herb College of Education, Department of Curriculum and Instruction, Toledo, OH 43606-3390. Offers art education (ME); career and technical education (ME, Ed S); curriculum and instruction (ME, PhD, Ed S); early childhood education (Ed S); education and anthropology (MAE); education and biology (MES); education and chemistry (MES); education and classics (MAE); education and economics (MAE); education and English (MAE); education and French (MAE); education and geology (MES); education and German (MAE); education and history (MAE); education and mathematics (MAE, MES); education and physics (MES); education and political science (MAE); education and sociology (MAE); education and Spanish (MAE); educational media (PhD); educational technology (ME); educational technology: virtual educator (Certificate); elementary education (PhD); English as a second language (MAE); gifted and talented education (PhD); middle childhood education (ME); secondary education (ME, PhD); special education (PhD). *Accreditation:* NCATE. *Program availability:* Part-time, evening/weekend. *Degree requirements:* For master's, comprehensive exam, thesis or alternative; for doctorate, comprehensive exam, thesis/dissertation; for other advanced degree, thesis optional. *Entrance requirements:* For master's, doctorate, and other advanced degree, minimum cumulative GPA of 2.7 for all previous academic work, letters of recommendation. Additional exam requirements/recommendations for international students: Required—TOEFL (minimum score 550 paper-based; 80 iBT). Electronic applications accepted.

University of Utah, Graduate School, College of Fine Arts, Department of Art and Art History, Salt Lake City, UT 84112-0380. Offers art history (MA); ceramics (MFA); community-based art education (MFA); drawing (MFA); graphic design (MFA); painting (MFA); photography/digital imaging (MFA); printmaking (MFA); sculpture/intermedia (MFA). *Faculty:* 18 full-time (10 women), 22 part-time/adjunct (11 women). *Students:* 6 full-time (2 women); includes 2 minority (both Hispanic/Latino). 48 applicants, 31% accepted, 10 enrolled. In 2016, 7 master's awarded. *Degree requirements:* For master's, variable foreign language requirement, comprehensive exam (for some programs), thesis or alternative, exhibit and final project paper (for MFA). *Entrance requirements:* For master's, CD portfolio (MFA), writing sample (MA), curriculum vitae, letters of recommendation, letter of intent. Additional exam requirements/recommendations for international students: Required—TOEFL (minimum score 575 paper-based; 75 iBT). *Application deadline:* For fall admission, 1/15 priority date for domestic and international students. Application fee: $55 ($65 for international students). Electronic applications accepted. *Expenses:* Contact institution. *Financial support:* In 2016–17, 6 students received support, including 2 fellowships, 6 research assistantships with partial tuition reimbursements available, 34 teaching assistantships with partial tuition reimbursements available; Federal Work-Study, institutionally sponsored loans, scholarships/grants, tuition waivers (partial), unspecified assistantships, and stipends also available. Financial award application deadline: 1/15; financial award applicants required to submit FAFSA. *Faculty research:* Studio art, European art history, Asian art history, Latin American art history, twentieth-century/contemporary art history. *Total annual research expenditures:* $54,906. *Unit head:* Prof. Brian Snapp, Chair, 801-581-8677, Fax: 801-585-6171, E-mail: b.snapp@utah.edu. *Application contact:* Prof. Kim Martinez, Director of Graduate Studies, 801-581-8677, Fax: 801-585-6171, E-mail: kim.martinez@art.utah.edu.
Website: http://www.art.utah.edu/

University of Victoria, Faculty of Graduate Studies, Faculty of Education, Department of Curriculum and Instruction, Victoria, BC V8W 2Y2, Canada. Offers art education (M Ed, PhD); curriculum studies (M Ed, MA, PhD); early childhood education (M Ed, PhD); educational studies (PhD); language and literacy (M Ed, MA, PhD); mathematics (M Ed, MA, PhD); music education (M Ed, MA, PhD); science (M Ed, MA, PhD); social studies (M Ed, MA); social, cultural and foundational studies (MA, PhD); technology and environmental education (PhD). *Program availability:* Part-time. *Degree requirements:* For master's, thesis, project (M Ed); for doctorate, comprehensive exam, thesis/dissertation. *Entrance requirements:* For master's, minimum B average. Additional exam requirements/recommendations for international students: Required—TOEFL (minimum score 575 paper-based), IELTS (minimum score 7). Electronic applications accepted. *Faculty research:* Elementary and secondary English, language arts, curriculum theory and practice, educational media and technology, educational administration and leadership, history and philosophy of education.

University of Wisconsin–Madison, Graduate School, School of Education, Department of Art and Department of Curriculum and Instruction, Program in Art Education, Madison, WI 53706-1380. Offers MA. *Accreditation:* NASAD.

University of Wisconsin–Madison, Graduate School, School of Education, Department of Curriculum and Instruction, Madison, WI 53706-1380. Offers art education (MA); curriculum and instruction (MS, PhD); education and mathematics (MA); French education (MA); German education (MA); music education (MS); science education (MS); Spanish education (MA). *Accreditation:* NASM (one or more programs are accredited). *Degree requirements:* For doctorate, thesis/dissertation.

University of Wisconsin–Milwaukee, Graduate School, School of Education, Department of Exceptional Education, Milwaukee, WI 53201-0413. Offers autism spectrum disorders (Graduate Certificate); exceptional education (MS); transition for students with disabilities (Graduate Certificate); urban education (PhD), including adult, continuing and higher education leadership, art education, curriculum and instruction, exceptional education, mathematics education, multicultural studies, social foundations of education. *Program availability:* Part-time. *Students:* 50 full-time (41 women), 66 part-time (51 women); includes 42 minority (24 Black or African American, non-Hispanic/Latino; 6 Asian, non-Hispanic/Latino; 1 Hispanic/Latino; 11 Two or more races, non-Hispanic/Latino), 4 international. Average age 39. 55 applicants, 51% accepted, 22 enrolled. In 2016, 14 master's, 10 doctorates, 3 other advanced degrees awarded. *Degree requirements:* For master's, thesis. *Entrance requirements:* Additional exam requirements/recommendations for international students: Required—TOEFL (minimum score 550 paper-based; 79 iBT), IELTS (minimum score 6.5). *Application deadline:* For fall admission, 1/1 priority date for domestic students; for spring admission, 9/1 for domestic students. Applications are processed on a rolling basis. Application fee: $56

($96 for international students). Electronic applications accepted. *Financial support:* Fellowships, research assistantships, teaching assistantships, career-related internships or fieldwork, health care benefits, and unspecified assistantships available. Support available to part-time students. Financial award application deadline: 4/15; financial award applicants required to submit FAFSA. *Faculty research:* Emotional disturbance, hearing impairment, learning disabilities, mental retardation. *Application contact:* General Information Contact, 414-229-4721, E-mail: soeinfo@uwm.edu.
Website: http://uwm.edu/education/academics/exceptional-edu-department/

University of Wisconsin–Superior, Graduate Division, Department of Visual Arts, Superior, WI 54880-4500. Offers art education (MA); art history (MA); art therapy (MA); studio arts (MA). *Program availability:* Part-time. *Degree requirements:* For master's, comprehensive exam, exhibit. *Entrance requirements:* For master's, minimum GPA of 2.75, portfolio. Electronic applications accepted.

Vermont College of Fine Arts, Graduate Studies in Art and Design Education, Montpelier, VT 05602. Offers MA, MAT. *Faculty:* 4 full-time (3 women). *Students:* 19 full-time (14 women), 1 part-time (0 women); includes 6 minority (3 Black or African American, non-Hispanic/Latino; 1 American Indian or Alaska Native, non-Hispanic/Latino; 1 Native Hawaiian or other Pacific Islander, non-Hispanic/Latino; 1 Two or more races, non-Hispanic/Latino). Average age 32. *Degree requirements:* For master's, thesis. *Expenses:* Contact institution. *Unit head:* Marni Leiken, Director, E-mail: marni.leiken@vcfa.edu. *Application contact:* David Markow, Director of Enrollment Management, 802-828-8535, E-mail: admissions@vcfa.edu.
Website: http://vcfa.edu/art-design-education

Virginia Commonwealth University, Graduate School, School of Education, Doctoral Program in Education, Richmond, VA 23284-9005. Offers art education (PhD); counselor education and supervision (PhD); curriculum, culture and change (PhD); educational leadership (PhD); educational psychology (PhD); leadership (Ed D); research and evaluation (PhD); special education and disability leadership (PhD); sport leadership (PhD); urban services leadership (PhD). *Accreditation:* NCATE. *Program availability:* Part-time. *Degree requirements:* For doctorate, thesis/dissertation. *Entrance requirements:* For doctorate, GRE (for PhD), MAT (for Ed D), interview, master's degree, writing sample. Additional exam requirements/recommendations for international students: Required—TOEFL (minimum score 600 paper-based; 100 iBT). *Application deadline:* For fall admission, 2/15 for domestic students. Application fee: $50. Electronic applications accepted. *Financial support:* Fellowships, research assistantships, career-related internships or fieldwork, Federal Work-Study, and institutionally sponsored loans available. Financial award application deadline: 3/1; financial award applicants required to submit FAFSA. *Unit head:* Dr. Kathleen Cauley, Interim Director, 804-827-2657, E-mail: kmcauley@vcu.edu. *Application contact:* Dr. Colleen A. Thoma, Administrative Assistant, 804-827-2651, E-mail: cathoma@vcu.edu.
Website: http://www.soe.vcu.edu/programs/doctoral-programs/

Virginia Commonwealth University, Graduate School, School of the Arts, Department of Art Education, Richmond, VA 23284-9005. Offers MAE, PhD. *Accreditation:* NASAD. *Degree requirements:* For master's, thesis optional. *Entrance requirements:* For master's, GRE if GPA is below 3.0, portfolio. Additional exam requirements/recommendations for international students: Required—TOEFL (minimum score 600 paper-based; 100 iBT). *Application deadline:* For fall admission, 1/15 for domestic students. Application fee: $50. Electronic applications accepted. *Financial support:* Fellowships, career-related internships or fieldwork, Federal Work-Study, and institutionally sponsored loans available. Financial award application deadline: 3/15. *Faculty research:* Teaching methods. *Unit head:* Dr. Sara Wilson McKay, Interim Chair, 804-828-7154, Fax: 804-828-6469, E-mail: arteducation@vcu.edu. *Application contact:* Dr. Melanie Buffington, Graduate Programs Coordinator, 804-828-3805, E-mail: mbuffington@vcu.edu.
Website: http://www.vcu.edu/artweb/ArtEd/

Wayne State University, College of Education, Division of Teacher Education, Detroit, MI 48202. Offers art education (M Ed); bilingual/bicultural education (M Ed, Certificate); career and technical education (M Ed); curriculum and instruction (Ed D, PhD, Ed S), including art education (Ed D, PhD), bilingual education (Ed D, Ed S), career and technical education (MAT, Ed D, PhD, Ed S), early childhood education (MAT, Ed D, PhD, Ed S), elementary education, English as a second language (MAT, Ed D, Ed S), English education (MAT, Ed D, PhD, Ed S), foreign language education (MAT, Ed D, PhD), K-12 curriculum, mathematics education (MAT, Ed D, PhD, Ed S), science education (MAT, Ed D, PhD, Ed S), secondary education, social studies education (MAT, Ed D, PhD, Ed S); early childhood education (M Ed); elementary education (M Ed, MAT), including bilingual/bicultural education (MAT), early childhood education (MAT, Ed D, PhD, Ed S), English as a second language (MAT, Ed D, Ed S), general elementary education (MAT), mathematics education (MAT, Ed D, PhD, Ed S), science education (MAT, Ed D, PhD, Ed S), social studies education (MAT, Ed D, PhD, Ed S); English as a second language (Certificate); English education (M Ed); foreign language education (M Ed); mathematics education (M Ed); reading (M Ed, Ed S); reading, language and literature (Ed D); science education (M Ed); secondary education (MAT), including art education (K-12), bilingual/bicultural education, career and technical education (MAT, Ed D, PhD, Ed S), English as a second language (MAT, Ed D, Ed S), English education (MAT, Ed D, PhD, Ed S), foreign language education (MAT, Ed D, PhD), kinesiology, mathematics education (MAT, Ed D, PhD, Ed S); social studies education (M Ed); special education (M Ed, MAT, Ed D, PhD, Ed S), including autism spectrum disorders (MAT), cognitive development (MAT), emotional impairment (MAT), learning disabilities (MAT). *Program availability:* Part-time, blended/hybrid learning. *Faculty:* 29. *Students:* 106 full-time (73 women), 351 part-time (276 women); includes 115 minority (76 Black or African American, non-Hispanic/Latino; 10 Asian, non-Hispanic/Latino; 20 Hispanic/Latino; 1 Native Hawaiian or other Pacific Islander, non-Hispanic/Latino; 8 Two or more races, non-Hispanic/Latino), 12 international. Average age 37. 242 applicants, 37% accepted, 72 enrolled. In 2016, 178 master's, 19 doctorates, 17 other advanced degrees awarded. *Degree requirements:* For master's, essay or project (for some M Ed programs), professional field experience (for MAT programs); for doctorate, thesis/dissertation. *Entrance requirements:* For master's, Michigan Test for Teacher Certification, verification of participation in group work with children, Michigan State Police criminal background check; for doctorate, minimum undergraduate GPA of 3.0, graduate 3.5; interview; curriculum vitae; references. Additional exam requirements/recommendations for international students: Required—TOEFL (minimum score 550 paper-based; 79 iBT), TWE (minimum score 5.5), Michigan English Language Assessment Battery (minimum score 85); Recommended—IELTS (minimum score 6.5). *Application deadline:* For fall admission, 6/1 priority date for domestic students, 5/1 priority date for international students; for winter admission, 10/1 priority date for domestic students, 9/1 priority date for international students; for spring admission, 2/1 priority date for domestic students, 1/1 priority date for international students. Applications are processed on a rolling basis. Application fee: $50. Electronic applications accepted. *Expenses:* $16,503 per year resident tuition and fees, $33,697 per year non-resident tuition and fees. *Financial support:* In 2016–17, 101 students received support, including 3 fellowships (averaging $11,409 per year); research assistantships with tuition reimbursements available, Federal Work-Study, scholarships/grants, and unspecified assistantships also available. Support available to part-time students. Financial award applicants required to submit FAFSA. *Faculty research:* Improving students' skill achievement in mathematics, improving elementary children's understanding of informational text, teachers' use of their pedagogical and mathematical knowledge in the interactive work of teaching, the intersection of identity construction in teaching and learning, identifying effective methods of literacy instruction and assessments for bilingual students in elementary language arts classrooms. *Unit head:* Dr. Kathleen Crawford-McKinney, Assistant Dean, 313-577-0122. *Application contact:* Janice Green, Assistant Dean, 313-577-1605, E-mail: jwgreen@wayne.edu.
Website: http://coe.wayne.edu/ted/index.php

Western Kentucky University, Graduate Studies, Potter College of Arts and Letters, Department of Art, Bowling Green, KY 42101. Offers art education (MA Ed). *Accreditation:* NASAD; NCATE. *Program availability:* Part-time, evening/weekend. *Degree requirements:* For master's, comprehensive exam, final exam. *Entrance requirements:* For master's, GRE General Test, minimum GPA of 2.75. Additional exam requirements/recommendations for international students: Required—TOEFL (minimum score 555 paper-based; 79 iBT). *Faculty research:* Nineteenth century Kentucky women artists.

Western Michigan University, Graduate College, College of Fine Arts, Gwen Frostic School of Art, Kalamazoo, MI 49008. Offers art education (MA). *Accreditation:* NASAD. *Degree requirements:* For master's, thesis or alternative.

West Virginia University, College of Creative Arts, School of Art and Design, Morgantown, WV 26506. Offers art education (MA); art history (MA); ceramics (MFA); graphic design (MFA); painting (MFA); printmaking (MFA); sculpture (MFA); studio art (MA). *Accreditation:* NASAD. *Degree requirements:* For master's, thesis, exhibit. *Entrance requirements:* For master's, minimum GPA of 2.75, portfolio. Additional exam requirements/recommendations for international students: Required—TOEFL. *Expenses:* Contact institution. *Faculty research:* Medieval art history.

Wilkes University, College of Graduate and Professional Studies, School of Education, Wilkes-Barre, PA 18766-0002. Offers 21st century teaching and learning (MS Ed); art and science of teaching (MS Ed); classroom technology (MS Ed); early childhood literacy (MS Ed); educational development and strategies (MS Ed); educational leadership (MS Ed, Ed D); effective teaching (MS Ed); instructional media (MS Ed); instructional technology (MS Ed); international school leadership (MS Ed); international teaching and learning (MS Ed); middle level education (MS Ed); online teaching (MS Ed); reading (MS Ed); school business leadership (MS Ed); special education (MS Ed); teaching English to speakers of other languages (MS Ed). *Program availability:* Part-time, evening/weekend, 100% online, blended/hybrid learning. *Students:* 87 full-time (70 women), 1,496 part-time (1,111 women); includes 77 minority (11 Black or African American, non-Hispanic/Latino; 2 American Indian or Alaska Native, non-Hispanic/Latino; 12 Asian, non-Hispanic/Latino; 28 Hispanic/Latino; 3 Native Hawaiian or other Pacific Islander, non-Hispanic/Latino; 21 Two or more races, non-Hispanic/Latino). Average age 33. In 2016, 524 master's, 21 doctorates awarded. *Entrance requirements:* Additional exam requirements/recommendations for international students: Required—TOEFL (minimum score 550 paper-based; 79 iBT). *Application deadline:* Applications are processed on a rolling basis. Application fee: $45. Electronic applications accepted. *Expenses:* Contact institution. *Financial support:* Unspecified assistantships available. Financial award application deadline: 3/1; financial award applicants required to submit FAFSA. *Unit head:* Dr. Rhonda Rabbitt, Dean, 570-408-4680, Fax: 570-408-7872, E-mail: rhonda.rabbitt@wilkes.edu. *Application contact:* Director of Graduate Education, 570-408-4234, Fax: 570-408-7846.
Website: http://www.wilkes.edu/academics/graduate-programs/masters-programs/graduate-education/index.aspx

William Carey University, School of Education, Hattiesburg, MS 39401-5499. Offers art education (M Ed); art of teaching (M Ed); elementary education (M Ed, Ed S); English education (M Ed); gifted education (M Ed); history and social science (M Ed); mild/moderate disabilities (M Ed); secondary education (M Ed). *Accreditation:* NCATE. *Program availability:* Part-time. *Degree requirements:* For master's, comprehensive exam. *Entrance requirements:* For master's, GRE, MAT, minimum GPA of 2.5, Class A teacher's license. Additional exam requirements/recommendations for international students: Required—TOEFL (minimum score 550 paper-based).

Winthrop University, College of Visual and Performing Arts, Department of Art, Rock Hill, SC 29733. Offers art (MFA); art administration (MA); art education (MA). *Accreditation:* NASAD. *Program availability:* Part-time. *Degree requirements:* For master's, comprehensive exam (for some programs), thesis (for some programs), documented exhibit, oral exam. *Entrance requirements:* For master's, GRE General Test or MAT, PRAXIS (for MA), minimum GPA of 3.0, resume, slide portfolio, teaching certificate (MA). Additional exam requirements/recommendations for international students: Required—TOEFL (minimum score 550 paper-based; 79 iBT), IELTS (minimum score 6). Electronic applications accepted. *Expenses:* Tuition, state resident: full-time $14,312; part-time $599 per credit hour. Tuition, nonresident: full-time $27,570; part-time $1153 per credit hour.

Business Education

Alabama Agricultural and Mechanical University, School of Graduate Studies, College of Education, Humanities, and Behavioral Sciences, Department of Educational Leadership and Secondary Education, Huntsville, AL 35811. Offers biology (M Ed); business/marketing education (M Ed, Ed S); chemistry (M Ed); collaborative teacher secondary education (M Ed, Ed S); education (M Ed, Ed S); English language arts (M Ed); family/consumer science education (M Ed, Ed S); general science (M Ed); general social science (M Ed); mathematics (M Ed, Ed S); physics (M Ed, Ed S); technology education (M Ed). *Accreditation:* NCATE. *Program availability:* Evening/weekend. *Degree requirements:* For master's, comprehensive exam; for Ed S, thesis. *Entrance requirements:* For master's, GRE General Test. Additional exam requirements/

recommendations for international students: Required—TOEFL (minimum score 500 paper-based; 61 iBT). *Application deadline:* For fall admission, 5/1 for domestic students. Applications are processed on a rolling basis. Application fee: $25. Electronic applications accepted. *Expenses:* Tuition, nonresident: part-time $826 per credit hour. Full-time tuition and fees vary according to course load and program. *Financial support:* Research assistantships, career-related internships or fieldwork, Federal Work-Study, institutionally sponsored loans, and traineeships available. Financial award application deadline: 4/1. *Faculty research:* World peace through education, computer-assisted instruction. *Unit head:* Dr. Derrick Davis, Chair, 256-372-4047, Fax: 256-372-5526.

Arkansas State University, Graduate School, College of Business, Department of Computer and Information Technology, State University, AR 72467. Offers business administration education (SCCT); business technology education (SCCT). *Program availability:* Part-time. *Entrance requirements:* Additional exam requirements/recommendations for international students: Required—TOEFL (minimum score 550 paper-based; 79 iBT), IELTS (minimum score 6), PTE (minimum score 56). Electronic applications accepted. *Expenses:* Contact institution.

Ball State University, Graduate School, Miller College of Business, Department of Information Systems and Operations Management, Muncie, IN 47306. Offers business education (MA); information systems security management (Certificate). *Accreditation:* NCATE (one or more programs are accredited). *Program availability:* Part-time, online only, 100% online. *Entrance requirements:* For master's, minimum baccalaureate GPA of 2.75 or 3.0 in latter half of baccalauareate. Additional exam requirements/recommendations for international students: Required—TOEFL (minimum score 550 paper-based; 79 iBT), IELTS (minimum score 6.5). Electronic applications accepted. *Expenses:* Contact institution.

Bloomsburg University of Pennsylvania, School of Graduate Studies, Zeigler College of Business, Program in Business Education, Bloomsburg, PA 17815-1301. Offers M Ed. *Program availability:* Part-time, evening/weekend. *Faculty:* 2 full-time (both women), 1 part-time/adjunct (0 women). *Students:* 3 full-time (1 woman), 1 part-time (0 women). Average age 29. 12 applicants, 58% accepted, 3 enrolled. In 2016, 2 master's awarded. *Degree requirements:* For master's, thesis optional, student teaching, minimum QPA of 3.0. *Entrance requirements:* For master's, PRAXIS, minimum QPA of 3.0, 2 letters of recommendation, personal statement, resume. Additional exam requirements/recommendations for international students: Required—TOEFL, IELTS. *Application deadline:* Applications are processed on a rolling basis. Application fee: $35 ($60 for international students). Electronic applications accepted. *Expenses:* Tuition, state resident: full-time $9660; part-time $483 per credit. Tuition, nonresident: full-time $14,500; part-time $725 per credit. *Required fees:* $2410; $107 per credit. $75 per term. Tuition and fees vary according to course load, degree level and program. *Financial support:* Federal Work-Study and unspecified assistantships available. *Unit head:* Dr. Margaret O'Connor, Chair, 570-389-4771, Fax: 570-389-3892, E-mail: moconno1@bloomu.edu. *Application contact:* Jennifer Kessler, Administrative Assistant, 570-389-4015, Fax: 570-389-3054, E-mail: jkessler@bloomu.edu.
Website: http://www.bloomu.edu/gradschool/business-education

Bowling Green State University, Graduate College, College of Education and Human Development, School of Teaching and Learning, Program in Workforce Education and Development, Bowling Green, OH 43403. Offers M Ed. *Accreditation:* NCATE. *Program availability:* Part-time. *Degree requirements:* For master's, thesis or alternative. *Entrance requirements:* For master's, GRE General Test. Additional exam requirements/recommendations for international students: Required—TOEFL. *Application deadline:* Applications are processed on a rolling basis. Application fee: $30. Electronic applications accepted. *Financial support:* Research assistantships with full tuition reimbursements, teaching assistantships with full tuition reimbursements, career-related internships or fieldwork, Federal Work-Study, and unspecified assistantships available. Financial award applicants required to submit FAFSA. *Faculty research:* School to work, workforce education, marketing education, contextual teaching and learning. *Unit head:* Dr. Cindy Hendricks, Director, 419-372-7341. *Application contact:* Dr. Bob Berns, Graduate Coordinator, 419-372-2904.

Buffalo State College, State University of New York, The Graduate School, Faculty of Applied Science and Education, Department of Business Studies, Buffalo, NY 14222-1095. Offers business and marketing education (MS Ed). *Program availability:* Part-time, evening/weekend. *Degree requirements:* For master's, thesis or alternative, project. *Entrance requirements:* For master's, minimum GPA of 2.5, New York teaching certificate.

Canisius College, Graduate Division, School of Education and Human Services, Department of Graduate Education and Leadership, Buffalo, NY 14208-1098. Offers business and marketing education (MS Ed); college student personnel (MS Ed); deaf education (MS Ed); deaf/adolescent education, grades 7-12 (MS Ed); deaf/childhood education, grades 1-6 (MS Ed); differentiated instruction (MS Ed); education administration (MS); educational administration (MS Ed); educational technologies (Certificate); gifted education extension (Certificate); literacy (MS Ed); reading (Certificate); school building leadership (MS Ed, Certificate); school district leadership (Certificate); teacher leader (Certificate); TESOL (MS Ed). *Accreditation:* NCATE. *Program availability:* Part-time, evening/weekend, 100% online, blended/hybrid learning. *Faculty:* 5 full-time (all women), 23 part-time/adjunct (16 women). *Students:* 95 full-time (78 women), 223 part-time (177 women); includes 31 minority (15 Black or African American, non-Hispanic/Latino; 2 American Indian or Alaska Native, non-Hispanic/Latino; 4 Asian, non-Hispanic/Latino; 9 Hispanic/Latino; 1 Two or more races, non-Hispanic/Latino), 1 international. Average age 30. 162 applicants, 89% accepted, 135 enrolled. In 2016, 135 master's, 39 other advanced degrees awarded. *Entrance requirements:* For master's, GRE (if cumulative GPA less than 2.7), transcripts, two letters of recommendation. Additional exam requirements/recommendations for international students: Required—TOEFL (minimum score 550 paper-based, 79 iBT), IELTS (minimum score 6.5), or CAEL (minimum score 70). *Application deadline:* Applications are processed on a rolling basis. Application fee: $25. Electronic applications accepted. Application fee is waived when completed online. *Expenses:* *Tuition:* Full-time $14,742. *Required fees:* $724. *Financial support:* Career-related internships or fieldwork, Federal Work-Study, scholarships/grants, tuition waivers (partial), and unspecified assistantships available. Support available to part-time students. Financial award application deadline: 4/30; financial award applicants required to submit FAFSA. *Faculty research:* Asperger's disease, autism, private higher education, reading strategies. *Unit head:* Dr. Rosemary K. Murray, Chair/Associate Professor of Graduate Education and Leadership, 716-888-3723, E-mail: murray1@canisius.edu. *Application contact:* Kathleen B. Davis, Vice President of Enrollment Management, 716-888-2500, Fax: 716-888-3195, E-mail: daviskb@canisius.edu.
Website: http://www.canisius.edu/graduate/

Capella University, School of Business and Technology, Doctoral Programs in Business, Minneapolis, MN 55402. Offers accounting (DBA, PhD); business intelligence (DBA); finance (DBA, PhD); general business management (PhD); human resource management (DBA, PhD); leadership (DBA, PhD); management education (PhD); marketing (DBA, PhD); project management (DBA, PhD); strategy and innovation (DBA, PhD). *Accreditation:* ACBSP.

Chadron State College, School of Professional and Graduate Studies, Department of Education, Chadron, NE 69337. Offers business (MA Ed); community counseling (MA Ed); educational administration (MS Ed, Sp Ed); elementary education (MS Ed); history (MA Ed); language and literature (MA Ed); secondary administration (MS Ed); secondary education (MS Ed). *Accreditation:* NCATE. *Program availability:* Part-time, evening/weekend, online learning. *Degree requirements:* For master's, thesis optional. *Entrance requirements:* For master's, GRE General Test, GRE Writing Test, minimum GPA of 2.75 or 12 graduate hours at CSC with minimum GPA of 3.25. Additional exam requirements/recommendations for international students: Required—TOEFL. Electronic applications accepted. *Faculty research:* Rural education, technology, mental health.

Clemson University, Graduate School, College of Business, Clemson, SC 29634. Offers MA, MBA, MP Acc, MS, PhD. *Program availability:* Part-time, evening/weekend. *Faculty:* 131 full-time (41 women), 25 part-time/adjunct (5 women). *Students:* 358 full-time (138 women), 348 part-time (114 women); includes 105 minority (55 Black or African American, non-Hispanic/Latino; 17 Asian, non-Hispanic/Latino; 21 Hispanic/Latino; 1 Native Hawaiian or other Pacific Islander, non-Hispanic/Latino; 11 Two or more races, non-Hispanic/Latino), 109 international. Average age 29. 743 applicants, 46% accepted, 233 enrolled. In 2016, 284 master's, 14 doctorates awarded. Terminal master's awarded for partial completion of doctoral program. *Degree requirements:* For master's, thesis optional; for doctorate, thesis/dissertation. *Entrance requirements:* For master's and doctorate, GRE General Test, GMAT, unofficial transcripts, letters of recommendation. Additional exam requirements/recommendations for international students: Required—TOEFL (minimum score 80 iBT), IELTS (minimum score 6.5). *Application deadline:* Applications are processed on a rolling basis. Application fee: $80 ($90 for international students). Electronic applications accepted. *Expenses:* Contact institution. *Financial support:* In 2016–17, 152 students received support, including 33 fellowships with partial tuition reimbursements available (averaging $6,876 per year), 5 research assistantships with partial tuition reimbursements available (averaging $18,557 per year), 53 teaching assistantships with partial tuition reimbursements available (averaging $20,528 per year); career-related internships or fieldwork and unspecified assistantships also available. *Faculty research:* Entrepreneurship, marketing, price theory, information systems, operations management. *Total annual research expenditures:* $164,260. *Unit head:* Dr. Robert McCormick, Interim Dean, 864-656-3178, E-mail: sixmile@clemson.edu. *Application contact:* Dr. Gregory Pickett, Senior Associate Dean, 864-656-3975, E-mail: pgregor@clemson.edu.
Website: http://www.clemson.edu/business/index.html

Colorado Christian University, Program in Curriculum and Instruction, Lakewood, CO 80226. Offers corporate education (MACI); early childhood educator (MACI); elementary educator (MACI); instructional technology (MACI); master educator (MACI); online course developer (MACI); online teaching and learning (MACI); special education generalist (MACI). *Program availability:* Part-time, evening/weekend. *Degree requirements:* For master's, thesis optional, practicum. *Entrance requirements:* For master's, interviews, letters of recommendation. Additional exam requirements/recommendations for international students: Required—TOEFL. Electronic applications accepted. *Expenses:* Contact institution.

East Carolina University, Graduate School, College of Education, Department of Interdisciplinary Professions, Greenville, NC 27858-4353. Offers adult education (MA Ed); business and marketing education (MA); career and technical education (MA Ed); counselor education (MS); library science (MLS); vocational education (MS). *Accreditation:* ACA; NCATE. *Program availability:* Part-time, evening/weekend. *Students:* 95 full-time (79 women), 427 part-time (374 women); includes 106 minority (68 Black or African American, non-Hispanic/Latino; 13 American Indian or Alaska Native, non-Hispanic/Latino; 4 Asian, non-Hispanic/Latino; 13 Hispanic/Latino; 8 Two or more races, non-Hispanic/Latino). Average age 37. 225 applicants, 93% accepted, 174 enrolled. In 2016, 86 master's awarded. *Degree requirements:* For master's, comprehensive exam, thesis optional. *Entrance requirements:* For master's, GRE General Test or MAT, interview, minimum GPA of 2.5, bachelor's degree in related field, teaching license (MA Ed). Additional exam requirements/recommendations for international students: Required—TOEFL. *Application deadline:* For fall admission, 5/15 priority date for domestic students. Applications are processed on a rolling basis. Application fee: $50. *Financial support:* Research assistantships with partial tuition reimbursements, teaching assistantships with partial tuition reimbursements, and Federal Work-Study available. Support available to part-time students. Financial award application deadline: 6/1. *Unit head:* Dr. Vivian W. Mott, Chair, 252-328-6177, Fax: 252-328-4368, E-mail: mottv@ecu.edu. *Application contact:* Dean of Graduate School, 252-328-6012, Fax: 252-328-6071, E-mail: gradschool@ecu.edu.
Website: http://www.ecu.edu/cs-educ/idp/index.cfm

Eastern Kentucky University, The Graduate School, College of Education, Department of Curriculum and Instruction, Program in Secondary and Higher Education, Richmond, KY 40475-3102. Offers secondary education (MA Ed), including agricultural education, art education, biological sciences education, business education, English education, geography education, history education, home economics education, industrial education, mathematical sciences education, physical education, school health education. *Accreditation:* NCATE. *Program availability:* Part-time. *Entrance requirements:* For master's, GRE General Test, minimum GPA of 2.5.

Emporia State University, Program in Business Education, Emporia, KS 66801-5415. Offers MS. *Program availability:* Part-time, evening/weekend, online learning. *Faculty:* 30 full-time (5 women). *Students:* 1 full-time (0 women), 10 part-time (8 women); includes 1 minority (Asian, non-Hispanic/Latino). 9 applicants, 100% accepted, 3 enrolled. In 2016, 9 master's awarded. *Entrance requirements:* For master's, GRE, 15 undergraduate credits in business; minimum undergraduate GPA of 2.7 over last 60 hours. Additional exam requirements/recommendations for international students: Required—TOEFL (minimum score 520 paper-based; 68 iBT). *Application deadline:* For fall admission, 8/15 priority date for domestic students. Applications are processed on a rolling basis. Application fee: $30 ($75 for international students). Electronic applications accepted. *Expenses:* Tuition, state resident: full-time $5922; part-time $246.75 per credit hour. Tuition, nonresident: full-time $18,414; part-time $767.25 per credit hour. *Required fees:* $1884; $78.50 per credit hour. *Financial support:* Career-related internships or fieldwork, institutionally sponsored loans, health care benefits, and unspecified assistantships available. Financial award application deadline: 3/15; financial award applicants required to submit FAFSA. *Unit head:* James Willingham, Coordinator, Graduate and Career Services, 620-341-5456, E-mail: jwilling@emporia.edu.

Florida Agricultural and Mechanical University, Division of Graduate Studies, Research, and Continuing Education, College of Education, Department of Vocational Education, Tallahassee, FL 32307-3200. Offers business education (MBE); industrial education (MS Ed); technology education (M Ed). *Accreditation:* NCATE. *Degree requirements:* For master's, thesis (for some programs). *Entrance requirements:* For master's, GRE General Test, minimum GPA of 3.0. Additional exam requirements/recommendations for international students: Required—TOEFL.

Hofstra University, School of Education, Programs in Teacher Education, Hempstead, NY 11549. Offers bilingual education (MA, Advanced Certificate); bilingual extension

(Advanced Certificate), including education/speech language pathology; business education (MS Ed); early childhood and childhood education (MS Ed); early childhood education (MA, MS Ed); education technology (Advanced Certificate); elementary education (MA, MS Ed), including science, technology, engineering, and mathematics (STEM) (MA); English education (MS Ed); family and consumer science (MS Ed); fine arts and music education (Advanced Certificate); fine arts education (MS Ed); foreign language and TESOL (MS Ed); foreign language education (MS Ed), including French, German, Russian, Spanish; learning and teaching (Ed D), including applied linguistics, art education, arts and humanities, early childhood education, English education, human development, math education, math, science, and technology, multicultural education, physical education, science education, social studies education, special education; mathematics education (MA, MS Ed); middle school extension (Advanced Certificate), including grades 5-6, grades 7-9; music education (MA, MS Ed); science education (MA, MS Ed), including biology, chemistry, earth science, geology, physics; secondary education (Advanced Certificate); social studies education (MA, MS Ed); teaching languages other than English and TESOL (MS Ed); TESOL (MS Ed, Advanced Certificate). *Program availability:* Part-time, evening/weekend, blended/hybrid learning. *Students:* 139 full-time (97 women), 145 part-time (106 women); includes 60 minority (15 Black or African American, non-Hispanic/Latino; 1 American Indian or Alaska Native, non-Hispanic/Latino; 12 Asian, non-Hispanic/Latino; 31 Hispanic/Latino; 1 Two or more races, non-Hispanic/Latino), 21 international. Average age 29. 255 applicants, 86% accepted, 122 enrolled. In 2016, 101 master's, 4 doctorates, 43 other advanced degrees awarded. *Degree requirements:* For master's, comprehensive exam, thesis (for some programs), exit project, student teaching, fieldwork, electronic portfolio, curriculum project, minimum GPA of 3.0; for doctorate, thesis/dissertation; for Advanced Certificate, 3 foreign languages, comprehensive exam (for some programs), thesis project. *Entrance requirements:* For master's, GRE, MAT, 2 letters of recommendation, portfolio, teacher certification (MA), interview, essay; for doctorate, GMAT, GRE, LSAT, or MAT; for Advanced Certificate, 2 letters of recommendation, essay, interview and/or portfolio, teaching certificate. Additional exam requirements/recommendations for international students: Required—TOEFL (minimum score 550 paper-based; 80 iBT). *Application deadline:* Applications are processed on a rolling basis. Application fee: $75. Electronic applications accepted. *Expenses: Tuition:* Full-time $1240. *Required fees:* $970. Tuition and fees vary according to program. *Financial support:* In 2016–17, 149 students received support, including 58 fellowships with full and partial tuition reimbursements available (averaging $5,309 per year), 5 research assistantships with full and partial tuition reimbursements available (averaging $7,073 per year); career-related internships or fieldwork, Federal Work-Study, institutionally sponsored loans, scholarships/grants, traineeships, tuition waivers (full and partial), and unspecified assistantships also available. Support available to part-time students. Financial award applicants required to submit FAFSA. *Faculty research:* Educational interventions that foster critical-thinking skills; teachers' attitudes about professional development; threats to teacher quality. *Unit head:* Dr. Eustace Thompson, Chairperson, 516-463-5749, Fax: 516-463-6275, E-mail: eustace.g.thompson@hofstra.edu. *Application contact:* Sunil Samuel, Assistant Vice President of Admissions, 516-463-4723, Fax: 516-463-4664, E-mail: graduateadmission@hofstra.edu.
Website: http://www.hofstra.edu/education/

Indiana University of Pennsylvania, School of Graduate Studies and Research, College of Education and Educational Technology, Department of Adult and Community Education, Program in Business/Business Specialist, Indiana, PA 15705. Offers M Ed. *Program availability:* Part-time. *Faculty:* 2 full-time (1 woman). *Students:* 1 full-time (0 women), 2 part-time (0 women). Average age 30. 3 applicants, 33% accepted, 1 enrolled. *Degree requirements:* For master's, thesis optional. *Entrance requirements:* For master's, GMAT or GRE. Additional exam requirements/recommendations for international students: Required—TOEFL (minimum score 540 paper-based). *Application deadline:* Applications are processed on a rolling basis. Application fee: $50. Electronic applications accepted. *Expenses:* Tuition, state resident: full-time $8694; part-time $483 per credit. Tuition, nonresident: full-time $13,050; part-time $725 per credit. *Required fees:* $157 per credit. $50 per term. Tuition and fees vary according to course load and program. *Financial support:* Research assistantships with tuition reimbursements, career-related internships or fieldwork, Federal Work-Study, scholarships/grants, and unspecified assistantships available. Financial award application deadline: 4/15; financial award applicants required to submit FAFSA. *Unit head:* Dr. Lucinda Willis, Graduate Coordinator, 724-357-4585, E-mail: lucinda.willis@iup.edu.
Website: http://www.iup.edu/ace/grad/default.aspx

Inter American University of Puerto Rico, Metropolitan Campus, Graduate Programs, Program in Commercial Education, San Juan, PR 00919-1293. Offers MA.

Inter American University of Puerto Rico, San Germán Campus, Graduate Studies Center, Program in Business Education, San Germán, PR 00683-5008. Offers MA. *Accreditation:* TEAC. *Program availability:* Part-time, evening/weekend. *Degree requirements:* For master's, comprehensive exam. *Entrance requirements:* For master's, GRE General Test or EXADEP, minimum GPA of 3.0.

International College of the Cayman Islands, Graduate Program in Management, Newlands, Cayman Islands. Offers business administration (MBA); management (MS), including education, human resources. *Program availability:* Part-time, evening/weekend. *Degree requirements:* For master's, comprehensive exam. *Entrance requirements:* Additional exam requirements/recommendations for international students: Recommended—TOEFL. *Faculty research:* International human resources administration.

Johnson & Wales University, Graduate Studies, MAT Program in Teacher Education, Providence, RI 02903-3703. Offers business education and secondary special education (MAT); culinary arts education (MAT); elementary education and elementary special education (MAT); elementary education and elementary/secondary special education (MAT); elementary education and secondary special education (MAT); food service education (MAT). *Program availability:* Part-time, evening/weekend. *Entrance requirements:* For master's, MAT, minimum GPA of 2.75. Additional exam requirements/recommendations for international students: Required—TOEFL (minimum score 550 paper-based) or IELTS (recommended). *Faculty research:* Secondary education, student teaching, educational reform, evaluation procedures.

Lehman College of the City University of New York, School of Education, Department of Middle and High School Education, Program in Business Education, Bronx, NY 10468-1589. Offers MS Ed. *Accreditation:* NCATE. *Program availability:* Part-time, evening/weekend. *Degree requirements:* For master's, thesis. *Entrance requirements:* For master's, minimum GPA of 2.7.

Lock Haven University of Pennsylvania, The Stephen Poorman College of Business, Information Systems, and Human Services, Lock Haven, PA 17745-2390. Offers clinical mental health counseling (MS); sport science (MS). *Program availability:* Online learning. *Degree requirements:* For master's, thesis. *Entrance requirements:* For master's, minimum undergraduate GPA of 3.0. Additional exam requirements/recommendations for international students: Required—TOEFL. Electronic applications accepted.

Louisiana State University and Agricultural & Mechanical College, Graduate School, College of Human Sciences and Education, School of Human Resource Education and Workforce Development, Baton Rouge, LA 70803. Offers agriculture and extension education and youth development (MS, PhD); career and technical education (MS, PhD); comprehensive vocational education (MS, PhD); extension and international education (MS, PhD); human resource and leadership development (MS, PhD); industrial education (MS); vocational agriculture education (MS, PhD); vocational business education (MS); vocational home economics education (MS). *Accreditation:* NCATE.

Manhattanville College, School of Business, Purchase, NY 10577. Offers MS. *Program availability:* Part-time, evening/weekend. *Faculty:* 32 part-time/adjunct (10 women). *Students:* 142 (91 women); includes 59 minority (26 Black or African American, non-Hispanic/Latino; 8 Asian, non-Hispanic/Latino; 20 Hispanic/Latino; 5 Two or more races, non-Hispanic/Latino). Average age 30. 154 applicants, 39% accepted, 40 enrolled. In 2016, 44 master's awarded. *Degree requirements:* For master's, thesis (for some programs), final project, internship, portfolio. *Entrance requirements:* For master's, transcripts, 2 letters of recommendation, resume. Additional exam requirements/recommendations for international students: Required—TOEFL (minimum score 563 paper-based; 85 iBT). *Application deadline:* Applications are processed on a rolling basis. Application fee: $75. Electronic applications accepted. *Expenses:* Contact institution. *Financial support:* Federal Work-Study, institutionally sponsored loans, scholarships/grants, and unspecified assistantships available. Financial award applicants required to submit FAFSA. *Unit head:* Steve Albanese, Interim Dean, 914-323-5469, E-mail: steve.albanese@mville.edu. *Application contact:* Monika Pottgen, Assistant Director, Recruitment and Admissions, 914-323-5150, E-mail: business@mville.edu.
Website: http://www.mville.edu/business

Maryville University of Saint Louis, The John E. Simon School of Business, St. Louis, MO 63141-7299. Offers accounting (MBA, Certificate); business studies (Certificate); cyber security (MBA); cybersecurity (Certificate); financial services (MBA, Certificate); healthcare practice management (MBA, Certificate); human resource management (MBA); information technology (MBA, Certificate); management (MBA, Certificate); management and leadership (MA); marketing (MBA, Certificate); project management (MBA); sport business management (MBA); supply chain management/logistics (MBA). *Accreditation:* ACBSP. *Program availability:* Part-time, evening/weekend, 100% online, blended/hybrid learning. *Faculty:* 7 full-time (3 women), 34 part-time/adjunct (9 women). *Students:* 84 full-time (40 women), 223 part-time (118 women); includes 67 minority (40 Black or African American, non-Hispanic/Latino; 2 American Indian or Alaska Native, non-Hispanic/Latino; 8 Asian, non-Hispanic/Latino; 12 Hispanic/Latino; 1 Native Hawaiian or other Pacific Islander, non-Hispanic/Latino; 4 Two or more races, non-Hispanic/Latino), 15 international. Average age 32. In 2016, 67 master's awarded. *Entrance requirements:* Additional exam requirements/recommendations for international students: Required—TOEFL (minimum score 563 paper-based; 85 iBT). *Application deadline:* Applications are processed on a rolling basis. Electronic applications accepted. *Expenses:* $650 per credit hour. *Financial support:* Career-related internships or fieldwork, Federal Work-Study, tuition waivers (partial), and campus employment available. Financial award application deadline: 3/1; financial award applicants required to submit FAFSA. *Faculty research:* Global business, e-marketing, strategic planning, interpersonal management skills, financial analysis. *Unit head:* Pam Horwitz, Interim Dean, 314-529-9680, Fax: 314-529-9975. *Application contact:* Dustin Loeffler, Director for Graduate Studies in Business, 314-529-9571, Fax: 314-529-9975, E-mail: dloeffler@maryville.edu.
Website: http://www.maryville.edu/bu/business-administration-masters/

Middle Tennessee State University, College of Graduate Studies, Jennings A. Jones College of Business, Department of Business Communication and Entrepreneurship, Murfreesboro, TN 37132. Offers business education (MBE). *Program availability:* Part-time, evening/weekend, online learning. *Degree requirements:* For master's, comprehensive exam. *Entrance requirements:* For master's, GRE or MAT. Additional exam requirements/recommendations for international students: Required—TOEFL (minimum score 525 paper-based; 71 iBT) or IELTS (minimum score 6). Electronic applications accepted.

Milwaukee School of Engineering, Rader School of Business, Program in Business Administration - Education Leadership, Milwaukee, WI 53202-3109. Offers MBA. *Faculty:* 1 (woman) full-time, 2 part-time/adjunct (0 women). *Students:* 15 full-time (6 women), 2 part-time (both women); includes 2 minority (1 Black or African American, non-Hispanic/Latino; 1 Hispanic/Latino). Average age 25. 1 applicant, 100% accepted, 1 enrolled. In 2016, 2 master's awarded. *Entrance requirements:* For master's, GRE or GMAT (top 25th percentile), minimum cumulative undergraduate GPA of 3.25, teaching license, three years of full-time classroom teaching experience, two letters of recommendation, Professional Educator License or eligibility. Additional exam requirements/recommendations for international students: Required—TOEFL (minimum score 79 iBT), IELTS (minimum score 6.5). *Application deadline:* For fall admission, 11/30 for domestic students. Applications are processed on a rolling basis. Electronic applications accepted. *Expenses: Tuition:* Full-time $31,440; part-time $655 per credit. *Financial support:* In 2016–17, 15 students received support, including 15 fellowships (averaging $45,552 per year); career-related internships or fieldwork and scholarships/grants also available. Financial award application deadline: 3/15; financial award applicants required to submit FAFSA. *Unit head:* Dr. Steven Bialek, Chairman, 414-277-7364, Fax: 414-277-7479, E-mail: bialek@msoe.edu. *Application contact:* Ian Dahlinghaus, Graduate Program Associate, 414-277-7208, E-mail: dahlinghaus@msoe.edu.
Website: http://www.msoe.edu/community/academics/business/page/2311/mba-in-education-leadership-overview

Mississippi College, Graduate School, School of Business, Clinton, MS 39058. Offers accounting (Certificate); business administration (MBA), including accounting; business education (M Ed); finance (MBA, Certificate); JD/MBA. *Accreditation:* ACBSP. *Program availability:* Part-time, evening/weekend. *Degree requirements:* For master's, comprehensive exam, thesis optional. *Entrance requirements:* For master's, GMAT, minimum GPA of 2.5, 24 hours of undergraduate course work in business. Additional exam requirements/recommendations for international students: Recommended—TOEFL, IELTS. Electronic applications accepted.

Mississippi College, Graduate School, School of Education, Department of Teacher Education and Leadership, Clinton, MS 39058. Offers art (M Ed); biological science (M Ed); business education (M Ed); computer science (M Ed); dyslexia therapy (M Ed); educational leadership (M Ed, Ed D, Ed S); elementary education (M Ed, Ed S); English (M Ed); higher education administration (MS); mathematics (M Ed); secondary education (M Ed); social studies (history) (M Ed); teaching arts (M Ed). *Program availability:* Part-time, online learning. *Degree requirements:* For master's, comprehensive exam, thesis optional. *Entrance requirements:* For master's, NTE. Additional exam requirements/recommendations for international students: Recommended—TOEFL, IELTS. Electronic applications accepted.

Morehead State University, Graduate Programs, College of Education, Department of Foundational and Graduate Studies in Education, Morehead, KY 40351. Offers adult and higher education (MA, Ed S); certified professional counselor (Ed S); counseling P-12 (MA); curriculum and instruction (Ed S); educational technology (MA Ed); instructional leadership (Ed S); school administration (MA); school counseling (Ed S); teacher leader business and marketing content (MA Ed); teacher leader business and marketing technology (MA Ed); teacher leader educational technology (MA Ed); teacher leader English (MA Ed); teacher leader gifted education (MA Ed); teacher leader IECE certification (MA Ed); teacher leader interdisciplinary education P-5 (MA Ed); teacher leader middle grades (MA Ed); teacher leader non IECE certification (MA Ed); teacher leader reading/writing - non-certification (MA Ed); teacher leader reading/writing certification (MA Ed); teacher leader school communication - certification (MA Ed); teacher leader school communication - non-certification (MA Ed); teacher leader social studies (MA Ed); teacher leader special education (MA Ed). *Accreditation:* NCATE. *Program availability:* Part-time, evening/weekend. *Degree requirements:* For master's, thesis optional, oral and/or written comprehensive exams; for Ed S, thesis, oral exam. *Entrance requirements:* For master's, GRE General Test, minimum overall undergraduate GPA of 2.5; for Ed S, GRE General Test, interview, master's degree, minimum GPA of 3.5, work experience. Additional exam requirements/recommendations for international students: Required—TOEFL (minimum score 500 paper-based). Electronic applications accepted. *Faculty research:* Character education, school accountability, computer applications for school administrators.

Morehead State University, Graduate Programs, College of Education, Department of Middle Grades and Secondary Education, Morehead, KY 40351. Offers business and marketing education (MAT); English/language arts 5-9 (MAT); French (MAT); health P-12 (MAT); mathematics 5-9 (MAT); physical education P-12 (MAT); science 5-9 (MAT); secondary biology (MAT); secondary chemistry (MAT); secondary earth science (MAT); secondary English (MAT); secondary math (MAT); secondary physics (MAT); secondary social studies (MAT); social studies 5-9 (MAT); Spanish (MAT). *Program availability:* Part-time, evening/weekend. *Degree requirements:* For master's, portfolio. *Entrance requirements:* For master's, GRE or PRAXIS II content exam, minimum overall undergraduate GPA of 2.5. Additional exam requirements/recommendations for international students: Required—TOEFL (minimum score 500 paper-based). Electronic applications accepted.

New York University, Steinhardt School of Culture, Education, and Human Development, Department of Administration, Leadership, and Technology, Program in Business Education, New York, NY 10012. Offers business and workplace education (MA, Advanced Certificate); workplace learning (Advanced Certificate). *Accreditation:* TEAC. *Program availability:* Part-time. *Degree requirements:* For master's, thesis (for some programs). *Entrance requirements:* For degree, master's degree. Additional exam requirements/recommendations for international students: Required—TOEFL (minimum score 100 iBT). Electronic applications accepted. *Faculty research:* Applications of technology to instruction, workplace and corporate education, adult learning.

North Carolina Agricultural and Technical State University, School of Graduate Studies, School of Business and Economics, Greensboro, NC 27411. Offers accounting (MBA); business education (MAT); human resources management (MBA); supply chain systems (MBA).

North Carolina State University, Graduate School, College of Education, Department of Curriculum and Instruction, Program in Business and Marketing Education, Raleigh, NC 27695. Offers M Ed, MS. *Entrance requirements:* For master's, MAT or GRE, minimum GPA of 3.0, teaching license, 3 letters of reference.

Nova Southeastern University, H. Wayne Huizenga College of Business and Entrepreneurship, Fort Lauderdale, FL 33314-7796. Offers accounting (M Acc); business intelligence/analytics (MBA); entrepreneurship (MBA); finance (MBA); human resource management (MBA); international business (MBA); management (MBA); marketing (MBA); process improvement (MBA); public administration (MPA); real estate development (MS); sport revenue generation (MBA); supply chain management (MBA); taxation (M Tax). *Program availability:* Part-time, evening/weekend, 100% online, blended/hybrid learning. *Faculty:* 65 full-time (26 women), 111 part-time/adjunct (74 women). *Students:* 2,242 full-time (1,400 women), 425 part-time (239 women); includes 1,798 minority (734 Black or African American, non-Hispanic/Latino; 5 American Indian or Alaska Native, non-Hispanic/Latino; 110 Asian, non-Hispanic/Latino; 890 Hispanic/Latino; 2 Native Hawaiian or other Pacific Islander, non-Hispanic/Latino; 57 Two or more races, non-Hispanic/Latino), 255 international. Average age 34. 1,422 applicants, 64% accepted, 672 enrolled. In 2016, 971 master's awarded. *Degree requirements:* For master's, thesis optional. *Entrance requirements:* For master's, GMAT or GRE (depending on undergraduate GPA), official transcripts from all schools attended while in pursuit of bachelor's degree; minimum GPA of 2.5 from regionally-accredited institution. Additional exam requirements/recommendations for international students: Required—TOEFL (minimum score 550 paper-based; 79 iBT), IELTS (minimum score 6), PTE (minimum score 54). *Application deadline:* For fall admission, 8/5 priority date for domestic students, 7/29 priority date for international students; for winter admission, 12/16 priority date for domestic students, 12/9 priority date for international students; for summer admission, 4/21 priority date for domestic and international students. Applications are processed on a rolling basis. Application fee: $50. Electronic applications accepted. *Expenses:* Contact institution. *Financial support:* In 2016–17, 325 students received support. Federal Work-Study and scholarships/grants available. Support available to part-time students. Financial award application deadline: 4/15; financial award applicants required to submit FAFSA. *Faculty research:* Reputation management, call centers, international social capital, corporate earnings guidance, corporate governance. *Unit head:* Dr. J. Preston Jones, Dean, 954-262-5127, E-mail: prestonj@nova.edu. *Application contact:* Zeida Rodriguez, Associate Director of Enrollment Services, 954-262-5163, Fax: 954-262-3822, E-mail: zeida@nova.edu.
Website: http://www.huizenga.nova.edu

Old Dominion University, Darden College of Education, Programs in STEM Education and Professional Studies, Norfolk, VA 23529. Offers community college teaching (MS); human resources training (PhD); technology education (PhD). *Accreditation:* NCATE (one or more programs are accredited). *Program availability:* Part-time, evening/weekend, blended/hybrid learning, mix of synchronous and asynchronous study. *Faculty:* 6 full-time (2 women). *Students:* 12 full-time (7 women), 33 part-time (20 women); includes 16 minority (15 Black or African American, non-Hispanic/Latino; 1 Two or more races, non-Hispanic/Latino), 2 international. Average age 42. 3 applicants, 100% accepted, 3 enrolled. In 2016, 6 master's, 6 doctorates awarded. Terminal master's awarded for partial completion of doctoral program. *Degree requirements:* For master's, comprehensive exam, thesis optional, writing exam, candidacy exam; for doctorate, comprehensive exam, thesis/dissertation, writing exam, candidacy exam. *Entrance requirements:* For master's, GRE General Test or MAT, minimum GPA of 2.8, 2 letters of reference; for doctorate, GRE, minimum GPA of 3.0, 3 letters of reference. Additional exam requirements/recommendations for international students: Required—TOEFL. *Application deadline:* For fall admission, 6/1 priority date for domestic students, 6/1 for international students; for winter admission, 11/1 priority date for domestic students, 11/1 for international students; for spring admission, 3/1 priority date for domestic students, 3/1 for international students. Applications are processed on a rolling basis. Application fee: $50. Electronic applications accepted. *Expenses:* Tuition, state resident: full-time $8604; part-time $478 per credit hour. Tuition, nonresident: full-time $21,510; part-time $1195 per credit hour. *Required fees:* $66 per semester. Tuition and fees vary according to campus/location, program and reciprocity agreements. *Financial support:* In 2016–17, 3 students received support, including 2 teaching assistantships with partial tuition reimbursements available (averaging $15,000 per year). Financial award application deadline: 2/15; financial award applicants required to submit FAFSA. *Faculty research:* Training and development, STEM education, visualization, leadership, technology literacy. *Total annual research expenditures:* $1 million. *Unit head:* Dr. Petros Katsioloudis, Graduate Program Director, 757-683-5323, E-mail: pkatsiol@odu.edu.
Website: http://education.odu.edu/ots/

Pace University, School of Education, New York, NY 10038. Offers adolescent education (MST), including biology, business education, chemistry, earth science, English, foreign languages, mathematics, physics, social studies, visual arts; childhood education (MST); early childhood development, learning and intervention (MST); educational technology studies (MS); inclusive adolescent education (MST), including biology, business education, chemistry, earth science, English, foreign languages, mathematics, physics, social studies, visual arts; integrated instruction for educational technology (Certificate); integrated instruction for literacy and technology (Certificate); literacy (MS Ed); special education (MS Ed). *Accreditation:* NCATE. *Program availability:* Part-time, evening/weekend, blended/hybrid learning. *Faculty:* 19 full-time (13 women), 86 part-time/adjunct (49 women). *Students:* 115 full-time (97 women), 543 part-time (381 women); includes 280 minority (137 Black or African American, non-Hispanic/Latino; 1 American Indian or Alaska Native, non-Hispanic/Latino; 40 Asian, non-Hispanic/Latino; 87 Hispanic/Latino; 15 Two or more races, non-Hispanic/Latino), 13 international. Average age 30. 181 applicants, 78% accepted, 72 enrolled. In 2016, 193 master's, 9 other advanced degrees awarded. *Degree requirements:* For master's, certification exams. *Entrance requirements:* For master's, GRE, interview, teaching certificate (except for MST). Additional exam requirements/recommendations for international students: Required—TOEFL (minimum score 88 iBT), IELTS or PTE. *Application deadline:* For fall admission, 8/1 priority date for domestic students, 6/1 for international students; for spring admission, 12/1 priority date for domestic students, 10/1 for international students. Applications are processed on a rolling basis. Application fee: $70. Electronic applications accepted. *Expenses:* Contact institution. *Financial support:* In 2016–17, 17 students received support, including 17 research assistantships with partial tuition reimbursements available (averaging $6,020 per year); career-related internships or fieldwork and Federal Work-Study also available. Financial award application deadline: 9/1; financial award applicants required to submit FAFSA. *Faculty research:* STEM education, TESOL, teacher education, special education, language and literary development. *Total annual research expenditures:* $290,153. *Unit head:* Dr. Xiao-Lei Wang, Dean, School of Education, 914-773-3876, E-mail: xwang@pace.edu. *Application contact:* Susan Ford-Goldschein, Director of Graduate Admissions, 212-346-1531, Fax: 212-346-1585, E-mail: graduateadmission@pace.edu.
Website: http://www.pace.edu/school-of-education

Pepperdine University, Seaver College, Division of Business, Malibu, CA 90263. Offers accounting (MS). *Students:* 1 full-time (0 women), 1 (woman) part-time, 1 international. Average age 22. In 2016, 2 master's awarded. *Entrance requirements:* For master's, GRE General Test, statement of purpose and intent for writing as a vocation, script writing sample, letters of recommendation. Additional exam requirements/recommendations for international students: Required—TOEFL. *Application deadline:* For fall admission, 2/1 priority date for domestic students. Application fee: $55. Electronic applications accepted. *Unit head:* Dr. Dean Baim, Divisional Dean/Professor of Economics and Finance, 310-506-4237, E-mail: dean.baim@pepperdine.edu. *Application contact:* Hayley Wolf, Director of Admission, 310-506-4392, E-mail: hayley.wolf@pepperdine.edu.
Website: http://seaver.pepperdine.edu/humanities/graduate/screenwriting/

Pontifical Catholic University of Puerto Rico, College of Education, Doctoral Program in Business Teacher Education, Ponce, PR 00717-0777. Offers PhD. *Degree requirements:* For doctorate, thesis/dissertation. *Entrance requirements:* For doctorate, EXADEP, GRE General Test or MAT, 3 letters of recommendation.

Pontifical Catholic University of Puerto Rico, College of Education, Master's Program in Business Teacher Education, Ponce, PR 00717-0777. Offers M Ed. *Degree requirements:* For master's, comprehensive exam, thesis (for some programs). *Entrance requirements:* For master's, GRE, 2 letters of recommendation, interview, minimum GPA of 2.75.

Regis University, College of Business and Economics, Denver, CO 80221-1099. Offers accounting (MS); executive leadership (Certificate); finance (MS); finance and accounting (MBA); health industry leadership (MBA); human resource management and leadership (MSOL); management (MBA); marketing (MBA); nonprofit leadership (Post-Graduate Certificate); nonprofit management (MNM); nonprofit organizational capacity building (Certificate); operations management (MBA); organizational leadership and management (MSOL); project leadership and management (MS, MSOL); strategic business management (Certificate); strategic human resource integration (Certificate); strategic management (MBA). Programs offered at Colorado Springs Campus, Northwest Denver Campus, Southeast Denver Campus, Fort Collins Campus, Broomfield Campus, Henderson (Nevada) Campus, and Summerlin (Nevada) Campus. *Program availability:* Part-time, evening/weekend, 100% online, blended/hybrid learning. *Faculty:* 15 full-time (5 women), 43 part-time/adjunct (16 women). *Students:* 622 full-time (350 women), 460 part-time (170 women); includes 317 minority (88 Black or African American, non-Hispanic/Latino; 7 American Indian or Alaska Native, non-Hispanic/Latino; 44 Asian, non-Hispanic/Latino; 151 Hispanic/Latino; 1 Native Hawaiian or other Pacific Islander, non-Hispanic/Latino; 26 Two or more races, non-Hispanic/Latino), 44 international. Average age 36. 307 applicants, 73% accepted, 134 enrolled. In 2016, 394 master's awarded. *Degree requirements:* For master's, thesis (for some programs), capstone or final research project. *Entrance requirements:* For master's, official transcript reflecting baccalaureate degree awarded from regionally-accredited college or university, interview, 2 years of full-time related work experience, resume, letters of recommendation. Additional exam requirements/recommendations for international students: Required—TOEFL (minimum score 550 paper-based; 82 iBT). *Application deadline:* For fall admission, 8/15 priority date for domestic students, 8/13 for international students; for winter admission, 10/10 priority date for domestic students, 9/8 for international students; for spring admission, 1/10 priority date for domestic students, 11/17 for international students; for summer admission, 5/1 priority date for domestic students. Applications are processed on a rolling basis. Application fee: $75. Electronic applications accepted. *Expenses:* $780 per credit hour. *Financial support:* Scholarships/grants available. Financial award application deadline: 4/15; financial award applicants required to submit FAFSA. *Faculty research:* Impact of information technology on small business regulation of accounting, international project financing, mineral development, delivery of healthcare to rural indigenous communities. *Unit head:* Dr. Timothy Keane, Academic Dean. *Application contact:* Cate Clark, Director of Admissions, 303-458-4900, Fax: 303-964-5534, E-mail: ruadmissions@regis.edu.
Website: http://www.regis.edu/CBE.aspx

Rider University, Department of Graduate Education, Leadership and Counseling, Teacher Certification Program, Lawrenceville, NJ 08648-3001. Offers business education (Certificate); elementary education (Certificate); English as a second language (Certificate); English education (Certificate); mathematics education (Certificate); preschool to grade 3 (Certificate); science education (Certificate); social studies education (Certificate); world languages (Certificate), including French, German, Spanish. *Program availability:* Part-time. *Degree requirements:* For Certificate, internship, professional portfolio. *Entrance requirements:* For degree, PRAXIS, resume. Additional exam requirements/recommendations for international students: Required—TOEFL (minimum score 550 paper-based). Electronic applications accepted. *Faculty research:* Conceptual foundations for optimal development of creativity; creative theory, cognitive processes in mathematics learning, teacher collaboration.

Robert Morris University, School of Education and Social Sciences, Moon Township, PA 15108-1189. Offers business education (MS); counseling psychology (MS); education (Postbaccalaureate Certificate); higher education (MS); instructional leadership (MS), including education; instructional management and leadership (PhD); literacy (MS); special education (MS). *Accreditation:* TEAC. *Program availability:* Part-time, evening/weekend, online learning. *Faculty:* 17 full-time (9 women), 4 part-time/adjunct (3 women). *Students:* 154 part-time (104 women); includes 18 minority (11 Black or African American, non-Hispanic/Latino; 2 Hispanic/Latino; 5 Two or more races, non-Hispanic/Latino), 1 international. Average age 26. 69 applicants, 26% accepted, 18 enrolled. In 2016, 40 master's, 15 doctorates awarded. *Degree requirements:* For doctorate, thesis/dissertation. *Entrance requirements:* Additional exam requirements/recommendations for international students: Required—TOEFL (minimum score 550 paper-based; 79 iBT). *Application deadline:* For fall admission, 7/1 priority date for domestic and international students; for spring admission, 11/1 priority date for domestic and international students. Applications are processed on a rolling basis. Application fee: $35. Electronic applications accepted. *Expenses:* $840 per credit (for master's degree). *Unit head:* Dr. Mary Ann Rafoth, Dean, 412-397-6020, Fax: 412-397-6044, E-mail: rafoth@rmu.edu.
Website: http://www.rmu.edu/web/cms/schools/sess/

South Carolina State University, College of Graduate and Professional Studies, Department of Education, Orangeburg, SC 29117-0001. Offers early childhood education (MAT); education (M Ed); elementary education (M Ed, MAT); English (MAT); general science/biology (MAT); mathematics (MAT); secondary education (M Ed), including biology education, business education, counselor education, English education, home economics education, industrial education, mathematics education, science education, social studies education; special education (M Ed), including emotionally handicapped, learning disabilities, mentally handicapped. *Accreditation:* NCATE. *Program availability:* Part-time, evening/weekend. *Faculty:* 12 full-time (8 women), 3 part-time/adjunct (1 woman). *Students:* 28 full-time (20 women), 20 part-time (17 women); includes 45 minority (44 Black or African American, non-Hispanic/Latino; 1 Two or more races, non-Hispanic/Latino). Average age 31. 22 applicants, 100% accepted, 16 enrolled. In 2016, 9 master's awarded. *Degree requirements:* For master's, thesis optional, departmental qualifying exam. *Entrance requirements:* For master's, GRE General Test, NTE, interview, teaching certificate. *Application deadline:* For fall admission, 6/15 priority date for domestic students, 6/15 for international students; for spring admission, 11/1 for domestic and international students. Application fee: $25. Electronic applications accepted. *Expenses:* Tuition, state resident: full-time $8938; part-time $579 per credit hour. Tuition, nonresident: full-time $19,018; part-time $1139 per credit hour. *Required fees:* $1482; $82 per credit hour. *Financial support:* Fellowships, career-related internships or fieldwork, Federal Work-Study, and scholarships/grants available. Financial award application deadline: 6/1. *Unit head:* Dr. Charlie Spell, Interim Chair, Department of Education, 803-536-8963, Fax: 803-516-4568, E-mail: cspell@scsu.edu. *Application contact:* Curtis Foskey, Coordinator of Graduate Studies, 803-536-8419, Fax: 803-536-8812, E-mail: cfoskey@scsu.edu.

Southern New Hampshire University, School of Education, Manchester, NH 03106-1045. Offers business education (M Ed); child development (M Ed); curriculum and instruction (M Ed), including education leadership, reading, special education, technology integration; education (M Ed); educational leadership (M Ed, Ed D); educational studies (M Ed); elementary education (M Ed); English (MAT); English for speakers of other languages (M Ed); reading and writing specialist (M Ed); school business administration (Certificate); secondary education (M Ed); special education (M Ed); technology integration specialist (M Ed). *Program availability:* Part-time, evening/weekend, online learning. *Degree requirements:* For master's, comprehensive exam (for some programs), thesis or alternative. *Entrance requirements:* For master's, PRAXIS I, minimum GPA of 2.75. Additional exam requirements/recommendations for international students: Required—TOEFL (minimum score 550 paper-based). Electronic applications accepted. *Expenses:* Contact institution.

Spalding University, Graduate Studies, College of Education, Programs in Education, Louisville, KY 40203-2188. Offers art teacher education (MAT); business teacher education (MAT); elementary school education (MAT); foreign language (MAT); high school education (MAT); middle school education (MAT); secondary education (MAT); special education (learning and behavioral disorders) (MAT); student guidance counselor (MA); teacher leader (M Ed). *Accreditation:* NCATE. *Program availability:* Part-time, evening/weekend. *Faculty:* 39 full-time (26 women), 13 part-time/adjunct (4 women). *Students:* 97 full-time (76 women), 31 part-time (23 women); includes 39 minority (33 Black or African American, non-Hispanic/Latino; 1 Asian, non-Hispanic/Latino; 3 Hispanic/Latino; 2 Two or more races, non-Hispanic/Latino). Average age 35. 62 applicants, 55% accepted, 33 enrolled. In 2016, 49 master's awarded. *Entrance requirements:* For master's, GRE General Test or MAT, interview, letters of recommendation, resume. Additional exam requirements/recommendations for international students: Required—TOEFL (minimum score 535 paper-based). *Application deadline:* Applications are processed on a rolling basis. Application fee: $30. Electronic applications accepted. *Expenses: Tuition:* Full-time $15,300. *Financial support:* Scholarships/grants, traineeships, and unspecified assistantships available. Financial award applicants required to submit FAFSA. *Faculty research:* Instructional technology, achievement gap, classroom management, assessment. *Unit head:* Dr. Chris Walsh, Associate Dean, 502-873-4272, Fax: 502-585-7123, E-mail: cwalsh@spalding.edu. *Application contact:* Valerie Anderson, Administrative Assistant, 502-873-4260, E-mail: vanderson@spalding.edu.

State University of New York at Oswego, Graduate Studies, School of Education, Department of Vocational Teacher Preparation, Oswego, NY 13126. Offers agriculture (MS Ed); business and marketing (MS Ed); family and consumer sciences (MS Ed); health careers (MS Ed); technical education (MS Ed); trade education (MS Ed). *Accreditation:* NCATE. *Program availability:* Part-time, evening/weekend. *Degree requirements:* For master's, comprehensive exam, thesis or alternative. *Entrance requirements:* Additional exam requirements/recommendations for international students: Required—TOEFL (minimum score 560 paper-based).

Temple University, College of Education, Department of Teaching and Learning, Philadelphia, PA 19122-6096. Offers career and technical education (Ed M), including business, computing, and information technology, industrial education, marketing education; middle grades education (Ed M), including math and language arts, math and science, science and language arts; secondary education (Ed M), including English, math, social studies; teaching English to speakers of other languages (MS Ed); urban education (Ed M). *Program availability:* Part-time, evening/weekend. *Faculty:* 26 full-time (16 women), 74 part-time/adjunct (54 women). *Students:* 204 full-time (139 women), 320 part-time (201 women); includes 112 minority (66 Black or African American, non-Hispanic/Latino; 17 Asian, non-Hispanic/Latino; 18 Hispanic/Latino; 11 Two or more races, non-Hispanic/Latino), 18 international. 300 applicants, 55% accepted, 99 enrolled. In 2016, 93 master's awarded. Terminal master's awarded for partial completion of doctoral program. *Degree requirements:* For master's, thesis or alternative. *Entrance requirements:* Additional exam requirements/recommendations for international students: Required—TOEFL (minimum score 550 paper-based; 79 iBT). *Application deadline:* For fall admission, 4/1 for domestic students, 12/15 for international students; for spring admission, 10/1 for domestic students, 8/1 for international students. Application fee: $60. Electronic applications accepted. *Expenses:* Contact institution. *Financial support:* Fellowships, research assistantships, and teaching assistantships available. Financial award application deadline: 1/15; financial award applicants required to submit FAFSA. *Faculty research:* Workforce development, vocational education, technical education, industrial education, professional development, literacy, classroom management, school communities, curriculum development, instruction, applied linguistics, cross linguistic influence, bilingual education, oral proficiency, multilingualism. *Unit head:* Dr. Christine Woyshner, Chairperson, 215-204-6387, E-mail: christine.woyshner@temple.edu. *Application contact:* Sarah Stapleton, Assistant Director, Academic Operations, 215-204-8220, E-mail: sarah.stapleton@temple.edu.
Website: http://education.temple.edu/tl

Thomas College, Graduate School, Programs in Business, Waterville, ME 04901-5097. Offers business (MBA); computer technology education (MS); education (MS); human resource management (MBA). *Program availability:* Part-time, evening/weekend. *Entrance requirements:* For master's, GMAT, GRE, MAT or minimum GPA of 3.3 in first 3 graduate-level courses. Additional exam requirements/recommendations for international students: Recommended—TOEFL.

University of Delaware, Alfred Lerner College of Business and Economics, Department of Economics, Newark, DE 19716. Offers economic education (PhD); economics (MA, MS, PhD); economics for entrepreneurship and educators (MA); MA/MBA. *Program availability:* Part-time. *Degree requirements:* For master's, comprehensive exam, thesis (for some programs), mathematics review exam, research project; for doctorate, comprehensive exam, thesis/dissertation, field exam. *Entrance requirements:* For master's, GMAT or GRE General Test, minimum GPA of 2.5; for doctorate, GRE General Test, minimum GPA of 3.5 in graduate economics course work. Additional exam requirements/recommendations for international students: Required—TOEFL (minimum score 550 paper-based). Electronic applications accepted. *Faculty research:* Applied quantitative economics, industrial organization, resource economics, monetary economics, labor economics.

University of Georgia, College of Education, Department of Career and Information Studies, Athens, GA 30602. Offers learning, design, and technology (M Ed, PhD, Ed S), including instructional design and development (M Ed, Ed S); workforce education (MAT, Ed D), including business education (MAT). *Accreditation:* NCATE. *Faculty:* 14 full-time (7 women). *Students:* 27 full-time (15 women), 70 part-time (46 women); includes 24 minority (23 Black or African American, non-Hispanic/Latino; 1 Native Hawaiian or other Pacific Islander, non-Hispanic/Latino), 5 international. Average age 37. 40 applicants, 63% accepted, 8 enrolled. In 2016, 16 master's, 23 doctorates, 5 other advanced degrees awarded. *Entrance requirements:* For master's, GRE General Test, MAT; for doctorate, GRE General Test; for Ed S, GRE General Test or MAT. *Application deadline:* For fall admission, 7/1 priority date for domestic students; for spring admission, 11/15 for domestic students. Application fee: $50. Electronic applications accepted. *Financial support:* Fellowships, research assistantships, teaching assistantships, and unspecified assistantships available. *Unit head:* Dr. Robert C. Branch, Head, 706-542-4100, Fax: 706-542-4054. *Application contact:* Dr. Robert C. Wicklein, Graduate Coordinator, 706-542-4503, Fax: 706-542-4054, E-mail: wickone@uga.edu.
Website: http://www.coe.uga.edu/cis/

University of Missouri, Office of Research and Graduate Studies, College of Education, Department of Learning, Teaching and Curriculum, Columbia, MO 65211. Offers agricultural education (M Ed, PhD, Ed S); art education (M Ed, PhD, Ed S); business and office education (M Ed, PhD, Ed S); early childhood education (M Ed, PhD, Ed S); elementary education (M Ed, PhD, Ed S); English education (M Ed, PhD, Ed S); foreign language education (M Ed, PhD, Ed S); health education and promotion (M Ed, PhD); learning and instruction (M Ed); marketing education (M Ed, PhD, Ed S); mathematics education (M Ed, PhD, Ed S); music education (M Ed, PhD, Ed S); reading education (M Ed, PhD, Ed S); science education (M Ed, PhD, Ed S); social studies education (M Ed, PhD, Ed S); vocational education (M Ed, PhD, Ed S). *Program availability:* Part-time. *Faculty:* 30 full-time (18 women), 1 (woman) part-time/adjunct. *Students:* 157 full-time (124 women), 157 part-time (125 women). Terminal master's awarded for partial completion of doctoral program. *Degree requirements:* For doctorate, thesis/dissertation. *Entrance requirements:* For master's and Ed S, GRE General Test or MAT, minimum GPA of 3.0; for doctorate, GRE General Test, minimum GPA of 3.0. Additional exam requirements/recommendations for international students: Required—TOEFL (minimum score 600 paper-based; 100 iBT). *Application deadline:* For fall admission, 12/1 priority date for domestic and international students. Applications are processed on a rolling basis. Application fee: $75 ($90 for international students). Electronic applications accepted. *Expenses:* Tuition, state resident: full-time $6347; part-time $352.60 per credit hour. Tuition, nonresident: full-time $17,379; part-time $965.50 per credit hour. *Required fees:* $1035. Tuition and fees vary according to course load, campus/location and program. *Financial support:* Fellowships, research assistantships, teaching assistantships, institutionally sponsored loans, traineeships, health care benefits, and unspecified assistantships available. Support available to part-time students.
Website: http://education.missouri.edu/LTC/index.php

The University of North Carolina at Charlotte, College of Computing and Informatics, Program in Computing and Information Systems, Charlotte, NC 28223-0001. Offers computing and information systems (PhD), including bioinformatics, business information systems and operations management, computer science, interdisciplinary, software and information systems. *Faculty:* 3 full-time (0 women). *Students:* 91 full-time (30 women), 23 part-time (3 women); includes 8 minority (2 Black or African American, non-Hispanic/Latino; 4 Asian, non-Hispanic/Latino; 1 Hispanic/Latino; 1 Two or more races, non-Hispanic/Latino), 76 international. Average age 31. 90 applicants, 41% accepted, 18 enrolled. In 2016, 13 doctorates awarded. *Degree requirements:* For doctorate, comprehensive exam, thesis/dissertation. *Entrance requirements:* For doctorate, GRE or GMAT, baccalaureate degree, minimum GPA of 3.0 on courses related to the chosen field of PhD study, essay, reference letters. Additional exam requirements/recommendations for international students: Required—TOEFL (minimum score 523 paper-based, 70 iBT) or IELTS (6.5). *Application deadline:* For fall admission, 2/1 for domestic and international students; for spring admission, 9/1 for domestic and international students. Applications are processed on a rolling basis. Application fee: $75. Electronic applications accepted. *Expenses:* Tuition, state resident: full-time

$4252. Tuition, nonresident: full-time $17,423. *Required fees:* $3026. Tuition and fees vary according to course load and program. *Financial support:* Career-related internships or fieldwork, institutionally sponsored loans, scholarships/grants, health care benefits, and unspecified assistantships available. Support available to part-time students. Financial award applicants required to submit FAFSA. *Unit head:* Manuel A. Perez Quinones, Director, 704-687-8553, E-mail: perez.quinones@uncc.edu. *Application contact:* Kathy B. Giddings, Director of Graduate Admissions, 704-687-5503, Fax: 704-687-1668, E-mail: gradadm@uncc.edu.

University of St. Francis, College of Business and Health Administration, School of Professional Studies, Joliet, IL 60435-6169. Offers e-learning (Certificate); management of training and development (Certificate); training and development (MS); training specialist (Certificate). *Accreditation:* ACBSP. *Program availability:* Part-time, evening/weekend, 100% online. *Faculty:* 1 (woman) full-time, 2 part-time/adjunct (both women). *Students:* 6 full-time (4 women), 49 part-time (37 women); includes 20 minority (13 Black or African American, non-Hispanic/Latino; 1 Asian, non-Hispanic/Latino; 5 Hispanic/Latino; 1 Native Hawaiian or other Pacific Islander, non-Hispanic/Latino). Average age 42. 36 applicants, 47% accepted, 13 enrolled. In 2016, 26 master's, 3 other advanced degrees awarded. *Entrance requirements:* Additional exam requirements/recommendations for international students: Required—TOEFL (minimum score 550 paper-based; 79 iBT), IELTS (minimum score 6). *Application deadline:* Applications are processed on a rolling basis. Application fee: $30. Electronic applications accepted. Application fee is waived when completed online. *Expenses: Tuition:* Part-time $739 per credit hour. *Required fees:* $125 per semester. Part-time tuition and fees vary according to degree level and program. *Financial support:* In 2016–17, 8 students received support. Tuition waivers (partial) and unspecified assistantships available. Support available to part-time students. Financial award applicants required to submit FAFSA. *Unit head:* Dr. Orlando Griego, Dean, 815-740-3395, Fax: 815-740-3537, E-mail: ogriego@stfrancis.edu. *Application contact:* Sandra Sloka, Director of Admissions for Graduate and Degree Completion Programs, 800-735-7500, Fax: 815-740-3431, E-mail: ssloka@stfrancis.edu.
Website: http://www.stfrancis.edu/academics/college-of-business-health-administration

University of South Carolina, The Graduate School, College of Education, Department of Instruction and Teacher Education, Program in Secondary Education, Columbia, SC 29208. Offers art education (IMA, MAT); business education (IMA, MAT); English (MAT); foreign language (MAT); health education (MAT); mathematics (MAT); science (IMA, MAT); secondary (Ed D); secondary education (MT, PhD); social studies (MAT); theatre and speech (MAT). IMA and MT offered jointly with the subject areas. *Accreditation:* NCATE. *Degree requirements:* For master's, comprehensive exam, thesis (for some programs), foreign language (MA); for doctorate, one foreign language, comprehensive exam, thesis/dissertation. *Entrance requirements:* For master's, GRE General Test or MAT, teaching certificate (IMA, M Ed), interview; for doctorate, GRE General Test or MAT, interview. *Faculty research:* Middle school programs, professional development, school collaboration.

University of the Cumberlands, Graduate Programs in Education, Williamsburg, KY 40769-1372. Offers all grades (P-12) (M Ed); business and marketing (MA Ed, MAT); counselor education and supervision (Ed D); director of pupil personnel (Certificate); director of special education (Certificate); educational administration and supervision (Ed S); educational leadership (Ed D); elementary education (MA Ed, MAT); instructional leadership - principalship (MA Ed); instructional leadership - school principal (Certificate); middle school education (MA Ed, MAT); reading and writing (MA Ed); school counseling (MA Ed); school superintendent (Certificate); secondary education (MA Ed, MAT); special education (MAT); supervisor of instruction (Certificate); teacher leader (MA Ed). *Program availability:* Part-time, evening/weekend, online learning. *Degree requirements:* For master's, comprehensive exam. Electronic applications accepted.

The University of Toledo, College of Graduate Studies, Judith Herb College of Education, Department of Curriculum and Instruction, Toledo, OH 43606-3390. Offers art education (ME); career and technical education (ME, Ed S); curriculum and instruction (ME, PhD, Ed S); early childhood education (Ed S); education and anthropology (MAE); education and biology (MES); education and chemistry (MES); education and classics (MAE); education and economics (MAE); education and English (MAE); education and French (MAE); education and geology (MES); education and German (MAE); education and history (MAE); education and mathematics (MAE, MES); education and physics (MES); education and political science (MAE); education and sociology (MAE); education and Spanish (MAE); educational media (PhD); educational technology (ME); educational technology: virtual educator (Certificate); elementary education (PhD); English as a second language (MAE); gifted and talented education (PhD); middle childhood education (ME); secondary education (ME, PhD); special education (PhD). *Accreditation:* NCATE. *Program availability:* Part-time, evening/weekend. *Degree requirements:* For master's, comprehensive exam, thesis or alternative; for doctorate, comprehensive exam, thesis/dissertation; for other advanced degree, thesis optional. *Entrance requirements:* For master's, doctorate, and other advanced degree, minimum cumulative GPA of 2.7 for all previous academic work, letters of recommendation. Additional exam requirements/recommendations for international students: Required—TOEFL (minimum score 550 paper-based; 80 iBT). Electronic applications accepted.

University of Washington, Graduate School, Michael G. Foster School of Business, Seattle, WA 98195-3200. Offers auditing and assurance (MP Acc); business administration (MBA, PhD); entrepreneurship (MS); executive business administration (MBA); global executive business administration (MBA); information systems (MSIS); supply chain management (MSSCM); taxation (MP Acc); technology management (MBA); JD/MBA; MBA/MAIS; MBA/MHA. *Accreditation:* AACSB. *Program availability:* Part-time, evening/weekend. Terminal master's awarded for partial completion of doctoral program. *Degree requirements:* For doctorate, comprehensive exam, thesis/dissertation. *Entrance requirements:* For master's and doctorate, GMAT, GRE. Additional exam requirements/recommendations for international students: Required—TOEFL (minimum score 600 paper-based; 100 iBT). Electronic applications accepted. *Expenses:* Contact institution. *Faculty research:* Finance, marketing, organizational behavior, information technology, strategy.

University of West Georgia, College of Education, Carrollton, GA 30118. Offers business education (M Ed); early childhood education (M Ed, Ed S); educational leadership (M Ed, Ed S); media (M Ed, Ed S); professional counseling (M Ed, Ed S); professional counseling and supervision (Ed D); reading instruction (M Ed); school improvement (Ed D); secondary education (M Ed); special education (M Ed, Ed S), including teaching (M Ed); speech language pathology (M Ed); teaching (MAT). *Accreditation:* NCATE. *Program availability:* Part-time, evening/weekend, 100% online, blended/hybrid learning. *Faculty:* 46 full-time (31 women). *Students:* 321 full-time (266 women), 1,007 part-time (813 women); includes 456 minority (389 Black or African American, non-Hispanic/Latino; 1 American Indian or Alaska Native, non-Hispanic/Latino; 13 Asian, non-Hispanic/Latino; 43 Hispanic/Latino; 10 Two or more races, non-Hispanic/Latino), 12 international. Average age 33. 541 applicants, 79% accepted, 305 enrolled. In 2016, 286 master's, 20 doctorates, 156 other advanced degrees awarded. *Entrance requirements:* Additional exam requirements/recommendations for international students: Required—TOEFL (minimum score 523 paper-based; 69 iBT); Recommended—IELTS (minimum score 6.5). *Application deadline:* For fall admission, 7/21 for domestic students, 6/1 for international students; for spring admission, 11/30 for domestic students, 10/15 for international students; for summer admission, 4/15 for domestic students, 3/30 for international students. Applications are processed on a rolling basis. Application fee: $40. Electronic applications accepted. *Expenses:* Tuition, state resident: full-time $5316; part-time $222 per semester hour. Tuition, nonresident: full-time $20,658; part-time $861 per semester hour. *Required fees:* $1962. Tuition and fees vary according to course load, degree level and program. *Financial support:* Fellowships, research assistantships, teaching assistantships, career-related internships or fieldwork, Federal Work-Study, institutionally sponsored loans, scholarships/grants, and unspecified assistantships available. Support available to part-time students. Financial award application deadline: 4/1; financial award applicants required to submit FAFSA. *Unit head:* Dr. Diane Hoff, Dean, College of Education, 678-839-6570, Fax: 678-839-6098, E-mail: dhoff@westga.edu. *Application contact:* Dr. Toby Ziglar, Assistant Dean of the Graduate School, 678-839-1394, Fax: 678-839-1395, E-mail: graduate@westga.edu.
Website: http://www.westga.edu/education/

University of Wisconsin–Whitewater, School of Graduate Studies, College of Business and Economics, Program in Business and Marketing Education, Whitewater, WI 53190-1790. Offers MS. *Accreditation:* NCATE. *Program availability:* Part-time, evening/weekend, online learning. *Degree requirements:* For master's, thesis or alternative. *Entrance requirements:* For master's, interview, teaching license. Additional exam requirements/recommendations for international students: Required—TOEFL (minimum score 550 paper-based; 80 iBT), IELTS (minimum score 6). Electronic applications accepted.

Utah State University, School of Graduate Studies, College of Business, Department of Business Information Systems, Logan, UT 84322. Offers business education (MS); business information systems (MS); business information systems and education (Ed D); education (PhD). *Program availability:* Part-time. Terminal master's awarded for partial completion of doctoral program. *Degree requirements:* For master's, thesis optional; for doctorate, thesis/dissertation. *Entrance requirements:* For master's, GMAT, minimum GPA of 3.2; for doctorate, GRE General Test, minimum GPA of 3.0. Additional exam requirements/recommendations for international students: Required—TOEFL. *Faculty research:* Oral and written communication, methods of teaching, CASE tools, object-oriented programming, decision support systems.

Utah State University, School of Graduate Studies, Emma Eccles Jones College of Education and Human Services, Doctoral Program in Education, Logan, UT 84322. Offers business information systems (Ed D, PhD); curriculum and instruction (Ed D, PhD); research and evaluation (PhD). *Degree requirements:* For doctorate, comprehensive exam, thesis/dissertation. *Entrance requirements:* For doctorate, GRE General Test, minimum GPA of 3.0, master's degree. Additional exam requirements/recommendations for international students: Required—TOEFL. Electronic applications accepted. *Faculty research:* Language and literacy development, math and science education, instructional technology, hearing problems/deafness, domestic violence and animal abuse.

Washington State University, College of Education, Department of Educational Leadership, Sports Studies, and Educational/Counseling Psychology, Pullman, WA 99164-2136. Offers counseling psychology (PhD); educational leadership (Ed M, MA, Ed D, PhD); educational psychology (MA, PhD); sport management (MA). Programs also offered at the Spokane, Tri-Cities, Vancouver and Global (online) campuses. *Program availability:* Part-time, online learning. *Degree requirements:* For master's, comprehensive exam (for some programs), thesis (for some programs), oral or written exam; for doctorate, comprehensive exam, thesis/dissertation, oral and written exam, internship. *Entrance requirements:* For master's and doctorate, GRE General Test, minimum GPA of 3.0, 3 letters of recommendation, transcripts showing all college or university course work, statement of professional objectives, current curriculum vitae/resume. Additional exam requirements/recommendations for international students: Required—TOEFL (minimum score 550 paper-based; 80 iBT). Electronic applications accepted. *Faculty research:* Multicultural counseling and career development, educational and psychological measurement issues, business decision-making process and power relationships, leadership practices and processes as suffused with and constituted by emotion work.

Wayne State College, School of Education and Counseling, Department of Educational Foundations and Leadership, Program in Curriculum and Instruction, Wayne, NE 68787. Offers alternative education (MSE); business and information technology education (MSE); communication arts education (MSE); early childhood education (MSE); elementary education (MSE); English as a second language (MSE); English education (MSE); family and consumer sciences education (MSE); industrial technology and vocational education (MSE); learning communities (MSE); mathematics education (MSE); music education (MSE); science education (MSE); social science education (MSE). *Accreditation:* NCATE. *Program availability:* Part-time, evening/weekend. *Degree requirements:* For master's, comprehensive exam, thesis optional. *Entrance requirements:* For master's, GRE General Test. Additional exam requirements/recommendations for international students: Required—TOEFL (minimum score 550 paper-based).

West Chester University of Pennsylvania, College of Business and Public Management, School of Business, West Chester, PA 19383. Offers business analytics (Certificate); business education (MBA); entrepreneurship (Certificate); project management (Certificate). *Accreditation:* AACSB. *Program availability:* Part-time, evening/weekend, 100% online. *Faculty:* 13 full-time (6 women), 2 part-time/adjunct (1 woman). *Students:* 44 full-time (23 women), 213 part-time (82 women); includes 37 minority (16 Black or African American, non-Hispanic/Latino; 11 Asian, non-Hispanic/Latino; 9 Hispanic/Latino; 1 Two or more races, non-Hispanic/Latino). Average age 32. 202 applicants, 83% accepted, 126 enrolled. In 2016, 41 master's, 10 other advanced degrees awarded. *Degree requirements:* For master's, minimum GPA of 3.0. *Entrance requirements:* For master's, GMAT or GRE, statement of professional goals, resume, two letters of recommendation, transcripts. Additional exam requirements/recommendations for international students: Required—TOEFL or IELTS. *Application deadline:* For fall admission, 5/15 for international students; for spring admission, 10/15 for international students. Applications are processed on a rolling basis. Application fee: $50. Electronic applications accepted. *Expenses:* Tuition, state resident: full-time $8694; part-time $483 per credit. Tuition, nonresident: full-time $13,050; part-time $725 per credit. *Required fees:* $2399; $119.05 per credit. Tuition and fees vary according to campus/location and program. *Financial support:* Scholarships/grants and unspecified assistantships available. Financial award application deadline: 2/15; financial award applicants required to submit FAFSA. *Unit head:* Dr. Brian Halsey, MBA Director/Graduate Coordinator, 610-425-5000 Ext. 4444, E-mail: mba@wcupa.edu. *Application contact:* Office of Graduate Studies and Extended Education, 610-436-2943, Fax: 610-436-2763, E-mail: gradstudy@wcupa.edu.
Website: http://www.wcupa.edu/mba

Computer Education

Arcadia University, School of Education, Glenside, PA 19038-3295. Offers art education (M Ed); computer education (CAS); curriculum (CAS); curriculum studies (M Ed); early childhood education (M Ed), including individualized, master teacher, research in child development; educational leadership (M Ed, Ed D, CAS); elementary education (M Ed); English education (MA Ed); environmental education (MA Ed); instructional technology (M Ed); language arts (M Ed); library science (M Ed); mathematics education (M Ed, MA Ed); music education (MA Ed); psychology (MA Ed); reading (M Ed, CAS); science education (M Ed, CAS); secondary education (M Ed, CAS); special education (M Ed, Ed D, CAS); theater arts (MA Ed); written communication (MA Ed). *Accreditation:* NASAD. *Program availability:* Part-time, evening/weekend, online learning. *Faculty:* 19 full-time (13 women), 3 part-time/adjunct (all women). *Students:* 22 full-time (16 women), 356 part-time (284 women); includes 84 minority (55 Black or African American, non-Hispanic/Latino; 2 American Indian or Alaska Native, non-Hispanic/Latino; 13 Asian, non-Hispanic/Latino; 11 Hispanic/Latino; 3 Two or more races, non-Hispanic/Latino), 4 international. Average age 34. 145 applicants, 73% accepted, 80 enrolled. In 2016, 95 master's, 11 doctorates awarded. *Application deadline:* Applications are processed on a rolling basis. Application fee: $50. Electronic applications accepted. *Expenses:* Contact institution. *Financial support:* Career-related internships or fieldwork, tuition waivers (partial), and unspecified assistantships available. *Unit head:* John T Groves, Interim Dean of the School of Education, 215-572-2940. *Application contact:* 215-572-2925, Fax: 215-572-2126, E-mail: grad@arcadia.edu.

Ball State University, Graduate School, Teachers College, Department of Educational Studies, Muncie, IN 47306. Offers adult education (MA, Ed D, Certificate), including adult and community education (MA), adult, higher and community education (Ed D); college and university teaching (Certificate); community college leadership (Certificate); community education (Certificate); computer education (Certificate); curriculum and educational technology (MA); diversity studies (Certificate); educational studies (PhD), including educational studies; executive development for public service (MA); middle-level education (Certificate); qualitative research in education (Certificate); secondary education (MA); student affairs administration in higher education (MA), including student affairs administration in higher education. *Accreditation:* NCATE. *Program availability:* Part-time, 100% online, blended/hybrid learning. *Degree requirements:* For doctorate, thesis/dissertation. *Entrance requirements:* For master's, minimum baccalaureate GPA of 2.75 or 3.0 in latter half of baccalauareate; for doctorate, minimum graduate GPA of 3.2. Additional exam requirements/recommendations for international students: Required—TOEFL (minimum score 550 paper-based; 79 iBT), IELTS (minimum score 6.5). Electronic applications accepted.

Eastern Washington University, Graduate Studies, College of Science, Technology, Engineering and Mathematics, Department of Computer Science, Cheney, WA 99004-2431. Offers computer science (MS). *Program availability:* Part-time. *Faculty:* 12 full-time (3 women). *Students:* 14 full-time (1 woman), 3 part-time (0 women); includes 3 minority (1 American Indian or Alaska Native, non-Hispanic/Latino; 1 Hispanic/Latino; 1 Native Hawaiian or other Pacific Islander, non-Hispanic/Latino). Average age 31. 27 applicants, 41% accepted, 5 enrolled. In 2016, 4 master's awarded. *Degree requirements:* For master's, comprehensive exam, thesis or alternative. *Entrance requirements:* For master's, minimum GPA of 3.0. Additional exam requirements/recommendations for international students: Required—TOEFL (minimum score 580 paper-based; 92 iBT), IELTS (minimum score 7), PTE (minimum score 63). *Application deadline:* For fall admission, 4/1 priority date for domestic students; for spring admission, 1/15 for domestic students. Applications are processed on a rolling basis. Application fee: $75. Electronic applications accepted. *Expenses:* Tuition, state resident: full-time $11,000; part-time $5500 per credit. Tuition, nonresident: full-time $24,000; part-time $12,000 per credit. *Required fees:* $1300. One-time fee: $50 full-time. Part-time tuition and fees vary according to course load, campus/location and program. *Financial support:* In 2016–17, 16 teaching assistantships with partial tuition reimbursements (averaging $12,000 per year) were awarded; career-related internships or fieldwork, Federal Work-Study, institutionally sponsored loans, scholarships/grants, health care benefits, tuition waivers (partial), and unspecified assistantships also available. Support available to part-time students. Financial award application deadline: 2/1. *Unit head:* Dr. Carol Taylor, Chair, 509-359-6065, Fax: 509-359-2215, E-mail: ctaylor@ewu.edu.
Website: http://www.ewu.edu/cshe/programs/computer-science.xml

Florida Institute of Technology, College of Science, Program in Computer Education, Melbourne, FL 32901-6975. Offers MS. *Program availability:* Part-time. *Students:* 2 full-time (1 woman), 1 (woman) part-time, all international. Average age 27. 14 applicants, 43% accepted, 1 enrolled. In 2016, 3 master's awarded. *Degree requirements:* For master's, thesis or final exam. *Entrance requirements:* For master's, 3 letters of recommendation, statement of objectives, resume. Additional exam requirements/recommendations for international students: Required—TOEFL (minimum score 550 paper-based; 79 iBT). *Application deadline:* Applications are processed on a rolling basis. Electronic applications accepted. *Expenses: Tuition:* Full-time $22,338; part-time $1241 per credit hour. *Required fees:* $250. Tuition and fees vary according to degree level, campus/location and program. *Financial support:* Applicants required to submit FAFSA. *Unit head:* Dr. Hamed Kastro, Department Head, 321-674-7206, E-mail: khamed@fit.edu. *Application contact:* Cheryl A. Brown, Associate Director of Graduate Admissions, 321-674-7581, Fax: 321-723-9468, E-mail: cbrown@fit.edu.
Website: http://admission.fit.edu/graduate/documents/doc_mgr/214/computer_education.pdf

Illinois Institute of Technology, Graduate College, College of Science, Department of Computer Science, Chicago, IL 60616. Offers business (MCS); computational intelligence (MCS); computer science (MCS, MS, PhD); cyber-physical systems (MCS); data analytics (MCS); data science (MAS); database systems (MCS); distributed and cloud computing (MCS); education (MCS); finance (MCS); information security and assurance (MCS); networking and communications (MCS); software engineering (MCS); telecommunications and software engineering (MAS); MS/MAS. *Program availability:* Part-time, evening/weekend, online learning. Terminal master's awarded for partial completion of doctoral program. *Degree requirements:* For master's, thesis optional; for doctorate, comprehensive exam, thesis/dissertation. *Entrance requirements:* For master's, GRE General Test with minimum scores of 298 Quantitative and Verbal, 3.0 Analytical Writing (for MS); GRE General Test with minimum scores of 292 Quantitative and Verbal, 2.5 Analytical Writing (for MAS), minimum undergraduate GPA of 3.0; for doctorate, GRE General Test (minimum scores: 304 Quantitative and Verbal, 3.5 Analytical Writing), minimum undergraduate GPA of 3.0. Additional exam requirements/recommendations for international students: Required—TOEFL (minimum score 523 paper-based; 70 iBT). Electronic applications accepted. *Faculty research:* Parallel and distributed processing, high-performance computing, computational linguistics, information retrieval, data mining, grid computing.

Kent State University, College of Education, Health and Human Services, School of Lifespan Development and Educational Sciences, Program in Instructional Technology, Kent, OH 44242-0001. Offers computer technology (M Ed); educational psychology (PhD), including instructional technology; general instructional technology (M Ed). *Accreditation:* NCATE. *Degree requirements:* For master's, thesis (for some programs). *Entrance requirements:* For master's, 2 letters of reference, goals statement, minimum GPA of 2.75. Additional exam requirements/recommendations for international students: Required—TOEFL (minimum score 550 paper-based; 80 iBT). *Expenses:* Tuition, state resident: full-time $10,864; part-time $495 per credit hour. Tuition, nonresident: full-time $18,380; part-time $837 per credit hour. *Faculty research:* Cooperative learning, aesthetics, computers in schools.

Lesley University, Graduate School of Education, Cambridge, MA 02138-2790. Offers arts, community, and education (M Ed); autism studies (Certificate); curriculum and instruction (M Ed, CAGS); early childhood education (M Ed); ecological teaching and learning (MS); educational studies (PhD), including adult learning, educational leadership, individually designed; elementary education (M Ed); emergent technologies for educators (Certificate); ESLArts: language learning through the arts (M Ed); high school education (M Ed); individually designed (M Ed); integrated teaching through the arts (M Ed); literacy for K-8 classroom teachers (M Ed); mathematics education (M Ed); middle school education (M Ed); moderate disabilities (M Ed); online learning (Certificate); reading (CAGS); science in education (M Ed); severe disabilities (M Ed); special needs (CAGS); specialist teacher of reading (M Ed); teacher of visual art (M Ed); technology in education (M Ed, CAGS). *Accreditation:* TEAC. *Program availability:* Part-time, evening/weekend, online learning. *Degree requirements:* For master's, practicum; for doctorate, thesis/dissertation. *Entrance requirements:* For master's, Massachusetts Tests for Educator Licensure (MTEL), transcripts, statement of purpose, recommendations; interview (for special education); for doctorate, GRE General Test, transcripts, statement of purpose, recommendations, interview, master's degree, resume; for other advanced degree, interview, master's degree. Additional exam requirements/recommendations for international students: Required—TOEFL (minimum score 550 paper-based; 80 iBT). Electronic applications accepted. *Faculty research:* Assessment in literacy, mathematics and science; autism spectrum disorders; instructional technology and online learning; multicultural education and English language learners.

Marlboro College, Graduate and Professional Studies, Program in Teaching with Technology, Marlboro, VT 05344. Offers educational technology (Certificate); teaching with technology (MAT). *Program availability:* Part-time, evening/weekend, blended/hybrid learning. *Faculty:* 1 full-time (0 women), 8 part-time/adjunct (5 women). *Students:* 6 full-time (3 women), 13 part-time (5 women); includes 3 minority (1 Black or African American, non-Hispanic/Latino; 2 Two or more races, non-Hispanic/Latino). Average age 44. 8 applicants, 88% accepted, 7 enrolled. In 2016, 5 master's awarded. *Degree requirements:* For master's, 36 credits including capstone project. *Entrance requirements:* For master's, statement of intent, 2 letters of recommendation, transcripts. *Application deadline:* For fall admission, 7/1 priority date for domestic students; for winter admission, 11/1 priority date for domestic students; for spring admission, 3/1 priority date for domestic students. Applications are processed on a rolling basis. Application fee: $0. Electronic applications accepted. *Expenses:* $765 per credit. *Financial support:* In 2016–17, 2 students received support. Scholarships/grants available. Financial award application deadline: 8/5; financial award applicants required to submit FAFSA. *Unit head:* Caleb Clark, Degree Chair, 802-258-9207, Fax: 802-258-9201, E-mail: cclark@gradschool.marlboro.edu. *Application contact:* Don Parker, Admissions Assistant, 802-451-7505, Fax: 802-258-9201, E-mail: graduateadmissions@marlboro.edu.
Website: https://www.marlboro.edu/academics/graduate/mat

Mississippi College, Graduate School, School of Education, Department of Teacher Education and Leadership, Clinton, MS 39058. Offers art (M Ed); biological science (M Ed); business education (M Ed); computer science (M Ed); dyslexia therapy (M Ed); educational leadership (M Ed, Ed D, Ed S); elementary education (M Ed, Ed S); English (M Ed); higher education administration (MS); mathematics (M Ed); secondary education (M Ed); social studies (history) (M Ed); teaching arts (M Ed). *Program availability:* Part-time, online learning. *Degree requirements:* For master's, comprehensive exam, thesis optional. *Entrance requirements:* For master's, NTE. Additional exam requirements/recommendations for international students: Recommended—TOEFL, IELTS. Electronic applications accepted.

Ohio University, Graduate College, Gladys W. and David H. Patton College of Education and Human Services, Department of Educational Studies, Athens, OH 45701-2979. Offers computer education and technology (M Ed); educational administration (M Ed, Ed D); educational research and evaluation (M Ed, PhD); instructional technology (PhD). *Program availability:* Part-time, evening/weekend, online learning. *Degree requirements:* For master's, thesis or alternative; for doctorate, comprehensive exam, thesis/dissertation. *Entrance requirements:* For master's, GRE General Test (if GPA less than 2.9); for doctorate, GRE General Test, GRE Subject Test, minimum GPA of 2.9, work experience, 3 letters of reference, autobiography. Additional exam requirements/recommendations for international students: Required—TOEFL (minimum score 550 paper-based; 80 iBT) or IELTS (minimum score 6.5). *Application deadline:* For fall admission, 3/1 priority date for domestic and international students; for winter admission, 10/1 priority date for domestic and international students; for spring admission, 1/30 priority date for domestic students, 1/1 priority date for international students. Applications are processed on a rolling basis. Application fee: $50 ($55 for international students). Electronic applications accepted. *Financial support:* Research assistantships with full tuition reimbursements, teaching assistantships with full tuition reimbursements, Federal Work-Study, institutionally sponsored loans, tuition waivers (partial), and unspecified assistantships available. Financial award application deadline: 3/1. *Faculty research:* Race, class and gender; computer programs; development and organization theory; evaluation/development of instruments, leadership. *Unit head:* Dr. David Richard Moore, Chair, 740-597-1322, Fax: 740-593-0477, E-mail: moored3@ohio.edu. *Application contact:* Floyd J. Doney, Director of Student Affairs, 740-593-4400, Fax: 740-593-9310, E-mail: doney@ohio.edu.
Website: http://www.cehs.ohio.edu/academics/es/

Stony Brook University, State University of New York, Graduate School, College of Engineering and Applied Sciences, Department of Technology and Society, Program in Educational Technology, Stony Brook, NY 11794. Offers MS. *Accreditation:* NCATE. *Entrance requirements:* For master's, GRE, minimum GPA of 3.0, statement of purpose. Additional exam requirements/recommendations for international students: Required—

TOEFL (minimum score 85 iBT), IELTS (minimum score 6.5). *Application deadline:* For fall admission, 8/2 for domestic students, 4/15 for international students; for spring admission, 12/1 for domestic students, 10/5 for international students. Electronic applications accepted. *Expenses:* Contact institution. *Financial support:* Research assistantships and teaching assistantships available. *Unit head:* Dr. David Ferguson, Chair, 631-632-8763, E-mail: david.ferguson@stonybrook.edu. *Application contact:* Marypat Taveras, Coordinator, 631-632-8762, Fax: 631-632-7809, E-mail: marypat.taveras@stonybrook.edu.
Website: http://www.stonybrook.edu/est/graduate/msedtech.shtml

Teachers College, Columbia University, Department of Mathematics, Science and Technology, New York, NY 10027-6696. Offers biology 7-12 (MA); chemistry 7-12 (MA); communication and education (MA, Ed D); computing in education (MA); earth science 7-12 (MA); instructional technology and media (Ed M, MA, Ed D); mathematics education (Ed M, MA, Ed D, Ed DCT, PhD); physics 7-12 (MA); science and dental education (MA); science education (Ed M, MS, Ed DCT, PhD); supervisor/teacher of science education (MA); technology specialist (MA). *Program availability:* Part-time, evening/weekend, online learning. *Students:* 195 full-time (133 women), 222 part-time (139 women); includes 152 minority (44 Black or African American, non-Hispanic/Latino; 66 Asian, non-Hispanic/Latino; 32 Hispanic/Latino; 10 Two or more races, non-Hispanic/Latino), 106 international. 368 applicants, 65% accepted, 123 enrolled. Terminal master's awarded for partial completion of doctoral program. *Degree requirements:* For doctorate, thesis/dissertation. *Expenses: Tuition:* Full-time $36,288; part-time $1512 per credit. *Required fees:* $438 per semester. One-time fee: $510 full-time. Full-time tuition and fees vary according to course load. *Unit head:* Dr. O. Roger Anderson, Chair, 212-678-3405, Fax: 212-678-8129, E-mail: ora@ldeo.columbia.edu. *Application contact:* David Estrella, Director of Admission, 212-678-3305, E-mail: estrella@tc.columbia.edu.
Website: http://www.tc.columbia.edu/mathematics-science-and-technology/

Thomas College, Graduate School, Programs in Business, Waterville, ME 04901-5097. Offers business (MBA); computer technology education (MS); education (MS); human resource management (MBA). *Program availability:* Part-time, evening/weekend. *Entrance requirements:* For master's, GMAT, GRE, MAT or minimum GPA of 3.3 in first 3 graduate-level courses. Additional exam requirements/recommendations for international students: Recommended—TOEFL.

University of Bridgeport, School of Education, Department of Education, Bridgeport, CT 06604. Offers education (MS); educational management (Ed D, Diploma), including intermediate administrator or supervisor (Diploma), leadership (Ed D); elementary education (MS, Diploma), including early childhood education, elementary education; middle school education (MS); music education (MS); remedial reading and language arts (Diploma); secondary education (MS, Diploma), including computer specialist (Diploma), international education (Diploma), reading specialist, secondary education. *Program availability:* Part-time, evening/weekend. *Degree requirements:* For master's, final exam, final project, or thesis; for doctorate, comprehensive exam, thesis/dissertation; for Diploma, thesis or alternative, final project. *Entrance requirements:* For master's, minimum undergraduate QPA of 2.67; for doctorate, GRE, MAT; for Diploma, GRE General Test or MAT, minimum graduate QPA of 3.0. Additional exam requirements/recommendations for international students: Recommended—TOEFL (minimum score 550 paper-based; 80 iBT), IELTS (minimum score 6.5). Electronic applications accepted. *Expenses:* Contact institution.

University of Illinois at Chicago, Program in Learning Sciences, Chicago, IL 60607-7128. Offers PhD.

University of Phoenix–Central Valley Campus, College of Education, Fresno, CA 93720-1552. Offers curriculum and instruction (MA Ed); curriculum and instruction-computer education (MA Ed); elementary teacher education (MA Ed); secondary teacher education (MA Ed).

University of Phoenix–North Florida Campus, College of Education, Jacksonville, FL 32216-0959. Offers administration and supervision (MA Ed); curriculum and instruction (MA Ed), including computer education, mathematics education; early childhood education (MA Ed); elementary teacher education (MA Ed); secondary teacher education (MA Ed). *Program availability:* Evening/weekend. *Degree requirements:* For master's, thesis (for some programs). *Entrance requirements:* For master's, 3 years of work experience, minimum undergraduate GPA of 2.5. Additional exam requirements/recommendations for international students: Required—TOEFL (minimum score 550 paper-based; 49 iBT). Electronic applications accepted.

University of Phoenix–Online Campus, College of Education, Phoenix, AZ 85034-7209. Offers administration and supervision (MAEd, Certificate); adult education and training (MAEd); curriculum and instruction (MAEd), including computer education, curriculum and instruction, English as a second language, language arts, mathematics, reading; early childhood education (MAEd); educational studies (MAEd); elementary teacher education (MAEd), including early childhood, elementary teacher education, high school middle level, middle level; principal licensure (Certificate); secondary teacher education (MAEd); special education (MAEd, Certificate); teacher education (MAEd), including middle level generalist; teacher education middle level mathematics (MAEd), including middle level mathematics; teacher education middle level science (MAEd), including middle level science; teacher education secondary mathematics (MAEd); teacher education secondary science (MAEd); teacher leadership (MAEd); teachers of English learners (Certificate); transition to teaching (Certificate), including elementary education, secondary education. *Program availability:* Evening/weekend, online learning. *Entrance requirements:* Additional exam requirements/recommendations for international students: Required—TOEFL, TOEIC (Test of English as an International Communication), Berlitz Online English Proficiency Exam, PTE, or IELTS. Electronic applications accepted. *Expenses:* Contact institution.

University of Phoenix–San Diego Campus, College of Education, San Diego, CA 92123. Offers curriculum and instruction (MA Ed), including computer education, curriculum and instruction, English as a second language; elementary teacher education (MA Ed); secondary teacher education (MA Ed). *Program availability:* Evening/weekend. *Degree requirements:* For master's, thesis (for some programs). *Entrance requirements:* For master's, 3 years of work experience, minimum undergraduate GPA of 3.0. Additional exam requirements/recommendations for international students: Required—TOEFL (minimum score 550 paper-based; 79 iBT). Electronic applications accepted.

University of Phoenix–South Florida Campus, College of Education, Miramar, FL 33027-4145. Offers administration and supervision (MA Ed); curriculum and instruction (MA Ed), including computer education, curriculum and instruction, mathematics education; early childhood education (MA Ed); elementary teacher education (MA Ed); secondary teacher education (MA Ed). *Program availability:* Evening/weekend. *Degree requirements:* For master's, thesis (for some programs). *Entrance requirements:* For master's, 3 years of work experience, minimum undergraduate GPA of 2.5. Additional exam requirements/recommendations for international students: Required—TOEFL (minimum score 550 paper-based; 79 iBT). Electronic applications accepted.

University of Phoenix–Washington D.C. Campus, College of Education, Washington, DC 20001. Offers administration and supervision (MA Ed); adult education and training (MA Ed); computer education (MA Ed); curriculum and instruction (MA Ed, Ed D); early childhood education (MA Ed); education (Ed S); educational leadership (Ed D); educational technology (Ed D); elementary teacher education (MA Ed); English and language arts education (MA Ed); English as a second language (MA Ed); higher education administration (PhD); mathematics education (MA Ed); secondary teacher education (MA Ed); special education (MA Ed); teacher leadership (MA Ed).

Counselor Education

Acadia University, Faculty of Professional Studies, School of Education, Program in Counseling, Wolfville, NS B4P 2R6, Canada. Offers M Ed. *Program availability:* Part-time. *Degree requirements:* For master's, thesis optional. *Entrance requirements:* For master's, B Ed, minimum B average in undergraduate course work, 2 years of teaching or related experience. Additional exam requirements/recommendations for international students: Required—TOEFL (minimum score 580 paper-based; 93 iBT), IELTS (minimum score 6.5). *Faculty research:* Computer-assisted supervision, rural/remote school counseling, non-custodial fathers, spirituality, counseling relationships.

Adams State University, The Graduate School, Department of Counselor Education, Alamosa, CO 81101. Offers counseling (MA). *Accreditation:* ACA. *Program availability:* Part-time. *Degree requirements:* For master's, internship, qualifying exam. *Entrance requirements:* For master's, GRE General Test or MAT, minimum undergraduate GPA of 2.75.

Adler Graduate School, Program in Adlerian Counseling and Psychotherapy, Richfield, MN 55423. Offers Adlerian studies (MA); art therapy (MA); clinical mental health counseling (MA); co-occurring mental health and substance abuse disorders (MA); marriage and family therapy (MA); school counseling (MA). *Program availability:* Part-time, evening/weekend. *Faculty:* 71 part-time/adjunct (55 women). *Students:* 298 part-time (225 women); includes 51 minority (40 Black or African American, non-Hispanic/Latino; 6 American Indian or Alaska Native, non-Hispanic/Latino; 5 Hispanic/Latino). *Degree requirements:* For master's, thesis or alternative, 500-700 hour internship (depending on license choice). *Entrance requirements:* For master's, interview, official transcripts, minimum cumulative GPA of 3.0. *Application deadline:* Applications are processed on a rolling basis. Application fee: $50. Electronic applications accepted. *Financial support:* Career-related internships or fieldwork and tuition waivers available. Support available to part-time students. Financial award applicants required to submit FAFSA. *Unit head:* Dr. Dan Haugen, President, 612-767-7048, Fax: 612-861-7559, E-mail: haugen@alfredadler.edu. *Application contact:* Evelyn B. Haas, Director of Admissions, 612-767-7044, Fax: 612-861-7559, E-mail: ev@alfredadler.edu.

Adler University, Programs in Psychology, Chicago, IL 60602. Offers advanced Adlerian psychotherapy (Certificate); art therapy (MA); clinical mental health counseling (MA); clinical neuropsychology (Certificate); clinical psychology (Psy D); community psychology (MA); counseling and organizational psychology (MA); counseling psychology (MA); counselor education and supervision (PhD); couple and family therapy (DCFT); criminology (MA); emergency management leadership (MA); forensic psychology (MA); marriage and family counseling (MA); marriage and family therapy (Certificate); military psychology (MA); nonprofit management (MA); organizational psychology (MA); police psychology (MA); public policy and administration (MA); rehabilitation counseling (MA); sport and health psychology (MA); substance abuse counseling (Certificate); Psy D/Certificate; Psy D/MACAT; Psy D/MACP; Psy D/MAMFC; Psy D/MASAC. *Accreditation:* APA. *Program availability:* Part-time, evening/weekend, online learning. Terminal master's awarded for partial completion of doctoral program. *Degree requirements:* For master's, thesis or alternative, oral exam, practicum; for doctorate, thesis/dissertation, clinical exam, internship, oral exam, practicum, written qualifying exam. *Entrance requirements:* For master's, 12 semester hours in psychology, minimum GPA of 3.0; for doctorate, 18 semester hours in psychology, minimum GPA of 3.25; for Certificate, appropriate master's or doctoral degree. Additional exam requirements/recommendations for international students: Required—TOEFL (minimum score 550 paper-based; 79 iBT). Electronic applications accepted.

Alabama Agricultural and Mechanical University, School of Graduate Studies, College of Education, Humanities, and Behavioral Sciences, Department of Social Work, Psychology and Counseling, Huntsville, AL 35811. Offers psychology and counseling (MS, Ed S), including clinical psychology (MS), counseling psychology (MS), guidance and counseling, rehabilitation counseling (MS), school counseling (MS), school psychology (MS), school psychometry (MS); social work (MSW). *Accreditation:* CORE; NCATE. *Program availability:* Part-time, evening/weekend. *Degree requirements:* For master's, comprehensive exam. *Entrance requirements:* For master's, GRE General Test. Additional exam requirements/recommendations for international students: Required—TOEFL (minimum score 500 paper-based; 61 iBT). *Application deadline:* For fall admission, 5/1 for domestic students. Application fee: $15 ($20 for international students). *Expenses:* Tuition, nonresident: part-time $826 per credit hour. Full-time tuition and fees vary according to course load and program. *Financial support:* Career-related internships or fieldwork available. Support available to part-time students. Financial award application deadline: 4/1. *Faculty research:* Increasing numbers of minorities in special education and speech-language pathology. *Unit head:* Dr. Shirley King, Chair, 256-372-5520, Fax: 256-372-5526.

Alabama State University, College of Education, Department of Instructional Support Programs, Montgomery, AL 36101-0271. Offers counselor education (M Ed, MS, Ed S), including general counseling (MS, Ed S), school counseling (M Ed, Ed S); educational administration (M Ed, Ed D, Ed S), including educational administration (Ed S), educational leadership, policy and law (Ed D), instructional leadership (M Ed); library education media (M Ed, Ed S). *Program availability:* Part-time. *Faculty:* 11 full-time (6 women), 7 part-time/adjunct (5 women). *Students:* 50 full-time (32 women), 128 part-time (95 women); includes 167 minority (166 Black or African American, non-Hispanic/Latino; 1 Two or more races, non-Hispanic/Latino), 3 international. Average age 37. 84

applicants, 50% accepted, 16 enrolled. In 2016, 39 master's, 19 doctorates, 5 other advanced degrees awarded. *Degree requirements:* For master's, comprehensive exam; for Ed S, comprehensive exam, thesis. *Entrance requirements:* For master's, GRE General Test, MAT, writing competency test, bachelor's degree or its equivalent from accredited college or university with minimum GPA of 2.5; for Ed S, GRE General Test, MAT, writing competency test, minimum GPA of 3.25. Additional exam requirements/ recommendations for international students: Required—TOEFL (minimum score 500 paper-based). *Application deadline:* For fall admission, 4/15 for domestic and international students; for spring admission, 11/15 for domestic and international students; for summer admission, 3/15 for domestic and international students. Applications are processed on a rolling basis. Application fee: $25. Electronic applications accepted. *Expenses:* Tuition, state resident: full-time $3087; part-time $2744 per credit. Tuition, nonresident: full-time $6174; part-time $5488 per credit. *Required fees:* $2284; $1142 per credit. $571 per semester. Tuition and fees vary according to class time, course level, course load, degree level, program and student level. *Financial support:* In 2016–17, 3 students received support. Research assistantships and unspecified assistantships available. Financial award application deadline: 6/30; financial award applicants required to submit FAFSA. *Unit head:* Dr. Necoal Driver, Chair, 334-229-4456, Fax: 334-229-6831, E-mail: ndriver@alasu.edu. *Application contact:* Dr. William Person, Dean of Graduate Studies, 334-229-4275, Fax: 334-229-4928, E-mail: wperson@alasu.edu.
Website: http://www.alasu.edu/academics/colleges—departments/college-of-education/instructional-support-programs/index.aspx

Albany State University, College of Education, Albany, GA 31705-2717. Offers early childhood education (M Ed); educational leadership (Ed S); health and physical education (M Ed); middle grades education (M Ed); school counseling (M Ed); special education (M Ed). *Accreditation:* NCATE. *Program availability:* Part-time, evening/ weekend, online learning. *Degree requirements:* For master's, comprehensive exam, internship, GACE Content Exam. *Entrance requirements:* For master's, GRE or MAT. *Application deadline:* For fall admission, 6/1 for domestic students, 5/1 for international students; for spring admission, 11/1 for domestic students, 10/1 for international students. Applications are processed on a rolling basis. Application fee: $20. Electronic applications accepted. *Financial support:* Scholarships/grants available. Financial award application deadline: 4/15; financial award applicants required to submit FAFSA. *Faculty research:* GACE preparation, STEM (science, technology, engineering, and mathematics), technology education, special education, professional teacher development, health implications liberation philosophy, NET-Q, learning community, disabled or at-risk students. *Unit head:* Dr. Rhonda C. Porter, Interim Dean, 229-430-1718, Fax: 229-430-4993. *Application contact:* Jeffrey Pierce, II, Graduate Admissions Counselor, 229-430-4646, Fax: 229-430-4105, E-mail: jeffrey.pierce@asurams.edu.
Website: https://www.asurams.edu/Academics/collegeofeducation/

Alcorn State University, School of Graduate Studies, School of Psychology and Education, Lorman, MS 39096-7500. Offers agricultural education (MS Ed); elementary education (MS Ed, Ed S); guidance and counseling (MS Ed); industrial education (MS Ed); secondary education (MS Ed), including health and physical education; special education (MS Ed). *Accreditation:* NCATE. *Degree requirements:* For master's, thesis optional.

Alfred University, Graduate School, Counseling and School Psychology Program, Alfred, NY 14802-1205. Offers mental health counseling (MS Ed); school counseling (MS Ed, CAS); school psychology (MA, Psy D, CAS). *Accreditation:* APA. *Faculty:* 10 full-time (3 women), 4 part-time/adjunct (2 women). *Students:* 43 full-time (35 women), 40 part-time (31 women); includes 11 minority (6 Black or African American, non-Hispanic/Latino; 1 Asian, non-Hispanic/Latino; 4 Hispanic/Latino), 1 international. Average age 25. 40 applicants, 80% accepted, 24 enrolled. In 2016, 85 master's, 8 doctorates, 18 other advanced degrees awarded. *Degree requirements:* For master's, internship; for doctorate, thesis/dissertation, internship. *Entrance requirements:* For master's and doctorate, GRE General Test. Additional exam requirements/ recommendations for international students: Required—TOEFL (minimum score 590 paper-based; 90 iBT), IELTS (minimum score 6.5). *Application deadline:* For fall admission, 1/15 priority date for domestic and international students. Application fee: $60. Electronic applications accepted. *Expenses: Tuition:* Full-time $38,020; part-time $810 per credit. *Required fees:* $970; $82 per semester. *Financial support:* Research assistantships with partial tuition reimbursements, career-related internships or fieldwork, and unspecified assistantships available. Financial award application deadline: 8/1; financial award applicants required to submit FAFSA. *Faculty research:* Family processes, alternative assessment approaches, behavior disorders in children, parent involvement, school psychology training issues. *Unit head:* Dr. Nancy Evangelista, Chair, 607-871-2212, E-mail: fevangel@alfred.edu. *Application contact:* Sara Love, Coordinator of Graduate Admissions, 607-871-2115, Fax: 607-871-2198, E-mail: gradinquiry@alfred.edu.

Alliant International University–San Francisco, California School of Professional Psychology, Program in Clinical Counseling, San Francisco, CA 94133. Offers MA. *Degree requirements:* For master's, comprehensive exam, project. *Entrance requirements:* For master's, minimum GPA of 3.0, recommendations, essay, interview. Additional exam requirements/recommendations for international students: Required—TOEFL (minimum score 550 paper-based; 80 iBT), TWE (minimum score 5). Electronic applications accepted. *Faculty research:* Systems of privilege and oppression, multicultural and social justice advocacy competence, rural issues, LGBTQ affirmative therapy and identity development, college student mental health.

American International College, School of Education, Springfield, MA 01109-3189. Offers early childhood education (M Ed, CAGS); elementary education (M Ed, CAGS); middle education/secondary education (M Ed, CAGS); moderate disabilities (M Ed, CAGS); reading specialist (M Ed, CAGS); school adjustment counseling (MAEP, CAGS); school guidance counseling (MAEP, CAGS); school leadership (M Ed, CAGS). *Program availability:* Evening/weekend. *Faculty:* 1 (woman) full-time, 90 part-time/ adjunct (63 women). *Students:* 1,194 full-time (970 women), 118 part-time (83 women); includes 108 minority (15 Black or African American, non-Hispanic/Latino; 4 American Indian or Alaska Native, non-Hispanic/Latino; 12 Asian, non-Hispanic/Latino; 55 Hispanic/Latino; 2 Native Hawaiian or other Pacific Islander, non-Hispanic/Latino; 20 Two or more races, non-Hispanic/Latino). Average age 34. 517 applicants, 417 enrolled. In 2016, 879 master's, 194 CAGSs awarded. Terminal master's awarded for partial completion of doctoral program. *Degree requirements:* For master's, comprehensive exam (for some programs), thesis (for some programs), practicum/culminating experience; for CAGS, practicum/culminating experience. *Entrance requirements:* For master's, Communication and Literacy portion of the Massachusetts Tests for Education Licensure, graduate of accredited four-year college with minimum B- average in undergraduate course work; for CAGS, M Ed or master's degree in field related to licensure from accredited institution. *Application deadline:* Applications are processed on a rolling basis. Application fee: $50. Electronic applications accepted. *Expenses:* $439 per credit. *Financial support:* Applicants required to submit FAFSA. *Unit head:* Sylvia Mason, Dean, 413-205-1743, Fax: 413-205-3943, E-mail: sylvia.mason@aic.edu. *Application contact:* Kerry Barnes, Dean of Graduate Admissions, 413-205-3703, Fax: 413-205-3051, E-mail: kerry.barnes@aic.edu.
Website: http://www.aic.edu/school-of-education/

Amridge University, Graduate and Professional Programs, Montgomery, AL 36117. Offers Biblical studies (MA, PhD); Christian ministry (MS); family therapy (D Min); human services (MS); leadership and management (MS); marriage and family therapy (M Div, MA, PhD); ministerial leadership (M Div, MS); New Testament studies (MA); Old Testament studies (MA); professional counseling (M Div, MA, PhD); theology (M Div, D Min). *Program availability:* Part-time, evening/weekend, online learning. *Faculty:* 22 full-time (3 women), 10 part-time/adjunct (6 women). *Students:* 81 full-time (49 women), 225 part-time (137 women); includes 81 minority (80 Black or African American, non-Hispanic/Latino; 1 Hispanic/Latino). Average age 41. 122 applicants, 100% accepted, 79 enrolled. *Degree requirements:* For master's, one foreign language, comprehensive exam (for some programs), thesis (for some programs); for doctorate, one foreign language, comprehensive exam (for some programs), thesis/dissertation (for some programs). *Entrance requirements:* For master's, official transcript showing an earned 4-year BA or BS from regionally- or nationally-accredited institution; for doctorate, official transcript showing earned graduate degree from regionally- or nationally-accredited institution; writing sample (e.g. career monograph, published journal article, term paper from master's degree or doctoral dissertation); interview. Additional exam requirements/ recommendations for international students: Required—TOEFL (minimum score 79 iBT). *Application deadline:* Applications are processed on a rolling basis. Application fee: $50. Electronic applications accepted. *Expenses: Tuition:* Full-time $12,870; part-time $715 per credit hour. *Required fees:* $1300; $650 per semester. *Financial support:* In 2016–17, 45 students received support. Federal Work-Study and scholarships/grants available. Support available to part-time students. Financial award applicants required to submit FAFSA. *Faculty research:* Technology and mental healthcare, resilience in black families, theology and congregational ministry. *Unit head:* Laina Costanza, Vice President, Student Affairs, 888-790-8080 Ext. 1, Fax: 334-387-3878, E-mail: cc@amridgeuniversity.edu. *Application contact:* Brooks Housley, Student Affairs Coordinator, 888-790-8080 Ext. 1, Fax: 334-387-3878, E-mail: admissions@amridgeuniversity.edu.

Angelo State University, College of Graduate Studies and Research, College of Education, Department of Curriculum and Instruction, San Angelo, TX 76909. Offers curriculum and instruction (MA); educational administration (M Ed); guidance and counseling (M Ed); student development and leadership in higher education (M Ed). *Program availability:* Part-time, evening/weekend, online learning. *Students:* 400 full-time (328 women), 396 part-time (325 women); includes 242 minority (80 Black or African American, non-Hispanic/Latino; 2 American Indian or Alaska Native, non-Hispanic/Latino; 6 Asian, non-Hispanic/Latino; 148 Hispanic/Latino; 6 Two or more races, non-Hispanic/Latino), 1 international. Average age 35. *Application deadline:* For fall admission, 7/15 priority date for domestic students, 6/10 for international students; for spring admission, 12/1 priority date for domestic students, 11/1 for international students. Application fee: $40 ($50 for international students). *Expenses:* Tuition, state resident: full-time $3726; part-time $2484 per year. Tuition, nonresident: full-time $10,746; part-time $7164 per year. *Required fees:* $2538; $1702 per unit. *Unit head:* Dr. Jim Summerlin, Chair, 325-942-2647, Fax: 325-942-2039, E-mail: james.summerlin@angelo.edu. *Application contact:* Lesley Casarez, Graduate Advisor, 325-486-6775, E-mail: lesley.casarez@angelo.edu.
Website: http://www.angelo.edu/dept/ci/

Appalachian State University, Cratis D. Williams Graduate School, Department of Human Development and Psychological Counseling, Boone, NC 28608. Offers clinical mental health counseling (MA); college student development (MA); marriage and family therapy (MA); school counseling (MA). *Accreditation:* AAMFT/COAMFTE; ACA; NCATE. *Program availability:* Part-time. *Degree requirements:* For master's, comprehensive exam (for some programs), thesis optional, internships. *Entrance requirements:* For master's, GRE General Test, 3 letters of recommendation. Additional exam requirements/recommendations for international students: Required—TOEFL (minimum score 570 paper-based; 79 iBT), IELTS (minimum score 6.5). *Application deadline:* For fall admission, 2/1 priority date for domestic students, 2/1 for international students; for spring admission, 2/1 for international students. Applications are processed on a rolling basis. Application fee: $55. Electronic applications accepted. *Expenses:* Tuition, state resident: full-time $4744. Tuition, nonresident: full-time $17,913. Full-time tuition and fees vary according to program. *Financial support:* Fellowships, research assistantships, teaching assistantships, career-related internships or fieldwork, Federal Work-Study, scholarships/grants, and unspecified assistantships available. Financial award application deadline: 4/1; financial award applicants required to submit FAFSA. *Faculty research:* Multicultural counseling, addictions counseling, play therapy, expressive arts, child and adolescent therapy, sexual abuse counseling. *Unit head:* Dr. Lee Baruth, Chairman, 828-262-2055, E-mail: baruthlg@appstate.edu. *Application contact:* Dr. Mark Schwarze, Program Director, 828-262-6046, E-mail: asucmhc@appstate.edu.
Website: http://www.ced.appstate.edu/departments/hpc

Argosy University, Atlanta, Georgia School of Professional Psychology, Atlanta, GA 30328. Offers clinical psychology (MA, Psy D, Postdoctoral Respecialization Certificate), including child and family psychology (Psy D), general adult clinical (Psy D), health psychology (Psy D), neuropsychology/geropsychology (Psy D); community counseling (MA), including marriage and family therapy; counselor education and supervision (Ed D); forensic psychology (MA); industrial organizational psychology (MA); marriage and family therapy (Certificate); sport-exercise psychology (MA). *Accreditation:* APA.

Argosy University, Chicago, Illinois School of Professional Psychology, Program in Counseling Psychology, Chicago, IL 60601. Offers counselor education and supervision (Ed D). *Accreditation:* ACA. *Program availability:* Online learning.

Argosy University, Dallas, College of Psychology and Behavioral Sciences, Program in Counselor Education and Supervision, Farmers Branch, TX 75244. Offers Ed D.

Argosy University, Denver, College of Psychology and Behavioral Sciences, Denver, CO 80231. Offers clinical mental health counseling (MA); clinical psychology (MA, Psy D); counseling psychology (Ed D); counselor education and supervision (Ed D); forensic psychology (MA); industrial organizational psychology (MA); marriage and family therapy (MA, DMFT).

Argosy University, Nashville, College of Psychology and Behavioral Sciences, Program in Counselor Education and Supervision, Nashville, TN 37214. Offers Ed D.

Argosy University, Northern Virginia, American School of Professional Psychology, Arlington, VA 22209. Offers clinical psychology (MA, Psy D), including child and family psychology (Psy D), diversity and multicultural psychology (Psy D), forensic psychology (Psy D), health and neuropsychology (Psy D); community counseling (MA); counseling psychology (Ed D), including counselor education and supervision; counselor education and supervision (Ed D); forensic psychology (MA).

Argosy University, Salt Lake City, College of Psychology and Behavioral Sciences, Draper, UT 84020. Offers counseling psychology (Ed D); counselor education and supervision (Ed D); forensic psychology (MA); marriage and family therapy (MA, DMFT); mental health counseling (MA).

Argosy University, Sarasota, College of Education, Sarasota, FL 34235. Offers community college executive leadership (Ed D); educational leadership (MA Ed, Ed D, Ed S), including higher education administration (Ed D), K-12 education (Ed D); school counseling (MA, Ed S); school psychology (MA); teaching and learning (MA Ed, Ed D, Ed S), including education technology (Ed D), higher education (Ed D), K-12 education (Ed D).

Argosy University, Sarasota, College of Psychology and Behavioral Sciences, Sarasota, FL 34235. Offers community counseling (MA); counseling psychology (Ed D); counselor education and supervision (Ed D); forensic psychology (MA); marriage and family therapy (MA); mental health counseling (MA); pastoral community counseling (Ed D).

Argosy University, Tampa, College of Education, Tampa, FL 33607. Offers community college executive leadership (Ed D); educational leadership (MA Ed, Ed D, Ed S), including higher education administration (Ed D), K-12 education (Ed D); school counseling (MA); teaching and learning (MA Ed, Ed D, Ed S), including higher education (Ed D), K-12 education (Ed D).

Argosy University, Tampa, Florida School of Professional Psychology, Tampa, FL 33607. Offers clinical psychology (MA, Psy D), including clinical psychology; counselor education and supervision (Ed D); industrial organizational psychology (MA); marriage and family therapy (MA); mental health counseling (MA).

Arizona State University at the Tempe campus, School of Letters and Sciences, Program in Counseling, Tempe, AZ 85287-0811. Offers MC. *Accreditation:* ACA. *Degree requirements:* For master's, comprehensive exam (for some programs), thesis (for some programs), interactive Program of Study (iPOS) submitted before completing 50 percent of required credit hours. *Entrance requirements:* For master's, GRE, minimum GPA of 3.0 or equivalent in last 2 years of work leading to bachelor's degree; 3 letters of recommendation; 3-5 page personal statement with information on significant life experiences, professional experiences and goals. Additional exam requirements/recommendations for international students: Required—TOEFL, IELTS, or PTE. Electronic applications accepted.

Arkansas State University, Graduate School, College of Education and Behavioral Science, Department of Psychology and Counseling, State University, AR 72467. Offers clinical mental health counseling (Graduate Certificate); college student personnel services (MS); dyslexia therapy (Graduate Certificate); psychological science (MS); psychology and counseling (Ed S); rehabilitation counseling (MRC); school counseling (MSE); student affairs (Graduate Certificate). *Accreditation:* ACA (one or more programs are accredited); CORE (one or more programs are accredited); NCATE. *Program availability:* Part-time. *Degree requirements:* For master's and other advanced degree, comprehensive exam, thesis or alternative. *Entrance requirements:* For master's, GRE General Test or MAT (for MSE), appropriate bachelor's degree, interview, letters of reference, official transcripts, immunization records, written statement, 2-3 page autobiography; for other advanced degree, GRE General Test, interview, master's degree, letters of reference, official transcript, personal statement, immunization records. Additional exam requirements/recommendations for international students: Required—TOEFL (minimum score 550 paper-based; 79 iBT), IELTS (minimum score 6), PTE (minimum score 56). Electronic applications accepted.

Arkansas Tech University, College of Education, Russellville, AR 72801. Offers college student personnel (MS); educational leadership (M Ed, Ed S); elementary education (M Ed); instructional improvement (M Ed); instructional technology (M Ed); school counseling and leadership (M Ed); school leadership (Ed D); strength and conditioning studies (MS); teaching (MAT); teaching, learning, and leadership (M Ed). *Accreditation:* NCATE. *Program availability:* Part-time, evening/weekend, online learning. *Students:* 72 full-time (43 women), 371 part-time (283 women); includes 108 minority (80 Black or African American, non-Hispanic/Latino; 1 American Indian or Alaska Native, non-Hispanic/Latino; 4 Asian, non-Hispanic/Latino; 13 Hispanic/Latino; 10 Two or more races, non-Hispanic/Latino), 6 international. Average age 33. In 2016, 181 master's, 1 other advanced degree awarded. *Degree requirements:* For master's, comprehensive exam, thesis optional, action research project. *Entrance requirements:* Additional exam requirements/recommendations for international students: Required—TOEFL (minimum score 550 paper-based; 79 iBT), IELTS (minimum score 6.5). *Application deadline:* For fall admission, 3/1 priority date for domestic students, 5/1 priority date for international students; for spring admission, 10/1 priority date for domestic and international students. Applications are processed on a rolling basis. Application fee: $25 ($75 for international students). Electronic applications accepted. *Expenses:* Tuition, state resident: full-time $4932; part-time $274 per credit hour. Tuition, nonresident: full-time $9864; part-time $548 per credit hour. *Required fees:* $513 per semester. Tuition and fees vary according to course load. *Financial support:* In 2016–17, research assistantships with full tuition reimbursements (averaging $4,800 per year), teaching assistantships with full tuition reimbursements (averaging $4,800 per year) were awarded; career-related internships or fieldwork, Federal Work-Study, scholarships/grants, health care benefits, and unspecified assistantships also available. Support available to part-time students. Financial award application deadline: 4/15; financial award applicants required to submit FAFSA. *Unit head:* Dr. Mary Gunter, Dean, 479-964-3217, E-mail: mgunter@atu.edu.
Website: http://www.atu.edu/education/

Ashland Theological Seminary, Graduate Programs, Ashland, OH 44805. Offers Biblical studies (MA); Christian ministries (MACM), including Black church studies (MACM, D Min), general Christian ministries, leadership, spiritual formation (MACM, D Min); clinical mental health counseling (MA); counseling (MAC); historical and theological studies (MA), including Anabaptism and Pietism, Christian theology, church history, New Testament, Old Testament; ministry (D Min), including Black church studies (MACM, D Min), chaplaincy (M Div, D Min), independent design, spiritual formation (MACM, D Min), transformational leadership; pastoral ministry (M Div), including chaplaincy (M Div, D Min), general ministry. MAC program offered in Detroit, MI. *Accreditation:* ATS. *Program availability:* Part-time. *Degree requirements:* For master's, 2 foreign languages, comprehensive exam (for some programs), thesis (for some programs); for doctorate, thesis/dissertation. *Entrance requirements:* For master's, bachelor's degree from accredited institution with a minimum undergraduate GPA of 2.75; for doctorate, M Div, minimum undergraduate GPA of 3.0. Additional exam requirements/recommendations for international students: Required—TOEFL (minimum score 500 paper-based; 65 iBT). *Application deadline:* For fall admission, 8/30 for domestic students. Applications are processed on a rolling basis. Application fee: $35. Electronic applications accepted. *Expenses: Tuition:* Full-time $15,120; part-time $630 per semester hour. Tuition and fees vary according to program. *Financial support:* Research assistantships, teaching assistantships, career-related internships or fieldwork, institutionally sponsored loans, scholarships/grants, and unspecified assistantships available. Support available to part-time students. Financial award application deadline: 5/15; financial award applicants required to submit FAFSA. *Faculty research:* Semitic languages and linguistics, rhetorical and social-scientific criticism, Anabaptist studies, inner spiritual healing, African-American clergy in film and literature. *Unit head:* Dr. Mark Harden, President, 419-289-5160, Fax: 419-289-5969, E-mail: mharden@ashland.edu. *Application contact:* Dr. Mark Harden, President, 419-289-5160, Fax: 419-289-5969, E-mail: mharden@ashland.edu.

Athabasca University, Program in Counseling, Athabasca, AB T9S 3A3, Canada. Offers applied psychology (Post Master's Certificate); art therapy (MC); career counseling (MC); counseling (Advanced Certificate); counseling psychology (MC); school counseling (MC).

Auburn University at Montgomery, College of Education, Department of Counselor, Leadership, and Special Education, Montgomery, AL 36124-4023. Offers counselor education (M Ed, Ed S), including clinical mental health counseling, school counseling; early childhood special education (M Ed); instructional leadership (M Ed, Ed S); special education/collaborative teacher (M Ed, Ed S). *Accreditation:* ACA; NCATE. *Program availability:* Part-time, evening/weekend. *Faculty:* 9 full-time (7 women), 3 part-time/adjunct (all women). *Students:* 7 full-time (5 women), 28 part-time (all women); includes 11 minority (10 Black or African American, non-Hispanic/Latino; 1 Asian, non-Hispanic/Latino). Average age 35. In 2016, 35 master's, 9 Ed Ss awarded. *Degree requirements:* For master's and Ed S, comprehensive exam. *Entrance requirements:* For master's, GRE General Test or MAT, certification, BS in teaching; for Ed S, GRE General Test or MAT, certification. Additional exam requirements/recommendations for international students: Recommended—TOEFL (minimum score 500 paper-based; 61 iBT), IELTS (minimum score 5.5), TSE (minimum score 44). *Application deadline:* Applications are processed on a rolling basis. Electronic applications accepted. *Expenses:* Tuition, state resident: full-time $6462; part-time $359 per credit hour. Tuition, nonresident: full-time $14,526; part-time $807 per credit hour. *Required fees:* $554. *Financial support:* Career-related internships or fieldwork and scholarships/grants available. Support available to part-time students. Financial award application deadline: 3/1; financial award applicants required to submit FAFSA. *Unit head:* Dr. Samuel Flynt, Head, 334-244-3835, Fax: 334-244-3101, E-mail: sflynt@aum.edu. *Application contact:* Dr. Rhonda Morton, Associate Dean/Graduate Coordinator, 334-244-3287, Fax: 334-244-3978, E-mail: rmorton@aum.edu.
Website: http://education.aum.edu/academic-departments/counselor-leadership-and-special-education

Augusta University, The Graduate School, College of Education, Department of Counselor Education, Leadership, and Research, Augusta, GA 30912. Offers counselor education (M Ed, Ed S), including clinical mental health counseling (M Ed), school counselor (M Ed). *Accreditation:* ACA; NCATE. *Program availability:* Part-time, evening/weekend. *Degree requirements:* For master's, comprehensive exam; for Ed S, comprehensive exam, thesis. *Entrance requirements:* For master's, GRE, MAT, minimum GPA of 2.5; for Ed S, GRE, MAT. *Application deadline:* For fall admission, 8/1 priority date for domestic students. Applications are processed on a rolling basis. Application fee: $20. *Financial support:* Career-related internships or fieldwork, Federal Work-Study, institutionally sponsored loans, and unspecified assistantships available. Support available to part-time students. Financial award application deadline: 4/15; financial award applicants required to submit FAFSA. *Faculty research:* Restructuring schools, financing education, student transition. *Unit head:* Dr. Richard Deaner, Director, 706-729-2443, E-mail: rdeaner@augusta.edu. *Application contact:* Dr. Richard Deaner, Director, 706-729-2443, E-mail: rdeaner@augusta.edu.

Austin Peay State University, College of Graduate Studies, College of Behavioral and Health Sciences, Department of Psychology, Program in School Counseling, Clarksville, TN 37044. Offers MS. *Degree requirements:* For master's, comprehensive exam. *Expenses:* Tuition, state resident: full-time $8300; part-time $415 per credit hour. Tuition, nonresident: full-time $22,280; part-time $1114 per credit hour. *Required fees:* $1473; $73.65 per credit hour. *Unit head:* Dr. Deborah Buchanan, Coordinator, 931-221-1247, E-mail: buchanand@apsu.edu. *Application contact:* Brad Averitt, Coordinator of Graduate Admissions, 800-859-4723, Fax: 931-221-7641, E-mail: gradadmissions@apsu.edu.
Website: http://www.apsu.edu/psychology/scclass

Austin Peay State University, College of Graduate Studies, College of Education, Department of Educational Specialties, Clarksville, TN 37044. Offers administration and supervision (Ed S); counseling and guidance (Ed S); curriculum and instruction (MA Ed); education leadership (MA Ed); elementary education (Ed S); reading (MA Ed); secondary education (Ed S). *Program availability:* Part-time, evening/weekend, online learning. *Faculty:* 7 full-time (4 women), 4 part-time/adjunct (3 women). *Students:* 4 full-time (3 women), 77 part-time (60 women); includes 13 minority (8 Black or African American, non-Hispanic/Latino; 1 Asian, non-Hispanic/Latino; 3 Hispanic/Latino; 1 Two or more races, non-Hispanic/Latino). Average age 37. 18 applicants, 89% accepted, 14 enrolled. In 2016, 34 master's, 9 Ed Ss awarded. *Degree requirements:* For master's, comprehensive exam, thesis optional. *Entrance requirements:* For master's, GRE General Test, MAT, minimum undergraduate GPA of 2.75. Additional exam requirements/recommendations for international students: Required—TOEFL (minimum score 500 paper-based). *Application deadline:* For fall admission, 8/9 priority date for domestic students. Applications are processed on a rolling basis. Application fee: $45 ($50 for international students). Electronic applications accepted. *Expenses:* Tuition, state resident: full-time $8300; part-time $415 per credit hour. Tuition, nonresident: full-time $22,280; part-time $1114 per credit hour. *Required fees:* $1473; $73.65 per credit hour. *Financial support:* Research assistantships with full tuition reimbursements, career-related internships or fieldwork, Federal Work-Study, institutionally sponsored loans, scholarships/grants, and unspecified assistantships available. Support available to part-time students. Financial award application deadline: 4/1; financial award applicants required to submit FAFSA. *Unit head:* Dr. Moniqueka Gold, Chair, 931-221-7696, Fax: 931-221-1292, E-mail: goldm@apsu.edu. *Application contact:* Brad Averitt, Coordinator of Graduate Admissions, 800-859-4723, Fax: 931-221-7641, E-mail: gradadmissions@apsu.edu.

Azusa Pacific University, School of Education, Department of School Counseling and School Psychology, Program in Educational Counseling, Azusa, CA 91702-7000. Offers MA.

Ball State University, Graduate School, Teachers College, Department of Counseling Psychology and Guidance Services, Program in Counseling Psychology, Muncie, IN 47306. Offers counseling (MA), including clinical mental health counseling, mental health counseling, rehabilitation counseling, school counseling; counseling psychology (PhD). *Accreditation:* ACA; APA. *Program availability:* Part-time. *Degree requirements:* For doctorate, thesis/dissertation. *Entrance requirements:* For master's, GRE General Test (minimum scores 144 quantitative, 153 verbal), minimum baccalaureate GPA of 2.75 or 3.0 in latter half of baccalauareate, minimum GPA of 3.0 in psychology coursework, three letters of recommendation; for doctorate, GRE General Test, interview, minimum graduate GPA of 3.2, resume. Additional exam requirements/recommendations for international students: Required—TOEFL (minimum score 550 paper-based; 79 iBT), IELTS (minimum score 6.5). Electronic applications accepted.

Barry University, School of Education, Program in Counseling, Miami Shores, FL 33161-6695. Offers MS, PhD, Ed S. *Accreditation:* ACA. *Program availability:* Part-time, evening/weekend. *Degree requirements:* For master's, comprehensive exam. *Entrance requirements:* For master's, GRE General Test or MAT, minimum GPA of 3.0; for doctorate, GRE, minimum GPA of 3.25; for Ed S, GRE General Test, minimum GPA of 3.0.

Counselor Education

Barry University, School of Education, Program in Mental Health Counseling, Miami Shores, FL 33161-6695. Offers MS, Ed S. *Accreditation:* ACA. *Program availability:* Part-time, evening/weekend. *Degree requirements:* For master's, comprehensive exam, scholarly paper; for Ed S, comprehensive exam. *Entrance requirements:* For master's, GRE General Test or MAT, minimum GPA of 3.0; for Ed S, GRE General Test, minimum GPA of 3.0. Electronic applications accepted.

Barry University, School of Education, Program in School Counseling, Miami Shores, FL 33161-6695. Offers MS, Ed S. *Accreditation:* ACA (one or more programs are accredited). *Program availability:* Part-time, evening/weekend. *Degree requirements:* For master's, comprehensive exam, scholarly paper; for Ed S, comprehensive exam. *Entrance requirements:* For master's, GRE General Test or MAT, minimum GPA of 3.0; for Ed S, GRE General Test, minimum GPA of 3.0. Electronic applications accepted.

Bayamón Central University, Graduate Programs, Program in Education, Bayamón, PR 00960-1725. Offers administration and supervision (MA Ed); commercial education (MA Ed); elementary education (K–3) (MA Ed); family counseling (Graduate Certificate); guidance and counseling (MA Ed); pre-elementary teacher (MA Ed); rehabilitation counseling (MA Ed); special education (MA Ed), including attention deficit disorder, education of the autistic, learning disabilities. *Program availability:* Part-time, evening/weekend. *Degree requirements:* For master's, comprehensive exam. *Entrance requirements:* For master's, EXADEP, bachelor's degree in education or related field.

Becker College, Program in Mental Health Counseling, Worcester, MA 01609. Offers community mental health (MA); school consultation (MA). *Entrance requirements:* For master's, GRE, interview, official transcript, three letters of recommendation, essay. Electronic applications accepted.

Bellevue University, Graduate School, College of Arts and Sciences, Bellevue, NE 68005-3098. Offers clinical counseling (MS); healthcare administration (MHA); human services (MA); international security and intelligence studies (MS); managerial communication (MA). *Program availability:* Online learning.

Bloomsburg University of Pennsylvania, School of Graduate Studies, College of Education, Department of Teaching and Learning, Program in Educational Leadership, Bloomsburg, PA 17815-1301. Offers college student affairs (M Ed); PreK-12 curriculum and instruction (M Ed); PreK-12 school counseling (M Ed); PreK-12 school principal (M Ed). *Faculty:* 6 full-time (2 women), 1 (woman) part-time/adjunct. *Students:* 64 full-time (42 women), 39 part-time (26 women); includes 18 minority (8 Black or African American, non-Hispanic/Latino; 4 Asian, non-Hispanic/Latino; 3 Hispanic/Latino; 1 Native Hawaiian or other Pacific Islander, non-Hispanic/Latino; 2 Two or more races, non-Hispanic/Latino), 1 international. Average age 27. 87 applicants, 60% accepted, 43 enrolled. In 2016, 39 master's awarded. *Degree requirements:* For master's, practicum. *Entrance requirements:* For master's, 3 letters of recommendation, resume, minimum QPA of 3.0, personal statement, interview. Additional exam requirements/recommendations for international students: Required—TOEFL, IELTS. Application fee: $35 ($60 for international students). Electronic applications accepted. *Expenses:* Tuition, state resident: full-time $9660; part-time $483 per credit. Tuition, nonresident: full-time $14,500; part-time $725 per credit. *Required fees:* $2410; $107 per credit. $75 per term. Tuition and fees vary according to course load, degree level and program. *Financial support:* Federal Work-Study and unspecified assistantships available. Financial award applicants required to submit FAFSA. *Unit head:* Dr. Ingrid Everett, Program Coordinator, 570-389-5120, Fax: 570-389-3030, E-mail: ieverett@bloomu.edu. *Application contact:* Jennifer Kessler, Administrative Assistant, 570-389-4015, Fax: 570-389-3054, E-mail: jkessler@bloomu.edu.

Bob Jones University, Graduate Programs, Greenville, SC 29614. Offers accountancy (MS); Bible (MA); Bible translation (MA); Biblical studies (Certificate); broadcast management (MS); business administration (MBA); church history (MA, PhD); church ministries (MA); church music (MM); cinema and video production (MA); counseling (MS); curriculum and instruction (Ed D); divinity (M Div); dramatic production (MA); educational leadership (MS, Ed D, Ed S); elementary education (M Ed, MAT); English (M Ed, MA, MAT); fine arts (MA); graphic design (MA); history (M Ed, MA); illustration (MA); interpretative speech (MA); mathematics (M Ed, MAT); medical missions (Certificate); ministry (MM, D Min); multi-categorical special education (M Ed, MAT); music (M Ed); New Testament interpretation (PhD); Old Testament interpretation (PhD); orchestral instrument performance (MM); organ performance (MM); pastoral studies (MA); personnel services (MS, Ed S); piano pedagogy (MM); piano performance (MM); platform arts (MA); radio and television broadcasting (MS); rhetoric and public address (MA); secondary education (M Ed); studio art (MA); teaching Bible (MA); theology (MA, PhD); voice performance (MM); youth ministries (MA); M Div/MM.

Boise State University, College of Education, Department of Counselor Education, Boise, ID 83725-1721. Offers MA, Graduate Certificate. *Accreditation:* ACA. *Program availability:* Part-time. *Faculty:* 14. *Students:* 36 full-time (30 women), 30 part-time (25 women); includes 8 minority (1 Asian, non-Hispanic/Latino; 6 Hispanic/Latino; 1 Two or more races, non-Hispanic/Latino). Average age 33. 74 applicants, 45% accepted, 20 enrolled. In 2016, 12 master's, 8 other advanced degrees awarded. *Degree requirements:* For master's, comprehensive exam, comprehensive portfolio, video-recorded evidence of skill. *Entrance requirements:* For master's, minimum GPA of 3.0. Additional exam requirements/recommendations for international students: Required—TOEFL (minimum score 550 paper-based; 80 iBT), IELTS (minimum score 6). *Application deadline:* For fall admission, 2/1 for domestic and international students. Application fee: $65 ($95 for international students). Electronic applications accepted. *Expenses:* Tuition, state resident: full-time $6058; part-time $358 per credit hour. Tuition, nonresident: full-time $20,108; part-time $608 per credit hour. *Required fees:* $2108. Tuition and fees vary according to program. *Financial support:* In 2016–17, 13 students received support. Scholarships/grants and unspecified assistantships available. Financial award application deadline: 2/1; financial award applicants required to submit FAFSA. *Unit head:* Dr. Diana Doumas, Department Chair, 208-426-2646, E-mail: dianadoumas@boisestate.edu. *Application contact:* Dr. Laura Gallo, Program Coordinator, 208-426-1219, E-mail: counseloreducation@boisestate.edu.
Website: http://education.boisestate.edu/counselored/

Bowie State University, Graduate Programs, Program in Guidance and Counseling, Bowie, MD 20715-9465. Offers M Ed. *Program availability:* Part-time, evening/weekend. *Degree requirements:* For master's, comprehensive exam, thesis optional, research paper. *Entrance requirements:* For master's, teaching experience, minimum GPA of 2.5, 3 recommendations. Electronic applications accepted.

Bowling Green State University, Graduate College, College of Education and Human Development, School of Intervention Services, Program in Clinical Mental Health Counseling, Bowling Green, OH 43403. Offers clinical mental health counseling (MA); school counseling (M Ed). *Accreditation:* ACA; NCATE. *Program availability:* Part-time. *Students:* 37 full-time (30 women), 24 part-time (18 women); includes 11 minority (7 Black or African American, non-Hispanic/Latino; 4 Hispanic/Latino), 1 international. Average age 30. 44 applicants, 64% accepted, 14 enrolled. In 2016, 34 degrees awarded. *Degree requirements:* For master's, thesis or alternative. *Entrance requirements:* For master's, GRE General Test. Additional exam requirements/recommendations for international students: Required—TOEFL. *Application deadline:* For fall admission, 3/1 priority date for domestic students. Applications are processed on a rolling basis. Application fee: $30. Electronic applications accepted. *Financial support:* In 2016–17, 15 research assistantships with full tuition reimbursements (averaging $5,323 per year) were awarded; teaching assistantships with full tuition reimbursements, career-related internships or fieldwork, and unspecified assistantships also available. Financial award applicants required to submit FAFSA. *Faculty research:* Perfectionism, multicultural counseling, suicide, ethics and legal issues related to counseling, play therapy. *Application contact:* Dr. Greg Garske, Graduate Coordinator, 415-372-7319.

Bradley University, The Graduate School, College of Education and Health Sciences, Department of Leadership in Education, Nonprofits and Counseling, Peoria, IL 61625-0002. Offers counseling (MA), including clinical mental health counseling, professional school counseling; leadership in educational administration (MA); nonprofit leadership (MA). *Accreditation:* ACA; NCATE. *Program availability:* Part-time, evening/weekend. *Degree requirements:* For master's, comprehensive exam, thesis optional. *Entrance requirements:* For master's, GRE General Test or MAT, interview, 3 letters of recommendation. Additional exam requirements/recommendations for international students: Required—TOEFL (minimum score 550 paper-based; 79 iBT), IELTS (minimum score 6.5). *Application deadline:* For fall admission, 5/15 priority date for domestic and international students; for spring admission, 10/15 priority date for domestic and international students. Applications are processed on a rolling basis. Application fee: $40 ($50 for international students). Electronic applications accepted. *Expenses: Tuition:* Full-time $7650; part-time $850 per credit. *Required fees:* $50 per credit. One-time fee: $100 full-time. *Financial support:* Research assistantships with full and partial tuition reimbursements, career-related internships or fieldwork, scholarships/grants, tuition waivers (partial), and unspecified assistantships available. Support available to part-time students. Financial award application deadline: 4/1. *Unit head:* Jenny Tripses, Interim Chair, 309-677-3593, E-mail: jtripses@bradley.edu. *Application contact:* Kayla Carroll, Director of International Admissions and Student Services, 309-677-2375, E-mail: klcarroll@fsmail.bradley.edu.
Website: http://www.bradley.edu/academic/departments/lenc/

Brandman University, School of Education, Irvine, CA 92618. Offers education (MA); elementary education (MAT); organizational leadership (Ed D); school counseling (MA); secondary education (MAT); special education (MA). *Expenses: Tuition:* Full-time $14,880; part-time $620 per credit hour. Tuition and fees vary according to degree level and program. *Unit head:* Dr. Christine G. Zeppos, Dean, 949-341-9948, E-mail: zeppos@brandman.edu.
Website: http://www.brandman.edu/education/

Brandon University, Faculty of Education, Brandon, MB R7A 6A9, Canada. Offers curriculum and instruction (M Ed, Diploma); educational administration (M Ed, Diploma); guidance and counseling (M Ed, Diploma); special education (M Ed, Diploma). *Degree requirements:* For master's, thesis. *Entrance requirements:* For master's, minimum GPA of 3.0, teaching certificate or equivalent. Additional exam requirements/recommendations for international students: Required—TOEFL. *Faculty research:* Comparative education, environmental studies, parent/school council.

Bridgewater State University, College of Graduate Studies, College of Education and Allied Studies, Department of Secondary Education and Professional Programs, Program in Counseling, Bridgewater, MA 02325. Offers M Ed, CAGS. *Accreditation:* ACA; NCATE. *Program availability:* Part-time, evening/weekend. *Entrance requirements:* For master's, GRE General Test.

Brooklyn College of the City University of New York, School of Education, Program in School Counseling, Brooklyn, NY 11210-2889. Offers MS Ed. *Accreditation:* ACA. *Program availability:* Part-time. *Degree requirements:* For master's, comprehensive exam, internship. *Entrance requirements:* For master's, interview, 2 letters of recommendation, resume, essay. Additional exam requirements/recommendations for international students: Required—TOEFL (minimum score 500 paper-based; 61 iBT). Electronic applications accepted. *Faculty research:* Urban school counseling, parent involvement, multicultural competence and counselor training.

Buena Vista University, School of Education, Storm Lake, IA 50588. Offers curriculum and instruction (M Ed), including effective teaching, TESL; school guidance and counseling (MS Ed). Program offered in summer only. *Program availability:* Part-time, evening/weekend, online learning. *Degree requirements:* For master's, thesis, fieldwork/practicum, capstone portfolio. *Entrance requirements:* For master's, Analytical Writing Assessment (in-house), minimum undergraduate GPA of 2.75. Electronic applications accepted. *Faculty research:* Reading, curriculum, educational psychology, special education.

Butler University, College of Education, Indianapolis, IN 46208-3485. Offers alternative special education licensure (Certificate); educational administration (MS); effective teaching and leadership (MS); international baccalaureate teaching and learning (Certificate); licensed mental health counselor (Certificate); school counseling (MS); teachers of the visually impaired (Certificate). *Accreditation:* ACA; NCATE. *Program availability:* Part-time. *Faculty:* 13 full-time (10 women), 5 part-time/adjunct (4 women). *Students:* 9 full-time (7 women), 119 part-time (85 women); includes 14 minority (10 Black or African American, non-Hispanic/Latino; 1 Asian, non-Hispanic/Latino; 2 Hispanic/Latino; 1 Two or more races, non-Hispanic/Latino). Average age 32. 79 applicants, 76% accepted, 63 enrolled. In 2016, 42 master's, 30 other advanced degrees awarded. *Entrance requirements:* For master's, GRE (minimum score 291) or MAT (minimum score 396) unless undergraduate GPA is a 3.0 or higher, two letters of recommendation, transcripts, interview, professional resume. Additional exam requirements/recommendations for international students: Required—TOEFL (minimum score 550 paper-based; 79 iBT), IELTS (minimum score 6). *Application deadline:* For fall admission, 2/1 for domestic and international students; for spring admission, 11/1 for domestic and international students; for summer admission, 4/1 for domestic and international students. Applications are processed on a rolling basis. Application fee: $0. Electronic applications accepted. *Expenses:* Contact institution. *Financial support:* In 2016–17, 60 students received support. Scholarships/grants and unspecified assistantships available. Financial award application deadline: 7/15; financial award applicants required to submit FAFSA. *Faculty research:* Principals role in school improvement, leadership and school climate, retention of teachers in special education, the neuro-diversity brain, school counseling intervention. *Unit head:* Dr. Ena Shelley, Dean, 317-940-9752, Fax: 317-940-6481. *Application contact:* Diane Dubord, Graduate Student Services Specialist, 317-940-8100, Fax: 317-940-8250, E-mail: ddubord@butler.edu.
Website: https://www.butler.edu/coe/graduate-programs

Caldwell University, Graduate Studies, Department of Psychology, Caldwell, NJ 07006-6195. Offers art therapy (MA); counseling (MA), including art therapy, mental health, school counseling; director of school counseling (Post-Master's Certificate); professional counselor (Post-Master's Certificate); school counselor (Post-Master's Certificate). *Accreditation:* ACA. *Program availability:* Part-time, evening/weekend. *Degree requirements:* For master's, comprehensive exam. *Entrance requirements:* For master's, GRE or MAT, interview. Electronic applications accepted. *Faculty research:* Counseling, school counseling, art therapy.

California Baptist University, Program in School Counseling, Riverside, CA 92504-3206. Offers MS. *Program availability:* Part-time, evening/weekend. *Faculty:* 2 full-time

(both women), 2 part-time/adjunct (1 woman). *Students:* 2 full-time (1 woman), 46 part-time (41 women); includes 25 minority (4 Black or African American, non-Hispanic/Latino; 1 American Indian or Alaska Native, non-Hispanic/Latino; 19 Hispanic/Latino; 1 Two or more races, non-Hispanic/Latino). Average age 33. 45 applicants, 56% accepted, 21 enrolled. In 2016, 1 master's awarded. *Degree requirements:* For master's, 100 hours of introductory fieldwork, 600 hours of field experience/internship, PRAXIS. *Entrance requirements:* For master's, California Basic Educational Skills Test, minimum GPA of 3.0, completion of prerequisite courses with minimum C grade, three letters of recommendation, 500-word essay. Additional exam requirements/recommendations for international students: Required—TOEFL (minimum score 80 iBT). *Application deadline:* For fall admission, 8/1 priority date for domestic students, 7/7 priority date for international students; for spring admission, 12/1 priority date for domestic students, 11/1 priority date for international students. Applications are processed on a rolling basis. Application fee: $45. Electronic applications accepted. *Expenses:* Contact institution. *Financial support:* In 2016–17, 17 students received support. Federal Work-Study and scholarships/grants available. Financial award applicants required to submit CSS PROFILE or FAFSA. *Faculty research:* Cultural competence, behavioral assessment, school neuropsychology, learning handicapped, cognitive development. *Unit head:* Dr. John Shoup, Dean, School of Education, 951-343-4205, E-mail: jshoup@calbaptist.edu. *Application contact:* Dr. Nona Cabral, Program Coordinator, School Counseling, 951-343-4804, E-mail: ncabral@calbaptist.edu.
Website: http://www.calbaptist.edu/academics/schools-colleges/school-education/programs/graduate/master-science-school-counseling/

California Lutheran University, Graduate Studies, Graduate School of Education, Thousand Oaks, CA 91360-2787. Offers counseling and guidance (MS), including college student personnel, counseling and guidance; educational leadership (MA, Ed D), including educational leadership (K-12) (Ed D), higher education leadership (Ed D); special education (MS); teacher leadership (M Ed); teaching (M Ed). *Accreditation:* NCATE. *Program availability:* Part-time, evening/weekend. *Faculty:* 23 full-time (17 women), 39 part-time/adjunct (26 women). *Students:* 518 full-time (411 women), 79 part-time (67 women); includes 252 minority (12 Black or African American, non-Hispanic/Latino; 3 American Indian or Alaska Native, non-Hispanic/Latino; 17 Asian, non-Hispanic/Latino; 108 Hispanic/Latino; 1 Native Hawaiian or other Pacific Islander, non-Hispanic/Latino; 111 Two or more races, non-Hispanic/Latino), 14 international. Average age 35. 319 applicants, 74% accepted, 192 enrolled. In 2016, 93 master's, 13 doctorates awarded. *Degree requirements:* For master's, comprehensive exam or thesis; for doctorate, thesis/dissertation. *Entrance requirements:* For master's, GRE General Test, interview, minimum GPA of 3.0. *Application deadline:* For fall admission, 7/1 priority date for domestic students; for spring admission, 11/1 priority date for domestic students; for summer admission, 4/1 priority date for domestic students. Applications are processed on a rolling basis. Application fee: $50. Electronic applications accepted. *Unit head:* Dr. Michael Hillis, Dean, 805-493-3421. *Application contact:* 805-493-3325, Fax: 805-493-3861, E-mail: clugrad@callutheran.edu.

California State University, Bakersfield, Division of Graduate Studies, School of Social Sciences and Education, Program in Counseling, Bakersfield, CA 93311. Offers school counseling (MS); student affairs (MS). *Accreditation:* NCATE. *Students:* 64 full-time (57 women), 7 part-time (6 women); includes 55 minority (1 Black or African American, non-Hispanic/Latino; 1 Asian, non-Hispanic/Latino; 49 Hispanic/Latino; 4 Two or more races, non-Hispanic/Latino), 1 international. Average age 28. 74 applicants, 59% accepted, 38 enrolled. In 2016, 35 master's awarded. *Degree requirements:* For master's, thesis or alternative, culminating projects. *Entrance requirements:* For master's, CBEST (for school counseling). *Application deadline:* Applications are processed on a rolling basis. Application fee: $55. *Expenses:* Tuition, state resident: full-time $2246; part-time $1302 per semester. *Financial support:* In 2016–17, fellowships (averaging $1,850 per year) were awarded; Federal Work-Study, scholarships/grants, and tuition waivers (full and partial) also available. Financial award application deadline: 3/2; financial award applicants required to submit FAFSA. *Unit head:* Dr. Yvonne Ortiz-Bush, Graduate Coordinator, 661-654-3087, Fax: 661-654-2479, E-mail: yortiz_bush@csub.edu. *Application contact:* Debbie Blowers, Assistant Director of Admissions and Evaluations, 661-664-3381, E-mail: dblowers@csub.edu.
Website: https://www.csub.edu/psychology/mscounselingpsych/index.html

California State University, Dominguez Hills, College of Education, Division of Graduate Education, Program in Counseling, Carson, CA 90747-0001. Offers college counseling (MS); school counseling (MS). *Program availability:* Part-time, evening/weekend. *Degree requirements:* For master's, comprehensive exam. *Entrance requirements:* For master's, minimum GPA of 3.0. Additional exam requirements/recommendations for international students: Required—TOEFL. *Faculty research:* Social development.

California State University, East Bay, Office of Graduate Studies, College of Education and Allied Studies, Department of Educational Psychology, Counseling Program, Hayward, CA 94542-3000. Offers marriage and family therapy (MS); school counseling (MS); school psychology (MS). *Accreditation:* NCATE. *Students:* 104 full-time (85 women), 2 part-time (both women); includes 54 minority (3 Black or African American, non-Hispanic/Latino; 15 Asian, non-Hispanic/Latino; 26 Hispanic/Latino; 10 Two or more races, non-Hispanic/Latino), 1 international. Average age 29. 178 applicants, 34% accepted, 50 enrolled. In 2016, 42 master's awarded. *Degree requirements:* For master's, comprehensive exam, project or thesis. *Entrance requirements:* For master's, GRE or MAT, interview, minimum GPA of 2.5 during previous 2 years of course work. Additional exam requirements/recommendations for international students: Required—TOEFL (minimum score 550 paper-based). *Application deadline:* For fall admission, 6/30 for domestic and international students. Application fee: $55. Electronic applications accepted. *Financial support:* Career-related internships or fieldwork, Federal Work-Study, and institutionally sponsored loans available. Support available to part-time students. Financial award application deadline: 3/2; financial award applicants required to submit FAFSA. *Unit head:* Dr. Jack Davis, Chair, Educational Psychology, 510-885-3011, Fax: 510-885-4642, E-mail: jack.davis@csueastbay.edu. *Application contact:* Prof. Greg Jennings, Graduate Coordinator, 510-885-2296, Fax: 510-885-4642, E-mail: greg.jennings@csueastbay.edu.
Website: http://www20.csueastbay.edu/ceas/departments/epsy/

California State University, Fresno, Division of Research and Graduate Studies, Kremen School of Education and Human Development, Department of Counselor Education and Rehabilitation, Program in Student Affairs and College Counseling, Fresno, CA 93740-8027. Offers MS. *Accreditation:* NCATE. *Program availability:* Part-time, evening/weekend. *Degree requirements:* For master's, thesis or alternative. *Entrance requirements:* For master's, GRE General Test, MAT, minimum GPA of 3.0. Additional exam requirements/recommendations for international students: Required—TOEFL. *Application deadline:* For fall admission, 5/1 for domestic and international students; for spring admission, 10/1 for domestic and international students. Applications are processed on a rolling basis. Application fee: $55. Electronic applications accepted. *Financial support:* Career-related internships or fieldwork, Federal Work-Study, scholarships/grants, and research awards available. Support available to part-time students. Financial award application deadline: 3/1; financial award applicants required to submit FAFSA. *Unit head:* Dr. Kyoung Mi Choi, Facilitator, 559-278-0070, Fax: 559-278-0045, E-mail: kchoi@csufresno.edu.

California State University, Fullerton, Graduate Studies, College of Health and Human Development, Department of Counseling, Fullerton, CA 92834-9480. Offers MS. *Accreditation:* ACA; NCATE. *Program availability:* Part-time. *Degree requirements:* For master's, comprehensive exam, project or thesis. *Entrance requirements:* For master's, minimum GPA of 3.0 in behavioral science and for undergraduate degree. Application fee: $55. *Expenses:* Tuition, state resident: full-time $3369; part-time $1953 per unit. Tuition, nonresident: full-time $3915; part-time $2499 per unit. Tuition and fees vary according to course load, degree level and program. *Financial support:* Career-related internships or fieldwork, Federal Work-Study, institutionally sponsored loans, and scholarships/grants available. Support available to part-time students. Financial award application deadline: 3/1; financial award applicants required to submit FAFSA. *Unit head:* Dr. Leah Brew, Chair, 657-278-8444. *Application contact:* Admissions/Applications, 657-278-2371.

California State University, Long Beach, Graduate Studies, College of Education, Department of Advanced Studies in Education and Counseling, Long Beach, CA 90840. Offers counseling (MS), including marriage and family therapy, school counseling, student development in higher education; education (MA, Ed D); educational administration (MA, Ed D); educational psychology (MA); special education (MS). *Program availability:* Part-time, evening/weekend. *Entrance requirements:* For master's, GRE General Test, minimum GPA of 2.75. *Application deadline:* For fall admission, 3/1 for domestic students. Applications are processed on a rolling basis. Application fee: $55. Electronic applications accepted. *Financial support:* Federal Work-Study, institutionally sponsored loans, and scholarships/grants available. Financial award application deadline: 3/2. *Unit head:* Dr. Hiromi Masunaga, Chair, 562-985-4517, E-mail: asec@csulb.edu.

California State University, Los Angeles, Graduate Studies, Charter College of Education, Division of Special Education and Counseling, Los Angeles, CA 90032-8530. Offers counseling (MS), including applied behavior analysis, community college counseling, rehabilitation counseling, school counseling, school psychology; special education (MA, PhD). *Accreditation:* ACA. *Program availability:* Part-time, evening/weekend. *Entrance requirements:* For master's, minimum GPA of 2.75 in last 90 units of course work, teaching certificate. Additional exam requirements/recommendations for international students: Required—TOEFL (minimum score 500 paper-based). Electronic applications accepted.

California State University, Northridge, Graduate Studies, Michael D. Eisner College of Education, Department of Educational Psychology and Counseling, Northridge, CA 91330. Offers counseling (MS), including career counseling, college counseling and student services, marriage and family therapy, school counseling, school psychology; educational psychology (MA Ed), including development, learning, and instruction, early childhood education. *Accreditation:* ACA (one or more programs are accredited); NCATE. *Program availability:* Part-time, evening/weekend. *Faculty:* 17 full-time (4 women), 46 part-time/adjunct (15 women). *Students:* 283 full-time (235 women), 79 part-time (72 women); includes 180 minority (8 Black or African American, non-Hispanic/Latino; 22 Asian, non-Hispanic/Latino; 132 Hispanic/Latino; 18 Two or more races, non-Hispanic/Latino), 13 international. Average age 29. 411 applicants, 36% accepted, 129 enrolled. *Entrance requirements:* For master's, GRE General Test or minimum GPA of 3.0. Additional exam requirements/recommendations for international students: Required—TOEFL. *Application deadline:* For fall admission, 11/30 for domestic students. Application fee: $55. *Expenses:* Tuition, state resident: full-time $4152. *Financial support:* Scholarships/grants available. Support available to part-time students. Financial award application deadline: 3/1. *Unit head:* Dr. Shari Tarver-Behring, Chair, 818-677-2599. *Application contact:* 818-677-3755.
Website: http://www.csun.edu/eisner-education/educational-psychology-counseling

California State University, Sacramento, Office of Graduate Studies, College of Education, Graduate and Professional Studies in Education, Sacramento, CA 95819. Offers child development (MA); counseling (MS); curriculum and instruction (MA); education (Ed D); education leadership and policy studies (MA), including higher education, PreK-12; educational technology (MA); gender equity (MA); language and literacy (MA); multicultural education (MA); school psychology (MA); special education (MA); workforce development advocacy (MA). *Program availability:* Part-time. *Students:* 446 full-time (335 women), 125 part-time (97 women); includes 298 minority (39 Black or African American, non-Hispanic/Latino; 3 American Indian or Alaska Native, non-Hispanic/Latino; 97 Asian, non-Hispanic/Latino; 153 Hispanic/Latino; 6 Native Hawaiian or other Pacific Islander, non-Hispanic/Latino). Average age 32. 540 applicants, 76% accepted, 250 enrolled. In 2016, 107 master's, 7 doctorates awarded. *Degree requirements:* For master's, thesis or project; writing proficiency exam. *Entrance requirements:* For master's, minimum GPA of 2.5, 3.0 in last 60 units. Additional exam requirements/recommendations for international students: Required—TOEFL (minimum score 550 paper-based; 80 iBT). *Application deadline:* For fall admission, 2/15 for domestic students, 1/15 for international students. Applications are processed on a rolling basis. Application fee: $55. Electronic applications accepted. *Expenses:* $4,302 full-time tuition and fees per semester, $2,796 part-time. *Financial support:* Career-related internships or fieldwork and Federal Work-Study available. Support available to part-time students. Financial award application deadline: 3/1; financial award applicants required to submit FAFSA. *Unit head:* Dr. Susan Heredia, Chair, 916-278-5942, E-mail: coe@csus.edu. *Application contact:* Jose Martinez, Graduate Admissions Supervisor, 916-278-7871, E-mail: martinj@skymail.csus.edu.
Website: http://www.csus.edu/coe/academics/graduate/index.html

California State University, San Bernardino, Graduate Studies, College of Education, Program in Counseling and Guidance, San Bernardino, CA 92407. Offers counseling and guidance (MS); rehabilitation counseling (MA). *Accreditation:* NCATE. *Program availability:* Part-time, evening/weekend. *Students:* 124 full-time (101 women), 15 part-time (10 women); includes 93 minority (6 Black or African American, non-Hispanic/Latino; 4 Asian, non-Hispanic/Latino; 81 Hispanic/Latino; 2 Two or more races, non-Hispanic/Latino), 3 international. 95 applicants, 62% accepted, 46 enrolled. In 2016, 39 master's awarded. *Degree requirements:* For master's, comprehensive exam, thesis or alternative. *Entrance requirements:* Additional exam requirements/recommendations for international students: Required—TOEFL. *Application deadline:* For fall admission, 7/16 for domestic students. Application fee: $55. *Expenses:* Tuition, state resident: full-time $7843; part-time $5011.20 per year. Tuition and fees vary according to course load, degree level, program and reciprocity agreements. *Unit head:* Dr. Judith Sylva, Chair, 909-537-5606, E-mail: jsylva@csusb.edu. *Application contact:* Dr. Francisca Beer, Dean of Graduate Studies, 909-537-5058, E-mail: fbeer@csusb.edu.

California State University, Stanislaus, College of Education, Program in Education (MA), Turlock, CA 95382. Offers curriculum and instruction (MA), including education technology, elementary education, multilingual education, physical education, reading, secondary education, special education; school administration (MA); school counseling (MA). *Program availability:* Part-time, evening/weekend. *Degree requirements:* For master's, comprehensive exam (for some programs), thesis (for some programs). *Entrance requirements:* For master's, MAT, GRE, or CBEST (varies by concentration), 3 letters of recommendation, personal statement. Additional exam requirements/

recommendations for international students: Required—TOEFL (minimum score 550 paper-based). Electronic applications accepted. *Faculty research:* Children's perspectives on historical events, method elementary schools dual language education, K-12 reading programs.

California University of Pennsylvania, School of Graduate Studies and Research, College of Education and Human Services, Department of Counselor Education, California, PA 15419-1394. Offers clinical mental health counseling (MS); school counseling (M Ed). *Accreditation:* ACA; NCATE. *Program availability:* Part-time, evening/weekend. *Degree requirements:* For master's, comprehensive exam, thesis optional. *Entrance requirements:* For master's, MAT, minimum GPA of 3.0, resume, letters of reference. Additional exam requirements/recommendations for international students: Required—TOEFL (minimum score 550 paper-based; 80 iBT). Electronic applications accepted. *Expenses:* Tuition, state resident: full-time $11,592; part-time $483 per credit. Tuition, nonresident: full-time $17,400; part-time $725 per credit. *Required fees:* $3916. Tuition and fees vary according to course load, degree level, campus/location and reciprocity agreements. *Faculty research:* Mind-body theories and practice, grief issues, career development, supervision, sports counseling.

Cambridge College, School of Education, Cambridge, MA 02138-5304. Offers autism specialist (M Ed); autism/behavior analyst (M Ed); behavior analyst (Post-Master's Certificate); behavioral management (M Ed); early childhood teacher (M Ed); education specialist in curriculum and instruction (CAGS); educational leadership (Ed D); elementary teacher (M Ed); English as a second language (M Ed, Certificate); general science (M Ed); health education (Post-Master's Certificate); health/family and consumer sciences (M Ed); history (M Ed); individualized (M Ed); information technology literacy (M Ed); instructional technology (M Ed); interdisciplinary studies (M Ed); library teacher (M Ed); literacy education (M Ed); mathematics (M Ed); mathematics specialist (Certificate); middle school mathematics and science (M Ed); school administration (M Ed, CAGS); school guidance counselor (M Ed); school nurse education (M Ed); school social worker/school adjustment counselor (M Ed); special education administrator (CAGS); special education/moderate disabilities (M Ed); teaching skills and methodologies (M Ed). *Program availability:* Part-time, evening/weekend, online learning. *Degree requirements:* For master's, thesis, internship/practicum (licensure program only); for doctorate, thesis/dissertation; for other advanced degree, thesis. *Entrance requirements:* For master's, interview, resume, documentation of licensure, 2 professional references; for doctorate, official transcripts, interview, resume, documentation of licensure (if any), written personal statement/essay, portfolio of scholarly and professional work, qualifying assessment, 2 professional references, health insurance, immunizations form; for other advanced degree, official transcripts, interview, resume, documentation of licensure (if any), written personal statement/essay, 2 professional references, health insurance, immunizations form. Additional exam requirements/recommendations for international students: Required—TOEFL (minimum score 550 paper-based; 79 iBT), Michigan English Language Assessment Battery (minimum score 85); Recommended—IELTS (minimum score 6). Electronic applications accepted. *Expenses:* Contact institution. *Faculty research:* Adult education, accelerated learning, mathematics education, brain compatible learning, special education and law.

Cambridge College, School of Psychology and Counseling, Cambridge, MA 02138-5304. Offers addiction counseling (M Ed); alcohol and drug counseling (Certificate); counseling psychology (M Ed, CAGS); counseling psychology: forensic counseling (M Ed); marriage and family therapy (M Ed); mental health and addiction counseling (M Ed); mental health counseling (M Ed); mental health counseling for school guidance counselors (Post Master's Certificate); psychological studies (M Ed); school adjustment and mental health counseling (M Ed); school adjustment, mental health and addiction counseling (M Ed); school guidance counselor (M Ed); trauma studies (Certificate). *Program availability:* Part-time, evening/weekend. *Degree requirements:* For master's and other advanced degree, thesis, practicum/internship. *Entrance requirements:* For master's, resume, 2 professional references; for other advanced degree, official transcripts, documents for transfer credit evaluation, resume, written personal statement/essay, 2 professional references, health insurance, immunizations form. Additional exam requirements/recommendations for international students: Required—TOEFL (minimum score 550 paper-based; 79 iBT), Michigan English Language Assessment Battery (minimum score 85); Recommended—IELTS (minimum score 6). Electronic applications accepted. *Expenses:* Contact institution. *Faculty research:* Trauma, drug and alcohol counseling, cross-cultural issues, school counseling, trauma in schools.

Campbell University, Graduate and Professional Programs, School of Education, Buies Creek, NC 27506. Offers elementary education (M Ed); interdisciplinary studies (M Ed); middle grades education (M Ed); physical education (M Ed); school administration (MSA); school counseling (M Ed); secondary education (M Ed). *Accreditation:* NCATE. *Program availability:* Part-time, evening/weekend. *Degree requirements:* For master's, comprehensive exam. *Entrance requirements:* For master's, GRE General Test, minimum GPA of 2.7. *Faculty research:* Spiritual values and wellness issues in counseling, stress and professional burnout among counselors, thinking strategies, leadership, adaptive technology.

Canisius College, Graduate Division, School of Education and Human Services, Programs in Counseling and Human Services, Buffalo, NY 14208-1098. Offers community mental health counseling (MS); counseling and human services (MS); school agency counseling (MS). *Accreditation:* ACA. *Program availability:* Part-time, evening/weekend. *Faculty:* 6 full-time (3 women), 10 part-time/adjunct (7 women). *Students:* 83 full-time (67 women), 39 part-time (33 women); includes 25 minority (13 Black or African American, non-Hispanic/Latino; 1 Asian, non-Hispanic/Latino; 6 Hispanic/Latino; 5 Two or more races, non-Hispanic/Latino), 5 international. Average age 26. 109 applicants, 86% accepted, 37 enrolled. In 2016, 48 master's awarded. *Degree requirements:* For master's, thesis, research project. *Entrance requirements:* For master's, GRE (if cumulative GPA less than 2.7), transcripts, two letters of recommendation, interview, BA. Additional exam requirements/recommendations for international students: Required—TOEFL (minimum score 550 paper-based, 79 iBT), IELTS (minimum score 6.5), or CAEL (minimum score 70). *Application deadline:* Applications are processed on a rolling basis. Application fee: $25. Electronic applications accepted. Application fee is waived when completed online. *Expenses: Tuition:* Full-time $14,742. *Required fees:* $724. *Financial support:* Career-related internships or fieldwork, Federal Work-Study, scholarships/grants, tuition waivers (partial), and unspecified assistantships available. Support available to part-time students. Financial award application deadline: 4/30; financial award applicants required to submit FAFSA. *Faculty research:* Impact of trauma on adults, long term psych-social impact on police officers. *Unit head:* Dr. Christine Moll, Chair, 716-888-3287, E-mail: moll@canisius.edu. *Application contact:* Kathleen B. Davis, Vice President of Enrollment Management, 716-888-2500, Fax: 716-888-3195, E-mail: daviskb@canisius.edu.
Website: http://www.canisius.edu/masters-counseling/

Capella University, Harold Abel School of Social and Behavioral Science, Doctoral Programs in Counseling, Minneapolis, MN 55402. Offers general counselor education and supervision (PhD); general social work (DSW). *Accreditation:* ACA.

Capella University, Harold Abel School of Social and Behavioral Science, Master's Programs in Counseling, Minneapolis, MN 55402. Offers child and adolescent development (MS); general addiction counseling (MS); general marriage and family counseling/therapy (MS); general mental health counseling (MS); general school counseling (MS).

Carlow University, College of Leadership and Social Change, Program in Professional Counseling, Pittsburgh, PA 15213-3165. Offers addictions (MS); adult/generalist (MS); child and family (MS); professional counseling (Certificate); trauma-informed (MS). *Program availability:* Part-time, evening/weekend. *Students:* 127 full-time (111 women), 23 part-time (19 women); includes 46 minority (34 Black or African American, non-Hispanic/Latino; 1 American Indian or Alaska Native, non-Hispanic/Latino; 2 Asian, non-Hispanic/Latino; 5 Hispanic/Latino; 4 Two or more races, non-Hispanic/Latino), 1 international. Average age 30. 49 applicants, 86% accepted, 26 enrolled. In 2016, 41 master's, 1 other advanced degree awarded. *Entrance requirements:* For master's, personal essay; resume or curriculum vitae; three recommendations; official transcripts; interview; minimum undergraduate GPA of 3.0. Additional exam requirements/recommendations for international students: Required—TOEFL (minimum score 550 paper-based). *Application deadline:* Applications are processed on a rolling basis. Electronic applications accepted. *Expenses: Tuition:* Full-time $11,855; part-time $801 per credit. *Required fees:* $182; $13 per credit. Tuition and fees vary according to course load, degree level and program. *Financial support:* Application deadline: 4/1; applicants required to submit FAFSA. *Unit head:* Dr. Travis W. Schermer, Director, 412-575-6650, Fax: 412-575-6357, E-mail: twschermer@carlow.edu.
Website: http://www.carlow.edu/Master_of_Science_in_Professional_Counseling.aspx

Carson-Newman University, Graduate Program in Education, Jefferson City, TN 37760. Offers curriculum and instruction (M Ed); educational leadership (M Ed); elementary education (MAT); school counseling (MS); secondary education (MAT); teaching English as a second language (MATESL). *Accreditation:* NCATE. *Program availability:* Part-time, evening/weekend, 100% online, blended/hybrid learning. *Degree requirements:* For master's, thesis or alternative. *Entrance requirements:* For master's, PRAXIS II or GRE with minimum score of 290 on the verbal and quantitative components (for MAT), minimum GPA of 3.0 in major, 2.5 overall. Additional exam requirements/recommendations for international students: Recommended—TOEFL (minimum score 79 iBT), IELTS (minimum score 6.5), TSE (minimum score 53). *Expenses: Tuition:* Full-time $10,142; part-time $461 per credit hour. *Required fees:* $300; $150 per semester. One-time fee: $150.

Carson-Newman University, Program in Counseling, Jefferson City, TN 37760. Offers MSC. *Accreditation:* ACA. *Program availability:* Part-time, evening/weekend. *Entrance requirements:* Additional exam requirements/recommendations for international students: Recommended—TOEFL (minimum score 79 iBT), IELTS (minimum score 6.5), TSE (minimum score 53). *Expenses: Tuition:* Full-time $10,142; part-time $461 per credit hour. *Required fees:* $300; $150 per semester. One-time fee: $150.

Carthage College, Division of Teacher Education, Kenosha, WI 53140. Offers classroom guidance and counseling (M Ed); creative arts (M Ed); gifted and talented children (M Ed); language arts (M Ed); modern language (M Ed); natural sciences (M Ed); reading (M Ed, Certificate); social sciences (M Ed); teacher leadership (M Ed). *Program availability:* Part-time, evening/weekend. *Degree requirements:* For master's, thesis optional. *Entrance requirements:* For master's, MAT, minimum B average, letters of reference.

Central Connecticut State University, School of Graduate Studies, School of Education and Professional Studies, Department of Counselor Education and Family Therapy, New Britain, CT 06050-4010. Offers marriage and family therapy (MS); professional counseling (MS, AC, Certificate); school counseling (MS); student development in higher education (MS). *Accreditation:* AAMFT/COAMFTE; ACA. *Program availability:* Part-time, evening/weekend. *Faculty:* 10 full-time (5 women), 23 part-time/adjunct (21 women). *Students:* 157 full-time (120 women), 193 part-time (151 women); includes 99 minority (41 Black or African American, non-Hispanic/Latino; 3 Asian, non-Hispanic/Latino; 46 Hispanic/Latino; 9 Two or more races, non-Hispanic/Latino). Average age 39. 201 applicants, 64% accepted, 95 enrolled. In 2016, 96 master's, 7 other advanced degrees awarded. *Degree requirements:* For master's, comprehensive exam, thesis or alternative; for other advanced degree, qualifying exam. *Entrance requirements:* For master's, minimum undergraduate GPA of 2.7, essay, interview, letters of recommendation. Additional exam requirements/recommendations for international students: Required—TOEFL (minimum score 550 paper-based; 79 iBT). *Application deadline:* For fall admission, 3/1 for domestic and international students; for spring admission, 11/1 for domestic and international students. Applications are processed on a rolling basis. Application fee: $50. Electronic applications accepted. *Expenses: Tuition, area resident:* Full-time $6497; part-time $606 per credit. Tuition, state resident: full-time $9748; part-time $622 per credit. Tuition, nonresident: full-time $18,102; part-time $622 per credit. *Required fees:* $4459; $246 per credit. *Financial support:* In 2016–17, 46 students received support. Career-related internships or fieldwork, Federal Work-Study, scholarships/grants, and unspecified assistantships available. Support available to part-time students. Financial award application deadline: 3/1; financial award applicants required to submit FAFSA. *Faculty research:* Elementary and secondary school counseling, marriage and family therapy, rehabilitation counseling, counseling in higher educational settings. *Unit head:* Dr. Connie Tait, Chair, 860-832-2154, E-mail: taitc@ccsu.edu. *Application contact:* Patricia Gardner, Associate Director of Graduate Studies, 860-832-2350, Fax: 860-832-2362.
Website: http://www.ccsu.edu/ceft/

Central Methodist University, College of Graduate and Extended Studies, Fayette, MO 65248-1198. Offers clinical counseling (MS); clinical nurse leader (MSN); education (M Ed); music education (MME); nurse educator (MSN). *Program availability:* Part-time, evening/weekend, online learning. *Degree requirements:* For master's, thesis. *Entrance requirements:* For master's, GRE General Test, minimum GPA of 2.75. Electronic applications accepted.

Central Michigan University, Central Michigan University Global Campus, Program in Counseling, Mount Pleasant, MI 48859. Offers professional counseling (MA); school counseling (MA). *Accreditation:* TEAC. *Program availability:* Part-time, evening/weekend. *Faculty:* 6 full-time (2 women), 12 part-time/adjunct (10 women). *Students:* 123 (103 women); includes 43 minority (30 Black or African American, non-Hispanic/Latino; 2 Asian, non-Hispanic/Latino; 1 Hispanic/Latino; 10 Two or more races, non-Hispanic/Latino). Average age 38. In 2016, 13 master's awarded. *Entrance requirements:* For master's, MAT, minimum GPA of 2.7. Additional exam requirements/recommendations for international students: Required—TOEFL. *Application deadline:* Applications are processed on a rolling basis. Application fee: $50. Electronic applications accepted. *Financial support:* Scholarships/grants available. Support available to part-time students. *Unit head:* Dr. Twinet Parmer, Chair, 989-774-3776, E-mail: parme1t@cmich.edu. *Application contact:* 877-268-4636, E-mail: cmuglobal@cmich.edu.

Central Michigan University, College of Graduate Studies, College of Education and Human Services, Department of Counseling and Special Education, Program in Counseling, Mount Pleasant, MI 48859. Offers counseling (MA), including professional counseling, school counseling. *Accreditation:* TEAC. *Program availability:* Part-time. *Degree requirements:* For master's, comprehensive exam, thesis or alternative. *Entrance requirements:* For master's, MAT, eligible for Michigan Teacher Certification (for school counseling). Electronic applications accepted. *Faculty research:* School counseling, professional counseling.

Central Washington University, Graduate Studies and Research, College of the Sciences, Department of Psychology, Program in School Counseling, Ellensburg, WA 98926. Offers M Ed. *Degree requirements:* For master's, thesis or alternative, internship. *Entrance requirements:* For master's, GRE General Test, minimum GPA of 3.0. Additional exam requirements/recommendations for international students: Required—TOEFL (minimum score 550 paper-based; 79 iBT). Electronic applications accepted.

Chadron State College, School of Professional and Graduate Studies, Department of Education, Chadron, NE 69337. Offers business (MA Ed); community counseling (MA Ed); educational administration (MS Ed, Sp Ed); elementary education (MS Ed); history (MA Ed); language and literature (MA Ed); secondary administration (MS Ed); secondary education (MS Ed). *Accreditation:* NCATE. *Program availability:* Part-time, evening/weekend, online learning. *Degree requirements:* For master's, thesis optional. *Entrance requirements:* For master's, GRE General Test, GRE Writing Test, minimum GPA of 2.75 or 12 graduate hours at CSC with minimum GPA of 3.25. Additional exam requirements/recommendations for international students: Required—TOEFL. Electronic applications accepted. *Faculty research:* Rural education, technology, mental health.

Chapman University, College of Educational Studies, Orange, CA 92866. Offers counseling (MA), including school counseling (MA, Credential); education (PhD), including cultural and curricular studies, disability studies, leadership studies, school psychology (PhD, Credential); educational psychology (MA); leadership development (MA); multiple subjects (Credential), including Spanish/English bilingual; pupil personnel services (Credential), including school counseling (MA, Credential), school psychology (PhD, Credential); school psychology (Ed S); single subject (Credential); special education (MA, Credential), including mild/moderate (Credential), moderate/severe (Credential); teaching (MA), including elementary education, secondary education, secondary music education. *Accreditation:* TEAC. *Program availability:* Part-time, evening/weekend. *Faculty:* 29 full-time (14 women), 36 part-time/adjunct (28 women). *Students:* 186 full-time (148 women), 186 part-time (134 women); includes 144 minority (9 Black or African American, non-Hispanic/Latino; 39 Asian, non-Hispanic/Latino; 78 Hispanic/Latino; 2 Native Hawaiian or other Pacific Islander, non-Hispanic/Latino; 16 Two or more races, non-Hispanic/Latino), 8 international. Average age 29. 143 applicants, 63% accepted, 64 enrolled. In 2016, 111 master's, 24 doctorates awarded. *Degree requirements:* For doctorate, thesis/dissertation. *Entrance requirements:* Additional exam requirements/recommendations for international students: Required—TOEFL (minimum score 550 paper-based, 80 iBT), IELTS (6.5), PTE Academic (53), or CAE. *Application deadline:* Applications are processed on a rolling basis. Application fee: $60. Electronic applications accepted. *Expenses:* Contact institution. *Financial support:* Fellowships and scholarships/grants available. Financial award application deadline: 3/2; financial award applicants required to submit FAFSA. *Unit head:* Dr. Margaret Grogan, Dean, 714-516-5968, E-mail: grogan@chapman.edu. *Application contact:* Sara Simon, Graduate Admission Counselor, 714-997-6770, E-mail: simon@chapman.edu.
Website: http://www.chapman.edu/CES/

Chicago State University, School of Graduate and Professional Studies, College of Arts and Sciences, Department of Psychology, Chicago, IL 60628. Offers counseling (MA). *Accreditation:* ACA; NCATE. *Degree requirements:* For master's, comprehensive exam, thesis optional. *Entrance requirements:* For master's, minimum GPA of 3.0 for last 60 semester hours of course work or essay; interview.

The Citadel, The Military College of South Carolina, Citadel Graduate College, School of Humanities and Social Sciences, Department of Psychology, Charleston, SC 29409. Offers psychology (MA), including clinical counseling; school psychology (Ed S). *Program availability:* Part-time, evening/weekend. *Faculty:* 4 full-time (1 woman), 4 part-time/adjunct (3 women). *Students:* 50 full-time (41 women), 50 part-time (45 women); includes 14 minority (6 Black or African American, non-Hispanic/Latino; 5 Hispanic/Latino; 1 Native Hawaiian or other Pacific Islander, non-Hispanic/Latino; 2 Two or more races, non-Hispanic/Latino). In 2016, 20 master's, 9 other advanced degrees awarded. *Degree requirements:* For master's, comprehensive exam, practicum; internship (written and oral presentation of a case study as part of internship); for Ed S, comprehensive exam, thesis (for some programs), practicum, internship. *Entrance requirements:* For master's, GRE (minimum combined score of 297, 150 on verbal reasoning and 141 on quantitative reasoning) or MAT (minimum score of 410), minimum undergraduate GPA of 3.0; 12 credit hours in psychology or minimum score on GRE Subject Test in psychology of 600; 2 letters of recommendation; for Ed S, GRE (minimum combined score of 297, 150 on verbal reasoning and 147 on quantitative reasoning) or MAT (minimum score of 410), minimum undergraduate or graduate GPA of 3.0; 2 letters of recommendation. Additional exam requirements/recommendations for international students: Required—TOEFL (minimum score 550 paper-based; 79 iBT). *Application deadline:* Applications are processed on a rolling basis. Application fee: $40. Electronic applications accepted. *Expenses:* Tuition, state resident: full-time $5121; part-time $569 per credit hour. Tuition, nonresident: full-time $8613; part-time $957 per credit hour. *Required fees:* $90 per term. *Financial support:* Fellowships and unspecified assistantships available. Support available to part-time students. Financial award application deadline: 7/1; financial award applicants required to submit FAFSA. *Unit head:* Dr. Steve A. Nida, Department Head, 843-953-5320, E-mail: steve.nida@citadel.edu. *Application contact:* Dr. Genelle K. Sawyer, Director of the MA in Clinical Counseling Program, 843-953-5427, E-mail: genelle.sawyer@citadel.edu.
Website: http://www.citadel.edu/root/psychology-graduateprograms

The Citadel, The Military College of South Carolina, Citadel Graduate College, Zucker Family School of Education, Charleston, SC 29409. Offers elementary/secondary school administration and supervision (M Ed); elementary/secondary school counseling (M Ed); interdisciplinary STEM education (M Ed); literacy education (M Ed, Graduate Certificate); middle grades (MAT), including English, mathematics, science, social studies; physical education (grades K-12) (MAT); school superintendency (Ed S); secondary education (MAT), including biology, English, mathematics, social studies; student affairs (Graduate Certificate); student affairs and college counseling (M Ed). *Accreditation:* NCATE. *Program availability:* Part-time, evening/weekend, 100% online, blended/hybrid learning. *Faculty:* 9 full-time (4 women), 9 part-time/adjunct (5 women). *Students:* 70 full-time (58 women), 249 part-time (200 women); includes 87 minority (70 Black or African American, non-Hispanic/Latino; 1 Asian, non-Hispanic/Latino; 9 Hispanic/Latino; 7 Two or more races, non-Hispanic/Latino), 2 international. 146 applicants, 98% accepted, 105 enrolled. In 2016, 85 master's, 7 other advanced degrees awarded. *Degree requirements:* For master's, comprehensive exam (for some programs). *Entrance requirements:* For master's, GRE (minimum combined verbal and quantitative score of 290) or MAT (minimum score 396). Additional exam requirements/recommendations for international students: Required—TOEFL (minimum score 550 paper-based; 79 iBT). *Application deadline:* Applications are processed on a rolling basis. Application fee: $40. Electronic applications accepted. *Expenses:* Tuition, state resident: full-time $5121; part-time $569 per credit hour. Tuition, nonresident: full-time $8613; part-time $957 per credit hour. *Required fees:* $90 per term. *Financial support:* Fellowships and unspecified assistantships available. Support available to part-time students. Financial award application deadline: 7/1; financial award applicants required to submit FAFSA. *Unit head:* Dr. Larry G. Daniel, Dean, 843-953-5097, E-mail: ldaniel@citadel.edu. *Application contact:* Dr. Tammy J. Graham, Associate Professor, 843-953-6854, E-mail: tammy.graham@citadel.edu.
Website: http://www.citadel.edu/root/education-graduate-programs

City University of Seattle, Graduate Division, Albright School of Education, Seattle, WA 98121. Offers administrator certification (Certificate); curriculum and instruction (M Ed); elementary education (MIT); guidance and counseling (M Ed); leadership (M Ed); reading and literacy (M Ed); school counseling (M Ed); special education (MIT); superintendent certification (Certificate). *Program availability:* Part-time, evening/weekend, online learning. *Degree requirements:* For master's, comprehensive exam (for some programs), thesis (for some programs). *Entrance requirements:* For master's, baccalaureate degree or equivalent from an accredited or otherwise recognized institution. Additional exam requirements/recommendations for international students: Required—TOEFL (minimum score 567 paper-based; 87 iBT); Recommended—IELTS. Electronic applications accepted. *Expenses:* Contact institution.

Clark Atlanta University, School of Education, Department of Counseling and Psychological Studies, Atlanta, GA 30314. Offers MA. *Accreditation:* ACA. *Program availability:* Part-time. *Faculty:* 4 full-time (2 women), 2 part-time/adjunct (both women). *Students:* 29 full-time (21 women), 8 part-time (4 women); includes 30 minority (all Black or African American, non-Hispanic/Latino), 1 international. Average age 28. 20 applicants, 100% accepted, 11 enrolled. In 2016, 26 master's awarded. *Degree requirements:* For master's, comprehensive exam. *Entrance requirements:* For master's, GRE General Test, minimum undergraduate GPA of 2.6. Additional exam requirements/recommendations for international students: Required—TOEFL (minimum score 500 paper-based; 61 iBT). *Application deadline:* For fall admission, 4/1 for domestic and international students; for spring admission, 11/1 for domestic and international students. Applications are processed on a rolling basis. Application fee: $40 ($55 for international students). Electronic applications accepted. *Expenses:* *Tuition:* Full-time $15,498; part-time $861 per credit hour. *Required fees:* $1326; $1326 per credit hour. Tuition and fees vary according to course load. *Financial support:* Career-related internships or fieldwork, Federal Work-Study, scholarships/grants, and unspecified assistantships available. Support available to part-time students. Financial award application deadline: 4/30; financial award applicants required to submit FAFSA. *Unit head:* Dr. Ken Sanders, Chairperson, 404-880-8519, E-mail: ksanders1@cau.edu. *Application contact:* Graduate Program Admissions, 404-880-8483, E-mail: graduateadmissions@cau.edu.

Clarks Summit University, Graduate Studies, South Abington Township, PA 18411. Offers Bible (MA); counseling (MA, MS); curriculum and instruction (M Ed); educational administration (M Ed); intercultural studies (MA); literature (MA); missions (MA); organizational leadership (MA); reading specialist (M Ed); secondary English/communications (M Ed); social entrepreneurship (MA); worldview studies (MA). MA in missions program available only for Association of Baptists for World Evangelism missionary personnel. *Program availability:* Part-time, evening/weekend, online learning. *Entrance requirements:* Additional exam requirements/recommendations for international students: Required—TOEFL (minimum score 500 paper-based).

Clemson University, Graduate School, College of Education, Department of Education and Human Development, Program in Counselor Education, Clemson, SC 29634. Offers counselor education (M Ed, Ed S), including clinical mental health counseling, school counseling. *Accreditation:* ACA; NCATE. *Program availability:* Part-time, evening/weekend. *Faculty:* 2 full-time (both women). *Students:* 142 full-time (114 women), 14 part-time (13 women); includes 39 minority (24 Black or African American, non-Hispanic/Latino; 4 Asian, non-Hispanic/Latino; 7 Hispanic/Latino; 4 Two or more races, non-Hispanic/Latino). Average age 26. 256 applicants, 46% accepted, 57 enrolled. In 2016, 73 master's, 38 Ed Ss awarded. *Degree requirements:* For master's, comprehensive exam. *Entrance requirements:* For master's, GRE General Test, unofficial transcripts, two letters of recommendation, essays. Additional exam requirements/recommendations for international students: Required—TOEFL (minimum score 80 iBT), IELTS (minimum score 6.5). *Application deadline:* For fall admission, 2/1 priority date for domestic and international students; for summer admission, 2/1 priority date for domestic and international students. Application fee: $80 ($90 for international students). Electronic applications accepted. *Expenses:* $4,027 per semester full-time resident, $8,013 per semester full-time non-resident, $437 per credit hour part-time resident, $874 per credit hour part-time non-resident. *Financial support:* Application deadline: 2/1. *Faculty research:* School counseling, disabilities, college readiness, transitions, counselor education. *Unit head:* Dr. Amy Milsom, Program Coordinator, 864-656-0927, E-mail: amilsom@clemson.edu.
Website: http://www.clemson.edu/education/departments/education-human-development/academics/index.html

Cleveland State University, College of Graduate Studies, College of Education and Human Services, Department of Counseling, Administration, Supervision and Adult Learning (CASAL), Cleveland, OH 44115. Offers adult learning and development (M Ed); counselor education (PhD); early childhood mental health counseling (Certificate); educational administration and supervision (M Ed). *Accreditation:* ACA (one or more programs are accredited). *Program availability:* Part-time, evening/weekend. *Faculty:* 15 full-time (8 women), 19 part-time/adjunct (10 women). *Students:* 104 full-time (85 women), 259 part-time (197 women); includes 138 minority (115 Black or African American, non-Hispanic/Latino; 1 American Indian or Alaska Native, non-Hispanic/Latino; 3 Asian, non-Hispanic/Latino; 16 Hispanic/Latino; 3 Two or more races, non-Hispanic/Latino), 8 international. Average age 34. 57 applicants, 93% accepted, 51 enrolled. In 2016, 102 master's awarded. *Degree requirements:* For master's, comprehensive exam (for some programs), thesis optional, internship. *Entrance requirements:* For master's, GRE General Test or MAT, letter of recommendation and minimum GPA of 2.75 (for counseling); 2 letters of recommendation and interviews (for organizational leadership). Additional exam requirements/recommendations for international students: Required—TOEFL (minimum score 550 paper-based; 78 iBT), IELTS (minimum score 6). *Application deadline:* For fall admission, 6/21 for domestic students, 5/15 for international students; for spring admission, 8/31 for domestic students, 11/1 for international students. Application fee: $40. Electronic applications accepted. *Expenses:* Tuition, state resident: full-time $9565. Tuition, nonresident: full-time $17,980. Tuition and fees vary according to program. *Financial support:* In 2016–17, 19 students received support, including 10 research assistantships with tuition reimbursements available (averaging $11,882 per year), 5 teaching assistantships with tuition reimbursements available (averaging $11,882 per year); scholarships/grants and unspecified assistantships also available. Support available to part-time students. *Faculty research:* Education law, career development, bullying, psychopharmacology, counseling and spirituality. *Total annual research expenditures:* $225,821. *Unit head:* Dr. Ann L. Bauer, Chairperson, 216-687-4582, Fax: 216-687-5378, E-mail: a.l.bauer@csuohio.edu. *Application contact:* Deborah L. Brown, Interim Assistant Director,

Graduate Admissions, 216-523-7572, Fax: 216-687-5400, E-mail: d.l.brown@csuohio.edu.
Website: http://www.csuohio.edu/cehs/departments/CASAL/casal_dept.html

The College at Brockport, State University of New York, School of Education, Health, and Human Services, Department of Counselor Education, Brockport, NY 14420-2997. Offers college counseling (MS Ed, CAS); mental health counseling (MS, CAS); school counseling (MS Ed, CAS); school counselor supervision (CAS). *Accreditation:* ACA (one or more programs are accredited). *Program availability:* Part-time. *Faculty:* 5 full-time (3 women), 6 part-time/adjunct (4 women). *Students:* 26 full-time (20 women), 75 part-time (60 women); includes 22 minority (12 Black or African American, non-Hispanic/Latino; 1 American Indian or Alaska Native, non-Hispanic/Latino; 1 Asian, non-Hispanic/Latino; 3 Hispanic/Latino; 5 Two or more races, non-Hispanic/Latino). 102 applicants, 34% accepted, 26 enrolled. In 2016, 20 master's, 4 other advanced degrees awarded. *Degree requirements:* For master's, thesis, internship. *Entrance requirements:* For master's, group interview, letters of recommendation, written objectives, audio response; for CAS, master's degree, New York state school counselor certificate. Additional exam requirements/recommendations for international students: Required—TOEFL (minimum score 550 paper-based; 79 iBT), IELTS (minimum score 6.5). *Application deadline:* For fall admission, 2/1 priority date for domestic and international students; for spring admission, 9/1 priority date for domestic and international students; for summer admission, 2/1 priority date for domestic and international students. Application fee: $80. Electronic applications accepted. *Expenses:* Contact institution. *Financial support:* In 2016–17, 1 fellowship with full tuition reimbursement (averaging $7,500 per year), 1 teaching assistantship with full tuition reimbursement (averaging $6,000 per year) were awarded; Federal Work-Study, scholarships/grants, and unspecified assistantships also available. Support available to part-time students. Financial award application deadline: 3/15; financial award applicants required to submit FAFSA. *Faculty research:* Gender and diversity issues; counseling outcomes; spirituality; school, college and mental health counseling; obesity. *Unit head:* Dr. Susan Seem, Chair, 585-395-5492, Fax: 585-395-2366, E-mail: sseem@brockport.edu. *Application contact:* Danielle A. Welch, Graduate Admissions Counselor, 585-395-5465, Fax: 585-395-2515.
Website: http://www.brockport.edu/edc/

The College of New Jersey, Office of Graduate and Advancing Education, School of Education, Department of Counselor Education, Program in Community Counseling: Human Services Specialization, Ewing, NJ 08628. Offers MA. *Accreditation:* ACA. *Program availability:* Part-time. *Degree requirements:* For master's, comprehensive exam. *Entrance requirements:* For master's, GRE General Test, minimum GPA of 3.0 in field or 2.75 overall, interview. Additional exam requirements/recommendations for international students: Required—TOEFL. Electronic applications accepted.

The College of New Jersey, Office of Graduate and Advancing Education, School of Education, Department of Counselor Education, Program in School Counseling, Ewing, NJ 08628. Offers MA. *Accreditation:* ACA; NCATE. *Program availability:* Part-time. *Degree requirements:* For master's, comprehensive exam. *Entrance requirements:* For master's, GRE General Test, minimum GPA of 3.0 in field or 2.75 overall, interview. Additional exam requirements/recommendations for international students: Required—TOEFL. Electronic applications accepted.

College of St. Joseph, Graduate Programs, Division of Psychology and Human Services, Rutland, VT 05701-3899. Offers alcohol and substance abuse counseling (MS); clinical mental health counseling (MS); clinical psychology (MS); community counseling (MS); school guidance counseling (MS). *Program availability:* Part-time, evening/weekend. *Degree requirements:* For master's, comprehensive exam, thesis optional. *Entrance requirements:* For master's, official college transcripts; 2 letters of reference. Additional exam requirements/recommendations for international students: Required—TOEFL (minimum score 550 paper-based). *Application deadline:* Applications are processed on a rolling basis. Application fee: $35. Electronic applications accepted. *Expenses: Tuition:* Full-time $13,800; part-time $560 per credit. *Required fees:* $75 per semester. Full-time tuition and fees vary according to course load. *Financial support:* Teaching assistantships with tuition reimbursements, career-related internships or fieldwork, Federal Work-Study, and unspecified assistantships available. Support available to part-time students. Financial award application deadline: 3/1. *Unit head:* Dr. Craig Knapp, Chair, 802-773-5900 Ext. 3219, Fax: 802-776-5258, E-mail: cknapp@csj.edu. *Application contact:* Alan Young, Dean of Admissions, 802-773-5900 Ext. 3227, Fax: 802-776-5310, E-mail: alanyoung@csj.edu.

The College of Saint Rose, Graduate Studies, Thelma P. Lally School of Education, Programs in Clinical Mental Health Counseling, Albany, NY 12203-1419. Offers clinical mental health counseling (Certificate); school counseling (MS Ed, Certificate), including mental health counseling (MS Ed). *Students:* 58 full-time (53 women), 23 part-time (19 women); includes 9 minority (5 Black or African American, non-Hispanic/Latino; 2 Asian, non-Hispanic/Latino; 1 Hispanic/Latino; 1 Two or more races, non-Hispanic/Latino), 1 international. Average age 28. 60 applicants, 78% accepted, 32 enrolled. In 2016, 1 Certificate awarded. *Entrance requirements:* For master's, minimum undergraduate GPA of 3.0. Additional exam requirements/recommendations for international students: Required—TOEFL (minimum score 550 paper-based; 80 iBT), IELTS (minimum score 6), PTE (minimum score 56). *Application deadline:* For fall admission, 4/1 for domestic and international students; for spring admission, 10/15 priority date for domestic and international students; for summer admission, 3/15 for domestic and international students. Applications are processed on a rolling basis. Application fee: $40. Electronic applications accepted. *Expenses: Tuition:* Full-time $14,382; part-time $799 per credit. *Required fees:* $814; $32 per credit. $88 per semester. Tuition and fees vary according to course load. *Financial support:* Career-related internships or fieldwork, scholarships/grants, tuition waivers (partial), and unspecified assistantships available. Support available to part-time students. Financial award application deadline: 4/15. *Unit head:* Dr. Claudia Lingertat-Putnam, Chair, 518-337-4311, E-mail: lingertc@strose.edu. *Application contact:* Cris Murray, Assistant Vice President for Graduate Recruitment and Enrollment, 518-485-3390, Fax: 518-458-5479, E-mail: grad@strose.edu.
Website: https://www.strose.edu/counseling/

The College of William and Mary, School of Education, Program in Counselor Education, Williamsburg, VA 23187-8795. Offers addictions counseling (M Ed); community counseling (M Ed); counselor education (PhD); family counseling (M Ed); school counseling (M Ed). *Accreditation:* ACA; NCATE. *Faculty:* 9 full-time (2 women), 6 part-time/adjunct (5 women). *Students:* 69 full-time (47 women), 4 part-time (3 women); includes 15 minority (4 Black or African American, non-Hispanic/Latino; 1 Asian, non-Hispanic/Latino; 6 Hispanic/Latino; 4 Two or more races, non-Hispanic/Latino), 5 international. Average age 27. 116 applicants, 48% accepted, 28 enrolled. In 2016, 24 master's, 6 doctorates awarded. *Degree requirements:* For doctorate, comprehensive exam, thesis/dissertation. *Entrance requirements:* For master's, GRE, minimum GPA of 3.0; for doctorate, GRE, minimum GPA of 3.5. Additional exam requirements/recommendations for international students: Required—TOEFL (minimum score 100 iBT), IELTS (minimum score 7). *Application deadline:* For fall admission, 1/15 for domestic and international students. Application fee: $50. Electronic applications accepted. *Expenses:* $14,258 per year in-state full-time, $275 per credit in-state part-time; $30,500 per year out-of-state full-time, $1,200 per credit out-of-state part-time. *Financial support:* In 2016–17, 37 students received support, including 29 research assistantships (averaging $17,725 per year); career-related internships or fieldwork, scholarships/grants, and unspecified assistantships also available. Financial award application deadline: 1/15; financial award applicants required to submit FAFSA. *Faculty research:* Sexuality, multicultural education, addiction counseling, transpersonal psychology, measurement and evaluation in counseling. *Unit head:* Dr. Charles F. Gressard, Department Chair, 757-221-2352, E-mail: cfgres@wm.edu. *Application contact:* Dorothy Smith Osborne, Assistant Dean for Academic Programs and Student Services, 757-221-2317, E-mail: dsosbo@wm.edu.
Website: http://education.wm.edu

Colorado State University, College of Health and Human Sciences, School of Education, Fort Collins, CO 80523-1588. Offers adult education and training (M Ed); counseling and career development (M Ed); education sciences (PhD); higher education leadership (PhD); organization learning, performance, and change (PhD); organizational learning, performance, and change (M Ed); student affairs in higher education (MS); teaching and learning (M Ed), including principal licensure, teacher licensure. *Accreditation:* ACA; TEAC. *Program availability:* Part-time, online only, 100% online, blended/hybrid learning, face-to-face off-campus courses. *Faculty:* 29 full-time (21 women), 23 part-time/adjunct (11 women). *Students:* 80 full-time (56 women), 541 part-time (353 women); includes 142 minority (26 Black or African American, non-Hispanic/Latino; 2 American Indian or Alaska Native, non-Hispanic/Latino; 22 Asian, non-Hispanic/Latino; 71 Hispanic/Latino; 21 Two or more races, non-Hispanic/Latino), 18 international. Average age 37. 483 applicants, 31% accepted, 137 enrolled. In 2016, 183 master's, 33 doctorates awarded. *Degree requirements:* For master's, thesis optional, professional portfolio; for doctorate, comprehensive exam, thesis/dissertation. *Entrance requirements:* For master's, bachelor's degree; minimum GPA of 3.0 in last degree earned; for doctorate, GRE or GMAT (depending upon specialization), master's degree; minimum GPA of 3.0 in last degree earned. Additional exam requirements/recommendations for international students: Required—TOEFL (minimum score 550 paper-based; 80 iBT), IELTS (minimum score 6.5), PTE (minimum score 58). *Application deadline:* Applications are processed on a rolling basis. Application fee: $60 ($70 for international students). Electronic applications accepted. *Expenses:* Contact institution. *Financial support:* In 2016–17, 3 students received support, including 7 research assistantships with full tuition reimbursements available (averaging $11,749 per year), 5 teaching assistantships with full tuition reimbursements available (averaging $15,886 per year); fellowships with full tuition reimbursements available, scholarships/grants, and unspecified assistantships also available. Financial award application deadline: 3/1; financial award applicants required to submit FAFSA. *Faculty research:* Higher education leadership; research methods; human resource development; K-16 education; diversity, equity, and inclusion. *Total annual research expenditures:* $499,898. *Unit head:* Dr. Louise Jennings, Co-Director, 970-491-6317, Fax: 970-491-1317, E-mail: louise.jennings@colostate.edu. *Application contact:* Kelli Clark, Graduate Programs Coordinator, 970-491-2093, Fax: 970-491-1317, E-mail: kelli.clark@colostate.edu.
Website: http://www.soe.chhs.colostate.edu/

Columbia International University, Columbia Graduate School, Columbia, SC 29230-3122. Offers Bible teaching (MABT); counseling (MACN); early childhood and elementary education (MAT); educational administration (M Ed); educational leadership (PhD); instruction and learning (M Ed); teaching English as a foreign language (Certificate); teaching English as a foreign language and intercultural studies (MATF). *Program availability:* Part-time, evening/weekend, online learning. *Degree requirements:* For master's, internships, professional project. *Entrance requirements:* For master's, MAT; GRE (for some programs), minimum GPA of 2.7. Additional exam requirements/recommendations for international students: Required—TOEFL. Electronic applications accepted.

Columbus State University, Graduate Studies, College of Education and Health Professions, Department of Counseling, Foundations, and Leadership, Columbus, GA 31907-5645. Offers clinical mental health counseling (MS); curriculum and leadership (Ed D), including curriculum, educational leadership, higher education (M Ed, Ed D); educational leadership (M Ed, Ed S), including higher education (M Ed, Ed D); school counseling (M Ed, Ed S). *Accreditation:* ACA; NCATE. *Program availability:* Part-time, evening/weekend, 100% online, blended/hybrid learning. *Faculty:* 14 full-time (4 women), 25 part-time/adjunct (14 women). *Students:* 226 full-time (159 women), 294 part-time (219 women); includes 298 minority (270 Black or African American, non-Hispanic/Latino; 1 American Indian or Alaska Native, non-Hispanic/Latino; 5 Asian, non-Hispanic/Latino; 13 Hispanic/Latino; 9 Two or more races, non-Hispanic/Latino), 1 international. Average age 39. 367 applicants, 57% accepted, 162 enrolled. In 2016, 20 master's, 7 doctorates, 121 other advanced degrees awarded. *Degree requirements:* For master's, thesis, exit exam; for doctorate, comprehensive exam, thesis/dissertation; for Ed S, thesis or alternative. *Entrance requirements:* For master's, GRE General Test, minimum undergraduate GPA of 2.75; for doctorate, GRE General Test, minimum graduate GPA of 3.5, four years of professional service; for Ed S, GRE General Test, minimum undergraduate GPA of 2.75, graduate 3.0. Additional exam requirements/recommendations for international students: Required—TOEFL (minimum score 550 paper-based; 79 iBT). *Application deadline:* For fall admission, 6/30 for domestic and international students; for spring admission, 11/1 for domestic and international students; for summer admission, 3/1 for domestic and international students. Applications are processed on a rolling basis. Application fee: $50. Electronic applications accepted. *Expenses:* Tuition, state resident: full-time $4804; part-time $2412 per semester hour. Tuition, nonresident: full-time $19,218; part-time $9612 per semester hour. *Required fees:* $1850; $1850 per semester hour. Tuition and fees vary according to program. *Financial support:* In 2016–17, 43 students received support, including 9 research assistantships with partial tuition reimbursements available (averaging $3,000 per year); career-related internships or fieldwork, Federal Work-Study, institutionally sponsored loans, scholarships/grants, tuition waivers (partial), and unspecified assistantships also available. Support available to part-time students. Financial award application deadline: 5/1; financial award applicants required to submit FAFSA. *Unit head:* Dr. Tom Hackett, Department Chair, 706-507-8968, Fax: 706-569-3134, E-mail: hackett_paul@columbusstate.edu. *Application contact:* Kristin Williams, Director of International and Graduate Recruitment, 706-507-8848, Fax: 706-568-5091, E-mail: williams_kristin@columbusstate.edu.
Website: http://cfl.columbusstate.edu/

Concordia University Chicago, College of Graduate and Innovative Programs, Program in School Counseling, River Forest, IL 60305-1499. Offers MA, CAS. *Accreditation:* ACA (one or more programs are accredited); NCATE. *Program availability:* Part-time, evening/weekend. *Degree requirements:* For master's, comprehensive exam, thesis optional; for CAS, thesis, final project. *Entrance requirements:* For master's, minimum GPA of 2.9; for CAS, master's degree. Additional exam requirements/recommendations for international students: Required—TOEFL (minimum score 550 paper-based). Electronic applications accepted. *Faculty research:* Development of comprehensive school counseling education, training of school counselors for parochial schools.

Concordia University Irvine, School of Education, Irvine, CA 92612-3299. Offers curriculum and instruction (MA); education and preliminary teaching credential (M Ed); educational administration and preliminary administrative services credential (MA); educational technology (MA); school counseling with pupil personnel services credential (MA). *Program availability:* Part-time, evening/weekend, online learning. *Degree requirements:* For master's, action research project. *Entrance requirements:* For master's, California Basic Educational Skills Test, California Subject Examinations for Teachers (M Ed and MA in educational administration and preliminary administrative services credential), official college transcript(s), signed statement of intent, two references, copy of credential. Additional exam requirements/recommendations for international students: Required—TOEFL. Electronic applications accepted. *Expenses:* Contact institution.

Concordia University Wisconsin, Graduate Programs, Department of Education, Mequon, WI 53097-2402. Offers art education (MS Ed); early childhood (MS Ed); educational administration (MS Ed); environmental education (MS Ed); family studies (MS Ed); literacy (MS Ed); school counseling (MS Ed); special education (MS Ed). *Program availability:* Part-time, evening/weekend, online learning. *Degree requirements:* For master's, comprehensive exam, thesis or alternative. *Entrance requirements:* For master's, minimum GPA of 3.0, teaching license. Additional exam requirements/recommendations for international students: Required—TOEFL. Application fee: $35. *Financial support:* Career-related internships or fieldwork and tuition waivers (partial) available. Financial award application deadline: 8/1. *Faculty research:* Motivation, developmental learning, learning styles. *Unit head:* Dr. James Juergensen, Director, 262-243-4214, E-mail: james.juergensen@cuw.edu. *Application contact:* Graduate Admissions, 262-243-4248, Fax: 262-243-4428.

Creighton University, Graduate School, College of Arts and Sciences, Department of Education, Program in School Counseling and Preventive Mental Health, Omaha, NE 68178-0001. Offers elementary school guidance (MS); secondary school guidance (MS). *Program availability:* Part-time, online only, 100% online, blended/hybrid learning. *Faculty:* 3 full-time (1 woman). *Students:* 12 full-time (10 women), 37 part-time (32 women); includes 1 minority (Asian, non-Hispanic/Latino). Average age 35. In 2016, 10 master's awarded. *Degree requirements:* For master's, comprehensive exam. *Entrance requirements:* For master's, resume, 3 letters of recommendation, personal statement, background check. Additional exam requirements/recommendations for international students: Required—TOEFL (minimum score 90 iBT). *Application deadline:* For fall admission, 7/1 for domestic students, 3/1 for international students; for winter admission, 10/1 for domestic students, 7/1 for international students; for spring admission, 3/1 for domestic students, 9/1 for international students; for summer admission, 3/1 for domestic and international students. Application fee: $50. Electronic applications accepted. *Expenses: Tuition:* Full-time $14,400; part-time $800 per credit hour. *Required fees:* $158 per semester. Tuition and fees vary according to course load, campus/location, program, reciprocity agreements and student's religious affiliation. *Financial support:* Scholarships/grants available. Support available to part-time students. Financial award applicants required to submit FAFSA. *Unit head:* Dr. Timothy Dickel, Professor of Education, 402-280-2230, E-mail: ctdickel@creighton.edu. *Application contact:* Lindsay Johnson, Director of Graduate and Adult Recruitment, 402-280-2703, Fax: 402-280-2423, E-mail: gradschool@creighton.edu.

Dallas Baptist University, Dorothy M. Bush College of Education, Program in School Counseling, Dallas, TX 75211-9299. Offers M Ed, Advanced Certificate. *Program availability:* Part-time, evening/weekend. *Application deadline:* Applications are processed on a rolling basis. Application fee: $25. Electronic applications accepted. Application fee is waived when completed online. *Expenses: Tuition:* Full-time $15,408; part-time $856 per credit hour. *Required fees:* $400 per semester. Tuition and fees vary according to course load and degree level. *Unit head:* Dr. Bonnie B. Bond, Director, 214-333-5413, E-mail: graduate@dbu.edu. *Application contact:* Bobby Soto, Director of Admissions, 214-333-5242, E-mail: graduate@dbu.edu.
Website: http://www3.dbu.edu/graduate/education_counseling.asp

Delta State University, Graduate Programs, College of Education, Division of Counselor Education and Psychology, Cleveland, MS 38733-0001. Offers counseling (M Ed). *Accreditation:* ACA (one or more programs are accredited); NCATE. *Program availability:* Part-time, evening/weekend. *Degree requirements:* For master's, thesis optional, practicum. Electronic applications accepted.

Delta State University, Graduate Programs, College of Education, Division of Teacher Education, Leadership, and Research, Program in Professional Studies, Cleveland, MS 38733-0001. Offers counselor education (Ed D); elementary education (Ed D); higher education (Ed D). *Program availability:* Part-time, evening/weekend. *Degree requirements:* For doctorate, thesis/dissertation. *Entrance requirements:* For doctorate, GRE General Test.

DePaul University, College of Education, Chicago, IL 60614. Offers bilingual bicultural education (M Ed, MA); counseling (M Ed, MA), including clinical mental health counseling, college student development, school counseling; curriculum studies (M Ed, MA, Ed D); early childhood education (M Ed, MA, Ed D); educating adults (MA); educational leadership (M Ed, MA, Ed D), including administration and supervision (M Ed, MA), principal preparation (M Ed, MA); elementary education (MA); mathematics education (MA); mathematics for teaching (MS); middle school mathematics education (MS); reading specialist (M Ed, MA); secondary education (M Ed); social and cultural foundations in education (MA); special education (M Ed, MA); world languages education (M Ed, MA). *Program availability:* Part-time, evening/weekend, online learning. *Degree requirements:* For doctorate, thesis/dissertation. Electronic applications accepted.

Doane University, Program in Counseling, Crete, NE 68333-2430. Offers MAC. *Program availability:* Evening/weekend. *Faculty:* 2 full-time (1 woman), 15 part-time/adjunct (11 women). *Students:* 71 full-time (55 women), 24 part-time (19 women); includes 11 minority (2 Black or African American, non-Hispanic/Latino; 1 American Indian or Alaska Native, non-Hispanic/Latino; 7 Hispanic/Latino; 1 Two or more races, non-Hispanic/Latino). Average age 33. In 2016, 45 master's awarded. *Degree requirements:* For master's, thesis. *Entrance requirements:* For master's, minimum GPA of 3.0. Additional exam requirements/recommendations for international students: Required—TOEFL. *Application deadline:* Applications are processed on a rolling basis. Application fee: $25. Electronic applications accepted. *Expenses:* Contact institution. *Financial support:* Unspecified assistantships available. Financial award application deadline: 6/1; financial award applicants required to submit FAFSA. *Unit head:* Associate Dean/Director of the Counseling Program, 402-466-4774, Fax: 402-466-4228. *Application contact:* Jean Kilnoski, Assistant Dean, 402-466-4774, Fax: 404-466-4228, E-mail: jean.kilnoski@doane.edu.
Website: http://www.doane.edu/master-of-arts-in-counseling-0

Duquesne University, School of Education, Department of Counseling, Psychology, and Special Education, Program in Counselor Education, Pittsburgh, PA 15282-0001. Offers clinical mental health counseling (MS Ed, Post-Master's Certificate); counselor education and supervision (Ed D); counselor licensure (Post-Master's Certificate); marriage and family counseling (MS Ed); school counseling (MS Ed). *Accreditation:* ACA (one or more programs are accredited). *Program availability:* Part-time, evening/weekend. *Faculty:* 8 full-time (3 women). *Students:* 188 full-time (139 women), 5 part-time (4 women); includes 39 minority (20 Black or African American, non-Hispanic/Latino; 5 Asian, non-Hispanic/Latino; 5 Hispanic/Latino; 9 Two or more races, non-Hispanic/Latino), 8 international. Average age 29. 152 applicants, 73% accepted, 69 enrolled. In 2016, 34 master's, 9 doctorates awarded. *Degree requirements:* For master's, thesis optional; for doctorate, thesis/dissertation. *Entrance requirements:* For master's, letters of recommendation, essay, interview, bachelor's degree; for doctorate, GRE, letters of recommendation, essay, interview, master's degree; for Post-Master's Certificate, GRE, letters of recommendation, essay, interview, bachelor's/master's degree. Additional exam requirements/recommendations for international students: Required—TOEFL (minimum score 550 paper-based), IELTS (minimum score 7). *Application deadline:* For fall admission, 3/1 for domestic students; for spring admission, 9/1 for domestic students. Applications are processed on a rolling basis. Application fee: $0. Electronic applications accepted. *Expenses: Tuition:* Full-time $22,212; part-time $1234 per credit. Tuition and fees vary according to program. *Financial support:* Research assistantships, teaching assistantships, and Federal Work-Study available. Support available to part-time students. *Unit head:* Dr. Jered Kolbert, Professor/Director, 412-396-4471, Fax: 412-396-1340, E-mail: kolbertj@duq.edu. *Application contact:* Michael Dolinger, Director of Student and Academic Services, 412-396-6647, Fax: 412-396-5585, E-mail: dolingerm@duq.edu.

East Carolina University, Graduate School, College of Allied Health Sciences, Department of Addictions and Rehabilitation Studies, Greenville, NC 27858-4353. Offers military and trauma counseling (Certificate); rehabilitation and career counseling (MS); rehabilitation counseling (Certificate); rehabilitation counseling and administration (PhD); substance abuse and clinical counseling (MS); substance abuse counseling (Certificate); vocational evaluation (Certificate). *Accreditation:* CORE. *Program availability:* Part-time, evening/weekend. *Students:* 86 full-time (73 women), 44 part-time (38 women); includes 39 minority (34 Black or African American, non-Hispanic/Latino; 1 American Indian or Alaska Native, non-Hispanic/Latino; 2 Asian, non-Hispanic/Latino; 2 Hispanic/Latino). Average age 32. 80 applicants, 85% accepted, 50 enrolled. In 2016, 22 master's, 2 doctorates awarded. *Degree requirements:* For master's, comprehensive exam, thesis or alternative, internship. *Entrance requirements:* For master's, GRE General Test or MAT. Additional exam requirements/recommendations for international students: Required—TOEFL. *Application deadline:* For fall admission, 3/1 priority date for domestic students; for spring admission, 10/1 priority date for domestic students. Applications are processed on a rolling basis. Application fee: $50. *Financial support:* Research assistantships with partial tuition reimbursements, teaching assistantships with partial tuition reimbursements, Federal Work-Study, and scholarships/grants available. Support available to part-time students. Financial award application deadline: 3/1. *Unit head:* Dr. Paul Toriello, Chair, 252-744-6292, E-mail: toriellop@ecu.edu.
Website: http://www.ecu.edu/rehb/

East Carolina University, Graduate School, College of Education, Department of Interdisciplinary Professions, Greenville, NC 27858-4353. Offers adult education (MA Ed); business and marketing education (MA); career and technical education (MA Ed); counselor education (MS); library science (MLS); vocational education (MS). *Accreditation:* ACA; NCATE. *Program availability:* Part-time, evening/weekend. *Students:* 95 full-time (79 women), 427 part-time (374 women); includes 106 minority (68 Black or African American, non-Hispanic/Latino; 13 American Indian or Alaska Native, non-Hispanic/Latino; 4 Asian, non-Hispanic/Latino; 13 Hispanic/Latino; 8 Two or more races, non-Hispanic/Latino). Average age 37. 225 applicants, 93% accepted, 174 enrolled. In 2016, 86 master's awarded. *Degree requirements:* For master's, comprehensive exam, thesis optional. *Entrance requirements:* For master's, GRE General Test or MAT, interview, minimum GPA of 2.5, bachelor's degree in related field, teaching license (MA Ed). Additional exam requirements/recommendations for international students: Required—TOEFL. *Application deadline:* For fall admission, 5/15 priority date for domestic students. Applications are processed on a rolling basis. Application fee: $50. *Financial support:* Research assistantships with partial tuition reimbursements, teaching assistantships with partial tuition reimbursements, and Federal Work-Study available. Support available to part-time students. Financial award application deadline: 6/1. *Unit head:* Dr. Vivian W. Mott, Chair, 252-328-6177, Fax: 252-328-4368, E-mail: mottv@ecu.edu. *Application contact:* Dean of Graduate School, 252-328-6012, Fax: 252-328-6071, E-mail: gradschool@ecu.edu.
Website: http://www.ecu.edu/cs-educ/idp/index.cfm

East Central University, School of Graduate Studies, Department of Human Resources, Ada, OK 74820. Offers administration (MSHR); counseling (MSHR); criminal justice (MSHR); human services (MSHR); rehabilitation counseling (MSHR). *Accreditation:* CORE. *Program availability:* Part-time, evening/weekend. *Degree requirements:* For master's, thesis optional. *Entrance requirements:* For master's, GRE General Test, MAT, minimum GPA of 2.5. Electronic applications accepted.

Eastern Illinois University, Graduate School, College of Education and Professional Studies, Department of Counseling and Student Development, Charleston, IL 61920. Offers college student affairs (MS); counseling (MS). *Accreditation:* ACA; NCATE. *Program availability:* Part-time, evening/weekend. *Degree requirements:* For master's, comprehensive exam (for some programs), thesis (for some programs). *Entrance requirements:* For master's, GMAT or GRE. Additional exam requirements/recommendations for international students: Required—TOEFL (minimum score 500 paper-based; 61 iBT), IELTS (minimum score 6). Electronic applications accepted.

Eastern Kentucky University, The Graduate School, College of Education, Department of Counseling and Educational Leadership, Richmond, KY 40475-3102. Offers human services (MA); instructional leadership (MA Ed); mental health counseling (MA); school counseling (MA Ed). *Accreditation:* ACA (one or more programs are accredited); NCATE. *Program availability:* Part-time, online learning. *Entrance requirements:* For master's, GRE General Test, minimum GPA of 2.5.

Eastern Mennonite University, Master of Arts in Counseling Program, Harrisonburg, VA 22802-2462. Offers MA, M Div/MA. *Accreditation:* ACA (one or more programs are accredited); ACIPE. *Program availability:* Part-time. *Degree requirements:* For master's, practicum, internship. *Entrance requirements:* For master's, minimum GPA of 3.0. Additional exam requirements/recommendations for international students: Required—TOEFL (minimum score 550 paper-based). Electronic applications accepted. *Expenses:* Contact institution. *Faculty research:* Career and gender, empathy and consciousness, emotion theory, education models.

Eastern Michigan University, Graduate School, College of Education, Department of Leadership and Counseling, Programs in Counseling, Ypsilanti, MI 48197. Offers clinical mental health counseling (MA); college counseling (MA); helping interventions in a multicultural society (Graduate Certificate); school counseling (MA); school counselor licensure (Post Master's Certificate). *Program availability:* Part-time, evening/weekend. *Students:* 15 full-time (14 women), 72 part-time (55 women); includes 26 minority (19 Black or African American, non-Hispanic/Latino; 2 Asian, non-Hispanic/Latino; 4 Hispanic/Latino; 1 Two or more races, non-Hispanic/Latino), 1 international. Average age 33. 63 applicants, 40% accepted, 16 enrolled. In 2016, 27 master's, 14 other advanced degrees awarded. *Degree requirements:* For master's, comprehensive exam, internship. *Entrance requirements:* Additional exam requirements/recommendations for international students: Required—TOEFL. *Application deadline:* For fall admission, 5/1 for domestic and international students; for winter admission, 9/15 for domestic and international students; for spring admission, 2/10 for domestic and international students. Applications are processed on a rolling basis. Application fee: $45. *Financial support:* Fellowships, research assistantships with full tuition reimbursements, teaching assistantships with full tuition reimbursements, career-related internships or fieldwork, Federal Work-Study, institutionally sponsored loans, scholarships/grants, tuition waivers (partial), and unspecified assistantships available. Support available to part-time students. Financial award applicants required to submit FAFSA. *Application contact:* Dr. Irene Ametrano, Coordinator of Advising for Programs in Counseling, 734-487-0255, Fax: 734-487-4608, E-mail: iametrano@emich.edu.

Eastern New Mexico University, Graduate School, College of Education and Technology, Department of Educational Studies, Program in Counseling, Portales, NM 88130. Offers MA. *Program availability:* Part-time. *Degree requirements:* For master's, comprehensive exam, thesis optional, 48-hour course work including a 600-hour internship in field placement. *Entrance requirements:* For master's, minimum GPA of 3.0, 3 letters of recommendation, interview. Additional exam requirements/recommendations for international students: Required—TOEFL (minimum score 550 paper-based; 79 iBT), IELTS (minimum score 6). Electronic applications accepted.

Eastern New Mexico University, Graduate School, College of Education and Technology, Department of Educational Studies, Program in School Counseling, Portales, NM 88130. Offers M Ed. *Program availability:* Part-time. *Degree requirements:* For master's, comprehensive exam, thesis optional, 48-hour curriculum, 600-hour internship in field placement. *Entrance requirements:* For master's, minimum GPA of 3.0, three letters of recommendation, interview. Additional exam requirements/recommendations for international students: Required—TOEFL (minimum score 550 paper-based; 79 iBT), IELTS (minimum score 6). Electronic applications accepted.

Eastern University, Department of Counseling Psychology, St. Davids, PA 19087-3696. Offers applied behavior analysis (MA, Certificate); counseling (MA); professional counseling (Certificate); school counseling (MA, Certificate); school psychology (MS, Certificate). *Program availability:* Part-time. *Students:* 104 full-time (92 women), 88 part-time (75 women); includes 83 minority (61 Black or African American, non-Hispanic/Latino; 1 American Indian or Alaska Native, non-Hispanic/Latino; 4 Asian, non-Hispanic/Latino; 13 Hispanic/Latino; 4 Two or more races, non-Hispanic/Latino), 3 international. Average age 29. In 2016, 46 master's awarded. *Degree requirements:* For master's, internship. *Entrance requirements:* Additional exam requirements/recommendations for international students: Required—TOEFL (minimum score 550 paper-based; 79 iBT). *Application deadline:* Applications are processed on a rolling basis. Application fee: $35. Electronic applications accepted. Application fee is waived when completed online. *Expenses:* $690 per credit. *Financial support:* Application deadline: 3/15. *Unit head:* Michael Dziedziak, Executive Director of Enrollment, 800-452-0996, E-mail: gpsadmissions@eastern.edu.
Website: http://www.eastern.edu/academics/programs/graduate-counseling-and-psychology-department

Eastern Washington University, Graduate Studies, College of Social Sciences, Department of Psychology, Program in School Counseling, Cheney, WA 99004-2431. Offers applied psychology (MS); school counseling (MS). *Accreditation:* ACA. *Students:* 13 full-time (6 women), 1 (woman) part-time; includes 6 minority (4 Asian, non-Hispanic/Latino; 2 Hispanic/Latino). Average age 26. 33 applicants, 42% accepted, 11 enrolled. In 2016, 2 master's awarded. *Degree requirements:* For master's, comprehensive exam, thesis or alternative. *Entrance requirements:* For master's, GRE General Test, minimum GPA of 3.0. Additional exam requirements/recommendations for international students: Required—TOEFL (minimum score 580 paper-based; 92 iBT), IELTS (minimum score 7), PTE (minimum score 63). *Application deadline:* For fall admission, 2/1 for domestic students. Applications are processed on a rolling basis. Application fee: $75. Electronic applications accepted. *Expenses:* Tuition, state resident: full-time $11,000; part-time $5500 per credit. Tuition, nonresident: full-time $24,000; part-time $12,000 per credit. *Required fees:* $1300. One-time fee: $50 full-time. Part-time tuition and fees vary according to course load, campus/location and program. *Financial support:* In 2016–17, teaching assistantships with partial tuition reimbursements (averaging $10,000 per year) were awarded; career-related internships or fieldwork, Federal Work-Study, institutionally sponsored loans, scholarships/grants, health care benefits, tuition waivers (partial), and unspecified assistantships also available. Support available to part-time students. Financial award application deadline: 2/1; financial award applicants required to submit FAFSA. *Unit head:* Dr. Keely Hope, Associate Professor/Director, Counselor Education, 509-359-2439, E-mail: khope@ewu.edu. *Application contact:* Kathy White, Advisor/Recruiter for Graduate Studies, 509-359-6656, E-mail: gradprograms@ewu.edu.
Website: http://www.ewu.edu/grad/programs/applied-psychology—school-counseling.xml

East Tennessee State University, School of Graduate Studies, College of Education, Department of Counseling and Human Services, Johnson City, TN 37614. Offers MA. *Accreditation:* ACA; NCATE. *Program availability:* Part-time. Terminal master's awarded for partial completion of doctoral program. *Degree requirements:* For master's, comprehensive exam, thesis optional, internship, student teaching, culminating experience. *Entrance requirements:* For master's, GRE General Test, minimum GPA of 3.0, three letters of recommendation, interview. Additional exam requirements/recommendations for international students: Required—TOEFL (minimum score 550 paper-based; 79 iBT). Electronic applications accepted. *Faculty research:* Intervention and assistance with at-risk and under-served youth and high conflict families; service and social justice; women and girls' issues in counseling; counseling competence with LGBTQ individuals; counselor education and supervision.

Edinboro University of Pennsylvania, Department of Counseling, School Psychology and Special Education, Edinboro, PA 16444. Offers counseling (MA), including art therapy, clinical mental health counseling, college counseling, rehabilitation counseling, school counseling; educational psychology (M Ed); school psychology (Ed S); special education (M Ed), including autism, behavior management. *Accreditation:* ACA. *Program availability:* Part-time, evening/weekend. *Degree requirements:* For master's, thesis or alternative, competency exam; for Ed S, thesis or alternative. *Entrance requirements:* For master's and Ed S, GRE or MAT, minimum QPA of 2.5. Electronic applications accepted.

Emporia State University, Program in School Counseling, Emporia, KS 66801-5415. Offers MS. *Accreditation:* ACA; NCATE. *Program availability:* Part-time. *Faculty:* 11 full-time (7 women), 1 (woman) part-time/adjunct. *Students:* 24 full-time (21 women), 77 part-time (68 women); includes 7 minority (1 Black or African American, non-Hispanic/Latino; 1 Asian, non-Hispanic/Latino; 4 Hispanic/Latino; 1 Two or more races, non-Hispanic/Latino), 1 international. 25 applicants, 100% accepted, 8 enrolled. In 2016, 28 master's awarded. *Degree requirements:* For master's, comprehensive exam or thesis, practicum. *Entrance requirements:* For master's, GRE or MAT, essay exam, appropriate bachelor's degree, interview, letters of recommendation. *Application deadline:* For fall admission, 8/15 priority date for domestic students. Applications are processed on a rolling basis. Application fee: $30 ($75 for international students). Electronic applications accepted. *Expenses:* Tuition, state resident: full-time $5922; part-time $246.75 per credit hour. Tuition, nonresident: full-time $18,414; part-time $767.25 per credit hour. *Required fees:* $1884; $78.50 per credit hour. *Financial support:* In 2016–17, 4 research assistantships with full tuition reimbursements (averaging $7,353 per year), 1 teaching assistantship with full tuition reimbursement (averaging $7,335 per year) were awarded; career-related internships or fieldwork, Federal Work-Study, institutionally sponsored loans, health care benefits, and unspecified assistantships also available. Financial award application deadline: 3/15; financial award applicants required to submit FAFSA. *Unit head:* Dr. Katrina Miller, Chair, 620-341-5791, E-mail: kmille12@emporia.edu. *Application contact:* Mary Sewell, Admissions Coordinator, 800-950-GRAD, Fax: 620-341-5909, E-mail: msewell@emporia.edu.

Evangel University, School Counseling Program, Springfield, MO 65802. Offers MS. *Program availability:* Part-time, evening/weekend. *Faculty:* 4 full-time (3 women), 4 part-time/adjunct (all women). *Students:* 25 full-time (22 women), 20 part-time (15 women); includes 2 minority (both Black or African American, non-Hispanic/Latino). Average age 31. 12 applicants, 100% accepted, 12 enrolled. In 2016, 20 master's awarded. *Degree requirements:* For master's, comprehensive exam. *Entrance requirements:* For master's, MAT (preferred) or GRE. Additional exam requirements/recommendations for international students: Required—TOEFL (minimum score 550 paper-based). *Application deadline:* For fall admission, 7/15 priority date for domestic students, 7/1 for international students; for spring admission, 11/15 priority date for domestic students, 12/1 for international students. Applications are processed on a rolling basis. Application fee: $25. Electronic applications accepted. *Expenses: Tuition:* Part-time $400 per credit hour. *Required fees:* $148 per trimester. One-time fee: $25. Tuition and fees vary according to course load, degree level and program. *Financial support:* In 2016–17, 2 students received support. Unspecified assistantships available. Financial award application deadline: 4/1; financial award applicants required to submit FAFSA. *Unit head:* Christine Arnzen, Program Coordinator, 417-865-2815 Ext. 8678, Fax: 417-575-5484, E-mail: arnzenc@evangel.edu. *Application contact:* Karen Benitez, Admissions Representative, Graduate Studies, 417-865-2815 Ext. 7416, Fax: 417-575-5484, E-mail: benitezk@evangel.edu.
Website: http://www.evangel.edu/academics/graduate-studies/graduate-programs

Fairfield University, Graduate School of Education and Allied Professions, Fairfield, CT 06824. Offers applied behavior analysis (ATC); applied psychology (MA); clinical mental health counseling (MA, CAS); educational technology (MA); elementary education (MA, CAS); family studies (MA); integration of spirituality and religion in counseling (ATC); marriage and family therapy (MA); reading and language development (Sixth Year Certificate); school counseling (MA, CAS); school psychology (MA, CAS); school-based marriage and family therapy (ATC); secondary education (MA); special education (MA, CAS); substance abuse counseling (ATC); teaching (Certificate); teaching and foundations (MA, CAS); TESOL, world languages, and bilingual education (MA, CAS). *Accreditation:* NCATE. *Program availability:* Part-time, evening/weekend. *Faculty:* 19 full-time (15 women), 38 part-time/adjunct (26 women). *Students:* 153 full-time (132 women), 302 part-time (252 women); includes 97 minority (24 Black or African American, non-Hispanic/Latino; 12 Asian, non-Hispanic/Latino; 55 Hispanic/Latino; 6 Two or more races, non-Hispanic/Latino), 6 international. Average age 32. 283 applicants, 61% accepted, 97 enrolled. In 2016, 130 master's awarded. *Degree requirements:* For master's, comprehensive exam. *Entrance requirements:* For master's, minimum GPA of 3.0, 2 recommendations, resume. Additional exam requirements/recommendations for international students: Required—TOEFL (minimum score 550 paper-based; 84 iBT) or IELTS (minimum score 7.5). *Application deadline:* For fall admission, 2/15 for international students; for spring admission, 10/1 for international students. Application fee: $60. Electronic applications accepted. *Expenses:* $725 per credit hour. *Financial support:* In 2016–17, 42 students received support. Career-related internships or fieldwork and unspecified assistantships available. Support available to part-time students. Financial award applicants required to submit FAFSA. *Faculty research:* Reading and literacy, writing, social justice and inequality in education, addictions and mental health issues, therapeutic relationships and clinical supervision. *Unit head:* Dr. Robert D. Hannafin, Dean, 203-254-4250, Fax: 203-254-4241, E-mail: rhannafin@fairfield.edu. *Application contact:* Marianne Gumpper, Director of Graduate Admission, 203-254-4184, Fax: 203-254-4073, E-mail: gradadmis@fairfield.edu.
Website: http://www.fairfield.edu/gseap

Faulkner University, Alabama Christian College of Arts and Sciences, Department of Social and Behavioral Sciences, Montgomery, AL 36109-3398. Offers counseling (MS). *Program availability:* Online learning.

Fitchburg State University, Division of Graduate and Continuing Education, Program in Interdisciplinary Studies, Fitchburg, MA 01420-2697. Offers applied communications (CAGS); counseling/psychology (CAGS); individualized track (CAGS); reading specialist (CAGS). *Program availability:* Part-time, evening/weekend. *Entrance requirements:* Additional exam requirements/recommendations for international students: Required—TOEFL (minimum score 550 paper-based; 79 iBT). Electronic applications accepted. *Expenses:* Tuition, state resident: full-time $2871; part-time $1914 per year. Tuition, nonresident: full-time $2871; part-time $1914 per year. *Required fees:* $3828. Tuition and fees vary according to program.

Fitchburg State University, Division of Graduate and Continuing Education, Programs in Counseling, Fitchburg, MA 01420-2697. Offers elementary school guidance counseling (MS); mental health counseling (MS); secondary school guidance counseling (MS). *Accreditation:* NCATE. *Program availability:* Part-time, evening/weekend. *Entrance requirements:* Additional exam requirements/recommendations for international students: Required—TOEFL (minimum score 550 paper-based; 79 iBT). Electronic applications accepted. *Expenses:* Tuition, state resident: full-time $2871; part-time $1914 per year. Tuition, nonresident: full-time $2871; part-time $1914 per year. *Required fees:* $3828. Tuition and fees vary according to program.

Florida Agricultural and Mechanical University, Division of Graduate Studies, Research, and Continuing Education, College of Education, Department of Educational Leadership and Human Services, Tallahassee, FL 32307-3200. Offers administration and supervision (M Ed, MS, PhD); adult education (M Ed, MS); educational leadership (PhD); guidance and counseling (M Ed, MS). *Accreditation:* NCATE. *Degree requirements:* For master's, thesis (for some programs); for doctorate, thesis/dissertation. *Entrance requirements:* For master's, GRE General Test, minimum GPA of 3.0. Additional exam requirements/recommendations for international students: Required—TOEFL.

Florida Atlantic University, College of Education, Department of Counselor Education, Boca Raton, FL 33431-0991. Offers MS, PhD. *Accreditation:* ACA; NCATE. *Program availability:* Part-time, evening/weekend. *Faculty:* 8 full-time (4 women), 1 (woman) part-time/adjunct. *Students:* 44 full-time (40 women), 76 part-time (61 women); includes 44 minority (24 Black or African American, non-Hispanic/Latino; 16 Hispanic/Latino; 4 Two or more races, non-Hispanic/Latino), 2 international. Average age 32. 151 applicants, 20% accepted, 24 enrolled. In 2016, 28 master's, 4 doctorates awarded. *Entrance requirements:* For master's, GRE General Test, minimum GPA of 3.0 during previous 2 years. Additional exam requirements/recommendations for international students: Required—TOEFL (minimum score 500 paper-based; 61 iBT), IELTS (minimum score 6). *Application deadline:* For fall admission, 3/1 for domestic students, 2/1 for international students; for spring admission, 9/15 for domestic students, 7/1 for

international students. Applications are processed on a rolling basis. Application fee: $30. *Expenses:* Tuition, state resident: full-time $7392; part-time $369.82 per credit hour. Tuition, nonresident: full-time $19,432; part-time $1024.81 per credit hour. *Financial support:* Research assistantships with partial tuition reimbursements, teaching assistantships, career-related internships or fieldwork, scholarships/grants, and unspecified assistantships available. *Faculty research:* Brief therapy, psychological type, marriage and family counseling, international programs, integrated services. *Unit head:* Dr. Paul Peluso, Interim Chair, 561-297-3625, Fax: 561-297-2309, E-mail: ppeluso@fau.edu.
Website: http://www.coe.fau.edu/academicdepartments/ce/

Florida International University, College of Arts, Sciences, and Education, Department of Leadership and Professional Studies, Miami, FL 33199. Offers adult education and human resource development (MS, Ed D); counseling (MS), including rehabilitation counseling, school counseling; counselor education (MS), including clinical mental health counseling; educational administration and supervision (Ed D); educational leadership (MS, Certificate, Ed S); higher education (Ed D); higher education administration (MS); international and comparative education (MS); recreation and sport management (MS), including recreation and sport management, recreational therapy; school psychology (Ed S); urban education (MS), including instruction in urban settings, learning technologies, multicultural/bilingual, multicultural/TESOL, urban education. *Program availability:* Part-time, evening/weekend. *Faculty:* 27 full-time (19 women), 38 part-time/adjunct (25 women). *Students:* 253 full-time (191 women), 306 part-time (241 women); includes 444 minority (129 Black or African American, non-Hispanic/Latino; 3 Asian, non-Hispanic/Latino; 304 Hispanic/Latino; 8 Two or more races, non-Hispanic/Latino), 18 international. Average age 31. 366 applicants, 60% accepted, 115 enrolled. In 2016, 193 master's, 8 doctorates awarded. *Degree requirements:* For doctorate, thesis/dissertation. *Entrance requirements:* For master's, minimum GPA of 3.0; for doctorate and other advanced degree, GRE General Test. Additional exam requirements/recommendations for international students: Required—TOEFL (minimum score 550 paper-based; 80 iBT), IELTS (minimum score 6.3). *Application deadline:* For fall admission, 6/1 priority date for domestic students, 4/1 for international students; for winter admission, 10/1 priority date for domestic students, 9/1 for international students; for spring admission, 3/1 priority date for domestic students, 2/1 for international students. Applications are processed on a rolling basis. Application fee: $30. Electronic applications accepted. *Expenses:* Tuition, state resident: full-time $8912; part-time $446 per credit hour. Tuition, nonresident: full-time $21,393; part-time $992 per credit hour. *Required fees:* $2185; $195 per semester. Tuition and fees vary according to program. *Financial support:* Fellowships, research assistantships with tuition reimbursements, teaching assistantships with tuition reimbursements, Federal Work-Study, and tuition waivers (full and partial) available. Support available to part-time students. Financial award applicants required to submit FAFSA. *Unit head:* Dr. Benjamin Baez, Chair, 305-348-3214, Fax: 305-348-1515, E-mail: benjamin.baez@fiu.edu. *Application contact:* Nanett Rojas, Assistant Director, Graduate Admissions, 305-348-7464, Fax: 305-348-7441, E-mail: gradadm@fiu.edu.
Website: http://education.fiu.edu

Fordham University, Graduate School of Education, Division of Psychological and Educational Services, New York, NY 10023. Offers counseling and personnel services (MSE); counseling psychology (PhD); school psychology (PhD). *Accreditation:* APA (one or more programs are accredited); NCATE. *Program availability:* Part-time, evening/weekend. Terminal master's awarded for partial completion of doctoral program. *Degree requirements:* For master's, comprehensive exam (for some programs); for doctorate, comprehensive exam (for some programs), thesis/dissertation. *Entrance requirements:* For doctorate, GRE General Test. Additional exam requirements/recommendations for international students: Required—TOEFL (minimum score 577 paper-based; 90 iBT), IELTS (minimum score 7). Electronic applications accepted.

Fort Hays State University, Graduate School, College of Education, Department of Educational Administration and Counseling, Program in Counseling, Hays, KS 67601-4099. Offers MS. *Accreditation:* NCATE. *Program availability:* Part-time. *Degree requirements:* For master's, comprehensive exam, thesis or alternative. *Entrance requirements:* For master's, GRE General Test or MAT, minimum undergraduate GPA of 3.0 in last 60 hours. Additional exam requirements/recommendations for international students: Required—TOEFL (minimum score 550 paper-based). Electronic applications accepted. *Faculty research:* Career education, evaluation and plans, counseling the disabled, marriage and family parenting, underemployment and work in the family.

Fort Valley State University, College of Graduate Studies and Extended Education, Department of Counseling Psychology, Fort Valley, GA 31030. Offers guidance and counseling (Ed S); mental health counseling (MS); rehabilitation counseling (MS). *Program availability:* Part-time. *Degree requirements:* For master's, comprehensive exam (for some programs), thesis optional. *Entrance requirements:* For master's and Ed S, GRE General Test or MAT.

Freed-Hardeman University, Program in Counseling, Henderson, TN 38340-2399. Offers MS. *Program availability:* Part-time, evening/weekend. *Degree requirements:* For master's, comprehensive exam, practicum. *Entrance requirements:* For master's, GRE General Test or MAT. Additional exam requirements/recommendations for international students: Required—TOEFL (minimum score 500 paper-based).

Freed-Hardeman University, Program in Education, Henderson, TN 38340-2399. Offers curriculum and instruction (M Ed); school counseling (M Ed), including administration and supervision, special education; school leadership (Ed S). *Accreditation:* NCATE. *Program availability:* Part-time, evening/weekend. *Degree requirements:* For master's, comprehensive exam, thesis optional; for Ed S, thesis. *Entrance requirements:* For master's, GRE General Test or NTE; for Ed S, 3 years of teaching experience. Additional exam requirements/recommendations for international students: Required—TOEFL (minimum score 500 paper-based).

Fresno Pacific University, Graduate Programs, School of Education, Division of Pupil Personnel Services, Program in School Counseling, Fresno, CA 93702-4709. Offers MA. *Program availability:* Part-time, evening/weekend. *Degree requirements:* For master's, thesis or alternative. *Entrance requirements:* Additional exam requirements/recommendations for international students: Required—TOEFL (minimum score 550 paper-based). *Expenses:* Contact institution.

Frostburg State University, Graduate School, College of Education, Department of Educational Professions, Program in School Counseling, Frostburg, MD 21532-1099. Offers M Ed. *Accreditation:* NCATE. *Program availability:* Part-time, evening/weekend. *Degree requirements:* For master's, comprehensive exam, thesis or alternative. *Entrance requirements:* For master's, GRE General Test or MAT, interview. Additional exam requirements/recommendations for international students: Required—TOEFL. Electronic applications accepted.

Gallaudet University, The Graduate School, Washington, DC 20002-3625. Offers American Sign Language/English bilingual early childhood deaf education: birth to 5 (Certificate); audiology (Au D); clinical psychology (PhD); deaf and hard of hearing infants, toddlers, and their families (Certificate); deaf education (MA, Ed S); deaf history (Certificate); deaf studies (Certificate); educating deaf students with disabilities (Certificate); education: teacher preparation (MA), including deaf education, early childhood education and deaf education, elementary education and deaf education, secondary education and deaf education; educational neuroscience (PhD); hearing, speech and language sciences (MS, PhD); international development (MA); interpretation (MA, PhD), including combined interpreting practice and research (MA), interpreting research (MA); linguistics (MA, PhD); mental health counseling (MA); peer mentoring (Certificate); public administration (MPA); school counseling (MA); school psychology (Psy S); sign language teaching (MA); social work (MSW); speech-language pathology (MS). *Program availability:* Part-time. *Students:* 297 full-time (231 women), 129 part-time (97 women); includes 105 minority (35 Black or African American, non-Hispanic/Latino; 20 Asian, non-Hispanic/Latino; 39 Hispanic/Latino; 11 Two or more races, non-Hispanic/Latino), 22 international. Average age 30. 471 applicants, 52% accepted, 147 enrolled. In 2016, 138 master's, 25 doctorates, 14 other advanced degrees awarded. Terminal master's awarded for partial completion of doctoral program. *Degree requirements:* For master's, comprehensive exam (for some programs), thesis optional; for doctorate, comprehensive exam, thesis/dissertation. *Entrance requirements:* For master's and doctorate, GRE General Test or MAT, letters of recommendation, interviews, goals statement, American Sign Language proficiency interview, written English competency. Additional exam requirements/recommendations for international students: Required—TOEFL. *Application deadline:* For fall admission, 2/15 for domestic students. Applications are processed on a rolling basis. Application fee: $75. Electronic applications accepted. *Expenses: Tuition:* Full-time $17,100; part-time $950 per credit hour. *Required fees:* $3725; $276 per semester. *Financial support:* Fellowships, research assistantships, teaching assistantships, career-related internships or fieldwork, Federal Work-Study, scholarships/grants, tuition waivers (partial), and unspecified assistantships available. Support available to part-time students. Financial award application deadline: 7/1; financial award applicants required to submit FAFSA. *Faculty research:* Signing math dictionaries, telecommunications access, cancer genetics, linguistics, visual language and visual learning, integrated quantum materials, deaf legal discourse, advance recruitment and retention in geosciences. *Unit head:* Dr. Gaurav Mathur, Dean, Graduate School and Continuing Studies, 202-250-2380, Fax: 202-651-5027, E-mail: gaurav.mathur@gallaudet.edu. *Application contact:* Wednesday Luria, Coordinator of Prospective Graduate Student Services, 202-651-5400, Fax: 202-651-5295, E-mail: graduate.school@gallaudet.edu.

Geneva College, Master of Arts in Counseling Program, Beaver Falls, PA 15010-3599. Offers clinical mental health counseling (MA); marriage and family counseling (MA); school counseling (MA). *Accreditation:* ACA. *Program availability:* Part-time, evening/weekend. *Faculty:* 6 full-time (3 women), 3 part-time/adjunct (2 women). *Students:* 35 full-time (28 women), 32 part-time (23 women); includes 11 minority (9 Black or African American, non-Hispanic/Latino; 2 Hispanic/Latino). Average age 34. 42 applicants, 71% accepted, 21 enrolled. In 2016, 24 master's awarded. *Degree requirements:* For master's, comprehensive exam, 50-60 credits (depending on program), practicum, internship. *Entrance requirements:* For master's, minimum GPA of 3.0 (preferred), 3 letters of recommendation, essay on career goals, resume of educational and professional experiences. Additional exam requirements/recommendations for international students: Required—TOEFL. *Application deadline:* For fall admission, 9/1 for domestic students; for spring admission, 1/10 for domestic students. Applications are processed on a rolling basis. Electronic applications accepted. *Expenses:* $670 per credit. *Financial support:* In 2016–17, 3 students received support. Research assistantships, teaching assistantships, career-related internships or fieldwork, and unspecified assistantships available. Financial award application deadline: 8/1; financial award applicants required to submit FAFSA. *Faculty research:* Blended family counseling; premarital and newlywed couples; religion in clinical supervision; conceptual mapping in research, supervision, and clinical work. *Unit head:* Dr. Shannan Shiderly, Program Director, 724-847-6649, Fax: 724-847-6101, E-mail: slshider@geneva.edu. *Application contact:* Marina Frazier, Graduate Program Manager, 724-847-6697, E-mail: counseling@geneva.edu.
Website: http://www.geneva.edu/page/grad_counseling

George Fox University, College of Education, Graduate Department of Counseling, Newberg, OR 97132-2697. Offers clinical mental health counseling (MA); marriage, couple and family counseling (MA, Certificate); school counseling (MA, Certificate); school psychology (Ed S). *Program availability:* Part-time. *Degree requirements:* For master's, clinical project. *Entrance requirements:* For master's, MAT or GRE, bachelor's degree from regionally-accredited college or university, minimum cumulative GPA of 3.0, 1 professional and 1 academic reference, resume, on-campus interview, official transcripts. Additional exam requirements/recommendations for international students: Required—TOEFL (minimum score 577 paper-based; 90 iBT), IELTS (minimum score 7). Electronic applications accepted. *Expenses:* Contact institution.

George Mason University, College of Education and Human Development, Program in Counseling and Development, Fairfax, VA 22030. Offers community agency counseling (M Ed); school counseling PK-12 (M Ed). *Accreditation:* NCATE. *Faculty:* 5 full-time (3 women), 17 part-time/adjunct (12 women). *Students:* 53 full-time (45 women), 106 part-time (87 women); includes 82 minority (28 Black or African American, non-Hispanic/Latino; 1 American Indian or Alaska Native, non-Hispanic/Latino; 19 Asian, non-Hispanic/Latino; 25 Hispanic/Latino; 1 Native Hawaiian or other Pacific Islander, non-Hispanic/Latino; 8 Two or more races, non-Hispanic/Latino), 3 international. Average age 31. 71 applicants, 59% accepted, 27 enrolled. In 2016, 37 master's awarded. *Degree requirements:* For master's, thesis (for some programs). *Entrance requirements:* For master's, bachelor's degree from regionally-accredited institution with minimum GPA of 3.0 overall or in last 60 credit hours; 2 copies of official transcripts; expanded goals statement; 3 letters of recommendation; 12 credits of undergraduate behavioral sciences; 1000 hours of counseling or related experience. Additional exam requirements/recommendations for international students: Required—TOEFL (minimum score 575 paper-based; 88 iBT), IELTS (minimum score 6.5), PTE (minimum score 59). *Application deadline:* For spring admission, 9/15 for domestic and international students. Application fee: $75 ($80 for international students). Electronic applications accepted. *Expenses:* Tuition, state resident: full-time $10,628; part-time $443 per credit. Tuition, nonresident: full-time $29,306; part-time $1221 per credit. *Required fees:* $3096; $129 per credit. Tuition and fees vary according to program. *Financial support:* In 2016–17, 3 students received support, including 2 research assistantships with tuition reimbursements available (averaging $5,300 per year), 1 teaching assistantship (averaging $2,300 per year); career-related internships or fieldwork, Federal Work-Study, scholarships/grants, unspecified assistantships, and health care benefits (for full-time research or teaching assistantship recipients) also available. Support available to part-time students. Financial award application deadline: 3/1; financial award applicants required to submit FAFSA. *Faculty research:* Leadership, multiculturalism, social justice, and advocacy; global well-being; social psychological, physical, and spiritual health of individuals, families, communities, and organizations. *Unit head:* Fred Bemak, Academic Program Coordinator, 703-993-3941, Fax: 703-993-5577, E-mail: fbemak@gmu.edu.
Website: http://gse.gmu.edu/programs/counseling/

The George Washington University, Graduate School of Education and Human Development, Department of Counseling and Human Development, Program in Counseling, Washington, DC 20052. Offers PhD, Ed S. *Accreditation:* ACA (one or more programs are accredited); NCATE. *Program availability:* Part-time, evening/weekend.

Counselor Education

Students: 16 full-time (13 women), 31 part-time (24 women); includes 16 minority (6 Black or African American, non-Hispanic/Latino; 1 American Indian or Alaska Native, non-Hispanic/Latino; 5 Asian, non-Hispanic/Latino; 4 Hispanic/Latino), 5 international. Average age 33. 37 applicants, 43% accepted, 8 enrolled. In 2016, 9 doctorates, 2 other advanced degrees awarded. *Degree requirements:* For doctorate, comprehensive exam, thesis/dissertation; for Ed S, comprehensive exam. *Entrance requirements:* For doctorate, GRE General Test, interview, minimum GPA of 3.3; for Ed S, GRE General Test or MAT, minimum GPA of 3.3. *Application deadline:* For fall admission, 1/15 priority date for domestic students; for spring admission, 10/1 for domestic students. Applications are processed on a rolling basis. Application fee: $75. *Financial support:* Fellowships, research assistantships, teaching assistantships, career-related internships or fieldwork, Federal Work-Study, and tuition waivers (partial) available. Financial award application deadline: 1/15; financial award applicants required to submit FAFSA. *Faculty research:* Values in counseling, religion and counseling. *Unit head:* Dr. Pat Schwallie-Giddis, Director, 202-994-6856, E-mail: drpat@gwu.edu. *Application contact:* Sarah Lang, Director of Graduate Admissions, 202-994-1447, Fax: 202-994-7207, E-mail: slang@gwu.edu.

The George Washington University, Graduate School of Education and Human Development, Department of Counseling and Human Development, Program in School Counseling, Washington, DC 20052. Offers MA Ed, Graduate Certificate. *Students:* 30 full-time (24 women), 11 part-time (10 women); includes 14 minority (8 Black or African American, non-Hispanic/Latino; 1 American Indian or Alaska Native, non-Hispanic/Latino; 2 Asian, non-Hispanic/Latino; 2 Hispanic/Latino; 1 Two or more races, non-Hispanic/Latino), 2 international. Average age 30. 67 applicants, 90% accepted, 19 enrolled. In 2016, 28 master's awarded. *Unit head:* Dr. Pat Schwallie-Giddis, Chair, 202-994-6856, E-mail: drpat@gwu.edu. *Application contact:* Sarah Lang, Director of Graduate Admissions, 202-994-1447, Fax: 202-994-7207, E-mail: slang@gwu.edu.

Georgian Court University, School of Arts and Sciences, Lakewood, NJ 08701-2697. Offers applied behavior analysis (MA); clinical mental health counseling (MA); holistic health studies (MA, Certificate); homeland security (MS, Certificate); mercy spirituality (Certificate); parish business management (Certificate); professional counselor (Certificate); school psychology (MA, Certificate); theology (MA, Certificate). *Program availability:* Part-time, evening/weekend. *Faculty:* 19 full-time (11 women), 6 part-time/adjunct (3 women). *Students:* 90 full-time (75 women), 107 part-time (79 women); includes 34 minority (9 Black or African American, non-Hispanic/Latino; 20 Hispanic/Latino; 5 Two or more races, non-Hispanic/Latino), 1 international. Average age 34. 187 applicants, 49% accepted, 60 enrolled. In 2016, 66 master's, 17 other advanced degrees awarded. *Degree requirements:* For master's, comprehensive exam (for some programs), thesis (for some programs). *Entrance requirements:* For master's, GRE, GMAT, or NTE/PRAXIS, 3 letters of recommendation. Additional exam requirements/recommendations for international students: Required—TOEFL (minimum score 550 paper-based). *Application deadline:* For fall admission, 8/15 for domestic students, 5/1 for international students; for spring admission, 1/15 for domestic students, 10/1 for international students. Applications are processed on a rolling basis. Application fee: $40. Electronic applications accepted. *Expenses: Tuition:* Full-time $15,079; part-time $839 per credit. *Required fees:* $968; $496 per credit. Tuition and fees vary according to campus/location and program. *Financial support:* Scholarships/grants, health care benefits, and unspecified assistantships available. Financial award application deadline: 4/15; financial award applicants required to submit FAFSA. *Unit head:* Dr. Mary Chinery, Dean, 732-987-2493, Fax: 732-987-2007, E-mail: mchinery@georgian.edu. *Application contact:* Patrick Givens, Director of Graduate and Professional Studies Admissions, 732-987-2736, Fax: 732-987-2000, E-mail: gps@georgian.edu.
Website: http://georgian.edu/academics/school-of-arts-sciences/

Georgia Southern University, Jack N. Averitt College of Graduate Studies, College of Education, Department of Leadership, Technology, and Human Development, Program in Counselor Education, Statesboro, GA 30460. Offers M Ed, Ed S. *Accreditation:* ACA; NCATE. *Program availability:* Part-time, evening/weekend. *Students:* 40 full-time (36 women), 14 part-time (10 women); includes 24 minority (22 Black or African American, non-Hispanic/Latino; 1 Hispanic/Latino; 1 Two or more races, non-Hispanic/Latino), 1 international. Average age 28. 24 applicants, 63% accepted, 11 enrolled. In 2016, 27 master's, 3 Ed Ss awarded. *Degree requirements:* For master's, comprehensive exam, transition point assessments; for Ed S, comprehensive exam. *Entrance requirements:* For master's, GRE General Test or MAT, minimum GPA of 2.5, letters of recommendation, interview; for Ed S, GRE General Test or MAT, minimum graduate GPA of 3.25, letters of recommendation. Additional exam requirements/recommendations for international students: Required—TOEFL (minimum score 550 paper-based; 80 iBT), IELTS (minimum score 6). *Application deadline:* For fall admission, 3/2 for domestic students, 3/15 for international students; for spring admission, 3/2 for domestic students, 10/1 for international students. Application fee: $50. Electronic applications accepted. *Expenses:* Tuition, state resident: full-time $7236; part-time $277 per semester hour. Tuition, nonresident: full-time $27,118; part-time $1105 per semester hour. *Required fees:* $2092. *Financial support:* In 2016–17, 20 students received support, including 2 fellowships with full tuition reimbursements available (averaging $7,750 per year), research assistantships with partial tuition reimbursements available (averaging $7,200 per year); career-related internships or fieldwork, scholarships/grants, tuition waivers (full), and unspecified assistantships also available. Financial award application deadline: 4/15; financial award applicants required to submit FAFSA. *Faculty research:* School counseling, test development, gender equity, career counseling, mental health counseling. *Unit head:* Dr. Brandon Hunt, Program Coordinator, 912-478-0502, Fax: 912-478-7104, E-mail: bhunt@georgiasouthern.edu. *Application contact:* Lydia Cross, Graduate Academic Services Center, 912-478-8664, E-mail: lcross@georgiasouthern.edu.
Website: http://coe.georgiasouthern.edu/coun/

Georgia State University, College of Education and Human Development, Department of Counseling and Psychological Services, Program in School Counseling, Atlanta, GA 30302-3083. Offers M Ed, Ed S. *Accreditation:* ACA (one or more programs are accredited); NCATE. *Degree requirements:* For master's, comprehensive exam. *Entrance requirements:* For master's, GRE, goal statement, resume, 3 letters of recommendation, transcripts. Additional exam requirements/recommendations for international students: Required—TOEFL. *Application deadline:* For fall admission, 12/1 for domestic and international students. Application fee: $50. Electronic applications accepted. *Expenses:* Tuition, state resident: full-time $6876; part-time $382 per credit hour. Tuition, nonresident: full-time $22,374; part-time $1243 per credit hour. *Required fees:* $2128; $1064 per term. Part-time tuition and fees vary according to course load and program. *Financial support:* Research assistantships with tuition reimbursements, teaching assistantships with tuition reimbursements, career-related internships or fieldwork, institutionally sponsored loans, scholarships/grants, health care benefits, and unspecified assistantships available. Financial award application deadline: 4/1. *Faculty research:* Mattering, adolescent counseling, school counselor identity, group leadership of school counselors, play therapy. *Unit head:* Dr. Brian Dew, Chairperson, 404-413-8168, Fax: 404-413-8013, E-mail: bdew@gsu.edu. *Application contact:* CPS Admissions Office, 404-413-8200, E-mail: nkeita@gsu.edu.
Website: http://cps.education.gsu.edu/programs/school-counseling/

Grambling State University, School of Graduate Studies and Research, College of Education, Department of Educational Leadership, Grambling, LA 71245. Offers developmental education (MS, Ed D, PMC), including curriculum and instructional design (Ed D), English (MS), guidance and counseling (MS), higher education administration and management (Ed D), mathematics (MS), reading (MS), science (MS), student development and personnel services (Ed D); educational leadership (M Ed). *Program availability:* Part-time, evening/weekend. *Degree requirements:* For master's, comprehensive exam, thesis (for some programs); for doctorate, comprehensive exam, thesis/dissertation. *Entrance requirements:* For master's, GRE, minimum GPA of 2.5 on last degree; for doctorate, GRE (minimum score 1000, 500 on Verbal), master's degree, minimum GPA of 3.0 on last degree. Additional exam requirements/recommendations for international students: Required—TOEFL (minimum score 500 paper-based; 62 iBT). Electronic applications accepted.

Gwynedd Mercy University, School of Education, Gwynedd Valley, PA 19437-0901. Offers educational administration (MS); master teacher (MS); school counseling (MS); special education (MS). *Program availability:* Part-time, evening/weekend, 100% online. *Faculty:* 8 full-time (5 women), 38 part-time/adjunct (24 women). *Students:* 466 full-time (355 women); includes 93 minority (66 Black or African American, non-Hispanic/Latino; 12 Asian, non-Hispanic/Latino; 15 Hispanic/Latino). Average age 36. 127 applicants, 18% accepted, 9 enrolled. In 2016, 86 master's awarded. *Degree requirements:* For master's, thesis, internship, practicum. *Entrance requirements:* For master's, GRE or MAT; PRAXIS I, minimum GPA of 3.0. *Application deadline:* Applications are processed on a rolling basis. *Expenses: Tuition:* Full-time $14,400; part-time $800 per credit hour. One-time fee: $165. Tuition and fees vary according to degree level and program. *Financial support:* In 2016–17, 2 research assistantships were awarded; career-related internships or fieldwork, Federal Work-Study, institutionally sponsored loans, tuition waivers (full and partial), and unspecified assistantships also available. Financial award applicants required to submit FAFSA. *Faculty research:* Learning and the brain, reading literacy, ethics and moral judgment, leadership, teaching and multicultural education. *Unit head:* Dr. Heather Pfleger, Dean, 215-646-7300 Ext. 21581, E-mail: pfleger.h@gmercyu.edu. *Application contact:* Graduate Program Coordinator, 877-499-6333, E-mail: graduate@gmercyu.edu.
Website: https://www.gmercyu.edu/academics/graduate-education-programs

Hampton University, School of Education and Human Development, Program in Counseling, Hampton, VA 23668. Offers college student development (MA); community agency counseling (MA); counseling (Ed S); counselor education and supervision (PhD); pastoral counseling (MA); school counseling (MA). *Accreditation:* ACA; NCATE. *Program availability:* Part-time, evening/weekend, online learning. *Faculty:* 4 full-time (2 women). *Students:* 37 full-time (34 women), 17 part-time (16 women); includes 49 minority (all Black or African American, non-Hispanic/Latino), 1 international. Average age 32. 55 applicants, 53% accepted, 19 enrolled. In 2016, 20 master's awarded. *Degree requirements:* For master's, comprehensive exam; for doctorate, comprehensive exam, thesis/dissertation. *Entrance requirements:* For master's, GRE General Test, personal statement, two letters of recommendation; for doctorate, GRE General Test, personal statement, writing sample, three letters of recommendation; for Ed S, personal statement, two letters of recommendation. Additional exam requirements/recommendations for international students: Required—TOEFL (minimum score 525 paper-based) or IELTS (6.5). *Application deadline:* For fall admission, 6/1 priority date for domestic students, 4/1 priority date for international students; for winter admission, 9/1 priority date for international students; for spring admission, 11/1 priority date for domestic students, 9/1 for international students; for summer admission, 4/1 priority date for domestic students, 2/1 priority date for international students. Applications are processed on a rolling basis. Application fee: $35. Electronic applications accepted. *Expenses: Tuition:* Full-time $10,776; part-time $548 per credit hour. *Required fees:* $35; $35 per credit hour. Tuition and fees vary according to course load and program. *Financial support:* Fellowships, research assistantships, teaching assistantships, career-related internships or fieldwork, Federal Work-Study, institutionally sponsored loans, and scholarships/grants available. Support available to part-time students. Financial award application deadline: 6/30; financial award applicants required to submit FAFSA. *Faculty research:* Personality development, temperament, post-traumatic stress disorder, continuum of normal to abnormal personality. *Unit head:* Dr. Spencer R. Baker, Chair, 757-637-2232, E-mail: spencer.baker@hamptonu.edu.
Website: http://edhd.hamptonu.edu/counseling/

Harding University, Cannon-Clary College of Education, Searcy, AR 72149-0001. Offers advanced studies in teaching and learning (M Ed); art (MSE); behavioral science (MSE); counseling (MS, Ed S); early childhood special education (M Ed, MSE); education (MSE); educational leadership (M Ed, Ed S); elementary education (M Ed); English (MSE); French (MSE); history/social science (MSE); kinesiology (MSE); math (MSE); reading (M Ed); secondary education (M Ed); Spanish (MSE); teaching (MAT); teaching English as a second language (MSE). *Accreditation:* NCATE. *Program availability:* Part-time, evening/weekend. *Faculty:* 22 full-time (9 women), 51 part-time/adjunct (37 women). *Students:* 130 full-time (94 women), 321 part-time (234 women); includes 83 minority (50 Black or African American, non-Hispanic/Latino; 4 American Indian or Alaska Native, non-Hispanic/Latino; 6 Asian, non-Hispanic/Latino; 13 Hispanic/Latino; 10 Two or more races, non-Hispanic/Latino), 11 international. Average age 35. 125 applicants, 88% accepted, 110 enrolled. In 2016, 124 master's, 27 other advanced degrees awarded. *Degree requirements:* For master's, comprehensive exam (for some programs), thesis optional, portfolio(s); for Ed S, comprehensive exam, portfolio, project. *Entrance requirements:* For master's, GRE, MAT, PRAXIS; for Ed S, MAT or GRE. Additional exam requirements/recommendations for international students: Required—TOEFL (minimum score 550 paper-based; 79 iBT). *Application deadline:* For fall admission, 8/1 for domestic and international students; for spring admission, 1/1 for domestic and international students. Applications are processed on a rolling basis. Application fee: $35. Tuition and fees vary according to degree level and program. *Financial support:* In 2016–17, 31 students received support. Unspecified assistantships available. *Faculty research:* Reading, comprehension, school violence, educational technology, behavior, college choice, differentiated instruction, brain-based teaching. *Unit head:* Dr. Clara Carroll, Chair, 501-279-4501, Fax: 501-279-4083, E-mail: ccarroll@harding.edu. *Application contact:* Information Contact, 501-279-4315, E-mail: gradstudiesedu@harding.edu.
Website: http://www.harding.edu/education

Hardin-Simmons University, Graduate School, Irvin School of Education, Department of Counseling and Human Development, Abilene, TX 79698-0001. Offers M Ed. *Program availability:* Part-time. *Faculty:* 3 full-time (1 woman), 2 part-time/adjunct (both women). *Students:* 19 full-time (13 women), 10 part-time (5 women); includes 8 minority (7 Black or African American, non-Hispanic/Latino; 1 Hispanic/Latino), 2 international. Average age 35. In 2016, 10 master's awarded. *Degree requirements:* For master's, comprehensive exam, practicum. *Entrance requirements:* For master's, minimum undergraduate GPA of 3.0 in major, 2.7 overall; interview; 3 letters of recommendation; resume. Additional exam requirements/recommendations for international students: Required—TOEFL (minimum score 550 paper-based; 75 iBT). *Application deadline:* For fall admission, 8/15 priority date for domestic students, 4/1 for international students; for spring admission, 1/5 priority date for domestic students, 9/1 for international students.

Applications are processed on a rolling basis. Application fee: $50. Electronic applications accepted. *Expenses: Tuition:* Full-time $12,510; part-time $695 per credit hour. *Required fees:* $325; $110 per semester. *Financial support:* In 2016–17, 25 students received support, including 4 fellowships (averaging $2,400 per year); career-related internships or fieldwork and scholarships/grants also available. Support available to part-time students. Financial award application deadline: 6/30; financial award applicants required to submit FAFSA. *Unit head:* Dr. Robert Barnes, Head, 325-670-1451, Fax: 325-670-5859, E-mail: rbarnes@hsutx.edu. *Application contact:* Dr. Nancy Kucinski, Dean of Graduate Studies, 325-670-1298, Fax: 325-670-1564, E-mail: gradoff@hsutx.edu.
Website: http://www.hsutx.edu/academics/irvin/graduate/counseling

Henderson State University, Graduate Studies, Teachers College, Department of Counselor Education, Arkadelphia, AR 71999-0001. Offers clinical mental health counseling (MS); developmental therapy (MS, Graduate Certificate); secondary school counseling (MSE). *Accreditation:* ACA; NCATE. *Program availability:* Part-time. *Faculty:* 6 full-time (2 women). *Students:* 46 full-time (33 women), 84 part-time (74 women); includes 48 minority (40 Black or African American, non-Hispanic/Latino; 1 American Indian or Alaska Native, non-Hispanic/Latino; 4 Hispanic/Latino; 3 Two or more races, non-Hispanic/Latino). Average age 34. 18 applicants, 100% accepted, 18 enrolled. In 2016, 36 master's awarded. *Entrance requirements:* For master's, GRE General Test or MAT, letters of recommendation, minimum GPA of 2.7, teacher certification. Additional exam requirements/recommendations for international students: Required—TOEFL (minimum score 600 paper-based); Recommended—IELTS (minimum score 6.5). *Application deadline:* For fall admission, 8/1 priority date for domestic students, 6/30 priority date for international students; for spring admission, 1/1 priority date for domestic students, 11/30 priority date for international students. Applications are processed on a rolling basis. Application fee: $25 ($75 for international students). *Expenses:* Tuition, state resident: full-time $6288; part-time $3144 per credit hour. Tuition, nonresident: full-time $12,888; part-time $6444 per credit hour. *Required fees:* $1429; $1024 per credit hour. Tuition and fees vary according to course load and student level. *Financial support:* In 2016–17, 1 teaching assistantship with partial tuition reimbursement (averaging $4,000 per year) was awarded; scholarships/grants and unspecified assistantships also available. Financial award application deadline: 4/15; financial award applicants required to submit FAFSA. *Unit head:* Dr. Mike Kelly, Interim Chairperson, 870-230-5216, Fax: 870-230-5459, E-mail: kellym@hsu.edu. *Application contact:* Dr. Ken Taylor, Graduate Dean, 870-230-5126, Fax: 870-230-5479, E-mail: taylorke@hsu.edu.
Website: http://www.hsu.edu/counselor-education/

Heritage University, Graduate Programs in Education, Program in Counseling, Toppenish, WA 98948-9599. Offers M Ed. *Program availability:* Part-time. *Degree requirements:* For master's, comprehensive exam. *Entrance requirements:* For master's, interview, letters of recommendation, at least 9 semester-credits of behavioral sciences.

Hofstra University, School of Health Professions and Human Services, Programs in Counseling, Hempstead, NY 11549. Offers counseling (MS Ed, PD); creative arts therapy (MA); interdisciplinary transition specialist (Advanced Certificate); marriage and family therapy (MA); mental health counseling (MA, Advanced Certificate), including alcohol and substance abuse (Advanced Certificate); rehabilitation administration (PD); rehabilitation counseling (MS Ed, Advanced Certificate); rehabilitation counseling in mental health (MS Ed, Advanced Certificate); school counselor bilingual extension (Advanced Certificate). *Accreditation:* ACA. *Program availability:* Part-time, evening/weekend. *Students:* 116 full-time (100 women), 66 part-time (59 women); includes 48 minority (18 Black or African American, non-Hispanic/Latino; 11 Asian, non-Hispanic/Latino; 17 Hispanic/Latino; 2 Two or more races, non-Hispanic/Latino), 5 international. Average age 29. 166 applicants, 81% accepted, 66 enrolled. In 2016, 71 master's, 7 other advanced degrees awarded. *Degree requirements:* For master's, comprehensive exam (for some programs), thesis (for some programs), internship, practicum, student teaching, seminars, minimum GPA of 3.0. *Entrance requirements:* For master's, GRE, interview, letters of recommendation, portfolio, essay, professional experience, certification; for other advanced degree, GRE, interview, letters of recommendation, essay, professional experience, resume, master's degree. Additional exam requirements/recommendations for international students: Required—TOEFL (minimum score 550 paper-based; 80 iBT). *Application deadline:* Applications are processed on a rolling basis. Application fee: $75. Electronic applications accepted. *Expenses: Tuition:* Full-time $1240. *Required fees:* $970. Tuition and fees vary according to program. *Financial support:* In 2016–17, 76 students received support, including 40 fellowships with full and partial tuition reimbursements available (averaging $3,465 per year), 5 research assistantships with full and partial tuition reimbursements available (averaging $6,939 per year); career-related internships or fieldwork, Federal Work-Study, institutionally sponsored loans, scholarships/grants, traineeships, tuition waivers (full and partial), and unspecified assistantships also available. Support available to part-time students. Financial award applicants required to submit FAFSA. *Faculty research:* The constructs of hope and grit; the efficacy of support groups in treating eating disorders; attitudes of primary care physicians related to providing integrated care with mental health counselors; expanding the counselor identity through disability cultural competence; vocational evaluation and assessment collaboration; disability cultural competence. *Unit head:* Dr. Jamie Mitus, Chairperson, 516-463-5759, E-mail: jamie.s.mitus@hofstra.edu. *Application contact:* Sunil Samuel, Assistant Vice President of Admissions, 516-463-4723, Fax: 516-463-4664, E-mail: graduateadmission@hofstra.edu.
Website: http://www.hofstra.edu/academics/colleges/healthscienceshumanservices/

Houston Baptist University, College of Education and Behavioral Sciences, Programs in Education, Houston, TX 77074-3298. Offers bilingual education (M Ed); counselor education (M Ed); curriculum and instruction (M Ed); educational administration (M Ed); educational diagnostician (M Ed), executive educational leadership (Ed D); reading education (M Ed). *Program availability:* Part-time, evening/weekend, 100% online, blended/hybrid learning. *Students:* 45 full-time (35 women), 158 part-time (136 women); includes 141 minority (87 Black or African American, non-Hispanic/Latino; 1 American Indian or Alaska Native, non-Hispanic/Latino; 5 Asian, non-Hispanic/Latino; 47 Hispanic/Latino; 1 Two or more races, non-Hispanic/Latino), 3 international. Average age 34. 320 applicants, 30% accepted, 61 enrolled. In 2016, 121 degrees awarded. *Degree requirements:* For master's, comprehensive exam; for doctorate, thesis/dissertation. *Entrance requirements:* For master's, minimum GPA of 2.75, two recommendations, resume, bachelor's degree conferred transcript; interview (for non-certified teachers); for doctorate, GRE, 3 letters of recommendation. Additional exam requirements/recommendations for international students: Required—TOEFL (minimum score 80 iBT), IELTS (minimum score 6.5). *Application deadline:* For fall admission, 8/1 for domestic students, 6/1 for international students; for spring admission, 1/1 for domestic students, 11/1 for international students; for summer admission, 5/1 for domestic students, 3/1 for international students. Applications are processed on a rolling basis. Application fee: $0 ($100 for international students). Electronic applications accepted. Application fee is waived when completed online. *Expenses:* $1,650 per 3-hour course; $1,275 annual general fee; $1,060 annual technology fee. *Financial support:* In 2016–17, 2 students received support. Research assistantships, teaching assistantships, Federal Work-Study, and scholarships/grants available. Support available to part-time students. Financial award application deadline: 4/1; financial award applicants required to submit FAFSA. *Faculty research:* Autism and inclusion, integrating technology into instruction, school change and leadership trust. *Unit head:* Dr. Charlotte Fontenot, Director, Graduate Programs, 281-649-3078, Fax: 281-649-3361, E-mail: cfontenot@hbu.edu. *Application contact:* Kristy Wright, Administrative Assistant for Graduate Programs, 281-649-3094, Fax: 281-649-3361, E-mail: kwright@hbu.edu.
Website: http://www.hbu.edu/MED

Howard University, School of Education, Department of Human Development and Psychoeducational Studies, Program in School Psychology and Counseling Services, Washington, DC 20059-0002. Offers M Ed. *Accreditation:* NCATE. *Program availability:* Part-time. *Degree requirements:* For master's, comprehensive exam, expository writing exam, practicum. *Entrance requirements:* Additional exam requirements/recommendations for international students: Required—TOEFL (minimum score 550 paper-based; 79 iBT). Electronic applications accepted. *Faculty research:* Law and forensic evaluation, juvenile justice, ethics, clinical assessment, personality disorders, substance abuse.

Hunter College of the City University of New York, Graduate School, School of Education, Department of Educational Foundations and Counseling, Program in School Counseling, New York, NY 10065-5085. Offers MS Ed. *Accreditation:* ACA; NCATE. *Degree requirements:* For master's, thesis, internship, practicum, research seminar. *Entrance requirements:* For master's, interview, minimum GPA of 2.7. Additional exam requirements/recommendations for international students: Required—TOEFL, TWE. *Application deadline:* For fall admission, 4/1 for domestic students, 2/1 for international students; for spring admission, 11/1 for domestic students, 9/1 for international students. Applications are processed on a rolling basis. *Financial support:* Federal Work-Study and tuition waivers (partial) available. Support available to part-time students. *Unit head:* Dr. Tamara Buckley, Coordinator, 212-772-4758, E-mail: tamara.buckley@hunter.cuny.edu. *Application contact:* Milena Solo, Director for Graduate Admissions, 212-772-4480, E-mail: admissions@hunter.cuny.edu.

Husson University, Graduate Programs in Counseling and Human Relations, Bangor, ME 04401-2999. Offers clinical mental health counseling (MS); human relations (MS); school counseling (MS). *Accreditation:* ACA. *Program availability:* Part-time, evening/weekend. *Faculty:* 3 full-time (2 women), 5 part-time/adjunct (all women). *Students:* 17 full-time (15 women), 55 part-time (48 women); includes 1 minority (Black or African American, non-Hispanic/Latino), 2 international. Average age 32. 50 applicants, 52% accepted, 20 enrolled. In 2016, 16 master's awarded. *Degree requirements:* For master's, comprehensive exam (for some programs), thesis optional. *Entrance requirements:* For master's, BS with minimum GPA of 3.0, letters of recommendation, interview. Additional exam requirements/recommendations for international students: Required—TOEFL (minimum score 550 paper-based; 80 iBT), IELTS (minimum score 6.5). *Application deadline:* For fall admission, 2/1 for domestic students. Application fee: $50. Electronic applications accepted. *Expenses:* $560 per credit tuition; $450 full-time fees, $220 part-time (6-9 credits), $110 part-time (less than 6 credits per year). *Financial support:* Federal Work-Study, scholarships/grants, and unspecified assistantships available. Financial award application deadline: 4/15; financial award applicants required to submit FAFSA. *Faculty research:* Challenges and rewards of counseling practice in rural, small town and neighborhood settings. *Unit head:* Dr. Deborah Drew, Director, Graduate Counseling Programs, 207-992-4912, Fax: 207-992-4952, E-mail: drewd@husson.edu. *Application contact:* Kristen Card, Director of Graduate Admissions, 207-404-5660, Fax: 207-941-7935, E-mail: cardk@husson.edu.
Website: http://www.husson.edu/college-of-health-and-education/school-of-education/graduate-programs/

Idaho State University, Office of Graduate Studies, Kasiska College of Health Professions, Department of Counseling, Pocatello, ID 83209-8120. Offers counseling (M Coun, Ed S), including marriage and family counseling (M Coun), mental health counseling (M Coun), school counseling (M Coun), student affairs and college counseling (M Coun); counselor education and counseling (PhD). *Accreditation:* ACA (one or more programs are accredited). *Program availability:* Part-time. *Degree requirements:* For master's, comprehensive exam, thesis, 4 semesters resident graduate study, practicum/internship; for doctorate, comprehensive exam, thesis/dissertation, 3 semesters internship, 4 consecutive semesters doctoral-level study on campus; for Ed S, comprehensive exam, thesis, case studies, oral exam. *Entrance requirements:* For master's, GRE General Test, MAT, minimum GPA of 3.0, bachelors degree, interview, 3 letters of recommendation; for doctorate, GRE General Test, MAT, minimum graduate GPA of 3.0, resume, interview, counseling license, master's degree; for Ed S, GRE General Test, minimum graduate GPA of 3.0, master's degree in counseling, 3 letters of recommendation, 2 years work experience. Additional exam requirements/recommendations for international students: Required—TOEFL (minimum score 600 paper-based; 80 iBT). Electronic applications accepted. *Faculty research:* Group counseling, multicultural counseling, family counseling, child therapy, supervision.

Indiana State University, College of Graduate and Professional Studies, Bayh College of Education, Department of Communication Disorders and Counseling, School, and Educational Psychology, Terre Haute, IN 47809. Offers clinical mental health counseling (MS); communication disorders (MS); school counseling (M Ed); school psychology (PhD, Ed S); MA/MS. *Accreditation:* ACA; ASHA; NCATE. *Program availability:* Part-time, evening/weekend. *Degree requirements:* For master's, thesis optional; for doctorate, thesis/dissertation, research tools proficiency tests. *Entrance requirements:* For master's, GRE General Test or MAT, minimum undergraduate GPA of 2.75; for doctorate, GRE General Test, master's degree, minimum undergraduate GPA of 3.5. Electronic applications accepted. *Faculty research:* Vocational development supervision.

Indiana University Bloomington, School of Education, Department of Counseling and Educational Psychology, Bloomington, IN 47405-1006. Offers counseling (MS, PhD, Ed S); counselor education (MS, Ed S); educational psychology (MS, PhD); inquiry methodology (PhD); learning and developmental sciences (MS, PhD); school psychology (PhD, Ed S). *Accreditation:* ACA (one or more programs are accredited); APA (one or more programs are accredited); NCATE. Terminal master's awarded for partial completion of doctoral program. *Degree requirements:* For master's, thesis optional; for doctorate, thesis/dissertation; for Ed S, comprehensive exam or project. *Entrance requirements:* For master's, doctorate, and Ed S, GRE General Test. Additional exam requirements/recommendations for international students: Required—TOEFL. Electronic applications accepted. *Faculty research:* Counseling psychology, inquiry methodology, school psychology, learning sciences, human development, educational psychology.

Indiana University of Pennsylvania, School of Graduate Studies and Research, College of Education and Educational Technology, Department of Counseling, Program in School Counseling, Indiana, PA 15705. Offers M Ed. *Program availability:* Part-time. *Faculty:* 12 full-time (10 women), 5 part-time/adjunct (all women). *Students:* 38 full-time (35 women), 21 part-time (14 women); includes 8 minority (4 Black or African American, non-Hispanic/Latino; 1 Hispanic/Latino; 3 Two or more races, non-Hispanic/Latino). Average age 27. 61 applicants, 61% accepted, 22 enrolled. In 2016, 21 master's

awarded. *Entrance requirements:* Additional exam requirements/recommendations for international students: Required—TOEFL (minimum score 540 paper-based). *Application deadline:* Applications are processed on a rolling basis. Application fee: $50. Electronic applications accepted. *Expenses:* Tuition, state resident: full-time $8694; part-time $483 per credit. Tuition, nonresident: full-time $13,050; part-time $725 per credit. *Required fees:* $157 per credit. $50 per term. Tuition and fees vary according to course load and program. *Financial support:* In 2016–17, 8 research assistantships with tuition reimbursements (averaging $3,033 per year) were awarded; fellowships with full tuition reimbursements, career-related internships or fieldwork, Federal Work-Study, scholarships/grants, and unspecified assistantships also available. Financial award application deadline: 4/15; financial award applicants required to submit FAFSA. *Unit head:* Dr. Claire Dandeneau, Chairperson/Graduate Coordinator, 724-357-2306, E-mail: candean@iup.edu.
Website: http://www.iup.edu/grad/schoolcounseling/default.aspx

Indiana University–Purdue University Fort Wayne, College of Education and Public Policy, Department of Professional Studies, Fort Wayne, IN 46805-1499. Offers couple and family counseling (MS Ed); educational leadership (MS Ed); school counseling (MS Ed); special education (MS Ed, Certificate). *Program availability:* Part-time. *Degree requirements:* For master's, comprehensive exam, practicum, internship, portfolio. *Entrance requirements:* For master's, minimum GPA of 2.5, three professional letters of recommendation. Additional exam requirements/recommendations for international students: Required—TOEFL (minimum score 550 paper-based; 79 iBT). *Faculty research:* Learning opportunities with deafness and the hearing impaired, adolescent emotion, student evaluation of teaching.

Indiana University–Purdue University Indianapolis, School of Education, Indianapolis, IN 46202-5155. Offers curriculum and instruction (MS); early childhood (MS); educational leadership (MS, Certificate); English as a second language (Certificate); kindergarten (Certificate); language education (MS); reading (Certificate); school counseling (MS); special education (MS, Certificate). *Program availability:* Part-time, evening/weekend. *Faculty:* 35 full-time (27 women), 56 part-time/adjunct (42 women). *Students:* 125 full-time (86 women), 181 part-time (139 women); includes 106 minority (78 Black or African American, non-Hispanic/Latino; 9 Asian, non-Hispanic/Latino; 12 Hispanic/Latino; 7 Two or more races, non-Hispanic/Latino), 3 international. Average age 32. 73 applicants, 93% accepted, 68 enrolled. In 2016, 73 master's awarded. Terminal master's awarded for partial completion of doctoral program. *Degree requirements:* For master's, thesis optional. *Entrance requirements:* For master's, GRE General Test, minimum GPA of 2.5; for Certificate, official transcripts. Additional exam requirements/recommendations for international students: Required—TOEFL (minimum score 60 iBT), IELTS (minimum score 5.5). *Application deadline:* For fall admission, 5/1 for domestic students; for spring admission, 11/1 for domestic students. Application fee: $60 ($65 for international students). Electronic applications accepted. *Expenses:* $1,262 tuition, $213 general fee. *Financial support:* Applicants required to submit FAFSA. *Faculty research:* Educational policies and school leaders' responses to these; issues of intersectionality in the experiences of African American lesbian, gay, and bisexual students attending historically black colleges and universities and those who belong to black Greek-letter organizations; students' experiential knowledge and their evolving disciplinary-specific literacy and understanding; innovative program development; urban ESL teacher preparation; target-based instructional coaching. *Total annual research expenditures:* $2.1 million. *Unit head:* Dr. Robin Hughes, Executive Associate Dean, 317-274-6817, E-mail: roblhugh@iupui.edu. *Application contact:* Ky Shaw, Graduate Admissions Coordinator, 317-278-6778, E-mail: kycshaw@iupui.edu.
Website: http://education.iupui.edu/

Indiana University South Bend, School of Education, South Bend, IN 46634-7111. Offers addiction counseling (MS Ed); alcohol and drug counseling (Graduate Certificate); clinical mental health counseling (MS Ed); educational leadership (MS Ed); elementary education (MS Ed); marriage, couple, and family counseling (MS Ed); school counseling (MS Ed); secondary education (MS Ed); special education (MAT, MS Ed), including intense intervention (MS Ed), mild intervention (MS Ed). *Accreditation:* NCATE. *Program availability:* Part-time, evening/weekend. *Faculty:* 21 full-time (11 women), 9 part-time/adjunct (3 women). *Students:* 26 full-time (19 women), 104 part-time (80 women); includes 22 minority (13 Black or African American, non-Hispanic/Latino; 5 Hispanic/Latino; 4 Two or more races, non-Hispanic/Latino). Average age 35. 51 applicants, 69% accepted, 22 enrolled. In 2016, 31 master's, 2 other advanced degrees awarded. *Degree requirements:* For master's, thesis or alternative, exit project. *Entrance requirements:* For master's, letters of recommendation, GRE or minimum GPA of 3.0. Additional exam requirements/recommendations for international students: Required—TOEFL. *Application deadline:* For fall admission, 7/1 for domestic students; for spring admission, 11/1 for domestic students. Applications are processed on a rolling basis. Application fee: $40 ($60 for international students). Electronic applications accepted. *Expenses:* $276.98 per credit hour in-state; $652.54 per credit hour out-of-state. *Financial support:* Career-related internships or fieldwork available. Support available to part-time students. Financial award application deadline: 3/1; financial award applicants required to submit FAFSA. *Faculty research:* Professional dispositions, early childhood literacy, online learning, program assessments, problem-based learning. *Unit head:* Dr. Marvin Lynn, Dean, 574-520-4339, E-mail: lynnm@iusb.edu. *Application contact:* Yvonne Walker, Student Services Representative, 574-520-4185, E-mail: ydwalker@iusb.edu.
Website: https://www.iusb.edu/education/index.php

Indiana University Southeast, School of Education, New Albany, IN 47150. Offers counselor education (MS Ed); elementary education (MS Ed); secondary education (MS Ed). *Accreditation:* NCATE. *Program availability:* Part-time, evening/weekend. *Students:* 13 full-time (10 women), 190 part-time (150 women); includes 29 minority (21 Black or African American, non-Hispanic/Latino; 5 Hispanic/Latino; 3 Two or more races, non-Hispanic/Latino). Average age 33. 61 applicants, 84% accepted, 43 enrolled. In 2016, 70 master's awarded. *Entrance requirements:* For master's, minimum undergraduate GPA of 2.5, graduate 3.0. *Application deadline:* Applications are processed on a rolling basis. Application fee: $40 ($60 for international students). Electronic applications accepted. *Financial support:* Career-related internships or fieldwork, Federal Work-Study, and institutionally sponsored loans available. Support available to part-time students. Financial award applicants required to submit FAFSA. *Faculty research:* Learning styles, technology, constructivism, group process, innovative math strategies. *Unit head:* Dr. Faye Marsha Camahalan, Director of Graduate Studies, 812-941-2136, Fax: 812-941-2667, E-mail: fcamahal@ius.edu. *Application contact:* Admissions Counselor, 812-941-2212, Fax: 812-941-2595, E-mail: admissions@ius.edu.
Website: http://www.ius.edu/education/graduate-programs/

Indiana Wesleyan University, Graduate School, College of Arts and Sciences, Marion, IN 46953. Offers addictions counseling (MS); clinical mental health counseling (MS); community counseling (MS); marriage and family therapy (MS); school counseling (MS); student development counseling and administration (MS). *Accreditation:* ACA. *Program availability:* Part-time. *Degree requirements:* For master's, thesis or alternative. *Entrance requirements:* For master's, GRE General Test. Additional exam requirements/recommendations for international students: Required—TOEFL. Electronic applications accepted. *Expenses:* Contact institution. *Faculty research:* Community counseling, multicultural counseling, addictions.

Inter American University of Puerto Rico, Arecibo Campus, Programs in Education, Arecibo, PR 00614-4050. Offers administration and educational supervision (MA Ed); counseling and guidance (MA Ed); curriculum and teaching (MA Ed), including biology education, English as a second language, history education, math education, Spanish; elementary education (MA Ed). *Accreditation:* TEAC. *Degree requirements:* For master's, comprehensive exam, thesis optional. *Entrance requirements:* For master's, GRE, EXADEP, bachelor's degree in education or teaching license (administration and supervision) or courses in education and psychology (counseling and guidance), minimum GPA of 2.5 in last 60 credits.

Inter American University of Puerto Rico, Metropolitan Campus, Graduate Programs, Program in Education, San Juan, PR 00919-1293. Offers curriculum and instruction (Ed D); educational administration (Ed D); guidance and counseling (MA, Ed D); special education administration (Ed D). *Accreditation:* TEAC. *Degree requirements:* For doctorate, comprehensive exam, thesis/dissertation. *Entrance requirements:* For doctorate, GRE, MAT, or EXADEP. Electronic applications accepted.

Inter American University of Puerto Rico, San Germán Campus, Graduate Studies Center, Program in Counseling and Guidance, San Germán, PR 00683-5008. Offers education: counseling (MA, PhD). *Accreditation:* TEAC. *Program availability:* Part-time, evening/weekend. *Degree requirements:* For master's, comprehensive exam. *Entrance requirements:* For master's, GRE General Test or EXADEP, minimum GPA of 3.0.

Iowa State University of Science and Technology, Department of Educational Leadership and Policy Studies, Ames, IA 50011. Offers counselor education (M Ed, MS); educational administration (M Ed, MS); educational leadership (PhD); higher education (M Ed, MS); organizational learning and human resource development (M Ed, MS); research and evaluation (MS); student affairs (MS). *Degree requirements:* For master's, thesis or alternative; for doctorate, thesis/dissertation. *Entrance requirements:* For master's and doctorate, GRE General Test. Additional exam requirements/recommendations for international students: Required—TOEFL (minimum score 560 paper-based; 83 iBT), IELTS (minimum score 6.5). *Application deadline:* For fall admission, 1/1 priority date for domestic and international students. Application fee: $60 ($90 for international students). Electronic applications accepted. *Application contact:* Robyn Goldy, Application Contact, 515-294-1241, Fax: 515-294-4942, E-mail: rgoldy@iastate.edu.
Website: http://www.elps.hs.iastate.edu/

Jackson State University, Graduate School, College of Education and Human Development, Department of Counseling, Rehabilitation and Psychometric Services, Jackson, MS 39217. Offers clinical mental health (MS); rehabilitation counseling (MS); school counseling (MS Ed). *Accreditation:* ACA; CORE (one or more programs are accredited); NCATE. *Program availability:* Part-time, evening/weekend, 100% online, blended/hybrid learning. *Faculty:* 9 full-time (6 women), 1 part-time/adjunct (0 women). *Students:* 48 full-time (7 women), 82 part-time (74 women); includes 121 minority (118 Black or African American, non-Hispanic/Latino; 1 American Indian or Alaska Native, non-Hispanic/Latino; 1 Hispanic/Latino; 1 Two or more races, non-Hispanic/Latino). Average age 37. 106 applicants, 64% accepted, 47 enrolled. In 2016, 26 master's awarded. *Degree requirements:* For master's, comprehensive exam, thesis. *Entrance requirements:* For master's, GRE General Test. Additional exam requirements/recommendations for international students: Required—TOEFL (minimum score 520 paper-based; 67 iBT). *Application deadline:* For fall admission, 3/1 priority date for domestic students, 2/1 for international students; for spring admission, 10/1 for domestic and international students. Applications are processed on a rolling basis. Application fee: $25. Electronic applications accepted. *Expenses:* Contact institution. *Financial support:* Career-related internships or fieldwork, Federal Work-Study, scholarships/grants, and unspecified assistantships available. Support available to part-time students. Financial award application deadline: 3/1; financial award applicants required to submit FAFSA. *Unit head:* Dr. Dion Porter, Chair, 601-979-3364, Fax: 601-979-2213, E-mail: dion.porter@jsums.edu. *Application contact:* Dr. Dion Porter, Chair, 601-979-3364, Fax: 601-979-2213, E-mail: dion.porter@jsums.edu.
Website: http://www.jsums.edu/commcounseling/

Jacksonville State University, College of Graduate Studies and Continuing Education, College of Education and Professional Studies, Program in Guidance and Counseling, Jacksonville, AL 36265-1602. Offers MS. *Accreditation:* ACA; NCATE. *Program availability:* Part-time, evening/weekend. *Faculty:* 10 full-time (6 women), 12 part-time/adjunct (5 women). *Students:* 23 full-time (20 women), 58 part-time (47 women); includes 29 minority (28 Black or African American, non-Hispanic/Latino; 1 American Indian or Alaska Native, non-Hispanic/Latino). Average age 36. 49 applicants, 59% accepted, 17 enrolled. In 2016, 16 master's awarded. *Degree requirements:* For master's, comprehensive exam, thesis (for some programs). *Entrance requirements:* For master's, GRE General Test or MAT. Additional exam requirements/recommendations for international students: Required—TOEFL (minimum score 500 paper-based; 61 iBT). *Application deadline:* Applications are processed on a rolling basis. Application fee: $35. Electronic applications accepted. *Financial support:* In 2016–17, 16 students received support. Available to part-time students. Application deadline: 4/1; applicants required to submit FAFSA. *Unit head:* Dr. Tommy Turner, Head, 256-782-5180, E-mail: tturner@jsu.edu. *Application contact:* Dr. Jean Pugliese, 256-782-8278, Fax: 256-782-5321, E-mail: pugliese@jsu.edu.

John Brown University, Graduate Counseling Programs, Siloam Springs, AR 72761-2121. Offers clinical mental health counseling (MS); marriage and family therapy (MS); play therapy (Graduate Certificate); school counseling (MS). *Accreditation:* NCATE. *Program availability:* Part-time, evening/weekend. *Faculty:* 9 full-time (2 women), 18 part-time/adjunct (6 women). *Students:* 157 full-time (124 women), 153 part-time (124 women); includes 94 minority (50 Black or African American, non-Hispanic/Latino; 7 American Indian or Alaska Native, non-Hispanic/Latino; 3 Asian, non-Hispanic/Latino; 21 Hispanic/Latino; 13 Two or more races, non-Hispanic/Latino), 1 international. Average age 32. 129 applicants, 74% accepted, 83 enrolled. In 2016, 68 master's awarded. *Degree requirements:* For master's, practica or internships. *Entrance requirements:* For master's, GRE (minimum score of 300), recommendation forms from three people, 200-word essay describing professional plans and reason for seeking acceptance. Additional exam requirements/recommendations for international students: Required—TOEFL (minimum score 550 paper-based; 79 iBT). *Application deadline:* Applications are processed on a rolling basis. Application fee: $35 ($100 for international students). Electronic applications accepted. *Expenses:* Contact institution. *Financial support:* Fellowships, institutionally sponsored loans, scholarships/grants, and unspecified assistantships available. Financial award applicants required to submit FAFSA. *Unit head:* Dr. John V. Carmack, Program Director, 479-524-8630, E-mail: jcarmack@jbu.edu. *Application contact:* Mark Bjornsen, Graduate Counseling Representative, 479-631-4665, E-mail: mbjornsen@jbu.edu.
Website: http://www.jbu.edu/

John Carroll University, Graduate Studies, Program in Clinical Mental Health Counseling, University Heights, OH 44118-4581. Offers clinical counseling (Certificate); community counseling (MA). *Accreditation:* ACA. *Program availability:* Part-time, evening/weekend. *Faculty:* 7 full-time (4 women), 15 part-time/adjunct (10 women). *Students:* 36 full-time (33 women), 12 part-time (8 women); includes 4 minority (3 Black or African American, non-Hispanic/Latino; 1 Hispanic/Latino). Average age 32. 53 applicants, 40% accepted, 21 enrolled. In 2016, 22 master's awarded. *Degree requirements:* For master's, comprehensive exam, internship, practicum. *Entrance requirements:* For master's, MAT or GRE, minimum GPA of 2.75, statement of volunteer experience, interview, 12-18 hours of social science course work. Additional exam requirements/recommendations for international students: Required—TOEFL. *Application deadline:* For fall admission, 8/15 priority date for domestic students; for spring admission, 1/3 for domestic students. Applications are processed on a rolling basis. Application fee: $25 ($35 for international students). Electronic applications accepted. *Expenses: Tuition:* Full-time $10,425; part-time $695 per credit hour. One-time fee: $200 full-time. Tuition and fees vary according to course load, campus/location and program. *Financial support:* In 2016–17, 20 students received support, including 1 teaching assistantship with full tuition reimbursement available (averaging $8,000 per year); career-related internships or fieldwork, institutionally sponsored loans, and unspecified assistantships also available. Financial award application deadline: 3/1; financial award applicants required to submit FAFSA. *Faculty research:* Child and adolescent development, HIV, hypnosis, wellness, women's issues. *Unit head:* Dr. Cecile Brennan, Coordinator, 216-397-1987, Fax: 216-397-3045, E-mail: counseladmin@jcu.edu. *Application contact:* Jennifer L. Tucker, Records Management Assistant, 216-397-1925, Fax: 216-397-1835, E-mail: jtucker@jcu.edu.

John Carroll University, Graduate Studies, Program in School Counseling, University Heights, OH 44118-4581. Offers M Ed. *Accreditation:* ACA; NCATE. *Program availability:* Part-time, evening/weekend. *Degree requirements:* For master's, comprehensive exam, research essay or thesis (MA only). *Entrance requirements:* For master's, GRE General Test or MAT, minimum GPA of 2.75, interview. Additional exam requirements/recommendations for international students: Required—TOEFL. *Application deadline:* For fall admission, 8/15 priority date for domestic students; for spring admission, 1/3 for domestic students. Applications are processed on a rolling basis. Application fee: $25 ($35 for international students). Electronic applications accepted. *Expenses: Tuition:* Full-time $10,425; part-time $695 per credit hour. One-time fee: $200 full-time. Tuition and fees vary according to course load, campus/location and program. *Financial support:* Scholarships/grants, tuition waivers (partial), and unspecified assistantships available. Financial award application deadline: 3/1; financial award applicants required to submit FAFSA. *Unit head:* Amy Zucca, Administrative Assistant, 216-397-1708, Fax: 216-397-3045, E-mail: azucca@jcu.edu. *Application contact:* Jennifer L. Tucker, Records Management Assistant, 216-397-1925, Fax: 216-397-1835, E-mail: jtucker@jcu.edu.

Johns Hopkins University, School of Education, Certificate Programs in Education, Baltimore, MD 21218. Offers advanced methods for differentiated instruction and inclusive education (Graduate Certificate); applied behavior analysis (Post-Master's Certificate); clinical mental health counseling (Post-Master's Certificate); counseling (Advanced Certificate); data-based decision making and organizational improvement (Graduate Certificate); early intervention/preschool special education specialist (Graduate Certificate); education of students with autism and other pervasive developmental disorders (Graduate Certificate); educational leadership for independent schools (Graduate Certificate); evidence-based teaching in the health professions (Post-Master's Certificate); gifted education (Graduate Certificate); leadership in technology integration (Graduate Certificate); mind, brain and teaching (Graduate Certificate); school administration and supervision (Graduate Certificate); urban education (Graduate Certificate). *Program availability:* Part-time-only, evening/weekend, 100% online, blended/hybrid learning. *Students:* 5 full-time (all women), 194 part-time (164 women); includes 46 minority (29 Black or African American, non-Hispanic/Latino; 2 American Indian or Alaska Native, non-Hispanic/Latino; 3 Asian, non-Hispanic/Latino; 8 Hispanic/Latino; 4 Two or more races, non-Hispanic/Latino), 7 international. Average age 37. 240 applicants, 75% accepted, 143 enrolled. In 2016, 167 Advanced Certificates awarded. *Entrance requirements:* For degree, minimum of bachelor's degree from regionally- or nationally-accredited institution (master's degree for some programs); minimum GPA of 3.0 in all previous programs of study; official transcripts from all post-secondary institutions attended; essay; curriculum vitae/resume; two letters of recommendation; dispositions survey. *Application deadline:* For fall admission, 4/1 priority date for domestic students; for spring admission, 10/1 priority date for domestic students; for summer admission, 2/1 priority date for domestic students. Applications are processed on a rolling basis. Application fee: $80. Electronic applications accepted. *Expenses:* Contact institution. *Financial support:* Application deadline: 4/1; applicants required to submit FAFSA. *Unit head:* Dr. Christopher C. Morphew, Dean. *Application contact:* Elisabeth Woodward, Director of Admissions, 410-516-9796, Fax: 410-516-9817, E-mail: soe.info@jhu.edu.
Website: http://education.jhu.edu

Johns Hopkins University, School of Education, Master's Programs in Education, Baltimore, MD 21218. Offers counseling (MS), including clinical mental health counseling, school counseling; education (MS), including educational studies, gifted education, reading, school administration and supervision, technology for educators; elementary education (MAT); health professions (M Ed); intelligence analysis (MS); organizational leadership (MS); secondary education (MAT), including biology, chemistry, earth/space science, English, physics, social studies; special education (MS), including early childhood special education, general special education studies, mild to moderate disabilities, severe disabilities. *Program availability:* Part-time, evening/weekend, 100% online, blended/hybrid learning. *Students:* 345 full-time (265 women), 1,601 part-time (1,245 women); includes 837 minority (392 Black or African American, non-Hispanic/Latino; 7 American Indian or Alaska Native, non-Hispanic/Latino; 141 Asian, non-Hispanic/Latino; 207 Hispanic/Latino; 7 Native Hawaiian or other Pacific Islander, non-Hispanic/Latino; 83 Two or more races, non-Hispanic/Latino), 55 international. Average age 27. 1,352 applicants, 76% accepted, 819 enrolled. In 2016, 042 master's awarded. *Degree requirements:* For master's, comprehensive exam (for some programs), portfolio, capstone project and/or internship; PRAXIS II (subject area assessments) for initial teacher preparation programs that lead to licensure. *Entrance requirements:* For master's, GRE (for full-time programs only); PRAXIS I/core or state-approved alternative (for initial teacher preparation programs that lead to licensure), minimum of bachelor's degree from regionally- or nationally-accredited institution; minimum GPA of 3.0 in all previous programs of study; official transcripts from all post-secondary institutions attended; essay; curriculum vitae/resume; letters of recommendation (3 for full-time programs, 2 for part-time programs); dispositions survey. Additional exam requirements/recommendations for international students: Required—TOEFL (minimum score 600 paper-based; 100 iBT), IELTS (minimum score 7). *Application deadline:* For fall admission, 4/1 priority date for domestic students, 4/1 for international students; for spring admission, 10/1 priority date for domestic students, 10/1 for international students; for summer admission, 2/1 priority date for domestic students, 2/1 for international students. Applications are processed on a rolling basis. Application fee: $80. Electronic applications accepted. *Expenses:* Contact institution. *Financial support:* Application deadline: 4/1; applicants required to submit FAFSA. *Unit head:* Dr. Christopher C. Morphew, Dean. *Application contact:* Elisabeth Woodward, Director of Admissions, 410-516-9796, Fax: 410-516-9817, E-mail: soe.info@jhu.edu.
Website: http://education.jhu.edu

Johnson State College, Program in Counseling, Johnson, VT 05656. Offers addictions counseling (MA); clinical mental health counseling (MA); general counseling (MA); school counseling (MA). *Program availability:* Part-time. *Degree requirements:* For master's, comprehensive exam. *Entrance requirements:* For master's, interview. Additional exam requirements/recommendations for international students: Required—TOEFL. *Application deadline:* For fall admission, 7/1 for domestic students, 2/1 for international students; for spring admission, 11/1 for domestic students, 7/1 for international students; for summer admission, 4/1 for domestic students. Applications are processed on a rolling basis. Electronic applications accepted. Application fee is waived when completed online. *Expenses:* Tuition, state resident: part-time $555 per credit. Tuition, nonresident: part-time $800 per credit. *Financial support:* Career-related internships or fieldwork and unspecified assistantships available. Support available to part-time students. Financial award application deadline: 3/1; financial award applicants required to submit FAFSA. *Unit head:* Dr. David Fink, Coordinator, 802-635-1383, Fax: 802-635-1465, E-mail: david.fink@jsc.edu. *Application contact:* Catherine H. Higley, Administrative Assistant, 800-635-2356 Ext. 1244, Fax: 802-635-1248, E-mail: catherine.higley@jsc.edu.

Johnson University, Graduate and Professional Programs, Knoxville, TN 37998-1001. Offers biblical interpretation (Graduate Certificate); business administration (MBA); Christian ministries (Graduate Certificate); clinical mental health counseling (MA); educational technology (MA); intercultural studies (MA); leadership (MBA); leadership studies (PhD); New Testament (MA); nonprofit management (MBA); school counseling (MA); spiritual formation and leadership (Graduate Certificate); strategic ministry (MA); teacher education (MA). *Program availability:* Part-time, evening/weekend, 100% online, blended/hybrid learning. *Faculty:* 26 full-time (10 women), 32 part-time/adjunct (9 women). *Students:* 126 full-time (46 women), 170 part-time (65 women); includes 33 minority (13 Black or African American, non-Hispanic/Latino; 1 American Indian or Alaska Native, non-Hispanic/Latino; 4 Asian, non-Hispanic/Latino; 8 Hispanic/Latino; 7 Two or more races, non-Hispanic/Latino), 21 international. Average age 35. In 2016, 106 master's, 3 doctorates awarded. *Degree requirements:* For master's, variable foreign language requirement, comprehensive exam, thesis (for some programs), internships; for doctorate, variable foreign language requirement, comprehensive exam, thesis/dissertation, internships. *Entrance requirements:* For master's, PRAXIS (for MA in teacher education); MAT (for counseling); GRE or GMAT (for MBA), interview, 3 references, transcripts, essay, minimum GPA of 2.5 or 3.0 (depending on program); for doctorate, GRE or MAT (taken not less than 5 years prior), interview, 3 references, transcripts, essay, minimum GPA of 3.0; for Graduate Certificate, interview, 3 references, transcripts, essay, minimum GPA of 3.0. Additional exam requirements/recommendations for international students: Required—TOEFL (minimum score 527 paper-based; 71 iBT). *Application deadline:* For fall admission, 7/1 for domestic students; for spring admission, 11/1 for domestic students; for summer admission, 4/1 for domestic students. Application fee: $50. Electronic applications accepted. *Expenses:* Contact institution. *Financial support:* Scholarships/grants available. Financial award application deadline: 4/15; financial award applicants required to submit FAFSA. *Unit head:* Richard Clark, Vice President for External Relations, 865-251-2327, E-mail: rclark@johnsonu.edu. *Application contact:* Lisa Tarwater, Director of Graduate Admissions, 865-251-3400, E-mail: ltarwater@johnsonu.edu.

Kansas State University, Graduate School, College of Education, Department of Special Education, Counseling and Student Affairs, Manhattan, KS 66506. Offers academic advising (MS, Certificate); counseling and student development (MS), including college student development, school counseling; special education (MS, Ed D); special education, counseling, and student affairs (PhD). *Accreditation:* ACA; NCATE. *Program availability:* Part-time, online learning. *Faculty:* 16 full-time (11 women), 11 part-time/adjunct (5 women). *Students:* 108 full-time (63 women), 252 part-time (193 women); includes 83 minority (33 Black or African American, non-Hispanic/Latino; 4 American Indian or Alaska Native, non-Hispanic/Latino; 7 Asian, non-Hispanic/Latino; 28 Hispanic/Latino; 2 Native Hawaiian or other Pacific Islander, non-Hispanic/Latino; 9 Two or more races, non-Hispanic/Latino), 6 international. Average age 33. 189 applicants, 82% accepted, 96 enrolled. In 2016, 134 master's, 4 doctorates, 70 other advanced degrees awarded. *Degree requirements:* For master's, comprehensive exam; for doctorate, comprehensive exam, thesis/dissertation. *Entrance requirements:* For master's, minimum undergraduate GPA of 3.0; for doctorate, GRE General Test, minimum GPA of 3.0 in last 60 hours. Additional exam requirements/recommendations for international students: Required—TOEFL. *Application deadline:* For fall admission, 2/1 for domestic students, 1/1 priority date for international students; for spring admission, 8/1 for domestic students, 8/1 priority date for international students; for summer admission, 12/1 priority date for international students. Applications are processed on a rolling basis. Application fee: $50 ($75 for international students). Electronic applications accepted. *Expenses:* Tuition, state resident: full-time $9670. Tuition, nonresident: full-time $21,828. *Required fees:* $862. *Financial support:* In 2016–17, 3 teaching assistantships (averaging $14,727 per year) were awarded; career-related internships or fieldwork, institutionally sponsored loans, and scholarships/grants also available. Financial award application deadline: 3/1; financial award applicants required to submit FAFSA. *Faculty research:* Counseling supervision, academic advising, career development, student development, universal design for learning, autism, learning disabilities. *Total annual research expenditures:* $17,900. *Unit head:* Dr. Kenneth Hughey, Head, 785-532-5541, Fax: 785-532-7304, E-mail: khughey@ksu.edu. *Application contact:* Cassandra Llewelyn, Application Contact, 785-532-5541, Fax: 785-532-7304, E-mail: cjwalker@ksu.edu.
Website: http://www.coe.k-state.edu/departments/secsa/

Kean University, Nathan Weiss Graduate College, Program in Counselor Education, Union, NJ 07083. Offers alcohol and drug abuse counseling (MA); clinical mental health counseling (MA); school counseling (MA). *Accreditation:* ACA; NCATE. *Program availability:* Part-time. *Faculty:* 8 full-time (5 women). *Students:* 130 full-time (105 women), 149 part-time (114 women); includes 114 minority (54 Black or African American, non-Hispanic/Latino; 1 American Indian or Alaska Native, non-Hispanic/Latino; 5 Asian, non-Hispanic/Latino; 49 Hispanic/Latino; 5 Two or more races, non-Hispanic/Latino), 3 international. Average age 32. 258 applicants, 30% accepted, 68 enrolled. In 2016, 71 master's awarded. *Degree requirements:* For master's, practicum, internship, portfolio. *Entrance requirements:* For master's, minimum GPA of 3.0, 2 letters of recommendation, personal statement, resume. Additional exam requirements/recommendations for international students: Required—TOEFL (minimum score 550 paper-based; 79 iBT), IELTS. *Application deadline:* For fall admission, 3/2 for domestic and international students; for spring admission, 10/31 for domestic and international students. Applications are processed on a rolling basis. Application fee: $75. Electronic applications accepted. *Expenses:* Tuition, state resident: full-time $13,156; part-time $640 per credit. Tuition, nonresident: full-time $17,831; part-time $785 per credit. *Required fees:* $3316; $151 per credit. Tuition and fees vary according to course level, course load, degree level and program. *Financial support:* Scholarships/grants and unspecified assistantships available. Financial award applicants required to submit FAFSA. *Unit head:* Dr. J. Barry Mascari, Program Coordinator, 908-737-5954, E-mail: jmascari@kean.edu. *Application contact:* Pedro Lopes, Admissions Counselor, 908-

737-7100, E-mail: grad-adm@kean.edu.
Website: http://grad.kean.edu/counseling

Keene State College, School of Professional and Graduate Studies, Keene, NH 03435. Offers curriculum and instruction (M Ed); education leadership (PMC); educational leadership (M Ed); safety and occupational health applied science (MS); school counselor (M Ed, PMC); special education (M Ed). *Accreditation:* NCATE. *Program availability:* Part-time, evening/weekend. *Faculty:* 9 full-time (4 women), 8 part-time/adjunct (3 women). *Students:* 24 full-time (17 women), 66 part-time (38 women); includes 3 minority (1 Black or African American, non-Hispanic/Latino; 1 Hispanic/Latino; 1 Two or more races, non-Hispanic/Latino), 1 international. Average age 33. 24 applicants, 100% accepted, 24 enrolled. In 2016, 26 master's, 1 other advanced degree awarded. *Degree requirements:* For master's, thesis (for some programs). *Entrance requirements:* For master's, PRAXIS I, 3 references; official transcripts; minimum GPA of 2.5; interview; essay; teacher/educator certificate; work/internship experience. Additional exam requirements/recommendations for international students: Required—TOEFL (minimum score 550 paper-based; 61 iBT). *Application deadline:* For fall admission, 4/1 for domestic and international students; for spring admission, 11/1 for domestic and international students; for summer admission, 3/1 for domestic and international students. Applications are processed on a rolling basis. Application fee: $50. Electronic applications accepted. *Expenses:* Tuition, state resident: full-time $9180; part-time $510 per credit. Tuition, nonresident: full-time $10,080; part-time $560 per credit. *Required fees:* $1908; $106 per credit. Tuition and fees vary according to course load. *Financial support:* In 2016–17, 27 students received support. Career-related internships or fieldwork, Federal Work-Study, institutionally sponsored loans, scholarships/grants, and unspecified assistantships available. Support available to part-time students. Financial award application deadline: 3/1; financial award applicants required to submit FAFSA. *Unit head:* Dr. Karrie Kalich, Dean of Professional and Graduate Studies, 603-358-2885, E-mail: kkalich@keene.edu. *Application contact:* Peter Tandy, Assistant Director for Graduate Studies, 603-358-2332, E-mail: kscgraduatestudies@keene.edu.
Website: http://www.keene.edu/academics/graduate/

Kent State University, College of Education, Health and Human Services, School of Lifespan Development and Educational Sciences, Program in Counseling, Kent, OH 44242-0001. Offers Ed S. *Accreditation:* ACA. *Entrance requirements:* For degree, 2 letters of reference, goals statement, interview. Additional exam requirements/recommendations for international students: Required—TOEFL (minimum score 550 paper-based; 80 iBT). Electronic applications accepted. *Expenses:* Tuition, state resident: full-time $10,864; part-time $495 per credit hour. Tuition, nonresident: full-time $18,380; part-time $837 per credit hour.

Kent State University, College of Education, Health and Human Services, School of Lifespan Development and Educational Sciences, Program in Counseling and Human Development Services, Kent, OH 44242-0001. Offers PhD. *Accreditation:* ACA; NCATE. *Degree requirements:* For doctorate, comprehensive exam, thesis/dissertation. *Entrance requirements:* For doctorate, GRE General Test, preliminary written exam, 2 letters of reference, resume, interview. Additional exam requirements/recommendations for international students: Required—TOEFL (minimum score 550 paper-based; 80 iBT). Electronic applications accepted. *Expenses:* Tuition, state resident: full-time $10,864; part-time $495 per credit hour. Tuition, nonresident: full-time $18,380; part-time $837 per credit hour. *Faculty research:* Family/child therapy, clinical supervision, group work, experiential training methods.

Kent State University, College of Education, Health and Human Services, School of Lifespan Development and Educational Sciences, Program in School Counseling, Kent, OH 44242-0001. Offers M Ed. *Accreditation:* ACA; NCATE. *Entrance requirements:* For master's, minimum undergraduate GPA of 2.75, 2 letters of reference, goals statement, moral character statement, interview. Additional exam requirements/recommendations for international students: Required—TOEFL (minimum score 550 paper-based; 80 iBT). Electronic applications accepted. *Expenses:* Tuition, state resident: full-time $10,864; part-time $495 per credit hour. Tuition, nonresident: full-time $18,380; part-time $837 per credit hour. *Faculty research:* Appraisal, diagnosis, group work.

Kutztown University of Pennsylvania, College of Education, Program in School Counseling, Kutztown, PA 19530-0730. Offers MS. *Accreditation:* NCATE. *Program availability:* Part-time, evening/weekend. *Faculty:* 4 full-time (3 women). *Students:* 24 full-time (20 women), 26 part-time (20 women); includes 5 minority (1 Black or African American, non-Hispanic/Latino; 3 Hispanic/Latino; 1 Two or more races, non-Hispanic/Latino). Average age 29. 26 applicants, 85% accepted, 14 enrolled. In 2016, 27 master's awarded. *Degree requirements:* For master's, comprehensive exam, thesis optional. *Entrance requirements:* For master's, GRE General Test, 3 letters of recommendation, minimum undergraduate GPA of 3.0, psychobiographical statement, resume. Additional exam requirements/recommendations for international students: Required—TOEFL (minimum score 550 paper-based, 79 iBT) or IELTS (minimum score 6.5). *Application deadline:* For fall admission, 3/1 for domestic and international students; for spring admission, 10/1 for domestic and international students. Application fee: $35. Electronic applications accepted. *Expenses:* Tuition, state resident: full-time $4347; part-time $483 per credit. Tuition, nonresident: full-time $6525; part-time $725 per credit. *Required fees:* $88 per credit. One-time fee: $50 full-time. *Financial support:* Career-related internships or fieldwork, Federal Work-Study, scholarships/grants, and unspecified assistantships available. Financial award application deadline: 3/1; financial award applicants required to submit FAFSA. *Faculty research:* Family addictions, family roles. *Unit head:* Dr. Helen S. Hamlet, Department Chair, 610-683-4204, Fax: 610-683-1585, E-mail: hamlet@kutztown.edu.
Website: https://www.kutztown.edu/academics/graduate-programs/counseling.htm

Lakeland University, Graduate Studies Division, Program in Counseling, Plymouth, WI 53073. Offers MA.

Lamar University, College of Graduate Studies, College of Education and Human Development, Department of Counseling and Special Populations, Beaumont, TX 77710. Offers clinical mental health counseling (M Ed); school counseling (M Ed); special education (M Ed), including special education. *Accreditation:* ACA. *Faculty:* 6 full-time (3 women), 29 part-time/adjunct (11 women). *Students:* 16 full-time (9 women), 1,586 part-time (1,424 women); includes 758 minority (373 Black or African American, non-Hispanic/Latino; 6 American Indian or Alaska Native, non-Hispanic/Latino; 20 Asian, non-Hispanic/Latino; 337 Hispanic/Latino; 2 Native Hawaiian or other Pacific Islander, non-Hispanic/Latino; 20 Two or more races, non-Hispanic/Latino), 5 international. Average age 37. 840 applicants, 96% accepted, 393 enrolled. In 2016, 703 master's awarded. *Entrance requirements:* Additional exam requirements/recommendations for international students: Required—TOEFL (minimum score 550 paper-based; 79 iBT), IELTS (minimum score 6.5). *Application deadline:* For fall admission, 8/10 for domestic students, 7/1 for international students; for spring admission, 1/5 for domestic students, 12/1 for international students. Applications are processed on a rolling basis. Application fee: $25 ($50 for international students). Electronic applications accepted. *Expenses:* $8,134 in-state full-time, $5,574 in-state part-time; $15,604 out-of-state full-time, $10,554 out-of-state part-time per year. *Financial support:* Applicants required to submit FAFSA. *Unit head:* Dr. Rebecca Weinbaum, Interim Chair, 409-880-8978, Fax: 409-880-2263. *Application contact:* Deidre Mayer, Interim Director, Admissions and Academic Services, 409-880-8888, Fax: 409-880-7419, E-mail: gradmissions@lamar.edu.
Website: http://education.lamar.edu/counseling-and-special-populations

Lancaster Bible College, Graduate School, Lancaster, PA 17601-5036. Offers adult ministries (MA); Bible (MA); children and family ministry (MA); church planting (MA); consulting resource teacher (M Ed); elementary school counseling (M Ed); leadership (PhD); leadership studies (MA); marriage and family counseling (MA); mental health counseling (MA); pastoral studies (MA); secondary school counseling (M Ed); sports ministry (MA); student ministry (MA); town and country ministry (MA). *Program availability:* Part-time, evening/weekend. *Degree requirements:* For master's, comprehensive exam (for some programs), thesis (for some programs). *Entrance requirements:* For master's, bachelor's degree with a minimum of 30 credits of course work in Bible, minimum undergraduate GPA of 3.0, interview. Additional exam requirements/recommendations for international students: Required—TOEFL.

La Sierra University, School of Education, Department of School Psychology and Counseling, Riverside, CA 92515. Offers counseling (MA); educational psychology (Ed S); school psychology (Ed S). *Program availability:* Part-time, evening/weekend. *Degree requirements:* For master's, thesis optional; for Ed S, practicum (educational psychology). *Entrance requirements:* For master's, California Basic Educational Skills Test, NTE, minimum GPA of 3.0; for Ed S, minimum GPA of 3.3. *Faculty research:* Equivalent score scales, self perception.

Lee University, Graduate Studies in Counseling, Cleveland, TN 37320-3450. Offers holistic child development (MS); marriage and family studies (MS); marriage and family therapy (MS); school counseling (MS). *Program availability:* Part-time, 100% online. *Faculty:* 8 full-time (3 women), 3 part-time/adjunct (0 women). *Students:* 86 full-time (65 women), 27 part-time (18 women); includes 46 minority (9 Black or African American, non-Hispanic/Latino; 1 American Indian or Alaska Native, non-Hispanic/Latino; 1 Asian, non-Hispanic/Latino; 33 Hispanic/Latino; 2 Two or more races, non-Hispanic/Latino), 8 international. Average age 31. 34 applicants, 65% accepted, 18 enrolled. In 2016, 31 master's awarded. *Degree requirements:* For master's, variable foreign language requirement, comprehensive exam (for some programs), thesis (for some programs), internship. *Entrance requirements:* For master's, GRE General Test or MAT (waived if undergraduate GPA is greater than 3.0 or if applicant already has a graduate degree), minimum undergraduate GPA of 3.0, 3 letters of recommendation, interview, official transcripts, essay. Additional exam requirements/recommendations for international students: Required—TOEFL (minimum score 61 iBT). *Application deadline:* For fall admission, 4/1 priority date for domestic and international students; for spring admission, 11/1 priority date for domestic and international students. Applications are processed on a rolling basis. Application fee: $25. Electronic applications accepted. *Expenses: Tuition:* Full-time $11,367; part-time $632 per credit hour. *Required fees:* $35 per term. One-time fee: $25. Tuition and fees vary according to program. *Financial support:* In 2016–17, 25 students received support. Career-related internships or fieldwork, Federal Work-Study, institutionally sponsored loans, scholarships/grants, and unspecified assistantships available. Financial award application deadline: 3/1; financial award applicants required to submit FAFSA. *Unit head:* Dr. Trevor Milliron, Director, 423-614-8126, Fax: 423-614-8124, E-mail: tmilliron@leeuniversity.edu.
Website: http://www.leeuniversity.edu/academics/graduate/counseling/

Lehigh University, College of Education, Program in Counseling Psychology, Bethlehem, PA 18015. Offers counseling and human services (M Ed); counseling psychology (PhD); international counseling (M Ed, Certificate); school counseling (M Ed). *Accreditation:* APA (one or more programs are accredited). *Program availability:* Blended/hybrid learning. *Faculty:* 8 full-time (5 women), 6 part-time/adjunct (all women). *Students:* 60 full-time (53 women), 31 part-time (26 women); includes 21 minority (7 Black or African American, non-Hispanic/Latino; 3 Asian, non-Hispanic/Latino; 11 Hispanic/Latino), 15 international. Average age 30. 167 applicants, 31% accepted, 19 enrolled. In 2016, 35 master's, 7 doctorates awarded. *Degree requirements:* For doctorate, comprehensive exam, thesis/dissertation. *Entrance requirements:* For master's, minimum GPA of 3.0, 2 letters of recommendation, essay, transcript; for doctorate, GRE General Test, 2 letters of recommendation, transcript, essay; for Certificate, minimum GPA of 3.0 (undergraduate), 3.5 (graduate). Additional exam requirements/recommendations for international students: Required—TOEFL (minimum score 600 paper-based; 93 iBT). *Application deadline:* For fall admission, 2/1 for domestic and international students. Application fee: $65. Electronic applications accepted. *Expenses:* $565 per credit. *Financial support:* In 2016–17, 23 students received support, including 4 research assistantships with partial tuition reimbursements available (averaging $15,800 per year); fellowships, career-related internships or fieldwork, scholarships/grants, tuition waivers, and unspecified assistantships also available. Financial award application deadline: 2/15; financial award applicants required to submit FAFSA. *Faculty research:* Maternal/infant attachment, multicultural training and counseling, career development and health interventions, intersection of identities, community based participatory research. *Total annual research expenditures:* $729,282. *Unit head:* Dr. Christpher Liang, Director, 610-758-3253, Fax: 610-758-3227, E-mail: ctl212@lehigh.edu. *Application contact:* Lauryn Woodman, Coordinator, Counseling, 610-758-3250, Fax: 610-758-6223, E-mail: laa314@lehigh.edu.
Website: http://coe.lehigh.edu/academics/disciplines/cp

Lehman College of the City University of New York, School of Education, Department of Specialized Services in Education, Program in Guidance and Counseling, Bronx, NY 10468-1589. Offers MS Ed. *Accreditation:* ACA; NCATE. *Program availability:* Part-time, evening/weekend. *Degree requirements:* For master's, thesis. *Entrance requirements:* For master's, minimum GPA of 2.7. *Faculty research:* Crisis intervention, domestic violence, alcohol abuse, gender issues.

Lenoir-Rhyne University, Graduate Programs, School of Counseling and Human Services, Program in School Counseling, Hickory, NC 28601. Offers MA. *Program availability:* Part-time, evening/weekend. *Degree requirements:* For master's, comprehensive exam, thesis optional. *Entrance requirements:* For master's, GRE General Test, minimum undergraduate GPA of 2.7, graduate 3.0; writing sample. Additional exam requirements/recommendations for international students: Required—TOEFL (minimum score 600 paper-based). Electronic applications accepted. *Expenses:* Contact institution.

Lewis University, College of Arts and Sciences, Program in School Counseling, Romeoville, IL 60446. Offers MA. *Program availability:* Part-time, evening/weekend. *Students:* 28 full-time (23 women), 38 part-time (31 women); includes 4 minority (1 Black or African American, non-Hispanic/Latino; 3 Hispanic/Latino). Average age 29. *Degree requirements:* For master's, comprehensive exam, internship; practicum. *Entrance requirements:* For master's, letters of recommendation, interview, minimum GPA of 2.75. Additional exam requirements/recommendations for international students: Required—TOEFL (minimum score 550 paper-based; 80 iBT). *Application deadline:* For fall admission, 5/1 priority date for international students; for spring admission, 11/15 priority date for international students. Applications are processed on a rolling basis. Application fee: $40. Electronic applications accepted. *Expenses: Tuition:* Full-time $13,860; part-time $770 per credit hour. *Required fees:* $75 per semester. Tuition and fees vary according to degree level and program. *Financial support:* Federal Work-Study, scholarships/grants, tuition waivers (full and partial), and unspecified assistantships available. Financial award application deadline: 5/1; financial award applicants required to submit FAFSA. *Unit head:* Dr. Judith Zito, Director, 815-838-0500 Ext. 5971, E-mail: zitoju@lewisu.edu. *Application contact:* Assistant Director, Graduate and Adult Admission, 815-836-5610, Fax: 815-836-5578, E-mail: grad@lewisu.edu.

Liberty University, School of Behavioral Sciences, Lynchburg, VA 24515. Offers clinical mental health counseling (MA); counselor education and supervision (PhD); human services counseling (MA), including addictions and recovery, business, child and family law, Christian ministries, criminal justice, crisis response and trauma, executive leadership, health and wellness, life coaching, marriage and family, military resilience; marriage and family therapy (MA); military resilience (Certificate); professional counseling (MA). *Program availability:* Part-time, online learning. *Students:* 2,041 full-time (1,612 women), 4,970 part-time (3,875 women); includes 1,991 minority (1,678 Black or African American, non-Hispanic/Latino; 33 American Indian or Alaska Native, non-Hispanic/Latino; 48 Asian, non-Hispanic/Latino; 80 Hispanic/Latino; 8 Native Hawaiian or other Pacific Islander, non-Hispanic/Latino; 144 Two or more races, non-Hispanic/Latino), 127 international. Average age 39. 5,496 applicants, 41% accepted, 1257 enrolled. In 2016, 2,813 master's, 11 doctorates, 20 other advanced degrees awarded. *Application deadline:* Applications are processed on a rolling basis. Application fee: $50. Electronic applications accepted. *Financial support:* Applicants required to submit FAFSA. *Unit head:* Dr. Ronald Hawkins, Founding Dean, School of Behavioral Sciences. *Application contact:* Jay Bridge, Director of Admissions, 800-424-9595, Fax: 800-628-7977, E-mail: gradadmissions@liberty.edu.

Lincoln Memorial University, Carter and Moyers School of Education, Harrogate, TN 37752-1901. Offers administration and supervision (M Ed, Ed S); counseling and guidance (M Ed); curriculum and instruction (M Ed, Ed D, Ed S); English (M Ed); executive leadership (Ed D); higher education administration (Ed D); human resource development (Ed D); leadership and administration (Ed D). *Program availability:* Part-time, evening/weekend, online learning. *Degree requirements:* For master's, comprehensive exam, thesis optional; for Ed S, comprehensive exam. *Entrance requirements:* For master's, PRAXIS, NTE, GRE, MAT, letters of recommendation; for Ed S, graduate transcripts. Additional exam requirements/recommendations for international students: Recommended—TOEFL. *Faculty research:* Brain compatible teaching and learning; poverty in Appalachia; leadership for change; ethics, moral responsibility and social justice; human and organizational learning.

Lincoln University, Graduate Studies, Jefferson City, MO 65101. Offers business administration (MBA), including accounting, management, management information systems, public administration/policy; elementary teaching (M Ed); environmental science (MS); guidance and counseling (M Ed), including community/agency counseling, elementary school, secondary school; higher education (MA); history (MA); integrated agricultural systems (MS); middle school (M Ed); natural sciences (MS); secondary teaching (M Ed); sociology (MA); sociology/criminal justice (MA). *Program availability:* Part-time, evening/weekend, 100% online, blended/hybrid learning. *Students:* 50 full-time (29 women), 68 part-time (39 women); includes 40 minority (37 Black or African American, non-Hispanic/Latino; 1 Asian, non-Hispanic/Latino; 2 Two or more races, non-Hispanic/Latino), 14 international. Average age 33. 75 applicants, 80% accepted, 34 enrolled. In 2016, 51 master's awarded. *Degree requirements:* For master's, comprehensive exam, thesis optional. *Entrance requirements:* For master's, GRE, MAT or GMAT, minimum GPA of 2.75 overall, 3.0 in courses related to specialization; 3 letters of recommendation; minimum C average in English composition; personal statement of purpose. Additional exam requirements/recommendations for international students: Required—TOEFL (minimum score 500 paper-based; 61 iBT), IELTS (minimum score 5.5), Michigan English Language Assessment Battery (minimum score 80). *Application deadline:* For fall admission, 7/1 priority date for domestic students, 5/1 priority date for international students; for spring admission, 11/1 priority date for domestic students, 10/1 priority date for international students; for summer admission, 6/1 priority date for domestic students. Applications are processed on a rolling basis. Application fee: $30. Electronic applications accepted. *Expenses:* Tuition, state resident: full-time $6840; part-time $5130 per year. Tuition, nonresident: full-time $12,720; part-time $9540 per year. *Required fees:* $852; $811 per unit. Tuition and fees vary according to course load. *Financial support:* In 2016–17, 2 fellowships with tuition reimbursements, 8 research assistantships with tuition reimbursements were awarded; Federal Work-Study, scholarships/grants, and unspecified assistantships also available. Support available to part-time students. Financial award application deadline: 3/1; financial award applicants required to submit FAFSA. *Unit head:* Dr. Rolundus R. Rice, Dean, 573-681-5247, Fax: 573-681-5106, E-mail: gradschool@lincolnu.edu. *Application contact:* Irasema Steck, Administrative Assistant, 573-681-5247, Fax: 573-681-5106, E-mail: gradschool@lincolnu.edu.
Website: http://www.lincolnu.edu/web/graduate-studies/graduate-studies

Lindenwood University–Belleville, Graduate Programs, Belleville, IL 62226. Offers business administration (MBA); communications (MA), including digital and multimedia, media management, promotions, training and development; counseling (MA); criminal justice administration (MS); education (MA); healthcare administration (MS); human resource management (MS); school administration (MA); teaching (MAT).

Lindsey Wilson College, School of Professional Counseling, Columbia, KY 42728. Offers counseling and human development (M Ed); counselor education and supervision (PhD). *Accreditation:* ACA (one or more programs are accredited). *Program availability:* Part-time, evening/weekend, online learning.

Loma Linda University, School of Behavioral Health, Department of Counseling and Family Sciences, Loma Linda, CA 92350. Offers child life specialist (MS); clinical mediation (Certificate); counseling (MS); drug and alcohol counseling (Certificate); family life education (Certificate); marital and family therapy (DMFT); school counseling (Certificate). *Degree requirements:* For master's, comprehensive exam, thesis optional; for doctorate, comprehensive exam, thesis/dissertation (for some programs). *Entrance requirements:* For master's, minimum GPA of 3.0; for doctorate, GRE. Additional exam requirements/recommendations for international students: Required—TOEFL (minimum score 550 paper-based). Electronic applications accepted.

Long Island University–Brentwood Campus, Graduate Programs, Brentwood, NY 11717. Offers childhood education (grades 1-6) (MS), including grades 1-6; childhood education/literacy (grades 1-6) (MS); childhood education/special education (grades 1-6) (MS); clinical mental health counseling (MS, Advanced Certificate); early childhood education (B-2) (MS); literacy (B-6) (MS Ed); school counselor (MS); special education (grades 1-6) (MS Ed); students with disabilities generalist (grades 7-12) (Advanced Certificate). *Program availability:* Part-time. *Faculty:* 54 part-time/adjunct (30 women). *Students:* 98 full-time (80 women), 57 part-time (47 women); includes 28 minority (7 Black or African American, non-Hispanic/Latino; 1 Asian, non-Hispanic/Latino; 20 Hispanic/Latino). 85 applicants, 89% accepted, 43 enrolled. In 2016, 99 master's, 11 other advanced degrees awarded. *Degree requirements:* For master's, comprehensive exam (for some programs), thesis optional. *Entrance requirements:* For master's and Advanced Certificate, GRE. Additional exam requirements/recommendations for international students: Required—TOEFL or IELTS. *Application deadline:* Applications are processed on a rolling basis. Application fee: $50. Electronic applications accepted. Application fee is waived when completed online. *Expenses:* *Tuition:* Full-time $28,272; part-time $1178 per credit. *Required fees:* $451 per term. *Financial support:* Scholarships/grants and unspecified assistantships available. Support available to part-time students. Financial award applicants required to submit FAFSA. *Unit head:* Donna Di Donato, Dean and Chief Operating Officer, 631-287-8010, Fax: 631-287-8575, E-mail: donna.didonato@liu.edu. *Application contact:* Scott Aug, Associate Director of Enrollment Management, 631-287-8500, Fax: 631-287-8575, E-mail: scott.aug@liu.edu.
Website: http://liu.edu/brentwood

Long Island University–Hudson, Graduate School, Purchase, NY 10577. Offers autism (Advanced Certificate); childhood education (MS Ed); early childhood education (MS Ed); educational leadership (MS Ed); finance (MBA); health administration (MPA); healthcare sector management (MBA); literacy (MS Ed); management (MBA); marriage and family therapy (MS); mental health counseling (MS), including credentialed alcoholism and substance abuse counselor; middle childhood and adolescence education (MS Ed); pharmaceutics (MS), including cosmetic science, industrial pharmacy; public administration (MPA); school counseling (MS Ed, Advanced Certificate); school psychology (MS Ed); special education (MS Ed); TESOL (all grades) (Advanced Certificate); TESOL and bilingual education (MS Ed); the business of pharmaceutics and biotechnology (MBA). *Program availability:* Part-time, evening/weekend, online learning. *Faculty:* 7 full-time (5 women), 42 part-time/adjunct (25 women). *Students:* 55 full-time (41 women), 158 part-time (123 women); includes 40 minority (8 Black or African American, non-Hispanic/Latino; 1 Asian, non-Hispanic/Latino; 31 Hispanic/Latino). Average age 35. *Entrance requirements:* Additional exam requirements/recommendations for international students: Required—TOEFL (minimum score 550 paper-based; 79 iBT). *Application deadline:* Applications are processed on a rolling basis. Application fee: $50. Electronic applications accepted. *Expenses:* Contact institution. *Unit head:* Dr. Sylvia Blake, Dean and Chief Operating Officer, 914-831-2700, E-mail: westchester@liu.edu. *Application contact:* Cindy Pagnotta, Director of Marketing and Enrollment, 914-831-2701, Fax: 914-251-5959, E-mail: cindy.pagnotta@liu.edu.

Long Island University–LIU Brooklyn, School of Education, Brooklyn, NY 11201-8423. Offers adolescence urban education (MS Ed); applied behavior analysis (Advanced Certificate); bilingual education (Advanced Certificate); bilingual school counselor (MS Ed, Advanced Certificate); childhood urban education (MS Ed); childhood/early childhood urban education (MS Ed); early childhood urban education (MS Ed, Advanced Certificate); educational leadership (Advanced Certificate); marriage and family therapy (MS, Advanced Certificate); mental health counseling (MS, Advanced Certificate); school building district leader (Advanced Certificate); school counselor (MS Ed, Advanced Certificate); school psychologist (MS Ed); teaching urban children/adolescents with disabilities (MS Ed); TESOL (MS Ed). *Accreditation:* TEAC. *Program availability:* Part-time, evening/weekend. *Faculty:* 23 full-time (17 women), 44 part-time/adjunct (32 women). *Students:* 161 full-time (144 women), 594 part-time (461 women); includes 493 minority (229 Black or African American, non-Hispanic/Latino; 1 American Indian or Alaska Native, non-Hispanic/Latino; 30 Asian, non-Hispanic/Latino; 218 Hispanic/Latino; 2 Native Hawaiian or other Pacific Islander, non-Hispanic/Latino; 13 Two or more races, non-Hispanic/Latino), 9 international. 513 applicants, 73% accepted, 272 enrolled. In 2016, 262 master's, 18 other advanced degrees awarded. *Degree requirements:* For master's, thesis optional, electronic portfolio. *Entrance requirements:* For master's, GRE (for MS Ed). Additional exam requirements/recommendations for international students: Required—TOEFL (minimum score 527 paper-based; 75 iBT). *Application deadline:* Applications are processed on a rolling basis. Application fee: $50. Electronic applications accepted. *Expenses:* *Tuition:* Full-time $28,272; part-time $1178 per credit. *Required fees:* $451 per term. Tuition and fees vary according to degree level, program and student level. *Financial support:* In 2016–17, 81 students received support. Career-related internships or fieldwork, Federal Work-Study, institutionally sponsored loans, scholarships/grants, and unspecified assistantships available. Support available to part-time students. Financial award application deadline: 2/15; financial award applicants required to submit FAFSA. *Faculty research:* Technology in education, teaching civics and sustainability, biliteracy and dual language instruction, diversity in organizations and leadership, counseling diverse couples and families. *Unit head:* Dr. Amy Ginsberg, Dean, 718-246-6308, E-mail: amy.ginsberg@liu.edu. *Application contact:* Gabrielle Gannon, Director of Graduate Admissions, 718-488-1011, Fax: 718-780-6110, E-mail: bkln-admissions@liu.edu.
Website: http://www.liu.edu/Brooklyn/Academics/School-of-Education

Longwood University, College of Graduate and Professional Studies, College of Education and Human Services, Farmville, VA 23909. Offers education (MS), including algebra and middle school mathematics, counselor education, elementary and middle school mathematics, elementary education, elementary education initial licensure, health and physical education, special education general curriculum, special education initial licensure; reading, literacy and learning (M Ed); school librarianship (M Ed); social work and communication sciences and disorders (MS), including communication sciences and disorders. *Accreditation:* NCATE. *Program availability:* Part-time, evening/weekend. *Degree requirements:* For master's, comprehensive exam (for some programs), thesis optional, professional portfolio, internship, clinical experience, or practicum. *Entrance requirements:* For master's, PRAXIS I (for initial teaching licensure programs); GRE (for some programs), bachelor's degree from regionally-accredited institution, 2 recommendations (3 for some programs), minimum 500-word personal essay, official transcripts, minimum GPA of 2.75, valid teaching license (for some programs). Additional exam requirements/recommendations for international students: Required—TOEFL (minimum score 570 paper-based), IELTS (minimum score 6.5). Electronic applications accepted. *Expenses:* Contact institution.

Louisiana State University and Agricultural & Mechanical College, Graduate School, College of Human Sciences and Education, Department of Educational Theory, Policy and Practice, Baton Rouge, LA 70803. Offers counseling (M Ed, MA, Ed S); educational administration (M Ed, MA, PhD, Ed S); educational technology (MA); elementary education (M Ed, MAT); higher education (PhD); research methodology (PhD); secondary education (M Ed, MAT). *Accreditation:* ACA (one or more programs are accredited); NCATE.

Louisiana State University in Shreveport, College of Business, Education, and Human Development, Program in Counseling, Shreveport, LA 71115-2399. Offers MS. *Students:* 21 full-time (18 women), 11 part-time (9 women); includes 11 minority (9 Black or African American, non-Hispanic/Latino; 2 Hispanic/Latino). Average age 30. 27 applicants, 96% accepted, 7 enrolled. In 2016, 9 master's awarded. *Degree requirements:* For master's, comprehensive exam, internship (600 clock hours). *Entrance requirements:* For master's, GRE, references, interview. Additional exam requirements/recommendations for international students: Required—TOEFL (minimum score 550 paper-based; 61 iBT). *Application deadline:* For fall admission, 6/30 for domestic and international students; for spring admission, 11/30 for domestic and international students; for summer admission, 4/30 for domestic and international students. Applications are processed on a rolling basis. Application fee: $20 ($30 for international students). Electronic applications accepted. *Expenses:* Tuition, state resident: full-time $5163; part-time $350 per credit hour. Tuition, nonresident: full-time $15,578; part-time $1038 per credit hour. *Required fees:* $63 per credit hour. Tuition and fees vary according to course load and program. *Financial support:* In 2016–17, 8 research assistantships (averaging $3,500 per year) were awarded. Financial award applicants required to submit FAFSA. *Unit head:* Dr. Meredith G. Nelson, Program

Counselor Education

Director, 318-797-5199, Fax: 318-798-4171, E-mail: mnelson@pilot.lsus.edu. *Application contact:* Mary Catherine Harvison, Director of Admissions, 318-797-2400, Fax: 318-797-5286, E-mail: mary.harvison@lsus.edu.

Louisiana Tech University, Graduate School, College of Education, Department of Psychology and Behavioral Sciences, Ruston, LA 71272. Offers counseling and guidance (MA); counseling psychology (PhD); industrial and organizational psychology (MA, PhD). *Accreditation:* APA (one or more programs are accredited). *Program availability:* Part-time. *Degree requirements:* For master's, thesis or alternative; for doctorate, thesis/dissertation. *Entrance requirements:* For master's and doctorate, GRE General Test. *Application deadline:* For fall admission, 7/29 for domestic students; for spring admission, 2/3 for domestic students. Application fee: $20 ($30 for international students). *Financial support:* Fellowships, research assistantships, teaching assistantships, and career-related internships or fieldwork available. Financial award application deadline: 2/1. *Unit head:* Dr. Donna Thomas, Chair, 318-257-5066, Fax: 318-257-2379, E-mail: dthomas@latech.edu. *Application contact:* Dr. Cathy Stockton, Associate Dean of Graduate Studies, 318-257-3229, Fax: 318-257-2379, E-mail: cstock@latech.edu.
Website: http://education.latech.edu/departments/psychology/

Loyola Marymount University, School of Education, Department of Educational Support Services, Program in Guidance and Counseling, Los Angeles, CA 90045-2659. Offers MA. *Program availability:* Part-time. *Students:* 37 full-time (27 women), 7 part-time (6 women); includes 32 minority (8 Black or African American, non-Hispanic/Latino; 4 Asian, non-Hispanic/Latino; 18 Hispanic/Latino; 2 Two or more races, non-Hispanic/Latino), 4 international. Average age 30. 18 applicants, 78% accepted, 12 enrolled. In 2016, 33 master's awarded. *Entrance requirements:* For master's, CBEST, 2 letters of recommendation, letter of intent. Additional exam requirements/recommendations for international students: Required—TOEFL (minimum score 600 paper-based; 100 iBT). *Application deadline:* For fall admission, 6/15 for domestic students; for spring admission, 11/15 for domestic students. Application fee: $50. Electronic applications accepted. *Financial support:* In 2016–17, 23 students received support, including 2 research assistantships, 1 teaching assistantship; scholarships/grants and unspecified assistantships also available. Support available to part-time students. Financial award application deadline: 6/30; financial award applicants required to submit FAFSA. *Unit head:* Dr. Sheri Atwater, Program Director, 310-568-6854, E-mail: satwater@lmu.edu. *Application contact:* Chake H. Kouyoumjian, Associate Dean of Graduate Studies, 310-338-2721, E-mail: ckouyoum@lmu.edu.
Website: http://soe.lmu.edu/academics/counseling/

Loyola Marymount University, School of Education, Department of Educational Support Services, Program in School Counseling, Los Angeles, CA 90045-2659. Offers MA. *Program availability:* Part-time. *Students:* 48 full-time (35 women), 6 part-time (4 women); includes 47 minority (5 Black or African American, non-Hispanic/Latino; 3 Asian, non-Hispanic/Latino; 38 Hispanic/Latino; 1 Two or more races, non-Hispanic/Latino). Average age 27. 37 applicants, 65% accepted, 18 enrolled. In 2016, 18 master's awarded. *Entrance requirements:* For master's, CBEST, 2 letters of recommendation, letter of intent. Additional exam requirements/recommendations for international students: Required—TOEFL (minimum score 600 paper-based; 100 iBT). *Application deadline:* For fall admission, 6/15 for domestic students; for spring admission, 11/15 for domestic students. Application fee: $50. Electronic applications accepted. *Financial support:* In 2016–17, 25 students received support, including 2 teaching assistantships; scholarships/grants and unspecified assistantships also available. Support available to part-time students. Financial award application deadline: 6/30; financial award applicants required to submit FAFSA. *Unit head:* Dr. Sheri Atwater, Director, 310-568-6854, E-mail: satwater@lmu.edu. *Application contact:* Chake H. Kouyoumjian, Associate Dean of Graduate Studies, 310-338-2721, E-mail: ckouyoum@lmu.edu.
Website: http://soe.lmu.edu/academics/counseling/

Loyola University Chicago, School of Education, Program in School Counseling, Chicago, IL 60660. Offers M Ed, Certificate. *Accreditation:* NCATE. *Faculty:* 6 full-time (2 women), 6 part-time/adjunct (4 women). *Students:* 22 full-time (21 women), 2 part-time (1 woman); includes 6 minority (2 Black or African American, non-Hispanic/Latino; 1 Asian, non-Hispanic/Latino; 2 Hispanic/Latino; 1 Two or more races, non-Hispanic/Latino). Average age 25. 31 applicants, 71% accepted, 8 enrolled. In 2016, 3 master's awarded. *Degree requirements:* For master's, comprehensive exam. *Entrance requirements:* For master's, GRE General Test, minimum GPA of 3.0, letters of recommendation, resume. Additional exam requirements/recommendations for international students: Required—TOEFL (minimum score 550 paper-based; 79 iBT). *Application deadline:* For fall admission, 1/1 for domestic and international students. Application fee: $50. Electronic applications accepted. Application fee is waived when completed online. *Expenses:* $949 per hour; $2,847 per course; $8,541-$11,388 per semester plus fees $432 per semester and $225 the first semester. *Financial support:* Career-related internships or fieldwork, institutionally sponsored loans, and scholarships/grants available. Support available to part-time students. Financial award application deadline: 2/1; financial award applicants required to submit FAFSA. *Faculty research:* Career development, group counseling, family therapy, child and adolescent development, multicultural counseling. *Unit head:* Dr. Steven Brown, Program Chair, 312-915-6311, E-mail: sbrown@luc.edu. *Application contact:* Thomas Ott, Information Contact, 312-915-8907, E-mail: tott@luc.edu.

Loyola University Maryland, Graduate Programs, School of Education, Program in School Counseling, Baltimore, MD 21210-2699. Offers M Ed, MA, CAS. *Accreditation:* ACA; NCATE. *Program availability:* Part-time. *Faculty:* 34 full-time (22 women), 30 part-time/adjunct (24 women). *Students:* 53 full-time (46 women), 121 part-time (107 women); includes 49 minority (37 Black or African American, non-Hispanic/Latino; 9 Hispanic/Latino; 3 Two or more races, non-Hispanic/Latino). Average age 30. 70 applicants, 66% accepted, 33 enrolled. In 2016, 58 master's awarded. *Degree requirements:* For master's, thesis. *Entrance requirements:* For master's, essay, transcript, 2 letters of recommendation. Additional exam requirements/recommendations for international students: Required—TOEFL (minimum score 550 paper-based), IELTS (minimum score 7). *Application deadline:* For fall admission, 6/15 priority date for domestic students, 3/1 for international students. Applications are processed on a rolling basis. Application fee: $60. Electronic applications accepted. *Expenses:* Contact institution. *Financial support:* In 2016–17, 6 students received support. Scholarships/grants and unspecified assistantships available. Financial award application deadline: 4/15; financial award applicants required to submit FAFSA. *Application contact:* Maureen Faux, Executive Director of Graduate Admission, 410-617-5817, E-mail: mwfaux@loyola.edu.

Lynchburg College, Graduate Studies, M Ed Program in School Counseling, Lynchburg, VA 24501-3199. Offers M Ed. *Accreditation:* ACA. *Program availability:* Part-time, evening/weekend. *Students:* 9 full-time (8 women), 15 part-time (13 women); includes 6 minority (5 Black or African American, non-Hispanic/Latino; 1 Hispanic/Latino). In 2016, 10 master's awarded. *Degree requirements:* For master's, counseling internship. *Entrance requirements:* For master's, GRE, minimum GPA of 3.0 (preferred), official transcripts (bachelor's, others as relevant), three letters of recommendation, career goals statement. Additional exam requirements/recommendations for international students: Required—TOEFL (minimum score 550 paper-based; 79 iBT), IELTS (minimum score 6.5). *Application deadline:* For fall admission, 7/31 for domestic students, 6/1 for international students; for spring admission, 11/30 for domestic students, 10/15 for international students. Applications are processed on a rolling basis. Application fee: $30. Electronic applications accepted. Application fee is waived when completed online. *Expenses:* Contact institution. *Financial support:* Federal Work-Study, scholarships/grants, health care benefits, and unspecified assistantships available. Support available to part-time students. Financial award application deadline: 7/31; financial award applicants required to submit FAFSA. *Unit head:* Dr. Jeanne Booth, Associate Professor/Coordinator of M Ed in School Counseling, 434-544-8551, E-mail: booth@lynchburg.edu.
Website: http://www.lynchburg.edu/graduate/master-of-education-in-counselor-education/school-counseling/

Lyndon State College, Graduate Programs in Education, Department of Education, Lyndonville, VT 05851-0919. Offers curriculum and instruction (M Ed); reading specialist (M Ed); special education (M Ed); teaching and counseling (M Ed). *Program availability:* Part-time, evening/weekend. *Degree requirements:* For master's, exam or major field project. *Entrance requirements:* Additional exam requirements/recommendations for international students: Recommended—TOEFL (minimum score 500 paper-based).

Malone University, Graduate Program in Counseling and Human Development, Canton, OH 44709. Offers clinical counseling (MA); school counseling (MA). *Accreditation:* ACA; NCATE. *Program availability:* Part-time, evening/weekend. *Entrance requirements:* For master's, minimum undergraduate GPA of 3.0. Additional exam requirements/recommendations for international students: Required—TOEFL (minimum score 550 paper-based; 79 iBT). *Faculty research:* Spirituality and clinical counseling supervision, ethical and legal issues in counseling regarding supervision, resilience in adolescent offenders, protective factors for suicidal clients.

Manhattan College, Graduate Programs, School of Education and Health, Program in Counseling, Riverdale, NY 10471. Offers bilingual pupil personnel services (Professional Diploma); mental health counseling (MS, Professional Diploma); school counseling (MA, Professional Diploma). *Program availability:* Part-time, evening/weekend. *Faculty:* 2 full-time (both women), 17 part-time/adjunct (8 women). *Students:* 70 full-time (55 women), 33 part-time (24 women); includes 56 minority (22 Black or African American, non-Hispanic/Latino; 2 Asian, non-Hispanic/Latino; 32 Hispanic/Latino). Average age 32. 51 applicants, 88% accepted, 38 enrolled. In 2016, 38 master's, 10 other advanced degrees awarded. *Degree requirements:* For master's, thesis, internship. *Entrance requirements:* For master's, minimum GPA of 3.0. Additional exam requirements/recommendations for international students: Required—TOEFL. *Application deadline:* For fall admission, 7/1 priority date for domestic students; for spring admission, 12/20 priority date for domestic students. Applications are processed on a rolling basis. Application fee: $75. Electronic applications accepted. *Expenses:* $925 per credit tuition; $175 per term information fee; $375 graduation fee; $105 per term registration fee. *Financial support:* Federal Work-Study, health care benefits, and unspecified assistantships available. Financial award application deadline: 2/1; financial award applicants required to submit FAFSA. *Faculty research:* Cognitive development, college and career readiness, group counseling, cultural attitudes, bullying, family social environments. *Unit head:* Dr. Corine Fitzpatrick, Director, 718-862-7497, Fax: 718-862-7472, E-mail: corine.fitzpatrick@manhattan.edu. *Application contact:* William Bisset, Vice President for Enrollment, 718-862-7199, Fax: 718-862-8019, E-mail: william.bisset@manhattan.edu.

Marquette University, Graduate School, College of Education, Department of Counselor Education and Counseling Psychology, Milwaukee, WI 53201-1881. Offers clinical mental health counseling (MS); community counseling (MA); counseling psychology (PhD); school counseling (MA). *Accreditation:* ACA. *Program availability:* Part-time. *Faculty:* 6 full-time (3 women), 5 part-time/adjunct (3 women). *Students:* 69 full-time (53 women), 13 part-time (10 women); includes 18 minority (6 Black or African American, non-Hispanic/Latino; 3 Asian, non-Hispanic/Latino; 7 Hispanic/Latino; 2 Two or more races, non-Hispanic/Latino), 3 international. Average age 26. 122 applicants, 47% accepted, 32 enrolled. In 2016, 24 master's, 2 doctorates awarded. Terminal master's awarded for partial completion of doctoral program. *Degree requirements:* For master's, comprehensive exam, thesis (for some programs); for doctorate, thesis/dissertation, qualifying exam. *Entrance requirements:* For master's, GRE General Test or MAT, official transcripts from all current and previous colleges/universities except Marquette, three letters of recommendation, statement of purpose; for doctorate, GRE General Test, MAT, sample of written work, official transcripts from all current and previous colleges/universities except Marquette, three letters of recommendation, statement of purpose, resume/curriculum vitae. Additional exam requirements/recommendations for international students: Required—TOEFL (minimum score 530 paper-based). *Application deadline:* For fall admission, 1/15 for domestic and international students. Application fee: $50. *Financial support:* Fellowships, research assistantships, scholarships/grants, health care benefits, tuition waivers (partial), and unspecified assistantships available. Support available to part-time students. Financial award application deadline: 2/15. *Faculty research:* Ethical and legal issues in education, anxiety disorders, multicultural counseling, child psychopathology, group counseling and dynamics. *Unit head:* Dr. Alan Burkard, Chair, 414-288-3434, E-mail: alan.burkard@marquette.edu. *Application contact:* Dr. Alan Burkard.

Marshall University, Academic Affairs Division, College of Education and Professional Development, Program in Counseling, Huntington, WV 25755. Offers MA, Ed S, Graduate Certificate. *Accreditation:* NCATE. *Program availability:* Part-time, evening/weekend. *Degree requirements:* For master's, thesis optional, comprehensive or oral assessment. *Entrance requirements:* For master's, GRE General Test, MAT.

Marymount University, School of Education and Human Services, Program in Counseling, Arlington, VA 22207-4299. Offers clinical mental health counseling (MA); pastoral counseling (MA); school counseling (MA). *Accreditation:* ACA. *Program availability:* Part-time, evening/weekend. *Faculty:* 29 full-time (21 women), 7 part-time/adjunct (all women). *Students:* 84 full-time (74 women), 57 part-time (51 women); includes 55 minority (28 Black or African American, non-Hispanic/Latino; 2 American Indian or Alaska Native, non-Hispanic/Latino; 3 Asian, non-Hispanic/Latino; 17 Hispanic/Latino; 5 Two or more races, non-Hispanic/Latino), 2 international. Average age 30. 83 applicants, 77% accepted, 45 enrolled. In 2016, 39 master's awarded. *Degree requirements:* For master's, thesis or alternative, capstone/internship. *Entrance requirements:* For master's, GRE, 2 letters of recommendation, interview, resume, personal statement. Additional exam requirements/recommendations for international students: Required—TOEFL (minimum score 600 paper-based; 96 iBT), IELTS (minimum score 6.5). *Application deadline:* For fall admission, 1/15 priority date for domestic and international students; for spring admission, 10/5 for domestic and international students. Applications are processed on a rolling basis. Application fee: $40. Electronic applications accepted. *Expenses: Tuition:* Full-time $8460; part-time $940 per credit hour. *Required fees:* $10 per credit hour. One-time fee: $240 part-time. Tuition and fees vary according to program. *Financial support:* In 2016–17, 15 students received support, including 8 research assistantships with tuition reimbursements available, 4 teaching assistantships with tuition reimbursements available; career-related internships or fieldwork, Federal Work-Study, scholarships/grants, and unspecified assistantships also available. Support available to part-time students.

Financial award applicants required to submit FAFSA. *Unit head:* Dr. Lisa Jackson-Cherry, Chair, Counseling, 703-284-1633, Fax: 703-284-5708, E-mail: lisa.jackson cherry@marymount.edu. *Application contact:* Francesca Reed, Director, Graduate Admissions, 703-284-5901, Fax: 703-527-3815, E-mail: grad.admissions@marymount.edu.
Website: http://www.marymount.edu/Academics/School-of-Education-Human-Services/Graduate-Programs/Counseling-(M-A-)

Marywood University, Academic Affairs, Reap College of Education and Human Development, Department of Psychology and Counseling, Program in Counselor Education, Scranton, PA 18509-1598. Offers MS. *Program availability:* Part-time. Electronic applications accepted.

McDaniel College, Graduate and Professional Studies, Program in Counseling, Westminster, MD 21157-4390. Offers MS. *Program availability:* Part-time, evening/weekend. *Faculty:* 5 full-time (3 women), 13 part-time/adjunct (6 women). *Students:* 39 full-time (31 women), 128 part-time (108 women); includes 34 minority (26 Black or African American, non-Hispanic/Latino; 3 Asian, non-Hispanic/Latino; 4 Hispanic/Latino; 1 Two or more races, non-Hispanic/Latino). Average age 30. 58 applicants, 95% accepted. In 2016, 45 master's awarded. *Degree requirements:* For master's, thesis optional, internship. *Entrance requirements:* For master's, 3 letters of reference; interview with program faculty. Additional exam requirements/recommendations for international students: Required—TOEFL (minimum score 79 iBT), IELTS (minimum score 6). *Application deadline:* For fall admission, 6/1 priority date for domestic students; for spring admission, 11/1 priority date for domestic students; for summer admission, 3/1 priority date for domestic students. Applications are processed on a rolling basis. Application fee: $75. Electronic applications accepted. *Expenses:* $525 per credit tuition and $75 per semester administrative fee(s). *Financial support:* Application deadline: 3/1; applicants required to submit FAFSA. *Unit head:* Fax: 410-857-2515, E-mail: gradadms@mcdaniel.edu. *Application contact:* Penny Pfeiffer, Senior Graduate Enrollment Management Specialist, 410-857-2513, Fax: 410-857-2515, E-mail: ppfeiffer@mcdaniel.edu.

McNeese State University, Doré School of Graduate Studies, Burton College of Education, Office of Graduate Education Programs, Program in School Counseling, Lake Charles, LA 70609. Offers M Ed. *Accreditation:* NCATE. *Program availability:* Evening/weekend. *Entrance requirements:* For master's, GRE, 18 hours in professional education.

McNeese State University, Doré School of Graduate Studies, Burton College of Education, Office of Student Teaching and Professional Education Services, Program in Counseling, Grades K-12, Lake Charles, LA 70609. Offers Graduate Certificate. *Entrance requirements:* For degree, bachelor's degree, teaching certificate.

Mercer University, Graduate Studies, Cecil B. Day Campus, Penfield College, Atlanta, GA 30341. Offers certified rehabilitation counseling (MS); clinical mental health (MS); counselor education and supervision (PhD); criminal justice and public safety leadership (MS); health informatics (MS); human services (MS), including child and adolescent services, gerontology services; organizational leadership (MS); school counseling (MS). *Program availability:* Part-time, evening/weekend, 100% online, blended/hybrid learning. *Faculty:* 15 full-time (8 women), 22 part-time/adjunct (18 women). *Students:* 168 full-time (136 women), 242 part-time (201 women); includes 231 minority (192 Black or African American, non-Hispanic/Latino; 1 American Indian or Alaska Native, non-Hispanic/Latino; 15 Asian, non-Hispanic/Latino; 19 Hispanic/Latino; 1 Native Hawaiian or other Pacific Islander, non-Hispanic/Latino; 3 Two or more races, non-Hispanic/Latino), 2 international. Average age 32. 300 applicants, 45% accepted, 114 enrolled. In 2016, 92 master's, 8 doctorates awarded. *Degree requirements:* For master's, comprehensive exam (for some programs), thesis (for some programs); for doctorate, thesis/dissertation. *Entrance requirements:* For master's, GRE or MAT, Georgia Professional Standards Commission (GPSC) Certification at the SC-5 level; for doctorate, GRE or MAT. Additional exam requirements/recommendations for international students: Recommended—TOEFL (minimum score 550 paper-based; 80 iBT), IELTS (minimum score 6.5). *Application deadline:* For fall admission, 7/1 priority date for domestic and international students; for spring admission, 11/1 priority date for domestic and international students; for summer admission, 4/1 priority date for domestic and international students. Application fee: $35. Electronic applications accepted. Application fee is waived when completed online. *Expenses:* $588 per credit hour. *Financial support:* In 2016–17, 32 students received support. Federal Work-Study, scholarships/grants, and unspecified assistantships available. Financial award applicants required to submit FAFSA. *Faculty research:* Marriage and families issues, leadership and ethics, cyber-bullying, trauma, narrative counseling and theory. *Total annual research expenditures:* $85,000. *Unit head:* Dr. Priscilla R. Danheiser, Dean, 678-547-6028, Fax: 678-547-6008, E-mail: danheiser_p@mercer.edu.
Website: http://penfield.mercer.edu/programs/graduate-professional/

Mercy College, School of Social and Behavioral Sciences, Dobbs Ferry, NY 10522-1189. Offers counseling (MS, Certificate), including counseling (MS), family counseling (Certificate); health services management (MPA, MS); marriage and family therapy (MS); mental health counseling (MS); psychology (MS); school counseling (Certificate); school psychology (MS). *Program availability:* Part-time, evening/weekend, 100% online, blended/hybrid learning. *Students:* 234 full-time (200 women), 292 part-time (240 women); includes 388 minority (169 Black or African American, non-Hispanic/Latino; 1 American Indian or Alaska Native, non-Hispanic/Latino; 19 Asian, non-Hispanic/Latino; 190 Hispanic/Latino; 2 Native Hawaiian or other Pacific Islander, non-Hispanic/Latino; 7 Two or more races, non-Hispanic/Latino), 5 international. Average age 34. 448 applicants, 48% accepted, 150 enrolled. In 2016, 150 master's, 2 other advanced degrees awarded. *Degree requirements:* For master's, comprehensive exam (for some programs), thesis (for some programs). *Entrance requirements:* For master's, essay, 2 letters of recommendation, interview, resume, undergraduate transcript. Additional exam requirements/recommendations for international students: Required—TOEFL (minimum score 600 paper-based; 100 iBT), IELTS (minimum score 8). *Application deadline:* For fall admission, 8/1 for international students. Applications are processed on a rolling basis. Application fee: $40. Electronic applications accepted. *Expenses: Tuition:* Full-time $15,156; part-time $842 per credit hour. *Required fees:* $620; $155 per term. Tuition and fees vary according to course load and program. *Financial support:* Career-related internships or fieldwork, Federal Work-Study, scholarships/grants, and unspecified assistantships available. Support available to part-time students. Financial award applicants required to submit FAFSA. *Unit head:* Dr. Karol Dean, Dean, School of Social and Behavioral Sciences, 914-674-7517, E-mail: kdean@mercy.edu. *Application contact:* Allison Gurdineer, Senior Director of Admissions, 877-637-2946, Fax: 914-674-7382, E-mail: admissions@mercy.edu.
Website: https://www.mercy.edu/social-and-behavioral-sciences/

Messiah College, Program in Counseling, Mechanicsburg, PA 17055. Offers clinical mental health counseling (MAC); counseling (CAGS); marriage, couple, and family counseling (MAC); school counseling (MAC). *Accreditation:* ACA. *Program availability:* Part-time, online learning. *Entrance requirements:* For master's, minimum undergraduate cumulative GPA of 3.0, 2 recommendations, resume or curriculum vitae, interview; for CAGS, bachelor's degree, minimum undergraduate cumulative GPA of 3.0, essay, two recommendations, resume or curriculum vitae, interview. Electronic applications accepted.

Michigan State University, The Graduate School, College of Education, Department of Counseling, Educational Psychology and Special Education, East Lansing, MI 48824. Offers counseling (MA); educational psychology and educational technology (PhD); educational technology (MA); measurement and quantitative methods (PhD); rehabilitation counseling (MA); rehabilitation counselor education (PhD); school psychology (MA, PhD, Ed S); special education (MA, PhD). *Accreditation:* APA (one or more programs are accredited); CORE (one or more programs are accredited). *Program availability:* Part-time. *Entrance requirements:* Additional exam requirements/recommendations for international students: Required—TOEFL. Electronic applications accepted.

Middle Tennessee State University, College of Graduate Studies, College of Education, Department of Educational Leadership, Program in Professional Counseling, Murfreesboro, TN 37132. Offers mental health counseling (M Ed); school counseling (M Ed). *Accreditation:* ACA; NCATE. *Program availability:* Part-time, evening/weekend, online learning. *Degree requirements:* For master's, comprehensive exam, thesis. *Entrance requirements:* For master's, GRE or MAT. Additional exam requirements/recommendations for international students: Required—TOEFL (minimum score 525 paper-based; 71 iBT) or IELTS (minimum score 6). Electronic applications accepted.

Midwestern State University, Billie Doris McAda Graduate School, West College of Education, Program in Counseling, Wichita Falls, TX 76308. Offers counseling (MA); human resource development (MA); school counseling (M Ed); training and development (MA). *Program availability:* Part-time, evening/weekend. *Degree requirements:* For master's, comprehensive exam, thesis (for some programs). *Entrance requirements:* For master's, GRE General Test, MAT, or GMAT, valid teaching certificate (M Ed). Additional exam requirements/recommendations for international students: Required—TOEFL (minimum score 550 paper-based). Electronic applications accepted. *Faculty research:* Social development of students with disabilities, autism, criminal justice counseling, conflict resolution issues, leadership.

Milligan College, Area of Social Learning, Milligan College, TN 37682. Offers clinical mental health counseling (MSC); counseling ministry (Graduate Certificate); school counseling (MSC). *Program availability:* Part-time. *Faculty:* 3 full-time (all women), 2 part-time/adjunct (0 women). *Students:* 25 full-time (22 women), 3 part-time (2 women); includes 2 minority (1 Black or African American, non-Hispanic/Latino; 1 Two or more races, non-Hispanic/Latino), 1 international. Average age 31. 29 applicants, 72% accepted, 14 enrolled. In 2016, 15 master's awarded. *Degree requirements:* For master's, thesis or alternative. *Entrance requirements:* For master's, GRE General Test if undergraduate degree is less than 3.0, undergraduate degree and supporting transcripts, essay/personal statement, professional recommendations, interview. Additional exam requirements/recommendations for international students: Required—TOEFL (minimum score 550 paper-based, 79 iBT) or IELTS (6.5). *Application deadline:* For fall admission, 8/1 for domestic students, 6/1 for international students. Applications are processed on a rolling basis. Application fee: $30. Electronic applications accepted. *Expenses:* $430 per hour tuition; $325 per semester tech/activity fees. *Financial support:* Scholarships/grants available. Financial award application deadline: 12/1; financial award applicants required to submit FAFSA. *Faculty research:* Parent-child interaction therapy/autism; childhood sexual abuse/trauma; poverty and homelessness; social justice advocacy and competence; school-based mental health. *Unit head:* Dr. Christine Browning, Director of Master of Science in Counseling Program, 423-461-3513, Fax: 423-461-8777, E-mail: cmbrowning@milligan.edu. *Application contact:* Jenni Duran, Graduate Admissions Recruiter, Healthcare Programs, 423-461-8424, Fax: 423-461-8789, E-mail: jduran@milligan.edu.
Website: http://www.Milligan.edu/GPS

Minnesota State University Mankato, College of Graduate Studies and Research, College of Education, Department of Counseling and Student Personnel, Mankato, MN 56001. Offers college student affairs (MS); counselor education and supervision (Ed D); mental health counseling (MS); professional school counseling (K-12) (MS). *Accreditation:* ACA (one or more programs are accredited); NCATE. *Students:* 77 full-time (68 women), 38 part-time (26 women). *Degree requirements:* For master's, comprehensive exam, thesis or alternative. *Entrance requirements:* For master's, GRE General Test or MAT (if GPA less than 3.0 for last 2 years), minimum GPA of 3.0 during previous 2 years, 3 letters of reference. Additional exam requirements/recommendations for international students: Required—TOEFL. *Application deadline:* For fall admission, 1/15 priority date for domestic students. Applications are processed on a rolling basis. Application fee: $40. Electronic applications accepted. *Financial support:* Research assistantships with full tuition reimbursements, teaching assistantships with full tuition reimbursements, career-related internships or fieldwork, Federal Work-Study, institutionally sponsored loans, and unspecified assistantships available. Support available to part-time students. Financial award application deadline: 3/15; financial award applicants required to submit FAFSA. *Unit head:* Dr. Jackie Lewis, Chair, E-mail: jacqueline.lewis@mnsu.edu.
Website: http://ed.mnsu.edu/csp/

Minnesota State University Moorhead, Graduate Studies, College of Education and Human Services, Moorhead, MN 56563. Offers counseling and student affairs (MS); curriculum and instruction (MS); educational leadership (MS, Ed S); special education (MS); speech-language pathology (MS). *Accreditation:* NCATE. *Program availability:* Part-time, 100% online, blended/hybrid learning. *Students:* 133 full-time (116 women), 363 part-time (274 women). Average age 32. 273 applicants, 49% accepted. In 2016, 114 master's awarded. *Degree requirements:* For master's, comprehensive exam (for some programs), thesis. *Entrance requirements:* For master's, GRE, essay, letter of intent, letters of reference, teaching license, teaching verification. Additional exam requirements/recommendations for international students: Required—TOEFL (minimum score 550 paper-based). *Application deadline:* For fall admission, 4/15 priority date for domestic students; for spring admission, 11/1 priority date for domestic students. Applications are processed on a rolling basis. Application fee: $20. Electronic applications accepted. *Expenses:* Tuition, state resident: full-time $9000; part-time $4500 per credit. Tuition, nonresident: full-time $18,000; part-time $9000 per credit. *Required fees:* $942; $39.25 per credit. One-time fee: $90 full-time. Full-time tuition and fees vary according to course load, degree level, program and reciprocity agreements. *Financial support:* Federal Work-Study and unspecified assistantships available. Financial award application deadline: 10/1; financial award applicants required to submit FAFSA. *Unit head:* Dr. Ok-Hee Lee, Dean, 218-477-2095, E-mail: okheelee@mnstate.edu. *Application contact:* Karla Wenger, Office Manager, 218-477-2344, Fax: 218-477-2482, E-mail: wengerk@mnstate.edu.
Website: http://www.mnstate.edu/cehs/

Mississippi College, Graduate School, School of Education, Department of Psychology and Counseling, Clinton, MS 39058. Offers counseling (Ed S); marriage and family counseling (MS); mental health counseling (MS); school counseling (M Ed). *Program availability:* Part-time. *Degree requirements:* For master's and Ed S, comprehensive exam, thesis optional. *Entrance requirements:* For master's, GRE or NTE. Additional exam requirements/recommendations for international students: Recommended—TOEFL, IELTS. Electronic applications accepted.

Counselor Education

Mississippi State University, College of Education, Department of Counseling, Educational Psychology, and Foundations, Mississippi State, MS 39762. Offers clinical mental health (MS); college counseling (MS); college/post secondary student counseling and personnel services (PhD); counselor education (Ed S); counselor education/student counseling and guidance services (PhD); general educational psychology (MS); psychometry (MS); rehabilitation (MS); school counseling (MS); school psychology (PhD, Ed S); student affairs (MS). *Accreditation:* ACA (one or more programs are accredited); APA; CORE (one or more programs are accredited); NCATE. *Program availability:* Part-time, blended/hybrid learning. *Faculty:* 21 full-time (14 women), 2 part-time/adjunct (both women). *Students:* 125 full-time (94 women), 70 part-time (60 women); includes 63 minority (48 Black or African American, non-Hispanic/Latino; 1 American Indian or Alaska Native, non-Hispanic/Latino; 4 Asian, non-Hispanic/Latino; 5 Hispanic/Latino; 5 Two or more races, non-Hispanic/Latino), 6 international. Average age 30. 151 applicants, 64% accepted, 70 enrolled. In 2016, 49 master's, 3 doctorates, 4 other advanced degrees awarded. Terminal master's awarded for partial completion of doctoral program. *Degree requirements:* For master's, comprehensive exam, thesis optional; for doctorate, thesis/dissertation, comprehensive oral and written exam. *Entrance requirements:* For master's, GRE (taken within the last five years), BS with minimum GPA of 2.75 on last 60 hours; for doctorate, GRE, MS from CACREP- or CORE-accredited program in counseling; for Ed S, GRE, MS in counseling or related field, minimum GPA of 3.3 on all graduate work. Additional exam requirements/ recommendations for international students: Required—TOEFL (minimum score 550 paper-based; 79 iBT); Recommended—IELTS (minimum score 6.5). *Application deadline:* For fall admission, 2/1 priority date for domestic and international students. Applications are processed on a rolling basis. Application fee: $60. Electronic applications accepted. *Expenses:* Tuition, state resident: full-time $7670; part-time $852.50 per credit hour. Tuition, nonresident: full-time $20,790; part-time $2310.50 per credit hour. Part-time tuition and fees vary according to course load. *Financial support:* In 2016–17, 9 teaching assistantships with full tuition reimbursements (averaging $8,401 per year) were awarded; career-related internships or fieldwork, Federal Work-Study, institutionally sponsored loans, and unspecified assistantships also available. Financial award application deadline: 2/1; financial award applicants required to submit FAFSA. *Faculty research:* HIV/AIDS in college population, substance abuse in youth and college students, ADHD and conduct disorders in youth, assessment and identification of early childhood disabilities, assessment and vocational transition of the disabled. *Unit head:* Dr. David Morse, Professor and Head, 662-325-3426, Fax: 662-325-3263, E-mail: dmorse@colled.msstate.edu. *Application contact:* Linda Bonner, Senior Admissions Assistant, 662-325-3363, E-mail: lbonner@grad.msstate.edu.
Website: http://www.cep.msstate.edu/

Missouri Baptist University, Graduate Programs, St. Louis, MO 63141-8660. Offers business administration (MBA); Christian ministries (MACM); counseling (MAC); education (MSE); education administration (MEA); educational leadership (MSE, Ed S); teaching (MAT).

Missouri State University, Graduate College, College of Education, Department of Counseling, Leadership, and Special Education, Program in Counseling, Springfield, MO 65897. Offers elementary school counseling (MS); mental health counseling (MS); secondary school counseling (MS). *Accreditation:* ACA. *Program availability:* Part-time, evening/weekend. *Students:* 67 full-time (51 women), 43 part-time (39 women); includes 16 minority (4 Black or African American, non-Hispanic/Latino; 7 Hispanic/Latino; 5 Two or more races, non-Hispanic/Latino), 3 international. Average age 30. 46 applicants, 50% accepted, 18 enrolled. In 2016, 35 master's awarded. *Degree requirements:* For master's, comprehensive exam, thesis or alternative. *Entrance requirements:* For master's, GRE or MAT, minimum GPA of 2.75. Additional exam requirements/ recommendations for international students: Required—TOEFL (minimum score 550 paper-based; 79 iBT), IELTS (minimum score 6). *Application deadline:* For fall admission, 2/1 priority date for domestic students, 1/1 priority date for international students; for spring admission, 10/1 priority date for domestic students, 9/1 priority date for international students. Application fee: $35 ($50 for international students). Electronic applications accepted. *Expenses:* Tuition, state resident: full-time $5830. Tuition, nonresident: full-time $10,708. *Required fees:* $1130. Tuition and fees vary according to class time, course level, course load and program. *Financial support:* Federal Work-Study, institutionally sponsored loans, scholarships/grants, and unspecified assistantships available. Financial award application deadline: 3/31; financial award applicants required to submit FAFSA. *Unit head:* Dr. James Satterfield, Department Head, 417-836-5392, Fax: 417-836-4918, E-mail: clse@missouristate.edu. *Application contact:* Michael Edwards, Coordinator of Graduate Admissions, 417-836-5300, Fax: 417-836-6200, E-mail: michaeledwards@missouristate.edu.
Website: http://education.missouristate.edu/clse/

Montana State University Billings, College of Education, Department of Educational Theory and Practice, Option in School Counseling, Billings, MT 59101. Offers M Ed. *Accreditation:* NCATE. *Program availability:* Part-time. *Faculty:* 2 full-time (1 woman). *Students:* 35. *Degree requirements:* For master's, thesis or professional paper and/or field experience. *Entrance requirements:* For master's, GRE General Test or MAT, minimum GPA of 3.0, letters of recommendation, resume, letter of intent. Additional exam requirements/recommendations for international students: Required—TOEFL (minimum score 79 iBT), IELTS (minimum score 6.5). *Application deadline:* Applications are processed on a rolling basis. Application fee: $40. Electronic applications accepted. *Expenses:* Tuition, state resident: full-time $5265; part-time $3436 per year. Tuition, nonresident: full-time $14,030; part-time $9280 per year. *International tuition:* $19,295 full-time. Tuition and fees vary according to degree level, campus/location and program. *Financial support:* Teaching assistantships with partial tuition reimbursements, career-related internships or fieldwork, Federal Work-Study, institutionally sponsored loans, scholarships/grants, tuition waivers (partial), and unspecified assistantships available. Support available to part-time students. Financial award application deadline: 5/1; financial award applicants required to submit FAFSA. *Unit head:* Dr. Ken Miller, Chair, 406-657-2034, E-mail: kmiller@msubillings.edu. *Application contact:* David M. Sullivan, Graduate Studies Counselor, 406-657-2053, Fax: 406-657-2299, E-mail: dsullivan@msubillings.edu.

Montana State University–Northern, Graduate Programs, Option in Counselor Education, Havre, MT 59501-7751. Offers M Ed. *Program availability:* Part-time, evening/weekend. *Degree requirements:* For master's, comprehensive exam, thesis optional, oral exams, internship. *Entrance requirements:* For master's, GRE General Test or MAT, minimum major and overall GPA of 3.0. *Application deadline:* For fall admission, 9/20 priority date for domestic students. Applications are processed on a rolling basis. Application fee: $30. Electronic applications accepted. *Financial support:* Research assistantships with partial tuition reimbursements, teaching assistantships with partial tuition reimbursements, Federal Work-Study, institutionally sponsored loans, and unspecified assistantships available. Support available to part-time students. Financial award application deadline: 4/1; financial award applicants required to submit FAFSA. *Unit head:* Dr. Darlene Sellers, Head, 406-265-3527. *Application contact:* Robert Kurtz, Program Advisor, 406-265-3700.

Montclair State University, The Graduate School, College of Education and Human Services, Doctoral Program in Counselor Education, Montclair, NJ 07043-1624. Offers PhD. *Accreditation:* ACA. *Program availability:* Part-time, evening/weekend. *Degree requirements:* For doctorate, comprehensive exam, thesis/dissertation. *Entrance requirements:* For doctorate, GRE General Test, interview, 3 letters of recommendation. Additional exam requirements/recommendations for international students: Required—TOEFL (minimum score 83 iBT), IELTS (minimum score 6.5). Electronic applications accepted. *Expenses:* Tuition, state resident: part-time $553 per credit. Tuition, nonresident: part-time $854 per credit. *Required fees:* $91 per credit. Tuition and fees vary according to program.

Montclair State University, The Graduate School, College of Education and Human Services, Program in Counseling, Montclair, NJ 07043-1624. Offers MA. *Accreditation:* ACA. *Program availability:* Part-time, evening/weekend. *Degree requirements:* For master's, comprehensive exam, thesis or alternative. *Entrance requirements:* For master's, GRE General Test, interview, 2 letters of recommendation. Additional exam requirements/recommendations for international students: Required—TOEFL (minimum score 83 iBT), IELTS (minimum score 6.5). Electronic applications accepted. *Expenses:* Tuition, state resident: part-time $553 per credit. Tuition, nonresident: part-time $854 per credit. *Required fees:* $91 per credit. Tuition and fees vary according to program.

Morehead State University, Graduate Programs, College of Education, Department of Foundational and Graduate Studies in Education, Morehead, KY 40351. Offers adult and higher education (MA, Ed S); certified professional counselor (Ed S); counseling P-12 (MA); curriculum and instruction (Ed S); educational technology (MA Ed); instructional leadership (Ed S); school administration (MA); school counseling (Ed S); teacher leader business and marketing content (MA Ed); teacher leader business and marketing technology (MA Ed); teacher leader educational technology (MA Ed); teacher leader English (MA Ed); teacher leader gifted education (MA Ed); teacher leader IECE certification (MA Ed); teacher leader interdisciplinary education P-5 (MA Ed); teacher leader middle grades (MA Ed); teacher leader non IECE certification (MA Ed); teacher leader reading/writing - non-certification (MA Ed); teacher leader reading/writing certification (MA Ed); teacher leader school communication - certification (MA Ed); teacher leader school communication - non-certification (MA Ed); teacher leader social studies (MA Ed); teacher leader special education (MA Ed). *Accreditation:* NCATE. *Program availability:* Part-time, evening/weekend. *Degree requirements:* For master's, thesis optional, oral and/or written comprehensive exams; for Ed S, thesis, oral exam. *Entrance requirements:* For master's, GRE General Test, minimum overall undergraduate GPA of 2.5; for Ed S, GRE General Test, interview, master's degree, minimum GPA of 3.5, work experience. Additional exam requirements/ recommendations for international students: Required—TOEFL (minimum score 500 paper-based). Electronic applications accepted. *Faculty research:* Character education, school accountability, computer applications for school administrators.

Mount Mary University, Graduate Programs, Program in Counseling, Milwaukee, WI 53222-4597. Offers clinical mental health counseling (MS, Certificate); clinical rehabilitation counseling (MS, Certificate); school counseling (MS, Certificate); vocational rehabilitation counseling (MS, Certificate). *Accreditation:* ACA. *Program availability:* Part-time, evening/weekend. *Faculty:* 6 full-time (all women), 12 part-time/ adjunct (10 women). *Students:* 91 full-time (84 women), 17 part-time (14 women); includes 25 minority (12 Black or African American, non-Hispanic/Latino; 1 Asian, non-Hispanic/Latino; 8 Hispanic/Latino; 1 Native Hawaiian or other Pacific Islander, non-Hispanic/Latino; 3 Two or more races, non-Hispanic/Latino). Average age 31. 68 applicants, 59% accepted, 29 enrolled. In 2016, 42 master's, 1 other advanced degree awarded. *Degree requirements:* For master's, comprehensive exam, thesis or alternative. *Entrance requirements:* For master's, minimum GPA of 3.0. Additional exam requirements/recommendations for international students: Required—TOEFL (minimum score 550 paper-based; 80 iBT); Recommended—IELTS (minimum score 6.5). *Application deadline:* For fall admission, 5/1 for domestic and international students; for spring admission, 10/1 for domestic and international students; for summer admission, 4/15 for domestic and international students. Applications are processed on a rolling basis. Application fee: $45. Electronic applications accepted. *Expenses:* Contact institution. *Financial support:* Career-related internships or fieldwork, Federal Work-Study, and unspecified assistantships available. Support available to part-time students. Financial award application deadline: 5/1; financial award applicants required to submit FAFSA. *Faculty research:* Cognitive behavioral interventions for depression, eating disorders and compliance, trauma-informed care. *Unit head:* Dr. Carrie King, Graduate Program Director, 414-258-4810 Ext. 318, E-mail: kingc@mtmary.edu. *Application contact:* Kirk Heller de Messer, Director, Graduate Admissions, 414-930-3221, E-mail: hellerk@mtmary.edu.
Website: http://www.mtmary.edu/majors-programs/graduate/counseling/index.html

Murray State University, College of Education, Department of Educational Studies, Leadership and Counseling, Program in Community and Agency Counseling, Murray, KY 42071. Offers Ed S. *Accreditation:* ACA; NCATE. *Program availability:* Part-time. *Degree requirements:* For Ed S, comprehensive exam, thesis. *Entrance requirements:* For degree, GRE General Test. Additional exam requirements/recommendations for international students: Required—TOEFL.

Murray State University, College of Education, Department of Educational Studies, Leadership and Counseling, Programs in School Guidance and Counseling, Murray, KY 42071. Offers MA Ed, Ed S. *Accreditation:* NCATE. *Program availability:* Part-time. *Degree requirements:* For master's, comprehensive exam, thesis (for some programs), portfolio; for Ed S, comprehensive exam, portfolio. *Entrance requirements:* For master's, GRE General Test or MAT. Additional exam requirements/recommendations for international students: Required—TOEFL.

Naropa University, Graduate Programs, Program in Clinical Mental Health Counseling, Concentration in Mindfulness-based Transpersonal Counseling, Boulder, CO 80302-6697. Offers MA. *Faculty:* 10 full-time (7 women), 23 part-time/adjunct (17 women). *Students:* 109 full-time (81 women), 35 part-time (21 women); includes 23 minority (2 Black or African American, non-Hispanic/Latino; 1 American Indian or Alaska Native, non-Hispanic/Latino; 2 Asian, non-Hispanic/Latino; 11 Hispanic/Latino; 7 Two or more races, non-Hispanic/Latino), 2 international. Average age 32. 94 applicants, 96% accepted, 63 enrolled. In 2016, 54 master's awarded. *Degree requirements:* For master's, internship, counseling practicum. *Entrance requirements:* For master's, interview, statement of interest, essay, professional experience, resume, 2 letters of recommendation, transcripts. Additional exam requirements/recommendations for international students: Required—TOEFL (minimum score 550 paper-based; 80 iBT). *Application deadline:* For fall admission, 1/15 priority date for domestic and international students. Applications are processed on a rolling basis. Application fee: $60. Electronic applications accepted. *Expenses:* $22,560 for first year in program. *Financial support:* In 2016–17, 73 students received support, including 1 research assistantship with partial tuition reimbursement available (averaging $3,000 per year), 2 teaching assistantships with partial tuition reimbursements available (averaging $3,000 per year); career-related internships or fieldwork, scholarships/grants, health care benefits, tuition waivers (partial), and unspecified assistantships also available. Support available to part-time students. Financial award application deadline: 3/1; financial award applicants required to submit FAFSA. *Unit head:* Dr. Deborah Bowman, Dean, Graduate School of Counseling and Psychology, 303-546-3559, E-mail: mjack@naropa.edu. *Application contact:* Office of Admissions, 303-546-3572, Fax: 303-546-3583, E-mail: admissions@

naropa.edu.
Website: http://www.naropa.edu/academics/masters/clinical-mental-health-counseling/mindfulness-based-counseling-psychology/index.php

National Louis University, College of Arts and Sciences, Chicago, IL 60603. Offers adult education (Ed D); counseling and human services (MS); language and academic development (M Ed, Certificate); psychology (MA, PhD, Certificate); public policy (MA); written communication (MS, Certificate). *Program availability:* Part-time, evening/weekend, online learning. *Degree requirements:* For master's and Certificate, comprehensive exam (for some programs), thesis (for some programs); for doctorate, thesis/dissertation. *Entrance requirements:* For master's, MAT or GRE, 3 professional or academic references, interview, minimum GPA of 3.0; for doctorate, GRE General Test, MAT, or Watson-Glaser Critical Thinking Appraisal, three professional or academic references, statement of academic and professional goals, 3 years of experience in field, interview, master's degree, resume, writing sample; for Certificate, GRE, MAT, or Watson-Glaser Critical Thinking Appraisal, three professional or academic references, statement of academic and professional goals, interview, minimum GPA of 3.0. Additional exam requirements/recommendations for international students: Required—Department of Language Studies Assessment or TOEFL (minimum score 550 paper-based; 79 iBT). Electronic applications accepted.

New Jersey City University, Debra Cannon Partridge Wolfe College of Education, Department of Educational Leadership and Counseling, Counselor Education Program, Jersey City, NJ 07305-1597. Offers MA. *Accreditation:* ACA. *Program availability:* Part-time, evening/weekend. *Entrance requirements:* Additional exam requirements/recommendations for international students: Required—TOEFL (minimum score 79 iBT).

New Mexico Highlands University, Graduate Studies, School of Education, Las Vegas, NM 87701. Offers curriculum and instruction (MA); educational leadership (MA); professional counseling (MA); special education (MA). *Accreditation:* NCATE. *Program availability:* Part time. *Degree requirements:* For master's, comprehensive exam, thesis or alternative. *Entrance requirements:* For master's, minimum undergraduate GPA of 3.0. Additional exam requirements/recommendations for international students: Required—TOEFL (minimum score 540 paper-based). *Faculty research:* Middle school curriculum, integrated computer applications for pre-service classroom teachers, adolescent literacy, narrative cognitive modes in New Mexico multicultural setting, math and math education.

New Mexico State University, College of Education, Department of Counseling and Educational Psychology, Las Cruces, NM 88003. Offers counseling psychology (PhD); educational diagnostics (MA), including counseling and guidance, educational diagnostics; school psychology (Ed S). *Accreditation:* ACA; APA (one or more programs are accredited); NCATE. *Program availability:* Part-time. *Faculty:* 11 full-time (9 women), 4 part-time/adjunct (2 women). *Students:* 74 full-time (56 women), 12 part-time (9 women); includes 58 minority (2 Black or African American, non-Hispanic/Latino; 1 American Indian or Alaska Native, non-Hispanic/Latino; 6 Asian, non-Hispanic/Latino; 48 Hispanic/Latino; 1 Two or more races, non-Hispanic/Latino), 1 international. Average age 29. 115 applicants, 36% accepted, 26 enrolled. In 2016, 12 master's, 6 doctorates, 9 other advanced degrees awarded. *Degree requirements:* For master's, comprehensive exam, thesis optional, internship; for doctorate, comprehensive exam, thesis/dissertation, internship; for Ed S, comprehensive exam, thesis or alternative, internship. *Entrance requirements:* For master's, doctorate, and Ed S, GRE General Test, minimum GPA of 3.0. Additional exam requirements/recommendations for international students: Required—TOEFL (minimum score 550 paper-based; 79 iBT), IELTS (minimum score 6.5). *Application deadline:* For fall admission, 12/15 for domestic and international students; for spring admission, 2/1 priority date for domestic students, 2/1 for international students. Application fee: $40 ($50 for international students). Electronic applications accepted. *Expenses:* Tuition, state resident: full-time $4086. Tuition, nonresident: full-time $14,254. *Required fees:* $853. Tuition and fees vary according to course load. *Financial support:* In 2016–17, 69 students received support, including 6 fellowships (averaging $4,088 per year), 5 research assistantships (averaging $12,036 per year), 23 teaching assistantships (averaging $12,358 per year); career-related internships or fieldwork, Federal Work-Study, scholarships/grants, traineeships, health care benefits, and unspecified assistantships also available. Support available to part-time students. Financial award application deadline: 3/1. *Faculty research:* Multicultural counseling and training, school and counseling psychology, social justice, integrated primary care behavioral health training, mental health disparities. *Total annual research expenditures:* $122,042. *Unit head:* Dr. Gladys DeNecochea, Interim Department Head, 575-646-2121, Fax: 575-646-8035, E-mail: gdenecoc@nmsu.edu. *Application contact:* Norma Arrieta, Student Program Coordinator, 575-646-2121, Fax: 575-646-8035, E-mail: cep@nmsu.edu.
Website: http://cep.education.nmsu.edu

New York Institute of Technology, School of Interdisciplinary Studies and Education, Department of School Counseling, Old Westbury, NY 11568-8000. Offers school counseling (MS); student behavior management (Advanced Certificate). *Accreditation:* ACA. *Program availability:* Part-time, evening/weekend, blended/hybrid learning. *Faculty:* 3 full-time (2 women), 4 part-time/adjunct (3 women). *Students:* 21 full-time (20 women), 25 part-time (24 women); includes 22 minority (8 Black or African American, non-Hispanic/Latino; 1 Asian, non-Hispanic/Latino; 13 Hispanic/Latino). Average age 30. 60 applicants, 58% accepted, 25 enrolled. In 2016, 18 master's awarded. *Degree requirements:* For master's, internship, practicum. *Entrance requirements:* For master's, GRE (minimum combined score of 300 from any two tests) or MAT (minimum score 400), minimum undergraduate GPA of 3.0; BS or equivalent with academic background in psychology, education, sociology, law, or related behavioral science, or work experience in school, social agency, hospital, criminal justice, or community action program; goal statement; 3 letters of reference; signed candidate statement of understanding. Additional exam requirements/recommendations for international students: Required—TOEFL (minimum score 79 iBT), IELTS (minimum score 6). *Application deadline:* Applications are processed on a rolling basis. Application fee: $50. Electronic applications accepted. *Expenses:* $1,215 per credit. *Financial support:* Career-related internships or fieldwork, Federal Work-Study, scholarships/grants, tuition waivers (full and partial), and unspecified assistantships available. Support available to part-time students. Financial award application deadline: 3/1; financial award applicants required to submit FAFSA. *Faculty research:* School counselor accountability, school counselor-principal relationship, comprehensive school counseling program design and evaluation, cultural competence, college and career readiness. *Unit head:* Dr. Carol Dahir, Department Chair, 516-686-7616, Fax: 516-686-7655, E-mail: cdahir@nyit.edu. *Application contact:* Alice Dolitsky, Director, Graduate Admissions, 516-686-7520, Fax: 516-686-1116, E-mail: nyitgrad@nyit.edu.
Website: http://www.nyit.edu/degrees/school_counseling

New York University, Steinhardt School of Culture, Education, and Human Development, Department of Applied Psychology, Programs in Counseling, New York, NY 10003. Offers counseling and guidance (MA, Advanced Certificate), including bilingual school counseling K-12 (MA), school counseling K-12 (MA); counseling for mental health and wellness (MA); counseling psychology (PhD); LGBT health, education, and social services (Advanced Certificate); Advanced Certificate/MPH; MA/Advanced Certificate. *Accreditation:* APA (one or more programs are accredited). *Program availability:* Part-time. *Degree requirements:* For master's, thesis (for some programs); for doctorate, thesis/dissertation. *Entrance requirements:* For doctorate, GRE General Test, interview. Additional exam requirements/recommendations for international students: Required—TOEFL (minimum score 100 iBT). Electronic applications accepted. *Faculty research:* Sexual and gender identities, group dynamics, psychopathy and personality, multicultural assessment, working people's lives.

Niagara University, Graduate Division of Education, Concentration in Mental Health Counseling, Niagara University, NY 14109. Offers MS, Certificate. *Accreditation:* ACA. *Program availability:* Part-time. *Students:* 41 full-time (36 women), 12 part-time (11 women); includes 2 minority (both Black or African American, non-Hispanic/Latino), 14 international. Average age 28. In 2016, 18 master's, 1 other advanced degree awarded. *Entrance requirements:* For master's, GRE General Test or MAT. Additional exam requirements/recommendations for international students: Required—TOEFL (minimum score 550 paper-based; 79 iBT), IELTS (minimum score 6). *Application deadline:* For fall admission, 8/1 for domestic students. Applications are processed on a rolling basis. Application fee: $30. *Expenses:* Contact institution. *Financial support:* Research assistantships with tuition reimbursements, teaching assistantships with tuition reimbursements, career-related internships or fieldwork, Federal Work-Study, scholarships/grants, and unspecified assistantships available. Financial award application deadline: 4/15; financial award applicants required to submit FAFSA. *Unit head:* Dr. Shannon Hodges, Chair, 716-286-8328. *Application contact:* Evan Pierce, Associate Director, Graduate Studies, 716-286-8327, E-mail: epierce@niagara.edu.
Website: http://www.niagara.edu/mental-health-counseling

Niagara University, Graduate Division of Education, Concentration in School Counseling, Niagara University, NY 14109. Offers MS Ed, Certificate. *Accreditation:* NCATE. *Program availability:* Part-time, evening/weekend. *Students:* 21 full-time (20 women), 7 part-time (5 women); includes 6 minority (5 Black or African American, non-Hispanic/Latino; 1 Two or more races, non-Hispanic/Latino), 1 international. Average age 27. In 2016, 3 master's awarded. *Entrance requirements:* For master's, GRE General Test or MAT; for Certificate, GRE General Test, GRE Subject Test or MAT. Additional exam requirements/recommendations for international students: Required—TOEFL (minimum score 550 paper-based; 79 iBT), IELTS (minimum score 6). *Application deadline:* For fall admission, 8/1 for domestic students. Applications are processed on a rolling basis. Application fee: $30. *Expenses:* Contact institution. *Financial support:* Research assistantships with tuition reimbursements, teaching assistantships with tuition reimbursements, career-related internships or fieldwork, Federal Work-Study, scholarships/grants, and unspecified assistantships available. Financial award application deadline: 4/15; financial award applicants required to submit FAFSA. *Unit head:* Dr. Kristine Augustyniak, Chair, 716-286-8548, E-mail: kma@niagara.edu. *Application contact:* Evan Pierce, Associate Director, Graduate Studies, 716-286-8327, E-mail: epierce@niagara.edu.
Website: http://www.niagara.edu/school-counseling

Nicholls State University, Graduate Studies, College of Education, Department of Psychology, Counseling and Family Studies, Thibodaux, LA 70310. Offers clinical mental health counseling (MA); school counseling (M Ed); school psychology (SSP). *Accreditation:* NCATE. *Program availability:* Part-time, evening/weekend. *Degree requirements:* For master's, comprehensive exam; for SSP, comprehensive exam, internship. *Entrance requirements:* For master's, GRE General Test. Electronic applications accepted.

North Carolina Agricultural and Technical State University, School of Graduate Studies, School of Education, Department of Human Development and Services, Greensboro, NC 27411. Offers adult education (MS); counseling (MS); school administration (MS). *Accreditation:* ACA. *Program availability:* Part-time, evening/weekend. *Degree requirements:* For master's, comprehensive exam, thesis, qualifying exam. *Entrance requirements:* For master's, GRE General Test, minimum GPA of 3.0.

North Carolina Central University, School of Education, Department of Counselor Education, Durham, NC 27707-3129. Offers career counseling (MA); school counseling (MA). *Accreditation:* ACA; NCATE. *Program availability:* Part-time, evening/weekend. *Degree requirements:* For master's, comprehensive exam, thesis or alternative. *Entrance requirements:* For master's, GRE, minimum GPA of 3.0 in major, 2.5 overall. Additional exam requirements/recommendations for international students: Required—TOEFL.

North Carolina State University, Graduate School, College of Education, Department of Curriculum and Instruction, Program in Counselor Education, Raleigh, NC 27695. Offers M Ed, MS, PhD. *Accreditation:* ACA. *Degree requirements:* For master's, thesis (for some programs). *Entrance requirements:* For master's, GRE or MAT. Electronic applications accepted. *Faculty research:* Career development, retention of at-risk students in higher education, psycho-social development, multicultural issues, cognitive-developmental interventions.

North Dakota State University, College of Graduate and Interdisciplinary Studies, College of Human Development and Education, School of Education, Program in Counselor Education, Fargo, ND 58102. Offers clinical mental health counseling (M Ed, MS); counselor education and supervision (PhD); school counseling (M Ed, MS). *Accreditation:* ACA; NCATE. *Program availability:* Part-time, online learning. *Degree requirements:* For master's, comprehensive exam, thesis or alternative; for doctorate, comprehensive exam, thesis/dissertation. *Entrance requirements:* For master's, GRE, MAT, interview. Additional exam requirements/recommendations for international students: Required—TOEFL. *Faculty research:* Supervision, program assessment, multicultural issues.

Northeastern Illinois University, College of Graduate Studies and Research, College of Education, Program in School Counseling, Chicago, IL 60625-4699. Offers MA. *Accreditation:* ACA.

Northeastern State University, College of Education, Department of Psychology and Counseling, Tahlequah, OK 74464-2399. Offers counseling psychology (MS); school counseling (M Ed); substance abuse counseling (MS). *Program availability:* Part-time, evening/weekend. *Faculty:* 16 full-time (7 women), 4 part-time/adjunct (3 women). *Students:* 80 full-time (61 women), 73 part-time (61 women); includes 66 minority (7 Black or African American, non-Hispanic/Latino; 23 American Indian or Alaska Native, non-Hispanic/Latino; 3 Asian, non-Hispanic/Latino; 5 Hispanic/Latino; 28 Two or more races, non-Hispanic/Latino), 1 international. Average age 32. In 2016, 43 master's awarded. *Degree requirements:* For master's, thesis (for some programs), written and oral examinations. *Entrance requirements:* For master's, GRE, minimum GPA of 2.5. Application fee: $25. *Expenses:* Tuition, state resident: full-time $2816; part-time $216.60 per credit hour. Tuition, nonresident: full-time $6365; part-time $489.60 per credit hour. *Required fees:* $37.40 per credit hour. *Financial support:* Teaching assistantships, career-related internships or fieldwork, and Federal Work-Study available. Financial award application deadline: 3/1. *Unit head:* Dr. Kenny Paris, Department Chair of Psychology and Counseling, 918-444-3021, E-mail: parisk@nsuok.edu. *Application contact:* Josh McCollum, Graduate Coordinator, 918-444-2093, E-mail: mccolluj@nsuok.edu.

Counselor Education

Website: https://academics.nsuok.edu/education/EducationHome/COEDepartments/PsychologyCounseling.aspx

Northern Arizona University, Graduate College, College of Education, Department of Educational Psychology, Flagstaff, AZ 86011. Offers counseling (MA); educational psychology (PhD), including counseling psychology, school psychology; human relations (M Ed); school counseling (M Ed); school psychology (Ed S); student affairs (M Ed). *Program availability:* Part-time, online learning. Terminal master's awarded for partial completion of doctoral program. *Degree requirements:* For master's, internship (for some programs); for doctorate, comprehensive exam, thesis/dissertation, internship. *Entrance requirements:* Additional exam requirements/recommendations for international students: Required—TOEFL (minimum score 550 paper-based; 80 iBT), IELTS (minimum score 7). Electronic applications accepted. *Expenses:* Tuition, state resident: full-time $8971; part-time $444 per credit hour. Tuition, nonresident: full-time $20,958; part-time $1164 per credit hour. *Required fees:* $1018; $644 per credit hour. Tuition and fees vary according to course load, campus/location and program.

Northern Illinois University, Graduate School, College of Education, Department of Counseling, Adult and Higher Education, De Kalb, IL 60115-2854. Offers adult and higher education (MS Ed, Ed D); counseling (MS Ed, Ed D). *Accreditation:* ACA. *Program availability:* Part-time, evening/weekend. *Faculty:* 19 full-time (11 women), 2 part-time/adjunct (1 woman). *Students:* 108 full-time (74 women), 205 part-time (146 women); includes 123 minority (68 Black or African American, non-Hispanic/Latino; 2 American Indian or Alaska Native, non-Hispanic/Latino; 10 Asian, non-Hispanic/Latino; 34 Hispanic/Latino; 9 Two or more races, non-Hispanic/Latino), 8 international. Average age 35. 126 applicants, 59% accepted, 36 enrolled. In 2016, 66 master's, 24 doctorates awarded. Terminal master's awarded for partial completion of doctoral program. *Degree requirements:* For master's, comprehensive exam, thesis optional; for doctorate, thesis/dissertation, candidacy exam, dissertation defense. *Entrance requirements:* For master's, GRE General Test or MAT, minimum undergraduate GPA of 2.75, interview (for counseling); for doctorate, GRE General Test, minimum undergraduate GPA of 2.75, 3.2 graduate; interview (for counseling). Additional exam requirements/recommendations for international students: Required—TOEFL (minimum score 550 paper-based). *Application deadline:* For fall admission, 6/1 for domestic students, 5/1 for international students; for spring admission, 11/1 for domestic students, 10/1 for international students. Applications are processed on a rolling basis. Application fee: $40. Electronic applications accepted. *Financial support:* In 2016–17, 12 research assistantships with full tuition reimbursements, 7 teaching assistantships with full tuition reimbursements were awarded; fellowships with full tuition reimbursements, career-related internships or fieldwork, Federal Work-Study, scholarships/grants, tuition waivers (full), and staff assistantships also available. Support available to part-time students. Financial award applicants required to submit FAFSA. *Unit head:* Dr. Suzanne Degges-White, Interim Chair, 815-753-1448, E-mail: cahe@niu.edu. *Application contact:* Graduate School Office, 815-753-0395, E-mail: gradsch@niu.edu.
Website: http://www.cedu.niu.edu/cahe/index.html

Northern Kentucky University, Office of Graduate Programs, College of Education and Human Services, Program in School Counseling, Highland Heights, KY 41099. Offers MA. *Accreditation:* ACA. *Program availability:* Part-time, evening/weekend. *Degree requirements:* For master's, portfolio, practicum, internship. *Entrance requirements:* For master's, GRE or MAT, official transcript(s), two essays, three letters of reference, professional resume, KY Statement of Eligibility or teaching certificate, criminal background check, interview. Additional exam requirements/recommendations for international students: Required—TOEFL (minimum score 79 iBT); Recommended—IELTS (minimum score 6.5). Electronic applications accepted. *Faculty research:* Counselor wellness, counseling preferences and expectations, creativity in counseling, integrating mindfulness-based approaches into counseling, evidence-based school counseling.

Northern State University, MS Ed Program in Counseling, Aberdeen, SD 57401-7198. Offers clinical mental health counseling (MS Ed); school counseling (MS Ed). *Accreditation:* NCATE. *Program availability:* Part-time, online learning. *Degree requirements:* For master's, comprehensive exam, thesis optional. *Entrance requirements:* For master's, minimum GPA of 2.75. Additional exam requirements/recommendations for international students: Required—TOEFL (minimum score 550 paper-based; 78 iBT), IELTS (minimum score 6). Electronic applications accepted.

Northwest Christian University, School of Education and Counseling, Eugene, OR 97401-3745. Offers clinical mental health counseling (MA); elementary teaching (MAT); English for speakers of other languages (ESOL) (MAT); school counseling (MA); secondary teaching (MAT). *Program availability:* Part-time, evening/weekend, online learning. *Faculty:* 9 full-time (5 women), 21 part-time/adjunct (14 women). *Students:* 87 full-time (64 women), 52 part-time (40 women); includes 22 minority (5 Black or African American, non-Hispanic/Latino; 2 American Indian or Alaska Native, non-Hispanic/Latino; 2 Asian, non-Hispanic/Latino; 7 Hispanic/Latino; 2 Native Hawaiian or other Pacific Islander, non-Hispanic/Latino; 4 Two or more races, non-Hispanic/Latino). Average age 36. In 2016, 76 master's awarded. *Degree requirements:* For master's, thesis (for some programs). *Entrance requirements:* For master's, MAT, minimum undergraduate GPA of 3.0, interview, 2-3 page statement of purpose, two letters of recommendation, resume, background check. Additional exam requirements/recommendations for international students: Required—TOEFL (minimum score 550 paper-based; 80 iBT). *Application deadline:* Applications are processed on a rolling basis. Electronic applications accepted. *Expenses:* Contact institution. *Unit head:* Gene James, Dean of Counseling, 541-684-7261, Fax: 541-684-7310, E-mail: gjames@nwcu.edu. *Application contact:* Billy Dorsch, Admission Counselor for Graduate Studies, 541-684-7279, Fax: 541-349-5281, E-mail: wdorsch@nwcu.edu.

Northwestern Oklahoma State University, School of Professional Studies, Program in School Counseling, Alva, OK 73717-2799. Offers M Ed. *Accreditation:* NCATE. *Program availability:* Part-time. *Degree requirements:* For master's, thesis optional, portfolio. *Entrance requirements:* For master's, GRE General Test or MAT, minimum GPA of 2.75.

Northwestern State University of Louisiana, Graduate Studies and Research, College of Education and Human Development, Program in School Counseling, Natchitoches, LA 71497. Offers MA. *Accreditation:* ACA. *Degree requirements:* For master's, comprehensive exam, thesis (for some programs). *Entrance requirements:* For master's, GRE General Test. Additional exam requirements/recommendations for international students: Required—TOEFL. Electronic applications accepted.

Northwestern State University of Louisiana, Graduate Studies and Research, College of Education and Human Development, Programs in Educational Leadership and Instruction, Natchitoches, LA 71497. Offers counseling (Ed S); educational leadership (M Ed, Ed S); educational technology (Ed S); elementary teaching (Ed S); reading (Ed S); secondary teaching (Ed S); special education (Ed S). *Accreditation:* NASAD. *Degree requirements:* For master's, comprehensive exam, thesis (for some programs). *Entrance requirements:* For master's and Ed S, GRE General Test. Additional exam requirements/recommendations for international students: Required—TOEFL. Electronic applications accepted.

Northwest Nazarene University, Program in Counselor Education, Nampa, ID 83686-5897. Offers clinical counseling (MS); marriage and family counseling (MS); school counseling (MS). *Program availability:* Part-time. *Faculty:* 6 full-time (4 women), 10 part-time/adjunct (6 women). *Students:* 92 full-time (74 women), 26 part-time (19 women); includes 10 minority (2 Black or African American, non-Hispanic/Latino; 6 Hispanic/Latino; 2 Two or more races, non-Hispanic/Latino), 1 international. Average age 35. 47 applicants, 66% accepted, 25 enrolled. In 2016, 33 master's awarded. *Degree requirements:* For master's, comprehensive exam. *Entrance requirements:* For master's, minimum GPA of 3.0, BA. Additional exam requirements/recommendations for international students: Required—TOEFL. *Application deadline:* For fall admission, 2/15 for domestic and international students; for spring admission, 9/15 for domestic and international students. Application fee: $50. Electronic applications accepted. *Expenses: Tuition:* Full-time $9315; part-time $4658 per credit hour. *Required fees:* $120. *Unit head:* Dr. Michael Pitts, Chair, 208-467-8040, Fax: 208-467-8339. *Application contact:* Lynette Kingsmore, Graduate Admissions Counselor, 208-467-8107, E-mail: lkingsmore@nnu.edu.

Nova Southeastern University, College of Psychology, Fort Lauderdale, FL 33314-7796. Offers clinical psychology (PhD, Psy D); counseling (MS); experimental psychology (MS); forensic psychology (MS); general psychology (MS); mental health counseling (MS); school counseling (MS); school psychology (Psy D, Psy S). *Accreditation:* APA (one or more programs are accredited). *Program availability:* 100% online, blended/hybrid learning. *Faculty:* 51 full-time (21 women), 120 part-time/adjunct (70 women). *Students:* 724 full-time (596 women), 918 part-time (792 women); includes 797 minority (276 Black or African American, non-Hispanic/Latino; 1 American Indian or Alaska Native, non-Hispanic/Latino; 44 Asian, non-Hispanic/Latino; 427 Hispanic/Latino; 2 Native Hawaiian or other Pacific Islander, non-Hispanic/Latino; 47 Two or more races, non-Hispanic/Latino), 41 international. Average age 31. 1,349 applicants, 61% accepted, 651 enrolled. In 2016, 377 master's, 177 doctorates, 26 other advanced degrees awarded. Terminal master's awarded for partial completion of doctoral program. *Degree requirements:* For master's, comprehensive exam, 3 practica; for doctorate, thesis/dissertation, clinical internship, competency exam; for Psy S, comprehensive exam, internship. *Entrance requirements:* For doctorate, GRE General Test, GRE Subject Test (recommended), minimum undergraduate GPA of 3.0; for Psy S, GRE General Test. Additional exam requirements/recommendations for international students: Required—TOEFL (minimum score 550 paper-based). *Application deadline:* Applications are processed on a rolling basis. Application fee: $50. Electronic applications accepted. *Expenses:* Contact institution. *Financial support:* In 2016–17, 197 students received support, including 15 research assistantships (averaging $5,600 per year), 68 teaching assistantships (averaging $2,000 per year); career-related internships or fieldwork, Federal Work-Study, institutionally sponsored loans, scholarships/grants, and unspecified assistantships also available. Support available to part-time students. Financial award application deadline: 4/15; financial award applicants required to submit FAFSA. *Faculty research:* Clinical health psychology, multicultural/diversity psychology, clinical neuropsychology, clinical child psychology, family violence. *Unit head:* Dr. Karen Grosby, Dean, 954-262-5712, Fax: 954-262-3859, E-mail: grosby@nova.edu. *Application contact:* Carlos Perez, Senior Manager of Outreach, 954-262-5702, Fax: 954-262-3893, E-mail: gradschool@nova.edu.
Website: http://psychology.nova.edu/

Nyack College, Alliance Graduate School of Counseling, Nyack, NY 10960. Offers marriage and family therapy (MA); mental health counseling (MA). *Program availability:* Part-time, evening/weekend, 100% online. *Students:* 84 full-time (69 women), 123 part-time (103 women); includes 152 minority (64 Black or African American, non-Hispanic/Latino; 44 Asian, non-Hispanic/Latino; 41 Hispanic/Latino; 3 Two or more races, non-Hispanic/Latino), 9 international. Average age 37. In 2016, 70 master's awarded. *Degree requirements:* For master's, comprehensive exam, counselor-in-training therapy, internship, CPCE exam. *Entrance requirements:* For master's, Millon Clinical Multiaxial Inventory-3, Minnesota Multiphasic Personality Inventory-2, transcripts, statement of Christian life and experience, statement of support systems. Additional exam requirements/recommendations for international students: Required—TOEFL (minimum score 550 paper-based; 80 iBT). *Application deadline:* For fall admission, 8/1 for domestic students, 2/15 for international students; for spring admission, 12/15 for domestic students, 7/15 for international students. Applications are processed on a rolling basis. Application fee: $30. Electronic applications accepted. *Expenses:* $775 per credit. *Financial support:* Career-related internships or fieldwork and scholarships/grants available. Financial award applicants required to submit FAFSA. *Unit head:* Dr. Carol Robles, Associate Dean, 845-770-5735. *Application contact:* Esther Guzman, Admissions Associate, 800-541-6891, E-mail: admissions.grad@nyack.edu.
Website: http://www.nyack.edu/agsc

Ohio University, Graduate College, Gladys W. and David H. Patton College of Education and Human Services, Department of Counseling and Higher Education, Athens, OH 45701-2979. Offers college student personnel (M Ed); community/agency counseling (M Ed); counselor education (PhD); higher education (PhD); rehabilitation counseling (M Ed); school counseling (M Ed). *Accreditation:* ACA; CORE. *Program availability:* Part-time, evening/weekend. *Degree requirements:* For master's, comprehensive exam (for some programs), thesis or alternative; for doctorate, comprehensive exam, thesis/dissertation. *Entrance requirements:* For master's, GRE General Test or MAT (if GPA less than 2.9), 3 letters of reference; for doctorate, GRE General Test, work experience, minimum GPA of 3.4. Additional exam requirements/recommendations for international students: Required—TOEFL (minimum score 550 paper-based; 80 iBT) or IELTS (minimum score 6.5). *Application deadline:* For fall admission, 1/15 for domestic and international students. Application fee: $50 ($55 for international students). Electronic applications accepted. *Financial support:* Research assistantships with full tuition reimbursements, teaching assistantships with full tuition reimbursements, Federal Work-Study, institutionally sponsored loans, tuition waivers (partial), and unspecified assistantships available. Financial award application deadline: 1/15. *Faculty research:* Youth violence, gender studies, student affairs, chemical dependency, disabilities issues. *Unit head:* Dr. Tracy Leinbaugh, Chair, 740-593-0846, Fax: 740-593-0477, E-mail: leinbaug@ohio.edu. *Application contact:* Floyd J. Doney, Director of Student Affairs, 740-593-4400, Fax: 740-593-9310, E-mail: doney@ohio.edu.
Website: http://www.cehs.ohio.edu/academics/che/

Oklahoma City University, Petree College of Arts and Sciences, Oklahoma City, OK 73106-1402. Offers applied behavioral studies (M Ed); applied sociology: nonprofit leadership (MA); creative writing (MFA); criminology (MS); early childhood education (M Ed); elementary education (M Ed); general studies (MLA); leadership/management (MLA); moving image arts (MFA); professional counseling (M Ed); teaching (MA); teaching English to speakers of other languages (MA). *Program availability:* Part-time, evening/weekend. *Faculty:* 11 full-time (5 women), 15 part-time/adjunct (6 women). *Students:* 77 full-time (55 women), 46 part-time (30 women); includes 32 minority (13 Black or African American, non-Hispanic/Latino; 1 American Indian or Alaska Native, non-Hispanic/Latino; 2 Asian, non-Hispanic/Latino; 12 Hispanic/Latino; 4 Two or more races, non-Hispanic/Latino), 37 international. Average age 34. 92 applicants, 74% accepted, 46 enrolled. In 2016, 72 master's awarded. *Degree requirements:* For master's, capstone/practicum. *Entrance requirements:* For master's, bachelor's degree

from accredited institution with minimum GPA of 3.0, essay, recommendation letters. Additional exam requirements/recommendations for international students: Required—TOEFL (minimum score 550 paper-based; 80 iBT). *Application deadline:* Applications are processed on a rolling basis. Application fee: $50. Electronic applications accepted. *Expenses:* Contact institution. *Financial support:* In 2016–17, 16 students received support. Federal Work-Study, institutionally sponsored loans, scholarships/grants, and tuition waivers (full and partial) available. Support available to part-time students. Financial award application deadline: 6/1; financial award applicants required to submit FAFSA. *Unit head:* Dr. Amy Cataldi, Dean, 405-208-5446, Fax: 405-208-5447, E-mail: acataldi@okcu.edu. *Application contact:* Michael Harrington, Director of Graduate Admissions, 800-633-7242, Fax: 405-208-5356, E-mail: gadmissions@okcu.edu.
Website: http://www.okcu.edu/petree/

Old Dominion University, Darden College of Education, Counseling Program, Norfolk, VA 23529. Offers clinical mental health counseling (MS Ed); college counseling (MS Ed); counseling (Ed S); counselor education (PhD); school counseling (MS Ed). *Accreditation:* ACA. *Program availability:* Part-time, evening/weekend. *Faculty:* 14 full-time (7 women), 9 part-time/adjunct (7 women). *Students:* 125 full-time (107 women), 58 part-time (43 women); includes 74 minority (44 Black or African American, non-Hispanic/Latino; 1 American Indian or Alaska Native, non-Hispanic/Latino; 5 Asian, non-Hispanic/Latino; 18 Hispanic/Latino; 6 Two or more races, non-Hispanic/Latino), 8 international. Average age 31. 195 applicants, 57% accepted, 79 enrolled. In 2016, 53 master's, 9 doctorates, 3 other advanced degrees awarded. *Degree requirements:* For master's and Ed S, comprehensive exam; for doctorate, comprehensive exam, thesis/dissertation. *Entrance requirements:* For master's and Ed S, GRE General Test, resume, essay, transcripts, recommendations; for doctorate, GRE General Test, resume, interview, essay, transcripts, recommendations. Additional exam requirements/recommendations for international students: Required—TOEFL. *Application deadline:* For fall admission, 3/1 for domestic and international students; for winter admission, 1/10 for domestic students; for spring admission, 10/1 for domestic and international students; for summer admission, 3/1 for domestic students, 2/1 for international students. Application fee: $50. Electronic applications accepted. *Expenses:* Tuition, state resident: full-time $8604; part-time $478 per credit hour. Tuition, nonresident: full-time $21,510; part-time $1195 per credit hour. *Required fees:* $66 per semester. Tuition and fees vary according to campus/location, program and reciprocity agreements. *Financial support:* In 2016–17, 20 students received support, including 2 fellowships with full tuition reimbursements available (averaging $15,000 per year), 13 research assistantships (averaging $9,000 per year), 20 teaching assistantships with full tuition reimbursements available (averaging $20,000 per year); career-related internships or fieldwork, Federal Work-Study, institutionally sponsored loans, scholarships/grants, tuition waivers (partial), and unspecified assistantships also available. Support available to part-time students. Financial award application deadline: 10/1; financial award applicants required to submit FAFSA. *Faculty research:* Group counseling, counselor education, career counseling, spirituality and counseling, school counseling, LGBT counseling, legal and ethical issues. *Total annual research expenditures:* $75,000. *Unit head:* Dr. Jeff Moe, Graduate Program Director, 757-683-6235, Fax: 757-683-5756, E-mail: jmoe@odu.edu. *Application contact:* Jeff Moe, Graduate Program Director, 757-683-6235, Fax: 757-683-5756, E-mail: jmoe@odu.edu.
Website: http://www.odu.edu/chs

Oregon State University, College of Education, Program in Counseling, Corvallis, OR 97331. Offers clinical mental health (M Coun); counseling (MS, PhD); school counseling (M Coun). *Accreditation:* ACA (one or more programs are accredited); NCATE. *Program availability:* Part-time, blended/hybrid learning. *Faculty:* 9 full-time (3 women), 13 part-time/adjunct (11 women). *Students:* 73 full-time (60 women), 105 part-time (80 women); includes 40 minority (6 Black or African American, non-Hispanic/Latino; 7 Asian, non-Hispanic/Latino; 17 Hispanic/Latino; 1 Native Hawaiian or other Pacific Islander, non-Hispanic/Latino; 9 Two or more races, non-Hispanic/Latino), 1 international. Average age 36. 177 applicants, 51% accepted, 66 enrolled. In 2016, 31 master's, 5 doctorates awarded. *Degree requirements:* For master's, thesis or alternative; for doctorate, one foreign language, thesis/dissertation. *Entrance requirements:* For master's, minimum GPA of 3.0 in last 90 hours; for doctorate, GRE or MAT, master's degree, minimum GPA of 3.0 in last 90 hours of course work, 2 years of teaching experience. Additional exam requirements/recommendations for international students: Required—TOEFL (minimum score 575 paper-based). *Application deadline:* For fall admission, 1/31 for domestic students. Application fee: $75 ($85 for international students). *Expenses:* Tuition, state resident: full-time $12,150; part-time $450 per credit. Tuition, nonresident: full-time $21,789; part-time $807 per credit. *Required fees:* $1651; $1507 per credit. One-time fee: $350. Tuition and fees vary according to course load, campus/location and program. *Financial support:* Teaching assistantships, career-related internships or fieldwork, Federal Work-Study, and institutionally sponsored loans available. Support available to part-time students. Financial award application deadline: 3/1. *Faculty research:* Counseling and guidance improvement in social services agencies, elementary and secondary schools. *Unit head:* Dr. Larry Flick, Dean. *Application contact:* Mary Aguilera, Advisor, 541-737-2232, E-mail: mary.aguilera@oregonstate.edu.
Website: http://education.oregonstate.edu/counseling

Ottawa University, Graduate Studies-Arizona, Program in Education, Ottawa, KS 66067-3399. Offers community college counseling (MA); curriculum and instruction (MA); early childhood (MA); education intervention (MA); education leadership (MA); education technology (MA); Montessori early childhood education (MA); Montessori elementary education (MA); professional development (MA); school guidance counseling (MA); special education - cross categorical (MA). Programs offered in Mesa, Phoenix, Tempe and West Valley, AZ. *Accreditation:* NCATE. *Program availability:* Part-time. *Degree requirements:* For master's, thesis or alternative. *Entrance requirements:* For master's, minimum undergraduate GPA of 3.0, copy of current state certification or teaching license. Additional exam requirements/recommendations for international students: Required—TOEFL (minimum score 550 paper-based). Electronic applications accepted. *Expenses:* Contact institution.

Our Lady of the Lake University, School of Professional Studies, Program in School Counseling, San Antonio, TX 78207-4689. Offers M Ed. *Program availability:* Part-time, online only, 100% online. *Faculty:* 2 full-time (1 woman), 6 part-time/adjunct (5 women). *Students:* 79 full-time (75 women), 7 part-time (all women); includes 57 minority (10 Black or African American, non-Hispanic/Latino; 1 Asian, non-Hispanic/Latino; 45 Hispanic/Latino; 1 Two or more races, non-Hispanic/Latino). Average age 33. 45 applicants, 100% accepted, 35 enrolled. In 2016, 5 master's awarded. *Degree requirements:* For master's, comprehensive exam, practicum. *Entrance requirements:* For master's, official transcripts, personal statement, reference form, FERPA Consent to Release Education Records and Information form, current teaching license. Additional exam requirements/recommendations for international students: Required—TOEFL. *Application deadline:* For fall admission, 6/15 priority date for domestic and international students; for spring admission, 11/15 priority date for domestic and international students; for summer admission, 4/15 priority date for domestic students, 4/15 for international students. Applications are processed on a rolling basis. Application fee: $40 ($50 for international students). Electronic applications accepted. Application fee is waived when completed online. *Expenses:* *Tuition:* Full-time $14,796. Tuition and fees vary according to course load, degree level, campus/location and program. *Financial support:* In 2016–17, 3 students received support. Federal Work-Study, scholarships/grants, unspecified assistantships, and tuition discounts available. Support available to part-time students. Financial award application deadline: 5/1; financial award applicants required to submit FAFSA. *Faculty research:* Multicultural issues, career counseling, counselor identity, ethics. *Unit head:* Dr. Alycia Maurer, Education Department Chair, 210-434-6711 Ext. 7152, E-mail: admaurer@ollusa.edu. *Application contact:* Office of Graduate Admissions, 210-431-3995 Ext. 2314, Fax: 210-431-3945, E-mail: gradadm@lake.ollusa.edu.
Website: http://onlineprograms.ollusa.edu/med-school-counseling

Palm Beach Atlantic University, School of Education and Behavioral Studies, West Palm Beach, FL 33416-4708. Offers counseling psychology (MS), including addictions/mental health, general counseling, marriage and family therapy, mental health counseling, school guidance counseling. *Program availability:* Part-time, evening/weekend. *Faculty:* 8 full-time (2 women), 17 part-time/adjunct (13 women). *Students:* 243 full-time (206 women), 29 part-time (24 women); includes 147 minority (67 Black or African American, non-Hispanic/Latino; 4 Asian, non-Hispanic/Latino; 60 Hispanic/Latino; 1 Native Hawaiian or other Pacific Islander, non-Hispanic/Latino; 15 Two or more races, non-Hispanic/Latino), 6 international. Average age 35. 81 applicants, 89% accepted, 53 enrolled. In 2016, 122 master's awarded. *Entrance requirements:* For master's, GRE or MAT, minimum GPA of 3.0; essay. Additional exam requirements/recommendations for international students: Required—TOEFL (minimum score 550 paper-based; 79 iBT). *Application deadline:* Applications are processed on a rolling basis. Application fee: $50. Electronic applications accepted. *Expenses:* *Tuition:* Full-time $6600; part-time $550 per credit hour. Full-time tuition and fees vary according to degree level, campus/location and program. *Financial support:* In 2016–17, 11 students received support. Career-related internships or fieldwork, scholarships/grants, and employee education grants available. Financial award application deadline: 5/1; financial award applicants required to submit FAFSA. *Faculty research:* Group dynamics, phenomenology, spirituality, multicultural psychology. *Unit head:* Dr. Gene Sale, Program Director, 561-803-2352. *Application contact:* Graduate Admissions, 888-468-6722, E-mail: grad@pba.edu.
Website: http://www.pba.edu/graduate-counseling-program

Penn State University Park, Graduate School, College of Education, Department of Educational Psychology, Counseling, and Special Education, University Park, PA 16802. Offers counselor education (M Ed, D Ed, PhD, Certificate); educational psychology (MS, PhD, Certificate); school psychology (M Ed, MS, PhD, Certificate); special education (M Ed, MS, PhD, Certificate). *Unit head:* Dr. David H. Monk, Dean, 814-865-2523, Fax: 814-865-0555. *Application contact:* Lori Hawn, Director, Graduate Student Services, 814-865-1795, Fax: 814-863-4627, E-mail: l-gswww@lists.psu.edu.
Website: http://ed.psu.edu/epcse

Phillips Graduate University, Programs in Marriage and Family Therapy and School Counseling, Chatsworth, CA 91311. Offers art therapy (MA); marriage and family therapy (MA); school counseling (MA). *Program availability:* Evening/weekend. *Degree requirements:* For master's, comprehensive exam, thesis. *Entrance requirements:* For master's, minimum GPA of 2.5. Electronic applications accepted. *Faculty research:* Integration of interpersonal psychological theory, systems approach, firsthand experiential learning.

Pittsburg State University, Graduate School, College of Education, Department of Psychology and Counseling, Program in Counselor Education, Pittsburg, KS 66762. Offers school counseling (MS). *Accreditation:* ACA; NCATE. *Students:* 35. In 2016, 18 master's awarded. *Degree requirements:* For master's, thesis or alternative. *Entrance requirements:* For master's, GRE General Test, minimum GPA of 2.8. Additional exam requirements/recommendations for international students: Required—TOEFL (minimum score 550 paper-based; 79 iBT), IELTS (minimum score 6.5), PTE (minimum score 53). *Application deadline:* Applications are processed on a rolling basis. Application fee: $35 ($60 for international students). Electronic applications accepted. *Expenses:* Contact institution. *Financial support:* Teaching assistantships, career-related internships or fieldwork, and Federal Work-Study available. Financial award application deadline: 2/1; financial award applicants required to submit FAFSA. *Unit head:* Dr. David Hurford, Chairperson, 620-235-4521. *Application contact:* Lisa Allen, Assistant Director of Graduate and Continuing Studies, 620-235-4218, Fax: 620-235-4219, E-mail: lallen@pittstate.edu.

Plymouth State University, College of Graduate Studies, Graduate Studies in Education, Programs in Counseling, Plymouth, NH 03264-1595. Offers human relations (M Ed); school counseling (M Ed); school psychology (M Ed). *Accreditation:* ACA; NCATE. *Program availability:* Part-time, evening/weekend. *Degree requirements:* For master's, PRAXIS I. *Entrance requirements:* For master's, MAT, minimum GPA of 3.0.

Point Loma Nazarene University, School of Education, Program in Education, San Diego, CA 92106-2899. Offers counseling and guidance (MA); educational administration (MA); leadership in learning (MA). *Program availability:* Part-time, evening/weekend. *Students:* 68 full-time (50 women), 146 part-time (116 women); includes 124 minority (8 Black or African American, non-Hispanic/Latino; 12 Asian, non-Hispanic/Latino; 96 Hispanic/Latino; 1 Native Hawaiian or other Pacific Islander, non-Hispanic/Latino; 7 Two or more races, non-Hispanic/Latino), 4 international. Average age 34. 91 applicants, 86% accepted, 67 enrolled. In 2016, 85 master's awarded. *Entrance requirements:* For master's, interview, letters of recommendation, essay. Additional exam requirements/recommendations for international students: Required—TOEFL. *Application deadline:* For fall admission, 8/4 priority date for domestic students; for spring admission, 12/8 priority date for domestic students; for summer admission, 4/12 priority date for domestic students. Applications are processed on a rolling basis. Application fee: $50. Electronic applications accepted. *Expenses:* $610 per credit (for San Diego campus), $595 per credit (for Bakersfield campus). *Financial support:* Federal Work-Study and scholarships/grants available. Support available to part-time students. Financial award applicants required to submit FAFSA. *Unit head:* Conni Campbell, Associate Dean of the School of Education, 619-849-2532, Fax: 619-849-2532, E-mail: connicampbell@pointloma.edu. *Application contact:* Claire Buckley, Director of Graduate Admission, 866-692-4723, E-mail: gradinfo@pointloma.edu.
Website: http://gps.pointloma.edu/education

Pontifical Catholic University of Puerto Rico, College of Education, Program in Counselor Education, Ponce, PR 00717-0777. Offers M Ed. *Degree requirements:* For master's, comprehensive exam, thesis (for some programs). *Entrance requirements:* For master's, GRE, 2 letters of recommendation, interview, minimum GPA of 2.75.

Prairie View A&M University, College of Education, Department of Educational Leadership and Counseling, Prairie View, TX 77446. Offers M Ed, MA, MS Ed, PhD. *Accreditation:* NCATE. *Program availability:* Part-time, evening/weekend. *Faculty:* 16 full-time (6 women), 10 part-time/adjunct (8 women). *Students:* 113 full-time (94 women), 318 part-time (250 women); includes 406 minority (383 Black or African American, non-Hispanic/Latino; 2 American Indian or Alaska Native, non-Hispanic/Latino; 1 Asian, non-Hispanic/Latino; 17 Hispanic/Latino; 3 Two or more races, non-Hispanic/Latino), 5 international. Average age 35. 270 applicants, 83% accepted, 176 enrolled. In 2016, 121 master's, 6 doctorates awarded. *Degree requirements:* For master's, thesis optional; for doctorate, comprehensive exam, thesis/dissertation. *Entrance requirements:* For master's, GRE General Test, 3 letters of reference, minimum undergraduate GPA of 2.5; for doctorate, GRE General Test, 3 letters of reference. Additional exam requirements/recommendations for international students: Required—TOEFL (minimum score 550 paper-based; 79 iBT). *Application deadline:* For fall admission, 5/1 priority date for domestic students, 5/1 for international students; for spring admission, 10/1 priority date for domestic students, 9/1 for international students; for summer admission, 3/1 for domestic students, 2/1 for international students. Applications are processed on a rolling basis. Application fee: $50. Electronic applications accepted. *Expenses:* Tuition, state resident: full-time $4362; part-time $273.48 per credit hour. Tuition, nonresident: full-time $12,390; part-time $534.10 per credit hour. *Required fees:* $2782; $178.26 per credit hour. *Financial support:* Career-related internships or fieldwork available. Support available to part-time students. Financial award application deadline: 4/1; financial award applicants required to submit FAFSA. *Faculty research:* Mentoring, personality assessment, holistic/humanistic education. *Unit head:* Dr. Abul Pitre, Department Head, 936-261-3530, Fax: 936-261-3617, E-mail: abpitre@pvamu.edu. *Application contact:* Pauline Walker, Administrative Assistant II, Research and Graduate Studies, 936-261-3521, Fax: 936-261-3529, E-mail: gradadmissions@pvamu.edu.

Prescott College, Graduate Programs, Program in Education, Prescott, AZ 86301. Offers early childhood education (MA); early childhood special education (MA); education (MA); elementary education (MA); environmental education leadership and administration (MA); equine-assisted learning (MA); school guidance counseling (MA); secondary education (MA); special education: learning disabilities (MA); special education: mental retardation (MA); special education: serious emotional disabilities (MA); student-directed independent study (MA); sustainability education (PhD). *Program availability:* Part-time, online learning. *Faculty:* 3 full-time (all women). *Students:* 9 full-time (8 women), 30 part-time (20 women); includes 11 minority (3 Black or African American, non-Hispanic/Latino; 2 American Indian or Alaska Native, non-Hispanic/Latino; 6 Hispanic/Latino). Average age 36. 66 applicants, 82% accepted, 32 enrolled. In 2016, 12 master's, 8 doctorates awarded. *Degree requirements:* For master's, thesis, fieldwork or internship, practicum; for doctorate, thesis/dissertation. *Entrance requirements:* For master's, 2 letters of recommendation, resume; for doctorate, 3 letters of recommendation, resume, official transcripts, personal statement, program proposal. Additional exam requirements/recommendations for international students: Required—TOEFL (minimum score 500 paper-based). *Application deadline:* For fall admission, 4/15 priority date for domestic and international students; for spring admission, 9/15 priority date for domestic and international students. Applications are processed on a rolling basis. Application fee: $40. Electronic applications accepted. *Expenses: Tuition:* Full-time $19,680. One-time fee: $260 part-time. *Financial support:* Fellowships, research assistantships, teaching assistantships, career-related internships or fieldwork, Federal Work-Study, institutionally sponsored loans, scholarships/grants, traineeships, health care benefits, tuition waivers, and unspecified assistantships available. Support available to part-time students. Financial award applicants required to submit FAFSA. *Unit head:* Bob Ellis, 928-350-2217, E-mail: bellis@prescott.edu. *Application contact:* Melanie Lefever, Assistant Director, Limited-residency Programs, 928-350-2106, Fax: 928-776-5242, E-mail: mlefever@prescott.edu.

Providence College, Program in Counseling, Providence, RI 02918. Offers M Ed. *Program availability:* Part-time, evening/weekend. *Faculty:* 6 full-time (4 women), 33 part-time/adjunct (21 women). *Students:* 60 full-time (40 women), 49 part-time (38 women); includes 18 minority (7 Black or African American, non-Hispanic/Latino; 6 Hispanic/Latino; 1 Native Hawaiian or other Pacific Islander, non-Hispanic/Latino; 4 Two or more races, non-Hispanic/Latino), 7 international. Average age 29. 50 applicants, 100% accepted, 46 enrolled. In 2016, 46 master's awarded. *Degree requirements:* For master's, comprehensive exam, portfolio. *Entrance requirements:* Additional exam requirements/recommendations for international students: Required—TOEFL (minimum score 577 paper-based; 90 iBT). *Application deadline:* For fall admission, 7/15 priority date for domestic and international students; for spring admission, 11/15 priority date for domestic and international students; for summer admission, 3/15 priority date for domestic students, 3/15 for international students. Application fee: $55. *Expenses: Tuition:* Part-time $1260 per course. One-time fee: $265. Tuition and fees vary according to course load and program. *Financial support:* Career-related internships or fieldwork, institutionally sponsored loans, and unspecified assistantships available. Support available to part-time students. Financial award application deadline: 8/1; financial award applicants required to submit FAFSA.
Website: http://www.providence.edu/professional-studies/graduate-degrees/Pages/master-education-counseling.aspx

Purdue University, Graduate School, College of Education, Department of Educational Studies, West Lafayette, IN 47907. Offers administration (MS Ed, PhD, Ed S); counseling and development (MS Ed, PhD); education of the gifted (MS Ed); educational psychology (MS Ed, PhD); foundations of education (MS Ed, PhD); higher education administration (MS Ed, PhD); special education (MS Ed, PhD). *Accreditation:* ACA (one or more programs are accredited); NCATE (one or more programs are accredited). *Program availability:* Part-time, evening/weekend. *Faculty:* 29 full-time (22 women), 1 part-time/adjunct (0 women). *Students:* 78 full-time (60 women), 226 part-time (162 women); includes 45 minority (16 Black or African American, non-Hispanic/Latino; 8 Asian, non-Hispanic/Latino; 15 Hispanic/Latino; 6 Two or more races, non-Hispanic/Latino), 45 international. Average age 32. 214 applicants, 53% accepted, 70 enrolled. In 2016, 38 master's, 20 doctorates, 4 other advanced degrees awarded. *Degree requirements:* For master's, thesis optional; for doctorate, thesis/dissertation, oral and written exams; for Ed S, oral presentation, project. *Entrance requirements:* For master's, GRE General Test (except for special education if undergraduate GPA is higher than a 3.0), minimum undergraduate GPA of 3.0; for doctorate and Ed S, GRE General Test (minimum combined score of 1000, 300 for new scoring), minimum undergraduate GPA of 3.0. Additional exam requirements/recommendations for international students: Required—TOEFL (minimum score 550 paper-based; 77 iBT), TWE (minimum score 5). *Application deadline:* Applications are processed on a rolling basis. Application fee: $60 ($75 for international students). Electronic applications accepted. *Financial support:* Fellowships with full tuition reimbursements, research assistantships with full tuition reimbursements, teaching assistantships with full tuition reimbursements, career-related internships or fieldwork, and tuition waivers (full) available. Support available to part-time students. Financial award application deadline: 3/1; financial award applicants required to submit FAFSA. *Faculty research:* Motivation, learning disabilities, school learning, group processes, cognitive development. *Unit head:* F. Richard Olenchak, Head, 765-494-9170, E-mail: olenchak@purdue.edu. *Application contact:* Heather Brinkman, Graduate Contact, 765-494-2345, Fax: 765-494-5832, E-mail: hbrinkma@purdue.edu.
Website: http://www.edst.purdue.edu/

Purdue University Northwest, Graduate Studies Office, School of Education, Program in Counseling, Hammond, IN 46323-2094. Offers human services (MS Ed); mental health counseling (MS Ed); school counseling (MS Ed). *Accreditation:* ACA. *Entrance requirements:* Additional exam requirements/recommendations for international students: Required—TOEFL.

Queens College of the City University of New York, Division of Education, Department of Educational and Community Programs, Queens, NY 11367-1597. Offers bilingual pupil personnel (AC); counselor education (MS Ed); mental health counseling (MS); school building leader (AC); school district leader (AC); school psychologist (MS Ed); special education-childhood education (AC); special education-early childhood (MS Ed); teacher of special education 1-6 (MS Ed); teacher of special education birth-2 (MS Ed); teaching students with disabilities, grades 7-12 (MS Ed, AC). *Program availability:* Part-time. *Faculty:* 20 full-time (14 women), 50 part-time/adjunct (26 women). *Students:* 101 full-time (85 women), 459 part-time (383 women); includes 230 minority (44 Black or African American, non-Hispanic/Latino; 3 American Indian or Alaska Native, non-Hispanic/Latino; 46 Asian, non-Hispanic/Latino; 128 Hispanic/Latino; 1 Native Hawaiian or other Pacific Islander, non-Hispanic/Latino; 8 Two or more races, non-Hispanic/Latino), 3 international. Average age 28. 515 applicants, 57% accepted, 230 enrolled. In 2016, 158 master's, 68 other advanced degrees awarded. *Degree requirements:* For master's, research project; for AC, internship. *Entrance requirements:* For master's, minimum GPA of 3.0. Additional exam requirements/recommendations for international students: Required—TOEFL, IELTS. *Application deadline:* For fall admission, 3/1 for domestic students. Applications are processed on a rolling basis. Application fee: $125. Electronic applications accepted. *Expenses:* Tuition, state resident: full-time $5065; part-time $425 per credit. Tuition, nonresident: part-time $780 per credit. *Required fees:* $522; $397 per credit. Part-time tuition and fees vary according to course load and program. *Financial support:* Career-related internships or fieldwork available. Financial award application deadline: 4/1; financial award applicants required to submit FAFSA. *Unit head:* Dr. Lynn Howell, Chairperson, 718-997-5250, E-mail: lynn.howell@qc.cuny.edu.

Quincy University, Master of Science in Education Counseling Program, Quincy, IL 62301-2699. Offers college personnel (MS Ed); counseling (MS Ed); school counseling (MS Ed). *Program availability:* Part-time, evening/weekend. *Degree requirements:* For master's, comprehensive exam, practicum, internship. *Entrance requirements:* For master's, MAT or GRE. Additional exam requirements/recommendations for international students: Required—TOEFL (minimum score 550 paper-based; 79 iBT). Electronic applications accepted.

Radford University, College of Graduate Studies and Research, Program in Counselor Education, Radford, VA 24142. Offers MS. *Accreditation:* ACA; NCATE. *Program availability:* Part-time, evening/weekend. *Faculty:* 6 full-time (2 women). *Students:* 52 full-time (38 women), 10 part-time (8 women); includes 11 minority (7 Black or African American, non-Hispanic/Latino; 1 Asian, non-Hispanic/Latino; 3 Two or more races, non-Hispanic/Latino). Average age 26. 69 applicants, 93% accepted, 38 enrolled. In 2016, 29 master's awarded. *Degree requirements:* For master's, comprehensive exam, thesis optional. *Entrance requirements:* For master's, GRE or MAT, minimum GPA of 2.75, 3 letters of reference, personal essay, resume, official transcripts. Additional exam requirements/recommendations for international students: Required—TOEFL (minimum score 550 paper-based; 79 iBT), IELTS (minimum score 6.5). *Application deadline:* For fall admission, 2/15 priority date for domestic students, 12/1 for international students; for spring admission, 7/1 for international students. Applications are processed on a rolling basis. Application fee: $50. Electronic applications accepted. *Expenses:* Tuition, state resident: full-time $7868; part-time $328 per credit hour. Tuition, nonresident: full-time $16,394; part-time $683 per credit hour. *Required fees:* $3090; $130 per credit hour. Tuition and fees vary according to course load and program. *Financial support:* In 2016–17, 23 students received support, including 1 research assistantship (averaging $11,000 per year), 3 teaching assistantships (averaging $11,000 per year); career-related internships or fieldwork, scholarships/grants, and unspecified assistantships also available. Support available to part-time students. Financial award application deadline: 3/1; financial award applicants required to submit FAFSA. *Unit head:* Dr. Nadine Hartig, Chair, 540-831-5214, Fax: 540-831-6755, E-mail: vgoad4@radford.edu.
Website: http://www.radford.edu/content/cehd/home/counselor-education.html

Regent University, Graduate School, School of Psychology and Counseling, Virginia Beach, VA 23464-9800. Offers clinical mental health counseling (MA); clinical psychology (Psy D); counseling and psychological studies (PhD); counseling studies (CAGS); counselor education and supervision (PhD); general psychology (MS); marriage, couple, and family counseling (MA); pastoral counseling (MA); school counseling (MA); M Div/MA; M Ed/MA; MBA/MA. *Accreditation:* ACA; APA (one or more programs are accredited). *Program availability:* Part-time, evening/weekend, 100% online, blended/hybrid learning. *Faculty:* 28 full-time (17 women), 45 part-time/adjunct (26 women). *Students:* 295 full-time (240 women), 331 part-time (252 women); includes 244 minority (186 Black or African American, non-Hispanic/Latino; 4 American Indian or Alaska Native, non-Hispanic/Latino; 11 Asian, non-Hispanic/Latino; 29 Hispanic/Latino; 14 Two or more races, non-Hispanic/Latino), 10 international. Average age 36. 1,192 applicants, 29% accepted, 235 enrolled. In 2016, 156 master's, 41 doctorates, 1 other advanced degree awarded. *Degree requirements:* For master's, thesis or alternative, internship, practicum, written competency exam; for doctorate, thesis/dissertation or alternative. *Entrance requirements:* For master's, GRE General Test (including writing exam) or MAT, minimum undergraduate GPA of 3.0, resume, transcripts, writing sample, personal goals statement; for doctorate, GRE General Test (including writing exam), minimum undergraduate GPA of 3.0, graduate 3.5; writing sample; 3 recommendations; resume; college transcripts; personal goals statement. Additional exam requirements/recommendations for international students: Required—TOEFL (minimum score 577 paper-based). *Application deadline:* For fall admission, 4/1 priority date for domestic students; for spring admission, 11/1 priority date for domestic students. Applications are processed on a rolling basis. Application fee: $50. Electronic applications accepted. *Expenses:* Contact institution. *Financial support:* In 2016–17, 446 students received support, including 5 fellowships (averaging $4,000 per year), 10 research assistantships (averaging $3,200 per year); career-related internships or fieldwork, scholarships/grants, and unspecified assistantships also available. Support available to part-time students. *Faculty research:* Marriage enrichment, clinical psychology, troubled youth, faith and learning, trauma. *Unit head:* Dr. William Hathaway, Dean, 757-352-4294, Fax: 757-352-4282, E-mail: willhat@regent.edu. *Application contact:* Heidi Cece, Assistant Vice President of Enrollment Management, 800-373-5504, Fax: 757-352-4381, E-mail: admissions@regent.edu.
Website: http://www.regent.edu/spc/

Regis University, Rueckert-Hartman College for Health Professions, Denver, CO 80221-1099. Offers advanced practice nurse (DNP); counseling (MA); counseling children and adolescents (Post-Graduate Certificate); counseling military families (Post-Graduate Certificate); depth psychotherapy (Post-Graduate Certificate); fellowship in orthopedic manual physical therapy (Certificate); health care business management (Certificate); health care quality and patient safety (Certificate); health industry leadership (MBA); health services administration (MS); marriage and family therapy (MA, Post-Graduate Certificate); neonatal nurse practitioner (MSN); nursing education (MSN); nursing leadership (MSN); occupational therapy (OTD); pharmacy (Pharm D); physical therapy (DPT). *Program availability:* Part-time, evening/weekend, 100% online, blended/hybrid learning. *Faculty:* 66 full-time (44 women), 33 part-time/adjunct (25 women). *Students:* 1,088 full-time (788 women), 316 part-time (253 women); includes 403 minority (59 Black or African American, non-Hispanic/Latino; 5 American Indian or Alaska Native, non-Hispanic/Latino; 101 Asian, non-Hispanic/Latino; 187 Hispanic/

Latino; 51 Two or more races, non-Hispanic/Latino), 11 international. Average age 33. 2,199 applicants, 25% accepted, 277 enrolled. In 2016, 428 master's, 160 doctorates awarded. *Degree requirements:* For master's, thesis (for some programs), internship. *Entrance requirements:* For master's, official transcript reflecting baccalaureate degree awarded from regionally-accredited college or university. Additional exam requirements/recommendations for international students: Required—TOEFL (minimum score 550 paper-based; 82 iBT). *Application deadline:* For fall admission, 8/15 priority date for domestic students; for spring admission, 1/10 priority date for domestic students; for summer admission, 5/1 priority date for domestic students. Applications are processed on a rolling basis. Application fee: $75. Electronic applications accepted. *Expenses:* Contact institution. *Financial support:* In 2016–17, 102 students received support. Federal Work-Study and scholarships/grants available. Financial award application deadline: 4/15; financial award applicants required to submit FAFSA. *Faculty research:* Normal and pathological balance and gait research, normal/pathological upper limb motor control/biomechanics, exercise energy/metabolism research, optical treatment protocols for therapeutic modalities. *Unit head:* Dr. Janet Houser, Academic Dean. *Application contact:* Cate Clark, Director of Admissions, 303-458-4900, Fax: 303-964-5534, E-mail: ruadmissions@regis.edu.
Website: http://www.regis.edu/RHCHP.aspx

Rhode Island College, School of Graduate Studies, Feinstein School of Education and Human Development, Department of Counseling, Educational Leadership, and School Psychology, Providence, RI 02908-1991. Offers advanced counseling (CGS); agency counseling (MA); clinical mental health counseling (MS); co-occurring disorders (MA, CGS); educational leadership (M Ed); mental health counseling (CAGS); school counseling (MA); school psychology (CAGS); teacher leadership (CGS). *Accreditation:* ACA; NCATE. *Program availability:* Part-time, evening/weekend. *Faculty:* 9 full-time (5 women), 10 part-time/adjunct (all women). *Students:* 34 full-time (28 women), 83 part-time (72 women); includes 16 minority (5 Black or African American, non-Hispanic/Latino; 1 Asian, non-Hispanic/Latino; 10 Hispanic/Latino). Average age 33. In 2016, 50 master's, 34 other advanced degrees awarded. *Degree requirements:* For master's and other advanced degree, comprehensive exam (for some programs), thesis (for some programs). *Entrance requirements:* For master's, GRE General Test or MAT, undergraduate transcripts; minimum undergraduate GPA of 3.0; for other advanced degree, GRE or MAT (for most programs), undergraduate transcripts; minimum undergraduate GPA of 3.0; 3 letters of recommendation; current resume. Additional exam requirements/recommendations for international students: Recommended—TOEFL (minimum score 550 paper-based; 79 iBT). *Application deadline:* For fall admission, 3/1 for domestic students; for spring admission, 11/1 for domestic students. Applications are processed on a rolling basis. Application fee: $50. Electronic applications accepted. *Expenses:* Tuition, state resident: full-time $8928; part-time $372 per credit. Tuition, nonresident: full-time $17,376; part-time $724 per credit. *Required fees:* $604; $22 per credit. One-time fee: $74. *Financial support:* In 2016–17, 3 teaching assistantships with full tuition reimbursements (averaging $2,500 per year) were awarded; career-related internships or fieldwork, Federal Work-Study, scholarships/grants, health care benefits, and unspecified assistantships also available. Support available to part-time students. Financial award application deadline: 5/15; financial award applicants required to submit FAFSA. *Unit head:* Dr. Andrew Snyder, Chair, 401-456-9633. *Application contact:* Graduate Studies, 401-456-8700.
Website: http://www.ric.edu/counselingEducationalLeadershipSchoolPsychology/index.php

Richmont Graduate University, School of Counseling, Atlanta, GA 30339. Offers clinical mental health counseling (MA); marriage and family therapy (MA). *Accreditation:* ACA. *Program availability:* Part-time, evening/weekend. *Degree requirements:* For master's, comprehensive exam, thesis optional. *Entrance requirements:* For master's, GRE or MAT. *Application deadline:* Applications are processed on a rolling basis. Application fee: $50. Electronic applications accepted. *Expenses: Tuition:* Part-time $665 per credit hour. *Required fees:* $200 per semester. One-time fee: $250. *Financial support:* Career-related internships or fieldwork, scholarships/grants, and unspecified assistantships available. Financial award application deadline: 5/1. *Unit head:* Dr. Stephen P. Bradshaw, Dean, E-mail: sbradshaw@richmont.edu. *Application contact:* Admissions, 888-924-6774, Fax: 866-363-4323, E-mail: admissions@richmont.edu.
Website: http://richmont.edu/academics/school-of-counseling/

Rider University, Department of Graduate Education, Leadership and Counseling, Program in Counseling Services, Lawrenceville, NJ 08648-3001. Offers counseling services (MA, Ed S); director of school counseling (Certificate); school counseling services (Certificate). *Accreditation:* ACA; NCATE. *Program availability:* Part-time, evening/weekend. *Degree requirements:* For master's, comprehensive exam, research project; for other advanced degree, specialty seminar. *Entrance requirements:* For master's, GRE or MAT, interview, resume, 2 letters of recommendation; for other advanced degree, GRE or MAT, interview, professional experience, 2 letters of recommendation. Additional exam requirements/recommendations for international students: Required—TOEFL (minimum score 550 paper-based). Electronic applications accepted. *Faculty research:* Diversity in counseling.

Rivier University, School of Graduate Studies, Department of Education, Nashua, NH 03060. Offers curriculum and instruction (M Ed); early childhood education (M Ed); educational administration (M Ed); educational studies (M Ed); elementary education (M Ed); elementary education and general special education (M Ed); emotional and behavioral disorders (M Ed); general social education (M Ed); leadership and learning (Ed D, CAGS); learning disabilities (M Ed); learning disabilities and reading (M Ed); mental health counseling (MA); reading (M Ed); school counseling (M Ed). *Program availability:* Part-time, evening/weekend. *Degree requirements:* For master's, comprehensive exam (for some programs), internships. *Entrance requirements:* For master's, GRE General Test or MAT.

Roberts Wesleyan College, Graduate Psychology Programs, Rochester, NY 14624-1997. Offers clinical/school psychology (Psy D); school counseling (MS); school psychology (MS). *Program availability:* Part-time, evening/weekend. *Degree requirements:* For master's, comprehensive exam, PRAXIS II (for school psychology). *Entrance requirements:* For master's, GRE. Electronic applications accepted. Application fee is waived when completed online. *Faculty research:* Counselor supervision, forgiveness, community health psychology, applied research in group process.

Rollins College, Hamilton Holt School, Master of Arts in Counseling Program, Winter Park, FL 32789-4499. Offers clinical mental health counseling (MA). *Accreditation:* ACA. *Program availability:* Part-time, evening/weekend. *Faculty:* 4 full-time (2 women), 4 part-time/adjunct (3 women). *Students:* 54 full-time (47 women), 39 part-time (30 women); includes 35 minority (7 Black or African American, non-Hispanic/Latino; 1 American Indian or Alaska Native, non-Hispanic/Latino; 4 Asian, non-Hispanic/Latino; 19 Hispanic/Latino; 4 Two or more races, non-Hispanic/Latino), 2 international. Average age 31. 60 applicants, 78% accepted, 33 enrolled. In 2016, 16 master's awarded. *Degree requirements:* For master's, satisfactory completion of pre-practicum, practicum, and internship (1,000 hours total). *Entrance requirements:* For master's, GRE General Test or MAT, official transcripts, minimum GPA of 3.0, three letters of recommendation, essay, current resume. Additional exam requirements/recommendations for international students: Required—TOEFL (minimum score 550 paper-based; 80 iBT). *Application deadline:* For fall admission, 3/15 for domestic students. Application fee: $50. *Expenses:* $630 per credit hour. *Financial support:* In 2016–17, 25 students received support. Federal Work-Study, scholarships/grants, and unspecified assistantships available. Support available to part-time students. Financial award applicants required to submit FAFSA. *Unit head:* Dr. Kathryn Norsworthy, Faculty Director, 407-646-2132, E-mail: knorsworthy@rollins.edu. *Application contact:* 407-646-1568, Fax: 407-975-6430, E-mail: graduateeducation@rollins.edu.

Roosevelt University, Graduate Division, College of Education, Program in Counseling and Human Services, Chicago, IL 60605. Offers clinical mental health counseling (MA); school counseling (MA). *Accreditation:* ACA. *Students:* 55 full-time (45 women), 42 part-time (38 women); includes 45 minority (26 Black or African American, non-Hispanic/Latino; 1 Asian, non-Hispanic/Latino; 15 Hispanic/Latino; 3 Two or more races, non-Hispanic/Latino), 2 international. Average age 30. 66 applicants, 97% accepted, 29 enrolled. In 2016, 34 master's awarded. *Expenses: Tuition, area resident:* Full-time $19,566; part-time $880 per credit hour. *Required fees:* $175 per semester. One-time fee: $200. Part-time tuition and fees vary according to course load, degree level and program. *Application contact:* Angela Ryan, Director of Graduate Enrollment, 312-341-2420, Fax: 312-281-3356, E-mail: aryan@roosevelt.edu.

Rosemont College, Schools of Graduate and Professional Studies, Counseling Psychology Program, Rosemont, PA 19010-1699. Offers human services (MA); school counseling (MA). *Program availability:* Part-time, evening/weekend. *Degree requirements:* For master's, thesis or alternative, practicum. *Entrance requirements:* For master's, minimum undergraduate GPA of 3.0, 3 letters of recommendation. Additional exam requirements/recommendations for international students: Required—TOEFL. Electronic applications accepted. Application fee is waived when completed online. *Expenses:* Contact institution. *Faculty research:* Addictions counseling.

Rowan University, Graduate School, College of Education, Department of Educational Services and Leadership, Program in Counseling in Educational Settings, Glassboro, NJ 08028-1701. Offers MA. *Accreditation:* ACA. *Program availability:* Part-time, evening/weekend. *Degree requirements:* For master's, thesis. *Entrance requirements:* For master's, GRE General Test, minimum GPA of 2.8, 1 year of teaching experience. Additional exam requirements/recommendations for international students: Required—TOEFL. Electronic applications accepted.

Rutgers University–New Brunswick, Graduate School of Education, Department of Educational Psychology, Programs in School Counseling and Counseling Psychology, Piscataway, NJ 08854-8097. Offers Ed M. *Program availability:* Part-time, evening/weekend. *Entrance requirements:* For master's, GRE General Test, 3 letters of recommendation. Additional exam requirements/recommendations for international students: Required—TOEFL (minimum score 550 paper-based; 83 iBT). Electronic applications accepted. *Faculty research:* Children and family in cross-cultural context, attachment theory, multicultural counseling, therapy relationship.

Sage Graduate School, Esteves School of Education, Professional School Counseling Program, Troy, NY 12180-4115. Offers MS, Post Master's Certificate. *Accreditation:* NCATE. *Program availability:* Part-time, evening/weekend. *Faculty:* 17 full-time (13 women), 18 part-time/adjunct (12 women). *Students:* 28 full-time (25 women), 13 part-time (8 women); includes 6 minority (2 Black or African American, non-Hispanic/Latino; 1 Asian, non-Hispanic/Latino; 3 Hispanic/Latino). Average age 27. 41 applicants, 39% accepted, 8 enrolled. In 2016, 27 master's, 4 other advanced degrees awarded. *Entrance requirements:* For master's, minimum GPA of 2.75, current resume, essay, official transcripts, 2 letters of recommendation. Additional exam requirements/recommendations for international students: Required—TOEFL (minimum score 550 paper-based). *Application deadline:* Applications are processed on a rolling basis. Application fee: $40. *Expenses: Tuition:* Full-time $12,240; part-time $680 per credit hour. Tuition and fees vary according to degree level and program. *Financial support:* Fellowships, research assistantships, Federal Work-Study, scholarships/grants, and unspecified assistantships available. Support available to part-time students. Financial award application deadline: 3/1; financial award applicants required to submit FAFSA. *Faculty research:* Roles and responsibilities of guidance personnel, projections of need for guidance counselors. *Unit head:* Dr. John Pelizza, Interim Dean, Esteves School of Education, 518-244-2051, Fax: 518-244-2334, E-mail: pelizj@sage.edu. *Application contact:* Dr. Laurae Coburn, Assistant Professor, Education, 518-244-2401, Fax: 518-244-2334, E-mail: wartil@sage.edu.

St. Bonaventure University, School of Graduate Studies, School of Education, Program in Counselor Education, St. Bonaventure, NY 14778-2284. Offers community mental health counseling (MS Ed); rehabilitation counseling (MS Ed); school counseling (MS Ed); school counselor (Adv C). *Accreditation:* ACA. *Program availability:* Part-time, evening/weekend, 100% online. *Faculty:* 5 full-time (1 woman), 8 part-time/adjunct (6 women). *Students:* 53 full-time (40 women), 21 part-time (14 women); includes 6 minority (3 Black or African American, non-Hispanic/Latino; 3 Two or more races, non-Hispanic/Latino), 2 international. Average age 29. 64 applicants, 69% accepted, 29 enrolled. In 2016, 20 master's, 2 Adv Cs awarded. *Degree requirements:* For master's, comprehensive exam, thesis optional, internship, portfolio; for Adv C, internship. *Entrance requirements:* For master's, statement of intent/writing sample, transcripts from all colleges previously attended; two references; interview; minimum undergraduate GPA of 3.0; for Adv C, interview, writing sample, minimum undergraduate GPA of 3.0, two letters of recommendation, master's degree, transcripts from all colleges previously attended. Additional exam requirements/recommendations for international students: Required—TOEFL (minimum score 550 paper-based; 79 iBT). *Application deadline:* For fall admission, 3/15 priority date for domestic students, 2/1 priority date for international students; for spring admission, 11/15 priority date for domestic students, 7/1 priority date for international students. Applications are processed on a rolling basis. Application fee: $0. Electronic applications accepted. *Expenses:* $733 per credit, $100 graduation fee. *Financial support:* Career-related internships or fieldwork, Federal Work-Study, scholarships/grants, health care benefits, and unspecified assistantships available. Support available to part-time students. Financial award application deadline: 4/15; financial award applicants required to submit FAFSA. *Faculty research:* Balance between technology and personal contact in counselor education, special education and cyberbullying, school response to child abuse. *Unit head:* Dr. S. Alan Silliker, Director, 716-375-2368, Fax: 716-375-2360, E-mail: silliker@sbu.edu. *Application contact:* Bruce Campbell, Director of Graduate Admissions, 716-375-2429, Fax: 716-375-4015, E-mail: gradsch@sbu.edu.
Website: http://www.sbu.edu/academics/schools/education

St. Cloud State University, School of Graduate Studies, School of Education, Department of Educational Leadership and Higher Education, Program in College Counseling and Student Development, St. Cloud, MN 56301-4498. Offers MS. *Degree requirements:* For master's, comprehensive exam, thesis or alternative. *Entrance requirements:* For master's, GRE General Test, minimum GPA of 2.75. Additional exam requirements/recommendations for international students: Required—Michigan English Language Assessment Battery; Recommended—TOEFL (minimum score 550 paper-based), IELTS (minimum score 6.5). Electronic applications accepted.

Counselor Education

St. Cloud State University, School of Graduate Studies, School of Education, Department of Educational Leadership and Higher Education, Program in School Counseling, St. Cloud, MN 56301-4498. Offers MS. *Accreditation:* ACA; NCATE. *Degree requirements:* For master's, comprehensive exam (for some programs), thesis or alternative. *Entrance requirements:* For master's, GRE General Test, minimum GPA of 2.75. Additional exam requirements/recommendations for international students: Required—Michigan English Language Assessment Battery; Recommended—TOEFL (minimum score 550 paper-based), IELTS. Electronic applications accepted.

St. Edward's University, School of Education, Austin, TX 78704. Offers counseling (MA); education (Certificate). *Program availability:* Part-time, evening/weekend. *Degree requirements:* For master's, completion of required 60 hrs of coursework with a cumulative GPA of 3.0. *Entrance requirements:* For master's, GRE General Test, minimum GPA of 3.0 in last 60 hours or 2.75 overall. Additional exam requirements/recommendations for international students: Required—TOEFL (minimum score 79 iBT), IELTS (minimum score 6). Electronic applications accepted. *Expenses: Tuition:* Full-time $25,092; part-time $1394 per credit hour. *Required fees:* $75 per trimester. Full-time tuition and fees vary according to course load and program.

St. John's University, The School of Education, Department of Counselor Education, Program in School Counseling, Queens, NY 11439. Offers MS Ed, Adv C. *Accreditation:* ACA (one or more programs are accredited). *Program availability:* Part-time, evening/weekend. *Degree requirements:* For master's, comprehensive exam. *Entrance requirements:* For master's, bachelor's degree from accredited college or university, minimum GPA of 3.0, 2 letters of recommendation, interview, minimum of 18 credits in behavioral or social science; for Adv C, master's degree in counseling or related field, essay, official transcript showing minimum GPA of 3.0, 2 letters of recommendation, interview. Additional exam requirements/recommendations for international students: Required—TOEFL (minimum score 600 paper-based; 100 iBT), IELTS (minimum score 7). Electronic applications accepted. *Faculty research:* Counseling/client engagement; counseling accountability; pipe-line mentoring from grade 4 to college; stress, coping and resilience for children and adults; helping parents deal with aggressive children; effects of bullying and cyber bullying with adolescents; creative connections through the arts.

St. John's University, The School of Education, Department of Counselor Education, Program in School Counseling with Bilingual Extension, Queens, NY 11439. Offers MS Ed. *Program availability:* Part-time, evening/weekend. *Degree requirements:* For master's, comprehensive exam. *Entrance requirements:* For master's, GRE, New York State Bilingual Assessment (BEA), bachelor's degree from an accredited college or university, minimum GPA of 3.0, 2 letters of recommendation, interview, minimum of 18 credits in behavioral or social science. Additional exam requirements/recommendations for international students: Required—TOEFL (minimum score 600 paper-based; 100 iBT), IELTS (minimum score 7). Electronic applications accepted. *Faculty research:* Cross-cultural comparisons of predictors of active coping.

St. John's University, The School of Education, Department of Education Specialties, Queens, NY 11439. Offers clinical mental health counseling (MS Ed, Adv C); literacy (MS Ed, PhD, Adv C), including literacy (PhD), teaching literacy (Adv C), teaching literacy 5-12 (MS Ed), teaching literacy B-12 (MS Ed), teaching literacy B-6 (MS Ed), teaching literacy B-6 and children with disabilities (MS Ed); school counseling (MS Ed, Adv C); school counseling with bilingual extension (MS Ed); teaching children with disabilities in childhood education (MS Ed, Adv C); teaching English to speakers of other languages and bilingual education (MS Ed, Adv C). *Program availability:* Part-time, evening/weekend, online learning. *Degree requirements:* For master's, one foreign language, comprehensive exam, thesis, internship; for doctorate, one foreign language, comprehensive exam, thesis/dissertation. *Entrance requirements:* For master's, minimum GPA of 3.0, 2 letters of recommendation, interview, minimum of 18 credits in behavioral science, bachelor's degree; for doctorate, MAT, GRE General Test (analytical), official transcript showing conferral of degree with minimum GPA of 3.2, 2 letters of recommendation, statement of goals, resume, evidence of teaching experience, interview; for Adv C, statement of goals, official transcript showing conferral of degree with minimum GPA of 3.0, 2 letters of recommendation, interview. Additional exam requirements/recommendations for international students: Required—TOEFL (minimum score 600 paper-based; 100 iBT), IELTS (minimum score 7). Electronic applications accepted. *Faculty research:* Assisting troubled children and teens with substance abuse, truancy, and coping skills; literacy development for ESL learners; investigating Caribbean and Creole language and culture.

St. Lawrence University, Department of Education, Program in Counseling and Human Development, Canton, NY 13617. Offers mental health counseling (MS); school counseling (M Ed, CAS). *Program availability:* Part-time, evening/weekend. *Entrance requirements:* For master's, GRE General Test. *Faculty research:* Defense mechanisms and mediation.

Saint Louis University, Graduate Education, College of Education and Public Service and Graduate Education, Department of Counseling and Family Therapy, St. Louis, MO 63103. Offers counseling and family therapy (PhD); human development counseling (MA); marriage and family therapy (Certificate); school counseling (MA, MA-R). *Accreditation:* AAMFT/COAMFTE; NCATE. *Program availability:* Part-time. *Degree requirements:* For master's, comprehensive exam, thesis (for some programs); for doctorate, comprehensive exam, thesis/dissertation, preliminary oral and written exams. *Entrance requirements:* For master's, GRE General Test, letters of recommendation, resume; for doctorate, GRE General Test, letters of recommendation, resumé, transcripts, goal statement. Additional exam requirements/recommendations for international students: Required—TOEFL (minimum score 550 paper-based). Electronic applications accepted. *Faculty research:* Medical family therapy/collaborative health care multicultural counseling, mental health needs of diverse, minority, or Immigrant/refugee populations, divorce, aging families.

Saint Mary's College of California, Kalmanovitz School of Education, Program in Counseling, Moraga, CA 94575. Offers career counseling (MA); college student services (Credential); general counseling (MA); marriage and family therapy (MA); pupil personnel services (Credential), including school counseling, school psychology; school counseling (MA); school psychology (MA). *Program availability:* Part-time, evening/weekend. *Degree requirements:* For master's, thesis or alternative. *Entrance requirements:* For master's, interview, minimum GPA of 3.0. *Faculty research:* Counselor training effectiveness, multicultural development, empathy, the interface of spirituality and psychotherapy, gender issues.

St. Mary's University, Graduate Studies, Program in Counselor Education and Supervision, San Antonio, TX 78228-8507. Offers PhD. *Accreditation:* ACA. *Program availability:* Part-time, evening/weekend. *Students:* 19 full-time (15 women), 31 part-time (22 women); includes 19 minority (3 Black or African American, non-Hispanic/Latino; 2 Asian, non-Hispanic/Latino; 14 Hispanic/Latino), 13 international. Average age 38. 9 applicants. In 2016, 9 doctorates awarded. *Degree requirements:* For doctorate, comprehensive exam, thesis/dissertation, internship. *Entrance requirements:* For doctorate, GRE General Test, master's degree in counseling or related area from accredited college or university; recommendations from past employers relating to professional counseling experience, as well as from faculties of previous undergraduate/graduate studies; recommendation from Graduate Admissions Committee. Additional exam requirements/recommendations for international students: Required—TOEFL (minimum score 550 paper-based; 80 iBT), IELTS (minimum score 6). *Application deadline:* For fall admission, 7/1 for domestic students; for spring admission, 11/15 for domestic students; for summer admission, 4/1 for domestic students. Applications are processed on a rolling basis. Application fee: $0. Electronic applications accepted. *Expenses: Tuition:* Full-time $15,600; part-time $865 per credit hour. *Required fees:* $148 per semester. *Financial support:* Fellowships, research assistantships, career-related internships or fieldwork, Federal Work-Study, institutionally sponsored loans, scholarships/grants, health care benefits, and unspecified assistantships available. Financial award application deadline: 3/31; financial award applicants required to submit FAFSA. *Faculty research:* Palliative care, neuroscience of psychology and religion, cranial electrotherapy, EEG biofeedback. *Unit head:* Dr. Melanie Harper, Program Director, 210-438-6400, E-mail: mharper@stmarytx.edu. *Application contact:* Kim Thornton, Director, Graduate and Adult Enrollment Services, 210-436-3101, E-mail: kthornton@stmarytx.edu.
Website: https://www.stmarytx.edu/academics/graduate/doctoral-programs/counselor-education/

Saint Peter's University, Graduate Programs in Education, Program in School Counseling, Jersey City, NJ 07306-5997. Offers MA, Certificate.

St. Thomas University, Biscayne College, Department of Social Sciences and Counseling, Program in Guidance and Counseling, Miami Gardens, FL 33054-6459. Offers MS, Post-Master's Certificate. *Program availability:* Part-time, evening/weekend. *Degree requirements:* For master's, comprehensive exam. *Entrance requirements:* For master's, interview, minimum GPA of 3.0 or GRE. Additional exam requirements/recommendations for international students: Required—TOEFL (minimum score 550 paper-based; 79 iBT). Electronic applications accepted.

Saint Xavier University, Graduate Studies, School of Education, Program in Counseling, Chicago, IL 60655-3105. Offers MA. *Degree requirements:* For master's, practicum, internship. *Entrance requirements:* For master's, 3 letters of recommendation, interview. Additional exam requirements/recommendations for international students: Required—TOEFL. Electronic applications accepted.

Salem College, Department of Education, Winston-Salem, NC 27101. Offers art education (MAT); elementary education (M Ed, MAT); language and literacy (M Ed); middle school education (MAT); school counseling (M Ed); second language studies (MAT); secondary education (MAT); special education (M Ed, MAT). *Accreditation:* NCATE. *Program availability:* Part-time, evening/weekend, online learning. *Degree requirements:* For master's, practicum (MAT), project (M Ed), oral and written comprehensive exams. *Entrance requirements:* For master's, minimum GPA of 2.5. *Faculty research:* Content area reading strategies, literacy development, brain compatible instruction.

Salem State University, School of Graduate Studies, Program in School Counseling, Salem, MA 01970-5353. Offers M Ed. *Accreditation:* NCATE. *Program availability:* Part-time, evening/weekend. *Entrance requirements:* For master's, GRE or MAT. Additional exam requirements/recommendations for international students: Required—TOEFL (minimum score 550 paper-based; 80 iBT) or IELTS (minimum score 5.5).

Sam Houston State University, College of Education, Department of Counseling, Huntsville, TX 77341. Offers M Ed, MA, PhD. *Accreditation:* NCATE. *Program availability:* Part-time, online learning. *Degree requirements:* For master's, thesis optional; for doctorate, comprehensive exam, thesis/dissertation. *Entrance requirements:* For master's, GRE General Test, 3.0 GPA, Three References, Essay, Face-to-Face interview; for doctorate, On-site interview, on-site professional presentation, and on-site writing prompt, Personal statement, Five References, Master's Degree with 3.5 GPA. Additional exam requirements/recommendations for international students: Required—TOEFL (minimum score 550 paper-based; 79 iBT), IELTS (minimum score 6.5). Electronic applications accepted. *Faculty research:* Family counseling, career counseling, business emergent counseling.

San Diego State University, Graduate and Research Affairs, College of Education, Department of Counseling and School Psychology, San Diego, CA 92182. Offers MS. *Accreditation:* NCATE. *Program availability:* Evening/weekend. *Degree requirements:* For master's, comprehensive exam (for some programs), thesis (for some programs). *Entrance requirements:* For master's, GRE General Test, interview, letters of reference. Additional exam requirements/recommendations for international students: Required—TOEFL. Electronic applications accepted. *Faculty research:* Multicultural and cross-cultural counseling and training, AIDS counseling.

San Francisco State University, Division of Graduate Studies, College of Health and Social Sciences, Department of Counseling, San Francisco, CA 94132-1722. Offers clinical rehabilitation and mental health counseling (MS); counseling (MS); marriage, family, and child counseling (MSC); school counseling (Credential). *Accreditation:* ACA (one or more programs are accredited). *Program availability:* Part-time. *Application deadline:* Applications are processed on a rolling basis. *Expenses:* Tuition, state resident: full-time $6738. Tuition, nonresident: full-time $15,666. *Required fees:* $1012. Tuition and fees vary according to degree level and program. *Unit head:* Dr. Graciela Orozco, Chair, 415-338-2005, Fax: 415-338-0594, E-mail: counsel@sfsu.edu. *Application contact:* Dr. Alison Cerezo, College Counseling Coordinator, 415-338-1064, Fax: 415-338-0594, E-mail: acerezo@sfsu.edu.
Website: http://counseling.sfsu.edu

San Jose State University, Graduate Studies and Research, Connie L. Lurie College of Education, San Jose, CA 95192-0001. Offers child and adolescent development (MA); common core mathematics (K-8) (Certificate, Credential); education (MA, Credential), including counseling and student personnel (MA), speech pathology (MA); educational leadership (MA, Ed D, Credential), including administration and supervision (MA), higher education (MA), preliminary administrative services (Credential), professional administrative services (Credential); elementary education (MA), including curriculum and instruction; K-12 school counseling (Credential); K-12 school counseling internship (Credential); school child welfare attendance (Credential); single subject (Credential). *Accreditation:* NCATE. *Program availability:* Evening/weekend. Electronic applications accepted.

Santa Clara University, School of Education and Counseling Psychology, Santa Clara, CA 95053. Offers Catholic school teaching (MA); counseling (MA); counseling psychology (MA); educational leadership (MA); interdisciplinary education (MA); teaching multiple subjects (MA); teaching single subjects (MA). *Program availability:* Part-time, evening/weekend. *Faculty:* 32 full-time (22 women), 40 part-time/adjunct (25 women). *Students:* 265 full-time (213 women), 333 part-time (270 women); includes 282 minority (16 Black or African American, non-Hispanic/Latino; 1 American Indian or Alaska Native, non-Hispanic/Latino; 78 Asian, non-Hispanic/Latino; 156 Hispanic/Latino; 31 Two or more races, non-Hispanic/Latino), 46 international. Average age 30. 266 applicants, 74% accepted, 126 enrolled. In 2016, 253 master's awarded. *Entrance requirements:* For master's, transcript, letters of recommendation, statement of purpose, resume. Additional exam requirements/recommendations for international students: Required—TOEFL (minimum score 90 iBT) or IELTS (6.5). *Application deadline:* Applications are processed on a rolling basis. Application fee: $50. Electronic

applications accepted. *Expenses:* $581 per unit. *Financial support:* Fellowships, research assistantships, teaching assistantships, career-related internships or fieldwork, Federal Work-Study, scholarships/grants, traineeships, health care benefits, and tuition waivers available. Support available to part-time students. Financial award applicants required to submit FAFSA. *Unit head:* Dr. Sabrina Zirkel, Dean, 408-551-3074, Fax: 408-554-4367, E-mail: szirkel@scu.edu. *Application contact:* Victoria Rodriguez, Graduate Admissions Advisor, 408-554-4723, E-mail: v1rodriguez@scu.edu.
Website: http://www.scu.edu/ecp/

Seattle Pacific University, Master of Education in School Counseling Program, Seattle, WA 98119-1997. Offers M Ed, Certificate. *Accreditation:* ACA; NCATE. *Program availability:* Part-time. *Degree requirements:* For master's, year-long internship. *Entrance requirements:* For master's, GRE General Test or MAT, copy of teaching certificate; official transcript(s) from each college/university attended; resume; personal statement, including long-term professional goals (maximum of 500 words); 2 letters of recommendation. Electronic applications accepted. *Expenses:* Contact institution.

Seattle Pacific University, PhD in Counselor Education Program, Seattle, WA 98119-1997. Offers PhD. *Entrance requirements:* For doctorate, GRE (minimum revised score of 153 Verbal, 152 Quantitative, taken within five years of application; minimum combined score of 1200 on old test), official transcripts, personal statement, four recent letters of recommendation, writing sample, resume.

Seattle University, College of Education, Program in Counseling and School Psychology, Seattle, WA 98122-1090. Offers MA, Certificate, Ed S. *Accreditation:* ACA; NCATE. *Program availability:* Part-time, evening/weekend. *Faculty:* 11 full-time (6 women), 3 part-time/adjunct (2 women). *Students:* 75 full-time (65 women), 142 part-time (119 women); includes 73 minority (13 Black or African American, non-Hispanic/Latino; 3 American Indian or Alaska Native, non-Hispanic/Latino; 15 Asian, non-Hispanic/Latino; 30 Hispanic/Latino; 12 Two or more races, non-Hispanic/Latino), 4 international. Average age 30. 207 applicants, 43% accepted, 52 enrolled. In 2016, 36 master's, 20 other advanced degrees awarded. *Degree requirements:* For master's, comprehensive exam. *Entrance requirements:* For master's, interview; GRE, MAT, or minimum GPA of 3.0; related work experience. Additional exam requirements/recommendations for international students: Required—TOEFL. *Application deadline:* For fall admission, 7/1 for domestic students; for winter admission, 10/20 for domestic students; for spring admission, 1/20 for domestic students. Application fee: $55. *Financial support:* In 2016–17, 20 students received support. *Unit head:* Hutch Haney, Director, 206-296-5750, E-mail: schpsy@seattleu.edu. *Application contact:* Janet Shandley, Associate Dean of Graduate Admissions, 206-296-5900, Fax: 206-298-5656, E-mail: grad_admissions@seattleu.edu.

Seton Hall University, College of Education and Human Services, Department of Professional Psychology and Family Therapy, Program in Counseling Psychology, South Orange, NJ 07079-2697. Offers counseling psychology (PhD); school counseling (MA). *Accreditation:* APA. *Faculty:* 10 full-time (7 women). *Students:* 40 full-time (30 women), 203 part-time (170 women). Average age 32. 133 applicants, 39% accepted, 28 enrolled. In 2016, 9 master's, 14 doctorates awarded. *Degree requirements:* For doctorate, comprehensive exam, thesis/dissertation, internship. *Entrance requirements:* For master's and doctorate, GRE, interview. *Application deadline:* For fall admission, 1/15 for domestic students. Application fee: $50. *Financial support:* In 2016–17, 1 research assistantship with full tuition reimbursement (averaging $4,500 per year) was awarded; career-related internships or fieldwork also available. Financial award application deadline: 2/1. *Faculty research:* Vocational indecision, coping skills, cognitive behavioral interventions, vocational development. *Unit head:* Dr. Ben Beitin, Chair, 973-761-9451, E-mail: beitinbe@shu.edu. *Application contact:* Diana Minakakis, Director of Graduate Admissions, 973-275-2824, Fax: 973-275-2181, E-mail: diana.minakakis@shu.edu.
Website: http://www.shu.edu/academics/education/professional-psychology/

Shippensburg University of Pennsylvania, School of Graduate Studies, College of Education and Human Services, Department of Counseling, Shippensburg, PA 17257-2299. Offers clinical mental health (MS); college counseling (MS); college student personnel (MS); counselor education and supervision (Ed D); couple and family counseling (Certificate); school counseling (M Ed). *Accreditation:* ACA (one or more programs are accredited); NCATE. *Program availability:* Part-time, evening/weekend, blended/hybrid learning. *Faculty:* 8 full-time (3 women), 6 part-time/adjunct (4 women). *Students:* 90 full-time (76 women), 57 part-time (45 women); includes 35 minority (21 Black or African American, non-Hispanic/Latino; 1 Asian, non-Hispanic/Latino; 10 Hispanic/Latino; 3 Two or more races, non-Hispanic/Latino), 5 international. Average age 28. 115 applicants, 44% accepted, 34 enrolled. In 2016, 51 master's awarded. *Degree requirements:* For master's, fieldwork, research project, internship, candidacy; for doctorate, thesis/dissertation, practicum, internship. *Entrance requirements:* For master's, GRE or MAT (for MS if GPA is less than 2.75), minimum GPA of 2.75 (3.0 for M Ed), resume, 3 letter of recommendation forms, one year of relevant work experience, on-campus interview, autobiographical statement; for doctorate, master's degree in counseling or related discipline; resume; three recommendation letters (1 from employer; 1 from clinical supervisor, 1 from prior graduate school faculty member); personal essay; interview with department chair. Additional exam requirements/recommendations for international students: Required—TOEFL (minimum score 550 paper-based, 68 iBT) or IELTS (minimum score 6). *Application deadline:* Applications are processed on a rolling basis. Application fee: $45. Electronic applications accepted. *Expenses:* Tuition, state resident: part-time $483 per credit. Tuition, nonresident: part-time $725 per credit. *Required fees:* $141 per credit. *Financial support:* In 2016–17, 62 students received support. Career-related internships or fieldwork, scholarships/grants, unspecified assistantships, and resident hall director and student payroll positions available. Support available to part-time students. Financial award application deadline: 3/1; financial award applicants required to submit FAFSA. *Unit head:* Dr. Kurt L. Kraus, Departmental Chair and Program Coordinator, 717-477-1603, Fax: 717-477-4016, E-mail: klkrau@ship.edu. *Application contact:* Megan N. Luft, Assistant Dean of Graduate Admissions, 717-477-1231, Fax: 717-477-4016, E-mail: mnluft@ship.edu.
Website: http://www.ship.edu/counsel/

Simon Fraser University, Office of Graduate Studies and Postdoctoral Fellows, Faculty of Education, Program in Counseling Psychology, Burnaby, BC V5A 1S6, Canada. Offers M Ed, MA. *Program availability:* Part-time, evening/weekend. *Faculty:* 6 full-time (3 women). *Students:* 11 full-time (9 women). 74 applicants, 26% accepted, 9 enrolled. *Degree requirements:* For master's, comprehensive exam (for some programs), thesis (for some programs), practicum. *Entrance requirements:* For master's, minimum GPA of 3.0 (on scale of 4.33) or 3.33 based on last 60 credits of undergraduate courses. Additional exam requirements/recommendations for international students: Recommended—TOEFL (minimum score 580 paper-based; 93 iBT), IELTS (minimum score 7), TWE (minimum score 5). *Application deadline:* For fall admission, 1/15 for domestic and international students. Application fee: $90 ($125 for international students). Electronic applications accepted. *Financial support:* In 2016–17, fellowships (averaging $6,250 per year) were awarded; research assistantships, teaching assistantships, career-related internships or fieldwork, and scholarships/grants also available. *Faculty research:* Cultural and personal dimensions in psychological development, and psychology of working; and career development, social justice and multicultural competence issues, traumatic stress studies, counselor education. *Unit head:* Dr. Shawn Bullock, Associate Dean, Graduate Studies in Education, 778-782-4102, Fax: 778-782-4320, E-mail: mesbit@sfu.ca. *Application contact:* Bridget Fox, Graduate Secretary, 778-782-4215, E-mail: educmast@sfu.ca.

Slippery Rock University of Pennsylvania, Graduate Studies (Recruitment), College of Education, Department of Counseling and Development, Slippery Rock, PA 16057-1383. Offers clinical mental health (MA); school counseling (M Ed); student affairs in higher education (MA); student affairs in higher education with college counseling (MA). *Accreditation:* ACA (one or more programs are accredited); NCATE. *Program availability:* Part-time, evening/weekend. *Faculty:* 7 full-time (5 women), 1 (woman) part-time/adjunct. *Students:* 86 full-time (55 women), 23 part-time (18 women); includes 13 minority (7 Black or African American, non-Hispanic/Latino; 4 Hispanic/Latino; 2 Two or more races, non-Hispanic/Latino), 1 international. Average age 28. 107 applicants, 57% accepted, 42 enrolled. In 2016, 39 master's awarded. *Degree requirements:* For master's, comprehensive exam, thesis (for some programs). *Entrance requirements:* For master's, GRE General Test or MAT, official transcripts, personal statement, three letters of recommendation, interview. Additional exam requirements/recommendations for international students: Required—TOEFL (minimum score 550 paper-based; 80 iBT). *Application deadline:* For fall admission, 1/15 priority date for domestic and international students. Applications are processed on a rolling basis. Application fee: $25 ($30 for international students). Electronic applications accepted. *Expenses:* $646.50 per credit in-state, $936.80 per credit out-of-state; $581.45 per online credit in-state, $648.65 per online credit out-of-state. *Financial support:* In 2016–17, 58 students received support. Career-related internships or fieldwork, Federal Work-Study, institutionally sponsored loans, scholarships/grants, tuition waivers (partial), and unspecified assistantships available. Support available to part-time students. Financial award application deadline: 5/1; financial award applicants required to submit FAFSA. *Unit head:* Dr. Stacy Jacob, Graduate Coordinator, 724-738-2758, Fax: 724-738-4859, E-mail: stacy.jacob@sru.edu. *Application contact:* Brandi Weber-Mortimer, Director of Graduate Admissions, 724-738-2051, Fax: 724-738-2146, E-mail: graduate.admissions@sru.edu.
Website: http://www.sru.edu/academics/colleges-and-departments/coe/departments/counseling-and-development

South Carolina State University, College of Graduate and Professional Studies, Department of Education, Orangeburg, SC 29117-0001. Offers early childhood education (MAT); education (M Ed); elementary education (M Ed, MAT); English (MAT); general science/biology (MAT); mathematics (MAT); secondary education (M Ed), including biology education, business education, counselor education, English education, home economics education, industrial education, mathematics education, science education, social studies education; special education (M Ed), including emotionally handicapped, learning disabilities, mentally handicapped. *Accreditation:* NCATE. *Program availability:* Part-time, evening/weekend. *Faculty:* 12 full-time (8 women), 3 part-time/adjunct (1 woman). *Students:* 28 full-time (20 women), 20 part-time (17 women); includes 45 minority (44 Black or African American, non-Hispanic/Latino; 1 Two or more races, non-Hispanic/Latino). Average age 31. 22 applicants, 100% accepted, 16 enrolled. In 2016, 9 master's awarded. *Degree requirements:* For master's, thesis optional, departmental qualifying exam. *Entrance requirements:* For master's, GRE General Test, NTE, interview, teaching certificate. *Application deadline:* For fall admission, 6/15 priority date for domestic students, 6/15 for international students; for spring admission, 11/1 for domestic and international students. Application fee: $25. Electronic applications accepted. *Expenses:* Tuition, state resident: full-time $8938; part-time $579 per credit hour. Tuition, nonresident: full-time $19,018; part-time $1139 per credit hour. *Required fees:* $1482; $82 per credit hour. *Financial support:* Fellowships, career-related internships or fieldwork, Federal Work-Study, and scholarships/grants available. Financial award application deadline: 6/1. *Unit head:* Dr. Charlie Spell, Interim Chair, Department of Education, 803-536-8963, Fax: 803-516-4568, E-mail: cspell@scsu.edu. *Application contact:* Curtis Foskey, Coordinator of Graduate Studies, 803-536-8419, Fax: 803-536-8812, E-mail: cfoskey@scsu.edu.

South Carolina State University, College of Graduate and Professional Studies, Department of Human Services, Orangeburg, SC 29117-0001. Offers counselor education (M Ed); rehabilitation counseling (MA). *Accreditation:* CORE. *Program availability:* Part-time, evening/weekend. *Faculty:* 8 full-time (6 women), 1 (woman) part-time/adjunct. *Students:* 81 full-time (65 women), 21 part-time (16 women); includes 97 minority (all Black or African American, non-Hispanic/Latino). Average age 33. 40 applicants, 85% accepted, 32 enrolled. In 2016, 54 master's awarded. *Degree requirements:* For master's, comprehensive exam (for some programs), departmental qualifying exam, internship. *Entrance requirements:* For master's, GRE, MAT, minimum GPA of 2.7. *Application deadline:* For fall admission, 6/15 priority date for domestic students, 6/15 for international students; for spring admission, 11/1 for domestic and international students. Application fee: $25. Electronic applications accepted. *Expenses:* Tuition, state resident: full-time $8938; part-time $579 per credit hour. Tuition, nonresident: full-time $19,018; part-time $1139 per credit hour. *Required fees:* $1482; $82 per credit hour. *Financial support:* Fellowships, career-related internships or fieldwork, scholarships/grants, and unspecified assistantships available. Financial award application deadline: 6/1. *Unit head:* Dr. Michelle Maultsby-Priester, Interim Chair, Department of Human Services, 803-536-7075, Fax: 803-533-3636, E-mail: mmaultsb@scsu.edu. *Application contact:* Curtis Foskey, Coordinator of Graduate Admissions, 803-536-8419, Fax: 803-536-8812, E-mail: cfoskey@scsu.edu.

South Dakota State University, Graduate School, College of Education and Human Sciences, Department of Counseling and Human Development, Brookings, SD 57007. Offers counseling and human resource development (M Ed, MS); human sciences (MS). *Accreditation:* ACA (one or more programs are accredited); NCATE. *Program availability:* Part-time, evening/weekend. *Degree requirements:* For master's, comprehensive exam, thesis (for some programs), oral exams. *Entrance requirements:* For master's, minimum GPA of 2.75. Additional exam requirements/recommendations for international students: Required—TOEFL (minimum score 525 paper-based; 71 iBT). *Faculty research:* Rural mental health, family issues, character education, student affairs, solution focused therapy.

Southeastern Louisiana University, College of Nursing and Health Sciences, Department of Health and Human Sciences, Hammond, LA 70402. Offers communication sciences and disorders (MS); counseling (MS). *Accreditation:* ACA; ASHA; NCATE. *Faculty:* 15 full-time (14 women), 4 part-time/adjunct (all women). *Students:* 98 full-time (89 women), 43 part-time (42 women); includes 33 minority (13 Black or African American, non-Hispanic/Latino; 1 American Indian or Alaska Native, non-Hispanic/Latino; 8 Hispanic/Latino; 1 Native Hawaiian or other Pacific Islander, non-Hispanic/Latino; 10 Two or more races, non-Hispanic/Latino), 1 international. Average age 27. 204 applicants, 58% accepted, 26 enrolled. In 2016, 44 master's awarded. *Degree requirements:* For master's, comprehensive exam, thesis optional, 25 clock hours of clinical observation. *Entrance requirements:* Additional exam requirements/recommendations for international students: Required—TOEFL (minimum score 500 paper-based; 61 iBT). *Application deadline:* For fall admission, 3/1 priority date for domestic students, 6/1 priority date for international students; for spring admission, 10/1 priority date for domestic and international students. Applications are processed on a rolling basis. Application fee: $20 ($30 for international students). Electronic applications

accepted. *Expenses:* Tuition, state resident: full-time $6540; part-time $465 per credit hour. Tuition, nonresident: full-time $19,017; part-time $1158 per credit hour. *Required fees:* $1829. *Financial support:* In 2016–17, 6 students received support. Research assistantships, teaching assistantships, career-related internships or fieldwork, Federal Work-Study, institutionally sponsored loans, scholarships/grants, and unspecified assistantships available. Support available to part-time students. Financial award application deadline: 5/1; financial award applicants required to submit FAFSA. *Faculty research:* School counseling, play therapy, family counseling, grief counseling, transformational teaching. *Unit head:* Dr. Jacqueline Guendouzi, Department Head, 985-549-2309, Fax: 985-549-3758, E-mail: jguendouzi@southeastern.edu. *Application contact:* Amanda Harper, Graduate Admissions Analyst, 985-549-5620, Fax: 985-549-5632, E-mail: admissions@southeastern.edu.
Website: http://www.southeastern.edu/acad_research/depts/hhs/index.html

Southeastern Oklahoma State University, School of Behavioral Sciences, Durant, OK 74701-0609. Offers clinical mental health counseling (MS). *Accreditation:* ACA. *Program availability:* Part-time, evening/weekend. *Degree requirements:* For master's, comprehensive exam, thesis optional. *Entrance requirements:* For master's, GRE General Test, minimum GPA of 3.0 in last 60 hours or 2.75 overall. Additional exam requirements/recommendations for international students: Required—TOEFL (minimum score 550 paper-based; 79 iBT). Electronic applications accepted.

Southeastern Oklahoma State University, School of Education, Durant, OK 74701-0609. Offers math specialist (M Ed); reading specialist (M Ed); school administration (M Ed); school counseling (M Ed). *Accreditation:* NCATE. *Program availability:* Part-time, evening/weekend. *Degree requirements:* For master's, comprehensive exam, thesis optional, portfolio (M Ed). *Entrance requirements:* For master's, GRE General Test (for school counseling), minimum GPA of 3.0 in last 60 hours or 2.75 overall. Additional exam requirements/recommendations for international students: Required—TOEFL (minimum score 550 paper-based; 79 iBT). Electronic applications accepted.

Southeastern University, College of Behavioral and Social Sciences, Lakeland, FL 33801-6099. Offers human services (MA); international community development (MA); marriage and family counseling (MS); professional counseling (MS); school counseling (MS); social work (MSW). *Program availability:* Evening/weekend. *Expenses: Tuition:* Full-time $9450; part-time $6300 per credit. *Required fees:* $500; $250 per semester. One-time fee: $150. Tuition and fees vary according to degree level, campus/location and program. *Unit head:* Erica H. Sirrine, Dean, 863-667-5341, E-mail: ehsirrine@seu.edu.
Website: http://www.seu.edu/behavior/

Southeast Missouri State University, School of Graduate Studies, Department of Educational Leadership and Counseling, Counseling Program, Cape Girardeau, MO 63701-4799. Offers career counseling (MA); mental health counseling (MA); school counseling (MA). *Accreditation:* ACA; NCATE. *Program availability:* Part-time, evening/weekend. *Faculty:* 5 full-time (4 women), 2 part-time/adjunct (both women). *Students:* 33 full-time (24 women), 39 part-time (36 women); includes 6 minority (4 Black or African American, non-Hispanic/Latino; 2 American Indian or Alaska Native, non-Hispanic/Latino), 1 international. Average age 33. 48 applicants, 67% accepted, 31 enrolled. In 2016, 44 master's, 7 other advanced degrees awarded. *Degree requirements:* For master's and Ed S, comprehensive exam, thesis or alternative. *Entrance requirements:* For master's, personal essay, interview, minimum GPA of 3.5; for Ed S, minimum graduate GPA of 3.7. Additional exam requirements/recommendations for international students: Required—TOEFL (minimum score 550 paper-based; 79 iBT), IELTS (minimum score 6), PTE (minimum score 53). *Application deadline:* For fall admission, 3/1 for domestic and international students; for spring admission, 11/21 for domestic students, 10/1 for international students; for summer admission, 3/1 for domestic students. Applications are processed on a rolling basis. Application fee: $30 ($40 for international students). Electronic applications accepted. *Expenses:* Tuition, state resident: full-time $3130; part-time $260.80 per credit hour. Tuition, nonresident: full-time $5842; part-time $486.80 per credit hour. *Required fees:* $33.70 per credit hour. *Financial support:* In 2016–17, 10 students received support. Career-related internships or fieldwork, Federal Work-Study, scholarships/grants, traineeships, tuition waivers (full), and unspecified assistantships available. Financial award application deadline: 6/30; financial award applicants required to submit FAFSA. *Faculty research:* School counseling, mental health, career and family counseling, social justice and spirituality in counseling. *Unit head:* Dr. C. P. Gause, Department Chair, 573-651-2137, Fax: 573-986-6512, E-mail: cpgause@semo.edu. *Application contact:* Dr. Melissa Odegard-Koester, Associate Professor, 573-651-2420, Fax: 573-986-6512, E-mail: modegard@semo.edu.
Website: http://www.semo.edu/eduleadcounsel/

Southern Adventist University, School of Education and Psychology, Collegedale, TN 37315-0370. Offers clinical mental health counseling (MS); inclusive education (MS Ed); instructional leadership (MS Ed); literacy education (MS Ed); outdoor teacher education (MS Ed); school counseling (MS). *Accreditation:* NCATE. *Program availability:* Part-time, evening/weekend. *Degree requirements:* For master's, comprehensive exam (for some programs), thesis optional, position paper (MS), portfolio (MS Ed in outdoor teacher education). *Entrance requirements:* For master's, interview (MS); 9 semester hours of upper-division course work in psychology or related field, including 1 course in psychology research or statistics; 9 semester hours of education (MS Ed). Additional exam requirements/recommendations for international students: Required—TOEFL (minimum score 600 paper-based; 100 iBT). Electronic applications accepted.

Southern Arkansas University–Magnolia, School of Graduate Studies, Magnolia, AR 71753. Offers agriculture (MS); business administration (MBA), including agri-business, social entrepreneurship, supply chain management; clinical and mental health counseling (MS); computer and information sciences (MS), including cyber security and privacy, data science, information technology; gifted and talented (M Ed), including curriculum and instruction, educational administration and supervision, gifted and talented P-8/7-12, instructional specialist P-4; higher, adult and lifelong education (M Ed); kinesiology (M Ed), including coaching; library media and information specialist (M Ed); public administration (MPA); school counseling K-12 (M Ed); student affairs and college counseling (M Ed); teaching (MAT). *Accreditation:* NCATE. *Program availability:* Part-time, 100% online, blended/hybrid learning. *Faculty:* 36 full-time (19 women), 33 part-time/adjunct (14 women). *Students:* 605 full-time (143 women), 879 part-time (352 women); includes 130 minority (113 Black or African American, non-Hispanic/Latino; 7 American Indian or Alaska Native, non-Hispanic/Latino; 2 Asian, non-Hispanic/Latino; 2 Hispanic/Latino; 6 Two or more races, non-Hispanic/Latino), 1,048 international. Average age 28. 904 applicants, 81% accepted, 262 enrolled. In 2016, 278 master's awarded. *Degree requirements:* For master's, comprehensive exam (for some programs), thesis optional. *Entrance requirements:* For master's, GRE, MAT or GMAT, minimum GPA of 2.5. Additional exam requirements/recommendations for international students: Required—TOEFL (minimum score 550 paper-based), IELTS (minimum score 6). *Application deadline:* For fall admission, 7/20 for domestic students, 7/10 for international students; for spring admission, 12/1 for domestic students, 11/15 for international students; for summer admission, 4/1 for domestic students, 5/1 for international students. Applications are processed on a rolling basis. Application fee: $25 ($50 for international students). Electronic applications accepted. *Expenses:* Tuition, state resident: full-time $2511; part-time $279 per credit hour. Tuition, nonresident: full-time $3726; part-time $414 per credit hour. *Required fees:* $307 per semester. Tuition and fees vary according to course load and program. *Financial support:* Career-related internships or fieldwork, Federal Work-Study, scholarships/grants, tuition waivers (full), and unspecified assistantships available. Financial award applicants required to submit FAFSA. *Faculty research:* Alternative certification for teachers, supervision of instruction, instructional leadership, counseling. *Unit head:* Dr. Kim Bloss, Dean, School of Graduate Studies, 870-235-4150, Fax: 870-235-5227, E-mail: kkbloss@saumag.edu. *Application contact:* Shrijana Malakar, Admissions Specialist, 870-235-4150, Fax: 870-235-5227, E-mail: smalakar@saumag.edu.
Website: http://www.saumag.edu/graduate

Southern Connecticut State University, School of Graduate Studies, School of Education, Department of Counseling and School Psychology, New Haven, CT 06515-1355. Offers community counseling (MS); counseling (Diploma); school counseling (MS); school psychology (MS, Diploma). *Accreditation:* ACA (one or more programs are accredited); NCATE. *Program availability:* Part-time, evening/weekend. *Faculty:* 10 full-time (8 women). *Students:* 71 full-time (62 women), 58 part-time (46 women); includes 27 minority (18 Black or African American, non-Hispanic/Latino; 8 Hispanic/Latino; 1 Two or more races, non-Hispanic/Latino). Average age 29. 202 applicants, 44% accepted, 54 enrolled. In 2016, 42 master's, 13 other advanced degrees awarded. *Degree requirements:* For master's, comprehensive exam. *Entrance requirements:* For master's, interview, previous course work in behavioral sciences, minimum QPA of 2.7. *Application deadline:* For fall admission, 1/15 for domestic students; for spring admission, 10/15 for domestic students. Application fee: $50. Electronic applications accepted. *Expenses:* Tuition, state resident: full-time $6497; part-time $519 per credit hour. Tuition, nonresident: full-time $18,102; part-time $535 per credit hour. *Required fees:* $4722; $55 per semester. Tuition and fees vary according to program. *Financial support:* Career-related internships or fieldwork, scholarships/grants, and unspecified assistantships available. Financial award application deadline: 4/15; financial award applicants required to submit FAFSA. *Unit head:* Dr. Margaret Generali, Chairperson, 203-392-5175, Fax: 203-392-5910, E-mail: generalim1@southernct.edu. *Application contact:* Lisa Galvin, Director of Graduate Admissions, 203-392-5240, Fax: 203-392-5235, E-mail: galvinl1@southernct.edu.

Southern Methodist University, Annette Caldwell Simmons School of Education and Human Development, Department of Dispute Resolution and Counseling, Dallas, TX 75275. Offers counseling (MS); dispute resolution (MA). *Program availability:* Part-time. *Degree requirements:* For master's, practica experience, 2 internships (counseling). *Entrance requirements:* For master's, minimum undergraduate GPA of 2.75 (for dispute resolution), 3.0 (for counseling); 3 letters of recommendation. Additional exam requirements/recommendations for international students: Required—TOEFL. Electronic applications accepted.

Southern University and Agricultural and Mechanical College, Graduate School, College of Education, Department of Behavioral Studies and Educational Leadership, Baton Rouge, LA 70813. Offers administration and supervision (M Ed); counselor education (MA); educational leadership (M Ed); mental health counseling (MA). *Accreditation:* ACA; NCATE. *Degree requirements:* For master's, comprehensive exam, thesis optional. *Entrance requirements:* For master's, GRE General Test. Additional exam requirements/recommendations for international students: Required—TOEFL (minimum score 525 paper-based). *Faculty research:* Mental health, computer assisted programs, families relations, head start improvements, careers.

Southwestern Oklahoma State University, College of Professional and Graduate Studies, School of Behavioral Sciences and Education, Specialization in Community Counseling, Weatherford, OK 73096-3098. Offers M Ed. M Ed distance learning degree program offered to Oklahoma residents only. *Accreditation:* NCATE. *Program availability:* Part-time, evening/weekend, online learning. *Degree requirements:* For master's, exam. *Entrance requirements:* For master's, GRE General Test or minimum undergraduate GPA of 3.0. Additional exam requirements/recommendations for international students: Required—TOEFL.

Southwestern Oklahoma State University, College of Professional and Graduate Studies, School of Behavioral Sciences and Education, Specialization in School Counseling, Weatherford, OK 73096-3098. Offers M Ed. M Ed distance learning degree program offered to Oklahoma residents only. *Accreditation:* NCATE. *Program availability:* Part-time, evening/weekend, online learning. *Degree requirements:* For master's, exam. *Entrance requirements:* For master's, GRE General Test or minimum undergraduate GPA of 3.0, portfolio. Additional exam requirements/recommendations for international students: Required—TOEFL.

Spalding University, Graduate Studies, College of Education, Programs in Education, Louisville, KY 40203-2188. Offers art teacher education (MAT); business teacher education (MAT); elementary school education (MAT); foreign language (MAT); high school education (MAT); middle school education (MAT); secondary education (MAT); special education (learning and behavioral disorders) (MAT); student guidance counselor (MA); teacher leader (M Ed). *Accreditation:* NCATE. *Program availability:* Part-time, evening/weekend. *Faculty:* 39 full-time (26 women), 13 part-time/adjunct (4 women). *Students:* 97 full-time (76 women), 31 part-time (23 women); includes 39 minority (33 Black or African American, non-Hispanic/Latino; 1 Asian, non-Hispanic/Latino; 3 Hispanic/Latino; 2 Two or more races, non-Hispanic/Latino). Average age 35. 62 applicants, 55% accepted, 33 enrolled. In 2016, 49 master's awarded. *Entrance requirements:* For master's, GRE General Test or MAT, interview, letters of recommendation, resume. Additional exam requirements/recommendations for international students: Required—TOEFL (minimum score 535 paper-based). *Application deadline:* Applications are processed on a rolling basis. Application fee: $30. Electronic applications accepted. *Expenses: Tuition:* Full-time $15,300. *Financial support:* Scholarships/grants, traineeships, and unspecified assistantships available. Financial award applicants required to submit FAFSA. *Faculty research:* Instructional technology, achievement gap, classroom management, assessment. *Unit head:* Dr. Chris Walsh, Associate Dean, 502-873-4272, Fax: 502-585-7123, E-mail: cwalsh@spalding.edu. *Application contact:* Valerie Anderson, Administrative Assistant, 502-873-4260, E-mail: vanderson@spalding.edu.

Springfield College, Graduate Programs, Programs in Education, Springfield, MA 01109-3797. Offers educational studies (M Ed); school guidance counseling (M Ed); secondary education (M Ed); special education (M Ed). *Program availability:* Part-time, evening/weekend. *Entrance requirements:* Additional exam requirements/recommendations for international students: Required—TOEFL (minimum score 550 paper-based); Recommended—IELTS (minimum score 6). Electronic applications accepted. *Expenses: Tuition:* Full-time $29,640; part-time $988 per credit. *Required fees:* $195.

Springfield College, Graduate Programs, Programs in Psychology, Springfield, MA 01109-3797. Offers athletic counseling (MS, CAGS); clinical mental health counseling (M Ed, CAGS); counseling psychology (Psy D); industrial and organizational psychology (M Ed, CAGS); school guidance counseling (M Ed, CAGS); student personnel administration in higher education (M Ed). *Accreditation:* APA. *Program availability:* Part-time. *Degree requirements:* For master's, research project, portfolio; for doctorate, dissertation project, 1500 hours of counseling psychology practicum, full-year internship. *Entrance requirements:* Additional exam requirements/recommendations for international students: Required—TOEFL (minimum score 550 paper-based). Electronic applications accepted. *Expenses: Tuition:* Full-time $29,640; part-time $988 per credit. *Required fees:* $195.

State University of New York at New Paltz, Graduate School, School of Liberal Arts and Sciences, Department of Psychology, New Paltz, NY 12561. Offers mental health counseling (MS, AC); psychology (MA); school counseling (MS). *Program availability:* Part-time, evening/weekend. *Students:* 52 full-time (40 women), 19 part-time (12 women); includes 13 minority (1 Black or African American, non-Hispanic/Latino; 1 Asian, non-Hispanic/Latino; 11 Hispanic/Latino), 1 international. 103 applicants, 50% accepted, 33 enrolled. In 2016, 22 master's awarded. *Degree requirements:* For master's, comprehensive exam, thesis. *Entrance requirements:* For master's, GRE General Test, minimum GPA of 3.0. Additional exam requirements/recommendations for international students: Required—TOEFL (minimum score 550 paper-based; 80 iBT), IELTS (minimum score 6.5). *Application deadline:* For fall admission, 2/1 priority date for domestic and international students; for spring admission, 11/15 priority date for domestic and international students. Application fee: $50. Electronic applications accepted. *Financial support:* In 2016–17, 6 teaching assistantships with partial tuition reimbursements (averaging $5,000 per year) were awarded. Financial award application deadline: 8/1. *Faculty research:* Disaster mental health, women's objectification, mate selection, cultural psychology, achievement motivation. *Unit head:* Dr. Glenn Geher, Chair, 845-257-3091, E-mail: geherg@newpaltz.edu. *Application contact:* Dr. Tabitha Holmes, Program Coordinator, 845-257-3955, E-mail: holmest@newpaltz.edu.
Website: http://www.newpaltz.edu/psychology/

State University of New York at Plattsburgh, School of Education, Health, and Human Services, Department of Counselor Education, Plattsburgh, NY 12901-2681. Offers clinical mental health counseling (MS, Advanced Certificate); school counselor (MS Ed, CAS); student affairs counseling (MS). *Accreditation:* ACA (one or more programs are accredited); TEAC. *Program availability:* Part-time. *Entrance requirements:* For master's, GRE General Test or MAT, minimum GPA of 2.8. Additional exam requirements/recommendations for international students: Required—TOEFL. *Faculty research:* Campus violence, program accreditation, substance abuse, vocational assessment, group counseling, divorce.

State University of New York College at Oneonta, Graduate Programs, Division of Education, Department of Educational Psychology, Counseling and Special Education, Oneonta, NY 13820-4015. Offers school counselor K-12 (MS Ed, CAS); special education (MS Ed). *Accreditation:* NCATE. *Program availability:* Part-time, evening/weekend. *Degree requirements:* For master's, comprehensive exam. *Entrance requirements:* For master's, GRE General Test. *Application deadline:* For fall admission, 3/1 for domestic students. Application fee: $50. *Unit head:* Dr. Dawn Hamlin, Chair, 607-436-3526, Fax: 607-436-3799, E-mail: dawn.hamlin@oneonta.edu. *Application contact:* Patrick J. Mente, Director of Graduate Studies, 607-436-2523, Fax: 607-436-3084, E-mail: gradstudies@oneonta.edu.
Website: http://www.oneonta.edu/academics/ed/edpsych/

Stephen F. Austin State University, Graduate School, College of Education, Department of Human Services, Nacogdoches, TX 75962. Offers counseling (MA); school psychology (MA); special education (M Ed); speech pathology (MS). *Accreditation:* ACA (one or more programs are accredited); ASHA (one or more programs are accredited); CORE; NCATE. *Degree requirements:* For master's, comprehensive exam, thesis (for some programs). *Entrance requirements:* For master's, GRE General Test, minimum GPA of 2.8. Additional exam requirements/recommendations for international students: Required—TOEFL.

Stephens College, Division of Graduate and Continuing Studies, Columbia, MO 65215-0002. Offers counseling (M Ed), including addictions counseling, clinical mental health counseling, school counseling; health information administration (Postbaccalaureate Certificate); physician assistant studies (MPAS); TV and screenwriting (MFA). *Program availability:* Part-time, evening/weekend, online learning. *Faculty:* 14 full-time (9 women), 30 part-time/adjunct (19 women). *Students:* 117 full-time (101 women), 107 part-time (96 women); includes 25 minority (2 Black or African American, non-Hispanic/Latino; 2 American Indian or Alaska Native, non-Hispanic/Latino; 1 Asian, non-Hispanic/Latino; 2 Hispanic/Latino; 1 Native Hawaiian or other Pacific Islander, non-Hispanic/Latino; 17 Two or more races, non-Hispanic/Latino), 1 international. Average age 35. 226 applicants, 43% accepted, 87 enrolled. In 2016, 44 master's awarded. *Entrance requirements:* For master's, minimum GPA of 3.0 in last 60 hours. Additional exam requirements/recommendations for international students: Required—TOEFL (minimum score 79 iBT). *Application deadline:* For fall admission, 8/15 priority date for domestic and international students; for winter admission, 1/9 priority date for domestic and international students; for spring admission, 6/5 priority date for domestic and international students. Applications are processed on a rolling basis. Application fee: $50. Electronic applications accepted. *Expenses: Tuition:* Full-time $3564; part-time $396 per credit hour. *Required fees:* $45 per credit hour. *Financial support:* In 2016–17, 5 fellowships with full tuition reimbursements (averaging $7,673 per year) were awarded; unspecified assistantships also available. Financial award applicants required to submit FAFSA. *Faculty research:* Educational psychology, outcomes assessment. *Unit head:* Dr. Brian Sajko, Vice President of Strategic Enrollment Management, 800-388-7579, Fax: 573-876-7237, E-mail: online@stephens.edu. *Application contact:* Lindsey Boudinot, Director of Graduate and Online Admissions, 800-388-7579, E-mail: online@stephens.edu.

Stetson University, College of Arts and Sciences, Division of Education, Department of Counselor Education, DeLand, FL 32723. Offers marriage, couple and family counseling (MS); mental health counseling (MS); school counseling (MS). *Accreditation:* ACA. *Program availability:* Evening/weekend. *Faculty:* 5 full-time (all women), 7 part-time/adjunct (6 women). *Students:* 114 full-time (102 women), 13 part-time (9 women); includes 36 minority (9 Black or African American, non-Hispanic/Latino; 1 Asian, non-Hispanic/Latino; 21 Hispanic/Latino; 5 Two or more races, non-Hispanic/Latino), 3 international. Average age 29. 61 applicants, 70% accepted, 37 enrolled. In 2016, 16 master's awarded. *Entrance requirements:* For master's, GRE or MAT, transcripts, three letters of recommendation, group interview. Additional exam requirements/recommendations for international students: Required—TOEFL (minimum score 90 iBT), IELTS (minimum score 7). *Application deadline:* For fall admission, 8/1 priority date for domestic students; for spring admission, 1/1 priority date for domestic students; for summer admission, 5/1 priority date for domestic students. Applications are processed on a rolling basis. Application fee: $50. Electronic applications accepted. *Expenses:* $886 per credit hour. *Financial support:* In 2016–17, 45 students received support. Federal Work-Study, scholarships/grants, unspecified assistantships, and tuition waivers for staff and dependents available. Support available to part-time students. *Faculty research:* Play therapy, trauma, wellness, infertility, counselor education training, gatekeeping and counselor education. *Unit head:* Dr. Leila Roach, Chair, 386-822-8992. *Application contact:* Jamie Vanderlip, Senior Associate Director of Graduate Admissions, 386-822-7100, Fax: 386-822-7112, E-mail: jlvander@stetson.edu.

Suffolk University, College of Arts and Sciences, Department of Psychology, Boston, MA 02108-2770. Offers clinical psychology (PhD); college admission counseling (Certificate); mental health counseling (MS); school counseling (MS, CAGS). *Accreditation:* APA. *Faculty:* 14 full-time (7 women), 7 part-time/adjunct (6 women). *Students:* 51 full-time (45 women), 42 part-time (38 women); includes 24 minority (3 Black or African American, non-Hispanic/Latino; 8 Asian, non-Hispanic/Latino; 11 Hispanic/Latino; 2 Two or more races, non-Hispanic/Latino), 6 international. Average age 27. 306 applicants, 25% accepted, 38 enrolled. In 2016, 22 master's, 10 doctorates, 14 other advanced degrees awarded. *Degree requirements:* For doctorate, thesis/dissertation, practicum. *Entrance requirements:* For doctorate, GRE General Test or MAT, 2 letters of recommendation, resume. Additional exam requirements/recommendations for international students: Required—TOEFL (minimum score 550 paper-based; 80 iBT). *Application deadline:* For fall admission, 12/1 for domestic and international students. Applications are processed on a rolling basis. Application fee: $50. Electronic applications accepted. *Expenses:* Contact institution. *Financial support:* In 2016–17, 54 students received support, including 53 fellowships (averaging $13,943 per year); career-related internships or fieldwork, Federal Work-Study, institutionally sponsored loans, scholarships/grants, and unspecified assistantships also available. Support available to part-time students. Financial award application deadline: 4/1; financial award applicants required to submit FAFSA. *Faculty research:* Assessing exposure in the context of a family-based cognitive behavioral treatment for pediatric OCD, a mindfulness approach to designing and testing the efficacy of a new sexual revictimization prevention program for college women, olfaction and decision-making in substance-dependent individuals, the role of experiential avoidance in Generalized Anxiety Disorder, ego development as a predictor of dogmatism and intolerance in the political right and left. *Unit head:* Dr. Gary Fireman, Chairperson, 617-305-6368, Fax: 617-367-2924, E-mail: gfireman@suffolk.edu. *Application contact:* Mara Marzocchi, Associate Director of Graduate Admissions, 617-573-8302, Fax: 617-305-1733, E-mail: grad.admission@suffolk.edu.
Website: http://www.suffolk.edu/college/graduate/69299.php

Sul Ross State University, College of Professional Studies, Department of Education, Program in Counseling, Alpine, TX 79832. Offers M Ed. *Program availability:* Part-time, evening/weekend. *Degree requirements:* For master's, thesis optional. *Entrance requirements:* For master's, GMAT or GRE General Test, minimum GPA of 2.5 in last 60 hours of undergraduate work.

Sul Ross State University, Rio Grande College of Sul Ross State University, Alpine, TX 79832. Offers business administration (MBA); teacher education (M Ed), including bilingual education, counseling, educational diagnostics, elementary education, general education, reading, school administration, secondary education. *Program availability:* Part-time, evening/weekend, online learning. *Degree requirements:* For master's, comprehensive exam, thesis optional, minimum GPA of 3.0. *Entrance requirements:* For master's, GMAT or GRE General Test, minimum GPA of 2.5 in last 60 hours of undergraduate work. Additional exam requirements/recommendations for international students: Required—TOEFL.

Syracuse University, School of Education, MS Program in Student Affairs Counseling, Syracuse, NY 13244. Offers MS. *Program availability:* Part-time. *Students:* Average age 28. *Entrance requirements:* For master's, GRE or MAT, baccalaureate degree from regionally-accredited college/university, three letters of recommendation, personal statement, transcripts, interview. Additional exam requirements/recommendations for international students: Required—TOEFL (minimum score 100 iBT). *Application deadline:* For fall admission, 6/15 priority date for domestic and international students; for spring admission, 10/15 priority date for domestic and international students; for summer admission, 1/15 priority date for domestic and international students. Applications are processed on a rolling basis. Application fee: $75. Electronic applications accepted. *Expenses: Tuition:* Full-time $25,974; part-time $1443 per credit hour. *Required fees:* $802; $50 per course. Tuition and fees vary according to course load and program. *Financial support:* Fellowships with full tuition reimbursements, research assistantships, teaching assistantships with tuition reimbursements, career-related internships or fieldwork, and scholarships/grants available. Financial award application deadline: 1/15. *Faculty research:* Group work in counseling, theories of counseling and psychotherapy, social and cultural dimensions of counseling, life-span human development, assessment in counseling. *Unit head:* Dr. Nicole Hill, Professor/Chair of the Department of Counseling and Human Service, 315-443-2266, E-mail: nrhill@syr.edu. *Application contact:* Speranza Migliore, Graduate Admissions Recruiter, 315-443-2505, E-mail: gradrcrt@syr.edu.
Website: http://soe.syr.edu/academic/counseling_and_human_services/graduate/masters/student_affairs_counseling/default.aspx

Syracuse University, School of Education, PhD Program in Counseling and Counselor Education, Syracuse, NY 13244. Offers PhD. *Accreditation:* ACA. *Program availability:* Part-time. *Degree requirements:* For doctorate, comprehensive exam, thesis/dissertation. *Entrance requirements:* For doctorate, GRE including Writing/Analytic Test, master's degree in counseling or rehabilitation counseling, personal interview, three letters of recommendation, transcripts of all undergraduate and graduate study, personal statement. Additional exam requirements/recommendations for international students: Required—TOEFL (minimum score 600 paper-based; 100 iBT), IELTS (minimum score 7). *Application deadline:* For fall admission, 11/1 for domestic and international students. Applications are processed on a rolling basis. Application fee: $75. Electronic applications accepted. *Expenses: Tuition:* Full-time $25,974; part-time $1443 per credit hour. *Required fees:* $802; $50 per course. Tuition and fees vary according to course load and program. *Financial support:* Fellowships with full tuition reimbursements, research assistantships, teaching assistantships with full tuition reimbursements, career-related internships or fieldwork, and scholarships/grants available. Financial award application deadline: 1/15; financial award applicants required to submit FAFSA. *Faculty research:* Clinical supervision, college mental health counseling, counseling people with disabilities, the future professoriate, social justice and urban youth. *Unit head:* Dr. Nicole Hill, Chair, 315-443-2266, Fax: 315-443-5732, E-mail: nrhill@syr.edu. *Application contact:* Speranza Migliore, Graduate Admissions Recruiter, 315-443-2505, E-mail: gradrcrt@syr.edu.
Website: http://soe.syr.edu/academic/counseling_and_human_services/graduate/phd/default.aspx

Texas A&M International University, Office of Graduate Studies and Research, College of Education, Department of Professional Programs, Laredo, TX 78041-1900. Offers educational administration (MS Ed); generic special education (MS Ed); school counseling (MS). *Entrance requirements:* Additional exam requirements/recommendations for international students: Required—TOEFL (minimum score 550 paper-based; 79 iBT).

Texas A&M University–Central Texas, Graduate Studies and Research, Killeen, TX 76549. Offers accounting (MS); business administration (MBA); clinical mental health counseling (MS); criminal justice (MCJ); curriculum and instruction (M Ed); educational administration (M Ed); educational psychology - experimental psychology (MS); history (MA); human resource management (MS); information systems (MS); liberal studies (MS); management and leadership (MS); marriage and family therapy (MS); mathematics (MS); political science (MA); school counseling (M Ed); school psychology (Ed S).

Counselor Education

Texas A&M University–Commerce, College of Education and Human Services, Commerce, TX 75429-3011. Offers counseling (MS); curriculum and instruction (M Ed, MS); early childhood education (M Ed, MS); educational administration (M Ed, Ed D); educational psychology (PhD); educational technology leadership (MS); educational technology library science (MS); health, kinesiology and sports studies (MS); higher education (MS, Ed D); organization, learning, and technology (MS); psychology (MS); reading (M Ed, MS); school psychology (SSP); secondary education (M Ed, MS); social work (MSW); special education (M Ed); supervision, curriculum and instruction-elementary education (Ed D). *Program availability:* Part-time, 100% online, blended/hybrid learning. *Faculty:* 88 full-time (52 women), 31 part-time/adjunct (24 women). *Students:* 341 full-time (276 women), 1,495 part-time (1,156 women); includes 762 minority (429 Black or African American, non-Hispanic/Latino; 4 American Indian or Alaska Native, non-Hispanic/Latino; 27 Asian, non-Hispanic/Latino; 247 Hispanic/Latino; 1 Native Hawaiian or other Pacific Islander, non-Hispanic/Latino; 54 Two or more races, non-Hispanic/Latino), 18 international. Average age 37. 1,070 applicants, 54% accepted, 452 enrolled. In 2016, 579 master's, 31 doctorates awarded. *Degree requirements:* For master's, one foreign language, comprehensive exam, thesis optional, departmental qualifying exams (for some programs); for doctorate, comprehensive exam, thesis/dissertation, departmental qualifying exam; for SSP, comprehensive exam, thesis optional. *Entrance requirements:* For master's and doctorate, GRE General Test. Additional exam requirements/recommendations for international students: Required—TOEFL (minimum score 550 paper-based; 79 iBT), IELTS (minimum score 6). *Application deadline:* For fall admission, 6/1 priority date for international students; for spring admission, 10/15 priority date for international students; for summer admission, 3/15 priority date for international students. Applications are processed on a rolling basis. Application fee: $50. Electronic applications accepted. *Expenses:* $2,254 resident; $4,744 non-resident. *Financial support:* In 2016–17, 301 students received support, including 39 research assistantships with partial tuition reimbursements available (averaging $9,000 per year), 17 teaching assistantships with partial tuition reimbursements available (averaging $9,000 per year); career-related internships or fieldwork, Federal Work-Study, institutionally sponsored loans, scholarships/grants, health care benefits, and unspecified assistantships also available. Financial award application deadline: 5/1; financial award applicants required to submit FAFSA. *Faculty research:* Cognitive and bilingual education, positive behavioral intervention, literacy, math readiness. *Total annual research expenditures:* $470,963. *Unit head:* Dr. Timothy Letzring, Dean, 903-886-5181, Fax: 903-886-5905, E-mail: tim.letzring@tamuc.edu. *Application contact:* Jennifer Faunce, Graduate Recruiter, 903-886-5030, Fax: 903-886-5905, E-mail: jennifer.faunce@tamuc.edu.
Website: http://www.tamuc.edu/academics/graduateSchool/programs/education/default.aspx

Texas A&M University–Corpus Christi, College of Graduate Studies, College of Education, Programs in Counseling, Corpus Christi, TX 78412-5503. Offers MS, PhD. *Accreditation:* ACA. *Program availability:* Part-time, evening/weekend. *Students:* 89 full-time (78 women), 75 part-time (65 women); includes 89 minority (13 Black or African American, non-Hispanic/Latino; 1 American Indian or Alaska Native, non-Hispanic/Latino; 3 Asian, non-Hispanic/Latino; 72 Hispanic/Latino), 11 international. Average age 33. 103 applicants, 54% accepted, 53 enrolled. In 2016, 52 master's, 9 doctorates awarded. *Degree requirements:* For master's, comprehensive exam; for doctorate, comprehensive exam, thesis/dissertation. *Entrance requirements:* For master's, minimum GPA of 3.0 in last 60 hours, essay (approximately 500-700 words in length), 3 letters of recommendation, interview; for doctorate, GRE (taken within 5 years), master's degree, essay (2 pages), resume, 3 reference forms, interview. Additional exam requirements/recommendations for international students: Required—TOEFL (minimum score 550 paper-based; 79 iBT), IELTS (minimum score 6.5). *Application deadline:* For fall admission, 6/15 priority date for domestic and international students; for spring admission, 10/15 priority date for domestic students, 9/1 priority date for international students; for summer admission, 2/15 priority date for domestic students, 2/1 priority date for international students. Applications are processed on a rolling basis. Application fee: $50 ($70 for international students). Electronic applications accepted. *Financial support:* Research assistantships, teaching assistantships, career-related internships or fieldwork, Federal Work-Study, institutionally sponsored loans, scholarships/grants, health care benefits, and unspecified assistantships available. Support available to part-time students. Financial award application deadline: 3/15; financial award applicants required to submit FAFSA. *Unit head:* Dr. Robert Smith, Chair, 361-825-2307, E-mail: robert.smith@tamucc.edu. *Application contact:* Graduate Admissions Coordinator, 361-825-2177, Fax: 361-825-2755, E-mail: gradweb@tamucc.edu.
Website: http://cnep.tamucc.edu/

Texas A&M University–Kingsville, College of Graduate Studies, College of Education and Human Performance, Department of Educational Leadership and Counseling, Kingsville, TX 78363. Offers adult education (M Ed); counseling and guidance (MA, MS); educational administration (MA, MS); educational leadership (Ed D); instructional technology (MS). *Program availability:* Part-time, evening/weekend, 100% online, blended/hybrid learning. *Entrance requirements:* Additional exam requirements/recommendations for international students: Required—TOEFL (minimum score 550 paper-based; 79 iBT); Recommended—IELTS. Electronic applications accepted.

Texas A&M University–Kingsville, College of Graduate Studies, College of Education and Human Performance, Program in Counseling and Guidance, Kingsville, TX 78363. Offers MA, MS. MS offered jointly with University of North Texas. *Program availability:* Part-time, evening/weekend. *Degree requirements:* For master's, variable foreign language requirement, comprehensive exam, thesis (for some programs). *Entrance requirements:* For master's, GRE, MAT, GMAT, minimum GPA of 2.6. Additional exam requirements/recommendations for international students: Required—TOEFL (minimum score 550 paper-based; 79 iBT). Electronic applications accepted. *Faculty research:* Diagnostician requirements for certification, teaching methods for adult learners.

Texas A&M University–San Antonio, Department of Leadership and Counseling, San Antonio, TX 78224. Offers counseling and guidance (MA); educational leadership (MA). *Program availability:* Part-time, evening/weekend. *Degree requirements:* For master's, comprehensive exam, thesis or alternative. *Entrance requirements:* For master's, MAT. Additional exam requirements/recommendations for international students: Required—TOEFL (minimum score 550 paper-based; 80 iBT), IELTS (minimum score 6). Electronic applications accepted.

Texas Christian University, College of Education, Doctoral Programs in Education, Fort Worth, TX 76129. Offers counseling and counselor education (PhD); curriculum studies (PhD); educational leadership (Ed D); higher educational leadership (Ed D); science education (PhD); MBA/Ed D. *Program availability:* Part-time, evening/weekend. *Faculty:* 29 full-time (21 women), 8 part-time/adjunct (5 women). *Students:* 77 full-time (56 women), 19 part-time (7 women); includes 33 minority (12 Black or African American, non-Hispanic/Latino; 5 Asian, non-Hispanic/Latino; 15 Hispanic/Latino; 1 Two or more races, non-Hispanic/Latino), 6 international. Average age 37. 34 applicants, 56% accepted, 13 enrolled. In 2016, 5 doctorates awarded. *Degree requirements:* For doctorate, comprehensive exam, thesis/dissertation. *Entrance requirements:* For doctorate, GRE General Test. Additional exam requirements/recommendations for international students: Required—TOEFL (minimum score 550 paper-based; 80 iBT). *Application deadline:* For fall admission, 2/1 for domestic and international students; for winter admission, 2/1 for domestic and international students; for spring admission, 11/16 for domestic and international students. Application fee: $60. Electronic applications accepted. *Expenses: Tuition:* Full-time $26,640; part-time $1480 per credit hour. *Required fees:* $48. Tuition and fees vary according to program. *Financial support:* In 2016–17, 57 students received support, including 1 fellowship with full tuition reimbursement available, 10 research assistantships with full tuition reimbursements available (averaging $18,500 per year), 7 teaching assistantships with full tuition reimbursements available (averaging $18,500 per year); career-related internships or fieldwork, scholarships/grants, health care benefits, and unspecified assistantships also available. Support available to part-time students. Financial award application deadline: 2/1; financial award applicants required to submit FAFSA. *Unit head:* Dr. Jan Lacina, Associate Dean, 817-257-6786, Fax: 817-257-7466, E-mail: j.lacina@tcu.edu. *Application contact:* Lori Kimball, Administrative Program Specialist, 817-257-7661, Fax: 817-257-7466, E-mail: l.kimball@tcu.edu.
Website: http://coe.tcu.edu/graduate-overview/

Texas Christian University, College of Education, Master's Programs in Education, Fort Worth, TX 76129. Offers counseling (M Ed); curriculum and instruction (M Ed), including curriculum studies, language and literacy, math education, science education; educational leadership (M Ed); special education (M Ed). *Program availability:* Part-time, evening/weekend. *Faculty:* 29 full-time (21 women), 8 part-time/adjunct (5 women). *Students:* 112 full-time (95 women), 12 part-time (11 women); includes 39 minority (6 Black or African American, non-Hispanic/Latino; 2 Asian, non-Hispanic/Latino; 27 Hispanic/Latino; 1 Native Hawaiian or other Pacific Islander, non-Hispanic/Latino; 3 Two or more races, non-Hispanic/Latino), 2 international. Average age 29. 107 applicants, 78% accepted, 66 enrolled. In 2016, 54 master's awarded. *Degree requirements:* For master's, comprehensive exam (for some programs), thesis (for some programs). *Entrance requirements:* For master's, GRE General Test. Additional exam requirements/recommendations for international students: Required—TOEFL (minimum score 550 paper-based; 80 iBT). *Application deadline:* For fall admission, 3/1 for domestic and international students; for spring admission, 11/16 for domestic and international students; for summer admission, 3/1 for domestic and international students. Application fee: $60. Electronic applications accepted. *Expenses: Tuition:* Full-time $26,640; part-time $1480 per credit hour. *Required fees:* $48. Tuition and fees vary according to program. *Financial support:* In 2016–17, 104 students received support, including 4 research assistantships with full tuition reimbursements available (averaging $15,000 per year), 31 teaching assistantships with full tuition reimbursements available (averaging $15,000 per year); career-related internships or fieldwork, scholarships/grants, and unspecified assistantships also available. Support available to part-time students. Financial award application deadline: 3/1; financial award applicants required to submit FAFSA. *Unit head:* Dr. Jan Lacina, Associate Dean, 817-257-6786, Fax: 817-257-7466, E-mail: j.lacina@tcu.edu. *Application contact:* Lori Kimball, Administrative Program Specialist, 817-257-7661, Fax: 817-257-7466, E-mail: l.kimball@tcu.edu.
Website: http://coe.tcu.edu/graduate-overview/

Texas Southern University, College of Education, Department of Counselor Education, Houston, TX 77004-4584. Offers counseling (M Ed); counselor education (Ed D). *Program availability:* Part-time, evening/weekend. *Degree requirements:* For master's, one foreign language, comprehensive exam; for doctorate, comprehensive exam, thesis/dissertation. *Entrance requirements:* For master's, GRE General Test, minimum GPA of 2.5; for doctorate, GRE General Test or MAT, master's degree, minimum B+ average. Additional exam requirements/recommendations for international students: Required—TOEFL. Electronic applications accepted. *Faculty research:* Clinical and urban psychology.

Texas State University, The Graduate College, College of Education, Program in Professional Counseling, San Marcos, TX 78666. Offers community counseling (MA); marital, couple and family counseling (MA); school counseling (MA). *Accreditation:* ACA. *Program availability:* Part-time. *Faculty:* 13 full-time (11 women), 6 part-time/adjunct (all women). *Students:* 94 full-time (77 women), 107 part-time (89 women); includes 53 minority (4 Black or African American, non-Hispanic/Latino; 7 Asian, non-Hispanic/Latino; 34 Hispanic/Latino; 8 Two or more races, non-Hispanic/Latino), 2 international. Average age 32. 114 applicants, 52% accepted, 29 enrolled. In 2016, 54 master's awarded. *Degree requirements:* For master's, comprehensive exam, thesis optional, internship. *Entrance requirements:* For master's, GRE General Test (minimum preferred score of 291 [150 verbal, 141 quantitative]), baccalaureate degree from regionally-accredited institution with minimum GPA of 3.0 in last 60 hours of undergraduate work; resume; statement of purpose addressing professional goals, reasoning for specified emphasis (i.e., community, school, marital), strengths and weaknesses, and perspective on diversity; 3 references. Additional exam requirements/recommendations for international students: Required—TOEFL (minimum score 550 paper-based; 78 iBT), IELTS (minimum score 6.5). *Application deadline:* For fall admission, 2/15 for domestic and international students; for spring admission, 10/1 for domestic and international students; for summer admission, 2/15 for domestic and international students. Applications are processed on a rolling basis. Application fee: $40 ($90 for international students). Electronic applications accepted. *Expenses:* $4,851 per semester. *Financial support:* In 2016–17, 105 students received support, including 8 research assistantships (averaging $8,504 per year); teaching assistantships, Federal Work-Study, institutionally sponsored loans, and scholarships/grants also available. Support available to part-time students. Financial award application deadline: 3/1; financial award applicants required to submit FAFSA. *Unit head:* Dr. Kevin Fall, Graduate Advisor, 512-245-2081, Fax: 512-245-8872, E-mail: kf22@txstate.edu. *Application contact:* Dr. Andrea Golato, Dean of Graduate School, 512-245-2581, Fax: 512-245-8365, E-mail: gradcollege@txstate.edu.

Texas Tech University, Graduate School, College of Education, Department of Educational Psychology and Leadership, Lubbock, TX 79409-1071. Offers counselor education (M Ed, PhD); distance education (M Ed); educational leadership (M Ed, Ed D, PhD); educational psychology (M Ed, PhD); higher education (M Ed, Ed D); higher education research (PhD); instructional technology (M Ed, Ed D); special education (M Ed, Ed D, PhD). *Accreditation:* ACA; NCATE. *Program availability:* Part-time, evening/weekend. *Faculty:* 59 full-time (29 women), 3 part-time/adjunct (all women). *Students:* 300 full-time (218 women), 656 part-time (482 women); includes 320 minority (87 Black or African American, non-Hispanic/Latino; 5 American Indian or Alaska Native, non-Hispanic/Latino; 5 Asian, non-Hispanic/Latino; 200 Hispanic/Latino; 23 Two or more races, non-Hispanic/Latino), 51 international. Average age 36. 668 applicants, 56% accepted, 285 enrolled. In 2016, 171 master's, 47 doctorates awarded. Terminal master's awarded for partial completion of doctoral program. *Degree requirements:* For master's, comprehensive exam, thesis optional; for doctorate, comprehensive exam, thesis/dissertation. *Entrance requirements:* For master's, GRE (for some programs); for doctorate, GRE. Additional exam requirements/recommendations for international students: Required—TOEFL (minimum score 550 paper-based; 79 iBT). *Application deadline:* For fall admission, 6/1 priority date for domestic students, 1/15 priority date for international students; for spring admission, 9/1 priority date for domestic students, 6/15 priority date for international students. Applications are processed on a rolling basis. Application fee: $75. Electronic applications accepted. *Expenses:* $285 per credit hour full-time resident tuition, $693 per credit hour full-time non-resident tuition; $50.50 per

credit hour fee plus $608 per term fee. *Financial support:* In 2016–17, 384 students received support, including 384 fellowships (averaging $3,632 per year); scholarships/grants and unspecified assistantships also available. Support available to part-time students. Financial award application deadline: 1/3; financial award applicants required to submit FAFSA. *Faculty research:* Cognitive, motivational, and developmental processes in learning; counseling education; instructional technology; generic special education and sensory impairment; community college administration; K-12 school administration. *Total annual research expenditures:* $1,371. *Unit head:* Dr. Hansel Burley, Chair, 806-834-5135, Fax: 806-742-2179, E-mail: hansel.burley@ttu.edu. *Application contact:* Pam Smith, Admissions Advisor, 806-834-2969, Fax: 806-742-2179, E-mail: pam.smith@ttu.edu.
Website: http://www.educ.ttu.edu/

Texas Wesleyan University, Graduate Programs, Programs in Education, Fort Worth, TX 76105. Offers education (M Ed, Ed D); marriage and family therapy (MSMFT, PhD); professional counseling (MA); school counseling (MS). *Program availability:* Part-time, evening/weekend. *Faculty:* 18 full-time (9 women), 10 part-time/adjunct (5 women). *Students:* 23 full-time (18 women), 217 part-time (190 women); includes 121 minority (61 Black or African American, non-Hispanic/Latino; 3 American Indian or Alaska Native, non-Hispanic/Latino; 2 Asian, non-Hispanic/Latino; 47 Hispanic/Latino; 8 Two or more races, non-Hispanic/Latino), 9 international. Average age 36. 194 applicants, 70% accepted, 118 enrolled. In 2016, 52 master's, 8 doctorates awarded. *Degree requirements:* For master's, comprehensive exam (for some programs); for doctorate, thesis/dissertation. *Entrance requirements:* For master's and doctorate, GRE General Test. Additional exam requirements/recommendations for international students: Required—TOEFL (minimum score 550 paper-based; 79 iBT), IELTS (minimum score 6.5). *Application deadline:* Applications are processed on a rolling basis. Application fee: $64. Electronic applications accepted. *Expenses:* Contact institution. *Financial support:* Career-related internships or fieldwork, Federal Work-Study, scholarships/grants, and tuition waivers (full and partial) available. Support available to part-time students. Financial award application deadline: 3/15; financial award applicants required to submit FAFSA. *Faculty research:* Teacher effectiveness, bilingual education, analytic teaching. *Unit head:* Dr. Carlos Martinez, Dean, School of Education, 817-531-4940, Fax: 817-531-4943. *Application contact:* Amy Orcutt, Interim Director of Graduate Admissions, 817-531-4288, Fax: 817-531-4261, E-mail: arorcutt@txwes.edu.
Website: https://txwes.edu/academics/school-of-education/

Texas Woman's University, Graduate School, College of Professional Education, Department of Family Sciences, Denton, TX 76204-5769. Offers child development (MS); counseling and development (MS); early childhood development and education (PhD); early childhood education (M Ed); family studies (MS, PhD); family therapy (MS, PhD). *Accreditation:* ACA (one or more programs are accredited). *Program availability:* Part-time, evening/weekend. *Students:* Average age 34. In 2016, 99 master's, 9 doctorates awarded. Terminal master's awarded for partial completion of doctoral program. *Degree requirements:* For master's, comprehensive exam (for some programs), thesis (for some programs); for doctorate, comprehensive exam, thesis/dissertation. *Entrance requirements:* Additional exam requirements/recommendations for international students: Required—TOEFL (minimum score 550 paper-based; 79 iBT). *Application deadline:* For fall admission, 7/1 priority date for domestic students, 2/15 for international students; for spring admission, 9/15 priority date for domestic students, 7/1 for international students. Applications are processed on a rolling basis. Application fee: $50 ($75 for international students). Electronic applications accepted. *Expenses:* Tuition, state resident: full-time $9046; part-time $251 per credit hour. Tuition, nonresident: full-time $22,922; part-time $614 per credit hour. *International tuition:* $23,046 full-time. *Required fees:* $2690; $1285 per credit hour. One-time fee: $50. Tuition and fees vary according to course level, course load, program and reciprocity agreements. *Financial support:* Research assistantships, teaching assistantships, career-related internships or fieldwork, Federal Work-Study, institutionally sponsored loans, scholarships/grants, traineeships, health care benefits, and unspecified assistantships available. Support available to part-time students. Financial award application deadline: 3/1; financial award applicants required to submit FAFSA. *Faculty research:* Parenting/parent education, military families, play therapy, family sexuality, diversity, healthy relationships/healthy marriages, childhood obesity, male communication. *Unit head:* Dr. Karen Petty, Chair, 940-898-2685, Fax: 940-898-2676, E-mail: famsci@twu.edu. *Application contact:* Dr. Samuel Wheeler, Assistant Director of Admissions, 940-898-3188, Fax: 940-898-3081, E-mail: wheelersr@twu.edu.
Website: http://www.twu.edu/family-sciences/

Trevecca Nazarene University, Graduate Counseling Program, Nashville, TN 37210-2877. Offers clinical counseling: teaching and supervision (PhD); clinical mental health counseling (MA); marriage and family counseling/therapy (MMFC/T). *Accreditation:* ACA. *Program availability:* Part-time, evening/weekend. *Faculty:* 5 full-time (1 woman), 10 part-time/adjunct (6 women). *Students:* 135 full-time (94 women), 76 part-time (63 women); includes 49 minority (40 Black or African American, non-Hispanic/Latino; 1 American Indian or Alaska Native, non-Hispanic/Latino; 2 Hispanic/Latino; 6 Two or more races, non-Hispanic/Latino). Average age 34. In 2016, 55 master's, 5 doctorates awarded. *Degree requirements:* For master's, comprehensive exam; for doctorate, comprehensive exam, thesis/dissertation. *Entrance requirements:* For master's, MAT (minimum score of 380) or GRE (minimum score of 290 combined verbal and quantitative), minimum GPA of 2.7, official transcript from regionally accredited institution, 2 reference assessment forms; for doctorate, GRE (minimum scores: 300 combined verbal and quantitative, 3.5 analytical writing), minimum GPA of 3.25, official transcript of master's degree from regionally-accredited institution, 3 recommendation forms, 400-word letter of intent, professional vita, interview. Additional exam requirements/recommendations for international students: Required—TOEFL (minimum score 600 paper-based). *Application deadline:* Applications are processed on a rolling basis. Application fee: $0. Electronic applications accepted. *Expenses:* $636 per credit hour (for MA and MMFC/T); $799 per credit hour (for PhD). *Financial support:* Applicants required to submit FAFSA. *Unit head:* Dr. Peter Wilson, Director, 615-248-1384, Fax: 615-248-1662, E-mail: admissions_gradcouns@trevecca.edu. *Application contact:* 615-248-1384, Fax: 615-248-1662, E-mail: admissions_gradcouns@trevecca.edu.
Website: http://trevecca.edu/gradcounseling

Trinity Washington University, School of Education, Washington, DC 20017-1094. Offers clinical mental health counseling (MA); early childhood education (MAT); educating for change (M Ed); educational administration (MSA); elementary education (MAT); reading (M Ed); school counseling (MA); secondary education (MAT), including English, social studies; special education (MAT). *Accreditation:* NCATE. *Program availability:* Part-time, evening/weekend. *Degree requirements:* For master's, thesis (for some programs), capstone project(s). *Entrance requirements:* For master's, PRAXIS I, minimum GPA of 2.8. Additional exam requirements/recommendations for international students: Required—TOEFL (minimum score 550 paper-based). *Faculty research:* Technology, literacy, special education, organizations, inclusion models.

Troy University, Graduate School, College of Education, Program in Counseling and Psychology, Troy, AL 36082. Offers community counseling (MS). *Accreditation:* ACA; CORE; NCATE. *Program availability:* Part-time, evening/weekend. *Faculty:* 41 full-time (19 women), 27 part-time/adjunct (15 women). *Students:* 49 full-time (42 women), 156 part-time (136 women); includes 134 minority (121 Black or African American, non-Hispanic/Latino; 2 American Indian or Alaska Native, non-Hispanic/Latino; 5 Hispanic/Latino; 6 Two or more races, non-Hispanic/Latino). Average age 34. 246 applicants, 99% accepted, 84 enrolled. In 2016, 296 master's awarded. *Degree requirements:* For master's, comprehensive exam, thesis. *Entrance requirements:* For master's, GRE (minimum score of 850 on old exam or 290 on new exam), GMAT (minimum score of 380), or MAT (minimum score of 385), bachelor's degree; minimum undergraduate GPA of 2.5 or 3.0 on last 30 semester hours, letter of recommendation. Additional exam requirements/recommendations for international students: Required—TOEFL (minimum score 523 paper-based; 70 iBT), IELTS (minimum score 6). *Application deadline:* Applications are processed on a rolling basis. Application fee: $50. Electronic applications accepted. *Expenses:* Tuition, state resident: full-time $7146; part-time $397 per credit hour. Tuition, nonresident: full-time $14,292; part-time $794 per credit hour. *Required fees:* $802; $50 per semester. Tuition and fees vary according to campus/location and program. *Financial support:* Fellowships, career-related internships or fieldwork, and scholarships/grants available. Support available to part-time students. *Unit head:* Dr. Andrew Creamer, Chair, 334-670-3350, Fax: 334-670-3291, E-mail: acreamer@troy.edu. *Application contact:* Jessica A. Kimbro, Director of Graduate Admissions, 334-670-3178, E-mail: jacord@troy.edu.

Troy University, Graduate School, College of Education, Program in School Counseling, Troy, AL 36082. Offers MS, Ed S. *Accreditation:* ACA; CORE; NCATE. *Program availability:* Part-time, evening/weekend. *Faculty:* 2 full-time (1 woman), 4 part-time/adjunct (all women). *Students:* 13 full-time (12 women), 17 part-time (13 women); includes 19 minority (17 Black or African American, non-Hispanic/Latino; 1 Hispanic/Latino; 1 Two or more races, non-Hispanic/Latino). Average age 32. 14 applicants, 93% accepted, 5 enrolled. In 2016, 3 other advanced degrees awarded. *Degree requirements:* For master's, comprehensive exam, thesis. *Entrance requirements:* For master's, GRE (minimum score of 850 on old exam or 290 on new exam), GMAT (minimum score of 380), or MAT (minimum score of 385), bachelor's degree, minimum undergraduate GPA of 2.5 or 3.0 on last 30 semester hours, letter of recommendation, teaching certification, 2 years of teaching experience. Additional exam requirements/recommendations for international students: Required—TOEFL (minimum score 523 paper-based; 70 iBT), IELTS (minimum score 6). *Application deadline:* Applications are processed on a rolling basis. Application fee: $50. Electronic applications accepted. *Expenses:* Tuition, state resident: full-time $7146; part-time $397 per credit hour. Tuition, nonresident: full-time $14,292; part-time $794 per credit hour. *Required fees:* $802; $50 per semester. Tuition and fees vary according to campus/location and program. *Financial support:* Fellowships, career-related internships or fieldwork, and scholarships/grants available. Support available to part-time students. *Unit head:* Dr. Andrew Creamer, Chair, 334-670-3350, Fax: 334-670-3291, E-mail: drcreamer@troy.edu. *Application contact:* Jessica A. Kimbro, Director of Graduate Admissions, 334-670-3178, E-mail: jacord@troy.edu.

Universidad del Turabo, Graduate Programs, Programs in Education, Program in Counseling, Gurabo, PR 00778-3030. Offers M Ed. *Program availability:* Part-time, evening/weekend. *Students:* 34 full-time (29 women), 42 part-time (26 women); all minorities (all Hispanic/Latino). Average age 31. 44 applicants, 86% accepted, 32 enrolled. In 2016, 21 master's awarded. *Entrance requirements:* For master's, GRE, EXADEP, GMAT, interview, official transcript, essay, recommendation letters. *Application deadline:* For fall admission, 8/5 for domestic students. Applications are processed on a rolling basis. Application fee: $25. Electronic applications accepted. *Financial support:* Institutionally sponsored loans available. Financial award applicants required to submit FAFSA. *Unit head:* Israel Rodríguez, Dean, 787-743-7979 Ext. 4627. *Application contact:* Diriee Rodríguez, Admissions Director, 787-743-7979 Ext. 4453, E-mail: admisiones-ut@suagm.edu.
Website: http://ut.suagm.edu/es/educacion

Université de Moncton, Faculty of Education, Graduate Studies in Education, Moncton, NB E1A 3E9, Canada. Offers educational psychology (M Ed, MA Ed); guidance (M Ed, MA Ed); school administration (M Ed, MA Ed); teaching (M Ed, MA Ed). *Program availability:* Part-time. *Degree requirements:* For master's, proficiency in English and French. *Entrance requirements:* For master's, minimum GPA of 3.0. *Faculty research:* Guidance, ethnolinguistic vitality, children's rights, ecological education, entrepreneurship.

Université Laval, Faculty of Education, Department of Foundations and Interventions in Education, Programs in Orientation Sciences, Québec, QC G1K 7P4, Canada. Offers MA, PhD. Terminal master's awarded for partial completion of doctoral program. *Degree requirements:* For master's, thesis (for some programs); for doctorate, comprehensive exam, thesis/dissertation. *Entrance requirements:* For master's, English test (comprehension of written English), knowledge of French; for doctorate, oral exam (subject of thesis), knowledge of French and English. Electronic applications accepted. *Faculty research:* Counseling psychology, psychological education, vocational guidance, growth and development.

University at Buffalo, the State University of New York, Graduate School, Graduate School of Education, Department of Counseling, School, and Educational Psychology, Buffalo, NY 14260. Offers applied statistical analysis (Advanced Certificate); counseling/school psychology (PhD); counselor education (PhD); education studies (Ed M); educational psychology (MA, PhD); mental health counseling (MS, Certificate); mindful counseling for wellness and engagement (Advanced Certificate); rehabilitation counseling (MS, Advanced Certificate); school counseling (Ed M, Certificate). *Accreditation:* CORE (one or more programs are accredited). *Program availability:* Part-time, 100% online. *Faculty:* 27 full-time (11 women), 52 part-time/adjunct (45 women). *Students:* 161 full-time (131 women), 140 part-time (109 women); includes 30 minority (22 Black or African American, non-Hispanic/Latino; 2 American Indian or Alaska Native, non-Hispanic/Latino; 3 Asian, non-Hispanic/Latino; 3 Hispanic/Latino), 20 international. Average age 30. 321 applicants, 56% accepted, 113 enrolled. In 2016, 62 master's, 10 doctorates, 47 other advanced degrees awarded. *Degree requirements:* For master's, comprehensive exam (for some programs), thesis (for some programs); for doctorate, comprehensive exam, thesis/dissertation. *Entrance requirements:* For master's, GRE General Test, interview, letters of reference; for doctorate, GRE General Test, interview, letters of reference, writing sample. Additional exam requirements/recommendations for international students: Required—TOEFL (minimum score 79 iBT). *Application deadline:* For fall admission, 2/1 priority date for domestic and international students. Application fee: $50. Electronic applications accepted. *Financial support:* In 2016–17, 20 fellowships (averaging $8,477 per year), 33 research assistantships with tuition reimbursements (averaging $10,419 per year) were awarded; teaching assistantships, career-related internships or fieldwork, Federal Work-Study, institutionally sponsored loans, scholarships/grants, tuition waivers (full and partial), and unspecified assistantships also available. Financial award application deadline: 2/1; financial award applicants required to submit FAFSA. *Faculty research:* Multicultural counseling, class size effects, good work in counseling, eating disorders, outcome assessment, change agents and therapeutic factors in group counseling. *Total annual research expenditures:* $1.3 million. *Unit head:* Dr. Jeremy Finn, Chair, 716-645-1126, Fax: 716-645-6616, E-mail: finn@buffalo.edu. *Application contact:* Joanne Laska, Admissions Assistant,

Counselor Education

716-645-2110, Fax: 716-645-7937, E-mail: jlaska@buffalo.edu.
Website: http://gse.buffalo.edu/csep

The University of Akron, Graduate School, College of Health Professions, School of Counseling, Program in Counselor Education and Supervision, Akron, OH 44325. Offers PhD. *Accreditation:* ACA. *Students:* 14 full-time (13 women), 11 part-time (8 women); includes 6 minority (5 Black or African American, non-Hispanic/Latino; 1 Asian, non-Hispanic/Latino), 1 international. Average age 35. 10 applicants, 40% accepted, 3 enrolled. In 2016, 1 doctorate awarded. *Degree requirements:* For doctorate, comprehensive exam, thesis/dissertation, written and oral exams. *Entrance requirements:* For doctorate, GRE, minimum GPA of 3.25 on all completed graduate coursework, three letters of recommendation, professional resume, interview. Additional exam requirements/recommendations for international students: Required—TOEFL (minimum score 550 paper-based; 79 iBT), IELTS (minimum score 6.5). *Application deadline:* For fall admission, 1/15 for domestic and international students. Application fee: $45 ($70 for international students). Electronic applications accepted. *Expenses:* Tuition, state resident: full-time $8618; part-time $359 per credit hour. Tuition, nonresident: full-time $17,149; part-time $715 per credit hour. *Required fees:* $1652.
Website: https://www.uakron.edu/soc/doctoral/

The University of Akron, Graduate School, College of Health Professions, School of Counseling, Program in School Counseling, Akron, OH 44325. Offers MA, MS. *Accreditation:* ACA; NCATE. *Students:* 19 full-time (15 women), 39 part-time (30 women); includes 17 minority (12 Black or African American, non-Hispanic/Latino; 1 American Indian or Alaska Native, non-Hispanic/Latino; 1 Asian, non-Hispanic/Latino; 1 Hispanic/Latino; 2 Two or more races, non-Hispanic/Latino). Average age 30. 28 applicants, 61% accepted, 9 enrolled. In 2016, 13 master's awarded. *Degree requirements:* For master's, comprehensive exam. *Entrance requirements:* For master's, minimum GPA of 2.75, three letters of recommendation, Bureau of Criminal Investigation clearance, interview. Additional exam requirements/recommendations for international students: Required—TOEFL (minimum score 550 paper-based; 79 iBT), IELTS (minimum score 6.5). *Application deadline:* For fall admission, 3/15 for domestic and international students; for spring admission, 10/1 for domestic and international students. Application fee: $45 ($70 for international students). Electronic applications accepted. *Expenses:* Tuition, state resident: full-time $8618; part-time $359 per credit hour. Tuition, nonresident: full-time $17,149; part-time $715 per credit hour. *Required fees:* $1652. *Application contact:* Dr. Delila Owens, Program Coordinator, 330-972-8635, E-mail: dowens1@uakron.edu.
Website: https://www.uakron.edu/soc/masters/school-counseling/index.dot

The University of Alabama, Graduate School, College of Education, Department of Educational Studies in Psychology, Research Methodology and Counseling, Tuscaloosa, AL 35487. Offers MA, Ed D, PhD, Ed S. *Accreditation:* ACA (one or more programs are accredited); CORE; NCATE. *Program availability:* Part-time. *Faculty:* 32 full-time (17 women). *Students:* 105 full-time (85 women), 98 part-time (86 women); includes 68 minority (47 Black or African American, non-Hispanic/Latino; 1 American Indian or Alaska Native, non-Hispanic/Latino; 5 Asian, non-Hispanic/Latino; 9 Hispanic/Latino; 6 Two or more races, non-Hispanic/Latino), 13 international. Average age 34. 165 applicants, 65% accepted, 64 enrolled. In 2016, 43 master's, 3 doctorates, 8 other advanced degrees awarded. *Degree requirements:* For master's, comprehensive exam, thesis optional; for doctorate, comprehensive exam, thesis/dissertation; for Ed S, comprehensive exam. *Entrance requirements:* For master's and doctorate, GRE General Test, MAT, or NTE, minimum GPA of 3.0; for Ed S, minimum GPA of 3.0 during previous 2 years. Additional exam requirements/recommendations for international students: Required—TOEFL (minimum score 550 paper-based), IELTS (minimum score 6.5). *Application deadline:* For fall admission, 7/1 for domestic students; for spring admission, 11/1 for domestic students. Applications are processed on a rolling basis. Application fee: $50 ($60 for international students). Electronic applications accepted. *Expenses:* Tuition, state resident: full-time $10,470. Tuition, nonresident: full-time $26,950. *Financial support:* Research assistantships with tuition reimbursements, teaching assistantships with tuition reimbursements, and career-related internships or fieldwork available. Financial award application deadline: 7/14; financial award applicants required to submit FAFSA. *Faculty research:* Moral development, positive psychology, children's fears, digital storytelling. *Total annual research expenditures:* $119,924. *Unit head:* Dr. Aaron Kuntz, Department Head, 205-348-5675, E-mail: amkuntz@ua.edu. *Application contact:* Marie S. Marshall, Office Associate II, 205-348-8362, Fax: 205-348-0683, E-mail: mmarshal@bamaed.ua.edu.
Website: http://education.ua.edu/departments/esprmc/

The University of Alabama at Birmingham, School of Education, Program in Counseling, Birmingham, AL 35294. Offers MA. *Accreditation:* ACA; CORE; NCATE. *Degree requirements:* For master's, comprehensive exam, thesis optional, practicum, internship. *Entrance requirements:* For master's, GRE General Test or MAT, minimum GPA of 2.75, interview. Electronic applications accepted. Full-time tuition and fees vary according to course load and program.

University of Alaska Anchorage, College of Education, Program in Counseling and Guidance, Anchorage, AK 99508. Offers M Ed. *Program availability:* Part-time. *Entrance requirements:* For master's, GRE or MAT, interview, resume. Additional exam requirements/recommendations for international students: Required—TOEFL (minimum score 550 paper-based).

University of Alaska Fairbanks, School of Education, Program in Counseling, Fairbanks, AK 99775. Offers community counseling (M Ed). *Program availability:* 100% online, blended/hybrid learning. *Students:* 11 full-time (9 women), 47 part-time (39 women); includes 12 minority (3 American Indian or Alaska Native, non-Hispanic/Latino; 2 Hispanic/Latino; 7 Two or more races, non-Hispanic/Latino), 1 international. Average age 38. 44 applicants, 52% accepted, 22 enrolled. In 2016, 14 master's, 1 other advanced degree awarded. *Degree requirements:* For master's, comprehensive exam, oral defense of project or thesis. *Entrance requirements:* For master's, bachelor's degree from accredited institution with minimum cumulative undergraduate and major GPA of 3.0; for Graduate Certificate, master's degree from accredited institution with minimum GPA of 3.0. Additional exam requirements/recommendations for international students: Required—TOEFL (minimum score 550 paper-based; 79 iBT), IELTS (minimum score 6.5). *Application deadline:* For fall admission, 3/1 for domestic and international students; for spring admission, 10/1 for domestic students, 9/1 for international students. Applications are processed on a rolling basis. Application fee: $60. Electronic applications accepted. *Expenses:* Tuition, state resident: full-time $7992; part-time $444 per credit. Tuition, nonresident: full-time $16,326; part-time $907 per credit. *Required fees:* $39 per credit. $322 per semester. Tuition and fees vary according to course level, course load, campus/location, program and reciprocity agreements. *Financial support:* In 2016–17, 1 teaching assistantship with full tuition reimbursement (averaging $4,247 per year) was awarded; fellowships with full tuition reimbursements, career-related internships or fieldwork, Federal Work-Study, scholarships/grants, health care benefits, and unspecified assistantships also available. Support available to part-time students. Financial award application deadline: 7/1; financial award applicants required to submit FAFSA. *Unit head:* Jane Monahan, Graduate Advisor, 907-474-5362, Fax: 907-474-5451, E-mail: jmmonahan@alaska.edu. *Application contact:* Mary Kreta, Director of Admissions, 907-474-7500, Fax: 907-474-7097, E-mail: admissions@uaf.edu.
Website: https://sites.google.com/a/alaska.edu/uaf-soe-graduate/home/potential-students——degree-programs/counseling

University of Alberta, Faculty of Graduate Studies and Research, Department of Educational Psychology, Edmonton, AB T6G 2E1, Canada. Offers counseling psychology (M Ed, PhD); educational psychology (M Ed, PhD); instructional technology (M Ed); school counseling (M Ed); school psychology (M Ed, PhD); special education (M Ed, PhD); special education-deafness studies (M Ed); teaching English as a second language (M Ed). *Program availability:* Part-time. *Degree requirements:* For master's, thesis optional; for doctorate, comprehensive exam, thesis/dissertation. *Entrance requirements:* For master's and doctorate, minimum GPA of 3.0. Additional exam requirements/recommendations for international students: Required—TOEFL. *Faculty research:* Human learning, development and assessment.

The University of Arizona, College of Education, Department of Disability and Psychoeducational Studies, Program in School Counseling, Tucson, AZ 85721. Offers MA. *Accreditation:* ACA. *Program availability:* Part-time. *Degree requirements:* For master's, presentation or thesis. *Entrance requirements:* Additional exam requirements/recommendations for international students: Required—TOEFL (minimum score 550 paper-based; 79 iBT). Electronic applications accepted.

University of Arkansas, Graduate School, College of Education and Health Professions, Department of Rehabilitation, Human Resources and Communication Disorders, Program in Counseling, Fayetteville, AR 72701. Offers MS, PhD, Ed S. *Accreditation:* ACA; NCATE. *Program availability:* Part-time, evening/weekend. *Students:* 130 part-time (96 women); includes 30 minority (9 Black or African American, non-Hispanic/Latino; 4 American Indian or Alaska Native, non-Hispanic/Latino; 2 Asian, non-Hispanic/Latino; 10 Hispanic/Latino; 5 Two or more races, non-Hispanic/Latino), 3 international. In 2016, 21 master's awarded. *Degree requirements:* For master's, thesis optional; for doctorate, thesis/dissertation. *Entrance requirements:* For master's, GRE General Test or MAT; for doctorate, GRE General Test. *Application deadline:* For fall admission, 3/15 for domestic students, 4/1 for international students; for spring admission, 10/15 for domestic students, 10/1 for international students. Applications are processed on a rolling basis. Application fee: $40 ($50 for international students). Electronic applications accepted. *Financial support:* In 2016–17, 15 research assistantships, 2 teaching assistantships were awarded; fellowships with tuition reimbursements, career-related internships or fieldwork, and Federal Work-Study also available. Support available to part-time students. Financial award application deadline: 4/1; financial award applicants required to submit FAFSA. *Unit head:* Dr. Kate Mamiseishvili, Unit Head, 479-575-4758, E-mail: kmamisei@uark.edu. *Application contact:* Dr. Kristin Higgins, Graduate Coordinator, 479-575-3329, E-mail: kkhiggi@uark.edu.
Website: http://cned.uark.edu

University of Arkansas at Little Rock, Graduate School, College of Education and Health Professions, Department of Counseling, Adult and Rehabilitation Education, Program in Counselor Education, Little Rock, AR 72204-1099. Offers M Ed. *Program availability:* Part-time, evening/weekend. *Degree requirements:* For master's, comprehensive exam, portfolio or thesis; PRAXIS II. *Entrance requirements:* For master's, minimum GPA of 2.75, teaching certificate, interview, current resume.

University of Central Arkansas, Graduate School, College of Education, Department of Leadership Studies, Program in School Counseling, Conway, AR 72035-0001. Offers MS. *Accreditation:* NCATE. *Program availability:* Part-time, evening/weekend, online learning. *Degree requirements:* For master's, comprehensive exam, thesis optional. *Entrance requirements:* For master's, GRE General Test, minimum GPA of 2.7. Additional exam requirements/recommendations for international students: Required—TOEFL (minimum score 550 paper-based). Electronic applications accepted.

University of Central Florida, College of Education and Human Performance, Department of Educational and Human Sciences, Program in Counselor Education, Orlando, FL 32816. Offers M Ed, MA, Certificate, Ed S. *Accreditation:* ACA. *Program availability:* Part-time, evening/weekend. *Students:* 128 full-time (109 women), 56 part-time (48 women); includes 55 minority (14 Black or African American, non-Hispanic/Latino; 5 Asian, non-Hispanic/Latino; 31 Hispanic/Latino; 5 Two or more races, non-Hispanic/Latino), 1 international. Average age 26. 188 applicants, 40% accepted, 52 enrolled. In 2016, 62 master's, 13 other advanced degrees awarded. *Degree requirements:* For master's, comprehensive exam, thesis or alternative. *Entrance requirements:* For master's, GRE General Test, interview, minimum GPA of 3.0. Additional exam requirements/recommendations for international students: Required—TOEFL. *Application deadline:* For fall admission, 2/1 for domestic students; for spring admission, 9/1 for domestic students. Application fee: $30. Electronic applications accepted. *Expenses:* Tuition, state resident: part-time $288.16 per credit hour. Tuition, nonresident: part-time $1071.31 per credit hour. *Financial support:* In 2016–17, 16 students received support, including 3 fellowships with partial tuition reimbursements available (averaging $6,487 per year), 12 research assistantships with partial tuition reimbursements available (averaging $8,729 per year), 2 teaching assistantships with partial tuition reimbursements available (averaging $5,036 per year); career-related internships or fieldwork, Federal Work-Study, institutionally sponsored loans, tuition waivers (partial), and unspecified assistantships also available. Financial award application deadline: 3/1; financial award applicants required to submit FAFSA. *Unit head:* Dr. W. Bryce Hagedorn, Program Coordinator, 407-823-2999, E-mail: bryce.hagedorn@ucf.edu. *Application contact:* Assistant Director, Graduate Admissions, 407-823-2766, Fax: 407-823-6442, E-mail: gradadmissions@ucf.edu.
Website: http://education.ucf.edu/counselored/

University of Central Missouri, The Graduate School, Warrensburg, MO 64093. Offers accountancy (MA); accounting (MBA); applied mathematics (MS); aviation safety (MA); biology (MS); business administration (MBA); career and technical education leadership (MS); college student personnel administration (MS); communication (MA); computer science (MS); counseling (MS); criminal justice (MS); educational leadership (Ed D); educational technology (MS); elementary and early childhood education (MSE); English (MA); environmental studies (MA); finance (MBA); history (MA); human services/educational technology (Ed S); human services/learning resources (Ed S); human services/professional counseling (Ed S); industrial hygiene (MS); industrial management (MS); information systems (MBA); information technology (MS); kinesiology (MS); library science and information services (MS); literacy education (MSE); marketing (MBA); mathematics (MS); music (MA); occupational safety management (MS); psychology (MS); rural family nursing (MS); school administration (MSE); social gerontology (MS); sociology (MA); special education (MSE); speech language pathology (MS); superintendency (Ed S); teaching (MAT); teaching English as a second language (MA); technology (MS); technology management (PhD); theatre (MA). *Program availability:* Part-time, 100% online, blended/hybrid learning. *Degree requirements:* For master's and Ed S, comprehensive exam (for some programs), thesis (for some programs). *Entrance requirements:* Additional exam requirements/recommendations for international students: Required—TOEFL (minimum score 550 paper-based; 79 iBT). Electronic applications accepted.

University of Central Oklahoma, The Jackson College of Graduate Studies, College of Education and Professional Studies, Department of Advanced Professional and Special Services, Edmond, OK 73034-5209. Offers educational leadership (M Ed); library media education (M Ed); reading (M Ed); school counseling (M Ed); special education (M Ed), including mild/moderate disabilities, severe-profound/multiple disabilities, special education; speech-language pathology (MS). *Accreditation:* ASHA. *Program availability:* Part-time. *Degree requirements:* For master's, comprehensive exam (for some programs), thesis (for some programs). *Entrance requirements:* For master's, GRE. Additional exam requirements/recommendations for international students: Required—TOEFL (minimum score 550 paper-based; 79 iBT), IELTS (minimum score 6.5). Electronic applications accepted. *Faculty research:* Intellectual freedom, fair use copyright, technology integration, young adult literature, distance learning.

University of Cincinnati, Graduate School, College of Education, Criminal Justice, and Human Services, School of Human Services, Counseling Program, Cincinnati, OH 45221. Offers counselor education (Ed D); mental health (MA); school counseling (M Ed); substance abuse prevention (Graduate Certificate). *Accreditation:* ACA (one or more programs are accredited); NCATE. *Program availability:* Part-time. Terminal master's awarded for partial completion of doctoral program. *Degree requirements:* For master's, comprehensive exam, thesis or alternative; for doctorate, comprehensive exam, thesis/dissertation. *Entrance requirements:* For master's and doctorate, GRE General Test, interview. Additional exam requirements/recommendations for international students: Required—TOEFL (minimum score 620 paper-based). *Application deadline:* For fall admission, 1/31 for domestic students. Application fee: $65 ($70 for international students). Electronic applications accepted. *Expenses: Tuition, area resident:* Full-time $12,790; part-time $389 per credit hour. Tuition, state resident: full-time $13,290; part-time $419 per credit hour. Tuition, nonresident: full-time $24,532; part-time $976 per credit hour. *International tuition:* $24,832 full-time. *Required fees:* $3958; $140 per credit hour. Tuition and fees vary according to course load, degree level, program and reciprocity agreements. *Financial support:* Teaching assistantships with full tuition reimbursements, career-related internships or fieldwork, scholarships/grants, tuition waivers (full), and unspecified assistantships available. Support available to part-time students. *Faculty research:* Group work, career development, ecology, prevention, multicultural. *Unit head:* Dr. Michael Brubaker, Program Director, 513-556-9196, Fax: 513-556-3898, E-mail: michael.brubaker@uc.edu. *Application contact:* Amanda Carlisle, Program Coordinator, 513-556-3335, Fax: 513-556-3898, E-mail: amanda.carlisle@uc.edu.
Website: http://cech.uc.edu/human-services/graduate-programs/counselor-ed-phd/about.html

University of Colorado Colorado Springs, College of Education, Colorado Springs, CO 80918. Offers counseling and human services (MA); curriculum and instruction (MA); educational leadership (MA); educational leadership, research and policy (PhD); special education (MA); teaching English to speakers of other languages (MA). *Accreditation:* ACA; NCATE. *Program availability:* Part-time, evening/weekend, 100% online, blended/hybrid learning. *Faculty:* 26 full-time (18 women), 33 part-time/adjunct (21 women). *Students:* 136 full-time (94 women), 264 part-time (177 women); includes 99 minority (17 Black or African American, non-Hispanic/Latino; 1 American Indian or Alaska Native, non-Hispanic/Latino; 8 Asian, non-Hispanic/Latino; 55 Hispanic/Latino; 18 Two or more races, non-Hispanic/Latino), 9 international. Average age 35. 152 applicants, 89% accepted, 88 enrolled. In 2016, 161 master's, 11 doctorates awarded. *Degree requirements:* For master's, comprehensive exam, thesis or alternative, microcomputer proficiency; for doctorate, comprehensive exam, thesis/dissertation, research lab. *Entrance requirements:* For master's and doctorate, GRE General Test. Additional exam requirements/recommendations for international students: Recommended—TOEFL (minimum score 550 paper-based; 80 iBT), IELTS (minimum score 6). *Application deadline:* For fall admission, 2/1 priority date for domestic students, 2/1 for international students; for spring admission, 10/15 for domestic students, 10/1 for international students. Applications are processed on a rolling basis. Application fee: $60 ($100 for international students). Electronic applications accepted. *Expenses:* Contact institution. *Financial support:* In 2016–17, 108 students received support. Career-related internships or fieldwork, Federal Work-Study, scholarships/grants, and unspecified assistantships available. Support available to part-time students. Financial award application deadline: 3/1; financial award applicants required to submit FAFSA. *Faculty research:* Linguistically diverse education (LDE), educational policy, evidence-based reading and writing instruction, relational and social aggression, positive behavior supports, inclusive schooling, K-12 education policy. *Total annual research expenditures:* $272,136. *Unit head:* Dr. Valerie Martin Conley, Dean, 719-255-4133, E-mail: vmconley@uccs.edu. *Application contact:* The College of Education Student Resource Office, 719-255-4996, E-mail: education@uccs.edu.
Website: http://www.uccs.edu/coe

University of Colorado Denver, School of Education and Human Development, Program in Counseling Psychology and Counselor Education, Denver, CO 80217. Offers counseling (MA), including clinical mental health counseling, couple and family counseling, multicultural counseling, school counseling; school counseling (MA). *Accreditation:* ACA; NCATE. *Program availability:* Part-time, evening/weekend. *Students:* 179 full-time (139 women), 42 part-time (32 women); includes 45 minority (10 Black or African American, non-Hispanic/Latino; 5 Asian, non-Hispanic/Latino; 25 Hispanic/Latino; 5 Two or more races, non-Hispanic/Latino), 1 international. Average age 30. 227 applicants, 28% accepted, 26 enrolled. In 2016, 61 master's awarded. *Degree requirements:* For master's, comprehensive exam (for some programs), thesis or alternative, 63-66 hours. *Entrance requirements:* For master's, GRE or MAT (unless applicant already holds a graduate degree), letters of recommendation, interview, resume, transcripts from all colleges/universities attended. Additional exam requirements/recommendations for international students: Required—TOEFL (minimum score 525 paper-based; 71 iBT); Recommended—IELTS (minimum score 6.3). *Application deadline:* For fall admission, 1/15 for domestic students, 1/1 for international students; for spring admission, 9/15 for domestic students, 9/1 for international students. Application fee: $50 ($75 for international students). Electronic applications accepted. *Expenses:* Contact institution. *Financial support:* In 2016–17, 16 students received support. Research assistantships, Federal Work-Study, institutionally sponsored loans, scholarships/grants, and traineeships available. Financial award application deadline: 4/1; financial award applicants required to submit FAFSA. *Faculty research:* Spiritual issues in counseling, multicultural and diversity issues in counseling, adolescent suicide, career development. *Unit head:* Farah Ibrahim, Counseling Professor, 303-315-6329, E-mail: farah.ibrahim@ucdenver.edu. *Application contact:* Student Services Coordinator, 303-315-6300, Fax: 303-315-6311, E-mail: education@ucdenver.edu.
Website: http://www.ucdenver.edu/academics/colleges/SchoolOfEducation/Academics/MASTERS/counseling/Pages/default.aspx

University of Connecticut, Graduate School, Neag School of Education, Department of Educational Psychology, Program in Counseling Psychology, Storrs, CT 06269. Offers counseling psychology (PhD); school counseling (MA). *Accreditation:* ACA. Terminal master's awarded for partial completion of doctoral program. *Degree requirements:* For master's, comprehensive exam, thesis or alternative; for doctorate, thesis/dissertation. *Entrance requirements:* For doctorate, GRE General Test. Additional exam requirements/recommendations for international students: Required—TOEFL (minimum score 550 paper-based). Electronic applications accepted.

University of Dayton, Department of Counselor Education and Human Services, Dayton, OH 45469. Offers clinical mental health counseling (MS Ed); college student personnel (MS Ed); higher education administration (MS Ed); human services (MS Ed); school counseling (MS Ed); school psychology (MS Ed, Ed S). *Accreditation:* ACA; NCATE. *Program availability:* Part-time, evening/weekend. *Faculty:* 10 full-time (6 women), 24 part-time/adjunct (15 women). *Students:* 198 full-time (155 women), 95 part-time (75 women); includes 15 minority (8 Black or African American, non-Hispanic/Latino; 2 Asian, non-Hispanic/Latino; 2 Hispanic/Latino; 3 Two or more races, non-Hispanic/Latino), 3 international. Average age 36. 426 applicants, 28% accepted. In 2016, 115 master's, 9 Ed Ss awarded. *Degree requirements:* For Ed S, thesis. *Entrance requirements:* For master's, MAT or GRE (if GPA less than 2.75), essays (for some programs). Additional exam requirements/recommendations for international students: Required—TOEFL (minimum score 550 paper-based; 80 iBT); Recommended—IELTS. *Application deadline:* For fall admission, 3/10 priority date for domestic and international students; for spring admission, 9/10 priority date for domestic and international students; for summer admission, 12/1 priority date for domestic and international students. Application fee: $0 ($50 for international students). Electronic applications accepted. *Expenses:* $620 per credit hour (for master's degree programs); $740 per credit hour (for Ed S). *Financial support:* In 2016–17, 7 research assistantships with partial tuition reimbursements (averaging $8,038 per year), 4 teaching assistantships with partial tuition reimbursements (averaging $9,390 per year) were awarded; career-related internships or fieldwork, institutionally sponsored loans, health care benefits, and unspecified assistantships also available. Financial award application deadline: 1/9; financial award applicants required to submit FAFSA. *Faculty research:* School bonding, traumatic brain injuries, second-year student experience, impact of physical space on learning, integrative health and mental health care. *Total annual research expenditures:* $1,500. *Unit head:* Dr. Alan Demmitt, Chair, 937-229-3644, Fax: 937-229-1055, E-mail: ademmitt1@udayton.edu. *Application contact:* Kathleen Brown, Administrative Assistant, 937-229-3644, Fax: 937-229-1055, E-mail: kbrown1@udayton.edu.
Website: https://www.udayton.edu/education/departments_and_programs/edc/

University of Florida, Graduate School, College of Education, School of Human Development and Organizational Studies in Education, Gainesville, FL 32611. Offers counseling and counselor education (Ed D, PhD), including counseling and counselor education, marriage and family counseling, mental health counseling, school counseling and guidance; educational leadership (M Ed, MAE, Ed D, PhD, Ed S), including educational leadership (Ed D, PhD), educational policy (Ed D, PhD); higher education administration (Ed D, PhD), including education policy (Ed D), educational policy, higher education administration; marriage and family counseling (M Ed, MAE, Ed D, PhD, Ed S); mental health counseling (M Ed, MAE, Ed D, PhD, Ed S); research and evaluation methodology (M Ed, MAE, Ed D, PhD); school counseling and guidance (M Ed, MAE, Ed D, PhD, Ed S); student personnel in higher education (M Ed, MAE). *Accreditation:* ACA (one or more programs are accredited); NCATE. *Program availability:* Part-time, online learning. Terminal master's awarded for partial completion of doctoral program. *Degree requirements:* For master's, thesis optional; for doctorate, comprehensive exam, thesis/dissertation. *Entrance requirements:* For master's and doctorate, GRE General Test, minimum GPA of 3.0 (undergraduate), 3.5 (graduate); for Ed S, GRE General Test. Additional exam requirements/recommendations for international students: Required—TOEFL (minimum score 550 paper-based; 80 iBT), IELTS (minimum score 6). Electronic applications accepted.

University of Georgia, College of Education, Department of Counseling and Human Development Services, Athens, GA 30602. Offers college student affairs administration (M Ed, PhD); professional school counseling (Ed S). *Accreditation:* ACA (one or more programs are accredited); APA (one or more programs are accredited); NCATE. *Degree requirements:* For master's, thesis (MA); for doctorate, variable foreign language requirement, thesis/dissertation. *Entrance requirements:* For master's, GRE General Test or MAT; for doctorate, GRE General Test. *Application deadline:* For fall admission, 7/1 priority date for domestic students; for spring admission, 11/15 for domestic students. Application fee: $50. Electronic applications accepted. *Financial support:* Fellowships, research assistantships, teaching assistantships, and unspecified assistantships available. *Unit head:* Dr. Rosemary E. Phelps, Head, 706-542-4221, Fax: 706-542-4130, E-mail: rephelps@uga.edu. *Application contact:* Merrilyn Dunn, Graduate Coordinator, 706-542-1812, E-mail: chdsgrad@uga.edu.
Website: http://www.coe.uga.edu/chds/

University of Guam, Office of Graduate Studies, School of Education, Program in Counseling, Mangilao, GU 96923. Offers MA. *Degree requirements:* For master's, comprehensive oral and written exams, special project or thesis. *Entrance requirements:* For master's, GRE General Test. Additional exam requirements/recommendations for international students: Required—TOEFL. *Faculty research:* Drugs in the local schools, standardized teaching procedures in the elementary school, how to address the dropout problems.

University of Hartford, College of Education, Nursing, and Health Professions, Program in Counseling, West Hartford, CT 06117-1599. Offers M Ed, MS, Sixth Year Certificate. *Accreditation:* NCATE. *Program availability:* Part-time, evening/weekend. *Degree requirements:* For master's and Sixth Year Certificate, comprehensive exam. *Entrance requirements:* For master's, GRE General Test or MAT, PRAXIS I or waiver, interview, 2 letters of recommendation; for Sixth Year Certificate, GRE General Test or MAT, PRAXIS I or waiver, interview. Additional exam requirements/recommendations for international students: Required—TOEFL (minimum score 550 paper-based). Electronic applications accepted.

University of Holy Cross, Program in Education and Counseling, New Orleans, LA 70131-7399. Offers administration and supervision (M Ed); curriculum and instruction (M Ed); marriage and family counseling (MA); school counseling (M Ed, MA). *Accreditation:* ACA; NCATE. *Program availability:* Part-time, evening/weekend. *Degree requirements:* For master's, thesis. *Entrance requirements:* For master's, GRE General Test, minimum GPA of 2.7.

University of Houston–Clear Lake, School of Education, Program in Foundations and Professional Studies, Houston, TX 77058-1002. Offers counseling (MS); instructional technology (MS); multicultural studies (MS). *Program availability:* Part-time, evening/weekend. *Degree requirements:* For master's, thesis optional. *Entrance requirements:* For master's, GRE or minimum GPA of 3.0 in last 60 hours. Additional exam requirements/recommendations for international students: Required—TOEFL (minimum score 550 paper-based). Electronic applications accepted.

University of Houston–Victoria, School of Education, Health Professions and Human Development, Victoria, TX 77901-4450. Offers administration and supervision (M Ed); adult and higher education (M Ed); counselor education (M Ed); curriculum and instruction (M Ed); educational technology (M Ed); special education (M Ed). *Program availability:* Part-time, evening/weekend, online learning. *Degree requirements:* For master's, comprehensive exam, project or thesis. *Entrance requirements:* For master's, GRE General Test. Additional exam requirements/recommendations for international students: Required—TOEFL. Electronic applications accepted. *Faculty research:*

Reading and language arts education, evaluation and diagnosis of special children's abilities.

University of Idaho, College of Graduate Studies, College of Education, Department of Leadership and Counseling, Boise, ID 83702. Offers adult/organizational learning and leadership (MS, Ed S); educational leadership (M Ed, Ed S); rehabilitation counseling and human services (M Ed, MS); school counseling (M Ed, MS); special education (M Ed). *Faculty:* 14 full-time, 7 part-time/adjunct. *Students:* 37 full-time (26 women), 154 part-time (84 women). Average age 39. In 2016, 75 master's, 21 other advanced degrees awarded. *Entrance requirements:* For master's, minimum GPA of 3.0. Additional exam requirements/recommendations for international students: Required—TOEFL. *Application deadline:* Applications are processed on a rolling basis. Application fee: $60. Electronic applications accepted. *Expenses:* Tuition, state resident: full-time $6460; part-time $414 per credit hour. Tuition, nonresident: full-time $21,268; part-time $1237 per credit hour. *Required fees:* $2070; $60 per credit hour. Full-time tuition and fees vary according to course load and reciprocity agreements. *Financial support:* Applicants required to submit FAFSA. *Unit head:* Dr. Kathy Canfield-Davis, Chair, 208-364-4047, E-mail: lead@uidaho.edu. *Application contact:* Sean Scoggin, Graduate Recruitment Coordinator, 208-885-4723, Fax: 208-885-4406, E-mail: graduateadmissions@uidaho.edu.
Website: https://www.uidaho.edu/ed/lc

University of Illinois at Urbana–Champaign, Graduate College, College of Education, Department of Educational Psychology, Champaign, IL 61820. Offers Ed M, MA, MS, PhD, CAS. *Accreditation:* APA (one or more programs are accredited). *Program availability:* Part-time, online learning.

The University of Iowa, Graduate College, College of Education, Department of Rehabilitation and Counselor Education, Iowa City, IA 52242-1316. Offers counselor education and supervision (PhD); couple and family therapy (PhD); rehabilitation and mental health counseling (MA); rehabilitation counselor education (PhD); school counseling (MA). *Accreditation:* ACA (one or more programs are accredited); CORE (one or more programs are accredited). *Degree requirements:* For master's, thesis optional, exam; for doctorate, comprehensive exam, thesis/dissertation. *Entrance requirements:* For master's and doctorate, GRE General Test, minimum GPA of 3.0. Additional exam requirements/recommendations for international students: Required—TOEFL (minimum score 550 paper-based; 81 iBT). Electronic applications accepted.

University of La Verne, LaFetra College of Education, Program in Educational Counseling, La Verne, CA 91750-4443. Offers educational counseling (MS); pupil personnel services (Credential); school psychology (MS). *Program availability:* Part-time. *Students:* 66 full-time (57 women), 98 part-time (79 women); includes 115 minority (8 Black or African American, non-Hispanic/Latino; 6 Asian, non-Hispanic/Latino; 100 Hispanic/Latino; 1 Two or more races, non-Hispanic/Latino). Average age 30. *Degree requirements:* For master's, thesis optional. *Entrance requirements:* For master's, California Basic Educational Skills Test, minimum undergraduate GPA of 2.75, graduate 3.0; interview; 1 year's experience working with children; 3 letters of reference. Additional exam requirements/recommendations for international students: Required—TOEFL (minimum score 550 paper-based). *Application deadline:* Applications are processed on a rolling basis. Application fee: $50. *Expenses:* Contact institution. *Financial support:* Scholarships/grants and traineeships available. Financial award application deadline: 3/2; financial award applicants required to submit FAFSA. *Unit head:* Laurie Schroeder, Chairperson, 909-448-4653, E-mail: lschroeder3@laverne.edu. *Application contact:* Kristen Ahn, Assistant Director of Graduate Admissions, 909-448-4480, E-mail: sahn@laverne.edu.
Website: http://www.laverne.edu/education/

University of La Verne, Regional and Online Campuses, Graduate Credential Program in Education, California Statewide Campus, La Verne, CA 91750-4443. Offers administration services (preliminary) (Credential); education specialist: mild/moderate (Credential); English (Certificate); multiple subject teaching (Credential); pupil personnel services: school counseling (Credential); single subject teaching (Credential); special education (MS); special emphasis (M Ed). *Accreditation:* NCATE. *Program availability:* Part-time. *Entrance requirements:* For degree, California Basic Educational Skills Test, minimum undergraduate GPA of 2.75, 3 letters of recommendation, interview. *Expenses:* Contact institution.

University of La Verne, Regional and Online Campuses, Graduate Programs, Central Coast/Vandenberg Air Force Base Campuses, La Verne, CA 91750-4443. Offers business administration for experienced professionals (MBA), including health services management, information technology; education (special emphasis) (M Ed); educational counseling (MS); educational leadership (M Ed); multiple subject (elementary) (Credential); preliminary administrative services (Credential); pupil personnel services (Credential); single subject (secondary) (Credential). *Program availability:* Part-time. *Expenses:* Contact institution.

University of La Verne, Regional and Online Campuses, Graduate Programs, High Desert Campus, Victorville, CA 92392. Offers business administration for experienced professionals (MBA); educational counseling (MS); educational leadership (M Ed); multiple subject (elementary) (Credential); preliminary administrative services (Credential); pupil personnel services (Credential); single subject (secondary) (Credential). *Expenses:* Contact institution.

University of La Verne, Regional and Online Campuses, Graduate Programs, Kern County Campus, Bakersfield, CA 93301. Offers business administration for experienced professionals (MBA-EP); education (special emphasis) (M Ed); educational counseling (MS); educational leadership (M Ed); health administration (MHA); leadership and management (MS); mild/moderate education specialist (Credential); multiple subject (elementary) (Credential); organizational leadership (Ed D); preliminary administrative services (Credential); single subject (secondary) (Credential); special education studies (MS). *Program availability:* Part-time, evening/weekend. *Expenses:* Contact institution.

University of La Verne, Regional and Online Campuses, Graduate Programs, Orange County Campus, Irvine, CA 92840. Offers business administration for experienced professionals (MBA); educational counseling (MS); educational leadership (M Ed); health administration (MHA); leadership and management (MS); preliminary administrative services (Credential); pupil personnel services (Credential). *Program availability:* Part-time. *Expenses:* Contact institution.

University of La Verne, Regional and Online Campuses, Graduate Programs, San Fernando Valley Campus, Burbank, CA 91505. Offers business administration for experienced professionals (MBA-EP); educational counseling (MS); educational leadership (M Ed); leadership and management (MS); preliminary administrative services (Credential); pupil personnel services (Credential). *Program availability:* Part-time, evening/weekend. *Expenses:* Contact institution.

University of La Verne, Regional and Online Campuses, Graduate Programs, Ventura County/Point Mugu Naval Air Station Campuses, Oxnard, CA 93036. Offers business administration for experienced professionals (MS); educational counseling (MS); educational leadership (M Ed); leadership and management (MS); multiple subject (elementary) (Credential); pupil personnel services (Credential); single subject (secondary) (Credential). *Program availability:* Part-time, evening/weekend. *Expenses:* Contact institution.

University of La Verne, Regional and Online Campuses, Master's Programs in Education, California Statewide Campus, La Verne, CA 91750-4443. Offers administration services (preliminary) (Credential); education specialist: mild/moderate (Credential); educational counseling (MS); educational leadership (M Ed); multiple subject teaching (Credential); pupil personnel services: school counseling (Credential); single subject teaching (Credential); special education studies (MS); special emphasis (M Ed). *Accreditation:* NCATE. *Entrance requirements:* For master's, California Basic Educational Skills Test, 3 letters of recommendation, teaching credential. *Expenses:* Contact institution.

University of Lethbridge, School of Graduate Studies, Lethbridge, AB T1K 3M4, Canada. Offers addictions counseling (M Sc); agricultural biotechnology (M Sc); agricultural studies (M Sc, MA); anthropology (MA); archaeology (M Sc, MA); art (MA, MFA); biochemistry (M Sc); biological sciences (M Sc); biomolecular science (PhD); biosystems and biodiversity (PhD); Canadian studies (MA); chemistry (M Sc); computer science (M Sc); computer science and geographical information science (M Sc); counseling (MC); counseling psychology (M Ed); dramatic arts (MA); earth, space, and physical science (PhD); economics (MA); education (MA, PhD); educational leadership (M Ed); English (MA); environmental science (M Sc); evolution and behavior (PhD); exercise science (M Sc); French (MA); French/German (MA); French/Spanish (MA); general education (M Ed); geography (M Sc, MA); German (MA); health sciences (M Sc); individualized multidisciplinary (M Sc, MA); kinesiology (M Sc, MA); management (M Sc), including accounting, finance, human resource management and labor relations, information systems, international management, marketing, policy and strategy; mathematics (M Sc); music (M Mus, MA); Native American studies (MA); neuroscience (M Sc, PhD); new media (MA, MFA); nursing (M Sc, MN); philosophy (MA); physics (M Sc); political science (MA); psychology (M Sc, MA); religious studies (MA); sociology (MA); theatre and dramatic arts (MFA); theoretical and computational science (PhD); urban and regional studies (MA); women and gender studies (MA). *Program availability:* Part-time, evening/weekend. *Degree requirements:* For master's, thesis (for some programs); for doctorate, comprehensive exam, thesis/dissertation. *Entrance requirements:* For master's, GMAT (for M Sc in management), bachelor's degree in related field, minimum GPA of 3.0 during previous 20 graded semester courses, 2 years' teaching or related experience (M Ed); for doctorate, master's degree, minimum graduate GPA of 3.5. Additional exam requirements/recommendations for international students: Required—TOEFL (minimum score 580 paper-based; 93 iBT). Electronic applications accepted. *Faculty research:* Movement and brain plasticity, gibberellin physiology, photosynthesis, carbon cycling, molecular properties of main-group ring components.

University of Louisiana at Lafayette, Department of Counselor Education, Lafayette, LA 70504. Offers MS. *Accreditation:* ACA. *Entrance requirements:* For master's, GRE General Test, minimum GPA of 2.75. Additional exam requirements/recommendations for international students: Required—TOEFL (minimum score 550 paper-based). Electronic applications accepted.

University of Louisiana at Monroe, Graduate School, College of Health and Pharmaceutical Sciences, Programs in Counseling Studies, Monroe, LA 71209-0001. Offers clinical mental health counseling (MS); school counseling (MS). *Accreditation:* ACA; NCATE. *Program availability:* Part-time, evening/weekend, online learning. *Faculty:* 4 full-time (3 women), 2 part-time/adjunct (1 woman). *Students:* 35 full-time (22 women), 16 part-time (7 women); includes 21 minority (20 Black or African American, non-Hispanic/Latino; 1 Asian, non-Hispanic/Latino), 1 international. Average age 30. 167 applicants, 13% accepted, 8 enrolled. In 2016, 13 master's awarded. *Degree requirements:* For master's, comprehensive exam, thesis. *Entrance requirements:* For master's, GRE General Test, minimum GPA of 2.8 in last 60 hours. Additional exam requirements/recommendations for international students: Required—TOEFL (minimum score 500 paper-based; 61 iBT). *Application deadline:* For fall admission, 8/24 priority date for domestic students, 7/1 for international students; for winter admission, 12/14 priority date for domestic students; for spring admission, 1/19 for domestic students, 11/1 for international students. Applications are processed on a rolling basis. Application fee: $20 ($30 for international students). Electronic applications accepted. *Expenses:* Tuition, state resident: full-time $6489. Tuition, nonresident: full-time $18,589. *Required fees:* $8984. Tuition and fees vary according to course level, course load, degree level and program. *Financial support:* Career-related internships or fieldwork, Federal Work-Study, and unspecified assistantships available. Financial award application deadline: 4/1; financial award applicants required to submit FAFSA. *Unit head:* Dr. Jana Sutton, Director, 318-342-1246, E-mail: sutton@ulm.edu.
Website: http://www.ulm.edu/counseling/

University of Louisville, Graduate School, College of Education and Human Development, Department of Counseling and Human Development, Louisville, KY 40292-0001. Offers counseling and personnel services (M Ed, PhD), including art therapy (M Ed), clinical mental health counseling (M Ed), college student personnel, counseling psychology, counselor education and supervision (PhD), educational psychology, measurement, and evaluation (PhD), school counseling (M Ed). *Accreditation:* APA; NCATE. *Program availability:* Part-time, evening/weekend. *Students:* 148 full-time (115 women), 58 part-time (42 women); includes 52 minority (36 Black or African American, non-Hispanic/Latino; 1 American Indian or Alaska Native, non-Hispanic/Latino; 4 Asian, non-Hispanic/Latino; 7 Hispanic/Latino; 4 Two or more races, non-Hispanic/Latino), 2 international. Average age 28. 206 applicants, 56% accepted, 73 enrolled. In 2016, 38 master's, 1 doctorate awarded. *Degree requirements:* For doctorate, comprehensive exam, thesis/dissertation. *Entrance requirements:* For master's and doctorate, GRE General Test. Application fee: $60. *Expenses:* Tuition, state resident: full-time $12,246; part-time $681 per credit hour. Tuition, nonresident: full-time $25,486; part-time $1417 per credit hour. *Required fees:* $196. Tuition and fees vary according to program and reciprocity agreements. *Financial support:* Fellowships, research assistantships, teaching assistantships, career-related internships or fieldwork, Federal Work-Study, scholarships/grants, health care benefits, and unspecified assistantships available. Financial award application deadline: 6/1; financial award applicants required to submit FAFSA. *Faculty research:* Mental health services and under-served populations; health disparities and outcomes; well-being identity development; measurement and evaluation. *Total annual research expenditures:* $295,684. *Unit head:* Dr. Mark M. Leach, Interim Chair/Professor, 502-852-0588, Fax: 502-852-0629, E-mail: m.leach@louisville.edu. *Application contact:* Betty Hampton, Director of Graduate Student Services, 502-852-5597, Fax: 502-852-1465, E-mail: edadvise@louisville.edu.
Website: http://www.louisville.edu/education/departments/ecpy

University of Manitoba, Faculty of Graduate Studies, Faculty of Education, Department of Educational Administration, Foundations and Psychology, Winnipeg, MB R3T 2N2, Canada. Offers adult and post-secondary education (M Ed); educational administration (M Ed); guidance and counseling (M Ed); inclusive special education (M Ed); social foundations of education (M Ed). *Degree requirements:* For master's, thesis or alternative.

University of Mary Hardin-Baylor, Graduate Studies in Counseling, Belton, TX 76513. Offers clinical and mental health counseling (MA); marriage, family and child counseling (MA); non-clinical professional studies (MA). *Accreditation:* ACA. *Program availability:* Part-time, evening/weekend. *Faculty:* 13 full-time (8 women), 8 part-time/adjunct (3 women). *Students:* 49 full-time (39 women), 22 part-time (16 women); includes 30 minority (17 Black or African American, non-Hispanic/Latino; 12 Hispanic/Latino; 1 Two or more races, non-Hispanic/Latino). Average age 32. 51 applicants, 71% accepted, 23 enrolled. In 2016, 25 master's awarded. *Degree requirements:* For master's, comprehensive exam. *Entrance requirements:* For master's, GRE General Test with minimum cumulative score of 300 on verbal and quantitative portions and minimum score of 3.0 on analytical section (if overall undergraduate GPA is below a 3.0), minimum cumulative undergraduate GPA of 2.75 or 3.0 on last 60 hours of course work; three letters of recommendation; interview with departmental graduate admissions committee. Additional exam requirements/recommendations for international students: Required—TOEFL (minimum score 60 iBT), IELTS (minimum score 4.5). *Application deadline:* For fall admission, 6/1 for domestic students, 4/30 priority date for international students; for spring admission, 11/1 for domestic students, 9/30 priority date for international students. Applications are processed on a rolling basis. Application fee: $35 ($135 for international students). Electronic applications accepted. *Expenses: Tuition:* Full-time $14,940; part-time $830 per credit hour. *Required fees:* $1350; $75 per credit hour. $50 per term. Tuition and fees vary according to course load and degree level. *Financial support:* In 2016–17, 41 students received support. Federal Work-Study, unspecified assistantships, and scholarships for some active duty military personnel available. Support available to part-time students. Financial award applicants required to submit FAFSA. *Faculty research:* Teaching mindfulness skills as part of an interdisciplinary training protocol for doctor of physical therapy students; using symbolic art cards and oracle cards in supervision as a method for teaching appropriate self-disclosure, clinical reflection and counselor development reflection; understanding integral breath therapy. *Unit head:* Dr. Dan Williamson, Director, Graduate Counseling, 254-295-5018, E-mail: dwilliamson@umhb.edu. *Application contact:* Sharon Aguilera, Assistant Director, Graduate Admissions, 254-295-4835, Fax: 254-295-5038, E-mail: saguilera@umhb.edu.
Website: http://graduate.umhb.edu/counseling/

University of Maryland, College Park, Academic Affairs, College of Education, Department of Counseling, Higher Education and Special Education, College Park, MD 20742. Offers college student personnel (M Ed, MA); college student personnel administration (PhD); community counseling (CAGS); community/career counseling (M Ed, MA); counseling and personnel services (M Ed, MA, PhD), including art therapy (M Ed), college student personnel (M Ed), counseling and personnel services (PhD), counseling psychology (M Ed), mental health counseling (M Ed), school counseling (M Ed); counseling psychology (PhD); counselor education (PhD); rehabilitation counseling (M Ed, MA, AGSC); school counseling (M Ed, MA); school psychology (M Ed, MA, PhD). *Accreditation:* ACA (one or more programs are accredited); APA (one or more programs are accredited); NCATE. *Program availability:* Part-time, evening/weekend, online learning. *Degree requirements:* For master's, thesis (for some programs); for doctorate, thesis/dissertation. *Entrance requirements:* For master's, GRE General Test or MAT, minimum GPA of 3.0, 3 letters of recommendation; for doctorate, GRE General Test or MAT, minimum GPA of 3.5, 3 letters of recommendation. Additional exam requirements/recommendations for international students: Required—TOEFL. Electronic applications accepted. *Faculty research:* Educational psychology, counseling, health.

University of Maryland Eastern Shore, Graduate Programs, Department of Education, Program in Guidance and Counseling, Princess Anne, MD 21853-1299. Offers M Ed. *Program availability:* Evening/weekend. *Degree requirements:* For master's, comprehensive exam, practicum, seminar paper. *Entrance requirements:* For master's, interview, minimum GPA of 3.0. Additional exam requirements/recommendations for international students: Required—TOEFL (minimum score 80 iBT). Electronic applications accepted.

University of Massachusetts Amherst, Graduate School, College of Education, Program in Education, Amherst, MA 01003. Offers bilingual, English as a second language, and multicultural education (M Ed, Ed S); child study and early education (M Ed); children, families and schools (Ed D, Ed S); early childhood and elementary teacher education (M Ed); educational leadership (M Ed); educational policy and leadership (Ed D); higher education (M Ed); international education (M Ed); language, literacy and culture (Ed D); learning, media and technology (M Ed, Ed S); mathematics, science, and learning technologies (Ed D); reading and writing (M Ed); research, educational measurement and psychometrics (Ed D); school counselor education (M Ed, Ed S); school psychology (Ed S); science education (Ed S); secondary teacher education (M Ed); social justice education (M Ed, Ed D, Ed S); special education (M Ed, Ed D, Ed S); teacher education and school improvement (Ed D, Ed S). *Accreditation:* NCATE. *Program availability:* Part-time, online learning. Terminal master's awarded for partial completion of doctoral program. *Degree requirements:* For doctorate, comprehensive exam, thesis/dissertation. *Entrance requirements:* Additional exam requirements/recommendations for international students: Required—TOEFL (minimum score 550 paper-based; 80 iBT), IELTS (minimum score 6.5). Electronic applications accepted.

University of Massachusetts Boston, College of Education and Human Development, Program in School Counseling, Boston, MA 02125-3393. Offers M Ed. *Students:* 58 full-time (51 women), 13 part-time (9 women); includes 9 minority (3 Black or African American, non-Hispanic/Latino; 2 Asian, non-Hispanic/Latino; 2 Hispanic/Latino; 2 Two or more races, non-Hispanic/Latino), 2 international. Average age 30. 44 applicants, 95% accepted, 33 enrolled. In 2016, 22 master's awarded. *Expenses:* Tuition, state resident: full-time $16,863. Tuition, nonresident: full-time $32,913. *Required fees:* $177. *Unit head:* Dr. Tim Poynton. *Application contact:* Peggy Roldan Patel, Graduate Admissions Coordinator, 617-287-6400, Fax: 617-287-6236, E-mail: bos.gadm@dpc.umassp.edu.

University of Memphis, Graduate School, College of Education, Department of Counseling, Educational Psychology and Research, Memphis, TN 38152. Offers counseling (MS, Ed D), including clinical mental health counseling (MS), clinical rehabilitation counseling (MS), rehabilitation counseling (MS), school counseling (MS); counseling psychology (PhD); educational psychology and research (MS, PhD), including educational psychology, educational research. *Accreditation:* ACA (one or more programs are accredited); APA (one or more programs are accredited); CORE (one or more programs are accredited); NCATE. *Program availability:* Blended/hybrid learning. *Faculty:* 26 full-time (18 women), 10 part-time/adjunct (7 women). *Students:* 124 full-time (99 women), 79 part-time (60 women); includes 64 minority (48 Black or African American, non-Hispanic/Latino; 3 Asian, non-Hispanic/Latino; 6 Hispanic/Latino; 7 Two or more races, non-Hispanic/Latino), 7 international. Average age 32. 82 applicants, 68% accepted, 39 enrolled. In 2016, 65 master's, 8 doctorates awarded. *Degree requirements:* For master's, comprehensive exam, thesis or alternative, internship; for doctorate, comprehensive exam, thesis/dissertation, practicum, internship, residency, scholarly work. *Entrance requirements:* For master's, GRE General Test or MAT, minimum GPA of 2.5, letters of reference, interview; for doctorate, GRE General Test, master's degree or equivalent, letters of reference, interview, curriculum vitae, personal statement. Additional exam requirements/recommendations for international students: Required—TOEFL (minimum score 550 paper-based; 79 iBT). *Application deadline:* For fall admission, 10/1 priority date for domestic students; for spring admission, 4/1 priority date for domestic students. Applications are processed on a rolling basis. Application fee: $35 ($60 for international students). Electronic applications accepted. *Expenses:* $5,231.50 per semester full-time in-state, $9,623.50 full-time out-of-state. *Financial support:* In 2016–17, 130 students received support, including 13 research assistantships with full tuition reimbursements available (averaging $14,820 per year), 11 teaching assistantships with full tuition reimbursements available (averaging $15,600 per year); fellowships with full tuition reimbursements available, career-related internships or fieldwork, Federal Work-Study, scholarships/grants, and unspecified assistantships also available. Financial award application deadline: 2/1; financial award applicants required to submit FAFSA. *Faculty research:* Anger management, aging and disability, supervision, multicultural counseling. *Unit head:* Dr. Steve West, Chair, 901-678-2841, Fax: 901-678-5114, E-mail: slwest@memphis.edu. *Application contact:* Dr. Suzanne Lease, Interim Assistant Dean of Education and Graduate Programs, 901-678-4476, Fax: 901-678-4778, E-mail: slease@memphis.edu.
Website: http://www.memphis.edu/cepr/

University of Miami, Graduate School, School of Education and Human Development, Department of Educational and Psychological Studies, Program in Counseling, Coral Gables, FL 33124. Offers counseling and research (MS Ed); Latino mental health (Certificate); marriage and family therapy (MS Ed); mental health counseling (MS Ed). *Program availability:* Part-time, evening/weekend. *Faculty:* 6 full-time (2 women). *Students:* 36 full-time (30 women), 8 part-time (all women); includes 28 minority (6 Black or African American, non-Hispanic/Latino; 22 Hispanic/Latino), 2 international. Average age 30. 60 applicants, 38% accepted, 17 enrolled. In 2016, 14 master's awarded. *Degree requirements:* For master's, comprehensive exam, personal growth experience. *Entrance requirements:* For master's, GRE General Test. Additional exam requirements/recommendations for international students: Required—TOEFL (minimum score 550 paper-based; 80 iBT); Recommended—IELTS (minimum score 6.5). *Application deadline:* For fall admission, 2/1 for domestic students. Application fee: $65. Electronic applications accepted. *Financial support:* Career-related internships or fieldwork and institutionally sponsored loans available. Support available to part-time students. Financial award application deadline: 3/1; financial award applicants required to submit FAFSA. *Faculty research:* Cocaine recidivism, HIV, non-traditional families, health psychology, diversity. *Unit head:* Dr. Anabel Bejarano, Assistant Professor of Professional Practice/Program Director, 305-284-4829, Fax: 305-284-3003, E-mail: bejarano@miami.edu. *Application contact:* Lois Heffernan, Graduate Admissions Coordinator, 305-284-2167, Fax: 305-284-9395, E-mail: lheffernan@miami.edu.
Website: http://www.education.miami.edu

University of Minnesota, Twin Cities Campus, Graduate School, College of Education and Human Development, Department of Educational Psychology, Program in Counseling and Student Personnel Psychology, Minneapolis, MN 55455-0213. Offers MA. *Students:* 77 full-time (58 women), 5 part-time (2 women); includes 11 minority (2 Asian, non-Hispanic/Latino; 5 Hispanic/Latino; 4 Two or more races, non-Hispanic/Latino), 6 international. Average age 27. 85 applicants, 42% accepted, 36 enrolled. In 2016, 33 master's awarded. Application fee: $75 ($95 for international students). *Unit head:* Dr. Geoffrey Maruyama, Chair, 612-624-1003, Fax: 612-625-5861, E-mail: geoff@umn.edu. *Application contact:* Dr. Ernest Davenport, Director of Graduate Studies, 612-624-1040, E-mail: lqr6576@umn.edu.
Website: http://www.cehd.umn.edu/EdPsych/Programs/CSPP/default.html

University of Missouri–Kansas City, School of Education, Kansas City, MO 64110-2499. Offers administration (Ed D); counseling and guidance (MA, Ed S), including mental health counseling (Ed S), school counseling (Ed S); counseling psychology (PhD); curriculum and instruction (MA, Ed S), including language and literacy (Ed S); education (PhD), including higher education administration, PK-12 education administration; educational administration (MA, Ed S), including advanced principal (Ed S), beginning principal (Ed S), district-level administration (Ed S); reading education (MA); special education (MA). PhD in education offered through the School of Graduate Studies. *Accreditation:* NCATE. *Program availability:* Part-time, evening/weekend. *Faculty:* 33 full-time (26 women), 51 part-time/adjunct (39 women). *Students:* 136 full-time (103 women), 275 part-time (194 women); includes 110 minority (71 Black or African American, non-Hispanic/Latino; 3 American Indian or Alaska Native, non-Hispanic/Latino; 8 Asian, non-Hispanic/Latino; 22 Hispanic/Latino; 6 Two or more races, non-Hispanic/Latino), 20 international. Average age 32. 324 applicants, 45% accepted, 108 enrolled. In 2016, 152 master's, 13 doctorates, 50 other advanced degrees awarded. *Degree requirements:* For doctorate, thesis/dissertation, internship, practicum. *Entrance requirements:* For master's, GRE, minimum GPA of 2.75, 2 letters of reference, written statement of purpose; for doctorate, GRE, minimum GPA of 3.0; for Ed S, minimum GPA of 3.0. Additional exam requirements/recommendations for international students: Required—TOEFL (minimum score 550 paper-based; 80 iBT). *Application deadline:* For fall admission, 4/1 priority date for domestic and international students; for spring admission, 11/1 priority date for domestic and international students. Applications are processed on a rolling basis. Application fee: $45 ($50 for international students). *Financial support:* In 2016–17, 12 research assistantships with partial tuition reimbursements (averaging $12,476 per year) were awarded; career-related internships or fieldwork, Federal Work-Study, institutionally sponsored loans, and tuition waivers (full and partial) also available. Support available to part-time students. Financial award application deadline: 3/1; financial award applicants required to submit FAFSA. *Faculty research:* Urban education, inquiry-based field study, theories of counseling and psychotherapy, school literacy, educational technology. *Unit head:* Justin Perry, Dean, 816-235-5663, Fax: 816-235-5270, E-mail: education@umkc.edu.
Website: http://education.umkc.edu

University of Missouri–St. Louis, College of Education, Department of Counseling and Family Therapy, St. Louis, MO 63121. Offers clinical mental health counseling (M Ed); counseling (PhD); elementary school counseling (M Ed); secondary school counseling (M Ed). *Accreditation:* ACA; NCATE. *Program availability:* Part-time, evening/weekend. *Faculty:* 8 full-time (4 women), 7 part-time/adjunct (6 women). *Students:* 58 full-time (48 women), 164 part-time (129 women); includes 61 minority (48 Black or African American, non-Hispanic/Latino; 2 American Indian or Alaska Native, non-Hispanic/Latino; 3 Asian, non-Hispanic/Latino; 4 Hispanic/Latino; 4 Two or more races, non-Hispanic/Latino), 4 international. Average age 32. 74 applicants, 72% accepted, 44 enrolled. *Degree requirements:* For master's, comprehensive exam. *Entrance requirements:* For master's, 3 letters of recommendation; for doctorate, GRE General Test, 3 letters of recommendation. Additional exam requirements/recommendations for international students: Recommended—TOEFL (minimum score 550 paper-based; 79 iBT), IELTS (minimum score 6.5). *Application deadline:* For fall admission, 5/1 for domestic and international students; for spring admission, 10/1 for domestic and international students. Application fee: $50 ($40 for international students). Electronic applications accepted. *Financial support:* Teaching assistantships with tuition reimbursements available. Financial award application deadline: 4/1; financial award applicants required to submit FAFSA. *Faculty research:* Vocational interests, self-concept, decision-making factors, developmental differences. *Unit head:* Dr. Mark Pope, Chair, 314-516-5782. *Application contact:* 314-516-5458, Fax: 314-516-6996, E-mail: gradadm@umsl.edu.

University of Missouri–St. Louis, College of Education, Interdisciplinary Doctoral Programs, St. Louis, MO 63121. Offers counseling (PhD); educational leadership and policy studies (PhD); educational psychology (PhD); leadership in educational practice (Ed D); teaching-learning processes (PhD). *Degree requirements:* For doctorate, thesis/dissertation. *Entrance requirements:* For doctorate, GRE General Test, 3 letters of recommendation; personal interview. Additional exam requirements/recommendations for international students: Recommended—TOEFL (minimum score 550 paper-based; 79 iBT), IELTS (minimum score 6.5). *Application deadline:* For fall admission, 3/1 for domestic and international students; for spring admission, 10/1 for domestic and international students. Application fee: $50 ($40 for international students). Electronic applications accepted. *Financial support:* Research assistantships and teaching assistantships available. Financial award application deadline: 4/1; financial award applicants required to submit FAFSA. *Faculty research:* Higher education law and policy, gender and higher education, student retention, lifelong learning orientation, school counselor's role in violence prevention. *Unit head:* Dr. Kathleen Haywood, Director of Graduate Studies, 314-516-5483, Fax: 314-516-5227, E-mail: kathleen_haywood@umsl.edu. *Application contact:* 314-516-5458, Fax: 314-516-6996, E-mail: gradadm@umsl.edu.

University of Montana, Graduate School, Phyllis J. Washington College of Education and Human Sciences, Department of Counselor Education, Missoula, MT 59812-0002. Offers clinical mental health counseling (MA); counseling and supervision (Ed D); counselor education (Ed S); intercultural youth and family development (MA); school counseling (MA). *Accreditation:* ACA. *Degree requirements:* For doctorate, thesis/dissertation. *Entrance requirements:* For master's, doctorate, and Ed S, GRE General Test. Additional exam requirements/recommendations for international students: Required—TOEFL.

University of Montevallo, College of Education, Program in Counseling, Montevallo, AL 35115. Offers M Ed. *Accreditation:* ACA; NCATE. *Program availability:* Part-time, evening/weekend. *Students:* 53 full-time (43 women), 54 part-time (42 women); includes 27 minority (21 Black or African American, non-Hispanic/Latino; 5 Hispanic/Latino; 1 Two or more races, non-Hispanic/Latino). In 2016, 35 master's awarded. *Entrance requirements:* For master's, GRE General Test or MAT, minimum undergraduate GPA of 2.75 in last 60 hours or 2.5 overall, interview. Additional exam requirements/recommendations for international students: Required—TOEFL (minimum score 550 paper-based). *Application deadline:* For fall admission, 7/15 for domestic students; for spring admission, 11/15 for domestic students. Application fee: $25. *Expenses:* Tuition, state resident: full-time $9936. Tuition, nonresident: full-time $20,592. *Required fees:* $640. *Financial support:* Federal Work-Study, scholarships/grants, and unspecified assistantships available. *Unit head:* Dr. Charlotte Daughhetee, Chair, 205-665-6358, E-mail: daughc@montevallo.edu. *Application contact:* Kevin Thornthwaite, Director, Graduate Admissions and Records, 205-665-6350, E-mail: graduate@montevallo.edu.
Website: http://www.montevallo.edu/education/college-of-education/traditional-masters-degrees/counseling/

University of Nebraska at Kearney, College of Education, Department of Counseling and School Psychology, Kearney, NE 68849-0001. Offers clinical mental health counseling (MS Ed); school counseling (MS Ed), including elementary, secondary; school psychology (Ed S); student affairs (MS Ed). *Accreditation:* ACA; NCATE. *Program availability:* Part-time, evening/weekend, 100% online. *Faculty:* 7 full-time (3 women). *Students:* 69 full-time (56 women), 102 part-time (81 women); includes 21 minority (2 Black or African American, non-Hispanic/Latino; 2 Asian, non-Hispanic/Latino; 12 Hispanic/Latino; 5 Two or more races, non-Hispanic/Latino), 4 international. Average age 30. 43 applicants, 100% accepted, 37 enrolled. In 2016, 24 master's, 13 Ed Ss awarded. *Degree requirements:* For master's, comprehensive exam, thesis optional; for Ed S, thesis. *Entrance requirements:* For master's and Ed S, personal statement, recommendations, resume, interview. Additional exam requirements/recommendations for international students: Recommended—TOEFL (minimum score 550 paper-based; 79 iBT), IELTS (minimum score 6.5). *Application deadline:* For fall admission, 6/15 for domestic and international students; for spring admission, 10/15 for domestic and international students; for summer admission, 3/15 for domestic and international students. Application fee: $45. Electronic applications accepted. *Expenses:* Tuition, state resident: full-time $4064; part-time $225.75 per credit hour. Tuition, nonresident: full-time $8915; part-time $495.25 per credit hour. *Required fees:* $772; $23 per credit hour. Part-time tuition and fees vary according to course load, campus/location, program and reciprocity agreements. *Financial support:* In 2016–17, 7 students received support, including 7 research assistantships with full tuition reimbursements available (averaging $10,500 per year); fellowships, career-related internships or fieldwork, scholarships/grants, health care benefits, and unspecified assistantships also available. Support available to part-time students. Financial award application deadline: 2/28; financial award applicants required to submit FAFSA. *Faculty research:* Multicultural counseling and diversity issues, team decision-making, adult development, women's issues, brief therapy. *Unit head:* Dr. Grace Mims, Chair, Counseling and School Psychology, 308-865-8508, E-mail: mimsga@unk.edu. *Application contact:* Linda Johnson, Director, Graduate Admissions and Programs, 800-717-7881, Fax: 308-865-8837, E-mail: gradstudies@unk.edu.
Website: http://www.unk.edu/academics/csp/

University of Nebraska at Omaha, Graduate Studies, College of Education, Department of Counseling, Omaha, NE 68182. Offers MA, MS. *Accreditation:* ACA (one or more programs are accredited); NCATE. *Program availability:* Part-time, evening/weekend. *Faculty:* 4 full-time (3 women). *Students:* 71 full-time (52 women), 88 part-time (73 women); includes 26 minority (6 Black or African American, non-Hispanic/Latino; 4 Asian, non-Hispanic/Latino; 12 Hispanic/Latino; 4 Two or more races, non-Hispanic/Latino), 1 international. Average age 30. 53 applicants, 57% accepted, 27 enrolled. In 2016, 39 master's awarded. *Degree requirements:* For master's, comprehensive exam, thesis (for some programs). *Entrance requirements:* For master's, GRE General Test, MAT, interview, minimum GPA of 3.0, 3 letters of recommendation, transcripts. Additional exam requirements/recommendations for international students: Required—TOEFL, IELTS, PTE. *Application deadline:* For fall admission, 3/1 for domestic and international students; for spring admission, 10/1 for domestic and international students; for summer admission, 3/1 for domestic and international students. Applications are processed on a rolling basis. Application fee: $45. Electronic applications accepted. *Financial support:* In 2016–17, 7 students received support, including 5 research assistantships with tuition reimbursements available, 2 teaching assistantships with tuition reimbursements available; fellowships, Federal Work-Study, institutionally sponsored loans, scholarships/grants, health care benefits, tuition waivers (partial), and unspecified assistantships also available. Support available to part-time students. Financial award application deadline: 3/1; financial award applicants required to submit FAFSA. *Unit head:* Dr. Daniel Kissinger, Chairperson and Graduate Program Chair, 402-554-2341, E-mail: graduate@unomaha.edu.

University of Nevada, Las Vegas, Graduate College, College of Education, Department of Educational and Clinical Studies, Las Vegas, NV 89154-3066. Offers addiction studies (Advanced Certificate); counselor education (M Ed, MS), including clinical mental health (MS), school counseling (M Ed); early childhood education (M Ed); early childhood special education (Certificate), including infancy, preschool; English language learning (M Ed); mental health counseling (Advanced Certificate); special education (M Ed, PhD); PhD/JD. *Program availability:* Part-time, evening/weekend. *Faculty:* 17 full-time (8 women), 28 part-time/adjunct (20 women). *Students:* 269 full-time (219 women), 174 part-time (138 women); includes 181 minority (51 Black or African American, non-Hispanic/Latino; 2 American Indian or Alaska Native, non-Hispanic/Latino; 15 Asian, non-Hispanic/Latino; 81 Hispanic/Latino; 3 Native Hawaiian or other Pacific Islander, non-Hispanic/Latino; 29 Two or more races, non-Hispanic/Latino), 23 international. Average age 34. 256 applicants, 72% accepted, 145 enrolled. In 2016, 178 master's, 3 doctorates awarded. *Degree requirements:* For master's, comprehensive exam (for some programs); for doctorate, comprehensive exam, thesis/dissertation; for other advanced degree, final project. *Entrance requirements:* For master's, bachelor's degree; letter of recommendation; statement of purpose; for doctorate, GRE General Test, statement of purpose; writing sample; 3 letters of recommendation. Additional exam requirements/recommendations for international students: Required—TOEFL (minimum score 550 paper-based; 80 iBT), IELTS (minimum score 7). *Application deadline:* For fall admission, 7/15 for domestic students, 5/1 for international students; for spring admission, 11/15 for domestic students, 10/1 for international students; for summer admission, 4/15 for domestic students. Application fee: $60 ($95 for international students). Electronic applications accepted. *Expenses:* $269.25 per credit, $792 per 3-credit course; $9,634 per year resident; $23,274 per year non-resident; $7,094 fees non-resident (7 credits or more); $1,307 annual health insurance fee. *Financial support:* In 2016–17, 12 research assistantships with partial tuition reimbursements (averaging $12,569 per year), 27 teaching assistantships with partial tuition reimbursements (averaging $13,759 per year) were awarded; institutionally sponsored loans, scholarships/grants, health care benefits, and unspecified assistantships also available. Financial award application deadline: 3/15. *Faculty research:* Multicultural issues in counseling, academic interventions for students with disabilities, establishment of pro-social skills in young children with severe disabilities, inclusive strategies for students with disabilities, language and literacy for English language learners. *Total annual research expenditures:* $768,906. *Unit head:* Dr. Monica Brown, Interim Department Chair/Professor, 702-895-3167, Fax: 702-895-3205, E-mail: monica.brown@unlv.edu. *Application contact:* Dr. Cori More, Graduate Coordinator, 702-895-3271, Fax: 702-895-3205, E-mail: cori.more@unlv.edu.
Website: http://education.unlv.edu/ecs/

University of Nevada, Reno, Graduate School, College of Education, Department of Counseling and Educational Psychology, Reno, NV 89557. Offers M Ed, MA, MS, Ed D, PhD, Ed S. *Accreditation:* ACA (one or more programs are accredited); NCATE. Terminal master's awarded for partial completion of doctoral program. *Degree requirements:* For master's, comprehensive exam, thesis optional; for doctorate, comprehensive exam, thesis/dissertation, qualifying exam. *Entrance requirements:* For master's, GRE, minimum GPA of 2.75; for doctorate, GRE, minimum GPA of 3.0. Additional exam requirements/recommendations for international students: Required—TOEFL (minimum score 500 paper-based; 61 iBT), IELTS (minimum score 6). Electronic applications accepted. *Faculty research:* Marriage and family counseling, substance abuse attitudes of teachers, current supply of counseling educators, HIV-positive services for patients, family counseling for youth at risk.

University of New Mexico, Graduate Studies, College of Education, Program in Counselor Education, Albuquerque, NM 87131. Offers counseling (MA); counselor education (PhD). *Accreditation:* ACA (one or more programs are accredited); NCATE. *Program availability:* Part-time. *Faculty:* 10 full-time (3 women), 2 part-time/adjunct (both women). *Students:* 50 full-time (43 women), 40 part-time (30 women); includes 42 minority (1 Black or African American, non-Hispanic/Latino; 3 American Indian or Alaska Native, non-Hispanic/Latino; 1 Asian, non-Hispanic/Latino; 36 Hispanic/Latino; 1 Two or more races, non-Hispanic/Latino), 1 international. Average age 33. 69 applicants, 26% accepted, 16 enrolled. In 2016, 30 master's, 3 doctorates awarded. *Degree requirements:* For master's, comprehensive exam; for doctorate, comprehensive exam, thesis/dissertation. *Entrance requirements:* For master's, 3 letters of recommendation, personal statement; for doctorate, GRE General Test, 3 letters of recommendation, writing sample, personal statement. Additional exam requirements/recommendations for international students: Required—TOEFL. *Application deadline:* For fall admission, 11/1 for domestic and international students; for spring admission, 9/15 for domestic and international students. Application fee: $50. Electronic applications accepted. *Financial support:* Unspecified assistantships available. Financial award application deadline: 3/1; financial award applicants required to submit FAFSA. *Faculty research:* Counselor education and supervision, school counseling, LGBTQQI, crisis and trauma, multiculturalism. *Unit head:* Dr. Jean Keim, Program Coordinator, 505-277-4535, Fax: 505-277-8361, E-mail: divbse@unm.edu. *Application contact:* Cynthia Salas, Department Administrator, 505-277-4535, Fax: 505-277-8361, E-mail: divbse@unm.edu.
Website: https://coe.unm.edu/departments-programs/ifce/counselor-education/index.html

University of New Orleans, Graduate School, College of Education and Human Development, Department of Educational Leadership, Counseling, and Foundations, Program in Counselor Education, New Orleans, LA 70148. Offers M Ed, PhD. *Accreditation:* ACA (one or more programs are accredited); NCATE. *Program availability:* Evening/weekend. Terminal master's awarded for partial completion of doctoral program. *Degree requirements:* For master's, thesis (for some programs); for doctorate, variable foreign language requirement, thesis/dissertation. *Entrance requirements:* For master's and doctorate, GRE General Test. Additional exam requirements/recommendations for international students: Required—TOEFL (minimum score 550 paper-based; 79 iBT). Electronic applications accepted.

University of North Alabama, College of Education, Department of Counselor Education, Florence, AL 35632-0001. Offers clinical mental health counseling (MA); counseling (MA Ed). *Accreditation:* ACA; NCATE. *Program availability:* Part-time. *Faculty:* 4 full-time (all women), 1 part-time/adjunct (0 women). *Students:* 14 full-time (11 women), 32 part-time (24 women); includes 7 minority (3 Black or African American, non-Hispanic/Latino; 1 Hispanic/Latino; 3 Two or more races, non-Hispanic/Latino). Average age 35. 25 applicants, 64% accepted, 12 enrolled. In 2016, 15 master's awarded. *Degree requirements:* For master's, comprehensive exam. *Entrance requirements:* For master's, GRE, MAT, or NTE, minimum GPA of 2.5, Alabama Class B Certificate or equivalent, teaching experience. Additional exam requirements/recommendations for international students: Required—TOEFL (minimum score 79 iBT), IELTS (minimum score 6), PTE (minimum score 54). *Application deadline:* Applications are processed on a rolling basis. Application fee: $50 ($100 for international students). Electronic applications accepted. *Expenses:* Tuition, state resident: full-time $2799; part-time $1866 per semester. Tuition, nonresident: full-time $5598; part-time $3732 per semester. *Required fees:* $915; $642 per semester. Tuition and fees vary according to course load. *Financial support:* In 2016–17, 1 student received support. Scholarships/grants available. Financial award application deadline: 2/1; financial award applicants required to submit FAFSA. *Unit head:* Dr. Sandra Loew, Chair, 256-765-4763, Fax: 256-765-4159, E-mail: saloew@una.edu. *Application contact:* Hillary N.

Coats, Graduate Admissions Coordinator, 256-765-4447, E-mail: graduate@una.edu.
Website: http://www.una.edu/education/departments/counselor-education.html

The University of North Carolina at Chapel Hill, Graduate School, School of Education, Program in School Counseling, Chapel Hill, NC 27599. Offers M Ed. *Accreditation:* ACA; NCATE. *Degree requirements:* For master's, comprehensive exam. *Entrance requirements:* For master's, GRE General Test, minimum GPA of 3.0 during last 2 years of undergraduate course work. Additional exam requirements/recommendations for international students: Required—TOEFL (minimum score 550 paper-based). Electronic applications accepted. *Faculty research:* Career counseling, development and assessment, multicultural counseling, measurement.

The University of North Carolina at Charlotte, Cato College of Education, Department of Counseling, Charlotte, NC 28223-0001. Offers counseling (MA); counselor education and supervision (PhD); play therapy (Postbaccalaureate Certificate); school counseling (Post-Master's Certificate); substance abuse counseling (Postbaccalaureate Certificate). *Accreditation:* ACA. *Program availability:* Part-time, evening/weekend. *Faculty:* 12 full-time (7 women), 5 part-time/adjunct (2 women). *Students:* 144 full-time (117 women), 94 part-time (76 women); includes 69 minority (49 Black or African American, non-Hispanic/Latino; 3 Asian, non-Hispanic/Latino; 15 Hispanic/Latino; 2 Two or more races, non-Hispanic/Latino), 3 international. Average age 31. 221 applicants, 63% accepted, 101 enrolled. In 2016, 45 master's, 3 doctorates, 22 other advanced degrees awarded. Terminal master's awarded for partial completion of doctoral program. *Degree requirements:* For master's, thesis or alternative, practicum, internship; for doctorate, thesis/dissertation; for other advanced degree, internship. *Entrance requirements:* For master's, GRE or MAT, bachelor's degree from regionally-accredited university, minimum overall GPA of 3.0, brief statement of purpose, professional references, official transcripts; for doctorate, GRE or MAT, master's degree in counseling from a CACREP-accredited program with minimum cumulative GPA of 3.5; one year of experience as a professional counselor (preferred); letters of reference; essay; interview; for other advanced degree, statement of purpose, three reference letters. Additional exam requirements/recommendations for international students: Required—TOEFL (minimum score 523 paper-based, 70 iBT) or IELTS (6.5). *Application deadline:* For fall admission, 12/1 for domestic and international students; for summer admission, 12/1 for domestic and international students. Applications are processed on a rolling basis. Application fee: $75. Electronic applications accepted. *Expenses:* Tuition, state resident: full-time $4252. Tuition, nonresident: full-time $17,423. *Required fees:* $3026. Tuition and fees vary according to course load and program. *Financial support:* In 2016–17, 9 students received support, including 2 research assistantships (averaging $11,800 per year), 7 teaching assistantships (averaging $6,357 per year); career-related internships or fieldwork, institutionally sponsored loans, scholarships/grants, and unspecified assistantships also available. Support available to part-time students. Financial award application deadline: 3/1; financial award applicants required to submit FAFSA. *Total annual research expenditures:* $28,946. *Unit head:* Dr. Henry L. Harris, Chair, 704-687-8960, E-mail: hharris2@uncc.edu. *Application contact:* Kathy B. Giddings, Director of Graduate Admissions, 704-687-5503, Fax: 704-687-1668, E-mail: gradadm@uncc.edu.
Website: http://counseling.uncc.edu/

The University of North Carolina at Greensboro, Graduate School, School of Education, Department of Counseling and Educational Development, Greensboro, NC 27412-5001. Offers advanced school counseling (PMC); counseling and counselor education (PhD); counseling and educational development (MS); couple and family counseling (PMC); school counseling (PMC); MS/Ed S. *Accreditation:* ACA (one or more programs are accredited); NCATE. *Degree requirements:* For master's, comprehensive exam, practicum, internship; for doctorate, comprehensive exam, thesis/dissertation. *Entrance requirements:* For master's, doctorate, and PMC, GRE General Test. Additional exam requirements/recommendations for international students: Required—TOEFL. Electronic applications accepted. *Faculty research:* Gerontology, invitational theory, career development, marriage and family therapy, drug and alcohol abuse prevention.

The University of North Carolina at Pembroke, The Graduate School, School of Education, Programs in Counseling, Pembroke, NC 28372-1510. Offers clinical mental health counseling (MA Ed); professional school counseling (MA Ed). *Accreditation:* NCATE. *Program availability:* Part-time, evening/weekend. *Degree requirements:* For master's, comprehensive exam, thesis optional. *Entrance requirements:* For master's, GRE General Test or MAT, minimum GPA of 3.0 in major, 2.5 overall. Additional exam requirements/recommendations for international students: Required—TOEFL.

University of Northern Colorado, Graduate School, College of Education and Behavioral Sciences, Department of Applied Psychology and Counselor Education, Program in School Counseling, Greeley, CO 80639. Offers MA. *Accreditation:* ACA. *Program availability:* Part-time. *Application deadline:* Applications are processed on a rolling basis. Application fee: $50 ($60 for international students). Electronic applications accepted. *Financial support:* Application deadline: 3/1; applicants required to submit FAFSA. *Unit head:* Heather Helm, Program Coordinator, 970-351-2731. *Application contact:* Linda Sisson, Graduate Student Admission Coordinator, 970-351-1807, Fax: 970-351-2371, E-mail: linda.sisson@unco.edu.
Website: http://www.unco.edu/cebs/applied-psychology-counselor-education/professional-counseling/programs/school-counseling/

University of Northern Iowa, Graduate College, College of Social and Behavioral Sciences, School of Applied Human Sciences, MA Program in Counseling, Cedar Falls, IA 50614. Offers mental health counseling (MA); school counseling (MA). *Accreditation:* ACA. *Program availability:* Part-time, evening/weekend. *Degree requirements:* For master's, comprehensive exam, thesis or alternative. *Entrance requirements:* For master's, minimum GPA of 3.0. Additional exam requirements/recommendations for international students: Required—TOEFL (minimum score 500 paper-based; 61 iBT). Electronic applications accepted.

University of North Florida, College of Education and Human Services, Department of Leadership, School Counseling and Sport Management, Jacksonville, FL 32224. Offers counselor education (M Ed), including school counseling; educational leadership (M Ed, Ed D), including athletic administration (M Ed), educational leadership, educational technology (M Ed), instructional leadership (M Ed). *Program availability:* Part-time, evening/weekend. *Faculty:* 18 full-time (10 women), 1 (woman) part-time/adjunct. *Students:* 74 full-time (61 women), 219 part-time (149 women); includes 93 minority (65 Black or African American, non-Hispanic/Latino; 1 American Indian or Alaska Native, non-Hispanic/Latino; 3 Asian, non-Hispanic/Latino; 15 Hispanic/Latino; 1 Native Hawaiian or other Pacific Islander, non-Hispanic/Latino; 8 Two or more races, non-Hispanic/Latino), 14 international. Average age 34. 128 applicants, 57% accepted, 55 enrolled. In 2016, 94 master's, 7 doctorates awarded. *Degree requirements:* For doctorate, thesis/dissertation. *Entrance requirements:* For master's, GRE General Test, minimum GPA of 3.0 in last 60 hours, interview, 3 letters of recommendation; for doctorate, GRE General Test, master's degree, interview, 3 letters of recommendation, writing sample. Additional exam requirements/recommendations for international students: Required—TOEFL (minimum score 500 paper-based). *Application deadline:* For fall admission, 5/1 priority date for domestic students, 5/1 for international students. Application fee: $30. Electronic applications accepted. Tuition and fees vary according to course load, campus/location and program. *Financial support:* In 2016–17, 48 students received support, including 1 research assistantship (averaging $4,445 per year), 1 teaching assistantship (averaging $5,378 per year); career-related internships or fieldwork, Federal Work-Study, scholarships/grants, tuition waivers (partial), and unspecified assistantships also available. Support available to part-time students. Financial award application deadline: 4/1; financial award applicants required to submit FAFSA. *Faculty research:* Counseling: ethics; lesbian, bisexual and transgender issues; educational leadership: school culture and climate; educational assessment and accountability; school safety and student discipline. *Total annual research expenditures:* $45,589. *Unit head:* Dr. Liz Gregg, Chair, 904-620-5199, E-mail: liz.gregg@unf.edu. *Application contact:* Dr. Amanda Pascale, Director, The Graduate School, 904-620-1360, Fax: 904-620-1362, E-mail: graduateschool@unf.edu.
Website: http://www.unf.edu/coehs/lscsm/

University of North Texas, Robert B. Toulouse School of Graduate Studies, Denton, TX 76203-5459. Offers accounting (MS); applied anthropology (MA, MS); applied behavior analysis (Certificate); applied geography (MA); applied technology and performance improvement (M Ed, MS); art education (MA); art history (MA); art museum education (Certificate); arts leadership (Certificate); audiology (Au D); behavior analysis (MS); behavioral science (PhD); biochemistry and molecular biology (MS); biology (MA, MS); biomedical engineering (MS); business analysis (MS); chemistry (MS); clinical health psychology (PhD); communication studies (MA, MS); computer engineering (MS); computer science (MS); counseling (M Ed, MS), including clinical mental health counseling (MS), college and university counseling, elementary school counseling, secondary school counseling; creative writing (MA); criminal justice (MS); curriculum and instruction (M Ed); decision sciences (MBA); design (MA, MFA), including fashion design (MFA), innovation studies, interior design (MFA); early childhood studies (MS); economics (MS); educational leadership (M Ed, Ed D); educational psychology (MS, PhD), including family studies (MS), gifted and talented (MS), human development (MS), learning and cognition (MS), research, measurement and evaluation (MS); electrical engineering (MS); emergency management (MPA); engineering technology (MS); English (MA); English as a second language (MA); environmental science (MS); finance (MBA, MS); financial management (MPA); French (MA); health services management (MBA); higher education (M Ed, Ed D); history (MA, MS); hospitality management (MS); human resources management (MPA); information science (MS); information systems (PhD); information technologies (MBA); interdisciplinary studies (MA, MS); international studies (MA); international sustainable tourism (MS); jazz studies (MM); journalism (MA, MJ, Graduate Certificate), including interactive and virtual digital communication (Graduate Certificate), narrative journalism (Graduate Certificate), public relations (Graduate Certificate); kinesiology (MS); linguistics (MA); local government management (MPA); logistics (PhD); logistics and supply chain management (MBA); long-term care, senior housing, and aging services (MA); management (PhD); marketing (MBA); mathematics (MA, MS); mechanical and energy engineering (MS, PhD); music (MA), including ethnomusicology, music theory, musicology, performance; music composition (PhD); music education (MM Ed, PhD); nonprofit management (MPA); operations and supply chain management (MBA); performance (MM, DMA); philosophy (MA); political science (MA); professional and technical communication (MA); radio, television and film (MA, MFA); rehabilitation counseling (Certificate); sociology (MA); Spanish (MA); special education (M Ed); speech-language pathology (MA); strategic management (MBA); studio art (MFA); teaching (M Ed); MBA/MS. *Program availability:* Part-time, evening/weekend, online learning. Terminal master's awarded for partial completion of doctoral program. *Degree requirements:* For master's, variable foreign language requirement, comprehensive exam (for some programs), thesis (for some programs); for doctorate, variable foreign language requirement, comprehensive exam (for some programs), thesis/dissertation; for other advanced degree, variable foreign language requirement, comprehensive exam (for some programs). *Entrance requirements:* For master's and doctorate, GRE, GMAT. Additional exam requirements/recommendations for international students: Required—TOEFL (minimum score 550 paper-based; 79 iBT). Electronic applications accepted.

University of North Texas at Dallas, Graduate School, Dallas, TX 75241. Offers accounting (MBA); counseling (M Ed, MS); criminal justice (MS); curriculum and instruction (M Ed); educational administration (M Ed); human resources and organizational behavior (MBA); public leadership (MS); strategic management (MBA).

University of Pennsylvania, Graduate School of Education, Division of Human Development and Quantitative Methods, Program in School and Mental Health Counseling, Philadelphia, PA 19104. Offers MS Ed. *Students:* 65 full-time (52 women); includes 20 minority (12 Black or African American, non-Hispanic/Latino; 1 Asian, non-Hispanic/Latino; 5 Hispanic/Latino; 1 Native Hawaiian or other Pacific Islander, non-Hispanic/Latino; 1 Two or more races, non-Hispanic/Latino), 3 international. Average age 31. 59 applicants, 80% accepted, 40 enrolled. In 2016, 29 master's awarded. *Expenses: Tuition:* Full-time $31,068; part-time $5762 per course. *Required fees:* $3200; $336 per course. Full-time tuition and fees vary according to degree level, program and student level. Part-time tuition and fees vary according to course load, degree level and program.

University of Phoenix–Las Vegas Campus, College of Human Services, Las Vegas, NV 89135. Offers marriage, family, and child therapy (MSC); mental health counseling (MSC); school counseling (MSC). *Program availability:* Online learning. *Entrance requirements:* For master's, minimum undergraduate GPA of 2.5, 3 years of work experience. Additional exam requirements/recommendations for international students: Required—TOEFL (minimum score 550 paper-based; 79 iBT). Electronic applications accepted.

University of Phoenix–New Mexico Campus, College of Education, Albuquerque, NM 87113-1570. Offers administration and supervision (MAEd); curriculum and instruction (MAEd); elementary teacher education (MAEd); school counseling (MSC); secondary teacher education (MAEd). *Program availability:* Evening/weekend. *Degree requirements:* For master's, thesis (for some programs). *Entrance requirements:* For master's, minimum undergraduate GPA of 2.5, 3 years of work experience. Additional exam requirements/recommendations for international students: Required—TOEFL (minimum score 550 paper-based; 79 iBT). Electronic applications accepted.

University of Phoenix–Phoenix Campus, College of Social Sciences, Tempe, AZ 85282-2371. Offers counseling (MS), including clinical mental health counseling, community counseling, counseling, marriage, family and child therapy; psychology (MS). *Program availability:* Evening/weekend, online learning. *Entrance requirements:* Additional exam requirements/recommendations for international students: Required—TOEFL, TOEIC (Test of English as an International Communication), Berlitz Online English Proficiency Exam, PTE, or IELTS. Electronic applications accepted. *Expenses:* Contact institution.

University of Phoenix–Southern Arizona Campus, College of Education, Tucson, AZ 85711. Offers administration and supervision (MA Ed); adult education and training (MA Ed); curriculum instruction (MA Ed); educational counseling (MA Ed); elementary teacher education (MA Ed); school counseling (MSC); secondary teacher education (MA Ed); special education (MA Ed, Certificate). *Program availability:* Evening/weekend. *Degree requirements:* For master's, thesis (for some programs). *Entrance requirements:* For master's, minimum undergraduate GPA of 2.5, 3 years of work experience.

Additional exam requirements/recommendations for international students: Required—TOEFL (minimum score 550 paper-based; 79 iBT). Electronic applications accepted.

University of Phoenix–Southern California Campus, College of Social Sciences, Costa Mesa, CA 92626. Offers counseling (MS), including counseling, marriage, family and child therapy; psychology (MS), including behavioral health. *Program availability:* Evening/weekend, online learning. *Entrance requirements:* Additional exam requirements/recommendations for international students: Required—TOEFL, TOEIC (Test of English as an International Communication), Berlitz Online English Proficiency Exam, PTE, or IELTS. Electronic applications accepted. *Expenses:* Contact institution.

University of Puerto Rico, Río Piedras Campus, College of Education, Program in Guidance and Counseling, San Juan, PR 00931-3300. Offers M Ed, Ed D. *Program availability:* Part-time. *Degree requirements:* For master's, thesis; for doctorate, thesis/dissertation, internship. *Entrance requirements:* For master's, PAEG or GRE, interview, minimum GPA of 3.0, letter of recommendation; for doctorate, GRE or PAEG, master's degree, minimum GPA of 3.0, letter of recommendation (2), interview.

University of Puget Sound, School of Education, Program in Counseling, Tacoma, WA 98416. Offers mental health counseling (M Ed); school counseling (M Ed). *Program availability:* Part-time. *Faculty:* 2 full-time (both women), 1 (woman) part-time/adjunct. *Students:* 27 part-time (25 women); includes 5 minority (1 Asian, non-Hispanic/Latino; 2 Hispanic/Latino; 2 Two or more races, non-Hispanic/Latino). Average age 31. 33 applicants, 61% accepted, 17 enrolled. In 2016, 9 master's awarded. *Degree requirements:* For master's, capstone course. *Entrance requirements:* For master's, GRE General Test, interview. Additional exam requirements/recommendations for international students: Required—TOEFL (minimum score 550 paper-based; 90 iBT). *Application deadline:* For fall admission, 3/1 priority date for domestic and international students. Applications are processed on a rolling basis. Application fee: $60. Electronic applications accepted. *Expenses:* Contact institution. *Financial support:* In 2016–17, 1 student received support. Scholarships/grants available. Financial award application deadline: 3/31; financial award applicants required to submit FAFSA. *Faculty research:* Suicide prevention. *Unit head:* Dr. Grace Kirchner, Director, 253-879-3785, Fax: 253-879-3926, E-mail: kirchner@pugetsound.edu. *Application contact:* Karen Stump, Certification Officer/Admission Coordinator, 253-879-3382, Fax: 253-879-3926, E-mail: kstump@pugetsound.edu.
Website: http://www.pugetsound.edu/academics/departments-and-programs/graduate/school-of-education/med/

University of Rochester, Margaret Warner Graduate School of Education and Human Development, Doctoral Programs in Education, Rochester, NY 14627. Offers counseling (Ed D); educational administration (Ed D); educational policy and theory (PhD); higher education (PhD); human development in educational context (PhD); teaching, curriculum, and change (PhD). *Expenses: Tuition:* Full-time $47,450; part-time $1482 per credit hour. *Required fees:* $528. Tuition and fees vary according to program.

University of Rochester, Margaret Warner Graduate School of Education and Human Development, Master's Program in Counseling, Rochester, NY 14627. Offers school and community counseling (MS); school counseling (MS). *Expenses: Tuition:* Full-time $47,450; part-time $1482 per credit hour. *Required fees:* $528. Tuition and fees vary according to program.

University of Saint Francis, Graduate School, Department of Behavioral and Social Sciences, Fort Wayne, IN 46808-3994. Offers clinical mental health counseling (MS, Post Master's Certificate); psychology (MS); school counseling (MS Ed). *Program availability:* Part-time, evening/weekend. *Faculty:* 3 full-time (1 woman). *Students:* 25 full-time (22 women), 10 part-time (6 women); includes 7 minority (6 Black or African American, non-Hispanic/Latino; 1 Hispanic/Latino), 2 international. Average age 31. 21 applicants, 95% accepted, 13 enrolled. In 2016, 19 master's awarded. *Entrance requirements:* For master's, GRE/MAT if undergraduate GPA is below 3.0 (for MS Ed), minimum undergraduate GPA of 3.0 (2.8 for MS Ed); undergraduate coursework in psychology; statement of professional goals (for MS); 2 professional recommendations; interview (for mental health counseling and school counseling). Additional exam requirements/recommendations for international students: Required—TOEFL (minimum score 550 paper-based) or IELTS (minimum score 6.5). *Application deadline:* Applications are processed on a rolling basis. Application fee: $0. Electronic applications accepted. *Expenses: Tuition:* Full-time $16,290; part-time $905 per credit hour. *Required fees:* $25 per credit hour. $140 per semester. Tuition and fees vary according to campus/location and program. *Financial support:* In 2016–17, 5 students received support. Federal Work-Study, scholarships/grants, and unspecified assistantships available. Support available to part-time students. Financial award application deadline: 3/10; financial award applicants required to submit FAFSA. *Unit head:* Dr. John Brinkman, Chair of Department of Behavioral and Social Sciences, 260-399-7700 Ext. 8425, Fax: 260-399-8170, E-mail: jbrinkman@sf.edu. *Application contact:* Kyle Richardson, Enrollment Services Specialist, 260-399-7700 Ext. 6310, Fax: 260-399-8152, E-mail: krichardson@sf.edu.
Website: http://bhvscience.sf.edu/

University of Saint Joseph, Department of Counseling and Applied Behavioral Studies, West Hartford, CT 06117-2700. Offers applied behavioral analysis (Graduate Certificate); clinical mental health counseling (MA); school counseling (MA). *Accreditation:* ACA. *Program availability:* Part-time, evening/weekend. *Degree requirements:* For master's, comprehensive exam, thesis optional. *Entrance requirements:* For master's, 2 letters of recommendation. Electronic applications accepted. Application fee is waived when completed online. *Expenses: Tuition:* Full-time $14,580; part-time $729 per credit hour. *Required fees:* $920; $46 per credit hour. Tuition and fees vary according to course load, degree level and program.

University of St. Thomas, School of Education and Human Services, Houston, TX 77006-4696. Offers all level education (M Ed); bilingual/dual language (M Ed); Catholic school teaching (M Ed); Catholic/private school leadership (M Ed); counselor education (M Ed); curriculum and instruction (M Ed); education (Ed D); educational leadership (M Ed); elementary teaching (M Ed); English as a second language (M Ed); exceptionality/educational diagnostician (M Ed); exceptionality/special education (M Ed); generalist (M Ed); reading (M Ed); secondary teaching (M Ed); teaching (MAT). *Accreditation:* TEAC. *Program availability:* Part-time, evening/weekend, online learning. *Faculty:* 44 full-time (29 women), 31 part-time/adjunct (17 women). *Students:* 65 full-time (61 women), 719 part-time (645 women); includes 515 minority (169 Black or African American, non-Hispanic/Latino; 25 Asian, non-Hispanic/Latino; 315 Hispanic/Latino; 2 Native Hawaiian or other Pacific Islander, non-Hispanic/Latino; 4 Two or more races, non-Hispanic/Latino), 24 international. Average age 36. 297 applicants, 92% accepted, 211 enrolled. In 2016, 403 master's awarded. *Degree requirements:* For master's, thesis, field experience. *Entrance requirements:* For master's, GRE or MAT if GPA is below 3.0, bachelor's degree; minimum GPA of 2.75 in bachelor's degree or last 60 credit hours; official transcripts from all institutions; goal statement of 250-300 words; 1 reference. Additional exam requirements/recommendations for international students: Required—TOEFL (minimum score 94 iBT), IELTS (minimum score 7), PTE (minimum score 53). *Application deadline:* Applications are processed on a rolling basis. Application fee: $35. Electronic applications accepted. *Expenses:* Contact institution. *Financial support:* In 2016–17, 52 students received support. Federal Work-Study, scholarships/grants, and state work-study, institutional employment available. Support available to part-time students. Financial award application deadline: 4/15; financial award applicants required to submit FAFSA. *Faculty research:* Leadership, diversity, personality traits, second language acquisition. *Unit head:* Dr. Robert LeBlanc, Dean, 713-525-3540, Fax: 713-525-3871, E-mail: education@stthom.edu. *Application contact:* Rita Paredes, Administrative Assistant, 713-525-3442, Fax: 713-525-3871, E-mail: rparede@stthom.edu.
Website: http://www.stthom.edu/Academics/School_of_Education_and_Human_Services/Index.aqf

University of San Diego, School of Leadership and Education Sciences, Department of Counseling and Marital and Family Therapy, San Diego, CA 92110-2492. Offers clinical mental health counseling (MA); marital and family therapy (MA). *Accreditation:* ACA. *Program availability:* Part-time, evening/weekend. *Faculty:* 11 full-time (5 women), 28 part-time/adjunct (18 women). *Students:* 144 full-time (129 women), 41 part-time (38 women); includes 80 minority (10 Black or African American, non-Hispanic/Latino; 1 American Indian or Alaska Native, non-Hispanic/Latino; 12 Asian, non-Hispanic/Latino; 50 Hispanic/Latino; 7 Two or more races, non-Hispanic/Latino), 2 international. Average age 27. 387 applicants, 43% accepted, 83 enrolled. In 2016, 72 master's awarded. *Degree requirements:* For master's, comprehensive exam, international experience. *Entrance requirements:* For master's, minimum GPA of 3.0, interview with faculty member. Additional exam requirements/recommendations for international students: Required—TOEFL (minimum score 580 paper-based; 83 iBT), TWE. *Application deadline:* For fall admission, 1/13 priority date for domestic and international students. Applications are processed on a rolling basis. Application fee: $45. Electronic applications accepted. *Financial support:* In 2016–17, 151 students received support. Career-related internships or fieldwork, Federal Work-Study, institutionally sponsored loans, unspecified assistantships, and stipends available. Support available to part-time students. Financial award application deadline: 4/1; financial award applicants required to submit FAFSA. *Faculty research:* Action research, collaboration between family therapists and medical professionals, family therapy training and supervision, multicultural counseling, school counseling. *Unit head:* Dr. Ann Garland, Director, 619-260-7879, E-mail: agarland@sandiego.edu. *Application contact:* Monica Mahon, Director of Admissions and Enrollment, 619-260-4524, Fax: 619-260-4158, E-mail: grads@sandiego.edu.
Website: http://www.sandiego.edu/soles/departments/school-family-mental-health-professions/

University of San Francisco, School of Education, Department of Counseling Psychology, San Francisco, CA 94117-1080. Offers counseling (MA), including educational counseling, life transitions counseling, marital and family therapy. *Program availability:* Part-time. *Faculty:* 9 full-time (7 women), 43 part-time/adjunct (23 women). *Students:* 240 full-time (204 women), 72 part-time (59 women); includes 181 minority (18 Black or African American, non-Hispanic/Latino; 46 Asian, non-Hispanic/Latino; 96 Hispanic/Latino; 3 Native Hawaiian or other Pacific Islander, non-Hispanic/Latino; 18 Two or more races, non-Hispanic/Latino), 6 international. Average age 29. 270 applicants, 69% accepted, 108 enrolled. In 2016, 94 master's awarded. *Entrance requirements:* Additional exam requirements/recommendations for international students: Required—TOEFL, IELTS, PTE. *Application deadline:* For fall admission, 3/1 priority date for domestic students, 3/1 for international students; for spring admission, 10/15 priority date for domestic students, 10/15 for international students. Applications are processed on a rolling basis. Application fee: $55 ($65 for international students). Electronic applications accepted. *Expenses:* Full-time $23,310; part-time $1295 per credit. Tuition and fees vary according to course load, degree level, campus/location and program. *Financial support:* In 2016–17, 34 students received support. Fellowships, research assistantships, and teaching assistantships available. Financial award application deadline: 3/2; financial award applicants required to submit FAFSA. *Unit head:* Dr. Christine Yeh, Chair, 415-422-6868. *Application contact:* Peter Cole, Admission Coordinator, 415-422-5467, E-mail: schoolofeducation@usfca.edu.

The University of Scranton, Panuska College of Professional Studies, Department of Counseling and Human Services, Program in School Counseling, Scranton, PA 18510. Offers MS. *Accreditation:* ACA; NCATE. *Program availability:* Part-time, evening/weekend. *Degree requirements:* For master's, comprehensive exam (for some programs), thesis (for some programs), capstone experience. *Entrance requirements:* For master's, minimum GPA of 3.0, three letters of reference. Additional exam requirements/recommendations for international students: Required—TOEFL (minimum score 500 paper-based; 80 iBT), IELTS (minimum score 6.5). Electronic applications accepted.

University of South Africa, College of Human Sciences, Pretoria, South Africa. Offers adult education (M Ed); African languages (MA, PhD); African politics (MA, PhD); Afrikaans (MA, PhD); ancient history (MA, PhD); ancient Near Eastern studies (MA, PhD); anthropology (MA, PhD); applied linguistics (MA); Arabic (MA, PhD); archaeology (MA); art history (MA); Biblical archaeology (MA); Biblical studies (M Th, D Th, PhD); Christian spirituality (M Th, D Th); church history (M Th, D Th); classical studies (MA, PhD); clinical psychology (MA); communication (MA, PhD); comparative education (M Ed, Ed D); consulting psychology (D Admin, D Com, PhD); curriculum studies (M Ed, Ed D); development studies (M Admin, MA, D Admin, PhD); didactics (M Ed, Ed D); education (M Tech); education management (M Ed, Ed D); educational psychology (M Ed); English (MA); environmental education (M Ed); French (MA, PhD); German (MA, PhD); Greek (MA); guidance and counseling (M Ed); health studies (MA, PhD), including health sciences education (MA), health services management (MA), medical and surgical nursing science (critical care general) (MA), midwifery and neonatal nursing science (MA), trauma and emergency care (MA); history (MA, PhD); history of education (Ed D); inclusive education (M Ed, Ed D); information and communications technology policy and regulation (MA); information science (MA, MIS, PhD); international politics (MA, PhD); Islamic studies (MA, PhD); Italian (MA, PhD); Judaica (MA, PhD); linguistics (MA, PhD); mathematical education (M Ed); mathematics education (MA); missiology (M Th, D Th); modern Hebrew (MA, PhD); musicology (MA, MMus, D Mus, PhD); natural science education (M Ed); New Testament (M Th, D Th); Old Testament (D Th); pastoral therapy (M Th, D Th); philosophy (MA); philosophy of education (M Ed, Ed D); politics (MA, PhD); Portuguese (MA, PhD); practical theology (M Th, D Th); psychology (MA, MS, PhD); psychology of education (M Ed, Ed D); public health (MA); religious studies (MA, D Th, PhD); Romance languages (MA); Russian (MA, PhD); Semitic languages (MA, PhD); social behavior studies in HIV/AIDS (MA); social science (mental health) (MA); social science in development studies (MA); social science in psychology (MA); social science in social work (MA); social science in sociology (MA); social work (MSW, DSW, PhD); socio-education (M Ed, Ed D); sociolinguistics (MA); sociology (MA, PhD); Spanish (MA, PhD); systematic theology (M Th, D Th); TESOL (teaching English to speakers of other languages) (MA); theological ethics (M Th, D Th); theory of literature (MA, PhD); urban ministries (D Th); urban ministry (M Th).

University of South Alabama, College of Education and Professional Studies, Department of Counseling and Instructional Sciences, Mobile, AL 36688. Offers clinical mental health counseling (MS); educational media (M Ed, MS); instructional design and development (MS, PhD); school counseling (M Ed). *Accreditation:* NCATE. *Program availability:* Part-time. *Faculty:* 12 full-time (8 women), 6 part-time/adjunct (5 women).

Students: 104 full-time (83 women), 67 part-time (56 women); includes 49 minority (35 Black or African American, non-Hispanic/Latino; 2 American Indian or Alaska Native, non-Hispanic/Latino; 2 Asian, non-Hispanic/Latino; 8 Hispanic/Latino; 1 Native Hawaiian or other Pacific Islander, non-Hispanic/Latino; 1 Two or more races, non-Hispanic/Latino), 4 international. Average age 35. 59 applicants, 51% accepted, 26 enrolled. In 2016, 28 master's, 8 doctorates awarded. *Degree requirements:* For master's, comprehensive exam; for doctorate, comprehensive exam, thesis/dissertation. *Entrance requirements:* For master's, GRE General Test or MAT, minimum GPA of 3.0, two letters of recommendation; for doctorate, GRE, three letters of recommendation, master's degree in field or completion of prerequisites, resume. Additional exam requirements/recommendations for international students: Required—TOEFL (minimum score 525 paper-based; 71 iBT). *Application deadline:* For fall admission, 6/15 for domestic students, 5/15 for international students; for spring admission, 12/1 for domestic students, 11/1 for international students; for summer admission, 4/1 for domestic students. Applications are processed on a rolling basis. Application fee: $35. Electronic applications accepted. *Expenses:* Tuition, state resident: full-time $9768; part-time $407 per credit hour. Tuition, nonresident: full-time $19,536; part-time $814 per credit hour. *Financial support:* Fellowships, research assistantships, teaching assistantships, career-related internships or fieldwork, Federal Work-Study, institutionally sponsored loans, scholarships/grants, and unspecified assistantships available. Support available to part-time students. Financial award application deadline: 5/31; financial award applicants required to submit FAFSA. *Faculty research:* Agency counseling, rehabilitation counseling, school psychometry. *Unit head:* Dr. Tres Stefurak, Department Chair, 251-380-2734, Fax: 251-380-2713, E-mail: jstefurak@southalabama.edu. *Application contact:* Dr. Susan Santoli, Director of Graduate Studies, 251-380-2836, Fax: 251-380-2758, E-mail: ssantoli@southalabama.edu.
Website: http://www.southalabama.edu/colleges/ceps/cins/

University of South Carolina, The Graduate School, College of Education, Department of Educational Studies, Program in Counseling Education, Columbia, SC 29208. Offers PhD, Ed S. *Accreditation:* ACA (one or more programs are accredited); NCATE. *Program availability:* Part-time. *Degree requirements:* For doctorate, one foreign language, comprehensive exam, thesis/dissertation; for Ed S, comprehensive exam. *Entrance requirements:* For doctorate, GRE General Test or MAT, interview, resume, references; for Ed S, GRE General Test or MAT, interview, resum&e, transcripts, letter of intent, references. Electronic applications accepted. *Faculty research:* Multicultural counseling, children's fears, career development, family counseling.

The University of South Dakota, Graduate School, School of Education, Division of Counseling and Psychology in Education, Vermillion, SD 57069. Offers counseling (MA, PhD, Ed S); human development and educational psychology (MA, PhD, Ed S); school psychology (PhD, Ed S). *Accreditation:* ACA (one or more programs are accredited); NCATE. *Program availability:* Part-time. *Degree requirements:* For master's and Ed S, comprehensive exam, thesis or alternative; for doctorate, comprehensive exam, thesis/dissertation. *Entrance requirements:* For master's and doctorate, GRE General Test, minimum GPA of 3.0. Additional exam requirements/recommendations for international students: Required—TOEFL (minimum score 550 paper-based; 79 iBT). Electronic applications accepted.

University of Southern California, Graduate School, Rossier School of Education, Master's Programs in Education, Los Angeles, CA 90089-4038. Offers educational counseling (ME); marriage, family and child counseling (MMFT); postsecondary administration and student affairs [PASA] (ME); school counseling (ME); teaching (online) (MAT); teaching and teaching credential (MAT); teaching English to speakers of other languages (MAT). *Program availability:* Part-time, evening/weekend, online learning. *Degree requirements:* For master's, thesis optional. *Entrance requirements:* For master's, GRE (for all programs except MAT). Additional exam requirements/recommendations for international students: Required—TOEFL (minimum score 100 iBT). Electronic applications accepted. *Faculty research:* College access and equity, preparing teachers for culturally diverse populations, sociocultural basis of learning as mediated by instruction with focus on reading and literacy in English learners, social and political aspects of teaching and learning English, school counselor development and training.

University of Southern Maine, College of Management and Human Service, School of Education and Human Development, Program in Counselor Education, Portland, ME 04103. Offers clinical mental health counseling (MS); counseling (CAS); culturally responsive practices in education and human development (CGS); mental health rehabilitation technician/community (CGS); rehabilitation counseling (MS); school counseling (MS); substance abuse counseling (CGS). *Accreditation:* ACA (one or more programs are accredited); CORE; TEAC. *Program availability:* Part-time, evening/weekend. *Degree requirements:* For master's, comprehensive exam, thesis or alternative; for other advanced degree, thesis or alternative. *Entrance requirements:* For master's, GRE General Test or MAT, interview; for other advanced degree, master's degree. Additional exam requirements/recommendations for international students: Required—TOEFL (minimum score 550 paper-based; 79 iBT). Electronic applications accepted. *Faculty research:* Counselor licensure, group dynamics, counseling theories, healthy adaptation, counselor educator well-being.

University of South Florida, College of Education, Department of Educational and Psychological Studies, Tampa, FL 33620-9951. Offers college student affairs (M Ed); counselor education (MA, PhD, Ed S); interdisciplinary (PhD, Ed S); school psychology (PhD, Ed S). *Faculty:* 25 full-time (12 women). *Students:* 97 full-time (66 women), 94 part-time (62 women); includes 52 minority (22 Black or African American, non-Hispanic/Latino; 8 Asian, non-Hispanic/Latino; 19 Hispanic/Latino; 3 Two or more races, non-Hispanic/Latino), 25 international. Average age 34. 132 applicants, 45% accepted, 46 enrolled. In 2016, 94 master's, 7 doctorates, 8 other advanced degrees awarded. Application fee: $30. *Expenses:* Tuition, state resident: full-time $7766; part-time $431.43 per credit hour. Tuition, nonresident: full-time $15,789; part-time $877.17 per credit hour. *Required fees:* $37 per term. *Faculty research:* College student affairs, counselor education, educational psychology, school psychology, social foundations. *Total annual research expenditures:* $11.1 million. *Unit head:* Dr. Barabara Shircliff, Chair, 813-974-4001, E-mail: shirclif@usf.edu.
Website: http://www.coedu.usf.edu/main/departments/psf/psf.html

University of South Florida, College of Education, Department of Leadership, Counseling, Adult, Career and Higher Education, Tampa, FL 33620-9951. Offers adult education (MA, Ed D, PhD, Ed S); career and technical education (MA); career and workforce education (PhD); higher education/community college teaching (MA, Ed D, PhD); vocational education (Ed S). *Faculty:* 17 full-time (10 women). *Students:* 137 full-time (96 women), 331 part-time (237 women); includes 170 minority (75 Black or African American, non-Hispanic/Latino; 2 American Indian or Alaska Native, non-Hispanic/Latino; 12 Asian, non-Hispanic/Latino; 71 Hispanic/Latino; 2 Native Hawaiian or other Pacific Islander, non-Hispanic/Latino; 8 Two or more races, non-Hispanic/Latino), 18 international. Average age 35. 175 applicants, 66% accepted, 93 enrolled. In 2016, 111 master's, 22 doctorates, 1 other advanced degree awarded. Application fee: $30. *Expenses:* Tuition, state resident: full-time $7766; part-time $431.43 per credit hour. Tuition, nonresident: full-time $15,789; part-time $877.17 per credit hour. *Required fees:* $37 per term. *Total annual research expenditures:* $545,936. *Unit head:* Dr. Judith Ponticell, Chair, 813-974-4897, Fax: 813-974-5423, E-mail: jponticell@usf.edu.
Website: http://www.coedu.usf.edu/main/departments/ache/ache.html

University of South Florida, Innovative Education, Tampa, FL 33620-9951. Offers adult, career and higher education (Graduate Certificate), including college teaching, leadership in developing human resources, leadership in higher education; Africana studies (Graduate Certificate), including diasporas and health disparities, genocide and human rights; aging studies (Graduate Certificate), including gerontology; art research (Graduate Certificate), including museum studies; business foundations (Graduate Certificate); chemical and biomedical engineering (Graduate Certificate), including materials science and engineering, water, health and sustainability; child and family studies (Graduate Certificate), including positive behavior support; civil and industrial engineering (Graduate Certificate), including transportation systems analysis; community and family health (Graduate Certificate), including maternal and child health, social marketing and public health, violence and injury: prevention and intervention, women's health; criminology (Graduate Certificate), including criminal justice administration; educational measurement and research (Graduate Certificate), including evaluation; English (Graduate Certificate), including comparative literary studies, creative writing, professional and technical communication; entrepreneurship (Graduate Certificate); environmental health (Graduate Certificate), including safety management; epidemiology and biostatistics (Graduate Certificate), including applied biostatistics, biostatistics, concepts and tools of epidemiology, epidemiology, epidemiology of infectious diseases; geography, environment and planning (Graduate Certificate), including community development, environmental policy and management, geographical information systems; geology (Graduate Certificate), including hydrogeology; global health (Graduate Certificate), including disaster management, global health and Latin American and Caribbean studies, global health practice, humanitarian assistance, infection control; government and international affairs (Graduate Certificate), including Cuban studies, globalization studies; health policy and management (Graduate Certificate), including health management and leadership, public health policy and programs; hearing specialist: early intervention (Graduate Certificate); industrial and management systems engineering (Graduate Certificate), including systems engineering, technology management; information studies (Graduate Certificate), including school library media specialist; information systems/decision sciences (Graduate Certificate), including analytics and business intelligence; instructional technology (Graduate Certificate), including distance education, Florida digital/virtual educator, instructional design, multimedia design, Web design; internal medicine, bioethics and medical humanities (Graduate Certificate), including biomedical ethics; Latin American and Caribbean studies (Graduate Certificate); mass communications (Graduate Certificate), including multimedia journalism; mathematics and statistics (Graduate Certificate), including mathematics; medicine (Graduate Certificate), including aging and neuroscience, bioinformatics, biotechnology, brain fitness and memory management, clinical investigation, health informatics, health sciences, integrative weight management, intellectual property, medicine and gender, metabolic and nutritional medicine, metabolic cardiology, pharmacy sciences; national and competitive intelligence (Graduate Certificate); psychological and social foundations (Graduate Certificate), including career counseling, college teaching, diversity in education, mental health counseling, school counseling; public affairs (Graduate Certificate), including nonprofit management, public management, research administration; public health (Graduate Certificate), including environmental health, health equity, public health generalist, translational research in adolescent behavioral health; public health practices (Graduate Certificate), including planning for healthy communities; rehabilitation and mental health counseling (Graduate Certificate), including integrative mental health care, marriage and family therapy, rehabilitation technology; secondary education (Graduate Certificate), including ESOL, foreign language education: culture and content, foreign language education: professional; social work (Graduate Certificate), including geriatric social work/clinical gerontology; special education (Graduate Certificate), including autism spectrum disorder, disabilities education: severe/profound; world languages (Graduate Certificate), including teaching English as a second language (TESL) or foreign language. *Expenses:* Tuition, state resident: full-time $7766; part-time $431.43 per credit hour. Tuition, nonresident: full-time $15,789; part-time $877.17 per credit hour. *Required fees:* $37 per term. *Unit head:* Kathy Barnes, Interdisciplinary Programs Coordinator, 813-974-8031, Fax: 813-974-7061, E-mail: barnesk@usf.edu. *Application contact:* Karen Tylinski, Metro Initiatives, 813-974-9943, Fax: 813-974-7061, E-mail: ktylinsk@usf.edu.
Website: http://www.usf.edu/innovative-education/

The University of Tennessee, Graduate School, College of Education, Health and Human Sciences, Department of Educational Psychology and Counseling, Knoxville, TN 37996. Offers adult education (MS); applied educational psychology (MS); collaborative learning (Ed D); college student personnel (MS); mental health counseling (MS); rehabilitation counseling (MS); school counseling (MS). *Accreditation:* ACA (one or more programs are accredited); CORE (one or more programs are accredited); NCATE. *Program availability:* Part-time, evening/weekend. *Degree requirements:* For master's, thesis optional. *Entrance requirements:* For master's, GRE General Test, minimum GPA of 2.7. Additional exam requirements/recommendations for international students: Required—TOEFL. Electronic applications accepted.

The University of Tennessee, Graduate School, College of Education, Health and Human Sciences, Program in Education, Knoxville, TN 37996. Offers art education (MS); counseling education (PhD); cultural studies in education (PhD); curriculum (MS, Ed S); curriculum, educational research and evaluation (Ed D, PhD); early childhood education (PhD); early childhood special education (MS); education of deaf and hard of hearing (MS); educational administration and policy studies (Ed D, PhD); educational administration and supervision (Ed S); educational psychology (Ed D, PhD); elementary education (MS, Ed S); elementary teaching (MS); English education (MS, Ed S); exercise science (PhD); foreign language/ESL education (MS, Ed S); instructional technology (MS, Ed D, PhD, Ed S); literacy, language and ESL education (PhD); literacy, language education, and ESL education (Ed D); mathematics education (MS, Ed S); modified and comprehensive special education (MS); reading education (MS, Ed S); school counseling (Ed S); school psychology (PhD, Ed S); science education (MS, Ed S); secondary teaching (MS); social foundations (MS); social science education (MS, Ed S); socio-cultural foundations of sports and education (PhD); special education (Ed S); teacher education (Ed D, PhD). *Accreditation:* NCATE. *Program availability:* Part-time, evening/weekend. *Degree requirements:* For master's and Ed S, thesis optional; for doctorate, variable foreign language requirement, thesis/dissertation. *Entrance requirements:* For master's, minimum GPA of 2.7; for doctorate and Ed S, GRE General Test, minimum GPA of 2.7. Additional exam requirements/recommendations for international students: Required—TOEFL. Electronic applications accepted.

The University of Tennessee at Chattanooga, School of Education, Chattanooga, TN 37403. Offers counseling (M Ed), including community counseling, school counseling; education (M Ed, Post-Master's Certificate), including elementary education (M Ed), school leadership, secondary education (M Ed), special education (M Ed); educational specialist (Ed S), including educational technology, school psychology; learning and leadership (Ed D), including educational leadership. *Accreditation:* ACA; NCATE. *Program availability:* Part-time. *Faculty:* 13 full-time (8 women), 2 part-time/adjunct (both

women). *Students:* 50 full-time (32 women), 157 part-time (107 women); includes 42 minority (28 Black or African American, non-Hispanic/Latino; 4 Asian, non-Hispanic/Latino; 2 Hispanic/Latino; 8 Two or more races, non-Hispanic/Latino), 1 international. Average age 36. 169 applicants, 76% accepted, 49 enrolled. In 2016, 77 master's, 5 other advanced degrees awarded. *Degree requirements:* For master's, comprehensive exam, thesis optional, culminating experience; for doctorate, comprehensive exam, thesis/dissertation; for other advanced degree, internship. *Entrance requirements:* For master's, GRE General Test, PPST 1, teaching certificate; for doctorate, GRE General Test, master's degree, two years of practical work experience in organizational environment; for other advanced degree, GRE General Test, letters of reference. Additional exam requirements/recommendations for international students: Required—TOEFL (minimum score 550 paper-based; 79 iBT), IELTS (minimum score 6). *Application deadline:* For fall admission, 6/15 for domestic students, 7/1 for international students; for spring admission, 11/1 for domestic and international students. Applications are processed on a rolling basis. Application fee: $35 ($40 for international students). Electronic applications accepted. *Expenses:* $9,876 full-time in-state; $25,994 full-time out-of-state; $450 per credit part-time in-state; $1,345 per credit part-time out-of-state. *Financial support:* In 2016–17, 18 research assistantships, 5 teaching assistantships were awarded; career-related internships or fieldwork, institutionally sponsored loans, scholarships/grants, and unspecified assistantships also available. Support available to part-time students. Financial award application deadline: 7/1; financial award applicants required to submit FAFSA. *Faculty research:* School counseling, community counseling, elementary and secondary education, school leadership and administration. *Total annual research expenditures:* $247,231. *Unit head:* Dr. Renee Murley, Director, 423-425-4684, Fax: 423-425-5380, E-mail: renee-murley@utc.edu. *Application contact:* Dr. Joanne Romagni, Dean of the Graduate School, 423-425-4478, Fax: 423-425-5223, E-mail: joanne-romagni@utc.edu.
Website: http://www.utc.edu/school-education/aboutheschool/gradprograms.php

The University of Tennessee at Martin, Graduate Programs, College of Education, Health and Behavioral Sciences, Program in Counseling, Martin, TN 38238. Offers addictions counseling (MS Ed); community counseling (MS Ed); school counseling (MS Ed); student affairs and college counseling (MS Ed). *Accreditation:* NCATE. *Program availability:* Part-time, online only, 100% online. *Students:* 14 full-time (12 women), 62 part-time (59 women); includes 10 minority (6 Black or African American, non-Hispanic/Latino; 3 Hispanic/Latino; 1 Two or more races, non-Hispanic/Latino). Average age 35. 40 applicants, 48% accepted, 18 enrolled. In 2016, 17 master's awarded. *Degree requirements:* For master's, comprehensive exam. *Entrance requirements:* For master's, GRE General Test, minimum GPA of 2.5, resume, letters of reference. Additional exam requirements/recommendations for international students: Required—TOEFL (minimum score 525 paper-based; 71 iBT). *Application deadline:* For fall admission, 7/27 priority date for domestic and international students; for spring admission, 12/17 priority date for domestic and international students; for summer admission, 5/10 priority date for domestic and international students. Applications are processed on a rolling basis. Application fee: $30 ($130 for international students). Electronic applications accepted. *Expenses:* Tuition, state resident: full-time $8254; part-time $459 per credit hour. Tuition, nonresident: full-time $22,198; part-time $1234 per credit hour. *Required fees:* $79 per credit hour. Part-time tuition and fees vary according to course load and campus/location. *Financial support:* Scholarships/grants and unspecified assistantships available. Financial award application deadline: 2/1; financial award applicants required to submit FAFSA. *Unit head:* Cynthia West, Dean, 731-881-7125, Fax: 731-881-7975, E-mail: cwest@utm.edu. *Application contact:* Jolene L. Cunningham, Student Services Specialist, 731-881-7012, Fax: 731-881-7499, E-mail: jcunningham@utm.edu.

The University of Texas at Austin, Graduate School, College of Education, Department of Educational Psychology, Austin, TX 78712-1111. Offers academic educational psychology (M Ed, MA); counseling psychology (PhD); counselor education (M Ed); human development, culture and learning sciences (PhD); program evaluation (MA); quantitative methods (M Ed, MA, PhD); school psychology (MA, PhD). *Accreditation:* APA (one or more programs are accredited). *Degree requirements:* For master's, thesis optional; for doctorate, thesis/dissertation. *Entrance requirements:* For master's and doctorate, GRE General Test, 3 letters of recommendation. Additional exam requirements/recommendations for international students: Required—TOEFL.

The University of Texas at El Paso, Graduate School, College of Education, Department of Educational Psychology and Special Services, El Paso, TX 79968-0001. Offers educational diagnostics (M Ed); guidance and counseling (M Ed); special education (M Ed). *Program availability:* Part-time, evening/weekend. *Degree requirements:* For master's, thesis optional. *Entrance requirements:* For master's, minimum GPA of 3.0. Additional exam requirements/recommendations for international students: Required—TOEFL. Electronic applications accepted.

The University of Texas at San Antonio, College of Education and Human Development, Department of Counseling, San Antonio, TX 78207. Offers counselor education and supervision (PhD); school counseling (M Ed). *Accreditation:* ACA. *Program availability:* Part-time, evening/weekend. *Faculty:* 15 full-time (8 women), 6 part-time/adjunct (4 women). *Students:* 191 full-time (167 women), 225 part-time (185 women); includes 237 minority (23 Black or African American, non-Hispanic/Latino; 1 American Indian or Alaska Native, non-Hispanic/Latino; 5 Asian, non-Hispanic/Latino; 203 Hispanic/Latino; 5 Two or more races, non-Hispanic/Latino), 3 international. Average age 31. 160 applicants, 70% accepted, 91 enrolled. In 2016, 109 master's, 8 doctorates awarded. *Degree requirements:* For master's, comprehensive exam, thesis; for doctorate, comprehensive exam, thesis/dissertation. *Entrance requirements:* For master's, minimum GPA of 3.0 during last 60 hours of undergraduate study; two-page narrative statement; for doctorate, GRE, minimum GPA of 3.0 in master's-level courses in counseling or in related mental health field; resume; three letters of recommendation; statement of purpose; interview. Additional exam requirements/recommendations for international students: Required—TOEFL (minimum score 550 paper-based; 79 iBT), IELTS (minimum score 6.5). *Application deadline:* For fall admission, 7/1 for domestic students, 4/1 for international students; for spring admission, 10/1 for domestic students, 9/1 for international students. Applications are processed on a rolling basis. Application fee: $45 ($80 for international students). Electronic applications accepted. *Expenses:* Contact institution. *Financial support:* In 2016–17, 10 students received support, including 9 research assistantships (averaging $12,468 per year); scholarships/grants and unspecified assistantships also available. *Faculty research:* Creativity in counseling, non-suicidal self-injury, family violence, counselor preparation and supervision, technology, ethics, cognitive complexity, counseling outcome research, trauma, body image resiliency. *Unit head:* Dr. Thelma Duffey, Department Chair, 210-458-2602, Fax: 210-458-2605, E-mail: thelma.duffey@utsa.edu. *Application contact:* Kristina Talamantez, Student Development Specialist III, 210-458-2723, Fax: 210-458-2605, E-mail: kristina.talamantez@utsa.edu.
Website: http://coehd.utsa.edu/counseling

The University of Texas of the Permian Basin, Office of Graduate Studies, School of Education, Program in Counseling, Odessa, TX 79762-0001. Offers MA. *Degree requirements:* For master's, comprehensive exam (for some programs), thesis (for some programs). *Entrance requirements:* For master's, GRE General Test. Additional exam requirements/recommendations for international students: Required—TOEFL (minimum score 550 paper-based).

The University of Texas Rio Grande Valley, College of Education and P-16 Integration, Department of Counseling and Guidance, Edinburg, TX 78539. Offers clinical mental health counseling (M Ed); school counseling (M Ed). Tuition and fees vary according to course load and program.

University of the Cumberlands, Graduate Programs in Education, Williamsburg, KY 40769-1372. Offers all grades (P-12) (M Ed); business and marketing (MA Ed, MAT); counselor education and supervision (Ed D); director of pupil personnel (Certificate); director of special education (Certificate); educational administration and supervision (Ed S); educational leadership (Ed D); elementary education (MA Ed, MAT); instructional leadership - principalship (MA Ed); instructional leadership - school principal (Certificate); middle school education (MA Ed, MAT); reading and writing (MA Ed); school counseling (MA Ed); school superintendent (Certificate); secondary education (MA Ed, MAT); special education (MAT); supervisor of instruction (Certificate); teacher leader (MA Ed). *Program availability:* Part-time, evening/weekend, online learning. *Degree requirements:* For master's, comprehensive exam. Electronic applications accepted.

University of the Southwest, Graduate Programs, Hobbs, NM 88240-9129. Offers business administration (MBA); curriculum and instruction (MSE); curriculum and instruction: bilingual (MSE); curriculum and instruction: TESOL (MSE); early childhood education (MSE); educational administration (MSE); mental health counseling (MSE); school counseling (MSE); special education (MSE); sports management (MBA). *Program availability:* Part-time, evening/weekend, online learning. *Degree requirements:* For master's, comprehensive exam, thesis (for some programs). *Entrance requirements:* Additional exam requirements/recommendations for international students: Recommended—TOEFL. Electronic applications accepted.

The University of Toledo, College of Graduate Studies, College of Social Justice and Human Service, Department of School Psychology, Higher Education and Counselor Education, Toledo, OH 43606-3390. Offers counselor education (MA, PhD); higher education (ME, PhD, Certificate); school psychology (MA, Ed S). *Program availability:* Part-time. *Degree requirements:* For master's, comprehensive exam, thesis or alternative; for doctorate, comprehensive exam, thesis/dissertation; for other advanced degree, thesis optional. *Entrance requirements:* For master's, doctorate, and other advanced degree, minimum cumulative GPA of 2.7 for all previous academic work, letters of recommendation. Additional exam requirements/recommendations for international students: Required—TOEFL (minimum score 550 paper-based; 80 iBT). Electronic applications accepted.

University of Utah, Graduate School, College of Education, Department of Educational Psychology, Salt Lake City, UT 84112. Offers clinical mental health counseling (M Ed); counseling psychology (PhD); elementary education (M Ed); instructional design and educational technology (M Ed); instructional design and technology (MS); learning and cognition (MS, PhD); reading and literacy (M Ed, PhD); school counseling (M Ed); school psychology (M Ed, PhD, Ed S); statistics (M Stat). *Accreditation:* APA (one or more programs are accredited). *Faculty:* 23 full-time (12 women), 15 part-time/adjunct (10 women). *Students:* 119 full-time (95 women), 106 part-time (74 women); includes 37 minority (2 Black or African American, non-Hispanic/Latino; 6 Asian, non-Hispanic/Latino; 22 Hispanic/Latino; 7 Two or more races, non-Hispanic/Latino), 6 international. Average age 31. 296 applicants, 27% accepted, 73 enrolled. In 2016, 47 master's, 8 doctorates awarded. Terminal master's awarded for partial completion of doctoral program. *Degree requirements:* For master's, variable foreign language requirement, comprehensive exam (for some programs), thesis (for some programs), projects; for doctorate, variable foreign language requirement, comprehensive exam, thesis/dissertation, oral exam. *Entrance requirements:* For master's and doctorate, GRE General Test, minimum GPA of 3.0. Additional exam requirements/recommendations for international students: Required—TOEFL (minimum score 80 iBT). *Application deadline:* For fall admission, 12/15 for domestic and international students; for winter admission, 11/1 for domestic and international students; for spring admission, 3/15 for domestic and international students. Application fee: $55 ($65 for international students). Electronic applications accepted. *Expenses:* Contact institution. *Financial support:* In 2016–17, 84 students received support, including 12 fellowships with full and partial tuition reimbursements available (averaging $18,000 per year), 21 research assistantships with full and partial tuition reimbursements available (averaging $14,500 per year), 57 teaching assistantships with full and partial tuition reimbursements available (averaging $14,500 per year); career-related internships or fieldwork, Federal Work-Study, institutionally sponsored loans, scholarships/grants, traineeships, health care benefits, and unspecified assistantships also available. Financial award application deadline: 4/1; financial award applicants required to submit FAFSA. *Faculty research:* Autism, computer technology and instruction, cognitive behavior, aging, group counseling. *Total annual research expenditures:* $620,935. *Unit head:* Dr. Anne E. Cook, Chair, 801-581-7148, Fax: 801-581-5566, E-mail: anne.cook@utah.edu. *Application contact:* JoLynn N. Yates, Academic Coordinator, 801-581-7148, Fax: 801-581-5566, E-mail: jo.yates@utah.edu.
Website: http://www.ed.utah.edu/edps/

University of Vermont, Graduate College, College of Education and Social Services, Department of Leadership and Developmental Sciences, Counseling Program, Burlington, VT 05405. Offers MS. *Accreditation:* ACA; NCATE. *Entrance requirements:* For master's, GRE General Test, resume. Additional exam requirements/recommendations for international students: Required—TOEFL (minimum score 550 paper-based; 80 iBT). Electronic applications accepted. *Expenses:* Tuition, state resident: full-time $5814. Tuition, nonresident: full-time $14,670. *Faculty research:* Women and tenure, counseling children and adolescents.

University of Victoria, Faculty of Graduate Studies, Faculty of Education, Department of Educational Psychology and Leadership Studies, Victoria, BC V8W 2Y2, Canada. Offers aboriginal communities counseling (M Ed); counseling (M Ed, MA); educational psychology (M Ed, MA, PhD), including counseling psychology (M Ed, MA), leadership studies (PhD), learning and development (MA, PhD), measurement and evaluation, special education (M Ed, MA); leadership studies (M Ed, MA). *Program availability:* Part-time. *Degree requirements:* For master's, thesis (for some programs), comprehensive exam (M Ed); for doctorate, comprehensive exam, thesis/dissertation, candidacy exam. *Entrance requirements:* For master's, 2 years of work experience in a relevant field; for doctorate, GRE, 2 years of work experience in a relevant field, minimum B average. Additional exam requirements/recommendations for international students: Required—TOEFL (minimum score 575 paper-based), IELTS (minimum score 7). *Faculty research:* Learning and development (child, adolescent and adult), special education and exceptional children.

University of Virginia, Curry School of Education, Department of Human Services, Program in Counselor Education, Charlottesville, VA 22903. Offers M Ed, Ed S. *Accreditation:* ACA (one or more programs are accredited). *Students:* 45 full-time (40 women); includes 11 minority (4 Black or African American, non-Hispanic/Latino; 1 Asian, non-Hispanic/Latino; 3 Hispanic/Latino; 3 Two or more races, non-Hispanic/Latino), 1 international. Average age 24. 58 applicants, 69% accepted, 25 enrolled. In

2016, 31 master's awarded. *Entrance requirements:* For master's, GRE General Test, 2 letters of recommendation; for Ed S, GRE General Test. Additional exam requirements/recommendations for international students: Required—TOEFL (minimum score 600 paper-based; 90 iBT), IELTS. *Application deadline:* For fall admission, 1/5 for domestic and international students. Applications are processed on a rolling basis. Application fee: $60. Electronic applications accepted. *Expenses:* Tuition, state resident: full-time $15,026; part-time $834 per credit hour. Tuition, nonresident: full-time $25,168; part-time $1378 per credit hour. *Required fees:* $2654. *Financial support:* Applicants required to submit FAFSA. *Unit head:* Derick J. Williams, Program Area Director, 434-924-4928, E-mail: dw4pd@virginia.edu. *Application contact:* Eric Molnar, Assistant Director, Admissions and Enrollment Reporting, 434-243-2085, E-mail: eric.molnar@virginia.edu.
Website: http://curry.edschool.virginia.edu/counselor-ed-home-counslered-347?task-view

University of Virginia, Curry School of Education, Program in Education, Charlottesville, VA 22903. Offers administration and supervision (PhD); applied developmental science (PhD); counselor education (PhD); curriculum and instruction (PhD); early childhood special education (MT); education evaluation (PhD); educational psychology (PhD); educational research (PhD); elementary education (MT); English education (MT, PhD); foreign language education (MT); higher education (PhD); instructional technology (PhD); kinesiology (MT, PhD); math education (PhD); reading education (PhD); research, statistics and evaluation (PhD); school psychology (PhD); science education (PhD); social studies education (MT, PhD); special education (PhD); world languages education (MT). *Students:* 452 full-time (357 women), 18 part-time (13 women); includes 100 minority (28 Black or African American, non-Hispanic/Latino; 39 Asian, non-Hispanic/Latino; 18 Hispanic/Latino; 15 Two or more races, non-Hispanic/Latino), 14 international. Average age 25. 309 applicants, 51% accepted, 87 enrolled. In 2016, 144 master's, 31 doctorates awarded. *Degree requirements:* For master's, comprehensive exam (for some programs), field project; for doctorate, comprehensive exam, thesis/dissertation. *Entrance requirements:* For doctorate, GRE General Test. Additional exam requirements/recommendations for international students: Required—TOEFL (minimum score 600 paper-based; 90 iBT), IELTS (minimum score 7). *Application deadline:* Applications are processed on a rolling basis. Application fee: $60. Electronic applications accepted. *Expenses:* Tuition, state resident: full-time $15,026; part-time $834 per credit hour. Tuition, nonresident: full-time $25,168; part-time $1378 per credit hour. *Required fees:* $2654. *Financial support:* Fellowships, research assistantships, and teaching assistantships available. Financial award application deadline: 1/5; financial award applicants required to submit FAFSA. *Unit head:* Robert C. Pianta, Dean, 434-924-3334, E-mail: pianta@virginia.edu. *Application contact:* Eric Molnar, Assistant Director, Admissions and Enrollment Reporting, 434-243-2085, E-mail: eric.molnar@virginia.edu.
Website: http://curry.virginia.edu/teacher-education

The University of West Alabama, School of Graduate Studies, College of Education, Departments of Instructional Leadership and Support/Curriculum and Instruction, Program in Continuing Education, Livingston, AL 35470. Offers counseling and psychology (MSCE); family counseling (MSCE); general (MSCE); guidance and counseling (MSCE); library media (MSCE); student affairs in higher education (MSCE). *Accreditation:* NCATE. *Program availability:* Part-time, evening/weekend, 100% online. *Faculty:* 14 full-time (11 women), 45 part-time/adjunct (31 women). *Students:* 352 (295 women); includes 247 minority (234 Black or African American, non-Hispanic/Latino; 3 American Indian or Alaska Native, non-Hispanic/Latino; 1 Asian, non-Hispanic/Latino; 3 Hispanic/Latino; 1 Native Hawaiian or other Pacific Islander, non-Hispanic/Latino; 5 Two or more races, non-Hispanic/Latino). Average age 34. 92 applicants, 90% accepted, 72 enrolled. In 2016, 117 master's awarded. *Degree requirements:* For master's, comprehensive exam, thesis optional. *Entrance requirements:* For master's, GRE General Test, MAT, minimum GPA of 2.75. Additional exam requirements/recommendations for international students: Required—TOEFL (minimum score 500 paper-based; 61 iBT). *Application deadline:* Applications are processed on a rolling basis. Application fee: $40. Electronic applications accepted. *Expenses:* Tuition, state resident: part-time $355 per credit hour. Tuition, nonresident: part-time $710 per credit hour. *Required fees:* $130 per semester. *Financial support:* Teaching assistantships, Federal Work-Study, scholarships/grants, and unspecified assistantships available. Support available to part-time students. Financial award applicants required to submit FAFSA. *Unit head:* Dr. Reenay Rogers, Chair of Instructional Leadership and Support, 205-652-5423, Fax: 205-652-3706, E-mail: rrogers@uwa.edu. *Application contact:* Dr. B. J. Kimbrough, Dean of Graduate Studies, 205-652-3647, Fax: 205-652-3670, E-mail: bkimbrough@uwa.edu.

The University of West Alabama, School of Graduate Studies, College of Education, Departments of Instructional Leadership and Support/Curriculum and Instruction, Program in School Counseling, Livingston, AL 35470. Offers M Ed, Ed S. *Accreditation:* NCATE. *Program availability:* Part-time, evening/weekend, 100% online. *Faculty:* 8 full-time (5 women), 20 part-time/adjunct (14 women). *Students:* 353 (324 women); includes 111 minority (99 Black or African American, non-Hispanic/Latino; 3 American Indian or Alaska Native, non-Hispanic/Latino; 1 Asian, non-Hispanic/Latino; 5 Hispanic/Latino; 3 Two or more races, non-Hispanic/Latino). Average age 36. 94 applicants, 86% accepted, 67 enrolled. In 2016, 101 master's, 40 Ed Ss awarded. *Degree requirements:* For master's, comprehensive exam, thesis optional; for Ed S, comprehensive exam. *Entrance requirements:* For master's, GRE General Test, MAT, minimum GPA of 2.75. Additional exam requirements/recommendations for international students: Required—TOEFL (minimum score 500 paper-based; 61 iBT). *Application deadline:* Applications are processed on a rolling basis. Application fee: $40. Electronic applications accepted. *Expenses:* Tuition, state resident: part-time $355 per credit hour. Tuition, nonresident: part-time $710 per credit hour. *Required fees:* $130 per semester. *Financial support:* Teaching assistantships, Federal Work-Study, scholarships/grants, and unspecified assistantships available. Support available to part-time students. Financial award application deadline: 3/1; financial award applicants required to submit FAFSA. *Unit head:* Dr. Reenay Rogers, Chair of Instructional Leadership and Support, 205-652-5423, Fax: 205-652-3706, E-mail: rrogers@uwa.edu. *Application contact:* Dr. B. J. Kimbrough, Dean of Graduate Studies, 205-652-3647, Fax: 205-652-3706, E-mail: bkimbrough@uwa.edu.
Website: http://www.uwa.edu/medschoolcounseling.aspx

University of West Georgia, College of Education, Carrollton, GA 30118. Offers business education (M Ed); early childhood education (M Ed, Ed S); educational leadership (M Ed, Ed S); media (M Ed, Ed S); professional counseling (M Ed, Ed S); professional counseling and supervision (Ed D); reading instruction (M Ed); school improvement (Ed D); secondary education (M Ed); special education (M Ed, Ed S), including teaching (M Ed); speech language pathology (M Ed); teaching (MAT). *Accreditation:* NCATE. *Program availability:* Part-time, evening/weekend, 100% online, blended/hybrid learning. *Faculty:* 46 full-time (31 women). *Students:* 321 full-time (266 women), 1,007 part-time (813 women); includes 456 minority (389 Black or African American, non-Hispanic/Latino; 1 American Indian or Alaska Native, non-Hispanic/Latino; 13 Asian, non-Hispanic/Latino; 43 Hispanic/Latino; 10 Two or more races, non-Hispanic/Latino), 12 international. Average age 33. 541 applicants, 79% accepted, 305 enrolled. In 2016, 286 master's, 20 doctorates, 156 other advanced degrees awarded. *Entrance requirements:* Additional exam requirements/recommendations for international students: Required—TOEFL (minimum score 523 paper-based; 69 iBT); Recommended—IELTS (minimum score 6.5). *Application deadline:* For fall admission, 7/21 for domestic students, 6/1 for international students; for spring admission, 11/30 for domestic students, 10/15 for international students; for summer admission, 4/15 for domestic students, 3/30 for international students. Applications are processed on a rolling basis. Application fee: $40. Electronic applications accepted. *Expenses:* Tuition, state resident: full-time $5316; part-time $222 per semester hour. Tuition, nonresident: full-time $20,658; part-time $861 per semester hour. *Required fees:* $1962. Tuition and fees vary according to course load, degree level and program. *Financial support:* Fellowships, research assistantships, teaching assistantships, career-related internships or fieldwork, Federal Work-Study, institutionally sponsored loans, scholarships/grants, and unspecified assistantships available. Support available to part-time students. Financial award application deadline: 4/1; financial award applicants required to submit FAFSA. *Unit head:* Dr. Diane Hoff, Dean, College of Education, 678-839-6570, Fax: 678-839-6098, E-mail: dhoff@westga.edu. *Application contact:* Dr. Toby Ziglar, Assistant Dean of the Graduate School, 678-839-1394, Fax: 678-839-1395, E-mail: graduate@westga.edu.
Website: http://www.westga.edu/education/

University of Wisconsin–Madison, Graduate School, School of Education, Department of Counseling Psychology, Program in Counseling, Madison, WI 53706-1380. Offers MS. *Entrance requirements:* For master's, GRE General Test. Electronic applications accepted.

University of Wisconsin–Milwaukee, Graduate School, School of Education, Department of Educational Psychology, Milwaukee, WI 53201-0413. Offers children's mental health for school professionals (Graduate Certificate); community counseling (MS); counseling psychology (PhD); educational statistics and measurement (MS, PhD); learning and development (MS, PhD); multicultural knowledge of mental health practices (Graduate Certificate); school counseling (MS); school counseling (Graduate Certificate); school psychology (MS, PhD, Ed S). *Accreditation:* APA. *Program availability:* Part-time. *Students:* 161 full-time (121 women), 53 part-time (39 women); includes 47 minority (12 Black or African American, non-Hispanic/Latino; 1 American Indian or Alaska Native, non-Hispanic/Latino; 5 Asian, non-Hispanic/Latino; 8 Hispanic/Latino; 1 Native Hawaiian or other Pacific Islander, non-Hispanic/Latino; 20 Two or more races, non-Hispanic/Latino), 6 international. Average age 30. 266 applicants, 45% accepted, 71 enrolled. In 2016, 73 master's, 9 doctorates, 18 other advanced degrees awarded. *Degree requirements:* For master's, comprehensive exam, thesis; for doctorate, thesis/dissertation. *Entrance requirements:* For master's, minimum GPA of 3.0; for doctorate, GRE General Test, minimum GPA of 3.0. Additional exam requirements/recommendations for international students: Required—TOEFL (minimum score 550 paper-based; 79 iBT), IELTS (minimum score 6.5). *Application deadline:* For fall admission, 1/1 priority date for domestic students; for spring admission, 9/1 for domestic students. Applications are processed on a rolling basis. Application fee: $56 ($96 for international students). Electronic applications accepted. *Financial support:* In 2016–17, 14 fellowships, 1 research assistantship, 8 teaching assistantships were awarded; career-related internships or fieldwork, health care benefits, unspecified assistantships, and project assistantships also available. Support available to part-time students. Financial award application deadline: 4/15; financial award applicants required to submit FAFSA. *Application contact:* General Information Contact, 414-229-4721, E-mail: soeinfo@uwm.edu.
Website: http://uwm.edu/education/academics/educational-psychology-department/

University of Wisconsin–Oshkosh, Graduate Studies, College of Education and Human Services, Department of Professional Counseling, Oshkosh, WI 54901. Offers counseling (MSE). *Accreditation:* ACA. *Program availability:* Part-time, evening/weekend. *Degree requirements:* For master's, thesis optional, practicum. *Entrance requirements:* For master's, MAT, interview, minimum GPA of 3.0, letters of recommendation. Additional exam requirements/recommendations for international students: Required—TOEFL (minimum score 550 paper-based; 79 iBT). Electronic applications accepted. *Faculty research:* Gender issues, grief and loss, addictions, career development, close relationships.

University of Wisconsin–Platteville, School of Graduate Studies, College of Liberal Arts and Education, Counselor Education Program, Platteville, WI 53818-3099. Offers MSE. *Accreditation:* NCATE. *Program availability:* Part-time. *Students:* 1 (woman) full-time, 1 part-time (0 women). In 2016, 16 master's awarded. *Degree requirements:* For master's, comprehensive exam, thesis or alternative. *Entrance requirements:* Additional exam requirements/recommendations for international students: Required—TOEFL (minimum score 550 paper-based; 79 iBT), IELTS (minimum score 6.5). Application fee: $56. *Financial support:* Research assistantships with partial tuition reimbursements, career-related internships or fieldwork, Federal Work-Study, institutionally sponsored loans, scholarships/grants, and unspecified assistantships available. Support available to part-time students. Financial award applicants required to submit FAFSA. *Unit head:* Betsy Klinger, Coordinator, 608-342-1294, E-mail: klingerb@uwplatt.edu. *Application contact:* Dee Dunbar, School of Graduate Studies, 608-342-1322, Fax: 608-342-1389, E-mail: gradstudies@uwplatt.edu.

University of Wisconsin–River Falls, Outreach and Graduate Studies, College of Education and Professional Studies, Department of Counseling and School Psychology, River Falls, WI 54022. Offers counseling (MSE); school psychology (MSE, Ed S). *Accreditation:* ACA. *Program availability:* Part-time. *Entrance requirements:* For master's, minimum GPA of 2.75, resume, 3 letters of reference, vita. Additional exam requirements/recommendations for international students: Required—TOEFL (minimum score 500 paper-based; 65 iBT), IELTS (minimum score 5.5). Electronic applications accepted.

University of Wisconsin–Stevens Point, College of Professional Studies, School of Education, Program in Guidance and Counseling, Stevens Point, WI 54481-3897. Offers MSE. Program offered jointly with University of Wisconsin–Oshkosh. *Degree requirements:* For master's, comprehensive exam, thesis or alternative.

University of Wisconsin–Superior, Graduate Division, Department of Counseling and Psychological Professions, Superior, WI 54880-4500. Offers community counseling (MSE); human relations (MSE); school counseling (MSE). *Program availability:* Part-time, evening/weekend. *Degree requirements:* For master's, position paper, practicum. *Entrance requirements:* For master's, GRE and/or MAT, minimum GPA of 2.75. Electronic applications accepted. *Faculty research:* Women and power, intrafamily dynamics.

University of Wyoming, College of Education, Programs in Counselor Education, Laramie, WY 82071. Offers community mental health (MS); counselor education and supervision (PhD); school counseling (MS); student affairs (MS). *Accreditation:* ACA (one or more programs are accredited). *Degree requirements:* For master's, comprehensive exam (for some programs), thesis optional; for doctorate, thesis/dissertation, video demonstration. *Entrance requirements:* For master's, interview, background check; for doctorate, video tape session, interview, writing sample, master's degree, background check. Additional exam requirements/recommendations for international students: Required—TOEFL. *Faculty research:* Wyoming SAGE photovoice project; accountable school counseling programs; GLBT issues; addictions; play therapy-early childhood mental health.

Utah State University, School of Graduate Studies, Emma Eccles Jones College of Education and Human Services, Department of Psychology, Logan, UT 84322. Offers clinical/counseling/school psychology (PhD); research and evaluation methodology (PhD); school counseling (MS); school psychology (MS). *Accreditation:* APA (one or more programs are accredited). *Program availability:* Part-time, evening/weekend, online learning. Terminal master's awarded for partial completion of doctoral program. *Degree requirements:* For master's, thesis (for some programs); for doctorate, thesis/dissertation. *Entrance requirements:* For master's, GRE General Test (school psychology), MAT (school counseling), minimum GPA of 3.5; for doctorate, GRE General Test, minimum GPA of 3.5. Additional exam requirements/recommendations for international students: Required—TOEFL. *Faculty research:* Hearing loss detection in infancy, ADHD, eating disorders, domestic violence, neuropsychology, bilingual/Spanish speaking students/parents.

Valdosta State University, Department of Psychology, Counseling, and Family Therapy, Valdosta, GA 31698. Offers school counseling (M Ed, Ed S). *Accreditation:* AAMFT/COAMFTE. *Program availability:* Part-time, evening/weekend, 100% online, blended/hybrid learning. *Degree requirements:* For master's, thesis or alternative, comprehensive written and/or oral exams; for Ed S, thesis. *Entrance requirements:* For master's, GRE General Test or MAT, GACE; for Ed S, GRE General Test or MAT. Additional exam requirements/recommendations for international students: Required—TOEFL (minimum score 523 paper-based); Recommended—IELTS. Electronic applications accepted. *Expenses:* Contact institution.

Vanderbilt University, Peabody College, Department of Human and Organizational Development, Nashville, TN 37240-1001. Offers community development and action (M Ed); human development counseling (M Ed). *Accreditation:* ACA; NCATE. *Program availability:* Part-time. *Faculty:* 30 full-time (18 women), 38 part-time/adjunct (26 women). *Students:* 113 full-time (94 women), 12 part-time (10 women); includes 19 minority (7 Black or African American, non-Hispanic/Latino; 2 Asian, non-Hispanic/Latino; 6 Hispanic/Latino; 4 Two or more races, non-Hispanic/Latino), 5 international. Average age 25. 217 applicants, 48% accepted, 53 enrolled. In 2016, 60 master's awarded. *Degree requirements:* For master's, comprehensive exam, thesis optional. *Entrance requirements:* For master's, GRE General Test, MAT. Additional exam requirements/recommendations for international students: Required—TOEFL (minimum score 550 paper-based; 80 iBT). *Application deadline:* For fall admission, 12/31 priority date for domestic and international students; for spring admission, 11/1 priority date for domestic and international students. Applications are processed on a rolling basis. Application fee: $0. Electronic applications accepted. *Expenses: Tuition:* Part-time $1854 per credit hour. *Financial support:* Fellowships with partial tuition reimbursements, research assistantships with partial tuition reimbursements, teaching assistantships with partial tuition reimbursements, Federal Work-Study, institutionally sponsored loans, scholarships/grants, tuition waivers (partial), and unspecified assistantships available. Support available to part-time students. Financial award application deadline: 1/15; financial award applicants required to submit FAFSA. *Faculty research:* Community psychology and community development; counseling and mental health services, prevention and positive youth development; organizational and community change; youth physical and behavioral health in schools and communities. *Unit head:* Dr. Paul Speer, Chair, 615-322-6881, Fax: 615-322-1141, E-mail: paul.w.speer@vanderbilt.edu. *Application contact:* Sherrie Lane, Educational Coordinator, 615-322-8484, Fax: 615-322-1141, E-mail: sherrie.a.lane@vanderbilt.edu.

Villanova University, Graduate School of Liberal Arts and Sciences, Department of Education and Counseling, Villanova, PA 19085-1699. Offers clinical mental health counseling (MS), including counseling and human relations; education (MA); education plus teacher certification (MA); elementary school counseling (MS), including counseling and human relations; secondary school counseling (MS), including counseling and human relations; teacher leadership (MA). *Program availability:* Part-time, evening/weekend. *Faculty:* 20. *Students:* 81 full-time (67 women), 35 part-time (24 women); includes 18 minority (5 Black or African American, non-Hispanic/Latino; 7 Asian, non-Hispanic/Latino; 6 Hispanic/Latino), 2 international. Average age 30. 71 applicants, 72% accepted, 38 enrolled. In 2016, 47 master's awarded. *Degree requirements:* For master's, comprehensive exam. *Entrance requirements:* For master's, GRE or MAT, minimum GPA of 3.0, statement of goals. Additional exam requirements/recommendations for international students: Required—TOEFL or IELTS. *Application deadline:* For fall admission, 3/1 priority date for domestic students, 5/1 for international students; for spring admission, 11/15 priority date for domestic students, 10/15 for international students; for summer admission, 5/1 for domestic students. Applications are processed on a rolling basis. Application fee: $50. Electronic applications accepted. *Financial support:* Research assistantships, teaching assistantships, scholarships/grants, and unspecified assistantships available. Financial award applicants required to submit FAFSA. *Unit head:* Dr. Edward Fierros, Chairperson, 610-519-4625. *Application contact:* Dean, Graduate School of Liberal Arts and Sciences.
Website: http://www.education.villanova.edu/

Virginia Commonwealth University, Graduate School, School of Education, Doctoral Program in Education, Richmond, VA 23284-9005. Offers art education (PhD); counselor education and supervision (PhD); curriculum, culture and change (PhD); educational leadership (PhD); educational psychology (PhD); leadership (Ed D); research and evaluation (PhD); special education and disability leadership (PhD); sport leadership (PhD); urban services leadership (PhD). *Accreditation:* NCATE. *Program availability:* Part-time. *Degree requirements:* For doctorate, thesis/dissertation. *Entrance requirements:* For doctorate, GRE (for PhD), MAT (for Ed D), interview, master's degree, writing sample. Additional exam requirements/recommendations for international students: Required—TOEFL (minimum score 600 paper-based; 100 iBT). *Application deadline:* For fall admission, 2/15 for domestic students. Application fee: $50. Electronic applications accepted. *Financial support:* Fellowships, research assistantships, career-related internships or fieldwork, Federal Work-Study, and institutionally sponsored loans available. Financial award application deadline: 3/1; financial award applicants required to submit FAFSA. *Unit head:* Dr. Kathleen Cauley, Interim Director, 804-827-2657, E-mail: kmcauley@vcu.edu. *Application contact:* Dr. Colleen A. Thoma, Administrative Assistant, 804-827-2651, E-mail: cathoma@vcu.edu.
Website: http://www.soe.vcu.edu/programs/doctoral-programs/

Virginia Commonwealth University, Graduate School, School of Education, Program in Counselor Education, Richmond, VA 23284-9005. Offers college student development and counseling (M Ed); school counseling (M Ed). *Accreditation:* ACA; NCATE. *Entrance requirements:* For master's, GRE General Test or MAT. Additional exam requirements/recommendations for international students: Required—TOEFL (minimum score 600 paper-based; 100 iBT). *Application deadline:* For fall admission, 3/15 for domestic students; for spring admission, 11/1 for domestic students. Application fee: $50. Electronic applications accepted. *Financial support:* Career-related internships or fieldwork and tuition waivers (full and partial) available. Support available to part-time students. Financial award application deadline: 3/1; financial award applicants required to submit FAFSA. *Unit head:* Dr. Mary A. Hermann, Chair, 804-827-2626, E-mail: mahermann@vcu.edu. *Application contact:* Dr. Donna Gibson, Graduate Program Director, 804-828-1333, E-mail: dgibson7@vcu.edu.
Website: http://www.soe.vcu.edu/departments/ce/index.html

Virginia Polytechnic Institute and State University, Graduate School, College of Liberal Arts and Human Sciences, Blacksburg, VA 24061. Offers career and technical education (MS Ed, Ed D, PhD, Ed S); communication (MA); counselor education (MA Ed, Ed D, PhD, Ed S); creative writing (MFA); curriculum and instruction (MA Ed, Ed D, PhD, Ed S); educational leadership and policy studies (MA Ed, Ed D, PhD, Ed S); educational research and evaluation (PhD); English (MA); foreign languages, cultures, and literatures (MA); higher education (PhD); higher education and student affairs (MA Ed); history (MA); human development (MS, PhD); material culture and public humanities (MA); philosophy (MA); political science (MA); rhetoric and writing (PhD); science and technology studies (MS, PhD); social, political, ethical, and cultural thought (PhD); sociology (MS, PhD); theater arts (MFA). *Faculty:* 408 full-time (204 women), 3 part-time/adjunct (2 women). *Students:* 657 full-time (446 women), 457 part-time (292 women); includes 213 minority (114 Black or African American, non-Hispanic/Latino; 3 American Indian or Alaska Native, non-Hispanic/Latino; 29 Asian, non-Hispanic/Latino; 44 Hispanic/Latino; 23 Two or more races, non-Hispanic/Latino), 93 international. Average age 33. 805 applicants, 55% accepted, 328 enrolled. In 2016, 270 master's, 91 doctorates awarded. *Degree requirements:* For master's, comprehensive exam (for some programs), thesis (for some programs); for doctorate, comprehensive exam (for some programs), thesis/dissertation (for some programs). *Entrance requirements:* For master's and doctorate, GRE/GMAT. Additional exam requirements/recommendations for international students: Required—TOEFL (minimum score 80 iBT). *Application deadline:* For fall admission, 8/1 for domestic students, 4/1 for international students; for spring admission, 1/1 for domestic students, 9/1 for international students. Applications are processed on a rolling basis. Application fee: $75. Electronic applications accepted. *Expenses:* Tuition, state resident: full-time $12,467; part-time $692.50 per credit hour. Tuition, nonresident: full-time $25,095; part-time $1394.25 per credit hour. *Required fees:* $2669; $491.50 per semester. Tuition and fees vary according to course load, campus/location and program. *Financial support:* In 2016–17, 21 research assistantships with full tuition reimbursements (averaging $19,817 per year), 237 teaching assistantships with full tuition reimbursements (averaging $15,497 per year) were awarded. Financial award application deadline: 3/1; financial award applicants required to submit FAFSA. *Total annual research expenditures:* $6.6 million. *Unit head:* Rosemary Blieszner, Interim Dean, 540-231-6779, Fax: 540-231-7157, E-mail: liberalartsdean@vt.edu. *Application contact:* Chelsea Blanchet, Executive Assistant, 540-231-6779, Fax: 540-231-7157, E-mail: bchels1@vt.edu.
Website: http://www.liberalarts.vt.edu/

Virginia State University, College of Graduate Studies, College of Education, Department of School and Community Counseling, Petersburg, VA 23806-0001. Offers M Ed, MS. *Accreditation:* NCATE. *Degree requirements:* For master's, thesis optional.

Wake Forest University, Graduate School of Arts and Sciences, Counseling Program, Winston-Salem, NC 27106. Offers MA, M Div/MA. *Accreditation:* ACA. *Entrance requirements:* For master's, GRE General Test. Additional exam requirements/recommendations for international students: Required—TOEFL (minimum score 79 iBT). Electronic applications accepted.

Walden University, Graduate Programs, School of Counseling, Minneapolis, MN 55401. Offers addiction counseling (MS), including addictions and public health, child and adolescent counseling, family studies and interventions, forensic counseling, general program, military families and culture, trauma and crisis counseling; clinical mental health counseling (MS), including addiction counseling, forensic counseling, military families and culture, trauma and crisis counseling; counselor education and supervision (PhD), including consultation, counseling and social change, forensic mental health counseling, leadership and program evaluation, trauma and crisis; marriage, couple, and family counseling (MS), including addiction counseling, career counseling, forensic counseling, military families and culture, trauma and crisis counseling; school counseling (MS), including addiction counseling, career counseling, crisis and trauma, military families and culture. *Accreditation:* ACA. *Program availability:* Part-time, evening/weekend, online only, 100% online. *Degree requirements:* For master's, residency, field experience, professional development plan, licensure plan; for doctorate, thesis/dissertation, residency, practicum, internship. *Entrance requirements:* For master's, bachelor's degree or higher; minimum GPA of 2.5; official transcripts; goal statement (for some programs); access to computer and Internet; for doctorate, master's degree or higher; three years of related professional or academic experience (preferred); minimum GPA of 3.0; goal statement and current resume (for select programs); official transcripts; access to computer and Internet. Additional exam requirements/recommendations for international students: Required—TOEFL (minimum score 550 paper-based, 79 iBT), IELTS (minimum score 6.5), Michigan English Language Assessment Battery (minimum score 82), or PTE (minimum score 53). Electronic applications accepted.

Walsh University, Graduate Programs, Program in Counseling and Human Development, North Canton, OH 44720-3396. Offers clinical mental health counseling (MA); school counseling (MA); student affairs in higher education (MA). *Accreditation:* ACA. *Program availability:* Part-time, evening/weekend. *Faculty:* 5 full-time (4 women), 10 part-time/adjunct (8 women). *Students:* 34 full-time (24 women), 66 part-time (51 women); includes 11 minority (6 Black or African American, non-Hispanic/Latino; 2 American Indian or Alaska Native, non-Hispanic/Latino; 2 Hispanic/Latino; 1 Two or more races, non-Hispanic/Latino), 1 international. Average age 30. 58 applicants, 69% accepted, 27 enrolled. In 2016, 24 master's awarded. *Degree requirements:* For master's, comprehensive exam, internship, practicum. *Entrance requirements:* For master's, GRE (minimum score of 145 verbal and 146 quantitative) or MAT (minimum score of 397), interview, minimum GPA of 3.0, writing sample, reference forms, notarized affidavit of good moral conduct. Additional exam requirements/recommendations for international students: Required—TOEFL (minimum score 500 paper-based; 61 iBT). *Application deadline:* For fall admission, 7/15 priority date for domestic students. Applications are processed on a rolling basis. Application fee: $25. Electronic applications accepted. Application fee is waived when completed online. *Expenses:* $665 per credit hour. *Financial support:* In 2016–17, 11 students received support, including 11 research assistantships with partial tuition reimbursements available (averaging $8,442 per year). Financial award application deadline: 12/31. *Faculty research:* Supervision of clinical mental health, clinical mental health practice/issues, clinical mental health skills development, advocacy, teaching and professional development, career development, refugee development in US, supervision in student affairs, offender treatment, domestic violence issues, alcohol and drug treatment issues, Professional identity and advocacy in school counseling, Efficacy in counseling clinic. *Unit head:* Dr. Ruthann Anderson, Program Director, 330-490-7338, Fax: 330-490-7323, E-mail: randerson@walsh.edu. *Application contact:* Audra Dice, Graduate and Transfer Admissions Counselor, 330-490-7181, Fax: 330-244-4925, E-mail: adice@walsh.edu.
Website: http://www.walsh.edu/counseling-graduate-program

Waynesburg University, Graduate and Professional Studies, Canonsburg, PA 15370. Offers business (MBA), including energy management, finance, health systems, human resources, leadership, market development; counseling (MA), including addictions counseling, clinical mental health; counselor education and supervision (PhD); criminal investigation (MA); education (M Ed), including autism, curriculum and instruction, educational leadership, online teaching; nursing (MSN), including administration, education, informatics; nursing practice (DNP); special education (M Ed); technology (M Ed); MSN/MBA. *Accreditation:* AACN. *Program availability:* Part-time, evening/weekend. *Degree requirements:* For doctorate, thesis/dissertation. *Entrance requirements:* Additional exam requirements/recommendations for international students: Required—TOEFL. Electronic applications accepted.

Wayne State College, School of Education and Counseling, Department of Counseling and Special Education, Program in Guidance and Counseling, Wayne, NE 68787. Offers counseling (MSE); counselor education (MSE); school counseling (MSE). *Accreditation:* ACA; NCATE. *Program availability:* Part-time, evening/weekend. *Degree requirements:* For master's, comprehensive exam, thesis optional. *Entrance requirements:* For master's, GRE General Test, minimum GPA of 3.0. Additional exam requirements/recommendations for international students: Required—TOEFL (minimum score 550 paper-based). Electronic applications accepted.

Wayne State University, College of Education, Division of Theoretical and Behavioral Foundations, Detroit, MI 48202. Offers applied behavior analysis (Certificate); counseling (M Ed, MA, Ed D, PhD, Ed S); counseling psychology (MA); education evaluation and research (M Ed, Ed D, PhD); educational psychology (M Ed, PhD), including learning and instruction sciences (PhD); rehabilitation counseling and community inclusion (MA); school and community psychology (MA); school psychology (Certificate). *Accreditation:* ACA (one or more programs are accredited); CORE (one or more programs are accredited). *Program availability:* Evening/weekend. *Faculty:* 12. *Students:* 211 full-time (179 women), 237 part-time (196 women); includes 167 minority (119 Black or African American, non-Hispanic/Latino; 1 American Indian or Alaska Native, non-Hispanic/Latino; 10 Asian, non-Hispanic/Latino; 17 Hispanic/Latino; 20 Two or more races, non-Hispanic/Latino), 24 international. Average age 32. 294 applicants, 34% accepted, 72 enrolled. In 2016, 87 master's, 12 doctorates, 14 other advanced degrees awarded. *Degree requirements:* For master's, thesis (for some programs); for doctorate, thesis/dissertation. *Entrance requirements:* For master's, GRE, interview, personal statement, portfolio (art therapy); for doctorate, GRE, department-written exam, interview, curriculum vitae, references, master's degree in closely-related field with minimum GPA of 3.5, demonstration of counseling skills (counseling); for other advanced degree, master's degree in counseling and counseling license (for Ed S); good standing in school and community psychology MA program (for Certificate). Additional exam requirements/recommendations for international students: Required—TOEFL (minimum score 550 paper-based; 79 iBT), Michigan English Language Assessment Battery (minimum score 85); Recommended—IELTS (minimum score 6.5), TWE (minimum score 5.5). *Application deadline:* For fall admission, 6/1 priority date for domestic students, 5/1 priority date for international students; for winter admission, 10/1 priority date for domestic students, 9/1 priority date for international students; for spring admission, 2/1 priority date for domestic students, 1/1 priority date for international students. Applications are processed on a rolling basis. Application fee: $50. Electronic applications accepted. *Expenses:* $16,503 per year resident tuition and fees, $33,697 per year non-resident tuition and fees. *Financial support:* In 2016–17, 92 students received support, including 2 research assistantships with tuition reimbursements available (averaging $17,994 per year); fellowships with tuition reimbursements available, teaching assistantships with tuition reimbursements available, Federal Work-Study, scholarships/grants, health care benefits, and unspecified assistantships also available. Support available to part-time students. Financial award applicants required to submit FAFSA. *Faculty research:* Adolescents at risk, supervision of counseling. *Unit head:* Dr. Cheryl Somers, Assistant Dean, 313-577-1670, E-mail: c.somers@wayne.edu. *Application contact:* Janice Green, Assistant Dean, 313-577-1605, E-mail: jwgreen@wayne.edu.
Website: http://coe.wayne.edu/tbf/index.php

West Chester University of Pennsylvania, College of Education and Social Work, Department of Counselor Education, West Chester, PA 19383. Offers clinical mental health counseling (MS); counseling (Certificate); higher education counseling (Post Master's Certificate); higher education counseling/student affairs (MS, Certificate); school counseling (M Ed). *Accreditation:* ACA; NCATE. *Program availability:* Part-time, evening/weekend. *Faculty:* 10 full-time (6 women), 5 part-time/adjunct (3 women). *Students:* 130 full-time (100 women), 65 part-time (55 women); includes 48 minority (27 Black or African American, non-Hispanic/Latino; 2 Asian, non-Hispanic/Latino; 13 Hispanic/Latino; 6 Two or more races, non-Hispanic/Latino), 1 international. Average age 27. 199 applicants, 56% accepted, 66 enrolled. In 2016, 78 master's, 3 other advanced degrees awarded. *Degree requirements:* For master's, comprehensive exam. *Entrance requirements:* For master's, minimum GPA of 3.0, three letters of reference. Additional exam requirements/recommendations for international students: Required—TOEFL or IELTS. *Application deadline:* For fall admission, 5/15 for international students; for spring admission, 10/15 for international students. Applications are processed on a rolling basis. Application fee: $50. Electronic applications accepted. *Expenses:* Tuition, state resident: full-time $8694; part-time $483 per credit. Tuition, nonresident: full-time $13,050; part-time $725 per credit. *Required fees:* $2399; $119.05 per credit. Tuition and fees vary according to campus/location and program. *Financial support:* Scholarships/grants and unspecified assistantships available. Financial award application deadline: 2/15; financial award applicants required to submit FAFSA. *Faculty research:* Teacher and student cognition, adolescent cognitive development, college counseling, motivational interviewing. *Unit head:* Dr. Eric Owens, Chair, 610-436-2559, Fax: 610-425-7432, E-mail: eowens@wcupa.edu. *Application contact:* Dr. Cheryl Neale-McFall, Graduate Coordinator, 610-436-2559, Fax: 610-425-7432, E-mail: cneale-mcfall@wcupa.edu.
Website: http://www.wcupa.edu/education-socialWork/counselorEducation/

Western Connecticut State University, Division of Graduate Studies, School of Professional Studies, Department of Education and Educational Psychology, Program in School Counseling, Danbury, CT 06810-6885. Offers MS. *Accreditation:* ACA. *Program availability:* Part-time. *Degree requirements:* For master's, practicum, internship, completion of program in 6 years. *Entrance requirements:* For master's, PRAXIS I, minimum GPA of 2.8, 3 letters of reference, essay, 6 hours of psychology. Additional exam requirements/recommendations for international students: Recommended—TOEFL (minimum score 550 paper-based; 79 iBT), IELTS (minimum score 6). *Faculty research:* The effect of affective factors on cognition and learning, statistics and research methods, interviewing, individual and multicultural counseling.

Western Illinois University, School of Graduate Studies, College of Education and Human Services, Department of Counselor Education, Macomb, IL 61455-1390. Offers counseling (MS Ed). *Accreditation:* ACA. *Program availability:* Part-time. *Students:* 26 full-time (24 women), 47 part-time (40 women); includes 8 minority (4 Black or African American, non-Hispanic/Latino; 1 Asian, non-Hispanic/Latino; 3 Hispanic/Latino). Average age 32. 41 applicants, 66% accepted, 10 enrolled. In 2016, 21 master's awarded. *Degree requirements:* For master's, thesis or alternative. *Entrance requirements:* For master's, GRE, interview. Additional exam requirements/recommendations for international students: Required—TOEFL (minimum score 550 paper-based; 80 iBT). Application fee: $30. Electronic applications accepted. *Financial support:* In 2016–17, 5 students received support. Unspecified assistantships available. Financial award applicants required to submit FAFSA. *Unit head:* Dr. Holly Nikels, Interim Chairperson, 309-762-1876. *Application contact:* Dr. Nancy Parsons, Assistant Director of Graduate Studies, 309-298-1806, Fax: 309-298-2345, E-mail: grad-office@wiu.edu.
Website: http://wiu.edu/counselored

Western Kentucky University, Graduate Studies, College of Education and Behavioral Sciences, Department of Counseling and Student Affairs, Bowling Green, KY 42101. Offers counseling (MA Ed), including marriage and family therapy, mental health counseling; school counseling (P-12) (MA Ed); student affairs in higher education (MA Ed). *Accreditation:* ACA; NCATE. *Program availability:* Part-time, evening/weekend. *Degree requirements:* For master's, comprehensive exam, thesis optional. *Entrance requirements:* For master's, GRE General Test. Additional exam requirements/recommendations for international students: Required—TOEFL (minimum score 555 paper-based; 79 iBT). *Faculty research:* Counselor education, research for residential workers.

Western Michigan University, Graduate College, College of Education and Human Development, Department of Counselor Education and Counseling Psychology, Kalamazoo, MI 49008. Offers counseling psychology (MA, PhD); counselor education (MA, PhD), including counselor education (MA). *Accreditation:* ACA (one or more programs are accredited); APA (one or more programs are accredited); CORE; NCATE. *Degree requirements:* For doctorate, thesis/dissertation.

Western Washington University, Graduate School, College of Humanities and Social Sciences, Department of Psychology, Program in School Counseling, Bellingham, WA 98225-5996. Offers M Ed. *Accreditation:* ACA. *Degree requirements:* For master's, comprehensive exam. *Entrance requirements:* For master's, GRE General Test, minimum GPA of 3.0 in last 60 semester hours or last 90 quarter hours. Additional exam requirements/recommendations for international students: Required—TOEFL (minimum score 567 paper-based). Electronic applications accepted.

Westfield State University, College of Graduate and Continuing Education, Department of Psychology, Program in Counseling, Westfield, MA 01086. Offers forensic mental health counseling (MA); mental health counseling (MA); school adjustment counseling (MA); school guidance counseling (MA). *Program availability:* Part-time, evening/weekend. *Degree requirements:* For master's, comprehensive exam, practicum. *Entrance requirements:* For master's, GRE General Test, MAT, minimum undergraduate GPA of 3.0. Additional exam requirements/recommendations for international students: Recommended—TOEFL (minimum score 550 paper-based; 79 iBT). *Expenses:* Tuition, state resident: part-time $318 per semester hour. Tuition, nonresident: part-time $318 per semester hour. *Required fees:* $75 per semester. Tuition and fees vary according to course load and program.

Westminster College, Graduate School, Program in School Counseling, New Wilmington, PA 16172-0001. Offers M Ed, Certificate. *Program availability:* Part-time, evening/weekend. *Degree requirements:* For master's, comprehensive exam. *Entrance requirements:* For master's, minimum GPA of 3.0. *Application deadline:* For fall admission, 8/15 priority date for domestic students; for spring admission, 1/8 priority date for domestic students. Applications are processed on a rolling basis. Application fee: $35. *Expenses: Tuition:* Full-time $1362; part-time $454 per semester hour. One-time fee: $235.50 full-time. *Financial support:* Career-related internships or fieldwork and scholarships/grants available. *Unit head:* Eric J. Perry, Coordinator, 724-946-7874, Fax: 724-946-6158. *Application contact:* Dr. Darwin W. Huey, Graduate Education Director, 724-946-7186, Fax: 724-946-6158, E-mail: hueydw@westminster.edu.

West Texas A&M University, College of Education and Social Sciences, Department of Education, Program in Counseling, Canyon, TX 79016-0001. Offers MA. *Program availability:* Part-time. *Degree requirements:* For master's, comprehensive exam. *Entrance requirements:* For master's, GRE General Test, interview, 12 semester hours in education and/or psychology, approval from the Counselor Admissions Committee. Additional exam requirements/recommendations for international students: Required—TOEFL (minimum score 550 paper-based). *Application deadline:* For fall admission, 8/1 for domestic students, 5/1 for international students; for spring admission, 12/1 for domestic students, 10/30 for international students; for summer admission, 5/1 for domestic students. Application fee: $40 ($75 for international students). Electronic applications accepted. *Financial support:* Research assistantships, teaching assistantships, career-related internships or fieldwork, Federal Work-Study, institutionally sponsored loans, and tuition waivers (partial) available. Support available to part-time students. Financial award applicants required to submit CSS PROFILE or FAFSA. *Unit head:* Dr. Ivette Castillo, Assistant Professor, 806-651-8233. *Application contact:* Dr. Ivette Castillo, Assistant Professor, 806-651-8233.
Website: http://www.wtamu.edu/academics/counseling-ma-graduate-program.aspx

West Virginia University, College of Education and Human Services, Department of Counseling, Rehabilitation Counseling, and Counseling Psychology, Program in Counseling, Morgantown, WV 26506. Offers MA. *Accreditation:* ACA; APA. *Degree requirements:* For master's, content exams. *Entrance requirements:* For master's, GRE General Test, minimum GPA of 2.8, interview 2.8. Additional exam requirements/recommendations for international students: Required—TOEFL (minimum score 550 paper-based; 65 iBT). Electronic applications accepted. *Faculty research:* Career development and placement, family therapy, conflict resolution, interviewing technique, multicultural counseling.

Whitworth University, School of Education, Graduate Studies in Education, Program in Counseling, Spokane, WA 99251-0001. Offers school counselors (M Ed); social agency/church setting (M Ed). *Accreditation:* NCATE. *Program availability:* Part-time, evening/weekend. *Degree requirements:* For master's, comprehensive exam, internship, practicum, research project, or thesis. *Entrance requirements:* For master's, GRE General Test, MAT. *Faculty research:* Church counseling service support.

Wichita State University, Graduate School, College of Education, Department of Counseling, Educational Leadership, Educational and School Psychology, Wichita, KS 67260. Offers counseling (M Ed); educational leadership (M Ed, Ed D); educational psychology (M Ed); school psychology (Ed S). *Accreditation:* NCATE. *Program availability:* Part-time, evening/weekend. Application fee: $50 ($65 for international students). *Unit head:* Dr. Jody Fiorini, Department Head, 316-978-3325, Fax: 316-978-3102, E-mail: jody.fiorini@wichita.edu. *Application contact:* Jordan Oleson, Admissions Coordinator, 316-978-3095, Fax: 316-978-3253, E-mail: jordan.oleson@wichita.edu.
Website: http://www.wichita.edu/cles

Widener University, School of Education, Hospitality, and Continuing Studies, Chester, PA 19013-5792. Offers adult education (M Ed); counseling in higher education (M Ed); counselor education (M Ed); early childhood education (M Ed); educational foundations (M Ed); educational leadership (M Ed); educational psychology (M Ed); elementary education (M Ed); English and language arts (M Ed); health education (M Ed); higher education leadership (Ed D); home and school visitor (M Ed); human sexuality (M Ed, PhD); mathematics education (M Ed); middle school education (M Ed); principalship (M Ed); reading and language arts (Ed D); reading education (M Ed); school administration (Ed D); science education (M Ed); social studies education (M Ed); special education (M Ed); technology education (M Ed). *Accreditation:* NCATE. *Program availability:* Part-time, evening/weekend. *Faculty:* 34 full-time (22 women), 37 part-time/

adjunct (14 women). *Students:* 97 full-time (64 women), 201 part-time (143 women); includes 56 minority (44 Black or African American, non-Hispanic/Latino; 1 American Indian or Alaska Native, non-Hispanic/Latino; 2 Asian, non-Hispanic/Latino; 8 Hispanic/Latino; 1 Two or more races, non-Hispanic/Latino), 32 international. Average age 39. 139 applicants, 88% accepted. In 2016, 45 master's, 21 doctorates awarded. Terminal master's awarded for partial completion of doctoral program. *Degree requirements:* For doctorate, thesis/dissertation. *Entrance requirements:* For master's, minimum GPA of 2.5; for doctorate, GRE or MAT, minimum GPA of 2.0 (undergraduate), 3.5 (graduate). *Application deadline:* Applications are processed on a rolling basis. Application fee: $25 ($300 for international students). Electronic applications accepted. *Expenses:* Contact institution. *Financial support:* Career-related internships or fieldwork, tuition waivers (full and partial), and unspecified assistantships available. Support available to part-time students. Financial award application deadline: 5/1. *Faculty research:* Reading and cognition, adult education, technology education, educational leadership, special education. *Unit head:* Dr. Shawn Fitzgerald, Dean, 610-499-4294, Fax: 610-499-4623, E-mail: smfitzgerald@widener.edu. *Application contact:* Dr. Roberta Nolan, Director of Graduate Admissions, 610-499-4125, E-mail: rdnolan@widener.edu.
Website: http://www.widener.edu/academics/schools/eics

William Paterson University of New Jersey, College of Education, Wayne, NJ 07470-8420. Offers curriculum and learning (M Ed); educational leadership (M Ed); elementary education (MAT); literacy (M Ed); professional counseling (M Ed); secondary education (MAT); special education (M Ed). *Accreditation:* NCATE. *Program availability:* Part-time, evening/weekend. *Faculty:* 36 full-time (25 women), 32 part-time/adjunct (27 women). *Students:* 74 full-time (51 women), 607 part-time (515 women); includes 194 minority (42 Black or African American, non-Hispanic/Latino; 21 Asian, non-Hispanic/Latino; 116 Hispanic/Latino; 15 Two or more races, non-Hispanic/Latino), 1 international. Average age 35. 390 applicants, 83% accepted, 263 enrolled. In 2016, 170 master's awarded. *Degree requirements:* For master's, comprehensive exam, thesis (for some programs), exit interview (for some programs); practicum/internship; minimum GPA of 3.0 (for some programs); exit portfolio (for some programs). *Entrance requirements:* For master's, GRE/MAT, minimum GPA of 2.75; teaching certificate; essay; interview; 2 letters of recommendation; personal statement. Additional exam requirements/recommendations for international students: Required—TOEFL (minimum score 550 paper-based; 79 iBT), IELTS (minimum score 6). *Application deadline:* For fall admission, 8/1 for domestic students, 4/1 for international students; for spring admission, 12/1 for domestic students, 11/1 for international students; for summer admission, 5/1 for domestic students, 2/1 for international students. Applications are processed on a rolling basis. Application fee: $50. Electronic applications accepted. *Expenses:* Tuition, state resident: full-time $12,480; part-time $611 per credit. Tuition, nonresident: full-time $20,263; part-time $992 per credit. *Required fees:* $1573; $77 per credit. Tuition and fees vary according to course load, degree level and program. *Financial support:* Career-related internships or fieldwork, Federal Work-Study, scholarships/grants, and unspecified assistantships available. Support available to part-time students. Financial award application deadline: 4/1; financial award applicants required to submit FAFSA. *Faculty research:* History of education, social media in classrooms and education, integrating environmental lessons into urban classrooms, minority student self-advocacy in higher education, factors affecting high school teacher retention. *Total annual research expenditures:* $289,197. *Unit head:* Dr. Candace Burns, Dean, 973-720-2137, Fax: 973-720-3467, E-mail: burnsc@wpunj.edu. *Application contact:* Liana Fornarotto, Director of Education Enrollment and Certification, 973-720-2206, Fax: 973-720-2989, E-mail: fornarottol@wpunj.edu.
Website: http://www.wpunj.edu/coe

Wilmington University, College of Education, New Castle, DE 19720-6491. Offers applied technology in education (M Ed); career and technical education (M Ed); educational leadership (Ed D); elementary and secondary school counseling (M Ed); elementary studies (M Ed); ESOL literacy (M Ed); higher education leadership (Ed D); instruction: gifted and talented (M Ed); instruction: teacher of reading (M Ed); instruction: teaching and learning (M Ed); organizational leadership (Ed D); school leadership (M Ed); secondary education (MAT); special education (M Ed). *Accreditation:* NCATE. *Program availability:* Part-time, evening/weekend. *Faculty:* 19 full-time (11 women), 178 part-time/adjunct (99 women). *Students:* 248 full-time (176 women), 999 part-time (738 women); includes 244 minority (193 Black or African American, non-Hispanic/Latino; 17 American Indian or Alaska Native, non-Hispanic/Latino; 9 Asian, non-Hispanic/Latino; 19 Hispanic/Latino; 2 Native Hawaiian or other Pacific Islander, non-Hispanic/Latino; 4 Two or more races, non-Hispanic/Latino), 7 international. Average age 34. 672 applicants, 96% accepted, 348 enrolled. In 2016, 529 master's, 87 doctorates awarded. *Entrance requirements:* For master's, 2 letters of recommendation, interview. Additional exam requirements/recommendations for international students: Required—TOEFL (minimum score 500 paper-based). *Application deadline:* For fall admission, 4/30 for domestic students. Applications are processed on a rolling basis. Application fee: $35. Electronic applications accepted. *Expenses: Tuition:* Full-time $8388; part-time $466 per credit. *Required fees:* $25 per semester. Tuition and fees vary according to degree level. *Financial support:* Applicants required to submit FAFSA. *Unit head:* Dr. John C. Gray, Dean. *Application contact:* Laura Morris, Director of Admissions, 877-967-5464, E-mail: infocenter@wilmu.edu.
Website: http://www.wilmu.edu/education/

Winona State University, College of Education, Counselor Education Department, Winona, MN 55987. Offers community counseling (MS); professional development (MS); school counseling (MS). *Accreditation:* ACA; NCATE. *Program availability:* Part-time, evening/weekend. *Degree requirements:* For master's, thesis or alternative. *Entrance requirements:* For master's, letters of reference, interview, group activity, on-site writing. Electronic applications accepted.

Winthrop University, College of Education, Program in Counseling and Development, Rock Hill, SC 29733. Offers agency counseling (M Ed); school counseling (M Ed). *Accreditation:* ACA; NCATE. *Program availability:* Part-time. *Degree requirements:* For master's, comprehensive exam. *Entrance requirements:* For master's, GRE General Test or MAT, interview. Additional exam requirements/recommendations for international students: Required—TOEFL (minimum score 550 paper-based; 79 iBT), IELTS (minimum score 6). Electronic applications accepted. *Expenses:* Tuition, state resident: full-time $14,312; part-time $599 per credit hour. Tuition, nonresident: full-time $27,570; part-time $1153 per credit hour.

Wright State University, Graduate School, College of Education and Human Services, Department of Human Services, Programs in Counseling, Dayton, OH 45435. Offers counseling (MA, MS), including business and industrial management; pupil personnel services (M Ed), including school counseling. *Accreditation:* ACA (one or more programs are accredited); NCATE. *Degree requirements:* For master's, comprehensive exam, thesis (for some programs). *Entrance requirements:* For master's, GRE General Test, MAT, interview. Additional exam requirements/recommendations for international students: Required—TOEFL. Application fee: $25. *Expenses:* Tuition, state resident: full-time $9952; part-time $622 per credit hour. Tuition, nonresident: full-time $16,960; part-time $1060 per credit hour. *Financial support:* Tuition waivers (full and partial) and unspecified assistantships available. Support available to part-time students. Financial award applicants required to submit FAFSA. *Unit head:* Dr. Stephen B. Fortson, Chair, 937-775-2075, Fax: 937-775-2042, E-mail: stephen.fortson@wright.edu. *Application contact:* John Kimble, Associate Director of Graduate Admissions and Records, 937-775-2957, Fax: 937-775-2453, E-mail: john.kimble@wright.edu.

Xavier University, College of Social Sciences, Health and Education, School of Education, Department of Counseling, Cincinnati, OH 45207. Offers clinical mental health counseling (MA); school counseling (MA). *Program availability:* Part-time, evening/weekend. *Degree requirements:* For master's, internship. *Entrance requirements:* For master's, GRE or MAT, minimum GPA of 3.0; 2 letters of recommendation; resume; official transcript; statement of purpose. Additional exam requirements/recommendations for international students: Required—TOEFL (minimum score 550 paper-based; 79 iBT). Electronic applications accepted. Application fee is waived when completed online. *Expenses:* Contact institution. *Faculty research:* Supervision, ethics, consultation, self-injury, bullying.

Xavier University of Louisiana, Graduate School, Programs in Education, New Orleans, LA 70125. Offers counseling (MA); curriculum and instruction (MA); educational leadership (MA). *Accreditation:* NCATE. *Program availability:* Part-time, evening/weekend. *Degree requirements:* For master's, comprehensive exam, thesis or alternative. *Entrance requirements:* For master's, GRE General Test, MAT, minimum GPA of 2.5. Additional exam requirements/recommendations for international students: Required—TOEFL.

Youngstown State University, Graduate School, Beeghly College of Education, Department of Counseling, Youngstown, OH 44555-0001. Offers community counseling (MS Ed); school counseling (MS Ed). *Accreditation:* ACA; NCATE. *Program availability:* Part-time, evening/weekend. *Degree requirements:* For master's, comprehensive exam. *Entrance requirements:* For master's, MAT, interview, minimum GPA of 2.7. Additional exam requirements/recommendations for international students: Required—TOEFL. *Faculty research:* Suicide, euthanasia, ethical issues, marriage and family.

Developmental Education

Austin Peay State University, College of Graduate Studies, College of Behavioral and Health Sciences, Department of Professional Studies, Clarksville, TN 37044. Offers human resources leadership (MPS); strategic leadership (MPS); training and development (MPS). *Program availability:* Part-time, online learning. *Faculty:* 3 full-time (all women), 1 (woman) part-time/adjunct. *Students:* 9 full-time (6 women), 25 part-time (20 women); includes 12 minority (8 Black or African American, non-Hispanic/Latino; 3 Hispanic/Latino; 1 Two or more races, non-Hispanic/Latino). Average age 43. 14 applicants, 71% accepted, 7 enrolled. In 2016, 4 master's awarded. *Degree requirements:* For master's, project. *Entrance requirements:* For master's, GRE General Test, minimum GPA of 2.75. Additional exam requirements/recommendations for international students: Required—TOEFL (minimum score 500 paper-based). *Application deadline:* For fall admission, 8/9 priority date for domestic students. Applications are processed on a rolling basis. Application fee: $45 ($50 for international students). Electronic applications accepted. *Expenses:* Tuition, state resident: full-time $8300; part-time $415 per credit hour. Tuition, nonresident: full-time $22,280; part-time $1114 per credit hour. *Required fees:* $1473; $73.65 per credit hour. *Financial support:* Career-related internships or fieldwork, Federal Work-Study, institutionally sponsored loans, scholarships/grants, and unspecified assistantships available. Support available to part-time students. Financial award application deadline: 4/1; financial award applicants required to submit FAFSA. *Unit head:* Dr. Robyn Hulsart, Department Chair, 931-221-1439, E-mail: hulsartr@apsu.edu. *Application contact:* Brad Averitt, Coordinator of Graduate Admissions, 800-859-4723, Fax: 931-221-7641, E-mail: gradadmissions@apsu.edu.
Website: http://www.apsu.edu/apfc/MPS

Ferris State University, College of Education and Human Services, School of Education, Big Rapids, MI 49307. Offers curriculum and instruction (M Ed), including special education, subject area; educational leadership (MS); instructor (MSCTE); post-secondary administration (MSCTE); training and development (MSCTE). *Program availability:* Part-time, evening/weekend, blended/hybrid learning. *Faculty:* 7 full-time (4 women), 9 part-time/adjunct (6 women). *Students:* 3 full-time (1 woman), 62 part-time (34 women); includes 8 minority (3 Black or African American, non-Hispanic/Latino; 1 Hispanic/Latino; 4 Two or more races, non-Hispanic/Latino), 9 international. Average age 37. 24 applicants, 71% accepted, 10 enrolled. In 2016, 36 master's awarded. *Degree requirements:* For master's, thesis, research paper or project. *Entrance requirements:* For master's, minimum undergraduate GPA of 3.0. Additional exam requirements/recommendations for international students: Required—TOEFL (minimum score 500 paper-based, 79 iBT) or IELTS. *Application deadline:* For fall admission, 7/1 priority date for domestic and international students; for spring admission, 11/1 priority date for domestic and international students; for summer admission, 3/1 priority date for domestic and international students. Applications are processed on a rolling basis. Application fee: $30. Electronic applications accepted. Application fee is waived when completed online. Tuition and fees vary according to degree level and program. *Financial support:* Career-related internships or fieldwork and scholarships/grants available. Support available to part-time students. Financial award applicants required to submit FAFSA. *Faculty research:* Suicide prevention, reading, women in education, special needs, administration. *Unit head:* Arrick L. Jackson, Dean, 231-591-2702, Fax: 231-591-2043, E-mail: arrickJackson@ferris.edu. *Application contact:* Liza Ing, Graduate Program Coordinator, 231-591-5362, Fax: 231-591-2043, E-mail: lizaIng@ferris.edu.
Website: http://www.ferris.edu/education/education/

Grambling State University, School of Graduate Studies and Research, College of Education, Department of Educational Leadership, Grambling, LA 71245. Offers developmental education (MS, Ed D, PMC), including curriculum and instructional design (Ed D), English (MS), guidance and counseling (MS), higher education administration and management (Ed D), mathematics (MS), reading (MS), science (MS), student development and personnel services (Ed D); educational leadership

(M Ed). *Program availability:* Part-time, evening/weekend. *Degree requirements:* For master's, comprehensive exam, thesis (for some programs); for doctorate, comprehensive exam, thesis/dissertation. *Entrance requirements:* For master's, GRE, minimum GPA of 2.5 on last degree; for doctorate, GRE (minimum score 1000, 500 on Verbal), master's degree, minimum GPA of 3.0 on last degree. Additional exam requirements/recommendations for international students: Required—TOEFL (minimum score 500 paper-based; 62 iBT). Electronic applications accepted.

Instituto Tecnológico y de Estudios Superiores de Monterrey, Campus Ciudad Obregón, Programs in Education, Program in Cognitive Development, Ciudad Obregón, Mexico. Offers ME.

National Louis University, College of Arts and Sciences, Chicago, IL 60603. Offers adult education (Ed D); counseling and human services (MS); language and academic development (M Ed, Certificate); psychology (MA, PhD, Certificate); public policy (MA); written communication (MS, Certificate). *Program availability:* Part-time, evening/weekend, online learning. *Degree requirements:* For master's and Certificate, comprehensive exam (for some programs), thesis (for some programs); for doctorate, thesis/dissertation. *Entrance requirements:* For master's, MAT or GRE, 3 professional or academic references, interview, minimum GPA of 3.0; for doctorate, GRE General Test, MAT, or Watson-Glaser Critical Thinking Appraisal, three professional or academic references, statement of academic and professional goals, 3 years of experience in field, interview, master's degree, resume, writing sample; for Certificate, GRE, MAT, or Watson-Glaser Critical Thinking Appraisal, three professional or academic references, statement of academic and professional goals, interview, minimum GPA of 3.0. Additional exam requirements/recommendations for international students: Required—Department of Language Studies Assessment or TOEFL (minimum score 550 paper-based; 79 iBT). Electronic applications accepted.

North Carolina State University, Graduate School, College of Education, Department of Adult and Higher Education, Program in Training and Development, Raleigh, NC 27695. Offers M Ed, Ed D, Certificate. *Program availability:* Online learning. *Degree requirements:* For master's, thesis optional. *Entrance requirements:* For master's, GRE General Test or MAT, minimum GPA of 3.0 in major. Electronic applications accepted.

Penn State Harrisburg, Graduate School, School of Behavioral Sciences and Education, Middletown, PA 17057. Offers adult education in the health and medical professions (Certificate); applied behavior analysis (MA); applied clinical psychology (MA); applied psychological research (MA); community psychology and social change (MA); English as a second language (ESL) program specialist and leadership (Certificate); folklore and ethnography (Certificate); health education (M Ed); lifelong learning and adult education (M Ed, D Ed); literacy education (M Ed); literacy leadership (Certificate); psychology: applications in clinical psychology (Certificate); psychology: health psychology (Certificate); teaching and curriculum (M Ed); training and development (M Ed, Certificate). *Program availability:* Part-time, evening/weekend. *Unit head:* Dr. Mukund S. Kulkarni, Chancellor, 717-948-6105, Fax: 717-948-6452. *Application contact:* Robert W. Coffman, Jr., Director of Enrollment Management, Recruitment and Admissions, 717-948-6250, Fax: 717-948-6325, E-mail: hbgadmit@psu.edu.
Website: https://harrisburg.psu.edu/behavioral-sciences-and-education/

Rutgers University–New Brunswick, Graduate School of Education, Department of Educational Psychology, Program in Learning, Cognition and Development, Piscataway, NJ 08854-8097. Offers Ed M. *Program availability:* Part-time, evening/weekend. *Entrance requirements:* For master's, GRE General Test, 3 letters of recommendation. Additional exam requirements/recommendations for international students: Required—TOEFL (minimum score 550 paper-based; 83 iBT). Electronic applications accepted. *Faculty research:* Cognitive development, gender roles, cognition and instruction, peer learning, infancy and early childhood.

Sam Houston State University, College of Education, Department of Educational Leadership, Huntsville, TX 77341. Offers administration (M Ed); developmental education administration (Ed D); educational leadership (Ed D); higher education administration (MA); instructional leadership (M Ed, MA). *Program availability:* Part-time, evening/weekend, online learning. *Degree requirements:* For master's, comprehensive exam (for some programs), thesis (for some programs); for doctorate, comprehensive exam, thesis/dissertation. *Entrance requirements:* For master's, GRE General Test, references, personal essay, resume, professional statement; for doctorate, GRE General Test, master's degree, references, personal essay, resume. Additional exam requirements/recommendations for international students: Required—TOEFL (minimum score 550 paper-based; 79 iBT), IELTS (minimum score 6.5). Electronic applications accepted.

Texas State University, The Graduate College, College of Education, Program in Developmental Education, San Marcos, TX 78666. Offers MA, PhD. *Program availability:* Part-time. *Faculty:* 5 full-time (4 women), 1 part-time/adjunct (0 women). *Students:* 29 full-time (23 women), 18 part-time (14 women); includes 20 minority (7 Black or African American, non-Hispanic/Latino; 1 Asian, non-Hispanic/Latino; 11 Hispanic/Latino; 1 Two or more races, non-Hispanic/Latino), 4 international. Average age 39. 29 applicants, 52% accepted, 7 enrolled. In 2016, 2 master's, 2 doctorates awarded. *Degree requirements:* For master's, comprehensive exam, thesis optional; for doctorate, comprehensive exam, thesis/dissertation. *Entrance requirements:* For master's, baccalaureate degree from regionally-accredited institution with minimum GPA of 2.75 on last 60 hours of undergraduate work, statement of purpose, 3 letters of reference from individuals with knowledge of the candidate as a student or professional; for doctorate, GRE (minimum preferred score of 299 with no less than 150 on the verbal section, 149 on the quantitative section and 4.0 on the analytical section), baccalaureate and master's degrees from regionally-accredited institution in area relevant to developmental education with minimum graduate GPA of 3.0; statement of purpose; resume; 3 letters of recommendation addressing the applicant's professional and academic background. Additional exam requirements/recommendations for international students: Required—TOEFL (minimum score 78 iBT), IELTS (minimum score 6.5). *Application deadline:* For fall admission, 1/15 priority date for domestic and international students; for spring admission, 10/15 for domestic students, 10/1 for international students; for summer admission, 4/15 for domestic students, 3/15 for international students. Application fee: $40 ($90 for international students). Electronic applications accepted. *Expenses:* $4,851 per semester. *Financial support:* In 2016–17, 33 students received support, including 16 research assistantships (averaging $25,544 per year), 6 teaching assistantships (averaging $27,132 per year); scholarships/grants and unspecified assistantships also available. Financial award application deadline: 3/1; financial award applicants required to submit FAFSA. *Unit head:* Dr. Sonya Armstrong, Doctoral Program Director, 512-245-7789, E-mail: sla113@txstate.edu. *Application contact:* Dr. Andrea Golato, Dean of Graduate School, 512-245-2581, Fax: 512-245-8365, E-mail: gradcollege@txstate.edu.

The University of Iowa, Graduate College, College of Education, Department of Teaching and Learning, Program in Education, Iowa City, IA 52242-1316. Offers art education (MA); developmental reading (MA); elementary education (MA); English education (MA, MAT); foreign and second language education (MAT); foreign language education (MA); foreign language/ESL education (PhD); language, literacy and culture (PhD); mathematics education (MA, MAT, PhD); music education (MM, PhD); science education (MA); secondary education (MA); social studies (MA, PhD). *Degree requirements:* For master's, thesis optional, exam; for doctorate, comprehensive exam, thesis/dissertation. *Entrance requirements:* For master's and doctorate, GRE General Test, minimum GPA of 3.0. Additional exam requirements/recommendations for international students: Required—TOEFL (minimum score 550 paper-based; 81 iBT). Electronic applications accepted.

University of St. Francis, College of Business and Health Administration, School of Business, Joliet, IL 60435-6169. Offers accounting (MBA, Certificate); business analytics (MBA, Certificate); finance (MBA, Certificate); health administration (MBA); human resource management (MBA); logistics (Certificate); management (MBA, MSM); training and development (MBA); transportation and logistics (MBA). *Accreditation:* ACBSP. *Program availability:* Part-time, evening/weekend, 100% online, blended/hybrid learning. *Faculty:* 6 full-time (3 women), 12 part-time/adjunct (6 women). *Students:* 78 full-time (28 women), 110 part-time (62 women); includes 41 minority (22 Black or African American, non-Hispanic/Latino; 3 Asian, non-Hispanic/Latino; 15 Hispanic/Latino; 1 Two or more races, non-Hispanic/Latino), 8 international. Average age 36. 171 applicants, 44% accepted, 58 enrolled. In 2016, 62 master's, 3 other advanced degrees awarded. *Entrance requirements:* For master's, GMAT or 2 years of managerial experience. Additional exam requirements/recommendations for international students: Required—TOEFL (minimum score 550 paper-based; 79 iBT), IELTS (minimum score 6). *Application deadline:* Applications are processed on a rolling basis. Application fee: $30. Electronic applications accepted. Application fee is waived when completed online. *Expenses:* $798 per credit. *Financial support:* In 2016–17, 51 students received support. Career-related internships or fieldwork, scholarships/grants, tuition waivers (partial), and unspecified assistantships available. Support available to part-time students. Financial award applicants required to submit FAFSA. *Unit head:* Dr. Orlando Griego, Dean, 815-740-3395, Fax: 815-740-3537, E-mail: ogriego@stfrancis.edu. *Application contact:* Sandra Sloka, Director of Admissions for Graduate and Degree Completion Programs, 800-735-7500, Fax: 815-740-3431, E-mail: ssloka@stfrancis.edu.
Website: http://www.stfrancis.edu/academics/college-of-business-health-administration/

Walden University, Graduate Programs, Richard W. Riley College of Education and Leadership, Minneapolis, MN 55401. Offers adult education (Post-Master's Certificate); adult learning (Graduate Certificate); college teaching and learning (Graduate Certificate); community college leadership (Ed D); curriculum, instruction and assessment (Ed D, Ed S, Graduate Certificate); developmental education (Graduate Certificate); early childhood administration, management, and leadership (Graduate Certificate); early childhood education (Ed D, Ed S); early childhood public policy and advocacy (Graduate Certificate); early childhood studies (MS), including administration, management and leadership, early childhood public policy and advocacy, teaching adults in the early childhood field, teaching and diversity in early childhood education; education (MS, PhD), including adolescent literacy and learning (MS), curriculum, instruction, and assessment (grades K-12) (MS), curriculum, instruction, assessment, and evaluation (PhD), early childhood leadership and advocacy (PhD), early childhood special education (PhD), educational leadership (MS), educational leadership and administration (principal preparation) (MS), educational technology and design (PhD), elementary reading and literacy (PreK-6) (MS), elementary reading and mathematics (grades K-6) (MS), global and comparative education (PhD), higher education leadership management and policy (PhD), integrating technology in the classroom (grades K-12) (MS), learning, instruction and innovation (PhD), mathematics (grades 5-8) (MS), mathematics (grades K-6) (MS), mathematics and science (grades K-8) (MS), organizational research, assessment, and evaluation (PhD), reading and literacy with a reading K-12 endorsement (MS), reading literacy assessment and evaluation (PhD), science (grades K-8) (MS), special education (non-licensure) (grades K-12) (MS), teacher leadership (grades K-12) (MS), teaching English language learners (grades K-12) (MS); educational administration and leadership (Ed D); educational leadership and administration (principal preparation) (Ed S); educational technology (Ed D, Ed S, Post Master's Certificate); elementary reading and literacy (Graduate Certificate); engaging culturally diverse learners (Graduate Certificate); enrollment management and institutional marketing (Graduate Certificate); higher education (MS), including adult learning, college teaching and learning, enrollment management and institutional marketing, global higher education, leadership for student success, online and distance learning; higher education and adult learning (Ed D); higher education leadership and management (Ed D); higher education leadership for student success (Graduate Certificate); instructional design and technology (MS, Postbaccalaureate Certificate), including general program (MS), online learning (MS), training and performance improvement (MS); integrating technology in the classroom (Graduate Certificate); mathematics 5-8 (Graduate Certificate); mathematics K-6 (Graduate Certificate); online teaching for adult educators (Graduate Certificate); reading, literacy, and assessment (Ed D, Ed S); science K-8 (Graduate Certificate); special education (Ed D, Ed S, Graduate Certificate); special education (K-age 21) (MAT); teacher leadership (Graduate Certificate); teaching adults English as a second language (Graduate Certificate); teaching adults in the early childhood field (Graduate Certificate); teaching and diversity in early childhood education (Graduate Certificate); teaching English language learners (grades K-12) (Graduate Certificate); teaching K-12 students online (Graduate Certificate). *Accreditation:* NCATE. *Program availability:* Part-time, evening/weekend, online only, 100% online. *Degree requirements:* For doctorate, thesis/dissertation (for some programs), residency; for other advanced degree, residency (for some programs). *Entrance requirements:* For master's, bachelor's degree or higher; minimum GPA of 2.5; official transcripts; goal statement (for some programs); access to computer and Internet; for doctorate, master's degree or higher; three years of related professional or academic experience (preferred); minimum GPA of 3.0; goal statement and current resume (for select programs); official transcripts; access to computer and Internet; for other advanced degree, relevant work experience; access to computer and Internet. Additional exam requirements/recommendations for international students: Required—TOEFL (minimum score 550 paper-based, 79 iBT), IELTS (minimum score 6.5), Michigan English Language Assessment Battery (minimum score 82), or PTE (minimum score 53). Electronic applications accepted.

Wayne State University, College of Education, Division of Teacher Education, Detroit, MI 48202. Offers art education (M Ed); bilingual/bicultural education (M Ed, Certificate); career and technical education (M Ed); curriculum and instruction (Ed D, PhD, Ed S), including art education (Ed D, PhD), bilingual education (Ed D, Ed S), career and technical education (MAT, Ed D, PhD, Ed S), early childhood education (MAT, Ed D, PhD, Ed S), elementary education, English as a second language (MAT, Ed D, Ed S), English education (MAT, Ed D, PhD, Ed S), foreign language education (MAT, Ed D, PhD), K-12 curriculum, mathematics education (MAT, Ed D, PhD, Ed S), science education (MAT, Ed D, PhD, Ed S), secondary education, social studies education (MAT, Ed D, PhD, Ed S); early childhood education (M Ed); elementary education (M Ed, MAT), including bilingual/bicultural education (MAT), early childhood education (MAT, Ed D, PhD, Ed S), English as a second language (MAT, Ed D, Ed S), general elementary education (MAT), mathematics education (MAT, Ed D, PhD, Ed S), science education (MAT, Ed D, PhD, Ed S), social studies education (MAT, Ed D, PhD, Ed S); English as a second language (Certificate); English education (M Ed); foreign language

education (M Ed); mathematics education (M Ed); reading (M Ed, Ed S); reading, language and literature (Ed D); science education (M Ed); secondary education (MAT), including art education (K-12), bilingual/bicultural education, career and technical education (MAT, Ed D, PhD, Ed S), English as a second language (MAT, Ed D, Ed S), English education (MAT, Ed D, PhD, Ed S), foreign language education (MAT, Ed D, PhD), kinesiology, mathematics education (MAT, Ed D, PhD, Ed S); social studies education (M Ed); special education (M Ed, MAT, Ed D, PhD, Ed S), including autism spectrum disorders (MAT), cognitive development (MAT), emotional impairment (MAT), learning disabilities (MAT). *Program availability:* Part-time, blended/hybrid learning. *Faculty:* 29. *Students:* 106 full-time (73 women), 351 part-time (276 women); includes 115 minority (76 Black or African American, non-Hispanic/Latino; 10 Asian, non-Hispanic/Latino; 20 Hispanic/Latino; 1 Native Hawaiian or other Pacific Islander, non-Hispanic/Latino; 8 Two or more races, non-Hispanic/Latino), 12 international. Average age 37. 242 applicants, 37% accepted, 72 enrolled. In 2016, 178 master's, 19 doctorates, 17 other advanced degrees awarded. *Degree requirements:* For master's, essay or project (for some M Ed programs), professional field experience (for MAT programs); for doctorate, thesis/dissertation. *Entrance requirements:* For master's, Michigan Test for Teacher Certification, verification of participation in group work with children, Michigan State Police criminal background check; for doctorate, minimum undergraduate GPA of 3.0, graduate 3.5; interview; curriculum vitae; references. Additional exam requirements/recommendations for international students: Required—TOEFL (minimum score 550 paper-based; 79 iBT), TWE (minimum score 5.5), Michigan English Language Assessment Battery (minimum score 85); Recommended—IELTS (minimum score 6.5). *Application deadline:* For fall admission, 6/1 priority date for domestic students, 5/1 priority date for international students; for winter admission, 10/1 priority date for domestic students, 9/1 priority date for international students; for spring admission, 2/1 priority date for domestic students, 1/1 priority date for international students. Applications are processed on a rolling basis. Application fee: $50. Electronic applications accepted. *Expenses:* $16,503 per year resident tuition and fees, $33,697 per year non-resident tuition and fees. *Financial support:* In 2016–17, 101 students received support, including 3 fellowships (averaging $11,409 per year); research assistantships with tuition reimbursements available, Federal Work-Study, scholarships/grants, and unspecified assistantships also available. Support available to part-time students. Financial award applicants required to submit FAFSA. *Faculty research:* Improving students' skill achievement in mathematics, improving elementary children's understanding of informational text, teachers' use of their pedagogical and mathematical knowledge in the interactive work of teaching, the intersection of identity construction in teaching and learning, identifying effective methods of literacy instruction and assessments for bilingual students in elementary language arts classrooms. *Unit head:* Dr. Kathleen Crawford-McKinney, Assistant Dean, 313-577-0122. *Application contact:* Janice Green, Assistant Dean, 313-577-1605, E-mail: jwgreen@wayne.edu.
Website: http://coe.wayne.edu/ted/index.php

English Education

Alabama Agricultural and Mechanical University, School of Graduate Studies, College of Education, Humanities, and Behavioral Sciences, Department of Educational Leadership and Secondary Education, Huntsville, AL 35811. Offers biology (M Ed); business/marketing education (M Ed, Ed S); chemistry (M Ed); collaborative teacher secondary education (M Ed, Ed S); education (M Ed, Ed S); English language arts (M Ed); family/consumer science education (M Ed, Ed S); general science (M Ed); general social science (M Ed); mathematics (M Ed, Ed S); physics (M Ed, Ed S); technology education (M Ed). *Accreditation:* NCATE. *Program availability:* Evening/weekend. *Degree requirements:* For master's, comprehensive exam; for Ed S, thesis. *Entrance requirements:* For master's, GRE General Test. Additional exam requirements/recommendations for international students: Required—TOEFL (minimum score 500 paper-based; 61 iBT). *Application deadline:* For fall admission, 5/1 for domestic students. Applications are processed on a rolling basis. Application fee: $25. Electronic applications accepted. *Expenses:* Tuition, nonresident: part-time $826 per credit hour. Full-time tuition and fees vary according to course load and program. *Financial support:* Research assistantships, career-related internships or fieldwork, Federal Work-Study, institutionally sponsored loans, and traineeships available. Financial award application deadline: 4/1. *Faculty research:* World peace through education, computer-assisted instruction. *Unit head:* Dr. Derrick Davis, Chair, 256-372-4047, Fax: 256-372-5526.

Alabama State University, College of Education, Department of Curriculum and Instruction, Montgomery, AL 36101-0271. Offers early childhood education (M Ed, Ed S); elementary education (M Ed, Ed S); secondary education (M Ed, Ed S), including biology education, English language arts education (M Ed), history education, math education, music education (M Ed), reading education (M Ed), social science education; special education (M Ed). *Program availability:* Part-time. *Faculty:* 7 full-time (4 women), 7 part-time/adjunct (4 women). *Students:* 37 full-time (30 women), 82 part-time (69 women); includes 117 minority (115 Black or African American, non-Hispanic/Latino; 2 Two or more races, non-Hispanic/Latino). Average age 33. 65 applicants, 55% accepted, 22 enrolled. In 2016, 25 master's, 5 Ed Ss awarded. *Degree requirements:* For master's, comprehensive exam, thesis optional; for Ed S, comprehensive exam, thesis. *Entrance requirements:* For master's, GRE General Test, MAT, writing competency test; for Ed S, writing competency test, GRE, MAT. Additional exam requirements/recommendations for international students: Required—TOEFL (minimum score 500 paper-based). *Application deadline:* For fall admission, 4/15 for domestic and international students; for spring admission, 11/15 for domestic and international students; for summer admission, 3/15 for domestic and international students. Applications are processed on a rolling basis. Application fee: $25. Electronic applications accepted. *Expenses:* Tuition, state resident: full-time $3087; part-time $2744 per credit. Tuition, nonresident: full-time $6174; part-time $5488 per credit. *Required fees:* $2284; $1142 per credit. $571 per semester. Tuition and fees vary according to class time, course level, course load, degree level, program and student level. *Financial support:* Research assistantships available. Financial award application deadline: 6/30; financial award applicants required to submit FAFSA. *Unit head:* Dr. Joyce Johnson, Acting Chairperson, 334-229-4485, Fax: 334-229-5603, E-mail: jjohnson@alasu.edu. *Application contact:* Dr. William Person, Dean of Graduate Studies, 334-229-4274, Fax: 334-229-4928, E-mail: wperson@alasu.edu.
Website: http://www.alasu.edu/academics/colleges—departments/college-of-education/curriculum—instruction/index.aspx

Albany State University, College of Arts and Humanities, Albany, GA 31705-2717. Offers criminal justice (MS); English education (M Ed); public administration (MPA), including community and economic development, criminal justice administration, health administration and policy, human resources management, public management, public policy, water resources management and policy; social work (MSW). *Program availability:* Part-time. *Degree requirements:* For master's, comprehensive exam, professional portfolio (for MPA), internship, capstone report. *Entrance requirements:* For master's, GRE, MAT, minimum GPA of 3.0, official transcript, pre-medical record/certificate of immunization, letters of reference. *Application deadline:* For fall admission, 6/1 for domestic students, 5/1 for international students; for spring admission, 11/1 for domestic students, 10/1 for international students. Applications are processed on a rolling basis. Application fee: $20. Electronic applications accepted. *Financial support:* Application deadline: 4/15; applicants required to submit FAFSA. *Faculty research:* HIV prevention for minority students. *Unit head:* Dr. Rani George, Dean, 229-430-1877, Fax: 229-430-4296. *Application contact:* Jeffrey Pierce, II, Graduate Admissions Counselor, 229-430-4646, Fax: 229-430-4105, E-mail: jeffrey.pierce@asurams.edu.
Website: https://www.asurams.edu/Academics/collegeofarthum/

Andrews University, School of Graduate Studies, College of Arts and Sciences, Department of English, Berrien Springs, MI 49104. Offers MA, MAT. *Program availability:* Part-time. *Faculty:* 8 full-time (4 women), 2 part-time/adjunct (1 woman). *Students:* 5 full-time (4 women), 5 part-time (4 women); includes 3 minority (2 Black or African American, non-Hispanic/Latino; 1 Hispanic/Latino), 2 international. Average age 30. In 2016, 5 master's awarded. *Degree requirements:* For master's, one foreign language, thesis optional. *Entrance requirements:* For master's, GRE Subject Test. Additional exam requirements/recommendations for international students: Required—TOEFL (minimum score 550 paper-based). *Application deadline:* For fall admission, 8/15 for domestic students. Applications are processed on a rolling basis. Application fee: $40. *Financial support:* Fellowships, research assistantships, teaching assistantships, career-related internships or fieldwork, and Federal Work-Study available. *Faculty research:* Shakespearean studies. *Unit head:* Dr. Meredith Jones-Gray, Chairperson, 269-471-3298.. *Application contact:* Justina Clayburn, Supervisor of Graduate Admission, 800-253-2874, Fax: 269-471-6321, E-mail: graduate@andrews.edu.

Andrews University, School of Graduate Studies, School of Education, Department of Teaching, Learning, and Curriculum, Berrien Springs, MI 49104. Offers curriculum and instruction (MA, Ed D, PhD, Ed S); elementary education (MAT); secondary education (MAT), including biology, education, English, English as a second language, French, history, physics; teacher education (MAT). *Faculty:* 7 full-time (5 women). *Students:* 17 full-time (12 women), 10 part-time (all women); includes 11 minority (6 Black or African American, non-Hispanic/Latino; 5 Hispanic/Latino), 7 international. Average age 38. In 2016, 9 master's, 7 doctorates awarded. *Entrance requirements:* For master's, GRE Subject Test. Additional exam requirements/recommendations for international students: Required—TOEFL (minimum score 550 paper-based). *Application deadline:* For fall admission, 8/15 for domestic students. Applications are processed on a rolling basis. Application fee: $40. *Unit head:* Dr. Lee C. Davidson, Chair, 269-471-6364. *Application contact:* Justina Clayburn, Supervisor of Graduate Admission, 800-253-2874, Fax: 269-471-6321, E-mail: graduate@andrews.edu.

Anna Maria College, Graduate Division, Program in Education, Paxton, MA 01612. Offers early childhood education (M Ed); education (CAGS); elementary education (M Ed); English language arts (M Ed); visual arts (M Ed). *Program availability:* Part-time, evening/weekend. *Entrance requirements:* For master's, bachelor's degree in liberal arts or sciences, minimum GPA of 3.0. Additional exam requirements/recommendations for international students: Required—TOEFL (minimum score 500 paper-based). Electronic applications accepted.

Appalachian State University, Cratis D. Williams Graduate School, Department of Curriculum and Instruction, Boone, NC 28608. Offers curriculum specialist (MA); educational media (MA); elementary education (MA); middle grades education (MA), including language arts, mathematics, science, social studies. *Accreditation:* NCATE. *Program availability:* Part-time, evening/weekend, online learning. *Degree requirements:* For master's, comprehensive exam, thesis or alternative. *Entrance requirements:* For master's, GRE General Test or MAT, 3 letters of recommendation. Additional exam requirements/recommendations for international students: Required—TOEFL (minimum score 570 paper-based; 79 iBT), IELTS (minimum score 6.5). *Application deadline:* For fall admission, 3/14 for domestic students, 2/1 for international students; for spring admission, 11/1 for domestic students, 7/1 for international students. Applications are processed on a rolling basis. Application fee: $55. Electronic applications accepted. *Expenses:* Tuition, state resident: full-time $4744. Tuition, nonresident: full-time $17,913. Full-time tuition and fees vary according to program. *Financial support:* Fellowships, research assistantships, teaching assistantships, career-related internships or fieldwork, Federal Work-Study, scholarships/grants, and unspecified assistantships available. Financial award application deadline: 4/1; financial award applicants required to submit FAFSA. *Faculty research:* Media literacy, elementary teaching, curriculum development, online learning environments. *Unit head:* Dr. Michael Jacobson, Chairperson, 828-262-2224. *Application contact:* Dr. Chrystal Dean, Program Director, 828-262-8009, E-mail: deanco@appstate.edu.
Website: http://www.ced.appstate.edu/departments/ci

Arcadia University, School of Education, Glenside, PA 19038-3295. Offers art education (M Ed); computer education (CAS); curriculum (CAS); curriculum studies (M Ed); early childhood education (M Ed), including individualized, master teacher, research in child development; educational leadership (M Ed, Ed D, CAS); elementary education (M Ed); English education (MA Ed); environmental education (MA Ed); instructional technology (M Ed); language arts (M Ed); library science (M Ed); mathematics education (M Ed, MA Ed); music education (MA Ed); psychology (MA Ed); reading (M Ed, CAS); science education (M Ed, CAS); secondary education (M Ed, CAS); special education (M Ed, Ed D, CAS); theater arts (MA Ed); written communication (MA Ed). *Accreditation:* NASAD. *Program availability:* Part-time, evening/weekend, online learning. *Faculty:* 19 full-time (13 women), 3 part-time/adjunct (all women). *Students:* 22 full-time (16 women), 356 part-time (284 women); includes 84 minority (55 Black or African American, non-Hispanic/Latino; 2 American Indian or Alaska Native, non-Hispanic/Latino; 13 Asian, non-Hispanic/Latino; 11 Hispanic/Latino; 3 Two or more races, non-Hispanic/Latino), 4 international. Average age 34. 145 applicants, 73% accepted, 80 enrolled. In 2016, 95 master's, 11 doctorates awarded. *Application deadline:* Applications are processed on a rolling basis. Application fee: $50. Electronic applications accepted. *Expenses:* Contact institution. *Financial support:* Career-related internships or fieldwork, tuition waivers (partial), and unspecified assistantships available. *Unit head:* John T Groves, Interim Dean of the School of Education, 215-572-2940. *Application contact:* 215-572-2925, Fax: 215-572-2126, E-mail: grad@arcadia.edu.

Arkansas State University, Graduate School, College of Humanities and Social Sciences, Department of English and Philosophy, State University, AR 72467. Offers English (MA); English education (MSE, SCCT). *Program availability:* Part-time. *Degree requirements:* For master's, variable foreign language requirement, comprehensive exam, thesis or alternative, preliminary exam; for SCCT, comprehensive exam. *Entrance requirements:* For master's, GRE General Test or MAT, appropriate bachelor's degree, official transcript, valid teaching certificate (for MSE), immunization records; for SCCT, GRE General Test or MAT, interview, master's degree, official transcript, immunization records. Additional exam requirements/recommendations for international students: Required—TOEFL (minimum score 550 paper-based; 79 iBT), IELTS (minimum score 6), PTE (minimum score 56). Electronic applications accepted.

Arkansas Tech University, College of Arts and Humanities, Russellville, AR 72801. Offers applied sociology (MS); English (M Ed, MA); history (MA); liberal arts (MLA); multi-media journalism (MA); psychology (MS); teaching English as a second language (MA). *Program availability:* Part-time. *Students:* 56 full-time (42 women), 121 part-time (85 women); includes 23 minority (7 Black or African American, non-Hispanic/Latino; 1 Asian, non-Hispanic/Latino; 11 Hispanic/Latino; 4 Two or more races, non-Hispanic/Latino), 34 international. Average age 32. In 2016, 90 master's awarded. *Degree requirements:* For master's, comprehensive exam (for some programs), thesis (for some programs), project. *Entrance requirements:* For master's, GRE General Test or GMAT. Additional exam requirements/recommendations for international students: Required—TOEFL (minimum score 550 paper-based; 79 iBT), IELTS (minimum score 6). *Application deadline:* For fall admission, 3/1 priority date for domestic students, 5/1 priority date for international students; for spring admission, 10/1 priority date for domestic and international students. Applications are processed on a rolling basis. Application fee: $25 ($75 for international students). Electronic applications accepted. *Expenses:* Tuition, state resident: full-time $4932; part-time $274 per credit hour. Tuition, nonresident: full-time $9864; part-time $548 per credit hour. *Required fees:* $513 per semester. Tuition and fees vary according to course load. *Financial support:* In 2016–17, research assistantships with full tuition reimbursements (averaging $4,800 per year), teaching assistantships with full tuition reimbursements (averaging $4,800 per year) were awarded; career-related internships or fieldwork, Federal Work-Study, scholarships/grants, health care benefits, and unspecified assistantships also available. Support available to part-time students. Financial award application deadline: 4/15; financial award applicants required to submit FAFSA. *Unit head:* Dr. Jeffrey Woods, Dean, 479-968-0274, Fax: 479-964-0812, E-mail: jwoods@atu.edu. *Application contact:* Dr. Mary B. Gunter, Dean of Graduate College, 479-968-0398, Fax: 479-964-0542, E-mail: gradcollege@atu.edu.
Website: http://www.atu.edu/humanities/

Binghamton University, State University of New York, Graduate School, Graduate School of Education, Program in Adolescence Education, Binghamton, NY 13902-6000. Offers biology education (MAT, MS Ed); chemistry education (MAT, MS Ed); earth science education (MAT, MS Ed); English education (MAT, MS Ed); French education (MAT, MS Ed); literacy education (MS Ed); mathematical sciences education (MAT, MS Ed); physics (MAT, MS Ed); social studies (MAT, MS Ed); Spanish education (MAT, MS Ed). *Accreditation:* TEAC. *Program availability:* Part-time, evening/weekend. *Students:* 59 full-time (36 women), 7 part-time (2 women); includes 10 minority (2 Black or African American, non-Hispanic/Latino; 1 American Indian or Alaska Native, non-Hispanic/Latino; 1 Asian, non-Hispanic/Latino; 5 Hispanic/Latino; 1 Two or more races, non-Hispanic/Latino). Average age 26. 46 applicants, 76% accepted, 25 enrolled. In 2016, 26 master's awarded. *Degree requirements:* For master's, portfolio. *Entrance requirements:* For master's, GRE General Test, teaching certification. Additional exam requirements/recommendations for international students: Required—TOEFL (minimum score 550 paper-based; 80 iBT). *Application deadline:* For fall admission, 2/1 priority date for domestic and international students; for spring admission, 10/15 priority date for domestic and international students. Application fee: $75. Electronic applications accepted. *Financial support:* In 2016–17, 6 students received support. Research assistantships, teaching assistantships, career-related internships or fieldwork, Federal Work-Study, institutionally sponsored loans, scholarships/grants, health care benefits, tuition waivers (full and partial), and unspecified assistantships available. Financial award applicants required to submit FAFSA. *Unit head:* Dr. Susan Strehle, Dean, 607-777-7329, E-mail: sstrehle@binghamton.edu. *Application contact:* Ben Balkaya, Assistant Dean and Director, 607-777-2151, Fax: 607-777-2501, E-mail: balkaya@binghamton.edu.

Bloomsburg University of Pennsylvania, School of Graduate Studies, College of Education, Department of Teaching and Learning, Program in Middle Level Education Grades 4-8, Bloomsburg, PA 17815-1301. Offers language arts (M Ed); math (M Ed); science (M Ed); social studies (M Ed). *Accreditation:* NCATE. *Faculty:* 6 full-time (1 woman). *Students:* 3 applicants, 67% accepted. In 2016, 2 master's awarded. *Degree requirements:* For master's, thesis optional, practicum, student teaching. *Entrance requirements:* For master's, MAT, GRE, or PRAXIS, minimum QPA of 3.0, teaching certificate, U.S. citizenship, related undergraduate coursework, professional liability insurance, recent TB test. Additional exam requirements/recommendations for international students: Required—TOEFL (minimum score 550 paper-based), IELTS. *Application deadline:* Applications are processed on a rolling basis. Application fee: $35 ($60 for international students). Electronic applications accepted. *Expenses:* Tuition, state resident: full-time $9660; part-time $483 per credit. Tuition, nonresident: full-time $14,500; part-time $725 per credit. *Required fees:* $2410; $107 per credit. $75 per term. Tuition and fees vary according to course load, degree level and program. *Financial support:* Federal Work-Study and unspecified assistantships available. Financial award applicants required to submit FAFSA. *Unit head:* Dr. Ingrid Everett, Program Coordinator, 570-389-5120, Fax: 570-389-3030, E-mail: ieverett@bloomu.edu. *Application contact:* Jennifer Kessler, Administrative Assistant, 570-389-4015, Fax: 570-389-3054, E-mail: jkessler@bloomu.edu.
Website: http://www.bloomu.edu/gradschool/middle-level-education

Bob Jones University, Graduate Programs, Greenville, SC 29614. Offers accountancy (MS); Bible (MA); Bible translation (MA); Biblical studies (Certificate); broadcast management (MS); business administration (MBA); church history (MA, PhD); church ministries (MA); church music (MM); cinema and video production (MA); counseling (MS); curriculum and instruction (Ed D); divinity (M Div); dramatic production (MA); educational leadership (MS, Ed D, Ed S); elementary education (M Ed, MAT); English (M Ed, MA, MAT); fine arts (MA); graphic design (MA); history (M Ed, MA); illustration (MA); interpretative speech (MA); mathematics (M Ed, MAT); medical missions (Certificate); ministry (MM, D Min); multi-categorical special education (M Ed, MAT); music (M Ed); New Testament interpretation (PhD); Old Testament interpretation (PhD); orchestral instrument performance (MM); organ performance (MM); pastoral studies (MA); personnel services (MS, Ed S); piano pedagogy (MM); piano performance (MM); platform arts (MA); radio and television broadcasting (MS); rhetoric and public address (MA); secondary education (M Ed); studio art (MA); teaching Bible (MA); theology (MA, PhD); voice performance (MM); youth ministries (MA); M Div/MM.

Boise State University, College of Arts and Sciences, Department of English, Boise, ID 83725-1525. Offers creative writing (MFA); English (MA); rhetoric and composition (MA); teaching English language (MA); technical communication (MA). *Program availability:* Part-time. *Faculty:* 26. *Students:* 44 full-time (28 women), 38 part-time (29 women); includes 6 minority (2 American Indian or Alaska Native, non-Hispanic/Latino; 2 Asian, non-Hispanic/Latino; 1 Hispanic/Latino; 1 Two or more races, non-Hispanic/Latino), 3 international. Average age 33. 242 applicants, 15% accepted, 28 enrolled. In 2016, 29 master's awarded. *Degree requirements:* For master's, thesis (for some programs). *Entrance requirements:* For master's, GRE General Test, minimum GPA of 3.0. Additional exam requirements/recommendations for international students: Required—TOEFL (minimum score 550 paper-based; 80 iBT), IELTS (minimum score 6). *Application deadline:* For fall admission, 4/15 for domestic and international students; for spring admission, 10/15 for domestic and international students. Application fee: $65 ($95 for international students). Electronic applications accepted. *Expenses:* Tuition, state resident: full-time $6058; part-time $358 per credit hour. Tuition, nonresident: full-time $20,108; part-time $608 per credit hour. *Required fees:* $2108. Tuition and fees vary according to program. *Financial support:* In 2016–17, 10 students received support, including 32 teaching assistantships (averaging $8,109 per year); scholarships/grants and unspecified assistantships also available. Financial award application deadline: 1/15; financial award applicants required to submit FAFSA. *Unit head:* Dr. Michelle Payne, Chair, 208-426-3426, Fax: 208-426-4373, E-mail: mpayne@boisestate.edu. *Application contact:* Dr. Tom Hillard, Director of English, 208-426-2991, E-mail: thomashillard@boisestate.edu.
Website: http://english.boisestate.edu/graduate-programs/

Brooklyn College of the City University of New York, School of Education, Program in Adolescence Science Education and Special Subjects, Brooklyn, NY 11210-2889. Offers adolescence science education (MAT); biology teacher (7-12) (MA); chemistry teacher (7-12) (MA); earth science teacher (7-12) (MAT); English teacher (7-12) (MA); French teacher (7-12) (MA); mathematics teacher (7-12) (MA); music teacher (MA); physics teacher (7-12) (MA); social studies teacher (7-12) (MA); Spanish teacher (7-12) (MA). *Program availability:* Part-time, evening/weekend. *Degree requirements:* For master's, comprehensive exam (for some programs), thesis (for some programs). *Entrance requirements:* For master's, LAST, previous course work in education, resume, 2 letters of recommendation, essay. Additional exam requirements/recommendations for international students: Required—TOEFL (minimum score 500 paper-based; 61 iBT). Electronic applications accepted. *Faculty research:* Interdisciplinary education, semiotics, discourse analysis, autobiography, teacher identity.

Brown University, Graduate School, Department of Education, Program in Teaching, Providence, RI 02912. Offers elementary education (MAT); English (MAT); history/social studies (MAT); science (MAT); secondary education (MAT). *Degree requirements:* For master's, student teaching, portfolio. *Entrance requirements:* For master's, GRE General Test, transcript, personal statement, 3 letters of recommendation, interview, writing sample (English applicants only). Additional exam requirements/recommendations for international students: Required—TOEFL (minimum score 577 paper-based). Electronic applications accepted. *Faculty research:* Literacy, English language learners, diversity, special education, biodiversity.

Buffalo State College, State University of New York, The Graduate School, Faculty of Arts and Humanities, Department of English, Buffalo, NY 14222-1095. Offers English (MA); secondary education (MS Ed), including English. *Program availability:* Part-time, evening/weekend. *Degree requirements:* For master's, thesis or project, 1 foreign language (MS Ed). *Entrance requirements:* For master's, minimum GPA of 2.75, 36 hours in English, New York teaching certificate (MS Ed). Additional exam requirements/recommendations for international students: Required—TOEFL (minimum score 550 paper-based).

California Baptist University, Program in English, Riverside, CA 92504-3206. Offers English pedagogy (MA); literature (MA); teaching English to speakers of other languages (TESOL) (MA). *Program availability:* Part-time, evening/weekend. *Faculty:* 9 full-time (7 women), 1 (woman) part-time/adjunct. *Students:* 3 full-time (2 women), 26 part-time (19 women); includes 14 minority (4 Black or African American, non-Hispanic/Latino; 1 Asian, non-Hispanic/Latino; 9 Hispanic/Latino), 3 international. Average age 28. 8 applicants, 88% accepted, 6 enrolled. In 2016, 4 master's awarded. *Degree requirements:* For master's, comprehensive exam, project, or thesis. *Entrance requirements:* For master's, GRE (for applicants with a GPA below 2.75) or CSET, minimum undergraduate GPA of 2.75; 18 semester hours of course work in English beyond freshman level; three recommendations; essay; demonstration of writing; interview. Additional exam requirements/recommendations for international students: Required—TOEFL (minimum score 80 iBT). *Application deadline:* For fall admission, 8/1 priority date for domestic students, 7/1 for international students; for spring admission, 12/1 priority date for domestic students, 11/1 for international students. Applications are processed on a rolling basis. Application fee: $45. Electronic applications accepted. *Expenses:* Contact institution. *Financial support:* In 2016–17, 5 students received support. Federal Work-Study and scholarships/grants available. Financial award applicants required to submit CSS PROFILE or FAFSA. *Faculty research:* Classical mythology and folklore, multicultural literature, genre studies, science fiction and fantasy literature, intercultural rhetoric. *Unit head:* Dr. Gayne Anacker, Dean, College of Arts and Sciences, 951-343-4682, E-mail: ganacker@calbaptist.edu. *Application contact:* Dr. Laura Veltman, Director, Master of Arts Program in English, 951-343-4276, Fax: 951-343-4661, E-mail: lveltman@calbaptist.edu.
Website: http://www.calbaptist.edu/maenglish/

California State University, Northridge, Graduate Studies, Michael D. Eisner College of Education, Department of Secondary Education, Northridge, CA 91330. Offers educational technology (MA); English education (MA); mathematics education (MA); secondary science education (MA); teaching and learning (MA). *Accreditation:* NCATE. *Program availability:* Part-time. *Faculty:* 10 full-time (5 women), 50 part-time/adjunct (24 women). *Students:* 17 full-time (10 women), 87 part-time (55 women); includes 41 minority (3 Black or African American, non-Hispanic/Latino; 11 Asian, non-Hispanic/Latino; 24 Hispanic/Latino; 1 Native Hawaiian or other Pacific Islander, non-Hispanic/Latino; 2 Two or more races, non-Hispanic/Latino), 4 international. Average age 37. 80 applicants, 80% accepted, 50 enrolled. *Degree requirements:* For master's, thesis optional. *Entrance requirements:* For master's, GRE General Test or minimum GPA of 3.0. Additional exam requirements/recommendations for international students: Required—TOEFL. *Application deadline:* For fall admission, 11/30 for domestic students. Application fee: $55. *Expenses:* Tuition, state resident: full-time $4152. *Financial support:* Application deadline: 3/1. *Unit head:* Dr. Julie Gainsburg, Chair, 818-677-2580. *Application contact:* Dr. Michael Rivas, Graduate Advisor, 818-677-6792, E-mail: michael.rivas@csun.edu.
Website: http://www.csun.edu/eisner-education/secondary-education

Caribbean University, Graduate School, Bayamón, PR 00960-0493. Offers administration and supervision (MA Ed); criminal justice (MA); curriculum and instruction (MA Ed, PhD), including elementary education (MA Ed), English education (MA Ed), history education (MA Ed), mathematics education (MA Ed), primary education (MA Ed), science education (MA Ed), Spanish education (MA Ed); educational technology in instructional systems (MA Ed); gerontology (MSN); human resources (MBA);

museology, archiving and art history (MA Ed); neonatal pediatrics (MSN); physical education (MA Ed); special education (MA Ed). *Entrance requirements:* For master's, interview, minimum GPA of 2.5.

Carthage College, Division of Teacher Education, Kenosha, WI 53140. Offers classroom guidance and counseling (M Ed); creative arts (M Ed); gifted and talented children (M Ed); language arts (M Ed); modern language (M Ed); natural sciences (M Ed); reading (M Ed, Certificate); social sciences (M Ed); teacher leadership (M Ed). *Program availability:* Part-time, evening/weekend. *Degree requirements:* For master's, thesis optional. *Entrance requirements:* For master's, MAT, minimum B average, letters of reference.

Chadron State College, School of Professional and Graduate Studies, Department of Education, Chadron, NE 69337. Offers business (MA Ed); community counseling (MA Ed); educational administration (MS Ed, Sp Ed); elementary education (MS Ed); history (MA Ed); language and literature (MA Ed); secondary administration (MS Ed); secondary education (MS Ed). *Accreditation:* NCATE. *Program availability:* Part-time, evening/weekend, online learning. *Degree requirements:* For master's, thesis optional. *Entrance requirements:* For master's, GRE General Test, GRE Writing Test, minimum GPA of 2.75 or 12 graduate hours at CSC with minimum GPA of 3.25. Additional exam requirements/recommendations for international students: Required—TOEFL. Electronic applications accepted. *Faculty research:* Rural education, technology, mental health.

Chatham University, Program in Education, Pittsburgh, PA 15232-2826. Offers early childhood education (MAT); elementary education (MAT); environmental education (K-12) (MAT); secondary art (MAT); secondary biology education (MAT); secondary chemistry education (MAT); secondary English education (MAT); secondary math education (MAT); secondary physics education (MAT); secondary social studies education (MAT); special education (MAT). *Degree requirements:* For master's, thesis, teaching experience. *Entrance requirements:* For master's, minimum GPA of 3.0, sample of written work, recommendation letters. Additional exam requirements/recommendations for international students: Required—TOEFL (minimum score 600 paper-based; 100 iBT), IELTS (minimum score 7), TWE. Electronic applications accepted. Application fee is waived when completed online. *Expenses: Tuition:* Full-time $16,254; part-time $903 per credit hour. *Required fees:* $468; $26 per credit hour. *Faculty research:* Gifted education, environmental education, technology in education, writing as learning, class size and achievement.

The Citadel, The Military College of South Carolina, Citadel Graduate College, Zucker Family School of Education, Charleston, SC 29409. Offers elementary/secondary school administration and supervision (M Ed); elementary/secondary school counseling (M Ed); interdisciplinary STEM education (M Ed); literacy education (M Ed, Graduate Certificate); middle grades (MAT), including English, mathematics, science, social studies; physical education (grades K-12) (MAT); school superintendency (Ed S); secondary education (MAT), including biology, English, mathematics, social studies; student affairs (Graduate Certificate); student affairs and college counseling (M Ed). *Accreditation:* NCATE. *Program availability:* Part-time, evening/weekend, 100% online, blended/hybrid learning. *Faculty:* 9 full-time (4 women), 9 part-time/adjunct (5 women). *Students:* 70 full-time (58 women), 249 part-time (200 women); includes 87 minority (70 Black or African American, non-Hispanic/Latino; 1 Asian, non-Hispanic/Latino; 9 Hispanic/Latino; 7 Two or more races, non-Hispanic/Latino), 2 international. 146 applicants, 98% accepted, 105 enrolled. In 2016, 85 master's, 7 other advanced degrees awarded. *Degree requirements:* For master's, comprehensive exam (for some programs). *Entrance requirements:* For master's, GRE (minimum combined verbal and quantitative score of 290) or MAT (minimum score 396). Additional exam requirements/recommendations for international students: Required—TOEFL (minimum score 550 paper-based; 79 iBT). *Application deadline:* Applications are processed on a rolling basis. Application fee: $40. Electronic applications accepted. *Expenses:* Tuition, state resident: full-time $5121; part-time $569 per credit hour. Tuition, nonresident: full-time $8613; part-time $957 per credit hour. *Required fees:* $90 per term. *Financial support:* Fellowships and unspecified assistantships available. Support available to part-time students. Financial award application deadline: 7/1; financial award applicants required to submit FAFSA. *Unit head:* Dr. Larry G. Daniel, Dean, 843-953-5097, E-mail: ldaniel@citadel.edu. *Application contact:* Dr. Tammy J. Graham, Associate Professor, 843-953-6854, E-mail: tammy.graham@citadel.edu.
Website: http://www.citadel.edu/root/education-graduate-programs

City College of the City University of New York, Graduate School, School of Education, Department of Secondary Education, New York, NY 10031-9198. Offers adolescent mathematics education (MA, AC); English education (MA); middle school mathematics education (MS); science education (MA); social studies education (AC). *Accreditation:* NCATE. *Entrance requirements:* For master's, Liberal Arts and Sciences Test (LAST), Content Specialty Test (CST). Additional exam requirements/recommendations for international students: Required—TOEFL. Tuition and fees vary according to course load, degree level and program.

Clayton State University, School of Graduate Studies, College of Arts and Sciences, Program in Education, Morrow, GA 30260-0285. Offers biology (MAT); English (MAT); history (MAT); mathematics (MAT). *Accreditation:* NCATE. *Entrance requirements:* For master's, GRE, GACE, 2 official copies of transcripts, 3 recommendation letters, statement of purpose. Additional exam requirements/recommendations for international students: Required—TOEFL (minimum score 550 paper-based). Electronic applications accepted. *Expenses:* Tuition, state resident: full-time $3528; part-time $196 per credit hour. Tuition, nonresident: full-time $13,176; part-time $732 per credit hour. *Required fees:* $1454; $1454 per credit hour. $727 per semester. Tuition and fees vary according to campus/location and program.

The College at Brockport, State University of New York, School of Education, Health, and Human Services, Department of Education and Human Development, Program in Adolescence Education, Brockport, NY 14420-2997. Offers adolescence biology education (MS Ed); adolescence chemistry education (MS Ed); adolescence earth science education (MS Ed); adolescence English education (MS Ed); adolescence mathematics education (MS Ed); adolescence physics education (MS Ed); adolescence social studies education (MS Ed). *Accreditation:* NCATE. *Program availability:* Part-time. *Students:* 4 full-time (1 woman), 35 part-time (23 women); includes 3 minority (2 Black or African American, non-Hispanic/Latino; 1 Two or more races, non-Hispanic/Latino). 21 applicants, 71% accepted, 11 enrolled. In 2016, 18 master's awarded. *Degree requirements:* For master's, thesis or alternative. *Entrance requirements:* For master's, minimum GPA of 3.0, letters of recommendation, statement of objectives, current resume. Additional exam requirements/recommendations for international students: Required—TOEFL (minimum score 550 paper-based; 79 iBT), IELTS (minimum score 6.5). *Application deadline:* For fall admission, 3/15 priority date for domestic and international students; for spring admission, 10/15 priority date for domestic and international students; for summer admission, 3/15 priority date for domestic students, 3/13 priority date for international students. Application fee: $80. Electronic applications accepted. *Expenses:* Contact institution. *Financial support:* Federal Work-Study, scholarships/grants, and unspecified assistantships available. Support available to part-time students. Financial award application deadline: 3/15; financial award applicants required to submit FAFSA. *Unit head:* Dr. Sue Robb, Chairperson, 585-395-5935, Fax: 585-395-2172, E-mail: srobb@brockport.edu. *Application contact:* Anne Walton, Coordinator of Certification and Graduate Advisement, 585-395-2326, Fax: 585-395-2172, E-mail: awalton@brockport.edu.
Website: http://www.brockport.edu/ehd/

The College at Brockport, State University of New York, School of Education, Health, and Human Services, Department of Education and Human Development, Program in Inclusive Generalist Education, Brockport, NY 14420-2997. Offers biology (MS Ed, AGC); chemistry (MS Ed, AGC); English (MS Ed, Advanced Certificate); mathematics (MS Ed, Advanced Certificate); science (MS Ed, Advanced Certificate); social studies (MS Ed, Advanced Certificate). *Students:* 28 full-time (15 women), 19 part-time (10 women); includes 9 minority (2 Black or African American, non-Hispanic/Latino; 3 Asian, non-Hispanic/Latino; 1 Hispanic/Latino; 3 Two or more races, non-Hispanic/Latino). 21 applicants, 52% accepted, 11 enrolled. In 2016, 12 master's, 3 AGCs awarded. *Degree requirements:* For master's, thesis or alternative. *Entrance requirements:* For master's, minimum GPA of 3.0, letters of recommendation, statement of objectives, academic major (or equivalent) in program discipline, current resume. Additional exam requirements/recommendations for international students: Required—TOEFL (minimum score 550 paper-based; 79 iBT), IELTS (minimum score 6.5). *Application deadline:* For fall admission, 3/15 priority date for domestic and international students; for spring admission, 10/15 priority date for domestic and international students; for summer admission, 3/15 for domestic and international students. Application fee: $80. Electronic applications accepted. *Expenses:* Contact institution. *Financial support:* Federal Work-Study, scholarships/grants, and unspecified assistantships available. Support available to part-time students. Financial award application deadline: 3/15; financial award applicants required to submit FAFSA. *Unit head:* Dr. Sue Robb, Chairperson, 585-395-5935, Fax: 585-395-2171, E-mail: awalton@brockport.edu. *Application contact:* Anne Walton, Coordinator of Certification and Graduate Advisement, 585-395-2326, Fax: 585-395-2172, E-mail: awalton@brockport.edu.
Website: http://www.brockport.edu/ehd/

College of St. Joseph, Graduate Programs, Division of Education, Program in Secondary Education, Rutland, VT 05701-3899. Offers English (M Ed); social studies (M Ed). *Program availability:* Part-time, evening/weekend. *Degree requirements:* For master's, comprehensive exam. *Entrance requirements:* For master's, PRAXIS I, official college transcripts; 2 letters of reference; minimum GPA of 3.0 (initial licensure) or 2.7 (nonlicensure); interview. Additional exam requirements/recommendations for international students: Required—TOEFL (minimum score 550 paper-based). *Application deadline:* Applications are processed on a rolling basis. Application fee: $35. Electronic applications accepted. *Expenses: Tuition:* Full-time $13,800; part-time $560 per credit. *Required fees:* $75 per semester. Full-time tuition and fees vary according to course load. *Financial support:* Career-related internships or fieldwork, Federal Work-Study, and unspecified assistantships available. Support available to part-time students. Financial award application deadline: 3/1. *Unit head:* Dr. Maria Bove, Chair, 802-773-5900 Ext. 3243, Fax: 802-776-5258, E-mail: mbove@csj.edu. *Application contact:* Alan Young, Director of Admissions, 802-773-5900 Ext. 3227, Fax: 802-776-5310, E-mail: alanyoung@csj.edu.

College of Staten Island of the City University of New York, Graduate Programs, School of Education, Program in Adolescence Education, Staten Island, NY 10314-6600. Offers biology (MS Ed); English (MS Ed); mathematics (MS Ed); social studies (MS Ed). *Program availability:* Part-time, evening/weekend. *Faculty:* 18 full-time, 8 part-time/adjunct. *Students:* 4 full-time, 84 part-time. Average age 29. 40 applicants, 88% accepted, 14 enrolled. In 2016, 41 master's awarded. *Degree requirements:* For master's, thesis, educational research project supervised by faculty; minimum of 33-38 credits distributed among 11 courses or minimum of 46-53 credits. *Entrance requirements:* For master's, GRE General Test or an approved equivalent examination, relevant bachelor's degree, minimum overall GPA of 3.0, two letters of recommendation, one- or two-page personal statement. Additional exam requirements/recommendations for international students: Required—TOEFL (minimum score 550 paper-based; 79 iBT), IELTS (minimum score 6.5). *Application deadline:* For fall admission, 4/25 for domestic and international students; for spring admission, 11/25 for domestic and international students. Applications are processed on a rolling basis. Application fee: $125. Electronic applications accepted. *Expenses:* Tuition, state resident: full-time $10,130; part-time $425 per credit. Tuition, nonresident: full-time $18,720; part-time $780 per credit. *Required fees:* $181.10 per semester. Tuition and fees vary according to program. *Faculty research:* Development and assessment of TPACK (technological pedagogical content knowledge), technology and differentiation in stem classrooms, teacher effectiveness and student achievement, teacher knowledge, knowledge transfer from college to classroom. *Unit head:* Dr. Bethany Rogers, Graduate Faculty Advisor, 718-982-4247, E-mail: bethany.rogers@csi.cuny.edu. *Application contact:* Sasha Spence, Associate Director for Graduate Admissions, 718-982-2019, Fax: 718-982-2500, E-mail: sasha.spence@csi.cuny.edu.
Website: http://www.csi.cuny.edu/catalog/graduate/graduate-programs-in-education.htm#o2608

The Colorado College, Education Department, Program in Secondary Education, Colorado Springs, CO 80903-3294. Offers art teaching (K-12) (MAT); English teaching (MAT); foreign language teaching (MAT); mathematics teaching (MAT); music teaching (MAT); science teaching (MAT); social studies teaching (MAT). *Degree requirements:* For master's, thesis, internship. Electronic applications accepted.

Columbus State University, Graduate Studies, College of Education and Health Professions, Department of Teacher Education, Columbus, GA 31907-5645. Offers curriculum and instruction in accomplished teaching (M Ed); early childhood education (M Ed, MAT, Ed S); middle grades education (M Ed, MAT, Ed S); secondary education (M Ed, MAT, Ed S), including biology (MAT), chemistry (MAT), earth and space science (MAT), English/language arts, general science (M Ed), history (MAT), mathematics, science (Ed S), social science (M Ed, Ed S); special education (M Ed, MAT, Ed S), including general curriculum (M Ed, MAT); teacher leadership (M Ed). *Accreditation:* NCATE. *Program availability:* Part-time, evening/weekend, 100% online, blended/hybrid learning. *Faculty:* 20 full-time (13 women), 19 part-time/adjunct (16 women). *Students:* 92 full-time (66 women), 212 part-time (179 women); includes 113 minority (104 Black or African American, non-Hispanic/Latino; 1 American Indian or Alaska Native, non-Hispanic/Latino; 2 Asian, non-Hispanic/Latino; 4 Hispanic/Latino; 2 Two or more races, non-Hispanic/Latino), 5 international. Average age 34. 209 applicants, 56% accepted, 79 enrolled. In 2016, 111 master's, 18 other advanced degrees awarded. *Degree requirements:* For Ed S, thesis or alternative. *Entrance requirements:* For master's, GRE General Test, minimum undergraduate GPA of 2.75; for Ed S, GRE General Test, minimum undergraduate GPA of 2.75, graduate 3.0. Additional exam requirements/recommendations for international students: Required—TOEFL (minimum score 550 paper-based; 79 iBT). *Application deadline:* For fall admission, 6/30 for domestic students, 5/1 for international students; for spring admission, 11/1 for domestic and international students; for summer admission, 3/1 for domestic and international students. Applications are processed on a rolling basis. Application fee: $50. Electronic applications accepted. *Expenses:* Tuition, state resident: full-time $4804; part-time $2412 per semester hour. Tuition, nonresident: full-time $19,218; part-time $9612 per

semester hour. *Required fees:* $1850 per semester hour. Tuition and fees vary according to program. *Financial support:* In 2016–17, 60 students received support, including 12 research assistantships with partial tuition reimbursements available (averaging $3,000 per year); career-related internships or fieldwork, Federal Work-Study, institutionally sponsored loans, scholarships/grants, tuition waivers (partial), and unspecified assistantships also available. Support available to part-time students. Financial award application deadline: 5/1; financial award applicants required to submit FAFSA. *Unit head:* Dr. Jan Burcham, Department Chair, 706-507-8519, Fax: 706-568-3134, E-mail: burcham_jan@columbusstate.edu. *Application contact:* Kristin Williams, Director of International and Graduate Recruitment, 706-507-8848, Fax: 706-568-5091, E-mail: williams_kristin@columbusstate.edu.
Website: http://te.columbusstate.edu/

Converse College, School of Education and Graduate Studies, Program in Secondary Education, Spartanburg, SC 29302. Offers biology (MAT); chemistry (MAT); English (M Ed, MAT); mathematics (M Ed, MAT); natural sciences (M Ed); social sciences (M Ed, MAT). *Program availability:* Part-time. *Degree requirements:* For master's, capstone paper. *Entrance requirements:* For master's, NTE or PRAXIS II (M Ed), minimum GPA of 2.75, 2 recommendations. *Application deadline:* For fall admission, 8/1 for domestic and international students; for winter admission, 11/15 for domestic and international students; for spring admission, 1/15 for domestic and international students. Applications are processed on a rolling basis. Application fee: $40. Electronic applications accepted. *Expenses: Tuition:* Full-time $3600; part-time $400 per credit hour. *Required fees:* $70 per term. *Financial support:* Available to part-time students. Applicants required to submit FAFSA. *Application contact:* 864-596-9404, E-mail: graduate@converse.edu.

Delta State University, Graduate Programs, College of Arts and Sciences, Division of Languages and Literature, Cleveland, MS 38733-0001. Offers secondary education (M Ed), including English. *Program availability:* Part-time. *Degree requirements:* For master's, thesis or alternative.

Duquesne University, School of Education, Department of Instruction and Leadership, Program in Secondary Education, Pittsburgh, PA 15282-0001. Offers biology (MS Ed); chemistry (MS Ed); English (MS Ed); K-12 education (MS Ed), including Latin; mathematics (MS Ed); physics (MS Ed); social studies (MS Ed). *Program availability:* Part-time, evening/weekend. *Faculty:* 5 full-time (4 women). *Students:* 21 full-time (8 women), 4 part-time (0 women); includes 3 minority (2 Black or African American, non-Hispanic/Latino; 1 Two or more races, non-Hispanic/Latino). Average age 28. 12 applicants, 100% accepted, 7 enrolled. In 2016, 19 master's awarded. *Degree requirements:* For master's, thesis optional. *Entrance requirements:* For master's, letters of recommendation, letter of intent, interview, bachelor's degree. Additional exam requirements/recommendations for international students: Required—TOEFL (minimum score 550 paper-based), IELTS (minimum score 7). *Application deadline:* For fall admission, 9/1 for domestic students; for spring admission, 1/1 for domestic students. Applications are processed on a rolling basis. Application fee: $0. Electronic applications accepted. *Expenses: Tuition:* Full-time $22,212; part-time $1234 per credit. Tuition and fees vary according to program. *Financial support:* Research assistantships and Federal Work-Study available. Support available to part-time students. *Unit head:* Dr. Melissa Boston, Associate Professor and Director, 412-396-6109, E-mail: bostonm@duq.edu. *Application contact:* Michael Dolinger, Director of Student and Academic Services, 412-396-6647, Fax: 412-396-5585, E-mail: dolingerm@duq.edu.
Website: http://www.duq.edu/academics/schools/education/graduate-programs-education/ms-ed-secondary-education

East Carolina University, Graduate School, College of Education, Department of Elementary and Middle Grades Education, Greenville, NC 27858-4353. Offers elementary education (MA Ed, MAT); English education (MAT); family and consumer science (MAT); health education (MAT); Hispanic studies (MAT); history education (MAT); middle grades education (MA Ed, MAT); music education (MAT); science education (MAT); special education (MAT), including general curriculum; vocational education (MAT). *Accreditation:* NCATE. *Program availability:* Part-time, evening/weekend, online learning. *Students:* 5 full-time (4 women), 18 part-time (16 women); includes 4 minority (3 Black or African American, non-Hispanic/Latino; 1 Hispanic/Latino). Average age 31. 19 applicants, 95% accepted, 13 enrolled. In 2016, 8 master's awarded. *Degree requirements:* For master's, comprehensive exam, thesis optional. *Entrance requirements:* For master's, GRE or MAT, minimum GPA of 2.5, bachelor's degree in related field, teaching license (MA Ed). Additional exam requirements/recommendations for international students: Required—TOEFL. *Application deadline:* For fall admission, 6/1 priority date for domestic students. Applications are processed on a rolling basis. Application fee: $70. *Financial support:* Federal Work-Study available. Support available to part-time students. Financial award application deadline: 6/1. *Unit head:* Dr. Ann Bullock, Chair, 252-328-1126, E-mail: bullockv@ecu.edu. *Application contact:* Dean of Graduate School, 252-328-6012, Fax: 252-328-6071, E-mail: gradschool@ecu.edu.
Website: http://www.ecu.edu/cs-educ/elmid/index.cfm

East Carolina University, Graduate School, Thomas Harriot College of Arts and Sciences, Department of English, Greenville, NC 27858-4353. Offers creative writing (MA); English studies (MA); linguistics (MA); literature (MA); multicultural and transnational literatures (MA, Certificate); rhetoric and composition (MA); rhetoric, writing, and professional communication (PhD); teaching English in the two-year college (Certificate); teaching English to speakers of other languages (MA, Certificate); technical and professional communication (MA). *Program availability:* Part-time, evening/weekend. *Students:* 54 full-time (36 women), 95 part-time (77 women); includes 32 minority (19 Black or African American, non-Hispanic/Latino; 3 Asian, non-Hispanic/Latino; 6 Hispanic/Latino; 4 Two or more races, non-Hispanic/Latino), 1 international. Average age 35. 78 applicants, 96% accepted, 50 enrolled. In 2016, 34 master's, 1 doctorate awarded. *Degree requirements:* For master's, one foreign language, comprehensive exam, thesis optional. *Entrance requirements:* For master's, GRE General Test, MAT (for MA Ed). Additional exam requirements/recommendations for international students: Required—TOEFL. *Application deadline:* For fall admission, 6/1 priority date for domestic students; for spring admission, 10/15 for domestic students. Applications are processed on a rolling basis. Application fee: $50. *Financial support:* Research assistantships with partial tuition reimbursements, teaching assistantships with partial tuition reimbursements, and Federal Work-Study available. Support available to part-time students. Financial award application deadline: 6/1. *Unit head:* Dr. Jeffrey Johnson, Chair, 252-328-6041, E-mail: johnsonj@ecu.edu. *Application contact:* Dean of Graduate School, 252-328-6012, Fax: 252-328-6071, E-mail: gradschool@ecu.edu.
Website: http://www.ecu.edu/cs-cas/engl/graduate/

Eastern Kentucky University, The Graduate School, College of Education, Department of Curriculum and Instruction, Program in Secondary and Higher Education, Richmond, KY 40475-3102. Offers secondary education (MA Ed), including agricultural education, art education, biological sciences education, business education, English education, geography education, history education, home economics education, industrial education, mathematical sciences education, physical education, school health education. *Accreditation:* NCATE. *Program availability:* Part-time. *Entrance requirements:* For master's, GRE General Test, minimum GPA of 2.5.

Eastern Michigan University, Graduate School, College of Arts and Sciences, Department of English Language and Literature, Program in English Studies for Teachers, Ypsilanti, MI 48197. Offers MA. *Program availability:* Part-time, evening/weekend. *Students:* 7 part-time (5 women); includes 1 minority (Black or African American, non-Hispanic/Latino). Average age 35. In 2016, 2 master's awarded. *Entrance requirements:* Additional exam requirements/recommendations for international students: Required—TOEFL. Application fee: $45. *Financial support:* Research assistantships with full tuition reimbursements, teaching assistantships with full tuition reimbursements, career-related internships or fieldwork, Federal Work-Study, institutionally sponsored loans, scholarships/grants, and unspecified assistantships available. Support available to part-time students. *Application contact:* Dr. John Staunton, Program Advisor, 734-487-0135, Fax: 734-487-9744, E-mail: jstaunto@emich.edu.

Eastern University, Loeb School of Education, St. Davids, PA 19087-3696. Offers ESL program specialist (K-12) (Certificate); general supervisor (PreK-12) (Certificate); health and physical education (K-12) (Certificate); middle level (4-8) (Certificate); multicultural education (M Ed); organizational leadership with education (PhD); Pre K-4 (Certificate); Pre K-4 with special education (Certificate); reading (M Ed); reading specialist (K-12) (Certificate); reading supervisor (K-12) (Certificate); school health supervisor (Certificate); school nurse (K-12) (Certificate); secondary biology education (7-12) (Certificate); secondary chemistry education (7-12) (Certificate); secondary communication education (7-12) (Certificate); secondary education (7-12) (Certificate); secondary English education (7-12) (Certificate); secondary math education (7-12) (Certificate); secondary social studies education (7-12) (Certificate); special education (M Ed); special education (7-12) (Certificate); special education (Pre K-8) (Certificate); special education supervisor (N-12) (Certificate); TESOL (M Ed); world language (Certificate), including French, Spanish. *Program availability:* Part-time, evening/weekend, online learning. *Students:* 41 full-time (32 women), 89 part-time (68 women); includes 54 minority (38 Black or African American, non-Hispanic/Latino; 3 Asian, non-Hispanic/Latino; 11 Hispanic/Latino; 2 Two or more races, non-Hispanic/Latino), 2 international. Average age 37. In 2016, 64 master's awarded. *Entrance requirements:* Additional exam requirements/recommendations for international students: Required—TOEFL. *Application deadline:* Applications are processed on a rolling basis. Application fee: $35. Electronic applications accepted. Application fee is waived when completed online. *Expenses:* $690 per credit. *Unit head:* Michael Dziedziak, Executive Director of Enrollment, 800-452-0996, E-mail: gpsadmissions@eastern.edu.
Website: http://www.eastern.edu/academics/programs/loeb-school-education-0

Elms College, Division of Education, Chicopee, MA 01013-2839. Offers early childhood education (MAT); education (M Ed, CAGS); elementary education (MAT); English as a second language (MAT); reading (MAT); secondary education (MAT), including biology education, English education, Spanish education; special education (MAT). *Program availability:* Part-time, evening/weekend. *Faculty:* 5 full-time (all women), 7 part-time/adjunct (6 women). *Students:* 6 full-time (all women), 136 part-time (111 women); includes 6 minority (1 Asian, non-Hispanic/Latino; 5 Hispanic/Latino). Average age 33. 27 applicants, 89% accepted, 20 enrolled. In 2016, 47 master's, 3 other advanced degrees awarded. *Degree requirements:* For master's, thesis (for some programs). *Entrance requirements:* For master's, Massachusetts Educators Certification Test, minimum GPA of 3.0; for CAGS, master's degree in education. Additional exam requirements/recommendations for international students: Required—TOEFL. *Application deadline:* For fall admission, 7/1 priority date for domestic students; for spring admission, 11/1 priority date for domestic students. Applications are processed on a rolling basis. Application fee: $30. *Expenses: Tuition:* Full-time $13,392. *Required fees:* $200. *Financial support:* In 2016–17, 2 teaching assistantships with partial tuition reimbursements were awarded; tuition waivers (partial) also available. Support available to part-time students. Financial award applicants required to submit FAFSA. *Unit head:* Dr. Mary Janeczek, Chair, Division of Education, 413-594-2761, Fax: 413-592-4871, E-mail: janeczeke@elms.edu. *Application contact:* Dr. Elizabeth Teahan Hukowicz, Dean, School of Graduate and Professional Studies, 413-265-2360, Fax: 413-265-2459, E-mail: hukowicze@elms.edu.

Fitchburg State University, Division of Graduate and Continuing Education, Programs in English and Teaching English (Secondary Level), Fitchburg, MA 01420-2697. Offers MA, MAT, Certificate. *Accreditation:* NCATE. *Program availability:* Part-time, evening/weekend. *Entrance requirements:* Additional exam requirements/recommendations for international students: Required—TOEFL (minimum score 550 paper-based; 79 iBT). Electronic applications accepted. *Expenses:* Tuition, state resident: full-time $2871; part-time $1914 per year. Tuition, nonresident: full-time $2871; part-time $1914 per year. *Required fees:* $3828. Tuition and fees vary according to program.

Florida Agricultural and Mechanical University, Division of Graduate Studies, Research, and Continuing Education, College of Education, Program in Secondary Education and Foundation, Tallahassee, FL 32307-3200. Offers biology (M Ed); chemistry (MS Ed); English (MS Ed); history (MS Ed); math (MS Ed); physics (MS Ed). *Accreditation:* NCATE. *Degree requirements:* For master's, thesis (for some programs). *Entrance requirements:* For master's, GRE General Test, minimum GPA of 3.0. Additional exam requirements/recommendations for international students: Required—TOEFL.

Florida Atlantic University, College of Education, Department of Teaching and Learning, Boca Raton, FL 33431-0991. Offers curriculum and instruction (M Ed), including art, biology, chemistry, English, French, German, mathematics, music, physics, Pre-K and primary education, reading, social sciences, Spanish; elementary education (M Ed); environmental education (M Ed); reading education (M Ed); social foundations of education (M Ed), including educational psychology, educational technology, multilingual education. *Accreditation:* NCATE. *Program availability:* Part-time, evening/weekend. *Faculty:* 15 full-time (12 women), 2 part-time/adjunct (1 woman). *Students:* 25 full-time (20 women), 41 part-time (37 women); includes 18 minority (9 Black or African American, non-Hispanic/Latino; 2 Asian, non-Hispanic/Latino; 7 Hispanic/Latino), 7 international. Average age 32. 54 applicants, 59% accepted, 18 enrolled. In 2016, 36 master's awarded. *Entrance requirements:* For master's, GRE General Test, minimum GPA of 3.0 in last 2 years of undergraduate course work. Additional exam requirements/recommendations for international students: Required—TOEFL (minimum score 500 paper-based; 61 iBT), IELTS (minimum score 6). *Application deadline:* For fall admission, 7/1 for domestic students, 2/15 for international students; for spring admission, 11/1 for domestic students, 7/15 for international students. Applications are processed on a rolling basis. Application fee: $30. *Expenses:* Tuition, state resident: full-time $7392; part-time $369.82 per credit hour. Tuition, nonresident: full-time $19,432; part-time $1024.81 per credit hour. *Financial support:* Fellowships with partial tuition reimbursements, research assistantships with partial tuition reimbursements, teaching assistantships with partial tuition reimbursements, career-related internships or fieldwork, scholarships/grants, and unspecified assistantships available. *Faculty research:* Technology, teaching English to speakers of other languages, math teaching, electronic portfolio assessment, global perspectives through social studies. *Unit head:* Dr. Barbara Ridener, Chairperson, 561-297-3588, E-mail: bridener@fau.edu. *Application contact:* Dr. Eliah Watlington,

Associate Dean, 561-296-8520, Fax: 261-297-2991, E-mail: ewatling@fau.edu.
Website: http://www.coe.fau.edu/academicdepartments/tl/

Florida Gulf Coast University, College of Education, Program in Curriculum and Instruction, Fort Myers, FL 33965-6565. Offers elementary education (M Ed); English education (M Ed); gifted education (M Ed); mathematics education (M Ed); middle school education (M Ed); science education (M Ed); social science education (M Ed). *Program availability:* Part-time, evening/weekend, online learning. *Faculty:* 26 full-time (18 women), 44 part-time/adjunct (32 women). *Students:* 1 (woman) full-time, 22 part-time (20 women); includes 49 minority (19 Black or African American, non-Hispanic/Latino; 4 Asian, non-Hispanic/Latino; 24 Hispanic/Latino; 2 Two or more races, non-Hispanic/Latino), 2 international. Average age 28. 9 applicants, 78% accepted, 2 enrolled. In 2016, 9 master's awarded. *Degree requirements:* For master's, final project or portfolio. *Entrance requirements:* For master's, GRE General Test, MAT, minimum undergraduate GPA of 3.0 in last 2 years. Additional exam requirements/recommendations for international students: Required—TOEFL (minimum score 550 paper-based). *Application deadline:* For fall admission, 7/1 priority date for domestic students; for spring admission, 10/15 for domestic students. Applications are processed on a rolling basis. Application fee: $30. Electronic applications accepted. *Expenses:* Tuition, state resident: full-time $6721. Tuition, nonresident: full-time $28,170. *Required fees:* $1987. Tuition and fees vary according to course load and degree level. *Financial support:* In 2016–17, 1 student received support. Application deadline: 3/1; applicants required to submit FAFSA. *Faculty research:* Internet in schools, technology in pre-service and in-service teacher training. *Unit head:* Dr. Diane Schmidt, Department Chair, 239-590-7741, Fax: 239-590-7801, E-mail: dschmidt@fgcu.edu. *Application contact:* Keiana Desmore, Adviser/Counselor, 239-590-7759, Fax: 239-590-7801, E-mail: kdesmore@fgcu.edu.
Website: http://coe.fgcu.edu/c-imed/

Florida International University, College of Arts, Sciences, and Education, Department of Teaching and Learning, Miami, FL 33199. Offers art education (MA, MS); curriculum and instruction (MS, Ed D, PhD, Ed S), including curriculum development (MS), elementary education (MS), English education (MS), learning technologies (MS), mathematics education (MS), modern language education (MS), physical education (MS), science education (MS), social studies education (MS), special education (MS); early childhood education (MS); exceptional student education (Ed D); foreign language education (MS), including foreign language education, teaching English to speakers of other languages (TESOL); international/intercultural education (MS); language, literacy and culture (PhD); mathematics, science, and learning technologies (PhD); physical education (MS), including sport and fitness; reading education (MS). *Program availability:* Part-time, evening/weekend. *Faculty:* 34 full-time (23 women), 64 part-time/adjunct (48 women). *Students:* 182 full-time (154 women), 231 part-time (190 women); includes 323 minority (69 Black or African American, non-Hispanic/Latino; 10 Asian, non-Hispanic/Latino; 237 Hispanic/Latino; 7 Two or more races, non-Hispanic/Latino), 19 international. Average age 34. 282 applicants, 58% accepted, 113 enrolled. In 2016, 184 master's, 12 doctorates awarded. *Degree requirements:* For doctorate, comprehensive exam, thesis/dissertation. *Entrance requirements:* For master's, GRE General Test, Florida General Knowledge Test or Florida College Level Academic Skills Test; for doctorate and Ed S, GRE General Test. Additional exam requirements/recommendations for international students: Required—TOEFL (minimum score 550 paper-based; 80 iBT), IELTS (minimum score 6.3). *Application deadline:* For fall admission, 6/1 priority date for domestic students, 4/1 for international students; for winter admission, 10/1 priority date for domestic students, 9/1 for international students; for spring admission, 3/1 priority date for domestic students, 2/1 for international students. Applications are processed on a rolling basis. Application fee: $30. Electronic applications accepted. *Expenses:* Tuition, state resident: full-time $8912; part-time $446 per credit hour. Tuition, nonresident: full-time $21,393; part-time $992 per credit hour. *Required fees:* $2185; $195 per semester. Tuition and fees vary according to program. *Financial support:* Research assistantships with tuition reimbursements and teaching assistantships with tuition reimbursements available. *Unit head:* Dr. Lynn Miller, Chair, 305-348-2005, Fax: 305-348-2086, E-mail: lynne.miller@fiu.edu. *Application contact:* Nanett Rojas, Assistant Director, Graduate Admissions, 305-348-7464, Fax: 305-348-7441, E-mail: gradadm@fiu.edu.
Website: http://education.fiu.edu

Florida State University, The Graduate School, College of Education, Program in Curriculum and Instruction, Tallahassee, FL 32306. Offers curriculum and instruction (MS, PhD, Ed S), including early childhood education, elementary education, English education, English teaching (MS), exceptional student education (MS), foreign and second language education, foreign and second language teaching (MS), mathematics education, mathematics teaching (MS), reading education and language arts, science education, social science education, social science teaching (MS), special education, special education studies (MS), visual disabilities (MS, Ed S). *Program availability:* Part-time, evening/weekend. Terminal master's awarded for partial completion of doctoral program. *Degree requirements:* For master's and Ed S, comprehensive exam, thesis optional; for doctorate, comprehensive exam, thesis/dissertation, diagnostic exam, preliminary exam, prospectus defense, dissertation defense. *Entrance requirements:* For master's, doctorate, and Ed S, GRE General Test, minimum upper-division GPA of 3.0. Additional exam requirements/recommendations for international students: Required—TOEFL (minimum score 550 paper-based, 80 iBT), IELTS (minimum score 6.5), Michigan English Language Assessment Battery (minimum score 77), or PTE (minimum score 55). Application fee: $30. Electronic applications accepted. *Expenses:* Tuition, state resident: full-time $7263; part-time $403.51 per credit hour. Tuition, nonresident: full-time $18,087; part-time $1004.85 per credit hour. *Required fees:* $1365; $75.81 per credit hour. $20 per semester. Tuition and fees vary according to campus/location. *Financial support:* Fellowships, research assistantships, teaching assistantships, scholarships/grants, tuition waivers (full and partial), and unspecified assistantships available. Financial award application deadline: 1/15; financial award applicants required to submit FAFSA. *Faculty research:* Identifying effective intervention strategies to improve reading skills; improving literacy teaching and learning through technology; understanding of student sense making, problem solving, the history and structure of STEM disciplines, and teacher education to support the development of ambitious instruction that supports the STEM learning of all students; examining practices of international education; identifying ways to support the professional development of teachers. *Unit head:* Dr. Sherry Southerland, Professor/Department Chair, 850-644-4880, Fax: 850-644-7736, E-mail: ssoutherland@admin.fsu.edu. *Application contact:* Libbie Crowley, Academic Support Specialist, 850-644-2122, Fax: 850-644-7736, E-mail: ecrowley@fsu.edu.
Website: http://education.fsu.edu/degrees-and-programs/graduate-programs

Framingham State University, Continuing Education, Program in English, Framingham, MA 01701-9101. Offers M Ed.

Gardner-Webb University, Graduate School, Department of English, Boiling Springs, NC 28017. Offers English (MA); English education (MA). *Program availability:* Part-time, evening/weekend. *Faculty:* 4 full-time (all women). *Students:* 16 part-time (11 women); includes 1 minority (Black or African American, non-Hispanic/Latino). Average age 29. 27 applicants, 37% accepted, 6 enrolled. In 2016, 6 master's awarded. *Degree requirements:* For master's, comprehensive exam. *Entrance requirements:* For master's, GRE General Test, MAT, or NTE; PRAXIS, minimum GPA of 2.5. *Application deadline:* For fall admission, 8/1 priority date for domestic students. Applications are processed on a rolling basis. Application fee: $0. Electronic applications accepted. *Expenses:* Contact institution. *Financial support:* Unspecified assistantships available. *Unit head:* Dr. David Parker, Chair, 704-406-4413, E-mail: dparker@gardner-webb.edu. *Application contact:* Office of Graduate Admissions, 877-498-4723, Fax: 704-406-3895, E-mail: gradinfo@gardner-webb.edu.

George Mason University, College of Education and Human Development, Programs in Curriculum and Instruction, Fairfax, VA 22030. Offers advanced international baccalaureate (M Ed); assistive technology (M Ed); designing digital learning in schools (M Ed); early childhood education (M Ed); early childhood education for diverse learners (M Ed); elementary education (M Ed); English as a second language (M Ed); gifted child education (M Ed); history (M Ed); literacy (M Ed), including PK-12 classroom teachers, reading specialist; literacy leadership for diverse schools (M Ed), including K-12 reading; physical education (M Ed); science K-12 (M Ed); secondary education (M Ed), including biology, chemistry, earth science, English, history/social science, math, physics; special education (M Ed); teacher leadership (M Ed); teaching culturally, linguistically diverse and exceptional learners (M Ed); transformative teaching (M Ed). *Faculty:* 41 full-time (35 women), 53 part-time/adjunct (46 women). *Students:* 155 full-time (127 women), 821 part-time (697 women); includes 267 minority (82 Black or African American, non-Hispanic/Latino; 5 American Indian or Alaska Native, non-Hispanic/Latino; 75 Asian, non-Hispanic/Latino; 88 Hispanic/Latino; 1 Native Hawaiian or other Pacific Islander, non-Hispanic/Latino; 16 Two or more races, non-Hispanic/Latino), 19 international. Average age 33. 513 applicants, 90% accepted, 352 enrolled. In 2016, 347 master's awarded. *Degree requirements:* For master's, comprehensive exam, thesis (for some programs). *Entrance requirements:* For master's, PRAXIS Core (for some programs), minimum GPA of 3.0 in last 60 hours, licensed as teacher or educational administrator, official transcripts, goals statement, 3 recommendation letters, interview or writing sample (depending on program), up to 3 years' teaching experience (depending on program). Additional exam requirements/recommendations for international students: Required—TOEFL (minimum score 575 paper-based; 88 iBT), IELTS (minimum score 6.5), PTE (minimum score 59). *Application deadline:* For spring admission, 11/1 priority date for domestic and international students. Application fee: $75 ($80 for international students). Electronic applications accepted. *Expenses:* Tuition, state resident: full-time $10,628; part-time $443 per credit. Tuition, nonresident: full-time $29,306; part-time $1221 per credit. *Required fees:* $3096; $129 per credit. Tuition and fees vary according to program. *Financial support:* In 2016–17, 1 student received support, including 1 teaching assistantship (averaging $4,060 per year); career-related internships or fieldwork, Federal Work-Study, scholarships/grants, unspecified assistantships, and health care benefits (for full-time research or teaching assistantship recipients) also available. Support available to part-time students. Financial award application deadline: 3/1; financial award applicants required to submit FAFSA. *Faculty research:* Achievement gaps and superintendent decisions, constructivist view of classroom teaching, cost of cheating, creating a critical literacy milieu in kindergarten. *Unit head:* Rebecca Fox, Professor and Academic Program Coordinator, 703-993-4123, E-mail: rfox@gmu.edu.
Website: http://gse.gmu.edu/programs/gsemasters

Georgia Southern University, Jack N. Averitt College of Graduate Studies, College of Education, Department of Teaching and Learning, Program in English Education, Statesboro, GA 30460. Offers MAT. *Accreditation:* NCATE. *Program availability:* Part-time, evening/weekend. *Students:* 8 full-time (5 women); includes 1 minority (Hispanic/Latino). Average age 30. 4 applicants, 100% accepted, 4 enrolled. *Degree requirements:* For master's, portfolio, transition point assessments, exit assessment. *Entrance requirements:* For master's, GRE General Test or MAT; GACE Basic Skills and Content Assessments (for MAT), minimum cumulative GPA of 2.5. Additional exam requirements/recommendations for international students: Required—TOEFL (minimum score 550 paper-based; 80 iBT), IELTS (minimum score 6). *Application deadline:* For fall admission, 3/1 priority date for domestic and international students; for spring admission, 10/1 priority date for domestic students, 10/1 for international students. Applications are processed on a rolling basis. Application fee: $50. Electronic applications accepted. *Expenses:* Tuition, state resident: full-time $7236; part-time $277 per semester hour. Tuition, nonresident: full-time $27,118; part-time $1105 per semester hour. *Required fees:* $2092. *Financial support:* In 2016–17, 4 fellowships with full tuition reimbursements (averaging $7,750 per year) were awarded; Federal Work-Study, scholarships/grants, tuition waivers (full), and unspecified assistantships also available. Support available to part-time students. Financial award application deadline: 4/15; financial award applicants required to submit FAFSA. *Faculty research:* Literacy for at-risk students. *Unit head:* Dr. Greg Chamblee, Coordinator, 912-478-5783, Fax: 912-478-0026, E-mail: gchamblee@georgiasouthern.edu. *Application contact:* Lydia Cross, Coordinator for Graduate Academic Services Center, 912-478-8664, E-mail: lcross@georgiasouthern.edu.
Website: http://coe.georgiasouthern.edu/ger/

Georgia Southwestern State University, School of Education, Americus, GA 31709-4693. Offers early childhood education (M Ed, Ed S); middle grades education (Ed S); middle grades language arts (M Ed); middle grades mathematics (M Ed); special education (M Ed). *Accreditation:* NCATE. *Faculty:* 13 full-time (8 women), 7 part-time/adjunct (6 women). *Students:* 209 full-time (199 women), 6 part-time (all women); includes 52 minority (45 Black or African American, non-Hispanic/Latino; 6 Hispanic/Latino; 1 Two or more races, non-Hispanic/Latino). Average age 33. In 2016, 57 master's awarded. *Degree requirements:* For master's, minimum cumulative GPA of 3.0; for Ed S, minimum GPA of 3.25 in all courses with no grade less than a B; degree must be completed within 7 calendar years from date of initial enrollment in graduate work. *Entrance requirements:* For master's, undergraduate degree from accredited institution; professional Georgia Teaching Certificate or eligibility; minimum undergraduate GPA of 2.75 as reported on official final transcripts from all accredited institutions attended; 2 confidential Administrative Recommendation Forms; for Ed S, master's degree from accredited college or university; professional Georgia Teaching Certificate or eligibility; minimum graduate GPA of 3.0 as reported on official final graduate transcripts from all accredited institutions attended; 2 confidential Administrative Recommendation Forms. *Application deadline:* For summer admission, 4/15 for domestic students. Application fee: $25. Electronic applications accepted. *Expenses:* $257 per credit hour for online program courses, plus fees, which vary according to enrolled credit hours. *Financial support:* Application deadline: 6/1; applicants required to submit FAFSA. *Unit head:* Dr. Rachel Abbott, Dean, 229-931-2145. *Application contact:* Whitney Ford, Admissions Specialist, Office of Graduate Admissions, 800-338-0082, Fax: 229-931-2983.
Website: https://gsw.edu/Academics/Schools-and-Departments/School-of-Education/index

Georgia State University, College of Education and Human Development, Department of Middle and Secondary Education, Atlanta, GA 30302-3083. Offers curriculum and instruction (Ed D); English education (MAT); mathematics education (M Ed, MAT); middle level education (MAT); reading, language and literacy education (M Ed, MAT), including reading instruction (M Ed); science education (M Ed, MAT), including biology (MAT), broad field science (MAT), chemistry (MAT), earth science (MAT), physics

(MAT); social studies education (M Ed, MAT), including economics (MAT), geography (MAT), history (MAT), political science (MAT); teaching and learning (PhD), including language and literacy, mathematics education, music education, science education, social studies education, teaching and teacher education. *Accreditation:* NCATE. *Program availability:* Part-time, evening/weekend, online learning. *Faculty:* 24 full-time (18 women). *Students:* 145 full-time (91 women), 151 part-time (102 women); includes 141 minority (104 Black or African American, non-Hispanic/Latino; 1 American Indian or Alaska Native, non-Hispanic/Latino; 16 Asian, non-Hispanic/Latino; 12 Hispanic/Latino; 8 Two or more races, non-Hispanic/Latino), 10 international. Average age 36. 115 applicants, 50% accepted, 41 enrolled. In 2016, 94 master's, 22 doctorates awarded. *Degree requirements:* For master's, comprehensive exam (for some programs), thesis or alternative, exit portfolio; for doctorate, comprehensive exam, thesis/dissertation. *Entrance requirements:* For master's, GRE; GACE I (for initial teacher preparation programs), baccalaureate degree or equivalent, resume, goals statement, two letters of recommendation, minimum undergraduate GPA of 2.5; proof of initial teacher certification in the content area (for M Ed); for doctorate, GRE, resume, goals statement, writing sample, two letters of recommendation, minimum graduate GPA of 3.3, interview. Additional exam requirements/recommendations for international students: Required—TOEFL (minimum score 550 paper-based; 79 iBT) or IELTS (minimum score 6.5). *Application deadline:* For fall admission, 1/15 priority date for domestic and international students; for spring admission, 10/1 for domestic and international students. Application fee: $50. Electronic applications accepted. *Expenses:* Tuition, state resident: full-time $6876; part-time $382 per credit hour. Tuition, nonresident: full-time $22,374; part-time $1243 per credit hour. *Required fees:* $2128; $1064 per term. Part-time tuition and fees vary according to course load and program. *Financial support:* In 2016–17, fellowships with full tuition reimbursements (averaging $19,667 per year), research assistantships with full tuition reimbursements (averaging $5,436 per year), teaching assistantships with full tuition reimbursements (averaging $2,779 per year) were awarded; career-related internships or fieldwork, Federal Work-Study, scholarships/grants, health care benefits, tuition waivers (full and partial), and unspecified assistantships also available. Financial award application deadline: 3/15. *Faculty research:* Teacher education in language and literacy, mathematics, science, and social studies in urban middle and secondary school settings; learning technologies in school, community, and corporate settings; multicultural education and education for social justice; urban education; international education. *Unit head:* Dr. Dana L. Fox, Chair, 404-413-8060, Fax: 404-413-8063, E-mail: dfox@gsu.edu. *Application contact:* Bobbie Turner, Administrative Coordinator I, 404-413-8405, Fax: 404-413-8063, E-mail: bnturner@gsu.edu.
Website: http://mse.education.gsu.edu/

Grand Valley State University, College of Education, Program in Reading and Language Arts, Allendale, MI 49401-9403. Offers M Ed. *Accreditation:* NCATE. *Program availability:* Part-time, evening/weekend. *Students:* 2 part-time (both women). Average age 35. In 2016, 3 master's awarded. *Degree requirements:* For master's, project or thesis. *Entrance requirements:* For master's, GRE General Test or minimum GPA of 3.0; last 60 credits from regionally-accredited college/university; 3 letters of recommendation. Additional exam requirements/recommendations for international students: Required—TOEFL (minimum score 550 paper-based, 80 iBT), IELTS (6.5), or Michigan English Language Assessment Battery. *Application deadline:* Applications are processed on a rolling basis. Application fee: $30. Electronic applications accepted. *Expenses:* $628 per credit hour. *Financial support:* Career-related internships or fieldwork, Federal Work-Study, scholarships/grants, and unspecified assistantships available. *Faculty research:* Culture of literacy, literacy acquisition, assessment, content area literacy, writing pedagogy. *Unit head:* Dr. Elizabeth Stolle, Graduate Program Director, 616-331-6242, E-mail: stollee@gvsu.edu. *Application contact:* Thomas Owens, Director, Student Information and Services Center, 616-331-6282, Fax: 616-331-6217, E-mail: owenst@gvsu.edu.

Harding University, Cannon-Clary College of Education, Searcy, AR 72149-0001. Offers advanced studies in teaching and learning (M Ed); art (MSE); behavioral science (MSE); counseling (MS, Ed S); early childhood special education (M Ed, MSE); education (MSE); educational leadership (M Ed, Ed S); elementary education (M Ed); English (MSE); French (MSE); history/social science (MSE); kinesiology (MSE); math (MSE); reading (M Ed); secondary education (M Ed); Spanish (MSE); teaching (MAT); teaching English as a second language (MSE). *Accreditation:* NCATE. *Program availability:* Part-time, evening/weekend. *Faculty:* 22 full-time (9 women), 51 part-time/adjunct (37 women). *Students:* 130 full-time (94 women), 321 part-time (234 women); includes 83 minority (50 Black or African American, non-Hispanic/Latino; 4 American Indian or Alaska Native, non-Hispanic/Latino; 6 Asian, non-Hispanic/Latino; 13 Hispanic/Latino; 10 Two or more races, non-Hispanic/Latino), 11 international. Average age 35. 125 applicants, 88% accepted, 110 enrolled. In 2016, 124 master's, 27 other advanced degrees awarded. *Degree requirements:* For master's, comprehensive exam (for some programs), thesis optional, portfolio(s); for Ed S, comprehensive exam, portfolio, project. *Entrance requirements:* For master's, GRE, MAT, PRAXIS; for Ed S, MAT or GRE. Additional exam requirements/recommendations for international students: Required—TOEFL (minimum score 550 paper-based; 79 iBT). *Application deadline:* For fall admission, 8/1 for domestic and international students; for spring admission, 1/1 for domestic and international students. Applications are processed on a rolling basis. Application fee: $35. Tuition and fees vary according to degree level and program. *Financial support:* In 2016–17, 31 students received support. Unspecified assistantships available. *Faculty research:* Reading, comprehension, school violence, educational technology, behavior, college choice, differentiated instruction, brain-based teaching. *Unit head:* Dr. Clara Carroll, Chair, 501-279-4501, Fax: 501-279-4083, E-mail: ccarroll@harding.edu. *Application contact:* Information Contact, 501-279-4315, E-mail: gradstudiesedu@harding.edu.
Website: http://www.harding.edu/education

Hofstra University, School of Education, Programs in Teacher Education, Hempstead, NY 11549. Offers bilingual education (MA, Advanced Certificate); bilingual extension (Advanced Certificate), including education/speech language pathology; business education (MS Ed); early childhood and childhood education (MS Ed), early childhood education (MA, MS Ed); education technology (Advanced Certificate); elementary education (MA, MS Ed), including science, technology, engineering, and mathematics (STEM) (MA); English education (MS Ed); family and consumer science (MS Ed); fine arts and music education (Advanced Certificate); fine arts education (MS Ed); foreign language and TESOL (MS Ed); foreign language education (MS Ed), including French, German, Russian, Spanish; learning and teaching (Ed D), including applied linguistics, art education, arts and humanities, early childhood education, English education, human development, math education, math, science, and technology, multicultural education, physical education, science education, social studies education, special education; mathematics education (MA, MS Ed); middle school extension (Advanced Certificate), including grades 5-6, grades 7-9; music education (MA, MS Ed); science education (MA, MS Ed), including biology, chemistry, earth science, geology, physics; secondary education (Advanced Certificate); social studies education (MA, MS Ed); teaching languages other than English and TESOL (MS Ed); TESOL (MS Ed, Advanced Certificate). *Program availability:* Part-time, evening/weekend, blended/hybrid learning. *Students:* 139 full-time (97 women), 145 part-time (106 women); includes 60 minority (15 Black or African American, non-Hispanic/Latino; 1 American Indian or Alaska Native, non-Hispanic/Latino; 12 Asian, non-Hispanic/Latino; 31 Hispanic/Latino; 1 Two or more races, non-Hispanic/Latino), 21 international. Average age 29. 255 applicants, 86% accepted, 122 enrolled. In 2016, 101 master's, 4 doctorates, 43 other advanced degrees awarded. *Degree requirements:* For master's, comprehensive exam, thesis (for some programs), exit project, student teaching, fieldwork, electronic portfolio, curriculum project, minimum GPA of 3.0; for doctorate, thesis/dissertation; for Advanced Certificate, 3 foreign languages, comprehensive exam (for some programs), thesis project. *Entrance requirements:* For master's, GRE, MAT, 2 letters of recommendation, portfolio, teacher certification (MA), interview, essay; for doctorate, GMAT, GRE, LSAT, or MAT; for Advanced Certificate, 2 letters of recommendation, essay, interview and/or portfolio, teaching certificate. Additional exam requirements/recommendations for international students: Required—TOEFL (minimum score 550 paper-based; 80 iBT). *Application deadline:* Applications are processed on a rolling basis. Application fee: $75. Electronic applications accepted. *Expenses: Tuition:* Full-time $1240. *Required fees:* $970. Tuition and fees vary according to program. *Financial support:* In 2016–17, 149 students received support, including 58 fellowships with full and partial tuition reimbursements available (averaging $5,309 per year), 5 research assistantships with full and partial tuition reimbursements available (averaging $7,073 per year); career-related internships or fieldwork, Federal Work-Study, institutionally sponsored loans, scholarships/grants, traineeships, tuition waivers (full and partial), and unspecified assistantships also available. Support available to part-time students. Financial award applicants required to submit FAFSA. *Faculty research:* Educational interventions that foster critical-thinking skills; teachers' attitudes about professional development; threats to teacher quality. *Unit head:* Dr. Eustace Thompson, Chairperson, 516-463-5749, Fax: 516-463-6275, E-mail: eustace.g.thompson@hofstra.edu. *Application contact:* Sunil Samuel, Assistant Vice President of Admissions, 516-463-4723, Fax: 516-463-4664, E-mail: graduateadmission@hofstra.edu.
Website: http://www.hofstra.edu/education/

Houston Baptist University, School of Christian Thought, Program in Divinity, Houston, TX 77074-3298. Offers Biblical languages (M Div); English languages (M Div). *Students:* 3 full-time (1 woman), 14 part-time (5 women); includes 5 minority (4 Black or African American, non-Hispanic/Latino; 1 Hispanic/Latino). Average age 37. 30 applicants, 77% accepted, 17 enrolled. *Entrance requirements:* For master's, bachelor's degree conferred transcript, resume, essay/personal statement. Additional exam requirements/recommendations for international students: Required—TOEFL (minimum score 80 iBT), IELTS (minimum score 6.5). *Application deadline:* For fall admission, 8/1 for domestic students, 6/1 for international students; for spring admission, 1/1 for domestic students, 11/1 for international students; for summer admission, 5/1 for domestic students, 3/1 for international students. Applications are processed on a rolling basis. Application fee: $0 ($100 for international students). Electronic applications accepted. Application fee is waived when completed online. *Expenses:* $1,500 per 3-hour course; $1,275 annual general fee; $1,060 annual technology fee. *Financial support:* Federal Work-Study and scholarships/grants available. Financial award application deadline: 4/1; financial award applicants required to submit FAFSA. *Unit head:* Dr. Jeffrey Green, Interim Dean, Fax: 281-649-3012, E-mail: jgreen@hbu.edu. *Application contact:* Celeste Risteski, Administrative Assistant to the Dean, 281-649-3383, Fax: 281-649-3012, E-mail: cristeski@hbu.edu.

Hunter College of the City University of New York, Graduate School, School of Education, Programs in Secondary Education, Concentration in English Education, New York, NY 10065-5085. Offers MA. *Accreditation:* NCATE. *Degree requirements:* For master's, thesis, professional teaching portfolio, New York State Teacher Certification Exam, research project. *Entrance requirements:* For master's, minimum GPA of 2.8, 2 letters of reference, minimum of 21 credits in English. Additional exam requirements/recommendations for international students: Required—TOEFL, TWE. *Application deadline:* For fall admission, 4/1 for domestic students, 2/1 for international students; for spring admission, 11/1 for domestic students, 9/1 for international students. Applications are processed on a rolling basis. *Financial support:* Federal Work-Study and tuition waivers (partial) available. Support available to part-time students. *Unit head:* Melissa Schieble, Education Program Coordinator, 212-772-4773, E-mail: mschiebl@hunter.cuny.edu. *Application contact:* Candice Jenkins, English Department Program Coordinator, 212-772-5172, E-mail: candice.jenkins@hunter.cuny.edu.

Indiana University of Pennsylvania, School of Graduate Studies and Research, College of Humanities and Social Sciences, Department of English, PhD Program in Composition and Teaching English to Speakers of Other Languages, Indiana, PA 15705. Offers PhD. *Program availability:* Part-time. *Faculty:* 20 full-time (9 women). *Students:* 28 full-time (13 women), 78 part-time (52 women); includes 9 minority (3 Black or African American, non-Hispanic/Latino; 1 Asian, non-Hispanic/Latino; 1 Hispanic/Latino; 4 Two or more races, non-Hispanic/Latino), 41 international. Average age 37. 113 applicants, 42% accepted, 13 enrolled. In 2016, 14 doctorates awarded. *Degree requirements:* For doctorate, one foreign language, comprehensive exam, thesis/dissertation. *Entrance requirements:* For doctorate, 2 letters of recommendation. Additional exam requirements/recommendations for international students: Required—TOEFL (minimum score 600 paper-based). *Application deadline:* For fall admission, 2/1 priority date for domestic students; for summer admission, 11/1 priority date for domestic students. Applications are processed on a rolling basis. Application fee: $50. Electronic applications accepted. *Expenses:* Contact institution. *Financial support:* In 2016–17, 18 research assistantships with tuition reimbursements (averaging $6,398 per year), 5 teaching assistantships with partial tuition reimbursements (averaging $11,652 per year) were awarded; fellowships with full tuition reimbursements, career-related internships or fieldwork, Federal Work-Study, scholarships/grants, and unspecified assistantships also available. Support available to part-time students. Financial award application deadline: 4/15; financial award applicants required to submit FAFSA. *Unit head:* Dr. Sharon Deckert, Graduate Coordinator, 724-357-2261, E-mail: sharon.deckert@iup.edu.
Website: http://www.iup.edu/english/grad/composition-tesol-phd/default.aspx

Indiana University of Pennsylvania, School of Graduate Studies and Research, College of Humanities and Social Sciences, Department of English, Program in Teaching English, Indiana, PA 15705. Offers MA. *Program availability:* Part-time. *Faculty:* 20 full-time (9 women). *Degree requirements:* For master's, thesis optional. *Entrance requirements:* For master's, two letters of recommendation. Additional exam requirements/recommendations for international students: Required—TOEFL (minimum score 540 paper-based). *Application deadline:* Applications are processed on a rolling basis. Application fee: $50. Electronic applications accepted. *Expenses:* Tuition, state resident: full-time $8694; part-time $483 per credit. Tuition, nonresident: full-time $13,050; part-time $725 per credit. *Required fees:* $157 per credit. $50 per term. Tuition and fees vary according to course load and program. *Financial support:* Fellowships with full tuition reimbursements, research assistantships with tuition reimbursements, career-related internships or fieldwork, Federal Work-Study, scholarships/grants, and unspecified assistantships available. Financial award application deadline: 4/15; financial award applicants required to submit FAFSA. *Unit head:* Dr. Linda Norris, Coordinator, 724-357-2263, E-mail: lnorris@iup.edu.
Website: http://www.iup.edu/english/grad/teaching-english-ma/default.aspx

Indiana University–Purdue University Fort Wayne, College of Arts and Sciences, Department of English and Linguistics, Fort Wayne, IN 46805-1499. Offers English (MA,

MAT); TENL (teaching English as a new language) (Certificate). *Program availability:* Part-time. *Degree requirements:* For master's, one foreign language, thesis (for some programs), teaching certificate (for MAT). *Entrance requirements:* For master's, GRE General Test, minimum GPA of 3.0, major or minor in English, 3 letters of recommendation; for Certificate, bachelor's degree with minimum GPA of 2.5. Additional exam requirements/recommendations for international students: Required—TOEFL (minimum score 600 paper-based; 79 iBT). *Faculty research:* Hebrew names and the vernacular Savior in Anglo-Saxon England.

Iona College, School of Arts and Science, Department of Education, New Rochelle, NY 10801-1890. Offers adolescence education: biology (MS Ed, MST); adolescence education: English (MS Ed); adolescence education: mathematics (MST); adolescence education: social studies (MS Ed, MST); adolescence education: Spanish (MS Ed); adolescence special education 5-12 (MST); childhood and special education (MST); early childhood and childhood (MST); educational leadership (MS Ed). *Accreditation:* NCATE. *Program availability:* Part-time, evening/weekend. *Faculty:* 7 full-time (6 women), 4 part-time/adjunct (2 women). *Students:* 27 full-time (19 women), 27 part-time (18 women); includes 18 minority (4 Black or African American, non-Hispanic/Latino; 1 Asian, non-Hispanic/Latino; 12 Hispanic/Latino; 1 Two or more races, non-Hispanic/Latino). Average age 26. 6 applicants, 67% accepted, 3 enrolled. In 2016, 25 master's awarded. *Degree requirements:* For master's, thesis or alternative. *Entrance requirements:* For master's, minimum GPA of 3.0, NY State teaching certificate and bachelor's degree (for MS Ed). Additional exam requirements/recommendations for international students: Required—TOEFL (minimum score 550 paper-based; 80 iBT), IELTS (minimum score 6.5). *Application deadline:* For fall admission, 8/1 priority date for domestic students, 5/1 priority date for international students; for spring admission, 1/1 priority date for domestic students, 9/1 priority date for international students. Applications are processed on a rolling basis. Application fee: $50. Electronic applications accepted. *Expenses: Tuition:* Full-time $19,692; part-time $1094 per credit. *Required fees:* $245 per term. Tuition and fees vary according to program. *Financial support:* In 2016–17, 3 students received support. Unspecified assistantships available. Support available to part-time students. Financial award application deadline: 4/15; financial award applicants required to submit FAFSA. *Faculty research:* Engaging teacher educators in scientific process, cross-national comparisons of mathematics teaching, questioning strategies in the classroom, research methods, literacy development. *Unit head:* Margaret Smith, PhD, Chair, 914-633-2210, Fax: 914-633-2608, E-mail: msmith@iona.edu. *Application contact:* Richard McMahon, Coordinator, Graduate School of Education, 914-633-2552, E-mail: rmcmahon@iona.edu.
Website: http://www.iona.edu/Academics/School-of-Arts-Science/Departments/Education/Graduate-Programs.aspx

Ithaca College, School of Humanities and Sciences, Program in Adolescence Education, Ithaca, NY 14850. Offers biology (MAT); chemistry (MAT); earth science (MAT); English (MAT); French (MAT); mathematics (MAT); physics (MAT); social studies (MAT); Spanish (MAT). *Program availability:* Part-time. *Faculty:* 26 full-time (12 women). *Students:* 11 full-time (4 women). Average age 26. 17 applicants, 94% accepted, 10 enrolled. *Degree requirements:* For master's, thesis or alternative. *Entrance requirements:* Additional exam requirements/recommendations for international students: Required—TOEFL (minimum score 550 paper-based; 80 iBT). *Application deadline:* For fall admission, 2/15 for domestic and international students; for spring admission, 12/1 for domestic and international students. Applications are processed on a rolling basis. Application fee: $40. Electronic applications accepted. *Expenses:* Contact institution. *Financial support:* In 2016–17, 5 students received support, including 5 research assistantships (averaging $13,259 per year); career-related internships or fieldwork, Federal Work-Study, scholarships/grants, and unspecified assistantships also available. Support available to part-time students. Financial award application deadline: 2/15; financial award applicants required to submit CSS PROFILE or FAFSA. *Unit head:* Peter Martin, Chair, 607-274-1076, E-mail: pmartin@ithaca.edu. *Application contact:* Nicole Eversley Bradwell, Director, Office of Admission, 607-274-3124, Fax: 607-274-1263, E-mail: admission@ithaca.edu.
Website: http://www.ithaca.edu/gradprograms/education/programs/aded

Jackson State University, Graduate School, College of Liberal Arts, Department of English and Modern Foreign Languages, Jackson, MS 39217. Offers English (MA); teaching English (MAT). *Program availability:* Part-time, evening/weekend. *Faculty:* 8 full-time (7 women). *Students:* 4 full-time (3 women); includes 1 minority (Black or African American, non-Hispanic/Latino), 1 international. Average age 26. 12 applicants, 75% accepted, 6 enrolled. In 2016, 14 master's awarded. *Degree requirements:* For master's, comprehensive exam, thesis or alternative. *Entrance requirements:* For master's, GRE General Test. Additional exam requirements/recommendations for international students: Required—TOEFL (minimum score 520 paper-based; 67 iBT). *Application deadline:* For fall admission, 3/1 priority date for domestic students, 3/1 for international students; for spring admission, 10/1 for domestic and international students. Applications are processed on a rolling basis. Application fee: $25. Electronic applications accepted. *Expenses:* Contact institution. *Financial support:* Career-related internships or fieldwork, Federal Work-Study, scholarships/grants, and unspecified assistantships available. Support available to part-time students. Financial award application deadline: 3/1; financial award applicants required to submit FAFSA. *Unit head:* Dr. Preselfannie McDaniels, Chair, 601-978-6928, Fax: 601-974-2249, E-mail: preselfannie.w.mcdaniels@jsums.edu. *Application contact:* Dr. Preselfannie McDaniels, Chair, 601-978-6928, Fax: 601-974-2249, E-mail: preselfannie.w.mcdaniels@jsums.edu.
Website: http://www.jsums.edu/english/

Kansas State University, Graduate School, College of Education, Department of Curriculum and Instruction, Manhattan, KS 66506. Offers curriculum and instruction (Ed D, PhD); digital teaching and learning (MS); educational computing, design and online learning (MS); elementary/middle level curriculum and instruction (MS); online learning (Certificate); reading specialist endorsement (MS); reading/language arts (MS); teacher leader/school improvement (MS); teaching and learning (Certificate). *Accreditation:* NCATE. *Program availability:* Part-time, online learning. *Faculty:* 36 full-time (22 women), 18 part-time/adjunct (9 women). *Students:* 59 full-time (40 women), 94 part-time (72 women); includes 21 minority (5 Black or African American, non-Hispanic/Latino; 3 Asian, non-Hispanic/Latino; 11 Hispanic/Latino; 2 Two or more races, non-Hispanic/Latino), 20 international. Average age 35. 70 applicants, 71% accepted, 36 enrolled. In 2016, 61 master's, 12 doctorates, 9 other advanced degrees awarded. *Degree requirements:* For master's, comprehensive exam, portfolio, project, report or thesis; for doctorate, comprehensive exam, thesis/dissertation, preliminary exam; for Certificate, comprehensive exam, portfolio. *Entrance requirements:* For master's, minimum GPA of 3.0, 3 letters of recommendation; for doctorate, GRE, minimum GPA of 3.0, 3 letters of recommendation, evidence of scholarly writing; for Certificate, minimum GPA of 3.0, letters of recommendation. Additional exam requirements/recommendations for international students: Required—TOEFL (minimum score 550 paper-based; 80 iBT) or IELTS. *Application deadline:* For fall admission, 3/1 priority date for domestic students, 2/1 priority date for international students; for spring admission, 10/1 priority date for domestic students, 8/1 priority date for international students. Applications are processed on a rolling basis. Application fee: $50 ($75 for international students). Electronic applications accepted. *Expenses:* Tuition, state resident: full-time $9670. Tuition, nonresident: full-time $21,828. *Required fees:* $862. *Financial support:* In 2016–17, 1 research assistantship (averaging $19,980 per year), 8 teaching assistantships (averaging $12,620 per year) were awarded; career-related internships or fieldwork, institutionally sponsored loans, scholarships/grants, and unspecified assistantships also available. Support available to part-time students. Financial award application deadline: 3/1; financial award applicants required to submit FAFSA. *Faculty research:* Literacy and technology, critical race theory and diversity, achievement gaps, school improvement, teacher education. *Total annual research expenditures:* $647,057. *Unit head:* Dr. F. Todd Goodson, Department Chair, 785-532-5904, Fax: 785-532-7304, E-mail: tgoodson@ksu.edu. *Application contact:* Dr. Kay Ann Taylor, Director, Curriculum and Instruction Graduate Programs, 785-532-6974, Fax: 785-532-7304, E-mail: ktaylor@ksu.edu.
Website: http://www.coe.ksu.edu/edci/index.html

Kennesaw State University, Leland and Clarice C. Bagwell College of Education, Program in Teaching, Kennesaw, GA 30144. Offers art education (MAT); biology (MAT); chemistry (MAT); foreign language education (Chinese and Spanish) (MAT); physics (MAT); secondary English (MAT); secondary mathematics (MAT); special education (MAT); teaching English to speakers of other languages (MAT). *Program availability:* Part-time, evening/weekend. *Entrance requirements:* For master's, GRE, GACE I (state certificate exam), minimum GPA of 2.75, 2 recommendations, resume. Additional exam requirements/recommendations for international students: Required—TOEFL (minimum score 550 paper-based; 80 iBT), IELTS (minimum score 6.5). Electronic applications accepted.

Kent State University, College of Arts and Sciences, Department of English, Kent, OH 44242-0001. Offers creative writing (MFA); English (MA, PhD); English for teachers (MA); literature and writing (MA); rhetoric and composition (PhD); teaching English as a second language (MA). MFA program offered jointly with Cleveland State University, The University of Akron, and Youngstown State University. *Program availability:* Part-time. *Faculty:* 45 full-time (29 women). *Students:* 111 full-time (75 women), 19 part-time (13 women); includes 8 minority (3 Black or African American, non-Hispanic/Latino; 1 Asian, non-Hispanic/Latino; 2 Hispanic/Latino; 2 Two or more races, non-Hispanic/Latino), 27 international. Average age 30. 98 applicants, 61% accepted, 19 enrolled. In 2016, 30 master's, 8 doctorates awarded. *Degree requirements:* For master's, one foreign language, thesis (for some programs), final portfolio, final exam, or thesis (for MA in teaching English as a second language); for doctorate, one foreign language, comprehensive exam, thesis/dissertation. *Entrance requirements:* For master's and doctorate, GRE General Test, statement of purpose, 3 letters of recommendation, writing sample or undergraduate/graduate paper, transcripts. Additional exam requirements/recommendations for international students: Required—TOEFL (minimum score of 600 paper-based, 100 iBT), IELTS (minimum score of 7.0), Michigan English Language Assessment Battery (minimum score of 85), or PTE (minimum score of 68). *Application deadline:* For fall admission, 1/15 for domestic and international students. Applications are processed on a rolling basis. Application fee: $45 ($70 for international students). Electronic applications accepted. *Expenses:* Tuition, state resident: full-time $10,864; part-time $495 per credit hour. Tuition, nonresident: full-time $18,380; part-time $837 per credit hour. *Financial support:* Fellowships with full tuition reimbursements, teaching assistantships with full tuition reimbursements, and unspecified assistantships available. Financial award application deadline: 1/15. *Unit head:* Dr. Robert Trogdon, Chair, 330-672-2676, E-mail: rtrogdon@kent.edu. *Application contact:* Kevin Floyd, Professor and Graduate Coordinator, 330-672-1708, E-mail: kfloyd@kent.edu.
Website: http://www.kent.edu/english/

Kutztown University of Pennsylvania, College of Education, Program in Secondary Education, Kutztown, PA 19530-0730. Offers biology (M Ed); curriculum and instruction (M Ed); English (M Ed); mathematics (M Ed); middle level (M Ed); social studies (M Ed); teaching (M Ed). *Accreditation:* NCATE. *Program availability:* Part-time, evening/weekend. *Faculty:* 4 full-time (2 women), 2 part-time/adjunct (0 women). *Students:* 35 full-time (23 women), 58 part-time (37 women); includes 4 minority (2 Black or African American, non-Hispanic/Latino; 2 Hispanic/Latino). Average age 31. 96 applicants, 86% accepted, 43 enrolled. In 2016, 35 master's awarded. *Degree requirements:* For master's, comprehensive exam, thesis optional. *Entrance requirements:* For master's, GRE General Test, minimum undergraduate major GPA of 3.0, 3 letters of recommendation, copy of PRAXIS II or valid instructional I or II teaching certificate. Additional exam requirements/recommendations for international students: Required—TOEFL (minimum score 550 paper-based, 79 iBT) or IELTS (minimum score 6.5). *Application deadline:* For fall admission, 8/1 for domestic and international students; for spring admission, 12/1 for domestic and international students. Application fee: $35. Electronic applications accepted. *Expenses:* Tuition, state resident: full-time $4347; part-time $483 per credit. Tuition, nonresident: full-time $6525; part-time $725 per credit. *Required fees:* $88 per credit. One-time fee: $50 full-time. *Financial support:* Career-related internships or fieldwork, Federal Work-Study, scholarships/grants, and unspecified assistantships available. Financial award application deadline: 3/1; financial award applicants required to submit FAFSA. *Unit head:* Dr. Theresa Stahler, Chairperson, 610-683-4259, Fax: 610-683-1338, E-mail: stahler@kutztown.edu. *Application contact:* Dr. Patricia Walsh Coates, Graduate Coordinator, 610-638-4289, Fax: 610-683-1338, E-mail: coates@kutztown.edu.
Website: https://www.kutztown.edu/academcs/graduate-programs/secondary-education.htm

Lake Forest College, Master of Arts in Teaching Program, Lake Forest, IL 60045. Offers elementary education (MAT); K-12 French (MAT); K-12 music (MAT); K-12 Spanish (MAT); K-12 visual art (MAT); secondary biology (MAT); secondary chemistry (MAT); secondary English (MAT); secondary history (MAT); secondary mathematics (MAT). *Degree requirements:* For master's, comprehensive exam, portfolio. *Entrance requirements:* For master's, GRE.

Lehman College of the City University of New York, School of Education, Department of Middle and High School Education, Program in English Education, Bronx, NY 10468-1589. Offers MS Ed. *Accreditation:* NCATE. *Entrance requirements:* For master's, minimum GPA of 3.0 in English, 2.8 overall; teaching certificate.

Le Moyne College, Department of Education, Syracuse, NY 13214. Offers adolescent education (MS Ed, MST); adolescent education/special education (MS Ed, MST); adolescent English (MST), including grades 7-12; adolescent English/special education (MST), including grades 7-12; adolescent foreign language (MST), including grades 7-12; adolescent history (MST), including grades 7-12; childhood education (MS Ed); childhood education/special education (MS Ed); elementary education (MS Ed); general education (MS Ed); inclusive childhood education (MST); literacy education (MS Ed), including birth to grade 6, grades 5-12; school building leader (MS Ed); school building leadership (CAS); school district business leader (MS Ed, CAS); school district leader (MS Ed); school district leadership (CAS); secondary education (MS Ed); special education (MS Ed); teaching English to speakers of other languages (MS Ed); urban studies (MS Ed). *Accreditation:* TEAC. *Program availability:* Part-time, evening/weekend. *Faculty:* 8 full-time (5 women), 20 part-time/adjunct (12 women). *Students:* 66 full-time (40 women), 155 part-time (117 women); includes 13 minority (4 Black or African American, non-Hispanic/Latino; 2 American Indian or Alaska Native, non-

Hispanic/Latino; 2 Asian, non-Hispanic/Latino; 5 Hispanic/Latino), 3 international. Average age 30. 74 applicants, 99% accepted, 66 enrolled. In 2016, 81 master's, 53 CASs awarded. *Degree requirements:* For master's, thesis. *Entrance requirements:* For master's, bachelor's degree with minimum undergraduate GPA of 3.0, 2 letters of recommendation, transcripts. Additional exam requirements/recommendations for international students: Required—TOEFL (minimum score 550 paper-based; 79 iBT); Recommended—IELTS (minimum score 6.5). *Application deadline:* For fall admission, 4/1 priority date for domestic and international students; for spring admission, 10/1 priority date for domestic and international students; for summer admission, 3/1 priority date for domestic and international students. Applications are processed on a rolling basis. Application fee: $50. Electronic applications accepted. *Expenses:* $700 per credit hour. *Financial support:* In 2016–17, 21 students received support. Career-related internships or fieldwork, scholarships/grants, and health care benefits available. Support available to part-time students. Financial award applicants required to submit FAFSA. *Faculty research:* Minority teachers, special education, multiculturalism, literacy, technology, media literacy learning, autism, school district organization, service-learning, higher level problem solving, teacher leadership. *Unit head:* Dr. Stephen C. Fleury, Chair, Department of Education, 315-445-4376, Fax: 315-445-4744, E-mail: fleurysc@lemoyne.edu. *Application contact:* Kristen P. Richards, Senior Director of Enrollment Management, 315-445-5444, Fax: 315-445-6092, E-mail: trapaskp@lemoyne.edu.
Website: http://www.lemoyne.edu/education

Lewis University, College of Education, Program in Secondary Education, Romeoville, IL 60446. Offers biology (MA); chemistry (MA); English (MA); history (MA); math (MA); physics (MA); psychology and social science (MA). *Program availability:* Part-time. *Students:* 12 full-time (7 women), 16 part-time (12 women); includes 6 minority (2 Black or African American, non-Hispanic/Latino; 3 Hispanic/Latino; 1 Two or more races, non-Hispanic/Latino). Average age 27. *Degree requirements:* For master's, departmental qualifying exam. *Entrance requirements:* For master's, writing exam, minimum GPA of 2.75, 2 letters of recommendation, interview. Additional exam requirements/recommendations for international students: Required—TOEFL (minimum score 550 paper-based; 80 iBT). *Application deadline:* For fall admission, 5/1 priority date for international students; for spring admission, 11/15 priority date for international students. Applications are processed on a rolling basis. Application fee: $40. Electronic applications accepted. *Expenses: Tuition:* Full-time $13,860; part-time $770 per credit hour. *Required fees:* $75 per semester. Tuition and fees vary according to degree level and program. *Financial support:* Federal Work-Study, scholarships/grants, and unspecified assistantships available. Financial award application deadline: 5/1; financial award applicants required to submit FAFSA. *Unit head:* Dr. Dorene Huvaere, Program Director, 815-838-0500 Ext. 5885, E-mail: huvaersdo@lewisu.edu. *Application contact:* Linda Campbell, Graduate Admissions Counselor, 815-836-5610, E-mail: campbeld@lewisu.edu.

Lincoln Memorial University, Carter and Moyers School of Education, Harrogate, TN 37752-1901. Offers administration and supervision (M Ed, Ed S); counseling and guidance (M Ed); curriculum and instruction (M Ed, Ed D, Ed S); English (M Ed); executive leadership (Ed D); higher education administration (Ed D); human resource development (Ed D); leadership and administration (Ed D). *Program availability:* Part-time, evening/weekend, online learning. *Degree requirements:* For master's, comprehensive exam, thesis optional; for Ed S, comprehensive exam. *Entrance requirements:* For master's, PRAXIS, NTE, GRE, MAT, letters of recommendation; for Ed S, graduate transcripts. Additional exam requirements/recommendations for international students: Recommended—TOEFL. *Faculty research:* Brain compatible teaching and learning; poverty in Appalachia; leadership for change; ethics, moral responsibility and social justice; human and organizational learning.

Lipscomb University, College of Education, Nashville, TN 37204-3951. Offers applied behavior analysis (MS, Certificate); educational leadership (M Ed, Ed S); English language learning (M Ed, Ed S); instructional coaching (M Ed, Certificate, Ed S); instructional practice (M Ed); learning organizations and strategic change (Ed D); literacy coaching (Certificate); reading specialty (M Ed, Ed S); special education (M Ed); teaching, learning, and leading (M Ed); technology integration (M Ed, Ed S); technology integration specialist (Certificate). *Accreditation:* NCATE. *Program availability:* Part-time, evening/weekend, 100% online. *Faculty:* 21 full-time (15 women), 38 part-time/adjunct (26 women). *Students:* 111 full-time (80 women), 345 part-time (292 women); includes 104 minority (70 Black or African American, non-Hispanic/Latino; 1 American Indian or Alaska Native, non-Hispanic/Latino; 3 Asian, non-Hispanic/Latino; 20 Hispanic/Latino; 10 Two or more races, non-Hispanic/Latino), 1 international. Average age 33. In 2016, 201 master's, 36 doctorates, 86 other advanced degrees awarded. *Degree requirements:* For master's, comprehensive exam, portfolio, research project and presentation; for doctorate, practical capstone project in experiential setting. *Entrance requirements:* For master's, MAT (minimum score 31) or GRE General Test (minimum score 294), 2 reference letters, goals statement, writing sample, interview; for doctorate, MAT or GRE General Test, 3 reference letters, artifact of demonstrated academic excellence, written personal statements, interview. Additional exam requirements/recommendations for international students: Required—TOEFL (minimum score 570 paper-based; 80 iBT). *Application deadline:* For fall admission, 8/29 priority date for domestic students; for spring admission, 1/15 priority date for domestic students. Applications are processed on a rolling basis. Application fee: $50 ($75 for international students). Electronic applications accepted. *Expenses:* $934 per hour; $570 per hour (Teach for America). *Financial support:* Scholarships/grants, unspecified assistantships, and partnerships with local school districts available. Financial award applicants required to submit FAFSA. *Faculty research:* Facilitative learning styles, leadership, student assessment, interactive multimedia inclusion, learning organizations and strategic change. *Unit head:* Dr. Deborah Boyd, Director of Graduate Studies, 615-966-6263, E-mail: deborah.boyd@lipscomb.edu. *Application contact:* Amanda Logsdon, Director of Enrollment and Outreach, 615-966-7199, E-mail: amanda.logsdon@lipscomb.edu.
Website: http://www.lipscomb.edu/education/graduate-programs

London Metropolitan University, Graduate Programs, London, United Kingdom. Offers applied psychology (M Sc); architecture (MA); biomedical science (M Sc); blood science (M Sc); cancer pharmacology (M Sc); computer networking and cyber security (M Sc); computing and information systems (M Sc); conference interpreting (MA); counter-terrorism studies (M Sc); creative, digital and professional writing (MA); crime, violence and prevention (M Sc); criminology (M Sc); curating contemporary art (MA); data analytics (M Sc); digital media (MA); early childhood studies (MA); education (MA, Ed D); financial services law, regulation and compliance (LL M); food science (M Sc); forensic psychology (M Sc); health and social care management and policy (M Sc); human nutrition (M Sc); human resource management (MA); human rights and international conflict (MA); information technology (M Sc); intelligence and security studies (M Sc); international oil, gas and energy law (LL M); international relations (MA); interpreting (MA); learning and teaching in higher education (MA); legal practice (LL M); media and entertainment law (LL M); organizational and consumer psychology (M Sc); psychological therapy (M Sc); psychology of mental health (M Sc); public health (M Sc); public policy and management (MPA); security studies (M Sc); social work (M Sc); spatial planning and urban design (MA); sports therapy (M Sc); supporting older children and young people with dyslexia (MA); teaching languages (MA), including Arabic, English; translation (MA); woman and child abuse (MA).

Manhattanville College, School of Education, Program in Middle Childhood/Adolescence Education (Grades 5-12), Purchase, NY 10577-2132. Offers biology (MAT); biology and special education (MPS); chemistry (MAT); chemistry and special education (MPS); English (MAT); English and special education (MPS); literacy and special education (MPS); literacy specialist (MPS); math and special education (MPS); mathematics (MAT); physics (MAT); social studies (MAT); social studies and special education (MPS); special education generalist (MPS); teaching languages other than English (MAT), including French, Italian, Latin, Spanish. *Program availability:* Part-time, evening/weekend. *Students:* 28 applicants, 86% accepted, 21 enrolled. In 2016, 23 master's awarded. *Degree requirements:* For master's, comprehensive exam (for some programs), thesis (for some programs), student teaching, research seminars, portfolios, internships, writing assessment. *Entrance requirements:* For master's, GRE or MAT, minimum undergraduate GPA of 3.0, 2 letters of recommendation. Additional exam requirements/recommendations for international students: Required—TOEFL (minimum score 85 iBT); Recommended—IELTS. *Application deadline:* For fall admission, 7/1 priority date for domestic and international students; for spring admission, 11/1 priority date for domestic and international students; for summer admission, 4/1 priority date for domestic and international students. Applications are processed on a rolling basis. Application fee: $75. Electronic applications accepted. *Expenses: Tuition:* Full-time $16,470; part-time $915 per credit. *Required fees:* $60 per semester. Part-time tuition and fees vary according to course load and program. *Financial support:* Teaching assistantships, career-related internships or fieldwork, Federal Work-Study, institutionally sponsored loans, scholarships/grants, and unspecified assistantships available. Financial award applicants required to submit FAFSA. *Unit head:* Victoria Fantozzi, Chairperson, Department of Curriculum and Instruction, 914-323-7138, E-mail: victoria.fantozzi@mville.edu. *Application contact:* Jeanine Pardey-Levine, Director of Graduate Enrollment Management, 914-323-3208, Fax: 914-694-1732, E-mail: edschool@mville.edu.
Website: http://www.mville.edu/programs#/search/19

Marymount University, School of Arts and Sciences, Program in English and the Humanities, Arlington, VA 22207-4299. Offers English and humanities (MA); teaching English at the community college (Certificate). *Program availability:* Part-time, evening/weekend. *Faculty:* 5 full-time (2 women). *Students:* 1 (woman) full-time, 7 part-time (4 women); includes 2 minority (both Two or more races, non-Hispanic/Latino), 1 international. Average age 28. 4 applicants, 75% accepted, 2 enrolled. In 2016, 2 master's, 2 other advanced degrees awarded. *Degree requirements:* For master's, thesis, capstone (final project, practicum). *Entrance requirements:* For master's, 2 letters of recommendation, resume, minimum undergraduate GPA of 3.0 with major in English or other humanities discipline, writing samples of 8-10 pages. Additional exam requirements/recommendations for international students: Required—TOEFL (minimum score 600 paper-based; 96 iBT), IELTS (minimum score 6.5). *Application deadline:* Applications are processed on a rolling basis. Application fee: $40. Electronic applications accepted. *Expenses: Tuition:* Full-time $8460; part-time $940 per credit hour. *Required fees:* $10 per credit hour. One-time fee: $240 part-time. Tuition and fees vary according to program. *Financial support:* In 2016–17, 1 student received support, including 1 teaching assistantship with tuition reimbursement available; career-related internships or fieldwork, Federal Work-Study, scholarships/grants, and unspecified assistantships also available. Support available to part-time students. Financial award applicants required to submit FAFSA. *Unit head:* Dr. David Brown, Director, English and the Humanities, 703-284-5762, Fax: 703-284-3859, E-mail: david.brown@marymount.edu. *Application contact:* Francesca Reed, Director, Graduate Admissions, 703-284-5901, Fax: 703-527-3815, E-mail: grad.admissions@marymount.edu.
Website: http://www.marymount.edu/Academics/School-of-Arts-Sciences/Graduate-Programs/English-Humanities-(M-A-)

Mississippi College, Graduate School, School of Education, Department of Teacher Education and Leadership, Clinton, MS 39058. Offers art (M Ed); biological science (M Ed); business education (M Ed); computer science (M Ed); dyslexia therapy (M Ed); educational leadership (M Ed, Ed D, Ed S); elementary education (M Ed, Ed S); English (M Ed); higher education administration (MS); mathematics (M Ed); secondary education (M Ed); social studies (history) (M Ed); teaching arts (M Ed). *Program availability:* Part-time, online learning. *Degree requirements:* For master's, comprehensive exam, thesis optional. *Entrance requirements:* For master's, NTE. Additional exam requirements/recommendations for international students: Recommended—TOEFL, IELTS. Electronic applications accepted.

Missouri State University, Graduate College, College of Arts and Letters, Department of English, Springfield, MO 65897. Offers applied second language acquisition (MASLA); English (MA); English education (MS Ed); teaching English to speakers of other languages (Certificate); writing (MA). MASLA offered with the Department of Modern and Classical Languages. *Program availability:* Part-time, evening/weekend. *Faculty:* 25 full-time (18 women), 5 part-time/adjunct (2 women). *Students:* 47 full-time (34 women), 44 part-time (32 women); includes 4 minority (1 Asian, non-Hispanic/Latino; 3 Two or more races, non-Hispanic/Latino), 17 international. Average age 29. 79 applicants, 63% accepted, 27 enrolled. In 2016, 49 master's awarded. *Degree requirements:* For master's, one foreign language, comprehensive exam, thesis or alternative. *Entrance requirements:* For master's, GRE (for MA), 9-12 teacher certification (MS Ed); minimum GPA of 3.0 (MA); personal statement (200- to 250-word description of reasons and goals behind interest in English graduate studies); at least two letters of recommendation from individuals able to speak of the applicant's academic achievements and potential; writing sample. Additional exam requirements/recommendations for international students: Required—TOEFL (minimum score 550 paper-based; 79 iBT), IELTS (minimum score 6). *Application deadline:* For fall admission, 3/1 priority date for domestic students, 3/1 for international students; for spring admission, 10/1 priority date for domestic students, 10/1 for international students. Applications are processed on a rolling basis. Application fee: $35 ($50 for international students). Electronic applications accepted. *Expenses:* Tuition, state resident: full-time $5830. Tuition, nonresident: full-time $10,708. *Required fees:* $1130. Tuition and fees vary according to class time, course level, course load and program. *Financial support:* In 2016–17, 2 teaching assistantships with full tuition reimbursements (averaging $8,772 per year) were awarded; Federal Work-Study, institutionally sponsored loans, scholarships/grants, and unspecified assistantships also available. Financial award application deadline: 3/31; financial award applicants required to submit FAFSA. *Faculty research:* History of rhetoric, modern poetry, African-American literature, digital writing, teaching English to speakers of other languages. *Unit head:* Dr. W. D. Blackmon, Department Head, 417-836-5107, Fax: 417-836-6940, E-mail: english@missouristate.edu. *Application contact:* Michael Edwards, Coordinator of Graduate Admissions, 417-836-5330, Fax: 417-836-6200, E-mail: michaeledwards@missouristate.edu.
Website: http://english.missouristate.edu/

Montclair State University, The Graduate School, College of Education and Human Services, MAT Program in Teaching, Montclair, NJ 07043-1624. Offers art (MAT); biology (MAT); chemistry (MAT); earth science (MAT); English (MAT); French (MAT);

health and physical education (MAT); health education (MAT); mathematics (MAT); music (MAT); physical education (MAT); physical science (MAT); social studies (MAT); Spanish (MAT); teacher of English as a second language (MAT). *Degree requirements:* For master's, comprehensive exam, thesis or alternative. *Entrance requirements:* For master's, interview, 2 letters of recommendation. Additional exam requirements/recommendations for international students: Required—TOEFL (minimum score 83 iBT), IELTS (minimum score 6.5). Electronic applications accepted. *Expenses:* Tuition, state resident: part-time $553 per credit. Tuition, nonresident: part-time $854 per credit. *Required fees:* $91 per credit. Tuition and fees vary according to program.

Montclair State University, The Graduate School, College of Humanities and Social Sciences, Teaching Writing Certificate Program, Montclair, NJ 07043-1624. Offers Certificate. *Program availability:* Part-time, evening/weekend. *Entrance requirements:* For degree, 2 letters of recommendation, essay. Additional exam requirements/recommendations for international students: Required—TOEFL (minimum score 83 iBT), IELTS (minimum score 6.5). Electronic applications accepted. *Expenses:* Tuition, state resident: part-time $553 per credit. Tuition, nonresident: part-time $854 per credit. *Required fees:* $91 per credit. Tuition and fees vary according to program. *Faculty research:* Pedagogy in writing.

Morehead State University, Graduate Programs, College of Education, Department of Foundational and Graduate Studies in Education, Morehead, KY 40351. Offers adult and higher education (MA, Ed S); certified professional counselor (Ed S); counseling P-12 (MA); curriculum and instruction (Ed S); educational technology (MA Ed); instructional leadership (Ed S); school administration (MA); school counseling (Ed S); teacher leader business and marketing content (MA Ed); teacher leader business and marketing technology (MA Ed); teacher leader educational technology (MA Ed); teacher leader English (MA Ed); teacher leader gifted education (MA Ed); teacher leader IECE certification (MA Ed); teacher leader interdisciplinary education P-5 (MA Ed); teacher leader middle grades (MA Ed); teacher leader non IECE certification (MA Ed); teacher leader reading/writing - non-certification (MA Ed); teacher leader reading/writing certification (MA Ed); teacher leader school communication - certification (MA Ed); teacher leader school communication - non-certification (MA Ed); teacher leader social studies (MA Ed); teacher leader special education (MA Ed). *Accreditation:* NCATE. *Program availability:* Part-time, evening/weekend. *Degree requirements:* For master's, thesis optional, oral and/or written comprehensive exams; for Ed S, thesis, oral exam. *Entrance requirements:* For master's, GRE General Test, minimum overall undergraduate GPA of 2.5; for Ed S, GRE General Test, interview, master's degree, minimum GPA of 3.5, work experience. Additional exam requirements/recommendations for international students: Required—TOEFL (minimum score 500 paper-based). Electronic applications accepted. *Faculty research:* Character education, school accountability, computer applications for school administrators.

Morehead State University, Graduate Programs, College of Education, Department of Middle Grades and Secondary Education, Morehead, KY 40351. Offers business and marketing education (MAT); English/language arts 5-9 (MAT); French (MAT); health P-12 (MAT); mathematics 5-9 (MAT); physical education P-12 (MAT); science 5-9 (MAT); secondary biology (MAT); secondary chemistry (MAT); secondary earth science (MAT); secondary English (MAT); secondary math (MAT); secondary physics (MAT); secondary social studies (MAT); social studies 5-9 (MAT); Spanish (MAT). *Program availability:* Part-time, evening/weekend. *Degree requirements:* For master's, portfolio. *Entrance requirements:* For master's, GRE or PRAXIS II content exam, minimum overall undergraduate GPA of 2.5. Additional exam requirements/recommendations for international students: Required—TOEFL (minimum score 500 paper-based). Electronic applications accepted.

National Louis University, National College of Education, Chicago, IL 60603. Offers administration and supervision (M Ed, Ed D, CAS, Ed S); curriculum and instruction (M Ed, MS Ed, CAS); early childhood administration (M Ed, CAS); early childhood education (M Ed, MAT, MS Ed, CAS); education (Ed D); educational psychology/human learning and development (M Ed, MS Ed, CAS, Ed S); elementary education (MAT); interdisciplinary curriculum and instruction (M Ed); mathematics education (M Ed, MS Ed, CAS); middle grades education (MAT); reading and language (M Ed, MS Ed, CAS); school psychology (M Ed, Ed S); science education (M Ed, MS Ed, CAS); secondary education (MAT); special education (M Ed, MAT, CAS); technology in education (M Ed, CAS). *Accreditation:* NCATE. *Program availability:* Part-time, evening/weekend. *Degree requirements:* For doctorate, comprehensive exam, thesis/dissertation. *Entrance requirements:* For master's, MAT or GRE, minimum GPA of 3.0; for doctorate, GRE General Test, minimum GPA of 3.25, interview, resume, writing sample, 4 recommendations. Additional exam requirements/recommendations for international students: Required—TOEFL (minimum score 550 paper-based; 79 iBT).

New Mexico State University, College of Arts and Sciences, Department of English, Las Cruces, NM 88003. Offers creative writing (MFA); English (MA), including creative writing, English studies for teachers, literature, rhetoric and professional communication; rhetoric and professional communication (PhD). *Program availability:* Part-time. *Faculty:* 19 full-time (9 women), 1 (woman) part-time/adjunct. *Students:* 48 full-time (33 women), 24 part-time (14 women); includes 19 minority (2 Asian, non-Hispanic/Latino; 15 Hispanic/Latino; 2 Two or more races, non-Hispanic/Latino), 6 international. Average age 34. 90 applicants, 32% accepted, 19 enrolled. In 2016, 21 master's, 5 doctorates awarded. *Degree requirements:* For master's, one foreign language, thesis (for some programs); for doctorate, comprehensive exam, thesis/dissertation, internship. *Entrance requirements:* For master's and doctorate, sample of written work. Additional exam requirements/recommendations for international students: Required—TOEFL (minimum score 550 paper-based; 79 iBT), IELTS (minimum score 6.5). *Application deadline:* For fall admission, 2/1 for domestic and international students. Application fee: $40 ($50 for international students). Electronic applications accepted. *Expenses:* Tuition, state resident: full-time $4086. Tuition, nonresident: full-time $14,254. *Required fees:* $853. Tuition and fees vary according to course load. *Financial support:* In 2016–17, 47 students received support, including 42 teaching assistantships (averaging $17,394 per year); career-related internships or fieldwork, Federal Work-Study, scholarships/grants, traineeships, health care benefits, and unspecified assistantships also available. Support available to part-time students. Financial award application deadline: 3/1. *Faculty research:* Composition research, history and theory of rhetoric, technical/professional communication, creative writing, English and American literature. *Total annual research expenditures:* $10,316. *Unit head:* Dr. Barry L. Thatcher, Department Head, 575-646-3931, Fax: 575-646-7725, E-mail: bathatch@nmsu.edu. *Application contact:* Dr. Tracey Eileen Miller-Tomlinson, Director of Graduate Studies, 575-646-2213, Fax: 575-646-7725, E-mail: tomlin@nmsu.edu.
Website: http://english.nmsu.edu

New York University, Steinhardt School of Culture, Education, and Human Development, Department of Music and Performing Arts Professions, Program in Educational Theatre, New York, NY 10012. Offers educational theatre and English 7-12 (MA); educational theatre and social studies 7-12 (MA); educational theatre in colleges and communities (MA, Ed D, PhD); educational theatre, all grades (MA). *Program availability:* Part-time. *Degree requirements:* For master's, thesis (for some programs); for doctorate, thesis/dissertation. *Entrance requirements:* For master's, audition; for doctorate, GRE General Test, interview. Additional exam requirements/recommendations for international students: Required—TOEFL (minimum score 100 iBT). Electronic applications accepted. *Faculty research:* Theatre for young audiences, drama in education, applied theatre, arts education assessment, reflective praxis.

New York University, Steinhardt School of Culture, Education, and Human Development, Department of Teaching and Learning, Program in English Education, New York, NY 10012-1019. Offers clinically-based English education, grades 7-12 (MA); English education (PhD, Advanced Certificate); English education, grades 7-12 (MA). *Accreditation:* TEAC. *Program availability:* Part-time. *Degree requirements:* For master's, thesis (for some programs); for doctorate, thesis/dissertation. *Entrance requirements:* For doctorate, GRE General Test, interview; for Advanced Certificate, master's degree. Additional exam requirements/recommendations for international students: Required—TOEFL (minimum score 100 iBT). Electronic applications accepted. *Faculty research:* Making meaning of literature, teaching of literature, urban adolescent literacy and equity, literacy development and globalization, digital media and literacy.

North Carolina Agricultural and Technical State University, School of Graduate Studies, College of Arts and Sciences, Department of English, Greensboro, NC 27411. Offers English (MA); English and African-American literature (MA); English education (MAT, MS). *Program availability:* Part-time, evening/weekend. *Degree requirements:* For master's, comprehensive exam, qualifying exam. *Entrance requirements:* For master's, GRE General Test, minimum GPA of 3.0.

North Carolina State University, Graduate School, College of Education, Department of Curriculum and Instruction, Program in Secondary English Education, Raleigh, NC 27695. Offers M Ed, MS Ed. *Degree requirements:* For master's, thesis optional.

Northern Arizona University, Graduate College, College of Arts and Letters, Department of English, Flagstaff, AZ 86011. Offers applied linguistics (PhD); creative writing (MFA), including creative writing; English (MA), including English education, literature, professional writing, rhetoric, writing, and digital media studies; professional writing (Certificate); teaching English as a second language (MA, Certificate). *Program availability:* Part-time. *Degree requirements:* For master's, comprehensive exam (for some programs), thesis (for some programs), departmental qualifying exam; for doctorate, comprehensive exam, thesis/dissertation, departmental qualifying exam. *Entrance requirements:* For master's, minimum GPA of 3.0 or GRE; for doctorate, GRE General Test. Additional exam requirements/recommendations for international students: Required—TOEFL (minimum score 550 paper-based; 80 iBT), IELTS (minimum score 7), TOEFL (minimum score 600 paper-based; 100 iBT) for PhD; TOEFL (minimum score 570 paper-based; 89 iBT) for MA. Electronic applications accepted. *Expenses:* Tuition, state resident: full-time $8971; part-time $444 per credit hour. Tuition, nonresident: full-time $20,958; part-time $1164 per credit hour. *Required fees:* $1018; $644 per credit hour. Tuition and fees vary according to course load, campus/location and program.

Northwest Missouri State University, Graduate School, College of Arts and Sciences, Maryville, MO 64468-6001. Offers biology (MS); elementary mathematics specialist (MS Ed); English (MA); English education (MS Ed); English pedagogy (MA); geographic information science (MS, Certificate); history (MS Ed); mathematics (MS); mathematics education (MS Ed); teaching: science (MS Ed). *Program availability:* Part-time. *Students:* 12 full-time (8 women), 69 part-time (31 women). *Degree requirements:* For master's, comprehensive exam. *Entrance requirements:* For master's, GRE General Test, writing sample. Additional exam requirements/recommendations for international students: Required—TOEFL (minimum score 550 paper-based). *Application deadline:* For fall admission, 7/1 for domestic and international students; for spring admission, 11/15 for domestic and international students. Applications are processed on a rolling basis. Application fee: $0 ($50 for international students). Electronic applications accepted. *Expenses:* Tuition, state resident: full-time $3447; part-time $383 per credit hour. Tuition, nonresident: full-time $5724; part-time $636 per credit hour. *Required fees:* $130 per credit hour. *Financial support:* Research assistantships with full tuition reimbursements, teaching assistantships with full tuition reimbursements, and administrative assistantships, tutorial assistantships available. Financial award application deadline: 4/1; financial award applicants required to submit FAFSA. *Unit head:* Dr. Michael Steiner, Dean, 660-562-1197.
Website: http://www.nwmissouri.edu/academics/arts/

Oregon State University, College of Education, Program in Teaching, Corvallis, OR 97331. Offers clinically based elementary education (MAT); elementary education (MAT); language arts (MAT); mathematics (MAT); music education (MAT); science (MAT); social studies (MAT). *Program availability:* Part-time, blended/hybrid learning. *Faculty:* 17 full-time (8 women), 2 part-time/adjunct (both women). *Students:* 57 full-time (39 women), 22 part-time (18 women); includes 11 minority (2 Hispanic/Latino; 1 Native Hawaiian or other Pacific Islander, non-Hispanic/Latino; 8 Two or more races, non-Hispanic/Latino). Average age 29. 131 applicants, 76% accepted, 76 enrolled. In 2016, 92 master's awarded. *Entrance requirements:* For master's, CBEST. Additional exam requirements/recommendations for international students: Required—TOEFL (minimum score 575 paper-based). *Application deadline:* For fall admission, 12/1 for domestic students. Application fee: $60. *Expenses:* Contact institution. *Unit head:* Dr. Larry Flick, Dean. *Application contact:* E-mail: askcoed@oregonstate.edu.
Website: http://education.oregonstate.edu/mat

Plymouth State University, College of Graduate Studies, Graduate Studies in Education, Program in English Education, Plymouth, NH 03264-1595. Offers M Ed. *Program availability:* Part-time, evening/weekend. *Degree requirements:* For master's, capstone, research, or thesis. *Entrance requirements:* For master's, MAT.

Purdue University, Graduate School, College of Education, Department of Curriculum and Instruction, West Lafayette, IN 47907. Offers agricultural and extension education (MS, MS Ed, PhD, Ed S); art education (PhD); career and technical education (MS Ed, PhD, Ed S); curriculum studies (MS Ed, PhD, Ed S); educational technology (MS Ed, PhD, Ed S); elementary education (MS Ed); family and consumer sciences education (MS Ed, PhD, Ed S); foreign language education (MS Ed, PhD, Ed S); industrial technology (PhD, Ed S); language arts (MS Ed, PhD, Ed S); literacy (MS Ed, PhD, Ed S); mathematics education (MS, MS Ed, PhD, Ed S); science education (MS, MS Ed, PhD, Ed S); social studies education (MS Ed, PhD, Ed S). *Accreditation:* NCATE. *Program availability:* Part-time, evening/weekend. *Faculty:* 37 full-time (27 women), 1 (woman) part-time/adjunct. *Students:* 78 full-time (50 women), 286 part-time (195 women); includes 68 minority (25 Black or African American, non-Hispanic/Latino; 3 American Indian or Alaska Native, non-Hispanic/Latino; 10 Asian, non-Hispanic/Latino; 22 Hispanic/Latino; 1 Native Hawaiian or other Pacific Islander, non-Hispanic/Latino; 7 Two or more races, non-Hispanic/Latino), 44 international. Average age 36. 150 applicants, 79% accepted, 73 enrolled. In 2016, 107 master's, 20 doctorates, 2 other advanced degrees awarded. *Degree requirements:* For master's, thesis optional; for doctorate, thesis/dissertation, oral and written exams; for Ed S, oral presentation, project. *Entrance requirements:* For master's, GRE General Test (if undergraduate GPA is below 3.0), minimum undergraduate GPA of 3.0 or equivalent; for doctorate, GRE General Test (minimum combined verbal and quantitative score of 1000, 300 for new scoring), minimum undergraduate GPA of 3.0 or equivalent; master's degree with minimum GPA of 3.0 or equivalent; for Ed S, GRE General Test (minimum combined

verbal and quantitative score of 1000, 300 for new scoring), minimum undergraduate GPA of 3.0 or equivalent; master's degree. Additional exam requirements/recommendations for international students: Required—TOEFL (minimum score 550 paper-based; 77 iBT). *Application deadline:* For fall admission, 12/15 for domestic students, 3/1 for international students; for spring admission, 9/15 for domestic students, 8/1 for international students. Application fee: $60 ($75 for international students). Electronic applications accepted. *Financial support:* Fellowships with full tuition reimbursements, research assistantships with full tuition reimbursements, teaching assistantships with full tuition reimbursements, career-related internships or fieldwork, and tuition waivers (full) available. Support available to part-time students. Financial award application deadline: 3/1; financial award applicants required to submit FAFSA. *Faculty research:* Literacy acquisition and development, teacher beliefs and knowledge, recruitment and retention of underrepresented students, economic education, literacy discourse. *Unit head:* Janet M. Alsup, Head, 765-494-9667, E-mail: alsupj@purdue.edu. *Application contact:* Heather Brinkman, Graduate Contact, 765-494-2345, E-mail: hbrinkma@purdue.edu.
Website: http://www.edci.purdue.edu/

Queens College of the City University of New York, Arts and Humanities Division, Department of Linguistics and Communication Disorders, Queens, NY 11367-1597. Offers applied linguistics (MA); English language teaching (Advanced Certificate); speech-language pathology (MA); teaching English to speakers of other languages (MS Ed); TESOL (MS Ed); TESOL and bilingual education (MS Ed). *Accreditation:* ASHA. *Program availability:* Part-time. *Faculty:* 22 full-time (16 women), 19 part-time/adjunct (13 women). *Students:* 44 full-time (42 women), 123 part-time (107 women); includes 64 minority (11 Black or African American, non-Hispanic/Latino; 20 Asian, non-Hispanic/Latino; 31 Hispanic/Latino; 2 Two or more races, non-Hispanic/Latino), 4 international. Average age 28. 390 applicants, 25% accepted, 81 enrolled. In 2016, 71 master's, 30 other advanced degrees awarded. *Entrance requirements:* For master's, minimum GPA of 3.0. Additional exam requirements/recommendations for international students: Required—TOEFL, IELTS. *Application deadline:* For fall admission, 4/1 for domestic students. Applications are processed on a rolling basis. Application fee: $125. Electronic applications accepted. *Expenses:* Tuition, state resident: full-time $5065; part-time $425 per credit. Tuition, nonresident: part-time $780 per credit. *Required fees:* $522; $397 per credit. Part-time tuition and fees vary according to course load and program. *Financial support:* Career-related internships or fieldwork available. Financial award application deadline: 4/1; financial award applicants required to submit FAFSA. *Unit head:* Dr. Robert Vago, Chairperson, 718-997-2875, E-mail: robert.vago@qc.cuny.edu.

Queens College of the City University of New York, Division of Education, Department of Secondary Education and Youth Services, Queens, NY 11367-1597. Offers adolescent biology (MAT); art (MS Ed); biology (MS Ed, AC); chemistry (MS Ed, AC); earth sciences (MS Ed, AC); English (MS Ed, AC); French (MS Ed); Italian (MS Ed, AC); literacy education (MS Ed); mathematics (MS Ed, AC); music (MS Ed, AC); physics (MS Ed, AC); social studies (MS Ed, AC); Spanish (MS Ed, AC). *Program availability:* Part-time, evening/weekend. *Faculty:* 22 full-time (14 women), 40 part-time/adjunct (26 women). *Students:* 31 full-time (21 women), 356 part-time (211 women); includes 164 minority (22 Black or African American, non-Hispanic/Latino; 54 Asian, non-Hispanic/Latino; 81 Hispanic/Latino; 7 Two or more races, non-Hispanic/Latino), 11 international. Average age 29. 236 applicants, 88% accepted, 121 enrolled. In 2016, 119 master's, 51 other advanced degrees awarded. *Degree requirements:* For master's, research project. *Entrance requirements:* For master's, minimum GPA of 3.0. Additional exam requirements/recommendations for international students: Required—TOEFL, IELTS. *Application deadline:* For fall admission, 4/1 for domestic students; for spring admission, 11/1 for domestic students. Applications are processed on a rolling basis. Application fee: $125. Electronic applications accepted. *Expenses:* Tuition, state resident: full-time $5065; part-time $425 per credit. Tuition, nonresident: part-time $780 per credit. *Required fees:* $522; $397 per credit. Part-time tuition and fees vary according to course load and program. *Financial support:* Career-related internships or fieldwork available. Financial award application deadline: 4/1; financial award applicants required to submit FAFSA. *Unit head:* Dr. Eleanor Armour-Thomas, Chairperson, 718-997-5150, E-mail: armourthomas@yahoo.com.

Quinnipiac University, School of Education, Program in Secondary Education, Hamden, CT 06518-1940. Offers biology (MAT); English (MAT); history/social studies (MAT); mathematics (MAT); Spanish (MAT). *Accreditation:* NCATE. *Faculty:* 6 full-time (2 women), 24 part-time/adjunct (16 women). *Students:* 43 full-time (29 women), 1 part-time (0 women); includes 6 minority (1 Asian, non-Hispanic/Latino; 4 Hispanic/Latino; 1 Two or more races, non-Hispanic/Latino). 43 applicants, 98% accepted, 36 enrolled. In 2016, 32 master's awarded. *Entrance requirements:* For master's, PRAXIS I or PRAXIS Core Academic Skills Exam, minimum GPA of 3.0, interview. *Application deadline:* For fall admission, 5/1 priority date for domestic students. Applications are processed on a rolling basis. Application fee: $45. Electronic applications accepted. *Expenses: Tuition:* Part-time $985 per credit. *Required fees:* $40 per credit. $150 per semester. Tuition and fees vary according to program. *Financial support:* Career-related internships or fieldwork, Federal Work-Study, and unspecified assistantships available. Financial award application deadline: 6/1; financial award applicants required to submit FAFSA. *Faculty research:* Multicultural and urban education/leadership, challenges of teaching diverse learners, scholarship of teaching and learning, technology and teaching, humor and education. *Unit head:* Mordechai Gordon, Program Director, 203-582-8442, E-mail: mordechai.gordon@qu.edu. *Application contact:* Office of Graduate Admissions, 203-582-8672, Fax: 203-582-3443, E-mail: graduate@qu.edu.
Website: http://www.qu.edu/gradeducation

Rhode Island College, School of Graduate Studies, Feinstein School of Education and Human Development, Department of Educational Studies, Providence, RI 02908-1991. Offers advanced studies in teaching and learning (M Ed); English (MAT); French (MAT); history (MAT); math (MAT); secondary education (MAT); Spanish (MAT); teaching English as a second language (M Ed). *Accreditation:* NCATE. *Program availability:* Part-time, evening/weekend. *Faculty:* 6 full-time (5 women), 8 part-time/adjunct (6 women). *Students:* 5 full-time (2 women), 53 part-time (48 women); includes 8 minority (2 Black or African American, non-Hispanic/Latino; 2 Asian, non-Hispanic/Latino; 3 Hispanic/Latino; 1 Two or more races, non-Hispanic/Latino). Average age 39. In 2016, 29 master's awarded. *Degree requirements:* For master's, capstone or comprehensive assessment. *Entrance requirements:* For master's, GRE or MAT (for most programs), minimum undergraduate GPA of 3.0; baccalaureate degree in English, French, history, math or Spanish; 3 letters of recommendation; interview. Additional exam requirements/recommendations for international students: Recommended—TOEFL (minimum score 550 paper-based; 79 iBT). *Application deadline:* For fall admission, 3/1 for domestic students; for spring admission, 11/1 for domestic students. Applications are processed on a rolling basis. Application fee: $50. Electronic applications accepted. *Expenses:* Tuition, state resident: full-time $8928; part-time $372 per credit. Tuition, nonresident: full-time $17,376; part-time $724 per credit. *Required fees:* $604; $22 per credit. One-time fee: $74. *Financial support:* In 2016–17, 1 teaching assistantship with full tuition reimbursement (averaging $3,000 per year) was awarded; career-related internships or fieldwork, Federal Work-Study, scholarships/grants, health care benefits, and unspecified assistantships also available. Support available to part-time students. Financial award application deadline: 5/15; financial award applicants required to submit FAFSA. *Unit head:* Dr. Gerri August, Chair, 401-456-8170. *Application contact:* Graduate Studies, 401-456-8700.
Website: http://www.ric.edu/educationalStudies/

Rider University, Department of Graduate Education, Leadership and Counseling, Teacher Certification Program, Lawrenceville, NJ 08648-3001. Offers business education (Certificate); elementary education (Certificate); English as a second language (Certificate); English education (Certificate); mathematics education (Certificate); preschool to grade 3 (Certificate); science education (Certificate); social studies education (Certificate); world languages (Certificate), including French, German, Spanish. *Program availability:* Part-time. *Degree requirements:* For Certificate, internship, professional portfolio. *Entrance requirements:* For degree, PRAXIS, resume. Additional exam requirements/recommendations for international students: Required—TOEFL (minimum score 550 paper-based). Electronic applications accepted. *Faculty research:* Conceptual foundations for optimal development of creativity; creative theory, cognitive processes in mathematics learning, teacher collaboration.

Rowan University, Graduate School, College of Communication and Creative Arts, Writing, Composition, and Rhetoric Certificate of Graduate Study Program, Glassboro, NJ 08028-1701. Offers CGS.

Rutgers University–New Brunswick, Graduate School of Education, Department of Learning and Teaching, Program in English Education, Piscataway, NJ 08854-8097. Offers Ed M. *Program availability:* Part-time. *Degree requirements:* For master's, comprehensive exam or paper. *Entrance requirements:* For master's, GRE General Test, minimum GPA of 3.0. Additional exam requirements/recommendations for international students: Required—TOEFL. Electronic applications accepted.

St. John Fisher College, Ralph C. Wilson Jr. School of Education, Program in Adolescence Education and Special Education, Rochester, NY 14618-3597. Offers adolescence education: biology with special education (MS Ed); adolescence education: chemistry with special education (MS Ed); adolescence education: English with special education (MS Ed); adolescence education: French with special education (MS Ed); adolescence education: math with special education (MS Ed); adolescence education: physics with special education (MS Ed); adolescence education: social studies with special education (MS Ed); adolescence education: Spanish with special education (MS Ed). *Program availability:* Part-time, evening/weekend. *Faculty:* 7 full-time (6 women), 5 part-time/adjunct (all women). *Students:* 15 full-time (6 women), 9 part-time (6 women); includes 3 minority (2 Black or African American, non-Hispanic/Latino; 1 Hispanic/Latino). Average age 28. 16 applicants, 56% accepted, 6 enrolled. In 2016, 8 master's awarded. *Degree requirements:* For master's, field experiences, student teaching, LAST. *Entrance requirements:* For master's, 2 letters of recommendation, personal statement, current resume. Additional exam requirements/recommendations for international students: Required—TOEFL (minimum score 575 paper-based; 80 iBT). *Application deadline:* Applications are processed on a rolling basis. Application fee: $30. Electronic applications accepted. *Expenses:* $885 per credit hour. *Financial support:* Scholarships/grants available. Financial award applicants required to submit FAFSA. *Faculty research:* Arts and humanities, urban schools, constructivist learning, at-risk students, mentoring. *Unit head:* Dr. Susan Hildenbrand, Program Director, 585-385-7297, E-mail: shildenbrand@sjfc.edu. *Application contact:* Michelle Gosier, Associate Director of Transfer and Graduate Admissions, 585-385-8064, E-mail: mgosier@sjfc.edu.

San Francisco State University, Division of Graduate Studies, College of Education, Department of Elementary Education, Program in Language and Literacy Education, San Francisco, CA 94132-1722. Offers language and literacy education (MA); reading (Certificate); reading and literacy leadership (Credential). *Expenses:* Tuition, state resident: full-time $6738. Tuition, nonresident: full-time $15,666. *Required fees:* $1012. Tuition and fees vary according to degree level and program. *Unit head:* Dr. Josephine Arce, Chair, 415-338-7636, Fax: 415-338-0567, E-mail: jarce@sfsu.edu. *Application contact:* Dr. Ali Borjian, MA Program Coordinator, 415-338-1838, Fax: 415-338-0567, E-mail: borjian@sfsu.edu.
Website: http://gcoe.sfsu.edu/

Simon Fraser University, Office of Graduate Studies and Postdoctoral Fellows, Faculty of Arts and Social Sciences, Department of English, Burnaby, BC V5A 1S6, Canada. Offers English (MA, PhD); teachers of English (MA). *Program availability:* Part-time. *Faculty:* 35 full-time (19 women). *Students:* 54 full-time (39 women). 56 applicants, 32% accepted, 16 enrolled. In 2016, 21 master's, 2 doctorates awarded. *Degree requirements:* For master's, one foreign language, thesis or alternative; for doctorate, one foreign language, thesis/dissertation, field exams. *Entrance requirements:* For master's, minimum GPA of 3.0 (on scale of 4.33) or 3.33 based on last 60 credits of undergraduate courses; for doctorate, minimum GPA of 3.5 (on scale of 4.33). Additional exam requirements/recommendations for international students: Recommended—TOEFL (minimum score 580 paper-based; 93 iBT), IELTS (minimum score 7), TWE (minimum score 5). *Application deadline:* For fall admission, 1/25 for domestic and international students; for spring admission, 2/1 for domestic students. Application fee: $90 ($125 for international students). Electronic applications accepted. *Financial support:* In 2016–17, 40 students received support, including 21 fellowships (averaging $5,571 per year), teaching assistantships (averaging $5,608 per year); research assistantships and scholarships/grants also available. *Faculty research:* Literary criticism, literature and psychoanalysis, Renaissance drama and poetry, Shakespeare, Canadian and American literature. *Unit head:* Dr. Michelle Levy, Graduate Chair, 778-782-5393, E-mail: engl-grad-chair@sfu.ca. *Application contact:* Christa Gruninger, Graduate Secretary, 778-782-4614, Fax: 778-782-3136, E-mail: englgrad@sfu.ca.
Website: http://www.english.sfu.ca/

Slippery Rock University of Pennsylvania, Graduate Studies (Recruitment), College of Education, Department of Secondary Education/Foundations of Education, Slippery Rock, PA 16057-1383. Offers secondary education (M Ed), including English, math/science, social studies. *Accreditation:* NCATE. *Program availability:* Part-time, evening/weekend, 100% online. *Faculty:* 7 full-time (2 women), 1 part-time/adjunct (0 women). *Students:* 43 full-time (23 women), 36 part-time (23 women); includes 2 minority (1 Black or African American, non-Hispanic/Latino; 1 Two or more races, non-Hispanic/Latino). Average age 29. 77 applicants, 79% accepted, 35 enrolled. In 2016, 36 master's awarded. *Degree requirements:* For master's, comprehensive exam, thesis (for some programs). *Entrance requirements:* For master's, copy of teaching certification and two letters of recommendation (for some programs). Additional exam requirements/recommendations for international students: Required—TOEFL (minimum score 550 paper-based; 80 iBT). *Application deadline:* For fall admission, 3/1 priority date for domestic students, 5/1 priority date for international students; for spring admission, 10/1 priority date for domestic students, 9/1 priority date for international students. Applications are processed on a rolling basis. Application fee: $25 ($30 for international students). Electronic applications accepted. *Expenses:* $646.50 per credit in-state, $936.80 per credit out-of-state; $581.45 per online credit in-state, $648.65 per online credit out-of-state. *Financial support:* In 2016–17, 12 students received support. Career-related internships or fieldwork, Federal Work-Study, institutionally sponsored loans, scholarships/grants, tuition waivers (partial), and unspecified assistantships available.

Support available to part-time students. Financial award application deadline: 5/1; financial award applicants required to submit FAFSA. *Unit head:* Dr. Jeffrey Lehman, Graduate Coordinator, 724-738-2311, Fax: 724-738-4987, E-mail: jeffrey.lehman@sru.edu. *Application contact:* Brandi Weber-Mortimer, Director of Graduate Studies, 724-738-2051, Fax: 724-738-2146, E-mail: graduate.admissions@sru.edu.
Website: http://www.sru.edu/academics/colleges-and-departments/coe/departments/secondary-education-/-foundations-of-education

Smith College, Graduate and Special Programs, Department of Education and Child Study, Program in Secondary Education, Northampton, MA 01063. Offers secondary education (MAT), including biological sciences education, chemistry education, English education, French education, geology education, government education, history education, mathematics education, physics education, Spanish education. *Program availability:* Part-time. *Students:* 3 full-time (2 women), 3 part-time (2 women). Average age 31. 14 applicants, 79% accepted, 4 enrolled. In 2016, 11 master's awarded. *Entrance requirements:* Additional exam requirements/recommendations for international students: Required—TOEFL (minimum score 595 paper-based; 97 iBT), IELTS. *Application deadline:* For fall admission, 4/1 for domestic students, 1/15 priority date for international students; for spring admission, 12/1 for domestic students. Application fee: $60. *Expenses: Tuition:* Full-time $34,560; part-time $1440 per credit. Tuition and fees vary according to course load and program. *Financial support:* In 2016–17, 5 students received support, including 1 fellowship with full tuition reimbursement available; scholarships/grants also available. Support available to part-time students. Financial award application deadline: 4/1; financial award applicants required to submit CSS PROFILE or FAFSA. *Unit head:* Rosetta Cohen, Graduate Student Advisor, 413-585-3266, E-mail: rcohen@smith.edu. *Application contact:* Ruth Morgan, Program Assistant, 413-585-3050, Fax: 413-585-3054, E-mail: gradstdy@smith.edu.
Website: http://www.smith.edu/educ/

Smith College, Graduate and Special Programs, Department of English Language and Literature, Northampton, MA 01063. Offers secondary education (MAT), including English education. *Program availability:* Part-time. *Students:* 1 (woman) full-time. Average age 23. 3 applicants, 67% accepted, 1 enrolled. In 2016, 6 master's awarded. *Entrance requirements:* Additional exam requirements/recommendations for international students: Required—TOEFL (minimum score 595 paper-based; 97 iBT), IELTS. *Application deadline:* For fall admission, 4/1 for domestic students, 1/15 for international students; for spring admission, 12/1 for domestic students. Application fee: $60. *Expenses: Tuition:* Full-time $34,560; part-time $1440 per credit. Tuition and fees vary according to course load and program. *Financial support:* In 2016–17, 1 student received support. Scholarships/grants available. Support available to part-time students. Financial award application deadline: 4/1; financial award applicants required to submit CSS PROFILE or FAFSA. *Unit head:* Craig Davis, Graduate Adviser, 413-585-3327, E-mail: crdavis@smith.edu. *Application contact:* Ruth Morgan, Program Assistant, 413-585-3050, Fax: 413-585-3054, E-mail: gradstdy@smith.edu.
Website: http://www.smith.edu/english/

South Carolina State University, College of Graduate and Professional Studies, Department of Education, Orangeburg, SC 29117-0001. Offers early childhood education (MAT); education (M Ed); elementary education (M Ed, MAT); English (MAT); general science/biology (MAT); mathematics (MAT); secondary education (M Ed), including biology education, business education, counselor education, English education, home economics education, industrial education, mathematics education, science education, social studies education; special education (M Ed), including emotionally handicapped, learning disabilities, mentally handicapped. *Accreditation:* NCATE. *Program availability:* Part-time, evening/weekend. *Faculty:* 12 full-time (8 women), 3 part-time/adjunct (1 woman). *Students:* 28 full-time (20 women), 20 part-time (17 women); includes 45 minority (44 Black or African American, non-Hispanic/Latino; 1 Two or more races, non-Hispanic/Latino). Average age 31. 22 applicants, 100% accepted, 16 enrolled. In 2016, 9 master's awarded. *Degree requirements:* For master's, thesis optional, departmental qualifying exam. *Entrance requirements:* For master's, GRE General Test, NTE, interview, teaching certificate. *Application deadline:* For fall admission, 6/15 priority date for domestic students, 6/15 for international students; for spring admission, 11/1 for domestic and international students. Application fee: $25. Electronic applications accepted. *Expenses:* Tuition, state resident: full-time $8938; part-time $579 per credit hour. Tuition, nonresident: full-time $19,018; part-time $1139 per credit hour. *Required fees:* $1482; $82 per credit hour. *Financial support:* Fellowships, career-related internships or fieldwork, Federal Work-Study, and scholarships/grants available. Financial award application deadline: 6/1. *Unit head:* Dr. Charlie Spell, Interim Chair, Department of Education, 803-536-8963, Fax: 803-516-4568, E-mail: cspell@scsu.edu. *Application contact:* Curtis Foskey, Coordinator of Graduate Studies, 803-536-8419, Fax: 803-536-8812, E-mail: cfoskey@scsu.edu.

Southeastern Louisiana University, College of Arts, Humanities and Social Sciences, Department of English, Hammond, LA 70402. Offers creative writing (MA); language and theory (MA); professional writing (MA); publishing studies (MA). *Program availability:* Part-time. *Faculty:* 12 full-time (4 women), 1 part-time/adjunct (0 women). *Students:* 12 full-time (9 women), 15 part-time (10 women); includes 4 minority (1 Black or African American, non-Hispanic/Latino; 2 Hispanic/Latino; 1 Two or more races, non-Hispanic/Latino). Average age 28. 10 applicants, 60% accepted, 4 enrolled. In 2016, 15 master's awarded. *Degree requirements:* For master's, comprehensive exam, thesis optional. *Entrance requirements:* Additional exam requirements/recommendations for international students: Required—TOEFL (minimum score 500 paper-based; 61 iBT), IELTS (minimum score 5.5). *Application deadline:* For fall admission, 7/15 priority date for domestic students, 6/1 priority date for international students; for spring admission, 12/1 priority date for domestic students, 10/1 priority date for international students. Applications are processed on a rolling basis. Application fee: $20 ($30 for international students). Electronic applications accepted. *Expenses:* Tuition, state resident: full-time $6540; part-time $465 per credit hour. Tuition, nonresident: full-time $19,017; part-time $1158 per credit hour. *Required fees:* $1829. *Financial support:* In 2016–17, 16 students received support, including 8 research assistantships (averaging $9,688 per year), 2 teaching assistantships (averaging $9,900 per year); institutionally sponsored loans, scholarships/grants, and unspecified assistantships also available. Support available to part-time students. Financial award application deadline: 5/1; financial award applicants required to submit FAFSA. *Faculty research:* John Ruskin, animal studies, linguistics, film studies. *Unit head:* Dr. David Hanson, Department Head, 985-549-2100, Fax: 985-549-5021, E-mail: dhanson@southeastern.edu. *Application contact:* Amanda Harper, Graduate Admissions Analyst, 985-549-5620, Fax: 985-549-5632, E-mail: admissions@southeastern.edu.
Website: http://www.southeastern.edu/acad_research/depts/engl

Southern Illinois University Edwardsville, Graduate School, College of Arts and Sciences, Department of English Language and Literature, Program in Teaching of Writing, Edwardsville, IL 62026-0001. Offers MA, Postbaccalaureate Certificate. *Program availability:* Part-time, evening/weekend. *Degree requirements:* For master's, thesis or alternative, final exam. *Entrance requirements:* Additional exam requirements/recommendations for international students: Required—TOEFL (minimum score 550 paper-based, 79 iBT), IELTS (minimum score 6.5), Michigan Test of English Language Proficiency or PTE. Electronic applications accepted.

Southern New Hampshire University, School of Education, Manchester, NH 03106-1045. Offers business education (M Ed); child development (M Ed); curriculum and instruction (M Ed), including education leadership, reading, special education, technology integration; education (M Ed); educational leadership (M Ed, Ed D); educational studies (M Ed); elementary education (M Ed); English (MAT); English for speakers of other languages (M Ed); reading and writing specialist (M Ed); school business administration (Certificate); secondary education (M Ed); special education (M Ed); technology integration specialist (M Ed). *Program availability:* Part-time, evening/weekend, online learning. *Degree requirements:* For master's, comprehensive exam (for some programs), thesis or alternative. *Entrance requirements:* For master's, PRAXIS I, minimum GPA of 2.75. Additional exam requirements/recommendations for international students: Required—TOEFL (minimum score 550 paper-based). Electronic applications accepted. *Expenses:* Contact institution.

Southwestern Oklahoma State University, College of Arts and Sciences, Specialization in English, Weatherford, OK 73096-3098. Offers M Ed. M Ed distance learning degree program offered to Oklahoma residents only. *Accreditation:* NCATE. *Program availability:* Part-time. *Degree requirements:* For master's, exam. *Entrance requirements:* For master's, GRE General Test or minimum undergraduate GPA of 3.0. Additional exam requirements/recommendations for international students: Required—TOEFL.

State University of New York at New Paltz, Graduate School, School of Education, Department of Secondary Education, New Paltz, NY 12561. Offers adolescence education: biology (MAT, MS Ed); adolescence education: chemistry (MAT, MS Ed); adolescence education: earth science (MAT, MS Ed); adolescence education: English (MAT, MS Ed); adolescence education: French (MAT, MS Ed); adolescence education: social studies (MAT, MS Ed); adolescence education: Spanish (MAT, MS Ed); second language education (MS Ed, AC), including second language education (MS Ed), teaching English language learners (AC). *Accreditation:* NCATE. *Program availability:* Part-time, evening/weekend. *Students:* 60 full-time (36 women), 59 part-time (48 women); includes 28 minority (2 Black or African American, non-Hispanic/Latino; 2 Asian, non-Hispanic/Latino; 22 Hispanic/Latino; 2 Two or more races, non-Hispanic/Latino). 96 applicants, 83% accepted, 54 enrolled. In 2016, 56 master's awarded. *Degree requirements:* For master's, comprehensive exam (for some programs), portfolio. *Entrance requirements:* For master's, minimum GPA of 3.0, New York state teaching certificate (MS Ed). Additional exam requirements/recommendations for international students: Required—TOEFL (minimum score 550 paper-based; 80 iBT), IELTS (minimum score 6.5). *Application deadline:* For fall admission, 3/1 priority date for domestic students, 3/1 for international students; for spring admission, 10/1 priority date for domestic students, 10/1 for international students. Application fee: $50. Electronic applications accepted. *Financial support:* Application deadline: 8/1. *Unit head:* Dr. Laura Dull, Chair, 845-257-2849, E-mail: dullj@newpaltz.edu. *Application contact:* Vika Shock, Director of Graduate Admissions, 845-257-3285, Fax: 845-257-3284, E-mail: gradschool@newpaltz.edu.
Website: http://www.newpaltz.edu/secondaryed/

State University of New York at Plattsburgh, School of Education, Health, and Human Services, Program in Teacher Education: Adolescence Education, Plattsburgh, NY 12901-2681. Offers adolescence education (MST); biology 7-12 (MST); chemistry 7-12 (MST); earth science 7-12 (MST); English 7-12 (MST); French 7-12 (MST); mathematics 7-12 (MST); physics 7-12 (MST); social studies 7-12 (MST); Spanish 7-12 (MST). *Accreditation:* TEAC. *Program availability:* Part-time, evening/weekend. *Entrance requirements:* For master's, minimum GPA of 2.75. Additional exam requirements/recommendations for international students: Required—TOEFL.

State University of New York College at Cortland, Graduate Studies, School of Arts and Sciences, Programs in Adolescence Education, Cortland, NY 13045. Offers biology (MAT); chemistry (MAT); English (MAT, MS Ed); mathematics (MAT); mathematics and physics (MS Ed); physics (MAT, MS Ed). *Accreditation:* NCATE. *Program availability:* Part-time, evening/weekend. *Degree requirements:* For master's, one foreign language, comprehensive exam (for some programs), thesis (for some programs). *Entrance requirements:* For master's, GRE General Test.

State University of New York College at Geneseo, Graduate Studies, School of Education, Program in Adolescence Education, Geneseo, NY 14454-1401. Offers English 7-12 (MS Ed); math 7-12 (MS Ed); Spanish 7-12 (MS Ed). *Program availability:* Part-time. *Faculty:* 8 full-time (4 women). *Students:* 5 part-time (4 women). Average age 30. 8 applicants, 13% accepted. In 2016, 4 master's awarded. *Degree requirements:* For master's, 2 foreign languages. *Entrance requirements:* For master's, initial certification to teach in New York state. Additional exam requirements/recommendations for international students: Required—TOEFL, IELTS, PTE. *Application deadline:* For fall admission, 4/1 priority date for domestic students; for spring admission, 11/1 priority date for domestic students. Applications are processed on a rolling basis. Application fee: $50. Electronic applications accepted. *Expenses:* Tuition, state resident: full-time $10,870; part-time $453 per credit. Tuition, nonresident: full-time $22,210; part-time $925 per credit. *Required fees:* $865; $35.85 per credit hour. *Financial support:* In 2016–17, 1 student received support, including 1 fellowship with partial tuition reimbursement available (averaging $10,000 per year); scholarships/grants, health care benefits, tuition waivers (partial), and unspecified assistantships also available. Support available to part-time students. Financial award application deadline: 4/1; financial award applicants required to submit FAFSA. *Unit head:* Dr. Anjoo Sikka, Dean of School of Education, 585-245-5151, Fax: 585-245-5220, E-mail: sikka@geneseo.edu. *Application contact:* Michael R. George, Graduate Enrollment Coordinator, 585-245-5148, Fax: 585-245-5550, E-mail: georgem@geneseo.edu.

State University of New York College at Old Westbury, School of Education, Old Westbury, NY 11568-0210. Offers biology (MAT, MS); chemistry (MAT, MS); English language arts (MAT, MS); math (MAT, MS); social studies (MAT, MS); Spanish (MAT, MS). *Program availability:* Part-time, evening/weekend. *Faculty:* 17 full-time (9 women), 5 part-time/adjunct (2 women). *Students:* 46 full-time (19 women), 26 part-time (17 women); includes 20 minority (1 Black or African American, non-Hispanic/Latino; 4 Asian, non-Hispanic/Latino; 15 Hispanic/Latino). Average age 30. 35 applicants, 77% accepted, 23 enrolled. In 2016, 25 master's awarded. *Entrance requirements:* For master's, Liberal Arts and Sciences Test, undergraduate degree with at least 30 semester hours of appropriate coursework as defined by the respective discipline; minimum cumulative undergraduate GPA of 3.0; two letters of recommendation (one from an academic source); essay. Additional exam requirements/recommendations for international students: Required—TOEFL (minimum score 550 paper-based); Recommended—IELTS. Application fee: $50. *Expenses:* Tuition, state resident: full-time $10,870; part-time $453 per credit. Tuition, nonresident: full-time $22,210; part-time $925 per credit. *Required fees:* $24.35 per credit. $76 per semester. Tuition and fees vary according to course load. *Financial support:* Applicants required to submit FAFSA. *Unit head:* Dr. Nancy Brown, Dean, School of Education, 516-876-3275, E-mail: brownn@oldwestbury.edu. *Application contact:* Philip D'Angelo, Graduate Admissions Office, 516-876-3073, E-mail: enroll@oldwestbury.edu.

State University of New York College at Potsdam, School of Education and Professional Studies, Program in Secondary Education, Potsdam, NY 13676. Offers English education (MST); mathematics education (MST); science education (MST), including biology, chemistry, earth science, physics; social studies education (MST). *Accreditation:* NCATE. *Degree requirements:* For master's, culminating experience. *Entrance requirements:* For master's, minimum GPA of 2.75 in last 60 hours of course work (3.0 for English program). Additional exam requirements/recommendations for international students: Required—TOEFL (minimum score 550 paper-based; 80 iBT), IELTS (minimum score 6). Electronic applications accepted.

Stony Brook University, State University of New York, Graduate School, College of Arts and Sciences, Department of English, Stony Brook, NY 11794. Offers English (MA, PhD); English education (MAT). MAT offered through the School of Professional Development. *Faculty:* 22 full-time (9 women), 4 part-time/adjunct (3 women). *Students:* 40 full-time (19 women), 11 part-time (8 women); includes 13 minority (1 Black or African American, non-Hispanic/Latino; 3 Asian, non-Hispanic/Latino; 6 Hispanic/Latino; 3 Two or more races, non-Hispanic/Latino), 5 international. Average age 31. 86 applicants, 34% accepted, 9 enrolled. In 2016, 12 master's, 12 doctorates awarded. Terminal master's awarded for partial completion of doctoral program. *Degree requirements:* For doctorate, thesis/dissertation. *Entrance requirements:* For master's and doctorate, GRE General Test. Additional exam requirements/recommendations for international students: Required—TOEFL. *Application deadline:* For fall admission, 1/15 for domestic students; for spring admission, 10/1 for domestic students. Application fee: $100. Electronic applications accepted. *Expenses:* Contact institution. *Financial support:* In 2016–17, 1 research assistantship, 26 teaching assistantships were awarded; fellowships also available. *Faculty research:* Humanities, poetry, literary theory, rhetoric, American literature. *Unit head:* Dr. Celia Marshik, Chair, 631-632-7356, E-mail: celia.marshik@stonybrook.edu. *Application contact:* Theresa Spadola, Coordinator, 631-632-7373, E-mail: theresa.spadola@stonybrook.edu.
Website: http://www.stonybrook.edu/english/

Stony Brook University, State University of New York, School of Professional Development, Stony Brook, NY 11794-443. Offers biology (MAT); chemistry (MAT); coaching (Graduate Certificate); earth science (MAT); educational computing (Graduate Certificate); educational leadership (Advanced Certificate); English (MAT); environmental management (MPS, Graduate Certificate); French (MAT); German (MAT); higher education administration (MA, Certificate); human resource management (MS, Graduate Certificate); industrial management (Graduate Certificate); information systems management (Graduate Certificate); Italian (MAT); liberal studies (MA); mathematics (MAT); operations research (Graduate Certificate); physics (MAT); school district business leadership (Advanced Certificate); social studies (MAT); Spanish (MAT). *Program availability:* Part-time, evening/weekend, online learning. *Faculty:* 4 full-time (3 women), 77 part-time/adjunct (34 women). *Students:* 197 full-time (125 women), 965 part-time (674 women); includes 222 minority (79 Black or African American, non-Hispanic/Latino; 2 American Indian or Alaska Native, non-Hispanic/Latino; 35 Asian, non-Hispanic/Latino; 87 Hispanic/Latino; 1 Native Hawaiian or other Pacific Islander, non-Hispanic/Latino; 18 Two or more races, non-Hispanic/Latino), 5 international. Average age 33. 462 applicants, 87% accepted, 317 enrolled. In 2016, 348 master's, 159 other advanced degrees awarded. *Degree requirements:* For master's, one foreign language, thesis or alternative. *Entrance requirements:* Additional exam requirements/recommendations for international students: Required—TOEFL (minimum score 85 iBT). *Application deadline:* For fall admission, 1/15 for domestic students, 6/1 for international students; for spring admission, 10/1 for domestic and international students. Applications are processed on a rolling basis. Application fee: $100. *Expenses:* Contact institution. *Financial support:* Fellowships, research assistantships, teaching assistantships, and career-related internships or fieldwork available. Support available to part-time students. *Unit head:* Dr. Ken Lindblom, Dean, 631-632-7049, Fax: 631-632-9046, E-mail: kenneth.lindblom@stonybrook.edu. *Application contact:* Melissa Jordan, Assistant Dean, 631-632-7751, E-mail: melissa.jordan@stonybrook.edu.
Website: http://www.stonybrook.edu/spd/

Syracuse University, School of Education, MS Program in English Education Preparation (Grades 7-12), Syracuse, NY 13244. Offers MS. *Program availability:* Part-time. *Degree requirements:* For master's, thesis or alternative. *Entrance requirements:* For master's, GRE, baccalaureate degree from regionally-accredited college/university with an English major or a 30-credit major equivalent determined via transcript review, at least nine credits of writing-intensive coursework, strong teacher and/or employer recommendations, personal statement. Additional exam requirements/recommendations for international students: Required—TOEFL (minimum score 100 iBT). *Application deadline:* For fall admission, 1/15 for domestic and international students. Applications are processed on a rolling basis. Application fee: $75. Electronic applications accepted. *Expenses: Tuition:* Full-time $25,974; part-time $1443 per credit hour. *Required fees:* $802; $50 per course. Tuition and fees vary according to course load and program. *Financial support:* Fellowships with full tuition reimbursements, research assistantships, teaching assistantships with tuition reimbursements, career-related internships or fieldwork, and scholarships/grants available. Financial award application deadline: 1/15. *Faculty research:* Educational theory, research in the field of English education, English and textual studies, composition and cultural rhetoric, teaching youth from diverse backgrounds. *Unit head:* Dr. Kelly Chandler-Olcott, Program Coordinator, 315-443-4755, E-mail: kpchandl@syr.edu. *Application contact:* Speranza Migliore, Graduate Admissions Recruiter, 315-443-2505, E-mail: gradrcrt@syr.edu.
Website: http://soe.syr.edu/academic/reading_language_arts/graduate/masters/english_ed_prep_7_12/default.aspx

Teachers College, Columbia University, Department of Arts and Humanities, New York, NY 10027. Offers applied linguistics (MA, Ed D); art and art education (Ed M, MA, Ed D, Ed DCT); arts administration (MA); bilingual and bicultural education (MA); global competence (Certificate); history and education (Ed D, PhD); music and music education (Ed DCT); philosophy and education (MA, Ed D, PhD); social studies education (Ed M, PhD); teaching English to speakers of other languages (Ed M); teaching of English and English education (Ed M, MA, Ed D, PhD), including English education (Ed M, Ed D, PhD), teaching of English (MA); teaching of social studies (MA); TESOL (MA, Ed D). *Program availability:* Part-time, evening/weekend. *Students:* 429 full-time (329 women), 467 part-time (332 women); includes 268 minority (62 Black or African American, non-Hispanic/Latino; 1 American Indian or Alaska Native, non-Hispanic/Latino; 108 Asian, non-Hispanic/Latino; 76 Hispanic/Latino; 21 Two or more races, non-Hispanic/Latino), 212 international. 1,068 applicants, 53% accepted, 272 enrolled. Terminal master's awarded for partial completion of doctoral program. *Expenses: Tuition:* Full-time $36,288; part-time $1512 per credit. *Required fees:* $438 per semester. One-time fee: $510 full-time. Full-time tuition and fees vary according to course load. *Financial support:* Fellowships, research assistantships, teaching assistantships, career-related internships or fieldwork, Federal Work-Study, institutionally sponsored loans, tuition waivers (full and partial), and unspecified assistantships available. Support available to part-time students. *Unit head:* Prof. William Gaudelli, Department Chair, 212-678-3150, E-mail: wg74@columbia.edu. *Application contact:* David Estrella, Director of Admissions, 212-678-3305, Fax: 212-678-4171, E-mail: estrella@tc.columbia.edu.
Website: http://www.tc.edu/a%26h/

Temple University, College of Education, Department of Teaching and Learning, Philadelphia, PA 19122-6096. Offers career and technical education (Ed M), including business, computing, and information technology, industrial education, marketing education; middle grades education (Ed M), including math and language arts, math and science, science and language arts; secondary education (Ed M), including English, math, social studies; teaching English to speakers of other languages (MS Ed); urban education (Ed M). *Program availability:* Part-time, evening/weekend. *Faculty:* 26 full-time (16 women), 74 part-time/adjunct (54 women). *Students:* 204 full-time (139 women), 320 part-time (201 women); includes 112 minority (66 Black or African American, non-Hispanic/Latino; 17 Asian, non-Hispanic/Latino; 18 Hispanic/Latino; 11 Two or more races, non-Hispanic/Latino), 18 international. 300 applicants, 55% accepted, 99 enrolled. In 2016, 93 master's awarded. Terminal master's awarded for partial completion of doctoral program. *Degree requirements:* For master's, thesis or alternative. *Entrance requirements:* Additional exam requirements/recommendations for international students: Required—TOEFL (minimum score 550 paper-based; 79 iBT). *Application deadline:* For fall admission, 4/1 for domestic students, 12/15 for international students; for spring admission, 10/1 for domestic students, 8/1 for international students. Application fee: $60. Electronic applications accepted. *Expenses:* Contact institution. *Financial support:* Fellowships, research assistantships, and teaching assistantships available. Financial award application deadline: 1/15; financial award applicants required to submit FAFSA. *Faculty research:* Workforce development, vocational education, technical education, industrial education, professional development, literacy, classroom management, school communities, curriculum development, instruction, applied linguistics, cross linguistic influence, bilingual education, oral proficiency, multilingualism. *Unit head:* Dr. Christine Woyshner, Chairperson, 215-204-6387, E-mail: christine.woyshner@temple.edu. *Application contact:* Sarah Stapleton, Assistant Director, Academic Operations, 215-204-8220, E-mail: sarah.stapleton@temple.edu.
Website: http://education.temple.edu/tl

Trinity Washington University, School of Education, Washington, DC 20017-1094. Offers clinical mental health counseling (MA); early childhood education (MAT); educating for change (M Ed); educational administration (MSA); elementary education (MAT); reading (M Ed); school counseling (MA); secondary education (MAT), including English, social studies; special education (MAT). *Accreditation:* NCATE. *Program availability:* Part-time, evening/weekend. *Degree requirements:* For master's, thesis (for some programs), capstone project(s). *Entrance requirements:* For master's, PRAXIS I, minimum GPA of 2.8. Additional exam requirements/recommendations for international students: Required—TOEFL (minimum score 550 paper-based). *Faculty research:* Technology, literacy, special education, organizations, inclusion models.

University at Buffalo, the State University of New York, Graduate School, Graduate School of Education, Department of Learning and Instruction, Buffalo, NY 14260. Offers biology education (Ed M, Certificate); chemistry education (Ed M, Certificate); childhood education (Ed M); childhood education with bilingual extension (Ed M); college teaching (Advanced Certificate); curriculum, instruction and the science of learning (PhD); early childhood education (Ed M); early childhood education with bilingual extension (Ed M); earth science education (Ed M, Certificate); education and technology (Ed M); education studies (Ed M); educational technology and new literacies (Certificate); educational technology and new literacies (Advanced Certificate); elementary education (Ed D); English education (Ed M, Certificate); English education studies (Ed M); English for speakers of other languages (Ed M); foreign and second language education (PhD); French education (Ed M, Certificate); German education (Ed M, Certificate); gifted education (Certificate); Latin education (Ed M, Certificate); literacy education studies (Ed M); literacy specialist (Ed M); literacy teaching and learning (Certificate); mathematics education (Ed M, Certificate); music education (Ed M, Certificate); music education studies (Ed M); music learning theory (Advanced Certificate); online education (Advanced Certificate); physics education (Ed M, Certificate); science and the public (Ed M); social studies education (Ed M, Certificate); Spanish education (Ed M, Certificate); special education (PhD); teaching English to speakers of other languages (Ed M). *Program availability:* Part-time, evening/weekend, 100% online. *Faculty:* 28 full-time (21 women), 67 part-time/adjunct (49 women). *Students:* 198 full-time (153 women), 312 part-time (220 women); includes 48 minority (28 Black or African American, non-Hispanic/Latino; 4 American Indian or Alaska Native, non-Hispanic/Latino; 15 Asian, non-Hispanic/Latino; 1 Hispanic/Latino), 66 international. Average age 33. 336 applicants, 86% accepted, 178 enrolled. In 2016, 137 master's, 24 doctorates, 25 other advanced degrees awarded. *Degree requirements:* For master's, comprehensive exam; for doctorate, thesis/dissertation, research analysis exam, research experience. *Entrance requirements:* For master's, letters of reference; for doctorate, GRE General Test or MAT, interview, writing sample, letters of recommendation. Additional exam requirements/recommendations for international students: Required—TOEFL (minimum score 600 paper-based; 96 iBT). *Application deadline:* For fall admission, 2/1 priority date for domestic and international students; for spring admission, 11/15 priority date for domestic students, 10/1 for international students. Applications are processed on a rolling basis. Application fee: $50. Electronic applications accepted. *Financial support:* In 2016–17, 44 fellowships (averaging $4,010 per year), 39 research assistantships with tuition reimbursements (averaging $9,897 per year) were awarded; teaching assistantships, career-related internships or fieldwork, Federal Work-Study, institutionally sponsored loans, scholarships/grants, tuition waivers (full and partial), and unspecified assistantships also available. Financial award application deadline: 2/28; financial award applicants required to submit FAFSA. *Faculty research:* Science assessment, foreign language teaching and learning, early learning, new literacies, gender and education. *Total annual research expenditures:* $534,880. *Unit head:* Dr. Deborah Moore-Russo, Chair, 716-645-4069, Fax: 716-645-3161, E-mail: dam29@buffalo.edu. *Application contact:* Luann Zak, Admissions Assistant, 716-645-2110, Fax: 716-645-7937, E-mail: luannzak@buffalo.edu.
Website: http://gse.buffalo.edu/lai

The University of Akron, Graduate School, College of Education, Department of Curricular and Instructional Studies, Program in Adolescent to Young Adult Education, Akron, OH 44325. Offers chemistry (MS); chemistry and physics (MS); earth science (MS); earth science and chemistry (MS); earth science and physics (MS); integrated language arts (MS); integrated mathematics (MS); integrated social studies (MS); life science (MS); life science and chemistry (MS); life science and earth science (MS); life science and physics (MS); physics (MS). *Accreditation:* NCATE. *Degree requirements:* For master's, comprehensive exam, portfolio. *Entrance requirements:* Additional exam requirements/recommendations for international students: Required—TOEFL (minimum score 550 paper-based, 79 iBT) or IELTS (minimum score 6.5). *Application deadline:* For fall admission, 3/1 for domestic and international students; for spring admission, 10/1 for domestic and international students. Applications are processed on a rolling basis. Application fee: $45 ($70 for international students). Electronic applications accepted. *Expenses:* Tuition, state resident: full-time $8618; part-time $359 per credit hour. Tuition, nonresident: full-time $17,149; part-time $715 per credit hour. *Required fees:* $1652. *Unit head:* Dr. Peggy McCann, Interim Chair, 330-972-5742, E-mail: plm@uakron.edu.

English Education

The University of Alabama in Huntsville, School of Graduate Studies, College of Arts, Humanities, and Social Sciences, Department of English, Huntsville, AL 35899. Offers education (MA); English (MA); technical writing (Certificate); TESOL (Certificate). *Program availability:* Part-time, evening/weekend. *Degree requirements:* For master's, one foreign language, comprehensive exam, thesis or alternative, oral and written exams. *Entrance requirements:* For master's and Certificate, GRE General Test, minimum GPA of 3.0. Additional exam requirements/recommendations for international students: Required—TOEFL (minimum score 500 paper-based; 80 iBT), IELTS (minimum score 6.5). Electronic applications accepted. *Expenses:* Tuition, state resident: full-time $9834; part-time $600 per credit hour. Tuition, nonresident: full-time $21,830; part-time $1325 per credit hour. *Faculty research:* Fiction and identity, Shakespeare, science fiction, eighteenth-century literature, technical writing.

The University of Alabama in Huntsville, School of Graduate Studies, College of Education, Huntsville, AL 35899. Offers autism spectrum disorders (M Ed, Graduate Certificate); biology (MAT); chemistry (MAT); differentiated instruction in elementary education (M Ed); English language arts (MAT); English speakers of other languages (M Ed, MAT); history (MAT); mathematics (MAT); physics (MAT); reading education (M Ed); secondary education (M Ed). *Expenses:* Tuition, state resident: full-time $9834; part-time $600 per credit hour. Tuition, nonresident: full-time $21,830; part-time $1325 per credit hour.

The University of Arizona, College of Humanities, Department of English, Rhetoric, Composition and the Teaching of English Program, Tucson, AZ 85721. Offers MA, PhD. *Accreditation:* NASM. *Degree requirements:* For master's, one foreign language, comprehensive exam; for doctorate, one foreign language, comprehensive exam, thesis/dissertation. *Entrance requirements:* For doctorate, GRE General Test, 3 letters of recommendation, writing sample. Additional exam requirements/recommendations for international students: Required—TOEFL (minimum score 550 paper-based; 79 iBT). Electronic applications accepted.

University of Arkansas at Pine Bluff, School of Education, Pine Bluff, AR 71601-2799. Offers elementary education (M Ed); secondary education (M Ed), including English education, mathematics education, science education, social studies education; teaching (MAT). *Accreditation:* NCATE. *Program availability:* Part-time, evening/weekend. *Degree requirements:* For master's, comprehensive exam. *Entrance requirements:* For master's, GRE, minimum GPA of 2.75, NTE or Standard Arkansas Teaching Certificate. Application fee: $25. *Expenses:* Tuition, state resident: full-time $4776. Tuition, nonresident: full-time $10,824. *Required fees:* $1612. Tuition and fees vary according to course load. *Financial support:* Research assistantships with full and partial tuition reimbursements, teaching assistantships with full and partial tuition reimbursements, institutionally sponsored loans, and scholarships/grants available. Support available to part-time students. *Faculty research:* Teacher certification, accreditation, assessment, standards, portfolio development, rehabilitation, technology. *Unit head:* Dr. George Herts, Dean, 870-575-8000, E-mail: johnson_c@uapb.edu.
Website: http://www.uapb.edu/academics/school_of_education.aspx

University of Central Florida, College of Education and Human Performance, School of Teaching, Learning, and Leadership, Program in Teacher Education, Orlando, FL 32816. Offers art education (MAT); English language (MAT); mathematics education (MAT); middle school mathematics (MAT); middle school science (MAT); science education (MAT), including biology, chemistry, physics; social science education (MAT). *Accreditation:* NCATE. *Program availability:* Part-time, evening/weekend. *Students:* 16 full-time (11 women), 28 part-time (23 women); includes 16 minority (6 Black or African American, non-Hispanic/Latino; 1 Asian, non-Hispanic/Latino; 8 Hispanic/Latino; 1 Two or more races, non-Hispanic/Latino), 1 international. Average age 31. 1 applicant, 100% accepted. In 2016, 33 master's awarded. *Entrance requirements:* For master's, GRE General Test. Additional exam requirements/recommendations for international students: Required—TOEFL. *Application deadline:* For spring admission, 12/1 for domestic students; for summer admission, 4/15 for domestic students. Application fee: $30. Electronic applications accepted. *Expenses:* Tuition, state resident: part-time $288.16 per credit hour. Tuition, nonresident: part-time $1071.31 per credit hour. *Financial support:* Fellowships, research assistantships, teaching assistantships, career-related internships or fieldwork, Federal Work-Study, institutionally sponsored loans, tuition waivers (partial), and unspecified assistantships available. Financial award application deadline: 3/1; financial award applicants required to submit FAFSA. *Unit head:* Dr. Michael Hynes, Director, 407-823-2005, E-mail: mychael.hynes@ucf.edu. *Application contact:* Assistant Director, Graduate Admissions, 407-823-2766, Fax: 407-823-6442, E-mail: gradadmissions@ucf.edu.
Website: http://education.ucf.edu/programs.cfm?pid=g&cat=2

University of Colorado Denver, College of Liberal Arts and Sciences, Department of English, Denver, CO 80217. Offers applied linguistics (MA); literature (MA); rhetoric and teaching of writing (MA). *Program availability:* Part-time, evening/weekend. *Faculty:* 22 full-time (13 women). *Students:* 18 full-time (12 women), 13 part-time (10 women); includes 3 minority (1 Black or African American, non-Hispanic/Latino; 2 Hispanic/Latino). Average age 31. 19 applicants, 68% accepted, 6 enrolled. In 2016, 10 master's awarded. *Degree requirements:* For master's, variable foreign language requirement, comprehensive exam (for some programs), thesis (for some programs), minimum of 33 credit hours (for literature program), 30 (for rhetoric and teaching of writing and applied linguistics programs). *Entrance requirements:* For master's, GRE General Test, minimum GPA of 3.0 in undergraduate courses, critical writing sample, letters of recommendation, completion of 24 semester hours in English courses (at least 16 at the upper-division level), statement of purpose. Additional exam requirements/recommendations for international students: Required—TOEFL (minimum score 537 paper-based; 75 iBT); Recommended—IELTS (minimum score 6.5). *Application deadline:* For fall admission, 4/1 for domestic and international students; for spring admission, 10/1 for domestic and international students; for summer admission, 4/1 for domestic and international students. Application fee: $50 ($75 for international students). Electronic applications accepted. *Expenses:* Tuition, state resident: full-time $11,006; part-time $474 per credit. Tuition, nonresident: full-time $28,212; part-time $1264 per credit hour. *Required fees:* $256 per semester. One-time fee: $94.32. Tuition and fees vary according to campus/location and program. *Financial support:* In 2016–17, 9 students received support. Fellowships, research assistantships, teaching assistantships, Federal Work-Study, institutionally sponsored loans, scholarships/grants, traineeships, and unspecified assistantships available. Financial award application deadline: 4/1; financial award applicants required to submit FAFSA. *Faculty research:* Literature, rhetoric, teaching of writing, applied linguistics. *Unit head:* Prof. Nancy Ciccone, Chair, 303-556-8395, E-mail: nancy.ciccone@ucdenver.edu. *Application contact:* Francine Olivas-Zarate, English Department, 303-556-2584, Fax: 303-556-2959.
Website: http://www.ucdenver.edu/academics/colleges/CLAS/Departments/english/Programs/Masters/Pages/Overview.aspx

University of Colorado Denver, School of Education and Human Development, Teacher Education Programs, Denver, CO 80217. Offers elementary linguistically diverse education (MA); elementary math and science education (MA); elementary math education (MA); elementary reading and writing (MA); elementary science education (MA); secondary English education (MA); secondary linguistically diverse education (MA); secondary math education (MA); secondary reading and writing (MA); secondary science education (MA); special education (MA). *Accreditation:* NCATE. *Program availability:* Part-time, evening/weekend. *Students:* 142 full-time (117 women), 184 part-time (159 women); includes 56 minority (6 Black or African American, non-Hispanic/Latino; 1 American Indian or Alaska Native, non-Hispanic/Latino; 4 Asian, non-Hispanic/Latino; 38 Hispanic/Latino; 1 Native Hawaiian or other Pacific Islander, non-Hispanic/Latino; 6 Two or more races, non-Hispanic/Latino), 1 international. Average age 30. 18 applicants, 67% accepted, 9 enrolled. In 2016, 134 master's awarded. *Degree requirements:* For master's, comprehensive exam. *Entrance requirements:* For master's, GRE or MAT (for those with GPA below 2.75), transcripts, resume, letters of recommendation. Additional exam requirements/recommendations for international students: Required—TOEFL (minimum score 537 paper-based; 75 iBT); Recommended—IELTS (minimum score 6.5). *Application deadline:* For fall admission, 4/15 for domestic students, 4/1 for international students; for spring admission, 9/15 for domestic students, 9/1 for international students; for summer admission, 2/15 for domestic students, 2/1 for international students. Applications are processed on a rolling basis. Application fee: $50 ($75 for international students). Electronic applications accepted. *Expenses:* Contact institution. *Financial support:* In 2016–17, 26 students received support. Fellowships, research assistantships, teaching assistantships, Federal Work-Study, institutionally sponsored loans, scholarships/grants, and traineeships available. Financial award application deadline: 4/1; financial award applicants required to submit FAFSA. *Faculty research:* Linguistically diverse education/ESL, elementary reading and writing, elementary teacher education, secondary teacher education, special education. *Unit head:* Cindy Gutierrez, Director, 303-315-4982, E-mail: cindy.gutierrez@ucdenver.edu. *Application contact:* 303-315-6300, E-mail: education@ucdenver.edu.
Website: http://www.ucdenver.edu/academics/colleges/SchoolOfEducation/Academics/MASTERS/Pages/default.aspx

University of Connecticut, Graduate School, Neag School of Education, Department of Curriculum and Instruction, Program in English Education, Storrs, CT 06269. Offers MA, PhD. *Accreditation:* NCATE. Terminal master's awarded for partial completion of doctoral program. *Degree requirements:* For master's, comprehensive exam, thesis or alternative; for doctorate, thesis/dissertation. *Entrance requirements:* For doctorate, GRE General Test. Additional exam requirements/recommendations for international students: Required—TOEFL (minimum score 550 paper-based). Electronic applications accepted.

University of Florida, Graduate School, College of Education, School of Teaching and Learning, Gainesville, FL 32611. Offers curriculum and instruction (M Ed, MAE, Ed D, PhD, Ed S); elementary education (M Ed, MAE); English education (M Ed, MAE); mathematics education (M Ed, MAE); reading education (M Ed, MAE); science education (M Ed, MAE); social studies education (M Ed, MAE). *Accreditation:* NCATE. *Program availability:* Part-time, evening/weekend, online learning. Terminal master's awarded for partial completion of doctoral program. *Degree requirements:* For master's, comprehensive exam (for some programs), thesis (for some programs); for doctorate, comprehensive exam (for some programs), thesis/dissertation (for some programs). *Entrance requirements:* For master's and doctorate, GRE General Test, minimum GPA of 3.0; for Ed S, GRE General Test. Additional exam requirements/recommendations for international students: Required—TOEFL (minimum score 550 paper-based; 80 iBT), IELTS (minimum score 6). Electronic applications accepted. *Faculty research:* STEM education; curriculum; teaching and teacher education; languages and literacy; schools, culture, and society; theories and processes of learning.

University of Georgia, College of Education, Department of Language and Literacy Education, Athens, GA 30602. Offers English education (M Ed); language and literacy education (PhD). *Accreditation:* NCATE. *Faculty:* 15 full-time (11 women). *Students:* 100 full-time (81 women), 94 part-time (80 women); includes 21 minority (17 Black or African American, non-Hispanic/Latino; 1 Asian, non-Hispanic/Latino; 2 Hispanic/Latino; 1 Two or more races, non-Hispanic/Latino), 31 international. Average age 33. 185 applicants, 61% accepted, 42 enrolled. In 2016, 43 master's, 15 doctorates awarded. *Degree requirements:* For doctorate, variable foreign language requirement. *Entrance requirements:* For master's, GRE General Test or MAT; for doctorate, GRE General Test. Additional exam requirements/recommendations for international students: Required—TOEFL (minimum score 550 paper-based). *Application deadline:* For fall admission, 7/1 priority date for domestic students; for spring admission, 11/15 for domestic students. Application fee: $50. Electronic applications accepted. *Faculty research:* Comprehension, critical literacy, literacy and technology, vocabulary instruction, content area reading. *Unit head:* Dr. Mark A. Faust, Head, 706-542-4515, Fax: 706-542-4509, E-mail: mfaust@uga.edu. *Application contact:* Dr. Elizabeth St. Pierre, Graduate Coordinator, 706-542-4520, E-mail: stpierre@uga.edu.
Website: http://www.coe.uga.edu/lle/

University of Illinois at Springfield, Graduate Programs, College of Liberal Arts and Sciences, Department of English and Modern Languages, Springfield, IL 62703-5407. Offers English (MA); teaching English (Graduate Certificate). *Program availability:* Part-time, evening/weekend. *Faculty:* 5 full-time (4 women). *Students:* 8 full-time (4 women), 9 part-time (5 women); includes 1 minority (Asian, non-Hispanic/Latino), 1 international. Average age 31. 11 applicants, 73% accepted, 6 enrolled. In 2016, 4 master's, 1 other advanced degree awarded. *Degree requirements:* For master's, thesis, critical project, or creative project. *Entrance requirements:* For master's, GRE General Test, minimum overall undergraduate GPA of 3.0; analytical writing sample or sample of creative work; two letters of recommendation. Additional exam requirements/recommendations for international students: Required—TOEFL (minimum score 500 paper-based; 61 iBT). *Application deadline:* Applications are processed on a rolling basis. Application fee: $60 ($75 for international students). Electronic applications accepted. *Expenses:* Tuition, state resident: part-time $329 per credit hour. Tuition, nonresident: part-time $675 per credit hour. *Financial support:* In 2016–17, fellowships with full tuition reimbursements (averaging $9,900 per year), research assistantships with full tuition reimbursements (averaging $9,991 per year), teaching assistantships with full tuition reimbursements (averaging $10,059 per year) were awarded; career-related internships or fieldwork, Federal Work-Study, scholarships/grants, health care benefits, and unspecified assistantships also available. Support available to part-time students. Financial award application deadline: 11/15; financial award applicants required to submit FAFSA. *Unit head:* Dr. Tena Helton, Program Administrator, 217-206-7441, Fax: 217-206-6217, E-mail: thelt2@uis.edu. *Application contact:* Dr. Cecelia Cornell, Associate Vice Chancellor for Graduate Education, 217-206-7230, E-mail: ccorn1@uis.edu.

University of Indianapolis, Graduate Programs, School of Education, Indianapolis, IN 46227-3697. Offers art education (MAT); biology (MAT); chemistry (MAT); curriculum and instruction (MA); earth sciences (MAT); education (MA, MAT); educational leadership (MA); elementary education (MA); English (MAT); French (MAT); math (MAT); physical education (MAT); physics (MAT); secondary education (MA), including art education, education, English education, social studies education; social studies (MAT); Spanish (MAT). *Accreditation:* NCATE. *Program availability:* Part-time, evening/weekend. *Entrance requirements:* For master's, GRE Subject Test, PRAXIS I, minimum GPA of 2.5, 3 letters of recommendation, interview. Additional exam requirements/recommendations for international students: Required—TOEFL (minimum score 550 paper-based). *Faculty research:* Assessment of teacher education, perceptions of prospective teachers by parents.

The University of Iowa, Graduate College, College of Education, Department of Teaching and Learning, Program in Education, Iowa City, IA 52242-1316. Offers art education (MA); developmental reading (MA); elementary education (MA); English education (MA, MAT); foreign and second language education (MAT); foreign language education (MA); foreign language/ESL education (PhD); language, literacy and culture (PhD); mathematics education (MA, MAT, PhD); music education (MM, PhD); science education (MA); secondary education (MA); social studies (MA, PhD). *Degree requirements:* For master's, thesis optional, exam; for doctorate, comprehensive exam, thesis/dissertation. *Entrance requirements:* For master's and doctorate, GRE General Test, minimum GPA of 3.0. Additional exam requirements/recommendations for international students: Required—TOEFL (minimum score 550 paper-based; 81 iBT). Electronic applications accepted.

University of Louisiana at Monroe, Graduate School, College of Arts, Education, and Sciences, School of Education, Program in Curriculum and Instruction, Monroe, LA 71209-0001. Offers art education (M Ed); biology education (M Ed); chemistry education (M Ed); curriculum and instruction (Ed D); early childhood education (M Ed); earth science education (M Ed); educational leadership (M Ed); elementary education (1-5) (M Ed); English as a second language (M Ed); English education (M Ed); family and consumer education (M Ed); French education (M Ed); history education (M Ed); math education (M Ed); middle school education (M Ed); music education (M Ed); reading education (K-12) (M Ed); Spanish education (M Ed); special education - academically gifted (M Ed); special education - early intervention (M Ed); special education - educational diagnostician (M Ed); special education - mild/moderate disabilities (M Ed); speech education (M Ed). *Accreditation:* NCATE. *Faculty:* 8 full-time (4 women), 4 part-time/adjunct (3 women). *Students:* 13 full-time (11 women), 80 part-time (65 women); includes 25 minority (19 Black or African American, non-Hispanic/Latino; 1 Asian, non-Hispanic/Latino; 3 Hispanic/Latino; 2 Two or more races, non-Hispanic/Latino). Average age 37. 118 applicants, 30% accepted, 16 enrolled. In 2016, 23 master's, 4 doctorates awarded. *Degree requirements:* For master's, comprehensive exam (for some programs), thesis; for doctorate, thesis/dissertation, internships. *Entrance requirements:* For master's, GRE General Test; for doctorate, GRE General Test, minimum undergraduate GPA of 2.75, graduate 3.25. Additional exam requirements/ recommendations for international students: Required—TOEFL (minimum score 500 paper-based; 61 iBT). *Application deadline:* For fall admission, 8/24 priority date for domestic students, 7/1 for international students; for winter admission, 12/14 priority date for domestic students; for spring admission, 1/19 for domestic students, 11/1 for international students. Applications are processed on a rolling basis. Application fee: $20 ($30 for international students). Electronic applications accepted. *Expenses:* Tuition, state resident: full-time $6489. Tuition, nonresident: full-time $18,589. *Required fees:* $8984. Tuition and fees vary according to course level, course load, degree level and program. *Financial support:* Research assistantships, career-related internships or fieldwork, Federal Work-Study, and unspecified assistantships available. Financial award application deadline: 4/1; financial award applicants required to submit FAFSA. *Unit head:* Dr. Dorothy Schween, Director, 318-342-1268, Fax: 318-342-3131, E-mail: schween@ulm.edu.

University of Manitoba, Faculty of Graduate Studies, Faculty of Education, Department of Curriculum, Teaching and Learning, Winnipeg, MB R3T 2N2, Canada. Offers language and literacy (M Ed); second language education (M Ed); studies in curriculum, teaching and learning (M Ed). *Degree requirements:* For master's, thesis or alternative.

University of Maryland, Baltimore County, The Graduate School, College of Arts, Humanities and Social Sciences, Department of Education, Program in Teaching, Baltimore, MD 21250. Offers early childhood education (MAT); elementary education (MAT); teaching (MAT), including art, biology, chemistry, choral music, classical foreign language, dance, earth/space science, English, instrumental music, mathematics, modern foreign language, physical science, physics, social studies, theatre. *Program availability:* Part-time, evening/weekend. *Faculty:* 24 full-time (18 women), 25 part-time/ adjunct (19 women). *Students:* 41 full-time (34 women), 27 part-time (18 women); includes 26 minority (6 Black or African American, non-Hispanic/Latino; 9 Asian, non-Hispanic/Latino; 7 Hispanic/Latino; 1 Native Hawaiian or other Pacific Islander, non-Hispanic/Latino; 3 Two or more races, non-Hispanic/Latino), 2 international. Average age 30. 54 applicants, 83% accepted, 35 enrolled. In 2016, 50 master's awarded. *Degree requirements:* For master's, comprehensive exam (for some programs), thesis (for some programs). *Entrance requirements:* For master's, PRAXIS Core Examination or GRE (minimum score of 1000), minimum GPA of 3.0. Additional exam requirements/ recommendations for international students: Required—TOEFL. *Application deadline:* For fall admission, 6/1 for domestic and international students; for spring admission, 11/ 1 for domestic and international students. Applications are processed on a rolling basis. Application fee: $50. Electronic applications accepted. *Expenses:* Tuition, state resident: full-time $13,294. Tuition, nonresident: full-time $20,286. *Financial support:* In 2016–17, 8 students received support, including teaching assistantships with tuition reimbursements available (averaging $12,000 per year); career-related internships or fieldwork, Federal Work-Study, scholarships/grants, tuition waivers, and unspecified assistantships also available. Financial award application deadline: 3/15. *Faculty research:* STEM teacher education, culturally sensitive pedagogy, ESOL/bilingual education, early childhood education, language, literacy and culture. *Total annual research expenditures:* $100,000. *Unit head:* Dr. Susan M. Blunck, Graduate Program Director, 410-455-2869, Fax: 410-455-3986, E-mail: blunck@umbc.edu. *Application contact:* Cheryl Johnson, MAT Program Specialist, 410-455-3388, E-mail: blackwel@ umbc.edu.
Website: http://www.umbc.edu/education/

University of Michigan, Rackham Graduate School, Joint PhD Program in English and Education, Ann Arbor, MI 48109. Offers PhD. *Accreditation:* TEAC. *Students:* 22 full-time (17 women); includes 2 minority (1 Asian, non-Hispanic/Latino; 1 Hispanic/Latino). Average age 34. 34 applicants, 24% accepted, 5 enrolled. In 2016, 3 doctorates awarded. *Degree requirements:* For doctorate, one foreign language, comprehensive exam, thesis/dissertation, 3 preliminary exams, oral defense of dissertation. *Entrance requirements:* For doctorate, GRE General Test, master's degree, teaching experience. Additional exam requirements/recommendations for international students: Required—TOEFL. *Application deadline:* For fall admission, 1/5 for domestic and international students. Application fee: $75 ($90 for international students). Electronic applications accepted. *Expenses:* Contact institution. *Financial support:* In 2016–17, 20 students received support, including 11 fellowships with full tuition reimbursements available, 4 research assistantships with full tuition reimbursements available, 28 teaching assistantships with full tuition reimbursements available; institutionally sponsored loans, scholarships/grants, and health care benefits also available. Financial award application deadline: 4/15. *Faculty research:* Literacy, teacher education, discourse analysis, rhetoric and composition studies. *Unit head:* Dr. Anne Ruggles Gere, Chair, 734-763-6643, Fax: 734-936-1606, E-mail: argere@umich.edu. *Application contact:* Jeanie Mahoney Laubenthal, Graduate Coordinator, 734-763-6643, Fax: 734-936-1606, E-mail: laubenth@umich.edu.
Website: https://jpee.lsa.umich.edu/

University of Minnesota, Twin Cities Campus, Graduate School, College of Education and Human Development, Department of Curriculum and Instruction, Program in Teaching, Minneapolis, MN 55455-0213. Offers teaching (M Ed), including arts in education, elementary education, English education, mathematics, science, second language education, social studies. *Students:* 237 full-time (169 women), 171 part-time (112 women); includes 91 minority (23 Black or African American, non-Hispanic/Latino; 3 American Indian or Alaska Native, non-Hispanic/Latino; 19 Asian, non-Hispanic/Latino; 25 Hispanic/Latino; 21 Two or more races, non-Hispanic/Latino), 10 international. Average age 27. 421 applicants, 72% accepted, 275 enrolled. In 2016, 584 master's awarded. Application fee: $75 ($95 for international students). *Unit head:* Dr. Cynthia Lewis, Chair, 612-625-6313, Fax: 612-624-8277, E-mail: lewis@umn.edu. *Application contact:* Dr. Kendall King, Director of Graduate Studies, 612-625-3692, E-mail: roehr013@umn.edu.
Website: http://www.cehd.umn.edu/ci/

University of Missouri, Office of Research and Graduate Studies, College of Education, Department of Learning, Teaching and Curriculum, Columbia, MO 65211. Offers agricultural education (M Ed, PhD, Ed S); art education (M Ed, PhD, Ed S); business and office education (M Ed, PhD, Ed S); early childhood education (M Ed, PhD, Ed S); elementary education (M Ed, PhD, Ed S); English education (M Ed, PhD, Ed S); foreign language education (M Ed, PhD, Ed S); health education and promotion (M Ed, PhD); learning and instruction (M Ed); marketing education (M Ed, PhD, Ed S); mathematics education (M Ed, PhD, Ed S); music education (M Ed, PhD, Ed S); reading education (M Ed, PhD, Ed S); science education (M Ed, PhD, Ed S); social studies education (M Ed, PhD, Ed S); vocational education (M Ed, PhD, Ed S). *Program availability:* Part-time. *Faculty:* 30 full-time (18 women), 1 (woman) part-time/adjunct. *Students:* 157 full-time (124 women), 157 part-time (125 women). Terminal master's awarded for partial completion of doctoral program. *Degree requirements:* For doctorate, thesis/dissertation. *Entrance requirements:* For master's and Ed S, GRE General Test or MAT, minimum GPA of 3.0; for doctorate, GRE General Test, minimum GPA of 3.0. Additional exam requirements/recommendations for international students: Required—TOEFL (minimum score 600 paper-based; 100 iBT). *Application deadline:* For fall admission, 12/1 priority date for domestic and international students. Applications are processed on a rolling basis. Application fee: $75 ($90 for international students). Electronic applications accepted. *Expenses:* Tuition, state resident: full-time $6347; part-time $352.60 per credit hour. Tuition, nonresident: full-time $17,379; part-time $965.50 per credit hour. *Required fees:* $1035. Tuition and fees vary according to course load, campus/location and program. *Financial support:* Fellowships, research assistantships, teaching assistantships, institutionally sponsored loans, traineeships, health care benefits, and unspecified assistantships available. Support available to part-time students.
Website: http://education.missouri.edu/LTC/index.php

University of Montana, Graduate School, College of Humanities and Sciences, Department of English, Program in Teaching, Missoula, MT 59812-0002. Offers MA. *Entrance requirements:* For master's, GRE General Test, sample of written work.

University of New Mexico, Graduate Studies, College of Education, Program in Language, Literacy and Sociocultural Studies, Albuquerque, NM 87131. Offers American Indian education (MA); bilingual education (MA, PhD); educational linguistics (PhD); educational thought and sociocultural studies (MA, PhD); literacy/language arts (MA, PhD); social studies (MA); TESOL (MA, PhD). *Faculty:* 17 full-time (10 women), 4 part-time/adjunct (3 women). *Students:* 57 full-time (38 women), 129 part-time (105 women); includes 102 minority (8 Black or African American, non-Hispanic/Latino; 16 American Indian or Alaska Native, non-Hispanic/Latino; 6 Asian, non-Hispanic/Latino; 67 Hispanic/Latino; 5 Two or more races, non-Hispanic/Latino), 32 international. Average age 39. 50 applicants, 60% accepted, 23 enrolled. In 2016, 36 master's, 4 doctorates awarded. *Degree requirements:* For master's, comprehensive exam, thesis optional; for doctorate, comprehensive exam, thesis/dissertation, research skills. *Entrance requirements:* For master's, letter of intent, 3 letters of recommendation, resume, BA/BS, department demographic form, transcripts; for doctorate, writing sample, letter of intent, 3 letters of recommendation, resume, BA/BS, MA, department demographic form, transcripts. Additional exam requirements/recommendations for international students: Required—TOEFL. *Application deadline:* For fall admission, 12/1 for domestic and international students; for spring admission, 9/15 for domestic and international students. Application fee: $50. Electronic applications accepted. *Financial support:* Fellowships, research assistantships, teaching assistantships with tuition reimbursements, career-related internships or fieldwork, institutionally sponsored loans, scholarships/grants, and unspecified assistantships available. Support available to part-time students. Financial award application deadline: 3/1; financial award applicants required to submit FAFSA. *Faculty research:* School reform, professional development, history of education, Native American education, politics of education, feminism and issues of sexual identity, critical race theory, bilingualism, literacy reading, adolescent literature, second language acquisition, critical theory and schooling, indigenous languages. *Unit head:* Dr. Lois M. Meyer, Chair, 505-277-7244, Fax: 505-277-8362, E-mail: lsmeyer@unm.edu. *Application contact:* Debra Schaffer, Administrative Assistant, 505-277-0437, Fax: 505-277-8362, E-mail: schaffer@unm.edu.
Website: http://coe.unm.edu/departments-programs/llss/index.html

The University of North Carolina at Chapel Hill, Graduate School, School of Education, Program in Secondary Education, Chapel Hill, NC 27599. Offers English (Grades 9-12) (MAT); English as a second language (MAT); French (Grades K-12) (MAT); German (Grades K-12) (MAT); Japanese (Grades K-12) (MAT); Latin (Grades 9-12) (MAT); mathematics (Grades 9-12) (MAT); music (Grades K-12) (MAT); science (Grades 9-12) (MAT); social studies (Grades 9-12) (MAT); Spanish (Grades K-12) (MAT). *Accreditation:* NCATE. *Degree requirements:* For master's, comprehensive exam. *Entrance requirements:* For master's, GRE General Test, minimum GPA of 3.0 during last 2 years of undergraduate course work. Additional exam requirements/ recommendations for international students: Required—TOEFL (minimum score 550 paper-based). Electronic applications accepted.

The University of North Carolina at Greensboro, Graduate School, College of Arts and Sciences, Department of English, Program in English, Greensboro, NC 27412-5001. Offers American literature (PhD); English (M Ed, MA); English literature (PhD); rhetoric and composition (PhD). *Degree requirements:* For master's, comprehensive exam, thesis or alternative; for doctorate, variable foreign language requirement, thesis/ dissertation, preliminary exam. *Entrance requirements:* For master's, GRE General Test, GRE Subject Test, minimum GPA of 3.0; for doctorate, GRE General Test, GRE Subject Test, critical writing sample, minimum GPA of 3.0. Additional exam requirements/recommendations for international students: Required—TOEFL. Electronic applications accepted.

The University of North Carolina at Pembroke, The Graduate School, Department of English, Theatre and Foreign Languages, Pembroke, NC 28372-1510. Offers English education (MA, MAT). *Program availability:* Part-time, evening/weekend. *Degree requirements:* For master's, comprehensive exam, thesis optional. *Entrance requirements:* For master's, GRE, MAT, or NTE, minimum GPA of 3.0 in major or 2.5 overall. Additional exam requirements/recommendations for international students: Required—TOEFL.

English Education

University of Northern Colorado, Graduate School, College of Education and Behavioral Sciences, School of Teacher Education, Greeley, CO 80639. Offers curriculum studies (MAT); educational studies (Ed D); elementary education (MAT); English education (MAT); literacy (MA); multilingual education (MA), including TESOL, world languages; teaching diverse learners (MA). *Accreditation:* NCATE. *Program availability:* Part-time, evening/weekend. *Degree requirements:* For master's, comprehensive exam, thesis or alternative; for doctorate, comprehensive exam, thesis/dissertation. *Entrance requirements:* For master's and doctorate, GRE General Test, 3 letters of recommendation. *Application deadline:* Applications are processed on a rolling basis. Application fee: $50 ($60 for international students). Electronic applications accepted. *Financial support:* Fellowships, research assistantships, teaching assistantships, and unspecified assistantships available. Financial award application deadline: 3/1; financial award applicants required to submit FAFSA. *Unit head:* Dr. Alexander Sidorkin, Director, 970-351-2908, Fax: 970-351-1877. *Application contact:* Linda Sisson, Graduate Student Admission Coordinator, 970-351-1807, Fax: 970-351-2371, E-mail: linda.sisson@unco.edu.
Website: http://www.unco.edu/cebs/teachered/

University of Northern Iowa, Graduate College, College of Humanities, Arts and Sciences, Department of Languages and Literatures, MA Program in Teaching English in Secondary Schools, Cedar Falls, IA 50614. Offers MA.

University of North Georgia, College of Education, Dahlonega, GA 30597. Offers early childhood education (M Ed); middle grades education (M Ed, MAT); physical education (MS); school leadership (Ed S); secondary education (M Ed), including English education, history education, mathematics education, physical education. *Accreditation:* NCATE. *Program availability:* Part-time, evening/weekend, online learning. *Faculty:* 16 full-time (12 women), 3 part-time/adjunct (all women). *Students:* 11 full-time (8 women), 146 part-time (107 women); includes 19 minority (10 Black or African American, non-Hispanic/Latino; 2 Asian, non-Hispanic/Latino; 6 Hispanic/Latino; 1 Two or more races, non-Hispanic/Latino). Average age 28. 77 applicants, 83% accepted, 47 enrolled. In 2016, 79 master's awarded. *Degree requirements:* For master's, comprehensive exam, thesis optional. *Entrance requirements:* For master's, GRE or MAT, GACE, minimum GPA of 2.75; for Ed S, GRE General Test or MAT, 3 years of teaching experience, master's degree, minimum graduate GPA of 3.25, leadership position in the school. Additional exam requirements/recommendations for international students: Required—TOEFL (minimum score 550 paper-based; 79 iBT), IELTS (minimum score 6.5). *Application deadline:* For fall admission, 8/1 priority date for domestic students, 7/1 priority date for international students; for spring admission, 12/1 priority date for domestic students, 11/1 priority date for international students. Applications are processed on a rolling basis. Application fee: $40. Electronic applications accepted. *Expenses:* Contact institution. *Financial support:* Teaching assistantships, career-related internships or fieldwork, scholarships/grants, and unspecified assistantships available. Financial award application deadline: 5/1; financial award applicants required to submit CSS PROFILE or FAFSA. *Unit head:* Dr. Susan Ayers, Dean, College of Education, 706-864-1998, E-mail: susan.ayres@ung.edu. *Application contact:* Regina Boling, Teacher Education Graduate Admissions, 706-864-1533, E-mail: regina.boling@ung.edu.
Website: http://ung.edu/college-of-education/

University of Oklahoma, Jeannine Rainbolt College of Education, Department of Instructional Leadership and Academic Curriculum, Norman, OK 73019. Offers instructional leadership and academic curriculum (M Ed, PhD), including biomedical education (PhD), early childhood education, elementary education (M Ed), English education, instructional leadership, mathematics education, reading education, science education, social studies education, world languages education (M Ed). *Accreditation:* NCATE. *Program availability:* Part-time. *Faculty:* 19 full-time (15 women), 1 (woman) part-time/adjunct. *Students:* 66 full-time (49 women), 116 part-time (88 women); includes 49 minority (12 Black or African American, non-Hispanic/Latino; 6 American Indian or Alaska Native, non-Hispanic/Latino; 6 Asian, non-Hispanic/Latino; 11 Hispanic/Latino; 1 Native Hawaiian or other Pacific Islander, non-Hispanic/Latino; 13 Two or more races, non-Hispanic/Latino), 13 international. Average age 35. 38 applicants, 97% accepted, 28 enrolled. In 2016, 33 master's, 10 doctorates awarded. Terminal master's awarded for partial completion of doctoral program. *Degree requirements:* For master's, comprehensive exam (for some programs), thesis (for some programs); for doctorate, comprehensive exam (for some programs), thesis/dissertation. *Entrance requirements:* For doctorate, GRE. Additional exam requirements/recommendations for international students: Required—TOEFL (minimum score 79 iBT) or IELTS (minimum score 6.5). Application fee: $50 ($100 for international students). Electronic applications accepted. *Expenses:* Tuition, state resident: full-time $4886; part-time $203.60 per credit hour. Tuition, nonresident: full-time $18,989; part-time $791.20 per credit hour. *Required fees:* $3283; $126.25 per credit hour. $126.50 per semester. *Financial support:* In 2016–17, 112 students received support, including 7 research assistantships with partial tuition reimbursements available (averaging $10,373 per year), 6 teaching assistantships with partial tuition reimbursements available (averaging $11,446 per year); fellowships, scholarships/grants, and unspecified assistantships also available. Financial award application deadline: 6/1; financial award applicants required to submit FAFSA. *Faculty research:* Teacher preparation; instruction; curriculum; learning; constructivist theory. *Total annual research expenditures:* $165,297. *Unit head:* Dr. Stacy Reeder, Chair, 405-325-1498, Fax: 405-325-4061, E-mail: reeder@ou.edu. *Application contact:* Anna Steele, Graduate Programs Officer, 405-325-4525, E-mail: anna.steele@ou.edu.
Website: http://www.ou.edu/education/ilac

University of Pennsylvania, Graduate School of Education, Division of Literacy, Culture, and International Education, Program in Reading/Writing/Literacy, Philadelphia, PA 19104. Offers MS Ed, Ed D, PhD. *Program availability:* Part-time. *Students:* 53 full-time (36 women), 26 part-time (21 women); includes 37 minority (19 Black or African American, non-Hispanic/Latino; 7 Asian, non-Hispanic/Latino; 6 Hispanic/Latino; 5 Two or more races, non-Hispanic/Latino), 5 international. Average age 32. 101 applicants, 53% accepted, 30 enrolled. In 2016, 15 master's, 7 doctorates awarded. *Expenses: Tuition:* Full-time $31,068; part-time $5762 per course. *Required fees:* $3200; $336 per course. Full-time tuition and fees vary according to degree level, program and student level. Part-time tuition and fees vary according to course load, degree level and program. *Financial support:* In 2016–17, 26 students received support.

University of Phoenix–Online Campus, College of Education, Phoenix, AZ 85034-7209. Offers administration and supervision (MAEd, Certificate); adult education and training (MAEd); curriculum and instruction (MAEd), including computer education, curriculum and instruction, English as a second language, language arts, mathematics, reading; early childhood education (MAEd); educational studies (MAEd); elementary teacher education (MAEd), including early childhood, elementary teacher education, high school middle level, middle level; principal licensure (Certificate); secondary teacher education (MAEd); special education (MAEd, Certificate); teacher education (MAEd), including middle level generalist; teacher education middle level mathematics (MAEd), including middle level mathematics; teacher education middle level science (MAEd), including middle level science; teacher education secondary mathematics (MAEd); teacher education secondary science (MAEd); teacher leadership (MAEd); teachers of English learners (Certificate); transition to teaching (Certificate), including elementary education, secondary education. *Program availability:* Evening/weekend, online learning. *Entrance requirements:* Additional exam requirements/recommendations for international students: Required—TOEFL, TOEIC (Test of English as an International Communication), Berlitz Online English Proficiency Exam, PTE, or IELTS. Electronic applications accepted. *Expenses:* Contact institution.

University of Phoenix–Washington D.C. Campus, College of Education, Washington, DC 20001. Offers administration and supervision (MA Ed); adult education and training (MA Ed); computer education (MA Ed); curriculum and instruction (MA Ed, Ed D); early childhood education (MA Ed); education (Ed S); educational leadership (Ed D); educational technology (Ed D); elementary teacher education (MA Ed); English and language arts education (MA Ed); English as a second language (MA Ed); higher education administration (PhD); mathematics education (MA Ed); secondary teacher education (MA Ed); special education (MA Ed); teacher leadership (MA Ed).

University of Pittsburgh, School of Education, Department of Instruction and Learning, Program in Secondary Education, Pittsburgh, PA 15260. Offers English and communications education (M Ed, MAT); foreign language education (M Ed, MAT); language, literacy and culture education (Ed D, PhD); mathematics education (M Ed, MAT, Ed D, PhD); science education (M Ed, MAT, Ed D, PhD); secondary education (PhD); social studies education (M Ed, MAT); STEM education (Ed D). *Program availability:* Part-time, evening/weekend. *Degree requirements:* For master's, thesis; for doctorate, thesis/dissertation. *Entrance requirements:* For master's, PRAXIS I; for doctorate, GRE General Test. Additional exam requirements/recommendations for international students: Required—TOEFL. Electronic applications accepted. Tuition and fees vary according to program.

University of Puerto Rico, Mayagüez Campus, Graduate Studies, College of Arts and Sciences, Department of English, Mayagüez, PR 00681-9000. Offers English education (MA). *Program availability:* Part-time. *Faculty:* 34 full-time (23 women), 3 part-time/adjunct (2 women). *Students:* 52 full-time (37 women), 3 part-time (all women); includes 50 minority (all Hispanic/Latino). Average age 25. 12 applicants, 67% accepted, 7 enrolled. In 2016, 7 master's awarded. *Degree requirements:* For master's, one foreign language, comprehensive exam, thesis. *Entrance requirements:* For master's, minimum GPA of 3.0; course work in linguistics or language, American literature, British literature, and structure/grammar or syntax. Additional exam requirements/recommendations for international students: Required—TOEFL (minimum score 550 paper-based; 79 iBT). *Application deadline:* For fall admission, 2/15 for domestic and international students; for spring admission, 9/15 for domestic and international students. Applications are processed on a rolling basis. Application fee: $25. Electronic applications accepted. *Expenses: Tuition, area resident:* Full-time $2466. *International tuition:* $7166 full-time. *Required fees:* $210. Tuition and fees vary according to course level, campus/location, program and student level. *Financial support:* In 2016–17, 46 students received support, including 2 research assistantships with full and partial tuition reimbursements available (averaging $2,200 per year), 46 teaching assistantships with full and partial tuition reimbursements available (averaging $4,145 per year); unspecified assistantships also available. *Faculty research:* Multiliteracies and multimodality theorizing and practice, second language writing, Afro-Puerto Rican studies, modern poetry, Puerto Rican culture and folklore. *Unit head:* Leonardo Flores, PhD, Interim Director, 787-832-4040 Ext. 3064, Fax: 787-265-3847, E-mail: leonardo.flores@upr.edu. *Application contact:* Paulette Almodóvar, Administrative Secretary, 787-265-3847, Fax: 787-265-3847, E-mail: paulette.almodovar@upr.edu.
Website: http://www.uprm.edu./english/

University of St. Francis, College of Education, Joliet, IL 60435-6169. Offers educational leadership (MS, Ed D); elementary education (M Ed); reading (MS); secondary education (M Ed), including English education, math education, science education, social studies education, visual arts education; special education (M Ed); teaching and learning (MS); TESOL (Certificate). *Accreditation:* NCATE. *Program availability:* Part-time, evening/weekend, 100% online, blended/hybrid learning. *Faculty:* 11 full-time (8 women), 60 part-time/adjunct (42 women). *Students:* 34 full-time (26 women), 420 part-time (318 women); includes 92 minority (51 Black or African American, non-Hispanic/Latino; 5 Asian, non-Hispanic/Latino; 31 Hispanic/Latino; 5 Two or more races, non-Hispanic/Latino), 4 international. Average age 36. 242 applicants, 48% accepted, 96 enrolled. In 2016, 229 master's, 44 doctorates, 10 other advanced degrees awarded. *Degree requirements:* For master's, comprehensive exam; for doctorate, thesis/dissertation. *Entrance requirements:* Additional exam requirements/recommendations for international students: Required—TOEFL (minimum score 550 paper-based; 79 iBT), IELTS (minimum score 6). *Application deadline:* Applications are processed on a rolling basis. Application fee: $30. Electronic applications accepted. Application fee is waived when completed online. *Expenses:* Contact institution. *Financial support:* In 2016–17, 48 students received support. Career-related internships or fieldwork and unspecified assistantships available. Support available to part-time students. Financial award applicants required to submit FAFSA. *Unit head:* Dr. John Gambro, Dean, 815-740-3829, Fax: 815-740-2264, E-mail: jgambro@stfrancis.edu. *Application contact:* Sandra Sloka, Director of Admissions for Graduate and Degree Completion Programs, 800-735-7500, Fax: 815-740-3431, E-mail: ssloka@stfrancis.edu.
Website: http://www.stfrancis.edu/academics/college-of-education/

University of South Carolina, The Graduate School, College of Arts and Sciences, Department of English Language and Literature, Columbia, SC 29208. Offers creative writing (MFA); English (MA, PhD); English education (MAT); MLIS/MA. MAT offered in cooperation with the College of Education. *Program availability:* Part-time. *Degree requirements:* For master's, one foreign language, comprehensive exam, thesis; for doctorate, 2 foreign languages, comprehensive exam, thesis/dissertation. *Entrance requirements:* For master's, GRE General Test (MFA), GRE Subject Test (MA, MAT), sample of written work; for doctorate, GRE General Test, GRE Subject Test, sample of written work. Additional exam requirements/recommendations for international students: Required—TOEFL. Electronic applications accepted. *Faculty research:* American literature, British literature, composition and rhetoric, linguistics, speech communication.

University of South Carolina, The Graduate School, College of Education, Department of Instruction and Teacher Education, Program in Secondary Education, Columbia, SC 29208. Offers art education (IMA, MAT); business education (IMA, MAT); English (MAT); foreign language (MAT); health education (MAT); mathematics (MAT); science (IMA, MAT); secondary (Ed D); secondary education (MT, PhD); social studies (MAT); theatre and speech (MAT). IMA and MT offered jointly with the subject areas. *Accreditation:* NCATE. *Degree requirements:* For master's, comprehensive exam, thesis (for some programs), foreign language (MA); for doctorate, one foreign language, comprehensive exam, thesis/dissertation. *Entrance requirements:* For master's, GRE General Test or MAT, teaching certificate (IMA, M Ed), interview; for doctorate, GRE General Test or MAT, interview. *Faculty research:* Middle school programs, professional development, school collaboration.

University of Southern Mississippi, Graduate School, College of Arts and Letters, Department of English, Hattiesburg, MS 39406-0001. Offers creative writing (MA, PhD); English education (MA); literature (MA, PhD). *Degree requirements:* For master's, one foreign language, comprehensive exam, thesis; for doctorate, 2 foreign languages, comprehensive exam, thesis/dissertation. *Entrance requirements:* For master's, GRE

General Test, minimum GPA of 3.0 in field of study, 2.75 in last 2 years; for doctorate, GRE General Test, minimum GPA of 3.5. Additional exam requirements/ recommendations for international students: Required—TOEFL, IELTS. *Application deadline:* For fall admission, 3/15 priority date for domestic students, 3/15 for international students. Application fee: $60. Electronic applications accepted. *Expenses: Tuition, area resident:* Full-time $15,708; part-time $437 per credit hour. *Financial support:* Fellowships, research assistantships with full tuition reimbursements, teaching assistantships with full tuition reimbursements, Federal Work-Study, institutionally sponsored loans, scholarships/grants, and unspecified assistantships available. Financial award application deadline: 3/15; financial award applicants required to submit FAFSA. *Faculty research:* English and American literature, critical theory and cultural studies, creative writing. *Unit head:* Dr. Luis Iglesias, Chair, 601-266-4060, Fax: 601-266-5757, E-mail: luis.iglesias@usm.edu. *Application contact:* Dr. Monika Gehlawat, Director, Graduate Studies, 601-266-4070, Fax: 601-266-5757, E-mail: monika.gehlawat@usm.edu.
Website: https://www.usm.edu/english

University of South Florida, St. Petersburg, College of Education, St. Petersburg, FL 33701. Offers educational leadership development (M Ed); elementary education (MA), including math/science; English education (MA); middle grades STEM education (MS); reading education (MA). *Program availability:* Part-time. *Degree requirements:* For master's, comprehensive exam, practicum, internship, comprehensive portfolio. *Entrance requirements:* For master's, State of Florida General Knowledge Test (GKT), Florida Teaching Certificate (for non-initial certification programs), letters of recommendation. Additional exam requirements/recommendations for international students: Required—TOEFL (minimum score 550 paper-based; 79 iBT); Recommended—IELTS. Electronic applications accepted.

University of South Florida Sarasota-Manatee, College of Liberal Arts and Social Sciences, Sarasota, FL 34243. Offers criminal justice (MA); education (MA); educational leadership (M Ed), including curriculum leadership, K-12 public school leadership, non-public/charter school leadership; elementary education (MAT); English education (MA); social work (MSW). *Program availability:* Part-time, 100% online, blended/hybrid learning. *Faculty:* 11 full-time (9 women), 7 part-time/adjunct (5 women). *Students:* 11 full-time (all women), 55 part-time (41 women); includes 18 minority (5 Black or African American, non-Hispanic/Latino; 1 American Indian or Alaska Native, non-Hispanic/ Latino; 2 Asian, non-Hispanic/Latino; 10 Hispanic/Latino). Average age 36. 40 applicants, 43% accepted, 17 enrolled. In 2016, 28 master's awarded. *Degree requirements:* For master's, comprehensive exam (for some programs). *Entrance requirements:* Additional exam requirements/recommendations for international students: Required—TOEFL (minimum score 550 paper-based; 79 iBT), IELTS (minimum score 6.5). *Application deadline:* For fall admission, 3/1 priority date for domestic students, 3/1 for international students; for spring admission, 10/1 priority date for domestic students, 10/1 for international students. Applications are processed on a rolling basis. Application fee: $30. Electronic applications accepted. *Expenses:* Contact institution. *Financial support:* In 2016–17, 9 students received support. Career-related internships or fieldwork, institutionally sponsored loans, scholarships/grants, health care benefits, and unspecified assistantships available. Support available to part-time students. Financial award application deadline: 3/1; financial award applicants required to submit FAFSA. *Faculty research:* Educational leadership, secondary education, elementary education, criminal justice, social work. *Unit head:* Dr. Jane Rose, Dean, 941-359-4469, Fax: 941-359-4778, E-mail: jane.rose@sar.usf.edu. *Application contact:* Brandon Avery, Assistant Director, Admissions, 941-359-4331, E-mail: bavery@ sar.usf.edu.
Website: http://usfsm.edu/college-of-liberal-arts-sciences/

The University of Tennessee, Graduate School, College of Education, Health and Human Sciences, Program in Education, Knoxville, TN 37996. Offers art education (MS); counseling education (PhD); cultural studies in education (PhD); curriculum (MS, Ed S); curriculum, educational research and evaluation (Ed D, PhD); early childhood education (PhD); early childhood special education (MS); education of deaf and hard of hearing (MS); educational administration and policy studies (Ed D, PhD); educational administration and supervision (Ed S); educational psychology (Ed D, PhD); elementary education (MS, Ed S); elementary teaching (MS); English education (MS, Ed S); exercise science (PhD); foreign language/ESL education (MS, Ed S); instructional technology (MS, Ed D, PhD, Ed S); literacy, language and ESL education (PhD); literacy, language education, and ESL education (Ed D); mathematics education (MS, Ed S); modified and comprehensive special education (MS); reading education (MS, Ed S); school counseling (Ed S); school psychology (PhD, Ed S); science education (MS, Ed S); secondary teaching (MS); social foundations (MS); social science education (MS, Ed S); socio-cultural foundations of sports and education (PhD); special education (Ed S); teacher education (Ed D, PhD). *Accreditation:* NCATE. *Program availability:* Part-time, evening/weekend. *Degree requirements:* For master's and Ed S, thesis optional; for doctorate, variable foreign language requirement, thesis/dissertation. *Entrance requirements:* For master's, minimum GPA of 2.7; for doctorate and Ed S, GRE General Test, minimum GPA of 2.7. Additional exam requirements/ recommendations for international students: Required—TOEFL. Electronic applications accepted.

The University of Texas at El Paso, Graduate School, College of Liberal Arts, Department of English, El Paso, TX 79968-0001. Offers bilingual professional writing (Certificate); English and American literature (MA); rhetoric and composition (PhD); rhetoric and writing studies (MA); teaching English (MAT). *Program availability:* Part-time, evening/weekend. *Degree requirements:* For master's, thesis optional. *Entrance requirements:* For master's, GRE General Test, minimum GPA of 3.0. Additional exam requirements/recommendations for international students: Required—TOEFL. Electronic applications accepted. *Faculty research:* Literature, creative writing, literary theory.

University of the District of Columbia, College of Arts and Sciences, Program in Teaching, Washington, DC 20008-1175. Offers elementary education (MAT); middle school mathematics (MAT); secondary English language arts (MAT); secondary social studies (MAT).

University of the Sacred Heart, Graduate Programs, Department of Education, San Juan, PR 00914-0383. Offers early childhood education (M Ed); information technology and multimedia (Certificate); instruction systems and education technology (M Ed), including English, information technology and multimedia, instructional design, mathematics, Spanish. *Program availability:* Part-time, evening/weekend. *Degree requirements:* For master's, thesis. *Entrance requirements:* For master's, EXADEP, minimum undergraduate GPA of 2.75, interview.

The University of Toledo, College of Graduate Studies, Judith Herb College of Education, Department of Curriculum and Instruction, Toledo, OH 43606-3390. Offers art education (ME); career and technical education (ME, Ed S); curriculum and instruction (ME, PhD, Ed S); early childhood education (Ed S); education and anthropology (MAE); education and biology (MES); education and chemistry (MES); education and classics (MAE); education and economics (MAE); education and English (MAE); education and French (MAE); education and geology (MES); education and German (MAE); education and history (MAE); education and mathematics (MAE, MES); education and physics (MES); education and political science (MAE); education and sociology (MAE); education and Spanish (MAE); educational media (PhD); educational technology (ME); educational technology: virtual educator (Certificate); elementary education (PhD); English as a second language (MAE); gifted and talented education (PhD); middle childhood education (ME); secondary education (ME, PhD); special education (PhD). *Accreditation:* NCATE. *Program availability:* Part-time, evening/ weekend. *Degree requirements:* For master's, comprehensive exam, thesis or alternative; for doctorate, comprehensive exam, thesis/dissertation; for other advanced degree, thesis optional. *Entrance requirements:* For master's, doctorate, and other advanced degree, minimum cumulative GPA of 2.7 for all previous academic work, letters of recommendation. Additional exam requirements/recommendations for international students: Required—TOEFL (minimum score 550 paper-based; 80 iBT). Electronic applications accepted.

The University of Tulsa, Graduate School, Kendall College of Arts and Sciences, School of Urban Education, Program in Teaching Arts, Tulsa, OK 74104-3189. Offers art (MTA); biology (MTA); English (MTA); history (MTA); mathematics (MTA). *Program availability:* Part-time. *Students:* 1 (woman) full-time. Average age 26. 4 applicants, 50% accepted, 1 enrolled. In 2016, 1 master's awarded. *Entrance requirements:* For master's, GRE General Test. Additional exam requirements/recommendations for international students: Required—TOEFL (minimum score 577 paper-based), IELTS (minimum score 6.5). *Application deadline:* Applications are processed on a rolling basis. Application fee: $55. Electronic applications accepted. *Expenses: Tuition:* Full-time $22,230; part-time $1235 per credit hour. *Required fees:* $990 per semester. Tuition and fees vary according to course load. *Financial support:* In 2016–17, 1 student received support, including 1 teaching assistantship with full tuition reimbursement available (averaging $13,410 per year); fellowships with tuition reimbursements available, research assistantships with tuition reimbursements available, career-related internships or fieldwork, Federal Work-Study, scholarships/grants, health care benefits, tuition waivers (full and partial), and unspecified assistantships also available. Support available to part-time students. Financial award application deadline: 2/1; financial award applicants required to submit FAFSA. *Unit head:* Dr. Sharon Baker, Chair, 918-631-2238, Fax: 918-631-3721, E-mail: sharon-baker@utulsa.edu. *Application contact:* Dr. David Brown, Advisor, 918-631-2719, Fax: 918-631-2133, E-mail: david-brown@ utulsa.edu.

University of Victoria, Faculty of Graduate Studies, Faculty of Education, Department of Curriculum and Instruction, Victoria, BC V8W 2Y2, Canada. Offers art education (M Ed, PhD); curriculum studies (M Ed, MA, PhD); early childhood education (M Ed, PhD); educational studies (PhD); language and literacy (M Ed, MA, PhD); mathematics (M Ed, MA, PhD); music education (M Ed, MA, PhD); science (M Ed, MA, PhD); social studies (M Ed, MA); social, cultural and foundational studies (MA, PhD); technology and environmental education (PhD). *Program availability:* Part-time. *Degree requirements:* For master's, thesis, project (M Ed); for doctorate, comprehensive exam, thesis/ dissertation. *Entrance requirements:* For master's, minimum B average. Additional exam requirements/recommendations for international students: Required—TOEFL (minimum score 575 paper-based), IELTS (minimum score 7). Electronic applications accepted. *Faculty research:* Elementary and secondary English, language arts, curriculum theory and practice, educational media and technology, educational administration and leadership, history and philosophy of education.

University of Virginia, Curry School of Education, Department of Curriculum, Instruction, and Special Education, Program in Curriculum and Instruction, Charlottesville, VA 22903. Offers curriculum and instruction (M Ed, Ed S); elementary education (M Ed, Ed D); English education (M Ed, Ed D); foreign language education (M Ed); mathematics education (M Ed, Ed D); science education (Ed D); social studies education (M Ed); MBA/M Ed. *Students:* 43 full-time (35 women), 24 part-time (16 women); includes 7 minority (1 Black or African American, non-Hispanic/Latino; 1 Asian, non-Hispanic/Latino; 2 Hispanic/Latino; 3 Two or more races, non-Hispanic/Latino), 4 international. Average age 33. 93 applicants, 78% accepted, 54 enrolled. In 2016, 52 master's, 14 other advanced degrees awarded. *Degree requirements:* For master's, comprehensive exam (for some programs); for doctorate, comprehensive exam, thesis/ dissertation; for Ed S, comprehensive exam. *Entrance requirements:* For master's, doctorate, and Ed S, GRE General Test, 2 letters of recommendation. Additional exam requirements/recommendations for international students: Required—TOEFL (minimum score 600 paper-based; 90 iBT), IELTS (minimum score 7). *Application deadline:* Applications are processed on a rolling basis. Application fee: $60. Electronic applications accepted. *Expenses:* Tuition, state resident: full-time $15,026; part-time $834 per credit hour. Tuition, nonresident: full-time $25,168; part-time $1378 per credit hour. *Required fees:* $2654. *Financial support:* Fellowships with tuition reimbursements, research assistantships with tuition reimbursements, and teaching assistantships with tuition reimbursements available. Financial award application deadline: 1/5; financial award applicants required to submit FAFSA. *Unit head:* Susan Mintz, Program Area Director, 434-924-3128, E-mail: slm4r@virginia.edu. *Application contact:* Eric Molnar, Assistant Director, Admissions and Enrollment Reporting, 434-243-2085, E-mail: eric.molnar@virginia.edu.
Website: http://curry.virginia.edu/academics/areas-of-study/curriculum-teaching-learning

University of Virginia, Curry School of Education, Program in Education, Charlottesville, VA 22903. Offers administration and supervision (PhD); applied developmental science (PhD); counselor education (PhD); curriculum and instruction (PhD); early childhood special education (MT); education evaluation (PhD); educational psychology (PhD); educational research (PhD); elementary education (MT); English education (MT, PhD); foreign language education (MT); higher education (PhD); instructional technology (PhD); kinesiology (MT, PhD); math education (PhD); reading education (PhD); research, statistics and evaluation (PhD); school psychology (PhD); science education (PhD); social studies education (MT, PhD); special education (PhD); world languages education (MT). *Students:* 452 full-time (357 women), 18 part-time (13 women); includes 100 minority (28 Black or African American, non-Hispanic/Latino; 39 Asian, non-Hispanic/Latino; 18 Hispanic/Latino; 15 Two or more races, non-Hispanic/ Latino), 14 international. Average age 25. 309 applicants, 51% accepted, 87 enrolled. In 2016, 144 master's, 31 doctorates awarded. *Degree requirements:* For master's, comprehensive exam (for some programs), field project; for doctorate, comprehensive exam, thesis/dissertation. *Entrance requirements:* For doctorate, GRE General Test. Additional exam requirements/recommendations for international students: Required—TOEFL (minimum score 600 paper-based; 90 iBT), IELTS (minimum score 7). *Application deadline:* Applications are processed on a rolling basis. Application fee: $60. Electronic applications accepted. *Expenses:* Tuition, state resident: full-time $15,026; part-time $834 per credit hour. Tuition, nonresident: full-time $25,168; part-time $1378 per credit hour. *Required fees:* $2654. *Financial support:* Fellowships, research assistantships, and teaching assistantships available. Financial award application deadline: 1/5; financial award applicants required to submit FAFSA. *Unit head:* Robert C. Pianta, Dean, 434-924-3334, E-mail: pianta@virginia.edu. *Application contact:* Eric Molnar, Assistant Director, Admissions and Enrollment Reporting, 434-243-2085, E-mail: eric.molnar@virginia.edu.
Website: http://curry.virginia.edu/teacher-education

English Education

University of Washington, Graduate School, College of Arts and Sciences, Department of English, Seattle, WA 98195. Offers creative writing (MFA); English as a second language (MAT); English literature and language (MA, MAT, PhD). *Program availability:* Part-time. Terminal master's awarded for partial completion of doctoral program. *Degree requirements:* For master's, one foreign language, thesis (for some programs); for doctorate, one foreign language, thesis/dissertation. *Entrance requirements:* For master's, GRE General Test, GRE Subject Test (MA and MAT in English), minimum GPA of 3.0; for doctorate, GRE General Test, GRE Subject Test. Additional exam requirements/recommendations for international students: Required—TOEFL. Electronic applications accepted. *Faculty research:* English and American literature, critical theory, creative writing, language theory.

University of Washington, Graduate School, College of Education, Seattle, WA 98195. Offers curriculum and instruction (M Ed, Ed D, PhD), including educational technology, general curriculum (Ed D, PhD), language, literacy, and culture, mathematics education, multicultural education, reading and language arts education (Ed D), science education, social studies education, teaching and curriculum (M Ed); educational leadership and policy studies (M Ed, Ed D, PhD), including administration (Ed D), educational policy, organization, and leadership (M Ed, PhD), higher education, leadership for learning (Ed D), social and cultural foundations of education (M Ed, PhD); educational psychology (M Ed, PhD), including educational psychology (PhD), human development and cognition (M Ed), learning sciences, measurement, statistics and research design (M Ed), school psychology (M Ed); instructional leadership (M Ed); intercollegiate athletic leadership (M Ed); special education (M Ed, Ed D, PhD), including early childhood special education (M Ed), emotional and behavioral disabilities (M Ed), learning disabilities (M Ed), low-incidence disabilities (M Ed), severe disabilities (M Ed), special education (Ed D, PhD); teacher education (MIT). *Accreditation:* APA. *Program availability:* Part-time, evening/weekend. *Degree requirements:* For master's, thesis optional; for doctorate, thesis/dissertation. *Entrance requirements:* For master's and doctorate, GRE General Test, minimum GPA of 3.0. Additional exam requirements/recommendations for international students: Required—TOEFL. Electronic applications accepted. *Faculty research:* School restructuring/effective schools, special education interventions, literacy and writing, technology, school partnerships, teacher preparation.

The University of West Alabama, School of Graduate Studies, College of Education, Departments of Instructional Leadership and Support/Curriculum and Instruction, Program in Secondary Education, Livingston, AL 35470. Offers biology (MAT); English language arts (MAT); high school 6-12 (M Ed); history (MAT); mathematics (MAT); science (MAT); social science (MAT). *Program availability:* Part-time, evening/weekend, 100% online. *Faculty:* 19 full-time (7 women), 7 part-time/adjunct (3 women). *Students:* 236 (159 women); includes 59 minority (53 Black or African American, non-Hispanic/Latino; 2 American Indian or Alaska Native, non-Hispanic/Latino; 1 Asian, non-Hispanic/Latino; 1 Hispanic/Latino; 2 Two or more races, non-Hispanic/Latino). Average age 32. 85 applicants, 88% accepted, 52 enrolled. In 2016, 84 master's awarded. *Degree requirements:* For master's, comprehensive exam, thesis optional. *Entrance requirements:* For master's, GRE General Test, MAT, minimum GPA of 2.75. Additional exam requirements/recommendations for international students: Required—TOEFL (minimum score 500 paper-based; 61 iBT). *Application deadline:* Applications are processed on a rolling basis. Application fee: $40. Electronic applications accepted. *Expenses:* Tuition, state resident: part-time $355 per credit hour. Tuition, nonresident: part-time $710 per credit hour. *Required fees:* $130 per semester. *Financial support:* Teaching assistantships, Federal Work-Study, scholarships/grants, and unspecified assistantships available. Support available to part-time students. Financial award application deadline: 3/1; financial award applicants required to submit FAFSA. *Faculty research:* Integrated arts in the curriculum, moral development of children. *Unit head:* Dr. Jodie Winship, Chair of Curriculum and Instruction, 205-652-5415, Fax: 205-652-3706, E-mail: jwinship@uwa.edu. *Application contact:* Dr. B. J. Kimbrough, Dean of Graduate Studies, 205-652-3647, Fax: 205-652-3706, E-mail: bkimbrough@uwa.edu. Website: http://www.uwa.edu/highschool612.aspx

University of Wisconsin–La Crosse, School of Education, La Crosse, WI 54601-3742. Offers English language arts elementary (Graduate Certificate); professional development (ME-PD); reading (MS Ed); special education (MS Ed). *Program availability:* Part-time, evening/weekend. *Faculty:* 5 full-time (3 women), 25 part-time/adjunct (17 women). *Students:* 85 part-time (74 women); includes 2 minority (1 Asian, non-Hispanic/Latino; 1 Hispanic/Latino). Average age 27. 32 applicants, 100% accepted, 23 enrolled. In 2016, 25 master's, 5 other advanced degrees awarded. *Entrance requirements:* For master's, GRE. Additional exam requirements/recommendations for international students: Required—TOEFL (minimum score 550 paper-based; 79 iBT). *Application deadline:* Applications are processed on a rolling basis. Electronic applications accepted. *Financial support:* Research assistantships, Federal Work-Study, scholarships/grants, health care benefits, and tuition waivers (partial) available. Support available to part-time students. Financial award application deadline: 3/15; financial award applicants required to submit FAFSA. *Unit head:* Marcie Wycoff-Horn, Dean, School of Education, 608-785-6786, E-mail: mwycoff-horn@uwlax.edu. *Application contact:* Brandon Schaller, Senior Graduate Student Status Examiner, 608-785-8941, E-mail: admissions@uwlax.edu. Website: https://www.uwlax.edu/soe/

University of Wisconsin–Milwaukee, Graduate School, School of Education, Department of Curriculum and Instruction, Milwaukee, WI 53201-0413. Offers curriculum and instruction (MS), including cross-curricular focus, early childhood education, English education, mathematics education, middle childhood/early adolescence education, reading education, science education, urban social studies education. *Program availability:* Part-time. *Students:* 21 full-time (13 women), 44 part-time (42 women); includes 10 minority (1 Black or African American, non-Hispanic/Latino; 1 Asian, non-Hispanic/Latino; 2 Hispanic/Latino; 6 Two or more races, non-Hispanic/Latino), 2 international. Average age 33. 42 applicants, 71% accepted, 20 enrolled. In 2016, 45 master's awarded. *Degree requirements:* For master's, thesis or alternative. *Entrance requirements:* Additional exam requirements/recommendations for international students: Required—TOEFL (minimum score 550 paper-based; 79 iBT), IELTS (minimum score 6.5). *Application deadline:* For fall admission, 1/1 priority date for domestic students; for spring admission, 9/1 for domestic students. Applications are processed on a rolling basis. Application fee: $56 ($96 for international students). Electronic applications accepted. *Financial support:* In 2016–17, 1 fellowship was awarded; research assistantships, teaching assistantships, career-related internships or fieldwork, health care benefits, unspecified assistantships, and project assistantships also available. Support available to part-time students. Financial award application deadline: 4/15; financial award applicants required to submit FAFSA. *Application contact:* General Information Contact, 414-229-4721, E-mail: soeinfo@uwm.edu. Website: http://uwm.edu/education/academics/curriculum-instruction-department/

Valdosta State University, Department of English, Valdosta, GA 31698. Offers literature (MA); rhetoric and composition (MA); studies for language arts teachers (MA). *Program availability:* Part-time, 100% online, blended/hybrid learning. *Degree requirements:* For master's, one foreign language, thesis, comprehensive written and/or oral exams. *Entrance requirements:* For master's, GRE General Test, minimum GPA of 3.0. Additional exam requirements/recommendations for international students: Required—TOEFL (minimum score 523 paper-based); Recommended—IELTS. Electronic applications accepted. *Expenses:* Contact institution. *Faculty research:* American literature, creative writing.

Valley City State University, Online Master of Education Program, Valley City, ND 58072. Offers elementary education (M Ed); English education (M Ed); library and information technologies (M Ed); teaching (MAT); teaching and technology (M Ed); teaching English language learners (M Ed); technology education (M Ed). *Accreditation:* NCATE. *Program availability:* Part-time, evening/weekend, online only, 100% online. *Faculty:* 21 full-time (12 women), 15 part-time/adjunct (11 women). *Students:* 4 full-time (3 women), 133 part-time (92 women); includes 9 minority (1 American Indian or Alaska Native, non-Hispanic/Latino; 4 Hispanic/Latino; 4 Two or more races, non-Hispanic/Latino), 1 international. Average age 34. 35 applicants, 91% accepted, 28 enrolled. In 2016, 45 master's awarded. *Degree requirements:* For master's, action research report, comprehensive portfolio. *Entrance requirements:* For master's, GRE, MAT, PRAXIS II or National Teaching Board for Professional Standards (if GPA is less than 3.0). Additional exam requirements/recommendations for international students: Required—TOEFL (minimum score 525 paper-based; 71 iBT); Recommended—IELTS (minimum score 5.5). *Application deadline:* For fall admission, 7/21 priority date for domestic and international students; for spring admission, 12/8 priority date for domestic and international students; for summer admission, 5/5 priority date for domestic and international students. Applications are processed on a rolling basis. Application fee: $35. Electronic applications accepted. *Expenses:* $373 per credit. *Financial support:* In 2016–17, 23 students received support. Scholarships/grants, tuition waivers (full and partial), and unspecified assistantships available. Financial award application deadline: 6/14; financial award applicants required to submit FAFSA. *Faculty research:* Universal accessibility, instructional design and technology, gender communication, STEM education in K-12. *Unit head:* Dr. Gary Thompson, Dean, 701-845-7197, E-mail: gary.thompson@vcsu.edu. *Application contact:* Misty Lindgren, Graduate Studies, 701-845-7303, Fax: 701-845-7190, E-mail: misty.lindgren@vcsu.edu. Website: http://www.vcsu.edu/graduate

Vanderbilt University, Peabody College, Department of Teaching and Learning, Nashville, TN 37240-1001. Offers elementary education (M Ed); English language learners (M Ed); learning and design (M Ed); learning, diversity, and urban studies (M Ed); reading education (M Ed); secondary education (M Ed). *Accreditation:* NCATE. *Program availability:* Part-time. *Faculty:* 44 full-time (34 women), 26 part-time/adjunct (21 women). *Students:* 120 full-time (106 women), 26 part-time (18 women); includes 22 minority (9 Black or African American, non-Hispanic/Latino; 6 Asian, non-Hispanic/Latino; 6 Hispanic/Latino; 1 Two or more races, non-Hispanic/Latino), 44 international. Average age 24. 328 applicants, 73% accepted, 76 enrolled. In 2016, 110 master's awarded. *Degree requirements:* For master's, comprehensive exam, thesis optional. *Entrance requirements:* For master's, GRE General Test, MAT. Additional exam requirements/recommendations for international students: Required—TOEFL (minimum score 550 paper-based; 80 iBT). *Application deadline:* For fall admission, 12/31 priority date for domestic and international students; for spring admission, 11/1 priority date for domestic and international students. Applications are processed on a rolling basis. Application fee: $0. Electronic applications accepted. *Expenses:* Tuition: Part-time $1854 per credit hour. *Financial support:* Fellowships with partial tuition reimbursements, research assistantships with partial tuition reimbursements, teaching assistantships with partial tuition reimbursements, Federal Work-Study, institutionally sponsored loans, scholarships/grants, tuition waivers (partial), and unspecified assistantships available. Support available to part-time students. Financial award application deadline: 1/15; financial award applicants required to submit FAFSA. *Faculty research:* Children's learning and development in core conceptual domains (STEM, English language arts, social studies); classroom discourse structures that teachers can learn and use to support students' learning and development K-6; intervention and design-based research on educational improvement at classroom, school, and district levels; design-based and learning sciences research on relations between learning in schools and other settings. *Unit head:* Dr. Rogers Hall, Chair, 615-322-8100, Fax: 615-322-8999, E-mail: rogers.hall@vanderbilt.edu. *Application contact:* Angela Saylor, Educational Coordinator, 615-322-8092, Fax: 615-322-8999, E-mail: angela.saylor@vanderbilt.edu.

Wagner College, Division of Graduate Studies, Education Department, Program in Secondary Education/Students with Disabilities, Staten Island, NY 10301-4495. Offers secondary education 7-12 (MS Ed), including language arts, languages other than English, mathematics and technology, science and technology, social studies. *Program availability:* Part-time, evening/weekend. *Degree requirements:* For master's, thesis (for some programs), completion of state certification exams before student teaching. *Entrance requirements:* For master's, minimum GPA of 3.0, interview, recommendations. Electronic applications accepted. Tuition and fees vary according to degree level.

Wayland Baptist University, Graduate Programs, Program in Education, Plainview, TX 79072-6998. Offers education administration (M Ed); education diagnostics (M Ed); education literacy (M Ed); elementary certification (M Ed); English (M Ed); English as a second language (M Ed); higher education administration (M Ed); human resources (M Ed); instructional leadership (M Ed); instructional technology (M Ed); leadership training and development (M Ed); science education (M Ed); secondary certification (M Ed); social studies (M Ed); special education (M Ed); sports administration and management (M Ed). *Program availability:* Part-time, evening/weekend, online learning. *Degree requirements:* For master's, comprehensive exam, capstone course. *Entrance requirements:* For master's, GRE, GMAT or MAT. Additional exam requirements/recommendations for international students: Required—TOEFL (minimum score 500 paper-based; 61 iBT). Electronic applications accepted.

Wayne State College, School of Education and Counseling, Department of Educational Foundations and Leadership, Program in Curriculum and Instruction, Wayne, NE 68787. Offers alternative education (MSE); business and information technology education (MSE); communication arts education (MSE); early childhood education (MSE); elementary education (MSE); English as a second language (MSE); English education (MSE); family and consumer sciences education (MSE); industrial technology and vocational education (MSE); learning communities (MSE); mathematics education (MSE); music education (MSE); science education (MSE); social science education (MSE). *Accreditation:* NCATE. *Program availability:* Part-time, evening/weekend. *Degree requirements:* For master's, comprehensive exam, thesis optional. *Entrance requirements:* For master's, GRE General Test. Additional exam requirements/recommendations for international students: Required—TOEFL (minimum score 550 paper-based).

Wayne State University, College of Education, Division of Teacher Education, Detroit, MI 48202. Offers art education (M Ed); bilingual/bicultural education (M Ed, Certificate); career and technical education (M Ed); curriculum and instruction (Ed D, PhD, Ed S), including art education (Ed D, PhD), bilingual education (Ed D, Ed S), career and technical education (MAT, Ed D, PhD, Ed S), early childhood education (MAT, Ed D, PhD, Ed S), elementary education, English as a second language (MAT, Ed D, Ed S), English education (MAT, Ed D, PhD, Ed S), foreign language education (MAT, Ed D, PhD), K-12 curriculum, mathematics education (MAT, Ed D, PhD, Ed S), science

education (MAT, Ed D, PhD, Ed S), secondary education, social studies education (MAT, Ed D, PhD, Ed S); early childhood education (M Ed); elementary education (M Ed, MAT), including bilingual/bicultural education (MAT), early childhood education (MAT, Ed D, PhD, Ed S), English as a second language (MAT, Ed D, Ed S), general elementary education (MAT), mathematics education (MAT, Ed D, PhD, Ed S), science education (MAT, Ed D, PhD, Ed S), social studies education (MAT, Ed D, PhD, Ed S); English as a second language (Certificate); English education (M Ed); foreign language education (M Ed); mathematics education (M Ed); reading (M Ed, Ed S); reading, language and literature (Ed D); science education (M Ed); secondary education (MAT), including art education (K-12), bilingual/bicultural education, career and technical education (MAT, Ed D, PhD, Ed S), English as a second language (MAT, Ed D, Ed S), English education (MAT, Ed D, PhD, Ed S), foreign language education (MAT, Ed D, PhD), kinesiology, mathematics education (MAT, Ed D, PhD, Ed S); social studies education (M Ed); special education (M Ed, MAT, Ed D, PhD, Ed S), including autism spectrum disorders (MAT), cognitive development (MAT), emotional impairment (MAT), learning disabilities (MAT). *Program availability:* Part-time, blended/hybrid learning. *Faculty:* 29. *Students:* 106 full-time (73 women), 351 part-time (276 women); includes 115 minority (76 Black or African American, non-Hispanic/Latino; 10 Asian, non-Hispanic/Latino; 20 Hispanic/Latino; 1 Native Hawaiian or other Pacific Islander, non-Hispanic/Latino; 8 Two or more races, non-Hispanic/Latino), 12 international. Average age 37. 242 applicants, 37% accepted, 72 enrolled. In 2016, 178 master's, 19 doctorates, 17 other advanced degrees awarded. *Degree requirements:* For master's, essay or project (for some M Ed programs), professional field experience (for MAT programs); for doctorate, thesis/dissertation. *Entrance requirements:* For master's, Michigan Test for Teacher Certification, verification of participation in group work with children, Michigan State Police criminal background check; for doctorate, minimum undergraduate GPA of 3.0, graduate 3.5; interview; curriculum vitae; references. Additional exam requirements/recommendations for international students: Required—TOEFL (minimum score 550 paper-based; 79 iBT), TWE (minimum score 5.5), Michigan English Language Assessment Battery (minimum score 85); Recommended—IELTS (minimum score 6.5). *Application deadline:* For fall admission, 6/1 priority date for domestic students, 5/1 priority date for international students; for winter admission, 10/1 priority date for domestic students, 9/1 priority date for international students; for spring admission, 2/1 priority date for domestic students, 1/1 priority date for international students. Applications are processed on a rolling basis. Application fee: $50. Electronic applications accepted. *Expenses:* $16,503 per year resident tuition and fees, $33,697 per year non-resident tuition and fees. *Financial support:* In 2016–17, 101 students received support, including 3 fellowships (averaging $11,409 per year); research assistantships with tuition reimbursements available, Federal Work-Study, scholarships/grants, and unspecified assistantships also available. Support available to part-time students. Financial award applicants required to submit FAFSA. *Faculty research:* Improving students' skill achievement in mathematics, improving elementary children's understanding of informational text, teachers' use of their pedagogical and mathematical knowledge in the interactive work of teaching, the intersection of identity construction in teaching and learning, identifying effective methods of literacy instruction and assessments for bilingual students in elementary language arts classrooms. *Unit head:* Dr. Kathleen Crawford-McKinney, Assistant Dean, 313-577-0122. *Application contact:* Janice Green, Assistant Dean, 313-577-1605, E-mail: jwgreen@wayne.edu.
Website: http://coe.wayne.edu/ted/index.php

West Chester University of Pennsylvania, College of Arts and Humanities, Department of English, West Chester, PA 19383. Offers English (MA), including creative writing, literature, writing, teaching, and criticism; publishing (Certificate); secondary English (Teaching Certificate). *Program availability:* Part-time, evening/weekend, blended/hybrid learning. *Faculty:* 12 full-time (8 women). *Students:* 21 full-time (14 women), 38 part-time (25 women); includes 3 minority (1 Black or African American, non-Hispanic/Latino; 2 Two or more races, non-Hispanic/Latino). Average age 28. 30 applicants, 97% accepted, 18 enrolled. In 2016, 13 master's, 2 other advanced degrees awarded. *Degree requirements:* For master's, thesis optional; for other advanced degree, capstone internship and e-portfolio (for Certificate). *Entrance requirements:* For master's, minimum GPA of 2.8, two letters of recommendation, writing sample, goals statement, official transcripts; for other advanced degree, undergraduate degree, statement of goals, and two letters of recommendation (for Certificate). Additional exam requirements/recommendations for international students: Required—TOEFL or IELTS. *Application deadline:* For fall admission, 5/15 for international students; for spring admission, 10/15 for international students. Applications are processed on a rolling basis. Application fee: $50. Electronic applications accepted. *Expenses:* Tuition, state resident: full-time $8694; part-time $483 per credit. Tuition, nonresident: full-time $13,050; part-time $725 per credit. *Required fees:* $2399; $119.05 per credit. Tuition and fees vary according to campus/location and program. *Financial support:* Scholarships/grants and unspecified assistantships available. Financial award application deadline: 2/15; financial award applicants required to submit FAFSA. *Faculty research:* Critical theory, cultural studies, literature, rhetoric and composition, creative writing. *Unit head:* Dr. Rodney Mader, Chair, 610-436-2822, Fax: 610-738-0516, E-mail: rmader@wcupa.edu. *Application contact:* Dr. Eleanor Shevlin, Graduate Coordinator for English, 610-436-2745, Fax: 610-738-0516, E-mail: eshevlin@wcupa.edu.
Website: http://www.wcupa.edu/arts-humanities/english/

Western Governors University, Teachers College, Salt Lake City, UT 84107. Offers curriculum and instruction (MS); educational leadership (MS); educational studies (MA); educational studies (5-12) (MA), including mathematics; elementary education (K-8) (MAT, Postbaccalaureate Certificate); elementary education (PreK-8) (MAT); English language learning (K-12) (MA); instructional design (MAT); learning and technology (M Ed, MA); management and innovation (M Ed); mathematics (5-12) (MAT, Postbaccalaureate Certificate); mathematics (5-9) (MAT, Postbaccalaureate Certificate); mathematics education (5-12) (MA); mathematics education (5-9) (MA); mathematics education (K-6) (MA); measurement and evaluation (M Ed); science (5-12) (Postbaccalaureate Certificate); science (5-9) (MAT, Postbaccalaureate Certificate); science education (5-12) (MA), including biology, chemistry, geology, physics; science education (5-9) (MA); social science (5-12) (MAT, Postbaccalaureate Certificate); special education (MAT, MS). *Accreditation:* NCATE. *Program availability:* Evening/weekend, online learning. *Degree requirements:* For master's, capstone project. *Entrance requirements:* For master's and Postbaccalaureate Certificate, Readiness Assessment, transcripts. Additional exam requirements/recommendations for international students: Required—TOEFL (minimum score 450 paper-based; 80 iBT). Electronic applications accepted. *Expenses:* Contact institution.

Western Kentucky University, Graduate Studies, Potter College of Arts and Letters, Department of English, Bowling Green, KY 42101. Offers education (MA); English (MA Ed); literature (MA), including American literature, British literature, literary theory, women writers, world literature; teaching English as a second language (MA); writing (MA). *Program availability:* Part-time, evening/weekend. *Degree requirements:* For master's, comprehensive exam, thesis optional, final exam. *Entrance requirements:* For master's, GRE General Test, minimum GPA of 2.75. Additional exam requirements/recommendations for international students: Required—TOEFL (minimum score 555 paper-based; 79 iBT). *Faculty research:* Improving writing, linking teacher knowledge and performance, Victorian women writers, Kentucky women writers, Kentucky poets.

Western Michigan University, Graduate College, College of Arts and Sciences, Department of English, Kalamazoo, MI 49008. Offers creative writing (MFA, PhD); English (MA, PhD); English teaching (MA). *Degree requirements:* For doctorate, one foreign language, thesis/dissertation.

Western New England University, College of Arts and Sciences, Program in English for Teachers, Springfield, MA 01119. Offers MAET. *Program availability:* Part-time, evening/weekend. *Faculty:* 12 full-time (6 women). *Students:* 14 part-time (11 women); includes 1 minority (Hispanic/Latino). Average age 31. 4 applicants, 50% accepted, 1 enrolled. In 2016, 7 master's awarded. *Entrance requirements:* For master's, two letters of recommendation, official transcript, personal statement, resume; provisional or standard state teaching certificate (preferred). Additional exam requirements/recommendations for international students: Required—TOEFL (minimum score 79 iBT). *Application deadline:* Applications are processed on a rolling basis. Application fee: $30. Electronic applications accepted. *Expenses:* Contact institution. *Financial support:* Application deadline: 4/15; applicants required to submit FAFSA. *Unit head:* Dr. Saeed Ghahramani, Dean, 413-782-1218, Fax: 413-796-2118, E-mail: sghahram@wne.edu. *Application contact:* Matthew Fox, Director of Admissions for Graduate Students and Adult Learners, 413-782-1410, Fax: 413-782-1777, E-mail: study@wne.edu.
Website: http://www1.wne.edu/academics/graduate/ma-english-teachers.cfm

Widener University, School of Education, Hospitality, and Continuing Studies, Chester, PA 19013-5792. Offers adult education (M Ed); counseling in higher education (M Ed); counselor education (M Ed); early childhood education (M Ed); educational foundations (M Ed); educational leadership (M Ed); educational psychology (M Ed); elementary education (M Ed); English and language arts (M Ed); health education (M Ed); higher education leadership (Ed D); home and school visitor (M Ed); human sexuality (M Ed, PhD); mathematics education (M Ed); middle school education (M Ed); principalship (M Ed); reading and language arts (Ed D); reading education (M Ed); school administration (Ed D); science education (M Ed); social studies education (M Ed); special education (M Ed); technology education (M Ed). *Accreditation:* NCATE. *Program availability:* Part-time, evening/weekend. *Faculty:* 34 full-time (22 women), 37 part-time/adjunct (14 women). *Students:* 97 full-time (64 women), 201 part-time (143 women); includes 56 minority (44 Black or African American, non-Hispanic/Latino; 1 American Indian or Alaska Native, non-Hispanic/Latino; 2 Asian, non-Hispanic/Latino; 8 Hispanic/Latino; 1 Two or more races, non-Hispanic/Latino), 32 international. Average age 39. 139 applicants, 88% accepted. In 2016, 45 master's, 21 doctorates awarded. Terminal master's awarded for partial completion of doctoral program. *Degree requirements:* For doctorate, thesis/dissertation. *Entrance requirements:* For master's, minimum GPA of 2.5; for doctorate, GRE or MAT, minimum GPA of 2.0 (undergraduate), 3.5 (graduate). *Application deadline:* Applications are processed on a rolling basis. Application fee: $25 ($300 for international students). Electronic applications accepted. *Expenses:* Contact institution. *Financial support:* Career-related internships or fieldwork, tuition waivers (full and partial), and unspecified assistantships available. Support available to part-time students. Financial award application deadline: 5/1. *Faculty research:* Reading and cognition, adult education, technology education, educational leadership, special education. *Unit head:* Dr. Shawn Fitzgerald, Dean, 610-499-4294, Fax: 610-499-4623, E-mail: smfitzgerald@widener.edu. *Application contact:* Dr. Roberta Nolan, Director of Graduate Admissions, 610-499-4125, E-mail: rdnolan@widener.edu.
Website: http://www.widener.edu/academics/schools/eics

William Carey University, School of Education, Hattiesburg, MS 39401-5499. Offers art education (M Ed); art of teaching (M Ed); elementary education (M Ed, Ed S); English education (M Ed); gifted education (M Ed); history and social science (M Ed); mild/moderate disabilities (M Ed); secondary education (M Ed). *Accreditation:* NCATE. *Program availability:* Part-time. *Degree requirements:* For master's, comprehensive exam. *Entrance requirements:* For master's, GRE, MAT, minimum GPA of 2.5, Class A teacher's license. Additional exam requirements/recommendations for international students: Required—TOEFL (minimum score 550 paper-based).

William Jessup University, Program in Teaching, Rocklin, CA 95765. Offers single subject English (MAT); single subject math (MAT). *Program availability:* Evening/weekend.

Worcester State University, Graduate Studies, Program in English, Worcester, MA 01602-2597. Offers MA. *Program availability:* Part-time, evening/weekend. *Faculty:* 3 full-time (1 woman). *Students:* 2 full-time (1 woman), 8 part-time (6 women). Average age 30. 11 applicants, 91% accepted, 5 enrolled. In 2016, 6 master's awarded. *Degree requirements:* For master's, comprehensive exam (for some programs), thesis or exam. *Entrance requirements:* For master's, GRE General Test or MAT, undergraduate degree in English or 18 undergraduate credits in English, excluding composition classes or English for English Language Learners. Additional exam requirements/recommendations for international students: Required—TOEFL (minimum score 550 paper-based; 79 iBT). *Application deadline:* For fall admission, 6/15 for domestic and international students; for spring admission, 11/1 for domestic and international students; for summer admission, 4/1 for domestic and international students. Applications are processed on a rolling basis. Application fee: $50. Electronic applications accepted. *Expenses:* Tuition, state resident: part-time $150 per credit. Tuition, nonresident: part-time $150 per credit. *Financial support:* Career-related internships or fieldwork, scholarships/grants, and unspecified assistantships available. Financial award application deadline: 3/1; financial award applicants required to submit FAFSA. *Unit head:* Dr. Dennis Quinn, Coordinator, 508-929-8705, Fax: 508-929-8174, E-mail: dwquinn@worcester.edu. *Application contact:* Sara Grady, Associate Dean, Graduate Studies and Professional Development, 508-929-8787, Fax: 508-929-8100, E-mail: sara.grady@worcester.edu.

Environmental Education

Alaska Pacific University, Graduate Programs, Environmental Science Department, Program in Outdoor and Environmental Education, Anchorage, AK 99508-4672. Offers MSOEE. *Program availability:* Part-time. *Degree requirements:* For master's, thesis. *Entrance requirements:* For master's, MAT or GRE, minimum GPA of 3.0. Additional exam requirements/recommendations for international students: Required—TOEFL (minimum score 550 paper-based).

Antioch University New England, Graduate School, Department of Environmental Studies, Program in Environmental Education, Keene, NH 03431-3552. Offers MS. *Degree requirements:* For master's, practicum. *Entrance requirements:* For master's, previous undergraduate course work in biology, chemistry, and mathematics; resume; 3 letters of recommendation. Additional exam requirements/recommendations for international students: Required—TOEFL (minimum score 550 paper-based). Electronic applications accepted. *Expenses:* Contact institution. *Faculty research:* Sustainability, natural resources inventory.

Arcadia University, School of Education, Glenside, PA 19038-3295. Offers art education (M Ed); computer education (CAS); curriculum (CAS); curriculum studies (M Ed); early childhood education (M Ed), including individualized, master teacher, research in child development; educational leadership (M Ed, Ed D, CAS); elementary education (M Ed); English education (MA Ed); environmental education (MA Ed); instructional technology (M Ed); language arts (M Ed); library science (M Ed); mathematics education (M Ed, MA Ed); music education (MA Ed); psychology (MA Ed); reading (M Ed, CAS); science education (M Ed, CAS); secondary education (M Ed, CAS); special education (M Ed, Ed D, CAS); theater arts (MA Ed); written communication (MA Ed). *Accreditation:* NASAD. *Program availability:* Part-time, evening/weekend, online learning. *Faculty:* 19 full-time (13 women), 3 part-time/adjunct (all women). *Students:* 22 full-time (16 women), 356 part-time (284 women); includes 84 minority (55 Black or African American, non-Hispanic/Latino; 2 American Indian or Alaska Native, non-Hispanic/Latino; 13 Asian, non-Hispanic/Latino; 11 Hispanic/Latino; 3 Two or more races, non-Hispanic/Latino), 4 international. Average age 34. 145 applicants, 73% accepted, 80 enrolled. In 2016, 95 master's, 11 doctorates awarded. *Application deadline:* Applications are processed on a rolling basis. Application fee: $50. Electronic applications accepted. *Expenses:* Contact institution. *Financial support:* Career-related internships or fieldwork, tuition waivers (partial), and unspecified assistantships available. *Unit head:* John T Groves, Interim Dean of the School of Education, 215-572-2940. *Application contact:* 215-572-2925, Fax: 215-572-2126, E-mail: grad@arcadia.edu.

Ball State University, Graduate School, College of Sciences and Humanities, Department of Natural Resources and Environmental Management, Muncie, IN 47306. Offers emergency management and homeland security (Certificate); natural resources and environmental management (MA, MS). *Program availability:* Part-time. *Degree requirements:* For master's, thesis (for some programs). *Entrance requirements:* For master's, GRE General Test, minimum baccalaureate GPA of 2.75 or 3.0 in latter half of baccalauareate, two letters of reference. Additional exam requirements/recommendations for international students: Required—TOEFL (minimum score 550 paper-based; 79 iBT), IELTS (minimum score 6.5). Electronic applications accepted. *Faculty research:* Acid rain, indoor air pollution, land reclamation.

Brooklyn College of the City University of New York, School of Education, Program in Childhood Education, Brooklyn, NY 11210-2889. Offers bilingual education (MS Ed); liberal arts (MS Ed); mathematics (MS Ed); science and environmental education (MS Ed). *Program availability:* Part-time, evening/weekend. *Entrance requirements:* For master's, LAST, interview, previous course work in education, writing sample, resume, 2 letters of recommendation. Additional exam requirements/recommendations for international students: Required—TOEFL (minimum score 500 paper-based; 61 iBT). Electronic applications accepted. *Faculty research:* Emotional intelligence, multiculturalism, arts immersion, the Holocaust.

Chatham University, Program in Education, Pittsburgh, PA 15232-2826. Offers early childhood education (MAT); elementary education (MAT); environmental education (K-12) (MAT); secondary art (MAT); secondary biology education (MAT); secondary chemistry education (MAT); secondary English education (MAT); secondary math education (MAT); secondary physics education (MAT); secondary social studies education (MAT); special education (MAT). *Degree requirements:* For master's, thesis, teaching experience. *Entrance requirements:* For master's, minimum GPA of 3.0, sample of written work, recommendation letters. Additional exam requirements/recommendations for international students: Required—TOEFL (minimum score 600 paper-based; 100 iBT), IELTS (minimum score 7), TWE. Electronic applications accepted. Application fee is waived when completed online. *Expenses: Tuition:* Full-time $16,254; part-time $903 per credit hour. *Required fees:* $468; $26 per credit hour. *Faculty research:* Gifted education, environmental education, technology in education, writing as learning, class size and achievement.

Concordia University, College of Education, Portland, OR 97211-6099. Offers career and technical education (M Ed); curriculum and instruction (M Ed), including adolescent literacy, career and technical education, e-learning/technology education, early childhood education, English for speakers of other languages, English language development, environmental education, mathematics, methods and curriculum, reading, science, teacher leadership, the inclusive classroom; early childhood (MAT); education leadership (Ed D); educational administration (M Ed); elementary education (MAT); secondary education (MAT); special education (M Ed); teacher leadership (Ed D). *Program availability:* Part-time, online learning. *Degree requirements:* For master's, comprehensive exam, work samples/portfolio. *Entrance requirements:* For master's, California Basic Educational Skills Test or PRAXIS I, minimum undergraduate GPA of 2.8, graduate 3.0; 2 letters of recommendation. Additional exam requirements/recommendations for international students: Required—TOEFL (minimum score 525 paper-based). Electronic applications accepted. *Faculty research:* Learner-centered classroom, brain-based learning, future of online learning.

Concordia University Wisconsin, Graduate Programs, Department of Education, Mequon, WI 53097-2402. Offers art education (MS Ed); early childhood (MS Ed); educational administration (MS Ed); environmental education (MS Ed); family studies (MS Ed); literacy (MS Ed); school counseling (MS Ed); special education (MS Ed). *Program availability:* Part-time, evening/weekend, online learning. *Degree requirements:* For master's, comprehensive exam, thesis or alternative. *Entrance requirements:* For master's, minimum GPA of 3.0, teaching license. Additional exam requirements/recommendations for international students: Required—TOEFL. Application fee: $35. *Financial support:* Career-related internships or fieldwork and tuition waivers (partial) available. Financial award application deadline: 8/1. *Faculty research:* Motivation, developmental learning, learning styles. *Unit head:* Dr. James Juergensen, Director, 262-243-4214, E-mail: james.juergensen@cuw.edu. *Application contact:* Graduate Admissions, 262-243-4248, Fax: 262-243-4428.

Florida Atlantic University, College of Education, Department of Teaching and Learning, Boca Raton, FL 33431-0991. Offers curriculum and instruction (M Ed), including art, biology, chemistry, English, French, German, mathematics, music, physics, Pre-K and primary education, reading, social sciences, Spanish; elementary education (M Ed); environmental education (M Ed); reading education (M Ed); social foundations of education (M Ed), including educational psychology, educational technology, multilingual education. *Accreditation:* NCATE. *Program availability:* Part-time, evening/weekend. *Faculty:* 15 full-time (12 women), 2 part-time/adjunct (1 woman). *Students:* 25 full-time (20 women), 41 part-time (37 women); includes 18 minority (9 Black or African American, non-Hispanic/Latino; 2 Asian, non-Hispanic/Latino; 7 Hispanic/Latino), 7 international. Average age 32. 54 applicants, 59% accepted, 18 enrolled. In 2016, 36 master's awarded. *Entrance requirements:* For master's, GRE General Test, minimum GPA of 3.0 in last 2 years of undergraduate course work. Additional exam requirements/recommendations for international students: Required—TOEFL (minimum score 500 paper-based; 61 iBT), IELTS (minimum score 6). *Application deadline:* For fall admission, 7/1 for domestic students, 2/15 for international students; for spring admission, 11/1 for domestic students, 7/15 for international students. Applications are processed on a rolling basis. Application fee: $30. *Expenses:* Tuition, state resident: full-time $7392; part-time $369.82 per credit hour. Tuition, nonresident: full-time $19,432; part-time $1024.81 per credit hour. *Financial support:* Fellowships with partial tuition reimbursements, research assistantships with partial tuition reimbursements, teaching assistantships with partial tuition reimbursements, career-related internships or fieldwork, scholarships/grants, and unspecified assistantships available. *Faculty research:* Technology, teaching English to speakers of other languages, math teaching, electronic portfolio assessment, global perspectives through social studies. *Unit head:* Dr. Barbara Ridener, Chairperson, 561-297-3588, E-mail: bridener@fau.edu. *Application contact:* Dr. Eliah Watlington, Associate Dean, 561-296-8520, Fax: 261-297-2991, E-mail: ewatling@fau.edu.
Website: http://www.coe.fau.edu/academicdepartments/tl/

Florida Institute of Technology, College of Science, Program in Environmental Education, Melbourne, FL 32901-6975. Offers MS. *Students:* 3 full-time (all women), 1 (woman) part-time. Average age 25. 5 applicants, 60% accepted, 1 enrolled. In 2016, 2 master's awarded. *Degree requirements:* For master's, comprehensive exam (for some programs), thesis optional, 30 credit hours. *Entrance requirements:* For master's, 3 letters of recommendation; resume; statement of objectives; bachelor's degree in science, environmental studies, environmental interpretation, psychology, or K-12 education. Additional exam requirements/recommendations for international students: Required—TOEFL (minimum score 550 paper-based; 79 iBT). *Application deadline:* Applications are processed on a rolling basis. Electronic applications accepted. *Expenses: Tuition:* Full-time $22,338; part-time $1241 per credit hour. *Required fees:* $250. Tuition and fees vary according to degree level, campus/location and program. *Financial support:* Applicants required to submit FAFSA. *Unit head:* Dr. Kastro Hamed, Department Head, 321-674-7206, E-mail: khamed@fit.edu. *Application contact:* Cheryl A. Brown, Associate Director of Graduate Admissions, 321-674-7581, Fax: 321-723-9468, E-mail: cbrown@fit.edu.
Website: http://www.fit.edu/programs/8119/ms-environmental-education#.VT_jzU10ypo

Goshen College, Merry Lea Environmental Learning Center, Goshen, IN 46526-4794. Offers MA. *Accreditation:* NCATE. *Faculty:* 6 full-time (0 women). *Students:* 5 full-time (4 women). Average age 31. 17 applicants, 53% accepted, 5 enrolled. In 2016, 3 master's awarded. *Degree requirements:* For master's, thesis. *Entrance requirements:* Additional exam requirements/recommendations for international students: Required—TOEFL (minimum score 600 paper-based; 100 iBT), IELTS (minimum score 6.5). *Application deadline:* For fall admission, 4/30 for domestic students. Applications are processed on a rolling basis. Application fee: $25. Electronic applications accepted. *Expenses: Tuition:* Full-time $15,000; part-time $750 per credit hour. Tuition and fees vary according to program. *Financial support:* Application deadline: 9/10. *Faculty research:* Environmental education, climate change, climate justice, landscape ecology, invasive species. *Unit head:* Dr. Luke Gascho, Executive Director, 260-799-5869, E-mail: lukeag@goshen.edu. *Application contact:* Dr. David Ostergren, Director of the Graduate Program in Environmental Education, 260-799-5869, E-mail: daveo@goshen.edu.
Website: http://www.goshen.edu/merrylea/

Hamline University, School of Education, St. Paul, MN 55104-1284. Offers education (MA Ed, Ed D); English as a second language (MA); literacy education (MA); natural science and environmental education (MA Ed); teaching (MAT); teaching English to speakers of other languages (MA). *Accreditation:* NCATE (one or more programs are accredited). *Program availability:* Part-time, evening/weekend, 100% online, blended/hybrid learning. *Faculty:* 29 full-time (23 women), 90 part-time/adjunct (70 women). *Students:* 277 full-time (201 women), 762 part-time (601 women); includes 122 minority (29 Black or African American, non-Hispanic/Latino; 1 American Indian or Alaska Native, non-Hispanic/Latino; 43 Asian, non-Hispanic/Latino; 29 Hispanic/Latino; 20 Two or more races, non-Hispanic/Latino), 12 international. Average age 34. 408 applicants, 77% accepted, 230 enrolled. In 2016, 279 master's, 14 doctorates awarded. *Degree requirements:* For master's, thesis (for some programs), thesis or capstone project; for doctorate, comprehensive exam, thesis/dissertation. *Entrance requirements:* For master's, official transcripts, essay, letters of recommendation, minimum GPA of 3.0 from bachelor's work; resume and/or writing samples (for some programs); for doctorate, personal statement, master's degree with minimum GPA of 3.0, letters of recommendation, writing sample. Additional exam requirements/recommendations for international students: Required—TOEFL. *Application deadline:* For fall admission, 6/1 for domestic and international students; for spring admission, 11/1 for domestic and international students; for summer admission, 3/1 for domestic and international students. Applications are processed on a rolling basis. Application fee: $0 ($100 for international students). Electronic applications accepted. *Expenses:* $466-$721 per credit. *Financial support:* Career-related internships or fieldwork, Federal Work-Study, and scholarships/grants available. Support available to part-time students. Financial award applicants required to submit FAFSA. *Faculty research:* Adult basic education, service-learning, teacher dispositions, diversity, technology. *Unit head:* Dr. Nancy Sorenson, Dean, 651-523-2600, Fax: 651-523-2489, E-mail: education@hamline.edu. *Application contact:* Shawn Skoog, Director of Graduate Recruitment and Admission, 651-523-2900, Fax: 651-523-3058, E-mail: gradprog@hamline.edu.
Website: http://www.hamline.edu/education

Instituto Tecnologico de Santo Domingo, Graduate School, Area of Basic And Environmental Sciences, Santo Domingo, Dominican Republic. Offers environmental science (M En S), including environmental education, environmental management, marine resources, natural resources management; mathematics (MS, PhD); renewable energy technology (MS, Certificate).

Montclair State University, The Graduate School, College of Science and Mathematics, Program in Environmental Studies, Montclair, NJ 07043-1624. Offers environmental education (MA); environmental management (MA); environmental science (MA). *Program availability:* Part-time, evening/weekend. *Degree requirements:* For master's, thesis. *Entrance requirements:* For master's, GRE General Test, 2 letters of recommendation, essay. Additional exam requirements/recommendations for international students: Required—TOEFL (minimum score 83 iBT), IELTS (minimum score 6.5). Electronic applications accepted. *Expenses:* Tuition, state resident: part-time $553 per credit. Tuition, nonresident: part-time $854 per credit. *Required fees:* $91 per credit. Tuition and fees vary according to program. *Faculty research:* Environmental geochemistry/remediation/forensics, environmental law and policy, regional climate modeling, remote sensing, Cenozoic marine sediment records from polar regions, sustainability science.

New York University, Steinhardt School of Culture, Education, and Human Development, Department of Teaching and Learning, Program in Environmental Conservation Education, New York, NY 10003. Offers MA. *Accreditation:* TEAC. *Program availability:* Part-time. *Degree requirements:* For master's, thesis (for some programs). *Entrance requirements:* Additional exam requirements/recommendations for international students: Required—TOEFL (minimum score 100 iBT). Electronic applications accepted. *Faculty research:* Environmental ethics, values and policy, philosophy and geography.

Oregon State University, Interdisciplinary/Institutional Programs, Program in Environmental Sciences, Corvallis, OR 97331. Offers biogeochemistry (MA, MS, PhD); ecology (MA, MS, PhD); environmental education (MA, MS, PhD); environmental sciences (PSM); natural resources (MA, MS, PhD); quantitative analysis (MA, MS, PhD); social science (MA, MS, PhD); water resources (MA, MS, PhD). *Program availability:* Part-time. *Students:* 22 full-time (16 women), 10 part-time (4 women); includes 5 minority (2 Asian, non-Hispanic/Latino; 1 Hispanic/Latino; 2 Two or more races, non-Hispanic/Latino), 4 international. Average age 33. 51 applicants, 33% accepted, 8 enrolled. In 2016, 4 master's, 6 doctorates awarded. *Degree requirements:* For master's, variable foreign language requirement, thesis; for doctorate, thesis/dissertation. *Entrance requirements:* For master's and doctorate, GRE. Additional exam requirements/recommendations for international students: Required—TOEFL (minimum score 80 iBT), IELTS (minimum score 6.5). *Application deadline:* For fall admission, 1/15 priority date for domestic and international students. Application fee: $75 ($85 for international students). *Expenses:* Tuition, state resident: full-time $12,150; part-time $450 per credit. Tuition, nonresident: full-time $21,789; part-time $807 per credit. *Required fees:* $1651; $1507 per credit. One-time fee: $350. Tuition and fees vary according to course load, campus/location and program. *Unit head:* Dr. Carolyn Fonyo Boggess, Interim Director, 541-760-4196, E-mail: carolyn.fonyo@oregonstate.edu.
Website: http://gradschool.oregonstate.edu/environmental-sciences-graduate-program-esgp

Prescott College, Graduate Programs, Program in Education, Prescott, AZ 86301. Offers early childhood education (MA); early childhood special education (MA); education (MA); elementary education (MA); environmental education leadership and administration (MA); equine-assisted learning (MA); school guidance counseling (MA); secondary education (MA); special education: learning disabilities (MA); special education: mental retardation (MA); special education: serious emotional disabilities (MA); student-directed independent study (MA); sustainability education (PhD). *Program availability:* Part-time, online learning. *Faculty:* 3 full-time (all women). *Students:* 9 full-time (8 women), 30 part-time (20 women); includes 11 minority (3 Black or African American, non-Hispanic/Latino; 2 American Indian or Alaska Native, non-Hispanic/Latino; 6 Hispanic/Latino). Average age 36. 66 applicants, 82% accepted, 32 enrolled. In 2016, 12 master's, 8 doctorates awarded. *Degree requirements:* For master's, thesis, fieldwork or internship, practicum; for doctorate, thesis/dissertation. *Entrance requirements:* For master's, 2 letters of recommendation, resume; for doctorate, 3 letters of recommendation, resume, official transcripts, personal statement, program proposal. Additional exam requirements/recommendations for international students: Required—TOEFL (minimum score 500 paper-based). *Application deadline:* For fall admission, 4/15 priority date for domestic and international students; for spring admission, 9/15 priority date for domestic and international students. Applications are processed on a rolling basis. Application fee: $40. Electronic applications accepted. *Expenses: Tuition:* Full-time $19,680. One-time fee: $260 part-time. *Financial support:* Fellowships, research assistantships, teaching assistantships, career-related internships or fieldwork, Federal Work-Study, institutionally sponsored loans, scholarships/grants, traineeships, health care benefits, tuition waivers, and unspecified assistantships available. Support available to part-time students. Financial award applicants required to submit FAFSA. *Unit head:* Bob Ellis, 928-350-2217, E-mail: bellis@prescott.edu. *Application contact:* Melanie Lefever, Assistant Director, Limited-residency Programs, 928-350-2106, Fax: 928-776-5242, E-mail: mlefever@prescott.edu.

Royal Roads University, Graduate Studies, Environment and Sustainability Program, Victoria, BC V9B 5Y2, Canada. Offers environment and management (M Sc, MA); environmental education and communication (MA, G Dip, Graduate Certificate); MA/MS. *Program availability:* Online learning. *Degree requirements:* For master's, thesis. *Entrance requirements:* For master's, 5-7 years of related work experience. Electronic applications accepted. *Faculty research:* Sustainable development, atmospheric processes, sustainable communities, chemical fate and transport of persistent organic pollutants, educational technology.

Slippery Rock University of Pennsylvania, Graduate Studies (Recruitment), College of Health, Environment, and Science, Department of Parks and Recreation, Slippery Rock, PA 16057-1383. Offers environmental education (M Ed); park and resource management (MS). *Program availability:* Part-time, evening/weekend, online only, 100% online. *Faculty:* 2 full-time (1 woman), 1 (woman) part-time/adjunct. *Students:* 8 full-time (4 women), 86 part-time (59 women); includes 7 minority (4 Black or African American, non-Hispanic/Latino; 1 Asian, non-Hispanic/Latino; 1 Hispanic/Latino; 1 Two or more races, non-Hispanic/Latino), 1 international. Average age 31. 66 applicants, 74% accepted, 31 enrolled. In 2016, 42 master's awarded. *Degree requirements:* For master's, comprehensive exam (for some programs), thesis (for some programs), internship. *Entrance requirements:* For master's, official transcripts, minimum GPA of 2.75, personal statement. Additional exam requirements/recommendations for international students: Required—TOEFL (minimum score 550 paper-based; 80 iBT). *Application deadline:* For fall admission, 3/1 priority date for domestic students, 5/1 priority date for international students; for spring admission, 10/1 priority date for domestic students, 9/1 priority date for international students. Applications are processed on a rolling basis. Application fee: $25 ($30 for international students). Electronic applications accepted. *Expenses:* $646.50 per credit in-state, $936.80 per credit out-of-state; $581.45 per online credit in-state, $648.65 per online credit out-of-state. *Financial support:* In 2016–17, 5 students received support. Career-related internships or fieldwork, Federal Work-Study, institutionally sponsored loans, scholarships/grants, tuition waivers (partial), and unspecified assistantships available. Support available to part-time students. Financial award application deadline: 5/1; financial award applicants required to submit FAFSA. *Unit head:* Dr. John Lisco, Graduate Coordinator, 724-738-2596, Fax: 724-738-2938, E-mail: john.lisco@sru.edu. *Application contact:* Brandi Weber-Mortimer, Director of Graduate Admissions, 724-738-2051, Fax: 724-738-2146, E-mail: graduate.admissions@sru.edu.
Website: http://www.sru.edu/academics/colleges-and-departments/ches/departments/parks-and-recreation

Southern Connecticut State University, School of Graduate Studies, School of Arts and Sciences, Department of Environment, Geography and Marine Sciences, New Haven, CT 06515-1355. Offers environmental education (MS); science education (MS, Diploma). *Accreditation:* NCATE. *Program availability:* Part-time, evening/weekend. *Faculty:* 3 full-time (1 woman), 1 part-time/adjunct (0 women). *Students:* 7 full-time (4 women), 27 part-time (14 women); includes 5 minority (1 Black or African American, non-Hispanic/Latino; 1 Asian, non-Hispanic/Latino; 2 Hispanic/Latino; 1 Two or more races, non-Hispanic/Latino). Average age 33. 26 applicants, 69% accepted, 15 enrolled. In 2016, 12 master's awarded. *Degree requirements:* For master's, thesis or alternative. *Entrance requirements:* For master's, interview; for Diploma, master's degree. *Application deadline:* For fall admission, 7/15 priority date for domestic students. Applications are processed on a rolling basis. Application fee: $50. Electronic applications accepted. *Expenses:* Tuition, state resident: full-time $6497; part-time $519 per credit hour. Tuition, nonresident: full-time $18,102; part-time $535 per credit hour. *Required fees:* $4722; $55 per semester. Tuition and fees vary according to program. *Financial support:* Career-related internships or fieldwork, scholarships/grants, and unspecified assistantships available. Financial award application deadline: 4/15; financial award applicants required to submit FAFSA. *Unit head:* Dr. Patrick Heidkamp, Chairman, 203-392-5919, Fax: 203-392-5834, E-mail: heidkampc1@southernct.edu. *Application contact:* Lisa Galvin, Director of Graduate Admissions, 203-392-5240, Fax: 203-392-5235, E-mail: galvinl1@southernct.edu.

Southern Oregon University, Graduate Studies, Program in Environmental Education, Ashland, OR 97520. Offers MS. *Program availability:* Part-time, online learning. *Faculty:* 11 full-time (5 women), 2 part-time/adjunct (0 women). *Students:* 27 full-time (22 women), 1 (woman) part-time; includes 3 minority (2 Hispanic/Latino; 1 Two or more races, non-Hispanic/Latino). Average age 28. 2 applicants, 100% accepted, 2 enrolled. In 2016, 13 master's awarded. *Degree requirements:* For master's, thesis (for some programs), comprehensive exam (for MA). *Entrance requirements:* For master's, GRE General Test, minimum cumulative GPA of 3.0 in the last 90 quarter credits (60 semester credits) of undergraduate coursework. Additional exam requirements/recommendations for international students: Required—TOEFL (minimum score 540 paper-based; 76 iBT), IELTS (minimum score 6), ELPT (minimum score 964) or ELS (minimum score 112). *Application deadline:* For fall admission, 7/31 priority date for domestic and international students; for winter admission, 11/15 priority date for domestic and international students; for spring admission, 1/7 priority date for domestic and international students. Applications are processed on a rolling basis. Application fee: $60. Electronic applications accepted. *Expenses:* Tuition, state resident: full-time $10,719; part-time $397 per credit. Tuition, nonresident: full-time $13,419; part-time $497 per credit. *Required fees:* $548. *Financial support:* In 2016–17, 3 students received support, including 3 research assistantships with partial tuition reimbursements available; career-related internships or fieldwork, scholarships/grants, and unspecified assistantships also available. *Unit head:* Dr. Stuart Janes, Graduate Program Coordinator, 541-552-6797, E-mail: janes@sou.edu. *Application contact:* Kelly Moutsatson, Director of Admissions, 541-552-6411, Fax: 541-552-8403, E-mail: admissions@sou.edu.
Website: http://www.sou.edu/ee/

State University of New York College at Cortland, Graduate Studies, School of Professional Studies, Department of Recreation, Parks and Leisure Studies, Cortland, NY 13045. Offers outdoor education (MS, MS Ed); recreation management (MS, MS Ed); therapeutic recreation (MS, MS Ed). *Program availability:* Part-time, evening/weekend. *Degree requirements:* For master's, comprehensive exam, thesis (for some programs). *Entrance requirements:* Additional exam requirements/recommendations for international students: Required—TOEFL.

Université du Québec à Montréal, Graduate Programs, Program in Education, Montréal, QC H3C 3P8, Canada. Offers education (M Ed, MA, PhD); education of the environmental sciences (Diploma). PhD offered jointly with Université du Québec à Chicoutimi, Université du Québec à Rimouski, Université du Québec à Trois-Rivières, Université du Québec en Outaouais, and Université du Québec en Abitibi-Témiscamingue. *Program availability:* Part-time. *Degree requirements:* For master's, thesis (for some programs); for doctorate, thesis/dissertation. *Entrance requirements:* For master's and Diploma, appropriate bachelor's degree or equivalent, proficiency in French; for doctorate, appropriate master's degree or equivalent, proficiency in French.

University of Colorado Denver, College of Liberal Arts and Sciences, Department of Geography and Environmental Sciences, Denver, CO 80217. Offers environmental sciences (MS), including air quality, ecosystems, environmental health, environmental science education, geospatial analysis, urban agriculture, water quality. *Program availability:* Part-time, evening/weekend. *Faculty:* 13 full-time (4 women), 5 part-time/adjunct (2 women). *Students:* 47 full-time (24 women), 6 part-time (2 women); includes 10 minority (1 Black or African American, non-Hispanic/Latino; 2 Asian, non-Hispanic/Latino; 5 Hispanic/Latino; 2 Two or more races, non-Hispanic/Latino), 1 international. Average age 30. 57 applicants, 72% accepted, 18 enrolled. In 2016, 23 master's awarded. *Degree requirements:* For master's, thesis or alternative, 30 credits including 21 of core requirements and 9 of environmental science electives. *Entrance requirements:* For master's, GRE General Test, BA in one of the natural/physical sciences or engineering (or equivalent background); prerequisite coursework in calculus and physics (one semester each); general chemistry with lab and general biology with lab (two semesters each); three letters of recommendation. Additional exam requirements/recommendations for international students: Required—TOEFL (minimum score 537 paper-based; 75 iBT); Recommended—IELTS (minimum score 6.5). *Application deadline:* For fall admission, 1/20 for domestic and international students; for spring admission, 10/1 for domestic and international students. Application fee: $50 ($75 for international students). Electronic applications accepted. *Expenses:* Tuition, state resident: full-time $11,006; part-time $474 per credit. Tuition, nonresident: full-time $28,212; part-time $1264 per credit hour. *Required fees:* $256 per semester. One-time fee: $94.32. Tuition and fees vary according to campus/location and program. *Financial support:* In 2016–17, 6 students received support. Fellowships, research assistantships, teaching assistantships, Federal Work-Study, institutionally sponsored loans, scholarships/grants, and traineeships available. Financial award application deadline: 4/1; financial award applicants required to submit FAFSA. *Faculty research:* Air quality, environmental health, ecosystems, hazardous waste, water quality, geospatial analysis and environmental science education. *Unit head:* Anne Chinn, Director of MS in Environmental Sciences Program, 303-556-3958, E-mail: ges@ucdenver.edu. *Application contact:* Sue Eddleman, Program Assistant, 303-352-3698, E-mail: sue.eddleman@ucdenver.edu.
Website: http://www.ucdenver.edu/academics/colleges/CLAS/Departments/ges/Programs/MasterofScience/Pages/MasterofScience.aspx

University of Florida, Graduate School, College of Agricultural and Life Sciences, Department of Wildlife Ecology and Conservation, Gainesville, FL 32611. Offers environmental education and communications (Certificate); wildlife ecology and conservation (MS, PhD), including geographic information systems, tropical conservation and development, wetland sciences. *Degree requirements:* For master's, comprehensive exam, thesis optional; for doctorate, comprehensive exam, thesis/dissertation. *Entrance requirements:* For master's and doctorate, GRE General Test (minimum 34th percentile for Quantitative), minimum GPA of 3.3. Additional exam requirements/recommendations for international students: Required—TOEFL (minimum score 550 paper-based; 80 iBT), IELTS (minimum score 6). Electronic applications accepted. *Faculty research:* Conservation biology, spatial ecology, wildlife conservation and management, wetlands ecology and conservation, human dimensions in wildlife conservation.

University of South Africa, College of Human Sciences, Pretoria, South Africa. Offers adult education (M Ed); African languages (MA, PhD); African politics (MA, PhD); Afrikaans (MA, PhD); ancient history (MA, PhD); ancient Near Eastern studies (MA, PhD); anthropology (MA, PhD); applied linguistics (MA); Arabic (MA, PhD); archaeology (MA); art history (MA); Biblical archaeology (MA); Biblical studies (M Th, D Th, PhD); Christian spirituality (M Th, D Th); church history (M Th, D Th); classical studies (MA, PhD); clinical psychology (MA); communication (MA, PhD); comparative education (M Ed, Ed D); consulting psychology (D Admin, D Com, PhD); curriculum studies (M Ed, Ed D); development studies (M Admin, MA, D Admin, PhD); didactics (M Ed, Ed D); education (M Tech); education management (M Ed, Ed D); educational psychology (M Ed); English (MA); environmental education (M Ed); French (MA, PhD); German (MA, PhD); Greek (MA); guidance and counseling (M Ed); health studies (MA, PhD), including health sciences education (MA), health services management (MA), medical and surgical nursing science (critical care general) (MA), midwifery and neonatal nursing science (MA), trauma and emergency care (MA); history (MA, PhD); history of education (Ed D); inclusive education (M Ed, Ed D); information and communications technology policy and regulation (MA); information science (MA, MIS, PhD); international politics (MA, PhD); Islamic studies (MA, PhD); Italian (MA, PhD); Judaica (MA, PhD); linguistics (MA, PhD); mathematical education (M Ed); mathematics education (MA); missiology (M Th, D Th); modern Hebrew (MA, PhD); musicology (MA, MMus, D Mus, PhD); natural science education (M Ed); New Testament (M Th, D Th); Old Testament (D Th); pastoral therapy (M Th, D Th); philosophy (MA); philosophy of education (M Ed, Ed D); politics (MA, PhD); Portuguese (MA, PhD); practical theology (M Th, D Th); psychology (MA, MS, PhD); psychology of education (M Ed, Ed D); public health (MA); religious studies (MA, D Th, PhD); Romance languages (MA); Russian (MA, PhD); Semitic languages (MA, PhD); social behavior studies in HIV/AIDS (MA); social science (mental health) (MA); social science in development studies (MA); social science in psychology (MA); social science in social work (MA); social science in sociology (MA); social work (MSW, DSW, PhD); socio-education (M Ed, Ed D); sociolinguistics (MA); sociology (MA, PhD); Spanish (MA, PhD); systematic theology (M Th, D Th); TESOL (teaching English to speakers of other languages) (MA); theological ethics (M Th, D Th); theory of literature (MA, PhD); urban ministries (D Th); urban ministry (M Th).

University of Victoria, Faculty of Graduate Studies, Faculty of Education, Department of Curriculum and Instruction, Victoria, BC V8W 2Y2, Canada. Offers art education (M Ed, PhD); curriculum studies (M Ed, MA, PhD); early childhood education (M Ed, PhD); educational studies (PhD); language and literacy (M Ed, MA, PhD); mathematics (M Ed, MA, PhD); music education (M Ed, MA, PhD); science (M Ed, MA, PhD); social studies (M Ed, MA); social, cultural and foundational studies (MA, PhD); technology and environmental education (PhD). *Program availability:* Part-time. *Degree requirements:* For master's, thesis, project (M Ed); for doctorate, comprehensive exam, thesis/dissertation. *Entrance requirements:* For master's, minimum B average. Additional exam requirements/recommendations for international students: Required—TOEFL (minimum score 575 paper-based), IELTS (minimum score 7). Electronic applications accepted. *Faculty research:* Elementary and secondary English, language arts, curriculum theory and practice, educational media and technology, educational administration and leadership, history and philosophy of education.

Western Washington University, Graduate School, Huxley College of the Environment, Department of Environmental Studies, Program in Environmental Education, Bellingham, WA 98225-5996. Offers M Ed. *Program availability:* Part-time. *Degree requirements:* For master's, comprehensive exam, thesis optional. *Entrance requirements:* For master's, GRE or MAT, minimum GPA of 3.0 in last 60 semester hours. Additional exam requirements/recommendations for international students: Required—TOEFL (minimum score 567 paper-based). Electronic applications accepted. *Faculty research:* Role of wilderness in national park history; history of the conservation movement and sense of place in environmental education; environmental care and responsibility; conservation psychology and environmental education.

West Virginia University, Davis College of Agriculture, Forestry and Consumer Sciences, Division of Resource Management and Sustainable Development, Program in Agricultural and Extension Education, Morgantown, WV 26506. Offers agricultural and extension education (MS, PhD); teaching vocational-agriculture (MS). *Accreditation:* NCATE. *Program availability:* Part-time. *Degree requirements:* For master's, thesis. *Entrance requirements:* For master's, GRE General Test, minimum GPA of 2.75. Additional exam requirements/recommendations for international students: Required—TOEFL. *Faculty research:* Program development in vocational agriculture, agricultural extension, supervised experience programs, leadership development.

Foreign Languages Education

Andrews University, School of Graduate Studies, School of Education, Department of Teaching, Learning, and Curriculum, Berrien Springs, MI 49104. Offers curriculum and instruction (MA, Ed D, PhD, Ed S); elementary education (MAT); secondary education (MAT), including biology, education, English, English as a second language, French, history, physics; teacher education (MAT). *Faculty:* 7 full-time (5 women). *Students:* 17 full-time (12 women), 10 part-time (all women); includes 11 minority (6 Black or African American, non-Hispanic/Latino; 5 Hispanic/Latino), 7 international. Average age 38. In 2016, 9 master's, 7 doctorates awarded. *Entrance requirements:* For master's, GRE Subject Test. Additional exam requirements/recommendations for international students: Required—TOEFL (minimum score 550 paper-based). *Application deadline:* For fall admission, 8/15 for domestic students. Applications are processed on a rolling basis. Application fee: $40. *Unit head:* Dr. Lee C. Davidson, Chair, 269-471-6364. *Application contact:* Justina Clayburn, Supervisor of Graduate Admission, 800-253-2874, Fax: 269-471-6321, E-mail: graduate@andrews.edu.

Appalachian State University, Cratis D. Williams Graduate School, Department of Languages, Literatures and Cultures, Boone, NC 28608. Offers romance languages (MA), including French teaching, Spanish teaching. *Program availability:* Part-time, online learning. *Degree requirements:* For master's, one foreign language, comprehensive exam, thesis optional. *Entrance requirements:* For master's, GRE General Test, 3 letters of recommendation. Additional exam requirements/recommendations for international students: Required—TOEFL (minimum score 570 paper-based; 79 iBT) or IELTS (minimum score 6.5). *Application deadline:* For fall admission, 3/15 priority date for domestic students, 2/1 for international students; for spring admission, 11/1 for domestic students, 7/1 for international students. Applications are processed on a rolling basis. Application fee: $55. Electronic applications accepted. *Expenses:* Tuition, state resident: full-time $4744. Tuition, nonresident: full-time $17,913. Full-time tuition and fees vary according to program. *Financial support:* Career-related internships or fieldwork available. Financial award application deadline: 4/1; financial award applicants required to submit FAFSA. *Faculty research:* French and Spanish literature, Latin American culture, teaching foreign languages. *Unit head:* Dr. James Fogelquist, Chairperson, 828-262-3096, Fax: 828-262-3095, E-mail: fogelquistjd@appstate.edu. *Application contact:* Dr. Beverly Moser, Graduate Coordinator, 828-262-2303, E-mail: moserba@appstate.edu.
Website: https://dllc.appstate.edu/

Arizona State University at the Tempe campus, College of Liberal Arts and Sciences, School of International Letters and Cultures, Program in Spanish, Tempe, AZ 85287-0202. Offers cultural studies (PhD); linguistics (MA), including second language acquisition/applied linguistics, sociolinguistics; literature (PhD); literature and culture (MA). *Program availability:* Part-time. Terminal master's awarded for partial completion of doctoral program. *Degree requirements:* For master's, thesis, oral defense; written comprehensive exam (literature and culture); portfolio review (linguistics); interactive Program of Study (iPOS) submitted before completing 50 percent of required credit hours; for doctorate, comprehensive exam, thesis/dissertation, interactive Program of Study (iPOS) submitted before completing 50 percent of required credit hours. *Entrance requirements:* For master's, GRE (recommended), BA in Spanish or close equivalent from accredited institution with minimum GPA of 3.5, 3 letters of recommendation, personal statement, academic writing sample; for doctorate, GRE (recommended), MA in Spanish or equivalent from accredited institution with minimum GPA of 3.75, 3 letters of recommendation, personal statement, academic writing sample. Additional exam requirements/recommendations for international students: Required—TOEFL (minimum score 550 paper-based; 83 iBT), IELTS (minimum score 6.5). Electronic applications accepted.

Augusta University, The Graduate School, College of Education, Program in Curriculum and Instruction, Augusta, GA 30912. Offers curriculum and instruction (Ed S); elementary education (MAT); foreign language education (MAT); instruction (M Ed); middle grades education (MAT); music education (MAT); secondary education (MAT); special education (MAT). *Degree requirements:* For master's, thesis, portfolio. *Entrance requirements:* For master's, GRE, MAT, minimum GPA of 2.5. Application fee: $20. *Financial support:* Career-related internships or fieldwork, Federal Work-Study, institutionally sponsored loans, and unspecified assistantships available. Support available to part-time students. Financial award application deadline: 4/15; financial award applicants required to submit FAFSA. *Unit head:* Dr. Gordon Eisenman, Director, 706-737-1496, Fax: 706-667-4706, E-mail: geisenman@augusta.edu. *Application contact:* Dr. Gordon Eisenman, Director, 706-737-1496, Fax: 706-667-4706, E-mail: geisenman@augusta.edu.

Binghamton University, State University of New York, Graduate School, Graduate School of Education, Program in Adolescence Education, Binghamton, NY 13902-6000. Offers biology education (MAT, MS Ed); chemistry education (MAT, MS Ed); earth science education (MAT, MS Ed); English education (MAT, MS Ed); French education (MAT, MS Ed); literacy education (MS Ed); mathematical sciences education (MAT, MS Ed); physics (MAT, MS Ed); social studies (MAT, MS Ed); Spanish education (MAT, MS Ed). *Accreditation:* TEAC. *Program availability:* Part-time, evening/weekend. *Students:* 59 full-time (36 women), 7 part-time (2 women); includes 10 minority (2 Black or African American, non-Hispanic/Latino; 1 American Indian or Alaska Native, non-Hispanic/Latino; 1 Asian, non-Hispanic/Latino; 5 Hispanic/Latino; 1 Two or more races, non-Hispanic/Latino). Average age 26. 46 applicants, 76% accepted, 25 enrolled. In 2016, 26 master's awarded. *Degree requirements:* For master's, portfolio. *Entrance requirements:* For master's, GRE General Test, teaching certification. Additional exam requirements/recommendations for international students: Required—TOEFL (minimum score 550 paper-based; 80 iBT). *Application deadline:* For fall admission, 2/1 priority date for domestic and international students; for spring admission, 10/15 priority date for domestic and international students. Application fee: $75. Electronic applications accepted. *Financial support:* In 2016–17, 6 students received support. Research assistantships, teaching assistantships, career-related internships or fieldwork, Federal Work-Study, institutionally sponsored loans, scholarships/grants, health care benefits, tuition waivers (full and partial), and unspecified assistantships available. Financial award applicants required to submit FAFSA. *Unit head:* Dr. Susan Strehle, Dean, 607-777-7329, E-mail: sstrehle@binghamton.edu. *Application contact:* Ben Balkaya, Assistant Dean and Director, 607-777-2151, Fax: 607-777-2501, E-mail: balkaya@binghamton.edu.

Brigham Young University, Graduate Studies, College of Humanities, Center for Language Studies, Provo, UT 84602-1001. Offers second language teaching (MA). *Faculty:* 26 full-time (7 women). *Students:* 6 full-time (4 women), 10 part-time (5 women); includes 2 minority (both Asian, non-Hispanic/Latino). Average age 33. 5 applicants, 100% accepted, 5 enrolled. In 2016, 4 master's awarded. *Degree requirements:* For master's, one foreign language, comprehensive exam, thesis. *Entrance requirements:* For master's, GRE General Test (minimum score in 50th percentile on the verbal section and a rating of 4 on the analytical/writing section); ACTFL OPI in language of specialization, English writing sample, minimum GPA of 3.0, three letters of recommendation, letter of intent, completion of a teaching method class. Additional exam requirements/recommendations for international students: Required—TOEFL (minimum score 85 iBT). *Application deadline:* For fall admission, 2/1 for domestic and international students. Application fee: $50. Electronic applications accepted. *Expenses:* Contact institution. *Financial support:* In 2016–17, 12 students received support, including 24 fellowships with partial tuition reimbursements available (averaging $2,082 per year); career-related internships or fieldwork, scholarships/

grants, tuition waivers (partial), and unspecified assistantships also available. Support available to part-time students. Financial award application deadline: 2/1. *Faculty research:* Test construct validation, strategy for attaining superior language proficiency, error correction strategies, direct versus indirect testing, eye tracking and reading proficiency. *Total annual research expenditures:* $92,000. *Unit head:* Dr. Ray T. Clifford, Director, 801-422-3263, E-mail: rayc@byu.edu. *Application contact:* Agnes Y. Welch, Graduate Program Manager, 801-422-5199, E-mail: agnes_welch@byu.edu.
Website: http://slat.byu.edu

Brigham Young University, Graduate Studies, College of Humanities, Department of Spanish and Portuguese, Provo, UT 84602. Offers Portuguese (MA), including Luso-Brazilian literatures, Portuguese linguistics, Portuguese pedagogy; Spanish (MA), including Hispanic linguistics, Hispanic literatures, Spanish pedagogy. *Faculty:* 31 full-time (6 women). *Students:* 20 full-time (9 women), 15 part-time (9 women); includes 12 minority (all Hispanic/Latino). Average age 32. 19 applicants, 79% accepted, 12 enrolled. In 2016, 9 master's awarded. *Degree requirements:* For master's, 2 foreign languages, comprehensive exam, thesis, 1 semester of teaching. *Entrance requirements:* For master's, minimum GPA of 3.5 in Spanish or Portuguese, 3.3 overall. Additional exam requirements/recommendations for international students: Required—TOEFL (minimum score 580 paper-based; 85 iBT). *Application deadline:* For fall admission, 2/1 for domestic and international students. Application fee: $50. Electronic applications accepted. *Expenses:* Contact institution. *Financial support:* In 2016–17, 25 students received support, including 7 research assistantships (averaging $1,895 per year), 81 teaching assistantships (averaging $3,200 per year); institutionally sponsored loans, scholarships/grants, tuition waivers (partial), and unspecified assistantships also available. Support available to part-time students. *Faculty research:* Mexican prose; Latin American theater, literature, phonetics, and phonology; pedagogy; classical Portuguese literature; Peninsular prose and theater. *Unit head:* Dr. David P. Laraway, Chair, 801-422-3807, Fax: 801-422-0628, E-mail: david_laraway@byu.edu. *Application contact:* Jessica C. Erickson, Graduate Program Manager, 801-422-2196, Fax: 801-422-0628, E-mail: jessica_erickson@byu.edu.
Website: http://spanport.byu.edu/

Brooklyn College of the City University of New York, School of Education, Program in Adolescence Science Education and Special Subjects, Brooklyn, NY 11210-2889. Offers adolescence science education (MAT); biology teacher (7-12) (MA); chemistry teacher (7-12) (MA); earth science teacher (7-12) (MAT); English teacher (7-12) (MA); French teacher (7-12) (MA); mathematics teacher (7-12) (MA); music teacher (MA); physics teacher (7-12) (MA); social studies teacher (7-12) (MA); Spanish teacher (7-12) (MA). *Program availability:* Part-time, evening/weekend. *Degree requirements:* For master's, comprehensive exam (for some programs), thesis (for some programs). *Entrance requirements:* For master's, LAST, previous course work in education, resume, 2 letters of recommendation, essay. Additional exam requirements/recommendations for international students: Required—TOEFL (minimum score 500 paper-based; 61 iBT). Electronic applications accepted. *Faculty research:* Interdisciplinary education, semiotics, discourse analysis, autobiography, teacher identity.

California State University, Sacramento, Office of Graduate Studies, College of Arts and Letters, Department of World Languages and Literatures, Sacramento, CA 95819. Offers MA. *Program availability:* Part-time. *Students:* 6 full-time (5 women), 26 part-time (19 women); includes 27 minority (1 Black or African American, non-Hispanic/Latino; 26 Hispanic/Latino). Average age 34. 11 applicants, 100% accepted, 10 enrolled. In 2016, 12 master's awarded. *Entrance requirements:* For master's, interview, minimum GPA of 3.0 during previous 2 years of course work. Additional exam requirements/recommendations for international students: Required—TOEFL (minimum score 550 paper-based; 80 iBT). *Application deadline:* For fall admission, 3/1 for domestic and international students; for spring admission, 9/30 for international students. Applications are processed on a rolling basis. Application fee: $55. Electronic applications accepted. *Expenses:* $4,302 full-time tuition and fees per semester, $2,796 part-time. *Financial support:* Teaching assistantships, career-related internships or fieldwork, and Federal Work-Study available. Support available to part-time students. Financial award application deadline: 3/1; financial award applicants required to submit FAFSA. *Unit head:* Dr. Curtis Smith, Chair, 916-278-6333, Fax: 916-278-5502, E-mail: curtis.smith@csus.edu. *Application contact:* Jose Martinez, Graduate Admissions Supervisor, 916-278-7871, E-mail: martinj@skymail.csus.edu.
Website: http://www.csus.edu/fl

Caribbean University, Graduate School, Bayamón, PR 00960-0493. Offers administration and supervision (MA Ed); criminal justice (MA); curriculum and instruction (MA Ed, PhD), including elementary education (MA Ed), English education (MA Ed), history education (MA Ed), mathematics education (MA Ed), primary education (MA Ed), science education (MA Ed), Spanish education (MA Ed); educational technology in instructional systems (MA Ed); gerontology (MSN); human resources (MBA); museology, archiving and art history (MA Ed); neonatal pediatrics (MSN); physical education (MA Ed); special education (MA Ed). *Entrance requirements:* For master's, interview, minimum GPA of 2.5.

Central Connecticut State University, School of Graduate Studies, College of Liberal Arts and Social Sciences, Department of Modern Languages, New Britain, CT 06050-4010. Offers modern language (MA, Certificate), including French, German (Certificate), Italian, Spanish (MA); Spanish (MS, Certificate). *Program availability:* Part-time, evening/weekend. *Faculty:* 8 full-time (6 women). *Students:* 7 full-time (6 women), 12 part-time (7 women); includes 10 minority (all Hispanic/Latino). Average age 32. 11 applicants, 91% accepted, 4 enrolled. In 2016, 9 master's, 1 other advanced degree awarded. *Degree requirements:* For master's, one foreign language, comprehensive exam, thesis or alternative; for Certificate, qualifying exam. *Entrance requirements:* For master's, minimum undergraduate GPA of 2.7, 24 credits of undergraduate courses in each language in which graduate work will be undertaken. Additional exam requirements/recommendations for international students: Required—TOEFL (minimum score 550 paper-based; 79 iBT). *Application deadline:* For fall admission, 6/1 for domestic students, 5/1 for international students; for spring admission, 11/1 for domestic and international students. Applications are processed on a rolling basis. Application fee: $50. Electronic applications accepted. *Expenses: Tuition, area resident:* Full-time $6497; part-time $606 per credit. Tuition, state resident: full-time $9748; part-time $622 per credit. Tuition, nonresident: full-time $18,102; part-time $622 per credit. *Required fees:* $4459; $246 per credit. *Financial support:* In 2016–17, 6 students received support. Career-related internships or fieldwork, Federal Work-Study, scholarships/grants, and unspecified assistantships available. Support available to part-time students. Financial award application deadline: 3/1; financial award applicants required to submit FAFSA. *Faculty research:* Quebecois literature, Caribbean literature, modern French/Spanish drama, Puerto Rican novel and drama. *Unit head:* Dr. Carmela Pesca, Chair, 860-832-2875, E-mail: pescac@ccsu.edu. *Application contact:* Patricia Gardner, Associate Director of Graduate Studies, 860-832-2350, Fax: 860-832-2362.
Website: http://web.ccsu.edu/modlang/

City College of the City University of New York, Graduate School, Division of Humanities and the Arts, Department of Classical and Modern Languages and Literatures, New York, NY 10031-9198. Offers Spanish (MA). *Degree requirements:* For master's, one foreign language, comprehensive exam, thesis or alternative. *Entrance requirements:* For master's, minimum GPA of 3.0. Additional exam requirements/recommendations for international students: Required—TOEFL (minimum score 500 paper-based; 61 iBT). Electronic applications accepted. Tuition and fees vary according to course load, degree level and program.

Cleveland State University, College of Graduate Studies, College of Education and Human Services, Department of Curriculum and Foundations, Cleveland, OH 44115. Offers art education (M Ed); early childhood education (M Ed); foreign language education (M Ed); middle childhood mathematics and science education (M Ed); special education (M Ed), including mild/moderate disabilities, moderate/intensive disabilities; teaching English to speakers of other languages (M Ed). *Program availability:* Part-time, evening/weekend. *Faculty:* 19 full-time (14 women), 32 part-time/adjunct (27 women). *Students:* 86 full-time (65 women), 369 part-time (301 women); includes 119 minority (89 Black or African American, non-Hispanic/Latino; 1 American Indian or Alaska Native, non-Hispanic/Latino; 2 Asian, non-Hispanic/Latino; 16 Hispanic/Latino; 11 Two or more races, non-Hispanic/Latino), 35 international. Average age 34. 177 applicants, 55% accepted, 68 enrolled. In 2016, 179 master's awarded. *Degree requirements:* For master's, comprehensive exam (for some programs), thesis or alternative. *Entrance requirements:* For master's, GRE General Test or MAT, minimum GPA of 2.75. Additional exam requirements/recommendations for international students: Required—TOEFL (minimum score 550 paper-based; 78 iBT), IELTS (minimum score 6). *Application deadline:* For fall admission, 7/1 priority date for domestic students, 5/15 for international students; for spring admission, 11/15 for domestic students, 11/1 for international students; for summer admission, 4/1 for domestic students, 3/15 for international students. Applications are processed on a rolling basis. Application fee: $30. *Expenses:* Tuition, state resident: full-time $9565. Tuition, nonresident: full-time $17,980. Tuition and fees vary according to program. *Financial support:* In 2016–17, 13 research assistantships with full tuition reimbursements (averaging $15,845 per year) were awarded; tuition waivers (partial) and unspecified assistantships also available. Financial award application deadline: 2/15; financial award applicants required to submit FAFSA. *Faculty research:* Early childhood education, literacy education, special education: mild/moderate, moderate/intensive, early childhood intervention specialist), teaching English to speakers of other languages (TESOL). *Total annual research expenditures:* $275,907. *Unit head:* Dr. Tachelle I. Banks, Chairperson, 216-687-4608, Fax: 216-687-5379, E-mail: t.i.banks@csuohio.edu. *Application contact:* Michael Almony, Senior Student Services Specialist, 216-875-9929, Fax: 216-687-5491, E-mail: m.almony@csuohio.edu.
Website: http://www.csuohio.edu/cehs/te/te

College of Charleston, Graduate School, School of Education, Health, and Human Performance, Program in Languages, Charleston, SC 29424-0001. Offers M Ed. *Program availability:* Part-time, evening/weekend. *Degree requirements:* For master's, comprehensive exam or portfolio. *Entrance requirements:* For master's, minimum GPA of 2.5. Additional exam requirements/recommendations for international students: Required—TOEFL (minimum score 81 iBT). *Application deadline:* For fall admission, 4/1 for domestic students; for spring admission, 11/1 for domestic students. Application fee: $45. Electronic applications accepted. *Financial support:* Fellowships, research assistantships, scholarships/grants, and unspecified assistantships available. Financial award application deadline: 4/1; financial award applicants required to submit FAFSA. *Unit head:* Silvia Rodriguez Sabater, Director, 843-953-5882, E-mail: rodriguezsabaters@cofc.edu. *Application contact:* Silvia Rodriguez Sabater, Director, 843-953-5882, E-mail: rodriguezsabaters@cofc.edu.
Website: http://teachered.cofc.edu/grad-progs/lale.php

The College of William and Mary, School of Education, Program in Curriculum and Instruction, Williamsburg, VA 23187-8795. Offers elementary education (MA Ed); gifted education (MA Ed); literacy leadership (MA Ed); math specialist (MA Ed); secondary education (MA Ed), including English, foreign language, math, science, social studies; special education (MA Ed). *Accreditation:* NCATE. *Program availability:* Part-time. *Faculty:* 30 full-time (21 women), 48 part-time/adjunct (38 women). *Students:* 60 full-time (47 women), 14 part-time (all women); includes 13 minority (1 Black or African American, non-Hispanic/Latino; 1 American Indian or Alaska Native, non-Hispanic/Latino; 2 Asian, non-Hispanic/Latino; 7 Hispanic/Latino; 2 Two or more races, non-Hispanic/Latino). Average age 26. 134 applicants, 79% accepted, 66 enrolled. In 2016, 77 master's awarded. *Degree requirements:* For master's, project. *Entrance requirements:* For master's, GRE, MAT, PRAXIS Core Academic Skills for Educators, minimum GPA of 2.5. Additional exam requirements/recommendations for international students: Required—TOEFL (minimum score 100 iBT), IELTS (minimum score 7). *Application deadline:* For fall admission, 1/15 for domestic and international students; for spring admission, 10/1 for domestic and international students. Application fee: $50. Electronic applications accepted. *Expenses:* $14,258 per year in-state full-time, $275 per credit in-state part-time; $30,500 per year out-of-state full-time, $1,200 per credit out-of-state part-time. *Financial support:* In 2016–17, 30 students received support, including 3 research assistantships (averaging $14,259 per year); scholarships/grants and unspecified assistantships also available. Financial award application deadline: 1/15; financial award applicants required to submit FAFSA. *Faculty research:* Educational technology, professional development and evaluation, inclusive education, rural education, education policy. *Unit head:* Dr. Jeremy D. Stoddard, Department Chair, 757-221-2348, E-mail: jdstod@wm.edu. *Application contact:* Dorothy Smith Osborne, Assistant Dean for Academic Programs and Student Services, 757-221-2317, E-mail: dsosbo@wm.edu.
Website: http://education.wm.edu

The Colorado College, Education Department, Program in Secondary Education, Colorado Springs, CO 80903-3294. Offers art teaching (K-12) (MAT); English teaching (MAT); foreign language teaching (MAT); mathematics teaching (MAT); music teaching (MAT); science teaching (MAT); social studies teaching (MAT). *Degree requirements:* For master's, thesis, internship. Electronic applications accepted.

Colorado State University–Pueblo, College of Education, Engineering and Professional Studies, Education Program, Pueblo, CO 81001-4901. Offers art education (M Ed); foreign language education (M Ed); health and physical education (M Ed); instructional technology (M Ed); linguistically diverse education (M Ed); music education (M Ed); special education (M Ed). *Accreditation:* TEAC. *Program availability:* Part-time. *Degree requirements:* For master's, portfolio. *Entrance requirements:* For master's, 3 recommendations, teaching license. Additional exam requirements/recommendations for international students: Required—TOEFL (minimum score 500 paper-based). Electronic applications accepted. *Faculty research:* Portfolio assessment, math education, science education.

Columbia University, Graduate School of Arts and Sciences, New York, NY 10027. Offers African-American studies (MA); American studies (MA); anthropology (MA, PhD); art history and archaeology (MA, PhD); astronomy (PhD); biological sciences (PhD); biotechnology (MA); chemical physics (PhD); chemistry (PhD); classical studies (MA, PhD); classics (MA, PhD); climate and society (MA); conservation biology (MA); earth and environmental sciences (PhD); East Asia: regional studies (MA); East Asian languages and cultures (MA, PhD); ecology, evolution and environmental biology (MA), including conservation biology; ecology, evolution, and environmental biology (PhD), including ecology and evolutionary biology, evolutionary primatology; economics (MA, PhD); English and comparative literature (MA, PhD); French and Romance philology (MA, PhD); Germanic languages (MA, PhD); global French studies (MA); global thought (MA); Hispanic cultural studies (MA); history (PhD); history and literature (MA); human rights studies (MA); Islamic studies (MA); Italian (MA, PhD); Japanese pedagogy (MA); Jewish studies (MA); Latin America and the Caribbean: regional studies (MA); Latin American and Iberian cultures (PhD); mathematics (MA, PhD), including finance (MA); medieval and Renaissance studies (MA); Middle Eastern, South Asian, and African studies (MA, PhD); modern art: critical and curatorial studies (MA); modern European studies (MA); museum anthropology (MA); music (DMA, PhD); oral history (MA); philosophical foundations of physics (MA); philosophy (MA, PhD); physics (PhD); political science (MA, PhD); psychology (PhD); quantitative methods in the social sciences (MA); religion (MA, PhD); Russia, Eurasia and East Europe: regional studies (MA); Russian translation (MA); Slavic cultures (MA); Slavic languages (MA, PhD); sociology (MA, PhD); South Asian studies (MA); statistics (MA, PhD); theatre (PhD). Dual-degree programs require admission to both Graduate School of Arts and Sciences and another Columbia school. *Program availability:* Part-time. Terminal master's awarded for partial completion of doctoral program. *Degree requirements:* For master's, variable foreign language requirement, comprehensive exam (for some programs), thesis (for some programs); for doctorate, variable foreign language requirement, comprehensive exam (for some programs), thesis/dissertation. *Entrance requirements:* For master's and doctorate, GRE General Test, GRE Subject Test (for some programs). Additional exam requirements/recommendations for international students: Required—TOEFL, IELTS. Electronic applications accepted.

Concordia College, Program in Education, Moorhead, MN 56562. Offers world language instruction (M Ed). *Degree requirements:* For master's, thesis/seminar. *Entrance requirements:* For master's, 2 professional references, 1 personal reference.

Cornell University, Graduate School, Graduate Fields of Arts and Sciences, Field of Linguistics, Ithaca, NY 14853. Offers applied linguistics (MA, PhD); East Asian linguistics (MA, PhD); English linguistics (MA, PhD); general linguistics (MA, PhD); Germanic linguistics (MA, PhD); Indo-European linguistics (MA, PhD); phonetics (MA, PhD); phonological theory (MA, PhD); Romance linguistics (MA, PhD); second language acquisition (MA, PhD); semantics (MA, PhD); Slavic linguistics (MA, PhD); sociolinguistics (MA, PhD); South Asian linguistics (MA, PhD); Southeast Asian linguistics (MA, PhD); syntactic theory (MA, PhD). Terminal master's awarded for partial completion of doctoral program. *Degree requirements:* For master's, one foreign language, thesis; for doctorate, one foreign language, comprehensive exam, thesis/dissertation. *Entrance requirements:* For master's and doctorate, GRE General Test, 2 letters of recommendation. Additional exam requirements/recommendations for international students: Required—TOEFL (minimum score 600 paper-based; 77 iBT). Electronic applications accepted. *Faculty research:* Phonology and phonetics, syntax and semantics, historical linguistics, philosophy of language, language acquisition.

Delaware State University, Graduate Programs, Department of English and Foreign Languages, Dover, DE 19901-2277. Offers French (MA); Spanish (MA). *Entrance requirements:* Additional exam requirements/recommendations for international students: Required—TOEFL (minimum score 550 paper-based). Electronic applications accepted.

DePaul University, College of Education, Chicago, IL 60614. Offers bilingual bicultural education (M Ed, MA); counseling (M Ed, MA), including clinical mental health counseling, college student development, school counseling; curriculum studies (M Ed, MA, Ed D); early childhood education (M Ed, MA, Ed D); educating adults (MA); educational leadership (M Ed, MA, Ed D), including administration and supervision (M Ed, MA), principal preparation (M Ed, MA); elementary education (MA); mathematics education (MA); mathematics for teaching (MS); middle school mathematics education (MS); reading specialist (M Ed, MA); secondary education (M Ed); social and cultural foundations in education (MA); special education (M Ed, MA); world languages education (M Ed, MA). *Program availability:* Part-time, evening/weekend, online learning. *Degree requirements:* For doctorate, thesis/dissertation. Electronic applications accepted.

Duquesne University, School of Education, Department of Instruction and Leadership, Program in Secondary Education, Pittsburgh, PA 15282-0001. Offers biology (MS Ed); chemistry (MS Ed); English (MS Ed); K-12 education (MS Ed), including Latin; mathematics (MS Ed); physics (MS Ed); social studies (MS Ed). *Program availability:* Part-time, evening/weekend. *Faculty:* 5 full-time (4 women). *Students:* 21 full-time (8 women), 4 part-time (0 women); includes 3 minority (2 Black or African American, non-Hispanic/Latino; 1 Two or more races, non-Hispanic/Latino). Average age 28. 12 applicants, 100% accepted, 7 enrolled. In 2016, 19 master's awarded. *Degree requirements:* For master's, thesis optional. *Entrance requirements:* For master's, letters of recommendation, letter of intent, interview, bachelor's degree. Additional exam requirements/recommendations for international students: Required—TOEFL (minimum score 550 paper-based), IELTS (minimum score 7). *Application deadline:* For fall admission, 9/1 for domestic students; for spring admission, 1/1 for domestic students. Applications are processed on a rolling basis. Application fee: $0. Electronic applications accepted. *Expenses: Tuition:* Full-time $22,212; part-time $1234 per credit. Tuition and fees vary according to program. *Financial support:* Research assistantships and Federal Work-Study available. Support available to part-time students. *Unit head:* Dr. Melissa Boston, Associate Professor and Director, 412-396-6109, E-mail: bostonm@duq.edu. *Application contact:* Michael Dolinger, Director of Student and Academic Services, 412-396-6647, Fax: 412-396-5585, E-mail: dolingerm@duq.edu.
Website: http://www.duq.edu/academics/schools/education/graduate-programs-education/ms-ed-secondary-education

East Carolina University, Graduate School, College of Education, Department of Elementary and Middle Grades Education, Greenville, NC 27858-4353. Offers elementary education (MA Ed, MAT); English education (MAT); family and consumer science (MAT); health education (MAT); Hispanic studies (MAT); history education (MAT); middle grades education (MA Ed, MAT); music education (MAT); science education (MAT); special education (MAT), including general curriculum; vocational education (MAT). *Accreditation:* NCATE. *Program availability:* Part-time, evening/weekend, online learning. *Students:* 5 full-time (4 women), 18 part-time (16 women); includes 4 minority (3 Black or African American, non-Hispanic/Latino; 1 Hispanic/Latino). Average age 31. 19 applicants, 95% accepted, 13 enrolled. In 2016, 8 master's awarded. *Degree requirements:* For master's, comprehensive exam, thesis optional. *Entrance requirements:* For master's, GRE or MAT, minimum GPA of 2.5, bachelor's degree in related field, teaching license (MA Ed). Additional exam requirements/recommendations for international students: Required—TOEFL. *Application deadline:* For fall admission, 6/1 priority date for domestic students. Applications are processed on a rolling basis. Application fee: $70. *Financial support:* Federal Work-Study available. Support available to part-time students. Financial award application deadline: 6/1. *Unit head:* Dr. Ann Bullock, Chair, 252-328-1126, E-mail: bullockv@ecu.edu. *Application contact:* Dean of Graduate School, 252-328-6012, Fax: 252-328-6071, E-mail: gradschool@ecu.edu.
Website: http://www.ecu.edu/cs-educ/elmid/index.cfm

Eastern Michigan University, Graduate School, College of Arts and Sciences, Department of World Languages, Programs in World Languages, Ypsilanti, MI 48197. Offers MA, Graduate Certificate. *Program availability:* Part-time, evening/weekend, online learning. *Students:* 6 full-time (all women), 13 part-time (10 women); includes 6 minority (1 Black or African American, non-Hispanic/Latino; 5 Hispanic/Latino). Average age 34. 14 applicants, 100% accepted, 8 enrolled. In 2016, 5 master's, 1 other advanced degree awarded. *Degree requirements:* For master's, one foreign language, thesis optional. *Entrance requirements:* Additional exam requirements/recommendations for international students: Required—TOEFL. *Application deadline:* Applications are processed on a rolling basis. Application fee: $45. *Financial support:* Fellowships, research assistantships with full tuition reimbursements, teaching assistantships with full tuition reimbursements, career-related internships or fieldwork, Federal Work-Study, institutionally sponsored loans, scholarships/grants, tuition waivers (partial), and unspecified assistantships available. Support available to part-time students. Financial award applicants required to submit FAFSA. *Application contact:* Dr. Genevieve Peden, Program Advisor, 734-487-1498, Fax: 734-487-3411, E-mail: gpeden@emich.edu.

Eastern University, Loeb School of Education, St. Davids, PA 19087-3696. Offers ESL program specialist (K-12) (Certificate); general supervisor (PreK-12) (Certificate); health and physical education (K-12) (Certificate); middle level (4-8) (Certificate); multicultural education (M Ed); organizational leadership with education (PhD); Pre K-4 (Certificate); Pre K-4 with special education (Certificate); reading (M Ed); reading specialist (K-12) (Certificate); reading supervisor (K-12) (Certificate); school health supervisor (Certificate); school nurse (K-12) (Certificate); secondary biology education (7-12) (Certificate); secondary chemistry education (7-12) (Certificate); secondary communication education (7-12) (Certificate); secondary education (7-12) (Certificate); secondary English education (7-12) (Certificate); secondary math education (7-12) (Certificate); secondary social studies education (7-12) (Certificate); special education (M Ed); special education (7-12) (Certificate); special education (Pre K-8) (Certificate); special education supervisor (N-12) (Certificate); TESOL (M Ed); world language (Certificate), including French, Spanish. *Program availability:* Part-time, evening/weekend, online learning. *Students:* 41 full-time (32 women), 89 part-time (68 women); includes 54 minority (38 Black or African American, non-Hispanic/Latino; 3 Asian, non-Hispanic/Latino; 11 Hispanic/Latino; 2 Two or more races, non-Hispanic/Latino), 2 international. Average age 37. In 2016, 64 master's awarded. *Entrance requirements:* Additional exam requirements/recommendations for international students: Required—TOEFL. *Application deadline:* Applications are processed on a rolling basis. Application fee: $35. Electronic applications accepted. Application fee is waived when completed online. *Expenses:* $690 per credit. *Unit head:* Michael Dziedziak, Executive Director of Enrollment, 800-452-0996, E-mail: gpsadmissions@eastern.edu.
Website: http://www.eastern.edu/academics/programs/loeb-school-education-0

Elms College, Division of Education, Chicopee, MA 01013-2839. Offers early childhood education (MAT); education (M Ed, CAGS); elementary education (MAT); English as a second language (MAT); reading (MAT); secondary education (MAT), including biology education, English education, Spanish education; special education (MAT). *Program availability:* Part-time, evening/weekend. *Faculty:* 5 full-time (all women), 7 part-time/adjunct (6 women). *Students:* 6 full-time (all women), 136 part-time (111 women); includes 6 minority (1 Asian, non-Hispanic/Latino; 5 Hispanic/Latino). Average age 33. 27 applicants, 89% accepted, 20 enrolled. In 2016, 47 master's, 3 other advanced degrees awarded. *Degree requirements:* For master's, thesis (for some programs). *Entrance requirements:* For master's, Massachusetts Educators Certification Test, minimum GPA of 3.0; for CAGS, master's degree in education. Additional exam requirements/recommendations for international students: Required—TOEFL. *Application deadline:* For fall admission, 7/1 priority date for domestic students; for spring admission, 11/1 priority date for domestic students. Applications are processed on a rolling basis. Application fee: $30. *Expenses: Tuition:* Full-time $13,392. *Required fees:* $200. *Financial support:* In 2016–17, 2 teaching assistantships with partial tuition reimbursements were awarded; tuition waivers (partial) also available. Support available to part-time students. Financial award applicants required to submit FAFSA. *Unit head:* Dr. Mary Janeczek, Chair, Division of Education, 413-594-2761, Fax: 413-592-4871, E-mail: janeczeke@elms.edu. *Application contact:* Dr. Elizabeth Teahan Hukowicz, Dean, School of Graduate and Professional Studies, 413-265-2360, Fax: 413-265-2459, E-mail: hukowiczе@elms.edu.

Florida International University, College of Arts, Sciences, and Education, Department of Teaching and Learning, Miami, FL 33199. Offers art education (MA, MS); curriculum and instruction (MS, Ed D, PhD, Ed S), including curriculum development (MS), elementary education (MS), English education (MS), learning technologies (MS), mathematics education (MS), modern language education (MS), physical education (MS), science education (MS), social studies education (MS), special education (MS); early childhood education (MS); exceptional student education (Ed D); foreign language education (MS), including foreign language education, teaching English to speakers of other languages (TESOL); international/intercultural education (MS); language, literacy and culture (PhD); mathematics, science, and learning technologies (PhD); physical education (MS), including sport and fitness; reading education (MS). *Program availability:* Part-time, evening/weekend. *Faculty:* 34 full-time (23 women), 64 part-time/adjunct (48 women). *Students:* 182 full-time (154 women), 231 part-time (190 women); includes 323 minority (69 Black or African American, non-Hispanic/Latino; 10 Asian, non-Hispanic/Latino; 237 Hispanic/Latino; 7 Two or more races, non-Hispanic/Latino), 19 international. Average age 34. 282 applicants, 58% accepted, 113 enrolled. In 2016, 184 master's, 12 doctorates awarded. *Degree requirements:* For doctorate, comprehensive exam, thesis/dissertation. *Entrance requirements:* For master's, GRE General Test, Florida General Knowledge Test or Florida College Level Academic Skills Test; for doctorate and Ed S, GRE General Test. Additional exam requirements/recommendations for international students: Required—TOEFL (minimum score 550 paper-based; 80 iBT), IELTS (minimum score 6.3). *Application deadline:* For fall admission, 6/1 priority date for domestic students, 4/1 for international students; for winter admission, 10/1 priority date for domestic students, 9/1 for international students; for spring admission, 3/1 priority date for domestic students, 2/1 for international students. Applications are processed on a rolling basis. Application fee: $30. Electronic applications accepted. *Expenses:* Tuition, state resident: full-time $8912; part-time $446 per credit hour. Tuition, nonresident: full-time $21,393; part-time $992 per credit hour. *Required fees:* $2185; $195 per semester. Tuition and fees vary according to program. *Financial support:* Research assistantships with tuition reimbursements and teaching assistantships with tuition reimbursements available. *Unit head:* Dr. Lynn Miller, Chair, 305-348-2005, Fax: 305-348-2086, E-mail: lynne.miller@fiu.edu. *Application contact:* Nanett Rojas, Assistant Director, Graduate Admissions, 305-348-7464, Fax: 305-348-7441, E-mail: gradadm@fiu.edu.
Website: http://education.fiu.edu

Florida State University, The Graduate School, College of Education, Program in Curriculum and Instruction, Tallahassee, FL 32306. Offers curriculum and instruction (MS, PhD, Ed S), including early childhood education, elementary education, English education, English teaching (MS), exceptional student education (MS), foreign and second language education, foreign and second language teaching (MS), mathematics education, mathematics teaching (MS), reading education and language arts, science

education, social science education, social science teaching (MS), special education, special education studies (MS), visual disabilities (MS, Ed S). *Program availability:* Part-time, evening/weekend. Terminal master's awarded for partial completion of doctoral program. *Degree requirements:* For master's and Ed S, comprehensive exam, thesis optional; for doctorate, comprehensive exam, thesis/dissertation, diagnostic exam, preliminary exam, prospectus defense, dissertation defense. *Entrance requirements:* For master's, doctorate, and Ed S, GRE General Test, minimum upper-division GPA of 3.0. Additional exam requirements/recommendations for international students: Required—TOEFL (minimum score 550 paper-based, 80 iBT), IELTS (minimum score 6.5), Michigan English Language Assessment Battery (minimum score 77), or PTE (minimum score 55). Application fee: $30. Electronic applications accepted. *Expenses:* Tuition, state resident: full-time $7263; part-time $403.51 per credit hour. Tuition, nonresident: full-time $18,087; part-time $1004.85 per credit hour. *Required fees:* $1365; $75.81 per credit hour. $20 per semester. Tuition and fees vary according to campus/location. *Financial support:* Fellowships, research assistantships, teaching assistantships, scholarships/grants, tuition waivers (full and partial), and unspecified assistantships available. Financial award application deadline: 1/15; financial award applicants required to submit FAFSA. *Faculty research:* Identifying effective intervention strategies to improve reading skills; improving literacy teaching and learning through technology; understanding of student sense making, problem solving, the history and structure of STEM disciplines, and teacher education to support the development of ambitious instruction that supports the STEM learning of all students; examining practices of international education; identifying ways to support the professional development of teachers. *Unit head:* Dr. Sherry Southerland, Professor/Department Chair, 850-644-4880, Fax: 850-644-7736, E-mail: ssoutherland@admin.fsu.edu. *Application contact:* Libbie Crowley, Academic Support Specialist, 850-644-2122, Fax: 850-644-7736, E-mail: ecrowley@fsu.edu.
Website: http://education.fsu.edu/degrees-and-programs/graduate-programs

Framingham State University, Continuing Education, Program in Spanish, Framingham, MA 01701-9101. Offers M Ed.

George Mason University, College of Humanities and Social Sciences, Department of Modern and Classical Languages, Fairfax, VA 22030. Offers foreign languages (MA), including French. *Faculty:* 30 full-time (21 women), 44 part-time/adjunct (29 women). *Students:* 4 full-time (all women), 22 part-time (18 women); includes 19 minority (1 Black or African American, non-Hispanic/Latino; 1 Asian, non-Hispanic/Latino; 16 Hispanic/Latino; 1 Two or more races, non-Hispanic/Latino), 1 international. Average age 36. 11 applicants, 91% accepted, 7 enrolled. In 2016, 7 master's awarded. *Degree requirements:* For master's, comprehensive exam, thesis optional. *Entrance requirements:* For master's, 3 letters of recommendation; official transcripts; goals statement; baccalaureate degree in French or Spanish with minimum GPA of 3.0 (recommended). Additional exam requirements/recommendations for international students: Required—TOEFL (minimum score 575 paper-based; 88 iBT), IELTS (minimum score 6.5), PTE (minimum score 59). *Application deadline:* For fall admission, 4/15 for domestic students. Application fee: $75 ($80 for international students). Electronic applications accepted. *Expenses:* Tuition, state resident: full-time $10,628; part-time $443 per credit. Tuition, nonresident: full-time $29,306; part-time $1221 per credit. *Required fees:* $3096; $129 per credit. Tuition and fees vary according to program. *Financial support:* In 2016–17, 3 students received support, including 3 teaching assistantships with tuition reimbursements available (averaging $10,723 per year); career-related internships or fieldwork, Federal Work-Study, scholarships/grants, unspecified assistantships, and health care benefits (for full-time research or teaching assistantship recipients) also available. Support available to part-time students. Financial award application deadline: 3/1; financial award applicants required to submit FAFSA. *Faculty research:* French Renaissance studies, early Modern (sixteenth- to eighteenth-centuries) literary and cultural studies, history, literature and philosophy, women's studies. *Total annual research expenditures:* $4,138. *Unit head:* Rei Berroa, Chair, 703-993-1220, Fax: 703-993-1245, E-mail: rberroa@gmu.edu. *Application contact:* Jen Barnard, Office Manager, 703-993-1230, Fax: 703-993-1245, E-mail: jbarnard@gmu.edu.
Website: http://mcl.gmu.edu/

The George Washington University, Graduate School of Education and Human Development, Department of Curriculum and Pedagogy, Program in Secondary Education, Washington, DC 20052. Offers Arabic (M Ed); Italian (M Ed); math (M Ed); physics (M Ed); Russian (M Ed). Programs also offered in Arlington and Ashburn, VA. *Accreditation:* NCATE. *Students:* 13 full-time (11 women), 21 part-time (15 women); includes 12 minority (4 Black or African American, non-Hispanic/Latino; 2 Asian, non-Hispanic/Latino; 4 Hispanic/Latino; 2 Two or more races, non-Hispanic/Latino). Average age 32. 50 applicants, 82% accepted, 25 enrolled. In 2016, 22 master's awarded. *Degree requirements:* For master's, comprehensive exam. *Entrance requirements:* For master's, GRE General Test or MAT, interview, minimum GPA of 2.75. *Application deadline:* For fall admission, 1/15 priority date for domestic students; for spring admission, 10/1 for domestic students. Applications are processed on a rolling basis. Application fee: $75. *Financial support:* Fellowships, career-related internships or fieldwork, Federal Work-Study, tuition waivers (full and partial), and stipends available. Financial award application deadline: 1/15; financial award applicants required to submit FAFSA. *Unit head:* Prof. Curtis Pyke, Chair, 202-994-4516, E-mail: cpyke@gwu.edu. *Application contact:* Sarah Lang, Director of Graduate Admissions, 202-994-1447, Fax: 202-994-7207, E-mail: slang@gwu.edu.

Georgia Southern University, Jack N. Averitt College of Graduate Studies, College of Education, Department of Teaching and Learning, Program in Spanish P-12 Education, Statesboro, GA 30458. Offers MAT. *Program availability:* Part-time. *Students:* 2 full-time (1 woman), 1 (woman) part-time; includes 1 minority (Black or African American, non-Hispanic/Latino). Average age 27. 3 applicants, 100% accepted. In 2016, 8 master's awarded. *Entrance requirements:* Additional exam requirements/recommendations for international students: Required—TOEFL (minimum score 80 iBT). *Application deadline:* For fall admission, 3/15 for domestic and international students; for spring admission, 10/1 for domestic and international students; for summer admission, 3/1 for domestic and international students. *Expenses:* Tuition, state resident: full-time $7236; part-time $277 per semester hour. Tuition, nonresident: full-time $27,118; part-time $1105 per semester hour. *Required fees:* $2092. *Financial support:* Applicants required to submit FAFSA. *Unit head:* Dr. Greg Chamblee, Program Coordinator, 912-478-5783, Fax: 912-478-0026, E-mail: gchamblee@georgiasouthern.edu. *Application contact:* Lydia Cross, Coordinator for Graduate Academic Services Center, 912-478-8664, E-mail: lcross@georgiasouthern.edu.

Georgia State University, College of Arts and Sciences, Department of World Languages and Cultures, Atlanta, GA 30302-3083. Offers French (MA), including applied linguistics and pedagogy, French studies, literature and culture; Latin American studies (Certificate); Spanish (MA); translation and interpretation (Certificate), including interpretation, translation. *Program availability:* Part-time. *Faculty:* 36 full-time (20 women). *Students:* 17 full-time (12 women), 4 part-time (2 women); includes 18 minority (7 Black or African American, non-Hispanic/Latino; 6 Asian, non-Hispanic/Latino; 5 Hispanic/Latino), 5 international. Average age 38. 18 applicants, 83% accepted, 11 enrolled. In 2016, 3 other advanced degrees awarded. *Degree requirements:* For master's, 2 foreign languages, comprehensive exam, thesis or alternative, Graduate Foreign Language Reading Exam. *Entrance requirements:* For master's, GRE, statement of purpose, writing sample in the target language, 2 letters of recommendation, official transcripts; for Certificate, entrance examination involving translating one passage from English to the target language and one passage from the target language to English, 3 letters of recommendation, resume/curriculum vitae, official transcripts. Additional exam requirements/recommendations for international students: Required—TOEFL (minimum score 79 iBT). *Application deadline:* For fall admission, 3/15 priority date for domestic and international students; for spring admission, 11/15 priority date for domestic and international students. Application fee: $50. Electronic applications accepted. *Expenses:* Tuition, state resident: full-time $6876; part-time $382 per credit hour. Tuition, nonresident: full-time $22,374; part-time $1243 per credit hour. *Required fees:* $2128; $1064 per term. Part-time tuition and fees vary according to course load and program. *Financial support:* Applicants required to submit FAFSA. *Faculty research:* French literature and culture, Francophone literature and culture, Latin American literature and culture, Spanish literature and culture, Hispanic linguistics. *Unit head:* Dr. Fernando Reati, Department Chair, 404-413-5984, Fax: 404-413-5982, E-mail: freati@gsu.edu. *Application contact:* Amber Amari, Director, Graduate and Scheduling Services, 404-413-5037, E-mail: aamari@gsu.edu.
Website: http://wlc.gsu.edu/

Harding University, Cannon-Clary College of Education, Searcy, AR 72149-0001. Offers advanced studies in teaching and learning (M Ed); art (MSE); behavioral science (MSE); counseling (MS, Ed S); early childhood special education (M Ed, MSE); education (MSE); educational leadership (M Ed, Ed S); elementary education (M Ed); English (MSE); French (MSE); history/social science (MSE); kinesiology (MSE); math (MSE); reading (M Ed); secondary education (M Ed); Spanish (MSE); teaching (MAT); teaching English as a second language (MSE). *Accreditation:* NCATE. *Program availability:* Part-time, evening/weekend. *Faculty:* 22 full-time (9 women), 51 part-time/adjunct (37 women). *Students:* 130 full-time (94 women), 321 part-time (234 women); includes 83 minority (50 Black or African American, non-Hispanic/Latino; 4 American Indian or Alaska Native, non-Hispanic/Latino; 6 Asian, non-Hispanic/Latino; 13 Hispanic/Latino; 10 Two or more races, non-Hispanic/Latino), 11 international. Average age 35. 125 applicants, 88% accepted, 110 enrolled. In 2016, 124 master's, 27 other advanced degrees awarded. *Degree requirements:* For master's, comprehensive exam (for some programs), thesis optional, portfolio(s); for Ed S, comprehensive exam, portfolio, project. *Entrance requirements:* For master's, GRE, MAT, PRAXIS; for Ed S, MAT or GRE. Additional exam requirements/recommendations for international students: Required—TOEFL (minimum score 550 paper-based; 79 iBT). *Application deadline:* For fall admission, 8/1 for domestic and international students; for spring admission, 1/1 for domestic and international students. Applications are processed on a rolling basis. Application fee: $35. Tuition and fees vary according to degree level and program. *Financial support:* In 2016–17, 31 students received support. Unspecified assistantships available. *Faculty research:* Reading, comprehension, school violence, educational technology, behavior, college choice, differentiated instruction, brain-based teaching. *Unit head:* Dr. Clara Carroll, Chair, 501-279-4501, Fax: 501-279-4083, E-mail: ccarroll@harding.edu. *Application contact:* Information Contact, 501-279-4315, E-mail: gradstudiesedu@harding.edu.
Website: http://www.harding.edu/education

Hofstra University, School of Education, Programs in Teacher Education, Hempstead, NY 11549. Offers bilingual education (MA, Advanced Certificate); bilingual extension (Advanced Certificate), including education/speech language pathology; business education (MS Ed); early childhood and childhood education (MS Ed); early childhood education (MA, MS Ed); education technology (Advanced Certificate); elementary education (MA, MS Ed), including science, technology, engineering, and mathematics (STEM) (MA); English education (MS Ed); family and consumer science (MS Ed); fine arts and music education (Advanced Certificate); fine arts education (MS Ed); foreign language and TESOL (MS Ed); foreign language education (MS Ed), including French, German, Russian, Spanish; learning and teaching (Ed D), including applied linguistics, art education, arts and humanities, early childhood education, English education, human development, math education, math, science, and technology, multicultural education, physical education, science education, social studies education, special education; mathematics education (MA, MS Ed); middle school extension (Advanced Certificate), including grades 5-6, grades 7-9; music education (MA, MS Ed); science education (MA, MS Ed), including biology, chemistry, earth science, geology, physics; secondary education (Advanced Certificate); social studies education (MA, MS Ed); teaching languages other than English and TESOL (MS Ed); TESOL (MS Ed, Advanced Certificate). *Program availability:* Part-time, evening/weekend, blended/hybrid learning. *Students:* 139 full-time (97 women), 145 part-time (106 women); includes 60 minority (15 Black or African American, non-Hispanic/Latino; 1 American Indian or Alaska Native, non-Hispanic/Latino; 12 Asian, non-Hispanic/Latino; 31 Hispanic/Latino; 1 Two or more races, non-Hispanic/Latino), 21 international. Average age 29. 255 applicants, 86% accepted, 122 enrolled. In 2016, 101 master's, 4 doctorates, 43 other advanced degrees awarded. *Degree requirements:* For master's, comprehensive exam, thesis (for some programs), exit project, student teaching, fieldwork, electronic portfolio, curriculum project, minimum GPA of 3.0; for doctorate, thesis/dissertation; for Advanced Certificate, 3 foreign languages, comprehensive exam (for some programs), thesis project. *Entrance requirements:* For master's, GRE, MAT, 2 letters of recommendation, portfolio, teacher certification (MA), interview, essay; for doctorate, GMAT, GRE, LSAT, or MAT; for Advanced Certificate, 2 letters of recommendation, essay, interview and/or portfolio, teaching certificate. Additional exam requirements/recommendations for international students: Required—TOEFL (minimum score 550 paper-based; 80 iBT). *Application deadline:* Applications are processed on a rolling basis. Application fee: $75. Electronic applications accepted. *Expenses: Tuition:* Full-time $1240. *Required fees:* $970. Tuition and fees vary according to program. *Financial support:* In 2016–17, 149 students received support, including 58 fellowships with full and partial tuition reimbursements available (averaging $5,309 per year), 5 research assistantships with full and partial tuition reimbursements available (averaging $7,073 per year); career-related internships or fieldwork, Federal Work-Study, institutionally sponsored loans, scholarships/grants, traineeships, tuition waivers (full and partial), and unspecified assistantships also available. Support available to part-time students. Financial award applicants required to submit FAFSA. *Faculty research:* Educational interventions that foster critical-thinking skills; teachers' attitudes about professional development; threats to teacher quality. *Unit head:* Dr. Eustace Thompson, Chairperson, 516-463-5749, Fax: 516-463-6275, E-mail: eustace.g.thompson@hofstra.edu. *Application contact:* Sunil Samuel, Assistant Vice President of Admissions, 516-463-4723, Fax: 516-463-4664, E-mail: graduateadmission@hofstra.edu.
Website: http://www.hofstra.edu/education/

Hunter College of the City University of New York, Graduate School, School of Education, Programs in Secondary Education, Concentration in French Education, New York, NY 10065-5085. Offers MA. *Accreditation:* NCATE. *Degree requirements:* For master's, thesis, professional teaching portfolio, New York State Teacher Certification Exam. *Entrance requirements:* For master's, 24 credits in French; minimum GPA of 3.0 in French, 2.8 overall; 2 letters of reference; interview. Additional exam requirements/recommendations for international students: Required—TOEFL, TWE. *Application* *deadline:* For fall admission, 4/1 for domestic students, 2/1 for international students; for spring admission, 11/1 for domestic students, 9/1 for international students. Applications are processed on a rolling basis. *Financial support:* Federal Work-Study and tuition waivers (partial) available. Support available to part-time students. *Unit head:* Prof. Jenny Castillo, Graduate Advisor, 212-772-4614, E-mail: jmcastil@hunter.cuny.edu. *Application contact:* Milena Solo, Director for Graduate Admissions, 212-772-4480, E-mail: admissions@hunter.cuny.edu.

Hunter College of the City University of New York, Graduate School, School of Education, Programs in Secondary Education, Concentration in Italian Education, New York, NY 10065-5085. Offers MA. *Accreditation:* NCATE. *Degree requirements:* For master's, thesis, professional teaching portfolio, New York State Teacher Certification Exam, research project. *Entrance requirements:* For master's, minimum GPA of 3.0 in Italian, 2.8 overall; 24 credits of course work in Italian; 2 letters of reference; interview. Additional exam requirements/recommendations for international students: Required—TOEFL, TWE. *Application deadline:* For fall admission, 4/1 for domestic students, 2/1 for international students; for spring admission, 11/1 for domestic students, 9/1 for international students. Applications are processed on a rolling basis. *Financial support:* Federal Work-Study and tuition waivers (partial) available. Support available to part-time students. *Unit head:* Prof. Jenny Castillo, Education Program Coordinator, 212-772-4614, Fax: 212-772-5094, E-mail: jmcasti@hunter.cuny.edu. *Application contact:* Milena Solo, Director for Graduate Admissions, 212-772-4482, E-mail: admissions@hunter.cuny.edu.
Website: http://www.hunter.cuny.edu/school-of-education/programs/graduate/adolescent/foreign-languages/italian

Hunter College of the City University of New York, Graduate School, School of Education, Programs in Secondary Education, Concentration in Spanish Education, New York, NY 10065-5085. Offers MA. *Accreditation:* NCATE. *Degree requirements:* For master's, thesis, professional teaching portfolio, New York State Teacher Certification Exam. *Entrance requirements:* For master's, minimum GPA of 3.0 in Spanish, 2.8 overall; 24 credits of course work in Spanish; 2 letters of reference; interview. Additional exam requirements/recommendations for international students: Required—TOEFL, TWE. *Application deadline:* For fall admission, 4/1 for domestic students, 2/1 for international students; for spring admission, 11/1 for domestic students, 9/1 for international students. Applications are processed on a rolling basis. *Financial support:* Federal Work-Study and tuition waivers (partial) available. Support available to part-time students. *Unit head:* Dr. Magdalena Perkowska, Advisor, 212-772-5132, E-mail: mperkowsk@hunter.cuny.edu. *Application contact:* Milena Solo, Director for Graduate Admissions, 212-772-4482, E-mail: admissions@hunter.cuny.edu.

Indiana State University, College of Graduate and Professional Studies, College of Arts and Sciences, Department of Languages, Literatures, and Linguistics, Terre Haute, IN 47809. Offers applied linguistics/teaching English as a second language (MA); language education (PhD); Spanish/teaching english as a second language (MA); TESL/TEFL (CAS). *Degree requirements:* For master's, comprehensive exam. Electronic applications accepted.

Indiana University Bloomington, University Graduate School, College of Arts and Sciences, Department of French and Italian, Bloomington, IN 47405. Offers French (MA, PhD), including French and Francophone studies (MA), French instruction (MA), French linguistics; Italian (MA, PhD). *Program availability:* Part-time. *Faculty:* 23 full-time (10 women). *Students:* 51 full-time (32 women), 6 part-time (3 women); includes 2 minority (1 Black or African American, non-Hispanic/Latino; 1 Hispanic/Latino), 27 international. Average age 31. 28 applicants, 71% accepted, 7 enrolled. In 2016, 8 master's, 4 doctorates awarded. Terminal master's awarded for partial completion of doctoral program. *Degree requirements:* For master's, variable foreign language requirement, comprehensive exam (for some programs), thesis or alternative; for doctorate, variable foreign language requirement, comprehensive exam, thesis/dissertation. *Entrance requirements:* For master's, GRE General Test, BA or equivalent undergraduate preparation in French or Italian; for doctorate, GRE General Test, MA from degree program at IU; MA in the specific field. Additional exam requirements/recommendations for international students: Required—TOEFL (minimum score 550 paper-based; 79 iBT), GRE General Test (recommended). *Application deadline:* For fall admission, 1/15 priority date for domestic students, 12/1 priority date for international students; for spring admission, 9/1 priority date for domestic and international students. Application fee: $55 ($65 for international students). Electronic applications accepted. *Financial support:* In 2016–17, 40 students received support, including 6 fellowships with partial tuition reimbursements available (averaging $18,000 per year), 2 research assistantships with partial tuition reimbursements available (averaging $15,750 per year), 31 teaching assistantships with partial tuition reimbursements available (averaging $15,750 per year); scholarships/grants, health care benefits, and unspecified assistantships also available. Financial award application deadline: 1/15. *Faculty research:* French and Italian literature, French linguistics, including the novel and political theory, literature and fine arts, literary theory, postcolonialism, French-Creole studies, French literature of Africa and its Diaspora, humanism, Medieval folklore and mythology, humor in Medieval and Renaissance literature, emigration, second language acquisition, syntax, sociolinguistics, phonology, lexicography, media and cultural studies, cinema, drama. *Unit head:* Prof. Massimo Scalabrini, Chair, 812-855-8044, Fax: 812-855-8877, E-mail: mscalabar@indiana.edu. *Application contact:* Lauren Anderson, Graduate Student Services Coordinator, 812-855-1088, Fax: 812-855-8877, E-mail: fritgs@indiana.edu.
Website: http://frit.indiana.edu

Indiana University Bloomington, University Graduate School, College of Arts and Sciences, Department of Germanic Studies, Bloomington, IN 47405-7000. Offers German philology and linguistics (PhD); German studies (MA, PhD), including German (MA), German literature and culture (MA), German literature and linguistics (MA); medieval German studies (PhD); teaching German (MAT). *Faculty:* 13 full-time (4 women), 6 part-time/adjunct (2 women). *Students:* 28 full-time (15 women), 2 part-time (both women), 5 international. Average age 32. 16 applicants, 56% accepted, 4 enrolled. In 2016, 2 master's, 3 doctorates awarded. *Degree requirements:* For master's, one foreign language, project; for doctorate, one foreign language, comprehensive exam, thesis/dissertation. *Entrance requirements:* For master's, GRE General Test, BA in German or equivalent; for doctorate, GRE General Test, MA in German or equivalent. Additional exam requirements/recommendations for international students: Required—TOEFL. *Application deadline:* For fall admission, 12/1 priority date for domestic students, 12/1 for international students; for spring admission, 9/1 priority date for domestic students, 9/1 for international students. Applications are processed on a rolling basis. Application fee: $55 ($65 for international students). Electronic applications accepted. *Financial support:* Application deadline: 1/15. *Faculty research:* German and other European literature: medieval to modern/postmodern, German and culture studies, Germanic philology, literary theory, literature and the other arts. *Unit head:* William Rasch, Department Chairman, 812-855-7947, Fax: 812-855-8292, E-mail: wrasch@indiana.edu. *Application contact:* Michelle Dunbar, Graduate Secretary, 812-855-7947, E-mail: midunbar@indiana.edu.
Website: http://germanic.indiana.edu/

Indiana University Bloomington, University Graduate School, College of Arts and Sciences, School of Global and International Studies, Department of East Asian Languages and Cultures, Bloomington, IN 47408. Offers Chinese (MA, PhD); Chinese language pedagogy (MA); East Asian studies (MA); Japanese (MA, PhD); Japanese language pedagogy (MA). *Program availability:* Part-time. *Degree requirements:* For master's, one foreign language, thesis; for doctorate, 2 foreign languages, comprehensive exam, thesis/dissertation. *Entrance requirements:* Additional exam requirements/recommendations for international students: Required—TOEFL (minimum score 93 iBT). Electronic applications accepted. *Faculty research:* Modern East Asian history; politics and society; traditional Chinese thought and society; medieval and premodern Japanese history, literature and society; modern Chinese and Japanese film and literature; Chinese, Japanese, Korean language and linguistics.

Indiana University of Pennsylvania, School of Graduate Studies and Research, College of Humanities and Social Sciences, Department of Foreign Languages, Program in Spanish/Applied Linguistics and Teaching Methodology, Indiana, PA 15705. Offers MA. Application fee: $50. *Expenses:* Tuition, state resident: full-time $8694; part-time $483 per credit. Tuition, nonresident: full-time $13,050; part-time $725 per credit. *Required fees:* $157 per credit. $50 per term. Tuition and fees vary according to course load and program. *Financial support:* Fellowships with full tuition reimbursements and research assistantships with tuition reimbursements available. *Unit head:* Dr. Sean McDaniel, Chairperson, 724-357-7532, E-mail: mcdaniel@iup.edu.

Indiana University–Purdue University Indianapolis, School of Education, Indianapolis, IN 46202-5155. Offers curriculum and instruction (MS); early childhood (MS); educational leadership (MS, Certificate); English as a second language (Certificate); kindergarten (Certificate); language education (MS); reading (Certificate); school counseling (MS); special education (MS, Certificate). *Program availability:* Part-time, evening/weekend. *Faculty:* 35 full-time (27 women), 56 part-time/adjunct (42 women). *Students:* 125 full-time (86 women), 181 part-time (139 women); includes 106 minority (78 Black or African American, non-Hispanic/Latino; 9 Asian, non-Hispanic/Latino; 12 Hispanic/Latino; 7 Two or more races, non-Hispanic/Latino), 3 international. Average age 32. 73 applicants, 93% accepted, 68 enrolled. In 2016, 73 master's awarded. Terminal master's awarded for partial completion of doctoral program. *Degree requirements:* For master's, thesis optional. *Entrance requirements:* For master's, GRE General Test, minimum GPA of 2.5; for Certificate, official transcripts. Additional exam requirements/recommendations for international students: Required—TOEFL (minimum score 60 iBT), IELTS (minimum score 5.5). *Application deadline:* For fall admission, 5/1 for domestic students; for spring admission, 11/1 for domestic students. Application fee: $60 ($65 for international students). Electronic applications accepted. *Expenses:* $1,262 tuition, $213 general fee. *Financial support:* Applicants required to submit FAFSA. *Faculty research:* Educational policies and school leaders' responses to these; issues of intersectionality in the experiences of African American lesbian, gay, and bisexual students attending historically black colleges and universities and those who belong to black Greek-letter organizations; students' experiential knowledge and their evolving disciplinary-specific literacy and understanding; innovative program development; urban ESL teacher preparation; target-based instructional coaching. *Total annual research expenditures:* $2.1 million. *Unit head:* Dr. Robin Hughes, Executive Associate Dean, 317-274-6817, E-mail: roblhugh@iupui.edu. *Application contact:* Ky Shaw, Graduate Admissions Coordinator, 317-278-6778, E-mail: kycshaw@iupui.edu.
Website: http://education.iupui.edu/

Inter American University of Puerto Rico, Arecibo Campus, Programs in Education, Arecibo, PR 00614-4050. Offers administration and educational supervision (MA Ed); counseling and guidance (MA Ed); curriculum and teaching (MA Ed), including biology education, English as a second language, history education, math education, Spanish; elementary education (MA Ed). *Accreditation:* TEAC. *Degree requirements:* For master's, comprehensive exam, thesis optional. *Entrance requirements:* For master's, GRE, EXADEP, bachelor's degree in education or teaching license (administration and supervision) or courses in education and psychology (counseling and guidance), minimum GPA of 2.5 in last 60 credits.

Inter American University of Puerto Rico, Barranquitas Campus, Program in Education, Barranquitas, PR 00794. Offers curriculum and teaching (M Ed), including biology education, English as a second language, history education, mathematics education, Spanish; educational leadership and management (MA); elementary education (M Ed); information and library service technology (M Ed); special education (MA). *Accreditation:* TEAC. *Degree requirements:* For master's, comprehensive exam, thesis optional. *Entrance requirements:* For master's, EXADEP, letter of recommendation. Electronic applications accepted.

Inter American University of Puerto Rico, Metropolitan Campus, Graduate Programs, Program in Spanish Education, San Juan, PR 00919-1293. Offers MA.

Iona College, School of Arts and Science, Department of Education, New Rochelle, NY 10801-1890. Offers adolescence education: biology (MS Ed, MST); adolescence education: English (MS Ed); adolescence education: mathematics (MST); adolescence education: social studies (MS Ed, MST); adolescence education: Spanish (MS Ed); adolescence special education 5-12 (MST); childhood and special education (MST); early childhood and childhood (MST); educational leadership (MS Ed). *Accreditation:* NCATE. *Program availability:* Part-time, evening/weekend. *Faculty:* 7 full-time (6 women), 4 part-time/adjunct (2 women). *Students:* 27 full-time (19 women), 27 part-time (18 women); includes 18 minority (4 Black or African American, non-Hispanic/Latino; 1 Asian, non-Hispanic/Latino; 12 Hispanic/Latino; 1 Two or more races, non-Hispanic/Latino). Average age 26. 6 applicants, 67% accepted, 3 enrolled. In 2016, 25 master's awarded. *Degree requirements:* For master's, thesis or alternative. *Entrance requirements:* For master's, minimum GPA of 3.0, NY State teaching certificate and bachelor's degree (for MS Ed). Additional exam requirements/recommendations for international students: Required—TOEFL (minimum score 550 paper-based; 80 iBT), IELTS (minimum score 6.5). *Application deadline:* For fall admission, 8/1 priority date for domestic students, 5/1 priority date for international students; for spring admission, 1/1 priority date for domestic students, 9/1 priority date for international students. Applications are processed on a rolling basis. Application fee: $50. Electronic applications accepted. *Expenses: Tuition:* Full-time $19,692; part-time $1094 per credit. *Required fees:* $245 per term. Tuition and fees vary according to program. *Financial support:* In 2016–17, 3 students received support. Unspecified assistantships available. Support available to part-time students. Financial award application deadline: 4/15; financial award applicants required to submit FAFSA. *Faculty research:* Engaging teacher educators in scientific process, cross-national comparisons of mathematics teaching, questioning strategies in the classroom, research methods, literacy development. *Unit head:* Margaret Smith, PhD, Chair, 914-633-2210, Fax: 914-633-2608, E-mail: msmith@iona.edu. *Application contact:* Richard McMahon, Coordinator, Graduate School of Education, 914-633-2552, E-mail: rmcmahon@iona.edu.
Website: http://www.iona.edu/Academics/School-of-Arts-Science/Departments/Education/Graduate-Programs.aspx

Ithaca College, School of Humanities and Sciences, Program in Adolescence Education, Ithaca, NY 14850. Offers biology (MAT); chemistry (MAT); earth science (MAT); English (MAT); French (MAT); mathematics (MAT); physics (MAT); social studies (MAT); Spanish (MAT). *Program availability:* Part-time. *Faculty:* 26 full-time (12 women). *Students:* 11 full-time (4 women). Average age 26. 17 applicants, 94% accepted, 10 enrolled. *Degree requirements:* For master's, thesis or alternative.

Entrance requirements: Additional exam requirements/recommendations for international students: Required—TOEFL (minimum score 550 paper-based; 80 iBT). *Application deadline:* For fall admission, 2/15 for domestic and international students; for spring admission, 12/1 for domestic and international students. Applications are processed on a rolling basis. Application fee: $40. Electronic applications accepted. *Expenses:* Contact institution. *Financial support:* In 2016–17, 5 students received support, including 5 research assistantships (averaging $13,259 per year); career-related internships or fieldwork, Federal Work-Study, scholarships/grants, and unspecified assistantships also available. Support available to part-time students. Financial award application deadline: 2/15; financial award applicants required to submit CSS PROFILE or FAFSA. *Unit head:* Peter Martin, Chair, 607-274-1076, E-mail: pmartin@ithaca.edu. *Application contact:* Nicole Eversley Bradwell, Director, Office of Admission, 607-274-3124, Fax: 607-274-1263, E-mail: admission@ithaca.edu.
Website: http://www.ithaca.edu/gradprograms/education/programs/aded

James Madison University, The Graduate School, College of Education, Program in Education, Harrisonburg, VA 22807. Offers early childhood education (preK-3) (MAT); educational leadership (M Ed); educational technology (M Ed); elementary education (MAT); equity and cultural diversity (M Ed); inclusive early childhood education (MAT); K-8 mathematics specialist (M Ed); middle education (MAT); reading education (M Ed); secondary education (MAT); Spanish language and culture for educators (M Ed); TESOL (MAT). *Accreditation:* NCATE. *Program availability:* Part-time, evening/weekend. *Faculty:* 21 full-time (12 women), 5 part-time/adjunct (2 women). *Students:* 249 full-time (220 women), 123 part-time (86 women); includes 43 minority (7 Black or African American, non-Hispanic/Latino; 7 Asian, non-Hispanic/Latino; 17 Hispanic/Latino; 12 Two or more races, non-Hispanic/Latino), 2 international. Average age 30. 355 applicants, 98% accepted, 312 enrolled. In 2016, 247 master's awarded. Application fee: $55. Electronic applications accepted. *Financial support:* In 2016–17, 16 students received support. Career-related internships or fieldwork, Federal Work-Study, and 22 assistantships (averaging $7911) available. Financial award application deadline: 3/1; financial award applicants required to submit FAFSA. *Unit head:* Dr. Phillip M. Wishon, Dean, 540-568-6572, E-mail: wishonpm@jmu.edu. *Application contact:* Lynette D. Michael, Director of Graduate Admissions, 540-568-6131 Ext. 6395, Fax: 540-568-7860, E-mail: michaeld@jmu.edu.
Website: http://www.jmu.edu/coe/index.shtml

Kean University, College of Education, Program in Hindi and Urdu Language Pedagogy, Union, NJ 07083. Offers MA. *Program availability:* 100% online. *Faculty:* 3 full-time. *Students:* 6 full-time (all women), 4 part-time (all women); includes 8 minority (all Asian, non-Hispanic/Latino). Average age 44. 16 applicants, 69% accepted, 10 enrolled. *Degree requirements:* For master's, thesis/action research project. *Entrance requirements:* For master's, ACTFL OPI and WPT in Hindi or Urdu, bachelor's degree, minimum cumulative GPA of 3.0, official transcripts, professional resume or curriculum vitae, personal statement, two letters of recommendation, interview, teaching experience. Additional exam requirements/recommendations for international students: Required—TOEFL (minimum score 550 paper-based, 79 iBT) or IELTS (6.5). *Application deadline:* For fall admission, 6/1 for domestic students. Application fee: $75. Electronic applications accepted. *Expenses:* Tuition, state resident: full-time $13,156; part-time $640 per credit. Tuition, nonresident: full-time $17,831; part-time $785 per credit. *Required fees:* $3316; $151 per credit. Tuition and fees vary according to course level, course load, degree level and program. *Financial support:* Scholarships/grants and unspecified assistantships available. Financial award applicants required to submit FAFSA. *Unit head:* Dr. Michael Searson, Director, 908-737-0550, E-mail: msearson@kean.edu. *Application contact:* Brittany Gerstenhaber, Admissions Counselor, 908-737-7100, E-mail: grad-adm@kean.edu.

Kennesaw State University, Leland and Clarice C. Bagwell College of Education, Program in Teaching, Kennesaw, GA 30144. Offers art education (MAT); biology (MAT); chemistry (MAT); foreign language education (Chinese and Spanish) (MAT); physics (MAT); secondary English (MAT); secondary mathematics (MAT); special education (MAT); teaching English to speakers of other languages (MAT). *Program availability:* Part-time, evening/weekend. *Entrance requirements:* For master's, GRE, GACE I (state certificate exam), minimum GPA of 2.75, 2 recommendations, resume. Additional exam requirements/recommendations for international students: Required—TOEFL (minimum score 550 paper-based; 80 iBT), IELTS (minimum score 6.5). Electronic applications accepted.

Lamar University, College of Graduate Studies, College of Arts and Sciences, Department of English and Modern Languages, Beaumont, TX 77710. Offers English (MA); teaching Spanish (MA). *Program availability:* Part-time, evening/weekend. *Faculty:* 10 full-time (5 women). *Students:* 7 full-time (all women), 23 part-time (20 women); includes 9 minority (1 Black or African American, non-Hispanic/Latino; 8 Hispanic/Latino), 1 international. Average age 40. 5 applicants, 100% accepted, 2 enrolled. In 2016, 12 master's awarded. *Degree requirements:* For master's, one foreign language, thesis optional, practicum. *Entrance requirements:* For master's, GRE General Test, minimum GPA of 2.5 in last 60 hours of undergraduate course work. Additional exam requirements/recommendations for international students: Required—TOEFL (minimum score 550 paper-based; 79 iBT), IELTS (minimum score 6.5). *Application deadline:* For fall admission, 8/10 for domestic students, 7/1 for international students; for spring admission, 1/5 for domestic students, 12/1 for international students. Applications are processed on a rolling basis. Application fee: $25 ($50 for international students). Electronic applications accepted. *Expenses:* $8,134 in-state full-time, $5,574 in-state part-time; $15,604 out-of-state full-time, $10,554 out-of-state part-time per year. *Financial support:* Teaching assistantships, career-related internships or fieldwork, Federal Work-Study, and institutionally sponsored loans available. Support available to part-time students. Financial award application deadline: 4/1; financial award applicants required to submit FAFSA. *Faculty research:* British, Renaissance, nineteenth-century, and American literature; creative writing; modern literature; African-American literature. *Unit head:* Dr. Jim Sanderson, Chair, 409-880-8558, Fax: 409-880-8591. *Application contact:* Deidre Mayer, Interim Director, Admissions and Academic Services, 409-880-8888, Fax: 409-880-7419, E-mail: gradmissions@lamar.edu.
Website: http://artssciences.lamar.edu/english-and-modern-languages

Le Moyne College, Department of Education, Syracuse, NY 13214. Offers adolescent education (MS Ed, MST); adolescent education/special education (MS Ed, MST); adolescent English (MST), including grades 7-12; adolescent English/special education (MST), including grades 7-12; adolescent foreign language (MST), including grades 7-12; adolescent history (MST), including grades 7-12; childhood education (MS Ed); childhood education/special education (MS Ed); elementary education (MS Ed); general education (MS Ed); inclusive childhood education (MST); literacy education (MS Ed), including birth to grade 6, grades 5-12; school building leader (MS Ed); school building leadership (CAS); school district business leader (MS Ed, CAS); school district leader (MS Ed); school district leadership (CAS); secondary education (MS Ed); special education (MS Ed); teaching English to speakers of other languages (MS Ed); urban studies (MS Ed). *Accreditation:* TEAC. *Program availability:* Part-time, evening/weekend. *Faculty:* 8 full-time (5 women), 20 part-time/adjunct (12 women). *Students:* 66 full-time (40 women), 155 part-time (117 women); includes 13 minority (4 Black or African American, non-Hispanic/Latino; 2 American Indian or Alaska Native, non-Hispanic/Latino; 2 Asian, non-Hispanic/Latino; 5 Hispanic/Latino), 3 international. Average age 30. 74 applicants, 99% accepted, 66 enrolled. In 2016, 81 master's, 53 CASs awarded. *Degree requirements:* For master's, thesis. *Entrance requirements:* For master's, bachelor's degree with minimum undergraduate GPA of 3.0, 2 letters of recommendation, transcripts. Additional exam requirements/recommendations for international students: Required—TOEFL (minimum score 550 paper-based; 79 iBT); Recommended—IELTS (minimum score 6.5). *Application deadline:* For fall admission, 4/1 priority date for domestic and international students; for spring admission, 10/1 priority date for domestic and international students; for summer admission, 3/1 priority date for domestic and international students. Applications are processed on a rolling basis. Application fee: $50. Electronic applications accepted. *Expenses:* $700 per credit hour. *Financial support:* In 2016–17, 21 students received support. Career-related internships or fieldwork, scholarships/grants, and health care benefits available. Support available to part-time students. Financial award applicants required to submit FAFSA. *Faculty research:* Minority teachers, special education, multiculturalism, literacy, technology, media literacy learning, autism, school district organization, service-learning, higher level problem solving, teacher leadership. *Unit head:* Dr. Stephen C. Fleury, Chair, Department of Education, 315-445-4376, Fax: 315-445-4744, E-mail: fleurysc@lemoyne.edu. *Application contact:* Kristen P. Richards, Senior Director of Enrollment Management, 315-445-5444, Fax: 315-445-6092, E-mail: trapaskp@lemoyne.edu.
Website: http://www.lemoyne.edu/education

London Metropolitan University, Graduate Programs, London, United Kingdom. Offers applied psychology (M Sc); architecture (MA); biomedical science (M Sc); blood science (M Sc); cancer pharmacology (M Sc); computer networking and cyber security (M Sc); computing and information systems (M Sc); conference interpreting (MA); counter-terrorism studies (M Sc); creative, digital and professional writing (MA); crime, violence and prevention (M Sc); criminology (M Sc); curating contemporary art (MA); data analytics (M Sc); digital media (MA); early childhood studies (MA); education (MA, Ed D); financial services law, regulation and compliance (LL M); food science (M Sc); forensic psychology (M Sc); health and social care management and policy (M Sc); human nutrition (M Sc); human resource management (MA); human rights and international conflict (MA); information technology (M Sc); intelligence and security studies (M Sc); international oil, gas and energy law (LL M); international relations (MA); interpreting (MA); learning and teaching in higher education (MA); legal practice (LL M); media and entertainment law (LL M); organizational and consumer psychology (M Sc); psychological therapy (M Sc); psychology of mental health (M Sc); public health (M Sc); public policy and management (MPA); security studies (M Sc); social work (M Sc); spatial planning and urban design (MA); sports therapy (M Sc); supporting older children and young people with dyslexia (MA); teaching languages (MA), including Arabic, English; translation (MA); woman and child abuse (MA).

Manhattanville College, School of Education, Program in Middle Childhood/Adolescence Education (Grades 5-12), Purchase, NY 10577-2132. Offers biology (MAT); biology and special education (MPS); chemistry (MAT); chemistry and special education (MPS); English (MAT); English and special education (MPS); literacy and special education (MPS); literacy specialist (MPS); math and special education (MPS); mathematics (MAT); physics (MAT); social studies (MAT); social studies and special education (MPS); special education generalist (MPS); teaching languages other than English (MAT), including French, Italian, Latin, Spanish. *Program availability:* Part-time, evening/weekend. *Students:* 28 applicants, 86% accepted, 21 enrolled. In 2016, 23 master's awarded. *Degree requirements:* For master's, comprehensive exam (for some programs), thesis (for some programs), student teaching, research seminars, portfolios, internships, writing assessment. *Entrance requirements:* For master's, GRE or MAT, minimum undergraduate GPA of 3.0, 2 letters of recommendation. Additional exam requirements/recommendations for international students: Required—TOEFL (minimum score 85 iBT); Recommended—IELTS. *Application deadline:* For fall admission, 7/1 priority date for domestic and international students; for spring admission, 11/1 priority date for domestic and international students; for summer admission, 4/1 priority date for domestic and international students. Applications are processed on a rolling basis. Application fee: $75. Electronic applications accepted. *Expenses: Tuition:* Full-time $16,470; part-time $915 per credit. *Required fees:* $60 per semester. Part-time tuition and fees vary according to course load and program. *Financial support:* Teaching assistantships, career-related internships or fieldwork, Federal Work-Study, institutionally sponsored loans, scholarships/grants, and unspecified assistantships available. Financial award applicants required to submit FAFSA. *Unit head:* Victoria Fantozzi, Chairperson, Department of Curriculum and Instruction, 914-323-7138, E-mail: victoria.fantozzi@mville.edu. *Application contact:* Jeanine Pardey-Levine, Director of Graduate Enrollment Management, 914-323-3208, Fax: 914-694-1732, E-mail: edschool@mville.edu.
Website: http://www.mville.edu/programs#/search/19

Marquette University, Graduate School, College of Arts and Sciences, Department of Foreign Languages and Literatures, Milwaukee, WI 53201-1881. Offers Spanish (MA). *Program availability:* Part-time, evening/weekend. *Faculty:* 25 full-time (17 women), 4 part-time/adjunct (2 women). *Students:* 7 full-time (5 women), 1 international. Average age 26. 7 applicants, 86% accepted, 2 enrolled. In 2016, 5 master's awarded. *Degree requirements:* For master's, one foreign language, comprehensive exam. *Entrance requirements:* For master's, official transcripts from all current and previous colleges/universities except Marquette, three letters of recommendation, tape recording of foreign speaking voice. Additional exam requirements/recommendations for international students: Required—TOEFL. *Application deadline:* For fall admission, 12/15 for domestic and international students. Application fee: $50. Electronic applications accepted. *Financial support:* Fellowships, teaching assistantships with full tuition reimbursements, institutionally sponsored loans, scholarships/grants, health care benefits, tuition waivers (full and partial), and unspecified assistantships available. Support available to part-time students. Financial award application deadline: 2/15. *Faculty research:* Latin American literature, Afro-Hispanic literature, descriptive Spanish linguistics, Inter-American studies, foreign language education. *Total annual research expenditures:* $22,516. *Unit head:* Dr. Anne Pasero, Chair, 414-288-7063. *Application contact:* Dr. Dinorah Cortes-Velez, Director of Graduate Studies, 414-288-7268, Fax: 414-288-1578.
Website: http://www.marquette.edu/fola/grad_director_intro.shtml

McGill University, Faculty of Graduate and Postdoctoral Studies, Faculty of Education, Department of Integrated Studies in Education, Montréal, QC H3A 2T5, Canada. Offers culture and values in education (MA, PhD); curriculum studies (MA); educational leadership (MA, Certificate); educational studies (PhD); integrated studies in education (M Ed); second language education (MA, PhD).

Michigan State University, The Graduate School, College of Arts and Letters, Program in Second Language Studies, East Lansing, MI 48824. Offers PhD. *Accreditation:* TEAC. *Entrance requirements:* Additional exam requirements/recommendations for international students: Required—TOEFL, Michigan State University ELT (minimum score 85), Michigan English Language Assessment Battery (minimum score 83). Electronic applications accepted.

Foreign Languages Education

Middlebury Institute of International Studies at Monterey, Graduate School of Translation, Interpretation and Language Education, Program in Teaching Foreign Language, Monterey, CA 93940-2691. Offers MATFL. *Degree requirements:* For master's, one foreign language, portfolio, oral defense. *Entrance requirements:* For master's, minimum GPA of 3.0, proficiency in foreign language. Additional exam requirements/recommendations for international students: Required—TOEFL (minimum score 600 paper-based; 100 iBT). Electronic applications accepted. *Expenses: Tuition:* Full-time $38,250; part-time $1820 per credit. *Required fees:* $78 per semester.

Middle Tennessee State University, College of Graduate Studies, College of Liberal Arts, Department of Foreign Languages and Literatures, Murfreesboro, TN 37132. Offers foreign languages (MAT), including French, German, Spanish. *Program availability:* Part-time, evening/weekend, online learning. *Degree requirements:* For master's, one foreign language, comprehensive exam, thesis optional. *Entrance requirements:* For master's, GRE. Additional exam requirements/recommendations for international students: Required—TOEFL (minimum score 525 paper-based; 71 iBT) or IELTS (minimum score 6). Electronic applications accepted.

Minnesota State University Mankato, College of Graduate Studies and Research, College of Arts and Humanities, Department of World Languages and Cultures, Program in French, Mankato, MN 56001. Offers French (MS); French education (MS). *Students:* 3 full-time (2 women), 1 (woman) part-time. *Degree requirements:* For master's, one foreign language, comprehensive exam, thesis or alternative. *Entrance requirements:* For master's, minimum GPA of 3.0 during previous 2 years. Additional exam requirements/recommendations for international students: Required—TOEFL. *Application deadline:* For fall admission, 7/1 priority date for domestic students; for spring admission, 11/1 for domestic students. Applications are processed on a rolling basis. Application fee: $40. Electronic applications accepted. *Financial support:* Research assistantships, teaching assistantships with full tuition reimbursements, and unspecified assistantships available. Financial award application deadline: 3/15; financial award applicants required to submit FAFSA.

Minnesota State University Mankato, College of Graduate Studies and Research, College of Arts and Humanities, Department of World Languages and Cultures, Program in Spanish, Mankato, MN 56001. Offers Spanish (MS); Spanish education (MS); Spanish for the professions (MS). *Students:* 6 part-time (5 women). *Degree requirements:* For master's, one foreign language, comprehensive exam, thesis. *Entrance requirements:* For master's, minimum GPA of 3.0 during previous 2 years. *Application deadline:* For fall admission, 7/1 priority date for domestic students; for spring admission, 11/1 for domestic students. Applications are processed on a rolling basis. Application fee: $40. Electronic applications accepted. *Financial support:* Research assistantships with full tuition reimbursements, teaching assistantships with full tuition reimbursements, career-related internships or fieldwork, Federal Work-Study, institutionally sponsored loans, and unspecified assistantships available. Support available to part-time students. Financial award application deadline: 3/15.

Mississippi State University, College of Arts and Sciences, Department of Classical and Modern Languages and Literatures, Mississippi State, MS 39762. Offers MA. *Program availability:* Part-time. *Faculty:* 12 full-time (3 women). *Students:* 9 full-time (7 women), 1 (woman) part-time; includes 5 minority (1 Black or African American, non-Hispanic/Latino; 3 Hispanic/Latino; 1 Two or more races, non-Hispanic/Latino), 3 international. Average age 30. 4 applicants, 75% accepted, 3 enrolled. In 2016, 6 master's awarded. *Degree requirements:* For master's, one foreign language, thesis optional, comprehensive oral or written exam. *Entrance requirements:* For master's, minimum GPA of 2.75 on last two years of undergraduate courses. Additional exam requirements/recommendations for international students: Required—TOEFL (minimum score 525 paper-based; 70 iBT); Recommended—IELTS (minimum score 6). *Application deadline:* For fall admission, 7/1 for domestic students, 5/1 for international students; for spring admission, 11/1 for domestic students, 9/1 for international students. Applications are processed on a rolling basis. Application fee: $60. Electronic applications accepted. *Expenses:* Tuition, state resident: full-time $7670; part-time $852.50 per credit hour. Tuition, nonresident: full-time $20,790; part-time $2310.50 per credit hour. Part-time tuition and fees vary according to course load. *Financial support:* In 2016–17, 8 teaching assistantships (averaging $8,766 per year) were awarded; Federal Work-Study, institutionally sponsored loans, and unspecified assistantships also available. Financial award application deadline: 4/1; financial award applicants required to submit FAFSA. *Faculty research:* French, German, Spanish literature from medieval era to present; gender and cultural studies in French; Spanish-American literature; foreign language methodology; linguistics. *Unit head:* Dr. Lynn Holt, Professor and Interim Department Head, 662-325-3480, Fax: 662-325-8209, E-mail: lholt@cmll.msstate.edu. *Application contact:* Lakan Drinker, Admissions and Enrollment Assistant, 662-325-8951, E-mail: ldrinker@grad.msstate.edu.
Website: http://www.cmll.msstate.edu/

Morehead State University, Graduate Programs, College of Education, Department of Middle Grades and Secondary Education, Morehead, KY 40351. Offers business and marketing education (MAT); English/language arts 5-9 (MAT); French (MAT); health P-12 (MAT); mathematics 5-9 (MAT); physical education P-12 (MAT); science 5-9 (MAT); secondary biology (MAT); secondary chemistry (MAT); secondary earth science (MAT); secondary English (MAT); secondary math (MAT); secondary physics (MAT); secondary social studies (MAT); social studies 5-9 (MAT); Spanish (MAT). *Program availability:* Part-time, evening/weekend. *Degree requirements:* For master's, portfolio. *Entrance requirements:* For master's, GRE or PRAXIS II content exam, minimum overall undergraduate GPA of 2.5. Additional exam requirements/recommendations for international students: Required—TOEFL (minimum score 500 paper-based). Electronic applications accepted.

New Mexico State University, College of Education, Department of Curriculum and Instruction, Las Cruces, NM 88003. Offers bilingual education (MA); curriculum and instruction (Ed D); early childhood education (MA); educational diagnostics (Ed S); language, literacy and culture (MA); learning design and technologies (MA); teaching (MAT), including Spanish; teaching English to speakers of other languages (MA). *Accreditation:* NCATE. *Program availability:* Part-time, evening/weekend, 100% online. *Faculty:* 23 full-time (17 women), 7 part-time/adjunct (5 women). *Students:* 114 full-time (81 women), 219 part-time (159 women); includes 190 minority (16 Black or African American, non-Hispanic/Latino; 2 American Indian or Alaska Native, non-Hispanic/Latino; 5 Asian, non-Hispanic/Latino; 160 Hispanic/Latino; 7 Two or more races, non-Hispanic/Latino), 33 international. Average age 37. 126 applicants, 75% accepted, 65 enrolled. In 2016, 92 master's, 19 doctorates awarded. *Degree requirements:* For master's, comprehensive exam, thesis optional; for doctorate, comprehensive exam, thesis/dissertation. *Entrance requirements:* For master's, minimum cumulative GPA of 3.0; for doctorate, portfolio, minimum cumulative GPA of 3.0. Additional exam requirements/recommendations for international students: Required—TOEFL (minimum score 550 paper-based; 79 iBT), IELTS (minimum score 6.5). *Application deadline:* For fall admission, 12/15 priority date for domestic and international students; for spring admission, 11/1 for domestic students. Applications are processed on a rolling basis. Application fee: $40 ($50 for international students). Electronic applications accepted. *Expenses:* Tuition, state resident: full-time $4086. Tuition, nonresident: full-time $14,254. *Required fees:* $853. Tuition and fees vary according to course load. *Financial support:* In 2016–17, 102 students received support, including 2 fellowships (averaging $4,076 per year), 2 research assistantships (averaging $18,070 per year), 16 teaching assistantships (averaging $16,454 per year); career-related internships or fieldwork, Federal Work-Study, scholarships/grants, traineeships, health care benefits, and unspecified assistantships also available. Support available to part-time students. Financial award application deadline: 3/1. *Faculty research:* STEM education, bilingual and English as a second language education, critical pedagogy/multicultural education, learning design and technology, early childhood education. *Total annual research expenditures:* $29,926. *Unit head:* Dr. David Rutledge, Department Head, 575-646-5411, Fax: 575-646-5436, E-mail: rutledge@nmsu.edu. *Application contact:* Dr. David Rutledge, Associate Department Head for Graduate Programs, 575-646-5411, Fax: 575-646-5436, E-mail: rutledge@nmsu.edu.
Website: http://ci.education.nmsu.edu

New York University, Steinhardt School of Culture, Education, and Human Development, Department of Teaching and Learning, Program in Multilingual/Multicultural Studies, New York, NY 10003. Offers bilingual education (MA, PhD, Advanced Certificate); foreign language education (MA); teaching English to speakers of other languages (MA, PhD); teaching foreign languages, 7-12 (MA), including Chinese, French, Italian, Japanese, Spanish; teaching French as a foreign language (MA), including teaching English to speakers of other languages; teaching Spanish as a foreign language (MA), including teaching English to speakers of other languages. *Accreditation:* TEAC. *Program availability:* Part-time, evening/weekend. *Degree requirements:* For master's, thesis (for some programs); for doctorate, thesis/dissertation. *Entrance requirements:* For doctorate, GRE General Test, interview; for Advanced Certificate, master's degree. Additional exam requirements/recommendations for international students: Required—TOEFL (minimum score 100 iBT). Electronic applications accepted. *Faculty research:* Second language acquisition, cross-cultural communication, technology-enhanced language learning, language variation, action learning.

Northern Arizona University, Graduate College, College of Arts and Letters, Department of Global Languages and Cultures, Flagstaff, AZ 86011. Offers Spanish (MAT); Spanish education (MAT). *Program availability:* Part-time. *Degree requirements:* For master's, comprehensive exam, thesis optional. *Entrance requirements:* For master's, bachelor's degree in Spanish (coupled with preparation in general or foreign language education courses) or Spanish secondary education, or degree/experience in related field (e.g., bilingual education); minimum GPA of 3.0 or equivalent. Additional exam requirements/recommendations for international students: Required—TOEFL (minimum score 550 paper-based; 80 iBT), IELTS (minimum score 7). Electronic applications accepted. *Expenses:* Tuition, state resident: full-time $8971; part-time $444 per credit hour. Tuition, nonresident: full-time $20,958; part-time $1164 per credit hour. *Required fees:* $1018; $644 per credit hour. Tuition and fees vary according to course load, campus/location and program.

Pace University, School of Education, New York, NY 10038. Offers adolescent education (MST), including biology, business education, chemistry, earth science, English, foreign languages, mathematics, physics, social studies, visual arts; childhood education (MST); early childhood development, learning and intervention (MST); educational technology studies (MS); inclusive adolescent education (MST), including biology, business education, chemistry, earth science, English, foreign languages, mathematics, physics, social studies, visual arts; integrated instruction for educational technology (Certificate); integrated instruction for literacy and technology (Certificate); literacy (MS Ed); special education (MS Ed). *Accreditation:* NCATE. *Program availability:* Part-time, evening/weekend, blended/hybrid learning. *Faculty:* 19 full-time (13 women), 86 part-time/adjunct (49 women). *Students:* 115 full-time (97 women), 543 part-time (381 women); includes 280 minority (137 Black or African American, non-Hispanic/Latino; 1 American Indian or Alaska Native, non-Hispanic/Latino; 40 Asian, non-Hispanic/Latino; 87 Hispanic/Latino; 15 Two or more races, non-Hispanic/Latino), 13 international. Average age 30. 181 applicants, 78% accepted, 72 enrolled. In 2016, 193 master's, 9 other advanced degrees awarded. *Degree requirements:* For master's, certification exams. *Entrance requirements:* For master's, GRE, interview, teaching certificate (except for MST). Additional exam requirements/recommendations for international students: Required—TOEFL (minimum score 88 iBT), IELTS or PTE. *Application deadline:* For fall admission, 8/1 priority date for domestic students, 6/1 for international students; for spring admission, 12/1 priority date for domestic students, 10/1 for international students. Applications are processed on a rolling basis. Application fee: $70. Electronic applications accepted. *Expenses:* Contact institution. *Financial support:* In 2016–17, 17 students received support, including 17 research assistantships with partial tuition reimbursements available (averaging $6,020 per year); career-related internships or fieldwork and Federal Work-Study also available. Financial award application deadline: 9/1; financial award applicants required to submit FAFSA. *Faculty research:* STEM education, TESOL, teacher education, special education, language and literary development. *Total annual research expenditures:* $290,153. *Unit head:* Dr. Xiao-Lei Wang, Dean, School of Education, 914-773-3876, E-mail: xwang@pace.edu. *Application contact:* Susan Ford-Goldschein, Director of Graduate Admissions, 212-346-1531, Fax: 212-346-1585, E-mail: graduateadmission@pace.edu.
Website: http://www.pace.edu/school-of-education

Plymouth State University, College of Graduate Studies, Graduate Studies in Education, Program in Secondary Education, Plymouth, NH 03264-1595. Offers curriculum and instruction (M Ed); language education (M Ed); library media (M Ed); physical education (M Ed); social studies education (M Ed); special education (M Ed). *Program availability:* Part-time, evening/weekend. *Entrance requirements:* For master's, MAT.

Portland State University, Graduate Studies, College of Liberal Arts and Sciences, Department of World Languages and Literatures, Portland, OR 97207-0751. Offers French (MA); German (MA); Japanese (MA); Spanish (MA); world literature and language (MA). *Program availability:* Part-time. *Faculty:* 45 full-time (25 women), 39 part-time/adjunct (27 women). *Students:* 22 full-time (13 women), 6 part-time (3 women); includes 8 minority (2 Asian, non-Hispanic/Latino; 6 Hispanic/Latino), 4 international. Average age 31. 19 applicants, 53% accepted, 8 enrolled. In 2016, 18 master's awarded. *Degree requirements:* For master's, one foreign language, thesis (for some programs). *Entrance requirements:* Additional exam requirements/recommendations for international students: Required—TOEFL (minimum score 550 paper-based; 80 iBT), IELTS (minimum score 6.5). *Application deadline:* For fall admission, 4/1 for domestic students, 3/1 for international students; for winter admission, 9/1 for domestic students, 7/1 for international students; for spring admission, 11/1 for domestic and international students. Applications are processed on a rolling basis. Application fee: $65. *Expenses:* Contact institution. *Financial support:* In 2016–17, 18 teaching assistantships with tuition reimbursements (averaging $10,805 per year) were awarded; research assistantships, Federal Work-Study, scholarships/grants, and unspecified assistantships also available. Support available to part-time students. Financial award application deadline: 3/1; financial award applicants required to submit FAFSA. *Faculty research:* Foreign language pedagogy, applied and social linguistics, literary history and criticism. *Total annual research expenditures:* $396,300. *Unit head:* Dr. Gina Greco, Chair, 503-725-5287, E-mail: grecog@pdx.edu. *Application contact:* Kelli Martin,

Graduate Admissions Coordinator, 503-725-3243, E-mail: kmarti@pdx.edu.
Website: http://www.pdx.edu/wll/

Purdue University, Graduate School, College of Education, Department of Curriculum and Instruction, West Lafayette, IN 47907. Offers agricultural and extension education (MS, MS Ed, PhD, Ed S); art education (PhD); career and technical education (MS Ed, PhD, Ed S); curriculum studies (MS Ed, PhD, Ed S); educational technology (MS Ed, PhD, Ed S); elementary education (MS Ed); family and consumer sciences education (MS Ed, PhD, Ed S); foreign language education (MS Ed, PhD, Ed S); industrial technology (PhD, Ed S); language arts (MS Ed, PhD, Ed S); literacy (MS Ed, PhD, Ed S); mathematics education (MS, MS Ed, PhD, Ed S); science education (MS, MS Ed, PhD, Ed S); social studies education (MS Ed, PhD, Ed S). *Accreditation:* NCATE. *Program availability:* Part-time, evening/weekend. *Faculty:* 37 full-time (27 women), 1 (woman) part-time/adjunct. *Students:* 78 full-time (50 women), 286 part-time (195 women); includes 68 minority (25 Black or African American, non-Hispanic/Latino; 3 American Indian or Alaska Native, non-Hispanic/Latino; 10 Asian, non-Hispanic/Latino; 22 Hispanic/Latino; 1 Native Hawaiian or other Pacific Islander, non-Hispanic/Latino; 7 Two or more races, non-Hispanic/Latino), 44 international. Average age 36. 150 applicants, 79% accepted, 73 enrolled. In 2016, 107 master's, 20 doctorates, 2 other advanced degrees awarded. *Degree requirements:* For master's, thesis optional; for doctorate, thesis/dissertation, oral and written exams; for Ed S, oral presentation, project. *Entrance requirements:* For master's, GRE General Test (if undergraduate GPA is below 3.0), minimum undergraduate GPA of 3.0 or equivalent; for doctorate, GRE General Test (minimum combined verbal and quantitative score of 1000, 300 for new scoring), minimum undergraduate GPA of 3.0 or equivalent; master's degree with minimum GPA of 3.0 or equivalent; for Ed S, GRE General Test (minimum combined verbal and quantitative score of 1000, 300 for new scoring), minimum undergraduate GPA of 3.0 or equivalent; master's degree. Additional exam requirements/recommendations for international students: Required—TOEFL (minimum score 550 paper-based; 77 iBT). *Application deadline:* For fall admission, 12/15 for domestic students, 3/1 for international students; for spring admission, 9/15 for domestic students, 8/1 for international students. Application fee: $60 ($75 for international students). Electronic applications accepted. *Financial support:* Fellowships with full tuition reimbursements, research assistantships with full tuition reimbursements, teaching assistantships with full tuition reimbursements, career-related internships or fieldwork, and tuition waivers (full) available. Support available to part-time students. Financial award application deadline: 3/1; financial award applicants required to submit FAFSA. *Faculty research:* Literacy acquisition and development, teacher beliefs and knowledge, recruitment and retention of underrepresented students, economic education, literacy discourse. *Unit head:* Janet M. Alsup, Head, 765-494-9667, E-mail: alsupj@purdue.edu. *Application contact:* Heather Brinkman, Graduate Contact, 765-494-2345, E-mail: hbrinkma@purdue.edu.
Website: http://www.edci.purdue.edu/

Purdue University, Graduate School, College of Liberal Arts, School of Languages and Cultures, West Lafayette, IN 47907. Offers French (MA, MAT, PhD), including French (MA, PhD), French education (MAT); German (MA, MAT, PhD), including German (MA, PhD), German education (MAT); Japanese pedagogy (MA); Spanish (MA, MAT, PhD), including Spanish (MA, PhD), Spanish education (MAT). *Faculty:* 44 full-time (22 women), 1 (woman) part-time/adjunct. *Students:* 37 full-time (18 women), 41 part-time (30 women); includes 9 minority (1 Asian, non-Hispanic/Latino; 8 Hispanic/Latino), 52 international. Average age 32. 49 applicants, 39% accepted, 14 enrolled. In 2016, 11 master's, 5 doctorates awarded. Terminal master's awarded for partial completion of doctoral program. *Degree requirements:* For master's, one foreign language; for doctorate, 2 foreign languages, thesis/dissertation. *Entrance requirements:* For master's, GRE General Test (minimum score 600, 160 for new scoring), two writing samples, one in English, one in language (French, German, Japanese, or Spanish); sample recording of English and language of study; for doctorate, GRE General Test (minimum score 600, 160 for new scoring), master's degree with minimum GPA of 3.5 or equivalent; two writing samples, one in English, one in language (French, German, Japanese, or Spanish); sample recording of English and language of study. Additional exam requirements/recommendations for international students: Required—TOEFL (minimum score 550 paper-based; 77 iBT); Recommended—TWE. *Application deadline:* For fall admission, 12/12 for domestic and international students; for spring admission, 10/1 for domestic and international students. Applications are processed on a rolling basis. Application fee: $60 ($75 for international students). Electronic applications accepted. *Financial support:* In 2016–17, fellowships with tuition reimbursements (averaging $15,750 per year), teaching assistantships with tuition reimbursements (averaging $13,463 per year) were awarded. Support available to part-time students. Financial award applicants required to submit FAFSA. *Faculty research:* Linguistics, semiotics, literary criticism, pedagogy. *Unit head:* Dr. Madeleine M. Henry, Head, 765-494-3828, E-mail: henry48@purdue.edu. *Application contact:* Joni L. Hipsher, Graduate Contact, 765-494-3841, E-mail: jlhipshe@purdue.edu.
Website: http://www.cla.purdue.edu/slc/main/

Queens College of the City University of New York, Division of Education, Department of Secondary Education and Youth Services, Queens, NY 11367-1597. Offers adolescent biology (MAT); art (MS Ed); biology (MS Ed, AC); chemistry (MS Ed, AC); earth sciences (MS Ed, AC); English (MS Ed, AC); French (MS Ed); Italian (MS Ed, AC); literacy education (MS Ed); mathematics (MS Ed, AC); music (MS Ed, AC); physics (MS Ed, AC); social studies (MS Ed, AC); Spanish (MS Ed, AC). *Program availability:* Part-time, evening/weekend. *Faculty:* 22 full-time (14 women), 40 part-time/adjunct (26 women). *Students:* 31 full-time (21 women), 356 part-time (211 women); includes 164 minority (22 Black or African American, non-Hispanic/Latino; 54 Asian, non-Hispanic/Latino; 81 Hispanic/Latino; 7 Two or more races, non-Hispanic/Latino), 11 international. Average age 29. 236 applicants, 88% accepted, 121 enrolled. In 2016, 119 master's, 51 other advanced degrees awarded. *Degree requirements:* For master's, research project. *Entrance requirements:* For master's, minimum GPA of 3.0. Additional exam requirements/recommendations for international students: Required—TOEFL, IELTS. *Application deadline:* For fall admission, 4/1 for domestic students; for spring admission, 11/1 for domestic students. Applications are processed on a rolling basis. Application fee: $125. Electronic applications accepted. *Expenses:* Tuition, state resident: full-time $5065; part-time $425 per credit. Tuition, nonresident: part-time $780 per credit. *Required fees:* $522; $397 per credit. Part-time tuition and fees vary according to course load and program. *Financial support:* Career-related internships or fieldwork available. Financial award application deadline: 4/1; financial award applicants required to submit FAFSA. *Unit head:* Dr. Eleanor Armour-Thomas, Chairperson, 718-997-5150, E-mail: armourthomas@yahoo.com.

Quinnipiac University, School of Education, Program in Secondary Education, Hamden, CT 06518-1940. Offers biology (MAT); English (MAT); history/social studies (MAT); mathematics (MAT); Spanish (MAT). *Accreditation:* NCATE. *Faculty:* 6 full-time (2 women), 24 part-time/adjunct (16 women). *Students:* 43 full-time (29 women), 1 part-time (0 women); includes 6 minority (1 Asian, non-Hispanic/Latino; 4 Hispanic/Latino; 1 Two or more races, non-Hispanic/Latino). 43 applicants, 98% accepted, 36 enrolled. In 2016, 32 master's awarded. *Entrance requirements:* For master's, PRAXIS I or PRAXIS Core Academic Skills Exam, minimum GPA of 3.0, interview. *Application deadline:* For fall admission, 5/1 priority date for domestic students. Applications are processed on a rolling basis. Application fee: $45. Electronic applications accepted. *Expenses: Tuition:* Part-time $985 per credit. *Required fees:* $40 per credit. $150 per semester. Tuition and fees vary according to program. *Financial support:* Career-related internships or fieldwork, Federal Work-Study, and unspecified assistantships available. Financial award application deadline: 6/1; financial award applicants required to submit FAFSA. *Faculty research:* Multicultural and urban education/leadership, challenges of teaching diverse learners, scholarship of teaching and learning, technology and teaching, humor and education. *Unit head:* Mordechai Gordon, Program Director, 203-582-8442, E-mail: mordechai.gordon@qu.edu. *Application contact:* Office of Graduate Admissions, 203-582-8672, Fax: 203-582-3443, E-mail: graduate@qu.edu.
Website: http://www.qu.edu/gradeducation

Rhode Island College, School of Graduate Studies, Feinstein School of Education and Human Development, Department of Educational Studies, Providence, RI 02908-1991. Offers advanced studies in teaching and learning (M Ed); English (MAT); French (MAT); history (MAT); math (MAT); secondary education (MAT); Spanish (MAT); teaching English as a second language (M Ed). *Accreditation:* NCATE. *Program availability:* Part-time, evening/weekend. *Faculty:* 6 full-time (5 women), 8 part-time/adjunct (6 women). *Students:* 5 full-time (2 women), 53 part-time (48 women); includes 8 minority (2 Black or African American, non-Hispanic/Latino; 2 Asian, non-Hispanic/Latino; 3 Hispanic/Latino; 1 Two or more races, non-Hispanic/Latino). Average age 39. In 2016, 29 master's awarded. *Degree requirements:* For master's, capstone or comprehensive assessment. *Entrance requirements:* For master's, GRE or MAT (for most programs), minimum undergraduate GPA of 3.0; baccalaureate degree in English, French, history, math or Spanish; 3 letters of recommendation; interview. Additional exam requirements/recommendations for international students: Recommended—TOEFL (minimum score 550 paper-based; 79 iBT). *Application deadline:* For fall admission, 3/1 for domestic students; for spring admission, 11/1 for domestic students. Applications are processed on a rolling basis. Application fee: $50. Electronic applications accepted. *Expenses:* Tuition, state resident: full-time $8928; part-time $372 per credit. Tuition, nonresident: full-time $17,376; part-time $724 per credit. *Required fees:* $604; $22 per credit. One-time fee: $74. *Financial support:* In 2016–17, 1 teaching assistantship with full tuition reimbursement (averaging $3,000 per year) was awarded; career-related internships or fieldwork, Federal Work-Study, scholarships/grants, health care benefits, and unspecified assistantships also available. Support available to part-time students. Financial award application deadline: 5/15; financial award applicants required to submit FAFSA. *Unit head:* Dr. Gerri August, Chair, 401-456-8170. *Application contact:* Graduate Studies, 401-456-8700.
Website: http://www.ric.edu/educationalStudies/

Rider University, Department of Graduate Education, Leadership and Counseling, Teacher Certification Program, Lawrenceville, NJ 08648-3001. Offers business education (Certificate); elementary education (Certificate); English as a second language (Certificate); English education (Certificate); mathematics education (Certificate); preschool to grade 3 (Certificate); science education (Certificate); social studies education (Certificate); world languages (Certificate), including French, German, Spanish. *Program availability:* Part-time. *Degree requirements:* For Certificate, internship, professional portfolio. *Entrance requirements:* For degree, PRAXIS, resume. Additional exam requirements/recommendations for international students: Required—TOEFL (minimum score 550 paper-based). Electronic applications accepted. *Faculty research:* Conceptual foundations for optimal development of creativity; creative theory, cognitive processes in mathematics learning, teacher collaboration.

Rivier University, School of Graduate Studies, Department of Modern Languages, Nashua, NH 03060. Offers Spanish (MAT). *Program availability:* Part-time, evening/weekend.

Rutgers University–New Brunswick, Graduate School-New Brunswick, Program in French, Piscataway, NJ 08854-8097. Offers French (MA, PhD); French studies (MAT). *Program availability:* Part-time, evening/weekend. Terminal master's awarded for partial completion of doctoral program. *Degree requirements:* For master's, one foreign language, written and oral exams (MA); for doctorate, 3 foreign languages, thesis/dissertation, qualifying exam. *Entrance requirements:* For master's and doctorate, GRE General Test. *Faculty research:* Literatures in French, literary history and theory, rhetoric and poetics.

Rutgers University–New Brunswick, Graduate School-New Brunswick, Program in Italian, Piscataway, NJ 08854-8097. Offers Italian (MA, PhD); Italian literature and literary criticism (MA); language, literature and culture (MAT). *Program availability:* Part-time, evening/weekend. Terminal master's awarded for partial completion of doctoral program. *Degree requirements:* For master's, one foreign language, comprehensive exam (for some programs), thesis optional; for doctorate, 2 foreign languages, thesis/dissertation, qualifying exam. *Entrance requirements:* For master's and doctorate, GRE General Test. Additional exam requirements/recommendations for international students: Required—TOEFL. *Faculty research:* Literature.

Rutgers University–New Brunswick, Graduate School-New Brunswick, Program in Spanish, Piscataway, NJ 08854-8097. Offers bilingualism and second language acquisition (MA, PhD); Spanish (MA, MAT, PhD); Spanish literature (MA, PhD); translation (MA). *Program availability:* Part-time. *Degree requirements:* For master's, comprehensive exam (for some programs), thesis (for some programs); for doctorate, 2 foreign languages, comprehensive exam, thesis/dissertation. *Entrance requirements:* For master's and doctorate, GRE General Test. Additional exam requirements/recommendations for international students: Required—TOEFL. Electronic applications accepted. *Faculty research:* Hispanic literature, Luso-Brazilian literature, Spanish linguistics, Spanish translation.

Rutgers University–New Brunswick, Graduate School of Education, Department of Learning and Teaching, Program in Language Education, Piscataway, NJ 08854-8097. Offers English as a second language education (Ed M); language education (Ed M, Ed D). *Program availability:* Part-time. Terminal master's awarded for partial completion of doctoral program. *Degree requirements:* For master's, comprehensive exam; for doctorate, thesis/dissertation, concept paper, qualifying exam. *Entrance requirements:* For master's, GRE General Test, minimum GPA of 3.0; for doctorate, GRE General Test, minimum GPA of 3.5. Additional exam requirements/recommendations for international students: Required—TOEFL. Electronic applications accepted. *Faculty research:* Linguistics, sociolinguistics, cross-cultural/international communication.

Saginaw Valley State University, College of Education, Program in Teaching Chinese as a Foreign Language, University Center, MI 48710. Offers MAT. *Program availability:* Part-time, evening/weekend. *Students:* 5 full-time (3 women), 4 international. Average age 30. 4 applicants, 25% accepted, 1 enrolled. In 2016, 4 master's awarded. *Entrance requirements:* For master's, minimum GPA of 3.0. Additional exam requirements/recommendations for international students: Required—TOEFL (minimum score 550 paper-based; 79 iBT). *Application deadline:* For fall admission, 7/15 for international students; for winter admission, 11/15 for international students; for spring admission, 4/15 for international students. Applications are processed on a rolling basis. Application fee: $30 ($90 for international students). Electronic applications accepted. *Expenses:* Tuition, state resident: full-time $9652; part-time $536 per credit hour. Tuition, nonresident: full-time $12,259; part-time $1022 per credit hour. *Required fees:* $263;

$14.60 per credit hour. Tuition and fees vary according to degree level. *Financial support:* Federal Work-Study and scholarships/grants available. Support available to part-time students. Financial award application deadline: 4/1; financial award applicants required to submit FAFSA. *Unit head:* Dr. Craig Douglas, Dean, 989-964-4057, Fax: 989-964-4563, E-mail: coeconnect@svsu.edu. *Application contact:* Jenna Briggs, Director, Graduate and International Admissions, 989-964-6096, Fax: 989-964-2788, E-mail: gradadm@svsu.edu.

St. John Fisher College, Ralph C. Wilson Jr. School of Education, Program in Adolescence Education and Special Education, Rochester, NY 14618-3597. Offers adolescence education: biology with special education (MS Ed); adolescence education: chemistry with special education (MS Ed); adolescence education: English with special education (MS Ed); adolescence education: French with special education (MS Ed); adolescence education: math with special education (MS Ed); adolescence education: physics with special education (MS Ed); adolescence education: social studies with special education (MS Ed); adolescence education: Spanish with special education (MS Ed). *Program availability:* Part-time, evening/weekend. *Faculty:* 7 full-time (6 women), 5 part-time/adjunct (all women). *Students:* 15 full-time (6 women), 9 part-time (6 women); includes 3 minority (2 Black or African American, non-Hispanic/Latino; 1 Hispanic/Latino). Average age 28. 16 applicants, 56% accepted, 6 enrolled. In 2016, 8 master's awarded. *Degree requirements:* For master's, field experiences, student teaching, LAST. *Entrance requirements:* For master's, 2 letters of recommendation, personal statement, current resume. Additional exam requirements/recommendations for international students: Required—TOEFL (minimum score 575 paper-based; 80 iBT). *Application deadline:* Applications are processed on a rolling basis. Application fee: $30. Electronic applications accepted. *Expenses:* $885 per credit hour. *Financial support:* Scholarships/grants available. Financial award applicants required to submit FAFSA. *Faculty research:* Arts and humanities, urban schools, constructivist learning, at-risk students, mentoring. *Unit head:* Dr. Susan Hildenbrand, Program Director, 585-385-7297, E-mail: shildenbrand@sjfc.edu. *Application contact:* Michelle Gosier, Associate Director of Transfer and Graduate Admissions, 585-385-8064, E-mail: mgosier@sjfc.edu.

Saint Xavier University, Graduate Studies, School of Education, Chicago, IL 60655-3105. Offers counseling (MA); curriculum and instruction (MA); early childhood education (MA); educational administration (MA); elementary education (MA); individualized studies (MA), including educational technology, English as a second language (ESL), ISTEM (integrative science, technology, engineering, and math), science education; music education (MA); reading (MA); secondary education (MA); Spanish education (MA); special education (MA); teaching and leadership (MA). *Accreditation:* NCATE. *Program availability:* Part-time, evening/weekend. *Degree requirements:* For master's, thesis or project. *Entrance requirements:* For master's, minimum GPA of 3.0. *Expenses:* Contact institution.

Shippensburg University of Pennsylvania, School of Graduate Studies, College of Education and Human Services, Department of Teacher Education, Shippensburg, PA 17257-2299. Offers curriculum and instruction (M Ed), including biology, early childhood education, elementary and middle level education, elementary education, geography/earth science, history, mathematics, middle school education, modern languages; literacy studies (Certificate); online instruction, learning, and technology (Certificate); reading (M Ed); teaching English as a second language (Certificate). *Accreditation:* NCATE. *Program availability:* Part-time, evening/weekend, 100% online, blended/hybrid learning. *Faculty:* 14 full-time (9 women), 5 part-time/adjunct (all women). *Students:* 11 full-time (10 women), 88 part-time (81 women); includes 8 minority (3 Black or African American, non-Hispanic/Latino; 2 Asian, non-Hispanic/Latino; 3 Hispanic/Latino), 4 international. Average age 32. 57 applicants, 60% accepted, 28 enrolled. In 2016, 18 master's awarded. *Degree requirements:* For master's, comprehensive exam (for some programs), thesis optional, practicum or internship; capstone seminar (for some programs). *Entrance requirements:* For master's, MAT or GRE (if GPA less than 2.75), interview, 3 letters of reference, questionnaire of teaching background and future goals, resume. Additional exam requirements/recommendations for international students: Required—TOEFL (minimum score 550 paper-based, 68 iBT) or IELTS (minimum score 6). *Application deadline:* For fall admission, 4/1 priority date for domestic students, 4/30 for international students; for spring admission, 9/1 priority date for domestic students, 9/30 for international students; for summer admission, 2/1 priority date for domestic students. Applications are processed on a rolling basis. Application fee: $45. Electronic applications accepted. *Expenses:* Tuition, state resident: part-time $483 per credit. Tuition, nonresident: part-time $725 per credit. *Required fees:* $141 per credit. *Financial support:* In 2016–17, 3 students received support. Career-related internships or fieldwork, scholarships/grants, unspecified assistantships, and resident hall director and student payroll positions available. Support available to part-time students. Financial award application deadline: 3/1; financial award applicants required to submit FAFSA. *Unit head:* Dr. Christine A. Royce, Chairperson, 717-477-1688, Fax: 717-477-4046, E-mail: caroyc@ship.edu. *Application contact:* Megan N. Luft, Assistant Dean of Graduate Admissions, 717-477-1231, Fax: 717-477-4016, E-mail: mnluft@ship.edu.
Website: http://www.ship.edu/teacher/

Smith College, Graduate and Special Programs, Department of Education and Child Study, Program in Secondary Education, Northampton, MA 01063. Offers secondary education (MAT), including biological sciences education, chemistry education, English education, French education, geology education, government education, history education, mathematics education, physics education, Spanish education. *Program availability:* Part-time. *Students:* 3 full-time (2 women), 3 part-time (2 women). Average age 31. 14 applicants, 79% accepted, 4 enrolled. In 2016, 11 master's awarded. *Entrance requirements:* Additional exam requirements/recommendations for international students: Required—TOEFL (minimum score 595 paper-based; 97 iBT), IELTS. *Application deadline:* For fall admission, 4/1 for domestic students, 1/15 priority date for international students; for spring admission, 12/1 for domestic students. Application fee: $60. *Expenses: Tuition:* Full-time $34,560; part-time $1440 per credit. Tuition and fees vary according to course load and program. *Financial support:* In 2016–17, 5 students received support, including 1 fellowship with full tuition reimbursement available; scholarships/grants also available. Support available to part-time students. Financial award application deadline: 4/1; financial award applicants required to submit CSS PROFILE or FAFSA. *Unit head:* Rosetta Cohen, Graduate Student Advisor, 413-585-3266, E-mail: rcohen@smith.edu. *Application contact:* Ruth Morgan, Program Assistant, 413-585-3050, Fax: 413-585-3054, E-mail: gradstdy@smith.edu.
Website: http://www.smith.edu/educ/

Smith College, Graduate and Special Programs, Department of French Language and Literature, Northampton, MA 01063. Offers secondary education (MAT), including French education. *Program availability:* Part-time. In 2016, 1 master's awarded. *Degree requirements:* For master's, one foreign language. *Entrance requirements:* Additional exam requirements/recommendations for international students: Required—TOEFL (minimum score 595 paper-based; 97 iBT), IELTS. *Application deadline:* For fall admission, 4/1 for domestic students, 1/15 for international students; for spring admission, 12/1 for domestic students. Application fee: $60. *Expenses: Tuition:* Full-time $34,560; part-time $1440 per credit. Tuition and fees vary according to course load and program. *Financial support:* In 2016–17, 1 student received support. Scholarships/grants available. Support available to part-time students. Financial award application deadline: 4/1; financial award applicants required to submit CSS PROFILE or FAFSA. *Unit head:* Helene Visentin, Chair, 413-585-3359, E-mail: hvisenti@smith.edu. *Application contact:* Ruth Morgan, Program Assistant, 413-585-3050, Fax: 413-585-3054, E-mail: gradstdy@smith.edu.
Website: http://www.smith.edu/french

Smith College, Graduate and Special Programs, Department of Spanish and Portuguese, Northampton, MA 01063. Offers secondary education (MAT), including Spanish education. *Program availability:* Part-time. *Degree requirements:* For master's, one foreign language. *Entrance requirements:* Additional exam requirements/recommendations for international students: Required—TOEFL (minimum score 595 paper-based; 97 iBT), IELTS. *Application deadline:* For fall admission, 4/1 for domestic students, 1/15 for international students; for spring admission, 12/1 for domestic students. Application fee: $60. *Expenses: Tuition:* Full-time $34,560; part-time $1440 per credit. Tuition and fees vary according to course load and program. *Financial support:* Scholarships/grants available. Support available to part-time students. Financial award application deadline: 4/1; financial award applicants required to submit CSS PROFILE or FAFSA. *Unit head:* Maria Helena Rueda, Chair, 413-585-3451, E-mail: mrueda@smith.edu. *Application contact:* Ruth Morgan, Program Assistant, 413-585-3050, Fax: 413-585-3054, E-mail: gradstdy@smith.edu.
Website: http://www.smith.edu/spp/

Southern Connecticut State University, School of Graduate Studies, School of Arts and Sciences, Department of World Languages and Literatures, New Haven, CT 06515-1355. Offers multicultural-bilingual education/teaching English to speakers of other languages (MS); romance languages (MA). *Program availability:* Part-time, evening/weekend. *Faculty:* 8 full-time (6 women). *Students:* 10 full-time (8 women), 41 part-time (36 women); includes 16 minority (2 Black or African American, non-Hispanic/Latino; 1 Asian, non-Hispanic/Latino; 13 Hispanic/Latino), 2 international. Average age 36. 41 applicants, 51% accepted, 15 enrolled. In 2016, 18 master's awarded. *Degree requirements:* For master's, one foreign language, thesis or alternative. *Entrance requirements:* For master's, interview, minimum undergraduate GPA of 2.7. *Application deadline:* For fall admission, 7/15 priority date for domestic students. Applications are processed on a rolling basis. Application fee: $50. Electronic applications accepted. *Expenses:* Tuition, state resident: full-time $6497; part-time $519 per credit hour. Tuition, nonresident: full-time $18,102; part-time $535 per credit hour. *Required fees:* $4722; $55 per semester. Tuition and fees vary according to program. *Financial support:* Career-related internships or fieldwork, scholarships/grants, and unspecified assistantships available. Financial award application deadline: 4/15; financial award applicants required to submit FAFSA. *Unit head:* Dr. Resha Cardone, Chairperson, 203-392-7170, Fax: 203-392-6136, E-mail: cardoner1@southernct.edu. *Application contact:* Lisa Galvin, Director of Graduate Admissions, 203-392-5240, Fax: 203-392-5235, E-mail: galvinl1@southernct.edu.
Website: http://www.southernct.edu/academics/schools/arts/departments/world-languages/

Southern Oregon University, Graduate Studies, Department of Foreign Languages and Literatures, Ashland, OR 97520. Offers French language teaching (MA); Spanish language teaching (MA). *Program availability:* Part-time, online learning. *Faculty:* 4 full-time (2 women), 6 part-time/adjunct (3 women). *Students:* 74 full-time (54 women), 18 part-time (14 women); includes 17 minority (2 Black or African American, non-Hispanic/Latino; 1 American Indian or Alaska Native, non-Hispanic/Latino; 1 Asian, non-Hispanic/Latino; 11 Hispanic/Latino; 2 Two or more races, non-Hispanic/Latino), 1 international. Average age 37. 49 applicants, 84% accepted, 37 enrolled. In 2016, 18 master's awarded. *Degree requirements:* For master's, thesis (for some programs). *Entrance requirements:* For master's, GRE General Test, minimum cumulative GPA of 3.0 in the last 90 quarter credits (60 semester credits) of undergraduate coursework. Additional exam requirements/recommendations for international students: Required—TOEFL (minimum score 540 paper-based; 76 iBT), IELTS (minimum score 6), ELPT (minimum score 964) or ELS (minimum score 112). *Application deadline:* For fall admission, 7/31 priority date for domestic and international students; for winter admission, 11/15 priority date for domestic and international students; for spring admission, 1/7 priority date for domestic and international students. Applications are processed on a rolling basis. Application fee: $60. Electronic applications accepted. *Expenses:* Tuition, state resident: full-time $10,719; part-time $397 per credit. Tuition, nonresident: full-time $13,419; part-time $497 per credit. *Required fees:* $548. *Financial support:* Career-related internships or fieldwork, institutionally sponsored loans, scholarships/grants, and unspecified assistantships available. *Unit head:* Dr. Dan Morris, Graduate French Language Program Coordinator, 541-552-6740, E-mail: morris@sou.edu. *Application contact:* Dr. Anne Connor, Graduate Spanish Language Program Coordinator, 541-552-6743, E-mail: connora@sou.edu.
Website: http://www.sou.edu/language/

Spalding University, Graduate Studies, College of Education, Programs in Education, Louisville, KY 40203-2188. Offers art teacher education (MAT); business teacher education (MAT); elementary school education (MAT); foreign language (MAT); high school education (MAT); middle school education (MAT); secondary education (MAT); special education (learning and behavioral disorders) (MAT); student guidance counselor (MA); teacher leader (M Ed). *Accreditation:* NCATE. *Program availability:* Part-time, evening/weekend. *Faculty:* 39 full-time (26 women), 13 part-time/adjunct (4 women). *Students:* 97 full-time (76 women), 31 part-time (23 women); includes 39 minority (33 Black or African American, non-Hispanic/Latino; 1 Asian, non-Hispanic/Latino; 3 Hispanic/Latino; 2 Two or more races, non-Hispanic/Latino). Average age 35. 62 applicants, 55% accepted, 33 enrolled. In 2016, 49 master's awarded. *Entrance requirements:* For master's, GRE General Test or MAT, interview, letters of recommendation, resume. Additional exam requirements/recommendations for international students: Required—TOEFL (minimum score 535 paper-based). *Application deadline:* Applications are processed on a rolling basis. Application fee: $30. Electronic applications accepted. *Expenses: Tuition:* Full-time $15,300. *Financial support:* Scholarships/grants, traineeships, and unspecified assistantships available. Financial award applicants required to submit FAFSA. *Faculty research:* Instructional technology, achievement gap, classroom management, assessment. *Unit head:* Dr. Chris Walsh, Associate Dean, 502-873-4272, Fax: 502-585-7123, E-mail: cwalsh@spalding.edu. *Application contact:* Valerie Anderson, Administrative Assistant, 502-873-4260, E-mail: vanderson@spalding.edu.

State University of New York at Plattsburgh, School of Education, Health, and Human Services, Program in Teacher Education: Adolescence Education, Plattsburgh, NY 12901-2681. Offers adolescence education (MST); biology 7-12 (MST); chemistry 7-12 (MST); earth science 7-12 (MST); English 7-12 (MST); French 7-12 (MST); mathematics 7-12 (MST); physics 7-12 (MST); social studies 7-12 (MST); Spanish 7-12 (MST). *Accreditation:* TEAC. *Program availability:* Part-time, evening/weekend. *Entrance requirements:* For master's, minimum GPA of 2.75. Additional exam requirements/recommendations for international students: Required—TOEFL.

State University of New York College at Geneseo, Graduate Studies, School of Education, Program in Adolescence Education, Geneseo, NY 14454-1401. Offers

English 7-12 (MS Ed); math 7-12 (MS Ed); Spanish 7-12 (MS Ed). *Program availability:* Part-time. *Faculty:* 8 full-time (4 women). *Students:* 5 part-time (4 women). Average age 30. 8 applicants, 13% accepted. In 2016, 4 master's awarded. *Degree requirements:* For master's, 2 foreign languages. *Entrance requirements:* For master's, initial certification to teach in New York state. Additional exam requirements/recommendations for international students: Required—TOEFL, IELTS, PTE. *Application deadline:* For fall admission, 4/1 priority date for domestic students; for spring admission, 11/1 priority date for domestic students. Applications are processed on a rolling basis. Application fee: $50. Electronic applications accepted. *Expenses:* Tuition, state resident: full-time $10,870; part-time $453 per credit. Tuition, nonresident: full-time $22,210; part-time $925 per credit. *Required fees:* $865; $35.85 per credit hour. *Financial support:* In 2016–17, 1 student received support, including 1 fellowship with partial tuition reimbursement available (averaging $10,000 per year); scholarships/grants, health care benefits, tuition waivers (partial), and unspecified assistantships also available. Support available to part-time students. Financial award application deadline: 4/1; financial award applicants required to submit FAFSA. *Unit head:* Dr. Anjoo Sikka, Dean of School of Education, 585-245-5151, Fax: 585-245-5220, E-mail: sikka@geneseo.edu. *Application contact:* Michael R. George, Graduate Enrollment Coordinator, 585-245-5148, Fax: 585-245-5550, E-mail: georgem@geneseo.edu.

State University of New York College at Old Westbury, School of Education, Old Westbury, NY 11568-0210. Offers biology (MAT, MS); chemistry (MAT, MS); English language arts (MAT, MS); math (MAT, MS); social studies (MAT, MS); Spanish (MAT, MS). *Program availability:* Part-time, evening/weekend. *Faculty:* 17 full-time (9 women), 5 part-time/adjunct (2 women). *Students:* 46 full-time (19 women), 26 part-time (17 women); includes 20 minority (1 Black or African American, non-Hispanic/Latino; 4 Asian, non-Hispanic/Latino; 15 Hispanic/Latino). Average age 30. 35 applicants, 77% accepted, 23 enrolled. In 2016, 25 master's awarded. *Entrance requirements:* For master's, Liberal Arts and Sciences Test, undergraduate degree with at least 30 semester hours of appropriate coursework as defined by the respective discipline; minimum cumulative undergraduate GPA of 3.0; two letters of recommendation (one from an academic source); essay. Additional exam requirements/recommendations for international students: Required—TOEFL (minimum score 550 paper-based); Recommended—IELTS. Application fee: $50. *Expenses:* Tuition, state resident: full-time $10,870; part-time $453 per credit. Tuition, nonresident: full-time $22,210; part-time $925 per credit. *Required fees:* $24.35 per credit. $76 per semester. Tuition and fees vary according to course load. *Financial support:* Applicants required to submit FAFSA. *Unit head:* Dr. Nancy Brown, Dean, School of Education, 516-876-3275, E-mail: brownn@oldwestbury.edu. *Application contact:* Philip D'Angelo, Graduate Admissions Office, 516-876-3073, E-mail: enroll@oldwestbury.edu.

Stony Brook University, State University of New York, School of Professional Development, Stony Brook, NY 11794-443. Offers biology (MAT); chemistry (MAT); coaching (Graduate Certificate); earth science (MAT); educational computing (Graduate Certificate); educational leadership (Advanced Certificate); English (MAT); environmental management (MPS, Graduate Certificate); French (MAT); German (MAT); higher education administration (MA, Certificate); human resource management (MS, Graduate Certificate); industrial management (Graduate Certificate); information systems management (Graduate Certificate); Italian (MAT); liberal studies (MA); mathematics (MAT); operations research (Graduate Certificate); physics (MAT); school district business leadership (Advanced Certificate); social studies (MAT); Spanish (MAT). *Program availability:* Part-time, evening/weekend, online learning. *Faculty:* 4 full-time (3 women), 77 part-time/adjunct (34 women). *Students:* 197 full-time (125 women), 965 part-time (674 women); includes 222 minority (79 Black or African American, non-Hispanic/Latino; 2 American Indian or Alaska Native, non-Hispanic/Latino; 35 Asian, non-Hispanic/Latino; 87 Hispanic/Latino; 1 Native Hawaiian or other Pacific Islander, non-Hispanic/Latino; 18 Two or more races, non-Hispanic/Latino), 5 international. Average age 33. 462 applicants, 87% accepted, 317 enrolled. In 2016, 348 master's, 159 other advanced degrees awarded. *Degree requirements:* For master's, one foreign language, thesis or alternative. *Entrance requirements:* Additional exam requirements/recommendations for international students: Required—TOEFL (minimum score 85 iBT). *Application deadline:* For fall admission, 1/15 for domestic students, 6/1 for international students; for spring admission, 10/1 for domestic and international students. Applications are processed on a rolling basis. Application fee: $100. *Expenses:* Contact institution. *Financial support:* Fellowships, research assistantships, teaching assistantships, and career-related internships or fieldwork available. Support available to part-time students. *Unit head:* Dr. Ken Lindblom, Dean, 631-632-7049, Fax: 631-632-9046, E-mail: kenneth.lindblom@stonybrook.edu. *Application contact:* Melissa Jordan, Assistant Dean, 631-632-7751, E-mail: melissa.jordan@stonybrook.edu.
Website: http://www.stonybrook.edu/spd/

Texas A&M International University, Office of Graduate Studies and Research, College of Arts and Sciences, Department of Humanities, Laredo, TX 78041-1900. Offers English (MA); Hispanic studies (PhD); history and political thought (MA); language, literature and translation (MA). *Degree requirements:* For master's, comprehensive exam (for some programs), thesis (for some programs). *Entrance requirements:* For master's, GRE General Test. Additional exam requirements/recommendations for international students: Required—TOEFL (minimum score 550 paper-based; 79 iBT).

Texas A&M University–Kingsville, College of Graduate Studies, College of Arts and Sciences, Department of Language and Literature, Kingsville, TX 78363. Offers cultural studies (MA); English (MA, MS); Spanish (MA). *Entrance requirements:* Additional exam requirements/recommendations for international students: Required—TOEFL (minimum score 550 paper-based; 79 iBT); Recommended—IELTS. Electronic applications accepted.

Universidad del Este, Graduate School, Carolina, PR 00984. Offers accounting (MBA); adult education (M Ed); agribusiness (MBA); criminal justice and criminology (MA); curriculum and instruction - early education (M Ed); curriculum and instruction - elementary (M Ed); curriculum and instruction - English (M Ed); curriculum and instruction - Spanish (M Ed); human resources (MBA); information security management (MBA); information technology and Web business development (MBA); management (MBA); public policy (MPA); social work (MA), including clinical social work; special education (M Ed); strategic leadership (MBA).

Université du Québec en Outaouais, Graduate Programs, Department of Language Studies, Gatineau, QC J8X 3X7, Canada. Offers second and foreign language teaching (Diploma).

University at Buffalo, the State University of New York, Graduate School, Graduate School of Education, Department of Learning and Instruction, Buffalo, NY 14260. Offers biology education (Ed M, Certificate); chemistry education (Ed M, Certificate); childhood education (Ed M); childhood education with bilingual extension (Ed M); college teaching (Advanced Certificate); curriculum, instruction and the science of learning (PhD); early childhood education (Ed M); early childhood education with bilingual extension (Ed M); earth science education (Ed M, Certificate); education and technology (Ed M); education studies (Ed M); educational technology and new literacies (Certificate); educational technology and new literacies (Advanced Certificate); elementary education (Ed D); English education (Ed M, Certificate); English education studies (Ed M); English for speakers of other languages (Ed M); foreign and second language education (PhD); French education (Ed M, Certificate); German education (Ed M, Certificate); gifted education (Certificate); Latin education (Ed M, Certificate); literacy education studies (Ed M); literacy specialist (Ed M); literacy teaching and learning (Certificate); mathematics education (Ed M, Certificate); music education (Ed M, Certificate); music education studies (Ed M); music learning theory (Advanced Certificate); online education (Advanced Certificate); physics education (Ed M, Certificate); science and the public (Ed M); social studies education (Ed M, Certificate); Spanish education (Ed M, Certificate); special education (PhD); teaching English to speakers of other languages (Ed M). *Program availability:* Part-time, evening/weekend, 100% online. *Faculty:* 28 full-time (21 women), 67 part-time/adjunct (49 women). *Students:* 198 full-time (153 women), 312 part-time (220 women); includes 48 minority (28 Black or African American, non-Hispanic/Latino; 4 American Indian or Alaska Native, non-Hispanic/Latino; 15 Asian, non-Hispanic/Latino; 1 Hispanic/Latino), 66 international. Average age 33. 336 applicants, 86% accepted, 178 enrolled. In 2016, 137 master's, 24 doctorates, 25 other advanced degrees awarded. *Degree requirements:* For master's, comprehensive exam; for doctorate, thesis/dissertation, research analysis exam, research experience. *Entrance requirements:* For master's, letters of reference; for doctorate, GRE General Test or MAT, interview, writing sample, letters of recommendation. Additional exam requirements/recommendations for international students: Required—TOEFL (minimum score 600 paper-based; 96 iBT). *Application deadline:* For fall admission, 2/1 priority date for domestic and international students; for spring admission, 11/15 priority date for domestic students, 10/1 for international students. Applications are processed on a rolling basis. Application fee: $50. Electronic applications accepted. *Financial support:* In 2016–17, 44 fellowships (averaging $4,010 per year), 39 research assistantships with tuition reimbursements (averaging $9,897 per year) were awarded; teaching assistantships, career-related internships or fieldwork, Federal Work-Study, institutionally sponsored loans, scholarships/grants, tuition waivers (full and partial), and unspecified assistantships also available. Financial award application deadline: 2/28; financial award applicants required to submit FAFSA. *Faculty research:* Science assessment, foreign language teaching and learning, early learning, new literacies, gender and education. *Total annual research expenditures:* $534,880. *Unit head:* Dr. Deborah Moore-Russo, Chair, 716-645-4069, Fax: 716-645-3161, E-mail: dam29@buffalo.edu. *Application contact:* Luann Zak, Admissions Assistant, 716-645-2110, Fax: 716-645-7937, E-mail: luannzak@buffalo.edu.
Website: http://gse.buffalo.edu/lai

University of Arkansas at Little Rock, Graduate School, College of Arts, Letters, and Sciences, Department of International and Second Language Studies, Little Rock, AR 72204-1099. Offers second languages (MA). *Degree requirements:* For master's, comprehensive exam, thesis. *Entrance requirements:* For master's, GRE or MAT, bachelor's degree; 3 letters of reference; personal interview; minimum overall undergraduate GPA of 2.75, 3.0 in last 60 hours.

University of California, Irvine, School of Humanities, Department of Spanish and Portuguese, Irvine, CA 92697. Offers Spanish (MA, MAT, PhD). *Students:* 30 full-time (18 women); includes 21 minority (all Hispanic/Latino), 2 international. Average age 38. 14 applicants, 43% accepted, 3 enrolled. In 2016, 1 master's, 3 doctorates awarded. *Degree requirements:* For doctorate, thesis/dissertation. *Entrance requirements:* For master's and doctorate, GRE General Test, minimum GPA of 3.0. Additional exam requirements/recommendations for international students: Required—TOEFL (minimum score 550 paper-based). *Application deadline:* For fall admission, 1/2 priority date for domestic students, 1/2 for international students. Applications are processed on a rolling basis. Application fee: $105 ($125 for international students). Electronic applications accepted. *Financial support:* Fellowships, teaching assistantships, institutionally sponsored loans, traineeships, health care benefits, and unspecified assistantships available. Financial award application deadline: 3/1; financial award applicants required to submit FAFSA. *Faculty research:* Latin American literature, Spanish literature, Spanish linguistics in Creole studies, Hispanic literature in the U.S., Luso-Brazilian literature. *Unit head:* Luis Aviles, Department Chair, 949-824-7268, Fax: 949-824-2803, E-mail: laviles@uci.edu. *Application contact:* Evelyn Flores, Graduate Program Coordinator, 949-824-8793, Fax: 949-824-2803, E-mail: evelynf@uci.edu.
Website: http://www.hnet.uci.edu/spanishandportuguese/

University of Central Arkansas, Graduate School, College of Liberal Arts, Department of Foreign Languages, Conway, AR 72035-0001. Offers MA. *Program availability:* Part-time. *Degree requirements:* For master's, one foreign language, comprehensive exam, thesis optional. *Entrance requirements:* For master's, GRE General Test, minimum GPA of 2.7. Additional exam requirements/recommendations for international students: Required—TOEFL (minimum score 550 paper-based). Electronic applications accepted.

University of Connecticut, Graduate School, Neag School of Education, Department of Curriculum and Instruction, Program in World Languages Education, Storrs, CT 06269. Offers MA, PhD. *Accreditation:* NCATE. Terminal master's awarded for partial completion of doctoral program. *Degree requirements:* For master's, comprehensive exam, thesis or alternative; for doctorate, thesis/dissertation. *Entrance requirements:* For doctorate, GRE General Test. Additional exam requirements/recommendations for international students: Required—TOEFL (minimum score 550 paper-based). Electronic applications accepted.

University of Delaware, College of Arts and Sciences, Department of Foreign Languages and Literatures, Newark, DE 19716. Offers foreign languages and literatures (MA), including French, German, Spanish; foreign languages pedagogy (MA), including French, German, Spanish; technical Chinese translation (MA). *Degree requirements:* For master's, one foreign language, comprehensive exam, thesis optional. *Entrance requirements:* For master's, GRE General Test, letters of recommendation, writing sample. Additional exam requirements/recommendations for international students: Required—TOEFL. Electronic applications accepted. *Faculty research:* Medieval to Modern French and Spanish literature, twentieth-century German, French, Spanish literature by women, computer-assisted instruction.

University of Florida, Graduate School, College of Liberal Arts and Sciences, Department of Spanish and Portuguese Studies, Gainesville, FL 32611. Offers Spanish (MA, MAT, PhD). *Program availability:* Part-time. Terminal master's awarded for partial completion of doctoral program. *Degree requirements:* For master's, one foreign language, comprehensive exam, thesis or extended research paper; for doctorate, 2 foreign languages, comprehensive exam, thesis/dissertation, qualifying exam. *Entrance requirements:* For master's and doctorate, GRE General Test, minimum GPA of 3.0. Additional exam requirements/recommendations for international students: Required—TOEFL (minimum score 550 paper-based; 80 iBT), IELTS (minimum score 6). Electronic applications accepted. *Faculty research:* Spanish linguistics; second language acquisition and teaching; Spanish literature, film and culture; Latin American literature, film and culture; Portuguese literature, film and culture.

University of Hawaii at Hilo, Program in Hawaiian and Indigenous Language and Culture Revitalization, Hilo, HI 96720-4091. Offers PhD. *Entrance requirements:* Additional exam requirements/recommendations for international students: Required—TOEFL, IELTS. Electronic applications accepted.

Foreign Languages Education

University of Hawaii at Hilo, Program in Hawaiian Language and Literature, Hilo, HI 96720-4091. Offers MA. *Entrance requirements:* Additional exam requirements/recommendations for international students: Required—TOEFL, IELTS. Electronic applications accepted.

University of Hawaii at Hilo, Program in Indigenous Language and Culture Education, Hilo, HI 96720-4091. Offers MA. *Entrance requirements:* Additional exam requirements/recommendations for international students: Required—TOEFL, IELTS. Electronic applications accepted.

University of Hawaii at Manoa, Graduate Division, College of Languages, Linguistics and Literature, Department of Second Language Studies, Honolulu, HI 96822. Offers English as a second language (MA, Graduate Certificate); second language acquisition (PhD). *Program availability:* Part-time. *Degree requirements:* For master's, 2 foreign languages, thesis optional; for doctorate, 2 foreign languages, comprehensive exam, thesis/dissertation. *Entrance requirements:* For master's, GRE General Test, minimum GPA of 3.0; for doctorate, GRE General Test, MA, scholarly publications. Additional exam requirements/recommendations for international students: Required—TOEFL (minimum score 600 paper-based; 100 iBT), IELTS (minimum score 7). *Faculty research:* Second language use, second language analysis, second language pedagogy and testing, second language learning, qualitative and quantitative research methods for second languages.

University of Hawaii at Manoa, Graduate Division, Hawai'inuiakea School of Hawaiian Knowledge, Program in Hawaiian, Honolulu, HI 96822. Offers MA. *Program availability:* Part-time. *Degree requirements:* For master's, thesis optional. *Entrance requirements:* Additional exam requirements/recommendations for international students: Required—TOEFL (minimum score 500 paper-based; 61 iBT), IELTS (minimum score 5).

University of Hawaii at Manoa, Graduate Division, Hawai'inuiakea School of Hawaiian Knowledge, Program in Hawaiian Studies, Honolulu, HI 96822. Offers MA. *Program availability:* Part-time. *Degree requirements:* For master's, thesis optional. *Entrance requirements:* Additional exam requirements/recommendations for international students: Required—TOEFL (minimum score 500 paper-based; 61 iBT), IELTS (minimum score 5).

University of Illinois at Chicago, College of Liberal Arts and Sciences, School of Literatures, Cultural Studies and Linguistics, Chicago, IL 60607-7128. Offers French and Francophone studies (MA); Germanic studies (MA); Hispanic and Italian studies (MAT, PhD), including Hispanic linguistics (PhD), Hispanic literary and cultural studies (PhD), teaching of Spanish (MAT); linguistics (MA), including teaching English to speakers of other languages/applied linguistics; Slavic and Baltic languages and literatures (MA), including Slavic studies (MA, PhD); Slavic and Baltic languages and literatures (PhD), including Slavic studies (MA, PhD). *Program availability:* Part-time. Terminal master's awarded for partial completion of doctoral program. *Degree requirements:* For master's, one foreign language, exam. *Entrance requirements:* For master's, minimum GPA of 2.75. Additional exam requirements/recommendations for international students: Required—TOEFL. Electronic applications accepted. *Faculty research:* International studies, religious (Catholic, Jewish) studies, moving image arts.

University of Illinois at Urbana–Champaign, Graduate College, College of Liberal Arts and Sciences, School of Literatures, Cultures and Linguistics, Department of Spanish, Italian and Portuguese, Champaign, IL 61820. Offers Italian (MA, PhD); Portuguese (MA, PhD); Spanish (MA, PhD).

University of Illinois at Urbana–Champaign, Graduate College, College of Liberal Arts and Sciences, School of Literatures, Cultures and Linguistics, Department of the Classics, Champaign, IL 61820. Offers classical philology (PhD); classics (MA); teaching of Latin (MA).

University of Indianapolis, Graduate Programs, School of Education, Indianapolis, IN 46227-3697. Offers art education (MAT); biology (MAT); chemistry (MAT); curriculum and instruction (MA); earth sciences (MAT); education (MA, MAT); educational leadership (MA); elementary education (MA); English (MAT); French (MAT); math (MAT); physical education (MAT); physics (MAT); secondary education (MA), including art education, education, English education, social studies education; social studies (MAT); Spanish (MAT). *Accreditation:* NCATE. *Program availability:* Part-time, evening/weekend. *Entrance requirements:* For master's, GRE Subject Test, PRAXIS I, minimum GPA of 2.5, 3 letters of recommendation, interview. Additional exam requirements/recommendations for international students: Required—TOEFL (minimum score 550 paper-based). *Faculty research:* Assessment of teacher education, perceptions of prospective teachers by parents.

The University of Iowa, Graduate College, College of Education, Department of Teaching and Learning, Program in Education, Iowa City, IA 52242-1316. Offers art education (MA); developmental reading (MA); elementary education (MA); English education (MA, MAT); foreign and second language education (MAT); foreign language education (MA); foreign language/ESL education (PhD); language, literacy and culture (PhD); mathematics education (MA, MAT, PhD); music education (MM, PhD); science education (MA); secondary education (MA); social studies (MA, PhD). *Degree requirements:* For master's, thesis optional, exam; for doctorate, comprehensive exam, thesis/dissertation. *Entrance requirements:* For master's and doctorate, GRE General Test, minimum GPA of 3.0. Additional exam requirements/recommendations for international students: Required—TOEFL (minimum score 550 paper-based; 81 iBT). Electronic applications accepted.

The University of Iowa, Graduate College, College of Liberal Arts and Sciences, Program in Second Language Acquisition, Iowa City, IA 52242-1316. Offers PhD. *Degree requirements:* For doctorate, comprehensive exam, thesis/dissertation. *Entrance requirements:* For doctorate, GRE General Test, minimum GPA of 3.0. Additional exam requirements/recommendations for international students: Required—TOEFL (minimum score 600 paper-based; 100 iBT). Electronic applications accepted.

University of Kentucky, Graduate School, College of Arts and Sciences and College of Education, Program in Teaching World Languages, Lexington, KY 40506-0032. Offers MA. *Entrance requirements:* For master's, GRE General Test, minimum undergraduate GPA of 2.75. Additional exam requirements/recommendations for international students: Required—TOEFL (minimum score 550 paper-based). Electronic applications accepted.

University of Louisiana at Monroe, Graduate School, College of Arts, Education, and Sciences, School of Education, Program in Curriculum and Instruction, Monroe, LA 71209-0001. Offers art education (M Ed); biology education (M Ed); chemistry education (M Ed); curriculum and instruction (Ed D); early childhood education (M Ed); earth science education (M Ed); educational leadership (M Ed); elementary education (1-5) (M Ed); English as a second language (M Ed); English education (M Ed); family and consumer education (M Ed); French education (M Ed); history education (M Ed); math education (M Ed); middle school education (M Ed); music education (M Ed); reading education (K-12) (M Ed); Spanish education (M Ed); special education - academically gifted (M Ed); special education - early intervention (M Ed); special education - educational diagnostician (M Ed); special education - mild/moderate disabilities (M Ed); speech education (M Ed). *Accreditation:* NCATE. *Faculty:* 8 full-time (4 women), 4 part-time/adjunct (3 women). *Students:* 13 full-time (11 women), 80 part-time (65 women); includes 25 minority (19 Black or African American, non-Hispanic/Latino; 1 Asian, non-Hispanic/Latino; 3 Hispanic/Latino; 2 Two or more races, non-Hispanic/Latino). Average age 37. 118 applicants, 30% accepted, 16 enrolled. In 2016, 23 master's, 4 doctorates awarded. *Degree requirements:* For master's, comprehensive exam (for some programs), thesis; for doctorate, thesis/dissertation, internships. *Entrance requirements:* For master's, GRE General Test; for doctorate, GRE General Test, minimum undergraduate GPA of 2.75, graduate 3.25. Additional exam requirements/recommendations for international students: Required—TOEFL (minimum score 500 paper-based; 61 iBT). *Application deadline:* For fall admission, 8/24 priority date for domestic students, 7/1 for international students; for winter admission, 12/14 priority date for domestic students; for spring admission, 1/19 for domestic students, 11/1 for international students. Applications are processed on a rolling basis. Application fee: $20 ($30 for international students). Electronic applications accepted. *Expenses:* Tuition, state resident: full-time $6489. Tuition, nonresident: full-time $18,589. *Required fees:* $8984. Tuition and fees vary according to course level, course load, degree level and program. *Financial support:* Research assistantships, career-related internships or fieldwork, Federal Work-Study, and unspecified assistantships available. Financial award application deadline: 4/1; financial award applicants required to submit FAFSA. *Unit head:* Dr. Dorothy Schween, Director, 318-342-1268, Fax: 318-342-3131, E-mail: schween@ulm.edu.

University of Maine, Graduate School, College of Liberal Arts and Sciences, Department of Modern Languages and Classics, Orono, ME 04469. Offers French (MA, MAT); Spanish (MAT). *Program availability:* Part-time. *Faculty:* 6 full-time (3 women), 1 (woman) part-time/adjunct. *Students:* 2 full-time (1 woman), 1 (woman) part-time. Average age 41. 2 applicants, 100% accepted, 1 enrolled. In 2016, 5 master's awarded. *Degree requirements:* For master's, one foreign language, thesis (for some programs). *Entrance requirements:* For master's, GRE General Test, Applicants for M.A.T. require PRAXIS II. Additional exam requirements/recommendations for international students: Required—TOEFL. *Application deadline:* For fall admission, 2/1 priority date for domestic and international students. Applications are processed on a rolling basis. Application fee: $65. Electronic applications accepted. *Expenses:* Tuition, state resident: full-time $7524; part-time $2508 per credit. Tuition, nonresident: full-time $24,498; part-time $8166 per credit. *Required fees:* $1148; $571 per credit. *Financial support:* In 2016–17, 2 students received support, including 2 teaching assistantships with tuition reimbursements available (averaging $14,600 per year); Federal Work-Study and tuition waivers (full and partial) also available. Financial award application deadline: 3/1. *Faculty research:* Latin American literature and culture, early modern and modern Spanish literature and culture, North American French linguistics, 20th century Quebec literature and culture, contemporary French philosophy. *Unit head:* Dr. Jane Smith, Chair, 207-581-2075, Fax: 207-581-1832. *Application contact:* Scott G. Delcourt, Assistant Vice President for Graduate Studies/Senior Associate Dean, 207-581-3291, Fax: 207-581-3232, E-mail: graduate@maine.edu.
Website: https://umaine.edu/mlandc/graduate-programs/

University of Maryland, Baltimore County, The Graduate School, College of Arts, Humanities and Social Sciences, Department of Education, Program in Teaching, Baltimore, MD 21250. Offers early childhood education (MAT); elementary education (MAT); teaching (MAT), including art, biology, chemistry, choral music, classical foreign language, dance, earth/space science, English, instrumental music, mathematics, modern foreign language, physical science, physics, social studies, theatre. *Program availability:* Part-time, evening/weekend. *Faculty:* 24 full-time (18 women), 25 part-time/adjunct (19 women). *Students:* 41 full-time (34 women), 27 part-time (18 women); includes 26 minority (6 Black or African American, non-Hispanic/Latino; 9 Asian, non-Hispanic/Latino; 7 Hispanic/Latino; 1 Native Hawaiian or other Pacific Islander, non-Hispanic/Latino; 3 Two or more races, non-Hispanic/Latino), 2 international. Average age 30. 54 applicants, 83% accepted, 35 enrolled. In 2016, 50 master's awarded. *Degree requirements:* For master's, comprehensive exam (for some programs), thesis (for some programs). *Entrance requirements:* For master's, PRAXIS Core Examination or GRE (minimum score of 1000), minimum GPA of 3.0. Additional exam requirements/recommendations for international students: Required—TOEFL. *Application deadline:* For fall admission, 6/1 for domestic and international students; for spring admission, 11/1 for domestic and international students. Applications are processed on a rolling basis. Application fee: $50. Electronic applications accepted. *Expenses:* Tuition, state resident: full-time $13,294. Tuition, nonresident: full-time $20,286. *Financial support:* In 2016–17, 8 students received support, including teaching assistantships with tuition reimbursements available (averaging $12,000 per year); career-related internships or fieldwork, Federal Work-Study, scholarships/grants, tuition waivers, and unspecified assistantships also available. Financial award application deadline: 3/15. *Faculty research:* STEM teacher education, culturally sensitive pedagogy, ESOL/bilingual education, early childhood education, language, literacy and culture. *Total annual research expenditures:* $100,000. *Unit head:* Dr. Susan M. Blunck, Graduate Program Director, 410-455-2869, Fax: 410-455-3986, E-mail: blunck@umbc.edu. *Application contact:* Cheryl Johnson, MAT Program Specialist, 410-455-3388, E-mail: blackwel@umbc.edu.
Website: http://www.umbc.edu/education/

University of Maryland, College Park, Academic Affairs, College of Arts and Humanities, School of Languages, Literatures, and Cultures, Program in Second Language Acquisition and Application, College Park, MD 20742. Offers second language instruction (PhD); second language learning (PhD); second language measurement and assessment (PhD); second language use (PhD). Electronic applications accepted. *Faculty research:* Second language acquisition, pedagogical perspectives, technological applications, language use in professional contexts.

University of Massachusetts Amherst, Graduate School, College of Humanities and Fine Arts, Department of Languages, Literatures, and Cultures, Program in French and Francophone Studies, Amherst, MA 01003. Offers French (MAT); French and Francophone studies (MA). *Program availability:* Part-time. *Degree requirements:* For master's, thesis or alternative. *Entrance requirements:* For master's, GRE General Test. Additional exam requirements/recommendations for international students: Required—TOEFL (minimum score 550 paper-based; 80 iBT), IELTS (minimum score 6.5). Electronic applications accepted.

University of Michigan, Rackham Graduate School, College of Literature, Science, and the Arts, Department of Classical Studies, Ann Arbor, MI 48109. Offers classical studies (PhD); teaching Latin (MAT). *Faculty:* 22 full-time (11 women), 6 part-time/adjunct (2 women). *Students:* 27 full-time (10 women); includes 3 minority (1 Hispanic/Latino; 2 Two or more races, non-Hispanic/Latino), 6 international. Average age 28. 54 applicants, 19% accepted, 6 enrolled. In 2016, 4 doctorates awarded. Terminal master's awarded for partial completion of doctoral program. *Degree requirements:* For master's, one foreign language, comprehensive exam; for doctorate, 4 foreign languages, comprehensive exam, thesis/dissertation, oral defense of dissertation, preliminary exams, qualifying exams. *Entrance requirements:* For master's, GRE General Test, 2-3 years of Latin (for the Latin MAT); for doctorate, GRE General Test, strict minimum of 3 years of college-level Latin and 2 years of college-level Greek. Additional exam requirements/recommendations for international students: Required—TOEFL (minimum score 560 paper-based). *Application deadline:* For fall admission, 12/15 for domestic and international students. Application fee: $75 ($90 for international students).

Electronic applications accepted. *Expenses:* Tuition, state resident: full-time $21,466; part-time $1152 per credit hour. Tuition, nonresident: full-time $43,346; part-time $2367 per credit hour. Part-time tuition and fees vary according to course load, degree level and program. *Financial support:* In 2016–17, 26 students received support, including 11 fellowships with full tuition reimbursements available (averaging $19,000 per year), 15 teaching assistantships with full tuition reimbursements available (averaging $19,000 per year); career-related internships or fieldwork, Federal Work-Study, institutionally sponsored loans, scholarships/grants, traineeships, tuition waivers (full), unspecified assistantships, and summer stipends, year-round health care also available. Financial award application deadline: 3/15. *Faculty research:* Greek and Latin literature, ancient history, papyrology, archaeology. *Unit head:* Prof. Artemis Leontis, Chair and Professor, 734-764-0360, Fax: 734-763-4959, E-mail: classics@umich.edu. *Application contact:* Sarah Kandell-Gritzmaker, Student Services Coordinator, 734-615-3181, Fax: 734-763-4959, E-mail: skandell@umich.edu.
Website: http://www.lsa.umich.edu/classics

University of Minnesota, Twin Cities Campus, Graduate School, College of Education and Human Development, Department of Curriculum and Instruction, Program in Teaching, Minneapolis, MN 55455-0213. Offers teaching (M Ed), including arts in education, elementary education, English education, mathematics, science, second language education, social studies. *Students:* 237 full-time (169 women), 171 part-time (112 women); includes 91 minority (23 Black or African American, non-Hispanic/Latino; 3 American Indian or Alaska Native, non-Hispanic/Latino; 19 Asian, non-Hispanic/Latino; 25 Hispanic/Latino; 21 Two or more races, non-Hispanic/Latino), 10 international. Average age 27. 421 applicants, 72% accepted, 275 enrolled. In 2016, 584 master's awarded. Application fee: $75 ($95 for international students). *Unit head:* Dr. Cynthia Lewis, Chair, 612-625-6313, Fax: 612-624-8277, E-mail: lewis@umn.edu. *Application contact:* Dr. Kendall King, Director of Graduate Studies, 612-625-3692, E-mail: roehr013@umn.edu.
Website: http://www.cehd.umn.edu/ci/

University of Mississippi, Graduate School, College of Liberal Arts, University, MS 38677. Offers anthropology (MA); biology (MS, PhD); chemistry (MS, PhD); economics (MA, PhD); English (MA, PhD); experimental psychology (PhD); history (MA, PhD); mathematics (MS, PhD); modern languages (MA); music (MM); philosophy (MA); physics (MA, MS, PhD); political science (MA, PhD); studio art (MFA). *Program availability:* Part-time. *Faculty:* 472 full-time (263 women), 75 part-time/adjunct (35 women). *Students:* 415 full-time (210 women), 57 part-time (20 women); includes 70 minority (35 Black or African American, non-Hispanic/Latino; 13 Asian, non-Hispanic/Latino; 14 Hispanic/Latino; 8 Two or more races, non-Hispanic/Latino), 102 international. Average age 27. *Degree requirements:* For doctorate, thesis/dissertation. *Entrance requirements:* For master's, GRE General Test, minimum GPA of 3.0; for doctorate, GRE General Test. Additional exam requirements/recommendations for international students: Required—TOEFL. *Application deadline:* For fall admission, 4/1 for domestic students; for spring admission, 10/1 for domestic students. Applications are processed on a rolling basis. Application fee: $40. Electronic applications accepted. *Financial support:* Fellowships, research assistantships, teaching assistantships, career-related internships or fieldwork, Federal Work-Study, institutionally sponsored loans, scholarships/grants, and unspecified assistantships available. Financial award application deadline: 3/1; financial award applicants required to submit FAFSA. *Unit head:* Dr. Lee Michael Cohen, Dean, 662-915-7177, Fax: 662-915-5792, E-mail: libarts@olemiss.edu. *Application contact:* Dr. Christy M. Wyandt, Associate Dean of Graduate School, 662-915-7474, Fax: 662-915-7577, E-mail: cwyandt@olemiss.edu.
Website: https://www.olemiss.edu

University of Missouri, Office of Research and Graduate Studies, College of Arts and Science, Department of Romance Languages and Literatures, Columbia, MO 65211. Offers French (MA, PhD); literature (MA); Spanish (MA, PhD); teaching (MA). *Faculty:* 25 full-time (15 women). *Students:* 22 full-time (16 women), 15 part-time (10 women); includes 11 minority (3 Black or African American, non-Hispanic/Latino; 6 Hispanic/Latino; 2 Two or more races, non-Hispanic/Latino), 13 international. Average age 35. Terminal master's awarded for partial completion of doctoral program. *Degree requirements:* For master's, one foreign language; for doctorate, 4 foreign languages, comprehensive exam, thesis/dissertation. *Entrance requirements:* For master's, GRE General Test, minimum GPA of 3.0 in field of major; bachelor's degree; for doctorate, GRE General Test, minimum GPA of 3.0 in field of major; master's degree. Additional exam requirements/recommendations for international students: Required—TOEFL (minimum score 500 paper-based; 61 iBT). *Application deadline:* For fall admission, 2/15 priority date for domestic students; for winter admission, 10/15 for domestic students. Applications are processed on a rolling basis. Application fee: $75 ($90 for international students). Electronic applications accepted. *Expenses:* Tuition, state resident: full-time $6347; part-time $352.60 per credit hour. Tuition, nonresident: full-time $17,379; part-time $965.50 per credit hour. *Required fees:* $1035. Tuition and fees vary according to course load, campus/location and program. *Financial support:* Research assistantships, teaching assistantships with full tuition reimbursements, institutionally sponsored loans, health care benefits, and unspecified assistantships available.
Website: http://romancelanguages.missouri.edu/grad.shtml

University of Missouri, Office of Research and Graduate Studies, College of Education, Department of Learning, Teaching and Curriculum, Columbia, MO 65211. Offers agricultural education (M Ed, PhD, Ed S); art education (M Ed, PhD, Ed S); business and office education (M Ed, PhD, Ed S); early childhood education (M Ed, PhD, Ed S); elementary education (M Ed, PhD, Ed S); English education (M Ed, PhD, Ed S); foreign language education (M Ed, PhD, Ed S); health education and promotion (M Ed, PhD); learning and instruction (M Ed); marketing education (M Ed, PhD, Ed S); mathematics education (M Ed, PhD, Ed S); music education (M Ed, PhD, Ed S); reading education (M Ed, PhD, Ed S); science education (M Ed, PhD, Ed S); social studies education (M Ed, PhD, Ed S); vocational education (M Ed, PhD, Ed S). *Program availability:* Part-time. *Faculty:* 30 full-time (18 women), 1 (woman) part-time/adjunct. *Students:* 157 full-time (124 women), 157 part-time (125 women). Terminal master's awarded for partial completion of doctoral program. *Degree requirements:* For doctorate, thesis/dissertation. *Entrance requirements:* For master's and Ed S, GRE General Test or MAT, minimum GPA of 3.0; for doctorate, GRE General Test, minimum GPA of 3.0. Additional exam requirements/recommendations for international students: Required—TOEFL (minimum score 600 paper-based; 100 iBT). *Application deadline:* For fall admission, 12/1 priority date for domestic and international students. Applications are processed on a rolling basis. Application fee: $75 ($90 for international students). Electronic applications accepted. *Expenses:* Tuition, state resident: full-time $6347; part-time $352.60 per credit hour. Tuition, nonresident: full-time $17,379; part-time $965.50 per credit hour. *Required fees:* $1035. Tuition and fees vary according to course load, campus/location and program. *Financial support:* Fellowships, research assistantships, teaching assistantships, institutionally sponsored loans, traineeships, health care benefits, and unspecified assistantships available. Support available to part-time students.
Website: http://education.missouri.edu/LTC/index.php

University of Nebraska at Kearney, College of Fine Arts and Humanities, Department of Modern Languages, Kearney, NE 68849-0001. Offers Spanish education (MA Ed). *Accreditation:* NCATE. *Program availability:* Part-time, evening/weekend. *Faculty:* 4 full-time (2 women). *Students:* 29 part-time (24 women); includes 10 minority (all Hispanic/Latino), 1 international. Average age 32. 4 applicants, 75% accepted, 2 enrolled. In 2016, 10 master's awarded. *Degree requirements:* For master's, comprehensive exam, thesis optional. *Entrance requirements:* For master's, 21 semester hours of upper-level Spanish; two-page Spanish essay; one-page English essay; two letters of recommendation. Additional exam requirements/recommendations for international students: Recommended—TOEFL (minimum score 550 paper-based; 79 iBT), IELTS (minimum score 6.5). *Application deadline:* For fall admission, 6/15 for domestic and international students; for spring admission, 10/15 for domestic and international students; for summer admission, 3/15 for domestic and international students. Application fee: $45. Electronic applications accepted. *Expenses:* Tuition, state resident: full-time $4064; part-time $225.75 per credit hour. Tuition, nonresident: full-time $8915; part-time $495.25 per credit hour. *Required fees:* $772; $23 per credit hour. Part-time tuition and fees vary according to course load, campus/location, program and reciprocity agreements. *Financial support:* In 2016–17, 1 student received support, including 1 teaching assistantship with full tuition reimbursement available (averaging $10,500 per year); career-related internships or fieldwork, health care benefits, and unspecified assistantships also available. Support available to part-time students. Financial award application deadline: 2/28; financial award applicants required to submit FAFSA. *Faculty research:* Translation theory, Spanish linguistics; symotolistic poetry, critical theory and Marxism, French and Francophone film, themes of culture, nationality and ethnicity. *Unit head:* Dr. Johnathan Dettman, Chair, 308-865-8493, Fax: 308-865-8806, E-mail: dettmanjc@unk.edu. *Application contact:* Linda Johnson, Director, Graduate Admissions and Programs, 800-717-7881, E-mail: gradstudies@unk.edu.
Website: http://www.unk.edu/academics/modern-languages/index.php

University of Nebraska at Omaha, Graduate Studies, College of Arts and Sciences, Program in Language Teaching, Omaha, NE 68182. Offers MA. *Program availability:* Part-time, evening/weekend. *Faculty:* 9 full-time (7 women). *Students:* 6 full-time (5 women), 14 part-time (11 women); includes 5 minority (1 Black or African American, non-Hispanic/Latino; 1 Asian, non-Hispanic/Latino; 2 Hispanic/Latino; 1 Two or more races, non-Hispanic/Latino). Average age 34. 7 applicants, 71% accepted, 2 enrolled. In 2016, 5 master's awarded. *Degree requirements:* For master's, comprehensive exam, thesis (for some programs). *Entrance requirements:* For master's, minimum GPA of 3.0, official transcripts, 2 letters of recommendation, oral language sample, writing sample. Additional exam requirements/recommendations for international students: Required—TOEFL, IELTS, PTE. *Application deadline:* For fall admission, 4/15 priority date for domestic and international students; for spring admission, 11/15 priority date for domestic and international students; for summer admission, 4/15 for domestic and international students. Applications are processed on a rolling basis. Application fee: $45. Electronic applications accepted. *Financial support:* In 2016–17, 1 student received support, including 1 teaching assistantship with tuition reimbursement available; research assistantships with tuition reimbursements available, health care benefits, and tuition waivers (partial) also available. Financial award application deadline: 3/1; financial award applicants required to submit FAFSA. *Unit head:* Dr. Melanie Bloom, Chairperson, 402-554-2341, E-mail: graduate@unomaha.edu. *Application contact:* Dr. Claudia Garcia, Graduate Program Chair, 402-554-2341, E-mail: graduate@unomaha.edu.

University of Nevada, Reno, Graduate School, College of Liberal Arts, Department of Foreign Languages and Literatures, Reno, NV 89557. Offers French (MA); German (MA); Spanish (MA). *Degree requirements:* For master's, one foreign language, thesis optional. *Entrance requirements:* For master's, GRE General Test, minimum GPA of 2.75. Additional exam requirements/recommendations for international students: Required—TOEFL (minimum score 500 paper-based; 61 iBT), IELTS (minimum score 6). *Faculty research:* Thirteenth century mysticism, contemporary Spanish and Latin American poetry and theater, French interrelation between narration and photography, exile literature and Holocaust.

The University of North Carolina at Chapel Hill, Graduate School, School of Education, Program in Secondary Education, Chapel Hill, NC 27599. Offers English (Grades 9-12) (MAT); English as a second language (MAT); French (Grades K-12) (MAT); German (Grades K-12) (MAT); Japanese (Grades K-12) (MAT); Latin (Grades 9-12) (MAT); mathematics (Grades 9-12) (MAT); music (Grades K-12) (MAT); science (Grades 9-12) (MAT); social studies (Grades 9-12) (MAT); Spanish (Grades K-12) (MAT). *Accreditation:* NCATE. *Degree requirements:* For master's, comprehensive exam. *Entrance requirements:* For master's, GRE General Test, minimum GPA of 3.0 during last 2 years of undergraduate course work. Additional exam requirements/recommendations for international students: Required—TOEFL (minimum score 550 paper-based). Electronic applications accepted.

The University of North Carolina at Charlotte, Cato College of Education, Interdisciplinary Education Programs, Charlotte, NC 28223-0001. Offers art education (Graduate Certificate); child and family development: early childhood education (MAT); curriculum and instruction (PhD); elementary education (MAT); foreign language education (MAT); middle grades education (MAT); secondary education (MAT); special education (MAT); teaching (Graduate Certificate); teaching English as a second language (MAT); theatre education (Graduate Certificate). *Program availability:* Part-time, 100% online, blended/hybrid learning. *Students:* 78 full-time (59 women), 619 part-time (484 women); includes 255 minority (186 Black or African American, non-Hispanic/Latino; 1 American Indian or Alaska Native, non-Hispanic/Latino; 16 Asian, non-Hispanic/Latino; 37 Hispanic/Latino; 15 Two or more races, non-Hispanic/Latino), 10 international. Average age 33. 380 applicants, 92% accepted, 264 enrolled. In 2016, 93 master's, 8 doctorates, 176 other advanced degrees awarded. *Degree requirements:* For master's, thesis or alternative, research project/portfolio. *Entrance requirements:* For master's, GRE or MAT, bachelor's degree, or its U.S. equivalent, from regionally-accredited college or university; minimum overall GPA of 3.0 on all previous work beyond high school; statement of purpose (essay); at least three recommendation forms; for doctorate, GRE or MAT, bachelor's degree (or its U.S. equivalent) from regionally-accredited college or university; minimum overall GPA of 3.5 in master's degree program; for Graduate Certificate, bachelor's degree from regionally-accredited university; minimum GPA of 2.75 on all post-secondary work attempted; transcripts; personal statement outlining why the applicant seeks admission to the program. Additional exam requirements/recommendations for international students: Required—TOEFL (minimum score 523 paper-based, 70 iBT) or IELTS (6.5). *Application deadline:* For fall admission, 3/1 priority date for domestic and international students; for spring admission, 10/1 priority date for domestic and international students; for summer admission, 4/1 priority date for domestic and international students. Applications are processed on a rolling basis. Application fee: $75. Electronic applications accepted. *Expenses:* Tuition, state resident: full-time $4252. Tuition, nonresident: full-time $17,423. *Required fees:* $3026. Tuition and fees vary according to course load and program. *Financial support:* Career-related internships or fieldwork, institutionally sponsored loans, scholarships/grants, and unspecified assistantships available. Support available to part-time students. Financial award application deadline: 3/1; financial award applicants required to submit FAFSA. *Unit head:* Dr. Ellen McIntyre, Dean, 704-687-8722, E-mail: ellen.mcintyre@uncc.edu. *Application contact:* Kathy B. Giddings, Director of Graduate Admissions, 704-687-5503, Fax: 704-687-1668, E-mail:

gradadm@uncc.edu.
Website: http://education.uncc.edu/academic-programs

The University of North Carolina at Greensboro, Graduate School, School of Education, Department of Teacher Education and Higher Education, Greensboro, NC 27412-5001. Offers college teaching and adult learning (Certificate); curriculum and instruction (M Ed), including chemistry education, elementary education, English as a second language, French education, instructional technology, mathematics education, middle grades education, reading education, science education, social studies education, Spanish education; curriculum and teaching (PhD), including higher education, teacher education and development; English as a second language (Certificate); higher education (M Ed); supervision (M Ed). *Accreditation:* NCATE. *Program availability:* Part-time. *Degree requirements:* For doctorate, thesis/dissertation. *Entrance requirements:* For master's and doctorate, GRE General Test. Additional exam requirements/recommendations for international students: Required—TOEFL. Electronic applications accepted. *Faculty research:* Community college literacy program, middle school mathematics/computer mathematics.

The University of North Carolina Wilmington, Watson College of Education, Department of Instructional Technology, Foundations and Secondary Education, Wilmington, NC 28403-3297. Offers academically or intellectually gifted (M Ed); English as a second language (M Ed, MAT); instructional technology (MS); physical education and health (M Ed, MAT); secondary education (M Ed, MAT); Spanish (MAT); Spanish education (MASS). *Program availability:* Part-time. *Faculty:* 17 full-time (11 women). *Students:* 36 full-time (22 women), 62 part-time (49 women); includes 17 minority (12 Black or African American, non-Hispanic/Latino; 3 Hispanic/Latino; 2 Two or more races, non-Hispanic/Latino), 5 international. Average age 34. 89 applicants, 89% accepted, 59 enrolled. In 2016, 36 master's awarded. *Degree requirements:* For master's, comprehensive exam (for some programs), thesis (for some programs), thesis or research project. *Entrance requirements:* For master's, GRE or MAT, statement of interest, 3 letters of recommendation, minimum GPA of 3.0 in undergraduate work. Additional exam requirements/recommendations for international students: Required—TOEFL (minimum score 79 iBT), IELTS (minimum score 6.5). *Application deadline:* For fall admission, 5/15 for domestic students; for spring admission, 10/15 for domestic students; for summer admission, 3/15 for domestic students. Applications are processed on a rolling basis. Application fee: $60. Electronic applications accepted. *Expenses:* Contact institution. *Financial support:* Scholarships/grants and unspecified assistantships available. Financial award application deadline: 3/15; financial award applicants required to submit FAFSA. *Unit head:* Dr. Donyell Roseboro, Chair, 910-962-2289, Fax: 910-962-3609, E-mail: roseborod@uncw.edu. *Application contact:* Dr. Mahnaz Moallem, Graduate Coordinator, 910-962-4183, E-mail: moallemm@uncw.edu.
Website: http://www.uncw.edu/ed/itfse/

University of Northern Colorado, Graduate School, College of Education and Behavioral Sciences, School of Teacher Education, Greeley, CO 80639. Offers curriculum studies (MAT); educational studies (Ed D); elementary education (MAT); English education (MAT); literacy (MA); multilingual education (MA), including TESOL, world languages; teaching diverse learners (MA). *Accreditation:* NCATE. *Program availability:* Part-time, evening/weekend. *Degree requirements:* For master's, comprehensive exam, thesis or alternative; for doctorate, comprehensive exam, thesis/dissertation. *Entrance requirements:* For master's and doctorate, GRE General Test, 3 letters of recommendation. *Application deadline:* Applications are processed on a rolling basis. Application fee: $50 ($60 for international students). Electronic applications accepted. *Financial support:* Fellowships, research assistantships, teaching assistantships, and unspecified assistantships available. Financial award application deadline: 3/1; financial award applicants required to submit FAFSA. *Unit head:* Dr. Alexander Sidorkin, Director, 970-351-2908, Fax: 970-351-1877. *Application contact:* Linda Sisson, Graduate Student Admission Coordinator, 970-351-1807, Fax: 970-351-2371, E-mail: linda.sisson@unco.edu.
Website: http://www.unco.edu/cebs/teachered/

University of Northern Iowa, Graduate College, College of Humanities, Arts and Sciences, Department of Languages and Literatures, MA Program in Spanish, Cedar Falls, IA 50614. Offers Spanish (MA); Spanish teaching (MA). *Program availability:* Part-time, evening/weekend. *Degree requirements:* For master's, one foreign language, comprehensive exam, thesis or alternative. *Entrance requirements:* For master's, minimum GPA of 3.0, valid teaching license, documentation of successful teaching experience. Additional exam requirements/recommendations for international students: Required—TOEFL (minimum score 600 paper-based; 100 iBT). Electronic applications accepted.

University of Northern Iowa, Graduate College, College of Humanities, Arts and Sciences, Department of Languages and Literatures, MA Program in TESOL/Spanish, Cedar Falls, IA 50614. Offers MA.

University of Oklahoma, Jeannine Rainbolt College of Education, Department of Instructional Leadership and Academic Curriculum, Norman, OK 73019. Offers instructional leadership and academic curriculum (M Ed, PhD), including biomedical education (PhD), early childhood education, elementary education (M Ed), English education, instructional leadership, mathematics education, reading education, science education, social studies education, world languages education (M Ed). *Accreditation:* NCATE. *Program availability:* Part-time. *Faculty:* 19 full-time (15 women), 1 (woman) part-time/adjunct. *Students:* 66 full-time (49 women), 116 part-time (88 women); includes 49 minority (12 Black or African American, non-Hispanic/Latino; 6 American Indian or Alaska Native, non-Hispanic/Latino; 6 Asian, non-Hispanic/Latino; 11 Hispanic/Latino; 1 Native Hawaiian or other Pacific Islander, non-Hispanic/Latino; 13 Two or more races, non-Hispanic/Latino), 13 international. Average age 35. 38 applicants, 97% accepted, 28 enrolled. In 2016, 33 master's, 10 doctorates awarded. Terminal master's awarded for partial completion of doctoral program. *Degree requirements:* For master's, comprehensive exam (for some programs), thesis (for some programs); for doctorate, comprehensive exam (for some programs), thesis/dissertation. *Entrance requirements:* For doctorate, GRE. Additional exam requirements/recommendations for international students: Required—TOEFL (minimum score 79 iBT) or IELTS (minimum score 6.5). Application fee: $50 ($100 for international students). Electronic applications accepted. *Expenses:* Tuition, state resident: full-time $4886; part-time $203.60 per credit hour. Tuition, nonresident: full-time $18,989; part-time $791.20 per credit hour. *Required fees:* $3283; $126.25 per credit hour. $126.50 per semester. *Financial support:* In 2016–17, 112 students received support, including 7 research assistantships with partial tuition reimbursements available (averaging $10,373 per year), 6 teaching assistantships with partial tuition reimbursements available (averaging $11,446 per year); fellowships, scholarships/grants, and unspecified assistantships also available. Financial award application deadline: 6/1; financial award applicants required to submit FAFSA. *Faculty research:* Teacher preparation; instruction; curriculum; learning; constructivist theory. *Total annual research expenditures:* $165,297. *Unit head:* Dr. Stacy Reeder, Chair, 405-325-1498, Fax: 405-325-4061, E-mail: reeder@ou.edu. *Application contact:* Anna Steele, Graduate Programs Officer, 405-325-4525, E-mail: anna.steele@ou.edu.
Website: http://www.ou.edu/education/ilac

University of Pittsburgh, School of Education, Department of Instruction and Learning, Program in Secondary Education, Pittsburgh, PA 15260. Offers English and communications education (M Ed, MAT); foreign language education (M Ed, MAT); language, literacy and culture education (Ed D, PhD); mathematics education (M Ed, MAT, Ed D, PhD); science education (M Ed, MAT, Ed D, PhD); secondary education (PhD); social studies education (M Ed, MAT); STEM education (Ed D). *Program availability:* Part-time, evening/weekend. *Degree requirements:* For master's, thesis; for doctorate, thesis/dissertation. *Entrance requirements:* For master's, PRAXIS I; for doctorate, GRE General Test. Additional exam requirements/recommendations for international students: Required—TOEFL. Electronic applications accepted. Tuition and fees vary according to program.

University of Puerto Rico, Río Piedras Campus, College of Education, Program in Curriculum and Teaching, San Juan, PR 00931-3300. Offers biology education (M Ed); chemistry education (M Ed); curriculum and teaching (Ed D); history education (M Ed); mathematics education (M Ed); physics education (M Ed); Spanish education (M Ed). *Program availability:* Part-time. *Degree requirements:* For master's, thesis; for doctorate, thesis/dissertation, internship. *Entrance requirements:* For master's, PAEG or GRE, minimum GPA of 3.0, letter of recommendation; for doctorate, GRE or PAEG, master's degree, minimum GPA of 3.0, letter of recommendation (2), interview. *Faculty research:* Curriculum, math teaching.

University of South Carolina, The Graduate School, College of Arts and Sciences, Department of Languages, Literatures, and Cultures, Columbia, SC 29208. Offers comparative literature (MA, PhD); foreign languages (MAT), including French, German, Spanish; French (MA); German (MA); Spanish (MA). MAT offered in cooperation with the College of Education. *Program availability:* Part-time. *Degree requirements:* For master's, one foreign language, comprehensive exam, thesis optional; for doctorate, 2 foreign languages, comprehensive exam, thesis/dissertation. *Entrance requirements:* For master's and doctorate, GRE General Test, writing sample. Additional exam requirements/recommendations for international students: Required—TOEFL (minimum score 75 iBT). Electronic applications accepted. *Faculty research:* Modern literature, linguistics, literature and culture, medieval literature, literary theory.

University of South Carolina, The Graduate School, College of Education, Department of Instruction and Teacher Education, Program in Secondary Education, Columbia, SC 29208. Offers art education (IMA, MAT); business education (IMA, MAT); English (MAT); foreign language (MAT); health education (MAT); mathematics (MAT); science (IMA, MAT); secondary (Ed D); secondary education (MT, PhD); social studies (MAT); theatre and speech (MAT). IMA and MT offered jointly with the subject areas. *Accreditation:* NCATE. *Degree requirements:* For master's, comprehensive exam, thesis (for some programs), foreign language (MA); for doctorate, one foreign language, comprehensive exam, thesis/dissertation. *Entrance requirements:* For master's, GRE General Test or MAT, teaching certificate (IMA, M Ed), interview; for doctorate, GRE General Test or MAT, interview. *Faculty research:* Middle school programs, professional development, school collaboration.

University of Southern Mississippi, Graduate School, College of Arts and Letters, Department of Foreign Languages and Literatures, Hattiesburg, MS 39406-0001. Offers French (MATL); Spanish (MATL); teaching English to speakers of other languages (TESOL) (MATL). *Program availability:* 100% online. *Degree requirements:* For master's, comprehensive exam. *Entrance requirements:* For master's, GRE General Test, minimum GPA of 3.0 in field of study, 2.75 in last 2 years. Additional exam requirements/recommendations for international students: Required—TOEFL, IELTS. *Application deadline:* For fall admission, 3/1 for domestic and international students. Applications are processed on a rolling basis. Application fee: $60. *Expenses: Tuition, area resident:* Full-time $15,708; part-time $437 per credit hour. *Financial support:* Teaching assistantships with full tuition reimbursements, Federal Work-Study, institutionally sponsored loans, scholarships/grants, health care benefits, and unspecified assistantships available. Financial award application deadline: 3/15; financial award applicants required to submit FAFSA. *Unit head:* Christopher Miles, Chair, 601-266-4964, Fax: 601-266-4583. *Application contact:* Carmen Carracelas-Juncal, Graduate Director, 601-266-4964.
Website: https://www.usm.edu/foreign-languages-literatures

University of South Florida, Innovative Education, Tampa, FL 33620-9951. Offers adult, career and higher education (Graduate Certificate), including college teaching, leadership in developing human resources, leadership in higher education; Africana studies (Graduate Certificate), including diasporas and health disparities, genocide and human rights; aging studies (Graduate Certificate), including gerontology; art research (Graduate Certificate), including museum studies; business foundations (Graduate Certificate); chemical and biomedical engineering (Graduate Certificate), including materials science and engineering, water, health and sustainability; child and family studies (Graduate Certificate), including positive behavior support; civil and industrial engineering (Graduate Certificate), including transportation systems analysis; community and family health (Graduate Certificate), including maternal and child health, social marketing and public health, violence and injury: prevention and intervention, women's health; criminology (Graduate Certificate), including criminal justice administration; educational measurement and research (Graduate Certificate), including evaluation; English (Graduate Certificate), including comparative literary studies, creative writing, professional and technical communication; entrepreneurship (Graduate Certificate); environmental health (Graduate Certificate), including safety management; epidemiology and biostatistics (Graduate Certificate), including applied biostatistics, biostatistics, concepts and tools of epidemiology, epidemiology, epidemiology of infectious diseases; geography, environment and planning (Graduate Certificate), including community development, environmental policy and management, geographical information systems; geology (Graduate Certificate), including hydrogeology; global health (Graduate Certificate), including disaster management, global health and Latin American and Caribbean studies, global health practice, humanitarian assistance, infection control; government and international affairs (Graduate Certificate), including Cuban studies, globalization studies; health policy and management (Graduate Certificate), including health management and leadership, public health policy and programs; hearing specialist: early intervention (Graduate Certificate); industrial and management systems engineering (Graduate Certificate), including systems engineering, technology management; information studies (Graduate Certificate), including school library media specialist; information systems/decision sciences (Graduate Certificate), including analytics and business intelligence; instructional technology (Graduate Certificate), including distance education, Florida digital/virtual educator, instructional design, multimedia design, Web design; internal medicine, bioethics and medical humanities (Graduate Certificate), including biomedical ethics; Latin American and Caribbean studies (Graduate Certificate); mass communications (Graduate Certificate), including multimedia journalism; mathematics and statistics (Graduate Certificate), including mathematics; medicine (Graduate Certificate), including aging and neuroscience, bioinformatics, biotechnology, brain fitness and memory management, clinical investigation, health informatics, health sciences, integrative weight management, intellectual property, medicine and gender, metabolic and nutritional medicine, metabolic cardiology, pharmacy sciences; national and competitive intelligence (Graduate Certificate); psychological and social foundations (Graduate Certificate), including career counseling, college teaching, diversity in education, mental health counseling, school counseling; public affairs (Graduate

Certificate), including nonprofit management, public management, research administration; public health (Graduate Certificate), including environmental health, health equity, public health generalist, translational research in adolescent behavioral health; public health practices (Graduate Certificate), including planning for healthy communities; rehabilitation and mental health counseling (Graduate Certificate), including integrative mental health care, marriage and family therapy, rehabilitation technology; secondary education (Graduate Certificate), including ESOL, foreign language education: culture and content, foreign language education: professional; social work (Graduate Certificate), including geriatric social work/clinical gerontology; special education (Graduate Certificate), including autism spectrum disorder, disabilities education: severe/profound; world languages (Graduate Certificate), including teaching English as a second language (TESL) or foreign language. *Expenses:* Tuition, state resident: full-time $7766; part-time $431.43 per credit hour. Tuition, nonresident: full-time $15,789; part-time $877.17 per credit hour. *Required fees:* $37 per term. *Unit head:* Kathy Barnes, Interdisciplinary Programs Coordinator, 813-974-8031, Fax: 813-974-7061, E-mail: barnesk@usf.edu. *Application contact:* Karen Tylinski, Metro Initiatives, 813-974-9943, Fax: 813-974-7061, E-mail: ktylinsk@usf.edu.
Website: http://www.usf.edu/innovative-education/

The University of Tennessee, Graduate School, College of Education, Health and Human Sciences, Program in Education, Knoxville, TN 37996. Offers art education (MS); counseling education (PhD); cultural studies in education (PhD); curriculum (MS, Ed S); curriculum, educational research and evaluation (Ed D, PhD); early childhood education (PhD); early childhood special education (MS); education of deaf and hard of hearing (MS); educational administration and policy studies (Ed D, PhD); educational administration and supervision (Ed S); educational psychology (Ed D, PhD); elementary education (MS, Ed S); elementary teaching (MS); English education (MS, Ed S); exercise science (PhD); foreign language/ESL education (MS, Ed S); instructional technology (MS, Ed D, PhD, Ed S); literacy, language and ESL education (PhD); literacy, language education, and ESL education (Ed D); mathematics education (MS, Ed S); modified and comprehensive special education (MS); reading education (MS, Ed S); school counseling (Ed S); school psychology (PhD, Ed S); science education (MS, Ed S); secondary teaching (MS); social foundations (MS); social science education (MS, Ed S); socio-cultural foundations of sports and education (PhD); special education (Ed S); teacher education (Ed D, PhD). *Accreditation:* NCATE. *Program availability:* Part-time, evening/weekend. *Degree requirements:* For master's and Ed S, thesis optional; for doctorate, variable foreign language requirement, thesis/dissertation. *Entrance requirements:* For master's, minimum GPA of 2.7; for doctorate and Ed S, GRE General Test, minimum GPA of 2.7. Additional exam requirements/recommendations for international students: Required—TOEFL. Electronic applications accepted.

University of the Sacred Heart, Graduate Programs, Department of Education, San Juan, PR 00914-0383. Offers early childhood education (M Ed); information technology and multimedia (Certificate); instruction systems and education technology (M Ed), including English, information technology and multimedia, instructional design, mathematics, Spanish. *Program availability:* Part-time, evening/weekend. *Degree requirements:* For master's, thesis. *Entrance requirements:* For master's, EXADEP, minimum undergraduate GPA of 2.75, interview.

The University of Toledo, College of Graduate Studies, Judith Herb College of Education, Department of Curriculum and Instruction, Toledo, OH 43606-3390. Offers art education (ME); career and technical education (ME, Ed S); curriculum and instruction (ME, PhD, Ed S); early childhood education (Ed S); education and anthropology (MAE); education and biology (MES); education and chemistry (MES); education and classics (MAE); education and economics (MAE); education and English (MAE); education and French (MAE); education and geology (MES); education and German (MAE); education and history (MAE); education and mathematics (MAE, MES); education and physics (MES); education and political science (MAE); education and sociology (MAE); education and Spanish (MAE); educational media (PhD); educational technology (ME); educational technology: virtual educator (Certificate); elementary education (PhD); English as a second language (MAE); gifted and talented education (PhD); middle childhood education (ME); secondary education (ME, PhD); special education (PhD). *Accreditation:* NCATE. *Program availability:* Part-time, evening/weekend. *Degree requirements:* For master's, comprehensive exam, thesis or alternative; for doctorate, comprehensive exam, thesis/dissertation; for other advanced degree, thesis optional. *Entrance requirements:* For master's, doctorate, and other advanced degree, minimum cumulative GPA of 2.7 for all previous academic work, letters of recommendation. Additional exam requirements/recommendations for international students: Required—TOEFL (minimum score 550 paper-based; 80 iBT). Electronic applications accepted.

University of Utah, Graduate School, College of Humanities, Department of World Languages and Cultures, Salt Lake City, UT 84112. Offers comparative literary and cultural studies (MA, PhD); French (MA); Spanish (MA, MALP); world languages (MA). *Program availability:* Part-time. *Faculty:* 27 full-time (17 women), 2 part-time/adjunct (both women). *Students:* 37 full-time (29 women), 3 part-time (1 woman); includes 9 minority (2 Asian, non-Hispanic/Latino; 6 Hispanic/Latino; 1 Two or more races, non-Hispanic/Latino), 9 international. Average age 37. 29 applicants, 62% accepted, 15 enrolled. In 2016, 13 master's awarded. Terminal master's awarded for partial completion of doctoral program. *Degree requirements:* For master's, variable foreign language requirement, comprehensive exam (for some programs), thesis (for some programs); for doctorate, 2 foreign languages, comprehensive exam, thesis/dissertation. *Entrance requirements:* For master's, bachelor's degree from regionally-accredited college or university with minimum undergraduate overall GPA of 3.0; for doctorate, MA from regionally-accredited college or university, advanced proficiency in target language. Additional exam requirements/recommendations for international students: Required—TOEFL (minimum score 550 paper-based; 80 iBT). *Application deadline:* For fall admission, 1/15 priority date for domestic students, 12/15 priority date for international students. Application fee: $55 ($65 for international students). Electronic applications accepted. *Expenses:* Tuition, state resident: full-time $7011; part-time $3918.24 per credit hour. Tuition, nonresident: full-time $22,154; part-time $11,665.42 per credit hour. *Financial support:* In 2016–17, 27 students received support, including 27 teaching assistantships with full and partial tuition reimbursements available (averaging $16,500 per year); health care benefits and unspecified assistantships also available. Financial award application deadline: 1/15. *Faculty research:* Literary study, literary theory, linguistics, cultural studies, comparative studies. *Unit head:* Dr. Katharina Gerstenberger, Chair, 801-585-7908, Fax: 801-581-7581, E-mail: katharina.gerstenberger@utah.edu. *Application contact:* Mackenzie Buie, Academic Coordinator, 801-581-7748, Fax: 801-581-7581, E-mail: mackenzie.buie@utah.edu.
Website: http://languages.utah.edu/

University of Victoria, Faculty of Graduate Studies, Faculty of Humanities, Department of French, Victoria, BC V8W 2Y2, Canada. Offers literature (MA); teaching emphasis (MA). *Program availability:* Part-time, evening/weekend. *Degree requirements:* For master's, 2 foreign languages, thesis optional. *Entrance requirements:* For master's, BA in French. Additional exam requirements/recommendations for international students: Required—TOEFL (minimum score 575 paper-based), IELTS (minimum score 7). Electronic applications accepted. *Faculty research:* French-Canadian literature, stylistics, comparative literature, Francophone literature.

University of Virginia, Curry School of Education, Department of Curriculum, Instruction, and Special Education, Program in Curriculum and Instruction, Charlottesville, VA 22903. Offers curriculum and instruction (M Ed, Ed S); elementary education (M Ed, Ed D); English education (M Ed, Ed D); foreign language education (M Ed); mathematics education (M Ed, Ed D); science education (Ed D); social studies education (M Ed); MBA/M Ed. *Students:* 43 full-time (35 women), 24 part-time (16 women); includes 7 minority (1 Black or African American, non-Hispanic/Latino; 1 Asian, non-Hispanic/Latino; 2 Hispanic/Latino; 3 Two or more races, non-Hispanic/Latino), 4 international. Average age 33. 93 applicants, 78% accepted, 54 enrolled. In 2016, 52 master's, 14 other advanced degrees awarded. *Degree requirements:* For master's, comprehensive exam (for some programs); for doctorate, comprehensive exam, thesis/dissertation; for Ed S, comprehensive exam. *Entrance requirements:* For master's, doctorate, and Ed S, GRE General Test, 2 letters of recommendation. Additional exam requirements/recommendations for international students: Required—TOEFL (minimum score 600 paper-based; 90 iBT), IELTS (minimum score 7). *Application deadline:* Applications are processed on a rolling basis. Application fee: $60. Electronic applications accepted. *Expenses:* Tuition, state resident: full-time $15,026; part-time $834 per credit hour. Tuition, nonresident: full-time $25,168; part-time $1378 per credit hour. *Required fees:* $2654. *Financial support:* Fellowships with tuition reimbursements, research assistantships with tuition reimbursements, and teaching assistantships with tuition reimbursements available. Financial award application deadline: 1/5; financial award applicants required to submit FAFSA. *Unit head:* Susan Mintz, Program Area Director, 434-924-3128, E-mail: slm4r@virginia.edu. *Application contact:* Eric Molnar, Assistant Director, Admissions and Enrollment Reporting, 434-243-2085, E-mail: eric.molnar@virginia.edu.
Website: http://curry.virginia.edu/academics/areas-of-study/curriculum-teaching-learning

University of Virginia, Curry School of Education, Program in Education, Charlottesville, VA 22903. Offers administration and supervision (PhD); applied developmental science (PhD); counselor education (PhD); curriculum and instruction (PhD); early childhood special education (MT); education evaluation (PhD); educational psychology (PhD); educational research (PhD); elementary education (MT); English education (MT, PhD); foreign language education (MT); higher education (PhD); instructional technology (PhD); kinesiology (MT, PhD); math education (PhD); reading education (PhD); research, statistics and evaluation (PhD); school psychology (PhD); science education (PhD); social studies education (MT, PhD); special education (PhD); world languages education (MT). *Students:* 452 full-time (357 women), 18 part-time (13 women); includes 100 minority (28 Black or African American, non-Hispanic/Latino; 39 Asian, non-Hispanic/Latino; 18 Hispanic/Latino; 15 Two or more races, non-Hispanic/Latino), 14 international. Average age 25. 309 applicants, 51% accepted, 87 enrolled. In 2016, 144 master's, 31 doctorates awarded. *Degree requirements:* For master's, comprehensive exam (for some programs), field project; for doctorate, comprehensive exam, thesis/dissertation. *Entrance requirements:* For doctorate, GRE General Test. Additional exam requirements/recommendations for international students: Required—TOEFL (minimum score 600 paper-based; 90 iBT), IELTS (minimum score 7). *Application deadline:* Applications are processed on a rolling basis. Application fee: $60. Electronic applications accepted. *Expenses:* Tuition, state resident: full-time $15,026; part-time $834 per credit hour. Tuition, nonresident: full-time $25,168; part-time $1378 per credit hour. *Required fees:* $2654. *Financial support:* Fellowships, research assistantships, and teaching assistantships available. Financial award application deadline: 1/5; financial award applicants required to submit FAFSA. *Unit head:* Robert C. Pianta, Dean, 434-924-3334, E-mail: pianta@virginia.edu. *Application contact:* Eric Molnar, Assistant Director, Admissions and Enrollment Reporting, 434-243-2085, E-mail: eric.molnar@virginia.edu.
Website: http://curry.virginia.edu/teacher-education

University of Wisconsin–Madison, Graduate School, School of Education, Department of Curriculum and Instruction, Madison, WI 53706-1380. Offers art education (MA); curriculum and instruction (MS, PhD); education and mathematics (MA); French education (MA); German education (MA); music education (MS); science education (MS); Spanish education (MA). *Accreditation:* NASM (one or more programs are accredited). *Degree requirements:* For doctorate, thesis/dissertation.

University of Wisconsin–Milwaukee, Graduate School, College of Letters and Science, Department of Foreign Languages and Literature, Milwaukee, WI 53201-0413. Offers classic Greek (MA); classics (MA); comparative literature (MA); foreign language and literature (MA); French (MA); German (MA); Latin (MA); linguistics (MA); Spanish (MA); translation (MA, Graduate Certificate). *Program availability:* Part-time. *Students:* 10 full-time (7 women), 19 part-time (16 women); includes 5 minority (2 Black or African American, non-Hispanic/Latino; 2 Hispanic/Latino; 1 Two or more races, non-Hispanic/Latino), 2 international. Average age 31. 41 applicants, 32% accepted, 9 enrolled. In 2016, 21 master's awarded. *Degree requirements:* For master's, 2 foreign languages, thesis or alternative. *Entrance requirements:* Additional exam requirements/recommendations for international students: Required—TOEFL (minimum score 550 paper-based; 79 iBT), IELTS (minimum score 6.5). *Application deadline:* For fall admission, 1/1 priority date for domestic students; for spring admission, 9/1 for domestic students. Applications are processed on a rolling basis. Application fee: $56 ($96 for international students). Electronic applications accepted. *Financial support:* In 2016–17, 1 fellowship, 2 research assistantships, 26 teaching assistantships were awarded; career-related internships or fieldwork, health care benefits, unspecified assistantships, and project assistantships also available. Support available to part-time students. Financial award application deadline: 4/15; financial award applicants required to submit FAFSA. *Unit head:* Kevin Muse, Department Chair, 414-229-5213, E-mail: kmuse@uwm.edu. *Application contact:* General Information Contact, 414-229-4982, Fax: 414-229-6967, E-mail: gradschool@uwm.edu.
Website: http://uwm.edu/foreign-languages-literature/

Valparaiso University, Graduate School and Continuing Education, Program in Chinese Studies, Valparaiso, IN 46383. Offers MA, JD/MA. *Program availability:* Part-time, evening/weekend. *Entrance requirements:* For master's, minimum GPA of 3.0, Chinese language proficiency. Additional exam requirements/recommendations for international students: Required—TOEFL (minimum score 550 paper-based; 80 iBT), IELTS (minimum score 6). Electronic applications accepted. *Expenses: Tuition:* Full-time $11,070; part-time $615 per credit hour. *Required fees:* $116 per semester. Tuition and fees vary according to course load, degree level and program.

Vanderbilt University, Department of French and Italian, Nashville, TN 37240-1001. Offers French (MA, MAT, PhD). *Faculty:* 12 full-time (6 women). *Students:* 13 full-time (10 women); includes 1 minority (Two or more races, non-Hispanic/Latino), 3 international. Average age 28. 10 applicants, 50% accepted, 5 enrolled. Terminal master's awarded for partial completion of doctoral program. *Degree requirements:* For master's, one foreign language, comprehensive exam; for doctorate, 2 foreign languages, comprehensive exam, thesis/dissertation, final and qualifying exams. *Entrance requirements:* For master's and doctorate, GRE General Test. Additional exam requirements/recommendations for international students: Required—TOEFL (minimum

score 570 paper-based; 88 iBT). *Application deadline:* For fall admission, 1/15 for domestic and international students. Electronic applications accepted. *Expenses: Tuition:* Part-time $1854 per credit hour. *Financial support:* Fellowships with tuition reimbursements, teaching assistantships with tuition reimbursements, career-related internships or fieldwork, Federal Work-Study, institutionally sponsored loans, scholarships/grants, and health care benefits available. Financial award application deadline: 1/15; financial award applicants required to submit CSS PROFILE or FAFSA. *Faculty research:* Baudelaire, Rabelais, voyage literature, postcolonial literature, medieval epic. *Unit head:* Dr. Laura Schneider, Chair, 615-322-6900, Fax: 615-343-6909, E-mail: laura.c.schneider@vanderbilt.edu. *Application contact:* Paul Miller, Director of Graduate Studies, 615-322-6900, Fax: 615-343-6909, E-mail: paul.miller@vanderbilt.edu.
Website: http://as.vanderbilt.edu/french-italian/

Vanderbilt University, Department of Germanic and Slavic Languages, Nashville, TN 37240-1001. Offers German (MA, MAT, PhD). *Faculty:* 5 full-time (2 women). *Students:* 24 full-time (16 women); includes 3 minority (1 Black or African American, non-Hispanic/Latino; 1 Hispanic/Latino; 1 Two or more races, non-Hispanic/Latino), 5 international. Average age 31. 8 applicants, 75% accepted, 4 enrolled. In 2016, 4 doctorates awarded. Terminal master's awarded for partial completion of doctoral program. *Degree requirements:* For master's, one foreign language, comprehensive exam; for doctorate, 2 foreign languages, comprehensive exam, thesis/dissertation, qualifying and final exams. *Entrance requirements:* For master's and doctorate, GRE General Test, sample of written work. Additional exam requirements/recommendations for international students: Required—TOEFL (minimum score 570 paper-based; 88 iBT). *Application deadline:* For fall admission, 1/15 for domestic and international students. Electronic applications accepted. *Expenses: Tuition:* Part-time $1854 per credit hour. *Financial support:* Fellowships with tuition reimbursements, teaching assistantships with tuition reimbursements, career-related internships or fieldwork, Federal Work-Study, institutionally sponsored loans, scholarships/grants, and health care benefits available. Financial award application deadline: 1/15; financial award applicants required to submit CSS PROFILE or FAFSA. *Faculty research:* 1750 to present, Middle Ages, Baroque, language pedagogy, linguistics. *Unit head:* Dr. Lutz Koepnick, Chair, 615-322-2611, Fax: 615-343-7258, E-mail: lutz.koepnick@vanderbilt.edu. *Application contact:* Christoph Zeller, Director of Graduate Studies, 615-875-9065, Fax: 615-343-7258, E-mail: christoph.zeller@vanderbilt.edu.
Website: http://www.vanderbilt.edu/german/graduate/

Vanderbilt University, Department of Spanish and Portuguese, Nashville, TN 37240-1001. Offers Portuguese (MA); Spanish (MA, MAT, PhD); Spanish and Portuguese (PhD). *Faculty:* 13 full-time (6 women). *Students:* 25 full-time (11 women); includes 5 minority (all Hispanic/Latino), 11 international. Average age 31. 39 applicants, 31% accepted, 7 enrolled. In 2016, 2 master's, 3 doctorates awarded. *Degree requirements:* For master's, one foreign language, thesis; for doctorate, 2 foreign languages, thesis/dissertation, final and qualifying exams. *Entrance requirements:* For master's, GRE General Test; for doctorate, GRE General Test, writing sample in Spanish. Additional exam requirements/recommendations for international students: Required—TOEFL (minimum score 570 paper-based; 88 iBT). *Application deadline:* For fall admission, 1/15 for domestic and international students. Electronic applications accepted. *Expenses: Tuition:* Part-time $1854 per credit hour. *Financial support:* Fellowships with tuition reimbursements, teaching assistantships with full tuition reimbursements, Federal Work-Study, institutionally sponsored loans, and health care benefits available. Financial award application deadline: 1/15; financial award applicants required to submit CSS PROFILE or FAFSA. *Faculty research:* Spanish, Portuguese, and Latin American literatures; foreign language pedagogy; Renaissance and Baroque poetry; nineteenth-century Spanish novel. *Unit head:* Dr. Benigno Trigo, Chair, 615-322-6930, Fax: 615-343-7260, E-mail: benigno.trigo@vanderbilt.edu. *Application contact:* Andres Zamora, Director of Graduate Studies, 615-322-6930, Fax: 615-343-7260, E-mail: andres.zamora@vanderbilt.edu.
Website: http://as.vanderbilt.edu/spanish-portuguese/graduate/index.php

Virginia Polytechnic Institute and State University, Graduate School, College of Liberal Arts and Human Sciences, Blacksburg, VA 24061. Offers career and technical education (MS Ed, Ed D, PhD, Ed S); communication (MA); counselor education (MA Ed, Ed D, PhD, Ed S); creative writing (MFA); curriculum and instruction (MA Ed, Ed D, PhD, Ed S); educational leadership and policy studies (MA Ed, Ed D, PhD, Ed S); educational research and evaluation (PhD); English (MA); foreign languages, cultures, and literatures (MA); higher education (PhD); higher education and student affairs (MA Ed); history (MA); human development (MS, PhD); material culture and public humanities (MA); philosophy (MA); political science (MA); rhetoric and writing (PhD); science and technology studies (MS, PhD); social, political, ethical, and cultural thought (PhD); sociology (MS, PhD); theater arts (MFA). *Faculty:* 408 full-time (204 women), 3 part-time/adjunct (2 women). *Students:* 657 full-time (446 women), 457 part-time (292 women); includes 213 minority (114 Black or African American, non-Hispanic/Latino; 3 American Indian or Alaska Native, non-Hispanic/Latino; 29 Asian, non-Hispanic/Latino; 44 Hispanic/Latino; 23 Two or more races, non-Hispanic/Latino), 93 international. Average age 33. 805 applicants, 55% accepted, 328 enrolled. In 2016, 270 master's, 91 doctorates awarded. *Degree requirements:* For master's, comprehensive exam (for some programs), thesis (for some programs); for doctorate, comprehensive exam (for some programs), thesis/dissertation (for some programs). *Entrance requirements:* For master's and doctorate, GRE/GMAT. Additional exam requirements/recommendations for international students: Required—TOEFL (minimum score 80 iBT). *Application deadline:* For fall admission, 8/1 for domestic students, 4/1 for international students; for spring admission, 1/1 for domestic students, 9/1 for international students. Applications are processed on a rolling basis. Application fee: $75. Electronic applications accepted. *Expenses:* Tuition, state resident: full-time $12,467; part-time $692.50 per credit hour. Tuition, nonresident: full-time $25,095; part-time $1394.25 per credit hour. *Required fees:* $2669; $491.50 per semester. Tuition and fees vary according to course load, campus/location and program. *Financial support:* In 2016–17, 21 research assistantships with full tuition reimbursements (averaging $19,817 per year), 237 teaching assistantships with full tuition reimbursements (averaging $15,497 per year) were awarded. Financial award application deadline: 3/1; financial award applicants required to submit FAFSA. *Total annual research expenditures:* $6.6 million. *Unit head:* Rosemary Blieszner, Interim Dean, 540-231-6779, Fax: 540-231-7157, E-mail: liberalartsdean@vt.edu. *Application contact:* Chelsea Blanchet, Executive Assistant, 540-231-6779, Fax: 540-231-7157, E-mail: bchels1@vt.edu.
Website: http://www.liberalarts.vt.edu/

Wagner College, Division of Graduate Studies, Education Department, Program in Secondary Education/Students with Disabilities, Staten Island, NY 10301-4495. Offers secondary education 7-12 (MS Ed), including language arts, languages other than English, mathematics and technology, science and technology, social studies. *Program availability:* Part-time, evening/weekend. *Degree requirements:* For master's, thesis (for some programs), completion of state certification exams before student teaching. *Entrance requirements:* For master's, minimum GPA of 3.0, interview, recommendations. Electronic applications accepted. Tuition and fees vary according to degree level.

Washington State University, College of Arts and Sciences, Department of Foreign Languages and Cultures, Pullman, WA 99164. Offers MA. Programs offered at the Pullman campus. *Degree requirements:* For master's, comprehensive exam (for some programs), thesis (for some programs), 4 written exams, oral exam, paper. *Entrance requirements:* For master's, three current letters of recommendation; all original transcripts including an official English translation; two writing samples; letter of application stating qualifications and personal goals; brief (3-5 minute) tape recordings of two informal dialogues between applicant and native speaker. Additional exam requirements/recommendations for international students: Required—TOEFL (minimum score 550 paper-based). Electronic applications accepted. *Faculty research:* Spanish and Latin American literature, film, and culture; pedagogy; computer-aided instruction.

Wayne State University, College of Education, Division of Teacher Education, Detroit, MI 48202. Offers art education (M Ed); bilingual/bicultural education (M Ed, Certificate); career and technical education (M Ed); curriculum and instruction (Ed D, PhD, Ed S), including art education (Ed D, PhD), bilingual education (Ed D, Ed S), career and technical education (MAT, Ed D, PhD, Ed S), early childhood education (MAT, Ed D, PhD, Ed S), elementary education, English as a second language (MAT, Ed D, Ed S), English education (MAT, Ed D, PhD, Ed S), foreign language education (MAT, Ed D, PhD), K-12 curriculum, mathematics education (MAT, Ed D, PhD, Ed S), science education (MAT, Ed D, PhD, Ed S), secondary education, social studies education (MAT, Ed D, PhD, Ed S); early childhood education (M Ed); elementary education (M Ed, MAT), including bilingual/bicultural education (MAT), early childhood education (MAT, Ed D, PhD, Ed S), English as a second language (MAT, Ed D, Ed S), general elementary education (MAT), mathematics education (MAT, Ed D, PhD, Ed S), science education (MAT, Ed D, PhD, Ed S), social studies education (MAT, Ed D, PhD, Ed S); English as a second language (Certificate); English education (M Ed); foreign language education (M Ed); mathematics education (M Ed); reading (M Ed, Ed S); reading, language and literature (Ed D); science education (M Ed); secondary education (MAT), including art education (K-12), bilingual/bicultural education, career and technical education (MAT, Ed D, PhD, Ed S), English as a second language (MAT, Ed D, Ed S), English education (MAT, Ed D, PhD, Ed S), foreign language education (MAT, Ed D, PhD), kinesiology, mathematics education (MAT, Ed D, PhD, Ed S); social studies education (M Ed); special education (M Ed, MAT, Ed D, PhD, Ed S), including autism spectrum disorders (MAT), cognitive development (MAT), emotional impairment (MAT), learning disabilities (MAT). *Program availability:* Part-time, blended/hybrid learning. *Faculty:* 29. *Students:* 106 full-time (73 women), 351 part-time (276 women); includes 115 minority (76 Black or African American, non-Hispanic/Latino; 10 Asian, non-Hispanic/Latino; 20 Hispanic/Latino; 1 Native Hawaiian or other Pacific Islander, non-Hispanic/Latino; 8 Two or more races, non-Hispanic/Latino), 12 international. Average age 37. 242 applicants, 37% accepted, 72 enrolled. In 2016, 178 master's, 19 doctorates, 17 other advanced degrees awarded. *Degree requirements:* For master's, essay or project (for some M Ed programs), professional field experience (for MAT programs); for doctorate, thesis/dissertation. *Entrance requirements:* For master's, Michigan Test for Teacher Certification, verification of participation in group work with children, Michigan State Police criminal background check; for doctorate, minimum undergraduate GPA of 3.0, graduate 3.5; interview; curriculum vitae; references. Additional exam requirements/recommendations for international students: Required—TOEFL (minimum score 550 paper-based; 79 iBT), TWE (minimum score 5.5), Michigan English Language Assessment Battery (minimum score 85); Recommended—IELTS (minimum score 6.5). *Application deadline:* For fall admission, 6/1 priority date for domestic students, 5/1 priority date for international students; for winter admission, 10/1 priority date for domestic students, 9/1 priority date for international students; for spring admission, 2/1 priority date for domestic students, 1/1 priority date for international students. Applications are processed on a rolling basis. Application fee: $50. Electronic applications accepted. *Expenses:* $16,503 per year resident tuition and fees, $33,697 per year non-resident tuition and fees. *Financial support:* In 2016–17, 101 students received support, including 3 fellowships (averaging $11,409 per year); research assistantships with tuition reimbursements available, Federal Work-Study, scholarships/grants, and unspecified assistantships also available. Support available to part-time students. Financial award applicants required to submit FAFSA. *Faculty research:* Improving students' skill achievement in mathematics, improving elementary children's understanding of informational text, teachers' use of their pedagogical and mathematical knowledge in the interactive work of teaching, the intersection of identity construction in teaching and learning, identifying effective methods of literacy instruction and assessments for bilingual students in elementary language arts classrooms. *Unit head:* Dr. Kathleen Crawford-McKinney, Assistant Dean, 313-577-0122. *Application contact:* Janice Green, Assistant Dean, 313-577-1605, E-mail: jwgreen@wayne.edu.
Website: http://coe.wayne.edu/ted/index.php

Wayne State University, College of Liberal Arts and Sciences, Department of Classical and Modern Languages, Literatures, and Cultures, Detroit, MI 48202. Offers classics (MA), including ancient Greek and Latin, ancient studies, classics, Latin; German (MA); language learning (MALL), including Arabic (MA, MALL), French (MA, MALL, PhD), German (MALL, PhD), Italian (MA, MALL), Spanish (MA, MALL, PhD); modern languages (PhD), including French (MA, MALL, PhD), German (MALL, PhD), Spanish (MA, MALL, PhD); Near Eastern languages (MA), including Arabic (MA, MALL), Hebrew; Romance languages (MA), including French (MA, MALL, PhD), Italian (MA, MALL), Spanish (MA, MALL, PhD). *Faculty:* 26. *Students:* 25 full-time (20 women), 14 part-time (8 women); includes 7 minority (2 Black or African American, non-Hispanic/Latino; 1 American Indian or Alaska Native, non-Hispanic/Latino; 1 Asian, non-Hispanic/Latino; 2 Hispanic/Latino; 1 Two or more races, non-Hispanic/Latino), 3 international. Average age 35. 29 applicants, 31% accepted, 5 enrolled. In 2016, 15 master's, 5 doctorates awarded. *Degree requirements:* For master's, variable foreign language requirement, comprehensive exam (for some programs), thesis (for some programs); for doctorate, one foreign language, comprehensive exam, thesis/dissertation. *Entrance requirements:* For master's, GRE (for some programs); for doctorate, GRE. Additional exam requirements/recommendations for international students: Required—TOEFL (minimum score 550 paper-based; 79 iBT), TWE (minimum score 5.5), Michigan English Language Assessment Battery (minimum score 85); Recommended—IELTS (minimum score 6.5). Application fee: $50. Electronic applications accepted. *Expenses:* $16,503 per year resident tuition and fees, $33,697 per year non-resident tuition and fees. *Financial support:* In 2016–17, 22 students received support, including 4 fellowships with tuition reimbursements available (averaging $13,500 per year), 17 teaching assistantships with tuition reimbursements available (averaging $17,994 per year); research assistantships, scholarships/grants, and unspecified assistantships also available. Financial award applicants required to submit FAFSA. *Faculty research:* Classical and modern literature and culture (Greek, Latin, Arabic, Chinese, French, German, Russian, Spanish) including colonial studies and exile and Holocaust studies; critical theory (French, German, Slavic, Spanish); theoretical and applied linguistics (Arabic, Chinese, French, Spanish); area studies (Arabic, Near Eastern, classical, Islamic, and Judaic studies). *Unit head:* Dr. Anne Duggan, Department Chair, 313-577-6244, Fax: 313-577-6243, E-mail: a.duggan@wayne.edu.
Website: http://clas.wayne.edu/languages/

West Chester University of Pennsylvania, College of Arts and Humanities, Department of Languages and Cultures, West Chester, PA 19383. Offers French

(Teaching Certificate); German (Teaching Certificate); languages and cultures (MA), including French, German, Spanish; Spanish (Teaching Certificate). *Program availability:* Part-time, evening/weekend, minimal on-campus study. *Faculty:* 12 full-time (9 women). *Students:* 7 full-time (6 women), 26 part-time (23 women); includes 7 minority (all Hispanic/Latino). Average age 31. 14 applicants, 100% accepted, 11 enrolled. In 2016, 8 master's, 2 other advanced degrees awarded. *Degree requirements:* For master's, one foreign language, comprehensive exam, portfolio, exit exam, capstone project; for Teaching Certificate, one foreign language. *Entrance requirements:* For master's and Teaching Certificate, ACTFL OPI and WPT, undergraduate major or equivalent. Additional exam requirements/recommendations for international students: Required—TOEFL or IELTS. *Application deadline:* For fall admission, 5/15 for international students; for spring admission, 10/15 for international students. Applications are processed on a rolling basis. Application fee: $45. Electronic applications accepted. *Expenses:* Tuition, state resident: full-time $8694; part-time $483 per credit. Tuition, nonresident: full-time $13,050; part-time $725 per credit. *Required fees:* $2399; $119.05 per credit. Tuition and fees vary according to campus/location and program. *Financial support:* Scholarships/grants and unspecified assistantships available. Financial award application deadline: 2/15; financial award applicants required to submit FAFSA. *Faculty research:* Language structure, literature, film, culture, pedagogy, technology. *Unit head:* Dr. Jerome Williams, Interim Chair, 610-436-2700, Fax: 610-436-3048, E-mail: isanchez@wcupa.edu. *Application contact:* Dr. Rebecca Pauly, Graduate Coordinator, 610-436-4746, Fax: 610-436-3048, E-mail: mvanliew@wcupa.edu.
Website: http://www.wcupa.edu/arts-humanities/languagesCultures/

Western Kentucky University, Graduate Studies, Potter College of Arts and Letters, Department of Modern Languages, Bowling Green, KY 42101. Offers French (MA Ed); German (MA Ed); Spanish (MA Ed).

Worcester State University, Graduate Studies, Program in Spanish, Worcester, MA 01602-2597. Offers MA. *Program availability:* Part-time. *Faculty:* 3 full-time (1 woman). *Students:* 14 part-time (11 women); includes 7 minority (all Hispanic/Latino). Average age 40. 7 applicants, 86% accepted, 4 enrolled. In 2016, 5 master's awarded. *Degree requirements:* For master's, one foreign language, thesis or comprehensive exam. *Entrance requirements:* For master's, GRE, MAT, BA in Spanish or related field and/or interview with faculty member. Additional exam requirements/recommendations for international students: Required—TOEFL (minimum score 550 paper-based; 79 iBT). *Application deadline:* For fall admission, 6/15 for domestic and international students; for spring admission, 11/1 for domestic and international students; for summer admission, 3/1 for domestic students, 4/1 for international students. Applications are processed on a rolling basis. Application fee: $50. Electronic applications accepted. *Expenses:* Tuition, state resident: part-time $150 per credit. Tuition, nonresident: part-time $150 per credit. *Financial support:* Career-related internships or fieldwork, scholarships/grants, and unspecified assistantships available. Financial award application deadline: 3/1; financial award applicants required to submit FAFSA. *Unit head:* Dr. Ana Perez-Manrique, Program Coordinator, 508-929-8577, E-mail: aperezmanrique@worcester.edu. *Application contact:* Sara Grady, Associate Dean, Graduate Studies and Professional Development, 508-929-8787, Fax: 508-929-8100, E-mail: sara.grady@worcester.edu.

Health Education

Adelphi University, Ruth S. Ammon School of Education, Program in Health Studies, Garden City, NY 11530-0701. Offers community health education (MA, Certificate); school health education (MA). *Program availability:* Part-time, evening/weekend. *Students:* 5 full-time (3 women), 22 part-time (12 women); includes 5 minority (1 Black or African American, non-Hispanic/Latino; 4 Hispanic/Latino). Average age 30. 11 applicants, 82% accepted, 8 enrolled. In 2016, 15 master's, 2 other advanced degrees awarded. *Degree requirements:* For master's, internship. *Entrance requirements:* For master's, 3 letters of recommendation, resume, minimum cumulative GPA of 2.75. Additional exam requirements/recommendations for international students: Required—TOEFL (minimum score 550 paper-based; 80 iBT), IELTS (minimum score 6.5). *Application deadline:* For fall admission, 4/1 for international students; for spring admission, 11/1 for international students. Applications are processed on a rolling basis. Application fee: $50. Electronic applications accepted. *Expenses:* Contact institution. *Financial support:* Research assistantships with partial tuition reimbursements, teaching assistantships, career-related internships or fieldwork, institutionally sponsored loans, scholarships/grants, traineeships, and unspecified assistantships available. Support available to part-time students. Financial award application deadline: 2/15; financial award applicants required to submit FAFSA. *Faculty research:* Alcohol abuse, tobacco cessation, drug abuse, healthy family lives, healthy personal living. *Unit head:* Dr. Ronald Feingold, Director, 516-877-4764, E-mail: feingold@adelphi.edu. *Application contact:* Christine Murphy, Director of Admissions, 516-877-3050, Fax: 516-877-3039, E-mail: graduateadmissions@adelphi.edu.

Alabama State University, College of Education, Department of Health, Physical Education, and Recreation, Montgomery, AL 36101-0271. Offers health education (M Ed); physical education (M Ed). *Program availability:* Part-time. *Students:* 6 full-time (3 women), 11 part-time (4 women); includes 16 minority (all Black or African American, non-Hispanic/Latino). Average age 29. 7 applicants, 71% accepted, 5 enrolled. In 2016, 3 master's awarded. *Degree requirements:* For master's, comprehensive exam. *Entrance requirements:* For master's, GRE General Test, MAT, writing competency test, bachelor's degree or its equivalent from accredited college or university with minimum GPA of 2.5. Additional exam requirements/recommendations for international students: Required—TOEFL (minimum score 500 paper-based). *Application deadline:* For fall admission, 4/15 for domestic and international students; for spring admission, 11/15 for domestic and international students; for summer admission, 3/15 for domestic and international students. Applications are processed on a rolling basis. Application fee: $25. Electronic applications accepted. *Expenses:* Tuition, state resident: full-time $3087; part-time $2744 per credit. Tuition, nonresident: full-time $6174; part-time $5488 per credit. *Required fees:* $2284; $1142 per credit. $571 per semester. Tuition and fees vary according to class time, course level, course load, degree level, program and student level. *Financial support:* Research assistantships available. Financial award application deadline: 6/30; financial award applicants required to submit FAFSA. *Faculty research:* Risk factors for heart disease in the college-age population, cardiovascular reactivity for the Cold Pressor Test. *Unit head:* Dr. Charlie Gibbons, Interim Chair, 334-229-4504, Fax: 334-229-4928, E-mail: cgibbons@alasu.edu. *Application contact:* Dr. William Person, Dean of Graduate Studies, 334-229-4274, Fax: 334-229-4928, E-mail: wperson@alasu.edu.
Website: http://www.alasu.edu/academics/colleges—departments/college-of-education/health-physical-education—recreation/index.aspx

Albany State University, College of Education, Albany, GA 31705-2717. Offers early childhood education (M Ed); educational leadership (Ed S); health and physical education (M Ed); middle grades education (M Ed); school counseling (M Ed); special education (M Ed). *Accreditation:* NCATE. *Program availability:* Part-time, evening/weekend, online learning. *Degree requirements:* For master's, comprehensive exam, internship, GACE Content Exam. *Entrance requirements:* For master's, GRE or MAT. *Application deadline:* For fall admission, 6/1 for domestic students, 5/1 for international students; for spring admission, 11/1 for domestic students, 10/1 for international students. Applications are processed on a rolling basis. Application fee: $20. Electronic applications accepted. *Financial support:* Scholarships/grants available. Financial award application deadline: 4/15; financial award applicants required to submit FAFSA. *Faculty research:* GACE preparation, STEM (science, technology, engineering, and mathematics), technology education, special education, professional teacher development, health implications liberation philosophy, NET-Q, learning community, disabled or at-risk students. *Unit head:* Dr. Rhonda C. Porter, Interim Dean, 229-430-1718, Fax: 229-430-4993. *Application contact:* Jeffrey Pierce, II, Graduate Admissions Counselor, 229-430-4646, Fax: 229-430-4105, E-mail: jeffrey.pierce@asurams.edu.
Website: https://www.asurams.edu/Academics/collegeofeducation/

Alcorn State University, School of Graduate Studies, School of Psychology and Education, Lorman, MS 39096-7500. Offers agricultural education (MS Ed); elementary education (MS Ed, Ed S); guidance and counseling (MS Ed); industrial education (MS Ed); secondary education (MS Ed), including health and physical education; special education (MS Ed). *Accreditation:* NCATE. *Degree requirements:* For master's, thesis optional.

Allen College, Graduate Programs, Waterloo, IA 50703. Offers adult-gerontology acute care nurse practitioner (MSN); community/public health nursing (MSN); family nurse practitioner (MSN); health sciences (Ed D); leadership in health care delivery (MSN); nursing (DNP); occupational therapy (MS). *Accreditation:* AACN; ACEN. *Program availability:* Part-time, blended/hybrid learning. *Faculty:* 9 full-time (all women), 24 part-time/adjunct (23 women). *Students:* 71 full-time (60 women), 171 part-time (148 women); includes 12 minority (6 Black or African American, non-Hispanic/Latino; 1 American Indian or Alaska Native, non-Hispanic/Latino; 2 Hispanic/Latino; 3 Two or more races, non-Hispanic/Latino), 3 international. Average age 34. 291 applicants, 59% accepted, 109 enrolled. In 2016, 49 master's, 2 doctorates awarded. *Entrance requirements:* For master's, minimum GPA of 3.0 in the last 60 hours of undergraduate coursework; for doctorate, minimum GPA of 3.25 in graduate coursework. *Application deadline:* For fall admission, 2/1 priority date for domestic students; for spring admission, 9/1 priority date for domestic students. Applications are processed on a rolling basis. Application fee: $50. Electronic applications accepted. *Expenses:* $797 per credit hour tuition, $51 per credit hour lab fees, $28 per credit hour student services fee. *Financial support:* In 2016–17, 99 students received support. Institutionally sponsored loans, scholarships/grants, and traineeships available. Support available to part-time students. Financial award application deadline: 8/15; financial award applicants required to submit FAFSA. *Unit head:* Dr. Nancy Kramer, Vice Chancellor for Academic Affairs, 319-226-2040, Fax: 319-226-2070, E-mail: nancy.kramer@allencollege.edu. *Application contact:* Molly Quinn, Director of Admissions, 319-226-2001, Fax: 319-226-2010, E-mail: molly.quinn@allencollege.edu.
Website: http://www.allencollege.edu/

American University, College of Arts and Sciences, Department of Health Studies, Program in Nutrition Education, Washington, DC 20016-8001. Offers MS, Certificate. *Program availability:* Part-time, online only, 100% online. *Students:* 79 part-time (72 women); includes 4 minority (2 Black or African American, non-Hispanic/Latino; 1 American Indian or Alaska Native, non-Hispanic/Latino; 1 Hispanic/Latino), 1 international. Average age 34. 59 applicants, 93% accepted, 38 enrolled. In 2016, 9 master's awarded. *Entrance requirements:* For master's, GRE; for Certificate, statement of purpose, transcripts, resume. Additional exam requirements/recommendations for international students: Required—TOEFL (minimum score 100 iBT), IELTS (minimum score 7), PTE (minimum score 68). Application fee: $55. *Expenses:* $1,579 per credit hour tuition; $690 mandatory fees. *Financial support:* Applicants required to submit FAFSA. *Unit head:* Dr. Anastasia Snelling, Chair, Department of Health Studies, 202-885-6278, Fax: 202-885-1187, E-mail: stacey@american.edu. *Application contact:* Kathleen Clowery, Associate Director, Graduate Enrollment Management, 202-885-3620, Fax: 202-885-1344, E-mail: clowery@american.edu.
Website: http://www.american.edu/cas/nutrition/nutrition-education-ms.cfm

Arcadia University, College of Health Sciences, Department of Public Health, Program in Health Education, Glenside, PA 19038-3295. Offers MSHE. *Program availability:* Part-time, evening/weekend. *Students:* 5 part-time (all women); Includes 2 minority (both Black or African American, non-Hispanic/Latino). Average age 32. 3 applicants, 67% accepted, 1 enrolled. In 2016, 3 master's awarded. *Application deadline:* Applications are processed on a rolling basis. Application fee: $50. *Expenses:* Contact institution. *Financial support:* Tuition waivers (partial) and unspecified assistantships available. *Unit head:* Dr. Andrea Crivelli-Kovach, Chair, 215-572-4014, E-mail: crivella@arcadia.edu. *Application contact:* 215-572-2910, Fax: 215-572-4049, E-mail: admiss@arcadia.edu.
Website: http://www.arcadia.edu/academic/master-of-health-education/

Arizona State University at the Tempe campus, College of Health Solutions, Program in Behavioral Health, Phoenix, AZ 85004-2135. Offers DBH. *Program availability:* Part-time, evening/weekend, online learning. *Degree requirements:* For doctorate, thesis/dissertation or alternative, 16 hours/week practicum (400 hours total), applied research paper focused on design, implementation and evaluation of a clinical intervention in primary care or related setting, interactive Program of Study (iPOS) submitted before completing 50 percent of required credit hours. *Entrance requirements:* For doctorate, minimum GPA of 3.0 or equivalent in last 2 years of work leading to bachelor's degree; 3 professional reference letters; copy of current clinical license(s) to practice behavioral health; interview. Additional exam requirements/recommendations for international students: Required—TOEFL, IELTS, or PTE. Electronic applications accepted. *Expenses:* Contact institution.

Arkansas State University, Graduate School, College of Nursing and Health Professions, School of Nursing, State University, AR 72467. Offers aging studies (Graduate Certificate); health care management (Graduate Certificate); health sciences (MS); health sciences education (Graduate Certificate); nurse anesthesia (MSN);

nursing (MSN); nursing practice (DNP). *Accreditation:* AANA/CANAEP (one or more programs are accredited); ACEN. *Program availability:* Part-time. *Degree requirements:* For master's and Graduate Certificate, comprehensive exam, thesis or alternative; for doctorate, comprehensive exam, thesis/dissertation. *Entrance requirements:* For master's, GRE General Test or MAT, appropriate bachelor's degree, current Arkansas nursing license, CPR certification, physical examination, professional liability insurance, critical care experience, ACLS Certification, PALS Certification, interview, immunization records, personal goal statement, health assessment; for doctorate, GRE or MAT, NCLEX-RN Exam, appropriate master's degree, current Arkansas nursing license, CPR certification, physical examination, professional liability insurance, critical care experience, ACLS Certification, PALS Certification, interview, immunization records, personal goal statement, health assessment, TB skin test, background check; for Graduate Certificate, GRE or MAT, appropriate bachelor's degree, official transcripts, immunization records, proof of employment in healthcare, TB Skin Test, TB Mask Fit Test, CPR Certification. Additional exam requirements/recommendations for international students: Required—TOEFL (minimum score 550 paper-based; 79 iBT), IELTS (minimum score 6), PTE (minimum score 56). Electronic applications accepted. *Expenses:* Contact institution.

Auburn University, Graduate School, College of Education, Department of Kinesiology, Auburn University, AL 36849. Offers exercise science (M Ed). *Accreditation:* NCATE. *Program availability:* Part-time. *Faculty:* 18 full-time (9 women), 1 part-time/adjunct (0 women). *Students:* 96 full-time (57 women), 28 part-time (11 women); includes 132 minority (114 Black or African American, non-Hispanic/Latino; 2 American Indian or Alaska Native, non-Hispanic/Latino; 4 Asian, non-Hispanic/Latino; 6 Hispanic/Latino; 1 Native Hawaiian or other Pacific Islander, non-Hispanic/Latino; 5 Two or more races, non-Hispanic/Latino), 14 international. Average age 26. 127 applicants, 66% accepted, 53 enrolled. In 2016, 63 master's, 4 doctorates, 1 other advanced degree awarded. *Degree requirements:* For master's, thesis (for some programs); for doctorate, thesis/dissertation; for Ed S, exam, field project. *Entrance requirements:* For master's, GRE General Test; for doctorate and Ed S, GRE General Test, interview, master's degree. *Application deadline:* Applications are processed on a rolling basis. Application fee: $50 ($60 for international students). Electronic applications accepted. *Expenses:* Tuition, state resident: full-time $9072; part-time $504 per credit hour. Tuition, nonresident: full-time $27,216; part-time $1512 per credit hour. *Required fees:* $812 per semester. Tuition and fees vary according to degree level and program. *Financial support:* Research assistantships, teaching assistantships, and Federal Work-Study available. Support available to part-time students. Financial award application deadline: 3/15; financial award applicants required to submit FAFSA. *Faculty research:* Biomechanics, exercise physiology, motor skill learning, school health, curriculum development. *Unit head:* Dr. Mary E. Rudisill, Director, 334-844-1458. *Application contact:* Dr. George Flowers, Dean of the Graduate School, 334-844-2125.

Austin Peay State University, College of Graduate Studies, College of Behavioral and Health Sciences, Department of Health and Human Performance, Clarksville, TN 37044. Offers public health education (MS); sports and wellness leadership (MS). *Program availability:* Part-time, evening/weekend, online learning. *Faculty:* 7 full-time (4 women). *Students:* 22 full-time (8 women), 36 part-time (26 women); includes 16 minority (10 Black or African American, non-Hispanic/Latino; 1 Asian, non-Hispanic/Latino; 2 Hispanic/Latino; 3 Two or more races, non-Hispanic/Latino), 2 international. Average age 29. 79 applicants, 70% accepted, 43 enrolled. In 2016, 27 master's awarded. *Degree requirements:* For master's, comprehensive exam, thesis optional. *Entrance requirements:* For master's, GRE General Test, 3 letters of recommendation, minimum undergraduate GPA of 2.5. Additional exam requirements/recommendations for international students: Required—TOEFL (minimum score 500 paper-based). *Application deadline:* For fall admission, 8/9 priority date for domestic students. Applications are processed on a rolling basis. Application fee: $45 ($50 for international students). Electronic applications accepted. *Expenses:* Tuition, state resident: full-time $8300; part-time $415 per credit hour. Tuition, nonresident: full-time $22,280; part-time $1114 per credit hour. *Required fees:* $1473; $73.65 per credit hour. *Financial support:* Research assistantships with full tuition reimbursements, career-related internships or fieldwork, Federal Work-Study, institutionally sponsored loans, scholarships/grants, and unspecified assistantships available. Support available to part-time students. Financial award application deadline: 4/1; financial award applicants required to submit FAFSA. *Unit head:* Dr. Marcy Maurer, Chair, 931-221-6105, Fax: 931-221-7040, E-mail: maurerm@apsu.edu. *Application contact:* Brad Averitt, Coordinator of Graduate Admissions, 800-859-4723, Fax: 931-221-7641, E-mail: gradadmissions@apsu.edu. Website: http://www.apsu.edu/hhp/

Baldwin Wallace University, Graduate Programs, Public Health Program, Berea, OH 44017-2088. Offers health education and disease prevention (MPH); population health leadership and management (MPH). Program offered in partnership with The MetroHealth System. *Program availability:* Part-time, evening/weekend, online learning. *Faculty:* 1 full-time (0 women), 2 part-time/adjunct (0 women). *Students:* 16 full-time (13 women), 1 (woman) part-time; includes 6 minority (2 Black or African American, non-Hispanic/Latino; 2 Asian, non-Hispanic/Latino; 2 Hispanic/Latino). Average age 41. 27 applicants, 85% accepted, 17 enrolled. *Entrance requirements:* For master's, GRE. Additional exam requirements/recommendations for international students: Required—TOEFL (minimum score 550 paper-based; 100 iBT). Electronic applications accepted. *Financial support:* Applicants required to submit FAFSA. *Unit head:* Stephen D. Stahl, Provost, Academic Affairs, 440-826-2251, Fax: 440-826-2329, E-mail: sstahl@bw.edu. *Application contact:* Winifred W. Gerhardt, Director of Transfer, Adult and Graduate Admission, 440-826-8002, E-mail: wgerhard@bw.edu.
Website: http://www.bw.edu/academics/master-public-health/

Baylor University, Graduate School, Robbins College of Health and Human Sciences, Department of Health, Human Performance and Recreation, Waco, TX 76798. Offers MPH, MS, PhD. *Accreditation:* NCATE. *Program availability:* Part-time. *Faculty:* 13 full-time (5 women), 3 part-time/adjunct (1 woman). *Students:* 71 full-time (43 women), 16 part-time (7 women); includes 18 minority (5 Black or African American, non-Hispanic/Latino; 3 Asian, non-Hispanic/Latino; 6 Hispanic/Latino; 4 Two or more races, non-Hispanic/Latino), 7 international. 109 applicants, 59% accepted, 44 enrolled. In 2016, 31 master's, 1 doctorate awarded. *Degree requirements:* For master's, comprehensive exam, thesis optional; for doctorate, comprehensive exam, thesis/dissertation. *Entrance requirements:* For master's and doctorate, GRE General Test. Additional exam requirements/recommendations for international students: Required—TOEFL (minimum score 550 paper-based; 80 iBT). *Application deadline:* For fall admission, 2/1 priority date for domestic students, 2/1 for international students; for spring admission, 10/1 for domestic and international students. Applications are processed on a rolling basis. Application fee: $25. Electronic applications accepted. *Expenses: Tuition:* Full-time $28,494; part-time $1583 per credit hour. *Required fees:* $167 per credit hour. Tuition and fees vary according to course load and program. *Financial support:* In 2016–17, 60 students received support, including 1 research assistantship with full tuition reimbursement available (averaging $12,700 per year), 33 teaching assistantships with full tuition reimbursements available (averaging $7,650 per year); career-related internships or fieldwork, Federal Work-Study, institutionally sponsored loans, scholarships/grants, tuition waivers (full), and unspecified assistantships also available. Financial award application deadline: 2/1. *Faculty research:* Behavior change theory, nutrition and enzyme therapy, exercise testing, health planning. *Unit head:* Dr. Jaeho Shim, Graduate Program Director, 254-710-4009, Fax: 254-710-3527, E-mail: joe_shim@baylor.edu. *Application contact:* Kathy Mirick, Administrative Assistant, 254-710-3526, Fax: 254-710-3527, E-mail: kathy_mirick@baylor.edu.
Website: http://www.baylor.edu/HHPR/

Benedictine University, Graduate Programs, Program in Public Health, Lisle, IL 60532. Offers administration of health care institutions (MPH); dietetics (MPH); disaster management (MPH); health education (MPH); health information systems (MPH); MBA/MPH; MPH/MS. *Accreditation:* CEPH. *Program availability:* Part-time, evening/weekend, online learning. *Students:* 89 full-time (72 women), 462 part-time (358 women); includes 129 minority (61 Black or African American, non-Hispanic/Latino; 5 American Indian or Alaska Native, non-Hispanic/Latino; 51 Asian, non-Hispanic/Latino; 11 Hispanic/Latino; 1 Native Hawaiian or other Pacific Islander, non-Hispanic/Latino), 12 international. 195 applicants, 86% accepted, 143 enrolled. In 2016, 190 master's awarded. *Entrance requirements:* For master's, MAT, GRE, or GMAT. Additional exam requirements/recommendations for international students: Required—TOEFL (minimum score 550 paper-based). *Application deadline:* For fall admission, 9/1 for domestic students; for winter admission, 12/1 for domestic students; for spring admission, 2/15 for domestic students. Application fee: $40. *Expenses: Tuition:* Full-time $15,600; part-time $650 per hour. *Required fees:* $300. One-time fee: $125 part-time. Tuition and fees vary according to class time, course load, campus/location and program. *Financial support:* Career-related internships or fieldwork and health care benefits available. Support available to part-time students. *Unit head:* Dr. Georgeen Polyak, Director, 630-829-6217, E-mail: gpolyak@ben.edu. *Application contact:* Kari Gibbons, Associate Vice President, Enrollment Center, 630-829-6200, Fax: 630-829-6584, E-mail: kgibbons@ben.edu.

Brandeis University, The Heller School for Social Policy and Management, Program in Social Policy, Waltham, MA 02454-9110. Offers assets and inequalities (PhD); children, youth and families (PhD); global health and development (PhD); health and behavioral health (PhD). *Degree requirements:* For doctorate, comprehensive exam, thesis/dissertation, qualifying paper, 2-year residency. *Entrance requirements:* For doctorate, GRE General Test, 3 letters of recommendation, statement of purpose, writing sample, at least 3-5 years of professional experience. Additional exam requirements/recommendations for international students: Required—TOEFL (minimum score 600 paper-based; 100 iBT). Electronic applications accepted. *Faculty research:* Health; mental health; substance abuse; children, youth, and families; aging; international and community development; disabilities; work and inequality; hunger and poverty.

California Baptist University, Program in Public Health, Riverside, CA 92504-3206. Offers health education and promotion (MPH); health policy and administration (MPH). *Program availability:* Part-time, evening/weekend. *Faculty:* 10 full-time (6 women), 4 part-time/adjunct (3 women). *Students:* 48 full-time (40 women), 27 part-time (23 women); includes 58 minority (8 Black or African American, non-Hispanic/Latino; 4 Asian, non-Hispanic/Latino; 40 Hispanic/Latino; 6 Two or more races, non-Hispanic/Latino). Average age 28. 61 applicants, 75% accepted, 28 enrolled. *Degree requirements:* For master's, capstone project; practicum. *Entrance requirements:* For master's, minimum undergraduate GPA of 2.75, two recommendations, 500-word essay, resume. Additional exam requirements/recommendations for international students: Required—TOEFL (minimum score 80 iBT). *Application deadline:* For fall admission, 8/1 priority date for domestic students, 7/1 for international students; for spring admission, 12/1 priority date for domestic students, 11/1 for international students. Applications are processed on a rolling basis. Application fee: $45. Electronic applications accepted. *Expenses:* Contact institution. *Financial support:* In 2016–17, 22 students received support. Federal Work-Study and scholarships/grants available. Financial award applicants required to submit CSS PROFILE or FAFSA. *Faculty research:* Epidemiology, statistical education, exercise and immunity, obesity and chronic disease. *Unit head:* Dr. David Pearson, Dean, College of Health Science, 951-343-4298, E-mail: dpearson@calbaptist.edu. *Application contact:* Dr. Robert LaChausse, Chair, Department of Public Health Sciences, 951-552-8484, E-mail: rlachausse@calbaptist.edu.
Website: http://www.calbaptist.edu/explore-cbu/schools-colleges/college-allied-health/health-sciences/master-public-health/

California Institute of Integral Studies, School of Professional Psychology and Health, San Francisco, CA 94103. Offers clinical psychology (Psy D); community mental health (MA); drama therapy (MA); expressive arts therapy (MA); human sexuality (PhD); integral counseling psychology (MA); integrative health studies (MA); psychological studies (MA); somatic psychology (MA). *Program availability:* Part-time, evening/weekend, 100% online, blended/hybrid learning. *Students:* 526 full-time (408 women), 113 part-time (96 women); includes 173 minority (34 Black or African American, non-Hispanic/Latino; 5 American Indian or Alaska Native, non-Hispanic/Latino; 31 Asian, non-Hispanic/Latino; 58 Hispanic/Latino; 1 Native Hawaiian or other Pacific Islander, non-Hispanic/Latino; 44 Two or more races, non-Hispanic/Latino), 52 international. Average age 38. 319 applicants, 85% accepted, 164 enrolled. In 2016, 157 master's, 21 doctorates awarded. *Degree requirements:* For doctorate, comprehensive exam, thesis/dissertation. *Entrance requirements:* For master's, minimum GPA of 3.0, letters of recommendation, writing sample; for doctorate, GRE, MA in psychology or social work with appropriate practical experience for advanced standing, or BA with a minimum GPA of 3.1; letters of recommendation; writing sample. Additional exam requirements/recommendations for international students: Required—TOEFL. *Application deadline:* For fall admission, 2/1 priority date for domestic and international students; for spring admission, 10/15 priority date for domestic and international students. Applications are processed on a rolling basis. Application fee: $65. Electronic applications accepted. *Expenses: Tuition:* Full-time $19,728; part-time $1098 per semester hour. *Required fees:* $320; $320 per semester hour. *Financial support:* Research assistantships with tuition reimbursements, teaching assistantships with tuition reimbursements, career-related internships or fieldwork, Federal Work-Study, and scholarships/grants available. Support available to part-time students. Financial award application deadline: 4/15; financial award applicants required to submit FAFSA. *Faculty research:* Transpersonal psychology, somatic psychology, expressive arts therapy, drama therapy, community mental health, ecopsychology, integrative health, human sexuality. *Application contact:* Ellen Durst, Director of Admissions, 415-575-6100, Fax: 415-575-1268, E-mail: admissions@ciis.edu.

California State University, Long Beach, Graduate Studies, College of Health and Human Services, Department of Health Science, Long Beach, CA 90840. Offers MPH. *Accreditation:* CEPH; NCATE. *Program availability:* Part-time. *Degree requirements:* For master's, thesis optional. *Entrance requirements:* For master's, GRE, minimum GPA of 3.0 in last 60 units. *Application deadline:* For fall admission, 3/1 for domestic students. Applications are processed on a rolling basis. Application fee: $55. Electronic applications accepted. *Financial support:* Federal Work-Study, institutionally sponsored loans, and scholarships/grants available. Financial award application deadline: 3/2. *Unit head:* Javier Lopez-Zetina, Chair, 562-985-4057.

California State University, Northridge, Graduate Studies, The Tseng College of Extended Learning, Northridge, CA 91330. Offers business administration (Graduate Certificate); health administration (MPA); health education (MPH); knowledge management (MKM); music industry administration (MA); nonprofit-sector management (Graduate Certificate); public administration (MPA); public sector management and leadership (MPA); social work (MSW); taxation (MS); tourism, hospitality and recreation management (MS). *Faculty:* 55 part-time/adjunct (28 women). *Students:* 1 (woman) full-time, 1 (woman) part-time. Average age 40. *Entrance requirements:* For master's, GRE (if cumulative undergraduate GPA less than 3.0). *Expenses:* Tuition, state resident: full-time $4152. *Unit head:* Joyce Feucht-Haviar, Dean, 866-873-6439.

See Display on page 1665 and Close-Up on page 1687.

California State University, San Marcos, College of Education, Health and Human Services, Department of Social Work, San Marcos, CA 92096-0001. Offers behavioral health (MSW); children, youth and families (MSW). *Accreditation:* CSWE. *Degree requirements:* For master's, thesis, capstone project. *Expenses:* Contact institution.

Cambridge College, School of Education, Cambridge, MA 02138-5304. Offers autism specialist (M Ed); autism/behavior analyst (M Ed); behavior analyst (Post-Master's Certificate); behavioral management (M Ed); early childhood teacher (M Ed); education specialist in curriculum and instruction (CAGS); educational leadership (Ed D); elementary teacher (M Ed); English as a second language (M Ed, Certificate); general science (M Ed); health education (Post-Master's Certificate); health/family and consumer sciences (M Ed); history (M Ed); individualized (M Ed); information technology literacy (M Ed); instructional technology (M Ed); interdisciplinary studies (M Ed); library teacher (M Ed); literacy education (M Ed); mathematics (M Ed); mathematics specialist (Certificate); middle school mathematics and science (M Ed); school administration (M Ed, CAGS); school guidance counselor (M Ed); school nurse education (M Ed); school social worker/school adjustment counselor (M Ed); special education administrator (CAGS); special education/moderate disabilities (M Ed); teaching skills and methodologies (M Ed). *Program availability:* Part-time, evening/weekend, online learning. *Degree requirements:* For master's, thesis, internship/practicum (licensure program only); for doctorate, thesis/dissertation; for other advanced degree, thesis. *Entrance requirements:* For master's, interview, resume, documentation of licensure, 2 professional references; for doctorate, official transcripts, interview, resume, documentation of licensure (if any), written personal statement/essay, portfolio of scholarly and professional work, qualifying assessment, 2 professional references, health insurance, immunizations form; for other advanced degree, official transcripts, interview, resume, documentation of licensure (if any), written personal statement/essay, 2 professional references, health insurance, immunizations form. Additional exam requirements/recommendations for international students: Required—TOEFL (minimum score 550 paper-based; 79 iBT), Michigan English Language Assessment Battery (minimum score 85); Recommended—IELTS (minimum score 6). Electronic applications accepted. *Expenses:* Contact institution. *Faculty research:* Adult education, accelerated learning, mathematics education, brain compatible learning, special education and law.

Central Washington University, Graduate Studies and Research, College of Education and Professional Studies, Department of Physical Education, School and Public Health, Ellensburg, WA 98926. Offers athletic administration (MS); health and physical education (MS). *Program availability:* Part-time. *Degree requirements:* For master's, comprehensive exam, thesis or alternative. *Entrance requirements:* For master's, minimum GPA of 3.0. Additional exam requirements/recommendations for international students: Required—TOEFL (minimum score 550 paper-based; 79 iBT), IELTS. Electronic applications accepted.

The Citadel, The Military College of South Carolina, Citadel Graduate College, School of Science and Mathematics, Department of Health, Exercise, and Sport Science, Charleston, SC 29409. Offers health, exercise, and sport science (MS); sport management (MA, Graduate Certificate). *Accreditation:* NCATE. *Program availability:* Part-time, evening/weekend. *Faculty:* 4 full-time (2 women), 1 (woman) part-time/adjunct. *Students:* 13 full-time (5 women), 17 part-time (9 women); includes 6 minority (4 Black or African American, non-Hispanic/Latino; 1 Hispanic/Latino; 1 Native Hawaiian or other Pacific Islander, non-Hispanic/Latino), 1 international. 11 applicants, 82% accepted, 8 enrolled. In 2016, 24 master's, 3 other advanced degrees awarded. *Degree requirements:* For master's, comprehensive exam (for some programs), internship and professional portfolio (for some programs). *Entrance requirements:* For master's, GRE (minimum combined verbal and quantitative score 290) or MAT (minimum score 396), official transcript reflecting highest degree earned from regionally accredited college or university, minimum undergraduate GPA of 2.5, 3 letters of recommendation, resume detailing previous work experience. Additional exam requirements/recommendations for international students: Required—TOEFL (minimum score 550 paper-based; 79 iBT). *Application deadline:* Applications are processed on a rolling basis. Application fee: $40. Electronic applications accepted. *Expenses:* Tuition, state resident: full-time $5121; part-time $569 per credit hour. Tuition, nonresident: full-time $8613; part-time $957 per credit hour. *Required fees:* $90 per term. *Financial support:* Fellowships and unspecified assistantships available. Support available to part-time students. Financial award application deadline: 7/1; financial award applicants required to submit FAFSA. *Unit head:* Dr. Harry D. Davakos, Department Head, 843-953-5060, E-mail: harry.davakos@citadel.edu. *Application contact:* Dr. Dena P. Garner, Program Director, 843-953-6323, E-mail: garnerd1@citadel.edu.
Website: http://www.citadel.edu/root/hess

Clark University, Graduate School, Department of International Development, Community, and Environment, Worcester, MA 01610-1477. Offers community and global health (MHS); community development and planning (MA); environmental science and policy (MS); geographic information science for development and environment (MS); international development and social change (MA); MA/MBA; MBA/MS. *Faculty:* 16 full-time (8 women), 8 part-time/adjunct (2 women). *Students:* 161 full-time (97 women), 21 part-time (7 women); includes 31 minority (13 Black or African American, non-Hispanic/Latino; 1 American Indian or Alaska Native, non-Hispanic/Latino; 8 Asian, non-Hispanic/Latino; 7 Hispanic/Latino; 2 Two or more races, non-Hispanic/Latino), 47 international. Average age 27. 364 applicants, 80% accepted, 110 enrolled. In 2016, 115 master's awarded. *Degree requirements:* For master's, thesis. *Entrance requirements:* For master's, 3 references, resume or curriculum vitae. Additional exam requirements/recommendations for international students: Required—TOEFL (minimum score 575 paper-based; 90 iBT) or IELTS (minimum score 6.5). *Application deadline:* For fall admission, 1/15 for domestic students. Application fee: $75. *Expenses: Tuition:* Full-time $44,050. *Required fees:* $80. Tuition and fees vary according to course load and program. *Financial support:* Fellowships with partial tuition reimbursements, research assistantships with partial tuition reimbursements, teaching assistantships with partial tuition reimbursements, institutionally sponsored loans, and scholarships/grants available. *Faculty research:* Community action research, gender analysis, environmental risk assessment, land-use planning, geographic information systems, HIV and AIDS, global health and social justice, environmental health, climate change and sustainability. *Total annual research expenditures:* $140,000. *Unit head:* Dr. Ed Carr, Director, 508-421-3895, Fax: 508-793-8820, E-mail: edcarr@clarku.edu. *Application contact:* Erika Paradis, Student and Academic Services Director, 508-793-7201, Fax: 508-793-8820, E-mail: eparadis@clarku.edu.
Website: http://www2.clarku.edu/departments/international-development-community-environment/

Cleveland State University, College of Graduate Studies, College of Education and Human Services, Department of Health and Human Performance, Cleveland, OH 44115. Offers physical education pedagogy (M Ed); public health (MPH). *Program availability:* Part-time. *Faculty:* 7 full-time (4 women), 3 part-time/adjunct (2 women). *Students:* 39 full-time (20 women), 63 part-time (38 women); includes 37 minority (26 Black or African American, non-Hispanic/Latino; 2 Asian, non-Hispanic/Latino; 5 Hispanic/Latino; 1 Native Hawaiian or other Pacific Islander, non-Hispanic/Latino; 3 Two or more races, non-Hispanic/Latino), 15 international. Average age 27. 103 applicants, 72% accepted, 43 enrolled. In 2016, 33 master's awarded. *Degree requirements:* For master's, comprehensive exam, thesis optional. *Entrance requirements:* For master's, GRE General Test or MAT (if undergraduate GPA less than 2.75), minimum undergraduate GPA of 2.75. Additional exam requirements/recommendations for international students: Required—TOEFL (minimum score 550 paper-based; 78 iBT), IELTS (minimum score 6). *Application deadline:* For fall admission, 7/15 priority date for domestic students; for spring admission, 12/15 priority date for domestic students. Applications are processed on a rolling basis. Application fee: $30. Electronic applications accepted. *Expenses:* Tuition, state resident: full-time $9565. Tuition, nonresident: full-time $17,980. Tuition and fees vary according to program. *Financial support:* In 2016–17, 6 research assistantships with tuition reimbursements (averaging $3,480 per year), 1 teaching assistantship with tuition reimbursement (averaging $3,480 per year) were awarded; career-related internships or fieldwork, tuition waivers (full), and unspecified assistantships also available. Financial award application deadline: 3/15; financial award applicants required to submit FAFSA. *Faculty research:* Bone density, marketing fitness centers, motor development of disabled, online learning and survey research. *Unit head:* Dr. Sheila M. Patterson, Chairperson, 216-687-4870, Fax: 216-687-5410, E-mail: s.m.patterson@csuohio.edu. *Application contact:* Deborah L. Brown, Interim Assistant Director, Graduate Admissions, 216-523-7572, Fax: 216-687-5400, E-mail: d.l.brown@csuohio.edu.
Website: http://www.csuohio.edu/cehs/departments/HPERD/hperd_dept.html

The College at Brockport, State University of New York, School of Education, Health, and Human Services, Department of Public Health and Health Education, Brockport, NY 14420-2997. Offers health education (MS Ed), including health education K-12. *Faculty:* 2 full-time (0 women), 3 part-time/adjunct (2 women). *Students:* 9 full-time (4 women), 11 part-time (5 women); includes 1 minority (Hispanic/Latino). 15 applicants, 73% accepted, 8 enrolled. In 2016, 4 master's awarded. *Degree requirements:* For master's, thesis or alternative. *Entrance requirements:* For master's, minimum GPA of 3.0, letters of recommendation. Additional exam requirements/recommendations for international students: Required—TOEFL (minimum score 550 paper-based; 79 iBT), IELTS (minimum score 6.5). *Application deadline:* For fall admission, 3/1 priority date for domestic and international students; for spring admission, 10/1 priority date for domestic and international students; for summer admission, 3/1 priority date for domestic and international students. Application fee: $80. Electronic applications accepted. *Expenses:* Contact institution. *Financial support:* In 2016–17, 1 teaching assistantship with full tuition reimbursement (averaging $6,000 per year) was awarded; Federal Work-Study, scholarships/grants, and unspecified assistantships also available. Support available to part-time students. Financial award application deadline: 3/15; financial award applicants required to submit FAFSA. *Faculty research:* Nutrition, substance use, HIV/AIDS, bioethics, worksite health. *Unit head:* Dr. Darson Rhodes, Graduate Director, 585-395-5901, Fax: 585-395-5246, E-mail: drhodes@brockport.edu. *Application contact:* Danielle A. Welch, Graduate Admissions Counselor, 585-395-5465, Fax: 585-395-2515.
Website: http://www.brockport.edu/healthsci/graduate/

The College of New Jersey, Office of Graduate and Advancing Education, School of Nursing, Health and Exercise Science, Department of Health and Exercise Science, Program in Health Education, Ewing, NJ 08628. Offers health (MAT); physical education (M Ed). *Accreditation:* NCATE. *Program availability:* Part-time. *Degree requirements:* For master's, comprehensive exam. *Entrance requirements:* For master's, GRE, minimum GPA of 3.0 in field or 2.75 overall. Additional exam requirements/recommendations for international students: Required—TOEFL. Electronic applications accepted.

College of Saint Mary, Program in Health Professions Education, Omaha, NE 68106. Offers Ed D. *Program availability:* Part-time.

Colorado State University–Pueblo, College of Education, Engineering and Professional Studies, Education Program, Pueblo, CO 81001-4901. Offers art education (M Ed); foreign language education (M Ed); health and physical education (M Ed); instructional technology (M Ed); linguistically diverse education (M Ed); music education (M Ed); special education (M Ed). *Accreditation:* TEAC. *Program availability:* Part-time. *Degree requirements:* For master's, portfolio. *Entrance requirements:* For master's, 3 recommendations, teaching license. Additional exam requirements/recommendations for international students: Required—TOEFL (minimum score 500 paper-based). Electronic applications accepted. *Faculty research:* Portfolio assessment, math education, science education.

Columbus State University, Graduate Studies, College of Education and Health Professions, Department of Health, Physical Education and Exercise Science, Columbus, GA 31907-5645. Offers exercise science (MS); health and physical education (M Ed, MAT). *Program availability:* Part-time, evening/weekend. *Faculty:* 5 full-time (3 women). *Students:* 21 full-time (11 women), 8 part-time (2 women); includes 17 minority (12 Black or African American, non-Hispanic/Latino; 1 Asian, non-Hispanic/Latino, 3 Hispanic/Latino; 1 Two or more races, non-Hispanic/Latino). Average age 28. 19 applicants, 37% accepted, 3 enrolled. In 2016, 12 master's awarded. *Degree requirements:* For master's, thesis optional. *Entrance requirements:* For master's, GRE, minimum undergraduate GPA of 2.75. Additional exam requirements/recommendations for international students: Required—TOEFL (minimum score 550 paper-based; 79 iBT). *Application deadline:* For fall admission, 5/1 for domestic students, 4/1 for international students; for spring admission, 11/1 for domestic and international students; for summer admission, 2/1 for domestic students, 3/1 for international students. Applications are processed on a rolling basis. Application fee: $50. Electronic applications accepted. *Expenses:* Tuition, state resident: full-time $4804; part-time $2412 per semester hour. Tuition, nonresident: full-time $19,218; part-time $9612 per semester hour. *Required fees:* $1850; $1850 per semester hour. Tuition and fees vary according to program. *Financial support:* In 2016–17, 3 students received support, including 4 research assistantships (averaging $3,000 per year). Financial award application deadline: 5/15; financial award applicants required to submit FAFSA. *Unit head:* Dr. Tara Underwood, Chair, 706-568-2485, E-mail: underwood_tara@columbusstate.edu. *Application contact:* Kristin Williams, Director of International and Graduate Admissions, 706-507-8848, Fax: 706-568-5091, E-mail: williams_kristin@columbusstate.edu.
Website: http://hpex.columbusstate.edu/

Concordia University Wisconsin, Graduate Programs, School of Health Professions, Mequon, WI 53097-2402. Offers MOT, MSRS, DPT. *Unit head:* Dr. Marsha K. Konz, Dean of Graduate Studies, 262-243-4253, Fax: 262-243-4428, E-mail: marsha.konz@cuw.edu. *Application contact:* Bill V. Mueller, Graduate Admissions Counselor, 262-243-4551, Fax: 262-243-4428, E-mail: williamvmueller@cuw.edu.

Health Education

Daemen College, Program in Public Health, Amherst, NY 14226-3592. Offers community health education (MPH); epidemiology (MPH); generalist (MPH). *Program availability:* Part-time, online learning. *Degree requirements:* For master's, practicum.

Dalhousie University, Faculty of Health Professions, School of Health and Human Performance, Program in Health Promotion, Halifax, NS B3H 3J5, Canada. Offers MA. *Program availability:* Part-time. *Degree requirements:* For master's, thesis. *Entrance requirements:* Additional exam requirements/recommendations for international students: Required—TOEFL, IELTS, CANTEST, CAEL, or Michigan English Language Assessment Battery. Electronic applications accepted. *Faculty research:* AIDS research, health knowledge of adolescents, evaluating health promotion, program evaluation.

Delta State University, Graduate Programs, College of Education, Division of Health, Physical Education, and Recreation, Cleveland, MS 38733-0001. Offers health, physical education, and recreation (M Ed); sport and human performance (MS). *Program availability:* Part-time, evening/weekend. *Degree requirements:* For master's, thesis optional. *Entrance requirements:* For master's, GRE General Test or MAT, Class A teaching certificate. *Faculty research:* Blood pressure, body fat, power and reaction time, learning disorders of athletes, effects of walking.

Drew University, Caspersen School of Graduate Studies, Madison, NJ 07940-1493. Offers conflict resolution and leadership (Certificate), including community leadership, moderation, peace building; history and culture (MA, PhD), including American history, book history, British history, European history, Holocaust and genocide (M Litt, MA, D Litt, PhD), intellectual history, Irish history, print culture, public history; K-12 education (MAT), including art, biology, chemistry, elementary education, English, French, Italian, math, secondary education, special education, teacher of students with disabilities; liberal studies (M Litt, D Litt), including history, Holocaust and genocide (M Litt, MA, D Litt, PhD), Irish/Irish-American studies, literature (M Litt, MMH, D Litt, DMH, CMH), religion, spirituality, teaching in the two-year college, writing; medical humanities (MMH, DMH, CMH), including arts, health, healthcare, literature (M Litt, MMH, D Litt, DMH, CMH), scientific research; poetry (MFA). *Program availability:* Part-time, evening/weekend. *Faculty:* 4 full-time (2 women), 31 part-time/adjunct (16 women). *Students:* 62 full-time (41 women), 199 part-time (130 women); includes 38 minority (17 Black or African American, non-Hispanic/Latino; 3 Asian, non-Hispanic/Latino; 17 Hispanic/Latino; 1 Two or more races, non-Hispanic/Latino), 3 international. Average age 27. 93 applicants, 81% accepted, 46 enrolled. In 2016, 39 master's, 27 doctorates, 26 other advanced degrees awarded. Terminal master's awarded for partial completion of doctoral program. *Degree requirements:* For master's and other advanced degree, thesis (for some programs); for doctorate, one foreign language, comprehensive exam (for some programs), thesis/dissertation. *Entrance requirements:* For master's, PRAXIS Core and Subject Area tests (for MAT), resume, transcripts, writing sample, personal statement, letters of recommendation; for doctorate, GRE (PhD in history and culture), resume, transcripts, writing sample, personal statement, letters of recommendation. Additional exam requirements/recommendations for international students: Required—TOEFL (minimum score 587 paper-based; 94 iBT), IELTS (minimum score 7), TWE (minimum score 4). *Application deadline:* For fall admission, 8/1 for domestic students, 6/1 for international students; for spring admission, 12/1 for domestic students, 10/1 for international students. Applications are processed on a rolling basis. Application fee: $35. Electronic applications accepted. Tuition and fees vary according to program. *Financial support:* Fellowships, research assistantships, teaching assistantships, career-related internships or fieldwork, Federal Work-Study, scholarships/grants, and unspecified assistantships available. Support available to part-time students. Financial award applicants required to submit FAFSA. *Application contact:* Leanne Horinko, Director of Caspersen Admissions, 973-408-3280, E-mail: gradm@drew.edu.
Website: http://www.drew.edu/caspersen

East Carolina University, Graduate School, College of Education, Department of Elementary and Middle Grades Education, Greenville, NC 27858-4353. Offers elementary education (MA Ed, MAT); English education (MAT); family and consumer science (MAT); health education (MAT); Hispanic studies (MAT); history education (MAT); middle grades education (MA Ed, MAT); music education (MAT); science education (MAT); special education (MAT), including general curriculum; vocational education (MAT). *Accreditation:* NCATE. *Program availability:* Part-time, evening/weekend, online learning. *Students:* 5 full-time (4 women), 18 part-time (16 women); includes 4 minority (3 Black or African American, non-Hispanic/Latino; 1 Hispanic/Latino). Average age 31. 19 applicants, 95% accepted, 13 enrolled. In 2016, 8 master's awarded. *Degree requirements:* For master's, comprehensive exam, thesis optional. *Entrance requirements:* For master's, GRE or MAT, minimum GPA of 2.5, bachelor's degree in related field, teaching license (MA Ed). Additional exam requirements/recommendations for international students: Required—TOEFL. *Application deadline:* For fall admission, 6/1 priority date for domestic students. Applications are processed on a rolling basis. Application fee: $70. *Financial support:* Federal Work-Study available. Support available to part-time students. Financial award application deadline: 6/1. *Unit head:* Dr. Ann Bullock, Chair, 252-328-1126, E-mail: bullockv@ecu.edu. *Application contact:* Dean of Graduate School, 252-328-6012, Fax: 252-328-6071, E-mail: gradschool@ecu.edu.
Website: http://www.ecu.edu/cs-educ/elmid/index.cfm

East Carolina University, Graduate School, College of Health and Human Performance, Department of Health Education and Promotion, Greenville, NC 27858-4353. Offers environmental health (MS); health education (MA Ed); health education and promotion (MA). *Accreditation:* CEPH; NCATE. *Students:* 26 full-time (22 women), 64 part-time (44 women); includes 22 minority (15 Black or African American, non-Hispanic/Latino; 1 Asian, non-Hispanic/Latino; 4 Hispanic/Latino; 2 Two or more races, non-Hispanic/Latino), 2 international. Average age 31. 28 applicants, 86% accepted, 22 enrolled. In 2016, 16 master's awarded. *Degree requirements:* For master's, comprehensive exam, thesis optional. *Entrance requirements:* For master's, GRE General Test or MAT. Additional exam requirements/recommendations for international students: Required—TOEFL. *Application deadline:* For fall admission, 6/1 priority date for domestic students. Applications are processed on a rolling basis. Application fee: $50. *Financial support:* Fellowships, research assistantships, teaching assistantships, and career-related internships or fieldwork available. Support available to part-time students. Financial award application deadline: 6/1. *Faculty research:* Community health education, worksite health promotion, school health education, environmental health. *Unit head:* Dr. J. Don Chaney, Chair, 252-737-4942, E-mail: chaneyj@ecu.edu.
Website: http://www.ecu.edu/hlth/

Eastern Kentucky University, The Graduate School, College of Education, Department of Curriculum and Instruction, Program in Secondary and Higher Education, Richmond, KY 40475-3102. Offers secondary education (MA Ed), including agricultural education, art education, biological sciences education, business education, English education, geography education, history education, home economics education, industrial education, mathematical sciences education, physical education, school health education. *Accreditation:* NCATE. *Program availability:* Part-time. *Entrance requirements:* For master's, GRE General Test, minimum GPA of 2.5.

Eastern Michigan University, Graduate School, College of Health and Human Services, School of Health Promotion and Human Performance, Program in Health Education, Ypsilanti, MI 48197. Offers MS, Graduate Certificate. *Program availability:* Part-time, evening/weekend. *Students:* 25 part-time (22 women); includes 8 minority (7 Black or African American, non-Hispanic/Latino; 1 Two or more races, non-Hispanic/Latino). Average age 32. 12 applicants, 17% accepted, 7 enrolled. In 2016, 6 master's awarded. *Degree requirements:* For master's, thesis or project. *Entrance requirements:* For master's, teaching credential. Additional exam requirements/recommendations for international students: Required—TOEFL. *Application deadline:* For fall admission, 8/1 for domestic students, 5/1 for international students; for winter admission, 12/1 for domestic students, 10/1 for international students; for spring admission, 4/15 for domestic students, 3/1 for international students. Application fee: $45. *Application contact:* Dr. Susan McCarthy, Program Coordinator, 734-487-0090, Fax: 734-487-2024, E-mail: smccarthy@emich.edu.

Eastern University, Department of Nursing, St. Davids, PA 19087-3696. Offers school health services (M Ed). *Students:* 1 (woman) full-time, 23 part-time (all women); includes 3 minority (1 Black or African American, non-Hispanic/Latino; 1 Asian, non-Hispanic/Latino; 1 Hispanic/Latino). Average age 45. In 2016, 7 master's awarded. *Application deadline:* Applications are processed on a rolling basis. Application fee: $35. Electronic applications accepted. Application fee is waived when completed online. *Expenses:* $690 per credit. *Unit head:* Michael Dziedzak, Executive Director of Enrollment, 800-452-0996, E-mail: gpsadmissions@eastern.edu.
Website: http://www.eastern.edu/academics/programs/department-nursing-adult-undergraduate-graduate

Eastern University, Loeb School of Education, St. Davids, PA 19087-3696. Offers ESL program specialist (K-12) (Certificate); general supervisor (PreK-12) (Certificate); health and physical education (K-12) (Certificate); middle level (4-8) (Certificate); multicultural education (M Ed); organizational leadership with education (PhD); Pre K-4 (Certificate); Pre K-4 with special education (Certificate); reading (M Ed); reading specialist (K-12) (Certificate); reading supervisor (K-12) (Certificate); school health supervisor (Certificate); school nurse (K-12) (Certificate); secondary biology education (7-12) (Certificate); secondary chemistry education (7-12) (Certificate); secondary communication education (7-12) (Certificate); secondary education (7-12) (Certificate); secondary English education (7-12) (Certificate); secondary math education (7-12) (Certificate); secondary social studies education (7-12) (Certificate); special education (M Ed); special education (7-12) (Certificate); special education (Pre K-8) (Certificate); special education supervisor (N-12) (Certificate); TESOL (M Ed); world language (Certificate), including French, Spanish. *Program availability:* Part-time, evening/weekend, online learning. *Students:* 41 full-time (32 women), 89 part-time (68 women); includes 54 minority (38 Black or African American, non-Hispanic/Latino; 3 Asian, non-Hispanic/Latino; 11 Hispanic/Latino; 2 Two or more races, non-Hispanic/Latino), 2 international. Average age 37. In 2016, 64 master's awarded. *Entrance requirements:* Additional exam requirements/recommendations for international students: Required—TOEFL. *Application deadline:* Applications are processed on a rolling basis. Application fee: $35. Electronic applications accepted. Application fee is waived when completed online. *Expenses:* $690 per credit. *Unit head:* Michael Dziedziak, Executive Director of Enrollment, 800-452-0996, E-mail: gpsadmissions@eastern.edu.
Website: http://www.eastern.edu/academics/programs/loeb-school-education-0

East Stroudsburg University of Pennsylvania, Graduate and Extended Studies, College of Health Sciences, Department of Exercise Science, East Stroudsburg, PA 18301-2999. Offers MS. *Program availability:* Part-time, evening/weekend, online learning. *Faculty:* 2 full-time, 5 part-time/adjunct. *Students:* 54 full-time (25 women), 2 part-time (0 women); includes 10 minority (3 Black or African American, non-Hispanic/Latino; 5 Hispanic/Latino; 1 Native Hawaiian or other Pacific Islander, non-Hispanic/Latino; 1 Two or more races, non-Hispanic/Latino), 2 international. *Degree requirements:* For master's, comprehensive exam, thesis or alternative, computer literacy. *Entrance requirements:* Additional exam requirements/recommendations for international students: Recommended—TOEFL (minimum score 560 paper-based; 83 iBT), IELTS. *Application deadline:* For fall admission, 3/1 priority date for domestic and international students; for spring admission, 11/30 for domestic students, 10/31 for international students. Applications are processed on a rolling basis. Application fee: $50. Electronic applications accepted. *Expenses:* Tuition, state resident: full-time $8694; part-time $5796 per year. Tuition, nonresident: full-time $13,050; part-time $8700 per year. *Required fees:* $2550; $1690 per unit. $845 per semester. Tuition and fees vary according to course load, campus/location and program. *Financial support:* Research assistantships with tuition reimbursements, Federal Work-Study, and unspecified assistantships available. Support available to part-time students. Financial award application deadline: 3/1. *Unit head:* Dr. Chad Witmer, Graduate Coordinator, 570-422-3362, E-mail: cwitmer@esu.edu. *Application contact:* Kevin Quintero, Associate Director, Graduate and Extended Studies, 570-422-3890, Fax: 570-422-2711, E-mail: kquintero@esu.edu.

East Stroudsburg University of Pennsylvania, Graduate and Extended Studies, College of Health Sciences, Department of Health Studies, East Stroudsburg, PA 18301-2999. Offers MPH, MS. *Accreditation:* CEPH (one or more programs are accredited). *Program availability:* Part-time, evening/weekend, online learning. *Students:* 23 full-time (20 women), 21 part-time (18 women); includes 16 minority (7 Black or African American, non-Hispanic/Latino; 7 Hispanic/Latino; 2 Two or more races, non-Hispanic/Latino), 2 international. *Degree requirements:* For master's, oral comprehensive exam. *Entrance requirements:* For master's, GRE General Test, minimum GPA of 3.0 in major, 2.8 overall; undergraduate prerequisites in anatomy and physiology; 3 verifiable letters of recommendation; professional resume. Additional exam requirements/recommendations for international students: Recommended—TOEFL (minimum score 560 paper-based; 83 iBT), IELTS. *Application deadline:* For fall admission, 7/31 priority date for domestic students, 6/30 priority date for international students; for spring admission, 11/30 for domestic students, 10/31 for international students. Applications are processed on a rolling basis. Application fee: $50. Electronic applications accepted. *Expenses:* Tuition, state resident: full-time $8694; part-time $5796 per year. Tuition, nonresident: full-time $13,050; part-time $8700 per year. *Required fees:* $2550; $1690 per unit. $845 per semester. Tuition and fees vary according to course load, campus/location and program. *Financial support:* Research assistantships with tuition reimbursements, Federal Work-Study, and unspecified assistantships available. Support available to part-time students. Financial award application deadline: 3/1; financial award applicants required to submit FAFSA. *Faculty research:* HIV prevention, wellness, international health issues. *Unit head:* Dr. Kim Razzano, Chair, 570-422-3693, Fax: 570-422-3848, E-mail: krazzano@esu.edu. *Application contact:* Kevin Quintero, Associate Director, Graduate and Extended Studies, 570-422-3890, Fax: 570-422-2711, E-mail: kquintero@esu.edu.

Emory University, Rollins School of Public Health, Department of Behavioral Sciences and Health Education, Atlanta, GA 30322-1100. Offers MPH, PhD. *Accreditation:* CEPH. *Program availability:* Part-time. *Degree requirements:* For master's, comprehensive exam (for some programs), thesis, practicum. *Entrance requirements:* For master's, GRE General Test. Additional exam requirements/recommendations for international students: Required—TOEFL (minimum score 550 paper-based; 80 iBT). Electronic applications accepted.

Excelsior College, School of Health Sciences, Albany, NY 12203-5159. Offers health administration (MS); health care informatics (Certificate); health professions education

(MSHS); healthcare informatics (MS); organizational development (MS); public health (MSHS). *Program availability:* Part-time, evening/weekend, online learning. *Faculty:* 5 part-time/adjunct (4 women). *Students:* 307 part-time (240 women); includes 176 minority (101 Black or African American, non-Hispanic/Latino; 2 American Indian or Alaska Native, non-Hispanic/Latino; 17 Asian, non-Hispanic/Latino; 39 Hispanic/Latino; 3 Native Hawaiian or other Pacific Islander, non-Hispanic/Latino; 14 Two or more races, non-Hispanic/Latino), 1 international. Average age 39. In 2016, 21 master's awarded. *Entrance requirements:* For degree, bachelor's degree in applicable field. *Application deadline:* Applications are processed on a rolling basis. Application fee: $50. Electronic applications accepted. *Expenses: Tuition:* Part-time $645 per credit. *Required fees:* $265 per credit. *Financial support:* Scholarships/grants available. *Unit head:* Dr. Laurie Carbo-Porter, Dean, 518-464-8500, Fax: 518-464-8777. *Application contact:* Admissions Counselor, 518-464-8500, Fax: 518-464-8777, E-mail: admissions@excelsior.edu.

Fairfield University, Marion Peckham Egan School of Nursing and Health Studies, Fairfield, CT 06824. Offers advanced practice (DNP); family nurse practitioner (MSN, DNP); nurse anesthesia (DNP); nursing leadership (MSN); psychiatric nurse practitioner (MSN, DNP). *Accreditation:* AACN; AANA/CANAEP. *Program availability:* Part-time, evening/weekend. *Faculty:* 8 full-time (all women), 7 part-time/adjunct (4 women). *Students:* 44 full-time (36 women), 172 part-time (154 women); includes 45 minority (17 Black or African American, non-Hispanic/Latino; 1 American Indian or Alaska Native, non-Hispanic/Latino; 10 Asian, non-Hispanic/Latino; 14 Hispanic/Latino; 3 Two or more races, non-Hispanic/Latino), 2 international. Average age 36. 107 applicants, 34% accepted, 21 enrolled. In 2016, 20 master's, 28 doctorates awarded. *Degree requirements:* For master's, capstone project. *Entrance requirements:* For master's, minimum QPA of 3.0, RN license, resume, 2 recommendations; for doctorate, MSN (minimum QPA of 3.2) or BSN (minimum QPA of 3.0); critical care nursing experience (for nurse anesthesia DNP candidates). Additional exam requirements/recommendations for international students: Required—TOEFL (minimum score 550 paper-based; 80 iBT) or IELTS (minimum score 6.5). *Application deadline:* For fall admission, 5/15 for international students; for spring admission, 10/15 for international students. Applications are processed on a rolling basis. Application fee: $60. Electronic applications accepted. *Expenses:* $900-$1,000 per credit (for DNP); $850 per credit (for MSN). *Financial support:* In 2016–17, 47 students received support. Scholarships/grants and unspecified assistantships available. Financial award applicants required to submit FAFSA. *Faculty research:* Aging, spiritual care, palliative and end of life care, psychiatric mental health, pediatric trauma. *Unit head:* Dr. Meredith Wallace Kazer, Dean, 203-254-4000 Ext. 2701, Fax: 203-254-4126, E-mail: mkazer@fairfield.edu. *Application contact:* Marianne Gumpper, Director of Graduate and Continuing Studies Admission, 203-254-4184, Fax: 203-254-4073, E-mail: gradadmis@fairfield.edu.
Website: http://fairfield.edu/son

Florida State University, The Graduate School, College of Human Sciences, Department of Nutrition, Food and Exercise Sciences, Tallahassee, FL 32306-1493. Offers exercise physiology (MS, PhD); nutrition and food science (MS, PhD), including clinical nutrition (MS), food science, human nutrition (PhD), nutrition education and health promotion (MS), nutrition science (MS); sports nutrition (MS); sports sciences (MS). *Program availability:* Part-time. *Faculty:* 20 full-time (8 women). *Students:* 84 full-time (49 women), 12 part-time (8 women); includes 17 minority (3 Black or African American, non-Hispanic/Latino; 1 Asian, non-Hispanic/Latino; 6 Hispanic/Latino; 7 Two or more races, non-Hispanic/Latino), 16 international. 125 applicants, 50% accepted, 37 enrolled. In 2016, 30 master's, 2 doctorates awarded. *Degree requirements:* For master's, thesis optional; for doctorate, thesis/dissertation. *Entrance requirements:* For master's and doctorate, GRE General Test, minimum upper-division GPA of 3.0. Additional exam requirements/recommendations for international students: Required—TOEFL (minimum score 550 paper-based; 80 iBT). *Application deadline:* For fall admission, 4/1 for domestic and international students; for spring admission, 10/1 for domestic and international students. Applications are processed on a rolling basis. Application fee: $30. Electronic applications accepted. *Expenses:* Tuition, state resident: full-time $7263; part-time $403.51 per credit hour. Tuition, nonresident: full-time $18,087; part-time $1004.85 per credit hour. *Required fees:* $1365; $75.81 per credit hour. $20 per semester. Tuition and fees vary according to campus/location. *Financial support:* In 2016–17, 50 students received support, including 22 research assistantships with full tuition reimbursements available (averaging $7,026 per year), 47 teaching assistantships with full tuition reimbursements available (averaging $8,508 per year); career-related internships or fieldwork, Federal Work-Study, institutionally sponsored loans, scholarships/grants, and unspecified assistantships also available. Financial award application deadline: 2/1; financial award applicants required to submit FAFSA. *Faculty research:* Body composition, functional food, chronic disease and aging response; food safety, food allergy, and safety/quality detection methods; sports nutrition, energy and human performance; strength training, functional performance, cardiovascular physiology, sarcopenia. *Total annual research expenditures:* $712,777. *Unit head:* Dr. Chester Ray, Department Chair, 850-644-1850, Fax: 850-645-5000, E-mail: caray@fsu.edu. *Application contact:* Ann R. Smith, Office Administrator, 850-644-1828, Fax: 850-645-5000, E-mail: asmith@fsu.edu.
Website: http://www.chs.fsu.edu/Departments/Nutrition-Food-Exercise-Sciences

Fort Hays State University, Graduate School, College of Health and Life Sciences, Department of Health and Human Performance, Hays, KS 67601-4099. Offers MS. *Program availability:* Part-time. *Degree requirements:* For master's, comprehensive exam, thesis optional. *Entrance requirements:* For master's, GRE General Test or MAT. Additional exam requirements/recommendations for international students: Required—TOEFL (minimum score 550 paper-based). Electronic applications accepted. *Faculty research:* Isoproterenol hydrochloride and exercise, dehydrogenase and high-density lipoprotein levels in athletics, venous blood parameters to adipose fat.

Framingham State University, Continuing Education, Programs in Food and Nutrition, Program in Human Nutrition: Education and Media Technologies, Framingham, MA 01701-9101. Offers MS.

Georgia College & State University, Graduate School, College of Health Sciences, School of Health and Human Performance, Milledgeville, GA 31061. Offers health and human performance (MS), including health promotion; kinesiology/health education (MAT). *Accreditation:* NCATE (one or more programs are accredited). *Program availability:* Part-time, evening/weekend, 100% online. *Students:* 43 full-time (25 women), 17 part-time (15 women); includes 6 minority (4 Black or African American, non-Hispanic/Latino; 1 Asian, non-Hispanic/Latino; 1 Hispanic/Latino), 1 international. Average age 28. 33 applicants, 100% accepted, 28 enrolled. In 2016, 23 master's awarded. *Degree requirements:* For master's, completed in 6 years with minimum GPA of 3.0, thesis or project (for MS); minimum GPA of 3.0, GACE Exam and Assessment, and electronic teaching portfolio (for MAT). *Entrance requirements:* For master's, GRE with minimum score of 297 or MAT with minimum score of 385 (for MS); SAT (minimum score of 1000), ACT (minimum score of 43), GRE (minimum score of 297), MAT (minimum score of 385), or GACE Program Admission Assessment (for MAT), resume, 3 professional references; minimum GPA of 2.75 in upper-level undergraduate courses and undergraduate statistics course (for MS); minimum GPA of 2.75 on upper-division major courses (for MAT). *Application deadline:* For fall admission, 7/15 priority date for domestic students, 4/1 for international students; for spring admission, 11/15 priority date for domestic students, 9/1 for international students; for summer admission, 4/15 priority date for domestic students. Applications are processed on a rolling basis. Application fee: $40. Electronic applications accepted. *Expenses:* $228 per credit hour in-state tuition, $1,027 per credit hour out-of-state tuition, $1,990 per year fees (for MAT); $338 per credit hour (for MS). *Financial support:* In 2016–17, 24 students received support. Unspecified assistantships available. Support available to part-time students. Financial award application deadline: 3/1; financial award applicants required to submit FAFSA. *Unit head:* Dr. Lisa Griffin, Director, School of Health and Human Performance, 478-445-4072, Fax: 478-445-4074, E-mail: lisa.griffin@gcsu.edu.
Website: http://www.gcsu.edu/health/shhp

Georgia Southern University, Jack N. Averitt College of Graduate Studies, Jiann-Ping Hsu College of Public Health, Program in Public Health, Statesboro, GA 30460. Offers biostatistics (MPH, Dr PH); community health behavior and education (Dr PH); community health education (MPH); environmental health sciences (MPH); epidemiology (MPH); health policy and management (MPH, Dr PH). *Accreditation:* CEPH. *Program availability:* Part-time. *Students:* 158 full-time (100 women), 56 part-time (48 women); includes 113 minority (97 Black or African American, non-Hispanic/Latino; 6 Asian, non-Hispanic/Latino; 6 Hispanic/Latino; 4 Two or more races, non-Hispanic/Latino), 44 international. Average age 31. 227 applicants, 87% accepted, 89 enrolled. In 2016, 38 master's, 12 doctorates awarded. *Degree requirements:* For master's, thesis optional, practicum; for doctorate, comprehensive exam, thesis/dissertation, practicum. *Entrance requirements:* For master's, GRE General Test, minimum GPA of 2.75, resume, 3 letters of reference; for doctorate, GRE, GMAT, MCAT, LSAT, 3 letters of reference, statement of purpose, resume or curriculum vitae. Additional exam requirements/recommendations for international students: Required—TOEFL (minimum score 550 paper-based; 80 iBT), IELTS (minimum score 6). *Application deadline:* For fall admission, 6/1 priority date for domestic and international students; for spring admission, 10/1 priority date for domestic students, 10/1 for international students. Applications are processed on a rolling basis. Application fee: $50. Electronic applications accepted. *Expenses:* Contact institution. *Financial support:* In 2016–17, 54 students received support, including 23 fellowships with full tuition reimbursements available (averaging $7,750 per year), 1 research assistantship with full tuition reimbursement available (averaging $7,750 per year), 1 teaching assistantship with full tuition reimbursement available (averaging $7,750 per year); career-related internships or fieldwork, Federal Work-Study, scholarships/grants, tuition waivers (full), and unspecified assistantships also available. Support available to part-time students. Financial award application deadline: 4/15; financial award applicants required to submit FAFSA. *Faculty research:* Rural public health best practices, health disparity elimination, community initiatives to enhance public health, cost effectiveness analysis, epidemiology of rural public health, environmental health issues, health care system assessment, rural health care, health policy and healthcare financing, survival analysis, nonparametric statistics and resampling methods, micro-arrays and genomics, data imputation techniques and clinical trial methodology. *Total annual research expenditures:* $281,707. *Unit head:* Dr. Shamia Garrett, Program Coordinator, 912-478-2393, E-mail: sgarrett@georgiasouthern.edu.
Website: http://chhs.georgiasouthern.edu/health/

Georgia State University, College of Education and Human Development, Department of Kinesiology and Health, Program in Health and Physical Education, Atlanta, GA 30302-3083. Offers M Ed. *Program availability:* Part-time, evening/weekend. *Degree requirements:* For master's, comprehensive exam. *Entrance requirements:* For master's, GRE General Test, minimum GPA of 2.5. *Application deadline:* For fall admission, 5/1 for domestic students; for spring admission, 10/1 for domestic students. Application fee: $50. *Expenses:* Tuition, state resident: full-time $6876; part-time $382 per credit hour. Tuition, nonresident: full-time $22,374; part-time $1243 per credit hour. *Required fees:* $2128; $1064 per term. Part-time tuition and fees vary according to course load and program. *Financial support:* Teaching assistantships and career-related internships or fieldwork available. *Faculty research:* Exercise science, teacher behavior. *Unit head:* Dr. Jacalyn Lea Lund, Chair, 404-413-8051, E-mail: jlund@gsu.edu. *Application contact:* Dr. Rachel Gurvitch, Program Coordinator, 404-413-8374, E-mail: rgurvitch@gsu.edu.
Website: http://education.gsu.edu/KIN/kh_programs.htm

Harding University, Cannon-Clary College of Education, Searcy, AR 72149-0001. Offers advanced studies in teaching and learning (M Ed); art (MSE); behavioral science (MSE); counseling (MS, Ed S); early childhood special education (M Ed, MSE); education (MSE); educational leadership (M Ed, Ed S); elementary education (M Ed); English (MSE); French (MSE); history/social science (MSE); kinesiology (MSE); math (MSE); reading (M Ed); secondary education (M Ed); Spanish (MSE); teaching (MAT); teaching English as a second language (MSE). *Accreditation:* NCATE. *Program availability:* Part-time, evening/weekend. *Faculty:* 22 full-time (9 women), 51 part-time/adjunct (37 women). *Students:* 130 full-time (94 women), 321 part-time (234 women); includes 83 minority (50 Black or African American, non-Hispanic/Latino; 4 American Indian or Alaska Native, non-Hispanic/Latino; 6 Asian, non-Hispanic/Latino; 13 Hispanic/Latino; 10 Two or more races, non-Hispanic/Latino), 11 international. Average age 35. 125 applicants, 88% accepted, 110 enrolled. In 2016, 124 master's, 27 other advanced degrees awarded. *Degree requirements:* For master's, comprehensive exam (for some programs), thesis optional, portfolio(s); for Ed S, comprehensive exam, portfolio, project. *Entrance requirements:* For master's, GRE, MAT, PRAXIS; for Ed S, MAT or GRE. Additional exam requirements/recommendations for international students: Required—TOEFL (minimum score 550 paper-based; 79 iBT). *Application deadline:* For fall admission, 8/1 for domestic and international students; for spring admission, 1/1 for domestic and international students. Applications are processed on a rolling basis. Application fee: $35. Tuition and fees vary according to degree level and program. *Financial support:* In 2016–17, 31 students received support. Unspecified assistantships available. *Faculty research:* Reading, comprehension, school violence, educational technology, behavior, college choice, differentiated instruction, brain-based teaching. *Unit head:* Dr. Clara Carroll, Chair, 501-279-4501, Fax: 501-279-4083, E-mail: ccarroll@harding.edu. *Application contact:* Information Contact, 501-279-4315, E-mail: gradstudiesedu@harding.edu.
Website: http://www.harding.edu/education

Hofstra University, School of Education, Specialized Programs in Education, Hempstead, NY 11549. Offers applied behavior analysis (Advanced Certificate); early childhood special education (MS Ed, Advanced Certificate); educational and policy leadership (Ed D); educational leadership (Advanced Certificate), including school building leader/school district business leader; educational leadership and policy studies (MS Ed), including K-12; gifted education (Advanced Certificate), including school building leader/school district business leader; health education PK-12 teaching certification (MS); inclusive early childhood special education (MS Ed); inclusive elementary special education (MS Ed); inclusive secondary special education (MS Ed); literacy studies (MS Ed, Ed D, PhD, Advanced Certificate), including birth-grade 6 (MS Ed, Advanced Certificate), birth-grade 6 and special education (birth-grade2) (MS Ed), grades 5-12 (MS Ed, Advanced Certificate); physical education (MS); secondary education generalist (MS Ed), including students with disabilities 7-12; special education (MS Ed, Advanced Certificate); special education assessment and

diagnosis (Advanced Certificate); special education generalist (MS Ed), including extension in secondary education; sport science (MS), including strength and conditioning; teaching students with severe or multiple disabilities (Advanced Certificate). *Program availability:* Part-time, evening/weekend, 100% online, blended/hybrid learning. *Students:* 149 full-time (115 women), 258 part-time (187 women); includes 97 minority (50 Black or African American, non-Hispanic/Latino; 1 American Indian or Alaska Native, non-Hispanic/Latino; 11 Asian, non-Hispanic/Latino; 34 Hispanic/Latino; 1 Native Hawaiian or other Pacific Islander, non-Hispanic/Latino), 5 international. Average age 32. 250 applicants, 88% accepted, 146 enrolled. In 2016, 85 master's, 13 doctorates, 35 other advanced degrees awarded. *Degree requirements:* For master's, one foreign language, comprehensive exam (for some programs), thesis (for some programs), electronic portfolio, capstone course, internship, practicum, student teaching, seminars, minimum GPA of 3.0; for doctorate, one foreign language, comprehensive exam, thesis/dissertation, qualifying hearing. *Entrance requirements:* For master's, GRE, interview, letters of recommendation, portfolio, essay, certification; for doctorate, GRE or MAT, interview, resume, essay, master's degree, 3 letters of recommendation, writing sample; for Advanced Certificate, GRE, interview, letters of recommendation, essay, professional experience, resume, master's degree. Additional exam requirements/recommendations for international students: Required—TOEFL (minimum score 550 paper-based; 80 iBT). *Application deadline:* Applications are processed on a rolling basis. Application fee: $75. Electronic applications accepted. *Expenses: Tuition:* Full-time $1240. *Required fees:* $970. Tuition and fees vary according to program. *Financial support:* In 2016–17, 244 students received support, including 117 fellowships with full and partial tuition reimbursements available (averaging $3,705 per year), 12 research assistantships with full and partial tuition reimbursements available (averaging $6,490 per year); career-related internships or fieldwork, Federal Work-Study, institutionally sponsored loans, scholarships/grants, traineeships, tuition waivers (full and partial), and unspecified assistantships also available. Support available to part-time students. Financial award applicants required to submit FAFSA. *Faculty research:* Collaborative teaching and learning; language and culture; new media literacies; applied behavior analysis; K-12 leadership development. *Unit head:* Dr. Elfreda Blue, Chairperson, 516-463-5762, Fax: 516-463-6184, E-mail: elfreda.blue@hofstra.edu. *Application contact:* Sunil Samuel, Assistant Vice President of Admissions, 516-463-4723, Fax: 516-463-4664, E-mail: graduateadmission@hofstra.edu.
Website: http://www.hofstra.edu/education/

Howard University, Graduate School, Department of Health, Human Performance and Leisure Studies, Washington, DC 20059-0002. Offers exercise physiology (MS); health education (MS); sports studies (MS), including sociology of sports, sports management; urban recreation (MS), including leisure studies. *Program availability:* Part-time, evening/weekend. *Degree requirements:* For master's, comprehensive exam, thesis. *Entrance requirements:* For master's, BS in human performance or related field. Additional exam requirements/recommendations for international students: Recommended—TOEFL. Electronic applications accepted. *Faculty research:* Health promotion, cardiovascular hypertension, physical activity, sport and human rights issues.

Idaho State University, Office of Graduate Studies, Kasiska College of Health Professions, Department of Health and Nutrition Sciences, Program in Health Education, Pocatello, ID 83209-8109. Offers MHE. *Program availability:* Part-time. *Degree requirements:* For master's, comprehensive exam, thesis or project. *Entrance requirements:* For master's, GRE General Test, previous coursework in statistics, natural sciences, tests and measurements. Additional exam requirements/recommendations for international students: Required—TOEFL (minimum score 600 paper-based). Electronic applications accepted. *Faculty research:* Health and wellness.

Illinois State University, Graduate School, College of Applied Science and Technology, School of Kinesiology and Recreation, Normal, IL 61790-2200. Offers health education (MS). *Degree requirements:* For master's, thesis or alternative. *Entrance requirements:* For master's, GRE General Test, minimum GPA of 2.6 in last 60 hours of course work. *Faculty research:* Influences on positive youth development through sport, country-wide health fitness project, graduate practicum in athletic training, perceived exertion and self-selected intensity during resistance exercise in younger and older.

Indiana State University, College of Graduate and Professional Studies, College of Nursing, Health, and Human Services, Department of Applied Health Sciences, Terre Haute, IN 47809. Offers MS, DHS. *Accreditation:* NCATE (one or more programs are accredited). *Degree requirements:* For master's, thesis or alternative. *Entrance requirements:* For master's, GRE General Test. Electronic applications accepted.

Indiana University Bloomington, School of Public Health, Department of Applied Health Science, Bloomington, IN 47405. Offers behavioral, social, and community health (MPH); family health (MPH); health behavior (PhD); nutrition science (MS); professional health education (MPH); public health administration (MPH); safety management (MS); school and college health education (MS). *Accreditation:* CEPH (one or more programs are accredited). *Degree requirements:* For master's, thesis optional; for doctorate, comprehensive exam, thesis/dissertation. *Entrance requirements:* For master's, GRE (for MS in nutrition science), 3 recommendations; for doctorate, GRE, 3 recommendations. Additional exam requirements/recommendations for international students: Required—TOEFL (minimum score 550 paper-based; 80 iBT). Electronic applications accepted. *Faculty research:* Cancer education, HIV/AIDS and drug education, public health, parent-child interactions, safety education, obesity, public health policy, public health administration, school health, health education, human development, nutrition, human sexuality, chronic disease, early childhood health.

Indiana University of Pennsylvania, School of Graduate Studies and Research, College of Health and Human Services, Department of Kinesiology, Health, and Sport Science, Program in Health and Physical Education, Indiana, PA 15705. Offers M Ed. *Program availability:* Part-time. *Faculty:* 10 full-time (3 women). *Students:* 23 full-time (12 women), 3 part-time (1 woman). Average age 25. 6 applicants, 100% accepted, 5 enrolled. In 2016, 12 master's awarded. *Entrance requirements:* Additional exam requirements/recommendations for international students: Required—TOEFL (minimum score 540 paper-based). *Application deadline:* Applications are processed on a rolling basis. Application fee: $50. Electronic applications accepted. *Expenses:* Tuition, state resident: full-time $8694; part-time $483 per credit. Tuition, nonresident: full-time $13,050; part-time $725 per credit. *Required fees:* $157 per credit. $50 per term. Tuition and fees vary according to course load and program. *Financial support:* In 2016–17, 7 research assistantships with tuition reimbursements (averaging $3,303 per year) were awarded; career-related internships or fieldwork, Federal Work-Study, scholarships/grants, and unspecified assistantships also available. Support available to part-time students. Financial award application deadline: 4/15; financial award applicants required to submit FAFSA. *Unit head:* Dr. Keri Kulik, Coordinator, 724-357-5656, E-mail: kskulik@iup.edu.
Website: http://www.iup.edu/grad/healthphysed/default.aspx

Indiana University–Purdue University Indianapolis, School of Health and Rehabilitation Sciences, Indianapolis, IN 46202-5119. Offers health and rehabilitation sciences (PhD); health sciences (MS); nutrition and dietetics (MS); occupational therapy (MS); physical therapy (DPT); physician assistant (MPAS). *Program availability:* Part-time, evening/weekend. *Degree requirements:* For master's, thesis (for some programs). *Entrance requirements:* For master's, GRE General Test, minimum GPA of 3.0 (for MS in health sciences, nutrition and dietetics), 3.2 (for MS in occupational therapy), 3.0 cumulative and prerequisite math/science (for MPAS); for doctorate, GRE, minimum cumulative and prerequisite math/science GPA of 3.2. Additional exam requirements/recommendations for international students: Required—TOEFL (minimum score 550 paper-based; 79 iBT), IELTS (minimum score 6.5), PTE (minimum score 54). Electronic applications accepted. *Expenses:* Contact institution. *Faculty research:* Function and mobility across the lifespan, pediatric nutrition, driving and mobility rehabilitation, neurorehabilitation and biomechanics, rehabilitation and integrative therapy.

Inter American University of Puerto Rico, Metropolitan Campus, Graduate Programs, Program in Physical Education, San Juan, PR 00919-1293. Offers teaching of physical education (MA); training and sport performance (MA). *Degree requirements:* For master's, comprehensive exam. *Entrance requirements:* For master's, GRE or EXADEP, interview. Electronic applications accepted.

Inter American University of Puerto Rico, San Germán Campus, Graduate Studies Center, Program in Health and Physical Education, San Germán, PR 00683-5008. Offers MA. *Program availability:* Part-time, evening/weekend. *Degree requirements:* For master's, comprehensive exam. *Entrance requirements:* For master's, GRE General Test or EXADEP, minimum GPA of 3.0.

Ithaca College, School of Health Sciences and Human Performance, Program in Health Education, Ithaca, NY 14850. Offers MS. *Program availability:* Part-time. *Faculty:* 9 full-time (6 women). *Students:* 6 full-time (4 women), 1 (woman) part-time; includes 2 minority (1 Black or African American, non-Hispanic/Latino; 1 Two or more races, non-Hispanic/Latino). Average age 23. 11 applicants, 82% accepted, 7 enrolled. In 2016, 11 master's awarded. *Degree requirements:* For master's, thesis optional. *Entrance requirements:* Additional exam requirements/recommendations for international students: Required—TOEFL (minimum score 550 paper-based; 80 iBT). *Application deadline:* For fall admission, 3/1 priority date for domestic and international students; for spring admission, 12/1 for domestic and international students. Applications are processed on a rolling basis. Application fee: $40. Electronic applications accepted. *Expenses:* Contact institution. *Financial support:* In 2016–17, 7 students received support, including 6 research assistantships (averaging $11,983 per year); career-related internships or fieldwork, Federal Work-Study, scholarships/grants, and unspecified assistantships also available. Support available to part-time students. Financial award application deadline: 3/1; financial award applicants required to submit CSS PROFILE or FAFSA. *Unit head:* Dr. Stewart Auyash, Chair, 607-274-1312, E-mail: auyash@ithaca.edu. *Application contact:* Nicole Eversley Bradwell, Director, Office of Admission, 607-274-3124, Fax: 607-274-1263, E-mail: admission@ithaca.edu.
Website: http://www.ithaca.edu/gradprograms/hppe/programs/healthed

Jackson State University, Graduate School, College of Education and Human Development, Department of Health, Physical Education and Recreation, Jackson, MS 39217. Offers physical education (MS Ed); sport science (MS). *Accreditation:* NCATE. *Program availability:* Part-time, evening/weekend, 100% online, blended/hybrid learning. *Faculty:* 4 full-time (1 woman). *Students:* 37 full-time (21 women), 66 part-time (37 women); includes 99 minority (98 Black or African American, non-Hispanic/Latino; 1 Two or more races, non-Hispanic/Latino), 2 international. Average age 32. 74 applicants, 70% accepted, 30 enrolled. In 2016, 21 master's awarded. *Degree requirements:* For master's, comprehensive exam, thesis or alternative. *Entrance requirements:* For master's, GRE General Test. Additional exam requirements/recommendations for international students: Required—TOEFL (minimum score 520 paper-based; 67 iBT). *Application deadline:* For fall admission, 3/1 priority date for domestic students, 3/1 for international students; for spring admission, 10/1 for domestic and international students. Applications are processed on a rolling basis. Application fee: $25. Electronic applications accepted. *Expenses:* Contact institution. *Financial support:* Career-related internships or fieldwork, Federal Work-Study, scholarships/grants, and unspecified assistantships available. Support available to part-time students. Financial award application deadline: 3/1; financial award applicants required to submit FAFSA. *Unit head:* Dr. Patricia Kennedy, Interim Chair, 601-979-2765, Fax: 601-979-2766, E-mail: patricia.r.kennedy@jsums.edu. *Application contact:* Dr. Hill Williams, Interim Director of Sport Science, 601-979-0275, Fax: 601-979-2766, E-mail: hill.williams@jsums.edu.
Website: http://www.jsums.edu/healthedu/

James Madison University, The Graduate School, College of Arts and Letters, Program in Communication and Advocacy, Harrisonburg, VA 22807. Offers environmental communication (MA); health communication (MA); strategic communication (MA). *Program availability:* Part-time, evening/weekend. *Faculty:* 22 full-time (13 women), 1 (woman) part-time/adjunct. *Students:* 20 full-time (15 women); includes 5 minority (3 Black or African American, non-Hispanic/Latino; 1 Asian, non-Hispanic/Latino; 1 Two or more races, non-Hispanic/Latino), 1 international. Average age 30. 18 applicants, 100% accepted, 9 enrolled. In 2016, 9 master's awarded. Application fee: $55. Electronic applications accepted. *Financial support:* In 2016–17, 16 students received support, including 6 teaching assistantships with full tuition reimbursements available (averaging $9,284 per year); fellowships, Federal Work-Study, and 10 assistantships (averaging $7911) also available. Financial award application deadline: 3/1; financial award applicants required to submit FAFSA. *Unit head:* Dr. Eric M. Fife, Director of the School of Communication Studies, 540-568-6449, E-mail: fifeem@jmu.edu. *Application contact:* Lynette D. Michael, Director of Graduate Admissions, 540-568-6131 Ext. 6395, Fax: 540-568-7860, E-mail: michaeld@jmu.edu.
Website: http://www.jmu.edu/commstudies/

James Madison University, The Graduate School, College of Health and Behavioral Sciences, Program in Kinesiology, Harrisonburg, VA 22802. Offers clinical exercise physiology (MS); exercise physiology (MS); kinesiology (MAT, MS); nutrition and exercise (MS); physical and health education (MAT); sport and recreation leadership (MS). *Program availability:* Part-time, evening/weekend. *Faculty:* 9 full-time (3 women), 2 part-time/adjunct (1 woman). *Students:* 64 full-time (27 women), 8 part-time (5 women); includes 6 minority (1 Black or African American, non-Hispanic/Latino; 1 Asian, non-Hispanic/Latino; 2 Hispanic/Latino; 2 Two or more races, non-Hispanic/Latino). Average age 30. 140 applicants, 70% accepted, 44 enrolled. In 2016, 42 master's awarded. Application fee: $55. Electronic applications accepted. *Financial support:* In 2016–17, 45 students received support, including 14 teaching assistantships with full tuition reimbursements available (averaging $8,837 per year); Federal Work-Study and 25 assistantships (averaging $7911), 20 athletic assistantships (averaging $9284) also available. Financial award application deadline: 3/1; financial award applicants required to submit FAFSA. *Unit head:* Dr. Christopher J. Womack, Department Head, 540-568-6145, E-mail: womackcx@jmu.edu. *Application contact:* Lynette D. Michael, Director of Graduate Admissions, 540-568-6131 Ext. 6395, Fax: 540-568-7860, E-mail: michaeld@jmu.edu.
Website: http://www.jmu.edu/kinesiology/

John F. Kennedy University, Graduate School of Holistic Studies, Department of Integral Studies, Program in Holistic Health Education, Pleasant Hill, CA 94523-4817. Offers MA. *Program availability:* Part-time, evening/weekend. *Degree requirements:* For master's, thesis or alternative. *Entrance requirements:* For master's, interview.

Additional exam requirements/recommendations for international students: Required—TOEFL.

Johns Hopkins University, Bloomberg School of Public Health, Department of Health, Behavior and Society, Baltimore, MD 21218. Offers genetic counseling (Sc M); health education and health communication (MSPH); social and behavioral sciences (Dr PH, PhD); social factors in health (MHS). *Degree requirements:* For master's, comprehensive exam (for some programs), thesis (for some programs); for doctorate, comprehensive exam, thesis/dissertation. *Entrance requirements:* For master's, GRE, curriculum vitae, 3 letters of recommendation; for doctorate, GRE, transcripts, curriculum vitae, 3 recommendation letters. Additional exam requirements/recommendations for international students: Required—TOEFL (minimum score 600 paper-based; 100 iBT). Electronic applications accepted. *Faculty research:* Social determinants of health and structural and community-level inventions to improve health, communication and health education, behavioral and social aspects of genetic counseling.

Johns Hopkins University, School of Education, Master's Programs in Education, Baltimore, MD 21218. Offers counseling (MS), including clinical mental health counseling, school counseling; education (MS), including educational studies, gifted education, reading, school administration and supervision, technology for educators; elementary education (MAT); health professions (M Ed); intelligence analysis (MS); organizational leadership (MS); secondary education (MAT), including biology, chemistry, earth/space science, English, physics, social studies; special education (MS), including early childhood special education, general special education studies, mild to moderate disabilities, severe disabilities. *Program availability:* Part-time, evening/weekend, 100% online, blended/hybrid learning. *Students:* 345 full-time (265 women), 1,601 part-time (1,245 women); includes 837 minority (392 Black or African American, non-Hispanic/Latino; 7 American Indian or Alaska Native, non-Hispanic/Latino; 141 Asian, non-Hispanic/Latino; 207 Hispanic/Latino; 7 Native Hawaiian or other Pacific Islander, non-Hispanic/Latino; 83 Two or more races, non-Hispanic/Latino), 55 international. Average age 27. 1,352 applicants, 76% accepted, 819 enrolled. In 2016, 642 master's awarded. *Degree requirements:* For master's, comprehensive exam (for some programs), portfolio, capstone project and/or internship; PRAXIS II (subject area assessments) for initial teacher preparation programs that lead to licensure. *Entrance requirements:* For master's, GRE (for full-time programs only); PRAXIS I/core or state-approved alternative (for initial teacher preparation programs that lead to licensure), minimum of bachelor's degree from regionally- or nationally-accredited institution; minimum GPA of 3.0 in all previous programs of study; official transcripts from all post-secondary institutions attended; essay; curriculum vitae/resume; letters of recommendation (3 for full-time programs, 2 for part-time programs); dispositions survey. Additional exam requirements/recommendations for international students: Required—TOEFL (minimum score 600 paper-based; 100 iBT), IELTS (minimum score 7). *Application deadline:* For fall admission, 4/1 priority date for domestic students, 4/1 for international students; for spring admission, 10/1 priority date for domestic students, 10/1 for international students; for summer admission, 2/1 priority date for domestic students, 2/1 for international students. Applications are processed on a rolling basis. Application fee: $80. Electronic applications accepted. *Expenses:* Contact institution. *Financial support:* Application deadline: 4/1; applicants required to submit FAFSA. *Unit head:* Dr. Christopher C. Morphew, Dean. *Application contact:* Elisabeth Woodward, Director of Admissions, 410-516-9796, Fax: 410-516-9817, E-mail: soe.info@jhu.edu.
Website: http://education.jhu.edu

Kansas State University, Graduate School, College of Human Ecology, Department of Food, Nutrition, Dietetics and Health, Manhattan, KS 66506. Offers dietetics (MS); human nutrition (PhD); nutrition, dietetics and sensory sciences (MS); nutritional sciences (PhD); public health nutrition (PhD); public health physical activity (PhD); sensory analysis and consumer behavior (PhD). *Program availability:* Part-time. *Faculty:* 17 full-time (11 women), 11 part-time/adjunct (3 women). *Students:* 27 full-time (20 women), 32 part-time (26 women); includes 5 minority (2 Black or African American, non-Hispanic/Latino; 1 Asian, non-Hispanic/Latino; 2 Hispanic/Latino), 17 international. Average age 31. 18 applicants, 50% accepted, 5 enrolled. In 2016, 15 master's, 5 doctorates awarded. *Degree requirements:* For master's, thesis or alternative, residency; for doctorate, thesis/dissertation, residency. *Entrance requirements:* For master's, GRE General Test, minimum undergraduate GPA of 3.0; for doctorate, GRE General Test, minimum graduate GPA of 3.0. Additional exam requirements/recommendations for international students: Required—TOEFL (minimum score 550 paper-based; 79 iBT), IELTS (minimum score 6.5). *Application deadline:* For fall admission, 2/1 priority date for domestic and international students; for spring admission, 8/1 priority date for domestic and international students. Applications are processed on a rolling basis. Application fee: $50 ($75 for international students). Electronic applications accepted. *Expenses:* Tuition, state resident: full-time $9670. Tuition, nonresident: full-time $21,828. *Required fees:* $862. *Financial support:* In 2016–17, 29 students received support, including 16 research assistantships with full and partial tuition reimbursements available (averaging $15,711 per year), 6 teaching assistantships with full and partial tuition reimbursements available (averaging $10,167 per year); career-related internships or fieldwork, Federal Work-Study, institutionally sponsored loans, scholarships/grants, health care benefits, and tuition waivers (full and partial) also available. Support available to part-time students. Financial award application deadline: 3/1; financial award applicants required to submit FAFSA. *Faculty research:* Cancer and immunology, obesity, sensory analysis and consumer behavior, nutrient metabolism, clinical and community interventions. *Total annual research expenditures:* $1.1 million. *Unit head:* Dr. Mark Haub, Head, 785-532-5508, Fax: 785-532-3132, E-mail: haub@ksu.edu. *Application contact:* Karen Rogers, Administrative Assistant, 785-532-0124, E-mail: karen39@k-state.edu.
Website: http://www.he.k-state.edu/fndh/

Keiser University, Master of Science in Education Program, Ft. Lauderdale, FL 33309. Offers allied health teaching and leadership (MS Ed); career college administration (MS Ed); leadership (MS Ed); online teaching and learning (MS Ed); teaching and learning (MS Ed). *Program availability:* Part-time, online learning.

Kent State University, College of Education, Health and Human Services, School of Health Sciences, Program in Health Education and Promotion, Kent, OH 44242-0001. Offers M Ed, PhD. *Accreditation:* NCATE. *Degree requirements:* For doctorate, comprehensive exam, thesis/dissertation. *Entrance requirements:* For master's, 2 letters of reference, goals statement; for doctorate, GRE General Test, goals statement, resume, interview. Additional exam requirements/recommendations for international students: Required—TOEFL (minimum score 550 paper-based; 80 iBT). Electronic applications accepted. *Expenses:* Tuition, state resident: full-time $10,864; part-time $495 per credit hour. Tuition, nonresident: full-time $18,380; part-time $837 per credit hour. *Faculty research:* Substance use/abuse, sexuality, community health assessment, epidemiology, HIV/AIDS.

Lake Erie College of Osteopathic Medicine, Professional Programs, Erie, PA 16509-1025. Offers biomedical sciences (Postbaccalaureate Certificate); medical education (MS); osteopathic medicine (DO); pharmacy (Pharm D). *Accreditation:* ACPE; AOsA. *Degree requirements:* For doctorate, comprehensive exam, National Osteopathic Medical Licensing Exam, Levels 1 and 2; for Postbaccalaureate Certificate, comprehensive exam, North American Pharmacist Licensure Examination (NAPLEX). *Entrance requirements:* For doctorate, MCAT, minimum GPA of 3.2, letters of recommendation; for Postbaccalaureate Certificate, PCAT, letters of recommendation, minimum GPA of 3.5. Electronic applications accepted. *Faculty research:* Cardiac smooth and skeletal muscle mechanics, chemotherapeutics and vitamins, osteopathic manipulation.

Lehman College of the City University of New York, School of Health Sciences, Human Services and Nursing, Department of Health Sciences, Program in Health Education and Promotion, Bronx, NY 10468-1589. Offers MA. *Accreditation:* CEPH; NCATE. *Program availability:* Part-time, evening/weekend. *Degree requirements:* For master's, thesis or alternative. *Entrance requirements:* For master's, minimum GPA of 2.7.

Lehman College of the City University of New York, School of Health Sciences, Human Services and Nursing, Department of Health Sciences, Program in Health N–12 Teacher, Bronx, NY 10468-1589. Offers MS Ed. *Accreditation:* NCATE. *Degree requirements:* For master's, thesis or alternative.

Lock Haven University of Pennsylvania, College of Natural, Behavioral and Health Sciences, Lock Haven, PA 17745-2390. Offers actuarial science (PSM); athletic training (MS); health promotion/education (MHS); healthcare management (MHS); physician assistant (MHS). Program also offered at the Clearfield, Coudersport, and Harrisburg campuses. *Accreditation:* ARC-PA. *Entrance requirements:* For master's, minimum undergraduate GPA of 3.0. Additional exam requirements/recommendations for international students: Required—TOEFL. Electronic applications accepted.

Logan University, College of Health Sciences, Chesterfield, MO 63017. Offers health informatics (MS); health professionals education (DHPE); nutrition and human performance (MS); sports science and rehabilitation (MS). *Program availability:* Part-time, online only, 100% online. *Faculty:* 2 full-time (1 woman), 14 part-time/adjunct (6 women). *Students:* 54 full-time (40 women), 255 part-time (182 women); includes 38 minority (16 Black or African American, non-Hispanic/Latino; 4 Asian, non-Hispanic/Latino; 10 Hispanic/Latino; 8 Two or more races, non-Hispanic/Latino), 14 international. Average age 35. 229 applicants, 88% accepted, 164 enrolled. In 2016, 89 master's awarded. *Entrance requirements:* For master's, minimum GPA of 2.5; 6 hours of biology and physical science; bachelor's degree and 9 hours of business health administration (for health informatics). Additional exam requirements/recommendations for international students: Required—TOEFL (minimum score 500 paper-based; 79 iBT); Recommended—IELTS (minimum score 6.5). *Application deadline:* Applications are processed on a rolling basis. Application fee: $50. Electronic applications accepted. *Expenses:* $650 tuition per credit hour (for DHPE), $450 tuition per credit hour (for MS); $80 fees per trimester. *Financial support:* In 2016–17, 4 students received support. Federal Work-Study and scholarships/grants available. Support available to part-time students. Financial award applicants required to submit FAFSA. *Faculty research:* Ankle injury prevention in high school athletes, low back pain in college football players, short arc banding and low back pain, the effects of enzymes on inflammatory blood markers, gait analysis in high school and college athletes. *Unit head:* Dr. Sherri Cole, Dean, College of Health Sciences, 636-227-2100 Ext. 2702, Fax: 636-207-2418, E-mail: sherri.cole@logan.edu. *Application contact:* Jordan LaMarca, Assistant Director of Admissions, 636-227-2100 Ext. 1973, Fax: 636-207-2425, E-mail: admissions@logan.edu.

Loma Linda University, School of Public Health, Programs in Health Education, Loma Linda, CA 92350. Offers MPH, Dr PH. *Accreditation:* CEPH (one or more programs are accredited). *Degree requirements:* For doctorate, thesis/dissertation. *Entrance requirements:* For doctorate, GRE General Test. Additional exam requirements/recommendations for international students: Required—Michigan English Language Assessment Battery or TOEFL. *Expenses:* Contact institution.

Longwood University, College of Graduate and Professional Studies, College of Education and Human Services, Farmville, VA 23909. Offers education (MS), including algebra and middle school mathematics, counselor education, elementary and middle school mathematics, elementary education, elementary education initial licensure, health and physical education, special education general curriculum, special education initial licensure; reading, literacy and learning (M Ed); school librarianship (M Ed); social work and communication sciences and disorders (MS), including communication sciences and disorders. *Accreditation:* NCATE. *Program availability:* Part-time, evening/weekend. *Degree requirements:* For master's, comprehensive exam (for some programs), thesis optional, professional portfolio, internship, clinical experience, or practicum. *Entrance requirements:* For master's, PRAXIS I (for initial teaching licensure programs); GRE (for some programs), bachelor's degree from regionally-accredited institution, 2 recommendations (3 for some programs), minimum 500-word personal essay, official transcripts, minimum GPA of 2.75, valid teaching license (for some programs). Additional exam requirements/recommendations for international students: Required—TOEFL (minimum score 570 paper-based), IELTS (minimum score 6.5). Electronic applications accepted. *Expenses:* Contact institution.

Marshall University, Academic Affairs Division, College of Information Technology and Engineering, Division of Applied Science and Technology, Program in Safety, Huntington, WV 25755. Offers MS. *Accreditation:* NCATE. *Degree requirements:* For master's, thesis optional, comprehensive assessment.

Marymount University, Malek School of Health Professions, Program in Health Education and Promotion, Arlington, VA 22207-4299. Offers MS. *Program availability:* Part-time, evening/weekend. *Faculty:* 3 full-time (2 women), 1 (woman) part-time/adjunct. *Students:* 3 full-time (all women), 6 part-time (5 women); includes 3 minority (2 Black or African American, non-Hispanic/Latino; 1 Asian, non-Hispanic/Latino). Average age 29. 6 applicants, 100% accepted, 2 enrolled. In 2016, 12 master's awarded. *Degree requirements:* For master's, internship. *Entrance requirements:* For master's, GRE or MAT, 2 letters of recommendation, interview, resume, personal statement. Additional exam requirements/recommendations for international students: Required—TOEFL (minimum score 600 paper-based; 96 iBT), IELTS (minimum score 6.5). *Application deadline:* Applications are processed on a rolling basis. Application fee: $40. Electronic applications accepted. *Expenses: Tuition:* Full-time $8460; part-time $940 per credit hour. *Required fees:* $10 per credit hour. One-time fee: $240 part-time. Tuition and fees vary according to program. *Financial support:* In 2016–17, 3 students received support, including 3 research assistantships with tuition reimbursements available; career-related internships or fieldwork, Federal Work-Study, scholarships/grants, and unspecified assistantships also available. Support available to part-time students. Financial award applicants required to submit FAFSA. *Unit head:* Dr. Jennifer Tripken, Chair, Health and Human Performance, 703-526-1597, Fax: 703-284-3819, E-mail: jennifer.tripken@marymount.edu. *Application contact:* Francesca Reed, Director, Graduate Admissions, 703-284-5901, Fax: 703-527-3815, E-mail: grad.admissions@marymount.edu.
Website: http://www.marymount.edu/Academics/Malek-School-of-Health-Professions/Graduate-Programs/Health-Education-Promotion-(M-S-)

Marywood University, Academic Affairs, Center for Interdisciplinary Studies, Scranton, PA 18509-1598. Offers human development (PhD), including educational administration, health promotion, higher education administration, instructional leadership, social work. *Program availability:* Part-time. Electronic applications accepted. *Expenses:* Contact institution.

Massachusetts College of Liberal Arts, Graduate Programs, North Adams, MA 01247-4100. Offers business (MBA); educational administration (M Ed); educational leadership (CAGS); instruction and curriculum (M Ed); instructional technology (M Ed); physical education and health (M Ed); reading (M Ed); special education (M Ed). *Program availability:* Part-time, evening/weekend. *Degree requirements:* For master's, thesis. *Entrance requirements:* For master's, writing sample.

Meredith College, School of Education, Health and Human Sciences, Raleigh, NC 27607-5298. Offers academically and intellectually gifted (M Ed); curriculum instruction specialist (M Ed); elementary education (M Ed, MAT); English as a second language (M Ed, MAT); health and physical education (MAT); nutrition, health and human performance (MS, Postbaccalaureate Certificate), including dietetic internship (Postbaccalaureate Certificate), nutrition (MS); reading (M Ed); special education (MAT). *Accreditation:* NCATE. *Program availability:* Part-time, evening/weekend. *Degree requirements:* For master's, thesis optional. *Entrance requirements:* For master's, GRE General Test or MAT, minimum GPA of 2.5, teaching license, recommendations. Additional exam requirements/recommendations for international students: Required—TOEFL. Electronic applications accepted. *Expenses:* Contact institution.

Middle Tennessee State University, College of Graduate Studies, College of Behavioral and Health Sciences, Department of Health and Human Performance, Program in Health, Physical Education and Recreation, Murfreesboro, TN 37132. Offers health and human performance (MS); leisure and sport management (MS). *Program availability:* Part-time, evening/weekend, online learning. *Degree requirements:* For master's, comprehensive exam, thesis optional. *Entrance requirements:* For master's, GRE. Additional exam requirements/recommendations for international students: Required—TOEFL (minimum score 525 paper-based; 71 iBT) or IELTS (minimum score 6). *Faculty research:* Kinesiometrics, leisure behavior, health, lifestyles.

Minnesota State University Mankato, College of Graduate Studies and Research, College of Allied Health and Nursing, Department of Health Science, Mankato, MN 56001. Offers community health education (MS); public health education (Postbaccalaureate Certificate); school health education (MS, Postbaccalaureate Certificate). *Program availability:* Part-time. *Students:* 3 full-time (all women), 36 part-time (26 women). *Degree requirements:* For master's, comprehensive exam, thesis or alternative. *Entrance requirements:* For master's, minimum GPA of 3.0 during previous 2 years; for Postbaccalaureate Certificate, teaching license. Additional exam requirements/recommendations for international students: Required—TOEFL (minimum score 500 paper-based; 61 iBT). *Application deadline:* For fall admission, 7/1 for domestic students, 5/1 for international students; for spring admission, 11/1 for domestic students, 10/1 for international students. Applications are processed on a rolling basis. Application fee: $40. Electronic applications accepted. *Financial support:* Research assistantships with full tuition reimbursements, teaching assistantships with full tuition reimbursements, career-related internships or fieldwork, and Federal Work-Study available. Support available to part-time students. Financial award application deadline: 3/15; financial award applicants required to submit FAFSA. *Unit head:* Dr. Marlene K. Tappe, Professor and Chair, 507-389-2686, E-mail: marlene.tappe@mnsu.edu.
Website: http://ahn.mnsu.edu/health/

Mississippi University for Women, Graduate School, Department of Health and Kinesiology, Columbus, MS 39701-9998. Offers health education (MS). *Degree requirements:* For master's, comprehensive exam.

Montana State University, The Graduate School, College of Education, Health, and Human Development, Department of Health and Human Development, Bozeman, MT 59717. Offers family and consumer sciences (MS). *Accreditation:* ACA. *Program availability:* Part-time, online learning. *Degree requirements:* For master's, comprehensive exam. *Entrance requirements:* For master's, GRE (minimum scores: verbal 480; quantitative 480). Additional exam requirements/recommendations for international students: Required—TOEFL (minimum score 550 paper-based). Electronic applications accepted. *Faculty research:* Community food systems, ethic of care for teachers and coaches, influence of public policy on families and communities, cost effectiveness of early childhood education, exercise metabolism, winter sport performance enhancement, assessment of physical activity.

Montclair State University, The Graduate School, College of Education and Human Services, MAT Program in Teaching, Montclair, NJ 07043-1624. Offers art (MAT); biology (MAT); chemistry (MAT); earth science (MAT); English (MAT); French (MAT); health and physical education (MAT); health education (MAT); mathematics (MAT); music (MAT); physical education (MAT); physical science (MAT); social studies (MAT); Spanish (MAT); teacher of English as a second language (MAT). *Degree requirements:* For master's, comprehensive exam, thesis or alternative. *Entrance requirements:* For master's, interview, 2 letters of recommendation. Additional exam requirements/recommendations for international students: Required—TOEFL (minimum score 83 iBT), IELTS (minimum score 6.5). Electronic applications accepted. *Expenses:* Tuition, state resident: part-time $553 per credit. Tuition, nonresident: part-time $854 per credit. *Required fees:* $91 per credit. Tuition and fees vary according to program.

Morehead State University, Graduate Programs, College of Education, Department of Middle Grades and Secondary Education, Morehead, KY 40351. Offers business and marketing education (MAT); English/language arts 5-9 (MAT); French (MAT); health P-12 (MAT); mathematics 5-9 (MAT); physical education P-12 (MAT); science 5-9 (MAT); secondary biology (MAT); secondary chemistry (MAT); secondary earth science (MAT); secondary English (MAT); secondary math (MAT); secondary physics (MAT); secondary social studies (MAT); social studies 5-9 (MAT); Spanish (MAT). *Program availability:* Part-time, evening/weekend. *Degree requirements:* For master's, portfolio. *Entrance requirements:* For master's, GRE or PRAXIS II content exam, minimum overall undergraduate GPA of 2.5. Additional exam requirements/recommendations for international students: Required—TOEFL (minimum score 500 paper-based). Electronic applications accepted.

Morehead State University, Graduate Programs, College of Science and Technology, Department of Health, Wellness and Human Performance, Morehead, KY 40351. Offers health/physical education (MA). *Accreditation:* NCATE. *Program availability:* Part-time, evening/weekend. *Degree requirements:* For master's, comprehensive exam, thesis, oral exam, written core exam. *Entrance requirements:* For master's, GRE General Test or MAT, minimum GPA of 2.5; undergraduate major/minor in health, physical education, or recreation. Additional exam requirements/recommendations for international students: Required—TOEFL (minimum score 500 paper-based). Electronic applications accepted. *Faculty research:* Child growth and performance, instructional strategies, outdoor leadership qualities, exercise science, athletic training.

New Jersey City University, College of Professional Studies, Department of Health Sciences, Jersey City, NJ 07305-1597. Offers community health education (MS); health administration (MS); school health education (MS). *Program availability:* Part-time, evening/weekend. *Degree requirements:* For master's, thesis or alternative, internship. *Entrance requirements:* Additional exam requirements/recommendations for international students: Required—TOEFL (minimum score 79 iBT).

New Mexico Highlands University, Graduate Studies, College of Arts and Sciences, Department of Exercise and Sport Sciences, Las Vegas, NM 87701. Offers human performance and sport (MA), including human performance and sport sciences, sports administration, teacher education. *Program availability:* Part-time. *Degree requirements:* For master's, comprehensive exam, thesis or alternative. *Entrance requirements:* For master's, minimum undergraduate GPA of 3.0. Additional exam requirements/recommendations for international students: Required—TOEFL (minimum score 540 paper-based). *Faculty research:* Child obesity and physical inactivity, body composition and fitness assessment, motor development, sport marketing, sport finance.

New York Medical College, School of Health Sciences and Practice, Valhalla, NY 10595. Offers behavioral sciences and health promotion (MPH); biostatistics (MS); children with special health care (Graduate Certificate); emergency preparedness (Graduate Certificate); environmental health science (MPH); epidemiology (MPH, MS); global health (Graduate Certificate); health education (Graduate Certificate); health policy and management (MPH, Dr PH); industrial hygiene (Graduate Certificate); pediatric dysphagia (Post-Graduate Certificate); physical therapy (DPT); public health (Graduate Certificate); speech-language pathology (MS). *Accreditation:* CEPH. *Program availability:* Part-time, evening/weekend, 100% online, blended/hybrid learning. *Faculty:* 42 full-time (31 women), 236 part-time/adjunct (138 women). *Students:* 235 full-time (165 women), 252 part-time (185 women); includes 188 minority (83 Black or African American, non-Hispanic/Latino; 1 American Indian or Alaska Native, non-Hispanic/Latino; 62 Asian, non-Hispanic/Latino; 36 Hispanic/Latino; 6 Two or more races, non-Hispanic/Latino), 26 international. Average age 27. In 2016, 110 master's, 37 doctorates awarded. *Degree requirements:* For master's, comprehensive exam (for some programs), thesis (for some programs); for doctorate, thesis/dissertation. *Expenses:* $1,070 per credit tuition, $105 fees. *Unit head:* Ben Watson, PhD, Vice Dean, 914-594-4531, E-mail: ben_watson@nymc.edu. *Application contact:* Veronica Jarek-Prinz, Associate Dean for Admissions and Enrollment Management, 914-594-3941, E-mail: veronica_jarekprinz@nymc.edu.
Website: http://www.nymc.edu/school-of-health-sciences-and-practice-shsp/

Nicholls State University, Graduate Studies, College of Education, Department of Teacher Education, Thibodaux, LA 70310. Offers curriculum and instruction (M Ed); educational leadership (M Ed); elementary education (MAT); human performance education (MAT); middle school education (MAT); secondary education (MAT). *Accreditation:* NCATE. *Program availability:* Part-time, evening/weekend, online learning. *Degree requirements:* For master's, comprehensive exam, portfolio. *Entrance requirements:* For master's, GRE General Test, teaching license. Electronic applications accepted.

North Carolina Agricultural and Technical State University, School of Graduate Studies, School of Education, Department of Human Performance and Leisure Studies, Greensboro, NC 27411. Offers physical education (MAT, MS). *Accreditation:* NCATE. *Program availability:* Part-time, evening/weekend. *Degree requirements:* For master's, comprehensive exam, thesis or alternative, qualifying exam. *Entrance requirements:* For master's, GRE General Test or MAT.

Northeastern State University, College of Education, Department of Health and Kinesiology, Tahlequah, OK 74464-2399. Offers MS. *Program availability:* Part-time, evening/weekend. *Faculty:* 3 full-time (all women). *Students:* 11 full-time (4 women), 22 part-time (11 women); includes 14 minority (2 Black or African American, non-Hispanic/Latino; 8 American Indian or Alaska Native, non-Hispanic/Latino; 1 Hispanic/Latino; 3 Two or more races, non-Hispanic/Latino), 3 international. Average age 27. In 2016, 14 master's awarded. *Entrance requirements:* For master's, MAT or GRE, minimum GPA of 2.5. Additional exam requirements/recommendations for international students: Required—TOEFL. *Application deadline:* For fall admission, 6/1 for domestic and international students; for winter admission, 11/1 for domestic and international students; for spring admission, 3/1 for domestic students, 2/1 for international students. Applications are processed on a rolling basis. Application fee: $25. Electronic applications accepted. *Expenses:* Tuition, state resident: full-time $2816; part-time $216.60 per credit hour. Tuition, nonresident: full-time $6365; part-time $489.60 per credit hour. *Required fees:* $37.40 per credit hour. *Unit head:* Dr. Sonia Tinsley, Department Chair, 918-444-3915, E-mail: tinsleys@nsuok.edu. *Application contact:* Josh McCollum, Graduate Coordinator, 918-444-2093, E-mail: mccolluj@nsuok.edu.
Website: http://academics.nsuok.edu/education/DegreePrograms/GraduatePrograms/HealthandKinesiology.aspx

Northwestern State University of Louisiana, Graduate Studies and Research, Department of Health and Human Performance, Natchitoches, LA 71497. Offers MS. *Degree requirements:* For master's, comprehensive exam, thesis or alternative. *Entrance requirements:* For master's, GRE General Test, minimum undergraduate GPA of 2.5. Additional exam requirements/recommendations for international students: Required—TOEFL. Electronic applications accepted.

Northwest Missouri State University, Graduate School, School of Health Science and Wellness, Maryville, MO 64468-6001. Offers applied health and sport sciences (MS); recreation (MS). *Accreditation:* NCATE. *Program availability:* Part-time. *Students:* 68 full-time (38 women), 27 part-time (19 women). *Degree requirements:* For master's, comprehensive exam. *Entrance requirements:* For master's, GRE General Test, minimum undergraduate GPA of 2.75, teaching certificate, writing sample. Additional exam requirements/recommendations for international students: Required—TOEFL (minimum score 550 paper-based). *Application deadline:* For fall admission, 7/1 for domestic and international students; for spring admission, 11/15 for domestic and international students. Applications are processed on a rolling basis. Application fee: $0 ($50 for international students). *Expenses:* Tuition, state resident: full-time $3447; part-time $383 per credit hour. Tuition, nonresident: full-time $5724; part-time $636 per credit hour. *Required fees:* $130 per credit hour. *Financial support:* Teaching assistantships with full tuition reimbursements and unspecified assistantships available. Financial award application deadline: 4/1; financial award applicants required to submit FAFSA. *Unit head:* Dr. Terry Long, Director, School of Health Science and Wellness, 660-562-1706, E-mail: tlong@nwmissouri.edu. *Application contact:* Cathie Hannigan, Office Manager, 660-562-1297, Fax: 660-562-1483, E-mail: channig@nwmissouri.edu.
Website: http://www.nwmissouri.edu/health/

Nova Southeastern University, College of Osteopathic Medicine, Fort Lauderdale, FL 33328. Offers biomedical informatics (MS, Graduate Certificate), including biomedical informatics (MS), clinical informatics (Graduate Certificate), public health informatics (Graduate Certificate); disaster and emergency management (MS); medical education (MS); nutrition (MS, Graduate Certificate), including functional nutrition and herbal therapy (Graduate Certificate); osteopathic medicine (DO); public health (MPH, Graduate Certificate), including health education (Graduate Certificate); social medicine (Graduate Certificate). *Accreditation:* AOsA. *Faculty:* 126 full-time (64 women), 1,411 part-time/adjunct (352 women). *Students:* 1,040 full-time (476 women), 196 part-time (135 women); includes 635 minority (95 Black or African American, non-Hispanic/Latino; 298 Asian, non-Hispanic/Latino; 208 Hispanic/Latino; 1 Native Hawaiian or other Pacific Islander, non-Hispanic/Latino; 33 Two or more races, non-Hispanic/Latino), 54 international. Average age 27. 5,383 applicants, 7% accepted, 248 enrolled. In 2016, 94 master's, 231 doctorates, 2 other advanced degrees awarded. *Degree requirements:* For master's, comprehensive exam (for MPH); field/special projects; for doctorate,

comprehensive exam, COMLEX Boards; for Graduate Certificate, thesis or alternative. *Entrance requirements:* For master's, GRE; for doctorate, MCAT, biology, chemistry, organic chemistry, physics (all with labs), biochemistry, and English. *Application deadline:* For fall admission, 1/15 for domestic students. Applications are processed on a rolling basis. Application fee: $50. Electronic applications accepted. *Expenses:* $49,639 residents, $54,806 non-residentsfor out-of-state students; $100 microscope/laboratory fee (for first-year students); $145 per year Health Professions Division student access fee; $1,050 per year student service fee. *Financial support:* In 2016–17, 46 students received support, including 8 fellowships (averaging $30,690 per year); research assistantships, teaching assistantships, Federal Work-Study, and scholarships/grants also available. Financial award application deadline: 6/1; financial award applicants required to submit FAFSA. *Faculty research:* Teaching strategies, simulated patient use, HIV/AIDS education, minority health issues, managed care education. *Unit head:* Elaine M. Wallace, Dean, 954-262-1457, Fax: 954-262-2250, E-mail: ewallace@nova.edu. *Application contact:* HPD Admissions, 877-640-0218, E-mail: hpdinfo@nova.edu.
Website: http://www.osteopathic.nova.edu/

Oklahoma State University, College of Education, School of Applied Health and Educational Psychology, Stillwater, OK 74078. Offers applied behavioral studies (Ed D); applied health and educational psychology (MS, PhD, Ed S). *Accreditation:* APA (one or more programs are accredited). *Program availability:* Part-time. *Faculty:* 38 full-time (22 women), 11 part-time/adjunct (6 women). *Students:* 168 full-time (122 women), 140 part-time (80 women); includes 86 minority (21 Black or African American, non-Hispanic/Latino; 10 American Indian or Alaska Native, non-Hispanic/Latino; 3 Asian, non-Hispanic/Latino; 24 Hispanic/Latino; 28 Two or more races, non-Hispanic/Latino), 13 international. Average age 30. 157 applicants, 51% accepted, 73 enrolled. In 2016, 73 master's, 21 doctorates awarded. *Degree requirements:* For master's, thesis (for some programs); for doctorate, comprehensive exam, thesis/dissertation. *Entrance requirements:* For master's and doctorate, GRE or GMAT. Additional exam requirements/recommendations for international students: Required—TOEFL (minimum score 550 paper-based; 79 iBT). *Application deadline:* For fall admission, 3/1 priority date for international students; for spring admission, 8/1 priority date for international students. Applications are processed on a rolling basis. Application fee: $40 ($75 for international students). Electronic applications accepted. *Expenses:* Tuition, state resident: full-time $3775; part-time $209.70 per credit hour. Tuition, nonresident: full-time $14,851; part-time $825.05 per credit hour. *Required fees:* $2027; $112.60 per credit hour. Tuition and fees vary according to campus/location. *Financial support:* In 2016–17, 31 research assistantships (averaging $9,791 per year), 64 teaching assistantships (averaging $11,347 per year) were awarded; career-related internships or fieldwork, Federal Work-Study, scholarships/grants, health care benefits, tuition waivers (partial), and unspecified assistantships also available. Support available to part-time students. Financial award application deadline: 3/1; financial award applicants required to submit FAFSA. *Unit head:* Dr. Aric Warren, Head, 405-744-6040, Fax: 405-744-6779, E-mail: aric.warren@okstate.edu.
Website: http://education.okstate.edu/sahep

Old Dominion University, Darden College of Education, Program in Physical Education, Curriculum and Instruction Emphasis, Norfolk, VA 23529. Offers human movement sciences (PhD), including health and sport pedagogy; physical education (MS Ed), including adapted physical education, coaching education, curriculum and instruction. *Program availability:* Part-time, evening/weekend. *Faculty:* 2 full-time (0 women), 1 (woman) part-time/adjunct. *Students:* 5 full-time (2 women), 2 part-time (1 woman); includes 1 minority (Hispanic/Latino). Average age 29. 8 applicants, 75% accepted, 4 enrolled. In 2016, 4 master's awarded. *Degree requirements:* For master's, comprehensive exam (for some programs), thesis or alternative, internship, research project. *Entrance requirements:* For master's, GRE, PRAXIS Core (for licensure only), minimum GPA of 2.8 overall, 3.0 in major. Additional exam requirements/recommendations for international students: Required—TOEFL (minimum score 500 paper-based; 97 iBT). *Application deadline:* For fall admission, 3/1 priority date for domestic students; for spring admission, 11/1 for domestic students. Applications are processed on a rolling basis. Application fee: $50. Electronic applications accepted. *Expenses:* Tuition, state resident: full-time $8604; part-time $478 per credit hour. Tuition, nonresident: full-time $21,510; part-time $1195 per credit hour. *Required fees:* $66 per semester. Tuition and fees vary according to campus/location, program and reciprocity agreements. *Financial support:* In 2016–17, 2 students received support, including 1 teaching assistantship (averaging $10,000 per year); unspecified assistantships also available. Financial award application deadline: 4/15. *Faculty research:* Motor development, physical activity and fitness, motivation and learning in physical education, curriculum and instruction. *Unit head:* Dr. Lynn Ridinger, Chair, 757-683-4995, E-mail: lridinge@odu.edu. *Application contact:* William Heffelfinger, Director of Graduate Admissions, 757-683-5554, Fax: 757-683-3255, E-mail: gradadmit@odu.edu.
Website: http://education.odu.edu/eci/ciphd/

Penn State Harrisburg, Graduate School, School of Behavioral Sciences and Education, Middletown, PA 17057. Offers adult education in the health and medical professions (Certificate); applied behavior analysis (MA); applied clinical psychology (MA); applied psychological research (MA); community psychology and social change (MA); English as a second language (ESL) program specialist and leadership (Certificate); folklore and ethnography (Certificate); health education (M Ed); lifelong learning and adult education (M Ed, D Ed); literacy education (M Ed); literacy leadership (Certificate); psychology: applications in clinical psychology (Certificate); psychology: health psychology (Certificate); teaching and curriculum (M Ed); training and development (M Ed, Certificate). *Program availability:* Part-time, evening/weekend. *Unit head:* Dr. Mukund S. Kulkarni, Chancellor, 717-948-6105, Fax: 717-948-6452. *Application contact:* Robert W. Coffman, Jr., Director of Enrollment Management, Recruitment and Admissions, 717-948-6250, Fax: 717-948-6325, E-mail: hbgadmit@psu.edu.
Website: https://harrisburg.psu.edu/behavioral-sciences-and-education/

Pennsylvania College of Health Sciences, Graduate Programs, Lancaster, PA 17601. Offers administration (MSN); education (MSHS, MSN); healthcare administration (MHA). *Degree requirements:* For master's, internship (for MHA, MSN in administration); practicum (for MSHS, MSN in education).

Pittsburg State University, Graduate School, College of Education, Department of Health, Physical Education and Recreation, Pittsburg, KS 66762. Offers health, human performance, and recreation (MS), including human performance and wellness, sport and leisure service management. *Program availability:* Part-time, online only, 100% online. *Students:* 65 (25 women); includes 16 minority (8 Black or African American, non-Hispanic/Latino; 1 American Indian or Alaska Native, non-Hispanic/Latino; 5 Hispanic/Latino; 2 Two or more races, non-Hispanic/Latino). In 2016, 33 master's awarded. *Degree requirements:* For master's, thesis or alternative. *Entrance requirements:* For master's, letter of intent. Additional exam requirements/recommendations for international students: Required—TOEFL (minimum score 520 paper-based; 68 iBT), IELTS (minimum score 6), PTE (minimum score 47). *Application deadline:* For fall admission, 6/1 for international students; for spring admission, 10/15 for international students; for summer admission, 4/1 for international students. Applications are processed on a rolling basis. Application fee: $35 ($60 for international students). Electronic applications accepted. *Expenses:* Contact institution. *Financial support:* In 2016–17, 9 teaching assistantships with full tuition reimbursements (averaging $5,500 per year) were awarded; career-related internships or fieldwork, Federal Work-Study, and unspecified assistantships also available. Financial award application deadline: 2/1; financial award applicants required to submit FAFSA. *Faculty research:* Personality of athletes, fitness activities for children, aerobic conditioning, fitness evaluation. *Unit head:* Dr. John Oppliger, Chairperson, 620-235-4668, E-mail: joppliger@pittstate.edu. *Application contact:* Lisa Allen, Assistant Director of Graduate and Continuing Studies, 620-235-4223, Fax: 620-235-4219, E-mail: lallen@pittstate.edu.

Plymouth State University, College of Graduate Studies, Graduate Studies in Education, Program in Health Education, Plymouth, NH 03264-1595. Offers M Ed. *Program availability:* Part-time, evening/weekend. *Degree requirements:* For master's, PRAXIS. *Entrance requirements:* For master's, MAT, minimum GPA of 3.0.

Portland State University, Graduate Studies, OHSU-PSU School of Public Health, Health Promotion Program, Portland, OR 97207-0751. Offers aging (Certificate); community health (PhD); health education (MA, MS); health promotion (MPH); health studies (MPA, MPH), including health administration. MPH offered jointly with Oregon Health & Science University. *Program availability:* Part-time. *Faculty:* 25 full-time (19 women), 4 part-time/adjunct (2 women). *Students:* 22 full-time (19 women), 27 part-time (23 women); includes 14 minority (2 American Indian or Alaska Native, non-Hispanic/Latino; 2 Asian, non-Hispanic/Latino; 4 Hispanic/Latino; 1 Native Hawaiian or other Pacific Islander, non-Hispanic/Latino; 5 Two or more races, non-Hispanic/Latino), 1 international. Average age 32. 35 applicants, 20% accepted, 5 enrolled. In 2016, 19 master's, 1 doctorate awarded. *Degree requirements:* For master's, comprehensive exam (for some programs), thesis (for some programs), internship/praticum, oral and written exams (depending on program; for doctorate, comprehensive exam, thesis/dissertation. *Entrance requirements:* For master's, GRE (for MPH program), 3 letters of recommendation, minimum GPA of 3.0, resume; for doctorate, GRE, transcripts, personal statement, resume, writing sample, 3 letters of recommendation. Additional exam requirements/recommendations for international students: Required—TOEFL (minimum score 550 paper-based; 80 iBT). *Application deadline:* For fall admission, 2/1 for domestic and international students. Applications are processed on a rolling basis. Application fee: $65. *Expenses:* Contact institution. *Financial support:* In 2016–17, 9 research assistantships with tuition reimbursements (averaging $7,556 per year) were awarded; teaching assistantships, career-related internships or fieldwork, Federal Work-Study, scholarships/grants, and unspecified assistantships also available. Support available to part-time students. Financial award application deadline: 3/1; financial award applicants required to submit FAFSA. *Unit head:* Dr. David Bangsberg, Founding Dean, 503-282-7537. *Application contact:* Dr. Jill Rissi, Dean for Academic Affairs, E-mail: jrissi@pdx.edu.
Website: http://www.healthed.pdx.edu/

Prairie View A&M University, College of Education, Department of Health and Kinesiology, Prairie View, TX 77446. Offers M Ed, MS. *Accreditation:* NCATE. *Program availability:* Part-time, evening/weekend. *Faculty:* 4 full-time (all women). *Students:* 23 full-time (14 women), 11 part-time (4 women); includes 33 minority (31 Black or African American, non-Hispanic/Latino; 2 Hispanic/Latino). Average age 26. 24 applicants, 96% accepted, 16 enrolled. In 2016, 7 master's awarded. *Degree requirements:* For master's, thesis. *Entrance requirements:* For master's, GRE General Test. Additional exam requirements/recommendations for international students: Required—TOEFL (minimum score 550 paper-based; 79 iBT). *Application deadline:* For fall admission, 5/1 priority date for domestic and international students; for spring admission, 10/1 priority date for domestic students, 9/1 priority date for international students; for summer admission, 3/1 priority date for domestic students, 2/1 priority date for international students. Applications are processed on a rolling basis. Application fee: $50. Electronic applications accepted. *Expenses:* Tuition, state resident: full-time $4362; part-time $273.48 per credit hour. Tuition, nonresident: full-time $12,390; part-time $534.10 per credit hour. *Required fees:* $2782; $178.26 per credit hour. *Financial support:* Career-related internships or fieldwork available. Support available to part-time students. Financial award application deadline: 4/1; financial award applicants required to submit FAFSA. *Unit head:* Dr. Angela Branch-Vital, Department Head, 936-261-3900, Fax: 936-261-3905, E-mail: abranch-vital@pvamu.edu. *Application contact:* Pauline Walker, Administrative Assistant II, Research and Graduate Studies, 936-261-3521, Fax: 936-261-3529, E-mail: gradadmissions@pvamu.edu.

Purdue University, Graduate School, College of Health and Human Sciences, Department of Health and Kinesiology, West Lafayette, IN 47907. Offers athletic training education administration (MS, PhD); biomechanics (MS, PhD); exercise physiology (MS, PhD); health education (MS, PhD); history/philosophy of sport (MS, PhD); motor control and development (MS, PhD); physical education pedagogy (PhD); physical education teacher education (MS); recreation and sport management (MS, PhD); sport and exercise psychology (MS, PhD). *Program availability:* Part-time. *Faculty:* 19 full-time (7 women). *Students:* 30 full-time (13 women), 10 part-time (5 women); includes 2 minority (1 Asian, non-Hispanic/Latino; 1 Two or more races, non-Hispanic/Latino), 6 international. Average age 26. 77 applicants, 29% accepted, 18 enrolled. In 2016, 18 master's, 9 doctorates awarded. *Degree requirements:* For master's, thesis optional; for doctorate, comprehensive exam, thesis/dissertation, qualifying examination, preliminary examination. *Entrance requirements:* For master's, GRE General Test (minimum score 1000 combined verbal and quantitative), minimum undergraduate GPA of 3.0 or equivalent; for doctorate, GRE General Test (minimum score 1100 combined verbal and quantitative), minimum undergraduate GPA of 3.0 or equivalent; master's degree with minimum GPA of 3.25 (recommended). Additional exam requirements/recommendations for international students: Required—TOEFL (minimum score 77 iBT); Recommended—TWE. *Application deadline:* For fall admission, 4/30 for domestic and international students; for spring admission, 10/15 for domestic and international students. Applications are processed on a rolling basis. Application fee: $60 ($75 for international students). Electronic applications accepted. *Financial support:* Fellowships with partial tuition reimbursements, research assistantships with partial tuition reimbursements, teaching assistantships with partial tuition reimbursements, and Federal Work-Study available. Support available to part-time students. Financial award applicants required to submit FAFSA. *Faculty research:* Wellness, motivation, teaching effectiveness, learning and development. *Unit head:* Dr. Timothy P. Gavin, Head of the Graduate Program, 765-494-3178, Fax: 765-494-1239, E-mail: gavin1@purdue.edu. *Application contact:* Christy F. Daugherty, Graduate Contact, 765-494-3162, E-mail: daugher2@purdue.edu.
Website: http://www.purdue.edu/hhs/hk/

Purdue University, Graduate School, College of Health and Human Sciences, Department of Nutrition Science, West Lafayette, IN 47907. Offers animal health (MS, PhD); biochemical and molecular nutrition (MS, PhD); growth and development (MS, PhD); human and clinical nutrition (MS, PhD); public health and education (MS, PhD). *Faculty:* 21 full-time (15 women), 1 part-time/adjunct (0 women). *Students:* 40 full-time (29 women), 9 part-time (7 women); includes 5 minority (3 Black or African American,

non-Hispanic/Latino; 1 Asian, non-Hispanic/Latino; 1 Two or more races, non-Hispanic/Latino), 20 international. Average age 28. 66 applicants, 33% accepted, 13 enrolled. In 2016, 2 master's, 6 doctorates awarded. *Degree requirements:* For master's, thesis; for doctorate, thesis/dissertation. *Entrance requirements:* For master's and doctorate, GRE General Test (minimum scores in verbal and quantitative areas of 1000 or 300 on new scoring), minimum undergraduate GPA of 3.0 or equivalent. Additional exam requirements/recommendations for international students: Required—TOEFL (minimum score 600 paper-based; 77 iBT). *Application deadline:* For fall admission, 1/10 for domestic and international students. Applications are processed on a rolling basis. Application fee: $60 ($75 for international students). Electronic applications accepted. *Financial support:* Fellowships, research assistantships, and teaching assistantships available. Support available to part-time students. Financial award applicants required to submit FAFSA. *Faculty research:* Nutrient requirements, nutrient metabolism, nutrition and disease prevention. *Unit head:* Michele R. Forman, Head, 765-494-9921, E-mail: mforman@purdue.edu. *Application contact:* James C. Fleet, Chair of the Graduate Committee, 765-494-0302, E-mail: fleet@purdue.edu.
Website: http://www.cfs.purdue.edu/fn/

Rhode Island College, School of Graduate Studies, Feinstein School of Education and Human Development, Department of Health and Physical Education, Providence, RI 02908-1991. Offers health education (M Ed); physical education (CGS). *Accreditation:* NCATE. *Program availability:* Part-time, evening/weekend. *Faculty:* 2 part-time/adjunct (1 woman). *Students:* 1 (woman) full-time, 5 part-time (all women). Average age 45. In 2016, 6 master's awarded. *Degree requirements:* For master's, comprehensive assessment. *Entrance requirements:* For master's, GRE General Test or MAT, undergraduate transcripts; minimum undergraduate GPA of 3.0; 3 letters of recommendation; for CGS, GRE or MAT (for most programs), undergraduate transcripts; minimum undergraduate GPA of 3.0; 3 letters of recommendation. Additional exam requirements/recommendations for international students: Recommended—TOEFL (minimum score 550 paper-based; 79 iBT). *Application deadline:* For fall admission, 3/1 for domestic students; for spring admission, 11/1 for domestic students. Applications are processed on a rolling basis. Application fee: $50. Electronic applications accepted. *Expenses:* Tuition, state resident: full-time $8928; part-time $372 per credit. Tuition, nonresident: full-time $17,376; part-time $724 per credit. *Required fees:* $604; $22 per credit. One-time fee: $74. *Financial support:* In 2016–17, 1 teaching assistantship with full tuition reimbursement (averaging $1,500 per year) was awarded; Federal Work-Study, scholarships/grants, health care benefits, and unspecified assistantships also available. Support available to part-time students. Financial award application deadline: 5/15; financial award applicants required to submit FAFSA. *Unit head:* Dr. Robin Auld, Chair, 401-456-8046. *Application contact:* Graduate Studies, 401-456-8700.
Website: http://www.ric.edu/healthPhysicalEducation/

Rosalind Franklin University of Medicine and Science, College of Health Professions, Department of Interprofessional Healthcare Studies, Health Professions Education Program, North Chicago, IL 60064-3095. Offers MS.

Rosalind Franklin University of Medicine and Science, College of Health Professions, Department of Nutrition, North Chicago, IL 60064-3095. Offers clinical nutrition (MS); health promotion and wellness (MS); nutrition education (MS). *Program availability:* Part-time, evening/weekend, online learning. *Degree requirements:* For master's, thesis optional, portfolio. *Entrance requirements:* For master's, minimum GPA of 2.75, registered dietitian (RD), professional certificate or license. Additional exam requirements/recommendations for international students: Required—TOEFL. *Expenses:* Contact institution. *Faculty research:* Nutrition education, distance learning, computer-based graduate education, childhood obesity, nutrition medical education.

Rutgers University–Newark, School of Health Related Professions, Department of Interdisciplinary Studies, Program in Health Sciences, Newark, NJ 07102. Offers health sciences (MS, PhD). *Program availability:* Part-time, evening/weekend, online learning. *Degree requirements:* For doctorate, thesis/dissertation. *Entrance requirements:* For master's, BS, 2 reference letters, statement of career goals, curriculum vitae; for doctorate, GRE, interview, writing sample, 3 reference letters, curriculum vitae. Additional exam requirements/recommendations for international students: Required—TOEFL. Electronic applications accepted.

Rutgers University–New Brunswick, School of Public Health, Piscataway, NJ 08854. Offers biostatistics (MPH, MS, Dr PH, PhD); clinical epidemiology (Certificate); environmental and occupational health (MPH, Dr PH, PhD, Certificate); epidemiology (MPH, Dr PH, PhD); general public health (Certificate); health education and behavioral science (MPH, Dr PH, PhD); health systems and policy (MPH, PhD); public health (MPH, Dr PH, PhD); public health preparedness (Certificate); DO/MPH; JD/MPH; MBA/MPH; MD/MPH; MPH/MBA; MPH/MSPA; MS/MPH; Psy D/MPH. *Accreditation:* CEPH. *Program availability:* Part-time, evening/weekend. *Degree requirements:* For master's, thesis, internship; for doctorate, comprehensive exam, thesis/dissertation. *Entrance requirements:* For master's, GRE General Test; for doctorate, GRE General Test, MPH (Dr PH); MA, MPH, or MS (PhD). Additional exam requirements/recommendations for international students: Required—TOEFL. Electronic applications accepted.

Sage Graduate School, Esteves School of Education, Program in School Health Education, Troy, NY 12180-4115. Offers MS. *Accreditation:* NCATE. *Program availability:* Part-time, evening/weekend. *Faculty:* 4 full-time (all women), 4 part-time/adjunct (2 women). *Students:* 4 full-time (2 women), 14 part-time (3 women); includes 3 minority (1 Black or African American, non-Hispanic/Latino; 1 Hispanic/Latino; 1 Two or more races, non-Hispanic/Latino). Average age 28. 7 applicants, 57% accepted, 2 enrolled. In 2016, 13 master's awarded. *Degree requirements:* For master's, thesis optional. *Entrance requirements:* For master's, interview with advisor, assessment of writing skills. Additional exam requirements/recommendations for international students: Required—TOEFL (minimum score 550 paper-based). *Application deadline:* Applications are processed on a rolling basis. Application fee: $40. Electronic applications accepted. *Expenses: Tuition:* Full-time $12,240; part-time $680 per credit hour. Tuition and fees vary according to degree level and program. *Financial support:* Fellowships, research assistantships, Federal Work-Study, scholarships/grants, and unspecified assistantships available. Support available to part-time students. Financial award application deadline: 3/1; financial award applicants required to submit FAFSA. *Faculty research:* Policy development in health education and health care. *Unit head:* Dr. John Pelizza, Interim Dean, Estevez School of Education, 518-244-2051, Fax: 518-244-2334, E-mail: pelizj@sage.edu. *Application contact:* Wendy D. Diefendorf, Director of Graduate and Adult Admission, 518-244-2443, Fax: 518-244-6880, E-mail: diefew@sage.edu.

Saint Francis University, Health Science Program, Loretto, PA 15940-0600. Offers MHS. *Program availability:* Part-time, evening/weekend, online learning. *Degree requirements:* For master's, minimum GPA of 2.8. *Entrance requirements:* For master's, undergraduate transcript, letters of reference, minimum QPA of 2.5, resume. Additional exam requirements/recommendations for international students: Recommended—TOEFL (minimum score 80 iBT). Electronic applications accepted. *Expenses:* Contact institution. *Faculty research:* Distance education, health sciences, medical sciences, communication, adult education.

Saint Joseph's College of Maine, Master of Science in Education Program, Standish, ME 04084. Offers adult education and training (MS Ed); Catholic school leadership (MS Ed); health care educator (MS Ed); school educator (MS Ed). Program available by correspondence. *Program availability:* Part-time, online learning. Electronic applications accepted.

Saint Joseph's University, College of Arts and Sciences, Department of Health Services, Philadelphia, PA 19131-1395. Offers health administration (MS); health education (MS); informatics (MS); organizations development and leadership (MS). *Program availability:* Part-time, evening/weekend. *Faculty:* 12 full-time (6 women), 32 part-time/adjunct (12 women). *Students:* 52 full-time (35 women), 469 part-time (346 women); includes 188 minority (117 Black or African American, non-Hispanic/Latino; 1 American Indian or Alaska Native, non-Hispanic/Latino; 38 Asian, non-Hispanic/Latino; 23 Hispanic/Latino; 1 Native Hawaiian or other Pacific Islander, non-Hispanic/Latino; 8 Two or more races, non-Hispanic/Latino), 34 international. Average age 32. 156 applicants, 72% accepted, 59 enrolled. In 2016, 204 master's awarded. *Entrance requirements:* For master's, GRE (if GPA less than 2.75), 2 letters of recommendation, resume, personal statement, official transcripts. Additional exam requirements/recommendations for international students: Required—TOEFL (minimum score 550 paper-based; 80 iBT), IELTS (minimum score 6.5). *Application deadline:* For fall admission, 7/15 for international students; for spring admission, 11/1 for international students. Applications are processed on a rolling basis. Application fee: $35. Electronic applications accepted. *Expenses:* $853 per credit. *Financial support:* In 2016–17, 12 students received support. Career-related internships or fieldwork and unspecified assistantships available. Financial award application deadline: 5/1; financial award applicants required to submit FAFSA. *Unit head:* Louis D. Horvath, Director, 610-660-3131, E-mail: gradcas@sju.edu. *Application contact:* Graduate Admissions, College of Arts and Sciences, 610-660-3131, E-mail: gradcas@sju.edu.
Website: http://sju.edu/majors-programs/graduate-arts-sciences/masters/health-administration-ms

San Francisco State University, Division of Graduate Studies, College of Health and Social Sciences, Human Sexuality Studies Program, San Francisco, CA 94132-1722. Offers MA. *Expenses:* Tuition, state resident: full-time $6738. Tuition, nonresident: full-time $15,666. *Required fees:* $1012. Tuition and fees vary according to degree level and program. *Unit head:* Dr. Andreana Clay, Chair, 415-338-1090, Fax: 415-338-2653, E-mail: andreana@sfsu.edu. *Application contact:* Dr. Jessica Fields, Graduate Coordinator, 415-405-0589, Fax: 415-338-2653, E-mail: jfields@sfsu.edu.
Website: http://sxs.sfsu.edu/

Shenandoah University, School of Education and Human Development, Winchester, VA 22601-5195. Offers administrative leadership (D Ed); educational administration (MSE); emphasis in teaching (MSE); health and physical education (Certificate); individual focus (MSE); literacy education (MS); middle school teacher education (Certificate); organizational leadership (MS, D Prof); secondary school teacher education (Certificate); special education (MSE). *Accreditation:* TEAC. *Program availability:* Part-time, evening/weekend. *Faculty:* 9 full-time (7 women), 43 part-time/adjunct (33 women). *Students:* 31 full-time (25 women), 236 part-time (160 women); includes 39 minority (19 Black or African American, non-Hispanic/Latino; 1 American Indian or Alaska Native, non-Hispanic/Latino; 10 Asian, non-Hispanic/Latino; 7 Hispanic/Latino; 1 Native Hawaiian or other Pacific Islander, non-Hispanic/Latino; 1 Two or more races, non-Hispanic/Latino), 4 international. Average age 37. 90 applicants, 97% accepted, 56 enrolled. In 2016, 113 master's, 13 doctorates, 38 other advanced degrees awarded. *Degree requirements:* For master's, comprehensive exam (for some programs), thesis (for some programs); for doctorate, comprehensive exam, thesis/dissertation. *Entrance requirements:* For degree, PRAXIS Academic Core, SAT/ACT, PRAXIS Academic Core Math, or VCLA, three letters of recommendation, writing sample, undergraduate degree. Additional exam requirements/recommendations for international students: Required—TOEFL (minimum score 550 paper-based; 79 iBT), IELTS (minimum score 6.5). *Application deadline:* For fall admission, 5/1 priority date for domestic students, 5/1 for international students; for spring admission, 10/15 priority date for domestic students, 10/15 for international students; for summer admission, 3/15 priority date for domestic students, 3/15 for international students. Application fee: $30. Electronic applications accepted. *Expenses:* Contact institution. *Financial support:* In 2016–17, 18 students received support. Scholarships/grants and unspecified assistantships available. Financial award applicants required to submit FAFSA. *Faculty research:* Exploring helplessness and anxiety in learning statistics, facilitating effective classroom group work, expert-novice dynamics in teaching, K-12 policy implementation and change, adult education, family-school-community relations, mentoring of first-year school principals. *Total annual research expenditures:* $2,000. *Unit head:* Dennis William Kellison, PhD, Director, 540-535-7324, Fax: 540-665-4726, E-mail: dkelliso@su.edu. *Application contact:* Andrew Woodall, Executive Director of Recruitment and Admissions, 540-665-4581, Fax: 540-665-4627, E-mail: admit@su.edu.
Website: http://www.su.edu/education/

Simmons College, School of Nursing and Health Sciences, Boston, MA 02115. Offers didactic dietetics (Certificate); dietetic internship (Certificate); health professions education (PhD, CAGS); nursing (MS, MSN), including family nurse practitioner (MS); nursing practice (DNP); nutrition and health promotion (MS); physical therapy (DPT); sports nutrition (Certificate). *Accreditation:* AACN. *Program availability:* Part-time, blended/hybrid learning. *Faculty:* 25 full-time (21 women), 243 part-time/adjunct (226 women). *Students:* 321 full-time (294 women), 1,211 part-time (1,110 women); includes 310 minority (119 Black or African American, non-Hispanic/Latino; 5 American Indian or Alaska Native, non-Hispanic/Latino; 71 Asian, non-Hispanic/Latino; 81 Hispanic/Latino; 4 Native Hawaiian or other Pacific Islander, non-Hispanic/Latino; 30 Two or more races, non-Hispanic/Latino), 8 international. Average age 34. 1,056 applicants, 68% accepted, 429 enrolled. In 2016, 181 master's, 28 doctorates, 40 other advanced degrees awarded. *Entrance requirements:* For doctorate, GRE. Additional exam requirements/recommendations for international students: Required—TOEFL (minimum score 570 paper-based; 88 iBT). *Application deadline:* For fall admission, 6/1 for international students. Application fee: $50. Electronic applications accepted. *Expenses:* $1,315 per credit; $105 activity fee per semester. *Financial support:* In 2016–17, 15 research assistantships with partial tuition reimbursements were awarded; scholarships/grants and unspecified assistantships also available. *Unit head:* Dr. Judy Beal, Dean, 617-521-2139. *Application contact:* Brett DiMarzo, Director of Graduate Admission, 617-521-2651, Fax: 617-521-3137, E-mail: brett.dimarzo@simmons.edu.
Website: http://www.simmons.edu/snhs/

Southeastern Louisiana University, College of Nursing and Health Sciences, Department of Kinesiology and Health Studies, Hammond, LA 70402. Offers health and kinesiology (MS), including exercise science, health promotion and exercise science, health studies, kinesiology. *Accreditation:* NCATE. *Program availability:* Part-time. *Faculty:* 7 full-time (3 women), 2 part-time/adjunct (1 woman). *Students:* 24 full-time (8 women), 14 part-time (11 women); includes 14 minority (8 Black or African American, non-Hispanic/Latino; 3 Hispanic/Latino; 3 Two or more races, non-Hispanic/Latino), 1 international. Average age 25. 32 applicants, 59% accepted, 9 enrolled. In 2016, 19 master's awarded. *Degree requirements:* For master's, comprehensive exam (for some programs), thesis (for some programs). *Entrance requirements:* Additional exam

requirements/recommendations for international students: Required—TOEFL (minimum score 500 paper-based; 61 iBT). *Application deadline:* For fall admission, 7/15 priority date for domestic students, 6/1 priority date for international students; for spring admission, 12/1 priority date for domestic students, 10/1 priority date for international students. Applications are processed on a rolling basis. Application fee: $20 ($30 for international students). Electronic applications accepted. *Expenses:* Tuition, state resident: full-time $6540; part-time $465 per credit hour. Tuition, nonresident: full-time $19,017; part-time $1158 per credit hour. *Required fees:* $1829. *Financial support:* In 2016–17, 27 students received support, including 8 research assistantships (averaging $9,413 per year), 4 teaching assistantships (averaging $9,275 per year); career-related internships or fieldwork, Federal Work-Study, institutionally sponsored loans, scholarships/grants, and unspecified assistantships also available. Support available to part-time students. Financial award application deadline: 5/1; financial award applicants required to submit FAFSA. *Faculty research:* Exercise physiology, motor learning, sport and exercise psychology. school health, health and aging. *Unit head:* Dr. Eddie Hebert, Department Head, 985-549-2129, Fax: 985-549-5119, E-mail: ehebert@southeastern.edu. *Application contact:* Amanda Harper, Graduate Admissions Analyst, 985-549-5620, Fax: 985-549-5632, E-mail: admissions@southeastern.edu.
Website: http://www.southeastern.edu/acad_research/depts/kin_hs/index.html

Southern Connecticut State University, School of Graduate Studies, School of Health and Human Services, Department of Exercise Science, Program in School Health Education, New Haven, CT 06515-1355. Offers MS. *Accreditation:* NCATE. *Program availability:* Part-time, evening/weekend. *Faculty:* 1 (woman) full-time, 1 (woman) part-time/adjunct. *Students:* 1 (woman) full-time, 18 part-time (9 women); includes 2 minority (1 Black or African American, non-Hispanic/Latino; 1 Hispanic/Latino). Average age 30. 5 applicants, 100% accepted, 5 enrolled. In 2016, 7 master's awarded. *Entrance requirements:* For master's, interview. *Application deadline:* For fall admission, 7/15 priority date for domestic students. Applications are processed on a rolling basis. Application fee: $50. Electronic applications accepted. *Expenses:* Tuition, state resident: full-time $6497; part-time $519 per credit hour. Tuition, nonresident: full-time $18,102; part-time $535 per credit hour. *Required fees:* $4722; $55 per semester. Tuition and fees vary according to program. *Financial support:* Career-related internships or fieldwork, scholarships/grants, and unspecified assistantships available. Financial award application deadline: 4/15; financial award applicants required to submit FAFSA. *Unit head:* Dr. Doris Marino, Graduate Coordinator, 203-392-6922, Fax: 203-392-6911, E-mail: marinod1@southernct.edu. *Application contact:* Lisa Galvin, Director of Graduate Admissions, 203-392-5240, Fax: 203-392-5235, E-mail: galvinl1@southernct.edu.

Southern Illinois University Carbondale, Graduate School, College of Education and Human Services, Department of Health Education and Recreation, Program in Community Health Education, Carbondale, IL 62901-4701. Offers MPH, MD/MPH, PhD/MPH. *Accreditation:* CEPH. *Entrance requirements:* Additional exam requirements/recommendations for international students: Required—TOEFL (minimum score 550 paper-based; 80 iBT).

Southern Illinois University Carbondale, Graduate School, College of Education and Human Services, Department of Health Education and Recreation, Program in Health Education, Carbondale, IL 62901-4701. Offers MS Ed, PhD. *Accreditation:* NCATE. *Program availability:* Part-time. *Degree requirements:* For master's, thesis; for doctorate, thesis/dissertation. *Entrance requirements:* For master's, MAT, minimum GPA of 2.7; for doctorate, MAT, minimum GPA of 3.25. Additional exam requirements/recommendations for international students: Required—TOEFL. *Faculty research:* Sexuality education, research design, injury control, program evaluation.

Southern Illinois University Edwardsville, Graduate School, College of Arts and Sciences, Department of Applied Communication Studies, Edwardsville, IL 62026. Offers corporate and organizational communication (MA); health communication (MA); interpersonal communication (MA); public relations (MA). *Program availability:* Part-time, evening/weekend. *Degree requirements:* For master's, comprehensive exam (for some programs), thesis (for some programs), final exam. *Entrance requirements:* Additional exam requirements/recommendations for international students: Required—TOEFL (minimum score 550 paper-based; 79 iBT), IELTS (minimum score 6.5). Electronic applications accepted.

Southern Illinois University Edwardsville, Graduate School, School of Education, Health, and Human Behavior, Edwardsville, IL 62062. Offers MA, MS, MS Ed, Ed D, Ed S, Post-Master's Certificate, Postbaccalaureate Certificate, SD. *Accreditation:* NCATE. *Program availability:* Part-time, evening/weekend. *Degree requirements:* For master's, comprehensive exam (for some programs), thesis (for some programs), final exam, portfolio. *Entrance requirements:* For master's, GRE. Additional exam requirements/recommendations for international students: Required—TOEFL (minimum score 550 paper-based; 79 iBT), IELTS (minimum score 6.5). Electronic applications accepted.

State University of New York College at Cortland, Graduate Studies, School of Professional Studies, Department of Health, Cortland, NY 13045. Offers community health (MS); health education (MST). *Accreditation:* NCATE. *Program availability:* Part-time, evening/weekend. *Entrance requirements:* Additional exam requirements/recommendations for international students: Required—TOEFL.

Teachers College, Columbia University, Department of Health and Behavior Studies, New York, NY 10027-6696. Offers applied behavior analysis (MA, PhD); applied educational psychology: school psychology (Ed M, PhD); behavioral nutrition (PhD), including nutrition (Ed D, PhD); community health education (MS); community nutrition education (Ed M), including community nutrition education; education of deaf and hard of hearing (MA, PhD); health education (MA, Ed D); hearing impairment (Ed D); intellectual disability/autism (MA, Ed D, PhD); nursing education (Ed D, Advanced Certificate); nutrition and education (MS); nutrition and exercise physiology (MS); nutrition and public health (MS); nutrition education (Ed D), including nutrition (Ed D, PhD); physical disabilities (Ed D); reading specialist (MA); severe or multiple disabilities (MA); special education (Ed M, MA, Ed D); teaching of sign language (MA). *Program availability:* Part-time, evening/weekend. *Students:* 282 full-time (262 women), 262 part-time (222 women); includes 180 minority (54 Black or African American, non-Hispanic/Latino; 1 American Indian or Alaska Native, non-Hispanic/Latino; 56 Asian, non-Hispanic/Latino; 56 Hispanic/Latino; 1 Native Hawaiian or other Pacific Islander, non-Hispanic/Latino; 12 Two or more races, non-Hispanic/Latino), 55 international. 503 applicants, 57% accepted, 146 enrolled. Terminal master's awarded for partial completion of doctoral program. *Expenses: Tuition:* Full-time $36,288; part-time $1512 per credit. *Required fees:* $438 per semester. One-time fee: $510 full-time. Full-time tuition and fees vary according to course load. *Unit head:* Prof. Stephen T. Peverly, Chair, 212-678-3964, Fax: 212-678-8259, E-mail: stp4@columbia.edu. *Application contact:* David Estrella, Director of Admission, 212-678-3305, E-mail: estrella@tc.columbia.edu.
Website: http://www.tc.columbia.edu/health-and-behavior-studies/

Tennessee Technological University, College of Graduate Studies, College of Education, Department of Exercise Science, Physical Education and Wellness, Cookeville, TN 38505. Offers adapted physical education (MA); elementary/middle school physical education (MA); lifetime wellness (MA); sport management (MA). *Accreditation:* NCATE. *Program availability:* Part-time, online learning. *Faculty:* 7 full-time (0 women). *Students:* 17 full-time (5 women), 32 part-time (17 women); includes 6 minority (4 Black or African American, non-Hispanic/Latino; 1 Hispanic/Latino; 1 Two or more races, non-Hispanic/Latino). Average age 27. 29 applicants, 59% accepted, 15 enrolled. In 2016, 24 master's awarded. *Degree requirements:* For master's, comprehensive exam, thesis or alternative. *Entrance requirements:* For master's, MAT or GRE. Additional exam requirements/recommendations for international students: Required—TOEFL (minimum score 527 paper-based; 71 iBT), IELTS (minimum score 5.5), PTE (minimum score 48), or TOEIC (Test of English as an International Communication). *Application deadline:* For fall admission, 8/1 for domestic students, 5/1 for international students; for spring admission, 12/1 for domestic students, 10/1 for international students; for summer admission, 5/1 for domestic students, 2/1 for international students. Applications are processed on a rolling basis. Application fee: $35 ($40 for international students). Electronic applications accepted. *Expenses:* Tuition, state resident: full-time $9375; part-time $534 per credit hour. Tuition, nonresident: full-time $22,443; part-time $1260 per credit hour. *Financial support:* In 2016–17, 2 research assistantships (averaging $4,400 per year), 9 teaching assistantships (averaging $4,400 per year) were awarded; fellowships and career-related internships or fieldwork also available. Financial award application deadline: 4/1. *Unit head:* Dr. Christy Killman, Chairperson, 931-372-3467, Fax: 931-372-6319, E-mail: ckillman@tntech.edu. *Application contact:* Shelia K. Kendrick, Coordinator of Graduate Studies, 931-372-3808, Fax: 931-372-3497, E-mail: skendrick@tntech.edu.

Texas A&M University, College of Education and Human Development, Department of Health and Kinesiology, College Station, TX 77843. Offers athletic training (MS); health education (M Ed, MS, Ed D, PhD); kinesiology (MS, PhD); sports management (MS). *Program availability:* Part-time. *Faculty:* 56. *Students:* 216 full-time (119 women), 116 part-time (55 women); includes 100 minority (37 Black or African American, non-Hispanic/Latino; 9 Asian, non-Hispanic/Latino; 49 Hispanic/Latino; 5 Two or more races, non-Hispanic/Latino), 28 international. Average age 29. 169 applicants, 72% accepted, 77 enrolled. In 2016, 104 master's, 24 doctorates awarded. *Degree requirements:* For master's, thesis (for some programs); for doctorate, comprehensive exam, thesis/dissertation. *Entrance requirements:* For master's and doctorate, GRE General Test. Additional exam requirements/recommendations for international students: Required—TOEFL (minimum score 550 paper-based; 80 iBT), IELTS (minimum score 6), PTE (minimum score 53). *Application deadline:* For fall admission, 1/15 for domestic students; for spring admission, 10/1 for domestic students. Applications are processed on a rolling basis. Application fee: $50 ($90 for international students). Electronic applications accepted. *Expenses:* Contact institution. *Financial support:* In 2016–17, 172 students received support, including 3 fellowships with tuition reimbursements available (averaging $18,412 per year), 43 research assistantships with tuition reimbursements available (averaging $5,089 per year), 76 teaching assistantships with tuition reimbursements available (averaging $8,295 per year); career-related internships or fieldwork, institutionally sponsored loans, scholarships/grants, traineeships, health care benefits, tuition waivers (full and partial), and unspecified assistantships also available. Support available to part-time students. Financial award application deadline: 3/15; financial award applicants required to submit FAFSA. *Unit head:* Dr. Richard Kreider, Head, 979-845-1333, Fax: 979-847-8987, E-mail: rkreider@hlkn.tamu.edu. *Application contact:* Jenny Bilski, Academic Advisor, 979-862-4052, E-mail: jenny.bilski@tamu.edu.
Website: http://hlknweb.tamu.edu/

Texas A&M University–Kingsville, College of Graduate Studies, College of Education and Human Performance, Department of Health and Kinesiology, Kingsville, TX 78363. Offers MA, MS. *Degree requirements:* For master's, variable foreign language requirement, comprehensive exam, thesis (for some programs). *Entrance requirements:* For master's, GRE, MAT, GMAT, essay. Additional exam requirements/recommendations for international students: Required—TOEFL (minimum score 550 paper-based; 79 iBT). Electronic applications accepted.

Texas Southern University, College of Education, Department of Health and Kinesiology, Houston, TX 77004-4584. Offers health education (MS); human performance (MS). *Program availability:* Part-time, evening/weekend. *Degree requirements:* For master's, comprehensive exam, thesis optional. *Entrance requirements:* For master's, GRE General Test, minimum GPA of 2.5. Additional exam requirements/recommendations for international students: Required—TOEFL. Electronic applications accepted.

Texas State University, The Graduate College, College of Education, Program in Health Education, San Marcos, TX 78666. Offers M Ed. *Program availability:* Part-time, evening/weekend. *Faculty:* 3 full-time (1 woman). *Students:* 26 full-time (20 women), 1 part-time (0 women); includes 12 minority (2 Black or African American, non-Hispanic/Latino; 1 Asian, non-Hispanic/Latino; 7 Hispanic/Latino; 2 Two or more races, non-Hispanic/Latino). Average age 27. 24 applicants, 83% accepted, 16 enrolled. In 2016, 10 master's awarded. *Degree requirements:* For master's, comprehensive exam, thesis optional. *Entrance requirements:* For master's, baccalaureate degree from regionally-accredited institution with minimum GPA of 2.75 in last 60 hours of course work, 18 hours of health education background courses, statement of purpose. Additional exam requirements/recommendations for international students: Required—TOEFL (minimum score 550 paper-based; 78 iBT), IELTS (minimum score 6.5). *Application deadline:* For fall admission, 2/15 priority date for domestic and international students; for spring admission, 10/15 priority date for domestic students, 10/1 for international students; for summer admission, 4/15 for domestic students, 3/15 for international students. Applications are processed on a rolling basis. Application fee: $40 ($90 for international students). Electronic applications accepted. *Expenses:* $4,851 per semester. *Financial support:* In 2016–17, 16 students received support, including 6 research assistantships (averaging $13,637 per year), 3 teaching assistantships (averaging $15,452 per year); career-related internships or fieldwork, Federal Work-Study, institutionally sponsored loans, scholarships/grants, and unspecified assistantships also available. Support available to part-time students. Financial award application deadline: 3/1; financial award applicants required to submit FAFSA. *Faculty research:* AIDS education, employee wellness, isometric strength evaluation. *Unit head:* Dr. David C. Wiley, Graduate Advisor, 512-245-2946, E-mail: dw13@txstate.edu. *Application contact:* Dr. Andrea Golato, Dean of the Graduate College, 512-245-2581, Fax: 512-245-8365, E-mail: gradcollege@txstate.edu.
Website: http://www.hhp.txstate.edu/Degree-Plans/Graduate/Master-of-Education-Degree-in-Health-Education.html

Texas Woman's University, Graduate School, College of Health Sciences, Department of Health Studies, Denton, TX 76201. Offers MS, PhD. *Program availability:* Part-time, evening/weekend. *Degree requirements:* For master's, comprehensive exam, thesis or alternative, for doctorate, comprehensive exam, thesis/dissertation, qualifying exam. *Entrance requirements:* For master's, GRE General Test (preferred minimum scores 150 [450 old version] Verbal, 140 [400 old version] Quantitative), 2 letters of recommendation, curriculum vitae, essay; for doctorate, GRE General Test (preferred minimum scores 152 [480 old version] Verbal, 140 [400 old version] Quantitative), minimum GPA of 3.5 on all master's course work, 2 letters of recommendation,

curriculum vitae, essay, writing sample. Additional exam requirements/ recommendations for international students: Required—TOEFL (minimum score 575 paper-based; 90 iBT). *Application deadline:* For fall admission, 4/1 for domestic students, 3/1 for international students; for spring admission, 10/1 for domestic students, 7/1 for international students. Applications are processed on a rolling basis. Application fee: $50 ($75 for international students). Electronic applications accepted. *Expenses:* Tuition, state resident: full-time $9046; part-time $251 per credit hour. Tuition, nonresident: full-time $22,922; part-time $614 per credit hour. *International tuition:* $23,046 full-time. *Required fees:* $2690; $1285 per credit hour. One-time fee: $50. Tuition and fees vary according to course level, course load, program and reciprocity agreements. *Financial support:* Research assistantships, teaching assistantships, career-related internships or fieldwork, Federal Work-Study, institutionally sponsored loans, scholarships/grants, traineeships, health care benefits, tuition waivers (partial), and unspecified assistantships available. Support available to part-time students. Financial award application deadline: 3/1; financial award applicants required to submit FAFSA. *Faculty research:* Body image and eating disorder prevention, health communication/health literacy, violence prevention, chronic diseases, HIV/AIDS prevention. *Unit head:* Dr. Roger Shipley, Interim Chair, 940-898-2831, Fax: 940-898-2859, E-mail: rshipley@twu.edu. *Application contact:* Dr. Samuel Wheeler, Assistant Director of Admissions, 940-898-3188, Fax: 940-898-3081, E-mail: wheelersr@twu.edu.
Website: http://www.twu.edu/health-studies/

Thomas Jefferson University, Jefferson School of Population Health, Philadelphia, PA 19107. Offers applied health economics and outcomes research (MS, PhD, Certificate); behavioral health science (PhD); health policy (MS, Certificate); healthcare quality and safety (MS, PhD); population health (Certificate); public health (MPH, Certificate). *Program availability:* Part-time, evening/weekend, online learning. Terminal master's awarded for partial completion of doctoral program. *Degree requirements:* For master's, thesis; for doctorate, comprehensive exam, thesis/dissertation. *Entrance requirements:* For master's, GRE or other graduate entrance exam (MCAT, LSAT, DAT, etc.), two letters of recommendation, curriculum vitae, transcripts from all undergraduate and graduate institutions; for doctorate, GRE (taken within the last 5 years), three letters of recommendation, curriculum vitae, transcripts from all undergraduate and graduate institutions. Additional exam requirements/recommendations for international students: Required—TOEFL. Electronic applications accepted. *Faculty research:* Applied health economics and outcomes research, behavioral and health sciences, chronic disease management, health policy, healthcare quality and patient safety, wellness and prevention.

Trident University International, College of Health Sciences, Program in Health Sciences, Cypress, CA 90630. Offers clinical research administration (MS, Certificate); emergency and disaster management (MS, Certificate); environmental health science (Certificate); health care administration (PhD); health care management (MS), including health informatics; health education (MS, Certificate); health informatics (Certificate); health sciences (PhD); international health (MS); international health: educator or researcher option (PhD); international health: practitioner option (PhD); law and expert witness studies (MS, Certificate); public health (MS); quality assurance (Certificate). *Program availability:* Part-time, evening/weekend, online learning. *Degree requirements:* For doctorate, comprehensive exam, thesis/dissertation, defense of dissertation. *Entrance requirements:* For master's, minimum GPA of 2.5 (students with GPA 3.0 or greater may transfer up to 30% of graduate level credits); for doctorate, minimum GPA of 3.4, curriculum vitae, course work in research methods or statistics. Additional exam requirements/recommendations for international students: Required—TOEFL. Electronic applications accepted.

Union College, Graduate Programs, Department of Education, Barbourville, KY 40906-1499. Offers elementary education (MA); health and physical education (MA); middle grades (MA); music education (MA); principalship (MA); reading specialist (MA); secondary education (MA); special education (MA). *Degree requirements:* For master's, thesis optional. *Entrance requirements:* For master's, GRE General Test, NTE.

Union College, Graduate Programs, Department of Health and Physical Education, Barbourville, KY 40906-1499. Offers health (MA Ed). *Degree requirements:* For master's, thesis optional. *Entrance requirements:* For master's, GRE General Test, NTE.

The University of Alabama, Graduate School, College of Human Environmental Sciences, Department of Health Science, Tuscaloosa, AL 35487-0311. Offers health education and promotion (PhD); health studies (MA). *Program availability:* Part-time, online learning. *Faculty:* 12 full-time (7 women). *Students:* 66 full-time (51 women), 102 part-time (85 women); includes 53 minority (40 Black or African American, non-Hispanic/ Latino; 2 American Indian or Alaska Native, non-Hispanic/Latino; 3 Asian, non-Hispanic/ Latino; 6 Hispanic/Latino; 2 Two or more races, non-Hispanic/Latino), 2 international. Average age 34. 108 applicants, 73% accepted, 57 enrolled. In 2016, 69 master's, 4 doctorates awarded. *Degree requirements:* For master's, comprehensive exam, thesis optional; for doctorate, one foreign language, comprehensive exam, thesis/dissertation. *Entrance requirements:* For master's, minimum GPA of 3.0; for doctorate, GRE General Test, minimum GPA of 3.0, prerequisites in health education. Additional exam requirements/recommendations for international students: Required—TOEFL. *Application deadline:* For fall admission, 3/15 priority date for domestic students, 3/15 for international students. Applications are processed on a rolling basis. Application fee: $50 ($60 for international students). Electronic applications accepted. *Expenses:* Tuition, state resident: full-time $10,470. Tuition, nonresident: full-time $26,950. *Financial support:* In 2016–17, 2 research assistantships with full tuition reimbursements (averaging $10,500 per year), 6 teaching assistantships with full tuition reimbursements (averaging $10,500 per year) were awarded; career-related internships or fieldwork, Federal Work-Study, institutionally sponsored loans, health care benefits, and unspecified assistantships also available. Financial award application deadline: 4/ 14. *Faculty research:* Program planning, substance abuse prevention, obesity prevention, nutrition, physical activity, athletic training, osteoporosis, health behavior. *Unit head:* Dr. David Birch, Department Head and Professor, 205-348-4751, E-mail: dabirch@ches.ua.edu. *Application contact:* Dr. Stuart Usdan, Associate Professor and Doctoral Program Coordinator, 205-348-8373, Fax: 205-348-7568, E-mail: susdan@ ches.ua.edu.
Website: http://ches.ua.edu/

The University of Alabama at Birmingham, School of Public Health, Program in Health Education and Promotion, Birmingham, AL 35294. Offers PhD. Program offered jointly with the School of Education and The University of Alabama (Tuscaloosa). *Degree requirements:* For doctorate, comprehensive exam, thesis/dissertation, research internship. *Entrance requirements:* For doctorate, GRE, letters of recommendation. Additional exam requirements/recommendations for international students: Recommended—TOEFL, IELTS. Full-time tuition and fees vary according to course load and program.

University of Arkansas, Graduate School, College of Education and Health Professions, Department of Health, Human Performance and Recreation, Fayetteville, AR 72701. Offers athletic training (MAT); community health promotion (MS, PhD); health science (MS, PhD); kinesiology (MS, PhD); physical education (M Ed, MAT); recreation and sports management (M Ed, Ed D). In 2016, 77 master's, 6 doctorates awarded. *Degree requirements:* For doctorate, thesis/dissertation. *Application deadline:* For fall admission, 4/1 for international students; for spring admission, 10/1 for international students. Applications are processed on a rolling basis. Application fee: $40 ($50 for international students). Electronic applications accepted. *Financial support:* In 2016–17, 13 research assistantships, 10 teaching assistantships were awarded; fellowships with tuition reimbursements, career-related internships or fieldwork, and Federal Work-Study also available. Support available to part-time students. Financial award application deadline: 4/1; financial award applicants required to submit FAFSA. *Unit head:* Dr. Bart Hammig, Departmental Chairperson, 479-575-2857, Fax: 479-575-5778, E-mail: bhammig@uark.edu. *Application contact:* Dr. Stephen Dittmore, Coordinator of Graduate Studies, 479-575-6625, E-mail: dittmore@uark.edu.
Website: http://hkrd.uark.edu/

University of Arkansas at Little Rock, Graduate School, College of Education and Health Professions, Department of Educational Leadership, Program in Higher Education, Little Rock, AR 72204-1099. Offers administration (MA); college student affairs (MA); health professions teaching and learning (MA); higher education (Ed D); two-year college teaching (MA). *Degree requirements:* For doctorate, comprehensive exam, oral defense of dissertation, residency. *Entrance requirements:* For master's, GRE General Test or MAT, interview, minimum graduate GPA of 3.0; for doctorate, GRE General Test, interview, minimum graduate GPA of 3.5, teaching certificate, three years of work experience.

University of Arkansas at Little Rock, Graduate School, College of Education and Health Professions, Department of Health, Human Performance and Sport Management, Little Rock, AR 72204-1099. Offers exercise science (MS); health education and promotion (MS); sport management (MS). *Program availability:* Part-time, evening/weekend. *Degree requirements:* For master's, directed study or residency. *Entrance requirements:* For master's, GRE General Test, minimum GPA of 3.0, 3 reference letters.

University of Arkansas for Medical Sciences, College of Public Health, Little Rock, AR 72205-7199. Offers biostatistics (MPH); environmental and occupational health (MPH, Certificate); epidemiology (MPH, PhD); health behavior and health education (MPH); health policy and management (MPH); health promotion and prevention research (PhD); health services administration (MHSA); health systems research (PhD); public health (Certificate); public health leadership (Dr PH). *Accreditation:* CEPH. *Program availability:* Part-time. *Degree requirements:* For master's, preceptorship, culminating experience, internship; for doctorate, comprehensive exam, capstone. *Entrance requirements:* For master's, GRE, GMAT, LSAT, PCAT, MCAT, DAT; for doctorate, GRE. Additional exam requirements/recommendations for international students: Required—TOEFL (minimum score 80 iBT), IELTS. Electronic applications accepted. *Expenses:* Contact institution. *Faculty research:* Health systems, tobacco prevention control, obesity prevention, environmental and occupational exposure, cancer prevention.

University of Central Arkansas, Graduate School, College of Health and Behavioral Sciences, Department of Health Sciences, Conway, AR 72035-0001. Offers health education (MS). *Program availability:* Part-time, evening/weekend, online learning. *Degree requirements:* For master's, comprehensive exam, thesis optional. *Entrance requirements:* For master's, GRE General Test, minimum GPA of 2.7. Additional exam requirements/recommendations for international students: Required—TOEFL (minimum score 550 paper-based). Electronic applications accepted.

University of Cincinnati, Graduate School, College of Education, Criminal Justice, and Human Services, School of Human Services, Health Promotion and Education Program, Cincinnati, OH 45221. Offers exercise and fitness (MS); health education (PhD); public and community health (MS); public health (MPH). *Accreditation:* NCATE. *Program availability:* Part-time, evening/weekend. *Degree requirements:* For master's, thesis or alternative; for doctorate, thesis/dissertation. *Entrance requirements:* For master's and doctorate, GRE General Test. Additional exam requirements/recommendations for international students: Required—TOEFL (minimum score 580 paper-based). *Application deadline:* For fall admission, 2/1 for domestic students, 12/1 for international students. Application fee: $65 ($70 for international students). Electronic applications accepted. *Expenses: Tuition, area resident:* Full-time $12,790; part-time $389 per credit hour. Tuition, state resident: full-time $13,290; part-time $419 per credit hour. Tuition, nonresident: full-time $24,532; part-time $976 per credit hour. *International tuition:* $24,832 full-time. *Required fees:* $3958; $140 per credit hour. Tuition and fees vary according to course load, degree level, program and reciprocity agreements. *Financial support:* Teaching assistantships with full tuition reimbursements, scholarships/grants, tuition waivers (full), and unspecified assistantships available. Support available to part-time students. Financial award application deadline: 4/15. *Unit head:* Dr. Rebecca Vidourek, Graduate Program Director, 513-556-3857, Fax: 513-556-3898, E-mail: rebecca.vidourek@uc.edu. *Application contact:* Amanda Carlisle, Program Coordinator, 513-556-3335, Fax: 513-556-3898, E-mail: amanda.carlisle@uc.edu.
Website: http://cech.uc.edu/human-services/graduate-programs/health-ed-phd.html

University of Colorado Denver, College of Liberal Arts and Sciences, Program in Health and Behavioral Sciences, Denver, CO 80217. Offers PhD. *Program availability:* Part-time, evening/weekend. *Faculty:* 8 full-time (6 women), 3 part-time/adjunct (all women). *Students:* 15 full-time (13 women), 9 part-time (8 women); includes 6 minority (2 Black or African American, non-Hispanic/Latino; 2 Asian, non-Hispanic/Latino; 2 Hispanic/Latino). Average age 35. 12 applicants, 50% accepted, 5 enrolled. In 2016, 5 doctorates awarded. *Degree requirements:* For doctorate, comprehensive exam, thesis/ dissertation, minimum of 62 credit hours of course work. *Entrance requirements:* For doctorate, GRE (minimum scores in the top 30th percentile), master's or equivalent graduate degree; prior coursework or experience in social or behavioral sciences (minimum 15 semester hours), human biology or physiology (minimum six semester hours), and statistics and epidemiology (minimum three semester hours each); minimum undergraduate GPA of 3.25, graduate 3.5; three letters of recommendation; essay. Additional exam requirements/recommendations for international students: Required—TOEFL (minimum score 525 paper-based; 71 iBT). *Application deadline:* For fall admission, 2/15 for domestic students, 1/15 priority date for international students. Application fee: $50 ($75 for international students). Electronic applications accepted. *Expenses:* Tuition, state resident: full-time $11,006; part-time $474 per credit. Tuition, nonresident: full-time $28,212; part-time $1264 per credit hour. *Required fees:* $256 per semester. One-time fee: $94.32. Tuition and fees vary according to campus/location and program. *Financial support:* In 2016–17, 24 students received support. Fellowships with tuition reimbursements available, research assistantships with tuition reimbursements available, teaching assistantships, Federal Work-Study, institutionally sponsored loans, scholarships/grants, and traineeships available. Financial award application deadline: 4/ 1; financial award applicants required to submit FAFSA. *Faculty research:* HIV/AIDS prevention, tobacco control, globalization and primary health care, social inequality and health, maternal and child health. *Unit head:* Dr. David Tracer, Director and Chair of Health and Behavioral Sciences, 303-556-6792, E-mail: david.tracer@ucdenver.edu. *Application contact:* Abby Fitch, Program Assistant, 303-556-4300, Fax: 303-556-8501, E-mail: abby.fitch@ucdenver.edu.
Website: http://www.ucdenver.edu/academics/colleges/CLAS/Departments/hbsc/ Pages/HealthBehavioralSciences.aspx

University of Colorado Denver, Colorado School of Public Health, Program in Public Health, Aurora, CO 80206. Offers community and behavioral health (MPH, Dr PH); environmental and occupational health (MPH); epidemiology (MPH); health systems, management and policy (MPH). *Accreditation:* CEPH. *Program availability:* Part-time, evening/weekend. *Faculty:* 17 full-time (16 women), 2 part-time/adjunct (both women). *Students:* 423 full-time (349 women), 73 part-time (61 women); includes 117 minority (19 Black or African American, non-Hispanic/Latino; 3 American Indian or Alaska Native, non-Hispanic/Latino; 27 Asian, non-Hispanic/Latino; 52 Hispanic/Latino; 1 Native Hawaiian or other Pacific Islander, non-Hispanic/Latino; 15 Two or more races, non-Hispanic/Latino), 14 international. Average age 32. 872 applicants, 71% accepted, 186 enrolled. In 2016, 181 master's, 1 doctorate awarded. *Degree requirements:* For master's, thesis or alternative, 42 credit hours; for doctorate, comprehensive exam, thesis/dissertation, 67 credit hours. *Entrance requirements:* For master's, GRE, MCAT, DAT, LSAT, PCAT, GMAT or master's degree from accredited institution, baccalaureate degree or equivalent; minimum GPA of 3.0; transcripts; references; resume; essay; for doctorate, GRE, MCAT, DAT, LSAT, PCAT or GMAT, MPH or master's or higher degree in related field or equivalent; 2 years of previous work experience in public health; essay; resume. Additional exam requirements/recommendations for international students: Required—TOEFL (minimum score 550 paper-based; 80 iBT). *Application deadline:* For fall admission, 12/15 priority date for domestic students, 12/1 priority date for international students. Application fee: $65. Electronic applications accepted. *Expenses:* Contact institution. *Financial support:* In 2016–17, 316 students received support. Fellowships, research assistantships, teaching assistantships, Federal Work-Study, institutionally sponsored loans, scholarships/grants, traineeships, and unspecified assistantships available. Financial award application deadline: 3/15; financial award applicants required to submit FAFSA. *Faculty research:* Cancer prevention by nutrition, cancer survivorship outcomes, social and cultural factors related to health. *Unit head:* Dr. Lori Crane, Chair, 303-724-4385, E-mail: lori.crane@ucdenver.edu. *Application contact:* 303-724-4613, E-mail: csph.studentaffairs@ucdenver.edu.
Website: http://www.ucdenver.edu/academics/colleges/PublicHealth/Academics/degreesandprograms/Pages/index.aspx

University of Colorado Denver, School of Medicine, Physician Assistant Program, Aurora, CO 80045. Offers child health associate (MPAS), including global health, leadership, education, advocacy, development, and scholarship, pediatric critical and acute care, rural health, urban/underserved populations. *Accreditation:* ARC-PA. *Students:* 132 full-time (108 women); includes 16 minority (2 Black or African American, non-Hispanic/Latino; 5 Asian, non-Hispanic/Latino; 8 Hispanic/Latino; 1 Two or more races, non-Hispanic/Latino), 1 international. Average age 27. 60 applicants, 83% accepted, 44 enrolled. In 2016, 40 master's awarded. *Degree requirements:* For master's, comprehensive exam. *Entrance requirements:* For master's, GRE General Test, minimum GPA of 2.8; 3 letters of recommendation; prerequisite courses in chemistry, biology, general genetics, psychology and statistics; interview. Additional exam requirements/recommendations for international students: Required—TOEFL (minimum score 550 paper-based; 80 iBT). *Application deadline:* For fall admission, 9/1 for domestic students, 8/15 for international students. Application fee: $170. Electronic applications accepted. *Expenses:* Contact institution. *Financial support:* In 2016–17, 142 students received support. Fellowships, research assistantships, teaching assistantships, career-related internships or fieldwork, Federal Work-Study, institutionally sponsored loans, scholarships/grants, traineeships, and unspecified assistantships available. Financial award application deadline: 3/15; financial award applicants required to submit FAFSA. *Faculty research:* Clinical genetics and genetic counseling, evidence-based medicine, pediatric allergy and asthma, childhood diabetes, standardized patient assessment. *Unit head:* Jonathan Bowser, Program Director, 303-724-1349, E-mail: jonathan.bowser@ucdenver.edu. *Application contact:* Kay Denler, Academic Services Program Manager, 303-724-7963, E-mail: kay.denler@ucdenver.edu.
Website: http://www.ucdenver.edu/academics/colleges/medicalschool/education/degree_programs/PAProgram/Pages/Home.aspx

University of Florida, Graduate School, College of Health and Human Performance, Department of Health Education and Behavior, Gainesville, FL 32611. Offers health and human performance (PhD), including health behavior; health communication (Graduate Certificate); health education and behavior (MS). *Accreditation:* NCATE (one or more programs are accredited). *Program availability:* Part-time. Terminal master's awarded for partial completion of doctoral program. *Degree requirements:* For master's, comprehensive exam, thesis (for some programs); for doctorate, comprehensive exam, thesis/dissertation. *Entrance requirements:* For master's and doctorate, GRE General Test (minimum score 293), minimum GPA of 3.0. Additional exam requirements/recommendations for international students: Required—TOEFL (minimum score 550 paper-based; 80 iBT), IELTS (minimum score 6). Electronic applications accepted. *Faculty research:* Community-based participatory research; health disparities issues; health; cancer prevention and control; obesity-related issues; community capacity building; training community health workers; use of community based research principles to design, implement, an evaluate community health worker interventions; obesity; weight management; health literacy; health disparities (ethnic, gender, age, urban/rural); tailored health messages; entertainment education; COPD.

University of Georgia, Biomedical and Health Sciences Institute, Athens, GA 30602. Offers neuroscience (PhD). *Entrance requirements:* For doctorate, GRE, official transcripts, 3 letters of recommendation, statement of interest. Additional exam requirements/recommendations for international students: Required—TOEFL. *Financial support:* Unspecified assistantships available. Financial award application deadline: 12/31. *Unit head:* Dr. Harry Dailey, Director, 706-542-5922, Fax: 706-542-5285, E-mail: hdailey@uga.edu. *Application contact:* James D. Launderdale, Graduate Coordinator, 706-542-5922, E-mail: neurophd@uga.edu.
Website: http://biomed.uga.edu

University of Georgia, College of Public Health, Department of Health Promotion and Behavior, Athens, GA 30602. Offers MA, MPH, Dr PH, PhD. *Accreditation:* CEPH; NCATE (one or more programs are accredited). *Degree requirements:* For master's, thesis (MA); for doctorate, thesis/dissertation. *Entrance requirements:* For master's, GRE General Test or MAT; for doctorate, GRE General Test. *Application deadline:* For fall admission, 7/1 priority date for domestic students; for spring admission, 11/15 for domestic students. Application fee: $50. Electronic applications accepted. *Financial support:* Fellowships, research assistantships, teaching assistantships, and unspecified assistantships available. *Unit head:* Dr. Mark G. Wilson, Head, 706-542-4364, Fax: 706-542-4956, E-mail: mwilson@uga.edu. *Application contact:* Jessica Muilenburg, Graduate Coordinator, 706-542-4365, E-mail: jlm@uga.edu.
Website: http://www.publichealth.uga.edu/hpb/

University of Houston, College of Liberal Arts and Social Sciences, Department of Health and Human Performance, Houston, TX 77204. Offers exercise science (MS); human nutrition (MS); human space exploration sciences (MS); kinesiology (PhD); physical education (M Ed). *Accreditation:* NCATE (one or more programs are accredited). *Program availability:* Part-time, evening/weekend. *Degree requirements:* For master's, comprehensive exam (for some programs), thesis (for some programs); for doctorate, comprehensive exam, thesis/dissertation, qualifying exam, candidacy paper. *Entrance requirements:* For master's, GRE (minimum 35th percentile on each section), minimum cumulative GPA of 3.0; for doctorate, GRE (minimum 35th percentile on each section), minimum cumulative GPA of 3.3. Additional exam requirements/recommendations for international students: Required—TOEFL (minimum score 550 paper-based; 79 iBT). Electronic applications accepted. *Faculty research:* Biomechanics, exercise physiology, obesity, nutrition, space exploration science.

University of Illinois at Chicago, College of Medicine and Graduate College, Graduate Programs in Medicine, Department of Medical Education, Chicago, IL 60607-7128. Offers MHPE. *Program availability:* Part-time. *Degree requirements:* For master's, thesis. *Entrance requirements:* For master's, GRE General Test. Additional exam requirements/recommendations for international students: Required—TOEFL. Electronic applications accepted.

University of Illinois at Springfield, Graduate Programs, College of Public Affairs and Administration, Program in Public Health, Springfield, IL 62703-5407. Offers community health education (Graduate Certificate); emergency preparedness and homeland security (Graduate Certificate); environmental health (Graduate Certificate); environmental risk assessment (Graduate Certificate); epidemiology (Graduate Certificate); public health (MPH). *Program availability:* Part-time, evening/weekend, 100% online. *Faculty:* 7 full-time (5 women). *Students:* 42 full-time (28 women), 53 part-time (32 women); includes 25 minority (14 Black or African American, non-Hispanic/Latino; 7 Asian, non-Hispanic/Latino; 3 Hispanic/Latino; 1 Two or more races, non-Hispanic/Latino), 21 international. Average age 32. 107 applicants, 40% accepted, 20 enrolled. In 2016, 38 master's, 17 other advanced degrees awarded. *Degree requirements:* For master's, comprehensive exam, internship. *Entrance requirements:* For master's, GRE, minimum undergraduate GPA of 3.0, 3 letters of recommendation, statement of personal goals. Additional exam requirements/recommendations for international students: Required—TOEFL (minimum score 500 paper-based; 61 iBT). *Application deadline:* Applications are processed on a rolling basis. Application fee: $60 ($75 for international students). Electronic applications accepted. *Expenses:* Tuition, state resident: part-time $329 per credit hour. Tuition, nonresident: part-time $675 per credit hour. *Financial support:* In 2016–17, fellowships with full tuition reimbursements (averaging $9,900 per year), research assistantships with full tuition reimbursements (averaging $9,991 per year), teaching assistantships with full tuition reimbursements (averaging $10,059 per year) were awarded; career-related internships or fieldwork, Federal Work-Study, scholarships/grants, health care benefits, and unspecified assistantships also available. Support available to part-time students. Financial award application deadline: 11/15; financial award applicants required to submit FAFSA. *Unit head:* Dr. Josiah Alamu, Program Administrator, 217-206-7874, Fax: 217-206-7279, E-mail: jalam3@uis.edu. *Application contact:* Dr. Cecelia Cornell, Associate Vice Chancellor for Graduate Education, 217-206-7230, E-mail: ccorn1@uis.edu.
Website: http://www.uis.edu/publichealth/

The University of Kansas, Graduate Studies, School of Education, Department of Health, Sport, and Exercise Sciences, Lawrence, KS 66045. Offers exercise science (MS Ed); health and physical education (MS Ed, PhD); sport management (MS Ed). *Accreditation:* NCATE. *Program availability:* Part-time, evening/weekend. *Students:* 53 full-time (21 women), 12 part-time (5 women); includes 5 minority (1 Black or African American, non-Hispanic/Latino; 1 American Indian or Alaska Native, non-Hispanic/Latino; 3 Two or more races, non-Hispanic/Latino), 3 international. Average age 27. 70 applicants, 64% accepted, 25 enrolled. In 2016, 19 master's, 6 doctorates awarded. *Entrance requirements:* For master's, GRE General Test (minimum score 1000, 450 verbal, 450 quantitative, 4.0 analytical), minimum GPA of 3.0, three letters of recommendation, personal statement, resume, writing sample; for doctorate, GRE General Test (minimum score 1100, verbal 500, quantitative 500, analytical 4.5), minimum graduate GPA of 3.5, undergraduate 3.0; three letters of recommendation; personal statement; resume; writing sample; interview with an advisor. Additional exam requirements/recommendations for international students: Required—TOEFL or IELTS. *Application deadline:* For fall admission, 3/15 for domestic and international students; for spring admission, 10/1 for domestic and international students; for summer admission, 3/15 for domestic and international students. Application fee: $65 ($85 for international students). Electronic applications accepted. *Financial support:* Research assistantships, teaching assistantships, Federal Work-Study, scholarships/grants, and unspecified assistantships available. Financial award application deadline: 2/21. *Faculty research:* Exercise and sport psychology, obesity prevention, sexuality health, sport ethics, skeletal muscle cell signaling and performance. *Unit head:* Dr. Joseph Weir, Chair, 785-864-0784, E-mail: joseph.weir@ku.edu. *Application contact:* Sarah Clopton, Graduate Admissions Coordinator, 785-864-7268, E-mail: sclopton@ku.edu.
Website: http://hses.soe.ku.edu/

The University of Kansas, University of Kansas Medical Center, School of Nursing, Kansas City, KS 66160. Offers adult/gerontological clinical nurse specialist (PMC); adult/gerontological nurse practitioner (PMC); health care informatics (PMC); health professions educator (PMC); nurse midwife (PMC); nursing (MS, DNP, PhD); organizational leadership (PMC); psychiatric/mental health nurse practitioner (PMC); public health nursing (PMC). *Accreditation:* AACN; ACNM/ACME. *Program availability:* Part-time, 100% online, blended/hybrid learning. *Faculty:* 53. *Students:* 41 full-time (40 women), 270 part-time (244 women); includes 47 minority (15 Black or African American, non-Hispanic/Latino; 2 American Indian or Alaska Native, non-Hispanic/Latino; 9 Asian, non-Hispanic/Latino; 10 Hispanic/Latino; 11 Two or more races, non-Hispanic/Latino), 1 international. Average age 37. 95 applicants, 97% accepted, 67 enrolled. In 2016, 87 master's, 25 doctorates, 9 other advanced degrees awarded. Terminal master's awarded for partial completion of doctoral program. *Degree requirements:* For master's, comprehensive exam, thesis (for some programs), general oral exam; for doctorate, thesis/dissertation or alternative, comprehensive oral exam (for DNP); comprehensive written and oral exam, or three publications (for PhD). *Entrance requirements:* For master's, bachelor's degree in nursing, minimum GPA of 3.0, 1 year of clinical experience, RN license in KS and MO; for doctorate, GRE General Test (for PhD only), bachelor's degree in nursing, minimum GPA of 3.5, RN license in KS and MO. Additional exam requirements/recommendations for international students: Required—TOEFL. *Application deadline:* For fall admission, 4/1 for domestic and international students; for spring admission, 9/1 for domestic and international students. Application fee: $60. Electronic applications accepted. *Financial support:* In 2016–17, 50 students received support, including 5 research assistantships with tuition reimbursements available (averaging $20,000 per year), 30 teaching assistantships with tuition reimbursements available (averaging $20,000 per year); scholarships/grants and traineeships also available. Financial award application deadline: 3/1; financial award applicants required to submit FAFSA. *Faculty research:* Breastfeeding practices of teen mothers, national database of nursing quality indicators, caregiving of families of patients using technology in the home, simulation in nursing education, diaphragm fatigue. *Total annual research expenditures:* $1.2 million. *Unit head:* Dr. Sally Maliski, Dean, 913-588-1601, Fax: 913-588-1660, E-mail: smaliski@kumc.edu. *Application contact:* Dr. Pamela K. Barnes, Associate Dean, Student Affairs, 913-588-1619, Fax: 913-588-1615, E-mail: pbarnes2@kumc.edu.
Website: http://nursing.kumc.edu

Health Education

University of Louisville, Graduate School, College of Education and Human Development, Department of Educational Leadership, Evaluation and Organizational Development, Louisville, KY 40292-0001. Offers educational leadership and organizational development (Ed D, PhD), including evaluation (PhD), human resource development (PhD), P-12 administration (PhD), post-secondary administration (PhD), sport administration (PhD); health professions education (Certificate); higher education administration (MA); human resources and organization development (MS), including health professions education, human resource leadership, workplace learning and performance; P-12 educational administration (Ed S), including principalship, supervisor of instruction. *Accreditation:* NCATE. *Program availability:* Part-time, evening/weekend, online learning. *Students:* 278 full-time (65 women), 409 part-time (260 women); includes 202 minority (121 Black or African American, non-Hispanic/Latino; 1 American Indian or Alaska Native, non-Hispanic/Latino; 13 Asian, non-Hispanic/Latino; 44 Hispanic/Latino; 3 Native Hawaiian or other Pacific Islander, non-Hispanic/Latino; 20 Two or more races, non-Hispanic/Latino), 5 international. Average age 36. 233 applicants, 78% accepted, 129 enrolled. In 2016, 58 master's, 4 doctorates, 17 other advanced degrees awarded. Application fee: $60. *Expenses:* Tuition, state resident: full-time $12,246; part-time $681 per credit hour. Tuition, nonresident: full-time $25,486; part-time $1417 per credit hour. *Required fees:* $196. Tuition and fees vary according to program and reciprocity agreements. *Financial support:* Application deadline: 6/1; applicants required to submit FAFSA. *Faculty research:* Urban educational leadership and policy, human resources, organizational development, program evaluation, military education, community partnerships, higher education administration. *Total annual research expenditures:* $256,111. *Unit head:* Dr. Jeffrey Sun, Chair and Professor, 502-852-0618, E-mail: jeffrey.sun@louisville.edu. *Application contact:* Betty Hampton, Director of Graduate Student Services, 502-852-5597, Fax: 502-852-1465, E-mail: edadvise@louisville.edu.
Website: http://louisville.edu/education/departments/eleod

University of Louisville, Graduate School, College of Education and Human Development, Department of Health and Sport Sciences, Louisville, KY 40292-0001. Offers community health education (M Ed); exercise physiology (MS), including health and sport sciences, strength and conditioning; health and physical education (MAT); sport administration (MS). *Program availability:* Part-time, evening/weekend. *Students:* 39 full-time (18 women), 10 part-time (8 women); includes 7 minority (4 Black or African American, non-Hispanic/Latino; 2 Hispanic/Latino; 1 Two or more races, non-Hispanic/Latino), 1 international. Average age 27. 73 applicants, 63% accepted, 23 enrolled. In 2016, 25 master's awarded. Application fee: $60. *Expenses:* Tuition, state resident: full-time $12,246; part-time $681 per credit hour. Tuition, nonresident: full-time $25,486; part-time $1417 per credit hour. *Required fees:* $196. Tuition and fees vary according to program and reciprocity agreements. *Financial support:* Applicants required to submit FAFSA. *Faculty research:* Sport administration; exercise physiology; exercise science; physical education; health education. *Total annual research expenditures:* $91,688. *Unit head:* Dr. Margaret Hancock, Interim Chair/Assistant Professor, 502-852-6645, E-mail: meg.hancock@louisville.edu. *Application contact:* Betty Hampton, Director of Graduate Student Services, 502-852-5597, Fax: 502-852-1465, E-mail: edadvise@louisville.edu.
Website: http://www.louisville.edu/education/departments/hss

University of Louisville, Graduate School, College of Education and Human Development, Department of Teaching and Learning, Louisville, KY 40292-0001. Offers art education (MAT); autism and applied behavior analysis (Certificate); curriculum and instruction (PhD); early elementary education (MAT); exercise physiology (MS); health and physical education (MAT); health professions education (Certificate); higher education (MA); human resources and organization development (MS); instructional technology (M Ed); interdisciplinary early childhood education (MAT); middle school education (MAT); music education (MAT); secondary education (MAT); special education (MAT); sport administration (MS); teacher leadership (M Ed). *Program availability:* Part-time, evening/weekend. *Students:* 116 full-time (68 women), 158 part-time (112 women); includes 46 minority (24 Black or African American, non-Hispanic/Latino; 8 Asian, non-Hispanic/Latino; 5 Hispanic/Latino; 9 Two or more races, non-Hispanic/Latino), 6 international. Average age 30. 114 applicants, 71% accepted, 57 enrolled. In 2016, 59 master's, 3 doctorates awarded. *Application deadline:* For spring admission, 1/1 priority date for international students. Application fee: $60. *Expenses:* Tuition, state resident: full-time $12,246; part-time $681 per credit hour. Tuition, nonresident: full-time $25,486; part-time $1417 per credit hour. *Required fees:* $196. Tuition and fees vary according to program and reciprocity agreements. *Financial support:* Application deadline: 6/1; applicants required to submit FAFSA. *Faculty research:* STEM teaching and learning; content literacy for English language learners; social justice in teacher education; adolescent literacy; mathematics teacher development. *Total annual research expenditures:* $1.7 million. *Unit head:* Dr. Ann E. Larson, Dean, College of Education and Human Development, 502-852-6411, Fax: 502-852-1464, E-mail: ann@louisville.edu. *Application contact:* Betty Hampton, Director of Graduate Student Services, 502-852-5597, Fax: 502-852-1465, E-mail: edadvise@louisville.edu.
Website: http://louisville.edu/delphi

University of Maryland, Baltimore County, The Graduate School, College of Arts, Humanities and Social Sciences, Department of Emergency Health Services, Baltimore, MD 21250. Offers administration, planning, and policy (MS); education (MS); emergency health services (MS); emergency management (Postbaccalaureate Certificate); preventive medicine and epidemiology (MS); public policy (PhD), including emergency management, emergency public health. *Program availability:* Part-time, evening/weekend, 100% online, blended/hybrid learning. *Faculty:* 4 full-time (2 women), 8 part-time/adjunct (3 women). *Students:* 15 full-time (11 women), 14 part-time (6 women); includes 11 minority (5 Black or African American, non-Hispanic/Latino; 3 Asian, non-Hispanic/Latino; 2 Hispanic/Latino; 1 Two or more races, non-Hispanic/Latino), 4 international. Average age 26. 25 applicants, 88% accepted, 19 enrolled. In 2016, 22 master's awarded. *Degree requirements:* For master's, comprehensive exam (for some programs), thesis optional, capstone project. *Entrance requirements:* For master's, GRE General Test if GPA is below 3.2, minimum GPA of 3.2. Additional exam requirements/recommendations for international students: Required—TOEFL (minimum score 85 iBT) or IELTS (minimum score 6.5). *Application deadline:* For fall admission, 6/15 for domestic students, 3/1 for international students; for spring admission, 11/1 for domestic students, 10/1 for international students. Applications are processed on a rolling basis. Application fee: $50. Electronic applications accepted. *Expenses:* $13,194 in-state full-time per year, $733 per credit in-state part-time; $1,127 out-of-state per credit. *Financial support:* In 2016–17, 6 students received support, including 5 research assistantships with full tuition reimbursements available (averaging $16,875 per year); career-related internships or fieldwork, Federal Work-Study, scholarships/grants, health care benefits, and unspecified assistantships also available. Financial award application deadline: 5/30; financial award applicants required to submit FAFSA. *Faculty research:* EMS management, disaster health services, emergency management, epidemiology, risk profiles, infectious disease control, stress management for care providers, climate change and public health. *Total annual research expenditures:* $50,000. *Unit head:* Dr. J. Lee Jenkins, Department Chair, 410-455-3216, Fax: 410-455-3045, E-mail: jleejenkins@umbc.edu. *Application contact:* Dr. Rick Bissell, Program Director, 410-455-3776, Fax: 410-455-3045, E-mail: bissell@umbc.edu.
Website: http://ehs.umbc.edu/

University of Maryland, College Park, Academic Affairs, School of Public Health, Department of Behavioral and Community Health, College Park, MD 20742. Offers community health education (MPH); public/community health (PhD). *Accreditation:* CEPH. *Program availability:* Part-time, evening/weekend. *Degree requirements:* For master's, thesis optional; for doctorate, comprehensive exam, thesis/dissertation. *Entrance requirements:* For master's, GRE General Test, minimum GPA of 3.0, 3 letters of recommendation; for doctorate, GRE General Test, minimum GPA of 3.5, 3 letters of recommendation. Additional exam requirements/recommendations for international students: Required—TOEFL. Electronic applications accepted. *Faculty research:* Controlling stress and tension, women's health, aging and public policy, adolescent health, long-term care.

University of Massachusetts Amherst, Graduate School, School of Public Health and Health Sciences, Department of Public Health, Amherst, MA 01003. Offers biostatistics (MPH, MS, PhD); community health education (MPH, MS, PhD); environmental health sciences (MPH, MS, PhD); epidemiology (MPH, MS, PhD); health policy and management (MPH, MS, PhD); nutrition (MPH, PhD); public health practice (MPH); MPH/MPPA. *Accreditation:* CEPH (one or more programs are accredited). *Program availability:* Part-time, evening/weekend, online learning. Terminal master's awarded for partial completion of doctoral program. *Degree requirements:* For master's, thesis (for some programs); for doctorate, comprehensive exam, thesis/dissertation. *Entrance requirements:* For master's and doctorate, GRE General Test. Additional exam requirements/recommendations for international students: Required—TOEFL (minimum score 550 paper-based; 80 iBT), IELTS (minimum score 6.5). Electronic applications accepted.

University of Michigan, School of Public Health, Department of Health Behavior and Health Education, Ann Arbor, MI 48109. Offers MPH, PhD, MPH/MSW. PhD offered through the Rackham Graduate School. *Accreditation:* CEPH (one or more programs are accredited). *Faculty:* 23 full-time (13 women), 23 part-time/adjunct (16 women). *Students:* 161 full-time (137 women), 1 (woman) part-time; includes 64 minority (24 Black or African American, non-Hispanic/Latino; 1 American Indian or Alaska Native, non-Hispanic/Latino; 13 Asian, non-Hispanic/Latino; 17 Hispanic/Latino; 9 Two or more races, non-Hispanic/Latino), 4 international. Average age 26. 397 applicants, 74% accepted, 98 enrolled. In 2016, 78 master's, 3 doctorates awarded. Terminal master's awarded for partial completion of doctoral program. *Degree requirements:* For doctorate, oral defense of dissertation, preliminary exam. *Entrance requirements:* For master's, GRE General Test (preferred); MCAT; for doctorate, GRE General Test. Additional exam requirements/recommendations for international students: Required—TOEFL (minimum score 100 iBT). *Application deadline:* For fall admission, 12/15 priority date for domestic students, 1/15 for international students. Applications are processed on a rolling basis. Application fee: $75. Electronic applications accepted. *Expenses:* Tuition, state resident: full-time $21,466; part-time $1152 per credit hour. Tuition, nonresident: full-time $43,346; part-time $2367 per credit hour. Part-time tuition and fees vary according to course load, degree level and program. *Financial support:* Fellowships, research assistantships, teaching assistantships, career-related internships or fieldwork, Federal Work-Study, institutionally sponsored loans, scholarships/grants, traineeships, health care benefits, and unspecified assistantships available. Financial award application deadline: 12/1; financial award applicants required to submit FAFSA. *Faculty research:* Empowerment theory; structure, culture, and health; health disparities; community-based participatory research; health and medical decision-making. *Unit head:* Dr. Cleopatra Caldwell, Chair, 734-763-7031. *Application contact:* Jackie Cormany, Student Services Coordinator, 734-763-9938, Fax: 734-763-7379, E-mail: sph.hbhe.inquiries@umich.edu.
Website: http://www.sph.umich.edu/hbhe/

University of Michigan–Flint, School of Health Professions and Studies, Program in Health Education, Flint, MI 48502. Offers MS. *Program availability:* Part-time. *Faculty:* 15 full-time (12 women), 36 part-time/adjunct (19 women). *Students:* 5 full-time (4 women), 6 part-time (all women); includes 5 minority (3 Black or African American, non-Hispanic/Latino; 2 Hispanic/Latino), 2 international. Average age 31. 11 applicants, 27% accepted, 1 enrolled. In 2016, 3 master's awarded. *Degree requirements:* For master's, thesis, internship or current employment as health educator. *Entrance requirements:* For master's, bachelor's degree from regionally-accredited institution, minimum overall undergraduate GPA of 3.0. Additional exam requirements/recommendations for international students: Required—TOEFL (minimum score 84 iBT), IELTS (minimum score 6.5). *Application deadline:* For fall admission, 8/1 for domestic students, 5/1 for international students; for winter admission, 11/15 for domestic students, 9/1 for international students; for spring admission, 3/15 for domestic students, 1/1 for international students. Applications are processed on a rolling basis. Application fee: $55. Electronic applications accepted. *Expenses:* Contact institution. *Financial support:* Federal Work-Study, scholarships/grants, and unspecified assistantships available. Support available to part-time students. Financial award application deadline: 3/1; financial award applicants required to submit FAFSA. *Faculty research:* Minority health, health disparities, cultural competency, HIV/AIDS, women's health. *Unit head:* Dr. Shan Parker, Associate Director, 810-762-3172, Fax: 810-762-3003, E-mail: shanpark@umich.edu. *Application contact:* Bradley T. Maki, Director of Graduate Admissions, 810-762-3171, Fax: 810-766-6789, E-mail: bmaki@umflint.edu.
Website: http://www.umflint.edu/graduateprograms/health-education-ms

University of Michigan–Flint, School of Health Professions and Studies, Program in Public Health, Flint, MI 48502. Offers health administration (MPH); health education (MPH). *Program availability:* Part-time. *Faculty:* 15 full-time (12 women), 36 part-time/adjunct (19 women). *Students:* 19 full-time (17 women), 44 part-time (36 women); includes 20 minority (12 Black or African American, non-Hispanic/Latino; 2 American Indian or Alaska Native, non-Hispanic/Latino; 4 Asian, non-Hispanic/Latino; 2 Two or more races, non-Hispanic/Latino), 7 international. Average age 31. 59 applicants, 51% accepted, 9 enrolled. In 2016, 11 master's awarded. *Degree requirements:* For master's, thesis, public health capstone. *Entrance requirements:* For master's, GRE, bachelor's degree from accredited institution with sufficient preparation in algebra to succeed in epidemiology and biostatistics; minimum overall undergraduate GPA of 3.0. Additional exam requirements/recommendations for international students: Required—TOEFL (minimum score 84 iBT), IELTS (minimum score 6.5). *Application deadline:* For fall admission, 8/1 for domestic students, 5/1 for international students; for winter admission, 11/15 for domestic students, 8/15 for international students; for spring admission, 3/15 for domestic students, 1/15 for international students. Applications are processed on a rolling basis. Application fee: $55. Electronic applications accepted. *Expenses:* Contact institution. *Financial support:* Federal Work-Study, scholarships/grants, and unspecified assistantships available. Support available to part-time students. Financial award application deadline: 3/1; financial award applicants required to submit FAFSA. *Unit head:* Dr. Suzanne Selig, Director, 810-762-3172, E-mail: sselig@umflint.edu. *Application contact:* Bradley T. Maki, Director of Graduate Admissions, 810-762-3171, Fax: 810-766-6789, E-mail: bmaki@umflint.edu.
Website: http://www.umflint.edu/graduateprograms/public-health-mph

University of Missouri, Office of Research and Graduate Studies, College of Education, Department of Learning, Teaching and Curriculum, Columbia, MO 65211. Offers agricultural education (M Ed, PhD, Ed S); art education (M Ed, PhD, Ed S); business and office education (M Ed, PhD, Ed S); early childhood education (M Ed, PhD, Ed S); elementary education (M Ed, PhD, Ed S); English education (M Ed, PhD, Ed S); foreign language education (M Ed, PhD, Ed S); health education and promotion (M Ed, PhD); learning and instruction (M Ed, PhD); marketing education (M Ed, PhD, Ed S); mathematics education (M Ed, PhD, Ed S); music education (M Ed, PhD, Ed S); reading education (M Ed, PhD, Ed S); science education (M Ed, PhD, Ed S); social studies education (M Ed, PhD, Ed S); vocational education (M Ed, PhD, Ed S). *Program availability:* Part-time. *Faculty:* 30 full-time (18 women), 1 (woman) part-time/adjunct. *Students:* 157 full-time (124 women), 157 part-time (125 women). Terminal master's awarded for partial completion of doctoral program. *Degree requirements:* For doctorate, thesis/dissertation. *Entrance requirements:* For master's and Ed S, GRE General Test or MAT, minimum GPA of 3.0; for doctorate, GRE General Test, minimum GPA of 3.0. Additional exam requirements/recommendations for international students: Required—TOEFL (minimum score 600 paper-based; 100 iBT). *Application deadline:* For fall admission, 12/1 priority date for domestic and international students. Applications are processed on a rolling basis. Application fee: $75 ($90 for international students). Electronic applications accepted. *Expenses:* Tuition, state resident: full-time $6347; part-time $352.60 per credit hour. Tuition, nonresident: full-time $17,379; part-time $965.50 per credit hour. *Required fees:* $1035. Tuition and fees vary according to course load, campus/location and program. *Financial support:* Fellowships, research assistantships, teaching assistantships, institutionally sponsored loans, traineeships, health care benefits, and unspecified assistantships available. Support available to part-time students.
Website: http://education.missouri.edu/LTC/index.php

University of Missouri–Kansas City, School of Medicine, Kansas City, MO 64110-2499. Offers health professions education (MS); MD/PhD. *Accreditation:* LCME/AMA. *Faculty:* 47 full-time (18 women), 29 part-time/adjunct (12 women). *Students:* 519 full-time (273 women), 35 part-time (22 women); includes 259 minority (34 Black or African American, non-Hispanic/Latino; 2 American Indian or Alaska Native, non-Hispanic/Latino; 159 Asian, non-Hispanic/Latino; 19 Hispanic/Latino; 1 Native Hawaiian or other Pacific Islander, non-Hispanic/Latino; 44 Two or more races, non-Hispanic/Latino), 8 international. Average age 24. 1,065 applicants, 12% accepted, 121 enrolled. In 2016, 37 master's, 94 doctorates awarded. *Degree requirements:* For doctorate, one foreign language, United States Medical Licensing Exam Step 1 and 2. *Entrance requirements:* For doctorate, interview. *Application deadline:* For fall admission, 11/15 for domestic and international students. Application fee: $50. *Expenses:* Contact institution. *Financial support:* In 2016–17, 4 fellowships (averaging $35,935 per year), 2 research assistantships (averaging $12,684 per year) were awarded; career-related internships or fieldwork, Federal Work-Study, institutionally sponsored loans, scholarships/grants, and tuition waivers (partial) also available. Financial award application deadline: 3/1; financial award applicants required to submit FAFSA. *Faculty research:* Cardiovascular disease, women's and children's health, trauma and infectious diseases, neurological, metabolic disease. *Unit head:* Dr. Steven L. Kanter, MD, Dean, 816-235-1803, E-mail: kantersl@umkc.edu.
Website: http://www.med.umkc.edu/

University of Montana, Graduate School, Phyllis J. Washington College of Education and Human Sciences, Department of Health and Human Performance, Missoula, MT 59812-0002. Offers community health (MS); exercise science (MS); health and human performance generalist (MS). *Program availability:* Part-time. *Entrance requirements:* For master's, GRE General Test. Additional exam requirements/recommendations for international students: Required—TOEFL. *Faculty research:* Exercise physiology, performance psychology, nutrition, pre-employment physical screening, program evaluation.

University of Nebraska at Omaha, Graduate Studies, College of Education, School of Health and Kinesiology, Omaha, NE 68182. Offers athletic training (MA); exercise science (PhD); health, physical education, and recreation (MA, MS). *Program availability:* Part-time, evening/weekend. *Faculty:* 7 full-time (2 women). *Students:* 79 full-time (31 women), 28 part-time (13 women); includes 8 minority (2 Black or African American, non-Hispanic/Latino; 1 Asian, non-Hispanic/Latino; 2 Hispanic/Latino; 3 Two or more races, non-Hispanic/Latino), 18 international. Average age 26. 65 applicants, 74% accepted, 34 enrolled. In 2016, 38 master's, 1 doctorate awarded. *Degree requirements:* For master's, comprehensive exam, thesis (for some programs). *Entrance requirements:* For master's, GRE; entrance exam, minimum GPA of 3.0, official transcripts, statement of purpose, 2 letters of recommendation; for doctorate, GRE, minimum GPA of 3.2, official transcripts, statement of purpose, 3 letters of recommendation, resume, writing sample. Additional exam requirements/recommendations for international students: Required—TOEFL, IELTS, PTE. *Application deadline:* For fall admission, 7/1 priority date for domestic and international students; for spring admission, 11/1 priority date for domestic and international students; for summer admission, 1/15 for domestic and international students. Applications are processed on a rolling basis. Application fee: $45. Electronic applications accepted. *Financial support:* In 2016–17, 47 students received support, including 34 research assistantships with tuition reimbursements available, 13 teaching assistantships with tuition reimbursements available; fellowships, Federal Work-Study, institutionally sponsored loans, scholarships/grants, health care benefits, tuition waivers (full), and unspecified assistantships also available. Support available to part-time students. Financial award application deadline: 3/1; financial award applicants required to submit FAFSA. *Unit head:* Dr. Roland Bulbulian, Director, 402-554-2341, E-mail: graduate@unomaha.edu. *Application contact:* Dr. Dustin Slivka, Graduate Program Chair, 402-554-2341, E-mail: graduate@unomaha.edu.

University of New Mexico, Graduate Studies, College of Education, Program in Health Education, Albuquerque, NM 87131-2039. Offers community health education (MS). *Accreditation:* NCATE. *Program availability:* Part-time. *Faculty:* 4 full-time (3 women), 2 part-time/adjunct (both women). *Students:* 9 full-time (8 women), 12 part-time (10 women); includes 14 minority (1 Black or African American, non-Hispanic/Latino; 5 American Indian or Alaska Native, non-Hispanic/Latino; 1 Asian, non-Hispanic/Latino; 7 Hispanic/Latino), 1 international. Average age 34. 9 applicants, 56% accepted, 4 enrolled. In 2016, 11 master's awarded. *Degree requirements:* For master's, comprehensive exam, thesis optional. *Entrance requirements:* For master's, 3 letters of reference, resume, minimum cumulative GPA of 3.0 in last 2 years of bachelor's degree, letter of intent. Additional exam requirements/recommendations for international students: Required—TOEFL (minimum score 550 paper-based). *Application deadline:* For fall admission, 6/15 priority date for domestic students; for spring admission, 11/1 priority date for domestic students. Applications are processed on a rolling basis. Application fee: $50. Electronic applications accepted. *Financial support:* Fellowships, teaching assistantships with full tuition reimbursements, career-related internships or fieldwork, institutionally sponsored loans, scholarships/grants, and health care benefits available. Financial award application deadline: 3/1; financial award applicants required to submit FAFSA. *Faculty research:* Alcohol and families, health behaviors and sexuality, multicultural health behavior, health promotion policy, school/community-based prevention, health and aging. *Unit head:* Dr. Elias Duryea, Coordinator, 505-277-5151, Fax: 505-277-6227, E-mail: duryea@unm.edu. *Application contact:* Carol Catania, Graduate Coordinator, 505-277-5151, Fax: 505-277-6227, E-mail: catania@unm.edu.

The University of North Carolina Wilmington, Watson College of Education, Department of Instructional Technology, Foundations and Secondary Education, Wilmington, NC 28403-3297. Offers academically or intellectually gifted (M Ed); English as a second language (M Ed, MAT); instructional technology (MS); physical education and health (M Ed, MAT); secondary education (M Ed, MAT); Spanish (MAT); Spanish education (MASS). *Program availability:* Part-time. *Faculty:* 17 full-time (11 women). *Students:* 36 full-time (22 women), 62 part-time (49 women); includes 17 minority (12 Black or African American, non-Hispanic/Latino; 3 Hispanic/Latino; 2 Two or more races, non-Hispanic/Latino), 5 international. Average age 34. 89 applicants, 89% accepted, 59 enrolled. In 2016, 36 master's awarded. *Degree requirements:* For master's, comprehensive exam (for some programs), thesis (for some programs), thesis or research project. *Entrance requirements:* For master's, GRE or MAT, statement of interest, 3 letters of recommendation, minimum GPA of 3.0 in undergraduate work. Additional exam requirements/recommendations for international students: Required—TOEFL (minimum score 79 iBT), IELTS (minimum score 6.5). *Application deadline:* For fall admission, 5/15 for domestic students; for spring admission, 10/15 for domestic students; for summer admission, 3/15 for domestic students. Applications are processed on a rolling basis. Application fee: $60. Electronic applications accepted. *Expenses:* Contact institution. *Financial support:* Scholarships/grants and unspecified assistantships available. Financial award application deadline: 3/15; financial award applicants required to submit FAFSA. *Unit head:* Dr. Donyell Roseboro, Chair, 910-962-2289, Fax: 910-962-3609, E-mail: roseborod@uncw.edu. *Application contact:* Dr. Mahnaz Moallem, Graduate Coordinator, 910-962-4183, E-mail: moallemm@uncw.edu.
Website: http://www.uncw.edu/ed/itfse/

University of Northern Colorado, Graduate School, College of Natural and Health Sciences, School of Human Sciences, Program in Public Health, Greeley, CO 80639. Offers community health education (MPH); global health and community health education (MPH); healthy aging and community health education (MPH). *Degree requirements:* For master's, comprehensive exam, thesis or alternative. *Entrance requirements:* For master's, GRE General Test, 2 letters of recommendation. *Application deadline:* Applications are processed on a rolling basis. Application fee: $50 ($60 for international students). Electronic applications accepted. *Financial support:* Fellowships, research assistantships, teaching assistantships, and unspecified assistantships available. Financial award application deadline: 3/1; financial award applicants required to submit FAFSA. *Unit head:* Dr. Deborah Givray, Program Coordinator, 970-351-2403. *Application contact:* Linda Sisson, Graduate Student Admission Coordinator, 970-351-1807, Fax: 970-351-2371, E-mail: linda.sisson@unco.edu.
Website: http://www.unco.edu/nhs/colorado-school-public-health/

University of Northern Iowa, Graduate College, College of Education, School of Kinesiology, Allied Health and Human Services, MA Program in Health Education, Cedar Falls, IA 50614. Offers community health education (MA); health promotion/fitness management (MA); school health education (MA). *Program availability:* Part-time, evening/weekend. *Degree requirements:* For master's, comprehensive exam, thesis or alternative. *Entrance requirements:* For master's, minimum GPA of 3.0. Additional exam requirements/recommendations for international students: Required—TOEFL (minimum score 500 paper-based; 61 iBT). Electronic applications accepted.

University of Oklahoma Health Sciences Center, Graduate College, College of Allied Health, Department of Allied Health Sciences, Oklahoma City, OK 73190. Offers PhD. *Degree requirements:* For doctorate, one foreign language, comprehensive exam, thesis/dissertation optional. *Entrance requirements:* For doctorate, GRE General Test, 3 letters of recommendation, master's degree. Additional exam requirements/recommendations for international students: Required—TOEFL (minimum score 550 paper-based).

University of Phoenix–Charlotte Campus, College of Nursing, Charlotte, NC 28273-3409. Offers education (MHA); gerontology (MHA); health administration (MHA); informatics (MHA, MSN); nursing (MSN); nursing/health care education (MSN). *Program availability:* Evening/weekend. *Degree requirements:* For master's, thesis (for some programs). *Entrance requirements:* For master's, minimum undergraduate GPA of 2.5, 3 years work experience. Additional exam requirements/recommendations for international students: Required—TOEFL (minimum score 550 paper-based; 79 iBT). Electronic applications accepted.

University of Phoenix–Colorado Springs Downtown Campus, College of Nursing, Colorado Springs, CO 80903. Offers education (MHA); gerontology (MHA); health administration (MHA); nursing (MSN); MSN/MBA. *Program availability:* Evening/weekend. *Degree requirements:* For master's, thesis (for some programs). *Entrance requirements:* For master's, minimum undergraduate GPA of 2.5, 3 years of work experience, RN license. Additional exam requirements/recommendations for international students: Required—TOEFL (minimum score 550 paper-based; 79 iBT). Electronic applications accepted.

University of Phoenix–Online Campus, College of Health Sciences and Nursing, Phoenix, AZ 85034-7209. Offers family nurse practitioner (Certificate); health care (Certificate); health care education (Certificate); health care informatics (Certificate); informatics (MSN); nursing (MSN); nursing and health care education (MSN); MSN/MBA; MSN/MHA. *Accreditation:* AACN. *Program availability:* Evening/weekend, online learning. *Entrance requirements:* Additional exam requirements/recommendations for international students: Required—TOEFL, TOEIC (Test of English as an International Communication), Berlitz Online English Proficiency Exam, PTE, or IELTS. Electronic applications accepted. *Expenses:* Contact institution.

University of Phoenix–Washington D.C. Campus, College of Nursing, Washington, DC 20001. Offers education (MHA); gerontology (MHA); health administration (MHA, DHA); informatics (MHA, MSN); nursing (MSN, PhD); nursing/health care education (MSN); MSN/MBA, MSN/MHA.

University of Pittsburgh, Graduate School of Public Health, Department of Infectious Diseases and Microbiology, Pittsburgh, PA 15261. Offers infectious disease management, intervention, and community practice (MPH); infectious disease pathogenesis, eradication, and laboratory practice (MPH); infectious diseases and microbiology (MS, PhD). *Program availability:* Part-time. *Faculty:* 20 full-time (6 women), 5 part-time/adjunct (2 women). *Students:* 70 full-time (47 women), 15 part-time (7 women); includes 19 minority (4 Black or African American, non-Hispanic/Latino; 6 Asian, non-Hispanic/Latino; 3 Hispanic/Latino; 6 Two or more races, non-Hispanic/Latino), 10 international. Average age 26. 178 applicants, 63% accepted, 32 enrolled. In 2016, 22 master's, 2 doctorates awarded. *Degree requirements:* For master's, comprehensive exam (for some programs), thesis; for doctorate, comprehensive exam, thesis/dissertation, preliminary exam, dissertation approval. *Entrance requirements:* For master's and doctorate, GRE General Test, MCAT, DAT, or GMAT. Additional exam requirements/recommendations for international students: Required—TOEFL (minimum score 550 paper-based, 80 iBT) or IELTS (minimum score 6.5). *Application deadline:* For fall admission, 1/15 priority date for domestic and international students. Applications are processed on a rolling basis. Application fee: $120. Electronic

applications accepted. *Expenses:* $12,750 full-time in-state per term, $21,065 full-time out-of-state per term, $415 full-time fees; $1,039 part-time in-state per credit, $1,726 part-time out-of-state per credit, $265 part-time fees. *Financial support:* In 2016–17, 7 students received support, including fellowships (averaging $19,210 per year), 7 research assistantships (averaging $16,556 per year); scholarships/grants, traineeships, health care benefits, and unspecified assistantships also available. Financial award applicants required to submit FAFSA. *Faculty research:* HIV, complications of antiretroviral therapy, Hepatitis C, emerging infections, clinical and molecular epidemiology, genetic basis of innate immune response, HIV prevention and care, AIDS education and training. *Total annual research expenditures:* $12.2 million. *Unit head:* Dr. Charles R. Rinaldo, Chair, 412-624-3928, Fax: 412-624-4953, E-mail: rinaldo@pitt.edu. *Application contact:* Abby Michael, Student Services Coordinator, 412-624-3331, Fax: 412-383-8926, E-mail: abm82@pitt.edu.
Website: http://www.idm.pitt.edu/

University of Puerto Rico, Medical Sciences Campus, Graduate School of Public Health, Department of Social Sciences, Program in Public Health Education, San Juan, PR 00936-5067. Offers MPHE. *Program availability:* Part-time, evening/weekend. *Degree requirements:* For master's, thesis. *Entrance requirements:* For master's, GRE, previous course work in education, social sciences, algebra, and natural sciences.

University of Rhode Island, Graduate School, College of Health Sciences, Department of Kinesiology, Kingston, RI 02881. Offers cultural studies of sport and physical culture (MS); exercise science (MS); psychosocial/behavioral aspects of physical activity (MS). *Accreditation:* NCATE. *Program availability:* Part-time. *Faculty:* 15 full-time (9 women). *Students:* 16 full-time (9 women), 8 part-time (5 women); includes 4 minority (1 Black or African American, non-Hispanic/Latino; 1 Asian, non-Hispanic/Latino; 2 Hispanic/Latino). In 2016, 8 master's awarded. *Degree requirements:* For master's, thesis optional. *Entrance requirements:* For master's, GRE, 2 letters of recommendation. Additional exam requirements/recommendations for international students: Required—TOEFL. *Application deadline:* For fall admission, 7/15 for domestic students, 2/1 for international students; for spring admission, 11/15 for domestic students, 7/15 for international students. Application fee: $65. Electronic applications accepted. *Expenses:* Tuition, state resident: full-time $11,796; part-time $655 per credit. Tuition, nonresident: full-time $24,206; part-time $1345 per credit. *Required fees:* $1546; $44 per credit. One-time fee: $155 full-time; $35 part-time. *Financial support:* In 2016–17, 5 teaching assistantships with tuition reimbursements (averaging $10,740 per year) were awarded; research assistantships also available. Financial award application deadline: 7/15; financial award applicants required to submit FAFSA. *Unit head:* Dr. Disa Hatfield, Interim Chair, 401-874-5183, E-mail: doch@uri.edu. *Application contact:* Dr. Matthew Delmonico, Graduate Program Director, 401-874-5440, E-mail: delmonico@uri.edu.
Website: http://web.uri.edu/kinesiology/

University of St. Augustine for Health Sciences, Graduate Programs, Master of Health Science Program, San Marcos, CA 92069. Offers athletic training (MHS); executive leadership (MHS); informatics (MHS); teaching and learning (MHS). *Program availability:* Online learning. *Degree requirements:* For master's, comprehensive project.

University of St. Augustine for Health Sciences, Graduate Programs, Post Professional Programs, San Marcos, CA 92069. Offers health science (DH Sc); health sciences education (Ed D); occupational therapy (TOTD); physical therapy (TDPT). *Program availability:* Part-time, online learning. *Entrance requirements:* For doctorate, GRE General Test, master's degree in related field. Additional exam requirements/recommendations for international students: Required—TOEFL.

University of South Africa, College of Human Sciences, Pretoria, South Africa. Offers adult education (M Ed); African languages (MA, PhD); African politics (MA, PhD); Afrikaans (MA, PhD); ancient history (MA, PhD); ancient Near Eastern studies (MA, PhD); anthropology (MA, PhD); applied linguistics (MA); Arabic (MA, PhD); archaeology (MA); art history (MA); Biblical archaeology (MA); Biblical studies (M Th, D Th, PhD); Christian spirituality (M Th, D Th); church history (M Th, D Th); classical studies (MA, PhD); clinical psychology (MA); communication (MA, PhD); comparative education (M Ed, Ed D); consulting psychology (D Admin, D Com, PhD); curriculum studies (M Ed, Ed D); development studies (M Admin, MA, D Admin, PhD); didactics (M Ed, Ed D); education (M Tech); education management (M Ed, Ed D); educational psychology (M Ed); English (MA); environmental education (M Ed); French (MA, PhD); German (MA, PhD); Greek (MA); guidance and counseling (M Ed); health studies (MA, PhD), including health sciences education (MA), health services management (MA), medical and surgical nursing science (critical care general) (MA), midwifery and neonatal nursing science (MA), trauma and emergency care (MA); history (MA, PhD); history of education (Ed D); inclusive education (M Ed, Ed D); information and communications technology policy and regulation (MA); information science (MA, MIS, PhD); international politics (MA, PhD); Islamic studies (MA, PhD); Italian (MA, PhD); Judaica (MA, PhD); linguistics (MA, PhD); mathematical education (M Ed); mathematics education (MA); missiology (M Th, D Th); modern Hebrew (MA, PhD); musicology (MA, MMus, D Mus, PhD); natural science education (M Ed); New Testament (M Th, D Th); Old Testament (D Th); pastoral therapy (M Th, D Th); philosophy (MA); philosophy of education (M Ed, Ed D); politics (MA, PhD); Portuguese (MA, PhD); practical theology (M Th, D Th); psychology (MA, MS, PhD); psychology of education (M Ed, Ed D); public health (MA); religious studies (MA, D Th, PhD); Romance languages (MA); Russian (MA, PhD); Semitic languages (MA, PhD); social behavior studies in HIV/AIDS (MA); social science (mental health) (MA); social science in development studies (MA); social science in psychology (MA); social science in social work (MA); social science in sociology (MA); social work (MSW, DSW, PhD); socio-education (M Ed, Ed D); sociolinguistics (MA); sociology (MA, PhD); Spanish (MA, PhD); systematic theology (M Th, D Th); TESOL (teaching English to speakers of other languages) (MA); theological ethics (M Th, D Th); theory of literature (MA, PhD); urban ministries (D Th); urban ministry (M Th).

University of South Alabama, College of Education and Professional Studies, Department of Health, Kinesiology, and Sport, Mobile, AL 36688. Offers exercise science (MS); health education (M Ed); physical education (M Ed); sport management (MS). *Accreditation:* NCATE (one or more programs are accredited). *Program availability:* Part-time. *Faculty:* 7 full-time (2 women). *Students:* 50 full-time (15 women), 4 part-time (2 women); includes 21 minority (17 Black or African American, non-Hispanic/Latino; 1 Asian, non-Hispanic/Latino; 1 Hispanic/Latino; 2 Two or more races, non-Hispanic/Latino), 3 international. Average age 27. 53 applicants, 57% accepted, 28 enrolled. In 2016, 16 master's awarded. *Degree requirements:* For master's, comprehensive exam, thesis optional. *Entrance requirements:* For master's, GRE General Test or MAT, Alabama Class B certificate or the equivalent (for students seeking the master's-level/Class A certification). Additional exam requirements/recommendations for international students: Required—TOEFL. *Application deadline:* For fall admission, 7/15 priority date for domestic students, 6/15 priority date for international students; for spring admission, 11/15 priority date for domestic students, 10/15 priority date for international students; for summer admission, 4/15 for domestic students. Applications are processed on a rolling basis. Application fee: $35. Electronic applications accepted. *Expenses:* Tuition, state resident: full-time $9768; part-time $407 per credit hour. Tuition, nonresident: full-time $19,536; part-time $814 per credit hour. *Financial support:* Fellowships, research assistantships, teaching assistantships with partial tuition reimbursements, career-related internships or fieldwork, Federal Work-Study, institutionally sponsored loans, scholarships/grants, and unspecified assistantships available. Support available to part-time students. Financial award application deadline: 5/31; financial award applicants required to submit FAFSA. *Unit head:* Dr. John Kovaleski, Department Chair, 251-461-1622, Fax: 251-460-7252, E-mail: jkovales@southalabama.edu. *Application contact:* Dr. Susan Santoli, Director of Graduate Studies, 251-380-2738, Fax: 251-380-2758, E-mail: ssantoli@southalabama.edu.
Website: http://www.southalabama.edu/colleges/coe/hks/index.html

University of South Carolina, The Graduate School, Arnold School of Public Health, Department of Health Promotion, Education, and Behavior, Columbia, SC 29208. Offers health education (MAT); health promotion, education, and behavior (MPH, MS, MSPH, Dr PH, PhD); school health education (Certificate); MSW/MPH. MAT offered in cooperation with the College of Education. *Accreditation:* CEPH (one or more programs are accredited); NCATE (one or more programs are accredited). *Program availability:* Part-time. *Degree requirements:* For master's, comprehensive exam, thesis or alternative, practicum (MPH), project (MS); for doctorate, comprehensive exam, thesis/dissertation. *Entrance requirements:* For master's and doctorate, GRE General Test. Additional exam requirements/recommendations for international students: Required—TOEFL (minimum score 570 paper-based; 75 iBT). Electronic applications accepted. *Faculty research:* Health disparities and inequalities in communities, global health and nutrition, cancer and HIV/AIDS prevention, health communication, policy and program design.

University of South Carolina, The Graduate School, College of Education, Department of Instruction and Teacher Education, Program in Secondary Education, Columbia, SC 29208. Offers art education (IMA, MAT); business education (IMA, MAT); English (MAT); foreign language (MAT); health education (MAT); mathematics (MAT); science (IMA, MAT); secondary (Ed D); secondary education (MT, PhD); social studies (MAT); theatre and speech (MAT). IMA and MT offered jointly with the subject areas. *Accreditation:* NCATE. *Degree requirements:* For master's, comprehensive exam, thesis (for some programs), foreign language (MA); for doctorate, one foreign language, comprehensive exam, thesis/dissertation. *Entrance requirements:* For master's, GRE General Test or MAT, teaching certificate (IMA, M Ed), interview; for doctorate, GRE General Test or MAT, interview. *Faculty research:* Middle school programs, professional development, school collaboration.

University of Southern California, Keck School of Medicine and Graduate School, Graduate Programs in Medicine, Department of Preventive Medicine, Master of Public Health Program, Los Angeles, CA 90032-3628. Offers biostatistics and epidemiology (MPH); child and family health (MPH); environmental health (MPH); global health leadership (MPH); health communication (MPH); health education and promotion (MPH); public health policy (MPH). *Accreditation:* CEPH. *Program availability:* Part-time, evening/weekend. *Faculty:* 22 full-time (12 women), 3 part-time/adjunct (0 women). *Students:* 168 full-time (124 women), 30 part-time (22 women); includes 104 minority (14 Black or African American, non-Hispanic/Latino; 64 Asian, non-Hispanic/Latino; 26 Hispanic/Latino), 37 international. Average age 24. 246 applicants, 67% accepted, 76 enrolled. In 2016, 89 master's awarded. *Degree requirements:* For master's, practicum, final report, oral presentation. *Entrance requirements:* For master's, GRE General Test, MCAT, GMAT, minimum GPA of 3.0. Additional exam requirements/recommendations for international students: Required—TOEFL (minimum score 600 paper-based; 90 iBT). *Application deadline:* For fall admission, 12/1 priority date for domestic students, 5/1 priority date for international students; for spring admission, 9/1 priority date for domestic and international students; for summer admission, 3/1 for domestic and international students. Applications are processed on a rolling basis. Application fee: $90. Electronic applications accepted. *Expenses:* Contact institution. *Financial support:* Career-related internships or fieldwork, Federal Work-Study, institutionally sponsored loans, and scholarships/grants available. Support available to part-time students. Financial award application deadline: 5/4; financial award applicants required to submit CSS PROFILE or FAFSA. *Faculty research:* Substance abuse prevention, cancer and heart disease prevention, mass media and health communication research, health promotion, treatment compliance. *Unit head:* Dr. Louise A. Rohrbach, Director, 323-442-8237, Fax: 323-442-8297, E-mail: rohrbac@usc.edu. *Application contact:* Valerie Burris, Admissions Counselor, 323-442-7257, Fax: 323-442-8297, E-mail: valeriem@usc.edu.
Website: http://mph.usc.edu/

University of Southern Mississippi, Graduate School, College of Health, Department of Public Health, Hattiesburg, MS 39406. Offers epidemiology and biostatistics (MPH); health education (MPH); health policy and administration (MPH). *Accreditation:* CEPH. *Program availability:* Part-time, evening/weekend. *Degree requirements:* For master's, comprehensive exam, thesis (for some programs). *Entrance requirements:* For master's, GRE General Test, minimum GPA of 2.75 in last 60 hours. Additional exam requirements/recommendations for international students: Required—TOEFL, IELTS. *Application deadline:* For fall admission, 3/1 priority date for domestic and international students; for spring admission, 1/10 priority date for domestic and international students. Applications are processed on a rolling basis. Application fee: $60. Electronic applications accepted. *Expenses: Tuition, area resident:* Full-time $15,708; part-time $437 per credit hour. *Financial support:* Research assistantships with full tuition reimbursements, teaching assistantships with full tuition reimbursements, career-related internships or fieldwork, Federal Work-Study, institutionally sponsored loans, scholarships/grants, health care benefits, and unspecified assistantships available. Financial award application deadline: 3/15; financial award applicants required to submit FAFSA. *Faculty research:* Rural health care delivery, school health, nutrition of pregnant teens, risk factor reduction, sexually transmitted diseases. *Unit head:* Charkarra Anderson-Lewis, Interim Chair, 601-266-5435, Fax: 601-266-5043, E-mail: charkarra.andersonlewis@usm.edu. *Application contact:* Shonna Breland, Manager of Graduate Admissions, 601-266-6563, Fax: 601-266-5138.
Website: http://www.usm.edu/community-public-health-sciences

University of South Florida, College of Pharmacy, Tampa, FL 33620-9951. Offers pharmaceutical nanotechnology (MS); pharmacy (Pharm D), including pharmacy and health education. *Accreditation:* ACPE. *Faculty:* 41 full-time (28 women), 2 part-time/adjunct (0 women). *Students:* 391 full-time (233 women), 1 (woman) part-time; includes 170 minority (29 Black or African American, non-Hispanic/Latino; 63 Asian, non-Hispanic/Latino; 62 Hispanic/Latino; 4 Native Hawaiian or other Pacific Islander, non-Hispanic/Latino; 12 Two or more races, non-Hispanic/Latino). Average age 26. 679 applicants, 29% accepted, 102 enrolled. In 2016, 53 doctorates awarded. *Degree requirements:* For master's, comprehensive exam, thesis optional. *Entrance requirements:* For master's, GRE, MCAT or DAT, minimum GPA of 3.0, letters of reference, resume; for doctorate, PCAT, minimum GPA of 2.75 overall (preferred); completion of 72 prerequisite credit hours; U.S. citizenship or permanent resident. Additional exam requirements/recommendations for international students: Required—TOEFL (minimum score 550 paper-based; 79 iBT), IELTS (minimum score 6.5). *Application deadline:* For fall admission, 2/15 for domestic and international students; for spring admission, 10/15 for domestic students, 9/15 for international students; for summer admission, 2/15 for domestic and international students. Electronic applications accepted. *Expenses:* Tuition, state resident: full-time $7766; part-time $431.43 per credit hour. Tuition, nonresident: full-time $15,789; part-time $877.17 per credit hour.

Required fees: $37 per term. *Financial support:* In 2016–17, 131 students received support. *Total annual research expenditures:* $1.1 million. *Unit head:* Dr. Kevin Sneed, Dean, 813-974-5699, E-mail: ksneed@health.usf.edu. *Application contact:* Dr. Amy Schwartz, Associate Dean, 813-974-2251, E-mail: aschwar1@health.usf.edu.

The University of Tennessee, Graduate School, College of Education, Health and Human Sciences, Program in Health Promotion and Health Education, Knoxville, TN 37996. Offers MS. *Program availability:* Part-time. *Degree requirements:* For master's, thesis optional. *Entrance requirements:* For master's, minimum GPA of 2.7. Additional exam requirements/recommendations for international students: Required—TOEFL. Electronic applications accepted.

The University of Tennessee, Graduate School, College of Education, Health and Human Sciences, Program in Safety, Knoxville, TN 37996. Offers MS. *Accreditation:* NCATE. *Program availability:* Part-time. *Degree requirements:* For master's, thesis optional. *Entrance requirements:* For master's, minimum GPA of 2.7. Additional exam requirements/recommendations for international students: Required—TOEFL. Electronic applications accepted.

The University of Texas at Austin, Graduate School, College of Education, Department of Kinesiology and Health Education, Austin, TX 78712-1111. Offers behavioral health (PhD); exercise and sport psychology (M Ed, MA); exercise science (M Ed, MS, PhD); health education (M Ed, MS, Ed D, PhD). *Program availability:* Part-time. Terminal master's awarded for partial completion of doctoral program. *Degree requirements:* For master's, thesis (for some programs); for doctorate, thesis/dissertation. *Entrance requirements:* For master's and doctorate, GRE General Test. Additional exam requirements/recommendations for international students: Required—TOEFL. Electronic applications accepted. *Faculty research:* Health promotion, human performance and exercise biochemistry, motor behavior and biomechanics, sport management, aging and pediatric development.

The University of Texas at San Antonio, College of Education and Human Development, Department of Kinesiology, Health, and Nutrition, San Antonio, TX 78249-0617. Offers health and kinesiology (MS). *Program availability:* Part-time, evening/weekend. *Faculty:* 13 full-time (6 women). *Students:* 76 full-time (41 women), 61 part-time (35 women); includes 97 minority (16 Black or African American, non-Hispanic/Latino; 7 Asian, non-Hispanic/Latino; 70 Hispanic/Latino; 4 Two or more races, non-Hispanic/Latino), 2 international. Average age 27. 70 applicants, 80% accepted, 37 enrolled. In 2016, 54 master's awarded. *Degree requirements:* For master's, comprehensive exam, thesis optional. *Entrance requirements:* For master's, bachelor's degree with minimum GPA of 3.0 in last 60 hours of coursework; resume; statement of purpose; two letters of recommendation. Additional exam requirements/recommendations for international students: Required—TOEFL (minimum score 550 paper-based; 79 iBT), IELTS (minimum score 6.5). *Application deadline:* For fall admission, 7/1 for domestic students, 4/1 for international students; for spring admission, 11/1 for domestic students, 9/1 for international students; for summer admission, 4/1 for domestic students, 3/1 for international students. Applications are processed on a rolling basis. Application fee: $45 ($80 for international students). Electronic applications accepted. *Expenses:* Contact institution. *Financial support:* In 2016–17, 10 students received support. Unspecified assistantships available. Financial award application deadline: 3/31; financial award applicants required to submit FAFSA. *Faculty research:* Childhood obesity, health disparities, community health, exercise physiology, sport psychology. *Total annual research expenditures:* $169,815. *Unit head:* Dr. William Cooke, Chair, 210-458-5642, E-mail: william.cooke@utsa.edu.
Website: http://education.utsa.edu/health_and_kinesiology

The University of Texas at Tyler, College of Nursing and Health Sciences, Department of Health and Kinesiology, Tyler, TX 75799-0001. Offers health and kinesiology (M Ed, MA); health sciences (MS); kinesiology (MS). *Accreditation:* TEAC. *Program availability:* Part-time, online learning. *Degree requirements:* For master's, comprehensive exam (for some programs), thesis (for some programs). *Entrance requirements:* Additional exam requirements/recommendations for international students: Required—TOEFL. Electronic applications accepted. *Faculty research:* Osteoporosis, muscle soreness, economy of locomotion, adoption of rehabilitation programs, effect of inactivity and aging on muscle blood vessels, territoriality.

The University of Toledo, College of Graduate Studies, College of Health and Human Services, Department of Health and Recreation Professions, Toledo, OH 43606-3390. Offers health education (PhD); recreation and leisure studies (MA). *Program availability:* Part-time. *Degree requirements:* For master's, comprehensive exam, thesis; for doctorate, thesis/dissertation. *Entrance requirements:* For master's and doctorate, minimum cumulative GPA of 2.7 for all previous academic work, letters of recommendation. Additional exam requirements/recommendations for international students: Required—TOEFL (minimum score 550 paper-based; 80 iBT). Electronic applications accepted.

The University of Toledo, College of Graduate Studies, College of Medicine and Life Sciences, Department of Public Health and Preventative Medicine, Toledo, OH 43606-3390. Offers biostatistics and epidemiology (Certificate); contemporary gerontological practice (Certificate); environmental and occupational health and safety (MPH); epidemiology (Certificate); global public health (Certificate); health promotion and education (MPH); industrial hygiene (MSOH); medical and health science teaching and learning (Certificate); occupational health (Certificate); public health administration (MPH); public health and emergency response (Certificate); public health epidemiology (MPH); public health nutrition (MPH); MD/MPH. *Program availability:* Part-time, evening/weekend. *Degree requirements:* For master's, thesis or alternative. *Entrance requirements:* For master's, GRE, minimum undergraduate GPA of 3.0, three letters of recommendation, statement of purpose, transcripts from all prior institutions attended, resume; for Certificate, minimum undergraduate GPA of 3.0, three letters of recommendation, statement of purpose, transcripts from all prior institutions attended, resume. Additional exam requirements/recommendations for international students: Required—TOEFL (minimum score 550 paper-based; 80 iBT), IELTS (minimum score 6.5). Electronic applications accepted.

University of Utah, Graduate School, College of Health, Health Promotion and Education Program, Salt Lake City, UT 84112. Offers M Phil, MS, Ed D, PhD. *Program availability:* Part-time. *Faculty:* 6 full-time (3 women), 9 part-time/adjunct (5 women). *Students:* 37 full-time (31 women), 13 part-time (8 women); includes 5 minority (1 Black or African American, non-Hispanic/Latino; 1 American Indian or Alaska Native, non-Hispanic/Latino; 1 Asian, non-Hispanic/Latino; 2 Hispanic/Latino), 4 international. Average age 29. 22 applicants, 64% accepted, 11 enrolled. In 2016, 50 master's, 15 doctorates awarded. Terminal master's awarded for partial completion of doctoral program. *Degree requirements:* For master's, comprehensive exam, thesis or alternative, field experience; for doctorate, comprehensive exam, thesis/dissertation, field experience. *Entrance requirements:* For master's, GRE (for thesis option), minimum GPA of 3.0; for doctorate, GRE, minimum GPA of 3.2. Additional exam requirements/recommendations for international students: Required—TOEFL (minimum score 550 paper-based; 80 iBT). *Application deadline:* For fall admission, 2/1 for domestic and international students; for spring admission, 2/15 for domestic and international students; for summer admission, 2/1 for domestic and international students. Application fee: $55 ($65 for international students). Electronic applications accepted. *Expenses:* Tuition, state resident: full-time $7011; part-time $3918.24 per credit hour. Tuition, nonresident: full-time $22,154; part-time $11,665.42 per credit hour. *Financial support:* In 2016–17, 9 students received support, including 3 research assistantships with full tuition reimbursements available (averaging $14,500 per year), 6 teaching assistantships with full tuition reimbursements available (averaging $14,500 per year); health care benefits and unspecified assistantships also available. Financial award application deadline: 3/1; financial award applicants required to submit FAFSA. *Faculty research:* Health behavior and counseling, health service administration, evaluation of health programs. *Unit head:* Leslie K. Chatelain, Program Director, 801-581-4512, Fax: 801-585-3646, E-mail: les.chatelain@utah.edu. *Application contact:* Dr. Glenn E. Richardson, Director of Graduate Studies, 801-581-8039, Fax: 801-585-3646, E-mail: glenn.richardson@health.utah.edu.
Website: http://www.health.utah.edu/healthed/index.htm

University of Waterloo, Graduate Studies, Faculty of Applied Health Sciences, School of Public Health and Health Systems, Waterloo, ON N2L 3G1, Canada. Offers health evaluation (MHE); health informatics (MHI); health studies and gerontology (M Sc, PhD); public health (MPH). *Program availability:* Part-time. *Degree requirements:* For master's, thesis; for doctorate, comprehensive exam, thesis/dissertation. *Entrance requirements:* For master's, honors degree, minimum B average, resume, writing sample; for doctorate, GRE (recommended), master's degree, minimum B average, resume, writing sample. Additional exam requirements/recommendations for international students: Required—TOEFL, IELTS, PTE. Electronic applications accepted. *Faculty research:* Population health, health promotion and disease prevention, healthy aging, health policy, planning and evaluation, health information management and health informatics, aging, health and well-being, work and health.

University of Wisconsin–La Crosse, College of Science and Health, Department of Health Education and Health Promotion, Program in Community Health Education, La Crosse, WI 54601-3742. Offers MPH, MS. *Accreditation:* CEPH. *Students:* 17 full-time (15 women), 13 part-time (11 women). Average age 32. 6 applicants, 100% accepted, 4 enrolled. In 2016, 10 master's awarded. *Degree requirements:* For master's, thesis. *Entrance requirements:* For master's, GRE General Test, GRE Subject Test (for MPH), 3 letters of recommendation. Additional exam requirements/recommendations for international students: Required—TOEFL (minimum score 550 paper-based; 79 iBT). Electronic applications accepted. *Financial support:* Research assistantships with partial tuition reimbursements, Federal Work-Study, scholarships/grants, health care benefits, and tuition waivers (partial) available. Support available to part-time students. Financial award applicants required to submit FAFSA. *Unit head:* Dr. Gary Gilmore, Director, 608-785-8163, E-mail: gilmore.gary@uwlax.edu. *Application contact:* Brandon Schaller, Senior Graduate Student Status Examiner, 608-785-8941, E-mail: admissions@uwlax.edu.

University of Wisconsin–La Crosse, College of Science and Health, Department of Health Education and Health Promotion, Program in School Health Education, La Crosse, WI 54601-3742. Offers MS. *Students:* 1 part-time (0 women). Average age 31. 2 applicants, 100% accepted, 2 enrolled. In 2016, 1 master's awarded. *Entrance requirements:* For master's, GRE General Test, minimum GPA of 2.85. Additional exam requirements/recommendations for international students: Required—TOEFL (minimum score 550 paper-based; 79 iBT). *Application deadline:* Applications are processed on a rolling basis. Electronic applications accepted. *Financial support:* Federal Work-Study and scholarships/grants available. Support available to part-time students. Financial award applicants required to submit FAFSA. *Faculty research:* Adolescent health issues, heath education, human sexuality, mental health, stress management, comprehensive school health pedagogy (curriculum, instructional methodology and assessment), PK-12 health literacy, K-12 education, relationship management, substance use and abuse, skill development within health education. *Unit head:* Dr. Tracy Caravella, Director, 608-785-6788, E-mail: caravell.trac@uwlax.edu. *Application contact:* Brandon Schaller, Senior Graduate Student Status Examiner, 608-785-8941, E-mail: admissions@uwlax.edu.
Website: http://www.uwlax.edu/sah/hehp/html/gr_she.htm

University of Wisconsin–Milwaukee, Graduate School, Joseph J. Zilber School of Public Health, Program in Public Health, Milwaukee, WI 53201-0413. Offers biostatistics (MPH); community and behavioral health promotion (MPH); environmental health sciences (MPH); epidemiology (MPH); public health (Graduate Certificate); public health policy and administration (MPH); public health: biostatistics (PhD); public health: community and behavioral health promotion (PhD). *Students:* 62 full-time (50 women), 23 part-time (16 women); includes 21 minority (6 Black or African American, non-Hispanic/Latino; 8 Asian, non-Hispanic/Latino; 1 Hispanic/Latino; 6 Two or more races, non-Hispanic/Latino), 10 international. Average age 30. 93 applicants, 68% accepted, 34 enrolled. In 2016, 20 master's awarded. *Application contact:* Darcie K. G. Warren, Graduate Program Manager, 414-229-5633, E-mail: darcie@uwm.edu.

University of Wyoming, College of Health Sciences, Division of Kinesiology and Health, Laramie, WY 82071. Offers MS. *Accreditation:* NCATE. *Program availability:* Part-time, online learning. *Degree requirements:* For master's, comprehensive exam (for some programs), thesis (for some programs). *Entrance requirements:* For master's, GRE General Test, minimum GPA of 3.0. Additional exam requirements/recommendations for international students: Required—TOEFL. Electronic applications accepted. *Faculty research:* Teacher effectiveness, effects of exercising on heart function, physiological responses of overtraining, psychological benefits of physical activity, health behavior.

Utah State University, School of Graduate Studies, Emma Eccles Jones College of Education and Human Services, Department of Health, Physical Education and Recreation, Logan, UT 84322. Offers M Ed, MS. *Program availability:* Part-time, evening/weekend, online learning. *Degree requirements:* For master's, thesis (for some programs). *Entrance requirements:* For master's, GRE General Test or MAT, minimum GPA of 3.0. Additional exam requirements/recommendations for international students: Required—TOEFL. *Faculty research:* Sport psychology intervention, motor learning biomechanics, pedagogy, physiology.

Virginia State University, College of Graduate Studies, College of Natural and Health Sciences, Department of Psychology, Petersburg, VA 23806-0001. Offers behavioral and community health sciences (PhD); clinical health psychology (PhD); clinical psychology (MS); general psychology (MS). *Degree requirements:* For master's, one foreign language, thesis. *Entrance requirements:* For master's, GRE General Test.

Walden University, Graduate Programs, School of Health Sciences, Minneapolis, MN 55401. Offers clinical research administration (MS, Graduate Certificate); health education and promotion (MS, PhD), including behavioral health (PhD), disease surveillance (PhD), emergency preparedness (MS), general (MHA, MS), global health (PhD), health policy (PhD), health policy and advocacy (MS), population health (PhD); health informatics (MS); health services (PhD), including community health, healthcare administration, leadership, public health policy, self-designed; healthcare administration (MHA, DHA), including general (MHA, MS); leadership and organizational development (MHA); public health (MPH, Dr PH, PhD, Graduate Certificate), including community health education (PhD), epidemiology (PhD); systems policy (MHA). *Program* *availability:* Part-time, evening/weekend, online only, 100% online. *Degree requirements:* For doctorate, thesis/dissertation, residency. *Entrance requirements:* For master's, bachelor's degree or higher; minimum GPA of 2.5; official transcripts; goal statement (for some programs); access to computer and Internet; for doctorate, master's degree or higher; three years of related professional or academic experience (preferred); minimum GPA of 3.0; goal statement and current resume (for select programs); official transcripts; access to computer and Internet; for Graduate Certificate, relevant work experience; access to computer and Internet. Additional exam requirements/recommendations for international students: Required—TOEFL (minimum score 550 paper-based, 79 iBT), IELTS (minimum score 6.5), Michigan English Language Assessment Battery (minimum score 82), or PTE (minimum score 53). Electronic applications accepted.

Washburn University, School of Applied Studies, Department of Allied Health, Topeka, KS 66621. Offers health care education (MHS). *Program availability:* Part-time. *Degree requirements:* For master's, internship, practicum. *Entrance requirements:* For master's, bachelor's degree, two years of professional work experience in a health care environment, official transcripts, minimum cumulative GPA of 3.0 in last 60 hours, personal statement, resume, college algebra course with grade no lower than a C. Additional exam requirements/recommendations for international students: Required—TOEFL (minimum score 80 iBT).

Wayne State University, College of Education, Division of Kinesiology, Health and Sports Studies, Detroit, MI 48202. Offers health education (M Ed); kinesiology (M Ed, PhD), including exercise and sport science (PhD), physical education and physical activity leadership (PhD); sports administration (MA). *Program availability:* Part-time, 100% online. *Faculty:* 10. *Students:* 57 full-time (30 women), 131 part-time (68 women); includes 72 minority (63 Black or African American, non-Hispanic/Latino; 1 American Indian or Alaska Native, non-Hispanic/Latino; 1 Asian, non-Hispanic/Latino; 3 Hispanic/Latino; 4 Two or more races, non-Hispanic/Latino), 10 international. Average age 29. 160 applicants, 56% accepted, 51 enrolled. In 2016, 66 master's awarded. *Degree requirements:* For master's, thesis (for some programs); for doctorate, thesis/dissertation. *Entrance requirements:* For master's, minimum undergraduate GPA of 3.0; undergraduate degree directly relating to the field of specialization being applied for or one accompanied by extensive educational background in closely-related field; teaching certificates in specific areas (for some programs); for doctorate, minimum undergraduate GPA of 3.0; undergraduate degree directly relating to the field of specialization being applied for or one accompanied by extensive educational background in closely-related field. Additional exam requirements/recommendations for international students: Required—TOEFL (minimum score 79 iBT), TWE (minimum score 5.5), Michigan English Language Assessment Battery (minimum score 85); Recommended—IELTS (minimum score 6.5). *Application deadline:* For fall admission, 6/1 priority date for domestic students, 5/1 priority date for international students; for winter admission, 10/1 priority date for domestic students, 9/1 priority date for international students; for spring admission, 2/1 priority date for domestic students, 1/1 priority date for international students. Application fee: $50. Electronic applications accepted. *Expenses:* $18,522 per year resident tuition and fees, $35,715 per year non-resident tuition and fees. *Financial support:* In 2016–17, 49 students received support, including 6 research assistantships with tuition reimbursements available (averaging $17,994 per year); fellowships with tuition reimbursements available, scholarships/grants, health care benefits, and unspecified assistantships also available. Support available to part-time students. Financial award applicants required to submit FAFSA. *Faculty research:* Exercise and sport science, nutrition and physical activity interventions, school and community health, obesity prevention. *Total annual research expenditures:* $974,985. *Unit head:* Dr. Nate McCaughtry, Assistant Dean, Division of Kinesiology, Health and Sport Studies/Director, Center for School Health, 313-577-0014, Fax: 313-577-5002, E-mail: aj4391@wayne.edu. *Application contact:* Janice Green, Assistant Dean, 313-577-1605, E-mail: jwgreen@wayne.edu.
Website: http://coe.wayne.edu/kinesiology/index.php

Wayne State University, School of Medicine, Office of Biomedical Graduate Programs, Detroit, MI 48202. Offers anatomy and cell biology (MS, PhD); basic medical sciences (MS); biochemistry and molecular biology (MS, PhD); cancer biology (MS, PhD); clinical and translational science (Graduate Certificate); family medicine and public health sciences (MPH, Graduate Certificate), including public health practice; genetic counseling (MS); immunology and microbiology (MS, PhD); medical physics (MS, PhD, Graduate Certificate); medical research (MS); molecular medicine and genomics (MS, PhD), including molecular genetics and genomics; pathology (PhD); pharmacology (MS, PhD); physiology (MS, PhD), including physiology, reproductive sciences (PhD); psychiatry and behavioral neurosciences (PhD), including translational neuroscience; MD/MPH; MD/PhD; MPH/MA; MSW/MPH. *Program availability:* Part-time, evening/weekend. *Students:* 301 full-time (150 women), 112 part-time (56 women); includes 114 minority (19 Black or African American, non-Hispanic/Latino; 1 American Indian or Alaska Native, non-Hispanic/Latino; 65 Asian, non-Hispanic/Latino; 12 Hispanic/Latino; 17 Two or more races, non-Hispanic/Latino), 62 international. Average age 27. 1,009 applicants, 22% accepted, 161 enrolled. In 2016, 65 master's, 22 doctorates, 8 other advanced degrees awarded. Terminal master's awarded for partial completion of doctoral program. *Degree requirements:* For master's, thesis (for some programs); for doctorate, thesis/dissertation. *Entrance requirements:* For master's, doctorate, and Graduate Certificate, GRE. Additional exam requirements/recommendations for international students: Required—TOEFL (minimum score 550 paper-based; 100 iBT), Michigan English Language Assessment Battery (minimum score 85); Recommended—IELTS (minimum score 6.5), TWE (minimum score 5.5). *Application deadline:* For fall admission, 2/1 for domestic and international students. Applications are processed on a rolling basis. Application fee: $50. Electronic applications accepted. *Expenses:* $20,126 per year resident tuition and fees, $36,434 per year non-resident tuition and fees. *Financial support:* In 2016–17, 197 students received support, including 67 fellowships with full tuition reimbursements available (averaging $24,294 per year), 94 research assistantships with full tuition reimbursements available (averaging $26,850 per year); scholarships/grants, traineeships, and health care benefits also available. *Faculty research:* Cancer biology, neurosciences, vision sciences, molecular biology, pathology, physiology, pharmacology, public health, medical physics. *Unit head:* Dr. Daniel A. Walz, Associate Dean for Biomedical Graduate Programs, 313-577-1455, Fax: 313-577-8796, E-mail: gradprogs@med.wayne.edu.
Website: https://www.med.wayne.edu/biomedical-graduate-programs/

West Chester University of Pennsylvania, College of Health Sciences, Department of Health, West Chester, PA 19383. Offers emergency preparedness (Certificate); gerontology (Certificate); health care management (Certificate); integrative health (Certificate); public health (MPH); school health (M Ed). *Accreditation:* CEPH. *Program availability:* Part-time, evening/weekend. *Faculty:* 13 full-time (8 women), 5 part-time/adjunct (3 women). *Students:* 89 full-time (70 women), 94 part-time (62 women); includes 76 minority (65 Black or African American, non-Hispanic/Latino; 6 Asian, non-Hispanic/Latino; 5 Hispanic/Latino), 17 international. Average age 30. 119 applicants, 89% accepted, 63 enrolled. In 2016, 64 master's, 2 other advanced degrees awarded. *Degree requirements:* For master's, research report (for M Ed); major project and practicum (for MPH); for Certificate, 18 credits (for gerontology). *Entrance requirements:* For master's, undergraduate introduction to statistics course; for Certificate, goal statement, two letters of recommendation, resume, and official transcripts from all previously completed coursework (for gerontology). Additional exam requirements/recommendations for international students: Required—TOEFL or IELTS. *Application deadline:* For fall admission, 5/15 for international students; for spring admission, 10/15 for international students. Applications are processed on a rolling basis. Application fee: $50. Electronic applications accepted. *Expenses:* Tuition, state resident: full-time $8694; part-time $483 per credit. Tuition, nonresident: full-time $13,050; part-time $725 per credit. *Required fees:* $2399; $119.05 per credit. Tuition and fees vary according to campus/location and program. *Financial support:* Scholarships/grants and unspecified assistantships available. Financial award application deadline: 2/15; financial award applicants required to submit FAFSA. *Faculty research:* Healthy school communities, community health issues and evidence-based programs, environment and health, nutrition and health, integrative health. *Unit head:* Dr. Bethann Cinelli, Chair, 610-436-2267, E-mail: bcinelli@wcupa.edu. *Application contact:* Dr. Lynn Carson, Graduate Coordinator, 610-436-2138, E-mail: lcarson@wcupa.edu.
Website: http://www.wcupa.edu/HealthSciences/health/

Western Illinois University, School of Graduate Studies, College of Education and Human Services, Department of Health Sciences, Macomb, IL 61455-1390. Offers health sciences (MS); health services administration (Certificate). *Accreditation:* NCATE. *Program availability:* Part-time. *Students:* 33 full-time (24 women), 11 part-time (all women); includes 11 minority (6 Black or African American, non-Hispanic/Latino; 1 Asian, non-Hispanic/Latino; 3 Hispanic/Latino; 1 Two or more races, non-Hispanic/Latino), 14 international. Average age 30. 42 applicants, 81% accepted, 16 enrolled. In 2016, 9 master's, 9 other advanced degrees awarded. *Degree requirements:* For master's, comprehensive exam, thesis or alternative. *Entrance requirements:* Additional exam requirements/recommendations for international students: Required—TOEFL (minimum score 550 paper-based; 80 iBT). *Application deadline:* Applications are processed on a rolling basis. Application fee: $30. Electronic applications accepted. *Financial support:* In 2016–17, 13 students received support. Unspecified assistantships available. Financial award applicants required to submit FAFSA. *Unit head:* Dr. Lorette Oden, Interim Chairperson, 309-298-1076. *Application contact:* Dr. Nancy Parsons, Associate Provost and Director of Graduate Studies, 309-298-1806, Fax: 309-298-2345, E-mail: grad-office@wiu.edu.
Website: http://wiu.edu/health

Western Michigan University, Graduate College, College of Health and Human Services, Department of Interdisciplinary Health and Human Services, Kalamazoo, MI 49008. Offers interdisciplinary health services (PhD).

Western Oregon University, Graduate Programs, College of Education, Division of Teacher Education, Program in Secondary Education, Monmouth, OR 97361. Offers bilingual education (MS Ed); health (MS Ed); humanities (MAT, MS Ed); initial licensure (MAT); mathematics (MAT, MS Ed); science (MAT, MS Ed); social science (MAT, MS Ed). *Accreditation:* NCATE. *Program availability:* Part-time, evening/weekend. *Degree requirements:* For master's, thesis optional, written exam. *Entrance requirements:* For master's, minimum GPA of 3.0, teaching license. Additional exam requirements/recommendations for international students: Required—TOEFL (minimum score 550 paper-based; 79 iBT), IELTS (minimum score 6.5). *Faculty research:* Literacy, science in primary grades, geography education, retention, teacher burnout.

Western University of Health Sciences, College of Allied Health Professions, Program in Health Sciences, Pomona, CA 91766-1854. Offers MS. *Program availability:* Part-time, evening/weekend. *Faculty:* 3 full-time (2 women). *Students:* 17 full-time (15 women), 13 part-time (9 women); includes 19 minority (4 Black or African American, non-Hispanic/Latino; 3 Asian, non-Hispanic/Latino; 6 Hispanic/Latino; 6 Two or more races, non-Hispanic/Latino), 4 international. Average age 29. 22 applicants, 41% accepted, 8 enrolled. In 2016, 3 master's awarded. *Entrance requirements:* For master's, GRE (minimum score of 3.5 on analytical writing), bachelor's degree (preferred); minimum undergraduate GPA of 2.7, graduate 3.0; letters of recommendation; statement of purpose; current curriculum vitae. Additional exam requirements/recommendations for international students: Required—TOEFL. *Application deadline:* For fall admission, 5/31 priority date for domestic students. Application fee: $35. Electronic applications accepted. *Expenses:* $608 per credit hout. *Financial support:* Scholarships/grants available. Financial award application deadline: 3/2; financial award applicants required to submit FAFSA. *Faculty research:* Women's health, community based participatory research, global health, central Asia health and politics. *Unit head:* Dr. Tina Meyer, Chair, 909-469-5397, Fax: 909-469-5407, E-mail: tmeyer@westernu.edu. *Application contact:* Susan Hanson, Executive Director of Admissions for the College of Osteopathic Medicine of the Pacific and for Health Professions Education, 909-469-5335, Fax: 909-469-5570, E-mail: admissions@westernu.edu.
Website: http://prospective.westernu.edu/health-sciences/welcome-3/

Widener University, School of Education, Hospitality, and Continuing Studies, Chester, PA 19013-5792. Offers adult education (M Ed); counseling in higher education (M Ed); counselor education (M Ed); early childhood education (M Ed); educational foundations (M Ed); educational leadership (M Ed); educational psychology (M Ed); elementary education (M Ed); English and language arts (M Ed); health education (M Ed); higher education leadership (Ed D); home and school visitor (M Ed); human sexuality (M Ed, PhD); mathematics education (M Ed); middle school education (M Ed); principalship (M Ed); reading and language arts (Ed D); reading education (M Ed); school administration (Ed D); science education (M Ed); social studies education (M Ed); special education (M Ed); technology education (M Ed). *Accreditation:* NCATE. *Program availability:* Part-time, evening/weekend. *Faculty:* 34 full-time (22 women), 37 part-time/adjunct (14 women). *Students:* 97 full-time (64 women), 201 part-time (143 women); includes 56 minority (44 Black or African American, non-Hispanic/Latino; 1 American Indian or Alaska Native, non-Hispanic/Latino; 2 Asian, non-Hispanic/Latino; 8 Hispanic/Latino; 1 Two or more races, non-Hispanic/Latino), 32 international. Average age 39. 139 applicants, 88% accepted. In 2016, 45 master's, 21 doctorates awarded. Terminal master's awarded for partial completion of doctoral program. *Degree requirements:* For doctorate, thesis/dissertation. *Entrance requirements:* For master's, minimum GPA of 2.5; for doctorate, GRE or MAT, minimum GPA of 2.0 (undergraduate), 3.5 (graduate). *Application deadline:* Applications are processed on a rolling basis. Application fee: $25 ($300 for international students). Electronic applications accepted. *Expenses:* Contact institution. *Financial support:* Career-related internships or fieldwork, tuition waivers (full and partial), and unspecified assistantships available. Support available to part-time students. Financial award application deadline: 5/1. *Faculty research:* Reading and cognition, adult education, technology education, educational leadership, special education. *Unit head:* Dr. Shawn Fitzgerald, Dean, 610-499-4294, Fax: 610-499-4623, E-mail: smfitzgerald@widener.edu. *Application contact:* Dr. Roberta Nolan, Director of Graduate Admissions, 610-499-4125, E-mail: rdnolan@widener.edu.
Website: http://www.widener.edu/academics/schools/eics

Worcester State University, Graduate Studies, Department of Education, Program in Health Education, Worcester, MA 01602-2597. Offers M Ed. *Program availability:* Part-time. *Faculty:* 13 full-time (12 women), 16 part-time/adjunct (7 women). *Students:* 6 part-time (3 women); includes 2 minority (1 Black or African American, non-Hispanic/Latino; 1 Hispanic/Latino). Average age 33. 7 applicants, 86% accepted, 4 enrolled. In 2016, 1 master's awarded. *Degree requirements:* For master's, comprehensive exam (for some programs), thesis optional, Certified Health Education Specialist exam. *Entrance requirements:* For master's, GRE General Test or MAT. Additional exam requirements/recommendations for international students: Required—TOEFL (minimum score 550 paper-based; 79 iBT). *Application deadline:* For fall admission, 6/15 for domestic and international students; for spring admission, 11/1 for domestic and international students; for summer admission, 4/1 for domestic and international students. Applications are processed on a rolling basis. Application fee: $50. Electronic applications accepted. *Expenses:* Tuition, state resident: part-time $150 per credit. Tuition, nonresident: part-time $150 per credit. *Financial support:* Career-related internships or fieldwork, scholarships/grants, and unspecified assistantships available. Financial award application deadline: 3/1; financial award applicants required to submit FAFSA. *Unit head:* Dr. Marianna Calle, Coordinator, 508-929-8739, Fax: 508-929-8164, E-mail: mcalle@worcester.edu. *Application contact:* Sara Grady, Associate Dean for Graduate Studies and Professional Development, 508-929-8787, Fax: 508-929-8100, E-mail: sara.grady@worcester.edu.

Wright State University, School of Medicine, Department of Population and Public Health Sciences, Dayton, OH 45435. Offers health promotion and education (MPH). *Accreditation:* CEPH. *Expenses:* Tuition, state resident: full-time $9952; part-time $622 per credit hour. Tuition, nonresident: full-time $16,960; part-time $1060 per credit hour. *Unit head:* Dr. Richard J. Schuster, Director, 937-258-5555, Fax: 937-258-5544, E-mail: richard.schuster@wright.edu. *Application contact:* Dr. Paul G. Carlson, Associate Dean for Student Affairs and Admissions, 937-775-2934, Fax: 937-775-3672, E-mail: paul.carlson@wright.edu.

Home Economics Education

Alabama Agricultural and Mechanical University, School of Graduate Studies, College of Education, Humanities, and Behavioral Sciences, Department of Educational Leadership and Secondary Education, Huntsville, AL 35811. Offers biology (M Ed); business/marketing education (M Ed, Ed S); chemistry (M Ed); collaborative teacher secondary education (M Ed, Ed S); education (M Ed, Ed S); English language arts (M Ed); family/consumer science education (M Ed, Ed S); general science (M Ed); general social science (M Ed); mathematics (M Ed, Ed S); physics (M Ed, Ed S); technology education (M Ed). *Accreditation:* NCATE. *Program availability:* Evening/weekend. *Degree requirements:* For master's, comprehensive exam; for Ed S, thesis. *Entrance requirements:* For master's, GRE General Test. Additional exam requirements/recommendations for international students: Required—TOEFL (minimum score 500 paper-based; 61 iBT). *Application deadline:* For fall admission, 5/1 for domestic students. Applications are processed on a rolling basis. Application fee: $25. Electronic applications accepted. *Expenses:* Tuition, nonresident: part-time $826 per credit hour. Full-time tuition and fees vary according to course load and program. *Financial support:* Research assistantships, career-related internships or fieldwork, Federal Work-Study, institutionally sponsored loans, and traineeships available. Financial award application deadline: 4/1. *Faculty research:* World peace through education, computer-assisted instruction. *Unit head:* Dr. Derrick Davis, Chair, 256-372-4047, Fax: 256-372-5526.

Cambridge College, School of Education, Cambridge, MA 02138-5304. Offers autism specialist (M Ed); autism/behavior analyst (M Ed); behavior analyst (Post-Master's Certificate); behavioral management (M Ed); early childhood teacher (M Ed); education specialist in curriculum and instruction (CAGS); educational leadership (Ed D); elementary teacher (M Ed); English as a second language (M Ed, Certificate); general science (M Ed); health education (Post-Master's Certificate); health/family and consumer sciences (M Ed); history (M Ed); individualized (M Ed); information technology literacy (M Ed); instructional technology (M Ed); interdisciplinary studies (M Ed); library teacher (M Ed); literacy education (M Ed); mathematics (M Ed); mathematics specialist (Certificate); middle school mathematics and science (M Ed); school administration (M Ed, CAGS); school guidance counselor (M Ed); school nurse education (M Ed); school social worker/school adjustment counselor (M Ed); special education administrator (CAGS); special education/moderate disabilities (M Ed); teaching skills and methodologies (M Ed). *Program availability:* Part-time, evening/weekend, online learning. *Degree requirements:* For master's, thesis, internship/practicum (licensure program only); for doctorate, thesis/dissertation; for other advanced degree, thesis. *Entrance requirements:* For master's, interview, resume, documentation of licensure, 2 professional references; for doctorate, official transcripts, interview, resume, documentation of licensure (if any), written personal statement/essay, portfolio of scholarly and professional work, qualifying assessment, 2 professional references, health insurance, immunizations form; for other advanced degree, official transcripts, interview, resume, documentation of licensure (if any), written personal statement/essay, 2 professional references, health insurance, immunizations form. Additional exam requirements/recommendations for international students: Required—TOEFL (minimum score 550 paper-based; 79 iBT), Michigan English Language Assessment Battery (minimum score 85); Recommended—IELTS (minimum score 6). Electronic applications accepted. *Expenses:* Contact institution. *Faculty research:* Adult education, accelerated learning, mathematics education, brain compatible learning, special education and law.

Central Washington University, Graduate Studies and Research, College of Education and Professional Studies, Department of Family and Consumer Sciences, Ellensburg, WA 98926. Offers career and technical education (MS); family and consumer sciences education (MS); family studies (MS). *Program availability:* Part-time. *Degree requirements:* For master's, thesis or alternative. *Entrance requirements:* For master's, minimum GPA of 3.0. Additional exam requirements/recommendations for international students: Required—TOEFL (minimum score 550 paper-based; 79 iBT). Electronic applications accepted.

Eastern Kentucky University, The Graduate School, College of Education, Department of Curriculum and Instruction, Program in Secondary and Higher Education, Richmond, KY 40475-3102. Offers secondary education (MA Ed), including agricultural education, art education, biological sciences education, business education, English education, geography education, history education, home economics education, industrial education, mathematical sciences education, physical education, school health education. *Accreditation:* NCATE. *Program availability:* Part-time. *Entrance requirements:* For master's, GRE General Test, minimum GPA of 2.5.

Louisiana State University and Agricultural & Mechanical College, Graduate School, College of Human Sciences and Education, School of Human Resource Education and Workforce Development, Baton Rouge, LA 70803. Offers agriculture and extension education and youth development (MS, PhD); career and technical education (MS, PhD); comprehensive vocational education (MS, PhD); extension and international education (MS, PhD); human resource and leadership development (MS, PhD); industrial education (MS); vocational agriculture education (MS, PhD); vocational business education (MS); vocational home economics education (MS). *Accreditation:* NCATE.

Montana State University, The Graduate School, College of Education, Health, and Human Development, Department of Health and Human Development, Bozeman, MT 59717. Offers family and consumer sciences (MS). *Accreditation:* ACA. *Program availability:* Part-time, online learning. *Degree requirements:* For master's, comprehensive exam. *Entrance requirements:* For master's, GRE (minimum scores: verbal 480; quantitative 480). Additional exam requirements/recommendations for international students: Required—TOEFL (minimum score 550 paper-based). Electronic applications accepted. *Faculty research:* Community food systems, ethic of care for teachers and coaches, influence of public policy on families and communities, cost effectiveness of early childhood education, exercise metabolism, winter sport performance enhancement, assessment of physical activity.

Purdue University, Graduate School, College of Education, Department of Curriculum and Instruction, West Lafayette, IN 47907. Offers agricultural and extension education (MS, MS Ed, PhD, Ed S); art education (PhD); career and technical education (MS Ed, PhD, Ed S); curriculum studies (MS Ed, PhD, Ed S); educational technology (MS Ed, PhD, Ed S); elementary education (MS Ed); family and consumer sciences education (MS Ed, PhD, Ed S); foreign language education (MS Ed, PhD, Ed S); industrial technology (PhD, Ed S); language arts (MS Ed, PhD, Ed S); literacy (MS Ed, PhD, Ed S); mathematics education (MS, MS Ed, PhD, Ed S); science education (MS, MS Ed, PhD, Ed S); social studies education (MS Ed, PhD, Ed S). *Accreditation:* NCATE. *Program availability:* Part-time, evening/weekend. *Faculty:* 37 full-time (27 women), 1 (woman) part-time/adjunct. *Students:* 78 full-time (50 women), 286 part-time (195 women); includes 68 minority (25 Black or African American, non-Hispanic/Latino; 3 American Indian or Alaska Native, non-Hispanic/Latino; 10 Asian, non-Hispanic/Latino; 22 Hispanic/Latino; 1 Native Hawaiian or other Pacific Islander, non-Hispanic/Latino; 7 Two or more races, non-Hispanic/Latino), 44 international. Average age 36. 150 applicants, 79% accepted, 73 enrolled. In 2016, 107 master's, 20 doctorates, 2 other advanced degrees awarded. *Degree requirements:* For master's, thesis optional; for doctorate, thesis/dissertation, oral and written exams; for Ed S, oral presentation, project. *Entrance requirements:* For master's, GRE General Test (if undergraduate GPA is below 3.0), minimum undergraduate GPA of 3.0 or equivalent; for doctorate, GRE General Test (minimum combined verbal and quantitative score of 1000, 300 for new scoring), minimum undergraduate GPA of 3.0 or equivalent; master's degree with minimum GPA of 3.0 or equivalent; for Ed S, GRE General Test (minimum combined verbal and quantitative score of 1000, 300 for new scoring), minimum undergraduate GPA of 3.0 or equivalent; master's degree. Additional exam requirements/recommendations for international students: Required—TOEFL (minimum score 550 paper-based; 77 iBT). *Application deadline:* For fall admission, 12/15 for domestic students, 3/1 for international students; for spring admission, 9/15 for domestic students, 8/1 for international students. Application fee: $60 ($75 for international students). Electronic applications accepted. *Financial support:* Fellowships with full tuition reimbursements, research assistantships with full tuition reimbursements, teaching assistantships with full tuition reimbursements, career-related internships or fieldwork, and tuition waivers (full) available. Support available to part-time students. Financial award application deadline: 3/1; financial award applicants required to submit FAFSA. *Faculty research:* Literacy acquisition and development, teacher beliefs and knowledge, recruitment and retention of underrepresented students, economic education, literacy discourse. *Unit head:* Janet M. Alsup, Head, 765-494-9667, E-mail: alsupj@purdue.edu. *Application contact:* Heather Brinkman, Graduate Contact, 765-494-2345, E-mail: hbrinkma@purdue.edu.
Website: http://www.edci.purdue.edu/

South Carolina State University, College of Graduate and Professional Studies, Department of Education, Orangeburg, SC 29117-0001. Offers early childhood education (MAT); education (M Ed); elementary education (M Ed, MAT); English (MAT); general science/biology (MAT); mathematics (MAT); secondary education (M Ed), including biology education, business education, counselor education, English education, home economics education, industrial education, mathematics education, science education, social studies education; special education (M Ed), including emotionally handicapped, learning disabilities, mentally handicapped. *Accreditation:* NCATE. *Program availability:* Part-time, evening/weekend. *Faculty:* 12 full-time (8 women), 3 part-time/adjunct (1 woman). *Students:* 28 full-time (20 women), 20 part-time (17 women); includes 45 minority (44 Black or African American, non-Hispanic/Latino; 1 Two or more races, non-Hispanic/Latino). Average age 31. 22 applicants, 100% accepted, 16 enrolled. In 2016, 9 master's awarded. *Degree requirements:* For master's, thesis optional, departmental qualifying exam. *Entrance requirements:* For master's, GRE General Test, NTE, interview, teaching certificate. *Application deadline:* For fall admission, 6/15 priority date for domestic students, 6/15 for international students; for spring admission, 11/1 for domestic and international students. Application fee: $25. Electronic applications accepted. *Expenses:* Tuition, state resident: full-time $8938; part-time $579 per credit hour. Tuition, nonresident: full-time $19,018; part-time $1139 per credit hour. *Required fees:* $1482; $82 per credit hour. *Financial support:* Fellowships, career-related internships or fieldwork, Federal Work-Study, and scholarships/grants available. Financial award application deadline: 6/1. *Unit head:* Dr. Charlie Spell, Interim Chair, Department of Education, 803-536-8963, Fax: 803-516-4568, E-mail: cspell@scsu.edu. *Application contact:* Curtis Foskey, Coordinator of Graduate Studies, 803-536-8419, Fax: 803-536-8812, E-mail: cfoskey@scsu.edu.

Texas Tech University, Graduate School, College of Human Sciences, Program in Family and Consumer Sciences Education, Lubbock, TX 79409. Offers MS, PhD. *Program availability:* Part-time, evening/weekend, 100% online, blended/hybrid learning. *Students:* 10 full-time (all women), 31 part-time (28 women); includes 7 minority (1 Asian, non-Hispanic/Latino; 6 Hispanic/Latino). Average age 35. 13 applicants, 85% accepted, 6 enrolled. In 2016, 7 master's, 1 doctorate awarded. *Degree requirements:* For master's, thesis or alternative; for doctorate, comprehensive exam, thesis/dissertation. *Entrance requirements:* For doctorate, GRE General Test. Additional exam requirements/recommendations for international students: Required—TOEFL (minimum score 550 paper-based; 79 iBT). *Application deadline:* For fall admission, 6/1 priority date for domestic students, 1/15 priority date for international students; for spring admission, 9/1 priority date for domestic students, 6/15 priority date for international

students. Applications are processed on a rolling basis. Application fee: $75. Electronic applications accepted. *Expenses:* $315 per credit hour full-time resident tuition, $723 per credit hour full-time non-resident tuition; $50.50 per credit hour fee plus $608 per term fee. *Financial support:* In 2016–17, 21 students received support, including 20 fellowships (averaging $3,779 per year), 4 teaching assistantships (averaging $13,674 per year); research assistantships and scholarships/grants also available. Financial award application deadline: 4/15; financial award applicants required to submit FAFSA. *Faculty research:* Content literacy, implementation of programs of study, instructional practices for working with limited English proficiency students in FCS, mobile technologies with FCS instruction. *Unit head:* Dr. Karen Alexander, Program Coordinator, 806-834-2212, E-mail: karen.alexander@ttu.edu.
Website: http://www.depts.ttu.edu/hs/fcse/

The University of British Columbia, Faculty of Education, Department of Curriculum and Pedagogy, Vancouver, BC V6T 1Z4, Canada. Offers art education (M Ed, MA); curriculum studies (M Ed, MA, PhD); home economics education (M Ed, MA); mathematics education (M Ed, MA); media and technology studies education (M Ed, MA); music education (M Ed, MA); physical education (M Ed, MA); science education (M Ed, MA); social studies education (M Ed, MA). *Program availability:* Part-time, online learning. *Degree requirements:* For master's, thesis (MA); for doctorate, comprehensive exam, thesis/dissertation. *Entrance requirements:* Additional exam requirements/recommendations for international students: Required—TOEFL, IELTS. Application fee: $100 Canadian dollars ($162 Canadian dollars for international students). Electronic applications accepted. *Expenses:* $6,865 per year tuition and fees domestic, $10,938 per year international (for MA and M Ed); $4,802 per year tuition and fees, $8,436 per year international (for PhD). *Financial support:* Fellowships with partial tuition reimbursements, research assistantships with partial tuition reimbursements, teaching assistantships with partial tuition reimbursements, and tuition waivers (partial) available. *Faculty research:* School subjects, teaching and learning. *Application contact:* Alan Jay, Graduate Programs Assistant, 604-822-5367, Fax: 604-822-4714, E-mail: edcp.grad@ubc.ca.
Website: http://www.edcp.educ.ubc.ca/

University of Nebraska–Lincoln, Graduate College, College of Education and Human Sciences, Department of Child, Youth and Family Studies, Lincoln, NE 68588. Offers child development/early childhood education (MS, PhD); child, youth and family studies (MS); family and consumer sciences education (MS, PhD); family financial planning (MS); family science (MS, PhD); gerontology (PhD); human sciences (PhD), including child, youth and family studies, gerontology, medical family therapy; marriage and family therapy (MS); medical family therapy (PhD); youth development (MS). *Accreditation:* AAMFT/COAMFTE (one or more programs are accredited). *Program availability:* Online learning. *Degree requirements:* For master's, thesis optional. *Entrance requirements:* For master's, GRE. Additional exam requirements/recommendations for international students: Required—TOEFL (minimum score 550 paper-based). Electronic applications accepted. *Faculty research:* Marriage and family therapy, child development/early childhood education, family financial management.

Utah State University, School of Graduate Studies, College of Agriculture, Department of Agricultural Systems Technology and Education, Logan, UT 84322. Offers agricultural systems technology (MS), including agricultural extension education, agricultural mechanization, international agricultural extension, secondary and postsecondary agricultural education; family and consumer sciences education (MS). *Program availability:* Part-time, online learning. *Degree requirements:* For master's, comprehensive exam (for some programs), thesis (for some programs). *Entrance requirements:* For master's, GRE General Test, MAT, BS in agricultural education, agricultural extension, or related agricultural or science discipline; minimum GPA of 3.0. Additional exam requirements/recommendations for international students: Required—TOEFL. *Faculty research:* Extension and adult education; structures and environment; low-input agriculture; farm safety, systems, and mechanizations.

Wayne State College, School of Education and Counseling, Department of Educational Foundations and Leadership, Program in Curriculum and Instruction, Wayne, NE 68787. Offers alternative education (MSE); business and information technology education (MSE); communication arts education (MSE); early childhood education (MSE); elementary education (MSE); English as a second language (MSE); English education (MSE); family and consumer sciences education (MSE); industrial technology and vocational education (MSE); learning communities (MSE); mathematics education (MSE); music education (MSE); science education (MSE); social science education (MSE). *Accreditation:* NCATE. *Program availability:* Part-time, evening/weekend. *Degree requirements:* For master's, comprehensive exam, thesis optional. *Entrance requirements:* For master's, GRE General Test. Additional exam requirements/recommendations for international students: Required—TOEFL (minimum score 550 paper-based).

Mathematics Education

Acadia University, Faculty of Professional Studies, School of Education, Program in Curriculum Studies, Wolfville, NS B4P 2R6, Canada. Offers cultural and media studies (M Ed); learning and technology (M Ed); science, math and technology (M Ed). *Program availability:* Part-time. *Degree requirements:* For master's, thesis optional. *Entrance requirements:* For master's, B Ed or the equivalent, minimum B average in undergraduate course work, 2 years of teaching experience. Additional exam requirements/recommendations for international students: Required—TOEFL (minimum score 580 paper-based; 93 iBT), IELTS (minimum score 6.5). *Faculty research:* Literacy development, postmodern philosophy and curriculum theory, historiography, philosophy of education, learning and technology.

Alabama Agricultural and Mechanical University, School of Graduate Studies, College of Education, Humanities, and Behavioral Sciences, Department of Educational Leadership and Secondary Education, Huntsville, AL 35811. Offers biology (M Ed); business/marketing education (M Ed, Ed S); chemistry (M Ed); collaborative teacher secondary education (M Ed, Ed S); education (M Ed, Ed S); English language arts (M Ed); family/consumer science education (M Ed, Ed S); general science (M Ed); general social science (M Ed); mathematics (M Ed, Ed S); physics (M Ed, Ed S); technology education (M Ed). *Accreditation:* NCATE. *Program availability:* Evening/weekend. *Degree requirements:* For master's, comprehensive exam; for Ed S, thesis. *Entrance requirements:* For master's, GRE General Test. Additional exam requirements/recommendations for international students: Required—TOEFL (minimum score 500 paper-based; 61 iBT). *Application deadline:* For fall admission, 5/1 for domestic students. Applications are processed on a rolling basis. Application fee: $25. Electronic applications accepted. *Expenses:* Tuition, nonresident: part-time $826 per credit hour. Full-time tuition and fees vary according to course load and program. *Financial support:* Research assistantships, career-related internships or fieldwork, Federal Work-Study, institutionally sponsored loans, and traineeships available. Financial award application deadline: 4/1. *Faculty research:* World peace through education, computer-assisted instruction. *Unit head:* Dr. Derrick Davis, Chair, 256-372-4047, Fax: 256-372-5526.

Alabama State University, College of Education, Department of Curriculum and Instruction, Montgomery, AL 36101-0271. Offers early childhood education (M Ed, Ed S); elementary education (M Ed, Ed S); secondary education (M Ed, Ed S), including biology education, English language arts education (M Ed), history education, math education, music education (M Ed), reading education (M Ed), social science education; special education (M Ed). *Program availability:* Part-time. *Faculty:* 7 full-time (4 women), 7 part-time/adjunct (4 women). *Students:* 37 full-time (30 women), 82 part-time (69 women); includes 117 minority (115 Black or African American, non-Hispanic/Latino; 2 Two or more races, non-Hispanic/Latino). Average age 33. 65 applicants, 55% accepted, 22 enrolled. In 2016, 25 master's, 5 Ed Ss awarded. *Degree requirements:* For master's, comprehensive exam, thesis optional; for Ed S, comprehensive exam, thesis. *Entrance requirements:* For master's, GRE General Test, MAT, writing competency test; for Ed S, writing competency test, GRE, MAT. Additional exam requirements/recommendations for international students: Required—TOEFL (minimum score 500 paper-based). *Application deadline:* For fall admission, 4/15 for domestic and international students; for spring admission, 11/15 for domestic and international students; for summer admission, 3/15 for domestic and international students. Applications are processed on a rolling basis. Application fee: $25. Electronic applications accepted. *Expenses:* Tuition, state resident: full-time $3087; part-time $2744 per credit. Tuition, nonresident: full-time $6174; part-time $5488 per credit. *Required fees:* $2284; $1142 per credit. $571 per semester. Tuition and fees vary according to class time, course level, course load, degree level, program and student level. *Financial support:* Research assistantships available. Financial award application deadline: 6/30; financial award applicants required to submit FAFSA. *Unit head:* Dr. Joyce Johnson, Acting Chairperson, 334-229-4485, Fax: 334-229-5603, E-mail: jjohnson@alasu.edu. *Application contact:* Dr. William Person, Dean of Graduate Studies, 334-229-4274, Fax: 334-229-4928, E-mail: wperson@alasu.edu.
Website: http://www.alasu.edu/academics/colleges—departments/college-of-education/curriculum—instruction/index.aspx

Appalachian State University, Cratis D. Williams Graduate School, Department of Curriculum and Instruction, Boone, NC 28608. Offers curriculum specialist (MA); educational media (MA); elementary education (MA); middle grades education (MA), including language arts, mathematics, science, social studies. *Accreditation:* NCATE. *Program availability:* Part-time, evening/weekend, online learning. *Degree requirements:* For master's, comprehensive exam, thesis or alternative. *Entrance requirements:* For master's, GRE General Test or MAT, 3 letters of recommendation. Additional exam requirements/recommendations for international students: Required—TOEFL (minimum score 570 paper-based; 79 iBT), IELTS (minimum score 6.5). *Application deadline:* For fall admission, 3/14 for domestic students, 2/1 for international students; for spring admission, 11/1 for domestic students, 7/1 for international students. Applications are processed on a rolling basis. Application fee: $55. Electronic applications accepted. *Expenses:* Tuition, state resident: full-time $4744. Tuition, nonresident: full-time $17,913. Full-time tuition and fees vary according to program. *Financial support:* Fellowships, research assistantships, teaching assistantships, career-related internships or fieldwork, Federal Work-Study, scholarships/grants, and unspecified assistantships available. Financial award application deadline: 4/1; financial award applicants required to submit FAFSA. *Faculty research:* Media literacy, elementary teaching, curriculum development, online learning environments. *Unit head:* Dr. Michael Jacobson, Chairperson, 828-262-2224. *Application contact:* Dr. Chrystal Dean, Program Director, 828-262-8009, E-mail: deanco@appstate.edu.
Website: http://www.ced.appstate.edu/departments/ci

Arcadia University, School of Education, Glenside, PA 19038-3295. Offers art education (M Ed); computer education (CAS); curriculum (CAS); curriculum studies (M Ed); early childhood education (M Ed), including individualized, master teacher, research in child development; educational leadership (M Ed, Ed D, CAS); elementary education (M Ed); English education (MA Ed); environmental education (MA Ed); instructional technology (M Ed); language arts (M Ed); library science (M Ed); mathematics education (M Ed, MA Ed); music education (MA Ed); psychology (MA Ed); reading (M Ed, CAS); science education (M Ed, CAS); secondary education (M Ed, CAS); special education (M Ed, Ed D, CAS); theater arts (MA Ed); written communication (MA Ed). *Accreditation:* NASAD. *Program availability:* Part-time, evening/weekend, online learning. *Faculty:* 19 full-time (13 women), 3 part-time/adjunct (all women). *Students:* 22 full-time (16 women), 356 part-time (284 women); includes 84 minority (55 Black or African American, non-Hispanic/Latino; 2 American Indian or Alaska Native, non-Hispanic/Latino; 13 Asian, non-Hispanic/Latino; 11 Hispanic/Latino; 3 Two or more races, non-Hispanic/Latino), 4 international. Average age 34. 145 applicants, 73% accepted, 80 enrolled. In 2016, 95 master's, 11 doctorates awarded. *Application deadline:* Applications are processed on a rolling basis. Application fee: $50. Electronic applications accepted. *Expenses:* Contact institution. *Financial support:* Career-related internships or fieldwork, tuition waivers (partial), and unspecified assistantships available. *Unit head:* John T Groves, Interim Dean of the School of Education, 215-572-2940. *Application contact:* 215-572-2925, Fax: 215-572-2126, E-mail: grad@arcadia.edu.

Arizona State University at the Tempe campus, College of Liberal Arts and Sciences, School of Mathematical and Statistical Sciences, Tempe, AZ 85287-1804. Offers applied mathematics (PhD); mathematics (MA, PhD); mathematics education (PhD); statistics (MS, PhD, Graduate Certificate). *Program availability:* Part-time. Terminal master's awarded for partial completion of doctoral program. *Degree requirements:* For master's, thesis or alternative, interactive Program of Study (iPOS) submitted before completing 50 percent of required credit hours; for doctorate, comprehensive exam, thesis/dissertation, interactive Program of Study (iPOS) submitted before completing 50 percent of required credit hours. *Entrance requirements:* For master's and doctorate, GRE General Test, minimum GPA of 3.0 or equivalent in last 2 years of work leading to bachelor's degree. Additional exam requirements/recommendations for international students: Required—TOEFL, IELTS, or PTE. Electronic applications accepted. *Expenses:* Contact institution.

Arkansas State University, Graduate School, College of Sciences and Mathematics, Department of Mathematics and Statistics, State University, AR 72467. Offers mathematics (MS); mathematics education (MSE). *Program availability:* Part-time. *Degree requirements:* For master's, comprehensive exam, thesis or alternative. *Entrance requirements:* For master's, GRE General Test or MAT, appropriate bachelor's degree, official transcripts, immunization records, valid teaching certificate (for MSE). Additional exam requirements/recommendations for international students: Required—TOEFL (minimum score 550 paper-based; 79 iBT), IELTS (minimum score 6), PTE (minimum score 56). Electronic applications accepted.

Asbury University, School of Graduate and Professional Studies, Wilmore, KY 40390-1198. Offers biology: alternative certificate (MA Ed); chemistry: alternative certificate (MA Ed); English (MA Ed); English as a second language (MA Ed); ESL (MA Ed); French (MA Ed); Latin: alternative certificate (MA Ed); mathematics: alternative certificate (MA Ed); reading/writing endorsement (MA Ed); social studies (MA Ed); social work (MSW), including child and family services; Spanish (MA Ed); special education (MA Ed); special education: alternative certificate (MA Ed); teacher as leader endorsement (MA Ed). *Accreditation:* NCATE. *Program availability:* Part-time. *Degree requirements:* For master's, action research project, portfolio. *Entrance requirements:* For master's, PRAXIS/NTE, minimum GPA of 2.75, letters of recommendation. Additional exam requirements/recommendations for international students: Required—TOEFL (minimum score 550 paper-based). Electronic applications accepted.

Ball State University, Graduate School, College of Sciences and Humanities, Department of Mathematical Sciences, Program in Mathematics Education, Muncie, IN 47306. Offers mathematics education (MA), including elementary and middle school mathematics, elementary and middle school mathematics specialist, secondary mathematics. *Program availability:* Part-time, 100% online, blended/hybrid learning. *Entrance requirements:* For master's, minimum baccalaureate GPA of 2.75 or 3.0 in latter half of baccalaureate. Additional exam requirements/recommendations for international students: Required—TOEFL (minimum score 550 paper-based; 79 iBT), IELTS (minimum score 6.5). Electronic applications accepted.

Bank Street College of Education, Graduate School, Programs in Educational Leadership, New York, NY 10025. Offers early childhood leadership (MS Ed); educational leadership (MS Ed); leadership for educational change (Ed M, MS Ed); leadership in community-based learning (MS Ed); leadership in mathematics education (MS Ed); leadership in museum education (MS Ed); leadership in the arts: creative writing (MS Ed); leadership in the arts: visual arts (MS Ed). *Degree requirements:* For master's, thesis. *Entrance requirements:* For master's, interview, essays, minimum of 2 years experience as a classroom teacher. Additional exam requirements/recommendations for international students: Required—TOEFL (minimum score 600 paper-based; 100 iBT), IELTS (minimum score 7). Electronic applications accepted. *Faculty research:* Leadership in urban schools, leadership in small schools, mathematics in elementary schools, professional development in early childhood, leadership in arts education, leadership in special education, museum leadership, community-based leadership.

Bard College, Master of Arts in Teaching Program, Annandale-on-Hudson, NY 12504. Offers secondary education (MAT), including biology, history, literature, mathematics, Spanish; MS/MAT. *Program availability:* Part-time. *Degree requirements:* For master's, year-long teaching residencies in area middle and high schools. *Entrance requirements:* For master's, GRE General Test, resume, 3 letters of recommendation, personal statement, official transcripts. Additional exam requirements/recommendations for international students: Required—TOEFL. *Application deadline:* For winter admission, 1/30 priority date for domestic students; for spring admission, 4/27 for domestic students, 4/30 for international students. Applications are processed on a rolling basis. Application fee: $65. Electronic applications accepted. Application fee is waived when completed online. *Financial support:* Fellowships, institutionally sponsored loans, and scholarships/grants available. Support available to part-time students. Financial award application deadline: 4/28; financial award applicants required to submit FAFSA. *Unit head:* Derek Furr, Director, 845-758-7136, Fax: 845-758-7149, E-mail: mat@bard.edu. *Application contact:* Cecilia Maple, Assistant Director for Admission and Student Affairs, 845-758-7145, E-mail: mat@bard.edu.
Website: http://www.bard.edu/mat/ny

Bemidji State University, School of Graduate Studies, Bemidji, MN 56601. Offers biology (MS); education (MS); English (MA, MS); environmental studies (MS); mathematics (MS); mathematics (elementary and middle level education) (MS); special education (M Sp Ed). *Program availability:* Part-time, online learning. *Degree requirements:* For master's, comprehensive exam, thesis (for some programs). *Entrance requirements:* For master's, GRE; GMAT, letters of recommendation, letters of interest. Additional exam requirements/recommendations for international students: Required—TOEFL (minimum score 550 paper-based; 80 iBT). Electronic applications accepted. *Expenses:* Contact institution. *Faculty research:* Human performance, sport, and health: physical education teacher education, continuum models, spiritual health, intellectual health, resiliency, health priorities; psychology: health psychology, college student drinking behavior, micro-aggressions, infant cognition, false memories, leadership assessment; biology: structure and dynamics of forest communities, aquatic and riverine ecology, interaction between animal populations and aquatic environments, cellular motility.

Binghamton University, State University of New York, Graduate School, Graduate School of Education, Program in Adolescence Education, Binghamton, NY 13902-6000. Offers biology education (MAT, MS Ed); chemistry education (MAT, MS Ed); earth science education (MAT, MS Ed); English education (MAT, MS Ed); French education (MAT, MS Ed); literacy education (MS Ed); mathematical sciences education (MAT, MS Ed); physics (MAT, MS Ed); social studies (MAT, MS Ed); Spanish education (MAT, MS Ed). *Accreditation:* TEAC. *Program availability:* Part-time, evening/weekend. *Students:* 59 full-time (36 women), 7 part-time (2 women); includes 10 minority (2 Black or African American, non-Hispanic/Latino; 1 American Indian or Alaska Native, non-Hispanic/Latino; 1 Asian, non-Hispanic/Latino; 5 Hispanic/Latino; 1 Two or more races, non-Hispanic/Latino). Average age 26. 46 applicants, 76% accepted, 25 enrolled. In 2016, 26 master's awarded. *Degree requirements:* For master's, portfolio. *Entrance requirements:* For master's, GRE General Test, teaching certification. Additional exam requirements/recommendations for international students: Required—TOEFL (minimum score 550 paper-based; 80 iBT). *Application deadline:* For fall admission, 2/1 priority date for domestic and international students; for spring admission, 10/15 priority date for domestic and international students. Application fee: $75. Electronic applications accepted. *Financial support:* In 2016–17, 6 students received support. Research assistantships, teaching assistantships, career-related internships or fieldwork, Federal Work-Study, institutionally sponsored loans, scholarships/grants, health care benefits, tuition waivers (full and partial), and unspecified assistantships available. Financial award applicants required to submit FAFSA. *Unit head:* Dr. Susan Strehle, Dean, 607-777-7329, E-mail: sstrehle@binghamton.edu. *Application contact:* Ben Balkaya, Assistant Dean and Director, 607-777-2151, Fax: 607-777-2501, E-mail: balkaya@binghamton.edu.

Bloomsburg University of Pennsylvania, School of Graduate Studies, College of Education, Department of Teaching and Learning, Program in Middle Level Education Grades 4-8, Bloomsburg, PA 17815-1301. Offers language arts (M Ed); math (M Ed); science (M Ed); social studies (M Ed). *Accreditation:* NCATE. *Faculty:* 6 full-time (1 woman). *Students:* 3 applicants, 67% accepted. In 2016, 2 master's awarded. *Degree requirements:* For master's, thesis optional, practicum, student teaching. *Entrance requirements:* For master's, MAT, GRE, or PRAXIS, minimum QPA of 3.0, teaching certificate, U.S. citizenship, related undergraduate coursework, professional liability insurance, recent TB test. Additional exam requirements/recommendations for international students: Required—TOEFL (minimum score 550 paper-based), IELTS. *Application deadline:* Applications are processed on a rolling basis. Application fee: $35 ($60 for international students). Electronic applications accepted. *Expenses:* Tuition, state resident: full-time $9660; part-time $483 per credit. Tuition, nonresident: full-time $14,500; part-time $725 per credit. *Required fees:* $2410; $107 per credit. $75 per term. Tuition and fees vary according to course load, degree level and program. *Financial support:* Federal Work-Study and unspecified assistantships available. Financial award applicants required to submit FAFSA. *Unit head:* Dr. Ingrid Everett, Program Coordinator, 570-389-5120, Fax: 570-389-3030, E-mail: ieverett@bloomu.edu. *Application contact:* Jennifer Kessler, Administrative Assistant, 570-389-4015, Fax: 570-389-3054, E-mail: jkessler@bloomu.edu.
Website: http://www.bloomu.edu/gradschool/middle-level-education

Bob Jones University, Graduate Programs, Greenville, SC 29614. Offers accountancy (MS); Bible (MA); Bible translation (MA); Biblical studies (Certificate); broadcast management (MS); business administration (MBA); church history (MA, PhD); church ministries (MA); church music (MM); cinema and video production (MA); counseling (MS); curriculum and instruction (Ed D); divinity (M Div); dramatic production (MA); educational leadership (MS, Ed D, Ed S); elementary education (M Ed, MAT); English (M Ed, MA, MAT); fine arts (MA); graphic design (MA); history (M Ed, MA); illustration (MA); interpretative speech (MA); mathematics (M Ed, MAT); medical missions (Certificate); ministry (MM, D Min); multi-categorical special education (M Ed, MAT); music (M Ed); New Testament interpretation (PhD); Old Testament interpretation (PhD); orchestral instrument performance (MM); organ performance (MM); pastoral studies (MA); personnel services (MS, Ed S); piano pedagogy (MM); piano performance (MM); platform arts (MA); radio and television broadcasting (MS); rhetoric and public address (MA); secondary education (M Ed); studio art (MA); teaching Bible (MA); theology (MA, PhD); voice performance (MM); youth ministries (MA); M Div/MM.

Boise State University, College of Arts and Sciences, Department of Mathematics, Boise, ID 83725-1555. Offers mathematics (MS); mathematics education (MS). *Program availability:* Part-time. *Faculty:* 12. *Students:* 16 full-time (8 women), 9 part-time (5 women); includes 3 minority (all Asian, non-Hispanic/Latino), 3 international. Average age 31. 33 applicants, 33% accepted, 10 enrolled. In 2016, 4 master's awarded. *Degree requirements:* For master's, thesis optional. *Entrance requirements:* For master's, GRE General Test. Additional exam requirements/recommendations for international students: Required—TOEFL (minimum score 550 paper-based; 80 iBT), IELTS (minimum score 6). *Application deadline:* For fall admission, 2/1 priority date for domestic and international students. Application fee: $65 ($95 for international students). Electronic applications accepted. *Expenses:* Tuition, state resident: full-time $6058; part-time $358 per credit hour. Tuition, nonresident: full-time $20,108; part-time $608 per credit hour. *Required fees:* $2108. Tuition and fees vary according to program. *Financial support:* In 2016–17, 8 students received support, including 12 teaching assistantships (averaging $8,314 per year); scholarships/grants and unspecified assistantships also available. Financial award application deadline: 2/1; financial award applicants required to submit FAFSA. *Unit head:* Dr. Leming Qu, Chair, 208-426-1172, E-mail: lqu@boisestate.edu. *Application contact:* Dr. Jens Harlander, Graduate Program Coordinator, 208-426-3312, E-mail: mathematicsgrad@boisestate.edu.
Website: http://math.boisestate.edu/

Bowling Green State University, Graduate College, College of Arts and Sciences, Department of Mathematics and Statistics, Bowling Green, OH 43403. Offers mathematics (MA, MAT, PhD); statistics (PhD). *Program availability:* Part-time. *Degree requirements:* For master's, thesis or alternative; for doctorate, comprehensive exam, thesis/dissertation. *Entrance requirements:* For master's and doctorate, GRE General Test. Additional exam requirements/recommendations for international students: Required—TOEFL. *Application deadline:* For fall admission, 1/31 priority date for domestic students. Application fee: $30. Electronic applications accepted. *Financial support:* Fellowships with full tuition reimbursements, research assistantships with full tuition reimbursements, teaching assistantships with full tuition reimbursements, Federal Work-Study, institutionally sponsored loans, and unspecified assistantships available. Financial award applicants required to submit FAFSA. *Faculty research:* Statistics and probability, algebra, analysis. *Unit head:* Dr. Henfeng Chen, Chair, 419-372-2636, Fax: 419-372-6092, E-mail: math-stat@bgsu.edu. *Application contact:* Dr. John Chen, Graduate Coordinator, 419-372-7461, Fax: 419-372-6092.

Bridgewater State University, College of Graduate Studies, Bartlett College of Science and Mathematics, Department of Mathematics, Bridgewater, MA 02325. Offers MAT. *Program availability:* Part-time, evening/weekend. *Entrance requirements:* For master's, GRE General Test.

Brigham Young University, Graduate Studies, College of Physical and Mathematical Sciences, Department of Mathematics Education, Provo, UT 84602-1001. Offers MA. *Program availability:* Part-time. *Faculty:* 8 full-time (2 women). *Students:* 8 full-time (6 women), 7 part-time (4 women); includes 4 minority (2 Asian, non-Hispanic/Latino; 1 Hispanic/Latino; 1 Native Hawaiian or other Pacific Islander, non-Hispanic/Latino). Average age 32. 9 applicants, 89% accepted, 7 enrolled. In 2016, 8 master's awarded. *Degree requirements:* For master's, comprehensive exam, project or thesis. *Entrance requirements:* For master's, GRE General Test, teaching certificate, bachelor's degree in math education or equivalent. Additional exam requirements/recommendations for international students: Required—TOEFL. *Application deadline:* For fall admission, 3/1 priority date for domestic and international students; for summer admission, 3/1 priority date for domestic and international students. Application fee: $50. Electronic applications accepted. *Expenses:* $000 per credit hour. *Financial support:* In 2016–17, 15 students received support, including 3 research assistantships with full tuition reimbursements available (averaging $13,000 per year), 12 teaching assistantships with full tuition reimbursements available (averaging $13,000 per year); scholarships/grants also available. Financial award application deadline: 3/1. *Faculty research:* Understanding the characteristics of high-quality mathematics instruction, teaching mathematics for social justice, applying mathematics to science and engineering, technology in teaching and learning mathematics, how preservice teachers learn to teach mathematics, discourse and literacy in mathematics classrooms, how national policy influences mathematics teachers. *Total annual research expenditures:* $150,000. *Unit head:* Dr. Blake E. Peterson, Chair, 801-422-7784, E-mail: blake@byu.edu. *Application contact:* Kathy Lee Garrett, Administrative Assistant, 801-422-1840, E-mail: kathylee@mathed.byu.edu.
Website: https://mathed.byu.edu/

Brooklyn College of the City University of New York, School of Education, Program in Adolescence Science Education and Special Subjects, Brooklyn, NY 11210-2889. Offers adolescence science education (MAT); biology teacher (7-12) (MA); chemistry teacher (7-12) (MA); earth science teacher (7-12) (MAT); English teacher (7-12) (MA);

French teacher (7-12) (MA); mathematics teacher (7-12) (MA); music teacher (MA); physics teacher (7-12) (MA); social studies teacher (7-12) (MA); Spanish teacher (7-12) (MA). *Program availability:* Part-time, evening/weekend. *Degree requirements:* For master's, comprehensive exam (for some programs), thesis (for some programs). *Entrance requirements:* For master's, LAST, previous course work in education, resume, 2 letters of recommendation, essay. Additional exam requirements/recommendations for international students: Required—TOEFL (minimum score 500 paper-based; 61 iBT). Electronic applications accepted. *Faculty research:* Interdisciplinary education, semiotics, discourse analysis, autobiography, teacher identity.

Brooklyn College of the City University of New York, School of Education, Program in Childhood Education, Brooklyn, NY 11210-2889. Offers bilingual education (MS Ed); liberal arts (MS Ed); mathematics (MS Ed); science and environmental education (MS Ed). *Program availability:* Part-time, evening/weekend. *Entrance requirements:* For master's, LAST, interview, previous course work in education, writing sample, resume, 2 letters of recommendation. Additional exam requirements/recommendations for international students: Required—TOEFL (minimum score 500 paper-based; 61 iBT). Electronic applications accepted. *Faculty research:* Emotional intelligence, multiculturalism, arts immersion, the Holocaust.

Brooklyn College of the City University of New York, School of Education, Program in Middle Childhood Mathematics Education, Brooklyn, NY 11210-2889. Offers MS Ed. *Entrance requirements:* For master's, LAST, 2 letters of recommendation, essay, resume. Additional exam requirements/recommendations for international students: Required—TOEFL (minimum score 500 paper-based; 61 iBT). Electronic applications accepted.

Buffalo State College, State University of New York, The Graduate School, Faculty of Natural and Social Sciences, Department of Mathematics, Buffalo, NY 14222-1095. Offers mathematics education (MS Ed). *Accreditation:* NCATE. *Program availability:* Part-time, evening/weekend. *Degree requirements:* For master's, thesis or alternative. *Entrance requirements:* For master's, 18 undergraduate hours in upper-level mathematics, minimum GPA of 2.5 in undergraduate math courses. Additional exam requirements/recommendations for international students: Required—TOEFL (minimum score 550 paper-based).

California State University, Bakersfield, Division of Graduate Studies, School of Natural Sciences, Mathematics, and Engineering, Program in Teaching Mathematics, Bakersfield, CA 93311. Offers MA. *Students:* 1 full-time (0 women); minority (Hispanic/Latino). *Entrance requirements:* For master's, minimum GPA of 2.5 for last 90 quarter units. *Expenses:* Tuition, state resident: full-time $2246; part-time $1302 per semester. *Unit head:* Sophia Raczkowski, Chair, 661-654-3151, Fax: 661-664-2039. *Application contact:* Debbie Blowers, Assistant Director of Admissions and Evaluations, 661-664-3381, E-mail: dblowers@csub.edu.
Website: https://www.csub.edu/math/info/index.html

California State University, Chico, Office of Graduate Studies, College of Natural Sciences, Program in Mathematics Education, Chico, CA 95929-0722. Offers mathematics in education (MS). *Program availability:* Part-time. *Faculty:* 15 full-time (6 women), 27 part-time/adjunct (10 women). In 2016, 1 master's awarded. *Degree requirements:* For master's, thesis or project. *Entrance requirements:* For master's, GRE, teaching credential in mathematics, statement of purpose. Additional exam requirements/recommendations for international students: Required—TOEFL (minimum score 550 paper-based; 80 iBT), IELTS (minimum score 6.5), PTE (minimum score 59). *Application deadline:* For fall admission, 3/1 priority date for domestic students, 3/1 for international students. Application fee: $55. Electronic applications accepted. *Financial support:* Teaching assistantships and scholarships/grants available. Financial award application deadline: 3/1; financial award applicants required to submit FAFSA. *Unit head:* Dr. Richard L. Ford, Chair, 530-898-6111, Fax: 530-898-3097, E-mail: math@csuchico.edu. *Application contact:* Judy L. Morris, Graduate Admissions Coordinator, 530-898-5416, Fax: 530-898-3342, E-mail: jlmorris@csuchico.edu.
Website: http://catalog.csuchico.edu/viewer/15/MATH/MATHNONEMS.html

California State University, Dominguez Hills, College of Natural and Behavioral Sciences, Program in Teaching of Mathematics, Carson, CA 90747-0001. Offers MA. *Program availability:* Part-time, evening/weekend. *Degree requirements:* For master's, comprehensive exam, thesis. *Entrance requirements:* For master's, 2 years of teaching experience. Additional exam requirements/recommendations for international students: Required—TOEFL. Electronic applications accepted.

California State University, East Bay, Office of Graduate Studies, College of Science, Department of Mathematics, Hayward, CA 94542-3000. Offers applied mathematics (MS); mathematics (MS); mathematics teaching (MS). *Program availability:* Part-time, evening/weekend. *Students:* 24 full-time (11 women), 21 part-time (7 women); includes 25 minority (13 Asian, non-Hispanic/Latino; 9 Hispanic/Latino; 1 Native Hawaiian or other Pacific Islander, non-Hispanic/Latino; 2 Two or more races, non-Hispanic/Latino), 5 international. Average age 35. 37 applicants, 68% accepted, 14 enrolled. In 2016, 19 master's awarded. *Degree requirements:* For master's, comprehensive exam or thesis. *Entrance requirements:* For master's, minimum GPA of 3.0 in field. Additional exam requirements/recommendations for international students: Required—TOEFL (minimum score 550 paper-based). *Application deadline:* For fall admission, 6/30 for domestic and international students. Application fee: $55. Electronic applications accepted. *Financial support:* Fellowships, teaching assistantships, Federal Work-Study, institutionally sponsored loans, and scholarships/grants available. Support available to part-time students. Financial award application deadline: 3/1; financial award applicants required to submit FAFSA. *Unit head:* Julie Glass, Chair, 510-885-2159, E-mail: julie.glass@csueastbay.edu. *Application contact:* Dr. Donald Wolitzer, Math Graduate Advisor, 510-885-3467, E-mail: donald.wolitzer@csueastbay.edu.
Website: http://www.csueastbay.edu/csci/departments/math/index.html

California State University, Fresno, Division of Research and Graduate Studies, College of Science and Mathematics, Department of Mathematics, Fresno, CA 93740-8027. Offers mathematics (MA); mathematics teaching (MA). *Program availability:* Part-time. *Degree requirements:* For master's, thesis or alternative. *Entrance requirements:* For master's, GRE General Test. Additional exam requirements/recommendations for international students: Required—TOEFL. *Application deadline:* For fall admission, 5/1 for domestic and international students; for spring admission, 10/1 for domestic and international students. Applications are processed on a rolling basis. Application fee: $55. Electronic applications accepted. *Financial support:* Teaching assistantships, career-related internships or fieldwork, Federal Work-Study, scholarships/grants, and unspecified assistantships available. Support available to part-time students. Financial award application deadline: 3/1; financial award applicants required to submit FAFSA. *Faculty research:* Diagnostic testing project. *Unit head:* Dr. Rajee Amarasinghe, Chair, 559-278-2992, Fax: 559-278-2872, E-mail: ramarasi@csufresno.edu. *Application contact:* Dr. Doreen De Leon, Graduate Coordinator, 559-278-4009, Fax: 559-278-2872, E-mail: doreendl@csufresno.edu.
Website: http://www.fresnostate.edu/csm/math/

California State University, Fullerton, Graduate Studies, College of Education, Department of Secondary Education, Fullerton, CA 92834-9480. Offers teacher instruction (MS); teaching foundational mathematics (MS). *Program availability:* Part-time. Application fee: $55. *Expenses:* Tuition, state resident: full-time $3369; part-time $1953 per unit. Tuition, nonresident: full-time $3915; part-time $2499 per unit. Tuition and fees vary according to course load, degree level and program. *Financial support:* Career-related internships or fieldwork, Federal Work-Study, institutionally sponsored loans, and scholarships/grants available. Support available to part-time students. Financial award application deadline: 3/1; financial award applicants required to submit FAFSA. *Unit head:* Dr. Grace Cho, Chair, 657-278-3283, E-mail: gcho@fullerton.edu. *Application contact:* Admissions/Applications, 657-278-2371.

California State University, Fullerton, Graduate Studies, College of Natural Science and Mathematics, Department of Mathematics, Fullerton, CA 92834-9480. Offers applied mathematics (MA); mathematics education (MA). *Program availability:* Part-time. *Degree requirements:* For master's, comprehensive exam or project. *Entrance requirements:* For master's, minimum GPA of 2.5 in last 60 units of course work, major in mathematics or related field. Application fee: $55. *Expenses:* Tuition, state resident: full-time $3369; part-time $1953 per unit. Tuition, nonresident: full-time $3915; part-time $2499 per unit. Tuition and fees vary according to course load, degree level and program. *Financial support:* Research assistantships, teaching assistantships, career-related internships or fieldwork, Federal Work-Study, institutionally sponsored loans, and scholarships/grants available. Support available to part-time students. Financial award application deadline: 3/1; financial award applicants required to submit FAFSA. *Unit head:* Dr. Stephen W. Goode, Chair, 657-278-3631. *Application contact:* Admissions/Applications, 657-278-2371.

California State University, Long Beach, Graduate Studies, College of Natural Sciences and Mathematics, Department of Mathematics and Statistics, Long Beach, CA 90840. Offers mathematics (MS), including applied mathematics, applied statistics, mathematics education for secondary school teachers. *Program availability:* Part-time. *Degree requirements:* For master's, comprehensive exam or thesis. *Application deadline:* For fall admission, 7/1 for domestic students; for spring admission, 12/1 for domestic students. Applications are processed on a rolling basis. Application fee: $55. Electronic applications accepted. *Financial support:* Teaching assistantships, Federal Work-Study, institutionally sponsored loans, scholarships/grants, and traineeships available. Financial award application deadline: 3/2. *Faculty research:* Algebra, functional analysis, partial differential equations, operator theory, numerical analysis. *Unit head:* Dr. Robert Mena, Chair, 562-985-4721, Fax: 562-985-8227, E-mail: rmena@csulb.edu. *Application contact:* Dr. Ngo Viet, Graduate Associate Chair, 562-985-4721, Fax: 562-985-8227, E-mail: viet@csulb.edu.

California State University, Northridge, Graduate Studies, Michael D. Eisner College of Education, Department of Secondary Education, Northridge, CA 91330. Offers educational technology (MA); English education (MA); mathematics education (MA); secondary science education (MA); teaching and learning (MA). *Accreditation:* NCATE. *Program availability:* Part-time. *Faculty:* 10 full-time (5 women), 50 part-time/adjunct (24 women). *Students:* 17 full-time (10 women), 87 part-time (55 women); includes 41 minority (3 Black or African American, non-Hispanic/Latino; 11 Asian, non-Hispanic/Latino; 24 Hispanic/Latino; 1 Native Hawaiian or other Pacific Islander, non-Hispanic/Latino; 2 Two or more races, non-Hispanic/Latino), 4 international. Average age 37. 80 applicants, 80% accepted, 50 enrolled. *Degree requirements:* For master's, thesis optional. *Entrance requirements:* For master's, GRE General Test or minimum GPA of 3.0. Additional exam requirements/recommendations for international students: Required—TOEFL. *Application deadline:* For fall admission, 11/30 for domestic students. Application fee: $55. *Expenses:* Tuition, state resident: full-time $4152. *Financial support:* Application deadline: 3/1. *Unit head:* Dr. Julie Gainsburg, Chair, 818-677-2580. *Application contact:* Dr. Michael Rivas, Graduate Advisor, 818-677-6792, E-mail: michael.rivas@csun.edu.
Website: http://www.csun.edu/eisner-education/secondary-education

California State University, San Bernardino, Graduate Studies, College of Natural Sciences, Program in Mathematics, San Bernardino, CA 92407. Offers mathematics (MA); teaching mathematics (MAT). *Program availability:* Part-time. *Faculty:* 8 full-time (1 woman), 1 (woman) part-time/adjunct. *Students:* 2 full-time (1 woman), 31 part-time (14 women); includes 23 minority (1 Black or African American, non-Hispanic/Latino; 22 Hispanic/Latino), 1 international. 18 applicants, 56% accepted, 8 enrolled. In 2016, 19 master's awarded. *Degree requirements:* For master's, advancement to candidacy. *Entrance requirements:* Additional exam requirements/recommendations for international students: Required—TOEFL. *Application deadline:* For fall admission, 7/16 for domestic students; for winter admission, 10/16 for domestic students; for spring admission, 1/22 for domestic students. Application fee: $55. *Expenses:* Tuition, state resident: full-time $7843; part-time $5011.20 per year. Tuition and fees vary according to course load, degree level, program and reciprocity agreements. *Faculty research:* Mathematics education, technology in education, algebra, combinatorics, real analysis. *Unit head:* Dr. Charles Stanton, Chair, 909-537-5361, E-mail: cstanton@csusb.edu. *Application contact:* Dr. Francisca Beer, Assistant Dean of Graduate Studies, 909-537-5058, E-mail: fbeer@csusb.edu.

Cambridge College, School of Education, Cambridge, MA 02138-5304. Offers autism specialist (M Ed); autism/behavior analyst (M Ed); behavior analyst (Post-Master's Certificate); behavioral management (M Ed); early childhood teacher (M Ed); education specialist in curriculum and instruction (CAGS); educational leadership (Ed D); elementary teacher (M Ed); English as a second language (M Ed, Certificate); general science (M Ed); health education (Post-Master's Certificate); health/family and consumer sciences (M Ed); history (M Ed); individualized (M Ed); information technology literacy (M Ed); instructional technology (M Ed); interdisciplinary studies (M Ed); library teacher (M Ed); literacy education (M Ed); mathematics (M Ed); mathematics specialist (Certificate); middle school mathematics and science (M Ed); school administration (M Ed, CAGS); school guidance counselor (M Ed); school nurse education (M Ed); school social worker/school adjustment counselor (M Ed); special education administrator (CAGS); special education/moderate disabilities (M Ed); teaching skills and methodologies (M Ed). *Program availability:* Part-time, evening/weekend, online learning. *Degree requirements:* For master's, thesis, internship/practicum (licensure program only); for doctorate, thesis/dissertation; for other advanced degree, thesis. *Entrance requirements:* For master's, interview, resume, documentation of licensure, 2 professional references; for doctorate, official transcripts, interview, resume, documentation of licensure (if any), written personal statement/essay, portfolio of scholarly and professional work, qualifying assessment, 2 professional references, health insurance, immunizations form; for other advanced degree, official transcripts, interview, resume, documentation of licensure (if any), written personal statement/essay, 2 professional references, health insurance, immunizations form. Additional exam requirements/recommendations for international students: Required—TOEFL (minimum score 550 paper-based; 79 iBT), Michigan English Language Assessment Battery (minimum score 85); Recommended—IELTS (minimum score 6). Electronic applications accepted. *Expenses:* Contact institution. *Faculty research:* Adult education, accelerated learning, mathematics education, brain compatible learning, special education and law.

Caribbean University, Graduate School, Bayamón, PR 00960-0493. Offers administration and supervision (MA Ed); criminal justice (MA); curriculum and instruction

(MA Ed, PhD), including elementary education (MA Ed), English education (MA Ed), history education (MA Ed), mathematics education (MA Ed), primary education (MA Ed), science education (MA Ed), Spanish education (MA Ed); educational technology in instructional systems (MA Ed); gerontology (MSN); human resources (MBA); museology, archiving and art history (MA Ed); neonatal pediatrics (MSN); physical education (MA Ed); special education (MA Ed). *Entrance requirements:* For master's, interview, minimum GPA of 2.5.

Central Michigan University, College of Graduate Studies, College of Science and Technology, Department of Mathematics, Mount Pleasant, MI 48859. Offers mathematics (MA, PhD), including teaching of college mathematics (PhD). *Program availability:* Part-time. *Degree requirements:* For master's, thesis or alternative; for doctorate, thesis/dissertation. *Entrance requirements:* For master's, minimum GPA of 2.7, 20 hours of course work in mathematics; for doctorate, GRE, minimum GPA of 3.0, 20 hours of course work in mathematics. Electronic applications accepted. *Faculty research:* Combinatorics, approximation theory, applied mathematics, statistics, functional analysis and operator theory.

Chatham University, Program in Education, Pittsburgh, PA 15232-2826. Offers early childhood education (MAT); elementary education (MAT); environmental education (K-12) (MAT); secondary art (MAT); secondary biology education (MAT); secondary chemistry education (MAT); secondary English education (MAT); secondary math education (MAT); secondary physics education (MAT); secondary social studies education (MAT); special education (MAT). *Degree requirements:* For master's, thesis, teaching experience. *Entrance requirements:* For master's, minimum GPA of 3.0, sample of written work, recommendation letters. Additional exam requirements/recommendations for international students: Required—TOEFL (minimum score 600 paper-based; 100 iBT), IELTS (minimum score 7), TWE. Electronic applications accepted. Application fee is waived when completed online. *Expenses: Tuition:* Full-time $16,254; part-time $903 per credit hour. *Required fees:* $468; $26 per credit hour. *Faculty research:* Gifted education, environmental education, technology in education, writing as learning, class size and achievement.

The Citadel, The Military College of South Carolina, Citadel Graduate College, Zucker Family School of Education, Charleston, SC 29409. Offers elementary/secondary school administration and supervision (M Ed); elementary/secondary school counseling (M Ed); interdisciplinary STEM education (M Ed); literacy education (M Ed, Graduate Certificate); middle grades (MAT), including English, mathematics, science, social studies; physical education (grades K-12) (MAT); school superintendency (Ed S); secondary education (MAT), including biology, English, mathematics, social studies; student affairs (Graduate Certificate); student affairs and college counseling (M Ed). *Accreditation:* NCATE. *Program availability:* Part-time, evening/weekend, 100% online, blended/hybrid learning. *Faculty:* 9 full-time (4 women), 9 part-time/adjunct (5 women). *Students:* 70 full-time (58 women), 249 part-time (200 women); includes 87 minority (70 Black or African American, non-Hispanic/Latino; 1 Asian, non-Hispanic/Latino; 9 Hispanic/Latino; 7 Two or more races, non-Hispanic/Latino), 2 international. 146 applicants, 98% accepted, 105 enrolled. In 2016, 85 master's, 7 other advanced degrees awarded. *Degree requirements:* For master's, comprehensive exam (for some programs). *Entrance requirements:* For master's, GRE (minimum combined verbal and quantitative score of 290) or MAT (minimum score 396). Additional exam requirements/recommendations for international students: Required—TOEFL (minimum score 550 paper-based; 79 iBT). *Application deadline:* Applications are processed on a rolling basis. Application fee: $40. Electronic applications accepted. *Expenses:* Tuition, state resident: full-time $5121; part-time $569 per credit hour. Tuition, nonresident: full-time $8613; part-time $957 per credit hour. *Required fees:* $90 per term. *Financial support:* Fellowships and unspecified assistantships available. Support available to part-time students. Financial award application deadline: 7/1; financial award applicants required to submit FAFSA. *Unit head:* Dr. Larry G. Daniel, Dean, 843-953-5097, E-mail: ldaniel@citadel.edu. *Application contact:* Dr. Tammy J. Graham, Associate Professor, 843-953-6854, E-mail: tammy.graham@citadel.edu.
Website: http://www.citadel.edu/root/education-graduate-programs

City College of the City University of New York, Graduate School, School of Education, Department of Secondary Education, New York, NY 10031-9198. Offers adolescent mathematics education (MA, AC); English education (MA); middle school mathematics education (MS); science education (MA); social studies education (AC). *Accreditation:* NCATE. *Entrance requirements:* For master's, Liberal Arts and Sciences Test (LAST), Content Specialty Test (CST). Additional exam requirements/recommendations for international students: Required—TOEFL. Tuition and fees vary according to course load, degree level and program.

Clarion University of Pennsylvania, Office of Transfer, Adult and Graduate Admissions, Master of Education Program, Clarion, PA 16214. Offers curriculum and instruction (M Ed); early childhood (M Ed); math education (M Ed); reading (M Ed); science education (M Ed); special education (M Ed); technology (M Ed). *Accreditation:* NCATE. *Program availability:* Part-time, evening/weekend, 100% online, blended/hybrid learning. *Faculty:* 12 full-time (8 women), 5 part-time/adjunct (all women). *Students:* 17 full-time (15 women), 97 part-time (78 women); includes 1 minority (Two or more races, non-Hispanic/Latino). Average age 29. 76 applicants, 99% accepted, 48 enrolled. In 2016, 34 master's awarded. *Degree requirements:* For master's, comprehensive exam, thesis, or portfolio. *Entrance requirements:* For master's, minimum QPA of 3.0. Additional exam requirements/recommendations for international students: Required—TOEFL (minimum score 550 paper-based; 80 iBT), IELTS (minimum score 7). *Application deadline:* For fall admission, 8/1 for domestic students, 4/15 for international students; for spring admission, 8/1 for domestic students, 9/15 for international students. Applications are processed on a rolling basis. Application fee: $40. Electronic applications accepted. *Expenses:* $632.35 per credit. *Financial support:* Career-related internships or fieldwork, Federal Work-Study, scholarships/grants, and unspecified assistantships available. Support available to part-time students. Financial award application deadline: 5/1; financial award applicants required to submit FAFSA. *Unit head:* Dr. John McCullough, Chair, Department of Education, 814-393-2104, Fax: 814-393-2446, E-mail: gradstudies@clarion.edu. *Application contact:* Dana Bearer, Associate Director for Transfer, Adult, and Graduate Programs, 814-393-2337, Fax: 814-393-2722, E-mail: gradstudies@clarion.edu.

Clark Atlanta University, School of Education, Department of Curriculum, Atlanta, GA 30314. Offers special education general curriculum (MA); teaching math and science (MAT). *Program availability:* Part-time. *Faculty:* 2 full-time (both women), 1 part-time/adjunct (0 women). *Students:* 6 full-time (1 woman), 2 part-time (1 woman); includes 6 minority (all Black or African American, non-Hispanic/Latino), 1 international. Average age 34. 17 applicants, 76% accepted, 2 enrolled. In 2016, 2 master's awarded. *Degree requirements:* For master's, one foreign language, comprehensive exam. *Entrance requirements:* For master's, GRE General Test, minimum undergraduate GPA of 2.6. Additional exam requirements/recommendations for international students: Required—TOEFL (minimum score 500 paper-based; 61 iBT). *Application deadline:* For fall admission, 4/1 for domestic and international students; for spring admission, 11/1 for domestic and international students. Applications are processed on a rolling basis. Application fee: $40 ($55 for international students). *Expenses: Tuition:* Full-time $15,498; part-time $861 per credit hour. *Required fees:* $1326; $1326 per credit hour. Tuition and fees vary according to course load. *Financial support:* Career-related internships or fieldwork, Federal Work-Study, scholarships/grants, and unspecified assistantships available. Support available to part-time students. Financial award application deadline: 4/30; financial award applicants required to submit FAFSA. *Unit head:* Dr. James Young, Chairperson, 404-880-6079, E-mail: jyoung@cau.edu. *Application contact:* Graduate Program Admissions, 404-880-8483, E-mail: graduateadmissions@cau.edu.
Website: http://www.cau.edu/school-of-education/Dept-of-Curriculum-and-Instruction/index.html

Clayton State University, School of Graduate Studies, College of Arts and Sciences, Program in Education, Morrow, GA 30260-0285. Offers biology (MAT); English (MAT); history (MAT); mathematics (MAT). *Accreditation:* NCATE. *Entrance requirements:* For master's, GRE, GACE, 2 official copies of transcripts, 3 recommendation letters, statement of purpose. Additional exam requirements/recommendations for international students: Required—TOEFL (minimum score 550 paper-based). Electronic applications accepted. *Expenses:* Tuition, state resident: full-time $3528; part-time $196 per credit hour. Tuition, nonresident: full-time $13,176; part-time $732 per credit hour. *Required fees:* $1454; $1454 per credit hour. $727 per semester. Tuition and fees vary according to campus/location and program.

Clemson University, Graduate School, College of Education, Department of Teaching and Learning, Program in Secondary Math and Science, Clemson, SC 29634. Offers MAT. *Accreditation:* NCATE. *Faculty:* 15 full-time (12 women). *Students:* 13 full-time (10 women); includes 1 minority (Black or African American, non-Hispanic/Latino). Average age 28. In 2016, 16 master's awarded. *Degree requirements:* For master's, comprehensive exam, student teaching. *Entrance requirements:* For master's, GRE General Test, unofficial transcripts, letters of recommendation. Additional exam requirements/recommendations for international students: Required—TOEFL (minimum score 540 paper-based; 80 iBT). *Application deadline:* For fall admission, 4/1 for domestic and international students. Applications are processed on a rolling basis. Application fee: $80 ($90 for international students). Electronic applications accepted. *Expenses:* $4,841 per semester full-time resident, $9,640 per semester full-time non-resident, $612 per credit hour part-time resident, $1,223 per credit hour part-time non-resident. *Financial support:* In 2016–17, 10 students received support, including 10 fellowships with partial tuition reimbursements available (averaging $6,862 per year). Financial award application deadline: 4/1. *Faculty research:* Hegemony, culture and mathematics; representations in science education, pre-service science teacher preparation, developing standards-based mathematics pedagogy, environmental sustainability perspectives. *Unit head:* Dr. Jeff Marshall, Department Chair, 864-656-2059, E-mail: marsha9@clemson.edu. *Application contact:* Alison Search, Student Services Coordinator, 864-250-8880, E-mail: alisonp@clemson.edu.
Website: http://www.clemson.edu/education/academics/masters-specialist-programs/masters-education-arts-teaching-mat-secondary-math-science/index.html

Clemson University, Graduate School, College of Education, Department of Teaching and Learning, Program in Teaching and Learning, Clemson, SC 29634. Offers science, technology, engineering, arts and mathematics education (Certificate); teaching and learning (M Ed), including early childhood, instructional coaching, science, technology, engineering, arts and mathematics. *Program availability:* Part-time, evening/weekend, online only, 100% online. *Faculty:* 24 full-time (19 women). *Students:* 19 part-time (17 women); includes 1 minority (Hispanic/Latino). Average age 32. 4 applicants, 50% accepted, 2 enrolled. In 2016, 27 master's awarded. *Entrance requirements:* For master's, GRE General Test, unofficial transcripts, teaching certificate, letters of recommendation. Additional exam requirements/recommendations for international students: Required—TOEFL (minimum score 80 iBT), IELTS (minimum score 7). *Application deadline:* Applications are processed on a rolling basis. Application fee: $80 ($90 for international students). Electronic applications accepted. *Expenses:* $394 per credit hour; $10 per credit hour information technology fee; $17 fee per session for matriculation and software; $22 fee for activities and career services for students taking over 6 credit hours. *Unit head:* Dr. Jeff Marshall, Department Head, Fax: 864-656-0311, E-mail: soedean@clemson.edu. *Application contact:* Julie Jones, Student Services Program Coordinator, 864-656-5096, E-mail: jgambre@clemson.edu.
Website: http://www.clemson.edu/education/academics/masters-specialist-programs/masters-education-teaching-learning/index.html

Cleveland State University, College of Graduate Studies, College of Education and Human Services, Department of Curriculum and Foundations, Cleveland, OH 44115. Offers art education (M Ed); early childhood education (M Ed); foreign language education (M Ed); middle childhood mathematics and science education (M Ed); special education (M Ed), including mild/moderate disabilities, moderate/intensive disabilities; teaching English to speakers of other languages (M Ed). *Program availability:* Part-time, evening/weekend. *Faculty:* 19 full-time (14 women), 32 part-time/adjunct (27 women). *Students:* 86 full-time (65 women), 369 part-time (301 women); includes 119 minority (89 Black or African American, non-Hispanic/Latino; 1 American Indian or Alaska Native, non-Hispanic/Latino; 2 Asian, non-Hispanic/Latino; 16 Hispanic/Latino; 11 Two or more races, non-Hispanic/Latino), 35 international. Average age 34. 177 applicants, 55% accepted, 68 enrolled. In 2016, 179 master's awarded. *Degree requirements:* For master's, comprehensive exam (for some programs), thesis or alternative. *Entrance requirements:* For master's, GRE General Test or MAT, minimum GPA of 2.75. Additional exam requirements/recommendations for international students: Required—TOEFL (minimum score 550 paper-based; 78 iBT), IELTS (minimum score 6). *Application deadline:* For fall admission, 7/1 priority date for domestic students, 5/15 for international students; for spring admission, 11/15 for domestic students, 11/1 for international students; for summer admission, 4/1 for domestic students, 3/15 for international students. Applications are processed on a rolling basis. Application fee: $30. *Expenses:* Tuition, state resident: full-time $9565. Tuition, nonresident: full-time $17,980. Tuition and fees vary according to program. *Financial support:* In 2016–17, 13 research assistantships with full tuition reimbursements (averaging $15,845 per year) were awarded; tuition waivers (partial) and unspecified assistantships also available. Financial award application deadline: 2/15; financial award applicants required to submit FAFSA. *Faculty research:* Early childhood education, literacy education, special education: mild/moderate, moderate/intensive, early childhood intervention specialist), teaching English to speakers of other languages (TESOL). *Total annual research expenditures:* $275,907. *Unit head:* Dr. Tachelle I. Banks, Chairperson, 216-687-4608, Fax: 216-687-5379, E-mail: t.i.banks@csuohio.edu. *Application contact:* Michael Almony, Senior Student Services Specialist, 216-875-9929, Fax: 216-687-5491, E-mail: m.almony@csuohio.edu.
Website: http://www.csuohio.edu/cehs/te/te

The College at Brockport, State University of New York, School of Education, Health, and Human Services, Department of Education and Human Development, Program in Adolescence Education, Brockport, NY 14420-2997. Offers adolescence biology education (MS Ed); adolescence chemistry education (MS Ed); adolescence earth science education (MS Ed); adolescence English education (MS Ed); adolescence mathematics education (MS Ed); adolescence physics education (MS Ed); adolescence social studies education (MS Ed). *Accreditation:* NCATE. *Program availability:* Part-time. *Students:* 4 full-time (1 woman), 35 part-time (23 women); includes 3 minority (2 Black or

African American, non-Hispanic/Latino; 1 Two or more races, non-Hispanic/Latino). 21 applicants, 71% accepted, 11 enrolled. In 2016, 18 master's awarded. *Degree requirements:* For master's, thesis or alternative. *Entrance requirements:* For master's, minimum GPA of 3.0, letters of recommendation, statement of objectives, current resume. Additional exam requirements/recommendations for international students: Required—TOEFL (minimum score 550 paper-based; 79 iBT), IELTS (minimum score 6.5). *Application deadline:* For fall admission, 3/15 priority date for domestic and international students; for spring admission, 10/15 priority date for domestic and international students; for summer admission, 3/15 priority date for domestic students, 3/13 priority date for international students. Application fee: $80. Electronic applications accepted. *Expenses:* Contact institution. *Financial support:* Federal Work-Study, scholarships/grants, and unspecified assistantships available. Support available to part-time students. Financial award application deadline: 3/15; financial award applicants required to submit FAFSA. *Unit head:* Dr. Sue Robb, Chairperson, 585-395-5935, Fax: 585-395-2172, E-mail: srobb@brockport.edu. *Application contact:* Anne Walton, Coordinator of Certification and Graduate Advisement, 585-395-2326, Fax: 585-395-2172, E-mail: awalton@brockport.edu.
Website: http://www.brockport.edu/ehd/

The College at Brockport, State University of New York, School of Education, Health, and Human Services, Department of Education and Human Development, Program in Inclusive Generalist Education, Brockport, NY 14420-2997. Offers biology (MS Ed, AGC); chemistry (MS Ed, AGC); English (MS Ed, Advanced Certificate); mathematics (MS Ed, Advanced Certificate); science (MS Ed, Advanced Certificate); social studies (MS Ed, Advanced Certificate). *Students:* 28 full-time (15 women), 19 part-time (10 women); includes 9 minority (2 Black or African American, non-Hispanic/Latino; 3 Asian, non-Hispanic/Latino; 1 Hispanic/Latino; 3 Two or more races, non-Hispanic/Latino). 21 applicants, 52% accepted, 11 enrolled. In 2016, 12 master's, 3 AGCs awarded. *Degree requirements:* For master's, thesis or alternative. *Entrance requirements:* For master's, minimum GPA of 3.0, letters of recommendation, statement of objectives, academic major (or equivalent) in program discipline, current resume. Additional exam requirements/recommendations for international students: Required—TOEFL (minimum score 550 paper-based; 79 iBT), IELTS (minimum score 6.5). *Application deadline:* For fall admission, 3/15 priority date for domestic and international students; for spring admission, 10/15 priority date for domestic and international students; for summer admission, 3/15 for domestic and international students. Application fee: $80. Electronic applications accepted. *Expenses:* Contact institution. *Financial support:* Federal Work-Study, scholarships/grants, and unspecified assistantships available. Support available to part-time students. Financial award application deadline: 3/15; financial award applicants required to submit FAFSA. *Unit head:* Dr. Sue Robb, Chairperson, 585-395-5935, Fax: 585-395-2171, E-mail: awalton@brockport.edu. *Application contact:* Anne Walton, Coordinator of Certification and Graduate Advisement, 585-395-2326, Fax: 585-395-2172, E-mail: awalton@brockport.edu.
Website: http://www.brockport.edu/ehd/

College of Charleston, Graduate School, School of Education, Health, and Human Performance, Program in Science and Mathematics for Teachers, Charleston, SC 29424-0001. Offers M Ed. *Accreditation:* NCATE. *Program availability:* Part-time, evening/weekend. *Degree requirements:* For master's, capstone project. *Entrance requirements:* For master's, GRE or PRAXIS, 2 letters of recommendation, copy of teaching certificate. Additional exam requirements/recommendations for international students: Required—TOEFL (minimum score 81 iBT). *Application deadline:* For fall admission, 4/1 for domestic students; for spring admission, 11/1 for domestic students. Application fee: $45. Electronic applications accepted. *Financial support:* Research assistantships, teaching assistantships, scholarships/grants, and unspecified assistantships available. Financial award application deadline: 4/1; financial award applicants required to submit FAFSA. *Unit head:* John Peters, Director, 843-953-1422, E-mail: petersj@cofc.edu. *Application contact:* John Peters, Director, 843-953-1422, E-mail: petersj@cofc.edu.
Website: http://teachered.cofc.edu/grad-progs/smft.php

College of Staten Island of the City University of New York, Graduate Programs, School of Education, Program in Adolescence Education, Staten Island, NY 10314-6600. Offers biology (MS Ed); English (MS Ed); mathematics (MS Ed); social studies (MS Ed). *Program availability:* Part-time, evening/weekend. *Faculty:* 18 full-time, 8 part-time/adjunct. *Students:* 4 full-time, 84 part-time. Average age 29. 40 applicants, 88% accepted, 14 enrolled. In 2016, 41 master's awarded. *Degree requirements:* For master's, thesis, educational research project supervised by faculty; minimum of 33-38 credits distributed among 11 courses or minimum of 46-53 credits. *Entrance requirements:* For master's, GRE General Test or an approved equivalent examination, relevant bachelor's degree, minimum overall GPA of 3.0, two letters of recommendation, one- or two-page personal statement. Additional exam requirements/recommendations for international students: Required—TOEFL (minimum score 550 paper-based; 79 iBT), IELTS (minimum score 6.5). *Application deadline:* For fall admission, 4/25 for domestic and international students; for spring admission, 11/25 for domestic and international students. Applications are processed on a rolling basis. Application fee: $125. Electronic applications accepted. *Expenses:* Tuition, state resident: full-time $10,130; part-time $425 per credit. Tuition, nonresident: full-time $18,720; part-time $780 per credit. *Required fees:* $181.10 per semester. Tuition and fees vary according to program. *Faculty research:* Development and assessment of TPACK (technological pedagogical content knowledge), technology and differentiation in stem classrooms, teacher effectiveness and student achievement, teacher knowledge, knowledge transfer from college to classroom. *Unit head:* Dr. Bethany Rogers, Graduate Faculty Advisor, 718-982-4247, E-mail: bethany.rogers@csi.cuny.edu. *Application contact:* Sasha Spence, Associate Director for Graduate Admissions, 718-982-2019, Fax: 718-982-2500, E-mail: sasha.spence@csi.cuny.edu.
Website: http://www.csi.cuny.edu/catalog/graduate/graduate-programs-in-education.htm#o2608

College of Staten Island of the City University of New York, Graduate Programs, School of Education, Program in Childhood Education, Staten Island, NY 10314-6600. Offers learning and development (MS Ed); literacy education (MS Ed); mathematics education (MS Ed); music education (MS Ed); science education (MS Ed); social foundations of education (MS Ed); social studies education (MS Ed). *Program availability:* Part-time, evening/weekend. *Faculty:* 2 full-time, 11 part-time/adjunct. *Students:* 16 full-time, 53 part-time. Average age 30. 40 applicants, 53% accepted, 13 enrolled. In 2016, 20 master's awarded. *Degree requirements:* For master's, educational research project; ten courses and a minimum of 32-38 credits in five required areas of study or minimum of 45-49 credits in six required core courses before selecting from array of advanced courses. *Entrance requirements:* For master's, GRE General Test or an approved equivalent examination, relevant bachelor's degree, letters of recommendation, one- or two-page personal statement. Additional exam requirements/recommendations for international students: Required—TOEFL (minimum score 550 paper-based; 79 iBT), IELTS (minimum score 6.5). *Application deadline:* For fall admission, 4/25 for domestic and international students; for spring admission, 11/25 for domestic and international students. Applications are processed on a rolling basis. Application fee: $125. Electronic applications accepted. *Expenses:* Tuition, state resident: full-time $10,130; part-time $425 per credit. Tuition, nonresident: full-time $18,720; part-time $780 per credit. *Required fees:* $181.10 per semester. Tuition and fees vary according to program. *Faculty research:* Preservice teacher preparation, music integration, music education through children's songs, literacy, emergent bilingual. *Unit head:* Dr. Vivian Shulman, Graduate Faculty Advisor, 718-982-4086, E-mail: vivian.shulman@csi.cuny.edu. *Application contact:* Sasha Spence, Associate Director for Graduate Admissions, 718-982-2019, Fax: 718-982-2500, E-mail: sasha.spence@csi.cuny.edu.
Website: http://www.csi.cuny.edu/admissions/grad/pdf/Education%20Fact%20Sheet.pdf

The College of William and Mary, School of Education, Program in Curriculum and Instruction, Williamsburg, VA 23187-8795. Offers elementary education (MA Ed); gifted education (MA Ed); literacy leadership (MA Ed); math specialist (MA Ed); secondary education (MA Ed), including English, foreign language, math, science, social studies; special education (MA Ed). *Accreditation:* NCATE. *Program availability:* Part-time. *Faculty:* 30 full-time (21 women), 48 part-time/adjunct (38 women). *Students:* 60 full-time (47 women), 14 part-time (all women); includes 13 minority (1 Black or African American, non-Hispanic/Latino; 1 American Indian or Alaska Native, non-Hispanic/Latino; 2 Asian, non-Hispanic/Latino; 7 Hispanic/Latino; 2 Two or more races, non-Hispanic/Latino). Average age 26. 134 applicants, 79% accepted, 66 enrolled. In 2016, 77 master's awarded. *Degree requirements:* For master's, project. *Entrance requirements:* For master's, GRE, MAT, PRAXIS Core Academic Skills for Educators, minimum GPA of 2.5. Additional exam requirements/recommendations for international students: Required—TOEFL (minimum score 100 iBT), IELTS (minimum score 7). *Application deadline:* For fall admission, 1/15 for domestic and international students; for spring admission, 10/1 for domestic and international students. Application fee: $50. Electronic applications accepted. *Expenses:* $14,258 per year in-state full-time, $275 per credit in-state part-time; $30,500 per year out-of-state full-time, $1,200 per credit out-of-state part-time. *Financial support:* In 2016–17, 30 students received support, including 3 research assistantships (averaging $14,259 per year); scholarships/grants and unspecified assistantships also available. Financial award application deadline: 1/15; financial award applicants required to submit FAFSA. *Faculty research:* Educational technology, professional development and evaluation, inclusive education, rural education, education policy. *Unit head:* Dr. Jeremy D. Stoddard, Department Chair, 757-221-2348, E-mail: jdstod@wm.edu. *Application contact:* Dorothy Smith Osborne, Assistant Dean for Academic Programs and Student Services, 757-221-2317, E-mail: dsosbo@wm.edu.
Website: http://education.wm.edu

The Colorado College, Education Department, Program in Secondary Education, Colorado Springs, CO 80903-3294. Offers art teaching (K-12) (MAT); English teaching (MAT); foreign language teaching (MAT); mathematics teaching (MAT); music teaching (MAT); science teaching (MAT); social studies teaching (MAT). *Degree requirements:* For master's, thesis, internship. Electronic applications accepted.

Columbus State University, Graduate Studies, College of Education and Health Professions, Department of Teacher Education, Columbus, GA 31907-5645. Offers curriculum and instruction in accomplished teaching (M Ed); early childhood education (M Ed, MAT, Ed S); middle grades education (M Ed, MAT, Ed S); secondary education (M Ed, MAT, Ed S), including biology (MAT), chemistry (MAT), earth and space science (MAT), English/language arts, general science (M Ed), history (MAT), mathematics, science (Ed S), social science (M Ed, Ed S); special education (M Ed, MAT, Ed S), including general curriculum (M Ed, MAT); teacher leadership (M Ed). *Accreditation:* NCATE. *Program availability:* Part-time, evening/weekend, 100% online, blended/hybrid learning. *Faculty:* 20 full-time (13 women), 19 part-time/adjunct (16 women). *Students:* 92 full-time (66 women), 212 part-time (179 women); includes 113 minority (104 Black or African American, non-Hispanic/Latino; 1 American Indian or Alaska Native, non-Hispanic/Latino; 2 Asian, non-Hispanic/Latino; 4 Hispanic/Latino; 2 Two or more races, non-Hispanic/Latino), 5 international. Average age 34. 209 applicants, 56% accepted, 79 enrolled. In 2016, 111 master's, 18 other advanced degrees awarded. *Degree requirements:* For Ed S, thesis or alternative. *Entrance requirements:* For master's, GRE General Test, minimum undergraduate GPA of 2.75; for Ed S, GRE General Test, minimum undergraduate GPA of 2.75, graduate 3.0. Additional exam requirements/recommendations for international students: Required—TOEFL (minimum score 550 paper-based; 79 iBT). *Application deadline:* For fall admission, 6/30 for domestic students, 5/1 for international students; for spring admission, 11/1 for domestic and international students; for summer admission, 3/1 for domestic and international students. Applications are processed on a rolling basis. Application fee: $50. Electronic applications accepted. *Expenses:* Tuition, state resident: full-time $4804; part-time $2412 per semester hour. Tuition, nonresident: full-time $19,218; part-time $9612 per semester hour. *Required fees:* $1850; $1850 per semester hour. Tuition and fees vary according to program. *Financial support:* In 2016–17, 60 students received support, including 12 research assistantships with partial tuition reimbursements available (averaging $3,000 per year); career-related internships or fieldwork, Federal Work-Study, institutionally sponsored loans, scholarships/grants, tuition waivers (partial), and unspecified assistantships also available. Support available to part-time students. Financial award application deadline: 5/1; financial award applicants required to submit FAFSA. *Unit head:* Dr. Jan Burcham, Department Chair, 706-507-8519, Fax: 706-568-3134, E-mail: burcham_jan@columbusstate.edu. *Application contact:* Kristin Williams, Director of International and Graduate Recruitment, 706-507-8848, Fax: 706-568-5091, E-mail: williams_kristin@columbusstate.edu.
Website: http://te.columbusstate.edu/

Concordia University, College of Education, Portland, OR 97211-6099. Offers career and technical education (M Ed); curriculum and instruction (M Ed), including adolescent literacy, career and technical education, e-learning/technology education, early childhood education, English for speakers of other languages, English language development, environmental education, mathematics, methods and curriculum, reading, science, teacher leadership, the inclusive classroom; early childhood (MAT); education leadership (Ed D); educational administration (M Ed); elementary education (MAT); secondary education (MAT); special education (M Ed); teacher leadership (Ed D). *Program availability:* Part-time, online learning. *Degree requirements:* For master's, comprehensive exam, work samples/portfolio. *Entrance requirements:* For master's, California Basic Educational Skills Test or PRAXIS I, minimum undergraduate GPA of 2.8, graduate 3.0; 2 letters of recommendation. Additional exam requirements/recommendations for international students: Required—TOEFL (minimum score 525 paper-based). Electronic applications accepted. *Faculty research:* Learner-centered classroom, brain-based learning, future of online learning.

Concordia University, School of Graduate Studies, Faculty of Arts and Science, Department of Mathematics and Statistics, Montréal, QC H3G 1M8, Canada. Offers mathematics (PhD); mathematics and statistics (M Sc, MA); teaching of mathematics (MTM). *Degree requirements:* For master's, thesis optional; for doctorate, comprehensive exam, thesis/dissertation. *Entrance requirements:* For master's, honors degree in mathematics or equivalent. *Faculty research:* Number theory, computational algebra, mathematical physics, differential geometry, dynamical systems and statistics.

Converse College, School of Education and Graduate Studies, Program in Middle Level Education, Spartanburg, SC 29302. Offers language arts/English (MAT); mathematics (MAT); middle level education (M Ed); science (MAT); social studies (MAT). *Expenses: Tuition:* Full-time $3600; part-time $400 per credit hour. *Required fees:* $70 per term. *Application contact:* 864-596-9404, E-mail: graduate@converse.edu.

Converse College, School of Education and Graduate Studies, Program in Secondary Education, Spartanburg, SC 29302. Offers biology (MAT); chemistry (MAT); English (M Ed, MAT); mathematics (M Ed, MAT); natural sciences (M Ed); social sciences (M Ed, MAT). *Program availability:* Part-time. *Degree requirements:* For master's, capstone paper. *Entrance requirements:* For master's, NTE or PRAXIS II (M Ed), minimum GPA of 2.75, 2 recommendations. *Application deadline:* For fall admission, 8/1 for domestic and international students; for winter admission, 11/15 for domestic and international students; for spring admission, 1/15 for domestic and international students. Applications are processed on a rolling basis. Application fee: $40. Electronic applications accepted. *Expenses: Tuition:* Full-time $3600; part-time $400 per credit hour. *Required fees:* $70 per term. *Financial support:* Available to part-time students. Applicants required to submit FAFSA. *Application contact:* 864-596-9404, E-mail: graduate@converse.edu.

Cornell University, Graduate School, Graduate Fields of Agriculture and Life Sciences, Field of Education, Ithaca, NY 14853. Offers adult and extension education (MPS, MS, PhD); learning, teaching, and social policy (MPS, MS, PhD); mathematics 7-12 (MS). Terminal master's awarded for partial completion of doctoral program. *Degree requirements:* For master's, thesis (MS); for doctorate, comprehensive exam, thesis/dissertation. *Entrance requirements:* For master's and doctorate, GRE General Test, sample of written work (recommended), 2 letters of recommendation. Additional exam requirements/recommendations for international students: Required—TOEFL (minimum score 550 paper-based; 77 iBT). Electronic applications accepted. *Faculty research:* Moral development and professional ethics, public issues education and community development, socio/political issues in public education, teacher education and curriculum in agricultural science and mathematics, extension research.

Delaware State University, Graduate Programs, Department of Mathematics, Program in Mathematics Education, Dover, DE 19901-2277. Offers MS. *Entrance requirements:* Additional exam requirements/recommendations for international students: Required—TOEFL (minimum score 550 paper-based). Electronic applications accepted.

DePaul University, College of Education, Chicago, IL 60614. Offers bilingual bicultural education (M Ed, MA); counseling (M Ed, MA), including clinical mental health counseling, college student development, school counseling; curriculum studies (M Ed, MA, Ed D); early childhood education (M Ed, MA, Ed D); educating adults (MA); educational leadership (M Ed, MA, Ed D), including administration and supervision (M Ed, MA), principal preparation (M Ed, MA); elementary education (MA); mathematics education (MA); mathematics for teaching (MS); middle school mathematics education (MS); reading specialist (M Ed, MA); secondary education (M Ed); social and cultural foundations in education (MA); special education (M Ed, MA); world languages education (M Ed, MA). *Program availability:* Part-time, evening/weekend, online learning. *Degree requirements:* For doctorate, thesis/dissertation. Electronic applications accepted.

DePaul University, College of Science and Health, Chicago, IL 60614. Offers applied mathematics (MS); applied statistics (MS); biological sciences (MA, MS); chemistry (MS); mathematics education (MA); mathematics for teaching (MS); nursing (MS); nursing practice (DNP); physics (MS); psychology (MS); pure mathematics (MS); science education (MS); MA/PhD. *Accreditation:* AACN. Electronic applications accepted.

Duquesne University, School of Education, Department of Instruction and Leadership, Program in Secondary Education, Pittsburgh, PA 15282-0001. Offers biology (MS Ed); chemistry (MS Ed); English (MS Ed); K-12 education (MS Ed), including Latin; mathematics (MS Ed); physics (MS Ed); social studies (MS Ed). *Program availability:* Part-time, evening/weekend. *Faculty:* 5 full-time (4 women). *Students:* 21 full-time (8 women), 4 part-time (0 women); includes 3 minority (2 Black or African American, non-Hispanic/Latino; 1 Two or more races, non-Hispanic/Latino). Average age 28. 12 applicants, 100% accepted, 7 enrolled. In 2016, 19 master's awarded. *Degree requirements:* For master's, thesis optional. *Entrance requirements:* For master's, letters of recommendation, letter of intent, interview, bachelor's degree. Additional exam requirements/recommendations for international students: Required—TOEFL (minimum score 550 paper-based), IELTS (minimum score 7). *Application deadline:* For fall admission, 9/1 for domestic students; for spring admission, 1/1 for domestic students. Applications are processed on a rolling basis. Application fee: $0. Electronic applications accepted. *Expenses: Tuition:* Full-time $22,212; part-time $1234 per credit. Tuition and fees vary according to program. *Financial support:* Research assistantships and Federal Work-Study available. Support available to part-time students. *Unit head:* Dr. Melissa Boston, Associate Professor and Director, 412-396-6109, E-mail: bostonm@duq.edu. *Application contact:* Michael Dolinger, Director of Student and Academic Services, 412-396-6647, Fax: 412-396-5585, E-mail: dolingerm@duq.edu.
Website: http://www.duq.edu/academics/schools/education/graduate-programs-education/ms-ed-secondary-education

East Carolina University, Graduate School, College of Education, Department of Mathematics, Science, and Instructional Technology Education, Greenville, NC 27858-4353. Offers elementary mathematics (Certificate); instructional technology (MA Ed, MS); mathematics education (MA Ed); science education (MA Ed, MAT). *Program availability:* Part-time, evening/weekend. *Students:* 15 full-time (10 women), 266 part-time (213 women); includes 52 minority (34 Black or African American, non-Hispanic/Latino; 3 American Indian or Alaska Native, non-Hispanic/Latino; 4 Asian, non-Hispanic/Latino; 9 Hispanic/Latino; 2 Two or more races, non-Hispanic/Latino), 1 international. Average age 37. 131 applicants, 100% accepted, 116 enrolled. In 2016, 30 master's awarded. *Degree requirements:* For master's, comprehensive exam, thesis optional. *Entrance requirements:* For master's, GRE General Test or MAT, interview, minimum GPA of 2.5, bachelor's degree in related field, teaching license (MA Ed). Additional exam requirements/recommendations for international students: Required—TOEFL. *Application deadline:* For fall admission, 6/1 priority date for domestic students. Applications are processed on a rolling basis. Application fee: $50. *Financial support:* Research assistantships, teaching assistantships, and Federal Work-Study available. Support available to part-time students. Financial award application deadline: 6/1. *Unit head:* Susan Ganter, Chair, 252-737-3001, E-mail: ganters@ecu.edu. *Application contact:* Dean of Graduate School, 252-328-6012, Fax: 252-328-6071, E-mail: gradschool@ecu.edu.
Website: http://www.ecu.edu/cs-educ/msite/

Eastern Illinois University, Graduate School, College of Sciences, Department of Mathematics and Computer Science, Charleston, IL 61920. Offers elementary/middle school mathematics education (MA); mathematics (MA). *Program availability:* Part-time, evening/weekend. *Degree requirements:* For master's, comprehensive exam (for some programs), thesis (for some programs). *Entrance requirements:* For master's, GMAT or GRE. Additional exam requirements/recommendations for international students: Required—TOEFL (minimum score 500 paper-based; 61 iBT), IELTS (minimum score 6). Electronic applications accepted.

Eastern Kentucky University, The Graduate School, College of Education, Department of Curriculum and Instruction, Program in Secondary and Higher Education, Richmond, KY 40475-3102. Offers secondary education (MA Ed), including agricultural education, art education, biological sciences education, business education, English education, geography education, history education, home economics education, industrial education, mathematical sciences education, physical education, school health education. *Accreditation:* NCATE. *Program availability:* Part-time. *Entrance requirements:* For master's, GRE General Test, minimum GPA of 2.5.

Eastern University, Loeb School of Education, St. Davids, PA 19087-3696. Offers ESL program specialist (K-12) (Certificate); general supervisor (PreK-12) (Certificate); health and physical education (K-12) (Certificate); middle level (4-8) (Certificate); multicultural education (M Ed); organizational leadership with education (PhD); Pre K-4 (Certificate); Pre K-4 with special education (Certificate); reading (M Ed); reading specialist (K-12) (Certificate); reading supervisor (K-12) (Certificate); school health supervisor (Certificate); school nurse (K-12) (Certificate); secondary biology education (7-12) (Certificate); secondary chemistry education (7-12) (Certificate); secondary communication education (7-12) (Certificate); secondary education (7-12) (Certificate); secondary English education (7-12) (Certificate); secondary math education (7-12) (Certificate); secondary social studies education (7-12) (Certificate); special education (M Ed); special education (7-12) (Certificate); special education (Pre K-8) (Certificate); special education supervisor (N-12) (Certificate); TESOL (M Ed); world language (Certificate), including French, Spanish. *Program availability:* Part-time, evening/weekend, online learning. *Students:* 41 full-time (32 women), 89 part-time (68 women); includes 54 minority (38 Black or African American, non-Hispanic/Latino; 3 Asian, non-Hispanic/Latino; 11 Hispanic/Latino; 2 Two or more races, non-Hispanic/Latino), 2 international. Average age 37. In 2016, 64 master's awarded. *Entrance requirements:* Additional exam requirements/recommendations for international students: Required—TOEFL. *Application deadline:* Applications are processed on a rolling basis. Application fee: $35. Electronic applications accepted. Application fee is waived when completed online. *Expenses:* $690 per credit. *Unit head:* Michael Dziedziak, Executive Director of Enrollment, 800-452-0996, E-mail: gpsadmissions@eastern.edu.
Website: http://www.eastern.edu/academics/programs/loeb-school-education-0

Elizabeth City State University, School of Mathematics, Science and Technology, Master of Science in Mathematics Program, Elizabeth City, NC 27909-7806. Offers applied mathematics (MS); community college teaching (MS); mathematics education (MS); remote sensing (MS). *Program availability:* Part-time, evening/weekend. *Degree requirements:* For master's, thesis. *Entrance requirements:* For master's, MAT and/or GRE, minimum GPA of 3.0, 3 letters of recommendation, two official transcripts from all undergraduate/graduate schools attended, typewritten one-page request for entry into program that includes description of student's educational preparation. Additional exam requirements/recommendations for international students: Required—TOEFL (minimum score 550 paper-based, 80 iBT) or IELTS (minimum score 6.5). Electronic applications accepted. *Faculty research:* Oceanic temperature effects, mathematics strategies in elementary schools, multimedia, Antarctic temperature mapping, computer networks, water quality, remote sensing, polar ice, satellite imagery.

Florida Agricultural and Mechanical University, Division of Graduate Studies, Research, and Continuing Education, College of Education, Program in Secondary Education and Foundation, Tallahassee, FL 32307-3200. Offers biology (M Ed); chemistry (MS Ed); English (MS Ed); history (MS Ed); math (MS Ed); physics (MS Ed). *Accreditation:* NCATE. *Degree requirements:* For master's, thesis (for some programs). *Entrance requirements:* For master's, GRE General Test, minimum GPA of 3.0. Additional exam requirements/recommendations for international students: Required—TOEFL.

Florida Atlantic University, College of Education, Department of Teaching and Learning, Boca Raton, FL 33431-0991. Offers curriculum and instruction (M Ed), including art, biology, chemistry, English, French, German, mathematics, music, physics, Pre-K and primary education, reading, social sciences, Spanish; elementary education (M Ed); environmental education (M Ed); reading education (M Ed); social foundations of education (M Ed), including educational psychology, educational technology, multilingual education. *Accreditation:* NCATE. *Program availability:* Part-time, evening/weekend. *Faculty:* 15 full-time (12 women), 2 part-time/adjunct (1 woman). *Students:* 25 full-time (20 women), 41 part-time (37 women); includes 18 minority (9 Black or African American, non-Hispanic/Latino; 2 Asian, non-Hispanic/Latino; 7 Hispanic/Latino), 7 international. Average age 32. 54 applicants, 59% accepted, 18 enrolled. In 2016, 36 master's awarded. *Entrance requirements:* For master's, GRE General Test, minimum GPA of 3.0 in last 2 years of undergraduate course work. Additional exam requirements/recommendations for international students: Required—TOEFL (minimum score 500 paper-based; 61 iBT), IELTS (minimum score 6). *Application deadline:* For fall admission, 7/1 for domestic students, 2/15 for international students; for spring admission, 11/1 for domestic students, 7/15 for international students. Applications are processed on a rolling basis. Application fee: $30. *Expenses:* Tuition, state resident: full-time $7392; part-time $369.82 per credit hour. Tuition, nonresident: full-time $19,432; part-time $1024.81 per credit hour. *Financial support:* Fellowships with partial tuition reimbursements, research assistantships with partial tuition reimbursements, teaching assistantships with partial tuition reimbursements, career-related internships or fieldwork, scholarships/grants, and unspecified assistantships available. *Faculty research:* Technology, teaching English to speakers of other languages, math teaching, electronic portfolio assessment, global perspectives through social studies. *Unit head:* Dr. Barbara Ridener, Chairperson, 561-297-3588, E-mail: bridener@fau.edu. *Application contact:* Dr. Eliah Watlington, Associate Dean, 561-296-8520, Fax: 261-297-2991, E-mail: ewatling@fau.edu.
Website: http://www.coe.fau.edu/academicdepartments/tl/

Florida Gulf Coast University, College of Education, Program in Curriculum and Instruction, Fort Myers, FL 33965-6565. Offers elementary education (M Ed); English education (M Ed); gifted education (M Ed); mathematics education (M Ed); middle school education (M Ed); science education (M Ed); social science education (M Ed). *Program availability:* Part-time, evening/weekend, online learning. *Faculty:* 26 full-time (18 women), 44 part-time/adjunct (32 women). *Students:* 1 (woman) full-time, 22 part-time (20 women); includes 49 minority (19 Black or African American, non-Hispanic/Latino; 4 Asian, non-Hispanic/Latino; 24 Hispanic/Latino; 2 Two or more races, non-Hispanic/Latino), 2 international. Average age 28. 9 applicants, 78% accepted, 2 enrolled. In 2016, 9 master's awarded. *Degree requirements:* For master's, final project or portfolio. *Entrance requirements:* For master's, GRE General Test, MAT, minimum undergraduate GPA of 3.0 in last 2 years. Additional exam requirements/recommendations for international students: Required—TOEFL (minimum score 550 paper-based). *Application deadline:* For fall admission, 7/1 priority date for domestic students; for spring admission, 10/15 for domestic students. Applications are processed on a rolling basis. Application fee: $30. Electronic applications accepted. *Expenses:* Tuition, state resident: full-time $6721. Tuition, nonresident: full-time $28,170. *Required fees:* $1987. Tuition and fees vary according to course load and degree level. *Financial support:* In 2016–17, 1 student received support. Application deadline: 3/1; applicants

required to submit FAFSA. *Faculty research:* Internet in schools, technology in pre-service and in-service teacher training. *Unit head:* Dr. Diane Schmidt, Department Chair, 239-590-7741, Fax: 239-590-7801, E-mail: dschmidt@fgcu.edu. *Application contact:* Keiana Desmore, Adviser/Counselor, 239-590-7759, Fax: 239-590-7801, E-mail: kdesmore@fgcu.edu.
Website: http://coe.fgcu.edu/c-imed/

Florida Institute of Technology, College of Science, Program in Mathematics Education, Melbourne, FL 32901-6975. Offers MS, PhD, Ed S. *Students:* 7 full-time (5 women), 3 part-time (1 woman); includes 3 minority (2 Black or African American, non-Hispanic/Latino; 1 Hispanic/Latino), 4 international. Average age 33. 15 applicants, 60% accepted, 2 enrolled. In 2016, 1 doctorate, 1 other advanced degree awarded. *Degree requirements:* For master's, comprehensive exam (for some programs), thesis optional, minimum of 30 credit hours; for doctorate, comprehensive exam, thesis/dissertation, minimum of 42 credit hours; for Ed S, comprehensive exam, minimum of 30 credit hours, minimum GPA of 3.0. *Entrance requirements:* For master's, resume, statement of objectives, bachelor's degree in either mathematics or middle/secondary school mathematics education; for doctorate, master's degree in mathematics or mathematics education with minimum GPA of 3.2, 3 letters of recommendation, resume, statement of objectives; for Ed S, master's degree in mathematics or mathematics education, 3 letters of recommendation, resume, statement of objectives. Additional exam requirements/recommendations for international students: Required—TOEFL (minimum score 550 paper-based; 79 iBT). *Application deadline:* Applications are processed on a rolling basis. Electronic applications accepted. *Expenses: Tuition:* Full-time $22,338; part-time $1241 per credit hour. *Required fees:* $250. Tuition and fees vary according to degree level, campus/location and program. *Unit head:* Dr. Kastro Hamed, Department Head, 321-674-7206, E-mail: khmed@fit.edu. *Application contact:* Cheryl A. Brown, Associate Director of Graduate Admissions, 321-674-7581, Fax: 321-723-9468, E-mail: cbrown@fit.edu.
Website: http://www.fit.edu/programs/8127/ms-mathematics-education/career#.VT_qdU10ypo

Florida International University, College of Arts, Sciences, and Education, Department of Teaching and Learning, Miami, FL 33199. Offers art education (MA, MS); curriculum and instruction (MS, Ed D, PhD, Ed S), including curriculum development (MS), elementary education (MS), English education (MS), learning technologies (MS), mathematics education (MS), modern language education (MS), physical education (MS), science education (MS), social studies education (MS), special education (MS); early childhood education (MS); exceptional student education (Ed D); foreign language education (MS), including foreign language education, teaching English to speakers of other languages (TESOL); international/intercultural education (MS); language, literacy and culture (PhD); mathematics, science, and learning technologies (PhD); physical education (MS), including sport and fitness; reading education (MS). *Program availability:* Part-time, evening/weekend. *Faculty:* 34 full-time (23 women), 64 part-time/adjunct (48 women). *Students:* 182 full-time (154 women), 231 part-time (190 women); includes 323 minority (69 Black or African American, non-Hispanic/Latino; 10 Asian, non-Hispanic/Latino; 237 Hispanic/Latino; 7 Two or more races, non-Hispanic/Latino), 19 international. Average age 34. 282 applicants, 58% accepted, 113 enrolled. In 2016, 184 master's, 12 doctorates awarded. *Degree requirements:* For doctorate, comprehensive exam, thesis/dissertation. *Entrance requirements:* For master's, GRE General Test, Florida General Knowledge Test or Florida College Level Academic Skills Test; for doctorate and Ed S, GRE General Test. Additional exam requirements/recommendations for international students: Required—TOEFL (minimum score 550 paper-based; 80 iBT), IELTS (minimum score 6.3). *Application deadline:* For fall admission, 6/1 priority date for domestic students, 4/1 for international students; for winter admission, 10/1 priority date for domestic students, 9/1 for international students; for spring admission, 3/1 priority date for domestic students, 2/1 for international students. Applications are processed on a rolling basis. Application fee: $30. Electronic applications accepted. *Expenses:* Tuition, state resident: full-time $8912; part-time $446 per credit hour. Tuition, nonresident: full-time $21,393; part-time $992 per credit hour. *Required fees:* $2185; $195 per semester. Tuition and fees vary according to program. *Financial support:* Research assistantships with tuition reimbursements and teaching assistantships with tuition reimbursements available. *Unit head:* Dr. Lynn Miller, Chair, 305-348-2005, Fax: 305-348-2086, E-mail: lynne.miller@fiu.edu. *Application contact:* Nanett Rojas, Assistant Director, Graduate Admissions, 305-348-7464, Fax: 305-348-7441, E-mail: gradadm@fiu.edu.
Website: http://education.fiu.edu

Florida State University, The Graduate School, College of Education, Program in Curriculum and Instruction, Tallahassee, FL 32306. Offers curriculum and instruction (MS, PhD, Ed S), including early childhood education, elementary education, English education, English teaching (MS), exceptional student education (MS), foreign and second language education, foreign and second language teaching (MS), mathematics education, mathematics teaching (MS), reading education and language arts, science education, social science education, social science teaching (MS), special education, special education studies (MS), visual disabilities (MS, Ed S). *Program availability:* Part-time, evening/weekend. Terminal master's awarded for partial completion of doctoral program. *Degree requirements:* For master's and Ed S, comprehensive exam, thesis optional; for doctorate, comprehensive exam, thesis/dissertation, diagnostic exam, preliminary exam, prospectus defense, dissertation defense. *Entrance requirements:* For master's, doctorate, and Ed S, GRE General Test, minimum upper-division GPA of 3.0. Additional exam requirements/recommendations for international students: Required—TOEFL (minimum score 550 paper-based, 80 iBT), IELTS (minimum score 6.5), Michigan English Language Assessment Battery (minimum score 77), or PTE (minimum score 55). Application fee: $30. Electronic applications accepted. *Expenses:* Tuition, state resident: full-time $7263; part-time $403.51 per credit hour. Tuition, nonresident: full-time $18,087; part-time $1004.85 per credit hour. *Required fees:* $1365; $75.81 per credit hour. $20 per semester. Tuition and fees vary according to campus/location. *Financial support:* Fellowships, research assistantships, teaching assistantships, scholarships/grants, tuition waivers (full and partial), and unspecified assistantships available. Financial award application deadline: 1/15; financial award applicants required to submit FAFSA. *Faculty research:* Identifying effective intervention strategies to improve reading skills; improving literacy teaching and learning through technology; understanding of student sense making, problem solving, the history and structure of STEM disciplines, and teacher education to support the development of ambitious instruction that supports the STEM learning of all students; examining practices of international education; identifying ways to support the professional development of teachers. *Unit head:* Dr. Sherry Southerland, Professor/Department Chair, 850-644-4880, Fax: 850-644-7736, E-mail: ssoutherland@admin.fsu.edu. *Application contact:* Libbie Crowley, Academic Support Specialist, 850-644-2122, Fax: 850-644-7736, E-mail: ecrowley@fsu.edu.
Website: http://education.fsu.edu/degrees-and-programs/graduate-programs

Framingham State University, Continuing Education, Program in Mathematics, Framingham, MA 01701-9101. Offers M Ed. *Entrance requirements:* For master's, GRE General Test, minimum GPA of 3.0.

Fresno Pacific University, Graduate Programs, School of Education, Program in STEM Education, Fresno, CA 93702-4709. Offers MA Ed. *Program availability:* Part-time, evening/weekend. *Degree requirements:* For master's, thesis or alternative. *Entrance requirements:* Additional exam requirements/recommendations for international students: Required—TOEFL (minimum score 550 paper-based). *Expenses:* Contact institution.

George Mason University, College of Education and Human Development, Programs in Curriculum and Instruction, Fairfax, VA 22030. Offers advanced international baccalaureate (M Ed); assistive technology (M Ed); designing digital learning in schools (M Ed); early childhood education (M Ed); early childhood education for diverse learners (M Ed); elementary education (M Ed); English as a second language (M Ed); gifted child education (M Ed); history (M Ed); literacy (M Ed), including PK-12 classroom teachers, reading specialist; literacy leadership for diverse schools (M Ed), including K-12 reading; physical education (M Ed); science K-12 (M Ed); secondary education (M Ed), including biology, chemistry, earth science, English, history/social science, math, physics; special education (M Ed); teacher leadership (M Ed); teaching culturally, linguistically diverse and exceptional learners (M Ed); transformative teaching (M Ed). *Faculty:* 41 full-time (35 women), 53 part-time/adjunct (46 women). *Students:* 155 full-time (127 women), 821 part-time (697 women); includes 267 minority (82 Black or African American, non-Hispanic/Latino; 5 American Indian or Alaska Native, non-Hispanic/Latino; 75 Asian, non-Hispanic/Latino; 88 Hispanic/Latino; 1 Native Hawaiian or other Pacific Islander, non-Hispanic/Latino; 16 Two or more races, non-Hispanic/Latino), 19 international. Average age 33. 513 applicants, 90% accepted, 352 enrolled. In 2016, 347 master's awarded. *Degree requirements:* For master's, comprehensive exam, thesis (for some programs). *Entrance requirements:* For master's, PRAXIS Core (for some programs), minimum GPA of 3.0 in last 60 hours, licensed as teacher or educational administrator, official transcripts, goals statement, 3 recommendation letters, interview or writing sample (depending on program), up to 3 years' teaching experience (depending on program). Additional exam requirements/recommendations for international students: Required—TOEFL (minimum score 575 paper-based; 88 iBT), IELTS (minimum score 6.5), PTE (minimum score 59). *Application deadline:* For spring admission, 11/1 priority date for domestic and international students. Application fee: $75 ($80 for international students). Electronic applications accepted. *Expenses:* Tuition, state resident: full-time $10,628; part-time $443 per credit. Tuition, nonresident: full-time $29,306; part-time $1221 per credit. *Required fees:* $3096; $129 per credit. Tuition and fees vary according to program. *Financial support:* In 2016–17, 1 student received support, including 1 teaching assistantship (averaging $4,060 per year); career-related internships or fieldwork, Federal Work-Study, scholarships/grants, unspecified assistantships, and health care benefits (for full-time research or teaching assistantship recipients) also available. Support available to part-time students. Financial award application deadline: 3/1; financial award applicants required to submit FAFSA. *Faculty research:* Achievement gaps and superintendent decisions, constructivist view of classroom teaching, cost of cheating, creating a critical literacy milieu in kindergarten. *Unit head:* Rebecca Fox, Professor and Academic Program Coordinator, 703-993-4123, E-mail: rfox@gmu.edu.
Website: http://gse.gmu.edu/programs/gsemasters

The George Washington University, Graduate School of Education and Human Development, Department of Curriculum and Pedagogy, Program in Secondary Education, Washington, DC 20052. Offers Arabic (M Ed); Italian (M Ed); math (M Ed); physics (M Ed); Russian (M Ed). Programs also offered in Arlington and Ashburn, VA. *Accreditation:* NCATE. *Students:* 13 full-time (11 women), 21 part-time (15 women); includes 12 minority (4 Black or African American, non-Hispanic/Latino; 2 Asian, non-Hispanic/Latino; 4 Hispanic/Latino; 2 Two or more races, non-Hispanic/Latino). Average age 32. 50 applicants, 82% accepted, 25 enrolled. In 2016, 22 master's awarded. *Degree requirements:* For master's, comprehensive exam. *Entrance requirements:* For master's, GRE General Test or MAT, interview, minimum GPA of 2.75. *Application deadline:* For fall admission, 1/15 priority date for domestic students; for spring admission, 10/1 for domestic students. Applications are processed on a rolling basis. Application fee: $75. *Financial support:* Fellowships, career-related internships or fieldwork, Federal Work-Study, tuition waivers (full and partial), and stipends available. Financial award application deadline: 1/15; financial award applicants required to submit FAFSA. *Unit head:* Prof. Curtis Pyke, Chair, 202-994-4516, E-mail: cpyke@gwu.edu. *Application contact:* Sarah Lang, Director of Graduate Admissions, 202-994-1447, Fax: 202-994-7207, E-mail: slang@gwu.edu.

Georgia Southwestern State University, School of Education, Americus, GA 31709-4693. Offers early childhood education (M Ed, Ed S); middle grades education (Ed S); middle grades language arts (M Ed); middle grades mathematics (M Ed); special education (M Ed). *Accreditation:* NCATE. *Faculty:* 13 full-time (8 women), 7 part-time/adjunct (6 women). *Students:* 209 full-time (199 women), 6 part-time (all women); includes 52 minority (45 Black or African American, non-Hispanic/Latino; 6 Hispanic/Latino; 1 Two or more races, non-Hispanic/Latino). Average age 33. In 2016, 57 master's awarded. *Degree requirements:* For master's, minimum cumulative GPA of 3.0; for Ed S, minimum GPA of 3.25 in all courses with no grade less than a B; degree must be completed within 7 calendar years from date of initial enrollment in graduate work. *Entrance requirements:* For master's, undergraduate degree from accredited institution; professional Georgia Teaching Certificate or eligibility; minimum undergraduate GPA of 2.75 as reported on official final transcripts from all accredited institutions attended; 2 confidential Administrative Recommendation Forms; for Ed S, master's degree from accredited college or university; professional Georgia Teaching Certificate or eligibility; minimum graduate GPA of 3.0 as reported on official final graduate transcripts from all accredited institutions attended; 2 confidential Administrative Recommendation Forms. *Application deadline:* For summer admission, 4/15 for domestic students. Application fee: $25. Electronic applications accepted. *Expenses:* $257 per credit hour for online program courses, plus fees, which vary according to enrolled credit hours. *Financial support:* Application deadline: 6/1; applicants required to submit FAFSA. *Unit head:* Dr. Rachel Abbott, Dean, 229-931-2145. *Application contact:* Whitney Ford, Admissions Specialist, Office of Graduate Admissions, 800-338-0082, Fax: 229-931-2983.
Website: https://gsw.edu/Academics/Schools-and-Departments/School-of-Education/index

Georgia State University, College of Education and Human Development, Department of Early Childhood Education, Atlanta, GA 30302-3083. Offers early childhood and elementary education (PhD); early childhood education (M Ed, Ed S); mathematics education (M Ed); urban education (M Ed). *Accreditation:* NCATE. *Program availability:* Part-time, evening/weekend. *Faculty:* 27 full-time (22 women). *Students:* 68 full-time (60 women), 7 part-time (all women); includes 40 minority (33 Black or African American, non-Hispanic/Latino; 1 Asian, non-Hispanic/Latino; 4 Hispanic/Latino; 2 Two or more races, non-Hispanic/Latino), 3 international. Average age 32. 16 applicants, 44% accepted, 6 enrolled. In 2016, 35 master's, 4 doctorates awarded. *Degree requirements:* For master's, comprehensive exam (for some programs), thesis (for some programs); for doctorate, comprehensive exam, thesis/dissertation (for some programs); for Ed S, comprehensive exam (for some programs). *Entrance requirements:* For master's, GRE, undergraduate diploma; for doctorate and Ed S, GRE, master's degree. Additional exam requirements/recommendations for international students: Required—TOEFL (minimum score 550 paper-based; 79 iBT) or IELTS (minimum score 6.5). *Application deadline:*

Applications are processed on a rolling basis. Application fee: $50. Electronic applications accepted. *Expenses:* Tuition, state resident: full-time $6876; part-time $382 per credit hour. Tuition, nonresident: full-time $22,374; part-time $1243 per credit hour. *Required fees:* $2128; $1064 per term. Part-time tuition and fees vary according to course load and program. *Financial support:* In 2016–17, fellowships with full tuition reimbursements (averaging $24,000 per year), research assistantships with tuition reimbursements (averaging $4,000 per year), teaching assistantships with full tuition reimbursements (averaging $2,000 per year) were awarded; career-related internships or fieldwork, Federal Work-Study, institutionally sponsored loans, scholarships/grants, traineeships, health care benefits, tuition waivers (partial), and unspecified assistantships also available. Support available to part-time students. Financial award applicants required to submit FAFSA. *Faculty research:* Teacher development; language arts/literacy education; mathematics education; intersection of science, urban, and multicultural education; diversity in education. *Unit head:* Dr. Barbara Meyers, Department Chair, 404-413-8021, Fax: 404-413-8023, E-mail: barbara@gsu.edu. *Application contact:* Elaine King Jones, Administrative Curriculum Specialist, 404-413-8234, Fax: 404-413-8023, E-mail: ekjones@gsu.edu.
Website: http://ecee.education.gsu.edu/

Georgia State University, College of Education and Human Development, Department of Middle and Secondary Education, Atlanta, GA 30302-3083. Offers curriculum and instruction (Ed D); English education (MAT); mathematics education (M Ed, MAT); middle level education (MAT); reading, language and literacy education (M Ed, MAT), including reading instruction (M Ed); science education (M Ed, MAT), including biology (MAT), broad field science (MAT), chemistry (MAT), earth science (MAT), physics (MAT); social studies education (M Ed, MAT), including economics (MAT), geography (MAT), history (MAT), political science (MAT); teaching and learning (PhD), including language and literacy, mathematics education, music education, science education, social studies education, teaching and teacher education. *Accreditation:* NCATE. *Program availability:* Part-time, evening/weekend, online learning. *Faculty:* 24 full-time (18 women). *Students:* 145 full-time (91 women), 151 part-time (102 women); includes 141 minority (104 Black or African American, non-Hispanic/Latino; 1 American Indian or Alaska Native, non-Hispanic/Latino; 16 Asian, non-Hispanic/Latino; 12 Hispanic/Latino; 8 Two or more races, non-Hispanic/Latino), 10 international. Average age 36. 115 applicants, 50% accepted, 41 enrolled. In 2016, 94 master's, 22 doctorates awarded. *Degree requirements:* For master's, comprehensive exam (for some programs), thesis or alternative, exit portfolio; for doctorate, comprehensive exam, thesis/dissertation. *Entrance requirements:* For master's, GRE; GACE I (for initial teacher preparation programs), baccalaureate degree or equivalent, resume, goals statement, two letters of recommendation, minimum undergraduate GPA of 2.5; proof of initial teacher certification in the content area (for M Ed); for doctorate, GRE, resume, goals statement, writing sample, two letters of recommendation, minimum graduate GPA of 3.3, interview. Additional exam requirements/recommendations for international students: Required—TOEFL (minimum score 550 paper-based; 79 iBT) or IELTS (minimum score 6.5). *Application deadline:* For fall admission, 1/15 priority date for domestic and international students; for spring admission, 10/1 for domestic and international students. Application fee: $50. Electronic applications accepted. *Expenses:* Tuition, state resident: full-time $6876; part-time $382 per credit hour. Tuition, nonresident: full-time $22,374; part-time $1243 per credit hour. *Required fees:* $2128; $1064 per term. Part-time tuition and fees vary according to course load and program. *Financial support:* In 2016–17, fellowships with full tuition reimbursements (averaging $19,667 per year), research assistantships with full tuition reimbursements (averaging $5,436 per year), teaching assistantships with full tuition reimbursements (averaging $2,779 per year) were awarded; career-related internships or fieldwork, Federal Work-Study, scholarships/grants, health care benefits, tuition waivers (full and partial), and unspecified assistantships also available. Financial award application deadline: 3/15. *Faculty research:* Teacher education in language and literacy, mathematics, science, and social studies in urban middle and secondary school settings; learning technologies in school, community, and corporate settings; multicultural education and education for social justice; urban education; international education. *Unit head:* Dr. Dana L. Fox, Chair, 404-413-8060, Fax: 404-413-8063, E-mail: dfox@gsu.edu. *Application contact:* Bobbie Turner, Administrative Coordinator I, 404-413-8405, Fax: 404-413-8063, E-mail: bnturner@gsu.edu.
Website: http://mse.education.gsu.edu/

Gordon College, Graduate Education Program, Wenham, MA 01984-1899. Offers early childhood (M Ed); educational leadership (M Ed, Ed S); elementary education (M Ed); English as a second language (M Ed, Ed S); math specialist (M Ed); mathematics specialist (Ed S); middle school education (M Ed); moderate disabilities (M Ed); Montessori education (M Ed); reading (M Ed, Ed S); secondary education (M Ed). *Program availability:* Part-time, evening/weekend. *Faculty:* 17 full-time (9 women), 41 part-time/adjunct (34 women). *Students:* 81 full-time (61 women), 109 part-time (87 women); includes 28 minority (2 Black or African American, non-Hispanic/Latino; 11 Asian, non-Hispanic/Latino; 13 Hispanic/Latino; 2 Two or more races, non-Hispanic/Latino), 12 international. Average age 34. 190 applicants, 100% accepted, 141 enrolled. In 2016, 110 master's, 16 Ed Ss awarded. *Degree requirements:* For master's, action research or clinical experience (for most programs); for Ed S, action research or clinical experience (for some programs). *Entrance requirements:* For master's, minimum undergraduate GPA of 3.0; 2 official undergraduate transcripts; professional resume; 3 recommendation letters (one professional reference, one academic reference, one personal reference); 500-700 word statement of purpose; for Ed S, minimum master's GPA of 3.3; 2 official transcripts from undergraduate and graduate schools; professional resume; 3 recommendation letters (one professional reference, one academic reference, one personal reference); 500-700 word statement of purpose. Additional exam requirements/recommendations for international students: Required—TOEFL (minimum score 550 paper-based, 80 iBT) or IELTS (minimum score 6.5). *Application deadline:* Applications are processed on a rolling basis. Application fee: $75. *Expenses:* $325 per credit tuition, $75 per term fee. *Financial support:* Applicants required to submit FAFSA. *Faculty research:* Reading, early childhood development, English language learners, universal design for learning. *Unit head:* Dr. Janet Arndt, Director of Graduate Studies, 978-867-4355, Fax: 978-867-4663. *Application contact:* Julie Lenocker, Program Administrator, 978-867-4322, Fax: 978-867-4663, E-mail: graduate-education@gordon.edu.
Website: http://www.gordon.edu/graduate

Grambling State University, School of Graduate Studies and Research, College of Education, Department of Educational Leadership, Grambling, LA 71245. Offers developmental education (MS, Ed D, PMC), including curriculum and instructional design (Ed D), English (MS), guidance and counseling (MS), higher education administration and management (Ed D), mathematics (MS), reading (MS), science (MS), student development and personnel services (Ed D); educational leadership (M Ed). *Program availability:* Part-time, evening/weekend. *Degree requirements:* For master's, comprehensive exam, thesis (for some programs); for doctorate, comprehensive exam, thesis/dissertation. *Entrance requirements:* For master's, GRE, minimum GPA of 2.5 on last degree; for doctorate, GRE (minimum score 1000, 500 on Verbal), master's degree, minimum GPA of 3.0 on last degree. Additional exam requirements/recommendations for international students: Required—TOEFL (minimum score 500 paper-based; 62 iBT). Electronic applications accepted.

Harding University, Cannon-Clary College of Education, Searcy, AR 72149-0001. Offers advanced studies in teaching and learning (M Ed); art (MSE); behavioral science (MSE); counseling (MS, Ed S); early childhood special education (M Ed, MSE); education (MSE); educational leadership (M Ed, Ed S); elementary education (M Ed); English (MSE); French (MSE); history/social science (MSE); kinesiology (MSE); math (MSE); reading (M Ed); secondary education (M Ed); Spanish (MSE); teaching (MAT); teaching English as a second language (MSE). *Accreditation:* NCATE. *Program availability:* Part-time, evening/weekend. *Faculty:* 22 full-time (9 women), 51 part-time/adjunct (37 women). *Students:* 130 full-time (94 women), 321 part-time (234 women); includes 83 minority (50 Black or African American, non-Hispanic/Latino; 4 American Indian or Alaska Native, non-Hispanic/Latino; 6 Asian, non-Hispanic/Latino; 13 Hispanic/Latino; 10 Two or more races, non-Hispanic/Latino), 11 international. Average age 35. 125 applicants, 88% accepted, 110 enrolled. In 2016, 124 master's, 27 other advanced degrees awarded. *Degree requirements:* For master's, comprehensive exam (for some programs), thesis optional, portfolio(s); for Ed S, comprehensive exam, portfolio, project. *Entrance requirements:* For master's, GRE, MAT, PRAXIS; for Ed S, MAT or GRE. Additional exam requirements/recommendations for international students: Required—TOEFL (minimum score 550 paper-based; 79 iBT). *Application deadline:* For fall admission, 8/1 for domestic and international students; for spring admission, 1/1 for domestic and international students. Applications are processed on a rolling basis. Application fee: $35. Tuition and fees vary according to degree level and program. *Financial support:* In 2016–17, 31 students received support. Unspecified assistantships available. *Faculty research:* Reading, comprehension, school violence, educational technology, behavior, college choice, differentiated instruction, brain-based teaching. *Unit head:* Dr. Clara Carroll, Chair, 501-279-4501, Fax: 501-279-4083, E-mail: ccarroll@harding.edu. *Application contact:* Information Contact, 501-279-4315, E-mail: gradstudiesedu@harding.edu.
Website: http://www.harding.edu/education

Harvard University, Extension School, Cambridge, MA 02138-3722. Offers applied sciences (CAS); biotechnology (ALM); educational technologies (ALM); educational technology (CET); English for graduate and professional studies (DGP); environmental management (ALM, CEM); information technology (ALM); journalism (ALM); liberal arts (ALM); management (ALM, CM); mathematics for teaching (ALM); museum studies (ALM); premedical studies (Diploma); publication and communication (CPC). *Program availability:* Part-time, evening/weekend. *Degree requirements:* For master's, thesis. *Entrance requirements:* For master's, 3 completed graduate courses with grade of B or higher. Additional exam requirements/recommendations for international students: Required—TOEFL (minimum score 600 paper-based), TWE (minimum score 5). *Expenses:* Contact institution.

High Point University, Norcross Graduate School, High Point, NC 27268. Offers business administration (MBA); educational leadership (M Ed); elementary education (M Ed); history (MA); nonprofit management (MA); secondary math (M Ed); special education (M Ed); strategic communication (MA); teaching elementary education k-6 (MAT); teaching secondary mathematics 9-12 (MAT). *Accreditation:* NCATE. *Program availability:* Part-time, evening/weekend. *Degree requirements:* For master's, comprehensive exam (for some programs), thesis (for some programs). *Entrance requirements:* For master's, GMAT (MBA), GRE, MAT, minimum GPA of 3.0. Additional exam requirements/recommendations for international students: Required—TOEFL (minimum score 550 paper-based). Electronic applications accepted.

Hofstra University, School of Education, Programs in Teacher Education, Hempstead, NY 11549. Offers bilingual education (MA, Advanced Certificate); bilingual extension (Advanced Certificate), including education/speech language pathology; business education (MS Ed); early childhood and childhood education (MS Ed); early childhood education (MA, MS Ed); education technology (Advanced Certificate); elementary education (MA, MS Ed), including science, technology, engineering, and mathematics (STEM) (MA); English education (MS Ed); family and consumer science (MS Ed); fine arts and music education (Advanced Certificate); fine arts education (MS Ed); foreign language and TESOL (MS Ed); foreign language education (MS Ed), including French, German, Russian, Spanish; learning and teaching (Ed D), including applied linguistics, art education, arts and humanities, early childhood education, English education, human development, math education, math, science, and technology, multicultural education, physical education, science education, social studies education, special education; mathematics education (MA, MS Ed); middle school extension (Advanced Certificate), including grades 5-6, grades 7-9; music education (MA, MS Ed); science education (MA, MS Ed), including biology, chemistry, earth science, geology, physics; secondary education (Advanced Certificate); social studies education (MA, MS Ed); teaching languages other than English and TESOL (MS Ed); TESOL (MS Ed, Advanced Certificate). *Program availability:* Part-time, evening/weekend, blended/hybrid learning. *Students:* 139 full-time (97 women), 145 part-time (106 women); includes 60 minority (15 Black or African American, non-Hispanic/Latino; 1 American Indian or Alaska Native, non-Hispanic/Latino; 12 Asian, non-Hispanic/Latino; 31 Hispanic/Latino; 1 Two or more races, non-Hispanic/Latino), 21 international. Average age 29. 255 applicants, 86% accepted, 122 enrolled. In 2016, 101 master's, 4 doctorates, 43 other advanced degrees awarded. *Degree requirements:* For master's, comprehensive exam, thesis (for some programs), exit project, student teaching, fieldwork, electronic portfolio, curriculum project, minimum GPA of 3.0; for doctorate, thesis/dissertation; for Advanced Certificate, 3 foreign languages, comprehensive exam (for some programs), thesis project. *Entrance requirements:* For master's, GRE, MAT, 2 letters of recommendation, portfolio, teacher certification (MA), interview, essay; for doctorate, GMAT, GRE, LSAT, or MAT; for Advanced Certificate, 2 letters of recommendation, essay, interview and/or portfolio, teaching certificate. Additional exam requirements/recommendations for international students: Required—TOEFL (minimum score 550 paper-based; 80 iBT). *Application deadline:* Applications are processed on a rolling basis. Application fee: $75. Electronic applications accepted. *Expenses: Tuition:* Full-time $1240. *Required fees:* $970. Tuition and fees vary according to program. *Financial support:* In 2016–17, 149 students received support, including 58 fellowships with full and partial tuition reimbursements available (averaging $5,300 per year), 5 research assistantships with full and partial tuition reimbursements available (averaging $7,073 per year); career-related internships or fieldwork, Federal Work-Study, institutionally sponsored loans, scholarships/grants, traineeships, tuition waivers (full and partial), and unspecified assistantships also available. Support available to part-time students. Financial award applicants required to submit FAFSA. *Faculty research:* Educational interventions that foster critical-thinking skills; teachers' attitudes about professional development; threats to teacher quality. *Unit head:* Dr. Eustace Thompson, Chairperson, 516-463-5749, Fax: 516-463-6275, E-mail: eustace.g.thompson@hofstra.edu. *Application contact:* Sunil Samuel, Assistant Vice President of Admissions, 516-463-4723, Fax: 516-463-4664, E-mail: graduateadmission@hofstra.edu.
Website: http://www.hofstra.edu/education/

Hood College, Graduate School, Department of Education, Frederick, MD 21701-8575. Offers curriculum and instruction (MS), including elementary education, elementary science and mathematics education, secondary education, special education; educational leadership (MS); reading specialization (MS); STEM education (Certificate). *Accreditation:* NCATE. *Program availability:* Part-time-only, evening/weekend. *Faculty:* 3 full-time, 37 part-time/adjunct. *Students:* 1 (woman) full-time, 357 part-time (283

women); includes 71 minority (41 Black or African American, non-Hispanic/Latino; 6 Asian, non-Hispanic/Latino; 15 Hispanic/Latino; 9 Two or more races, non-Hispanic/Latino). Average age 33. 96 applicants, 95% accepted, 83 enrolled. In 2016, 47 master's awarded. *Degree requirements:* For master's, action research project, portfolio (for reading specialization); for Certificate, STEM capstone activity. *Entrance requirements:* For master's, minimum GPA of 2.75, teaching certification, writing sample during interview, letter of recommendation from principal (for educational leadership program only). Additional exam requirements/recommendations for international students: Required—TOEFL (minimum score 575 paper-based; 89 iBT), IELTS (minimum score 6.5). *Application deadline:* For fall admission, 8/15 priority date for domestic students, 8/5 for international students; for spring admission, 12/1 priority date for domestic students, 12/1 for international students; for summer admission, 5/1 priority date for domestic students, 4/15 for international students. Applications are processed on a rolling basis. Application fee: $35. Electronic applications accepted. *Expenses:* $450 per credit; $105 comprehensive fee per semester. *Financial support:* Tuition waivers (partial) and unspecified assistantships available. Financial award applicants required to submit FAFSA. *Faculty research:* Leadership, action research, brain research, learning styles. *Unit head:* April Boulton, Interim Dean of the Graduate School, E-mail: gofurther@hood.edu. *Application contact:* Jan Marcus, Assistant Director of Graduate Admissions, 301-696-3600, E-mail: gofurther@hood.edu.
Website: http://www.hood.edu/academics/education/index.html

Hood College, Graduate School, Program in Secondary Mathematics Education, Frederick, MD 21701-8575. Offers Certificate. *Program availability:* Part-time, evening/weekend. *Faculty:* 2 full-time, 1 part-time/adjunct. *Students:* 26 part-time (17 women); includes 2 minority (1 Black or African American, non-Hispanic/Latino; 1 Hispanic/Latino). Average age 33. 5 applicants, 100% accepted, 5 enrolled. *Entrance requirements:* Additional exam requirements/recommendations for international students: Required—TOEFL (minimum score 575 paper-based; 89 iBT), IELTS (minimum score 6.5). *Application deadline:* For fall admission, 8/15 priority date for domestic students, 8/15 for international students; for spring admission, 12/1 priority date for domestic students, 12/1 for international students; for summer admission, 5/1 priority date for domestic students, 4/15 for international students. Applications are processed on a rolling basis. Application fee: $35. Electronic applications accepted. *Expenses:* $450 per credit hour; $105 comprehensive fee per semester. *Financial support:* Tuition waivers (partial) and unspecified assistantships available. Financial award applicants required to submit FAFSA. *Unit head:* April Boulton, Interim Dean of the Graduate School, 301-696-3600, E-mail: gofurther@hood.edu. *Application contact:* Jan Marcus, Assistant Director of Graduate Admissions, 301-696-3600, E-mail: gofurther@hood.edu.
Website: http://www.hood.edu/graduate

Hunter College of the City University of New York, Graduate School, School of Arts and Sciences, Department of Mathematics and Statistics, New York, NY 10065-5085. Offers adolescent mathematics education (MA); applied mathematics (MA); bioinformatics (MA); pure mathematics (MA); statistics (MA). *Program availability:* Part-time, evening/weekend. *Students:* 1 full-time (0 women), 47 part-time (19 women); includes 14 minority (4 Black or African American, non-Hispanic/Latino; 8 Asian, non-Hispanic/Latino; 2 Hispanic/Latino), 8 international. Average age 32. 41 applicants, 73% accepted, 13 enrolled. In 2016, 8 master's awarded. *Degree requirements:* For master's, one foreign language, comprehensive exam, thesis (for some programs). *Entrance requirements:* For master's, GRE General Test, 24 credits in mathematics. Additional exam requirements/recommendations for international students: Required—TOEFL. *Application deadline:* For fall admission, 4/1 for domestic students, 2/1 for international students; for spring admission, 11/1 for domestic students, 9/1 for international students. *Financial support:* Federal Work-Study, institutionally sponsored loans, scholarships/grants, and tuition waivers (partial) available. Support available to part-time students. *Faculty research:* Data analysis, dynamical systems, computer graphics, topology, statistical decision theory. *Unit head:* Robert Thompson, Chair, 212-650-3831, Fax: 212-772-4858, E-mail: robert.thompson@hunter.cuny.edu. *Application contact:* Ada Peluso, Director for Graduate Admissions, 212-772-4632, Fax: 212-772-4858, E-mail: peluso@math.hunter.cuny.edu.
Website: http://math.hunter.cuny.edu/

Hunter College of the City University of New York, Graduate School, School of Education, Programs in Secondary Education, Concentration in Mathematics Education, New York, NY 10065-5085. Offers MA. *Accreditation:* NCATE. *Degree requirements:* For master's, thesis, professional teaching portfolio, New York State Teacher Certification Exam, research project. *Entrance requirements:* For master's, minimum GPA of 2.8 overall, 2.7 in mathematics courses; 24 credits of course work in mathematics. Additional exam requirements/recommendations for international students: Required—TOEFL, TWE. *Application deadline:* For fall admission, 4/1 for domestic students, 2/1 for international students; for spring admission, 11/1 for domestic students, 9/1 for international students. Applications are processed on a rolling basis. *Financial support:* Federal Work-Study and tuition waivers (partial) available. Support available to part-time students. *Unit head:* Dr. Patrick Burke, Program Coordinator, 212-396-6043, E-mail: patrick.burke@hunter.cuny.edu. *Application contact:* Milena Solo, Director for Graduate Admissions, 212-772-4480, E-mail: admissions@hunter.cuny.edu.
Website: http://www.hunter.cuny.edu/school-of-education/programs/graduate/adolescent/mathematics

Idaho State University, Office of Graduate Studies, College of Science and Engineering, Department of Mathematics, Pocatello, ID 83209-8085. Offers mathematics (MS, DA); mathematics for secondary teachers (MA). *Program availability:* Part-time. *Degree requirements:* For master's, comprehensive exam, thesis (for some programs), oral and written exams; for doctorate, comprehensive exam, thesis/dissertation, teaching internships. *Entrance requirements:* For master's, GRE General Test, GRE Subject Test, course work in modern algebra, differential equations, advanced calculus, introductory analysis; for doctorate, GRE General Test, GRE Subject Test, minimum graduate GPA of 3.5, MS in mathematics, teaching experience, 3 letters of recommendation. Additional exam requirements/recommendations for international students: Required—TOEFL (minimum score 550 paper-based; 80 iBT). Electronic applications accepted. *Faculty research:* Algebra, analysis geometry, statistics, applied mathematics.

Illinois Institute of Technology, Graduate College, College of Science, Department of Mathematics and Science Education, Chicago, IL 60616. Offers mathematics education (MAS, PhD); science education (MAS, PhD). *Degree requirements:* For master's, comprehensive exam (for some programs), thesis optional; for doctorate, comprehensive exam, thesis/dissertation. *Entrance requirements:* For master's, GRE General Test (minimum score 900 quantitative and verbal; 2.5 analytical writing), minimum undergraduate GPA of 3.0; two-page professional statement of goals/objectives; curriculum vita; three letters of recommendation; for doctorate, GRE General Test (minimum score 1000 quantitative and verbal; 3.0 analytical writing), minimum GPA of 3.0, 3 years of teaching experience. Additional exam requirements/recommendations for international students: Required—TOEFL (minimum score 600 paper-based; 80 iBT). Electronic applications accepted. *Faculty research:* Informal science/math education, curriculum development, integration of science/math disciplines and across disciplines, instructional methods, students' and teachers' conceptions of scientific/mathematical inquiry and the nature of science/math, instructional models, evaluation, and research design.

Illinois State University, Graduate School, College of Arts and Sciences, Department of Mathematics, Program in Mathematics Education, Normal, IL 61790-2200. Offers MA, PhD. *Degree requirements:* For doctorate, variable foreign language requirement, comprehensive exam, thesis/dissertation, 2 terms of residency. *Entrance requirements:* For doctorate, GRE General Test.

Indiana University Bloomington, School of Education, Department of Curriculum and Instruction, Bloomington, IN 47405-7000. Offers art education (MS, Ed D, PhD); curriculum studies (Ed D, PhD); elementary education (MS, Ed D, PhD, Ed S); mathematics education (MS, Ed D, PhD); science education (MS, Ed D, PhD); secondary education (MS, Ed D, PhD); social studies education (MS, PhD); special education (PhD, Ed S). *Accreditation:* NCATE. *Program availability:* Part-time, evening/weekend. Terminal master's awarded for partial completion of doctoral program. *Degree requirements:* For doctorate, thesis/dissertation; for Ed S, comprehensive exam or project. *Entrance requirements:* For master's, doctorate, and Ed S, GRE General Test. Electronic applications accepted.

Indiana University Bloomington, University Graduate School, College of Arts and Sciences, Department of Mathematics, Bloomington, IN 47405. Offers applied mathematics (MA); mathematical physics (PhD); mathematics education (MAT); pure mathematics (MA, PhD). *Faculty:* 49 full-time (3 women). *Students:* 111 full-time (21 women), 1 (woman) part-time; includes 10 minority (3 Black or African American, non-Hispanic/Latino; 5 Asian, non-Hispanic/Latino; 2 Hispanic/Latino), 72 international. Average age 27. 178 applicants, 19% accepted, 20 enrolled. In 2016, 15 master's, 11 doctorates awarded. Terminal master's awarded for partial completion of doctoral program. *Degree requirements:* For doctorate, one foreign language, thesis/dissertation. *Entrance requirements:* For master's and doctorate, GRE General Test, GRE Subject Test. Additional exam requirements/recommendations for international students: Required—TOEFL. *Application deadline:* For fall admission, 1/15 for domestic and international students. Application fee: $55 ($65 for international students). Electronic applications accepted. *Expenses:* Contact institution. *Financial support:* In 2016–17, 108 students received support, including 22 fellowships with full tuition reimbursements available (averaging $20,000 per year), 4 research assistantships with full tuition reimbursements available (averaging $18,750 per year), 82 teaching assistantships with full tuition reimbursements available (averaging $18,150 per year); scholarships/grants, health care benefits, and unspecified assistantships also available. Financial award application deadline: 1/15. *Faculty research:* Topology, geometry, algebra, applied mathematics, analysis. *Total annual research expenditures:* $749,256. *Unit head:* Elizabeth Housworth, Chair, 812-855-2200. *Application contact:* Kate Forrest, Graduate Secretary, 812-855-2645, Fax: 812-855-0046, E-mail: gradmath@indiana.edu.
Website: http://www.math.indiana.edu/

Indiana University of Pennsylvania, School of Graduate Studies and Research, College of Natural Sciences and Mathematics, Department of Mathematics, Program in Elementary and Middle School Mathematics Education, Indiana, PA 15705. Offers M Ed. *Accreditation:* NCATE. *Program availability:* Part-time. *Faculty:* 11 full-time (3 women). *Students:* 1 full-time (0 women), 11 part-time (10 women). Average age 28. 11 applicants, 82% accepted, 5 enrolled. In 2016, 4 master's awarded. *Degree requirements:* For master's, comprehensive exam (for some programs), thesis optional. *Entrance requirements:* For master's, 2 letters of recommendation. Additional exam requirements/recommendations for international students: Required—TOEFL (minimum score 540 paper-based). *Application deadline:* Applications are processed on a rolling basis. Application fee: $50. Electronic applications accepted. *Expenses:* Tuition, state resident: full-time $8694; part-time $483 per credit. Tuition, nonresident: full-time $13,050; part-time $725 per credit. *Required fees:* $157 per credit. $50 per term. Tuition and fees vary according to course load and program. *Financial support:* In 2016–17, 1 research assistantship with tuition reimbursement (averaging $6,360 per year) was awarded; career-related internships or fieldwork and Federal Work-Study also available. Support available to part-time students. Financial award application deadline: 4/15; financial award applicants required to submit FAFSA. *Unit head:* Dr. Mary Lou Metz, Graduate Coordinator, 724-357-4759, E-mail: mlmetz@iup.edu.
Website: http://www.iup.edu/grad/mathed/default.aspx

Indiana University of Pennsylvania, School of Graduate Studies and Research, College of Natural Sciences and Mathematics, Department of Mathematics, Program in Secondary Mathematics Education, Indiana, PA 15705. Offers M Ed. *Accreditation:* NCATE. *Program availability:* Part-time. *Faculty:* 11 full-time (3 women). *Students:* 2 full-time (1 woman), 14 part-time (7 women); includes 1 minority (Two or more races, non-Hispanic/Latino), 1 international. Average age 32. 11 applicants, 73% accepted, 5 enrolled. *Degree requirements:* For master's, thesis optional. *Entrance requirements:* For master's, 2 letters of recommendation. Additional exam requirements/recommendations for international students: Required—TOEFL (minimum score 540 paper-based). *Application deadline:* Applications are processed on a rolling basis. Application fee: $50. Electronic applications accepted. *Expenses:* Tuition, state resident: full-time $8694; part-time $483 per credit. Tuition, nonresident: full-time $13,050; part-time $725 per credit. *Required fees:* $157 per credit. $50 per term. Tuition and fees vary according to course load and program. *Financial support:* In 2016–17, 2 research assistantships (averaging $4,770 per year) were awarded; fellowships, career-related internships or fieldwork, Federal Work-Study, scholarships/grants, and unspecified assistantships also available. Support available to part-time students. Financial award application deadline: 4/15; financial award applicants required to submit FAFSA. *Unit head:* Dr. Margaret Stempien, Graduate Coordinator, 724-357-3791, E-mail: margaret.stempien@iup.edu. *Application contact:* Dr. Yu-Ju Kuo, Graduate Coordinator, 724-357-3797, E-mail: yjkuo@iup.edu.
Website: http://www.iup.edu/math/grad/mathematics-education-med/

Indiana University–Purdue University Fort Wayne, College of Arts and Sciences, Department of Mathematical Sciences, Fort Wayne, IN 46805-1499. Offers applied mathematics (MS); applied statistics (Certificate); mathematics (MS); operations research (MS); teaching (MAT). *Program availability:* Part-time, evening/weekend. *Entrance requirements:* For master's, minimum GPA of 3.0, major or minor in mathematics, three letters of recommendation. Additional exam requirements/recommendations for international students: Required—TOEFL (minimum score 550 paper-based; 79 iBT); Recommended—TWE. Electronic applications accepted. *Faculty research:* Eves' Theorem, paired-placements for student teaching, holomorphic maps.

Indiana University–Purdue University Indianapolis, School of Science, Department of Mathematical Sciences, Indianapolis, IN 46202-3216. Offers mathematics (MS, PhD), including applied mathematics, applied statistics (MS), mathematical statistics (PhD), mathematics, mathematics education (MS). *Program availability:* Part-time, evening/weekend. *Faculty:* 33 full-time (5 women), 2 part-time/adjunct (0 women). *Students:* 49 full-time (12 women), 29 part-time (12 women); includes 17 minority (5 Black or African American, non-Hispanic/Latino; 10 Asian, non-Hispanic/Latino; 2 Hispanic/Latino), 30 international. Average age 32. 41 applicants, 39% accepted, 13 enrolled. In 2016, 13 master's, 6 doctorates awarded. *Degree requirements:* For master's, thesis optional; for doctorate, one foreign language, comprehensive exam, thesis/dissertation. *Entrance*

requirements: For doctorate, GRE General Test (recommended). Additional exam requirements/recommendations for international students: Required—TOEFL (minimum score 79 iBT), IELTS (minimum score 6.5), GRE General Test. *Application deadline:* For fall admission, 3/1 for domestic students; for spring admission, 11/15 for domestic students; for summer admission, 4/1 for domestic students. Applications are processed on a rolling basis. Application fee: $60 ($65 for international students). Electronic applications accepted. *Financial support:* In 2016–17, 14 students received support, including fellowships with tuition reimbursements available (averaging $20,000 per year), 18 research assistantships with tuition reimbursements available (averaging $20,000 per year), 11 teaching assistantships with tuition reimbursements available (averaging $18,500 per year); health care benefits, tuition waivers (full), and unspecified assistantships also available. Financial award application deadline: 2/1. *Faculty research:* Mathematical physics, integral systems, partial differential equations, noncommutative geometry, biomathematics, computational neurosciences. *Total annual research expenditures:* $1 million. *Unit head:* Dr. Jeffery Xavier Watt, Chair, 317-274-6918, Fax: 317-274-3460, E-mail: jwatt@math.iupui.edu. *Application contact:* Alex Duncan, Academic Advisor and Graduate Programs Coordinator, 317-278-4127, E-mail: duncalex@iupui.edu.
Website: http://www.math.iupui.edu/

Instituto Tecnológico y de Estudios Superiores de Monterrey, Campus Ciudad Obregón, Programs in Education, Program in Mathematics, Ciudad Obregón, Mexico. Offers ME.

Inter American University of Puerto Rico, Arecibo Campus, Programs in Education, Arecibo, PR 00614-4050. Offers administration and educational supervision (MA Ed); counseling and guidance (MA Ed); curriculum and teaching (MA Ed), including biology education, English as a second language, history education, math education, Spanish; elementary education (MA Ed). *Accreditation:* TEAC. *Degree requirements:* For master's, comprehensive exam, thesis optional. *Entrance requirements:* For master's, GRE, EXADEP, bachelor's degree in education or teaching license (administration and supervision) or courses in education and psychology (counseling and guidance), minimum GPA of 2.5 in last 60 credits.

Inter American University of Puerto Rico, Barranquitas Campus, Program in Education, Barranquitas, PR 00794. Offers curriculum and teaching (M Ed), including biology education, English as a second language, history education, mathematics education, Spanish; educational leadership and management (MA); elementary education (M Ed); information and library service technology (M Ed); special education (MA). *Accreditation:* TEAC. *Degree requirements:* For master's, comprehensive exam, thesis optional. *Entrance requirements:* For master's, EXADEP, letter of recommendation. Electronic applications accepted.

Inter American University of Puerto Rico, Metropolitan Campus, Graduate Programs, Program in Teaching of Math, San Juan, PR 00919-1293. Offers MA.

Inter American University of Puerto Rico, Ponce Campus, Graduate School, Mercedita, PR 00715-1602. Offers accounting (MBA); biology (M Ed); chemistry (M Ed); criminal justice (MA); elementary education (M Ed); English as a Second Language (M Ed); finance (MBA); history (M Ed); human resources (MBA); marketing (MBA); mathematics (M Ed); Spanish (M Ed). *Entrance requirements:* For master's, minimum GPA of 2.5.

Inter American University of Puerto Rico, San Germán Campus, Graduate Studies Center, Program in Mathematics Education, San Germán, PR 00683-5008. Offers applied mathematics (MA). *Program availability:* Part-time, evening/weekend. *Degree requirements:* For master's, comprehensive exam. *Entrance requirements:* For master's, EXADEP or GRE General Test, minimum GPA of 3.0.

Iona College, School of Arts and Science, Department of Education, New Rochelle, NY 10801-1890. Offers adolescence education: biology (MS Ed, MST); adolescence education: English (MS Ed); adolescence education: mathematics (MST); adolescence education: social studies (MS Ed, MST); adolescence education: Spanish (MS Ed); adolescence special education 5-12 (MST); childhood and special education (MST); early childhood and childhood (MST); educational leadership (MS Ed). *Accreditation:* NCATE. *Program availability:* Part-time, evening/weekend. *Faculty:* 7 full-time (6 women), 4 part-time/adjunct (2 women). *Students:* 27 full-time (19 women), 27 part-time (18 women); includes 18 minority (4 Black or African American, non-Hispanic/Latino; 1 Asian, non-Hispanic/Latino; 12 Hispanic/Latino; 1 Two or more races, non-Hispanic/Latino). Average age 26. 6 applicants, 67% accepted, 3 enrolled. In 2016, 25 master's awarded. *Degree requirements:* For master's, thesis or alternative. *Entrance requirements:* For master's, minimum GPA of 3.0, NY State teaching certificate and bachelor's degree (for MS Ed). Additional exam requirements/recommendations for international students: Required—TOEFL (minimum score 550 paper-based; 80 iBT), IELTS (minimum score 6.5). *Application deadline:* For fall admission, 8/1 priority date for domestic students, 5/1 priority date for international students; for spring admission, 1/1 priority date for domestic students, 9/1 priority date for international students. Applications are processed on a rolling basis. Application fee: $50. Electronic applications accepted. *Expenses: Tuition:* Full-time $19,692; part-time $1094 per credit. *Required fees:* $245 per term. Tuition and fees vary according to program. *Financial support:* In 2016–17, 3 students received support. Unspecified assistantships available. Support available to part-time students. Financial award application deadline: 4/15; financial award applicants required to submit FAFSA. *Faculty research:* Engaging teacher educators in scientific process, cross-national comparisons of mathematics teaching, questioning strategies in the classroom, research methods, literacy development. *Unit head:* Margaret Smith, PhD, Chair, 914-633-2210, Fax: 914-633-2608, E-mail: msmith@iona.edu. *Application contact:* Richard McMahon, Coordinator, Graduate School of Education, 914-633-2552, E-mail: rmcmahon@iona.edu.
Website: http://www.iona.edu/Academics/School-of-Arts-Science/Departments/Education/Graduate-Programs.aspx

Iowa State University of Science and Technology, Department of Mathematics, Ames, IA 50011. Offers applied mathematics (MS, PhD); mathematics (MS, PhD), school mathematics (MSM). *Degree requirements:* For master's, thesis or alternative; for doctorate, thesis/dissertation. *Entrance requirements:* For master's and doctorate, GRE General Test. Additional exam requirements/recommendations for international students: Required—TOEFL (minimum score 550 paper-based; 79 iBT), IELTS (minimum score 6.5). *Application deadline:* For fall admission, 2/1 priority date for domestic and international students. Application fee: $60 ($90 for international students). Electronic applications accepted. *Financial support:* Scholarships/grants, health care benefits, and unspecified assistantships available. *Application contact:* Melanie Erickson, Application Contact, 515-294-0393, Fax: 515-294-5454, E-mail: gradmath@iastate.edu.
Website: http://www.math.iastate.edu/Graduate/Programs.html

Iowa State University of Science and Technology, Program in School Mathematics, Ames, IA 50011. Offers MSM. *Entrance requirements:* For master's, official academic transcripts, resume, three letters of recommendation, statement of purpose. Additional exam requirements/recommendations for international students: Required—TOEFL (minimum score 550 paper-based; 79 iBT), IELTS (minimum score 6.5). Application fee: $60 ($90 for international students). Electronic applications accepted. *Application contact:* Melanie Erickson, Application Contact, 515-294-0393, Fax: 515-294-5454, E-mail: msm@iastate.edu.
Website: http://www.math.iastate.edu/MSM/MSMhome.html

Ithaca College, School of Humanities and Sciences, Program in Adolescence Education, Ithaca, NY 14850. Offers biology (MAT); chemistry (MAT); earth science (MAT); English (MAT); French (MAT); mathematics (MAT); physics (MAT); social studies (MAT); Spanish (MAT). *Program availability:* Part-time. *Faculty:* 26 full-time (12 women). *Students:* 11 full-time (4 women). Average age 26. 17 applicants, 94% accepted, 10 enrolled. *Degree requirements:* For master's, thesis or alternative. *Entrance requirements:* Additional exam requirements/recommendations for international students: Required—TOEFL (minimum score 550 paper-based; 80 iBT). *Application deadline:* For fall admission, 2/15 for domestic and international students; for spring admission, 12/1 for domestic and international students. Applications are processed on a rolling basis. Application fee: $40. Electronic applications accepted. *Expenses:* Contact institution. *Financial support:* In 2016–17, 5 students received support, including 5 research assistantships (averaging $13,259 per year); career-related internships or fieldwork, Federal Work-Study, scholarships/grants, and unspecified assistantships also available. Support available to part-time students. Financial award application deadline: 2/15; financial award applicants required to submit CSS PROFILE or FAFSA. *Unit head:* Peter Martin, Chair, 607-274-1076, E-mail: pmartin@ithaca.edu. *Application contact:* Nicole Eversley Bradwell, Director, Office of Admission, 607-274-3124, Fax: 607-274-1263, E-mail: admission@ithaca.edu.
Website: http://www.ithaca.edu/gradprograms/education/programs/aded

Jackson State University, Graduate School, College of Science, Engineering and Technology, Department of Mathematics and Statistical Sciences, Jackson, MS 39217. Offers applied mathematics (MS); mathematics education (MST); pure mathematics (MS). *Program availability:* Part-time, evening/weekend. *Degree requirements:* For master's, comprehensive exam, thesis (for some programs). *Entrance requirements:* For master's, GRE General Test. Additional exam requirements/recommendations for international students: Required—TOEFL (minimum score 520 paper-based; 67 iBT). *Application deadline:* For fall admission, 3/1 priority date for domestic students, 3/1 for international students; for spring admission, 10/1 for domestic and international students. Applications are processed on a rolling basis. Application fee: $25. *Expenses:* Tuition, state resident: full-time $7141. Tuition, nonresident: full-time $17,494. *Required fees:* $1080. Tuition and fees vary according to class time, course level, course load, degree level, campus/location, program and student level. *Financial support:* Career-related internships or fieldwork, Federal Work-Study, scholarships/grants, and unspecified assistantships available. Support available to part-time students. Financial award application deadline: 3/1; financial award applicants required to submit FAFSA. *Unit head:* Dr. Tor A. Kwembe, Chair, 601-979-2161, E-mail: tor.a.kwembe@jsums.edu. *Application contact:* Fatoumatta Sisay, Manager of Graduate Admissions, 601-979-0342, Fax: 601-979-4325, E-mail: fatoumatta.sisay@jsums.edu.
Website: http://www.jsums.edu/math/

James Madison University, The Graduate School, College of Education, Program in Education, Harrisonburg, VA 22807. Offers early childhood education (preK-3) (MAT); educational leadership (M Ed); educational technology (M Ed); elementary education (MAT); equity and cultural diversity (M Ed); inclusive early childhood education (MAT); K-8 mathematics specialist (M Ed); middle education (MAT); reading education (M Ed); secondary education (MAT); Spanish language and culture for educators (M Ed); TESOL (MAT). *Accreditation:* NCATE. *Program availability:* Part-time, evening/weekend. *Faculty:* 21 full-time (12 women), 5 part-time/adjunct (2 women). *Students:* 249 full-time (220 women), 123 part-time (86 women); includes 43 minority (7 Black or African American, non-Hispanic/Latino; 7 Asian, non-Hispanic/Latino; 17 Hispanic/Latino; 12 Two or more races, non-Hispanic/Latino), 2 international. Average age 30. 355 applicants, 98% accepted, 312 enrolled. In 2016, 247 master's awarded. Application fee: $55. Electronic applications accepted. *Financial support:* In 2016–17, 16 students received support. Career-related internships or fieldwork, Federal Work-Study, and 22 assistantships (averaging $7911) available. Financial award application deadline: 3/1; financial award applicants required to submit FAFSA. *Unit head:* Dr. Phillip M. Wishon, Dean, 540-568-6572, E-mail: wishonpm@jmu.edu. *Application contact:* Lynette D. Michael, Director of Graduate Admissions, 540-568-6131 Ext. 6395, Fax: 540-568-7860, E-mail: michaeld@jmu.edu.
Website: http://www.jmu.edu/coe/index.shtml

James Madison University, The Graduate School, College of Education, Program in Mathematics Education, Harrisonburg, VA 22807. Offers K-8 math specialist (M Ed); mathematics (M Ed). *Students:* Average age 27. Application fee: $55. Electronic applications accepted. *Financial support:* In 2016–17, 17 students received support, including 6 fellowships; 11 assistantships (averaging $4450) also available. Financial award application deadline: 3/1; financial award applicants required to submit FAFSA. *Unit head:* Dr. Steven L. Purcell, Department Head, 540-568-6793. *Application contact:* Lynette D. Michael, Director of Graduate Admissions and Student Records, 540-568-6131 Ext. 6395, Fax: 540-568-7860, E-mail: michaeld@jmu.edu.
Website: http://www.jmu.edu/coe/msme/index.shtml

James Madison University, The Graduate School, College of Science and Mathematics, Program in Mathematics, Harrisonburg, VA 22807. Offers M Ed. *Program availability:* Part-time. *Faculty:* 12 full-time (5 women). *Students:* 9 part-time (5 women); includes 1 minority (Asian, non-Hispanic/Latino). Average age 30. 2 applicants, 100% accepted, 2 enrolled. In 2016, 3 master's awarded. Application fee: $55. Electronic applications accepted. *Financial support:* Federal Work-Study and unspecified assistantships available. Financial award application deadline: 3/1; financial award applicants required to submit FAFSA. *Unit head:* Dr. David C. Carothers, Department Head, 540-568-6184, E-mail: carothdc@jmu.edu. *Application contact:* Lynette D. Michael, Director of Graduate Admissions, 540-568-6395, Fax: 540-568-7860, E-mail: michaeld@jmu.edu.
Website: http://www.jmu.edu/mathstat/

Kaplan University, Davenport Campus, School of Teacher Education, Davenport, IA 52807. Offers education (M Ed); secondary education (M Ed); teaching and learning (MA); teaching literacy and language: grades 6-12 (MA); teaching literacy and language: grades K-6 (MA); teaching mathematics: grades 6-8 (MA); teaching mathematics: grades 9-12 (MA); teaching mathematics: grades K-5 (MA); teaching science: grades 6-12 (MA); teaching science: grades K-6 (MA); teaching students with special needs (MA); teaching with technology (MA). *Program availability:* Part-time, evening/weekend, online learning. *Entrance requirements:* Additional exam requirements/recommendations for international students: Required—TOEFL (minimum score 550 paper-based; 80 iBT).

Kennesaw State University, Leland and Clarice C. Bagwell College of Education, Program in Teaching, Kennesaw, GA 30144. Offers art education (MAT); biology (MAT); chemistry (MAT); foreign language education (Chinese and Spanish) (MAT); physics (MAT); secondary English (MAT); secondary mathematics (MAT); special education (MAT); teaching English to speakers of other languages (MAT). *Program availability:* Part-time, evening/weekend. *Entrance requirements:* For master's, GRE, GACE I (state certificate exam), minimum GPA of 2.75, 2 recommendations, resume. Additional exam requirements/recommendations for international students: Required—TOEFL (minimum score 550 paper-based; 80 iBT), IELTS (minimum score 6.5). Electronic applications accepted.

Kent State University, College of Arts and Sciences, Department of Mathematical Sciences, Kent, OH 44242-0001. Offers applied mathematics (MA, MS, PhD); mathematics for secondary teachers (MA); pure mathematics (MA, MS, PhD). *Program availability:* Part-time. *Faculty:* 41 full-time (16 women). *Students:* 69 full-time (24 women), 41 part-time (19 women); includes 6 minority (2 Black or African American, non-Hispanic/Latino; 4 Asian, non-Hispanic/Latino), 46 international. Average age 30. 86 applicants, 67% accepted, 17 enrolled. In 2016, 18 master's, 4 doctorates awarded. *Degree requirements:* For master's, comprehensive exam (for some programs), thesis (for some programs); for doctorate, comprehensive exam, thesis/dissertation. *Entrance requirements:* For master's, bachelor's degree in mathematics or similar field, minimum GPA of 3.0, personal statement, resume, 3 letters of recommendation; for doctorate, master's degree, minimum GPA of 3.0, personal statement, resume, 3 letters of recommendation. Additional exam requirements/recommendations for international students: Required—TOEFL (minimum score of 525 paper-based, 71 iBT), IELTS (minimum score of 6), Michigan English Language Assessment Battery (minimum score of 75), or PTE (minimum score of 48). *Application deadline:* For fall admission, 5/1 for domestic and international students; for spring admission, 10/1 for domestic and international students; for summer admission, 2/1 for domestic and international students. Applications are processed on a rolling basis. Application fee: $45 ($70 for international students). Electronic applications accepted. *Expenses:* Tuition, state resident: full-time $10,864; part-time $495 per credit hour. Tuition, nonresident: full-time $18,380; part-time $837 per credit hour. *Financial support:* Fellowships with full tuition reimbursements, research assistantships with full tuition reimbursements, teaching assistantships with full tuition reimbursements, scholarships/grants, and unspecified assistantships available. Financial award application deadline: 1/31. *Unit head:* Dr. Andrew Tonge, Professor and Chair, 330-672-9046, E-mail: tonge@math.kent.edu. *Application contact:* Artem Zvavitch, Professor and Graduate Coordinator, 330-672-9054, E-mail: jackn@math.kent.edu.
Website: http://www.kent.edu/math/

Lake Forest College, Master of Arts in Teaching Program, Lake Forest, IL 60045. Offers elementary education (MAT); K-12 French (MAT); K-12 music (MAT); K-12 Spanish (MAT); K-12 visual art (MAT); secondary biology (MAT); secondary chemistry (MAT); secondary English (MAT); secondary history (MAT); secondary mathematics (MAT). *Degree requirements:* For master's, comprehensive exam, portfolio. *Entrance requirements:* For master's, GRE.

Lebanon Valley College, Program in Science Education, Annville, PA 17003-1400. Offers Integrative STEM Education (Certificate); STEM education (MSE). *Program availability:* Part-time-only, evening/weekend. *Faculty:* 11 part-time/adjunct (6 women). *Students:* 1 full-time (0 women), 14 part-time (9 women). Average age 35. 10 applicants, 70% accepted, 7 enrolled. In 2016, 6 master's awarded. *Degree requirements:* For master's, thesis or capstone project. *Entrance requirements:* For master's, baccalaureate degree, minimum GPA of 3.0, teacher certification, 3 letters of recommendation, transcripts, goal statement. Additional exam requirements/recommendations for international students: Required—TOEFL (minimum score 80 iBT). *Application deadline:* Applications are processed on a rolling basis. Application fee: $0. Electronic applications accepted. *Expenses:* $595 per credit hour. *Financial support:* Scholarships/grants available. Financial award application deadline: 3/1; financial award applicants required to submit FAFSA. *Faculty research:* Teacher quality and student achievement, STEM reform, STEM education. *Unit head:* Carrie Coryer, Director of MSE and STEM-based programs, 717-867-6190, Fax: 717-867-6018, E-mail: coryer@lvc.edu.
Website: http://www.lvc.edu/academics/graduate-studies/master-of-science-in-stem-education/

Lee University, Program in Education, Cleveland, TN 37320-3450. Offers art (MAT); curriculum and instruction (M Ed, Ed S); early childhood (MAT); educational leadership (M Ed, Ed S); elementary education (MAT); English and math (MAT); English and science (MAT); English and social studies (MAT); higher education administration (MS); history (MAT); history and economics (MAT); math and science (MAT); math and social studies (MAT); middle grades (MAT); science and social studies (MASW); secondary education (MAT); Spanish (MAT); special education (M Ed, MAT); TESOL (MAT). *Accreditation:* NCATE. *Program availability:* Part-time. *Faculty:* 13 full-time (6 women), 9 part-time/adjunct (4 women). *Students:* 35 full-time (27 women), 50 part-time (32 women); includes 12 minority (5 Black or African American, non-Hispanic/Latino; 5 Hispanic/Latino; 2 Two or more races, non-Hispanic/Latino), 4 international. Average age 30. 43 applicants, 79% accepted, 28 enrolled. In 2016, 42 master's, 6 other advanced degrees awarded. *Degree requirements:* For master's, variable foreign language requirement, thesis optional, internship. *Entrance requirements:* For master's, MAT or GRE General Test, minimum undergraduate GPA of 2.75, 3 letters of recommendation, interview, writing sample, official transcripts, background check; for Ed S, minimum undergraduate and master's GPA of 2.75, official transcripts for undergraduate and master's degrees. Additional exam requirements/recommendations for international students: Required—TOEFL (minimum score 61 iBT). *Application deadline:* For fall admission, 6/1 priority date for domestic and international students; for spring admission, 11/1 priority date for domestic and international students; for summer admission, 4/1 priority date for domestic and international students. Applications are processed on a rolling basis. Application fee: $25. Electronic applications accepted. *Expenses: Tuition:* Full-time $11,367; part-time $632 per credit hour. *Required fees:* $35 per term. One-time fee: $25. Tuition and fees vary according to program. *Financial support:* In 2016–17, 42 students received support. Career-related internships or fieldwork, Federal Work-Study, institutionally sponsored loans, scholarships/grants, and unspecified assistantships available. Financial award application deadline: 3/1; financial award applicants required to submit FAFSA. *Unit head:* Dr. William Kamm, Director, 423-614-8544, E-mail: wkamm@leeuniversity.edu. *Application contact:* Crystal Keeter, Graduate Education Secretary, 423-614-8544, E-mail: ckeeter@leeuniversity.edu.
Website: http://www.leeuniversity.edu/academics/graduate/education

Lehman College of the City University of New York, School of Education, Department of Middle and High School Education, Program in Mathematics 7–12, Bronx, NY 10468-1589. Offers MS Ed. *Accreditation:* NCATE. *Program availability:* Part-time, evening/weekend. *Degree requirements:* For master's, comprehensive exam or thesis. *Entrance requirements:* For master's, 18 credits in mathematics, 12 credits in education. *Faculty research:* Mathematical problem solving, Piagetian cognitive theory.

Lesley University, Graduate School of Education, Cambridge, MA 02138-2790. Offers arts, community, and education (M Ed); autism studies (Certificate); curriculum and instruction (M Ed, CAGS); early childhood education (M Ed); ecological teaching and learning (MS); educational studies (PhD), including adult learning, educational leadership, individually designed; elementary education (M Ed); emergent technologies for educators (Certificate); ESLArts: language learning through the arts (M Ed); high school education (M Ed); individually designed (M Ed); integrated teaching through the arts (M Ed); literacy for K-8 classroom teachers (M Ed); mathematics education (M Ed); middle school education (M Ed); moderate disabilities (M Ed); online learning (Certificate); reading (CAGS); science in education (M Ed); severe disabilities (M Ed); special needs (CAGS); specialist teacher of reading (M Ed); teacher of visual art (M Ed); technology in education (M Ed, CAGS). *Accreditation:* TEAC. *Program availability:* Part-time, evening/weekend, online learning. *Degree requirements:* For master's, practicum; for doctorate, thesis/dissertation. *Entrance requirements:* For master's, Massachusetts Tests for Educator Licensure (MTEL), transcripts, statement of purpose, recommendations; interview (for special education); for doctorate, GRE General Test, transcripts, statement of purpose, recommendations, interview, master's degree, resume; for other advanced degree, interview, master's degree. Additional exam requirements/recommendations for international students: Required—TOEFL (minimum score 550 paper-based; 80 iBT). Electronic applications accepted. *Faculty research:* Assessment in literacy, mathematics and science; autism spectrum disorders; instructional technology and online learning; multicultural education and English language learners.

Lewis University, College of Education, Program in Secondary Education, Romeoville, IL 60446. Offers biology (MA); chemistry (MA); English (MA); history (MA); math (MA); physics (MA); psychology and social science (MA). *Program availability:* Part-time. *Students:* 12 full-time (7 women), 16 part-time (12 women); includes 6 minority (2 Black or African American, non-Hispanic/Latino; 3 Hispanic/Latino; 1 Two or more races, non-Hispanic/Latino). Average age 27. *Degree requirements:* For master's, departmental qualifying exam. *Entrance requirements:* For master's, writing exam, minimum GPA of 2.75, 2 letters of recommendation, interview. Additional exam requirements/recommendations for international students: Required—TOEFL (minimum score 550 paper-based; 80 iBT). *Application deadline:* For fall admission, 5/1 priority date for international students; for spring admission, 11/15 priority date for international students. Applications are processed on a rolling basis. Application fee: $40. Electronic applications accepted. *Expenses: Tuition:* Full-time $13,860; part-time $770 per credit hour. *Required fees:* $75 per semester. Tuition and fees vary according to degree level and program. *Financial support:* Federal Work-Study, scholarships/grants, and unspecified assistantships available. Financial award application deadline: 5/1; financial award applicants required to submit FAFSA. *Unit head:* Dr. Dorene Huvaere, Program Director, 815-838-0500 Ext. 5885, E-mail: huvaersdo@lewisu.edu. *Application contact:* Linda Campbell, Graduate Admissions Counselor, 815-836-5610, E-mail: campbeld@lewisu.edu.

Liberty University, School of Education, Lynchburg, VA 24515. Offers educational leadership (Ed D); gifted education (Certificate); math specialist (M Ed); middle grades (MAT, Certificate); reading specialist (M Ed); school leadership (Certificate); secondary education (MAT); sport management (MS), including administration, outdoor recreation, sport management, tourism. *Accreditation:* NCATE. *Program availability:* Part-time, online learning. *Students:* 1,910 full-time (1,427 women), 4,420 part-time (3,311 women); includes 1,451 minority (1,182 Black or African American, non-Hispanic/Latino; 33 American Indian or Alaska Native, non-Hispanic/Latino; 44 Asian, non-Hispanic/Latino; 46 Hispanic/Latino; 11 Native Hawaiian or other Pacific Islander, non-Hispanic/Latino; 135 Two or more races, non-Hispanic/Latino), 87 international. Average age 37. 5,120 applicants, 44% accepted, 1193 enrolled. In 2016, 1,378 master's, 151 doctorates, 497 other advanced degrees awarded. *Degree requirements:* For doctorate, comprehensive exam, thesis/dissertation. *Entrance requirements:* For master's, GRE General Test or MAT (if taken in or before 1999), 2 letters of recommendation, minimum undergraduate GPA of 3.0, curriculum vitae; for doctorate and Certificate, GRE General Test or MAT (if taken before 1999), minimum master's GPA of 3.0, 3 years of teaching experience. Additional exam requirements/recommendations for international students: Required—TOEFL (minimum score 600 paper-based; 100 iBT). *Application deadline:* For fall admission, 6/1 for domestic students; for spring admission, 11/1 for domestic students. Applications are processed on a rolling basis. Application fee: $50. Electronic applications accepted. *Expenses:* Contact institution. *Financial support:* Federal Work-Study and tuition waivers (partial) available. *Faculty research:* Self-determination, character education, bibliotherapy, learning styles, distance education. *Unit head:* Dr. Heather Schoffstall, Dean, 434-582-2445, Fax: 434-582-2468, E-mail: awgunter@liberty.edu. *Application contact:* Jay Bridge, Director of Graduate Admissions, 800-424-9595, Fax: 800-628-7977, E-mail: gradadmissions@liberty.edu.
Website: http://www.liberty.edu/academics/education/graduate/

Longwood University, College of Graduate and Professional Studies, College of Education and Human Services, Farmville, VA 23909. Offers education (MS), including algebra and middle school mathematics, counselor education, elementary and middle school mathematics, elementary education, elementary education initial licensure, health and physical education, special education general curriculum, special education initial licensure; reading, literacy and learning (M Ed); school librarianship (M Ed); social work and communication sciences and disorders (MS), including communication sciences and disorders. *Accreditation:* NCATE. *Program availability:* Part-time, evening/weekend. *Degree requirements:* For master's, comprehensive exam (for some programs), thesis optional, professional portfolio, internship, clinical experience, or practicum. *Entrance requirements:* For master's, PRAXIS I (for initial teaching licensure programs); GRE (for some programs), bachelor's degree from regionally-accredited institution, 2 recommendations (3 for some programs), minimum 500-word personal essay, official transcripts, minimum GPA of 2.75, valid teaching license (for some programs). Additional exam requirements/recommendations for international students: Required—TOEFL (minimum score 570 paper-based), IELTS (minimum score 6.5). Electronic applications accepted. *Expenses:* Contact institution.

Loyola Marymount University, College of Science and Engineering, Department of Mathematics, Program in Teaching in Mathematics, Los Angeles, CA 90045-2659. Offers MAT. *Program availability:* Part-time. *Students:* 1 (woman) full-time, 5 part-time (all women); includes 1 minority (Hispanic/Latino). Average age 36. 2 applicants, 100% accepted, 2 enrolled. In 2016, 2 master's awarded. *Entrance requirements:* For master's, letter of recommendation, personal statement. Additional exam requirements/recommendations for international students: Required—TOEFL (minimum score 550 paper-based; 80 iBT). Application fee: $50. Electronic applications accepted. *Financial support:* In 2016–17, 4 students received support. Scholarships/grants and unspecified assistantships available. Financial award application deadline: 6/30; financial award applicants required to submit FAFSA. *Unit head:* Dr. Anne E. Bargagliotti, Graduate Program Director, 310-338-4582, E-mail: abargagl@lmu.edu. *Application contact:* Chake H. Kouyoumjian, Associate Dean of Graduate Studies, 310-338-2721, E-mail: ckouyoum@lmu.edu.
Website: http://cse.lmu.edu/graduateprograms/teachingmathematics/

Manhattanville College, School of Education, Program in Middle Childhood/Adolescence Education (Grades 5-12), Purchase, NY 10577-2132. Offers biology (MAT); biology and special education (MPS); chemistry (MAT); chemistry and special education (MPS); English (MAT); English and special education (MPS); literacy and special education (MPS); literacy specialist (MPS); math and special education (MPS); mathematics (MAT); physics (MAT); social studies (MAT); social studies and special education (MPS); special education generalist (MPS); teaching languages other than English (MAT), including French, Italian, Latin, Spanish. *Program availability:* Part-time, evening/weekend. *Students:* 28 applicants, 86% accepted, 21 enrolled. In 2016, 23 master's awarded. *Degree requirements:* For master's, comprehensive exam (for some programs), thesis (for some programs), student teaching, research seminars, portfolios,

internships, writing assessment. *Entrance requirements:* For master's, GRE or MAT, minimum undergraduate GPA of 3.0, 2 letters of recommendation. Additional exam requirements/recommendations for international students: Required—TOEFL (minimum score 85 iBT); Recommended—IELTS. *Application deadline:* For fall admission, 7/1 priority date for domestic and international students; for spring admission, 11/1 priority date for domestic and international students; for summer admission, 4/1 priority date for domestic and international students. Applications are processed on a rolling basis. Application fee: $75. Electronic applications accepted. *Expenses: Tuition:* Full-time $16,470; part-time $915 per credit. *Required fees:* $60 per semester. Part-time tuition and fees vary according to course load and program. *Financial support:* Teaching assistantships, career-related internships or fieldwork, Federal Work-Study, institutionally sponsored loans, scholarships/grants, and unspecified assistantships available. Financial award applicants required to submit FAFSA. *Unit head:* Victoria Fantozzi, Chairperson, Department of Curriculum and Instruction, 914-323-7138, E-mail: victoria.fantozzi@mville.edu. *Application contact:* Jeanine Pardey-Levine, Director of Graduate Enrollment Management, 914-323-3208, Fax: 914-694-1732, E-mail: edschool@mville.edu.
Website: http://www.mville.edu/programs#/search/19

Marquette University, Graduate School, College of Arts and Sciences, Department of Mathematics, Statistics, and Computer Science, Milwaukee, WI 53201-1881. Offers bioinformatics (MS); computational sciences (MS, PhD); computing (MS); mathematics education (MS). *Program availability:* Part-time, evening/weekend, online learning. *Faculty:* 33 full-time (9 women), 8 part-time/adjunct (1 woman). *Students:* 21 full-time (5 women), 20 part-time (9 women); includes 6 minority (4 Asian, non-Hispanic/Latino; 2 Two or more races, non-Hispanic/Latino), 21 international. Average age 31. 40 applicants, 55% accepted, 10 enrolled. In 2016, 6 master's, 6 doctorates awarded. Terminal master's awarded for partial completion of doctoral program. *Degree requirements:* For master's, thesis (for some programs), essay with oral presentation; for doctorate, comprehensive exam, thesis/dissertation, qualifying examination. *Entrance requirements:* For master's, official transcripts from all current and previous colleges/universities except Marquette, three letters of recommendation; for doctorate, GRE General Test, official transcripts from all current and previous colleges/universities except Marquette, three letters of recommendation. Additional exam requirements/recommendations for international students: Required—TOEFL (minimum score 530 paper-based). *Application deadline:* For fall admission, 1/15 for domestic and international students. Applications are processed on a rolling basis. Application fee: $50. Electronic applications accepted. *Financial support:* Fellowships, research assistantships with full tuition reimbursements, teaching assistantships with full tuition reimbursements, scholarships/grants, health care benefits, tuition waivers (full and partial), and unspecified assistantships available. Support available to part-time students. Financial award application deadline: 2/15. *Faculty research:* Models of physiological systems, mathematical immunology, computational group theory, mathematical logic, computational science. *Total annual research expenditures:* $836,671. *Unit head:* Dr. Rebecca Sanders, Chair, 414-288-7573, Fax: 414-288-1578. *Application contact:* Dr. Gary Krenz.
Website: http://www.marquette.edu/mscs/grad.shtml

McDaniel College, Graduate and Professional Studies, Program in Elementary and Secondary Education, Westminster, MD 21157-4390. Offers elementary education (MS); elementary STEM instructional leader (Postbaccalaureate Certificate); equity and excellence in education (Postbaccalaureate Certificate); learning technology specialist (Postbaccalaureate Certificate); secondary education (MS). *Accreditation:* NCATE. *Program availability:* Part-time, evening/weekend. *Faculty:* 3 full-time (2 women), 27 part-time/adjunct (22 women). *Students:* 8 full-time (5 women), 179 part-time (143 women); includes 60 minority (31 Black or African American, non-Hispanic/Latino; 3 American Indian or Alaska Native, non-Hispanic/Latino; 13 Asian, non-Hispanic/Latino; 11 Hispanic/Latino; 2 Two or more races, non-Hispanic/Latino), 1 international. Average age 36. 79 applicants, 94% accepted. In 2016, 23 master's, 48 other advanced degrees awarded. *Degree requirements:* For master's, comprehensive exam (for some programs), thesis optional. *Entrance requirements:* For master's, PRAXIS, 2 references. Additional exam requirements/recommendations for international students: Required—TOEFL (minimum score 79 iBT), IELTS (minimum score 6). *Application deadline:* For fall admission, 6/1 priority date for domestic students; for spring admission, 11/1 priority date for domestic students; for summer admission, 3/1 priority date for domestic students. Applications are processed on a rolling basis. Application fee: $75. Electronic applications accepted. *Expenses: Tuition:* Full-time $8370; part-time $465 per credit. *Required fees:* $75 per semester. Tuition and fees vary according to course load, program and reciprocity agreements. *Financial support:* Application deadline: 3/1; applicants required to submit FAFSA. *Unit head:* Fax: 410-857-2515, E-mail: gradadms@mcdaniel.edu. *Application contact:* Penny Pfeiffer, Senior Graduate Enrollment Management Specialist, 410-857-2513, Fax: 410-857-2515, E-mail: ppfeiffer@mcdaniel.edu.

Miami University, College of Arts and Science, Department of Mathematics, Oxford, OH 45056. Offers MA, MAT, MS. *Students:* 20 full-time (4 women), 10 part-time (5 women), 4 international. Average age 26. In 2016, 13 master's awarded. *Expenses:* Tuition, state resident: full-time $12,890; part-time $564 per credit hour. Tuition, nonresident: full-time $29,604; part-time $1260 per credit hour. *Required fees:* $638. Part-time tuition and fees vary according to course load and program. *Unit head:* Dr. Patrick Dowling, Department Chair, 513-529-5818, E-mail: dowlinpn@miamioh.edu. *Application contact:* Dr. Doug Ward, Director of Graduate Studies, 513-529-3534, E-mail: wardde@miamioh.edu.
Website: http://www.MiamiOH.edu/mathematics

Michigan State University, The Graduate School, College of Natural Science, Department of Mathematics, East Lansing, MI 48824. Offers applied mathematics (MS, PhD); industrial mathematics (MS); mathematics (MAT, MS, PhD). *Entrance requirements:* Additional exam requirements/recommendations for international students: Required—TOEFL. Electronic applications accepted.

Michigan State University, The Graduate School, College of Natural Science and College of Education, Division of Science and Mathematics Education, East Lansing, MI 48824. Offers biological, physical and general science for teachers (MAT, MS), including biological science (MS), general science (MAT), physical science (MS); mathematics education (MS, PhD).

Middle Tennessee State University, College of Graduate Studies, College of Basic and Applied Sciences, Department of Mathematical Sciences, Murfreesboro, TN 37132. Offers mathematics (MS, MST). *Program availability:* Part-time, evening/weekend, online learning. *Degree requirements:* For master's, comprehensive exam, thesis optional. *Entrance requirements:* For master's, GRE General Test or MAT. Additional exam requirements/recommendations for international students: Required—TOEFL (minimum score 525 paper-based; 71 iBT) or IELTS (minimum score 6). Electronic applications accepted.

Middle Tennessee State University, College of Graduate Studies, Interdisciplinary Program in Mathematics and Science Education, Murfreesboro, TN 37132. Offers PhD. *Program availability:* Part-time, evening/weekend, online learning. *Entrance requirements:* For doctorate, GRE. Additional exam requirements/recommendations for international students: Required—TOEFL (minimum score 525 paper-based; 71 iBT) or IELTS (minimum score 6). Electronic applications accepted.

Millersville University of Pennsylvania, College of Graduate Studies and Adult Learning, College of Education and Human Services, Department of Educational Foundations, Program in Assessment, Curriculum and Teaching - STEM Education Option, Millersville, PA 17551-0302. Offers M Ed. *Program availability:* Part-time, online only, 100% online. *Faculty:* 20 full-time (13 women), 2 part-time/adjunct (both women). *Students:* 14 part-time (8 women). Average age 32. 13 applicants, 100% accepted, 10 enrolled. *Degree requirements:* For master's, thesis/capstone. *Entrance requirements:* For master's, GRE or MAT (if undergraduate cumulative GPA is lower than 2.8), teaching certificate. Additional exam requirements/recommendations for international students: Required—TOEFL (minimum score 600 paper-based), IELTS (minimum score 6). *Application deadline:* Applications are processed on a rolling basis. Application fee: $40. Electronic applications accepted. *Expenses:* $483 per credit resident tuition; $566 per credit non-resident tuition. *Financial support:* Unspecified assistantships available. Financial award application deadline: 3/15; financial award applicants required to submit FAFSA. *Faculty research:* STEM education, instructional technology, on-line teaching. *Unit head:* Dr. Tim E. Mahoney, Coordinator, 717-871-7202, E-mail: tim.mahoney@millersville.edu. *Application contact:* Dr. Victor S. DeSantis, Dean of College of Graduate Studies and Adult Learning/Associate Provost for Civic and Community Engagement, 717-871-7619, Fax: 717-871-7954, E-mail: victor.desantis@millersville.edu.
Website: http://millersville.edu/academics/educ/edfoundations/master-stem.php

Millersville University of Pennsylvania, College of Graduate Studies and Adult Learning, College of Science and Technology, Department of Mathematics, Millersville, PA 17551-0302. Offers M Ed. *Accreditation:* NCATE. *Program availability:* Part-time, evening/weekend. *Faculty:* 20 full-time (7 women). *Students:* 2 full-time (both women), 4 part-time (3 women); includes 1 minority (Black or African American, non-Hispanic/Latino). Average age 36. 5 applicants, 80% accepted, 1 enrolled. In 2016, 6 master's awarded. *Degree requirements:* For master's, field experience (thesis or research project). *Entrance requirements:* For master's, prerequisite math courses, three letters of recommendation, written statement of academic and professional goals. Additional exam requirements/recommendations for international students: Required—TOEFL (minimum score 600 paper-based), IELTS (minimum score 6). *Application deadline:* Applications are processed on a rolling basis. Application fee: $40. Electronic applications accepted. *Expenses:* $483 per credit resident tuition; $725 per credit non-resident tuition. *Financial support:* In 2016–17, 2 students received support. Unspecified assistantships available. Financial award application deadline: 3/15; financial award applicants required to submit FAFSA. *Faculty research:* Training of secondary mathematic teachers, the use of technology in mathematics classes, equity in mathematics, middle school mathematics, questioning techniques of teacher educators. *Unit head:* Dr. Delray J. Schultz, Chair, 717-871-7668, Fax: 717-871-7948, E-mail: delray.schultz@millersville.edu. *Application contact:* Dr. Victor S. DeSantis, Dean of College of Graduate Studies and Adult Learning/Associate Provost for Civic and Community Engagement, 717-871-7619, Fax: 717-871-7954, E-mail: victor.desantis@millersville.edu.
Website: http://www.millersville.edu/math/

Minnesota State University Mankato, College of Graduate Studies and Research, College of Science, Engineering and Technology, Department of Mathematics and Statistics, Program in Mathematics, Mankato, MN 56001. Offers mathematics (MA); mathematics education (MS). *Students:* 20 full-time (3 women), 24 part-time (6 women). *Degree requirements:* For master's, one foreign language, comprehensive exam (for some programs), thesis or alternative. *Entrance requirements:* For master's, GRE General Test, minimum GPA of 3.0 during previous 2 years. Additional exam requirements/recommendations for international students: Required—TOEFL. *Application deadline:* For fall admission, 7/1 priority date for domestic students; for spring admission, 11/1 for domestic students. Applications are processed on a rolling basis. Application fee: $40. Electronic applications accepted. *Financial support:* Research assistantships with partial tuition reimbursements, teaching assistantships with partial tuition reimbursements, and unspecified assistantships available. Financial award application deadline: 3/15; financial award applicants required to submit FAFSA.
Website: http://cset.mnsu.edu/mathstat/program/grad.html

Minot State University, Graduate School, Department of Mathematics and Computer Science, Minot, ND 58707-0002. Offers mathematics (MAT). *Degree requirements:* For master's, thesis or alternative. *Entrance requirements:* For master's, GRE General Test, minimum GPA of 2.75, undergraduate major in mathematics, teaching certificate. Additional exam requirements/recommendations for international students: Required—TOEFL (minimum score 79 iBT), IELTS (minimum score 6). *Faculty research:* Mathematics education.

Mississippi College, Graduate School, School of Education, Department of Teacher Education and Leadership, Clinton, MS 39058. Offers art (M Ed); biological science (M Ed); business education (M Ed); computer science (M Ed); dyslexia therapy (M Ed); educational leadership (M Ed, Ed D, Ed S); elementary education (M Ed, Ed S); English (M Ed); higher education administration (MS); mathematics (M Ed); secondary education (M Ed); social studies (history) (M Ed); teaching arts (M Ed). *Program availability:* Part-time, online learning. *Degree requirements:* For master's, comprehensive exam, thesis optional. *Entrance requirements:* For master's, NTE. Additional exam requirements/recommendations for international students: Recommended—TOEFL, IELTS. Electronic applications accepted.

Missouri State University, Graduate College, College of Natural and Applied Sciences, Department of Mathematics, Springfield, MO 65897. Offers mathematics (MS); natural and applied science (MNAS), including mathematics (MNAS, MS Ed); secondary education (MS Ed), including mathematics (MNAS, MS Ed). *Program availability:* Part-time. *Faculty:* 21 full-time (4 women). *Students:* 5 full-time (1 woman), 20 part-time (10 women), 7 international. Average age 27. 23 applicants, 43% accepted, 3 enrolled. In 2016, 17 master's awarded. *Degree requirements:* For master's, comprehensive exam, thesis or alternative. *Entrance requirements:* For master's, GRE (MS, MNAS), minimum undergraduate GPA of 3.0 (MS, MNAS), 9-12 teacher certification (MS Ed). Additional exam requirements/recommendations for international students: Required—TOEFL (minimum score 550 paper-based; 79 iBT), IELTS (minimum score 6). *Application deadline:* For fall admission, 7/20 priority date for domestic students, 5/1 for international students; for spring admission, 12/20 priority date for domestic students, 9/1 for international students. Applications are processed on a rolling basis. Application fee: $35 ($50 for international students). Electronic applications accepted. *Expenses:* Tuition, state resident: full-time $5830. Tuition, nonresident: full-time $10,708. *Required fees:* $1130. Tuition and fees vary according to class time, course level, course load and program. *Financial support:* In 2016–17, 11 teaching assistantships with full tuition reimbursements (averaging $10,672 per year) were awarded; Federal Work-Study, institutionally sponsored loans, scholarships/grants, and unspecified assistantships also available. Financial award application deadline: 3/31; financial award applicants required to submit FAFSA. *Faculty research:* Harmonic analysis, commutative algebra, number theory, K-theory, probability. *Unit head:* Dr. William Bray, Department Head, 417-836-5112, Fax: 417-836-6966, E-mail: mathematics@missouristate.edu. *Application contact:*

Michael Edwards, Coordinator of Graduate Admissions, 417-836-5330, Fax: 417-836-6200, E-mail: michaeledwards@missouristate.edu.
Website: http://math.missouristate.edu/

Missouri University of Science and Technology, Graduate School, Department of Mathematics and Statistics, Rolla, MO 65409. Offers applied mathematics (MS); mathematics (MST, PhD), including mathematics (PhD), mathematics education (MST), statistics (PhD). Terminal master's awarded for partial completion of doctoral program. *Degree requirements:* For master's, thesis or alternative; for doctorate, one foreign language, thesis/dissertation. *Entrance requirements:* For master's and doctorate, GRE General Test, GRE Subject Test. Additional exam requirements/recommendations for international students: Required—TOEFL (minimum score 550 paper-based). Electronic applications accepted. *Faculty research:* Analysis, differential equations, topology, statistics.

Montana State University, The Graduate School, College of Letters and Science, Department of Mathematical Sciences, Bozeman, MT 59717. Offers mathematics (MS, PhD), including mathematics education option (MS); statistics (MS, PhD). *Program availability:* Part-time, online learning. *Degree requirements:* For master's, comprehensive exam, thesis (for some programs); for doctorate, comprehensive exam, thesis/dissertation. *Entrance requirements:* For master's and doctorate, GRE General Test. Additional exam requirements/recommendations for international students: Required—TOEFL (minimum score 550 paper-based). Electronic applications accepted. *Faculty research:* Applied mathematics, dynamical systems, statistics, mathematics education, mathematical and computational biology.

Montclair State University, The Graduate School, College of Education and Human Services, MAT Program in Teaching, Montclair, NJ 07043-1624. Offers art (MAT); biology (MAT); chemistry (MAT); earth science (MAT); English (MAT); French (MAT); health and physical education (MAT); health education (MAT); mathematics (MAT); music (MAT); physical education (MAT); physical science (MAT); social studies (MAT); Spanish (MAT); teacher of English as a second language (MAT). *Degree requirements:* For master's, comprehensive exam, thesis or alternative. *Entrance requirements:* For master's, interview, 2 letters of recommendation. Additional exam requirements/recommendations for international students: Required—TOEFL (minimum score 83 iBT), IELTS (minimum score 6.5). Electronic applications accepted. *Expenses:* Tuition, state resident: part-time $553 per credit. Tuition, nonresident: part-time $854 per credit. *Required fees:* $91 per credit. Tuition and fees vary according to program.

Montclair State University, The Graduate School, College of Science and Mathematics, Program in Mathematics, Montclair, NJ 07043-1624. Offers mathematics education (MS); pure and applied mathematics (MS). *Program availability:* Part-time, evening/weekend. *Degree requirements:* For master's, comprehensive exam. *Entrance requirements:* For master's, GRE General Test, 2 letters of recommendation, essay. Additional exam requirements/recommendations for international students: Required—TOEFL (minimum score 83 iBT), IELTS (minimum score 6.5). Electronic applications accepted. *Expenses:* Tuition, state resident: part-time $553 per credit. Tuition, nonresident: part-time $854 per credit. *Required fees:* $91 per credit. Tuition and fees vary according to program. *Faculty research:* Computation, applied analysis.

Montclair State University, The Graduate School, College of Science and Mathematics, Program in Mathematics Education, Montclair, NJ 07043-1624. Offers Ed D. *Degree requirements:* For doctorate, thesis/dissertation. *Entrance requirements:* For doctorate, GRE General Test, 2 letters of recommendation, essay. Additional exam requirements/recommendations for international students: Required—TOEFL (minimum score 83 iBT), IELTS (minimum score 6.5). Electronic applications accepted. *Expenses:* Tuition, state resident: part-time $553 per credit. Tuition, nonresident: part-time $854 per credit. *Required fees:* $91 per credit. Tuition and fees vary according to program. *Faculty research:* Teacher development, student thinking.

Montclair State University, The Graduate School, College of Science and Mathematics, Program in Teaching Middle Grades Mathematics, Montclair, NJ 07043-1624. Offers MA. *Program availability:* Part-time, evening/weekend. *Degree requirements:* For master's, comprehensive exam, thesis or alternative. *Entrance requirements:* For master's, GRE General Test, 2 letters of recommendation, essay. Additional exam requirements/recommendations for international students: Required—TOEFL (minimum score 83 iBT), IELTS (minimum score 6.5). Electronic applications accepted. *Expenses:* Tuition, state resident: part-time $553 per credit. Tuition, nonresident: part-time $854 per credit. *Required fees:* $91 per credit. Tuition and fees vary according to program. *Faculty research:* Teacher knowledge, curriculum.

Montclair State University, The Graduate School, College of Science and Mathematics, Teaching Middle Grades Mathematics Certificate Program, Montclair, NJ 07043-1624. Offers Certificate. *Expenses:* Tuition, state resident: part-time $553 per credit. Tuition, nonresident: part-time $854 per credit. *Required fees:* $91 per credit. Tuition and fees vary according to program.

Morehead State University, Graduate Programs, College of Education, Department of Middle Grades and Secondary Education, Morehead, KY 40351. Offers business and marketing education (MAT); English/language arts 5-9 (MAT); French (MAT); health P-12 (MAT); mathematics 5-9 (MAT); physical education P-12 (MAT); science 5-9 (MAT); secondary biology (MAT); secondary chemistry (MAT); secondary earth science (MAT); secondary English (MAT); secondary math (MAT); secondary physics (MAT); secondary social studies (MAT); social studies 5-9 (MAT); Spanish (MAT). *Program availability:* Part-time, evening/weekend. *Degree requirements:* For master's, portfolio. *Entrance requirements:* For master's, GRE or PRAXIS II content exam, minimum overall undergraduate GPA of 2.5. Additional exam requirements/recommendations for international students: Required—TOEFL (minimum score 500 paper-based). Electronic applications accepted.

Morgan State University, School of Graduate Studies, School of Education and Urban Studies, Department of Advanced Studies, Leadership and Policy, Program in Mathematics Education, Baltimore, MD 21251. Offers MS, Ed D. *Degree requirements:* For doctorate, comprehensive exam, thesis/dissertation. *Entrance requirements:* For doctorate, GRE General Test or MAT. Additional exam requirements/recommendations for international students: Required—TOEFL (minimum score 550 paper-based).

Mount Holyoke College, Professional and Graduate Education (PaGE), South Hadley, MA 01075. Offers mathematics teaching (MAMT); teacher leadership (MATL); teaching (MAT). *Program availability:* Part-time, 100% online, blended/hybrid learning. *Faculty:* 4 full-time (3 women), 12 part-time/adjunct (10 women). *Students:* 23 full-time (21 women), 84 part-time (76 women); includes 11 minority (4 Black or African American, non-Hispanic/Latino; 2 Asian, non-Hispanic/Latino; 4 Hispanic/Latino; 1 Two or more races, non-Hispanic/Latino), 7 international. Average age 37. In 2016, 30 master's awarded. *Degree requirements:* For master's, practicum (for MAT); capstone course (for MATL); capstone portfolio (for MAMT). *Entrance requirements:* For master's, Massachusetts Tests for Education Licensure (MTEL), bachelor's degree; subject area knowledge in desired teaching discipline; personal statement; essay; official transcripts; two letters of recommendation; history of effective classroom teaching (for MATL). *Application deadline:* Applications are processed on a rolling basis. Application fee: $0. Electronic applications accepted. *Expenses: Tuition:* Full-time $24,500; part-time $770 per credit hour. *Required fees:* $117. Tuition and fees vary according to course load and program. *Financial support:* Scholarships/grants available. Financial award applicants required to submit FAFSA. *Faculty research:* Teacher leadership, state education policy, novice teacher development, global immersion experiences, mathematics education. *Unit head:* Dr. Tiffany Espinosa, Executive Director of Professional and Graduate Education, 413-538-3478, Fax: 413-538-3098.
Website: https://www.mtholyoke.edu/professional-graduate

National Louis University, National College of Education, Chicago, IL 60603. Offers administration and supervision (M Ed, Ed D, CAS, Ed S); curriculum and instruction (M Ed, MS Ed, CAS); early childhood administration (M Ed, CAS); early childhood education (M Ed, MAT, MS Ed, CAS); education (Ed D); educational psychology/human learning and development (M Ed, MS Ed, CAS, Ed S); elementary education (MAT); interdisciplinary curriculum and instruction (M Ed); mathematics education (M Ed, MS Ed, CAS); middle grades education (MAT); reading and language (M Ed, MS Ed, CAS); school psychology (M Ed, Ed S); science education (M Ed, MS Ed, CAS); secondary education (MAT); special education (M Ed, MAT, CAS); technology in education (M Ed, CAS). *Accreditation:* NCATE. *Program availability:* Part-time, evening/weekend. *Degree requirements:* For doctorate, comprehensive exam, thesis/dissertation. *Entrance requirements:* For master's, MAT or GRE, minimum GPA of 3.0; for doctorate, GRE General Test, minimum GPA of 3.25, interview, resume, writing sample, 4 recommendations. Additional exam requirements/recommendations for international students: Required—TOEFL (minimum score 550 paper-based; 79 iBT).

New Jersey City University, William J. Maxwell College of Arts and Sciences, Department of Mathematics, Jersey City, NJ 07305-1597. Offers mathematics education (MA). *Accreditation:* TEAC. *Program availability:* Part-time, evening/weekend. *Degree requirements:* For master's, comprehensive exam, thesis optional. *Entrance requirements:* Additional exam requirements/recommendations for international students: Required—TOEFL (minimum score 79 iBT).

New York Institute of Technology, School of Interdisciplinary Studies and Education, Department of Instructional Technology, Old Westbury, NY 11568-8000. Offers emerging technologies for trainers (Advanced Certificate); instructional design for global e-learning (Advanced Certificate); instructional technology (MS); school leadership and technology (Advanced Diploma); STEM education (Advanced Certificate). *Program availability:* Part-time, evening/weekend, 100% online, blended/hybrid learning. *Faculty:* 6 full-time (3 women), 6 part-time/adjunct (4 women). *Students:* 15 full-time (10 women), 192 part-time (132 women); includes 44 minority (15 Black or African American, non-Hispanic/Latino; 8 Asian, non-Hispanic/Latino; 17 Hispanic/Latino; 4 Two or more races, non-Hispanic/Latino), 1 international. Average age 33. 127 applicants, 82% accepted, 79 enrolled. In 2016, 47 master's, 13 other advanced degrees awarded. *Entrance requirements:* For master's, GRE (minimum combined score of 300) or MAT (minimum score of 400) within the last five years, bachelor's degree; minimum undergraduate GPA of 3.0; demonstrated proficiency in basic uses of instructional technologies; for other advanced degree, GRE or MAT within last 5 years, minimum undergraduate GPA of 3.0; demonstrated proficiency in basic uses of instructional technologies; master's degree, minimum 3 years' successful teaching experience, and permanent or provisional NY State teaching certification (for Advanced Diploma). Additional exam requirements/recommendations for international students: Required—TOEFL (minimum score 79 iBT), IELTS (minimum score 6). *Application deadline:* Applications are processed on a rolling basis. Application fee: $50. Electronic applications accepted. *Expenses:* $1,215 per credit. *Financial support:* Research assistantships with partial tuition reimbursements, career-related internships or fieldwork, scholarships/grants, health care benefits, tuition waivers (full and partial), and unspecified assistantships available. Support available to part-time students. Financial award application deadline: 3/1; financial award applicants required to submit FAFSA. *Faculty research:* Integration of information and communication technologies (ICTs) and media literacy education into learning environments; urban K-12 teachers' effective use of technology to enhance student achievement; instructional design and transdisciplinary curriculum studies for online instruction; STEM + computing partnerships for K-12 teachers; experiential, collaborative, and performance-based approaches to pedagogy and technology integration in the K-12 classroom. *Unit head:* Dr. Melda Yildiz, Department Chair, 516-686-1053, Fax: 516-686-7655, E-mail: myildiz@nyit.edu. *Application contact:* Alice Dolitsky, Director, Graduate Admissions, 516-686-7520, Fax: 516-686-1116, E-mail: nyitgrad@nyit.edu.
Website: http://www.nyit.edu/interdisciplinary/department_instructional_technology

New York University, Steinhardt School of Culture, Education, and Human Development, Department of Teaching and Learning, Program in Mathematics Education, New York, NY 10003. Offers MA. *Accreditation:* TEAC. *Program availability:* Part-time, evening/weekend. *Degree requirements:* For master's, thesis (for some programs). *Entrance requirements:* Additional exam requirements/recommendations for international students: Required—TOEFL (minimum score 100 iBT). Electronic applications accepted. *Faculty research:* Race, gender and mathematics learning; developing mathematical concepts through activity; innovative secondary school mathematics materials.

North Carolina Central University, College of Science and Technology, Department of Mathematics and Computer Science, Durham, NC 27707-3129. Offers applied mathematics (MS); mathematics education (MS); pure mathematics (MS). *Program availability:* Part-time, evening/weekend. *Degree requirements:* For master's, one foreign language, comprehensive exam, thesis. *Entrance requirements:* For master's, minimum GPA of 3.0 in major, 2.5 overall. Additional exam requirements/recommendations for international students: Required—TOEFL.

North Carolina State University, Graduate School, College of Education, Department of Mathematics, Science, and Technology Education, Program in Mathematics Education, Raleigh, NC 27695. Offers M Ed, MS, PhD. *Accreditation:* NCATE. *Program availability:* Part-time. *Degree requirements:* For master's, thesis (for some programs), oral exam; for doctorate, one foreign language, thesis/dissertation, oral and written exams. *Entrance requirements:* For master's, GRE General Test or MAT, minimum GPA of 3.0; for doctorate, GRE General Test, minimum GPA of 3.0, interview. Electronic applications accepted. *Faculty research:* Teacher education using technology, curriculum development, scientific visualization, problem solving.

North Dakota State University, College of Graduate and Interdisciplinary Studies, College of Engineering, Doctoral Program in Engineering, Fargo, ND 58102. Offers environmental and conservation science (PhD); materials and nanotechnology (PhD); natural resource management (PhD); science, technology, engineering, mathematics education (STEM) (PhD); transportation and logistics (PhD). *Degree requirements:* For doctorate, comprehensive exam, thesis/dissertation. *Entrance requirements:* For doctorate, bachelor's degree in engineering, minimum GPA of 3.0. Additional exam requirements/recommendations for international students: Required—TOEFL. Electronic applications accepted. *Expenses:* Contact institution.

North Dakota State University, College of Graduate and Interdisciplinary Studies, College of Human Development and Education, School of Education, Fargo, ND 58102. Offers agricultural education (M Ed, MS), including agricultural education; counselor education (M Ed, MS, PhD), including clinical mental health counseling (M Ed, MS), counselor education and supervision (PhD), school counseling (M Ed, MS); curriculum and instruction (M Ed, MS); education (PhD); educational leadership (M Ed, MS, Ed S); family and consumer sciences education (M Ed, MS); history education (M Ed, MS); institutional analysis (Ed D); mathematics education (M Ed, MS); music education (M Ed, MS); occupational and adult education (Ed D); science education (M Ed, MS). *Accreditation:* NCATE. *Program availability:* Part-time, evening/weekend, online learning. *Degree requirements:* For master's, comprehensive exam; for doctorate, thesis/dissertation; for Ed S, thesis. *Entrance requirements:* For degree, GRE General Test, master's degree, minimum GPA of 3.25. Additional exam requirements/ recommendations for international students: Required—TOEFL.

North Dakota State University, College of Graduate and Interdisciplinary Studies, Program in STEM Education, Fargo, ND 58102. Offers PhD. Electronic applications accepted.

Northeastern Illinois University, College of Graduate Studies and Research, College of Arts and Sciences, Program in Pedagogical Content Knowledge for Teaching Elementary and Middle School Mathematics, Chicago, IL 60625-4699. Offers MA. *Degree requirements:* For master's, portfolio, exit exam. *Entrance requirements:* For master's, current Illinois teaching certificate for teaching elementary or middle school; 6 or more credit hours of college mathematics content courses; essay.

Northeastern Illinois University, College of Graduate Studies and Research, College of Arts and Sciences, Program in Secondary Education Mathematics, Chicago, IL 60625-4699. Offers MS.

Northeastern State University, College of Science and Health Professions, Program in Mathematics Education, Tahlequah, OK 74464-2399. Offers M Ed. *Faculty:* 3 full-time (1 woman), 1 (woman) part-time/adjunct. *Students:* 7 full-time (all women), 24 part-time (22 women); includes 9 minority (3 American Indian or Alaska Native, non-Hispanic/Latino; 1 Asian, non-Hispanic/Latino; 1 Hispanic/Latino; 4 Two or more races, non-Hispanic/ Latino). Average age 36. In 2016, 8 master's awarded. *Entrance requirements:* For master's, GRE or MAT, minimum GPA of 2.5. Additional exam requirements/ recommendations for international students: Required—TOEFL. *Application deadline:* For fall admission, 8/19 for domestic students; for spring admission, 1/7 for domestic students. Applications are processed on a rolling basis. Application fee: $25. Electronic applications accepted. *Expenses:* Tuition, state resident: full-time $2816; part-time $216.60 per credit hour. Tuition, nonresident: full-time $6365; part-time $489.60 per credit hour. *Required fees:* $37.40 per credit hour. *Unit head:* Dr. Darryl Linde, Department Chair, 918-444-3809, E-mail: linded@nsuok.edu. *Application contact:* Josh McCollum, Graduate Coordinator, 918-444-2093, E-mail: mccolluj@nsuok.edu.
Website: http://academics.nsuok.edu/mathematics/DegreesMajors/Graduate/ MEdMathematicsEducation.aspx

Northern Arizona University, Graduate College, College of Engineering, Forestry, and Natural Sciences, Department of Mathematics and Statistics, Flagstaff, AZ 86011. Offers applied statistics (Certificate); mathematics (MS); mathematics education (MS); statistics (MS). *Program availability:* Part-time. *Degree requirements:* For master's, comprehensive exam (for some programs), thesis (for some programs). *Entrance requirements:* For master's, minimum GPA of 3.0. Additional exam requirements/ recommendations for international students: Required—TOEFL (minimum score 550 paper-based; 80 iBT), IELTS (minimum score 7). Electronic applications accepted. *Expenses:* Tuition, state resident: full-time $8971; part-time $444 per credit hour. Tuition, nonresident: full-time $20,958; part-time $1164 per credit hour. *Required fees:* $1018; $644 per credit hour. Tuition and fees vary according to course load, campus/ location and program. *Faculty research:* Topology, statistics, groups, ring theory, number theory.

Northwest Missouri State University, Graduate School, College of Arts and Sciences, Maryville, MO 64468-6001. Offers biology (MS); elementary mathematics specialist (MS Ed); English (MA); English education (MS Ed); English pedagogy (MA); geographic information science (MS, Certificate); history (MS Ed); mathematics (MS); mathematics education (MS Ed); teaching: science (MS Ed). *Program availability:* Part-time. *Students:* 12 full-time (8 women), 69 part-time (31 women). *Degree requirements:* For master's, comprehensive exam. *Entrance requirements:* For master's, GRE General Test, writing sample. Additional exam requirements/recommendations for international students: Required—TOEFL (minimum score 550 paper-based). *Application deadline:* For fall admission, 7/1 for domestic and international students; for spring admission, 11/ 15 for domestic and international students. Applications are processed on a rolling basis. Application fee: $0 ($50 for international students). Electronic applications accepted. *Expenses:* Tuition, state resident: full-time $3447; part-time $383 per credit hour. Tuition, nonresident: full-time $5724; part-time $636 per credit hour. *Required fees:* $130 per credit hour. *Financial support:* Research assistantships with full tuition reimbursements, teaching assistantships with full tuition reimbursements, and administrative assistantships, tutorial assistantships available. Financial award application deadline: 4/1; financial award applicants required to submit FAFSA. *Unit head:* Dr. Michael Steiner, Dean, 660-562-1197.
Website: http://www.nwmissouri.edu/academics/arts/

Northwest Missouri State University, Graduate School, School of Education, Maryville, MO 64468-6001. Offers early childhood education (MS Ed); education leadership (MS Ed), including elementary, K-12, secondary; educational leadership (Ed S), including elementary school principalship, secondary school principalship, superintendency; educational leadership and policy analysis (Ed D); elementary education (MS Ed); elementary mathematics (MS Ed); higher education leadership (MS); middle school education (MS Ed); reading (MS Ed); special education (MS Ed); teacher leadership (MS Ed); teaching English language learners (MS Ed). *Accreditation:* NCATE. *Program availability:* Part-time. *Students:* 15 full-time (11 women), 150 part-time (103 women). In 2016, 46 master's awarded. *Degree requirements:* For master's, comprehensive exam; for Ed S, comprehensive exam, thesis. *Entrance requirements:* For master's, GRE General Test, writing sample; for Ed S, minimum graduate GPA of 3.25. Additional exam requirements/recommendations for international students: Required—TOEFL (minimum score 550 paper-based). *Application deadline:* For fall admission, 7/1 for domestic and international students; for spring admission, 11/15 for domestic and international students. Applications are processed on a rolling basis. Application fee: $0 ($50 for international students). Electronic applications accepted. *Expenses:* Tuition, state resident: full-time $3447; part-time $383 per credit hour. Tuition, nonresident: full-time $5724; part-time $636 per credit hour. *Required fees:* $130 per credit hour. *Financial support:* Research assistantships with full tuition reimbursements, teaching assistantships with full tuition reimbursements, and unspecified assistantships available. Financial award application deadline: 4/1; financial award applicants required to submit FAFSA. *Faculty research:* Great books of educational administration. *Unit head:* Dr. Tim Wall, Dean, 660-562-1179, E-mail: timwall@nwmissouri.edu.
Website: http://www.nwmissouri.edu/academics/ed/

The Ohio State University, Graduate School, College of Arts and Sciences, Division of Natural and Mathematical Sciences, Department of Mathematics, Columbus, OH 43210. Offers actuarial and quantitative risk management (MAQRM); computational sciences (MMS); mathematical biosciences (MMS); mathematics (PhD); mathematics for educators (MMS). *Faculty:* 63. *Students:* 142 full-time (24 women), 1 (woman) part-time; includes 17 minority (7 Asian, non-Hispanic/Latino; 4 Hispanic/Latino; 6 Two or more races, non-Hispanic/Latino), 64 international. Average age 25. In 2016, 32 master's, 12 doctorates awarded. *Degree requirements:* For master's, thesis optional; for doctorate, one foreign language, thesis/dissertation. *Entrance requirements:* For master's, GRE General Test; for doctorate, GRE General Test (recommended), GRE Subject Test (mathematics). Additional exam requirements/recommendations for international students: Required—TOEFL (minimum score 550 paper-based; 79 iBT), Michigan English Language Assessment Battery (minimum score 82); Recommended—IELTS (minimum score 7). *Application deadline:* For fall admission, 12/15 priority date for domestic and international students. Applications are processed on a rolling basis. Application fee: $60 ($70 for international students). Electronic applications accepted. *Financial support:* Fellowships with tuition reimbursements, research assistantships with tuition reimbursements, teaching assistantships with tuition reimbursements, Federal Work-Study, institutionally sponsored loans, and unspecified assistantships available. Support available to part-time students. *Unit head:* Luis Casian, Chair, 614-292-7173, E-mail: casian.1@osu.edu. *Application contact:* Erin Anthony, Graduate Studies Coordinator, 614-292-6274, Fax: 614-292-1479, E-mail: grad-info@ math.osu.edu.
Website: http://www.math.osu.edu/

Oklahoma State University, College of Arts and Sciences, Department of Mathematics, Stillwater, OK 74078. Offers applied mathematics (MS, PhD); mathematics education (MS, PhD); pure mathematics (MS, PhD). *Faculty:* 44 full-time (11 women), 5 part-time/adjunct (4 women). *Students:* 6 full-time (2 women), 36 part-time (11 women); includes 3 minority (1 Black or African American, non-Hispanic/Latino; 2 Two or more races, non-Hispanic/Latino), 15 international. Average age 29. 65 applicants, 23% accepted, 14 enrolled. In 2016, 7 master's, 3 doctorates awarded. *Degree requirements:* For master's, thesis, creative component, or report; for doctorate, comprehensive exam, thesis/dissertation. *Entrance requirements:* For master's and doctorate, GRE (recommended). Additional exam requirements/recommendations for international students: Required—TOEFL (minimum score 550 paper-based; 79 iBT). *Application deadline:* For fall admission, 3/1 for domestic and international students; for spring admission, 10/15 for domestic students, 10/15 priority date for international students. Applications are processed on a rolling basis. Application fee: $40 ($75 for international students). Electronic applications accepted. *Expenses:* Tuition, state resident: full-time $3775; part-time $209.70 per credit hour. Tuition, nonresident: full-time $14,851; part-time $825.05 per credit hour. *Required fees:* $2027; $112.60 per credit hour. Tuition and fees vary according to campus/location. *Financial support:* In 2016–17, 2 research assistantships (averaging $23,112 per year), 43 teaching assistantships (averaging $18,080 per year) were awarded; health care benefits and tuition waivers (partial) also available. Financial award application deadline: 3/1; financial award applicants required to submit FAFSA. *Unit head:* Dr. Willam Jaco, Department Head, 405-744-5688, Fax: 405-744-8225, E-mail: william.jaco@ okstate.edu.
Website: http://math.okstate.edu/

Oregon State University, College of Education, Program in Education, Corvallis, OR 97331. Offers advanced science and mathematics education (Ed M); agricultural education (PhD); education (Ed D); free-choice learning (Ed M); language equity and educational policy (PhD); mathematics education (MS); pre-K-12 English to speakers of other languages (ESOL) (Ed M); science education (MS); science/mathematics education (PhD); social justice in education (Ed M). *Program availability:* Part-time, 100% online, blended/hybrid learning. *Faculty:* 9 full-time (8 women), 6 part-time/adjunct (2 women). *Students:* 14 full-time (8 women), 76 part-time (53 women); includes 25 minority (6 Black or African American, non-Hispanic/Latino; 2 American Indian or Alaska Native, non-Hispanic/Latino; 5 Asian, non-Hispanic/Latino; 10 Hispanic/Latino; 2 Two or more races, non-Hispanic/Latino), 3 international. Average age 38. 72 applicants, 69% accepted, 40 enrolled. In 2016, 14 master's, 21 doctorates awarded. Terminal master's awarded for partial completion of doctoral program. *Degree requirements:* For master's, variable foreign language requirement, thesis (for some programs); for doctorate, variable foreign language requirement, thesis/dissertation. *Entrance requirements:* Additional exam requirements/recommendations for international students: Required—TOEFL (minimum score 575 paper-based). Application fee: $75 ($85 for international students). *Expenses:* Tuition, state resident: full-time $12,150; part-time $450 per credit. Tuition, nonresident: full-time $21,789; part-time $807 per credit. *Required fees:* $1651; $1507 per credit. One-time fee: $350. Tuition and fees vary according to course load, campus/location and program. *Financial support:* Fellowships, research assistantships, teaching assistantships, career-related internships or fieldwork, Federal Work-Study, and institutionally sponsored loans available. Support available to part-time students. *Faculty research:* School administration, educational foundations, research methodology, education policy development, higher education administration. *Unit head:* Dr. Larry Flick, Dean. *Application contact:* E-mail: askcoed@oregonstate.edu.

Oregon State University, College of Science, Program in Mathematics, Corvallis, OR 97331. Offers actuarial science (MA, MS, PhD); algebra (MA, MS, PhD); analysis (MA, MS, PhD); applied mathematics (MA, MS, PhD); computational mathematics (MA, MS, PhD); differential equations (MA, MS, PhD); financial mathematics (MA, MS, PhD); geometry (MA, MS, PhD); mathematics education (MA). *Faculty:* 25 full-time (8 women), 6 part-time/adjunct (2 women). *Students:* 65 full-time (18 women), 4 part-time (1 woman); includes 13 minority (1 Black or African American, non-Hispanic/Latino; 2 Asian, non-Hispanic/Latino; 6 Hispanic/Latino; 4 Two or more races, non-Hispanic/ Latino), 16 international. Average age 28. 140 applicants, 30% accepted, 16 enrolled. In 2016, 16 master's, 6 doctorates awarded. Terminal master's awarded for partial completion of doctoral program. *Degree requirements:* For master's, thesis or alternative; for doctorate, thesis/dissertation, qualifying exams. *Entrance requirements:* For master's and doctorate, GRE. Additional exam requirements/recommendations for international students: Required—TOEFL (minimum score 100 iBT). *Application deadline:* For fall admission, 1/15 for domestic and international students. Application fee: $75 ($85 for international students). Electronic applications accepted. *Expenses:* Tuition, state resident: full-time $12,150; part-time $450 per credit. Tuition, nonresident: full-time $21,789; part-time $807 per credit. *Required fees:* $1651; $1507 per credit. One-time fee: $350. Tuition and fees vary according to course load, campus/location and program. *Financial support:* Research assistantships, teaching assistantships, Federal Work-Study, and institutionally sponsored loans available. Support available to part-time students. Financial award application deadline: 1/15. *Unit head:* Dr. Enrique A. Thomann, Professor and Department Head. *Application contact:* Mathematics Advisor, 541-737-4686, E-mail: gradinfo@math.oregonstate.edu.
Website: http://www.math.oregonstate.edu/

Plymouth State University, College of Graduate Studies, Graduate Studies in Education, Program in Mathematics Education, Plymouth, NH 03264-1595. Offers M Ed. *Program availability:* Part-time, evening/weekend. *Degree requirements:* For master's, comprehensive exam, thesis optional, internship or practicum. *Entrance requirements:* For master's, MAT, minimum GPA of 3.0.

Portland State University, Graduate Studies, College of Liberal Arts and Sciences, Department of Mathematics and Statistics, Portland, OR 97207-0751. Offers mathematical sciences (PhD); mathematics education (PhD); statistics (MS); MA/MS.

Faculty: 35 full-time (10 women), 18 part-time/adjunct (7 women). *Students:* 79 full-time (28 women), 55 part-time (21 women); includes 25 minority (2 Black or African American, non-Hispanic/Latino; 4 American Indian or Alaska Native, non-Hispanic/Latino; 8 Asian, non-Hispanic/Latino; 6 Hispanic/Latino; 5 Two or more races, non-Hispanic/Latino), 14 international. Average age 33. 79 applicants, 65% accepted, 39 enrolled. In 2016, 18 master's, 7 doctorates awarded. *Degree requirements:* For master's, thesis or alternative, exams; for doctorate, 2 foreign languages, thesis/dissertation, exams. *Entrance requirements:* For master's, GRE General Test, GRE Subject Test, minimum GPA of 3.0 in upper-division course work or 2.75 overall; for doctorate, GRE General Test. Additional exam requirements/recommendations for international students: Required—TOEFL (minimum score 550 paper-based; 80 iBT). *Application deadline:* For fall admission, 4/1 for domestic students, 3/1 for international students; for winter admission, 9/1 for domestic students, 7/1 for international students; for spring admission, 11/1 for domestic and international students; for summer admission, 2/1 for domestic and international students. Applications are processed on a rolling basis. Application fee: $65. *Expenses:* Contact institution. *Financial support:* In 2016–17, 13 research assistantships with full tuition reimbursements (averaging $15,353 per year), 43 teaching assistantships with full tuition reimbursements (averaging $11,301 per year) were awarded; Federal Work-Study, scholarships/grants, tuition waivers (partial), and unspecified assistantships also available. Support available to part-time students. Financial award application deadline: 3/1; financial award applicants required to submit FAFSA. *Faculty research:* Algebra, topology, statistical distribution theory, control theory, statistical robustness. *Total annual research expenditures:* $518,084. *Unit head:* Dr. John Caughman, Chair, 503-725-3634, E-mail: caughman@pdx.edu. *Application contact:* Kathie Leck, Graduate Program Administrator, 503-725-3604, Fax: 503-725-8244, E-mail: leck@pdx.edu.
Website: https://www.pdx.edu/math/

Providence College, Program in Teaching Mathematics, Providence, RI 02918. Offers MA. *Program availability:* Part-time, evening/weekend. *Faculty:* 6 full-time (4 women), 33 part-time/adjunct (21 women). *Students:* 9 part-time (5 women); includes 1 minority (Black or African American, non-Hispanic/Latino). Average age 33. 1 applicant, 100% accepted, 1 enrolled. In 2016, 13 master's awarded. *Entrance requirements:* Additional exam requirements/recommendations for international students: Required—TOEFL (minimum score 577 paper-based; 90 iBT). *Application deadline:* For fall admission, 7/15 priority date for domestic and international students; for spring admission, 11/15 priority date for domestic and international students; for summer admission, 3/15 priority date for domestic students, 3/15 for international students. Application fee: $55. *Expenses:* Contact institution. *Financial support:* Career-related internships or fieldwork, institutionally sponsored loans, and unspecified assistantships available. Support available to part-time students. Financial award application deadline: 8/1; financial award applicants required to submit FAFSA.
Website: http://www.providence.edu/academics/Pages/master-teaching-math.aspx

Purdue University, Graduate School, College of Education, Department of Curriculum and Instruction, West Lafayette, IN 47907. Offers agricultural and extension education (MS, MS Ed, PhD, Ed S); art education (PhD); career and technical education (MS Ed, PhD, Ed S); curriculum studies (MS Ed, PhD, Ed S); educational technology (MS Ed, PhD, Ed S); elementary education (MS Ed); family and consumer sciences education (MS Ed, PhD, Ed S); foreign language education (MS Ed, PhD, Ed S); industrial technology (PhD, Ed S); language arts (MS Ed, PhD, Ed S); literacy (MS Ed, PhD, Ed S); mathematics education (MS, MS Ed, PhD, Ed S); science education (MS, MS Ed, PhD, Ed S); social studies education (MS Ed, PhD, Ed S). *Accreditation:* NCATE. *Program availability:* Part-time, evening/weekend. *Faculty:* 37 full-time (27 women), 1 (woman) part-time/adjunct. *Students:* 78 full-time (50 women), 286 part-time (195 women); includes 68 minority (25 Black or African American, non-Hispanic/Latino; 3 American Indian or Alaska Native, non-Hispanic/Latino; 10 Asian, non-Hispanic/Latino; 22 Hispanic/Latino; 1 Native Hawaiian or other Pacific Islander, non-Hispanic/Latino; 7 Two or more races, non-Hispanic/Latino), 44 international. Average age 36. 150 applicants, 79% accepted, 73 enrolled. In 2016, 107 master's, 20 doctorates, 2 other advanced degrees awarded. *Degree requirements:* For master's, thesis optional; for doctorate, thesis/dissertation, oral and written exams; for Ed S, oral presentation, project. *Entrance requirements:* For master's, GRE General Test (if undergraduate GPA is below 3.0), minimum undergraduate GPA of 3.0 or equivalent; for doctorate, GRE General Test (minimum combined verbal and quantitative score of 1000, 300 for new scoring), minimum undergraduate GPA of 3.0 or equivalent; master's degree with minimum GPA of 3.0 or equivalent; for Ed S, GRE General Test (minimum combined verbal and quantitative score of 1000, 300 for new scoring), minimum undergraduate GPA of 3.0 or equivalent; master's degree. Additional exam requirements/recommendations for international students: Required—TOEFL (minimum score 550 paper-based; 77 iBT). *Application deadline:* For fall admission, 12/15 for domestic students, 3/1 for international students; for spring admission, 9/15 for domestic students, 8/1 for international students. Application fee: $60 ($75 for international students). Electronic applications accepted. *Financial support:* Fellowships with full tuition reimbursements, research assistantships with full tuition reimbursements, teaching assistantships with full tuition reimbursements, career-related internships or fieldwork, and tuition waivers (full) available. Support available to part-time students. Financial award application deadline: 3/1; financial award applicants required to submit FAFSA. *Faculty research:* Literacy acquisition and development, teacher beliefs and knowledge, recruitment and retention of underrepresented students, economic education, literacy discourse. *Unit head:* Janet M. Alsup, Head, 765-494-9667, E-mail: alsupj@purdue.edu. *Application contact:* Heather Brinkman, Graduate Contact, 765-494-2345, E-mail: hbrinkma@purdue.edu.
Website: http://www.edci.purdue.edu/

Purdue University Northwest, Graduate Studies Office, School of Engineering, Mathematics, and Science, Department of Mathematics, Computer Science, and Statistics, Hammond, IN 46323-2094. Offers computer science (MS); mathematics (MAT, MS). *Program availability:* Part-time. *Entrance requirements:* Additional exam requirements/recommendations for international students: Required—TOEFL. *Faculty research:* Topology, analysis, algebra, mathematics education.

Queens College of the City University of New York, Division of Education, Department of Secondary Education and Youth Services, Queens, NY 11367-1597. Offers adolescent biology (MAT); art (MS Ed); biology (MS Ed, AC); chemistry (MS Ed, AC); earth sciences (MS Ed, AC); English (MS Ed, AC); French (MS Ed); Italian (MS Ed, AC); literacy education (MS Ed); mathematics (MS Ed, AC); music (MS Ed, AC); physics (MS Ed, AC); social studies (MS Ed, AC); Spanish (MS Ed, AC). *Program availability:* Part-time, evening/weekend. *Faculty:* 22 full-time (14 women), 40 part-time/adjunct (26 women). *Students:* 31 full-time (21 women), 356 part-time (211 women); includes 164 minority (22 Black or African American, non-Hispanic/Latino; 54 Asian, non-Hispanic/Latino; 81 Hispanic/Latino; 7 Two or more races, non-Hispanic/Latino), 11 international. Average age 29. 236 applicants, 88% accepted, 121 enrolled. In 2016, 119 master's, 51 other advanced degrees awarded. *Degree requirements:* For master's, research project. *Entrance requirements:* For master's, minimum GPA of 3.0. Additional exam requirements/recommendations for international students: Required—TOEFL, IELTS. *Application deadline:* For fall admission, 4/1 for domestic students; for spring admission, 11/1 for domestic students. Applications are processed on a rolling basis. Application fee: $125. Electronic applications accepted. *Expenses:* Tuition, state resident: full-time $5065; part-time $425 per credit. Tuition, nonresident: part-time $780 per credit. *Required fees:* $522; $397 per credit. Part-time tuition and fees vary according to course load and program. *Financial support:* Career-related internships or fieldwork available. Financial award application deadline: 4/1; financial award applicants required to submit FAFSA. *Unit head:* Dr. Eleanor Armour-Thomas, Chairperson, 718-997-5150, E-mail: armourthomas@yahoo.com.

Quinnipiac University, School of Education, Program in Secondary Education, Hamden, CT 06518-1940. Offers biology (MAT); English (MAT); history/social studies (MAT); mathematics (MAT); Spanish (MAT). *Accreditation:* NCATE. *Faculty:* 6 full-time (2 women), 24 part-time/adjunct (16 women). *Students:* 43 full-time (29 women), 1 part-time (0 women); includes 6 minority (1 Asian, non-Hispanic/Latino; 4 Hispanic/Latino; 1 Two or more races, non-Hispanic/Latino). 43 applicants, 98% accepted, 36 enrolled. In 2016, 32 master's awarded. *Entrance requirements:* For master's, PRAXIS I or PRAXIS Core Academic Skills Exam, minimum GPA of 3.0, interview. *Application deadline:* For fall admission, 5/1 priority date for domestic students. Applications are processed on a rolling basis. Application fee: $45. Electronic applications accepted. *Expenses: Tuition:* Part-time $985 per credit. *Required fees:* $40 per credit. $150 per semester. Tuition and fees vary according to program. *Financial support:* Career-related internships or fieldwork, Federal Work-Study, and unspecified assistantships available. Financial award application deadline: 6/1; financial award applicants required to submit FAFSA. *Faculty research:* Multicultural and urban education/leadership, challenges of teaching diverse learners, scholarship of teaching and learning, technology and teaching, humor and education. *Unit head:* Mordechai Gordon, Program Director, 203-582-8442, E-mail: mordechai.gordon@qu.edu. *Application contact:* Office of Graduate Admissions, 203-582-8672, Fax: 203-582-3443, E-mail: graduate@qu.edu.
Website: http://www.qu.edu/gradeducation

Radford University, College of Graduate Studies and Research, Program in Education, Radford, VA 24142. Offers early childhood education (MS); math education content area studies (MS). *Accreditation:* NCATE. *Program availability:* Part-time, evening/weekend. *Faculty:* 12 full-time (8 women). *Students:* 39 full-time (33 women), 53 part-time (39 women); includes 7 minority (3 Black or African American, non-Hispanic/Latino; 2 Hispanic/Latino; 2 Two or more races, non-Hispanic/Latino). Average age 30. 32 applicants, 94% accepted, 26 enrolled. In 2016, 46 master's awarded. *Degree requirements:* For master's, comprehensive exam. *Entrance requirements:* For master's, GRE (waived for any applicant with advanced degree), minimum GPA of 3.0, 2 letters of professional reference, personal statement, resume, official transcripts. Additional exam requirements/recommendations for international students: Required—TOEFL (minimum score 550 paper-based; 79 iBT), IELTS (minimum score 6.5). *Application deadline:* For fall admission, 2/15 priority date for domestic students, 12/1 for international students; for spring admission, 7/1 for international students. Applications are processed on a rolling basis. Application fee: $50. Electronic applications accepted. *Expenses:* Tuition, state resident: full-time $7868; part-time $328 per credit hour. Tuition, nonresident: full-time $16,394; part-time $683 per credit hour. *Required fees:* $3090; $130 per credit hour. Tuition and fees vary according to course load and program. *Financial support:* In 2016–17, 15 students received support. Career-related internships or fieldwork, scholarships/grants, and unspecified assistantships available. Support available to part-time students. Financial award application deadline: 3/1; financial award applicants required to submit FAFSA. *Unit head:* Dr. Wendy Eckenrod-Green, Coordinator, 540-831-5302, E-mail: stel@radford.edu.
Website: http://www.radford.edu/content/cehd/home/teacher-ed/programs/education-master.html

Regent University, Graduate School, School of Education, Virginia Beach, VA 23464-9800. Offers adult education (Ed D, PhD, Ed S); advanced educational leadership (Ed D, PhD, Ed S); career switcher (M Ed); character education (Ed D, PhD, Ed S); Christian education leadership (Ed D, PhD, Ed S); Christian school administration (M Ed); curriculum and instruction (M Ed), including adult education, Christian school, gifted and talented education, STEM education, teacher leader; educational leadership (M Ed); educational psychology (Ed D, PhD, Ed S); educational technology and online learning (Ed D, PhD, Ed S); elementary education (M Ed); exceptional education executive leadership (Ed D, PhD, Ed S); higher education (Ed D, PhD, Ed S); higher education leadership and management (Ed D, PhD, Ed S); individualized degree plan (M Ed); K-12 school leadership (Ed D, PhD, Ed S); K-12 special education (M Ed); K-8 leadership in mathematics education (M Ed); leadership in mathematics education (Ed S); reading specialist (M Ed); special education (Ed D, PhD, Ed S); student affairs (M Ed); TESOL (M Ed), including adult education - collegiate, K-12. *Accreditation:* TEAC. *Program availability:* Part-time, evening/weekend, 100% online, blended/hybrid learning. *Faculty:* 22 full-time (10 women), 42 part-time/adjunct (31 women). *Students:* 89 full-time (62 women), 1,035 part-time (823 women); includes 466 minority (381 Black or African American, non-Hispanic/Latino; 3 American Indian or Alaska Native, non-Hispanic/Latino; 19 Asian, non-Hispanic/Latino; 50 Hispanic/Latino; 13 Two or more races, non-Hispanic/Latino), 11 international. Average age 39. 976 applicants, 59% accepted, 449 enrolled. In 2016, 241 master's, 22 doctorates, 4 other advanced degrees awarded. *Degree requirements:* For master's, thesis or alternative; for doctorate, comprehensive exam, thesis/dissertation. *Entrance requirements:* For master's, Virginia Communication and Literacy Assessment (VCLA), PRAXIS, college transcripts, writing sample, interview; for doctorate, GRE, writing sample, resume, transcripts, interview. Additional exam requirements/recommendations for international students: Required—TOEFL (minimum score 577 paper-based). *Application deadline:* For fall admission, 4/1 priority date for domestic students; for spring admission, 10/15 priority date for domestic students. Applications are processed on a rolling basis. Application fee: $50. Electronic applications accepted. *Expenses:* Contact institution. *Financial support:* In 2016–17, 622 students received support, including 1 fellowship (averaging $5,000 per year); career-related internships or fieldwork, scholarships/grants, and unspecified assistantships also available. Support available to part-time students. *Faculty research:* Christian school administration, curriculum and instruction, educational technology and online learning, higher education, special education. *Unit head:* Dr. Donald Finn, Dean, 757-352-4278, Fax: 757-352-4318, E-mail: dfinn@regent.edu. *Application contact:* Heidi Cece, Assistant Vice President of Enrollment Management, 800-373-5504, Fax: 757-352-4381, E-mail: admissions@regent.edu.
Website: http://www.regent.edu/soe/

Rhode Island College, School of Graduate Studies, Feinstein School of Education and Human Development, Department of Educational Studies, Providence, RI 02908-1991. Offers advanced studies in teaching and learning (M Ed); English (MAT); French (MAT); history (MAT); math (MAT); secondary education (MAT); Spanish (MAT); teaching English as a second language (M Ed). *Accreditation:* NCATE. *Program availability:* Part-time, evening/weekend. *Faculty:* 6 full-time (5 women), 8 part-time/adjunct (6 women). *Students:* 5 full-time (2 women), 53 part-time (48 women); includes 8 minority (2 Black or African American, non-Hispanic/Latino; 2 Asian, non-Hispanic/Latino; 3 Hispanic/Latino; 1 Two or more races, non-Hispanic/Latino). Average age 39. In 2016, 29 master's awarded. *Degree requirements:* For master's, capstone or comprehensive assessment. *Entrance requirements:* For master's, GRE or MAT (for most programs), minimum undergraduate GPA of 3.0; baccalaureate degree in English, French, history, math or Spanish; 3 letters of recommendation; interview. Additional exam requirements/

recommendations for international students: Recommended—TOEFL (minimum score 550 paper-based; 79 iBT). *Application deadline:* For fall admission, 3/1 for domestic students; for spring admission, 11/1 for domestic students. Applications are processed on a rolling basis. Application fee: $50. Electronic applications accepted. *Expenses:* Tuition, state resident: full-time $8928; part-time $372 per credit. Tuition, nonresident: full-time $17,376; part-time $724 per credit. *Required fees:* $604; $22 per credit. One-time fee: $74. *Financial support:* In 2016–17, 1 teaching assistantship with full tuition reimbursement (averaging $3,000 per year) was awarded; career-related internships or fieldwork, Federal Work-Study, scholarships/grants, health care benefits, and unspecified assistantships also available. Support available to part-time students. Financial award application deadline: 5/15; financial award applicants required to submit FAFSA. *Unit head:* Dr. Gerri August, Chair, 401-456-8170. *Application contact:* Graduate Studies, 401-456-8700.
Website: http://www.ric.edu/educationalStudies/

Rider University, Department of Graduate Education, Leadership and Counseling, Teacher Certification Program, Lawrenceville, NJ 08648-3001. Offers business education (Certificate); elementary education (Certificate); English as a second language (Certificate); English education (Certificate); mathematics education (Certificate); preschool to grade 3 (Certificate); science education (Certificate); social studies education (Certificate); world languages (Certificate), including French, German, Spanish. *Program availability:* Part-time. *Degree requirements:* For Certificate, internship, professional portfolio. *Entrance requirements:* For degree, PRAXIS, resume. Additional exam requirements/recommendations for international students: Required—TOEFL (minimum score 550 paper-based). Electronic applications accepted. *Faculty research:* Conceptual foundations for optimal development of creativity; creative theory, cognitive processes in mathematics learning, teacher collaboration.

Rowan University, Graduate School, College of Education, Department of Interdisciplinary and Inclusive Education, Program in Teaching STEM, Glassboro, NJ 08028-1701. Offers MA. *Program availability:* Part-time, evening/weekend. *Degree requirements:* For master's, thesis. *Entrance requirements:* For master's, GRE General Test. Additional exam requirements/recommendations for international students: Required—TOEFL. Electronic applications accepted.

Rowan University, Graduate School, College of Science and Mathematics, Department of Mathematics, Program in Middle Grades Math Education, Glassboro, NJ 08028-1701. Offers CGS. Electronic applications accepted.

Rutgers University–Camden, Graduate School of Arts and Sciences, Program in Mathematical Sciences, Camden, NJ 08102. Offers industrial mathematics (MBS); industrial/applied mathematics (MS); mathematical computer science (MS); pure mathematics (MS); teaching in mathematical sciences (MS). *Program availability:* Part-time, evening/weekend. *Degree requirements:* For master's, comprehensive exam, thesis optional, survey paper, 30 credits. *Entrance requirements:* For master's, GRE, BS/BA in math or related subject, 2 letters of recommendation. Additional exam requirements/recommendations for international students: Required—TOEFL (minimum score 550 paper-based), IELTS. Electronic applications accepted. *Faculty research:* Differential geometry, dynamical systems, vertex operator algebra, automorphic forms, CR-structures.

Rutgers University–New Brunswick, Graduate School of Education, Department of Learning and Teaching, Program in Mathematics Education, Piscataway, NJ 08854-8097. Offers Ed M, Ed D. *Program availability:* Part-time. Terminal master's awarded for partial completion of doctoral program. *Degree requirements:* For master's, comprehensive exam (for some programs); for doctorate, thesis/dissertation, qualifying exam. *Entrance requirements:* For master's, GRE General Test, minimum GPA of 3.0; for doctorate, GRE General Test, minimum GPA of 3.5. Additional exam requirements/recommendations for international students: Required—TOEFL. Electronic applications accepted.

Rutgers University–New Brunswick, Graduate School of Education, Doctoral Program in Education, New Brunswick, NJ 08901. Offers educational policy (PhD); educational psychology (PhD); literacy education (PhD); mathematics education (PhD). *Program availability:* Part-time. *Degree requirements:* For doctorate, thesis/dissertation, qualifying exam. *Entrance requirements:* For doctorate, GRE General Test, GRE Subject Test (mathematics education). Additional exam requirements/recommendations for international students: Required—TOEFL (minimum score 575 paper-based; 83 iBT). Electronic applications accepted. *Faculty research:* Literacy education, math education, educational psychology, educational policy, learning sciences.

St. John Fisher College, Ralph C. Wilson Jr. School of Education, Program in Adolescence Education and Special Education, Rochester, NY 14618-3597. Offers adolescence education: biology with special education (MS Ed); adolescence education: chemistry with special education (MS Ed); adolescence education: English with special education (MS Ed); adolescence education: French with special education (MS Ed); adolescence education: math with special education (MS Ed); adolescence education: physics with special education (MS Ed); adolescence education: social studies with special education (MS Ed); adolescence education: Spanish with special education (MS Ed). *Program availability:* Part-time, evening/weekend. *Faculty:* 7 full-time (6 women), 5 part-time/adjunct (all women). *Students:* 15 full-time (6 women), 9 part-time (6 women); includes 3 minority (2 Black or African American, non-Hispanic/Latino; 1 Hispanic/Latino). Average age 28. 16 applicants, 56% accepted, 6 enrolled. In 2016, 8 master's awarded. *Degree requirements:* For master's, field experiences, student teaching, LAST. *Entrance requirements:* For master's, 2 letters of recommendation, personal statement, current resume. Additional exam requirements/recommendations for international students: Required—TOEFL (minimum score 575 paper-based; 80 iBT). *Application deadline:* Applications are processed on a rolling basis. Application fee: $30. Electronic applications accepted. *Expenses:* $885 per credit hour. *Financial support:* Scholarships/grants available. Financial award applicants required to submit FAFSA. *Faculty research:* Arts and humanities, urban schools, constructivist learning, at-risk students, mentoring. *Unit head:* Dr. Susan Hildenbrand, Program Director, 585-385-7297, E-mail: shildenbrand@sjfc.edu. *Application contact:* Michelle Gosier, Associate Director of Transfer and Graduate Admissions, 585-385-8064, E-mail: mgosier@sjfc.edu.

St. Joseph's College, Long Island Campus, Programs in Education, Field in Mathematics Education, Patchogue, NY 11772-2399. Offers MA. *Program availability:* Evening/weekend. *Entrance requirements:* For master's, recommendation letter. *Expenses: Tuition:* Full-time $16,182; part-time $899 per credit. *Required fees:* $440.

Saint Peter's University, Graduate Programs in Education, Jersey City, NJ 07306-5997. Offers director of school counseling services (Certificate); educational leadership (MA Ed, Ed D); higher education (Ed D); middle school mathematics (Certificate); professional/associate counselor (Certificate); reading (MA Ed); school business administrator (Certificate); school counseling (MA, Certificate); special education (MA Ed, Certificate), including applied behavioral analysis (MA Ed), literacy (MA Ed), teacher of students with disabilities (Certificate); teaching (MA Ed, Certificate), including 6-8 middle school education, K-12 secondary education, K-5 elementary education. *Accreditation:* TEAC. *Program availability:* Part-time, evening/weekend. *Degree requirements:* For master's, comprehensive exam; for doctorate, comprehensive exam, thesis/dissertation. *Entrance requirements:* For master's and doctorate, GRE or MAT. Additional exam requirements/recommendations for international students: Required—TOEFL. Electronic applications accepted.

Salem State University, School of Graduate Studies, Program in Middle School Education, Salem, MA 01970-5353. Offers humanities (M Ed); math/science (MAT). *Program availability:* Part-time, evening/weekend. *Entrance requirements:* For master's, GRE or MAT. Additional exam requirements/recommendations for international students: Required—TOEFL (minimum score 550 paper-based; 80 iBT) or IELTS (minimum score 5.5).

Salem State University, School of Graduate Studies, Program in Middle School Math, Salem, MA 01970-5353. Offers MAT. *Program availability:* Part-time, evening/weekend. *Entrance requirements:* For master's, GRE or MAT. Additional exam requirements/recommendations for international students: Required—TOEFL (minimum score 550 paper-based; 80 iBT) or IELTS (minimum score 5.5).

Salisbury University, Program in Mathematics Education, Salisbury, MD 21801-6837. Offers mathematics (MSME), including high school, middle school. *Program availability:* Part-time. *Faculty:* 3 full-time (1 woman). *Students:* 2 full-time (1 woman), 8 part-time (5 women); includes 1 minority (Two or more races, non-Hispanic/Latino). Average age 27. 2 applicants, 100% accepted, 2 enrolled. In 2016, 2 master's awarded. *Entrance requirements:* Additional exam requirements/recommendations for international students: Required—TOEFL (minimum score 550 paper-based, 79 iBT) or IELTS (6.5). *Application deadline:* For fall admission, 5/15 priority date for domestic and international students; for spring admission, 10/1 priority date for domestic and international students. Applications are processed on a rolling basis. Application fee: $65. Electronic applications accepted. *Expenses:* $381 per credit hour resident tuition, $670 per credit hour non-resident tuition; $84 per credit hour fees. *Financial support:* In 2016–17, 1 teaching assistantship with full tuition reimbursement (averaging $8,000 per year) was awarded; career-related internships or fieldwork and scholarships/grants also available. Support available to part-time students. Financial award application deadline: 3/1; financial award applicants required to submit FAFSA. *Faculty research:* Conceptual development of multiplicative reasoning; early childhood mathematics; teachers' attitudes towards mathematics. *Unit head:* Dr. Jennifer Bergner, Graduate Program Director, Mathematics Education, 410-677-5429, E-mail: jabergner@salisbury.edu.
Website: http://www.salisbury.edu/gsr/gradstudies/MSMEpage.html

San Diego State University, Graduate and Research Affairs, College of Sciences, Department of Mathematics and Statistics, San Diego, CA 92182. Offers applied mathematics (MS); mathematics (MA); mathematics and science education (PhD); statistics (MS). PhD offered jointly wtih University of California, San Diego. *Program availability:* Part-time. *Degree requirements:* For doctorate, thesis/dissertation. *Entrance requirements:* For master's, GRE General Test; for doctorate, GRE, minimum GPA of 3.25 in last 30 undergraduate semester units, minimum graduate GPA of 3.5, MSE recommendation form, 3 letters of recommendation. Additional exam requirements/recommendations for international students: Required—TOEFL. Electronic applications accepted. *Faculty research:* Teacher education in mathematics.

San Francisco State University, Division of Graduate Studies, College of Education, Department of Elementary Education, Program in Mathematics Education, San Francisco, CA 94132-1722. Offers MA. *Accreditation:* NCATE. *Expenses:* Tuition, state resident: full-time $6738. Tuition, nonresident: full-time $15,666. *Required fees:* $1012. Tuition and fees vary according to degree level and program. *Unit head:* Dr. Josephine Arce, Chair, 415-338-7636, Fax: 415-338-0567, E-mail: jarce@sfsu.edu. *Application contact:* Dr. Maria Zavala, MA Program Coordinator, 415-405-0465, Fax: 415-338-0567, E-mail: mza@sfsu.edu.
Website: http://gcoe.sfsu.edu/

San Francisco State University, Division of Graduate Studies, College of Education, Department of Secondary Education, San Francisco, CA 94132-1722. Offers mathematics education (MA); secondary education (MA, Credential). *Accreditation:* NCATE. *Expenses:* Tuition, state resident: full-time $6738. Tuition, nonresident: full-time $15,666. *Required fees:* $1012. Tuition and fees vary according to degree level and program. *Unit head:* Dr. Maika Watanabe, Chair, 415-338-1622, Fax: 415-338-0914, E-mail: watanabe@sfsu.edu. *Application contact:* Administrative Office Coordinator, 415-338-7649, Fax: 415-338-0914, E-mail: seced@sfsu.edu.
Website: http://secondaryed.sfsu.edu/

San Jose State University, Graduate Studies and Research, College of Science, San Jose, CA 95192-0001. Offers biological sciences (MA, MS), including molecular biology and microbiology (MS), organismal biology, conservation and ecology (MS), physiology (MS); biotechnology (MBT); chemistry (MA, MS); computer science (MS); cybersecurity (Certificate); cybersecurity: core technologies (Certificate); geology (MS); marine science (MS); mathematics (MA, MS), including mathematics education (MA), science; meteorology (MS); physics (MS), including computational physics, modern optics, science (MA, MS); science education (MA); statistics (MS); Unix system administration (Certificate). *Program availability:* Part-time, evening/weekend. *Entrance requirements:* For master's, GRE. Electronic applications accepted. *Faculty research:* Radiochemistry/environmental analysis, health physics, radiation effects.

Seattle Pacific University, Program in Teaching Mathematics and Science, Seattle, WA 98119-1997. Offers MTMS. *Degree requirements:* For master's, internship.

Shippensburg University of Pennsylvania, School of Graduate Studies, College of Education and Human Services, Department of Teacher Education, Shippensburg, PA 17257-2299. Offers curriculum and instruction (M Ed), including biology, early childhood education, elementary and middle level education, elementary education, geography/earth science, history, mathematics, middle school education, modern languages; literacy studies (Certificate); online instruction, learning, and technology (Certificate); reading (M Ed); teaching English as a second language (Certificate). *Accreditation:* NCATE. *Program availability:* Part-time, evening/weekend, 100% online, blended/hybrid learning. *Faculty:* 14 full-time (9 women), 5 part-time/adjunct (all women). *Students:* 11 full-time (10 women), 88 part-time (81 women); includes 8 minority (3 Black or African American, non-Hispanic/Latino; 2 Asian, non-Hispanic/Latino; 3 Hispanic/Latino), 4 international. Average age 32. 57 applicants, 60% accepted, 28 enrolled. In 2016, 18 master's awarded. *Degree requirements:* For master's, comprehensive exam (for some programs), thesis optional, practicum or internship; capstone seminar (for some programs). *Entrance requirements:* For master's, MAT or GRE (if GPA less than 2.75), interview, 3 letters of reference, questionnaire of teaching background and future goals, resume. Additional exam requirements/recommendations for international students: Required—TOEFL (minimum score 550 paper-based, 68 iBT) or IELTS (minimum score 6). *Application deadline:* For fall admission, 4/1 priority date for domestic students, 4/30 for international students; for spring admission, 9/1 priority date for domestic students, 9/30 for international students; for summer admission, 2/1 priority date for domestic students. Applications are processed on a rolling basis. Application fee: $45. Electronic applications accepted. *Expenses:* Tuition, state resident: part-time $483 per credit. Tuition, nonresident: part-time $725 per credit. *Required fees:* $141 per credit. *Financial support:* In 2016–17, 3 students received support. Career-related internships or fieldwork, scholarships/grants, unspecified assistantships, and resident hall director and student payroll positions available. Support available to part-time students. Financial

award application deadline: 3/1; financial award applicants required to submit FAFSA. *Unit head:* Dr. Christine A. Royce, Chairperson, 717-477-1688, Fax: 717-477-4046, E-mail: caroyc@ship.edu. *Application contact:* Megan N. Luft, Assistant Dean of Graduate Admissions, 717-477-1231, Fax: 717-477-4016, E-mail: mnluft@ship.edu.
Website: http://www.ship.edu/teacher/

Simon Fraser University, Office of Graduate Studies and Postdoctoral Fellows, Faculty of Education, Program in Mathematics Education, Burnaby, BC V5A 1S6, Canada. Offers mathematics education (PhD); secondary mathematics education (M Ed, M Sc). *Program availability:* Part-time, evening/weekend. *Faculty:* 4 full-time (2 women). *Degree requirements:* For master's, comprehensive exam (for some programs), thesis; for doctorate, comprehensive exam, thesis/dissertation. *Entrance requirements:* For master's, minimum GPA of 3.0 (on scale of 4.33) or 3.33 based on last 60 credits of undergraduate courses; for doctorate, minimum GPA of 3.5 (on scale of 4.33). Additional exam requirements/recommendations for international students: Recommended—TOEFL (minimum score 580 paper-based; 93 iBT), IELTS (minimum score 7), TWE (minimum score 5). *Application deadline:* For fall admission, 1/31 for domestic and international students. Application fee: $90 ($125 for international students). Electronic applications accepted. *Financial support:* In 2016–17, fellowships (averaging $6,250 per year), teaching assistantships (averaging $5,608 per year) were awarded; research assistantships, career-related internships or fieldwork, and scholarships/grants also available. *Faculty research:* Historical and psychological development of mathematical thinking, math anxiety and concept formation, mathematical problem solving, numeracy, instructional design, cognition in mathematics thinking and learning, undergraduate math education. *Unit head:* Dr. Shawn Bullock, Graduate Chair, 778-782-4102. *Application contact:* Graduate Secretary, 778-782-3984, E-mail: educmast@sfu.ca.
Website: http://www.educ.sfu.ca/gs/areas-of-study/matheducation.html

Slippery Rock University of Pennsylvania, Graduate Studies (Recruitment), College of Education, Department of Elementary Education and Early Childhood, Slippery Rock, PA 16057-1383. Offers instructional coach (M Ed); K-12 reading (M Ed); K-12 science and math (M Ed); reading specialist (M Ed). *Accreditation:* NCATE. *Program availability:* Part-time, evening/weekend, online only, 100% online. *Faculty:* 9 full-time (8 women). *Students:* 6 full-time (all women), 128 part-time (124 women); includes 1 minority (Two or more races, non-Hispanic/Latino). Average age 28. 100 applicants, 77% accepted, 54 enrolled. In 2016, 49 master's awarded. *Degree requirements:* For master's, comprehensive exam (for some programs), thesis optional. *Entrance requirements:* For master's, minimum GPA of 3.0, resume, teaching certification, transcripts, letters of recommendation (depending on program). Additional exam requirements/recommendations for international students: Required—TOEFL (minimum score 550 paper-based; 80 iBT). *Application deadline:* For fall admission, 3/1 priority date for domestic students, 5/1 priority date for international students; for spring admission, 10/1 priority date for domestic students, 9/1 priority date for international students. Applications are processed on a rolling basis. Application fee: $25 ($30 for international students). Electronic applications accepted. *Expenses:* $646.50 per credit in-state, $936.80 per credit out-of-state; $581.45 per online credit in-state, $648.65 per online credit out-of-state. *Financial support:* Career-related internships or fieldwork, Federal Work-Study, institutionally sponsored loans, scholarships/grants, tuition waivers (partial), and unspecified assistantships available. Support available to part-time students. Financial award application deadline: 5/1; financial award applicants required to submit FAFSA. *Unit head:* Dr. Suzanne Rose, Graduate Coordinator, 724-738-2042, Fax: 724-738-2779, E-mail: suzanne.rose@sru.edu. *Application contact:* Brandi Weber-Mortimer, Director of Graduate Admissions, 724-738-2051, Fax: 724-738-2146, E-mail: graduate.admissions@sru.edu.
Website: http://www.sru.edu/academics/colleges-and-departments/coe/departments/elementary-education-/-early-childhood/graduate-programs

Slippery Rock University of Pennsylvania, Graduate Studies (Recruitment), College of Education, Department of Secondary Education/Foundations of Education, Slippery Rock, PA 16057-1383. Offers secondary education (M Ed), including English, math/science, social studies. *Accreditation:* NCATE. *Program availability:* Part-time, evening/weekend, 100% online. *Faculty:* 7 full-time (2 women), 1 part-time/adjunct (0 women). *Students:* 43 full-time (23 women), 36 part-time (23 women); includes 2 minority (1 Black or African American, non-Hispanic/Latino; 1 Two or more races, non-Hispanic/Latino). Average age 29. 77 applicants, 79% accepted, 35 enrolled. In 2016, 36 master's awarded. *Degree requirements:* For master's, comprehensive exam, thesis (for some programs). *Entrance requirements:* For master's, copy of teaching certification and two letters of recommendation (for some programs). Additional exam requirements/recommendations for international students: Required—TOEFL (minimum score 550 paper-based; 80 iBT). *Application deadline:* For fall admission, 3/1 priority date for domestic students, 5/1 priority date for international students; for spring admission, 10/1 priority date for domestic students, 9/1 priority date for international students. Applications are processed on a rolling basis. Application fee: $25 ($30 for international students). Electronic applications accepted. *Expenses:* $646.50 per credit in-state, $936.80 per credit out-of-state; $581.45 per online credit in-state, $648.65 per online credit out-of-state. *Financial support:* In 2016–17, 12 students received support. Career-related internships or fieldwork, Federal Work-Study, institutionally sponsored loans, scholarships/grants, tuition waivers (partial), and unspecified assistantships available. Support available to part-time students. Financial award application deadline: 5/1; financial award applicants required to submit FAFSA. *Unit head:* Dr. Jeffrey Lehman, Graduate Coordinator, 724-738-2311, Fax: 724-738-4987, E-mail: jeffrey.lehman@sru.edu. *Application contact:* Brandi Weber-Mortimer, Director of Graduate Studies, 724-738-2051, Fax: 724-738-2146, E-mail: graduate.admissions@sru.edu.
Website: http://www.sru.edu/academics/colleges-and-departments/coe/departments/secondary-education-/-foundations-of-education

Smith College, Graduate and Special Programs, Department of Education and Child Study, Program in Secondary Education, Northampton, MA 01063. Offers secondary education (MAT), including biological sciences education, chemistry education, English education, French education, geology education, government education, history education, mathematics education, physics education, Spanish education. *Program availability:* Part-time. *Students:* 3 full-time (2 women), 3 part-time (2 women). Average age 31. 14 applicants, 79% accepted, 4 enrolled. In 2016, 11 master's awarded. *Entrance requirements:* Additional exam requirements/recommendations for international students: Required—TOEFL (minimum score 595 paper-based; 97 iBT), IELTS. *Application deadline:* For fall admission, 4/1 for domestic students, 1/15 priority date for international students; for spring admission, 12/1 for domestic students. Application fee: $60. *Expenses: Tuition:* Full-time $34,560; part-time $1440 per credit. Tuition and fees vary according to course load and program. *Financial support:* In 2016–17, 5 students received support, including 1 fellowship with full tuition reimbursement available; scholarships/grants also available. Support available to part-time students. Financial award application deadline: 4/1; financial award applicants required to submit CSS PROFILE or FAFSA. *Unit head:* Rosetta Cohen, Graduate Student Advisor, 413-585-3266, E-mail: rcohen@smith.edu. *Application contact:* Ruth Morgan, Program Assistant, 413-585-3050, Fax: 413-585-3054, E-mail: gradstdy@smith.edu.
Website: http://www.smith.edu/educ/

Smith College, Graduate and Special Programs, Department of Mathematics, Northampton, MA 01063. Offers secondary education (MAT), including mathematics education. *Program availability:* Part-time. *Students:* 1 (woman) part-time. Average age 52. *Entrance requirements:* Additional exam requirements/recommendations for international students: Required—TOEFL (minimum score 595 paper-based; 97 iBT), IELTS. *Application deadline:* For fall admission, 4/1 for domestic students, 1/15 for international students; for spring admission, 12/1 for domestic students. Application fee: $60. *Expenses: Tuition:* Full-time $34,560; part-time $1440 per credit. Tuition and fees vary according to course load and program. *Financial support:* Scholarships/grants available. Support available to part-time students. Financial award application deadline: 4/1; financial award applicants required to submit CSS PROFILE or FAFSA. *Unit head:* Julianna Tymoczko, Department Chair, 413-585-3775, E-mail: jtymoczko@smith.edu. *Application contact:* Ruth Morgan, Program Assistant, 413-585-3050, Fax: 413-585-3054, E-mail: gradstdy@smith.edu.
Website: http://www.math.smith.edu/

South Carolina State University, College of Graduate and Professional Studies, Department of Education, Orangeburg, SC 29117-0001. Offers early childhood education (MAT); education (M Ed); elementary education (M Ed, MAT); English (MAT); general science/biology (MAT); mathematics (MAT); secondary education (M Ed), including biology education, business education, counselor education, English education, home economics education, industrial education, mathematics education, science education, social studies education; special education (M Ed), including emotionally handicapped, learning disabilities, mentally handicapped. *Accreditation:* NCATE. *Program availability:* Part-time, evening/weekend. *Faculty:* 12 full-time (8 women), 3 part-time/adjunct (1 woman). *Students:* 28 full-time (20 women), 20 part-time (17 women); includes 45 minority (44 Black or African American, non-Hispanic/Latino; 1 Two or more races, non-Hispanic/Latino). Average age 31. 22 applicants, 100% accepted, 16 enrolled. In 2016, 9 master's awarded. *Degree requirements:* For master's, thesis optional, departmental qualifying exam. *Entrance requirements:* For master's, GRE General Test, NTE, interview, teaching certificate. *Application deadline:* For fall admission, 6/15 priority date for domestic students, 6/15 for international students; for spring admission, 11/1 for domestic and international students. Application fee: $25. Electronic applications accepted. *Expenses:* Tuition, state resident: full-time $8938; part-time $579 per credit hour. Tuition, nonresident: full-time $19,018; part-time $1139 per credit hour. *Required fees:* $1482; $82 per credit hour. *Financial support:* Fellowships, career-related internships or fieldwork, Federal Work-Study, and scholarships/grants available. Financial award application deadline: 6/1. *Unit head:* Dr. Charlie Spell, Interim Chair, Department of Education, 803-536-8963, Fax: 803-516-4568, E-mail: cspell@scsu.edu. *Application contact:* Curtis Foskey, Coordinator of Graduate Studies, 803-536-8419, Fax: 803-536-8812, E-mail: cfoskey@scsu.edu.

Southeastern Oklahoma State University, School of Education, Durant, OK 74701-0609. Offers math specialist (M Ed); reading specialist (M Ed); school administration (M Ed); school counseling (M Ed). *Accreditation:* NCATE. *Program availability:* Part-time, evening/weekend. *Degree requirements:* For master's, comprehensive exam, thesis optional, portfolio (M Ed). *Entrance requirements:* For master's, GRE General Test (for school counseling), minimum GPA of 3.0 in last 60 hours or 2.75 overall. Additional exam requirements/recommendations for international students: Required—TOEFL (minimum score 550 paper-based; 79 iBT). Electronic applications accepted.

Southern Illinois University Edwardsville, Graduate School, College of Arts and Sciences, Department of Mathematics and Statistics, Program in Postsecondary Mathematics Education, Edwardsville, IL 62026. Offers MS. *Program availability:* Part-time. *Degree requirements:* For master's, thesis (for some programs), special project. *Entrance requirements:* Additional exam requirements/recommendations for international students: Required—TOEFL (minimum score 550 paper-based, 79 iBT), IELTS (minimum score 6.5), Michigan Test of English Language Proficiency or PTE. Electronic applications accepted.

Southern University and Agricultural and Mechanical College, Graduate School, Department of Science/Mathematics Education, Baton Rouge, LA 70813. Offers PhD. *Accreditation:* NCATE. *Degree requirements:* For doctorate, thesis/dissertation. *Entrance requirements:* For doctorate, GRE General Test. Additional exam requirements/recommendations for international students: Required—TOEFL (minimum score 525 paper-based). *Faculty research:* Performance assessment in science/mathematics education, equity in science/mathematics education, technology and distance learning, science/mathematics concept formation, cognitive themes, problem solving in science/mathematics education.

Southwestern Oklahoma State University, College of Arts and Sciences, Department of Mathematics, Weatherford, OK 73096-3098. Offers M Ed. *Program availability:* Part-time. *Degree requirements:* For master's, exam. *Entrance requirements:* For master's, GRE General Test or minimum undergraduate GPA of 3.0. Additional exam requirements/recommendations for international students: Required—TOEFL.

Southwest Minnesota State University, Department of Education, Marshall, MN 56258. Offers ESL (MS); math (MS); reading (MS); special education (MS), including developmental disabilities, early childhood education, emotional behavioral disorders, learning disabilities; teaching, learning and leadership (MS). *Program availability:* Part-time, evening/weekend, online learning. *Entrance requirements:* Additional exam requirements/recommendations for international students: Required—TOEFL or IELTS; Recommended—TOEFL (minimum score 550 paper-based; 80 iBT), IELTS.

State University of New York at New Paltz, Graduate School, School of Education, Department of Elementary Education, New Paltz, NY 12561. Offers childhood education 1-6 (MS Ed, MST), including childhood education 1-6 (MST), early childhood B-2 (MS Ed), mathematics, science and technology (MS Ed), reading/literacy (MS Ed); literacy education 5-12 (MS Ed); literacy education and childhood special education (MS Ed); literacy education B-6 (MS Ed). *Accreditation:* NCATE. *Program availability:* Part-time, evening/weekend. *Students:* 32 full-time (29 women), 100 part-time (91 women); includes 22 minority (5 Black or African American, non-Hispanic/Latino; 1 American Indian or Alaska Native, non-Hispanic/Latino; 2 Asian, non-Hispanic/Latino; 10 Hispanic/Latino; 4 Two or more races, non-Hispanic/Latino). 30 applicants, 73% accepted, 14 enrolled. In 2016, 70 master's awarded. *Degree requirements:* For master's, comprehensive exam (for some programs), portfolio. *Entrance requirements:* For master's, GRE or MAT (for MST), minimum GPA of 3.0 (3.2 for literacy and special education), New York state teaching certificate (for MS Ed). Additional exam requirements/recommendations for international students: Required—TOEFL (minimum score 550 paper-based; 80 iBT), IELTS (minimum score 6.5). *Application deadline:* For fall admission, 4/1 for domestic and international students; for spring admission, 11/1 priority date for domestic and international students; for summer admission, 4/15 priority date for domestic and international students. Applications are processed on a rolling basis. Application fee: $50. Electronic applications accepted. *Financial support:* Application deadline: 8/1. *Faculty research:* Multi-sensory teaching methods, volunteer tutoring programs for struggling readers, school readiness and transition, math/science/technology, university-school partnerships. *Unit head:* Dr. Aaron Isabelle, Chair, 845-257-2837, E-mail: isabella@newpaltz.edu. *Application contact:* Vika Shock, Assistant

Director of Graduate Admissions, 845-257-3285, Fax: 845-257-3284, E-mail: gradschool@newpaltz.edu.
Website: http://www.newpaltz.edu/elementaryed/

State University of New York at Plattsburgh, School of Education, Health, and Human Services, Program in Teacher Education: Adolescence Education, Plattsburgh, NY 12901-2681. Offers adolescence education (MST); biology 7-12 (MST); chemistry 7-12 (MST); earth science 7-12 (MST); English 7-12 (MST); French 7-12 (MST); mathematics 7-12 (MST); physics 7-12 (MST); social studies 7-12 (MST); Spanish 7-12 (MST). *Accreditation:* TEAC. *Program availability:* Part-time, evening/weekend. *Entrance requirements:* For master's, minimum GPA of 2.75. Additional exam requirements/recommendations for international students: Required—TOEFL.

State University of New York College at Cortland, Graduate Studies, School of Arts and Sciences, Programs in Adolescence Education, Cortland, NY 13045. Offers biology (MAT); chemistry (MAT); English (MAT, MS Ed); mathematics (MAT); mathematics and physics (MS Ed); physics (MAT, MS Ed). *Accreditation:* NCATE. *Program availability:* Part-time, evening/weekend. *Degree requirements:* For master's, one foreign language, comprehensive exam (for some programs), thesis (for some programs). *Entrance requirements:* For master's, GRE General Test.

State University of New York College at Old Westbury, School of Education, Old Westbury, NY 11568-0210. Offers biology (MAT, MS); chemistry (MAT, MS); English language arts (MAT, MS); math (MAT, MS); social studies (MAT, MS); Spanish (MAT, MS). *Program availability:* Part-time, evening/weekend. *Faculty:* 17 full-time (9 women), 5 part-time/adjunct (2 women). *Students:* 46 full-time (19 women), 26 part-time (17 women); includes 20 minority (1 Black or African American, non-Hispanic/Latino; 4 Asian, non-Hispanic/Latino; 15 Hispanic/Latino). Average age 30. 35 applicants, 77% accepted, 23 enrolled. In 2016, 25 master's awarded. *Entrance requirements:* For master's, Liberal Arts and Sciences Test, undergraduate degree with at least 30 semester hours of appropriate coursework as defined by the respective discipline; minimum cumulative undergraduate GPA of 3.0; two letters of recommendation (one from an academic source); essay. Additional exam requirements/recommendations for international students: Required—TOEFL (minimum score 550 paper-based); Recommended—IELTS. Application fee: $50. *Expenses:* Tuition, state resident: full-time $10,870; part-time $453 per credit. Tuition, nonresident: full-time $22,210; part-time $925 per credit. *Required fees:* $24.35 per credit. $76 per semester. Tuition and fees vary according to course load. *Financial support:* Applicants required to submit FAFSA. *Unit head:* Dr. Nancy Brown, Dean, School of Education, 516-876-3275, E-mail: brownn@oldwestbury.edu. *Application contact:* Philip D'Angelo, Graduate Admissions Office, 516-876-3073, E-mail: enroll@oldwestbury.edu.

State University of New York College at Potsdam, School of Education and Professional Studies, Program in Secondary Education, Potsdam, NY 13676. Offers English education (MST); mathematics education (MST); science education (MST), including biology, chemistry, earth science, physics; social studies education (MST). *Accreditation:* NCATE. *Degree requirements:* For master's, culminating experience. *Entrance requirements:* For master's, minimum GPA of 2.75 in last 60 hours of course work (3.0 for English program). Additional exam requirements/recommendations for international students: Required—TOEFL (minimum score 550 paper-based; 80 iBT), IELTS (minimum score 6). Electronic applications accepted.

Stephen F. Austin State University, Graduate School, College of Sciences and Mathematics, Department of Mathematics and Statistics, Nacogdoches, TX 75962. Offers mathematics (MS); mathematics education (MS); statistics (MS). *Degree requirements:* For master's, comprehensive exam, thesis optional. *Entrance requirements:* For master's, GRE General Test, minimum GPA of 2.8 in last 60 hours, 2.5 overall. Additional exam requirements/recommendations for international students: Required—TOEFL. *Faculty research:* Kernel type estimators, fractal mappings, spline curve fitting, robust regression continua theory.

Stevenson University, Master of Arts in Teaching Program, Stevenson, MD 21153. Offers secondary biology (MAT); secondary chemistry (MAT); secondary mathematics (MAT). *Program availability:* Part-time, blended/hybrid learning. *Faculty:* 3 part-time/adjunct (all women). *Students:* 17 part-time (10 women); includes 3 minority (2 Black or African American, non-Hispanic/Latino; 1 Asian, non-Hispanic/Latino). Average age 29. 13 applicants, 85% accepted, 10 enrolled. In 2016, 8 master's awarded. *Degree requirements:* For master's, internship, portfolio, action research project. *Entrance requirements:* For master's, PRAXIS, GRE, SAT, or ACT, official transcripts from each college or university attended verifying completion of baccalaureate degree in a science or math discipline from regionally-accredited institution. *Application deadline:* Applications are processed on a rolling basis. Electronic applications accepted. *Expenses:* $475 per credit hour. *Financial support:* Unspecified assistantships available. Financial award applicants required to submit FAFSA. *Unit head:* Anne P. Davis, Associate Dean of Teacher Education. *Application contact:* Amanda Courter, Senior Enrollment Counselor, 443-352-4243, Fax: 443-352-4440, E-mail: acourter@stevenson.edu.
Website: http://www.stevenson.edu/graduate-professional-studies/graduate-programs/master-of-arts-in-teaching/

Stony Brook University, State University of New York, School of Professional Development, Stony Brook, NY 11794-443. Offers biology (MAT); chemistry (MAT); coaching (Graduate Certificate); earth science (MAT); educational computing (Graduate Certificate); educational leadership (Advanced Certificate); English (MAT); environmental management (MPS, Graduate Certificate); French (MAT); German (MAT); higher education administration (MA, Certificate); human resource management (MS, Graduate Certificate); industrial management (Graduate Certificate); information systems management (Graduate Certificate); Italian (MAT); liberal studies (MA); mathematics (MAT); operations research (Graduate Certificate); physics (MAT); school district business leadership (Advanced Certificate); social studies (MAT); Spanish (MAT). *Program availability:* Part-time, evening/weekend, online learning. *Faculty:* 4 full-time (3 women), 77 part-time/adjunct (34 women). *Students:* 197 full-time (125 women), 965 part-time (674 women); includes 222 minority (79 Black or African American, non-Hispanic/Latino; 2 American Indian or Alaska Native, non-Hispanic/Latino; 35 Asian, non-Hispanic/Latino; 87 Hispanic/Latino; 1 Native Hawaiian or other Pacific Islander, non-Hispanic/Latino; 18 Two or more races, non-Hispanic/Latino), 5 international. Average age 33. 462 applicants, 87% accepted, 317 enrolled. In 2016, 348 master's, 159 other advanced degrees awarded. *Degree requirements:* For master's, one foreign language, thesis or alternative. *Entrance requirements:* Additional exam requirements/recommendations for international students: Required—TOEFL (minimum score 85 iBT). *Application deadline:* For fall admission, 1/15 for domestic students, 6/1 for international students; for spring admission, 10/1 for domestic and international students. Applications are processed on a rolling basis. Application fee: $100. *Expenses:* Contact institution. *Financial support:* Fellowships, research assistantships, teaching assistantships, and career-related internships or fieldwork available. Support available to part-time students. *Unit head:* Dr. Ken Lindblom, Dean, 631-632-7049, Fax: 631-632-9046, E-mail: kenneth.lindblom@stonybrook.edu. *Application contact:* Melissa Jordan, Assistant Dean, 631-632-7751, E-mail: melissa.jordan@stonybrook.edu.
Website: http://www.stonybrook.edu/spd/

Syracuse University, College of Arts and Sciences, Programs in Mathematics, Syracuse, NY 13244. Offers mathematics (PhD); mathematics education (MS). *Program availability:* Part-time. In 2016, 11 master's, 3 doctorates awarded. Terminal master's awarded for partial completion of doctoral program. *Degree requirements:* For doctorate, 2 foreign languages, comprehensive exam, thesis/dissertation. *Entrance requirements:* For master's and doctorate, GRE General Test, GRE Subject Test (recommended), brief (about 500 words) statement indicating why applicant wishes to pursue graduate study and why Syracuse is a good fit, curriculum vitae or resume, transcripts from each post-secondary institution, three letters of recommendation. Additional exam requirements/recommendations for international students: Required—TOEFL (minimum score 100 iBT). *Application deadline:* For fall admission, 1/20 priority date for domestic and international students. Application fee: $75. Electronic applications accepted. *Expenses: Tuition:* Full-time $25,974; part-time $1443 per credit hour. *Required fees:* $802; $50 per course. Tuition and fees vary according to course load and program. *Financial support:* Fellowships with full tuition reimbursements, research assistantships with tuition reimbursements, teaching assistantships with tuition reimbursements, and scholarships/grants available. Financial award application deadline: 1/1; financial award applicants required to submit FAFSA. *Faculty research:* Pure mathematics, numerical mathematics, computing statistics. *Unit head:* Dr. Uday Banerjee, Chair, 315-443-1471, E-mail: banerjee@syr.edu. *Application contact:* Graham Leuschke, Professor and Associate Chair for Graduate Affairs, 315-443-1500, E-mail: gjleusch@syr.edu.
Website: http://math.syr.edu

Syracuse University, School of Education, Programs in Mathematics Education, Syracuse, NY 13244. Offers MS, PhD. *Program availability:* Part-time. *Students:* Average age 30. *Degree requirements:* For master's, thesis or alternative; for doctorate, comprehensive exam, thesis/dissertation. *Entrance requirements:* For master's, GRE or MAT, baccalaureate degree from regionally-accredited college/university, transcripts, personal essay; for doctorate, GRE, master's degree, transcripts. Additional exam requirements/recommendations for international students: Required—TOEFL (minimum score 100 iBT). *Application deadline:* For fall admission, 1/15 priority date for domestic and international students; for spring admission, 10/15 priority date for domestic and international students. Applications are processed on a rolling basis. Application fee: $75. Electronic applications accepted. *Expenses: Tuition:* Full-time $25,974; part-time $1443 per credit hour. *Required fees:* $802; $50 per course. Tuition and fees vary according to course load and program. *Financial support:* Fellowships with full tuition reimbursements, research assistantships, teaching assistantships with tuition reimbursements, career-related internships or fieldwork, and scholarships/grants available. Financial award application deadline: 1/15. *Unit head:* Dr. Joanna Masingila, Dean and Professor, 315-443-4751, E-mail: jomasing@syr.edu. *Application contact:* Speranza Migliore, Graduate Admissions Recruiter, 315-443-2505, E-mail: gradrcrt@syr.edu.
Website: http://soe.syr.edu/

Teachers College, Columbia University, Department of Mathematics, Science and Technology, New York, NY 10027-6696. Offers biology 7-12 (MA); chemistry 7-12 (MA); communication and education (MA, Ed D); computing in education (MA); earth science 7-12 (MA); instructional technology and media (Ed M, MA, Ed D); mathematics education (Ed M, MA, Ed D, Ed DCT, PhD); physics 7-12 (MA); science and dental education (MA); science education (Ed M, MS, Ed DCT, PhD); supervisor/teacher of science education (MA); technology specialist (MA). *Program availability:* Part-time, evening/weekend, online learning. *Students:* 195 full-time (133 women), 222 part-time (139 women); includes 152 minority (44 Black or African American, non-Hispanic/Latino; 66 Asian, non-Hispanic/Latino; 32 Hispanic/Latino; 10 Two or more races, non-Hispanic/Latino), 106 international. 368 applicants, 65% accepted, 123 enrolled. Terminal master's awarded for partial completion of doctoral program. *Degree requirements:* For doctorate, thesis/dissertation. *Expenses: Tuition:* Full-time $36,288; part-time $1512 per credit. *Required fees:* $438 per semester. One-time fee: $510 full-time. Full-time tuition and fees vary according to course load. *Unit head:* Dr. O. Roger Anderson, Chair, 212-678-3405, Fax: 212-678-8129, E-mail: ora@ldeo.columbia.edu. *Application contact:* David Estrella, Director of Admission, 212-678-3305, E-mail: estrella@tc.columbia.edu.
Website: http://www.tc.columbia.edu/mathematics-science-and-technology/

Temple University, College of Education, Department of Teaching and Learning, Philadelphia, PA 19122-6096. Offers career and technical education (Ed M), including business, computing, and information technology, industrial education, marketing education; middle grades education (Ed M), including math and language arts, math and science, science and language arts; secondary education (Ed M), including English, math, social studies; teaching English to speakers of other languages (MS Ed); urban education (Ed M). *Program availability:* Part-time, evening/weekend. *Faculty:* 26 full-time (16 women), 74 part-time/adjunct (54 women). *Students:* 204 full-time (139 women), 320 part-time (201 women); includes 112 minority (66 Black or African American, non-Hispanic/Latino; 17 Asian, non-Hispanic/Latino; 18 Hispanic/Latino; 11 Two or more races, non-Hispanic/Latino), 18 international. 300 applicants, 55% accepted, 99 enrolled. In 2016, 93 master's awarded. Terminal master's awarded for partial completion of doctoral program. *Degree requirements:* For master's, thesis or alternative. *Entrance requirements:* Additional exam requirements/recommendations for international students: Required—TOEFL (minimum score 550 paper-based; 79 iBT). *Application deadline:* For fall admission, 4/1 for domestic students, 12/15 for international students; for spring admission, 10/1 for domestic students, 8/1 for international students. Application fee: $60. Electronic applications accepted. *Expenses:* Contact institution. *Financial support:* Fellowships, research assistantships, and teaching assistantships available. Financial award application deadline: 1/15; financial award applicants required to submit FAFSA. *Faculty research:* Workforce development, vocational education, technical education, industrial education, professional development, literacy, classroom management, school communities, curriculum development, instruction, applied linguistics, cross linguistic influence, bilingual education, oral proficiency, multilingualism. *Unit head:* Dr. Christine Woyshner, Chairperson, 215-204-6387, E-mail: christine.woyshner@temple.edu. *Application contact:* Sarah Stapleton, Assistant Director, Academic Operations, 215-204-8220, E-mail: sarah.stapleton@temple.edu.
Website: http://education.temple.edu/tl

Tennessee Technological University, College of Graduate Studies, College of Education, Department of Curriculum and Instruction, Program in STEM Education, Cookeville, TN 38505. Offers MA, Ed S. *Program availability:* Part-time, evening/weekend. *Students:* 2 full-time (1 woman), 3 part-time (2 women). 3 applicants, 100% accepted, 2 enrolled. *Degree requirements:* For master's, comprehensive exam, thesis or alternative. *Entrance requirements:* For master's, GRE, MAT. Additional exam requirements/recommendations for international students: Required—TOEFL (minimum score 527 paper-based; 71 iBT), IELTS (minimum score 5.5) or PTE (48). *Application deadline:* For fall admission, 8/1 for domestic students, 5/1 for international students; for spring admission, 2/1 for domestic students, 10/1 for international students; for summer admission, 5/1 for domestic students, 2/1 for international students. Applications are processed on a rolling basis. Application fee: $35 ($40 for international students). Electronic applications accepted. *Expenses:* Tuition, state resident: full-time $9375; part-time $534 per credit hour. Tuition, nonresident: full-time $22,443; part-time $1260 per credit hour. *Financial support:* Application deadline: 4/1. *Unit head:* Dr. Jeremy

Wendt, Interim Chairperson, 931-372-3181, E-mail: jwendt@tntech.edu. *Application contact:* Shelia K. Kendrick, Coordinator of Graduate Studies, 931-372-3808, Fax: 931-372-3497, E-mail: skendrick@tntech.edu.

Texas Christian University, College of Education, Master's Programs in Education, Fort Worth, TX 76129. Offers counseling (M Ed); curriculum and instruction (M Ed), including curriculum studies, language and literacy, math education, science education; educational leadership (M Ed); special education (M Ed). *Program availability:* Part-time, evening/weekend. *Faculty:* 29 full-time (21 women), 8 part-time/adjunct (5 women). *Students:* 112 full-time (95 women), 12 part-time (11 women); includes 39 minority (6 Black or African American, non-Hispanic/Latino; 2 Asian, non-Hispanic/Latino; 27 Hispanic/Latino; 1 Native Hawaiian or other Pacific Islander, non-Hispanic/Latino; 3 Two or more races, non-Hispanic/Latino), 2 international. Average age 29. 107 applicants, 78% accepted, 66 enrolled. In 2016, 54 master's awarded. *Degree requirements:* For master's, comprehensive exam (for some programs), thesis (for some programs). *Entrance requirements:* For master's, GRE General Test. Additional exam requirements/recommendations for international students: Required—TOEFL (minimum score 550 paper-based; 80 iBT). *Application deadline:* For fall admission, 3/1 for domestic and international students; for spring admission, 11/16 for domestic and international students; for summer admission, 3/1 for domestic and international students. Application fee: $60. Electronic applications accepted. *Expenses: Tuition:* Full-time $26,640; part-time $1480 per credit hour. *Required fees:* $48. Tuition and fees vary according to program. *Financial support:* In 2016–17, 104 students received support, including 4 research assistantships with full tuition reimbursements available (averaging $15,000 per year), 31 teaching assistantships with full tuition reimbursements available (averaging $15,000 per year); career-related internships or fieldwork, scholarships/grants, and unspecified assistantships also available. Support available to part-time students. Financial award application deadline: 3/1; financial award applicants required to submit FAFSA. *Unit head:* Dr. Jan Lacina, Associate Dean, 817-257-6786, Fax: 817-257-7466, E-mail: j.lacina@tcu.edu. *Application contact:* Lori Kimball, Administrative Program Specialist, 817-257-7661, Fax: 817-257-7466, E-mail: l.kimball@tcu.edu.
Website: http://coe.tcu.edu/graduate-overview/

Texas State University, The Graduate College, College of Science and Engineering, PhD Program in Mathematics Education, San Marcos, TX 78666. Offers PhD. *Program availability:* Part-time. *Faculty:* 19 full-time (9 women). *Students:* 19 full-time (11 women), 7 part-time (3 women); includes 4 minority (1 Black or African American, non-Hispanic/Latino; 1 Hispanic/Latino; 2 Two or more races, non-Hispanic/Latino), 4 international. Average age 33. 17 applicants, 53% accepted, 3 enrolled. In 2016, 6 doctorates awarded. *Degree requirements:* For doctorate, comprehensive exam, thesis/dissertation. *Entrance requirements:* For doctorate, GRE (minimum preferred score of 300 verbal and quantitative combined), baccalaureate degree from regionally-accredited university with minimum GPA of 3.0 on last 60 undergraduate semester hours, 500-word statement of purpose, current curriculum vitae, 3 letters of recommendation, interview with faculty, 2 years of teaching experience. Additional exam requirements/recommendations for international students: Required—TOEFL (minimum score 550 paper-based; 78 iBT), IELTS (minimum score 6.5). *Application deadline:* For fall admission, 1/10 for domestic and international students; for spring admission, 8/10 for domestic and international students. Application fee: $40 ($90 for international students). Electronic applications accepted. *Expenses:* $4,851 per semester. *Financial support:* In 2016–17, 18 students received support, including 1 research assistantship (averaging $15,324 per year), 18 teaching assistantships (averaging $28,648 per year); Federal Work-Study, institutionally sponsored loans, scholarships/grants, health care benefits, and unspecified assistantships also available. Support available to part-time students. Financial award application deadline: 3/1; financial award applicants required to submit FAFSA. *Faculty research:* Dynamic geometry in classrooms, mathematics instruction for English language learners. *Total annual research expenditures:* $248,262. *Unit head:* Dr. Alexander White, PhD Program Director, 512-245-2551, E-mail: aw22@txstate.edu. *Application contact:* Dr. Andrea Golato, Dean of the Graduate College, 512-245-2581, Fax: 512-245-8365, E-mail: gradcollege@txstate.edu.
Website: http://www.math.txstate.edu/degrees-programs/phd.html

Texas State University, The Graduate College, College of Science and Engineering, Program in Middle School Mathematics Teaching, San Marcos, TX 78666. Offers M Ed. *Program availability:* Part-time. *Faculty:* 8 full-time (3 women). *Students:* 1 full-time (0 women), 2 part-time (1 woman); includes 1 minority (Hispanic/Latino), 1 international. Average age 38. In 2016, 3 master's awarded. *Degree requirements:* For master's, comprehensive exam. *Entrance requirements:* For master's, GRE (minimum preferred score of 300 verbal and quantitative combined), baccalaureate degree in mathematics or related field from regionally-accredited university with minimum GPA of 2.75 on last 60 undergraduate semester hours. Additional exam requirements/recommendations for international students: Required—TOEFL (minimum score 550 paper-based; 78 iBT), IELTS (minimum score 6.5). *Application deadline:* For fall admission, 6/15 for domestic students, 6/1 for international students; for spring admission, 10/15 for domestic students, 10/1 for international students; for summer admission, 4/15 for domestic students, 3/15 for international students. Applications are processed on a rolling basis. Application fee: $40 ($90 for international students). Electronic applications accepted. *Expenses:* $4,851 per semester. *Financial support:* Teaching assistantships, Federal Work-Study, and institutionally sponsored loans available. Support available to part-time students. Financial award application deadline: 3/1; financial award applicants required to submit FAFSA. *Unit head:* Dr. Gregory Passty, Graduate Advisor, 512-245-2551, Fax: 512-245-3425, E-mail: gp02@txstate.edu. *Application contact:* Dr. Andrea Golato, Dean of the Graduate College, 512-245-2581, E-mail: gradcollege@txstate.edu.
Website: http://www.txstate.edu/math/degrees-programs/masters/middle-school.html

Texas Woman's University, Graduate School, College of Arts and Sciences, Department of Mathematics and Computer Science, Denton, TX 76201. Offers informatics (MS); mathematics (MS); mathematics teaching (MS). *Program availability:* Part-time, evening/weekend. *Students:* Average age 38. In 2016, 10 master's awarded. *Degree requirements:* For master's, comprehensive exam, thesis. *Entrance requirements:* For master's, 2 letters of reference. Additional exam requirements/recommendations for international students: Required—TOEFL (minimum score 550 paper-based; 79 iBT). *Application deadline:* For fall admission, 7/1 priority date for domestic students, 3/1 for international students; for spring admission, 12/1 priority date for domestic students, 7/1 for international students. Applications are processed on a rolling basis. Application fee: $50 ($75 for international students). Electronic applications accepted. *Expenses:* Tuition, state resident: full-time $9046; part-time $251 per credit hour. Tuition, nonresident: full-time $22,922; part-time $614 per credit hour. *International tuition:* $23,046 full-time. *Required fees:* $2690; $1285 per credit hour. One-time fee: $50. Tuition and fees vary according to course level, course load, program and reciprocity agreements. *Financial support:* Research assistantships, teaching assistantships, career-related internships or fieldwork, Federal Work-Study, institutionally sponsored loans, scholarships/grants, traineeships, health care benefits, and unspecified assistantships available. Support available to part-time students. Financial award application deadline: 3/1; financial award applicants required to submit FAFSA. *Faculty research:* Biopharmaceutical statistics, dynamic systems and control theory, Bayesian inference, math and computer science curriculum innovation, computer modeling of physical phenomenon. *Unit head:* Dr. Don E. Edwards, Chair, 940-898-3275, Fax: 940-898-2179, E-mail: mathcs@twu.edu. *Application contact:* Dr. Samuel Wheeler, Assistant Director of Admissions, 940-898-3188, Fax: 940-898-3081, E-mail: wheelersr@twu.edu.
Website: http://www.twu.edu/math-computer-science/

Touro College, Graduate School of Education, New York, NY 10010. Offers education and special education (MS); education biology (MS); instructional technology (MS); mathematics education (MS); school leadership (MS); teaching English to speakers of other languages (MS); teaching literacy (MS). *Accreditation:* TEAC. *Program availability:* Part-time, evening/weekend, online learning. *Faculty:* 52 full-time (34 women), 199 part-time/adjunct (136 women). *Students:* 578 full-time (483 women), 1,932 part-time (1,626 women); includes 749 minority (318 Black or African American, non-Hispanic/Latino; 5 American Indian or Alaska Native, non-Hispanic/Latino; 108 Asian, non-Hispanic/Latino; 288 Hispanic/Latino; 2 Native Hawaiian or other Pacific Islander, non-Hispanic/Latino; 28 Two or more races, non-Hispanic/Latino), 17 international. Average age 32. 1,422 applicants, 50% accepted, 675 enrolled. In 2016, 6 master's awarded. *Entrance requirements:* Additional exam requirements/recommendations for international students: Required—TOEFL (minimum score 83 iBT), IELTS (minimum score 6.5). *Application deadline:* For fall admission, 8/26 for domestic students, 7/15 for international students; for spring admission, 12/31 for domestic students, 12/15 for international students. Applications are processed on a rolling basis. Application fee: $50. *Financial support:* Federal Work-Study available. Financial award applicants required to submit FAFSA. *Faculty research:* Equity assistance, language development, scholarly communications, Latin American studies and cultural sensitivity, behavior management techniques and strategies in special education. *Unit head:* Dr. Arnold Spinner, Dean, 212-463-0400 Ext. 5561, Fax: 212-462-4889, E-mail: aspinner@touro.edu. *Application contact:* Luna Feliciano, Admissions, 212-463-0400.

Towson University, Program in Mathematics Education, Towson, MD 21252-0001. Offers MS. *Accreditation:* NCATE. *Program availability:* Part-time, evening/weekend. *Students:* 1 (woman) full-time, 34 part-time (27 women); includes 4 minority (1 Black or African American, non-Hispanic/Latino; 2 Asian, non-Hispanic/Latino; 1 Two or more races, non-Hispanic/Latino). *Entrance requirements:* For master's, undergraduate degree in mathematics or elementary education, current certification for teaching secondary school or elementary school mathematics, minimum GPA of 3.0. *Application deadline:* Applications are processed on a rolling basis. Application fee: $45. Electronic applications accepted. *Expenses:* Tuition, state resident: full-time $7580; part-time $379 per unit. Tuition, nonresident: full-time $15,700; part-time $785 per unit. *Required fees:* $2480. *Financial support:* Application deadline: 4/1. *Unit head:* Dr. Maureen Yarnevich, Graduate Program Director, 410-704-2988, E-mail: myarnevich@towson.edu. *Application contact:* Coverley Beidleman, Assistant Director of Graduate Admissions, 410-704-2113, Fax: 410-704-3030, E-mail: grads@towson.edu.
Website: http://www.towson.edu/fcsm/departments/mathematics/grad/education/

Tufts University, Graduate School of Arts and Sciences, Department of Education, Program in Education, Medford, MA 02155. Offers educational studies (MA); elementary education (MAT); middle and secondary education (MAT); museum education (MA); secondary education (MA); STEM education (MS, PhD). *Program availability:* Part-time. *Students:* 67 full-time (49 women), 14 part-time (12 women); includes 17 minority (4 Black or African American, non-Hispanic/Latino; 6 Asian, non-Hispanic/Latino; 6 Hispanic/Latino; 1 Two or more races, non-Hispanic/Latino), 6 international. Average age 28. 120 applicants, 71% accepted, 49 enrolled. In 2016, 25 master's awarded. *Degree requirements:* For master's, thesis optional. *Entrance requirements:* For master's, GRE General Test, portfolio (for art education only); for doctorate, GRE General Test, writing sample. Additional exam requirements/recommendations for international students: Required—TOEFL (minimum score 550 paper-based; 80 iBT), IELTS (minimum score 6.5). *Application deadline:* For fall admission, 1/2 for domestic and international students; for spring admission, 10/15 for domestic and international students. Applications are processed on a rolling basis. Application fee: $85. Electronic applications accepted. *Expenses:* Contact institution. *Financial support:* In 2016–17, 69 students received support. Research assistantships, teaching assistantships, Federal Work-Study, scholarships/grants, and tuition waivers (full and partial) available. Support available to part-time students. Financial award application deadline: 1/2. *Unit head:* Dr. Sabina Vaught, Graduate Program Director. *Application contact:* Office of Graduate Admissions, 617-627-3395, E-mail: gradadmissions@tufts.edu.

Tusculum College, Graduate and Professional Studies, Program in Curriculum and Instruction, Greeneville, TN 37743-9997. Offers mathematics education (MA Ed); special education (MA Ed). *Program availability:* Evening/weekend. *Degree requirements:* For master's, thesis or alternative. *Entrance requirements:* For master's, NTE, PRAXIS II, GRE, MAT, 3 years of work experience, minimum GPA of 3.0, bachelor's degree. Additional exam requirements/recommendations for international students: Required—TOEFL (minimum score 540 paper-based; 73 iBT). *Application deadline:* Applications are processed on a rolling basis. Application fee: $0. *Expenses: Tuition:* Full-time $7497; part-time $357 per credit hour. *Unit head:* Dr. Tricia Hunsader, Dean, School of Education, 423-636-7300 Ext. 5693, E-mail: thunsader@tusculum.edu. *Application contact:* Lindsey Seal, Director of Enrollment, 423-636-7300 Ext. 5006, E-mail: lseal@tusculum.edu.
Website: http://home.tusculum.edu/gps/graduate-degrees/master-arts-education-curriculum-instruction/

Universidad Autonoma de Guadalajara, Graduate Programs, Guadalajara, Mexico. Offers administrative law and justice (LL M); advertising and corporate communications (MA); architecture (M Arch); business (MBA); computational science (MCC); education (Ed M, Ed D); English-Spanish translation (MA); entrepreneurship and management (MBA); integrated management of digital animation (MA); international business (MIB); international corporate law (LL M); internet technologies (MS); manufacturing systems (MMS); occupational health (MS); philosophy (MA, PhD); power electronics (MS); quality systems (MQS); renewable energy (MS); social evaluation of projects (MBA); strategic market research (MBA); tax law (MA); teaching mathematics (MA).

University at Buffalo, the State University of New York, Graduate School, Graduate School of Education, Department of Learning and Instruction, Buffalo, NY 14260. Offers biology education (Ed M, Certificate); chemistry education (Ed M, Certificate); childhood education (Ed M); childhood education with bilingual extension (Ed M); college teaching (Advanced Certificate); curriculum, instruction and the science of learning (PhD); early childhood education (Ed M); early childhood education with bilingual extension (Ed M); earth science education (Ed M, Certificate); education and technology (Ed M); education studies (Ed M); educational technology and new literacies (Certificate); educational technology and new literacies (Advanced Certificate); elementary education (Ed D); English education (Ed M, Certificate); English education studies (Ed M); English for speakers of other languages (Ed M); foreign and second language education (PhD); French education (Ed M, Certificate); German education (Ed M, Certificate); gifted education (Certificate); Latin education (Ed M, Certificate); literacy education studies (Ed M); literacy specialist (Ed M); literacy teaching and learning (Certificate); mathematics education (Ed M, Certificate); music education (Ed M, Certificate); music education studies (Ed M); music learning theory (Advanced Certificate); online education (Advanced Certificate); physics education (Ed M, Certificate); science and the public (Ed M); social studies education (Ed M, Certificate); Spanish education (Ed M,

Certificate); special education (PhD); teaching English to speakers of other languages (Ed M). *Program availability:* Part-time, evening/weekend, 100% online. *Faculty:* 28 full-time (21 women), 67 part-time/adjunct (49 women). *Students:* 198 full-time (153 women), 312 part-time (220 women); includes 48 minority (28 Black or African American, non-Hispanic/Latino; 4 American Indian or Alaska Native, non-Hispanic/Latino; 15 Asian, non-Hispanic/Latino; 1 Hispanic/Latino), 66 international. Average age 33. 336 applicants, 86% accepted, 178 enrolled. In 2016, 137 master's, 24 doctorates, 25 other advanced degrees awarded. *Degree requirements:* For master's, comprehensive exam; for doctorate, thesis/dissertation, research analysis exam, research experience. *Entrance requirements:* For master's, letters of reference; for doctorate, GRE General Test or MAT, interview, writing sample, letters of recommendation. Additional exam requirements/recommendations for international students: Required—TOEFL (minimum score 600 paper-based; 96 iBT). *Application deadline:* For fall admission, 2/1 priority date for domestic and international students; for spring admission, 11/15 priority date for domestic students, 10/1 for international students. Applications are processed on a rolling basis. Application fee: $50. Electronic applications accepted. *Financial support:* In 2016–17, 44 fellowships (averaging $4,010 per year), 39 research assistantships with tuition reimbursements (averaging $9,897 per year) were awarded; teaching assistantships, career-related internships or fieldwork, Federal Work-Study, institutionally sponsored loans, scholarships/grants, tuition waivers (full and partial), and unspecified assistantships also available. Financial award application deadline: 2/28; financial award applicants required to submit FAFSA. *Faculty research:* Science assessment, foreign language teaching and learning, early learning, new literacies, gender and education. *Total annual research expenditures:* $534,880. *Unit head:* Dr. Deborah Moore-Russo, Chair, 716-645-4069, Fax: 716-645-3161, E-mail: dam29@buffalo.edu. *Application contact:* Luann Zak, Admissions Assistant, 716-645-2110, Fax: 716-645-7937, E-mail: luannzak@buffalo.edu.
Website: http://gse.buffalo.edu/lai

The University of Akron, Graduate School, College of Education, Department of Curricular and Instructional Studies, Program in Adolescent to Young Adult Education, Akron, OH 44325. Offers chemistry (MS); chemistry and physics (MS); earth science (MS); earth science and chemistry (MS); earth science and physics (MS); integrated language arts (MS); integrated mathematics (MS); integrated social studies (MS); life science (MS); life science and chemistry (MS); life science and earth science (MS); life science and physics (MS); physics (MS). *Accreditation:* NCATE. *Degree requirements:* For master's, comprehensive exam, portfolio. *Entrance requirements:* Additional exam requirements/recommendations for international students: Required—TOEFL (minimum score 550 paper-based, 79 iBT) or IELTS (minimum score 6.5). *Application deadline:* For fall admission, 3/1 for domestic and international students; for spring admission, 10/1 for domestic and international students. Applications are processed on a rolling basis. Application fee: $45 ($70 for international students). Electronic applications accepted. *Expenses:* Tuition, state resident: full-time $8618; part-time $359 per credit hour. Tuition, nonresident: full-time $17,149; part-time $715 per credit hour. *Required fees:* $1652. *Unit head:* Dr. Peggy McCann, Interim Chair, 330-972-5742, E-mail: plm@uakron.edu.

The University of Alabama in Huntsville, School of Graduate Studies, College of Education, Huntsville, AL 35899. Offers autism spectrum disorders (M Ed, Graduate Certificate); biology (MAT); chemistry (MAT); differentiated instruction in elementary education (M Ed); English language arts (MAT); English speakers of other languages (M Ed, MAT); history (MAT); mathematics (MAT); physics (MAT); reading education (M Ed); secondary education (M Ed). *Expenses:* Tuition, state resident: full-time $9834; part-time $600 per credit hour. Tuition, nonresident: full-time $21,830; part-time $1325 per credit hour.

The University of Alabama in Huntsville, School of Graduate Studies, College of Science, Department of Mathematical Sciences, Huntsville, AL 35899. Offers applied mathematics (PhD); education (MA); mathematics (MA, MS). PhD offered jointly with The University of Alabama (Tuscaloosa) and The University of Alabama at Birmingham. *Program availability:* Part-time, evening/weekend. *Degree requirements:* For master's, comprehensive exam, thesis or alternative, oral and written exams; for doctorate, comprehensive exam, thesis/dissertation, oral and written exams. *Entrance requirements:* For master's and doctorate, GRE General Test, minimum GPA of 3.0. Additional exam requirements/recommendations for international students: Required—TOEFL (minimum score 550 paper-based; 80 iBT), IELTS (minimum score 6.5). Electronic applications accepted. *Expenses:* Tuition, state resident: full-time $9834; part-time $600 per credit hour. Tuition, nonresident: full-time $21,830; part-time $1325 per credit hour. *Faculty research:* Combinatorics and graph theory, computational mathematics, differential equations and applications, mathematical biology, probability and stochastic processes.

University of Alaska Southeast, Graduate Programs, Program in Education, Juneau, AK 99801. Offers educational leadership (M Ed); elementary education (MAT); learning design and technology (M Ed); mathematics education (M Ed); reading specialist (M Ed); secondary education (MAT); special education (M Ed, MAT). *Accreditation:* NCATE. *Program availability:* Part-time, evening/weekend, online learning. *Degree requirements:* For master's, comprehensive exam or project, portfolio. *Entrance requirements:* For master's, PRAXIS, minimum GPA of 3.0, writing sample, letters of recommendation. *Application deadline:* For fall admission, 3/8 for domestic students. Applications are processed on a rolling basis. Application fee: $60. Electronic applications accepted. *Expenses:* Tuition, state resident: part-time $466 per credit. Tuition, nonresident: part-time $979 per credit. *Required fees:* $19 per credit. Part-time tuition and fees vary according to course level, campus/location and reciprocity agreements. *Financial support:* Federal Work-Study, scholarships/grants, and tuition waivers (full and partial) available. Support available to part-time students. Financial award applicants required to submit FAFSA. *Faculty research:* Applied classroom research, culturally responsive practices, action research, teaching effectiveness. *Unit head:* Dr. Larry Harris, Dean, 907-796-6551, Fax: 907-796-6550, E-mail: larry.harris@uas.alaska.edu. *Application contact:* Susan A. Stuck, Administrative Assistant, 866-465-6424, Fax: 866-465-5159, E-mail: jnsas@uas.alaska.edu.

The University of Arizona, College of Science, Department of Mathematics, Program in Secondary Mathematics Education, Tucson, AZ 85721. Offers MA. *Program availability:* Part-time. *Degree requirements:* For master's, thesis, internships, colloquium, business courses. *Entrance requirements:* For master's, GRE, minimum GPA of 3.0, statement of purpose. Additional exam requirements/recommendations for international students: Required—TOEFL (minimum score 550 paper-based). *Faculty research:* Algebra, coding theory, graph theory, combinatorics, probability.

University of Arkansas, Graduate School, J. William Fulbright College of Arts and Sciences, Department of Mathematical Sciences, Program in Secondary Mathematics, Fayetteville, AR 72701. Offers MA. *Accreditation:* NCATE. In 2016, 2 master's awarded. *Degree requirements:* For master's, written exam. *Application deadline:* For fall admission, 4/1 for international students; for spring admission, 10/1 for international students. Applications are processed on a rolling basis. Application fee: $40 ($50 for international students). Electronic applications accepted. *Financial support:* In 2016–17, 1 teaching assistantship was awarded; fellowships, research assistantships, career-related internships or fieldwork, and Federal Work-Study also available. Support available to part-time students. Financial award application deadline: 4/1; financial award applicants required to submit FAFSA. *Unit head:* Dr. Mark Johnson, Chair, 479-575-3351, Fax: 479-575-8630, E-mail: markj@uark.edu. *Application contact:* Dr. Maria Tjani, Graduate Coordinator, 479-575-3351, Fax: 479-575-8630, E-mail: mtjani@uark.edu.
Website: http://math.uark.edu/

University of Arkansas at Pine Bluff, School of Education, Pine Bluff, AR 71601-2799. Offers elementary education (M Ed); secondary education (M Ed), including English education, mathematics education, science education, social studies education; teaching (MAT). *Accreditation:* NCATE. *Program availability:* Part-time, evening/weekend. *Degree requirements:* For master's, comprehensive exam. *Entrance requirements:* For master's, GRE, minimum GPA of 2.75, NTE or Standard Arkansas Teaching Certificate. Application fee: $25. *Expenses:* Tuition, state resident: full-time $4776. Tuition, nonresident: full-time $10,824. *Required fees:* $1612. Tuition and fees vary according to course load. *Financial support:* Research assistantships with full and partial tuition reimbursements, teaching assistantships with full and partial tuition reimbursements, institutionally sponsored loans, and scholarships/grants available. Support available to part-time students. *Faculty research:* Teacher certification, accreditation, assessment, standards, portfolio development, rehabilitation, technology. *Unit head:* Dr. George Herts, Dean, 870-575-8000, E-mail: johnson_c@uapb.edu.
Website: http://www.uapb.edu/academics/school_of_education.aspx

The University of British Columbia, Faculty of Education, Department of Curriculum and Pedagogy, Vancouver, BC V6T 1Z4, Canada. Offers art education (M Ed, MA); curriculum studies (M Ed, MA, PhD); home economics education (M Ed, MA); mathematics education (M Ed, MA); media and technology studies education (M Ed, MA); music education (M Ed, MA); physical education (M Ed, MA); science education (M Ed, MA); social studies education (M Ed, MA). *Program availability:* Part-time, online learning. *Degree requirements:* For master's, thesis (MA); for doctorate, comprehensive exam, thesis/dissertation. *Entrance requirements:* Additional exam requirements/recommendations for international students: Required—TOEFL, IELTS. Application fee: $100 Canadian dollars ($162 Canadian dollars for international students). Electronic applications accepted. *Expenses:* $6,865 per year tuition and fees domestic, $10,938 per year international (for MA and M Ed); $4,802 per year tuition and fees, $8,436 per year international (for PhD). *Financial support:* Fellowships with partial tuition reimbursements, research assistantships with partial tuition reimbursements, teaching assistantships with partial tuition reimbursements, and tuition waivers (partial) available. *Faculty research:* School subjects, teaching and learning. *Application contact:* Alan Jay, Graduate Programs Assistant, 604-822-5367, Fax: 604-822-4714, E-mail: edcp.grad@ubc.ca.
Website: http://www.edcp.educ.ubc.ca/

University of California, Berkeley, Graduate Division, School of Education, Group in Science and Mathematics Education, Berkeley, CA 94720-1500. Offers PhD, MA/Credential. *Students:* 17 full-time (15 women); includes 1 minority (Hispanic/Latino), 3 international. Average age 30. 12 applicants, 4 enrolled. In 2016, 5 doctorates awarded. *Application deadline:* For fall admission, 12/1 for domestic students. Application fee: $105 ($125 for international students). Electronic applications accepted. *Financial support:* Fellowships, research assistantships, teaching assistantships, institutionally sponsored loans, health care benefits, and unspecified assistantships available. *Application contact:* Kate Capps, Graduate Student Services Advisor, 510-642-4207, E-mail: sme_info@lists.berkeley.edu.
Website: https://gse.berkeley.edu/sesame

University of California, Berkeley, Graduate Division, School of Education, Programs in Education, Berkeley, CA 94720-1500. Offers development in mathematics and science (MA); education in mathematics, science, and technology (MA, PhD); human development and education (MA, PhD); leadership education (MA); special education (PhD); teacher education (MA); MA/Credential; PhD/Credential; PhD/MA. *Students:* 286 full-time (207 women); includes 133 minority (31 Black or African American, non-Hispanic/Latino; 2 American Indian or Alaska Native, non-Hispanic/Latino; 44 Asian, non-Hispanic/Latino; 56 Hispanic/Latino), 29 international. Average age 33. 643 applicants, 84 enrolled. In 2016, 105 master's, 31 doctorates awarded. Terminal master's awarded for partial completion of doctoral program. *Degree requirements:* For master's, exam or thesis; for doctorate, thesis/dissertation, oral qualifying exam. *Entrance requirements:* For master's and doctorate, GRE General Test, minimum GPA of 3.0 during last 2 years of undergraduate course work. *Application deadline:* For fall admission, 12/16 for domestic students. Application fee: $105 ($125 for international students). Electronic applications accepted. *Financial support:* Fellowships, research assistantships, teaching assistantships, institutionally sponsored loans, health care benefits, and unspecified assistantships available. *Faculty research:* Human development, social and moral educational psychology, developmental teacher preparation. *Unit head:* Prof. Prudence L. Carter, Dean, 510-642-3726, E-mail: gsedeansoffice@lists.berkeley.edu.
Website: https://gse.berkeley.edu

University of California, San Diego, Graduate Division, Program in Mathematics and Science Education, La Jolla, CA 92093. Offers PhD. Program offered jointly with San Diego State University. *Students:* 3 full-time (0 women), 8 part-time (7 women). In 2016, 3 doctorates awarded. *Degree requirements:* For doctorate, thesis/dissertation, teaching practicum. *Entrance requirements:* For doctorate, GRE General Test, minimum GPA of 3.25. Additional exam requirements/recommendations for international students: Required—TOEFL (minimum score 550 paper-based; 80 iBT), IELTS (minimum score 7). Electronic applications accepted. *Expenses:* Tuition, state resident: full-time $11,220. Tuition, nonresident: full-time $26,322. *Required fees:* $1864. *Financial support:* Scholarships/grants and stipends available. Financial award applicants required to submit FAFSA. *Faculty research:* Effective teaching of rational numbers, teacher development, development of number sense and estimation. *Unit head:* Gabriele Wienhausen, Chair, 858-534-3105, E-mail: gwienhausen@ucsd.edu. *Application contact:* Sherry Seethaler, Graduate Coordinator, 858-534-4656, E-mail: sseethaler@ucsd.edu.
Website: http://sci.sdsu.edu/CRMSE/msed/

University of Central Arkansas, Graduate School, College of Natural Sciences and Math, Department of Mathematics, Conway, AR 72035-0001. Offers applied mathematics (MS); math education (MA). *Program availability:* Part-time. *Degree requirements:* For master's, comprehensive exam, thesis optional. *Entrance requirements:* For master's, GRE General Test, minimum GPA of 2.7. Additional exam requirements/recommendations for international students: Required—TOEFL (minimum score 550 paper-based; 80 iBT). Electronic applications accepted.

University of Central Florida, College of Education and Human Performance, Education Doctoral Programs, Orlando, FL 32816. Offers communication sciences and disorders (PhD); curriculum and instruction (Ed D); early childhood education (PhD); educational leadership (Ed D); elementary education (PhD); exceptional education (PhD); exercise physiology (PhD); higher education (PhD); instructional technology (PhD); mathematics education (PhD); methodology, measurement and analysis (PhD); reading education (PhD); science education (PhD); social science education (PhD); TESOL (PhD). *Students:* 127 full-time (91 women), 43 part-time (29 women); includes

33 minority (17 Black or African American, non-Hispanic/Latino; 5 Asian, non-Hispanic/Latino; 7 Hispanic/Latino; 4 Two or more races, non-Hispanic/Latino), 26 international. Average age 37. 163 applicants, 40% accepted, 52 enrolled. In 2016, 57 doctorates awarded. Application fee: $30. Electronic applications accepted. *Expenses:* Tuition, state resident: part-time $288.16 per credit hour. Tuition, nonresident: part-time $1071.31 per credit hour. *Financial support:* In 2016–17, 78 students received support, including 41 fellowships with partial tuition reimbursements available (averaging $5,916 per year), 44 research assistantships with partial tuition reimbursements available (averaging $7,637 per year), 48 teaching assistantships with partial tuition reimbursements available (averaging $9,633 per year). Financial award application deadline: 3/1; financial award applicants required to submit FAFSA. *Unit head:* Dr. Edward Robinson, Director of Doctoral Programs, 407-823-6106, E-mail: edward.robinson@ucf.edu. *Application contact:* Assistant Director, Graduate Admissions, 407-823-2766, Fax: 407-823-6442, E-mail: gradadmissions@ucf.edu.
Website: http://education.ucf.edu/programs.cfm?pid=g&cat=2

University of Central Florida, College of Education and Human Performance, School of Teaching, Learning, and Leadership, Program in K-8 Mathematics and Science Education, Orlando, FL 32816. Offers M Ed, Certificate. *Accreditation:* NCATE. *Program availability:* Part-time. *Students:* 21 part-time (18 women); includes 11 minority (4 Black or African American, non-Hispanic/Latino; 7 Hispanic/Latino). Average age 35. 3 applicants, 100% accepted, 2 enrolled. In 2016, 4 master's awarded. *Degree requirements:* For master's, thesis or alternative. *Entrance requirements:* Additional exam requirements/recommendations for international students: Required—TOEFL. *Application deadline:* For summer admission, 4/15 for domestic students. Application fee: $30. Electronic applications accepted. *Expenses:* Tuition, state resident: part-time $288.16 per credit hour. Tuition, nonresident: part-time $1071.31 per credit hour. *Financial support:* Application deadline: 3/1; applicants required to submit FAFSA. *Unit head:* Dr. Erhan Haciomeroglu, Program Coordinator, 407-823-4336, E-mail: erhan.haciomeroglu@ucf.edu. *Application contact:* Assistant Director, Graduate Admissions, 407-823-2766, Fax: 407-823-6442, E-mail: gradadmissions@ucf.edu.
Website: http://education.ucf.edu/mathed/

University of Central Florida, College of Education and Human Performance, School of Teaching, Learning, and Leadership, Program in Teacher Education, Orlando, FL 32816. Offers art education (MAT); English language (MAT); mathematics education (MAT); middle school mathematics (MAT); middle school science (MAT); science education (MAT), including biology, chemistry, physics; social science education (MAT). *Accreditation:* NCATE. *Program availability:* Part-time, evening/weekend. *Students:* 16 full-time (11 women), 28 part-time (23 women); includes 16 minority (6 Black or African American, non-Hispanic/Latino; 1 Asian, non-Hispanic/Latino; 8 Hispanic/Latino; 1 Two or more races, non-Hispanic/Latino), 1 international. Average age 31. 1 applicant, 100% accepted. In 2016, 33 master's awarded. *Entrance requirements:* For master's, GRE General Test. Additional exam requirements/recommendations for international students: Required—TOEFL. *Application deadline:* For spring admission, 12/1 for domestic students; for summer admission, 4/15 for domestic students. Application fee: $30. Electronic applications accepted. *Expenses:* Tuition, state resident: part-time $288.16 per credit hour. Tuition, nonresident: part-time $1071.31 per credit hour. *Financial support:* Fellowships, research assistantships, teaching assistantships, career-related internships or fieldwork, Federal Work-Study, institutionally sponsored loans, tuition waivers (partial), and unspecified assistantships available. Financial award application deadline: 3/1; financial award applicants required to submit FAFSA. *Unit head:* Dr. Michael Hynes, Director, 407-823-2005, E-mail: mychael.hynes@ucf.edu. *Application contact:* Assistant Director, Graduate Admissions, 407-823-2766, Fax: 407-823-6442, E-mail: gradadmissions@ucf.edu.
Website: http://education.ucf.edu/programs.cfm?pid=g&cat=2

University of Cincinnati, Graduate School, McMicken College of Arts and Sciences, Department of Mathematical Sciences, Cincinnati, OH 45221. Offers applied mathematics (MS, PhD); mathematics education (MAT); pure mathematics (MS, PhD); statistics (MS, PhD). *Program availability:* Part-time. Terminal master's awarded for partial completion of doctoral program. *Degree requirements:* For master's, comprehensive exam, thesis or alternative; for doctorate, one foreign language, comprehensive exam, thesis/dissertation. *Entrance requirements:* For master's, GRE, teacher certification (for MAT); for doctorate, GRE. Additional exam requirements/recommendations for international students: Required—TOEFL. Electronic applications accepted. *Expenses: Tuition, area resident:* Full-time $12,790; part-time $389 per credit hour. Tuition, state resident: full-time $13,290; part-time $419 per credit hour. Tuition, nonresident: full-time $24,532; part-time $976 per credit hour. *International tuition:* $24,832 full-time. *Required fees:* $3958; $140 per credit hour. Tuition and fees vary according to course load, degree level, program and reciprocity agreements. *Faculty research:* Algebra, analysis, differential equations, numerical analysis, statistics.

University of Colorado Denver, College of Liberal Arts and Sciences, Department of Mathematical and Statistical Sciences, Denver, CO 80217. Offers applied mathematics (MS, PhD), including applied mathematics, applied probability (MS), applied statistics (MS), computational biology, computational mathematics (PhD), discrete mathematics, finite geometry (PhD), mathematics education (PhD), mathematics of engineering and science (MS), numerical analysis, operations research (MS), optimization and operations research (PhD), probability (PhD), statistics (PhD). *Program availability:* Part-time. *Faculty:* 20 full-time (3 women), 4 part-time/adjunct (0 women). *Students:* 49 full-time (22 women), 10 part-time (4 women); includes 11 minority (1 Black or African American, non-Hispanic/Latino; 1 American Indian or Alaska Native, non-Hispanic/Latino; 3 Asian, non-Hispanic/Latino; 5 Hispanic/Latino; 1 Two or more races, non-Hispanic/Latino), 12 international. Average age 32. 88 applicants, 66% accepted, 12 enrolled. In 2016, 13 master's, 2 doctorates awarded. *Degree requirements:* For master's, comprehensive exam, thesis optional, 30 hours of course work with minimum GPA of 3.0; for doctorate, comprehensive exam, thesis/dissertation, 42 hours of course work with minimum GPA of 3.25. *Entrance requirements:* For master's, GRE General Test; GRE Subject Test in math (recommended), 30 hours of course work in mathematics (24 of which must be upper-division mathematics), bachelor's degree with minimum GPA of 3.0; for doctorate, GRE General Test; GRE Subject Test in math (recommended), 30 hours of course work in mathematics (24 of which must be upper-division mathematics), master's degree with minimum GPA of 3.25. Additional exam requirements/recommendations for international students: Required—TOEFL (minimum score 537 paper-based; 75 iBT); Recommended—IELTS (minimum score 6.5). *Application deadline:* For fall admission, 4/1 for domestic and international students; for spring admission, 10/1 for domestic and international students; for summer admission, 4/1 for domestic and international students. Application fee: $50 ($75 for international students). Electronic applications accepted. *Expenses:* Tuition, state resident: full-time $11,006; part-time $474 per credit. Tuition, nonresident: full-time $28,212; part-time $1264 per credit hour. *Required fees:* $256 per semester. One-time fee: $94.32. Tuition and fees vary according to campus/location and program. *Financial support:* In 2016–17, 35 students received support. Fellowships with partial tuition reimbursements available, research assistantships with full tuition reimbursements available, teaching assistantships with full tuition reimbursements available, Federal Work-Study, institutionally sponsored loans, scholarships/grants, and traineeships available. Financial award application deadline: 4/1; financial award applicants required to submit FAFSA. *Faculty research:* Computational mathematics, computational biology, discrete mathematics and geometry, probability and statistics, optimization. *Unit head:* Dr. Michael Ferrara, Graduate Chair, 303-315-1705, E-mail: michael.ferrara@ucdenver.edu. *Application contact:* Julie Blunck, Program Assistant, 303-315-1743, E-mail: julie.blunck@ucdenver.edu.
Website: http://www.ucdenver.edu/academics/colleges/CLAS/Departments/math/Pages/MathStats.aspx

University of Colorado Denver, School of Education and Human Development, Program in Educational Leadership and Innovation, Denver, CO 80217. Offers educational studies and research (PhD), including administrative leadership and policy, early childhood special education, math education, research, assessment and evaluation, science education, urban ecologies. *Program availability:* Part-time, evening/weekend. *Students:* 30 full-time (25 women), 14 part-time (11 women); includes 16 minority (7 Black or African American, non-Hispanic/Latino; 1 American Indian or Alaska Native, non-Hispanic/Latino; 1 Asian, non-Hispanic/Latino; 6 Hispanic/Latino; 1 Two or more races, non-Hispanic/Latino), 5 international. Average age 40. 21 applicants, 67% accepted, 8 enrolled. In 2016, 3 doctorates awarded. *Degree requirements:* For doctorate, comprehensive exam, thesis/dissertation, 75 credit hours (for PhD). *Entrance requirements:* For doctorate, GRE or equivalent, resume or curriculum vitae, letters of recommendation, master's degree or equivalent, completion of basic or advanced statistics course with minimum B grade. Additional exam requirements/recommendations for international students: Required—TOEFL (minimum score 537 paper-based; 75 iBT); Recommended—IELTS (minimum score 6.5). *Application deadline:* For fall admission, 12/1 priority date for domestic students, 11/1 priority date for international students. Applications are processed on a rolling basis. Application fee: $50 ($75 for international students). Electronic applications accepted. *Expenses:* Contact institution. *Financial support:* In 2016–17, 45 students received support. Fellowships, research assistantships, teaching assistantships, Federal Work-Study, institutionally sponsored loans, scholarships/grants, and traineeships available. Financial award application deadline: 4/1; financial award applicants required to submit FAFSA. *Faculty research:* Administrative leadership and policy studies, early childhood education, research in diversity, paraprofessionals in education, urban schools lab. *Unit head:* 303-315-6300, E-mail: education@ucdenver.edu. *Application contact:* 303-315-6300, E-mail: education@ucdenver.edu.
Website: http://www.ucdenver.edu/academics/colleges/SchoolOfEducation/Academics/Doctorate/Pages/PhD%20in%20Education%20and%20Human%20Development.aspx

University of Colorado Denver, School of Education and Human Development, Program in Mathematics Education, Denver, CO 80217. Offers MS Ed. *Students:* 6 full-time (4 women), 8 part-time (4 women); includes 4 minority (1 Black or African American, non-Hispanic/Latino; 1 Asian, non-Hispanic/Latino; 1 Hispanic/Latino; 1 Two or more races, non-Hispanic/Latino). Average age 32. 3 applicants, 67% accepted, 2 enrolled. In 2016, 6 master's awarded. *Degree requirements:* For master's, thesis or alternative, 36 semester hours. *Entrance requirements:* For master's, GRE or MAT, resume or curriculum vitae, three letters of recommendation, transcripts from all colleges/universities attended. Additional exam requirements/recommendations for international students: Required—TOEFL (minimum score 75 iBT). *Application deadline:* For fall admission, 4/1 for domestic and international students; for spring admission, 9/1 for domestic and international students; for summer admission, 2/15 for domestic and international students. Application fee: $50 ($75 for international students). Electronic applications accepted. *Expenses:* Tuition, state resident: full-time $11,006; part-time $474 per credit. Tuition, nonresident: full-time $28,212; part-time $1264 per credit hour. *Required fees:* $256 per semester. One-time fee: $94.32. Tuition and fees vary according to campus/location and program. *Financial support:* In 2016–17, 1 student received support. Federal Work-Study, institutionally sponsored loans, scholarships/grants, and traineeships available. Financial award application deadline: 4/1. *Unit head:* Rebecca Kantor, Dean, 303-315-6343, E-mail: rebecca.kantor@ucdenver.edu. *Application contact:* Academic Services, 303-315-6300, E-mail: education@ucdenver.edu.
Website: http://www.ucdenver.edu/academics/colleges/SchoolOfEducation/Academics/MASTERS/Pages/Master-of-Science-in-Education.aspx

University of Colorado Denver, School of Education and Human Development, Teacher Education Programs, Denver, CO 80217. Offers elementary linguistically diverse education (MA); elementary math and science education (MA); elementary math education (MA); elementary reading and writing (MA); elementary science education (MA); secondary English education (MA); secondary linguistically diverse education (MA); secondary math education (MA); secondary reading and writing (MA); secondary science education (MA); special education (MA). *Accreditation:* NCATE. *Program availability:* Part-time, evening/weekend. *Students:* 142 full-time (117 women), 184 part-time (159 women); includes 56 minority (6 Black or African American, non-Hispanic/Latino; 1 American Indian or Alaska Native, non-Hispanic/Latino; 4 Asian, non-Hispanic/Latino; 38 Hispanic/Latino; 1 Native Hawaiian or other Pacific Islander, non-Hispanic/Latino; 6 Two or more races, non-Hispanic/Latino), 1 international. Average age 30. 18 applicants, 67% accepted, 9 enrolled. In 2016, 134 master's awarded. *Degree requirements:* For master's, comprehensive exam. *Entrance requirements:* For master's, GRE or MAT (for those with GPA below 2.75), transcripts, resume, letters of recommendation. Additional exam requirements/recommendations for international students: Required—TOEFL (minimum score 537 paper-based; 75 iBT); Recommended—IELTS (minimum score 6.5). *Application deadline:* For fall admission, 4/15 for domestic students, 4/1 for international students; for spring admission, 9/15 for domestic students, 9/1 for international students; for summer admission, 2/15 for domestic students, 2/1 for international students. Applications are processed on a rolling basis. Application fee: $50 ($75 for international students). Electronic applications accepted. *Expenses:* Contact institution. *Financial support:* In 2016–17, 26 students received support. Fellowships, research assistantships, teaching assistantships, Federal Work-Study, institutionally sponsored loans, scholarships/grants, and traineeships available. Financial award application deadline: 4/1; financial award applicants required to submit FAFSA. *Faculty research:* Linguistically diverse education/ESL, elementary reading and writing, elementary teacher education, secondary teacher education, special education. *Unit head:* Cindy Gutierrez, Director, 303-315-4982, E-mail: cindy.gutierrez@ucdenver.edu. *Application contact:* 303-315-6300, E-mail: education@ucdenver.edu.
Website: http://www.ucdenver.edu/academics/colleges/SchoolOfEducation/Academics/MASTERS/Pages/default.aspx

University of Connecticut, Graduate School, Neag School of Education, Department of Curriculum and Instruction, Program in Mathematics Education, Storrs, CT 06269. Offers MA, PhD. *Accreditation:* NCATE. Terminal master's awarded for partial completion of doctoral program. *Degree requirements:* For master's, comprehensive exam; for doctorate, thesis/dissertation. *Entrance requirements:* For doctorate, GRE General Test. Additional exam requirements/recommendations for international students: Required—TOEFL (minimum score 550 paper-based). Electronic applications accepted.

University of Dayton, Department of Mathematics, Dayton, OH 45469. Offers applied mathematics (MAS); financial mathematics (MFM); mathematics education (MME).

Program availability: Part-time, evening/weekend. *Faculty:* 19 full-time (7 women). *Students:* 31 full-time (13 women), 5 part-time (2 women); includes 3 minority (2 Black or African American, non-Hispanic/Latino; 1 Hispanic/Latino), 27 international. Average age 26. 112 applicants, 20% accepted. In 2016, 26 master's awarded. *Entrance requirements:* For master's, minimum undergraduate GPA of 2.8 (MAS), 3.0 (MFM, MME). Additional exam requirements/recommendations for international students: Required—TOEFL (minimum score 550 paper-based; 80 iBT). *Application deadline:* Applications are processed on a rolling basis. Application fee: $0 ($50 for international students). Electronic applications accepted. *Expenses:* $890 per credit hour, $25 registration fee per term. *Financial support:* In 2016–17, 6 students received support, including 6 teaching assistantships with full tuition reimbursements available (averaging $14,750 per year); institutionally sponsored loans and health care benefits also available. Financial award application deadline: 3/1; financial award applicants required to submit FAFSA. *Faculty research:* Jump diffusion with regime switching in finance models, dynamical systems, boundary value problems for ordinary differential equations, decompositions of graphs and multigraphs. *Unit head:* Dr. Joe D. Mashburn, Chair, 937-229-2511, Fax: 937-229-2566, E-mail: jmashburn1@udayton.edu. *Application contact:* Dr. Paul W. Eloe, Graduate Program Director/Professor, 937-229-2016, E-mail: peloe1@udayton.edu.
Website: https://www.udayton.edu/artssciences/academics/mathematics/welcome/index.php

University of Dayton, Department of Teacher Education, Dayton, OH 45469. Offers early childhood leadership and advocacy (MS Ed); interdisciplinary education studies (MS Ed); leadership in educational systems (MS Ed); literacy (MS Ed); mathematics education (MS Ed); music education (MS Ed); teacher as leader (MS Ed); teacher education (MS Ed); technology-enhanced learning (MS Ed); trans-disciplinary early childhood education (MS Ed). *Program availability:* Part-time, evening/weekend, blended/hybrid learning. *Faculty:* 23 full-time (18 women), 49 part-time/adjunct (42 women). *Students:* 52 full-time (47 women), 89 part-time (76 women); includes 6 minority (2 Black or African American, non-Hispanic/Latino; 2 Hispanic/Latino; 2 Two or more races, non-Hispanic/Latino), 24 international. Average age 31. 106 applicants, 28% accepted. In 2016, 69 master's awarded. *Degree requirements:* For master's, variable foreign language requirement, thesis optional. *Entrance requirements:* For master's, GRE (minimum score of 149 verbal, 4 on writing) or MAT (minimum score of 396) if undergraduate GPA was under 2.75, minimum GPA of 2.75, 3 letters of recommendation, personal statement or resume, official transcripts. Additional exam requirements/recommendations for international students: Required—TOEFL (minimum score 550 paper-based; 80 iBT); Recommended—IELTS (minimum score 6.5). *Application deadline:* Applications are processed on a rolling basis. Application fee: $0 ($50 for international students). Electronic applications accepted. *Expenses:* $620 per credit hour, $25 registration fee per term. *Financial support:* Institutionally sponsored loans available. Financial award application deadline: 3/1; financial award applicants required to submit FAFSA. *Faculty research:* Educational technology; facilitating teacher reflection; teacher preparation in dyslexia. *Unit head:* Dr. Connie L. Bowman, Chair, 937-229-3305, E-mail: cbowman1@udayton.edu. *Application contact:* Gina Seiter, Graduate Program Advisor, 937-229-3103, E-mail: gseiter1@udayton.edu.
Website: https://www.udayton.edu/education/departments_and_programs/edt

University of Detroit Mercy, College of Engineering and Science, Detroit, MI 48221. Offers chemistry (MS); civil and environmental engineering (DE); electrical and computer engineering (ME); electrical engineering (DE); engineering management (M Eng Mgt); environmental engineering (MEE); mechanical engineering (MME, DE); product development (MS); software engineering (MSSE); teaching of mathematics (MATM). *Program availability:* Part-time, evening/weekend. *Degree requirements:* For doctorate, thesis/dissertation. Electronic applications accepted. Application fee is waived when completed online. *Expenses:* Contact institution.

University of Florida, Graduate School, College of Education, School of Teaching and Learning, Gainesville, FL 32611. Offers curriculum and instruction (M Ed, MAE, Ed D, PhD, Ed S); elementary education (M Ed, MAE); English education (M Ed, MAE); mathematics education (M Ed, MAE); reading education (M Ed, MAE); science education (M Ed, MAE); social studies education (M Ed, MAE). *Accreditation:* NCATE. *Program availability:* Part-time, evening/weekend, online learning. Terminal master's awarded for partial completion of doctoral program. *Degree requirements:* For master's, comprehensive exam (for some programs), thesis (for some programs); for doctorate, comprehensive exam (for some programs), thesis/dissertation (for some programs). *Entrance requirements:* For master's and doctorate, GRE General Test, minimum GPA of 3.0; for Ed S, GRE General Test. Additional exam requirements/recommendations for international students: Required—TOEFL (minimum score 550 paper-based; 80 iBT), IELTS (minimum score 6). Electronic applications accepted. *Faculty research:* STEM education; curriculum; teaching and teacher education; languages and literacy; schools, culture, and society; theories and processes of learning.

University of Georgia, College of Education, Department of Mathematics and Science Education, Athens, GA 30602. Offers mathematics education (M Ed, PhD, Ed S). *Application deadline:* For fall admission, 7/1 priority date for domestic students; for spring admission, 11/15 for domestic students. Application fee: $50. *Unit head:* Dr. Denise A. Spangler, Head, 706-542-4548, Fax: 706-542-4551, E-mail: dspangle@uga.edu. *Application contact:* Kevin Moore, Graduate Coordinator, 706-542-3211, E-mail: kvcmoore@uga.edu.
Website: http://www.coe.uga.edu/mse/

University of Illinois at Chicago, College of Liberal Arts and Sciences, Department of Mathematics, Statistics, and Computer Science, Program in Secondary School Mathematics, Chicago, IL 60607-7128. Offers MST. *Program availability:* Part-time. *Degree requirements:* For master's, comprehensive exam. *Entrance requirements:* For master's, GRE General Test, minimum GPA of 2.75. Additional exam requirements/recommendations for international students: Required—TOEFL. Electronic applications accepted.

University of Illinois at Chicago, Program in Learning Sciences, Chicago, IL 60607-7128. Offers PhD.

University of Illinois at Urbana–Champaign, Graduate College, College of Liberal Arts and Sciences, Department of Mathematics, Champaign, IL 61820. Offers applied mathematics (MS); applied mathematics: actuarial science (MS); mathematics (MS, PhD); teaching of mathematics (MS).

University of Indianapolis, Graduate Programs, School of Education, Indianapolis, IN 46227-3697. Offers art education (MAT); biology (MAT); chemistry (MAT); curriculum and instruction (MA); earth sciences (MAT); education (MA, MAT); educational leadership (MA); elementary education (MA); English (MAT); French (MAT); math (MAT); physical education (MAT); physics (MAT); secondary education (MA), including art education, education, English education, social studies education; social studies (MAT); Spanish (MAT). *Accreditation:* NCATE. *Program availability:* Part-time, evening/weekend. *Entrance requirements:* For master's, GRE Subject Test, PRAXIS I, minimum GPA of 2.5, 3 letters of recommendation, interview. Additional exam requirements/recommendations for international students: Required—TOEFL (minimum score 550 paper-based). *Faculty research:* Assessment of teacher education, perceptions of prospective teachers by parents.

The University of Iowa, Graduate College, College of Education, Department of Teaching and Learning, Program in Education, Iowa City, IA 52242-1316. Offers art education (MA); developmental reading (MA); elementary education (MA); English education (MA, MAT); foreign and second language education (MAT); foreign language education (MA); foreign language/ESL education (PhD); language, literacy and culture (PhD); mathematics education (MA, MAT, PhD); music education (MM, PhD); science education (MA); secondary education (MA); social studies (MA, PhD). *Degree requirements:* For master's, thesis optional, exam; for doctorate, comprehensive exam, thesis/dissertation. *Entrance requirements:* For master's and doctorate, GRE General Test, minimum GPA of 3.0. Additional exam requirements/recommendations for international students: Required—TOEFL (minimum score 550 paper-based; 81 iBT). Electronic applications accepted.

University of Louisiana at Monroe, Graduate School, College of Arts, Education, and Sciences, School of Education, Program in Curriculum and Instruction, Monroe, LA 71209-0001. Offers art education (M Ed); biology education (M Ed); chemistry education (M Ed); curriculum and instruction (Ed D); early childhood education (M Ed); earth science education (M Ed); educational leadership (M Ed); elementary education (1-5) (M Ed); English as a second language (M Ed); English education (M Ed); family and consumer education (M Ed); French education (M Ed); history education (M Ed); math education (M Ed); middle school education (M Ed); music education (M Ed); reading education (K-12) (M Ed); Spanish education (M Ed); special education - academically gifted (M Ed); special education - early intervention (M Ed); special education - educational diagnostician (M Ed); special education - mild/moderate disabilities (M Ed); speech education (M Ed). *Accreditation:* NCATE. *Faculty:* 8 full-time (4 women), 4 part-time/adjunct (3 women). *Students:* 13 full-time (11 women), 80 part-time (65 women); includes 25 minority (19 Black or African American, non-Hispanic/Latino; 1 Asian, non-Hispanic/Latino; 3 Hispanic/Latino; 2 Two or more races, non-Hispanic/Latino). Average age 37. 118 applicants, 30% accepted, 16 enrolled. In 2016, 23 master's, 4 doctorates awarded. *Degree requirements:* For master's, comprehensive exam (for some programs), thesis; for doctorate, thesis/dissertation, internships. *Entrance requirements:* For master's, GRE General Test; for doctorate, GRE General Test, minimum undergraduate GPA of 2.75, graduate 3.25. Additional exam requirements/recommendations for international students: Required—TOEFL (minimum score 500 paper-based; 61 iBT). *Application deadline:* For fall admission, 8/24 priority date for domestic students, 7/1 for international students; for winter admission, 12/14 priority date for domestic students; for spring admission, 1/19 for domestic students, 11/1 for international students. Applications are processed on a rolling basis. Application fee: $20 ($30 for international students). Electronic applications accepted. *Expenses:* Tuition, state resident: full-time $6489. Tuition, nonresident: full-time $18,589. *Required fees:* $8984. Tuition and fees vary according to course level, course load, degree level and program. *Financial support:* Research assistantships, career-related internships or fieldwork, Federal Work-Study, and unspecified assistantships available. Financial award application deadline: 4/1; financial award applicants required to submit FAFSA. *Unit head:* Dr. Dorothy Schween, Director, 318-342-1268, Fax: 318-342-3131, E-mail: schween@ulm.edu.

University of Maryland, Baltimore County, The Graduate School, College of Arts, Humanities and Social Sciences, Department of Education, Master of Arts in Education Program, Baltimore, MD 21250. Offers K-8 mathematics instructional leadership (MAE); K-8 science education (MAE); K-8 STEM education (MAE); secondary mathematics education (MAE); secondary science education (MAE); secondary STEM education (MAE). *Program availability:* Part-time-only, evening/weekend, 100% online, blended/hybrid learning. *Faculty:* 5 full-time (4 women), 5 part-time/adjunct (4 women). *Students:* 1 (woman) full-time, 137 part-time (100 women); includes 18 minority (7 Black or African American, non-Hispanic/Latino; 1 American Indian or Alaska Native, non-Hispanic/Latino; 7 Asian, non-Hispanic/Latino; 2 Hispanic/Latino; 1 Two or more races, non-Hispanic/Latino). Average age 32. 20 applicants, 95% accepted, 17 enrolled. In 2016, 17 master's awarded. *Degree requirements:* For master's, comprehensive exam (for some programs), thesis (for some programs). *Application deadline:* For fall admission, 6/1 for domestic students; for spring admission, 11/1 for domestic students. Application fee: $50. Electronic applications accepted. *Expenses:* Tuition, state resident: full-time $13,294. Tuition, nonresident: full-time $20,286. *Financial support:* In 2016–17, 1 student received support. Application deadline: 3/1. *Unit head:* Jerri Frick, Graduate Program Director, 410-455-1356, Fax: 410-455-6182, E-mail: frick@umbc.edu.
Website: http://www.umbc.edu/education/mae

University of Maryland, Baltimore County, The Graduate School, College of Arts, Humanities and Social Sciences, Department of Education, Program in Teaching, Baltimore, MD 21250. Offers early childhood education (MAT); elementary education (MAT); teaching (MAT), including art, biology, chemistry, choral music, classical foreign language, dance, earth/space science, English, instrumental music, mathematics, modern foreign language, physical science, physics, social studies, theatre. *Program availability:* Part-time, evening/weekend. *Faculty:* 24 full-time (18 women), 25 part-time/adjunct (19 women). *Students:* 41 full-time (34 women), 27 part-time (18 women); includes 26 minority (6 Black or African American, non-Hispanic/Latino; 9 Asian, non-Hispanic/Latino; 7 Hispanic/Latino; 1 Native Hawaiian or other Pacific Islander, non-Hispanic/Latino; 3 Two or more races, non-Hispanic/Latino), 2 international. Average age 30. 54 applicants, 83% accepted, 35 enrolled. In 2016, 50 master's awarded. *Degree requirements:* For master's, comprehensive exam (for some programs), thesis (for some programs). *Entrance requirements:* For master's, PRAXIS Core Examination or GRE (minimum score of 1000), minimum GPA of 3.0. Additional exam requirements/recommendations for international students: Required—TOEFL. *Application deadline:* For fall admission, 6/1 for domestic and international students; for spring admission, 11/1 for domestic and international students. Applications are processed on a rolling basis. Application fee: $50. Electronic applications accepted. *Expenses:* Tuition, state resident: full-time $13,294. Tuition, nonresident: full-time $20,286. *Financial support:* In 2016–17, 8 students received support, including teaching assistantships with tuition reimbursements available (averaging $12,000 per year); career-related internships or fieldwork, Federal Work-Study, scholarships/grants, tuition waivers, and unspecified assistantships also available. Financial award application deadline: 3/15. *Faculty research:* STEM teacher education, culturally sensitive pedagogy, ESOL/bilingual education, early childhood education, language, literacy and culture. *Total annual research expenditures:* $100,000. *Unit head:* Dr. Susan M. Blunck, Graduate Program Director, 410-455-2869, Fax: 410-455-3986, E-mail: blunck@umbc.edu. *Application contact:* Cheryl Johnson, MAT Program Specialist, 410-455-3388, E-mail: blackwel@umbc.edu.
Website: http://www.umbc.edu/education/

University of Massachusetts Dartmouth, Graduate School, College of Arts and Sciences, School of Education, Department of STEM Education and Teacher Development, North Dartmouth, MA 02747-2300. Offers education ESL preK-12 (Postbaccalaureate Certificate); mathematics education (PhD); middle school education (MAT); secondary school education (Postbaccalaureate Certificate); teaching secondary school education (MAT). *Program availability:* Part-time. *Faculty:* 9 full-time (6 women),

6 part-time/adjunct (3 women). *Students:* 25 full-time (12 women), 87 part-time (55 women); includes 15 minority (3 Black or African American, non-Hispanic/Latino; 2 Asian, non-Hispanic/Latino; 7 Hispanic/Latino; 3 Two or more races, non-Hispanic/Latino), 3 international. Average age 32. 53 applicants, 91% accepted, 38 enrolled. In 2016, 67 master's awarded. *Degree requirements:* For doctorate, thesis/dissertation. *Entrance requirements:* For master's, Massachusetts Tests for Educator Licensure (MTEL) Communication and Literacy Test and Subject Matter Test, statement of purpose (minimum of 300 words), resume, 2 letters of recommendation, official transcripts; for doctorate, GRE, statement of purpose (minimum of 300 words), resume, official transcripts, 3 letters of recommendation; for Postbaccalaureate Certificate, statement of purpose (minimum of 300 words), resume, 2 letters of recommendation, official transcripts. Additional exam requirements/recommendations for international students: Required—TOEFL (minimum score 533 paper-based; 72 iBT). *Application deadline:* For fall admission, 2/15 priority date for domestic students, 1/15 priority date for international students; for spring admission, 12/15 priority date for domestic students, 11/15 priority date for international students. Application fee: $60. Electronic applications accepted. *Expenses:* Tuition, state resident: full-time $14,994; part-time $624.75 per credit. Tuition, nonresident: full-time $27,068; part-time $1127.83 per credit. *Required fees:* $405; $25.88 per credit. Tuition and fees vary according to course load and reciprocity agreements. *Financial support:* In 2016–17, 3 fellowships (averaging $6,250 per year), 3 research assistantships (averaging $5,027 per year), 2 teaching assistantships (averaging $8,000 per year) were awarded; institutionally sponsored loans, scholarships/grants, unspecified assistantships, and instructional assistants, Fulbright scholarships also available. Financial award application deadline: 3/1; financial award applicants required to submit FAFSA. *Faculty research:* Reading/special education, education reform, English education, literacy, language arts K-12. *Total annual research expenditures:* $1.3 million. *Unit head:* Traci Almeida, Graduate Program Director, 508-999-8098, Fax: 508-910-8183, E-mail: talmeida@umassd.edu. *Application contact:* Steven Briggs, Director of Marketing and Recruitment for Graduate Studies, 508-999-8604, Fax: 508-999-8183, E-mail: graduate@umassd.edu.
Website: http://www.umassd.edu/cas/schoolofeducation/departments/stemeducationandteacherdevelopment/

University of Memphis, Graduate School, College of Arts and Sciences, Department of Mathematical Sciences, Memphis, TN 38152. Offers applied mathematics (MS); applied statistics (PhD); mathematics (MS, PhD); statistics (MS); teaching of mathematics (MS). *Program availability:* Part-time. *Faculty:* 15 full-time (6 women), 1 part-time/adjunct (0 women). *Students:* 35 full-time (6 women), 17 part-time (4 women); includes 18 minority (10 Black or African American, non-Hispanic/Latino; 6 Asian, non-Hispanic/Latino; 2 Hispanic/Latino), 16 international. Average age 33. 33 applicants, 91% accepted, 12 enrolled. In 2016, 9 master's, 8 doctorates awarded. Terminal master's awarded for partial completion of doctoral program. *Degree requirements:* For master's, comprehensive exam, thesis or alternative; for doctorate, one foreign language, comprehensive exam, thesis/dissertation, qualifying exam, final exam. *Entrance requirements:* For master's, GRE General Test, minimum GPA of 2.5, undergraduate degree in math or statistics, two letters of recommendation; for doctorate, GRE General Test, minimum GPA of 2.5, three letters of recommendation. Additional exam requirements/recommendations for international students: Required—TOEFL (minimum score 550 paper-based; 79 iBT). *Application deadline:* For fall admission, 8/1 for domestic students, 5/1 priority date for international students; for spring admission, 12/1 for domestic students, 9/1 priority date for international students. Applications are processed on a rolling basis. Application fee: $35 ($60 for international students). Electronic applications accepted. *Expenses:* $5,231.50 per semester full-time in-state, $9,623.50 full-time out-of-state. *Financial support:* In 2016–17, 22 students received support, including 4 research assistantships with full tuition reimbursements available (averaging $25,500 per year), 21 teaching assistantships with full tuition reimbursements available (averaging $24,438 per year); fellowships with full tuition reimbursements available, career-related internships or fieldwork, Federal Work-Study, scholarships/grants, and unspecified assistantships also available. Financial award application deadline: 2/1; financial award applicants required to submit FAFSA. *Faculty research:* Combinatorics, ergodic theory, graph theory, Ramsey theory, applied statistics. *Unit head:* Dr. Irena Lasiecka, Chair, 901-678-2482, Fax: 901-678-2480, E-mail: lasiecka@memphis.edu. *Application contact:* Dr. Fernanda Botelho, Director of Graduate Studies, 901-678-3131, Fax: 901-678-2480, E-mail: mbotelho@memphis.edu.
Website: http://www.MSCI.memphis.edu/

University of Miami, Graduate School, School of Education and Human Development, Department of Teaching and Learning, Program in Teaching and Learning, Coral Gables, FL 33124. Offers language and literacy learning in multilingual settings (PhD); science, technology, engineering and mathematics (PhD); special education (PhD). *Faculty:* 14 full-time (10 women), 9 part-time/adjunct (all women). *Students:* 21 full-time (16 women); includes 6 minority (2 Black or African American, non-Hispanic/Latino; 3 Hispanic/Latino; 1 Two or more races, non-Hispanic/Latino), 7 international. Average age 33. 20 applicants, 30% accepted, 4 enrolled. In 2016, 1 doctorate awarded. *Degree requirements:* For doctorate, thesis/dissertation, qualifying exam, electronic portfolio. *Entrance requirements:* For doctorate, GRE General Test. Additional exam requirements/recommendations for international students: Required—TOEFL (minimum score 550 paper-based; 80 iBT); Recommended—IELTS (minimum score 6.5). *Application deadline:* For fall admission, 2/15 for domestic students, 10/1 for international students. Application fee: $65. Electronic applications accepted. *Financial support:* Fellowships, research assistantships, teaching assistantships, health care benefits, tuition waivers (full and partial), and unspecified assistantships available. Financial award application deadline: 3/1; financial award applicants required to submit FAFSA. *Faculty research:* Teacher education, multicultural education, special education, second language acquisition, math and science education. *Unit head:* Dr. Luciana de Oliveira, Department Chairperson/Associate Professor, 305-284-4961, Fax: 305-284-6998, E-mail: ludeoliveira@miami.edu. *Application contact:* Lois Heffernan, Graduate Admission Coordinator, 305-284-2167, Fax: 305-284-9395, E-mail: lheffernan@miami.edu.
Website: http://www.education.miami.edu

University of Minnesota, Twin Cities Campus, Graduate School, College of Education and Human Development, Department of Curriculum and Instruction, Minneapolis, MN 55455-0213. Offers art education (M Ed, MA, PhD); curriculum and instruction (M Ed, MA, PhD); elementary education (MA, PhD); English education (PhD); language and immersion education (Certificate); learning technologies (MA, PhD); literacy education (MA, PhD); second language education (MA, PhD); social studies education (MA, PhD); STEM education (MA, PhD); teaching (M Ed), including mathematics, science, social studies, teaching; teaching English to speakers of other languages (MA); technology enhanced learning (Certificate). *Faculty:* 37 full-time (20 women). *Students:* 411 full-time (288 women), 317 part-time (223 women); includes 153 minority (37 Black or African American, non-Hispanic/Latino; 7 American Indian or Alaska Native, non-Hispanic/Latino; 31 Asian, non-Hispanic/Latino; 48 Hispanic/Latino; 1 Native Hawaiian or other Pacific Islander, non-Hispanic/Latino; 29 Two or more races, non-Hispanic/Latino), 53 international. Average age 32. 672 applicants, 66% accepted, 400 enrolled. In 2016, 645 master's, 33 doctorates, 27 other advanced degrees awarded. Application fee: $75 ($95 for international students). *Financial support:* In 2016–17, 13 fellowships, 36 research assistantships with full tuition reimbursements (averaging $8,454 per year), 61 teaching assistantships with full tuition reimbursements (averaging $11,406 per year) were awarded. *Faculty research:* Teaching and learning; influence of cultural, linguistic, social, political, and technological factors on teaching, learning and educational research; relationship between educational practice and a democratic and just society; urban education; immigrant education, racial justice and education. *Total annual research expenditures:* $684,005. *Unit head:* Dr. Cynthia Lewis, Chair, 612-625-6313, E-mail: lewis@umn.edu. *Application contact:* Dr. Gillian Roehrig, Director of Graduate Studies, 612-625-0561, E-mail: roehr013@umn.edu.
Website: http://www.cehd.umn.edu/ci

University of Missouri, Office of Research and Graduate Studies, College of Arts and Science, Department of Mathematics, Columbia, MO 65211. Offers applied mathematics (MS); mathematics (MA, MST, PhD). *Faculty:* 35 full-time (5 women), 1 part-time/adjunct (0 women). *Students:* 70 full-time (18 women), 9 part-time (2 women). *Degree requirements:* For doctorate, 2 foreign languages, comprehensive exam, thesis/dissertation. *Entrance requirements:* For master's and doctorate, GRE General Test, minimum GPA of 3.0; bachelor's degree from accredited institution. Additional exam requirements/recommendations for international students: Required—TOEFL (minimum score 500 paper-based; 61 iBT). *Application deadline:* For fall admission, 1/15 priority date for domestic and international students. Applications are processed on a rolling basis. Application fee: $75 ($90 for international students). Electronic applications accepted. *Expenses:* Tuition, state resident: full-time $6347; part-time $352.60 per credit hour. Tuition, nonresident: full-time $17,379; part-time $965.50 per credit hour. *Required fees:* $1035. Tuition and fees vary according to course load, campus/location and program. *Financial support:* Fellowships with full tuition reimbursements, research assistantships with full tuition reimbursements, teaching assistantships with full tuition reimbursements, institutionally sponsored loans, health care benefits, and unspecified assistantships available. Financial award applicants required to submit FAFSA. *Faculty research:* Algebraic geometry, analysis (real, complex, functional and harmonic), analytic functions, applied mathematics, financial mathematics and mathematics of insurance, commutative rings, scattering theory, differential equations (ordinary and partial), differential geometry, dynamical systems, general relativity, mathematical physics, number theory, probabilistic analysis and topology.
Website: https://www.math.missouri.edu/grad/index

University of Missouri, Office of Research and Graduate Studies, College of Education, Department of Learning, Teaching and Curriculum, Columbia, MO 65211. Offers agricultural education (M Ed, PhD, Ed S); art education (M Ed, PhD, Ed S); business and office education (M Ed, PhD, Ed S); early childhood education (M Ed, PhD, Ed S); elementary education (M Ed, PhD, Ed S); English education (M Ed, PhD, Ed S); foreign language education (M Ed, PhD, Ed S); health education and promotion (M Ed, PhD); learning and instruction (M Ed); marketing education (M Ed, PhD, Ed S); mathematics education (M Ed, PhD, Ed S); music education (M Ed, PhD, Ed S); reading education (M Ed, PhD, Ed S); science education (M Ed, PhD, Ed S); social studies education (M Ed, PhD, Ed S); vocational education (M Ed, PhD, Ed S). *Program availability:* Part-time. *Faculty:* 30 full-time (18 women), 1 (woman) part-time/adjunct. *Students:* 157 full-time (124 women), 157 part-time (125 women). Terminal master's awarded for partial completion of doctoral program. *Degree requirements:* For doctorate, thesis/dissertation. *Entrance requirements:* For master's and Ed S, GRE General Test or MAT, minimum GPA of 3.0; for doctorate, GRE General Test, minimum GPA of 3.0. Additional exam requirements/recommendations for international students: Required—TOEFL (minimum score 600 paper-based; 100 iBT). *Application deadline:* For fall admission, 12/1 priority date for domestic and international students. Applications are processed on a rolling basis. Application fee: $75 ($90 for international students). Electronic applications accepted. *Expenses:* Tuition, state resident: full-time $6347; part-time $352.60 per credit hour. Tuition, nonresident: full-time $17,379; part-time $965.50 per credit hour. *Required fees:* $1035. Tuition and fees vary according to course load, campus/location and program. *Financial support:* Fellowships, research assistantships, teaching assistantships, institutionally sponsored loans, traineeships, health care benefits, and unspecified assistantships available. Support available to part-time students.
Website: http://education.missouri.edu/LTC/index.php

University of Montana, Graduate School, College of Humanities and Sciences, Department of Mathematical Sciences, Missoula, MT 59812-0002. Offers mathematics (MA, PhD), including college mathematics teaching (PhD), mathematical sciences research (PhD); mathematics education (MA). *Program availability:* Part-time. Terminal master's awarded for partial completion of doctoral program. *Degree requirements:* For doctorate, thesis/dissertation. *Entrance requirements:* For master's and doctorate, GRE General Test. Additional exam requirements/recommendations for international students: Required—TOEFL (minimum score 525 paper-based).

University of Nebraska at Kearney, College of Natural and Social Sciences, Department of Biology, Kearney, NE 68849. Offers biology (MS); science/math education (MA Ed). *Program availability:* Part-time, evening/weekend, 100% online. *Faculty:* 17 full-time (6 women). *Students:* 27 full-time (21 women), 222 part-time (153 women); includes 44 minority (11 Black or African American, non-Hispanic/Latino; 2 American Indian or Alaska Native, non-Hispanic/Latino; 5 Asian, non-Hispanic/Latino; 17 Hispanic/Latino; 9 Two or more races, non-Hispanic/Latino), 3 international. Average age 32. 86 applicants, 83% accepted, 49 enrolled. In 2016, 57 master's awarded. *Degree requirements:* For master's, comprehensive exam, thesis optional. *Entrance requirements:* For master's, GRE (for thesis option and for online program applicants if undergraduate GPA is below 2.75), letter of interest. Additional exam requirements/recommendations for international students: Recommended—TOEFL (minimum score 550 paper-based; 79 iBT), IELTS (minimum score 6.5). *Application deadline:* For fall admission, 6/15 for domestic and international students; for spring admission, 10/15 for domestic and international students; for summer admission, 3/15 for domestic and international students. Application fee: $45. Electronic applications accepted. *Expenses:* $285 per hour resident; $507 per hour non-resident. *Financial support:* In 2016–17, 11 students received support, including 3 research assistantships with full tuition reimbursements available (averaging $10,500 per year), 8 teaching assistantships with full tuition reimbursements available (averaging $10,500 per year); career-related internships or fieldwork, scholarships/grants, health care benefits, and unspecified assistantships also available. Support available to part-time students. Financial award application deadline: 2/28; financial award applicants required to submit FAFSA. *Faculty research:* Pollution injury, molecular biology-viral gene expression, prairie range condition modeling, evolution of symbiotic nitrogen fixation, geographic information systems (GIS), molecular genetics of aging. *Unit head:* Dr. Paul Twig, Graduate Program Chair, 308-865-8315, E-mail: twiggp@unk.edu. *Application contact:* Brian Peterson, Coordinator, Online MA Program, 308-865-1589, E-mail: msbiology@unk.edu.
Website: http://unkcms.unk.edu/academics/biology/index.php

University of Nevada, Reno, Graduate School, College of Science, Department of Mathematics and Statistics, Reno, NV 89557. Offers mathematics (MS); teaching mathematics (MATM). *Degree requirements:* For master's, thesis optional. *Entrance requirements:* For master's, GRE General Test, minimum GPA of 2.75. Additional exam requirements/recommendations for international students: Required—TOEFL (minimum score 500 paper-based; 61 iBT), IELTS (minimum score 6). Electronic applications accepted. *Faculty research:* Operator algebra, nonlinear systems, differential equations.

University of New Hampshire, Graduate School, College of Engineering and Physical Sciences, Department of Mathematics and Statistics, Durham, NH 03824. Offers applied mathematics (PhD); industrial statistics (Certificate); mathematics (MS, MST, PhD); mathematics education (PhD); mathematics: applied mathematics (MS); mathematics: statistics (PhD). Terminal master's awarded for partial completion of doctoral program. *Degree requirements:* For doctorate, 2 foreign languages, thesis/dissertation. *Entrance requirements:* Additional exam requirements/recommendations for international students: Required—TOEFL (minimum score 550 paper-based; 80 iBT). *Application deadline:* For fall admission, 4/1 priority date for domestic students, 4/1 for international students; for spring admission, 12/1 for domestic students. Applications are processed on a rolling basis. Application fee: $65. Electronic applications accepted. *Financial support:* Fellowships, research assistantships, teaching assistantships, Federal Work-Study, scholarships/grants, and tuition waivers (full and partial) available. Support available to part-time students. Financial award application deadline: 2/15. *Faculty research:* Operator theory, complex analysis, algebra, nonlinear dynamics, statistics. *Unit head:* Dr. Edward Hinson, Chairperson, 603-862-2688. *Application contact:* Jennifer Cooke, Administrative Assistant, 603-862-2320, E-mail: jennifer.cooke@unh.edu.
Website: http://www.ceps.unh.edu/mathematics-statistics

The University of North Carolina at Chapel Hill, Graduate School, School of Education, Program in Secondary Education, Chapel Hill, NC 27599. Offers English (Grades 9-12) (MAT); English as a second language (MAT); French (Grades K-12) (MAT); German (Grades K-12) (MAT); Japanese (Grades K-12) (MAT); Latin (Grades 9-12) (MAT); mathematics (Grades 9-12) (MAT); music (Grades K-12) (MAT); science (Grades 9-12) (MAT); social studies (Grades 9-12) (MAT); Spanish (Grades K-12) (MAT). *Accreditation:* NCATE. *Degree requirements:* For master's, comprehensive exam. *Entrance requirements:* For master's, GRE General Test, minimum GPA of 3.0 during last 2 years of undergraduate course work. Additional exam requirements/recommendations for international students: Required—TOEFL (minimum score 550 paper-based). Electronic applications accepted.

The University of North Carolina at Greensboro, Graduate School, School of Education, Department of Teacher Education and Higher Education, Greensboro, NC 27412-5001. Offers college teaching and adult learning (Certificate); curriculum and instruction (M Ed), including chemistry education, elementary education, English as a second language, French education, instructional technology, mathematics education, middle grades education, reading education, science education, social studies education, Spanish education; curriculum and teaching (PhD), including higher education, teacher education and development; English as a second language (Certificate); higher education (M Ed); supervision (M Ed). *Accreditation:* NCATE. *Program availability:* Part-time. *Degree requirements:* For doctorate, thesis/dissertation. *Entrance requirements:* For master's and doctorate, GRE General Test. Additional exam requirements/recommendations for international students: Required—TOEFL. Electronic applications accepted. *Faculty research:* Community college literacy program, middle school mathematics/computer mathematics.

The University of North Carolina at Pembroke, The Graduate School, Department of Mathematics and Computer Science, Pembroke, NC 28372-1510. Offers mathematics education (MA). *Program availability:* Part-time, evening/weekend. *Degree requirements:* For master's, comprehensive exam, thesis optional. *Entrance requirements:* For master's, GRE General Test or MAT, bachelor's degree in mathematics or mathematics education; minimum GPA of 3.0 in major, 2.5 overall. Additional exam requirements/recommendations for international students: Required—TOEFL.

University of Northern Colorado, Graduate School, College of Natural and Health Sciences, School of Mathematical Sciences, Greeley, CO 80639. Offers educational mathematics (PhD); mathematical teaching (MA); mathematics (MA). *Program availability:* Part-time. *Degree requirements:* For master's, comprehensive exam, thesis or alternative; for doctorate, comprehensive exam, thesis/dissertation. *Entrance requirements:* For master's, GRE General Test (liberal arts), 3 letters of recommendation; for doctorate, GRE General Test, 3 letters of recommendation. *Application deadline:* Applications are processed on a rolling basis. Application fee: $50 ($60 for international students). Electronic applications accepted. *Financial support:* Fellowships, research assistantships, teaching assistantships, and unspecified assistantships available. Financial award application deadline: 3/1; financial award applicants required to submit FAFSA. *Unit head:* Dr. Dean Allison, Director, 970-351-2820, Fax: 970-351-2155. *Application contact:* Linda Sisson, Graduate Student Admission Coordinator, 970-351-1807, Fax: 970-351-2371, E-mail: linda.sisson@unco.edu.
Website: http://www.unco.edu/nhs/mathematical-sciences/

University of Northern Iowa, Graduate College, College of Humanities, Arts and Sciences, Department of Mathematics, MA Program in Mathematics, Cedar Falls, IA 50614. Offers community college teaching (MA); mathematics (MA); secondary teaching (MA).

University of Northern Iowa, Graduate College, College of Humanities, Arts and Sciences, Department of Mathematics, MA Program in Mathematics for the Middle Grades, Cedar Falls, IA 50614. Offers MA.

University of North Georgia, College of Education, Dahlonega, GA 30597. Offers early childhood education (M Ed); middle grades education (M Ed, MAT); physical education (MS); school leadership (Ed S); secondary education (M Ed), including English education, history education, mathematics education, physical education. *Accreditation:* NCATE. *Program availability:* Part-time, evening/weekend, online learning. *Faculty:* 16 full-time (12 women), 3 part-time/adjunct (all women). *Students:* 11 full-time (8 women), 146 part-time (107 women); includes 19 minority (10 Black or African American, non-Hispanic/Latino; 2 Asian, non-Hispanic/Latino; 6 Hispanic/Latino; 1 Two or more races, non-Hispanic/Latino). Average age 28. 77 applicants, 83% accepted, 47 enrolled. In 2016, 79 master's awarded. *Degree requirements:* For master's, comprehensive exam, thesis optional. *Entrance requirements:* For master's, GRE or MAT, GACE, minimum GPA of 2.75; for Ed S, GRE General Test or MAT, 3 years of teaching experience, master's degree, minimum graduate GPA of 3.25, leadership position in the school. Additional exam requirements/recommendations for international students: Required—TOEFL (minimum score 550 paper-based; 79 iBT), IELTS (minimum score 6.5). *Application deadline:* For fall admission, 8/1 priority date for domestic students, 7/1 priority date for international students; for spring admission, 12/1 priority date for domestic students, 11/1 priority date for international students. Applications are processed on a rolling basis. Application fee: $40. Electronic applications accepted. *Expenses:* Contact institution. *Financial support:* Teaching assistantships, career-related internships or fieldwork, scholarships/grants, and unspecified assistantships available. Financial award application deadline: 5/1; financial award applicants required to submit CSS PROFILE or FAFSA. *Unit head:* Dr. Susan Ayers, Dean, College of Education, 706-864-1998, E-mail: susan.ayres@ung.edu. *Application contact:* Regina Boling, Teacher Education Graduate Admissions, 706-864-1533, E-mail: regina.boling@ung.edu.
Website: http://ung.edu/college-of-education/

University of Oklahoma, Jeannine Rainbolt College of Education, Department of Instructional Leadership and Academic Curriculum, Norman, OK 73019. Offers instructional leadership and academic curriculum (M Ed, PhD), including biomedical education (PhD), early childhood education, elementary education (M Ed), English education, instructional leadership, mathematics education, reading education, science education, social studies education, world languages education (M Ed). *Accreditation:* NCATE. *Program availability:* Part-time. *Faculty:* 19 full-time (15 women), 1 (woman) part-time/adjunct. *Students:* 66 full-time (49 women), 116 part-time (88 women); includes 49 minority (12 Black or African American, non-Hispanic/Latino; 6 American Indian or Alaska Native, non-Hispanic/Latino; 6 Asian, non-Hispanic/Latino; 11 Hispanic/Latino; 1 Native Hawaiian or other Pacific Islander, non-Hispanic/Latino; 13 Two or more races, non-Hispanic/Latino), 13 international. Average age 35. 38 applicants, 97% accepted, 28 enrolled. In 2016, 33 master's, 10 doctorates awarded. Terminal master's awarded for partial completion of doctoral program. *Degree requirements:* For master's, comprehensive exam (for some programs), thesis (for some programs); for doctorate, comprehensive exam (for some programs), thesis/dissertation. *Entrance requirements:* For doctorate, GRE. Additional exam requirements/recommendations for international students: Required—TOEFL (minimum score 79 iBT) or IELTS (minimum score 6.5). Application fee: $50 ($100 for international students). Electronic applications accepted. *Expenses:* Tuition, state resident: full-time $4886; part-time $203.60 per credit hour. Tuition, nonresident: full-time $18,989; part-time $791.20 per credit hour. *Required fees:* $3283; $126.25 per credit hour. $126.50 per semester. *Financial support:* In 2016–17, 112 students received support, including 7 research assistantships with partial tuition reimbursements available (averaging $10,373 per year), 6 teaching assistantships with partial tuition reimbursements available (averaging $11,446 per year); fellowships, scholarships/grants, and unspecified assistantships also available. Financial award application deadline: 6/1; financial award applicants required to submit FAFSA. *Faculty research:* Teacher preparation; instruction; curriculum; learning; constructivist theory. *Total annual research expenditures:* $165,297. *Unit head:* Dr. Stacy Reeder, Chair, 405-325-1498, Fax: 405-325-4061, E-mail: reeder@ou.edu. *Application contact:* Anna Steele, Graduate Programs Officer, 405-325-4525, E-mail: anna.steele@ou.edu.
Website: http://www.ou.edu/education/ilac

University of Phoenix–North Florida Campus, College of Education, Jacksonville, FL 32216-0959. Offers administration and supervision (MA Ed); curriculum and instruction (MA Ed), including computer education, mathematics education; early childhood education (MA Ed); elementary teacher education (MA Ed); secondary teacher education (MA Ed). *Program availability:* Evening/weekend. *Degree requirements:* For master's, thesis (for some programs). *Entrance requirements:* For master's, 3 years of work experience, minimum undergraduate GPA of 2.5. Additional exam requirements/recommendations for international students: Required—TOEFL (minimum score 550 paper-based; 49 iBT). Electronic applications accepted.

University of Phoenix–Online Campus, College of Education, Phoenix, AZ 85034-7209. Offers administration and supervision (MAEd, Certificate); adult education and training (MAEd); curriculum and instruction (MAEd), including computer education, curriculum and instruction, English as a second language, language arts, mathematics, reading; early childhood education (MAEd); educational studies (MAEd); elementary teacher education (MAEd), including early childhood, elementary teacher education, high school middle level, middle level; principal licensure (Certificate); secondary teacher education (MAEd); special education (MAEd, Certificate); teacher education (MAEd), including middle level generalist; teacher education middle level mathematics (MAEd), including middle level mathematics; teacher education middle level science (MAEd), including middle level science; teacher education secondary mathematics (MAEd); teacher education secondary science (MAEd); teacher leadership (MAEd); teachers of English learners (Certificate); transition to teaching (Certificate), including elementary education, secondary education. *Program availability:* Evening/weekend, online learning. *Entrance requirements:* Additional exam requirements/recommendations for international students: Required—TOEFL, TOEIC (Test of English as an International Communication), Berlitz Online English Proficiency Exam, PTE, or IELTS. Electronic applications accepted. *Expenses:* Contact institution.

University of Phoenix–South Florida Campus, College of Education, Miramar, FL 33027-4145. Offers administration and supervision (MA Ed); curriculum and instruction (MA Ed), including computer education, curriculum and instruction, mathematics education; early childhood education (MA Ed); elementary teacher education (MA Ed); secondary teacher education (MA Ed). *Program availability:* Evening/weekend. *Degree requirements:* For master's, thesis (for some programs). *Entrance requirements:* For master's, 3 years of work experience, minimum undergraduate GPA of 2.5. Additional exam requirements/recommendations for international students: Required—TOEFL (minimum score 550 paper-based; 79 iBT). Electronic applications accepted.

University of Phoenix–Washington D.C. Campus, College of Education, Washington, DC 20001. Offers administration and supervision (MA Ed); adult education and training (MA Ed); computer education (MA Ed); curriculum and instruction (MA Ed, Ed D); early childhood education (MA Ed); education (Ed S); educational leadership (Ed D); educational technology (Ed D); elementary teacher education (MA Ed); English and language arts education (MA Ed); English as a second language (MA Ed); higher education administration (PhD); mathematics education (MA Ed); secondary teacher education (MA Ed); special education (MA Ed); teacher leadership (MA Ed).

University of Pittsburgh, School of Education, Department of Instruction and Learning, Program in Secondary Education, Pittsburgh, PA 15260. Offers English and communications education (M Ed, MAT); foreign language education (M Ed, MAT); language, literacy and culture education (Ed D, PhD); mathematics education (M Ed, MAT, Ed D, PhD); science education (M Ed, MAT, Ed D, PhD); secondary education (PhD); social studies education (M Ed, MAT); STEM education (Ed D). *Program availability:* Part-time, evening/weekend. *Degree requirements:* For master's, thesis; for doctorate, thesis/dissertation. *Entrance requirements:* For master's, PRAXIS I; for doctorate, GRE General Test. Additional exam requirements/recommendations for international students: Required—TOEFL. Electronic applications accepted. Tuition and fees vary according to program.

University of Puerto Rico, Mayagüez Campus, Graduate Studies, College of Arts and Sciences, Department of Mathematical Sciences, Mayagüez, PR 00681-9000. Offers applied mathematics (MS); pre-college math education (MS); pure mathematics (MS); scientific computing (MS); statistics (MS). *Program availability:* Part-time. *Faculty:* 39 full-time (6 women). *Students:* 62 full-time (18 women), 2 part-time (0 women); includes 37 minority (all Hispanic/Latino), 22 international. Average age 27. 29 applicants, 45% accepted, 11 enrolled. In 2016, 3 master's awarded. *Degree requirements:* For master's, one foreign language, comprehensive exam, thesis. *Entrance requirements:* For master's, undergraduate degree in mathematics or its equivalent. *Application deadline:* For fall admission, 2/15 for domestic and international students; for spring admission, 9/15 for domestic and international students. Applications are processed on a rolling basis. Application fee: $25. Electronic applications accepted. *Expenses: Tuition, area resident:* Full-time $2466. *International tuition:* $7166 full-time. *Required fees:* $210. Tuition and fees vary according to course level, campus/location, program and student

level. *Financial support:* In 2016–17, 71 students received support, including 8 research assistantships with full and partial tuition reimbursements available (averaging $2,642 per year), 68 teaching assistantships with full and partial tuition reimbursements available (averaging $4,775 per year); unspecified assistantships also available. *Faculty research:* Automata theory, linear algebra, logic. *Unit head:* Olgamary Rivera, PhD, Director, 787-832-4040 Ext. 3848, Fax: 787-265-5454, E-mail: olgamary.rivera@upr.edu. *Application contact:* Carmen L. Gonzlez, Secretary, 787-832-4040 Ext. 3285, Fax: 787-265-5454, E-mail: carmen.gonzalez23@upr.edu.
Website: http://math.uprm.edu/

University of Puerto Rico, Río Piedras Campus, College of Education, Program in Curriculum and Teaching, San Juan, PR 00931-3300. Offers biology education (M Ed); chemistry education (M Ed); curriculum and teaching (Ed D); history education (M Ed); mathematics education (M Ed); physics education (M Ed); Spanish education (M Ed). *Program availability:* Part-time. *Degree requirements:* For master's, thesis; for doctorate, thesis/dissertation, internship. *Entrance requirements:* For master's, PAEG or GRE, minimum GPA of 3.0, letter of recommendation; for doctorate, GRE or PAEG, master's degree, minimum GPA of 3.0, letter of recommendation (2), interview. *Faculty research:* Curriculum, math teaching.

University of St. Francis, College of Education, Joliet, IL 60435-6169. Offers educational leadership (MS, Ed D); elementary education (M Ed); reading (MS); secondary education (M Ed), including English education, math education, science education, social studies education, visual arts education; special education (M Ed); teaching and learning (MS); TESOL (Certificate). *Accreditation:* NCATE. *Program availability:* Part-time, evening/weekend, 100% online, blended/hybrid learning. *Faculty:* 11 full-time (8 women), 60 part-time/adjunct (42 women). *Students:* 34 full-time (26 women), 420 part-time (318 women); includes 92 minority (51 Black or African American, non-Hispanic/Latino; 5 Asian, non-Hispanic/Latino; 31 Hispanic/Latino; 5 Two or more races, non-Hispanic/Latino), 4 international. Average age 36. 242 applicants, 48% accepted, 96 enrolled. In 2016, 229 master's, 44 doctorates, 10 other advanced degrees awarded. *Degree requirements:* For master's, comprehensive exam; for doctorate, thesis/dissertation. *Entrance requirements:* Additional exam requirements/recommendations for international students: Required—TOEFL (minimum score 550 paper-based; 79 iBT), IELTS (minimum score 6). *Application deadline:* Applications are processed on a rolling basis. Application fee: $30. Electronic applications accepted. Application fee is waived when completed online. *Expenses:* Contact institution. *Financial support:* In 2016–17, 48 students received support. Career-related internships or fieldwork and unspecified assistantships available. Support available to part-time students. Financial award applicants required to submit FAFSA. *Unit head:* Dr. John Gambro, Dean, 815-740-3829, Fax: 815-740-2264, E-mail: jgambro@stfrancis.edu. *Application contact:* Sandra Sloka, Director of Admissions for Graduate and Degree Completion Programs, 800-735-7500, Fax: 815-740-3431, E-mail: ssloka@stfrancis.edu.
Website: http://www.stfrancis.edu/academics/college-of-education/

University of South Africa, College of Human Sciences, Pretoria, South Africa. Offers adult education (M Ed); African languages (MA, PhD); African politics (MA, PhD); Afrikaans (MA, PhD); ancient history (MA, PhD); ancient Near Eastern studies (MA, PhD); anthropology (MA, PhD); applied linguistics (MA); Arabic (MA, PhD); archaeology (MA); art history (MA); Biblical archaeology (MA); Biblical studies (M Th, D Th, PhD); Christian spirituality (M Th, D Th); church history (M Th, D Th); classical studies (MA, PhD); clinical psychology (MA); communication (MA, PhD); comparative education (M Ed, Ed D); consulting psychology (D Admin, D Com, PhD); curriculum studies (M Ed, Ed D); development studies (M Admin, MA, D Admin, PhD); didactics (M Ed, Ed D); education (M Tech); education management (M Ed, Ed D); educational psychology (M Ed); English (MA); environmental education (M Ed); French (MA, PhD); German (MA, PhD); Greek (MA); guidance and counseling (M Ed); health studies (MA, PhD), including health sciences education (MA), health services management (MA), medical and surgical nursing science (critical care general) (MA), midwifery and neonatal nursing science (MA), trauma and emergency care (MA); history (MA, PhD); history of education (Ed D); inclusive education (M Ed, Ed D); information and communications technology policy and regulation (MA); information science (MA, MIS, PhD); international politics (MA, PhD); Islamic studies (MA, PhD); Italian (MA, PhD); Judaica (MA, PhD); linguistics (MA, PhD); mathematical education (M Ed); mathematics education (MA); missiology (M Th, D Th); modern Hebrew (MA, PhD); musicology (MA, MMus, D Mus, PhD); natural science education (M Ed); New Testament (M Th, D Th); Old Testament (D Th); pastoral therapy (M Th, D Th); philosophy (MA); philosophy of education (M Ed, Ed D); politics (MA, PhD); Portuguese (MA, PhD); practical theology (M Th, D Th); psychology (MA, MS, PhD); psychology of education (M Ed, Ed D); public health (MA); religious studies (MA, D Th, PhD); Romance languages (MA); Russian (MA, PhD); Semitic languages (MA, PhD); social behavior studies in HIV/AIDS (MA); social science (mental health) (MA); social science in development studies (MA); social science in psychology (MA); social science in social work (MA); social science in sociology (MA); social work (MSW, DSW, PhD); socio-education (M Ed, Ed D); sociolinguistics (MA); sociology (MA, PhD); Spanish (MA, PhD); systematic theology (M Th, D Th); TESOL (teaching English to speakers of other languages) (MA); theological ethics (M Th, D Th); theory of literature (MA, PhD); urban ministries (D Th); urban ministry (M Th).

University of South Africa, Institute for Science and Technology Education, Pretoria, South Africa. Offers mathematics, science and technology education (M Sc, PhD).

University of South Carolina, The Graduate School, College of Arts and Sciences, Department of Mathematics, Columbia, SC 29208. Offers mathematics (MA, MS, PhD); mathematics education (M Math, MAT). MAT offered in cooperation with the College of Education. *Program availability:* Part-time. Terminal master's awarded for partial completion of doctoral program. *Degree requirements:* For master's, comprehensive exam, thesis (for some programs); for doctorate, one foreign language, comprehensive exam, thesis/dissertation, admission to candidacy exam, residency. *Entrance requirements:* For master's and doctorate, GRE General Test. Additional exam requirements/recommendations for international students: Required—TOEFL (minimum score 600 paper-based; 100 iBT). Electronic applications accepted. *Faculty research:* Computational mathematics, analysis (classical/modern), discrete mathematics, algebra, number theory.

University of South Carolina, The Graduate School, College of Education, Department of Instruction and Teacher Education, Program in Secondary Education, Columbia, SC 29208. Offers art education (IMA, MAT); business education (IMA, MAT); English (MAT); foreign language (MAT); health education (MAT); mathematics (MAT); science (IMA, MAT); secondary (Ed D); secondary education (MT, PhD); social studies (MAT); theatre and speech (MAT). IMA and MT offered jointly with the subject areas. *Accreditation:* NCATE. *Degree requirements:* For master's, comprehensive exam, thesis (for some programs), foreign language (MA); for doctorate, one foreign language, comprehensive exam, thesis/dissertation. *Entrance requirements:* For master's, GRE General Test or MAT, teaching certificate (IMA, M Ed), interview; for doctorate, GRE General Test or MAT, interview. *Faculty research:* Middle school programs, professional development, school collaboration.

University of Southern Indiana, Graduate Studies, Pott College of Science, Engineering, and Education, Department of Teacher Education, Program in Mathematics Teaching, Evansville, IN 47712-3590. Offers MSE. *Program availability:* Part-time, evening/weekend. *Faculty:* 7 full-time (2 women). *Students:* 1 full-time (0 women), 4 part-time (2 women). Average age 36. *Entrance requirements:* For master's, PRAXIS II, bachelor's degree with minimum cumulative GPA of 2.75 from college or university accredited by NCATE or comparable association; minimum GPA of 3.0 in all courses taken at graduate level at all schools attended; teaching license. Additional exam requirements/recommendations for international students: Required—TOEFL (minimum score 550 paper-based; 79 iBT), IELTS (minimum score 6). *Application deadline:* Applications are processed on a rolling basis. Application fee: $40. Electronic applications accepted. *Expenses:* Tuition, state resident: full-time $8497. Tuition, nonresident: full-time $16,691. *Required fees:* $500. *Financial support:* In 2016–17, 3 students received support. Federal Work-Study, scholarships/grants, tuition waivers (full and partial), and unspecified assistantships available. Financial award application deadline: 3/1; financial award applicants required to submit FAFSA. *Unit head:* Dr. Bonnie Beach, Associate Dean, 812-465-1620, E-mail: blbeach@usi.edu. *Application contact:* Dr. Mayola Rowser, Director, Graduate Studies, 812-465-7015, Fax: 812-464-1956, E-mail: mrowser@usi.edu.
Website: http://www.usi.edu/science/teacher-education/programs/mse

University of Southern Mississippi, Graduate School, College of Science and Technology, Center for Science and Mathematics Education, Hattiesburg, MS 39406. Offers MS, PhD. *Program availability:* Part-time. *Degree requirements:* For master's, comprehensive exam, thesis or alternative; for doctorate, comprehensive exam, thesis/dissertation. *Entrance requirements:* For master's, GRE General Test, minimum GPA of 2.75 in last 60 hours; for doctorate, GRE General Test, minimum GPA of 3.5. Additional exam requirements/recommendations for international students: Required—TOEFL, IELTS. *Application deadline:* For fall admission, 3/15 priority date for domestic students, 3/15 for international students; for spring admission, 1/10 priority date for domestic and international students. Applications are processed on a rolling basis. Application fee: $60. *Expenses: Tuition, area resident:* Full-time $15,708; part-time $437 per credit hour. *Financial support:* Fellowships with full tuition reimbursements, research assistantships with full tuition reimbursements, teaching assistantships with full tuition reimbursements, Federal Work-Study, scholarships/grants, health care benefits, and unspecified assistantships available. Financial award application deadline: 3/15; financial award applicants required to submit FAFSA. *Unit head:* Dr. Sherry Herron, Director, 601-266-4739, Fax: 601-266-4741, E-mail: sherry.herron@usm.edu. *Application contact:* Shonna Breland, Manager of Graduate School Admissions, 601-266-6567, Fax: 601-266-5138.
Website: https://www.usm.edu/science-math-education

University of South Florida, St. Petersburg, College of Education, St. Petersburg, FL 33701. Offers educational leadership development (M Ed); elementary education (MA), including math/science; English education (MA); middle grades STEM education (MS); reading education (MA). *Program availability:* Part-time. *Degree requirements:* For master's, comprehensive exam, practicum, internship, comprehensive portfolio. *Entrance requirements:* For master's, State of Florida General Knowledge Test (GKT), Florida Teaching Certificate (for non-initial certification programs), letters of recommendation. Additional exam requirements/recommendations for international students: Required—TOEFL (minimum score 550 paper-based; 79 iBT); Recommended—IELTS. Electronic applications accepted.

The University of Tennessee, Graduate School, College of Education, Health and Human Sciences, Program in Education, Knoxville, TN 37996. Offers art education (MS); counseling education (PhD); cultural studies in education (PhD); curriculum (MS, Ed S); curriculum, educational research and evaluation (Ed D, PhD); early childhood education (PhD); early childhood special education (MS); education of deaf and hard of hearing (MS); educational administration and policy studies (Ed D, PhD); educational administration and supervision (Ed S); educational psychology (Ed D, PhD); elementary education (MS, Ed S); elementary teaching (MS); English education (MS, Ed S); exercise science (PhD); foreign language/ESL education (MS, Ed S); instructional technology (MS, Ed D, PhD, Ed S); literacy, language and ESL education (PhD); literacy, language education, and ESL education (Ed D); mathematics education (MS, Ed S); modified and comprehensive special education (MS); reading education (MS, Ed S); school counseling (Ed S); school psychology (PhD, Ed S); science education (MS, Ed S); secondary teaching (MS); social foundations (MS); social science education (MS, Ed S); socio-cultural foundations of sports and education (PhD); special education (Ed S); teacher education (Ed D, PhD). *Accreditation:* NCATE. *Program availability:* Part-time, evening/weekend. *Degree requirements:* For master's and Ed S, thesis optional; for doctorate, variable foreign language requirement, thesis/dissertation. *Entrance requirements:* For master's, minimum GPA of 2.7; for doctorate and Ed S, GRE General Test, minimum GPA of 2.7. Additional exam requirements/recommendations for international students: Required—TOEFL. Electronic applications accepted.

The University of Tennessee at Chattanooga, Program in Mathematics, Chattanooga, TN 37403. Offers applied mathematics (MS); applied statistics (MS); mathematics education (MS); pre-professional mathematics (MS). *Program availability:* Part-time. *Faculty:* 17 full-time (1 woman). *Students:* 15 full-time (3 women), 6 part-time (1 woman); includes 5 minority (1 Asian, non-Hispanic/Latino; 1 Native Hawaiian or other Pacific Islander, non-Hispanic/Latino; 3 Two or more races, non-Hispanic/Latino), 1 international. Average age 27. 16 applicants, 81% accepted, 8 enrolled. In 2016, 4 master's awarded. *Degree requirements:* For master's, thesis optional. *Entrance requirements:* For master's, GRE (if applying for an assistantship), two letters of recommendation. Additional exam requirements/recommendations for international students: Required—TOEFL (minimum score 550 paper-based; 61 iBT), IELTS (minimum score 6). *Application deadline:* For fall admission, 6/15 for domestic students, 7/1 for international students; for spring admission, 11/1 for domestic and international students. Applications are processed on a rolling basis. Application fee: $35 ($40 for international students). Electronic applications accepted. *Expenses:* $9,876 full-time in-state; $25,994 full-time out-of-state; $450 per credit part-time in-state; $1,345 per credit part-time out-of-state. *Financial support:* In 2016–17, 1 research assistantship, 11 teaching assistantships were awarded. Financial award application deadline: 7/1; financial award applicants required to submit FAFSA. *Total annual research expenditures:* $611,696. *Unit head:* Dr. Francesco Barioli, Graduate Program Coordinator, 423-425-2198, E-mail: francesco-barioli@utc.edu. *Application contact:* Dr. Joanne Romagni, Dean of the Graduate School, 423-425-4478, Fax: 423-425-5223, E-mail: joanne-romagni@utc.edu.
Website: http://www.utc.edu/mathematics/

The University of Texas at Arlington, Graduate School, College of Education, Department of Curriculum and Instruction, Arlington, TX 76019. Offers curriculum and instruction (M Ed), including literacy studies, mathematics education, mind, brain, and education, science education; teaching (with certification) (M Ed T). *Accreditation:* NCATE. *Program availability:* Part-time, evening/weekend, online learning. *Degree requirements:* For master's, comprehensive exam (for some programs), comprehensive activity, research project. *Entrance requirements:* For master's, GRE General Test, minimum undergraduate GPA of 3.0 in last 60 hours of course work, writing sample, 3 letters of recommendation. Additional exam requirements/recommendations for international students: Required—TOEFL (minimum score 550 paper-based).

Application deadline: For fall admission, 6/1 priority date for domestic students, 4/1 priority date for international students; for spring admission, 10/15 priority date for domestic students, 9/15 priority date for international students. Applications are processed on a rolling basis. Application fee: $50. Electronic applications accepted. *Financial support:* Research assistantships, teaching assistantships, career-related internships or fieldwork, Federal Work-Study, scholarships/grants, and unspecified assistantships available. Financial award application deadline: 6/1; financial award applicants required to submit FAFSA. *Unit head:* Daniel H. Robinson, Chair, 817-272-0116, Fax: 817-272-2618, E-mail: daniel.robinson@uta.edu. *Application contact:* Caitlin Guerrero, Graduate Academic Advisor, 817-272-2956, Fax: 817-272-7624, E-mail: caitling@uta.edu.
Website: http://www.uta.edu/coed/curricandinstruct/index.php

The University of Texas at Arlington, Graduate School, College of Science, Department of Mathematics, Arlington, TX 76019. Offers applied math (MS); mathematics (PhD); mathematics education (MA). *Program availability:* Part-time, evening/weekend. *Degree requirements:* For master's, comprehensive exam, thesis or alternative; for doctorate, comprehensive exam, thesis/dissertation, preliminary examinations. *Entrance requirements:* For master's, GRE General Test (minimum score 350 verbal, 650 quantitative); for doctorate, GRE General Test (minimum score 350 verbal, 700 quantitative), 30 hours of graduate course work in mathematics, minimum GPA of 3.0 in last 60 hours of course work. Additional exam requirements/recommendations for international students: Required—TOEFL (minimum score 550 paper-based; 79 iBT). *Application deadline:* For fall admission, 6/1 priority date for domestic students, 4/1 for international students; for winter admission, 10/15 priority date for domestic students, 9/15 for international students. Applications are processed on a rolling basis. Application fee: $35 ($50 for international students). Electronic applications accepted. *Financial support:* Fellowships with full tuition reimbursements, research assistantships with partial tuition reimbursements, teaching assistantships with partial tuition reimbursements, Federal Work-Study, institutionally sponsored loans, scholarships/grants, health care benefits, and unspecified assistantships available. Financial award application deadline: 2/1; financial award applicants required to submit FAFSA. *Faculty research:* Algebra, combinatorics and geometry, applied mathematics and mathematical biology, computational mathematics, mathematics education, probability and statistics. *Unit head:* Dr. Zhu Jiaping, Chair, 817-272-1114, E-mail: jpzhu@uta.edu. *Application contact:* Dr. Jianzhong Su, Graduate Advisor, 817-272-5684, Fax: 817-272-5802, E-mail: su@uta.edu.
Website: http://www.uta.edu/math

The University of Texas at Dallas, School of Natural Sciences and Mathematics, Department of Science/Mathematics Education, Richardson, TX 75080. Offers mathematics education (MAT); science education (MAT). *Program availability:* Part-time, evening/weekend, online learning. *Faculty:* 4 full-time (1 woman). *Students:* 7 full-time (5 women), 25 part-time (16 women); includes 8 minority (4 Black or African American, non-Hispanic/Latino; 3 Asian, non-Hispanic/Latino; 1 Hispanic/Latino), 3 international. Average age 36. 13 applicants, 77% accepted, 5 enrolled. In 2016, 9 master's awarded. *Degree requirements:* For master's, thesis optional. *Entrance requirements:* For master's, GRE General Test, minimum GPA of 3.0 in upper-level coursework in field. Additional exam requirements/recommendations for international students: Required—TOEFL (minimum score 550 paper-based). *Application deadline:* For fall admission, 7/15 for domestic students, 5/1 priority date for international students; for spring admission, 11/15 for domestic students, 9/1 priority date for international students. Applications are processed on a rolling basis. Application fee: $50 ($100 for international students). Electronic applications accepted. *Expenses:* Tuition, state resident: full-time $12,418; part-time $690 per semester hour. Tuition, nonresident: full-time $24,150; part-time $1342 per semester hour. Tuition and fees vary according to course load. *Financial support:* In 2016–17, 15 students received support, including 1 fellowship (averaging $1,000 per year), 3 teaching assistantships with partial tuition reimbursements available (averaging $17,100 per year); research assistantships with partial tuition reimbursements available, career-related internships or fieldwork, Federal Work-Study, institutionally sponsored loans, scholarships/grants, and unspecified assistantships also available. Support available to part-time students. Financial award application deadline: 4/30; financial award applicants required to submit FAFSA. *Faculty research:* Innovative science/math education programs. *Unit head:* Dr. Mary Urquhart Kelly, Department Head, 972-883-2499, Fax: 972-883-6796, E-mail: scimathed@utdallas.edu. *Application contact:* 972-883-2496, Fax: 972-883-6796, E-mail: barbc@utdallas.edu.
Website: http://www.utdallas.edu/sme/

The University of Texas at El Paso, Graduate School, College of Science, Department of Mathematical Sciences, El Paso, TX 79968-0001. Offers mathematical sciences (MS); mathematics (teaching) (MAT); statistics (MS). *Program availability:* Part-time, evening/weekend. *Degree requirements:* For master's, thesis optional. *Entrance requirements:* For master's, minimum GPA of 3.0, letters of recommendation. Additional exam requirements/recommendations for international students: Required—TOEFL; Recommended—IELTS. Electronic applications accepted.

The University of Texas at San Antonio, College of Sciences, Department of Mathematics, San Antonio, TX 78249-0617. Offers applied mathematics (MS), including industrial mathematics; mathematics (MS); mathematics education (MS). *Program availability:* Part-time, evening/weekend. *Faculty:* 12 full-time (1 woman). *Students:* 11 full time (7 women), 21 part-time (10 women); includes 21 minority (1 Black or African American, non-Hispanic/Latino; 3 Asian, non-Hispanic/Latino; 16 Hispanic/Latino; 1 Two or more races, non-Hispanic/Latino), 1 international. Average age 30. 18 applicants, 72% accepted, 8 enrolled. In 2016, 13 master's awarded. *Degree requirements:* For master's, comprehensive exam (for some programs), thesis or alternative. *Entrance requirements:* For master's, GRE General Test, minimum GPA of 3.0 in last 60 hours. Additional exam requirements/recommendations for international students: Required—TOEFL (minimum score 550 paper-based; 79 iBT), IELTS (minimum score 6.5). *Application deadline:* For fall admission, 7/1 for domestic students, 4/1 for international students; for spring admission, 11/1 for domestic students, 9/1 for international students. Applications are processed on a rolling basis. Application fee: $45 ($80 for international students). Electronic applications accepted. *Financial support:* Applicants required to submit FAFSA. *Faculty research:* Differential equations, functional analysis, numerical analysis, number theory, logic. *Total annual research expenditures:* $456,204. *Unit head:* Dr. Sandy Norman, Department Chair, 210-458-8665, Fax: 210-458-4439, E-mail: sandy.norman@utsa.edu. *Application contact:* Monica Rodriguez, Director of Graduate Admissions, 210-458-4331, Fax: 210-458-4332, E-mail: graduatestudies@utsa.edu.
Website: http://math.utsa.edu/

University of the District of Columbia, College of Arts and Sciences, Program in Teaching, Washington, DC 20008-1175. Offers elementary education (MAT); middle school mathematics (MAT); secondary English language arts (MAT); secondary social studies (MAT).

University of the Incarnate Word, School of Graduate Studies and Research, School of Mathematics, Science, and Engineering, San Antonio, TX 78209-6397. Offers applied statistics (MS); biology (MA, MS); mathematics (MA), including teaching; nutrition (MS). *Program availability:* Part-time, evening/weekend. *Faculty:* 9 full-time (4 women), 4 part-time/adjunct (3 women). *Students:* 23 full-time (18 women), 26 part-time (22 women); includes 26 minority (2 Black or African American, non-Hispanic/Latino; 1 American Indian or Alaska Native, non-Hispanic/Latino; 22 Hispanic/Latino; 1 Two or more races, non-Hispanic/Latino), 8 international. In 2016, 18 master's awarded. *Degree requirements:* For master's, comprehensive exam (for some programs), thesis optional, capstone. *Entrance requirements:* For master's, GRE, recommendation letter. Additional exam requirements/recommendations for international students: Required—TOEFL (minimum score 560 paper-based; 83 iBT). *Application deadline:* Applications are processed on a rolling basis. Application fee: $20. Electronic applications accepted. *Expenses: Tuition:* Full-time $7965; part-time $885 per credit hour. *Required fees:* $40 per credit hour. Tuition and fees vary according to course load, degree level, campus/location, program and student level. *Financial support:* In 2016–17, 1 research assistantship (averaging $5,000 per year) was awarded; Federal Work-Study, scholarships/grants, tuition waivers (partial), and unspecified assistantships also available. Financial award applicants required to submit FAFSA. *Faculty research:* Biology, mathematics, multidisciplinary sciences, nutrition, research statistics, chemistry. *Total annual research expenditures:* $1.7 million. *Unit head:* Dr. Carlos A. Garcia, Dean, 210-829-2717, Fax: 210-829-3153, E-mail: cagarci9@uiwtx.edu. *Application contact:* Johnny Garcia, Graduate Admissions Counselor, 210-805-3554, Fax: 210-829-3921, E-mail: admis@uiwtx.edu.
Website: http://www.uiw.edu/smse/index.htm

University of the Sacred Heart, Graduate Programs, Department of Education, San Juan, PR 00914-0383. Offers early childhood education (M Ed); information technology and multimedia (Certificate); instruction systems and education technology (M Ed), including English, information technology and multimedia, instructional design, mathematics, Spanish. *Program availability:* Part-time, evening/weekend. *Degree requirements:* For master's, thesis. *Entrance requirements:* For master's, EXADEP, minimum undergraduate GPA of 2.75, interview.

University of the Virgin Islands, College of Science and Mathematics, St. Thomas, VI 00802. Offers marine and environmental science (MS); mathematics for secondary teachers (MA). *Program availability:* Part-time, online learning. *Faculty:* 5 full-time (4 women), 7 part-time/adjunct (2 women). *Students:* 12 full-time (10 women), 26 part-time (19 women); includes 7 minority (6 Black or African American, non-Hispanic/Latino; 1 Hispanic/Latino). Average age 27. 25 applicants, 80% accepted, 11 enrolled. In 2016, 6 master's awarded. *Degree requirements:* For master's, comprehensive exam, thesis. *Entrance requirements:* For master's, GRE, minimum GPA of 2.5. Additional exam requirements/recommendations for international students: Required—TOEFL (minimum score 550 paper-based). *Application deadline:* For fall admission, 4/30 for domestic and international students; for spring admission, 10/30 for domestic and international students. Application fee: $30. Electronic applications accepted. *Expenses:* Tuition, state resident: part-time $386 per credit hour. Tuition, nonresident: part-time $735 per credit hour. *Financial support:* Career-related internships or fieldwork and scholarships/grants available. Financial award application deadline: 4/15; financial award applicants required to submit FAFSA. *Unit head:* Dr. Sandra Romano, Dean, 340-693-1230, Fax: 340-693-1245, E-mail: sromano@uvi.edu. *Application contact:* Dr. Xuri M. Allen, Director of Admissions, 340-693-1224, Fax: 340-693-1167, E-mail: xallen@uvi.edu.

The University of Toledo, College of Graduate Studies, Judith Herb College of Education, Department of Curriculum and Instruction, Toledo, OH 43606-3390. Offers art education (ME); career and technical education (ME, Ed S); curriculum and instruction (ME, PhD, Ed S); early childhood education (Ed S); education and anthropology (MAE); education and biology (MES); education and chemistry (MES); education and classics (MAE); education and economics (MAE); education and English (MAE); education and French (MAE); education and geology (MES); education and German (MAE); education and history (MAE); education and mathematics (MAE, MES); education and physics (MES); education and political science (MAE); education and sociology (MAE); education and Spanish (MAE); educational media (PhD); educational technology (ME); educational technology: virtual educator (Certificate); elementary education (PhD); English as a second language (MAE); gifted and talented education (PhD); middle childhood education (ME); secondary education (ME, PhD); special education (PhD). *Accreditation:* NCATE. *Program availability:* Part-time, evening/weekend. *Degree requirements:* For master's, comprehensive exam, thesis or alternative; for doctorate, comprehensive exam, thesis/dissertation; for other advanced degree, thesis optional. *Entrance requirements:* For master's, doctorate, and other advanced degree, minimum cumulative GPA of 2.7 for all previous academic work, letters of recommendation. Additional exam requirements/recommendations for international students: Required—TOEFL (minimum score 550 paper-based; 80 iBT). Electronic applications accepted.

The University of Tulsa, Graduate School, Kendall College of Arts and Sciences, School of Urban Education, Program in Mathematics and Science Education, Tulsa, OK 74104-3189. Offers MSMSE. *Program availability:* Part-time. *Students:* 8 full-time (3 women), 2 part-time (0 women); includes 4 minority (2 Black or African American, non-Hispanic/Latino; 1 Asian, non-Hispanic/Latino; 1 Hispanic/Latino). Average age 26. 15 applicants, 73% accepted, 8 enrolled. In 2016, 6 master's awarded. *Entrance requirements:* For master's, GRE General Test. Additional exam requirements/recommendations for international students: Required—TOEFL (minimum score 577 paper-based), IELTS (minimum score 6.5). *Application deadline:* Applications are processed on a rolling basis. Application fee: $55. Electronic applications accepted. *Expenses: Tuition:* Full-time $22,230; part-time $1235 per credit hour. *Required fees:* $990 per semester. Tuition and fees vary according to course load. *Financial support:* In 2016–17, 3 students received support, including 3 teaching assistantships with full tuition reimbursements available (averaging $13,410 per year); fellowships with tuition reimbursements available, research assistantships, career-related internships or fieldwork, Federal Work-Study, scholarships/grants, health care benefits, tuition waivers (full and partial), and unspecified assistantships also available. Support available to part-time students. Financial award application deadline: 2/1; financial award applicants required to submit FAFSA. *Unit head:* Dr. Sharon Baker, Chair, 918-631-2238, Fax: 918-631-3721, E-mail: sharon-baker@utulsa.edu. *Application contact:* Dr. David Brown, Advisor, 918-631-2719, Fax: 918-631-2133, E-mail: david-brown@utulsa.edu.

University of Utah, Graduate School, College of Science, Department of Mathematics, Salt Lake City, UT 84112-0090. Offers mathematics (MA, MS, PhD); mathematics teaching (MS); statistics (M Stat). *Program availability:* Part-time. *Faculty:* 41 full-time (4 women), 37 part-time/adjunct (9 women). *Students:* 93 full-time (30 women), 50 part-time (18 women); includes 11 minority (6 Asian, non-Hispanic/Latino; 3 Hispanic/Latino; 2 Two or more races, non-Hispanic/Latino), 41 international. Average age 28. 195 applicants, 32% accepted, 27 enrolled. In 2016, 32 master's, 6 doctorates awarded. *Degree requirements:* For master's, comprehensive exam, thesis or alternative, written or oral exam; for doctorate, comprehensive exam, thesis/dissertation, written and oral exams. *Entrance requirements:* For master's and doctorate, GRE Subject Test in math (recommended), minimum undergraduate GPA of 3.0. Additional exam requirements/recommendations for international students: Required—TOEFL (minimum score 550 paper-based; 80 iBT), GRE (recommended). *Application deadline:* For fall admission, 3/15 for domestic and international students; for spring admission, 11/1 for domestic and international students; for summer admission, 3/15 for domestic and international

students. Application fee: $55 ($65 for international students). Electronic applications accepted. *Expenses:* Contact institution. *Financial support:* In 2016–17, 118 students received support, including 1 fellowship (averaging $34,000 per year), 29 research assistantships with full tuition reimbursements available (averaging $19,350 per year), 81 teaching assistantships with full tuition reimbursements available (averaging $17,000 per year); health care benefits and unspecified assistantships also available. Financial award application deadline: 1/1; financial award applicants required to submit FAFSA. *Faculty research:* Algebraic geometry, geometry and topology materials and microstructure, mathematical biology, probability and statistics. *Total annual research expenditures:* $3.4 million. *Unit head:* Dr. Peter Trapa, Chairman, 801-581-6851, Fax: 801-581-4148, E-mail: ptrapa@math.utah.edu. *Application contact:* Dr. Karl Schwede, Director of Graduate Studies, 801-581-7916, Fax: 801-581-6841, E-mail: schwede@math.utah.edu.
Website: http://www.math.utah.edu/

University of Vermont, Graduate College, College of Engineering and Mathematics, Department of Mathematics and Statistics, Program in Mathematics, Burlington, VT 05405. Offers mathematics (MS); mathematics education (MST). *Entrance requirements:* For master's, GRE General Test. Additional exam requirements/recommendations for international students: Required—TOEFL (minimum score 550 paper-based; 80 iBT). Electronic applications accepted. *Expenses:* Tuition, state resident: full-time $5814. Tuition, nonresident: full-time $14,670.

University of Victoria, Faculty of Graduate Studies, Faculty of Education, Department of Curriculum and Instruction, Victoria, BC V8W 2Y2, Canada. Offers art education (M Ed, PhD); curriculum studies (M Ed, MA, PhD); early childhood education (M Ed, PhD); educational studies (PhD); language and literacy (M Ed, MA, PhD); mathematics (M Ed, MA, PhD); music education (M Ed, MA, PhD); science (M Ed, MA, PhD); social studies (M Ed, MA); social, cultural and foundational studies (MA, PhD); technology and environmental education (PhD). *Program availability:* Part-time. *Degree requirements:* For master's, thesis, project (M Ed); for doctorate, comprehensive exam, thesis/dissertation. *Entrance requirements:* For master's, minimum B average. Additional exam requirements/recommendations for international students: Required—TOEFL (minimum score 575 paper-based), IELTS (minimum score 7). Electronic applications accepted. *Faculty research:* Elementary and secondary English, language arts, curriculum theory and practice, educational media and technology, educational administration and leadership, history and philosophy of education.

University of Virginia, Curry School of Education, Department of Curriculum, Instruction, and Special Education, Program in Curriculum and Instruction, Charlottesville, VA 22903. Offers curriculum and instruction (M Ed, Ed S); elementary education (M Ed, Ed D); English education (M Ed, Ed D); foreign language education (M Ed); mathematics education (M Ed, Ed D); science education (Ed D); social studies education (M Ed); MBA/M Ed. *Students:* 43 full-time (35 women), 24 part-time (16 women); includes 7 minority (1 Black or African American, non-Hispanic/Latino; 1 Asian, non-Hispanic/Latino; 2 Hispanic/Latino; 3 Two or more races, non-Hispanic/Latino), 4 international. Average age 33. 93 applicants, 78% accepted, 54 enrolled. In 2016, 52 master's, 14 other advanced degrees awarded. *Degree requirements:* For master's, comprehensive exam (for some programs); for doctorate, comprehensive exam, thesis/dissertation; for Ed S, comprehensive exam. *Entrance requirements:* For master's, doctorate, and Ed S, GRE General Test, 2 letters of recommendation. Additional exam requirements/recommendations for international students: Required—TOEFL (minimum score 600 paper-based; 90 iBT), IELTS (minimum score 7). *Application deadline:* Applications are processed on a rolling basis. Application fee: $60. Electronic applications accepted. *Expenses:* Tuition, state resident: full-time $15,026; part-time $834 per credit hour. Tuition, nonresident: full-time $25,168; part-time $1378 per credit hour. *Required fees:* $2654. *Financial support:* Fellowships with tuition reimbursements, research assistantships with tuition reimbursements, and teaching assistantships with tuition reimbursements available. Financial award application deadline: 1/5; financial award applicants required to submit FAFSA. *Unit head:* Susan Mintz, Program Area Director, 434-924-3128, E-mail: slm4r@virginia.edu. *Application contact:* Eric Molnar, Assistant Director, Admissions and Enrollment Reporting, 434-243-2085, E-mail: eric.molnar@virginia.edu.
Website: http://curry.virginia.edu/academics/areas-of-study/curriculum-teaching-learning

University of Virginia, Curry School of Education, Program in Education, Charlottesville, VA 22903. Offers administration and supervision (PhD); applied developmental science (PhD); counselor education (PhD); curriculum and instruction (PhD); early childhood special education (MT); education evaluation (PhD); educational psychology (PhD); educational research (PhD); elementary education (MT); English education (MT, PhD); foreign language education (MT); higher education (PhD); instructional technology (PhD); kinesiology (MT, PhD); math education (PhD); reading education (PhD); research, statistics and evaluation (PhD); school psychology (PhD); science education (PhD); social studies education (MT, PhD); special education (PhD); world languages education (MT). *Students:* 452 full-time (357 women), 18 part-time (13 women); includes 100 minority (28 Black or African American, non-Hispanic/Latino; 39 Asian, non-Hispanic/Latino; 18 Hispanic/Latino; 15 Two or more races, non-Hispanic/Latino), 14 international. Average age 25. 309 applicants, 51% accepted, 87 enrolled. In 2016, 144 master's, 31 doctorates awarded. *Degree requirements:* For master's, comprehensive exam (for some programs), field project; for doctorate, comprehensive exam, thesis/dissertation. *Entrance requirements:* For doctorate, GRE General Test. Additional exam requirements/recommendations for international students: Required—TOEFL (minimum score 600 paper-based; 90 iBT), IELTS (minimum score 7). *Application deadline:* Applications are processed on a rolling basis. Application fee: $60. Electronic applications accepted. *Expenses:* Tuition, state resident: full-time $15,026; part-time $834 per credit hour. Tuition, nonresident: full-time $25,168; part-time $1378 per credit hour. *Required fees:* $2654. *Financial support:* Fellowships, research assistantships, and teaching assistantships available. Financial award application deadline: 1/5; financial award applicants required to submit FAFSA. *Unit head:* Robert C. Pianta, Dean, 434-924-3334, E-mail: pianta@virginia.edu. *Application contact:* Eric Molnar, Assistant Director, Admissions and Enrollment Reporting, 434-243-2085, E-mail: eric.molnar@virginia.edu.
Website: http://curry.virginia.edu/teacher-education

University of Washington, Graduate School, College of Education, Seattle, WA 98195. Offers curriculum and instruction (M Ed, Ed D, PhD), including educational technology, general curriculum (Ed D, PhD), language, literacy, and culture, mathematics education, multicultural education, reading and language arts education (Ed D), science education, social studies education, teaching and curriculum (M Ed); educational leadership and policy studies (M Ed, Ed D, PhD), including administration (Ed D), educational policy, organization, and leadership (M Ed, PhD), higher education, leadership for learning (Ed D), social and cultural foundations of education (M Ed, PhD); educational psychology (M Ed, PhD), including educational psychology (PhD), human development and cognition (M Ed), learning sciences, measurement, statistics and research design (M Ed), school psychology (M Ed); instructional leadership (M Ed); intercollegiate athletic leadership (M Ed); special education (M Ed, Ed D, PhD), including early childhood special education (M Ed), emotional and behavioral disabilities (M Ed), learning disabilities (M Ed), low-incidence disabilities (M Ed), severe disabilities (M Ed), special education (Ed D, PhD); teacher education (MIT). *Accreditation:* APA. *Program availability:* Part-time, evening/weekend. *Degree requirements:* For master's, thesis optional; for doctorate, thesis/dissertation. *Entrance requirements:* For master's and doctorate, GRE General Test, minimum GPA of 3.0. Additional exam requirements/recommendations for international students: Required—TOEFL. Electronic applications accepted. *Faculty research:* School restructuring/effective schools, special education interventions, literacy and writing, technology, school partnerships, teacher preparation.

University of Washington, Tacoma, Graduate Programs, Program in Education, Tacoma, WA 98402-3100. Offers education (M Ed); educational administration (principal or program administrator certification) (M Ed); elementary education teacher certification (M Ed); elementary education/special education teacher certification (M Ed); secondary science or math teacher certification (M Ed). *Program availability:* Part-time, evening/weekend. *Degree requirements:* For master's, culminating project. *Entrance requirements:* For master's, WEST-B, WEST-E (teacher certification programs only), official sealed transcript from every college/university attended, personal goal statement, letters of recommendation, copy of valid teaching certificate. Additional exam requirements/recommendations for international students: Required—TOEFL (minimum score 580 paper-based; 92 iBT). Electronic applications accepted. *Faculty research:* Global learning communities for English/Chinese languages, evaluation of mathematics and reading intervention programs, response to intervention, school-wide behavioral and emotional support, mathematics education and culturally responsive mathematics education.

The University of West Alabama, School of Graduate Studies, College of Education, Departments of Instructional Leadership and Support/Curriculum and Instruction, Program in Secondary Education, Livingston, AL 35470. Offers biology (MAT); English language arts (MAT); high school 6-12 (M Ed); history (MAT); mathematics (MAT); science (MAT); social science (MAT). *Program availability:* Part-time, evening/weekend, 100% online. *Faculty:* 19 full-time (7 women), 7 part-time/adjunct (3 women). *Students:* 236 (159 women); includes 59 minority (53 Black or African American, non-Hispanic/Latino; 2 American Indian or Alaska Native, non-Hispanic/Latino; 1 Asian, non-Hispanic/Latino; 1 Hispanic/Latino; 2 Two or more races, non-Hispanic/Latino). Average age 32. 85 applicants, 88% accepted, 52 enrolled. In 2016, 84 master's awarded. *Degree requirements:* For master's, comprehensive exam, thesis optional. *Entrance requirements:* For master's, GRE General Test, MAT, minimum GPA of 2.75. Additional exam requirements/recommendations for international students: Required—TOEFL (minimum score 500 paper-based; 61 iBT). *Application deadline:* Applications are processed on a rolling basis. Application fee: $40. Electronic applications accepted. *Expenses:* Tuition, state resident: part-time $355 per credit hour. Tuition, nonresident: part-time $710 per credit hour. *Required fees:* $130 per semester. *Financial support:* Teaching assistantships, Federal Work-Study, scholarships/grants, and unspecified assistantships available. Support available to part-time students. Financial award application deadline: 3/1; financial award applicants required to submit FAFSA. *Faculty research:* Integrated arts in the curriculum, moral development of children. *Unit head:* Dr. Jodie Winship, Chair of Curriculum and Instruction, 205-652-5415, Fax: 205-652-3706, E-mail: jwinship@uwa.edu. *Application contact:* Dr. B. J. Kimbrough, Dean of Graduate Studies, 205-652-3647, Fax: 205-652-3706, E-mail: bkimbrough@uwa.edu.
Website: http://www.uwa.edu/highschool612.aspx

University of Wisconsin–Madison, Graduate School, School of Education, Department of Curriculum and Instruction, Madison, WI 53706-1380. Offers art education (MA); curriculum and instruction (MS, PhD); education and mathematics (MA); French education (MA); German education (MA); music education (MS); science education (MS); Spanish education (MA). *Accreditation:* NASM (one or more programs are accredited). *Degree requirements:* For doctorate, thesis/dissertation.

University of Wisconsin–Milwaukee, Graduate School, School of Education, Department of Curriculum and Instruction, Milwaukee, WI 53201-0413. Offers curriculum and instruction (MS), including cross-curricular focus, early childhood education, English education, mathematics education, middle childhood/early adolescence education, reading education, science education, urban social studies education. *Program availability:* Part-time. *Students:* 21 full-time (13 women), 44 part-time (42 women); includes 10 minority (1 Black or African American, non-Hispanic/Latino; 1 Asian, non-Hispanic/Latino; 2 Hispanic/Latino; 6 Two or more races, non-Hispanic/Latino), 2 international. Average age 33. 42 applicants, 71% accepted, 20 enrolled. In 2016, 45 master's awarded. *Degree requirements:* For master's, thesis or alternative. *Entrance requirements:* Additional exam requirements/recommendations for international students: Required—TOEFL (minimum score 550 paper-based; 79 iBT), IELTS (minimum score 6.5). *Application deadline:* For fall admission, 1/1 priority date for domestic students; for spring admission, 9/1 for domestic students. Applications are processed on a rolling basis. Application fee: $56 ($96 for international students). Electronic applications accepted. *Financial support:* In 2016–17, 1 fellowship was awarded; research assistantships, teaching assistantships, career-related internships or fieldwork, health care benefits, unspecified assistantships, and project assistantships also available. Support available to part-time students. Financial award application deadline: 4/15; financial award applicants required to submit FAFSA. *Application contact:* General Information Contact, 414-229-4721, E-mail: soeinfo@uwm.edu.
Website: http://uwm.edu/education/academics/curriculum-instruction-department/

University of Wisconsin–Milwaukee, Graduate School, School of Education, Department of Exceptional Education, Milwaukee, WI 53201-0413. Offers autism spectrum disorders (Graduate Certificate); exceptional education (MS); transition for students with disabilities (Graduate Certificate); urban education (PhD), including adult, continuing and higher education leadership, art education, curriculum and instruction, exceptional education, mathematics education, multicultural studies, social foundations of education. *Program availability:* Part-time. *Students:* 50 full-time (41 women), 66 part-time (51 women); includes 42 minority (24 Black or African American, non-Hispanic/Latino; 6 Asian, non-Hispanic/Latino; 1 Hispanic/Latino; 11 Two or more races, non-Hispanic/Latino), 4 international. Average age 39. 55 applicants, 51% accepted, 22 enrolled. In 2016, 14 master's, 10 doctorates, 3 other advanced degrees awarded. *Degree requirements:* For master's, thesis. *Entrance requirements:* Additional exam requirements/recommendations for international students: Required—TOEFL (minimum score 550 paper-based; 79 iBT), IELTS (minimum score 6.5). *Application deadline:* For fall admission, 1/1 priority date for domestic students; for spring admission, 9/1 for domestic students. Applications are processed on a rolling basis. Application fee: $56 ($96 for international students). Electronic applications accepted. *Financial support:* Fellowships, research assistantships, teaching assistantships, career-related internships or fieldwork, health care benefits, and unspecified assistantships available. Support available to part-time students. Financial award application deadline: 4/15; financial award applicants required to submit FAFSA. *Faculty research:* Emotional disturbance, hearing impairment, learning disabilities, mental retardation. *Application contact:* General Information Contact, 414-229-4721, E-mail: soeinfo@uwm.edu.
Website: http://uwm.edu/education/academics/exceptional-edu-department/

University of Wisconsin–Oshkosh, Graduate Studies, College of Letters and Science, Department of Mathematics, Oshkosh, WI 54901. Offers mathematics education (MS). *Program availability:* Part-time. *Degree requirements:* For master's, comprehensive exam, thesis optional. *Entrance requirements:* For master's, 30 undergraduate credits in mathematics. Additional exam requirements/recommendations for international students: Required—TOEFL (minimum score 550 paper-based; 79 iBT). Electronic applications accepted. *Faculty research:* Problem solving, number theory, discrete mathematics, statistics.

University of Wisconsin–River Falls, Outreach and Graduate Studies, College of Arts and Science, Program in Mathematics, River Falls, WI 54022. Offers mathematics education (MSE). *Program availability:* Part-time. *Degree requirements:* For master's, thesis (for some programs). *Entrance requirements:* For master's, minimum GPA of 2.75. Additional exam requirements/recommendations for international students: Required—TOEFL (minimum score 500 paper-based; 65 iBT), IELTS (minimum score 5.5). Electronic applications accepted.

University of Wyoming, College of Arts and Sciences, Department of Mathematics, Laramie, WY 82071. Offers mathematics (MA, MAT, MS, MST, PhD); mathematics/computer science (PhD). *Program availability:* Part-time. Terminal master's awarded for partial completion of doctoral program. *Degree requirements:* For master's, comprehensive exam, thesis, qualifying exam; for doctorate, comprehensive exam, thesis/dissertation, preliminary exam. *Entrance requirements:* For master's and doctorate, GRE General Test, minimum GPA of 3.0. Additional exam requirements/recommendations for international students: Required—TOEFL (minimum score 540 paper-based; 76 iBT). *Faculty research:* Numerical analysis, classical analysis, mathematical modeling, algebraic combinations.

Utah Valley University, Program in Education, Orem, UT 84058-5999. Offers educational technology (M Ed); elementary mathematics (M Ed); elementary STEM (M Ed); English as a second language (M Ed); reading (M Ed); teachers as leaders (M Ed). *Accreditation:* TEAC. *Program availability:* Part-time. *Degree requirements:* For master's, project. *Entrance requirements:* For master's, GRE, 3 letters of recommendation, interview, essay. Additional exam requirements/recommendations for international students: Required—TOEFL (minimum score 83 iBT). Electronic applications accepted. *Expenses:* Contact institution.

Virginia Polytechnic Institute and State University, Graduate School, College of Engineering, Blacksburg, VA 24061. Offers aerospace engineering (ME, MS, PhD); biological systems engineering (ME, MS, PhD); biomedical engineering (MS, PhD); chemical engineering (ME, MS, PhD); civil engineering (ME, MS, PhD); computer engineering (ME, MS, PhD); computer science (MS, PhD); electrical engineering (ME, PhD); engineering education (PhD); engineering mechanics (ME, MS, PhD); environmental engineering (MS); environmental science and engineering (MS); industrial and systems engineering (ME, MS, PhD); materials science and engineering (ME, MS, PhD); mechanical engineering (ME, MS, PhD); mining and minerals engineering (PhD); mining engineering (ME, MS); nuclear engineering (MS, PhD); ocean engineering (MS); systems engineering (ME, MS). *Faculty:* 400 full-time (73 women), 3 part-time/adjunct (2 women). *Students:* 1,949 full-time (487 women), 393 part-time (69 women); includes 251 minority (56 Black or African American, non-Hispanic/Latino; 3 American Indian or Alaska Native, non-Hispanic/Latino; 87 Asian, non-Hispanic/Latino; 70 Hispanic/Latino; 35 Two or more races, non-Hispanic/Latino), 1,354 international. Average age 27. 4,903 applicants, 19% accepted, 569 enrolled. In 2016, 364 master's, 200 doctorates awarded. *Degree requirements:* For master's, comprehensive exam (for some programs), thesis (for some programs); for doctorate, comprehensive exam (for some programs), thesis/dissertation (for some programs). *Entrance requirements:* For master's and doctorate, GRE/GMAT. Additional exam requirements/recommendations for international students: Required—TOEFL (minimum score 80 iBT). *Application deadline:* For fall admission, 8/1 for domestic students, 4/1 for international students; for spring admission, 1/1 for domestic students, 9/1 for international students. Applications are processed on a rolling basis. Application fee: $75. Electronic applications accepted. *Expenses:* Tuition, state resident: full-time $12,467; part-time $692.50 per credit hour. Tuition, nonresident: full-time $25,095; part-time $1394.25 per credit hour. *Required fees:* $2669; $491.50 per semester. Tuition and fees vary according to course load, campus/location and program. *Financial support:* In 2016–17, 160 fellowships with full tuition reimbursements (averaging $7,387 per year), 872 research assistantships with full tuition reimbursements (averaging $22,329 per year), 313 teaching assistantships with full tuition reimbursements (averaging $18,714 per year) were awarded. Financial award application deadline: 3/1; financial award applicants required to submit FAFSA. *Total annual research expenditures:* $91.8 million. *Unit head:* Dr. Julia Ross, Dean, 540-231-9752, Fax: 540-231-3031, E-mail: deaneng@vt.edu. *Application contact:* Linda Perkins, Executive Assistant, 540-231-9752, Fax: 540-231-3031, E-mail: lperkins@vt.edu.
Website: http://www.eng.vt.edu/

Virginia State University, College of Graduate Studies, College of Engineering and Technology, Department of Mathematics and Computer Science, Petersburg, VA 23806-0001. Offers computer science (MS); mathematics (MS); mathematics education (MS). *Degree requirements:* For master's, thesis (for some programs).

Wagner College, Division of Graduate Studies, Education Department, Program in Secondary Education/Students with Disabilities, Staten Island, NY 10301-4495. Offers secondary education 7-12 (MS Ed), including language arts, languages other than English, mathematics and technology, science and technology, social studies. *Program availability:* Part-time, evening/weekend. *Degree requirements:* For master's, thesis (for some programs), completion of state certification exams before student teaching. *Entrance requirements:* For master's, minimum GPA of 3.0, interview, recommendations. Electronic applications accepted. Tuition and fees vary according to degree level.

Walden University, Graduate Programs, Richard W. Riley College of Education and Leadership, Minneapolis, MN 55401. Offers adult education (Post-Master's Certificate); adult learning (Graduate Certificate); college teaching and learning (Graduate Certificate); community college leadership (Ed D); curriculum, instruction and assessment (Ed D, Ed S, Graduate Certificate); developmental education (Graduate Certificate); early childhood administration, management, and leadership (Graduate Certificate); early childhood education (Ed D, Ed S); early childhood public policy and advocacy (Graduate Certificate); early childhood studies (MS), including administration, management and leadership, early childhood public policy and advocacy, teaching adults in the early childhood field, teaching and diversity in early childhood education; education (MS, PhD), including adolescent literacy and learning (MS), curriculum, instruction, and assessment (grades K-12) (MS), curriculum, instruction, assessment, and evaluation (PhD), early childhood leadership and advocacy (PhD), early childhood special education (PhD), educational leadership (MS), educational leadership and administration (principal preparation) (MS), educational technology and design (PhD), elementary reading and literacy (PreK-6) (MS), elementary reading and mathematics (grades K-6) (MS), global and comparative education (PhD), higher education leadership management and policy (PhD), integrating technology in the classroom (grades K-12) (MS), learning, instruction and innovation (PhD), mathematics (grades 5-8) (MS), mathematics (grades K-6) (MS), mathematics and science (grades K-8) (MS), organizational research, assessment, and evaluation (PhD), reading and literacy with a reading K-12 endorsement (MS), reading literacy assessment and evaluation (PhD), science (grades K-8) (MS), special education (non-licensure) (grades K-12) (MS), teacher leadership (grades K-12) (MS), teaching English language learners (grades K-12) (MS); educational administration and leadership (Ed D); educational leadership and administration (principal preparation) (Ed S); educational technology (Ed D, Ed S, Post Master's Certificate); elementary reading and literacy (Graduate Certificate); engaging culturally diverse learners (Graduate Certificate); enrollment management and institutional marketing (Graduate Certificate); higher education (MS), including adult learning, college teaching and learning, enrollment management and institutional marketing, global higher education, leadership for student success, online and distance learning; higher education and adult learning (Ed D); higher education leadership and management (Ed D); higher education leadership for student success (Graduate Certificate); instructional design and technology (MS, Postbaccalaureate Certificate), including general program (MS), online learning (MS), training and performance improvement (MS); integrating technology in the classroom (Graduate Certificate); mathematics 5-8 (Graduate Certificate); mathematics K-6 (Graduate Certificate); online teaching for adult educators (Graduate Certificate); reading, literacy, and assessment (Ed D, Ed S); science K-8 (Graduate Certificate); special education (Ed D, Ed S, Graduate Certificate); special education (K-age 21) (MAT); teacher leadership (Graduate Certificate); teaching adults English as a second language (Graduate Certificate); teaching adults in the early childhood field (Graduate Certificate); teaching and diversity in early childhood education (Graduate Certificate); teaching English language learners (grades K-12) (Graduate Certificate); teaching K-12 students online (Graduate Certificate). *Accreditation:* NCATE. *Program availability:* Part-time, evening/weekend, online only, 100% online. *Degree requirements:* For doctorate, thesis/dissertation (for some programs), residency; for other advanced degree, residency (for some programs). *Entrance requirements:* For master's, bachelor's degree or higher; minimum GPA of 2.5; official transcripts; goal statement (for some programs); access to computer and Internet; for doctorate, master's degree or higher; three years of related professional or academic experience (preferred); minimum GPA of 3.0; goal statement and current resume (for select programs); official transcripts; access to computer and Internet; for other advanced degree, relevant work experience; access to computer and Internet. Additional exam requirements/recommendations for international students: Required—TOEFL (minimum score 550 paper-based, 79 iBT), IELTS (minimum score 6.5), Michigan English Language Assessment Battery (minimum score 82), or PTE (minimum score 53). Electronic applications accepted.

Washington State University, College of Arts and Sciences, Department of Mathematics, Pullman, WA 99164. Offers applied mathematics (MS, PhD); mathematics (MS, PhD); mathematics teaching (MS, PhD). Programs offered at the Pullman campus. *Program availability:* Part-time. Terminal master's awarded for partial completion of doctoral program. *Degree requirements:* For master's, comprehensive exam (for some programs), thesis or alternative, oral exam, project; for doctorate, 2 foreign languages, comprehensive exam, thesis/dissertation, oral exam, written exam. *Entrance requirements:* For master's and doctorate, minimum GPA of 3.0, 3 letters of recommendation. Additional exam requirements/recommendations for international students: Required—TOEFL (minimum score 600 paper-based; 100 iBT) or IELTS (minimum score 7). Electronic applications accepted. *Faculty research:* Computational mathematics, operations research, modeling in the natural sciences, applied statistics.

Washington State University, College of Education, Department of Teaching and Learning, Pullman, WA 99164-2132. Offers cultural studies and social thought in education (PhD); curriculum and instruction (Ed M, MA); English language learners (Ed M, MA); language, literacy and technology (PhD); literacy education (Ed M, MA); mathematics education (PhD); special education (Ed M, MA, PhD); teacher leadership (Ed D); teaching (MIT), including elementary education, secondary education. Programs offered at the Pullman, Spokane, Tri-cities, Vancouver and Global (online) campuses. *Program availability:* Part-time, online learning. *Degree requirements:* For master's, comprehensive exam, thesis, oral or written exam; for doctorate, comprehensive exam, thesis/dissertation, oral and written exam. *Entrance requirements:* For master's, GRE General Test, minimum GPA of 3.0, 3 letters of recommendation, letter of intent, transcripts, resume/curriculum vitae; for doctorate, GRE General Test, minimum GPA of 3.0, 3 letters of recommendation, letter of intent, transcripts, writing sample, resume/curriculum vitae. Additional exam requirements/recommendations for international students: Required—TOEFL (minimum score 550 paper-based; 80 iBT). Electronic applications accepted. *Faculty research:* Intersection of gender, youth cultures and schooling; examination of ideology of power in children's literature; early childhood special education; analyzing pre-service and in-service teacher development; second language acquisition.

Wayne State College, School of Education and Counseling, Department of Educational Foundations and Leadership, Program in Curriculum and Instruction, Wayne, NE 68787. Offers alternative education (MSE); business and information technology education (MSE); communication arts education (MSE); early childhood education (MSE); elementary education (MSE); English as a second language (MSE); English education (MSE); family and consumer sciences education (MSE); industrial technology and vocational education (MSE); learning communities (MSE); mathematics education (MSE); music education (MSE); science education (MSE); social science education (MSE). *Accreditation:* NCATE. *Program availability:* Part-time, evening/weekend. *Degree requirements:* For master's, comprehensive exam, thesis optional. *Entrance requirements:* For master's, GRE General Test. Additional exam requirements/recommendations for international students: Required—TOEFL (minimum score 550 paper-based).

Wayne State University, College of Education, Division of Teacher Education, Detroit, MI 48202. Offers art education (M Ed); bilingual/bicultural education (M Ed, Certificate); career and technical education (M Ed); curriculum and instruction (Ed D, PhD, Ed S), including art education (Ed D, PhD), bilingual education (Ed D, Ed S), career and technical education (MAT, Ed D, PhD, Ed S), early childhood education (MAT, Ed D, PhD, Ed S), elementary education, English as a second language (MAT, Ed D, Ed S), English education (MAT, Ed D, PhD, Ed S), foreign language education (MAT, Ed D, PhD), K-12 curriculum, mathematics education (MAT, Ed D, PhD, Ed S), science education (MAT, Ed D, PhD, Ed S), secondary education, social studies education (MAT, Ed D, PhD, Ed S); early childhood education (M Ed); elementary education (M Ed, MAT), including bilingual/bicultural education (MAT), early childhood education (MAT, Ed D, PhD, Ed S), English as a second language (MAT, Ed D, Ed S), general elementary education (MAT), mathematics education (MAT, Ed D, PhD, Ed S), science education (MAT, Ed D, PhD, Ed S), social studies education (MAT, Ed D, PhD, Ed S); English as a second language (Certificate); English education (M Ed); foreign language education (M Ed); mathematics education (M Ed); reading (M Ed, Ed S); reading, language and literature (Ed D); science education (M Ed); secondary education (MAT), including art education (K-12), bilingual/bicultural education, career and technical education (MAT, Ed D, PhD, Ed S), English as a second language (MAT, Ed D, Ed S), English education (MAT, Ed D, PhD, Ed S), foreign language education (MAT, Ed D, PhD), kinesiology, mathematics education (MAT, Ed D, PhD, Ed S); social studies education (M Ed); special education (M Ed, MAT, Ed D, PhD, Ed S), including autism spectrum disorders (MAT), cognitive development (MAT), emotional impairment (MAT), learning disabilities (MAT). *Program availability:* Part-time, blended/hybrid learning. *Faculty:* 29. *Students:* 106 full-time (73 women), 351 part-time (276 women); includes 115 minority (76 Black or African American, non-Hispanic/Latino; 10 Asian, non-

Hispanic/Latino; 20 Hispanic/Latino; 1 Native Hawaiian or other Pacific Islander, non-Hispanic/Latino; 8 Two or more races, non-Hispanic/Latino), 12 international. Average age 37. 242 applicants, 37% accepted, 72 enrolled. In 2016, 178 master's, 19 doctorates, 17 other advanced degrees awarded. *Degree requirements:* For master's, essay or project (for some M Ed programs), professional field experience (for MAT programs); for doctorate, thesis/dissertation. *Entrance requirements:* For master's, Michigan Test for Teacher Certification, verification of participation in group work with children, Michigan State Police criminal background check; for doctorate, minimum undergraduate GPA of 3.0, graduate 3.5; interview; curriculum vitae; references. Additional exam requirements/recommendations for international students: Required—TOEFL (minimum score 550 paper-based; 79 iBT), TWE (minimum score 5.5), Michigan English Language Assessment Battery (minimum score 85); Recommended—IELTS (minimum score 6.5). *Application deadline:* For fall admission, 6/1 priority date for domestic students, 5/1 priority date for international students; for winter admission, 10/1 priority date for domestic students, 9/1 priority date for international students; for spring admission, 2/1 priority date for domestic students, 1/1 priority date for international students. Applications are processed on a rolling basis. Application fee: $50. Electronic applications accepted. *Expenses:* $16,503 per year resident tuition and fees, $33,697 per year non-resident tuition and fees. *Financial support:* In 2016–17, 101 students received support, including 3 fellowships (averaging $11,409 per year); research assistantships with tuition reimbursements available, Federal Work-Study, scholarships/grants, and unspecified assistantships also available. Support available to part-time students. Financial award applicants required to submit FAFSA. *Faculty research:* Improving students' skill achievement in mathematics, improving elementary children's understanding of informational text, teachers' use of their pedagogical and mathematical knowledge in the interactive work of teaching, the intersection of identity construction in teaching and learning, identifying effective methods of literacy instruction and assessments for bilingual students in elementary language arts classrooms. *Unit head:* Dr. Kathleen Crawford-McKinney, Assistant Dean, 313-577-0122. *Application contact:* Janice Green, Assistant Dean, 313-577-1605, E-mail: jwgreen@wayne.edu.
Website: http://coe.wayne.edu/ted/index.php

Webster University, School of Education, Department of Multidisciplinary Studies, St. Louis, MO 63119-3194. Offers applied educational psychology (MA, Ed S); communication arts (MA); early childhood education (MA, MAT); education and innovation (MA); educational technology (MET); elementary education (MAT); mathematics for educators (MA); middle school education (MAT); multidisciplinary studies (MAT); multimodal literacy for global impact (MA); reading (MA); secondary school education (MAT); special education (MA, MAT); teaching English as a second language (MA); transformative learning in the global community (Ed S). *Program availability:* Part-time. *Entrance requirements:* For master's, minimum GPA of 2.5. Additional exam requirements/recommendations for international students: Required—TOEFL. *Application deadline:* Applications are processed on a rolling basis. Application fee: $35 ($50 for international students). *Expenses: Tuition:* Full-time $21,900; part-time $730 per credit hour. Tuition and fees vary according to campus/location and program. *Financial support:* Federal Work-Study available. Support available to part-time students. Financial award application deadline: 4/1; financial award applicants required to submit FAFSA. *Unit head:* Dr. Deborah Stiles, Chair, 314-968-7056, Fax: 314-968-7118, E-mail: stilesda@webster.edu.

West Chester University of Pennsylvania, College of the Sciences and Mathematics, Department of Mathematics, West Chester, PA 19383. Offers applied and computational mathematics (MS); applied statistics (MS, Certificate); mathematics (MA, Teaching Certificate); mathematics education (MA). *Program availability:* Part-time, evening/weekend. *Faculty:* 13 full-time (2 women). *Students:* 18 full-time (3 women), 101 part-time (46 women); includes 28 minority (5 Black or African American, non-Hispanic/Latino; 22 Asian, non-Hispanic/Latino; 1 Two or more races, non-Hispanic/Latino), 14 international. Average age 32. 71 applicants, 100% accepted, 51 enrolled. In 2016, 39 master's, 2 other advanced degrees awarded. *Degree requirements:* For master's, thesis (for all but MS in applied mathematics). *Entrance requirements:* For master's, GMAT or GRE General Test (for MA in mathematics), interview (for MA in mathematics); for other advanced degree, GMAT or GRE General Test (for Teaching Certificate). Additional exam requirements/recommendations for international students: Required—TOEFL or IELTS. *Application deadline:* For fall admission, 5/15 for international students; for spring admission, 10/15 for international students. Applications are processed on a rolling basis. Application fee: $50. Electronic applications accepted. *Expenses:* Tuition, state resident: full-time $8694; part-time $483 per credit. Tuition, nonresident: full-time $13,050; part-time $725 per credit. *Required fees:* $2399; $119.05 per credit. Tuition and fees vary according to campus/location and program. *Financial support:* Scholarships/grants and unspecified assistantships available. Financial award application deadline: 2/15; financial award applicants required to submit FAFSA. *Faculty research:* Teachers teaching with technology in service training program, biostatistics, hierarchical linear models, clustered binary outcome date, mathematics biology. *Unit head:* Dr. Peter Glidden, Chair, 610-436-2440, Fax: 610-738-0578, E-mail: pglidden@wcupa.edu. *Application contact:* Dr. Gail Gallitano, Graduate Coordinator, 610-436-2452, Fax: 610-738-0578, E-mail: ggallitano@wcupa.edu.
Website: http://www.wcupa.edu/sciences-mathematics/mathematics/

Western Governors University, Teachers College, Salt Lake City, UT 84107. Offers curriculum and instruction (MS); educational leadership (MS); educational studies (MA); educational studies (5-12) (MA), including mathematics; elementary education (K-8) (MAT, Postbaccalaureate Certificate); elementary education (PreK-8) (MAT); English language learning (K-12) (MA); instructional design (MAT); learning and technology (M Ed, MA); management and innovation (M Ed); mathematics (5-12) (MAT, Postbaccalaureate Certificate); mathematics (5-9) (MAT, Postbaccalaureate Certificate); mathematics education (5-12) (MA); mathematics education (5-9) (MA); mathematics education (K-6) (MA); measurement and evaluation (M Ed); science (5-12) (Postbaccalaureate Certificate); science (5-9) (MAT, Postbaccalaureate Certificate); science education (5-12) (MA), including biology, chemistry, geology, physics; science education (5-9) (MA); social science (5-12) (MAT, Postbaccalaureate Certificate); special education (MAT, MS). *Accreditation:* NCATE. *Program availability:* Evening/weekend, online learning. *Degree requirements:* For master's, capstone project. *Entrance requirements:* For master's and Postbaccalaureate Certificate, Readiness Assessment, transcripts. Additional exam requirements/recommendations for international students: Required—TOEFL (minimum score 450 paper-based; 80 iBT). Electronic applications accepted. *Expenses:* Contact institution.

Western Michigan University, Graduate College, College of Arts and Sciences, Department of Mathematics, Kalamazoo, MI 49008. Offers applied and computational mathematics (MS); mathematics education (MA, PhD), including collegiate mathematics education (PhD). *Degree requirements:* For doctorate, one foreign language, thesis/dissertation.

Western New England University, College of Arts and Sciences, Program in Mathematics for Teachers, Springfield, MA 01119. Offers MAMT. *Program availability:* Part-time, evening/weekend. *Faculty:* 13 full-time (4 women). *Students:* 13 part-time (10 women), 1 international. Average age 35. 9 applicants, 89% accepted, 6 enrolled. In 2016, 4 master's awarded. *Entrance requirements:* For master's, two letters of recommendation, official transcript, personal statement, resume. Additional exam requirements/recommendations for international students: Required—TOEFL (minimum score 79 iBT). *Application deadline:* Applications are processed on a rolling basis. Application fee: $30. Electronic applications accepted. *Expenses:* Contact institution. *Financial support:* Application deadline: 4/15; applicants required to submit FAFSA. *Unit head:* Dr. David Mazur, Chair and Professor of Mathematics, 413-782-1696, E-mail: dmazur@wne.edu. *Application contact:* Matthew Fox, Director of Admissions for Graduate Students and Adult Learners, 413-782-1410, Fax: 413-782-1777, E-mail: study@wne.edu.
Website: http://www1.wne.edu/academics/graduate/ma-mathematics-teachers.cfm

Western Oregon University, Graduate Programs, College of Education, Division of Teacher Education, Program in Secondary Education, Monmouth, OR 97361. Offers bilingual education (MS Ed); health (MS Ed); humanities (MAT, MS Ed); initial licensure (MAT); mathematics (MAT, MS Ed); science (MAT, MS Ed); social science (MAT, MS Ed). *Accreditation:* NCATE. *Program availability:* Part-time, evening/weekend. *Degree requirements:* For master's, thesis optional, written exam. *Entrance requirements:* For master's, minimum GPA of 3.0, teaching license. Additional exam requirements/recommendations for international students: Required—TOEFL (minimum score 550 paper-based; 79 iBT), IELTS (minimum score 6.5). *Faculty research:* Literacy, science in primary grades, geography education, retention, teacher burnout.

Westfield State University, College of Graduate and Continuing Education, Department of Education, Westfield, MA 01086. Offers early childhood education (M Ed); elementary education (M Ed); reading specialist (M Ed); secondary education (M Ed), including biology teacher education, chemistry teacher education, general science teacher education, history teacher education, mathematics teacher education, physical education teacher education; special education (M Ed), including moderate disabilities, 5-12, moderate disabilities, preK-8; vocational technical education (M Ed). *Accreditation:* NCATE. *Program availability:* Part-time, evening/weekend. *Faculty:* 16 full-time (7 women), 33 part-time/adjunct (24 women). *Students:* 21 full-time (10 women), 168 part-time (126 women); includes 6 minority (2 Black or African American, non-Hispanic/Latino; 2 Hispanic/Latino; 2 Two or more races, non-Hispanic/Latino), 1 international. Average age 32. 47 applicants, 85% accepted, 30 enrolled. In 2016, 51 master's awarded. *Degree requirements:* For master's, comprehensive exam, practicum. *Entrance requirements:* For master's, GRE General Test or MAT, minimum undergraduate GPA of 2.8. Additional exam requirements/recommendations for international students: Recommended—TOEFL (minimum score 550 paper-based; 79 iBT). *Application deadline:* For fall admission, 6/30 for domestic students; for spring admission, 10/31 for domestic students; for summer admission, 3/31 for domestic students. Applications are processed on a rolling basis. Application fee: $50. Electronic applications accepted. *Expenses:* Tuition, state resident: part-time $318 per semester hour. Tuition, nonresident: part-time $318 per semester hour. *Required fees:* $75 per semester. Tuition and fees vary according to course load and program. *Financial support:* Unspecified assistantships and SOS scholarships for education majors only available. Financial award application deadline: 3/1; financial award applicants required to submit FAFSA. *Faculty research:* Collaborative teacher education, developmental early childhood education. *Unit head:* Dr. Sandra Berkowitz, Department Chair, 413-572-5323, E-mail: sberkowitz@westfield.ma.edu. *Application contact:* Shelly Henrichon, Coordinator of DGCE Admissions, 413-572-8022, Fax: 413-572-5227, E-mail: mhenrichon@westfield.ma.edu.
Website: http://www.westfield.ma.edu/academics/degrees/education-graduate-programs

Westfield State University, College of Graduate and Continuing Education, Department of Education, Programs in Secondary Education, Program in Mathematics Teacher Education, Westfield, MA 01086. Offers secondary education-mathematics (M Ed). *Program availability:* Part-time, evening/weekend. *Faculty:* 4 full-time (0 women). *Students:* 1 (woman) full-time, 11 part-time (6 women); includes 2 minority (1 Black or African American, non-Hispanic/Latino; 1 Two or more races, non-Hispanic/Latino). 2 applicants, 100% accepted. In 2016, 2 master's awarded. *Degree requirements:* For master's, comprehensive exam, thesis (for some programs). *Entrance requirements:* For master's, GRE General Test or MAT, minimum undergraduate GPA of 2.8. Additional exam requirements/recommendations for international students: Recommended—TOEFL (minimum score 550 paper-based; 79 iBT). *Application deadline:* For fall admission, 6/30 for domestic students; for spring admission, 10/31 for domestic students; for summer admission, 3/31 for domestic students. Applications are processed on a rolling basis. Application fee: $50. *Expenses:* Tuition, state resident: part-time $318 per semester hour. Tuition, nonresident: part-time $318 per semester hour. *Required fees:* $75 per semester. Tuition and fees vary according to course load and program. *Financial support:* Unspecified assistantships and SOS scholarships for education majors only available. Financial award application deadline: 3/1; financial award applicants required to submit FAFSA. *Unit head:* Dr. Sandra Berkowitz, Chair, 413-572-5323. *Application contact:* Shelly Henrichon, Coordinator of DGCE Admissions, 413-572-8022, Fax: 413-572-5227, E-mail: mhenrichon@westfield.ma.edu.

West Virginia University, Eberly College of Arts and Sciences, Department of Mathematics, Morgantown, WV 26506. Offers applied mathematics (MS, PhD); discrete mathematics (PhD); interdisciplinary mathematics (MS); mathematics for secondary education (MS); pure mathematics (MS). *Program availability:* Part-time. Terminal master's awarded for partial completion of doctoral program. *Degree requirements:* For master's, comprehensive exam (for some programs), thesis optional; for doctorate, one foreign language, comprehensive exam, thesis/dissertation. *Entrance requirements:* For master's, GRE Subject Test (recommended), minimum GPA of 2.5; for doctorate, GRE Subject Test (recommended), master's degree in mathematics. Additional exam requirements/recommendations for international students: Required—TOEFL (paper-based 550) or IELTS (6). *Faculty research:* Combinatorics and graph theory, differential equations, applied and computational mathematics.

Widener University, School of Education, Hospitality, and Continuing Studies, Chester, PA 19013-5792. Offers adult education (M Ed); counseling in higher education (M Ed); counselor education (M Ed); early childhood education (M Ed); educational foundations (M Ed); educational leadership (M Ed); educational psychology (M Ed); elementary education (M Ed); English and language arts (M Ed); health education (M Ed); higher education leadership (Ed D); home and school visitor (M Ed); human sexuality (M Ed, PhD); mathematics education (M Ed); middle school education (M Ed); principalship (M Ed); reading and language arts (Ed D); reading education (M Ed); school administration (Ed D); science education (M Ed); social studies education (M Ed); special education (M Ed); technology education (M Ed). *Accreditation:* NCATE. *Program availability:* Part-time, evening/weekend. *Faculty:* 34 full-time (22 women), 37 part-time/adjunct (14 women). *Students:* 97 full-time (64 women), 201 part-time (143 women); includes 56 minority (44 Black or African American, non-Hispanic/Latino; 1 American Indian or Alaska Native, non-Hispanic/Latino; 2 Asian, non-Hispanic/Latino; 8 Hispanic/Latino; 1 Two or more races, non-Hispanic/Latino), 32 international. Average age 39. 139 applicants, 88% accepted. In 2016, 45 master's, 21 doctorates awarded. Terminal master's awarded for partial completion of doctoral program. *Degree requirements:* For doctorate, thesis/dissertation. *Entrance requirements:* For master's, minimum GPA of 2.5; for doctorate, GRE or MAT, minimum GPA of 2.0 (undergraduate), 3.5 (graduate).

Application deadline: Applications are processed on a rolling basis. Application fee: $25 ($300 for international students). Electronic applications accepted. *Expenses:* Contact institution. *Financial support:* Career-related internships or fieldwork, tuition waivers (full and partial), and unspecified assistantships available. Support available to part-time students. Financial award application deadline: 5/1. *Faculty research:* Reading and cognition, adult education, technology education, educational leadership, special education. *Unit head:* Dr. Shawn Fitzgerald, Dean, 610-499-4294, Fax: 610-499-4623, E-mail: smfitzgerald@widener.edu. *Application contact:* Dr. Roberta Nolan, Director of Graduate Admissions, 610-499-4125, E-mail: rdnolan@widener.edu.
Website: http://www.widener.edu/academics/schools/eics

William Jessup University, Program in Teaching, Rocklin, CA 95765. Offers single subject English (MAT); single subject math (MAT). *Program availability:* Evening/ weekend.

Wright State University, Graduate School, College of Science and Mathematics, Interdisciplinary Program in Science and Mathematics, Dayton, OH 45435. Offers PhD. *Expenses:* Tuition, state resident: full-time $9952; part-time $622 per credit hour. Tuition, nonresident: full-time $16,960; part-time $1060 per credit hour. *Unit head:* Dr. Beth Basista, Director, 937-775-2954, Fax: 937-775-2571, E-mail: beth.basista@wright.edu. *Application contact:* John Kimble, Associate Director of Graduate Admissions and Records, 937-775-2957, Fax: 937-775-2453, E-mail: john.kimble@wright.edu.

Youngstown State University, Graduate School, College of Science, Technology, Engineering and Mathematics, Department of Mathematics and Statistics, Youngstown, OH 44555-0001. Offers applied mathematics (MS); computer science (MS); secondary mathematics (MS); statistics (MS). *Program availability:* Part-time. *Degree requirements:* For master's, comprehensive exam, thesis optional. *Entrance requirements:* For master's, minimum GPA of 2.7 in computer science and mathematics. Additional exam requirements/recommendations for international students: Required—TOEFL. *Faculty research:* Regression analysis, numerical analysis, statistics, Markov chain, topology and fuzzy sets.

Museum Education

Bank Street College of Education, Graduate School, Program in Museum Education, New York, NY 10025. Offers museum education (MS Ed); museum education: elementary education certification (MS Ed). *Degree requirements:* For master's, thesis. *Entrance requirements:* For master's, interview, essays. Additional exam requirements/ recommendations for international students: Required—TOEFL (minimum score 600 paper-based; 100 iBT), IELTS (minimum score 7). Electronic applications accepted. *Faculty research:* Equitable access and openness to diversity in museum settings, exhibition display and development, museum and school partnerships.

Bank Street College of Education, Graduate School, Programs in Educational Leadership, New York, NY 10025. Offers early childhood leadership (MS Ed); educational leadership (MS Ed); leadership for educational change (Ed M, MS Ed); leadership in community-based learning (MS Ed); leadership in mathematics education (MS Ed); leadership in museum education (MS Ed); leadership in the arts: creative writing (MS Ed); leadership in the arts: visual arts (MS Ed). *Degree requirements:* For master's, thesis. *Entrance requirements:* For master's, interview, essays, minimum of 2 years experience as a classroom teacher. Additional exam requirements/ recommendations for international students: Required—TOEFL (minimum score 600 paper-based; 100 iBT), IELTS (minimum score 7). Electronic applications accepted. *Faculty research:* Leadership in urban schools, leadership in small schools, mathematics in elementary schools, professional development in early childhood, leadership in arts education, leadership in special education, museum leadership, community-based leadership.

Eastern Michigan University, Graduate School, College of Arts and Sciences, Department of Sociology, Anthropology and Criminology, Program in Cultural Museum Studies, Ypsilanti, MI 48197. Offers Graduate Certificate. *Program availability:* Part-time, evening/weekend, online learning. *Students:* 1 applicant, 100% accepted. In 2016, 5 Graduate Certificates awarded. *Entrance requirements:* Additional exam requirements/ recommendations for international students: Required—TOEFL. *Application deadline:* Applications are processed on a rolling basis. Application fee: $45. *Financial support:* Fellowships, research assistantships with full tuition reimbursements, teaching assistantships with full tuition reimbursements, career-related internships or fieldwork, Federal Work-Study, institutionally sponsored loans, scholarships/grants, tuition waivers (partial), and unspecified assistantships available. Support available to part-time students. Financial award applicants required to submit FAFSA. *Application contact:* Dr. Liza Cerroni-Long, Advisor, 734-487-0012, Fax: 734-487-9666, E-mail: liza.cerroni-long@emich.edu.

The George Washington University, Graduate School of Education and Human Development, Department of Educational Leadership, Program in Museum Education, Washington, DC 20052. Offers MAT. *Students:* 15 full-time (14 women); includes 5 minority (1 Black or African American, non-Hispanic/Latino; 4 Hispanic/Latino), 1 international. Average age 26. 36 applicants, 81% accepted, 15 enrolled. In 2016, 14 master's awarded. *Degree requirements:* For master's, comprehensive exam. *Entrance requirements:* For master's, GRE General Test or MAT, minimum GPA of 2.75. *Application deadline:* For fall admission, 1/15 priority date for domestic students; for spring admission, 10/1 for domestic students. Applications are processed on a rolling basis. Application fee: $75. *Financial support:* In 2016–17, 7 students received support. Fellowships, career-related internships or fieldwork, Federal Work-Study, and tuition waivers available. Financial award application deadline: 1/15; financial award applicants required to submit FAFSA. *Unit head:* Michael Feuer, Dean, 202-994-6161, E-mail: mjfeuer@gwu.edu. *Application contact:* Sarah Lang, Director of Graduate Admissions, 202-994-1447, Fax: 202-994-7207, E-mail: slang@gwu.edu.
Website: http://gsehd.gwu.edu/MEP

Seton Hall University, College of Communication and the Arts, South Orange, NJ 07079-2697. Offers museum professions (MA), including exhibition development, museum education, museum management, museum registration; public relations (MA); strategic communication (MA). *Program availability:* Part-time, evening/weekend, online learning. *Degree requirements:* For master's, thesis. *Entrance requirements:* Additional exam requirements/recommendations for international students: Required—TOEFL. Electronic applications accepted. *Faculty research:* Managerial communication, communication consulting, communication and development.

Tufts University, Graduate School of Arts and Sciences, Department of Education, Program in Education, Medford, MA 02155. Offers educational studies (MA); elementary education (MAT); middle and secondary education (MAT); museum education (MA); secondary education (MA); STEM education (MS, PhD). *Program availability:* Part-time. *Students:* 67 full-time (49 women), 14 part-time (12 women); includes 17 minority (4 Black or African American, non-Hispanic/Latino; 6 Asian, non-Hispanic/Latino; 6 Hispanic/Latino; 1 Two or more races, non-Hispanic/Latino), 6 international. Average age 28. 120 applicants, 71% accepted, 49 enrolled. In 2016, 25 master's awarded. *Degree requirements:* For master's, thesis optional. *Entrance requirements:* For master's, GRE General Test, portfolio (for art education only); for doctorate, GRE General Test, writing sample. Additional exam requirements/recommendations for international students: Required—TOEFL (minimum score 550 paper-based; 80 iBT), IELTS (minimum score 6.5). *Application deadline:* For fall admission, 1/2 for domestic and international students; for spring admission, 10/15 for domestic and international students. Applications are processed on a rolling basis. Application fee: $85. Electronic applications accepted. *Expenses:* Contact institution. *Financial support:* In 2016–17, 69 students received support. Research assistantships, teaching assistantships, Federal Work-Study, scholarships/grants, and tuition waivers (full and partial) available. Support available to part-time students. Financial award application deadline: 1/2. *Unit head:* Dr. Sabina Vaught, Graduate Program Director. *Application contact:* Office of Graduate Admissions, 617-627-3395, E-mail: gradadmissions@tufts.edu.

The University of the Arts, College of Art, Media and Design, Department of Museum Studies, Philadelphia, PA 19102-4944. Offers museum communication (MA); museum education (MA); museum exhibition planning and design (MFA). *Accreditation:* NASAD. *Degree requirements:* For master's, thesis, internship. *Entrance requirements:* For master's, official transcripts, three letters of recommendation, one- to two-page statement, personal interview; academic writing sample and examples of work (for museum communication); two examples of academic and professional writing (for museum education); portfolio and/or writing samples (for museum exhibition planning and design). Additional exam requirements/recommendations for international students: Required—TOEFL (minimum score 580 paper-based, 92 iBT) or IELTS (minimum score 6.5).

Music Education

Alabama Agricultural and Mechanical University, School of Graduate Studies, College of Education, Humanities, and Behavioral Sciences, Department of Visual, Performing, and Communication Arts, Huntsville, AL 35811. Offers art education (MS); music education (M Ed). *Accreditation:* NCATE. *Program availability:* Part-time, evening/ weekend. *Degree requirements:* For master's, comprehensive exam. *Entrance requirements:* For master's, GRE General Test. Additional exam requirements/ recommendations for international students: Required—TOEFL (minimum score 500 paper-based; 61 iBT). *Application deadline:* For fall admission, 5/1 for domestic students. Applications are processed on a rolling basis. Application fee: $25. Electronic applications accepted. *Expenses:* Tuition, nonresident: part-time $826 per credit hour. Full-time tuition and fees vary according to course load and program. *Financial support:* Career-related internships or fieldwork and traineeships available. Financial award application deadline: 4/1. *Faculty research:* Jazz and black music, Alabama folk music. *Unit head:* Dr. Horace Carney, Chair, 256-372-5512.

Alabama State University, College of Education, Department of Curriculum and Instruction, Montgomery, AL 36101-0271. Offers early childhood education (M Ed, Ed S); elementary education (M Ed, Ed S); secondary education (M Ed, Ed S), including biology education, English language arts education (M Ed), history education, math education, music education (M Ed), reading education (M Ed), social science education; special education (M Ed). *Program availability:* Part-time. *Faculty:* 7 full-time (4 women), 7 part-time/adjunct (4 women). *Students:* 37 full-time (30 women), 82 part-time (69 women); includes 117 minority (115 Black or African American, non-Hispanic/Latino; 2 Two or more races, non-Hispanic/Latino). Average age 33. 65 applicants, 55% accepted, 22 enrolled. In 2016, 25 master's, 5 Ed Ss awarded. *Degree requirements:* For master's, comprehensive exam, thesis optional; for Ed S, comprehensive exam, thesis. *Entrance requirements:* For master's, GRE General Test, MAT, writing competency test; for Ed S, writing competency test, GRE, MAT. Additional exam requirements/recommendations for international students: Required—TOEFL (minimum score 500 paper-based). *Application deadline:* For fall admission, 4/15 for domestic and international students; for spring admission, 11/15 for domestic and international students; for summer admission, 3/15 for domestic and international students. Applications are processed on a rolling basis. Application fee: $25. Electronic applications accepted. *Expenses:* Tuition, state resident: full-time $3087; part-time $2744 per credit. Tuition, nonresident: full-time $6174; part-time $5488 per credit. *Required fees:* $2284; $1142 per credit. $571 per semester. Tuition and fees vary according to class time, course level, course load, degree level, program and student level. *Financial support:* Research assistantships available. Financial award application deadline: 6/30; financial award applicants required to submit FAFSA. *Unit head:* Dr. Joyce Johnson, Acting Chairperson, 334-229-4485, Fax: 334-229-5603, E-mail: jjohnson@alasu.edu. *Application contact:* Dr. William Person, Dean of Graduate Studies, 334-229-4274, Fax: 334-229-4928, E-mail: wperson@alasu.edu.
Website: http://www.alasu.edu/academics/colleges—departments/college-of-education/curriculum—instruction/index.aspx

Music Education

Arcadia University, School of Education, Glenside, PA 19038-3295. Offers art education (M Ed); computer education (CAS); curriculum (CAS); curriculum studies (M Ed); early childhood education (M Ed), including individualized, master teacher, research in child development; educational leadership (M Ed, Ed D, CAS); elementary education (M Ed); English education (MA Ed); environmental education (MA Ed); instructional technology (M Ed); language arts (M Ed); library science (M Ed); mathematics education (M Ed, MA Ed); music education (MA Ed); psychology (MA Ed); reading (M Ed, CAS); science education (M Ed, CAS); secondary education (M Ed, CAS); special education (M Ed, Ed D, CAS); theater arts (MA Ed); written communication (MA Ed). *Accreditation:* NASAD. *Program availability:* Part-time, evening/weekend, online learning. *Faculty:* 19 full-time (13 women), 3 part-time/adjunct (all women). *Students:* 22 full-time (16 women), 356 part-time (284 women); includes 84 minority (55 Black or African American, non-Hispanic/Latino; 2 American Indian or Alaska Native, non-Hispanic/Latino; 13 Asian, non-Hispanic/Latino; 11 Hispanic/Latino; 3 Two or more races, non-Hispanic/Latino), 4 international. Average age 34. 145 applicants, 73% accepted, 80 enrolled. In 2016, 95 master's, 11 doctorates awarded. *Application deadline:* Applications are processed on a rolling basis. Application fee: $50. Electronic applications accepted. *Expenses:* Contact institution. *Financial support:* Career-related internships or fieldwork, tuition waivers (partial), and unspecified assistantships available. *Unit head:* John T Groves, Interim Dean of the School of Education, 215-572-2940. *Application contact:* 215-572-2925, Fax: 215-572-2126, E-mail: grad@arcadia.edu.

Arizona State University at the Tempe campus, Herberger Institute for Design and the Arts, School of Music, Tempe, AZ 85287-0405. Offers composition (MM, DMA); conducting (DMA); ethnomusicology (MA); interdisciplinary digital media/performance (DMA); music education (MM, PhD); music history and literature (MA); music therapy (MM); performance (MM, DMA). *Accreditation:* NASM. Terminal master's awarded for partial completion of doctoral program. *Degree requirements:* For master's, thesis (for some programs), interactive Program of Study (iPOS) submitted before completing 50 percent of required credit hours; for doctorate, comprehensive exam, thesis/dissertation, interactive Program of Study (iPOS) submitted before completing 50 percent of required credit hours. *Entrance requirements:* For master's, minimum GPA of 3.0 or equivalent in last 2 years of work leading to bachelor's degree, 3 letters of recommendation, resume; for doctorate, GRE or MAT, minimum GPA of 3.0 or equivalent in last 2 years of work leading to bachelor's degree, 3 letters of recommendation, curriculum vitae, statement of intent. Additional exam requirements/recommendations for international students: Required—TOEFL, IELTS, or PTE. Electronic applications accepted.

Arkansas State University, Graduate School, College of Fine Arts, Department of Music, State University, AR 72467. Offers music education (MME, SCCT); music performance (MM). *Accreditation:* NASM (one or more programs are accredited). *Program availability:* Part-time. *Degree requirements:* For master's, 2 foreign languages, comprehensive exam, thesis or alternative; for SCCT, comprehensive exam. *Entrance requirements:* For master's, GRE General Test or MAT, university entrance exam, appropriate bachelor's degree, audition, letters of recommendation, teaching experience, official transcripts, immunization records, valid teaching certificate; for SCCT, GRE General Test or MAT, interview, master's degree, official transcript, immunization records, letters of recommendation. Additional exam requirements/recommendations for international students: Required—TOEFL (minimum score 550 paper-based; 79 iBT), IELTS (minimum score 6), PTE (minimum score 56). Electronic applications accepted.

Augusta University, The Graduate School, College of Education, Program in Curriculum and Instruction, Augusta, GA 30912. Offers curriculum and instruction (Ed S); elementary education (MAT); foreign language education (MAT); instruction (M Ed); middle grades education (MAT); music education (MAT); secondary education (MAT); special education (MAT). *Degree requirements:* For master's, thesis, portfolio. *Entrance requirements:* For master's, GRE, MAT, minimum GPA of 2.5. Application fee: $20. *Financial support:* Career-related internships or fieldwork, Federal Work-Study, institutionally sponsored loans, and unspecified assistantships available. Support available to part-time students. Financial award application deadline: 4/15; financial award applicants required to submit FAFSA. *Unit head:* Dr. Gordon Eisenman, Director, 706-737-1496, Fax: 706-667-4706, E-mail: geisenman@augusta.edu. *Application contact:* Dr. Gordon Eisenman, Director, 706-737-1496, Fax: 706-667-4706, E-mail: geisenman@augusta.edu.

Austin Peay State University, College of Graduate Studies, College of Arts and Letters, Department of Music, Clarksville, TN 37044. Offers music education (M Mu); music performance (M Mu). *Accreditation:* NASM. *Program availability:* Part-time. *Faculty:* 15 full-time (7 women), 1 part-time/adjunct (0 women). *Students:* 13 full-time (4 women), 1 part-time (0 women); includes 1 minority (Black or African American, non-Hispanic/Latino), 1 international. Average age 28. 17 applicants, 24% accepted, 4 enrolled. In 2016, 9 master's awarded. *Degree requirements:* For master's, comprehensive exam, thesis optional. *Entrance requirements:* For master's, GRE General Test, diagnostic exams, audition, interview, bachelor's degree, 3 letters of recommendation. Additional exam requirements/recommendations for international students: Required—TOEFL (minimum score 500 paper-based). *Application deadline:* For fall admission, 8/9 priority date for domestic students. Applications are processed on a rolling basis. Application fee: $45 ($50 for international students). Electronic applications accepted. *Expenses:* Tuition, state resident: full-time $8300; part-time $415 per credit hour. Tuition, nonresident: full-time $22,280; part-time $1114 per credit hour. *Required fees:* $1473; $73.65 per credit hour. *Financial support:* Research assistantships with full tuition reimbursements, career-related internships or fieldwork, Federal Work-Study, institutionally sponsored loans, scholarships/grants, and unspecified assistantships available. Support available to part-time students. Financial award application deadline: 4/1; financial award applicants required to submit FAFSA. *Unit head:* Dr. Douglas Rose, Chair, 931-221-7808, Fax: 931-221-7529, E-mail: rosed@apsu.edu. *Application contact:* Brad Averitt, Coordinator of Graduate Admissions, 800-859-4723, Fax: 931-221-7641, E-mail: gradadmissions@apsu.edu.
Website: http://www.apsu.edu/music/

Azusa Pacific University, School of Music, Azusa, CA 91702-7000. Offers education (M Mus); performance (M Mus). *Accreditation:* NASM. *Program availability:* Part-time, evening/weekend. *Degree requirements:* For master's, recital. *Entrance requirements:* For master's, interview, audition. Additional exam requirements/recommendations for international students: Required—TOEFL (minimum score 550 paper-based).

Ball State University, Graduate School, College of Fine Arts, School of Music, Muncie, IN 47306. Offers music (MA, MM, DA, Artist Diploma), including conducting (MM, DA), music education (MA, MM, DA), music history and musicology (MA, MM, DA), music performance (MA, MM, DA), music theory (MA), music theory and composition (DA), piano chamber music/accompanying (MM, DA), piano performance and pedagogy (MM), woodwinds (MM). *Accreditation:* NASM; NCATE (one or more programs are accredited). *Degree requirements:* For doctorate, thesis/dissertation. *Entrance requirements:* For master's, placement tests in history and theory, minimum baccalaureate GPA of 2.75 or 3.0 in latter half of baccalauareate, resume, audition; for doctorate, GRE General Test, minimum graduate GPA of 3.2, interview, audition, resume, three professional letters of reference. Additional exam requirements/recommendations for international students: Required—TOEFL (minimum score 550 paper-based; 79 iBT), IELTS (minimum score 6.5). Electronic applications accepted. *Expenses:* Contact institution.

Bob Jones University, Graduate Programs, Greenville, SC 29614. Offers accountancy (MS); Bible (MA); Bible translation (MA); Biblical studies (Certificate); broadcast management (MS); business administration (MBA); church history (MA, PhD); church ministries (MA); church music (MM); cinema and video production (MA); counseling (MS); curriculum and instruction (Ed D); divinity (M Div); dramatic production (MA); educational leadership (MS, Ed D, Ed S); elementary education (M Ed, MAT); English (M Ed, MA, MAT); fine arts (MA); graphic design (MA); history (M Ed, MA); illustration (MA); interpretative speech (MA); mathematics (M Ed, MAT); medical missions (Certificate); ministry (MM, D Min); multi-categorical special education (M Ed, MAT); music (M Ed); New Testament interpretation (PhD); Old Testament interpretation (PhD); orchestral instrument performance (MM); organ performance (MM); pastoral studies (MA); personnel services (MS, Ed S); piano pedagogy (MM); piano performance (MM); platform arts (MA); radio and television broadcasting (MS); rhetoric and public address (MA); secondary education (M Ed); studio art (MA); teaching Bible (MA); theology (MA, PhD); voice performance (MM); youth ministries (MA); M Div/MM.

Boise State University, College of Arts and Sciences, Department of Music, Boise, ID 8325-1560. Offers music education (MM); performance (MM). *Accreditation:* NASM. *Program availability:* Part-time. *Faculty:* 14. *Students:* 11 full-time (3 women), 6 part-time (3 women); includes 2 minority (1 Asian, non-Hispanic/Latino; 1 Hispanic/Latino), 2 international. Average age 27. 9 applicants, 78% accepted, 5 enrolled. In 2016, 10 master's awarded. *Degree requirements:* For master's, thesis optional. *Entrance requirements:* For master's, minimum GPA of 3.0, performance demonstration. Additional exam requirements/recommendations for international students: Required—TOEFL (minimum score 550 paper-based; 80 iBT), IELTS (minimum score 6). *Application deadline:* For fall admission, 2/9 priority date for domestic and international students. Application fee: $65 ($95 for international students). Electronic applications accepted. *Expenses:* Tuition, state resident: full-time $6058; part-time $358 per credit hour. Tuition, nonresident: full-time $20,108; part-time $608 per credit hour. *Required fees:* $2108. Tuition and fees vary according to program. *Financial support:* In 2016–17, 6 students received support, including 4 teaching assistantships (averaging $9,352 per year); scholarships/grants and unspecified assistantships also available. Financial award application deadline: 2/9; financial award applicants required to submit FAFSA. *Unit head:* Dr. Linda Kline Lamar, Chair, 208-426-3665, E-mail: lkline@boisestate.edu. *Application contact:* Dr. Jeanne Belfy, Graduate Program Coordinator, 208-426-1216, E-mail: jbelfy@boisestate.edu.
Website: http://music.boisestate.edu/graduate/

Boston University, College of Fine Arts, School of Music, Program in Music Education, Boston, MA 02215. Offers MM, DMA. *Accreditation:* NASM. *Program availability:* Part-time, 100% online. *Faculty:* 9 full-time (3 women). *Students:* 426 full-time (201 women), 17 part-time (8 women); includes 72 minority (29 Black or African American, non-Hispanic/Latino; 1 American Indian or Alaska Native, non-Hispanic/Latino; 11 Asian, non-Hispanic/Latino; 24 Hispanic/Latino; 1 Native Hawaiian or other Pacific Islander, non-Hispanic/Latino; 6 Two or more races, non-Hispanic/Latino), 29 international. Average age 37. 36 applicants, 56% accepted, 7 enrolled. In 2016, 68 master's, 24 doctorates awarded. *Degree requirements:* For master's, thesis; for doctorate, 2 foreign languages, thesis/dissertation. *Entrance requirements:* Additional exam requirements/recommendations for international students: Required—TOEFL (minimum score 90 iBT), IELTS (minimum score 7). *Application deadline:* For fall admission, 12/1 priority date for domestic and international students. Application fee: $95. Electronic applications accepted. *Expenses:* Contact institution. *Financial support:* Fellowships, teaching assistantships, scholarships/grants, and unspecified assistantships available. Financial award application deadline: 12/1. *Unit head:* Shiela Kibbe, Director, 617-353-8789, Fax: 617-353-7455, E-mail: rdodson@bu.edu. *Application contact:* Shaun Ramsay, Assistant Director, School of Music Admissions and Student Affairs, 617-353-3341, E-mail: arts@bu.edu.

Bowling Green State University, Graduate College, College of Musical Arts, Bowling Green, OH 43403. Offers composition (MM); contemporary music (DMA), including composition, performance; ethnomusicology (MM); music education (MM), including choral music education, comprehensive music education, instrumental music education; music history (MM); music theory (MM); performance (MM). *Accreditation:* NASM. *Program availability:* Part-time. *Degree requirements:* For master's, thesis or alternative, recitals; for doctorate, comprehensive exam, thesis/dissertation. *Entrance requirements:* For master's, GRE General Test, diagnostic placement exams in music history and theory, audition, interview. Additional exam requirements/recommendations for international students: Required—TOEFL. *Application deadline:* For fall admission, 3/1 priority date for domestic students. Application fee: $30. Electronic applications accepted. *Financial support:* Research assistantships with full tuition reimbursements, teaching assistantships with full tuition reimbursements, career-related internships or fieldwork, Federal Work-Study, and unspecified assistantships available. Financial award applicants required to submit FAFSA. *Faculty research:* Ethnomusicology. *Unit head:* Dr. Richard Kennell, Dean, 419-372-2188. *Application contact:* Dr. Robert Satterlee, Graduate Coordinator, 419-372-2360.

Brandon University, School of Music, Brandon, MB R7A 6A9, Canada. Offers composition (M Mus); music education (M Mus); performance and literature (M Mus), including clarinet, conducting, jazz, low brass, piano, strings, trumpet. *Program availability:* Part-time. *Degree requirements:* For master's, comprehensive exam (for some programs), thesis (for some programs), 2 recitals. *Entrance requirements:* For master's, B Mus. Additional exam requirements/recommendations for international students: Required—TOEFL (minimum score 580 paper-based), IELTS (minimum score 7). Electronic applications accepted. *Expenses:* Contact institution. *Faculty research:* Composition, evaluation and assessment, performance anxiety, philosophy of music, teacher education.

Brigham Young University, Graduate Studies, College of Fine Arts and Communications, School of Music, Provo, UT 84602-1001. Offers composition (MM); conducting (MM), including band and orchestral conducting, choral conducting; music education (MA, MM); performance (MM), including keyboard performance, orchestral instrument, vocal performance. *Accreditation:* NASM. *Faculty:* 50 full-time (9 women), 58 part-time/adjunct (33 women). *Students:* 39 full-time (23 women), 8 part-time (7 women); includes 8 minority (1 American Indian or Alaska Native, non-Hispanic/Latino; 5 Asian, non-Hispanic/Latino; 1 Hispanic/Latino; 1 Native Hawaiian or other Pacific Islander, non-Hispanic/Latino). Average age 30. 47 applicants, 47% accepted, 16 enrolled. In 2016, 22 master's awarded. *Degree requirements:* For master's, comprehensive exam (for some programs), thesis (for some programs), recital, project, or composition (for some programs). *Entrance requirements:* For master's, School of Music Entrance Exam, minimum GPA of 3.0, BM. Additional exam requirements/recommendations for international students: Required—TOEFL (minimum score 85 iBT). *Application deadline:* For fall admission, 12/15 priority date for domestic and international students. Application fee: $50. Electronic applications accepted. *Expenses:* Contact institution. *Financial support:* In 2016–17, 44 students received support, including 44 research assistantships (averaging $3,000 per year), 44 teaching

assistantships (averaging $3,500 per year); career-related internships or fieldwork, institutionally sponsored loans, scholarships/grants, tuition waivers (partial), and unspecified assistantships also available. Support available to part-time students. Financial award application deadline: 12/15; financial award applicants required to submit FAFSA. *Faculty research:* Algorithmic composition; string quartet repertoire; Summer of Love 50th Anniversary (through lens of music). *Unit head:* Dr. Kirt R. Saville, Director, 801-422-6304, Fax: 801-422-0533, E-mail: kirt_saville@byu.edu. *Application contact:* Dr. A. Claudine Bigelow, Graduate Coordinator, 801-422-1315, Fax: 801-422-0533, E-mail: claudine_bigelow@byu.edu.
Website: https://cfac.byu.edu/music/

Brooklyn College of the City University of New York, School of Education, Program in Adolescence Science Education and Special Subjects, Brooklyn, NY 11210-2889. Offers adolescence science education (MAT); biology teacher (7-12) (MA); chemistry teacher (7-12) (MA); earth science teacher (7-12) (MAT); English teacher (7-12) (MA); French teacher (7-12) (MA); mathematics teacher (7-12) (MA); music teacher (MA); physics teacher (7-12) (MA); social studies teacher (7-12) (MA); Spanish teacher (7-12) (MA). *Program availability:* Part-time, evening/weekend. *Degree requirements:* For master's, comprehensive exam (for some programs), thesis (for some programs). *Entrance requirements:* For master's, LAST, previous course work in education, resume, 2 letters of recommendation, essay. Additional exam requirements/recommendations for international students: Required—TOEFL (minimum score 500 paper-based; 61 iBT). Electronic applications accepted. *Faculty research:* Interdisciplinary education, semiotics, discourse analysis, autobiography, teacher identity.

Brooklyn College of the City University of New York, School of Visual, Media and Performing Arts, Conservatory of Music, Brooklyn, NY 11210-2889. Offers composition (MM); music teacher (MA); musicology (MA); performance (MM). *Program availability:* Part-time. *Degree requirements:* For master's, one foreign language, comprehensive exam, thesis. *Entrance requirements:* For master's, placement exam, 36 credits in music, audition, completed composition, writing sample. Additional exam requirements/recommendations for international students: Required—TOEFL (minimum score 550 paper-based; 79 iBT). Electronic applications accepted. *Faculty research:* American music, computer music.

Butler University, Jordan College of the Arts, Indianapolis, IN 46208-3485. Offers composition (MM); conducting (MM); music education (MM); music history (MM). *Accreditation:* NASM. *Program availability:* Part-time. *Faculty:* 29 full-time (10 women), 36 part-time/adjunct (18 women). *Students:* 16 full-time (5 women), 21 part-time (4 women); includes 7 minority (3 Black or African American, non-Hispanic/Latino; 1 Asian, non-Hispanic/Latino; 1 Hispanic/Latino; 2 Two or more races, non-Hispanic/Latino), 1 international. Average age 26. 41 applicants, 66% accepted, 13 enrolled. In 2016, 16 master's awarded. *Degree requirements:* For master's, variable foreign language requirement, comprehensive exam, thesis (for some programs). *Entrance requirements:* For master's, GRE General Test (for MA in musicology), audition, interview, three letters of recommendation, transcripts, sample works. Additional exam requirements/recommendations for international students: Required—TOEFL (minimum score 550 paper-based; 79 iBT), IELTS (minimum score 6). *Application deadline:* For fall admission, 2/1 for domestic and international students; for spring admission, 12/15 for domestic and international students; for summer admission, 4/15 for domestic and international students. Applications are processed on a rolling basis. Application fee: $0. Electronic applications accepted. *Expenses:* Contact institution. *Financial support:* Scholarships/grants, tuition waivers (full and partial), and unspecified assistantships available. Financial award application deadline: 7/15; financial award applicants required to submit FAFSA. *Faculty research:* Music neuroscience; woodwind pedagogy and repertoire; music of the Renaissance; Johannes Kepler and Johannes Ockeghem; music criticism in early 20th-century Germany and Austria; Arabic choral music; pedagogy of music theory. *Unit head:* Michele Jarvis, Interim Dean, 317-940-9231, E-mail: mjarvis@butler.edu. *Application contact:* Diane Dubord, Graduate Student Services Specialist, 317-940-8107, E-mail: ddubord@butler.edu.
Website: http://www.butler.edu/jca/

California Baptist University, Program in Music, Riverside, CA 92504-3206. Offers conducting (MM); music education (MM); performance (MM). *Accreditation:* NASM. *Program availability:* Part-time, evening/weekend. *Faculty:* 14 full-time (8 women), 18 part-time/adjunct (7 women). *Students:* 12 full-time (6 women), 8 part-time (6 women); includes 8 minority (2 Black or African American, non-Hispanic/Latino; 3 Asian, non-Hispanic/Latino; 3 Hispanic/Latino), 8 international. Average age 26. 7 applicants, 57% accepted, 3 enrolled. In 2016, 7 master's awarded. *Degree requirements:* For master's, comprehensive exam or thesis. *Entrance requirements:* For master's, minimum undergraduate GPA of 2.75; bachelor's degree in music; three recommendations; comprehensive essay; interview/audition. Additional exam requirements/recommendations for international students: Required—TOEFL (minimum score 80 iBT). *Application deadline:* For fall admission, 8/1 priority date for domestic students, 7/1 for international students; for spring admission, 12/1 priority date for domestic students, 11/1 for international students. Applications are processed on a rolling basis. Application fee: $45. Electronic applications accepted. *Expenses:* Contact institution. *Financial support:* In 2016–17, 8 students received support. Federal Work-Study and scholarships/grants available. Financial award applicants required to submit CSS PROFILE or FAFSA. *Faculty research:* Choral conducting, church music, choir building, hymnology, music technology. *Unit head:* Dr. Joseph Bolin, Dean, School of Music, 951-343-4714, Fax: 951-343-4570, E-mail: jbolin@calbaptist.edu. *Application contact:* Stephanie Fluitt, Graduate Admissions Counselor, 952-343-4696, E-mail: sfluitt@calbaptist.edu.
Website: http://www.calbaptist.edu/masterofmusic/

California State University, Fresno, Division of Research and Graduate Studies, College of Arts and Humanities, Department of Music, Fresno, CA 93740-8027. Offers music (MA); music education (MA); performance (MA). *Accreditation:* NASM. *Program availability:* Part-time. *Degree requirements:* For master's, thesis or alternative. *Entrance requirements:* For master's, GRE General Test, BA in music, minimum GPA of 3.0. Additional exam requirements/recommendations for international students: Required—TOEFL. *Application deadline:* For fall admission, 5/1 for domestic and international students; for spring admission, 10/1 for domestic and international students. Applications are processed on a rolling basis. Application fee: $55. Electronic applications accepted. *Financial support:* Teaching assistantships, career-related internships or fieldwork, Federal Work-Study, and scholarships/grants available. Support available to part-time students. Financial award application deadline: 3/1; financial award applicants required to submit FAFSA. *Faculty research:* Technology transfer, folk art. *Unit head:* Matthew Darling, Chair, 559-278-2654, Fax: 559-278-6800, E-mail: matthewd@csufresno.edu. *Application contact:* Dr. Teresa Beaman, Graduate Program Coordinator, 559-278-3975, Fax: 559-278-6800, E-mail: teresab@csufresno.edu.
Website: http://www.fresnostate.edu/artshum/music/

California State University, Fullerton, Graduate Studies, College of the Arts, Department of Music, Fullerton, CA 92834-9480. Offers music education (MA); performance (MM). *Accreditation:* NASM. *Program availability:* Part-time. *Degree requirements:* For master's, comprehensive exam, project or thesis. *Entrance requirements:* For master's, audition, major in music or related field, minimum GPA of 2.5 in last 60 units of course work. Application fee: $55. *Expenses:* Tuition, state resident: full-time $3369; part-time $1953 per unit. Tuition, nonresident: full-time $3915; part-time $2499 per unit. Tuition and fees vary according to course load, degree level and program. *Financial support:* Career-related internships or fieldwork, Federal Work-Study, institutionally sponsored loans, and scholarships/grants available. Support available to part-time students. Financial award application deadline: 3/1; financial award applicants required to submit FAFSA. *Unit head:* Dr. Marc Dickey, Chair, 657-278-3511. *Application contact:* Admissions/Applications, 657-278-2371.

California State University, Los Angeles, Graduate Studies, College of Arts and Letters, Department of Music, Los Angeles, CA 90032-8530. Offers music composition (MM); music education (MA); musicology (MA); performance (MM). *Accreditation:* NASM. *Program availability:* Part-time, evening/weekend. *Degree requirements:* For master's, comprehensive exam, project or thesis. *Entrance requirements:* For master's, audition. Additional exam requirements/recommendations for international students: Required—TOEFL (minimum score 500 paper-based). Electronic applications accepted. *Faculty research:* Gregorian semiology, Baroque opera.

California State University, Northridge, Graduate Studies, College of Arts, Media, and Communication, Department of Music, Northridge, CA 91330. Offers composition (MM); conducting (MM); music education (MA); performance (MM). *Accreditation:* NASM. *Faculty:* 24 full-time (7 women), 66 part-time/adjunct (18 women). *Students:* 35 full-time (18 women), 44 part-time (28 women); includes 23 minority (2 Black or African American, non-Hispanic/Latino; 1 American Indian or Alaska Native, non-Hispanic/Latino; 5 Asian, non-Hispanic/Latino; 11 Hispanic/Latino; 4 Two or more races, non-Hispanic/Latino), 25 international. Average age 28. 162 applicants, 46% accepted, 29 enrolled. *Degree requirements:* For master's, thesis. *Entrance requirements:* For master's, audition, GRE General Test or minimum GPA of 3.0. Additional exam requirements/recommendations for international students: Required—TOEFL. *Application deadline:* For fall admission, 11/30 for domestic students. Application fee: $55. *Expenses:* Tuition, state resident: full-time $4152. *Financial support:* Application deadline: 3/1. *Unit head:* Rick Alviso, Chair, 816-677-4752. *Application contact:* Diane Roscetti Heinen, 818-677-3184, E-mail: diane.roscetti@csun.edu.
Website: http://www.csun.edu/music/

Campbellsville University, School of Music, Campbellsville, KY 42718-2799. Offers church music (MM); conducting (MM); instrumental performance (MM); music (MA); music education (MM); musicology (MA); pedagogy and performance (MM), including piano and vocal; worship (MA). *Accreditation:* NASM. *Program availability:* Part-time, 100% online, blended/hybrid learning. *Faculty:* 13 full-time (6 women), 10 part-time/adjunct (4 women). *Students:* 1 (woman) full-time, 26 part-time (13 women), 14 international. Average age 30. 17 applicants, 76% accepted, 12 enrolled. In 2016, 10 master's awarded. *Degree requirements:* For master's, comprehensive exam, thesis (for some programs), paper or recital. *Entrance requirements:* For master's, GRE General Test or PRAXIS, minimum GPA of 2.75, college transcripts. Additional exam requirements/recommendations for international students: Required—TOEFL (minimum score 550 paper-based; 79 iBT); Recommended—IELTS (minimum score 6). *Application deadline:* Applications are processed on a rolling basis. Application fee: $25. Electronic applications accepted. Application fee is waived when completed online. *Expenses:* $399 per credit hour. *Financial support:* Application deadline: 6/1; applicants required to submit FAFSA. *Unit head:* Dr. Tony Cunha, Dean, 270-789-5240, Fax: 270-789-5524, E-mail: accunha@campbellsville.edu. *Application contact:* Monica Bamwine, Assistant Director of Graduate Admissions, 270-789-5221, Fax: 270-789-5071, E-mail: mkbamwine@campbellsville.edu.
Website: http://www.campbellsville.edu/music

Capital University, Conservatory of Music, Columbus, OH 43209-2394. Offers music education (MM), including instrumental emphasis, Kodály emphasis. Program offered only in summer. *Accreditation:* NASM. *Program availability:* Part-time. *Degree requirements:* For master's, comprehensive exam, thesis or alternative, chamber performance exam. *Entrance requirements:* For master's, music theory exam, minimum undergraduate GPA of 3.0. Additional exam requirements/recommendations for international students: Required—TOEFL (minimum score 550 paper-based; 80 iBT). Electronic applications accepted. *Expenses:* Contact institution. *Faculty research:* Folk song research, Kodály method, performance, composition.

Carnegie Mellon University, College of Fine Arts, School of Music, Pittsburgh, PA 15213-3891. Offers collaborative piano (MM); composition (MM); instrumental performance (MM); music and technology (MS); music education (MM); vocal performance (MM). *Accreditation:* NASM. *Program availability:* Part-time. *Degree requirements:* For master's, comprehensive exam, recital. *Entrance requirements:* For master's, audition. *Faculty research:* Computer music, music history.

Case Western Reserve University, School of Graduate Studies, Department of Music, Program in Music Education, Cleveland, OH 44106. Offers MA, PhD. *Accreditation:* NASM; TEAC. *Faculty:* 4 full-time (2 women). *Students:* 12 full-time (9 women), 9 part-time (3 women); includes 1 minority (Hispanic/Latino), 2 international. Average age 31. 10 applicants, 70% accepted, 7 enrolled. In 2016, 3 master's, 2 doctorates awarded. *Degree requirements:* For master's, comprehensive exam (for some programs), thesis (for some programs); for doctorate, comprehensive exam, thesis/dissertation. *Entrance requirements:* For master's, GRE, resume, PDF of teaching license/certificate, audition/interview, writing sample, 1 year of teaching; for doctorate, GRE, resume, PDF of teaching license/certificate, audition/interview, writing sample, 3 years of teaching. Additional exam requirements/recommendations for international students: Required—TOEFL (minimum score 577 paper-based; 90 iBT); Recommended—IELTS (minimum score 7). *Application deadline:* For fall admission, 1/15 priority date for domestic students. Application fee: $50. Electronic applications accepted. *Expenses: Tuition:* Full-time $42,576; part-time $1774 per credit hour. *Required fees:* $34. Tuition and fees vary according to course load and program. *Financial support:* Fellowships, teaching assistantships, career-related internships or fieldwork, tuition waivers (full), unspecified assistantships, and stipends available. Financial award application deadline: 1/15; financial award applicants required to submit CSS PROFILE or FAFSA. *Faculty research:* Psychology of music, creative thinking, computer applications, educational psychology. *Unit head:* David J. Rothenberg, Associate Professor/Department Chair, 216-368-6046, Fax: 216-368-6557, E-mail: music@case.edu. *Application contact:* Laura Stauffer, Department Administrator, 216-368-0117, Fax: 216-368-6557, E-mail: music@case.edu.
Website: http://music.case.edu/

The Catholic University of America, Benjamin T. Rome School of Music, Washington, DC 20064. Offers cello (Artist Diploma); chamber music (piano) (MM, DMA); composition (MM, DMA), including concert music (MM), stage music (MM); music (MAT); musicology (MA, PhD); orchestral conducting (MM, DMA, Artist Diploma); orchestral instruments/guitar (MM, DMA); piano (Artist Diploma); piano pedagogy (MM, DMA); piano performance (MM, DMA); sacred music (MMSM, DMA); violin (Artist Diploma); vocal accompanying (MM, DMA); vocal pedagogy (MM, DMA); vocal performance (MM, DMA); voice (Artist Diploma); MA/MSLIS. MA/MSLIS offered in partnership with Department of Library and Information Science. *Accreditation:* NASM.

Music Education

Program availability: Part-time. *Faculty:* 20 full-time (4 women), 53 part-time/adjunct (21 women). *Students:* 29 full-time (15 women), 71 part-time (31 women); includes 26 minority (7 Black or African American, non-Hispanic/Latino; 13 Asian, non-Hispanic/Latino; 6 Hispanic/Latino), 22 international. Average age 33. 80 applicants, 73% accepted, 24 enrolled. In 2016, 15 master's, 9 doctorates awarded. *Degree requirements:* For master's, variable foreign language requirement, comprehensive exam (for some programs), thesis (for some programs), final recital (for some programs); for doctorate, variable foreign language requirement, comprehensive exam (for some programs), thesis/dissertation (for some programs), final recital (for some programs); for Artist Diploma, variable foreign language requirement, final recital (for some programs). *Entrance requirements:* For master's, music theory and music history placement examinations, statement of purpose, 2 letters of recommendation, minimum undergraduate B average, audition (for all performance degrees), official copy of academic transcript showing completed and conferred BM; for doctorate, music theory and music history placement examinations, 2 letters of recommendation, minimum B average in all previous course work and degrees, official copies of academic transcripts showing completion and conferral of all previous degrees, audition (for all performance degrees); for Artist Diploma, music theory and music history placement examinations, statement of purpose, 2 letters of recommendation, minimum B average in all previous course work and degrees, BM, audition, official copies of academic transcripts showing completion and conferral of all previous degrees. Additional exam requirements/recommendations for international students: Required—TOEFL (minimum score 580 paper-based). *Application deadline:* For fall admission, 7/15 priority date for domestic students, 7/1 for international students; for spring admission, 11/15 priority date for domestic students, 11/1 for international students. Applications are processed on a rolling basis. Application fee: $55. Electronic applications accepted. *Expenses:* $42,850 per year; $1,170 per credit; $200 per semester part-time fees. *Financial support:* Fellowships, research assistantships, teaching assistantships, Federal Work-Study, scholarships/grants, tuition waivers (full and partial), and unspecified assistantships available. Financial award application deadline: 2/1; financial award applicants required to submit FAFSA. *Faculty research:* Composition, sacred music, orchestral instruments, piano and vocal performance, piano and vocal pedagogy. *Total annual research expenditures:* $10,650. *Unit head:* Dr. Grayson Wagstaff, Dean, 202-319-5417, Fax: 202-319-6280, E-mail: cua-music@cua.edu. *Application contact:* Director of Graduate Admissions, 202-319-5057, Fax: 202-319-6533, E-mail: cua-admissions@cua.edu.
Website: http://music.cua.edu/

Central Connecticut State University, School of Graduate Studies, College of Liberal Arts and Social Sciences, Department of Music, New Britain, CT 06050-4010. Offers music education (MS, Certificate). *Accreditation:* NASM. *Program availability:* Part-time, evening/weekend. *Faculty:* 1 (woman) full-time. *Students:* 3 full-time (2 women), 11 part-time (4 women); includes 1 minority (Black or African American, non-Hispanic/Latino). Average age 28. 9 applicants, 56% accepted, 3 enrolled. In 2016, 5 master's, 3 other advanced degrees awarded. *Degree requirements:* For master's, comprehensive exam, thesis or alternative, special project; for Certificate, qualifying exam. *Entrance requirements:* For master's, theory examination, audition, minimum undergraduate GPA of 2.7, essay, portfolio. Additional exam requirements/recommendations for international students: Required—TOEFL (minimum score 550 paper-based; 79 iBT). *Application deadline:* For fall admission, 6/1 for domestic students, 5/1 for international students; for spring admission, 11/1 for domestic and international students. Applications are processed on a rolling basis. Application fee: $50. Electronic applications accepted. *Expenses: Tuition, area resident:* Full-time $6497; part-time $606 per credit. Tuition, state resident: full-time $9748; part-time $622 per credit. Tuition, nonresident: full-time $18,102; part-time $622 per credit. *Required fees:* $4459; $246 per credit. *Financial support:* Unspecified assistantships available. Financial award application deadline: 3/1. *Faculty research:* Applied music. *Unit head:* Dr. Carlotta Parr, Chair, 860-832-2912, E-mail: parrc@ccsu.edu. *Application contact:* Patricia Gardner, Associate Director of Graduate Studies, 860-832-2350, Fax: 860-832-2362.
Website: http://www.ccsu.edu/music/

Central Methodist University, College of Graduate and Extended Studies, Fayette, MO 65248-1198. Offers clinical counseling (MS); clinical nurse leader (MSN); education (M Ed); music education (MME); nurse educator (MSN). *Program availability:* Part-time, evening/weekend, online learning. *Degree requirements:* For master's, thesis. *Entrance requirements:* For master's, GRE General Test, minimum GPA of 2.75. Electronic applications accepted.

Central Michigan University, College of Graduate Studies, College of Communication and Fine Arts, School of Music, Mount Pleasant, MI 48859. Offers composition (MM); conducting (MM); music education (MM); performance (MM). *Accreditation:* NASM. *Program availability:* Part-time. *Degree requirements:* For master's, thesis or alternative. Electronic applications accepted. *Faculty research:* Music education, music composition, conducting, music performance.

Cleveland State University, College of Graduate Studies, College of Liberal Arts and Social Sciences, Department of Music, Cleveland, OH 44115. Offers composition (MM); music education (MM). *Accreditation:* NASM. *Program availability:* Part-time, evening/weekend. *Faculty:* 9 full-time (2 women), 19 part-time/adjunct (6 women). *Students:* 9 full-time (3 women), 20 part-time (8 women); includes 6 minority (1 Black or African American, non-Hispanic/Latino; 1 Asian, non-Hispanic/Latino; 2 Hispanic/Latino; 2 Two or more races, non-Hispanic/Latino), 4 international. Average age 26. 34 applicants, 91% accepted, 19 enrolled. In 2016, 10 master's awarded. *Degree requirements:* For master's, comprehensive exam (for some programs), thesis or recital. *Entrance requirements:* For master's, departmental assessment in music history, minimum undergraduate GPA of 2.75, audition on primary instrument, or submission of composition portfolio or written samples (for music education). Additional exam requirements/recommendations for international students: Required—TOEFL (minimum score 550 paper-based; 78 iBT). *Application deadline:* For fall admission, 7/1 priority date for domestic students, 5/15 for international students; for spring admission, 11/15 for domestic students, 11/1 for international students; for summer admission, 4/1 for domestic students, 3/15 for international students. Applications are processed on a rolling basis. Application fee: $40. Electronic applications accepted. *Expenses:* Tuition, state resident: full-time $9565. Tuition, nonresident: full-time $17,980. Tuition and fees vary according to program. *Financial support:* In 2016–17, 14 students received support. Scholarships/grants, tuition waivers (partial), and unspecified assistantships available. Financial award application deadline: 3/15; financial award applicants required to submit FAFSA. *Faculty research:* Performance, music education, music composition. *Total annual research expenditures:* $162,000. *Unit head:* Dr. John Perrine, Chairperson/Associate Professor, 216-687-3959, Fax: 216-687-9279, E-mail: j.m.perrine@csuohio.edu. *Application contact:* Kate Bill, Music Admission Specialist, 216-687-5039, Fax: 216-687-9279, E-mail: m.c.bill@csuohio.edu.
Website: http://www.csuohio.edu/music/

College of Charleston, Graduate School, School of Education, Health, and Human Performance, Department of Foundations, Secondary, and Special Education, Program in Performing Arts Education, Charleston, SC 29424-0001. Offers MAT. *Accreditation:* NASM. *Program availability:* Part-time, evening/weekend. *Entrance requirements:* For master's, GRE, minimum GPA of 2.5 overall, 3.0 in last 60 hours of undergraduate coursework; 2 letters of recommendation; audition/interview. Additional exam requirements/recommendations for international students: Required—TOEFL (minimum score 81 iBT). *Application deadline:* For fall admission, 7/1 for domestic students; for spring admission, 11/1 for domestic students. Application fee: $45. Electronic applications accepted. *Financial support:* Scholarships/grants and unspecified assistantships available. Financial award application deadline: 4/1; financial award applicants required to submit FAFSA. *Unit head:* Laura Turner, Program Director and Coordinator for Concentration in Theatre, 843-953-6306, E-mail: turnerl@cofc.edu. *Application contact:* Laura Turner, Program Director and Coordinator for Concentration in Theatre, 843-953-6306, E-mail: turnerl@cofc.edu.

College of Staten Island of the City University of New York, Graduate Programs, School of Education, Program in Childhood Education, Staten Island, NY 10314-6600. Offers learning and development (MS Ed); literacy education (MS Ed); mathematics education (MS Ed); music education (MS Ed); science education (MS Ed); social foundations of education (MS Ed); social studies education (MS Ed). *Program availability:* Part-time, evening/weekend. *Faculty:* 2 full-time, 11 part-time/adjunct. *Students:* 16 full-time, 53 part-time. Average age 30. 40 applicants, 53% accepted, 13 enrolled. In 2016, 20 master's awarded. *Degree requirements:* For master's, educational research project; ten courses and a minimum of 32-38 credits in five required areas of study or minimum of 45-49 credits in six required core courses before selecting from array of advanced courses. *Entrance requirements:* For master's, GRE General Test or an approved equivalent examination, relevant bachelor's degree, letters of recommendation, one- or two-page personal statement. Additional exam requirements/recommendations for international students: Required—TOEFL (minimum score 550 paper-based; 79 iBT), IELTS (minimum score 6.5). *Application deadline:* For fall admission, 4/25 for domestic and international students; for spring admission, 11/25 for domestic and international students. Applications are processed on a rolling basis. Application fee: $125. Electronic applications accepted. *Expenses:* Tuition, state resident: full-time $10,130; part-time $425 per credit. Tuition, nonresident: full-time $18,720; part-time $780 per credit. *Required fees:* $181.10 per semester. Tuition and fees vary according to program. *Faculty research:* Preservice teacher preparation, music integration, music education through children's songs, literacy, emergent bilingual. *Unit head:* Dr. Vivian Shulman, Graduate Faculty Advisor, 718-982-4086, E-mail: vivian.shulman@csi.cuny.edu. *Application contact:* Sasha Spence, Associate Director for Graduate Admissions, 718-982-2019, Fax: 718-982-2500, E-mail: sasha.spence@csi.cuny.edu.
Website: http://www.csi.cuny.edu/admissions/grad/pdf/Education%20Fact%20Sheet.pdf

The Colorado College, Education Department, Program in Secondary Education, Colorado Springs, CO 80903-3294. Offers art teaching (K-12) (MAT); English teaching (MAT); foreign language teaching (MAT); mathematics teaching (MAT); music teaching (MAT); science teaching (MAT); social studies teaching (MAT). *Degree requirements:* For master's, thesis, internship. Electronic applications accepted.

Colorado State University, College of Liberal Arts, School of Music, Theatre and Dance, Fort Collins, CO 80523-1779. Offers choral conducting (MM); collaborative piano (MM); instrumental conducting (MM); music education (MM), including conducting; music performance (MM); music therapy (MM). *Accreditation:* NASM. *Program availability:* Part-time. *Faculty:* 25 full-time (7 women), 9 part-time/adjunct (5 women). *Students:* 54 full-time (31 women), 100 part-time (77 women); includes 16 minority (2 Black or African American, non-Hispanic/Latino; 4 Asian, non-Hispanic/Latino; 8 Hispanic/Latino; 2 Two or more races, non-Hispanic/Latino), 13 international. Average age 30. 77 applicants, 79% accepted, 43 enrolled. In 2016, 69 master's awarded. *Degree requirements:* For master's, comprehensive exam, thesis, recital. *Entrance requirements:* For master's, minimum GPA of 3.0, audition, bachelor's degree, 3 letters of recommendation, transcripts, statement of purpose, curriculum vitae. Additional exam requirements/recommendations for international students: Required—TOEFL (minimum score 550 paper-based; 80 iBT), IELTS (minimum score 6.5). *Application deadline:* For fall admission, 2/15 for domestic and international students. Applications are processed on a rolling basis. Application fee: $60 ($70 for international students). Electronic applications accepted. *Expenses:* Contact institution. *Financial support:* In 2016–17, 25 students received support, including 24 teaching assistantships with full and partial tuition reimbursements available (averaging $8,998 per year); research assistantships, scholarships/grants, traineeships, and unspecified assistantships also available. Financial award application deadline: 2/15; financial award applicants required to submit FAFSA. *Faculty research:* Musical creativity in children with autism spectrum disorder; music therapy; cognitive, sensorimotor, speech and language and psychosocial functioning techniques; study/analysis/ear training strategies. *Total annual research expenditures:* $12,966. *Unit head:* Dr. Daniel Goble, Director, 970-491-5529, E-mail: dan.goble@colostate.edu. *Application contact:* Dr. G. Murray Oliver, Graduate Program Coordinator, 970-491-5193, Fax: 970-491-7541, E-mail: murray.oliver@colostate.edu.
Website: http://smtd.colostate.edu/

Colorado State University–Pueblo, College of Education, Engineering and Professional Studies, Education Program, Pueblo, CO 81001-4901. Offers art education (M Ed); foreign language education (M Ed); health and physical education (M Ed); instructional technology (M Ed); linguistically diverse education (M Ed); music education (M Ed); special education (M Ed). *Accreditation:* TEAC. *Program availability:* Part-time. *Degree requirements:* For master's, portfolio. *Entrance requirements:* For master's, 3 recommendations, teaching license. Additional exam requirements/recommendations for international students: Required—TOEFL (minimum score 500 paper-based). Electronic applications accepted. *Faculty research:* Portfolio assessment, math education, science education.

Columbus State University, Graduate Studies, College of the Arts, Schwob School of Music, Columbus, GA 31907-5645. Offers music (Artist Diploma); music education (MM); music performance (MM). *Accreditation:* NASM; NCATE (one or more programs are accredited). *Program availability:* Part-time. *Faculty:* 25 full-time (10 women), 2 part-time/adjunct (both women). *Students:* 46 full-time (21 women), 11 part-time (2 women); includes 8 minority (3 Black or African American, non-Hispanic/Latino; 1 Asian, non-Hispanic/Latino; 3 Hispanic/Latino; 1 Native Hawaiian or other Pacific Islander, non-Hispanic/Latino), 26 international. Average age 26. 67 applicants, 51% accepted, 28 enrolled. In 2016, 8 master's, 7 Artist Diplomas awarded. *Degree requirements:* For master's, exit exam. *Entrance requirements:* For master's, audition, letters of recommendation, undergraduate degree in music with a minimum GPA of 2.5. Additional exam requirements/recommendations for international students: Required—TOEFL (minimum score 550 paper-based; 79 iBT). *Application deadline:* For fall admission, 6/30 for domestic students, 5/1 for international students; for spring admission, 11/1 for domestic and international students; for summer admission, 3/1 for domestic and international students. Applications are processed on a rolling basis. Application fee: $50. Electronic applications accepted. *Expenses:* Tuition, state resident: full-time $4804; part-time $2412 per semester hour. Tuition, nonresident: full-time $19,218; part-time $9612 per semester hour. *Required fees:* $1850; $1850 per semester hour. Tuition and fees vary according to program. *Financial support:* In 2016–17, 44 students received support, including 32 research assistantships with partial tuition reimbursements available (averaging $3,000 per year); career-related internships or

fieldwork, Federal Work-Study, institutionally sponsored loans, scholarships/grants, tuition waivers (partial), and unspecified assistantships also available. Support available to part-time students. Financial award application deadline: 5/1; financial award applicants required to submit FAFSA. *Unit head:* Dr. Edwin Scott Harris, Director, 706-507-8419, E-mail: harris_scott@columbusstate.edu. *Application contact:* Kristin Williams, Director of International and Graduate Recruitment, 706-507-8848, Fax: 706-568-5091, E-mail: williams_kristin@columbusstate.edu.
Website: http://music.columbusstate.edu/

Conservatorio de Musica de Puerto Rico, Program in Music Education, San Juan, PR 00907. Offers MM Ed. *Accreditation:* NASM. *Entrance requirements:* For master's, EXADEP, 3 letters of recommendation, audition, bachelor's degree in music education, interview, minimum GPA of 2.5, performance video, teaching video. Additional exam requirements/recommendations for international students: Required—TOEFL.

Converse College, School of Education and Graduate Studies, Petrie School of Music, Spartanburg, SC 29302. Offers music education (M Mus); performance (M Mus). *Accreditation:* NASM. *Program availability:* Part-time, evening/weekend. *Degree requirements:* For master's, variable foreign language requirement, comprehensive exam, thesis (for some programs), recitals. *Entrance requirements:* For master's, NTE (music education), audition, 3 letters of recommendation. Additional exam requirements/recommendations for international students: Required—TOEFL. *Application deadline:* For spring admission, 3/1 priority date for domestic and international students. Applications are processed on a rolling basis. Application fee: $40. Electronic applications accepted. *Expenses: Tuition:* Full-time $3600; part-time $400 per credit hour. *Required fees:* $70 per term. *Financial support:* Career-related internships or fieldwork, Federal Work-Study, institutionally sponsored loans, and unspecified assistantships available. Support available to part-time students. Financial award application deadline: 4/15. *Faculty research:* Chamber music, opera, performance, composition, recording. *Unit head:* Patricia S. Foy, Director, 864-596-9172, E-mail: patti.foy@converse.edu. *Application contact:* 864-596-9404, E-mail: graduate@converse.edu.
Website: http://www.converse.edu/academics/school-arts/petrie-school-music

DePaul University, School of Music, Chicago, IL 60614. Offers composition (MM); jazz studies (MM); music education (MM); music performance (MM); performance (Certificate). *Accreditation:* NASM (one or more programs are accredited). *Program availability:* Part-time, evening/weekend. *Degree requirements:* For master's, comprehensive exam. *Entrance requirements:* For master's, bachelor's degree in music or related field, minimum GPA of 3.0, auditions (performance), scores (composition); for Certificate, master's degree in performance or related field, auditions (for performance majors). Additional exam requirements/recommendations for international students: Required—TOEFL (minimum score 550 paper-based; 80 iBT). Electronic applications accepted. *Expenses:* Contact institution.

Duquesne University, Mary Pappert School of Music, Pittsburgh, PA 15282-0001. Offers music education (MM). *Accreditation:* NASM. *Program availability:* Part-time. *Faculty:* 26 full-time (9 women), 77 part-time/adjunct (22 women). *Students:* 69 full-time (27 women), 16 part-time (6 women); includes 7 minority (3 Black or African American, non-Hispanic/Latino; 1 Asian, non-Hispanic/Latino; 1 Hispanic/Latino; 2 Two or more races, non-Hispanic/Latino), 24 international. Average age 26. 94 applicants, 93% accepted, 29 enrolled. In 2016, 19 master's, 9 ADs awarded. *Degree requirements:* For master's, comprehensive exam, thesis (for some programs), recital (music performance); for AD, recital. *Entrance requirements:* For master's, audition, minimum undergraduate QPA of 3.0 in music, portfolio of original compositions, or music education experience; for AD, audition. Additional exam requirements/recommendations for international students: Required—TOEFL (minimum score 550 paper-based; 79 iBT), IELTS (minimum score 6.5). *Application deadline:* For fall admission, 7/1 for domestic and international students; for spring admission, 12/1 for domestic and international students; for summer admission, 6/1 for domestic students, 5/1 for international students. Applications are processed on a rolling basis. Application fee: $50. Electronic applications accepted. Application fee is waived when completed online. *Expenses:* $1,469 per credit. *Financial support:* In 2016–17, 76 students received support. Scholarships/grants and unspecified assistantships available. Financial award application deadline: 4/1. *Faculty research:* Assessment of music education and professional dispositions; music philosophy; curricular design, pedagogy, and assessment; music composition; music performance. *Unit head:* Dr. Seth Beckman, Dean/Professor, 412-396-6082, Fax: 412-396-1524, E-mail: beckmans@duq.edu. *Application contact:* Katherine Shields, Director of Music Admissions, 412-396-5983, Fax: 412-396-5719, E-mail: shieldsk1@duq.edu.
Website: http://duq.edu/music

East Carolina University, Graduate School, College of Education, Department of Elementary and Middle Grades Education, Greenville, NC 27858-4353. Offers elementary education (MA Ed, MAT); English education (MAT); family and consumer science (MAT); health education (MAT); Hispanic studies (MAT); history education (MAT); middle grades education (MA Ed, MAT); music education (MAT); science education (MAT); special education (MAT), including general curriculum; vocational education (MAT). *Accreditation:* NCATE. *Program availability:* Part-time, evening/weekend, online learning. *Students:* 5 full-time (4 women), 18 part-time (16 women); includes 4 minority (3 Black or African American, non-Hispanic/Latino; 1 Hispanic/Latino). Average age 31. 19 applicants, 95% accepted, 13 enrolled. In 2016, 8 master's awarded. *Degree requirements:* For master's, comprehensive exam, thesis optional. *Entrance requirements:* For master's, GRE or MAT, minimum GPA of 2.5, bachelor's degree in related field, teaching license (MA Ed). Additional exam requirements/recommendations for international students: Required—TOEFL. *Application deadline:* For fall admission, 6/1 priority date for domestic students. Applications are processed on a rolling basis. Application fee: $70. *Financial support:* Federal Work-Study available. Support available to part-time students. Financial award application deadline: 6/1. *Unit head:* Dr. Ann Bullock, Chair, 252-328-1120, E-mail: bullockv@ecu.edu. *Application contact:* Dean of Graduate School, 252-328-6012, Fax: 252-328-6071, E-mail: gradschool@ecu.edu.
Website: http://www.ecu.edu/cs-educ/elmid/index.cfm

East Carolina University, Graduate School, College of Fine Arts and Communication, School of Music, Greenville, NC 27858-4353. Offers advanced performance studies (Certificate); music education (MM); music therapy (MM); performance (MM), including accompanying, choral conducting, instrumental conducting, jazz studies, organ, percussion, piano, piano pedagogy, sacred music, strings, Suzuki string pedagogy, vocal pedagogy, voice, woodwind specialist; Suzuki pedagogy (Certificate); theory and composition (MM). *Accreditation:* NASM. *Program availability:* Part-time. *Students:* 29 full-time (15 women), 19 part-time (9 women); includes 4 minority (2 Black or African American, non-Hispanic/Latino; 2 Asian, non-Hispanic/Latino), 1 international. Average age 27. 39 applicants, 100% accepted, 28 enrolled. In 2016, 10 master's awarded. *Degree requirements:* For master's, comprehensive exam, thesis optional. *Entrance requirements:* For master's, GRE General Test or MAT. Additional exam requirements/recommendations for international students: Required—TOEFL. *Application deadline:* For fall admission, 6/1 priority date for domestic students. Applications are processed on a rolling basis. Application fee: $50. *Financial support:* Fellowships, research assistantships, teaching assistantships, and Federal Work-Study available. Support available to part-time students. Financial award application deadline: 6/1. *Unit head:* Christopher Ulffers, Director, 252-328-4270, E-mail: ulffersj@ecu.edu. *Application contact:* Dean of Graduate School, 252-328-6012, Fax: 252-328-6071, E-mail: gradschool@ecu.edu.
Website: http://www.music.ecu.edu/

Eastern Kentucky University, The Graduate School, College of Education, Department of Curriculum and Instruction, Richmond, KY 40475-3102. Offers elementary education (MA Ed), including early elementary education, reading; library science (MA Ed); music education (MA Ed); secondary and higher education (MA Ed), including secondary education; teaching (MAT). *Accreditation:* NCATE. *Program availability:* Part-time. *Degree requirements:* For master's, portfolio is part of exam. *Entrance requirements:* For master's, GRE General Test, PRAXIS II (KY), minimum GPA of 2.5. *Faculty research:* Technology in education, reading instruction, e-portfolios, induction to teacher education, dispositions of teachers.

Eastern Washington University, Graduate Studies, College of Arts, Letters and Education, Department of Music, Cheney, WA 99004-2431. Offers composition (MA); general (MA); instrumental/vocal performance (MA); jazz pedagogy (MA); music education (MA). *Accreditation:* NASM. *Program availability:* Part-time. *Faculty:* 17 full-time (9 women), 14 part-time/adjunct (5 women). *Students:* 10 full-time (3 women), 6 part-time (2 women); includes 3 minority (1 Hispanic/Latino; 2 Native Hawaiian or other Pacific Islander, non-Hispanic/Latino), 2 international. Average age 31. 13 applicants, 77% accepted, 9 enrolled. In 2016, 9 master's awarded. *Degree requirements:* For master's, comprehensive exam, thesis or alternative. *Entrance requirements:* For master's, GRE General Test, minimum GPA of 3.0. Additional exam requirements/recommendations for international students: Required—TOEFL (minimum score 580 paper-based; 92 iBT), IELTS (minimum score 7), TWE, PTE (minimum score 63). *Application deadline:* For fall admission, 4/1 priority date for domestic students; for spring admission, 1/15 for domestic students. Applications are processed on a rolling basis. Application fee: $75. Electronic applications accepted. *Expenses:* Tuition, state resident: full-time $11,000; part-time $5500 per credit. Tuition, nonresident: full-time $24,000; part-time $12,000 per credit. *Required fees:* $1300. One-time fee: $50 full-time. Part-time tuition and fees vary according to course load, campus/location and program. *Financial support:* In 2016–17, 8 students received support, including 8 teaching assistantships with partial tuition reimbursements available (averaging $10,000 per year); career-related internships or fieldwork, Federal Work-Study, institutionally sponsored loans, scholarships/grants, health care benefits, tuition waivers (partial), and unspecified assistantships also available. Support available to part-time students. Financial award application deadline: 2/1; financial award applicants required to submit FAFSA. *Unit head:* Dr. Sheila Woodward, Director and Chair of Music Education, 509-359-7073, Fax: 509-359-7028. *Application contact:* Dr. Jane Ellsworth, Assistant Professor, 509-359-7076, E-mail: gradprograms@ewu.edu.
Website: http://www.ewu.edu/cale/programs/music.xml

Five Towns College, Graduate Programs, Dix Hills, NY 11746-6055. Offers childhood education (MS Ed); composition and arranging (DMA); jazz/commercial music (MM); music education (MM, DMA); music history and literature (DMA); music performance (DMA). *Program availability:* Part-time. *Faculty:* 12 full-time (3 women), 6 part-time/adjunct (0 women). *Students:* 18 full-time (7 women), 6 part-time (2 women); includes 9 minority (3 Black or African American, non-Hispanic/Latino; 4 Asian, non-Hispanic/Latino; 1 Hispanic/Latino; 1 Two or more races, non-Hispanic/Latino), 1 international. Average age 35. 63 applicants, 11% accepted, 7 enrolled. In 2016, 4 master's, 2 doctorates awarded. *Degree requirements:* For master's, thesis, exams, major composition or capstone project, recital; for doctorate, comprehensive exam, thesis/dissertation, final oral exam. *Entrance requirements:* For master's, audition (for MM); New York state teaching certification (for MS Ed); personal statement, two letters of recommendation; for doctorate, 3 letters of recommendation, audition, essay. Additional exam requirements/recommendations for international students: Required—TOEFL (minimum score 520 paper-based; 85 iBT); Recommended—IELTS (minimum score 7). *Application deadline:* For fall admission, 9/1 for domestic and international students; for spring admission, 1/25 for domestic and international students. Applications are processed on a rolling basis. Application fee: $50. Electronic applications accepted. *Expenses: Tuition:* Full-time $15,000; part-time $625 per credit. *Required fees:* $600; $150 per semester. Tuition and fees vary according to degree level. *Financial support:* Fellowships with tuition reimbursements, teaching assistantships with tuition reimbursements, and tuition waivers (partial) available. Financial award applicants required to submit FAFSA. *Faculty research:* Teaching methods, teaching strategies and techniques, analysis of modern music, jazz. *Application contact:* Ronnie MacDonald, Director of Admissions, 631-656-2110, Fax: 631-656-2172, E-mail: admissions@ftc.edu.
Website: http://www.ftc.edu

Florida Atlantic University, College of Education, Department of Teaching and Learning, Boca Raton, FL 33431-0991. Offers curriculum and instruction (M Ed), including art, biology, chemistry, English, French, German, mathematics, music, physics, Pre-K and primary education, reading, social sciences, Spanish; elementary education (M Ed); environmental education (M Ed); reading education (M Ed); social foundations of education (M Ed), including educational psychology, educational technology, multilingual education. *Accreditation:* NCATE. *Program availability:* Part-time, evening/weekend. *Faculty:* 15 full-time (12 women), 2 part-time/adjunct (1 woman). *Students:* 25 full-time (20 women), 41 part-time (37 women); includes 18 minority (9 Black or African American, non-Hispanic/Latino; 2 Asian, non-Hispanic/Latino; 7 Hispanic/Latino), 7 international. Average age 32. 54 applicants, 59% accepted, 18 enrolled. In 2016, 36 master's awarded. *Entrance requirements:* For master's, GRE General Test, minimum GPA of 3.0 in last 2 years of undergraduate course work. Additional exam requirements/recommendations for international students: Required—TOEFL (minimum score 500 paper-based; 61 iBT), IELTS (minimum score 6). *Application deadline:* For fall admission, 7/1 for domestic students, 2/15 for international students; for spring admission, 11/1 for domestic students, 7/15 for international students. Applications are processed on a rolling basis. Application fee: $30. *Expenses:* Tuition, state resident: full-time $7392; part-time $369.82 per credit hour. Tuition, nonresident: full-time $19,432; part-time $1024.81 per credit hour. *Financial support:* Fellowships with partial tuition reimbursements, research assistantships with partial tuition reimbursements, teaching assistantships with partial tuition reimbursements, career-related internships or fieldwork, scholarships/grants, and unspecified assistantships available. *Faculty research:* Technology, teaching English to speakers of other languages, math teaching, electronic portfolio assessment, global perspectives through social studies. *Unit head:* Dr. Barbara Ridener, Chairperson, 561-297-3588, E-mail: bridener@fau.edu. *Application contact:* Dr. Eliah Watlington, Associate Dean, 561-296-8520, Fax: 261-297-2991, E-mail: ewatling@fau.edu.
Website: http://www.coe.fau.edu/academicdepartments/tl/

Florida International University, College of Communication, Architecture and The Arts, School of Music, Miami, FL 33199. Offers music (MM); music education (MS). *Program availability:* Part-time, evening/weekend. *Faculty:* 21 full-time (3 women), 25 part-time/adjunct (5 women). *Students:* 31 full-time (13 women), 18 part-time (8 women);

includes 34 minority (7 Black or African American, non-Hispanic/Latino; 1 Asian, non-Hispanic/Latino; 24 Hispanic/Latino; 2 Two or more races, non-Hispanic/Latino), 3 international. Average age 29. 48 applicants, 56% accepted, 16 enrolled. In 2016, 18 master's awarded. *Degree requirements:* For master's, thesis (for some programs). *Entrance requirements:* For master's, GRE (depending on program), statement of intent; 2 letters of recommendation; audition, interview and/or writing sample (depending on the area). Additional exam requirements/recommendations for international students: Required—TOEFL (minimum score 550 paper-based; 80 iBT). *Application deadline:* For fall admission, 6/1 for domestic students, 4/1 for international students; for spring admission, 10/1 for domestic students, 9/1 for international students. Applications are processed on a rolling basis. Application fee: $30. Electronic applications accepted. *Expenses:* Tuition, state resident: full-time $8912; part-time $446 per credit hour. Tuition, nonresident: full-time $21,393; part-time $992 per credit hour. *Required fees:* $2185; $195 per semester. Tuition and fees vary according to program. *Financial support:* Institutionally sponsored loans and scholarships/grants available. Financial award application deadline: 3/1; financial award applicants required to submit FAFSA. *Unit head:* Robert Dundas, Interim Chair, 305-348-3587, Fax: 305-348-4073, E-mail: robert.dundas@fiu.edu. *Application contact:* Joel Galand, Graduate Program Director, 305-348-7078, E-mail: galandj@fiu.edu.
Website: http://carta.fiu.edu/music/

George Mason University, College of Visual and Performing Arts, School of Music, Program in Music, Fairfax, VA 22030. Offers composition (MM); conducting (MM); jazz studies (MM); music education (MM); pedagogy (MM); performance (MM). *Accreditation:* NASM. *Faculty:* 20 full-time (8 women), 34 part-time/adjunct (13 women). *Students:* 14 full-time (9 women), 26 part-time (15 women); includes 11 minority (3 Black or African American, non-Hispanic/Latino; 4 Asian, non-Hispanic/Latino; 3 Hispanic/Latino; 1 Native Hawaiian or other Pacific Islander, non-Hispanic/Latino), 2 international. Average age 31. 33 applicants, 70% accepted, 10 enrolled. In 2016, 28 master's awarded. *Degree requirements:* For master's, comprehensive exam. *Entrance requirements:* For master's, expanded goals statement; 2 letters of recommendation; official transcript. Additional exam requirements/recommendations for international students: Required—TOEFL (minimum score 575 paper-based; 88 iBT), IELTS (minimum score 6.5), PTE (minimum score 59). Application fee: $75 ($80 for international students). Electronic applications accepted. *Expenses:* Tuition, state resident: full-time $10,628; part-time $443 per credit. Tuition, nonresident: full-time $29,306; part-time $1221 per credit. *Required fees:* $3096; $129 per credit. Tuition and fees vary according to program. *Financial support:* Career-related internships or fieldwork, Federal Work-Study, scholarships/grants, and unspecified assistantships available. Financial award application deadline: 3/1; financial award applicants required to submit FAFSA. *Unit head:* Dr. Linda Apple Monson, Managing Director, 703-993-3580, Fax: 703-993-1394, E-mail: lmonson@gmu.edu. *Application contact:* Dr. Lisa A. Billingham, Director of Graduate Studies, 703-993-3778, Fax: 703-993-1394, E-mail: lbillin1@gmu.edu.
Website: http://music.gmu.edu

Georgia College & State University, Graduate School, College of Arts and Sciences, Department of Music, Milledgeville, GA 31061. Offers MM Ed. *Accreditation:* NASM. *Program availability:* Part-time. *Students:* 2 full-time (both women), 5 part-time (2 women); includes 3 minority (2 Black or African American, non-Hispanic/Latino; 1 Hispanic/Latino). Average age 32. In 2016, 3 master's awarded. *Degree requirements:* For master's, comprehensive exam, thesis optional. *Entrance requirements:* For master's, GA teaching certificate, GACE II, PRAXIS II music test, or GRE (less than 10 years old), bachelor's degree in music (education), 3 letters of recommendation, interview, resume, video recorded lesson or rehearsal with written lesson plan, transcript. *Application deadline:* For fall admission, 8/1 priority date for domestic students; for spring admission, 11/1 priority date for domestic students; for summer admission, 4/1 priority date for domestic students. Applications are processed on a rolling basis. Application fee: $40. Electronic applications accepted. *Expenses:* $288 per credit hour in-state, $1,027 per credit hour out-of-state, $1,990 full-time annual fees. *Financial support:* In 2016–17, 1 student received support. Unspecified assistantships available. Financial award applicants required to submit FAFSA. *Unit head:* Dr. Jennifer Flory, Graduate Coordinator for Music Education, 478-445-4839, Fax: 478-445-1633, E-mail: jennifer.flory@gcsu.edu. *Application contact:* Kate Marshall, Graduate Admissions Coordinator, 478-445-1184, Fax: 478-445-1336, E-mail: grad-admit@gcsu.edu.
Website: http://www.gcsu.edu/artsandsciences/music/music-education-mmed

Georgia Southern University, Jack N. Averitt College of Graduate Studies, College of Liberal Arts and Social Sciences, Program in Music, Statesboro, GA 30460. Offers composition (MM); conducting (MM); music education (MM); music technology (MM); performance (MM). *Accreditation:* NASM. *Program availability:* Part-time, evening/weekend. *Students:* 15 full-time (5 women), 11 part-time (6 women); includes 6 minority (4 Black or African American, non-Hispanic/Latino; 1 Hispanic/Latino; 1 Two or more races, non-Hispanic/Latino), 3 international. Average age 27. 23 applicants, 87% accepted, 11 enrolled. In 2016, 16 master's awarded. *Degree requirements:* For master's, comprehensive exam, recital or final project. *Entrance requirements:* For master's, minimum GPA of 2.5, audition, letters of recommendation. Additional exam requirements/recommendations for international students: Required—TOEFL (minimum score 550 paper-based; 80 iBT), IELTS (minimum score 6). *Application deadline:* For fall admission, 3/1 priority date for domestic and international students; for spring admission, 10/1 priority date for domestic students, 10/1 for international students. Applications are processed on a rolling basis. Application fee: $50. Electronic applications accepted. *Expenses:* Tuition, state resident: full-time $7236; part-time $277 per semester hour. Tuition, nonresident: full-time $27,118; part-time $1105 per semester hour. *Required fees:* $2092. *Financial support:* In 2016–17, 10 fellowships with full tuition reimbursements (averaging $7,750 per year), 3 teaching assistantships with full tuition reimbursements (averaging $7,750 per year) were awarded; Federal Work-Study, scholarships/grants, tuition waivers (full), and unspecified assistantships also available. Support available to part-time students. Financial award application deadline: 4/15; financial award applicants required to submit FAFSA. *Faculty research:* Performance, conducting, composition, technology, education. *Unit head:* Dr. Greg Harwood, Graduate Director, 912-478-5813, Fax: 912-478-1295, E-mail: gharwood@georgiasouthern.edu.
Website: http://class.georgiasouthern.edu/music/

Georgia State University, College of Arts and Sciences, School of Music, Atlanta, GA 30303. Offers choral conducting (MM); jazz studies (MM); music (Certificate); music composition (MM); music education (PhD); orchestral conducting (MM); performance (MM), including orchestral, piano, vocal; piano pedagogy (MM); wind band conducting (MM). *Accreditation:* NASM. *Program availability:* Part-time, evening/weekend. *Faculty:* 40 full-time (13 women). *Students:* 80 full-time (36 women), 10 part-time (4 women); includes 32 minority (19 Black or African American, non-Hispanic/Latino; 5 Asian, non-Hispanic/Latino; 8 Hispanic/Latino), 13 international. Average age 30. 84 applicants, 69% accepted, 42 enrolled. In 2016, 25 master's, 2 other advanced degrees awarded. *Degree requirements:* For master's, comprehensive exam, thesis (for some programs), recital; for doctorate, comprehensive exam, thesis/dissertation; for Certificate, recital. *Entrance requirements:* For master's, GRE (for music education, composition only), BM; for doctorate, GRE, MM; for Certificate, MM. Additional exam requirements/recommendations for international students: Required—TOEFL (minimum score 550 paper-based; 80 iBT). *Application deadline:* For fall admission, 3/1 priority date for domestic and international students; for spring admission, 10/1 priority date for domestic and international students. Applications are processed on a rolling basis. Application fee: $50. Electronic applications accepted. *Expenses:* Tuition, state resident: full-time $6876; part-time $382 per credit hour. Tuition, nonresident: full-time $22,374; part-time $1243 per credit hour. *Required fees:* $2128; $1064 per term. Part-time tuition and fees vary according to course load and program. *Financial support:* In 2016–17, research assistantships with full tuition reimbursements (averaging $4,000 per year) were awarded; Federal Work-Study, scholarships/grants, health care benefits, tuition waivers (partial), and unspecified assistantships also available. Financial award application deadline: 3/1; financial award applicants required to submit FAFSA. *Faculty research:* Male changing voice, nineteenth-century chamber music, improvisation and learning, Garibunda, African-American classical musicians. *Unit head:* William Dwight Coleman, Director, School of Music, 404-413-5953, Fax: 404-413-5910, E-mail: wcoleman@gsu.edu. *Application contact:* Dr. Steven Andrew Harper, Graduate Director, 404-413-5943, Fax: 404-413-5910, E-mail: sharper@gsu.edu.
Website: http://www.music.gsu.edu/

Georgia State University, College of Education and Human Development, Department of Middle and Secondary Education, Atlanta, GA 30302-3083. Offers curriculum and instruction (Ed D); English education (MAT); mathematics education (M Ed, MAT); middle level education (MAT); reading, language and literacy education (M Ed, MAT), including reading instruction (M Ed); science education (M Ed, MAT), including biology (MAT), broad field science (MAT), chemistry (MAT), earth science (MAT), physics (MAT); social studies education (M Ed, MAT), including economics (MAT), geography (MAT), history (MAT), political science (MAT); teaching and learning (PhD), including language and literacy, mathematics education, music education, science education, social studies education, teaching and teacher education. *Accreditation:* NCATE. *Program availability:* Part-time, evening/weekend, online learning. *Faculty:* 24 full-time (18 women). *Students:* 145 full-time (91 women), 151 part-time (102 women); includes 141 minority (104 Black or African American, non-Hispanic/Latino; 1 American Indian or Alaska Native, non-Hispanic/Latino; 16 Asian, non-Hispanic/Latino; 12 Hispanic/Latino; 8 Two or more races, non-Hispanic/Latino), 10 international. Average age 36. 115 applicants, 50% accepted, 41 enrolled. In 2016, 94 master's, 22 doctorates awarded. *Degree requirements:* For master's, comprehensive exam (for some programs), thesis or alternative, exit portfolio; for doctorate, comprehensive exam, thesis/dissertation. *Entrance requirements:* For master's, GRE; GACE I (for initial teacher preparation programs), baccalaureate degree or equivalent, resume, goals statement, two letters of recommendation, minimum undergraduate GPA of 2.5; proof of initial teacher certification in the content area (for M Ed); for doctorate, GRE, resume, goals statement, writing sample, two letters of recommendation, minimum graduate GPA of 3.3, interview. Additional exam requirements/recommendations for international students: Required—TOEFL (minimum score 550 paper-based; 79 iBT) or IELTS (minimum score 6.5). *Application deadline:* For fall admission, 1/15 priority date for domestic and international students; for spring admission, 10/1 for domestic and international students. Application fee: $50. Electronic applications accepted. *Expenses:* Tuition, state resident: full-time $6876; part-time $382 per credit hour. Tuition, nonresident: full-time $22,374; part-time $1243 per credit hour. *Required fees:* $2128; $1064 per term. Part-time tuition and fees vary according to course load and program. *Financial support:* In 2016–17, fellowships with full tuition reimbursements (averaging $19,667 per year), research assistantships with full tuition reimbursements (averaging $5,436 per year), teaching assistantships with full tuition reimbursements (averaging $2,779 per year) were awarded; career-related internships or fieldwork, Federal Work-Study, scholarships/grants, health care benefits, tuition waivers (full and partial), and unspecified assistantships also available. Financial award application deadline: 3/15. *Faculty research:* Teacher education in language and literacy, mathematics, science, and social studies in urban middle and secondary school settings; learning technologies in school, community, and corporate settings; multicultural education and education for social justice; urban education; international education. *Unit head:* Dr. Dana L. Fox, Chair, 404-413-8060, Fax: 404-413-8063, E-mail: dfox@gsu.edu. *Application contact:* Bobbie Turner, Administrative Coordinator I, 404-413-8405, Fax: 404-413-8063, E-mail: bnturner@gsu.edu.
Website: http://mse.education.gsu.edu/

Gordon College, Graduate Music Education Program, Wenham, MA 01984-1899. Offers MM Ed. *Accreditation:* NASM. *Program availability:* Part-time. *Faculty:* 2 full-time (1 woman), 7 part-time/adjunct (4 women). *Students:* 20 full-time (11 women), 45 part-time (27 women); includes 10 minority (2 Black or African American, non-Hispanic/Latino; 2 American Indian or Alaska Native, non-Hispanic/Latino; 3 Asian, non-Hispanic/Latino; 2 Hispanic/Latino; 1 Two or more races, non-Hispanic/Latino). Average age 35. 19 applicants, 100% accepted, 17 enrolled. In 2016, 16 master's awarded. *Degree requirements:* For master's, comprehensive exam, thesis or alternative, field-based experience, capstone research project. *Entrance requirements:* For master's, music theory and music history diagnostic exams, 15-20 minute video-recorded demonstration of current classroom teaching, undergraduate degree in music education with minimum GPA of 2.85, at least one year of teaching experience, initial license in music (for professional licensure), professional resume, 3-4 page essay, two letters of recommendation. Additional exam requirements/recommendations for international students: Required—TOEFL (minimum score 550 paper-based, 80 iBT) or IELTS (minimum score 6.5). *Application deadline:* For summer admission, 4/1 for domestic and international students. Applications are processed on a rolling basis. Application fee: $50. *Expenses:* Contact institution. *Financial support:* Applicants required to submit FAFSA. *Faculty research:* Medium-high security prison education through choral music instruction; healthy vocal development in adolescents; healthy use of the singing voice; national common music assessment initiative; choral literature and techniques to incorporate the new national standards for music education. *Unit head:* Dr. Sandra Doneski, Associate Professor, 978-867-4818, E-mail: sandra.doneski@gordon.edu. *Application contact:* Kristen Harrington, Program Administrator, 978-867-4429, Fax: 978-867-4663, E-mail: kristen.harrington@gordon.edu.
Website: http://www.gordon.edu/gradmusic

Hampton University, School of Education and Human Development, Program in Teaching, Hampton, VA 23668. Offers music education (MT); secondary education (MT). *Program availability:* Part-time. *Faculty:* 5 full-time (4 women), 2 part-time/adjunct (both women). *Students:* 8 full-time (4 women); all minorities (all Black or African American, non-Hispanic/Latino). Average age 23. 7 applicants, 57% accepted, 4 enrolled. In 2016, 2 master's awarded. *Entrance requirements:* For master's, GRE General Test. Additional exam requirements/recommendations for international students: Required—TOEFL (minimum score 525 paper-based) or IELTS (6.5). *Application deadline:* For fall admission, 6/1 priority date for domestic students, 4/1 for international students; for spring admission, 11/1 priority date for domestic students, 9/1 for international students; for summer admission, 4/1 priority date for domestic students, 2/1 priority date for international students. Applications are processed on a rolling basis. Application fee: $35. Electronic applications accepted. *Expenses: Tuition:* Full-time $10,776; part-time $548 per credit hour. *Required fees:* $35; $35 per credit hour. Tuition and fees vary according to course load and program. *Financial support:* Application deadline: 6/30; applicants required to submit FAFSA. *Unit head:* Dr. Ava Marrow, Program Coordinator, 757-727-2072.

Hardin-Simmons University, Graduate School, College of Fine Arts, Abilene, TX 79698-0001. Offers church music (MM); music education (MM); music performance (MM); theory and composition (MM). *Accreditation:* NASM. *Program availability:* Part-time. *Faculty:* 9 full-time (3 women), 3 part-time/adjunct (1 woman). *Students:* 4 full-time (2 women), 4 part-time (1 woman); includes 4 minority (1 Black or African American, non-Hispanic/Latino; 2 Hispanic/Latino; 1 Two or more races, non-Hispanic/Latino). Average age 28. In 2016, 2 master's awarded. *Degree requirements:* For master's, one foreign language, comprehensive exam, thesis (for some programs). *Entrance requirements:* For master's, minimum undergraduate GPA of 3.0 in major, 2.7 overall; writing sample; demonstrated knowledge in chosen area. Additional exam requirements/recommendations for international students: Required—TOEFL (minimum score 550 paper-based; 75 iBT). *Application deadline:* For fall admission, 8/15 priority date for domestic students, 4/1 for international students; for spring admission, 1/5 priority date for domestic students, 9/1 for international students. Applications are processed on a rolling basis. Application fee: $50. Electronic applications accepted. *Expenses: Tuition:* Full-time $12,510; part-time $695 per credit hour. *Required fees:* $325; $110 per semester. *Financial support:* In 2016–17, 6 students received support, including 4 fellowships (averaging $2,700 per year); career-related internships or fieldwork and scholarships/grants also available. Support available to part-time students. Financial award application deadline: 6/30; financial award applicants required to submit FAFSA. *Unit head:* Dr. Lynnette Chambers, Program Director, 325-670-1430, Fax: 325-670-5873, E-mail: lchambers@hsutx.edu. *Application contact:* Dr. Nancy Kucinski, Dean of Graduate Studies, 325-670-1298, Fax: 325-670-1564, E-mail: gradoff@hsutx.edu.
Website: http://www.hsutx.edu/academics/cofa/

Hebrew College, Program in Jewish Studies, Newton Centre, MA 02459. Offers Jewish liturgical music (Certificate); Jewish music education (Certificate); Jewish studies (MA). *Program availability:* Part-time, evening/weekend, online learning. *Degree requirements:* For master's, one foreign language. *Entrance requirements:* For master's, GRE, interview. Additional exam requirements/recommendations for international students: Required—TOEFL.

Heidelberg University, Master of Music Education Program, Tiffin, OH 44883-2462. Offers MME. Summer program only. *Accreditation:* NASM. *Program availability:* Part-time. In 2016, 5 master's awarded. *Entrance requirements:* For master's, bachelor's degree in music education, minimum cumulative GPA of 2.9, three letters of recommendation, copy of U.S. teaching license in music education, interview. Additional exam requirements/recommendations for international students: Required—TOEFL (minimum score 550 paper-based; 79 iBT), IELTS (minimum score 6.5). *Application deadline:* For fall admission, 6/1 for domestic students. Applications are processed on a rolling basis. Application fee: $0. Electronic applications accepted. *Expenses:* $510 per semester hour. *Financial support:* Applicants required to submit FAFSA. *Unit head:* Dr. Carol Dusdieker, Director, 419-448-2080, E-mail: cdusdiek@heidelberg.edu. *Application contact:* Katie Slosser, Graduate Studies Coordinator, 419-448-2602, Fax: 419-448-2565, E-mail: kslosser@heidelberg.edu.
Website: https://www.heidelberg.edu/academics/programs/master-music-education

Hofstra University, School of Education, Programs in Teacher Education, Hempstead, NY 11549. Offers bilingual education (MA, Advanced Certificate); bilingual extension (Advanced Certificate), including education/speech language pathology; business education (MS Ed); early childhood and childhood education (MS Ed); early childhood education (MA, MS Ed); education technology (Advanced Certificate); elementary education (MA, MS Ed), including science, technology, engineering, and mathematics (STEM) (MA); English education (MS Ed); family and consumer science (MS Ed); fine arts and music education (Advanced Certificate); fine arts education (MS Ed); foreign language and TESOL (MS Ed); foreign language education (MS Ed), including French, German, Russian, Spanish; learning and teaching (Ed D), including applied linguistics, art education, arts and humanities, early childhood education, English education, human development, math education, math, science, and technology, multicultural education, physical education, science education, social studies education, special education; mathematics education (MA, MS Ed); middle school extension (Advanced Certificate), including grades 5-6, grades 7-9; music education (MA, MS Ed); science education (MA, MS Ed), including biology, chemistry, earth science, geology, physics; secondary education (Advanced Certificate); social studies education (MA, MS Ed); teaching languages other than English and TESOL (MS Ed); TESOL (MS Ed, Advanced Certificate). *Program availability:* Part-time, evening/weekend, blended/hybrid learning. *Students:* 139 full-time (97 women), 145 part-time (106 women); includes 60 minority (15 Black or African American, non-Hispanic/Latino; 1 American Indian or Alaska Native, non-Hispanic/Latino; 12 Asian, non-Hispanic/Latino; 31 Hispanic/Latino; 1 Two or more races, non-Hispanic/Latino), 21 international. Average age 29. 255 applicants, 86% accepted, 122 enrolled. In 2016, 101 master's, 4 doctorates, 43 other advanced degrees awarded. *Degree requirements:* For master's, comprehensive exam, thesis (for some programs), exit project, student teaching, fieldwork, electronic portfolio, curriculum project, minimum GPA of 3.0; for doctorate, thesis/dissertation; for Advanced Certificate, 3 foreign languages, comprehensive exam (for some programs), thesis project. *Entrance requirements:* For master's, GRE, MAT, 2 letters of recommendation, portfolio, teacher certification (MA), interview, essay; for doctorate, GMAT, GRE, LSAT, or MAT; for Advanced Certificate, 2 letters of recommendation, essay, interview and/or portfolio, teaching certificate. Additional exam requirements/recommendations for international students: Required—TOEFL (minimum score 550 paper-based; 80 iBT). *Application deadline:* Applications are processed on a rolling basis. Application fee: $75. Electronic applications accepted. *Expenses: Tuition:* Full-time $1240. *Required fees:* $970. Tuition and fees vary according to program. *Financial support:* In 2016–17, 149 students received support, including 58 fellowships with full and partial tuition reimbursements available (averaging $5,309 per year), 5 research assistantships with full and partial tuition reimbursements available (averaging $7,073 per year); career-related internships or fieldwork, Federal Work-Study, institutionally sponsored loans, scholarships/grants, traineeships, tuition waivers (full and partial), and unspecified assistantships also available. Support available to part-time students. Financial award applicants required to submit FAFSA. *Faculty research:* Educational interventions that foster critical-thinking skills; teachers' attitudes about professional development; threats to teacher quality. *Unit head:* Dr. Eustace Thompson, Chairperson, 516-463-5749, Fax: 516-463-6275, E-mail: eustace.g.thompson@hofstra.edu. *Application contact:* Sunil Samuel, Assistant Vice President of Admissions, 516-463-4723, Fax: 516-463-4664, E-mail: graduateadmission@hofstra.edu.
Website: http://www.hofstra.edu/education/

Holy Names University, Graduate Division, Department of Music, Oakland, CA 94619-1699. Offers Kodaly (Certificate); music education with Kodaly emphasis (MM); piano pedagogy (MM); vocal pedagogy (MM). *Students:* 1 (woman) full-time, 12 part-time (10 women); includes 5 minority (1 Black or African American, non-Hispanic/Latino; 2 Asian, non-Hispanic/Latino; 1 Native Hawaiian or other Pacific Islander, non-Hispanic/Latino; 1 Two or more races, non-Hispanic/Latino). Average age 37. 10 applicants, 60% accepted, 4 enrolled. In 2016, 4 master's, 2 Certificates awarded. *Degree requirements:* For master's, comprehensive exam, recital. *Entrance requirements:* For master's, audition; minimum undergraduate GPA of 2.6 overall, 3.0 in major. Additional exam requirements/recommendations for international students: Required—TOEFL (minimum score 550 paper-based; 79 iBT). *Application deadline:* For fall admission, 8/1 priority date for domestic students, 7/15 for international students; for spring admission, 12/1 priority date for domestic students, 12/1 for international students; for summer admission, 5/1 priority date for domestic students, 5/1 for international students. Applications are processed on a rolling basis. Application fee: $65. Electronic applications accepted. *Expenses: Tuition:* Full-time $17,532; part-time $974 per credit hour. *Required fees:* $500; $250 per credit hour. *Financial support:* Career-related internships or fieldwork, Federal Work-Study, scholarships/grants, and unspecified assistantships available. Support available to part-time students. Financial award application deadline: 3/2; financial award applicants required to submit FAFSA. *Faculty research:* Performance practice with special interest in Baroque, Romantic, and twentieth-century instrumental and vocal music; choral pedagogy; Hungarian music education. *Unit head:* Dr. Steven Hofer, Chair of Music Department, 510-436-1244, E-mail: hofer@hnu.edu. *Application contact:* 800-430-1321, Fax: 510-436-1325, E-mail: graduateadmissions@hnu.edu.

Howard University, Graduate School, Division of Fine Arts, Department of Music, Washington, DC 20059-0002. Offers applied music (MM); instrument (MM Ed); jazz studies (MM); organ (MM Ed); piano (MM Ed); voice (MM Ed). *Accreditation:* NASM. *Program availability:* Part-time. *Degree requirements:* For master's, comprehensive exam, thesis or alternative, departmental qualifying exam, recital. *Entrance requirements:* For master's, minimum GPA of 3.0, bachelor's degree in music or music education. Additional exam requirements/recommendations for international students: Required—TOEFL.

Hunter College of the City University of New York, Graduate School, School of Education, Program in Music Education, New York, NY 10065-5085. Offers MA. *Accreditation:* NCATE. *Degree requirements:* For master's, one foreign language, comprehensive exam, thesis, professional teaching portfolio, New York State Teacher Certification Exams. *Entrance requirements:* For master's, minimum GPA of 2.8, 2 letters of reference. Additional exam requirements/recommendations for international students: Required—TOEFL, TWE. *Application deadline:* For fall admission, 4/1 for domestic students, 2/1 for international students; for spring admission, 11/1 for domestic students, 9/1 for international students. Applications are processed on a rolling basis. *Financial support:* Federal Work-Study and tuition waivers (partial) available. Support available to part-time students. *Unit head:* Matthew Caballero, Education Program Coordinator, 212-772-4621, E-mail: mc1360@hunter.cuny.edu.

Indiana State University, College of Graduate and Professional Studies, College of Arts and Sciences, School of Music, Terre Haute, IN 47809. Offers conducting (MM); music education (MM); music performance (MM). *Accreditation:* NASM. *Degree requirements:* For master's, comprehensive exam, thesis, qualifying exam. Electronic applications accepted.

Indiana University of Pennsylvania, School of Graduate Studies and Research, College of Fine Arts, Department of Music, Program in Music Education, Indiana, PA 15705. Offers MA. *Faculty:* 14 full-time (4 women). *Students:* 7 part-time (4 women). Average age 26. 4 applicants, 100% accepted, 3 enrolled. In 2016, 3 master's awarded. *Application deadline:* Applications are processed on a rolling basis. Application fee: $50. Electronic applications accepted. *Expenses:* Tuition, state resident: full-time $8694; part-time $483 per credit. Tuition, nonresident: full-time $13,050; part-time $725 per credit. *Required fees:* $157 per credit. $50 per term. Tuition and fees vary according to course load and program. *Financial support:* Federal Work-Study and scholarships/grants available. *Unit head:* Dr. Matthew Baumer, Coordinator, 724-357-5646, E-mail: mbaumer@iup.edu. *Application contact:* Dr. Matthew Baumer, Graduate Coordinator, 724-357-5646, E-mail: matthew.baumer@iup.edu.
Website: http://www.iup.edu/music/grad/music-education-ma/

Inter American University of Puerto Rico, Metropolitan Campus, Graduate Programs, Program in Music Education, San Juan, PR 00919-1293. Offers MM.

Inter American University of Puerto Rico, San Germán Campus, Graduate Studies Center, Program in Music Education, San Germán, PR 00683-5008. Offers music (MA); music teacher education (MA). *Accreditation:* TEAC. *Program availability:* Part-time, evening/weekend.

Ithaca College, School of Music, Programs in Music and Music Education, Ithaca, NY 14850. Offers composition (MM); conducting (MM); music education (MM, MS); performance (MM); Suzuki pedagogy (MM). *Accreditation:* NASM. *Program availability:* Part-time. *Faculty:* 57 full-time (19 women), 4 part-time/adjunct (3 women). *Students:* 22 full-time (7 women), 28 part-time (14 women); includes 11 minority (1 Black or African American, non-Hispanic/Latino; 6 Asian, non-Hispanic/Latino; 2 Hispanic/Latino; 2 Two or more races, non-Hispanic/Latino), 7 international. Average age 25. 155 applicants, 36% accepted, 25 enrolled. In 2016, 20 master's awarded. *Degree requirements:* For master's, comprehensive exam (for some programs), thesis (for some programs). *Entrance requirements:* Additional exam requirements/recommendations for international students: Required—TOEFL (minimum score 550 paper-based; 80 iBT). *Application deadline:* For fall admission, 1/15 for domestic and international students; for spring admission, 12/1 for domestic and international students. Applications are processed on a rolling basis. Application fee: $40. Electronic applications accepted. *Expenses:* Contact institution. *Financial support:* In 2016–17, 47 students received support, including 46 teaching assistantships (averaging $9,458 per year); career-related internships or fieldwork, Federal Work-Study, scholarships/grants, and unspecified assistantships also available. Support available to part-time students. Financial award application deadline: 1/15; financial award applicants required to submit CSS PROFILE or FAFSA. *Unit head:* Dr. Les Black, Chair, Graduate Studies in Music, 607-274-7997, E-mail: lblack@ithaca.edu. *Application contact:* Nicole Eversley Bradwell, Director, Office of Admission, 607-274-3124, Fax: 607-274-1263, E-mail: admission@ithaca.edu.
Website: http://www.ithaca.edu/gradprograms/music

Jackson State University, Graduate School, College of Liberal Arts, Department of Music, Jackson, MS 39217. Offers music education (MM Ed). *Accreditation:* NASM. *Program availability:* Part-time, evening/weekend. *Degree requirements:* For master's, comprehensive exam, thesis or alternative. *Entrance requirements:* For master's, GRE General Test. Additional exam requirements/recommendations for international students: Required—TOEFL (minimum score 520 paper-based; 67 iBT). *Application deadline:* For fall admission, 3/1 priority date for domestic students, 3/1 for international students; for spring admission, 10/1 for domestic and international students. Applications are processed on a rolling basis. Application fee: $25. *Expenses:* Tuition, state resident: full-time $7141. Tuition, nonresident: full-time $17,494. *Required fees:* $1080. Tuition and fees vary according to class time, course level, course load, degree level, campus/location, program and student level. *Financial support:* Career-related internships or fieldwork, Federal Work-Study, scholarships/grants, and unspecified assistantships available. Support available to part-time students. Financial award application deadline: 3/1; financial award applicants required to submit FAFSA. *Unit head:* Dr. David Akombo, Interim Chair, 601-979-2141, Fax: 601-979-2568. *Application contact:* Fatoumatta Sisay, Manager of Graduate Admissions, 601-979-0342, Fax: 601-

979-4325, E-mail: fatoumatta.sisay@jsums.edu.
Website: http://www.jsums.edu/music/

James Madison University, The Graduate School, College of Visual and Performing Arts, Master of Music Program, Harrisonburg, VA 22802. Offers composition (MM); conducting (MM); music education (MM); performance (MM). *Accreditation:* NASM. *Program availability:* Part-time. *Faculty:* 39 full-time (12 women), 9 part-time/adjunct (3 women). *Students:* 18 full-time (9 women), 3 part-time (0 women); includes 5 minority (1 Black or African American, non-Hispanic/Latino; 3 Hispanic/Latino; 1 Two or more races, non-Hispanic/Latino), 2 international. Average age 30. 38 applicants, 68% accepted, 12 enrolled. In 2016, 10 master's awarded. Application fee: $55. Electronic applications accepted. *Financial support:* In 2016–17, 12 students received support, including 2 teaching assistantships with full tuition reimbursements available (averaging $8,837 per year); fellowships, Federal Work-Study, and 12 assistantships (averaging $7911) also available. Financial award application deadline: 3/1; financial award applicants required to submit FAFSA. *Unit head:* Dr. Jeffrey Bush, Director of the School of Music, 540-568-3614, E-mail: bushje@jmu.edu. *Application contact:* Lynette D. Michael, Director of Graduate Admissions, 540-568-6131 Ext. 6395, Fax: 540-568-7860, E-mail: michaeld@jmu.edu.
Website: http://www.jmu.edu/music/

Kent State University, College of the Arts, Hugh A. Glauser School of Music, Kent, OH 44242-0001. Offers conducting (MM); ethnomusicology (MA); music composition (MA); music education (MM, PhD); music theory (MA); music theory-composition (PhD); performance (MM), including chamber music. *Accreditation:* NASM. *Program availability:* Part-time, online learning. *Faculty:* 33 full-time (12 women). *Students:* 51 full-time (23 women), 167 part-time (120 women); includes 18 minority (8 Black or African American, non-Hispanic/Latino; 1 American Indian or Alaska Native, non-Hispanic/Latino; 1 Asian, non-Hispanic/Latino; 4 Hispanic/Latino; 1 Native Hawaiian or other Pacific Islander, non-Hispanic/Latino; 3 Two or more races, non-Hispanic/Latino), 25 international. Average age 32. 90 applicants, 86% accepted, 51 enrolled. In 2016, 95 master's, 2 doctorates awarded. *Degree requirements:* For master's, comprehensive exam (for some programs), thesis (for some programs), capstone project or thesis (for MM in music education); for doctorate, comprehensive exam, thesis/dissertation. *Entrance requirements:* For master's, transcripts; minimum GPA of 3.0; 3 letters of recommendation; goal statement; resume; writing sample (for MA in ethnomusicology); portfolio of original composition (for MA in composition); audition (for MM in conducting, performance); prior degree, teaching certificate, and 1 year of teaching experience (for MM in music education); for doctorate, writing sample; 3 letters of recommendation; curriculum vitae/resume; transcripts; minimum GPA of 3.0; prior degree in music education, teaching license, statement of purpose, video of teaching sample, 3 years of teaching, and interview (for music education); goal statement and 3 original compositions (for music theory-composition). Additional exam requirements/recommendations for international students: Required—TOEFL (minimum score of 525 paper-based, 71 iBT), IELTS (minimum score of 6), Michigan English Language Assessment Battery (minimum score of 75), or PTE (minimum score of 48). *Application deadline:* Applications are processed on a rolling basis. Application fee: $45 ($70 for international students). Electronic applications accepted. *Expenses:* Tuition, state resident: full-time $10,864; part-time $495 per credit hour. Tuition, nonresident: full-time $18,380; part-time $837 per credit hour. *Financial support:* Unspecified assistantships available. Financial award application deadline: 4/1. *Unit head:* Dr. Ralph Lorenz, Interim Director, 330-672-2172, E-mail: rlorenz@kent.edu. *Application contact:* Michael Chunn, Graduate Coordinator/Trumpet Professor, 330-672-9234, Fax: 330-672-7837, E-mail: mchunn@kent.edu.
Website: http://www.kent.edu/music/

Lake Forest College, Master of Arts in Teaching Program, Lake Forest, IL 60045. Offers elementary education (MAT); K-12 French (MAT); K-12 music (MAT); K-12 Spanish (MAT); K-12 visual art (MAT); secondary biology (MAT); secondary chemistry (MAT); secondary English (MAT); secondary history (MAT); secondary mathematics (MAT). *Degree requirements:* For master's, comprehensive exam, portfolio. *Entrance requirements:* For master's, GRE.

Lebanon Valley College, Program in Music Education, Annville, PA 17003-1400. Offers MME. *Accreditation:* NASM. *Program availability:* Part-time-only, evening/weekend. *Faculty:* 10 part-time/adjunct (2 women). *Students:* 18 part-time (11 women); includes 1 minority (Black or African American, non-Hispanic/Latino). Average age 34. 4 applicants, 100% accepted, 4 enrolled. In 2016, 16 master's awarded. *Degree requirements:* For master's, thesis or project. *Entrance requirements:* For master's, teaching certification, 2 years of teaching experience. Additional exam requirements/recommendations for international students: Required—TOEFL (minimum score 80 iBT). *Application deadline:* Applications are processed on a rolling basis. Application fee: $0. Electronic applications accepted. *Expenses:* $595 per credit hour. *Financial support:* Career-related internships or fieldwork and scholarships/grants available. Financial award application deadline: 3/1; financial award applicants required to submit FAFSA. *Faculty research:* Modern band, popular music pedagogy. *Unit head:* Cherie Van Zant, Graduate and Community Programs Administrator, 717-867-6383, E-mail: vanzant@lvc.edu. *Application contact:* Cherie VanZant, Graduate and Community Programs Administrator, 717-867-6383, E-mail: vanzant@lvc.edu.
Website: http://www.lvc.edu/academics/graduate-studies/master-of-music-education

Lee University, Program in Music, Cleveland, TN 37320-3450. Offers conducting (MM); music education (MM); music performance (MM); religious studies (MCM); sacred music (MCM). *Accreditation:* NASM. *Program availability:* Part-time. *Faculty:* 21 full-time (5 women), 5 part-time/adjunct (2 women). *Students:* 25 full-time (13 women), 9 part-time (7 women); includes 5 minority (3 Black or African American, non-Hispanic/Latino; 2 Asian, non-Hispanic/Latino), 10 international. Average age 28. 21 applicants, 67% accepted, 8 enrolled. In 2016, 17 master's awarded. *Degree requirements:* For master's, variable foreign language requirement, comprehensive exam, thesis, internship. *Entrance requirements:* For master's, placement exercises in music theory, music history, diction, and piano proficiency, audition, resume, interview, minimum GPA of 2.75, official transcripts, essay, 3 recommendations, immunization forms. Additional exam requirements/recommendations for international students: Required—TOEFL (minimum score 61 iBT). *Application deadline:* For fall admission, 4/1 priority date for domestic and international students; for spring admission, 10/1 priority date for domestic and international students. Applications are processed on a rolling basis. Application fee: $25. Electronic applications accepted. *Expenses: Tuition:* Full-time $11,367; part-time $632 per credit hour. *Required fees:* $35 per term. One-time fee: $25. Tuition and fees vary according to program. *Financial support:* In 2016–17, 30 students received support. Career-related internships or fieldwork, Federal Work-Study, institutionally sponsored loans, scholarships/grants, and unspecified assistantships available. Financial award application deadline: 3/1; financial award applicants required to submit FAFSA. *Unit head:* Dr. Brad J. Moffett, Director, 423-614-8240, Fax: 423-614-8245, E-mail: gradmusic@leeuniversity.edu.
Website: http://www.leeuniversity.edu/academics/graduate/music

Lehman College of the City University of New York, School of Arts and Humanities, Department of Music, Bronx, NY 10468-1589. Offers MAT. *Accreditation:* NCATE. *Program availability:* Part-time, evening/weekend. *Entrance requirements:* For master's, audition. *Faculty research:* Music and music education.

Lehman College of the City University of New York, School of Education, Department of Middle and High School Education, Program in Music Education, Bronx, NY 10468-1589. Offers MS Ed. *Program availability:* Part-time, evening/weekend.

Liberty University, School of Music, Lynchburg, VA 24515. Offers ethnomusicology (MA); music and worship (MA); music education (MA); worship studies (MA, DWS), including ethnomusicology (MA), leadership (MA). *Accreditation:* NASM. *Program availability:* Part-time, online learning. *Students:* 58 full-time (26 women), 184 part-time (90 women); includes 52 minority (42 Black or African American, non-Hispanic/Latino; 3 Asian, non-Hispanic/Latino; 2 Hispanic/Latino; 5 Two or more races, non-Hispanic/Latino), 8 international. Average age 38. 323 applicants, 24% accepted, 49 enrolled. In 2016, 39 master's, 1 doctorate awarded. *Entrance requirements:* For master's, minimum GPA of 3.0; interview; letter of recommendation; statement of purpose; bachelor's/master's degree in music, worship, or related field, or 5 years of experience. Additional exam requirements/recommendations for international students: Required—TOEFL (minimum score 600 paper-based; 100 iBT). *Application deadline:* Applications are processed on a rolling basis. Application fee: $50. Electronic applications accepted. *Financial support:* Applicants required to submit FAFSA. *Unit head:* Dr. Vernon Whaley, Dean, 434-592-3463, E-mail: vwhaley@liberty.edu. *Application contact:* Jay Bridge, Director of Admissions, 800-424-9595, Fax: 800-628-7977, E-mail: gradadmissions@liberty.edu.
Website: http://www.liberty.edu/academics/music/

Long Island University–LIU Post, College of Education, Information and Technology, Brookville, NY 11548-1300. Offers adolescence education (MS); adolescence education 7-12 (MS); archives and records management (AC); art education (MS); childhood education (MS); childhood teaching literacy B-6 (MS); childhood/special education (MS); clinical mental health counseling (MS, AC); early childhood education (MS); early childhood education/childhood education (MS); educational leadership (AC); educational technology (MS); information studies (PhD); interdisciplinary educational studies (Ed D); middle childhood education (MS); music education (MS); school counselor (MS); special education (MS Ed); speech-language pathology (MA); students with disabilities, 7-12 generalist (AC); TESOL (MA). *Accreditation:* TEAC. *Program availability:* Part-time, 100% online, blended/hybrid learning. *Faculty:* 55 full-time (35 women), 104 part-time/adjunct (57 women). *Students:* 464 full-time (390 women), 740 part-time (580 women); includes 265 minority (99 Black or African American, non-Hispanic/Latino; 45 Asian, non-Hispanic/Latino; 113 Hispanic/Latino; 1 Native Hawaiian or other Pacific Islander, non-Hispanic/Latino; 7 Two or more races, non-Hispanic/Latino), 33 international. 928 applicants, 76% accepted, 406 enrolled. In 2016, 334 master's, 10 doctorates, 137 other advanced degrees awarded. Terminal master's awarded for partial completion of doctoral program. *Degree requirements:* For master's, variable foreign language requirement, comprehensive exam (for some programs), thesis optional; for doctorate, comprehensive exam, thesis/dissertation. *Entrance requirements:* For master's and AC, GRE. Additional exam requirements/recommendations for international students: Required—PTE, TOEFL (minimum score 550 paper-based, 75 iBT) or IELTS. *Application deadline:* Applications are processed on a rolling basis. Application fee: $50. Electronic applications accepted. *Expenses: Tuition:* Full-time $28,272; part-time $1178 per credit. *Required fees:* $451 per term. Tuition and fees vary according to degree level and program. *Financial support:* Career-related internships or fieldwork, Federal Work-Study, institutionally sponsored loans, scholarships/grants, tuition waivers (partial), and unspecified assistantships available. Support available to part-time students. Financial award application deadline: 2/15; financial award applicants required to submit FAFSA. *Faculty research:* English language learners, early childhood literacy development through play, sleep, social justice through education, using a structured protocol for discussing bad news. *Total annual research expenditures:* $575,000. *Unit head:* Dr. Albert Inserra, Dean, 516-299-2210, E-mail: albert.inserra@liu.edu. *Application contact:* Carol Zerah, Director of Graduate Admissions, 516-299-2900, Fax: 516-299-2137, E-mail: post-enroll@liu.edu.
Website: http://liu.edu/CWPost/Academics/College-of-Education-Information-and-Technology

Louisiana State University and Agricultural & Mechanical College, Graduate School, College of Music and Dramatic Arts, School of Music, Baton Rouge, LA 70803. Offers music (MM, DMA, PhD); music education (PhD). *Accreditation:* NASM.

Loyola University Maryland, Graduate Programs, School of Education, Program in Kodaly Music Education, Baltimore, MD 21210-2699. Offers M Ed. *Faculty:* 34 full-time (22 women), 30 part-time/adjunct (24 women). *Students:* 42 full-time (34 women); includes 3 minority (all Black or African American, non-Hispanic/Latino). Average age 31. 22 applicants, 95% accepted, 20 enrolled. In 2016, 14 master's awarded. *Entrance requirements:* For master's, essay, letter of recommendation, resume, transcript. Additional exam requirements/recommendations for international students: Required—TOEFL (minimum score 550 paper-based), IELTS (minimum score 7). *Application deadline:* For fall admission, 5/1 for domestic students, 3/1 for international students. Applications are processed on a rolling basis. Application fee: $60. Electronic applications accepted. *Expenses:* Contact institution. *Financial support:* In 2016–17, 3 students received support. Scholarships/grants available. Financial award application deadline: 4/15; financial award applicants required to submit FAFSA. *Application contact:* Maureen Faux, Executive Director, Graduate Admissions, 410-617-5020, Fax: 410-617-2002, E-mail: graduate@loyola.edu.
Website: http://www.loyola.edu/soe/academics/graduate/kodaly.aspx

Manhattanville College, School of Education, Program in Music Education, Purchase, NY 10577-2132. Offers MAT. *Program availability:* Part-time, evening/weekend. *Students:* 4 applicants, 50% accepted, 1 enrolled. In 2016, 8 master's awarded. *Degree requirements:* For master's, comprehensive exam (for some programs), thesis (for some programs), student teaching, research seminars, portfolios, internships, writing assessment. *Entrance requirements:* For master's, audition, minimum undergraduate GPA of 3.0, 2 letters of recommendation. Additional exam requirements/recommendations for international students: Required—TOEFL (minimum score 85 iBT); Recommended—IELTS. *Application deadline:* For fall admission, 7/1 priority date for domestic and international students; for spring admission, 11/1 priority date for domestic and international students; for summer admission, 4/1 priority date for domestic and international students. Applications are processed on a rolling basis. Application fee: $75. Electronic applications accepted. *Expenses: Tuition:* Full-time $16,470; part-time $915 per credit. *Required fees:* $60 per semester. Part-time tuition and fees vary according to course load and program. *Financial support:* Teaching assistantships, career-related internships or fieldwork, Federal Work-Study, institutionally sponsored loans, scholarships/grants, and unspecified assistantships available. Financial award applicants required to submit FAFSA. *Unit head:* Jerry Kerlin, Program Director, 914-323-5256, E-mail: jerry.kerlin@mville.edu. *Application contact:* Jeanine Pardey-Levine, Director of Graduate Enrollment Management, 914-323-3208, Fax: 914-694-1732, E-mail: edschool@mville.edu.
Website: http://www.mville.edu/programs/music-education-graduate

Marywood University, Academic Affairs, Insalaco College of Creative and Performing Arts, Music, Theatre and Dance Department, Scranton, PA 18509-1598. Offers music education (MA). *Accreditation:* NASM. *Program availability:* Part-time. Electronic applications accepted.

McGill University, Faculty of Graduate and Postdoctoral Studies, Schulich School of Music, Montréal, QC H3A 2T5, Canada. Offers composition (M Mus, D Mus, PhD); music education (MA, PhD); music technology (MA, PhD); musicology (MA, PhD); performance (M Mus); performance studies (D Mus); sound recording (M Mus, PhD); theory (MA, PhD).

McKendree University, Graduate Programs, Programs in Education, Lebanon, IL 62254-1299. Offers curriculum design and instruction (Ed D, Ed S); educational administration and leadership (MA Ed); educational studies (MA Ed); higher education administrative services (MA Ed); music education (MA Ed); reading (MA Ed); special education (MA Ed); teacher leadership (MA Ed); teaching certification (MA Ed). *Accreditation:* NCATE. *Program availability:* Part-time, evening/weekend, online learning. *Entrance requirements:* For master's, official transcripts from all institutions previously attended, minimum GPA of 3.0, resume, references; for doctorate, GRE (within the past 5 years), master's degree in education and Ed S, or the equivalent, from regionally-accredited institution; official transcripts from all institutions previously attended; curriculum vitae/resume; essay/personal statement; two years of teaching/professional experience; for Ed S, GRE (within the past 5 years), master's degree in education from regionally-accredited institution of higher education; official transcripts from all institutions previously attended; curriculum vitae/resume; essay/personal statement; two years of teaching/professional experience. Additional exam requirements/recommendations for international students: Required—TOEFL. Electronic applications accepted.

McNeese State University, Doré School of Graduate Studies, College of Liberal Arts, Department of Performing Arts, Lake Charles, LA 70609. Offers music education (Postbaccalaureate Certificate), including Kodaly studies. *Program availability:* Evening/weekend. *Entrance requirements:* For degree, GRE.

Miami University, College of Creative Arts, Department of Music, Oxford, OH 45056. Offers music education (MM); music performance (MM). *Accreditation:* NASM. *Students:* 18 full-time (13 women), 1 (woman) part-time; includes 2 minority (both Hispanic/Latino), 8 international. Average age 26. In 2016, 6 master's awarded. *Expenses:* Tuition, state resident: full-time $12,890; part-time $564 per credit hour. Tuition, nonresident: full-time $29,604; part-time $1260 per credit hour. *Required fees:* $638. Part-time tuition and fees vary according to course load and program. *Unit head:* Dr. Bruce Murray, Chair and Professor, 513-529-3014, E-mail: bruce.murray@miamioh.edu. *Application contact:* Dr. Brenda Mitchell, Associate Professor of Music/Director of Graduate Studies, 513-529-1228, E-mail: mitchebs@miamioh.edu.
Website: http://www.miamioh.edu/music

Michigan State University, The Graduate School, College of Music, East Lansing, MI 48824. Offers collaborative piano (M Mus); jazz studies (M Mus); music (PhD); music composition (M Mus, DMA); music conducting (M Mus, DMA); music education (M Mus); music performance (M Mus, DMA); music theory (M Mus); music therapy (M Mus); musicology (MA); piano pedagogy (M Mus). *Accreditation:* NASM. *Entrance requirements:* Additional exam requirements/recommendations for international students: Required—TOEFL. Electronic applications accepted.

Minnesota State University Mankato, College of Graduate Studies and Research, College of Arts and Humanities, Department of Music, Mankato, MN 56001. Offers choral conducting (MM); music education (MAT); piano performance (MM); wind band conducting (MM). *Accreditation:* NASM. *Students:* 1 full-time (0 women), 7 part-time (4 women). *Degree requirements:* For master's, comprehensive exam, thesis or alternative. *Entrance requirements:* For master's, minimum GPA of 3.0 during previous 2 years, audition or test. Additional exam requirements/recommendations for international students: Required—TOEFL. *Application deadline:* For fall admission, 7/1 priority date for domestic students; for spring admission, 11/1 for domestic students. Applications are processed on a rolling basis. Application fee: $40. Electronic applications accepted. *Financial support:* Research assistantships with full tuition reimbursements, teaching assistantships with full tuition reimbursements, career-related internships or fieldwork, Federal Work-Study, and institutionally sponsored loans available. Support available to part-time students. Financial award application deadline: 3/15. *Unit head:* John Lindberg, Chairperson, E-mail: john.lindberg@mnsu.edu.
Website: http://www.mnsu.edu/music/

Mississippi College, Graduate School, College of Arts and Sciences, School of Christian Studies and the Arts, Department of Music, Clinton, MS 39058. Offers applied music performance (MM); conducting (MM); music education (MM); music performance: organ (MM); vocal pedagogy (MM). *Accreditation:* NASM. *Program availability:* Part-time, evening/weekend. *Degree requirements:* For master's, comprehensive exam, recital. *Entrance requirements:* For master's, GRE, minimum GPA of 2.5. Additional exam requirements/recommendations for international students: Recommended—TOEFL, IELTS. Electronic applications accepted.

Montclair State University, The Graduate School, College of Education and Human Services, MAT Program in Teaching, Montclair, NJ 07043-1624. Offers art (MAT); biology (MAT); chemistry (MAT); earth science (MAT); English (MAT); French (MAT); health and physical education (MAT); health education (MAT); mathematics (MAT); music (MAT); physical education (MAT); physical science (MAT); social studies (MAT); Spanish (MAT); teacher of English as a second language (MAT). *Degree requirements:* For master's, comprehensive exam, thesis or alternative. *Entrance requirements:* For master's, interview, 2 letters of recommendation. Additional exam requirements/recommendations for international students: Required—TOEFL (minimum score 83 iBT), IELTS (minimum score 6.5). Electronic applications accepted. *Expenses:* Tuition, state resident: part-time $553 per credit. Tuition, nonresident: part-time $854 per credit. *Required fees:* $91 per credit. Tuition and fees vary according to program.

Montclair State University, The Graduate School, College of the Arts, John J. Cali School of Music, Program in Music, Montclair, NJ 07043-1624. Offers music education (MA), music therapy (MA); performance (MA); theory/composition (MA). *Program availability:* Part-time, evening/weekend. *Degree requirements:* For master's, thesis. *Entrance requirements:* For master's, GRE General Test, 2 letters of recommendation, essay. Additional exam requirements/recommendations for international students: Required—TOEFL (minimum score 83 iBT), IELTS (minimum score 6.5). Electronic applications accepted. *Expenses:* Tuition, state resident: part-time $553 per credit. Tuition, nonresident: part-time $854 per credit. *Required fees:* $91 per credit. Tuition and fees vary according to program.

Morehead State University, Graduate Programs, Caudill College of Arts, Humanities and Social Sciences, Department of Music, Theatre and Dance, Morehead, KY 40351. Offers music education (MM); music performance (MM). *Accreditation:* NASM. *Program availability:* Part-time, evening/weekend. *Degree requirements:* For master's, comprehensive exam, oral and written exams. *Entrance requirements:* For master's, music entrance exam, BA in music with minimum GPA of 3.0, 2.5 overall; audition. Additional exam requirements/recommendations for international students: Required—TOEFL (minimum score 550 paper-based). Electronic applications accepted. *Faculty research:* Musical instrument digital interface (MIDI) applications, tonal concepts of euphonium and baritone horn, digital synthesis, computer-assisted instruction in music, musical composition.

Murray State University, College of Humanities and Fine Arts, Program in Music, Murray, KY 42071. Offers music education (MME). *Accreditation:* NASM. *Program availability:* Part-time. *Entrance requirements:* For master's, GRE General Test or MAT. Additional exam requirements/recommendations for international students: Required—TOEFL.

Nazareth College of Rochester, Graduate Studies, Department of Music, Program in Music Education, Rochester, NY 14618. Offers MS Ed. *Accreditation:* NASM; TEAC. *Program availability:* Part-time, evening/weekend. *Entrance requirements:* For master's, audition, minimum GPA of 3.0. Additional exam requirements/recommendations for international students: Required—TOEFL or IELTS. *Application deadline:* For fall admission, 4/1 for domestic students; for spring admission, 10/1 for domestic students. Application fee: $40. *Expenses: Tuition:* Part-time $880 per credit hour. Part-time tuition and fees vary according to course load, degree level and program. *Financial support:* Unspecified assistantships available. Financial award application deadline: 3/1; financial award applicants required to submit FAFSA. *Unit head:* Dr. Mary Carlson, Director, 585-389-2697, Fax: 585-389-2698, E-mail: mccarlso3@naz.edu. *Application contact:* Judith Baker, Director, Transfer and Graduate Admissions, 585-531-1154, Fax: 585-389-2826, E-mail: gradadmissions@naz.edu.
Website: http://www.naz.edu

New Jersey City University, William J. Maxwell College of Arts and Sciences, Department of Music, Dance and Theatre, Jersey City, NJ 07305-1597. Offers music education (MA); performance (MM). *Accreditation:* NASM. *Program availability:* Part-time, evening/weekend. *Degree requirements:* For master's, thesis optional, recital. *Entrance requirements:* Additional exam requirements/recommendations for international students: Required—TOEFL (minimum score 79 iBT).

New Mexico State University, College of Arts and Sciences, Department of Music, Las Cruces, NM 88003. Offers conducting (MM); music education (MM); performance (MM). *Accreditation:* NASM. *Program availability:* Part-time. *Faculty:* 16 full-time (6 women), 3 part-time/adjunct (0 women). *Students:* 12 full-time (6 women), 12 part-time (4 women); includes 9 minority (all Hispanic/Latino), 4 international. Average age 31. 17 applicants, 59% accepted, 8 enrolled. In 2016, 6 master's awarded. *Degree requirements:* For master's, comprehensive exam (for some programs), thesis (for some programs), recital. *Entrance requirements:* For master's, diagnostic exam, audition, bachelor's degree or equivalent from an accredited institution. Additional exam requirements/recommendations for international students: Required—TOEFL (minimum score 550 paper-based; 79 iBT), IELTS (minimum score 6.5). *Application deadline:* For fall admission, 7/1 priority date for domestic students; for spring admission, 11/1 for domestic students. Applications are processed on a rolling basis. Application fee: $40 ($50 for international students). Electronic applications accepted. *Expenses:* Tuition, state resident: full-time $4086. Tuition, nonresident: full-time $14,254. *Required fees:* $853. Tuition and fees vary according to course load. *Financial support:* In 2016–17, 10 students received support, including 1 fellowship (averaging $812 per year), 8 teaching assistantships (averaging $13,960 per year); career-related internships or fieldwork, Federal Work-Study, scholarships/grants, traineeships, health care benefits, and unspecified assistantships also available. Support available to part-time students. Financial award application deadline: 3/1. *Faculty research:* Music education, contemporary wind band literature, performance, music history, composition. *Total annual research expenditures:* $6,480. *Unit head:* Dr. Lon W. Chaffin, Department Head, 575-646-2421, Fax: 575-646-8199, E-mail: lchaffin@nmsu.edu. *Application contact:* Dr. James Shearer, Coordinator of Graduate Studies, 575-646-2601, Fax: 575-646-8199, E-mail: jshearer@nmsu.edu.
Website: http://music.nmsu.edu

New York University, Steinhardt School of Culture, Education, and Human Development, Department of Music and Performing Arts Professions, Program in Music Education, New York, NY 10010. Offers MA, Ed D, PhD. *Accreditation:* TEAC. *Program availability:* Part-time. *Degree requirements:* For master's, thesis (for some programs); for doctorate, thesis/dissertation. *Entrance requirements:* For master's, audition; for doctorate, GRE General Test, interview. Additional exam requirements/recommendations for international students: Required—TOEFL (minimum score 100 iBT). Electronic applications accepted. *Faculty research:* Music education philosophy; community music education; integrated curriculum; multiple intelligences; technology in arts education; cognition, emotion, and music.

New York University, Steinhardt School of Culture, Education, and Human Development, Department of Music and Performing Arts Professions, Program in Music Performance and Composition, New York, NY 10012. Offers instrumental performance (MM), including instrumental performance, jazz instrumental performance; music performance and composition (PhD), including music performance and composition; music theory and composition (MM), including composition for film and multimedia, composition for music theater, computer music composition, music theory and composition, songwriting; piano performance (MM), including collaborative piano, solo piano; vocal pedagogy (Advanced Certificate); vocal performance (MM), including classical voice, musical theatre performance. *Program availability:* Part-time. *Degree requirements:* For master's, thesis (for some programs); for doctorate, thesis/dissertation. *Entrance requirements:* For master's, audition; for doctorate, GRE General Test, audition, interview. Additional exam requirements/recommendations for international students: Required—TOEFL (minimum score 100 iBT). Electronic applications accepted. *Faculty research:* Aesthetics, performance analysis, twentieth century music, music methodologies for arts criticism and analysis.

Norfolk State University, School of Graduate Studies, School of Liberal Arts, Department of Music, Norfolk, VA 23504. Offers music (MM); music education (MM); performance (MM); theory and composition (MM). *Accreditation:* NASM. *Program availability:* Part-time. *Degree requirements:* For master's, thesis or alternative. *Entrance requirements:* For master's, minimum GPA of 2.7, letters of recommendation. Additional exam requirements/recommendations for international students: Required—TOEFL.

North Dakota State University, College of Graduate and Interdisciplinary Studies, College of Arts, Humanities and Social Sciences, Challey School of Music, Fargo, ND 58102. Offers conducting (MM, DMA); music education (MM); performance (MM, DMA). *Accreditation:* NASM. *Degree requirements:* For master's, 2 foreign languages, comprehensive exam, thesis or alternative, recitals; for doctorate, 2 foreign languages, comprehensive exam, thesis/dissertation or alternative, recitals. *Entrance requirements:* For master's and doctorate, music history, music theory, performance audition. Additional exam requirements/recommendations for international students: Required—TOEFL (minimum score 525 paper-based; 71 iBT). Electronic applications accepted. *Faculty research:* Performance, conducting.

North Dakota State University, College of Graduate and Interdisciplinary Studies, College of Human Development and Education, School of Education, Fargo, ND 58102. Offers agricultural education (M Ed, MS), including agricultural education; counselor education (M Ed, MS, PhD), including clinical mental health counseling (M Ed, MS), counselor education and supervision (PhD), school counseling (M Ed, MS); curriculum and instruction (M Ed, MS); education (PhD); educational leadership (M Ed, MS, Ed S);

family and consumer sciences education (M Ed, MS); history education (M Ed, MS); institutional analysis (Ed D); mathematics education (M Ed, MS); music education (M Ed, MS); occupational and adult education (Ed D); science education (M Ed, MS). *Accreditation:* NCATE. *Program availability:* Part-time, evening/weekend, online learning. *Degree requirements:* For master's, comprehensive exam; for doctorate, thesis/dissertation; for Ed S, thesis. *Entrance requirements:* For degree, GRE General Test, master's degree, minimum GPA of 3.25. Additional exam requirements/recommendations for international students: Required—TOEFL.

Northern State University, MME Program in Music Education, Aberdeen, SD 57401-7198. Offers MME. *Accreditation:* NASM. *Program availability:* Part-time, online learning. *Entrance requirements:* For master's, minimum GPA of 2.75. Additional exam requirements/recommendations for international students: Required—TOEFL (minimum score 550 paper-based; 78 iBT), IELTS (minimum score 6). Electronic applications accepted.

Northwestern University, Henry and Leigh Bienen School of Music, Department of Music Performance, Evanston, IL 60208. Offers brass performance (MM, DMA); conducting (MM, DMA); jazz studies (MM); percussion performance (MM, DMA); performance (MM); piano pedagogy (MME); piano performance (MM, DMA); piano performance and collaborative arts (MM, DMA); piano performance and pedagogy (MM, DMA); string performance (MM, DMA); voice and opera performance (MM, DMA); woodwind performance (MM, DMA). *Accreditation:* NASM. *Degree requirements:* For master's, recital; for doctorate, comprehensive exam, thesis/dissertation, 3 recitals. *Entrance requirements:* For master's, audition, prescreening auditions where required; for doctorate, audition, preliminary tapes. Additional exam requirements/recommendations for international students: Required—TOEFL (minimum score 80 iBT).

Northwestern University, Henry and Leigh Bienen School of Music, Department of Music Studies, Evanston, IL 60208. Offers composition (DMA); music education (MME, PhD); music theory and cognition (PhD); musicology (MM, PhD); theory (MM). PhD admissions and degree offered through The Graduate School. *Accreditation:* NASM. *Degree requirements:* For doctorate, comprehensive exam, thesis/dissertation. *Entrance requirements:* For master's, portfolio or research papers; for doctorate, GRE General Test (for PhD), portfolio, research papers. Additional exam requirements/recommendations for international students: Required—TOEFL (minimum score 600 paper-based; 80 iBT). *Faculty research:* Music cognition, cognitive learning, aesthetic education, computer music, technology in education.

Oakland University, Graduate Study and Lifelong Learning, College of Arts and Sciences, Department of Music, Rochester, MI 48309-4401. Offers music (MM); music education (PhD). *Accreditation:* NASM. *Entrance requirements:* For master's, minimum GPA of 3.0. Additional exam requirements/recommendations for international students: Required—TOEFL (minimum score 550 paper-based). Electronic applications accepted. *Expenses:* Contact institution.

Ohio University, Graduate College, College of Fine Arts, School of Music, Athens, OH 45701-2979. Offers accompanying (MM); composition (MM); conducting (MM); history/literature (MM); music education (MM); music therapy (MM); performance (MM, Certificate); performance/pedagogy (MM); theory (MM). *Accreditation:* NASM. *Program availability:* Part-time, evening/weekend, online learning. *Degree requirements:* For master's, comprehensive exam, thesis (for some programs), oral exam. *Entrance requirements:* For master's, audition, interview, portfolio, recordings (varies by program). Additional exam requirements/recommendations for international students: Required—TOEFL (minimum score 550 paper-based; 80 iBT) or IELTS (minimum score 6.5). *Application deadline:* For fall admission, 1/1 priority date for domestic and international students. Application fee: $50 ($55 for international students). Electronic applications accepted. *Financial support:* Teaching assistantships with full and partial tuition reimbursements, career-related internships or fieldwork, Federal Work-Study, institutionally sponsored loans, and tuition waivers (full and partial) available. Financial award application deadline: 1/1. *Unit head:* Dr. Christopher Hayes, Director, 740-593-4244, E-mail: hayesc1@ohio.edu. *Application contact:* Dr. Richard Wetzel, Graduate Chair, 740-593-1652, Fax: 740-593-1429, E-mail: wetzel@ohio.edu.
Website: http://www.finearts.ohio.edu/music

Oklahoma State University, College of Arts and Sciences, Department of Music, Stillwater, OK 74078. Offers pedagogy and performance (MM). *Accreditation:* NASM. *Faculty:* 31 full-time (12 women), 5 part-time/adjunct (4 women). *Students:* 10 full-time (4 women), 6 part-time (1 woman); includes 1 minority (Hispanic/Latino), 1 international. Average age 25. 39 applicants, 36% accepted, 10 enrolled. In 2016, 10 master's awarded. *Degree requirements:* For master's, final project, oral exam. *Entrance requirements:* For master's, GRE, audition. Additional exam requirements/recommendations for international students: Required—TOEFL (minimum score 550 paper-based; 79 iBT). *Application deadline:* For fall admission, 3/1 priority date for international students; for spring admission, 8/1 priority date for international students. Applications are processed on a rolling basis. Application fee: $40 ($75 for international students). Electronic applications accepted. *Expenses:* Tuition, state resident: full-time $3775; part-time $209.70 per credit hour. Tuition, nonresident: full-time $14,851; part-time $825.05 per credit hour. *Required fees:* $2027; $112.60 per credit hour. Tuition and fees vary according to campus/location. *Financial support:* In 2016–17, 14 teaching assistantships (averaging $11,411 per year) were awarded; career-related internships or fieldwork, Federal Work-Study, scholarships/grants, health care benefits, tuition waivers (partial), and unspecified assistantships also available. Support available to part-time students. Financial award application deadline: 3/1; financial award applicants required to submit FAFSA. *Faculty research:* Discovery and presentation of music literature of other countries, transportation of ancient music literature to modern notation. *Unit head:* Dr. Howard Potter, Department Head, 405-744-8997, Fax: 405-744-9324, E-mail: osumusic@okstate.edu.
Website: http://music.okstate.edu/

Old Dominion University, College of Arts and Letters, Master's in Music Education Program, Norfolk, VA 23529. Offers MME. *Accreditation:* NASM. *Program availability:* Part-time, evening/weekend. *Faculty:* 12 full-time (3 women), 2 part-time/adjunct (1 woman). *Students:* 9 full-time (5 women), 13 part-time (8 women); includes 8 minority (4 Black or African American, non-Hispanic/Latino; 1 Asian, non-Hispanic/Latino; 1 Hispanic/Latino; 2 Two or more races, non-Hispanic/Latino), 1 international. Average age 34. 8 applicants, 88% accepted, 7 enrolled. In 2016, 6 master's awarded. *Degree requirements:* For master's, comprehensive exam, thesis (for some programs), recital, ePortfolio. *Entrance requirements:* For master's, music theory exam, diagnostic examination, GRE, baccalaureate degree in music theory, history, education, or applied music; audition. Additional exam requirements/recommendations for international students: Required—TOEFL. *Application deadline:* Applications are processed on a rolling basis. Application fee: $50. Electronic applications accepted. *Expenses:* $478 per credit. *Financial support:* In 2016–17, 6 students received support, including 6 teaching assistantships (averaging $10,000 per year); scholarships/grants and unspecified assistantships also available. Financial award application deadline: 5/30; financial award applicants required to submit FAFSA. *Faculty research:* Performance, composition, conducting, music education research. *Unit head:* Dr. Nancy K. Klein, Graduate Program Director, 757-683-4061, E-mail: nklein@odu.edu. *Application contact:* Dr. David C. Earnest, Associate Dean, 757-683-6077, Fax: 757-683-5746, E-mail: dearnest@odu.edu.
Website: http://al.odu.edu/music/academics/grad.shtml

Oregon State University, College of Education, Program in Teaching, Corvallis, OR 97331. Offers clinically based elementary education (MAT); elementary education (MAT); language arts (MAT); mathematics (MAT); music education (MAT); science (MAT); social studies (MAT). *Program availability:* Part-time, blended/hybrid learning. *Faculty:* 17 full-time (8 women), 2 part-time/adjunct (both women). *Students:* 57 full-time (39 women), 22 part-time (18 women); includes 11 minority (2 Hispanic/Latino; 1 Native Hawaiian or other Pacific Islander, non-Hispanic/Latino; 8 Two or more races, non-Hispanic/Latino). Average age 29. 131 applicants, 76% accepted, 76 enrolled. In 2016, 92 master's awarded. *Entrance requirements:* For master's, CBEST. Additional exam requirements/recommendations for international students: Required—TOEFL (minimum score 575 paper-based). *Application deadline:* For fall admission, 12/1 for domestic students. Application fee: $60. *Expenses:* Contact institution. *Unit head:* Dr. Larry Flick, Dean. *Application contact:* E-mail: askcoed@oregonstate.edu.
Website: http://education.oregonstate.edu/mat

Penn State University Park, Graduate School, College of Arts and Architecture, School of Music, University Park, PA 16802. Offers composition-theory (M Mus); conducting (M Mus); music (MA); music education (MME, PhD, Certificate); pedagogy and performance (M Mus); performance (M Mus); piano performance (DMA). *Accreditation:* NASM. *Unit head:* Dr. Barbara O. Korner, Dean, 814-865-2592, Fax: 814-865-2018. *Application contact:* Lori Hawn, Director, Graduate Student Services, 814-865-1795, Fax: 814-863-4627, E-mail: l-gswww@lists.psu.edu.
Website: http://music.psu.edu/

Piedmont College, School of Education, Demorest, GA 30535. Offers art education (MAT); curriculum and instruction (Ed S); early childhood education (MA, MAT); instructional technology (MAT); middle grades education (MA, MAT); music education (MAT); secondary education (MA, MAT); special education (MA, MAT). *Program availability:* Part-time, evening/weekend. *Students:* 290 full-time (217 women), 614 part-time (508 women); includes 131 minority (97 Black or African American, non-Hispanic/Latino; 4 American Indian or Alaska Native, non-Hispanic/Latino; 5 Asian, non-Hispanic/Latino; 11 Hispanic/Latino; 6 Native Hawaiian or other Pacific Islander, non-Hispanic/Latino; 8 Two or more races, non-Hispanic/Latino), 6 international. Average age 37. 257 applicants, 64% accepted, 160 enrolled. In 2016, 288 master's, 243 other advanced degrees awarded. *Degree requirements:* For master's, thesis, field experience in the classroom teaching. *Entrance requirements:* For master's, GRE General Test, MAT, minimum undergraduate GPA of 2.5; for Ed S, minimum graduate GPA of 3.5, valid teaching certificate. Additional exam requirements/recommendations for international students: Required—TOEFL (minimum score 550 paper-based). *Application deadline:* For fall admission, 7/15 for domestic students; for spring admission, 12/1 for domestic students. Applications are processed on a rolling basis. Electronic applications accepted. *Expenses: Tuition:* Full-time $8910. *Financial support:* Career-related internships or fieldwork, Federal Work-Study, and unspecified assistantships available. Support available to part-time students. Financial award applicants required to submit FAFSA. *Unit head:* Dr. Don Gnecco, Dean, 706-778-3000 Ext. 1201, Fax: 706-776-9608, E-mail: dgnecco@piedmont.edu. *Application contact:* Kathleen Anderson, Director of Graduate Enrollment Management, 706-778-8500 Ext. 1181, Fax: 706-778-0150, E-mail: kanderson@piedmont.edu.

Pittsburg State University, Graduate School, College of Arts and Sciences, Department of Music, Pittsburg, KS 66762. Offers conducting (MM), including choral, instrumental - orchestral, instrumental - wind, organ, piano, voice; education (MM), including instrumental, vocal; performance (MM), including harpsichord, percussion, strings, winds. *Accreditation:* NASM. *Students:* 16 (11 women); includes 1 minority (Two or more races, non-Hispanic/Latino), 7 international. In 2016, 7 master's awarded. *Degree requirements:* For master's, thesis or alternative. *Entrance requirements:* Additional exam requirements/recommendations for international students: Required—TOEFL (minimum score 520 paper-based; 68 iBT), IELTS (minimum score 6), PTE (minimum score 47). *Application deadline:* For fall admission, 7/15 for domestic students, 6/1 for international students; for spring admission, 12/15 for domestic students, 10/15 for international students; for summer admission, 5/15 for domestic students, 4/1 for international students. Applications are processed on a rolling basis. Application fee: $35 ($60 for international students). Electronic applications accepted. *Expenses:* Contact institution. *Financial support:* In 2016–17, 5 teaching assistantships with full tuition reimbursements (averaging $5,500 per year) were awarded; career-related internships or fieldwork, Federal Work-Study, and unspecified assistantships also available. Financial award application deadline: 2/1; financial award applicants required to submit FAFSA. *Unit head:* Dr. Susan Marchant, Chairperson, 620-235-4466, E-mail: smarchant@pittstate.edu. *Application contact:* Lisa Allen, Assistant Director of Graduate and Continuing Studies, 620-235-4223, Fax: 620-235-4219, E-mail: lallen@pittstate.edu.

Plymouth State University, College of Graduate Studies, Graduate Studies in Education, Program in Music Education, Plymouth, NH 03264-1595. Offers M Ed. *Program availability:* Evening/weekend.

Portland State University, Graduate Studies, College of the Arts, School of Music, Portland, OR 97207-0751. Offers conducting (MMC); music education (MAT, MST); performance (MMP). *Accreditation:* NASM. *Program availability:* Part-time. *Faculty:* 25 full-time (8 women), 52 part-time/adjunct (18 women). *Students:* 31 full-time (13 women), 7 part-time (4 women); includes 5 minority (1 Asian, non-Hispanic/Latino; 4 Two or more races, non-Hispanic/Latino), 5 international. Average age 30. 40 applicants, 65% accepted, 16 enrolled. In 2016, 12 master's awarded. *Degree requirements:* For master's, variable foreign language requirement, exit exam. *Entrance requirements:* For master's, GRE General Test, departmental exam, minimum GPA of 3.0 in upper-division course work or 2.75 overall. Additional exam requirements/recommendations for international students: Required—TOEFL (minimum score 550 paper-based). *Application deadline:* For fall admission, 4/15 priority date for domestic students, 4/15 for international students; for winter admission, 10/1 for domestic and international students; for spring admission, 12/1 for domestic and international students; for summer admission, 1/15 for domestic and international students. Application fee: $65. *Expenses:* Contact institution. *Financial support:* Teaching assistantships, Federal Work-Study, scholarships/grants, and unspecified assistantships available. Support available to part-time students. Financial award application deadline: 3/1; financial award applicants required to submit FAFSA. *Faculty research:* Composition, music analysis, music history, jazz. *Unit head:* Bonnie Miksch, Director, 503-725-3063, Fax: 503-725-8215, E-mail: bonnie@pdx.edu. *Application contact:* Ron Babcock, Graduate Coordinator, 503-725-3181, E-mail: babcocr@pdx.edu.
Website: https://www.pdx.edu/music/

Queens College of the City University of New York, Arts and Humanities Division, Aaron Copland School of Music, Queens, NY 11367-1597. Offers classical performance (MM, Advanced Diploma); jazz studies (MM); music (MA); music (PreK-12) (MS Ed); performance (Advanced Certificate). *Program availability:* Part-time. *Faculty:* 26 full-time (7 women), 67 part-time/adjunct (32 women). *Students:* 17 full-time (4 women), 166 part-time (73 women); includes 58 minority (8 Black or African American, non-Hispanic/Latino; 19 Asian, non-Hispanic/Latino; 23 Hispanic/Latino; 8 Two or more races, non-Hispanic/Latino), 54 international. Average age 30. 197 applicants, 57% accepted, 61 enrolled. In 2016, 97 master's, 16 other advanced degrees awarded. *Degree requirements:* For master's, qualifying exams, recital. *Entrance requirements:* For master's, audition, bachelor's degree in music, minimum GPA of 3.0. Additional exam requirements/recommendations for international students: Required—TOEFL, IELTS. *Application deadline:* For fall admission, 4/1 for domestic students; for spring admission, 11/1 for domestic students. Applications are processed on a rolling basis. Application fee: $125. Electronic applications accepted. *Expenses:* Tuition, state resident: full-time $5065; part-time $425 per credit. Tuition, nonresident: part-time $780 per credit. *Required fees:* $522; $397 per credit. Part-time tuition and fees vary according to course load and program. *Financial support:* Career-related internships or fieldwork, Federal Work-Study, institutionally sponsored loans, and tuition waivers (partial) available. Support available to part-time students. Financial award application deadline: 4/1; financial award applicants required to submit FAFSA. *Unit head:* Dr. Edward Smaldone, Chair/Director, 718-997-3800, E-mail: edward.smaldone@qc.cuny.edu.

Queens College of the City University of New York, Division of Education, Department of Secondary Education and Youth Services, Queens, NY 11367-1597. Offers adolescent biology (MAT); art (MS Ed); biology (MS Ed, AC); chemistry (MS Ed, AC); earth sciences (MS Ed, AC); English (MS Ed, AC); French (MS Ed); Italian (MS Ed, AC); literacy education (MS Ed); mathematics (MS Ed, AC); music (MS Ed, AC); physics (MS Ed, AC); social studies (MS Ed, AC); Spanish (MS Ed, AC). *Program availability:* Part-time, evening/weekend. *Faculty:* 22 full-time (14 women), 40 part-time/adjunct (26 women). *Students:* 31 full-time (21 women), 356 part-time (211 women); includes 164 minority (22 Black or African American, non-Hispanic/Latino; 54 Asian, non-Hispanic/Latino; 81 Hispanic/Latino; 7 Two or more races, non-Hispanic/Latino), 11 international. Average age 29. 236 applicants, 88% accepted, 121 enrolled. In 2016, 119 master's, 51 other advanced degrees awarded. *Degree requirements:* For master's, research project. *Entrance requirements:* For master's, minimum GPA of 3.0. Additional exam requirements/recommendations for international students: Required—TOEFL, IELTS. *Application deadline:* For fall admission, 4/1 for domestic students; for spring admission, 11/1 for domestic students. Applications are processed on a rolling basis. Application fee: $125. Electronic applications accepted. *Expenses:* Tuition, state resident: full-time $5065; part-time $425 per credit. Tuition, nonresident: part-time $780 per credit. *Required fees:* $522; $397 per credit. Part-time tuition and fees vary according to course load and program. *Financial support:* Career-related internships or fieldwork available. Financial award application deadline: 4/1; financial award applicants required to submit FAFSA. *Unit head:* Dr. Eleanor Armour-Thomas, Chairperson, 718-997-5150, E-mail: armourthomas@yahoo.com.

Rhode Island College, School of Graduate Studies, Faculty of Arts and Sciences, Department of Music, Theatre, and Dance, Providence, RI 02908-1991. Offers music education (MAT, MM Ed). *Program availability:* Part-time, evening/weekend. *Faculty:* 9 full-time (4 women), 2 part-time/adjunct (0 women). *Students:* 2 full-time (both women), 1 part-time (0 women). Average age 35. In 2016, 4 master's awarded. *Degree requirements:* For master's, comprehensive exam, thesis, final project (MFA). *Entrance requirements:* For master's, GRE General Test or MAT; exams in music education, theory, history and literature, audition, 3 letters of recommendation, evidence of musicianship, interview. Additional exam requirements/recommendations for international students: Recommended—TOEFL (minimum score 550 paper-based; 79 iBT). *Application deadline:* For fall admission, 3/1 for domestic students; for spring admission, 11/1 for domestic students. Applications are processed on a rolling basis. Application fee: $50. Electronic applications accepted. *Expenses:* Tuition, state resident: full-time $8928; part-time $372 per credit. Tuition, nonresident: full-time $17,376; part-time $724 per credit. *Required fees:* $604; $22 per credit. One-time fee: $74. *Financial support:* In 2016–17, 1 teaching assistantship with full tuition reimbursement (averaging $3,500 per year) was awarded; Federal Work-Study, scholarships/grants, health care benefits, and unspecified assistantships also available. Support available to part-time students. Financial award application deadline: 5/15; financial award applicants required to submit FAFSA. *Unit head:* Prof. Ian Greitzer, Chair, 401-456-4654. *Application contact:* Graduate Studies, 401-456-8700.
Website: http://www.ric.edu/mtd/index.php

Rider University, Westminster Choir College, Program in Music Education, Lawrenceville, NJ 08648-3001. Offers MAT, MM, MME. *Entrance requirements:* For master's, audition, interview, repertoire list, 2 letters of reference, resume. Additional exam requirements/recommendations for international students: Required—TOEFL (minimum score 525 paper-based). Electronic applications accepted.

Rider University, Westminster Choir College, Programs in Music, Lawrenceville, NJ 08648-3001. Offers choral conducting (MM); composition (MM); organ performance (MM); piano accompanying and coaching (MM); piano pedagogy and performance (MM); piano performance (MM); sacred music (MM); vocal pedagogy and performance (MM); vocal training (MVP). *Accreditation:* NASM. *Program availability:* Part-time. *Degree requirements:* For master's, variable foreign language requirement, departmental qualifying exam. *Entrance requirements:* For master's, audition, interview, repertoire list, 2 letters of reference, resume. Additional exam requirements/recommendations for international students: Required—TOEFL (minimum score 525 paper-based). Electronic applications accepted.

Rutgers University–New Brunswick, Mason Gross School of the Arts, Music Department, New Brunswick, NJ 08901. Offers collaborative piano (MM, DMA); conducting: choral (MM, DMA); conducting: instrumental (MM, DMA); conducting: orchestral (MM, DMA); jazz studies (MM); music (DMA, AD); music education (MM, DMA); music performance (MM). *Accreditation:* NASM. *Degree requirements:* For doctorate, one foreign language. *Entrance requirements:* For master's and doctorate, audition. Additional exam requirements/recommendations for international students: Required—TOEFL (minimum score 550 paper-based), IELTS (minimum score 7). Electronic applications accepted. *Faculty research:* Performance, twentieth century music, jazz, music education.

St. Cloud State University, School of Graduate Studies, College of Liberal Arts, Department of Music, St. Cloud, MN 56301-4498. Offers conducting and literature (MM); music education (MM); piano pedagogy (MM). *Degree requirements:* For master's, comprehensive exam (for some programs), thesis or alternative. *Entrance requirements:* For master's, GRE General Test, minimum GPA of 2.75. Additional exam requirements/recommendations for international students: Required—TOEFL (minimum score 550 paper-based; 79 iBT), IELTS (minimum score 6.5), Michigan English Language Assessment Battery. Electronic applications accepted.

Saint Xavier University, Graduate Studies, School of Education, Chicago, IL 60655-3105. Offers counseling (MA); curriculum and instruction (MA); early childhood education (MA); educational administration (MA); elementary education (MA); individualized studies (MA), including educational technology, English as a second language (ESL), ISTEM (integrative science, technology, engineering, and math), science education; music education (MA); reading (MA); secondary education (MA); Spanish education (MA); special education (MA); teaching and leadership (MA). *Accreditation:* NCATE. *Program availability:* Part-time, evening/weekend. *Degree requirements:* For master's, thesis or project. *Entrance requirements:* For master's, minimum GPA of 3.0. *Expenses:* Contact institution.

Samford University, School of the Arts, Birmingham, AL 35229. Offers design studies (MS); music (MM); music education (MME). MME program offered in traditional, fifth year non-traditional, and national board cohort formats. *Accreditation:* NASM. *Program availability:* Part-time, evening/weekend, online learning. *Faculty:* 9 full-time (4 women), 3 part-time/adjunct (1 woman). *Students:* 11 full-time (5 women); includes 4 minority (all Black or African American, non-Hispanic/Latino), 1 international. Average age 30. 9 applicants, 100% accepted, 5 enrolled. In 2016, 7 master's awarded. Terminal master's awarded for partial completion of doctoral program. *Degree requirements:* For master's, comprehensive exam, recital. *Entrance requirements:* For master's, audition. Additional exam requirements/recommendations for international students: Required—TOEFL (minimum score 90 iBT). *Application deadline:* For fall admission, 11/15 for domestic and international students; for spring admission, 4/15 for domestic and international students; for summer admission, 8/1 for domestic and international students. Applications are processed on a rolling basis. Application fee: $35. Electronic applications accepted. *Expenses: Tuition:* Full-time $18,530; part-time $789 per credit hour. *Required fees:* $610. Tuition and fees vary according to course load, degree level, program and student level. *Financial support:* In 2016–17, 10 students received support. Federal Work-Study, scholarships/grants, and unspecified assistantships available. Financial award application deadline: 3/1; financial award applicants required to submit FAFSA. *Unit head:* Dr. Joseph Hopkin, Dean of the School of the Arts/Professor, 205-726-2778, Fax: 205-726-2615, E-mail: jhopkins@samford.edu. *Application contact:* Dr. Demondrae L. Thurman, Director of Graduate Studies/Professor of Music, 205-726-2389, Fax: 205-726-2615, E-mail: dthurman@samford.edu.
Website: http://www.samford.edu/arts

San Diego State University, Graduate and Research Affairs, College of Professional Studies and Fine Arts, School of Music and Dance, San Diego, CA 92182. Offers composition (acoustic and electronic) (MM); conducting (MM); ethnomusicology (MA); jazz studies (MM); musicology (MA); performance (MM); piano pedagogy (MA); theory (MA). *Degree requirements:* For master's, comprehensive exam (for some programs), thesis (for some programs). *Entrance requirements:* For master's, GRE General Test, bachelor's degree in related field, 2 letters of reference. Additional exam requirements/recommendations for international students: Required—TOEFL. Electronic applications accepted.

San Francisco Conservatory of Music, Graduate Division, San Francisco, CA 94102. Offers brass (MM), including bass trombone, horn, tenor trombone, trumpet, tuba; chamber music (MM, Artist Certificate), including cello, piano, preformed string quartet, viola, violin; composition (MM); conducting (MM); guitar (MM); harp (MM); percussion (MM), including marimba, timpani; piano (MM, MM), including harpsichord (MM), historical keyboard (MM), organ (MM). *Faculty:* 26 full-time (7 women), 94 part-time/adjunct (31 women). *Students:* 211 full-time (122 women), 2 part-time (0 women); includes 42 minority (6 Black or African American, non-Hispanic/Latino; 1 American Indian or Alaska Native, non-Hispanic/Latino; 20 Asian, non-Hispanic/Latino; 8 Hispanic/Latino; 1 Native Hawaiian or other Pacific Islander, non-Hispanic/Latino; 6 Two or more races, non-Hispanic/Latino), 83 international. Average age 25. 684 applicants, 39% accepted, 131 enrolled. In 2016, 99 master's, 29 other advanced degrees awarded. *Degree requirements:* For master's and Artist Certificate, variable foreign language requirement, 1-2 recitals, 1-3 juried performances. *Entrance requirements:* For master's and Artist Certificate, recommendations, transcripts, audition. Additional exam requirements/recommendations for international students: Required—TOEFL (minimum score 500 paper-based; 80 iBT). *Application deadline:* For fall admission, 12/1 for domestic and international students; for spring admission, 10/1 for domestic and international students. Application fee: $110. Electronic applications accepted. *Expenses: Tuition:* Full-time $42,400; part-time $1868 per credit. *Required fees:* $1010; $1010 per credit. One-time fee: $50 full-time. Tuition and fees vary according to course load. *Financial support:* In 2016–17, 212 students received support. Federal Work-Study, scholarships/grants, tuition waivers (partial), and unspecified assistantships available. Financial award application deadline: 2/15; financial award applicants required to submit FAFSA. *Unit head:* Kate Sheeran, Provost and Dean, 415-503-6251, Fax: 415-503-6205, E-mail: lnickels@sfcm.edu. *Application contact:* Melissa Cocco-Mitten, Director of Admission, 415-503-6231, Fax: 415-503-6299, E-mail: admit@sfcm.edu.
Website: http://www.sfcm.edu/

San Francisco State University, Division of Graduate Studies, College of Liberal and Creative Arts, School of Music, San Francisco, CA 94132-1722. Offers chamber music (MM); classical performance (MM); composition (MA); conducting (MM); music education (MA); music history (MA). *Accreditation:* NASM. *Expenses:* Tuition, state resident: full-time $6738. Tuition, nonresident: full-time $15,666. *Required fees:* $1012. Tuition and fees vary according to degree level and program. *Unit head:* Dr. Cyrus Ginwala, Director, 415-405-0486, Fax: 415-338-3294, E-mail: cginwala@sfsu.edu. *Application contact:* Easther Oh, Academic Office Coordinator, 415-338-7613, Fax: 415-338-3294, E-mail: music@sfsu.edu.
Website: http://music.sfsu.edu/

Shenandoah University, Shenandoah Conservatory, Winchester, VA 22601-5195. Offers church music (MM, Certificate); collaborative piano (MM); composition (MM); conducting (MM); music (Artist Diploma); music education (MME); music therapy (MMT); pedagogy - voice (MM, DMA); performance (MM, DMA); performing arts leadership and management (MS). *Accreditation:* NASM. *Program availability:* Part-time. *Faculty:* 36 full-time (13 women), 12 part-time/adjunct (6 women). *Students:* 70 full-time (40 women), 71 part-time (43 women); includes 25 minority (7 Black or African American, non-Hispanic/Latino; 2 American Indian or Alaska Native, non-Hispanic/Latino; 5 Asian, non-Hispanic/Latino; 11 Hispanic/Latino), 21 international. Average age 31. 121 applicants, 79% accepted, 47 enrolled. In 2016, 29 master's, 7 doctorates, 9 other advanced degrees awarded. *Degree requirements:* For master's, comprehensive exam, minimum GPA of 3.0, internship (MS), recital (MM), research teaching project or thesis (MME), project (MA); for doctorate, comprehensive exam, minimum GPA of 3.0, dissertation or teaching project, recital; for other advanced degree, minimum GPA of 3.0, research project, recital. *Entrance requirements:* For master's, music theory diagnostic exam, bachelor's degree with minimum of GPA of 2.5, performance audition, writing sample, resume, all academic transcripts; for doctorate, music theory diagnostic exam; music history diagnostic exam; vocal diction proficiency exam, master's degree with minimum GPA of 3.25, performance audition, 2 letters of recommendation, writing sample, resume, all academic transcripts; for other advanced degree, bachelor's or master's degree; minimum GPA of 2.5; performance audition (for Artist Diploma). Additional exam requirements/recommendations for international students: Required—TOEFL (minimum score 550 paper-based; 79 iBT), IELTS (minimum score 6.5). *Application deadline:* For fall and spring admission, 1/15 for domestic and international students; for summer admission, 4/15 for domestic and international students. Application fee: $30. Electronic applications accepted. *Expenses:* Contact institution. *Financial support:* In 2016–17, 43 students received support. Scholarships/grants and unspecified assistantships available. Financial award applicants required to submit FAFSA. *Faculty research:* Brahms, Scriabin, arts as inquiry. *Unit head:* Dr. Michael J. Stepniak, Dean, 540-542.6201, Fax: 540-665-5402, E-mail: mstepnia@su.edu.

Music Education

Application contact: Andrew Woodall, Executive Director of Recruitment and Advancement, 540-665-4581, Fax: 540-665-4627, E-mail: admit@su.edu.
Website: http://www.su.edu/conservatory/

Southern Illinois University Edwardsville, Graduate School, College of Arts and Sciences, Department of Music, Program in Music, Edwardsville, IL 62026-0001. Offers music education (MM); music performance (MM). *Accreditation:* NASM. *Program availability:* Part-time. *Degree requirements:* For master's, one foreign language, thesis (for some programs), recital. *Entrance requirements:* Additional exam requirements/recommendations for international students: Required—TOEFL (minimum score 550 paper-based; 79 iBT), IELTS (minimum score 6.5). Electronic applications accepted.

Southern Illinois University Edwardsville, Graduate School, College of Arts and Sciences, Department of Music, Program in Piano Pedagogy, Edwardsville, IL 62026. Offers Postbaccalaureate Certificate. *Program availability:* Part-time. *Entrance requirements:* Additional exam requirements/recommendations for international students: Required—TOEFL (minimum score 550 paper-based; 79 iBT), IELTS (minimum score 6.5). Electronic applications accepted.

Southern Illinois University Edwardsville, Graduate School, College of Arts and Sciences, Department of Music, Program in Vocal Pedagogy, Edwardsville, IL 62026. Offers Postbaccalaureate Certificate. *Program availability:* Part-time. *Entrance requirements:* Additional exam requirements/recommendations for international students: Required—TOEFL (minimum score 550 paper-based; 79 iBT), IELTS (minimum score 6.5). Electronic applications accepted.

Southern Methodist University, Meadows School of the Arts, Division of Music, Dallas, TX 75275. Offers composition (MM); conducting (MM), including choral, instrumental; music education (MM); music history and literature (MM); performance (MM), including harpsichord, orchestral instrument, organ, piano, voice; piano performance and pedagogy (MM); theory pedagogy (MM). *Accreditation:* NASM. *Program availability:* Part-time. *Degree requirements:* For master's, variable foreign language requirement, comprehensive exam, project, recital, or thesis. *Entrance requirements:* For master's, placement exams in music history and theory, audition; bachelor's degree in music or equivalent; minimum GPA of 3.0; research paper in history, theory, education. Additional exam requirements/recommendations for international students: Required—TOEFL (minimum score 550 paper-based; 80 iBT). Electronic applications accepted. *Faculty research:* Music perception and cognition, computer-based instruction, music medicine and therapy, theoretical and historical analysis-medieval to contemporary.

Southern Utah University, Program in Music, Cedar City, UT 84720-2498. Offers music education (MM Ed); music technology (MM). *Program availability:* Part-time, 100% online. *Faculty:* 2 full-time (1 woman), 3 part-time/adjunct (0 women). *Students:* 13 full-time (4 women), 8 part-time (2 women); includes 1 minority (Hispanic/Latino). Average age 30. 15 applicants, 100% accepted, 14 enrolled. *Entrance requirements:* Additional exam requirements/recommendations for international students: Required—TOEFL (minimum score 550 paper-based; 79 iBT), IELTS (minimum score 6). Application fee: $60 ($65 for international students). *Expenses:* $7,692 per year resident or online full-time; $23,384 per year on-campus non-resident full-time. *Unit head:* Dr. Keith Bradshaw, Department Chair, 435-586-7891, E-mail: bradshaw@suu.edu.

Southwestern Oklahoma State University, College of Arts and Sciences, Department of Music, Weatherford, OK 73096-3098. Offers music education (MM); performance (MM). *Accreditation:* NASM. *Program availability:* Part-time. *Degree requirements:* For master's, comprehensive exam, recital (music performance). *Entrance requirements:* For master's, minimum GPA of 2.5. Additional exam requirements/recommendations for international students: Required—TOEFL.

State University of New York at Fredonia, School of Music, Fredonia, NY 14063. Offers music education (MM); music performance (MM); music theory/composition (MM); music therapy (MM). *Accreditation:* NASM. *Program availability:* Part-time. *Faculty:* 44 full-time (17 women), 58 part-time/adjunct (31 women). *Students:* 31 full-time (21 women), 14 part-time (11 women); includes 4 minority (2 Asian, non-Hispanic/Latino; 1 Hispanic/Latino; 1 Two or more races, non-Hispanic/Latino), 12 international. Average age 25. 46 applicants, 72% accepted, 14 enrolled. In 2016, 16 master's awarded. *Degree requirements:* For master's, comprehensive exam (for some programs), thesis or final project/recital. *Entrance requirements:* For master's, audition. Additional exam requirements/recommendations for international students: Required—TOEFL (minimum score 79 iBT), IELTS (minimum score 6.5). *Application deadline:* For fall admission, 4/1 priority date for domestic and international students; for spring admission, 11/1 priority date for domestic students, 11/1 for international students. Applications are processed on a rolling basis. Application fee: $75. Electronic applications accepted. *Expenses:* Tuition, state resident: full-time $10,370; part-time $453 per credit. Tuition, nonresident: full-time $20,190; part-time $925 per credit. *Required fees:* $1619; $67.30 per credit hour. $403.80 per semester. *Financial support:* In 2016–17, 14 students received support, including 4 fellowships (averaging $7,314 per year). Financial award application deadline: 3/15; financial award applicants required to submit FAFSA. *Unit head:* Dr. Melvin Unger, Director, School of Music, 716-673-3151, E-mail: melvin.unger@fredonia.edu. *Application contact:* Dr. Barry Kilpatrick, Admissions Coordinator, School of Music, 716-673-4635, E-mail: barry.kilpatrick@fredonia.edu.
Website: http://www.fredonia.edu/music/

State University of New York College at Potsdam, Crane School of Music, Potsdam, NY 13676. Offers music education (MM); music performance (MM). *Program availability:* Part-time. *Degree requirements:* For master's, variable foreign language requirement, thesis (for some programs). *Entrance requirements:* For master's, audition, minimum GPA of 3.0. Additional exam requirements/recommendations for international students: Required—TOEFL (minimum score 550 paper-based; 80 iBT), IELTS (minimum score 6). Electronic applications accepted.

Syracuse University, School of Education, MM/MS Programs in Music Education, Syracuse, NY 13244. Offers MM, MS. *Accreditation:* NASM. *Program availability:* Part-time. *Students:* Average age 23. *Degree requirements:* For master's, thesis or alternative. *Entrance requirements:* For master's, GRE, bachelor's degree in music from institution accredited by the National Association of Schools of Music (NASM). Additional exam requirements/recommendations for international students: Required—TOEFL (minimum score 100 iBT). *Application deadline:* For fall admission, 1/15 priority date for domestic and international students; for spring admission, 10/15 priority date for domestic and international students; for summer admission, 4/1 priority date for domestic and international students. Applications are processed on a rolling basis. Application fee: $75. Electronic applications accepted. *Expenses: Tuition:* Full-time $25,974; part-time $1443 per credit hour. *Required fees:* $802; $50 per course. Tuition and fees vary according to course load and program. *Financial support:* Fellowships with full tuition reimbursements, research assistantships, teaching assistantships with tuition reimbursements, career-related internships or fieldwork, and scholarships/grants available. Financial award application deadline: 1/15. *Faculty research:* Developing optimal teaching competencies, artistry and musicianship, philosophical perspectives of music, theoretical and historical perspectives of music and music education. *Unit head:* Elisa Macedo Dekaney, Coordinator, 315-443-4854, E-mail: emdekane@syr.edu. *Application contact:* Speranza Migliore, Graduate Admissions Recruiter, 315-443-2505, E-mail: gradrcrt@syr.edu.
Website: http://soe.syr.edu/academic/teaching_and_leadership/graduate/masters/music_education/default.aspx

Tarleton State University, College of Graduate Studies, College of Liberal and Fine Arts, Department of Fine Arts, Stephenville, TX 76402. Offers music education (MM). *Accreditation:* NASM. *Program availability:* Part-time, evening/weekend. *Faculty:* 2 full-time (both women). *Students:* 3 full-time (all women), 8 part-time (all women); includes 4 minority (1 Black or African American, non-Hispanic/Latino; 3 Hispanic/Latino). 3 applicants, 100% accepted, 3 enrolled. In 2016, 8 master's awarded. *Degree requirements:* For master's, comprehensive exam, thesis optional. *Entrance requirements:* For master's, GRE, minimum GPA of 3.0. Additional exam requirements/recommendations for international students: Required—TOEFL (minimum score 550 paper-based; 80 iBT). *Application deadline:* For fall admission, 8/15 priority date for domestic students; for spring admission, 1/7 for domestic students. Applications are processed on a rolling basis. Application fee: $45 ($145 for international students). Electronic applications accepted. *Expenses:* $3,672 tuition; $2,437 fees. *Financial support:* Research assistantships, institutionally sponsored loans, and scholarships/grants available. Financial award application deadline: 5/1; financial award applicants required to submit FAFSA. *Unit head:* Dr. Teresa Davidian, Head, 254-968-9245, Fax: 254-968-9239, E-mail: davidian@tarleton.edu. *Application contact:* Information Contact, 254-968-9104, Fax: 254-968-9670, E-mail: gradoffice@tarleton.edu.

Teachers College, Columbia University, Department of Arts and Humanities, New York, NY 10027. Offers applied linguistics (MA, Ed D); art and art education (Ed M, MA, Ed D, Ed DCT); arts administration (MA); bilingual and bicultural education (MA); global competence (Certificate); history and education (Ed D, PhD); music and music education (Ed DCT); philosophy and education (MA, Ed D, PhD); social studies education (Ed M, PhD); teaching English to speakers of other languages (Ed M); teaching of English and English education (Ed M, MA, Ed D, PhD), including English education (Ed M, Ed D, PhD), teaching of English (MA); teaching of social studies (MA); TESOL (MA, Ed D). *Program availability:* Part-time, evening/weekend. *Students:* 429 full-time (329 women), 467 part-time (332 women); includes 268 minority (62 Black or African American, non-Hispanic/Latino; 1 American Indian or Alaska Native, non-Hispanic/Latino; 108 Asian, non-Hispanic/Latino; 76 Hispanic/Latino; 21 Two or more races, non-Hispanic/Latino), 212 international. 1,068 applicants, 53% accepted, 272 enrolled. Terminal master's awarded for partial completion of doctoral program. *Expenses: Tuition:* Full-time $36,288; part-time $1512 per credit. *Required fees:* $438 per semester. One-time fee: $510 full-time. Full-time tuition and fees vary according to course load. *Financial support:* Fellowships, research assistantships, teaching assistantships, career-related internships or fieldwork, Federal Work-Study, institutionally sponsored loans, tuition waivers (full and partial), and unspecified assistantships available. Support available to part-time students. *Unit head:* Prof. William Gaudelli, Department Chair, 212-678-3150, E-mail: wg74@columbia.edu. *Application contact:* David Estrella, Director of Admissions, 212-678-3305, Fax: 212-678-4171, E-mail: estrella@tc.columbia.edu.
Website: http://www.tc.edu/a%26h/

Temple University, Center for the Performing and Cinematic Arts, Boyer College of Music and Dance, Department of Music, Philadelphia, PA 19122-6096. Offers choral conducting (MM); collaborative piano/chamber music (MM); collaborative piano/opera coaching (MM); composition (MM, PhD); instrumental conducting (MM); music education (MM, PhD); music history (MM); music performance (MM, DMA), including instrumental studies (MM), keyboard (DMA), keyboard studies (MM), voice (DMA), voice and opera (MM); music studies (PhD); music theory (MM, PhD); music therapy (MMT, PhD); musicology (MM, PhD); opera (MM); piano pedagogy (MM); string pedagogy (MM). *Accreditation:* NASM. *Program availability:* Part-time, online learning. *Faculty:* 39 full-time (17 women), 38 part-time/adjunct (16 women). *Students:* 205 full-time (121 women), 37 part-time (23 women); includes 39 minority (10 Black or African American, non-Hispanic/Latino; 12 Asian, non-Hispanic/Latino; 10 Hispanic/Latino; 7 Two or more races, non-Hispanic/Latino), 89 international. 379 applicants, 66% accepted, 95 enrolled. In 2016, 54 master's, 10 doctorates awarded. Terminal master's awarded for partial completion of doctoral program. *Degree requirements:* For doctorate, thesis/dissertation. *Entrance requirements:* Additional exam requirements/recommendations for international students: Required—TOEFL. *Application deadline:* For fall admission, 11/15 for international students; for spring admission, 8/1 for international students. Applications are processed on a rolling basis. Application fee: $60. Electronic applications accepted. *Financial support:* Fellowships with tuition reimbursements, research assistantships with tuition reimbursements, teaching assistantships with tuition reimbursements, career-related internships or fieldwork, Federal Work-Study, scholarships/grants, health care benefits, and unspecified assistantships available. Financial award application deadline: 3/1; financial award applicants required to submit FAFSA. *Unit head:* Dr. Robert Stroker, Dean, 215-204-8598, Fax: 215-204-4957, E-mail: rstroker@temple.edu. *Application contact:* James Short, Assistant Dean, Undergraduate and Graduate Admissions, 215-204-8301, Fax: 215-204-8598, E-mail: james.short@temple.edu.
Website: http://www.temple.edu/boyer/academicprograms/

Tennessee Technological University, College of Graduate Studies, College of Education, Department of Curriculum and Instruction, Program in Music, Cookeville, TN 38505. Offers MA. *Accreditation:* NASM. *Program availability:* Part-time, evening/weekend. *Students:* 3 full-time (1 woman). 1 applicant. *Degree requirements:* For master's, comprehensive exam, thesis or alternative. *Entrance requirements:* For master's, MAT or GRE. Additional exam requirements/recommendations for international students: Required—TOEFL (minimum score 527 paper-based; 71 iBT), IELTS (minimum score 5.5), PTE (minimum score 48), or TOEIC (Test of English as an International Communication). *Application deadline:* For fall admission, 8/1 for domestic students, 5/1 for international students; for spring admission, 12/1 for domestic students, 10/1 for international students; for summer admission, 5/1 for domestic students, 2/1 for international students. Applications are processed on a rolling basis. Application fee: $35 ($40 for international students). Electronic applications accepted. *Expenses:* Tuition, state resident: full-time $9375; part-time $534 per credit hour. Tuition, nonresident: full-time $22,443; part-time $1260 per credit hour. *Financial support:* Career-related internships or fieldwork available. *Unit head:* Dr. Jeremy Wendt, Interim Chairperson, 931-372-3181, Fax: 931-372-6270, E-mail: jwendt@tntech.edu. *Application contact:* Shelia K. Kendrick, Coordinator of Graduate Studies, 931-372-3808, Fax: 931-372-3497, E-mail: skendrick@tntech.edu.

Texas A&M University–Kingsville, College of Graduate Studies, College of Arts and Sciences, Department of Music, Program in Music Education, Kingsville, TX 78363. Offers elementary music (MM); instrumental (MM); vocal (MM).

Texas Christian University, College of Fine Arts, School of Music, Doctoral Programs in Music, Fort Worth, TX 76129. Offers composition (DMA), including music history; conducting (DMA), including music history, music theory; performance (DMA), including music history, music theory, piano pedagogy; piano pedagogy (DMA). *Accreditation:* NASM. *Faculty:* 38 full-time (6 women), 12 part-time/adjunct (4 women). *Students:* 10 full-time (1 woman), 6 part-time (3 women); includes 1 minority (Two or more races, non-

Hispanic/Latino), 4 international. Average age 32. 27 applicants, 30% accepted, 5 enrolled. In 2016, 2 doctorates awarded. *Degree requirements:* For doctorate, comprehensive exam, thesis/dissertation. *Entrance requirements:* For doctorate, GRE General Test. Additional exam requirements/recommendations for international students: Required—TOEFL (minimum score 100 iBT). *Application deadline:* For spring admission, 12/1 for domestic and international students. Application fee: $80. Electronic applications accepted. *Expenses: Tuition:* Full-time $26,640; part-time $1480 per credit hour. *Required fees:* $48. Tuition and fees vary according to program. *Financial support:* In 2016–17, 9 students received support, including 10 research assistantships with full tuition reimbursements available (averaging $10,000 per year); career-related internships or fieldwork, institutionally sponsored loans, scholarships/grants, tuition waivers (full and partial), and unspecified assistantships also available. Financial award application deadline: 12/1; financial award applicants required to submit CSS PROFILE or FAFSA. *Unit head:* Dr. Richard C. Gipson, Director, 817-257-6606, Fax: 817-257-5818, E-mail: r.gipson@tcu.edu. *Application contact:* Donna Smolik, TCU College of Fine Arts Graduate Office, 817-257-7603, Fax: 817-257-5672, E-mail: cfagradinfo@tcu.edu.
Website: http://www.music.tcu.edu

Texas Christian University, College of Fine Arts, School of Music, Master's Programs in Music, Fort Worth, TX 76129. Offers conducting (M Mus); music education (MM Ed); music theory (M Mus); musicology (M Mus); performance (M Mus), including piano, strings, voice, winds/percussion; piano pedagogy (M Mus); voice pedagogy (M Mus). *Faculty:* 38 full-time (6 women), 12 part-time/adjunct (4 women). *Students:* 41 full-time (20 women); includes 5 minority (2 Asian, non-Hispanic/Latino; 2 Hispanic/Latino; 1 Two or more races, non-Hispanic/Latino), 11 international. Average age 25. 60 applicants, 45% accepted, 19 enrolled. In 2016, 22 master's awarded. *Degree requirements:* For master's, comprehensive exam. *Entrance requirements:* For master's, GRE General Test. Additional exam requirements/recommendations for international students: Required—TOEFL (minimum score 80 iBT). *Application deadline:* For fall admission, 3/1 for domestic and international students. Application fee: $80. Electronic applications accepted. *Expenses: Tuition:* Full-time $26,640; part-time $1480 per credit hour. *Required fees:* $48. Tuition and fees vary according to program. *Financial support:* In 2016–17, 41 students received support, including 41 research assistantships with full tuition reimbursements available (averaging $6,000 per year); career-related internships or fieldwork, institutionally sponsored loans, scholarships/grants, tuition waivers (full and partial), and unspecified assistantships also available. Financial award application deadline: 3/1; financial award applicants required to submit CSS PROFILE or FAFSA. *Unit head:* Dr. Richard C. Gipson, Director, 817-257-6606, Fax: 817-257-5818, E-mail: music@tcu.edu. *Application contact:* Donna Smolik, TCU College of Fine Arts Graduate Office, 817-257-7603, Fax: 817-257-5672, E-mail: cfagradinfo@tcu.edu.
Website: http://www.music.tcu.edu

Texas State University, The Graduate College, College of Fine Arts and Communication, Program in Music Education, San Marcos, TX 78666. Offers MM. *Accreditation:* NASM. *Program availability:* Part-time. *Faculty:* 6 full-time (1 woman), 3 part-time/adjunct (1 woman). *Students:* 6 full-time (3 women), 5 part-time (2 women); includes 2 minority (both Hispanic/Latino). Average age 31. 8 applicants, 63% accepted, 3 enrolled. In 2016, 4 master's awarded. *Degree requirements:* For master's, comprehensive exam. *Entrance requirements:* For master's, baccalaureate degree from regionally-accredited institution with minimum GPA of 2.75 in last 60 hours of undergraduate course work, statement of purpose, resume, 3 letters of reference, music portfolio. Additional exam requirements/recommendations for international students: Required—TOEFL (minimum score 550 paper-based; 78 iBT), IELTS (minimum score 6.5). *Application deadline:* For fall admission, 1/15 priority date for domestic students, 1/1 priority date for international students; for spring admission, 10/15 priority date for domestic students, 10/1 for international students; for summer admission, 4/15 for domestic students, 3/15 for international students. Applications are processed on a rolling basis. Application fee: $40 ($90 for international students). Electronic applications accepted. *Expenses:* $4,851 per semester. *Financial support:* In 2016–17, 8 students received support, including 5 teaching assistantships (averaging $8,436 per year); career-related internships or fieldwork, Federal Work-Study, institutionally sponsored loans, scholarships/grants, and unspecified assistantships also available. Support available to part-time students. Financial award application deadline: 3/1; financial award applicants required to submit FAFSA. *Unit head:* Dr. Jason Kwak, Graduate Advisor, 512-245-3390, Fax: 512-245-8181, E-mail: jk45@txstate.edu. *Application contact:* Dr. Andrea Golato, Dean of Graduate School, 512-245-2581, Fax: 512-245-8365, E-mail: gradcollege@txstate.edu.
Website: http://www.finearts.txstate.edu/music/

Texas Tech University, Graduate School, J.T. and Margaret Talkington College of Visual and Performing Arts, School of Music, Lubbock, TX 79409-2033. Offers music (MM, DMA); music education (MM Ed). *Accreditation:* NASM. *Program availability:* Part-time. *Faculty:* 55 full-time (20 women), 6 part-time/adjunct (4 women). *Students:* 97 full-time (37 women), 27 part-time (16 women); includes 22 minority (4 Black or African American, non-Hispanic/Latino; 16 Hispanic/Latino; 2 Two or more races, non-Hispanic/Latino), 36 international. Average age 30. 119 applicants, 53% accepted, 37 enrolled. In 2016, 34 master's, 25 doctorates awarded. *Degree requirements:* For master's, thesis or alternative; for doctorate, comprehensive exam (for some programs), thesis/dissertation. *Entrance requirements:* For master's, GRE General Test. Additional exam requirements/recommendations for international students: Required—TOEFL (minimum score 550 paper-based; 79 iBT). *Application deadline:* For fall admission, 6/1 priority date for domestic students, 1/15 priority date for international students; for spring admission, 9/1 priority date for domestic students, 6/15 priority date for international students. Applications are processed on a rolling basis. Application fee: $75. Electronic applications accepted. *Expenses:* $325 per credit hour full-time resident tuition, $733 per credit hour full-time non-resident tuition; $53.75 per credit hour fee plus $608 per term fee. *Financial support:* In 2016–17, 143 students received support, including 125 fellowships (averaging $2,194 per year), 4 research assistantships (averaging $7,011 per year), 101 teaching assistantships (averaging $10,736 per year); Federal Work-Study, institutionally sponsored loans, scholarships/grants, health care benefits, tuition waivers (partial), and unspecified assistantships also available. Financial award application deadline: 4/15; financial award applicants required to submit FAFSA. *Faculty research:* Strategies for music pedagogy in grades K-12, performance practice of traditional music, role of the woman piano virtuoso, vernacular music center, voice health and culture. *Total annual research expenditures:* $23,000. *Unit head:* Prof. William Ballenger, Director, 806-834-1724, Fax: 806-742-2294, E-mail: william.ballenger@ttu.edu. *Application contact:* Emily Gifford, Admissions and Scholarship Coordinator, 806-834-5076, Fax: 806-742-2294, E-mail: emily.gifford@ttu.edu.
Website: http://www.depts.ttu.edu/music

Texas Woman's University, Graduate School, College of Arts and Sciences, School of the Arts, Department of Music and Drama, Denton, TX 76201. Offers instrumental pedagogy (MA); instrumental performance (MA); music (MA); music education (MA); piano performance (MA); vocal pedagogy (MA); vocal performance (MA). *Accreditation:* NASM. *Program availability:* Part-time. *Students:* 44 full-time (31 women), 29 part-time (21 women); includes 22 minority (4 Black or African American, non-Hispanic/Latino; 3 Asian, non-Hispanic/Latino; 13 Hispanic/Latino; 2 Two or more races, non-Hispanic/Latino), 3 international. Average age 29. In 2016, 18 master's awarded. *Degree requirements:* For master's, comprehensive exam, thesis (for some programs), project recital, professional paper. *Entrance requirements:* For master's, music history/theory placement exam (for music only), audition and/or design portfolio, interview, resume, writing sample (for drama only). Additional exam requirements/recommendations for international students: Required—TOEFL (minimum score 550 paper-based; 79 iBT). *Application deadline:* For fall admission, 7/1 priority date for domestic students, 3/1 for international students; for spring admission, 12/1 priority date for domestic students, 7/1 for international students. Applications are processed on a rolling basis. Application fee: $50 ($75 for international students). Electronic applications accepted. *Expenses:* Tuition, state resident: full-time $9046; part-time $251 per credit hour. Tuition, nonresident: full-time $22,922; part-time $614 per credit hour. *International tuition:* $23,046 full-time. *Required fees:* $2690; $1285 per credit hour. One-time fee: $50. Tuition and fees vary according to course level, course load, program and reciprocity agreements. *Financial support:* Research assistantships, career-related internships or fieldwork, Federal Work-Study, institutionally sponsored loans, scholarships/grants, traineeships, health care benefits, tuition waivers (partial), and unspecified assistantships available. Support available to part-time students. Financial award application deadline: 3/1; financial award applicants required to submit FAFSA. *Faculty research:* Musical development in early childhood, little known or neglected compositions for flute (especially by women composers), relationship of visual art to piano music, pedagogical development of the singing voice, guided imagery and music. *Unit head:* Dr. Pamela Youngblood, Chair, 940-898-2495, Fax: 940-898-2494, E-mail: pyoungblood@twu.edu. *Application contact:* Dr. Samuel Wheeler, Assistant Director of Admissions, 940-898-3188, Fax: 940-898-3081, E-mail: wheelersr@twu.edu.

Towson University, Program in Music Education, Towson, MD 21252-0001. Offers MS, Postbaccalaureate Certificate. *Accreditation:* NASM; NCATE. *Program availability:* Part-time, evening/weekend. *Students:* 6 full-time (2 women), 17 part-time (13 women); includes 2 minority (both Hispanic/Latino). *Degree requirements:* For master's, thesis optional. *Entrance requirements:* For master's, placement examination in music history and music theory, bachelor's degree in music education or certification as public school music teacher, minimum GPA of 3.0; for Postbaccalaureate Certificate, bachelor's degree with certification as a public school music teacher or a degree in music. *Application deadline:* Applications are processed on a rolling basis. Application fee: $45. Electronic applications accepted. *Expenses:* Tuition, state resident: full-time $7580; part-time $379 per unit. Tuition, nonresident: full-time $15,700; part-time $785 per unit. *Required fees:* $2480. *Financial support:* Application deadline: 4/1. *Unit head:* Dr. Melissa McCabe, Graduate Program Director, 410-704-5175, E-mail: mmccabe@towson.edu. *Application contact:* Coverley Beidleman, Assistant Director of Graduate Admissions, 410-704-2113, Fax: 410-704-3030, E-mail: grads@towson.edu.
Website: http://www.towson.edu/cofac/departments/music/grad/education/

Union College, Graduate Programs, Department of Education, Barbourville, KY 40906-1499. Offers elementary education (MA); health and physical education (MA); middle grades (MA); music education (MA); principalship (MA); reading specialist (MA); secondary education (MA); special education (MA). *Degree requirements:* For master's, thesis optional. *Entrance requirements:* For master's, GRE General Test, NTE.

Université Laval, Faculty of Music, Programs in Music, Québec, QC G1K 7P4, Canada. Offers composition (M Mus); instrumental didactics (M Mus); interpretation (M Mus); music education (M Mus, PhD); musicology (M Mus, PhD). Terminal master's awarded for partial completion of doctoral program. *Degree requirements:* For master's, thesis (for some programs); for doctorate, comprehensive exam, thesis/dissertation. *Entrance requirements:* For master's, English exam, audition, knowledge of French; for doctorate, English exam, knowledge of French, third language. Electronic applications accepted.

University at Buffalo, the State University of New York, Graduate School, Graduate School of Education, Department of Learning and Instruction, Buffalo, NY 14260. Offers biology education (Ed M, Certificate); chemistry education (Ed M, Certificate); childhood education (Ed M); childhood education with bilingual extension (Ed M); college teaching (Advanced Certificate); curriculum, instruction and the science of learning (PhD); early childhood education (Ed M); early childhood education with bilingual extension (Ed M); earth science education (Ed M, Certificate); education and technology (Ed M); education studies (Ed M); educational technology and new literacies (Certificate); educational technology and new literacies (Advanced Certificate); elementary education (Ed D); English education (Ed M, Certificate); English education studies (Ed M); English for speakers of other languages (Ed M); foreign and second language education (PhD); French education (Ed M, Certificate); German education (Ed M, Certificate); gifted education (Certificate); Latin education (Ed M, Certificate); literacy education studies (Ed M); literacy specialist (Ed M); literacy teaching and learning (Certificate); mathematics education (Ed M, Certificate); music education (Ed M, Certificate); music education studies (Ed M); music learning theory (Advanced Certificate); online education (Advanced Certificate); physics education (Ed M, Certificate); science and the public (Ed M); social studies education (Ed M, Certificate); Spanish education (Ed M, Certificate); special education (PhD); teaching English to speakers of other languages (Ed M). *Program availability:* Part-time, evening/weekend, 100% online. *Faculty:* 28 full-time (21 women), 67 part-time/adjunct (49 women). *Students:* 198 full-time (153 women), 312 part-time (220 women); includes 48 minority (28 Black or African American, non-Hispanic/Latino; 4 American Indian or Alaska Native, non-Hispanic/Latino; 15 Asian, non-Hispanic/Latino; 1 Hispanic/Latino), 66 international. Average age 33. 330 applicants, 80% accepted, 178 enrolled. In 2016, 137 master's, 24 doctorates, 25 other advanced degrees awarded. *Degree requirements:* For master's, comprehensive exam; for doctorate, thesis/dissertation, research analysis exam, research experience. *Entrance requirements:* For master's, letters of reference; for doctorate, GRE General Test or MAT, interview, writing sample, letters of recommendation. Additional exam requirements/recommendations for international students: Required—TOEFL (minimum score 600 paper-based; 96 iBT). *Application deadline:* For fall admission, 2/1 priority date for domestic and international students; for spring admission, 11/15 priority date for domestic students, 10/1 for international students. Applications are processed on a rolling basis. Application fee: $50. Electronic applications accepted. *Financial support:* In 2016–17, 44 fellowships (averaging $4,010 per year), 39 research assistantships with tuition reimbursements (averaging $9,897 per year) were awarded; teaching assistantships, career-related internships or fieldwork, Federal Work-Study, institutionally sponsored loans, scholarships/grants, tuition waivers (full and partial), and unspecified assistantships also available. Financial award application deadline: 2/28; financial award applicants required to submit FAFSA. *Faculty research:* Science assessment, foreign language teaching and learning, early learning, new literacies, gender and education. *Total annual research expenditures:* $534,880. *Unit head:* Dr. Deborah Moore-Russo, Chair, 716-645-4069, Fax: 716-645-3161, E-mail: dam29@buffalo.edu. *Application contact:* Luann Zak, Admissions Assistant, 716-645-2110, Fax: 716-645-7937, E-mail: luannzak@buffalo.edu.
Website: http://gse.buffalo.edu/lai

The University of Akron, Graduate School, Buchtel College of Arts and Sciences, School of Music, Program in Music Education, Akron, OH 44325. Offers MM. *Accreditation:* NCATE. *Students:* 8 full-time (4 women), 5 part-time (3 women); includes

1 minority (Hispanic/Latino). Average age 28. 12 applicants, 92% accepted, 8 enrolled. In 2016, 8 master's awarded. *Degree requirements:* For master's, comprehensive exam, thesis optional. *Entrance requirements:* For master's, minimum GPA of 2.75, interview, three letters of recommendation. Additional exam requirements/recommendations for international students: Required—TOEFL (minimum score 550 paper-based; 79 iBT), IELTS (minimum score 6.5). *Application deadline:* Applications are processed on a rolling basis. Application fee: $45 ($70 for international students). Electronic applications accepted. *Expenses:* Tuition, state resident: full-time $8618; part-time $359 per credit hour. Tuition, nonresident: full-time $17,149; part-time $715 per credit hour. *Required fees:* $1652. *Unit head:* Dr. J. Thomas Dukes, Interim Director, 330-972-5761, E-mail: jtdukes@uakron.edu. *Application contact:* Dr. Ann Usher, Graduate Coordinator, 330-972-6923, E-mail: ausher@uakron.edu.

The University of Alabama, Graduate School, College of Arts and Sciences, School of Music, Tuscaloosa, AL 35487. Offers arranging (MM); choral conducting (MM, DMA); church music (MM); composition (MM, DMA); music education (MA, PhD); musicology (MM); performance (MM, DMA); theory (MM); wind conducting (MM, DMA). *Accreditation:* NASM. *Faculty:* 38 full-time (13 women), 1 (woman) part-time/adjunct. *Students:* 57 full-time (20 women), 11 part-time (4 women); includes 15 minority (7 Black or African American, non-Hispanic/Latino; 1 American Indian or Alaska Native, non-Hispanic/Latino; 5 Hispanic/Latino; 2 Two or more races, non-Hispanic/Latino), 9 international. Average age 29. 82 applicants, 60% accepted, 25 enrolled. In 2016, 13 master's, 7 doctorates awarded. *Degree requirements:* For master's, variable foreign language requirement, comprehensive exam (for some programs), thesis (for some programs), recital; for doctorate, variable foreign language requirement, comprehensive exam, thesis/dissertation, oral exam; recital (for some majors). *Entrance requirements:* For master's and doctorate, audition exam, audition in the major instrument or area. Additional exam requirements/recommendations for international students: Required—PTE (minimum score 59), TOEFL (minimum score 550 paper-based, 79 iBT) or IELTS (minimum score 6.5). *Application deadline:* For fall admission, 3/15 priority date for domestic and international students; for winter admission, 9/1 priority date for domestic and international students; for spring admission, 9/1 priority date for domestic and international students. Applications are processed on a rolling basis. Application fee: $50 ($60 for international students). Electronic applications accepted. *Expenses:* Tuition, state resident: full-time $10,470. Tuition, nonresident: full-time $26,950. *Financial support:* In 2016–17, 50 students received support, including 1 fellowship with full tuition reimbursement available (averaging $10,000 per year), 44 teaching assistantships with tuition reimbursements available (averaging $10,161 per year); institutionally sponsored loans, scholarships/grants, health care benefits, and unspecified assistantships also available. Financial award application deadline: 3/15. *Faculty research:* Performance practice, musicology, theory, composition. *Unit head:* Charles G. Snead, Director, 205-348-7110, Fax: 205-348-1473, E-mail: ssnead@music.ua.edu. *Application contact:* Dr. Jon Noffsinger, Director of Graduate Studies, 205-348-1475, Fax: 205-348-1473, E-mail: jnoffsin@ua.edu.
Website: http://music.ua.edu/

The University of Alabama, Graduate School, College of Education, Department of Music Education, Tuscaloosa, AL 35487-0366. Offers choral music education (MA); instrumental music education (MA); music education (Ed D, PhD, Ed S). *Accreditation:* NASM. *Faculty:* 3 full-time (1 woman). *Degree requirements:* For master's, comprehensive exam, thesis optional; for doctorate, comprehensive exam, thesis/dissertation, oral exam (for PhD). *Entrance requirements:* For master's, GRE or MAT, video of teaching, letters of recommendation; for doctorate, GRE or MAT, interview, writing sample, video of teaching, letters of recommendation; for Ed S, GRE or MAT. Additional exam requirements/recommendations for international students: Required—TOEFL (minimum score 550 paper-based). *Application deadline:* For fall admission, 7/1 priority date for domestic students; for spring admission, 11/1 priority date for domestic students. Applications are processed on a rolling basis. Application fee: $50 ($60 for international students). Electronic applications accepted. *Expenses:* Tuition, state resident: full-time $10,470. Tuition, nonresident: full-time $26,950. *Financial support:* Research assistantships with tuition reimbursements and teaching assistantships with tuition reimbursements available. Financial award application deadline: 3/1. *Faculty research:* Elementary music, music for students with special needs, choral music. *Unit head:* Dr. Marvin E. Latimer, Department Head and Associate Professor, 205-348-0393, Fax: 205-348-1675, E-mail: mlatimer@music.ua.edu. *Application contact:* Jessica M. Westbrook, Office Associate II, 205-348-6054, Fax: 205-348-1675, E-mail: jessica.westbrook@ua.edu.
Website: http://www.musiceducation.ua.edu

The University of Arizona, College of Fine Arts, School of Music, Program in Music, Tucson, AZ 85721. Offers composition (MM); ethnomusicology (MM); music education (MM, PhD); music theory (MM, PhD); musicology (MM); performance (MM), including conducting - choral, conducting - instrumental, instrumental, keyboard, piano accompanying, piano and dance accompanying, vocal. *Entrance requirements:* Additional exam requirements/recommendations for international students: Required—TOEFL (minimum score 550 paper-based; 79 iBT). Electronic applications accepted. *Faculty research:* Music in general education, psychology of music learning, innovation in string music education, Zarzuela, Franz Liszt's work.

University of Bridgeport, School of Education, Department of Education, Bridgeport, CT 06604. Offers education (MS); educational management (Ed D, Diploma), including intermediate administrator or supervisor (Diploma), leadership (Ed D); elementary education (MS, Diploma), including early childhood education, elementary education; middle school education (MS); music education (MS); remedial reading and language arts (Diploma); secondary education (MS, Diploma), including computer specialist (Diploma), international education (Diploma), reading specialist, secondary education. *Program availability:* Part-time, evening/weekend. *Degree requirements:* For master's, final exam, final project, or thesis; for doctorate, comprehensive exam, thesis/dissertation; for Diploma, thesis or alternative, final project. *Entrance requirements:* For master's, minimum undergraduate QPA of 2.67; for doctorate, GRE, MAT; for Diploma, GRE General Test or MAT, minimum graduate QPA of 3.0. Additional exam requirements/recommendations for international students: Recommended—TOEFL (minimum score 550 paper-based; 80 iBT), IELTS (minimum score 6.5). Electronic applications accepted. *Expenses:* Contact institution.

The University of British Columbia, Faculty of Education, Department of Curriculum and Pedagogy, Vancouver, BC V6T 1Z4, Canada. Offers art education (M Ed, MA); curriculum studies (M Ed, MA, PhD); home economics education (M Ed, MA); mathematics education (M Ed, MA); media and technology studies education (M Ed, MA); music education (M Ed, MA); physical education (M Ed, MA); science education (M Ed, MA); social studies education (M Ed, MA). *Program availability:* Part-time, online learning. *Degree requirements:* For master's, thesis (MA); for doctorate, comprehensive exam, thesis/dissertation. *Entrance requirements:* Additional exam requirements/recommendations for international students: Required—TOEFL, IELTS. Application fee: $100 Canadian dollars ($162 Canadian dollars for international students). Electronic applications accepted. *Expenses:* $6,865 per year tuition and fees domestic, $10,938 per year international (for MA and M Ed); $4,802 per year tuition and fees, $8,436 per year international (for PhD). *Financial support:* Fellowships with partial tuition reimbursements, research assistantships with partial tuition reimbursements, teaching assistantships with partial tuition reimbursements, and tuition waivers (partial) available. *Faculty research:* School subjects, teaching and learning. *Application contact:* Alan Jay, Graduate Programs Assistant, 604-822-5367, Fax: 604-822-4714, E-mail: edcp.grad@ubc.ca.
Website: http://www.edcp.educ.ubc.ca/

University of Central Arkansas, Graduate School, College of Fine Arts and Communication, Department of Music, Conway, AR 72035-0001. Offers choral conducting (MM); instrumental conducting (MM); music (PC); music education (MM); music theory (MM); performance (MM). *Accreditation:* NASM. *Program availability:* Part-time. *Degree requirements:* For master's, comprehensive exam, thesis optional. *Entrance requirements:* For master's, GRE General Test, minimum GPA of 2.7. Additional exam requirements/recommendations for international students: Required—TOEFL (minimum score 550 paper-based). Electronic applications accepted.

University of Cincinnati, Graduate School, College-Conservatory of Music, Division of Music Education, Cincinnati, OH 45221. Offers MM. *Accreditation:* NASM; NCATE. *Degree requirements:* For master's, comprehensive exam, paper or thesis. *Entrance requirements:* For master's, GRE General Test, interview. Additional exam requirements/recommendations for international students: Required—TOEFL (minimum score 520 paper-based). Electronic applications accepted. *Expenses: Tuition, area resident:* Full-time $12,790; part-time $389 per credit hour. Tuition, state resident: full-time $13,290; part-time $419 per credit hour. Tuition, nonresident: full-time $24,532; part-time $976 per credit hour. *International tuition:* $24,832 full-time. *Required fees:* $3958; $140 per credit hour. Tuition and fees vary according to course load, degree level, program and reciprocity agreements. *Faculty research:* Choral, orchestral, and wind conducting; Kodaly; Orff-Schulwerk; jazz studies; string education.

University of Colorado Boulder, Graduate School, College of Music, Boulder, CO 80309. Offers composition (M Mus, D Mus A); conducting (M Mus); instrumental conducting and literature (D Mus A); literature and performance of choral music (D Mus A); music education (M Mus Ed, PhD), including choral or wind instrument conducting (M Mus Ed), general (M Mus Ed), Kodaly concepts (M Mus Ed), piano pedagogy (M Mus Ed), primary instruments (M Mus Ed), secondary instruments (M Mus Ed), voice pedagogy (M Mus Ed); music theory (M Mus); performance (M Mus, D Mus A); performance and pedagogy (M Mus, D Mus A). *Accreditation:* NASM. *Faculty:* 62 full-time (19 women). *Students:* 163 full-time (77 women), 43 part-time (25 women); includes 26 minority (4 Black or African American, non-Hispanic/Latino; 7 Asian, non-Hispanic/Latino; 9 Hispanic/Latino; 6 Two or more races, non-Hispanic/Latino), 18 international. Average age 30. 458 applicants, 38% accepted, 51 enrolled. In 2016, 39 master's, 27 doctorates awarded. Terminal master's awarded for partial completion of doctoral program. *Degree requirements:* For master's, variable foreign language requirement, comprehensive exam, thesis or alternative, recital; for doctorate, variable foreign language requirement, thesis/dissertation. *Entrance requirements:* For master's, GRE General Test, GRE Subject Test (music literature), minimum undergraduate GPA of 2.75; for doctorate, GRE General Test, GRE Subject Test, audition, sample of research. *Application deadline:* For fall admission, 12/1 for domestic and international students; for spring admission, 10/1 for domestic and international students. Applications are processed on a rolling basis. Application fee: $60 ($80 for international students). Electronic applications accepted. Application fee is waived when completed online. *Financial support:* In 2016–17, 496 students received support, including 234 fellowships (averaging $2,277 per year), 1 research assistantship with full and partial tuition reimbursement available (averaging $6,020 per year), 108 teaching assistantships with full and partial tuition reimbursements available (averaging $22,460 per year); institutionally sponsored loans, scholarships/grants, health care benefits, and unspecified assistantships also available. Financial award application deadline: 3/1; financial award applicants required to submit FAFSA. *Faculty research:* Music, instrumental music, performing arts, chamber music, musicology/music theory. *Total annual research expenditures:* $90,364. *Application contact:* E-mail: gradmusc@colorado.edu.
Website: http://music.colorado.edu/

University of Connecticut, Graduate School, Neag School of Education, Department of Curriculum and Instruction, Storrs, CT 06269. Offers agriculture (MA), including agriculture education; agriculture education (PhD); bilingual and bicultural education (MA, PhD); elementary education (MA, PhD); English education (MA, PhD); history and social sciences education (MA, PhD); mathematics education (MA, PhD); music education (MA); reading education (MA, PhD); science education (MA, PhD); secondary education (MA, PhD); world languages education (MA, PhD). *Accreditation:* NCATE. Terminal master's awarded for partial completion of doctoral program. *Degree requirements:* For master's, comprehensive exam, thesis or alternative; for doctorate, thesis/dissertation. *Entrance requirements:* For doctorate, GRE General Test. Additional exam requirements/recommendations for international students: Required—TOEFL (minimum score 550 paper-based). Electronic applications accepted.

University of Dayton, Department of Teacher Education, Dayton, OH 45469. Offers early childhood leadership and advocacy (MS Ed); interdisciplinary education studies (MS Ed); leadership in educational systems (MS Ed); literacy (MS Ed); mathematics education (MS Ed); music education (MS Ed); teacher as leader (MS Ed); teacher education (MS Ed); technology-enhanced learning (MS Ed); trans-disciplinary early childhood education (MS Ed). *Program availability:* Part-time, evening/weekend, blended/hybrid learning. *Faculty:* 23 full-time (18 women), 49 part-time/adjunct (42 women). *Students:* 52 full-time (47 women), 89 part-time (76 women); includes 6 minority (2 Black or African American, non-Hispanic/Latino; 2 Hispanic/Latino; 2 Two or more races, non-Hispanic/Latino), 24 international. Average age 31. 106 applicants, 28% accepted. In 2016, 69 master's awarded. *Degree requirements:* For master's, variable foreign language requirement, thesis optional. *Entrance requirements:* For master's, GRE (minimum score of 149 verbal, 4 on writing) or MAT (minimum score of 396) if undergraduate GPA was under 2.75, minimum GPA of 2.75, 3 letters of recommendation, personal statement or resume, official transcripts. Additional exam requirements/recommendations for international students: Required—TOEFL (minimum score 550 paper-based; 80 iBT); Recommended—IELTS (minimum score 6.5). *Application deadline:* Applications are processed on a rolling basis. Application fee: $0 ($50 for international students). Electronic applications accepted. *Expenses:* $620 per credit hour, $25 registration fee per term. *Financial support:* Institutionally sponsored loans available. Financial award application deadline: 3/1; financial award applicants required to submit FAFSA. *Faculty research:* Educational technology; facilitating teacher reflection; teacher preparation in dyslexia. *Unit head:* Dr. Connie L. Bowman, Chair, 937-229-3305, E-mail: cbowman1@udayton.edu. *Application contact:* Gina Seiter, Graduate Program Advisor, 937-229-3103, E-mail: gseiter1@udayton.edu.
Website: https://www.udayton.edu/education/departments_and_programs/edt

University of Delaware, College of Arts and Sciences, Department of Music, Newark, DE 19716. Offers composition (MM); music education (MM); performance (MM). *Accreditation:* NASM. *Program availability:* Part-time. *Entrance requirements:* For master's, audition. Additional exam requirements/recommendations for international students: Required—TOEFL. Electronic applications accepted. *Faculty research:* Teaching of music.

University of Denver, Division of Arts, Humanities and Social Sciences, Lamont School of Music, Denver, CO 80208. Offers composition (MM); composition - jazz emphasis (MM); conducting (MM, Certificate); jazz studies (Certificate); music theory (MA); musicology (MA); orchestral studies (Certificate); pedagogy (MM); performance (MM, Certificate); performance - jazz emphasis (MM); Suzuki teaching (Certificate). *Accreditation:* NASM. *Program availability:* Part-time. *Faculty:* 32 full-time (9 women), 33 part-time/adjunct (15 women). *Students:* 30 full-time (9 women), 71 part-time (35 women); includes 16 minority (2 Black or African American, non-Hispanic/Latino; 1 American Indian or Alaska Native, non-Hispanic/Latino; 2 Asian, non-Hispanic/Latino; 7 Hispanic/Latino; 4 Two or more races, non-Hispanic/Latino), 16 international. Average age 27. 150 applicants, 81% accepted, 58 enrolled. In 2016, 24 master's, 2 other advanced degrees awarded. *Degree requirements:* For master's, one foreign language, comprehensive exam, recital or project (for performance), thesis (for musicology, music theory, piano pedagogy). *Entrance requirements:* For master's, GRE General Test (for MA only), bachelor's degree, transcripts, personal statement, resume, three letters of recommendation, pre-screen audition (for performance), portfolio (for composition), essay or research paper (for MA only); for Certificate, bachelor's degree, transcripts, personal statement, resume, letters of recommendation, pre-screen video recording or music audition. Additional exam requirements/recommendations for international students: Required—TOEFL (minimum score 550 paper-based; 80 iBT). *Application deadline:* For fall admission, 1/15 priority date for domestic and international students. Applications are processed on a rolling basis. Application fee: $65. Electronic applications accepted. *Expenses:* $29,022 per year full-time. *Financial support:* In 2016–17, 89 students received support, including 25 teaching assistantships with tuition reimbursements available (averaging $6,933 per year); career-related internships or fieldwork, Federal Work-Study, institutionally sponsored loans, scholarships/grants, tuition waivers, and unspecified assistantships also available. Support available to part-time students. Financial award application deadline: 2/15; financial award applicants required to submit FAFSA. *Faculty research:* Performance, jazz studies and commercial music, musicology, music theory, composition, music pedagogy, music recording and production. *Unit head:* Dr. Nancy Cochran, Professor and Director, 303-871-6986, Fax: 303-871-3118, E-mail: nancy.cochran@du.edu. *Application contact:* Stephen Campbell, Director of Admission, 303-871-6973, Fax: 303-871-3118, E-mail: stephen.l.campbell@du.edu.
Website: http://www.du.edu/ahss/lamont/index.html

University of Florida, Graduate School, College of The Arts, School of Music, Gainesville, FL 32611. Offers choral conducting (MM); composition (MM, PhD); electronic music (MM); ethnomusicology (MM); instrumental conducting (MM); music (MM, PhD); music education (MM, PhD), including choral conducting (MM), composition (MM), electronic music (MM), ethnomusicology (MM), instrumental conducting (MM), music education (MM), music history and literature (MM), music theory (MM), performance (MM), piano pedagogy (MM); music history and literature (MM, PhD); music theory (MM); performance (MM); sacred music (MM). *Accreditation:* NASM. *Degree requirements:* For master's, variable foreign language requirement, comprehensive exam, thesis, recital; for doctorate, thesis/dissertation. *Entrance requirements:* For master's and doctorate, GRE General Test, audition, minimum GPA of 3.0. Additional exam requirements/recommendations for international students: Required—TOEFL (minimum score 550 paper-based; 80 iBT), IELTS (minimum score 6). Electronic applications accepted.

University of Georgia, Franklin College of Arts and Sciences, Hugh Hodgson School of Music, Athens, GA 30602. Offers composition (MM, DMA); conducting (MM, DMA); music (PhD); music education (MM Ed, Ed D); musicology (MA); performance (MM, DMA). Ed D offered jointly with College of Education. *Accreditation:* NASM. *Degree requirements:* For master's, variable foreign language requirement, thesis (MA); for doctorate, variable foreign language requirement, thesis/dissertation. *Entrance requirements:* For master's and doctorate, GRE General Test. *Application deadline:* For fall admission, 7/1 priority date for domestic students; for spring admission, 11/15 for domestic students. Application fee: $50. Electronic applications accepted. *Financial support:* Fellowships, research assistantships, teaching assistantships, and unspecified assistantships available. *Unit head:* Dr. Dale Monson, Director, 706-542-2776, Fax: 706-542-2773, E-mail: dmonson@uga.edu. *Application contact:* Peter Jutras, Graduate Coordinator, 206-542-2765, E-mail: pjutras@uga.edu.
Website: http://www.music.uga.edu

University of Hartford, The Hartt School, West Hartford, CT 06117-1599. Offers choral conducting (MM Ed); composition (MM, DMA, Artist Diploma, Diploma); conducting (MM, DMA, Artist Diploma, Diploma), including choral (MM, Diploma), instrumental (MM, Diploma); early childhood education (MM Ed); instrumental conducting (MM Ed); Kodály (MM Ed); music (CAGS); music education (DMA, PhD); music history (MM); music theory (MM); pedagogy (MM Ed); performance (MM, MM Ed, DMA, Artist Diploma, Diploma); research (MM Ed); technology (MM Ed). *Program availability:* Part-time. *Degree requirements:* For master's, variable foreign language requirement, thesis (for some programs), recital; for doctorate, variable foreign language requirement, thesis/dissertation (for some programs), recital; for other advanced degree, recital. *Entrance requirements:* For master's, audition, letters of recommendation; for doctorate, proficiency exam, audition, interview, research paper; for other advanced degree, audition. Additional exam requirements/recommendations for international students: Required—TOEFL. Electronic applications accepted. *Expenses:* Contact institution.

University of Houston, College of Liberal Arts and Social Sciences, Moores School of Music, Houston, TX 77204. Offers accompanying and chamber music (MM); applied music (MM); composition (MM); music education (DMA); music theory (MM); performance (DMA). *Accreditation:* NASM. *Program availability:* Part-time. *Degree requirements:* For master's, one foreign language, comprehensive exam, recital; for doctorate, one foreign language, comprehensive exam, thesis/dissertation. *Entrance requirements:* For master's, audition, resume, 3 letters of recommendation; for doctorate, writing sample, audition, statement of purpose, resume. Additional exam requirements/recommendations for international students: Required—TOEFL (minimum score 550 paper-based, 79 iBT), IELTS (minimum score 6.5). Electronic applications accepted. *Faculty research:* Twentieth century music, Baroque music, history of music theory, music analysis.

University of Illinois at Urbana–Champaign, Graduate College, College of Fine and Applied Arts, School of Music, Champaign, IL 61820. Offers music (M Mus, AD, DMA); music education (MME, PhD); musicology (PhD). *Accreditation:* NASM.

The University of Iowa, Graduate College, College of Education, Department of Teaching and Learning, Program in Education, Iowa City, IA 52242-1316. Offers art education (MA); developmental reading (MA); elementary education (MA); English education (MA, MAT); foreign and second language education (MAT); foreign language education (MA); foreign language/ESL education (PhD); language, literacy and culture (PhD); mathematics education (MA, MAT, PhD); music education (MM, PhD); science education (MA); secondary education (MA); social studies (MA, PhD). *Degree requirements:* For master's, thesis optional, exam; for doctorate, comprehensive exam, thesis/dissertation. *Entrance requirements:* For master's and doctorate, GRE General Test, minimum GPA of 3.0. Additional exam requirements/recommendations for international students: Required—TOEFL (minimum score 550 paper-based; 81 iBT). Electronic applications accepted.

The University of Kansas, Graduate Studies, School of Music, Program in Music Education, Lawrence, KS 66045. Offers MMF, PhD. *Accreditation:* NASM. *Program availability:* Part-time. *Students:* 14 full-time (11 women), 9 part-time (2 women); includes 1 minority (Asian, non-Hispanic/Latino), 3 international. Average age 33. 18 applicants, 83% accepted, 12 enrolled. In 2016, 10 master's, 4 doctorates awarded. *Entrance requirements:* For master's, GRE General Test, minimum undergraduate GPA of 3.0, video, letters of reference, transcripts; for doctorate, GRE General Test, MEMT Diagnostic Exam, minimum graduate GPA of 3.5, video, reference letters, transcripts, writing sample, proof of professional experience. Additional exam requirements/recommendations for international students: Required—TOEFL (minimum score 570 paper-based; 92 iBT) or IELTS (minimum score 6). *Application deadline:* For fall admission, 12/1 priority date for domestic students, 12/15 priority date for international students. Application fee: $65 ($85 for international students). Electronic applications accepted. *Financial support:* Fellowships, research assistantships, teaching assistantships, institutionally sponsored loans, scholarships/grants, and unspecified assistantships available. Financial award application deadline: 12/15; financial award applicants required to submit FAFSA. *Faculty research:* Philosophy of music and music education; choral/voice pedagogy, choir acoustics; classroom management, teacher stress; the child voice, children's choirs; string pedagogy, history of string education in American public school systems. *Unit head:* Dr. Chris Johnson, Director, 785-864-9633, E-mail: cmj@ku.edu. *Application contact:* Lois Elmer, Administrative Professional, 785-864-4748, Fax: 785-864-9640, E-mail: elmer@ku.edu.
Website: http://music.ku.edu/memt

University of Kentucky, Graduate School, College of Fine Arts, Program in Music, Lexington, KY 40506-0032. Offers composition (MM, DMA); conducting (MM, DMA); music education (MM, PhD); music theory (MA, PhD); music therapy (MM); musicology (MA, PhD); performance (MM, DMA); sacred music (MM). *Accreditation:* NASM. *Program availability:* Part-time, evening/weekend. *Degree requirements:* For master's, variable foreign language requirement, comprehensive exam, thesis (for some programs); for doctorate, variable foreign language requirement, comprehensive exam, thesis/dissertation. *Entrance requirements:* For master's, GRE General Test, minimum undergraduate GPA of 2.75; for doctorate, GRE General Test, minimum undergraduate GPA of 2.75, graduate 3.0. Additional exam requirements/recommendations for international students: Required—TOEFL (minimum score 550 paper-based). Electronic applications accepted. *Faculty research:* Musicology, music theory, jazz, music education, performance and conducting.

University of Louisiana at Lafayette, College of the Arts, School of Music, Lafayette, LA 70504. Offers conducting (MM); pedagogy (MM); vocal and instrumental performance (MM). *Accreditation:* NASM. *Degree requirements:* For master's, thesis or alternative. *Entrance requirements:* For master's, GRE General Test, minimum GPA of 2.75. Additional exam requirements/recommendations for international students: Required—TOEFL (minimum score 550 paper-based). Electronic applications accepted. *Faculty research:* Nineteenth century American music, trumpet pedagogy, fifteenth century Renaissance polyphony, Charles Ives.

University of Louisiana at Monroe, Graduate School, College of Arts, Education, and Sciences, School of Education, Program in Curriculum and Instruction, Monroe, LA 71209-0001. Offers art education (M Ed); biology education (M Ed); chemistry education (M Ed); curriculum and instruction (Ed D); early childhood education (M Ed); earth science education (M Ed); educational leadership (M Ed); elementary education (1-5) (M Ed); English as a second language (M Ed); English education (M Ed); family and consumer education (M Ed); French education (M Ed); history education (M Ed); math education (M Ed); middle school education (M Ed); music education (M Ed); reading education (K-12) (M Ed); Spanish education (M Ed); special education - academically gifted (M Ed); special education - early intervention (M Ed); special education - educational diagnostician (M Ed); special education - mild/moderate disabilities (M Ed); speech education (M Ed). *Accreditation:* NCATE. *Faculty:* 8 full-time (4 women), 4 part-time/adjunct (3 women). *Students:* 13 full-time (11 women), 80 part-time (65 women); includes 25 minority (19 Black or African American, non-Hispanic/Latino; 1 Asian, non-Hispanic/Latino; 3 Hispanic/Latino; 2 Two or more races, non-Hispanic/Latino). Average age 37. 118 applicants, 30% accepted, 16 enrolled. In 2016, 23 master's, 4 doctorates awarded. *Degree requirements:* For master's, comprehensive exam (for some programs), thesis; for doctorate, thesis/dissertation, internships. *Entrance requirements:* For master's, GRE General Test; for doctorate, GRE General Test, minimum undergraduate GPA of 2.75, graduate 3.25. Additional exam requirements/recommendations for international students: Required—TOEFL (minimum score 500 paper-based; 61 iBT). *Application deadline:* For fall admission, 8/24 priority date for domestic students, 7/1 for international students; for winter admission, 12/14 priority date for domestic students; for spring admission, 1/19 for domestic students, 11/1 for international students. Applications are processed on a rolling basis. Application fee: $20 ($30 for international students). Electronic applications accepted. *Expenses:* Tuition, state resident: full-time $6489. Tuition, nonresident: full-time $18,589. *Required fees:* $8984. Tuition and fees vary according to course level, course load, degree level and program. *Financial support:* Research assistantships, career-related internships or fieldwork, Federal Work-Study, and unspecified assistantships available. Financial award application deadline: 4/1; financial award applicants required to submit FAFSA. *Unit head:* Dr. Dorothy Schween, Director, 318-342-1268, Fax: 318-342-3131, E-mail: schween@ulm.edu.

University of Louisville, Graduate School, College of Education and Human Development, Department of Teaching and Learning, Louisville, KY 40292-0001. Offers art education (MAT); autism and applied behavior analysis (Certificate); curriculum and instruction (PhD); early elementary education (MAT); exercise physiology (MS); health and physical education (MAT); health professions education (Certificate); higher education (MA); human resources and organization development (MS); instructional technology (M Ed); interdisciplinary early childhood education (MAT); middle school education (MAT); music education (MAT); secondary education (MAT); special education (MAT); sport administration (MS); teacher leadership (M Ed). *Program availability:* Part-time, evening/weekend. *Students:* 116 full-time (68 women), 158 part-time (112 women); includes 46 minority (24 Black or African American, non-Hispanic/Latino; 8 Asian, non-Hispanic/Latino; 5 Hispanic/Latino; 9 Two or more races, non-Hispanic/Latino), 6 international. Average age 30. 114 applicants, 71% accepted, 57 enrolled. In 2016, 59 master's, 3 doctorates awarded. *Application deadline:* For spring admission, 1/1 priority date for international students. Application fee: $60. *Expenses:* Tuition, state resident: full-time $12,246; part-time $681 per credit hour. Tuition, nonresident: full-time $25,486; part-time $1417 per credit hour. *Required fees:* $196. Tuition and fees vary according to program and reciprocity agreements. *Financial support:* Application deadline: 6/1; applicants required to submit FAFSA. *Faculty research:* STEM teaching and learning; content literacy for English language learners; social justice in teacher education; adolescent literacy; mathematics teacher development. *Total annual research expenditures:* $1.7 million. *Unit head:* Dr. Ann E. Larson, Dean, College of Education and Human Development, 502-852-6411, Fax: 502-852-1464, E-mail: ann@louisville.edu. *Application contact:* Betty Hampton, Director of

Music Education

Graduate Student Services, 502-852-5597, Fax: 502-852-1465, E-mail: edadvise@louisville.edu.
Website: http://louisville.edu/delphi

University of Louisville, Graduate School, School of Music, Louisville, KY 40292-0001. Offers composition (MM); electronic composition (MM); music education (MME); music history and literature (MM); music performance (MM), including choral conducting, instrumental, jazz composition, jazz performance, orchestral conducting, organ performance, piano pedagogy, piano performance, string pedagogy, vocal performance, wind band performance, wind conducting; music theory (MM). *Accreditation:* NASM. *Program availability:* Part-time. *Faculty:* 36 full-time (10 women), 39 part-time/adjunct (18 women). *Students:* 54 full-time (20 women), 5 part-time (3 women); includes 5 minority (2 Black or African American, non-Hispanic/Latino; 1 Hispanic/Latino; 2 Two or more races, non-Hispanic/Latino), 7 international. Average age 25. 62 applicants, 66% accepted, 25 enrolled. In 2016, 31 master's awarded. *Degree requirements:* For master's, variable foreign language requirement, comprehensive exam, thesis (for some programs), recital (for performance), paper or thesis (for music education), major composition (for composition). *Entrance requirements:* For master's, music history and theory entrance exams, jazz history and theory entrance exam (for jazz majors), audition, portfolio. Additional exam requirements/recommendations for international students: Required—TOEFL (minimum score 79 iBT) or IELTS (6.5). Application fee: $60. Electronic applications accepted. *Expenses:* Contact institution. *Financial support:* In 2016–17, 1 fellowship with full tuition reimbursement (averaging $12,000 per year), 12 teaching assistantships with full tuition reimbursements (averaging $12,000 per year) were awarded; Federal Work-Study, scholarships/grants, health care benefits, and unspecified assistantships also available. Financial award application deadline: 3/1. *Faculty research:* Composition, musicology, performance, pedagogy, analysis and theoretical application. *Total annual research expenditures:* $87,500. *Unit head:* Dr. Christopher P. Doane, Dean, 502-852-6907, Fax: 502-852-0520, E-mail: c0doan01@louisville.edu. *Application contact:* Laura Angermeier, Admissions Counselor/Senior Advising Counselor, 502-852-1623, Fax: 502-852-0520, E-mail: leange01@louisville.edu.
Website: http://www.louisville.edu/music/

University of Maryland, Baltimore County, The Graduate School, College of Arts, Humanities and Social Sciences, Department of Education, Program in Teaching, Baltimore, MD 21250. Offers early childhood education (MAT); elementary education (MAT); teaching (MAT), including art, biology, chemistry, choral music, classical foreign language, dance, earth/space science, English, instrumental music, mathematics, modern foreign language, physical science, physics, social studies, theatre. *Program availability:* Part-time, evening/weekend. *Faculty:* 24 full-time (18 women), 25 part-time/adjunct (19 women). *Students:* 41 full-time (34 women), 27 part-time (18 women); includes 26 minority (6 Black or African American, non-Hispanic/Latino; 9 Asian, non-Hispanic/Latino; 7 Hispanic/Latino; 1 Native Hawaiian or other Pacific Islander, non-Hispanic/Latino; 3 Two or more races, non-Hispanic/Latino), 2 international. Average age 30. 54 applicants, 83% accepted, 35 enrolled. In 2016, 50 master's awarded. *Degree requirements:* For master's, comprehensive exam (for some programs), thesis (for some programs). *Entrance requirements:* For master's, PRAXIS Core Examination or GRE (minimum score of 1000), minimum GPA of 3.0. Additional exam requirements/recommendations for international students: Required—TOEFL. *Application deadline:* For fall admission, 6/1 for domestic and international students; for spring admission, 11/1 for domestic and international students. Applications are processed on a rolling basis. Application fee: $50. Electronic applications accepted. *Expenses:* Tuition, state resident: full-time $13,294. Tuition, nonresident: full-time $20,286. *Financial support:* In 2016–17, 8 students received support, including teaching assistantships with tuition reimbursements available (averaging $12,000 per year); career-related internships or fieldwork, Federal Work-Study, scholarships/grants, tuition waivers, and unspecified assistantships also available. Financial award application deadline: 3/15. *Faculty research:* STEM teacher education, culturally sensitive pedagogy, ESOL/bilingual education, early childhood education, language, literacy and culture. *Total annual research expenditures:* $100,000. *Unit head:* Dr. Susan M. Blunck, Graduate Program Director, 410-455-2869, Fax: 410-455-3986, E-mail: blunck@umbc.edu. *Application contact:* Cheryl Johnson, MAT Program Specialist, 410-455-3388, E-mail: blackwel@umbc.edu.
Website: http://www.umbc.edu/education/

University of Maryland, College Park, Academic Affairs, College of Arts and Humanities, School of Music, Program in Music, College Park, MD 20742. Offers M Ed, MA, MM, DMA, Ed D, PhD. *Accreditation:* NASM. *Entrance requirements:* For master's, GRE General Test (for ethnomusicology, historical musicology and music theory), 3 letters of recommendation, audition/interview. Additional exam requirements/recommendations for international students: Required—TOEFL.

University of Massachusetts Amherst, Graduate School, College of Humanities and Fine Arts, Department of Music and Dance, Amherst, MA 01003. Offers collaborative piano (MM); composition (MM); conducting (MM); jazz composition/arranging (MM); music education (MM, PhD); music history (MM); music theory (PhD); performance (MM). *Accreditation:* NASM. *Program availability:* Part-time. Terminal master's awarded for partial completion of doctoral program. *Degree requirements:* For master's, thesis or alternative; for doctorate, comprehensive exam, thesis/dissertation. *Entrance requirements:* For master's and doctorate, placement tests, original scores, research, audition or tape. Additional exam requirements/recommendations for international students: Required—TOEFL (minimum score 550 paper-based; 80 iBT), IELTS (minimum score 6.5). Electronic applications accepted.

University of Massachusetts Lowell, College of Fine Arts, Humanities and Social Sciences, Department of Music, Lowell, MA 01854. Offers music education (MM). *Accreditation:* NASM. *Program availability:* Part-time. *Degree requirements:* For master's, one foreign language, thesis. *Entrance requirements:* For master's, MAT, audition. Electronic applications accepted.

University of Memphis, Graduate School, College of Communication and Fine Arts, Rudi E. Scheidt School of Music, Memphis, TN 38152. Offers composition (M Mu, DMA); conducting (M Mu, DMA); jazz and studio music (M Mu); music education (M Mu, PhD); music theory (DCC); musicology (PhD); Orff-Schulwerk (M Mu); pedagogy (M Mu); performance (M Mu, DMA). *Accreditation:* NASM. *Program availability:* Part-time. *Faculty:* 35 full-time (8 women), 6 part-time/adjunct (2 women). *Students:* 72 full-time (31 women), 47 part-time (24 women); includes 24 minority (11 Black or African American, non-Hispanic/Latino; 4 Asian, non-Hispanic/Latino; 6 Hispanic/Latino; 3 Two or more races, non-Hispanic/Latino), 15 international. Average age 32. 76 applicants, 83% accepted, 33 enrolled. In 2016, 25 master's, 18 doctorates awarded. Terminal master's awarded for partial completion of doctoral program. *Degree requirements:* For master's, variable foreign language requirement, comprehensive exam, thesis or alternative; for doctorate, one foreign language, comprehensive exam, thesis/dissertation, qualifying exam. *Entrance requirements:* For master's, audition; for doctorate, GRE General Test or MAT, proficiency exam, audition, work sample, master's degree. Additional exam requirements/recommendations for international students: Required—TOEFL (minimum score 550 paper-based; 79 iBT). *Application deadline:* For fall admission, 8/1 for domestic students; for spring admission, 12/1 for domestic students. Applications are processed on a rolling basis. Application fee: $35 ($60 for international students). Electronic applications accepted. *Expenses:* $5,231.50 per semester full-time in-state, $9,623.50 full-time out-of-state. *Financial support:* In 2016–17, 73 students received support, including 5 research assistantships with tuition reimbursements available (averaging $9,600 per year), 28 teaching assistantships with tuition reimbursements available (averaging $12,142 per year); Federal Work-Study, scholarships/grants, and unspecified assistantships also available. Financial award application deadline: 2/1; financial award applicants required to submit FAFSA. *Faculty research:* Spanish Renaissance, twentieth-century music, Project OPTIMUS, composition, musical performance, regional music, performance, performance practice, composition. *Unit head:* Dr. John Chiego, Director, 901-678-3773, Fax: 901-678-3096, E-mail: jchiego@memphis.edu. *Application contact:* Dr. Dave Spencer, Assistant Director for Graduate Studies, 901-678-3779, Fax: 901-678-3096, E-mail: dspencer@memphis.edu.
Website: http://www.memphis.edu/music/

University of Miami, Graduate School, Frost School of Music, Department of Music Education and Music Therapy, Coral Gables, FL 33124. Offers music education (MM, PhD, Spec M); music therapy (MM). *Accreditation:* NASM. *Degree requirements:* For master's, thesis; for doctorate, thesis/dissertation, 2 research tools; for Spec M, thesis, research project. *Entrance requirements:* For master's and doctorate, GRE General Test. Additional exam requirements/recommendations for international students: Required—TOEFL (minimum score 550 paper-based; 59 iBT). Electronic applications accepted. *Faculty research:* Motivation, quantitative research, early childhood, instrumental music, elementary music.

University of Michigan, Rackham Graduate School, School of Music, Theatre, and Dance, Program in Music Education, Ann Arbor, MI 48109-2085. Offers MM, PhD, Spec M. *Accreditation:* NASM; TEAC. *Degree requirements:* For doctorate, thesis/dissertation, oral and preliminary exams. *Entrance requirements:* For doctorate, MAT, writing sample, portfolio. Additional exam requirements/recommendations for international students: Required—TOEFL. Electronic applications accepted. *Expenses:* Tuition, state resident: full-time $21,466; part-time $1152 per credit hour. Tuition, nonresident: full-time $43,346; part-time $2367 per credit hour. Part-time tuition and fees vary according to course load, degree level and program.

University of Minnesota, Duluth, Graduate School, School of Fine Arts, Department of Music, Duluth, MN 55812-2496. Offers music education (MM); performance (MM). *Accreditation:* NASM. *Program availability:* Part-time. *Degree requirements:* For master's, comprehensive exam, thesis (for some programs), recital (MM in performance). *Entrance requirements:* For master's, audition, minimum GPA of 3.0, sample of written work, interview, bachelor's degree in music, video of teaching. Additional exam requirements/recommendations for international students: Required—TOEFL (minimum score 550 paper-based). *Faculty research:* Band composition, music aesthetics, learning theory, value theory, music advocacy.

University of Missouri, Office of Research and Graduate Studies, College of Education, Department of Learning, Teaching and Curriculum, Columbia, MO 65211. Offers agricultural education (M Ed, PhD, Ed S); art education (M Ed, PhD, Ed S); business and office education (M Ed, PhD, Ed S); early childhood education (M Ed, PhD, Ed S); elementary education (M Ed, PhD, Ed S); English education (M Ed, PhD, Ed S); foreign language education (M Ed, PhD, Ed S); health education and promotion (M Ed, PhD); learning and instruction (M Ed); marketing education (M Ed, PhD, Ed S); mathematics education (M Ed, PhD, Ed S); music education (M Ed, PhD, Ed S); reading education (M Ed, PhD, Ed S); science education (M Ed, PhD, Ed S); social studies education (M Ed, PhD, Ed S); vocational education (M Ed, PhD, Ed S). *Program availability:* Part-time. *Faculty:* 30 full-time (18 women), 1 (woman) part-time/adjunct. *Students:* 157 full-time (124 women), 157 part-time (125 women). Terminal master's awarded for partial completion of doctoral program. *Degree requirements:* For doctorate, thesis/dissertation. *Entrance requirements:* For master's and Ed S, GRE General Test or MAT, minimum GPA of 3.0; for doctorate, GRE General Test, minimum GPA of 3.0. Additional exam requirements/recommendations for international students: Required—TOEFL (minimum score 600 paper-based; 100 iBT). *Application deadline:* For fall admission, 12/1 priority date for domestic and international students. Applications are processed on a rolling basis. Application fee: $75 ($90 for international students). Electronic applications accepted. *Expenses:* Tuition, state resident: full-time $6347; part-time $352.60 per credit hour. Tuition, nonresident: full-time $17,379; part-time $965.50 per credit hour. *Required fees:* $1035. Tuition and fees vary according to course load, campus/location and program. *Financial support:* Fellowships, research assistantships, teaching assistantships, institutionally sponsored loans, traineeships, health care benefits, and unspecified assistantships available. Support available to part-time students.
Website: http://education.missouri.edu/LTC/index.php

University of Missouri–Kansas City, Conservatory of Music and Dance, Kansas City, MO 64110-2499. Offers composition (MM, DMA); conducting (MM, DMA); music (MA); music education (MME, PhD); music history and literature (MM); music theory (MM); music therapy (MA); performance (MM, DMA). PhD (interdisciplinary) offered through the School of Graduate Studies. *Accreditation:* NASM. *Program availability:* Part-time. *Faculty:* 55 full-time (24 women), 39 part-time/adjunct (12 women). *Students:* 165 full-time (67 women), 64 part-time (34 women); includes 21 minority (4 Black or African American, non-Hispanic/Latino; 7 Asian, non-Hispanic/Latino; 7 Hispanic/Latino; 3 Two or more races, non-Hispanic/Latino), 49 international. Average age 28. 368 applicants, 49% accepted, 88 enrolled. In 2016, 49 master's, 26 doctorates awarded. *Degree requirements:* For master's, variable foreign language requirement, comprehensive exam, thesis (for some programs); for doctorate, variable foreign language requirement, comprehensive exam, thesis/dissertation or alternative. *Entrance requirements:* For master's, minimum GPA of 3.0 in major, auditions (for MM in performance); for doctorate, minimum graduate GPA of 3.5, auditions (for DMA in performance), portfolio of compositions. Additional exam requirements/recommendations for international students: Required—TOEFL (minimum score 550 paper-based; 80 iBT). *Application deadline:* For fall admission, 1/15 priority date for domestic students, 1/15 for international students. Application fee: $45 ($50 for international students). *Financial support:* In 2016–17, 32 teaching assistantships with partial tuition reimbursements (averaging $8,238 per year) were awarded; career-related internships or fieldwork, Federal Work-Study, institutionally sponsored loans, scholarships/grants, tuition waivers (partial), and unspecified assistantships also available. Support available to part-time students. Financial award application deadline: 3/1; financial award applicants required to submit FAFSA. *Faculty research:* Electro-acoustic composition, affective music responses, American music theatre, Russian choral music, music therapy and Alzheimer's. *Unit head:* Peter Witte, Dean, 816-235-2731, Fax: 816-235-5265, E-mail: wittep@umkc.edu. *Application contact:* William Everett, Associate Dean for Graduate Studies, 816-235-2857, Fax: 816-235-5264, E-mail: everettw@umkc.edu.
Website: http://conservatory.umkc.edu/

University of Missouri–St. Louis, College of Arts and Sciences, School of Fine and Performing Arts, Department of Music, St. Louis, MO 63121. Offers music education (MME). *Accreditation:* NASM. *Program availability:* Part-time, evening/weekend. *Faculty:* 1 full-time (0 women). *Students:* 4 part-time (all women). *Entrance*

requirements: For master's, 3 letters of recommendation, BA in music education. Additional exam requirements/recommendations for international students: Recommended—TOEFL (minimum score 550 paper-based; 79 iBT), IELTS (minimum score 6.5). *Application deadline:* For fall admission, 7/1 priority date for domestic and international students; for spring admission, 12/1 for domestic students, 12/1 priority date for international students. Applications are processed on a rolling basis. Application fee: $50 ($40 for international students). Electronic applications accepted. *Financial support:* Scholarships/grants available. Financial award applicants required to submit FAFSA. *Faculty research:* Music technology, musicology, music education methods, history of music education, psychology of music. *Unit head:* Gary Brandes, Chair, 314-516-5980, Fax: 314-516-6593, E-mail: brandesg@umsl.edu. *Application contact:* 314-516-5458, Fax: 314-516-6996, E-mail: gradadm@umsl.edu.
Website: http://music.umsl.edu/

University of Nebraska at Kearney, College of Fine Arts and Humanities, Department of Music, Kearney, NE 68849-0001. Offers music education (MA Ed). *Accreditation:* NCATE. *Program availability:* Part-time, evening/weekend, 100% online. *Faculty:* 17 full-time (7 women). *Students:* 1 (woman) full-time, 27 part-time (15 women); includes 2 minority (1 Black or African American, non-Hispanic/Latino; 1 Two or more races, non-Hispanic/Latino). Average age 32. 3 applicants, 67% accepted, 2 enrolled. In 2016, 8 master's awarded. *Degree requirements:* For master's, comprehensive exam, thesis optional. *Entrance requirements:* For master's, undergraduate degree in music, resume, philosophy of teaching, three letters of recommendation. Additional exam requirements/recommendations for international students: Recommended—TOEFL (minimum score 550 paper-based; 79 iBT), IELTS (minimum score 6.5). *Application deadline:* For fall admission, 6/15 for domestic and international students; for spring admission, 10/15 for domestic and international students; for summer admission, 3/15 for domestic and international students. Application fee: $45. Electronic applications accepted. *Expenses:* Tuition, state resident: full-time $4064; part-time $225.75 per credit hour. Tuition, nonresident: full-time $8915; part-time $495.25 per credit hour. *Required fees:* $772; $23 per credit hour. Part-time tuition and fees vary according to course load, campus/location, program and reciprocity agreements. *Financial support:* Career-related internships or fieldwork and scholarships/grants available. Support available to part-time students. Financial award application deadline: 2/28; financial award applicants required to submit FAFSA. *Faculty research:* Contemporary American music, musical theater, opera, woodwind performance and pedagogy, percussion pedagogy, historic and contemporary American piano, dramatic mezzo-soprano, violin performance, piano performance and pedagogy, music composition, opera, healing effects of music, Chamber music, diction. *Unit head:* Dr. Janet Harriott, Committee Chair, 308-865-8608, E-mail: harriottjm@unk.edu. *Application contact:* Linda Johnson, Director, Graduate Admissions, 800-717-7881, E-mail: gradstudies@unk.edu.
Website: http://aaunk.unk.edu/gradcatalogs/14-15cat/prog/progmus.asp

University of Nebraska–Lincoln, Graduate College, College of Fine and Performing Arts, School of Music, Lincoln, NE 68588. Offers composition (MM, DMA); conducting (MM, DMA); music education (MM, PhD); music history (MM); music theory (MM); performance (MM, DMA); piano pedagogy (MM); woodwind specialties (MM). *Accreditation:* NASM. *Degree requirements:* For master's, thesis optional; for doctorate, comprehensive exam, thesis/dissertation. *Entrance requirements:* For master's and doctorate, audition. Additional exam requirements/recommendations for international students: Required—TOEFL. Electronic applications accepted. *Faculty research:* Mozart, Tchaikovsky, Josquin des Prez, practice of J.S. Bach's organ works, instructional strategies in music education.

University of New Mexico, Graduate Studies, College of Fine Arts, Program in Music, Albuquerque, NM 87131. Offers collaborative piano (M Mu); conducting (M Mu); music education (M Mu); music history and literature (M Mu); performance (M Mu); theory and composition (M Mu). *Accreditation:* NASM. *Program availability:* Part-time. *Faculty:* 33 full-time (12 women), 8 part-time/adjunct (6 women). *Students:* 39 full-time (19 women), 54 part-time (29 women); includes 17 minority (1 Black or African American, non-Hispanic/Latino; 1 American Indian or Alaska Native, non-Hispanic/Latino; 3 Asian, non-Hispanic/Latino; 9 Hispanic/Latino; 3 Two or more races, non-Hispanic/Latino), 17 international. Average age 29. 75 applicants, 76% accepted, 36 enrolled. In 2016, 30 master's awarded. *Degree requirements:* For master's, variable foreign language requirement, comprehensive exam, thesis (for some programs), recital (for some programs). *Entrance requirements:* For master's, placement exams in music history and theory. Additional exam requirements/recommendations for international students: Required—TOEFL (minimum score 550 paper-based). *Application deadline:* For fall admission, 7/1 for domestic students, 5/1 for international students; for spring admission, 11/1 for domestic students, 10/1 for international students. Applications are processed on a rolling basis. Application fee: $50. Electronic applications accepted. *Financial support:* Research assistantships, teaching assistantships with tuition reimbursements, Federal Work-Study, scholarships/grants, and unspecified assistantships available. Support available to part-time students. Financial award application deadline: 2/1; financial award applicants required to submit FAFSA. *Faculty research:* Opera, twentieth-century and contemporary music, performance, conducting. *Unit head:* Dr. Steven Block, Chair, 505-277-2127, Fax: 505-277-4202, E-mail: sblock@unm.edu. *Application contact:* Colleen M. Sheinberg, Graduate Coordinator, 505-277-8401, Fax: 505-277-4202, E-mail: colleens@unm.edu.
Website: http://music.unm.edu/

The University of North Carolina at Chapel Hill, Graduate School, School of Education, Program in Secondary Education, Chapel Hill, NC 27599. Offers English (Grades 9-12) (MAT); English as a second language (MAT); French (Grades K-12) (MAT); German (Grades K-12) (MAT); Japanese (Grades K-12) (MAT); Latin (Grades 9-12) (MAT); mathematics (Grades 9-12) (MAT); music (Grades K-12) (MAT); science (Grades 9-12) (MAT); social studies (Grades 9-12) (MAT); Spanish (Grades K-12) (MAT). *Accreditation:* NCATE. *Degree requirements:* For master's, comprehensive exam. *Entrance requirements:* For master's, GRE General Test, minimum GPA of 3.0 during last 2 years of undergraduate course work. Additional exam requirements/recommendations for international students: Required—TOEFL (minimum score 550 paper-based). Electronic applications accepted.

The University of North Carolina at Greensboro, Graduate School, School of Music, Theatre and Dance, Greensboro, NC 27412-5001. Offers composition (MM); dance (MA, MFA); education (MM); music education (PhD); performance (MM, DMA); theatre (M Ed, MFA), including acting (MFA), design (MFA), directing (MFA), theatre education (M Ed), theatre for youth (MFA); theory (MM). *Accreditation:* NASM. *Degree requirements:* For master's, variable foreign language requirement, thesis (for some programs), recital; for doctorate, comprehensive exam, thesis/dissertation, diagnostic exam, recital. *Entrance requirements:* For master's, GRE General Test, NTE, audition; for doctorate, GRE General Test, GRE Subject Test (music), audition. Additional exam requirements/recommendations for international students: Required—TOEFL. Electronic applications accepted.

University of North Dakota, Graduate School, College of Arts and Sciences, Department of Music, Grand Forks, ND 58202. Offers music (MM); music education (PhD). *Accreditation:* NASM. *Program availability:* Part-time. *Degree requirements:* For master's, comprehensive exam, thesis or alternative. *Entrance requirements:* For master's, minimum GPA of 3.0. Additional exam requirements/recommendations for international students: Required—TOEFL (minimum score 550 paper-based; 79 iBT), IELTS (minimum score 6.5). *Application deadline:* For fall admission, 8/1 priority date for domestic students, 5/1 priority date for international students; for spring admission, 12/1 priority date for domestic students, 9/1 priority date for international students. Applications are processed on a rolling basis. Application fee: $35. Electronic applications accepted. *Financial support:* Fellowships with full and partial tuition reimbursements, research assistantships with full and partial tuition reimbursements, teaching assistantships with full tuition reimbursements, Federal Work-Study, institutionally sponsored loans, scholarships/grants, health care benefits, tuition waivers (full and partial), and unspecified assistantships available. Support available to part-time students. Financial award application deadline: 3/15; financial award applicants required to submit FAFSA. *Unit head:* Dr. Michael Wittgraf, Graduate Director, 701-777-2644, Fax: 701-777-3320, E-mail: michael.wittgraf@und.edu. *Application contact:* Debbie Ford, Admissions Specialist, 701-777-0749, Fax: 701-777-3619, E-mail: debra.ford@gradschool.und.edu.
Website: http://arts-sciences.und.edu/music/

University of Northern Colorado, Graduate School, College of Performing and Visual Arts, School of Music, Greeley, CO 80639. Offers collaborative piano (MM, DA); composition (DA); conducting (MM, DA); instrumental performance (MM); jazz studies (MM, DA); music education (MM, DA); music history and literature (MM, DA); music theory and composition (MM); performance (DA); vocal performance (MM). *Accreditation:* NASM; NCATE (one or more programs are accredited). *Program availability:* Part-time. *Degree requirements:* For master's, comprehensive exam, thesis or alternative; for doctorate, comprehensive exam, thesis/dissertation. *Entrance requirements:* For master's, audition; for doctorate, GRE General Test, audition, 3 letters of recommendation. *Application deadline:* Applications are processed on a rolling basis. Application fee: $50 ($60 for international students). Electronic applications accepted. *Financial support:* Fellowships, research assistantships, teaching assistantships, and unspecified assistantships available. Financial award application deadline: 3/1; financial award applicants required to submit FAFSA. *Unit head:* David Caffey, Director, 970-351-2679. *Application contact:* Linda Sisson, Graduate Student Admission Coordinator, 970-351-1807, Fax: 970-351-2371, E-mail: linda.sisson@unco.edu.
Website: http://www.arts.unco.edu/

University of Northern Iowa, Graduate College, College of Humanities, Arts and Sciences, School of Music, MM Program in Jazz Pedagogy, Cedar Falls, IA 50614. Offers MM. *Degree requirements:* For master's, comprehensive exam. *Entrance requirements:* For master's, audition, interview, essay.

University of Northern Iowa, Graduate College, College of Humanities, Arts and Sciences, School of Music, MM Program in Music Education, Cedar Falls, IA 50614. Offers MM. *Accreditation:* NASM. *Program availability:* Part-time, evening/weekend. *Degree requirements:* For master's, comprehensive exam, thesis or alternative. *Entrance requirements:* For master's, written diagnostic exam in theory, music history, expository writing skills, and in the area of claimed competency, portfolio, tape recordings of compositions, in-person auditions, minimum GPA of 3.0. Additional exam requirements/recommendations for international students: Required—TOEFL (minimum score 500 paper-based; 61 iBT). Electronic applications accepted.

University of Northern Iowa, Graduate College, College of Humanities, Arts and Sciences, School of Music, MM Program in Piano Performance and Pedagogy, Cedar Falls, IA 50614. Offers MM.

University of North Texas, Robert B. Toulouse School of Graduate Studies, Denton, TX 76203-5459. Offers accounting (MS); applied anthropology (MA, MS); applied behavior analysis (Certificate); applied geography (MA); applied technology and performance improvement (M Ed, MS); art education (MA); art history (MA); art museum education (Certificate); arts leadership (Certificate); audiology (Au D); behavior analysis (MS); behavioral science (PhD); biochemistry and molecular biology (MS); biology (MA, MS); biomedical engineering (MS); business analysis (MS); chemistry (MS); clinical health psychology (PhD); communication studies (MA, MS); computer engineering (MS); computer science (MS); counseling (M Ed, MS), including clinical mental health counseling (MS), college and university counseling, elementary school counseling, secondary school counseling; creative writing (MA); criminal justice (MS); curriculum and instruction (M Ed); decision sciences (MBA); design (MA, MFA), including fashion design (MFA), innovation studies, interior design (MFA); early childhood studies (MS); economics (MS); educational leadership (M Ed, Ed D); educational psychology (MS, PhD), including family studies (MS), gifted and talented (MS), human development (MS), learning and cognition (MS), research, measurement and evaluation (MS); electrical engineering (MS); emergency management (MPA); engineering technology (MS); English (MA); English as a second language (MA); environmental science (MS); finance (MBA, MS); financial management (MPA); French (MA); health services management (MBA); higher education (M Ed, Ed D); history (MA, MS); hospitality management (MS); human resources management (MPA); information science (MS); information systems (PhD); information technologies (MBA); interdisciplinary studies (MA, MS); international studies (MA); international sustainable tourism (MS); jazz studies (MM); journalism (MA, MJ, Graduate Certificate), including interactive and virtual digital communication (Graduate Certificate), narrative journalism (Graduate Certificate), public relations (Graduate Certificate); kinesiology (MS); linguistics (MA); local government management (MPA); logistics (PhD); logistics and supply chain management (MBA); long-term care, senior housing, and aging services (MA); management (PhD); marketing (MBA); mathematics (MA, MS); mechanical and energy engineering (MS, PhD); music (MA), including ethnomusicology, music theory, musicology, performance; music composition (PhD); music education (MM Ed, PhD); nonprofit management (MPA); operations and supply chain management (MBA); performance (MM, DMA); philosophy (MA); political science (MA); professional and technical communication (MA); radio, television and film (MA, MFA); rehabilitation counseling (Certificate); sociology (MA); Spanish (MA); special education (M Ed); speech-language pathology (MA); strategic management (MBA); studio art (MFA); teaching (M Ed); MBA/MS. *Program availability:* Part-time, evening/weekend, online learning. Terminal master's awarded for partial completion of doctoral program. *Degree requirements:* For master's, variable foreign language requirement, comprehensive exam (for some programs), thesis (for some programs); for doctorate, variable foreign language requirement, comprehensive exam (for some programs), thesis/dissertation; for other advanced degree, variable foreign language requirement, comprehensive exam (for some programs). *Entrance requirements:* For master's and doctorate, GRE, GMAT. Additional exam requirements/recommendations for international students: Required—TOEFL (minimum score 550 paper-based; 79 iBT). Electronic applications accepted.

University of Oklahoma, Weitzenhoffer Family College of Fine Arts, School of Music, Norman, OK 73019. Offers choral conducting (M Mus), including church music (M Mus, DMA), standard (M Mus, DMA); composition (M Mus, DMA); conducting (M Mus Ed, DMA), including choral, church music (M Mus, DMA), instrumental (M Mus Ed), orchestral (DMA), wind band (DMA); general music education (M Mus Ed), including Kodaly concepts; instrumental (M Mus Ed), including primary instrument, secondary instrument; instrumental conducting (M Mus); music education (PhD); music performance (Graduate Certificate); music theory (M Mus); musicology (M Mus); organ

(M Mus, DMA), including church music, organ technology (M Mus), standard; piano (M Mus, DMA), including performance, performance and pedagogy; piano pedagogy (M Mus Ed); voice (M Mus, DMA), including opera (M Mus), performance; wind/percussion/string instruments (M Mus, DMA). *Accreditation:* NASM. *Faculty:* 61 full-time (17 women), 1 part-time/adjunct (0 women). *Students:* 113 full-time (49 women), 68 part-time (32 women); includes 32 minority (5 Black or African American, non-Hispanic/Latino; 4 American Indian or Alaska Native, non-Hispanic/Latino; 7 Asian, non-Hispanic/Latino; 11 Hispanic/Latino; 5 Two or more races, non-Hispanic/Latino), 26 international. Average age 29. 161 applicants, 43% accepted, 50 enrolled. In 2016, 35 master's, 13 doctorates awarded. *Degree requirements:* For master's, variable foreign language requirement, comprehensive exam (for some programs), thesis (for some programs); for doctorate, variable foreign language requirement, comprehensive exam, thesis/dissertation, three recitals and/or workshops (two recitals for DMA in composition); for Graduate Certificate, variable foreign language requirement, two recitals. *Entrance requirements:* For master's, bachelor's degree in music, music education, or the equivalent; transcripts; resume; personal statement; 3 letters of recommendation; audition and/or other practical application materials as appropriate to intended degree; sample of scholarly writing (for M Mus in musicology and M Mus in music theory); for doctorate, master's degree in music, music education, or the equivalent; transcripts; resume; personal statement; 3 letters of recommendation; sample of scholarly writing; audition and/or other practical application materials as appropriate to intended degree; for Graduate Certificate, bachelor's degree in music, music education, or the equivalent; transcripts; resume; personal statement; 3 letters of recommendation; audition. Additional exam requirements/recommendations for international students: Required—TOEFL (minimum score 79 iBT) or IELTS (minimum score 6.5). *Application deadline:* For fall admission, 2/1 for domestic and international students; for spring admission, 10/1 for domestic students, 9/1 for international students; for summer admission, 2/1 for domestic and international students. Applications are processed on a rolling basis. Application fee: $50 ($100 for international students). Electronic applications accepted. *Expenses:* Tuition, state resident: full-time $4886; part-time $203.60 per credit hour. Tuition, nonresident: full-time $18,989; part-time $791.20 per credit hour. *Required fees:* $3283; $126.25 per credit hour. $126.50 per semester. *Financial support:* In 2016–17, 121 students received support, including 3 fellowships with full tuition reimbursements available (averaging $5,000 per year), 31 research assistantships with full tuition reimbursements available (averaging $10,557 per year), 64 teaching assistantships with full tuition reimbursements available (averaging $10,494 per year); health care benefits and unspecified assistantships also available. Financial award application deadline: 6/1; financial award applicants required to submit FAFSA. *Faculty research:* Piano pedagogy, performance practice, music education, musicology, music theory. *Unit head:* Dr. Roland Barrett, Interim Director, 405-325-2081, Fax: 405-325-7574, E-mail: rebarrett@ou.edu. *Application contact:* Jan Russell, Graduate Admissions and Recruiting Advisor, 405-325-5393, Fax: 405-325-7574, E-mail: jrussell@ou.edu.
Website: http://www.ou.edu/finearts/music/

University of Oregon, Graduate School, School of Music, Program in Music Education, Eugene, OR 97403. Offers M Mus, DMA, PhD. *Accreditation:* NASM. *Program availability:* Part-time. Terminal master's awarded for partial completion of doctoral program. *Degree requirements:* For master's, variable foreign language requirement, thesis (for some programs); for doctorate, one foreign language, comprehensive exam, thesis/dissertation. *Entrance requirements:* For master's, minimum GPA of 3.0, videotape or interview; for doctorate, GRE General Test, minimum GPA of 3.0, videotape or interview. Additional exam requirements/recommendations for international students: Required—TOEFL. *Faculty research:* Psalms of DeLasso, stress and muscular tension in stringed instrument performance, piano music of Stravinsky, learning aptitudes in elementary music.

University of Ottawa, Faculty of Graduate and Postdoctoral Studies, Faculty of Arts, Department of Music, Ottawa, ON K1N 6N5, Canada. Offers music (M Mus, MA); orchestral studies (Certificate); piano pedagogy research (Certificate). *Degree requirements:* For master's, thesis optional. *Entrance requirements:* For master's, honors degree or equivalent, minimum B+ average. Electronic applications accepted. *Faculty research:* Performance, theory, musicology.

University of Rhode Island, Graduate School, College of Arts and Sciences, Department of Music, Kingston, RI 02881. Offers music education (MM); music performance (MM). Program offered in partnership with School of Education. *Accreditation:* NASM. *Program availability:* Part-time. *Faculty:* 12 full-time (6 women). *Students:* 6 full-time (3 women), 2 part-time (both women); includes 2 minority (both Black or African American, non-Hispanic/Latino). In 2016, 3 master's awarded. *Entrance requirements:* For master's, 2 letters of recommendation, audition. Additional exam requirements/recommendations for international students: Required—TOEFL. *Application deadline:* For fall admission, 7/15 for domestic students, 2/1 for international students; for spring admission, 11/15 for domestic students, 7/15 for international students; for summer admission, 4/15 for domestic students. Application fee: $65. Electronic applications accepted. *Expenses:* Tuition, state resident: full-time $11,796; part-time $655 per credit. Tuition, nonresident: full-time $24,206; part-time $1345 per credit. *Required fees:* $1546; $44 per credit. One-time fee: $155 full-time; $35 part-time. *Financial support:* In 2016–17, 3 teaching assistantships with tuition reimbursements (averaging $10,310 per year) were awarded; research assistantships also available. Financial award application deadline: 3/15; financial award applicants required to submit FAFSA. *Unit head:* Dr. Mark Conley, Chair, 401-874-2431, E-mail: mconley@uri.edu. *Application contact:* Dr. Joe Parillo, Director of Graduate Studies, 401-874-2431, E-mail: jmparillo@uri.edu.
Website: http://www.uri.edu/artsci/mus/

University of Rochester, Eastman School of Music, Programs in Music Education, Rochester, NY 14627. Offers MA, MM, DMA, PhD. *Accreditation:* NASM. *Expenses: Tuition:* Full-time $47,450; part-time $1482 per credit hour. *Required fees:* $528. Tuition and fees vary according to program.

University of St. Thomas, Graduate Studies, College of Arts and Sciences, Graduate Programs in Music Education, St. Paul, MN 55105-1096. Offers choral (MA); instrumental (MA); Kodaly (MA); leadership in music education (Ed D); Orff Schulwerk (MA); piano pedagogy (MA). *Accreditation:* NASM; NCATE. *Program availability:* Part-time. *Degree requirements:* For master's, comprehensive exam, thesis, music history theory and diagnostic exam, piano recital (for piano pedagogy students). *Entrance requirements:* For master's, performance assessment hearing, interview. Additional exam requirements/recommendations for international students: Required—TOEFL (minimum score 550 paper-based; 80 iBT). *Application deadline:* For fall admission, 7/1 for domestic and international students; for winter admission, 12/1 for domestic and international students; for spring admission, 4/1 for domestic and international students. Applications are processed on a rolling basis. Application fee: $0. Electronic applications accepted. *Expenses:* Contact institution. *Financial support:* Federal Work-Study, institutionally sponsored loans, and scholarships/grants available. Financial award application deadline: 4/1; financial award applicants required to submit FAFSA. *Faculty research:* Kodaly, choral, piano pedagogy, Orff, instrumental, world music. *Unit head:* Dr. Douglas C. Orzolek, Director, 651-962-5878, Fax: 651-962-5886, E-mail: dcorzolek@stthomas.edu. *Application contact:* Bev Johnson, Program Coordinator, 651-962-5870, Fax: 651-962-5886, E-mail: bhjohnson@stthomas.edu.
Website: http://www.stthomas.edu/music/graduate

University of South Alabama, College of Arts and Sciences, Department of Music, Mobile, AL 36688. Offers collaborative keyboard (MM); music education (MM); performance (MM). *Faculty:* 6 full-time (1 woman). *Students:* 1 full-time (0 women), 3 part-time (0 women). Average age 29. 4 applicants, 50% accepted, 2 enrolled. In 2016, 5 master's awarded. *Degree requirements:* For master's, comprehensive exam, final project. *Entrance requirements:* For master's, GRE/GMAT, undergraduate degree in music with minimum GPA of 3.0, official transcript, resume, 3 recommendation letters; teaching certificate (for music education). Additional exam requirements/recommendations for international students: Required—TOEFL (minimum score 525 paper-based; 71 iBT). *Application deadline:* For fall admission, 7/1 priority date for domestic students, 6/1 priority date for international students; for spring admission, 12/1 priority date for domestic students, 11/1 priority date for international students; for summer admission, 5/1 priority date for domestic students, 4/1 priority date for international students. Applications are processed on a rolling basis. Application fee: $35. Electronic applications accepted. *Expenses:* Tuition, state resident: full-time $9768; part-time $407 per credit hour. Tuition, nonresident: full-time $19,536; part-time $814 per credit hour. *Financial support:* Fellowships, research assistantships, teaching assistantships, career-related internships or fieldwork, Federal Work-Study, institutionally sponsored loans, scholarships/grants, and unspecified assistantships available. Support available to part-time students. Financial award application deadline: 5/31; financial award applicants required to submit FAFSA. *Unit head:* Dr. Greg Gruner, Chair, Music, 251-460-6804, Fax: 251-460-7328, E-mail: ggruner@southalabama.edu. *Application contact:* Dr. Jeannette Fresne, Graduate Coordinator, Music, 251-460-6697, Fax: 251-460-7328, E-mail: jfresne@southalabama.edu.
Website: http://www.southalabama.edu/colleges/music/

University of South Carolina, The Graduate School, School of Music, Columbia, SC 29208. Offers composition (MM, DMA); conducting (MM, DMA); jazz studies (MM); music education (MM Ed, PhD); music history (MM); music performance (Certificate); music theory (MM); opera theater (MM); performance (MM, DMA); piano pedagogy (MM, DMA). *Program availability:* Part-time. *Degree requirements:* For master's, 5 foreign languages, comprehensive exam, thesis (for some programs); for doctorate, one foreign language, comprehensive exam, thesis/dissertation; for Certificate, recitals. *Entrance requirements:* For master's and doctorate, GRE General Test or MAT, music diagnostic exam. Additional exam requirements/recommendations for international students: Required—TOEFL (minimum score 570 paper-based). Electronic applications accepted. *Expenses:* Contact institution. *Faculty research:* Music skills in pre-school children, evaluation of school performing ensembles.

The University of South Dakota, Graduate School, College of Fine Arts, Department of Music, Vermillion, SD 57069. Offers collaborative piano (MM); conducting (MM); history of musical instruments (MM); music education (MM); music history (MM); music performance (MM). *Accreditation:* NASM. *Degree requirements:* For master's, thesis or alternative. *Entrance requirements:* For master's, minimum GPA of 2.7, audition or performance tape. Additional exam requirements/recommendations for international students: Required—TOEFL (minimum score 550 paper-based; 79 iBT). Electronic applications accepted.

University of Southern California, Graduate School, Thornton School of Music, Los Angeles, CA 90089. Offers brass performance (MM, DMA, Graduate Certificate); choral and sacred music (MM, DMA); classical guitar (MM, DMA, Graduate Certificate); composition (MM, DMA); early music (MA, DMA); harp performance (MM, DMA, Graduate Certificate); historical musicology (PhD); jazz studies (MM, DMA, Graduate Certificate); keyboard collaborative arts (MM, DMA, Graduate Certificate); music education (MM, DMA); organ performance (MM, DMA, Graduate Certificate); percussion performance (MM, DMA, Graduate Certificate); piano performance (MM, DMA, Graduate Certificate); scoring for motion pictures and television (Graduate Certificate); strings performance (MM, DMA, Graduate Certificate); studio jazz guitar (MM, DMA, Graduate Certificate); teaching music (MA); vocal arts (classical voice/opera) (MM, DMA, Graduate Certificate); woodwind performance (MM, DMA, Graduate Certificate). *Accreditation:* NASM. *Program availability:* Part-time, evening/weekend. Terminal master's awarded for partial completion of doctoral program. *Degree requirements:* For master's, variable foreign language requirement, comprehensive exam (for some programs), thesis (for some programs); for doctorate, variable foreign language requirement, comprehensive exam, thesis/dissertation (for some programs). *Entrance requirements:* For master's, GRE (for MA in early music and MM in music education); for doctorate, GRE (for DMA). Additional exam requirements/recommendations for international students: Required—TOEFL (minimum score 560 paper-based; 83 iBT). Electronic applications accepted. *Expenses:* Contact institution. *Faculty research:* Early Modern musical improvisation and composition, maternal sound stimulation of the premature infant, physiological characteristics of jazz guitarists, the musical experience of the very young child, electronic music.

University of Southern Maine, College of Arts, Humanities, and Social Sciences, School of Music, Portland, ME 04103. Offers composition (MM); conducting (MM); jazz studies (MM); music education (MM); performance (MM). *Accreditation:* NASM.

University of Southern Mississippi, Graduate School, College of Arts and Letters, School of Music, Hattiesburg, MS 39406. Offers conducting (MM, DMA); history and literature (MM); music education (MME, PhD); performance (MM); performance and pedagogy (DMA); piano accompanying (MM); theory (MM); woodwind performance and pedagogy (MM). *Accreditation:* NASM. *Program availability:* Blended/hybrid learning. Terminal master's awarded for partial completion of doctoral program. *Degree requirements:* For master's, comprehensive exam, thesis (for some programs); for doctorate, comprehensive exam, thesis/dissertation. *Entrance requirements:* For master's, GRE General Test, minimum GPA of 2.75 in last 60 hours; for doctorate, GRE General Test, minimum GPA of 3.5. Additional exam requirements/recommendations for international students: Required—TOEFL, IELTS. *Application deadline:* For fall admission, 6/1 for domestic students; for spring admission, 11/1 for domestic students; for summer admission, 3/1 for domestic students. Applications are processed on a rolling basis. Application fee: $60. *Expenses: Tuition, area resident:* Full-time $15,708; part-time $437 per credit hour. *Financial support:* Fellowships with full tuition reimbursements, research assistantships, teaching assistantships with full tuition reimbursements, Federal Work-Study, institutionally sponsored loans, scholarships/grants, health care benefits, tuition waivers (partial), and unspecified assistantships available. Financial award application deadline: 2/1; financial award applicants required to submit FAFSA. *Faculty research:* Music theory, composition, music performance. *Unit head:* Dr. Richard Kravchak, Director, 601-266-5543, Fax: 601-266-6427.
Website: https://www.usm.edu/music

University of South Florida, College of The Arts, School of Music, Tampa, FL 33620-9951. Offers music (MM, PhD), including chamber music (MM), choral conducting (MM), composition (MM), electro-acoustic music (MM), instrumental conducting (MM), jazz composition (MM), jazz performance (MM), music education (PhD), performance (MM), piano pedagogy (MM), theory (MM); music education (MA). *Accreditation:* NASM. *Program availability:* Part-time, evening/weekend. *Faculty:* 26 full-time (9 women), 1 part-time/adjunct (0 women). *Students:* 66 full-time (27 women), 19 part-time (6 women);

includes 15 minority (6 Black or African American, non-Hispanic/Latino; 2 Asian, non-Hispanic/Latino; 5 Hispanic/Latino; 2 Two or more races, non-Hispanic/Latino), 21 international. Average age 29. 93 applicants, 56% accepted, 38 enrolled. In 2016, 29 master's, 3 doctorates awarded. *Degree requirements:* For master's, comprehensive exam, thesis optional; for doctorate, comprehensive exam, thesis/dissertation. *Entrance requirements:* For master's, minimum GPA of 3.0 in upper-division courses and music courses for bachelor's degree; resume; three letters of recommendation; at least 2 years of K-12 music teaching experience (for MA in music education); audition or interview (for MM); for doctorate, GRE General Test, master's degree from accredited institution with minimum GPA of 3.5, 3.0 in upper-division undergraduate courses; at least 2 years of K-12 music teaching experience; interview with faculty; 3 letters of recommendation; academic writing sample; curriculum vitae; personal goals statement; 15-20 minute video of applicant teaching music. Additional exam requirements/recommendations for international students: Required—TOEFL (minimum score 550 paper-based; 79 iBT) or IELTS (minimum score 6.5). *Application deadline:* For fall admission, 2/15 priority date for domestic students, 2/1 for international students; for spring admission, 10/15 for domestic students, 9/15 for international students; for summer admission, 2/15 for domestic students, 1/15 for international students. Application fee: $30. Electronic applications accepted. *Expenses:* Tuition, state resident: full-time $7766; part-time $431.43 per credit hour. Tuition, nonresident: full-time $15,789; part-time $877.17 per credit hour. *Required fees:* $37 per term. *Financial support:* In 2016–17, 48 students received support, including 1 research assistantship with tuition reimbursement available (averaging $15,724 per year), 46 teaching assistantships with tuition reimbursements available (averaging $10,099 per year); unspecified assistantships also available. Financial award application deadline: 2/15. *Faculty research:* Music education: alternate methods, community collaboration, contemporary changes, early childhood, general music, international perspectives, multicultural issues, technology, teacher behaviors, philosophy, psychology, sociology; music: chamber music, composition, conducting, jazz studies, music performance, music theory, pedagogy, electronic music. *Total annual research expenditures:* $18,982. *Unit head:* Dr. Karen Bryan, Director, 813-974-2311, Fax: 813-974-8721, E-mail: kmbryan@usf.edu. *Application contact:* Dr. William Hayden, Associate Professor and Graduate Program Director, 813-974-1753, Fax: 813-974-8721, E-mail: wphayden@usf.edu.
Website: http://music.arts.usf.edu/

The University of Tennessee, Graduate School, College of Arts and Sciences, School of Music, Knoxville, TN 37996. Offers accompanying (MM); choral conducting (MM); composition (MM); instrumental conducting (MM); jazz (MM); music education (MM); music theory (MM); musicology (MM); performance (MM); piano pedagogy and literature (MM). *Accreditation:* NASM. *Program availability:* Part-time. *Degree requirements:* For master's, thesis (for some programs). *Entrance requirements:* For master's, audition, minimum GPA of 2.7. Additional exam requirements/recommendations for international students: Required—TOEFL. Electronic applications accepted.

The University of Tennessee at Chattanooga, Program in Music, Chattanooga, TN 37403. Offers music education (MM); performance (MM). *Accreditation:* NASM. *Faculty:* 5 full-time (3 women). *Students:* 5 part-time (3 women); includes 1 minority (Black or African American, non-Hispanic/Latino). Average age 29. 1 applicant, 100% accepted. In 2016, 7 master's awarded. *Degree requirements:* For master's, comprehensive exam, thesis or alternative, recital. *Entrance requirements:* For master's, GRE General Test or MAT, bachelor's degree in music, audition for placement. Additional exam requirements/recommendations for international students: Required—TOEFL (minimum score 550 paper-based; 79 iBT), IELTS (minimum score 6). *Application deadline:* For fall admission, 6/15 priority date for domestic students, 7/1 for international students; for spring admission, 11/1 priority date for domestic students, 11/1 for international students. Applications are processed on a rolling basis. Application fee: $35 ($40 for international students). Electronic applications accepted. *Expenses:* $9,876 full-time in-state; $25,994 full-time out-of-state; $450 per credit part-time in-state; $1,345 per credit part-time out-of-state. *Financial support:* Research assistantships, Federal Work-Study, scholarships/grants, and unspecified assistantships available. Financial award application deadline: 7/1; financial award applicants required to submit FAFSA. *Faculty research:* Music education, conducting, opera, vocal instruction, orchestras. *Total annual research expenditures:* $1,400. *Unit head:* Dr. Lee Harris, Department Head, 423-425-4601, Fax: 423-425-4603, E-mail: lee-harris@utc.edu. *Application contact:* Dr. Joanne Romagni, Dean of the Graduate School, 423-425-4478, Fax: 423-425-5223, E-mail: joanne-romagni@utc.edu.
Website: http://www.utc.edu/music/

The University of Texas at Arlington, Graduate School, College of Liberal Arts, Department of Music, Arlington, TX 76019. Offers education (MM); performance (MM). *Accreditation:* NASM. *Program availability:* Part-time, evening/weekend. *Degree requirements:* For master's, comprehensive exam, thesis optional. *Entrance requirements:* For master's, GRE, 3 letters of recommendation, minimum GPA of 3.0 in last 60 hours of course work. Additional exam requirements/recommendations for international students: Required—TOEFL (minimum score 550 paper-based). *Application deadline:* For fall admission, 6/1 priority date for domestic students. Applications are processed on a rolling basis. Application fee: $35 ($50 for international students). Electronic applications accepted. *Financial support:* Fellowships with full tuition reimbursements, teaching assistantships with partial tuition reimbursements, and scholarships/grants available. *Unit head:* Dr. Rick Bogard, Chair, 817-272-3471, Fax: 817-272-3434, E-mail: bogard@uta.edu. *Application contact:* Dr. Clifton Evans, Graduate Advisor, 817-272-5027, Fax: 817-272-3434, E-mail: cevans@uta.edu.
Website: http://www.uta.edu/music/

The University of Texas at Austin, Graduate School, College of Fine Arts, Sarah and Ernest Butler School of Music, Austin, TX 78712-1111. Offers band and wind conducting (M Music, DMA); brass/woodwind/percussion (MM, DMA); chamber music (MM); choral conducting (MM, DMA); collaborative piano (MM, DMA); composition (MM, DMA), including composition, jazz, jazz (DMA); ethnomusicology (MM, PhD); literature and pedagogy (MM), music and human learning (MM, PhD); music and human learning (DMA), including jazz (MM, DMA), piano pedagogy; musicology (MM, PhD); opera performance (MM, DMA); orchestral conducting (MM, DMA); organ (MM), including sacred music; organ performance (MM, DMA); performance (MM), including jazz (MM, DMA); performance (DMA), including jazz (MM, DMA); piano (DMA), including jazz (MM, DMA); piano literature and pedagogy (MM); piano performance (MM, DMA); string performance (MM, DMA); theory (MM, PhD); vocal performance (MM, DMA); voice (DMA), including opera; voice performance pedagogy (DMA); woodwind, brass, percussion performance (MM). *Accreditation:* NASM. *Program availability:* Part-time. *Degree requirements:* For master's, one foreign language, comprehensive exam, thesis (for some programs), recital (performance or composition majors); for doctorate, one foreign language, comprehensive exam, thesis/dissertation (for some programs), recital (for performance or composition majors). *Entrance requirements:* For master's and doctorate, GRE General Test (except for performance or composition majors), audition (performance majors). Electronic applications accepted.

The University of Texas at El Paso, Graduate School, College of Liberal Arts, Department of Music, El Paso, TX 79968-0001. Offers music education (MM); music performance (MM). *Accreditation:* NASM. *Program availability:* Part-time, evening/weekend. *Degree requirements:* For master's, thesis optional. *Entrance requirements:* For master's, audition, interview, letters of recommendation. Additional exam requirements/recommendations for international students: Required—TOEFL; Recommended—IELTS. Electronic applications accepted.

The University of Texas Rio Grande Valley, College of Fine Arts, School of Music, Edinburg, TX 78539. Offers ethnomusicology (M Mus); interdisciplinary studies (MAIS); music education (M Mus); performance (M Mus). *Accreditation:* NASM. *Program availability:* Part-time. *Degree requirements:* For master's, comprehensive exam, thesis optional, recital (performance). *Entrance requirements:* For master's, audition for performance area, bachelor's degree in music. Tuition and fees vary according to course load and program. *Faculty research:* Music history, instrumental pedagogy, vocal pedagogy, music education, ethnomusicology.

The University of the Arts, College of Performing Arts, School of Music, Division of Music Education, Philadelphia, PA 19102-4944. Offers MAT, MM. MM program offered in conjunction with Villanova University's Summer Music Studies program with summer enrollment only and priority application date of January 1. *Accreditation:* NASM. *Degree requirements:* For master's, student teaching (for MAT); thesis/project (for MM). *Entrance requirements:* For master's, official transcripts, three letters of recommendation, one- to two-page statement, personal interview, undergraduate degree with minimum cumulative GPA of 3.0, DVD/CD or link to uploaded film on YouTube or related site (or VHS video tape for MM), live or taped performance audition (for MAT). Additional exam requirements/recommendations for international students: Required—TOEFL (minimum score 580 paper-based, 92 iBT) or IELTS (minimum score 6.5).

University of the Pacific, Conservatory of Music, Stockton, CA 95211-0197. Offers music education (MM); music therapy (MA). *Students:* 10 full-time (7 women), 23 part-time (15 women); includes 8 minority (3 Asian, non-Hispanic/Latino; 4 Hispanic/Latino; 1 Two or more races, non-Hispanic/Latino), 4 international. Average age 33. 24 applicants, 129% accepted, 13 enrolled. In 2016, 4 master's awarded. *Entrance requirements:* For master's, GRE General Test. Additional exam requirements/recommendations for international students: Required—TOEFL. *Application deadline:* For fall admission, 3/1 priority date for domestic students; for spring admission, 10/1 priority date for domestic students. Applications are processed on a rolling basis. Application fee: $75. *Financial support:* Teaching assistantships and institutionally sponsored loans available. Support available to part-time students. Financial award application deadline: 3/1; financial award applicants required to submit FAFSA. *Unit head:* Dr. Daniel Ebbers, Interim Dean, 209-946-2415, E-mail: musicdean@pacific.edu. *Application contact:* 209-946-2415, Fax: 209-946-2770.

The University of Toledo, College of Graduate Studies, College of Communication and the Arts, Toledo, OH 43606-3390. Offers ME, MME, MMP, Certificate. *Accreditation:* NASM. *Degree requirements:* For master's, comprehensive exam, diagnostic theory and history exam. *Entrance requirements:* For master's, GRE if GPA is less than 3.0, minimum cumulative point-hour ratio of 2.7 for all previous academic work, audition. Additional exam requirements/recommendations for international students: Required—TOEFL (minimum score 550 paper-based; 80 iBT). Electronic applications accepted.

University of Toronto, School of Graduate Studies, Faculty of Music, Toronto, ON M5S 1A1, Canada. Offers composition (M Mus, DMA); ethnomusicology (MA, PhD); jazz (M Mus); music education (MA, PhD); musicology/theory (MA, PhD); opera (M Mus); performance (M Mus, DMA). *Program availability:* Part-time. *Degree requirements:* For master's, comprehensive exam (for some programs), oral examination (M Mus in composition), 1 foreign language (MA); for doctorate, recital of original works (DMA), thesis (PhD). *Entrance requirements:* For master's, BM in area of specialization with minimum B average in final 2 years, original compositions (M Mus in composition); for doctorate, master's degree in area of specialization, minimum B+ average, at least 2 extended compositions (DMA). Additional exam requirements/recommendations for international students: Required—TOEFL (minimum score 580 paper-based; 93 iBT), TWE (minimum score 5). Electronic applications accepted.

University of Utah, Graduate School, College of Fine Arts, School of Music, Salt Lake City, UT 84112. Offers choral conducting (M Mus, DMA); collaborative piano (M Mus); composition (M Mus, PhD); instrumental conducting (M Mus, DMA); instrumental performance (M Mus, DMA); jazz studies (M Mus); music education (M Mus, PhD); music history and literature (M Mus); musicology (MA); organ performance (M Mus); piano performance (M Mus, DMA); piano performance and pedagogy (M Mus); string performance and pedagogy (M Mus); theory (M Mus); vocal performance (DMA). *Accreditation:* NASM. *Faculty:* 33 full-time (11 women), 53 part-time/adjunct (20 women). *Students:* 83 full-time (44 women), 24 part-time (12 women); includes 27 minority (1 American Indian or Alaska Native, non-Hispanic/Latino; 13 Asian, non-Hispanic/Latino; 6 Hispanic/Latino; 7 Two or more races, non-Hispanic/Latino). Average age 32. 121 applicants, 55% accepted, 31 enrolled. In 2016, 10 master's, 13 doctorates awarded. *Degree requirements:* For master's, variable foreign language requirement, comprehensive exam (for some programs), thesis (for some programs), 1-2 recitals (MM), final oral exam; for doctorate, variable foreign language requirement, comprehensive exam (for some programs), thesis/dissertation, 4 recitals (DMA), thesis/dissertation defense. *Entrance requirements:* For master's, placement exams, minimum GPA of 3.0, audition, bachelor's degree in music; for doctorate, placement exams, minimum GPA of 3.0, audition, master's degree in music. Additional exam requirements/recommendations for international students: Required—TOEFL (minimum score 85 iBT). *Application deadline:* For fall admission, 2/15 for domestic students, 1/15 for international students; for spring admission, 10/1 for domestic students, 9/1 for international students; for summer admission, 3/15 for domestic students, 2/15 for international students. Applications are processed on a rolling basis. Application fee: $55 ($65 for international students). Electronic applications accepted. *Expenses:* Contact institution. *Financial support:* In 2016–17, 64 students received support, including 56 teaching assistantships with tuition reimbursements available (averaging $10,292 per year); fellowships with tuition reimbursements available, research assistantships with tuition reimbursements available, scholarships/grants, health care benefits, and unspecified assistantships also available. Financial award application deadline: 2/1. *Faculty research:* Music education, conducting, musicology, composition, performance. *Total annual research expenditures:* $25,000. *Unit head:* Miguel Chuaqui, Director, 801-585-3720, E-mail: m.chauqui@utah.edu. *Application contact:* Cassie Wagstaff, Academic Coordinator, 801-585-6972, Fax: 801-581-5683, E-mail: cassandra.wagstaff@utah.edu.
Website: http://www.music.utah.edu/

University of Victoria, Faculty of Graduate Studies, Faculty of Education, Department of Curriculum and Instruction, Victoria, BC V8W 2Y2, Canada. Offers art education (M Ed, PhD); curriculum studies (M Ed, MA, PhD); early childhood education (M Ed, PhD); educational studies (PhD); language and literacy (M Ed, MA, PhD); mathematics (M Ed, MA, PhD); music education (M Ed, MA, PhD); science (M Ed, MA, PhD); social studies (M Ed, MA); social, cultural and foundational studies (MA, PhD); technology and environmental education (PhD). *Program availability:* Part-time. *Degree requirements:* For master's, thesis, project (M Ed); for doctorate, comprehensive exam, thesis/dissertation. *Entrance requirements:* For master's, minimum B average. Additional exam requirements/recommendations for international students: Required—TOEFL (minimum score 575 paper-based), IELTS (minimum score 7). Electronic applications accepted. *Faculty research:* Elementary and secondary English, language arts, curriculum theory and practice, educational media and technology, educational administration and leadership, history and philosophy of education.

University of Washington, Graduate School, College of Arts and Sciences, School of Music, Concentration in Music Education, Seattle, WA 98195. Offers MA, PhD. *Degree requirements:* For doctorate, thesis/dissertation. *Entrance requirements:* For master's, GRE General Test, GRE Subject Test, minimum GPA of 3.0; for doctorate, GRE General Test, GRE Subject Test, minimum GPA of 3.0, sample of scholarly writing, videotape of teaching, 1 year of teaching experience. Additional exam requirements/recommendations for international students: Required—TOEFL. Electronic applications accepted. *Faculty research:* Multiethnic issues in music instruction, affective responses to music.

University of West Georgia, College of Arts and Humanities, Carrollton, GA 30118. Offers English (MA); history (MA); museum studies (Postbaccalaureate Certificate); music performance (M Mus); music teacher education (M Mus); public history (Postbaccalaureate Certificate). *Program availability:* Part-time, evening/weekend, 100% online, blended/hybrid learning. *Faculty:* 70 full-time (39 women). *Students:* 23 full-time (16 women), 55 part-time (33 women); includes 18 minority (10 Black or African American, non-Hispanic/Latino; 1 American Indian or Alaska Native, non-Hispanic/Latino; 5 Hispanic/Latino; 2 Two or more races, non-Hispanic/Latino), 1 international. Average age 31. 24 applicants, 100% accepted, 23 enrolled. In 2016, 34 master's, 6 other advanced degrees awarded. *Entrance requirements:* Additional exam requirements/recommendations for international students: Required—TOEFL (minimum score 523 paper-based; 69 iBT); Recommended—IELTS (minimum score 6.5). *Application deadline:* For fall admission, 8/1 for domestic students, 6/1 for international students; for spring admission, 11/15 for domestic students, 10/15 for international students; for summer admission, 5/15 for domestic students, 3/30 for international students. Applications are processed on a rolling basis. Application fee: $40. Electronic applications accepted. *Expenses:* Tuition, state resident: full-time $5316; part-time $222 per semester hour. Tuition, nonresident: full-time $20,658; part-time $861 per semester hour. *Required fees:* $1962. Tuition and fees vary according to course load, degree level and program. *Financial support:* Fellowships, research assistantships, teaching assistantships, career-related internships or fieldwork, Federal Work-Study, institutionally sponsored loans, scholarships/grants, and unspecified assistantships available. Support available to part-time students. Financial award application deadline: 4/1; financial award applicants required to submit FAFSA. *Unit head:* Dr. Pauline D. Gagnon, Dean of Arts and Humanities, 678-839-5450, Fax: 678-839-5451, E-mail: pgagnon@westga.edu. *Application contact:* Dr. Toby Ziglar, Assistant Dean of the Graduate School, 678-839-1394, Fax: 678-839-1395, E-mail: graduate@westga.edu.
Website: http://www.westga.edu/coah

University of Wisconsin–Madison, Graduate School, College of Letters and Science, School of Music, Program in Music Education, Madison, WI 53706-1380. Offers curriculum and instruction (MS, PhD); music education (MM). *Accreditation:* NASM. *Degree requirements:* For doctorate, 2 foreign languages, thesis/dissertation. *Entrance requirements:* For doctorate, GRE General Test.

University of Wisconsin–Madison, Graduate School, School of Education, Department of Curriculum and Instruction, Madison, WI 53706-1380. Offers art education (MA); curriculum and instruction (MS, PhD); education and mathematics (MA); French education (MA); German education (MA); music education (MS); science education (MS); Spanish education (MA). *Accreditation:* NASM (one or more programs are accredited). *Degree requirements:* For doctorate, thesis/dissertation.

University of Wisconsin–Stevens Point, College of Fine Arts and Communication, Department of Music, Stevens Point, WI 54481-3897. Offers elementary/secondary (MM Ed); studio pedagogy (MM Ed); Suzuki talent education (MM Ed). *Accreditation:* NASM. *Program availability:* Part-time. *Degree requirements:* For master's, thesis or alternative. *Entrance requirements:* For master's, teaching certificate. *Faculty research:* Music education, music composition, music performance.

University of Wyoming, College of Arts and Sciences, Department of Music, Laramie, WY 82071. Offers music education (MME); performance (MM). *Accreditation:* NASM. *Degree requirements:* For master's, comprehensive exam, thesis or alternative. *Entrance requirements:* For master's, minimum GPA of 3.0. Additional exam requirements/recommendations for international students: Required—TOEFL (minimum score 540 paper-based). Electronic applications accepted.

VanderCook College of Music, Master of Music Education Program, Chicago, IL 60616-3731. Offers MM Ed. *Accreditation:* NASM. *Program availability:* Part-time. *Degree requirements:* For master's, thesis, written comprehensive exam or professional teaching portfolio. *Entrance requirements:* For master's, minimum of one year of teaching experience, or its equivalent, in music; official transcripts; 3 letters of recommendation; bachelor's degree in music education from accredited college or university or minimum of 60 credits in undergraduate music and music education coursework. Additional exam requirements/recommendations for international students: Required—TOEFL (minimum score 500 paper-based; 70 iBT).

Virginia Commonwealth University, Graduate School, School of the Arts, Department of Music, Richmond, VA 23284-9005. Offers music education (MM). *Accreditation:* NASM. *Degree requirements:* For master's, departmental qualifying exam, recital. *Entrance requirements:* For master's, department examination, audition or tapes, portfolio. Additional exam requirements/recommendations for international students: Required—TOEFL (minimum score 600 paper-based; 100 iBT). *Application deadline:* For fall admission, 4/1 for domestic students. Application fee: $50. Electronic applications accepted. *Financial support:* Fellowships, teaching assistantships, career-related internships or fieldwork, Federal Work-Study, and institutionally sponsored loans available. Support available to part-time students. Financial award application deadline: 3/15. *Faculty research:* Composition, conducting, education, performance. *Unit head:* Darryl Harper, Interim Chair, 804-828-1166, Fax: 804-828-6469, E-mail: dharper2@vcu.edu. *Application contact:* Dr. David A. Greennagel, Graduate Program Director, 804-828-8523, E-mail: djgreennagel@vcu.edu.
Website: http://www.vcu.edu/arts/music/dept/index.html

Wayne State College, School of Education and Counseling, Department of Educational Foundations and Leadership, Program in Curriculum and Instruction, Wayne, NE 68787. Offers alternative education (MSE); business and information technology education (MSE); communication arts education (MSE); early childhood education (MSE); elementary education (MSE); English as a second language (MSE); English education (MSE); family and consumer sciences education (MSE); industrial technology and vocational education (MSE); learning communities (MSE); mathematics education (MSE); music education (MSE); science education (MSE); social science education (MSE). *Accreditation:* NCATE. *Program availability:* Part-time, evening/weekend. *Degree requirements:* For master's, comprehensive exam, thesis optional. *Entrance requirements:* For master's, GRE General Test. Additional exam requirements/recommendations for international students: Required—TOEFL (minimum score 550 paper-based).

Wayne State University, College of Fine, Performing and Communication Arts, Department of Music, Detroit, MI 48202. Offers composition/theory (MM); conducting (MM); jazz performance (MM); music (MA); music education (MM); orchestral studies (Certificate); performance (MM). *Accreditation:* NASM. *Faculty:* 14. *Students:* 14 full-time (6 women), 8 part-time (3 women); includes 6 minority (3 Black or African American, non-Hispanic/Latino; 2 Hispanic/Latino; 1 Two or more races, non-Hispanic/Latino), 1 international. Average age 27. 23 applicants, 39% accepted, 9 enrolled. In 2016, 7 master's awarded. *Degree requirements:* For master's, thesis (for some programs), oral examination (for some programs), recital with program notes (for some programs). *Entrance requirements:* For master's, diagnostic exam in theory and history, undergraduate degree in same field as desired field of graduate study or equivalent in course work, private study, or experience; audition/interview; for Certificate, undergraduate degree in same field as desired field of graduate study or equivalent in course work, private study, or experience; audition/interview. Additional exam requirements/recommendations for international students: Required—TOEFL (minimum score 550 paper-based; 79 iBT), Michigan English Language Assessment Battery (minimum score 85); Recommended—IELTS (minimum score 6.5), TWE (minimum score 5.5). *Application deadline:* Applications are processed on a rolling basis. Application fee: $50. Electronic applications accepted. *Expenses:* $17,240 per year resident tuition and fees, $34,434 per year non-resident tuition and fees. *Financial support:* In 2016–17, 17 students received support. Career-related internships or fieldwork, institutionally sponsored loans, and scholarships/grants available. Support available to part-time students. Financial award applicants required to submit FAFSA. *Faculty research:* Teacher training, pedagogy, musicology, composition/theory, conducting/performance practice. *Unit head:* Dr. Norah Duncan, Professor and Chair, 313-577-1775, E-mail: norah.duncan@wayne.edu. *Application contact:* E-mail: music@wayne.edu.
Website: http://music.wayne.edu/

Webster University, Leigh Gerdine College of Fine Arts, Department of Music, St. Louis, MO 63119-3194. Offers church music (MM); composition (MM); jazz studies (MM); music (MA); music education (MM); organ (MM); performance (MM); piano (MM); voice (MM). *Accreditation:* NASM. *Entrance requirements:* Additional exam requirements/recommendations for international students: Required—TOEFL. *Application deadline:* Applications are processed on a rolling basis. Application fee: $25 ($50 for international students). *Expenses: Tuition:* Full-time $21,900; part-time $730 per credit hour. Tuition and fees vary according to campus/location and program. *Financial support:* Teaching assistantships and Federal Work-Study available. Support available to part-time students. Financial award application deadline: 4/1; financial award applicants required to submit FAFSA. *Unit head:* Dr. Jeffrey Carter, Chair, 314-968-7033, E-mail: jeffreycarter67@webster.edu. *Application contact:* Jean Huber, Department Representative, 314-968-7032, E-mail: huberje@webster.edu.

West Chester University of Pennsylvania, College of Arts and Humanities, Department of Applied Music, West Chester, PA 19383. Offers performance (MM), including conducting, instrumental, keyboard, voice; piano pedagogy (MM, Certificate). *Program availability:* Part-time, evening/weekend. *Faculty:* 22 full-time (7 women), 4 part-time/adjunct (2 women). *Students:* 17 full-time (6 women), 13 part-time (3 women); includes 2 minority (1 Native Hawaiian or other Pacific Islander, non-Hispanic/Latino; 1 Two or more races, non-Hispanic/Latino), 5 international. Average age 30. 15 applicants, 87% accepted, 9 enrolled. In 2016, 14 master's awarded. *Degree requirements:* For master's, comprehensive exam, thesis optional, recital. *Entrance requirements:* For master's and Certificate, School of Music Graduate Placement Test (GPT), audition, interview. Additional exam requirements/recommendations for international students: Required—TOEFL or IELTS. *Application deadline:* For fall admission, 5/15 for international students; for spring admission, 10/15 for international students. Applications are processed on a rolling basis. Application fee: $50. Electronic applications accepted. *Expenses:* Tuition, state resident: full-time $8694; part-time $483 per credit. Tuition, nonresident: full-time $13,050; part-time $725 per credit. *Required fees:* $2399; $119.05 per credit. Tuition and fees vary according to campus/location and program. *Financial support:* Scholarships/grants and unspecified assistantships available. Financial award application deadline: 2/15; financial award applicants required to submit FAFSA. *Faculty research:* Performance, historical perspective, pedagogy. *Unit head:* Dr. Chris Hanning, Chair, 610-436-4178, Fax: 610-436-2873, E-mail: channing@wcupa.edu. *Application contact:* Dr. M. Gregory Martin, Graduate Coordinator, 610-436-2070, Fax: 610-436-2873, E-mail: mmartin@wcupa.edu.
Website: http://www.wcupa.edu/arts-humanities/music/appliedMusic/

West Chester University of Pennsylvania, College of Arts and Humanities, Department of Music Education, West Chester, PA 19383. Offers Kodaly methodology (Certificate); music education (MM, Teaching Certificate), including Kodaly methodology (MM), music technology (MM), Orff-Schulwerk (MM), performance (MM); music technology (Certificate); Orff-Schulwerk (Certificate). *Accreditation:* NASM; NCATE. *Program availability:* Part-time. *Faculty:* 3 full-time (1 woman). *Students:* 4 full-time (2 women), 18 part-time (13 women). Average age 29. 14 applicants, 93% accepted, 7 enrolled. In 2016, 10 master's, 3 Certificates awarded. *Degree requirements:* For master's, comprehensive exam, thesis (for some programs), recital (performance option only). *Entrance requirements:* For master's, School of Music Graduate Placement Test (GPT), audition (performance track only), interview; for other advanced degree, School of Music Graduate Placement Test (GPT), audition, interview. Additional exam requirements/recommendations for international students: Required—TOEFL or IELTS. *Application deadline:* For fall admission, 5/15 for international students; for spring admission, 10/15 for international students. Applications are processed on a rolling basis. Application fee: $50. Electronic applications accepted. *Expenses:* Tuition, state resident: full-time $8694; part-time $483 per credit. Tuition, nonresident: full-time $13,050; part-time $725 per credit. *Required fees:* $2399; $119.05 per credit. Tuition and fees vary according to campus/location and program. *Financial support:* Scholarships/grants and unspecified assistantships available. Financial award application deadline: 2/15; financial award applicants required to submit FAFSA. *Faculty research:* Music education in other cultures, educational advocacy and pedagogy, research in music education, special needs learners in music education, developing music listening skills. *Unit head:* Dr. Marci Major, Chair, 610-436-3030, Fax: 610-436-2873, E-mail: mmajor@wcupa.edu. *Application contact:* Dr. M. Gregory Martin, Graduate Coordinator, 610-436-2070, E-mail: mmartin@wcupa.edu.
Website: http://www.wcupa.edu/arts-humanities/music/musicEducation/

Western Connecticut State University, Division of Graduate Studies, School of Visual and Performing Arts, Department of Music, Danbury, CT 06810-6885. Offers music education (MS). *Accreditation:* NASM. *Program availability:* Part-time. *Degree requirements:* For master's, thesis or comprehensive exam, completion of program within 6 years. *Entrance requirements:* For master's, minimum GPA of 2.8, teaching certificate. Additional exam requirements/recommendations for international students: Recommended—TOEFL (minimum score 550 paper-based; 79 iBT), IELTS (minimum score 6). *Faculty research:* Ear training.

Western Kentucky University, Graduate Studies, Potter College of Arts and Letters, Department of Music, Bowling Green, KY 42101. Offers MA Ed. *Accreditation:* NASM; NCATE. *Program availability:* Part-time, evening/weekend. *Degree requirements:* For master's, comprehensive exam, written exam. *Entrance requirements:* For master's, GRE General Test, minimum GPA of 3.0. Additional exam requirements/recommendations for international students: Required—TOEFL (minimum score 555 paper-based; 79 iBT). *Faculty research:* Music education, music technology, performance.

Western Michigan University, Graduate College, College of Fine Arts, School of Music, Kalamazoo, MI 49008. Offers music (MA); music composition (MM); music conducting (MM); music education (MM); music performance (MM); music therapy (MM). *Accreditation:* NASM.

West Virginia University, College of Creative Arts, School of Music, Morgantown, WV 26506. Offers music composition (MM, DMA); music education (MM, PhD); music history (MM); music industry (MA); music performance (MM, DMA); music theory (MM). *Accreditation:* NASM. *Degree requirements:* For master's, comprehensive exam, thesis (for some programs), recitals; for doctorate, variable foreign language requirement, comprehensive exam, thesis/dissertation, recitals (DMA). *Entrance requirements:* For master's, GRE General Test (music history), minimum GPA of 3.0, audition; for doctorate, GRE General Test (music education), minimum GPA of 3.0, audition. Additional exam requirements/recommendations for international students: Required—TOEFL. *Faculty research:* Jazz history, seventeenth century French court music, nineteenth century composition theory.

Wichita State University, Graduate School, College of Fine Arts, School of Music, Wichita, KS 67260. Offers music (MM); music education (MME). *Accreditation:* NASM. *Program availability:* Part-time. *Unit head:* Prof. Russ Widener, Director, 316-978-6435, Fax: 316-978-3625, E-mail: russ.widener@wichita.edu. *Application contact:* Jordan Oleson, Admissions Coordinator, 316-978-3095, Fax: 316-978-3253, E-mail: jordan.oleson@wichita.edu.
Website: http://www.wichita.edu/music

Winthrop University, College of Visual and Performing Arts, Department of Music, Rock Hill, SC 29733. Offers conducting (MM); music education (MME); performance (MM). *Accreditation:* NASM. *Program availability:* Part-time. *Degree requirements:* For master's, comprehensive exam (for some programs), oral and written exams, recital (MM). *Entrance requirements:* For master's, GRE General Test, audition, minimum GPA of 3.0, 2 recitals. Additional exam requirements/recommendations for international students: Required—TOEFL (minimum score 550 paper-based; 79 iBT), IELTS (minimum score 6). Electronic applications accepted. *Expenses:* Tuition, state resident: full-time $14,312; part-time $599 per credit hour. Tuition, nonresident: full-time $27,570; part-time $1153 per credit hour.

Wright State University, Graduate School, College of Liberal Arts, Department of Music, Dayton, OH 45435. Offers MM. *Accreditation:* NASM. *Program availability:* Part-time. *Degree requirements:* For master's, thesis or alternative, oral exam. *Entrance requirements:* For master's, theory placement test, BA in music. Additional exam requirements/recommendations for international students: Required—TOEFL. Application fee: $25. *Expenses:* Tuition, state resident: full-time $9952; part-time $622 per credit hour. Tuition, nonresident: full-time $16,960; part-time $1060 per credit hour. *Financial support:* Fellowships, research assistantships, teaching assistantships, and unspecified assistantships available. Support available to part-time students. Financial award applicants required to submit FAFSA. *Faculty research:* General music, current needs, role of teacher, expectations in music education. *Unit head:* Dr. Herbert E. Dregalla, Jr., Chair, 937-775-2346, Fax: 937-775-3786, E-mail: herbert.dregalla@wright.edu. *Application contact:* John Kimble, Associate Director of Graduate Admissions and Records, 937-775-2957, Fax: 937-775-2453, E-mail: john.kimble@wright.edu.

Youngstown State University, Graduate School, College of Fine and Performing Arts, Dana School of Music, Youngstown, OH 44555-0001. Offers jazz studies (MM); music education (MM); music history and literature (MM); music theory and composition (MM); performance (MM). *Accreditation:* NASM. *Program availability:* Part-time, evening/weekend. *Degree requirements:* For master's, one foreign language, thesis optional, final qualifying exam. *Entrance requirements:* For master's, audition; GRE General Test or minimum GPA of 2.7. Additional exam requirements/recommendations for international students: Required—TOEFL. *Faculty research:* Teaching education, use of computers, conducting.

Reading Education

Adelphi University, Ruth S. Ammon School of Education, Program in Literacy, Garden City, NY 11530-0701. Offers birth-grade 12 (MS); birth-grade 6 (MS); grades 5-12 (MS). *Program availability:* Part-time, evening/weekend. *Students:* 3 full-time (all women), 11 part-time (10 women); includes 3 minority (2 Black or African American, non-Hispanic/Latino; 1 Hispanic/Latino). Average age 36. 15 applicants, 20% accepted, 2 enrolled. In 2016, 6 master's awarded. *Entrance requirements:* For master's, 2 letters of recommendation, resume, valid New York state teaching certification. Additional exam requirements/recommendations for international students: Required—TOEFL (minimum score 550 paper-based; 80 iBT), IELTS (minimum score 6.5). *Application deadline:* For fall admission, 4/1 priority date for domestic students, 4/1 for international students; for spring admission, 11/1 priority date for domestic students, 11/1 for international students. Applications are processed on a rolling basis. Application fee: $50. Electronic applications accepted. *Expenses:* Contact institution. *Financial support:* Research assistantships, teaching assistantships, career-related internships or fieldwork, institutionally sponsored loans, scholarships/grants, traineeships, and unspecified assistantships available. Support available to part-time students. Financial award application deadline: 2/15; financial award applicants required to submit FAFSA. *Faculty research:* Assessment and intervention, literacy education and development, higher and teacher education, human and adult development, achieving styles and human motivation. *Unit head:* Dr. Lori Wolf, Director, 516-877-4104, E-mail: wolf@adelphi.edu. *Application contact:* Christine Murphy, Director of Admissions, 516-877-3050, Fax: 516-877-3039, E-mail: graduateadmissions@adelphi.edu.

Alabama Agricultural and Mechanical University, School of Graduate Studies, College of Education, Humanities, and Behavioral Sciences, Department of Reading, Elementary, Early Childhood and Special Education, Huntsville, AL 35811. Offers early childhood education (MS Ed, Ed S); elementary education (MS Ed, Ed S); reading/literacy (PhD); special education collaborative teacher training (MS Ed, Ed S). *Accreditation:* NCATE. *Program availability:* Evening/weekend. *Degree requirements:* For master's, comprehensive exam; for Ed S, thesis. *Entrance requirements:* For master's, GRE General Test. Additional exam requirements/recommendations for international students: Required—TOEFL (minimum score 500 paper-based; 61 iBT). *Application deadline:* For fall admission, 5/1 for domestic students. Applications are processed on a rolling basis. Application fee: $25. Electronic applications accepted. *Expenses:* Tuition, nonresident: part-time $826 per credit hour. Full-time tuition and fees vary according to course load and program. *Financial support:* Research assistantships with tuition reimbursements and career-related internships or fieldwork available. Financial award application deadline: 4/1. *Faculty research:* Multicultural education, learning styles, diagnostic-prescriptive instruction. *Unit head:* Dr. Derrick Davis, Interim Chair, 256-372-4047.

Alabama State University, College of Education, Department of Curriculum and Instruction, Montgomery, AL 36101-0271. Offers early childhood education (M Ed, Ed S); elementary education (M Ed, Ed S); secondary education (M Ed, Ed S), including biology education, English language arts education (M Ed), history education, math education, music education (M Ed), reading education (M Ed), social science education; special education (M Ed). *Program availability:* Part-time. *Faculty:* 7 full-time (4 women), 7 part-time/adjunct (4 women). *Students:* 37 full-time (30 women), 82 part-time (69 women); includes 117 minority (115 Black or African American, non-Hispanic/Latino; 2 Two or more races, non-Hispanic/Latino). Average age 33. 65 applicants, 55% accepted, 22 enrolled. In 2016, 25 master's, 5 Ed Ss awarded. *Degree requirements:* For master's, comprehensive exam, thesis optional; for Ed S, comprehensive exam, thesis. *Entrance requirements:* For master's, GRE General Test, MAT, writing competency test; for Ed S, writing competency test, GRE, MAT. Additional exam requirements/recommendations for international students: Required—TOEFL (minimum score 500 paper-based). *Application deadline:* For fall admission, 4/15 for domestic and international students; for spring admission, 11/15 for domestic and international students; for summer admission, 3/15 for domestic and international students. Applications are processed on a rolling basis. Application fee: $25. Electronic applications accepted. *Expenses:* Tuition, state resident: full-time $3087; part-time $2744 per credit. Tuition, nonresident: full-time $6174; part-time $5488 per credit. *Required fees:* $2284; $1142 per credit. $571 per semester. Tuition and fees vary according to class time, course level, course load, degree level, program and student level. *Financial support:* Research assistantships available. Financial award application deadline: 6/30; financial award applicants required to submit FAFSA. *Unit head:* Dr. Joyce Johnson, Acting Chairperson, 334-229-4485, Fax: 334-229-5603, E-mail: jjohnson@alasu.edu. *Application contact:* Dr. William Person, Dean of Graduate Studies, 334-229-4274, Fax: 334-229-4928, E-mail: wperson@alasu.edu.
Website: http://www.alasu.edu/academics/colleges—departments/college-of-education/curriculum—instruction/index.aspx

Alfred University, Graduate School, Division of Education, Alfred, NY 14802-1205. Offers college student development (MS Ed); literacy (MS Ed). *Accreditation:* TEAC. *Program availability:* Part-time. *Faculty:* 4 full-time (3 women), 3 part-time/adjunct (2 women). *Students:* 50 full-time (38 women), 245 part-time (195 women); includes 169 minority (91 Black or African American, non-Hispanic/Latino; 2 American Indian or Alaska Native, non-Hispanic/Latino; 7 Asian, non-Hispanic/Latino; 69 Hispanic/Latino). Average age 34. In 2016, 21 master's awarded. *Entrance requirements:* For master's, Liberal Arts and Sciences Test (LAST), Assessment of Teaching Skills (written) (ATS-W), Content Specialty Test (CST). Additional exam requirements/recommendations for international students: Required—TOEFL (minimum score 590 paper-based; 90 iBT), IELTS (minimum score 6.5). *Application deadline:* For fall admission, 8/1 for domestic students, 3/15 for international students; for spring admission, 12/1 for domestic students, 10/1 for international students. Applications are processed on a rolling basis. Application fee: $60. Electronic applications accepted. *Expenses: Tuition:* Full-time $38,020; part-time $810 per credit. *Required fees:* $970; $82 per semester. *Financial support:* Research assistantships with partial tuition reimbursements, tuition waivers (partial), and unspecified assistantships available. Financial award applicants required to submit FAFSA. *Unit head:* Kevin Curtin, Program Director, 607-871-2699. *Application contact:* Sara Love, Coordinator of Graduate Admissions, 607-871-2115, Fax: 607-871-2198, E-mail: gradinquiry@alfred.edu.
Website: http://www.alfred.edu/gradschool/education/

Alverno College, School of Education, Milwaukee, WI 53234-3922. Offers adaptive education (MA); administrative leadership (MA); adult education and organizational development (MA); adult educational and instructional design (MA); adult educational and instructional technology (MA); global connections in the humanities (MA); instructional leadership (MA); instructional technology for K-12 settings (MA); professional development (MA); reading education (MA); reading education with adaptive education (MA); science education (MA); special education (MA); teaching in alternative schools (MA). *Accreditation:* NCATE. *Program availability:* Part-time, evening/weekend. *Faculty:* 4 full-time (3 women), 23 part-time/adjunct (17 women). *Students:* 58 full-time (57 women), 62 part-time (54 women); includes 32 minority (22 Black or African American, non-Hispanic/Latino; 2 Asian, non-Hispanic/Latino; 8 Hispanic/Latino), 1 international. Average age 39. 77 applicants, 99% accepted, 61 enrolled. In 2016, 85 master's awarded. *Degree requirements:* For master's, presentation/defense of proposal, conference presentation of inquiry projects. *Entrance requirements:* For master's, bachelor's degree in related field, communication samples from work setting, 3 letters of recommendation. Additional exam requirements/recommendations for international students: Required—TOEFL. *Application deadline:* For fall admission, 7/15 priority date for domestic and international students; for spring admission, 12/15 priority date for domestic and international students. Applications are processed on a rolling basis. Application fee: $0. Electronic applications accepted. *Expenses:* Contact institution. *Financial support:* In 2016–17, 17 students received support. Federal Work-Study and scholarships/grants available. Support available to part-time students. Financial award applicants required to submit FAFSA. *Faculty research:* Student self-assessment, self-reflection, integration of curriculum, identifying needs of students in strategic situations and designing appropriate classroom strategies. *Unit head:* Dr. Desiree Pointer Mace, Associate Dean, Graduate Program, 414-382-6345, Fax: 414-382-6332, E-mail: desiree.pointer-mace@alverno.edu. *Application contact:* Katie Kipp, Graduate Admissions Counselor, 414-382-6045, Fax: 414-382-6354, E-mail: katie.kipp@alverno.edu.

American International College, School of Education, Springfield, MA 01109-3189. Offers early childhood education (M Ed, CAGS); elementary education (M Ed, CAGS); middle education/secondary education (M Ed, CAGS); moderate disabilities (M Ed, CAGS); reading specialist (M Ed, CAGS); school adjustment counseling (MAEP, CAGS); school guidance counseling (MAEP, CAGS); school leadership (M Ed, CAGS).

Program availability: Evening/weekend. *Faculty:* 1 (woman) full-time, 90 part-time/adjunct (63 women). *Students:* 1,194 full-time (970 women), 118 part-time (83 women); includes 108 minority (15 Black or African American, non-Hispanic/Latino; 4 American Indian or Alaska Native, non-Hispanic/Latino; 12 Asian, non-Hispanic/Latino; 55 Hispanic/Latino; 2 Native Hawaiian or other Pacific Islander, non-Hispanic/Latino; 20 Two or more races, non-Hispanic/Latino). Average age 34. 517 applicants, 417 enrolled. In 2016, 879 master's, 194 CAGSs awarded. Terminal master's awarded for partial completion of doctoral program. *Degree requirements:* For master's, comprehensive exam (for some programs), thesis (for some programs), practicum/culminating experience; for CAGS, practicum/culminating experience. *Entrance requirements:* For master's, Communication and Literacy portion of the Massachusetts Tests for Education Licensure, graduate of accredited four-year college with minimum B- average in undergraduate course work; for CAGS, M Ed or master's degree in field related to licensure from accredited institution. *Application deadline:* Applications are processed on a rolling basis. Application fee: $50. Electronic applications accepted. *Expenses:* $439 per credit. *Financial support:* Applicants required to submit FAFSA. *Unit head:* Sylvia Mason, Dean, 413-205-1743, Fax: 413-205-3943, E-mail: sylvia.mason@aic.edu. *Application contact:* Kerry Barnes, Dean of Graduate Admissions, 413-205-3703, Fax: 413-205-3051, E-mail: kerry.barnes@aic.edu.
Website: http://www.aic.edu/school-of-education/

American Public University System, AMU/APU Graduate Programs, Charles Town, WV 25414. Offers accounting (MBA, MS); applied business analytics (MBA, MS); criminal justice (MA), including business administration, emergency and disaster management, general (MA, MS); educational leadership (M Ed); emergency and disaster management (MA); entrepreneurship (MBA); environmental policy and management (MS), including environmental planning, environmental sustainability, fish and wildlife management, general (MA, MS), global environmental management; finance (MBA); general (MBA); government contracting and acquisition (MBA); health care administration (MBA); health information management (MS); history (MA), including American history, ancient and classical history, European history, global history, public history; homeland security (MA), including business administration, counterterrorism studies, criminal justice, cyber, emergency management and public health, intelligence studies, transportation security; homeland security resource allocation (MBA); humanities (MA); information technology (MS), including digital forensics, enterprise software development, information assurance and security, IT project management; information technology management (MBA); intelligence studies (MA), including criminal intelligence, cyber, general (MA, MS), homeland security, intelligence analysis, intelligence collection, intelligence management, intelligence operations, terrorism studies; international relations and conflict resolution (MA), including comparative and security issues, conflict resolution, international and transnational security issues, peacekeeping; legal studies (MA); management (MA), including strategic consulting; marketing (MBA); military history (MA), including American military history, American Revolution, civil war, war since 1945, World War II; military studies (MA), including joint warfare, strategic leadership; national security studies (MA), including cyber, general (MA, MS), homeland security, regional security studies, security and intelligence analysis, terrorism studies; nonprofit management (MBA); political science (MA), including American politics and government, comparative government and development, general (MA, MS), international relations, public policy; psychology (MA); public administration (MPA), including disaster management, environmental policy, health policy, human resources, national security, organizational management, security management; public health (MPH); reverse logistics management (MA); security management (MA); space studies (MS), including aerospace science, general (MA, MS), planetary science; sports and health sciences (MS); sports management (MBA); teaching (M Ed), including autism spectrum disorder, curriculum and instruction for elementary teachers, elementary reading, English language learners, instructional leadership, online learning, special education, STEAM (STEM plus the arts); transportation and logistics management (MA). *Program availability:* Part-time, evening/weekend, online only, 100% online. *Faculty:* 401 full-time (228 women), 1,678 part-time/adjunct (781 women). *Students:* 378 full-time (184 women), 8,455 part-time (3,484 women); includes 2,972 minority (1,552 Black or African American, non-Hispanic/Latino; 52 American Indian or Alaska Native, non-Hispanic/Latino; 211 Asian, non-Hispanic/Latino; 791 Hispanic/Latino; 70 Native Hawaiian or other Pacific Islander, non-Hispanic/Latino; 296 Two or more races, non-Hispanic/Latino), 109 international. Average age 37. In 2016, 3,185 master's awarded. *Degree requirements:* For master's, comprehensive exam or practicum. *Entrance requirements:* For master's, official transcript showing earned bachelor's degree from institution accredited by recognized accrediting body. Additional exam requirements/recommendations for international students: Required—TOEFL (minimum score 550 paper-based), IELTS (minimum score 6.5). *Application deadline:* Applications are processed on a rolling basis. Application fee: $0. Electronic applications accepted. *Expenses: Tuition:* Part-time $350 per credit hour. *Required fees:* $50 per course. *Financial support:* Scholarships/grants available. Financial award applicants required to submit FAFSA. *Unit head:* Dr. Karan Powell, President, 877-468-6268, Fax: 304-724-3780. *Application contact:* Terry Grant, Vice President of Enrollment Management, 877-468-6268, Fax: 304-724-3780, E-mail: info@apus.edu.
Website: http://www.apus.edu

Appalachian State University, Cratis D. Williams Graduate School, Department of Reading Education and Special Education, Boone, NC 28608. Offers reading education (MA); special education (MA). *Accreditation:* ASHA. *Program availability:* Part-time, evening/weekend, online learning. *Degree requirements:* For master's, comprehensive exam, thesis optional. *Entrance requirements:* For master's, GRE General Test or MAT, 3 letters of recommendation. Additional exam requirements/recommendations for international students: Required—TOEFL (minimum score 570 paper-based; 79 iBT), IELTS (minimum score 6.5). *Application deadline:* For fall admission, 3/15 priority date for domestic students, 2/1 for international students; for spring admission, 11/1 for domestic students, 7/1 for international students. Applications are processed on a rolling basis. Application fee: $55. Electronic applications accepted. *Expenses:* Tuition, state resident: full-time $4744. Tuition, nonresident: full-time $17,913. Full-time tuition and fees vary according to program. *Financial support:* Research assistantships, Federal Work-Study, scholarships/grants, and unspecified assistantships available. Financial award application deadline: 4/1; financial award applicants required to submit FAFSA. *Faculty research:* Special education, language arts, reading. *Unit head:* Dr. Monica Lambert, Chairperson, 828-262-7173, Fax: 828-262-6767, E-mail: lambertma@appstate.edu. *Application contact:* Dr. David Koppenhaver, Program Director, E-mail: koppenhaverd@appstate.edu.
Website: https://rese.appstate.edu/

Arcadia University, School of Education, Glenside, PA 19038-3295. Offers art education (M Ed); computer education (CAS); curriculum (CAS); curriculum studies (M Ed); early childhood education (M Ed), including individualized, master teacher, research in child development; educational leadership (M Ed, Ed D, CAS); elementary education (M Ed); English education (MA Ed); environmental education (MA Ed); instructional technology (M Ed); language arts (M Ed); library science (M Ed); mathematics education (M Ed, MA Ed); music education (MA Ed); psychology (MA Ed); reading (M Ed, CAS); science education (M Ed, CAS); secondary education (M Ed, CAS); special education (M Ed, Ed D, CAS); theater arts (MA Ed); written communication (MA Ed). *Accreditation:* NASAD. *Program availability:* Part-time, evening/weekend, online learning. *Faculty:* 19 full-time (13 women), 3 part-time/adjunct (all women). *Students:* 22 full-time (16 women), 356 part-time (284 women); includes 84 minority (55 Black or African American, non-Hispanic/Latino; 2 American Indian or Alaska Native, non-Hispanic/Latino; 13 Asian, non-Hispanic/Latino; 11 Hispanic/Latino; 3 Two or more races, non-Hispanic/Latino), 4 international. Average age 34. 145 applicants, 73% accepted, 80 enrolled. In 2016, 95 master's, 11 doctorates awarded. *Application deadline:* Applications are processed on a rolling basis. Application fee: $50. Electronic applications accepted. *Expenses:* Contact institution. *Financial support:* Career-related internships or fieldwork, tuition waivers (partial), and unspecified assistantships available. *Unit head:* John T Groves, Interim Dean of the School of Education, 215-572-2940. *Application contact:* 215-572-2925, Fax: 215-572-2126, E-mail: grad@arcadia.edu.

Arkansas State University, Graduate School, College of Education and Behavioral Science, School of Teacher Education and Leadership, State University, AR 72467. Offers community college administration (SCCT); curriculum and instruction (MSE); early childhood education (MSE); early childhood services (MS); educational leadership (MSE, Ed D, Ed S); educational theory and practice (MSE); middle level education (MAT, MSE); reading (MSE, Ed S); special education - gifted, talented, and creative (MSE); special education - instructional specialist grades 4-12 (MSE); special education - instructional specialist grades P-4 (MSE); special education, K-12 (MSE). *Accreditation:* NCATE. *Program availability:* Part-time, online learning. *Degree requirements:* For master's, comprehensive exam, thesis or alternative; for doctorate, comprehensive exam, thesis/dissertation; for other advanced degree, comprehensive exam. *Entrance requirements:* For master's, GRE General Test or MAT, appropriate bachelor's degree, official transcripts, immunization records, letters of reference, interview; for doctorate, GRE General Test or MAT, interview, master's degree, letters of reference, official transcript, personal statement, writing sample, immunization records; for other advanced degree, GRE General Test or MAT, interview, master's degree, official transcript, immunization records, letters of reference, 3 years of teaching experience, teaching license. Additional exam requirements/recommendations for international students: Required—TOEFL (minimum score 550 paper-based; 79 iBT), IELTS (minimum score 6), PTE (minimum score 56). Electronic applications accepted.

Armstrong State University, School of Graduate Studies, Department of Childhood and Exceptional Student Education, Savannah, GA 31419-1997. Offers early childhood education (M Ed, MAT); reading (Certificate); special education (M Ed, MAT); special education transition specialist (Certificate). *Accreditation:* NCATE. *Program availability:* Part-time, evening/weekend. *Faculty:* 14 full-time (12 women), 1 (woman) part-time/adjunct. *Students:* 10 full-time (9 women), 199 part-time (177 women); includes 67 minority (55 Black or African American, non-Hispanic/Latino; 1 Asian, non-Hispanic/Latino; 5 Hispanic/Latino; 6 Two or more races, non-Hispanic/Latino). Average age 34. 131 applicants, 42% accepted, 45 enrolled. In 2016, 72 master's, 24 other advanced degrees awarded. *Degree requirements:* For master's, portfolio. *Entrance requirements:* For master's, MAT, Georgia Assessment for the Certification of Educators. Additional exam requirements/recommendations for international students: Required—TOEFL (minimum score 523 paper-based; 70 iBT). *Application deadline:* For fall admission, 7/1 priority date for domestic students, 5/1 priority date for international students; for spring admission, 11/15 priority date for domestic students, 9/15 priority date for international students; for summer admission, 4/15 priority date for domestic students, 9/15 for international students. Applications are processed on a rolling basis. Application fee: $30. Electronic applications accepted. *Expenses:* Tuition, state resident: full-time $1781; part-time $161.93 per credit hour. Tuition, nonresident: full-time $6482; part-time $589.27 per credit hour. *Required fees:* $1224 per unit. $612 per semester. Tuition and fees vary according to course load, campus/location and program. *Financial support:* In 2016–17, research assistantships with full tuition reimbursements (averaging $5,000 per year) were awarded; career-related internships or fieldwork, Federal Work-Study, and scholarships/grants also available. Support available to part-time students. Financial award application deadline: 3/15; financial award applicants required to submit FAFSA. *Faculty research:* Literacy, instructional design, poetry, working with local schools. *Unit head:* Dr. John Hobe, Department Head, 912-344-2619, Fax: 912-344-3443, E-mail: john.hobe@armstrong.edu. *Application contact:* McKenzie Peterman, Assistant Director of Graduate Admissions, 912-344-2503, Fax: 912-344-3417, E-mail: graduate@armstrong.edu.
Website: https://www.armstrong.edu/academic-departments/education-ceed

Asbury University, School of Graduate and Professional Studies, Wilmore, KY 40390-1198. Offers biology: alternative certificate (MA Ed); chemistry: alternative certificate (MA Ed); English (MA Ed); English as a second language (MA Ed); ESL (MA Ed); French (MA Ed); Latin: alternative certificate (MA Ed); mathematics: alternative certificate (MA Ed); reading/writing endorsement (MA Ed); social studies (MA Ed); social work (MSW), including child and family services; Spanish (MA Ed); special education (MA Ed); special education: alternative certificate (MA Ed); teacher as leader endorsement (MA Ed). *Accreditation:* NCATE. *Program availability:* Part-time. *Degree requirements:* For master's, action research project, portfolio. *Entrance requirements:* For master's, PRAXIS/NTE, minimum GPA of 2.75, letters of recommendation. Additional exam requirements/recommendations for international students: Required—TOEFL (minimum score 550 paper-based). Electronic applications accepted.

Ashland University, Dwight Schar College of Education, Department of Educational Foundations and Instruction, Ashland, OH 44805-3702. Offers educational technology (M Ed); literacy (M Ed); teaching and learning in the 21st century (M Ed). *Program availability:* Part-time, evening/weekend. *Degree requirements:* For master's, inquiry seminar, internship, or thesis. *Entrance requirements:* For master's, teaching certificate or license, bachelor's degree, minimum cumulative GPA of 2.75. Additional exam requirements/recommendations for international students: Required—TOEFL. *Application deadline:* Applications are processed on a rolling basis. Application fee: $30. Electronic applications accepted. *Financial support:* Application deadline: 4/15. *Faculty research:* Character education, teacher reflection, religion and education, professional education, environmental education. *Unit head:* Dr. Louise Fleming, Chair, 419-289-5347, E-mail: lfleming@ashland.edu. *Application contact:* Dr. Linda Billman, Associate Dean, 419-289-5369, Fax: 419-289-5331, E-mail: lbillman@ashland.edu.
Website: http://www.ashland.edu/academics/education/edfoundations/

Augustana University, MA in Education Program, Sioux Falls, SD 57197. Offers instructional strategies (MA); reading (MA); special populations (MA); STEM (MA); technology (MA). *Accreditation:* NCATE. *Program availability:* Part-time, evening/weekend, online only, 100% online. *Degree requirements:* For master's, thesis. *Entrance requirements:* For master's, appropriate bachelor's degree, minimum GPA of 3.0, teaching certificate. Additional exam requirements/recommendations for international students: Required—TOEFL (minimum score 550 paper-based). *Application deadline:* For fall admission, 8/1 for domestic and international students; for spring admission, 11/1 for domestic and international students; for summer admission, 4/1 for domestic and international students. Applications are processed on a rolling basis. Application fee: $50. Electronic applications accepted. *Expenses:* Contact institution. *Financial support:* Application deadline: 3/1; applicants required to submit FAFSA. *Unit head:* Dr. Laurie Daily, Chair, 605-274-5211, E-mail: laurie.daily@

augie.edu. *Application contact:* Jody Nitz, Graduate Coordinator, 605-274-4043, Fax: 605-274-4450, E-mail: graduate@augie.edu.
Website: http://www.augie.edu/master-arts-education

Aurora University, School of Education and Human Performance, Aurora, IL 60506-4892. Offers bilingual-ESL education (MA); educational leadership (MA); educational technology (MA); leadership in administration (Ed D); leadership in adult learning and higher education (Ed D); leadership in curriculum and instruction (Ed D); reading instruction (MA); special education (MA). *Accreditation:* NCATE. *Program availability:* Part-time, evening/weekend. *Faculty:* 22 full-time (12 women), 46 part-time/adjunct (27 women). *Students:* 36 full-time (30 women), 559 part-time (372 women); includes 68 minority (27 Black or African American, non-Hispanic/Latino; 1 American Indian or Alaska Native, non-Hispanic/Latino; 6 Asian, non-Hispanic/Latino; 29 Hispanic/Latino; 2 Native Hawaiian or other Pacific Islander, non-Hispanic/Latino; 3 Two or more races, non-Hispanic/Latino). Average age 37. 126 applicants, 98% accepted, 72 enrolled. In 2016, 178 master's, 27 doctorates awarded. *Degree requirements:* For master's, student teaching; for doctorate, comprehensive exam, thesis/dissertation. *Entrance requirements:* For master's, 2 years of teaching experience, valid teaching certificate; for doctorate, appropriate master's degree, two references, curriculum vitae, personal statement, professional project, reflective essay. Additional exam requirements/recommendations for international students: Required—TOEFL (minimum score 550 paper-based; 79 iBT). *Application deadline:* For fall admission, 6/1 for international students; for spring admission, 10/1 for international students. Applications are processed on a rolling basis. Application fee: $0. Electronic applications accepted. *Expenses:* Contact institution. *Financial support:* In 2016–17, 10 students received support. Federal Work-Study, scholarships/grants, and unspecified assistantships available. Support available to part-time students. Financial award applicants required to submit FAFSA. *Unit head:* Dr. Jen Buckley, Executive Director of the School of Education and Human Performance, 630-844-1542, Fax: 630-844-6155, E-mail: jbuckley@aurora.edu. *Application contact:* Elizabeth Botica, Graduate Education Recruiter, 630-947-8918, E-mail: ebotica@aurora.edu.
Website: http://aurora.edu/education

Austin Peay State University, College of Graduate Studies, College of Education, Department of Educational Specialties, Clarksville, TN 37044. Offers administration and supervision (Ed S); counseling and guidance (Ed S); curriculum and instruction (MA Ed); education leadership (MA Ed); elementary education (Ed S); reading (MA Ed); secondary education (Ed S). *Program availability:* Part-time, evening/weekend, online learning. *Faculty:* 7 full-time (4 women), 4 part-time/adjunct (3 women). *Students:* 4 full-time (3 women), 77 part-time (60 women); includes 13 minority (8 Black or African American, non-Hispanic/Latino; 1 Asian, non-Hispanic/Latino; 3 Hispanic/Latino; 1 Two or more races, non-Hispanic/Latino). Average age 37. 18 applicants, 89% accepted, 14 enrolled. In 2016, 34 master's, 9 Ed Ss awarded. *Degree requirements:* For master's, comprehensive exam, thesis optional. *Entrance requirements:* For master's, GRE General Test, MAT, minimum undergraduate GPA of 2.75. Additional exam requirements/recommendations for international students: Required—TOEFL (minimum score 500 paper-based). *Application deadline:* For fall admission, 8/9 priority date for domestic students. Applications are processed on a rolling basis. Application fee: $45 ($50 for international students). Electronic applications accepted. *Expenses:* Tuition, state resident: full-time $8300; part-time $415 per credit hour. Tuition, nonresident: full-time $22,280; part-time $1114 per credit hour. *Required fees:* $1473; $73.65 per credit hour. *Financial support:* Research assistantships with full tuition reimbursements, career-related internships or fieldwork, Federal Work-Study, institutionally sponsored loans, scholarships/grants, and unspecified assistantships available. Support available to part-time students. Financial award application deadline: 4/1; financial award applicants required to submit FAFSA. *Unit head:* Dr. Moniqueka Gold, Chair, 931-221-7696, Fax: 931-221-1292, E-mail: goldm@apsu.edu. *Application contact:* Brad Averitt, Coordinator of Graduate Admissions, 800-859-4723, Fax: 931-221-7641, E-mail: gradadmissions@apsu.edu.

Austin Peay State University, College of Graduate Studies, College of Education, Department of Teaching and Learning, Clarksville, TN 37044. Offers elementary education K-6 (MAT); reading (MA Ed); secondary education 7-12 (MAT); special education K-12 (MAT). *Program availability:* Part-time, evening/weekend, online learning. *Faculty:* 12 full-time (8 women), 1 (woman) part-time/adjunct. *Students:* 62 full-time (39 women), 79 part-time (72 women); includes 31 minority (16 Black or African American, non-Hispanic/Latino; 1 Asian, non-Hispanic/Latino; 8 Hispanic/Latino; 6 Two or more races, non-Hispanic/Latino), 2 international. Average age 33. 60 applicants, 80% accepted, 33 enrolled. In 2016, 53 master's awarded. *Degree requirements:* For master's, comprehensive exam, thesis optional. *Entrance requirements:* For master's, GRE General Test, minimum undergraduate GPA of 2.75. Additional exam requirements/recommendations for international students: Required—TOEFL (minimum score 500 paper-based). *Application deadline:* For fall admission, 8/9 priority date for domestic students. Applications are processed on a rolling basis. Application fee: $45 ($50 for international students). Electronic applications accepted. *Expenses:* Tuition, state resident: full-time $8300; part-time $415 per credit hour. Tuition, nonresident: full-time $22,280; part-time $1114 per credit hour. *Required fees:* $1473; $73.65 per credit hour. *Financial support:* Research assistantships, career-related internships or fieldwork, Federal Work-Study, institutionally sponsored loans, scholarships/grants, and unspecified assistantships available. Support available to part-time students. Financial award application deadline: 4/1; financial award applicants required to submit FAFSA. *Unit head:* Dr. Benita Bruster, Interim Chair, 931-221-6491, Fax: 931-221-1292, E-mail: brusterb@apsu.edu. *Application contact:* Brad Averitt, Coordinator of Graduate Admissions, 800-859-4723, Fax: 931-221-7641, E-mail: gradadmissions@apsu.edu.

Avila University, School of Education, Kansas City, MO 64145-1698. Offers English language learners (Advanced Certificate); international advocacy and leadership (MA, Certificate); literacy (MA); special reading (Advanced Certificate); teaching and learning (MA); TESL (MA). *Program availability:* Part-time, evening/weekend, online learning. *Faculty:* 0 full-time (5 women), 11 part-time/adjunct (6 women). *Students:* 65 full-time (50 women), 23 part-time (17 women); includes 12 minority (8 Black or African American, non-Hispanic/Latino; 2 Asian, non-Hispanic/Latino; 1 Hispanic/Latino; 1 Two or more races, non-Hispanic/Latino), 3 international. Average age 34. 135 applicants, 44% accepted, 33 enrolled. In 2016, 29 master's awarded. *Entrance requirements:* For master's, minimum GPA of 3.0, writing sample, recommendation, interview; for other advanced degree, foreign language. Additional exam requirements/recommendations for international students: Required—TOEFL (minimum score 580 paper-based; 92 iBT). *Application deadline:* Applications are processed on a rolling basis. Electronic applications accepted. *Expenses:* $483 per credit hour. *Financial support:* In 2016–17, 6 students received support. Unspecified assistantships available. Financial award applicants required to submit FAFSA. *Unit head:* Dr. Stacy Keith, Director of Graduate Education, 816-501-2440, Fax: 816-501-2915, E-mail: stacy.keith@avila.edu. *Application contact:* Cory Roup, Graduate Education Enrollment and Academic Advisor, 816-501-2464, E-mail: cory.roup@avila.edu.
Website: https://www.avila.edu/academics/graduate-studies/grad-education

Baldwin Wallace University, Graduate Programs, School of Education, Specialization in Literacy, Berea, OH 44017-2088. Offers MA Ed. *Accreditation:* NCATE. *Program availability:* Part-time, evening/weekend, blended/hybrid learning. *Students:* 23 full-time (21 women), 26 part-time (24 women); includes 5 minority (3 Black or African American, non-Hispanic/Latino; 1 Hispanic/Latino; 1 Two or more races, non-Hispanic/Latino). Average age 29. 6 applicants, 67% accepted, 4 enrolled. In 2016, 11 master's awarded. *Degree requirements:* For master's, comprehensive exam, capstone practicum. *Entrance requirements:* For master's, bachelor's degree in field, MAT or minimum GPA of 3.0. Additional exam requirements/recommendations for international students: Required—TOEFL (minimum score 550 paper-based; 79 iBT). *Application deadline:* For fall admission, 8/15 priority date for domestic students; for spring admission, 12/15 priority date for domestic students. Applications are processed on a rolling basis. Application fee: $25. Electronic applications accepted. Application fee is waived when completed online. *Expenses:* $721 per credit hour. *Financial support:* Career-related internships or fieldwork available. Financial award applicants required to submit FAFSA. *Faculty research:* Metacognition and the reading process, language acquisition, genres and the reader response theory, cultural responsiveness, content area literacy. *Unit head:* Dr. Karen Kaye, Chair, 440-826-2168, Fax: 440-826-3779, E-mail: kkaye@bw.edu. *Application contact:* Winifred W. Gerhardt, Director of Transfer, Adult and Graduate Admission, 440-826-2222, Fax: 440-826-3830, E-mail: admission@bw.edu.
Website: http://www.bw.edu/academics/master-of-arts-in-education/maed-in-literacy/

Ball State University, Graduate School, Teachers College, Department of Elementary Education, Muncie, IN 47306. Offers early childhood administration (Certificate); elementary education (MAE, Ed D, PhD); enhanced teaching practice for elementary teachers (Certificate); literacy instruction (Certificate); response to intervention (Certificate). *Accreditation:* NCATE. *Program availability:* Part-time, 100% online. *Degree requirements:* For doctorate, thesis/dissertation. *Entrance requirements:* For master's, minimum baccalaureate GPA of 2.75 or 3.0 in latter half of baccalaureate; for doctorate, GRE General Test, minimum graduate GPA of 3.2. Additional exam requirements/recommendations for international students: Required—TOEFL (minimum score 550 paper-based; 79 iBT), IELTS (minimum score 6.5). Electronic applications accepted.

Bank Street College of Education, Graduate School, Program in Reading and Literacy, New York, NY 10025. Offers advanced literacy specialization (Ed M); reading and literacy (MS Ed); teaching literacy (MS Ed); teaching literacy and childhood general education (MS Ed). *Degree requirements:* For master's, thesis. *Entrance requirements:* For master's, interview, essays. Additional exam requirements/recommendations for international students: Required—TOEFL (minimum score 600 paper-based; 100 iBT), IELTS (minimum score 7). Electronic applications accepted. *Faculty research:* Language development, children's literature, whole language, the reading and writing processes, reading difficulties in multicultural classrooms.

Barry University, School of Education, Program in Curriculum and Instruction, Miami Shores, FL 33161-6695. Offers accomplished teacher (Ed S); culture, language and literacy (TESOL) (PhD); curriculum evaluation and research (PhD); early childhood (Ed S); early childhood education (PhD); elementary (Ed S); elementary education (PhD); ESOL (Ed S); gifted (Ed S); Montessori (Ed S); PKP/elementary (Ed S); reading (Ed S); reading, language and cognition (PhD). *Entrance requirements:* For doctorate, GRE, minimum GPA of 3.25.

Barry University, School of Education, Program in Reading, Miami Shores, FL 33161-6695. Offers MS, Ed S. *Program availability:* Part-time, evening/weekend. *Degree requirements:* For master's, comprehensive exam, practicum; for Ed S, practicum. *Entrance requirements:* For master's, GRE General Test or MAT, minimum GPA of 3.0, course work in children's literature; for Ed S, GRE General Test, minimum GPA of 3.0. Electronic applications accepted.

Belhaven University, School of Education, Jackson, MS 39202-1789. Offers educational technology (M Ed); elementary education (M Ed, MAT); reading literacy (M Ed); secondary education (M Ed, MAT). *Program availability:* Part-time, evening/weekend, 100% online, blended/hybrid learning. *Faculty:* 36 full-time (27 women), 9 part-time/adjunct (6 women). *Students:* 319 full-time (270 women), 403 part-time (318 women); includes 502 minority (486 Black or African American, non-Hispanic/Latino; 2 Asian, non-Hispanic/Latino; 3 Hispanic/Latino; 11 Two or more races, non-Hispanic/Latino). Average age 35. In 2016, 78 master's awarded. *Degree requirements:* For master's, comprehensive exam, portfolio. *Entrance requirements:* For master's, PRAXIS I and II, minimum GPA of 2.8. *Application deadline:* Applications are processed on a rolling basis. Application fee: $25. Electronic applications accepted. *Expenses:* $495 per credit hour plus $75 technology fee per course. *Financial support:* Applicants required to submit FAFSA. *Unit head:* Dr. David Hand, Dean, 601-965-7020, E-mail: dhand@belhaven.edu. *Application contact:* Sean Kirnan, Assistant Vice President for Adult and Graduate Enrollment and Student Services, 601-968-8727, Fax: 601-968-5953, E-mail: gradadmission@belhaven.edu.
Website: http://graduateed.belhaven.edu

Bellarmine University, Annsley Frazier Thornton School of Education, Louisville, KY 40205. Offers education and district leadership (Ed D); education and social change (PhD); elementary education (MA Ed, MAT); leadership in higher education (PhD); learning and behavior disorders (MA Ed, MAT); middle grades education (MA Ed, MAT); principalship (Ed S); reading and writing (MA Ed); secondary education (MAT); teacher leadership (MA Ed). *Accreditation:* NCATE. *Program availability:* Part-time, evening/weekend. *Faculty:* 15 full-time (7 women), 44 part-time/adjunct (36 women). *Students:* 39 full-time (28 women), 211 part-time (164 women); includes 46 minority (35 Black or African American, non-Hispanic/Latino; 3 Asian, non-Hispanic/Latino; 5 Hispanic/Latino; 3 Two or more races, non-Hispanic/Latino). Average age 34. In 2016, 66 master's, 3 doctorates, 43 other advanced degrees awarded. *Degree requirements:* For master's, thesis (for some programs); for doctorate, thesis/dissertation. *Entrance requirements:* For master's, GRE, baccalaureate degree from accredited institution; minimum cumulative GPA of 2.75; recommendations from employers, supervisors, or professors attesting to applicant's potential as graduate student; statement of intent to pursue graduate degree; for doctorate, GRE, minimum GPA of 3.5 in all graduate coursework; baccalaureate and master's degrees in education or fields directly relevant to education; three letters of recommendation; two essays (no more than 1,000 words each); interview. Additional exam requirements/recommendations for international students: Required—TOEFL (minimum score 550 paper-based, 68 iBT), IELTS (minimum score 6), or Michigan English Language Assessment Battery. *Application deadline:* For fall admission, 8/1 priority date for domestic and international students; for spring admission, 12/1 priority date for domestic and international students; for summer admission, 4/10 priority date for domestic and international students. Applications are processed on a rolling basis. Application fee: $40. Electronic applications accepted. Tuition and fees vary according to program. *Financial support:* Scholarships/grants available. Financial award applicants required to submit FAFSA. *Faculty research:* Literacy, service-learning, dispositions, educational technology, special education. *Unit head:* Dr. Robert Cooter, Dean, 502-272-8191, Fax: 502-272-8189, E-mail: rcooter@bellarmine.edu. *Application contact:* Sarah Shumway Schuble, Senior Graduate Recruiter, 502-272-8271, Fax: 502-272-8002, E-mail: sshumway@bellarmine.edu.
Website: http://www.bellarmine.edu/education/graduate

Benedictine University, Graduate Programs, Program in Education, Lisle, IL 60532. Offers curriculum and instruction and collaborative teaching (M Ed); elementary education (MA Ed); leadership and administration (M Ed); reading and literacy (M Ed); secondary education (MA Ed); special education (MA Ed). *Program availability:* Part-time, evening/weekend. *Students:* 17 full-time (16 women), 30 part-time (26 women); includes 2 minority (both Black or African American, non-Hispanic/Latino). 21 applicants, 62% accepted, 8 enrolled. In 2016, 68 master's awarded. *Degree requirements:* For master's, comprehensive exam, thesis (for some programs). *Entrance requirements:* For master's, GRE or MAT. Additional exam requirements/recommendations for international students: Required—TOEFL (minimum score 550 paper-based). *Application deadline:* For fall admission, 9/1 for domestic students; for winter admission, 12/1 for domestic students; for spring admission, 2/15 for domestic students. Applications are processed on a rolling basis. Application fee: $40. Electronic applications accepted. *Expenses:* Contact institution. *Financial support:* Career-related internships or fieldwork and health care benefits available. Support available to part-time students. *Unit head:* MeShelda Jackson, Director, 630-829-6282, E-mail: mjackson@ben.edu. *Application contact:* Kari Gibbons, Associate Vice President, Enrollment Center, 630-829-6200, Fax: 630-829-6584, E-mail: kgibbons@ben.edu.

Berry College, Graduate Programs, Graduate Programs in Education, Program in Middle-Grades Education and Reading, Mount Berry, GA 30149-0159. Offers middle grades education (MAT); middle-grades education (M Ed); reading (M Ed). *Accreditation:* NCATE. *Program availability:* Part-time. *Faculty:* 6 part-time/adjunct (4 women). *Students:* 1 part-time (0 women). Average age 40. *Degree requirements:* For master's, thesis, portfolio, oral exams. *Entrance requirements:* For master's, GRE General Test or MAT, minimum GPA of 2.5. Additional exam requirements/recommendations for international students: Required—TOEFL (minimum score 550 paper-based). *Application deadline:* For fall admission, 7/21 for domestic students, 5/1 for international students; for spring admission, 12/1 for domestic students, 10/1 for international students. Applications are processed on a rolling basis. Application fee: $25 ($30 for international students). Electronic applications accepted. *Expenses:* Contact institution. *Financial support:* In 2016–17, 1 student received support. Research assistantships with full tuition reimbursements available, scholarships/grants, tuition waivers (partial), and unspecified assistantships available. Support available to part-time students. Financial award application deadline: 3/1; financial award applicants required to submit FAFSA. *Unit head:* Dr. Jacqueline McDowell, Dean, 706-236-1717, Fax: 706-238-5827, E-mail: jmcdowell@berry.edu. *Application contact:* Brett Kennedy, Assistant Vice President of Enrollment Management, 706-236-2215, Fax: 706-290-2178, E-mail: admissions@berry.edu.
Website: http://www.berry.edu/academics/education/graduate/

Binghamton University, State University of New York, Graduate School, Graduate School of Education, Program in Adolescence Education, Binghamton, NY 13902-6000. Offers biology education (MAT, MS Ed); chemistry education (MAT, MS Ed); earth science education (MAT, MS Ed); English education (MAT, MS Ed); French education (MAT, MS Ed); literacy education (MS Ed); mathematical sciences education (MAT, MS Ed); physics (MAT, MS Ed); social studies (MAT, MS Ed); Spanish education (MAT, MS Ed). *Accreditation:* TEAC. *Program availability:* Part-time, evening/weekend. *Students:* 59 full-time (36 women), 7 part-time (2 women); includes 10 minority (2 Black or African American, non-Hispanic/Latino; 1 American Indian or Alaska Native, non-Hispanic/Latino; 1 Asian, non-Hispanic/Latino; 5 Hispanic/Latino; 1 Two or more races, non-Hispanic/Latino). Average age 26. 46 applicants, 76% accepted, 25 enrolled. In 2016, 26 master's awarded. *Degree requirements:* For master's, portfolio. *Entrance requirements:* For master's, GRE General Test, teaching certification. Additional exam requirements/recommendations for international students: Required—TOEFL (minimum score 550 paper-based; 80 iBT). *Application deadline:* For fall admission, 2/1 priority date for domestic and international students; for spring admission, 10/15 priority date for domestic and international students. Application fee: $75. Electronic applications accepted. *Financial support:* In 2016–17, 6 students received support. Research assistantships, teaching assistantships, career-related internships or fieldwork, Federal Work-Study, institutionally sponsored loans, scholarships/grants, health care benefits, tuition waivers (full and partial), and unspecified assistantships available. Financial award applicants required to submit FAFSA. *Unit head:* Dr. Susan Strehle, Dean, 607-777-7329, E-mail: sstrehle@binghamton.edu. *Application contact:* Ben Balkaya, Assistant Dean and Director, 607-777-2151, Fax: 607-777-2501, E-mail: balkaya@binghamton.edu.

Binghamton University, State University of New York, Graduate School, Graduate School of Education, Program in Literacy Education, Binghamton, NY 13902-6000. Offers MS Ed. *Accreditation:* TEAC. *Program availability:* Part-time, evening/weekend. *Students:* 9 full-time (8 women), 19 part-time (14 women). Average age 26. 20 applicants, 95% accepted, 8 enrolled. In 2016, 16 master's awarded. *Degree requirements:* For master's, thesis. *Entrance requirements:* For master's, GRE General Test, teaching certification. Additional exam requirements/recommendations for international students: Required—TOEFL (minimum score 550 paper-based; 80 iBT). *Application deadline:* For fall admission, 2/1 priority date for domestic and international students; for spring admission, 10/15 priority date for domestic and international students. Application fee: $75. Electronic applications accepted. *Financial support:* In 2016–17, 2 students received support. Teaching assistantships, career-related internships or fieldwork, Federal Work-Study, institutionally sponsored loans, scholarships/grants, health care benefits, tuition waivers (full and partial), and unspecified assistantships available. Financial award applicants required to submit FAFSA. *Unit head:* Dr. Susan Strehle, Dean, 607-777-7329, E-mail: sstrehle@binghamton.edu. *Application contact:* Ben Balkaya, Assistant Dean and Director, 607-777-2151, Fax: 607-777-2501, E-mail: balkaya@binghamton.edu.

Bloomsburg University of Pennsylvania, School of Graduate Studies, College of Education, Department of Teaching and Learning, Program in Reading, Bloomsburg, PA 17815-1301. Offers M Ed. *Faculty:* 3 full-time (all women). *Students:* 1 (woman) full-time, 27 part-time (all women); includes 2 minority (both Two or more races, non-Hispanic/Latino). Average age 31. 21 applicants, 90% accepted, 16 enrolled. In 2016, 11 master's awarded. *Degree requirements:* For master's, thesis, PRAXIS II. *Entrance requirements:* For master's, baccalaureate degree, letter of intent, two letters of recommendation, teaching certificate. Additional exam requirements/recommendations for international students: Required—TOEFL, IELTS. *Application deadline:* Applications are processed on a rolling basis. Application fee: $35 ($60 for international students). Electronic applications accepted. *Expenses:* Tuition, state resident: full-time $9660; part-time $483 per credit. Tuition, nonresident: full-time $14,500; part-time $725 per credit. *Required fees:* $2410; $107 per credit. $75 per term. Tuition and fees vary according to course load, degree level and program. *Financial support:* Federal Work-Study and unspecified assistantships available. Financial award applicants required to submit FAFSA. *Unit head:* Dr. Ingrid Everett, Program Coordinator, 570-389-5120, Fax: 570-389-3030, E-mail: ieverett@bloomu.edu. *Application contact:* Jennifer Kessler, Administrative Assistant, 570-389-4015, Fax: 570-389-3054, E-mail: jkessler@bloomu.edu.
Website: http://www.bloomu.edu/gradschool/reading

Blue Mountain College, Program in Literacy/Reading (K-12), Blue Mountain, MS 38610. Offers M Ed. *Program availability:* Part-time, evening/weekend. *Degree requirements:* For master's, comprehensive exam. *Entrance requirements:* For master's, PRAXIS, GRE or MAT, official transcripts, bachelor's degree in a field of education from an accredited university or college, permanent teaching license, three recommendations. Additional exam requirements/recommendations for international students: Required—TOEFL (minimum score 550 paper-based). Electronic applications accepted.

Bluffton University, Programs in Education, Bluffton, OH 45817. Offers faith-based education (MA Ed); intervention specialist (MA Ed); leadership (MA Ed); reading (MA Ed). *Accreditation:* NCATE. *Program availability:* Part-time. *Faculty:* 6 full-time (3 women), 1 part-time/adjunct (0 women). *Students:* 9 full-time (all women), 10 part-time (9 women); includes 1 minority (Black or African American, non-Hispanic/Latino). Average age 34. 14 applicants, 50% accepted, 6 enrolled. In 2016, 1 master's awarded. *Degree requirements:* For master's, action research project, public presentation. *Entrance requirements:* For master's, PRAXIS I, bachelor's degree, minimum GPA of 3.0. Additional exam requirements/recommendations for international students: Required—TOEFL. *Application deadline:* For fall admission, 8/15 priority date for domestic students, 6/15 priority date for international students; for spring admission, 12/15 priority date for domestic students, 9/15 priority date for international students. Applications are processed on a rolling basis. Application fee: $25. Electronic applications accepted. Application fee is waived when completed online. *Expenses:* $453 per credit. *Financial support:* Health care benefits available. Support available to part-time students. Financial award application deadline: 9/15; financial award applicants required to submit FAFSA. *Faculty research:* Mentoring. *Unit head:* Dr. Gayle M. Trollinger, Director of Graduate Programs in Education, 419-358-3341, E-mail: trollingerg@bluffton.edu. *Application contact:* Nancey Schortgen, Program Representative, 419-358-3202, Fax: 419-358-3399, E-mail: schortgenn@bluffton.edu.
Website: http://www.bluffton.edu/grad/

Boise State University, College of Education, Department of Literacy, Language and Culture, Boise, ID 83725-1725. Offers bilingual education (M Ed); English as a new language (M Ed); literacy (MA). *Accreditation:* NCATE. *Program availability:* Part-time, evening/weekend. *Faculty:* 11 full-time (6 women). *Students:* 10 full-time (9 women), 53 part-time (46 women); includes 9 minority (1 Black or African American, non-Hispanic/Latino; 2 Asian, non-Hispanic/Latino; 5 Hispanic/Latino; 1 Native Hawaiian or other Pacific Islander, non-Hispanic/Latino), 6 international. Average age 36. 20 applicants, 75% accepted, 12 enrolled. In 2016, 26 master's awarded. *Degree requirements:* For master's, thesis optional. *Entrance requirements:* For master's, minimum GPA of 3.0. Additional exam requirements/recommendations for international students: Required—TOEFL (minimum score 550 paper-based; 80 iBT), IELTS (minimum score 6). Application fee: $65 ($95 for international students). Electronic applications accepted. *Expenses:* Tuition, state resident: full-time $6058; part-time $358 per credit hour. Tuition, nonresident: full-time $20,108; part-time $608 per credit hour. *Required fees:* $2108. Tuition and fees vary according to program. *Financial support:* In 2016–17, 4 students received support. Scholarships/grants and unspecified assistantships available. Financial award applicants required to submit FAFSA. *Unit head:* Dr. Maggie Chase, Department Chair, 208-426-3206, E-mail: maggiechase@boisestate.edu. *Application contact:* Dr. Arturo Rodriguez, Program Coordinator, 208-426-2243, E-mail: arturorodriguez@boisestate.edu.
Website: http://education.boisestate.edu/literacy/graduate/

Boston College, Lynch School of Education, Program in Reading and Literacy, Chestnut Hill, MA 02467-3800. Offers M Ed, MAT, CAES. *Accreditation:* TEAC. *Program availability:* Part-time, evening/weekend. *Faculty:* 9 full-time (5 women). *Students:* 2 full-time (both women), 8 part-time (all women). Average age 25. 14 applicants, 86% accepted, 2 enrolled. In 2016, 3 master's, 2 other advanced degrees awarded. *Degree requirements:* For master's and CAES, comprehensive exam. *Entrance requirements:* For master's, GRE General Test or MAT, general licensure, one year of teaching experience; for CAES, GRE General Test or MAT. Additional exam requirements/recommendations for international students: Required—TOEFL (minimum score 100 iBT). *Application deadline:* For fall admission, 12/1 priority date for domestic students, 12/1 for international students; for spring admission, 11/1 priority date for domestic and international students. Application fee: $65. Electronic applications accepted. Tuition and fees vary according to program. *Financial support:* Fellowships with tuition reimbursements, research assistantships with tuition reimbursements, teaching assistantships with tuition reimbursements, Federal Work-Study, scholarships/grants, and tuition waivers (full and partial) available. Financial award applicants required to submit FAFSA. *Unit head:* Dr. Susan Bruce, Chairperson, 617-552-4214, Fax: 617-552-0398. *Application contact:* Kimberly Rose, Graduate Admission Assistant, 617-552-4214, Fax: 617-552-0398, E-mail: roseki@bc.edu.

Bowie State University, Graduate Programs, Program in Reading Education, Bowie, MD 20715-9465. Offers M Ed. *Accreditation:* NCATE. *Program availability:* Part-time, evening/weekend. *Degree requirements:* For master's, comprehensive exam, thesis optional, research paper. *Entrance requirements:* For master's, minimum GPA of 2.5, teaching certificate, teaching experience. *Faculty research:* Literacy education, multicultural education.

Bowling Green State University, Graduate College, College of Education and Human Development, School of Teaching and Learning, Program in Reading, Bowling Green, OH 43403. Offers M Ed, Ed S. *Accreditation:* NCATE. *Program availability:* Part-time. *Degree requirements:* For master's, thesis or alternative; for Ed S, practicum or field experience. *Entrance requirements:* For master's and Ed S, GRE General Test. Additional exam requirements/recommendations for international students: Required—TOEFL. *Application deadline:* For fall admission, 2/15 priority date for domestic students. Applications are processed on a rolling basis. Application fee: $30. Electronic applications accepted. *Financial support:* Research assistantships with full tuition reimbursements, teaching assistantships with full tuition reimbursements, career-related internships or fieldwork, Federal Work-Study, institutionally sponsored loans, and unspecified assistantships available. Financial award applicants required to submit FAFSA. *Faculty research:* Children's literature, attention deficit disorder (ADD)/reading correlation, content area reading, reading instruction, reading/writing connection. *Unit head:* Dr. Cindy Hendricks, Director, 419-372-7341. *Application contact:* Dr. Cindy Hendricks, Graduate Coordinator, 419-372-7341.

Bridgewater State University, College of Graduate Studies, College of Education and Allied Studies, Department of Elementary and Early Childhood Education, Program in Reading, Bridgewater, MA 02325. Offers M Ed, CAGS. *Accreditation:* NCATE. *Program availability:* Part-time, evening/weekend. *Entrance requirements:* For master's, GRE General Test, 1 year of teaching experience.

Brigham Young University, Graduate Studies, David O. McKay School of Education, Department of Teacher Education, Provo, UT 84602. Offers integrative science-technology-engineering-mathematics (STEM) (MA); literacy education (MA); physical education teacher education (MA); teacher education (MA). *Program availability:* Part-time-only, evening/weekend. *Faculty:* 28 full-time (15 women). *Students:* 22 part-time (19 women); includes 2 minority (both Native Hawaiian or other Pacific Islander, non-Hispanic/Latino). Average age 34. 24 applicants, 79% accepted, 17 enrolled. In 2016, 6 master's awarded. *Degree requirements:* For master's, thesis. *Entrance requirements:* For master's, GRE General Test, minimum 1 year of teaching experience (preferred), minimum cumulative GPA of 3.25. Additional exam requirements/recommendations for

international students: Required—TOEFL. *Application deadline:* For fall admission, 2/1 for international students; for winter admission, 2/1 for international students; for summer admission, 2/1 priority date for domestic students, 2/1 for international students. Application fee: $50. Electronic applications accepted. *Expenses:* Contact institution. *Financial support:* In 2016–17, 20 students received support. Tuition waivers (full and partial) available. *Faculty research:* Multicultural education, physical education teacher education, curriculum and instructional education, teacher education, teaching English language learners. *Unit head:* Ramona Cutri, Graduate Coordinator, 801-422-4982, Fax: 801-422-0652, E-mail: ramona_cutri@byu.edu. *Application contact:* Hannah Nelson, Graduate Program Manager, 801-422-2089, Fax: 801-422-0652, E-mail: hannah_nelson@byu.edu.
Website: http://education.byu.edu/ted/

Buffalo State College, State University of New York, The Graduate School, Faculty of Applied Science and Education, Department of Elementary Education and Reading, Programs in Literacy Specialist, Buffalo, NY 14222-1095. Offers literacy specialist (birth-grade 6) (MS Ed); literacy specialist (grades 5-12) (MPS). *Accreditation:* NCATE. *Program availability:* Part-time, evening/weekend. *Degree requirements:* For master's, project. *Entrance requirements:* For master's, minimum GPA of 3.0 in last 60 hours. Additional exam requirements/recommendations for international students: Required—TOEFL (minimum score 550 paper-based).

Caldwell University, Graduate Studies, Division of Education, Caldwell, NJ 07006-6195. Offers curriculum and instruction (MA); education (Ed D, Postbaccalaureate Certificate); educational administration (MA); learning disabilities teacher-consultant (Post-Master's Certificate); literacy instruction (MA); principal (Post-Master's Certificate); reading specialist (Post-Master's Certificate); special education (MA), including special education, teaching of students with disabilities, teaching of students with disabilities and learning disabilities teacher-consultant; superintendent (Post-Master's Certificate); supervisor (Post-Master's Certificate). *Program availability:* Part-time, evening/weekend. *Degree requirements:* For master's, comprehensive exam (for some programs). *Entrance requirements:* For master's, PRAXIS, 3 years of work experience, prior teaching certification. Additional exam requirements/recommendations for international students: Required—TOEFL (minimum score 580 paper-based). Electronic applications accepted. *Faculty research:* Curriculum and instruction, secondary education, special education, education and technology.

California Baptist University, Program in Education, Riverside, CA 92504-3206. Offers educational leadership (MS); educational leadership for faith-based institutions (MS); educational leadership for public institutions (MS); educational technology (MS); instructional computer applications (MS); international education (MS); leadership and adult learning (MS); leadership and organizational studies (MS); online teaching and learning (MS); reading (MS); science education (MA); special education in mild/moderate disabilities (MS); special education in moderate/severe disabilities (MS); teacher leadership (MS); teaching (MS); teaching and learning (MS). *Program availability:* Part-time, evening/weekend, 100% online, blended/hybrid learning. *Faculty:* 20 full-time (8 women), 11 part-time/adjunct (7 women). *Students:* 191 full-time (148 women), 234 part-time (178 women); includes 194 minority (23 Black or African American, non-Hispanic/Latino; 5 American Indian or Alaska Native, non-Hispanic/Latino; 15 Asian, non-Hispanic/Latino; 131 Hispanic/Latino; 4 Native Hawaiian or other Pacific Islander, non-Hispanic/Latino; 16 Two or more races, non-Hispanic/Latino), 2 international. Average age 31. 277 applicants, 61% accepted, 150 enrolled. In 2016, 280 master's awarded. *Degree requirements:* For master's, comprehensive exam, project, or thesis. *Entrance requirements:* For master's, minimum undergraduate GPA of 2.75; 500-word essay; three letters of recommendation; two prerequisite courses completed with minimum C grade. Additional exam requirements/recommendations for international students: Required—TOEFL (minimum score 80 iBT). *Application deadline:* For fall admission, 8/1 priority date for domestic students, 7/1 for international students; for spring admission, 12/1 priority date for domestic students, 11/1 for international students. Applications are processed on a rolling basis. Application fee: $45. Electronic applications accepted. *Expenses:* Contact institution. *Financial support:* In 2016–17, 162 students received support. Federal Work-Study and scholarships/grants available. Financial award applicants required to submit CSS PROFILE or FAFSA. *Faculty research:* Leadership development, complexity theory, faith and learning, special education, social and philosophical contexts of education. *Unit head:* Dr. John Shoup, Dean, School of Education, 951-343-4516, E-mail: jshoup@calbaptist.edu.
Website: http://www.calbaptist.edu/mastersined/

California State Polytechnic University, Pomona, Master's Programs in Education, Pomona, CA 91768-2557. Offers curriculum and instruction (MA), including literacy studies. *Program availability:* Part-time, evening/weekend. *Students:* 21 full-time (14 women), 95 part-time (67 women); includes 69 minority (8 Black or African American, non-Hispanic/Latino; 1 American Indian or Alaska Native, non-Hispanic/Latino; 10 Asian, non-Hispanic/Latino; 48 Hispanic/Latino; 2 Two or more races, non-Hispanic/Latino), 4 international. Average age 34. 27 applicants, 93% accepted, 14 enrolled. In 2016, 50 master's awarded. *Entrance requirements:* Additional exam requirements/recommendations for international students: Required—TOEFL. *Application deadline:* Applications are processed on a rolling basis. Application fee: $55. Electronic applications accepted. *Expenses:* Contact institution. *Financial support:* Application deadline: 3/2; applicants required to submit FAFSA. *Unit head:* Kelly Mitchell, Graduate Studies Coordinator, 909-869-2358, Fax: 909-869-2722, E-mail: klmitchell@cpp.edu. *Application contact:* Andrew M Wright, Director of Admissions, 909-869-3130, Fax: 909-869-4529, E-mail: awright@cpp.edu.
Website: http://www.cpp.edu/~ceis/education/masters-programs/index.shtml

California State University, East Bay, Office of Graduate Studies, College of Education and Allied Studies, Department of Teacher Education, Hayward, CA 94542-3000. Offers education (MS), including curriculum, early childhood education, educational technology and leadership, reading instruction. *Program availability:* Online learning. *Students:* 55 full-time (43 women), 21 part-time (15 women); includes 34 minority (5 Black or African American, non-Hispanic/Latino; 1 American Indian or Alaska Native, non-Hispanic/Latino; 14 Asian, non-Hispanic/Latino; 10 Hispanic/Latino; 1 Native Hawaiian or other Pacific Islander, non-Hispanic/Latino; 3 Two or more races, non-Hispanic/Latino), 6 international. Average age 33. 65 applicants, 91% accepted, 11 enrolled. In 2016, 67 master's awarded. *Degree requirements:* For master's, project or thesis. *Entrance requirements:* For master's, minimum GPA of 3.0 in field, 2.5 overall; teaching experience; baccalaureate degree; 3 letters of recommendation. Additional exam requirements/recommendations for international students: Required—TOEFL (minimum score 550 paper-based), IELTS. *Application deadline:* For fall admission, 6/30 for domestic and international students. Application fee: $55. Electronic applications accepted. *Financial support:* Career-related internships or fieldwork, Federal Work-Study, and institutionally sponsored loans available. Support available to part-time students. Financial award application deadline: 3/2; financial award applicants required to submit FAFSA. *Faculty research:* Online, pedagogy, writing, learning, teaching. *Unit head:* Dr. Eric Engdahl, Chair, 510-885-4599, E-mail: eric.engdahl@csueastbay.edu. *Application contact:* Prof. Valerie Helgren-Lempesis, Education Graduate Advisor, 510-885-3006, Fax: 510-885-4632, E-mail: valerie.helgren-lempesis@csueastbay.edu.
Website: http://www20.csueastbay.edu/ceas/departments/ted/index.html

California State University, Fresno, Division of Research and Graduate Studies, Kremen School of Education and Human Development, Department of Literacy, Early, Bilingual, and Special Education, Fresno, CA 93740-8027. Offers education (MA), including early childhood education, reading/language arts; special education (MA). *Accreditation:* NCATE. *Program availability:* Part-time, evening/weekend. *Degree requirements:* For master's, thesis or alternative. *Entrance requirements:* For master's, GRE General Test, MAT, minimum GPA of 2.75. Additional exam requirements/recommendations for international students: Required—TOEFL. *Application deadline:* For fall admission, 5/1 for domestic and international students; for spring admission, 10/1 for domestic and international students. Applications are processed on a rolling basis. Application fee: $55. Electronic applications accepted. *Financial support:* Career-related internships or fieldwork, Federal Work-Study, scholarships/grants, and research awards available. Support available to part-time students. Financial award application deadline: 3/1; financial award applicants required to submit FAFSA. *Faculty research:* Reading recovery, monitoring/tutoring programs, character and academics, professional ethics, low-performing partnership schools. *Unit head:* Dr. Laura Alamillo, Chair, 559-278-0250, Fax: 559-278-0107. *Application contact:* Dr. Monica Billen, Coordinator, Early Childhood Education, 559-278-0267, E-mail: mbillen@csufresno.edu.
Website: http://www.fresnostate.edu/kremen/departments/lebse.html

California State University, Northridge, Graduate Studies, Michael D. Eisner College of Education, Department of Elementary Education, Northridge, CA 91330. Offers curriculum and instruction (MA); language and literacy (MA); multilingual/multicultural education (MA). *Accreditation:* NCATE. *Program availability:* Part-time, evening/weekend. *Faculty:* 12 full-time (4 women), 17 part-time/adjunct (7 women). *Students:* 37 part-time (33 women); includes 21 minority (1 Asian, non-Hispanic/Latino; 17 Hispanic/Latino; 3 Two or more races, non-Hispanic/Latino). Average age 29. 44 applicants, 55% accepted, 20 enrolled. *Degree requirements:* For master's, comprehensive exam. *Entrance requirements:* For master's, GRE General Test or minimum GPA of 3.0. Additional exam requirements/recommendations for international students: Required—TOEFL. *Application deadline:* For fall admission, 11/30 for domestic students. Application fee: $55. *Expenses:* Tuition, state resident: full-time $4152. *Financial support:* Federal Work-Study available. Financial award application deadline: 3/1. *Unit head:* Dr. Joyce Burstein, Chair, 818-677-2621.
Website: http://www.csun.edu/eisner-education/elementary-education

California State University, Sacramento, Office of Graduate Studies, College of Education, Graduate and Professional Studies in Education, Sacramento, CA 95819. Offers child development (MA); counseling (MS); curriculum and instruction (MA); education (Ed D); education leadership and policy studies (MA), including higher education, PreK-12; educational technology (MA); gender equity (MA); language and literacy (MA); multicultural education (MA); school psychology (MA); special education (MA); workforce development advocacy (MA). *Program availability:* Part-time. *Students:* 446 full-time (335 women), 125 part-time (97 women); includes 298 minority (39 Black or African American, non-Hispanic/Latino; 3 American Indian or Alaska Native, non-Hispanic/Latino; 97 Asian, non-Hispanic/Latino; 153 Hispanic/Latino; 6 Native Hawaiian or other Pacific Islander, non-Hispanic/Latino). Average age 32. 540 applicants, 76% accepted, 250 enrolled. In 2016, 107 master's, 7 doctorates awarded. *Degree requirements:* For master's, thesis or project; writing proficiency exam. *Entrance requirements:* For master's, minimum GPA of 2.5, 3.0 in last 60 units. Additional exam requirements/recommendations for international students: Required—TOEFL (minimum score 550 paper-based; 80 iBT). *Application deadline:* For fall admission, 2/15 for domestic students, 1/15 for international students. Applications are processed on a rolling basis. Application fee: $55. Electronic applications accepted. *Expenses:* $4,302 full-time tuition and fees per semester, $2,796 part-time. *Financial support:* Career-related internships or fieldwork and Federal Work-Study available. Support available to part-time students. Financial award application deadline: 3/1; financial award applicants required to submit FAFSA. *Unit head:* Dr. Susan Heredia, Chair, 916-278-5942, E-mail: coe@csus.edu. *Application contact:* Jose Martinez, Graduate Admissions Supervisor, 916-278-7871, E-mail: martinj@skymail.csus.edu.
Website: http://www.csus.edu/coe/academics/graduate/index.html

California State University, San Marcos, College of Education, Health and Human Services, School of Education, San Marcos, CA 92096-0001. Offers educational administration (MA); educational leadership (Ed D); general education (MA); literacy education (MA); special education (MA). *Accreditation:* NCATE (one or more programs are accredited). *Program availability:* Part-time, evening/weekend. *Degree requirements:* For master's, thesis. *Entrance requirements:* For master's, minimum GPA of 3.0, teaching credentials, 1 year of teaching experience. *Expenses:* Tuition, state resident: full-time $6738. Tuition, nonresident: full-time $13,434. *Required fees:* $1906. Tuition and fees vary according to campus/location and program. *Faculty research:* Multicultural literature, art as knowledge, poetry and second language acquisition, restructuring K–12 education and improving the training of K–8 science teachers.

California State University, Stanislaus, College of Education, Program in Education (MA), Turlock, CA 95382. Offers curriculum and instruction (MA), including education technology, elementary education, multilingual education, physical education, reading, secondary education, special education; school administration (MA); school counseling (MA). *Program availability:* Part-time, evening/weekend. *Degree requirements:* For master's, comprehensive exam (for some programs), thesis (for some programs). *Entrance requirements:* For master's, MAT, GRE, or CBEST (varies by concentration), 3 letters of recommendation, personal statement. Additional exam requirements/recommendations for international students: Required—TOEFL (minimum score 550 paper-based). Electronic applications accepted. *Faculty research:* Children's perspectives on historical events, method elementary schools dual language education, K-12 reading programs.

California University of Pennsylvania, School of Graduate Studies and Research, College of Education and Human Services, Program in Reading Specialist, California, PA 15419-1394. Offers M Ed. *Accreditation:* NCATE. *Program availability:* Part-time, evening/weekend. *Degree requirements:* For master's, comprehensive exam, thesis optional, practicum. *Entrance requirements:* For master's, MAT, PRAXIS, minimum GPA of 3.0, teaching certificate. Additional exam requirements/recommendations for international students: Required—TOEFL (minimum score 550 paper-based; 80 iBT). Electronic applications accepted. *Expenses:* Tuition, state resident: full-time $11,592; part-time $483 per credit. Tuition, nonresident: full-time $17,400; part-time $725 per credit. *Required fees:* $3916. Tuition and fees vary according to course load, degree level, campus/location and reciprocity agreements. *Faculty research:* Online education in reading supervision, phonetics education, remedial reading, injury and reading remediation in brain patients.

Cambridge College, School of Education, Cambridge, MA 02138-5304. Offers autism specialist (M Ed); autism/behavior analyst (M Ed); behavior analyst (Post-Master's Certificate), behavioral management (M Ed); early childhood teacher (M Ed); education specialist in curriculum and instruction (CAGS); educational leadership (Ed D); elementary teacher (M Ed); English as a second language (M Ed, Certificate); general science (M Ed); health education (Post-Master's Certificate); health/family and consumer sciences (M Ed); history (M Ed); individualized (M Ed); information technology literacy (M Ed); instructional technology (M Ed); interdisciplinary studies

(M Ed); library teacher (M Ed); literacy education (M Ed); mathematics (M Ed); mathematics specialist (Certificate); middle school mathematics and science (M Ed); school administration (M Ed, CAGS); school guidance counselor (M Ed); school nurse education (M Ed); school social worker/school adjustment counselor (M Ed); special education administrator (CAGS); special education/moderate disabilities (M Ed); teaching skills and methodologies (M Ed). *Program availability:* Part-time, evening/weekend, online learning. *Degree requirements:* For master's, thesis, internship/practicum (licensure program only); for doctorate, thesis/dissertation; for other advanced degree, thesis. *Entrance requirements:* For master's, interview, resume, documentation of licensure, 2 professional references; for doctorate, official transcripts, interview, resume, documentation of licensure (if any), written personal statement/essay, portfolio of scholarly and professional work, qualifying assessment, 2 professional references, health insurance, immunizations form; for other advanced degree, official transcripts, interview, resume, documentation of licensure (if any), written personal statement/essay, 2 professional references, health insurance, immunizations form. Additional exam requirements/recommendations for international students: Required—TOEFL (minimum score 550 paper-based; 79 iBT), Michigan English Language Assessment Battery (minimum score 85); Recommended—IELTS (minimum score 6). Electronic applications accepted. *Expenses:* Contact institution. *Faculty research:* Adult education, accelerated learning, mathematics education, brain compatible learning, special education and law.

Canisius College, Graduate Division, School of Education and Human Services, Department of Graduate Education and Leadership, Buffalo, NY 14208-1098. Offers business and marketing education (MS Ed); college student personnel (MS Ed); deaf education (MS Ed); deaf/adolescent education, grades 7-12 (MS Ed); deaf/childhood education, grades 1-6 (MS Ed); differentiated instruction (MS Ed); education administration (MS); educational administration (MS Ed); educational technologies (Certificate); gifted education extension (Certificate); literacy (MS Ed); reading (Certificate); school building leadership (MS Ed, Certificate); school district leadership (Certificate); teacher leader (Certificate); TESOL (MS Ed). *Accreditation:* NCATE. *Program availability:* Part-time, evening/weekend, 100% online, blended/hybrid learning. *Faculty:* 5 full-time (all women), 23 part-time/adjunct (16 women). *Students:* 95 full-time (78 women), 223 part-time (177 women); includes 31 minority (15 Black or African American, non-Hispanic/Latino; 2 American Indian or Alaska Native, non-Hispanic/Latino; 4 Asian, non-Hispanic/Latino; 9 Hispanic/Latino; 1 Two or more races, non-Hispanic/Latino), 1 international. Average age 30. 162 applicants, 89% accepted, 135 enrolled. In 2016, 135 master's, 39 other advanced degrees awarded. *Entrance requirements:* For master's, GRE (if cumulative GPA less than 2.7), transcripts, two letters of recommendation. Additional exam requirements/recommendations for international students: Required—TOEFL (minimum score 550 paper-based, 79 iBT), IELTS (minimum score 6.5), or CAEL (minimum score 70). *Application deadline:* Applications are processed on a rolling basis. Application fee: $25. Electronic applications accepted. Application fee is waived when completed online. *Expenses: Tuition:* Full-time $14,742. *Required fees:* $724. *Financial support:* Career-related internships or fieldwork, Federal Work-Study, scholarships/grants, tuition waivers (partial), and unspecified assistantships available. Support available to part-time students. Financial award application deadline: 4/30; financial award applicants required to submit FAFSA. *Faculty research:* Asperger's disease, autism, private higher education, reading strategies. *Unit head:* Dr. Rosemary K. Murray, Chair/Associate Professor of Graduate Education and Leadership, 716-888-3723, E-mail: murray1@canisius.edu. *Application contact:* Kathleen B. Davis, Vice President of Enrollment Management, 716-888-2500, Fax: 716-888-3195, E-mail: daviskb@canisius.edu.
Website: http://www.canisius.edu/graduate/

Capella University, School of Education, Doctoral Programs in Education, Minneapolis, MN 55402. Offers curriculum and instruction (PhD); educational leadership and management (Ed D); instructional design for online learning (PhD); K-12 studies in education (PhD); leadership for higher education (PhD); leadership in educational administration (PhD); postsecondary and adult education (PhD); professional studies in education (PhD); reading and literacy (Ed D); special education leadership (PhD); training and performance improvement (PhD).

Capella University, School of Education, Master's Programs in Education, Minneapolis, MN 55402. Offers adult education (MS); curriculum and instruction (MS); early childhood education (MS); enrollment management (MS); higher education leadership and management (MS); instructional design for online learning (MS); integrative studies (MS); K-12 studies in education (MS); leadership in educational administration (MS); reading and literacy (MS); special education teaching (MS).

Cardinal Stritch University, College of Education and Leadership, Department of Literacy, Milwaukee, WI 53217-3985. Offers language and literacy (MA, PhD). *Accreditation:* NCATE. *Program availability:* Part-time, evening/weekend. *Degree requirements:* For master's, comprehensive exam, thesis, faculty recommendation, research project. *Entrance requirements:* For master's, 2 letters of recommendation, minimum GPA of 2.75. *Application deadline:* For fall admission, 7/15 priority date for domestic students; for spring admission, 12/15 priority date for domestic students. Applications are processed on a rolling basis. Application fee: $25. *Expenses: Tuition:* Full-time $11,890; part-time $765 per credit hour. Tuition and fees vary according to class time, course load, degree level, program and student's religious affiliation. *Financial support:* Research assistantships with partial tuition reimbursements, Federal Work-Study, and scholarships/grants available. Financial award applicants required to submit FAFSA. *Unit head:* Janice Strop, Chair, 414-410-4487. *Application contact:* 800-347-8822 Ext. 4042, E-mail: gradadm@stritch.edu.

Carthage College, Division of Teacher Education, Kenosha, WI 53140. Offers classroom guidance and counseling (M Ed); creative arts (M Ed); gifted and talented children (M Ed); language arts (M Ed); modern language (M Ed); natural sciences (M Ed); reading (M Ed, Certificate); social sciences (M Ed); teacher leadership (M Ed). *Program availability:* Part-time, evening/weekend. *Degree requirements:* For master's, thesis optional. *Entrance requirements:* For master's, MAT, minimum B average, letters of reference.

Castleton University, Division of Graduate Studies, Department of Education, Program in Language Arts and Reading, Castleton, VT 05735. Offers MA Ed, CAGS. *Program availability:* Part-time, evening/weekend. *Degree requirements:* For master's, thesis or alternative; for CAGS, publishable paper, written exams. *Entrance requirements:* For master's, GRE General Test, MAT, interview, minimum undergraduate GPA of 3.0; for CAGS, educational research, master's degree, minimum undergraduate GPA of 3.0.

Centenary University, Program in Education, Hackettstown, NJ 07840-2100. Offers education practice (M Ed); educational leadership (MA, Ed D); instructional leadership (MA); reading (M Ed); special education (MA). *Accreditation:* TEAC. *Program availability:* Part-time, evening/weekend, online learning. *Degree requirements:* For master's, thesis. *Entrance requirements:* For master's, interview, minimum undergraduate GPA of 2.8.

Central Connecticut State University, School of Graduate Studies, School of Education and Professional Studies, Department of Literacy, Elementary, and Early Childhood Education, New Britain, CT 06050-4010. Offers MS, AC, Sixth Year Certificate. *Program availability:* Part-time, evening/weekend. *Faculty:* 5 full-time (3 women), 2 part-time/adjunct (both women). *Students:* 11 full-time (8 women), 120 part-time (114 women); includes 9 minority (2 Black or African American, non-Hispanic/Latino; 5 Hispanic/Latino; 2 Two or more races, non-Hispanic/Latino), 1 international. Average age 30. 47 applicants, 81% accepted, 25 enrolled. In 2016, 44 master's, 11 other advanced degrees awarded. *Degree requirements:* For master's, comprehensive exam, thesis or alternative; for other advanced degree, qualifying exam. *Entrance requirements:* For master's, minimum undergraduate GPA of 2.7, teacher certification, interview, essay, letters of recommendation; for other advanced degree, master's degree, essay, teacher certification, interview, letters of recommendation. Additional exam requirements/recommendations for international students: Required—TOEFL (minimum score 550 paper-based; 79 iBT). *Application deadline:* For fall admission, 5/1 for domestic and international students; for spring admission, 11/1 for domestic and international students. Applications are processed on a rolling basis. Application fee: $50. Electronic applications accepted. *Expenses: Tuition, area resident:* Full-time $6497; part-time $606 per credit. Tuition, state resident: full-time $9748; part-time $622 per credit. Tuition, nonresident: full-time $18,102; part-time $622 per credit. *Required fees:* $4459; $246 per credit. *Financial support:* In 2016–17, 4 students received support. Career-related internships or fieldwork, Federal Work-Study, and scholarships/grants available. Support available to part-time students. Financial award application deadline: 3/1. *Faculty research:* Developmental, clinical, and administrative aspects of reading and language arts instruction. *Unit head:* Dr. Helen Abadiano, Chair, 860-832-2175, E-mail: abadiano@ccsu.edu. *Application contact:* Patricia Gardner, Associate Director of Graduate Studies, 860-832-2350, Fax: 860-832-2362.
Website: http://www.ccsu.edu/leece/index.html

Central Michigan University, Central Michigan University Global Campus, Program in Education, Mount Pleasant, MI 48859. Offers college teaching (Graduate Certificate); community college (MA); curriculum and instruction (MA); educational technology (MA, DET); reading and literacy K-12 (MA); school principalship (MA), including charter school leadership; training and development (MA). *Accreditation:* TEAC. *Program availability:* Part-time, evening/weekend. *Faculty:* 24 full-time (14 women), 24 part-time/adjunct (8 women). *Students:* 888 (620 women); includes 225 minority (142 Black or African American, non-Hispanic/Latino; 8 American Indian or Alaska Native, non-Hispanic/Latino; 16 Asian, non-Hispanic/Latino; 13 Hispanic/Latino; 46 Two or more races, non-Hispanic/Latino). Average age 37. In 2016, 76 master's awarded. *Entrance requirements:* For master's, minimum GPA of 2.7 in major. Additional exam requirements/recommendations for international students: Required—TOEFL. *Application deadline:* Applications are processed on a rolling basis. Application fee: $50. Electronic applications accepted. *Financial support:* Scholarships/grants available. Support available to part-time students. *Unit head:* Kaleb Patrick, Director, 989-774-3144, E-mail: patri1kg@cmich.edu. *Application contact:* 877-268-4636, E-mail: cmuglobal@cmich.edu.

Central Michigan University, College of Graduate Studies, College of Education and Human Services, Department of Teacher Education and Professional Development, Mount Pleasant, MI 48859. Offers educational technology (MA, Graduate Certificate); elementary education (MA), including classroom teaching, early childhood; reading and literacy K-12 (MA); secondary education (MA). *Program availability:* Part-time, evening/weekend. *Degree requirements:* For master's, thesis or alternative. Electronic applications accepted. *Faculty research:* Integrating literacy across the curriculum, science teaching and aesthetic learning in science, diversity education, educational technology, educational psychology and child development.

Central Washington University, Graduate Studies and Research, College of Education and Professional Studies, Department of Language, Literacy and Special Education, Program in Reading Education, Ellensburg, WA 98926. Offers M Ed. *Program availability:* Part-time. *Degree requirements:* For master's, thesis or alternative. *Entrance requirements:* For master's, minimum GPA of 3.0. Additional exam requirements/recommendations for international students: Required—TOEFL (minimum score 550 paper-based; 79 iBT), IELTS (minimum score 6.5). Electronic applications accepted.

Chestnut Hill College, School of Graduate Studies, Department of Education, Program in Reading, Philadelphia, PA 19118-2693. Offers reading specialist (M Ed), including K-12, special education 7-12, special education PreK-8. *Program availability:* Part-time, evening/weekend. *Degree requirements:* For master's, thesis optional. *Entrance requirements:* Additional exam requirements/recommendations for international students: Required—TOEFL (minimum score 500 paper-based) or IELTS (minimum score 6). Electronic applications accepted. *Expenses:* Contact institution. *Faculty research:* Inclusive education, cultural issues in education.

Chicago State University, School of Graduate and Professional Studies, College of Education, Department of Reading, Elementary Education, Library Information and Media Studies, Program in Reading, Chicago, IL 60628. Offers teaching of reading (MS Ed). *Accreditation:* NCATE. *Entrance requirements:* For master's, minimum GPA of 2.75.

The Citadel, The Military College of South Carolina, Citadel Graduate College, Zucker Family School of Education, Charleston, SC 29409. Offers elementary/secondary school administration and supervision (M Ed); elementary/secondary school counseling (M Ed); interdisciplinary STEM education (M Ed); literacy education (M Ed, Graduate Certificate); middle grades (MAT), including English, mathematics, science, social studies; physical education (grades K-12) (MAT); school superintendency (Ed S); secondary education (MAT), including biology, English, mathematics, social studies; student affairs (Graduate Certificate); student affairs and college counseling (M Ed). *Accreditation:* NCATE. *Program availability:* Part-time, evening/weekend, 100% online, blended/hybrid learning. *Faculty:* 9 full-time (4 women), 9 part-time/adjunct (5 women). *Students:* 70 full-time (58 women), 249 part-time (200 women); includes 87 minority (70 Black or African American, non-Hispanic/Latino; 1 Asian, non-Hispanic/Latino; 9 Hispanic/Latino; 7 Two or more races, non-Hispanic/Latino), 2 international. 146 applicants, 98% accepted, 105 enrolled. In 2016, 85 master's, 7 other advanced degrees awarded. *Degree requirements:* For master's, comprehensive exam (for some programs). *Entrance requirements:* For master's, GRE (minimum combined verbal and quantitative score of 290) or MAT (minimum score 396). Additional exam requirements/recommendations for international students: Required—TOEFL (minimum score 550 paper-based; 79 iBT). *Application deadline:* Applications are processed on a rolling basis. Application fee: $40. Electronic applications accepted. *Expenses:* Tuition, state resident: full-time $5121; part-time $569 per credit hour. Tuition, nonresident: full-time $8613; part-time $957 per credit hour. *Required fees:* $90 per term. *Financial support:* Fellowships and unspecified assistantships available. Support available to part-time students. Financial award application deadline: 7/1; financial award applicants required to submit FAFSA. *Unit head:* Dr. Larry G. Daniel, Dean, 843-953-5097, E-mail: ldaniel@citadel.edu. *Application contact:* Dr. Tammy J. Graham, Associate Professor, 843-953-6854, E-mail: tammy.graham@citadel.edu.
Website: http://www.citadel.edu/root/education-graduate-programs

City College of the City University of New York, Graduate School, Division of Humanities and the Arts, Department of English, Program in Language and Literacy, New York, NY 10031-9198. Offers MA. *Accreditation:* NCATE. *Entrance requirements:*

For master's, 2 writing samples. Additional exam requirements/recommendations for international students: Required—TOEFL (minimum score 600 paper-based; 100 iBT). Electronic applications accepted. Tuition and fees vary according to course load, degree level and program.

City College of the City University of New York, Graduate School, School of Education, Department of Teaching, Learning and Culture, New York, NY 10031-9198. Offers bilingual education (MS); childhood education (MS); early childhood education (MS); educational theatre (MS); literacy (MS); TESOL (MS). *Accreditation:* NCATE. *Degree requirements:* For master's, thesis. *Entrance requirements:* For master's, Liberal Arts and Sciences Test (LAST), Content Specialty Test (CST). Additional exam requirements/recommendations for international students: Required—TOEFL. Tuition and fees vary according to course load, degree level and program.

City University of Seattle, Graduate Division, Albright School of Education, Seattle, WA 98121. Offers administrator certification (Certificate); curriculum and instruction (M Ed); elementary education (MIT); guidance and counseling (M Ed); leadership (M Ed); reading and literacy (M Ed); school counseling (M Ed); special education (MIT); superintendent certification (Certificate). *Program availability:* Part-time, evening/weekend, online learning. *Degree requirements:* For master's, comprehensive exam (for some programs), thesis (for some programs). *Entrance requirements:* For master's, baccalaureate degree or equivalent from an accredited or otherwise recognized institution. Additional exam requirements/recommendations for international students: Required—TOEFL (minimum score 567 paper-based; 87 iBT); Recommended—IELTS. Electronic applications accepted. *Expenses:* Contact institution.

Clarion University of Pennsylvania, Office of Transfer, Adult and Graduate Admissions, Master of Education Program, Clarion, PA 16214. Offers curriculum and instruction (M Ed); early childhood (M Ed); math education (M Ed); reading (M Ed); science education (M Ed); special education (M Ed); technology (M Ed). *Accreditation:* NCATE. *Program availability:* Part-time, evening/weekend, 100% online, blended/hybrid learning. *Faculty:* 12 full-time (8 women), 5 part-time/adjunct (all women). *Students:* 17 full-time (15 women), 97 part-time (78 women); includes 1 minority (Two or more races, non-Hispanic/Latino). Average age 29. 76 applicants, 99% accepted, 48 enrolled. In 2016, 34 master's awarded. *Degree requirements:* For master's, comprehensive exam, thesis, or portfolio. *Entrance requirements:* For master's, minimum QPA of 3.0. Additional exam requirements/recommendations for international students: Required—TOEFL (minimum score 550 paper-based; 80 iBT), IELTS (minimum score 7). *Application deadline:* For fall admission, 8/1 for domestic students, 4/15 for international students; for spring admission, 8/1 for domestic students, 9/15 for international students. Applications are processed on a rolling basis. Application fee: $40. Electronic applications accepted. *Expenses:* $632.35 per credit. *Financial support:* Career-related internships or fieldwork, Federal Work-Study, scholarships/grants, and unspecified assistantships available. Support available to part-time students. Financial award application deadline: 3/1; financial award applicants required to submit FAFSA. *Unit head:* Dr. John McCullough, Chair, Department of Education, 814-393-2104, Fax: 814-393-2446, E-mail: gradstudies@clarion.edu. *Application contact:* Dana Bearer, Associate Director for Transfer, Adult, and Graduate Programs, 814-393-2337, Fax: 814-393-2722, E-mail: gradstudies@clarion.edu.

Clarks Summit University, Graduate Studies, South Abington Township, PA 18411. Offers Bible (MA); counseling (MA, MS); curriculum and instruction (M Ed); educational administration (M Ed); intercultural studies (MA); literature (MA); missions (MA); organizational leadership (MA); reading specialist (M Ed); secondary English/communications (M Ed); social entrepreneurship (MA); worldview studies (MA). MA in missions program available only for Association of Baptists for World Evangelism missionary personnel. *Program availability:* Part-time, evening/weekend, online learning. *Entrance requirements:* Additional exam requirements/recommendations for international students: Required—TOEFL (minimum score 500 paper-based).

Clemson University, Graduate School, College of Education, Department of Education and Human Development, Program in Literacy, Clemson, SC 29634. Offers M Ed. *Accreditation:* NCATE. *Program availability:* Part-time, evening/weekend. *Faculty:* 7 full-time (5 women). *Students:* 13 part-time (all women); includes 1 minority (Hispanic/Latino). Average age 32. *Degree requirements:* For master's, comprehensive exam, electronic portfolio. *Entrance requirements:* For master's, GRE General Test, valid teaching certificate from a regionally accredited institution, statement of purpose, unofficial transcripts, two letters of recommendation. Additional exam requirements/recommendations for international students: Required—TOEFL (minimum score 80 iBT), IELTS (minimum score 7). *Application deadline:* For fall admission, 7/1 for domestic and international students. Applications are processed on a rolling basis. Application fee: $80 ($90 for international students). Electronic applications accepted. *Expenses:* $4,027 per semester full-time resident, $8,013 per semester full-time non-resident, $437 per credit hour part-time resident, $874 per credit hour part-time non-resident. *Financial support:* Application deadline: 7/1. *Faculty research:* Adolescent literacy, struggling readers, reading comprehension, literacy motivation, African American children's literature. *Unit head:* Dr. Susan Fullerton, Program Coordinator, 864-656-1869, E-mail: susanf@clemson.edu. *Application contact:* Julie Jones, Student Services Program Coordinator, 864-656-5096, E-mail: jgambre@clemson.edu.
Website: http://www.clemson.edu/education/academics/masters-specialist-programs/masters-education-literacy/index.html

Clemson University, Graduate School, College of Education, Department of Education and Human Development, Program in Literacy, Language and Culture, Clemson, SC 29634. Offers PhD. *Program availability:* Part-time. *Faculty:* 14 full-time (11 women). *Students:* 9 full-time (7 women), 4 part-time (all women); includes 2 minority (both Hispanic/Latino), 1 international. Average age 34. 11 applicants, 55% accepted, 5 enrolled. *Degree requirements:* For doctorate, comprehensive exam, thesis/dissertation. *Entrance requirements:* For doctorate, GRE General Test, unofficial transcripts, three letters of recommendation, master's degree with minimum GPA of 3.5, professional writing sample, resume/curriculum vitae, letter of intent, minimum of two years teaching experience. Additional exam requirements/recommendations for international students: Required—TOEFL (minimum score 80 iBT), IELTS (minimum score 7). *Application deadline:* For fall admission, 3/1 for domestic and international students; for spring admission, 10/1 for domestic and international students. Applications are processed on a rolling basis. Application fee: $80 ($90 for international students). Electronic applications accepted. *Expenses:* $4,264 per semester full-time resident, $8,485 per semester full-time non-resident, $471 per credit hour part-time resident, $942 per credit hour part-time non-resident. *Financial support:* In 2016–17, 10 students received support, including 1 fellowship with partial tuition reimbursement available (averaging $5,000 per year), 8 teaching assistantships with partial tuition reimbursements available (averaging $13,053 per year); unspecified assistantships also available. Financial award application deadline: 3/1. *Unit head:* Dr. David Reinking, Program Coordinator, 864-656-5103, E-mail: reinkin@clemson.edu. *Application contact:* Julie Jones, Student Services Program Coordinator, 864-656-5096, E-mail: jgambre@clemson.edu.
Website: http://www.clemson.edu/education/academics/doctoral-programs/phd-doctorate-literacy-language-culture/index.html

Coker College, Graduate Programs, Hartsville, SC 29550. Offers athletic administration (MS); literacy studies (M Ed). *Program availability:* Part-time, 100% online. *Degree requirements:* For master's, comprehensive exam, portfolio. *Entrance requirements:* For master's, GRE or GMAT, minimum overall GPA of 2.85 in bachelor's program, official transcripts, resume, three letters of recommendation, teacher licensure. Electronic applications accepted.

The College at Brockport, State University of New York, School of Education, Health, and Human Services, Department of Education and Human Development, Literacy Education B-12 Program, Brockport, NY 14420-2997. Offers MS Ed. *Accreditation:* NCATE. *Program availability:* Part-time. *Students:* 24 full-time (20 women), 107 part-time (92 women); includes 2 minority (1 Black or African American, non-Hispanic/Latino; 1 Hispanic/Latino). 43 applicants, 98% accepted, 35 enrolled. In 2016, 41 master's awarded. *Degree requirements:* For master's, thesis or alternative. *Entrance requirements:* For master's, minimum GPA of 3.0, letters of recommendation, interview. Additional exam requirements/recommendations for international students: Required—TOEFL (minimum score 550 paper-based; 79 iBT), IELTS (minimum score 6.5). *Application deadline:* For fall admission, 3/15 priority date for domestic and international students; for spring admission, 10/15 priority date for domestic and international students; for summer admission, 3/15 priority date for domestic and international students. Application fee: $80. Electronic applications accepted. *Expenses:* Contact institution. *Financial support:* Federal Work-Study and scholarships/grants available. Support available to part-time students. Financial award application deadline: 3/15; financial award applicants required to submit FAFSA. *Unit head:* Dr. Sue Robb, Chairperson, 585-395-5935, Fax: 585-395-2172, E-mail: srobb@brockport.edu. *Application contact:* Anne Walton, Coordinator of Certification and Graduate Advisement, 585-395-2326, Fax: 585-395-2172, E-mail: mharriso@brockport.edu.
Website: http://www.brockport.edu/ehd

The College of New Jersey, Office of Graduate and Advancing Education, School of Education, Department of Special Education, Language and Literacy, Program in Developmental Reading, Ewing, NJ 08628. Offers M Ed. *Accreditation:* NCATE. *Program availability:* Part-time. *Degree requirements:* For master's, comprehensive exam. *Entrance requirements:* For master's, GRE General Test, minimum GPA of 3.0 in field or 2.75 overall. Additional exam requirements/recommendations for international students: Required—TOEFL. Electronic applications accepted.

The College of New Jersey, Office of Graduate and Advancing Education, School of Education, Department of Special Education, Language and Literacy, Program in Reading Certification, Ewing, NJ 08628. Offers Certificate. *Program availability:* Part-time. *Entrance requirements:* Additional exam requirements/recommendations for international students: Required—TOEFL. Electronic applications accepted.

The College of New Rochelle, Graduate School, Division of Education, Program in Literacy Education, New Rochelle, NY 10805-2308. Offers MS Ed. *Program availability:* Part-time, evening/weekend. *Degree requirements:* For master's, practicum. *Entrance requirements:* For master's, interview, minimum GPA of 3.0 in field, 2.7 overall, early elementary teacher certification.

College of St. Joseph, Graduate Programs, Division of Education, Program in Reading, Rutland, VT 05701-3899. Offers M Ed. *Program availability:* Part-time, evening/weekend. *Degree requirements:* For master's, comprehensive exam. *Entrance requirements:* For master's, PRAXIS I, official college transcripts; 2 letters of reference; minimum GPA of 3.0 (initial licensure) or 2.7 (nonlicensure); interview. Additional exam requirements/recommendations for international students: Required—TOEFL (minimum score 550 paper-based). *Application deadline:* Applications are processed on a rolling basis. Application fee: $35. Electronic applications accepted. *Expenses:* *Tuition:* Full-time $13,800; part-time $560 per credit. *Required fees:* $75 per semester. Full-time tuition and fees vary according to course load. *Financial support:* Career-related internships or fieldwork, Federal Work-Study, and unspecified assistantships available. Support available to part-time students. Financial award application deadline: 3/1. *Unit head:* Dr. Maria Bove, Chair, 802-773-5900 Ext. 3243, Fax: 802-776-5258, E-mail: mbove@csj.edu. *Application contact:* Alan Young, Director of Admissions, 802-773-5900 Ext. 3227, Fax: 802-776-5310, E-mail: alanyoung@csj.edu.

The College of Saint Rose, Graduate Studies, Thelma P. Lally School of Education, Programs in Literacy, Albany, NY 12203-1419. Offers literacy: birth-grade 6 (MS Ed, Advanced Certificate); literacy: grades 5-12 (MS Ed, Advanced Certificate). *Students:* 11 full-time (10 women), 22 part-time (all women); includes 6 minority (3 Black or African American, non-Hispanic/Latino; 2 Hispanic/Latino; 1 Two or more races, non-Hispanic/Latino). Average age 27. 18 applicants, 83% accepted, 10 enrolled. In 2016, 41 master's, 2 Advanced Certificates awarded. *Degree requirements:* For master's, field and clinical experiences. *Entrance requirements:* For master's, minimum undergraduate GPA of 3.0, current classroom teaching certification, baccalaureate degree from accredited institution, official transcripts from all colleges/universities attended. Additional exam requirements/recommendations for international students: Required—TOEFL (minimum score 550 paper-based; 80 iBT), IELTS (minimum score 6), PTE (minimum score 56). *Application deadline:* For fall admission, 4/1 priority date for domestic and international students; for spring admission, 10/15 priority date for domestic and international students. Applications are processed on a rolling basis. Application fee: $40. Electronic applications accepted. *Expenses:* *Tuition:* Full-time $14,382; part-time $799 per credit. *Required fees:* $814; $32 per credit. $88 per semester. Tuition and fees vary according to course load. *Financial support:* Career-related internships or fieldwork, scholarships/grants, tuition waivers (partial), and unspecified assistantships available. Support available to part-time students. Financial award application deadline: 4/15. *Unit head:* Ekaterina Midgette, Co-Chair, 518-485-3797, E-mail: midgette@strose.edu. *Application contact:* Cris Murray, Assistant Vice President for Graduate Recruitment and Enrollment, 518-485-3390, E-mail: grad@strose.edu.
Website: https://www.strose.edu/literacy/

College of Staten Island of the City University of New York, Graduate Programs, School of Education, Program in Childhood Education, Staten Island, NY 10314-6600. Offers learning and development (MS Ed); literacy education (MS Ed); mathematics education (MS Ed); music education (MS Ed); science education (MS Ed); social foundations of education (MS Ed); social studies education (MS Ed). *Program availability:* Part-time, evening/weekend. *Faculty:* 2 full-time, 11 part-time/adjunct. *Students:* 16 full-time, 53 part-time. Average age 30. 40 applicants, 53% accepted, 13 enrolled. In 2016, 20 master's awarded. *Degree requirements:* For master's, educational research project; ten courses and a minimum of 32-38 credits in five required areas of study or minimum of 45-49 credits in six required core courses before selecting from array of advanced courses. *Entrance requirements:* For master's, GRE General Test or an approved equivalent examination, relevant bachelor's degree, letters of recommendation, one- or two-page personal statement. Additional exam requirements/recommendations for international students: Required—TOEFL (minimum score 550 paper-based; 79 iBT), IELTS (minimum score 6.5). *Application deadline:* For fall admission, 4/25 for domestic and international students; for spring admission, 11/25 for domestic and international students. Applications are processed on a rolling basis. Application fee: $125. Electronic applications accepted. *Expenses:* Tuition, state resident: full-time $10,130; part-time $425 per credit. Tuition, nonresident: full-time $18,720; part-time $780 per credit. *Required fees:* $181.10 per semester. Tuition and fees vary according to program. *Faculty research:* Preservice teacher preparation,

music integration, music education through children's songs, literacy, emergent bilingual. *Unit head:* Dr. Vivian Shulman, Graduate Faculty Advisor, 718-982-4086, E-mail: vivian.shulman@csi.cuny.edu. *Application contact:* Sasha Spence, Associate Director for Graduate Admissions, 718-982-2019, Fax: 718-982-2500, E-mail: sasha.spence@csi.cuny.edu.
Website: http://www.csi.cuny.edu/admissions/grad/pdf/Education%20Fact%20Sheet.pdf

The College of William and Mary, School of Education, Program in Curriculum and Instruction, Williamsburg, VA 23187-8795. Offers elementary education (MA Ed); gifted education (MA Ed); literacy leadership (MA Ed); math specialist (MA Ed); secondary education (MA Ed), including English, foreign language, math, science, social studies; special education (MA Ed). *Accreditation:* NCATE. *Program availability:* Part-time. *Faculty:* 30 full-time (21 women), 48 part-time/adjunct (38 women). *Students:* 60 full-time (47 women), 14 part-time (all women); includes 13 minority (1 Black or African American, non-Hispanic/Latino; 1 American Indian or Alaska Native, non-Hispanic/Latino; 2 Asian, non-Hispanic/Latino; 7 Hispanic/Latino; 2 Two or more races, non-Hispanic/Latino). Average age 26. 134 applicants, 79% accepted, 66 enrolled. In 2016, 77 master's awarded. *Degree requirements:* For master's, project. *Entrance requirements:* For master's, GRE, MAT, PRAXIS Core Academic Skills for Educators, minimum GPA of 2.5. Additional exam requirements/recommendations for international students: Required—TOEFL (minimum score 100 iBT), IELTS (minimum score 7). *Application deadline:* For fall admission, 1/15 for domestic and international students; for spring admission, 10/1 for domestic and international students. Application fee: $50. Electronic applications accepted. *Expenses:* $14,258 per year in-state full-time, $275 per credit in-state part-time; $30,500 per year out-of-state full-time, $1,200 per credit out-of-state part-time. *Financial support:* In 2016–17, 30 students received support, including 3 research assistantships (averaging $14,259 per year); scholarships/grants and unspecified assistantships also available. Financial award application deadline: 1/15; financial award applicants required to submit FAFSA. *Faculty research:* Educational technology, professional development and evaluation, inclusive education, rural education, education policy. *Unit head:* Dr. Jeremy D. Stoddard, Department Chair, 757-221-2348, E-mail: jdstod@wm.edu. *Application contact:* Dorothy Smith Osborne, Assistant Dean for Academic Programs and Student Services, 757-221-2317, E-mail: dsosbo@wm.edu.
Website: http://education.wm.edu

Concordia University, College of Education, Portland, OR 97211-6099. Offers career and technical education (M Ed); curriculum and instruction (M Ed), including adolescent literacy, career and technical education, e-learning/technology education, early childhood education, English for speakers of other languages, English language development, environmental education, mathematics, methods and curriculum, reading, science, teacher leadership, the inclusive classroom; early childhood (MAT); education leadership (Ed D); educational administration (M Ed); elementary education (MAT); secondary education (MAT); special education (M Ed); teacher leadership (Ed D). *Program availability:* Part-time, online learning. *Degree requirements:* For master's, comprehensive exam, work samples/portfolio. *Entrance requirements:* For master's, California Basic Educational Skills Test or PRAXIS I, minimum undergraduate GPA of 2.8, graduate 3.0; 2 letters of recommendation. Additional exam requirements/recommendations for international students: Required—TOEFL (minimum score 525 paper-based). Electronic applications accepted. *Faculty research:* Learner-centered classroom, brain-based learning, future of online learning.

Concordia University Chicago, College of Education, Program in Reading Education, River Forest, IL 60305-1499. Offers MA. *Program availability:* Part-time, evening/weekend. *Degree requirements:* For master's, comprehensive exam, thesis optional. *Entrance requirements:* For master's, minimum GPA of 2.9. Additional exam requirements/recommendations for international students: Required—TOEFL (minimum score 550 paper-based). Electronic applications accepted. *Faculty research:* Early literacy, classroom management and organization in reading, minority students and reading.

Concordia University, Nebraska, Graduate Programs in Education, Program in Reading Education, Seward, NE 68434-1556. Offers M Ed. *Accreditation:* NCATE. *Program availability:* Part-time. *Degree requirements:* For master's, thesis or alternative. *Entrance requirements:* For master's, GRE, MAT, or NTE, minimum GPA of 3.0, BS in education or equivalent.

Concordia University, St. Paul, College of Education, St. Paul, MN 55104-5494. Offers classroom instruction (MA Ed), including K-12 reading; differentiated instruction (MA Ed); education (Ed D); educational leadership (MA Ed); educational technology (MA Ed); K-12 principal licensure (Ed S); special education (MA Ed, Certificate), including autism spectrum disorder (MA Ed), emotional and behavioral disorders (MA Ed), learning disabilities (MA Ed); superintendent (Ed S); teaching (MAT). *Accreditation:* NCATE. *Program availability:* Part-time, evening/weekend, 100% online, blended/hybrid learning. *Faculty:* 9 full-time (5 women), 88 part-time/adjunct (52 women). *Students:* 994 full-time (745 women), 40 part-time (34 women); includes 118 minority (40 Black or African American, non-Hispanic/Latino; 7 American Indian or Alaska Native, non-Hispanic/Latino; 33 Asian, non-Hispanic/Latino; 20 Hispanic/Latino; 18 Two or more races, non-Hispanic/Latino), 15 international. Average age 34. 549 applicants, 82% accepted, 372 enrolled. In 2016, 399 master's, 108 other advanced degrees awarded. *Degree requirements:* For master's, thesis (for some programs); for doctorate, thesis/dissertation, capstone projects; for other advanced degree, e-folio review of competencies. *Entrance requirements:* For master's, official transcripts from regionally-accredited institution stating the conferral of a bachelor's degree with minimum cumulative GPA of 3.0; personal statement; professional resume; practitioner in field through work or volunteerism; resume; for doctorate, minimum master's or specialist degree GPA of 3.25; transcript; writing sample; three letters of recommendation; current resume; on-campus interview; for other advanced degree, at least three years of teaching experience; master's degree; valid MN teaching license; writing sample; two letters of recommendation; resume. Additional exam requirements/recommendations for international students: Recommended—TOEFL (minimum score 547 paper-based; 78 iBT), IELTS (minimum score 6). *Application deadline:* For fall admission, 8/1 for domestic and international students; for spring admission, 12/1 for domestic and international students; for summer admission, 5/1 for domestic and international students. Applications are processed on a rolling basis. Application fee: $50. Electronic applications accepted. *Expenses:* Contact institution. *Financial support:* In 2016–17, 112 students received support. Scholarships/grants and unspecified assistantships available. Financial award applicants required to submit FAFSA. *Faculty research:* Differentiated instruction in K-12 educational settings; educational leadership; effective online pedagogy in higher education; equine-assisted learning; faculty development in higher education. *Unit head:* Lonn Maly, Dean, 651-641-8203, E-mail: maly@csp.edu. *Application contact:* Kimberly Craig, Associate Vice President, Cohort Enrollment Management, 651-603-6223, Fax: 651-603-6320, E-mail: craig@csp.edu.

Concordia University Wisconsin, Graduate Programs, Department of Education, Program in Literacy, Mequon, WI 53097-2402. Offers MS Ed. *Program availability:* Part-time, evening/weekend, online learning. *Degree requirements:* For master's, comprehensive exam, thesis or alternative. *Entrance requirements:* For master's, minimum GPA of 3.0. Additional exam requirements/recommendations for international students: Required—TOEFL. Application fee: $35. *Financial support:* Application deadline: 8/1. *Unit head:* Dr. Steven Witt, Director, 262-243-4253, E-mail: steven.witt@cuw.edu.

Concord University, Graduate Studies, Athens, WV 24712-1000. Offers educational leadership and supervision (M Ed); health promotion (MA); reading specialist (M Ed); social work (MSW); special education (M Ed); teaching (MAT). *Program availability:* Part-time, evening/weekend, online learning. *Faculty:* 16 full-time (10 women), 7 part-time/adjunct (4 women). *Students:* 129 full-time (105 women), 220 part-time (169 women); includes 28 minority (26 Black or African American, non-Hispanic/Latino; 1 American Indian or Alaska Native, non-Hispanic/Latino; 1 Hispanic/Latino), 2 international. *Degree requirements:* For master's, thesis (for some programs). *Entrance requirements:* For master's, GRE or MAT, baccalaureate degree with minimum GPA of 2.5 from regionally-accredited institution; teaching license; 2 letters of recommendation; completed disposition assessment form. *Application deadline:* Applications are processed on a rolling basis. Application fee: $30. Electronic applications accepted. *Expenses:* Tuition, state resident: full-time $3800; part-time $2539 per semester. Tuition, nonresident: full-time $6627; part-time $4416 per semester. Tuition and fees vary according to course load. *Financial support:* Tuition waivers and unspecified assistantships available. Financial award applicants required to submit FAFSA. *Unit head:* Dr. Cheryl Barnes, Director, 304-384-6306, E-mail: cbarnes@concord.edu. *Application contact:* Debra Moore, Special Events Assistant, 304-384-5113, E-mail: dlm@concord.edu.
Website: http://www.concord.edu/graduate

Converse College, School of Education and Graduate Studies, Education Specialist Program, Spartanburg, SC 29302. Offers administration and leadership (Ed S); administration and supervision (Ed S); literacy (Ed S). *Accreditation:* AAMFT/COAMFTE. *Program availability:* Part-time. *Entrance requirements:* For degree, GRE or MAT (marriage and family therapy), minimum GPA of 3.0. *Application deadline:* For fall admission, 8/1 for domestic and international students; for winter admission, 11/15 for domestic and international students; for spring admission, 1/15 for domestic and international students. Applications are processed on a rolling basis. Application fee: $40. Electronic applications accepted. *Expenses: Tuition:* Full-time $3600; part-time $400 per credit hour. *Required fees:* $70 per term. *Unit head:* Dr. Kathy Good, Dean of the School of Education and Graduate Studies, 864-596-9082, E-mail: kathy.good@converse.edu. *Application contact:* Jill Feist, Administrative Assistant to the Dean of the School of Education and Graduate Studies, 864-596-9220, Fax: 864-596-9221, E-mail: jill.feist@converse.edu.

Coppin State University, Division of Graduate Studies, Division of Education, Department of Curriculum and Instruction, Program in Reading Education, Baltimore, MD 21216-3698. Offers MS. *Program availability:* Part-time. *Degree requirements:* For master's, 3 hours of capstone experience in urban literacy. *Entrance requirements:* For master's, MAT or GRE, resume, references, teacher certification, 3 years of teaching experience.

Crandall University, Graduate Programs, Moncton, NB E1C 9L7, Canada. Offers literacy education (M Ed); organizational management (MOM); resource education (M Ed).

Curry College, Graduate Studies, Program in Education, Milton, MA 02186-9984. Offers elementary education (M Ed); foundations (non-license) (M Ed); reading (M Ed, Certificate); special education (M Ed). *Program availability:* Part-time, evening/weekend. *Degree requirements:* For master's, project or thesis. *Entrance requirements:* For master's, interview, recommendations, resume, written statement. Additional exam requirements/recommendations for international students: Required—TOEFL (minimum score 550 paper-based; 80 iBT). *Expenses:* Contact institution. *Faculty research:* Classroom trauma, therapeutic writing, inclusionary practices.

Dallas Baptist University, Dorothy M. Bush College of Education, Program in Reading and English as a Second Language, Dallas, TX 75211-9299. Offers bilingual education (M Ed); English as a second language (M Ed); master reading teacher (M Ed); reading specialist (M Ed). *Program availability:* Part-time, evening/weekend. *Application deadline:* Applications are processed on a rolling basis. Application fee: $25. Electronic applications accepted. Application fee is waived when completed online. *Expenses: Tuition:* Full-time $15,408; part-time $856 per credit hour. *Required fees:* $400 per semester. Tuition and fees vary according to course load and degree level. *Unit head:* Dr. Carolyn Spain, Director, 214-333-5200, E-mail: carolyns@dbu.edu. *Application contact:* Bobby Soto, Director of Admissions, 214-333-5242, E-mail: graduate@dbu.edu.
Website: http://www3.dbu.edu/graduate/english_reading.asp

Delaware State University, Graduate Programs, College of Education, Health and Public Policy, Program in Adult Literacy and Basic Education, Dover, DE 19901-2277. Offers MA. *Entrance requirements:* Additional exam requirements/recommendations for international students: Required—TOEFL (minimum score 550 paper-based). Electronic applications accepted.

DePaul University, College of Education, Chicago, IL 60614. Offers bilingual bicultural education (M Ed, MA); counseling (M Ed, MA), including clinical mental health counseling, college student development, school counseling; curriculum studies (M Ed, MA, Ed D); early childhood education (M Ed, MA, Ed D); educating adults (MA); educational leadership (M Ed, MA, Ed D), including administration and supervision (M Ed, MA), principal preparation (M Ed, MA); elementary education (MA); mathematics education (MA); mathematics for teaching (MS); middle school mathematics education (MS); reading specialist (M Ed, MA); secondary education (M Ed); social and cultural foundations in education (MA); special education (M Ed, MA); world languages education (M Ed, MA). *Program availability:* Part-time, evening/weekend, online learning. *Degree requirements:* For doctorate, thesis/dissertation. Electronic applications accepted.

Dominican University, School of Education, River Forest, IL 60305-1099. Offers early childhood education (MS); education (MAT); elementary education (MA Ed); English as a second language (MA Ed); reading (MA Ed); special education (MS). *Accreditation:* NCATE. *Program availability:* Part-time, evening/weekend, 100% online, blended/hybrid learning. *Faculty:* 12 full-time (8 women), 64 part-time/adjunct (57 women). *Students:* 13 full-time (all women), 500 part-time (385 women); includes 88 minority (40 Black or African American, non-Hispanic/Latino; 3 American Indian or Alaska Native, non-Hispanic/Latino; 18 Asian, non-Hispanic/Latino; 11 Hispanic/Latino; 2 Native Hawaiian or other Pacific Islander, non-Hispanic/Latino; 14 Two or more races, non-Hispanic/Latino), 1 international. Average age 32. 162 applicants, 96% accepted, 104 enrolled. In 2016, 200 master's awarded. *Entrance requirements:* For master's, Illinois Test of Basic Skills. Additional exam requirements/recommendations for international students: Required—TOEFL (minimum score 550 paper-based; 79 iBT). *Application deadline:* Applications are processed on a rolling basis. Application fee: $25. *Expenses:* $550 per credit hour. *Financial support:* Career-related internships or fieldwork, scholarships/grants, tuition waivers (partial), and unspecified assistantships available. Support available to part-time students. Financial award application deadline: 8/15; financial award applicants required to submit FAFSA. *Faculty research:* Governance of private

education institutions, reading and language arts, inclusion, organizational planning, leadership and vision. *Unit head:* Dr. Colleen Reardon, Interim Executive Director, School of Education, 708-524-6643, Fax: 708-524-6665, E-mail: creardon@dom.edu. *Application contact:* Keven Hanson, Coordinator of Recruitment and Admissions, 708-524-6921, Fax: 708-524-6665, E-mail: educate@dom.edu.
Website: http://educate.dom.edu/

Drury University, Master in Education Program, Springfield, MO 5802. Offers curriculum and instruction (M Ed), including elementary, middle school, secondary; gifted education (M Ed); instructional leadership (M Ed); instructional technology (M Ed); integrated learning (M Ed); online teaching (M Ed); special education (M Ed); special reading (M Ed). *Accreditation:* NCATE. *Program availability:* Part-time, evening/weekend, 100% online, blended/hybrid learning. *Students:* 146 full-time (111 women); includes 6 minority (1 Asian, non-Hispanic/Latino; 3 Hispanic/Latino; 2 Two or more races, non-Hispanic/Latino), 1 international. Average age 34. 42 applicants, 74% accepted. In 2016, 74 master's awarded. *Entrance requirements:* For master's, GRE, bachelor's degree with minimum GPA of 2.75. Additional exam requirements/recommendations for international students: Recommended—TOEFL (minimum score 80 iBT), IELTS (minimum score 6.5). *Application deadline:* For fall admission, 8/4 priority date for domestic and international students; for spring admission, 1/5 priority date for domestic and international students; for summer admission, 5/26 priority date for domestic and international students. Applications are processed on a rolling basis. Application fee: $25 ($50 for international students). Electronic applications accepted. *Expenses:* $352 tuition per credit hour; $7 per credit hour technology fee; $100 graduation fee; $59 portfolio fee (one-time). *Financial support:* In 2016–17, 20 students received support. Career-related internships or fieldwork, scholarships/grants, tuition waivers (partial), and unspecified assistantships available. Financial award application deadline: 6/30; financial award applicants required to submit FAFSA. *Faculty research:* Gifted students, instructional technology, autism, diversity and social justice. *Unit head:* Dr. Asikaa Cosgrove, Director, Master in Education, 417-873-7806, E-mail: acosgrov@drury.edu.
Website: http://www.drury.edu/education-masters

Duquesne University, School of Education, Department of Instruction and Leadership, Program in Reading and Language Arts, Pittsburgh, PA 15282-0001. Offers MS Ed. *Program availability:* Part-time, evening/weekend. *Faculty:* 1 (woman) full-time. *Students:* 13 full-time (12 women), 1 (woman) part-time. Average age 29. 14 applicants, 100% accepted, 5 enrolled. In 2016, 12 master's awarded. *Degree requirements:* For master's, thesis optional. *Entrance requirements:* For master's, bachelor's degree. Additional exam requirements/recommendations for international students: Required—TOEFL (minimum score 550 paper-based), IELTS (minimum score 7). *Application deadline:* For fall admission, 9/1 for domestic students; for spring admission, 1/1 for domestic students. Applications are processed on a rolling basis. Application fee: $0. Electronic applications accepted. *Expenses: Tuition:* Full-time $22,212; part-time $1234 per credit. Tuition and fees vary according to program. *Financial support:* Research assistantships and Federal Work-Study available. Support available to part-time students. *Unit head:* Dr. Rosemary T. Mautino, Assistant Professor/Director, 412-396-6089, Fax: 412-396-1759, E-mail: mautino@duq.edu. *Application contact:* Michael Dolinger, Director of Student and Academic Services, 412-396-6647, Fax: 412-396-5585, E-mail: dolingerm@duq.edu.
Website: http://www.duq.edu/academics/schools/education/graduate-programs-education/ms-reading-language-arts

East Carolina University, Graduate School, College of Education, Department of Literacy Studies, English and History Education, Greenville, NC 27858-4353. Offers history education (MA Ed); reading education (MA Ed). *Accreditation:* NCATE. *Program availability:* Part-time, evening/weekend, online learning. *Students:* 3 full-time (2 women), 44 part-time (42 women); includes 5 minority (4 Black or African American, non-Hispanic/Latino; 1 Hispanic/Latino). Average age 31. 23 applicants, 100% accepted, 20 enrolled. In 2016, 20 master's awarded. *Degree requirements:* For master's, comprehensive exam, thesis optional. *Entrance requirements:* For master's, GRE General Test or MAT, interview, minimum GPA of 2.5, bachelor's degree in related field, teaching license (MA Ed). Additional exam requirements/recommendations for international students: Required—TOEFL. *Application deadline:* For fall admission, 6/1 priority date for domestic students. Applications are processed on a rolling basis. Application fee: $50. *Financial support:* Research assistantships, teaching assistantships, and Federal Work-Study available. Support available to part-time students. Financial award application deadline: 6/1. *Unit head:* Katherine Misulis, Chair, 252-328-6128, E-mail: misulisk@ecu.edu. *Application contact:* Dean of Graduate School, 252-328-6012, Fax: 252-328-6071, E-mail: gradschool@ecu.edu.
Website: http://www.ecu.edu/cs-educ/libs/index.cfm

Eastern Connecticut State University, School of Education and Professional Studies/Graduate Division, Program in Reading and Language Arts, Willimantic, CT 06226-2295. Offers MS. *Accreditation:* NCATE. *Program availability:* Part-time, evening/weekend. *Faculty:* 1 (woman) full-time, 2 part-time/adjunct (both women). *Students:* 7 full-time (all women). Average age 25. 3 applicants, 33% accepted, 1 enrolled. In 2016, 4 master's awarded. *Degree requirements:* For master's, comprehensive exam or thesis. *Entrance requirements:* For master's, minimum GPA of 3.0, teaching certificate, bachelor's degree from accredited institution. Additional exam requirements/recommendations for international students: Required—TOEFL (minimum score 550 paper-based; 79 iBT); Recommended—IELTS (minimum score 6). *Application deadline:* For fall admission, 7/6 priority date for domestic and international students; for spring admission, 11/3 priority date for domestic and international students. Applications are processed on a rolling basis. Application fee: $50. Electronic applications accepted. *Expenses: Tuition, area resident:* Full-time $11,781; part-time $560 per credit. Tuition, state resident: full-time $15,031; part-time $568 per credit. Tuition, nonresident: full-time $24,581; part-time $568 per credit. *Required fees:* $40 per semester. Full-time tuition and fees vary according to course level, course load and reciprocity agreements. *Financial support:* Research assistantships, teaching assistantships, career-related internships or fieldwork, institutionally sponsored loans, scholarships/grants, and unspecified assistantships available. Financial award application deadline: 3/1; financial award applicants required to submit FAFSA. *Unit head:* Dr. Susannah Richards, Advisor, 860-465-4533, Fax: 860-465-5099, E-mail: richardss@easternct.edu. *Application contact:* Paula Goyette, Graduate Division, School of Education and Professional Studies, 860-465-5292, Fax: 860-465-4538, E-mail: graduateadmissions@easternct.edu.

Eastern Michigan University, Graduate School, College of Education, Department of Teacher Education, Program in Reading, Ypsilanti, MI 48197. Offers MA. *Accreditation:* NCATE. *Program availability:* Part-time, evening/weekend, online learning. *Students:* 20 part-time (all women); includes 2 minority (1 Black or African American, non-Hispanic/Latino; 1 Hispanic/Latino). Average age 31. 11 applicants, 73% accepted, 6 enrolled. In 2016, 28 master's awarded. *Entrance requirements:* For master's, GRE. Additional exam requirements/recommendations for international students: Required—TOEFL. *Application deadline:* Applications are processed on a rolling basis. Application fee: $45. *Financial support:* Fellowships, research assistantships with full tuition reimbursements, teaching assistantships with full tuition reimbursements, career-related internships or fieldwork, Federal Work-Study, institutionally sponsored loans, scholarships/grants, tuition waivers (partial), and unspecified assistantships available. Support available to part-time students. Financial award applicants required to submit FAFSA. *Application contact:* Dr. Linda Lewis-White, Coordinator, 734-487-3260, Fax: 734-487-2101, E-mail: llewiswh@emich.edu.

Eastern Michigan University, Graduate School, College of Education, Department of Teacher Education, Programs in Curriculum and Instruction, Ypsilanti, MI 48197. Offers advanced teaching and learning (MA); early literacy instruction (Graduate Certificate); instructional leadership (MA); learning, motivation and creativity (Graduate Certificate); literacy coaching (Graduate Certificate); online teaching (Certificate); secondary literacy instruction (Graduate Certificate); urban and diversity education (MA). *Students:* 1 (woman) full-time, 31 part-time (29 women); includes 6 minority (2 Black or African American, non-Hispanic/Latino; 2 Asian, non-Hispanic/Latino; 2 Two or more races, non-Hispanic/Latino), 1 international. Average age 33. 11 applicants, 73% accepted, 4 enrolled. In 2016, 8 master's, 1 other advanced degree awarded. Application fee: $45. *Application contact:* Dr. Virginia Harder, Graduate Coordinator/Advisor, 734-487-2729, Fax: 734-487-2101, E-mail: vharder1@emich.edu.

Eastern Nazarene College, Adult and Graduate Studies, Division of Teacher Education, Quincy, MA 02170. Offers administration (M Ed); early childhood education (M Ed, Certificate); elementary education (M Ed, Certificate); English as a second language (Certificate); instructional enrichment and development (Certificate); middle school education (M Ed, Certificate); moderate special needs education (Certificate); principal (Certificate); program development and supervision (Certificate); secondary education (M Ed, Certificate); special education administrator (Certificate); special needs (M Ed); supervisor (Certificate); teacher of reading (M Ed, Certificate). M Ed also available through weekend program for administration, special needs, and teacher of reading only. *Program availability:* Part-time, evening/weekend. *Entrance requirements:* Additional exam requirements/recommendations for international students: Required—TOEFL (minimum score 550 paper-based).

Eastern New Mexico University, Graduate School, College of Education and Technology, Department of Curriculum and Instruction, Portales, NM 88130. Offers bilingual education (M Ed); educational technology (M Ed); elementary education (M Ed); English as a second language (M Ed); pedagogy and learning (M Ed); professional technical education (M Ed); reading/literacy (M Ed). *Program availability:* Part-time, online learning. *Degree requirements:* For master's, comprehensive exam, thesis optional. *Entrance requirements:* For master's, minimum GPA of 3.0, photocopy of teaching license, writing assessment, letter of recommendation. Additional exam requirements/recommendations for international students: Required—TOEFL (minimum score 550 paper-based; 79 iBT), IELTS (minimum score 6). Electronic applications accepted.

Eastern University, Loeb School of Education, St. Davids, PA 19087-3696. Offers ESL program specialist (K-12) (Certificate); general supervisor (PreK-12) (Certificate); health and physical education (K-12) (Certificate); middle level (4-8) (Certificate); multicultural education (M Ed); organizational leadership with education (PhD); Pre K-4 (Certificate); Pre K-4 with special education (Certificate); reading (M Ed); reading specialist (K-12) (Certificate); reading supervisor (K-12) (Certificate); school health supervisor (Certificate); school nurse (K-12) (Certificate); secondary biology education (7-12) (Certificate); secondary chemistry education (7-12) (Certificate); secondary communication education (7-12) (Certificate); secondary education (7-12) (Certificate); secondary English education (7-12) (Certificate); secondary math education (7-12) (Certificate); secondary social studies education (7-12) (Certificate); special education (M Ed); special education (7-12) (Certificate); special education (Pre K-8) (Certificate); special education supervisor (N-12) (Certificate); TESOL (M Ed); world language (Certificate), including French, Spanish. *Program availability:* Part-time, evening/weekend, online learning. *Students:* 41 full-time (32 women), 89 part-time (68 women); includes 54 minority (38 Black or African American, non-Hispanic/Latino; 3 Asian, non-Hispanic/Latino; 11 Hispanic/Latino; 2 Two or more races, non-Hispanic/Latino), 2 international. Average age 37. In 2016, 64 master's awarded. *Entrance requirements:* Additional exam requirements/recommendations for international students: Required—TOEFL. *Application deadline:* Applications are processed on a rolling basis. Application fee: $35. Electronic applications accepted. Application fee is waived when completed online. *Expenses:* $690 per credit. *Unit head:* Michael Dziedziak, Executive Director of Enrollment, 800-452-0996, E-mail: gpsadmissions@eastern.edu.
Website: http://www.eastern.edu/academics/programs/loeb-school-education-0

Eastern Washington University, Graduate Studies, College of Arts, Letters and Education, Department of Education, Program in Literacy, Cheney, WA 99004-2431. Offers M Ed. *Students:* 2 full-time (1 woman), 1 (woman) part-time. Average age 27. 3 applicants, 100% accepted, 1 enrolled. In 2016, 3 master's awarded. *Degree requirements:* For master's, comprehensive exam. *Entrance requirements:* For master's, minimum GPA of 3.0. Additional exam requirements/recommendations for international students: Required—TOEFL (minimum score 580 paper-based; 92 iBT), IELTS (minimum score 7), PTE (minimum score 63). *Application deadline:* For fall admission, 4/1 priority date for domestic students; for spring admission, 1/15 for domestic students. Applications are processed on a rolling basis. Application fee: $75. Electronic applications accepted. *Expenses:* Tuition, state resident: full-time $11,000; part-time $5500 per credit. Tuition, nonresident: full-time $24,000; part-time $12,000 per credit. *Required fees:* $1300. One-time fee: $50 full-time. Part-time tuition and fees vary according to course load, campus/location and program. *Financial support:* In 2016–17, teaching assistantships with partial tuition reimbursements (averaging $10,000 per year) were awarded; career-related internships or fieldwork, Federal Work-Study, institutionally sponsored loans, scholarships/grants, health care benefits, tuition waivers (partial), and unspecified assistantships also available. Support available to part-time students. Financial award application deadline: 2/1; financial award applicants required to submit FAFSA. *Unit head:* Robin Showalter, Program Coordinator, 509-359-6492, E-mail: rshowalter@mail.ewu.edu.

East Stroudsburg University of Pennsylvania, Graduate and Extended Studies, College of Education, Department of Reading, East Stroudsburg, PA 18301-2999. Offers M Ed. *Program availability:* Part-time, evening/weekend, online only, 100% online. *Students:* 4 full-time (all women), 64 part-time (59 women); includes 3 minority (1 Hispanic/Latino; 2 Two or more races, non-Hispanic/Latino). *Degree requirements:* For master's, comprehensive exam, research paper, electronic program portfolio. *Entrance requirements:* For master's, PRAXIS/teacher certification, letter of recommendation, Pennsylvania Department of Education requirements. Additional exam requirements/recommendations for international students: Recommended—TOEFL (minimum score 560 paper-based; 83 iBT), IELTS. *Application deadline:* For fall admission, 7/31 priority date for domestic students, 6/30 priority date for international students; for spring admission, 11/30 for domestic students, 10/31 for international students. Applications are processed on a rolling basis. Application fee: $50. Electronic applications accepted. *Expenses:* Tuition, state resident: full-time $8694; part-time $5796 per year. Tuition, nonresident: full-time $13,050; part-time $8700 per year. *Required fees:* $2550; $1690 per unit. $845 per semester. Tuition and fees vary according to course load, campus/location and program. *Financial support:* Research assistantships with tuition reimbursements, Federal Work-Study, and unspecified assistantships available. Support available to part-time students. Financial award application deadline: 3/1; financial award applicants required to submit FAFSA. *Faculty research:* Portfolio assessment, reading assessment. *Unit head:* Mary Beth Allen, Graduate Coordinator, 570-422-3411, Fax: 570-422-3920, E-mail: mballen@esu.edu. *Application contact:* Kevin Quintero, Associate Director, Graduate and Extended Studies, 570-422-3890, Fax: 570-422-2711, E-mail: kquintero@esu.edu.

East Tennessee State University, School of Graduate Studies, College of Education, Department of Curriculum and Instruction, Johnson City, TN 37614. Offers educational technology (M Ed), including educational communications and technology, school library media; elementary education (M Ed); reading (MA), including reading education; school library professional (Post-Master's Certificate); secondary education (M Ed), including classroom technology; teacher education with multiple levels (MAT), including elementary education, middle grades education, secondary education. *Accreditation:* NCATE. *Program availability:* Part-time, evening/weekend, online learning. *Degree requirements:* For master's, comprehensive exam, thesis optional, student teaching, practicum; for Post-Master's Certificate, field work (school library); culminating experience (storytelling). *Entrance requirements:* For master's, GRE, SAT, ACT, PRAXIS, minimum GPA of 3.0; for Post-Master's Certificate, master's degree, TN teaching license. Additional exam requirements/recommendations for international students: Required—TOEFL (minimum score 550 paper-based; 79 iBT). Electronic applications accepted. *Faculty research:* Critical thinking; curriculum development in reading, math, and science education; cultural diversity; cognitive processes; effective teaching strategies.

Edinboro University of Pennsylvania, Department of Early Childhood and Reading, Edinboro, PA 16444. Offers arts infusion (Graduate Certificate); early childhood education (M Ed); reading (M Ed); reading specialist (Graduate Certificate). *Program availability:* Part-time, evening/weekend. *Degree requirements:* For master's, thesis or alternative, competency exam; for Graduate Certificate, thesis or alternative. *Entrance requirements:* For master's and Graduate Certificate, GRE or MAT, minimum QPA of 2.5. Electronic applications accepted.

Elms College, Division of Education, Chicopee, MA 01013-2839. Offers early childhood education (MAT); education (M Ed, CAGS); elementary education (MAT); English as a second language (MAT); reading (MAT); secondary education (MAT), including biology education, English education, Spanish education; special education (MAT). *Program availability:* Part-time, evening/weekend. *Faculty:* 5 full-time (all women), 7 part-time/adjunct (6 women). *Students:* 6 full-time (all women), 136 part-time (111 women); includes 6 minority (1 Asian, non-Hispanic/Latino; 5 Hispanic/Latino). Average age 33. 27 applicants, 89% accepted, 20 enrolled. In 2016, 47 master's, 3 other advanced degrees awarded. *Degree requirements:* For master's, thesis (for some programs). *Entrance requirements:* For master's, Massachusetts Educators Certification Test, minimum GPA of 3.0; for CAGS, master's degree in education. Additional exam requirements/recommendations for international students: Required—TOEFL. *Application deadline:* For fall admission, 7/1 priority date for domestic students; for spring admission, 11/1 priority date for domestic students. Applications are processed on a rolling basis. Application fee: $30. *Expenses: Tuition:* Full-time $13,392. *Required fees:* $200. *Financial support:* In 2016–17, 2 teaching assistantships with partial tuition reimbursements were awarded; tuition waivers (partial) also available. Support available to part-time students. Financial award applicants required to submit FAFSA. *Unit head:* Dr. Mary Janeczek, Chair, Division of Education, 413-594-2761, Fax: 413-592-4871, E-mail: janeczeke@elms.edu. *Application contact:* Dr. Elizabeth Teahan Hukowicz, Dean, School of Graduate and Professional Studies, 413-265-2360, Fax: 413-265-2459, E-mail: hukowicze@elms.edu.

Emory & Henry College, Graduate Programs, Emory, VA 24327-0947. Offers American history (MA Ed); organizational leadership (MCOL); professional studies (M Ed); reading specialist (MA Ed). *Program availability:* Part-time, evening/weekend. *Entrance requirements:* For master's, GRE or PRAXIS I, recommendations, writing sample. Additional exam requirements/recommendations for international students: Recommended—TOEFL.

Emporia State University, Program in Instructional Specialist, Emporia, KS 66801-5415. Offers elementary subject matter (MS); reading (MS). *Accreditation:* NCATE. *Program availability:* Part-time. *Faculty:* 29 full-time (21 women), 3 part-time/adjunct (2 women). *Students:* 7 full-time (all women), 65 part-time (58 women). 23 applicants, 100% accepted, 16 enrolled. In 2016, 27 master's awarded. *Degree requirements:* For master's, comprehensive exam or thesis, practicum. *Entrance requirements:* For master's, GRE General Test or MAT, essay exam, appropriate bachelor's degree, letters of recommendation. Additional exam requirements/recommendations for international students: Required—TOEFL (minimum score 520 paper-based; 68 iBT). *Application deadline:* For fall admission, 8/15 priority date for domestic students. Applications are processed on a rolling basis. Application fee: $30 ($75 for international students). Electronic applications accepted. *Expenses:* Tuition, state resident: full-time $5922; part-time $246.75 per credit hour. Tuition, nonresident: full-time $18,414; part-time $767.25 per credit hour. *Required fees:* $1884; $78.50 per credit hour. *Financial support:* Federal Work-Study, institutionally sponsored loans, health care benefits, and unspecified assistantships available. Financial award application deadline: 3/15; financial award applicants required to submit FAFSA. *Unit head:* Dr. Matt Siemears, Chair, 620-341-6057, E-mail: msiemear@emporia.edu. *Application contact:* Mary Sewell, Admissions Coordinator, 800-950-GRAD, Fax: 620-341-5909, E-mail: msewell@emporia.edu.

Endicott College, Van Loan School of Graduate and Professional Studies, Program in Reading and Literacy, Beverly, MA 01915-2096. Offers M Ed. *Program availability:* Part-time, evening/weekend, 100% online, blended/hybrid learning. *Faculty:* 4 full-time (2 women), 6 part-time/adjunct (all women). *Students:* 16 full-time (all women), 11 part-time (all women); includes 1 minority (Two or more races, non-Hispanic/Latino). Average age 28. 2 applicants, 100% accepted, 1 enrolled. In 2016, 9 master's awarded. *Degree requirements:* For master's, comprehensive exam, practicum, seminar. *Entrance requirements:* For master's, MAT or GRE, Massachusetts Tests for Educator Licensure (MTEL), Massachusetts teaching certificate, letters of recommendation. Additional exam requirements/recommendations for international students: Required—TOEFL. *Application deadline:* Applications are processed on a rolling basis. Application fee: $50. Electronic applications accepted. *Expenses:* Contact institution. *Financial support:* Career-related internships or fieldwork available. Financial award applicants required to submit FAFSA. *Unit head:* Dr. Aubry Threlkeld, Director of Graduate Licensure Programs, 978-232-2408, E-mail: athrelke@endicott.edu. *Application contact:* Ian Menchini, Director, Graduate Enrollment and Advising, 978-232-5292, Fax: 978-232-3000, E-mail: imenchin@endicott.edu.
Website: http://www.endicott.edu/VanLoan/Graduate-Studies/Master-Education.aspx

Evangel University, Department of Education, Springfield, MO 65802. Offers curriculum and instruction (M Ed); educational leadership (M Ed); literacy (M Ed); secondary teaching (M Ed). *Accreditation:* NCATE. *Program availability:* Part-time, evening/weekend, 100% online, blended/hybrid learning. *Faculty:* 3 full-time (2 women), 4 part-time/adjunct (2 women). *Students:* 2 full-time (1 woman), 33 part-time (29 women); includes 1 minority (Asian, non-Hispanic/Latino). Average age 30. 10 applicants, 90% accepted, 9 enrolled. In 2016, 28 master's awarded. *Degree requirements:* For master's, comprehensive exam, thesis optional. *Entrance requirements:* For master's, PRAXIS II (preferred) or GRE, minimum undergraduate GPA of 3.0. Additional exam requirements/recommendations for international students: Required—TOEFL (minimum score 550 paper-based). *Application deadline:* For fall admission, 7/15 priority date for domestic students, 8/1 for international students; for spring admission, 11/15 priority date for domestic students, 12/1 for international students. Applications are processed on a rolling basis. Application fee: $25. Electronic applications accepted. Application fee is waived when completed online. *Expenses: Tuition:* Part-time $400 per credit hour. *Required fees:* $148 per trimester. One-time fee: $25. Tuition and fees vary according to course load, degree level and program. *Financial support:* In 2016–17, 11 students received support. Scholarships/grants and unspecified assistantships available. Financial award application deadline: 4/1; financial award applicants required to submit FAFSA. *Unit head:* Dr. Susan Langston, Program Coordinator, 417-865-2815 Ext. 8552, E-mail: langstons@evangel.edu. *Application contact:* Karen Benitez, Admissions Representative, Graduate Studies, 417-865-2815 Ext. 7416, Fax: 417-575-5484, E-mail: benitezk@evangel.edu.
Website: http://www.evangel.edu/academics/graduate-studies/graduate-programs

Fairleigh Dickinson University, College at Florham, University College: Arts, Sciences, and Professional Studies, Peter Sammartino School of Education, Madison, NJ 07940-1099. Offers education for certified teachers (MA, Certificate); educational leadership (MA); instructional technology (Certificate); literacy/reading (Certificate); teaching (MAT).

Fairleigh Dickinson University, Metropolitan Campus, University College: Arts, Sciences, and Professional Studies, Peter Sammartino School of Education, Teaneck, NJ 07666-1914. Offers dyslexia specialist (Certificate); education for certified teachers (MA); educational leadership (MA); instructional technology (Certificate); learning disabilities (MA); literacy/reading (Certificate); multilingual education (MA); teacher of the handicapped (Certificate); teaching (MAT). *Accreditation:* TEAC. *Program availability:* Part-time. *Degree requirements:* For master's, research project (MAT).

Fairmont State University, Programs in Education, Fairmont, WV 26554. Offers digital media, new literacies and learning (M Ed); education (MAT); exercise science, fitness and wellness (M Ed); professional studies (M Ed); reading (M Ed); special education (M Ed). *Accreditation:* NCATE. *Program availability:* Part-time, evening/weekend, 100% online. *Faculty:* 18 full-time (11 women), 5 part-time/adjunct (3 women). *Students:* 62 full-time (52 women), 102 part-time (82 women); includes 6 minority (2 Black or African American, non-Hispanic/Latino; 1 American Indian or Alaska Native, non-Hispanic/Latino; 1 Hispanic/Latino; 2 Two or more races, non-Hispanic/Latino). Average age 33. 68 applicants, 84% accepted, 47 enrolled. In 2016, 44 degrees awarded. *Entrance requirements:* For master's, GRE. Additional exam requirements/recommendations for international students: Required—TOEFL (minimum score 80 iBT), IELTS (minimum score 6.5). *Application deadline:* For fall admission, 5/1 for domestic and international students. Applications are processed on a rolling basis. Application fee: $40. Electronic applications accepted. *Expenses:* Tuition, state resident: full-time $7504; part-time $405 per credit hour. Tuition, nonresident: full-time $16,060; part-time $880 per credit hour. Part-time tuition and fees vary according to course load. *Financial support:* In 2016–17, 20 students received support. Research assistantships, teaching assistantships, scholarships/grants, and unspecified assistantships available. Financial award applicants required to submit FAFSA. *Unit head:* Dr. Carolyn Crislip-Tacy, Interim Dean, School of Education, 304-367-4143, Fax: 304-367-4599, E-mail: carolyn.crislip-tacy@fairmontstate.edu. *Application contact:* Jack Kirby, Director of Graduate Studies, 304-367-4101, E-mail: jack.kirby@fairmontstate.edu.
Website: http://www.fairmontstate.edu/graduatestudies/

Fitchburg State University, Division of Graduate and Continuing Education, Program in Interdisciplinary Studies, Fitchburg, MA 01420-2697. Offers applied communications (CAGS); counseling/psychology (CAGS); individualized track (CAGS); reading specialist (CAGS). *Program availability:* Part-time, evening/weekend. *Entrance requirements:* Additional exam requirements/recommendations for international students: Required—TOEFL (minimum score 550 paper-based; 79 iBT). Electronic applications accepted. *Expenses:* Tuition, state resident: full-time $2871; part-time $1914 per year. Tuition, nonresident: full-time $2871; part-time $1914 per year. *Required fees:* $3828. Tuition and fees vary according to program.

Florida Atlantic University, College of Education, Department of Teaching and Learning, Boca Raton, FL 33431-0991. Offers curriculum and instruction (M Ed), including art, biology, chemistry, English, French, German, mathematics, music, physics, Pre-K and primary education, reading, social sciences, Spanish; elementary education (M Ed); environmental education (M Ed); reading education (M Ed); social foundations of education (M Ed), including educational psychology, educational technology, multilingual education. *Accreditation:* NCATE. *Program availability:* Part-time, evening/weekend. *Faculty:* 15 full-time (12 women), 2 part-time/adjunct (1 woman). *Students:* 25 full-time (20 women), 41 part-time (37 women); includes 18 minority (9 Black or African American, non-Hispanic/Latino; 2 Asian, non-Hispanic/Latino; 7 Hispanic/Latino), 7 international. Average age 32. 54 applicants, 59% accepted, 18 enrolled. In 2016, 36 master's awarded. *Entrance requirements:* For master's, GRE General Test, minimum GPA of 3.0 in last 2 years of undergraduate course work. Additional exam requirements/recommendations for international students: Required—TOEFL (minimum score 500 paper-based; 61 iBT), IELTS (minimum score 6). *Application deadline:* For fall admission, 7/1 for domestic students, 2/15 for international students; for spring admission, 11/1 for domestic students, 7/15 for international students. Applications are processed on a rolling basis. Application fee: $30. *Expenses:* Tuition, state resident: full-time $7392; part-time $369.82 per credit hour. Tuition, nonresident: full-time $19,432; part-time $1024.81 per credit hour. *Financial support:* Fellowships with partial tuition reimbursements, research assistantships with partial tuition reimbursements, teaching assistantships with partial tuition reimbursements, career-related internships or fieldwork, scholarships/grants, and unspecified assistantships available. *Faculty research:* Technology, teaching English to speakers of other languages, math teaching, electronic portfolio assessment, global perspectives through social studies. *Unit head:* Dr. Barbara Ridener, Chairperson, 561-297-3588, E-mail: bridener@fau.edu. *Application contact:* Dr. Eliah Watlington, Associate Dean, 561-296-8520, Fax: 261-297-2991, E-mail: ewatling@fau.edu.
Website: http://www.coe.fau.edu/academicdepartments/tl/

Florida International University, College of Arts, Sciences, and Education, Department of Teaching and Learning, Miami, FL 33199. Offers art education (MA, MS); curriculum and instruction (MS, Ed D, PhD, Ed S), including curriculum development (MS), elementary education (MS), English education (MS), learning technologies (MS), mathematics education (MS), modern language education (MS), physical education (MS), science education (MS), social studies education (MS), special education (MS); early childhood education (MS); exceptional student education (Ed D); foreign language education (MS), including foreign language education, teaching English to speakers of other languages (TESOL); international/intercultural education (MS); language, literacy and culture (PhD); mathematics, science, and learning technologies (PhD); physical education (MS), including sport and fitness; reading education (MS). *Program availability:* Part-time, evening/weekend. *Faculty:* 34 full-time (23 women), 64 part-time/adjunct (48 women). *Students:* 182 full-time (154 women), 231 part-time (190 women);

includes 323 minority (69 Black or African American, non-Hispanic/Latino; 10 Asian, non-Hispanic/Latino; 237 Hispanic/Latino; 7 Two or more races, non-Hispanic/Latino), 19 international. Average age 34. 282 applicants, 58% accepted, 113 enrolled. In 2016, 184 master's, 12 doctorates awarded. *Degree requirements:* For doctorate, comprehensive exam, thesis/dissertation. *Entrance requirements:* For master's, GRE General Test, Florida General Knowledge Test or Florida College Level Academic Skills Test; for doctorate and Ed S, GRE General Test. Additional exam requirements/recommendations for international students: Required—TOEFL (minimum score 550 paper-based; 80 iBT), IELTS (minimum score 6.3). *Application deadline:* For fall admission, 6/1 priority date for domestic students, 4/1 for international students; for winter admission, 10/1 priority date for domestic students, 9/1 for international students; for spring admission, 3/1 priority date for domestic students, 2/1 for international students. Applications are processed on a rolling basis. Application fee: $30. Electronic applications accepted. *Expenses:* Tuition, state resident: full-time $8912; part-time $446 per credit hour. Tuition, nonresident: full-time $21,393; part-time $992 per credit hour. *Required fees:* $2185; $195 per semester. Tuition and fees vary according to program. *Financial support:* Research assistantships with tuition reimbursements and teaching assistantships with tuition reimbursements available. *Unit head:* Dr. Lynn Miller, Chair, 305-348-2005, Fax: 305-348-2086, E-mail: lynne.miller@fiu.edu. *Application contact:* Nanett Rojas, Assistant Director, Graduate Admissions, 305-348-7464, Fax: 305-348-7441, E-mail: gradadm@fiu.edu.
Website: http://education.fiu.edu

Florida Memorial University, School of Education, Miami-Dade, FL 33054. Offers elementary education (MS); exceptional student education (MS); reading (MS). *Degree requirements:* For master's, comprehensive exam or thesis, field and clinical experiences, exit exam. *Entrance requirements:* For master's, GRE, CLAST, PRAXIS I, baccalaureate or graduate degree with minimum GPA of 3.0 in last 60 hours, 3 recommendations. Additional exam requirements/recommendations for international students: Recommended—TOEFL.

Florida State University, The Graduate School, College of Education, Program in Curriculum and Instruction, Tallahassee, FL 32306. Offers curriculum and instruction (MS, PhD, Ed S), including early childhood education, elementary education, English education, English teaching (MS), exceptional student education (MS), foreign and second language education, foreign and second language teaching (MS), mathematics education, mathematics teaching (MS), reading education and language arts, science education, social science education, social science teaching (MS), special education, special education studies (MS), visual disabilities (MS, Ed S). *Program availability:* Part-time, evening/weekend. Terminal master's awarded for partial completion of doctoral program. *Degree requirements:* For master's and Ed S, comprehensive exam, thesis optional; for doctorate, comprehensive exam, thesis/dissertation, diagnostic exam, preliminary exam, prospectus defense, dissertation defense. *Entrance requirements:* For master's, doctorate, and Ed S, GRE General Test, minimum upper-division GPA of 3.0. Additional exam requirements/recommendations for international students: Required—TOEFL (minimum score 550 paper-based, 80 iBT), IELTS (minimum score 6.5), Michigan English Language Assessment Battery (minimum score 77), or PTE (minimum score 55). Application fee: $30. Electronic applications accepted. *Expenses:* Tuition, state resident: full-time $7263; part-time $403.51 per credit hour. Tuition, nonresident: full-time $18,087; part-time $1004.85 per credit hour. *Required fees:* $1365; $75.81 per credit hour. $20 per semester. Tuition and fees vary according to campus/location. *Financial support:* Fellowships, research assistantships, teaching assistantships, scholarships/grants, tuition waivers (full and partial), and unspecified assistantships available. Financial award application deadline: 1/15; financial award applicants required to submit FAFSA. *Faculty research:* Identifying effective intervention strategies to improve reading skills; improving literacy teaching and learning through technology; understanding of student sense making, problem solving, the history and structure of STEM disciplines, and teacher education to support the development of ambitious instruction that supports the STEM learning of all students; examining practices of international education; identifying ways to support the professional development of teachers. *Unit head:* Dr. Sherry Southerland, Professor/Department Chair, 850-644-4880, Fax: 850-644-7736, E-mail: ssoutherland@admin.fsu.edu. *Application contact:* Libbie Crowley, Academic Support Specialist, 850-644-2122, Fax: 850-644-7736, E-mail: ecrowley@fsu.edu.
Website: http://education.fsu.edu/degrees-and-programs/graduate-programs

Fontbonne University, Graduate Programs, St. Louis, MO 63105-3098. Offers accounting (MBA, MS); art (MA); art (K-12) (MAT); business (MBA); computer science (MS); deaf education (MA); early intervention in deaf education (MA); education (MA), including autism spectrum disorders, curriculum and instruction, diverse learners, early childhood education, reading, special education; elementary education (MAT); family and consumer sciences (MA), including multidisciplinary health communication studies; fine arts (MFA); instructional design and technology (MS); management and leadership (MM); middle school education (MAT); secondary education (MAT); special education (MAT); speech-language pathology (MS); supply chain management (MS); theatre (MA). *Program availability:* Part-time, evening/weekend, online learning. *Faculty:* 32 full-time (24 women), 43 part-time/adjunct (26 women). *Students:* 456 full-time (313 women), 102 part-time (77 women); includes 138 minority (118 Black or African American, non-Hispanic/Latino; 1 American Indian or Alaska Native, non-Hispanic/Latino; 7 Asian, non-Hispanic/Latino; 9 Hispanic/Latino; 3 Two or more races, non-Hispanic/Latino), 37 international. *Degree requirements:* For master's, comprehensive exam (for some programs), thesis (for some programs). *Entrance requirements:* Additional exam requirements/recommendations for international students: Required—TOEFL (minimum score 500 paper-based; 65 iBT). *Application deadline:* For fall admission, 8/1 for international students; for spring admission, 12/1 for international students. Applications are processed on a rolling basis. Application fee: $25 ($30 for international students). Electronic applications accepted. *Expenses: Tuition:* Full-time $8436; part-time $703 per credit hour. *Required fees:* $18 per credit hour. Tuition and fees vary according to course load. *Financial support:* Teaching assistantships with partial tuition reimbursements and scholarships/grants available. Support available to part-time students. Financial award application deadline: 4/1; financial award applicants required to submit FAFSA. *Unit head:* Dr. Carey Adams, Vice President for Academic Affairs, 314-719-3609, E-mail: cadams@fontbonne.edu. *Application contact:* Lauryn Filip, Coordinator, Graduate Admission and Professional Studies, 314-889-4650, E-mail: admissions@fontbonne.edu.
Website: https://www.fontbonne.edu/academics/graduate-programs/

Framingham State University, Continuing Education, Program in Literacy and Language, Framingham, MA 01701-9101. Offers M Ed. *Program availability:* Part-time, evening/weekend. *Entrance requirements:* For master's, MAT.

Fresno Pacific University, Graduate Programs, School of Education, Program in Reading and Language Arts, Fresno, CA 93702-4709. Offers reading (Certificate); reading/English as a second language (MA Ed); reading/language arts (MA Ed). *Program availability:* Part-time, evening/weekend. *Degree requirements:* For master's, thesis or alternative. *Entrance requirements:* For master's, three references. Additional exam requirements/recommendations for international students: Required—TOEFL (minimum score 550 paper-based). Electronic applications accepted. *Expenses:* Contact institution.

Frostburg State University, Graduate School, College of Education, Department of Educational Professions, Program in Reading, Frostburg, MD 21532-1099. Offers M Ed. *Accreditation:* NCATE. *Degree requirements:* For master's, thesis or alternative, in-service. *Entrance requirements:* For master's, teaching certificate. Additional exam requirements/recommendations for international students: Required—TOEFL. Electronic applications accepted.

Furman University, Graduate Division, Department of Education, Greenville, SC 29613. Offers curriculum and instruction (MA); early childhood education (MA); educational leadership (Ed S); English as a second language (MA); literacy (MA); school leadership (MA); special education (MA). *Accreditation:* NCATE. *Program availability:* Part-time, online learning. *Degree requirements:* For master's, comprehensive exam (for some programs), thesis or alternative. *Entrance requirements:* For master's, PRAXIS II. *Faculty research:* Literacy, pedagogy and practice, social justice, advanced leadership, achievement in high poverty schools.

Gannon University, School of Graduate Studies, College of Humanities, Education, and Social Sciences, School of Education, Program in Reading, Erie, PA 16541-0001. Offers M Ed. *Program availability:* Part-time, evening/weekend, 100% online. *Students:* 1 (woman) full-time, 29 part-time (28 women). Average age 34. 26 applicants, 96% accepted, 21 enrolled. In 2016, 9 master's awarded. *Degree requirements:* For master's, comprehensive exam, thesis or alternative, portfolio project. *Entrance requirements:* For master's, 3 letters of recommendation, transcript, bachelor's degree from regionally-accredited college or university with minimum GPA of 3.0. Additional exam requirements/recommendations for international students: Required—TOEFL (minimum score 79 iBT). *Application deadline:* Applications are processed on a rolling basis. Application fee: $25. Electronic applications accepted. Application fee is waived when completed online. *Expenses:* Contact institution. *Financial support:* Federal Work-Study available. Financial award application deadline: 7/1; financial award applicants required to submit FAFSA. *Unit head:* Dr. Robin Quick, Director, 814-871-5399, E-mail: quick003@gannon.edu. *Application contact:* Bridget Philip, Director of Graduate Admissions, 814-871-7412, E-mail: graduate@gannon.edu.

Gannon University, School of Graduate Studies, College of Humanities, Education, and Social Sciences, School of Education, Program in Reading Specialist, Erie, PA 16541-0001. Offers Certificate. *Program availability:* Part-time, evening/weekend, 100% online. *Students:* 4 part-time (all women). Average age 48. 1 applicant, 100% accepted, 1 enrolled. In 2016, 12 Certificates awarded. *Entrance requirements:* For degree, 3 letters of recommendation, transcript, bachelor's degree from regionally-accredited college or university with minimum GPA of 3.0, valid instructional I or II teaching certificate. Additional exam requirements/recommendations for international students: Required—TOEFL (minimum score 79 iBT). Application fee: $25. Application fee is waived when completed online. *Expenses: Tuition:* Full-time $17,370. *Required fees:* $550. Tuition and fees vary according to course load and program. *Financial support:* Federal Work-Study available. Financial award application deadline: 7/1; financial award applicants required to submit FAFSA. *Unit head:* Dr. Robin Quick, Director, 814-871-5399, E-mail: quick003@gannon.edu. *Application contact:* Bridget Philip, Director of Graduate Admissions, 814-871-7412, E-mail: graduate@gannon.edu.

George Fox University, College of Education, Graduate Teaching and Leading Program, Newberg, OR 97132-2697. Offers administrative leadership (Ed S); continuing administrator license (Certificate); educational leadership (M Ed); educational technology (M Ed); English for speakers of other languages (M Ed); ESOL (Certificate); initial administrator license (Certificate); reading (M Ed, Certificate); special education (M Ed); teaching (MAT). *Accreditation:* NCATE. *Program availability:* Part-time, evening/weekend, online learning. *Degree requirements:* For master's, thesis (for some programs). *Entrance requirements:* For master's, minimum undergraduate GPA of 3.0 during previous 2 years of course work, resume, 3 professional recommendations on university forms, official transcripts. Additional exam requirements/recommendations for international students: Required—TOEFL (minimum score 577 paper-based; 90 iBT). Electronic applications accepted. *Expenses:* Contact institution.

George Mason University, College of Education and Human Development, Programs in Curriculum and Instruction, Fairfax, VA 22030. Offers advanced international baccalaureate (M Ed); assistive technology (M Ed); designing digital learning in schools (M Ed); early childhood education (M Ed); early childhood education for diverse learners (M Ed); elementary education (M Ed); English as a second language (M Ed); gifted child education (M Ed); history (M Ed); literacy (M Ed), including PK-12 classroom teachers, reading specialist; literacy leadership for diverse schools (M Ed), including K-12 reading; physical education (M Ed); science K-12 (M Ed); secondary education (M Ed), including biology, chemistry, earth science, English, history/social science, math, physics; special education (M Ed); teacher leadership (M Ed); teaching culturally, linguistically diverse and exceptional learners (M Ed); transformative teaching (M Ed). *Faculty:* 41 full-time (35 women), 53 part-time/adjunct (46 women). *Students:* 155 full-time (127 women), 821 part-time (697 women); includes 267 minority (82 Black or African American, non-Hispanic/Latino; 5 American Indian or Alaska Native, non-Hispanic/Latino; 75 Asian, non-Hispanic/Latino; 88 Hispanic/Latino; 1 Native Hawaiian or other Pacific Islander, non-Hispanic/Latino; 16 Two or more races, non-Hispanic/Latino), 19 international. Average age 33. 513 applicants, 90% accepted, 352 enrolled. In 2016, 347 master's awarded. *Degree requirements:* For master's, comprehensive exam, thesis (for some programs). *Entrance requirements:* For master's, PRAXIS Core (for some programs), minimum GPA of 3.0 in last 60 hours, licensed as teacher or educational administrator, official transcripts, goals statement, 3 recommendation letters, interview or writing sample (depending on program), up to 3 years' teaching experience (depending on program). Additional exam requirements/recommendations for international students: Required—TOEFL (minimum score 575 paper-based; 88 iBT), IELTS (minimum score 6.5), PTE (minimum score 59). *Application deadline:* For spring admission, 11/1 priority date for domestic and international students. Application fee: $75 ($80 for international students). Electronic applications accepted. *Expenses:* Tuition, state resident: full-time $10,628; part-time $443 per credit. Tuition, nonresident: full-time $29,306; part-time $1221 per credit. *Required fees:* $3096; $129 per credit. Tuition and fees vary according to program. *Financial support:* In 2016–17, 1 student received support, including 1 teaching assistantship (averaging $4,060 per year); career-related internships or fieldwork, Federal Work-Study, scholarships/grants, unspecified assistantships, and health care benefits (for full-time research or teaching assistantship recipients) also available. Support available to part-time students. Financial award application deadline: 3/1; financial award applicants required to submit FAFSA. *Faculty research:* Achievement gaps and superintendent decisions, constructivist view of classroom teaching, cost of cheating, creating a critical literacy milieu in kindergarten. *Unit head:* Rebecca Fox, Professor and Academic Program Coordinator, 703-993-4123, E-mail: rfox@gmu.edu.
Website: http://gse.gmu.edu/programs/gsemasters

Georgetown College, Department of Education, Georgetown, KY 40324-1696. Offers reading and writing (MA Ed); special education (MA Ed); teaching (MA Ed). *Accreditation:* NCATE. *Program availability:* Part-time. *Degree requirements:* For master's, portfolio. *Entrance requirements:* For master's, teaching certificate, minimum GPA of 2.7 or GRE General Test.

Georgia College & State University, Graduate School, The John H. Lounsbury College of Education, Program in Reading, Literacy, and Language, Milledgeville, GA 31061. Offers M Ed. *Program availability:* Part-time, evening/weekend. *Students:* 1 (woman) part-time. Average age 38. In 2016, 3 master's awarded. *Degree requirements:* For master's, comprehensive exam, minimum GPA of 3.0 on all work, complete program within 6 years. *Entrance requirements:* For master's, on-site writing assessment, GRE General Test taken within six years (minimum scores 1,000 verbal and quantitative combined if taken before August 1, 2011, 305 if taken on or after August 1, 2011), or MAT (minimum score 400), two professional recommendations, level 4 teaching certificate, official transcripts, verification of immunization, minimum GPA of 2.75. *Application deadline:* For fall admission, 7/1 priority date for domestic students; for spring admission, 11/1 priority date for domestic students; for summer admission, 4/1 priority date for domestic students. Applications are processed on a rolling basis. Application fee: $40. Electronic applications accepted. *Expenses:* $288 per credit hour in-state tuition; $1,027 per credit hour out-of-state; fees vary by hours enrolled. *Financial support:* Application deadline: 3/1; applicants required to submit FAFSA. *Unit head:* Dr. Joseph Peters, Dean, College of Education, 478-445-2518, Fax: 478-445-6582, E-mail: joseph.peters@gcsu.edu. *Application contact:* Shanda Brand, Graduate Admissions Advisor, 478-445-1383, Fax: 478-445-6582, E-mail: shanda.brand@gcsu.edu.

Georgia Southern University, Jack N. Averitt College of Graduate Studies, College of Education, Department of Curriculum, Foundations, and Reading, Program in Reading Education, Statesboro, GA 30460. Offers M Ed, Ed S. *Accreditation:* NCATE. *Program availability:* Part-time, evening/weekend. *Students:* 4 full-time (3 women), 22 part-time (all women); includes 6 minority (5 Black or African American, non-Hispanic/Latino; 1 Two or more races, non-Hispanic/Latino). Average age 35. 11 applicants, 91% accepted, 7 enrolled. In 2016, 9 master's, 1 Ed S awarded. *Degree requirements:* For master's, comprehensive exam, transition point assessments. *Entrance requirements:* For master's, GRE General Test or MAT, minimum GPA of 2.5. Additional exam requirements/recommendations for international students: Required—TOEFL (minimum score 550 paper-based; 80 iBT), IELTS (minimum score 6). *Application deadline:* For fall admission, 3/15 priority date for domestic students, 3/1 priority date for international students; for spring admission, 10/1 priority date for domestic students, 10/1 for international students; for summer admission, 3/1 for domestic students. Applications are processed on a rolling basis. Application fee: $50. Electronic applications accepted. *Expenses:* Tuition, state resident: full-time $7236; part-time $277 per semester hour. Tuition, nonresident: full-time $27,118; part-time $1105 per semester hour. *Required fees:* $2092. *Financial support:* In 2016–17, 2 students received support, including 1 teaching assistantship with full tuition reimbursement available (averaging $7,750 per year); research assistantships with partial tuition reimbursements available, career-related internships or fieldwork, Federal Work-Study, scholarships/grants, tuition waivers (full), and unspecified assistantships also available. Support available to part-time students. Financial award application deadline: 4/15; financial award applicants required to submit FAFSA. *Faculty research:* Emerging literacy, content literacy, digital literacies, English language learners, literature groups, phonics/whole language, interpreting literacy policy. *Unit head:* Dr. Michael Moore, Coordinator, 912-478-0211, Fax: 912-478-5382, E-mail: mmoore@georgiasouthern.edu. *Application contact:* Lydia Cross, Coordinator for Graduate Student Recruitment, 912-478-8664, E-mail: lcross@georgiasouthern.edu.
Website: http://coe.georgiasouthern.edu/reading

Georgia State University, College of Education and Human Development, Department of Middle and Secondary Education, Atlanta, GA 30302-3083. Offers curriculum and instruction (Ed D); English education (MAT); mathematics education (M Ed, MAT); middle level education (MAT); reading, language and literacy education (M Ed, MAT), including reading instruction (M Ed); science education (M Ed, MAT), including biology (MAT), broad field science (MAT), chemistry (MAT), earth science (MAT), physics (MAT); social studies education (M Ed, MAT), including economics (MAT), geography (MAT), history (MAT), political science (MAT); teaching and learning (PhD), including language and literacy, mathematics education, music education, science education, social studies education, teaching and teacher education. *Accreditation:* NCATE. *Program availability:* Part-time, evening/weekend, online learning. *Faculty:* 24 full-time (18 women). *Students:* 145 full-time (91 women), 151 part-time (102 women); includes 141 minority (104 Black or African American, non-Hispanic/Latino; 1 American Indian or Alaska Native, non-Hispanic/Latino; 16 Asian, non-Hispanic/Latino; 12 Hispanic/Latino; 8 Two or more races, non-Hispanic/Latino), 10 international. Average age 36. 115 applicants, 50% accepted, 41 enrolled. In 2016, 94 master's, 22 doctorates awarded. *Degree requirements:* For master's, comprehensive exam (for some programs), thesis or alternative, exit portfolio; for doctorate, comprehensive exam, thesis/dissertation. *Entrance requirements:* For master's, GRE; GACE I (for initial teacher preparation programs), baccalaureate degree or equivalent, resume, goals statement, two letters of recommendation, minimum undergraduate GPA of 2.5; proof of initial teacher certification in the content area (for M Ed); for doctorate, GRE, resume, goals statement, writing sample, two letters of recommendation, minimum graduate GPA of 3.3, interview. Additional exam requirements/recommendations for international students: Required—TOEFL (minimum score 550 paper-based; 79 iBT) or IELTS (minimum score 6.5). *Application deadline:* For fall admission, 1/15 priority date for domestic and international students; for spring admission, 10/1 for domestic and international students. Application fee: $50. Electronic applications accepted. *Expenses:* Tuition, state resident: full-time $6876; part-time $382 per credit hour. Tuition, nonresident: full-time $22,374; part-time $1243 per credit hour. *Required fees:* $2128; $1064 per term. Part-time tuition and fees vary according to course load and program. *Financial support:* In 2016–17, fellowships with full tuition reimbursements (averaging $19,667 per year), research assistantships with full tuition reimbursements (averaging $5,436 per year), teaching assistantships with full tuition reimbursements (averaging $2,779 per year) were awarded; career-related internships or fieldwork, Federal Work-Study, scholarships/grants, health care benefits, tuition waivers (full and partial), and unspecified assistantships also available. Financial award application deadline: 3/15. *Faculty research:* Teacher education in language and literacy, mathematics, science, and social studies in urban middle and secondary school settings; learning technologies in school, community, and corporate settings; multicultural education and education for social justice; urban education; international education. *Unit head:* Dr. Dana L. Fox, Chair, 404-413-8060, Fax: 404-413-8063, E-mail: dfox@gsu.edu. *Application contact:* Bobbie Turner, Administrative Coordinator I, 404-413-8405, Fax: 404-413-8063, E-mail: bnturner@gsu.edu.
Website: http://mse.education.gsu.edu/

Gordon College, Graduate Education Program, Wenham, MA 01984-1899. Offers early childhood (M Ed); educational leadership (M Ed, Ed S); elementary education (M Ed); English as a second language (M Ed, Ed S); math specialist (M Ed); mathematics specialist (Ed S); middle school education (M Ed); moderate disabilities (M Ed); Montessori education (M Ed); reading (M Ed, Ed S); secondary education (M Ed). *Program availability:* Part-time, evening/weekend. *Faculty:* 17 full-time (9 women), 41 part-time/adjunct (34 women). *Students:* 81 full-time (61 women), 109 part-time (87 women); includes 28 minority (2 Black or African American, non-Hispanic/Latino; 11 Asian, non-Hispanic/Latino; 13 Hispanic/Latino; 2 Two or more races, non-Hispanic/Latino), 12 international. Average age 34. 190 applicants, 100% accepted, 141 enrolled. In 2016, 110 master's, 16 Ed Ss awarded. *Degree requirements:* For master's, action research or clinical experience (for most programs); for Ed S, action research or clinical experience (for some programs). *Entrance requirements:* For master's, minimum undergraduate GPA of 3.0; 2 official undergraduate transcripts; professional resume; 3 recommendation letters (one professional reference, one academic reference, one personal reference); 500-700 word statement of purpose; for Ed S, minimum master's GPA of 3.3; 2 official transcripts from undergraduate and graduate schools; professional resume; 3 recommendation letters (one professional reference, one academic reference, one personal reference); 500-700 word statement of purpose. Additional exam requirements/recommendations for international students: Required—TOEFL (minimum score 550 paper-based, 80 iBT) or IELTS (minimum score 6.5). *Application deadline:* Applications are processed on a rolling basis. Application fee: $75. *Expenses:* $325 per credit tuition, $75 per term fee. *Financial support:* Applicants required to submit FAFSA. *Faculty research:* Reading, early childhood development, English language learners, universal design for learning. *Unit head:* Dr. Janet Arndt, Director of Graduate Studies, 978-867-4355, Fax: 978-867-4663. *Application contact:* Julie Lenocker, Program Administrator, 978-867-4322, Fax: 978-867-4663, E-mail: graduate-education@gordon.edu.
Website: http://www.gordon.edu/graduate

Goucher College, Graduate Programs in Education, Baltimore, MD 21204-2794. Offers at-risk and diverse learners (M Ed, Certificate); athletic program leadership and administration (M Ed, Certificate); elementary and special education (MAT); elementary education (MAT); literacy strategies for content learning (M Ed, Certificate); middle school (M Ed, Certificate); Montessori studies (M Ed); reading instruction (M Ed, Certificate); school improvement leadership (M Ed, Certificate); school mediation (M Ed, Certificate); secondary and special education (MAT); secondary education (MAT); special education (MAT), including elementary education, secondary education; special education for certified teachers (M Ed, Certificate); teacher as leader in technology (M Ed, Certificate). *Program availability:* Part-time, evening/weekend. *Faculty:* 3 full-time (all women), 52 part-time/adjunct (40 women). *Students:* 29 full-time (20 women), 285 part-time (217 women); includes 54 minority (41 Black or African American, non-Hispanic/Latino; 3 Asian, non-Hispanic/Latino; 7 Hispanic/Latino; 3 Two or more races, non-Hispanic/Latino), 1 international. Average age 34. 85 applicants, 100% accepted, 61 enrolled. In 2016, 207 master's awarded. *Degree requirements:* For master's, thesis (M Ed), final presentation (MAT). *Entrance requirements:* For master's, minimum GPA of 3.0. Additional exam requirements/recommendations for international students: Required—TOEFL (minimum score 560 paper-based). *Application deadline:* For fall admission, 9/1 for domestic students; for spring admission, 1/15 for domestic students. Applications are processed on a rolling basis. Application fee: $75. Electronic applications accepted. *Expenses:* Contact institution. *Financial support:* Career-related internships or fieldwork and unspecified assistantships available. Support available to part-time students. Financial award application deadline: 4/15; financial award applicants required to submit FAFSA. *Faculty research:* Urban education, middle school, school improvement, teacher education, at-risk student achievement. *Unit head:* Dr. Phyllis Sunshine, Assistant Provost, 410-337-6047, Fax: 410-337-6394, E-mail: psunshin@goucher.edu. *Application contact:* Shelby Hillers, Admissions Coordinator, 410-337-6200, Fax: 410-337-6085, E-mail: shelby.hillers@goucher.edu.
Website: http://www.goucher.edu/graduate-programs/graduate-programs-in-education

Governors State University, College of Education, Program in Reading, University Park, IL 60484. Offers MA. *Accreditation:* NCATE. *Program availability:* Part-time. *Faculty:* 47 full-time (31 women), 49 part-time/adjunct (39 women). *Students:* 4 part-time (3 women). Average age 28. 8 applicants, 63% accepted, 1 enrolled. *Entrance requirements:* Additional exam requirements/recommendations for international students: Required—TOEFL (minimum score 550 paper-based; 80 iBT), IELTS. *Application deadline:* For fall admission, 4/1 for domestic students. Application fee: $50. Electronic applications accepted. *Expenses:* $307 per credit hour; $38 per term or $76 per credit hour fees. *Financial support:* Application deadline: 5/1; applicants required to submit FAFSA. *Unit head:* Timothy Harrington, Chair, Division of Education, 708-534-4361, E-mail: tharrington2@govst.edu. *Application contact:* Yakeea Daniels, Assistant Vice President for Enrollment Services/Director of Admission, 708-534-4510, E-mail: ydaniels@govst.edu.

Graceland University, Gleazer School of Education, Independence, MO 64050. Offers curriculum and instruction (M Ed); differentiated instruction (M Ed); instructional leadership (M Ed); literacy and instruction (M Ed); management in the inclusive classroom (M Ed); special education (M Ed); technology integration (M Ed). *Accreditation:* NCATE. *Program availability:* Part-time, evening/weekend, online learning. *Faculty:* 2 full-time (both women), 9 part-time/adjunct (5 women). *Students:* 115 full-time (96 women), 20 part-time (17 women); includes 10 minority (5 Black or African American, non-Hispanic/Latino; 1 Asian, non-Hispanic/Latino; 1 Hispanic/Latino; 1 Native Hawaiian or other Pacific Islander, non-Hispanic/Latino; 2 Two or more races, non-Hispanic/Latino), 2 international. 155 applicants, 61% accepted, 85 enrolled. In 2016, 61 master's awarded. *Degree requirements:* For master's, action research project. *Entrance requirements:* For master's, minimum GPA of 3.0, teaching certificate, current teaching contract. Additional exam requirements/recommendations for international students: Required—TOEFL. *Application deadline:* For fall admission, 10/1 for domestic students; for winter admission, 11/15 for domestic students; for spring admission, 2/15 priority date for domestic students; for summer admission, 6/1 for domestic students. Applications are processed on a rolling basis. Application fee: $50. Electronic applications accepted. *Expenses:* Contact institution. *Financial support:* Institutionally sponsored loans and scholarships/grants available. Financial award application deadline: 12/15; financial award applicants required to submit FAFSA. *Faculty research:* Literacy, technology, faculty mentoring, adult literacy, e-learning, online teaching. *Unit head:* Dr. Lee Bash, Interim Dean, 641-784-5072, E-mail: bash@graceland.edu. *Application contact:* Jeanette Calipetro, Admissions Representative, 816-423-4716, Fax: 816-833-2990, E-mail: jcali1@graceland.edu.
Website: http://www.graceland.edu/education

Grambling State University, School of Graduate Studies and Research, College of Education, Department of Educational Leadership, Grambling, LA 71245. Offers developmental education (MS, Ed D, PMC), including curriculum and instructional design (Ed D), English (MS), guidance and counseling (MS), higher education administration and management (Ed D), mathematics (MS), reading (MS), science (MS), student development and personnel services (Ed D); educational leadership (M Ed). *Program availability:* Part-time, evening/weekend. *Degree requirements:* For master's, comprehensive exam, thesis (for some programs); for doctorate, comprehensive exam, thesis/dissertation. *Entrance requirements:* For master's, GRE, minimum GPA of 2.5 on last degree; for doctorate, GRE (minimum score 1000, 500 on Verbal), master's degree, minimum GPA of 3.0 on last degree. Additional exam requirements/recommendations for international students: Required—TOEFL (minimum score 500 paper-based; 62 iBT). Electronic applications accepted.

Grand Canyon University, College of Education, Phoenix, AZ 85017-1097. Offers autism spectrum disorders (MA); curriculum and instruction (MA); early childhood education (M Ed); educational administration (M Ed); educational leadership (M Ed);

elementary education (M Ed); gifted education (MA); instructional technology (MS); K-12 leadership (Ed S); reading (MA); secondary education (M Ed); secondary humanities education (M Ed); secondary STEM education (M Ed); special education (M Ed); teaching and learning (Ed D); teaching English to speakers of other languages (MA). *Program availability:* Part-time, evening/weekend, online learning. *Degree requirements:* For master's, publishable research paper (M Ed), e-portfolio. *Entrance requirements:* For master's, undergraduate degree from accredited, GCU-approved college, university, or program with minimum GPA 2.8. Additional exam requirements/recommendations for international students: Required—TOEFL (minimum score 550 paper-based; 79 iBT), IELTS (minimum score 6). *Application deadline:* For fall admission, 8/21 for domestic students, 7/2 for international students; for spring admission, 12/24 for domestic students, 11/1 for international students. Applications are processed on a rolling basis. Application fee: $100. Electronic applications accepted. *Financial support:* Federal Work-Study available. Support available to part-time students. Financial award applicants required to submit FAFSA. *Unit head:* Dr. Kimberly L. LaPrade, Dean, 602-639-6360, E-mail: kimberly.laprade@gcu.edu. *Application contact:* Dr. Kimberly L. LaPrade, Dean, 602-639-6360, E-mail: kimberly.laprade@gcu.edu.
Website: https://www.gcu.edu/college-of-education.php

Grand Valley State University, College of Education, Program in Literacy Studies, Allendale, MI 49401-9403. Offers M Ed. *Program availability:* Part-time. *Students:* 3 full-time (1 woman), 100 part-time (94 women); includes 3 minority (2 Black or African American, non-Hispanic/Latino; 1 Two or more races, non-Hispanic/Latino). Average age 30. 30 applicants, 100% accepted, 12 enrolled. In 2016, 46 master's awarded. *Degree requirements:* For master's, project or thesis. *Entrance requirements:* For master's, minimum GPA of 3.0 or GRE General Test, last 60 credits from regionally-accredited college/university, 3 letters of recommendation. Additional exam requirements/recommendations for international students: Required—TOEFL (minimum score 550 paper-based, 80 iBT), IELTS (6.5), or Michigan English Language Assessment Battery. *Application deadline:* Applications are processed on a rolling basis. Application fee: $30. Electronic applications accepted. *Expenses:* $628 per credit hour. *Financial support:* In 2016–17, 14 students received support. Unspecified assistantships available. *Unit head:* Dr. Elizabeth Stolle, Program Coordinator, 616-331-6241, Fax: 616-331-6515, E-mail: stollee@gvsu.edu. *Application contact:* Thomas Owens, Director, Student Information and Services Center, 616-331-6282, Fax: 616-331-6217, E-mail: owenst@gvsu.edu.
Website: http://www.gvsu.edu/grad/literacy/

Grand Valley State University, College of Education, Program in Reading and Language Arts, Allendale, MI 49401-9403. Offers M Ed. *Accreditation:* NCATE. *Program availability:* Part-time, evening/weekend. *Students:* 2 part-time (both women). Average age 35. In 2016, 3 master's awarded. *Degree requirements:* For master's, project or thesis. *Entrance requirements:* For master's, GRE General Test or minimum GPA of 3.0; last 60 credits from regionally-accredited college/university; 3 letters of recommendation. Additional exam requirements/recommendations for international students: Required—TOEFL (minimum score 550 paper-based, 80 iBT), IELTS (6.5), or Michigan English Language Assessment Battery. *Application deadline:* Applications are processed on a rolling basis. Application fee: $30. Electronic applications accepted. *Expenses:* $628 per credit hour. *Financial support:* Career-related internships or fieldwork, Federal Work-Study, scholarships/grants, and unspecified assistantships available. *Faculty research:* Culture of literacy, literacy acquisition, assessment, content area literacy, writing pedagogy. *Unit head:* Dr. Elizabeth Stolle, Graduate Program Director, 616-331-6242, E-mail: stollee@gvsu.edu. *Application contact:* Thomas Owens, Director, Student Information and Services Center, 616-331-6282, Fax: 616-331-6217, E-mail: owenst@gvsu.edu.

Hamline University, School of Education, St. Paul, MN 55104-1284. Offers education (MA Ed, Ed D); English as a second language (MA); literacy education (MA); natural science and environmental education (MA Ed); teaching (MAT); teaching English to speakers of other languages (MA). *Accreditation:* NCATE (one or more programs are accredited). *Program availability:* Part-time, evening/weekend, 100% online, blended/hybrid learning. *Faculty:* 29 full-time (23 women), 90 part-time/adjunct (70 women). *Students:* 277 full-time (201 women), 762 part-time (601 women); includes 122 minority (29 Black or African American, non-Hispanic/Latino; 1 American Indian or Alaska Native, non-Hispanic/Latino; 43 Asian, non-Hispanic/Latino; 29 Hispanic/Latino; 20 Two or more races, non-Hispanic/Latino), 12 international. Average age 34. 408 applicants, 77% accepted, 230 enrolled. In 2016, 279 master's, 14 doctorates awarded. *Degree requirements:* For master's, thesis (for some programs), thesis or capstone project; for doctorate, comprehensive exam, thesis/dissertation. *Entrance requirements:* For master's, official transcripts, essay, letters of recommendation, minimum GPA of 3.0 from bachelor's work; resume and/or writing samples (for some programs); for doctorate, personal statement, master's degree with minimum GPA of 3.0, letters of recommendation, writing sample. Additional exam requirements/recommendations for international students: Required—TOEFL. *Application deadline:* For fall admission, 6/1 for domestic and international students; for spring admission, 11/1 for domestic and international students; for summer admission, 3/1 for domestic and international students. Applications are processed on a rolling basis. Application fee: $0 ($100 for international students). Electronic applications accepted. *Expenses:* $466-$721 per credit. *Financial support:* Career-related internships or fieldwork, Federal Work-Study, and scholarships/grants available. Support available to part-time students. Financial award applicants required to submit FAFSA. *Faculty research:* Adult basic education, service-learning, teacher dispositions, diversity, technology. *Unit head:* Dr. Nancy Sorenson, Dean, 651-523-2600, Fax: 651-523-2489, E-mail: education@hamline.edu. *Application contact:* Shawn Skoog, Director of Graduate Recruitment and Admission, 651-523-2900, Fax: 651-523-3058, E-mail: gradprog@hamline.edu.
Website: http://www.hamline.edu/education

Hannibal-LaGrange University, Program in Education, Hannibal, MO 63401-1999. Offers literacy (MS Ed); teaching and learning (MS Ed). *Program availability:* Part-time, evening/weekend. *Degree requirements:* For master's, thesis, portfolio, documenting of program outcomes, public sharing of research. *Entrance requirements:* For master's, copy of current teaching certificate; minimum GPA of 2.75. *Faculty research:* Reading assessment, reading remediation, handwriting instruction, early childhood intervention.

Harding University, Cannon-Clary College of Education, Searcy, AR 72149-0001. Offers advanced studies in teaching and learning (M Ed); art (MSE); behavioral science (MSE); counseling (MS, Ed S); early childhood special education (M Ed, MSE); education (MSE); educational leadership (M Ed, Ed S); elementary education (M Ed); English (MSE); French (MSE); history/social science (MSE); kinesiology (MSE); math (MSE); reading (M Ed); secondary education (M Ed); Spanish (MSE); teaching (MAT); teaching English as a second language (MSE). *Accreditation:* NCATE. *Program availability:* Part-time, evening/weekend. *Faculty:* 22 full-time (9 women), 51 part-time/adjunct (37 women). *Students:* 130 full-time (91 women), 321 part-time (234 women); includes 83 minority (50 Black or African American, non-Hispanic/Latino; 4 American Indian or Alaska Native, non-Hispanic/Latino; 6 Asian, non-Hispanic/Latino; 13 Hispanic/Latino; 10 Two or more races, non-Hispanic/Latino), 11 international. Average age 35. 125 applicants, 88% accepted, 110 enrolled. In 2016, 124 master's, 27 other advanced degrees awarded. *Degree requirements:* For master's, comprehensive exam (for some programs), thesis optional, portfolio(s); for Ed S, comprehensive exam, portfolio, project. *Entrance requirements:* For master's, GRE, MAT, PRAXIS; for Ed S, MAT or GRE. Additional exam requirements/recommendations for international students: Required—TOEFL (minimum score 550 paper-based; 79 iBT). *Application deadline:* For fall admission, 8/1 for domestic and international students; for spring admission, 1/1 for domestic and international students. Applications are processed on a rolling basis. Application fee: $35. Tuition and fees vary according to degree level and program. *Financial support:* In 2016–17, 31 students received support. Unspecified assistantships available. *Faculty research:* Reading, comprehension, school violence, educational technology, behavior, college choice, differentiated instruction, brain-based teaching. *Unit head:* Dr. Clara Carroll, Chair, 501-279-4501, Fax: 501-279-4083, E-mail: ccarroll@harding.edu. *Application contact:* Information Contact, 501-279-4315, E-mail: gradstudiesedu@harding.edu.
Website: http://www.harding.edu/education

Hardin-Simmons University, Graduate School, Irvin School of Education, Department of Educational Studies, Program in Reading Specialist Education, Abilene, TX 79698-0001. Offers M Ed. *Program availability:* Part-time. *Faculty:* 1 (woman) full-time. *Students:* 2 part-time (both women); includes 1 minority (Hispanic/Latino). Average age 47. *Degree requirements:* For master's, comprehensive exam. *Entrance requirements:* For master's, minimum undergraduate GPA of 3.0 in major, 2.7 overall. Additional exam requirements/recommendations for international students: Required—TOEFL (minimum score 550 paper-based; 75 iBT). *Application deadline:* For fall admission, 8/15 priority date for domestic students, 4/1 for international students; for spring admission, 1/5 priority date for domestic students, 9/1 for international students. Applications are processed on a rolling basis. Application fee: $50. Electronic applications accepted. *Expenses: Tuition:* Full-time $12,510; part-time $695 per credit hour. *Required fees:* $325; $110 per semester. *Financial support:* In 2016–17, 1 student received support, including 1 fellowship (averaging $1,600 per year); scholarships/grants also available. Support available to part-time students. Financial award application deadline: 6/30; financial award applicants required to submit FAFSA. *Faculty research:* Social networking as a gatekeeper, reflective process of teachers, growth of reflective practice in pre-service teachers, multicultural children's literature. *Unit head:* Dr. Emily Dean, Director, 325-671-5784, Fax: 325-670-5859, E-mail: emily.o.dean@hsutx.edu. *Application contact:* Dr. Nancy Kucinski, Dean of Graduate Studies, 325-670-1298, Fax: 325-670-1564, E-mail: gradoff@hsutx.edu.
Website: http://www.hsutx.edu/academics/irvin/graduate/readinged

Harvard University, Harvard Graduate School of Education, Master's Programs in Education, Cambridge, MA 02138. Offers arts in education (Ed M); education policy and management (Ed M); higher education (Ed M); human development and psychology (Ed M); international education policy (Ed M); language and literacy (Ed M); learning and teaching (Ed M); mind, brain, and education (Ed M); prevention science and practice (Ed M); school leadership (Ed M); special studies (Ed M); teacher education (Ed M); technology, innovation, and education (Ed M). *Program availability:* Part-time. *Entrance requirements:* For master's, GRE General Test, statement of purpose, 3 letters of recommendation, resume, official transcripts. Additional exam requirements/recommendations for international students: Required—TOEFL (minimum score 613 paper-based; 104 iBT), TWE (minimum score 5). Electronic applications accepted. *Faculty research:* Learning and development, educational leadership and organizations, education policy analysis.

Heritage University, Graduate Programs in Education, Program in Professional Studies, Toppenish, WA 98948-9599. Offers bilingual education/ESL (M Ed); biology (M Ed); English and literature (M Ed); reading/literacy (M Ed); special education (M Ed). *Program availability:* Part-time, evening/weekend. *Degree requirements:* For master's, comprehensive exam (for some programs), thesis (for some programs).

Hofstra University, School of Education, Specialized Programs in Education, Hempstead, NY 11549. Offers applied behavior analysis (Advanced Certificate); early childhood special education (MS Ed, Advanced Certificate); educational and policy leadership (Ed D); educational leadership (Advanced Certificate), including school building leader/school district business leader; educational leadership and policy studies (MS Ed), including K-12; gifted education (Advanced Certificate), including school building leader/school district business leader; health education PK-12 teaching certification (MS); inclusive early childhood special education (MS Ed); inclusive elementary special education (MS Ed); inclusive secondary special education (MS Ed); literacy studies (MS Ed, Ed D, PhD, Advanced Certificate), including birth-grade 6 (MS Ed, Advanced Certificate), birth-grade 6 and special education (birth-grade2) (MS Ed), grades 5-12 (MS Ed, Advanced Certificate); physical education (MS); secondary education generalist (MS Ed), including students with disabilities 7-12; special education (MS Ed, Advanced Certificate); special education assessment and diagnosis (Advanced Certificate); special education generalist (MS Ed), including extension in secondary education; sport science (MS), including strength and conditioning; teaching students with severe or multiple disabilities (Advanced Certificate). *Program availability:* Part-time, evening/weekend, 100% online, blended/hybrid learning. *Students:* 149 full-time (115 women), 258 part-time (187 women); includes 97 minority (50 Black or African American, non-Hispanic/Latino; 1 American Indian or Alaska Native, non-Hispanic/Latino; 11 Asian, non-Hispanic/Latino; 34 Hispanic/Latino; 1 Native Hawaiian or other Pacific Islander, non-Hispanic/Latino), 5 international. Average age 32. 250 applicants, 88% accepted, 146 enrolled. In 2016, 85 master's, 13 doctorates, 35 other advanced degrees awarded. *Degree requirements:* For master's, one foreign language, comprehensive exam (for some programs), thesis (for some programs), electronic portfolio, capstone course, internship, practicum, student teaching, seminars, minimum GPA of 3.0; for doctorate, one foreign language, comprehensive exam, thesis/dissertation, qualifying hearing. *Entrance requirements:* For master's, GRE, interview, letters of recommendation, portfolio, essay, certification; for doctorate, GRE or MAT, interview, resume, essay, master's degree, 3 letters of recommendation, writing sample; for Advanced Certificate, GRE, interview, letters of recommendation, essay, professional experience, resume, master's degree. Additional exam requirements/recommendations for international students: Required—TOEFL (minimum score 550 paper-based; 80 iBT). *Application deadline:* Applications are processed on a rolling basis. Application fee: $75. Electronic applications accepted. *Expenses: Tuition:* Full-time $1240. *Required fees:* $970. Tuition and fees vary according to program. *Financial support:* In 2016–17, 244 students received support, including 117 fellowships with full and partial tuition reimbursements available (averaging $3,705 per year), 12 research assistantships with full and partial tuition reimbursements available (averaging $6,490 per year); career-related internships or fieldwork, Federal Work-Study, institutionally sponsored loans, scholarships/grants, traineeships, tuition waivers (full and partial), and unspecified assistantships also available. Support available to part-time students. Financial award applicants required to submit FAFSA. *Faculty research:* Collaborative teaching and learning; language and culture; new media literacies; applied behavior analysis; K-12 leadership development. *Unit head:* Dr. Elfreda Blue, Chairperson, 516-463-5762, Fax: 516-463-6184, E-mail: elfreda.blue@hofstra.edu. *Application contact:* Sunil Samuel, Assistant Vice President of Admissions, 516-463-4723, Fax: 516-463-4664, E-mail: graduateadmission@hofstra.edu.
Website: http://www.hofstra.edu/education/

Reading Education

Holy Family University, Graduate and Professional Programs, School of Education, Master of Education Programs, Philadelphia, PA 19114. Offers early elementary education (PreK-Grade 4) (M Ed); education leadership (M Ed); general education (M Ed); reading specialist (M Ed); special education (M Ed); TESOL and literacy (M Ed). *Program availability:* Part-time. *Students:* 202 full-time, 58 part-time. 209 applicants, 77% accepted, 140 enrolled. In 2016, 123 master's awarded. *Degree requirements:* For master's, thesis optional. *Application deadline:* Applications are processed on a rolling basis. Application fee: $25. Electronic applications accepted. *Expenses: Tuition:* Part-time $751 per hour. *Required fees:* $140 per semester. One-time fee: $165 part-time. Part-time tuition and fees vary according to degree level and program. *Unit head:* Dr. Kevin Zook, Dean, 267-341-3246, Fax: 215-824-2438, E-mail: kzook@holyfamily.edu. *Application contact:* Donald Reimold, Director of Graduate Admissions, 267-341-5001, Fax: 215-637-1478, E-mail: dreimold@holyfamily.edu.

Hood College, Graduate School, Department of Education, Frederick, MD 21701-8575. Offers curriculum and instruction (MS), including elementary education, elementary science and mathematics education, secondary education, special education; educational leadership (MS); reading specialization (MS); STEM education (Certificate). *Accreditation:* NCATE. *Program availability:* Part-time-only, evening/weekend. *Faculty:* 3 full-time, 37 part-time/adjunct. *Students:* 1 (woman) full-time, 357 part-time (283 women); includes 71 minority (41 Black or African American, non-Hispanic/Latino; 6 Asian, non-Hispanic/Latino; 15 Hispanic/Latino; 9 Two or more races, non-Hispanic/ Latino). Average age 33. 96 applicants, 95% accepted, 83 enrolled. In 2016, 47 master's awarded. *Degree requirements:* For master's, action research project, portfolio (for reading specialization); for Certificate, STEM capstone activity. *Entrance requirements:* For master's, minimum GPA of 2.75, teaching certification, writing sample during interview, letter of recommendation from principal (for educational leadership program only). Additional exam requirements/recommendations for international students: Required—TOEFL (minimum score 575 paper-based; 89 iBT), IELTS (minimum score 6.5). *Application deadline:* For fall admission, 8/15 priority date for domestic students, 8/ 5 for international students; for spring admission, 12/1 priority date for domestic students, 12/1 for international students; for summer admission, 5/1 priority date for domestic students, 4/15 for international students. Applications are processed on a rolling basis. Application fee: $35. Electronic applications accepted. *Expenses:* $450 per credit; $105 comprehensive fee per semester. *Financial support:* Tuition waivers (partial) and unspecified assistantships available. Financial award applicants required to submit FAFSA. *Faculty research:* Leadership, action research, brain research, learning styles. *Unit head:* April Boulton, Interim Dean of the Graduate School, E-mail: gofurther@hood.edu. *Application contact:* Jan Marcus, Assistant Director of Graduate Admissions, 301-696-3600, E-mail: gofurther@hood.edu.
Website: http://www.hood.edu/academics/education/index.html

Houston Baptist University, College of Education and Behavioral Sciences, Programs in Education, Houston, TX 77074-3298. Offers bilingual education (M Ed); counselor education (M Ed); curriculum and instruction (M Ed); educational administration (M Ed); educational diagnostician (M Ed); executive educational leadership (Ed D); reading education (M Ed). *Program availability:* Part-time, evening/weekend, 100% online, blended/hybrid learning. *Students:* 45 full-time (35 women), 158 part-time (136 women); includes 141 minority (87 Black or African American, non-Hispanic/Latino; 1 American Indian or Alaska Native, non-Hispanic/Latino; 5 Asian, non-Hispanic/Latino; 47 Hispanic/ Latino; 1 Two or more races, non-Hispanic/Latino), 3 international. Average age 34. 320 applicants, 30% accepted, 61 enrolled. In 2016, 121 degrees awarded. *Degree requirements:* For master's, comprehensive exam; for doctorate, thesis/dissertation. *Entrance requirements:* For master's, minimum GPA of 2.75, two recommendations, resume, bachelor's degree conferred transcript; interview (for non-certified teachers); for doctorate, GRE, 3 letters of recommendation. Additional exam requirements/ recommendations for international students: Required—TOEFL (minimum score 80 iBT), IELTS (minimum score 6.5). *Application deadline:* For fall admission, 8/1 for domestic students, 6/1 for international students; for spring admission, 1/1 for domestic students, 11/1 for international students; for summer admission, 5/1 for domestic students, 3/1 for international students. Applications are processed on a rolling basis. Application fee: $0 ($100 for international students). Electronic applications accepted. Application fee is waived when completed online. *Expenses:* $1,650 per 3-hour course; $1,275 annual general fee; $1,060 annual technology fee. *Financial support:* In 2016–17, 2 students received support. Research assistantships, teaching assistantships, Federal Work-Study, and scholarships/grants available. Support available to part-time students. Financial award application deadline: 4/1; financial award applicants required to submit FAFSA. *Faculty research:* Autism and inclusion, integrating technology into instruction, school change and leadership trust. *Unit head:* Dr. Charlotte Fontenot, Director, Graduate Programs, 281-649-3078, Fax: 281-649-3361, E-mail: cfontenot@ hbu.edu. *Application contact:* Kristy Wright, Administrative Assistant for Graduate Programs, 281-649-3094, Fax: 281-649-3361, E-mail: kwright@hbu.edu.
Website: http://www.hbu.edu/MED

Idaho State University, Office of Graduate Studies, College of Education, Department of Educational Foundations, Pocatello, ID 83209-8059. Offers child and family studies (M Ed); curriculum leadership (M Ed); education (M Ed); educational administration (M Ed); educational foundations (5th Year Certificate); elementary education (M Ed), including K-12 education, literacy, secondary education. *Program availability:* Part-time. *Degree requirements:* For master's, comprehensive exam, thesis optional, oral exam, written exam; for 5th Year Certificate, comprehensive exam, thesis (for some programs), oral exam, written exam. *Entrance requirements:* For master's, GRE General Test or MAT, minimum undergraduate GPA of 3.0; for 5th Year Certificate, GRE General Test, minimum undergraduate GPA of 3.0, master's degree. Additional exam requirements/ recommendations for international students: Required—TOEFL (minimum score 550 paper-based; 80 iBT). Electronic applications accepted. *Faculty research:* Child and families studies; business education; special education; math, science, and technology education.

Idaho State University, Office of Graduate Studies, College of Education, Department of School Psychology, Literacy, and Special Education, Pocatello, ID 83209-8059. Offers deaf education (M Ed); human exceptionality (M Ed); literacy (M Ed); school psychology (Ed S); special education (Ed S). *Program availability:* Part-time. *Degree requirements:* For master's, comprehensive exam, thesis (for some programs), oral thesis defense or written comprehensive exam and oral exam; for Ed S, comprehensive exam, thesis (for some programs), oral exam, specialist paper or portfolio. *Entrance requirements:* For master's, GRE or MAT, minimum undergraduate GPA of 3.0, bachelor's degree, professional experience in an educational context; for Ed S, GRE or MAT, master's degree in related field. Additional exam requirements/recommendations for international students: Required—TOEFL (minimum score 550 paper-based; 80 iBT). Electronic applications accepted. *Faculty research:* Literacy, school psychology, special education.

Illinois State University, Graduate School, College of Education, Department of Curriculum and Instruction, Program in Reading, Normal, IL 61790-2200. Offers MS Ed. *Accreditation:* NCATE. *Degree requirements:* For master's, practicum. *Entrance requirements:* For master's, GRE General Test, minimum GPA of 3.0 in last 60 hours of course work, course work in reading.

Indiana University Bloomington, School of Education, Department of Literacy, Culture, and Language Education, Bloomington, IN 47405-7000. Offers MS, Ed D, PhD, Ed S. *Accreditation:* NCATE. *Program availability:* Part-time, evening/weekend, online learning. Terminal master's awarded for partial completion of doctoral program. *Degree requirements:* For doctorate, thesis/dissertation, internship; for Ed S, comprehensive exam or project. *Entrance requirements:* For master's, GRE General Test or minimum GPA of 3.0; for doctorate, GRE General Test, minimum graduate GPA of 3.5; for Ed S, GRE General Test. Additional exam requirements/recommendations for international students: Required—TOEFL. *Faculty research:* Discourse analysis, sociolinguistics, critical literacy, cultural studies.

Indiana University of Pennsylvania, School of Graduate Studies and Research, College of Education and Educational Technology, Department of Professional Studies in Education, Program in Literacy, Indiana, PA 15705. Offers literacy (M Ed); reading (Certificate). *Accreditation:* NCATE. *Program availability:* Part-time. *Faculty:* 15 full-time (11 women), 3 part-time/adjunct (2 women). *Students:* 13 full-time (all women), 14 part-time (13 women); includes 1 minority (Black or African American, non-Hispanic/Latino). Average age 27. 25 applicants, 80% accepted, 17 enrolled. In 2016, 6 master's awarded. *Degree requirements:* For master's, thesis optional. *Entrance requirements:* For master's, 2 letters of recommendation. Additional exam requirements/ recommendations for international students: Required—TOEFL (minimum score 540 paper-based). *Application deadline:* For fall admission, 7/1 for domestic students; for spring admission, 11/1 for domestic students. Applications are processed on a rolling basis. Application fee: $50. Electronic applications accepted. *Expenses:* Tuition, state resident: full-time $8694; part-time $483 per credit. Tuition, nonresident: full-time $13,050; part-time $725 per credit. *Required fees:* $157 per credit. $50 per term. Tuition and fees vary according to course load and program. *Financial support:* In 2016–17, 12 research assistantships with tuition reimbursements (averaging $5,679 per year) were awarded; fellowships, career-related internships or fieldwork, Federal Work-Study, scholarships/grants, and unspecified assistantships also available. Support available to part-time students. Financial award application deadline: 4/15; financial award applicants required to submit FAFSA. *Unit head:* Dr. Deanna Laverick, Graduate Co-Coordinator, 724-357-5597, E-mail: d.m.laverick@iup.edu. *Application contact:* Dr. Kelli Paquette, Graduate Co-Coordinator, 724-357-2400, E-mail: kpaquette@iup.edu.
Website: http://www.iup.edu/pse/grad/literacy-med-reading-specialist-certification/ default.aspx

Indiana University–Purdue University Indianapolis, School of Education, Indianapolis, IN 46202-5155. Offers curriculum and instruction (MS); early childhood (MS); educational leadership (MS, Certificate); English as a second language (Certificate); kindergarten (Certificate); language education (MS); reading (Certificate); school counseling (MS); special education (MS, Certificate). *Program availability:* Part-time, evening/weekend. *Faculty:* 35 full-time (27 women), 56 part-time/adjunct (42 women). *Students:* 125 full-time (86 women), 181 part-time (139 women); includes 106 minority (78 Black or African American, non-Hispanic/Latino; 9 Asian, non-Hispanic/ Latino; 12 Hispanic/Latino; 7 Two or more races, non-Hispanic/Latino), 3 international. Average age 32. 73 applicants, 93% accepted, 68 enrolled. In 2016, 73 master's awarded. Terminal master's awarded for partial completion of doctoral program. *Degree requirements:* For master's, thesis optional. *Entrance requirements:* For master's, GRE General Test, minimum GPA of 2.5; for Certificate, official transcripts. Additional exam requirements/recommendations for international students: Required—TOEFL (minimum score 60 iBT), IELTS (minimum score 5.5). *Application deadline:* For fall admission, 5/1 for domestic students; for spring admission, 11/1 for domestic students. Application fee: $60 ($65 for international students). Electronic applications accepted. *Expenses:* $1,262 tuition, $213 general fee. *Financial support:* Applicants required to submit FAFSA. *Faculty research:* Educational policies and school leaders' responses to these; issues of intersectionality in the experiences of African American lesbian, gay, and bisexual students attending historically black colleges and universities and those who belong to black Greek-letter organizations; students' experiential knowledge and their evolving disciplinary-specific literacy and understanding; innovative program development; urban ESL teacher preparation; target-based instructional coaching. *Total annual research expenditures:* $2.1 million. *Unit head:* Dr. Robin Hughes, Executive Associate Dean, 317-274-6817, E-mail: roblhugh@iupui.edu. *Application contact:* Ky Shaw, Graduate Admissions Coordinator, 317-278-6778, E-mail: kycshaw@iupui.edu.
Website: http://education.iupui.edu/

Jackson State University, Graduate School, College of Education and Human Development, Department of Elementary and Early Childhood Education, Jackson, MS 39217. Offers early childhood education (MS Ed, Ed D); elementary education (MS Ed, Ed S); reading education (MS Ed). *Accreditation:* NCATE. *Program availability:* Part-time, evening/weekend, 100% online, blended/hybrid learning. *Faculty:* 10 full-time (4 women). *Students:* 90 full-time (86 women), 132 part-time (123 women); includes 210 minority (207 Black or African American, non-Hispanic/Latino; 2 Hispanic/Latino; 1 Two or more races, non-Hispanic/Latino), 9 international. Average age 37. 137 applicants, 72% accepted, 58 enrolled. In 2016, 41 master's, 9 doctorates, 2 other advanced degrees awarded. Terminal master's awarded for partial completion of doctoral program. *Degree requirements:* For master's, comprehensive exam, thesis or alternative; for doctorate, comprehensive exam, thesis/dissertation. *Entrance requirements:* For master's, GRE General Test; for doctorate, MAT, teaching experience. Additional exam requirements/recommendations for international students: Required—TOEFL (minimum score 520 paper-based; 67 iBT). *Application deadline:* For fall admission, 3/1 priority date for domestic students, 3/1 for international students; for spring admission, 10/1 for domestic and international students. Applications are processed on a rolling basis. Application fee: $25. Electronic applications accepted. *Expenses:* Contact institution. *Financial support:* Career-related internships or fieldwork, Federal Work-Study, scholarships/grants, and unspecified assistantships available. Support available to part-time students. Financial award application deadline: 3/1; financial award applicants required to submit FAFSA. *Unit head:* Dr. Thea Williams-Black, Chair, 601-979-2341, E-mail: thea.h.williams-black@jsums.edu. *Application contact:* Dr. Thea Williams-Black, Chair, 601-979-2341, E-mail: thea.h.williams-black@ jsums.edu.
Website: http://www.jsums.edu/earlyeducation/

Jacksonville State University, College of Graduate Studies and Continuing Education, College of Education and Professional Studies, Program in Reading Specialist, Jacksonville, AL 36265-1602. Offers MS Ed. *Program availability:* Part-time, evening/ weekend. *Faculty:* 11 full-time (9 women), 1 (woman) part-time/adjunct. *Students:* 1 (woman) part-time. Average age 25. 3 applicants. In 2016, 1 master's awarded. *Degree requirements:* For master's, comprehensive exam, thesis (for some programs). *Entrance requirements:* Additional exam requirements/recommendations for international students: Required—TOEFL (minimum score 500 paper-based; 61 iBT). *Application deadline:* Applications are processed on a rolling basis. Application fee: $35. Electronic applications accepted. *Financial support:* Available to part-time students. Application deadline: 4/1; applicants required to submit FAFSA. *Unit head:* Dr. Janet Bavonese, Head, 256-782-8340, E-mail: jbavonese@jsu.edu. *Application contact:* Dr. Jean Pugliese, Associate Dean, 256-782-8278, Fax: 256-782-5321, E-mail: pugliese@ jsu.edu.

James Madison University, The Graduate School, College of Education, Program in Education, Harrisonburg, VA 22807. Offers early childhood education (preK-3) (MAT); educational leadership (M Ed); educational technology (M Ed); elementary education (MAT); equity and cultural diversity (M Ed); inclusive early childhood education (MAT); K-8 mathematics specialist (M Ed); middle education (MAT); reading education (M Ed); secondary education (MAT); Spanish language and culture for educators (M Ed); TESOL (MAT). *Accreditation:* NCATE. *Program availability:* Part-time, evening/weekend. *Faculty:* 21 full-time (12 women), 5 part-time/adjunct (2 women). *Students:* 249 full-time (220 women), 123 part-time (86 women); includes 43 minority (7 Black or African American, non-Hispanic/Latino; 7 Asian, non-Hispanic/Latino; 17 Hispanic/Latino; 12 Two or more races, non-Hispanic/Latino), 2 international. Average age 30. 355 applicants, 98% accepted, 312 enrolled. In 2016, 247 master's awarded. Application fee: $55. Electronic applications accepted. *Financial support:* In 2016–17, 16 students received support. Career-related internships or fieldwork, Federal Work-Study, and 22 assistantships (averaging $7911) available. Financial award application deadline: 3/1; financial award applicants required to submit FAFSA. *Unit head:* Dr. Phillip M. Wishon, Dean, 540-568-6572, E-mail: wishonpm@jmu.edu. *Application contact:* Lynette D. Michael, Director of Graduate Admissions, 540-568-6131 Ext. 6395, Fax: 540-568-7860, E-mail: michaeld@jmu.edu.
Website: http://www.jmu.edu/coe/index.shtml

James Madison University, The Graduate School, College of Education, Program in Reading Education, Harrisonburg, VA 22807. Offers M Ed. *Accreditation:* NCATE. *Program availability:* Part-time. *Students:* Average age 27. *Entrance requirements:* For master's, GRE General Test. Additional exam requirements/recommendations for international students: Required—TOEFL. *Application deadline:* For fall admission, 5/1 priority date for domestic students; for spring admission, 9/1 priority date for domestic students. Applications are processed on a rolling basis. Application fee: $55. Electronic applications accepted. *Financial support:* Federal Work-Study and unspecified assistantships available. Financial award application deadline: 3/1; financial award applicants required to submit FAFSA. *Unit head:* Dr. Martha Ross, Academic Unit Head, 540-568-6255. *Application contact:* Lynette M. Bible, Director of Graduate Admissions, 540-568-6395, Fax: 540-568-7860, E-mail: biblelm@jmu.edu.

Johns Hopkins University, School of Education, Master's Programs in Education, Baltimore, MD 21218. Offers counseling (MS), including clinical mental health counseling, school counseling; education (MS), including educational studies, gifted education, reading, school administration and supervision, technology for educators; elementary education (MAT); health professions (M Ed); intelligence analysis (MS); organizational leadership (MS); secondary education (MAT), including biology, chemistry, earth/space science, English, physics, social studies; special education (MS), including early childhood special education, general special education studies, mild to moderate disabilities, severe disabilities. *Program availability:* Part-time, evening/weekend, 100% online, blended/hybrid learning. *Students:* 345 full-time (265 women), 1,601 part-time (1,245 women); includes 837 minority (392 Black or African American, non-Hispanic/Latino; 7 American Indian or Alaska Native, non-Hispanic/Latino; 141 Asian, non-Hispanic/Latino; 207 Hispanic/Latino; 7 Native Hawaiian or other Pacific Islander, non-Hispanic/Latino; 83 Two or more races, non-Hispanic/Latino), 55 international. Average age 27. 1,352 applicants, 76% accepted, 819 enrolled. In 2016, 642 master's awarded. *Degree requirements:* For master's, comprehensive exam (for some programs), portfolio, capstone project and/or internship; PRAXIS II (subject area assessments) for initial teacher preparation programs that lead to licensure. *Entrance requirements:* For master's, GRE (for full-time programs only); PRAXIS I/core or state-approved alternative (for initial teacher preparation programs that lead to licensure), minimum of bachelor's degree from regionally- or nationally-accredited institution; minimum GPA of 3.0 in all previous programs of study; official transcripts from all post-secondary institutions attended; essay; curriculum vitae/resume; letters of recommendation (3 for full-time programs, 2 for part-time programs); dispositions survey. Additional exam requirements/recommendations for international students: Required—TOEFL (minimum score 600 paper-based; 100 iBT), IELTS (minimum score 7). *Application deadline:* For fall admission, 4/1 priority date for domestic students, 4/1 for international students; for spring admission, 10/1 priority date for domestic students, 10/1 for international students; for summer admission, 2/1 priority date for domestic students, 2/1 for international students. Applications are processed on a rolling basis. Application fee: $80. Electronic applications accepted. *Expenses:* Contact institution. *Financial support:* Application deadline: 4/1; applicants required to submit FAFSA. *Unit head:* Dr. Christopher C. Morphew, Dean. *Application contact:* Elisabeth Woodward, Director of Admissions, 410-516-9796, Fax: 410-516-9817, E-mail: soe.info@jhu.edu.
Website: http://education.jhu.edu

Judson University, Doctor of Education in Literacy Program, Elgin, IL 60123-1498. Offers Ed D. *Program availability:* Evening/weekend. *Faculty:* 6 full-time, 8 part-time/adjunct. *Students:* 37 full-time (32 women); includes 2 minority (1 Black or African American, non-Hispanic/Latino; 1 Two or more races, non-Hispanic/Latino). Average age 40. 10 applicants, 90% accepted, 8 enrolled. *Degree requirements:* For doctorate, thesis/dissertation, 4 authentic benchmark assessments. *Entrance requirements:* For doctorate, resume/curriculum vitae; official transcript(s) of all master's work; minimum GPA of 3.35. *Application deadline:* For fall admission, 11/1 for domestic and international students. Application fee: $200. *Expenses:* Contact institution. *Financial support:* Application deadline: 4/1; applicants required to submit FAFSA. *Faculty research:* Literacy, social justice, linguistics, communication theory, higher education. *Unit head:* Dr. Steven L. Layne, Director, 847-628-1093, E-mail: slayne@judsonu.edu. *Application contact:* Maria Aguirre, Student Academic Advisor, 847-628-1160, E-mail: maguirre@judsonu.edu.
Website: http://www.judsonu.edu/literacydoctor/

Judson University, Master of Education in Literacy Program, Elgin, IL 60123-1498. Offers M Ed. *Faculty:* 4 full-time (2 women), 9 part-time/adjunct (all women). *Students:* 14 full-time (13 women). Average age 33. 17 applicants, 100% accepted, 17 enrolled. In 2016, 17 master's awarded. *Degree requirements:* For master's, completion and submission of a feature article to a peer-reviewed journal in the field. *Entrance requirements:* For master's, copy of official teaching certificate, bachelor's degree with minimum GPA of 3.0, 2 letters of reference, essay, interview, live writing sample. *Application deadline:* Applications are processed on a rolling basis. Application fee: $40. *Expenses:* Contact institution. *Financial support:* Application deadline: 4/15; applicants required to submit FAFSA. *Faculty research:* Affective domain in reading, children's and adolescent literature, cross-curricular writing, critical thinking, administration in higher education, linguistics. *Unit head:* Dr. Steven L. Layne, Director, 847-628-1093, E-mail: slayne@judsonu.edu. *Application contact:* Maria Aguirre, Student Academic Advisor, 847-628-1160, E-mail: maguirre@judsonu.edu.

Kansas State University, Graduate School, College of Education, Department of Curriculum and Instruction, Manhattan, KS 66506. Offers curriculum and instruction (Ed D, PhD); digital teaching and learning (MS); educational computing, design and online learning (MS); elementary/middle level curriculum and instruction (MS); online learning (Certificate); reading specialist endorsement (MS); reading/language arts (MS); teacher leader/school improvement (MS); teaching and learning (Certificate). *Accreditation:* NCATE. *Program availability:* Part-time, online learning. *Faculty:* 36 full-time (22 women), 18 part-time/adjunct (9 women). *Students:* 59 full-time (40 women), 94 part-time (72 women); includes 21 minority (5 Black or African American, non-Hispanic/Latino; 3 Asian, non-Hispanic/Latino; 11 Hispanic/Latino; 2 Two or more races, non-Hispanic/Latino), 20 international. Average age 35. 70 applicants, 71% accepted, 36 enrolled. In 2016, 61 master's, 12 doctorates, 9 other advanced degrees awarded. *Degree requirements:* For master's, comprehensive exam, portfolio, project, report or thesis; for doctorate, comprehensive exam, thesis/dissertation, preliminary exam; for Certificate, comprehensive exam, portfolio. *Entrance requirements:* For master's, minimum GPA of 3.0, 3 letters of recommendation; for doctorate, GRE, minimum GPA of 3.0, 3 letters of recommendation, evidence of scholarly writing; for Certificate, minimum GPA of 3.0, letters of recommendation. Additional exam requirements/recommendations for international students: Required—TOEFL (minimum score 550 paper-based; 80 iBT) or IELTS. *Application deadline:* For fall admission, 3/1 priority date for domestic students, 2/1 priority date for international students; for spring admission, 10/1 priority date for domestic students, 8/1 priority date for international students. Applications are processed on a rolling basis. Application fee: $50 ($75 for international students). Electronic applications accepted. *Expenses:* Tuition, state resident: full-time $9670. Tuition, nonresident: full-time $21,828. *Required fees:* $862. *Financial support:* In 2016–17, 1 research assistantship (averaging $19,980 per year), 8 teaching assistantships (averaging $12,620 per year) were awarded; career-related internships or fieldwork, institutionally sponsored loans, scholarships/grants, and unspecified assistantships also available. Support available to part-time students. Financial award application deadline: 3/1; financial award applicants required to submit FAFSA. *Faculty research:* Literacy and technology, critical race theory and diversity, achievement gaps, school improvement, teacher education. *Total annual research expenditures:* $647,057. *Unit head:* Dr. F. Todd Goodson, Department Chair, 785-532-5904, Fax: 785-532-7304, E-mail: tgoodson@ksu.edu. *Application contact:* Dr. Kay Ann Taylor, Director, Curriculum and Instruction Graduate Programs, 785-532-6974, Fax: 785-532-7304, E-mail: ktaylor@ksu.edu.
Website: http://www.coe.ksu.edu/edci/index.html

Kaplan University, Davenport Campus, School of Teacher Education, Davenport, IA 52807. Offers education (M Ed); secondary education (M Ed); teaching and learning (MA); teaching literacy and language: grades 6-12 (MA); teaching literacy and language: grades K-6 (MA); teaching mathematics: grades 6-8 (MA); teaching mathematics: grades 9-12 (MA); teaching mathematics: grades K-5 (MA); teaching science: grades 6-12 (MA); teaching science: grades K-6 (MA); teaching students with special needs (MA); teaching with technology (MA). *Program availability:* Part-time, evening/weekend, online learning. *Entrance requirements:* Additional exam requirements/recommendations for international students: Required—TOEFL (minimum score 550 paper-based; 80 iBT).

Kean University, College of Education, Program in Reading Specialization, Union, NJ 07083. Offers MA. *Program availability:* Part-time. *Faculty:* 12 full-time (11 women). *Students:* 16 part-time (all women); includes 2 minority (both Hispanic/Latino). Average age 31. 6 applicants, 83% accepted, 5 enrolled. In 2016, 9 master's awarded. *Degree requirements:* For master's, thesis, practicum, clinical, research seminar, 2 years of teaching experience by end of program (for certification). *Entrance requirements:* For master's, GRE General Test or MAT, minimum cumulative GPA of 3.0, official transcripts from all institutions attended, two letters of recommendation, professional resume/curriculum vitae, personal statement, teacher certification (for some programs). Additional exam requirements/recommendations for international students: Required—TOEFL (minimum score 550 paper-based; 79 iBT), IELTS (minimum score 6.5). *Application deadline:* For fall admission, 6/1 for domestic and international students; for spring admission, 12/1 for domestic and international students. Applications are processed on a rolling basis. Application fee: $75. Electronic applications accepted. *Expenses:* Tuition, state resident: full-time $13,156; part-time $640 per credit. Tuition, nonresident: full-time $17,831; part-time $785 per credit. *Required fees:* $3316; $151 per credit. Tuition and fees vary according to course level, course load, degree level and program. *Financial support:* Scholarships/grants and unspecified assistantships available. Financial award applicants required to submit FAFSA. *Unit head:* Dr. Diane Tracey, Program Coordinator, 908-737-3944, E-mail: dtracey@kean.edu. *Application contact:* Brittany Gerstenhaber, Admission Counselor, 908-737-7100, E-mail: grad-adm@kean.edu.
Website: http://grad.kean.edu/masters-programs/reading-specialist

Kennesaw State University, Leland and Clarice C. Bagwell College of Education, Program in Graduate Education, Kennesaw, GA 30144. Offers educational leadership (M Ed); educational leadership technology (M Ed); elementary and early childhood education (M Ed); instructional technology (M Ed); middle grades education (M Ed); reading (M Ed); secondary education (M Ed); special education (M Ed); teaching English to speakers of other languages (M Ed). *Accreditation:* NCATE. *Program availability:* Part-time. *Degree requirements:* For master's, thesis or alternative. *Entrance requirements:* For master's, GRE General Test, T-4 state certification, minimum GPA of 2.75. Additional exam requirements/recommendations for international students: Required—TOEFL (minimum score 550 paper-based; 80 iBT), IELTS (minimum score 6.5). Electronic applications accepted.

Kent State University, College of Education, Health and Human Services, School of Teaching, Learning and Curriculum Studies, Program in Reading Specialization, Kent, OH 44242-0001. Offers M Ed, MA. *Accreditation:* NCATE. *Program availability:* Part-time, evening/weekend. *Degree requirements:* For master's, thesis (for some programs). *Entrance requirements:* For master's, 2 letters of reference, goals statement. Additional exam requirements/recommendations for international students: Required—TOEFL (minimum score 550 paper-based; 80 iBT). Electronic applications accepted. *Expenses:* Tuition, state resident: full-time $10,864; part-time $495 per credit hour. Tuition, nonresident: full-time $18,380; part-time $837 per credit hour. *Faculty research:* Adolescent literacy, adult and family literacy, school change in literacy education, struggling readers.

Kutztown University of Pennsylvania, College of Education, Program in Reading, Kutztown, PA 19530-0730. Offers M Ed. *Accreditation:* NCATE. *Program availability:* Part-time, evening/weekend. *Students:* 55 part-time (53 women); includes 1 minority (Asian, non-Hispanic/Latino). Average age 31. 33 applicants, 97% accepted, 27 enrolled. In 2016, 25 master's awarded. *Degree requirements:* For master's, comprehensive project. *Entrance requirements:* For master's, GRE General Test, PRAXIS II, NTE, or 10 years' experience in elementary or secondary school with appropriate certification, valid PA instructional I or II teaching certificate, 3 graduate evaluation forms from professionals in education. Additional exam requirements/recommendations for international students: Required—TOEFL (minimum score 550 paper-based, 79 iBT) or IELTS (minimum score 6.5). *Application deadline:* For fall admission, 8/1 for domestic and international students; for spring admission, 12/1 for domestic and international students. Application fee: $35. Electronic applications accepted. *Expenses:* Tuition, state resident: full-time $4347; part-time $483 per credit. Tuition, nonresident: full-time $6525; part-time $725 per credit. *Required fees:* $88 per credit. One-time fee: $50 full-time. *Financial support:* Career-related internships or fieldwork, Federal Work-Study, scholarships/grants, and unspecified assistantships available. Financial award application deadline: 3/1; financial award applicants required to submit FAFSA. *Unit head:* Dr. Jeanie Burnett, Chairperson, 610-683-4286, Fax: 610-

683-1327, E-mail: burnett@kutztown.edu. *Application contact:* Dr. Mary Ann O'Neil, 484-646-4224, E-mail: oneil@kutztown.edu.
Website: https://www.kutztown.edu/academics/graduate-programs/reading.htm

La Salle University, School of Arts and Sciences, Program in Education, Philadelphia, PA 19141-1199. Offers autism spectrum disorders (MA, Certificate); bilingual/bicultural studies (MA); classroom management (MA); dual early childhood and special education (MA); dual middle-level science and math and special education (MA); education (MA); English (MA); English as a second language (Certificate); history (MA); instructional coach (Certificate); instructional leadership (MA); reading specialist (MA, Certificate); secondary education (MA); special education (MA, Certificate). *Program availability:* Part-time, evening/weekend. *Faculty:* 5 full-time (4 women), 12 part-time/adjunct (8 women). *Students:* 10 full-time (all women), 98 part-time (74 women); includes 28 minority (13 Black or African American, non-Hispanic/Latino; 1 American Indian or Alaska Native, non-Hispanic/Latino; 1 Asian, non-Hispanic/Latino; 10 Hispanic/Latino; 3 Two or more races, non-Hispanic/Latino). Average age 34. 128 applicants, 84% accepted, 69 enrolled. In 2016, 53 master's awarded. *Degree requirements:* For master's, comprehensive exam. *Entrance requirements:* For master's, MAT or GRE, 2 letters of recommendation; for Certificate, GMAT or GRE, 2 letters of recommendation. Additional exam requirements/recommendations for international students: Required—TOEFL. *Application deadline:* For fall admission, 8/15 priority date for domestic students, 7/15 for international students; for spring admission, 12/15 priority date for domestic students, 11/15 for international students; for summer admission, 4/15 priority date for domestic students, 3/15 for international students. Applications are processed on a rolling basis. Application fee: $35. Electronic applications accepted. Application fee is waived when completed online. *Expenses:* Contact institution. *Financial support:* In 2016–17, 27 students received support. Scholarships/grants available. Support available to part-time students. Financial award application deadline: 8/31; financial award applicants required to submit FAFSA. *Unit head:* Dr. Greer Richardson, Director, 215-951-1806, Fax: 215-951-1843, E-mail: graded@lasalle.edu. *Application contact:* Elizabeth Heenan, Director, Graduate and Adult Enrollment, 215-951-1100, Fax: 215-951-1462, E-mail: heenan@lasalle.edu.
Website: http://www.lasalle.edu/grad-education-programs/

Lehman College of the City University of New York, School of Education, Department of Specialized Services in Education, Program in Reading Teacher, Bronx, NY 10468-1589. Offers MS Ed. *Accreditation:* NCATE. *Program availability:* Evening/weekend. *Entrance requirements:* For master's, interview, minimum GPA of 2.7. *Faculty research:* Emergent literacy, language-based classrooms, primary and secondary social contexts of language and literacy, innovative in-service education models, adult literacy.

Le Moyne College, Department of Education, Syracuse, NY 13214. Offers adolescent education (MS Ed, MST); adolescent education/special education (MS Ed, MST); adolescent English (MST), including grades 7-12; adolescent English/special education (MST), including grades 7-12; adolescent foreign language (MST), including grades 7-12; adolescent history (MST), including grades 7-12; childhood education (MS Ed); childhood education/special education (MS Ed); elementary education (MS Ed); general education (MS Ed); inclusive childhood education (MST); literacy education (MS Ed), including birth to grade 6, grades 5-12; school building leader (MS Ed); school building leadership (CAS); school district business leader (MS Ed, CAS); school district leader (MS Ed); school district leadership (CAS); secondary education (MS Ed); special education (MS Ed); teaching English to speakers of other languages (MS Ed); urban studies (MS Ed). *Accreditation:* TEAC. *Program availability:* Part-time, evening/weekend. *Faculty:* 8 full-time (5 women), 20 part-time/adjunct (12 women). *Students:* 66 full-time (40 women), 155 part-time (117 women); includes 13 minority (4 Black or African American, non-Hispanic/Latino; 2 American Indian or Alaska Native, non-Hispanic/Latino; 2 Asian, non-Hispanic/Latino; 5 Hispanic/Latino), 3 international. Average age 30. 74 applicants, 99% accepted, 66 enrolled. In 2016, 81 master's, 53 CASs awarded. *Degree requirements:* For master's, thesis. *Entrance requirements:* For master's, bachelor's degree with minimum undergraduate GPA of 3.0, 2 letters of recommendation, transcripts. Additional exam requirements/recommendations for international students: Required—TOEFL (minimum score 550 paper-based; 79 iBT); Recommended—IELTS (minimum score 6.5). *Application deadline:* For fall admission, 4/1 priority date for domestic and international students; for spring admission, 10/1 priority date for domestic and international students; for summer admission, 3/1 priority date for domestic and international students. Applications are processed on a rolling basis. Application fee: $50. Electronic applications accepted. *Expenses:* $700 per credit hour. *Financial support:* In 2016–17, 21 students received support. Career-related internships or fieldwork, scholarships/grants, and health care benefits available. Support available to part-time students. Financial award applicants required to submit FAFSA. *Faculty research:* Minority teachers, special education, multiculturalism, literacy, technology, media literacy learning, autism, school district organization, service-learning, higher level problem solving, teacher leadership. *Unit head:* Dr. Stephen C. Fleury, Chair, Department of Education, 315-445-4376, Fax: 315-445-4744, E-mail: fleurysc@lemoyne.edu. *Application contact:* Kristen P. Richards, Senior Director of Enrollment Management, 315-445-5444, Fax: 315-445-6092, E-mail: trapaskp@lemoyne.edu.
Website: http://www.lemoyne.edu/education

Lesley University, Graduate School of Education, Cambridge, MA 02138-2790. Offers arts, community, and education (M Ed); autism studies (Certificate); curriculum and instruction (M Ed, CAGS); early childhood education (M Ed); ecological teaching and learning (MS); educational studies (PhD), including adult learning, educational leadership, individually designed; elementary education (M Ed); emergent technologies for educators (Certificate); ESLArts: language learning through the arts (M Ed); high school education (M Ed); individually designed (M Ed); integrated teaching through the arts (M Ed); literacy for K-8 classroom teachers (M Ed); mathematics education (M Ed); middle school education (M Ed); moderate disabilities (M Ed); online learning (Certificate); reading (CAGS); science in education (M Ed); severe disabilities (M Ed); special needs (CAGS); specialist teacher of reading (M Ed); teacher of visual art (M Ed); technology in education (M Ed, CAGS). *Accreditation:* TEAC. *Program availability:* Part-time, evening/weekend, online learning. *Degree requirements:* For master's, practicum; for doctorate, thesis/dissertation. *Entrance requirements:* For master's, Massachusetts Tests for Educator Licensure (MTEL), transcripts, statement of purpose, recommendations; interview (for special education); for doctorate, GRE General Test, transcripts, statement of purpose, recommendations, interview, master's degree, resume; for other advanced degree, interview, master's degree. Additional exam requirements/recommendations for international students: Required—TOEFL (minimum score 550 paper-based; 80 iBT). Electronic applications accepted. *Faculty research:* Assessment in literacy, mathematics and science; autism spectrum disorders; instructional technology and online learning; multicultural education and English language learners.

Lewis University, College of Education, Programs in Reading and Literacy, Romeoville, IL 60446. Offers M Ed, MA. *Program availability:* Part-time, evening/weekend. *Students:* 44 part-time (38 women); includes 6 minority (4 Black or African American, non-Hispanic/Latino; 1 Asian, non-Hispanic/Latino; 1 Hispanic/Latino), 1 international. Average age 30. *Degree requirements:* For master's, departmental qualifying exam. *Entrance requirements:* For master's, writing exam, minimum GPA of 2.75, 2 letters of recommendation, interview. Additional exam requirements/recommendations for international students: Required—TOEFL (minimum score 550 paper-based; 80 iBT). *Application deadline:* For fall admission, 5/1 priority date for international students; for spring admission, 11/15 priority date for international students. Applications are processed on a rolling basis. Application fee: $40. Electronic applications accepted. *Expenses: Tuition:* Full-time $13,860; part-time $770 per credit hour. *Required fees:* $75 per semester. Tuition and fees vary according to degree level and program. *Financial support:* Federal Work-Study, scholarships/grants, and unspecified assistantships available. Financial award application deadline: 5/1; financial award applicants required to submit FAFSA. *Unit head:* Dr. Deborah Augsburger, Program Director, 815-838-0500 Ext. 5883, E-mail: augsbude@lewisu.edu. *Application contact:* Kathy Lisak, Graduate Admission Counselor, 815-836-5610, E-mail: grad@lewisu.edu.

Liberty University, School of Education, Lynchburg, VA 24515. Offers educational leadership (Ed D); gifted education (Certificate); math specialist (M Ed); middle grades (MAT, Certificate); reading specialist (M Ed); school leadership (Certificate); secondary education (MAT); sport management (MS), including administration, outdoor recreation, sport management, tourism. *Accreditation:* NCATE. *Program availability:* Part-time, online learning. *Students:* 1,910 full-time (1,427 women), 4,420 part-time (3,311 women); includes 1,451 minority (1,182 Black or African American, non-Hispanic/Latino; 33 American Indian or Alaska Native, non-Hispanic/Latino; 44 Asian, non-Hispanic/Latino; 46 Hispanic/Latino; 11 Native Hawaiian or other Pacific Islander, non-Hispanic/Latino; 135 Two or more races, non-Hispanic/Latino), 87 international. Average age 37. 5,120 applicants, 44% accepted, 1193 enrolled. In 2016, 1,378 master's, 151 doctorates, 497 other advanced degrees awarded. *Degree requirements:* For doctorate, comprehensive exam, thesis/dissertation. *Entrance requirements:* For master's, GRE General Test or MAT (if taken in or before 1999), 2 letters of recommendation, minimum undergraduate GPA of 3.0, curriculum vitae; for doctorate and Certificate, GRE General Test or MAT (if taken before 1999), minimum master's GPA of 3.0, 3 years of teaching experience. Additional exam requirements/recommendations for international students: Required—TOEFL (minimum score 600 paper-based; 100 iBT). *Application deadline:* For fall admission, 6/1 for domestic students; for spring admission, 11/1 for domestic students. Applications are processed on a rolling basis. Application fee: $50. Electronic applications accepted. *Expenses:* Contact institution. *Financial support:* Federal Work-Study and tuition waivers (partial) available. *Faculty research:* Self-determination, character education, bibliotherapy, learning styles, distance education. *Unit head:* Dr. Heather Schoffstall, Dean, 434-582-2445, Fax: 434-582-2468, E-mail: awgunter@liberty.edu. *Application contact:* Jay Bridge, Director of Graduate Admissions, 800-424-9595, Fax: 800-628-7977, E-mail: gradadmissions@liberty.edu.
Website: http://www.liberty.edu/academics/education/graduate/

Lipscomb University, College of Education, Nashville, TN 37204-3951. Offers applied behavior analysis (MS, Certificate); educational leadership (M Ed, Ed S); English language learning (M Ed, Ed S); instructional coaching (M Ed, Certificate, Ed S); instructional practice (M Ed); learning organizations and strategic change (Ed D); literacy coaching (Certificate); reading specialty (M Ed, Ed S); special education (M Ed); teaching, learning, and leading (M Ed); technology integration (M Ed, Ed S); technology integration specialist (Certificate). *Accreditation:* NCATE. *Program availability:* Part-time, evening/weekend, 100% online. *Faculty:* 21 full-time (15 women), 38 part-time/adjunct (26 women). *Students:* 111 full-time (80 women), 345 part-time (292 women); includes 104 minority (70 Black or African American, non-Hispanic/Latino; 1 American Indian or Alaska Native, non-Hispanic/Latino; 3 Asian, non-Hispanic/Latino; 20 Hispanic/Latino; 10 Two or more races, non-Hispanic/Latino), 1 international. Average age 33. In 2016, 201 master's, 36 doctorates, 86 other advanced degrees awarded. *Degree requirements:* For master's, comprehensive exam, portfolio, research project and presentation; for doctorate, practical capstone project in experiential setting. *Entrance requirements:* For master's, MAT (minimum score 31) or GRE General Test (minimum score 294), 2 reference letters, goals statement, writing sample, interview; for doctorate, MAT or GRE General Test, 3 reference letters, artifact of demonstrated academic excellence, written personal statements, interview. Additional exam requirements/recommendations for international students: Required—TOEFL (minimum score 570 paper-based; 80 iBT). *Application deadline:* For fall admission, 8/29 priority date for domestic students; for spring admission, 1/15 priority date for domestic students. Applications are processed on a rolling basis. Application fee: $50 ($75 for international students). Electronic applications accepted. *Expenses:* $934 per hour; $570 per hour (Teach for America). *Financial support:* Scholarships/grants, unspecified assistantships, and partnerships with local school districts available. Financial award applicants required to submit FAFSA. *Faculty research:* Facilitative learning styles, leadership, student assessment, interactive multimedia inclusion, learning organizations and strategic change. *Unit head:* Dr. Deborah Boyd, Director of Graduate Studies, 615-966-6263, E-mail: deborah.boyd@lipscomb.edu. *Application contact:* Amanda Logsdon, Director of Enrollment and Outreach, 615-966-7199, E-mail: amanda.logsdon@lipscomb.edu.
Website: http://www.lipscomb.edu/education/graduate-programs

Long Island University–Brentwood Campus, Graduate Programs, Brentwood, NY 11717. Offers childhood education (grades 1-6) (MS), including grades 1-6; childhood education/literacy (grades 1-6) (MS); childhood education/special education (grades 1-6) (MS); clinical mental health counseling (MS, Advanced Certificate); early childhood education (B-2) (MS); literacy (B-6) (MS Ed); school counselor (MS); special education (grades 1-6) (MS Ed); students with disabilities generalist (grades 7-12) (Advanced Certificate). *Program availability:* Part-time. *Faculty:* 54 part-time/adjunct (30 women). *Students:* 98 full-time (80 women), 57 part-time (47 women); includes 28 minority (7 Black or African American, non-Hispanic/Latino; 1 Asian, non-Hispanic/Latino; 20 Hispanic/Latino). 85 applicants, 89% accepted, 43 enrolled. In 2016, 99 master's, 11 other advanced degrees awarded. *Degree requirements:* For master's, comprehensive exam (for some programs), thesis optional. *Entrance requirements:* For master's and Advanced Certificate, GRE. Additional exam requirements/recommendations for international students: Required—TOEFL or IELTS. *Application deadline:* Applications are processed on a rolling basis. Application fee: $50. Electronic applications accepted. Application fee is waived when completed online. *Expenses: Tuition:* Full-time $28,272; part-time $1178 per credit. *Required fees:* $451 per term. *Financial support:* Scholarships/grants and unspecified assistantships available. Support available to part-time students. Financial award applicants required to submit FAFSA. *Unit head:* Donna Di Donato, Dean and Chief Operating Officer, 631-287-8010, Fax: 631-287-8575, E-mail: donna.didonato@liu.edu. *Application contact:* Scott Aug, Associate Director of Enrollment Management, 631-287-8500, Fax: 631-287-8575, E-mail: scott.aug@liu.edu.
Website: http://liu.edu/brentwood

Long Island University–Hudson, Graduate School, Purchase, NY 10577. Offers autism (Advanced Certificate); childhood education (MS Ed); early childhood education (MS Ed); educational leadership (MS Ed); finance (MBA); health administration (MPA); healthcare sector management (MBA); literacy (MS Ed); management (MBA); marriage and family therapy (MS); mental health counseling (MS), including credentialed alcoholism and substance abuse counselor; middle childhood and adolescence education (MS Ed); pharmaceutics (MS), including cosmetic science, industrial pharmacy; public administration (MPA); school counseling (MS Ed, Advanced Certificate); school psychology (MS Ed); special education (MS Ed); TESOL (all grades) (Advanced Certificate); TESOL and bilingual education (MS Ed); the business of pharmaceutics and biotechnology (MBA). *Program availability:* Part-time, evening/weekend, online learning. *Faculty:* 7 full-time (5 women), 42 part-time/adjunct (25 women). *Students:* 55 full-time (41 women), 158 part-time (123 women); includes 40 minority (8 Black or African American, non-Hispanic/Latino; 1 Asian, non-Hispanic/Latino; 31 Hispanic/Latino). Average age 35. *Entrance requirements:* Additional exam requirements/recommendations for international students: Required—TOEFL (minimum score 550 paper-based; 79 iBT). *Application deadline:* Applications are processed on a rolling basis. Application fee: $50. Electronic applications accepted. *Expenses:* Contact institution. *Unit head:* Dr. Sylvia Blake, Dean and Chief Operating Officer, 914-831-2700, E-mail: westchester@liu.edu. *Application contact:* Cindy Pagnotta, Director of Marketing and Enrollment, 914-831-2701, Fax: 914-251-5959, E-mail: cindy.pagnotta@liu.edu.

Long Island University–LIU Post, College of Education, Information and Technology, Brookville, NY 11548-1300. Offers adolescence education (MS); adolescence education 7-12 (MS); archives and records management (AC); art education (MS); childhood education (MS); childhood teaching literacy B-6 (MS); childhood/special education (MS); clinical mental health counseling (MS, AC); early childhood education (MS); early childhood education/childhood education (MS); educational leadership (AC); educational technology (MS); information studies (PhD); interdisciplinary educational studies (Ed D); middle childhood education (MS); music education (MS); school counselor (MS); special education (MS Ed); speech-language pathology (MA); students with disabilities, 7-12 generalist (AC); TESOL (MA). *Accreditation:* TEAC. *Program availability:* Part-time, 100% online, blended/hybrid learning. *Faculty:* 55 full-time (35 women), 104 part-time/adjunct (57 women). *Students:* 464 full-time (390 women), 740 part-time (580 women); includes 265 minority (99 Black or African American, non-Hispanic/Latino; 45 Asian, non-Hispanic/Latino; 113 Hispanic/Latino; 1 Native Hawaiian or other Pacific Islander, non-Hispanic/Latino; 7 Two or more races, non-Hispanic/Latino), 33 international. 928 applicants, 76% accepted, 406 enrolled. In 2016, 334 master's, 10 doctorates, 137 other advanced degrees awarded. Terminal master's awarded for partial completion of doctoral program. *Degree requirements:* For master's, variable foreign language requirement, comprehensive exam (for some programs), thesis optional; for doctorate, comprehensive exam, thesis/dissertation. *Entrance requirements:* For master's and AC, GRE. Additional exam requirements/recommendations for international students: Required—PTE, TOEFL (minimum score 550 paper-based, 75 iBT) or IELTS. *Application deadline:* Applications are processed on a rolling basis. Application fee: $50. Electronic applications accepted. *Expenses: Tuition:* Full-time $28,272; part-time $1178 per credit. *Required fees:* $451 per term. Tuition and fees vary according to degree level and program. *Financial support:* Career-related internships or fieldwork, Federal Work-Study, institutionally sponsored loans, scholarships/grants, tuition waivers (partial), and unspecified assistantships available. Support available to part-time students. Financial award application deadline: 2/15; financial award applicants required to submit FAFSA. *Faculty research:* English language learners, early childhood literacy development through play, sleep, social justice through education, using a structured protocol for discussing bad news. *Total annual research expenditures:* $575,000. *Unit head:* Dr. Albert Inserra, Dean, 516-299-2210, E-mail: albert.inserra@liu.edu. *Application contact:* Carol Zerah, Director of Graduate Admissions, 516-299-2900, Fax: 516-299-2137, E-mail: post-enroll@liu.edu.
Website: http://liu.edu/CWPost/Academics/College-of-Education-Information-and-Technology

Long Island University–Riverhead, Graduate Programs, Riverhead, NY 11901. Offers childhood education (MS), including grades 1-6; homeland security management (MS); literacy education (MS); teaching students with disabilities (MS), including grades 1-6, grades 7-12; TESOL (Advanced Certificate). *Accreditation:* TEAC. *Program availability:* Part-time. *Degree requirements:* For master's, thesis (for some programs); for Advanced Certificate, comprehensive exam (for some programs). *Entrance requirements:* Additional exam requirements/recommendations for international students: Required—TOEFL (minimum score 550 paper-based; 79 iBT), IELTS (minimum score 6). *Application deadline:* Applications are processed on a rolling basis. Application fee: $50. Electronic applications accepted. *Expenses:* Contact institution. *Financial support:* Institutionally sponsored loans, scholarships/grants, tuition waivers (partial), and unspecified assistantships available. Support available to part-time students. Financial award application deadline: 2/15; financial award applicants required to submit FAFSA. *Unit head:* Donna Di Donato, Dean and Chief Operating Officer, LIU Brentwood and LIU Riverhead, 631-287-8010, Fax: 631-287-8575, E-mail: donna.didonato@liu.edu. *Application contact:* Christina Seifert, Director of Admission, LIU Brentwood and LIU Riverhead, 631-287-8505, Fax: 631-287-8253, E-mail: christina.seifert@liu.edu.

Longwood University, College of Graduate and Professional Studies, College of Education and Human Services, Program in Reading, Literacy and Learning, Farmville, VA 23909. Offers M Ed. *Program availability:* Part-time, evening/weekend. *Degree requirements:* For master's, professional portfolio. *Entrance requirements:* For master's, bachelor's degree from regionally-accredited institution, 2 recommendations, minimum 500-word personal essay, official transcripts, minimum GPA of 2.75, valid teaching license. Additional exam requirements/recommendations for international students: Required—TOEFL (minimum score 570 paper-based; 80 iBT), IELTS (minimum score 6.5). Electronic applications accepted. *Expenses:* Contact institution.

Lourdes University, Graduate School, Sylvania, OH 43560-2898. Offers business (MBA); leadership (M Ed); nurse anesthesia (MSN); nurse educator (MSN), nurse leader (MSN); organizational leadership (MOL); reading (M Ed); teaching and curriculum (M Ed); theology (MA). *Program availability:* Evening/weekend. *Entrance requirements:* Additional exam requirements/recommendations for international students: Required—TOEFL.

Loyola Marymount University, School of Education, Department of Elementary and Secondary Education, Program in Literacy Education, Los Angeles, CA 90045-2659. Offers MA. *Program availability:* Part-time, evening/weekend. *Students:* 3 full-time (all women), 3 part-time (all women); includes 4 minority (all Hispanic/Latino). Average age 30. In 2016, 1 master's awarded. *Entrance requirements:* For master's, CBEST. Additional exam requirements/recommendations for international students: Required—TOEFL (minimum score 600 paper-based; 100 iBT). *Application deadline:* For fall admission, 6/15 for domestic students; for spring admission, 11/15 for domestic students. Application fee: $50. Electronic applications accepted. *Financial support:* In 2016–17, 2 students received support. Scholarships/grants and unspecified assistantships available. Support available to part-time students. Financial award application deadline: 6/30; financial award applicants required to submit FAFSA. *Unit head:* Dr. Candace Poindexter, Program Director, 310-338-7314, E-mail: cpoindex@lmu.edu. *Application contact:* Chake H. Kouyoumjian, Associate Dean of Graduate Studies, 310-338-2721, E-mail: ckouyoum@lmu.edu.
Website: http://soe.lmu.edu/

Loyola Marymount University, School of Education, Department of Elementary and Secondary Education, Program in Literacy/Language Arts, Los Angeles, CA 90045-2659. Offers MA. *Program availability:* Part-time, evening/weekend. *Students:* 7 full-time (5 women), 2 part-time (both women); includes 6 minority (1 Black or African American, non-Hispanic/Latino; 4 Hispanic/Latino; 1 Two or more races, non-Hispanic/Latino). Average age 30. 3 applicants, 67% accepted, 2 enrolled. In 2016, 2 master's awarded. *Degree requirements:* For master's, comprehensive exam. *Entrance requirements:* For master's, CBEST, CSET, RICA, 3 letters of recommendation. Additional exam requirements/recommendations for international students: Required—TOEFL (minimum score 600 paper-based; 100 iBT). *Application deadline:* For fall admission, 6/15 for domestic students; for spring admission, 11/15 for domestic students. Application fee: $50. Electronic applications accepted. *Financial support:* In 2016–17, 2 students received support. Scholarships/grants and unspecified assistantships available. Support available to part-time students. Financial award application deadline: 6/30; financial award applicants required to submit FAFSA. *Unit head:* Dr. Candace Poindexter, Chair, 310-338-7314, E-mail: cpoindex@lmu.edu. *Application contact:* Chake H. Kouyoumjian, Associate Dean of Graduate Studies, 310-338-2721, E-mail: ckouyoum@lmu.edu.

Loyola Marymount University, School of Education, Department of Elementary and Secondary Education, Program in Reading Instruction, Los Angeles, CA 90045-2659. Offers MA. *Students:* 20 full-time (all women), 4 part-time (all women); includes 9 minority (1 Asian, non-Hispanic/Latino; 7 Hispanic/Latino; 1 Native Hawaiian or other Pacific Islander, non-Hispanic/Latino). Average age 29. 11 applicants, 82% accepted, 9 enrolled. In 2016, 15 master's awarded. *Entrance requirements:* For master's, statement of intent, 2 letters of recommendation. Additional exam requirements/recommendations for international students: Required—TOEFL (minimum score 600 paper-based; 100 iBT). *Application deadline:* For fall admission, 6/15 for domestic students. Application fee: $50. Electronic applications accepted. *Financial support:* In 2016–17, 21 students received support. Application deadline: 6/30; applicants required to submit FAFSA. *Unit head:* Dr. Candace Poindexter, Director, 310-338-7314, E-mail: cpoindex@lmu.edu. *Application contact:* Chake H. Kouyoumjian, Associate Dean of Graduate Studies, 310-338-2721, E-mail: ckouyoum@lmu.edu.
Website: http://soe.lmu.edu/academics/readinginstruction/

Loyola University Maryland, Graduate Programs, School of Education, Program in Literacy/Reading, Baltimore, MD 21210-2699. Offers literacy teacher (M Ed); reading specialist (M Ed). *Accreditation:* NCATE. *Program availability:* Part-time. *Faculty:* 34 full-time (22 women), 30 part-time/adjunct (24 women). *Students:* 2 full-time (both women), 130 part-time (126 women); includes 42 minority (28 Black or African American, non-Hispanic/Latino; 4 Asian, non-Hispanic/Latino; 3 Hispanic/Latino; 1 Native Hawaiian or other Pacific Islander, non-Hispanic/Latino; 6 Two or more races, non-Hispanic/Latino), 1 international. Average age 34. 86 applicants, 91% accepted, 60 enrolled. In 2016, 16 master's awarded. *Entrance requirements:* For master's, essay, 2 letters of recommendation, resume, transcripts. Additional exam requirements/recommendations for international students: Required—TOEFL (minimum score 550 paper-based), IELTS (minimum score 7). *Application deadline:* For fall admission, 6/15 for domestic students; for winter admission, 11/1 for domestic students; for spring admission, 3/15 for domestic students. Applications are processed on a rolling basis. Application fee: $60. Electronic applications accepted. *Expenses:* Contact institution. *Financial support:* Unspecified assistantships available. Financial award application deadline: 4/15; financial award applicants required to submit FAFSA. *Application contact:* Maureen Faux, Director of Graduate Admission, 410-617-5817, E-mail: mwfaux@loyola.edu.
Website: http://www.loyola.edu/soe/academics/graduate/literacy-reading.aspx

Lynchburg College, Graduate Studies, M Ed Program in Reading, Lynchburg, VA 24501-3199. Offers reading instruction (M Ed); reading specialist (M Ed). *Program availability:* Part-time, evening/weekend. *Students:* 1 (woman) full-time, 16 part-time (all women); includes 2 minority (both Black or African American, non-Hispanic/Latino). In 2016, 1 master's awarded. *Degree requirements:* For master's, comprehensive exam (for some programs), practicum; portfolio or comprehensive exam. *Entrance requirements:* For master's, GRE, minimum GPA of 3.0 (preferred), three letters of recommendation, official transcripts (bachelor's, others as relevant), career goals statement. Additional exam requirements/recommendations for international students: Required—TOEFL (minimum score 550 paper-based; 79 iBT), IELTS (minimum score 6.5). *Application deadline:* For fall admission, 7/31 for domestic students, 6/1 for international students; for spring admission, 11/30 for domestic students, 10/15 for international students. Applications are processed on a rolling basis. Application fee: $30. Electronic applications accepted. Application fee is waived when completed online. *Expenses:* Contact institution. *Financial support:* Federal Work-Study, scholarships/grants, health care benefits, and unspecified assistantships available. Support available to part-time students. Financial award application deadline: 7/31; financial award applicants required to submit FAFSA. *Unit head:* Dr. Susan Thompson, Professor/Director of M Ed in Reading, 434-544-8510, E-mail: thompson.s@lynchburg.edu.
Website: http://www.lynchburg.edu/graduate/master-of-education-in-reading/

Lyndon State College, Graduate Programs in Education, Department of Education, Lyndonville, VT 05851-0919. Offers curriculum and instruction (M Ed); reading specialist (M Ed); special education (M Ed); teaching and counseling (M Ed). *Program availability:* Part-time, evening/weekend. *Degree requirements:* For master's, exam or major field project. *Entrance requirements:* Additional exam requirements/recommendations for international students: Recommended—TOEFL (minimum score 500 paper-based).

Madonna University, Programs in Education, Livonia, MI 48150-1173. Offers Catholic school leadership (MSA); educational leadership (MSA); learning disabilities (MAT); literacy education (MAT); teaching and learning (MAT). *Accreditation:* NCATE. *Program availability:* Part-time, evening/weekend. *Degree requirements:* For master's, thesis or alternative. Electronic applications accepted.

Manhattanville College, School of Education, Program in Literacy Education, Purchase, NY 10577-2132. Offers MPS. *Program availability:* Part-time, evening/weekend. *Students:* 29 applicants, 59% accepted, 14 enrolled. In 2016, 22 master's awarded. *Degree requirements:* For master's, comprehensive exam (for some programs), thesis (for some programs), student teaching, research seminars, portfolios, internships, writing assessment. *Entrance requirements:* For master's, GRE or MAT, minimum undergraduate GPA of 3.0, 2 letters of recommendation. Additional exam requirements/recommendations for international students: Required—TOEFL (minimum score 85 iBT); Recommended—IELTS. *Application deadline:* For fall admission, 7/1 priority date for domestic and international students; for spring admission, 11/1 priority date for domestic and international students; for summer admission, 4/1 priority date for domestic and international students. Applications are processed on a rolling basis. Application fee: $75. Electronic applications accepted. *Expenses: Tuition:* Full-time $16,470; part-time $915 per credit. *Required fees:* $60 per semester. Part-time tuition and fees vary according to course load and program. *Financial support:* Teaching assistantships, career-related internships or fieldwork, Federal Work-Study, institutionally sponsored loans, scholarships/grants, and unspecified assistantships available. Financial award applicants required to submit FAFSA. *Faculty research:* Power of story for literacy development. *Unit head:* Courtney Kelly, Chairperson, Department of Literacy, 914-798-2745, E-mail: courtney.kelly@mville.edu. *Application contact:* Jeanine Pardey-Levine, Director of Graduate Enrollment Management, 914-323-3208, Fax: 914-694-1732, E-mail: edschool@mville.edu.
Website: http://www.mville.edu/programs/literacy-education

Manhattanville College, School of Education, Program in Middle Childhood/Adolescence Education (Grades 5-12), Purchase, NY 10577-2132. Offers biology

(MAT); biology and special education (MPS); chemistry (MAT); chemistry and special education (MPS); English (MAT); English and special education (MPS); literacy and special education (MPS); literacy specialist (MPS); math and special education (MPS); mathematics (MAT); physics (MAT); social studies (MAT); social studies and special education (MPS); special education generalist (MPS); teaching languages other than English (MAT), including French, Italian, Latin, Spanish. *Program availability:* Part-time, evening/weekend. *Students:* 28 applicants, 86% accepted, 21 enrolled. In 2016, 23 master's awarded. *Degree requirements:* For master's, comprehensive exam (for some programs), thesis (for some programs), student teaching, research seminars, portfolios, internships, writing assessment. *Entrance requirements:* For master's, GRE or MAT, minimum undergraduate GPA of 3.0, 2 letters of recommendation. Additional exam requirements/recommendations for international students: Required—TOEFL (minimum score 85 iBT); Recommended—IELTS. *Application deadline:* For fall admission, 7/1 priority date for domestic and international students; for spring admission, 11/1 priority date for domestic and international students; for summer admission, 4/1 priority date for domestic and international students. Applications are processed on a rolling basis. Application fee: $75. Electronic applications accepted. *Expenses: Tuition:* Full-time $16,470; part-time $915 per credit. *Required fees:* $60 per semester. Part-time tuition and fees vary according to course load and program. *Financial support:* Teaching assistantships, career-related internships or fieldwork, Federal Work-Study, institutionally sponsored loans, scholarships/grants, and unspecified assistantships available. Financial award applicants required to submit FAFSA. *Unit head:* Victoria Fantozzi, Chairperson, Department of Curriculum and Instruction, 914-323-7138, E-mail: victoria.fantozzi@mville.edu. *Application contact:* Jeanine Pardey-Levine, Director of Graduate Enrollment Management, 914-323-3208, Fax: 914-694-1732, E-mail: edschool@mville.edu.
Website: http://www.mville.edu/programs#/search/19

Marquette University, Graduate School, College of Education, Department of Educational Policy and Leadership, Milwaukee, WI 53201-1881. Offers college student personnel administration (M Ed); curriculum and instruction (MA); education (MA); educational administration (M Ed); educational policy and foundations (MA); elementary education (Certificate); literacy (MA); principal (Certificate); reading specialist (Certificate); reading teacher (Certificate); secondary education (Certificate); superintendent (Certificate). *Program availability:* Part-time, evening/weekend. *Faculty:* 17 full-time (14 women), 28 part-time/adjunct (23 women). *Students:* 31 full-time (23 women), 103 part-time (66 women); includes 22 minority (7 Black or African American, non-Hispanic/Latino; 1 American Indian or Alaska Native, non-Hispanic/Latino; 6 Asian, non-Hispanic/Latino; 6 Hispanic/Latino; 2 Two or more races, non-Hispanic/Latino). Average age 31. 96 applicants, 92% accepted, 67 enrolled. In 2016, 47 master's, 3 other advanced degrees awarded. Terminal master's awarded for partial completion of doctoral program. *Degree requirements:* For master's, comprehensive exam, thesis (for some programs); for doctorate, thesis/dissertation, qualifying exam. *Entrance requirements:* For master's, GRE General Test or MAT, official transcripts from all current and previous colleges/universities except Marquette, three letters of recommendation, statement of purpose; for doctorate, GRE General Test, MAT, sample of written work, official transcripts from all current and previous colleges/universities except Marquette, three letters of recommendation, statement of purpose, resume/ curriculum vitae; for Certificate, GRE General Test or MAT, master's degree. Additional exam requirements/recommendations for international students: Required—TOEFL (minimum score 530 paper-based). *Application deadline:* For fall admission, 1/15 for domestic and international students. Application fee: $50. *Expenses:* Contact institution. *Financial support:* Fellowships, research assistantships, health care benefits, tuition waivers (partial), and unspecified assistantships available. Support available to part-time students. Financial award application deadline: 2/15. *Faculty research:* Leadership; social justice in education; development of lifelong learners; race, class, and schooling in historical perspective; urban teacher education. *Unit head:* Dr. Ellen Eckman, Chair, 414-288-1561. *Application contact:* Dr. Cynthia Ellwood.

Marshall University, Academic Affairs Division, College of Education and Professional Development, Program in Literacy Education, Huntington, WV 25755. Offers MA, Ed S. *Accreditation:* NCATE. *Program availability:* Part-time, evening/weekend. *Degree requirements:* For master's, thesis optional, comprehensive or oral assessment, final project; for Ed S, thesis optional, research project. *Entrance requirements:* For master's, GRE General Test or MAT; for Ed S, master's degree in reading, minimum GPA of 3.0.

Marygrove College, Graduate Division, Program in Reading and Literacy, Detroit, MI 48221-2599. Offers M Ed. *Accreditation:* TEAC. *Program availability:* Part-time, evening/ weekend. *Degree requirements:* For master's, practicum, research project. *Entrance requirements:* For master's, MAT, interview, minimum undergraduate GPA of 3.0, teaching certificate.

Maryville University of Saint Louis, School of Education, St. Louis, MO 63141-7299. Offers early childhood education (MA Ed); educational leadership (Ed D); educational leadership: principal certification (MA Ed); elementary education (MA Ed); gifted education (MA Ed); higher education leadership (Ed D); literacy specialist (MA Ed); middle grades education (MA Ed); secondary teaching and inquiry (MA Ed); teacher as leader (MA Ed); teacher leadership (Ed D). *Accreditation:* NCATE. *Program availability:* Part-time, evening/weekend. *Faculty:* 17 full-time (11 women), 21 part-time/adjunct (17 women). *Students:* 12 full-time (11 women), 297 part-time (208 women); includes 92 minority (79 Black or African American, non-Hispanic/Latino; 4 Asian, non-Hispanic/ Latino; 4 Hispanic/Latino; 5 Two or more races, non-Hispanic/Latino), 4 international. Average age 38. In 2016, 32 master's, 61 doctorates awarded. *Degree requirements:* For master's, thesis, project. *Entrance requirements:* For master's, minimum cumulative GPA of 3.0, 3 professional recommendations, essays, interview with program faculty; for doctorate, minimum GPA of 3.0, 3 professional recommendations, essay, interview, on-site writing sample. Additional exam requirements/recommendations for international students: Required—TOEFL (minimum score 550 paper-based). *Application deadline:* Applications are processed on a rolling basis. Electronic applications accepted. *Expenses:* $879 per credit (for Ed D); $781 per credit (for master's). *Financial support:* Career-related internships or fieldwork, Federal Work-Study, tuition waivers (partial), and professional educator discounts available. Financial award application deadline: 3/ 1; financial award applicants required to submit FAFSA. *Faculty research:* Collaboration with public schools, pre-service program development, mathematics, diversity, literacy. *Unit head:* Dr. Cathy Bear, Dean, 314-529-9692, Fax: 314-529-9921, E-mail: cbear@ maryville.edu. *Application contact:* Stacey Ruffin, Coordinator of Clinical Experiences and Graduate Programs, 314-529-9542, Fax: 314-529-9921, E-mail: teachered@ maryville.edu.
Website: http://www.maryville.edu/ed/graduate-programs/

Marywood University, Academic Affairs, Reap College of Education and Human Development, Department of Education, Program in Reading Education, Scranton, PA 18509-1598. Offers MS. *Accreditation:* NCATE. *Program availability:* Part-time. Electronic applications accepted.

Massachusetts College of Liberal Arts, Graduate Programs, North Adams, MA 01247-4100. Offers business (MBA); educational administration (M Ed); educational leadership (CAGS); instruction and curriculum (M Ed); instructional technology (M Ed); physical education and health (M Ed); reading (M Ed); special education (M Ed). *Program availability:* Part-time, evening/weekend. *Degree requirements:* For master's, thesis. *Entrance requirements:* For master's, writing sample.

McDaniel College, Graduate and Professional Studies, Program for Reading Specialists: Literacy Leadership, Westminster, MD 21157-4390. Offers MS. *Accreditation:* NCATE. *Program availability:* Part-time-only, evening/weekend. *Faculty:* 2 full-time (both women), 3 part-time/adjunct (all women). *Students:* 26 part-time (all women); includes 1 minority (Black or African American, non-Hispanic/Latino). Average age 30. 3 applicants, 100% accepted. In 2016, 11 master's awarded. *Degree requirements:* For master's, comprehensive exam, thesis optional. *Entrance requirements:* For master's, PRAXIS I, 3 references, teaching certificate. Additional exam requirements/recommendations for international students: Required—TOEFL (minimum score 79 iBT), IELTS (minimum score 6). *Application deadline:* For fall admission, 6/1 priority date for domestic students; for spring admission, 11/1 priority date for domestic students; for summer admission, 3/1 priority date for domestic students. Applications are processed on a rolling basis. Application fee: $75. Electronic applications accepted. *Expenses: Tuition:* Full-time $8370; part-time $465 per credit. *Required fees:* $75 per semester. Tuition and fees vary according to course load, program and reciprocity agreements. *Financial support:* Application deadline: 3/1; applicants required to submit FAFSA. *Unit head:* Fax: 410-857-2515, E-mail: gradadms@mcdaniel.edu. *Application contact:* Penny Pfeiffer, Senior Graduate Enrollment Management Specialist, 410-857-2513, Fax: 410-857-2515, E-mail: ppfeiffer@mcdaniel.edu.

McKendree University, Graduate Programs, Programs in Education, Lebanon, IL 62254-1299. Offers curriculum design and instruction (Ed D, Ed S); educational administration and leadership (MA Ed); educational studies (MA Ed); higher education administrative services (MA Ed); music education (MA Ed); reading (MA Ed); special education (MA Ed); teacher leadership (MA Ed); teaching certification (MA Ed). *Accreditation:* NCATE. *Program availability:* Part-time, evening/weekend, online learning. *Entrance requirements:* For master's, official transcripts from all institutions previously attended, minimum GPA of 3.0, resume, references; for doctorate, GRE (within the past 5 years), master's degree in education and Ed S, or the equivalent, from regionally-accredited institution; official transcripts from all institutions previously attended; curriculum vitae/resume; essay/personal statement; two years of teaching/ professional experience; for Ed S, GRE (within the past 5 years), master's degree in education from regionally-accredited institution of higher education; official transcripts from all institutions previously attended; curriculum vitae/resume; essay/personal statement; two years of teaching/professional experience. Additional exam requirements/recommendations for international students: Required—TOEFL. Electronic applications accepted.

McNeese State University, Doré School of Graduate Studies, Burton College of Education, Office of Graduate Education Programs, Program in Curriculum and Instruction, Lake Charles, LA 70609. Offers early childhood education (M Ed); elementary education (M Ed); reading (M Ed); secondary education (M Ed). *Program availability:* Evening/weekend. *Entrance requirements:* For master's, GRE, teaching certificate.

McNeese State University, Doré School of Graduate Studies, Burton College of Education, Office of Student Teaching and Professional Education Services, Program in Reading Specialist, Lake Charles, LA 70609. Offers Graduate Certificate. *Entrance requirements:* For degree, bachelor's degree, teaching certificate.

Medaille College, Program in Education, Buffalo, NY 14214-2695. Offers adolescent education (MS Ed); curriculum and instruction (MS Ed); education preparation (MS Ed); literacy (MS Ed); special education (MS). *Accreditation:* TEAC. *Program availability:* Part-time, evening/weekend. *Degree requirements:* For master's, comprehensive exam (for some programs), thesis or alternative. *Entrance requirements:* For master's, minimum undergraduate GPA of 2.7. Additional exam requirements/recommendations for international students: Required—TOEFL (minimum score 550 paper-based). Electronic applications accepted. *Faculty research:* Curriculum planning, truancy, tracking minority students, curriculum design, mentoring students.

Mercer University, Graduate Studies, Cecil B. Day Campus, Tift College of Education (Atlanta), Macon, GA 31207. Offers curriculum and instruction (PhD); early childhood education (M Ed, MAT, Ed S); educational leadership (PhD), including higher education leadership, P-12 school leadership; educational leadership P-12 (M Ed, Ed S); higher education leadership (M Ed); independent and charter school leadership (M Ed); middle grades education (M Ed, MAT); reading specialist (M Ed); secondary education (M Ed, MAT); teacher leadership (Ed S). *Accreditation:* NCATE. *Program availability:* Part-time, evening/weekend. *Faculty:* 28 full-time (15 women), 30 part-time/adjunct (27 women). *Students:* 177 full-time (150 women), 324 part-time (264 women); includes 288 minority (256 Black or African American, non-Hispanic/Latino; 1 American Indian or Alaska Native, non-Hispanic/Latino; 7 Asian, non-Hispanic/Latino; 17 Hispanic/Latino; 1 Native Hawaiian or other Pacific Islander, non-Hispanic/Latino; 6 Two or more races, non-Hispanic/Latino), 1 international. Average age 35. In 2016, 173 master's, 34 doctorates, 54 other advanced degrees awarded. *Degree requirements:* For master's and Ed S, research project; for doctorate, comprehensive exam, thesis/dissertation. *Entrance requirements:* For master's, GRE or MAT, minimum undergraduate GPA of 2.75; for doctorate, GRE; for Ed S, GRE or MAT, minimum GPA of 3.25; 3 years of certified teaching experience (for educational leadership and teacher leadership). Additional exam requirements/recommendations for international students: Required—TOEFL (minimum score 80 iBT). *Application deadline:* For fall admission, 8/1 for domestic and international students; for spring admission, 12/1 for domestic and international students; for summer admission, 5/1 for domestic and international students. Applications are processed on a rolling basis. Application fee: $25 ($50 for international students). Electronic applications accepted. *Expenses:* $590 per credit, $1,770 per course (for M Ed); $595 per credit, $1,785 per course (for MAT); $615 per credit, $1,845 per course (for Ed S); $717 per credit, $2,151 per course (for PhD); $150 per semester technology fee. *Financial support:* Federal Work-Study and unspecified assistantships available. Support available to part-time students. Financial award application deadline: 5/1; financial award applicants required to submit FAFSA. *Faculty research:* Educational technology, multicultural and minority issues in education, educational leadership (P-12 and higher education), school discipline and school bullying, standards-based mathematics education. *Unit head:* Dr. James Barta, Dean, 478-301-5355, Fax: 478-301-2280, E-mail: barta_jj@mercer.edu. *Application contact:* Renee Slaton, Associate Director of Graduate Admissions, 678-547-6084, Fax: 678-547-6055, E-mail: mercereducation@mercer.edu.
Website: http://education.mercer.edu/

Mercy College, School of Education, Program in Teaching Literacy, Dobbs Ferry, NY 10522-1189. Offers teaching literacy (Advanced Certificate); teaching literacy, birth-6 (MS); teaching literacy, grades 5-12 (MS). *Program availability:* Part-time, evening/ weekend, blended/hybrid learning. *Students:* 7 full-time (6 women), 92 part-time (82 women); includes 51 minority (12 Black or African American, non-Hispanic/Latino; 3 Asian, non-Hispanic/Latino; 35 Hispanic/Latino; 1 Two or more races, non-Hispanic/ Latino). Average age 32. 28 applicants, 43% accepted, 8 enrolled. In 2016, 25 master's awarded. *Degree requirements:* For master's, comprehensive exam (for some programs), thesis (for some programs). *Entrance requirements:* For master's, GRE,

resume, undergraduate transcript. Additional exam requirements/recommendations for international students: Required—TOEFL (minimum score 600 paper-based; 100 iBT), IELTS (minimum score 8). *Application deadline:* For fall admission, 8/1 for international students. Applications are processed on a rolling basis. Application fee: $40. Electronic applications accepted. *Expenses: Tuition:* Full-time $15,156; part-time $842 per credit hour. *Required fees:* $620; $155 per term. Tuition and fees vary according to course load and program. *Financial support:* Career-related internships or fieldwork, Federal Work-Study, scholarships/grants, and unspecified assistantships available. Support available to part-time students. Financial award applicants required to submit FAFSA. *Unit head:* Dr. Rose Rudnitski, Dean for the School of Education, 914-674-7447, Fax: 914-674-7352, E-mail: rrudnitski@mercy.edu. *Application contact:* Allison Gurdineer, Senior Director of Admissions, 877-637-2946, Fax: 914-674-7382, E-mail: admissions@mercy.edu.
Website: https://www.mercy.edu/education/literacy-and-multilingual-studies

Meredith College, School of Education, Health and Human Sciences, Raleigh, NC 27607-5298. Offers academically and intellectually gifted (M Ed); curriculum instruction specialist (M Ed); elementary education (M Ed, MAT); English as a second language (M Ed, MAT); health and physical education (MAT); nutrition, health and human performance (MS, Postbaccalaureate Certificate), including dietetic internship (Postbaccalaureate Certificate), nutrition (MS); reading (M Ed); special education (MAT). *Accreditation:* NCATE. *Program availability:* Part-time, evening/weekend. *Degree requirements:* For master's, thesis optional. *Entrance requirements:* For master's, GRE General Test or MAT, minimum GPA of 2.5, teaching license, recommendations. Additional exam requirements/recommendations for international students: Required—TOEFL. Electronic applications accepted. *Expenses:* Contact institution.

MGH Institute of Health Professions, School of Health and Rehabilitation Sciences, Department of Communication Sciences and Disorders, Boston, MA 02129. Offers reading (Certificate); speech-language pathology (MS). *Accreditation:* ASHA (one or more programs are accredited). *Program availability:* Part-time. *Degree requirements:* For master's, thesis or alternative, research proposal. *Entrance requirements:* For master's, GRE General Test, bachelor's degree from regionally-accredited college or university. Additional exam requirements/recommendations for international students: Required—TOEFL (minimum score 550 paper-based; 80 iBT). Electronic applications accepted. *Faculty research:* Children's language disorders, reading, speech disorders, voice disorders, augmentative communication, autism.

Michigan State University, The Graduate School, College of Education, Program in Literacy Instruction, East Lansing, MI 48824. Offers MA. *Accreditation:* TEAC. *Program availability:* Part-time. *Degree requirements:* For master's, comprehensive exam (for some programs), final exam or portfolio. *Entrance requirements:* Additional exam requirements/recommendations for international students: Required—TOEFL, Michigan State University ELT (minimum score 85), Michigan English Language Assessment Battery (minimum score 83). Electronic applications accepted.

MidAmerica Nazarene University, Professional and Graduate Studies in Education, Olathe, KS 66062-1899. Offers ESOL (M Ed); reading specialist (M Ed); technology enhanced teaching (M Ed). *Accreditation:* NCATE. *Program availability:* Part-time, evening/weekend, online only, 100% online. *Faculty:* 5 full-time (3 women), 12 part-time/adjunct (7 women). *Students:* 22 full-time (16 women), 43 part-time (38 women); includes 6 minority (3 Black or African American, non-Hispanic/Latino; 1 Asian, non-Hispanic/Latino; 2 Two or more races, non-Hispanic/Latino). Average age 32. 18 applicants, 22% accepted, 2 enrolled. In 2016, 41 master's awarded. *Entrance requirements:* For master's, bachelor's degree from an accredited college or university, minimum undergraduate GPA of 3.0, valid teaching license. Additional exam requirements/recommendations for international students: Required—TOEFL (minimum score 81 iBT), IELTS (minimum score 6). *Application deadline:* For fall admission, 8/6 for domestic students; for spring admission, 12/15 for domestic students; for summer admission, 5/7 for domestic students. Applications are processed on a rolling basis. Electronic applications accepted. *Expenses:* Contact institution. *Financial support:* Scholarships/grants available. Financial award applicants required to submit FAFSA. *Unit head:* Dr. Ramona Stowe, Chair, 913-971-3524, Fax: 913-971-3407, E-mail: rsstowe@mnu.edu. *Application contact:* Glenna Murray, Administrative Assistant, 913-971-3292, Fax: 913-971-3002, E-mail: gkmurray@mnu.edu.
Website: http://www.mnu.edu/education.html

Middle Tennessee State University, College of Graduate Studies, College of Education, Department of Elementary and Special Education, Major in Reading, Murfreesboro, TN 37132. Offers M Ed. *Accreditation:* NCATE. *Program availability:* Part-time, evening/weekend, online learning. *Degree requirements:* For master's, comprehensive exam. *Entrance requirements:* For master's, GRE, MAT or PRAXIS. Additional exam requirements/recommendations for international students: Required—TOEFL (minimum score 525 paper-based; 71 iBT) or IELTS (minimum score 6). Electronic applications accepted.

Middle Tennessee State University, College of Graduate Studies, College of Education, PhD in Literacy Studies Program, Murfreesboro, TN 37132. Offers PhD. *Program availability:* Part-time, evening/weekend, online learning. *Degree requirements:* For doctorate, comprehensive exam, thesis/dissertation. *Entrance requirements:* For doctorate, GRE. Additional exam requirements/recommendations for international students: Required—TOEFL (minimum score 525 paper-based; 71 iBT) or IELTS (minimum score 6).

Middle Tennessee State University, College of Graduate Studies, University College, Murfreesboro, TN 37132. Offers advanced studies in teaching and learning (M Ed); human resources leadership (MPS); nursing administration (MSN); nursing education (MSN); strategic leadership (MPS); training and development (MPS). *Program availability:* Part-time, evening/weekend, online learning. *Entrance requirements:* Additional exam requirements/recommendations for international students: Required—TOEFL (minimum score 525 paper-based; 71 iBT) or IELTS (minimum score 6).

Midwestern State University, Billie Doris McAda Graduate School, West College of Education, Program in Reading, Wichita Falls, TX 76308. Offers M Ed. *Program availability:* Part-time, evening/weekend. *Degree requirements:* For master's, comprehensive exam. *Entrance requirements:* For master's, GRE General Test, MAT or GMAT. Additional exam requirements/recommendations for international students: Required—TOEFL (minimum score 550 paper-based). Electronic applications accepted. *Faculty research:* Collective learning, school culture, early literacy development, family literacy, brain-based learning.

Millersville University of Pennsylvania, College of Graduate Studies and Adult Learning, College of Education and Human Services, Department of Early, Middle, and Exceptional Education, Program in Language and Literacy: Reading Specialist, Millersville, PA 17551-0302. Offers M Ed. *Accreditation:* NCATE. *Program availability:* Part-time, evening/weekend. *Faculty:* 14 full-time (9 women). *Students:* 58 part-time (55 women); includes 1 minority (Asian, non-Hispanic/Latino). Average age 29. 18 applicants, 100% accepted, 10 enrolled. In 2016, 26 master's awarded. *Degree requirements:* For master's, thesis optional. *Entrance requirements:* For master's, GRE or MAT if undergraduate cumulative GPA is lower than 3.0, teaching certificate. Additional exam requirements/recommendations for international students: Required—TOEFL (minimum score 600 paper-based), IELTS (minimum score 6). *Application deadline:* Applications are processed on a rolling basis. Application fee: $40. Electronic applications accepted. *Expenses:* $483 per credit resident tuition; $725 per credit non-resident tuition. *Financial support:* In 2016–17, 2 students received support. Unspecified assistantships available. Financial award application deadline: 3/15; financial award applicants required to submit FAFSA. *Faculty research:* Digital literacy, comprehension, diagnosis and remediation, content area reading, total participation techniques. *Unit head:* Dr. Judith K. Wenrich, Coordinator, 717-871-7348, E-mail: judith.wenrich@millersville.edu. *Application contact:* Dr. Victor S. DeSantis, Dean of College of Graduate Studies and Adult Learning/Associate Provost for Civic and Community Engagement, 717-871-7619, Fax: 717-871-7954, E-mail: victor.desantis@millersville.edu.
Website: http://www.millersville.edu/academics/educ/eled/graduate-programs/language-and-literacy.php

Misericordia University, College of Health Sciences and Education, Program in Education, Dallas, PA 18612-1098. Offers instructional technology (MS); reading specialist (MS); special education (MS). *Program availability:* Part-time, evening/weekend. *Entrance requirements:* For master's, minimum undergraduate GPA of 3.0. Additional exam requirements/recommendations for international students: Required—TOEFL. Electronic applications accepted.

Mississippi State University, College of Education, Department of Curriculum, Instruction and Special Education, Mississippi State, MS 39762. Offers early childhood education (PhD); elementary education (MS, PhD, Ed S), including early childhood education (MS), general elementary education (MS), middle level education (MS); general curriculum and instruction (PhD); middle level (MAT); reading education (PhD); secondary education (MAT, MS, PhD, Ed S); special education (MAT, MS, PhD, Ed S). *Accreditation:* NCATE. *Program availability:* Part-time, evening/weekend. *Faculty:* 21 full-time (16 women), 1 (woman) part-time/adjunct. *Students:* 39 full-time (26 women), 168 part-time (128 women); includes 49 minority (43 Black or African American, non-Hispanic/Latino; 2 American Indian or Alaska Native, non Hispanic/Latino; 1 Hispanic/Latino; 1 Native Hawaiian or other Pacific Islander, non-Hispanic/Latino; 2 Two or more races, non-Hispanic/Latino), 4 international. Average age 33. 98 applicants, 56% accepted, 47 enrolled. In 2016, 69 master's, 6 doctorates, 10 other advanced degrees awarded. *Degree requirements:* For master's, comprehensive exam; for doctorate, thesis/dissertation; for Ed S, comprehensive exam, thesis or alternative. *Entrance requirements:* For master's, GRE, minimum GPA of 2.75 in junior and senior year, eligibility for initial teacher certification; for doctorate, GRE, minimum GPA of 3.4 on previous graduate work; for Ed S, GRE, minimum GPA of 3.2 on master's degree. Additional exam requirements/recommendations for international students: Required—TOEFL (minimum score 550 paper-based; 79 iBT); Recommended—IELTS (minimum score 6.5). *Application deadline:* For fall admission, 3/1 priority date for domestic students, 5/1 for international students; for spring admission, 9/1 priority date for domestic students, 9/1 for international students. Applications are processed on a rolling basis. Application fee: $60. Electronic applications accepted. *Expenses:* Tuition, state resident: full-time $7670; part-time $852.50 per credit hour. Tuition, nonresident: full-time $20,790; part-time $2310.50 per credit hour. Part-time tuition and fees vary according to course load. *Financial support:* In 2016–17, 8 research assistantships with partial tuition reimbursements (averaging $11,381 per year) were awarded; Federal Work-Study, institutionally sponsored loans, scholarships/grants, and unspecified assistantships also available. Financial award application deadline: 4/1; financial award applicants required to submit FAFSA. *Faculty research:* Early childhood education, reading, rural schools, multicultural education, use of technology in instruction. *Unit head:* Dr. Janice Nicholson, Interim Department Head, 662-325-3704, Fax: 662-325-7857, E-mail: jin4@msstate.edu. *Application contact:* Linda Bonner, Senior Admissions Assistant, 662-325-3363, E-mail: lbonner@grad.msstate.edu.
Website: http://www.cise.msstate.edu/

Mississippi University for Women, Graduate School, College of Education and Human Sciences, Columbus, MS 39701-9998. Offers differentiated instruction (M Ed); educational leadership (M Ed); gifted studies (M Ed); reading/literacy (M Ed); teaching (MAT). *Accreditation:* ASHA; NCATE. *Program availability:* Part-time. *Degree requirements:* For master's, comprehensive exam, thesis optional. *Entrance requirements:* For master's, GRE General Test or NTE (M Ed in gifted education or MS in speech/language pathology), MAT (M Ed in instructional management), minimum QPA of 3.0.

Missouri State University, Graduate College, College of Education, Department of Reading, Foundations, and Technology, Program in Literacy, Springfield, MO 65897. Offers MS Ed. *Program availability:* Part-time, 100% online, blended/hybrid learning. *Students:* 7 full-time (all women), 75 part-time (72 women); includes 3 minority (all Hispanic/Latino). Average age 32. 25 applicants, 92% accepted, 13 enrolled. In 2016, 18 master's awarded. *Degree requirements:* For master's, comprehensive exam, thesis or alternative. *Entrance requirements:* For master's, GRE or minimum GPA of 3.0, teaching certificate. Additional exam requirements/recommendations for international students: Required—TOEFL (minimum score 550 paper-based; 79 iBT), IELTS (minimum score 6). *Application deadline:* For fall admission, 7/20 priority date for domestic students, 5/1 for international students; for spring admission, 12/20 priority date for domestic students, 9/1 for international students; for summer admission, 5/20 priority date for domestic students. Applications are processed on a rolling basis. Application fee: $35 ($50 for international students). Electronic applications accepted. *Expenses:* Tuition, state resident: full-time $5830. Tuition, nonresident: full-time $10,708. *Required fees:* $1130. Tuition and fees vary according to class time, course level, course load and program. *Financial support:* Federal Work-Study, institutionally sponsored loans, scholarships/grants, and unspecified assistantships available. Financial award application deadline: 3/31; financial award applicants required to submit FAFSA. *Unit head:* Dr. Cathy Pearman, Department Head, 417-836-6769, E-mail: deannecamp@missouristate.edu. *Application contact:* Michael Edwards, Coordinator of Graduate Admissions, 417-836-5330, Fax: 417-836-6200, E-mail: michaeledwards@missouristate.edu.
Website: http://education.missouristate.edu/rft/

Monmouth University, Graduate Studies, School of Education, West Long Branch, NJ 07764-1898. Offers applied behavior analysis (Certificate); autism (Certificate); director of school counseling services (Post-Master's Certificate); early childhood (M Ed); educational leadership (Ed D); elementary education (MAT), including elementary level, secondary level; English as a second language (M Ed); learning disabilities teacher-consultant (Post-Master's Certificate); literacy (MS Ed); school counseling (MS Ed); special education (MS Ed), including autism, learning disabilities teacher-consultant, teacher of students with disabilities, teaching in inclusive settings; speech-language pathology (MS Ed); student affairs and college counseling (MS Ed); supervisor (Post-Master's Certificate); teaching English to speakers of other languages (Certificate). *Accreditation:* NCATE. *Program availability:* Part-time, evening/weekend, 100% online, blended/hybrid learning. *Faculty:* 23 full-time (19 women), 33 part-time/adjunct (25 women). *Students:* 191 full-time (172 women), 141 part-time (122 women); includes 56 minority (10 Black or African American, non-Hispanic/Latino; 9 Asian, non-Hispanic/Latino; 31 Hispanic/Latino; 6 Two or more races, non-Hispanic/Latino). Average age 26.

423 applicants, 53% accepted, 139 enrolled. In 2016, 148 master's, 4 other advanced degrees awarded. *Entrance requirements:* For master's, GRE taken within last 5 years (for MS Ed in speech-language pathology); SAT (minimum combined score of 1660 in 3 sections), ACT (23), GRE (minimum score of 4.0 on analytical writing section and minimum combined score of 310 on quantitative and verbal sections), or passing scores on 3 parts of Core Academic Skills Educators, minimum GPA of 3.0 in major; 2 letters of recommendation (for some programs); resume, personal statement or essay (depending on program). Additional exam requirements/recommendations for international students: Required—TOEFL (minimum score 550 paper-based; 79 iBT), IELTS (minimum score 6), Michigan English Language Assessment Battery (minimum score 77) or Certificate of Advanced English (minimum score B2). *Application deadline:* For fall admission, 7/15 priority date for domestic students, 7/1 for international students; for spring admission, 12/1 priority date for domestic students, 11/1 for international students; for summer admission, 5/1 for domestic students. Applications are processed on a rolling basis. Application fee: $50. Electronic applications accepted. *Expenses: Tuition, area resident:* Full-time $19,764; part-time $1098 per credit hour. *Required fees:* $175 per semester. Tuition and fees vary according to program. *Financial support:* In 2016–17, 349 students received support, including 305 fellowships (averaging $3,558 per year), 48 teaching assistantships (averaging $9,619 per year); research assistantships, institutionally sponsored loans, scholarships/grants, and unspecified assistantships also available. Support available to part-time students. Financial award application deadline: 2/1; financial award applicants required to submit FAFSA. *Faculty research:* Multicultural literacy, science and mathematics teaching strategies, teacher as reflective practitioner, children with disabilities. *Unit head:* Dr. John E. Henning, Dean, 732-263-5513, Fax: 732-263-5277. *Application contact:* Laurie Kuhn, Associate Director of Graduate Admission, 732-571-3452, Fax: 732-263-5123, E-mail: gradadm@monmouth.edu.
Website: http://www.monmouth.edu/academics/schools/education/default.asp

Montana State University Billings, College of Education, Department of Educational Theory and Practice, Option in Reading, Billings, MT 59101. Offers M Ed. *Accreditation:* NCATE. *Program availability:* Part-time. *Faculty:* 2 full-time (both women). *Degree requirements:* For master's, thesis or professional paper and/or field experience. *Entrance requirements:* For master's, GRE General Test or MAT, minimum GPA of 3.0. Additional exam requirements/recommendations for international students: Required—TOEFL (minimum score 79 iBT), IELTS (minimum score 6.5). *Application deadline:* Applications are processed on a rolling basis. Application fee: $40. Electronic applications accepted. *Expenses:* Tuition, state resident: full-time $5265; part-time $3436 per year. Tuition, nonresident: full-time $14,030; part-time $9280 per year. *International tuition:* $19,295 full-time. Tuition and fees vary according to degree level, campus/location and program. *Financial support:* Teaching assistantships with partial tuition reimbursements, career-related internships or fieldwork, Federal Work-Study, institutionally sponsored loans, scholarships/grants, tuition waivers (partial), and unspecified assistantships available. Support available to part-time students. Financial award application deadline: 5/1; financial award applicants required to submit FAFSA. *Unit head:* Rachael Waller, Assistant Professor, 406-657-2167, E-mail: rachael.waller@msubillings.edu. *Application contact:* David M. Sullivan, Graduate Studies Counselor, 406-657-2053, Fax: 406-657-2299, E-mail: dsullivan@msubillings.edu.

Montclair State University, The Graduate School, College of Education and Human Services, Program in Reading, Montclair, NJ 07043-1624. Offers MA. *Program availability:* Part-time, evening/weekend. *Entrance requirements:* For master's, GRE General Test, interview, essay, 2 letters of recommendation. Additional exam requirements/recommendations for international students: Required—TOEFL (minimum score 83 iBT), IELTS (minimum score 6.5). Electronic applications accepted. *Expenses:* Tuition, state resident: part-time $553 per credit. Tuition, nonresident: part-time $854 per credit. *Required fees:* $91 per credit. Tuition and fees vary according to program.

Morehead State University, Graduate Programs, College of Education, Department of Curriculum and Instruction, Morehead, KY 40351. Offers curriculum and instruction (Ed S); elementary education (MA Ed), including elementary education, international education, middle school education, reading; secondary education (MA Ed); special education (MA Ed); teaching (MAT). *Program availability:* Part-time, evening/weekend. *Degree requirements:* For master's, comprehensive exam, thesis optional; for Ed S, thesis, oral exam. *Entrance requirements:* For master's, GRE General Test, minimum GPA of 2.75, teaching certificate; for Ed S, GRE General Test, interview, master's degree, minimum GPA of 3.5, work experience. Additional exam requirements/recommendations for international students: Required—TOEFL (minimum score 500 paper-based). Electronic applications accepted. *Faculty research:* Communicative competence of learning-disabled students, teaching social studies in elementary schools, ungraded primary school organization, study skills.

Morehead State University, Graduate Programs, College of Education, Department of Foundational and Graduate Studies in Education, Morehead, KY 40351. Offers adult and higher education (MA, Ed S); certified professional counselor (Ed S); counseling P-12 (MA); curriculum and instruction (Ed S); educational technology (MA Ed); instructional leadership (Ed S); school administration (MA); school counseling (Ed S); teacher leader business and marketing content (MA Ed); teacher leader business and marketing technology (MA Ed); teacher leader educational technology (MA Ed); teacher leader English (MA Ed); teacher leader gifted education (MA Ed); teacher leader IECE certification (MA Ed); teacher leader interdisciplinary education P-5 (MA Ed); teacher leader middle grades (MA Ed); teacher leader non IECE certification (MA Ed); teacher leader reading/writing - non-certification (MA Ed); teacher leader reading/writing certification (MA Ed); teacher leader school communication - certification (MA Ed); teacher leader school communication - non-certification (MA Ed); teacher leader social studies (MA Ed); teacher leader special education (MA Ed). *Accreditation:* NCATE. *Program availability:* Part-time, evening/weekend. *Degree requirements:* For master's, thesis optional, oral and/or written comprehensive exams; for Ed S, thesis, oral exam. *Entrance requirements:* For master's, GRE General Test, minimum overall undergraduate GPA of 2.5; for Ed S, GRE General Test, interview, master's degree, minimum GPA of 3.5, work experience. Additional exam requirements/recommendations for international students: Required—TOEFL (minimum score 500 paper-based). Electronic applications accepted. *Faculty research:* Character education, school accountability, computer applications for school administrators.

Mount Mercy University, Program in Education, Cedar Rapids, IA 52402-4797. Offers reading (MA Ed); special education (MA Ed); teacher leadership (MA Ed). *Entrance requirements:* For master's, minimum cumulative GPA of 3.0, 2 letters of recommendation, resume, valid teaching license. Additional exam requirements/recommendations for international students: Required—TOEFL (minimum score 570 paper-based; 88 iBT). Electronic applications accepted.

Mount St. Joseph University, Graduate Education Program, Cincinnati, OH 45233-1670. Offers adolescent to young adult education (MA); dyslexia (Certificate); inclusive early childhood education (MA); middle childhood education (MA); multicultural special education (MA); reading science (MA). *Accreditation:* TEAC. *Program availability:* Part-time, evening/weekend, online learning. *Faculty:* 7 full-time (5 women), 12 part-time/adjunct (10 women). *Students:* 44 full-time (33 women), 112 part-time (104 women); includes 16 minority (15 Black or African American, non-Hispanic/Latino; 1 Two or more races, non-Hispanic/Latino). Average age 34. In 2016, 60 master's awarded. *Degree requirements:* For master's, comprehensive exam, thesis, research project, student teaching, clinical and field-based experiences. *Entrance requirements:* For master's, GRE (if GPA is below 3.0), letter of intent, 2 referrals, background check, interview, resume, minimum undergraduate GPA of 3.0. Additional exam requirements/recommendations for international students: Required—TOEFL (minimum score 560 paper-based; 83 iBT). *Application deadline:* Applications are processed on a rolling basis. Application fee: $50. Electronic applications accepted. *Expenses:* $580 per credit hour. *Financial support:* Applicants required to submit FAFSA. *Faculty research:* Foreign and second language learning problems/reading disabilities, multicultural/bilingual special education, science education, pedagogical content knowledge, early childhood, response to intervention. *Unit head:* Dr. Laura Saylor, Dean, 513-244-3263, E-mail: laura.saylor@msj.edu. *Application contact:* Mary Brigham, Assistant Director of Graduate Recruitment, 513-244-4233, Fax: 513-244-4629, E-mail: mary.brigham@msj.edu.
Website: http://www.msj.edu/academics/graduate-programs/master-of-arts-initial-teacher-licensure-programs/

Mount Saint Mary College, Division of Education, Newburgh, NY 12550-3494. Offers adolescence and special education (MS Ed); childhood education (MS Ed); literacy education (MS Ed); middle school (7-9) (MS Ed). *Accreditation:* NCATE. *Program availability:* Part-time, evening/weekend. *Faculty:* 12 full-time (10 women), 3 part-time/adjunct (all women). *Students:* 27 full-time (19 women), 78 part-time (59 women); includes 12 minority (1 Black or African American, non-Hispanic/Latino; 1 Asian, non-Hispanic/Latino; 7 Hispanic/Latino; 3 Two or more races, non-Hispanic/Latino). Average age 28. 30 applicants, 100% accepted, 16 enrolled. In 2016, 62 master's awarded. *Entrance requirements:* Additional exam requirements/recommendations for international students: Required—TOEFL (minimum score 80 iBT). *Application deadline:* Applications are processed on a rolling basis. Application fee: $45. Electronic applications accepted. Application fee is waived when completed online. *Expenses: Tuition:* Full-time $13,914; part-time $773 per credit. *Required fees:* $82 per semester. *Financial support:* In 2016–17, 18 students received support. Unspecified assistantships available. Financial award application deadline: 4/15; financial award applicants required to submit FAFSA. *Faculty research:* Learning and teaching styles, computers in special education, language development. *Unit head:* Dr. Monica Merritt, Graduate Coordinator, 845-569-3430, Fax: 845-569-3535, E-mail: monica.merritt@msmc.edu. *Application contact:* Lisa Gallina, Director of Admissions for Graduate Programs and Adult Degree Completion, 845-569-3166, Fax: 845-569-3450, E-mail: lisa.gallina@msmc.edu.
Website: http://www.msmc.edu/Academics/Graduate_Programs/Master_of_Science_in_Education

Mount Saint Vincent University, Graduate Programs, Faculty of Education, Program in Literacy Education, Halifax, NS B3M 2J6, Canada. Offers M Ed, MA Ed, MA-R. *Program availability:* Part-time, evening/weekend, online learning. *Degree requirements:* For master's, thesis (for some programs). *Entrance requirements:* For master's, minimum B average, 1 year of teaching experience, bachelor's degree in related field. Electronic applications accepted. *Faculty research:* Writing processes and instruction, assessment and evaluation of literacy education, critical literacy, early literacy development, gender and literacy.

Murray State University, College of Education, Department of Early Childhood and Elementary Education, Programs in Elementary Education/Reading and Writing, Murray, KY 42071. Offers elementary education (MA Ed, Ed S); reading and writing (MA Ed). *Accreditation:* NCATE. *Program availability:* Part-time. *Degree requirements:* For master's, comprehensive exam, thesis optional; for Ed S, comprehensive exam. *Entrance requirements:* For master's, minimum GPA of 2.5 for conditional admittance, 3.0 for unconditional; for Ed S, GRE General Test or MAT. Additional exam requirements/recommendations for international students: Required—TOEFL.

National Louis University, National College of Education, Chicago, IL 60603. Offers administration and supervision (M Ed, Ed D, CAS, Ed S); curriculum and instruction (M Ed, MS Ed, CAS); early childhood administration (M Ed, CAS); early childhood education (M Ed, MAT, MS Ed, CAS); education (Ed D); educational psychology/human learning and development (M Ed, MS Ed, CAS, Ed S); elementary education (MAT); interdisciplinary curriculum and instruction (M Ed); mathematics education (M Ed, MS Ed, CAS); middle grades education (MAT); reading and language (M Ed, MS Ed, CAS); school psychology (M Ed, Ed S); science education (M Ed, MS Ed, CAS); secondary education (MAT); special education (M Ed, MAT, CAS); technology in education (M Ed, CAS). *Accreditation:* NCATE. *Program availability:* Part-time, evening/weekend. *Degree requirements:* For doctorate, comprehensive exam, thesis/dissertation. *Entrance requirements:* For master's, MAT or GRE, minimum GPA of 3.0; for doctorate, GRE General Test, minimum GPA of 3.25, interview, resume, writing sample, 4 recommendations. Additional exam requirements/recommendations for international students: Required—TOEFL (minimum score 550 paper-based; 79 iBT).

Nazareth College of Rochester, Graduate Studies, Department of Education, Program in Literacy Education, Rochester, NY 14618. Offers MS Ed. *Accreditation:* TEAC. *Program availability:* Part-time, evening/weekend. *Entrance requirements:* For master's, minimum GPA of 3.0. Additional exam requirements/recommendations for international students: Required—TOEFL or IELTS. *Application deadline:* For fall admission, 4/1 priority date for domestic students; for spring admission, 10/1 priority date for domestic students. Application fee: $40. *Expenses: Tuition:* Part-time $880 per credit hour. Part-time tuition and fees vary according to course load, degree level and program. *Financial support:* Unspecified assistantships available. Financial award application deadline: 3/1; financial award applicants required to submit FAFSA. *Unit head:* Dr. Naomi Erdmann, Director, 585-389-2614, E-mail: nerdman0@naz.edu. *Application contact:* Judith Baker, Director, Transfer and Graduate Admissions, 585-531-1154, Fax: 585-389-2826, E-mail: gradadmissions@naz.edu.

Newman University, Master of Science in Education Program, Wichita, KS 67213-2097. Offers building leadership (MS Ed); curriculum and instruction (MS Ed), including English as a second language, reading specialist; organizational leadership (MS Ed). *Accreditation:* NCATE. *Program availability:* Part-time, evening/weekend, online learning. *Degree requirements:* For master's, thesis optional. *Entrance requirements:* For master's, 3 years' full-time teaching experience, minimum GPA of 3.0, writing sample, 2 letters of recommendation, evidence of teaching certification. Additional exam requirements/recommendations for international students: Required—TOEFL (minimum score 600 paper-based; 100 iBT). Electronic applications accepted. *Expenses:* Contact institution. *Faculty research:* Online course design and deliver, staff engagement, classroom action.

New Mexico State University, College of Education, Department of Curriculum and Instruction, Las Cruces, NM 88003. Offers bilingual education (MA); curriculum and instruction (Ed D); early childhood education (MA); educational diagnostics (Ed S); language, literacy and culture (MA); learning design and technologies (MA); teaching (MAT), including Spanish; teaching English to speakers of other languages (MA). *Accreditation:* NCATE. *Program availability:* Part-time, evening/weekend, 100% online. *Faculty:* 23 full-time (17 women), 7 part-time/adjunct (5 women). *Students:* 114 full-time (81 women), 219 part-time (159 women); includes 190 minority (16 Black or African American, non-Hispanic/Latino; 2 American Indian or Alaska Native, non-Hispanic/

Latino; 5 Asian, non-Hispanic/Latino; 160 Hispanic/Latino; 7 Two or more races, non-Hispanic/Latino), 33 international. Average age 37. 126 applicants, 75% accepted, 65 enrolled. In 2016, 92 master's, 19 doctorates awarded. *Degree requirements:* For master's, comprehensive exam, thesis optional; for doctorate, comprehensive exam, thesis/dissertation. *Entrance requirements:* For master's, minimum cumulative GPA of 3.0; for doctorate, portfolio, minimum cumulative GPA of 3.0. Additional exam requirements/recommendations for international students: Required—TOEFL (minimum score 550 paper-based; 79 iBT), IELTS (minimum score 6.5). *Application deadline:* For fall admission, 12/15 priority date for domestic and international students; for spring admission, 11/1 for domestic students. Applications are processed on a rolling basis. Application fee: $40 ($50 for international students). Electronic applications accepted. *Expenses:* Tuition, state resident: full-time $4086. Tuition, nonresident: full-time $14,254. *Required fees:* $853. Tuition and fees vary according to course load. *Financial support:* In 2016–17, 102 students received support, including 2 fellowships (averaging $4,076 per year), 2 research assistantships (averaging $18,070 per year), 16 teaching assistantships (averaging $16,454 per year); career-related internships or fieldwork, Federal Work-Study, scholarships/grants, traineeships, health care benefits, and unspecified assistantships also available. Support available to part-time students. Financial award application deadline: 3/1. *Faculty research:* STEM education, bilingual and English as a second language education, critical pedagogy/multicultural education, learning design and technology, early childhood education. *Total annual research expenditures:* $29,926. *Unit head:* Dr. David Rutledge, Department Head, 575-646-5411, Fax: 575-646-5436, E-mail: rutledge@nmsu.edu. *Application contact:* Dr. David Rutledge, Associate Department Head for Graduate Programs, 575-646-5411, Fax: 575-646-5436, E-mail: rutledge@nmsu.edu.
Website: http://ci.education.nmsu.edu

New York University, Steinhardt School of Culture, Education, and Human Development, Department of Teaching and Learning, Program in Literacy Education, New York, NY 10012-1019. Offers MA. *Accreditation:* TEAC. *Program availability:* Part-time. *Degree requirements:* For master's, thesis (for some programs), fieldwork. *Entrance requirements:* For master's, teacher certification. Additional exam requirements/recommendations for international students: Required—TOEFL (minimum score 100 iBT). Electronic applications accepted. *Faculty research:* Early literacy intervention and development, psycho and sociolinguistics, multicultural education, literacy assessment and instruction.

Niagara University, Graduate Division of Education, Concentration in Literacy Instruction, Niagara University, NY 14109. Offers MS Ed. *Program availability:* Part-time. *Students:* 13 full-time (12 women), 24 part-time (all women); includes 1 minority (Hispanic/Latino), 1 international. Average age 24. In 2016, 19 master's awarded. *Entrance requirements:* For master's, GRE. Additional exam requirements/recommendations for international students: Required—TOEFL (minimum score 550 paper-based; 79 iBT), IELTS (minimum score 6). *Application deadline:* For fall admission, 8/1 for domestic students. Application fee: $30. *Expenses:* Contact institution. *Financial support:* Research assistantships with tuition reimbursements, teaching assistantships with tuition reimbursements, career-related internships or fieldwork, Federal Work-Study, scholarships/grants, and unspecified assistantships available. Financial award application deadline: 4/15. *Unit head:* Dr. Robin Erwin, Chair, 716-286-8551, E-mail: rerwin@niagara.edu. *Application contact:* Evan Pierce, Associate Director for Graduate Recruitment, 716-286-8769, Fax: 716-286-8170, E-mail: epierce@niagara.edu.
Website: http://www.niagara.edu/literacy-instruction

North Carolina Agricultural and Technical State University, School of Graduate Studies, School of Education, Department of Curriculum and Instruction, Program in Reading Education, Greensboro, NC 27411. Offers MA Ed. *Accreditation:* NCATE. *Program availability:* Part-time, evening/weekend. *Degree requirements:* For master's, comprehensive exam, comprehensive portfolio. *Entrance requirements:* For master's, GRE General Test, minimum GPA of 3.0.

Northeastern Illinois University, College of Graduate Studies and Research, College of Education, Program in Literacy Education, Chicago, IL 60625-4699. Offers MA. *Program availability:* Part-time, evening/weekend. *Degree requirements:* For master's, comprehensive exam, thesis optional. *Entrance requirements:* For master's, previous course work in psychology or tests and measurements, minimum GPA of 2.75. Additional exam requirements/recommendations for international students: Required—TOEFL (minimum score 550 paper-based; 79 iBT). Electronic applications accepted. *Faculty research:* Early literacy, reading disabilities, cognitive processes, multicultural and linguistic diversity, use of literature in the classroom.

Northeastern State University, College of Education, Department of Curriculum and Instruction, Program in Reading, Tahlequah, OK 74464-2399. Offers M Ed. *Program availability:* Part-time, evening/weekend. *Faculty:* 12 full-time (9 women). *Students:* 13 full-time (12 women), 68 part-time (67 women); includes 30 minority (14 American Indian or Alaska Native, non-Hispanic/Latino; 1 Asian, non-Hispanic/Latino; 1 Hispanic/Latino; 14 Two or more races, non-Hispanic/Latino), 1 international. Average age 36. In 2016, 34 master's awarded. *Degree requirements:* For master's, thesis. *Entrance requirements:* For master's, MAT or GRE, minimum GPA of 2.5. Additional exam requirements/recommendations for international students: Required—TOEFL. *Application deadline:* For fall admission, 6/1 priority date for domestic students. Applications are processed on a rolling basis. Application fee: $25. Electronic applications accepted. *Expenses:* Tuition, state resident: full-time $2816; part-time $216.60 per credit hour. Tuition, nonresident: full-time $6365, part-time $489.60 per credit hour. *Required fees:* $37.40 per credit hour. *Financial support:* Teaching assistantships and Federal Work-Study available. Financial award application deadline: 3/1. *Unit head:* Dr. Mindy Smith, Associate Professor, 918-449-6587, Fax: 918-458-2351, E-mail: smith071@nsuok.edu. *Application contact:* Josh McCollum, Graduate Coordinator, 918-444-2093, E-mail: mccolluj@nsuok.edu.
Website: https://academics.nsuok.edu/education/EducationHome/COEDepartments/CurriculumInstruction.aspx

Northern Illinois University, Graduate School, College of Education, Department of Literacy Education, De Kalb, IL 60115-2854. Offers curriculum and instruction (Ed D), including reading; literacy education (MS Ed). *Program availability:* Part-time, evening/weekend. *Faculty:* 12 full-time (10 women), 1 part-time/adjunct (0 women). *Students:* 11 full-time (9 women), 219 part-time (200 women); includes 43 minority (8 Black or African American, non-Hispanic/Latino; 3 Asian, non-Hispanic/Latino; 28 Hispanic/Latino; 4 Two or more races, non-Hispanic/Latino), 2 international. Average age 34. 85 applicants, 75% accepted, 35 enrolled. In 2016, 84 master's, 5 doctorates awarded. *Degree requirements:* For master's, comprehensive exam, thesis optional; for doctorate, thesis/dissertation, candidacy exam, dissertation defense. *Entrance requirements:* For master's, GRE General Test or MAT, minimum undergraduate GPA of 2.75; for doctorate, GRE General Test, minimum GPA of 2.75 (undergraduate), 3.2 (graduate). Additional exam requirements/recommendations for international students: Required—TOEFL (minimum score 550 paper-based). *Application deadline:* For fall admission, 3/1 priority date for domestic students, 5/1 for international students; for spring admission, 11/1 for domestic students, 10/1 for international students. Applications are processed on a rolling basis. Application fee: $40. Electronic applications accepted. *Financial support:* In 2016–17, 3 research assistantships with full tuition reimbursements, 12 teaching assistantships with full tuition reimbursements were awarded; fellowships with full tuition reimbursements, career-related internships or fieldwork, Federal Work-Study, scholarships/grants, tuition waivers (full), and staff assistantships also available. Support available to part-time students. Financial award applicants required to submit FAFSA. *Faculty research:* Early reading development, literacy for bilingual students, family literacy, expository writing, fluency. *Unit head:* Dr. Anne E. Gregory, Chair, 815-753-8556, E-mail: ltcy@niu.edu. *Application contact:* Graduate School Office, 815-753-0395, E-mail: gradsch@niu.edu.
Website: http://cedu.niu.edu/leed/programs/masters1.shtml

Northern Michigan University, Office of Graduate Education and Research, College of Health Sciences and Professional Studies, School of Education, Leadership and Public Service, Marquette, MI 49855-5301. Offers administration and supervision (MAE); elementary education (MAE); higher education in student affairs (MA); instruction (MAE); learning disabilities (MAE); public administration (MPA), including criminal justice administration, human resource administration, public administration, public management, state and local government; reading education (MAE), including reading, reading specialist; science education (MS); secondary education (MAE). *Accreditation:* TEAC. *Program availability:* Part-time, online learning. *Degree requirements:* For master's, thesis (for some programs). *Entrance requirements:* For master's, minimum GPA of 3.0. Additional exam requirements/recommendations for international students: Required—TOEFL (minimum score 550 paper-based; 79 iBT), IELTS (minimum score 6.5). Electronic applications accepted.

Northwestern Oklahoma State University, School of Professional Studies, Reading Specialist Program, Alva, OK 73717-2799. Offers M Ed. *Accreditation:* NCATE. *Program availability:* Part-time. *Degree requirements:* For master's, thesis optional, portfolio. *Entrance requirements:* For master's, GRE General Test or MAT, minimum GPA of 2.75.

Northwestern State University of Louisiana, Graduate Studies and Research, College of Education and Human Development, Programs in Educational Leadership and Instruction, Natchitoches, LA 71497. Offers counseling (Ed S); educational leadership (M Ed, Ed S); educational technology (Ed S); elementary teaching (Ed S); reading (Ed S); secondary teaching (Ed S); special education (Ed S). *Accreditation:* NASAD. *Degree requirements:* For master's, comprehensive exam, thesis (for some programs). *Entrance requirements:* For master's and Ed S, GRE General Test. Additional exam requirements/recommendations for international students: Required—TOEFL. Electronic applications accepted.

Northwest Missouri State University, Graduate School, School of Education, Maryville, MO 64468-6001. Offers early childhood education (MS Ed); education leadership (MS Ed), including elementary, K-12, secondary; educational leadership (Ed S), including elementary school principalship, secondary school principalship, superintendency; educational leadership and policy analysis (Ed D); elementary education (MS Ed); elementary mathematics (MS Ed); higher education leadership (MS); middle school education (MS Ed); reading (MS Ed); special education (MS Ed); teacher leadership (MS Ed); teaching English language learners (MS Ed). *Accreditation:* NCATE. *Program availability:* Part-time. *Students:* 15 full-time (11 women), 150 part-time (103 women). In 2016, 46 master's awarded. *Degree requirements:* For master's, comprehensive exam; for Ed S, comprehensive exam, thesis. *Entrance requirements:* For master's, GRE General Test, writing sample; for Ed S, minimum graduate GPA of 3.25. Additional exam requirements/recommendations for international students: Required—TOEFL (minimum score 550 paper-based). *Application deadline:* For fall admission, 7/1 for domestic and international students; for spring admission, 11/15 for domestic and international students. Applications are processed on a rolling basis. Application fee: $0 ($50 for international students). Electronic applications accepted. *Expenses:* Tuition, state resident: full-time $3447; part-time $383 per credit hour. Tuition, nonresident: full-time $5724; part-time $636 per credit hour. *Required fees:* $130 per credit hour. *Financial support:* Research assistantships with full tuition reimbursements, teaching assistantships with full tuition reimbursements, and unspecified assistantships available. Financial award application deadline: 4/1; financial award applicants required to submit FAFSA. *Faculty research:* Great books of educational administration. *Unit head:* Dr. Tim Wall, Dean, 660-562-1179, E-mail: timwall@nwmissouri.edu.
Website: http://www.nwmissouri.edu/academics/ed/

Notre Dame College, Graduate Programs, South Euclid, OH 44121-4293. Offers mild/moderate needs (M Ed); reading (M Ed); security policy studies (MA, Graduate Certificate); technology (M Ed). *Program availability:* Part-time, evening/weekend. *Degree requirements:* For master's, thesis. *Entrance requirements:* For master's, GRE General Test, MAT, minimum undergraduate GPA of 2.75, valid teaching certificate, bachelor's degree in an education-related field from accredited college or university, official transcripts of most recent college work. *Faculty research:* Cognitive psychology, teaching critical thinking in the classroom.

Oakland University, Graduate Study and Lifelong Learning, School of Education and Human Services, Department of Reading and Language Arts, Rochester, MI 48309-4401. Offers advanced microcomputer applications (Graduate Certificate); digital literacies and learning (Graduate Certificate); microcomputer applications (Graduate Certificate); reading and language arts (MAT); reading education (PhD); reading, language arts and literature (PMC). *Accreditation:* TEAC. *Degree requirements:* For doctorate, thesis/dissertation. *Entrance requirements:* For master's, minimum GPA of 3.0; for doctorate, MAT, minimum GPA of 3.0. Electronic applications accepted.

Ohio University, Graduate College, Gladys W. and David H. Patton College of Education and Human Services, Department of Teacher Education, Athens, OH 45701-2979. Offers adolescent to young adult education (M Ed); curriculum and instruction (M Ed, PhD); early childhood/special education (M Ed); intervention specialist/mild-moderate needs (M Ed); intervention specialist/moderate-intensive needs (M Ed); middle childhood education (M Ed); reading education (M Ed). *Program availability:* Part-time, evening/weekend. *Degree requirements:* For master's, thesis or alternative; for doctorate, comprehensive exam, thesis/dissertation. *Entrance requirements:* For master's, GRE General Test or MAT (if GPA is below 2.9); for doctorate, GRE General Test, minimum GPA of 3.4, work experience. Additional exam requirements/recommendations for international students: Required—TOEFL (minimum score 550 paper-based; 80 iBT) or IELTS (minimum score 6.5). *Application deadline:* For fall admission, 5/1 priority date for domestic students, 4/1 priority date for international students; for winter admission, 11/1 priority date for domestic students, 10/1 priority date for international students; for spring admission, 2/15 priority date for domestic students, 1/1 priority date for international students. Applications are processed on a rolling basis. Application fee: $50 ($55 for international students). Electronic applications accepted. *Financial support:* Research assistantships with full tuition reimbursements, teaching assistantships with full tuition reimbursements, Federal Work-Study, institutionally sponsored loans, tuition waivers (partial), and unspecified assistantships available. Financial award application deadline: 3/1. *Faculty research:* Cognition literacy, character education, teacher's education reform, disabilities. *Unit head:* Dr. John Henning, Chair, 740-597-1830, Fax: 740-593-0477, E-mail: henningj@ohio.edu. *Application contact:* Floyd J. Doney, Director of Student Affairs, 740-593-4400, Fax: 740-593-9310, E-mail:

doney@ohio.edu.
Website: http://www.cehs.ohio.edu/academics/te/index.htm

Old Dominion University, Darden College of Education, Program in Literacy Leadership, Norfolk, VA 23529. Offers PhD. *Program availability:* Part-time, evening/weekend. *Faculty:* 6 full-time (4 women). *Students:* 1 (woman) full-time, 4 part-time (all women); includes 1 minority (Black or African American, non-Hispanic/Latino). Average age 37. 2 applicants, 100% accepted, 2 enrolled. In 2016, 1 doctorate awarded. *Degree requirements:* For doctorate, comprehensive exam, thesis/dissertation. *Entrance requirements:* For doctorate, GRE, minimum GPA of 3.0, MS in reading or related degree, letters of recommendation. Additional exam requirements/recommendations for international students: Required—TOEFL (minimum score 600 paper-based). *Application deadline:* For fall admission, 6/1 for domestic students, 4/15 for international students; for winter admission, 11/1 for domestic students, 10/1 for international students; for spring admission, 11/1 for domestic students, 10/1 for international students; for summer admission, 2/1 for domestic and international students. Applications are processed on a rolling basis. Application fee: $50. Electronic applications accepted. *Expenses:* Tuition, state resident: full-time $8604; part-time $478 per credit hour. Tuition, nonresident: full-time $21,510; part-time $1195 per credit hour. *Required fees:* $66 per semester. Tuition and fees vary according to campus/location, program and reciprocity agreements. *Financial support:* In 2016–17, 1 teaching assistantship with full tuition reimbursement (averaging $20,000 per year) was awarded. Financial award applicants required to submit FAFSA. *Faculty research:* Literacy for students with special needs, children's reading first instruction, reading in the content area. *Unit head:* Dr. Sue Kimmel, Graduate Program Director, 757-683-3284, E-mail: skimmel@odu.edu. *Application contact:* William Heffelfinger, Director of Graduate Admissions, 757-683-5554, Fax: 757-683-3255, E-mail: gradadmit@odu.edu.
Website: http://education.odu.edu/eci/litphd/

Old Dominion University, Darden College of Education, Program in Reading Education, Norfolk, VA 23529. Offers reading specialist (MS Ed). *Accreditation:* NCATE. *Program availability:* Part-time, evening/weekend, 100% online, blended/hybrid learning. *Faculty:* 7 full-time (6 women), 12 part-time/adjunct (11 women). *Students:* 2 full-time (both women), 34 part-time (33 women); includes 8 minority (7 Black or African American, non-Hispanic/Latino; 1 Asian, non-Hispanic/Latino). Average age 36. 33 applicants, 55% accepted, 18 enrolled. In 2016, 12 master's awarded. *Degree requirements:* For master's, thesis optional. *Entrance requirements:* For master's, minimum GPA of 3.0 in major, 2.8 overall; 5-year teaching certificate; official transcripts; 2 letters of reference; essay. Additional exam requirements/recommendations for international students: Required—TOEFL. *Application deadline:* For fall admission, 6/1 for domestic students, 4/15 for international students; for spring admission, 11/1 for domestic students, 10/1 for international students; for summer admission, 3/1 for domestic students. Applications are processed on a rolling basis. Application fee: $50. Electronic applications accepted. *Expenses:* Tuition, state resident: full-time $8604; part-time $478 per credit hour. Tuition, nonresident: full-time $21,510; part-time $1195 per credit hour. *Required fees:* $66 per semester. Tuition and fees vary according to campus/location, program and reciprocity agreements. *Financial support:* In 2016–17, 7 students received support. Unspecified assistantships available. Financial award application deadline: 2/15; financial award applicants required to submit FAFSA. *Faculty research:* Metacognition and reading, strategies for improving comprehension in reading science, reading in content areas, vocabulary instruction for adolescents, literacy with special needs children, Reading First instruction, reading in the content area, vocabulary, diversity and literacy. *Total annual research expenditures:* $150,000. *Unit head:* Dr. Tami Al-Hazza, Graduate Program Director, 757-683-3228, Fax: 757-683-5862, E-mail: reading@odu.edu.
Website: https://www.odu.edu/teaching/academics/reading/masters

Olivet Nazarene University, Graduate School, Division of Education, Program in Reading Specialist, Bourbonnais, IL 60914. Offers MAE.

Pace University, School of Education, New York, NY 10038. Offers adolescent education (MST), including biology, business education, chemistry, earth science, English, foreign languages, mathematics, physics, social studies, visual arts; childhood education (MST); early childhood development, learning and intervention (MST); educational technology studies (MS); inclusive adolescent education (MST), including biology, business education, chemistry, earth science, English, foreign languages, mathematics, physics, social studies, visual arts; integrated instruction for educational technology (Certificate); integrated instruction for literacy and technology (Certificate); literacy (MS Ed); special education (MS Ed). *Accreditation:* NCATE. *Program availability:* Part-time, evening/weekend, blended/hybrid learning. *Faculty:* 19 full-time (13 women), 86 part-time/adjunct (49 women). *Students:* 115 full-time (97 women), 543 part-time (381 women); includes 280 minority (137 Black or African American, non-Hispanic/Latino; 1 American Indian or Alaska Native, non-Hispanic/Latino; 40 Asian, non-Hispanic/Latino; 87 Hispanic/Latino; 15 Two or more races, non-Hispanic/Latino), 13 international. Average age 30. 181 applicants, 78% accepted, 72 enrolled. In 2016, 193 master's, 9 other advanced degrees awarded. *Degree requirements:* For master's, certification exams. *Entrance requirements:* For master's, GRE, interview, teaching certificate (except for MST). Additional exam requirements/recommendations for international students: Required—TOEFL (minimum score 88 iBT), IELTS or PTE. *Application deadline:* For fall admission, 8/1 priority date for domestic students, 6/1 for international students; for spring admission, 12/1 priority date for domestic students, 10/1 for international students. Applications are processed on a rolling basis. Application fee: $70. Electronic applications accepted. *Expenses:* Contact institution. *Financial support:* In 2016–17, 17 students received support, including 17 research assistantships with partial tuition reimbursements available (averaging $6,020 per year); career-related internships or fieldwork and Federal Work-Study also available. Financial award application deadline: 9/1; financial award applicants required to submit FAFSA. *Faculty research:* STEM education, TESOL, teacher education, special education, language and literary development. *Total annual research expenditures:* $290,153. *Unit head:* Dr. Xiao-Lei Wang, Dean, School of Education, 914-773-3876, E-mail: xwang@pace.edu. *Application contact:* Susan Ford-Goldschein, Director of Graduate Admissions, 212-346-1531, Fax: 212-346-1585, E-mail: graduateadmission@pace.edu.
Website: http://www.pace.edu/school-of-education

Park University, School of Graduate and Professional Studies, Kansas City, MO 54105. Offers adult education (M Ed); business and government leadership (Graduate Certificate); business, government, and global society (MPA); communication and leadership (MA); creative and life writing (Graduate Certificate); disaster and emergency management (MPA, Graduate Certificate); educational leadership (M Ed); finance (MBA, Graduate Certificate); general business (MBA); global business (Graduate Certificate); healthcare administration (MHA); healthcare services management and leadership (Graduate Certificate); international business (MBA); language and literacy (M Ed), including English for speakers of other languages, special reading teacher/literacy coach; leadership of international healthcare organizations (Graduate Certificate); management information systems (MBA, Graduate Certificate); music performance (ADP, Graduate Certificate), including cello (MM, ADP), piano (MM, ADP), viola (MM, ADP), violin (MM, ADP); nonprofit and community services management (MPA); nonprofit leadership (Graduate Certificate); performance (MM), including cello (MM, ADP), piano (MM, ADP), viola (MM, ADP), violin (MM, ADP); public management (MPA); social work (MSW); teacher leadership (M Ed), including curriculum and assessment, instructional leader. *Program availability:* Part-time, evening/weekend, online learning. *Degree requirements:* For master's, comprehensive exam (for some programs), thesis (for some programs), internship (for some programs); exam (for some programs). *Entrance requirements:* For master's, GRE or GMAT (for some programs), teacher certification (for some M Ed programs), letters of recommendation, essay, resume (for some programs). Additional exam requirements/recommendations for international students: Required—TOEFL (minimum score 550 paper-based; 79 iBT), IELTS (minimum score 6). Electronic applications accepted.

Penn State Harrisburg, Graduate School, School of Behavioral Sciences and Education, Middletown, PA 17057. Offers adult education in the health and medical professions (Certificate); applied behavior analysis (MA); applied clinical psychology (MA); applied psychological research (MA); community psychology and social change (MA); English as a second language (ESL) program specialist and leadership (Certificate); folklore and ethnography (Certificate); health education (M Ed); lifelong learning and adult education (M Ed, D Ed); literacy education (M Ed); literacy leadership (Certificate); psychology: applications in clinical psychology (Certificate); psychology: health psychology (Certificate); teaching and curriculum (M Ed); training and development (M Ed, Certificate). *Program availability:* Part-time, evening/weekend. *Unit head:* Dr. Mukund S. Kulkarni, Chancellor, 717-948-6105, Fax: 717-948-6452. *Application contact:* Robert W. Coffman, Jr., Director of Enrollment Management, Recruitment and Admissions, 717-948-6250, Fax: 717-948-6325, E-mail: hbgadmit@psu.edu.
Website: https://harrisburg.psu.edu/behavioral-sciences-and-education/

Plymouth State University, College of Graduate Studies, Graduate Studies in Education, Program in Reading and Writing, Plymouth, NH 03264-1595. Offers M Ed. *Program availability:* Part-time, evening/weekend. *Degree requirements:* For master's, PRAXIS. *Entrance requirements:* For master's, GRE General Test or MAT, minimum GPA of 3.0.

Providence College, Program in Literacy, Providence, RI 02918. Offers M Ed. *Program availability:* Part-time, evening/weekend. *Faculty:* 6 full-time (4 women), 33 part-time/adjunct (21 women). *Students:* 7 full-time (all women), 27 part-time (26 women). Average age 29. 16 applicants, 88% accepted, 11 enrolled. In 2016, 10 master's awarded. *Degree requirements:* For master's, portfolio. *Entrance requirements:* Additional exam requirements/recommendations for international students: Required—TOEFL (minimum score 577 paper-based; 90 iBT). *Application deadline:* For fall admission, 7/15 priority date for domestic and international students; for spring admission, 11/15 priority date for domestic and international students; for summer admission, 3/15 priority date for domestic students, 3/15 for international students. Application fee: $55. *Expenses: Tuition:* Part-time $1260 per course. One-time fee: $265. Tuition and fees vary according to course load and program. *Financial support:* Career-related internships or fieldwork, institutionally sponsored loans, and unspecified assistantships available. Support available to part-time students. Financial award application deadline: 8/1; financial award applicants required to submit FAFSA.
Website: http://www.providence.edu/professional-studies/graduate-degrees/Pages/master-education-literacy.aspx

Purdue University, Graduate School, College of Education, Department of Curriculum and Instruction, West Lafayette, IN 47907. Offers agricultural and extension education (MS, MS Ed, PhD, Ed S); art education (PhD); career and technical education (MS Ed, PhD, Ed S); curriculum studies (MS Ed, PhD, Ed S); educational technology (MS Ed, PhD, Ed S); elementary education (MS Ed); family and consumer sciences education (MS Ed, PhD, Ed S); foreign language education (MS Ed, PhD, Ed S); industrial technology (PhD, Ed S); language arts (MS Ed, PhD, Ed S); literacy (MS Ed, PhD, Ed S); mathematics education (MS, MS Ed, PhD, Ed S); science education (MS, MS Ed, PhD, Ed S); social studies education (MS Ed, PhD, Ed S). *Accreditation:* NCATE. *Program availability:* Part-time, evening/weekend. *Faculty:* 37 full-time (27 women), 1 (woman) part-time/adjunct. *Students:* 78 full-time (50 women), 286 part-time (195 women); includes 68 minority (25 Black or African American, non-Hispanic/Latino; 3 American Indian or Alaska Native, non-Hispanic/Latino; 10 Asian, non-Hispanic/Latino; 22 Hispanic/Latino; 1 Native Hawaiian or other Pacific Islander, non-Hispanic/Latino; 7 Two or more races, non-Hispanic/Latino), 44 international. Average age 36. 150 applicants, 79% accepted, 73 enrolled. In 2016, 107 master's, 20 doctorates, 2 other advanced degrees awarded. *Degree requirements:* For master's, thesis optional; for doctorate, thesis/dissertation, oral and written exams; for Ed S, oral presentation, project. *Entrance requirements:* For master's, GRE General Test (if undergraduate GPA is below 3.0), minimum undergraduate GPA of 3.0 or equivalent; for doctorate, GRE General Test (minimum combined verbal and quantitative score of 1000, 300 for new scoring), minimum undergraduate GPA of 3.0 or equivalent; master's degree with minimum GPA of 3.0 or equivalent; for Ed S, GRE General Test (minimum combined verbal and quantitative score of 1000, 300 for new scoring), minimum undergraduate GPA of 3.0 or equivalent; master's degree. Additional exam requirements/recommendations for international students: Required—TOEFL (minimum score 550 paper-based; 77 iBT). *Application deadline:* For fall admission, 12/15 for domestic students, 3/1 for international students; for spring admission, 9/15 for domestic students, 8/1 for international students. Application fee: $60 ($75 for international students). Electronic applications accepted. *Financial support:* Fellowships with full tuition reimbursements, research assistantships with full tuition reimbursements, teaching assistantships with full tuition reimbursements, career-related internships or fieldwork, and tuition waivers (full) available. Support available to part-time students. Financial award application deadline: 3/1; financial award applicants required to submit FAFSA. *Faculty research:* Literacy acquisition and development, teacher beliefs and knowledge, recruitment and retention of underrepresented students, economic education, literacy discourse. *Unit head:* Janet M. Alsup, Head, 765-494-9667, E-mail: alsupj@purdue.edu. *Application contact:* Heather Brinkman, Graduate Contact, 765-494-2345, E-mail: hbrinkma@purdue.edu.
Website: http://www.edci.purdue.edu/

Queens College of the City University of New York, Division of Education, Department of Elementary and Early Childhood Education, Queens, NY 11367-1597. Offers bilingual education (MS Ed); child development psychology (AC); childhood education (MAT, MS Ed); childhood education and special education (MAT); childhood education-bilingual education (MAT, MS Ed, AC); children's literacy (AC); early childhood education (MAT); early childhood education birth-2 (MS Ed, AC); elementary education (MS Ed); literacy birth-grade 6 (AC); literacy technology birth-grade 6 (MS Ed); social studies education grades 1-6 (AC). *Program availability:* Part-time, evening/weekend. *Faculty:* 25 full-time (19 women), 33 part-time/adjunct (28 women). *Students:* 134 full-time (119 women), 374 part-time (349 women); includes 251 minority (55 Black or African American, non-Hispanic/Latino; 1 American Indian or Alaska Native, non-Hispanic/Latino; 82 Asian, non-Hispanic/Latino; 103 Hispanic/Latino; 10 Two or more races, non-Hispanic/Latino), 12 international. Average age 29. 364 applicants, 72% accepted, 224 enrolled. In 2016, 184 master's, 62 other advanced degrees awarded. *Degree requirements:* For master's, research project. *Entrance requirements:* For master's, minimum GPA of 3.0. Additional exam requirements/recommendations for international students: Required—TOEFL, IELTS. *Application deadline:* For fall admission, 4/1 for domestic students. Applications are processed on a rolling basis. Application fee: $125. Electronic applications accepted. *Expenses:* Tuition, state resident: full-time $5065; part-time $425 per credit. Tuition, nonresident: part-time $780 per credit. *Required fees:* $522; $397 per credit. Part-time tuition and fees vary according to course load and program. *Financial support:* Career-related internships or fieldwork available. Financial award application deadline: 4/1; financial award applicants required to submit FAFSA. *Unit head:* Dr. Mary Bushnell Greiner, Chairperson, 718-997-5328, E-mail: mary.greiner@qc.cuny.edu.

Queens College of the City University of New York, Division of Education, Department of Secondary Education and Youth Services, Queens, NY 11367-1597. Offers adolescent biology (MAT); art (MS Ed); biology (MS Ed, AC); chemistry (MS Ed, AC); earth sciences (MS Ed, AC); English (MS Ed, AC); French (MS Ed); Italian (MS Ed, AC); literacy education (MS Ed); mathematics (MS Ed, AC); music (MS Ed, AC); physics (MS Ed, AC); social studies (MS Ed, AC); Spanish (MS Ed, AC). *Program availability:* Part-time, evening/weekend. *Faculty:* 22 full-time (14 women), 40 part-time/adjunct (26 women). *Students:* 31 full-time (21 women), 356 part-time (211 women); includes 164 minority (22 Black or African American, non-Hispanic/Latino; 54 Asian, non-Hispanic/Latino; 81 Hispanic/Latino; 7 Two or more races, non-Hispanic/Latino), 11 international. Average age 29. 236 applicants, 88% accepted, 121 enrolled. In 2016, 119 master's, 51 other advanced degrees awarded. *Degree requirements:* For master's, research project. *Entrance requirements:* For master's, minimum GPA of 3.0. Additional exam requirements/recommendations for international students: Required—TOEFL, IELTS. *Application deadline:* For fall admission, 4/1 for domestic students; for spring admission, 11/1 for domestic students. Applications are processed on a rolling basis. Application fee: $125. Electronic applications accepted. *Expenses:* Tuition, state resident: full-time $5065; part-time $425 per credit. Tuition, nonresident: part-time $780 per credit. *Required fees:* $522; $397 per credit. Part-time tuition and fees vary according to course load and program. *Financial support:* Career-related internships or fieldwork available. Financial award application deadline: 4/1; financial award applicants required to submit FAFSA. *Unit head:* Dr. Eleanor Armour-Thomas, Chairperson, 718-997-5150, E-mail: armourthomas@yahoo.com.

Queens University of Charlotte, Wayland H. Cato, Jr. School of Education, Charlotte, NC 28274-0002. Offers educational leadership (MA); K-6 (MAT); literacy K-12 (M Ed). *Accreditation:* NCATE. *Program availability:* Part-time, evening/weekend, online learning. *Degree requirements:* For master's, comprehensive exam. *Entrance requirements:* For master's, GRE General Test. *Expenses:* Contact institution.

Quincy University, Master of Science in Education Programs, Quincy, IL 62301-2699. Offers curriculum and instruction (MS Ed), including bilingual/English as a second language; leadership (MS Ed); reading education (MS Ed); special education (MS Ed); teacher leader (MS Ed). *Program availability:* Part-time, evening/weekend, online learning. *Degree requirements:* For master's, comprehensive exam (for some programs), thesis optional. *Entrance requirements:* For master's, MAT or GRE. Additional exam requirements/recommendations for international students: Required—TOEFL (minimum score 550 paper-based; 79 iBT). Electronic applications accepted. Application fee is waived when completed online.

Radford University, College of Graduate Studies and Research, Program in Literacy Education, Radford, VA 24142. Offers MS. *Accreditation:* NCATE. *Program availability:* Part-time, evening/weekend. *Students:* 10 part-time (9 women). Average age 34. 5 applicants, 100% accepted, 4 enrolled. In 2016, 4 master's awarded. *Degree requirements:* For master's, comprehensive exam. *Entrance requirements:* For master's, minimum GPA of 2.75; copy of teaching license; 2 letters of reference; personal essay; resume; official transcripts. Additional exam requirements/recommendations for international students: Required—TOEFL (minimum score 550 paper-based; 79 iBT), IELTS (minimum score 6.5). *Application deadline:* For fall admission, 2/15 priority date for domestic students, 12/1 for international students; for spring admission, 7/1 for international students. Applications are processed on a rolling basis. Application fee: $50. Electronic applications accepted. *Expenses:* Tuition, state resident: full-time $7868; part-time $328 per credit hour. Tuition, nonresident: full-time $16,394; part-time $683 per credit hour. *Required fees:* $3090; $130 per credit hour. Tuition and fees vary according to course load and program. *Financial support:* In 2016–17, 1 student received support. Career-related internships or fieldwork, scholarships/grants, and unspecified assistantships available. Support available to part-time students. Financial award application deadline: 3/1; financial award applicants required to submit FAFSA. *Unit head:* Dr. Jennifer Jones-Powell, Interim Director, 540-831-5302, E-mail: stel@radford.edu.
Website: http://www.radford.edu/content/cehd/home/teacher-ed/programs/master-literacy.html

Regent University, Graduate School, School of Education, Virginia Beach, VA 23464-9800. Offers adult education (Ed D, PhD, Ed S); advanced educational leadership (Ed D, PhD, Ed S); career switcher (M Ed); character education (Ed D, PhD, Ed S); Christian education leadership (Ed D, PhD, Ed S); Christian school administration (M Ed); curriculum and instruction (M Ed), including adult education, Christian school, gifted and talented education, STEM education, teacher leader; educational leadership (M Ed); educational psychology (Ed D, PhD, Ed S); educational technology and online learning (Ed D, PhD, Ed S); elementary education (M Ed); exceptional education executive leadership (Ed D, PhD, Ed S); higher education (Ed D, PhD, Ed S); higher education leadership and management (Ed D, PhD, Ed S); individualized degree plan (M Ed); K-12 school leadership (Ed D, PhD, Ed S); K-12 special education (M Ed); K-8 leadership in mathematics education (M Ed); leadership in mathematics education (Ed S); reading specialist (M Ed); special education (Ed D, PhD, Ed S); student affairs (M Ed); TESOL (M Ed), including adult education - collegiate, K-12. *Accreditation:* TEAC. *Program availability:* Part-time, evening/weekend, 100% online, blended/hybrid learning. *Faculty:* 22 full-time (10 women), 42 part-time/adjunct (31 women). *Students:* 89 full-time (62 women), 1,035 part-time (823 women); includes 466 minority (381 Black or African American, non-Hispanic/Latino; 3 American Indian or Alaska Native, non-Hispanic/Latino; 19 Asian, non-Hispanic/Latino; 50 Hispanic/Latino; 13 Two or more races, non-Hispanic/Latino), 11 international. Average age 39. 976 applicants, 59% accepted, 449 enrolled. In 2016, 241 master's, 22 doctorates, 4 other advanced degrees awarded. *Degree requirements:* For master's, thesis or alternative; for doctorate, comprehensive exam, thesis/dissertation. *Entrance requirements:* For master's, Virginia Communication and Literacy Assessment (VCLA), PRAXIS, college transcripts, writing sample, interview; for doctorate, GRE, writing sample, resume, transcripts, interview. Additional exam requirements/recommendations for international students: Required—TOEFL (minimum score 577 paper-based). *Application deadline:* For fall admission, 4/1 priority date for domestic students; for spring admission, 10/15 priority date for domestic students. Applications are processed on a rolling basis. Application fee: $50. Electronic applications accepted. *Expenses:* Contact institution. *Financial support:* In 2016–17, 622 students received support, including 1 fellowship (averaging $5,000 per year); career-related internships or fieldwork, scholarships/grants, and unspecified assistantships also available. Support available to part-time students. *Faculty research:* Christian school administration, curriculum and instruction, educational technology and online learning, higher education, special education. *Unit head:* Dr. Donald Finn, Dean, 757-352-4278, Fax: 757-352-4318, E-mail: dfinn@regent.edu. *Application contact:* Heidi Cece, Assistant Vice President of Enrollment Management, 800-373-5504, Fax: 757-352-4381, E-mail: admissions@regent.edu.
Website: http://www.regent.edu/soe/

Regis College, Department of Education, Weston, MA 02493. Offers elementary teacher (MAT); higher education leadership (Ed D); reading (MAT); special education (MAT). *Program availability:* Part-time, evening/weekend, blended/hybrid learning. *Degree requirements:* For master's, thesis. *Entrance requirements:* For master's, GRE or MAT. Additional exam requirements/recommendations for international students: Required—TOEFL; Recommended—IELTS. *Application deadline:* Applications are processed on a rolling basis. Application fee: $50. Electronic applications accepted. *Financial support:* Federal Work-Study, scholarships/grants, and unspecified assistantships available. Financial award applicants required to submit FAFSA. *Unit head:* Dr. Priscilla Boerger, Department Chair/Graduate Program Director, 781-768-7422, E-mail: priscilla.boerger@regiscollege.edu.

Regis University, College of Contemporary Liberal Studies, Denver, CO 80221-1099. Offers creative writing (MFA); criminology (M Sc); curriculum, instruction and assessment (M Ed); education - teacher leadership (M Ed); educational leadership (M Ed); elementary education (M Ed); literacy (Certificate); reading (M Ed); secondary education (M Ed); special education (M Ed); teacher academic leadership (Certificate); teacher leadership (MA); teacher/educational leadership (M Ed); teaching the linguistically diverse (M Ed). *Program availability:* Part-time, evening/weekend, 100% online, blended/hybrid learning. *Faculty:* 18 full-time (12 women), 42 part-time/adjunct (26 women). *Students:* 302 full-time (234 women), 270 part-time (218 women); includes 148 minority (33 Black or African American, non-Hispanic/Latino; 3 American Indian or Alaska Native, non-Hispanic/Latino; 13 Asian, non-Hispanic/Latino; 83 Hispanic/Latino; 16 Two or more races, non-Hispanic/Latino), 3 international. Average age 36. 431 applicants, 90% accepted, 110 enrolled. In 2016, 308 master's awarded. *Degree requirements:* For master's, thesis (for some programs). *Entrance requirements:* For master's, official transcript reflecting baccalaureate degree awarded from regionally-accredited college or university, work experience, resume, letters of recommendation. Additional exam requirements/recommendations for international students: Required—TOEFL (minimum score 550 paper-based; 82 iBT). *Application deadline:* For fall admission, 8/15 priority date for domestic students, 7/13 for international students; for winter admission, 10/10 priority date for domestic students, 9/8 for international students; for spring admission, 1/10 priority date for domestic students, 11/17 for international students; for summer admission, 5/1 priority date for domestic students. Applications are processed on a rolling basis. Application fee: $75. Electronic applications accepted. *Expenses:* $485 per credit hour. *Financial support:* Scholarships/grants available. Financial award application deadline: 4/15; financial award applicants required to submit FAFSA. *Unit head:* Dr. Elisa Robyn, Academic Dean. *Application contact:* Cate Clark, Director of Admissions, 303-458-4900, Fax: 303-964-5534, E-mail: ruadmissions@regis.edu.
Website: http://www.regis.edu/CCLS.aspx

Rhode Island College, School of Graduate Studies, Feinstein School of Education and Human Development, Department of Elementary Education, Providence, RI 02908-1991. Offers early childhood education (M Ed); elementary education (M Ed, MAT); reading (M Ed). *Accreditation:* NCATE. *Program availability:* Part-time, evening/weekend. *Faculty:* 11 full-time (9 women), 1 (woman) part-time/adjunct. *Students:* 14 full-time (all women), 24 part-time (22 women); includes 3 minority (all Hispanic/Latino). Average age 32. In 2016, 16 master's awarded. *Degree requirements:* For master's, comprehensive exam (for some programs), comprehensive assessment. *Entrance requirements:* For master's, GRE General Test or MAT, PRAXIS II (elementary content knowledge), undergraduate transcripts; minimum undergraduate GPA of 3.0; 3 letters of recommendation. Additional exam requirements/recommendations for international students: Recommended—TOEFL (minimum score 550 paper-based; 79 iBT). *Application deadline:* For fall admission, 3/1 for domestic students; for spring admission, 11/1 for domestic students. Applications are processed on a rolling basis. Application fee: $50. Electronic applications accepted. *Expenses:* Tuition, state resident: full-time $8928; part-time $372 per credit. Tuition, nonresident: full-time $17,376; part-time $724 per credit. *Required fees:* $604; $22 per credit. One-time fee: $74. *Financial support:* Teaching assistantships with full tuition reimbursements, Federal Work-Study, scholarships/grants, and health care benefits available. Support available to part-time students. Financial award application deadline: 5/15; financial award applicants required to submit FAFSA. *Unit head:* Dr. Patricia Cordeiro, Chair, 401-456-8016. *Application contact:* Graduate Studies, 401-456-8700.
Website: http://www.ric.edu/elementaryEducation/

Rider University, Department of Graduate Education, Leadership and Counseling, Program in Reading/Language Arts, Lawrenceville, NJ 08648-3001. Offers reading specialist (Certificate); reading/language arts (MA). *Accreditation:* NCATE. *Program availability:* Part-time, evening/weekend. *Degree requirements:* For master's, comprehensive exam, research project. *Entrance requirements:* For master's, interview, resume. Additional exam requirements/recommendations for international students: Required—TOEFL (minimum score 550 paper-based). Electronic applications accepted. *Faculty research:* Ethnography in the reading/language arts process.

Rivier University, School of Graduate Studies, Department of Education, Nashua, NH 03060. Offers curriculum and instruction (M Ed); early childhood education (M Ed); educational administration (M Ed); educational studies (M Ed); elementary education (M Ed), elementary education and general special education (M Ed); emotional and behavioral disorders (M Ed); general social education (M Ed); leadership and learning (Ed D, CAGS); learning disabilities (M Ed); learning disabilities and reading (M Ed); mental health counseling (MA); reading (M Ed); school counseling (M Ed). *Program availability:* Part-time, evening/weekend. *Degree requirements:* For master's, comprehensive exam (for some programs), internships. *Entrance requirements:* For master's, GRE General Test or MAT.

Robert Morris University, School of Education and Social Sciences, Moon Township, PA 15108-1189. Offers business education (MS); counseling psychology (MS); education (Postbaccalaureate Certificate); higher education (MS); instructional leadership (MS), including education; instructional management and leadership (PhD); literacy (MS); special education (MS). *Accreditation:* TEAC. *Program availability:* Part-time, evening/weekend, online learning. *Faculty:* 17 full-time (9 women), 4 part-time/adjunct (3 women). *Students:* 154 part-time (104 women); includes 18 minority (11 Black or African American, non-Hispanic/Latino; 2 Hispanic/Latino; 5 Two or more races, non-Hispanic/Latino), 1 international. Average age 26. 69 applicants, 26% accepted, 18 enrolled. In 2016, 40 master's, 15 doctorates awarded. *Degree requirements:* For doctorate, thesis/dissertation. *Entrance requirements:* Additional exam requirements/recommendations for international students: Required—TOEFL (minimum score 550 paper-based; 79 iBT). *Application deadline:* For fall admission, 7/1 priority date for domestic and international students; for spring admission, 11/1 priority date for domestic and international students. Applications are processed on a rolling basis. Application fee: $35. Electronic applications accepted. *Expenses:* $840 per credit (for master's degree). *Unit head:* Dr. Mary Ann Rafoth, Dean, 412-397-6020, Fax: 412-397-6044,

E-mail: rafoth@rmu.edu.
Website: http://www.rmu.edu/web/cms/schools/sess/

Roberts Wesleyan College, Graduate Teacher Education Programs, Rochester, NY 14624-1997. Offers adolescence and special education (M Ed); childhood and special education (M Ed); literacy education (M Ed); special education (M Ed). *Program availability:* Part-time, evening/weekend. *Degree requirements:* For master's, thesis. Electronic applications accepted.

Rockford University, Graduate Studies, Department of Education, Program in Reading, Rockford, IL 61108-2393. Offers MAT. *Program availability:* Part-time, evening/weekend. *Degree requirements:* For master's, thesis optional. *Entrance requirements:* For master's, GRE General Test, 3 letters of recommendation. Additional exam requirements/recommendations for international students: Required—TOEFL (minimum score 550 paper-based; 79 iBT). *Application deadline:* Applications are processed on a rolling basis. Application fee: $50. Electronic applications accepted. *Expenses: Tuition:* Part-time $710 per credit. *Required fees:* $50 per semester. *Financial support:* Scholarships/grants and unspecified assistantships available. Support available to part-time students. Financial award application deadline: 3/1; financial award applicants required to submit FAFSA. *Application contact:* Michele Mehren, Assistant Director, Office of Graduate Studies, 815-226-4040, Fax: 815-394-3706, E-mail: mmehren@rockford.edu.
Website: https://www.rockford.edu/admission/graduate/mat/

Roger Williams University, School of Education, Bristol, RI 02809. Offers literacy education (MA). *Program availability:* Part-time, evening/weekend. *Faculty:* 1 (woman) full-time, 2 part-time/adjunct (1 woman). *Students:* 7 full-time (all women), 10 part-time (all women); includes 1 minority (Hispanic/Latino). Average age 34. 4 applicants, 100% accepted, 2 enrolled. In 2016, 3 master's awarded. *Entrance requirements:* For master's, resume, 2 letters of recommendation, college transcript, letter of intent, verification of active teaching license. Additional exam requirements/recommendations for international students: Required—TOEFL (minimum score 85 iBT), IELTS (minimum score 6.5). *Application deadline:* Applications are processed on a rolling basis. Application fee: $50. Electronic applications accepted. Application fee is waived when completed online. *Expenses:* $552 per credit hour. *Financial support:* Application deadline: 4/1; applicants required to submit FAFSA. *Unit head:* Robert McKenna, Interim Dean of School of Education, 401-254-3715, Fax: 401-254-3710, E-mail: rmckenna@rwu.edu. *Application contact:* Marcus Hanscom, Director of Graduate Admissions, 401-254-3345, Fax: 401-254-3557, E-mail: gradadmit@rwu.edu.
Website: http://www.rwu.edu/academics/schools/sed/

Roosevelt University, Graduate Division, College of Education, Program in Reading, Chicago, IL 60605. Offers reading teacher education (MA). *Students:* 22 part-time (18 women); includes 7 minority (2 Black or African American, non-Hispanic/Latino; 2 Asian, non-Hispanic/Latino; 3 Hispanic/Latino), 2 international. Average age 30. 16 applicants, 100% accepted, 6 enrolled. In 2016, 6 master's awarded. *Expenses: Tuition, area resident:* Full-time $19,566; part-time $880 per credit hour. *Required fees:* $175 per semester. One-time fee: $200. Part-time tuition and fees vary according to course load, degree level and program. *Unit head:* Margaret Policastro, Director, 312-281-3199. *Application contact:* Angela Ryan, Director of Graduate Enrollment, 312-341-2420, Fax: 312-281-3356, E-mail: aryan@roosevelt.edu.
Website: https://www.roosevelt.edu/academics/programs/masters-in-reading-ma

Rowan University, Graduate School, College of Education, Department of Language, Literacy, and Sociocultural Education, Program in Reading Education, Glassboro, NJ 08028-1701. Offers MA, CGS. Electronic applications accepted.

Rutgers University–New Brunswick, Graduate School of Education, Department of Learning and Teaching, Program in Literacy Education, Piscataway, NJ 08854-8097. Offers Ed M, Ed D. *Program availability:* Part-time. Terminal master's awarded for partial completion of doctoral program. *Degree requirements:* For master's, comprehensive exam; for doctorate, thesis/dissertation, qualifying exam. *Entrance requirements:* For master's, GRE General Test, minimum undergraduate GPA of 3.0; for doctorate, GRE General Test, 2 years of teaching experience, certification, minimum graduate GPA of 3.5. Additional exam requirements/recommendations for international students: Required—TOEFL. Electronic applications accepted. *Faculty research:* Early childhood literacy development, discourse analysis-adult literacy.

Rutgers University–New Brunswick, Graduate School of Education, Department of Learning and Teaching, Program in Reading Education, Piscataway, NJ 08854-8097. Offers Ed M. *Program availability:* Part-time. *Degree requirements:* For master's, comprehensive exam or paper. *Entrance requirements:* For master's, GRE General Test. Electronic applications accepted.

Rutgers University–New Brunswick, Graduate School of Education, Doctoral Program in Education, New Brunswick, NJ 08901. Offers educational policy (PhD); educational psychology (PhD); literacy education (PhD); mathematics education (PhD). *Program availability:* Part-time. *Degree requirements:* For doctorate, thesis/dissertation, qualifying exam. *Entrance requirements:* For doctorate, GRE General Test, GRE Subject Test (mathematics education). Additional exam requirements/recommendations for international students: Required—TOEFL (minimum score 575 paper-based; 83 iBT). Electronic applications accepted. *Faculty research:* Literacy education, math education, educational psychology, educational policy, learning sciences.

Sacred Heart University, Graduate Programs, Isabelle Farrington College of Education, Department of Leadership/Literacy, Fairfield, CT 06825. Offers advanced studies in administration (Professional Certificate); advanced studies in literacy (Professional Certificate). *Program availability:* Part-time, evening/weekend. *Faculty:* 8 full-time (2 women), 18 part-time/adjunct (9 women). *Students:* 52 part-time (49 women). Average age 41. 16 applicants, 100% accepted, 8 enrolled. In 2016, 25 Professional Certificates awarded. *Degree requirements:* For Professional Certificate, thesis or alternative. *Entrance requirements:* For degree, proof of teacher certification. Additional exam requirements/recommendations for international students: Required—TOEFL (minimum score 570 paper-based, 80 iBT), TWE, or IELTS (6.5); Recommended—TSE. *Application deadline:* Applications are processed on a rolling basis. Application fee: $75. Electronic applications accepted. *Expenses:* $705 per credit. *Financial support:* Unspecified assistantships available. Financial award applicants required to submit FAFSA. *Unit head:* Ann Clark, Chair/Associate Clinical Professor, 203-365-4876, E-mail: clarka@sacredheart.edu. *Application contact:* William Sweeney, Director of Graduate Admissions Operations, 203-365-4827, E-mail: sweeneyw@sacredheart.edu.

Sage Graduate School, Esteves School of Education, Program in Childhood Education/Literacy, Troy, NY 12180-4115. Offers MS. *Program availability:* Part-time, evening/weekend. *Faculty:* 17 full-time (13 women), 18 part-time/adjunct (12 women). *Students:* 6 full-time (all women), 3 part-time (all women). Average age 25. 8 applicants, 88% accepted, 5 enrolled. In 2016, 1 master's awarded. *Degree requirements:* For master's, thesis optional. *Entrance requirements:* For master's, GRE (minimum scores: Verbal Reasoning 145, Quantitative Reasoning 145, Analytical Writing 3.5) or MAT (minimum score: 350), bachelor's degree in a liberal arts or science area, minimum cumulative GPA of 3.0. Additional exam requirements/recommendations for international students: Required—TOEFL (minimum score 550 paper-based). *Application deadline:* Applications are processed on a rolling basis. Application fee: $40. Electronic applications accepted. *Expenses: Tuition:* Full-time $12,240; part-time $680 per credit hour. Tuition and fees vary according to degree level and program. *Financial support:* Fellowships, research assistantships, Federal Work-Study, scholarships/grants, and unspecified assistantships available. Support available to part-time students. Financial award application deadline: 3/1; financial award applicants required to submit FAFSA. *Unit head:* Dr. John Pelizza, Interim Dean, Esteves School of Education, 518-244-2051, Fax: 518-244-2334, E-mail: pelizj@sage.edu. *Application contact:* Dr. Kathleen Gormley, Chair and Professor of Education, 518-244-2403, Fax: 518-244-2334, E-mail: gormlk@sage.edu.

Sage Graduate School, Esteves School of Education, Program in Literacy, Troy, NY 12180-4115. Offers MS Ed. *Accreditation:* NCATE. *Program availability:* Part-time, evening/weekend. *Faculty:* 4 full-time (all women), 4 part-time/adjunct (2 women). *Students:* 6 full-time (all women), 1 (woman) part-time. Average age 25. 6 applicants, 33% accepted, 2 enrolled. In 2016, 9 master's awarded. *Entrance requirements:* For master's, minimum GPA of 2.75, resume, 2 letters of recommendation. Additional exam requirements/recommendations for international students: Required—TOEFL (minimum score 550 paper-based). *Application deadline:* Applications are processed on a rolling basis. Application fee: $40. *Expenses: Tuition:* Full-time $12,240; part-time $680 per credit hour. Tuition and fees vary according to degree level and program. *Financial support:* Fellowships, research assistantships, Federal Work-Study, scholarships/grants, and unspecified assistantships available. Support available to part-time students. Financial award application deadline: 3/1; financial award applicants required to submit FAFSA. *Faculty research:* Literacy development in at-risk children. *Unit head:* Dr. John Pelizza, Interim Dean, Esteves School of Education, 518-244-2051, Fax: 518-244-2334, E-mail: pelizj@sage.edu. *Application contact:* Dr. Kathleen Gormley, Chair/Professor of Education, 518-244-2403, Fax: 518-244-2334, E-mail: gormlk@sage.edu.

Sage Graduate School, Esteves School of Education, Program in Literacy/Childhood Special Education, Troy, NY 12180-4115. Offers MS Ed. *Accreditation:* NCATE. *Program availability:* Part-time, evening/weekend. *Faculty:* 4 full-time (all women), 4 part-time/adjunct (2 women). *Students:* 8 full-time (all women), 5 part-time (all women). Average age 26. 4 applicants, 25% accepted. In 2016, 10 master's awarded. *Entrance requirements:* For master's, current teacher certification, interview with appropriate advisor, assessment of writing. Additional exam requirements/recommendations for international students: Required—TOEFL (minimum score 550 paper-based). *Application deadline:* Applications are processed on a rolling basis. Application fee: $40. Electronic applications accepted. *Expenses: Tuition:* Full-time $12,240; part-time $680 per credit hour. Tuition and fees vary according to degree level and program. *Financial support:* Fellowships, research assistantships, Federal Work-Study, scholarships/grants, and unspecified assistantships available. Support available to part-time students. Financial award application deadline: 3/1; financial award applicants required to submit FAFSA. *Faculty research:* Commonalities in the roles of reading specialists and resource/consultant teachers. *Unit head:* Dr. John Pelizza, Interim Dean, Esteves School of Education, 518-244-2051, Fax: 518-244-2334, E-mail: pelizj@sage.edu. *Application contact:* Dr. Kathleen Gormley, Chair and Professor of Education, 518-244-2403, Fax: 518-244-2334, E-mail: gormlk@sage.edu.

Saginaw Valley State University, College of Education, Program in K-12 Literacy Specialist, University Center, MI 48710. Offers MAT. *Program availability:* Part-time, evening/weekend. *Students:* 2 full-time (both women), 35 part-time (all women); includes 3 minority (1 Black or African American, non-Hispanic/Latino; 2 Hispanic/Latino). Average age 33. 6 applicants, 100% accepted, 6 enrolled. In 2016, 16 master's awarded. *Degree requirements:* For master's, capstone course. *Entrance requirements:* For master's, minimum GPA of 3.0. Additional exam requirements/recommendations for international students: Required—TOEFL (minimum score 550 paper-based; 79 iBT). *Application deadline:* For fall admission, 7/15 for international students; for winter admission, 11/15 for international students; for spring admission, 4/15 for international students. Applications are processed on a rolling basis. Application fee: $30 ($90 for international students). Electronic applications accepted. *Expenses:* Tuition, state resident: full-time $9652; part-time $536 per credit hour. Tuition, nonresident: full-time $12,259; part-time $1022 per credit hour. *Required fees:* $263; $14.60 per credit hour. Tuition and fees vary according to degree level. *Financial support:* Federal Work-Study and scholarships/grants available. Support available to part-time students. Financial award applicants required to submit FAFSA. *Unit head:* Dr. Gretchen Owocki, Professor of Teacher Education, 989-964-7393, Fax: 989-964-4563, E-mail: coeconnect@svsu.edu. *Application contact:* Jenna Briggs, Director, Graduate and International Admissions, 989-964-6096, Fax: 989-964-2788, E-mail: gradadm@svsu.edu.

Saginaw Valley State University, College of Education, Program in Reading Education, University Center, MI 48710. Offers MAT. *Accreditation:* NCATE. *Program availability:* Part-time, evening/weekend. In 2016, 1 master's awarded. *Degree requirements:* For master's, capstone course, practicum. *Entrance requirements:* For master's, minimum GPA of 3.0, teaching certificate. Additional exam requirements/recommendations for international students: Required—TOEFL (minimum score 550 paper-based; 79 iBT). *Application deadline:* For fall admission, 7/15 for international students; for winter admission, 11/15 for international students; for spring admission, 4/15 for international students. Applications are processed on a rolling basis. Application fee: $30 ($90 for international students). Electronic applications accepted. *Expenses:* Tuition, state resident: full-time $9652; part-time $536 per credit hour. Tuition, nonresident: full-time $12,259; part-time $1022 per credit hour. *Required fees:* $263; $14.60 per credit hour. Tuition and fees vary according to degree level. *Financial support:* Federal Work-Study and scholarships/grants available. Support available to part-time students. Financial award applicants required to submit FAFSA. *Faculty research:* Pre-service, middle school, secondary teacher, literacy education. *Unit head:* Dr. Craig Douglas, Dean, 989-964-4057, Fax: 989-964-4385, E-mail: coeconnect@svsu.edu. *Application contact:* Jenna Briggs, Director, Graduate and International Admissions, 989-964-6096, Fax: 989-964-2788, E-mail: gradadm@svsu.edu.

St. Bonaventure University, School of Graduate Studies, School of Education, Literacy Programs, St. Bonaventure, NY 14778-2284. Offers adolescent literacy 5-12 (MS Ed); childhood literacy B-6 (MS Ed). *Accreditation:* NCATE. *Program availability:* Part-time, evening/weekend. *Faculty:* 2 full-time (both women), 2 part-time/adjunct (both women). *Students:* 7 full-time (all women), 6 part-time (all women); includes 1 minority (Hispanic/Latino). Average age 25. 10 applicants, 70% accepted, 4 enrolled. In 2016, 14 master's awarded. *Degree requirements:* For master's, comprehensive exam, thesis optional, minimum cumulative GPA of 3.0, clinical practicum, literacy coaching internship, electronic portfolio. *Entrance requirements:* For master's, GRE or MAT, teaching certificate in matching area in-hand or pending, transcripts from all previous colleges, minimum GPA of 3.0, 2 references, interview, writing sample. Additional exam requirements/recommendations for international students: Required—TOEFL (minimum score 550 paper-based; 80 iBT). *Application deadline:* For fall admission, 6/15 priority date for domestic students, 2/1 for international students; for spring admission, 11/15 priority date for domestic students, 7/1 for international students. Applications are processed on a rolling basis. Application fee: $0. Electronic applications accepted. *Expenses:* $733 per credit, $100 graduation fee. *Financial support:* Federal Work-Study, scholarships/grants, health care benefits, and unspecified assistantships available. Support available to part-time students. Financial award application deadline:

4/15; financial award applicants required to submit FAFSA. *Faculty research:* Gifted education, curriculum and instruction, theory and language. *Unit head:* Kayla Zimmer, Program Director, 716-375-2167, Fax: 716-375-2360, E-mail: kzimmer@sbu.edu. *Application contact:* Bruce Campbell, Director of Graduate Admissions, 716-375-2429, Fax: 716-375-4015, E-mail: gradsch@sbu.edu.
Website: http://www.sbu.edu/academics/schools/education/graduate-degrees-certificates/msed-in-childhood-literacy

Saint Francis University, Graduate Education Program, Loretto, PA 15940-0600. Offers education (M Ed); leadership (M Ed); reading (M Ed). *Program availability:* Part-time, 100% online, blended/hybrid learning. *Degree requirements:* For master's, comprehensive exam, thesis optional. *Entrance requirements:* For master's, GRE or MAT (if undergraduate GPA less than 3.0). Additional exam requirements/recommendations for international students: Required—TOEFL (minimum score 550 paper-based; 75 iBT), IELTS (minimum score 6.5), International Test of English Proficiency (minimum score 4). *Expenses:* Contact institution.

St. John Fisher College, Ralph C. Wilson Jr. School of Education, Program in Literacy Education, Rochester, NY 14618-3597. Offers literacy birth to grade 6 (MS); literacy grades 5 to 12 (MS). *Program availability:* Part-time, evening/weekend. *Faculty:* 3 full-time (all women), 4 part-time/adjunct (3 women). *Students:* 1 (woman) full-time, 33 part-time (27 women); includes 1 minority (Hispanic/Latino). Average age 24. 14 applicants, 86% accepted, 4 enrolled. In 2016, 25 master's awarded. *Degree requirements:* For master's, capstone project, practicum. *Entrance requirements:* For master's, teacher certification, 2 letters of recommendation, personal statement, current resume. Additional exam requirements/recommendations for international students: Required—TOEFL (minimum score 575 paper-based; 80 iBT). *Application deadline:* Applications are processed on a rolling basis. Application fee: $30. Electronic applications accepted. *Expenses:* $885 per credit hour. *Financial support:* Scholarships/grants available. Financial award applicants required to submit FAFSA. *Faculty research:* Adolescent use of new literacies (instant messaging), referral practices, at risk early literacy, new literacies (Internet, technology), equity in education. *Unit head:* Dr. Kathleen Broikou, Program Director, 585-385-8112, E-mail: kbroikou@sjfc.edu. *Application contact:* Michelle Gosier, Associate Director of Transfer and Graduate Admissions, 585-385-8064, E-mail: mgosier@sjfc.edu.
Website: https://www.sjfc.edu/graduate-programs/ms-in-literacy-education/

St. John's University, The School of Education, Department of Education Specialties, Literacy Program, Queens, NY 11439. Offers literacy (PhD); teaching literacy (Adv C); teaching literacy 5-12 (MS Ed); teaching literacy B-12 (MS Ed); teaching literacy B-6 (MS Ed); teaching literacy B-6 and children with disabilities (MS Ed). *Program availability:* Part-time, evening/weekend. *Degree requirements:* For master's, comprehensive exam; for doctorate, thesis/dissertation, residency; for Adv C, 50-hour practicum, content specialty test in literacy. *Entrance requirements:* For master's, minimum GPA of 3.0, transcript, personal statement; for doctorate, MAT, GRE General Test (analytical), statement of goals, official transcripts showing conferral of degree, minimum GPA of 3.2, 2 letters of recommendation, resume, evidence of teaching experience, interview; for Adv C, master's degree, initial teaching certification, minimum GPA of 3.0. Additional exam requirements/recommendations for international students: Required—TOEFL (minimum score 600 paper-based; 100 iBT), IELTS (minimum score 7). Electronic applications accepted. *Faculty research:* Higher order reading comprehension development and instruction, children's literature theory and children's reading interests, critical comprehension development, early writing development at the primary level, self-efficacy with textbook formats, out of school time program effects for at-risk students, teacher training effects for low performing parochial school students.

St. Joseph's College, Long Island Campus, Programs in Education, Field of Literacy and Cognition, Patchogue, NY 11772-2399. Offers MA. *Entrance requirements:* For master's, 1 course in child development, 6 credits of reading methods, minimum undergraduate GPA of 3.0, New York state teaching certificate, writing sample, resume, 2 letters of recommendation, interview. Additional exam requirements/recommendations for international students: Recommended—TOEFL (minimum score 550 paper-based; 79 iBT), IELTS (minimum score 7). Electronic applications accepted. *Expenses: Tuition:* Full-time $16,182; part-time $899 per credit. *Required fees:* $440.

St. Joseph's College, New York, Programs in Education, Field of Literacy and Cognition, Brooklyn, NY 11205-3688. Offers MA. *Program availability:* Part-time, evening/weekend. *Faculty:* 2 part-time/adjunct (both women). *Students:* 17 part-time (all women); includes 3 minority (all Hispanic/Latino). Average age 23. 17 applicants, 76% accepted, 9 enrolled. In 2016, 15 master's awarded. *Entrance requirements:* For master's, GRE, PRAXIS or MAT, official transcripts, two letters of recommendation, resume, copy of teaching certification. Additional exam requirements/recommendations for international students: Required—TOEFL (minimum score 80 iBT). *Application deadline:* Applications are processed on a rolling basis. Application fee: $25. Electronic applications accepted. *Expenses:* Contact institution. *Financial support:* In 2016–17, 16 students received support. *Unit head:* Susan Straut-Collard, Professor/Associate Chair/Director of the Special Education Program, 718-940-5689, E-mail: sstrautcollard@sjcny.edu.
Website: http://www.sjcny.edu

Saint Joseph's University, College of Arts and Sciences, Graduate Programs in Education, Philadelphia, PA 19131-1395. Offers curriculum supervisor (Certificate); educational leadership (MS, Ed D); elementary education (MS, Certificate); elementary/middle school education (Certificate); instructional technology (MS, Certificate); organizational development and leadership (MS); principal (Certificate); professional education (MS); reading specialist (MS, Certificate); reading supervisor (Certificate); secondary education (MS, Certificate); special education (MS); special education 7-12 (Certificate); special education PK-8 (Certificate); superintendent's letter of eligibility (Certificate); supervisor of special education (Certificate); teacher of the deaf and hard of hearing (Certificate). *Program availability:* Part-time, evening/weekend, blended/hybrid learning. *Faculty:* 26 full-time (21 women), 74 part-time/adjunct (45 women). *Students:* 107 full-time (88 women), 826 part-time (622 women); includes 170 minority (115 Black or African American, non-Hispanic/Latino; 2 American Indian or Alaska Native, non-Hispanic/Latino; 11 Asian, non-Hispanic/Latino; 31 Hispanic/Latino; 1 Native Hawaiian or other Pacific Islander, non-Hispanic/Latino; 10 Two or more races, non-Hispanic/Latino), 18 international. Average age 33. 338 applicants, 76% accepted, 173 enrolled. In 2016, 419 master's, 16 doctorates, 24 other advanced degrees awarded. *Degree requirements:* For master's, thesis or alternative; for doctorate, comprehensive exam, thesis/dissertation. *Entrance requirements:* For master's, 2 letters of recommendation, minimum GPA of 3.0, official transcripts, personal statement; for doctorate, GRE, master's degree from accredited institution, minimum graduate GPA of 3.5, computer competence, interview with program director. Additional exam requirements/recommendations for international students: Required—TOEFL (minimum score 550 paper-based; 80 iBT), IELTS (minimum score 6.5), PTE (minimum score 60). *Application deadline:* For fall admission, 7/15 for international students; for spring admission, 11/1 for international students. Applications are processed on a rolling basis. Application fee: $35. Electronic applications accepted. *Expenses:* $750 per credit, $100 education fee, $360 online organization development and leadership residency fee. *Financial support:* In 2016–17, 25 students received support. Unspecified assistantships available. Financial award application deadline: 5/1; financial award applicants required to submit FAFSA. *Faculty research:* Factors predicting early mathematics skills for low income children, early child care and development, preschool quality, parent communication and home-school collaboration issues, education of terminally ill children, preparing literacy teachers for urban schools. *Total annual research expenditures:* $18,118. *Unit head:* Dr. John Vacca, Associate Dean, Education, 610-660-3131, E-mail: gradcas@sju.edu. *Application contact:* Graduate Admissions, College of Arts and Sciences, 610-660-3131, E-mail: gradcas@sju.edu.
Website: http://sju.edu/int/academics/cas/grad/education/index.html

Saint Leo University, Graduate Studies in Education, Saint Leo, FL 33574-6665. Offers educational leadership (M Ed), including Catholic school administration; exceptional student education (M Ed); instructional design (MS, Certificate); instructional leadership (M Ed); reading (M Ed, Certificate); school leadership (Ed S). *Program availability:* Part-time, evening/weekend, online learning. *Faculty:* 11 full-time (10 women), 22 part-time/adjunct (15 women). *Students:* 424 part-time (335 women); includes 94 minority (54 Black or African American, non-Hispanic/Latino; 2 Asian, non-Hispanic/Latino; 32 Hispanic/Latino; 6 Two or more races, non-Hispanic/Latino), 1 international. Average age 37. 260 applicants, 76% accepted, 107 enrolled. In 2016, 166 master's, 6 other advanced degrees awarded. *Degree requirements:* For master's, appropriate State of Florida certification tests. *Entrance requirements:* For master's, GRE (minimum score of 1000), MAT (minimum score of 410), or minimum undergraduate GPA of 3.0 in final 2 years, official transcripts, current resumé, 2 professional recommendations, personal statement, bachelor's degree from regionally-accredited university, valid professional teaching certificate; for other advanced degree, valid professional teaching certificate (for Ed S). Additional exam requirements/recommendations for international students: Required—TOEFL (minimum score 550 paper-based; 80 iBT). *Application deadline:* For fall admission, 7/1 priority date for domestic students, 7/1 for international students; for winter admission, 7/1 for international students; for spring admission, 11/1 priority date for domestic students. Applications are processed on a rolling basis. Application fee: $80. Electronic applications accepted. *Expenses:* $465 per semester hour (for MS); $480 per semester hour (for M Ed); $670 per semester hour (for Ed S). *Financial support:* In 2016–17, 17 students received support. Career-related internships or fieldwork, scholarships/grants, and health care benefits available. Financial award application deadline: 3/1; financial award applicants required to submit FAFSA. *Faculty research:* Student achievement in literacy, leadership, instructional technology. *Unit head:* Dr. Fern Aefsky, Director of Graduate Studies in Education, 352-588-8309, Fax: 352-588-8861, E-mail: kara.winkler@saintleo.edu. *Application contact:* Jennifer Shelley, Senior Associate Director of Graduate Admissions, 800-707-8846, Fax: 352-588-7873, E-mail: grad.admissions@saintleo.edu.
Website: http://www.saintleo.edu/academics/graduate.aspx

Saint Mary's University of Minnesota, Schools of Graduate and Professional Programs, Graduate School of Education, Literacy Education Program, Winona, MN 55987-1399. Offers K-12 reading teacher (Certificate); literacy education (MA). Tuition and fees vary according to degree level and program. *Unit head:* Cindy Kronebusch, Assistant Program Director, 507-457-6637, E-mail: ckronebu@smumn.edu. *Application contact:* James Callinan, Director of Admissions for Graduate and Professional Programs, 612-728-5185, Fax: 612-728-5121, E-mail: jcallina@smumn.edu.
Website: http://www.smumn.edu/graduate-home/areas-of-study/graduate-school-of-education/ma-in-literacy-education

Saint Michael's College, Graduate Programs, Program in Education, Colchester, VT 05439. Offers arts in education (CAGS); literacy (M Ed); school leadership (CAGS); special education (M Ed). *Program availability:* Part-time, evening/weekend. *Students:* 5 full-time (4 women), 239 part-time (199 women); includes 9 minority (2 Black or African American, non-Hispanic/Latino; 1 American Indian or Alaska Native, non-Hispanic/Latino; 1 Asian, non-Hispanic/Latino; 4 Hispanic/Latino; 1 Two or more races, non-Hispanic/Latino), 1 international. Average age 36. In 2016, 31 master's awarded. *Degree requirements:* For master's, thesis. *Entrance requirements:* For master's, minimum GPA of 3.0, official transcripts, essay, interview. *Application deadline:* Applications are processed on a rolling basis. Application fee: $50. Electronic applications accepted. *Expenses: Tuition:* Full-time $10,620; part-time $590 per credit. Part-time tuition and fees vary according to course load and program. *Financial support:* Fellowships with partial tuition reimbursements and scholarships/grants available. Support available to part-time students. Financial award applicants required to submit FAFSA. *Faculty research:* Integrative curriculum, moral and spiritual dimensions of education, learning styles, multiple intelligences, integrating technology into the curriculum. *Unit head:* Jonathan Silverman, Department Chair, 802-654-2306, Fax: 802-654-2664, E-mail: jsilverman@smcvt.edu. *Application contact:* Lindsay A. Damici, Marketing Communications Manager, 802-654-2556, Fax: 802-654-2732.
Website: http://www.smcvt.edu/graduate-programs/academic-programs/education.aspx

Saint Peter's University, Graduate Programs in Education, Program in Special Education, Jersey City, NJ 07306-5997. Offers literacy (MA Ed). *Program availability:* Part-time, evening/weekend. *Degree requirements:* For master's, comprehensive exam. *Entrance requirements:* For master's, GRE or MAT. Additional exam requirements/recommendations for international students: Required—TOEFL. Electronic applications accepted.

Saint Peter's University, Graduate Programs in Education, Reading Program, Jersey City, NJ 07306-5997. Offers MA Ed. *Accreditation:* TEAC. *Program availability:* Part-time, evening/weekend. *Degree requirements:* For master's, comprehensive exam. *Entrance requirements:* For master's, GRE or MAT. Additional exam requirements/recommendations for international students: Required—TOEFL. Electronic applications accepted.

St. Thomas Aquinas College, Division of Teacher Education, Sparkill, NY 10976. Offers adolescence education (MST); childhood and special education (MST); childhood education (MST); educational leadership (MS Ed); reading (MS Ed, PMC); special education (MS Ed, PMC); teaching (MS Ed), including elementary education, middle school education, secondary education. *Accreditation:* NCATE. *Program availability:* Part-time, evening/weekend. *Degree requirements:* For master's, comprehensive exam, comprehensive professional portfolio; for PMC, action research project. *Entrance requirements:* For master's, New York State Qualifying Exam, GRE General Test or minimum GPA of 3.0, teaching certificate; for PMC, GRE General Test or minimum GPA of 3.0. Electronic applications accepted. *Faculty research:* Computer applications in education, adolescent special education students, literacy development, inclusive practices for special education students.

St. Thomas University, School of Leadership Studies, Institute for Education, Miami Gardens, FL 33054-6459. Offers earth/space science (Certificate); educational administration (MS, Certificate); educational leadership (Ed D); elementary education (MS); ESOL (Certificate); gifted education (Certificate); instructional technology (MS, Certificate); professional/studies (Certificate), reading (MS, Certificate); special education (MS). *Program availability:* Part-time, evening/weekend. *Degree requirements:* For master's, comprehensive exam; for doctorate, comprehensive exam, thesis/dissertation. *Entrance requirements:* For master's, interview, minimum GPA of 3.0 or GRE; for doctorate, GRE or MAT. Additional exam requirements/recommendations for international students: Required—TOEFL (minimum score 550 paper-based; 79 iBT). Electronic applications accepted.

Saint Xavier University, Graduate Studies, School of Education, Chicago, IL 60655-3105. Offers counseling (MA); curriculum and instruction (MA); early childhood education (MA); educational administration (MA); elementary education (MA); individualized studies (MA), including educational technology, English as a second language (ESL), ISTEM (integrative science, technology, engineering, and math), science education; music education (MA); reading (MA); secondary education (MA); Spanish education (MA); special education (MA); teaching and leadership (MA). *Accreditation:* NCATE. *Program availability:* Part-time, evening/weekend. *Degree requirements:* For master's, thesis or project. *Entrance requirements:* For master's, minimum GPA of 3.0. *Expenses:* Contact institution.

Salem College, Department of Education, Winston-Salem, NC 27101. Offers art education (MAT); elementary education (M Ed, MAT); language and literacy (M Ed); middle school education (MAT); school counseling (M Ed); second language studies (MAT); secondary education (MAT); special education (M Ed, MAT). *Accreditation:* NCATE. *Program availability:* Part-time, evening/weekend, online learning. *Degree requirements:* For master's, practicum (MAT), project (M Ed), oral and written comprehensive exams. *Entrance requirements:* For master's, minimum GPA of 2.5. *Faculty research:* Content area reading strategies, literacy development, brain compatible instruction.

Salem State University, School of Graduate Studies, Program in Reading, Salem, MA 01970-5353. Offers M Ed. *Accreditation:* NCATE. *Program availability:* Part-time, evening/weekend. *Entrance requirements:* For master's, GRE or MAT. Additional exam requirements/recommendations for international students: Required—TOEFL (minimum score 550 paper-based; 80 iBT) or IELTS (minimum score 5.5).

Salisbury University, Program in Contemporary Curriculum Theory and Instruction: Literacy, Salisbury, MD 21801-6837. Offers Ed D. *Program availability:* Part-time. *Faculty:* 4 full-time (2 women). *Students:* 18 full-time (16 women), 15 part-time (11 women); includes 1 minority (Two or more races, non-Hispanic/Latino). Average age 37. 17 applicants, 88% accepted, 13 enrolled. *Degree requirements:* For doctorate, comprehensive exam, thesis/dissertation. *Entrance requirements:* Additional exam requirements/recommendations for international students: Required—TOEFL (minimum score 550 paper-based, 79 iBT) or IELTS (6.5). *Application deadline:* For fall admission, 3/31 priority date for domestic and international students. Applications are processed on a rolling basis. Application fee: $65. Electronic applications accepted. *Expenses:* $540 per credit hour resident tuition, $940 per credit hour non-resident tuition; $84 per credit hour fees. *Financial support:* In 2016–17, 9 students received support, including 1 teaching assistantship with full tuition reimbursement available (averaging $10,000 per year); career-related internships or fieldwork and scholarships/grants also available. Support available to part-time students. Financial award application deadline: 3/1; financial award applicants required to submit FAFSA. *Faculty research:* Education policy; rural literacies; eye movement miscue analysis; writing pedagogy. *Unit head:* Dr. Judith Franzak, Graduate Program Director, 410-677-0238, E-mail: jkfranzak@salisbury.edu. *Application contact:* Stefani Hoffman, Administrative Assistant II, 410-677-0236, E-mail: slhoffman@salisbury.edu.
Website: http://www.salisbury.edu/gsr/gradstudies/EDDpage.html

Salisbury University, Program in Reading Specialist, Salisbury, MD 21801-6837. Offers M Ed. *Program availability:* Part-time, evening/weekend. *Faculty:* 2 full-time (both women), 1 part-time/adjunct. *Students:* 32 part-time (29 women); includes 3 minority (2 Black or African American, non-Hispanic/Latino; 1 Asian, non-Hispanic/Latino). Average age 30. 8 applicants, 75% accepted, 6 enrolled. In 2016, 3 master's awarded. *Entrance requirements:* Additional exam requirements/recommendations for international students: Required—TOEFL (minimum score 550 paper-based, 79 iBT) or IELTS (6.5). *Application deadline:* For fall admission, 3/1 priority date for domestic and international students; for spring admission, 10/1 priority date for domestic and international students; for summer admission, 3/1 priority date for domestic and international students. Applications are processed on a rolling basis. Application fee: $65. Electronic applications accepted. *Expenses:* $381 per credit hour resident tuition, $670 per credit hour non-resident tuition; $84 per credit hour fees. *Financial support:* In 2016–17, 3 students received support, including 4 teaching assistantships with full tuition reimbursements available (averaging $8,500 per year); career-related internships or fieldwork and scholarships/grants also available. Support available to part-time students. Financial award application deadline: 3/1; financial award applicants required to submit FAFSA. *Faculty research:* Literacy intervention; literacy assessment; digital literacies; diversity and literacy; early literacy prevention and intervention. *Unit head:* Dr. Patricia Richards, Graduate Program Director, Reading Specialist, 410-543-6379, E-mail: porichards@salisbury.edu.
Website: http://www.salisbury.edu/gsr/gradstudies/MEDpage.html

Sam Houston State University, College of Education, Department of Language, Literacy, and Special Populations, Huntsville, TX 77341. Offers international literacy (M Ed); reading (M Ed); special education (M Ed, MA), including low incidence disabilities and autism. *Program availability:* Part-time, evening/weekend, online learning. *Degree requirements:* For master's, comprehensive exam (for some programs), thesis optional, comprehensive portfolio; for doctorate, comprehensive exam, thesis/dissertation. *Entrance requirements:* For master's, GRE General Test, MAT, writing sample, recommendations; for doctorate, GRE General Test, MAT, master's degree, personal statement, recommendations. Additional exam requirements/recommendations for international students: Required—TOEFL (minimum score 550 paper-based; 79 iBT), IELTS (minimum score 6.5). Electronic applications accepted.

San Diego State University, Graduate and Research Affairs, College of Education, School of Teacher Education, Program in Reading Education, San Diego, CA 92182. Offers MA. *Accreditation:* NCATE. *Program availability:* Part-time. *Entrance requirements:* For master's, GRE General Test, letters of reference. Additional exam requirements/recommendations for international students: Required—TOEFL. Electronic applications accepted. *Faculty research:* Literacy, writing, reading/writing connection, class size reduction in reading, book clubs, evaluation instruments in reading/language arts.

San Francisco State University, Division of Graduate Studies, College of Education, Department of Elementary Education, Program in Language and Literacy Education, San Francisco, CA 94132-1722. Offers language and literacy education (MA); reading (Certificate); reading and literacy leadership (Credential). *Expenses:* Tuition, state resident: full-time $6738. Tuition, nonresident: full-time $15,666. *Required fees:* $1012. Tuition and fees vary according to degree level and program. *Unit head:* Dr. Josephine Arce, Chair, 415-338-7636, Fax: 415-338-0567, E-mail: jarce@sfsu.edu. *Application contact:* Dr. Ali Borjian, MA Program Coordinator, 415-338-1838, Fax: 415-338-0567, E-mail: borjian@sfsu.edu.
Website: http://gcoe.sfsu.edu/

San Francisco State University, Division of Graduate Studies, College of Liberal and Creative Arts, Department of English Language and Literature, San Francisco, CA 94132-1722. Offers composition (MA, Certificate); immigrant literacies (Certificate); linguistics (MA); literature (MA); teaching English to speakers of other languages (MA); teaching post-secondary reading (Certificate). *Program availability:* Part-time. *Application deadline:* Applications are processed on a rolling basis. *Expenses:* Tuition, state resident: full-time $6738. Tuition, nonresident: full-time $15,666. *Required fees:* $1012. Tuition and fees vary according to degree level and program. *Unit head:* Dr. Sugie Goen-Salter, Chair, 415-338-7582, Fax: 415-338-6159, E-mail: sgoen@sfsu.edu. *Application contact:* Cynthia Losinsky, Graduate Programs Coordinator, 415-338-2660, Fax: 415-338-6159, E-mail: cynthial@sfsu.edu.
Website: http://english.sfsu.edu/

Seattle Pacific University, Master of Education in Literacy Program, Seattle, WA 98119-1997. Offers M Ed. *Program availability:* Part-time. *Degree requirements:* For master's, comprehensive exam. *Entrance requirements:* For master's, MAT or GRE (unless minimum undergraduate GPA of 3.4 or master's degree from accredited university), copy of teaching certificate, official transcript(s) from each college/university attended, personal statement (1-2 pages), two letters of recommendation, moral and character fitness policy form, resume. Electronic applications accepted.

Shenandoah University, School of Education and Human Development, Winchester, VA 22601-5195. Offers administrative leadership (D Ed); educational administration (MSE); emphasis in teaching (MSE); health and physical education (Certificate); individual focus (MSE); literacy education (MS); middle school teacher education (Certificate); organizational leadership (MS, D Prof); secondary school teacher education (Certificate); special education (MSE). *Accreditation:* TEAC. *Program availability:* Part-time, evening/weekend. *Faculty:* 9 full-time (7 women), 43 part-time/adjunct (33 women). *Students:* 31 full-time (25 women), 236 part-time (160 women); includes 39 minority (19 Black or African American, non-Hispanic/Latino; 1 American Indian or Alaska Native, non-Hispanic/Latino; 10 Asian, non-Hispanic/Latino; 7 Hispanic/Latino; 1 Native Hawaiian or other Pacific Islander, non-Hispanic/Latino; 1 Two or more races, non-Hispanic/Latino), 4 international. Average age 37. 90 applicants, 97% accepted, 56 enrolled. In 2016, 113 master's, 13 doctorates, 38 other advanced degrees awarded. *Degree requirements:* For master's, comprehensive exam (for some programs), thesis (for some programs); for doctorate, comprehensive exam, thesis/dissertation. *Entrance requirements:* For degree, PRAXIS Academic Core, SAT/ACT, PRAXIS Academic Core Math, or VCLA, three letters of recommendation, writing sample, undergraduate degree. Additional exam requirements/recommendations for international students: Required—TOEFL (minimum score 550 paper-based; 79 iBT), IELTS (minimum score 6.5). *Application deadline:* For fall admission, 5/1 priority date for domestic students, 5/1 for international students; for spring admission, 10/15 priority date for domestic students, 10/15 for international students; for summer admission, 3/15 priority date for domestic students, 3/15 for international students. Application fee: $30. Electronic applications accepted. *Expenses:* Contact institution. *Financial support:* In 2016–17, 18 students received support. Scholarships/grants and unspecified assistantships available. Financial award applicants required to submit FAFSA. *Faculty research:* Exploring helplessness and anxiety in learning statistics, facilitating effective classroom group work, expert-novice dynamics in teaching, K-12 policy implementation and change, adult education, family-school-community relations, mentoring of first-year school principals. *Total annual research expenditures:* $2,000. *Unit head:* Dennis William Kellison, PhD, Director, 540-535-7324, Fax: 540-665-4726, E-mail: dkelliso@su.edu. *Application contact:* Andrew Woodall, Executive Director of Recruitment and Admissions, 540-665-4581, Fax: 540-665-4627, E-mail: admit@su.edu.
Website: http://www.su.edu/education/

Shippensburg University of Pennsylvania, School of Graduate Studies, College of Education and Human Services, Department of Teacher Education, Shippensburg, PA 17257-2299. Offers curriculum and instruction (M Ed), including biology, early childhood education, elementary and middle level education, elementary education, geography/earth science, history, mathematics, middle school education, modern languages; literacy studies (Certificate); online instruction, learning, and technology (Certificate); reading (M Ed); teaching English as a second language (Certificate). *Accreditation:* NCATE. *Program availability:* Part-time, evening/weekend, 100% online, blended/hybrid learning. *Faculty:* 14 full-time (9 women), 5 part-time/adjunct (all women). *Students:* 11 full-time (10 women), 88 part-time (81 women); includes 8 minority (3 Black or African American, non-Hispanic/Latino; 2 Asian, non-Hispanic/Latino; 3 Hispanic/Latino), 4 international. Average age 32. 57 applicants, 60% accepted, 28 enrolled. In 2016, 18 master's awarded. *Degree requirements:* For master's, comprehensive exam (for some programs), thesis optional, practicum or internship; capstone seminar (for some programs). *Entrance requirements:* For master's, MAT or GRE (if GPA less than 2.75), interview, 3 letters of reference, questionnaire of teaching background and future goals, resume. Additional exam requirements/recommendations for international students: Required—TOEFL (minimum score 550 paper-based, 68 iBT) or IELTS (minimum score 6). *Application deadline:* For fall admission, 4/1 priority date for domestic students, 4/30 for international students; for spring admission, 9/1 priority date for domestic students, 9/30 for international students; for summer admission, 2/1 priority date for domestic students. Applications are processed on a rolling basis. Application fee: $45. Electronic applications accepted. *Expenses:* Tuition, state resident: part-time $483 per credit. Tuition, nonresident: part-time $725 per credit. *Required fees:* $141 per credit. *Financial support:* In 2016–17, 3 students received support. Career-related internships or fieldwork, scholarships/grants, unspecified assistantships, and resident hall director and student payroll positions available. Support available to part-time students. Financial award application deadline: 3/1; financial award applicants required to submit FAFSA. *Unit head:* Dr. Christine A. Royce, Chairperson, 717-477-1688, Fax: 717-477-4046, E-mail: caroyc@ship.edu. *Application contact:* Megan N. Luft, Assistant Dean of Graduate Admissions, 717-477-1231, Fax: 717-477-4016, E-mail: mnluft@ship.edu.
Website: http://www.ship.edu/teacher/

Siena Heights University, Graduate College, Adrian, MI 49221-1796. Offers clinical mental health counseling (MA); educational leadership (Specialist); leadership (MA), including health care leadership, organizational leadership; teacher education (MA), including early childhood education, early childhood education: Montessori, education leadership: principal, elementary education: reading K-12, leadership: higher education, secondary education: reading K-12, special education: cognitive impairment, special education: learning disabilities. *Program availability:* Part-time, evening/weekend. *Degree requirements:* For master's, thesis, presentation. *Entrance requirements:* For master's, minimum GPA of 3.0, current resume, essay, all post-secondary transcripts, 3 letters of reference, conviction disclosure form; copy of teaching certificate (for some education programs); for Specialist, master's degree, minimum GPA of 3.0, current resume, essay, all post-secondary transcripts, 3 letters of reference, conviction disclosure form; copy of teaching certificate (for some education programs). Electronic applications accepted.

Simmons College, School of Library and Information Science, Boston, MA 02115. Offers children's literature (MA); library and information science (MS, PhD, Certificate), including archives management (MS), cultural heritage (MS), information science and technology (MS), school library teacher (MS); writing for children (MFA); MA/MA; MA/MAT; MA/MFA; MS/MA. *Accreditation:* ALA (one or more programs are accredited). *Program availability:* Part-time, evening/weekend, 100% online, blended/hybrid learning. *Faculty:* 23 full-time (17 women), 23 part-time/adjunct (16 women). *Students:* 313 full-time (262 women), 511 part-time (420 women); includes 88 minority (13 Black or African

American, non-Hispanic/Latino; 10 Asian, non-Hispanic/Latino; 41 Hispanic/Latino; 24 Two or more races, non-Hispanic/Latino), 19 international. Average age 30. 568 applicants, 98% accepted, 319 enrolled. In 2016, 245 master's, 3 doctorates, 4 other advanced degrees awarded. *Degree requirements:* For master's, thesis optional, capstone project experience; for doctorate, comprehensive exam, thesis/dissertation, 36 credit hours. *Entrance requirements:* For doctorate, GRE, transcripts, personal statement, resume, recommendations, master's degree. Additional exam requirements/recommendations for international students: Required—TOEFL (minimum score 550 paper-based; 79 iBT), IELTS (minimum score 7). *Application deadline:* For fall admission, 3/1 for domestic and international students; for spring admission, 9/1 for domestic and international students; for summer admission, 2/1 for domestic and international students. Applications are processed on a rolling basis. Application fee: $65. Electronic applications accepted. *Expenses:* $1,210 per credit, $3,630 per course, $52 activity fee per semester. *Financial support:* In 2016–17, 10 fellowships with partial tuition reimbursements were awarded; scholarships/grants, tuition waivers, and unspecified assistantships also available. Support available to part-time students. Financial award application deadline: 2/1; financial award applicants required to submit FAFSA. *Faculty research:* Archives and social justice, information-seeking behavior, information retrieval, organization of information, cultural heritage informatics. *Unit head:* Dr. Eileen G. Abels, Dean, 617-521-2869. *Application contact:* Sarah Petrakos, Assistant Dean for Admission and Recruitment, 617-521-2868, Fax: 617-521-3192, E-mail: gslisadm@simmons.edu.
Website: http://www.simmons.edu/slis/

Simon Fraser University, Office of Graduate Studies and Postdoctoral Fellows, Faculty of Education, Program in Languages, Cultures, and Literacies, Burnaby, BC V5A 1S6, Canada. Offers PhD. *Unit head:* Dr. Shawn Bullock, Associate Dean, Graduate Studies in Education, 778-782-4102, Fax: 778-782-4320, E-mail: mesbit@sfu.ca. *Application contact:* Administrative Assistant, 778-782-9488, Fax: 778-782-4320, E-mail: gse-sec@sfu.ca.

Slippery Rock University of Pennsylvania, Graduate Studies (Recruitment), College of Education, Department of Elementary Education and Early Childhood, Slippery Rock, PA 16057-1383. Offers instructional coach (M Ed); K-12 reading (M Ed); K-12 science and math (M Ed); reading specialist (M Ed). *Accreditation:* NCATE. *Program availability:* Part-time, evening/weekend, online only, 100% online. *Faculty:* 9 full-time (8 women). *Students:* 6 full-time (all women), 128 part-time (124 women); includes 1 minority (Two or more races, non-Hispanic/Latino). Average age 28. 100 applicants, 77% accepted, 54 enrolled. In 2016, 49 master's awarded. *Degree requirements:* For master's, comprehensive exam (for some programs), thesis optional. *Entrance requirements:* For master's, minimum GPA of 3.0, resume, teaching certification, transcripts, letters of recommendation (depending on program). Additional exam requirements/recommendations for international students: Required—TOEFL (minimum score 550 paper-based; 80 iBT). *Application deadline:* For fall admission, 3/1 priority date for domestic students, 5/1 priority date for international students; for spring admission, 10/1 priority date for domestic students, 9/1 priority date for international students. Applications are processed on a rolling basis. Application fee: $25 ($30 for international students). Electronic applications accepted. *Expenses:* $646.50 per credit in-state, $936.80 per credit out-of-state; $581.45 per online credit in-state, $648.65 per online credit out-of-state. *Financial support:* Career-related internships or fieldwork, Federal Work-Study, institutionally sponsored loans, scholarships/grants, tuition waivers (partial), and unspecified assistantships available. Support available to part-time students. Financial award application deadline: 5/1; financial award applicants required to submit FAFSA. *Unit head:* Dr. Suzanne Rose, Graduate Coordinator, 724-738-2042, Fax: 724-738-2779, E-mail: suzanne.rose@sru.edu. *Application contact:* Brandi Weber-Mortimer, Director of Graduate Admissions, 724-738-2051, Fax: 724-738-2146, E-mail: graduate.admissions@sru.edu.
Website: http://www.sru.edu/academics/colleges-and-departments/coe/departments/elementary-education-/-early-childhood/graduate-programs

Sonoma State University, School of Education, Rohnert Park, CA 94928-3609. Offers administrative services (Credential); curriculum, teaching, and learning (MA); early childhood education (MA); education specialist (Credential); educational leadership (MA); multiple subject (Credential); reading and literacy (MA, Credential); single subject (Credential); special education (MA). *Accreditation:* NCATE. *Program availability:* Part-time, evening/weekend. *Degree requirements:* For master's, thesis or alternative. *Entrance requirements:* For master's, minimum GPA of 2.5. Additional exam requirements/recommendations for international students: Required—TOEFL (minimum score 500 paper-based). Application fee: $55. *Expenses:* Tuition, state resident: full-time $6738; part-time $3906 per unit. *Required fees:* $1916; $1916 per year. Tuition and fees vary according to course load, degree level and program. *Financial support:* Fellowships, research assistantships, career-related internships or fieldwork, and Federal Work-Study available. Support available to part-time students. Financial award application deadline: 3/2; financial award applicants required to submit FAFSA. *Unit head:* Dr. Carlos Ayala, Dean, 707-664-4412, E-mail: carlos.ayala@sonoma.edu. *Application contact:* Dr. Jennifer Mahdavi, Coordinator of Graduate Studies, 707-664-3311, E-mail: jennifer.mahdavi@sonoma.edu.
Website: http://www.sonoma.edu/education/

Southeastern Louisiana University, College of Arts, Humanities and Social Sciences, Department of English, Hammond, LA 70402. Offers creative writing (MA); language and theory (MA); professional writing (MA); publishing studies (MA). *Program availability:* Part-time. *Faculty:* 12 full-time (4 women), 1 part-time/adjunct (0 women). *Students:* 12 full-time (9 women), 15 part-time (10 women); includes 4 minority (1 Black or African American, non-Hispanic/Latino; 2 Hispanic/Latino; 1 Two or more races, non-Hispanic/Latino). Average age 28. 10 applicants, 60% accepted, 4 enrolled. In 2016, 15 master's awarded. *Degree requirements:* For master's, comprehensive exam, thesis optional. *Entrance requirements:* Additional exam requirements/recommendations for international students: Required—TOEFL (minimum score 500 paper-based; 61 iBT), IELTS (minimum score 5.5). *Application deadline:* For fall admission, 7/15 priority date for domestic students, 6/1 priority date for international students; for spring admission, 12/1 priority date for domestic students, 10/1 priority date for international students. Applications are processed on a rolling basis. Application fee: $20 ($30 for international students). Electronic applications accepted. *Expenses:* Tuition, state resident: full-time $6540; part-time $465 per credit hour. Tuition, nonresident: full-time $19,017; part-time $1158 per credit hour. *Required fees:* $1829. *Financial support:* In 2016–17, 16 students received support, including 8 research assistantships (averaging $9,688 per year), 2 teaching assistantships (averaging $9,900 per year); institutionally sponsored loans, scholarships/grants, and unspecified assistantships also available. Support available to part-time students. Financial award application deadline: 5/1; financial award applicants required to submit FAFSA. *Faculty research:* John Ruskin, animal studies, linguistics, film studies. *Unit head:* Dr. David Hanson, Department Head, 985-549-2100, Fax: 985-549-5021, E-mail: dhanson@southeastern.edu. *Application contact:* Amanda Harper, Graduate Admissions Analyst, 985-549-5620, Fax: 985-549-5632, E-mail: admissions@southeastern.edu.
Website: http://www.southeastern.edu/acad_research/depts/engl

Southeastern Oklahoma State University, School of Education, Durant, OK 74701-0609. Offers math specialist (M Ed); reading specialist (M Ed); school administration (M Ed); school counseling (M Ed). *Accreditation:* NCATE. *Program availability:* Part-time, evening/weekend. *Degree requirements:* For master's, comprehensive exam, thesis optional, portfolio (M Ed). *Entrance requirements:* For master's, GRE General Test (for school counseling), minimum GPA of 3.0 in last 60 hours or 2.75 overall. Additional exam requirements/recommendations for international students: Required—TOEFL (minimum score 550 paper-based; 79 iBT). Electronic applications accepted.

Southeastern University, College of Education, Lakeland, FL 33801-6099. Offers curriculum and instruction (Ed D); educational leadership (M Ed); elementary education (M Ed); exceptional student education (M Ed); exceptional student education/educational therapy (M Ed); organizational leadership (Ed D); reading education (M Ed); teaching English to speakers of other languages (M Ed). *Expenses: Tuition:* Full-time $9450; part-time $6300 per credit. *Required fees:* $500; $250 per semester. One-time fee: $150. Tuition and fees vary according to degree level, campus/location and program. *Unit head:* Amy N. Bratten, Dean, 863-667-5238, E-mail: anbratten@seu.edu.
Website: http://www.seu.edu/education/

Southern Adventist University, School of Education and Psychology, Collegedale, TN 37315-0370. Offers clinical mental health counseling (MS); inclusive education (MS Ed); instructional leadership (MS Ed); literacy education (MS Ed); outdoor teacher education (MS Ed); school counseling (MS). *Accreditation:* NCATE. *Program availability:* Part-time, evening/weekend. *Degree requirements:* For master's, comprehensive exam (for some programs), thesis optional, position paper (MS), portfolio (MS Ed in outdoor teacher education). *Entrance requirements:* For master's, interview (MS); 9 semester hours of upper-division course work in psychology or related field, including 1 course in psychology research or statistics; 9 semester hours of education (MS Ed). Additional exam requirements/recommendations for international students: Required—TOEFL (minimum score 600 paper-based; 100 iBT). Electronic applications accepted.

Southern Connecticut State University, School of Graduate Studies, School of Education, Program in Reading, New Haven, CT 06515-1355. Offers MS, Diploma. *Program availability:* Part-time, evening/weekend. *Faculty:* 3 full-time (all women), 5 part-time/adjunct (4 women). *Students:* 29 full-time (all women), 60 part-time (56 women); includes 6 minority (3 Black or African American, non-Hispanic/Latino; 1 Asian, non-Hispanic/Latino; 1 Hispanic/Latino; 1 Two or more races, non-Hispanic/Latino). Average age 32. 59 applicants, 61% accepted, 36 enrolled. In 2016, 29 master's, 10 other advanced degrees awarded. *Degree requirements:* For master's, thesis or alternative. *Entrance requirements:* For master's, interview, teaching certificate; for Diploma, master's degree. *Application deadline:* For fall admission, 7/15 priority date for domestic students. Applications are processed on a rolling basis. Application fee: $50. Electronic applications accepted. *Expenses:* Tuition, state resident: full-time $6497; part-time $519 per credit hour. Tuition, nonresident: full-time $18,102; part-time $535 per credit hour. *Required fees:* $4722; $55 per semester. Tuition and fees vary according to program. *Financial support:* Career-related internships or fieldwork, scholarships/grants, and unspecified assistantships available. Financial award application deadline: 4/15; financial award applicants required to submit FAFSA. *Unit head:* Dr. Ruth Eren, Chairperson, 203-392-5947, Fax: 203-392-5927, E-mail: erenr1@southernct.edu. *Application contact:* Lisa Galvin, Director of Graduate Admissions, 203-392-5240, Fax: 203-392-5235, E-mail: galvinl1@southernct.edu.

Southern Illinois University Edwardsville, Graduate School, School of Education, Health, and Human Behavior, Department of Curriculum and Instruction, Program in Literacy Education, Edwardsville, IL 62026. Offers MS Ed. *Program availability:* Part-time, evening/weekend. *Degree requirements:* For master's, comprehensive exam, research paper. *Entrance requirements:* Additional exam requirements/recommendations for international students: Required—TOEFL (minimum score 550 paper-based; 79 iBT), IELTS (minimum score 6.5). Electronic applications accepted.

Southern Illinois University Edwardsville, Graduate School, School of Education, Health, and Human Behavior, Department of Curriculum and Instruction, Program in Literacy Specialist, Edwardsville, IL 62026. Offers Post-Master's Certificate. *Program availability:* Part-time. *Entrance requirements:* Additional exam requirements/recommendations for international students: Required—TOEFL (minimum score 550 paper-based; 79 iBT), IELTS (minimum score 6.5). Electronic applications accepted.

Southern Methodist University, Annette Caldwell Simmons School of Education and Human Development, Department of Teaching and Learning, Dallas, TX 75275. Offers bilingual/ESL education (MBE); education (M Ed, PhD); gifted education (MBE); reading and writing (M Ed); special education (M Ed). *Program availability:* Part-time, evening/weekend. Terminal master's awarded for partial completion of doctoral program. *Degree requirements:* For master's, comprehensive exam, minimum GPA of 3.0; for doctorate, thesis/dissertation, qualifying exams, major area paper, evidence of teaching competency, dissemination of research (e.g., conference presentation), professional portfolio. *Entrance requirements:* For master's, minimum GPA of 3.0 or GRE, 3 letters of recommendation; for doctorate, GRE, minimum GPA of 3.3, 3 years of full-time teaching, 3 letters of recommendation, interview. Additional exam requirements/recommendations for international students: Required—TOEFL. Electronic applications accepted. *Faculty research:* Reading intervention, mathematics intervention, bilingual education, new literacies.

Southern New Hampshire University, School of Education, Manchester, NH 03106-1045. Offers business education (M Ed); child development (M Ed); curriculum and instruction (M Ed), including education leadership, reading, special education, technology integration; education (M Ed); educational leadership (M Ed, Ed D); educational studies (M Ed); elementary education (M Ed); English (MAT); English for speakers of other languages (M Ed); reading and writing specialist (M Ed); school business administration (Certificate); secondary education (M Ed); special education (M Ed); technology integration specialist (M Ed). *Program availability:* Part-time, evening/weekend, online learning. *Degree requirements:* For master's, comprehensive exam (for some programs), thesis or alternative. *Entrance requirements:* For master's, PRAXIS I, minimum GPA of 2.75. Additional exam requirements/recommendations for international students: Required—TOEFL (minimum score 550 paper-based). Electronic applications accepted. *Expenses:* Contact institution.

Southern Oregon University, Graduate Studies, School of Education, Ashland, OR 97520. Offers elementary education (MA Ed, MS Ed), including classroom teacher, early childhood, handicapped learner, reading, supervision; secondary education (MA Ed, MS Ed), including classroom teacher, handicapped learner, reading, supervision; teaching (MAT). *Program availability:* Online learning. *Faculty:* 15 full-time (10 women), 27 part-time/adjunct (21 women). *Students:* 116 full-time (82 women), 86 part-time (68 women); includes 22 minority (1 American Indian or Alaska Native, non-Hispanic/Latino; 4 Asian, non-Hispanic/Latino; 8 Hispanic/Latino; 9 Two or more races, non-Hispanic/Latino). Average age 34. 81 applicants, 80% accepted, 49 enrolled. In 2016, 107 master's awarded. *Degree requirements:* For master's, thesis optional. *Entrance requirements:* For master's, GRE General Test, minimum cumulative GPA of 3.0 in the last 90 quarter credits (60 semester credits) of undergraduate coursework. Additional exam requirements/recommendations for international students: Required—TOEFL (minimum score 540 paper-based; 76 iBT), IELTS (minimum score 6), ELPT (minimum

score 964) or ELS (minimum score 112). *Application deadline:* For fall admission, 7/31 priority date for domestic and international students; for winter admission, 11/15 priority date for domestic and international students; for spring admission, 1/7 priority date for domestic and international students. Applications are processed on a rolling basis. Application fee: $60. Electronic applications accepted. *Expenses:* Tuition, state resident: full-time $10,719; part-time $397 per credit. Tuition, nonresident: full-time $13,419; part-time $497 per credit. *Required fees:* $548. *Financial support:* In 2016–17, 2 students received support. Career-related internships or fieldwork, institutionally sponsored loans, scholarships/grants, and unspecified assistantships available. *Unit head:* Dr. Gerry McCain, Graduate Program Coordinator, 541-552-6934, E-mail: mccaing@sou.edu. *Application contact:* Kelly Moutsatson, Director of Admissions, 541-552-6411, Fax: 541-552-8403, E-mail: admissions@sou.edu.
Website: http://www.sou.edu/education/

Southwestern Adventist University, Education Department, Keene, TX 76059. Offers curriculum and instruction with reading emphasis (M Ed); educational leadership (M Ed). *Program availability:* Part-time, evening/weekend. *Degree requirements:* For master's, thesis or alternative, professional paper. *Entrance requirements:* For master's, GRE General Test.

Southwest Minnesota State University, Department of Education, Marshall, MN 56258. Offers ESL (MS); math (MS); reading (MS); special education (MS), including developmental disabilities, early childhood education, emotional behavioral disorders, learning disabilities; teaching, learning and leadership (MS). *Program availability:* Part-time, evening/weekend, online learning. *Entrance requirements:* Additional exam requirements/recommendations for international students: Required—TOEFL or IELTS; Recommended—TOEFL (minimum score 550 paper-based; 80 iBT), IELTS.

Spring Arbor University, School of Education, Spring Arbor, MI 49283-9799. Offers education (MAE); reading (MAR); special education (MSE). *Accreditation:* TEAC. *Program availability:* Part-time, evening/weekend, online learning. *Degree requirements:* For master's, thesis. *Entrance requirements:* For master's, official transcripts from all institutions attended, including evidence of an earned bachelor's degree from regionally-accredited college or university with minimum cumulative GPA of 3.0 for the last two years of the bachelor's degree; two professional letters of recommendation. Additional exam requirements/recommendations for international students: Required—TOEFL (minimum score 600 paper-based). Electronic applications accepted.

State University of New York at Fredonia, College of Education, Fredonia, NY 14063. Offers curriculum and instruction (MS Ed); literacy education (MS Ed), including birth-grade 12, grades 5-12; TESOL (MS Ed). *Accreditation:* NCATE. *Program availability:* Part-time. *Faculty:* 21 full-time (17 women), 11 part-time/adjunct (9 women). *Students:* 39 full-time (32 women), 54 part-time (33 women); includes 8 minority (1 Black or African American, non-Hispanic/Latino; 4 Asian, non-Hispanic/Latino; 2 Hispanic/Latino; 1 Two or more races, non-Hispanic/Latino). Average age 29. 60 applicants, 97% accepted, 39 enrolled. In 2016, 56 master's awarded. *Degree requirements:* For master's, thesis. *Entrance requirements:* For master's, GRE, minimum undergraduate GPA of 3.0. Additional exam requirements/recommendations for international students: Required—TOEFL (minimum score 79 iBT), IELTS (minimum score 6.5). *Application deadline:* For fall admission, 4/1 priority date for domestic and international students; for spring admission, 11/1 priority date for domestic students, 11/1 for international students. Applications are processed on a rolling basis. Application fee: $75. Electronic applications accepted. *Expenses:* Tuition, state resident: full-time $10,370; part-time $453 per credit. Tuition, nonresident: full-time $20,190; part-time $925 per credit. *Required fees:* $1619; $67.30 per credit hour. $403.80 per semester. *Financial support:* In 2016–17, 4 teaching assistantships with full and partial tuition reimbursements (averaging $7,075 per year) were awarded. Financial award application deadline: 3/15; financial award applicants required to submit FAFSA. *Faculty research:* Positive behavioral intervention and support (PBIS), place-based science education, peer support for education, primary source material for social studies education, policies and practices in learning English language. *Unit head:* Dr. Christine Givner, Dean, 716-673-3311, E-mail: christine.givner@fredonia.edu. *Application contact:* Wendy S. Dunst, Interim Graduate Recruitment and Admissions Associate, 716-673-3808, Fax: 716-673-3712, E-mail: wendy.dunst@fredonia.edu.
Website: http://www.fredonia.edu/coe/

State University of New York at New Paltz, Graduate School, School of Education, Department of Educational Studies, Program in Special Education, New Paltz, NY 12561. Offers adolescence special education (7-12) (MS Ed); adolescence special education and literacy (MS Ed); childhood special education (1-6) (MS Ed); childhood special education and literacy (MS Ed); early childhood special education (B-2) (MS Ed). *Accreditation:* NCATE. *Program availability:* Part-time, evening/weekend. *Students:* 25 full-time (19 women), 39 part-time (29 women); includes 9 minority (2 Asian, non-Hispanic/Latino; 7 Hispanic/Latino). 13 applicants, 85% accepted, 10 enrolled. In 2016, 36 master's awarded. *Entrance requirements:* For master's, minimum GPA of 3.0 (3.2 for special education and literacy programs), New York state teaching certificate. Additional exam requirements/recommendations for international students: Required—TOEFL (minimum score 550 paper-based; 80 iBT), IELTS (minimum score 6.5). *Application deadline:* For fall admission, 3/15 priority date for domestic students, 3/15 for international students; for spring admission, 11/1 for domestic and international students. Application fee: $50. Electronic applications accepted. *Financial support:* Application deadline: 8/1. *Unit head:* Dr. Jane Sileo, Coordinator, 845-257-2835, E-mail: sileoj@newpaltz.edu. *Application contact:* Vika Shock, Director of Graduate Admissions, 845-257-3286, E-mail: gradschool@newpaltz.edu.
Website: http://www.newpaltz.edu/schoolofed/department-of-teaching—learning/special_ed.html

State University of New York at New Paltz, Graduate School, School of Education, Department of Elementary Education, New Paltz, NY 12561. Offers childhood education 1-6 (MS Ed, MST), including childhood education 1-6 (MST), early childhood B-2 (MS Ed), mathematics, science and technology (MS Ed), reading/literacy (MS Ed); literacy education 5-12 (MS Ed); literacy education and childhood special education (MS Ed); literacy education B-6 (MS Ed). *Accreditation:* NCATE. *Program availability:* Part-time, evening/weekend. *Students:* 32 full-time (29 women), 100 part-time (91 women); includes 22 minority (5 Black or African American, non-Hispanic/Latino; 1 American Indian or Alaska Native, non-Hispanic/Latino; 2 Asian, non-Hispanic/Latino; 10 Hispanic/Latino; 4 Two or more races, non-Hispanic/Latino). 30 applicants, 73% accepted, 14 enrolled. In 2016, 70 master's awarded. *Degree requirements:* For master's, comprehensive exam (for some programs), portfolio. *Entrance requirements:* For master's, GRE or MAT (for MST), minimum GPA of 3.0 (3.2 for literacy and special education), New York state teaching certificate (for MS Ed). Additional exam requirements/recommendations for international students: Required—TOEFL (minimum score 550 paper-based; 80 iBT), IELTS (minimum score 6.5). *Application deadline:* For fall admission, 4/1 for domestic and international students; for spring admission, 11/1 priority date for domestic and international students; for summer admission, 4/15 priority date for domestic and international students. Applications are processed on a rolling basis. Application fee: $50. Electronic applications accepted. *Financial support:* Application deadline: 8/1. *Faculty research:* Multi-sensory teaching methods, volunteer tutoring programs for struggling readers, school readiness and transition, math/science/technology, university-school partnerships. *Unit head:* Dr. Aaron Isabelle, Chair, 845-257-2837, E-mail: isabella@newpaltz.edu. *Application contact:* Vika Shock, Assistant Director of Graduate Admissions, 845-257-3285, Fax: 845-257-3284, E-mail: gradschool@newpaltz.edu.
Website: http://www.newpaltz.edu/elementaryed/

State University of New York at Oswego, Graduate Studies, School of Education, Department of Curriculum and Instruction, Oswego, NY 13126. Offers adolescence education (MST); art education (MAT); childhood education (MST); curriculum and instruction (MS Ed); literacy education (MS Ed); special education (MS Ed). *Program availability:* Part-time, evening/weekend. *Degree requirements:* For master's, comprehensive exam (for some programs), thesis optional. *Entrance requirements:* For master's, GRE General Test, minimum GPA of 2.7, provisional teaching certificate. Additional exam requirements/recommendations for international students: Required—TOEFL (minimum score 560 paper-based). *Faculty research:* Classroom applications for microcomputers; classroom questioning, wait-time, and achievement; values clarification and academic achievement.

State University of New York at Plattsburgh, School of Education, Health, and Human Services, Program in Teacher Education: Literacy Education, Plattsburgh, NY 12901-2681. Offers birth-grade 6 (MS Ed); grades 5-12 (MS Ed). *Accreditation:* TEAC. *Program availability:* Part-time, evening/weekend. *Entrance requirements:* For master's, minimum GPA of 2.75. Additional exam requirements/recommendations for international students: Required—TOEFL. *Faculty research:* Reading pedagogy, early childhood literacy, children's literature, integrated language arts.

State University of New York College at Cortland, Graduate Studies, School of Education, Program in Literacy Education, Cortland, NY 13045. Offers MS Ed. *Accreditation:* NCATE. *Program availability:* Part-time, evening/weekend. *Degree requirements:* For master's, one foreign language, comprehensive exam, thesis (for some programs). *Entrance requirements:* Additional exam requirements/recommendations for international students: Required—TOEFL.

State University of New York College at Geneseo, Graduate Studies, School of Education, Program in Reading and Literacy, Geneseo, NY 14454-1401. Offers MS Ed. *Program availability:* Part-time. *Faculty:* 8 full-time (6 women), 2 part-time/adjunct (both women). *Students:* 16 full-time (15 women), 40 part-time (32 women); includes 7 minority (3 Black or African American, non-Hispanic/Latino; 1 American Indian or Alaska Native, non-Hispanic/Latino; 2 Asian, non-Hispanic/Latino; 1 Hispanic/Latino). Average age 26. 18 applicants, 72% accepted, 11 enrolled. In 2016, 35 master's awarded. *Degree requirements:* For master's, thesis optional, reading clinics, action research project. *Entrance requirements:* For master's, initial teaching certification in New York state. Additional exam requirements/recommendations for international students: Required—TOEFL, IELTS, PTE. *Application deadline:* For fall admission, 4/1 priority date for domestic students; for spring admission, 11/1 for domestic students. Applications are processed on a rolling basis. Application fee: $50. Electronic applications accepted. *Expenses:* Tuition, state resident: full-time $10,870; part-time $453 per credit. Tuition, nonresident: full-time $22,210; part-time $925 per credit. *Required fees:* $865; $35.85 per credit hour. *Financial support:* In 2016–17, 8 students received support. Fellowships, career-related internships or fieldwork, scholarships/grants, health care benefits, tuition waivers (full), and unspecified assistantships available. Support available to part-time students. Financial award application deadline: 4/1; financial award applicants required to submit FAFSA. *Unit head:* Dr. Anjoo Sikka, Dean of School of Education, 585-245-5151, Fax: 585-245-5220, E-mail: sikka@geneseo.edu. *Application contact:* Michael R. George, Graduate Enrollment Coordinator, 585-245-5148, Fax: 585-245-5550, E-mail: georgem@geneseo.edu.

State University of New York College at Oneonta, Graduate Programs, Division of Education, Department of Elementary Education and Reading, Oneonta, NY 13820-4015. Offers childhood education (MS Ed); literacy education (MS Ed). *Accreditation:* NCATE. *Program availability:* Part-time, evening/weekend. *Entrance requirements:* For master's, GRE General Test. *Application deadline:* For fall admission, 3/25 priority date for domestic students; for spring admission, 10/1 priority date for domestic students. Applications are processed on a rolling basis. Application fee: $50. *Unit head:* Dr. Cindy Lassonde, Chair, 607-436-3176, Fax: 607-436-2554, E-mail: lassonc@oneonta.edu. *Application contact:* Patrick J. Mente, Director of Graduate Studies, 607-436-2523, Fax: 607-436-3084, E-mail: gradstudies@oneonta.edu.
Website: http://www.oneonta.edu/academics/ed/eled/

State University of New York College at Potsdam, School of Education and Professional Studies, Program in Literacy, Potsdam, NY 13676. Offers literacy educator (MS Ed); literacy specialist (MS Ed), including birth-grade 6, grades 5-12. *Accreditation:* NCATE. *Program availability:* Part-time, online learning. *Entrance requirements:* For master's, minimum GPA of 2.75 in last 60 hours of course work. Additional exam requirements/recommendations for international students: Required—TOEFL (minimum score 550 paper-based; 80 iBT), IELTS (minimum score 6). Electronic applications accepted.

Sul Ross State University, College of Professional Studies, Department of Education, Program in Reading Specialist, Alpine, TX 79832. Offers master reading teacher (Certificate); Texas reading specialist (M Ed). *Program availability:* Part-time, evening/weekend. *Degree requirements:* For master's, thesis optional. *Entrance requirements:* For master's, GMAT or GRE General Test, minimum GPA of 2.5 in last 60 hours of undergraduate work.

Sul Ross State University, Rio Grande College of Sul Ross State University, Alpine, TX 79832. Offers business administration (MBA); teacher education (M Ed), including bilingual education, counseling, educational diagnostics, elementary education, general education, reading, school administration, secondary education. *Program availability:* Part-time, evening/weekend, online learning. *Degree requirements:* For master's, comprehensive exam, thesis optional, minimum GPA of 3.0. *Entrance requirements:* For master's, GMAT or GRE General Test, minimum GPA of 2.5 in last 60 hours of undergraduate work. Additional exam requirements/recommendations for international students: Required—TOEFL.

Syracuse University, College of Arts and Sciences, MA Program in Spanish Literature and Culture, Syracuse, NY 13244. Offers MA. *Program availability:* Part-time. *Students:* Average age 26. In 2016, 6 master's awarded. *Degree requirements:* For master's, comprehensive exam, thesis (for some programs). *Entrance requirements:* For master's, GRE General Test, official transcripts, resume, three letters of recommendation. Additional exam requirements/recommendations for international students: Required—TOEFL (minimum score 100 iBT). *Application deadline:* For fall admission, 2/1 priority date for domestic and international students. Application fee: $75. Electronic applications accepted. *Expenses: Tuition:* Full-time $25,974; part-time $1443 per credit hour. *Required fees:* $802; $50 per course. Tuition and fees vary according to course load and program. *Financial support:* Fellowships with full tuition reimbursements, teaching assistantships with tuition reimbursements, scholarships/grants, and tuition waivers available. Financial award application deadline: 1/1. *Faculty research:* Literature and culture of the Hispanic world, Hispanic linguistics, literatures and cultures of contemporary Spain, methodological approaches and to the orientations of contemporary theory. *Unit head:* Alicia Ríos, Associate Professor/Program Coordinator,

315-443-5385, E-mail: abrios@syr.edu. *Application contact:* Kathryn Clinton, Information Contact, 315-443-5494, E-mail: kclinton@syr.edu.
Website: http://lang.syr.edu/academics/Spanish/MA-Spanish.html

Syracuse University, School of Education, MS Program in Literacy Education (Birth - Grade 12), Syracuse, NY 13244. Offers MS. *Program availability:* Part-time. *Students:* Average age 24. *Degree requirements:* For master's, thesis or alternative. *Entrance requirements:* For master's, GRE, baccalaureate degree from regionally-accredited college/university, New York State teaching certification, strong writing skills, letters of recommendation, personal statement. Additional exam requirements/recommendations for international students: Required—TOEFL (minimum score 100 iBT). *Application deadline:* For fall admission, 1/15 priority date for domestic and international students. Applications are processed on a rolling basis. Application fee: $75. Electronic applications accepted. *Expenses: Tuition:* Full-time $25,974; part-time $1443 per credit hour. *Required fees:* $802; $50 per course. Tuition and fees vary according to course load and program. *Financial support:* Fellowships with full tuition reimbursements, research assistantships, teaching assistantships with tuition reimbursements, career-related internships or fieldwork, and scholarships/grants available. Financial award application deadline: 1/15. *Faculty research:* Literacy, knowledge modeling, assessment, teaching of literature, writing. *Unit head:* Dr. Marcelle Haddix, Chair of Reading and Language Arts/Associate Professor, 315-443-7642, E-mail: mhaddix@syr.edu. *Application contact:* Speranza Migliore, Graduate Admissions Recruiter, 315-443-2505, E-mail: gradrcrt@syr.edu.
Website: http://soe.syr.edu/academic/reading_language_arts/graduate/masters/literacy_education/default.aspx

Syracuse University, School of Education, PhD Program in Literacy Education, Syracuse, NY 13244. Offers PhD. *Program availability:* Part-time. *Degree requirements:* For doctorate, thesis/dissertation. *Entrance requirements:* For doctorate, GRE, master's degree, three references, personal statement, college/university transcripts. Additional exam requirements/recommendations for international students: Required—TOEFL (minimum score 100 iBT). *Application deadline:* For fall admission, 1/15 priority date for domestic and international students; for spring admission, 10/15 priority date for domestic and international students. Applications are processed on a rolling basis. Application fee: $75. Electronic applications accepted. *Expenses: Tuition:* Full-time $25,974; part-time $1443 per credit hour. *Required fees:* $802; $50 per course. Tuition and fees vary according to course load and program. *Financial support:* Fellowships with full tuition reimbursements, research assistantships with tuition reimbursements, teaching assistantships with tuition reimbursements, career-related internships or fieldwork, and scholarships/grants available. Financial award application deadline: 1/15. *Faculty research:* Social and critical perspectives toward language and literacy development, instruction and teacher education, programs and curriculum development related to childhood or adolescent reading and writing instruction, literacy across the curriculum, or multimodal literacies. *Unit head:* Dr. Marcelle Haddix, Chair of Reading and Language Arts/Associate Professor, 315-443-7642, E-mail: mhaddix@syr.edu. *Application contact:* Speranza Migliore, Graduate Admissions Recruiter, 315-443-2505, E-mail: gradrcrt@syr.edu.
Website: http://soe.syr.edu/academic/reading_language_arts/graduate/phd/default.aspx

Tarleton State University, College of Graduate Studies, College of Education, Department of Curriculum and Instruction, Stephenville, TX 76402. Offers educational diagnostician (M Ed); elementary education (M Ed); instructional design and technology (M Ed); instructional leadership (M Ed); professional reading specialist (M Ed); secondary education (M Ed); special education (M Ed); technology applications (M Ed); technology director (M Ed). *Program availability:* Part-time, evening/weekend. *Faculty:* 9 full-time (7 women), 6 part-time/adjunct (4 women). *Students:* 17 full-time (0 women), 104 part-time (101 women); includes 28 minority (5 Black or African American, non-Hispanic/Latino; 1 American Indian or Alaska Native, non-Hispanic/Latino; 19 Hispanic/Latino; 3 Two or more races, non-Hispanic/Latino). 62 applicants, 94% accepted, 35 enrolled. In 2016, 34 master's awarded. *Degree requirements:* For master's, comprehensive exam. *Entrance requirements:* For master's, GRE General Test, minimum GPA of 3.0. Additional exam requirements/recommendations for international students: Required—TOEFL (minimum score 550 paper-based; 80 iBT). *Application deadline:* For fall admission, 8/15 priority date for domestic students; for spring admission, 1/7 for domestic students. Applications are processed on a rolling basis. Application fee: $45 ($145 for international students). Electronic applications accepted. *Expenses:* $3,672 tuition; $2,437 fees. *Financial support:* Research assistantships, teaching assistantships, career-related internships or fieldwork, Federal Work-Study, and institutionally sponsored loans available. Support available to part-time students. Financial award application deadline: 5/1; financial award applicants required to submit FAFSA. *Unit head:* Dr. Jordan Barkley, Department Head, 254-968-9089, E-mail: jbarkley@tarleton.edu. *Application contact:* Information Contact, 254-968-9104, Fax: 254-968-9670, E-mail: gradoffice@tarleton.edu.
Website: http://www.tarleton.edu/cimasters/

Teachers College, Columbia University, Department of Curriculum and Teaching, New York, NY 10027-6696. Offers curriculum and teaching (Ed M, MA, Ed D); curriculum and teaching: elementary education (MA); curriculum and teaching: secondary education (MA); early childhood education (MA, Ed D); early childhood education: special education (MA); elementary education-gifted extension (MA); elementary inclusive education (MA); gifted education (MA); literacy specialist (MA); secondary inclusive education (MA); special inclusive elementary education (MA). *Program availability:* Part-time, evening/weekend. *Students:* 236 full-time (219 women), 198 part-time (176 women); includes 160 minority (53 Black or African American, non-Hispanic/Latino; 1 American Indian or Alaska Native, non-Hispanic/Latino; 43 Asian, non-Hispanic/Latino; 41 Hispanic/Latino; 22 Two or more races, non-Hispanic/Latino), 38 international. 399 applicants, 66% accepted, 104 enrolled. Terminal master's awarded for partial completion of doctoral program. *Degree requirements:* For doctorate, thesis/dissertation. *Expenses: Tuition:* Full-time $36,288; part-time $1512 per credit. *Required fees:* $438 per semester. One-time fee: $510 full-time. Full-time tuition and fees vary according to course load. *Unit head:* Prof. Nancy Lesko, Chair, 212-678-3264, E-mail: lesko@tc.columbia.edu. *Application contact:* David Estrella, Director of Admission, 212-678-3305, Fax: 212-678-4171, E-mail: estrella@tc.columbia.edu.

Teachers College, Columbia University, Department of Health and Behavior Studies, New York, NY 10027-6696. Offers applied behavior analysis (MA, PhD); applied educational psychology: school psychology (Ed M, PhD); behavioral nutrition (PhD), including nutrition (Ed D, PhD); community health education (MS); community nutrition education (Ed M), including community nutrition education; education of deaf and hard of hearing (MA, PhD); health education (MA, Ed D); hearing impairment (Ed D); intellectual disability/autism (MA, Ed D, PhD); nursing education (Ed D, Advanced Certificate); nutrition and education (MS); nutrition and exercise physiology (MS); nutrition and public health (MS); nutrition education (Ed D), including nutrition (Ed D, PhD); physical disabilities (Ed D); reading specialist (MA); severe or multiple disabilities (MA); special education (Ed M, MA, Ed D); teaching of sign language (MA). *Program availability:* Part-time, evening/weekend. *Students:* 282 full-time (262 women), 262 part-time (222 women); includes 180 minority (54 Black or African American, non-Hispanic/Latino; 1 American Indian or Alaska Native, non-Hispanic/Latino; 56 Asian, non-Hispanic/Latino; 56 Hispanic/Latino; 1 Native Hawaiian or other Pacific Islander, non-Hispanic/Latino; 12 Two or more races, non-Hispanic/Latino), 55 international. 503 applicants, 57% accepted, 146 enrolled. Terminal master's awarded for partial completion of doctoral program. *Expenses: Tuition:* Full-time $36,288; part-time $1512 per credit. *Required fees:* $438 per semester. One-time fee: $510 full-time. Full-time tuition and fees vary according to course load. *Unit head:* Prof. Stephen T. Peverly, Chair, 212-678-3964, Fax: 212-678-8259, E-mail: stp4@columbia.edu. *Application contact:* David Estrella, Director of Admission, 212-678-3305, E-mail: estrella@tc.columbia.edu.
Website: http://www.tc.columbia.edu/health-and-behavior-studies/

Tennessee Technological University, College of Graduate Studies, College of Education, Department of Curriculum and Instruction, Program in Exceptional Learning, Cookeville, TN 38505. Offers applied behavior analysis (PhD); literacy (PhD); program planning and evaluation (PhD); STEM education (PhD). *Program availability:* Part-time, evening/weekend. *Students:* 10 full-time (6 women), 28 part-time (21 women); includes 2 minority (1 Black or African American, non-Hispanic/Latino; 1 Two or more races, non-Hispanic/Latino), 2 international. 15 applicants, 67% accepted, 7 enrolled. In 2016, 5 doctorates awarded. *Degree requirements:* For doctorate, comprehensive exam, thesis/dissertation. *Entrance requirements:* For doctorate, GRE, minimum GPA of 3.0. Additional exam requirements/recommendations for international students: Required—TOEFL (minimum score 550 paper-based; 79 iBT), IELTS (minimum score 5.5), PTE (minimum score 53), or TOEIC (Test of English as an International Communication). *Application deadline:* For fall admission, 8/1 for domestic students, 5/1 for international students; for spring admission, 12/1 for domestic students, 10/1 for international students; for summer admission, 5/1 for domestic students, 2/1 for international students. Applications are processed on a rolling basis. Application fee: $35 ($40 for international students). Electronic applications accepted. *Expenses:* Tuition, state resident: full-time $9375; part-time $534 per credit hour. Tuition, nonresident: full-time $22,443; part-time $1260 per credit hour. *Financial support:* In 2016–17, 4 fellowships (averaging $8,000 per year), 9 research assistantships (averaging $12,000 per year), 2 teaching assistantships (averaging $12,000 per year) were awarded. Financial award application deadline: 4/1. *Unit head:* Dr. Lisa Zagumny, Director, 931-372-3078, Fax: 931-372-3517, E-mail: lzagumny@tntech.edu. *Application contact:* Shelia K. Kendrick, Coordinator of Graduate Studies, 931-372-3808, Fax: 931-372-3497, E-mail: skendrick@tntech.edu.
Website: https://www.tntech.edu/education/elphd/

Tennessee Technological University, College of Graduate Studies, College of Education, Department of Curriculum and Instruction, Program in Reading, Cookeville, TN 38505. Offers MA, Ed S. *Accreditation:* NCATE. *Program availability:* Part-time, evening/weekend. *Faculty:* 2 full-time (both women). *Students:* 10 part-time (all women). Average age 27. 4 applicants, 75% accepted, 2 enrolled. In 2016, 2 master's, 1 other advanced degree awarded. *Degree requirements:* For master's and Ed S, comprehensive exam, thesis or alternative. *Entrance requirements:* For master's and Ed S, MAT or GRE. Additional exam requirements/recommendations for international students: Required—TOEFL (minimum score 527 paper-based; 71 iBT), IELTS (minimum score 5.5), PTE (minimum score 48), or TOEIC (Test of English as an International Communication). *Application deadline:* For fall admission, 8/1 for domestic students, 5/1 for international students; for spring admission, 12/1 for domestic students, 10/1 for international students; for summer admission, 5/1 for domestic students, 2/1 for international students. Applications are processed on a rolling basis. Application fee: $35 ($40 for international students). Electronic applications accepted. *Expenses:* Tuition, state resident: full-time $9375; part-time $534 per credit hour. Tuition, nonresident: full-time $22,443; part-time $1260 per credit hour. *Financial support:* Fellowships, research assistantships, teaching assistantships, and career-related internships or fieldwork available. Financial award application deadline: 4/1. *Unit head:* Dr. Jeremy Wendt, Interim Chairperson, 931-372-3181, Fax: 931-372-6270, E-mail: jwendt@tntech.edu. *Application contact:* Shelia K. Kendrick, Coordinator of Graduate Studies, 931-372-3808, Fax: 931-372-3497, E-mail: skendrick@tntech.edu.

Texas A&M University–Commerce, College of Education and Human Services, Commerce, TX 75429-3011. Offers counseling (MS); curriculum and instruction (M Ed, MS); early childhood education (M Ed, MS); educational administration (M Ed, Ed D); educational psychology (PhD); educational technology leadership (MS); educational technology library science (MS); health, kinesiology and sports studies (MS); higher education (MS, Ed D); organization, learning, and technology (MS); psychology (MS); reading (M Ed, MS); school psychology (SSP); secondary education (M Ed, MS); social work (MSW); special education (M Ed); supervision, curriculum and instruction-elementary education (Ed D). *Program availability:* Part-time, 100% online, blended/hybrid learning. *Faculty:* 88 full-time (52 women), 31 part-time/adjunct (24 women). *Students:* 341 full-time (276 women), 1,495 part-time (1,156 women); includes 762 minority (429 Black or African American, non-Hispanic/Latino; 4 American Indian or Alaska Native, non-Hispanic/Latino; 27 Asian, non-Hispanic/Latino; 247 Hispanic/Latino; 1 Native Hawaiian or other Pacific Islander, non-Hispanic/Latino; 54 Two or more races, non-Hispanic/Latino), 18 international. Average age 37. 1,070 applicants, 54% accepted, 452 enrolled. In 2016, 579 master's, 31 doctorates awarded. *Degree requirements:* For master's, one foreign language, comprehensive exam, thesis optional, departmental qualifying exams (for some programs); for doctorate, comprehensive exam, thesis/dissertation, departmental qualifying exam; for SSP, comprehensive exam, thesis optional. *Entrance requirements:* For master's and doctorate, GRE General Test. Additional exam requirements/recommendations for international students: Required—TOEFL (minimum score 550 paper-based; 79 iBT), IELTS (minimum score 6). *Application deadline:* For fall admission, 6/1 priority date for international students; for spring admission, 10/15 priority date for international students; for summer admission, 3/15 priority date for international students. Applications are processed on a rolling basis. Application fee: $50. Electronic applications accepted. *Expenses:* $2,254 resident; $4,744 non-resident. *Financial support:* In 2016–17, 301 students received support, including 39 research assistantships with partial tuition reimbursements available (averaging $9,000 per year), 17 teaching assistantships with partial tuition reimbursements available (averaging $9,000 per year); career-related internships or fieldwork, Federal Work-Study, institutionally sponsored loans, scholarships/grants, health care benefits, and unspecified assistantships also available. Financial award application deadline: 5/1; financial award applicants required to submit FAFSA. *Faculty research:* Cognitive and bilingual education, positive behavioral intervention, literacy, math readiness. *Total annual research expenditures:* $470,963. *Unit head:* Dr. Timothy Letzring, Dean, 903-886-5181, Fax: 903-886-5905, E-mail: tim.letzring@tamuc.edu. *Application contact:* Jennifer Faunce, Graduate Recruiter, 903-886-5030, Fax: 903-886-5905, E-mail: jennifer.faunce@tamuc.edu.
Website: http://www.tamuc.edu/academics/graduateSchool/programs/education/default.aspx

Texas A&M University–Corpus Christi, College of Graduate Studies, College of Education, Corpus Christi, TX 78412-5503. Offers counseling (MS), including counseling; counselor education (PhD); curriculum and instruction (MS, PhD); early childhood education (MS); educational administration (MS); educational leadership (Ed D); elementary education (MS); instructional design and educational technology (MS); kinesiology (MS); reading (MS); secondary education (MS); special education

(MS). *Program availability:* Part-time, evening/weekend, online learning. *Faculty:* 50 full-time (29 women), 29 part-time/adjunct (18 women). *Students:* 158 full-time (130 women), 344 part-time (281 women); includes 288 minority (28 Black or African American, non-Hispanic/Latino; 2 American Indian or Alaska Native, non-Hispanic/Latino; 8 Asian, non-Hispanic/Latino; 246 Hispanic/Latino; 4 Two or more races, non-Hispanic/Latino), 22 international. Average age 35. 273 applicants, 60% accepted, 142 enrolled. In 2016, 67 master's, 13 doctorates awarded. *Degree requirements:* For master's, comprehensive exam, capstone; for doctorate, thesis/dissertation. *Entrance requirements:* For master's, GRE General Test, essay (300 words); for doctorate, GRE, essay, resume, 3-4 reference forms. *Application deadline:* For fall admission, 7/15 priority date for domestic students, 5/1 priority date for international students; for spring admission, 11/15 priority date for domestic students, 9/1 priority date for international students. Applications are processed on a rolling basis. Application fee: $50 ($70 for international students). Electronic applications accepted. *Financial support:* Research assistantships, teaching assistantships, career-related internships or fieldwork, Federal Work-Study, institutionally sponsored loans, scholarships/grants, health care benefits, and unspecified assistantships available. Support available to part-time students. Financial award application deadline: 3/15; financial award applicants required to submit FAFSA. *Unit head:* Dr. Arthur Hernandez, Dean, 361-825-2660, E-mail: art.hernandez@tamucc.edu. *Application contact:* Graduate Admissions Coordinator, 361-825-2177, Fax: 361-825-2755, E-mail: gradweb@tamucc.edu.
Website: http://education.tamucc.edu/

Texas A&M University–Kingsville, College of Graduate Studies, College of Education and Human Performance, Department of Teacher and Bilingual Education, Program in Reading Specialization, Kingsville, TX 78363. Offers MS. *Program availability:* Part-time, evening/weekend. *Degree requirements:* For master's, variable foreign language requirement, comprehensive exam, thesis (for some programs). *Entrance requirements:* For master's, GRE, MAT, GMAT. Additional exam requirements/recommendations for international students: Required—TOEFL (minimum score 550 paper-based; 79 iBT). Electronic applications accepted.

Texas A&M University–San Antonio, Department of Curriculum and Kinesiology, San Antonio, TX 78224. Offers bilingual education (MA); early childhood education (M Ed); kinesiology (MS); reading (MS); special education (M Ed), including educational diagnostician, instructional specialist. *Program availability:* Part-time, evening/weekend. *Degree requirements:* For master's, comprehensive exam, thesis or alternative. *Entrance requirements:* For master's, MAT. Additional exam requirements/recommendations for international students: Required—TOEFL (minimum score 550 paper-based; 80 iBT), IELTS (minimum score 6). Electronic applications accepted.

Texas Christian University, College of Education, Master's Programs in Education, Fort Worth, TX 76129. Offers counseling (M Ed); curriculum and instruction (M Ed), including curriculum studies, language and literacy, math education, science education; educational leadership (M Ed); special education (M Ed). *Program availability:* Part-time, evening/weekend. *Faculty:* 29 full-time (21 women), 8 part-time/adjunct (5 women). *Students:* 112 full-time (95 women), 12 part-time (11 women); includes 39 minority (6 Black or African American, non-Hispanic/Latino; 2 Asian, non-Hispanic/Latino; 27 Hispanic/Latino; 1 Native Hawaiian or other Pacific Islander, non-Hispanic/Latino; 3 Two or more races, non-Hispanic/Latino), 2 international. Average age 29. 107 applicants, 78% accepted, 66 enrolled. In 2016, 54 master's awarded. *Degree requirements:* For master's, comprehensive exam (for some programs), thesis (for some programs). *Entrance requirements:* For master's, GRE General Test. Additional exam requirements/recommendations for international students: Required—TOEFL (minimum score 550 paper-based; 80 iBT). *Application deadline:* For fall admission, 3/1 for domestic and international students; for spring admission, 11/16 for domestic and international students; for summer admission, 3/1 for domestic and international students. Application fee: $60. Electronic applications accepted. *Expenses: Tuition:* Full-time $26,640; part-time $1480 per credit hour. *Required fees:* $48. Tuition and fees vary according to program. *Financial support:* In 2016–17, 104 students received support, including 4 research assistantships with full tuition reimbursements available (averaging $15,000 per year), 31 teaching assistantships with full tuition reimbursements available (averaging $15,000 per year); career-related internships or fieldwork, scholarships/grants, and unspecified assistantships also available. Support available to part-time students. Financial award application deadline: 3/1; financial award applicants required to submit FAFSA. *Unit head:* Dr. Jan Lacina, Associate Dean, 817-257-6786, Fax: 817-257-7466, E-mail: j.lacina@tcu.edu. *Application contact:* Lori Kimball, Administrative Program Specialist, 817-257-7661, Fax: 817-257-7466, E-mail: l.kimball@tcu.edu.
Website: http://coe.tcu.edu/graduate-overview/

Texas State University, The Graduate College, College of Education, Program in Reading Education, San Marcos, TX 78666. Offers M Ed. *Program availability:* Part-time, evening/weekend. *Faculty:* 10 full-time (9 women), 1 (woman) part-time/adjunct. *Students:* 3 full-time (all women), 32 part-time (31 women); includes 18 minority (all Hispanic/Latino). Average age 36. 23 applicants, 91% accepted, 15 enrolled. In 2016, 5 master's awarded. *Degree requirements:* For master's, comprehensive exam. *Entrance requirements:* For master's, GRE (preferred), baccalaureate degree from regionally-accredited institution with minimum GPA of 3.0 in last 60 hours of course work, statement of purpose, official teaching certificate. Additional exam requirements/recommendations for international students: Required—TOEFL (minimum score 550 paper-based; 78 iBT), IELTS (minimum score 6.5). *Application deadline:* For fall admission, 2/15 priority date for domestic and international students; for spring admission, 10/15 priority date for domestic students, 10/1 for international students; for summer admission, 4/15 for domestic students, 3/15 for international students. Applications are processed on a rolling basis. Application fee: $40 ($90 for international students). Electronic applications accepted. *Expenses:* $4,851 per semester. *Financial support:* In 2016–17, 17 students received support. Research assistantships, teaching assistantships, career-related internships or fieldwork, Federal Work-Study, institutionally sponsored loans, and scholarships/grants available. Support available to part-time students. Financial award application deadline: 3/1; financial award applicants required to submit FAFSA. *Unit head:* Dr. Jane Saunders, Graduate Advisor, 512-245-1512, Fax: 512-245-8365, E-mail: js99@txstate.edu. *Application contact:* Dr. Andrea Golato, Dean of Graduate School, 512-245-2581, Fax: 512-245-8365, E-mail: gradcollege@txstate.edu.
Website: http://www.education.txstate.edu/ci/degrees-certifications/graduate/reading.html

Texas Tech University, Graduate School, College of Education, Department of Curriculum and Instruction, Lubbock, TX 79409-1071. Offers bilingual education (M Ed); curriculum and instruction (M Ed); elementary education (M Ed); language/literacy education (M Ed); multidisciplinary science (MS); secondary education (M Ed). *Accreditation:* NCATE. *Program availability:* Part-time, evening/weekend, online learning. *Faculty:* 24 full-time (17 women), 1 part-time/adjunct (0 women). *Students:* 65 full-time (52 women), 237 part-time (191 women); includes 97 minority (30 Black or African American, non-Hispanic/Latino; 1 American Indian or Alaska Native, non-Hispanic/Latino; 10 Asian, non-Hispanic/Latino; 47 Hispanic/Latino; 9 Two or more races, non-Hispanic/Latino), 41 international. Average age 39. 181 applicants, 54% accepted, 78 enrolled. In 2016, 20 master's, 28 doctorates awarded. Terminal master's awarded for partial completion of doctoral program. *Degree requirements:* For master's, comprehensive exam (for some programs), thesis optional; for doctorate, comprehensive exam, thesis/dissertation. *Entrance requirements:* For master's, bachelor's degree; resume; letter of intent; academic writing sample; 2 letters of recommendation; for doctorate, GRE, master's degree; resume; letter of intent; academic writing sample; 3 letters of recommendation. Additional exam requirements/recommendations for international students: Required—TOEFL (minimum score 550 paper-based; 79 iBT). *Application deadline:* For fall admission, 6/1 priority date for domestic students, 1/15 priority date for international students; for spring admission, 9/1 priority date for domestic students, 6/15 priority date for international students. Applications are processed on a rolling basis. Application fee: $75. Electronic applications accepted. *Expenses:* $285 per credit hour full-time resident tuition, $693 per credit hour full-time non-resident tuition; $50.50 per credit hour fee plus $608 per term fee. *Financial support:* In 2016–17, 110 students received support, including 110 fellowships (averaging $3,132 per year); research assistantships, Federal Work-Study, institutionally sponsored loans, scholarships/grants, health care benefits, and unspecified assistantships also available. Support available to part-time students. Financial award application deadline: 2/1; financial award applicants required to submit FAFSA. *Faculty research:* Teacher education, curriculum studies, bilingual education, science and math education, language and literacy education. *Total annual research expenditures:* $120,552. *Unit head:* Dr. Jian Wang, Department Chair, Curriculum and Instruction, 806-834-5165, Fax: 806-742-2179, E-mail: jian.wang@ttu.edu. *Application contact:* Brianna Sanchez, Coordinator, 806-834-2353, Fax: 806-742-2179, E-mail: brianna.sanchez@ttu.edu.
Website: http://www.educ.ttu.edu

Texas Woman's University, Graduate School, College of Professional Education, Department of Reading, Denton, TX 76204-5769. Offers reading education (M Ed, MA, PhD). *Program availability:* Part-time, evening/weekend. *Students:* 2 full-time (both women), 63 part-time (61 women); includes 21 minority (4 Black or African American, non-Hispanic/Latino; 15 Hispanic/Latino; 2 Two or more races, non-Hispanic/Latino). Average age 41. In 2016, 18 master's, 1 doctorate awarded. Terminal master's awarded for partial completion of doctoral program. *Degree requirements:* For master's, comprehensive exam, thesis (for some programs); for doctorate, comprehensive exam, thesis/dissertation. *Entrance requirements:* For master's, GRE General Test (preferred minimum score 143 [350 old version] Verbal, 138 [350 old version] Quantitative); for doctorate, GRE General Test (preferred minimum score 153 [500 old version] Verbal, 144 [500 old version] Quantitative), master's degree, minimum GPA of 3.5, on-site writing sample, interview, 3 letters of reference, curriculum vitae/resume, 1-2 page statement of professional experience and goals, 3 years of teaching experience. Additional exam requirements/recommendations for international students: Required—TOEFL (minimum score 550 paper-based; 79 iBT). *Application deadline:* For fall admission, 7/1 priority date for domestic students, 3/1 for international students; for spring admission, 12/1 priority date for domestic students, 7/1 for international students. Applications are processed on a rolling basis. Application fee: $50 ($75 for international students). Electronic applications accepted. *Expenses:* Tuition, state resident: full-time $9046; part-time $251 per credit hour. Tuition, nonresident: full-time $22,922; part-time $614 per credit hour. *International tuition:* $23,046 full-time. *Required fees:* $2690; $1285 per credit hour. One-time fee: $50. Tuition and fees vary according to course level, course load, program and reciprocity agreements. *Financial support:* Research assistantships, career-related internships or fieldwork, Federal Work-Study, institutionally sponsored loans, scholarships/grants, traineeships, health care benefits, and unspecified assistantships available. Support available to part-time students. Financial award application deadline: 3/1; financial award applicants required to submit FAFSA. *Faculty research:* Teacher change, home/school partnerships, literacy (middle grades), early literacy, language acquisitions, new literacies, multicultural education, children's literature, literacy leadership and coaching. *Unit head:* Dr. Connie Briggs, Chair, 940-898-2233, Fax: 940-898-2224, E-mail: reading@twu.edu. *Application contact:* Dr. Samuel Wheeler, Assistant Director of Admissions, 940-898-3188, Fax: 940-898-3081, E-mail: wheelersr@twu.edu.
Website: http://www.twu.edu/reading/

Touro College, Graduate School of Education, New York, NY 10010. Offers education and special education (MS); education biology (MS); instructional technology (MS); mathematics education (MS); school leadership (MS); teaching English to speakers of other languages (MS); teaching literacy (MS). *Accreditation:* TEAC. *Program availability:* Part-time, evening/weekend, online learning. *Faculty:* 52 full-time (34 women), 199 part-time/adjunct (136 women). *Students:* 578 full-time (483 women), 1,932 part-time (1,626 women); includes 749 minority (318 Black or African American, non-Hispanic/Latino; 5 American Indian or Alaska Native, non-Hispanic/Latino; 108 Asian, non-Hispanic/Latino; 288 Hispanic/Latino; 2 Native Hawaiian or other Pacific Islander, non-Hispanic/Latino; 28 Two or more races, non-Hispanic/Latino), 17 international. Average age 32. 1,422 applicants, 50% accepted, 675 enrolled. In 2016, 6 master's awarded. *Entrance requirements:* Additional exam requirements/recommendations for international students: Required—TOEFL (minimum score 83 iBT), IELTS (minimum score 6.5). *Application deadline:* For fall admission, 8/26 for domestic students, 7/15 for international students; for spring admission, 12/31 for domestic students, 12/15 for international students. Applications are processed on a rolling basis. Application fee: $50. *Financial support:* Federal Work-Study available. Financial award applicants required to submit FAFSA. *Faculty research:* Equity assistance, language development, scholarly communications, Latin American studies and cultural sensitivity, behavior management techniques and strategies in special education. *Unit head:* Dr. Arnold Spinner, Dean, 212-463-0400 Ext. 5561, Fax: 212-462-4889, E-mail: aspinner@touro.edu. *Application contact:* Luna Feliciano, Admissions, 212-463-0400.

Towson University, Program in Reading, Towson, MD 21252-0001. Offers reading (M Ed); reading education (CAS). *Accreditation:* NCATE. *Program availability:* Part-time, evening/weekend. *Students:* 1 (woman) full-time, 159 part-time (149 women); includes 14 minority (7 Black or African American, non-Hispanic/Latino; 3 Hispanic/Latino; 4 Two or more races, non-Hispanic/Latino). *Entrance requirements:* For master's, minimum GPA of 3.0, essay; for CAS, 3 letters of reference, portfolio, master's degree in reading or related field. *Application deadline:* Applications are processed on a rolling basis. Application fee: $45. Electronic applications accepted. *Expenses:* Tuition, state resident: full-time $7580; part-time $379 per unit. Tuition, nonresident: full-time $15,700; part-time $785 per unit. *Required fees:* $2480. *Financial support:* Application deadline: 4/1. *Unit head:* Dr. Gilda Martinez-Alba, Graduate Program Director, 410-704-2480, E-mail: gmartinez@towson.edu. *Application contact:* Coverley Beidleman, Assistant Director of Graduate Admissions, 410-704-2113, Fax: 410-704-3030, E-mail: grads@towson.edu.
Website: http://www.towson.edu/coe/departments/elementary/grad/reading/

Trident University International, College of Education, Program in Education, Cypress, CA 90630. Offers adult education (MA Ed); aviation education (MA Ed); children's literacy development (MA Ed); e-learning (MA Ed); early childhood education (MA Ed); enrollment management (MA Ed); higher education (MA Ed); teaching and instruction (MA Ed); training and development (MA Ed). *Program availability:* Part-time, evening/weekend, online learning. *Degree requirements:* For master's, capstone project with integrative paper. *Entrance requirements:* For master's, minimum GPA of 2.5

(students with GPA 3.0 or greater may transfer up to 30% of graduate level credits). Additional exam requirements/recommendations for international students: Required—TOEFL (minimum score 525 paper-based). Electronic applications accepted.

Trinity Washington University, School of Education, Washington, DC 20017-1094. Offers clinical mental health counseling (MA); early childhood education (MAT); educating for change (M Ed); educational administration (MSA); elementary education (MAT); reading (M Ed); school counseling (MA); secondary education (MAT), including English, social studies; special education (MAT). *Accreditation:* NCATE. *Program availability:* Part-time, evening/weekend. *Degree requirements:* For master's, thesis (for some programs), capstone project(s). *Entrance requirements:* For master's, PRAXIS I, minimum GPA of 2.8. Additional exam requirements/recommendations for international students: Required—TOEFL (minimum score 550 paper-based). *Faculty research:* Technology, literacy, special education, organizations, inclusion models.

Union College, Graduate Programs, Department of Education, Barbourville, KY 40906-1499. Offers elementary education (MA); health and physical education (MA); middle grades (MA); music education (MA); principalship (MA); reading specialist (MA); secondary education (MA); special education (MA). *Degree requirements:* For master's, thesis optional. *Entrance requirements:* For master's, GRE General Test, NTE.

University at Albany, State University of New York, School of Education, Department of Literacy Teaching and Learning, Albany, NY 12222-0001. Offers MS, PhD, CAS. *Program availability:* Evening/weekend. *Faculty:* 3 full-time (all women), 6 part-time/adjunct (5 women). *Students:* 22 full-time (all women), 150 part-time (144 women); includes 7 minority (2 Black or African American, non-Hispanic/Latino; 1 Asian, non-Hispanic/Latino; 4 Hispanic/Latino), 1 international. Average age 33. 55 applicants, 85% accepted, 59 enrolled. In 2016, 79 master's, 3 doctorates, 4 other advanced degrees awarded. *Degree requirements:* For doctorate, one foreign language, thesis/dissertation. *Entrance requirements:* For doctorate, GRE General Test. Additional exam requirements/recommendations for international students: Required—TOEFL (minimum score 550 paper-based). *Application deadline:* For fall admission, 3/1 for domestic students. Applications are processed on a rolling basis. Application fee: $75. Electronic applications accepted. *Expenses:* Tuition, state resident: full-time $10,870; part-time $453 per credit hour. Tuition, nonresident: full-time $22,210; part-time $925 per credit hour. *International tuition:* $21,550 full-time. *Required fees:* $1864; $96 per credit hour. *Financial support:* Fellowships available. Financial award application deadline: 4/15. *Total annual research expenditures:* $534,813. *Unit head:* Dr. Virginia Goatley, Chair, 518-442-5104, E-mail: vgoatley@albany.edu.

University at Buffalo, the State University of New York, Graduate School, Graduate School of Education, Department of Learning and Instruction, Buffalo, NY 14260. Offers biology education (Ed M, Certificate); chemistry education (Ed M, Certificate); childhood education (Ed M); childhood education with bilingual extension (Ed M); college teaching (Advanced Certificate); curriculum, instruction and the science of learning (PhD); early childhood education (Ed M); early childhood education with bilingual extension (Ed M); earth science education (Ed M, Certificate); education and technology (Ed M); education studies (Ed M); educational technology and new literacies (Certificate); educational technology and new literacies (Advanced Certificate); elementary education (Ed D); English education (Ed M, Certificate); English education studies (Ed M); English for speakers of other languages (Ed M); foreign and second language education (PhD); French education (Ed M, Certificate); German education (Ed M, Certificate); gifted education (Certificate); Latin education (Ed M, Certificate); literacy education studies (Ed M); literacy specialist (Ed M); literacy teaching and learning (Certificate); mathematics education (Ed M, Certificate); music education (Ed M, Certificate); music education studies (Ed M); music learning theory (Advanced Certificate); online education (Advanced Certificate); physics education (Ed M, Certificate); science and the public (Ed M); social studies education (Ed M, Certificate); Spanish education (Ed M, Certificate); special education (PhD); teaching English to speakers of other languages (Ed M). *Program availability:* Part-time, evening/weekend, 100% online. *Faculty:* 28 full-time (21 women), 67 part-time/adjunct (49 women). *Students:* 198 full-time (153 women), 312 part-time (220 women); includes 48 minority (28 Black or African American, non-Hispanic/Latino; 4 American Indian or Alaska Native, non-Hispanic/Latino; 15 Asian, non-Hispanic/Latino; 1 Hispanic/Latino), 66 international. Average age 33. 336 applicants, 86% accepted, 178 enrolled. In 2016, 137 master's, 24 doctorates, 25 other advanced degrees awarded. *Degree requirements:* For master's, comprehensive exam; for doctorate, thesis/dissertation, research analysis exam, research experience. *Entrance requirements:* For master's, letters of reference; for doctorate, GRE General Test or MAT, interview, writing sample, letters of recommendation. Additional exam requirements/recommendations for international students: Required—TOEFL (minimum score 600 paper-based; 96 iBT). *Application deadline:* For fall admission, 2/1 priority date for domestic and international students; for spring admission, 11/15 priority date for domestic students, 10/1 for international students. Applications are processed on a rolling basis. Application fee: $50. Electronic applications accepted. *Financial support:* In 2016–17, 44 fellowships (averaging $4,010 per year), 39 research assistantships with tuition reimbursements (averaging $9,897 per year) were awarded; teaching assistantships, career-related internships or fieldwork, Federal Work-Study, institutionally sponsored loans, scholarships/grants, tuition waivers (full and partial), and unspecified assistantships also available. Financial award application deadline: 2/28; financial award applicants required to submit FAFSA. *Faculty research:* Science assessment, foreign language teaching and learning, early learning, new literacies, gender and education. *Total annual research expenditures:* $534,880. *Unit head:* Dr. Deborah Moore-Russo, Chair, 716-645-4069, Fax: 716-645-3161, E-mail: dam29@buffalo.edu. *Application contact:* Luann Zak, Admissions Assistant, 716-645-2110, Fax: 716-645-7937, E-mail: luannzak@buffalo.edu.
Website: http://gse.buffalo.edu/lai

The University of Akron, Graduate School, College of Education, Department of Curricular and Instructional Studies, Program in Elementary Education - Literacy Option, Akron, OH 44325. Offers MA. *Accreditation:* NCATE. *Students:* 7 full-time (4 women), 36 part-time (31 women); includes 6 minority (4 Black or African American, non-Hispanic/Latino; 1 Hispanic/Latino, 1 Two or more races, non-Hispanic/Latino), 6 international. Average age 35. 12 applicants, 100% accepted, 7 enrolled. In 2016, 14 master's awarded. *Degree requirements:* For master's, comprehensive exam, thesis optional. *Entrance requirements:* For master's, valid teaching license. Additional exam requirements/recommendations for international students: Required—TOEFL (minimum score 550 paper-based; 79 iBT), IELTS (minimum score 6.5). *Application deadline:* Applications are processed on a rolling basis. Application fee: $45 ($70 for international students). Electronic applications accepted. *Expenses:* Tuition, state resident: full-time $8618; part-time $359 per credit hour. Tuition, nonresident: full-time $17,149; part-time $715 per credit hour. *Required fees:* $1652. *Unit head:* Dr. Susan Clark, Interim Chair, 330-972-7780, E-mail: sclark1@uakron.edu. *Application contact:* Kelly Chaff, College Program Specialist, 330-972-7028, E-mail: klchaff@uakron.edu.

The University of Alabama at Birmingham, School of Education, Program in Reading, Birmingham, AL 35294. Offers MA Ed. *Program availability:* Online learning. *Entrance requirements:* For master's, two years' teaching experience, teaching certificate. Full-time tuition and fees vary according to course load and program.

The University of Alabama in Huntsville, School of Graduate Studies, College of Education, Huntsville, AL 35899. Offers autism spectrum disorders (M Ed, Graduate Certificate); biology (MAT); chemistry (MAT); differentiated instruction in elementary education (M Ed); English language arts (MAT); English speakers of other languages (M Ed, MAT); history (MAT); mathematics (MAT); physics (MAT); reading education (M Ed); secondary education (M Ed). *Expenses:* Tuition, state resident: full-time $9834; part-time $600 per credit hour. Tuition, nonresident: full-time $21,830; part-time $1325 per credit hour.

University of Alaska Southeast, Graduate Programs, Program in Education, Juneau, AK 99801. Offers educational leadership (M Ed); elementary education (MAT); learning design and technology (M Ed); mathematics education (M Ed); reading specialist (M Ed); secondary education (MAT); special education (M Ed, MAT). *Accreditation:* NCATE. *Program availability:* Part-time, evening/weekend, online learning. *Degree requirements:* For master's, comprehensive exam or project, portfolio. *Entrance requirements:* For master's, PRAXIS, minimum GPA of 3.0, writing sample, letters of recommendation. *Application deadline:* For fall admission, 3/8 for domestic students. Applications are processed on a rolling basis. Application fee: $60. Electronic applications accepted. *Expenses:* Tuition, state resident: part-time $466 per credit. Tuition, nonresident: part-time $979 per credit. *Required fees:* $19 per credit. Part-time tuition and fees vary according to course level, campus/location and reciprocity agreements. *Financial support:* Federal Work-Study, scholarships/grants, and tuition waivers (full and partial) available. Support available to part-time students. Financial award applicants required to submit FAFSA. *Faculty research:* Applied classroom research, culturally responsive practices, action research, teaching effectiveness. *Unit head:* Dr. Larry Harris, Dean, 907-796-6551, Fax: 907-796-6550, E-mail: larry.harris@uas.alaska.edu. *Application contact:* Susan A. Stuck, Administrative Assistant, 866-465-6424, Fax: 866-465-5159, E-mail: jnsas@uas.alaska.edu.

The University of Arizona, College of Education, Department of Teaching, Learning and Sociocultural Studies, Program in Language, Reading and Culture, Tucson, AZ 85721. Offers MA, Ed D, PhD, Ed S. *Program availability:* Part-time. *Entrance requirements:* Additional exam requirements/recommendations for international students: Required—TOEFL (minimum score 550 paper-based; 79 iBT); Recommended—IELTS (minimum score 7). Electronic applications accepted. *Faculty research:* Literacy acquisition, sociocultural theory, indigenous education, heritage-language revitalization, the study of households and community settings, children's and adolescent literatures and literacy.

University of Arkansas at Little Rock, Graduate School, College of Education and Health Professions, Department of Teacher Education, Program in Reading Education, Little Rock, AR 72204-1099. Offers M Ed, PhD, Ed S.

University of Bridgeport, School of Education, Department of Education, Bridgeport, CT 06604. Offers education (MS); educational management (Ed D, Diploma), including intermediate administrator or supervisor (Diploma), leadership (Ed D); elementary education (MS, Diploma), including early childhood education, elementary education; middle school education (MS); music education (MS); remedial reading and language arts (Diploma); secondary education (MS, Diploma), including computer specialist (Diploma), international education (Diploma), reading specialist, secondary education. *Program availability:* Part-time, evening/weekend. *Degree requirements:* For master's, final exam, final project, or thesis; for doctorate, comprehensive exam, thesis/dissertation; for Diploma, thesis or alternative, final project. *Entrance requirements:* For master's, minimum undergraduate QPA of 2.67; for doctorate, GRE, MAT; for Diploma, GRE General Test or MAT, minimum graduate QPA of 3.0. Additional exam requirements/recommendations for international students: Recommended—TOEFL (minimum score 550 paper-based; 80 iBT), IELTS (minimum score 6.5). Electronic applications accepted. *Expenses:* Contact institution.

The University of British Columbia, Faculty of Education, Department of Language and Literacy Education, Vancouver, BC V6T 1Z2, Canada. Offers literacy education (M Ed, MA, PhD); modern languages education (M Ed, MA); teaching English as a second language (M Ed, MA, PhD). *Program availability:* Part-time, evening/weekend. *Degree requirements:* For master's, thesis (MA); for doctorate, thesis/dissertation. *Entrance requirements:* For master's and doctorate, minimum B+ average in last 2 years with minimum 2 courses at A standing. Additional exam requirements/recommendations for international students: Required—TOEFL, TWE. *Application deadline:* Applications are processed on a rolling basis. Application fee: $100 Canadian dollars ($162 Canadian dollars for international students). Electronic applications accepted. *Expenses:* $6,865 per year tuition and fees domestic, $10,938 per year international (for MA and M Ed); $4,802 per year tuition and fees, $8,436 per year international (for PhD). *Financial support:* Fellowships with partial tuition reimbursements, research assistantships, teaching assistantships, institutionally sponsored loans, scholarships/grants, tuition waivers (full and partial), and unspecified assistantships available. *Faculty research:* Language and literacy development, second language acquisition, Asia Pacific language curriculum, children's literature, whole language instruction. *Application contact:* Christopher Fernandez, Graduate Program Staff, 604-822-8259, Fax: 604-822-3154, E-mail: lled.educ@ubc.ca.
Website: http://www.lled.educ.ubc.ca/

University of California, Riverside, Graduate Division, Graduate School of Education, Riverside, CA 92521-0102. Offers autism (M Ed); diversity and equity (M Ed); education specialist (Credential); education, society, and culture (MA, PhD); educational psychology (MA, PhD); general education (M Ed); higher education administration and policy (M Ed, PhD); multiple subject (Credential); reading (M Ed); school psychology (PhD); single subject (Credential); special education (M Ed, MA, PhD); TESOL (M Ed). Terminal master's awarded for partial completion of doctoral program. *Degree requirements:* For master's, thesis optional, comprehensive exams or thesis (MA), case study or analytical report (M Ed); for doctorate, thesis/dissertation, written and oral qualifying exams, college teaching practicum. *Entrance requirements:* For master's, GRE General Test (for MA); CBEST and CSET (for M Ed in general education only), UCR Extension TESOL certificate (for M Ed with TESOL emphasis only); for doctorate, GRE General Test, writing sample; for Credential, CBEST, CSET. Additional exam requirements/recommendations for international students: Required—TOEFL (minimum score 550 paper-based; 80 iBT), IELTS (minimum score 7). Electronic applications accepted. *Expenses:* Tuition, state resident: full-time $16,666. Tuition, nonresident: full-time $31,768. *Required fees:* $11,055.54 per quarter. $3685.18 per quarter. Tuition and fees vary according to campus/location and program. *Faculty research:* Responsiveness to intervention, faculty core, response to intervention of English language learners, advanced modeling techniques, study on social capital, trust, and motivation.

University of Central Arkansas, Graduate School, College of Education, Department of Early Childhood and Special Education, Program in Reading Education, Conway, AR 72035-0001. Offers MSE. *Accreditation:* NCATE. *Program availability:* Part-time, evening/weekend, online learning. *Degree requirements:* For master's, comprehensive exam, thesis optional. *Entrance requirements:* For master's, GRE General Test, minimum GPA of 2.7. Additional exam requirements/recommendations for international students: Required—TOEFL (minimum score 550 paper-based; 80 iBT).

Reading Education

University of Central Florida, College of Education and Human Performance, Education Doctoral Programs, Orlando, FL 32816. Offers communication sciences and disorders (PhD); curriculum and instruction (Ed D); early childhood education (PhD); educational leadership (Ed D); elementary education (PhD); exceptional education (PhD); exercise physiology (PhD); higher education (PhD); instructional technology (PhD); mathematics education (PhD); methodology, measurement and analysis (PhD); reading education (PhD); science education (PhD); social science education (PhD); TESOL (PhD). *Students:* 127 full-time (91 women), 43 part-time (29 women); includes 33 minority (17 Black or African American, non-Hispanic/Latino; 5 Asian, non-Hispanic/Latino; 7 Hispanic/Latino; 4 Two or more races, non-Hispanic/Latino), 26 international. Average age 37. 163 applicants, 40% accepted, 52 enrolled. In 2016, 57 doctorates awarded. Application fee: $30. Electronic applications accepted. *Expenses:* Tuition, state resident: part-time $288.16 per credit hour. Tuition, nonresident: part-time $1071.31 per credit hour. *Financial support:* In 2016–17, 78 students received support, including 41 fellowships with partial tuition reimbursements available (averaging $5,916 per year), 44 research assistantships with partial tuition reimbursements available (averaging $7,637 per year), 48 teaching assistantships with partial tuition reimbursements available (averaging $9,633 per year). Financial award application deadline: 3/1; financial award applicants required to submit FAFSA. *Unit head:* Dr. Edward Robinson, Director of Doctoral Programs, 407-823-6106, E-mail: edward.robinson@ucf.edu. *Application contact:* Assistant Director, Graduate Admissions, 407-823-2766, Fax: 407-823-6442, E-mail: gradadmissions@ucf.edu.
Website: http://education.ucf.edu/programs.cfm?pid=g&cat=2

University of Central Florida, College of Education and Human Performance, School of Teaching, Learning, and Leadership, Program in Reading Education, Orlando, FL 32816. Offers M Ed, Certificate. *Accreditation:* NCATE. *Program availability:* Part-time, evening/weekend. *Students:* 2 full-time (both women), 28 part-time (27 women); includes 10 minority (4 Black or African American, non-Hispanic/Latino; 1 Asian, non-Hispanic/Latino; 5 Hispanic/Latino). Average age 30. 21 applicants, 76% accepted, 7 enrolled. In 2016, 22 master's, 1 Certificate awarded. *Degree requirements:* For master's, comprehensive exam, thesis or alternative, portfolio, Reading K-12 Subject Area Exam of the Florida Teacher Certification Examination. *Entrance requirements:* For master's, GRE General Test. Additional exam requirements/recommendations for international students: Required—TOEFL. *Application deadline:* For fall admission, 7/15 for domestic students; for spring admission, 12/1 for domestic students. Application fee: $30. Electronic applications accepted. *Expenses:* Tuition, state resident: part-time $288.16 per credit hour. Tuition, nonresident: part-time $1071.31 per credit hour. *Financial support:* In 2016–17, 1 student received support, including 1 research assistantship with partial tuition reimbursement available (averaging $9,562 per year); career-related internships or fieldwork, Federal Work-Study, institutionally sponsored loans, tuition waivers (partial), and unspecified assistantships also available. Financial award application deadline: 3/1; financial award applicants required to submit FAFSA. *Unit head:* Dr. Karri J. Williams, Program Coordinator, 321-433-7922, E-mail: karri.williams@ucf.edu. *Application contact:* Assistant Director, Graduate Admissions, 407-823-2766, Fax: 407-823-6442, E-mail: gradadmissions@ucf.edu.
Website: http://www.education.ucf.edu/readinged/

University of Central Missouri, The Graduate School, Warrensburg, MO 64093. Offers accountancy (MA); accounting (MBA); applied mathematics (MS); aviation safety (MA); biology (MS); business administration (MBA); career and technical education leadership (MS); college student personnel administration (MS); communication (MA); computer science (MS); counseling (MS); criminal justice (MS); educational leadership (Ed D); educational technology (MS); elementary and early childhood education (MSE); English (MA); environmental studies (MA); finance (MBA); history (MA); human services/educational technology (Ed S); human services/learning resources (Ed S); human services/professional counseling (Ed S); industrial hygiene (MS); industrial management (MS); information systems (MBA); information technology (MS); kinesiology (MS); library science and information services (MS); literacy education (MSE); marketing (MBA); mathematics (MS); music (MA); occupational safety management (MS); psychology (MS); rural family nursing (MS); school administration (MSE); social gerontology (MS); sociology (MA); special education (MSE); speech language pathology (MS); superintendency (Ed S); teaching (MAT); teaching English as a second language (MA); technology (MS); technology management (PhD); theatre (MA). *Program availability:* Part-time, 100% online, blended/hybrid learning. *Degree requirements:* For master's and Ed S, comprehensive exam (for some programs), thesis (for some programs). *Entrance requirements:* Additional exam requirements/recommendations for international students: Required—TOEFL (minimum score 550 paper-based; 79 iBT). Electronic applications accepted.

University of Central Oklahoma, The Jackson College of Graduate Studies, College of Education and Professional Studies, Department of Advanced Professional and Special Services, Edmond, OK 73034-5209. Offers educational leadership (M Ed); library media education (M Ed); reading (M Ed); school counseling (M Ed); special education (M Ed), including mild/moderate disabilities, severe-profound/multiple disabilities, special education; speech-language pathology (MS). *Accreditation:* ASHA. *Program availability:* Part-time. *Degree requirements:* For master's, comprehensive exam (for some programs), thesis (for some programs). *Entrance requirements:* For master's, GRE. Additional exam requirements/recommendations for international students: Required—TOEFL (minimum score 550 paper-based; 79 iBT), IELTS (minimum score 6.5). Electronic applications accepted. *Faculty research:* Intellectual freedom, fair use copyright, technology integration, young adult literature, distance learning.

University of Cincinnati, Graduate School, College of Education, Criminal Justice, and Human Services, Division of Teacher Education, Program in Reading/Literacy, Cincinnati, OH 45221. Offers M Ed, Ed D. *Accreditation:* NCATE. *Program availability:* Part-time. *Degree requirements:* For master's, thesis or alternative; for doctorate, thesis/dissertation. *Entrance requirements:* For master's, GRE General Test. Additional exam requirements/recommendations for international students: Required—TOEFL (minimum score 550 paper-based), TWE (minimum score 4.5), OEPT. Electronic applications accepted. *Expenses: Tuition, area resident:* Full-time $12,790; part-time $389 per credit hour. Tuition, state resident: full-time $13,290; part-time $419 per credit hour. Tuition, nonresident: full-time $24,532; part-time $976 per credit hour. *International tuition:* $24,832 full-time. *Required fees:* $3958; $140 per credit hour. Tuition and fees vary according to course load, degree level, program and reciprocity agreements.

University of Colorado Denver, School of Education and Human Development, Teacher Education Programs, Denver, CO 80217. Offers elementary linguistically diverse education (MA); elementary math and science education (MA); elementary math education (MA); elementary reading and writing (MA); elementary science education (MA); secondary English education (MA); secondary linguistically diverse education (MA); secondary math education (MA); secondary reading and writing (MA); secondary science education (MA); special education (MA). *Accreditation:* NCATE. *Program availability:* Part-time, evening/weekend. *Students:* 142 full-time (117 women), 184 part-time (159 women); includes 56 minority (6 Black or African American, non-Hispanic/Latino; 1 American Indian or Alaska Native, non-Hispanic/Latino; 4 Asian, non-Hispanic/Latino; 38 Hispanic/Latino; 1 Native Hawaiian or other Pacific Islander, non-Hispanic/Latino; 6 Two or more races, non-Hispanic/Latino), 1 international. Average age 30. 18 applicants, 67% accepted, 9 enrolled. In 2016, 134 master's awarded. *Degree requirements:* For master's, comprehensive exam. *Entrance requirements:* For master's, GRE or MAT (for those with GPA below 2.75), transcripts, resume, letters of recommendation. Additional exam requirements/recommendations for international students: Required—TOEFL (minimum score 537 paper-based; 75 iBT); Recommended—IELTS (minimum score 6.5). *Application deadline:* For fall admission, 4/15 for domestic students, 4/1 for international students; for spring admission, 9/15 for domestic students, 9/1 for international students; for summer admission, 2/15 for domestic students, 2/1 for international students. Applications are processed on a rolling basis. Application fee: $50 ($75 for international students). Electronic applications accepted. *Expenses:* Contact institution. *Financial support:* In 2016–17, 26 students received support. Fellowships, research assistantships, teaching assistantships, Federal Work-Study, institutionally sponsored loans, scholarships/grants, and traineeships available. Financial award application deadline: 4/1; financial award applicants required to submit FAFSA. *Faculty research:* Linguistically diverse education/ESL, elementary reading and writing, elementary teacher education, secondary teacher education, special education. *Unit head:* Cindy Gutierrez, Director, 303-315-4982, E-mail: cindy.gutierrez@ucdenver.edu. *Application contact:* 303-315-6300, E-mail: education@ucdenver.edu.
Website: http://www.ucdenver.edu/academics/colleges/SchoolOfEducation/Academics/MASTERS/Pages/default.aspx

University of Connecticut, Graduate School, Neag School of Education, Department of Curriculum and Instruction, Program in Reading Education, Storrs, CT 06269. Offers MA, PhD. *Accreditation:* NCATE. Terminal master's awarded for partial completion of doctoral program. *Degree requirements:* For master's, comprehensive exam, thesis or alternative; for doctorate, thesis/dissertation. *Entrance requirements:* For doctorate, GRE General Test. Additional exam requirements/recommendations for international students: Required—TOEFL (minimum score 550 paper-based). Electronic applications accepted.

University of Dayton, Department of Teacher Education, Dayton, OH 45469. Offers early childhood leadership and advocacy (MS Ed); interdisciplinary education studies (MS Ed); leadership in educational systems (MS Ed); literacy (MS Ed); mathematics education (MS Ed); music education (MS Ed); teacher as leader (MS Ed); teacher education (MS Ed); technology-enhanced learning (MS Ed); trans-disciplinary early childhood education (MS Ed). *Program availability:* Part-time, evening/weekend, blended/hybrid learning. *Faculty:* 23 full-time (18 women), 49 part-time/adjunct (42 women). *Students:* 52 full-time (47 women), 89 part-time (76 women); includes 6 minority (2 Black or African American, non-Hispanic/Latino; 2 Hispanic/Latino; 2 Two or more races, non-Hispanic/Latino), 24 international. Average age 31. 106 applicants, 28% accepted. In 2016, 69 master's awarded. *Degree requirements:* For master's, variable foreign language requirement, thesis optional. *Entrance requirements:* For master's, GRE (minimum score of 149 verbal, 4 on writing) or MAT (minimum score of 396) if undergraduate GPA was under 2.75, minimum GPA of 2.75, 3 letters of recommendation, personal statement or resume, official transcripts. Additional exam requirements/recommendations for international students: Required—TOEFL (minimum score 550 paper-based; 80 iBT); Recommended—IELTS (minimum score 6.5). *Application deadline:* Applications are processed on a rolling basis. Application fee: $0 ($50 for international students). Electronic applications accepted. *Expenses:* $620 per credit hour, $25 registration fee per term. *Financial support:* Institutionally sponsored loans available. Financial award application deadline: 3/1; financial award applicants required to submit FAFSA. *Faculty research:* Educational technology; facilitating teacher reflection; teacher preparation in dyslexia. *Unit head:* Dr. Connie L. Bowman, Chair, 937-229-3305, E-mail: cbowman1@udayton.edu. *Application contact:* Gina Seiter, Graduate Program Advisor, 937-229-3103, E-mail: gseiter1@udayton.edu.
Website: https://www.udayton.edu/education/departments_and_programs/edt

The University of Findlay, Office of Graduate Admissions, Findlay, OH 45840-3653. Offers applied security and analytics (MSAS); athletic training (MAT); business (MBA), including certified management accountant, certified public accountant, health care management, hospitality management; education (MA Ed, Ed D), including children's literature (MA Ed), curriculum and teaching (MA Ed), education (MA Ed), educational administration (MA Ed), human resource development (MA Ed), reading (MA Ed), science education (MA Ed), superintendent (Ed D), teaching (Ed D), technology (MA Ed); environmental, safety and health management (MSEM); health informatics (MS); occupational therapy (MOT); pharmacy (Pharm D); physical therapy (DPT); physician assistant (MPA); rhetoric and writing (MA); teaching English to speakers of other languages (TESOL) and bilingual education (MA). *Program availability:* Part-time, evening/weekend, 100% online, blended/hybrid learning. *Faculty:* 114 full-time (63 women), 44 part-time/adjunct (18 women). *Students:* 751 full-time (452 women), 573 part-time (323 women); includes 164 minority (82 Black or African American, non-Hispanic/Latino; 1 American Indian or Alaska Native, non-Hispanic/Latino; 27 Asian, non-Hispanic/Latino; 37 Hispanic/Latino; 17 Two or more races, non-Hispanic/Latino), 280 international. Average age 28. 661 applicants, 52% accepted, 288 enrolled. In 2016, 366 master's, 137 doctorates awarded. *Degree requirements:* For master's, comprehensive exam (for some programs), thesis, cumulative project, capstone project; for doctorate, thesis/dissertation. *Entrance requirements:* For master's, GRE (for some programs), bachelor's degree from accredited institution, minimum undergraduate GPA of 3.0 in last 64 hours of course work; for doctorate, MAT, minimum cumulative GPA of 3.0, master's degree. Additional exam requirements/recommendations for international students: Recommended—TOEFL (minimum score 79 iBT), IELTS (minimum score 7). *Application deadline:* For fall admission, 6/15 for international students; for spring admission, 12/1 for international students; for summer admission, 4/1 for international students. Applications are processed on a rolling basis. Electronic applications accepted. *Expenses:* Contact institution. *Financial support:* In 2016–17, 139 students received support, including 15 research assistantships with partial tuition reimbursements available (averaging $7,200 per year), 25 teaching assistantships with partial tuition reimbursements available (averaging $7,200 per year); Federal Work-Study, institutionally sponsored loans, and unspecified assistantships also available. Financial award application deadline: 4/1; financial award applicants required to submit FAFSA. *Unit head:* Christopher M. Harris, Director of Admissions, 419-434-4347, E-mail: harrisc1@findlay.edu. *Application contact:* Madeline Fauser Brennan, Graduate Admissions Counselor, 419-434-4636, Fax: 419-434-4898, E-mail: fauserbrennan@findlay.edu.
Website: http://www.findlay.edu/admissions/graduate/Pages/default.aspx

University of Florida, Graduate School, College of Education, School of Teaching and Learning, Gainesville, FL 32611. Offers curriculum and instruction (M Ed, MAE, Ed D, PhD, Ed S); elementary education (M Ed, MAE); English education (M Ed, MAE); mathematics education (M Ed, MAE); reading education (M Ed, MAE); science education (M Ed, MAE); social studies education (M Ed, MAE). *Accreditation:* NCATE. *Program availability:* Part-time, evening/weekend, online learning. Terminal master's awarded for partial completion of doctoral program. *Degree requirements:* For master's, comprehensive exam (for some programs), thesis (for some programs); for doctorate, comprehensive exam (for some programs), thesis/dissertation (for some programs). *Entrance requirements:* For master's and doctorate, GRE General Test, minimum GPA of 3.0; for Ed S, GRE General Test. Additional exam requirements/recommendations for international students: Required—TOEFL (minimum score 550 paper-based; 80 iBT), IELTS (minimum score 6). Electronic applications accepted. *Faculty research:* STEM education; curriculum; teaching and teacher education; languages and literacy; schools, culture, and society; theories and processes of learning.

University of Georgia, College of Education, Department of Language and Literacy Education, Athens, GA 30602. Offers English education (M Ed); language and literacy education (PhD). *Accreditation:* NCATE. *Faculty:* 15 full-time (11 women). *Students:* 100 full-time (81 women), 94 part-time (80 women); includes 21 minority (17 Black or African American, non-Hispanic/Latino; 1 Asian, non-Hispanic/Latino; 2 Hispanic/Latino; 1 Two or more races, non-Hispanic/Latino), 31 international. Average age 33. 185 applicants, 61% accepted, 42 enrolled. In 2016, 43 master's, 15 doctorates awarded. *Degree requirements:* For doctorate, variable foreign language requirement. *Entrance requirements:* For master's, GRE General Test or MAT; for doctorate, GRE General Test. Additional exam requirements/recommendations for international students: Required—TOEFL (minimum score 550 paper-based). *Application deadline:* For fall admission, 7/1 priority date for domestic students; for spring admission, 11/15 for domestic students. Application fee: $50. Electronic applications accepted. *Faculty research:* Comprehension, critical literacy, literacy and technology, vocabulary instruction, content area reading. *Unit head:* Dr. Mark A. Faust, Head, 706-542-4515, Fax: 706-542-4509, E-mail: mfaust@uga.edu. *Application contact:* Dr. Elizabeth St. Pierre, Graduate Coordinator, 706-542-4520, E-mail: stpierre@uga.edu.
Website: http://www.coe.uga.edu/lle/

University of Guam, Office of Graduate Studies, School of Education, Program in Language and Literacy, Mangilao, GU 96923. Offers M Ed. *Program availability:* Part-time. *Degree requirements:* For master's, comprehensive oral and written exams, special project or thesis. *Entrance requirements:* For master's, GRE General Test. Additional exam requirements/recommendations for international students: Required—TOEFL.

University of Houston–Clear Lake, School of Education, Program in Curriculum and Instruction, Houston, TX 77058-1002. Offers curriculum and instruction (MS); early childhood education (MS); reading (MS); school library and information science (MS). *Program availability:* Part-time, evening/weekend. *Degree requirements:* For master's, thesis (for some programs). *Entrance requirements:* For master's, GRE or minimum GPA of 3.0 in last 60 hours. Additional exam requirements/recommendations for international students: Required—TOEFL (minimum score 550 paper-based). Electronic applications accepted.

University of Kentucky, Graduate School, College of Education, Program in Curriculum and Instruction, Lexington, KY 40506-0032. Offers curriculum and instruction (Ed D, PhD); elementary education (MA Ed); instructional system design (MS Ed); literacy (MA Ed); middle school education (MA Ed, MS Ed); secondary education (MA Ed, MS Ed). *Accreditation:* NCATE. *Degree requirements:* For master's, comprehensive exam, thesis optional; for doctorate, comprehensive exam, thesis/dissertation. *Entrance requirements:* For master's, GRE General Test, minimum undergraduate GPA of 2.75; for doctorate, GRE General Test, minimum graduate GPA of 3.0. Additional exam requirements/recommendations for international students: Required—TOEFL (minimum score 550 paper-based). Electronic applications accepted. *Faculty research:* Educational reform, multicultural education, classroom instructional practices, performance based assessment, primary school programs.

University of La Verne, LaFetra College of Education, Program in Reading, La Verne, CA 91750-4443. Offers reading (M Ed, Certificate); reading and language arts specialist (Credential). *Students:* 1 (woman) full-time, 21 part-time (18 women); includes 13 minority (2 Black or African American, non-Hispanic/Latino; 11 Hispanic/Latino). Average age 44. *Degree requirements:* For master's, thesis optional. *Entrance requirements:* For master's, MAT, California Basic Educational Skills Test, minimum GPA of 3.0, basic teaching credential, interview, 3 letters of reference. *Application deadline:* Applications are processed on a rolling basis. Application fee: $50. *Expenses:* Contact institution. *Financial support:* Institutionally sponsored loans and scholarships/grants available. Financial award application deadline: 3/2; financial award applicants required to submit FAFSA. *Unit head:* Sarah Pfenninger, Program Chairperson, 909-448-4677, E-mail: spfenninger@laverne.edu. *Application contact:* Kristen Ahn, Assistant Director of Graduate Admission, 909-448-4480, Fax: 909-971-2295, E-mail: sahn@laverne.edu.
Website: http://www.laverne.edu/education/

University of Louisiana at Monroe, Graduate School, College of Arts, Education, and Sciences, School of Education, Program in Curriculum and Instruction, Monroe, LA 71209-0001. Offers art education (M Ed); biology education (M Ed); chemistry education (M Ed); curriculum and instruction (Ed D); early childhood education (M Ed); earth science education (M Ed); educational leadership (M Ed); elementary education (1-5) (M Ed); English as a second language (M Ed); English education (M Ed); family and consumer education (M Ed); French education (M Ed); history education (M Ed); math education (M Ed); middle school education (M Ed); music education (M Ed); reading education (K-12) (M Ed); Spanish education (M Ed); special education - academically gifted (M Ed); special education - early intervention (M Ed); special education - educational diagnostician (M Ed); special education - mild/moderate disabilities (M Ed); speech education (M Ed). *Accreditation:* NCATE. *Faculty:* 8 full-time (4 women), 4 part-time/adjunct (3 women). *Students:* 13 full-time (11 women), 80 part-time (65 women); includes 25 minority (19 Black or African American, non-Hispanic/Latino; 1 Asian, non-Hispanic/Latino; 3 Hispanic/Latino; 2 Two or more races, non Hispanic/Latino). Average age 37. 118 applicants, 30% accepted, 16 enrolled. In 2016, 23 master's, 4 doctorates awarded. *Degree requirements:* For master's, comprehensive exam (for some programs), thesis; for doctorate, thesis/dissertation, internships. *Entrance requirements:* For master's, GRE General Test; for doctorate, GRE General Test, minimum undergraduate GPA of 2.75, graduate 3.25. Additional exam requirements/recommendations for international students: Required—TOEFL (minimum score 500 paper-based; 61 iBT). *Application deadline:* For fall admission, 8/24 priority date for domestic students, 7/1 for international students; for winter admission, 12/14 priority date for domestic students; for spring admission, 1/19 for domestic students, 11/1 for international students. Applications are processed on a rolling basis. Application fee: $20 ($30 for international students). Electronic applications accepted. *Expenses:* Tuition, state resident: full-time $6489. Tuition, nonresident: full-time $18,589. *Required fees:* $8984. Tuition and fees vary according to course level, course load, degree level and program. *Financial support:* Research assistantships, career-related internships or fieldwork, Federal Work-Study, and unspecified assistantships available. Financial award application deadline: 4/1; financial award applicants required to submit FAFSA. *Unit head:* Dr. Dorothy Schween, Director, 318-342-1268, Fax: 318-342-3131, E-mail: schween@ulm.edu.

University of Maine, Graduate School, College of Education and Human Development, School of Learning and Teaching, Orono, ME 04469. Offers counselor education (M Ed, MA, MS, CAS); early childhood teacher (CGS); education (PhD), including counselor education, literacy education, prevention and intervention studies; elementary education (M Ed, CAS); individualized education (M Ed); literacy education (CAS); response to intervention for behavior (CGS); secondary education (M Ed, CAS); social studies education (M Ed); special education (M Ed, CAS). *Program availability:* Part-time. *Students:* 89 full-time (82 women), 184 part-time (162 women); includes 13 minority (8 American Indian or Alaska Native, non-Hispanic/Latino; 3 Hispanic/Latino; 1 Native Hawaiian or other Pacific Islander, non-Hispanic/Latino; 1 Two or more races, non-Hispanic/Latino), 4 international. Average age 37. 132 applicants, 97% accepted, 100 enrolled. In 2016, 50 master's, 3 doctorates, 19 other advanced degrees awarded. *Degree requirements:* For master's, thesis (for some programs); for doctorate, comprehensive exam, thesis/dissertation. *Entrance requirements:* For master's, GRE General Test, MAT. Additional exam requirements/recommendations for international students: Required—TOEFL. *Application deadline:* For fall admission, 2/1 priority date for domestic students. Applications are processed on a rolling basis. Application fee: $65. Electronic applications accepted. *Expenses:* Tuition, state resident: full-time $7524; part-time $2508 per credit. Tuition, nonresident: full-time $24,498; part-time $8166 per credit. *Required fees:* $1148; $571 per credit. *Financial support:* In 2016–17, 20 students received support, including 12 teaching assistantships (averaging $14,600 per year); Federal Work-Study, scholarships/grants, and unspecified assistantships also available. Financial award application deadline: 3/1. *Unit head:* Dr. Jim Artesani, Associate Dean of Accreditation and Graduate Affairs, 207-581-4061. *Application contact:* Scott G. Delcourt, Assistant Vice President for Graduate Studies and Senior Associate Dean, 207-581-3291, Fax: 207-581-3232, E-mail: graduate@maine.edu.
Website: http://umaine.edu/edhd/

University of Mary, Liffrig Family School of Education and Behavioral Sciences, Department of Education, Bismarck, ND 58504-9652. Offers curriculum, instruction and assessment (M Ed); education (Ed D); elementary administration (M Ed); reading (M Ed); secondary administration (M Ed); special education strategist (M Ed). *Program availability:* Part-time. *Degree requirements:* For master's, portfolio or thesis. *Entrance requirements:* For master's, interview, letters of reference, minimum GPA of 2.5. Additional exam requirements/recommendations for international students: Required—TOEFL (minimum score 500 paper-based; 71 iBT). Electronic applications accepted.

University of Maryland, College Park, Academic Affairs, College of Education, Department of Teaching, Learning, Policy and Leadership, College Park, MD 20742. Offers reading (M Ed, MA, PhD, CAGS); secondary education (M Ed, MA, Ed D, PhD, CAGS); teaching English to speakers of other languages (M Ed). *Accreditation:* NCATE. *Program availability:* Part-time, evening/weekend, online learning. *Degree requirements:* For master's, comprehensive exam, seminar paper; for doctorate, comprehensive exam, thesis/dissertation, published paper, oral exam. *Entrance requirements:* For master's, GRE General Test or MAT, minimum GPA of 3.0, 3 letters of recommendation; for doctorate, GRE General Test or MAT, minimum undergraduate GPA of 3.0, graduate 3.5; 3 letters of recommendation. Electronic applications accepted. *Faculty research:* Teacher preparation, curriculum study, in-service education.

University of Massachusetts Amherst, Graduate School, College of Education, Program in Education, Amherst, MA 01003. Offers bilingual, English as a second language, and multicultural education (M Ed, Ed S); child study and early education (M Ed); children, families and schools (Ed D, Ed S); early childhood and elementary teacher education (M Ed); educational leadership (M Ed); educational policy and leadership (Ed D); higher education (M Ed); international education (M Ed); language, literacy and culture (Ed D); learning, media and technology (M Ed, Ed S); mathematics, science, and learning technologies (Ed D); reading and writing (M Ed); research, educational measurement and psychometrics (Ed D); school counselor education (M Ed, Ed S); school psychology (Ed S); science education (Ed S); secondary teacher education (M Ed); social justice education (M Ed, Ed D, Ed S); special education (M Ed, Ed D, Ed S); teacher education and school improvement (Ed D, Ed S). *Accreditation:* NCATE. *Program availability:* Part-time, online learning. Terminal master's awarded for partial completion of doctoral program. *Degree requirements:* For doctorate, comprehensive exam, thesis/dissertation. *Entrance requirements:* Additional exam requirements/recommendations for international students: Required—TOEFL (minimum score 550 paper-based; 80 iBT), IELTS (minimum score 6.5). Electronic applications accepted.

University of Memphis, Graduate School, College of Education, Department of Instruction and Curriculum Leadership, Memphis, TN 38152. Offers advanced studies in teaching and learning (M Ed); applied behavior analysis (Graduate Certificate); autism studies (Graduate Certificate); early childhood education (MAT, MS, Ed D); elementary education (MAT); instruction and curriculum (MS, Ed D); instruction design and technology (MS, Ed D); instructional design and technology (Graduate Certificate); literacy, leadership, and coaching (Graduate Certificate); reading (MS, Ed D); school library information specialist (Graduate Certificate); secondary education (MAT); special education (MAT, MS, Ed D); STEM teacher leadership (Graduate Certificate); urban education (Graduate Certificate). *Accreditation:* NCATE (one or more programs are accredited). *Program availability:* Part-time. *Faculty:* 24 full-time (14 women), 17 part-time/adjunct (12 women). *Students:* 66 full-time (52 women), 315 part-time (243 women); includes 163 minority (132 Black or African American, non-Hispanic/Latino; 1 American Indian or Alaska Native, non-Hispanic/Latino; 6 Asian, non-Hispanic/Latino; 13 Hispanic/Latino; 1 Native Hawaiian or other Pacific Islander, non-Hispanic/Latino; 10 Two or more races, non-Hispanic/Latino), 4 international. Average age 35. 215 applicants, 78% accepted, 120 enrolled. In 2016, 111 master's, 21 doctorates, 8 other advanced degrees awarded. Terminal master's awarded for partial completion of doctoral program. *Degree requirements:* For master's, comprehensive exam, thesis or alternative; for doctorate, comprehensive exam, thesis/dissertation. *Entrance requirements:* For master's, GRE General Test, PRAXIS, minimum GPA of 2.5, letters of reference; for doctorate, GRE General Test, GRE Subject Test, 2 years of teaching experience, letters of reference, statement of purpose, interview. Additional exam requirements/recommendations for international students: Required—TOEFL (minimum score 550 paper-based; 79 iBT). *Application deadline:* For fall admission, 4/1 priority date for domestic students; for spring admission, 10/1 priority date for domestic students; for summer admission, 2/1 priority date for domestic students. Applications are processed on a rolling basis. Application fee: $35 ($60 for international students). Electronic applications accepted. *Expenses:* $5,231.50 per semester full-time in-state, $9,623.50 full-time out-of-state. *Financial support:* In 2016–17, 2 research assistantships with full tuition reimbursements (averaging $10,000 per year), 3 teaching assistantships with full tuition reimbursements (averaging $10,666 per year) were awarded; career-related internships or fieldwork, Federal Work-Study, institutionally sponsored loans, scholarships/grants, traineeships, and unspecified assistantships also available. Support available to part-time students. Financial award application deadline: 2/1; financial award applicants required to submit FAFSA. *Faculty research:* Effective urban teachers, preparation and retention of urban teachers, technology utilization in schools, field-based teacher preparation programs, effective use of online instruction. *Unit head:* Dr. Angiline Powell, Interim Chair, 901-678-3310, E-mail: apowell3@memphis.edu. *Application contact:* Dr. James Meindl, Coordinator of Graduate Studies, 901-678-3310, E-mail: jnmeindl@memphis.edu.
Website: http://www.memphis.edu/icl/

University of Miami, Graduate School, School of Education and Human Development, Department of Teaching and Learning, Program in Teaching and Learning, Coral Gables, FL 33124. Offers language and literacy learning in multilingual settings (PhD); science, technology, engineering and mathematics (PhD); special education (PhD).

Faculty: 14 full-time (10 women), 9 part-time/adjunct (all women). *Students:* 21 full-time (16 women); includes 6 minority (2 Black or African American, non-Hispanic/Latino; 3 Hispanic/Latino; 1 Two or more races, non-Hispanic/Latino), 7 international. Average age 33. 20 applicants, 30% accepted, 4 enrolled. In 2016, 1 doctorate awarded. *Degree requirements:* For doctorate, thesis/dissertation, qualifying exam, electronic portfolio. *Entrance requirements:* For doctorate, GRE General Test. Additional exam requirements/recommendations for international students: Required—TOEFL (minimum score 550 paper-based; 80 iBT); Recommended—IELTS (minimum score 6.5). *Application deadline:* For fall admission, 2/15 for domestic students, 10/1 for international students. Application fee: $65. Electronic applications accepted. *Financial support:* Fellowships, research assistantships, teaching assistantships, health care benefits, tuition waivers (full and partial), and unspecified assistantships available. Financial award application deadline: 3/1; financial award applicants required to submit FAFSA. *Faculty research:* Teacher education, multicultural education, special education, second language acquisition, math and science education. *Unit head:* Dr. Luciana de Oliveira, Department Chairperson/Associate Professor, 305-284-4961, Fax: 305-284-6998, E-mail: ludeoliveira@miami.edu. *Application contact:* Lois Heffernan, Graduate Admission Coordinator, 305-284-2167, Fax: 305-284-9395, E-mail: lheffernan@miami.edu.
Website: http://www.education.miami.edu

University of Michigan–Flint, School of Education and Human Services, Department of Education, Flint, MI 48502. Offers curriculum and instruction (Ed S); early childhood education (MA); education (Ed D); educational leadership (Ed S); educational technology (MA), including curriculum and instruction, developer; literacy education (MA); secondary education with certification (MA). *Program availability:* Part-time, evening/weekend, 100% online, mixed mode format (for some programs). *Faculty:* 14 full-time (9 women), 30 part-time/adjunct (17 women). *Students:* 31 full-time (18 women), 199 part-time (144 women); includes 61 minority (48 Black or African American, non-Hispanic/Latino; 1 Asian, non-Hispanic/Latino; 6 Hispanic/Latino; 1 Native Hawaiian or other Pacific Islander, non-Hispanic/Latino; 5 Two or more races, non-Hispanic/Latino), 2 international. Average age 39. 124 applicants, 86% accepted, 75 enrolled. In 2016, 77 master's, 1 doctorate awarded. *Degree requirements:* For master's, thesis optional; for doctorate, thesis/dissertation. *Entrance requirements:* For master's, bachelor's degree from regionally-accredited institution, minimum overall undergraduate GPA of 3.0; for doctorate, Ed S; minimum overall graduate GPA of 3.3 (6.0 on a 9.0 scale) or equivalent; at least 3 years of work experience in a P-16 educational institution or in an education-related position; for Ed S, MA or MS in education-related field from accredited institution; minimum overall graduate GPA of 3.0 (6.0 on a 9.0 scale) or equivalent; at least 3 years of work experience in an educational setting. Additional exam requirements/recommendations for international students: Required—TOEFL (minimum score 84 iBT), IELTS (minimum score 6.5). *Application deadline:* For fall admission, 8/1 for domestic students, 5/1 for international students; for winter admission, 11/15 for domestic students, 9/15 for international students; for spring admission, 3/15 for domestic students, 1/15 for international students; for summer admission, 5/15 for domestic students. Applications are processed on a rolling basis. Application fee: $55. Electronic applications accepted. *Expenses:* Contact institution. *Financial support:* Federal Work-Study, scholarships/grants, and unspecified assistantships available. Support available to part-time students. Financial award application deadline: 3/1; financial award applicants required to submit FAFSA. *Unit head:* Dr. Mary Jo Finney, Department Chair/Associate Professor, 810-766-6617, E-mail: mjfinney@umflint.edu. *Application contact:* Bradley T. Maki, Director of Graduate Admissions, 810-762-3171, Fax: 810-766-6789, E-mail: bmaki@umflint.edu.
Website: https://www.umflint.edu/education/graduate-programs

University of Minnesota, Twin Cities Campus, Graduate School, College of Education and Human Development, Department of Curriculum and Instruction, Minneapolis, MN 55455-0213. Offers art education (M Ed, MA, PhD); curriculum and instruction (M Ed, MA, PhD); elementary education (MA, PhD); English education (PhD); language and immersion education (Certificate); learning technologies (MA, PhD); literacy education (MA, PhD); second language education (MA, PhD); social studies education (MA, PhD); STEM education (MA, PhD); teaching (M Ed), including mathematics, science, social studies, teaching; teaching English to speakers of other languages (MA); technology enhanced learning (Certificate). *Faculty:* 37 full-time (20 women). *Students:* 411 full-time (288 women), 317 part-time (223 women); includes 153 minority (37 Black or African American, non-Hispanic/Latino; 7 American Indian or Alaska Native, non-Hispanic/Latino; 31 Asian, non-Hispanic/Latino; 48 Hispanic/Latino; 1 Native Hawaiian or other Pacific Islander, non-Hispanic/Latino; 29 Two or more races, non-Hispanic/Latino), 53 international. Average age 32. 672 applicants, 66% accepted, 400 enrolled. In 2016, 645 master's, 33 doctorates, 27 other advanced degrees awarded. Application fee: $75 ($95 for international students). *Financial support:* In 2016–17, 13 fellowships, 36 research assistantships with full tuition reimbursements (averaging $8,454 per year), 61 teaching assistantships with full tuition reimbursements (averaging $11,406 per year) were awarded. *Faculty research:* Teaching and learning; influence of cultural, linguistic, social, political, and technological factors on teaching, learning and educational research; relationship between educational practice and a democratic and just society; urban education; immigrant education, racial justice and education. *Total annual research expenditures:* $684,005. *Unit head:* Dr. Cynthia Lewis, Chair, 612-625-6313, E-mail: lewis@umn.edu. *Application contact:* Dr. Gillian Roehrig, Director of Graduate Studies, 612-625-0561, E-mail: roehr013@umn.edu.
Website: http://www.cehd.umn.edu/ci

University of Minnesota, Twin Cities Campus, Graduate School, College of Education and Human Development, Department of Organizational Leadership, Policy and Development, Minneapolis, MN 55455-0213. Offers adult education (M Ed, Certificate); adult literacy (Certificate); comparative and international development education (MA, PhD); disability policy and services (Certificate); education policy and leadership (M Ed, MA, Ed D, PhD), including educational policy and leadership (MA, Ed D, PhD), leadership in education (M Ed); evaluation studies (MA, PhD); higher education (MA, Ed D, PhD), including higher education (MA, PhD), multicultural college teaching and learning (MA); human resource development (M Ed, MA, Ed D, PhD, Certificate); PK-12 administrative licensure (Certificate); private college leadership (Certificate); professional development (Certificate); program evaluation (Certificate); technical education (Certificate); undergraduate multicultural teaching and learning (Certificate); work and human resource education (M Ed). *Faculty:* 33 full-time (15 women). *Students:* 281 full-time (186 women), 240 part-time (147 women); includes 110 minority (43 Black or African American, non-Hispanic/Latino; 3 American Indian or Alaska Native, non-Hispanic/Latino; 23 Asian, non-Hispanic/Latino; 29 Hispanic/Latino; 12 Two or more races, non-Hispanic/Latino), 63 international. Average age 37. 422 applicants, 59% accepted, 225 enrolled. In 2016, 76 master's, 56 doctorates, 37 other advanced degrees awarded. Application fee: $75 ($95 for international students). *Financial support:* In 2016–17, 7 fellowships, 41 research assistantships with full tuition reimbursements (averaging $10,156 per year), 28 teaching assistantships with full tuition reimbursements (averaging $9,170 per year) were awarded. *Faculty research:* Organizational issues in schools, universities, and other organizations; international education and development; program evaluation and research on applied evaluation methods; international human resource development and change; gender and race/ethnicity in relation to learning and leadership. *Total annual research expenditures:* $987,854. *Unit head:* Dr. Heidi Barajas, Chair, 612-625-4823, Fax: 612-624-3377, E-mail: hbarajas@umn.edu. *Application contact:* Dr. Jeremy J. Hernandez, Coordinator of Graduate Studies, 612-626-9377, E-mail: herna220@umn.edu.
Website: http://www.cehd.umn.edu/olpd/

University of Missouri, Office of Research and Graduate Studies, College of Education, Department of Learning, Teaching and Curriculum, Columbia, MO 65211. Offers agricultural education (M Ed, PhD, Ed S); art education (M Ed, PhD, Ed S); business and office education (M Ed, PhD, Ed S); early childhood education (M Ed, PhD, Ed S); elementary education (M Ed, PhD, Ed S); English education (M Ed, PhD, Ed S); foreign language education (M Ed, PhD, Ed S); health education and promotion (M Ed, PhD); learning and instruction (M Ed); marketing education (M Ed, PhD, Ed S); mathematics education (M Ed, PhD, Ed S); music education (M Ed, PhD, Ed S); reading education (M Ed, PhD, Ed S); science education (M Ed, PhD, Ed S); social studies education (M Ed, PhD, Ed S); vocational education (M Ed, PhD, Ed S). *Program availability:* Part-time. *Faculty:* 30 full-time (18 women), 1 (woman) part-time/adjunct. *Students:* 157 full-time (124 women), 157 part-time (125 women). Terminal master's awarded for partial completion of doctoral program. *Degree requirements:* For doctorate, thesis/dissertation. *Entrance requirements:* For master's and Ed S, GRE General Test or MAT, minimum GPA of 3.0; for doctorate, GRE General Test, minimum GPA of 3.0. Additional exam requirements/recommendations for international students: Required—TOEFL (minimum score 600 paper-based; 100 iBT). *Application deadline:* For fall admission, 12/1 priority date for domestic and international students. Applications are processed on a rolling basis. Application fee: $75 ($90 for international students). Electronic applications accepted. *Expenses:* Tuition, state resident: full-time $6347; part-time $352.60 per credit hour. Tuition, nonresident: full-time $17,379; part-time $965.50 per credit hour. *Required fees:* $1035. Tuition and fees vary according to course load, campus/location and program. *Financial support:* Fellowships, research assistantships, teaching assistantships, institutionally sponsored loans, traineeships, health care benefits, and unspecified assistantships available. Support available to part-time students.
Website: http://education.missouri.edu/LTC/index.php

University of Missouri–Kansas City, School of Education, Kansas City, MO 64110-2499. Offers administration (Ed D); counseling and guidance (MA, Ed S), including mental health counseling (Ed S), school counseling (Ed S); counseling psychology (PhD); curriculum and instruction (MA, Ed S), including language and literacy (Ed S); education (PhD), including higher education administration, PK-12 education administration; educational administration (MA, Ed S), including advanced principal (Ed S), beginning principal (Ed S), district-level administration (Ed S); reading education (MA); special education (MA). PhD in education offered through the School of Graduate Studies. *Accreditation:* NCATE. *Program availability:* Part-time, evening/weekend. *Faculty:* 33 full-time (26 women), 51 part-time/adjunct (39 women). *Students:* 136 full-time (103 women), 275 part-time (194 women); includes 110 minority (71 Black or African American, non-Hispanic/Latino; 3 American Indian or Alaska Native, non-Hispanic/Latino; 8 Asian, non-Hispanic/Latino; 22 Hispanic/Latino; 6 Two or more races, non-Hispanic/Latino), 20 international. Average age 32. 324 applicants, 45% accepted, 108 enrolled. In 2016, 152 master's, 13 doctorates, 50 other advanced degrees awarded. *Degree requirements:* For doctorate, thesis/dissertation, internship, practicum. *Entrance requirements:* For master's, GRE, minimum GPA of 2.75, 2 letters of reference, written statement of purpose; for doctorate, GRE, minimum GPA of 3.0; for Ed S, minimum GPA of 3.0. Additional exam requirements/recommendations for international students: Required—TOEFL (minimum score 550 paper-based; 80 iBT). *Application deadline:* For fall admission, 4/1 priority date for domestic and international students; for spring admission, 11/1 priority date for domestic and international students. Applications are processed on a rolling basis. Application fee: $45 ($50 for international students). *Financial support:* In 2016–17, 12 research assistantships with partial tuition reimbursements (averaging $12,476 per year) were awarded; career-related internships or fieldwork, Federal Work-Study, institutionally sponsored loans, and tuition waivers (full and partial) also available. Support available to part-time students. Financial award application deadline: 3/1; financial award applicants required to submit FAFSA. *Faculty research:* Urban education, inquiry-based field study, theories of counseling and psychotherapy, school literacy, educational technology. *Unit head:* Justin Perry, Dean, 816-235-5663, Fax: 816-235-5270, E-mail: education@umkc.edu.
Website: http://education.umkc.edu

University of Missouri–St. Louis, College of Education, Department of Educator Preparation, Innovation and Research, St. Louis, MO 63121. Offers elementary education (M Ed), including early childhood, general, reading; secondary education (M Ed), including curriculum and instruction, general, middle level education, reading, teaching English to speakers of other languages (TESOL); special education (M Ed), including autism and developmental disabilities, early childhood special education. *Program availability:* Part-time, evening/weekend. *Faculty:* 26 full-time (14 women), 22 part-time/adjunct (14 women). *Students:* 151 full-time (127 women), 728 part-time (564 women); includes 222 minority (165 Black or African American, non-Hispanic/Latino; 1 American Indian or Alaska Native, non-Hispanic/Latino; 16 Asian, non-Hispanic/Latino; 31 Hispanic/Latino; 1 Native Hawaiian or other Pacific Islander, non-Hispanic/Latino; 8 Two or more races, non-Hispanic/Latino), 6 international. Average age 29. 363 applicants, 84% accepted, 211 enrolled. *Degree requirements:* For master's, comprehensive exam. *Entrance requirements:* Additional exam requirements/recommendations for international students: Recommended—TOEFL (minimum score 550 paper-based; 79 iBT), IELTS (minimum score 6.5). *Application deadline:* For fall admission, 7/1 priority date for domestic and international students; for spring admission, 12/1 priority date for domestic and international students. Application fee: $50 ($40 for international students). Electronic applications accepted. *Financial support:* Application deadline: 4/1; applicants required to submit FAFSA. *Unit head:* Dr. Gayle Wilkinson, Chair, 314-516-5791. *Application contact:* 314-516-5458, Fax: 314-516-6996, E-mail: gadadm@umsl.edu.
Website: https://coe.umsl.edu/dept/epir.html

University of Nebraska at Kearney, College of Education, Department of Teacher Education, Kearney, NE 68849-0001. Offers curriculum and instruction (MA Ed), including early childhood education, elementary education, English as a second language, instructional effectiveness, reading/special education, secondary education; instructional technology (MS Ed), including information technology, instructional technology, school librarian; reading PK-12 (MA Ed); special education (MA Ed), including advanced practitioner: assistive technology specialist, advanced practitioner: behavioral interventionist, advanced practitioner: inclusive collaboration specialist, gifted, teacher education. *Program availability:* Part-time, evening/weekend, online only, 100% online. *Faculty:* 18 full-time (13 women). *Students:* 21 full-time (15 women), 296 part-time (240 women); includes 21 minority (3 Black or African American, non-Hispanic/Latino; 1 Asian, non-Hispanic/Latino; 14 Hispanic/Latino; 1 Native Hawaiian or other Pacific Islander, non-Hispanic/Latino; 2 Two or more races, non-Hispanic/Latino), 1 international. Average age 32. 81 applicants, 100% accepted, 61 enrolled. In 2016, 129 master's awarded. *Degree requirements:* For master's, comprehensive exam, thesis optional. *Entrance requirements:* For master's, portfolio or GRE. Additional exam requirements/recommendations for international students: Recommended—TOEFL

(minimum score 550 paper-based; 79 iBT), IELTS (minimum score 6.5). *Application deadline:* For fall admission, 6/15 for domestic students, 5/15 for international students; for spring admission, 10/15 for domestic and international students; for summer admission, 3/15 for domestic and international students. Application fee: $45. Electronic applications accepted. *Expenses:* $285 per credit hour resident tuition, $415 per credit hour non-resident tuition (online). *Financial support:* In 2016–17, 6 students received support, including 6 research assistantships with full tuition reimbursements available (averaging $10,500 per year); career-related internships or fieldwork, scholarships/grants, health care benefits, and unspecified assistantships also available. Support available to part-time students. Financial award application deadline: 2/28; financial award applicants required to submit FAFSA. *Unit head:* Sarah Bartling, Administrative Assistant, 308-865-8513, E-mail: bartlingseg@unk.edu. *Application contact:* Linda Johnson, Director, Graduate Admissions and Programs, 308-865-8841, Fax: 308-865-8837, E-mail: johnsonli@unk.edu.
Website: http://www.unk.edu/academics/ted/index.php

University of Nevada, Reno, Graduate School, College of Education, Department of Educational Specialties, Program in Literacy Studies, Reno, NV 89557. Offers M Ed, MA, Ed D, PhD. Terminal master's awarded for partial completion of doctoral program. *Degree requirements:* For master's, thesis optional; for doctorate, thesis/dissertation. *Entrance requirements:* For master's, minimum GPA of 2.75; for doctorate, GRE General Test, minimum GPA of 3.0. Additional exam requirements/recommendations for international students: Required—TOEFL (minimum score 500 paper-based; 61 iBT), IELTS (minimum score 6). Electronic applications accepted. *Faculty research:* Cognitive language process, literacy.

University of New England, College of Graduate and Professional Studies, Portland, ME 04103. Offers applied nutrition (MS); career and technical education (MS Ed); curriculum and instruction (MS Ed); education (CAGS, Post-Master's Certificate); education leadership (Ed D); educational leadership (MS Ed); generalist (MS Ed); health informatics (MS, Graduate Certificate); inclusion education (MS Ed); literacy K-12 (MS Ed); medical education leadership (MMEL); public health (Graduate Certificate); reading specialist (MS Ed); social work (MSW). *Program availability:* Part-time, evening/weekend, online only, 100% online. *Faculty:* 67 part-time/adjunct (46 women). *Students:* 891 full-time (667 women), 359 part-time (261 women); includes 309 minority (215 Black or African American, non-Hispanic/Latino; 2 American Indian or Alaska Native, non-Hispanic/Latino; 63 Asian, non-Hispanic/Latino; 18 Hispanic/Latino; 2 Native Hawaiian or other Pacific Islander, non-Hispanic/Latino; 9 Two or more races, non-Hispanic/Latino). Average age 36. 777 applicants, 50% accepted, 316 enrolled. In 2016, 292 master's, 34 doctorates, 130 other advanced degrees awarded. *Application deadline:* Applications are processed on a rolling basis. Electronic applications accepted. Tuition and fees vary according to degree level, program and student level. *Financial support:* Application deadline: 5/1; applicants required to submit FAFSA. *Unit head:* Dr. Martha Wilson, Associate Provost for Online Worldwide Learning/Dean of the College of Graduate and Professional Studies, 207-221-4985, E-mail: mwilson13@une.edu.
Website: http://online.une.edu

University of New Mexico, Graduate Studies, College of Education, Program in Language, Literacy and Sociocultural Studies, Albuquerque, NM 87131. Offers American Indian education (MA); bilingual education (MA, PhD); educational linguistics (PhD); educational thought and sociocultural studies (MA, PhD); literacy/language arts (MA, PhD); social studies (MA); TESOL (MA, PhD). *Faculty:* 17 full-time (10 women), 4 part-time/adjunct (3 women). *Students:* 57 full-time (38 women), 129 part-time (105 women); includes 102 minority (8 Black or African American, non-Hispanic/Latino; 16 American Indian or Alaska Native, non-Hispanic/Latino; 6 Asian, non-Hispanic/Latino; 67 Hispanic/Latino; 5 Two or more races, non-Hispanic/Latino), 32 international. Average age 39. 50 applicants, 60% accepted, 23 enrolled. In 2016, 36 master's, 4 doctorates awarded. *Degree requirements:* For master's, comprehensive exam, thesis optional; for doctorate, comprehensive exam, thesis/dissertation, research skills. *Entrance requirements:* For master's, letter of intent, 3 letters of recommendation, resume, BA/BS, department demographic form, transcripts; for doctorate, writing sample, letter of intent, 3 letters of recommendation, resume, BA/BS, MA, department demographic form, transcripts. Additional exam requirements/recommendations for international students: Required—TOEFL. *Application deadline:* For fall admission, 12/1 for domestic and international students; for spring admission, 9/15 for domestic and international students. Application fee: $50. Electronic applications accepted. *Financial support:* Fellowships, research assistantships, teaching assistantships with tuition reimbursements, career-related internships or fieldwork, institutionally sponsored loans, scholarships/grants, and unspecified assistantships available. Support available to part-time students. Financial award application deadline: 3/1; financial award applicants required to submit FAFSA. *Faculty research:* School reform, professional development, history of education, Native American education, politics of education, feminism and issues of sexual identity, critical race theory, bilingualism, literacy reading, adolescent literature, second language acquisition, critical theory and schooling, indigenous languages. *Unit head:* Dr. Lois M. Meyer, Chair, 505-277-7244, Fax: 505-277-8362, E-mail: lsmeyer@unm.edu. *Application contact:* Debra Schaffer, Administrative Assistant, 505-277-0437, Fax: 505-277-8362, E-mail: schaffer@unm.edu.
Website: http://coe.unm.edu/departments-programs/llss/index.html

The University of North Carolina at Chapel Hill, Graduate School, School of Education, Program in Education, Chapel Hill, NC 27599. Offers culture, curriculum and change (MA, PhD); early childhood, intervention and literacy (MA, PhD); educational psychology, measurement and evaluation (MA, PhD). *Accreditation:* NCATE. *Degree requirements:* For master's, thesis; for doctorate, comprehensive exam, thesis/dissertation. *Entrance requirements:* For master's, GRE General Test, minimum GPA of 3.0 during last 2 years of undergraduates course work; for doctorate, GRE General Test, minimum GPA of 3.0 during last 2 years of undergraduate course work. Additional exam requirements/recommendations for international students: Required—TOEFL (minimum score 550 paper-based). Electronic applications accepted.

The University of North Carolina at Charlotte, Cato College of Education, Department of Reading and Elementary Education, Charlotte, NC 28223-0001. Offers elementary education (M Ed, Graduate Certificate); elementary mathematics education (Graduate Certificate); reading education (M Ed). *Program availability:* Part-time, evening/weekend, 100% online, blended/hybrid learning. *Faculty:* 25 full-time (13 women), 3 part-time/adjunct (all women). *Students:* 5 full-time (all women), 72 part-time (69 women); includes 13 minority (8 Black or African American, non-Hispanic/Latino; 4 Hispanic/Latino; 1 Two or more races, non-Hispanic/Latino), 1 international. Average age 30. 55 applicants, 98% accepted, 51 enrolled. In 2016, 24 master's awarded. *Degree requirements:* For master's, thesis or alternative, capstone project. *Entrance requirements:* For master's, GRE or MAT, three letters of recommendation, official transcripts, academic and professional goals statement, valid teacher's license, bachelor's degree in elementary education; NC A-level license or its equivalent in another state (for reading education). Additional exam requirements/recommendations for international students: Required—TOEFL (minimum score 523 paper-based, 70 iBT) or IELTS (6.5). *Application deadline:* For fall admission, 3/1 priority date for domestic students, 3/1 for international students; for spring admission, 10/1 priority date for domestic students, 10/1 for international students; for summer admission, 4/1 priority date for domestic students, 4/1 for international students. Applications are processed on a rolling basis. Application fee: $75. Electronic applications accepted. *Expenses:* Tuition, state resident: full-time $4252. Tuition, nonresident: full-time $17,423. *Required fees:* $3026. Tuition and fees vary according to course load and program. *Financial support:* In 2016–17, 4 students received support, including 4 research assistantships (averaging $16,437 per year); career-related internships or fieldwork, institutionally sponsored loans, scholarships/grants, and unspecified assistantships also available. Support available to part-time students. Financial award application deadline: 3/1; financial award applicants required to submit FAFSA. *Total annual research expenditures:* $44,142. *Unit head:* Dr. Mike Putman, Chair, 704-687-8019, E-mail: michael.putman@uncc.edu. *Application contact:* Kathy B. Giddings, Director of Graduate Admissions, 704-687-5503, Fax: 704-687-1668, E-mail: gradadm@uncc.edu.
Website: http://reel.uncc.edu/

The University of North Carolina at Greensboro, Graduate School, School of Education, Department of Teacher Education and Higher Education, Greensboro, NC 27412-5001. Offers college teaching and adult learning (Certificate); curriculum and instruction (M Ed), including chemistry education, elementary education, English as a second language, French education, instructional technology, mathematics education, middle grades education, reading education, science education, social studies education, Spanish education; curriculum and teaching (PhD), including higher education, teacher education and development; English as a second language (Certificate); higher education (M Ed); supervision (M Ed). *Accreditation:* NCATE. *Program availability:* Part-time. *Degree requirements:* For doctorate, thesis/dissertation. *Entrance requirements:* For master's and doctorate, GRE General Test. Additional exam requirements/recommendations for international students: Required—TOEFL. Electronic applications accepted. *Faculty research:* Community college literacy program, middle school mathematics/computer mathematics.

The University of North Carolina at Pembroke, The Graduate School, School of Education, Program in Reading Education, Pembroke, NC 28372-1510. Offers MA Ed. *Accreditation:* NCATE. *Program availability:* Part-time, evening/weekend. *Degree requirements:* For master's, comprehensive exam, thesis optional. *Entrance requirements:* For master's, GRE General Test or MAT, minimum GPA of 3.0 in major, 2.5 overall; teaching license; one year of teaching experience; three professional references. Additional exam requirements/recommendations for international students: Required—TOEFL.

The University of North Carolina Wilmington, Watson College of Education, Department of Early Childhood, Elementary, Middle, Literacy and Special Education, Wilmington, NC 28403-3297. Offers educational leadership, policy, and advocacy (M Ed); elementary education (M Ed, MAT); language and literacy (M Ed); middle grades education (M Ed, MAT). *Accreditation:* NCATE. *Program availability:* Part-time. *Faculty:* 26 full-time (19 women). *Students:* 121 full-time (89 women), 139 part-time (135 women); includes 70 minority (47 Black or African American, non-Hispanic/Latino; 1 Asian, non-Hispanic/Latino; 14 Hispanic/Latino; 8 Two or more races, non-Hispanic/Latino). Average age 34. 109 applicants, 78% accepted, 65 enrolled. In 2016, 83 master's awarded. *Degree requirements:* For master's, comprehensive exam, capstone experience. *Entrance requirements:* For master's, GRE General Test, MAT, minimum GPA of 3.0 in undergraduate work, 3 letters of recommendations, NC Class A teacher license in related field, statement of interest. *Application deadline:* For fall admission, 5/15 for domestic students; for spring admission, 10/15 for domestic students; for summer admission, 3/15 for domestic students. Applications are processed on a rolling basis. Application fee: $60. Electronic applications accepted. *Expenses:* Contact institution. *Financial support:* Scholarships/grants and unspecified assistantships available. Support available to part-time students. Financial award application deadline: 3/15; financial award applicants required to submit FAFSA. *Unit head:* Dr. Kathy Fox, Chair, 910-962-3240, Fax: 910-962-3988, E-mail: foxk@uncw.edu. *Application contact:* Dr. Elizabeth Crawford, Graduate Program Coordinator, 910-962-2916, Fax: 910-962-3988, E-mail: crawforde@uncw.edu.
Website: http://www.uncw.edu/ed/eemls/index.html

University of North Dakota, Graduate School, College of Education and Human Development, Program in Reading Education, Grand Forks, ND 58202. Offers M Ed, MS. *Accreditation:* NCATE. *Program availability:* Part-time, online learning. *Degree requirements:* For master's, comprehensive exam, thesis or alternative. *Entrance requirements:* For master's, minimum GPA of 3.0. Additional exam requirements/recommendations for international students: Required—TOEFL (minimum score 550 paper-based; 79 iBT), IELTS (minimum score 6.5). *Application deadline:* For fall admission, 8/1 priority date for domestic students, 5/1 priority date for international students; for spring admission, 12/1 priority date for domestic students, 9/1 priority date for international students. Applications are processed on a rolling basis. Application fee: $35. Electronic applications accepted. *Financial support:* Fellowships with full and partial tuition reimbursements, research assistantships with full and partial tuition reimbursements, teaching assistantships with full and partial tuition reimbursements, career-related internships or fieldwork, Federal Work-Study, institutionally sponsored loans, scholarships/grants, health care benefits, and tuition waivers (full and partial) available. Support available to part-time students. Financial award application deadline: 3/15; financial award applicants required to submit FAFSA. *Faculty research:* Whole language, multicultural education, child-focused learning, experiential science, cooperative learning. *Unit head:* Dr. Shellay Baurentine, Director, 701-777-3162, Fax: 701-777-4393, E-mail: shellay.baurentine@und.edu. *Application contact:* Staci Wells, Admissions Associate, 701-777-2945, Fax: 701-777-3619, E-mail: staci.wells@gradschool.und.edu.
Website: http://education.und.edu/teaching-and-learning/grad-reading.cfm

University of Northern Colorado, Graduate School, College of Education and Behavioral Sciences, School of Teacher Education, Program in Literacy, Greeley, CO 80639. Offers MA. *Accreditation:* NCATE. *Program availability:* Part-time, evening/weekend, online learning. *Faculty:* 3 full-time (2 women). *Students:* 1 (woman) full-time. Average age 44. 1 applicant, 100% accepted. In 2016, 8 degrees awarded. *Degree requirements:* For master's, comprehensive exam, thesis or alternative. *Entrance requirements:* For master's, GRE General Test (if undergraduate GPA less than 3.0), resume, letters of reference. *Application deadline:* Applications are processed on a rolling basis. Application fee: $50 ($60 for international students). Electronic applications accepted. *Financial support:* Fellowships, research assistantships, teaching assistantships, and unspecified assistantships available. Financial award application deadline: 3/1; financial award applicants required to submit FAFSA. *Unit head:* Dr. Michael Opitz, Program Coordinator, 970-351-1605. *Application contact:* Linda Sisson, Graduate Student Admission Coordinator, 970-351-1807, Fax: 970-351-2371, E-mail: linda.sisson@unco.edu.
Website: http://www.unco.edu/cebs/teachered/graduate/reading/

University of Northern Iowa, Graduate College, College of Education, Department of Curriculum and Instruction, MAE Program in Literacy Education, Cedar Falls, IA 50614. Offers MAE. *Program availability:* Part-time, evening/weekend. *Degree requirements:* For master's, comprehensive exam, thesis or alternative. *Entrance requirements:* For master's, writing exam, minimum GPA of 3.0, two recommendations from professional educators. Additional exam requirements/recommendations for international students:

Required—TOEFL (minimum score 500 paper-based; 61 iBT). Electronic applications accepted.

University of North Florida, College of Education and Human Services, Department of Childhood Education, Literacy, and TESOL, Jacksonville, FL 32224. Offers literacy (M Ed); professional education (M Ed); TESOL (M Ed). *Accreditation:* NCATE. *Program availability:* Part-time, evening/weekend. *Faculty:* 10 full-time (8 women). *Students:* 9 full-time (7 women), 27 part-time (all women); includes 14 minority (7 Black or African American, non-Hispanic/Latino; 2 Asian, non-Hispanic/Latino; 2 Hispanic/Latino; 3 Two or more races, non-Hispanic/Latino), 2 international. Average age 31. 34 applicants, 50% accepted, 12 enrolled. In 2016, 22 master's awarded. *Entrance requirements:* For master's, GRE General Test, minimum GPA of 3.0 in last 60 hours, 3 letters of recommendation, interview. Additional exam requirements/recommendations for international students: Required—TOEFL (minimum score 500 paper-based). *Application deadline:* For fall admission, 8/1 priority date for domestic students, 5/1 for international students; for spring admission, 12/1 priority date for domestic students, 10/1 for international students; for summer admission, 3/15 priority date for domestic students, 2/1 for international students. Application fee: $30. Electronic applications accepted. Tuition and fees vary according to course load, campus/location and program. *Financial support:* In 2016–17, 3 students received support. Research assistantships, Federal Work-Study, tuition waivers (partial), and unspecified assistantships available. Support available to part-time students. Financial award application deadline: 4/1; financial award applicants required to submit FAFSA. *Faculty research:* Social context of and processes in learning, inter-disciplinary instruction, cross-cultural conflict resolution, the Vygotskian perspective on literacy diagnosis and instruction, performance poetry and teaching the language arts through drama. *Total annual research expenditures:* $2,531. *Unit head:* Dr. Paul Parkison, Chair, 904-620-5352, Fax: 904-620-1025, E-mail: n01230143@unf.edu. *Application contact:* Dr. Amanda Pascale, Director, The Graduate School, 904-620-1360, Fax: 904-620-1362, E-mail: graduateschool@unf.edu.
Website: http://www.unf.edu/coehs/celt/

University of Oklahoma, College of Arts and Sciences, Department of English, Norman, OK 73019. Offers composition and rhetoric (MA, PhD); literary and cultural studies (MA, PhD). *Program availability:* Part-time. *Faculty:* 31 full-time (15 women). *Students:* 26 full-time (16 women), 18 part-time (9 women); includes 9 minority (2 American Indian or Alaska Native, non-Hispanic/Latino; 2 Asian, non-Hispanic/Latino; 3 Hispanic/Latino; 2 Two or more races, non-Hispanic/Latino), 1 international. Average age 32. 38 applicants, 34% accepted, 3 enrolled. In 2016, 7 master's, 7 doctorates awarded. *Degree requirements:* For master's, one foreign language, comprehensive exam (for some programs), thesis (for some programs), exam or thesis; for doctorate, one foreign language, comprehensive exam, thesis/dissertation. *Entrance requirements:* For master's, BA in English or related field; for doctorate, MA in English or related field. Additional exam requirements/recommendations for international students: Required—TOEFL (minimum score 79 iBT) or IELTS (minimum score 6.5). *Application deadline:* For fall admission, 1/5 priority date for domestic and international students. Application fee: $50 ($100 for international students). Electronic applications accepted. *Expenses:* Tuition, state resident: full-time $4886; part-time $203.60 per credit hour. Tuition, nonresident: full-time $18,989; part-time $791.20 per credit hour. *Required fees:* $3283; $126.25 per credit hour. $126.50 per semester. *Financial support:* In 2016–17, 40 students received support, including 5 research assistantships (averaging $13,011 per year), 32 teaching assistantships (averaging $12,550 per year); fellowships, scholarships/grants, health care benefits, and unspecified assistantships also available. Financial award application deadline: 6/1; financial award applicants required to submit FAFSA. *Faculty research:* American Indian literature and culture; composition and rhetoric; American literature; British literature; postcolonial literature and culture. *Unit head:* Dr. Daniela Garofalo, Professor and Chair, 405-325-4661, Fax: 405-325-0831, E-mail: dg@ou.edu. *Application contact:* Sara Day, Graduate Assistant, 405-325-0489, Fax: 405-325-0831, E-mail: redpanda@ou.edu.
Website: http://cas.ou.edu/english

University of Oklahoma, Jeannine Rainbolt College of Education, Department of Instructional Leadership and Academic Curriculum, Norman, OK 73019. Offers instructional leadership and academic curriculum (M Ed, PhD), including biomedical education (PhD), early childhood education, elementary education (M Ed), English education, instructional leadership, mathematics education, reading education, science education, social studies education, world languages education (M Ed). *Accreditation:* NCATE. *Program availability:* Part-time. *Faculty:* 19 full-time (15 women), 1 (woman) part-time/adjunct. *Students:* 66 full-time (49 women), 116 part-time (88 women); includes 49 minority (12 Black or African American, non-Hispanic/Latino; 6 American Indian or Alaska Native, non-Hispanic/Latino; 6 Asian, non-Hispanic/Latino; 11 Hispanic/Latino; 1 Native Hawaiian or other Pacific Islander, non-Hispanic/Latino; 13 Two or more races, non-Hispanic/Latino), 13 international. Average age 35. 38 applicants, 97% accepted, 28 enrolled. In 2016, 33 master's, 10 doctorates awarded. Terminal master's awarded for partial completion of doctoral program. *Degree requirements:* For master's, comprehensive exam (for some programs), thesis (for some programs); for doctorate, comprehensive exam (for some programs), thesis/dissertation. *Entrance requirements:* For doctorate, GRE. Additional exam requirements/recommendations for international students: Required—TOEFL (minimum score 79 iBT) or IELTS (minimum score 6.5). Application fee: $50 ($100 for international students). Electronic applications accepted. *Expenses:* Tuition, state resident: full-time $4886; part-time $203.60 per credit hour. Tuition, nonresident: full-time $18,989; part-time $791.20 per credit hour. *Required fees:* $3283; $126.25 per credit hour. $126.50 per semester. *Financial support:* In 2016–17, 112 students received support, including 7 research assistantships with partial tuition reimbursements available (averaging $10,373 per year), 6 teaching assistantships with partial tuition reimbursements available (averaging $11,446 per year); fellowships, scholarships/grants, and unspecified assistantships also available. Financial award application deadline: 6/1; financial award applicants required to submit FAFSA. *Faculty research:* Teacher preparation; instruction; curriculum; learning; constructivist theory. *Total annual research expenditures:* $165,297. *Unit head:* Dr. Stacy Reeder, Chair, 405-325-1498, Fax: 405-325-4061, E-mail: reeder@ou.edu. *Application contact:* Anna Steele, Graduate Programs Officer, 405-325-4525, E-mail: anna.steele@ou.edu.
Website: http://www.ou.edu/education/ilac

University of Oklahoma Health Sciences Center, Graduate College, College of Allied Health, Department of Communication Sciences and Disorders, Oklahoma City, OK 73190. Offers audiology (MS, Au D, PhD); communication sciences and disorders (Certificate), including reading, speech-language pathology; education of the deaf (MS); speech-language pathology (MS, PhD). *Accreditation:* ASHA (one or more programs are accredited). *Program availability:* Part-time. Terminal master's awarded for partial completion of doctoral program. *Degree requirements:* For master's, comprehensive exam, thesis optional; for doctorate, one foreign language, comprehensive exam, thesis/dissertation. *Entrance requirements:* For master's and doctorate, GRE General Test, 3 letters of recommendation. Additional exam requirements/recommendations for international students: Required—TOEFL (minimum score 550 paper-based). *Faculty research:* Event-related potentials, cleft palate, fluency disorders, language disorders, hearing and speech science.

University of Pennsylvania, Graduate School of Education, Division of Literacy, Culture, and International Education, Program in Language and Literacy, Philadelphia, PA 19104. Offers MS Ed. *Students:* 3 full-time (all women), 1 (woman) part-time; includes 1 minority (Asian, non-Hispanic/Latino), 2 international. Average age 27. 15 applicants, 67% accepted, 2 enrolled. In 2016, 2 master's awarded. *Expenses: Tuition:* Full-time $31,068; part-time $5762 per course. *Required fees:* $3200; $336 per course. Full-time tuition and fees vary according to degree level, program and student level. Part-time tuition and fees vary according to course load, degree level and program.

University of Phoenix–Online Campus, College of Education, Phoenix, AZ 85034-7209. Offers administration and supervision (MAEd, Certificate); adult education and training (MAEd); curriculum and instruction (MAEd), including computer education, curriculum and instruction, English as a second language, language arts, mathematics, reading; early childhood education (MAEd); educational studies (MAEd); elementary teacher education (MAEd), including early childhood, elementary teacher education, high school middle level, middle level; principal licensure (Certificate); secondary teacher education (MAEd); special education (MAEd, Certificate); teacher education (MAEd), including middle level generalist; teacher education middle level mathematics (MAEd), including middle level mathematics; teacher education middle level science (MAEd), including middle level science; teacher education secondary mathematics (MAEd); teacher education secondary science (MAEd); teacher leadership (MAEd); teachers of English learners (Certificate); transition to teaching (Certificate), including elementary education, secondary education. *Program availability:* Evening/weekend, online learning. *Entrance requirements:* Additional exam requirements/recommendations for international students: Required—TOEFL, TOEIC (Test of English as an International Communication), Berlitz Online English Proficiency Exam, PTE, or IELTS. Electronic applications accepted. *Expenses:* Contact institution.

University of Phoenix–Phoenix Campus, College of Education, Tempe, AZ 85282-2371. Offers administration and supervision (MA Ed); adult education and training (MA Ed); curriculum and instruction reading (MA Ed); early childhood education (MA Ed); education studies (MA Ed); elementary teacher education (MA Ed); secondary teacher education (MA Ed); special education (MA Ed); teacher leadership (MA Ed). *Program availability:* Evening/weekend, online learning. *Entrance requirements:* Additional exam requirements/recommendations for international students: Required—TOEFL, TOEIC (Test of English as an International Communication), Berlitz Online English Proficiency Exam, PTE, or IELTS. Electronic applications accepted. *Expenses:* Contact institution.

University of Pittsburgh, School of Education, Department of Instruction and Learning, Program in Reading Education, Pittsburgh, PA 15260. Offers M Ed, Ed D, PhD. *Degree requirements:* For master's, thesis; for doctorate, thesis/dissertation. *Entrance requirements:* For master's, PRAXIS I; for doctorate, GRE General Test. Additional exam requirements/recommendations for international students: Required—TOEFL. Tuition and fees vary according to program.

University of Pittsburgh, School of Education, Department of Instruction and Learning, Program in Secondary Education, Pittsburgh, PA 15260. Offers English and communications education (M Ed, MAT); foreign language education (M Ed, MAT); language, literacy and culture education (Ed D, PhD); mathematics education (M Ed, MAT, Ed D, PhD); science education (M Ed, MAT, Ed D, PhD); secondary education (PhD); social studies education (M Ed, MAT); STEM education (Ed D). *Program availability:* Part-time, evening/weekend. *Degree requirements:* For master's, thesis; for doctorate, thesis/dissertation. *Entrance requirements:* For master's, PRAXIS I; for doctorate, GRE General Test. Additional exam requirements/recommendations for international students: Required—TOEFL. Electronic applications accepted. Tuition and fees vary according to program.

University of Portland, School of Education, Portland, OR 97203-5798. Offers education (MA, MAT); educational leadership (M Ed); English for speakers of other languages (M Ed); initial administrator licensure (M Ed); neuroeducation (M Ed, Ed D); organizational leadership and development (Ed D); reading (M Ed); school leadership and development (Ed D); special education (M Ed). M Ed also available through the Graduate Outreach Program for teachers residing in the Oregon and Washington state areas. *Accreditation:* NCATE. *Program availability:* Part-time, evening/weekend. *Entrance requirements:* For master's, minimum GPA of 3.0, teaching certificate, letters of recommendation, resume, statement of goals, official transcripts. Additional exam requirements/recommendations for international students: Required—TOEFL (minimum score 550 paper-based; 80 iBT), IELTS (minimum score 7). *Faculty research:* Multicultural education, supervision/leadership.

University of Rhode Island, Graduate School, Alan Shawn Feinstein College of Education and Professional Studies, School of Education, Kingston, RI 02881. Offers education (PhD); reading (MA); special education (MA). *Accreditation:* NCATE. *Program availability:* Part-time, evening/weekend. *Faculty:* 18 full-time (13 women). *Students:* 65 full-time (51 women), 147 part-time (108 women); includes 27 minority (7 Black or African American, non-Hispanic/Latino; 6 American Indian or Alaska Native, non-Hispanic/Latino; 7 Asian, non-Hispanic/Latino; 6 Hispanic/Latino; 1 Two or more races, non-Hispanic/Latino), 10 international. In 2016, 26 master's, 7 doctorates awarded. *Degree requirements:* For master's, comprehensive exam (for some programs), thesis optional; for doctorate, comprehensive exam, thesis/dissertation. *Entrance requirements:* For master's, 2 letters of recommendation; interview (for special education applicants); for doctorate, GRE, 3 letters of recommendation, resume. Additional exam requirements/recommendations for international students: Required—TOEFL. *Application deadline:* For fall admission, 1/15 for domestic students, 1/31 for international students; for spring admission, 11/15 for domestic students; for summer admission, 4/15 for domestic students. Application fee: $65. Electronic applications accepted. *Expenses:* Tuition, state resident: full-time $11,796; part-time $655 per credit. Tuition, nonresident: full-time $24,206; part-time $1345 per credit. *Required fees:* $1546; $44 per credit. One-time fee: $155 full-time; $35 part-time. *Financial support:* In 2016–17, 1 research assistantship with tuition reimbursement (averaging $8,592 per year), 4 teaching assistantships with tuition reimbursements (averaging $15,036 per year) were awarded. Financial award application deadline: 1/31; financial award applicants required to submit FAFSA. *Unit head:* Dr. David Byrd, Director, School of Education, 401-874-5484, Fax: 401-874-5471, E-mail: dbyrd@uri.edu. *Application contact:* Graduate Admissions, 401-874-2872, E-mail: gradadm@etal.uri.edu.
Website: http://www.uri.edu/hss/education/

University of St. Francis, College of Education, Joliet, IL 60435-6169. Offers educational leadership (MS, Ed D); elementary education (M Ed); reading (MS); secondary education (M Ed), including English education, math education, science education, social studies education, visual arts education; special education (M Ed); teaching and learning (MS); TESOL (Certificate). *Accreditation:* NCATE. *Program availability:* Part-time, evening/weekend, 100% online, blended/hybrid learning. *Faculty:* 11 full-time (8 women), 60 part-time/adjunct (42 women). *Students:* 34 full-time (26 women), 420 part-time (318 women); includes 92 minority (51 Black or African American, non-Hispanic/Latino; 5 Asian, non-Hispanic/Latino; 31 Hispanic/Latino; 5 Two or more races, non-Hispanic/Latino), 4 international. Average age 36. 242 applicants, 48% accepted, 96 enrolled. In 2016, 229 master's, 44 doctorates, 10 other advanced degrees awarded. *Degree requirements:* For master's, comprehensive exam; for

doctorate, thesis/dissertation. *Entrance requirements:* Additional exam requirements/recommendations for international students: Required—TOEFL (minimum score 550 paper-based; 79 iBT), IELTS (minimum score 6). *Application deadline:* Applications are processed on a rolling basis. Application fee: $30. Electronic applications accepted. Application fee is waived when completed online. *Expenses:* Contact institution. *Financial support:* In 2016–17, 48 students received support. Career-related internships or fieldwork and unspecified assistantships available. Support available to part-time students. Financial award applicants required to submit FAFSA. *Unit head:* Dr. John Gambro, Dean, 815-740-3829, Fax: 815-740-2264, E-mail: jgambro@stfrancis.edu. *Application contact:* Sandra Sloka, Director of Admissions for Graduate and Degree Completion Programs, 800-735-7500, Fax: 815-740-3431, E-mail: ssloka@stfrancis.edu.
Website: http://www.stfrancis.edu/academics/college-of-education/

University of Saint Joseph, Department of Education, West Hartford, CT 06117-2700. Offers curriculum and instruction (MA); educational technology (MA); literacy internship (MA); multiple intelligences (MA); reading/language (MA); TESOL (MA). *Program availability:* Part-time, evening/weekend. *Degree requirements:* For master's, comprehensive exam, thesis or alternative. *Entrance requirements:* For master's, 2 letters of recommendation. Electronic applications accepted. Application fee is waived when completed online. *Expenses: Tuition:* Full-time $14,580; part-time $729 per credit hour. *Required fees:* $920; $46 per credit hour. Tuition and fees vary according to course load, degree level and program.

University of St. Thomas, School of Education and Human Services, Houston, TX 77006-4696. Offers all level education (M Ed); bilingual/dual language (M Ed); Catholic school teaching (M Ed); Catholic/private school leadership (M Ed); counselor education (M Ed); curriculum and instruction (M Ed); education (Ed D); educational leadership (M Ed); elementary teaching (M Ed); English as a second language (M Ed); exceptionality/educational diagnostician (M Ed); exceptionality/special education (M Ed); generalist (M Ed); reading (M Ed); secondary teaching (M Ed); teaching (MAT). *Accreditation:* TEAC. *Program availability:* Part-time, evening/weekend, online learning. *Faculty:* 44 full-time (29 women), 31 part-time/adjunct (17 women). *Students:* 65 full-time (61 women), 719 part-time (645 women); includes 515 minority (169 Black or African American, non-Hispanic/Latino; 25 Asian, non-Hispanic/Latino; 315 Hispanic/Latino; 2 Native Hawaiian or other Pacific Islander, non-Hispanic/Latino; 4 Two or more races, non-Hispanic/Latino), 24 international. Average age 36. 297 applicants, 92% accepted, 211 enrolled. In 2016, 403 master's awarded. *Degree requirements:* For master's, thesis, field experience. *Entrance requirements:* For master's, GRE or MAT if GPA is below 3.0, bachelor's degree; minimum GPA of 2.75 in bachelor's degree or last 60 credit hours; official transcripts from all institutions; goal statement of 250-300 words; 1 reference. Additional exam requirements/recommendations for international students: Required—TOEFL (minimum score 94 iBT), IELTS (minimum score 7), PTE (minimum score 53). *Application deadline:* Applications are processed on a rolling basis. Application fee: $35. Electronic applications accepted. *Expenses:* Contact institution. *Financial support:* In 2016–17, 52 students received support. Federal Work-Study, scholarships/grants, and state work-study, institutional employment available. Support available to part-time students. Financial award application deadline: 4/15; financial award applicants required to submit FAFSA. *Faculty research:* Leadership, diversity, personality traits, second language acquisition. *Unit head:* Dr. Robert LeBlanc, Dean, 713-525-3540, Fax: 713-525-3871, E-mail: education@stthom.edu. *Application contact:* Rita Paredes, Administrative Assistant, 713-525-3442, Fax: 713-525-3871, E-mail: rparede@stthom.edu.
Website: http://www.stthom.edu/Academics/School_of_Education_and_Human_Services/Index.aqf

University of San Diego, School of Leadership and Education Sciences, Department of Learning and Teaching, San Diego, CA 92110-2492. Offers inclusive learning (M Ed); literacy and digital learning (M Ed); school leadership (M Ed); special education with deaf and hard of hearing (M Ed); STEAM (science, technology, engineering, arts, and mathematics) (M Ed); teaching (MAT); TESOL, literacy and culture (M Ed). *Program availability:* Part-time, evening/weekend. *Faculty:* 9 full-time (7 women), 29 part-time/adjunct (19 women). *Students:* 161 full-time (126 women), 188 part-time (153 women); includes 127 minority (4 Black or African American, non-Hispanic/Latino; 24 Asian, non-Hispanic/Latino; 86 Hispanic/Latino; 1 Native Hawaiian or other Pacific Islander, non-Hispanic/Latino; 12 Two or more races, non-Hispanic/Latino), 20 international. Average age 33. 383 applicants, 83% accepted, 194 enrolled. In 2016, 114 master's awarded. *Degree requirements:* For master's, thesis (for some programs), international experience. *Entrance requirements:* For master's, California Basic Educational Skills Test, California Subject Examination for Teachers, minimum GPA of 2.75. Additional exam requirements/recommendations for international students: Required—TOEFL (minimum score 580 paper-based; 83 iBT), TWE. *Application deadline:* Applications are processed on a rolling basis. Application fee: $45. Electronic applications accepted. *Financial support:* In 2016–17, 46 students received support. Career-related internships or fieldwork, Federal Work-Study, institutionally sponsored loans, and stipends available. Financial award application deadline: 4/1; financial award applicants required to submit FAFSA. *Faculty research:* Action research methodology, cultural studies, instructional theories and practices, second language acquisition, school reform. *Unit head:* Dr. Maya Kalyanpur, Chair, 619-260-7655, E-mail: mkalyanpur@sandiego.edu. *Application contact:* Monica Mahon, Associate Director of Graduate Admissions, 619-260-4524, Fax: 619-260-4158, E-mail: grads@sandiego.edu.
Website: http://www.sandiego.edu/soles/departments/learning-and-teaching/

University of San Francisco, School of Education, Department of Learning and Instruction, San Francisco, CA 94117-1080. Offers digital technologies for teaching and learning (MA); learning and instruction (MA, Ed D); special education (MA, Ed D); teaching reading (MA). *Program availability:* Part-time, evening/weekend. *Faculty:* 9 full-time (5 women), 2 part-time/adjunct (both women). *Students:* 79 full-time (61 women), 30 part-time (23 women); includes 41 minority (12 Black or African American, non-Hispanic/Latino; 12 Asian, non-Hispanic/Latino; 14 Hispanic/Latino; 3 Two or more races, non-Hispanic/Latino), 7 international. Average age 37. 64 applicants, 94% accepted, 41 enrolled. In 2016, 20 master's, 8 doctorates awarded. *Degree requirements:* For doctorate, thesis/dissertation. *Entrance requirements:* Additional exam requirements/recommendations for international students: Required—TOEFL, IELTS, PTE. *Application deadline:* For fall admission, 3/1 priority date for domestic and international students; for spring admission, 11/1 priority date for domestic and international students. Applications are processed on a rolling basis. Application fee: $55 ($65 for international students). Electronic applications accepted. *Expenses: Tuition:* Full-time $23,310; part-time $1295 per credit. Tuition and fees vary according to course load, degree level, campus/location and program. *Financial support:* In 2016–17, 13 students received support. Fellowships, research assistantships, and teaching assistantships available. Financial award application deadline: 3/2; financial award applicants required to submit FAFSA. *Unit head:* Dr. Kevin Oh, Chair, 415-422-2099. *Application contact:* Amy Fogliani, Admission Coordinator, 415-422-5467, E-mail: schoolofeducation@usfca.edu.

University of San Francisco, School of Education, Department of Teacher Education, San Francisco, CA 94117-1080. Offers digital media and learning (MA); teaching (MA); teaching reading (MA); teaching urban education and social justice (MA). *Program availability:* Part-time. *Faculty:* 6 full-time (2 women), 50 part-time/adjunct (33 women). *Students:* 212 full-time (154 women), 25 part-time (20 women); includes 106 minority (16 Black or African American, non-Hispanic/Latino; 30 Asian, non-Hispanic/Latino; 48 Hispanic/Latino; 2 Native Hawaiian or other Pacific Islander, non-Hispanic/Latino; 10 Two or more races, non-Hispanic/Latino), 1 international. Average age 29. 246 applicants, 95% accepted, 125 enrolled. In 2016, 127 master's awarded. *Entrance requirements:* Additional exam requirements/recommendations for international students: Required—TOEFL, IELTS, PTE. *Application deadline:* For fall admission, 3/1 priority date for domestic and international students; for spring admission, 10/15 priority date for domestic students, 10/1 for international students. Applications are processed on a rolling basis. Electronic applications accepted. *Expenses: Tuition:* Full-time $23,310; part-time $1295 per credit. Tuition and fees vary according to course load, degree level, campus/location and program. *Financial support:* In 2016–17, 25 students received support. Applicants required to submit FAFSA. *Unit head:* Dr. Noah Borrero, Chair, 415-422-6481. *Application contact:* Peter Cole, Admission Coordinator, 415-422-5467, E-mail: schoolofeducation@usfca.edu.
Website: https://www.usfca.edu/catalog/graduate/school-of-education/programs-teacher-education

The University of Scranton, Panuska College of Professional Studies, Department of Education, Program in Reading Education, Scranton, PA 18510. Offers MS. *Accreditation:* NCATE. *Program availability:* Part-time, evening/weekend. *Degree requirements:* For master's, comprehensive exam (for some programs), thesis (for some programs), capstone experience. *Entrance requirements:* For master's, minimum GPA of 3.0, three letters of reference. Additional exam requirements/recommendations for international students: Required—TOEFL (minimum score 500 paper-based; 80 iBT), IELTS (minimum score 6.5). Electronic applications accepted.

University of Sioux Falls, Fredrikson School of Education, Sioux Falls, SD 57105-1699. Offers educational administration (Ed S), including principal leadership, superintendent and district leadership; leadership in reading (M Ed); leadership in schools (M Ed); leadership in technology (M Ed); teaching (M Ed). Admission in summer only. *Accreditation:* NCATE. *Program availability:* Part-time, evening/weekend. *Degree requirements:* For master's, comprehensive exam (for some programs), research application project; for Ed S, comprehensive exam, portfolio. *Entrance requirements:* For master's, minimum GPA of 3.0, 1 year of teaching experience; for Ed S, minimum 3 years of teaching experience, minimum cumulative GPA of 3.5, 1 year of administrative experience. Additional exam requirements/recommendations for international students: Required—TOEFL. *Faculty research:* Reading, literacy, leadership.

University of South Alabama, College of Education and Professional Studies, Department of Leadership and Teacher Education, Mobile, AL 36688. Offers art education (M Ed); early childhood education (M Ed); educational leadership (M Ed, Ed D); elementary education (M Ed); reading education (M Ed); science education (M Ed); secondary education (M Ed); special education (M Ed). *Accreditation:* NCATE. *Program availability:* Part-time, 100% online, blended/hybrid learning. *Faculty:* 16 full-time (12 women), 6 part-time/adjunct (3 women). *Students:* 198 full-time (150 women), 77 part-time (58 women); includes 77 minority (61 Black or African American, non-Hispanic/Latino; 2 American Indian or Alaska Native, non-Hispanic/Latino; 2 Asian, non-Hispanic/Latino; 7 Hispanic/Latino; 1 Native Hawaiian or other Pacific Islander, non-Hispanic/Latino; 4 Two or more races, non-Hispanic/Latino). Average age 34. 153 applicants, 53% accepted, 69 enrolled. In 2016, 80 master's, 1 doctorate awarded. *Degree requirements:* For master's, comprehensive exam, thesis (for some programs); for doctorate, comprehensive exam, thesis/dissertation. *Entrance requirements:* For master's, GRE General Test or MAT, minimum GPA of 3.0; for doctorate, GRE, minimum graduate GPA of 3.25, 3 years of experience in field, 3 letters of recommendation, interview, official transcripts. Additional exam requirements/recommendations for international students: Required—TOEFL. *Application deadline:* For fall admission, 7/15 for domestic students; for spring admission, 11/15 for domestic students; for summer admission, 4/15 for domestic students. Applications are processed on a rolling basis. Application fee: $35. Electronic applications accepted. *Expenses:* Tuition, state resident: full-time $9768; part-time $407 per credit hour. Tuition, nonresident: full-time $19,536; part-time $814 per credit hour. *Financial support:* Fellowships, research assistantships, teaching assistantships, career-related internships or fieldwork, Federal Work-Study, institutionally sponsored loans, scholarships/grants, and unspecified assistantships available. Support available to part-time students. Financial award application deadline: 5/31; financial award applicants required to submit FAFSA. *Unit head:* Dr. Susan Santoli, Department Chair, 251-380-2836, Fax: 251-380-2758, E-mail: ssantoli@southalabama.edu. *Application contact:* Dr. Susan Santoli, Director of Graduate Studies, 251-380-2836, Fax: 251-380-2758, E-mail: ssantoli@southalabama.edu.
Website: http://www.southalabama.edu/colleges/coe/lte/index.html

University of South Carolina, The Graduate School, College of Education, Department of Instruction and Teacher Education, Program in Language and Literacy, Columbia, SC 29208. Offers M Ed, PhD. *Accreditation:* NCATE. *Degree requirements:* For master's, comprehensive exam; for doctorate, one foreign language, comprehensive exam, thesis/dissertation. *Entrance requirements:* For master's, GRE General Test, Miller Analogies Test, teaching certificate, resume, letters of reference, letter of intent; for doctorate, GRE General Test, Miller Analogies Test, resumé, letters of reference, letter of intent, interview. *Faculty research:* Remedial and compensatory education, metacognition and learning, literacy, learning, teacher change.

The University of South Dakota, Graduate School, School of Education, Division of Curriculum and Instruction, Program in Elementary Education, Vermillion, SD 57069. Offers elementary education (MA), including early childhood education, English language learning, reading specialist/literacy coach, science, technology or math (STM). *Accreditation:* NCATE. *Program availability:* Part-time, 100% online, blended/hybrid learning. *Degree requirements:* For master's, comprehensive exam, thesis or alternative. *Entrance requirements:* For master's, GRE General Test, MAT, minimum GPA of 2.7. Additional exam requirements/recommendations for international students: Required—TOEFL (minimum score 550 paper-based; 79 iBT). Electronic applications accepted.

University of Southern Maine, College of Management and Human Service, School of Education and Human Development, Program in Literacy Education, Portland, ME 04103. Offers applied literacy (MS Ed); English as a second language (MS Ed, CAS, CGS); literacy education (MS Ed, CAS, CGS). *Accreditation:* TEAC. *Program availability:* Part-time, evening/weekend. *Degree requirements:* For master's, comprehensive exam, thesis or alternative; for other advanced degree, thesis or alternative. *Entrance requirements:* For master's, teacher certification; for other advanced degree, master's degree. Additional exam requirements/recommendations for international students: Required—TOEFL (minimum score 550 paper-based; 79 iBT). Electronic applications accepted. *Faculty research:* Teacher research in literacy, multiliteracies, learning to teach culturally and linguistically diverse students, motivation to read.

University of South Florida, College of Education, Department of Teaching and Learning, Tampa, FL 33620-9951. Offers early childhood education (M Ed, MA, PhD);

elementary education (MA, MAT, PhD); reading/language arts (MA, PhD, Ed S). *Accreditation:* NCATE. *Faculty:* 40 full-time (29 women), 2 part-time/adjunct (both women). *Students:* 205 full-time (143 women), 263 part-time (207 women); includes 108 minority (45 Black or African American, non-Hispanic/Latino; 10 Asian, non-Hispanic/Latino; 48 Hispanic/Latino; 5 Two or more races, non-Hispanic/Latino), 62 international. Average age 34. 153 applicants, 78% accepted, 100 enrolled. In 2016, 142 master's, 22 doctorates, 1 other advanced degree awarded. Application fee: $30. *Expenses:* Tuition, state resident: full-time $7766; part-time $431.43 per credit hour. Tuition, nonresident: full-time $15,789; part-time $877.17 per credit hour. *Required fees:* $37 per term. *Total annual research expenditures:* $2.8 million. *Unit head:* Dr. Denisse Thompson, Chair, 813-974-4110.
Website: http://www.coedu.usf.edu/main/departments/ce/ce.html

University of South Florida, St. Petersburg, College of Education, St. Petersburg, FL 33701. Offers educational leadership development (M Ed); elementary education (MA), including math/science; English education (MA); middle grades STEM education (MS); reading education (MA). *Program availability:* Part-time. *Degree requirements:* For master's, comprehensive exam, practicum, internship, comprehensive portfolio. *Entrance requirements:* For master's, State of Florida General Knowledge Test (GKT), Florida Teaching Certificate (for non-initial certification programs), letters of recommendation. Additional exam requirements/recommendations for international students: Required—TOEFL (minimum score 550 paper-based; 79 iBT); Recommended—IELTS. Electronic applications accepted.

The University of Tennessee, Graduate School, College of Education, Health and Human Sciences, Program in Education, Knoxville, TN 37996. Offers art education (MS); counseling education (PhD); cultural studies in education (PhD); curriculum (MS, Ed S); curriculum, educational research and evaluation (Ed D, PhD); early childhood education (PhD); early childhood special education (MS); education of deaf and hard of hearing (MS); educational administration and policy studies (Ed D, PhD); educational administration and supervision (Ed S); educational psychology (Ed D, PhD); elementary education (MS, Ed S); elementary teaching (MS); English education (MS, Ed S); exercise science (PhD); foreign language/ESL education (MS, Ed S); instructional technology (MS, Ed D, PhD, Ed S); literacy, language and ESL education (PhD); literacy, language education, and ESL education (Ed D); mathematics education (MS, Ed S); modified and comprehensive special education (MS); reading education (MS, Ed S); school counseling (Ed S); school psychology (PhD, Ed S); science education (MS, Ed S); secondary teaching (MS); social foundations (MS); social science education (MS, Ed S); socio-cultural foundations of sports and education (PhD); special education (Ed S); teacher education (Ed D, PhD). *Accreditation:* NCATE. *Program availability:* Part-time, evening/weekend. *Degree requirements:* For master's and Ed S, thesis optional; for doctorate, variable foreign language requirement, thesis/dissertation. *Entrance requirements:* For master's, minimum GPA of 2.7; for doctorate and Ed S, GRE General Test, minimum GPA of 2.7. Additional exam requirements/recommendations for international students: Required—TOEFL. Electronic applications accepted.

The University of Texas at Arlington, Graduate School, College of Education, Department of Curriculum and Instruction, Arlington, TX 76019. Offers curriculum and instruction (M Ed), including literacy studies, mathematics education, mind, brain, and education, science education; teaching (with certification) (M Ed T). *Accreditation:* NCATE. *Program availability:* Part-time, evening/weekend, online learning. *Degree requirements:* For master's, comprehensive exam (for some programs), comprehensive activity, research project. *Entrance requirements:* For master's, GRE General Test, minimum undergraduate GPA of 3.0 in last 60 hours of course work, writing sample, 3 letters of recommendation. Additional exam requirements/recommendations for international students: Required—TOEFL (minimum score 550 paper-based). *Application deadline:* For fall admission, 6/1 priority date for domestic students, 4/1 priority date for international students; for spring admission, 10/15 priority date for domestic students, 9/15 priority date for international students. Applications are processed on a rolling basis. Application fee: $50. Electronic applications accepted. *Financial support:* Research assistantships, teaching assistantships, career-related internships or fieldwork, Federal Work-Study, scholarships/grants, and unspecified assistantships available. Financial award application deadline: 6/1; financial award applicants required to submit FAFSA. *Unit head:* Daniel H. Robinson, Chair, 817-272-0116, Fax: 817-272-2618, E-mail: daniel.robinson@uta.edu. *Application contact:* Caitlin Guerrero, Graduate Academic Advisor, 817-272-2956, Fax: 817-272-7624, E-mail: caitling@uta.edu.
Website: http://www.uta.edu/coed/curricandinstruct/index.php

The University of Texas at Austin, Graduate School, College of Education, Department of Curriculum and Instruction, Austin, TX 78712-1111. Offers bilingual/bicultural education (M Ed, MA, PhD); cultural studies in education (M Ed, MA, PhD); early childhood education (M Ed, MA, PhD); language and literacy studies (M Ed, PhD); learning technologies (M Ed, MA, PhD); physical education (M Ed, MA, PhD). Terminal master's awarded for partial completion of doctoral program. *Degree requirements:* For doctorate, thesis/dissertation. *Entrance requirements:* For master's and doctorate, GRE General Test. Electronic applications accepted.

The University of Texas at El Paso, Graduate School, College of Education, Department of Teacher Education, El Paso, TX 79968-0001. Offers education (MA); instruction (M Ed); reading education (M Ed); teaching, learning, and culture (PhD). *Program availability:* Part-time, evening/weekend. *Degree requirements:* For master's, thesis optional. *Entrance requirements:* For master's, GRE General Test, minimum GPA of 3.0. Additional exam requirements/recommendations for international students: Required—TOEFL. Electronic applications accepted.

The University of Texas at San Antonio, College of Education and Human Development, Department of Bicultural and Bilingual Studies, San Antonio, TX 78249-0617. Offers bicultural and bilingual studies (MA), including bicultural and bilingual education, bicultural studies; culture, literacy, and language (PhD); teaching English as a second language (MA). *Program availability:* Part-time, evening/weekend. *Faculty:* 19 full-time (13 women), 2 part-time/adjunct (1 woman). *Students:* 32 full-time (21 women), 109 part-time (86 women); includes 80 minority (3 Black or African American, non-Hispanic/Latino; 4 Asian, non-Hispanic/Latino; 72 Hispanic/Latino; 1 Two or more races, non-Hispanic/Latino), 11 international. Average age 37. 70 applicants, 77% accepted, 36 enrolled. In 2016, 28 master's, 10 doctorates awarded. *Degree requirements:* For master's, one foreign language, comprehensive exam, thesis optional; for doctorate, one foreign language, comprehensive exam, thesis/dissertation. *Entrance requirements:* For master's, bachelor's degree with 18 credit hours in field of study or in another appropriate field of study; for doctorate, GRE General Test, resume or curriculum vitae, 3 letters of recommendation, statement of purpose, master's degree. Additional exam requirements/recommendations for international students: Required—TOEFL (minimum score 550 paper-based; 79 iBT), IELTS (minimum score 6.5). *Application deadline:* For fall admission, 7/1 for domestic students, 4/1 for international students; for spring admission, 11/1 for domestic students, 9/1 for international students. Applications are processed on a rolling basis. Application fee: $45 ($80 for international students). Electronic applications accepted. *Expenses:* Contact institution. *Financial support:* In 2016–17, 18 students received support, including 18 fellowships (averaging $28,000 per year), 2 research assistantships (averaging $12,468 per year), 16 teaching assistantships (averaging $11,000 per year); scholarships/grants and unspecified assistantships also available. Financial award application deadline: 4/15. *Faculty research:* Bilingual and ESL teacher preparation; transnational communities; applied linguistics; cultural studies; bilingualism, biliteracy and second language acquisition. *Total annual research expenditures:* $300,234. *Unit head:* Dr. Belinda Flores, Chair, 210-458-5570, Fax: 210-458-5962, E-mail: belinda.flores@utsa.edu. *Application contact:* Rahnuma Islam, Student Development Specialist, 210-458-6619, Fax: 210-458-5576, E-mail: rahnuma.islam@utsa.edu.
Website: http://education.utsa.edu/bicultural-bilingual_studies

The University of Texas at San Antonio, College of Education and Human Development, Department of Interdisciplinary Learning and Teaching, San Antonio, TX 78249-0617. Offers education (MA), including curriculum and instruction, early childhood and elementary education, instructional technology, reading and literacy, special education; interdisciplinary learning and teaching (PhD). *Program availability:* Part-time, evening/weekend. *Faculty:* 25 full-time (18 women), 4 part-time/adjunct (2 women). *Students:* 70 full-time (53 women), 256 part-time (222 women); includes 185 minority (22 Black or African American, non-Hispanic/Latino; 10 Asian, non-Hispanic/Latino; 148 Hispanic/Latino; 1 Native Hawaiian or other Pacific Islander, non-Hispanic/Latino; 4 Two or more races, non-Hispanic/Latino), 4 international. Average age 34. 145 applicants, 88% accepted, 100 enrolled. In 2016, 90 master's, 4 doctorates awarded. *Degree requirements:* For master's, comprehensive exam, thesis optional, 36 hours of course work without thesis (33 with thesis); for doctorate, comprehensive exam, thesis/dissertation, minimum of 60 semester credit hours. *Entrance requirements:* For master's, bachelor's degree with minimum GPA of 3.0 in last 60 hours of coursework; 18 hours of undergraduate coursework in education or related field; for doctorate, GRE, transcripts from all colleges and universities attended, professional vitae demonstrating experience in work environment where education was primary professional emphasis, 3 letters of recommendation, statement of purpose, minimum GPA of 3.5. Additional exam requirements/recommendations for international students: Required—TOEFL (minimum score 550 paper-based; 79 iBT), IELTS (minimum score 6.5). *Application deadline:* For fall admission, 7/1 for domestic students, 4/1 for international students; for spring admission, 11/1 for domestic students, 9/1 for international students. Applications are processed on a rolling basis. Application fee: $45 ($80 for international students). Electronic applications accepted. *Financial support:* Career-related internships or fieldwork, Federal Work-Study, and scholarships/grants available. Support available to part-time students. *Faculty research:* Explorations of science, learning and teaching, family involvement in early childhood, culturally-responsive literacy instruction in diverse settings, STEM education, autism spectrum disorder. *Total annual research expenditures:* $766,662. *Unit head:* Dr. Maria R. Cortez, Department Chair, 210-458-4413, Fax: 210-458-7281, E-mail: mari.cortez@utsa.edu. *Application contact:* Elizabeth Narvaes, Student Development Specialist, 210-458-7443, Fax: 210-458-7281, E-mail: elizabeth.narvaez@utsa.edu.
Website: http://education.utsa.edu/interdisciplinary_learning_and_teaching/

The University of Texas at Tyler, College of Education and Psychology, School of Education, Tyler, TX 75799-0001. Offers early childhood education (M Ed, MA); reading (M Ed, MA); special education (M Ed, MA). *Program availability:* Part-time, evening/weekend. *Degree requirements:* For master's, comprehensive exam, thesis (for some programs), research project. *Entrance requirements:* For master's, GRE General Test. Additional exam requirements/recommendations for international students: Required—TOEFL. Electronic applications accepted. *Faculty research:* Improving quality in childcare settings, play and creativity, teacher interactions, effects of modeling on early childhood teachers, biofeedback, literacy instruction.

The University of Texas of the Permian Basin, Office of Graduate Studies, School of Education, Program in Reading, Odessa, TX 79762-0001. Offers MA. *Degree requirements:* For master's, comprehensive exam (for some programs), thesis (for some programs). *Entrance requirements:* For master's, GRE General Test. Additional exam requirements/recommendations for international students: Required—TOEFL (minimum score 550 paper-based).

The University of Texas Rio Grande Valley, College of Education and P-16 Integration, Department of Bilingual and Literacy Studies, Edinburg, TX 78539. Offers bilingual education (M Ed); reading and literacy (M Ed). Tuition and fees vary according to course load and program.

University of the Cumberlands, Graduate Programs in Education, Williamsburg, KY 40769-1372. Offers all grades (P-12) (M Ed); business and marketing (MA Ed, MAT); counselor education and supervision (Ed D); director of pupil personnel (Certificate); director of special education (Certificate); educational administration and supervision (Ed S); educational leadership (Ed D); elementary education (MA Ed, MAT); instructional leadership - principalship (MA Ed); instructional leadership - school principal (Certificate); middle school education (MA Ed, MAT); reading and writing (MA Ed); school counseling (MA Ed); school superintendent (Certificate); secondary education (MA Ed, MAT); special education (MAT); supervisor of instruction (Certificate); teacher leader (MA Ed). *Program availability:* Part-time, evening/weekend, online learning. *Degree requirements:* For master's, comprehensive exam. Electronic applications accepted.

University of Utah, Graduate School, College of Education, Department of Educational Psychology, Salt Lake City, UT 84112. Offers clinical mental health counseling (M Ed); counseling psychology (PhD); elementary education (M Ed); instructional design and educational technology (M Ed); instructional design and technology (MS); learning and cognition (MS, PhD); reading and literacy (M Ed, PhD); school counseling (M Ed); school psychology (M Ed, PhD, Ed S); statistics (M Stat). *Accreditation:* APA (one or more programs are accredited). *Faculty:* 23 full-time (12 women), 15 part-time/adjunct (10 women). *Students:* 119 full-time (95 women), 106 part-time (74 women); includes 37 minority (2 Black or African American, non-Hispanic/Latino; 6 Asian, non-Hispanic/Latino; 22 Hispanic/Latino; 7 Two or more races, non-Hispanic/Latino), 6 international. Average age 31. 296 applicants, 27% accepted, 73 enrolled. In 2016, 47 master's, 8 doctorates awarded. Terminal master's awarded for partial completion of doctoral program. *Degree requirements:* For master's, variable foreign language requirement, comprehensive exam (for some programs), thesis (for some programs), projects; for doctorate, variable foreign language requirement, comprehensive exam, thesis/dissertation, oral exam. *Entrance requirements:* For master's and doctorate, GRE General Test, minimum GPA of 3.0. Additional exam requirements/recommendations for international students: Required—TOEFL (minimum score 80 iBT). *Application deadline:* For fall admission, 12/15 for domestic and international students; for winter admission, 11/1 for domestic and international students; for spring admission, 3/15 for domestic and international students. Application fee: $55 ($65 for international students). Electronic applications accepted. *Expenses:* Contact institution. *Financial support:* In 2016–17, 84 students received support, including 12 fellowships with full and partial tuition reimbursements available (averaging $18,000 per year), 21 research assistantships with full and partial tuition reimbursements available (averaging $14,500 per year), 57 teaching assistantships with full and partial tuition reimbursements available (averaging $14,500 per year); career-related internships or fieldwork, Federal Work-Study, institutionally sponsored loans, scholarships/grants, traineeships, health care benefits,

and unspecified assistantships also available. Financial award application deadline: 4/1; financial award applicants required to submit FAFSA. *Faculty research:* Autism, computer technology and instruction, cognitive behavior, aging, group counseling. *Total annual research expenditures:* $620,935. *Unit head:* Dr. Anne E. Cook, Chair, 801-581-7148, Fax: 801-581-5566, E-mail: anne.cook@utah.edu. *Application contact:* JoLynn N. Yates, Academic Coordinator, 801-581-7148, Fax: 801-581-5566, E-mail: jo.yates@utah.edu.
Website: http://www.ed.utah.edu/edps/

University of Victoria, Faculty of Graduate Studies, Faculty of Education, Department of Curriculum and Instruction, Victoria, BC V8W 2Y2, Canada. Offers art education (M Ed, PhD); curriculum studies (M Ed, MA, PhD); early childhood education (M Ed, PhD); educational studies (PhD); language and literacy (M Ed, MA, PhD); mathematics (M Ed, MA, PhD); music education (M Ed, MA, PhD); science (M Ed, MA, PhD); social studies (M Ed, MA); social, cultural and foundational studies (MA, PhD); technology and environmental education (PhD). *Program availability:* Part-time. *Degree requirements:* For master's, thesis, project (M Ed); for doctorate, comprehensive exam, thesis/dissertation. *Entrance requirements:* For master's, minimum B average. Additional exam requirements/recommendations for international students: Required—TOEFL (minimum score 575 paper-based), IELTS (minimum score 7). Electronic applications accepted. *Faculty research:* Elementary and secondary English, language arts, curriculum theory and practice, educational media and technology, educational administration and leadership, history and philosophy of education.

University of Virginia, Curry School of Education, Program in Education, Charlottesville, VA 22903. Offers administration and supervision (PhD); applied developmental science (PhD); counselor education (PhD); curriculum and instruction (PhD); early childhood special education (MT); education evaluation (PhD); educational psychology (PhD); educational research (PhD); elementary education (MT); English education (MT, PhD); foreign language education (MT); higher education (PhD); instructional technology (PhD); kinesiology (MT, PhD); math education (PhD); reading education (PhD); research, statistics and evaluation (PhD); school psychology (PhD); science education (PhD); social studies education (MT, PhD); special education (PhD); world languages education (MT). *Students:* 452 full-time (357 women), 18 part-time (13 women); includes 100 minority (28 Black or African American, non-Hispanic/Latino; 39 Asian, non-Hispanic/Latino; 18 Hispanic/Latino; 15 Two or more races, non-Hispanic/Latino), 14 international. Average age 25. 309 applicants, 51% accepted, 87 enrolled. In 2016, 144 master's, 31 doctorates awarded. *Degree requirements:* For master's, comprehensive exam (for some programs), field project; for doctorate, comprehensive exam, thesis/dissertation. *Entrance requirements:* For doctorate, GRE General Test. Additional exam requirements/recommendations for international students: Required—TOEFL (minimum score 600 paper-based; 90 iBT), IELTS (minimum score 7). *Application deadline:* Applications are processed on a rolling basis. Application fee: $60. Electronic applications accepted. *Expenses:* Tuition, state resident: full-time $15,026; part-time $834 per credit hour. Tuition, nonresident: full-time $25,168; part-time $1378 per credit hour. *Required fees:* $2654. *Financial support:* Fellowships, research assistantships, and teaching assistantships available. Financial award application deadline: 1/5; financial award applicants required to submit FAFSA. *Unit head:* Robert C. Pianta, Dean, 434-924-3334, E-mail: pianta@virginia.edu. *Application contact:* Eric Molnar, Assistant Director, Admissions and Enrollment Reporting, 434-243-2085, E-mail: eric.molnar@virginia.edu.
Website: http://curry.virginia.edu/teacher-education

University of Washington, Graduate School, College of Education, Seattle, WA 98195. Offers curriculum and instruction (M Ed, Ed D, PhD), including educational technology, general curriculum (Ed D, PhD), language, literacy, and culture, mathematics education, multicultural education, reading and language arts education (Ed D), science education, social studies education, teaching and curriculum (M Ed); educational leadership and policy studies (M Ed, Ed D, PhD), including administration (Ed D), educational policy, organization, and leadership (M Ed, PhD), higher education, leadership for learning (Ed D), social and cultural foundations of education (M Ed, PhD); educational psychology (M Ed, PhD), including educational psychology (PhD), human development and cognition (M Ed), learning sciences, measurement, statistics and research design (M Ed), school psychology (M Ed); instructional leadership (M Ed); intercollegiate athletic leadership (M Ed); special education (M Ed, Ed D, PhD), including early childhood special education (M Ed), emotional and behavioral disabilities (M Ed), learning disabilities (M Ed), low-incidence disabilities (M Ed), severe disabilities (M Ed), special education (Ed D, PhD); teacher education (MIT). *Accreditation:* APA. *Program availability:* Part-time, evening/weekend. *Degree requirements:* For master's, thesis optional; for doctorate, thesis/dissertation. *Entrance requirements:* For master's and doctorate, GRE General Test, minimum GPA of 3.0. Additional exam requirements/recommendations for international students: Required—TOEFL. Electronic applications accepted. *Faculty research:* School restructuring/effective schools, special education interventions, literacy and writing, technology, school partnerships, teacher preparation.

University of West Florida, College of Education and Professional Studies, Department of Teacher Education and Educational Leadership, Program in Reading Education, Pensacola, FL 32514-5750. Offers M Ed. *Program availability:* Part-time, evening/weekend. *Degree requirements:* For master's, portfolio, teacher certification exams (general knowledge, professional, reading subject area). *Entrance requirements:* For master's, GRE (minimum score 450 verbal) or MAT (minimum score 396) if bachelor's GPA less than 3.0, state teaching certification; letter of intent; two professional references. Additional exam requirements/recommendations for international students: Required—TOEFL (minimum score 550 paper-based). *Application deadline:* For fall admission, 6/1 for domestic and international students; for spring admission, 10/1 for domestic and international students. Applications are processed on a rolling basis. Application fee: $30. *Expenses:* Tuition, state resident: full-time $5316.12. Tuition, nonresident: full-time $11,308. *Required fees:* $583.92. Tuition and fees vary according to course load and program. *Financial support:* Fellowships, teaching assistantships, career-related internships or fieldwork, Federal Work-Study, scholarships/grants, and unspecified assistantships available. Financial award application deadline: 4/15; financial award applicants required to submit FAFSA. *Unit head:* Dr. William H. Evans, Acting Director, 850-474-2892, Fax: 850-474-2844, E-mail: wevans@uwf.edu. *Application contact:* Terry McCray, Assistant Director of Graduate Admissions, 850-473-7718, Fax: 850-473-7714, E-mail: gradadmissions@uwf.edu.

University of West Georgia, College of Education, Carrollton, GA 30118. Offers business education (M Ed); early childhood education (M Ed, Ed S); educational leadership (M Ed, Ed S); media (M Ed, Ed S); professional counseling (M Ed, Ed S); professional counseling and supervision (Ed D); reading instruction (M Ed); school improvement (Ed D); secondary education (M Ed); special education (M Ed, Ed S), including teaching (M Ed); speech language pathology (M Ed); teaching (MAT). *Accreditation:* NCATE. *Program availability:* Part-time, evening/weekend, 100% online, blended/hybrid learning. *Faculty:* 46 full-time (31 women). *Students:* 321 full-time (266 women), 1,007 part-time (813 women); includes 456 minority (389 Black or African American, non-Hispanic/Latino; 1 American Indian or Alaska Native, non-Hispanic/Latino; 13 Asian, non-Hispanic/Latino; 43 Hispanic/Latino; 10 Two or more races, non-Hispanic/Latino), 12 international. Average age 33. 541 applicants, 79% accepted, 305 enrolled. In 2016, 286 master's, 20 doctorates, 156 other advanced degrees awarded. *Entrance requirements:* Additional exam requirements/recommendations for international students: Required—TOEFL (minimum score 523 paper-based; 69 iBT); Recommended—IELTS (minimum score 6.5). *Application deadline:* For fall admission, 7/21 for domestic students, 6/1 for international students; for spring admission, 11/30 for domestic students, 10/15 for international students; for summer admission, 4/15 for domestic students, 3/30 for international students. Applications are processed on a rolling basis. Application fee: $40. Electronic applications accepted. *Expenses:* Tuition, state resident: full-time $5316; part-time $222 per semester hour. Tuition, nonresident: full-time $20,658; part-time $861 per semester hour. *Required fees:* $1962. Tuition and fees vary according to course load, degree level and program. *Financial support:* Fellowships, research assistantships, teaching assistantships, career-related internships or fieldwork, Federal Work-Study, institutionally sponsored loans, scholarships/grants, and unspecified assistantships available. Support available to part-time students. Financial award application deadline: 4/1; financial award applicants required to submit FAFSA. *Unit head:* Dr. Diane Hoff, Dean, College of Education, 678-839-6570, Fax: 678-839-6098, E-mail: dhoff@westga.edu. *Application contact:* Dr. Toby Ziglar, Assistant Dean of the Graduate School, 678-839-1394, Fax: 678-839-1395, E-mail: graduate@westga.edu.
Website: http://www.westga.edu/education/

University of Wisconsin–Eau Claire, College of Education and Human Sciences, Program in Reading, Eau Claire, WI 54702-4004. Offers MST. *Program availability:* Part-time. *Degree requirements:* For master's, comprehensive exam, portfolio with an oral examination. *Entrance requirements:* For master's, certification to teach. Additional exam requirements/recommendations for international students: Required—TOEFL (minimum score 79 iBT).

University of Wisconsin–La Crosse, School of Education, La Crosse, WI 54601-3742. Offers English language arts elementary (Graduate Certificate); professional development (ME-PD); reading (MS Ed); special education (MS Ed). *Program availability:* Part-time, evening/weekend. *Faculty:* 5 full-time (3 women), 25 part-time/adjunct (17 women). *Students:* 85 part-time (74 women); includes 2 minority (1 Asian, non-Hispanic/Latino; 1 Hispanic/Latino). Average age 27. 32 applicants, 100% accepted, 23 enrolled. In 2016, 25 master's, 5 other advanced degrees awarded. *Entrance requirements:* For master's, GRE. Additional exam requirements/recommendations for international students: Required—TOEFL (minimum score 550 paper-based; 79 iBT). *Application deadline:* Applications are processed on a rolling basis. Electronic applications accepted. *Financial support:* Research assistantships, Federal Work-Study, scholarships/grants, health care benefits, and tuition waivers (partial) available. Support available to part-time students. Financial award application deadline: 3/15; financial award applicants required to submit FAFSA. *Unit head:* Marcie Wycoff-Horn, Dean, School of Education, 608-785-6786, E-mail: mwycoff-horn@uwlax.edu. *Application contact:* Brandon Schaller, Senior Graduate Student Status Examiner, 608-785-8941, E-mail: admissions@uwlax.edu.
Website: https://www.uwlax.edu/soe/

University of Wisconsin–Milwaukee, Graduate School, School of Education, Department of Curriculum and Instruction, Milwaukee, WI 53201-0413. Offers curriculum and instruction (MS), including cross-curricular focus, early childhood education, English education, mathematics education, middle childhood/early adolescence education, reading education, science education, urban social studies education. *Program availability:* Part-time. *Students:* 21 full-time (13 women), 44 part-time (42 women); includes 10 minority (1 Black or African American, non-Hispanic/Latino; 1 Asian, non-Hispanic/Latino; 2 Hispanic/Latino; 6 Two or more races, non-Hispanic/Latino), 2 international. Average age 33. 42 applicants, 71% accepted, 20 enrolled. In 2016, 45 master's awarded. *Degree requirements:* For master's, thesis or alternative. *Entrance requirements:* Additional exam requirements/recommendations for international students: Required—TOEFL (minimum score 550 paper-based; 79 iBT), IELTS (minimum score 6.5). *Application deadline:* For fall admission, 1/1 priority date for domestic students; for spring admission, 9/1 for domestic students. Applications are processed on a rolling basis. Application fee: $56 ($96 for international students). Electronic applications accepted. *Financial support:* In 2016–17, 1 fellowship was awarded; research assistantships, teaching assistantships, career-related internships or fieldwork, health care benefits, unspecified assistantships, and project assistantships also available. Support available to part-time students. Financial award application deadline: 4/15; financial award applicants required to submit FAFSA. *Application contact:* General Information Contact, 414-229-4721, E-mail: soeinfo@uwm.edu.
Website: http://uwm.edu/education/academics/curriculum-instruction-department/

University of Wisconsin–Oshkosh, Graduate Studies, College of Education and Human Services, Department of Reading Education, Oshkosh, WI 54901. Offers MSE. Program offered jointly with University of Wisconsin–Green Bay. *Program availability:* Part-time. *Degree requirements:* For master's, thesis or alternative, reflective journey course. *Entrance requirements:* For master's, interview, teaching certificate, undergraduate degree in teacher education, letters of recommendation. Additional exam requirements/recommendations for international students: Required—TOEFL (minimum score 550 paper-based; 79 iBT). Electronic applications accepted. *Faculty research:* Writing and reading, assessment, learner-centered instruction, multicultural literature, family literacy.

University of Wisconsin–River Falls, Outreach and Graduate Studies, College of Education and Professional Studies, Department of Teacher Education, River Falls, WI 54022. Offers elementary education (MSE); professional development shared inquiry communities (MSE); reading (MSE). *Program availability:* Part-time. *Degree requirements:* For master's, comprehensive exam, thesis or alternative. *Entrance requirements:* For master's, minimum GPA of 2.75. Additional exam requirements/recommendations for international students: Required—TOEFL (minimum score 500 paper-based; 65 iBT), IELTS (minimum score 5.5). Electronic applications accepted.

University of Wisconsin–Stevens Point, College of Professional Studies, School of Education, Program in Education—General/Reading, Stevens Point, WI 54481-3897. Offers MSE. *Program availability:* Part-time. *Degree requirements:* For master's, comprehensive exam, thesis or alternative. *Entrance requirements:* For master's, minimum undergraduate GPA of 3.0, teacher certification, 2 years teaching experience, letters of recommendation. Additional exam requirements/recommendations for international students: Required—TOEFL (minimum score 523 paper-based). *Faculty research:* Reading strategies in the content areas, gifted education, curriculum and instruction, standards-based education.

University of Wisconsin–Superior, Graduate Division, Department of Teacher Education, Program in Teaching Reading, Superior, WI 54880-4500. Offers MSE. *Program availability:* Part-time, evening/weekend. *Degree requirements:* For master's, comprehensive exam, thesis or alternative, research project. *Entrance requirements:* For master's, minimum GPA of 2.75, teaching certificate. Electronic applications accepted.

Reading Education

Upper Iowa University, Master of Education Program, Fayette, IA 52142-1857. Offers early childhood (M Ed); English as a second language (M Ed); higher education (M Ed); instructional strategist (M Ed); reading (M Ed); teacher leadership (M Ed).

Utah Valley University, Program in Education, Orem, UT 84058-5999. Offers educational technology (M Ed); elementary mathematics (M Ed); elementary STEM (M Ed); English as a second language (M Ed); reading (M Ed); teachers as leaders (M Ed). *Accreditation:* TEAC. *Program availability:* Part-time. *Degree requirements:* For master's, project. *Entrance requirements:* For master's, GRE, 3 letters of recommendation, interview, essay. Additional exam requirements/recommendations for international students: Required—TOEFL (minimum score 83 iBT). Electronic applications accepted. *Expenses:* Contact institution.

Vanderbilt University, Peabody College, Department of Teaching and Learning, Nashville, TN 37240-1001. Offers elementary education (M Ed); English language learners (M Ed); learning and design (M Ed); learning, diversity, and urban studies (M Ed); reading education (M Ed); secondary education (M Ed). *Accreditation:* NCATE. *Program availability:* Part-time. *Faculty:* 44 full-time (34 women), 26 part-time/adjunct (21 women). *Students:* 120 full-time (106 women), 26 part-time (18 women); includes 22 minority (9 Black or African American, non-Hispanic/Latino; 6 Asian, non-Hispanic/Latino; 6 Hispanic/Latino; 1 Two or more races, non-Hispanic/Latino), 44 international. Average age 24. 328 applicants, 73% accepted, 76 enrolled. In 2016, 110 master's awarded. *Degree requirements:* For master's, comprehensive exam, thesis optional. *Entrance requirements:* For master's, GRE General Test, MAT. Additional exam requirements/recommendations for international students: Required—TOEFL (minimum score 550 paper-based; 80 iBT). *Application deadline:* For fall admission, 12/31 priority date for domestic and international students; for spring admission, 11/1 priority date for domestic and international students. Applications are processed on a rolling basis. Application fee: $0. Electronic applications accepted. *Expenses: Tuition:* Part-time $1854 per credit hour. *Financial support:* Fellowships with partial tuition reimbursements, research assistantships with partial tuition reimbursements, teaching assistantships with partial tuition reimbursements, Federal Work-Study, institutionally sponsored loans, scholarships/grants, tuition waivers (partial), and unspecified assistantships available. Support available to part-time students. Financial award application deadline: 1/15; financial award applicants required to submit FAFSA. *Faculty research:* Children's learning and development in core conceptual domains (STEM, English language arts, social studies); classroom discourse structures that teachers can learn and use to support students' learning and development K-6; intervention and design-based research on educational improvement at classroom, school, and district levels; design-based and learning sciences research on relations between learning in schools and other settings. *Unit head:* Dr. Rogers Hall, Chair, 615-322-8100, Fax: 615-322-8999, E-mail: rogers.hall@vanderbilt.edu. *Application contact:* Angela Saylor, Educational Coordinator, 615-322-8092, Fax: 615-322-8999, E-mail: angela.saylor@vanderbilt.edu.

Virginia Commonwealth University, Graduate School, School of Education, Program in Adult Learning, Richmond, VA 23284-9005. Offers adult literacy (M Ed); human resource development (M Ed); teaching and learning with technology (M Ed). *Accreditation:* NCATE. *Program availability:* Part-time. *Entrance requirements:* For master's, GRE General Test or MAT. Additional exam requirements/recommendations for international students: Required—TOEFL (minimum score 600 paper-based; 100 iBT). *Application deadline:* For fall admission, 3/15 for domestic students; for spring admission, 11/1 for domestic students. Applications are processed on a rolling basis. Application fee: $50. Electronic applications accepted. *Financial support:* Career-related internships or fieldwork and Federal Work-Study available. Financial award application deadline: 3/1; financial award applicants required to submit FAFSA. *Faculty research:* Adult development and learning, program planning and evaluation. *Unit head:* Dr. Leila Christenbury, Interim Department Chair, 804-828-1306, Fax: 804-827-0676, E-mail: lchriste@vcu.edu. *Application contact:* Dr. Robin R. Hurst, Graduate Program Director, 804-828-8021, E-mail: rrhurst@vcu.edu.
Website: http://www.soe.vcu.edu/programs.html#graduate

Virginia Commonwealth University, Graduate School, School of Education, Program in Reading, Richmond, VA 23284-9005. Offers reading (M Ed); reading specialist (Certificate). *Accreditation:* NCATE. *Degree requirements:* For master's, comprehensive exam. *Entrance requirements:* For master's, GRE General Test or MAT. Additional exam requirements/recommendations for international students: Required—TOEFL (minimum score 600 paper-based; 100 iBT). *Application deadline:* For fall admission, 3/15 for domestic students; for spring admission, 11/1 for domestic students. Applications are processed on a rolling basis. Application fee: $50. Electronic applications accepted. *Financial support:* Federal Work-Study, institutionally sponsored loans, and tuition waivers (partial) available. Financial award application deadline: 3/1; financial award applicants required to submit FAFSA. *Unit head:* Dr. Michael D. Davis, Chair, Department of Teaching and Learning, 804-828-1305, E-mail: mddavis@vcu.edu. *Application contact:* Dr. Valarie J. Robnolt, Graduate Program Director, 804-828-1305, E-mail: vjrobnolt@vcu.edu.
Website: http://www.vcu.edu/ebuweb/

Viterbo University, Graduate Programs in Education, La Crosse, WI 54601-4797. Offers cross-categorical special education (Certificate); director of instruction (Certificate); director of special education and pupil services (Certificate); early childhood (Certificate); education (MAE); literacy coaching (Certificate); PreK-12 principal/supervisor of special education (Certificate); principal (Certificate); reading specialist endorsement (Certificate); reading teacher (Certificate); reading teacher 5-12 endorsement (Certificate); reading teacher K-8 endorsement (Certificate); superintendent (Certificate); talented and gifted endorsement (Certificate); Wisconsin school business administrator (Certificate). Weekend courses available in summer. *Accreditation:* NCATE. *Program availability:* Part-time, evening/weekend. *Degree requirements:* For master's, comprehensive exam, thesis, 30 credits of course work. *Entrance requirements:* For master's, BS, transcripts, teaching license, written narrative. Electronic applications accepted. *Expenses:* Contact institution.

Wagner College, Division of Graduate Studies, Education Department, Program in Literacy (B-6), Staten Island, NY 10301-4495. Offers MS Ed. *Program availability:* Part-time, evening/weekend. *Degree requirements:* For master's, thesis. *Entrance requirements:* For master's, minimum GPA of 3.0, valid initial NY State Certificate or equivalent, interview, recommendations. Electronic applications accepted. Tuition and fees vary according to degree level.

Walden University, Graduate Programs, Richard W. Riley College of Education and Leadership, Minneapolis, MN 55401. Offers adult education (Post-Master's Certificate); adult learning (Graduate Certificate); college teaching and learning (Graduate Certificate); community college leadership (Ed D); curriculum, instruction and assessment (Ed D, Ed S, Graduate Certificate); developmental education (Graduate Certificate); early childhood administration, management, and leadership (Graduate Certificate); early childhood education (Ed D, Ed S); early childhood public policy and advocacy (Graduate Certificate); early childhood studies (MS), including administration, management and leadership, early childhood public policy and advocacy, teaching adults in the early childhood field, teaching and diversity in early childhood education; education (MS, PhD), including adolescent literacy and learning (MS), curriculum, instruction, and assessment (grades K-12) (MS), curriculum, instruction, assessment, and evaluation (PhD), early childhood leadership and advocacy (PhD), early childhood special education (PhD), educational leadership (MS), educational leadership and administration (principal preparation) (MS), educational technology and design (PhD), elementary reading and literacy (PreK-6) (MS), elementary reading and mathematics (grades K-6) (MS), global and comparative education (PhD), higher education leadership management and policy (PhD), integrating technology in the classroom (grades K-12) (MS), learning, instruction and innovation (PhD), mathematics (grades 5-8) (MS), mathematics (grades K-6) (MS), mathematics and science (grades K-8) (MS), organizational research, assessment, and evaluation (PhD), reading and literacy with a reading K-12 endorsement (MS), reading literacy assessment and evaluation (PhD), science (grades K-8) (MS), special education (non-licensure) (grades K-12) (MS), teacher leadership (grades K-12) (MS), teaching English language learners (grades K-12) (MS); educational administration and leadership (Ed D); educational leadership and administration (principal preparation) (Ed S); educational technology (Ed D, Ed S, Post Master's Certificate); elementary reading and literacy (Graduate Certificate); engaging culturally diverse learners (Graduate Certificate); enrollment management and institutional marketing (Graduate Certificate); higher education (MS), including adult learning, college teaching and learning, enrollment management and institutional marketing, global higher education, leadership for student success, online and distance learning; higher education and adult learning (Ed D); higher education leadership and management (Ed D); higher education leadership for student success (Graduate Certificate); instructional design and technology (MS, Postbaccalaureate Certificate), including general program (MS), online learning (MS), training and performance improvement (MS); integrating technology in the classroom (Graduate Certificate); mathematics 5-8 (Graduate Certificate); mathematics K-6 (Graduate Certificate); online teaching for adult educators (Graduate Certificate); reading, literacy, and assessment (Ed D, Ed S); science K-8 (Graduate Certificate); special education (Ed D, Ed S, Graduate Certificate); special education (K-age 21) (MAT); teacher leadership (Graduate Certificate); teaching adults English as a second language (Graduate Certificate); teaching adults in the early childhood field (Graduate Certificate); teaching and diversity in early childhood education (Graduate Certificate); teaching English language learners (grades K-12) (Graduate Certificate); teaching K-12 students online (Graduate Certificate). *Accreditation:* NCATE. *Program availability:* Part-time, evening/weekend, online only, 100% online. *Degree requirements:* For doctorate, thesis/dissertation (for some programs), residency; for other advanced degree, residency (for some programs). *Entrance requirements:* For master's, bachelor's degree or higher; minimum GPA of 2.5; official transcripts; goal statement (for some programs); access to computer and Internet; for doctorate, master's degree or higher; three years of related professional or academic experience (preferred); minimum GPA of 3.0; goal statement and current resume (for select programs); official transcripts; access to computer and Internet; for other advanced degree, relevant work experience; access to computer and Internet. Additional exam requirements/recommendations for international students: Required—TOEFL (minimum score 550 paper-based, 79 iBT), IELTS (minimum score 6.5), Michigan English Language Assessment Battery (minimum score 82), or PTE (minimum score 53). Electronic applications accepted.

Walla Walla University, Graduate Studies, School of Education and Psychology, College Place, WA 99324. Offers curriculum and instruction (M Ed, MA, MAT); educational leadership (M Ed, MA, MAT); literacy instruction (M Ed, MA, MAT); students at risk (M Ed, MA, MAT); teaching (MAT). *Program availability:* Part-time. *Entrance requirements:* For master's, GRE General Test, minimum GPA of 2.75. Additional exam requirements/recommendations for international students: Required—TOEFL (minimum score 550 paper-based; 79 iBT). *Application deadline:* For fall admission, 4/1 priority date for domestic students. Applications are processed on a rolling basis. Application fee: $50. Electronic applications accepted. *Expenses: Tuition:* Part-time $592 per quarter hour. *Financial support:* Research assistantships, teaching assistantships, Federal Work-Study, and tuition waivers (partial) available. Support available to part-time students. Financial award application deadline: 4/30; financial award applicants required to submit FAFSA. *Faculty research:* Admissions/retention, instructional psychology, moral development, teaching of reading. *Unit head:* Denise Dunzweiler, Dean, 509-527-2212, Fax: 509-527-2248, E-mail: denise.dunzweiler@wallawalla.edu. *Application contact:* Dr. Joe G. Galusha, Dean of Graduate Studies, 509-527-2421, Fax: 509-527-2237, E-mail: joe.galusha@wallawalla.edu.
Website: https://wallawalla.edu/academics/areas-of-study/undergraduate-programs/education-and-psychology/

Walsh University, Graduate Programs, Program in Education, North Canton, OH 44720-3396. Offers leadership with principal license (MA Ed); reading literacy (MA Ed). *Accreditation:* NCATE. *Program availability:* Part-time, evening/weekend. *Faculty:* 5 full-time (3 women), 5 part-time/adjunct (4 women). *Students:* 27 full-time (15 women), 53 part-time (45 women); includes 2 minority (both Black or African American, non-Hispanic/Latino), 1 international. Average age 34. 27 applicants, 70% accepted, 19 enrolled. In 2016, 26 master's awarded. *Degree requirements:* For master's, comprehensive exam (for some programs), thesis optional, action research project or comprehensive exam. *Entrance requirements:* For master's, MAT (minimum score 396), GRE (minimum scores: verbal 145, quantitative 146, combined 291, writing 3.0), or minimum GPA of 3.0 on the baccalaureate transcript, interview, minimum GPA of 3.0, writing sample, 3 recommendation forms, notarized affidavit of good moral character. Additional exam requirements/recommendations for international students: Required—TOEFL (minimum score 500 paper-based; 61 iBT). *Application deadline:* For fall admission, 7/15 priority date for domestic students. Applications are processed on a rolling basis. Application fee: $25. Electronic applications accepted. Application fee is waived when completed online. *Expenses:* $664 per credit hour. *Financial support:* In 2016–17, 5 students received support, including 5 research assistantships (averaging $10,917 per year). Financial award application deadline: 12/31; financial award applicants required to submit FAFSA. *Faculty research:* Learning and the brain, primary STEM, effective assessment practices, literacy. *Unit head:* Dr. Alan Digianantonio, Director, 330-490-7336, Fax: 330-244-4777, E-mail: adigianantonio@walsh.edu. *Application contact:* Audra Dice, Graduate and Transfer Admissions Counselor, 330-490-7181, Fax: 330-244-4680, E-mail: adice@walsh.edu.

Washburn University, College of Arts and Sciences, Department of Education, Topeka, KS 66621. Offers curriculum and instruction (M Ed); educational leadership (M Ed); reading (M Ed); special education (M Ed). *Accreditation:* NCATE. *Program availability:* Part-time. *Degree requirements:* For master's, comprehensive exam, thesis or alternative, portfolio, comprehensive paper, or action research project. *Entrance requirements:* For master's, department exam, GRE General Test, or MAT, minimum GPA of 3.0 in graduate coursework or last 60 hours of undergraduate coursework. Additional exam requirements/recommendations for international students: Required—TOEFL (minimum score 80 iBT). *Faculty research:* Reading/literature/literacy, foundations, special education, diversity, teaching and technology.

Washington State University, College of Education, Department of Teaching and Learning, Pullman, WA 99164-2132. Offers cultural studies and social thought in education (PhD); curriculum and instruction (Ed M, MA); English language learners (Ed M, MA); language, literacy and technology (PhD); literacy education (Ed M, MA); mathematics education (PhD); special education (Ed M, MA, PhD); teacher leadership

(Ed D); teaching (MIT), including elementary education, secondary education. Programs offered at the Pullman, Spokane, Tri-cities, Vancouver and Global (online) campuses. *Program availability:* Part-time, online learning. *Degree requirements:* For master's, comprehensive exam, thesis, oral or written exam; for doctorate, comprehensive exam, thesis/dissertation, oral and written exam. *Entrance requirements:* For master's, GRE General Test, minimum GPA of 3.0, 3 letters of recommendation, letter of intent, transcripts, resume/curriculum vitae; for doctorate, GRE General Test, minimum GPA of 3.0, 3 letters of recommendation, letter of intent, transcripts, writing sample, resume/curriculum vitae. Additional exam requirements/recommendations for international students: Required—TOEFL (minimum score 550 paper-based; 80 iBT). Electronic applications accepted. *Faculty research:* Intersection of gender, youth cultures and schooling; examination of ideology of power in children's literature; early childhood special education; analyzing pre-service and in-service teacher development; second language acquisition.

Wayne State University, College of Education, Division of Teacher Education, Detroit, MI 48202. Offers art education (M Ed); bilingual/bicultural education (M Ed, Certificate); career and technical education (M Ed); curriculum and instruction (Ed D, PhD, Ed S), including art education (Ed D, PhD), bilingual education (Ed D, Ed S), career and technical education (MAT, Ed D, PhD, Ed S), early childhood education (MAT, Ed D, PhD, Ed S), elementary education, English as a second language (MAT, Ed D, Ed S), English education (MAT, Ed D, PhD, Ed S), foreign language education (MAT, Ed D, PhD), K-12 curriculum, mathematics education (MAT, Ed D, PhD, Ed S), science education (MAT, Ed D, PhD, Ed S), secondary education, social studies education (MAT, Ed D, PhD, Ed S); early childhood education (M Ed); elementary education (M Ed, MAT), including bilingual/bicultural education (MAT), early childhood education (MAT, Ed D, PhD, Ed S), English as a second language (MAT, Ed D, Ed S), general elementary education (MAT), mathematics education (MAT, Ed D, PhD, Ed S), science education (MAT, Ed D, PhD, Ed S), social studies education (MAT, Ed D, PhD, Ed S); English as a second language (Certificate); English education (M Ed); foreign language education (M Ed); mathematics education (M Ed); reading (M Ed, Ed S); reading, language and literature (Ed D); science education (M Ed); secondary education (MAT), including art education (K-12), bilingual/bicultural education, career and technical education (MAT, Ed D, PhD, Ed S), English as a second language (MAT, Ed D, Ed S), English education (MAT, Ed D, PhD, Ed S), foreign language education (MAT, Ed D, PhD), kinesiology, mathematics education (MAT, Ed D, PhD, Ed S); social studies education (M Ed); special education (M Ed, MAT, Ed D, PhD, Ed S), including autism spectrum disorders (MAT), cognitive development (MAT), emotional impairment (MAT), learning disabilities (MAT). *Program availability:* Part-time, blended/hybrid learning. *Faculty:* 29. *Students:* 106 full-time (73 women), 351 part-time (276 women); includes 115 minority (76 Black or African American, non-Hispanic/Latino; 10 Asian, non-Hispanic/Latino; 20 Hispanic/Latino; 1 Native Hawaiian or other Pacific Islander, non-Hispanic/Latino; 8 Two or more races, non-Hispanic/Latino), 12 international. Average age 37. 242 applicants, 37% accepted, 72 enrolled. In 2016, 178 master's, 19 doctorates, 17 other advanced degrees awarded. *Degree requirements:* For master's, essay or project (for some M Ed programs), professional field experience (for MAT programs); for doctorate, thesis/dissertation. *Entrance requirements:* For master's, Michigan Test for Teacher Certification, verification of participation in group work with children, Michigan State Police criminal background check; for doctorate, minimum undergraduate GPA of 3.0, graduate 3.5; interview; curriculum vitae; references. Additional exam requirements/recommendations for international students: Required—TOEFL (minimum score 550 paper-based; 79 iBT), TWE (minimum score 5.5), Michigan English Language Assessment Battery (minimum score 85); Recommended—IELTS (minimum score 6.5). *Application deadline:* For fall admission, 6/1 priority date for domestic students, 5/1 priority date for international students; for winter admission, 10/1 priority date for domestic students, 9/1 priority date for international students; for spring admission, 2/1 priority date for domestic students, 1/1 priority date for international students. Applications are processed on a rolling basis. Application fee: $50. Electronic applications accepted. *Expenses:* $16,503 per year resident tuition and fees, $33,697 per year non-resident tuition and fees. *Financial support:* In 2016–17, 101 students received support, including 3 fellowships (averaging $11,409 per year); research assistantships with tuition reimbursements available, Federal Work-Study, scholarships/grants, and unspecified assistantships also available. Support available to part-time students. Financial award applicants required to submit FAFSA. *Faculty research:* Improving students' skill achievement in mathematics, improving elementary children's understanding of informational text, teachers' use of their pedagogical and mathematical knowledge in the interactive work of teaching, the intersection of identity construction in teaching and learning, identifying effective methods of literacy instruction and assessments for bilingual students in elementary language arts classrooms. *Unit head:* Dr. Kathleen Crawford-McKinney, Assistant Dean, 313-577-0122. *Application contact:* Janice Green, Assistant Dean, 313-577-1605, E-mail: jwgreen@wayne.edu.
Website: http://coe.wayne.edu/ted/index.php

Webster University, School of Education, Department of Communication Arts, Reading and Early Childhood, St. Louis, MO 63119-3194. Offers communication arts (MAT); reading (MA). *Entrance requirements:* For master's, minimum GPA of 2.5. Additional exam requirements/recommendations for international students: Required—TOEFL. *Application deadline:* Applications are processed on a rolling basis. Application fee: $35 ($50 for international students). *Expenses: Tuition:* Full-time $21,900; part-time $730 per credit hour. Tuition and fees vary according to campus/location and program. *Financial support:* Federal Work-Study available. Support available to part-time students. Financial award application deadline: 4/1; financial award applicants required to submit FAFSA. *Unit head:* Dr. Thomas Cornell, Chairperson, 314-246-7087, E-mail: thomascornell28@webster.edu. *Application contact:* Lisa Davis, Department Representative, 314-246-7090, E-mail: lisadavis98@webster.edu.

Webster University, School of Education, Department of Multidisciplinary Studies, St. Louis, MO 63119-3194. Offers applied educational psychology (MA, Ed S); communication arts (MA); early childhood education (MA, MAT); education and innovation (MA); educational technology (MET); elementary education (MAT); mathematics for educators (MA); middle school education (MAT); multidisciplinary studies (MAT); multimodal literacy for global impact (MA); reading (MA); secondary school education (MAT); special education (MA, MAT); teaching English as a second language (MA); transformative learning in the global community (Ed S). *Program availability:* Part-time. *Entrance requirements:* For master's, minimum GPA of 2.5. Additional exam requirements/recommendations for international students: Required—TOEFL. *Application deadline:* Applications are processed on a rolling basis. Application fee: $35 ($50 for international students). *Expenses: Tuition:* Full-time $21,900; part-time $730 per credit hour. Tuition and fees vary according to campus/location and program. *Financial support:* Federal Work-Study available. Support available to part-time students. Financial award application deadline: 4/1; financial award applicants required to submit FAFSA. *Unit head:* Dr. Deborah Stiles, Chair, 314-968-7056, Fax: 314-968-7118, E-mail: stilesda@webster.edu.

West Chester University of Pennsylvania, College of Education and Social Work, Department of Literacy, West Chester, PA 19383. Offers literacy (Certificate); literacy coaching (Certificate); reading (M Ed, Teaching Certificate). *Program availability:* Part-time, evening/weekend. *Faculty:* 9 full-time (8 women), 3 part-time/adjunct (2 women). *Students:* 4 full-time (all women), 127 part-time (122 women); includes 5 minority (2 Black or African American, non-Hispanic/Latino; 3 Hispanic/Latino). Average age 30. 35 applicants, 71% accepted, 1 enrolled. In 2016, 28 master's awarded. *Degree requirements:* For master's, minimum GPA of 3.0, portfolio assessment; for other advanced degree, portfolio assessment. *Entrance requirements:* For master's, GRE or MAT if GPA is below 3.0, minimum GPA of 3.0, teaching certificate, two letters of reference. Additional exam requirements/recommendations for international students: Required—TOEFL or IELTS. *Application deadline:* For fall admission, 5/15 for international students; for spring admission, 10/15 for international students. Applications are processed on a rolling basis. Application fee: $50. Electronic applications accepted. *Expenses:* Tuition, state resident: full-time $8694; part-time $483 per credit. Tuition, nonresident: full-time $13,050; part-time $725 per credit. *Required fees:* $2399; $119.05 per credit. Tuition and fees vary according to campus/location and program. *Financial support:* Scholarships/grants and unspecified assistantships available. Financial award application deadline: 2/15; financial award applicants required to submit FAFSA. *Faculty research:* Teaching and mentoring pre-service and in-service teachers to teach literacy in urban settings, literacy and technology, children's and young adult literature, literacy and diversity, developmental word knowledge. *Unit head:* Dr. Carol Smith, Chair, 610-436-5642, Fax: 610-436-3102, E-mail: csmith@wcupa.edu. *Application contact:* Dr. Kevin Flanigan, Graduate Coordinator, 610-430-5642, Fax: 610-436-3102, E-mail: kflanigan@wcupa.edu.
Website: http://www.wcupa.edu/education-socialWork/literacy/

Western Connecticut State University, Division of Graduate Studies, School of Professional Studies, Department of Education and Educational Psychology, Reading Option, Danbury, CT 06810-6885. Offers MS. *Program availability:* Part-time. *Degree requirements:* For master's, thesis or research project, completion of program in 6 years. *Entrance requirements:* For master's, minimum GPA of 2.8, teaching certificate in elementary education. Additional exam requirements/recommendations for international students: Recommended—TOEFL (minimum score 550 paper-based; 79 iBT), IELTS (minimum score 6). *Faculty research:* Training guides for educators.

Western Illinois University, School of Graduate Studies, College of Education and Human Services, Department of Curriculum and Instruction, Program in Reading, Macomb, IL 61455-1390. Offers MS Ed. *Accreditation:* NCATE. *Program availability:* Part-time. *Students:* 1 (woman) full-time, 38 part-time (35 women). Average age 33. 7 applicants, 100% accepted, 5 enrolled. In 2016, 19 master's awarded. *Degree requirements:* For master's, thesis or alternative. *Entrance requirements:* For master's, teacher certification. Additional exam requirements/recommendations for international students: Required—TOEFL (minimum score 550 paper-based; 80 iBT). *Application deadline:* Applications are processed on a rolling basis. Application fee: $30. Electronic applications accepted. *Financial support:* In 2016–17, 1 student received support. Applicants required to submit FAFSA. *Unit head:* Dr. Barry Witten, Interim Chairperson, 309-298-1961. *Application contact:* Dr. Nancy Parsons, Assistant Director of Graduate Studies, 309-298-1806, Fax: 309-298-2345, E-mail: grad-office@wiu.edu.
Website: http://wiu.edu/curriculum

Western Kentucky University, Graduate Studies, College of Education and Behavioral Sciences, School of Teacher Education, Bowling Green, KY 42101. Offers elementary education (MAE, Ed S); exceptional education: learning and behavioral disorders (MAE); exceptional education: moderate and severe disabilities (MAE); instructional design (MS); interdisciplinary early childhood education (MAE); library media education (MS); literacy education (MAE); middle grades education (MAE); secondary education (MAE, Ed S). *Program availability:* Part-time, evening/weekend, online learning. *Degree requirements:* For master's, comprehensive exam. *Entrance requirements:* For master's, GRE General Test. Additional exam requirements/recommendations for international students: Required—TOEFL (minimum score 555 paper-based; 79 iBT). *Faculty research:* Teacher preparation in moderate/severe disabilities.

Western Michigan University, Graduate College, College of Education and Human Development, Department of Special Education and Literacy Studies, Kalamazoo, MI 49008. Offers literacy studies (MA); special education (MA, Ed D), including clinical teacher (MA); teaching children with visual impairments (MA).

Western New Mexico University, Graduate Division, School of Education, Silver City, NM 88062-0680. Offers bilingual education (MAT); educational leadership (MA); elementary education (MAT); reading (MAT); secondary education (MAT); special education (MAT); TESOL (teaching English to speakers of other languages) (MAT). *Accreditation:* NCATE. *Program availability:* Part-time, online learning. *Degree requirements:* For master's, comprehensive exam. *Entrance requirements:* For master's, minimum GPA of 3.0 in last 64 hours of undergraduate study. Additional exam requirements/recommendations for international students: Required—TOEFL (minimum score 550 paper-based; 79 iBT). Electronic applications accepted. *Faculty research:* International education, electronic reading assessment, developing STEM teachers.

Western State Colorado University, Graduate Programs in Education, Gunnison, CO 81231. Offers education administrator leadership (MA); reading leadership (MA); teacher leadership (MA). *Program availability:* Online learning. *Degree requirements:* For master's, capstone.

Westfield State University, College of Graduate and Continuing Education, Department of Education, Program in Reading Specialist, Westfield, MA 01086. Offers M Ed. *Accreditation:* NCATE. *Program availability:* Part-time, evening/weekend. *Faculty:* 1 (woman) full-time, 3 part-time/adjunct (2 women). *Students:* 22 part-time (21 women). Average age 28. 3 applicants, 100% accepted, 2 enrolled. In 2016, 6 master's awarded. *Degree requirements:* For master's, comprehensive exam, practicum. *Entrance requirements:* For master's, GRE General Test or MAT, minimum undergraduate GPA of 2.8. Additional exam requirements/recommendations for international students: Recommended—TOEFL (minimum score 550 paper-based; 79 iBT). *Application deadline:* For fall admission, 6/30 for domestic students; for spring admission, 10/31 for domestic students; for summer admission, 3/31 for domestic students. Applications are processed on a rolling basis. Application fee: $50. *Expenses:* Tuition, state resident: part-time $318 per semester hour. Tuition, nonresident: part-time $310 per semester hour. *Required fees:* $75 per semester. Tuition and fees vary according to course load and program. *Financial support:* Unspecified assistantships and SOS scholarships for education majors only available. Financial award application deadline: 3/1; financial award applicants required to submit FAFSA. *Unit head:* Dr. Sandra Berkowitz, Head, 413-572-5323. *Application contact:* Shelly Henrichon, Coordinator of DGCE Admissions, 413-572-8022, Fax: 413-572-5227, E-mail: mhenrichon@westfield.ma.edu.

Westminster College, Graduate School, Program in Special Education and Reading Specialist, New Wilmington, PA 16172-0001. Offers M Ed, Certificate. *Program availability:* Part-time, evening/weekend. *Degree requirements:* For master's, comprehensive exam, portfolio. *Entrance requirements:* For master's, minimum GPA of 3.0. *Application deadline:* For fall admission, 8/15 priority date for domestic students; for spring admission, 1/8 priority date for domestic students. Applications are processed on a rolling basis. Application fee: $35. *Expenses: Tuition:* Full-time $1362; part-time $454 per semester hour. One-time fee: $235.50 full-time. *Financial support:* Career-related internships or fieldwork and scholarships/grants available. *Unit head:* Dr. Amy Camardese, Co-Coordinator, 724-946-7183. *Application contact:* Dr. Darwin W. Huey,

Graduate Education Director, 724-946-7186, Fax: 724-946-6158, E-mail: hueydw@westminster.edu.

West Texas A&M University, College of Education and Social Sciences, Department of Education, Program in Reading Education, Canyon, TX 79016-0001. Offers M Ed. *Program availability:* Part-time, evening/weekend. *Degree requirements:* For master's, comprehensive exam. *Entrance requirements:* For master's, GRE General Test, interview with master's committee chairperson, state certification as a reading specialist with 3 years of teaching experience. *Application deadline:* For fall admission, 8/1 for domestic students, 5/1 for international students; for spring admission, 12/1 for domestic students, 10/30 for international students; for summer admission, 5/1 for domestic students. Applications are processed on a rolling basis. Application fee: $40 ($75 for international students). Electronic applications accepted. *Financial support:* Research assistantships, teaching assistantships, Federal Work-Study, and institutionally sponsored loans available. Support available to part-time students. Financial award applicants required to submit FAFSA. *Faculty research:* Multicultural child and adolescent literature, bilingual, dual language, monolingual classrooms. *Application contact:* Dr. Sang Hwang, Associate Professor, 806-651-2617, E-mail: shwang@wtamu.edu.
Website: http://www.wtamu.edu/academics/education-curriculum-and-instruction-graduate-program3.aspx

West Virginia University, College of Education and Human Services, Department of Curriculum and Instruction/Literacy Studies, Program in Reading, Morgantown, WV 26506. Offers MA. *Accreditation:* NCATE. *Program availability:* Part-time. *Degree requirements:* For master's, thesis optional, content exams. *Entrance requirements:* For master's, minimum GPA of 2.75. Additional exam requirements/recommendations for international students: Required—TOEFL. Electronic applications accepted. *Faculty research:* Teacher education, current practices, protocol research, metacognitive studies.

Wheelock College, Graduate Programs, Division of Education, Boston, MA 02215. Offers early childhood education (MS); education leadership (MS); elementary education (MS); language, literacy, and reading (MS); teaching students with moderate disabilities (MS). *Accreditation:* NCATE. *Program availability:* Online learning. *Degree requirements:* For master's, comprehensive exam. *Entrance requirements:* Additional exam requirements/recommendations for international students: Required—TOEFL. Electronic applications accepted. *Faculty research:* Symbolic learning, emergent literacy, diversity inclusion, beginning reading language and culture, math education.

Widener University, School of Education, Hospitality, and Continuing Studies, Chester, PA 19013-5792. Offers adult education (M Ed); counseling in higher education (M Ed); counselor education (M Ed); early childhood education (M Ed); educational foundations (M Ed); educational leadership (M Ed); educational psychology (M Ed); elementary education (M Ed); English and language arts (M Ed); health education (M Ed); higher education leadership (Ed D); home and school visitor (M Ed); human sexuality (M Ed, PhD); mathematics education (M Ed); middle school education (M Ed); principalship (M Ed); reading and language arts (Ed D); reading education (M Ed); school administration (Ed D); science education (M Ed); social studies education (M Ed); special education (M Ed); technology education (M Ed). *Accreditation:* NCATE. *Program availability:* Part-time, evening/weekend. *Faculty:* 34 full-time (22 women), 37 part-time/adjunct (14 women). *Students:* 97 full-time (64 women), 201 part-time (143 women); includes 56 minority (44 Black or African American, non-Hispanic/Latino; 1 American Indian or Alaska Native, non-Hispanic/Latino; 2 Asian, non-Hispanic/Latino; 8 Hispanic/Latino; 1 Two or more races, non-Hispanic/Latino), 32 international. Average age 39. 139 applicants, 88% accepted. In 2016, 45 master's, 21 doctorates awarded. Terminal master's awarded for partial completion of doctoral program. *Degree requirements:* For doctorate, thesis/dissertation. *Entrance requirements:* For master's, minimum GPA of 2.5; for doctorate, GRE or MAT, minimum GPA of 2.0 (undergraduate), 3.5 (graduate). *Application deadline:* Applications are processed on a rolling basis. Application fee: $25 ($300 for international students). Electronic applications accepted. *Expenses:* Contact institution. *Financial support:* Career-related internships or fieldwork, tuition waivers (full and partial), and unspecified assistantships available. Support available to part-time students. Financial award application deadline: 5/1. *Faculty research:* Reading and cognition, adult education, technology education, educational leadership, special education. *Unit head:* Dr. Shawn Fitzgerald, Dean, 610-499-4294, Fax: 610-499-4623, E-mail: smfitzgerald@widener.edu. *Application contact:* Dr. Roberta Nolan, Director of Graduate Admissions, 610-499-4125, E-mail: rdnolan@widener.edu.
Website: http://www.widener.edu/academics/schools/eics

Wilkes University, College of Graduate and Professional Studies, School of Education, Wilkes-Barre, PA 18766-0002. Offers 21st century teaching and learning (MS Ed); art and science of teaching (MS Ed); classroom technology (MS Ed); early childhood literacy (MS Ed); educational development and strategies (MS Ed); educational leadership (MS Ed, Ed D); effective teaching (MS Ed); instructional media (MS Ed); instructional technology (MS Ed); international school leadership (MS Ed); international teaching and learning (MS Ed); middle level education (MS Ed); online teaching (MS Ed); reading (MS Ed); school business leadership (MS Ed); special education (MS Ed); teaching English to speakers of other languages (MS Ed). *Program availability:* Part-time, evening/weekend, 100% online, blended/hybrid learning. *Students:* 87 full-time (70 women), 1,496 part-time (1,111 women); includes 77 minority (11 Black or African American, non-Hispanic/Latino; 2 American Indian or Alaska Native, non-Hispanic/Latino; 12 Asian, non-Hispanic/Latino; 28 Hispanic/Latino; 3 Native Hawaiian or other Pacific Islander, non-Hispanic/Latino; 21 Two or more races, non-Hispanic/Latino). Average age 33. In 2016, 524 master's, 21 doctorates awarded. *Entrance requirements:* Additional exam requirements/recommendations for international students: Required—TOEFL (minimum score 550 paper-based; 79 iBT). *Application deadline:* Applications are processed on a rolling basis. Application fee: $45. Electronic applications accepted. *Expenses:* Contact institution. *Financial support:* Unspecified assistantships available. Financial award application deadline: 3/1; financial award applicants required to submit FAFSA. *Unit head:* Dr. Rhonda Rabbitt, Dean, 570-408-4680, Fax: 570-408-7872, E-mail: rhonda.rabbitt@wilkes.edu. *Application contact:* Director of Graduate Education, 570-408-4234, Fax: 570-408-7846.
Website: http://www.wilkes.edu/academics/graduate-programs/masters-programs/graduate-education/index.aspx

William Paterson University of New Jersey, College of Education, Wayne, NJ 07470-8420. Offers curriculum and learning (M Ed); educational leadership (M Ed); elementary education (MAT); literacy (M Ed); professional counseling (M Ed); secondary education (MAT); special education (M Ed). *Accreditation:* NCATE. *Program availability:* Part-time, evening/weekend. *Faculty:* 36 full-time (25 women), 32 part-time/adjunct (27 women). *Students:* 74 full-time (51 women), 607 part-time (515 women); includes 194 minority (42 Black or African American, non-Hispanic/Latino; 21 Asian, non-Hispanic/Latino; 116 Hispanic/Latino; 15 Two or more races, non-Hispanic/Latino), 1 international. Average age 35. 390 applicants, 83% accepted, 263 enrolled. In 2016, 170 master's awarded. *Degree requirements:* For master's, comprehensive exam, thesis (for some programs), exit interview (for some programs); practicum/internship; minimum GPA of 3.0 (for some programs); exit portfolio (for some programs). *Entrance requirements:* For master's, GRE/MAT, minimum GPA of 2.75; teaching certificate; essay; interview; 2 letters of recommendation; personal statement. Additional exam requirements/recommendations for international students: Required—TOEFL (minimum score 550 paper-based; 79 iBT), IELTS (minimum score 6). *Application deadline:* For fall admission, 8/1 for domestic students, 4/1 for international students; for spring admission, 12/1 for domestic students, 11/1 for international students; for summer admission, 5/1 for domestic students, 2/1 for international students. Applications are processed on a rolling basis. Application fee: $50. Electronic applications accepted. *Expenses:* Tuition, state resident: full-time $12,480; part-time $611 per credit. Tuition, nonresident: full-time $20,263; part-time $992 per credit. *Required fees:* $1573; $77 per credit. Tuition and fees vary according to course load, degree level and program. *Financial support:* Career-related internships or fieldwork, Federal Work-Study, scholarships/grants, and unspecified assistantships available. Support available to part-time students. Financial award application deadline: 4/1; financial award applicants required to submit FAFSA. *Faculty research:* History of education, social media in classrooms and education, integrating environmental lessons into urban classrooms, minority student self-advocacy in higher education, factors affecting high school teacher retention. *Total annual research expenditures:* $289,197. *Unit head:* Dr. Candace Burns, Dean, 973-720-2137, Fax: 973-720-3467, E-mail: burnsc@wpunj.edu. *Application contact:* Liana Fornarotto, Director of Education Enrollment and Certification, 973-720-2206, Fax: 973-720-2989, E-mail: fornarottol@wpunj.edu.
Website: http://www.wpunj.edu/coe

Wilmington College, Department of Education, Wilmington, OH 45177. Offers reading (M Ed); special education (M Ed). *Accreditation:* TEAC. *Program availability:* Part-time. *Degree requirements:* For master's, comprehensive exam. *Entrance requirements:* For master's, GRE or MAT, minimum GPA of 3.0, 2 letters of recommendation. Additional exam requirements/recommendations for international students: Required—TOEFL. *Faculty research:* Reading instruction, special education practices, conflict resolution in the schools, models of higher education for teachers.

Wilmington University, College of Education, New Castle, DE 19720-6491. Offers applied technology in education (M Ed); career and technical education (M Ed); educational leadership (Ed D); elementary and secondary school counseling (M Ed); elementary studies (M Ed); ESOL literacy (M Ed); higher education leadership (Ed D); instruction: gifted and talented (M Ed); instruction: teacher of reading (M Ed); instruction: teaching and learning (M Ed); organizational leadership (Ed D); school leadership (M Ed); secondary education (MAT); special education (M Ed). *Accreditation:* NCATE. *Program availability:* Part-time, evening/weekend. *Faculty:* 19 full-time (11 women), 178 part-time/adjunct (99 women). *Students:* 248 full-time (176 women), 999 part-time (738 women); includes 244 minority (193 Black or African American, non-Hispanic/Latino; 17 American Indian or Alaska Native, non-Hispanic/Latino; 9 Asian, non-Hispanic/Latino; 19 Hispanic/Latino; 2 Native Hawaiian or other Pacific Islander, non-Hispanic/Latino; 4 Two or more races, non-Hispanic/Latino), 7 international. Average age 34. 672 applicants, 96% accepted, 348 enrolled. In 2016, 529 master's, 87 doctorates awarded. *Entrance requirements:* For master's, 2 letters of recommendation, interview. Additional exam requirements/recommendations for international students: Required—TOEFL (minimum score 500 paper-based). *Application deadline:* For fall admission, 4/30 for domestic students. Applications are processed on a rolling basis. Application fee: $35. Electronic applications accepted. *Expenses: Tuition:* Full-time $8388; part-time $466 per credit. *Required fees:* $25 per semester. Tuition and fees vary according to degree level. *Financial support:* Applicants required to submit FAFSA. *Unit head:* Dr. John C. Gray, Dean. *Application contact:* Laura Morris, Director of Admissions, 877-967-5464, E-mail: infocenter@wilmu.edu.
Website: http://www.wilmu.edu/education/

Worcester State University, Graduate Studies, Department of Education, Program in Reading, Worcester, MA 01602-2597. Offers M Ed, CAGS, Ed S, Postbaccalaureate Certificate. *Program availability:* Part-time, evening/weekend. *Faculty:* 13 full-time (12 women), 16 part-time/adjunct (7 women). *Students:* 1 (woman) full-time, 12 part-time (11 women). Average age 30. 12 applicants, 58% accepted, 6 enrolled. In 2016, 3 master's, 3 CAGSs awarded. *Degree requirements:* For master's, comprehensive exam (for some programs), thesis optional, portfolio; capstone. *Entrance requirements:* For master's, GRE General Test or MAT, MTEL Communication and Literacy test, teaching license at the initial or professional level; for other advanced degree, Massachusetts Teacher Education Licensure (MTEL), M Ed or master's degree in related field. Additional exam requirements/recommendations for international students: Required—TOEFL (minimum score 550 paper-based; 79 iBT). *Application deadline:* For fall admission, 6/15 for domestic and international students; for spring admission, 11/1 for domestic and international students; for summer admission, 4/1 for domestic and international students. Applications are processed on a rolling basis. Application fee: $50. Electronic applications accepted. *Expenses:* Tuition, state resident: part-time $150 per credit. Tuition, nonresident: part-time $150 per credit. *Financial support:* Career-related internships or fieldwork, scholarships/grants, and unspecified assistantships available. Financial award application deadline: 3/1; financial award applicants required to submit FAFSA. *Unit head:* Dr. Pamela Hollander, Coordinator, 508-929-8347, Fax: 508-929-8164, E-mail: phollander@worcester.edu. *Application contact:* Sara Grady, Associate Dean for Graduate Studies and Professional Development, 508-929-8787, Fax: 508-929-8100, E-mail: sara.grady@worcester.edu.

Xavier University, College of Social Sciences, Health and Education, School of Education, Department of Childhood Education and Literacy, Cincinnati, OH 45207. Offers children's multicultural literature (M Ed); elementary education (M Ed); Montessori education (M Ed); reading (M Ed). *Program availability:* Part-time. *Degree requirements:* For master's, comprehensive exam, thesis, 30 semester hours. *Entrance requirements:* For master's, GRE, MAT, official transcript; 3 letters of recommendation (for Montessori education); resume; statement of purpose. Additional exam requirements/recommendations for international students: Required—TOEFL (minimum score 550 paper-based; 79 iBT). Electronic applications accepted. Application fee is waived when completed online. *Expenses:* Contact institution. *Faculty research:* Multicultural literacy/fluency, early literacy development, writing/creative and across curriculum, assessment of reading abilities.

York College of Pennsylvania, Master of Education Program, York, PA 17403. Offers educational leadership (M Ed); educational technology (M Ed); reading specialist (M Ed). *Program availability:* Part-time, evening/weekend. *Faculty:* 3 full-time (2 women), 5 part-time/adjunct (2 women). *Students:* 54 part-time (39 women), 1 international. Average age 33. 51 applicants, 67% accepted, 30 enrolled. In 2016, 4 master's awarded. *Degree requirements:* For master's, comprehensive exam (for some programs), thesis (for some programs). *Entrance requirements:* For master's, PRAXIS, GRE, or MAT (within past 10 years), statement of applicant's professional and academic goals, 2 letters of recommendation, letter from current supervisor, official undergraduate and graduate transcript(s), copy of teaching certificate(s), current professional resume, interview. Additional exam requirements/recommendations for international students: Required—TOEFL. *Application deadline:* For fall admission, 7/15 priority date for domestic students; for spring admission, 11/15 priority date for domestic students; for summer admission, 4/15 priority date for domestic students. Applications are processed on a rolling basis. Application fee: $0. Electronic applications accepted. *Expenses:* $620 per credit. *Financial support:* Scholarships/grants available. Financial award applicants required to submit FAFSA. *Faculty research:* Classroom technology, assessment, educational leadership, professional development. *Unit head:* Dr. Joshua D. DeSantis, Director, Master of Education Program, 717-815-1936, E-mail: jdesant1@ycp.edu. Website: https://www.ycp.edu/med

Youngstown State University, Graduate School, Beeghly College of Education, Department of Teacher Education, Youngstown, OH 44555-0001. Offers adolescent/young adult education (MS Ed); content area concentration (MS Ed); early childhood education (MS Ed); educational technology (MS Ed); literacy (MS Ed); middle childhood education (MS Ed); special education (MS Ed), including gifted and talented education, special education. *Accreditation:* NCATE. *Program availability:* Part-time, evening/weekend. *Degree requirements:* For master's, comprehensive exam. *Entrance requirements:* For master's, GRE, MAT, or teaching certificate; minimum GPA of 2.7. Additional exam requirements/recommendations for international students: Required—TOEFL. *Faculty research:* Multicultural literacy, hands-on mathematics teaching, integrated instruction, reading comprehension, emergent curriculum.

Religious Education

Andrews University, School of Graduate Studies, Seventh-day Adventist Theological Seminary, Program in Religious Education, Berrien Springs, MI 49104. Offers MA, Ed D, PhD, Ed S. *Program availability:* Part-time. *Faculty:* 3 full-time (1 woman). *Students:* 4 full-time (3 women), 5 part-time (2 women); includes 3 minority (1 Black or African American, non-Hispanic/Latino; 1 Asian, non-Hispanic/Latino; 1 Hispanic/Latino), 5 international. Average age 43. In 2016, 5 master's, 1 doctorate awarded. Terminal master's awarded for partial completion of doctoral program. *Degree requirements:* For doctorate, thesis/dissertation. *Entrance requirements:* For master's, GRE Subject Test. Additional exam requirements/recommendations for international students: Required—TOEFL (minimum score 550 paper-based). *Application deadline:* For fall admission, 8/31 for domestic students. Applications are processed on a rolling basis. Application fee: $40. *Financial support:* Fellowships, research assistantships, teaching assistantships, and career-related internships or fieldwork available. Financial award application deadline: 6/1. *Faculty research:* Marriage and family, spiritual gifts and temperament. *Unit head:* Coordinator, 269-471-8618. *Application contact:* Justina Clayburn, Supervisor of Graduate Admission, 800-253-2874, Fax: 269-471-6321, E-mail: graduate@andrews.edu.

Asbury Theological Seminary, Graduate and Professional Programs, Wilmore, KY 40390-1199. Offers M Div, MA, MAAS, MACE, MACL, MACM, MACP, MAMFC, MAMHC, MAPC, MASF, MAYM, Th M, D Min, PhD, Certificate. *Accreditation:* ATS. *Program availability:* Part-time, online learning. Terminal master's awarded for partial completion of doctoral program. *Degree requirements:* For master's, thesis (for some programs); for doctorate, thesis/dissertation, qualifying exam. *Entrance requirements:* For master's, minimum GPA of 2.75; for doctorate, minimum GPA of 3.0. Additional exam requirements/recommendations for international students: Required—TOEFL, IELTS. Electronic applications accepted.

Azusa Pacific University, Haggard Graduate School of Theology, Program in Pastoral Studies, Concentration in Christian Education in Youth Ministry, Azusa, CA 91702-7000. Offers MA. *Accreditation:* NCATE.

Baptist Theological Seminary at Richmond, Graduate and Professional Programs, Richmond, VA 23228. Offers Biblical interpretation (M Div); Christian education formation (M Div); Christian ministry (MCM); justice and peacebuilding (M Div); ministry (D Min); religious freedom (M Div); theological studies (MTS, Graduate Certificate); theology (M Div); youth and student ministries (M Div); M Div/MBA; M Div/MS; M Div/MSW. *Accreditation:* ATS. *Program availability:* Part-time, 100% online, blended/hybrid learning. *Faculty:* 5 full-time (1 woman), 11 part-time/adjunct (2 women). *Students:* 42 full-time (23 women), 34 part-time (19 women); includes 11 minority (all Black or African American, non-Hispanic/Latino), 2 international. Average age 46. In 2016, 8 master's, 2 doctorates awarded. *Degree requirements:* For master's and Graduate Certificate, thesis optional; for doctorate, comprehensive exam, thesis/dissertation, field study, independent study. *Entrance requirements:* For master's, BA/BS, minimum GPA of 2.2, 2 references, resume, official transcripts, writing sample; for doctorate, MAT (minimum score of 400), M Div with minimum GPA of 2.75, 3 years of full-time ministry experience, 3 references, resume, official transcripts, writing sample, personal statement. Additional exam requirements/recommendations for international students: Required—TOEFL (minimum score 550 paper-based), IELTS (minimum score 5.5). *Application deadline:* For fall admission, 7/1 for domestic students, 5/1 for international students; for winter admission, 12/15 for domestic students, 9/1 for international students; for spring admission, 1/15 for domestic students, 10/1 for international students. Applications are processed on a rolling basis. Application fee: $35. Electronic applications accepted. *Expenses:* $19,800 per 12 credit hours for both semesters; $1,650 per 3 semester hour course. *Financial support:* In 2016–17, 46 students received support, including 11 teaching assistantships (averaging $3,300 per year); scholarships/grants also available. Financial award application deadline: 2/1. *Faculty research:* Biblical studies, pastoral care, church history, theology, ministry. *Unit head:* Dr. Ronald W. Crawford, President, 804-204-1201, Fax: 804-355-8182, E-mail: rcrawford@btsr.edu. *Application contact:* Melissa Fallen, Director of Admissions and Recruitment, 804-204-1208, E-mail: admissions@btsr.edu.
Website: http://www.btsr.edu/programs/degree-programs/

Biola University, Talbot School of Theology, La Mirada, CA 90639-0001. Offers adult/family ministry (MACE); Bible exposition (MA, Th M); Biblical and theological studies (Certificate); biblical and theological studies/diversified (MA); children's ministry (MACE); Christian education (M Div); cross-cultural education ministry (MACE); educational studies (Ed D, PhD); evangelism and discipleship (M Div); general Christian education (MACE); Messianic Jewish studies (M Div, Certificate); missions and intercultural studies (M Div); New Testament (MA, Th M); Old Testament (MA); Old Testament and Semitics (Th M); pastoral and general ministry (M Div); pastoral care and counseling (M Div, MACML); philosophy (MA); preaching and pastoral ministry (MACML); spiritual formation (M Div, Certificate); spiritual formation and soul care (MA), sports ministry (MACML); theology (MA, Th M, D Min, Certificate); youth ministry (MACE). *Accreditation:* ATS. *Program availability:* Part-time, evening/weekend. *Entrance requirements:* For master's, bachelor's degree from accredited college or university; minimum GPA of 2.6 (for M Div), 3.0 (for MA); for doctorate, M Div or MA. Additional exam requirements/recommendations for international students: Required—TOEFL (minimum score 600 paper-based; 88 iBT). Electronic applications accepted. *Faculty research:* New Testament, Old Testament, spiritual formation, Christian education, theological studies, Christian ministry, preaching and pastoral ministry, language and literature, bible exposition, Christian leadership.

Boston College, School of Theology and Ministry, Chestnut Hill, MA 02467-3800. Offers church leadership (MA); divinity (M Div); pastoral ministry (MA), including Hispanic ministry, liturgy and worship, pastoral care and counseling, spirituality; religious education (MA, PhD); sacred theology (STD, STL); social justice/social ministry (MA); spiritual direction (MA); theological studies (MTS); theology (Th M, PhD); youth ministry (MA); MA/MA; MS/MA; MSW/MA. *Accreditation:* TEAC. *Program availability:* Part-time. *Degree requirements:* For doctorate, one foreign language, thesis/dissertation. *Entrance requirements:* For doctorate, GRE. Additional exam requirements/recommendations for international students: Required—TOEFL (minimum score 550 paper-based). Electronic applications accepted. Tuition and fees vary according to program. *Faculty research:* Philosophy and practice of religious education, pastoral psychology, liturgical and spiritual theology, spiritual formation for the practice of ministry.

Boston University, School of Theology, Boston, MA 02118. Offers chaplaincy (M Div); choral conducting (MSM); church and the arts (M Div); constructive theology and ethics (PhD), including constructive theology, theological ethics; ecological theology and ethics (MTS); global and community engagement (M Div); history and hermeneutics (PhD), including Biblical studies, church history, liturgical studies, mission studies; organ (MSM); pastoral ministry (M Div); practical theology (PhD), including church and society, congregation and community, evangelism and missiology, homiletics, leadership and administration, pastoral theology and psychology, religious education, spirituality studies, worship; religion and conflict transformation (MTS); religion and science (MTS); religion and the academy (M Div); spirituality studies (MTS); theology (MTS, STM); transcultural studies (MTS); transformational leadership (D Min); M Div/MSM; M Div/MSW; MTS/MSW. PhD in history and hermeneutics: mission studies offered in collaboration with Gordon-Conwell Theological Seminary. *Accreditation:* ACIPE; ATS. *Program availability:* Part-time, blended/hybrid learning. *Faculty:* 34 full-time (14 women), 7 part-time/adjunct (3 women). *Students:* 260 full-time (131 women), 69 part-time (30 women); includes 69 minority (36 Black or African American, non-Hispanic/Latino; 10 Asian, non-Hispanic/Latino; 16 Hispanic/Latino; 7 Two or more races, non-Hispanic/Latino), 53 international. Average age 35. 234 applicants, 71% accepted, 106 enrolled. In 2016, 78 master's, 9 doctorates awarded. *Degree requirements:* For master's, comprehensive exam (for some programs), thesis optional, contextual education; for doctorate, 2 foreign languages, comprehensive exam, thesis/dissertation. *Entrance requirements:* For master's, minimum GPA of 3.0; for doctorate, GRE General Test, minimum GPA of 3.3. Additional exam requirements/recommendations for international students: Required—TOEFL (minimum score 570 paper-based; 89 iBT). *Application deadline:* For fall admission, 1/15 priority date for domestic and international students; for spring admission, 10/15 priority date for domestic and international students. Applications are processed on a rolling basis. Application fee: $95. Electronic applications accepted. *Expenses:* $19,500 per year tuition; $156 per semester student service fee; $54 per semester community service fee; $199 per semester health and wellness fee. *Financial support:* In 2016–17, 252 students received support, including 78 fellowships with full tuition reimbursements available (averaging $4,537 per year), 32 research assistantships (averaging $6,000 per year), 32 teaching assistantships with full and partial tuition reimbursements available (averaging $20,000 per year); career-related internships or fieldwork, Federal Work-Study, institutionally sponsored loans, scholarships/grants, traineeships, health care benefits, tuition waivers (full and partial), and unspecified assistantships also available. Support available to part-time students. Financial award application deadline: 7/15; financial award applicants required to submit FAFSA. *Faculty research:* Practical theology, Biblical studies, theology and ethical, history of Christianity. *Total annual research expenditures:* $2.5 million. *Unit head:* Rev. Dr. Mary Elizabeth Moore, Dean, 617-353-3050, Fax: 617-353-3061, E-mail: memoore@bu.edu. *Application contact:* Rev. Anastasia Kidd, Director of Admissions and College Relations, 617-353-3036, Fax: 617-358-0140, E-mail: sthadmis@bu.edu.
Website: http://www.bu.edu/sth

Brandeis University, Graduate School of Arts and Sciences, Teaching Program, Waltham, MA 02454-9110. Offers Jewish day school (MAT); public elementary education (MAT); secondary education (MAT), including Bible, biology, chemistry, Chinese, English, history, math, physics; teacher leadership (Ed M, CAGS). *Faculty:* 4 full-time (2 women), 11 part-time/adjunct (10 women). *Students:* 26 full-time (19 women), 32 part-time (26 women); includes 3 minority (all Hispanic/Latino), 10 international. 106 applicants, 70% accepted, 53 enrolled. In 2016, 39 master's awarded. *Degree requirements:* For master's, internship; research project. *Entrance requirements:* For master's, GRE General Test or MAT, official transcript(s), 2 letters of recommendation, resume, statement of purpose. Additional exam requirements/recommendations for international students: Required—TOEFL (minimum score 600 paper-based; 100 iBT); Recommended—IELTS (minimum score 7), TSE (minimum score 68). *Application deadline:* Applications are processed on a rolling basis. Application fee: $75. Electronic applications accepted. *Expenses:* Contact institution. *Financial support:* Scholarships/grants and tuition waivers (partial) available. Financial award application deadline: 4/15; financial award applicants required to submit FAFSA. *Faculty research:* Teacher education, education, teaching, elementary education, secondary education, Jewish education, English, history, biology, chemistry, physics, math, Chinese, Bible/Tanakh. *Unit head:* Prof. Marya Levenson, Director, 781-736-2002, Fax: 781-736-5020, E-mail: mlevenso@brandeis.edu. *Application contact:* Manuel Tuan, Department Coordinator, 781-736-2002, Fax: 781-736-5020, E-mail: tuan@brandeis.edu.
Website: http://www.brandeis.edu/programs/mat

Brigham Young University, Graduate Studies, College of Religious Education, Provo, UT 84602. Offers MA. *Faculty:* 42 full-time (4 women), 2 part-time/adjunct (0 women). *Students:* 17 full-time (2 women). Average age 32. 7 applicants, 43% accepted, 3 enrolled. In 2016, 8 master's awarded. *Degree requirements:* For master's, thesis. *Entrance requirements:* For master's, GRE, minimum GPA of 3.0 in last 60 hours, letter of recommendation. *Application deadline:* For fall admission, 12/1 for domestic and international students. Application fee: $50. Electronic applications accepted. *Expenses:* Contact institution. *Financial support:* In 2016–17, 6 students received support. Scholarships/grants available. *Unit head:* Dr. Brent L. Top, Dean, 801-422-2736, Fax: 801-422-0616, E-mail: brent_top@byu.edu. *Application contact:* Dr. Terry B. Ball, Professor of Ancient Scripture, 801-422-3357, Fax: 801-422-0616, E-mail: terry_ball@byu.edu.

Calvary University, Graduate School and Seminary, Kansas City, MO 64147. Offers Bible and theology (MS); Biblical counseling (MA); education (MS), including

administration and leadership, Christian education, curriculum and instruction, elementary education; organization development (MS); pastoral studies (M Div). *Program availability:* Part-time, evening/weekend. *Faculty:* 6 full-time (2 women), 2 part-time/adjunct (1 woman). *Students:* 11 full-time (3 women), 29 part-time (15 women); includes 12 minority (4 Black or African American, non-Hispanic/Latino; 1 American Indian or Alaska Native, non-Hispanic/Latino; 6 Asian, non-Hispanic/Latino; 1 Native Hawaiian or other Pacific Islander, non-Hispanic/Latino). Average age 39. In 2016, 19 master's awarded. *Degree requirements:* For master's, variable foreign language requirement, comprehensive exam, thesis or alternative. *Entrance requirements:* For master's, minimum GPA of 2.5, BA or BS, doctrine agreement. Additional exam requirements/recommendations for international students: Required—TOEFL (minimum score 550 paper-based). *Application deadline:* Applications are processed on a rolling basis. Application fee: $0. Electronic applications accepted. *Expenses: Tuition:* Full-time $7200; part-time $4800 per credit. *Required fees:* $640; $520 per credit. $140 per semester. One-time fee: $100. Tuition and fees vary according to program. *Financial support:* In 2016–17, 8 students received support. Scholarships/grants available. Financial award application deadline: 11/5; financial award applicants required to submit FAFSA. *Unit head:* Dr. Thomas Baurain, Director of Seminary, 816-322-0110 Ext. 1502, Fax: 816-331-4474, E-mail: thomas.baurain@calvary.edu. *Application contact:* Ann Rogers, Admissions Office Assistant, 800-326-3960 Ext. 1321, Fax: 816-331-4474, E-mail: admissions@calvary.edu.
Website: http://www.calvary.edu

Calvin Theological Seminary, Graduate and Professional Programs, Grand Rapids, MI 49546-4387. Offers Bible and theology (MA); divinity (M Div), including ancient near eastern languages and literature, contextual ministry, evangelism and teaching, history of Christianity, new church development, New Testament, Old Testament, pastoral care and leadership, preaching and worship, theological studies, youth and family ministries; educational ministry (MA); historical theology (PhD); missions and evangelism (MA); pastoral care (MA); philosophical and moral theology (PhD); systematic theology (PhD); theological studies (MTS); theology (Th M); worship (MA); youth and family ministries (MA). *Accreditation:* ACIPE; ATS. *Program availability:* Part-time. *Degree requirements:* For master's, variable foreign language requirement, thesis (for some programs); for doctorate, 4 foreign languages, comprehensive exam, thesis/dissertation. *Entrance requirements:* For doctorate, GRE General Test, Hebrew, Greek, and a modern foreign language. Additional exam requirements/recommendations for international students: Required—TOEFL (minimum score 550 paper-based), TWE (minimum score 4). Electronic applications accepted. *Faculty research:* Recent Trinity theory, Christian anthropology, Proverbs, reformed confessions, Paul's view of law.

Carolina Christian College, Program in Religious Education, Winston-Salem, NC 27102-0777. Offers Christian education (MRE); pastoral care (MRE). *Entrance requirements:* For master's, bachelor's degree from accredited institution, minimum undergraduate "B" average.

Claremont School of Theology, Graduate and Professional Programs, Program in Religion, Claremont, CA 91711-3199. Offers practical theology (PhD), including religious education and formation, spiritual care and counseling; religion (MA, PhD), including comparative theology and philosophy (PhD), Hebrew Bible and Jewish studies (PhD), New Testament and Christian origins (PhD), process studies (PhD), religion, ethics, and society (PhD). *Accreditation:* ACIPE; ATS. Terminal master's awarded for partial completion of doctoral program. *Degree requirements:* For master's, thesis; for doctorate, 2 foreign languages, thesis/dissertation. *Entrance requirements:* For doctorate, GRE General Test. Additional exam requirements/recommendations for international students: Required—TOEFL. *Application deadline:* For fall admission, 1/15 for domestic and international students. Application fee: $50. Electronic applications accepted. *Expenses: Tuition:* Full-time $21,120. Tuition and fees vary according to course level, course load and degree level. *Financial support:* Research assistantships, teaching assistantships, career-related internships or fieldwork, Federal Work-Study, institutionally sponsored loans, scholarships/grants, and tuition waivers (full and partial) available. Support available to part-time students. Financial award application deadline: 4/1; financial award applicants required to submit FAFSA. *Unit head:* Sheryl A. Kujawa-Holbrook, Vice President for Academic Affairs/Dean, 909-447-2520, Fax: 909-447-6274, E-mail: skujawaholbrook@cst.edu. *Application contact:* Director of Admissions, 866-274-6500, Fax: 909-447-6389, E-mail: admission@cst.edu.
Website: https://cst.edu/academics/m-a/

Clarks Summit University, Baptist Bible Seminary, South Abington Township, PA 18411. Offers Biblical apologetics (MA); church education (M Div, M Min); church planting (M Div, M Min); global ministry (M Div, M Min); leadership in communication (D Min); leadership in counseling and spiritual development (D Min); leadership in global ministry (D Min); leadership in pastoral ministry (D Min); leadership in theological studies (D Min); military chaplaincy (M Div); ministry (PhD); organizational leadership (M Min); outreach pastor (M Div, M Min); pastoral counseling (M Div, M Min); pastoral leadership (M Div, M Min); theology (Th M); worship ministries leadership (M Div, M Min); youth pastor (M Div, M Min). *Program availability:* Part-time, evening/weekend, online learning. Terminal master's awarded for partial completion of doctoral program. *Degree requirements:* For master's, 2 foreign languages, thesis, oral exam (for M Div); for doctorate, 2 foreign languages, comprehensive exam (for some programs), thesis/dissertation, oral exam. *Entrance requirements:* For doctorate, Greek and Hebrew entrance exams (for PhD). Electronic applications accepted.

Clarks Summit University, Graduate Studies, South Abington Township, PA 18411. Offers Bible (MA); counseling (MA, MS); curriculum and instruction (M Ed); educational administration (M Ed); intercultural studies (MA); literature (MA); missions (MA); organizational leadership (MA); reading specialist (M Ed); secondary English/communications (M Ed); social entrepreneurship (MA); worldview studies (MA). MA in missions program available only for Association of Baptists for World Evangelism missionary personnel. *Program availability:* Part-time, evening/weekend, online learning. *Entrance requirements:* Additional exam requirements/recommendations for international students: Required—TOEFL (minimum score 500 paper-based).

Columbia International University, Columbia Graduate School, Columbia, SC 29230-3122. Offers Bible teaching (MABT); counseling (MACN); early childhood and elementary education (MAT); educational administration (M Ed); educational leadership (PhD); instruction and learning (M Ed); teaching English as a foreign language (Certificate); teaching English as a foreign language and intercultural studies (MATF). *Program availability:* Part-time, evening/weekend, online learning. *Degree requirements:* For master's, internships, professional project. *Entrance requirements:* For master's, MAT; GRE (for some programs), minimum GPA of 2.7. Additional exam requirements/recommendations for international students: Required—TOEFL. Electronic applications accepted.

Concordia University Chicago, College of Education, Program in Christian Education, River Forest, IL 60305-1499. Offers MA. *Entrance requirements:* Additional exam requirements/recommendations for international students: Required—TOEFL (minimum score 550 paper-based). Electronic applications accepted.

Concordia University, Nebraska, Graduate Programs in Education, Program in Parish Education, Seward, NE 68434-1556. Offers MPE. *Accreditation:* NCATE. *Program availability:* Part-time, evening/weekend. *Degree requirements:* For master's, thesis or alternative. *Entrance requirements:* For master's, GRE, MAT, or NTE, minimum GPA of 3.0, BS in education or equivalent.

Dallas Baptist University, Graduate School of Ministry, Program in Children's Ministry, Dallas, TX 75211-9299. Offers general (MA); special needs children ministry (MA). *Program availability:* Part-time, evening/weekend, 100% online, blended/hybrid learning. *Application deadline:* Applications are processed on a rolling basis. Application fee: $25. Electronic applications accepted. Application fee is waived when completed online. *Expenses: Tuition:* Full-time $15,408; part-time $856 per credit hour. *Required fees:* $400 per semester. Tuition and fees vary according to course load and degree level. *Unit head:* Dr. Shelly Melia, Director, 214-333-5246, E-mail: shelly@dbu.edu. *Application contact:* Bobby Soto, Director of Admissions, 214-333-5242, E-mail: graduate@dbu.edu.
Website: http://www3.dbu.edu/gsom/Childrens-Ministry/

Dallas Baptist University, Graduate School of Ministry, Program in Student Ministry, Dallas, TX 75211-9299. Offers MA. *Program availability:* Part-time, evening/weekend, 100% online, blended/hybrid learning. *Application deadline:* Applications are processed on a rolling basis. Application fee: $25. Electronic applications accepted. Application fee is waived when completed online. *Expenses: Tuition:* Full-time $15,408; part-time $856 per credit hour. *Required fees:* $400 per semester. Tuition and fees vary according to course load and degree level. *Unit head:* Dr. Chris Shirley, Director, 214-333-5256, E-mail: crissh@dbu.edu. *Application contact:* Bobby Soto, Director of Admissions, 214-333-5242, E-mail: graduate@dbu.edu.
Website: http://www3.dbu.edu/gsom/student-ministry/

Dallas Theological Seminary, Graduate Programs, Dallas, TX 75204-6499. Offers adult education (Th M); apologetics (Th M); Bible backgrounds (Th M); Bible translation (Th M); Biblical and theological studies (Certificate); biblical counseling (MA); biblical exegesis and linguistics (MA); biblical exposition (PhD); biblical studies (MA); Biblical theology (Th M); children's education (Th M); Christian education (MA, D Min); Christian leadership (MA); cross-cultural ministries (MA); educational administration (Th M); educational leadership (Th M); evangelism and discipleship (Th M); exposition of Biblical books (Th M); family life education (Th M); general studies (Th M); Hebrew and cognate studies (Th M); hermeneutics (Th M); historical theology (Th M); homiletics (Th M); intercultural ministries (Th M); Jesus studies (Th M); leadership studies (Th M); media and communication (MA); media arts (Th M); ministry (D Min); ministry with women (Th M); New Testament studies (Th M, PhD); Old Testament studies (Th M, PhD); parachurch ministries (Th M); pastoral care and counseling (Th M); pastoral theology and practice (Th M); philosophy (Th M); sacred theology (STM); spiritual formation (Th M); systematic theology (Th M); teaching in Christian institutions (Th M); theological studies (PhD); urban ministries (Th M); worship studies (Th M); youth education (Th M). *Program availability:* Part-time, online learning. *Degree requirements:* For master's, variable foreign language requirement, thesis (for some programs); for doctorate, 2 foreign languages, thesis/dissertation. *Entrance requirements:* For master's, GRE or MAT (if minimum undergraduate cumulative GPA is below 2.5 or undergraduate degree is unaccredited). Additional exam requirements/recommendations for international students: Required—TOEFL (minimum score 575 paper-based; 85 iBT), TWE. Electronic applications accepted.

Felician University, Program in Religious Education, Lodi, NJ 07644-2117. Offers MA, Certificate. *Accreditation:* TEAC. *Program availability:* Part-time, evening/weekend, online only, 100% online. *Faculty:* 1 (woman) full-time, 5 part-time/adjunct (2 women). *Students:* 1 (woman) full-time, 16 part-time (11 women); includes 6 minority (1 Black or African American, non-Hispanic/Latino; 3 Asian, non-Hispanic/Latino; 2 Hispanic/Latino). Average age 45. 10 applicants, 70% accepted, 4 enrolled. In 2016, 8 master's awarded. *Degree requirements:* For master's, thesis, presentation; for Certificate, capstone project. *Entrance requirements:* For master's, letter of recommendation, interview, reading/writing sample, ministerial discount form, notarized copy of valid passport, graduation from accredited baccalaureate program. Additional exam requirements/recommendations for international students: Required—TOEFL (minimum score 650 paper-based; 79 iBT), IELTS (minimum score 6.5). *Application deadline:* Applications are processed on a rolling basis. Application fee: $40. Electronic applications accepted. Application fee is waived when completed online. *Expenses:* $1,000 per credit and $55 mandatory fee per term. *Financial support:* Federal Work-Study, scholarships/grants, and tuition waivers (partial) available. Financial award applicants required to submit FAFSA. *Faculty research:* Catechesis and evangelization, education ministry, religious education, church leadership, faith formation. *Unit head:* Dr. Dolores M. Henchy, Director, 201-559-6053, Fax: 973-472-8936, E-mail: henchyd@felician.edu. *Application contact:* Michael Szarek, Director, Graduate Admissions, 201-559-1451, E-mail: szarekm@felician.edu.

Fordham University, Graduate School of Religion and Religious Education, New York, NY 10458. Offers pastoral counseling and spiritual care (MA); pastoral ministry/spirituality/pastoral counseling (D Min); religion and religious education (MA); religious education (MS, PhD, PD); spiritual direction (Certificate). *Program availability:* Part-time. Terminal master's awarded for partial completion of doctoral program. *Degree requirements:* For master's, research paper; for doctorate, comprehensive exam, thesis/dissertation. *Entrance requirements:* For doctorate, MAT. Electronic applications accepted. *Expenses:* Contact institution. *Faculty research:* Spirituality and spiritual direction, pastoral care and counseling, adult family and community, growth and young adult.

Gardner-Webb University, School of Divinity, Boiling Springs, NC 28017. Offers biblical studies (M Div); Christian education and formation (M Div); intercultural studies (M Div); ministry (D Min); missiology (M Div); pastoral care and counseling (M Div); pastoral care and counseling/member care for missionaries (D Min); pastoral studies (M Div); M Div/MA; M Div/MBA. *Accreditation:* ACIPE. *Program availability:* Part-time. *Faculty:* 12 full-time (2 women), 3 part-time/adjunct (1 woman). *Students:* 115 full-time (59 women), 68 part-time (27 women); includes 86 minority (80 Black or African American, non-Hispanic/Latino; 5 Asian, non-Hispanic/Latino; 1 Hispanic/Latino). Average age 40. 86 applicants, 44% accepted, 16 enrolled. In 2016, 40 master's, 3 doctorates awarded. *Entrance requirements:* For master's, minimum GPA of 2.6; for doctorate, minimum GPA of 2.75. Additional exam requirements/recommendations for international students: Required—TOEFL (minimum score 500 paper-based; 61 iBT). *Application deadline:* Applications are processed on a rolling basis. Electronic applications accepted. *Expenses:* Contact institution. *Financial support:* Fellowships, institutionally sponsored loans, and unspecified assistantships available. Support available to part-time students. Financial award application deadline: 5/15. *Faculty research:* Jewish-Christian dialogue, Islam. *Unit head:* Dr. Robert W. Canoy, Sr., Dean, 704-406-4400, Fax: 704-406-3935, E-mail: rcanoy@gardner-webb.edu. *Application contact:* Kheresa Harmon, Director of Admissions, 704-406-3205, Fax: 704-406-3895, E-mail: kharmon@gardner-webb.edu.
Website: http://gardner-webb.edu/academic-programs-and-resources/colleges-and-schools/divinity/index

Garrett-Evangelical Theological Seminary, Graduate and Professional Programs, Evanston, IL 60201-3298. Offers Bible and culture (PhD); Christian education (MA); Christian education and congregational studies (PhD); contemporary theology and culture (PhD); divinity (M Div); ethics, church, and society (MA); liturgical studies (PhD); ministry (D Min); music ministry (MA); pastoral care and counseling (MA); pastoral theology, personality, and culture (PhD); spiritual formation and evangelism (MA); theological studies (MTS); M Div/MSW. M Div/MSW offered jointly with Loyola University Chicago. *Accreditation:* ACIPE; ATS (one or more programs are accredited). *Program availability:* Part-time. *Degree requirements:* For master's, thesis (for some programs); for doctorate, thesis/dissertation. *Entrance requirements:* For doctorate, GRE (PhD). Additional exam requirements/recommendations for international students: Required—TOEFL (minimum score 560 paper-based). Electronic applications accepted.

Global University, Graduate School of Theology, Springfield, MO 65804. Offers bible and theology (D Min); biblical language (M Div); biblical studies (MA); Christian ministry (M Div, D Min); ministerial studies (MA), including education, leadership, missions, New Testament, Old Testament. *Program availability:* Part-time, evening/weekend, online learning. *Degree requirements:* For master's, thesis (for some programs). *Entrance requirements:* For master's, minimum undergraduate GPA of 3.0. Electronic applications accepted. *Faculty research:* Higher education, cross-cultural missions.

Grand Rapids Theological Seminary of Cornerstone University, Graduate Programs, Grand Rapids, MI 49525-5897. Offers biblical counseling (MA); Biblical counseling (M Div); chaplaincy (M Div); Christian education (M Div, MA); intercultural studies (M Div, MA); New Testament (MA, Th M); Old Testament (MA, Th M); pastoral studies (M Div); systematic theology (MA); theology (Th M). *Accreditation:* ATS. *Program availability:* Part-time, online learning. *Entrance requirements:* Additional exam requirements/recommendations for international students: Required—TOEFL (minimum score 577 paper-based; 90 iBT). Electronic applications accepted.

Gratz College, Graduate Programs, Program in Jewish Education, Melrose Park, PA 19027. Offers education leadership (Ed D); Jewish instructional education (MA); MA/MA. *Program availability:* Part-time, evening/weekend, online learning. *Degree requirements:* For master's, one foreign language, internship. *Entrance requirements:* For master's, interview. *Application deadline:* Applications are processed on a rolling basis. Application fee: $50. *Financial support:* Fellowships, career-related internships or fieldwork, Federal Work-Study, and unspecified assistantships available. Support available to part-time students. Financial award application deadline: 4/15; financial award applicants required to submit FAFSA. *Unit head:* Coordinator, 215-635-7300, Fax: 215-635-7320. *Application contact:* Joanna Boeing Bratton, Director of Admissions, 215-635-7300 Ext. 140, Fax: 215-635-7399, E-mail: admissions@gratz.edu.
Website: https://www.gratz.edu/academics/jewish-education-graduate

Hebrew College, Shoolman Graduate School of Jewish Education, Newton Centre, MA 02459. Offers early childhood Jewish education (Certificate); Jewish day school education (Certificate); Jewish education (MJ Ed); Jewish family education (Certificate); Jewish special education (Certificate); Jewish youth education, informal education and camping (Certificate). *Program availability:* Part-time, evening/weekend, online learning. *Degree requirements:* For master's, one foreign language. *Entrance requirements:* For master's, GRE, interview. Additional exam requirements/recommendations for international students: Required—TOEFL.

Hebrew Union College–Jewish Institute of Religion, School of Education, New York, NY 10012-1186. Offers MARE. *Program availability:* Part-time. *Degree requirements:* For master's, one foreign language, thesis. *Entrance requirements:* For master's, GRE, minimum 2 years of college-level Hebrew.

Inter American University of Puerto Rico, Metropolitan Campus, Graduate Programs, Program in Christian Education, San Juan, PR 00919-1293. Offers PhD.

Interdenominational Theological Center, Graduate and Professional Programs, Atlanta, GA 30314-4112. Offers Christian education (MACE); ministry (D Min); pastoral counseling (Th D); theology (M Div); M Div/MACE. D Min and Th D programs offered in collaboration with the Atlanta Theological Association. *Accreditation:* ACIPE; ATS (one or more programs are accredited). *Program availability:* Part-time, evening/weekend, blended/hybrid learning. *Faculty:* 15 full-time (6 women), 12 part-time/adjunct (5 women). *Students:* 119 full-time (45 women), 137 part-time (60 women); includes 249 minority (248 Black or African American, non-Hispanic/Latino; 1 Two or more races, non-Hispanic/Latino), 2 international. *Degree requirements:* For doctorate, thesis/dissertation. *Entrance requirements:* For doctorate, master's degree. *Application deadline:* For fall admission, 7/1 for domestic and international students; for spring admission, 10/1 for domestic and international students. Applications are processed on a rolling basis. Application fee: $50. Electronic applications accepted. *Expenses: Tuition:* Full-time $13,000; part-time $9324 per credit. *Required fees:* $938; $938 per credit. Full-time tuition and fees vary according to course load. *Financial support:* Research assistantships, career-related internships or fieldwork, and Federal Work-Study available. Support available to part-time students. Financial award application deadline: 6/15; financial award applicants required to submit FAFSA. *Unit head:* Edward Lorenza Wheeler, President, 404-527-7702, Fax: 404-527-7770. *Application contact:* Michelle Davis, Office of Admission and Recruitment, 404-527-7793, E-mail: lmdavis@itc.edu.
Website: http://www.itc.edu/academics/degreeprograms/

The Jewish Theological Seminary, William Davidson Graduate School of Jewish Education, New York, NY 10027-4649. Offers MA, Ed D. Offered in conjunction with The Rabbinical School; H. L. Miller Cantorial School and College of Jewish Music; Teacher's College, Columbia University; and Union Theological Seminary. *Program availability:* Part-time, online learning. *Degree requirements:* For master's, one foreign language, thesis optional; for doctorate, one foreign language, comprehensive exam, thesis/dissertation. *Entrance requirements:* For master's, GRE or MAT, 3 letters of recommendation; for doctorate, GRE or MAT, writing sample, 3 letters of recommendation. Additional exam requirements/recommendations for international students: Recommended—TOEFL.

Lancaster Theological Seminary, Graduate and Professional Programs, Lancaster, PA 17603-2812. Offers biblical studies (MAR); Christian education (MAR); Christianity and the arts (MAR); church history (MAR); congregational life (MAR); lay leadership (Certificate); theological studies (M Div); theology (D Min); theology and ethics (MAR). *Accreditation:* ACIPE; ATS. *Degree requirements:* For doctorate, thesis/dissertation.

La Sierra University, School of Religion, Riverside, CA 92515. Offers pastoral ministry (M Div); religion (MA); religious education (MA); religious studies (MA). *Program availability:* Part-time. *Degree requirements:* For master's, one foreign language, thesis or alternative. *Entrance requirements:* For master's, GRE General Test, minimum GPA of 3.0.

Liberty University, School of Divinity, Lynchburg, VA 24515. Offers Biblical studies (M Div); church history (MAR, Th M); discipleship and church ministry (M Div, MAR, MCM); evangelism and church planting (M Div, MAR, MCM); global studies (M Div, MCM, MGS); homiletics (M Div, MAR, Th M, D Min); leadership (M Div, D Min); marketplace chaplaincy (M Div, MCM); ministry (D Min); pastoral counseling (M Div, MA, MAR, D Min), including addictions and recovery (MA), crisis response and trauma (MA), discipleship and church ministries (MA), leadership (MA), life coaching (MA), marketplace chaplaincy (MA), marriage and family (MA), military resilience (MA), pastoral counseling (MA); pastoral ministries (M Div, MCM); religious education (MRE); theology (M Div, MAR, MTS); theology and apologetics (PhD); worship (M Div, MAR, MCM, D Min). *Program availability:* Part-time, online learning. *Students:* 2,140 full-time (615 women), 3,020 part-time (906 women); includes 1,312 minority (1,016 Black or African American, non-Hispanic/Latino; 9 American Indian or Alaska Native, non-Hispanic/Latino; 100 Asian, non-Hispanic/Latino; 90 Hispanic/Latino; 7 Native Hawaiian or other Pacific Islander, non-Hispanic/Latino; 90 Two or more races, non-Hispanic/Latino), 158 international. Average age 42. 3,651 applicants, 37% accepted, 909 enrolled. In 2016, 1,551 master's, 39 doctorates, 168 other advanced degrees awarded. *Degree requirements:* For master's, 2 foreign languages, thesis (for some programs); for doctorate, 2 foreign languages, thesis/dissertation. *Entrance requirements:* For master's, minimum undergraduate GPA of 2.0; for doctorate, GRE General Test or MAT, minimum graduate GPA of 3.0. Additional exam requirements/recommendations for international students: Required—TOEFL (minimum score 600 paper-based; 100 iBT). *Application deadline:* For fall admission, 6/1 for domestic students; for spring admission, 11/1 for domestic students. Applications are processed on a rolling basis. Application fee: $50. Electronic applications accepted. *Expenses:* Contact institution. *Financial support:* Teaching assistantships with tuition reimbursements, career-related internships or fieldwork, and Federal Work-Study available. Financial award applicants required to submit FAFSA. *Unit head:* Dr. Ed Hindson, Dean, 434-592-4140, Fax: 434-522-0415, E-mail: ehindson@liberty.edu. *Application contact:* Jay Bridge, Director of Graduate Admissions, 800-424-9595, Fax: 800-628-7977, E-mail: gradadmissions@liberty.edu.
Website: https://www.liberty.edu/divinity/

Lincoln Christian Seminary, Graduate and Professional Programs, Lincoln, IL 62656-2167. Offers Bible and theology (MA); Christian ministries (MA); counseling (MA); divinity (M Div); leadership ministry (D Min); religious education (MRE). *Accreditation:* ACIPE; ATS. *Program availability:* Part-time. *Degree requirements:* For master's, 2 foreign languages, thesis; for doctorate, thesis/dissertation. *Entrance requirements:* For master's, minimum GPA of 2.5; for doctorate, M Div or equivalent. Additional exam requirements/recommendations for international students: Required—TOEFL (minimum score 550 paper-based). Electronic applications accepted.

Loyola Marymount University, School of Education, Department of Educational Support Services, Los Angeles, CA 90045-2659. Offers Catholic inclusive education (MA); counseling (MA); guidance and counseling (MA); school counseling (MA); school psychology (MA). *Unit head:* Dr. William Parham, Chair, 310-258-5591, E-mail: wparham@lmu.edu. *Application contact:* Chake H. Kouyoumjian, Associate Dean of Graduate Studies, 310-338-2721, Fax: 310-338-6086, E-mail: ckouyoum@lmu.edu.

Loyola University Chicago, Institute of Pastoral Studies, Chicago, IL 60611. Offers Christian spirituality (MA), including spiritual direction; church management (Certificate); counseling for ministry (MA); health care ministry leadership (Certificate); health care mission leadership (MA); pastoral counseling (MA, Certificate); pastoral studies (M Div, MA); religious education (Certificate); social justice (MA, Certificate); spiritual direction (Certificate); M Div/MA; M Div/MSW; MSW/MA. MSW/MA offered with School of Social Work. *Accreditation:* ACIPE. *Program availability:* Part-time, evening/weekend, 100% online, blended/hybrid learning. *Faculty:* 11 full-time (4 women), 25 part-time/adjunct (11 women). *Students:* 79 full-time (58 women), 120 part-time (76 women); includes 54 minority (22 Black or African American, non-Hispanic/Latino; 1 American Indian or Alaska Native, non-Hispanic/Latino; 6 Asian, non-Hispanic/Latino; 23 Hispanic/Latino; 2 Two or more races, non-Hispanic/Latino), 23 international. Average age 42. 116 applicants, 83% accepted, 71 enrolled. In 2016, 63 master's, 4 other advanced degrees awarded. *Degree requirements:* For master's, thesis optional, project. *Entrance requirements:* Additional exam requirements/recommendations for international students: Required—TOEFL (minimum score 550 paper-based; 79 iBT), IELTS (minimum score 6.5). *Application deadline:* Applications are processed on a rolling basis. Application fee: $50. Electronic applications accepted. Application fee is waived when completed online. *Expenses:* Contact institution. *Financial support:* In 2016–17, 84 students received support. Career-related internships or fieldwork, Federal Work-Study, institutionally sponsored loans, scholarships/grants, tuition waivers (partial), and unspecified assistantships available. Support available to part-time students. Financial award application deadline: 3/1; financial award applicants required to submit FAFSA. *Faculty research:* Catholic theology, skills of religious ministry, family ministries, spirituality and divorced men. *Unit head:* Dr. Brian J. Schmisek, Dean, 312-915-7400, Fax: 312-915-7410, E-mail: bschmisek@luc.edu. *Application contact:* Dr. M. Therese Lysaught, Associate Dean, 312-915-7485, Fax: 312-915-7410, E-mail: mlysaught@luc.edu.
Website: http://www.luc.edu/ips/

Maple Springs Baptist Bible College and Seminary, Graduate and Professional Programs, Capitol Heights, MD 20743. Offers biblical studies (MA, Certificate); Christian counseling (MA); church administration (MA); divinity (M Div); ministry (D Min); religious education (MRE).

Midwestern Baptist Theological Seminary, Graduate and Professional Programs, Kansas City, MO 64118-4697. Offers Christian education (MACE); Christian foundations (Graduate Certificate); church music (MCM); counseling (MA); ministry (D Ed Min, D Min); Old or New Testament studies (PhD); theology (M Div). *Accreditation:* ATS. *Program availability:* Part-time, online learning. *Degree requirements:* For doctorate, thesis/dissertation. *Entrance requirements:* For doctorate, MAT. Electronic applications accepted. *Faculty research:* Ministerial studies, Biblical and theological studies, missions, counseling.

Milligan College, Emmanuel Christian Seminary at Milligan College, Milligan College, TN 37682. Offers Christian care and counseling (M Div); Christian education (M Div); Christian ministries (MACM, Graduate Certificate); Christian ministry (M Div); Christian theology (M Div, MAR); church history (MAR); church history/historical theology (M Div); general studies (M Div); ministry (D Min); New Testament (M Div, MAR); Old Testament (M Div, MAR); urban ministry (M Div); world missions (M Div). *Accreditation:* ACIPE; ATS. *Program availability:* Part-time, blended/hybrid learning. *Faculty:* 9 full-time (1 woman), 11 part-time/adjunct (0 women). *Students:* 55 full-time (16 women), 44 part-time (17 women); includes 7 minority (6 Black or African American, non-Hispanic/Latino; 1 Hispanic/Latino), 6 international. Average age 33. In 2016, 21 master's, 3 doctorates awarded. *Degree requirements:* For master's, 2 foreign languages, thesis or alternative, portfolio; for doctorate, thesis/dissertation. *Entrance requirements:* For master's, undergraduate degree and supporting transcripts, essay/personal statement, professional recommendations, interview; for doctorate, M Div or equivalent, essay/personal statement, professional recommendations. Additional exam requirements/recommendations for international students: Required—TOEFL (minimum score 550 paper-based, 79 iBT) or IELTS (6.5). *Application deadline:* For fall admission, 8/1 for domestic students, 6/1 for international students; for spring admission, 12/15 for domestic students, 8/1 for international students. Applications are processed on a rolling basis. Application fee: $30 ($0 for international students). Electronic applications accepted. *Expenses:* $470 per hour tuition; $325 per semester tech/activity fees. *Financial support:* In 2016–17, 124 students received support. Scholarships/grants and unspecified assistantships available. Financial award application deadline: 12/1; financial award applicants required to submit FAFSA. *Faculty research:* Theology of Old Testament prophets; performance criticism of New Testament texts; practical theology and spiritual formation for Christian leaders; church history and missions; constructive

theology, art and imagination. *Unit head:* Dr. Rollin Ramsaran, Academic Dean, Emmanuel Christian Seminary, 423-461-1524, Fax: 423-926-6198, E-mail: raramsaran@milligan.edu. *Application contact:* Lauren Gullett, Director of Admissions and Recruitment for Emmanuel Christian Seminary, 423-461-1535, Fax: 423-926-6198, E-mail: lwgullett@milligan.edu.
Website: http://ecs.milligan.edu/

Moody Theological Seminary–Michigan, Graduate Programs, Plymouth, MI 48170. Offers Bible (Graduate Certificate); Christian education (MA); counseling psychology (MA); divinity (M Div); theological studies (MA). *Program availability:* Part-time, evening/weekend. *Degree requirements:* For master's, one foreign language, thesis. *Faculty research:* Judaism, cults, world religions.

Newman Theological College, Religious Education Programs, Edmonton, AB T6V 1H3, Canada. Offers MRE, Graduate Certificate. *Program availability:* Part-time, blended/hybrid learning. *Faculty:* 2 full-time (1 woman), 11 part-time/adjunct (3 women). *Students:* 87 part-time (61 women). 20 applicants, 100% accepted, 20 enrolled. In 2016, 8 master's awarded. *Degree requirements:* For master's, thesis or alternative. *Entrance requirements:* For master's, 2 years of teaching experience, graduate diploma in religious education; for Graduate Certificate, bachelor's degree in education, teaching certificate. Additional exam requirements/recommendations for international students: Required—TOEFL (minimum score 560 paper-based; 86 iBT), IELTS (minimum score 6.5). *Application deadline:* For fall admission, 8/21 priority date for domestic students; for winter admission, 11/22 priority date for domestic students; for spring admission, 4/18 priority date for domestic students. Applications are processed on a rolling basis. Application fee: $45 ($250 for international students). *Expenses:* $639 per course. *Financial support:* In 2016–17, 9,041 students received support. Tuition bursaries available. Support available to part-time students. Financial award application deadline: 5/31. *Unit head:* Sandra Talarico, Director, 780-392-2450 Ext. 2214, Fax: 780-462-4013, E-mail: sandra.talarico@newman.edu. *Application contact:* Maria Saulnier, Registrar, 780-392-2451, Fax: 780-462-4013, E-mail: registrar@newman.edu.
Website: http://www.newman.edu/

New Orleans Baptist Theological Seminary, Graduate and Professional Programs, Division of Christian Education Ministries, New Orleans, LA 70126-4858. Offers Christian education (M Div, MACE, D Min, DEM, PhD). *Program availability:* Evening/weekend, online learning. *Degree requirements:* For master's, 2 foreign languages; for doctorate, 3 foreign languages, comprehensive exam, thesis/dissertation. *Entrance requirements:* For doctorate, GRE General Test.

Oral Roberts University, School of Theology and Missions, Tulsa, OK 74171. Offers biblical literature (MA), including advanced languages, Judaic-Christian studies; Christian counseling (MA), including marriage and family therapy; divinity (M Div); missions (MA); practical theology (MA); theological/historical studies (MA); theology (D Min). *Accreditation:* ATS. *Program availability:* Part-time, online learning. *Degree requirements:* For master's, thesis (for some programs), practicum/internship; for doctorate, thesis/dissertation, applied research project. *Entrance requirements:* For master's, GRE General Test or MAT, minimum GPA of 2.5; for doctorate, M Div, minimum GPA of 3.0, 3 years of full-time ministry experience. Additional exam requirements/recommendations for international students: Required—TOEFL (minimum score 550 paper-based; 79 iBT). Electronic applications accepted.

Palm Beach Atlantic University, School of Ministry, West Palm Beach, FL 33416-4708. Offers Christian studies (MA); ministry (M Div). *Program availability:* Part-time. *Faculty:* 10 part-time/adjunct (2 women). *Students:* 36 full-time (12 women), 1 part-time (0 women); includes 10 minority (2 Black or African American, non-Hispanic/Latino; 7 Hispanic/Latino; 1 Two or more races, non-Hispanic/Latino), 1 international. Average age 28. 26 applicants, 88% accepted, 16 enrolled. In 2016, 7 master's awarded. *Degree requirements:* For master's, one foreign language, comprehensive exam (for some programs), thesis optional, 8 credits of biblical language (for M Div). *Entrance requirements:* For master's, minimum GPA of 2.75; writing samples. Additional exam requirements/recommendations for international students: Required—TOEFL (minimum score 550 paper-based; 79 iBT). *Application deadline:* Applications are processed on a rolling basis. Application fee: $50. Electronic applications accepted. *Expenses: Tuition:* Full-time $6600; part-time $550 per credit hour. Full-time tuition and fees vary according to degree level, campus/location and program. *Financial support:* In 2016–17, 25 students received support. Scholarships/grants, unspecified assistantships, and employee education grants available. Financial award application deadline: 5/1; financial award applicants required to submit FAFSA. *Faculty research:* Ethics, apologetics, spiritual formation, theology. *Unit head:* Dr. Jonathan Grenz, Director of the M Div Program, 561-803-2622. *Application contact:* Graduate Admissions, 888-468-6722, E-mail: grad@pba.edu.
Website: http://www.pba.edu/school-of-ministry

Pfeiffer University, Program in Practical Theology, Misenheimer, NC 28109-0960. Offers MA. *Program availability:* Part-time, evening/weekend. *Entrance requirements:* For master's, minimum GPA of 2.75.

Phillips Theological Seminary, Programs in Theology, Tulsa, OK 74116. Offers administration of church agencies (M Div); campus ministry (M Div); church-related social work (M Div); college and seminary teaching (M Div); global mission work (M Div); institutional chaplaincy (M Div); ministerial vocations in Christian education (M Div); ministry (D Min), including parish ministry, pastoral counseling, practices of ministry; ministry and culture (MAMC), including Christian education, congregational leadership, history and practice of Christian spirituality, theology, ethics, and culture; ministry of music (M Div); pastoral care and counseling (M Div); pastoral ministry (M Div); theological studies (MTS). *Accreditation:* ATS. *Program availability:* Part-time, online learning. *Degree requirements:* For master's, thesis (for some programs); for doctorate, thesis/dissertation. *Entrance requirements:* For master's, minimum GPA of 2.5; for doctorate, M Div, minimum GPA of 3.0. *Faculty research:* Biblical studies, historical studies, theology and culture, practical theology, theology and film.

Pontifical Catholic University of Puerto Rico, College of Education, Program in Religious Education, Ponce, PR 00717-0777. Offers MRE.

Providence University College & Theological Seminary, Theological Seminary, Otterburne, MB R0A 1G0, Canada. Offers children's ministry (Certificate); Christian studies (MA, Certificate); counseling (MA); cross-cultural discipleship (Certificate); divinity (M Div); educational studies (MA), including counseling psychology, educational ministries, student development, teaching English to speakers of other languages, training teachers of English to speakers of other languages; global studies (MA); lay counseling (Diploma); ministry (D Min); teaching English to speakers of other languages (Certificate); theological studies (MA); training teacher of English to speakers of other languages (Certificate); youth ministry (Certificate). *Accreditation:* ATS. *Program availability:* Part-time. *Degree requirements:* For master's, variable foreign language requirement, thesis (for some programs); for doctorate, thesis/dissertation. *Entrance requirements:* Additional exam requirements/recommendations for international students: Recommended—TOEFL (minimum score 550 paper-based). *Faculty research:* Studies in Isaiah, theology of sin.

Reformed Theological Seminary–Jackson Campus, Graduate and Professional Programs, Jackson, MS 39209-3004. Offers Bible, theology, and missions (Certificate); Biblical exegesis (M Div); biblical studies (MA); Christian education (MA); counseling (M Div); marriage and family therapy (MA); ministry (D Min); missions (M Div, MA, D Min); theological studies (MA). *Accreditation:* AAMFT/COAMFTE (one or more programs are accredited); ATS (one or more programs are accredited). *Degree requirements:* For master's, thesis (for some programs), fieldwork; for doctorate, 2 foreign languages, thesis/dissertation. *Entrance requirements:* For master's, minimum GPA of 2.6; for doctorate, minimum GPA of 3.0. Additional exam requirements/recommendations for international students: Required—TOEFL.

Regent University, Graduate School, School of Divinity, Virginia Beach, VA 23464-9800. Offers divinity (M Div), including Biblical studies (M Div, MTS, PhD), chaplain ministry, Christian theology (M Div, MTS, PhD), church and ministry (M Div, MA), history of Christianity (M Div, MTS, PhD), inter-cultural studies (M Div, MA), interdisciplinary studies (M Div, MA, MTS), marketplace ministry, worship and media (M Div, MA); leadership and renewal (D Min), including Christian leadership and renewal, clinical pastoral education, community transformation, military ministry, ministry leadership coaching; practical theology (MA), including church and ministry (M Div, MA), inter-cultural studies (M Div, MA), interdisciplinary studies (M Div, MA, MTS), worship and media (M Div, MA); theological studies (MTS, PhD), including Biblical studies (M Div, MTS, PhD), Christian theology (M Div, MTS, PhD), history of Christianity (M Div, MTS, PhD), interdisciplinary studies (M Div, MA, MTS). *Accreditation:* ACIPE; ATS. *Program availability:* Part-time, evening/weekend, 100% online, blended/hybrid learning. *Faculty:* 15 full-time (3 women), 51 part-time/adjunct (6 women). *Students:* 148 full-time (60 women), 787 part-time (321 women); includes 506 minority (416 Black or African American, non-Hispanic/Latino; 1 American Indian or Alaska Native, non-Hispanic/Latino; 23 Asian, non-Hispanic/Latino; 54 Hispanic/Latino; 1 Native Hawaiian or other Pacific Islander, non-Hispanic/Latino; 11 Two or more races, non-Hispanic/Latino), 31 international. Average age 43. 1,020 applicants, 42% accepted, 276 enrolled. In 2016, 127 master's, 25 doctorates awarded. *Degree requirements:* For master's, comprehensive exam, thesis or alternative, internship; for doctorate, thesis/dissertation or alternative. *Entrance requirements:* For master's, minimum undergraduate GPA of 2.75, writing sample, personal goal statement, college transcripts; for doctorate, GRE, minimum graduate GPA of 3.5 (PhD), 3.0 (D Min); clergy recommendations; writing sample; transcripts; resume; interview. Additional exam requirements/recommendations for international students: Required—TOEFL (minimum score 577 paper-based). *Application deadline:* For fall admission, 5/1 priority date for domestic students. Applications are processed on a rolling basis. Application fee: $50. Electronic applications accepted. *Expenses:* Contact institution. *Financial support:* In 2016–17, 602 students received support. Career-related internships or fieldwork, scholarships/grants, and unspecified assistantships available. Support available to part-time students. *Faculty research:* Greek and Hebrew, theology, spiritual formation, global missions and world Christianity, women in ministry leadership. *Unit head:* Dr. Cornelius Bekker, Dean, 757-352-4401, Fax: 757-352-4597, E-mail: clbekker@regent.edu. *Application contact:* Heidi Cece, Assistant Vice President of Enrollment Management, 800-373-5504, Fax: 757-352-4381, E-mail: admissions@regent.edu.
Website: http://www.regent.edu/sod/

Regent University, Graduate School, School of Education, Virginia Beach, VA 23464-9800. Offers adult education (Ed D, PhD, Ed S); advanced educational leadership (Ed D, PhD, Ed S); career switcher (M Ed); character education (Ed D, PhD, Ed S); Christian education leadership (Ed D, PhD, Ed S); Christian school administration (M Ed); curriculum and instruction (M Ed), including adult education, Christian school, gifted and talented education, STEM education, teacher leader; educational leadership (M Ed); educational psychology (Ed D, PhD, Ed S); educational technology and online learning (Ed D, PhD, Ed S); elementary education (M Ed); exceptional education executive leadership (Ed D, PhD, Ed S); higher education (Ed D, PhD, Ed S); higher education leadership and management (Ed D, PhD, Ed S); individualized degree plan (M Ed); K-12 school leadership (Ed D, PhD, Ed S); K-12 special education (M Ed); K-8 leadership in mathematics education (M Ed); leadership in mathematics education (Ed S); reading specialist (M Ed); special education (Ed D, PhD, Ed S); student affairs (M Ed); TESOL (M Ed), including adult education - collegiate, K-12. *Accreditation:* TEAC. *Program availability:* Part-time, evening/weekend, 100% online, blended/hybrid learning. *Faculty:* 22 full-time (10 women), 42 part-time/adjunct (31 women). *Students:* 89 full-time (62 women), 1,035 part-time (823 women); includes 466 minority (381 Black or African American, non-Hispanic/Latino; 3 American Indian or Alaska Native, non-Hispanic/Latino; 19 Asian, non-Hispanic/Latino; 50 Hispanic/Latino; 13 Two or more races, non-Hispanic/Latino), 11 international. Average age 39. 976 applicants, 59% accepted, 449 enrolled. In 2016, 241 master's, 22 doctorates, 4 other advanced degrees awarded. *Degree requirements:* For master's, thesis or alternative; for doctorate, comprehensive exam, thesis/dissertation. *Entrance requirements:* For master's, Virginia Communication and Literacy Assessment (VCLA), PRAXIS, college transcripts, writing sample, interview; for doctorate, GRE, writing sample, resume, transcripts, interview. Additional exam requirements/recommendations for international students: Required—TOEFL (minimum score 577 paper-based). *Application deadline:* For fall admission, 4/1 priority date for domestic students; for spring admission, 10/15 priority date for domestic students. Applications are processed on a rolling basis. Application fee: $50. Electronic applications accepted. *Expenses:* Contact institution. *Financial support:* In 2016–17, 622 students received support, including 1 fellowship (averaging $5,000 per year); career-related internships or fieldwork, scholarships/grants, and unspecified assistantships also available. Support available to part-time students. *Faculty research:* Christian school administration, curriculum and instruction, educational technology and online learning, higher education, special education. *Unit head:* Dr. Donald Finn, Dean, 757-352-4278, Fax: 757-352-4318, E-mail: dfinn@regent.edu. *Application contact:* Heidi Cece, Assistant Vice President of Enrollment Management, 800-373-5504, Fax: 757-352-4381, E-mail: admissions@regent.edu.
Website: http://www.regent.edu/soe/

Rochester College, Center for Missional Leadership, Rochester Hills, MI 48307-2764. Offers MRE.

St. Augustine's Seminary of Toronto, Graduate and Professional Programs, Scarborough, ON M1M 1M3, Canada. Offers divinity (M Div); lay ministry (Diploma); religious education (MRE); theological studies (MTS, Diploma). *Accreditation:* ATS. *Program availability:* Part-time, evening/weekend. *Entrance requirements:* Additional exam requirements/recommendations for international students: Required—TOEFL (minimum score 580 paper-based), TWE (minimum score 5).

Saint Mary's University of Minnesota, Schools of Graduate and Professional Programs, Graduate School of Education, Institute for LaSallian Studies, Winona, MN 55987-1399. Offers LaSallian leadership (MA); LaSallian studies (MA). Tuition and fees vary according to degree level and program. *Unit head:* Dr. Roxanne Eubank, Director, 612-728-5217, E-mail: reubank@smumn.edu. *Application contact:* James Callinan, Director of Admissions for Graduate and Professional Programs, 612-728-5185, Fax: 612-728-5121, E-mail: jcallina@smumn.edu.
Website: http://www.smumn.edu/graduate-home/areas-of-study/graduate-school-of-education/ma-in-lasallian-studies

Saints Cyril and Methodius Seminary, Graduate and Professional Programs, Orchard Lake, MI 48324. Offers pastoral ministry (MAPM); religious education (MARE); theology (M Div, MA). *Program availability:* Part-time.

Selma University, Graduate Programs, Selma, AL 36701-5299. Offers Bible and Christian education (MA); Bible and pastoral ministry (MA).

Shasta Bible College, Program in Biblical Counseling, Redding, CA 96002. Offers biblical counseling and Christian family life education (MA). *Program availability:* Part-time. *Degree requirements:* For master's, comprehensive exam (for some programs), thesis or alternative. *Entrance requirements:* For master's, minimum GPA of 2.5. Additional exam requirements/recommendations for international students: Required—TOEFL (minimum score 550 paper-based).

Southeastern Baptist Theological Seminary, Graduate and Professional Programs, Wake Forest, NC 27588-1889. Offers advanced biblical studies (M Div); Christian education (M Div, MACE); Christian ethics (PhD); Christian ministry (M Div); Christian planting (M Div); church music (MACM); counseling (MACO); evangelism (PhD); language (M Div); ministry (D Min); New Testament (PhD); Old Testament (PhD); philosophy (PhD); theology (Th M, PhD); women's studies (M Div). *Accreditation:* ACIPE; ATS (one or more programs are accredited). *Degree requirements:* For master's, thesis (for some programs), oral exam; for doctorate, thesis/dissertation, fieldwork. *Entrance requirements:* For master's, Cooperative English Test, minimum GPA of 2.0, M Div or equivalent (Th M); for doctorate, GRE General Test or MAT, Cooperative English Test, M Div or equivalent, 3 years of professional experience.

Southern Adventist University, School of Religion, Collegedale, TN 37315-0370. Offers Biblical and theological studies (MA); church leadership and management (M Min); church ministry and homiletics (M Min); evangelism and world mission (M Min); religious studies (MA). *Program availability:* Part-time. *Degree requirements:* For master's, comprehensive exam, thesis (for some programs). *Entrance requirements:* For master's, GRE. Additional exam requirements/recommendations for international students: Required—TOEFL (minimum score 600 paper-based). *Faculty research:* Biblical archaeology.

Southern Evangelical Seminary, Graduate Programs, Matthews, NC 28105. Offers apologetics (MA, D Min, Certificate); Christian education (MA); church ministry (MA, Certificate); divinity (Certificate), including apologetics (M Div, Certificate); Islamic studies (MA, Certificate); Jewish studies (MA); philosophy (MA); philosophy of religion (PhD); religion (MA); theology (M Div), including apologetics (M Div, Certificate), Biblical studies; youth ministry (MA). *Program availability:* Part-time, evening/weekend, online learning. *Degree requirements:* For master's, thesis (for some programs); for doctorate, 2 foreign languages, comprehensive exam (for some programs), thesis/dissertation. *Entrance requirements:* Additional exam requirements/recommendations for international students: Required—TOEFL (minimum score 600 paper-based).

Southwestern Assemblies of God University, Thomas F. Harrison School of Graduate Studies, Program in Education, Waxahachie, TX 75165-5735. Offers Christian school administration (MS); curriculum development (MS); early education administration (M Ed); middle and secondary education (M Ed). *Degree requirements:* For master's, comprehensive written and oral exams. *Entrance requirements:* For master's, GRE General Test, minimum GPA of 2.5. Electronic applications accepted.

Southwestern Baptist Theological Seminary, Jack D. Terry School of Church and Family Ministries, Fort Worth, TX 76122-0000. Offers MA, MACE, MACSE, DEM, PhD. *Program availability:* Part-time, evening/weekend. Terminal master's awarded for partial completion of doctoral program. *Degree requirements:* For master's, thesis; for doctorate, thesis/dissertation, statistics comprehensive exam. *Entrance requirements:* For doctorate, GRE or MAT, MACE or equivalent, minimum GPA of 3.0. Additional exam requirements/recommendations for international students: Required—TOEFL, TWE. Electronic applications accepted.

Towson University, Baltimore Hebrew Institute, Towson, MD 21252-0001. Offers Jewish communal service (MAJCS, Postbaccalaureate Certificate); Jewish education (Postbaccalaureate Certificate); Jewish studies (MAJS). *Students:* 6 full-time (5 women), 11 part-time (6 women); includes 2 minority (1 Black or African American, non-Hispanic/Latino; 1 Hispanic/Latino), 1 international. *Entrance requirements:* For master's, bachelor's degree, minimum GPA of 3.0, letters of recommendation, statement of intent, sample of work, interview, resume; for Postbaccalaureate Certificate, bachelor's degree, minimum GPA of 3.0, statement of intent, sample of work, interview, 2 letters of recommendation, resume. Additional exam requirements/recommendations for international students: Required—TOEFL. *Application deadline:* Applications are processed on a rolling basis. Application fee: $45. Electronic applications accepted. *Expenses:* Tuition, state resident: full-time $7580; part-time $379 per unit. Tuition, nonresident: full-time $15,700; part-time $785 per unit. *Required fees:* $2480. *Unit head:* Jill Max, Director, 410-704-7120, E-mail: jmax@towson.edu. *Application contact:* Coverley Beidleman, Assistant Director of Graduate Admissions, 410-704-2113, Fax: 410-704-3030, E-mail: grads@towson.edu.
Website: http://www.towson.edu/cla/centers/baltimorehebrewinstitute

Trinity International University, Trinity Evangelical Divinity School, Deerfield, IL 60015-1284. Offers academic ministry (M Div); Biblical and Near Eastern archaeology and languages (MA); chaplaincy and ministry care (MA); Christian studies (Certificate); church and parachurch ministry (M Div); church history (MA, Th M); counseling (Th M); educational ministries (MA); educational ministry (Th M); educational studies (PhD); intercultural studies (MA, PhD); leadership and management (D Min); mental health counseling (MA); military chaplaincy (D Min); ministry (MA); missions (Th M); missions and evangelism (D Min); New Testament (MA, Th M); Old Testament (Th M); Old Testament and Semitic languages (MA); pastoral ministry and care (D Min); pastoral theology (Th M); preaching and teaching (D Min); spiritual formation and education (D Min); systematic theology (MA, Th M); theological studies (MA, PhD); urban ministry (MA). *Program availability:* Part-time, online learning. *Students:* 578 full-time (141 women), 711 part-time (202 women). *Degree requirements:* For master's, comprehensive exam, thesis, fieldwork; for doctorate, comprehensive exam (for some programs), thesis/dissertation; for Certificate, comprehensive exam, integrative papers. *Entrance requirements:* For master's, GRE, MAT, minimum cumulative undergraduate GPA of 3.0; for doctorate, GRE, minimum cumulative graduate GPA of 3.2; for Certificate, GRE, MAT, minimum undergraduate GPA of 2.5. Additional exam requirements/recommendations for international students: Required—TOEFL (minimum score 580 paper-based), TWE (minimum score 4). *Application deadline:* For fall admission, 7/15 priority date for domestic and international students. Applications are processed on a rolling basis. Application fee: $25. Electronic applications accepted. *Expenses: Tuition:* Full-time $19,898. *Required fees:* $200. *Financial support:* Fellowships with partial tuition reimbursements, teaching assistantships with partial tuition reimbursements, career-related internships or fieldwork, Federal Work-Study, scholarships/grants, and tuition waivers (partial) available. Financial award application deadline: 4/1; financial award applicants required to submit FAFSA. *Unit head:* Dr. Tite Tienou, Academic Dean, 847-317-8086, Fax: 847-317-8014, E-mail: ttienou@teds.edu. *Application contact:* Ron Campbell, Director of Admissions, 800-345-8337, Fax: 847-317-8097, E-mail: rcampbel@tiu.edu.
Website: https://divinity.tiu.edu/

Trinity Lutheran Seminary, Graduate and Professional Programs, Columbus, OH 43209-2334. Offers African American studies (MTS); Biblical studies (MTS, STM); Christian education (MA); Christian spirituality (STM); church in the world (MTS); church music (MA); divinity (M Div); general theological studies (MTS); mission and evangelism (STM); pastoral leadership and practice (STM); youth and family ministry (MA); MSN/MTS; MTS/JD. *Accreditation:* ACIPE; ATS. *Program availability:* Part-time. *Degree requirements:* For master's, variable foreign language requirement, comprehensive exam (for some programs), thesis (for some programs), field experience (for some programs). *Entrance requirements:* For master's, BA or equivalent (for MA, M Div, MTS); M Div, MTS, or equivalent (for STM); audition (for MACM). Additional exam requirements/recommendations for international students: Required—TOEFL. Electronic applications accepted. *Expenses:* Contact institution.

Unification Theological Seminary, Graduate Program, Main Campus, Barrytown, NY 12507. Offers divinity (M Div); ministry (D Min); religious education (MRE), including interfaith peacebuilding (MA, MRE); religious studies (MA), including interfaith peacebuilding (MA, MRE), non-profit leadership, theological studies, unification studies. *Program availability:* Part-time, evening/weekend. *Faculty:* 3 full-time (1 woman), 3 part-time/adjunct (0 women). *Students:* 27 full-time (8 women); includes 15 minority (11 Black or African American, non-Hispanic/Latino; 2 Asian, non-Hispanic/Latino; 1 Hispanic/Latino; 1 Two or more races, non-Hispanic/Latino), 6 international. Average age 50. In 2016, 12 master's, 5 doctorates awarded. *Degree requirements:* For master's, variable foreign language requirement, thesis (for some programs); for doctorate, thesis/dissertation. *Entrance requirements:* For master's, bachelor's degree; for doctorate, M Div or equivalency. Additional exam requirements/recommendations for international students: Required—TOEFL (minimum score 450 paper-based; 45 iBT). *Application deadline:* For fall admission, 3/15 priority date for domestic and international students; for spring admission, 9/15 priority date for domestic and international students. Applications are processed on a rolling basis. Application fee: $30. Electronic applications accepted. *Expenses:* Contact institution. *Financial support:* In 2016–17, 2 students received support. Scholarships/grants available. Financial award application deadline: 6/15; financial award applicants required to submit FAFSA. *Faculty research:* Church leadership, church history, world religions, ecumenism, interfaith peace building, service-learning. *Unit head:* Dr. Kathy Winings, Vice-President for Academic Affairs, 845-752-3000 Ext. 228, Fax: 845-752-3014, E-mail: academics@uts.edu. *Application contact:* Henry Christopher, Director of Admissions, 212-563-6647 Ext. 105, Fax: 845-752-3014, E-mail: h.christopher@uts.edu.
Website: http://www.uts.edu

Unification Theological Seminary, New York Extension Center, New York, NY 10036. Offers divinity (M Div); religious education (MRE), including interfaith peacebuilding (MA, MRE); religious studies (MA), including interfaith peacebuilding (MA, MRE), non-profit leadership, theological studies, unification studies. *Program availability:* Part-time, evening/weekend. *Faculty:* 4 full-time (0 women), 7 part-time/adjunct (1 woman). *Students:* 25 full-time (9 women), 23 part-time (6 women); includes 24 minority (8 Black or African American, non-Hispanic/Latino; 9 Asian, non-Hispanic/Latino; 3 Hispanic/Latino; 4 Two or more races, non-Hispanic/Latino), 14 international. Average age 43. *Degree requirements:* For master's, variable foreign language requirement, thesis (for some programs). *Entrance requirements:* For master's, bachelor's degree. Additional exam requirements/recommendations for international students: Required—TOEFL (minimum score 450 paper-based; 45 iBT). *Application deadline:* For fall admission, 8/15 for domestic students, 3/15 priority date for international students; for spring admission, 1/15 for domestic students, 9/15 priority date for international students. Applications are processed on a rolling basis. Application fee: $30. Electronic applications accepted. *Expenses: Tuition:* Full-time $11,760; part-time $490 per credit. *Required fees:* $320; $250 per credit. $125 per semester. Tuition and fees vary according to degree level. *Financial support:* In 2016–17, 48 students received support. Career-related internships or fieldwork, scholarships/grants, tuition waivers (partial), and on-campus employment (for international students) available. Support available to part-time students. Financial award application deadline: 6/15; financial award applicants required to submit FAFSA. *Faculty research:* Church history, world religions, ecumenism, interfaith peace building, service-learning. *Unit head:* Dr. Kathy Winings, Vice-President for Academic Affairs, 212-563-6647 Ext. 101, Fax: 212-563-6431, E-mail: academics@uts.edu. *Application contact:* Joy Theriot, Recruiter, 212-563-6647 Ext. 110, Fax: 212-563-6431, E-mail: j.theriot@uts.edu.
Website: http://www.uts.edu

Union Presbyterian Seminary, Graduate and Professional Programs, Richmond, VA 23227-4597. Offers M Div, MACE, Th M, PhD, M Div/MACE. *Program availability:* Part-time, evening/weekend, online learning. *Degree requirements:* For master's, oral and written exams. *Entrance requirements:* For master's, three references, transcripts, background check; for doctorate, GRE General Test, three references, transcripts, background check, statement of goals, essay. Additional exam requirements/recommendations for international students: Required—TOEFL (minimum score 550 paper-based), TWE (minimum score 4). Electronic applications accepted.

University of Detroit Mercy, College of Liberal Arts and Education, Detroit, MI 48221. Offers addiction counseling (MA); addiction studies (Certificate); clinical mental health counseling (MA); clinical psychology (MA, PhD); computer and information systems (MS); criminal justice (MA); curriculum and instruction (MA); economics (MA); educational administration (MA); financial economics (MA); industrial/organizational psychology (MA); information assurance (MS); intelligence analysis (MS); liberal studies (MALS); religious studies (MA); school counseling (MA, Certificate); school psychology (Spec); security administration (MS); special education: emotionally impaired/behaviorally disordered (MA); special education: learning disabilities (MA). *Program availability:* Part-time, evening/weekend. *Degree requirements:* For doctorate, departmental qualifying exam. *Faculty research:* Psychology of aging, history of technology, Renaissance humanism, U.S. and Japanese economic relations.

University of St. Michael's College, Faculty of Theology, Toronto, ON M5S 1J4, Canada. Offers Catholic leadership (MA); eastern Christian studies (Diploma); religious education (Diploma), theological studies (Diploma); theology (M Div, MA, MRE, MTS, D Min, PhD, Th D); theology and Jewish studies (MA). Th D offered jointly with University of Toronto. *Accreditation:* ATS (one or more programs are accredited). *Program availability:* Part-time. *Degree requirements:* For master's, thesis (for some programs), 1 foreign language (MA), 2 foreign languages (Th M); for doctorate, 3 foreign languages, comprehensive exam, thesis/dissertation; for other advanced degree, thesis optional. *Entrance requirements:* For master's, M Div or BA, course work in an ancient or modern language, minimum GPA of 3.3; for doctorate, MA in theology, Th M, or M Div with thesis, minimum GPA of 3.7; for other advanced degree, minimum GPA of 2.7. Additional exam requirements/recommendations for international students: Required—TOEFL (minimum score 600 paper-based). Electronic applications accepted. *Expenses:* Contact institution. *Faculty research:* Patristics, eastern Christianity, ecology and theology, ecumenism, Jewish Christian studies.

University of St. Thomas, Graduate Studies, The Saint Paul Seminary School of Divinity, St. Paul, MN 55105. Offers pastoral ministry (MAPM); religious education (MARE); theology (MA). *Accreditation:* ACIPE; ATS. *Program availability:* Part-time, evening/weekend. *Degree requirements:* For master's, one foreign language,

comprehensive exam (for some programs), thesis (for some programs). *Entrance requirements:* For master's, GRE, 3 letters of recommendation, interview. Additional exam requirements/recommendations for international students: Required—TOEFL (minimum score 550 paper-based). *Application deadline:* For fall admission, 6/1 priority date for domestic students. Applications are processed on a rolling basis. Application fee: $40. Electronic applications accepted. *Expenses:* Contact institution. *Financial support:* Fellowships, research assistantships, institutionally sponsored loans, and scholarships/grants available. Support available to part-time students. Financial award application deadline: 4/1; financial award applicants required to submit FAFSA. *Faculty research:* Theological education. *Unit head:* Rev. Msgr. Aloysius R. Callaghan, Rector/Vice President, 651-962-5052, Fax: 651-962-5790, E-mail: arcallaghan@stthomas.edu. *Application contact:* Rev. Peter Williams, Vice Rector for Formation, 651-962-5775, Fax: 651-962-5790, E-mail: will2750@stthomas.edu.
Website: http://www.stthomas.edu/spssod/

University of St. Thomas, School of Education and Human Services, Houston, TX 77006-4696. Offers all level education (M Ed); bilingual/dual language (M Ed); Catholic school teaching (M Ed); Catholic/private school leadership (M Ed); counselor education (M Ed); curriculum and instruction (M Ed); education (Ed D); educational leadership (M Ed); elementary teaching (M Ed); English as a second language (M Ed); exceptionality/educational diagnostician (M Ed); exceptionality/special education (M Ed); generalist (M Ed); reading (M Ed); secondary teaching (M Ed); teaching (MAT). *Accreditation:* TEAC. *Program availability:* Part-time, evening/weekend, online learning. *Faculty:* 44 full-time (29 women), 31 part-time/adjunct (17 women). *Students:* 65 full-time (61 women), 719 part-time (645 women); includes 515 minority (169 Black or African American, non-Hispanic/Latino; 25 Asian, non-Hispanic/Latino; 315 Hispanic/Latino; 2 Native Hawaiian or other Pacific Islander, non-Hispanic/Latino; 4 Two or more races, non-Hispanic/Latino), 24 international. Average age 36. 297 applicants, 92% accepted, 211 enrolled. In 2016, 403 master's awarded. *Degree requirements:* For master's, thesis, field experience. *Entrance requirements:* For master's, GRE or MAT if GPA is below 3.0, bachelor's degree; minimum GPA of 2.75 in bachelor's degree or last 60 credit hours; official transcripts from all institutions; goal statement of 250-300 words; 1 reference. Additional exam requirements/recommendations for international students: Required—TOEFL (minimum score 94 iBT), IELTS (minimum score 7), PTE (minimum score 53). *Application deadline:* Applications are processed on a rolling basis. Application fee: $35. Electronic applications accepted. *Expenses:* Contact institution. *Financial support:* In 2016–17, 52 students received support. Federal Work-Study, scholarships/grants, and state work-study, institutional employment available. Support available to part-time students. Financial award application deadline: 4/15; financial award applicants required to submit FAFSA. *Faculty research:* Leadership, diversity, personality traits, second language acquisition. *Unit head:* Dr. Robert LeBlanc, Dean, 713-525-3540, Fax: 713-525-3871, E-mail: education@stthom.edu. *Application contact:* Rita Paredes, Administrative Assistant, 713-525-3442, Fax: 713-525-3871, E-mail: rparede@stthom.edu.
Website: http://www.stthom.edu/Academics/School_of_Education_and_Human_Services/Index.aqf

University of San Francisco, School of Education, Catholic Educational Leadership Program, San Francisco, CA 94117-1080. Offers Catholic school leadership (Ed D). *Program availability:* Part-time, evening/weekend. *Faculty:* 1 (woman) part-time/adjunct. *Students:* 14 full-time (6 women), 15 part-time (6 women); includes 6 minority (1 Black or African American, non-Hispanic/Latino; 2 Asian, non-Hispanic/Latino; 2 Hispanic/Latino; 1 Two or more races, non-Hispanic/Latino), 7 international. Average age 38. 7 applicants, 100% accepted, 4 enrolled. In 2016, 16 master's, 5 doctorates awarded. *Degree requirements:* For doctorate, thesis/dissertation. *Entrance requirements:* Additional exam requirements/recommendations for international students: Required—TOEFL, IELTS, PTE. Application fee: $55 ($65 for international students). Electronic applications accepted. *Expenses: Tuition:* Full-time $23,310; part-time $1295 per credit. Tuition and fees vary according to course load, degree level, campus/location and program. *Financial support:* In 2016–17, 9 students received support. Fellowships, research assistantships, and teaching assistantships available. Financial award application deadline: 3/2; financial award applicants required to submit FAFSA. *Unit head:* Dr. Patricia Mitchell, Chair, 415-422-6226. *Application contact:* Peter Cole, Admission Coordinator, 415-422-5467, E-mail: schoolofeducation@usfca.edu.
Website: https://www.usfca.edu/catalog/graduate/school-of-education/programs-catholic-educational-leadership

Walsh University, Graduate Programs, Master of Arts in Theology Program, North Canton, OH 44720-3396. Offers parish administration (MA); pastoral ministry (MA); religious education (MA). *Program availability:* Part-time, evening/weekend. *Faculty:* 4 full-time (0 women). *Students:* 5 full-time (2 women), 10 part-time (3 women); includes 1 minority (Black or African American, non-Hispanic/Latino), 1 international. Average age 41. 6 applicants, 67% accepted, 4 enrolled. In 2016, 7 master's awarded. *Degree requirements:* For master's, thesis or alternative, culminating assignment. *Entrance requirements:* For master's, MAT or GRE (minimum scores: Verbal 145, Quantitative 146, Combined 291, Writing 3.0), minimum GPA of 3.0. Additional exam requirements/recommendations for international students: Required—TOEFL. *Application deadline:* For fall admission, 7/15 for domestic students. Applications are processed on a rolling basis. Application fee: $25. Electronic applications accepted. Application fee is waived when completed online. *Expenses:* $332 per credit hour tuition. *Financial support:* Research assistantships available. Financial award application deadline: 12/31; financial award applicants required to submit FAFSA. *Faculty research:* Cardinal Newman, phenomenological method, Flavius Josephus, post-conciliar moral teaching. *Unit head:* Dr. Bradley Beach, Chair, 330-244-4732, Fax: 330-244-4955, E-mail: bbeach@walsh.edu. *Application contact:* Audra Dice, Graduate Admissions Counselor, 330-490-7181, Fax: 330-244-4925, E-mail: adice@walsh.edu.

Wesley Biblical Seminary, Graduate Programs, Jackson, MS 39206. Offers apologetics (MA); Biblical languages (M Div); Biblical literature (MA); Christian studies (MA); context and mission (M Div); honors research (M Div); interpretation (M Div); ministry (M Div); spiritual formation (M Div); teaching (M Div); theology (MA). *Accreditation:* ATS. *Program availability:* Part-time. *Degree requirements:* For master's, thesis. *Entrance requirements:* Additional exam requirements/recommendations for international students: Required—TOEFL. Electronic applications accepted. *Faculty research:* Patristics, missiology, culture, hermeneutics.

Wheaton College, Graduate School, Department of Christian Formation and Ministry, Wheaton, IL 60187-5593. Offers MA. *Program availability:* Part-time. *Faculty:* 1 full-time (0 women). *Students:* 25 full-time (19 women), 23 part-time (11 women); includes 8 minority (2 Black or African American, non-Hispanic/Latino; 1 Asian, non-Hispanic/Latino; 3 Hispanic/Latino; 2 Two or more races, non-Hispanic/Latino), 4 international. Average age 27. 33 applicants, 94% accepted, 15 enrolled. In 2016, 17 master's awarded. *Degree requirements:* For master's, thesis or alternative. *Entrance requirements:* For master's, GRE General Test or MAT. Additional exam requirements/recommendations for international students: Required—TOEFL (minimum score 550 paper-based; 80 iBT), IELTS (minimum score 6.5). *Application deadline:* For fall admission, 5/1 for domestic students, 1/1 for international students; for spring admission, 11/1 for domestic students. Applications are processed on a rolling basis. Application fee: $30. Electronic applications accepted. *Expenses: Tuition:* Full-time $19,080; part-time $795 per credit hour. Tuition and fees vary according to degree level and program. *Financial support:* Career-related internships or fieldwork, scholarships/grants, and unspecified assistantships available. Financial award application deadline: 3/1; financial award applicants required to submit FAFSA. *Unit head:* Dr. Laura Barwegen, Chair, 630-752-5196, E-mail: cfm@wheaton.edu. *Application contact:* Dusty Di Santo, Director of Graduate Admissions, 630-752-5195, Fax: 630-752-7047, E-mail: graduate.admissions@wheaton.edu.
Website: http://www.wheaton.edu/Academics/Departments/CFM/MA-in-CFM

Xavier University, College of Arts and Sciences, Department of Theology, Cincinnati, OH 45207. Offers health care mission integration (MA); theology (MA), including religious education, social and pastoral ministry, theology. *Program availability:* Part-time, evening/weekend. *Degree requirements:* For master's, final paper (or thesis) and defense or comprehension exam. *Entrance requirements:* For master's, MAT or GRE, 2 letters of recommendation; statement of reasons and goals for enrolling in program (1,000-2,000 words); resume; transcript. Additional exam requirements/recommendations for international students: Required—TOEFL (minimum score 550 paper-based; 79 iBT). Electronic applications accepted. Application fee is waived when completed online. *Expenses:* Contact institution. *Faculty research:* Scripture, ethics, constructive theology, historical theology.

Yeshiva University, Azrieli Graduate School of Jewish Education and Administration, New York, NY 10033-4391. Offers MS, Ed D, Specialist. *Accreditation:* TEAC. *Program availability:* Part-time, evening/weekend. Terminal master's awarded for partial completion of doctoral program. *Degree requirements:* For master's, one foreign language, student teaching experience, comprehensive exam or thesis; for doctorate, one foreign language, comprehensive exam, thesis/dissertation, certifying exams, internship; for Specialist, one foreign language, comprehensive exam, certifying exams, internship. *Entrance requirements:* For master's, GRE General Test, BA in Jewish studies or equivalent; for doctorate and Specialist, GRE General Test, master's degree in Jewish education, 2 years of teaching experience. *Expenses:* Contact institution. *Faculty research:* Social patterns of American and Israeli Jewish population, special education, adult education, technology in education, return to religious values.

Science Education

Acadia University, Faculty of Professional Studies, School of Education, Program in Curriculum Studies, Wolfville, NS B4P 2R6, Canada. Offers cultural and media studies (M Ed); learning and technology (M Ed); science, math and technology (M Ed). *Program availability:* Part-time. *Degree requirements:* For master's, thesis optional. *Entrance requirements:* For master's, B Ed or the equivalent, minimum B average in undergraduate course work, 2 years of teaching experience. Additional exam requirements/recommendations for international students: Required—TOEFL (minimum score 580 paper-based; 93 iBT), IELTS (minimum score 6.5). *Faculty research:* Literacy development, postmodern philosophy and curriculum theory, historiography, philosophy of education, learning and technology.

Alabama Agricultural and Mechanical University, School of Graduate Studies, College of Education, Humanities, and Behavioral Sciences, Department of Educational Leadership and Secondary Education, Huntsville, AL 35811. Offers biology (M Ed); business/marketing education (M Ed, Ed S); chemistry (M Ed); collaborative teacher secondary education (M Ed, Ed S); education (M Ed, Ed S); English language arts (M Ed); family/consumer science education (M Ed, Ed S); general science (M Ed); general social science (M Ed); mathematics (M Ed, Ed S); physics (M Ed, Ed S); technology education (M Ed). *Accreditation:* NCATE. *Program availability:* Evening/weekend. *Degree requirements:* For master's, comprehensive exam; for Ed S, thesis. *Entrance requirements:* For master's, GRE General Test. Additional exam requirements/recommendations for international students: Required—TOEFL (minimum score 500 paper-based; 61 iBT). *Application deadline:* For fall admission, 5/1 for domestic students. Applications are processed on a rolling basis. Application fee: $25. Electronic applications accepted. *Expenses:* Tuition, nonresident: part-time $826 per credit hour. Full-time tuition and fees vary according to course load and program. *Financial support:* Research assistantships, career-related internships or fieldwork, Federal Work-Study, institutionally sponsored loans, and traineeships available. Financial award application deadline: 4/1. *Faculty research:* World peace through education, computer-assisted instruction. *Unit head:* Dr. Derrick Davis, Chair, 256-372-4047, Fax: 256-372-5526.

Alabama State University, College of Education, Department of Curriculum and Instruction, Montgomery, AL 36101-0271. Offers early childhood education (M Ed, Ed S); elementary education (M Ed, Ed S); secondary education (M Ed, Ed S), including biology education, English language arts education (M Ed), history education, math education, music education (M Ed), reading education (M Ed), social science education; special education (M Ed). *Program availability:* Part-time. *Faculty:* 7 full-time (4 women), 7 part-time/adjunct (4 women). *Students:* 37 full-time (30 women), 82 part-time (69 women); includes 117 minority (115 Black or African American, non-Hispanic/Latino; 2 Two or more races, non-Hispanic/Latino). Average age 33. 65 applicants, 55% accepted, 22 enrolled. In 2016, 25 master's, 5 Ed Ss awarded. *Degree requirements:* For master's, comprehensive exam, thesis optional; for Ed S, comprehensive exam, thesis. *Entrance requirements:* For master's, GRE General Test, MAT, writing competency test; for Ed S, writing competency test, GRE, MAT. Additional exam requirements/recommendations for international students: Required—TOEFL (minimum score 500 paper-based). *Application deadline:* For fall admission, 4/15 for domestic and international students; for spring admission, 11/15 for domestic and international students; for summer admission, 3/15 for domestic and international students. Applications are processed on a rolling basis. Application fee: $25. Electronic applications accepted. *Expenses:* Tuition, state resident: full-time $3087; part-time $2744 per credit. Tuition, nonresident: full-time $6174; part-time $5488 per credit. *Required fees:* $2284; $1142 per credit. $571 per semester. Tuition and fees vary

according to class time, course level, course load, degree level, program and student level. *Financial support:* Research assistantships available. Financial award application deadline: 6/30; financial award applicants required to submit FAFSA. *Unit head:* Dr. Joyce Johnson, Acting Chairperson, 334-229-4485, Fax: 334-229-5603, E-mail: jjohnson@alasu.edu. *Application contact:* Dr. William Person, Dean of Graduate Studies, 334-229-4274, Fax: 334-229-4928, E-mail: wperson@alasu.edu.
Website: http://www.alasu.edu/academics/colleges—departments/college-of-education/curriculum—instruction/index.aspx

Alverno College, School of Education, Milwaukee, WI 53234-3922. Offers adaptive education (MA); administrative leadership (MA); adult education and organizational development (MA); adult educational and instructional design (MA); adult educational and instructional technology (MA); global connections in the humanities (MA); instructional leadership (MA); instructional technology for K-12 settings (MA); professional development (MA); reading education (MA); reading education with adaptive education (MA); science education (MA); special education (MA); teaching in alternative schools (MA). *Accreditation:* NCATE. *Program availability:* Part-time, evening/weekend. *Faculty:* 4 full-time (3 women), 23 part-time/adjunct (17 women). *Students:* 58 full-time (57 women), 62 part-time (54 women); includes 32 minority (22 Black or African American, non-Hispanic/Latino; 2 Asian, non-Hispanic/Latino; 8 Hispanic/Latino), 1 international. Average age 39. 77 applicants, 99% accepted, 61 enrolled. In 2016, 85 master's awarded. *Degree requirements:* For master's, presentation/defense of proposal, conference presentation of inquiry projects. *Entrance requirements:* For master's, bachelor's degree in related field, communication samples from work setting, 3 letters of recommendation. Additional exam requirements/recommendations for international students: Required—TOEFL. *Application deadline:* For fall admission, 7/15 priority date for domestic and international students; for spring admission, 12/15 priority date for domestic and international students. Applications are processed on a rolling basis. Application fee: $0. Electronic applications accepted. *Expenses:* Contact institution. *Financial support:* In 2016–17, 17 students received support. Federal Work-Study and scholarships/grants available. Support available to part-time students. Financial award applicants required to submit FAFSA. *Faculty research:* Student self-assessment, self-reflection, integration of curriculum, identifying needs of students in strategic situations and designing appropriate classroom strategies. *Unit head:* Dr. Desiree Pointer Mace, Associate Dean, Graduate Program, 414-382-6345, Fax: 414-382-6332, E-mail: desiree.pointer-mace@alverno.edu. *Application contact:* Katie Kipp, Graduate Admissions Counselor, 414-382-6045, Fax: 414-382-6354, E-mail: katie.kipp@alverno.edu.

American University of Puerto Rico, Program in Education, Bayamon, PR 00960-2037. Offers art education (M Ed); elementary education 4-6 (M Ed); elementary education K-3 (M Ed); general science education (M Ed); physical education (M Ed); special education (M Ed). *Program availability:* Part-time, evening/weekend. *Faculty:* 17 part-time/adjunct (7 women). *Students:* 22 full-time (18 women), 54 part-time (42 women); all minorities (all Hispanic/Latino). Average age 33. 22 applicants, 86% accepted, 19 enrolled. In 2016, 53 master's awarded. *Entrance requirements:* For master's, EXADEP, GRE, or MAT, 2 letters of recommendation, minimum GPA of 2.5. *Application deadline:* For fall admission, 8/1 for domestic students; for winter admission, 10/18 for domestic students; for spring admission, 3/15 for domestic students. Applications are processed on a rolling basis. Application fee: $25. *Financial support:* In 2016–17, 79 students received support, including 76 fellowships (averaging $400 per year), 55 teaching assistantships (averaging $1,741 per year). Financial award applicants required to submit FAFSA. *Unit head:* Prof. Bolivar Ramirez-Carlo, III, Dean of Faculty, 787-620-2040 Ext. 2010, Fax: 787-620-2958, E-mail: bramirez@aupr.edu. *Application contact:* Keren I. Llanos-Figueroa, Information Contact, 787-620-2040 Ext. 2021, Fax: 787-785-7377, E-mail: oficnaadmisiones@aupr.edu.

Andrews University, School of Graduate Studies, College of Arts and Sciences, Department of Biology, Berrien Springs, MI 49104. Offers MAT, MS. *Faculty:* 7 full-time (3 women). *Students:* 5 full-time (4 women), 1 international. Average age 31. In 2016, 2 master's awarded. *Degree requirements:* For master's, comprehensive exam, thesis. *Entrance requirements:* For master's, GRE Subject Test. Additional exam requirements/recommendations for international students: Required—TOEFL (minimum score 550 paper-based). *Application deadline:* Applications are processed on a rolling basis. Application fee: $40. *Financial support:* Fellowships, research assistantships, teaching assistantships, career-related internships or fieldwork, Federal Work-Study, and institutionally sponsored loans available. Financial award application deadline: 3/15. *Faculty research:* Manatee habitat characterization, seabird habitat dynamics. *Unit head:* Dr. Thomas Goodwin, Chairman, 269-471-3243. *Application contact:* Justina Clayburn, Supervisor of Graduate Admission, 800-253-2874, Fax: 269-471-6321, E-mail: graduate@andrews.edu.

Andrews University, School of Graduate Studies, School of Education, Department of Teaching, Learning, and Curriculum, Berrien Springs, MI 49104. Offers curriculum and instruction (MA, Ed D, PhD, Ed S); elementary education (MAT); secondary education (MAT), including biology, education, English, English as a second language, French, history, physics; teacher education (MAT). *Faculty:* 7 full-time (5 women). *Students:* 17 full-time (12 women), 10 part-time (all women); includes 11 minority (6 Black or African American, non-Hispanic/Latino; 5 Hispanic/Latino), 7 international. Average age 38. In 2016, 9 master's, 7 doctorates awarded. *Entrance requirements:* For master's, GRE Subject Test. Additional exam requirements/recommendations for international students: Required—TOEFL (minimum score 550 paper-based). *Application deadline:* For fall admission, 8/15 for domestic students. Applications are processed on a rolling basis. Application fee: $40. *Unit head:* Dr. Lee C. Davidson, Chair, 269-471-6364. *Application contact:* Justina Clayburn, Supervisor of Graduate Admission, 800-253-2874, Fax: 269-471-6321, E-mail: graduate@andrews.edu.

Angelo State University, College of Graduate Studies and Research, College of Science and Engineering, Department of Biology, San Angelo, TX 76909. Offers biology (MS); science education (MS). *Program availability:* Part-time, evening/weekend. *Students:* 4 full-time (1 woman), 11 part-time (8 women). Average age 25. *Degree requirements:* For master's, comprehensive exam, thesis optional. *Entrance requirements:* For master's, GRE General Test, essay. Additional exam requirements/recommendations for international students: Required—TOEFL or IELTS. *Application deadline:* For fall admission, 7/15 priority date for domestic students, 6/10 for international students; for spring admission, 12/1 priority date for domestic students, 11/1 for international students. Applications are processed on a rolling basis. Application fee: $40 ($50 for international students). Electronic applications accepted. *Expenses:* Tuition, state resident: full-time $3726; part-time $2484 per year. Tuition, nonresident: full-time $10,746; part-time $7164 per year. *Required fees:* $2538; $1702 per unit. *Financial support:* Research assistantships, teaching assistantships, career-related internships or fieldwork, Federal Work-Study, scholarships/grants, and unspecified assistantships available. Support available to part-time students. Financial award application deadline: 3/1. *Faculty research:* Texas poppy-mallow project, Chisos hedgehog cactus, skunks, reptiles, amphibians, rodents, seed germination, mammals. *Unit head:* Dr. Russell Wilke, Chair, 325-486-6638, Fax: 325-942-2184, E-mail: russell.wilke@angelo.edu. *Application contact:* Dr. Russell Wilke, Chair, 325-486-6638, Fax: 325-942-2184, E-mail: russell.wilke@angelo.edu.
Website: http://www.angelo.edu/dept/biology/

Antioch University New England, Graduate School, Department of Education, Integrated Learning Program, Keene, NH 03431-3552. Offers early childhood education (M Ed); elementary education (M Ed), including arts and humanities, science and environmental education; special education (M Ed). *Degree requirements:* For master's, internship. *Entrance requirements:* For master's, previous course work or work experience in education. Additional exam requirements/recommendations for international students: Required—TOEFL (minimum score 550 paper-based). Electronic applications accepted. *Expenses:* Contact institution. *Faculty research:* Problem-based learning, place-based education, mathematics education, democratic classrooms, art education.

Antioch University New England, Graduate School, Department of Environmental Studies, Science Teacher Certification Program, Keene, NH 03431-3552. Offers MS. *Degree requirements:* For master's, practicum, seminar, student teaching. *Entrance requirements:* Additional exam requirements/recommendations for international students: Required—TOEFL (minimum score 550 paper-based). Electronic applications accepted.

Appalachian State University, Cratis D. Williams Graduate School, Department of Curriculum and Instruction, Boone, NC 28608. Offers curriculum specialist (MA); educational media (MA); elementary education (MA); middle grades education (MA), including language arts, mathematics, science, social studies. *Accreditation:* NCATE. *Program availability:* Part-time, evening/weekend, online learning. *Degree requirements:* For master's, comprehensive exam, thesis or alternative. *Entrance requirements:* For master's, GRE General Test or MAT, 3 letters of recommendation. Additional exam requirements/recommendations for international students: Required—TOEFL (minimum score 570 paper-based; 79 iBT), IELTS (minimum score 6.5). *Application deadline:* For fall admission, 3/14 for domestic students, 2/1 for international students; for spring admission, 11/1 for domestic students, 7/1 for international students. Applications are processed on a rolling basis. Application fee: $55. Electronic applications accepted. *Expenses:* Tuition, state resident: full-time $4744. Tuition, nonresident: full-time $17,913. Full-time tuition and fees vary according to program. *Financial support:* Fellowships, research assistantships, teaching assistantships, career-related internships or fieldwork, Federal Work-Study, scholarships/grants, and unspecified assistantships available. Financial award application deadline: 4/1; financial award applicants required to submit FAFSA. *Faculty research:* Media literacy, elementary teaching, curriculum development, online learning environments. *Unit head:* Dr. Michael Jacobson, Chairperson, 828-262-2224. *Application contact:* Dr. Chrystal Dean, Program Director, 828-262-8009, E-mail: deanco@appstate.edu.
Website: http://www.ced.appstate.edu/departments/ci

Arcadia University, School of Education, Glenside, PA 19038-3295. Offers art education (M Ed); computer education (CAS); curriculum (CAS); curriculum studies (M Ed); early childhood education (M Ed), including individualized, master teacher, research in child development; educational leadership (M Ed, Ed D, CAS); elementary education (M Ed); English education (MA Ed); environmental education (MA Ed); instructional technology (M Ed); language arts (M Ed); library science (M Ed); mathematics education (M Ed, MA Ed); music education (MA Ed); psychology (MA Ed); reading (M Ed, CAS); science education (M Ed, CAS); secondary education (M Ed, CAS); special education (M Ed, Ed D, CAS); theater arts (MA Ed); written communication (MA Ed). *Accreditation:* NASAD. *Program availability:* Part-time, evening/weekend, online learning. *Faculty:* 19 full-time (13 women), 3 part-time/adjunct (all women). *Students:* 22 full-time (16 women), 356 part-time (284 women); includes 84 minority (55 Black or African American, non-Hispanic/Latino; 2 American Indian or Alaska Native, non-Hispanic/Latino; 13 Asian, non-Hispanic/Latino; 11 Hispanic/Latino; 3 Two or more races, non-Hispanic/Latino), 4 international. Average age 34. 145 applicants, 73% accepted, 80 enrolled. In 2016, 95 master's, 11 doctorates awarded. *Application deadline:* Applications are processed on a rolling basis. Application fee: $50. Electronic applications accepted. *Expenses:* Contact institution. *Financial support:* Career-related internships or fieldwork, tuition waivers (partial), and unspecified assistantships available. *Unit head:* John T Groves, Interim Dean of the School of Education, 215-572-2940. *Application contact:* 215-572-2925, Fax: 215-572-2126, E-mail: grad@arcadia.edu.

Arkansas State University, Graduate School, College of Sciences and Mathematics, Department of Biological Sciences, State University, AR 72467. Offers biological sciences (MA); biology (MS); biology education (MSE, SCCT); biotechnology (PSM). *Program availability:* Part-time. *Degree requirements:* For master's, comprehensive exam, thesis (for some programs); for SCCT, comprehensive exam. *Entrance requirements:* For master's, GRE General Test, appropriate bachelor's degree, letters of reference, interview, official transcripts, immunization records, statement of educational objectives and career goals, teaching certificate (for MSE); for SCCT, GRE General Test or MAT, interview, master's degree, letters of reference, official transcript, personal statement, immunization records. Additional exam requirements/recommendations for international students: Required—TOEFL (minimum score 550 paper-based; 79 iBT), IELTS (minimum score 6), PTE (minimum score 56). Electronic applications accepted.

Arkansas State University, Graduate School, College of Sciences and Mathematics, Department of Chemistry and Physics, State University, AR 72467. Offers chemistry (MS); chemistry education (MSE, SCCT). *Program availability:* Part-time. *Degree requirements:* For master's, comprehensive exam, thesis or alternative; for SCCT, comprehensive exam. *Entrance requirements:* For master's, GRE General Test or MAT, appropriate bachelor's degree, official transcript, immunization records, valid teaching certificate (for MSE); for SCCT, GRE General Test or MAT, interview, master's degree, official transcript, immunization records. Additional exam requirements/recommendations for international students: Required—TOEFL (minimum score 550 paper-based; 79 iBT), IELTS (minimum score 6), PTE (minimum score 56). Electronic applications accepted.

Asbury University, School of Graduate and Professional Studies, Wilmore, KY 40390-1198. Offers biology: alternative certificate (MA Ed); chemistry: alternative certificate (MA Ed); English (MA Ed); English as a second language (MA Ed); ESL (MA Ed); French (MA Ed); Latin: alternative certificate (MA Ed); mathematics: alternative certificate (MA Ed); reading/writing endorsement (MA Ed); social studies (MA Ed); social work (MSW), including child and family services; Spanish (MA Ed); special education (MA Ed); special education: alternative certificate (MA Ed); teacher as leader endorsement (MA Ed). *Accreditation:* NCATE. *Program availability:* Part-time. *Degree requirements:* For master's, action research project, portfolio. *Entrance requirements:* For master's, PRAXIS/NTE, minimum GPA of 2.75, letters of recommendation. Additional exam requirements/recommendations for international students: Required—TOEFL (minimum score 550 paper-based). Electronic applications accepted.

Athabasca University, Faculty of Science and Technology, Athabasca, AB T9S 3A3, Canada. Offers architecture (Postgraduate Diploma); information systems (M Sc). *Program availability:* Part-time, online learning. *Degree requirements:* For master's, thesis optional. *Entrance requirements:* For master's, B Sc in computing or other bachelor's degree and IT experience. Electronic applications accepted. *Expenses:*

Contact institution. *Faculty research:* Distributed systems multimedia, computer science education, e-services.

Augustana University, MA in Education Program, Sioux Falls, SD 57197. Offers instructional strategies (MA); reading (MA); special populations (MA); STEM (MA); technology (MA). *Accreditation:* NCATE. *Program availability:* Part-time, evening/weekend, online only, 100% online. *Degree requirements:* For master's, thesis. *Entrance requirements:* For master's, appropriate bachelor's degree, minimum GPA of 3.0, teaching certificate. Additional exam requirements/recommendations for international students: Required—TOEFL (minimum score 550 paper-based). *Application deadline:* For fall admission, 8/1 for domestic and international students; for spring admission, 11/1 for domestic and international students; for summer admission, 4/1 for domestic and international students. Applications are processed on a rolling basis. Application fee: $50. Electronic applications accepted. *Expenses:* Contact institution. *Financial support:* Application deadline: 3/1; applicants required to submit FAFSA. *Unit head:* Dr. Laurie Daily, Chair, 605-274-5211, E-mail: laurie.daily@augie.edu. *Application contact:* Jody Nitz, Graduate Coordinator, 605-274-4043, Fax: 605-274-4450, E-mail: graduate@augie.edu.
Website: http://www.augie.edu/master-arts-education

Bard College, Master of Arts in Teaching Program, Annandale-on-Hudson, NY 12504. Offers secondary education (MAT), including biology, history, literature, mathematics, Spanish; MS/MAT. *Program availability:* Part-time. *Degree requirements:* For master's, year-long teaching residencies in area middle and high schools. *Entrance requirements:* For master's, GRE General Test, resume, 3 letters of recommendation, personal statement, official transcripts. Additional exam requirements/recommendations for international students: Required—TOEFL. *Application deadline:* For winter admission, 1/30 priority date for domestic students; for spring admission, 4/27 for domestic students, 4/30 for international students. Applications are processed on a rolling basis. Application fee: $65. Electronic applications accepted. Application fee is waived when completed online. *Financial support:* Fellowships, institutionally sponsored loans, and scholarships/grants available. Support available to part-time students. Financial award application deadline: 4/28; financial award applicants required to submit FAFSA. *Unit head:* Derek Furr, Director, 845-758-7136, Fax: 845-758-7149, E-mail: mat@bard.edu. *Application contact:* Cecilia Maple, Assistant Director for Admission and Student Affairs, 845-758-7145, E-mail: mat@bard.edu.
Website: http://www.bard.edu/mat/ny

Benedictine University, Graduate Programs, Program in Science Content and Process, Lisle, IL 60532. Offers MS. *Application deadline:* For fall admission, 9/1 for domestic students; for winter admission, 12/1 for domestic students; for spring admission, 2/15 for domestic students. Application fee: $40. *Expenses: Tuition:* Full-time $15,600; part-time $650 per hour. *Required fees:* $300. One-time fee: $125 part-time. Tuition and fees vary according to class time, course load, campus/location and program. *Unit head:* Dr. Allison Wilson, Director, 630-829-6520, E-mail: awilson@ben.edu. *Application contact:* Kari Gibbons, Associate Vice President, Enrollment Center, 630-829-6200, Fax: 630-829-6584, E-mail: kgibbons@ben.edu.

Binghamton University, State University of New York, Graduate School, Graduate School of Education, Program in Adolescence Education, Binghamton, NY 13902-6000. Offers biology education (MAT, MS Ed); chemistry education (MAT, MS Ed); earth science education (MAT, MS Ed); English education (MAT, MS Ed); French education (MAT, MS Ed); literacy education (MS Ed); mathematical sciences education (MAT, MS Ed); physics (MAT, MS Ed); social studies (MAT, MS Ed); Spanish education (MAT, MS Ed). *Accreditation:* TEAC. *Program availability:* Part-time, evening/weekend. *Students:* 59 full-time (36 women), 7 part-time (2 women); includes 10 minority (2 Black or African American, non-Hispanic/Latino; 1 American Indian or Alaska Native, non-Hispanic/Latino; 1 Asian, non-Hispanic/Latino; 5 Hispanic/Latino; 1 Two or more races, non-Hispanic/Latino). Average age 26. 46 applicants, 76% accepted, 25 enrolled. In 2016, 26 master's awarded. *Degree requirements:* For master's, portfolio. *Entrance requirements:* For master's, GRE General Test, teaching certification. Additional exam requirements/recommendations for international students: Required—TOEFL (minimum score 550 paper-based; 80 iBT). *Application deadline:* For fall admission, 2/1 priority date for domestic and international students; for spring admission, 10/15 priority date for domestic and international students. Application fee: $75. Electronic applications accepted. *Financial support:* In 2016–17, 6 students received support. Research assistantships, teaching assistantships, career-related internships or fieldwork, Federal Work-Study, institutionally sponsored loans, scholarships/grants, health care benefits, tuition waivers (full and partial), and unspecified assistantships available. Financial award applicants required to submit FAFSA. *Unit head:* Dr. Susan Strehle, Dean, 607-777-7329, E-mail: sstrehle@binghamton.edu. *Application contact:* Ben Balkaya, Assistant Dean and Director, 607-777-2151, Fax: 607-777-2501, E-mail: balkaya@binghamton.edu.

Biola University, School of Arts and Sciences, La Mirada, CA 90639-0001. Offers Christian apologetics (MA, Certificate); science and religion (MA); speech language pathology (MA). *Program availability:* Part-time, evening/weekend, online learning. *Entrance requirements:* For master's, minimum GPA of 3.0, bachelor's degree from accredited college or university (in science-related field for science and religion program). Additional exam requirements/recommendations for international students: Required—TOEFL (minimum score 600 paper-based; 100 iBT). Electronic applications accepted. *Faculty research:* Apologetics, science and religion, intelligent design.

Bloomsburg University of Pennsylvania, School of Graduate Studies, College of Education, Department of Teaching and Learning, Program in Middle Level Education Grades 4-8, Bloomsburg, PA 17815-1301. Offers language arts (M Ed); math (M Ed); science (M Ed); social studies (M Ed). *Accreditation:* NCATE. *Faculty:* 6 full-time (1 woman). *Students:* 3 applicants, 67% accepted. In 2016, 2 master's awarded. *Degree requirements:* For master's, thesis optional, practicum, student teaching. *Entrance requirements:* For master's, MAT, GRE, or PRAXIS, minimum QPA of 3.0, teaching certificate, U.S. citizenship, related undergraduate coursework, professional liability insurance, recent TB test. Additional exam requirements/recommendations for international students: Required—TOEFL (minimum score 550 paper-based), IELTS. *Application deadline:* Applications are processed on a rolling basis. Application fee: $35 ($60 for international students). Electronic applications accepted. *Expenses:* Tuition, state resident: full-time $9660; part-time $483 per credit. Tuition, nonresident: full-time $14,500; part-time $725 per credit. *Required fees:* $2410; $107 per credit. $75 per term. Tuition and fees vary according to course load, degree level and program. *Financial support:* Federal Work-Study and unspecified assistantships available. Financial award applicants required to submit FAFSA. *Unit head:* Dr. Ingrid Everett, Program Coordinator, 570-389-5120, Fax: 570-389-3030, E-mail: ieverett@bloomu.edu. *Application contact:* Jennifer Kessler, Administrative Assistant, 570-389-4015, Fax: 570-389-3054, E-mail: jkessler@bloomu.edu.
Website: http://www.bloomu.edu/gradschool/middle-level-education

Boise State University, College of Arts and Sciences, Department of Geosciences, Boise, ID 83725-1535. Offers earth science (M E Sci); geophysics (MS, PhD); geosciences (MS, PhD); hydrology (MS). *Program availability:* Part-time. *Faculty:* 20. *Students:* 52 full-time (21 women), 13 part-time (3 women); includes 7 minority (1 Black or African American, non-Hispanic/Latino; 5 Hispanic/Latino; 1 Two or more races, non-Hispanic/Latino), 7 international. Average age 29. 73 applicants, 29% accepted, 14 enrolled. In 2016, 4 master's, 1 doctorate awarded. Terminal master's awarded for partial completion of doctoral program. *Degree requirements:* For master's, thesis (for some programs); for doctorate, thesis/dissertation. *Entrance requirements:* For master's, GRE General Test, BS in related field, minimum GPA of 3.0; for doctorate, GRE General Test. Additional exam requirements/recommendations for international students: Required—TOEFL (minimum score 550 paper-based; 80 iBT), IELTS (minimum score 6). *Application deadline:* For fall admission, 2/1 for domestic and international students; for spring admission, 10/15 for domestic and international students. Application fee: $65 ($95 for international students). Electronic applications accepted. *Expenses:* Tuition, state resident: full-time $6058; part-time $358 per credit hour. Tuition, nonresident: full-time $20,108; part-time $608 per credit hour. *Required fees:* $2108. Tuition and fees vary according to program. *Financial support:* In 2016–17, 6 students received support, including 17 research assistantships with full tuition reimbursements available (averaging $10,119 per year), 15 teaching assistantships (averaging $9,024 per year); scholarships/grants and unspecified assistantships also available. Financial award application deadline: 2/1; financial award applicants required to submit FAFSA. *Faculty research:* Seismology, geothermal aquifers, sedimentation, tectonics, seismo-acoustic propagation. *Unit head:* Dr. James McNamara, Department Chair, 208-426-1354, E-mail: jmcnamar@boisestate.edu. *Application contact:* Dr. Mark Schmitz, Graduate Program Coordinator, 208-426-5907, E-mail: markschmitz@boisestate.edu. Website: http://earth.boisestate.edu/degrees/graduate/

Boston College, Graduate School of Arts and Sciences, Department of Chemistry, Chestnut Hill, MA 02467-3800. Offers biochemistry (PhD); inorganic chemistry (PhD); organic chemistry (PhD); physical chemistry (PhD); science education (MST). *Faculty:* 23 full-time. *Students:* 121 full-time (55 women); includes 14 minority (1 Black or African American, non-Hispanic/Latino; 8 Asian, non-Hispanic/Latino; 4 Hispanic/Latino; 1 Two or more races, non-Hispanic/Latino), 55 international. 215 applicants, 33% accepted, 24 enrolled. In 2016, 5 master's, 16 doctorates awarded. *Degree requirements:* For doctorate, thesis/dissertation, qualifying exam. *Entrance requirements:* For doctorate, GRE General Test, GRE Subject Test. Additional exam requirements/recommendations for international students: Required—TOEFL (minimum score 600 paper-based; 100 iBT), IELTS (minimum score 8). *Application deadline:* For fall admission, 1/2 for domestic and international students. Application fee: $75. Electronic applications accepted. Tuition and fees vary according to program. *Financial support:* In 2016–17, 121 students received support, including fellowships with full tuition reimbursements available (averaging $30,000 per year), research assistantships with full tuition reimbursements available (averaging $30,000 per year), teaching assistantships with full tuition reimbursements available (averaging $30,000 per year); Federal Work-Study, scholarships/grants, health care benefits, and unspecified assistantships also available. Support available to part-time students. Financial award application deadline: 1/2. *Faculty research:* Organic and organometallic chemistry, chemical biology and biochemistry, physical and theoretical chemistry, inorganic chemistry. *Unit head:* Dr. Marc Snapper, Chairperson, 617-552-8.96, E-mail: marc.snapper@bc.edu. *Application contact:* Dr. Jianmin Gao, Graduate Program Director, 617-552-0326, Fax: 617-552-0833, E-mail: gaojc@bc.edu. Website: http://www.bc.edu/chemistry

Bowling Green State University, Graduate College, College of Arts and Sciences, Department of Physics and Astronomy, Bowling Green, OH 43403. Offers geophysics (MS); physics (MAT, MS). *Degree requirements:* For master's, thesis or alternative. *Entrance requirements:* For master's, GRE General Test. Additional exam requirements/recommendations for international students: Required—TOEFL. *Application deadline:* For fall admission, 2/15 priority date for domestic students. Application fee: $30. Electronic applications accepted. *Financial support:* Research assistantships with full tuition reimbursements, teaching assistantships with full tuition reimbursements, career-related internships or fieldwork, institutionally sponsored loans, and unspecified assistantships available. Financial award applicants required to submit FAFSA. *Faculty research:* Computational physics, solid-state physics, materials science, theoretical physics. *Unit head:* Dr. John Laird, Chair, 419-372-7244. *Application contact:* Dr. Lewis Fulcher, Graduate Coordinator, 419-372-2635.

Bridgewater State University, College of Graduate Studies, Bartlett College of Science and Mathematics, Department of Biological Sciences, Bridgewater, MA 02325. Offers biology (MAT). *Program availability:* Part-time, evening/weekend. *Entrance requirements:* For master's, GRE General Test.

Bridgewater State University, College of Graduate Studies, Bartlett College of Science and Mathematics, Department of Physics, Bridgewater, MA 02325. Offers MAT. *Accreditation:* NCATE. *Program availability:* Part-time, evening/weekend. *Entrance requirements:* For master's, GRE General Test.

Bridgewater State University, College of Graduate Studies, College of Humanities and Social Sciences, Program in Physical Sciences, Bridgewater, MA 02325. Offers MAT. *Accreditation:* NCATE. *Program availability:* Part-time, evening/weekend. *Entrance requirements:* For master's, GRE General Test.

Brigham Young University, Graduate Studies, College of Life Sciences, Department of Biology, Provo, UT 84602. Offers biological science education (MS); biology (MS, PhD). *Faculty:* 23 full-time (2 women). *Students:* 37 full-time (13 women); includes 5 minority (3 Hispanic/Latino; 2 Native Hawaiian or other Pacific Islander, non-Hispanic/Latino), 4 international. Average age 29. 24 applicants, 50% accepted, 8 enrolled. In 2016, 3 master's, 6 doctorates awarded. *Degree requirements:* For master's, comprehensive exam, thesis, prospectus, defense of research, defense of thesis; for doctorate, comprehensive exam, thesis/dissertation, prospectus, defense of research, defense of dissertation. *Entrance requirements:* For master's and doctorate, GRE General Test, minimum cumulative GPA of 3.0 for undergraduate degree. Additional exam requirements/recommendations for international students: Required—TOEFL (minimum score 580 paper-based; 85 iBT). *Application deadline:* For fall admission, 1/15 for domestic and international students. Application fee: $50. Electronic applications accepted. *Expenses:* Contact institution. *Financial support:* In 2016–17, 32 students received support, including 3 fellowships with full and partial tuition reimbursements available (averaging $25,000 per year), 26 research assistantships with full and partial tuition reimbursements available (averaging $6,645 per year), 31 teaching assistantships with full and partial tuition reimbursements available (averaging $6,612 per year); career-related internships or fieldwork, institutionally sponsored loans, scholarships/grants, health care benefits, tuition waivers (full and partial), and unspecified assistantships also available. Financial award application deadline: 3/1; financial award applicants required to submit FAFSA. *Faculty research:* Systematics, bioinformatics, ecology, evolution. *Total annual research expenditures:* $1.8 million. *Unit head:* Dr. Dennis K. Shiozawa, Chair, 801-422-4972, Fax: 801-422-0004, E-mail: dennis_shiozawa@byu.edu. *Application contact:* Gentri Glaittli, Graduate Program Manager, 801-422-7137, Fax: 801-422-0004, E-mail: biogradmanager@byu.edu.
Website: http://biology.byu.edu/

Brooklyn College of the City University of New York, School of Education, Program in Adolescence Science Education and Special Subjects, Brooklyn, NY 11210-2889. Offers adolescence science education (MAT); biology teacher (7-12) (MA); chemistry teacher (7-12) (MA); earth science teacher (7-12) (MAT); English teacher (7-12) (MA); French teacher (7-12) (MA); mathematics teacher (7-12) (MA); music teacher (MA);

physics teacher (7-12) (MA); social studies teacher (7-12) (MA); Spanish teacher (7-12) (MA). *Program availability:* Part-time, evening/weekend. *Degree requirements:* For master's, comprehensive exam (for some programs), thesis (for some programs). *Entrance requirements:* For master's, LAST, previous course work in education, resume, 2 letters of recommendation, essay. Additional exam requirements/recommendations for international students: Required—TOEFL (minimum score 500 paper-based; 61 iBT). Electronic applications accepted. *Faculty research:* Interdisciplinary education, semiotics, discourse analysis, autobiography, teacher identity.

Brooklyn College of the City University of New York, School of Education, Program in Childhood Education, Brooklyn, NY 11210-2889. Offers bilingual education (MS Ed); liberal arts (MS Ed); mathematics (MS Ed); science and environmental education (MS Ed). *Program availability:* Part-time, evening/weekend. *Entrance requirements:* For master's, LAST, interview, previous course work in education, writing sample, resume, 2 letters of recommendation. Additional exam requirements/recommendations for international students: Required—TOEFL (minimum score 500 paper-based; 61 iBT). Electronic applications accepted. *Faculty research:* Emotional intelligence, multiculturalism, arts immersion, the Holocaust.

Brooklyn College of the City University of New York, School of Education, Program in Middle Childhood Science Education, Brooklyn, NY 11210-2889. Offers biology (MA); chemistry (MA); earth science (MA); general science (MA); physics (MA). *Program availability:* Part-time, evening/weekend. *Entrance requirements:* For master's, LAST, interview, previous course work in education and mathematics, resume, 2 letters of recommendation, essay. Additional exam requirements/recommendations for international students: Required—TOEFL (minimum score 500 paper-based; 61 iBT). Electronic applications accepted. *Faculty research:* Geometric thinking, mastery of basic facts, problem-solving strategies, history of mathematics.

Brown University, Graduate School, Department of Education, Program in Teaching, Providence, RI 02912. Offers elementary education (MAT); English (MAT); history/social studies (MAT); science (MAT); secondary education (MAT). *Degree requirements:* For master's, student teaching, portfolio. *Entrance requirements:* For master's, GRE General Test, transcript, personal statement, 3 letters of recommendation, interview, writing sample (English applicants only). Additional exam requirements/recommendations for international students: Required—TOEFL (minimum score 577 paper-based). Electronic applications accepted. *Faculty research:* Literacy, English language learners, diversity, special education, biodiversity.

Buffalo State College, State University of New York, The Graduate School, Faculty of Natural and Social Sciences, Department of Biology, Buffalo, NY 14222-1095. Offers biology (MA); secondary education (MS Ed), including biology. *Program availability:* Evening/weekend. *Degree requirements:* For master's, thesis (for some programs), project. *Entrance requirements:* For master's, minimum GPA of 2.75. Additional exam requirements/recommendations for international students: Required—TOEFL (minimum score 550 paper-based).

Buffalo State College, State University of New York, The Graduate School, Faculty of Natural and Social Sciences, Department of Chemistry, Buffalo, NY 14222-1095. Offers chemistry (MA); secondary education (MS Ed), including chemistry. *Program availability:* Part-time, evening/weekend. *Degree requirements:* For master's, thesis (for some programs), project. *Entrance requirements:* For master's, minimum GPA of 2.6, New York teaching certificate (MS Ed). Additional exam requirements/recommendations for international students: Required—TOEFL (minimum score 550 paper-based).

Buffalo State College, State University of New York, The Graduate School, Faculty of Natural and Social Sciences, Department of Earth Science and Science Education, Buffalo, NY 14222-1095. Offers secondary education (MS Ed), including geoscience, science. *Accreditation:* NCATE. *Program availability:* Part-time, evening/weekend. *Degree requirements:* For master's, thesis or alternative, project. *Entrance requirements:* For master's, 36 undergraduate hours in mathematics and science. Additional exam requirements/recommendations for international students: Required—TOEFL (minimum score 550 paper-based).

Buffalo State College, State University of New York, The Graduate School, Faculty of Natural and Social Sciences, Department of Physics, Buffalo, NY 14222-1095. Offers secondary education physics (MS Ed). *Degree requirements:* For master's, project. *Entrance requirements:* For master's, minimum GPA of 2.5, New York State teaching certification. Additional exam requirements/recommendations for international students: Required—TOEFL (minimum score 550 paper-based).

California Baptist University, Program in Education, Riverside, CA 92504-3206. Offers educational leadership (MS); educational leadership for faith-based institutions (MS); educational leadership for public institutions (MS); educational technology (MS); instructional computer applications (MS); international education (MS); leadership and adult learning (MS); leadership and organizational studies (MS); online teaching and learning (MS); reading (MS); science education (MA); special education in mild/moderate disabilities (MS); special education in moderate/severe disabilities (MS); teacher leadership (MS); teaching (MS); teaching and learning (MS). *Program availability:* Part-time, evening/weekend, 100% online, blended/hybrid learning. *Faculty:* 20 full-time (8 women), 11 part-time/adjunct (7 women). *Students:* 191 full-time (148 women), 234 part-time (178 women); includes 194 minority (23 Black or African American, non-Hispanic/Latino; 5 American Indian or Alaska Native, non-Hispanic/Latino; 15 Asian, non-Hispanic/Latino; 131 Hispanic/Latino; 4 Native Hawaiian or other Pacific Islander, non-Hispanic/Latino; 16 Two or more races, non-Hispanic/Latino), 2 international. Average age 31. 277 applicants, 61% accepted, 150 enrolled. In 2016, 280 master's awarded. *Degree requirements:* For master's, comprehensive exam, project, or thesis. *Entrance requirements:* For master's, minimum undergraduate GPA of 2.75; 500-word essay; three letters of recommendation; two prerequisite courses completed with minimum C grade. Additional exam requirements/recommendations for international students: Required—TOEFL (minimum score 80 iBT). *Application deadline:* For fall admission, 8/1 priority date for domestic students, 7/1 for international students; for spring admission, 12/1 priority date for domestic students, 11/1 for international students. Applications are processed on a rolling basis. Application fee: $45. Electronic applications accepted. *Expenses:* Contact institution. *Financial support:* In 2016–17, 162 students received support. Federal Work-Study and scholarships/grants available. Financial award applicants required to submit CSS PROFILE or FAFSA. *Faculty research:* Leadership development, complexity theory, faith and learning, special education, social and philosophical contexts of education. *Unit head:* Dr. John Shoup, Dean, School of Education, 951-343-4516, E-mail: jshoup@calbaptist.edu.
Website: http://www.calbaptist.edu/mastersined/

California State University, Bakersfield, Division of Graduate Studies, School of Natural Sciences, Mathematics, and Engineering, Program in Geological Sciences, Bakersfield, CA 93311. Offers geological sciences (MS); hydrogeology (MS); petroleum geology (MS); science education (MS). *Program availability:* Part-time, evening/weekend. *Students:* 7 full-time (1 woman), 17 part-time (4 women); includes 11 minority (1 Black or African American, non-Hispanic/Latino; 3 Asian, non-Hispanic/Latino; 6 Hispanic/Latino; 1 Two or more races, non-Hispanic/Latino). Average age 30. 11 applicants, 82% accepted, 7 enrolled. In 2016, 21 master's awarded. *Degree requirements:* For master's, thesis. *Entrance requirements:* For master's, GRE General Test, BS in geology. *Application deadline:* Applications are processed on a rolling basis. Application fee: $55. *Expenses:* Tuition, state resident: full-time $2246; part-time $1302 per semester. *Financial support:* In 2016–17, fellowships (averaging $1,850 per year) were awarded; Federal Work-Study, scholarships/grants, and tuition waivers (full and partial) also available. Financial award application deadline: 3/2; financial award applicants required to submit FAFSA. *Unit head:* Dr. William Krugh, Graduate Coordinator, 661-654-3126, Fax: 661-664-2040, E-mail: wkrugh@csub.edu. *Application contact:* Debbie Blowers, Assistant Director of Admissions and Evaluations, 661-664-3381, E-mail: dblowers@csub.edu.
Website: https://www.csub.edu/geology/Academic%20Programs%20in%20Geology/Graduate%20Students/index.html

California State University, Dominguez Hills, College of Education, Division of Graduate Education, Program in Curriculum and Instruction: Science Education, Carson, CA 90747-0001. Offers MA. *Program availability:* Part-time, evening/weekend. *Degree requirements:* For master's, comprehensive exam. *Entrance requirements:* For master's, minimum GPA of 2.75. Additional exam requirements/recommendations for international students: Required—TOEFL.

California State University, Fullerton, Graduate Studies, College of Natural Science and Mathematics, Program in Science Education, Fullerton, CA 92834-9480. Offers teaching science (MAT). *Program availability:* Part-time. *Degree requirements:* For master's, project or thesis. *Entrance requirements:* For master's, diagnostic exam, minimum GPA of 2.5 in last 60 units of course work, teaching credential, bachelor's degree in science. Application fee: $55. *Expenses:* Tuition, state resident: full-time $3369; part-time $1953 per unit. Tuition, nonresident: full-time $3915; part-time $2499 per unit. Tuition and fees vary according to course load, degree level and program. *Financial support:* Teaching assistantships, career-related internships or fieldwork, Federal Work-Study, institutionally sponsored loans, and scholarships/grants available. Support available to part-time students. Financial award application deadline: 3/1; financial award applicants required to submit FAFSA. *Faculty research:* Earth and space science education. *Unit head:* Monica Azimioara, Director, 657-278-2817. *Application contact:* Admissions/Applications, 657-278-2731.

California State University, Long Beach, Graduate Studies, College of Natural Sciences and Mathematics, Department of Science Education, Long Beach, CA 90840. Offers MS. *Unit head:* Laura Henriques, Chair, 562-985-4801, E-mail: lhenriqu@csulb.edu. *Application contact:* Dr. Henry Fung, Associate Dean for Curriculum and Instruction, 562-985-7898, Fax: 562-985-2315, E-mail: hcfung@csulb.edu.
Website: http://www.cnsm.csulb.edu/depts/scied/

California State University, Northridge, Graduate Studies, Michael D. Eisner College of Education, Department of Secondary Education, Northridge, CA 91330. Offers educational technology (MA); English education (MA); mathematics education (MA); secondary science education (MA); teaching and learning (MA). *Accreditation:* NCATE. *Program availability:* Part-time. *Faculty:* 10 full-time (5 women), 50 part-time/adjunct (24 women). *Students:* 17 full-time (10 women), 87 part-time (55 women); includes 41 minority (3 Black or African American, non-Hispanic/Latino; 11 Asian, non-Hispanic/Latino; 24 Hispanic/Latino; 1 Native Hawaiian or other Pacific Islander, non-Hispanic/Latino; 2 Two or more races, non-Hispanic/Latino), 4 international. Average age 37. 80 applicants, 80% accepted, 50 enrolled. *Degree requirements:* For master's, thesis optional. *Entrance requirements:* For master's, GRE General Test or minimum GPA of 3.0. Additional exam requirements/recommendations for international students: Required—TOEFL. *Application deadline:* For fall admission, 11/30 for domestic students. Application fee: $55. *Expenses:* Tuition, state resident: full-time $4152. *Financial support:* Application deadline: 3/1. *Unit head:* Dr. Julie Gainsburg, Chair, 818-677-2580. *Application contact:* Dr. Michael Rivas, Graduate Advisor, 818-677-6792, E-mail: michael.rivas@csun.edu.
Website: http://www.csun.edu/eisner-education/secondary-education

Cambridge College, School of Education, Cambridge, MA 02138-5304. Offers autism specialist (M Ed); autism/behavior analyst (M Ed); behavior analyst (Post-Master's Certificate); behavioral management (M Ed); early childhood teacher (M Ed); education specialist in curriculum and instruction (CAGS); educational leadership (Ed D); elementary teacher (M Ed); English as a second language (M Ed, Certificate); general science (M Ed); health education (Post-Master's Certificate); health/family and consumer sciences (M Ed); history (M Ed); individualized (M Ed); information technology literacy (M Ed); instructional technology (M Ed); interdisciplinary studies (M Ed); library teacher (M Ed); literacy education (M Ed); mathematics (M Ed); mathematics specialist (Certificate); middle school mathematics and science (M Ed); school administration (M Ed, CAGS); school guidance counselor (M Ed); school nurse education (M Ed); school social worker/school adjustment counselor (M Ed); special education administrator (CAGS); special education/moderate disabilities (M Ed); teaching skills and methodologies (M Ed). *Program availability:* Part-time, evening/weekend, online learning. *Degree requirements:* For master's, thesis, internship/practicum (licensure program only); for doctorate, thesis/dissertation; for other advanced degree, thesis. *Entrance requirements:* For master's, interview, resume, documentation of licensure, 2 professional references; for doctorate, official transcripts, interview, resume, documentation of licensure (if any), written personal statement/essay, portfolio of scholarly and professional work, qualifying assessment, 2 professional references, health insurance, immunizations form; for other advanced degree, official transcripts, interview, resume, documentation of licensure (if any), written personal statement/essay, 2 professional references, health insurance, immunizations form. Additional exam requirements/recommendations for international students: Required—TOEFL (minimum score 550 paper-based; 79 iBT), Michigan English Language Assessment Battery (minimum score 85); Recommended—IELTS (minimum score 6). Electronic applications accepted. *Expenses:* Contact institution. *Faculty research:* Adult education, accelerated learning, mathematics education, brain compatible learning, special education and law.

Caribbean University, Graduate School, Bayamón, PR 00960-0493. Offers administration and supervision (MA Ed); criminal justice (MA); curriculum and instruction (MA Ed, PhD), including elementary education (MA Ed), English education (MA Ed), history education (MA Ed), mathematics education (MA Ed), primary education (MA Ed), science education (MA Ed), Spanish education (MA Ed); educational technology in instructional systems (MA Ed); gerontology (MSN); human resources (MBA); museology, archiving and art history (MA Ed); neonatal pediatrics (MSN); physical education (MA Ed); special education (MA Ed). *Entrance requirements:* For master's, interview, minimum GPA of 2.5.

Carthage College, Division of Teacher Education, Kenosha, WI 53140. Offers classroom guidance and counseling (M Ed); creative arts (M Ed); gifted and talented children (M Ed); language arts (M Ed); modern language (M Ed); natural sciences (M Ed); reading (M Ed, Certificate); social sciences (M Ed); teacher leadership (M Ed). *Program availability:* Part-time, evening/weekend. *Degree requirements:* For master's, thesis optional. *Entrance requirements:* For master's, MAT, minimum B average, letters of reference.

Science Education

Catawba College, Department of Teacher Education, Salisbury, NC 28144-2488. Offers elementary education (M Ed); STEM education (M Ed). *Accreditation:* NCATE. *Program availability:* Part-time-only. *Faculty:* 4 full-time (3 women), 1 part-time/adjunct (0 women). *Students:* 9 part-time (all women). Average age 30. 9 applicants, 100% accepted, 9 enrolled. In 2016, 3 master's awarded. *Degree requirements:* For master's, portfolio. *Entrance requirements:* For master's, NTE, PRAXIS II, minimum undergraduate GPA of 3.0, valid teaching license, official transcripts, 3 references, essay, interview, practicing teacher. *Application deadline:* For spring admission, 10/1 for domestic students. Applications are processed on a rolling basis. Application fee: $25. Electronic applications accepted. *Expenses:* $185 per semester hour; $25 per semester parking fee. *Financial support:* In 2016–17, 9 students received support. Scholarships/grants and free tuition (for Rowan-Salisbury teachers only) available. Financial award application deadline: 10/1. *Unit head:* Dr. Kimberly Creamer, Director, Graduate Program, 704-637-4462, Fax: 704-637-4732, E-mail: kcreamer14@catawba.edu. *Application contact:* Jane V. Snider, Administrative Assistant, 704-637-4461, Fax: 704-637-4732, E-mail: jvsnider@catawba.edu.
Website: http://catawba.edu/academics/schools/education/teacher-education/

Central Connecticut State University, School of Graduate Studies, School of Engineering, Science and Technology, Department of Geological Sciences, New Britain, CT 06050-4010. Offers STEM education (MS). *Program availability:* Part-time, evening/weekend. *Degree requirements:* For master's, thesis or alternative, special project. *Entrance requirements:* For master's, minimum undergraduate GPA of 2.7. Additional exam requirements/recommendations for international students: Required—TOEFL (minimum score 550 paper-based; 79 iBT). *Application deadline:* For fall admission, 6/1 for domestic students, 5/1 for international students; for spring admission, 11/1 for domestic and international students. Applications are processed on a rolling basis. Application fee: $50. Electronic applications accepted. *Expenses: Tuition, area resident:* Full-time $6497; part-time $606 per credit. Tuition, state resident: full-time $9748; part-time $622 per credit. Tuition, nonresident: full-time $18,102; part-time $622 per credit. *Required fees:* $4459; $246 per credit. *Financial support:* Application deadline: 3/1; applicants required to submit FAFSA. *Unit head:* Dr. Mark Evans, Chair, 860-832-2930, E-mail: evansmaa@ccsu.edu. *Application contact:* Patricia Gardner, Associate Director of Graduate Studies, 860-832-2350, Fax: 860-832-2362.
Website: http://www.ccsu.edu/geolsci/

Central Connecticut State University, School of Graduate Studies, School of Engineering, Science and Technology, Department of Technology and Engineering Education, New Britain, CT 06050-4010. Offers STEM education (MS). *Program availability:* Part-time, evening/weekend. *Faculty:* 4 full-time (1 woman). *Students:* 4 full-time (1 woman), 50 part-time (24 women); includes 1 minority (Hispanic/Latino). Average age 36. 17 applicants, 82% accepted, 10 enrolled. In 2016, 4 master's awarded. *Degree requirements:* For master's, thesis or alternative, special project. *Entrance requirements:* For master's, minimum undergraduate GPA of 2.7. Additional exam requirements/recommendations for international students: Required—TOEFL (minimum score 550 paper-based; 79 iBT). *Application deadline:* For fall admission, 6/1 for domestic students, 5/1 for international students; for spring admission, 11/1 for domestic and international students. Applications are processed on a rolling basis. Application fee: $50. Electronic applications accepted. *Expenses: Tuition, area resident:* Full-time $6497; part-time $606 per credit. Tuition, state resident: full-time $9748; part-time $622 per credit. Tuition, nonresident: full-time $18,102; part-time $622 per credit. *Required fees:* $4459; $246 per credit. *Financial support:* In 2016–17, 7 students received support. Career-related internships or fieldwork, Federal Work-Study, and scholarships/grants available. Support available to part-time students. Financial award application deadline: 3/1; financial award applicants required to submit FAFSA. *Faculty research:* Instruction, curriculum development, administration, occupational training. *Unit head:* Dr. James DeLaura, Chair, 860-832-1850, E-mail: delaura@ccsu.edu. *Application contact:* Patricia Gardner, Associate Director of Graduate Studies, 860-832-2350, Fax: 860-832-2362.
Website: http://www.ccsu.edu/teched/

Central Michigan University, College of Graduate Studies, College of Science and Technology, Department of Chemistry, Mount Pleasant, MI 48859. Offers chemistry (MS); teaching chemistry (MA), including teaching college chemistry, teaching high school chemistry. *Program availability:* Part-time. *Degree requirements:* For master's, comprehensive exam, thesis or alternative. *Entrance requirements:* For master's, GRE. Electronic applications accepted. *Faculty research:* Analytical and organic-inorganic chemistry, biochemistry, catalysis, dendrimer and polymer studies, nanotechnology.

Chatham University, Program in Education, Pittsburgh, PA 15232-2826. Offers early childhood education (MAT); elementary education (MAT); environmental education (K-12) (MAT); secondary art (MAT); secondary biology education (MAT); secondary chemistry education (MAT); secondary English education (MAT); secondary math education (MAT); secondary physics education (MAT); secondary social studies education (MAT); special education (MAT). *Degree requirements:* For master's, thesis, teaching experience. *Entrance requirements:* For master's, minimum GPA of 3.0, sample of written work, recommendation letters. Additional exam requirements/recommendations for international students: Required—TOEFL (minimum score 600 paper-based; 100 iBT), IELTS (minimum score 7), TWE. Electronic applications accepted. Application fee is waived when completed online. *Expenses: Tuition:* Full-time $16,254; part-time $903 per credit hour. *Required fees:* $468; $26 per credit hour. *Faculty research:* Gifted education, environmental education, technology in education, writing as learning, class size and achievement.

The Citadel, The Military College of South Carolina, Citadel Graduate College, Zucker Family School of Education, Charleston, SC 29409. Offers elementary/secondary school administration and supervision (M Ed); elementary/secondary school counseling (M Ed); interdisciplinary STEM education (M Ed); literacy education (M Ed, Graduate Certificate); middle grades (MAT), including English, mathematics, science, social studies; physical education (grades K-12) (MAT); school superintendency (Ed S); secondary education (MAT), including biology, English, mathematics, social studies; student affairs (Graduate Certificate); student affairs and college counseling (M Ed). *Accreditation:* NCATE. *Program availability:* Part-time, evening/weekend, 100% online, blended/hybrid learning. *Faculty:* 9 full-time (4 women), 9 part-time/adjunct (5 women). *Students:* 70 full-time (58 women), 249 part-time (200 women); includes 87 minority (70 Black or African American, non-Hispanic/Latino; 1 Asian, non-Hispanic/Latino; 9 Hispanic/Latino; 7 Two or more races, non-Hispanic/Latino), 2 international. 146 applicants, 98% accepted, 105 enrolled. In 2016, 85 master's, 7 other advanced degrees awarded. *Degree requirements:* For master's, comprehensive exam (for some programs). *Entrance requirements:* For master's, GRE (minimum combined verbal and quantitative score of 290) or MAT (minimum score 396). Additional exam requirements/recommendations for international students: Required—TOEFL (minimum score 550 paper-based; 79 iBT). *Application deadline:* Applications are processed on a rolling basis. Application fee: $40. Electronic applications accepted. *Expenses:* Tuition, state resident: full-time $5121; part-time $569 per credit hour. Tuition, nonresident: full-time $8613; part-time $957 per credit hour. *Required fees:* $90 per term. *Financial support:* Fellowships and unspecified assistantships available. Support available to part-time students. Financial award application deadline: 7/1; financial award applicants required to submit FAFSA. *Unit head:* Dr. Larry G. Daniel, Dean, 843-953-5097, E-mail: ldaniel@citadel.edu. *Application contact:* Dr. Tammy J. Graham, Associate Professor, 843-953-6854, E-mail: tammy.graham@citadel.edu.
Website: http://www.citadel.edu/root/education-graduate-programs

City College of the City University of New York, Graduate School, School of Education, Department of Secondary Education, Program in Science Education, New York, NY 10031-9198. Offers MA. *Accreditation:* NCATE. *Entrance requirements:* For master's, Liberal Arts and Sciences Test (LAST), Content Specialty Test (CST). Additional exam requirements/recommendations for international students: Required—TOEFL. Tuition and fees vary according to course load, degree level and program.

Clarion University of Pennsylvania, Office of Transfer, Adult and Graduate Admissions, Master of Education Program, Clarion, PA 16214. Offers curriculum and instruction (M Ed); early childhood (M Ed); math education (M Ed); reading (M Ed); science education (M Ed); special education (M Ed); technology (M Ed). *Accreditation:* NCATE. *Program availability:* Part-time, evening/weekend, 100% online, blended/hybrid learning. *Faculty:* 12 full-time (8 women), 5 part-time/adjunct (all women). *Students:* 17 full-time (15 women), 97 part-time (78 women); includes 1 minority (Two or more races, non-Hispanic/Latino). Average age 29. 76 applicants, 99% accepted, 48 enrolled. In 2016, 34 master's awarded. *Degree requirements:* For master's, comprehensive exam, thesis, or portfolio. *Entrance requirements:* For master's, minimum QPA of 3.0. Additional exam requirements/recommendations for international students: Required—TOEFL (minimum score 550 paper-based; 80 iBT), IELTS (minimum score 7). *Application deadline:* For fall admission, 8/1 for domestic students, 4/15 for international students; for spring admission, 8/1 for domestic students, 9/15 for international students. Applications are processed on a rolling basis. Application fee: $40. Electronic applications accepted. *Expenses:* $632.35 per credit. *Financial support:* Career-related internships or fieldwork, Federal Work-Study, scholarships/grants, and unspecified assistantships available. Support available to part-time students. Financial award application deadline: 3/1; financial award applicants required to submit FAFSA. *Unit head:* Dr. John McCullough, Chair, Department of Education, 814-393-2104, Fax: 814-393-2446, E-mail: gradstudies@clarion.edu. *Application contact:* Dana Bearer, Associate Director for Transfer, Adult, and Graduate Programs, 814-393-2337, Fax: 814-393-2722, E-mail: gradstudies@clarion.edu.

Clark Atlanta University, School of Education, Department of Curriculum, Atlanta, GA 30314. Offers special education general curriculum (MA); teaching math and science (MAT). *Program availability:* Part-time. *Faculty:* 2 full-time (both women), 1 part-time/adjunct (0 women). *Students:* 6 full-time (1 woman), 2 part-time (1 woman); includes 6 minority (all Black or African American, non-Hispanic/Latino), 1 international. Average age 34. 17 applicants, 76% accepted, 2 enrolled. In 2016, 2 master's awarded. *Degree requirements:* For master's, one foreign language, comprehensive exam. *Entrance requirements:* For master's, GRE General Test, minimum undergraduate GPA of 2.6. Additional exam requirements/recommendations for international students: Required—TOEFL (minimum score 500 paper-based; 61 iBT). *Application deadline:* For fall admission, 4/1 for domestic and international students; for spring admission, 11/1 for domestic and international students. Applications are processed on a rolling basis. Application fee: $40 ($55 for international students). *Expenses: Tuition:* Full-time $15,498; part-time $861 per credit hour. *Required fees:* $1326; $1326 per credit hour. Tuition and fees vary according to course load. *Financial support:* Career-related internships or fieldwork, Federal Work-Study, scholarships/grants, and unspecified assistantships available. Support available to part-time students. Financial award application deadline: 4/30; financial award applicants required to submit FAFSA. *Unit head:* Dr. James Young, Chairperson, 404-880-6079, E-mail: jyoung@cau.edu. *Application contact:* Graduate Program Admissions, 404-880-8483, E-mail: graduateadmissions@cau.edu.
Website: http://www.cau.edu/school-of-education/Dept-of-Curriculum-and-Instruction/index.html

Clemson University, Graduate School, College of Education, Department of Teaching and Learning, Program in Secondary Math and Science, Clemson, SC 29634. Offers MAT. *Accreditation:* NCATE. *Faculty:* 15 full-time (12 women). *Students:* 13 full-time (10 women); includes 1 minority (Black or African American, non-Hispanic/Latino). Average age 28. In 2016, 16 master's awarded. *Degree requirements:* For master's, comprehensive exam, student teaching. *Entrance requirements:* For master's, GRE General Test, unofficial transcripts, letters of recommendation. Additional exam requirements/recommendations for international students: Required—TOEFL (minimum score 540 paper-based; 80 iBT). *Application deadline:* For fall admission, 4/1 for domestic and international students. Applications are processed on a rolling basis. Application fee: $80 ($90 for international students). Electronic applications accepted. *Expenses:* $4,841 per semester full-time resident, $9,640 per semester full-time non-resident, $612 per credit hour part-time resident, $1,223 per credit hour part-time non-resident. *Financial support:* In 2016–17, 10 students received support, including 10 fellowships with partial tuition reimbursements available (averaging $6,862 per year). Financial award application deadline: 4/1. *Faculty research:* Hegemony, culture and mathematics; representations in science education, pre-service science teacher preparation, developing standards-based mathematics pedagogy, environmental sustainability perspectives. *Unit head:* Dr. Jeff Marshall, Department Chair, 864-656-2059, E-mail: marsha9@clemson.edu. *Application contact:* Alison Search, Student Services Coordinator, 864-250-8880, E-mail: alisonp@clemson.edu.
Website: http://www.clemson.edu/education/academics/masters-specialist-programs/masters-education-arts-teaching-mat-secondary-math-science/index.html

Clemson University, Graduate School, College of Education, Department of Teaching and Learning, Program in Teaching and Learning, Clemson, SC 29634. Offers science, technology, engineering, arts and mathematics education (Certificate); teaching and learning (M Ed), including early childhood, instructional coaching, science, technology, engineering, arts and mathematics. *Program availability:* Part-time, evening/weekend, online only, 100% online. *Faculty:* 24 full-time (19 women). *Students:* 19 part-time (17 women); includes 1 minority (Hispanic/Latino). Average age 32. 4 applicants, 50% accepted, 2 enrolled. In 2016, 27 master's awarded. *Entrance requirements:* For master's, GRE General Test, unofficial transcripts, teaching certificate, letters of recommendation. Additional exam requirements/recommendations for international students: Required—TOEFL (minimum score 80 iBT), IELTS (minimum score 7). *Application deadline:* Applications are processed on a rolling basis. Application fee: $80 ($90 for international students). Electronic applications accepted. *Expenses:* $394 per credit hour; $10 per credit hour information technology fee; $17 fee per session for matriculation and software; $22 fee for activities and career services for students taking over 6 credit hours. *Unit head:* Dr. Jeff Marshall, Department Head, Fax: 864-656-0311, E-mail: soedean@clemson.edu. *Application contact:* Julie Jones, Student Services Program Coordinator, 864-656-5096, E-mail: jgambre@clemson.edu.
Website: http://www.clemson.edu/education/academics/masters-specialist-programs/masters-education-teaching-learning/index.html

Clemson University, Graduate School, College of Engineering, Computing and Applied Sciences, Department of Engineering and Science Education, Clemson, SC 29634. Offers PhD, Certificate. *Faculty:* 5 full-time (all women). *Students:* 11 full-time (9 women), 1 part-time (0 women), 1 international. Average age 28. 2 applicants, 100%

accepted, 2 enrolled. In 2016, 7 doctorates awarded. *Degree requirements:* For doctorate, comprehensive exam, thesis/dissertation, qualifying exam. *Entrance requirements:* For doctorate and Certificate, GRE General Test, unofficial transcripts, letters of recommendation. Additional exam requirements/recommendations for international students: Required—TOEFL (minimum score 550 paper-based; 80 iBT), IELTS (minimum score 6.5). *Application deadline:* Applications are processed on a rolling basis. Application fee: $80 ($90 for international students). Electronic applications accepted. *Expenses:* $4,841 per semester full-time resident, $9,640 per semester full-time non-resident, $612 per credit hour part-time resident, $1,223 per credit hour part-time non-resident. *Financial support:* In 2016–17, 12 students received support, including 2 fellowships with partial tuition reimbursements available (averaging $5,667 per year), 7 research assistantships with partial tuition reimbursements available (averaging $23,505 per year), 1 teaching assistantship with partial tuition reimbursement available (averaging $22,000 per year); unspecified assistantships also available. *Total annual research expenditures:* $402,221. *Unit head:* Dr. Cindy Lee, Department Chair, 864-656-1006, E-mail: lc@clemson.edu. *Application contact:* Dr. Lisa Benson, Program Coordinator, 864-656-0417, E-mail: lbenson@clemson.edu.
Website: http://www.clemson.edu/cecas/departments/ese/

Cleveland State University, College of Graduate Studies, College of Education and Human Services, Department of Curriculum and Foundations, Cleveland, OH 44115. Offers art education (M Ed); early childhood education (M Ed); foreign language education (M Ed); middle childhood mathematics and science education (M Ed); special education (M Ed), including mild/moderate disabilities, moderate/intensive disabilities; teaching English to speakers of other languages (M Ed). *Program availability:* Part-time, evening/weekend. *Faculty:* 19 full-time (14 women), 32 part-time/adjunct (27 women). *Students:* 86 full-time (65 women), 369 part-time (301 women); includes 119 minority (89 Black or African American, non-Hispanic/Latino; 1 American Indian or Alaska Native, non-Hispanic/Latino; 2 Asian, non-Hispanic/Latino; 16 Hispanic/Latino; 11 Two or more races, non-Hispanic/Latino), 35 international. Average age 34. 177 applicants, 55% accepted, 68 enrolled. In 2016, 179 master's awarded. *Degree requirements:* For master's, comprehensive exam (for some programs), thesis or alternative. *Entrance requirements:* For master's, GRE General Test or MAT, minimum GPA of 2.75. Additional exam requirements/recommendations for international students: Required—TOEFL (minimum score 550 paper-based; 78 iBT), IELTS (minimum score 6). *Application deadline:* For fall admission, 7/1 priority date for domestic students, 5/15 for international students; for spring admission, 11/15 for domestic students, 11/1 for international students; for summer admission, 4/1 for domestic students, 3/15 for international students. Applications are processed on a rolling basis. Application fee: $30. *Expenses:* Tuition, state resident: full-time $9565. Tuition, nonresident: full-time $17,980. Tuition and fees vary according to program. *Financial support:* In 2016–17, 13 research assistantships with full tuition reimbursements (averaging $15,845 per year) were awarded; tuition waivers (partial) and unspecified assistantships also available. Financial award application deadline: 2/15; financial award applicants required to submit FAFSA. *Faculty research:* Early childhood education, literacy education, special education: mild/moderate, moderate/intensive, early childhood intervention specialist), teaching English to speakers of other languages (TESOL). *Total annual research expenditures:* $275,907. *Unit head:* Dr. Tachelle I. Banks, Chairperson, 216-687-4608, Fax: 216-687-5379, E-mail: t.i.banks@csuohio.edu. *Application contact:* Michael Almony, Senior Student Services Specialist, 216-875-9929, Fax: 216-687-5491, E-mail: m.almony@csuohio.edu.
Website: http://www.csuohio.edu/cehs/te/te

The College at Brockport, State University of New York, School of Education, Health, and Human Services, Department of Education and Human Development, Program in Adolescence Education, Brockport, NY 14420-2997. Offers adolescence biology education (MS Ed); adolescence chemistry education (MS Ed); adolescence earth science education (MS Ed); adolescence English education (MS Ed); adolescence mathematics education (MS Ed); adolescence physics education (MS Ed); adolescence social studies education (MS Ed). *Accreditation:* NCATE. *Program availability:* Part-time. *Students:* 4 full-time (1 woman), 35 part-time (23 women); includes 3 minority (2 Black or African American, non-Hispanic/Latino; 1 Two or more races, non-Hispanic/Latino). 21 applicants, 71% accepted, 11 enrolled. In 2016, 18 master's awarded. *Degree requirements:* For master's, thesis or alternative. *Entrance requirements:* For master's, minimum GPA of 3.0, letters of recommendation, statement of objectives, current resume. Additional exam requirements/recommendations for international students: Required—TOEFL (minimum score 550 paper-based; 79 iBT), IELTS (minimum score 6.5). *Application deadline:* For fall admission, 3/15 priority date for domestic and international students; for spring admission, 10/15 priority date for domestic and international students; for summer admission, 3/15 priority date for domestic students, 3/13 priority date for international students. Application fee: $80. Electronic applications accepted. *Expenses:* Contact institution. *Financial support:* Federal Work-Study, scholarships/grants, and unspecified assistantships available. Support available to part-time students. Financial award application deadline: 3/15; financial award applicants required to submit FAFSA. *Unit head:* Dr. Sue Robb, Chairperson, 585-395-5935, Fax: 585-395-2172, E-mail: srobb@brockport.edu. *Application contact:* Anne Walton, Coordinator of Certification and Graduate Advisement, 585-395-2326, Fax: 585-395-2172, E-mail: awalton@brockport.edu.
Website: http://www.brockport.edu/ehd/

The College at Brockport, State University of New York, School of Education, Health, and Human Services, Department of Education and Human Development, Program in Inclusive Generalist Education, Brockport, NY 14420-2997. Offers biology (MS Ed, AGC); chemistry (MS Ed, AGC); English (MS Ed, Advanced Certificate); mathematics (MS Ed, Advanced Certificate); science (MS Ed, Advanced Certificate); social studies (MS Ed, Advanced Certificate). *Students:* 28 full-time (15 women), 19 part-time (10 women); includes 9 minority (2 Black or African American, non-Hispanic/Latino; 3 Asian, non-Hispanic/Latino; 1 Hispanic/Latino; 3 Two or more races, non-Hispanic/Latino). 21 applicants, 52% accepted, 11 enrolled. In 2016, 12 master's, 3 AGCs awarded. *Degree requirements:* For master's, thesis or alternative. *Entrance requirements:* For master's, minimum GPA of 3.0, letters of recommendation, statement of objectives, academic major (or equivalent) in program discipline, current resume. Additional exam requirements/recommendations for international students: Required—TOEFL (minimum score 550 paper-based; 79 iBT), IELTS (minimum score 6.5). *Application deadline:* For fall admission, 3/15 priority date for domestic and international students; for spring admission, 10/15 priority date for domestic and international students; for summer admission, 3/15 for domestic and international students. Application fee: $80. Electronic applications accepted. *Expenses:* Contact institution. *Financial support:* Federal Work-Study, scholarships/grants, and unspecified assistantships available. Support available to part-time students. Financial award application deadline: 3/15; financial award applicants required to submit FAFSA. *Unit head:* Dr. Sue Robb, Chairperson, 585-395-5935, Fax: 585-395-2171, E-mail: awalton@brockport.edu. *Application contact:* Anne Walton, Coordinator of Certification and Graduate Advisement, 585-395-2326, Fax: 585-395-2172, E-mail: awalton@brockport.edu.
Website: http://www.brockport.edu/ehd/

College of Charleston, Graduate School, School of Education, Health, and Human Performance, Program in Science and Mathematics for Teachers, Charleston, SC 29424-0001. Offers M Ed. *Accreditation:* NCATE. *Program availability:* Part-time, evening/weekend. *Degree requirements:* For master's, capstone project. *Entrance requirements:* For master's, GRE or PRAXIS, 2 letters of recommendation, copy of teaching certificate. Additional exam requirements/recommendations for international students: Required—TOEFL (minimum score 81 iBT). *Application deadline:* For fall admission, 4/1 for domestic students; for spring admission, 11/1 for domestic students. Application fee: $45. Electronic applications accepted. *Financial support:* Research assistantships, teaching assistantships, scholarships/grants, and unspecified assistantships available. Financial award application deadline: 4/1; financial award applicants required to submit FAFSA. *Unit head:* John Peters, Director, 843-953-1422, E-mail: petersj@cofc.edu. *Application contact:* John Peters, Director, 843-953-1422, E-mail: petersj@cofc.edu.
Website: http://teachered.cofc.edu/grad-progs/smft.php

College of Staten Island of the City University of New York, Graduate Programs, School of Education, Program in Adolescence Education, Staten Island, NY 10314-6600. Offers biology (MS Ed); English (MS Ed); mathematics (MS Ed); social studies (MS Ed). *Program availability:* Part-time, evening/weekend. *Faculty:* 18 full-time, 8 part-time/adjunct. *Students:* 4 full-time, 84 part-time. Average age 29. 40 applicants, 88% accepted, 14 enrolled. In 2016, 41 master's awarded. *Degree requirements:* For master's, thesis, educational research project supervised by faculty; minimum of 33-38 credits distributed among 11 courses or minimum of 46-53 credits. *Entrance requirements:* For master's, GRE General Test or an approved equivalent examination, relevant bachelor's degree, minimum overall GPA of 3.0, two letters of recommendation, one- or two-page personal statement. Additional exam requirements/recommendations for international students: Required—TOEFL (minimum score 550 paper-based; 79 iBT), IELTS (minimum score 6.5). *Application deadline:* For fall admission, 4/25 for domestic and international students; for spring admission, 11/25 for domestic and international students. Applications are processed on a rolling basis. Application fee: $125. Electronic applications accepted. *Expenses:* Tuition, state resident: full-time $10,130; part-time $425 per credit. Tuition, nonresident: full-time $18,720; part-time $780 per credit. *Required fees:* $181.10 per semester. Tuition and fees vary according to program. *Faculty research:* Development and assessment of TPACK (technological pedagogical content knowledge), technology and differentiation in stem classrooms, teacher effectiveness and student achievement, teacher knowledge, knowledge transfer from college to classroom. *Unit head:* Dr. Bethany Rogers, Graduate Faculty Advisor, 718-982-4247, E-mail: bethany.rogers@csi.cuny.edu. *Application contact:* Sasha Spence, Associate Director for Graduate Admissions, 718-982-2019, Fax: 718-982-2500, E-mail: sasha.spence@csi.cuny.edu.
Website: http://www.csi.cuny.edu/catalog/graduate/graduate-programs-in-education.htm#o2608

College of Staten Island of the City University of New York, Graduate Programs, School of Education, Program in Childhood Education, Staten Island, NY 10314-6600. Offers learning and development (MS Ed); literacy education (MS Ed); mathematics education (MS Ed); music education (MS Ed); science education (MS Ed); social foundations of education (MS Ed); social studies education (MS Ed). *Program availability:* Part-time, evening/weekend. *Faculty:* 2 full-time, 11 part-time/adjunct. *Students:* 16 full-time, 53 part-time. Average age 30. 40 applicants, 53% accepted, 13 enrolled. In 2016, 20 master's awarded. *Degree requirements:* For master's, educational research project; ten courses and a minimum of 32-38 credits in five required areas of study or minimum of 45-49 credits in six required core courses before selecting from array of advanced courses. *Entrance requirements:* For master's, GRE General Test or an approved equivalent examination, relevant bachelor's degree, letters of recommendation, one- or two-page personal statement. Additional exam requirements/recommendations for international students: Required—TOEFL (minimum score 550 paper-based; 79 iBT), IELTS (minimum score 6.5). *Application deadline:* For fall admission, 4/25 for domestic and international students; for spring admission, 11/25 for domestic and international students. Applications are processed on a rolling basis. Application fee: $125. Electronic applications accepted. *Expenses:* Tuition, state resident: full-time $10,130; part-time $425 per credit. Tuition, nonresident: full-time $18,720; part-time $780 per credit. *Required fees:* $181.10 per semester. Tuition and fees vary according to program. *Faculty research:* Preservice teacher preparation, music integration, music education through children's songs, literacy, emergent bilingual. *Unit head:* Dr. Vivian Shulman, Graduate Faculty Advisor, 718-982-4086, E-mail: vivian.shulman@csi.cuny.edu. *Application contact:* Sasha Spence, Associate Director for Graduate Admissions, 718-982-2019, Fax: 718-982-2500, E-mail: sasha.spence@csi.cuny.edu.
Website: http://www.csi.cuny.edu/admissions/grad/pdf/Education%20Fact%20Sheet.pdf

The College of William and Mary, School of Education, Program in Curriculum and Instruction, Williamsburg, VA 23187-8795. Offers elementary education (MA Ed); gifted education (MA Ed); literacy leadership (MA Ed); math specialist (MA Ed); secondary education (MA Ed), including English, foreign language, math, science, social studies; special education (MA Ed). *Accreditation:* NCATE. *Program availability:* Part-time. *Faculty:* 30 full-time (21 women), 48 part-time/adjunct (38 women). *Students:* 60 full-time (47 women), 14 part-time (all women); includes 13 minority (1 Black or African American, non-Hispanic/Latino; 1 American Indian or Alaska Native, non-Hispanic/Latino; 2 Asian, non-Hispanic/Latino; 7 Hispanic/Latino; 2 Two or more races, non-Hispanic/Latino). Average age 26. 134 applicants, 79% accepted, 66 enrolled. In 2016, 77 master's awarded. *Degree requirements:* For master's, project. *Entrance requirements:* For master's, GRE, MAT, PRAXIS Core Academic Skills for Educators, minimum GPA of 2.5. Additional exam requirements/recommendations for international students: Required—TOEFL (minimum score 100 iBT), IELTS (minimum score 7). *Application deadline:* For fall admission, 1/15 for domestic and international students; for spring admission, 10/1 for domestic and international students. Application fee: $50. Electronic applications accepted. *Expenses:* $14,258 per year in-state full-time, $275 per credit in-state part-time; $30,500 per year out-of-state full-time, $1,200 per credit out-of-state part-time. *Financial support:* In 2016–17, 30 students received support, including 3 research assistantships (averaging $14,259 per year); scholarships/grants and unspecified assistantships also available. Financial award application deadline: 1/15; financial award applicants required to submit FAFSA. *Faculty research:* Educational technology, professional development and evaluation, inclusive education, rural education, education policy. *Unit head:* Dr. Jeremy D. Stoddard, Department Chair, 757-221-2348, E-mail: jdstod@wm.edu. *Application contact:* Dorothy Smith Osborne, Assistant Dean for Academic Programs and Student Services, 757-221-2317, E-mail: dsosbo@wm.edu.
Website: http://education.wm.edu

The Colorado College, Education Department, Experienced Teacher Program, Colorado Springs, CO 80903-3294. Offers arts and humanities (MAT); integrated natural sciences (MAT); liberal arts (MAT); Southwest studies (MAT). Programs offered during summer only. *Program availability:* Part-time. *Degree requirements:* For master's, thesis, oral exam, 50-page paper. *Expenses:* Contact institution.

Science Education

The Colorado College, Education Department, Program in Secondary Education, Colorado Springs, CO 80903-3294. Offers art teaching (K-12) (MAT); English teaching (MAT); foreign language teaching (MAT); mathematics teaching (MAT); music teaching (MAT); science teaching (MAT); social studies teaching (MAT). *Degree requirements:* For master's, thesis, internship. Electronic applications accepted.

Columbia University, College of Dental Medicine and Graduate School of Arts and Sciences, Programs in Dental Specialties, New York, NY 10027. Offers advanced education in general dentistry (Certificate); biomedical informatics (MA, PhD); endodontics (Certificate); orthodontics (MS, Certificate); periodontics (MS, Certificate); prosthodontics (MS, Certificate); science education (MA). *Degree requirements:* For master's, thesis, presentation of seminar. *Entrance requirements:* For master's, GRE General Test, DDS or equivalent. *Expenses:* Contact institution. *Faculty research:* Analysis of growth/form, pulpal microcirculation, implants, microbiology of oral environment, calcified tissues.

Columbus State University, Graduate Studies, College of Education and Health Professions, Department of Teacher Education, Columbus, GA 31907-5645. Offers curriculum and instruction in accomplished teaching (M Ed); early childhood education (M Ed, MAT, Ed S); middle grades education (M Ed, MAT, Ed S); secondary education (M Ed, MAT, Ed S), including biology (MAT), chemistry (MAT), earth and space science (MAT), English/language arts, general science (M Ed), history (MAT), mathematics, science (Ed S), social science (M Ed, Ed S); special education (M Ed, MAT, Ed S), including general curriculum (M Ed, MAT); teacher leadership (M Ed). *Accreditation:* NCATE. *Program availability:* Part-time, evening/weekend, 100% online, blended/hybrid learning. *Faculty:* 20 full-time (13 women), 19 part-time/adjunct (16 women). *Students:* 92 full-time (66 women), 212 part-time (179 women); includes 113 minority (104 Black or African American, non-Hispanic/Latino; 1 American Indian or Alaska Native, non-Hispanic/Latino; 2 Asian, non-Hispanic/Latino; 4 Hispanic/Latino; 2 Two or more races, non-Hispanic/Latino), 5 international. Average age 34. 209 applicants, 56% accepted, 79 enrolled. In 2016, 111 master's, 18 other advanced degrees awarded. *Degree requirements:* For Ed S, thesis or alternative. *Entrance requirements:* For master's, GRE General Test, minimum undergraduate GPA of 2.75; for Ed S, GRE General Test, minimum undergraduate GPA of 2.75, graduate 3.0. Additional exam requirements/recommendations for international students: Required—TOEFL (minimum score 550 paper-based; 79 iBT). *Application deadline:* For fall admission, 6/30 for domestic students, 5/1 for international students; for spring admission, 11/1 for domestic and international students; for summer admission, 3/1 for domestic and international students. Applications are processed on a rolling basis. Application fee: $50. Electronic applications accepted. *Expenses:* Tuition, state resident: full-time $4804; part-time $2412 per semester hour. Tuition, nonresident: full-time $19,218; part-time $9612 per semester hour. *Required fees:* $1850; $1850 per semester hour. Tuition and fees vary according to program. *Financial support:* In 2016–17, 60 students received support, including 12 research assistantships with partial tuition reimbursements available (averaging $3,000 per year); career-related internships or fieldwork, Federal Work-Study, institutionally sponsored loans, scholarships/grants, tuition waivers (partial), and unspecified assistantships also available. Support available to part-time students. Financial award application deadline: 5/1; financial award applicants required to submit FAFSA. *Unit head:* Dr. Jan Burcham, Department Chair, 706-507-8519, Fax: 706-568-3134, E-mail: burcham_jan@columbusstate.edu. *Application contact:* Kristin Williams, Director of International and Graduate Recruitment, 706-507-8848, Fax: 706-568-5091, E-mail: williams_kristin@columbusstate.edu.
Website: http://te.columbusstate.edu/

Columbus State University, Graduate Studies, College of Letters and Sciences, Department of Earth and Space Sciences, Columbus, GA 31907-5645. Offers natural sciences (MS), including biology, chemistry, environmental science, geosciences. *Program availability:* Part-time, evening/weekend. *Faculty:* 5 full-time (1 woman), 5 part-time/adjunct (0 women). *Students:* 18 full-time (11 women), 3 part-time (1 woman); includes 6 minority (3 Black or African American, non-Hispanic/Latino; 1 American Indian or Alaska Native, non-Hispanic/Latino; 1 Asian, non-Hispanic/Latino; 1 Two or more races, non-Hispanic/Latino). Average age 26. 28 applicants, 36% accepted, 6 enrolled. In 2016, 4 master's awarded. *Degree requirements:* For master's, thesis. *Entrance requirements:* For master's, GRE General Test, minimum GPA of 3.0. Additional exam requirements/recommendations for international students: Required—TOEFL (minimum score 550 paper-based; 79 iBT). *Application deadline:* For fall admission, 6/30 priority date for domestic students, 5/1 for international students; for spring admission, 11/1 for domestic and international students; for summer admission, 3/1 for domestic and international students. Applications are processed on a rolling basis. Application fee: $50. Electronic applications accepted. *Expenses:* Tuition, state resident: full-time $4804; part-time $2412 per semester hour. Tuition, nonresident: full-time $19,218; part-time $9612 per semester hour. *Required fees:* $1850; $1850 per semester hour. Tuition and fees vary according to program. *Financial support:* In 2016–17, 1 student received support, including 15 research assistantships with partial tuition reimbursements available (averaging $3,000 per year); career-related internships or fieldwork, Federal Work-Study, institutionally sponsored loans, scholarships/grants, and unspecified assistantships also available. Support available to part-time students. Financial award application deadline: 5/1; financial award applicants required to submit FAFSA. *Unit head:* Dr. Clint Barineau, Department Chair, 706-569-3026, E-mail: barineau_clinton@columbusstate.edu. *Application contact:* Kristin Williams, Director of International and Graduate Recruitment, 706-507-8848, Fax: 706-568-5091, E-mail: williams_kristin@columbusstate.edu.
Website: http://ess.columbusstate.edu/

Concordia University, College of Education, Portland, OR 97211-6099. Offers career and technical education (M Ed); curriculum and instruction (M Ed), including adolescent literacy, career and technical education, e-learning/technology education, early childhood education, English for speakers of other languages, English language development, environmental education, mathematics, methods and curriculum, reading, science, teacher leadership, the inclusive classroom; early childhood (MAT); education leadership (Ed D); educational administration (M Ed); elementary education (MAT); secondary education (MAT); special education (M Ed); teacher leadership (Ed D). *Program availability:* Part-time, online learning. *Degree requirements:* For master's, comprehensive exam, work samples/portfolio. *Entrance requirements:* For master's, California Basic Educational Skills Test or PRAXIS I, minimum undergraduate GPA of 2.8, graduate 3.0; 2 letters of recommendation. Additional exam requirements/recommendations for international students: Required—TOEFL (minimum score 525 paper-based). Electronic applications accepted. *Faculty research:* Learner-centered classroom, brain-based learning, future of online learning.

Converse College, School of Education and Graduate Studies, Program in Middle Level Education, Spartanburg, SC 29302. Offers language arts/English (MAT); mathematics (MAT); middle level education (M Ed); science (MAT); social studies (MAT). *Expenses: Tuition:* Full-time $3600; part-time $400 per credit hour. *Required fees:* $70 per term. *Application contact:* 864-596-9404, E-mail: graduate@converse.edu.

Converse College, School of Education and Graduate Studies, Program in Secondary Education, Spartanburg, SC 29302. Offers biology (MAT); chemistry (MAT); English (M Ed, MAT); mathematics (M Ed, MAT); natural sciences (M Ed); social sciences (M Ed, MAT). *Program availability:* Part-time. *Degree requirements:* For master's, capstone paper. *Entrance requirements:* For master's, NTE or PRAXIS II (M Ed), minimum GPA of 2.75, 2 recommendations. *Application deadline:* For fall admission, 8/1 for domestic and international students; for winter admission, 11/15 for domestic and international students; for spring admission, 1/15 for domestic and international students. Applications are processed on a rolling basis. Application fee: $40. Electronic applications accepted. *Expenses: Tuition:* Full-time $3600; part-time $400 per credit hour. *Required fees:* $70 per term. *Financial support:* Available to part-time students. Applicants required to submit FAFSA. *Application contact:* 864-596-9404, E-mail: graduate@converse.edu.

Delaware State University, Graduate Programs, College of Education, Health and Public Policy, Program in Science Education, Dover, DE 19901-2277. Offers MA. *Program availability:* Part-time, evening/weekend. *Degree requirements:* For master's, comprehensive exam, thesis optional. *Entrance requirements:* For master's, GRE General Test, minimum GPA of 3.0 in major, 2.75 overall. Electronic applications accepted. *Faculty research:* Science reform in schools, inquiry science.

Delaware State University, Graduate Programs, Department of Biological Sciences, Program in Biology Education, Dover, DE 19901-2277. Offers MS. *Entrance requirements:* Additional exam requirements/recommendations for international students: Required—TOEFL (minimum score 550 paper-based).

Delaware State University, Graduate Programs, Department of Physics, Dover, DE 19901-2277. Offers applied optics (MS); optics (PhD); physics (MS); physics teaching (MS). *Program availability:* Part-time, evening/weekend. *Entrance requirements:* For master's, minimum GPA of 3.0 in major, 2.75 overall. Additional exam requirements/recommendations for international students: Required—TOEFL. Electronic applications accepted. *Faculty research:* Thermal properties of solids, nuclear physics, radiation damage in solids.

DePaul University, College of Science and Health, Chicago, IL 60614. Offers applied mathematics (MS); applied statistics (MS); biological sciences (MA, MS); chemistry (MS); mathematics education (MA); mathematics for teaching (MS); nursing (MS); nursing practice (DNP); physics (MS); psychology (MS); pure mathematics (MS); science education (MS); MA/PhD. *Accreditation:* AACN. Electronic applications accepted.

Duquesne University, School of Education, Department of Instruction and Leadership, Program in Secondary Education, Pittsburgh, PA 15282-0001. Offers biology (MS Ed); chemistry (MS Ed); English (MS Ed); K-12 education (MS Ed), including Latin; mathematics (MS Ed); physics (MS Ed); social studies (MS Ed). *Program availability:* Part-time, evening/weekend. *Faculty:* 5 full-time (4 women). *Students:* 21 full-time (8 women), 4 part-time (0 women); includes 3 minority (2 Black or African American, non-Hispanic/Latino; 1 Two or more races, non-Hispanic/Latino). Average age 28. 12 applicants, 100% accepted, 7 enrolled. In 2016, 19 master's awarded. *Degree requirements:* For master's, thesis optional. *Entrance requirements:* For master's, letters of recommendation, letter of intent, interview, bachelor's degree. Additional exam requirements/recommendations for international students: Required—TOEFL (minimum score 550 paper-based), IELTS (minimum score 7). *Application deadline:* For fall admission, 9/1 for domestic students; for spring admission, 1/1 for domestic students. Applications are processed on a rolling basis. Application fee: $0. Electronic applications accepted. *Expenses: Tuition:* Full-time $22,212; part-time $1234 per credit. Tuition and fees vary according to program. *Financial support:* Research assistantships and Federal Work-Study available. Support available to part-time students. *Unit head:* Dr. Melissa Boston, Associate Professor and Director, 412-396-6109, E-mail: bostonm@duq.edu. *Application contact:* Michael Dolinger, Director of Student and Academic Services, 412-396-6647, Fax: 412-396-5585, E-mail: dolingerm@duq.edu.
Website: http://www.duq.edu/academics/schools/education/graduate-programs-education/ms-ed-secondary-education

East Carolina University, Graduate School, College of Education, Department of Elementary and Middle Grades Education, Greenville, NC 27858-4353. Offers elementary education (MA Ed, MAT); English education (MAT); family and consumer science (MAT); health education (MAT); Hispanic studies (MAT); history education (MAT); middle grades education (MA Ed, MAT); music education (MAT); science education (MAT); special education (MAT), including general curriculum; vocational education (MAT). *Accreditation:* NCATE. *Program availability:* Part-time, evening/weekend, online learning. *Students:* 5 full-time (4 women), 18 part-time (16 women); includes 4 minority (3 Black or African American, non-Hispanic/Latino; 1 Hispanic/Latino). Average age 31. 19 applicants, 95% accepted, 13 enrolled. In 2016, 8 master's awarded. *Degree requirements:* For master's, comprehensive exam, thesis optional. *Entrance requirements:* For master's, GRE or MAT, minimum GPA of 2.5, bachelor's degree in related field, teaching license (MA Ed). Additional exam requirements/recommendations for international students: Required—TOEFL. *Application deadline:* For fall admission, 6/1 priority date for domestic students. Applications are processed on a rolling basis. Application fee: $70. *Financial support:* Federal Work-Study available. Support available to part-time students. Financial award application deadline: 6/1. *Unit head:* Dr. Ann Bullock, Chair, 252-328-1126, E-mail: bullockv@ecu.edu. *Application contact:* Dean of Graduate School, 252-328-6012, Fax: 252-328-6071, E-mail: gradschool@ecu.edu.
Website: http://www.ecu.edu/cs-educ/elmid/index.cfm

East Carolina University, Graduate School, College of Education, Department of Mathematics, Science, and Instructional Technology Education, Greenville, NC 27858-4353. Offers elementary mathematics (Certificate); instructional technology (MA Ed, MS); mathematics education (MA Ed); science education (MA Ed, MAT). *Program availability:* Part-time, evening/weekend. *Students:* 15 full-time (10 women), 266 part-time (213 women); includes 52 minority (34 Black or African American, non-Hispanic/Latino; 3 American Indian or Alaska Native, non-Hispanic/Latino; 4 Asian, non-Hispanic/Latino; 9 Hispanic/Latino; 2 Two or more races, non-Hispanic/Latino), 1 international. Average age 37. 131 applicants, 100% accepted, 116 enrolled. In 2016, 30 master's awarded. *Degree requirements:* For master's, comprehensive exam, thesis optional. *Entrance requirements:* For master's, GRE General Test or MAT, interview, minimum GPA of 2.5, bachelor's degree in related field, teaching license (MA Ed). Additional exam requirements/recommendations for international students: Required—TOEFL. *Application deadline:* For fall admission, 6/1 priority date for domestic students. Applications are processed on a rolling basis. Application fee: $50. *Financial support:* Research assistantships, teaching assistantships, and Federal Work-Study available. Support available to part-time students. Financial award application deadline: 6/1. *Unit head:* Susan Ganter, Chair, 252-737-3001, E-mail: ganters@ecu.edu. *Application contact:* Dean of Graduate School, 252-328-6012, Fax: 252-328-6071, E-mail: gradschool@ecu.edu.
Website: http://www.ecu.edu/cs-educ/msite/

Eastern Kentucky University, The Graduate School, College of Education, Department of Curriculum and Instruction, Program in Secondary and Higher Education, Richmond, KY 40475-3102. Offers secondary education (MA Ed), including agricultural education, art education, biological sciences education, business education, English education, geography education, history education, home economics education, industrial education, mathematical sciences education, physical education, school health education. *Accreditation:* NCATE. *Program availability:* Part-time. *Entrance requirements:* For master's, GRE General Test, minimum GPA of 2.5.

Eastern Michigan University, Graduate School, College of Arts and Sciences, Department of Biology, Ypsilanti, MI 48197. Offers cell and molecular biology (MS); community college biology teaching (MS); ecology and organismal biology (MS); general biology (MS); water resources (MS). *Program availability:* Part-time, evening/weekend, online learning. *Faculty:* 23 full-time (6 women). *Students:* 9 full-time (4 women), 34 part-time (15 women); includes 11 minority (3 Black or African American, non-Hispanic/Latino; 5 Asian, non-Hispanic/Latino; 1 Hispanic/Latino; 2 Two or more races, non-Hispanic/Latino), 2 international. Average age 27. 46 applicants, 52% accepted, 14 enrolled. In 2016, 17 master's awarded. *Entrance requirements:* For master's, GRE General Test, GRE Subject Test. Additional exam requirements/recommendations for international students: Required—TOEFL. *Application deadline:* Applications are processed on a rolling basis. Application fee: $45. *Financial support:* Fellowships, research assistantships with full tuition reimbursements, teaching assistantships with full tuition reimbursements, career-related internships or fieldwork, Federal Work-Study, institutionally sponsored loans, scholarships/grants, tuition waivers (partial), and unspecified assistantships available. Support available to part-time students. Financial award applicants required to submit FAFSA. *Unit head:* Dr. Marianne Laporte, Department Head, 734-487-4242, Fax: 734-487-9235, E-mail: mlaporte@emich.edu. *Application contact:* Dr. David Kass, Graduate Coordinator, 734-487-4242, Fax: 734-487-9235, E-mail: dkass@emich.edu.
Website: http://www.emich.edu/biology

Eastern Michigan University, Graduate School, College of Arts and Sciences, Department of Physics and Astronomy, Ypsilanti, MI 48197. Offers general science (MS); physics (MS). *Program availability:* Part-time, evening/weekend, online learning. *Faculty:* 10 full-time (2 women). *Students:* 3 full-time (0 women), 7 part-time (2 women); includes 3 minority (2 Black or African American, non-Hispanic/Latino; 1 Two or more races, non-Hispanic/Latino). Average age 26. 28 applicants, 54% accepted, 5 enrolled. In 2016, 2 master's awarded. *Entrance requirements:* Additional exam requirements/recommendations for international students: Required—TOEFL. *Application deadline:* Applications are processed on a rolling basis. Application fee: $45. *Financial support:* Fellowships, research assistantships with full tuition reimbursements, teaching assistantships with full tuition reimbursements, career-related internships or fieldwork, Federal Work-Study, institutionally sponsored loans, scholarships/grants, tuition waivers, and unspecified assistantships available. Support available to part-time students. Financial award applicants required to submit FAFSA. *Unit head:* Dr. Alexandria Oakes, Department Head, 734-487-4144, Fax: 734-487-0989, E-mail: aoakes@emich.edu.
Website: http://www.emich.edu/physics/

Eastern University, Loeb School of Education, St. Davids, PA 19087-3696. Offers ESL program specialist (K-12) (Certificate); general supervisor (PreK-12) (Certificate); health and physical education (K-12) (Certificate); middle level (4-8) (Certificate); multicultural education (M Ed); organizational leadership with education (PhD); Pre K-4 (Certificate); Pre K-4 with special education (Certificate); reading (M Ed); reading specialist (K-12) (Certificate); reading supervisor (K-12) (Certificate); school health supervisor (Certificate); school nurse (K-12) (Certificate); secondary biology education (7-12) (Certificate); secondary chemistry education (7-12) (Certificate); secondary communication education (7-12) (Certificate); secondary education (7-12) (Certificate); secondary English education (7-12) (Certificate); secondary math education (7-12) (Certificate); secondary social studies education (7-12) (Certificate); special education (M Ed); special education (7-12) (Certificate); special education (Pre K-8) (Certificate); special education supervisor (N-12) (Certificate); TESOL (M Ed); world language (Certificate), including French, Spanish. *Program availability:* Part-time, evening/weekend, online learning. *Students:* 41 full-time (32 women), 89 part-time (68 women); includes 54 minority (38 Black or African American, non-Hispanic/Latino; 3 Asian, non-Hispanic/Latino; 11 Hispanic/Latino; 2 Two or more races, non-Hispanic/Latino), 2 international. Average age 37. In 2016, 64 master's awarded. *Entrance requirements:* Additional exam requirements/recommendations for international students: Required—TOEFL. *Application deadline:* Applications are processed on a rolling basis. Application fee: $35. Electronic applications accepted. Application fee is waived when completed online. *Expenses:* $690 per credit. *Unit head:* Michael Dziedziak, Executive Director of Enrollment, 800-452-0996, E-mail: gpsadmissions@eastern.edu.
Website: http://www.eastern.edu/academics/programs/loeb-school-education-0

Elizabeth City State University, School of Mathematics, Science and Technology, Master of Science in Biology/Biological Science Program, Elizabeth City, NC 27909-7806. Offers biological sciences (MS); biology education (MS). *Program availability:* Part-time, evening/weekend. *Degree requirements:* For master's, thesis. *Entrance requirements:* For master's, GRE, minimum GPA of 3.0, 3 letters of recommendation, 2 official transcripts from all undergraduate/graduate schools attended, typewritten one-page expository description of student educational preparation, research interests and career aspirations. Additional exam requirements/recommendations for international students: Required—TOEFL (minimum score 550 paper-based, 80 iBT) or IELTS (minimum score 6.5). Electronic applications accepted. *Faculty research:* Apoptosis and cancer, plant bioengineering, development of biofuels, microbial degradation, developmental toxicology.

Elms College, Division of Education, Chicopee, MA 01013-2839. Offers early childhood education (MAT); education (M Ed, CAGS); elementary education (MAT); English as a second language (MAT); reading (MAT); secondary education (MAT), including biology education, English education, Spanish education; special education (MAT). *Program availability:* Part-time, evening/weekend. *Faculty:* 5 full-time (all women), 7 part-time/adjunct (6 women). *Students:* 6 full-time (all women), 136 part-time (111 women); includes 6 minority (1 Asian, non-Hispanic/Latino; 5 Hispanic/Latino). Average age 33. 27 applicants, 89% accepted, 20 enrolled. In 2016, 47 master's, 3 other advanced degrees awarded. *Degree requirements:* For master's, thesis (for some programs). *Entrance requirements:* For master's, Massachusetts Educators Certification Test, minimum GPA of 3.0; for CAGS, master's degree in education. Additional exam requirements/recommendations for international students: Required—TOEFL. *Application deadline:* For fall admission, 7/1 priority date for domestic students; for spring admission, 11/1 priority date for domestic students. Applications are processed on a rolling basis. Application fee: $30. *Expenses: Tuition:* Full-time $13,392. *Required fees:* $200. *Financial support:* In 2016–17, 2 teaching assistantships with partial tuition reimbursements were awarded; tuition waivers (partial) also available. Support available to part-time students. Financial award applicants required to submit FAFSA. *Unit head:* Dr. Mary Janeczek, Chair, Division of Education, 413-594-2761, Fax: 413-592-4871, E-mail: janeczeke@elms.edu. *Application contact:* Dr. Elizabeth Teahan Hukowicz, Dean, School of Graduate and Professional Studies, 413-265-2360, Fax: 413-265-2459, E-mail: hukowiczе@elms.edu.

Fairleigh Dickinson University, Metropolitan Campus, University College: Arts, Sciences, and Professional Studies, School of Natural Sciences, Program in Science, Teaneck, NJ 07666-1914. Offers MA. *Accreditation:* TEAC.

Fitchburg State University, Division of Graduate and Continuing Education, Program in Science Education, Fitchburg, MA 01420-2697. Offers M Ed. *Accreditation:* NCATE. *Program availability:* Part-time, evening/weekend. *Entrance requirements:* Additional exam requirements/recommendations for international students: Required—TOEFL (minimum score 550 paper-based; 79 iBT). Electronic applications accepted. *Expenses:* Tuition, state resident: full-time $2871; part-time $1914 per year. Tuition, nonresident: full-time $2871; part-time $1914 per year. *Required fees:* $3828. Tuition and fees vary according to program.

Fitchburg State University, Division of Graduate and Continuing Education, Programs in Biology and Teaching Biology (Secondary Level), Fitchburg, MA 01420-2697. Offers MA, MAT, Certificate. *Accreditation:* NCATE. *Program availability:* Part-time, evening/weekend. *Entrance requirements:* Additional exam requirements/recommendations for international students: Required—TOEFL (minimum score 550 paper-based; 79 iBT). Electronic applications accepted. *Expenses:* Tuition, state resident: full-time $2871; part-time $1914 per year. Tuition, nonresident: full-time $2871; part-time $1914 per year. *Required fees:* $3828. Tuition and fees vary according to program.

Florida Agricultural and Mechanical University, Division of Graduate Studies, Research, and Continuing Education, College of Education, Program in Secondary Education and Foundation, Tallahassee, FL 32307-3200. Offers biology (M Ed); chemistry (MS Ed); English (MS Ed); history (MS Ed); math (MS Ed); physics (MS Ed). *Accreditation:* NCATE. *Degree requirements:* For master's, thesis (for some programs). *Entrance requirements:* For master's, GRE General Test, minimum GPA of 3.0. Additional exam requirements/recommendations for international students: Required—TOEFL.

Florida Atlantic University, Charles E. Schmidt College of Science, Department of Biological Sciences, Boca Raton, FL 33431-0991. Offers biology (MS, MST). *Program availability:* Part-time. *Faculty:* 41 full-time (15 women), 1 part-time/adjunct (0 women). *Students:* 86 full-time (49 women), 65 part-time (41 women); includes 41 minority (7 Black or African American, non-Hispanic/Latino; 7 Asian, non-Hispanic/Latino; 21 Hispanic/Latino; 6 Two or more races, non-Hispanic/Latino), 14 international. Average age 28. 49 applicants, 51% accepted, 6 enrolled. In 2016, 49 master's awarded. *Degree requirements:* For master's, thesis (for some programs). *Entrance requirements:* For master's, GRE General Test, minimum GPA of 3.0. Additional exam requirements/recommendations for international students: Required—TOEFL (minimum score 500 paper-based; 61 iBT), IELTS (minimum score 6). *Application deadline:* For fall admission, 3/15 for domestic and international students; for spring admission, 10/1 for domestic and international students. Application fee: $30. *Expenses:* Tuition, state resident: full-time $7392; part-time $369.82 per credit hour. Tuition, nonresident: full-time $19,432; part-time $1024.81 per credit hour. *Financial support:* Fellowships, research assistantships, teaching assistantships, career-related internships or fieldwork, and Federal Work-Study available. *Faculty research:* Ecology of the Everglades, molecular biology and biotechnology, marine biology.
Website: http://www.science.fau.edu/biology/

Florida Atlantic University, Charles E. Schmidt College of Science, Department of Physics, Boca Raton, FL 33431-0991. Offers physics (MS, MST, PhD). *Program availability:* Part-time. *Faculty:* 10 full-time (1 woman), 2 part-time/adjunct (1 woman). *Students:* 16 full-time (4 women), 17 part-time (3 women); includes 2 minority (1 Black or African American, non-Hispanic/Latino; 1 Asian, non-Hispanic/Latino), 22 international. Average age 30. 14 applicants, 100% accepted, 9 enrolled. In 2016, 8 master's, 5 doctorates awarded. *Degree requirements:* For master's, thesis; for doctorate, thesis/dissertation. *Entrance requirements:* For master's, GRE General Test, minimum GPA of 3.0; for doctorate, GRE General Test. Additional exam requirements/recommendations for international students: Required—TOEFL (minimum score 500 paper-based; 61 iBT), IELTS (minimum score 6). *Application deadline:* For fall admission, 7/1 for domestic students, 2/15 for international students; for spring admission, 11/1 for domestic students, 7/15 for international students. Applications are processed on a rolling basis. Application fee: $30. *Expenses:* Tuition, state resident: full-time $7392; part-time $369.82 per credit hour. Tuition, nonresident: full-time $19,432; part-time $1024.81 per credit hour. *Financial support:* Fellowships, research assistantships with tuition reimbursements, teaching assistantships with tuition reimbursements, Federal Work-Study, and unspecified assistantships available. *Faculty research:* Astrophysics, spectroscopy, mathematical physics, theory of metals, superconductivity. *Application contact:* Zia Smith, 561-297-3380, E-mail: zasmith@fau.edu.
Website: http://physics.fau.edu/

Florida Atlantic University, College of Education, Department of Teaching and Learning, Boca Raton, FL 33431-0991. Offers curriculum and instruction (M Ed), including art, biology, chemistry, English, French, German, mathematics, music, physics, Pre-K and primary education, reading, social sciences, Spanish; elementary education (M Ed); environmental education (M Ed); reading education (M Ed); social foundations of education (M Ed), including educational psychology, educational technology, multilingual education. *Accreditation:* NCATE. *Program availability:* Part-time, evening/weekend. *Faculty:* 15 full-time (12 women), 2 part-time/adjunct (1 woman). *Students:* 25 full-time (20 women), 41 part-time (37 women); includes 18 minority (9 Black or African American, non-Hispanic/Latino; 2 Asian, non-Hispanic/Latino; 7 Hispanic/Latino), 7 international. Average age 32. 54 applicants, 59% accepted, 18 enrolled. In 2016, 36 master's awarded. *Entrance requirements:* For master's, GRE General Test, minimum GPA of 3.0 in last 2 years of undergraduate course work. Additional exam requirements/recommendations for international students: Required—TOEFL (minimum score 500 paper-based; 61 iBT), IELTS (minimum score 6). *Application deadline:* For fall admission, 7/1 for domestic students, 2/15 for international students; for spring admission, 11/1 for domestic students, 7/15 for international students. Applications are processed on a rolling basis. Application fee: $30. *Expenses:* Tuition, state resident: full-time $7392; part-time $369.82 per credit hour. Tuition, nonresident: full-time $19,432; part-time $1024.81 per credit hour. *Financial support:* Fellowships with partial tuition reimbursements, research assistantships with partial tuition reimbursements, teaching assistantships with partial tuition reimbursements, career-related internships or fieldwork, scholarships/grants, and unspecified assistantships available. *Faculty research:* Technology, teaching English to speakers of other languages, math teaching, electronic portfolio assessment, global perspectives through social studies. *Unit head:* Dr. Barbara Ridener, Chairperson, 561-297-3588, E-mail: bridener@fau.edu. *Application contact:* Dr. Eliah Watlington, Associate Dean, 561-296-8520, Fax: 261-297-2991, E-mail: ewatling@fau.edu.
Website: http://www.coe.fau.edu/academicdepartments/tl/

Florida Gulf Coast University, College of Education, Program in Curriculum and Instruction, Fort Myers, FL 33965-6565. Offers elementary education (M Ed); English education (M Ed); gifted education (M Ed); mathematics education (M Ed); middle school education (M Ed); science education (M Ed); social science education (M Ed). *Program availability:* Part-time, evening/weekend, online learning. *Faculty:* 26 full-time (18 women), 44 part-time/adjunct (32 women). *Students:* 1 (woman) full-time, 22 part-time (20 women); includes 49 minority (19 Black or African American, non-Hispanic/Latino; 4 Asian, non-Hispanic/Latino; 24 Hispanic/Latino; 2 Two or more races, non-Hispanic/Latino), 2 international. Average age 28. 9 applicants, 78% accepted, 2 enrolled. In 2016, 9 master's awarded. *Degree requirements:* For master's, final project

Science Education

or portfolio. *Entrance requirements:* For master's, GRE General Test, MAT, minimum undergraduate GPA of 3.0 in last 2 years. Additional exam requirements/ recommendations for international students: Required—TOEFL (minimum score 550 paper-based). *Application deadline:* For fall admission, 7/1 priority date for domestic students; for spring admission, 10/15 for domestic students. Applications are processed on a rolling basis. Application fee: $30. Electronic applications accepted. *Expenses:* Tuition, state resident: full-time $6721. Tuition, nonresident: full-time $28,170. *Required fees:* $1987. Tuition and fees vary according to course load and degree level. *Financial support:* In 2016–17, 1 student received support. Application deadline: 3/1; applicants required to submit FAFSA. *Faculty research:* Internet in schools, technology in pre-service and in-service teacher training. *Unit head:* Dr. Diane Schmidt, Department Chair, 239-590-7741, Fax: 239-590-7801, E-mail: dschmidt@fgcu.edu. *Application contact:* Keiana Desmore, Adviser/Counselor, 239-590-7759, Fax: 239-590-7801, E-mail: kdesmore@fgcu.edu.
Website: http://coe.fgcu.edu/c-imed/

Florida Institute of Technology, College of Science, Program in Elementary Science Education, Melbourne, FL 32901-6975. Offers M Ed. *Program availability:* Part-time. *Students:* 1 (woman) full-time. Average age 25. 2 applicants. *Degree requirements:* For master's, comprehensive exam, thesis or alternative, 30 credit hours, minimum GPA of 3.0. *Entrance requirements:* For master's, minimum GPA of 3.0, 3 letters of recommendation, resume, statement of objectives. Additional exam requirements/ recommendations for international students: Required—TOEFL (minimum score 550 paper-based; 79 iBT). *Application deadline:* Applications are processed on a rolling basis. Electronic applications accepted. *Expenses: Tuition:* Full-time $22,338; part-time $1241 per credit hour. *Required fees:* $250. Tuition and fees vary according to degree level, campus/location and program. *Financial support:* Applicants required to submit FAFSA. *Unit head:* Dr. Kastro Hamed, Department Head, 321-674-7206, E-mail: khamed@fit.edu. *Application contact:* Cheryl A. Brown, Associate Director of Graduate Admissions, 321-674-7581, Fax: 321-723-9468, E-mail: cbrown@fit.edu.
Website: http://www.fit.edu/programs/8118/med-elementary-science-education#.VT_jIU10ypo

Florida Institute of Technology, College of Science, Program in Science Education, Melbourne, FL 32901-6975. Offers MS, PhD, Ed S. *Students:* 19 full-time (7 women), 10 part-time (6 women); includes 6 minority (1 Black or African American, non-Hispanic/ Latino; 2 Asian, non-Hispanic/Latino; 3 Hispanic/Latino), 10 international. Average age 38. 24 applicants, 46% accepted, 6 enrolled. In 2016, 1 master's, 3 doctorates, 2 other advanced degrees awarded. *Degree requirements:* For master's, comprehensive exam (for some programs), thesis optional, minimum of 30 credit hours; for doctorate, comprehensive exam, thesis/dissertation, minimum of 42 credit hours; for Ed S, comprehensive exam, thesis or alternative, minimum GPA of 3.0, minimum of 30 credit hours. *Entrance requirements:* For master's, resume, statement of objectives; for doctorate, master's degree in science, technology, aeronautics, or science education with minimum GPA of 3.2 (aeronautics degree must have FAA certification and experience); 3 letters of recommendation; resume; statement of objectives; for Ed S, master's degree in science or education, 3 letters of recommendation, resume, statement of objectives. Additional exam requirements/recommendations for international students: Required—TOEFL (minimum score 550 paper-based; 79 iBT). *Application deadline:* Applications are processed on a rolling basis. Electronic applications accepted. *Expenses: Tuition:* Full-time $22,338; part-time $1241 per credit hour. *Required fees:* $250. Tuition and fees vary according to degree level, campus/ location and program. *Financial support:* Applicants required to submit FAFSA. *Unit head:* Dr. Kastro Hamed, Department Head, 321-674-7206, E-mail: khamed@fit.edu. *Application contact:* Cheryl A. Brown, Associate Director of Graduate Admissions, 321-674-7581, Fax: 321-723-9468, E-mail: cbrown@fit.edu.
Website: http://cos.fit.edu/education/

Florida Institute of Technology, College of Science, Program in Science Education: Informal Science Education, Melbourne, FL 32901-6975. Offers MS. *Students:* 2 applicants, 50% accepted. *Degree requirements:* For master's, comprehensive exam (for some programs), thesis optional, minimum of 30 credit hours. *Entrance requirements:* For master's, resume, statement of objectives, bachelor's degree in either science or secondary school science education. Additional exam requirements/ recommendations for international students: Required—TOEFL (minimum score 550 paper-based; 79 iBT). *Application deadline:* Applications are processed on a rolling basis. Electronic applications accepted. *Expenses: Tuition:* Full-time $22,338; part-time $1241 per credit hour. *Required fees:* $250. Tuition and fees vary according to degree level, campus/location and program. *Financial support:* Applicants required to submit FAFSA. *Unit head:* Dr. Kastro Hamed, Department Head, 321-674-7206, E-mail: khamed@fit.edu. *Application contact:* Cheryl A. Brown, Associate Director of Graduate Admissions, 321-674-7581, Fax: 321-723-9468, E-mail: cbrown@fit.edu.
Website: http://cos.fit.edu/education/

Florida International University, College of Arts, Sciences, and Education, Department of Teaching and Learning, Miami, FL 33199. Offers art education (MA, MS); curriculum and instruction (MS, Ed D, PhD, Ed S), including curriculum development (MS), elementary education (MS), English education (MS), learning technologies (MS), mathematics education (MS), modern language education (MS), physical education (MS), science education (MS), social studies education (MS), special education (MS); early childhood education (MS); exceptional student education (Ed D); foreign language education (MS), including foreign language education, teaching English to speakers of other languages (TESOL); international/intercultural education (MS); language, literacy and culture (PhD); mathematics, science, and learning technologies (PhD); physical education (MS), including sport and fitness; reading education (MS). *Program availability:* Part-time, evening/weekend. *Faculty:* 34 full-time (23 women), 64 part-time/ adjunct (48 women). *Students:* 182 full-time (154 women), 231 part-time (190 women); includes 323 minority (69 Black or African American, non-Hispanic/Latino; 10 Asian, non-Hispanic/Latino; 237 Hispanic/Latino; 7 Two or more races, non-Hispanic/Latino), 19 international. Average age 34. 282 applicants, 58% accepted, 113 enrolled. In 2016, 184 master's, 12 doctorates awarded. *Degree requirements:* For doctorate, comprehensive exam, thesis/dissertation. *Entrance requirements:* For master's, GRE General Test, Florida General Knowledge Test or Florida College Level Academic Skills Test; for doctorate and Ed S, GRE General Test. Additional exam requirements/ recommendations for international students: Required—TOEFL (minimum score 550 paper-based; 80 iBT), IELTS (minimum score 6.3). *Application deadline:* For fall admission, 6/1 priority date for domestic students, 4/1 for international students; for winter admission, 10/1 priority date for domestic students, 9/1 for international students; for spring admission, 3/1 priority date for domestic students, 2/1 for international students. Applications are processed on a rolling basis. Application fee: $30. Electronic applications accepted. *Expenses:* Tuition, state resident: full-time $8912; part-time $446 per credit hour. Tuition, nonresident: full-time $21,393; part-time $992 per credit hour. *Required fees:* $2185; $195 per semester. Tuition and fees vary according to program. *Financial support:* Research assistantships with tuition reimbursements and teaching assistantships with tuition reimbursements available. *Unit head:* Dr. Lynn Miller, Chair, 305-348-2005, Fax: 305-348-2086, E-mail: lynne.miller@fiu.edu. *Application contact:* Nanett Rojas, Assistant Director, Graduate Admissions, 305-348-7464, Fax: 305-348-7441, E-mail: gradadm@fiu.edu.
Website: http://education.fiu.edu

Florida State University, The Graduate School, College of Arts and Sciences, Department of Biological Science, Master's in Science Teaching Program, Tallahassee, FL 32306. Offers community college science teaching (MST). *Faculty:* 2 full-time (both women). *Students:* 8 full-time (7 women); includes 2 minority (1 American Indian or Alaska Native, non-Hispanic/Latino; 1 Hispanic/Latino), 1 international. Average age 27. In 2016, 2 master's awarded. *Degree requirements:* For master's, thesis or alternative, teacher work sample (action research). *Entrance requirements:* For master's, GRE, minimum upper-level undergraduate GPA of 3.0. *Application deadline:* For fall admission, 7/1 for domestic students; for spring admission, 11/1 for domestic students; for summer admission, 3/1 for domestic students. Applications are processed on a rolling basis. Application fee: $30. Electronic applications accepted. *Expenses:* Tuition, state resident: full-time $7263; part-time $403.51 per credit hour. Tuition, nonresident: full-time $18,087; part-time $1004.85 per credit hour. *Required fees:* $1365; $75.81 per credit hour. $20 per semester. Tuition and fees vary according to campus/location. *Faculty research:* Science and mathematics education, science and mathematics teacher preparation. *Unit head:* Dr. D. Ellen Granger, Director, Office of Science Teaching Activities, 850-644-6747, Fax: 850-644-0643, E-mail: granger@bio.fsu.edu. *Application contact:* Dr. Erica M. Staehling, Director, Master's in Science Teaching Program, 850-644-6747, Fax: 850-644-0643, E-mail: staehling@bio.fsu.edu.
Website: http://bio.fsu.edu/osta/tpp.php

Florida State University, The Graduate School, College of Education, Program in Curriculum and Instruction, Tallahassee, FL 32306. Offers curriculum and instruction (MS, PhD, Ed S), including early childhood education, elementary education, English education, English teaching (MS), exceptional student education (MS), foreign and second language education, foreign and second language teaching (MS), mathematics education, mathematics teaching (MS), reading education and language arts, science education, social science education, social science teaching (MS), special education, special education studies (MS), visual disabilities (MS, Ed S). *Program availability:* Part-time, evening/weekend. Terminal master's awarded for partial completion of doctoral program. *Degree requirements:* For master's and Ed S, comprehensive exam, thesis optional; for doctorate, comprehensive exam, thesis/dissertation, diagnostic exam, preliminary exam, prospectus defense, dissertation defense. *Entrance requirements:* For master's, doctorate, and Ed S, GRE General Test, minimum upper-division GPA of 3.0. Additional exam requirements/recommendations for international students: Required—TOEFL (minimum score 550 paper-based, 80 iBT), IELTS (minimum score 6.5), Michigan English Language Assessment Battery (minimum score 77), or PTE (minimum score 55). Application fee: $30. Electronic applications accepted. *Expenses:* Tuition, state resident: full-time $7263; part-time $403.51 per credit hour. Tuition, nonresident: full-time $18,087; part-time $1004.85 per credit hour. *Required fees:* $1365; $75.81 per credit hour. $20 per semester. Tuition and fees vary according to campus/location. *Financial support:* Fellowships, research assistantships, teaching assistantships, scholarships/grants, tuition waivers (full and partial), and unspecified assistantships available. Financial award application deadline: 1/15; financial award applicants required to submit FAFSA. *Faculty research:* Identifying effective intervention strategies to improve reading skills; improving literacy teaching and learning through technology; understanding of student sense making, problem solving, the history and structure of STEM disciplines, and teacher education to support the development of ambitious instruction that supports the STEM learning of all students; examining practices of international education; identifying ways to support the professional development of teachers. *Unit head:* Dr. Sherry Southerland, Professor/Department Chair, 850-644-4880, Fax: 850-644-7736, E-mail: ssoutherland@admin.fsu.edu. *Application contact:* Libbie Crowley, Academic Support Specialist, 850-644-2122, Fax: 850-644-7736, E-mail: ecrowley@fsu.edu.
Website: http://education.fsu.edu/degrees-and-programs/graduate-programs

Fresno Pacific University, Graduate Programs, School of Education, Program in STEM Education, Fresno, CA 93702-4709. Offers MA Ed. *Program availability:* Part-time, evening/weekend. *Degree requirements:* For master's, thesis or alternative. *Entrance requirements:* Additional exam requirements/recommendations for international students: Required—TOEFL (minimum score 550 paper-based). *Expenses:* Contact institution.

George Mason University, College of Education and Human Development, Programs in Curriculum and Instruction, Fairfax, VA 22030. Offers advanced international baccalaureate (M Ed); assistive technology (M Ed); designing digital learning in schools (M Ed); early childhood education (M Ed); early childhood education for diverse learners (M Ed); elementary education (M Ed); English as a second language (M Ed); gifted child education (M Ed); history (M Ed); literacy (M Ed), including PK-12 classroom teachers, reading specialist; literacy leadership for diverse schools (M Ed), including K-12 reading; physical education (M Ed); science K-12 (M Ed); secondary education (M Ed), including biology, chemistry, earth science, English, history/social science, math, physics; special education (M Ed); teacher leadership (M Ed); teaching culturally, linguistically diverse and exceptional learners (M Ed); transformative teaching (M Ed). *Faculty:* 41 full-time (35 women), 53 part-time/adjunct (46 women). *Students:* 155 full-time (127 women), 821 part-time (697 women); includes 267 minority (82 Black or African American, non-Hispanic/Latino; 5 American Indian or Alaska Native, non-Hispanic/Latino; 75 Asian, non-Hispanic/Latino; 88 Hispanic/Latino; 1 Native Hawaiian or other Pacific Islander, non-Hispanic/Latino; 16 Two or more races, non-Hispanic/Latino), 19 international. Average age 33. 513 applicants, 90% accepted, 352 enrolled. In 2016, 347 master's awarded. *Degree requirements:* For master's, comprehensive exam, thesis (for some programs). *Entrance requirements:* For master's, PRAXIS Core (for some programs), minimum GPA of 3.0 in last 60 hours, licensed as teacher or educational administrator, official transcripts, goals statement, 3 recommendation letters, interview or writing sample (depending on program), up to 3 years' teaching experience (depending on program). Additional exam requirements/recommendations for international students: Required—TOEFL (minimum score 575 paper-based; 88 iBT), IELTS (minimum score 6.5), PTE (minimum score 59). *Application deadline:* For spring admission, 11/1 priority date for domestic and international students. Application fee: $75 ($80 for international students). Electronic applications accepted. *Expenses:* Tuition, state resident: full-time $10,628; part-time $443 per credit. Tuition, nonresident: full-time $29,306; part-time $1221 per credit. *Required fees:* $3096; $129 per credit. Tuition and fees vary according to program. *Financial support:* In 2016–17, 1 student received support, including 1 teaching assistantship (averaging $4,060 per year); career-related internships or fieldwork, Federal Work-Study, scholarships/grants, unspecified assistantships, and health care benefits (for full-time research or teaching assistantship recipients) also available. Support available to part-time students. Financial award application deadline: 3/1; financial award applicants required to submit FAFSA. *Faculty research:* Achievement gaps and superintendent decisions, constructivist view of classroom teaching, cost of cheating, creating a critical literacy milieu in kindergarten. *Unit head:* Rebecca Fox, Professor and Academic Program Coordinator, 703-993-4123, E-mail: rfox@gmu.edu.
Website: http://gse.gmu.edu/programs/gsemasters

The George Washington University, Graduate School of Education and Human Development, Department of Curriculum and Pedagogy, Program in Secondary Education, Washington, DC 20052. Offers Arabic (M Ed); Italian (M Ed); math (M Ed); physics (M Ed); Russian (M Ed). Programs also offered in Arlington and Ashburn, VA. *Accreditation:* NCATE. *Students:* 13 full-time (11 women), 21 part-time (15 women); includes 12 minority (4 Black or African American, non-Hispanic/Latino; 2 Asian, non-Hispanic/Latino; 4 Hispanic/Latino; 2 Two or more races, non-Hispanic/Latino). Average age 32. 50 applicants, 82% accepted, 25 enrolled. In 2016, 22 master's awarded. *Degree requirements:* For master's, comprehensive exam. *Entrance requirements:* For master's, GRE General Test or MAT, interview, minimum GPA of 2.75. *Application deadline:* For fall admission, 1/15 priority date for domestic students; for spring admission, 10/1 for domestic students. Applications are processed on a rolling basis. Application fee: $75. *Financial support:* Fellowships, career-related internships or fieldwork, Federal Work-Study, tuition waivers (full and partial), and stipends available. Financial award application deadline: 1/15; financial award applicants required to submit FAFSA. *Unit head:* Prof. Curtis Pyke, Chair, 202-994-4516, E-mail: cpyke@gwu.edu. *Application contact:* Sarah Lang, Director of Graduate Admissions, 202-994-1447, Fax: 202-994-7207, E-mail: slang@gwu.edu.

Georgia State University, College of Education and Human Development, Department of Middle and Secondary Education, Atlanta, GA 30302-3083. Offers curriculum and instruction (Ed D); English education (MAT); mathematics education (M Ed, MAT); middle level education (MAT); reading, language and literacy education (M Ed, MAT), including reading instruction (M Ed); science education (M Ed, MAT), including biology (MAT), broad field science (MAT), chemistry (MAT), earth science (MAT), physics (MAT); social studies education (M Ed, MAT), including economics (MAT), geography (MAT), history (MAT), political science (MAT); teaching and learning (PhD), including language and literacy, mathematics education, music education, science education, social studies education, teaching and teacher education. *Accreditation:* NCATE. *Program availability:* Part-time, evening/weekend, online learning. *Faculty:* 24 full-time (18 women). *Students:* 145 full-time (91 women), 151 part-time (102 women); includes 141 minority (104 Black or African American, non-Hispanic/Latino; 1 American Indian or Alaska Native, non-Hispanic/Latino; 16 Asian, non-Hispanic/Latino; 12 Hispanic/Latino; 8 Two or more races, non-Hispanic/Latino), 10 international. Average age 36. 115 applicants, 50% accepted, 41 enrolled. In 2016, 94 master's, 22 doctorates awarded. *Degree requirements:* For master's, comprehensive exam (for some programs), thesis or alternative, exit portfolio; for doctorate, comprehensive exam, thesis/dissertation. *Entrance requirements:* For master's, GRE; GACE I (for initial teacher preparation programs), baccalaureate degree or equivalent, resume, goals statement, two letters of recommendation, minimum undergraduate GPA of 2.5; proof of initial teacher certification in the content area (for M Ed); for doctorate, GRE, resume, goals statement, writing sample, two letters of recommendation, minimum graduate GPA of 3.3, interview. Additional exam requirements/recommendations for international students: Required—TOEFL (minimum score 550 paper-based; 79 iBT) or IELTS (minimum score 6.5). *Application deadline:* For fall admission, 1/15 priority date for domestic and international students; for spring admission, 10/1 for domestic and international students. Application fee: $50. Electronic applications accepted. *Expenses:* Tuition, state resident: full-time $6876; part-time $382 per credit hour. Tuition, nonresident: full-time $22,374; part-time $1243 per credit hour. *Required fees:* $2128; $1064 per term. Part-time tuition and fees vary according to course load and program. *Financial support:* In 2016–17, fellowships with full tuition reimbursements (averaging $19,667 per year), research assistantships with full tuition reimbursements (averaging $5,436 per year), teaching assistantships with full tuition reimbursements (averaging $2,779 per year) were awarded; career-related internships or fieldwork, Federal Work-Study, scholarships/grants, health care benefits, tuition waivers (full and partial), and unspecified assistantships also available. Financial award application deadline: 3/15. *Faculty research:* Teacher education in language and literacy, mathematics, science, and social studies in urban middle and secondary school settings; learning technologies in school, community, and corporate settings; multicultural education and education for social justice; urban education; international education. *Unit head:* Dr. Dana L. Fox, Chair, 404-413-8060, Fax: 404-413-8063, E-mail: dfox@gsu.edu. *Application contact:* Bobbie Turner, Administrative Coordinator I, 404-413-8405, Fax: 404-413-8063, E-mail: bnturner@gsu.edu.
Website: http://mse.education.gsu.edu/

Grambling State University, School of Graduate Studies and Research, College of Education, Department of Educational Leadership, Grambling, LA 71245. Offers developmental education (MS, Ed D, PMC), including curriculum and instructional design (Ed D), English (MS), guidance and counseling (MS), higher education administration and management (Ed D), mathematics (MS), reading (MS), science (MS), student development and personnel services (Ed D); educational leadership (M Ed). *Program availability:* Part-time, evening/weekend. *Degree requirements:* For master's, comprehensive exam, thesis (for some programs); for doctorate, comprehensive exam, thesis/dissertation. *Entrance requirements:* For master's, GRE, minimum GPA of 2.5 on last degree; for doctorate, GRE (minimum score 1000, 500 on Verbal), master's degree, minimum GPA of 3.0 on last degree. Additional exam requirements/recommendations for international students: Required—TOEFL (minimum score 500 paper-based; 62 iBT). Electronic applications accepted.

Grand Canyon University, College of Education, Phoenix, AZ 85017-1097. Offers autism spectrum disorders (MA); curriculum and instruction (MA); early childhood education (M Ed); educational administration (M Ed); educational leadership (M Ed); elementary education (M Ed); gifted education (MA); instructional technology (MS); K-12 leadership (Ed S); reading (MA); secondary education (M Ed); secondary humanities education (M Ed); secondary STEM education (M Ed); special education (M Ed); teaching and learning (Ed D); teaching English to speakers of other languages (MA). *Program availability:* Part-time, evening/weekend, online learning. *Degree requirements:* For master's, publishable research paper (M Ed), e-portfolio. *Entrance requirements:* For master's, undergraduate degree from accredited, GCU-approved college, university, or program with minimum GPA 2.8. Additional exam requirements/recommendations for international students: Required—TOEFL (minimum score 550 paper-based; 79 iBT), IELTS (minimum score 6). *Application deadline:* For fall admission, 8/21 for domestic students, 7/2 for international students; for spring admission, 12/24 for domestic students, 11/1 for international students. Applications are processed on a rolling basis. Application fee: $100. Electronic applications accepted. *Financial support:* Federal Work-Study available. Support available to part-time students. Financial award applicants required to submit FAFSA. *Unit head:* Dr. Kimberly L. LaPrade, Dean, 602-639-6360, E-mail: kimberly.laprade@gcu.edu. *Application contact:* Dr. Kimberly L. LaPrade, Dean, 602-639-6360, E-mail: kimberly.laprade@gcu.edu.
Website: https://www.gcu.edu/college-of-education.php

Hamline University, School of Education, St. Paul, MN 55104-1284. Offers education (MA Ed, Ed D); English as a second language (MA); literacy education (MA); natural science and environmental education (MA Ed); teaching (MAT); teaching English to speakers of other languages (MA). *Accreditation:* NCATE (one or more programs are accredited). *Program availability:* Part-time, evening/weekend, 100% online, blended/hybrid learning. *Faculty:* 29 full-time (23 women), 90 part-time/adjunct (70 women). *Students:* 277 full-time (201 women), 762 part-time (601 women); includes 122 minority (29 Black or African American, non-Hispanic/Latino; 1 American Indian or Alaska Native, non-Hispanic/Latino; 43 Asian, non-Hispanic/Latino; 29 Hispanic/Latino; 20 Two or more races, non-Hispanic/Latino), 12 international. Average age 34. 408 applicants, 77% accepted, 230 enrolled. In 2016, 279 master's, 14 doctorates awarded. *Degree requirements:* For master's, thesis (for some programs), thesis or capstone project; for doctorate, comprehensive exam, thesis/dissertation. *Entrance requirements:* For master's, official transcripts, essay, letters of recommendation, minimum GPA of 3.0 from bachelor's work; resume and/or writing samples (for some programs); for doctorate, personal statement, master's degree with minimum GPA of 3.0, letters of recommendation, writing sample. Additional exam requirements/recommendations for international students: Required—TOEFL. *Application deadline:* For fall admission, 6/1 for domestic and international students; for spring admission, 11/1 for domestic and international students; for summer admission, 3/1 for domestic and international students. Applications are processed on a rolling basis. Application fee: $0 ($100 for international students). Electronic applications accepted. *Expenses:* $466-$721 per credit. *Financial support:* Career-related internships or fieldwork, Federal Work-Study, and scholarships/grants available. Support available to part-time students. Financial award applicants required to submit FAFSA. *Faculty research:* Adult basic education, service-learning, teacher dispositions, diversity, technology. *Unit head:* Dr. Nancy Sorenson, Dean, 651-523-2600, Fax: 651-523-2489, E-mail: education@hamline.edu. *Application contact:* Shawn Skoog, Director of Graduate Recruitment and Admission, 651-523-2900, Fax: 651-523-3058, E-mail: gradprog@hamline.edu.
Website: http://www.hamline.edu/education

Hardin-Simmons University, Graduate School, Holland School of Sciences and Mathematics, Abilene, TX 79698-0001. Offers MS, DPT. *Program availability:* Part-time. *Faculty:* 5 full-time (2 women), 1 part-time/adjunct (0 women). *Students:* 4 full-time (2 women), 15 part-time (12 women); includes 3 minority (all Hispanic/Latino). Average age 35. In 2016, 9 master's awarded. *Degree requirements:* For master's, comprehensive exam, thesis or alternative, internship; for doctorate, comprehensive exam, thesis/dissertation or alternative. *Entrance requirements:* For master's, minimum undergraduate GPA of 3.0 in major, 2.7 overall; 2 semesters of course work each in biology, chemistry and geology; interview; writing sample; occupational experience; for doctorate, letters of recommendation, interview, writing sample. Additional exam requirements/recommendations for international students: Required—TOEFL (minimum score 550 paper-based; 75 iBT). *Application deadline:* For fall admission, 8/15 priority date for domestic students, 4/1 for international students; for spring admission, 1/5 priority date for domestic students, 9/1 for international students. Applications are processed on a rolling basis. Application fee: $50. Electronic applications accepted. *Expenses: Tuition:* Full-time $12,510; part-time $695 per credit hour. *Required fees:* $325; $110 per semester. *Financial support:* In 2016–17, 9 students received support. Fellowships, career-related internships or fieldwork, and scholarships/grants available. Support available to part-time students. Financial award application deadline: 6/30; financial award applicants required to submit FAFSA. *Unit head:* Dr. Christopher McNair, Dean, 325-670-1401, Fax: 325-670-1385, E-mail: cmcnair@hsutx.edu. *Application contact:* Dr. Nancy Kucinski, Dean of Graduate Studies, 325-670-1298, Fax: 325-670-1564, E-mail: gradoff@hsutx.edu.
Website: http://www.hsutx.edu/academics/holland

Harrison Middleton University, Graduate Program, Tempe, AZ 85282. Offers education (MA, Ed D); humanities (MA); imaginative literature (MA); interdisciplinary studies (DA); jurisprudence (MA); natural science (MA); philosophy and religion (MA); social science (MA). *Program availability:* Part-time, evening/weekend, online learning. *Degree requirements:* For master's and doctorate, capstone project. *Entrance requirements:* For master's, interview; for doctorate, 2 academic letters of reference, interview, essay. Additional exam requirements/recommendations for international students: Required—TOEFL (minimum score 550 paper-based; 80 iBT). Electronic applications accepted. *Faculty research:* Japanese animation, educational leadership, war art, John Muir's wilderness.

Heritage University, Graduate Programs in Education, Program in Professional Studies, Toppenish, WA 98948-9599. Offers bilingual education/ESL (M Ed); biology (M Ed); English and literature (M Ed); reading/literacy (M Ed); special education (M Ed). *Program availability:* Part-time, evening/weekend. *Degree requirements:* For master's, comprehensive exam (for some programs), thesis (for some programs).

Hofstra University, School of Education, Programs in Teacher Education, Hempstead, NY 11549. Offers bilingual education (MA, Advanced Certificate); bilingual extension (Advanced Certificate), including education/speech language pathology; business education (MS Ed); early childhood and childhood education (MS Ed); early childhood education (MA, MS Ed); education technology (Advanced Certificate); elementary education (MA, MS Ed), including science, technology, engineering, and mathematics (STEM) (MA); English education (MS Ed); family and consumer science (MS Ed); fine arts and music education (Advanced Certificate); fine arts education (MS Ed); foreign language and TESOL (MS Ed); foreign language education (MS Ed), including French, German, Russian, Spanish; learning and teaching (Ed D), including applied linguistics, art education, arts and humanities, early childhood education, English education, human development, math education, math, science, and technology, multicultural education, physical education, science education, social studies education, special education; mathematics education (MA, MS Ed); middle school extension (Advanced Certificate), including grades 5-6, grades 7-9; music education (MA, MS Ed); science education (MA, MS Ed), including biology, chemistry, earth science, geology, physics; secondary education (Advanced Certificate); social studies education (MA, MS Ed); teaching languages other than English and TESOL (MS Ed); TESOL (MS Ed, Advanced Certificate). *Program availability:* Part-time, evening/weekend, blended/hybrid learning. *Students:* 139 full-time (97 women), 145 part-time (106 women); includes 60 minority (15 Black or African American, non-Hispanic/Latino; 1 American Indian or Alaska Native, non-Hispanic/Latino; 12 Asian, non-Hispanic/Latino; 31 Hispanic/Latino; 1 Two or more races, non-Hispanic/Latino), 21 international. Average age 29. 255 applicants, 86% accepted, 122 enrolled. In 2016, 101 master's, 4 doctorates, 43 other advanced degrees awarded. *Degree requirements:* For master's, comprehensive exam, thesis (for some programs), exit project, student teaching, fieldwork, electronic portfolio, curriculum project, minimum GPA of 3.0; for doctorate, thesis/dissertation; for Advanced Certificate, 3 foreign languages, comprehensive exam (for some programs), thesis project. *Entrance requirements:* For master's, GRE, MAT, 2 letters of recommendation, portfolio, teacher certification (MA), interview, essay; for doctorate, GMAT, GRE, LSAT, or MAT; for Advanced Certificate, 2 letters of recommendation, essay, interview and/or portfolio, teaching certificate. Additional exam requirements/recommendations for international students: Required—TOEFL (minimum score 550 paper-based; 80 iBT). *Application deadline:* Applications are processed on a rolling basis. Application fee: $75. Electronic applications accepted. *Expenses: Tuition:* Full-time $1240. *Required fees:* $970. Tuition and fees vary according to program. *Financial support:* In 2016–17, 149 students received support, including 58 fellowships with full and partial tuition reimbursements available (averaging $5,309 per year), 5 research assistantships with full and partial tuition reimbursements available (averaging $7,073 per year); career-related internships or fieldwork, Federal Work-Study, institutionally sponsored loans, scholarships/grants, traineeships, tuition waivers (full and partial), and unspecified assistantships also available. Support available to part-time students. Financial award applicants required to submit FAFSA. *Faculty research:* Educational interventions that foster critical-thinking

skills; teachers' attitudes about professional development; threats to teacher quality. *Unit head:* Dr. Eustace Thompson, Chairperson, 516-463-5749, Fax: 516-463-6275, E-mail: eustace.g.thompson@hofstra.edu. *Application contact:* Sunil Samuel, Assistant Vice President of Admissions, 516-463-4723, Fax: 516-463-4664, E-mail: graduateadmission@hofstra.edu.
Website: http://www.hofstra.edu/education/

Hood College, Graduate School, Department of Education, Frederick, MD 21701-8575. Offers curriculum and instruction (MS), including elementary education, elementary science and mathematics education, secondary education, special education; educational leadership (MS); reading specialization (MS); STEM education (Certificate). *Accreditation:* NCATE. *Program availability:* Part-time-only, evening/weekend. *Faculty:* 3 full-time, 37 part-time/adjunct. *Students:* 1 (woman) full-time, 357 part-time (283 women); includes 71 minority (41 Black or African American, non-Hispanic/Latino; 6 Asian, non-Hispanic/Latino; 15 Hispanic/Latino; 9 Two or more races, non-Hispanic/Latino). Average age 33. 96 applicants, 95% accepted, 83 enrolled. In 2016, 47 master's awarded. *Degree requirements:* For master's, action research project, portfolio (for reading specialization); for Certificate, STEM capstone activity. *Entrance requirements:* For master's, minimum GPA of 2.75, teaching certification, writing sample during interview, letter of recommendation from principal (for educational leadership program only). Additional exam requirements/recommendations for international students: Required—TOEFL (minimum score 575 paper-based; 89 iBT), IELTS (minimum score 6.5). *Application deadline:* For fall admission, 8/15 priority date for domestic students, 8/5 for international students; for spring admission, 12/1 priority date for domestic students, 12/1 for international students; for summer admission, 5/1 priority date for domestic students, 4/15 for international students. Applications are processed on a rolling basis. Application fee: $35. Electronic applications accepted. *Expenses:* $450 per credit; $105 comprehensive fee per semester. *Financial support:* Tuition waivers (partial) and unspecified assistantships available. Financial award applicants required to submit FAFSA. *Faculty research:* Leadership, action research, brain research, learning styles. *Unit head:* April Boulton, Interim Dean of the Graduate School, E-mail: gofurther@hood.edu. *Application contact:* Jan Marcus, Assistant Director of Graduate Admissions, 301-696-3600, E-mail: gofurther@hood.edu.
Website: http://www.hood.edu/academics/education/index.html

Hunter College of the City University of New York, Graduate School, School of Education, Programs in Secondary Education, Concentration in Biology Education, New York, NY 10065-5085. Offers MA. *Accreditation:* NCATE. *Degree requirements:* For master's, thesis, professional teaching portfolio, New York State Teacher Certification Exams, research project. *Entrance requirements:* For master's, minimum GPA of 2.8, 2 letters of reference, 21 credits of course work in biology. Additional exam requirements/recommendations for international students: Required—TOEFL, TWE. *Application deadline:* For fall admission, 4/1 for domestic students, 2/1 for international students; for spring admission, 11/1 for domestic students, 9/1 for international students. *Financial support:* Federal Work-Study and tuition waivers (partial) available. Support available to part-time students. *Unit head:* Dr. Steve Demeo, Program Advisor, 212-772-4776, E-mail: sdemeo@hunter.cuny.edu. *Application contact:* Milena Solo, Director for Graduate Admissions, 212-772-4482, E-mail: admissions@hunter.cuny.edu.

Hunter College of the City University of New York, Graduate School, School of Education, Programs in Secondary Education, Concentration in Chemistry Education, New York, NY 10065-5085. Offers MA. *Accreditation:* NCATE. *Degree requirements:* For master's, thesis, professional teaching portfolio, New York State Teacher Certification Exam. *Entrance requirements:* For master's, minimum GPA of 2.8, 2 letters of reference, minimum of 29 credits in science and mathematics. *Application deadline:* For fall admission, 4/1 for domestic students, 2/1 for international students; for spring admission, 11/1 for domestic students, 9/1 for international students. *Financial support:* Federal Work-Study and tuition waivers (partial) available. Support available to part-time students. *Unit head:* Dr. Stephen DeMeo, Education Advisor, 212-772-4776, E-mail: sdemeo@hunter.cuny.edu. *Application contact:* Pamela Mills, Chemistry Department Advisor, 212-772-5331, E-mail: pam.mills@hunter.cuny.edu.

Illinois Institute of Technology, Graduate College, College of Science, Department of Mathematics and Science Education, Chicago, IL 60616. Offers mathematics education (MAS, PhD); science education (MAS, PhD). *Degree requirements:* For master's, comprehensive exam (for some programs), thesis optional; for doctorate, comprehensive exam, thesis/dissertation. *Entrance requirements:* For master's, GRE General Test (minimum score 900 quantitative and verbal; 2.5 analytical writing), minimum undergraduate GPA of 3.0; two-page professional statement of goals/objectives; curriculum vita; three letters of recommendation; for doctorate, GRE General Test (minimum score 1000 quantitative and verbal; 3.0 analytical writing), minimum GPA of 3.0, 3 years of teaching experience. Additional exam requirements/recommendations for international students: Required—TOEFL (minimum score 600 paper-based; 80 iBT). Electronic applications accepted. *Faculty research:* Informal science/math education, curriculum development, integration of science/math disciplines and across disciplines, instructional methods, students' and teachers' conceptions of scientific/mathematical inquiry and the nature of science/math, instructional models, evaluation, and research design.

Indiana State University, College of Graduate and Professional Studies, College of Arts and Sciences, Department of Biology, Terre Haute, IN 47809. Offers cellular and molecular biology (PhD); ecology, systematics and evolution (PhD); life sciences (MS); physiology (PhD); science education (MS). *Degree requirements:* For master's, thesis optional; for doctorate, comprehensive exam, thesis/dissertation. *Entrance requirements:* For master's and doctorate, GRE General Test. Electronic applications accepted.

Indiana University Bloomington, School of Education, Department of Curriculum and Instruction, Bloomington, IN 47405-7000. Offers art education (MS, Ed D, PhD); curriculum studies (Ed D, PhD); elementary education (MS, Ed D, PhD, Ed S); mathematics education (MS, Ed D, PhD); science education (MS, Ed D, PhD); secondary education (MS, Ed D, PhD); social studies education (MS, PhD); special education (PhD, Ed S). *Accreditation:* NCATE. *Program availability:* Part-time, evening/weekend. Terminal master's awarded for partial completion of doctoral program. *Degree requirements:* For doctorate, thesis/dissertation; for Ed S, comprehensive exam or project. *Entrance requirements:* For master's, doctorate, and Ed S, GRE General Test. Electronic applications accepted.

Indiana University Bloomington, University Graduate School, College of Arts and Sciences, Department of Biology, Bloomington, IN 47405. Offers biology teaching (MAT); biotechnology (MA); evolution, ecology, and behavior (MA, PhD); genetics (PhD); microbiology (MA, PhD); molecular, cellular, and developmental biology (PhD); plant sciences (MA, PhD); zoology (MA, PhD). Terminal master's awarded for partial completion of doctoral program. *Degree requirements:* For master's, thesis, oral defense; for doctorate, thesis/dissertation, oral defense. *Entrance requirements:* For master's and doctorate, GRE General Test. Additional exam requirements/recommendations for international students: Required—TOEFL (minimum score 100 iBT). Electronic applications accepted. *Faculty research:* Evolution, ecology and behavior; microbiology; molecular biology and genetics; plant biology.

Indiana University Bloomington, University Graduate School, College of Arts and Sciences, Department of Chemistry, Bloomington, IN 47405. Offers analytical chemistry (PhD); chemical biology (PhD); chemistry (MAT); inorganic chemistry (PhD); materials chemistry (PhD); organic chemistry (PhD); physical chemistry (PhD); MSES/MS. Terminal master's awarded for partial completion of doctoral program. *Degree requirements:* For master's, thesis; for doctorate, thesis/dissertation. *Entrance requirements:* For master's and doctorate, GRE General Test, GRE Subject Test. Additional exam requirements/recommendations for international students: Required—TOEFL. Electronic applications accepted. *Faculty research:* Synthesis of complex natural products, organic reaction mechanisms, organic electrochemistry, transitive-metal chemistry, solid-state and surface chemistry.

Instituto Tecnológico y de Estudios Superiores de Monterrey, Campus Monterrey, Graduate and Research Division, Program in Natural and Social Sciences, Monterrey, Mexico. Offers biotechnology (MS); chemistry (MS, PhD); communications (MS); education (MA). *Program availability:* Part-time. *Degree requirements:* For master's, one foreign language, thesis; for doctorate, one foreign language, thesis/dissertation. *Entrance requirements:* For master's, EXADEP; for doctorate, EXADEP, master's degree in related field. Additional exam requirements/recommendations for international students: Required—TOEFL. *Faculty research:* Cultural industries, mineral substances, bioremediation, food processing, CQ in industrial chemical processing.

Inter American University of Puerto Rico, Arecibo Campus, Programs in Education, Arecibo, PR 00614-4050. Offers administration and educational supervision (MA Ed); counseling and guidance (MA Ed); curriculum and teaching (MA Ed), including biology education, English as a second language, history education, math education, Spanish; elementary education (MA Ed). *Accreditation:* TEAC. *Degree requirements:* For master's, comprehensive exam, thesis optional. *Entrance requirements:* For master's, GRE, EXADEP, bachelor's degree in education or teaching license (administration and supervision) or courses in education and psychology (counseling and guidance), minimum GPA of 2.5 in last 60 credits.

Inter American University of Puerto Rico, Barranquitas Campus, Program in Education, Barranquitas, PR 00794. Offers curriculum and teaching (M Ed), including biology education, English as a second language, history education, mathematics education, Spanish; educational leadership and management (MA); elementary education (M Ed); information and library service technology (M Ed); special education (MA). *Accreditation:* TEAC. *Degree requirements:* For master's, comprehensive exam, thesis optional. *Entrance requirements:* For master's, EXADEP, letter of recommendation. Electronic applications accepted.

Inter American University of Puerto Rico, Metropolitan Campus, Graduate Programs, Program in Teaching of Science, San Juan, PR 00919-1293. Offers MA. *Degree requirements:* For master's, comprehensive exam. *Entrance requirements:* For master's, GRE or EXADEP, interview. Electronic applications accepted.

Inter American University of Puerto Rico, Ponce Campus, Graduate School, Mercedita, PR 00715-1602. Offers accounting (MBA); biology (M Ed); chemistry (M Ed); criminal justice (MA); elementary education (M Ed); English as a Second Language (M Ed); finance (MBA); history (M Ed); human resources (MBA); marketing (MBA); mathematics (M Ed); Spanish (M Ed). *Entrance requirements:* For master's, minimum GPA of 2.5.

Inter American University of Puerto Rico, San Germán Campus, Graduate Studies Center, Program in Science Education, San Germán, PR 00683-5008. Offers MA. *Accreditation:* TEAC. *Program availability:* Part-time, evening/weekend. *Degree requirements:* For master's, comprehensive exam. *Entrance requirements:* For master's, GRE General Test or EXADEP, minimum GPA of 3.0.

Iona College, School of Arts and Science, Department of Education, New Rochelle, NY 10801-1890. Offers adolescence education: biology (MS Ed, MST); adolescence education: English (MS Ed); adolescence education: mathematics (MST); adolescence education: social studies (MS Ed, MST); adolescence education: Spanish (MS Ed); adolescence special education 5-12 (MST); childhood and special education (MST); early childhood and childhood (MST); educational leadership (MS Ed). *Accreditation:* NCATE. *Program availability:* Part-time, evening/weekend. *Faculty:* 7 full-time (6 women), 4 part-time/adjunct (2 women). *Students:* 27 full-time (19 women), 27 part-time (18 women); includes 18 minority (4 Black or African American, non-Hispanic/Latino; 1 Asian, non-Hispanic/Latino; 12 Hispanic/Latino; 1 Two or more races, non-Hispanic/Latino). Average age 26. 6 applicants, 67% accepted, 3 enrolled. In 2016, 25 master's awarded. *Degree requirements:* For master's, thesis or alternative. *Entrance requirements:* For master's, minimum GPA of 3.0, NY State teaching certificate and bachelor's degree (for MS Ed). Additional exam requirements/recommendations for international students: Required—TOEFL (minimum score 550 paper-based; 80 iBT), IELTS (minimum score 6.5). *Application deadline:* For fall admission, 8/1 priority date for domestic students, 5/1 priority date for international students; for spring admission, 1/1 priority date for domestic students, 9/1 priority date for international students. Applications are processed on a rolling basis. Application fee: $50. Electronic applications accepted. *Expenses: Tuition:* Full-time $19,692; part-time $1094 per credit. *Required fees:* $245 per term. Tuition and fees vary according to program. *Financial support:* In 2016–17, 3 students received support. Unspecified assistantships available. Support available to part-time students. Financial award application deadline: 4/15; financial award applicants required to submit FAFSA. *Faculty research:* Engaging teacher educators in scientific process, cross-national comparisons of mathematics teaching, questioning strategies in the classroom, research methods, literacy development. *Unit head:* Margaret Smith, PhD, Chair, 914-633-2210, Fax: 914-633-2608, E-mail: msmith@iona.edu. *Application contact:* Richard McMahon, Coordinator, Graduate School of Education, 914-633-2552, E-mail: rmcmahon@iona.edu.
Website: http://www.iona.edu/Academics/School-of-Arts-Science/Departments/Education/Graduate-Programs.aspx

Iowa State University of Science and Technology, Program in Science Education, Ames, IA 50011. Offers MAT. *Entrance requirements:* For master's, GRE, three letters of recommendation, undergraduate degree in sciences (preferred). Additional exam requirements/recommendations for international students: Required—TOEFL (minimum score 560 paper-based; 83 iBT), IELTS (minimum score 6.5). *Application deadline:* For fall admission, 2/1 for domestic students. Application fee: $60 ($90 for international students). Electronic applications accepted. *Application contact:* Robyn Goldy, Application Contact, 515-294-1241, Fax: 515-294-6206, E-mail: rgoldy@iastate.edu.
Website: http://www.admissions.iastate.edu/apply/index.php

Jackson State University, Graduate School, College of Science, Engineering and Technology, Department of Physics, Atmospheric Sciences, and Geoscience, Jackson, MS 39217. Offers physical science (MS, PhD); science education (MST). *Program availability:* Part-time, evening/weekend. *Degree requirements:* For master's, comprehensive exam. *Entrance requirements:* For master's, GRE General Test. Additional exam requirements/recommendations for international students: Required—TOEFL (minimum score 520 paper-based; 67 iBT). *Application deadline:* For fall admission, 3/1 priority date for domestic students, 3/1 for international students; for spring admission, 10/1 for domestic and international students. Applications are processed on a rolling basis. Application fee: $25. *Expenses:* Tuition, state resident:

full-time $7141. Tuition, nonresident: full-time $17,494. *Required fees:* $1080. Tuition and fees vary according to class time, course level, course load, degree level, campus/location, program and student level. *Financial support:* Application deadline: 3/1. *Unit head:* Dr. Mehri Fadavi, Chair, 601-979-3634, Fax: 601-979-6196, E-mail: mehri.fadavi@jsums.edu. *Application contact:* Fatoumatta Sisay, Manager of Graduate Admissions, 601-979-0342, Fax: 601-979-4325, E-mail: fatoumatta.sisay@jsums.edu.
Website: http://www.jsums.edu/physics/

Kaplan University, Davenport Campus, School of Teacher Education, Davenport, IA 52807. Offers education (M Ed); secondary education (M Ed); teaching and learning (MA); teaching literacy and language: grades 6-12 (MA); teaching literacy and language: grades K-6 (MA); teaching mathematics: grades 6-8 (MA); teaching mathematics: grades 9-12 (MA); teaching mathematics: grades K-5 (MA); teaching science: grades 6-12 (MA); teaching science: grades K-6 (MA); teaching students with special needs (MA); teaching with technology (MA). *Program availability:* Part-time, evening/weekend, online learning. *Entrance requirements:* Additional exam requirements/recommendations for international students: Required—TOEFL (minimum score 550 paper-based; 80 iBT).

Lake Forest College, Master of Arts in Teaching Program, Lake Forest, IL 60045. Offers elementary education (MAT); K-12 French (MAT); K-12 music (MAT); K-12 Spanish (MAT); K-12 visual art (MAT); secondary biology (MAT); secondary chemistry (MAT); secondary English (MAT); secondary history (MAT); secondary mathematics (MAT). *Degree requirements:* For master's, comprehensive exam, portfolio. *Entrance requirements:* For master's, GRE.

Laurentian University, School of Graduate Studies and Research, Programme in Science Communication, Sudbury, ON P3E 2C6, Canada. Offers G Dip.

Lebanon Valley College, Program in Science Education, Annville, PA 17003-1400. Offers Integrative STEM Education (Certificate); STEM education (MSE). *Program availability:* Part-time-only, evening/weekend. *Faculty:* 11 part-time/adjunct (6 women). *Students:* 1 full-time (0 women), 14 part-time (9 women). Average age 35. 10 applicants, 70% accepted, 7 enrolled. In 2016, 6 master's awarded. *Degree requirements:* For master's, thesis or capstone project. *Entrance requirements:* For master's, baccalaureate degree, minimum GPA of 3.0, teacher certification, 3 letters of recommendation, transcripts, goal statement. Additional exam requirements/recommendations for international students: Required—TOEFL (minimum score 80 iBT). *Application deadline:* Applications are processed on a rolling basis. Application fee: $0. Electronic applications accepted. *Expenses:* $595 per credit hour. *Financial support:* Scholarships/grants available. Financial award application deadline: 3/1; financial award applicants required to submit FAFSA. *Faculty research:* Teacher quality and student achievement, STEM reform, STEM education. *Unit head:* Carrie Coryer, Director of MSE and STEM-based programs, 717-867-6190, Fax: 717-867-6018, E-mail: coryer@lvc.edu.
Website: http://www.lvc.edu/academics/graduate-studies/master-of-science-in-stem-education/

Lehman College of the City University of New York, School of Education, Department of Middle and High School Education, Program in Science Education, Bronx, NY 10468-1589. Offers MS Ed. *Accreditation:* NCATE.

Lesley University, Graduate School of Education, Cambridge, MA 02138-2790. Offers arts, community, and education (M Ed); autism studies (Certificate); curriculum and instruction (M Ed, CAGS); early childhood education (M Ed); ecological teaching and learning (MS); educational studies (PhD), including adult learning, educational leadership, individually designed; elementary education (M Ed); emergent technologies for educators (Certificate); ESLArts: language learning through the arts (M Ed); high school education (M Ed); individually designed (M Ed); integrated teaching through the arts (M Ed); literacy for K-8 classroom teachers (M Ed); mathematics education (M Ed); middle school education (M Ed); moderate disabilities (M Ed); online learning (Certificate); reading (CAGS); science in education (M Ed); severe disabilities (M Ed); special needs (CAGS); specialist teacher of reading (M Ed); teacher of visual art (M Ed); technology in education (M Ed, CAGS). *Accreditation:* TEAC. *Program availability:* Part-time, evening/weekend, online learning. *Degree requirements:* For master's, practicum; for doctorate, thesis/dissertation. *Entrance requirements:* For master's, Massachusetts Tests for Educator Licensure (MTEL), transcripts, statement of purpose, recommendations; interview (for special education); for doctorate, GRE General Test, transcripts, statement of purpose, recommendations, interview, master's degree, resume; for other advanced degree, interview, master's degree. Additional exam requirements/recommendations for international students: Required—TOEFL (minimum score 550 paper-based; 80 iBT). Electronic applications accepted. *Faculty research:* Assessment in literacy, mathematics and science; autism spectrum disorders; instructional technology and online learning; multicultural education and English language learners.

Lewis University, College of Education, Program in Secondary Education, Romeoville, IL 60446. Offers biology (MA); chemistry (MA); English (MA); history (MA); math (MA); physics (MA); psychology and social science (MA). *Program availability:* Part-time. *Students:* 12 full-time (7 women), 16 part-time (12 women); includes 6 minority (2 Black or African American, non-Hispanic/Latino; 3 Hispanic/Latino; 1 Two or more races, non-Hispanic/Latino). Average age 27. *Degree requirements:* For master's, departmental qualifying exam. *Entrance requirements:* For master's, writing exam, minimum GPA of 2.75, 2 letters of recommendation, interview. Additional exam requirements/recommendations for international students: Required—TOEFL (minimum score 550 paper-based; 80 iBT). *Application deadline:* For fall admission, 5/1 priority date for international students; for spring admission, 11/15 priority date for international students. Applications are processed on a rolling basis. Application fee: $40. Electronic applications accepted. *Expenses: Tuition:* Full-time $13,860; part-time $770 per credit hour. *Required fees:* $75 per semester. Tuition and fees vary according to degree level and program. *Financial support:* Federal Work-Study, scholarships/grants, and unspecified assistantships available. Financial award application deadline: 5/1; financial award applicants required to submit FAFSA. *Unit head:* Dr. Dorene Huvaere, Program Director, 815-838-0500 Ext. 5885, E-mail: huvaersdo@lewisu.edu. *Application contact:* Linda Campbell, Graduate Admissions Counselor, 815-836-5610, E-mail: campbold@lewisu.edu.

Lynchburg College, Graduate Studies, M Ed Program in Science Education, Lynchburg, VA 24501-3199. Offers M Ed. *Program availability:* Part-time, evening/weekend. *Students:* 7 full-time (6 women), 4 part-time (3 women); includes 1 minority (Black or African American, non-Hispanic/Latino), 3 international. In 2016, 1 master's awarded. *Degree requirements:* For master's, comprehensive exam. *Entrance requirements:* For master's, GRE, minimum GPA of 3.0 (preferred), official transcripts (bachelor's, others as relevant), three letters of recommendation, career goals statement. Additional exam requirements/recommendations for international students: Required—TOEFL (minimum score 550 paper-based; 79 iBT), IELTS (minimum score 6.5). *Application deadline:* For fall admission, 7/31 for domestic students, 6/1 for international students; for spring admission, 11/30 for domestic students, 10/15 for international students. Applications are processed on a rolling basis. Application fee: $30. Electronic applications accepted. Application fee is waived when completed online. *Expenses:* Contact institution. *Financial support:* Federal Work-Study, scholarships/grants, health care benefits, and unspecified assistantships available. Support available to part-time students. Financial award application deadline: 7/31; financial award applicants required to submit FAFSA. *Unit head:* Dr. David Perault, Professor/Director of M Ed in Science Education, 434-544-8370, E-mail: perault@lynchburg.edu.
Website: http://www.lynchburg.edu/graduate/master-of-education-in-science-education/

Lyndon State College, Graduate Programs in Education, Department of Natural Sciences, Lyndonville, VT 05851-0919. Offers science education (MST). *Program availability:* Part-time. *Degree requirements:* For master's, exam or major field project. *Entrance requirements:* Additional exam requirements/recommendations for international students: Recommended—TOEFL (minimum score 500 paper-based). *Faculty research:* Fern genetics, comparative butterfly research.

Manhattanville College, School of Education, Program in Middle Childhood/Adolescence Education (Grades 5-12), Purchase, NY 10577-2132. Offers biology (MAT); biology and special education (MPS); chemistry (MAT); chemistry and special education (MPS); English (MAT); English and special education (MPS); literacy and special education (MPS); literacy specialist (MPS); math and special education (MPS); mathematics (MAT); physics (MAT); social studies (MAT); social studies and special education (MPS); special education generalist (MPS); teaching languages other than English (MAT), including French, Italian, Latin, Spanish. *Program availability:* Part-time, evening/weekend. *Students:* 28 applicants, 86% accepted, 21 enrolled. In 2016, 23 master's awarded. *Degree requirements:* For master's, comprehensive exam (for some programs), thesis (for some programs), student teaching, research seminars, portfolios, internships, writing assessment. *Entrance requirements:* For master's, GRE or MAT, minimum undergraduate GPA of 3.0, 2 letters of recommendation. Additional exam requirements/recommendations for international students: Required—TOEFL (minimum score 85 iBT); Recommended—IELTS. *Application deadline:* For fall admission, 7/1 priority date for domestic and international students; for spring admission, 11/1 priority date for domestic and international students; for summer admission, 4/1 priority date for domestic and international students. Applications are processed on a rolling basis. Application fee: $75. Electronic applications accepted. *Expenses: Tuition:* Full-time $16,470; part-time $915 per credit. *Required fees:* $60 per semester. Part-time tuition and fees vary according to course load and program. *Financial support:* Teaching assistantships, career-related internships or fieldwork, Federal Work-Study, institutionally sponsored loans, scholarships/grants, and unspecified assistantships available. Financial award applicants required to submit FAFSA. *Unit head:* Victoria Fantozzi, Chairperson, Department of Curriculum and Instruction, 914-323-7138, E-mail: victoria.fantozzi@mville.edu. *Application contact:* Jeanine Pardey-Levine, Director of Graduate Enrollment Management, 914-323-3208, Fax: 914-694-1732, E-mail: edschool@mville.edu.
Website: http://www.mville.edu/programs#/search/19

McDaniel College, Graduate and Professional Studies, Program in Elementary and Secondary Education, Westminster, MD 21157-4390. Offers elementary education (MS); elementary STEM instructional leader (Postbaccalaureate Certificate); equity and excellence in education (Postbaccalaureate Certificate); learning technology specialist (Postbaccalaureate Certificate); secondary education (MS). *Accreditation:* NCATE. *Program availability:* Part-time, evening/weekend. *Faculty:* 3 full-time (2 women), 27 part-time/adjunct (22 women). *Students:* 8 full-time (5 women), 179 part-time (143 women); includes 60 minority (31 Black or African American, non-Hispanic/Latino; 3 American Indian or Alaska Native, non-Hispanic/Latino; 13 Asian, non-Hispanic/Latino; 11 Hispanic/Latino; 2 Two or more races, non-Hispanic/Latino), 1 international. Average age 36. 79 applicants, 94% accepted. In 2016, 23 master's, 48 other advanced degrees awarded. *Degree requirements:* For master's, comprehensive exam (for some programs), thesis optional. *Entrance requirements:* For master's, PRAXIS, 2 references. Additional exam requirements/recommendations for international students: Required—TOEFL (minimum score 79 iBT), IELTS (minimum score 6). *Application deadline:* For fall admission, 6/1 priority date for domestic students; for spring admission, 11/1 priority date for domestic students; for summer admission, 3/1 priority date for domestic students. Applications are processed on a rolling basis. Application fee: $75. Electronic applications accepted. *Expenses: Tuition:* Full-time $8370; part-time $465 per credit. *Required fees:* $75 per semester. Tuition and fees vary according to course load, program and reciprocity agreements. *Financial support:* Application deadline: 3/1; applicants required to submit FAFSA. *Unit head:* Fax: 410-857-2515, E-mail: gradadms@mcdaniel.edu. *Application contact:* Penny Pfeiffer, Senior Graduate Enrollment Management Specialist, 410-857-2513, Fax: 410-857-2515, E-mail: ppfeiffer@mcdaniel.edu.

McNeese State University, Doré School of Graduate Studies, College of Science, Department of Chemistry, Program in Environmental and Chemical Sciences, Lake Charles, LA 70609. Offers chemistry (MS); chemistry/environmental science education (MS). *Program availability:* Evening/weekend. *Degree requirements:* For master's, comprehensive exam, thesis or alternative. *Entrance requirements:* For master's, GRE.

Michigan State University, The Graduate School, College of Natural Science and College of Education, Division of Science and Mathematics Education, East Lansing, MI 48824. Offers biological, physical and general science for teachers (MAT, MS), including biological science (MS), general science (MAT), physical science (MS); mathematics education (MS, PhD).

Michigan Technological University, Graduate School, College of Sciences and Arts, Department of Cognitive and Learning Sciences, Houghton, MI 49931. Offers applied cognitive science and human factors (MS, PhD); applied science education (MS); post-secondary STEM education (Graduate Certificate). *Program availability:* Part-time, blended/hybrid learning. *Faculty:* 24 full-time (9 women), 11 part-time/adjunct (3 women). *Students:* 12 full-time (8 women), 21 part-time (10 women); includes 2 minority (1 Black or African American, non-Hispanic/Latino; 1 Two or more races, non-Hispanic/Latino), 3 international. Average age 35. 46 applicants, 20% accepted, 5 enrolled. In 2016, 6 master's, 4 doctorates awarded. Terminal master's awarded for partial completion of doctoral program. *Degree requirements:* For master's, comprehensive exam (for some programs), thesis (for some programs); for doctorate, comprehensive exam, thesis/dissertation, applied internship experience. *Entrance requirements:* For master's, GRE (for applied cognitive science and human factors program only), statement of purpose, personal statement, official transcripts, 3 letters of recommendation, resume/curriculum vitae; for doctorate, GRE, statement of purpose, personal statement, official transcripts, 3 letters of recommendation, resume/curriculum vitae. Additional exam requirements/recommendations for international students: Required—TOEFL (recommended minimum score 90 iBT) or IELTS. *Application deadline:* For fall admission, 2/15 priority date for domestic and international students. Applications are processed on a rolling basis. Electronic applications accepted. *Expenses:* Tuition, state resident: full-time $16,290; part-time $905 per credit. Tuition, nonresident: full-time $16,290; part-time $905 per credit. *Required fees:* $248; $124 per term. Tuition and fees vary according to course load and program. *Financial support:* In 2016–17, 14 students received support, including 2 fellowships (averaging $15,242 per year), 7 research assistantships with tuition reimbursements available (averaging $15,242 per year), teaching assistantships (averaging $15,242 per year); career-related internships or fieldwork, Federal Work-Study, scholarships/grants, health care benefits, unspecified assistantships, and adjunct instructor positions also available. Financial

award applicants required to submit FAFSA. *Faculty research:* Physical ergonomics, applied science education, applied cognitive science, human factors, educational technology cognitive modeling. *Total annual research expenditures:* $308,969. *Unit head:* Dr. Susan L. Amato-Henderson, Chair, 906-487-2536, Fax: 906-487-2468, E-mail: slamato@mtu.edu. *Application contact:* Carol T. Wingerson, Senior Staff Assistant, 906-487-2328, Fax: 906-487-2284, E-mail: gradadms@mtu.edu.
Website: http://www.mtu.edu/cls/

Middle Tennessee State University, College of Graduate Studies, College of Basic and Applied Sciences, Department of Aerospace, Murfreesboro, TN 37132. Offers aerospace education (M Ed); aviation administration (MS). *Program availability:* Part-time, evening/weekend, online learning. *Degree requirements:* For master's, comprehensive exam, thesis optional. *Entrance requirements:* For master's, GRE General Test or MAT. Additional exam requirements/recommendations for international students: Required—TOEFL (minimum score 525 paper-based; 71 iBT) or IELTS (minimum score 6). Electronic applications accepted.

Middle Tennessee State University, College of Graduate Studies, Interdisciplinary Program in Mathematics and Science Education, Murfreesboro, TN 37132. Offers PhD. *Program availability:* Part-time, evening/weekend, online learning. *Entrance requirements:* For doctorate, GRE. Additional exam requirements/recommendations for international students: Required—TOEFL (minimum score 525 paper-based; 71 iBT) or IELTS (minimum score 6). Electronic applications accepted.

Millersville University of Pennsylvania, College of Graduate Studies and Adult Learning, College of Education and Human Services, Department of Educational Foundations, Program in Assessment, Curriculum and Teaching - STEM Education Option, Millersville, PA 17551-0302. Offers M Ed. *Program availability:* Part-time, online only, 100% online. *Faculty:* 20 full-time (13 women), 2 part-time/adjunct (both women). *Students:* 14 part-time (8 women). Average age 32. 13 applicants, 100% accepted, 10 enrolled. *Degree requirements:* For master's, thesis/capstone. *Entrance requirements:* For master's, GRE or MAT (if undergraduate cumulative GPA is lower than 2.8), teaching certificate. Additional exam requirements/recommendations for international students: Required—TOEFL (minimum score 600 paper-based), IELTS (minimum score 6). *Application deadline:* Applications are processed on a rolling basis. Application fee: $40. Electronic applications accepted. *Expenses:* $483 per credit resident tuition; $566 per credit non-resident tuition. *Financial support:* Unspecified assistantships available. Financial award application deadline: 3/15; financial award applicants required to submit FAFSA. *Faculty research:* STEM education, instructional technology, on-line teaching. *Unit head:* Dr. Tim E. Mahoney, Coordinator, 717-871-7202, E-mail: tim.mahoney@millersville.edu. *Application contact:* Dr. Victor S. DeSantis, Dean of College of Graduate Studies and Adult Learning/Associate Provost for Civic and Community Engagement, 717-871-7619, Fax: 717-871-7954, E-mail: victor.desantis@millersville.edu.
Website: http://millersville.edu/academics/educ/edfoundations/master-stem.php

Millersville University of Pennsylvania, College of Graduate Studies and Adult Learning, College of Science and Technology, Millersville, PA 17551-0302. Offers M Ed, MS, MSN, DNP. *Program availability:* Part-time, evening/weekend, 100% online. *Faculty:* 54 full-time (21 women), 1 part-time/adjunct (0 women). *Students:* 20 full-time (12 women), 166 part-time (102 women); includes 25 minority (5 Black or African American, non-Hispanic/Latino; 1 American Indian or Alaska Native, non-Hispanic/Latino; 6 Asian, non-Hispanic/Latino; 10 Hispanic/Latino; 2 Native Hawaiian or other Pacific Islander, non-Hispanic/Latino; 1 Two or more races, non-Hispanic/Latino), 4 international. Average age 34. 112 applicants, 64% accepted, 52 enrolled. In 2016, 78 master's awarded. *Degree requirements:* For master's, comprehensive exam (for some programs), thesis optional, graded portfolio (educational foundations); field practicum; internship; applied research or scholarly project; for doctorate, comprehensive exam, scholarly project. *Entrance requirements:* For master's, GRE or MAT (if undergraduate cumulative GPA is 3.0 or lower). Additional exam requirements/recommendations for international students: Required—TOEFL (minimum score 600 paper-based), IELTS (minimum score 6). *Application deadline:* Applications are processed on a rolling basis. Application fee: $40. Electronic applications accepted. *Expenses:* $483 per credit resident tuition; $725 per credit non-resident tuition. *Financial support:* In 2016–17, 20 students received support. Unspecified assistantships available. Financial award application deadline: 3/15; financial award applicants required to submit FAFSA. *Unit head:* Dr. Michael Jackson, Dean, College of Science and Technology, 717-871-4292, E-mail: michael.jackson@millersville.edu. *Application contact:* Dr. Victor S. DeSantis, Dean of College of Graduate Studies and Adult Learning/Associate Provost for Civic and Community Engagement, 717-871-7619, Fax: 717-871-7954, E-mail: victor.desantis@millersville.edu.
Website: http://www.millersville.edu/academics/scma/scienceandmath/index.php

Minnesota State University Mankato, College of Graduate Studies and Research, College of Science, Engineering and Technology, Department of Biological Sciences, Mankato, MN 56001. Offers biology (MS); biology education (MS); environmental sciences (MS). *Program availability:* Part-time. *Students:* 8 full-time (4 women), 13 part-time (10 women). *Degree requirements:* For master's, one foreign language, comprehensive exam, thesis or alternative. *Entrance requirements:* For master's, minimum GPA of 3.0 during previous 2 years of course work. Additional exam requirements/recommendations for international students: Required—TOEFL. *Application deadline:* For fall admission, 7/1 priority date for domestic students; for spring admission, 11/1 for domestic students. Applications are processed on a rolling basis. Application fee: $40. Electronic applications accepted. *Financial support:* Fellowships, research assistantships with full tuition reimbursements, teaching assistantships with full tuition reimbursements, career-related internships or fieldwork, Federal Work-Study, institutionally sponsored loans, and unspecified assistantships available. Support available to part-time students. Financial award application deadline: 3/15; financial award applicants required to submit FAFSA.
Website: http://cset.mnsu.edu/biology/

Minnesota State University Mankato, College of Graduate Studies and Research, College of Science, Engineering and Technology, Department of Physics and Astronomy, Mankato, MN 56001. Offers physics (MS); physics education (MS). *Students:* 4 full-time (all women), 4 part-time (2 women). *Degree requirements:* For master's, one foreign language, comprehensive exam, thesis or alternative. *Entrance requirements:* For master's, minimum GPA of 2.75, two recommendation letters, one-page personal statement. Additional exam requirements/recommendations for international students: Required—TOEFL (minimum score 530 paper-based; 72 iBT). *Application deadline:* For fall admission, 7/1 priority date for domestic students; for spring admission, 11/1 for domestic students. Applications are processed on a rolling basis. Application fee: $40. Electronic applications accepted. *Financial support:* Research assistantships, teaching assistantships with full tuition reimbursements, Federal Work-Study, and unspecified assistantships available. Support available to part-time students. Financial award application deadline: 3/15; financial award applicants required to submit FAFSA. *Unit head:* Dr. Thomas Brown, Chair, 507-389-2096, Fax: 507-389-1095, E-mail: thomas.brown@mnsu.edu.
Website: http://cset.mnsu.edu/pa/

Minot State University, Graduate School, Program in Biological and Agricultural Sciences, Minot, ND 58707-0002. Offers science (MAT). *Degree requirements:* For master's, thesis. *Entrance requirements:* For master's, minimum GPA of 3.0 or GRE General Test, secondary teaching certificate. Additional exam requirements/recommendations for international students: Required—TOEFL (minimum score 79 iBT), IELTS (minimum score 6). *Faculty research:* Science education.

Mississippi College, Graduate School, School of Education, Department of Teacher Education and Leadership, Clinton, MS 39058. Offers art (M Ed); biological science (M Ed); business education (M Ed); computer science (M Ed); dyslexia therapy (M Ed); educational leadership (M Ed, Ed D, Ed S); elementary education (M Ed, Ed S); English (M Ed); higher education administration (MS); mathematics (M Ed); secondary education (M Ed); social studies (history) (M Ed); teaching arts (M Ed). *Program availability:* Part-time, online learning. *Degree requirements:* For master's, comprehensive exam, thesis optional. *Entrance requirements:* For master's, NTE. Additional exam requirements/recommendations for international students: Recommended—TOEFL, IELTS. Electronic applications accepted.

Missouri State University, Graduate College, College of Natural and Applied Sciences, Department of Biology, Springfield, MO 65897. Offers biology (MS); natural and applied science (MNAS), including biology (MNAS, MS Ed); secondary education (MS Ed), including biology (MNAS, MS Ed). *Faculty:* 18 full-time (3 women), 7 part-time/adjunct (2 women). *Students:* 11 full-time (7 women), 30 part-time (22 women); includes 4 minority (1 Asian, non-Hispanic/Latino; 2 Hispanic/Latino; 1 Two or more races, non-Hispanic/Latino), 7 international. Average age 26. 34 applicants, 41% accepted, 10 enrolled. In 2016, 23 master's awarded. *Degree requirements:* For master's, comprehensive exam, thesis or alternative. *Entrance requirements:* For master's, GRE (MS, MNAS), 24 hours of course work in biology (MS); minimum GPA of 3.0 (MS, MNAS); 9-12 teacher certification (MS Ed). Additional exam requirements/recommendations for international students: Required—TOEFL (minimum score 550 paper-based; 79 iBT), IELTS (minimum score 6). *Application deadline:* For fall admission, 7/20 priority date for domestic students, 5/1 for international students; for spring admission, 12/20 priority date for domestic students, 9/1 for international students; for summer admission, 5/20 priority date for domestic students. Applications are processed on a rolling basis. Application fee: $35 ($50 for international students). Electronic applications accepted. *Expenses:* Tuition, state resident: full-time $5830. Tuition, nonresident: full-time $10,708. *Required fees:* $1130. Tuition and fees vary according to class time, course level, course load and program. *Financial support:* In 2016–17, 2 research assistantships with full tuition reimbursements (averaging $10,672 per year), 26 teaching assistantships with full tuition reimbursements (averaging $9,746 per year) were awarded; Federal Work-Study, institutionally sponsored loans, scholarships/grants, and unspecified assistantships also available. Financial award application deadline: 3/31; financial award applicants required to submit FAFSA. *Faculty research:* Hibernation physiology of bats, behavioral ecology of salamanders, mussel conservation, plant evolution and systematics, cellular/molecular mechanisms involved in migraine pathology. *Unit head:* Dr. S. Alicia Mathis, Department Head, 417-836-5126, Fax: 417-836-6934, E-mail: biology@missouristate.edu. *Application contact:* Michael Edwards, Coordinator of Graduate Admissions, 417-836-5330, Fax: 417-836-6200, E-mail: michaeledwards@missouristate.edu.
Website: http://biology.missouristate.edu/

Missouri State University, Graduate College, College of Natural and Applied Sciences, Department of Geography, Geology, and Planning, Springfield, MO 65897. Offers natural and applied science (MNAS), including geography, geology and planning; secondary education (MS Ed), including earth science, physical geography. *Program availability:* Part-time, evening/weekend. *Faculty:* 18 full-time (4 women), 1 part-time/adjunct (0 women). *Students:* 18 full-time (6 women), 15 part-time (9 women); includes 2 minority (both Hispanic/Latino), 4 international. Average age 30. 36 applicants, 67% accepted, 19 enrolled. In 2016, 5 master's awarded. *Degree requirements:* For master's, comprehensive exam, thesis (for some programs). *Entrance requirements:* For master's, GRE General Test (MS, MNAS), minimum undergraduate GPA of 3.0 (MS, MNAS), 9-12 teacher certification (MS Ed). Additional exam requirements/recommendations for international students: Required—TOEFL (minimum score 550 paper-based; 79 iBT), IELTS (minimum score 6). *Application deadline:* For fall admission, 7/20 priority date for domestic students, 5/1 for international students; for spring admission, 12/20 priority date for domestic students, 9/1 for international students. Applications are processed on a rolling basis. Application fee: $35 ($50 for international students). Electronic applications accepted. *Expenses:* Tuition, state resident: full-time $5830. Tuition, nonresident: full-time $10,708. *Required fees:* $1130. Tuition and fees vary according to class time, course level, course load and program. *Financial support:* In 2016–17, 3 research assistantships with full tuition reimbursements (averaging $11,574 per year), 15 teaching assistantships with full tuition reimbursements (averaging $9,365 per year) were awarded; career-related internships or fieldwork, Federal Work-Study, institutionally sponsored loans, scholarships/grants, and unspecified assistantships also available. Financial award application deadline: 3/31; financial award applicants required to submit FAFSA. *Faculty research:* Stratigraphy and ancient meteorite impacts, environmental geochemistry of karst, hyperspectral image processing, water quality, small town planning. *Unit head:* Dr. Toby Dogwiler, Department Head, 417-836-5800, Fax: 417-836-6934, E-mail: tobydogwiler@missouristate.edu. *Application contact:* Michael Edwards, Coordinator of Graduate Admissions, 417-836-5330, Fax: 417-836-6200, E-mail: michaeledwards@missouristate.edu.
Website: http://geosciences.missouristate.edu/

Missouri State University, Graduate College, College of Natural and Applied Sciences, Department of Physics, Astronomy, and Materials Science, Springfield, MO 65897. Offers materials science (MS); natural and applied science (MNAS), including physics (MNAS, MS Ed); secondary education (MS Ed), including physics (MNAS, MS Ed). *Program availability:* Part-time. *Faculty:* 9 full-time (0 women). *Students:* 17 full-time (2 women), 3 part-time (0 women), 15 international. Average age 26. 36 applicants, 44% accepted, 7 enrolled. In 2016, 5 master's awarded. *Degree requirements:* For master's, comprehensive exam, thesis. *Entrance requirements:* For master's, GRE (MS, MNAS), minimum undergraduate GPA of 3.0 (MS and MNAS), 9-12 teaching certification (MS Ed). Additional exam requirements/recommendations for international students: Required—TOEFL (minimum score 550 paper-based; 79 iBT), IELTS (minimum score 6). *Application deadline:* For fall admission, 7/20 priority date for domestic students, 5/1 for international students; for spring admission, 12/20 priority date for domestic students, 9/1 for international students. Applications are processed on a rolling basis. Application fee: $35 ($50 for international students). Electronic applications accepted. *Expenses:* Tuition, state resident: full-time $5830. Tuition, nonresident: full-time $10,708. *Required fees:* $1130. Tuition and fees vary according to class time, course level, course load and program. *Financial support:* In 2016–17, 6 research assistantships with full tuition reimbursements (averaging $10,672 per year), 11 teaching assistantships with full tuition reimbursements (averaging $10,672 per year) were awarded; Federal Work-Study, institutionally sponsored loans, scholarships/grants, and unspecified assistantships also available. Financial award application deadline: 3/31; financial award applicants required to submit FAFSA. *Faculty research:* Nanocomposites, ferroelectricity, infrared focal plane array sensors, biosensors, pulsating stars. *Unit head:* Dr. David Cornelison, Department Head, 417-836-4467, Fax: 417-836-6226, E-mail: physics@missouristate.edu. *Application contact:* Michael Edwards, Coordinator

of Graduate Admissions, 417-836-5330, Fax: 417-836-6200, E-mail: michaeledwards@missouristate.edu.
Website: http://physics.missouristate.edu/

Montclair State University, The Graduate School, College of Education and Human Services, MAT Program in Teaching, Montclair, NJ 07043-1624. Offers art (MAT); biology (MAT); chemistry (MAT); earth science (MAT); English (MAT); French (MAT); health and physical education (MAT); health education (MAT); mathematics (MAT); music (MAT); physical education (MAT); physical science (MAT); social studies (MAT); Spanish (MAT); teacher of English as a second language (MAT). *Degree requirements:* For master's, comprehensive exam, thesis or alternative. *Entrance requirements:* For master's, interview, 2 letters of recommendation. Additional exam requirements/recommendations for international students: Required—TOEFL (minimum score 83 iBT), IELTS (minimum score 6.5). Electronic applications accepted. *Expenses:* Tuition, state resident: part-time $553 per credit. Tuition, nonresident: part-time $854 per credit. *Required fees:* $91 per credit. Tuition and fees vary according to program.

Montclair State University, The Graduate School, College of Science and Mathematics, Program in Biology, Montclair, NJ 07043-1624. Offers biological science/education (MS); biology (MS); ecology and evolution (MS); physiology (MS). *Expenses:* Tuition, state resident: part-time $553 per credit. Tuition, nonresident: part-time $854 per credit. *Required fees:* $91 per credit. Tuition and fees vary according to program.

Morehead State University, Graduate Programs, College of Education, Department of Middle Grades and Secondary Education, Morehead, KY 40351. Offers business and marketing education (MAT); English/language arts 5-9 (MAT); French (MAT); health P-12 (MAT); mathematics 5-9 (MAT); physical education P-12 (MAT); science 5-9 (MAT); secondary biology (MAT); secondary chemistry (MAT); secondary earth science (MAT); secondary English (MAT); secondary math (MAT); secondary physics (MAT); secondary social studies (MAT); social studies 5-9 (MAT); Spanish (MAT). *Program availability:* Part-time, evening/weekend. *Degree requirements:* For master's, portfolio. *Entrance requirements:* For master's, GRE or PRAXIS II content exam, minimum overall undergraduate GPA of 2.5. Additional exam requirements/recommendations for international students: Required—TOEFL (minimum score 500 paper-based). Electronic applications accepted.

Morgan State University, School of Graduate Studies, School of Computer, Mathematical, and Natural Sciences, Department of Biology, Baltimore, MD 21251. Offers bioenvironmental science (PhD); biology (MS); science education (MS). *Degree requirements:* For master's, comprehensive exam, thesis. *Entrance requirements:* For master's, minimum GPA of 3.0.

Morgan State University, School of Graduate Studies, School of Education and Urban Studies, Department of Advanced Studies, Leadership and Policy, Program in Science Education, Baltimore, MD 21251. Offers MS, Ed D. *Entrance requirements:* Additional exam requirements/recommendations for international students: Required—TOEFL (minimum score 550 paper-based).

National Louis University, National College of Education, Chicago, IL 60603. Offers administration and supervision (M Ed, Ed D, CAS, Ed S); curriculum and instruction (M Ed, MS Ed, CAS); early childhood administration (M Ed, CAS); early childhood education (M Ed, MAT, MS Ed, CAS); education (Ed D); educational psychology/human learning and development (M Ed, MS Ed, CAS, Ed S); elementary education (MAT); interdisciplinary curriculum and instruction (M Ed); mathematics education (M Ed, MS Ed, CAS); middle grades education (MAT); reading and language (M Ed, MS Ed, CAS); school psychology (M Ed, Ed S); science education (M Ed, MS Ed, CAS); secondary education (MAT); special education (M Ed, MAT, CAS); technology in education (M Ed, CAS). *Accreditation:* NCATE. *Program availability:* Part-time, evening/weekend. *Degree requirements:* For doctorate, comprehensive exam, thesis/dissertation. *Entrance requirements:* For master's, MAT or GRE, minimum GPA of 3.0; for doctorate, GRE General Test, minimum GPA of 3.25, interview, resume, writing sample, 4 recommendations. Additional exam requirements/recommendations for international students: Required—TOEFL (minimum score 550 paper-based; 79 iBT).

New Mexico Institute of Mining and Technology, Center for Graduate Studies, Department of Management, Socorro, NM 87801. Offers STEM education (MEM). *Program availability:* Part-time.

New Mexico Institute of Mining and Technology, Center for Graduate Studies, Master of Science for Teachers Interdepartmental Program, Socorro, NM 87801. Offers MST. *Degree requirements:* For master's, thesis optional. *Entrance requirements:* For master's, GRE General Test. Additional exam requirements/recommendations for international students: Required—TOEFL (minimum score 540 paper-based). Electronic applications accepted. *Faculty research:* Teaching secondary school science and/or mathematics.

New York Institute of Technology, School of Interdisciplinary Studies and Education, Department of Instructional Technology, Old Westbury, NY 11568-8000. Offers emerging technologies for trainers (Advanced Certificate); instructional design for global e-learning (Advanced Certificate); instructional technology (MS); school leadership and technology (Advanced Diploma); STEM education (Advanced Certificate). *Program availability:* Part-time, evening/weekend, 100% online, blended/hybrid learning. *Faculty:* 6 full-time (3 women), 6 part-time/adjunct (4 women). *Students:* 15 full-time (10 women), 192 part-time (132 women); includes 44 minority (15 Black or African American, non-Hispanic/Latino; 8 Asian, non-Hispanic/Latino; 17 Hispanic/Latino; 4 Two or more races, non-Hispanic/Latino), 1 international. Average age 33. 127 applicants, 82% accepted, 79 enrolled. In 2016, 47 master's, 13 other advanced degrees awarded. *Entrance requirements:* For master's, GRE (minimum combined score of 300) or MAT (minimum score of 400) within the last five years, bachelor's degree; minimum undergraduate GPA of 3.0; demonstrated proficiency in basic uses of instructional technologies; for other advanced degree, GRE or MAT within last 5 years, minimum undergraduate GPA of 3.0; demonstrated proficiency in basic uses of instructional technologies; master's degree, minimum 3 years' successful teaching experience, and permanent or provisional NY State teaching certification (for Advanced Diploma). Additional exam requirements/recommendations for international students: Required—TOEFL (minimum score 79 iBT), IELTS (minimum score 6). *Application deadline:* Applications are processed on a rolling basis. Application fee: $50. Electronic applications accepted. *Expenses:* $1,215 per credit. *Financial support:* Research assistantships with partial tuition reimbursements, career-related internships or fieldwork, scholarships/grants, health care benefits, tuition waivers (full and partial), and unspecified assistantships available. Support available to part-time students. Financial award application deadline: 3/1; financial award applicants required to submit FAFSA. *Faculty research:* Integration of information and communication technologies (ICTs) and media literacy education into learning environments; urban K-12 teachers' effective use of technology to enhance student achievement; instructional design and transdisciplinary curriculum studies for online instruction; STEM + computing partnerships for K-12 teachers; experiential, collaborative, and performance-based approaches to pedagogy and technology integration in the K-12 classroom. *Unit head:* Dr. Melda Yildiz, Department Chair, 516-686-1053, Fax: 516-686-7655, E-mail: myildiz@nyit.edu. *Application contact:* Alice Dolitsky, Director, Graduate Admissions, 516-686-7520, Fax: 516-686-1116, E-mail: nyitgrad@nyit.edu.
Website: http://www.nyit.edu/interdisciplinary/department_instructional_technology

New York Institute of Technology, School of Interdisciplinary Studies and Education, Department of Teacher Education, Old Westbury, NY 11568-8000. Offers adolescence education (MS), including mathematics, science; childhood education (MS); early childhood (MS). *Program availability:* Part-time, evening/weekend, 100% online, blended/hybrid learning. *Faculty:* 2 full-time (both women), 7 part-time/adjunct (3 women). *Students:* 19 full-time (15 women), 41 part-time (35 women); includes 18 minority (5 Black or African American, non-Hispanic/Latino; 4 Asian, non-Hispanic/Latino; 8 Hispanic/Latino; 1 Two or more races, non-Hispanic/Latino). Average age 33. 57 applicants, 74% accepted, 29 enrolled. In 2016, 12 master's awarded. *Entrance requirements:* For master's, GRE (minimum combined score of 300 from any two tests), MAT (minimum score 400), LAST (taken within past five years), BS or equivalent; minimum cumulative undergraduate GPA of 3.0; NY state provisional or initial certification (for adolescence education); BS with major in biology, chemistry, economics, English, history, life sciences, math, physics, or psychology (for childhood and early childhood education). Additional exam requirements/recommendations for international students: Required—TOEFL (minimum score 79 iBT), IELTS (minimum score 6). *Application deadline:* Applications are processed on a rolling basis. Application fee: $50. Electronic applications accepted. *Expenses:* $1,215 per credit. *Financial support:* Career-related internships or fieldwork, Federal Work-Study, scholarships/grants, tuition waivers (full and partial), and unspecified assistantships available. Support available to part-time students. Financial award application deadline: 3/1; financial award applicants required to submit FAFSA. *Faculty research:* Evolving definition of new literacies and its impact on teaching and learning (twenty-first century skills), new literacies practices in teacher education, teachers' professional development, English language and literacy learning through mobile learning, teaching reading to culturally and linguistically diverse children. *Unit head:* Dr. Hui-Yin Hsu, Department Chair, 516-686-1322, Fax: 516-686-7655, E-mail: hhsu02@nyit.edu. *Application contact:* Alice Dolitsky, Director, Graduate Admissions, 516-686-7520, Fax: 516-686-1116, E-mail: nyitgrad@nyit.edu.
Website: http://www.nyit.edu/interdisciplinary/department_teacher_education

New York University, Steinhardt School of Culture, Education, and Human Development, Department of Teaching and Learning, New York, NY 10003. Offers clinically rich integrated science (MA), including clinically rich integrated science, teaching biology grades 7-12, teaching chemistry 7-12, teaching physics 7-12; early childhood and childhood education (MA), including childhood education, early childhood education, early childhood education/early childhood special education; English education (MA, PhD, Advanced Certificate), including clinically-based English education, grades 7-12 (MA), English education (PhD, Advanced Certificate), English education, grades 7-12 (MA); environmental conservation education (MA); literacy education (MA), including literacy 5-12, literacy B-6; mathematics education (MA), including teachers of mathematics 7-12; multilingual/multicultural studies (MA, PhD, Advanced Certificate), including bilingual education, foreign language education (MA), teaching English to speakers of other languages (MA, PhD), teaching foreign languages, 7-12 (MA), teaching French as a foreign language (MA), teaching Spanish as a foreign language (MA); social studies education (MA), including teaching art/social studies 7-12, teaching social studies 7-12; special education (MA), including childhood, early childhood; teaching and learning (Ed D, PhD). *Program availability:* Part-time. *Degree requirements:* For doctorate, thesis/dissertation. *Entrance requirements:* For doctorate, GRE General Test, interview; for Advanced Certificate, master's degree. Additional exam requirements/recommendations for international students: Required—TOEFL (minimum score 100 iBT). Electronic applications accepted. *Faculty research:* Cultural contexts for literacy learning, school restructuring, parenting and education, teacher learning, language assessment.

North Carolina Agricultural and Technical State University, School of Graduate Studies, College of Arts and Sciences, Department of Biology, Greensboro, NC 27411. Offers biology (MS); biology education (MAT). *Program availability:* Part-time, evening/weekend. *Degree requirements:* For master's, comprehensive exam, thesis (for some programs), qualifying exam. *Entrance requirements:* For master's, GRE General Test, personal statement. *Faculty research:* Physical ecology, cytochemistry, botany, parasitology, microbiology.

North Carolina State University, Graduate School, College of Education, Department of Mathematics, Science, and Technology Education, Program in Science Education, Raleigh, NC 27695. Offers M Ed, MS, PhD. *Accreditation:* NCATE. *Program availability:* Part-time. *Degree requirements:* For master's, thesis (for some programs), oral exam; for doctorate, one foreign language, thesis/dissertation, oral and written exams. *Entrance requirements:* For master's, GRE General Test or MAT, minimum GPA of 3.0; for doctorate, GRE General Test, minimum GPA of 3.0, interview. Electronic applications accepted. *Faculty research:* Teacher development, sociocultural issues in learning, student science misconceptions, technical applications to science teaching.

North Dakota State University, College of Graduate and Interdisciplinary Studies, College of Engineering, Doctoral Program in Engineering, Fargo, ND 58102. Offers environmental and conservation science (PhD); materials and nanotechnology (PhD); natural resource management (PhD); science, technology, engineering, mathematics education (STEM) (PhD); transportation and logistics (PhD). *Degree requirements:* For doctorate, comprehensive exam, thesis/dissertation. *Entrance requirements:* For doctorate, bachelor's degree in engineering, minimum GPA of 3.0. Additional exam requirements/recommendations for international students: Required—TOEFL. Electronic applications accepted. *Expenses:* Contact institution.

North Dakota State University, College of Graduate and Interdisciplinary Studies, College of Human Development and Education, School of Education, Fargo, ND 58102. Offers agricultural education (M Ed, MS), including agricultural education; counselor education (M Ed, MS, PhD), including clinical mental health counseling (M Ed, MS), counselor education and supervision (PhD), school counseling (M Ed, MS); curriculum and instruction (M Ed, MS); education (PhD); educational leadership (M Ed, MS, Ed S); family and consumer sciences education (M Ed, MS); history education (M Ed, MS); institutional analysis (Ed D); mathematics education (M Ed, MS); music education (M Ed, MS); occupational and adult education (Ed D); science education (M Ed, MS). *Accreditation:* NCATE. *Program availability:* Part-time, evening/weekend, online learning. *Degree requirements:* For master's, comprehensive exam; for doctorate, thesis/dissertation; for Ed S, thesis. *Entrance requirements:* For degree, GRE General Test, master's degree, minimum GPA of 3.25. Additional exam requirements/recommendations for international students: Required—TOEFL.

North Dakota State University, College of Graduate and Interdisciplinary Studies, Program in STEM Education, Fargo, ND 58102. Offers PhD. Electronic applications accepted.

Northeastern State University, College of Science and Health Professions, Department of Natural Sciences, Program in Science Education, Tahlequah, OK 74464-2399. Offers M Ed. *Program availability:* Part-time, evening/weekend. *Faculty:* 14 full-time (9 women). *Students:* 7 full-time (6 women), 30 part-time (23 women); includes 6 minority (3 American Indian or Alaska Native, non-Hispanic/Latino; 2 Hispanic/Latino; 1

Two or more races, non-Hispanic/Latino). Average age 39. In 2016, 12 master's awarded. *Entrance requirements:* For master's, MAT or GRE, minimum GPA of 2.5. *Application deadline:* For fall admission, 6/1 for domestic students. Application fee: $25. *Expenses:* Tuition, state resident: full-time $2816; part-time $216.60 per credit hour. Tuition, nonresident: full-time $6365; part-time $489.60 per credit hour. *Required fees:* $37.40 per credit hour. *Unit head:* Dr. April Adams, Program Chair, 918-444-3819, E-mail: adams001@nsuok.edu. *Application contact:* Josh McCollum, Graduate Coordinator, 918-444-2093, E-mail: mccolluj@nsuok.edu.
Website: http://academics.nsuok.edu/naturalsciences/Degrees/Graduate/MEdScienceEducation.aspx

Northern Arizona University, Graduate College, College of Engineering, Forestry, and Natural Sciences, Center for Science Teaching and Learning, Flagstaff, AZ 86011. Offers science teaching (MAST, Certificate); teaching science (MAT). *Program availability:* Part-time, online learning. *Entrance requirements:* Additional exam requirements/recommendations for international students: Required—TOEFL (minimum score 550 paper-based; 80 iBT), IELTS (minimum score 7). *Expenses:* Tuition, state resident: full-time $8971; part-time $444 per credit hour. Tuition, nonresident: full-time $20,958; part-time $1164 per credit hour. *Required fees:* $1018; $644 per credit hour. Tuition and fees vary according to course load, campus/location and program.

Northern Michigan University, Office of Graduate Education and Research, College of Health Sciences and Professional Studies, School of Education, Leadership and Public Service, Marquette, MI 49855-5301. Offers administration and supervision (MAE); elementary education (MAE); higher education in student affairs (MA); instruction (MAE); learning disabilities (MAE); public administration (MPA), including criminal justice administration, human resource administration, public administration, public management, state and local government; reading education (MAE), including reading, reading specialist; science education (MS); secondary education (MAE). *Accreditation:* TEAC. *Program availability:* Part-time, online learning. *Degree requirements:* For master's, thesis (for some programs). *Entrance requirements:* For master's, minimum GPA of 3.0. Additional exam requirements/recommendations for international students: Required—TOEFL (minimum score 550 paper-based; 79 iBT), IELTS (minimum score 6.5). Electronic applications accepted.

Northwest Missouri State University, Graduate School, College of Arts and Sciences, Maryville, MO 64468-6001. Offers biology (MS); elementary mathematics specialist (MS Ed); English (MA); English education (MS Ed); English pedagogy (MA); geographic information science (MS, Certificate); history (MS Ed); mathematics (MS); mathematics education (MS Ed); teaching: science (MS Ed). *Program availability:* Part-time. *Students:* 12 full-time (8 women), 69 part-time (31 women). *Degree requirements:* For master's, comprehensive exam. *Entrance requirements:* For master's, GRE General Test, writing sample. Additional exam requirements/recommendations for international students: Required—TOEFL (minimum score 550 paper-based). *Application deadline:* For fall admission, 7/1 for domestic and international students; for spring admission, 11/15 for domestic and international students. Applications are processed on a rolling basis. Application fee: $0 ($50 for international students). Electronic applications accepted. *Expenses:* Tuition, state resident: full-time $3447; part-time $383 per credit hour. Tuition, nonresident: full-time $5724; part-time $636 per credit hour. *Required fees:* $130 per credit hour. *Financial support:* Research assistantships with full tuition reimbursements, teaching assistantships with full tuition reimbursements, and administrative assistantships, tutorial assistantships available. Financial award application deadline: 4/1; financial award applicants required to submit FAFSA. *Unit head:* Dr. Michael Steiner, Dean, 660-562-1197.
Website: http://www.nwmissouri.edu/academics/arts/

Oregon State University, College of Education, Program in Education, Corvallis, OR 97331. Offers advanced science and mathematics education (Ed M); agricultural education (PhD); education (Ed D); free-choice learning (Ed M); language equity and educational policy (PhD); mathematics education (MS); pre-K-12 English to speakers of other languages (ESOL) (Ed M); science education (MS); science/mathematics education (PhD); social justice in education (Ed M). *Program availability:* Part-time, 100% online, blended/hybrid learning. *Faculty:* 9 full-time (8 women), 6 part-time/adjunct (2 women). *Students:* 14 full-time (8 women), 76 part-time (53 women); includes 25 minority (6 Black or African American, non-Hispanic/Latino; 2 American Indian or Alaska Native, non-Hispanic/Latino; 5 Asian, non-Hispanic/Latino; 10 Hispanic/Latino; 2 Two or more races, non-Hispanic/Latino), 3 international. Average age 38. 72 applicants, 69% accepted, 40 enrolled. In 2016, 14 master's, 21 doctorates awarded. Terminal master's awarded for partial completion of doctoral program. *Degree requirements:* For master's, variable foreign language requirement, thesis (for some programs); for doctorate, variable foreign language requirement, thesis/dissertation. *Entrance requirements:* Additional exam requirements/recommendations for international students: Required—TOEFL (minimum score 575 paper-based). Application fee: $75 ($85 for international students). *Expenses:* Tuition, state resident: full-time $12,150; part-time $450 per credit. Tuition, nonresident: full-time $21,789; part-time $807 per credit. *Required fees:* $1651; $1507 per credit. One-time fee: $350. Tuition and fees vary according to course load, campus/location and program. *Financial support:* Fellowships, research assistantships, teaching assistantships, career-related internships or fieldwork, Federal Work-Study, and institutionally sponsored loans available. Support available to part-time students. *Faculty research:* School administration, educational foundations, research methodology, education policy development, higher education administration. *Unit head:* Dr. Larry Flick, Dean. *Application contact:* E-mail: askcoed@oregonstate.edu.

Oregon State University, College of Education, Program in Teaching, Corvallis, OR 97331. Offers clinically based elementary education (MAT); elementary education (MAT); language arts (MAT); mathematics (MAT); music education (MAT); science (MAT); social studies (MAT). *Program availability:* Part-time, blended/hybrid learning. *Faculty:* 17 full-time (8 women), 2 part-time/adjunct (both women). *Students:* 57 full-time (39 women), 22 part-time (18 women); includes 11 minority (2 Hispanic/Latino; 1 Native Hawaiian or other Pacific Islander, non-Hispanic/Latino; 8 Two or more races, non-Hispanic/Latino). Average age 29. 131 applicants, 76% accepted, 76 enrolled. In 2016, 92 master's awarded. *Entrance requirements:* For master's, CBEST. Additional exam requirements/recommendations for international students: Required—TOEFL (minimum score 575 paper-based). *Application deadline:* For fall admission, 12/1 for domestic students. Application fee: $60. *Expenses:* Contact institution. *Unit head:* Dr. Larry Flick, Dean. *Application contact:* E-mail: askcoed@oregonstate.edu.
Website: http://education.oregonstate.edu/mat

Our Lady of the Lake University, School of Professional Studies, Program in Curriculum and Instruction, San Antonio, TX 78207-4689. Offers integrated science teaching (M Ed). *Program availability:* Part-time, evening/weekend. *Faculty:* 4 full-time (all women), 3 part-time/adjunct (2 women). *Students:* 22 part-time (19 women); includes 16 minority (all Hispanic/Latino). Average age 38. 1 applicant. In 2016, 4 master's awarded. *Degree requirements:* For master's, comprehensive exam. *Entrance requirements:* For master's, GRE General Test or MAT, official transcripts demonstrating bachelor's degree with minimum cumulative GPA of 2.75, personal statement, 2 references, completed FERPA Consent to Release Education Records and Information form, interview. Additional exam requirements/recommendations for international students: Required—TOEFL. *Application deadline:* For fall admission, 6/15 for domestic and international students; for spring admission, 11/15 for domestic and international students; for summer admission, 4/15 for domestic and international students. Applications are processed on a rolling basis. Application fee: $40 ($50 for international students). Electronic applications accepted. Application fee is waived when completed online. *Expenses: Tuition:* Full-time $14,796. Tuition and fees vary according to course load, degree level, campus/location and program. *Financial support:* Federal Work-Study, scholarships/grants, unspecified assistantships, and tuition discounts available. Support available to part-time students. Financial award application deadline: 5/1; financial award applicants required to submit FAFSA. *Faculty research:* Multicultural Issues, technology integration, mentoring teachers, teacher retention. *Unit head:* Dr. Alycia Maurer, Chair, Education Department, 210-434-6711 Ext. 7152, E-mail: admaurer@ollusa.edu. *Application contact:* Office of Graduate Admissions, 210-431-3995, Fax: 210-431-3945, E-mail: gradadm@lake.ollusa.edu.
Website: http://www.ollusa.edu/s/1190/hybrid/default-hybrid-ollu.aspx?sid-1190&gid-1&pgid-7883

Pacific University, College of Education, Forest Grove, OR 97116-1797. Offers early childhood education (MAT); education (MAE); elementary education (MAT); ESOL (MAT); high school education (MAT); middle school education (MAT); special education (MAT); speech-language pathology (MS); STEM education (MAT); talented and gifted (M Ed); visual function in learning (M Ed). *Accreditation:* NCATE. *Program availability:* Part-time, evening/weekend. *Degree requirements:* For master's, research project. *Entrance requirements:* For master's, California Basic Educational Skills Test, PRAXIS II, minimum undergraduate GPA of 2.75, 3.0 graduate. Additional exam requirements/recommendations for international students: Required—TOEFL. Electronic applications accepted. *Expenses:* Contact institution. *Faculty research:* Defining a culturally competent classroom, technology in the k-12 classroom, Socratic seminars, social studies education.

Pepperdine University, Graduate School of Education and Psychology, Division of Education, Los Angeles, CA 90045. Offers administration and preliminary administrative services (MS); education (MA); educational leadership, administration, and policy (Ed D); global leadership and change (PhD); learning technologies (MA, Ed D); organizational leadership (Ed D); social entrepreneurship and change (MA); teaching (MA); teaching: TESOL (MA). *Program availability:* Part-time, evening/weekend, online learning. *Students:* 262 full-time (169 women), 385 part-time (264 women); includes 286 minority (123 Black or African American, non-Hispanic/Latino; 4 American Indian or Alaska Native, non-Hispanic/Latino; 59 Asian, non-Hispanic/Latino; 77 Hispanic/Latino; 6 Native Hawaiian or other Pacific Islander, non-Hispanic/Latino; 17 Two or more races, non-Hispanic/Latino), 46 international. Average age 38. 372 applicants, 95% accepted, 200 enrolled. In 2016, 142 master's, 66 doctorates awarded. *Degree requirements:* For doctorate, thesis/dissertation. *Entrance requirements:* For master's, GRE General Test; for doctorate, GRE General Test, MAT. Additional exam requirements/recommendations for international students: Required—TOEFL. *Application deadline:* Applications are processed on a rolling basis. Application fee: $55. *Expenses:* $1,165 per unit (for master's); $1,460 per unit (for doctorate). *Financial support:* Research assistantships, teaching assistantships, career-related internships or fieldwork, institutionally sponsored loans, and scholarships/grants available. Support available to part-time students. Financial award application deadline: 7/1; financial award applicants required to submit FAFSA. *Unit head:* Dr. Martine Jago, Associate Dean, Education Division, 310-568-2828, E-mail: martine.jago@pepperdine.edu. *Application contact:* Chris Costa, Director of Enrollment, 310-568-2850, E-mail: chris.costa@pepperdine.edu.
Website: http://gsep.pepperdine.edu/masters-education/

Plymouth State University, College of Graduate Studies, Graduate Studies in Education, Program in Science, Plymouth, NH 03264-1595. Offers applied meteorology (MS); biology (MS); clinical mental health counseling (MS); environmental science and policy (MS); science education (MS).

Plymouth State University, College of Graduate Studies, Graduate Studies in Education, Program in Teaching, Plymouth, NH 03264-1595. Offers art education (MAT); science education (MAT). *Program availability:* Evening/weekend. *Degree requirements:* For master's, internship or teaching experience.

Portland State University, Graduate Studies, College of Liberal Arts and Sciences, Department of Geology, Portland, OR 97207-0751. Offers environmental sciences and resources (PhD); geology (MA, MS); science/geology (MAT, MST). *Program availability:* Part-time. *Faculty:* 10 full-time (2 women), 6 part-time/adjunct (2 women). *Students:* 19 full-time (12 women), 11 part-time (5 women); includes 5 minority (1 American Indian or Alaska Native, non-Hispanic/Latino; 1 Asian, non-Hispanic/Latino; 3 Hispanic/Latino), 1 international. Average age 33. 39 applicants, 28% accepted, 10 enrolled. In 2016, 9 master's awarded. *Degree requirements:* For master's, comprehensive exam, thesis or alternative, field comprehensive; for doctorate, thesis/dissertation. *Entrance requirements:* For master's, GRE General Test, GRE Subject Test, BA/BS in geology, minimum GPA of 3.0 in geology-related and allied sciences, resume, statement of intent, 2 letters of recommendation. Additional exam requirements/recommendations for international students: Required—TOEFL (minimum score 550 paper-based; 80 iBT). *Application deadline:* 1/31 priority date for domestic and international students. Application fee: $65. Electronic applications accepted. *Expenses:* Contact institution. *Financial support:* In 2016–17, 4 research assistantships with tuition reimbursements (averaging $12,661 per year), 9 teaching assistantships with full tuition reimbursements (averaging $5,000 per year) were awarded; career-related internships or fieldwork, Federal Work-Study, scholarships/grants, and unspecified assistantships also available. Support available to part-time students. Financial award application deadline: 3/1; financial award applicants required to submit FAFSA. *Faculty research:* Sediment transport, volcanic environmental geology, coastal and fluvial processes. *Total annual research expenditures:* $1.3 million. *Unit head:* Dr. Martin Streck, Chair, 503-725-3379, Fax: 503-725-3025, E-mail: streckm@pdx.edu. *Application contact:* Dr. Andrew Fountain, Graduate Committee Chair, 503-725-3386, Fax: 503-725-3025, E-mail: andrew@pdx.edu.
Website: https://www.pdx.edu/geology/

Portland State University, Graduate Studies, College of Liberal Arts and Sciences, Interdisciplinary Programs in General Science, General Social Science, and General Arts and Letters, Portland, OR 97207-0751. Offers general arts and letters education (MAT, MST); general science education (MAT, MST); general social science education (MAT, MST). *Program availability:* Part-time, evening/weekend. *Degree requirements:* For master's, variable foreign language requirement, written exam. *Entrance requirements:* For master's, minimum GPA of 3.0 in upper-division course work or 2.75 overall. Additional exam requirements/recommendations for international students: Required—TOEFL (minimum score 550 paper-based; 80 iBT), IELTS (minimum score 6.5). *Application deadline:* For fall admission, 4/1 priority date for domestic students, 3/1 priority date for international students. *Expenses:* Contact institution. *Financial support:* Federal Work-Study and unspecified assistantships available. Support available to part-time students. Financial award application deadline: 3/1; financial award applicants required to submit FAFSA. *Unit head:* Robert Mercer, Associate Dean, 503-725-5059, Fax: 503-725-3693, E-mail: mercerr@pdx.edu. *Application contact:* 503-725-3511, Fax: 503-725-5525.

Portland State University, Graduate Studies, College of Liberal Arts and Sciences, Program in Environmental Sciences and Management, Portland, OR 97207-0751. Offers environmental management (MEM); environmental sciences/biology (PhD); environmental sciences/chemistry (PhD); environmental sciences/civil engineering (PhD); environmental sciences/geography (PhD); environmental sciences/geology (PhD); environmental sciences/physics (PhD); environmental studies (MS); science/ environmental science (MST). *Program availability:* Part-time. *Faculty:* 20 full-time (8 women), 5 part-time/adjunct (1 woman). *Students:* 49 full-time (32 women), 38 part-time (20 women); includes 7 minority (1 Black or African American, non-Hispanic/Latino; 2 Hispanic/Latino; 1 Native Hawaiian or other Pacific Islander, non-Hispanic/Latino; 3 Two or more races, non-Hispanic/Latino), 4 international. Average age 34. 65 applicants, 48% accepted, 26 enrolled. In 2016, 11 master's, 5 doctorates awarded. *Degree requirements:* For master's, thesis or alternative; for doctorate, variable foreign language requirement, comprehensive exam, thesis/dissertation, oral and qualifying exams. *Entrance requirements:* For master's, GRE General Test, 3 letters of recommendation; for doctorate, minimum GPA of 3.0 in upper-division course work or 2.75 overall. Additional exam requirements/recommendations for international students: Required—TOEFL (minimum score 550 paper-based; 80 iBT), IELTS (minimum score 6.5). *Application deadline:* For fall admission, 2/1 for domestic and international students. Applications are processed on a rolling basis. Application fee: $65. *Expenses:* Contact institution. *Financial support:* In 2016–17, 8 research assistantships with full tuition reimbursements (averaging $17,598 per year), 16 teaching assistantships with full tuition reimbursements (averaging $14,426 per year) were awarded; Federal Work-Study, scholarships/grants, tuition waivers (partial), and unspecified assistantships also available. Support available to part-time students. Financial award application deadline: 3/1; financial award applicants required to submit FAFSA. *Faculty research:* Environmental aspects of biology, chemistry, civil engineering, geology, physics. *Unit head:* Dr. John Rueter, Chair, 503-725-8038, Fax: 503-725-9040, E-mail: rueterj@pdx.edu. *Application contact:* Dr. Robert Scheller, Chair, Graduate Admissions, 503-725-4982, Fax: 503-725-9040, E-mail: rmschell@pdx.edu.
Website: https://www.pdx.edu/esm

Purdue University, College of Engineering, School of Engineering Education, West Lafayette, IN 47907. Offers PhD. *Faculty:* 34. *Students:* 62. In 2016, 12 doctorates awarded. *Degree requirements:* For doctorate, thesis/dissertation. *Entrance requirements:* For doctorate, GRE General Test, minimum GPA of 3.0. *Application deadline:* For fall admission, 12/15 for domestic and international students. Applications are processed on a rolling basis. Application fee: $60 ($75 for international students). Electronic applications accepted. *Financial support:* Fellowships with full and partial tuition reimbursements, research assistantships with full and partial tuition reimbursements, teaching assistantships with full and partial tuition reimbursements, health care benefits, and unspecified assistantships available. Financial award applicants required to submit FAFSA. *Faculty research:* Engineering teaching and learning, learning environments, problem solving, technology, teaming, diversity. *Application contact:* Loretta McKinniss, Secretary V, E-mail: enegrad@purdue.edu.
Website: https://engineering.purdue.edu/ENE

Purdue University, Graduate School, College of Education, Department of Curriculum and Instruction, West Lafayette, IN 47907. Offers agricultural and extension education (MS, MS Ed, PhD, Ed S); art education (PhD); career and technical education (MS Ed, PhD, Ed S); curriculum studies (MS Ed, PhD, Ed S); educational technology (MS Ed, PhD, Ed S); elementary education (MS Ed); family and consumer sciences education (MS Ed, PhD, Ed S); foreign language education (MS Ed, PhD, Ed S); industrial technology (PhD, Ed S); language arts (MS Ed, PhD, Ed S); literacy (MS Ed, PhD, Ed S); mathematics education (MS, MS Ed, PhD, Ed S); science education (MS, MS Ed, PhD, Ed S); social studies education (MS Ed, PhD, Ed S). *Accreditation:* NCATE. *Program availability:* Part-time, evening/weekend. *Faculty:* 37 full-time (27 women), 1 (woman) part-time/adjunct. *Students:* 78 full-time (50 women), 286 part-time (195 women); includes 68 minority (25 Black or African American, non-Hispanic/Latino; 3 American Indian or Alaska Native, non-Hispanic/Latino; 10 Asian, non-Hispanic/Latino; 22 Hispanic/Latino; 1 Native Hawaiian or other Pacific Islander, non-Hispanic/Latino; 7 Two or more races, non-Hispanic/Latino), 44 international. Average age 36. 150 applicants, 79% accepted, 73 enrolled. In 2016, 107 master's, 20 doctorates, 2 other advanced degrees awarded. *Degree requirements:* For master's, thesis optional; for doctorate, thesis/dissertation, oral and written exams; for Ed S, oral presentation, project. *Entrance requirements:* For master's, GRE General Test (if undergraduate GPA is below 3.0), minimum undergraduate GPA of 3.0 or equivalent; for doctorate, GRE General Test (minimum combined verbal and quantitative score of 1000, 300 for new scoring), minimum undergraduate GPA of 3.0 or equivalent; master's degree with minimum GPA of 3.0 or equivalent; for Ed S, GRE General Test (minimum combined verbal and quantitative score of 1000, 300 for new scoring), minimum undergraduate GPA of 3.0 or equivalent; master's degree. Additional exam requirements/ recommendations for international students: Required—TOEFL (minimum score 550 paper-based; 77 iBT). *Application deadline:* For fall admission, 12/15 for domestic students, 3/1 for international students; for spring admission, 9/15 for domestic students, 8/1 for international students. Application fee: $60 ($75 for international students). Electronic applications accepted. *Financial support:* Fellowships with full tuition reimbursements, research assistantships with full tuition reimbursements, teaching assistantships with full tuition reimbursements, career-related internships or fieldwork, and tuition waivers (full) available. Support available to part-time students. Financial award application deadline: 3/1; financial award applicants required to submit FAFSA. *Faculty research:* Literacy acquisition and development, teacher beliefs and knowledge, recruitment and retention of underrepresented students, economic education, literacy discourse. *Unit head:* Janet M. Alsup, Head, 765-494-9667, E-mail: alsupj@purdue.edu. *Application contact:* Heather Brinkman, Graduate Contact, 765-494-2345, E-mail: hbrinkma@purdue.edu.
Website: http://www.edci.purdue.edu/

Purdue University, Graduate School, College of Science, Department of Chemistry, West Lafayette, IN 47907. Offers analytical chemistry (MS, PhD); biochemistry (MS, PhD); chemical education (MS, PhD); inorganic chemistry (MS, PhD); organic chemistry (MS, PhD); physical chemistry (MS, PhD). *Faculty:* 46 full-time (14 women), 2 part-time/ adjunct (0 women). *Students:* 320 full-time (129 women), 11 part-time (3 women); includes 60 minority (15 Black or African American, non-Hispanic/Latino; 18 Asian, non-Hispanic/Latino; 20 Hispanic/Latino; 7 Two or more races, non-Hispanic/Latino), 114 international. Average age 26. 719 applicants, 22% accepted, 57 enrolled. In 2016, 11 master's, 53 doctorates awarded. Terminal master's awarded for partial completion of doctoral program. *Degree requirements:* For master's, thesis; for doctorate, comprehensive exam, thesis/dissertation. *Entrance requirements:* For master's and doctorate, minimum undergraduate GPA of 3.0. Additional exam requirements/ recommendations for international students: Required—TOEFL (minimum score 550 paper-based; 77 iBT); Recommended—TWE. *Application deadline:* For fall admission, 2/15 priority date for domestic students, 1/1 for international students. Applications are processed on a rolling basis. Application fee: $60 ($75 for international students). Electronic applications accepted. *Financial support:* In 2016–17, 2 fellowships with partial tuition reimbursements (averaging $18,000 per year), 55 teaching assistantships with partial tuition reimbursements (averaging $18,000 per year) were awarded; research assistantships with partial tuition reimbursements and tuition waivers (partial) also available. Support available to part-time students. Financial award applicants required to submit FAFSA. *Unit head:* Timothy S. Zwier, Head, 765-494-5278, E-mail: zwier@purdue.edu. *Application contact:* Betty L. Hatfield, Director of Graduate Admissions, 765-494-5208, E-mail: bettyh@purdue.edu.
Website: https://www.chem.purdue.edu/

Purdue University Northwest, Graduate Studies Office, School of Engineering, Mathematics, and Science, Department of Biological Sciences, Hammond, IN 46323-2094. Offers biology (MS); biology teaching (MS); biotechnology (MS). *Entrance requirements:* For master's, GRE. Additional exam requirements/recommendations for international students: Required—TOEFL. Electronic applications accepted. *Faculty research:* Cell biology, molecular biology, genetics, microbiology, neurophysiology.

Queens College of the City University of New York, Division of Education, Department of Secondary Education and Youth Services, Queens, NY 11367-1597. Offers adolescent biology (MAT); art (MS Ed); biology (MS Ed, AC); chemistry (MS Ed, AC); earth sciences (MS Ed, AC); English (MS Ed, AC); French (MS Ed); Italian (MS Ed, AC); literacy education (MS Ed); mathematics (MS Ed, AC); music (MS Ed, AC); physics (MS Ed, AC); social studies (MS Ed, AC); Spanish (MS Ed, AC). *Program availability:* Part-time, evening/weekend. *Faculty:* 22 full-time (14 women), 40 part-time/adjunct (26 women). *Students:* 31 full-time (21 women), 356 part-time (211 women); includes 164 minority (22 Black or African American, non-Hispanic/Latino; 54 Asian, non-Hispanic/ Latino; 81 Hispanic/Latino; 7 Two or more races, non-Hispanic/Latino), 11 international. Average age 29. 236 applicants, 88% accepted, 121 enrolled. In 2016, 119 master's, 51 other advanced degrees awarded. *Degree requirements:* For master's, research project. *Entrance requirements:* For master's, minimum GPA of 3.0. Additional exam requirements/recommendations for international students: Required—TOEFL, IELTS. *Application deadline:* For fall admission, 4/1 for domestic students; for spring admission, 11/1 for domestic students. Applications are processed on a rolling basis. Application fee: $125. Electronic applications accepted. *Expenses:* Tuition, state resident: full-time $5065; part-time $425 per credit. Tuition, nonresident: part-time $780 per credit. *Required fees:* $522; $397 per credit. Part-time tuition and fees vary according to course load and program. *Financial support:* Career-related internships or fieldwork available. Financial award application deadline: 4/1; financial award applicants required to submit FAFSA. *Unit head:* Dr. Eleanor Armour-Thomas, Chairperson, 718-997-5150, E-mail: armourthomas@yahoo.com.

Quinnipiac University, School of Education, Program in Secondary Education, Hamden, CT 06518-1940. Offers biology (MAT); English (MAT); history/social studies (MAT); mathematics (MAT); Spanish (MAT). *Accreditation:* NCATE. *Faculty:* 6 full-time (2 women), 24 part-time/adjunct (16 women). *Students:* 43 full-time (29 women), 1 part-time (0 women); includes 6 minority (1 Asian, non-Hispanic/Latino; 4 Hispanic/Latino; 1 Two or more races, non-Hispanic/Latino). 43 applicants, 98% accepted, 36 enrolled. In 2016, 32 master's awarded. *Entrance requirements:* For master's, PRAXIS I or PRAXIS Core Academic Skills Exam, minimum GPA of 3.0, interview. *Application deadline:* For fall admission, 5/1 priority date for domestic students. Applications are processed on a rolling basis. Application fee: $45. Electronic applications accepted. *Expenses: Tuition:* Part-time $985 per credit. *Required fees:* $40 per credit. $150 per semester. Tuition and fees vary according to program. *Financial support:* Career-related internships or fieldwork, Federal Work-Study, and unspecified assistantships available. Financial award application deadline: 6/1; financial award applicants required to submit FAFSA. *Faculty research:* Multicultural and urban education/leadership, challenges of teaching diverse learners, scholarship of teaching and learning, technology and teaching, humor and education. *Unit head:* Mordechai Gordon, Program Director, 203-582-8442, E-mail: mordechai.gordon@qu.edu. *Application contact:* Office of Graduate Admissions, 203-582-8672, Fax: 203-582-3443, E-mail: graduate@qu.edu.
Website: http://www.qu.edu/gradeducation

Regent University, Graduate School, School of Education, Virginia Beach, VA 23464-9800. Offers adult education (Ed D, PhD, Ed S); advanced educational leadership (Ed D, PhD, Ed S); career switcher (M Ed); character education (Ed D, PhD, Ed S); Christian education leadership (Ed D, PhD, Ed S); Christian school administration (M Ed); curriculum and instruction (M Ed), including adult education, Christian school, gifted and talented education, STEM education, teacher leader; educational leadership (M Ed); educational psychology (Ed D, PhD, Ed S); educational technology and online learning (Ed D, PhD, Ed S); elementary education (M Ed); exceptional education executive leadership (Ed D, PhD, Ed S); higher education (Ed D, PhD, Ed S); higher education leadership and management (Ed D, PhD, Ed S); individualized degree plan (M Ed); K-12 school leadership (Ed D, PhD, Ed S); K-12 special education (M Ed); K-8 leadership in mathematics education (M Ed); leadership in mathematics education (Ed S); reading specialist (M Ed); special education (Ed D, PhD, Ed S); student affairs (M Ed); TESOL (M Ed), including adult education - collegiate, K-12. *Accreditation:* TEAC. *Program availability:* Part-time, evening/weekend, 100% online, blended/hybrid learning. *Faculty:* 22 full-time (10 women), 42 part-time/adjunct (31 women). *Students:* 89 full-time (62 women), 1,035 part-time (823 women); includes 466 minority (381 Black or African American, non-Hispanic/Latino; 3 American Indian or Alaska Native, non-Hispanic/Latino; 19 Asian, non-Hispanic/Latino; 50 Hispanic/Latino; 13 Two or more races, non-Hispanic/Latino), 11 international. Average age 39. 976 applicants, 59% accepted, 449 enrolled. In 2016, 241 master's, 22 doctorates, 4 other advanced degrees awarded. *Degree requirements:* For master's, thesis or alternative; for doctorate, comprehensive exam, thesis/dissertation. *Entrance requirements:* For master's, Virginia Communication and Literacy Assessment (VCLA), PRAXIS, college transcripts, writing sample, interview; for doctorate, GRE, writing sample, resume, transcripts, interview. Additional exam requirements/recommendations for international students: Required—TOEFL (minimum score 577 paper-based). *Application deadline:* For fall admission, 4/1 priority date for domestic students; for spring admission, 10/15 priority date for domestic students. Applications are processed on a rolling basis. Application fee: $50. Electronic applications accepted. *Expenses:* Contact institution. *Financial support:* In 2016–17, 622 students received support, including 1 fellowship (averaging $5,000 per year); career-related internships or fieldwork, scholarships/grants, and unspecified assistantships also available. Support available to part-time students. *Faculty research:* Christian school administration, curriculum and instruction, educational technology and online learning, higher education, special education. *Unit head:* Dr. Donald Finn, Dean, 757-352-4278, Fax: 757-352-4318, E-mail: dfinn@regent.edu. *Application contact:* Heidi Cece, Assistant Vice President of Enrollment Management, 800-373-5504, Fax: 757-352-4381, E-mail: admissions@regent.edu.
Website: http://www.regent.edu/soe/

Rice University, Graduate Programs, Wiess School of Natural Sciences, Department of Physics and Astronomy, Houston, TX 77251-1892. Offers nanoscale physics (MS); physics and astronomy (PhD); science teaching (MST). *Program availability:* Part-time. *Degree requirements:* For master's, thesis (for some programs); for doctorate, thesis/ dissertation, minimum B average. *Entrance requirements:* For master's, GRE General Test; for doctorate, GRE General Test, GRE Subject Test. Additional exam requirements/recommendations for international students: Required—TOEFL (minimum score 600 paper-based; 90 iBT). Electronic applications accepted. *Faculty research:*

Science Education

Optical physics; ultra cold atoms; membrane electr-statics, peptides, proteins and lipids; solar astrophysics; stellar activity; magnetic fields; young stars.

Rider University, Department of Graduate Education, Leadership and Counseling, Teacher Certification Program, Lawrenceville, NJ 08648-3001. Offers business education (Certificate); elementary education (Certificate); English as a second language (Certificate); English education (Certificate); mathematics education (Certificate); preschool to grade 3 (Certificate); science education (Certificate); social studies education (Certificate); world languages (Certificate), including French, German, Spanish. *Program availability:* Part-time. *Degree requirements:* For Certificate, internship, professional portfolio. *Entrance requirements:* For degree, PRAXIS, resume. Additional exam requirements/recommendations for international students: Required—TOEFL (minimum score 550 paper-based). Electronic applications accepted. *Faculty research:* Conceptual foundations for optimal development of creativity; creative theory, cognitive processes in mathematics learning, teacher collaboration.

Rowan University, Graduate School, College of Education, Department of Interdisciplinary and Inclusive Education, Program in Teaching STEM, Glassboro, NJ 08028-1701. Offers MA. *Program availability:* Part-time, evening/weekend. *Degree requirements:* For master's, thesis. *Entrance requirements:* For master's, GRE General Test. Additional exam requirements/recommendations for international students: Required—TOEFL. Electronic applications accepted.

Rutgers University–New Brunswick, Graduate School of Education, Department of Learning and Teaching, Program in Science Education, Piscataway, NJ 08854-8097. Offers Ed M, Ed D. *Program availability:* Part-time. Terminal master's awarded for partial completion of doctoral program. *Degree requirements:* For master's, comprehensive exam (for some programs); for doctorate, thesis/dissertation, qualifying exam. *Entrance requirements:* For master's, GRE General Test, minimum GPA of 3.0; for doctorate, GRE General Test, minimum GPA of 3.5. Additional exam requirements/recommendations for international students: Required—TOEFL. Electronic applications accepted.

Saginaw Valley State University, College of Education, Program in Natural Science Teaching, University Center, MI 48710. Offers MAT. *Accreditation:* NCATE. *Program availability:* Part-time, evening/weekend. In 2016, 1 master's awarded. *Degree requirements:* For master's, capstone course. *Entrance requirements:* For master's, minimum GPA of 3.0, teaching certificate. Additional exam requirements/recommendations for international students: Required—TOEFL (minimum score 550 paper-based; 79 iBT). *Application deadline:* For fall admission, 7/15 for international students; for winter admission, 11/15 for international students; for spring admission, 4/15 for international students. Applications are processed on a rolling basis. Application fee: $30 ($90 for international students). Electronic applications accepted. *Expenses:* Tuition, state resident: full-time $9652; part-time $536 per credit hour. Tuition, nonresident: full-time $12,259; part-time $1022 per credit hour. *Required fees:* $263; $14.60 per credit hour. Tuition and fees vary according to degree level. *Financial support:* Federal Work-Study and scholarships/grants available. Support available to part-time students. Financial award applicants required to submit FAFSA. *Unit head:* Dr. Craig Douglas, Dean, 989-964-4057, Fax: 989-964-4385, E-mail: coeconnect@svsu.edu. *Application contact:* Jenna Briggs, Director, Graduate and International Admissions, 989-964-6096, Fax: 989-964-2788, E-mail: gradadm@svsu.edu.

Saint Xavier University, Graduate Studies, School of Education, Chicago, IL 60655-3105. Offers counseling (MA); curriculum and instruction (MA); early childhood education (MA); educational administration (MA); elementary education (MA); individualized studies (MA), including educational technology, English as a second language (ESL), ISTEM (integrative science, technology, engineering, and math), science education; music education (MA); reading (MA); secondary education (MA); Spanish education (MA); special education (MA); teaching and leadership (MA). *Accreditation:* NCATE. *Program availability:* Part-time, evening/weekend. *Degree requirements:* For master's, thesis or project. *Entrance requirements:* For master's, minimum GPA of 3.0. *Expenses:* Contact institution.

Salem State University, School of Graduate Studies, Program in Chemistry, Salem, MA 01970-5353. Offers MAT. *Program availability:* Part-time, evening/weekend. *Entrance requirements:* For master's, GRE or MAT. Additional exam requirements/recommendations for international students: Required—TOEFL (minimum score 550 paper-based; 80 iBT) or IELTS (minimum score 5.5).

Salem State University, School of Graduate Studies, Program in Middle School General Science, Salem, MA 01970-5353. Offers MAT. *Program availability:* Part-time, evening/weekend. *Entrance requirements:* For master's, GRE or MAT. Additional exam requirements/recommendations for international students: Required—TOEFL (minimum score 550 paper-based; 80 iBT) or IELTS (minimum score 5.5).

San Diego State University, Graduate and Research Affairs, College of Sciences, Department of Mathematics and Statistics, San Diego, CA 92182. Offers applied mathematics (MS); mathematics (MA); mathematics and science education (PhD); statistics (MS). PhD offered jointly wtih University of California, San Diego. *Program availability:* Part-time. *Degree requirements:* For doctorate, thesis/dissertation. *Entrance requirements:* For master's, GRE General Test; for doctorate, GRE, minimum GPA of 3.25 in last 30 undergraduate semester units, minimum graduate GPA of 3.5, MSE recommendation form, 3 letters of recommendation. Additional exam requirements/recommendations for international students: Required—TOEFL. Electronic applications accepted. *Faculty research:* Teacher education in mathematics.

San Jose State University, Graduate Studies and Research, College of Science, San Jose, CA 95192-0001. Offers biological sciences (MA, MS), including molecular biology and microbiology (MS), organismal biology, conservation and ecology (MS), physiology (MS); biotechnology (MBT); chemistry (MA, MS); computer science (MS); cybersecurity (Certificate); cybersecurity: core technologies (Certificate); geology (MS); marine science (MS); mathematics (MA, MS), including mathematics education (MA), science; meteorology (MS); physics (MS), including computational physics, modern optics, science (MA, MS); science education (MA); statistics (MS); Unix system administration (Certificate). *Program availability:* Part-time, evening/weekend. *Entrance requirements:* For master's, GRE. Electronic applications accepted. *Faculty research:* Radiochemistry/environmental analysis, health physics, radiation effects.

Seattle Pacific University, Program in Teaching Mathematics and Science, Seattle, WA 98119-1997. Offers MTMS. *Degree requirements:* For master's, internship.

Shippensburg University of Pennsylvania, School of Graduate Studies, College of Education and Human Services, Department of Teacher Education, Shippensburg, PA 17257-2299. Offers curriculum and instruction (M Ed), including biology, early childhood education, elementary and middle level education, elementary education, geography/earth science, history, mathematics, middle school education, modern languages; literacy studies (Certificate); online instruction, learning, and technology (Certificate); reading (M Ed); teaching English as a second language (Certificate). *Accreditation:* NCATE. *Program availability:* Part-time, evening/weekend, 100% online, blended/hybrid learning. *Faculty:* 14 full-time (9 women), 5 part-time/adjunct (all women). *Students:* 11 full-time (10 women), 88 part-time (81 women); includes 8 minority (3 Black or African American, non-Hispanic/Latino; 2 Asian, non-Hispanic/Latino; 3 Hispanic/Latino), 4 international. Average age 32. 57 applicants, 60% accepted, 28 enrolled. In 2016, 18 master's awarded. *Degree requirements:* For master's, comprehensive exam (for some programs), thesis optional, practicum or internship; capstone seminar (for some programs). *Entrance requirements:* For master's, MAT or GRE (if GPA less than 2.75), interview, 3 letters of reference, questionnaire of teaching background and future goals, resume. Additional exam requirements/recommendations for international students: Required—TOEFL (minimum score 550 paper-based, 68 iBT) or IELTS (minimum score 6). *Application deadline:* For fall admission, 4/1 priority date for domestic students, 4/30 for international students; for spring admission, 9/1 priority date for domestic students, 9/30 for international students; for summer admission, 2/1 priority date for domestic students. Applications are processed on a rolling basis. Application fee: $45. Electronic applications accepted. *Expenses:* Tuition, state resident: part-time $483 per credit. Tuition, nonresident: part-time $725 per credit. *Required fees:* $141 per credit. *Financial support:* In 2016–17, 3 students received support. Career-related internships or fieldwork, scholarships/grants, unspecified assistantships, and resident hall director and student payroll positions available. Support available to part-time students. Financial award application deadline: 3/1; financial award applicants required to submit FAFSA. *Unit head:* Dr. Christine A. Royce, Chairperson, 717-477-1688, Fax: 717-477-4046, E-mail: caroyc@ship.edu. *Application contact:* Megan N. Luft, Assistant Dean of Graduate Admissions, 717-477-1231, Fax: 717-477-4016, E-mail: mnluft@ship.edu.
Website: http://www.ship.edu/teacher/

Shippensburg University of Pennsylvania, School of Graduate Studies, College of Education and Human Services, Master of Arts in Teaching STEM Education Program, Shippensburg, PA 17257-2299. Offers MAT. *Program availability:* Part-time, evening/weekend, blended/hybrid learning. *Students:* 10 part-time (3 women); includes 1 minority (Hispanic/Latino). Average age 30. 14 applicants, 86% accepted, 10 enrolled. In 2016, 8 master's awarded. *Degree requirements:* For master's, 12-week student teaching practicum (12 credits), two capstone projects which include professional portfolio and the results of a research project. *Entrance requirements:* For master's, Pre-Service Academic Performance Assessment (PAPA), PRAXIS II Subject Assessment, statement of intent summarizing motivations and goals for entering the teaching profession, two letters of recommendation. Additional exam requirements/recommendations for international students: Required—TOEFL (minimum score 550 paper-based, 68 iBT) or IELTS (minimum score 6). *Application deadline:* For fall admission, 4/30 for international students; for spring admission, 9/30 for international students. Applications are processed on a rolling basis. Application fee: $45. Electronic applications accepted. *Expenses:* Tuition, state resident: part-time $483 per credit. Tuition, nonresident: part-time $725 per credit. *Required fees:* $141 per credit. *Financial support:* Career-related internships or fieldwork and resident hall director and student payroll positions available. Support available to part-time students. Financial award application deadline: 3/1; financial award applicants required to submit FAFSA. *Unit head:* Dr. Joseph W. Shane, Associate Professor of Chemistry and Science Education, 717-477-1572, Fax: 717-477-4048, E-mail: jwshan@ship.edu. *Application contact:* Megan N. Luft, Assistant Dean of Graduate Admissions, 717-477-1231, Fax: 717-477-4016, E-mail: mnluft@ship.edu.
Website: http://www.ship.edu/STEM/

Slippery Rock University of Pennsylvania, Graduate Studies (Recruitment), College of Education, Department of Elementary Education and Early Childhood, Slippery Rock, PA 16057-1383. Offers instructional coach (M Ed); K-12 reading (M Ed); K-12 science and math (M Ed); reading specialist (M Ed). *Accreditation:* NCATE. *Program availability:* Part-time, evening/weekend, online only, 100% online. *Faculty:* 9 full-time (8 women). *Students:* 6 full-time (all women), 128 part-time (124 women); includes 1 minority (Two or more races, non-Hispanic/Latino). Average age 28. 100 applicants, 77% accepted, 54 enrolled. In 2016, 49 master's awarded. *Degree requirements:* For master's, comprehensive exam (for some programs), thesis optional. *Entrance requirements:* For master's, minimum GPA of 3.0, resume, teaching certification, transcripts, letters of recommendation (depending on program). Additional exam requirements/recommendations for international students: Required—TOEFL (minimum score 550 paper-based; 80 iBT). *Application deadline:* For fall admission, 3/1 priority date for domestic students, 5/1 priority date for international students; for spring admission, 10/1 priority date for domestic students, 9/1 priority date for international students. Applications are processed on a rolling basis. Application fee: $25 ($30 for international students). Electronic applications accepted. *Expenses:* $646.50 per credit in-state, $936.80 per credit out-of-state; $581.45 per online credit in-state, $648.65 per online credit out-of-state. *Financial support:* Career-related internships or fieldwork, Federal Work-Study, institutionally sponsored loans, scholarships/grants, tuition waivers (partial), and unspecified assistantships available. Support available to part-time students. Financial award application deadline: 5/1; financial award applicants required to submit FAFSA. *Unit head:* Dr. Suzanne Rose, Graduate Coordinator, 724-738-2042, Fax: 724-738-2779, E-mail: suzanne.rose@sru.edu. *Application contact:* Brandi Weber-Mortimer, Director of Graduate Admissions, 724-738-2051, Fax: 724-738-2146, E-mail: graduate.admissions@sru.edu.
Website: http://www.sru.edu/academics/colleges-and-departments/coe/departments/elementary-education-/-early-childhood/graduate-programs

Slippery Rock University of Pennsylvania, Graduate Studies (Recruitment), College of Education, Department of Secondary Education/Foundations of Education, Slippery Rock, PA 16057-1383. Offers secondary education (M Ed), including English, math/science, social studies. *Accreditation:* NCATE. *Program availability:* Part-time, evening/weekend, 100% online. *Faculty:* 7 full-time (2 women), 1 part-time/adjunct (0 women). *Students:* 43 full-time (23 women), 36 part-time (23 women); includes 2 minority (1 Black or African American, non-Hispanic/Latino; 1 Two or more races, non-Hispanic/Latino). Average age 29. 77 applicants, 79% accepted, 35 enrolled. In 2016, 36 master's awarded. *Degree requirements:* For master's, comprehensive exam, thesis (for some programs). *Entrance requirements:* For master's, copy of teaching certification and two letters of recommendation (for some programs). Additional exam requirements/recommendations for international students: Required—TOEFL (minimum score 550 paper-based; 80 iBT). *Application deadline:* For fall admission, 3/1 priority date for domestic students, 5/1 priority date for international students; for spring admission, 10/1 priority date for domestic students, 9/1 priority date for international students. Applications are processed on a rolling basis. Application fee: $25 ($30 for international students). Electronic applications accepted. *Expenses:* $646.50 per credit in-state, $936.80 per credit out-of-state; $581.45 per online credit in-state, $648.65 per online credit out-of-state. *Financial support:* In 2016–17, 12 students received support. Career-related internships or fieldwork, Federal Work-Study, institutionally sponsored loans, scholarships/grants, tuition waivers (partial), and unspecified assistantships available. Support available to part-time students. Financial award application deadline: 5/1; financial award applicants required to submit FAFSA. *Unit head:* Dr. Jeffrey Lehman, Graduate Coordinator, 724-738-2311, Fax: 724-738-4987, E-mail: jeffrey.lehman@sru.edu. *Application contact:* Brandi Weber-Mortimer, Director of Graduate Studies, 724-738-2051, Fax: 724-738-2146, E-mail: graduate.admissions@sru.edu.
Website: http://www.sru.edu/academics/colleges-and-departments/coe/departments/secondary-education-/-foundations-of-education

Smith College, Graduate and Special Programs, Department of Education and Child Study, Program in Secondary Education, Northampton, MA 01063. Offers secondary

education (MAT), including biological sciences education, chemistry education, English education, French education, geology education, government education, history education, mathematics education, physics education, Spanish education. *Program availability:* Part-time. *Students:* 3 full-time (2 women), 3 part-time (2 women). Average age 31. 14 applicants, 79% accepted, 4 enrolled. In 2016, 11 master's awarded. *Entrance requirements:* Additional exam requirements/recommendations for international students: Required—TOEFL (minimum score 595 paper-based; 97 iBT), IELTS. *Application deadline:* For fall admission, 4/1 for domestic students, 1/15 priority date for international students; for spring admission, 12/1 for domestic students. Application fee: $60. *Expenses: Tuition:* Full-time $34,560; part-time $1440 per credit. Tuition and fees vary according to course load and program. *Financial support:* In 2016–17, 5 students received support, including 1 fellowship with full tuition reimbursement available; scholarships/grants also available. Support available to part-time students. Financial award application deadline: 4/1; financial award applicants required to submit CSS PROFILE or FAFSA. *Unit head:* Rosetta Cohen, Graduate Student Advisor, 413-585-3266, E-mail: rcohen@smith.edu. *Application contact:* Ruth Morgan, Program Assistant, 413-585-3050, Fax: 413-585-3054, E-mail: gradstdy@smith.edu.
Website: http://www.smith.edu/educ/

Smith College, Graduate and Special Programs, Department of Physics, Northampton, MA 01063. Offers secondary education (MAT), including physics education. *Program availability:* Part-time. *Students:* 1 (woman) part-time. Average age 24. 1 applicant, 100% accepted. *Entrance requirements:* Additional exam requirements/recommendations for international students: Required—TOEFL (minimum score 595 paper-based; 97 iBT), IELTS. *Application deadline:* For fall admission, 4/1 for domestic students, 1/15 for international students; for spring admission, 12/1 for domestic students. Application fee: $60. *Expenses: Tuition:* Full-time $34,560; part-time $1440 per credit. Tuition and fees vary according to course load and program. *Financial support:* Scholarships/grants available. Support available to part-time students. Financial award application deadline: 4/1; financial award applicants required to submit CSS PROFILE or FAFSA. *Unit head:* Gary Felder, Chair, 413-585-4489, E-mail: gfelder@smith.edu. *Application contact:* Ruth Morgan, Program Assistant, 413-585-3050, Fax: 413-585-3054, E-mail: gradstdy@smith.edu.

South Carolina State University, College of Graduate and Professional Studies, Department of Education, Orangeburg, SC 29117-0001. Offers early childhood education (MAT); education (M Ed); elementary education (M Ed, MAT); English (MAT); general science/biology (MAT); mathematics (MAT); secondary education (M Ed), including biology education, business education, counselor education, English education, home economics education, industrial education, mathematics education, science education, social studies education; special education (M Ed), including emotionally handicapped, learning disabilities, mentally handicapped. *Accreditation:* NCATE. *Program availability:* Part-time, evening/weekend. *Faculty:* 12 full-time (8 women), 3 part-time/adjunct (1 woman). *Students:* 28 full-time (20 women), 20 part-time (17 women); includes 45 minority (44 Black or African American, non-Hispanic/Latino; 1 Two or more races, non-Hispanic/Latino). Average age 31. 22 applicants, 100% accepted, 16 enrolled. In 2016, 9 master's awarded. *Degree requirements:* For master's, thesis optional, departmental qualifying exam. *Entrance requirements:* For master's, GRE General Test, NTE, interview, teaching certificate. *Application deadline:* For fall admission, 6/15 priority date for domestic students, 6/15 for international students; for spring admission, 11/1 for domestic and international students. Application fee: $25. Electronic applications accepted. *Expenses:* Tuition, state resident: full-time $8938; part-time $579 per credit hour. Tuition, nonresident: full-time $19,018; part-time $1139 per credit hour. *Required fees:* $1482; $82 per credit hour. *Financial support:* Fellowships, career-related internships or fieldwork, Federal Work-Study, and scholarships/grants available. Financial award application deadline: 6/1. *Unit head:* Dr. Charlie Spell, Interim Chair, Department of Education, 803-536-8963, Fax: 803-516-4568, E-mail: cspell@scsu.edu. *Application contact:* Curtis Foskey, Coordinator of Graduate Studies, 803-536-8419, Fax: 803-536-8812, E-mail: cfoskey@scsu.edu.

Southern Connecticut State University, School of Graduate Studies, School of Arts and Sciences, Department of Environment, Geography and Marine Sciences, New Haven, CT 06515-1355. Offers environmental education (MS); science education (MS, Diploma). *Accreditation:* NCATE. *Program availability:* Part-time, evening/weekend. *Faculty:* 3 full-time (1 woman), 1 part-time/adjunct (0 women). *Students:* 7 full-time (4 women), 27 part-time (14 women); includes 5 minority (1 Black or African American, non-Hispanic/Latino; 1 Asian, non-Hispanic/Latino; 2 Hispanic/Latino; 1 Two or more races, non-Hispanic/Latino). Average age 33. 26 applicants, 69% accepted, 15 enrolled. In 2016, 12 master's awarded. *Degree requirements:* For master's, thesis or alternative. *Entrance requirements:* For master's, interview; for Diploma, master's degree. *Application deadline:* For fall admission, 7/15 priority date for domestic students. Applications are processed on a rolling basis. Application fee: $50. Electronic applications accepted. *Expenses:* Tuition, state resident: full-time $6497; part-time $519 per credit hour. Tuition, nonresident: full-time $18,102; part-time $535 per credit hour. *Required fees:* $4722; $55 per semester. Tuition and fees vary according to program. *Financial support:* Career-related internships or fieldwork, scholarships/grants, and unspecified assistantships available. Financial award application deadline: 4/15; financial award applicants required to submit FAFSA. *Unit head:* Dr. Patrick Heidkamp, Chairman, 203-392-5919, Fax: 203-392-5834, E-mail: heidkampc1@southernct.edu. *Application contact:* Lisa Galvin, Director of Graduate Admissions, 203-392-5240, Fax: 203-392-5235, E-mail: galvinl1@southernct.edu.

Southern University and Agricultural and Mechanical College, Graduate School, Department of Science/Mathematics Education, Baton Rouge, LA 70813. Offers PhD. *Accreditation:* NCATE. *Degree requirements:* For doctorate, thesis/dissertation. *Entrance requirements:* For doctorate, GRE General Test. Additional exam requirements/recommendations for international students: Required—TOEFL (minimum score 525 paper-based). *Faculty research:* Performance assessment in science/mathematics education, equity in science/mathematics education, technology and distance learning, science/mathematics concept formation, cognitive themes, problem solving in science/mathematics education.

Southwestern Oklahoma State University, College of Arts and Sciences, Specialization in Natural Sciences, Weatherford, OK 73096-3098. Offers M Ed. *Program availability:* Part-time. *Degree requirements:* For master's, exam. *Entrance requirements:* For master's, GRE General Test or minimum undergraduate GPA of 3.0. Additional exam requirements/recommendations for international students: Required—TOEFL.

State University of New York at New Paltz, Graduate School, School of Education, Department of Elementary Education, New Paltz, NY 12561. Offers childhood education 1-6 (MS Ed, MST), including childhood education 1-6 (MST), early childhood B-2 (MS Ed), mathematics, science and technology (MS Ed), reading/literacy (MS Ed); literacy education 5-12 (MS Ed); literacy education and childhood special education (MS Ed); literacy education B-6 (MS Ed). *Accreditation:* NCATE. *Program availability:* Part-time, evening/weekend. *Students:* 32 full-time (29 women), 100 part-time (91 women); includes 22 minority (5 Black or African American, non-Hispanic/Latino; 1 American Indian or Alaska Native, non-Hispanic/Latino; 2 Asian, non-Hispanic/Latino; 10 Hispanic/Latino; 4 Two or more races, non-Hispanic/Latino). 30 applicants, 73% accepted, 14 enrolled. In 2016, 70 master's awarded. *Degree requirements:* For master's, comprehensive exam (for some programs), portfolio. *Entrance requirements:* For master's, GRE or MAT (for MST), minimum GPA of 3.0 (3.2 for literacy and special education), New York state teaching certificate (for MS Ed). Additional exam requirements/recommendations for international students: Required—TOEFL (minimum score 550 paper-based; 80 iBT), IELTS (minimum score 6.5). *Application deadline:* For fall admission, 4/1 for domestic and international students; for spring admission, 11/1 priority date for domestic and international students; for summer admission, 4/15 priority date for domestic and international students. Applications are processed on a rolling basis. Application fee: $50. Electronic applications accepted. *Financial support:* Application deadline: 8/1. *Faculty research:* Multi-sensory teaching methods, volunteer tutoring programs for struggling readers, school readiness and transition, math/science/technology, university-school partnerships. *Unit head:* Dr. Aaron Isabelle, Chair, 845-257-2837, E-mail: isabella@newpaltz.edu. *Application contact:* Vika Shock, Assistant Director of Graduate Admissions, 845-257-3285, Fax: 845-257-3284, E-mail: gradschool@newpaltz.edu.
Website: http://www.newpaltz.edu/elementaryed/

State University of New York at New Paltz, Graduate School, School of Education, Department of Secondary Education, New Paltz, NY 12561. Offers adolescence education: biology (MAT, MS Ed); adolescence education: chemistry (MAT, MS Ed); adolescence education: earth science (MAT, MS Ed); adolescence education: English (MAT, MS Ed); adolescence education: French (MAT, MS Ed); adolescence education: social studies (MAT, MS Ed); adolescence education: Spanish (MAT, MS Ed); second language education (MS Ed, AC), including second language education (MS Ed), teaching English language learners (AC). *Accreditation:* NCATE. *Program availability:* Part-time, evening/weekend. *Students:* 60 full-time (36 women), 59 part-time (48 women); includes 28 minority (2 Black or African American, non-Hispanic/Latino; 2 Asian, non-Hispanic/Latino; 22 Hispanic/Latino; 2 Two or more races, non-Hispanic/Latino). 96 applicants, 83% accepted, 54 enrolled. In 2016, 56 master's awarded. *Degree requirements:* For master's, comprehensive exam (for some programs), portfolio. *Entrance requirements:* For master's, minimum GPA of 3.0, New York state teaching certificate (MS Ed). Additional exam requirements/recommendations for international students: Required—TOEFL (minimum score 550 paper-based; 80 iBT), IELTS (minimum score 6.5). *Application deadline:* For fall admission, 3/1 priority date for domestic students, 3/1 for international students; for spring admission, 10/1 priority date for domestic students, 10/1 for international students. Application fee: $50. Electronic applications accepted. *Financial support:* Application deadline: 8/1. *Unit head:* Dr. Laura Dull, Chair, 845-257-2849, E-mail: dullj@newpaltz.edu. *Application contact:* Vika Shock, Director of Graduate Admissions, 845-257-3285, Fax: 845-257-3284, E-mail: gradschool@newpaltz.edu.
Website: http://www.newpaltz.edu/secondaryed/

State University of New York at Plattsburgh, School of Arts and Sciences, Program in Natural Science, Plattsburgh, NY 12901-2681. Offers MS, PSM. *Accreditation:* TEAC. *Program availability:* Part-time. *Entrance requirements:* For master's, GRE General Test (minimum score of 1200), bachelor's degree in science discipline, minimum GPA of 3.0. Additional exam requirements/recommendations for international students: Required—TOEFL.

State University of New York at Plattsburgh, School of Education, Health, and Human Services, Program in Teacher Education: Adolescence Education, Plattsburgh, NY 12901-2681. Offers adolescence education (MST); biology 7-12 (MST); chemistry 7-12 (MST); earth science 7-12 (MST); English 7-12 (MST); French 7-12 (MST); mathematics 7-12 (MST); physics 7-12 (MST); social studies 7-12 (MST); Spanish 7-12 (MST). *Accreditation:* TEAC. *Program availability:* Part-time, evening/weekend. *Entrance requirements:* For master's, minimum GPA of 2.75. Additional exam requirements/recommendations for international students: Required—TOEFL.

State University of New York College at Cortland, Graduate Studies, School of Arts and Sciences, Programs in Adolescence Education, Cortland, NY 13045. Offers biology (MAT); chemistry (MAT); English (MAT, MS Ed); mathematics (MAT); mathematics and physics (MS Ed); physics (MAT, MS Ed). *Accreditation:* NCATE. *Program availability:* Part-time, evening/weekend. *Degree requirements:* For master's, one foreign language, comprehensive exam (for some programs), thesis (for some programs). *Entrance requirements:* For master's, GRE General Test.

State University of New York College at Geneseo, Graduate Studies, School of Education, Program in Adolescence Education, Geneseo, NY 14454-1401. Offers English 7-12 (MS Ed); math 7-12 (MS Ed); Spanish 7-12 (MS Ed). *Program availability:* Part-time. *Faculty:* 8 full-time (4 women). *Students:* 5 part-time (4 women). Average age 30. 8 applicants, 13% accepted. In 2016, 4 master's awarded. *Degree requirements:* For master's, 2 foreign languages. *Entrance requirements:* For master's, initial certification to teach in New York state. Additional exam requirements/recommendations for international students: Required—TOEFL, IELTS, PTE. *Application deadline:* For fall admission, 4/1 priority date for domestic students; for spring admission, 11/1 priority date for domestic students. Applications are processed on a rolling basis. Application fee: $50. Electronic applications accepted. *Expenses:* Tuition, state resident: full-time $10,870; part-time $453 per credit. Tuition, nonresident: full-time $22,210; part-time $925 per credit. *Required fees:* $865; $35.85 per credit hour. *Financial support:* In 2016–17, 1 student received support, including 1 fellowship with partial tuition reimbursement available (averaging $10,000 per year); scholarships/grants, health care benefits, tuition waivers (partial), and unspecified assistantships also available. Support available to part-time students. Financial award application deadline: 4/1; financial award applicants required to submit FAFSA. *Unit head:* Dr. Anjoo Sikka, Dean of School of Education, 585-245-5151, Fax: 585-245-5220, E-mail: sikka@geneseo.edu. *Application contact:* Michael R. George, Graduate Enrollment Coordinator, 585-245-5148, Fax: 585-245-5550, E-mail: georgem@geneseo.edu.

State University of New York College at Old Westbury, School of Education, Old Westbury, NY 11568-0210. Offers biology (MAT, MS); chemistry (MAT, MS); English language arts (MAT, MS); math (MAT, MS); social studies (MAT, MS); Spanish (MAT, MS). *Program availability:* Part-time, evening/weekend. *Faculty:* 17 full-time (9 women), 5 part-time/adjunct (2 women). *Students:* 46 full-time (19 women), 26 part-time (17 women); includes 20 minority (1 Black or African American, non-Hispanic/Latino; 4 Asian, non-Hispanic/Latino; 15 Hispanic/Latino). Average age 30. 35 applicants, 77% accepted, 23 enrolled. In 2016, 25 master's awarded. *Entrance requirements:* For master's, Liberal Arts and Sciences Test, undergraduate degree with at least 30 semester hours of appropriate coursework as defined by the respective discipline; minimum cumulative undergraduate GPA of 3.0; two letters of recommendation (one from an academic source); essay. Additional exam requirements/recommendations for international students: Required—TOEFL (minimum score 550 paper-based); Recommended—IELTS. Application fee: $50. *Expenses:* Tuition, state resident: full-time $10,870; part-time $453 per credit. Tuition, nonresident: full-time $22,210; part-time $925 per credit. *Required fees:* $24.35 per credit. $76 per semester. Tuition and fees vary according to course load. *Financial support:* Applicants required to submit FAFSA. *Unit head:* Dr. Nancy Brown, Dean, School of Education, 516-876-3275, E-mail:

brownn@oldwestbury.edu. *Application contact:* Philip D'Angelo, Graduate Admissions Office, 516-876-3073, E-mail: enroll@oldwestbury.edu.

State University of New York College at Potsdam, School of Education and Professional Studies, Program in Secondary Education, Potsdam, NY 13676. Offers English education (MST); mathematics education (MST); science education (MST), including biology, chemistry, earth science, physics; social studies education (MST). *Accreditation:* NCATE. *Degree requirements:* For master's, culminating experience. *Entrance requirements:* For master's, minimum GPA of 2.75 in last 60 hours of course work (3.0 for English program). Additional exam requirements/recommendations for international students: Required—TOEFL (minimum score 550 paper-based; 80 iBT), IELTS (minimum score 6). Electronic applications accepted.

Stevenson University, Master of Arts in Teaching Program, Stevenson, MD 21153. Offers secondary biology (MAT); secondary chemistry (MAT); secondary mathematics (MAT). *Program availability:* Part-time, blended/hybrid learning. *Faculty:* 3 part-time/adjunct (all women). *Students:* 17 part-time (10 women); includes 3 minority (2 Black or African American, non-Hispanic/Latino; 1 Asian, non-Hispanic/Latino). Average age 29. 13 applicants, 85% accepted, 10 enrolled. In 2016, 8 master's awarded. *Degree requirements:* For master's, internship, portfolio, action research project. *Entrance requirements:* For master's, PRAXIS, GRE, SAT, or ACT, official transcripts from each college or university attended verifying completion of baccalaureate degree in a science or math discipline from regionally-accredited institution. *Application deadline:* Applications are processed on a rolling basis. Electronic applications accepted. *Expenses:* $475 per credit hour. *Financial support:* Unspecified assistantships available. Financial award applicants required to submit FAFSA. *Unit head:* Anne P. Davis, Associate Dean of Teacher Education. *Application contact:* Amanda Courter, Senior Enrollment Counselor, 443-352-4243, Fax: 443-352-4440, E-mail: acourter@stevenson.edu.
Website: http://www.stevenson.edu/graduate-professional-studies/graduate-programs/master-of-arts-in-teaching/

Stony Brook University, State University of New York, Graduate School, College of Arts and Sciences, Department of Physics and Astronomy, Program in Physics, Stony Brook, NY 11794. Offers modern research instrumentation (MS); physics (MA, PhD); physics education (MAT). *Faculty:* 51 full-time (6 women), 5 part-time/adjunct (0 women). *Students:* 174 full-time (33 women), 4 part-time (0 women); includes 16 minority (2 Black or African American, non-Hispanic/Latino; 9 Asian, non-Hispanic/Latino; 4 Hispanic/Latino; 1 Two or more races, non-Hispanic/Latino), 118 international. 592 applicants, 36% accepted, 43 enrolled. In 2016, 17 master's, 27 doctorates awarded. *Degree requirements:* For doctorate, one foreign language, thesis/dissertation. *Entrance requirements:* For master's and doctorate, GRE General Test. Additional exam requirements/recommendations for international students: Required—TOEFL (minimum score 90 iBT). *Application deadline:* For fall admission, 1/15 for domestic students; for spring admission, 10/1 for domestic students. Application fee: $100. Electronic applications accepted. *Expenses:* Contact institution. *Financial support:* In 2016–17, 7 fellowships, 55 research assistantships, 49 teaching assistantships were awarded. Financial award application deadline: 2/1. *Total annual research expenditures:* $11 million. *Unit head:* Dr. Axel Drees, Chair, 631-632-8114, E-mail: axel.drees@stonybrook.edu. *Application contact:* Donald Sheehan, Coordinator, 631-632-1046, Fax: 631-632-8176, E-mail: donald.j.sheehan@stonybrook.edu.

Stony Brook University, State University of New York, Graduate School, College of Arts and Sciences, Institute for STEM Education, Stony Brook, NY 11794-5233. Offers PhD. *Faculty:* 3 full-time (2 women), 4 part-time/adjunct (1 woman). *Students:* 1 (woman) full-time, 34 part-time (24 women); includes 3 minority (all Black or African American, non-Hispanic/Latino). Average age 43. In 2016, 1 doctorate awarded. *Degree requirements:* For doctorate, comprehensive exam, thesis/dissertation. *Entrance requirements:* For doctorate, GRE. Additional exam requirements/recommendations for international students: Required—TOEFL (minimum score 550 paper-based; 90 iBT), IELTS (minimum score 6.5). *Application deadline:* For fall admission, 1/15 for domestic students; for spring admission, 10/1 for domestic students. Application fee: $100. *Expenses:* Contact institution. *Faculty research:* Educational evaluation or assessment, educational improvement, educational psychology. *Unit head:* Dr. Keith Sheppard, Director, 631-632-2989, E-mail: keith.sheppard@stonybrook.edu. *Application contact:* Judith Nimmo, Coordinator, 631-632-9750, E-mail: judith.nimmo@stonybrook.edu.
Website: http://istem.stonybrook.edu/

Stony Brook University, State University of New York, School of Professional Development, Stony Brook, NY 11794-443. Offers biology (MAT); chemistry (MAT); coaching (Graduate Certificate); earth science (MAT); educational computing (Graduate Certificate); educational leadership (Advanced Certificate); English (MAT); environmental management (MPS, Graduate Certificate); French (MAT); German (MAT); higher education administration (MA, Certificate); human resource management (MS, Graduate Certificate); industrial management (Graduate Certificate); information systems management (Graduate Certificate); Italian (MAT); liberal studies (MA); mathematics (MAT); operations research (Graduate Certificate); physics (MAT); school district business leadership (Advanced Certificate); social studies (MAT); Spanish (MAT). *Program availability:* Part-time, evening/weekend, online learning. *Faculty:* 4 full-time (3 women), 77 part-time/adjunct (34 women). *Students:* 197 full-time (125 women), 965 part-time (674 women); includes 222 minority (79 Black or African American, non-Hispanic/Latino; 2 American Indian or Alaska Native, non-Hispanic/Latino; 35 Asian, non-Hispanic/Latino; 87 Hispanic/Latino; 1 Native Hawaiian or other Pacific Islander, non-Hispanic/Latino; 18 Two or more races, non-Hispanic/Latino), 5 international. Average age 33. 462 applicants, 87% accepted, 317 enrolled. In 2016, 348 master's, 159 other advanced degrees awarded. *Degree requirements:* For master's, one foreign language, thesis or alternative. *Entrance requirements:* Additional exam requirements/recommendations for international students: Required—TOEFL (minimum score 85 iBT). *Application deadline:* For fall admission, 1/15 for domestic students, 6/1 for international students; for spring admission, 10/1 for domestic and international students. Applications are processed on a rolling basis. Application fee: $100. *Expenses:* Contact institution. *Financial support:* Fellowships, research assistantships, teaching assistantships, and career-related internships or fieldwork available. Support available to part-time students. *Unit head:* Dr. Ken Lindblom, Dean, 631-632-7049, Fax: 631-632-9046, E-mail: kenneth.lindblom@stonybrook.edu. *Application contact:* Melissa Jordan, Assistant Dean, 631-632-7751, E-mail: melissa.jordan@stonybrook.edu.
Website: http://www.stonybrook.edu/spd/

Syracuse University, College of Arts and Sciences, Program in College Science Teaching, Syracuse, NY 13244. Offers PhD. *Program availability:* Part-time. *Degree requirements:* For doctorate, comprehensive exam, thesis/dissertation. *Entrance requirements:* For doctorate, GRE General Test, three letters of recommendation, personal statement, transcripts. Additional exam requirements/recommendations for international students: Required—TOEFL (minimum score 100 iBT). *Application deadline:* For fall admission, 2/1 priority date for domestic and international students. Applications are processed on a rolling basis. Application fee: $75. Electronic applications accepted. *Expenses: Tuition:* Full-time $25,974; part-time $1443 per credit hour. *Required fees:* $802; $50 per course. Tuition and fees vary according to course load and program. *Financial support:* Fellowships with full tuition reimbursements, research assistantships with tuition reimbursements, teaching assistantships with tuition reimbursements, and scholarships/grants available. Financial award application deadline: 1/15; financial award applicants required to submit FAFSA. *Faculty research:* Philosophy of science, methods of teaching science in higher education, research focused on the problems of college teaching, curriculum development. *Unit head:* Dr. Sharon Dotger, Program Coordinator, 315-443-9138. *Application contact:* Michelle Mondo, Office Coordinator, 315-443-2685, E-mail: mrmondo@syr.edu.
Website: http://sciteach.syr.edu/

Syracuse University, School of Education, Programs in Science Education, Syracuse, NY 13244. Offers biology (MS); chemistry (MS, PhD). *Program availability:* Part-time. *Students:* Average age 38. In 2016, 4 doctorates awarded. *Degree requirements:* For doctorate, comprehensive exam, thesis/dissertation. *Entrance requirements:* For master's, GRE General Test or MAT, official transcripts from previous academic institutions, 3 letters of recommendation (preferably from faculty), personal statement that makes a clear and compelling argument for why applicant wants to teach secondary science; for doctorate, GRE General Test or MAT, master's degree, interview. Additional exam requirements/recommendations for international students: Required—TOEFL (minimum score 100 iBT). *Application deadline:* For fall admission, 1/15 priority date for domestic and international students; for spring admission, 10/15 priority date for domestic and international students. Applications are processed on a rolling basis. Application fee: $75. Electronic applications accepted. *Expenses: Tuition:* Full-time $25,974; part-time $1443 per credit hour. *Required fees:* $802; $50 per course. Tuition and fees vary according to course load and program. *Financial support:* Fellowships with full tuition reimbursements, research assistantships with tuition reimbursements, teaching assistantships with tuition reimbursements, and scholarships/grants available. Financial award application deadline: 1/15. *Faculty research:* Diverse field experiences and theoretical and practical knowledge in research-based science teaching, biology, chemistry, earth science, and physics. *Unit head:* Dr. Sharon Dotger, Program Coordinator, 315-443-9138, E-mail: sdotger@syr.edu. *Application contact:* Speranza Migliore, Graduate Admissions Recruiter, 315-443-2505, E-mail: gradrcrt@syr.edu.
Website: http://soeweb.syr.edu/

Teachers College, Columbia University, Department of Mathematics, Science and Technology, New York, NY 10027-6696. Offers biology 7-12 (MA); chemistry 7-12 (MA); communication and education (MA, Ed D); computing in education (MA); earth science 7-12 (MA); instructional technology and media (Ed M, MA, Ed D); mathematics education (Ed M, MA, Ed D, Ed DCT, PhD); physics 7-12 (MA); science and dental education (MA); science education (Ed M, MS, Ed DCT, PhD); supervisor/teacher of science education (MA); technology specialist (MA). *Program availability:* Part-time, evening/weekend, online learning. *Students:* 195 full-time (133 women), 222 part-time (139 women); includes 152 minority (44 Black or African American, non-Hispanic/Latino; 66 Asian, non-Hispanic/Latino; 32 Hispanic/Latino; 10 Two or more races, non-Hispanic/Latino), 106 international. 368 applicants, 65% accepted, 123 enrolled. Terminal master's awarded for partial completion of doctoral program. *Degree requirements:* For doctorate, thesis/dissertation. *Expenses: Tuition:* Full-time $36,288; part-time $1512 per credit. *Required fees:* $438 per semester. One-time fee: $510 full-time. Full-time tuition and fees vary according to course load. *Unit head:* Dr. O. Roger Anderson, Chair, 212-678-3405, Fax: 212-678-8129, E-mail: ora@ldeo.columbia.edu. *Application contact:* David Estrella, Director of Admission, 212-678-3305, E-mail: estrella@tc.columbia.edu.
Website: http://www.tc.columbia.edu/mathematics-science-and-technology/

Temple University, College of Education, Department of Teaching and Learning, Philadelphia, PA 19122-6096. Offers career and technical education (Ed M), including business, computing, and information technology, industrial education, marketing education; middle grades education (Ed M), including math and language arts, math and science, science and language arts; secondary education (Ed M), including English, math, social studies; teaching English to speakers of other languages (MS Ed); urban education (Ed M). *Program availability:* Part-time, evening/weekend. *Faculty:* 26 full-time (16 women), 74 part-time/adjunct (54 women). *Students:* 204 full-time (139 women), 320 part-time (201 women); includes 112 minority (66 Black or African American, non-Hispanic/Latino; 17 Asian, non-Hispanic/Latino; 18 Hispanic/Latino; 11 Two or more races, non-Hispanic/Latino), 18 international. 300 applicants, 55% accepted, 99 enrolled. In 2016, 93 master's awarded. Terminal master's awarded for partial completion of doctoral program. *Degree requirements:* For master's, thesis or alternative. *Entrance requirements:* Additional exam requirements/recommendations for international students: Required—TOEFL (minimum score 550 paper-based; 79 iBT). *Application deadline:* For fall admission, 4/1 for domestic students, 12/15 for international students; for spring admission, 10/1 for domestic students, 8/1 for international students. Application fee: $60. Electronic applications accepted. *Expenses:* Contact institution. *Financial support:* Fellowships, research assistantships, and teaching assistantships available. Financial award application deadline: 1/15; financial award applicants required to submit FAFSA. *Faculty research:* Workforce development, vocational education, technical education, industrial education, professional development, literacy, classroom management, school communities, curriculum development, instruction, applied linguistics, cross linguistic influence, bilingual education, oral proficiency, multilingualism. *Unit head:* Dr. Christine Woyshner, Chairperson, 215-204-6387, E-mail: christine.woyshner@temple.edu. *Application contact:* Sarah Stapleton, Assistant Director, Academic Operations, 215-204-8220, E-mail: sarah.stapleton@temple.edu.
Website: http://education.temple.edu/tl

Tennessee Technological University, College of Graduate Studies, College of Education, Department of Curriculum and Instruction, Program in STEM Education, Cookeville, TN 38505. Offers MA, Ed S. *Program availability:* Part-time, evening/weekend. *Students:* 2 full-time (1 woman), 3 part-time (2 women). 3 applicants, 100% accepted, 2 enrolled. *Degree requirements:* For master's, comprehensive exam, thesis or alternative. *Entrance requirements:* For master's, GRE, MAT. Additional exam requirements/recommendations for international students: Required—TOEFL (minimum score 527 paper-based; 71 iBT), IELTS (minimum score 5.5) or PTE (48). *Application deadline:* For fall admission, 8/1 for domestic students, 5/1 for international students; for spring admission, 2/1 for domestic students, 10/1 for international students; for summer admission, 5/1 for domestic students, 2/1 for international students. Applications are processed on a rolling basis. Application fee: $35 ($40 for international students). Electronic applications accepted. *Expenses:* Tuition, state resident: full-time $9375; part-time $534 per credit hour. Tuition, nonresident: full-time $22,443; part-time $1260 per credit hour. *Financial support:* Application deadline: 4/1. *Unit head:* Dr. Jeremy Wendt, Interim Chairperson, 931-372-3181, E-mail: jwendt@tntech.edu. *Application contact:* Shelia K. Kendrick, Coordinator of Graduate Studies, 931-372-3808, Fax: 931-372-3497, E-mail: skendrick@tntech.edu.

Texas Christian University, College of Education, Doctoral Programs in Education, Fort Worth, TX 76129. Offers counseling and counselor education (PhD); curriculum studies (PhD); educational leadership (Ed D); higher educational leadership (Ed D); science education (PhD); MBA/Ed D. *Program availability:* Part-time, evening/weekend. *Faculty:* 29 full-time (21 women), 8 part-time/adjunct (5 women). *Students:* 77 full-time (56 women), 19 part-time (7 women); includes 33 minority (12 Black or African American, non-Hispanic/Latino; 5 Asian, non-Hispanic/Latino; 15 Hispanic/Latino; 1 Two

or more races, non-Hispanic/Latino), 6 international. Average age 37. 34 applicants, 56% accepted, 13 enrolled. In 2016, 5 doctorates awarded. *Degree requirements:* For doctorate, comprehensive exam, thesis/dissertation. *Entrance requirements:* For doctorate, GRE General Test. Additional exam requirements/recommendations for international students: Required—TOEFL (minimum score 550 paper-based; 80 iBT). *Application deadline:* For fall admission, 2/1 for domestic and international students; for winter admission, 2/1 for domestic and international students; for spring admission, 11/16 for domestic and international students. Application fee: $60. Electronic applications accepted. *Expenses: Tuition:* Full-time $26,640; part-time $1480 per credit hour. *Required fees:* $48. Tuition and fees vary according to program. *Financial support:* In 2016–17, 57 students received support, including 1 fellowship with full tuition reimbursement available, 10 research assistantships with full tuition reimbursements available (averaging $18,500 per year), 7 teaching assistantships with full tuition reimbursements available (averaging $18,500 per year); career-related internships or fieldwork, scholarships/grants, health care benefits, and unspecified assistantships also available. Support available to part-time students. Financial award application deadline: 2/1; financial award applicants required to submit FAFSA. *Unit head:* Dr. Jan Lacina, Associate Dean, 817-257-6786, Fax: 817-257-7466, E-mail: j.lacina@tcu.edu. *Application contact:* Lori Kimball, Administrative Program Specialist, 817-257-7661, Fax: 817-257-7466, E-mail: l.kimball@tcu.edu.
Website: http://coe.tcu.edu/graduate-overview/

Texas Christian University, College of Education, Master's Programs in Education, Fort Worth, TX 76129. Offers counseling (M Ed); curriculum and instruction (M Ed), including curriculum studies, language and literacy, math education, science education; educational leadership (M Ed); special education (M Ed). *Program availability:* Part-time, evening/weekend. *Faculty:* 29 full-time (21 women), 8 part-time/adjunct (5 women). *Students:* 112 full-time (95 women), 12 part-time (11 women); includes 39 minority (6 Black or African American, non-Hispanic/Latino; 2 Asian, non-Hispanic/Latino; 27 Hispanic/Latino; 1 Native Hawaiian or other Pacific Islander, non-Hispanic/Latino; 3 Two or more races, non-Hispanic/Latino), 2 international. Average age 29. 107 applicants, 78% accepted, 66 enrolled. In 2016, 54 master's awarded. *Degree requirements:* For master's, comprehensive exam (for some programs), thesis (for some programs). *Entrance requirements:* For master's, GRE General Test. Additional exam requirements/recommendations for international students: Required—TOEFL (minimum score 550 paper-based; 80 iBT). *Application deadline:* For fall admission, 3/1 for domestic and international students; for spring admission, 11/16 for domestic and international students; for summer admission, 3/1 for domestic and international students. Application fee: $60. Electronic applications accepted. *Expenses: Tuition:* Full-time $26,640; part-time $1480 per credit hour. *Required fees:* $48. Tuition and fees vary according to program. *Financial support:* In 2016–17, 104 students received support, including 4 research assistantships with full tuition reimbursements available (averaging $15,000 per year), 31 teaching assistantships with full tuition reimbursements available (averaging $15,000 per year); career-related internships or fieldwork, scholarships/grants, and unspecified assistantships also available. Support available to part-time students. Financial award application deadline: 3/1; financial award applicants required to submit FAFSA. *Unit head:* Dr. Jan Lacina, Associate Dean, 817-257-6786, Fax: 817-257-7466, E-mail: j.lacina@tcu.edu. *Application contact:* Lori Kimball, Administrative Program Specialist, 817-257-7661, Fax: 817-257-7466, E-mail: l.kimball@tcu.edu.
Website: http://coe.tcu.edu/graduate-overview/

Texas Tech University, Graduate School, College of Education, Department of Curriculum and Instruction, Lubbock, TX 79409-1071. Offers bilingual education (M Ed); curriculum and instruction (M Ed); elementary education (M Ed); language/literacy education (M Ed); multidisciplinary science (MS); secondary education (M Ed). *Accreditation:* NCATE. *Program availability:* Part-time, evening/weekend, online learning. *Faculty:* 24 full-time (17 women), 1 part-time/adjunct (0 women). *Students:* 65 full-time (52 women), 237 part-time (191 women); includes 97 minority (30 Black or African American, non-Hispanic/Latino; 1 American Indian or Alaska Native, non-Hispanic/Latino; 10 Asian, non-Hispanic/Latino; 47 Hispanic/Latino; 9 Two or more races, non-Hispanic/Latino), 41 international. Average age 39. 181 applicants, 54% accepted, 78 enrolled. In 2016, 20 master's, 28 doctorates awarded. Terminal master's awarded for partial completion of doctoral program. *Degree requirements:* For master's, comprehensive exam (for some programs), thesis optional; for doctorate, comprehensive exam, thesis/dissertation. *Entrance requirements:* For master's, bachelor's degree; resume; letter of intent; academic writing sample; 2 letters of recommendation; for doctorate, GRE, master's degree; resume; letter of intent; academic writing sample; 3 letters of recommendation. Additional exam requirements/recommendations for international students: Required—TOEFL (minimum score 550 paper-based; 79 iBT). *Application deadline:* For fall admission, 6/1 priority date for domestic students, 1/15 priority date for international students; for spring admission, 9/1 priority date for domestic students, 6/15 priority date for international students. Applications are processed on a rolling basis. Application fee: $75. Electronic applications accepted. *Expenses:* $285 per credit hour full-time resident tuition, $693 per credit hour full-time non-resident tuition; $50.50 per credit hour fee plus $608 per term fee. *Financial support:* In 2016–17, 110 students received support, including 110 fellowships (averaging $3,132 per year); research assistantships, Federal Work-Study, institutionally sponsored loans, scholarships/grants, health care benefits, and unspecified assistantships also available. Support available to part-time students. Financial award application deadline: 2/1; financial award applicants required to submit FAFSA. *Faculty research:* Teacher education, curriculum studies, bilingual education, science and math education, language and literacy education. *Total annual research expenditures:* $120,552. *Unit head:* Dr. Jian Wang, Department Chair, Curriculum and Instruction, 806-834-5165, Fax: 806-742-2179, E-mail: jian.wang@ttu.edu. *Application contact:* Brianna Sanchez, Coordinator, 806-834-2353, Fax: 806-742-2179, E-mail: brianna.sanchez@ttu.edu.
Website: http://www.educ.ttu.edu

Touro College, Graduate School of Education, New York, NY 10010. Offers education and special education (MS); education biology (MS); instructional technology (MS); mathematics education (MS); school leadership (MS); teaching English to speakers of other languages (MS); teaching literacy (MS). *Accreditation:* TEAC. *Program availability:* Part-time, evening/weekend, online learning. *Faculty:* 52 full-time (34 women), 199 part-time/adjunct (136 women). *Students:* 578 full-time (483 women), 1,932 part-time (1,626 women); includes 749 minority (318 Black or African American, non-Hispanic/Latino; 5 American Indian or Alaska Native, non-Hispanic/Latino; 108 Asian, non-Hispanic/Latino; 288 Hispanic/Latino; 2 Native Hawaiian or other Pacific Islander, non-Hispanic/Latino; 28 Two or more races, non-Hispanic/Latino), 17 international. Average age 32. 1,422 applicants, 50% accepted, 675 enrolled. In 2016, 6 master's awarded. *Entrance requirements:* Additional exam requirements/recommendations for international students: Required—TOEFL (minimum score 83 iBT), IELTS (minimum score 6.5). *Application deadline:* For fall admission, 8/26 for domestic students, 7/15 for international students; for spring admission, 12/31 for domestic students, 12/15 for international students. Applications are processed on a rolling basis. Application fee: $50. *Financial support:* Federal Work-Study available. Financial award applicants required to submit FAFSA. *Faculty research:* Equity assistance, language development, scholarly communications, Latin American studies and cultural sensitivity, behavior management techniques and strategies in special education. *Unit head:* Dr. Arnold Spinner, Dean, 212-463-0400 Ext. 5561, Fax: 212-462-4889, E-mail: aspinner@touro.edu. *Application contact:* Luna Feliciano, Admissions, 212-463-0400.

Tufts University, Graduate School of Arts and Sciences, Department of Education, Program in Education, Medford, MA 02155. Offers educational studies (MA); elementary education (MAT); middle and secondary education (MAT); museum education (MA); secondary education (MA); STEM education (MS, PhD). *Program availability:* Part-time. *Students:* 67 full-time (49 women), 14 part-time (12 women); includes 17 minority (4 Black or African American, non-Hispanic/Latino; 6 Asian, non-Hispanic/Latino; 6 Hispanic/Latino; 1 Two or more races, non-Hispanic/Latino), 6 international. Average age 28. 120 applicants, 71% accepted, 49 enrolled. In 2016, 25 master's awarded. *Degree requirements:* For master's, thesis optional. *Entrance requirements:* For master's, GRE General Test, portfolio (for art education only); for doctorate, GRE General Test, writing sample. Additional exam requirements/recommendations for international students: Required—TOEFL (minimum score 550 paper-based; 80 iBT), IELTS (minimum score 6.5). *Application deadline:* For fall admission, 1/2 for domestic and international students; for spring admission, 10/15 for domestic and international students. Applications are processed on a rolling basis. Application fee: $85. Electronic applications accepted. *Expenses:* Contact institution. *Financial support:* In 2016–17, 69 students received support. Research assistantships, teaching assistantships, Federal Work-Study, scholarships/grants, and tuition waivers (full and partial) available. Support available to part-time students. Financial award application deadline: 1/2. *Unit head:* Dr. Sabina Vaught, Graduate Program Director. *Application contact:* Office of Graduate Admissions, 617-627-3395, E-mail: gradadmissions@tufts.edu.

Tufts University, Graduate School of Arts and Sciences, Department of Physics and Astronomy, Medford, MA 02155. Offers astrophysics (MS, PhD); chemical physics (PhD); physics (MS, PhD); physics education (PhD). *Students:* 33 full-time (7 women), 15 international. Average age 27. 126 applicants, 17% accepted, 9 enrolled. In 2016, 4 master's, 1 doctorate awarded. Terminal master's awarded for partial completion of doctoral program. *Degree requirements:* For master's, thesis optional; for doctorate, thesis/dissertation, oral qualifying exam. *Entrance requirements:* For master's and doctorate, GRE General Test. Additional exam requirements/recommendations for international students: Required—TOEFL (minimum score 550 paper-based; 80 iBT), IELTS (minimum score 6.5). *Application deadline:* For fall admission, 1/15 for domestic and international students. Applications are processed on a rolling basis. Application fee: $85. Electronic applications accepted. *Expenses:* $49,982 full-time tuition (for MS); $29,936 full-time tuition (for PhD). *Financial support:* In 2016–17, 33 students received support. Fellowships, research assistantships, teaching assistantships, Federal Work-Study, scholarships/grants, tuition waivers (full and partial), and unspecified assistantships available. Financial award application deadline: 1/15. *Unit head:* Dr. Danilo Marchesini, Graduate Program Director. *Application contact:* Office of Graduate Admissions, 617-627-3395, E-mail: gradadmissions@tufts.edu.
Website: http://www.tufts.edu/as/physics/

Universidad Nacional Pedro Henriquez Urena, Graduate School, Santo Domingo, Dominican Republic. Offers agricultural diversity (MS), including horticultural/fruit production, tropical animal production; conservation of monuments and cultural assets (M Arch); ecology and environment (MS); environmental engineering (MEE); international relations (MA); natural resource management (MS); political science (MA); project optimization (MPM); project feasibility (MPM); project management (MPM); sanitation engineering (ME); science for teachers (MS); tropical Caribbean architecture (M Arch).

University at Buffalo, the State University of New York, Graduate School, Graduate School of Education, Department of Learning and Instruction, Buffalo, NY 14260. Offers biology education (Ed M, Certificate); chemistry education (Ed M, Certificate); childhood education (Ed M); childhood education with bilingual extension (Ed M); college teaching (Advanced Certificate); curriculum, instruction and the science of learning (PhD); early childhood education (Ed M); early childhood education with bilingual extension (Ed M); earth science education (Ed M, Certificate); education and technology (Ed M); education studies (Ed M); educational technology and new literacies (Certificate); educational technology and new literacies (Advanced Certificate); elementary education (Ed D); English education (Ed M, Certificate); English education studies (Ed M); English for speakers of other languages (Ed M); foreign and second language education (PhD); French education (Ed M, Certificate); German education (Ed M, Certificate); gifted education (Certificate); Latin education (Ed M, Certificate); literacy education studies (Ed M); literacy specialist (Ed M); literacy teaching and learning (Certificate); mathematics education (Ed M, Certificate); music education (Ed M, Certificate); music education studies (Ed M); music learning theory (Advanced Certificate); online education (Advanced Certificate); physics education (Ed M, Certificate); science and the public (Ed M); social studies education (Ed M, Certificate); Spanish education (Ed M, Certificate); special education (PhD); teaching English to speakers of other languages (Ed M). *Program availability:* Part-time, evening/weekend, 100% online. *Faculty:* 28 full-time (21 women), 67 part-time/adjunct (49 women). *Students:* 198 full-time (153 women), 312 part-time (220 women); includes 48 minority (28 Black or African American, non-Hispanic/Latino; 4 American Indian or Alaska Native, non-Hispanic/Latino; 15 Asian, non-Hispanic/Latino; 1 Hispanic/Latino), 66 international. Average age 33. 336 applicants, 86% accepted, 178 enrolled. In 2016, 137 master's, 24 doctorates, 25 other advanced degrees awarded. *Degree requirements:* For master's, comprehensive exam; for doctorate, thesis/dissertation, research analysis exam, research experience. *Entrance requirements:* For master's, letters of reference; for doctorate, GRE General Test or MAT, interview, writing sample, letters of recommendation. Additional exam requirements/recommendations for international students: Required—TOEFL (minimum score 600 paper-based; 96 iBT). *Application deadline:* For fall admission, 2/1 priority date for domestic and international students; for spring admission, 11/15 priority date for domestic students, 10/1 for international students. Applications are processed on a rolling basis. Application fee: $50. Electronic applications accepted. *Financial support:* In 2016–17, 44 fellowships (averaging $4,010 per year), 39 research assistantships with tuition reimbursements (averaging $9,897 per year) were awarded; teaching assistantships, career-related internships or fieldwork, Federal Work-Study, institutionally sponsored loans, scholarships/grants, tuition waivers (full and partial), and unspecified assistantships also available. Financial award application deadline: 2/28; financial award applicants required to submit FAFSA. *Faculty research:* Science assessment, foreign language teaching and learning, early learning, new literacies, gender and education. *Total annual research expenditures:* $534,880. *Unit head:* Dr. Deborah Moore-Russo, Chair, 716-645-4069, Fax: 716-645-3161, E-mail: dam29@buffalo.edu. *Application contact:* Luann Zak, Admissions Assistant, 716-645-2110, Fax: 716-645-7937, E-mail: luannzak@buffalo.edu.
Website: http://gse.buffalo.edu/lai

The University of Akron, Graduate School, College of Education, Department of Curricular and Instructional Studies, Program in Adolescent to Young Adult Education, Akron, OH 44325. Offers chemistry (MS); chemistry and physics (MS); earth science (MS); earth science and chemistry (MS); earth science and physics (MS); integrated language arts (MS); integrated mathematics (MS); integrated social studies (MS); life science (MS); life science and chemistry (MS); life science and earth science (MS); life science and physics (MS); physics (MS). *Accreditation:* NCATE. *Degree requirements:* For master's, comprehensive exam, portfolio. *Entrance requirements:* Additional exam requirements/recommendations for international students: Required—TOEFL (minimum score 550 paper-based, 79 iBT) or IELTS (minimum score 6.5). *Application deadline:* For fall admission, 3/1 for domestic and international students; for spring admission, 10/1 for domestic and international students. Applications are processed on a rolling basis. Application fee: $45 ($70 for international students). Electronic applications accepted. *Expenses:* Tuition, state resident: full-time $8618; part-time $359 per credit hour. Tuition, nonresident: full-time $17,149; part-time $715 per credit hour. *Required fees:* $1652. *Unit head:* Dr. Peggy McCann, Interim Chair, 330-972-5742, E-mail: plm@uakron.edu.

The University of Alabama in Huntsville, School of Graduate Studies, College of Education, Huntsville, AL 35899. Offers autism spectrum disorders (M Ed, Graduate Certificate); biology (MAT); chemistry (MAT); differentiated instruction in elementary education (M Ed); English language arts (MAT); English speakers of other languages (M Ed, MAT); history (MAT); mathematics (MAT); physics (MAT); reading education (M Ed); secondary education (M Ed). *Expenses:* Tuition, state resident: full-time $9834; part-time $600 per credit hour. Tuition, nonresident: full-time $21,830; part-time $1325 per credit hour.

The University of Alabama in Huntsville, School of Graduate Studies, College of Science, Department of Biological Sciences, Huntsville, AL 35899. Offers biology (MS); biotechnology science and engineering (PhD); education (MS). *Program availability:* Part-time, evening/weekend. *Degree requirements:* For master's, comprehensive exam, thesis or alternative, oral and written exams. *Entrance requirements:* For master's, GRE General Test, previous course work in biochemistry and organic chemistry, minimum GPA of 3.0. Additional exam requirements/recommendations for international students: Required—TOEFL (minimum score 550 paper-based; 80 iBT), IELTS (minimum score 6.5). Electronic applications accepted. *Expenses:* Tuition, state resident: full-time $9834; part-time $600 per credit hour. Tuition, nonresident: full-time $21,830; part-time $1325 per credit hour. *Faculty research:* Physiology, microbiology, genomics and protemics, ecology and evolution, drug discovery.

The University of Alabama in Huntsville, School of Graduate Studies, College of Science, Department of Chemistry, Huntsville, AL 35899. Offers biotechnology science and engineering (PhD); chemistry (MS); education (MS); materials science (MS, PhD). *Program availability:* Part-time, evening/weekend. *Degree requirements:* For master's, comprehensive exam, thesis or alternative, oral and written exams. *Entrance requirements:* For master's, GRE General Test, minimum GPA of 3.0. Additional exam requirements/recommendations for international students: Required—TOEFL (minimum score 550 paper-based; 80 iBT), IELTS (minimum score 6.5). Electronic applications accepted. *Expenses:* Tuition, state resident: full-time $9834; part-time $600 per credit hour. Tuition, nonresident: full-time $21,830; part-time $1325 per credit hour. *Faculty research:* Natural products drug discovery, protein biochemistry, macromolecular biophysics, polymer synthesis, surface modification and analysis of materials.

The University of Alabama in Huntsville, School of Graduate Studies, College of Science, Department of Physics, Huntsville, AL 35899. Offers education (MS); optics and photonics technology (MS); physics (MS, PhD). *Program availability:* Part-time, evening/weekend. *Degree requirements:* For master's, comprehensive exam, thesis or alternative, oral and written exams; for doctorate, comprehensive exam, thesis/dissertation, oral and written exams. *Entrance requirements:* For master's and doctorate, GRE General Test, minimum GPA of 3.0. Additional exam requirements/recommendations for international students: Required—TOEFL (minimum score 550 paper-based; 80 iBT), IELTS (minimum score 6.5). Electronic applications accepted. *Expenses:* Tuition, state resident: full-time $9834; part-time $600 per credit hour. Tuition, nonresident: full-time $21,830; part-time $1325 per credit hour. *Faculty research:* Space and solar physics, computational physics, optics, high energy astrophysics.

University of Arkansas at Pine Bluff, School of Education, Pine Bluff, AR 71601-2799. Offers elementary education (M Ed); secondary education (M Ed), including English education, mathematics education, science education, social studies education; teaching (MAT). *Accreditation:* NCATE. *Program availability:* Part-time, evening/weekend. *Degree requirements:* For master's, comprehensive exam. *Entrance requirements:* For master's, GRE, minimum GPA of 2.75, NTE or Standard Arkansas Teaching Certificate. Application fee: $25. *Expenses:* Tuition, state resident: full-time $4776. Tuition, nonresident: full-time $10,824. *Required fees:* $1612. Tuition and fees vary according to course load. *Financial support:* Research assistantships with full and partial tuition reimbursements, teaching assistantships with full and partial tuition reimbursements, institutionally sponsored loans, and scholarships/grants available. Support available to part-time students. *Faculty research:* Teacher certification, accreditation, assessment, standards, portfolio development, rehabilitation, technology. *Unit head:* Dr. George Herts, Dean, 870-575-8000, E-mail: johnson_c@uapb.edu.
Website: http://www.uapb.edu/academics/school_of_education.aspx

The University of British Columbia, Faculty of Education, Department of Curriculum and Pedagogy, Vancouver, BC V6T 1Z4, Canada. Offers art education (M Ed, MA); curriculum studies (M Ed, MA, PhD); home economics education (M Ed, MA); mathematics education (M Ed, MA); media and technology studies education (M Ed, MA); music education (M Ed, MA); physical education (M Ed, MA); science education (M Ed, MA); social studies education (M Ed, MA). *Program availability:* Part-time, online learning. *Degree requirements:* For master's, thesis (MA); for doctorate, comprehensive exam, thesis/dissertation. *Entrance requirements:* Additional exam requirements/recommendations for international students: Required—TOEFL, IELTS. Application fee: $100 Canadian dollars ($162 Canadian dollars for international students). Electronic applications accepted. *Expenses:* $6,865 per year tuition and fees domestic, $10,938 per year international (for MA and M Ed); $4,802 per year tuition and fees, $8,436 per year international (for PhD). *Financial support:* Fellowships with partial tuition reimbursements, research assistantships with partial tuition reimbursements, teaching assistantships with partial tuition reimbursements, and tuition waivers (partial) available. *Faculty research:* School subjects, teaching and learning. *Application contact:* Alan Jay, Graduate Programs Assistant, 604-822-5367, Fax: 604-822-4714, E-mail: edcp.grad@ubc.ca.
Website: http://www.edcp.educ.ubc.ca/

University of California, Berkeley, Graduate Division, School of Education, Group in Science and Mathematics Education, Berkeley, CA 94720-1500. Offers PhD, MA/Credential. *Students:* 17 full-time (15 women); includes 1 minority (Hispanic/Latino), 3 international. Average age 30. 12 applicants, 4 enrolled. In 2016, 5 doctorates awarded. *Application deadline:* For fall admission, 12/1 for domestic students. Application fee: $105 ($125 for international students). Electronic applications accepted. *Financial support:* Fellowships, research assistantships, teaching assistantships, institutionally sponsored loans, health care benefits, and unspecified assistantships available. *Application contact:* Kate Capps, Graduate Student Services Advisor, 510-642-4207, E-mail: sme_info@lists.berkeley.edu.
Website: https://gse.berkeley.edu/sesame

University of California, Berkeley, Graduate Division, School of Education, Programs in Education, Berkeley, CA 94720-1500. Offers development in mathematics and science (MA); education in mathematics, science, and technology (MA, PhD); human development and education (MA, PhD); leadership education (MA); special education (PhD); teacher education (MA); MA/Credential; PhD/Credential; PhD/MA. *Students:* 286 full-time (207 women); includes 133 minority (31 Black or African American, non-Hispanic/Latino; 2 American Indian or Alaska Native, non-Hispanic/Latino; 44 Asian, non-Hispanic/Latino; 56 Hispanic/Latino), 29 international. Average age 33. 643 applicants, 84 enrolled. In 2016, 105 master's, 31 doctorates awarded. Terminal master's awarded for partial completion of doctoral program. *Degree requirements:* For master's, exam or thesis; for doctorate, thesis/dissertation, oral qualifying exam. *Entrance requirements:* For master's and doctorate, GRE General Test, minimum GPA of 3.0 during last 2 years of undergraduate course work. *Application deadline:* For fall admission, 12/16 for domestic students. Application fee: $105 ($125 for international students). Electronic applications accepted. *Financial support:* Fellowships, research assistantships, teaching assistantships, institutionally sponsored loans, health care benefits, and unspecified assistantships available. *Faculty research:* Human development, social and moral educational psychology, developmental teacher preparation. *Unit head:* Prof. Prudence L. Carter, Dean, 510-642-3726, E-mail: gsedeansoffice@lists.berkeley.edu.
Website: https://gse.berkeley.edu

University of California, San Diego, Graduate Division, Program in Mathematics and Science Education, La Jolla, CA 92093. Offers PhD. Program offered jointly with San Diego State University. *Students:* 3 full-time (0 women), 8 part-time (7 women). In 2016, 3 doctorates awarded. *Degree requirements:* For doctorate, thesis/dissertation, teaching practicum. *Entrance requirements:* For doctorate, GRE General Test, minimum GPA of 3.25. Additional exam requirements/recommendations for international students: Required—TOEFL (minimum score 550 paper-based; 80 iBT), IELTS (minimum score 7). Electronic applications accepted. *Expenses:* Tuition, state resident: full-time $11,220. Tuition, nonresident: full-time $26,322. *Required fees:* $1864. *Financial support:* Scholarships/grants and stipends available. Financial award applicants required to submit FAFSA. *Faculty research:* Effective teaching of rational numbers, teacher development, development of number sense and estimation. *Unit head:* Gabriele Wienhausen, Chair, 858-534-3105, E-mail: gwienhausen@ucsd.edu. *Application contact:* Sherry Seethaler, Graduate Coordinator, 858-534-4656, E-mail: sseethaler@ucsd.edu.
Website: http://sci.sdsu.edu/CRMSE/msed/

University of Central Florida, College of Education and Human Performance, Education Doctoral Programs, Orlando, FL 32816. Offers communication sciences and disorders (PhD); curriculum and instruction (Ed D); early childhood education (PhD); educational leadership (Ed D); elementary education (PhD); exceptional education (PhD); exercise physiology (PhD); higher education (PhD); instructional technology (PhD); mathematics education (PhD); methodology, measurement and analysis (PhD); reading education (PhD); science education (PhD); social science education (PhD); TESOL (PhD). *Students:* 127 full-time (91 women), 43 part-time (29 women); includes 33 minority (17 Black or African American, non-Hispanic/Latino; 5 Asian, non-Hispanic/Latino; 7 Hispanic/Latino; 4 Two or more races, non-Hispanic/Latino), 26 international. Average age 37. 163 applicants, 40% accepted, 52 enrolled. In 2016, 57 doctorates awarded. Application fee: $30. Electronic applications accepted. *Expenses:* Tuition, state resident: part-time $288.16 per credit hour. Tuition, nonresident: part-time $1071.31 per credit hour. *Financial support:* In 2016–17, 78 students received support, including 41 fellowships with partial tuition reimbursements available (averaging $5,916 per year), 44 research assistantships with partial tuition reimbursements available (averaging $7,637 per year), 48 teaching assistantships with partial tuition reimbursements available (averaging $9,633 per year). Financial award application deadline: 3/1; financial award applicants required to submit FAFSA. *Unit head:* Dr. Edward Robinson, Director of Doctoral Programs, 407-823-6106, E-mail: edward.robinson@ucf.edu. *Application contact:* Assistant Director, Graduate Admissions, 407-823-2766, Fax: 407-823-6442, E-mail: gradadmissions@ucf.edu.
Website: http://education.ucf.edu/programs.cfm?pid=g&cat=2

University of Central Florida, College of Education and Human Performance, School of Teaching, Learning, and Leadership, Program in K-8 Mathematics and Science Education, Orlando, FL 32816. Offers M Ed, Certificate. *Accreditation:* NCATE. *Program availability:* Part-time. *Students:* 21 part-time (18 women); includes 11 minority (4 Black or African American, non-Hispanic/Latino; 7 Hispanic/Latino). Average age 35. 3 applicants, 100% accepted, 2 enrolled. In 2016, 4 master's awarded. *Degree requirements:* For master's, thesis or alternative. *Entrance requirements:* Additional exam requirements/recommendations for international students: Required—TOEFL. *Application deadline:* For summer admission, 4/15 for domestic students. Application fee: $30. Electronic applications accepted. *Expenses:* Tuition, state resident: part-time $288.16 per credit hour. Tuition, nonresident: part-time $1071.31 per credit hour. *Financial support:* Application deadline: 3/1; applicants required to submit FAFSA. *Unit head:* Dr. Erhan Haciomeroglu, Program Coordinator, 407-823-4336, E-mail: erhan.haciomeroglu@ucf.edu. *Application contact:* Assistant Director, Graduate Admissions, 407-823-2766, Fax: 407-823-6442, E-mail: gradadmissions@ucf.edu.
Website: http://education.ucf.edu/mathed/

University of Central Florida, College of Education and Human Performance, School of Teaching, Learning, and Leadership, Program in Teacher Education, Orlando, FL 32816. Offers art education (MAT); English language (MAT); mathematics education (MAT); middle school mathematics (MAT); middle school science (MAT); science education (MAT), including biology, chemistry, physics; social science education (MAT). *Accreditation:* NCATE. *Program availability:* Part-time, evening/weekend. *Students:* 16 full-time (11 women), 28 part-time (23 women); includes 16 minority (6 Black or African American, non-Hispanic/Latino; 1 Asian, non-Hispanic/Latino; 8 Hispanic/Latino; 1 Two or more races, non-Hispanic/Latino), 1 international. Average age 31. 1 applicant, 100% accepted. In 2016, 33 master's awarded. *Entrance requirements:* For master's, GRE General Test. Additional exam requirements/recommendations for international students: Required—TOEFL. *Application deadline:* For spring admission, 12/1 for domestic students; for summer admission, 4/15 for domestic students. Application fee: $30. Electronic applications accepted. *Expenses:* Tuition, state resident: part-time $288.16 per credit hour. Tuition, nonresident: part-time $1071.31 per credit hour. *Financial support:* Fellowships, research assistantships, teaching assistantships, career-related internships or fieldwork, Federal Work-Study, institutionally sponsored loans, tuition waivers (partial), and unspecified assistantships available. Financial award application deadline: 3/1; financial award applicants required to submit FAFSA. *Unit head:* Dr. Michael Hynes, Director, 407-823-2005, E-mail: mychael.hynes@ucf.edu. *Application contact:* Assistant Director, Graduate Admissions, 407-823-2766, Fax: 407-823-6442, E-mail: gradadmissions@ucf.edu.
Website: http://education.ucf.edu/programs.cfm?pid=g&cat=2

University of Chicago, Division of the Social Sciences, Committee on Conceptual and Historical Studies of Science, Chicago, IL 60637. Offers PhD. *Students:* 9 full-time (5 women); includes 1 minority (Hispanic/Latino), 3 international. 25 applicants, 20% accepted, 2 enrolled. *Degree requirements:* For doctorate, one foreign language, thesis/

dissertation, 2 oral exams. *Entrance requirements:* For doctorate, GRE General Test. Additional exam requirements/recommendations for international students: Required—TOEFL (minimum score 104 iBT), IELTS (minimum score 7). *Application deadline:* For fall admission, 12/15 for domestic and international students. Application fee: $90. Electronic applications accepted. *Financial support:* In 2016–17, 2 students received support, including 2 fellowships with full tuition reimbursements available (averaging $23,000 per year); career-related internships or fieldwork, Federal Work-Study, institutionally sponsored loans, scholarships/grants, and health care benefits also available. Financial award application deadline: 12/15. *Unit head:* Prof. Adrian Johns, Chair, E-mail: johns@uchicago.edu. *Application contact:* Office of the Dean of Students, 773-702-8415, E-mail: admissions@ssd.uchicago.edu.
Website: http://chss.uchicago.edu/

University of Cincinnati, Graduate School, College of Education, Criminal Justice, and Human Services, Division of Teacher Education, Cincinnati, OH 45221. Offers curriculum and instruction (M Ed, Ed D); deaf studies (Certificate); early childhood education (M Ed); middle childhood education (M Ed); postsecondary literacy instruction (Certificate); reading/literacy (M Ed, Ed D); secondary education (M Ed); special education (M Ed, Ed D); teaching English as a second language (Ed D, Certificate); teaching science (MS). *Program availability:* Part-time. *Degree requirements:* For doctorate, thesis/dissertation. *Entrance requirements:* For master's, GRE General Test. Additional exam requirements/recommendations for international students: Required—TOEFL (minimum score 550 paper-based). Electronic applications accepted. *Expenses: Tuition, area resident:* Full-time $12,790; part-time $389 per credit hour. Tuition, state resident: full-time $13,290; part-time $419 per credit hour. Tuition, nonresident: full-time $24,532; part-time $976 per credit hour. *International tuition:* $24,832 full-time. *Required fees:* $3958; $140 per credit hour. Tuition and fees vary according to course load, degree level, program and reciprocity agreements.

University of Colorado Denver, School of Education and Human Development, Program in Educational Leadership and Innovation, Denver, CO 80217. Offers educational studies and research (PhD), including administrative leadership and policy, early childhood special education, math education, research, assessment and evaluation, science education, urban ecologies. *Program availability:* Part-time, evening/weekend. *Students:* 30 full-time (25 women), 14 part-time (11 women); includes 16 minority (7 Black or African American, non-Hispanic/Latino; 1 American Indian or Alaska Native, non-Hispanic/Latino; 1 Asian, non-Hispanic/Latino; 6 Hispanic/Latino; 1 Two or more races, non-Hispanic/Latino), 5 international. Average age 40. 21 applicants, 67% accepted, 8 enrolled. In 2016, 3 doctorates awarded. *Degree requirements:* For doctorate, comprehensive exam, thesis/dissertation, 75 credit hours (for PhD). *Entrance requirements:* For doctorate, GRE or equivalent, resume or curriculum vitae, letters of recommendation, master's degree or equivalent, completion of basic or advanced statistics course with minimum B grade. Additional exam requirements/recommendations for international students: Required—TOEFL (minimum score 537 paper-based; 75 iBT); Recommended—IELTS (minimum score 6.5). *Application deadline:* For fall admission, 12/1 priority date for domestic students, 11/1 priority date for international students. Applications are processed on a rolling basis. Application fee: $50 ($75 for international students). Electronic applications accepted. *Expenses:* Contact institution. *Financial support:* In 2016–17, 45 students received support. Fellowships, research assistantships, teaching assistantships, Federal Work-Study, institutionally sponsored loans, scholarships/grants, and traineeships available. Financial award application deadline: 4/1; financial award applicants required to submit FAFSA. *Faculty research:* Administrative leadership and policy studies, early childhood education, research in diversity, paraprofessionals in education, urban schools lab. *Unit head:* 303-315-6300, E-mail: education@ucdenver.edu. *Application contact:* 303-315-6300, E-mail: education@ucdenver.edu.
Website: http://www.ucdenver.edu/academics/colleges/SchoolOfEducation/Academics/Doctorate/Pages/PhD%20in%20Education%20and%20Human%20Development.aspx

University of Colorado Denver, School of Education and Human Development, Teacher Education Programs, Denver, CO 80217. Offers elementary linguistically diverse education (MA); elementary math and science education (MA); elementary math education (MA); elementary reading and writing (MA); elementary science education (MA); secondary English education (MA); secondary linguistically diverse education (MA); secondary math education (MA); secondary reading and writing (MA); secondary science education (MA); special education (MA). *Accreditation:* NCATE. *Program availability:* Part-time, evening/weekend. *Students:* 142 full-time (117 women), 184 part-time (159 women); includes 56 minority (6 Black or African American, non-Hispanic/Latino; 1 American Indian or Alaska Native, non-Hispanic/Latino; 4 Asian, non-Hispanic/Latino; 38 Hispanic/Latino; 1 Native Hawaiian or other Pacific Islander, non-Hispanic/Latino; 6 Two or more races, non-Hispanic/Latino), 1 international. Average age 30. 18 applicants, 67% accepted, 9 enrolled. In 2016, 134 master's awarded. *Degree requirements:* For master's, comprehensive exam. *Entrance requirements:* For master's, GRE or MAT (for those with GPA below 2.75), transcripts, resume, letters of recommendation. Additional exam requirements/recommendations for international students: Required—TOEFL (minimum score 537 paper-based; 75 iBT); Recommended—IELTS (minimum score 6.5). *Application deadline:* For fall admission, 4/15 for domestic students, 4/1 for international students; for spring admission, 9/15 for domestic students, 9/1 for international students; for summer admission, 2/15 for domestic students, 2/1 for international students. Applications are processed on a rolling basis. Application fee: $50 ($75 for international students). Electronic applications accepted. *Expenses:* Contact institution. *Financial support:* In 2016–17, 26 students received support. Fellowships, research assistantships, teaching assistantships, Federal Work-Study, institutionally sponsored loans, scholarships/grants, and traineeships available. Financial award application deadline: 4/1; financial award applicants required to submit FAFSA. *Faculty research:* Linguistically diverse education/ESL, elementary reading and writing, elementary teacher education, secondary teacher education, special education. *Unit head:* Cindy Gutierrez, Director, 303-315-4982, E-mail: cindy.gutierrez@ucdenver.edu. *Application contact:* 303-315-6300, E-mail: education@ucdenver.edu.
Website: http://www.ucdenver.edu/academics/colleges/SchoolOfEducation/Academics/MASTERS/Pages/default.aspx

University of Connecticut, Graduate School, Neag School of Education, Department of Curriculum and Instruction, Program in Science Education, Storrs, CT 06269. Offers MA, PhD. *Accreditation:* NCATE. Terminal master's awarded for partial completion of doctoral program. *Degree requirements:* For master's, comprehensive exam, thesis or alternative; for doctorate, thesis/dissertation. *Entrance requirements:* For doctorate, GRE General Test. Additional exam requirements/recommendations for international students: Required—TOEFL (minimum score 550 paper-based). Electronic applications accepted.

The University of Findlay, Office of Graduate Admissions, Findlay, OH 45840-3653. Offers applied security and analytics (MSAS); athletic training (MAT); business (MBA), including certified management accountant, certified public accountant, health care management, hospitality management; education (MA Ed, Ed D), including children's literature (MA Ed), curriculum and teaching (MA Ed), education (MA Ed), educational administration (MA Ed), human resource development (MA Ed), reading (MA Ed), science education (MA Ed), superintendent (Ed D), teaching (Ed D), technology (MA Ed); environmental, safety and health management (MSEM); health informatics (MS); occupational therapy (MOT); pharmacy (Pharm D); physical therapy (DPT); physician assistant (MPA); rhetoric and writing (MA); teaching English to speakers of other languages (TESOL) and bilingual education (MA). *Program availability:* Part-time, evening/weekend, 100% online, blended/hybrid learning. *Faculty:* 114 full-time (63 women), 44 part-time/adjunct (18 women). *Students:* 751 full-time (452 women), 573 part-time (323 women); includes 164 minority (82 Black or African American, non-Hispanic/Latino; 1 American Indian or Alaska Native, non-Hispanic/Latino; 27 Asian, non-Hispanic/Latino; 37 Hispanic/Latino; 17 Two or more races, non-Hispanic/Latino), 280 international. Average age 28. 661 applicants, 52% accepted, 288 enrolled. In 2016, 366 master's, 137 doctorates awarded. *Degree requirements:* For master's, comprehensive exam (for some programs), thesis, cumulative project, capstone project; for doctorate, thesis/dissertation. *Entrance requirements:* For master's, GRE (for some programs), bachelor's degree from accredited institution, minimum undergraduate GPA of 3.0 in last 64 hours of course work; for doctorate, MAT, minimum cumulative GPA of 3.0, master's degree. Additional exam requirements/recommendations for international students: Recommended—TOEFL (minimum score 79 iBT), IELTS (minimum score 7). *Application deadline:* For fall admission, 6/15 for international students; for spring admission, 12/1 for international students; for summer admission, 4/1 for international students. Applications are processed on a rolling basis. Electronic applications accepted. *Expenses:* Contact institution. *Financial support:* In 2016–17, 139 students received support, including 15 research assistantships with partial tuition reimbursements available (averaging $7,200 per year), 25 teaching assistantships with partial tuition reimbursements available (averaging $7,200 per year); Federal Work-Study, institutionally sponsored loans, and unspecified assistantships also available. Financial award application deadline: 4/1; financial award applicants required to submit FAFSA. *Unit head:* Christopher M. Harris, Director of Admissions, 419-434-4347, E-mail: harrisc1@findlay.edu. *Application contact:* Madeline Fauser Brennan, Graduate Admissions Counselor, 419-434-4636, Fax: 419-434-4898, E-mail: fauserbrennan@findlay.edu.
Website: http://www.findlay.edu/admissions/graduate/Pages/default.aspx

University of Florida, Graduate School, College of Education, School of Teaching and Learning, Gainesville, FL 32611. Offers curriculum and instruction (M Ed, MAE, Ed D, PhD, Ed S); elementary education (M Ed, MAE); English education (M Ed, MAE); mathematics education (M Ed, MAE); reading education (M Ed, MAE); science education (M Ed, MAE); social studies education (M Ed, MAE). *Accreditation:* NCATE. *Program availability:* Part-time, evening/weekend, online learning. Terminal master's awarded for partial completion of doctoral program. *Degree requirements:* For master's, comprehensive exam (for some programs), thesis (for some programs); for doctorate, comprehensive exam (for some programs), thesis/dissertation (for some programs). *Entrance requirements:* For master's and doctorate, GRE General Test, minimum GPA of 3.0; for Ed S, GRE General Test. Additional exam requirements/recommendations for international students: Required—TOEFL (minimum score 550 paper-based; 80 iBT), IELTS (minimum score 6). Electronic applications accepted. *Faculty research:* STEM education; curriculum; teaching and teacher education; languages and literacy; schools, culture, and society; theories and processes of learning.

University of Georgia, College of Education, Department of Mathematics and Science Education, Athens, GA 30602. Offers mathematics education (M Ed, PhD, Ed S). *Application deadline:* For fall admission, 7/1 priority date for domestic students; for spring admission, 11/15 for domestic students. Application fee: $50. *Unit head:* Dr. Denise A. Spangler, Head, 706-542-4548, Fax: 706-542-4551, E-mail: dspangle@uga.edu. *Application contact:* Kevin Moore, Graduate Coordinator, 706-542-3211, E-mail: kvcmoore@uga.edu.
Website: http://www.coe.uga.edu/mse/

University of Illinois at Chicago, Program in Learning Sciences, Chicago, IL 60607-7128. Offers PhD.

University of Illinois at Urbana–Champaign, Graduate College, College of Engineering, Department of Physics, Champaign, IL 61820. Offers physics (MS, PhD); teaching of physics (MS).

University of Illinois at Urbana–Champaign, Graduate College, College of Liberal Arts and Sciences, School of Chemical Sciences, Department of Chemistry, Champaign, IL 61820. Offers astrochemistry (PhD); chemical physics (PhD); chemistry (MA, MS, PhD); teaching of chemistry (MS); MS/JD; MS/MBA.

University of Illinois at Urbana–Champaign, Graduate College, College of Liberal Arts and Sciences, School of Earth, Society and Environment, Department of Geology, Champaign, IL 61820. Offers geology (MS, PhD); teaching of earth sciences (MS). Terminal master's awarded for partial completion of doctoral program.

University of Indianapolis, Graduate Programs, School of Education, Indianapolis, IN 46227-3697. Offers art education (MAT); biology (MAT); chemistry (MAT); curriculum and instruction (MA); earth sciences (MAT); education (MA, MAT); educational leadership (MA); elementary education (MA); English (MAT); French (MAT); math (MAT); physical education (MAT); physics (MAT); secondary education (MA), including art education, education, English education, social studies education; social studies (MAT); Spanish (MAT). *Accreditation:* NCATE. *Program availability:* Part-time, evening/weekend. *Entrance requirements:* For master's, GRE Subject Test, PRAXIS I, minimum GPA of 2.5, 3 letters of recommendation, interview. Additional exam requirements/recommendations for international students: Required—TOEFL (minimum score 550 paper-based). *Faculty research:* Assessment of teacher education, perceptions of prospective teachers by parents.

The University of Iowa, Graduate College, College of Education, Department of Teaching and Learning, Program in Education, Iowa City, IA 52242-1316. Offers art education (MA); developmental reading (MA); elementary education (MA); English education (MA, MAT); foreign and second language education (MAT); foreign language education (MA); foreign language/ESL education (PhD); language, literacy and culture (PhD); mathematics education (MA, MAT, PhD); music education (MM, PhD); science education (MA); secondary education (MA); social studies (MA, PhD). *Degree requirements:* For master's, thesis optional, exam; for doctorate, comprehensive exam, thesis/dissertation. *Entrance requirements:* For master's and doctorate, GRE General Test, minimum GPA of 3.0. Additional exam requirements/recommendations for international students: Required—TOEFL (minimum score 550 paper-based; 81 iBT). Electronic applications accepted.

University of Louisiana at Monroe, Graduate School, College of Arts, Education, and Sciences, School of Education, Program in Curriculum and Instruction, Monroe, LA 71209-0001. Offers art education (M Ed); biology education (M Ed); chemistry education (M Ed); curriculum and instruction (Ed D); early childhood education (M Ed); earth science education (M Ed); educational leadership (M Ed); elementary education (1-5) (M Ed); English as a second language (M Ed); English education (M Ed); family and consumer education (M Ed); French education (M Ed); history education (M Ed); math education (M Ed); middle school education (M Ed); music education (M Ed); reading education (K-12) (M Ed); Spanish education (M Ed); special education - academically gifted (M Ed); special education - early intervention (M Ed); special education -

educational diagnostician (M Ed); special education - mild/moderate disabilities (M Ed); speech education (M Ed). *Accreditation:* NCATE. *Faculty:* 8 full-time (4 women), 4 part-time/adjunct (3 women). *Students:* 13 full-time (11 women), 80 part-time (65 women); includes 25 minority (19 Black or African American, non-Hispanic/Latino; 1 Asian, non-Hispanic/Latino; 3 Hispanic/Latino; 2 Two or more races, non-Hispanic/Latino). Average age 37. 118 applicants, 30% accepted, 16 enrolled. In 2016, 23 master's, 4 doctorates awarded. *Degree requirements:* For master's, comprehensive exam (for some programs), thesis; for doctorate, thesis/dissertation, internships. *Entrance requirements:* For master's, GRE General Test; for doctorate, GRE General Test, minimum undergraduate GPA of 2.75, graduate 3.25. Additional exam requirements/recommendations for international students: Required—TOEFL (minimum score 500 paper-based; 61 iBT). *Application deadline:* For fall admission, 8/24 priority date for domestic students, 7/1 for international students; for winter admission, 12/14 priority date for domestic students; for spring admission, 1/19 for domestic students, 11/1 for international students. Applications are processed on a rolling basis. Application fee: $20 ($30 for international students). Electronic applications accepted. *Expenses:* Tuition, state resident: full-time $6489. Tuition, nonresident: full-time $18,589. *Required fees:* $8984. Tuition and fees vary according to course level, course load, degree level and program. *Financial support:* Research assistantships, career-related internships or fieldwork, Federal Work-Study, and unspecified assistantships available. Financial award application deadline: 4/1; financial award applicants required to submit FAFSA. *Unit head:* Dr. Dorothy Schween, Director, 318-342-1268, Fax: 318-342-3131, E-mail: schween@ulm.edu.

University of Maryland, Baltimore County, The Graduate School, College of Arts, Humanities and Social Sciences, Department of Education, Master of Arts in Education Program, Baltimore, MD 21250. Offers K-8 mathematics instructional leadership (MAE); K-8 science education (MAE); K-8 STEM education (MAE); secondary mathematics education (MAE); secondary science education (MAE); secondary STEM education (MAE). *Program availability:* Part-time-only, evening/weekend, 100% online, blended/hybrid learning. *Faculty:* 5 full-time (4 women), 5 part-time/adjunct (4 women). *Students:* 1 (woman) full-time, 137 part-time (100 women); includes 18 minority (7 Black or African American, non-Hispanic/Latino; 1 American Indian or Alaska Native, non-Hispanic/Latino; 7 Asian, non-Hispanic/Latino; 2 Hispanic/Latino; 1 Two or more races, non-Hispanic/Latino). Average age 32. 20 applicants, 95% accepted, 17 enrolled. In 2016, 17 master's awarded. *Degree requirements:* For master's, comprehensive exam (for some programs), thesis (for some programs). *Application deadline:* For fall admission, 6/1 for domestic students; for spring admission, 11/1 for domestic students. Application fee: $50. Electronic applications accepted. *Expenses:* Tuition, state resident: full-time $13,294. Tuition, nonresident: full-time $20,286. *Financial support:* In 2016–17, 1 student received support. Application deadline: 3/1. *Unit head:* Jerri Frick, Graduate Program Director, 410-455-1356, Fax: 410-455-6182, E-mail: frick@umbc.edu.
Website: http://www.umbc.edu/education/mae

University of Maryland, Baltimore County, The Graduate School, College of Arts, Humanities and Social Sciences, Department of Education, Program in Teaching, Baltimore, MD 21250. Offers early childhood education (MAT); elementary education (MAT); teaching (MAT), including art, biology, chemistry, choral music, classical foreign language, dance, earth/space science, English, instrumental music, mathematics, modern foreign language, physical science, physics, social studies, theatre. *Program availability:* Part-time, evening/weekend. *Faculty:* 24 full-time (18 women), 25 part-time/adjunct (19 women). *Students:* 41 full-time (34 women), 27 part-time (18 women); includes 26 minority (6 Black or African American, non-Hispanic/Latino; 9 Asian, non-Hispanic/Latino; 7 Hispanic/Latino; 1 Native Hawaiian or other Pacific Islander, non-Hispanic/Latino; 3 Two or more races, non-Hispanic/Latino), 2 international. Average age 30. 54 applicants, 83% accepted, 35 enrolled. In 2016, 50 master's awarded. *Degree requirements:* For master's, comprehensive exam (for some programs), thesis (for some programs). *Entrance requirements:* For master's, PRAXIS Core Examination or GRE (minimum score of 1000), minimum GPA of 3.0. Additional exam requirements/recommendations for international students: Required—TOEFL. *Application deadline:* For fall admission, 6/1 for domestic and international students; for spring admission, 11/1 for domestic and international students. Applications are processed on a rolling basis. Application fee: $50. Electronic applications accepted. *Expenses:* Tuition, state resident: full-time $13,294. Tuition, nonresident: full-time $20,286. *Financial support:* In 2016–17, 8 students received support, including teaching assistantships with tuition reimbursements available (averaging $12,000 per year); career-related internships or fieldwork, Federal Work-Study, scholarships/grants, tuition waivers, and unspecified assistantships also available. Financial award application deadline: 3/15. *Faculty research:* STEM teacher education, culturally sensitive pedagogy, ESOL/bilingual education, early childhood education, language, literacy and culture. *Total annual research expenditures:* $100,000. *Unit head:* Dr. Susan M. Blunck, Graduate Program Director, 410-455-2869, Fax: 410-455-3986, E-mail: blunck@umbc.edu. *Application contact:* Cheryl Johnson, MAT Program Specialist, 410-455-3388, E-mail: blackwel@umbc.edu.
Website: http://www.umbc.edu/education/

University of Massachusetts Amherst, Graduate School, College of Education, Program in Education, Amherst, MA 01003. Offers bilingual, English as a second language, and multicultural education (M Ed, Ed S); child study and early education (M Ed); children, families and schools (Ed D, Ed S); early childhood and elementary teacher education (M Ed); educational leadership (M Ed); educational policy and leadership (Ed D); higher education (M Ed); international education (M Ed); language, literacy and culture (Ed D); learning, media and technology (M Ed, Ed S); mathematics, science, and learning technologies (Ed D); reading and writing (M Ed); research, educational measurement and psychometrics (Ed D); school counselor education (M Ed, Ed S); school psychology (Ed S); science education (Ed S); secondary teacher education (M Ed); social justice education (M Ed, Ed D, Ed S); special education (M Ed, Ed D, Ed S); teacher education and school improvement (Ed D, Ed S). *Accreditation:* NCATE. *Program availability:* Part-time, online learning. Terminal master's awarded for partial completion of doctoral program. *Degree requirements:* For doctorate, comprehensive exam, thesis/dissertation. *Entrance requirements:* Additional exam requirements/recommendations for international students: Required—TOEFL (minimum score 550 paper-based; 80 iBT), IELTS (minimum score 6.5). Electronic applications accepted.

University of Massachusetts Dartmouth, Graduate School, College of Arts and Sciences, School of Education, Department of STEM Education and Teacher Development, North Dartmouth, MA 02747-2300. Offers education ESL preK-12 (Postbaccalaureate Certificate); mathematics education (PhD); middle school education (MAT); secondary school education (Postbaccalaureate Certificate); teaching secondary school education (MAT). *Program availability:* Part-time. *Faculty:* 9 full-time (6 women), 6 part-time/adjunct (3 women). *Students:* 25 full-time (12 women), 87 part-time (55 women); includes 15 minority (3 Black or African American, non-Hispanic/Latino; 2 Asian, non-Hispanic/Latino; 7 Hispanic/Latino; 3 Two or more races, non-Hispanic/Latino), 3 international. Average age 32. 53 applicants, 91% accepted, 38 enrolled. In 2016, 67 master's awarded. *Degree requirements:* For doctorate, thesis/dissertation. *Entrance requirements:* For master's, Massachusetts Tests for Educator Licensure (MTEL) Communication and Literacy Test and Subject Matter Test, statement of purpose (minimum of 300 words), resume, 2 letters of recommendation, official transcripts; for doctorate, GRE, statement of purpose (minimum of 300 words), resume, official transcripts, 3 letters of recommendation; for Postbaccalaureate Certificate, statement of purpose (minimum of 300 words), resume, 2 letters of recommendation, official transcripts. Additional exam requirements/recommendations for international students: Required—TOEFL (minimum score 533 paper-based; 72 iBT). *Application deadline:* For fall admission, 2/15 priority date for domestic students, 1/15 priority date for international students; for spring admission, 12/15 priority date for domestic students, 11/15 priority date for international students. Application fee: $60. Electronic applications accepted. *Expenses:* Tuition, state resident: full-time $14,994; part-time $624.75 per credit. Tuition, nonresident: full-time $27,068; part-time $1127.83 per credit. *Required fees:* $405; $25.88 per credit. Tuition and fees vary according to course load and reciprocity agreements. *Financial support:* In 2016–17, 3 fellowships (averaging $6,250 per year), 3 research assistantships (averaging $5,027 per year), 2 teaching assistantships (averaging $8,000 per year) were awarded; institutionally sponsored loans, scholarships/grants, unspecified assistantships, and instructional assistants, Fulbright scholarships also available. Financial award application deadline: 3/1; financial award applicants required to submit FAFSA. *Faculty research:* Reading/special education, education reform, English education, literacy, language arts K-12. *Total annual research expenditures:* $1.3 million. *Unit head:* Traci Almeida, Graduate Program Director, 508-999-8098, Fax: 508-910-8183, E-mail: talmeida@umassd.edu. *Application contact:* Steven Briggs, Director of Marketing and Recruitment for Graduate Studies, 508-999-8604, Fax: 508-999-8183, E-mail: graduate@umassd.edu.
Website: http://www.umassd.edu/cas/schoolofeducation/departments/stemeducationandteacherdevelopment/

University of Memphis, Graduate School, College of Education, Department of Instruction and Curriculum Leadership, Memphis, TN 38152. Offers advanced studies in teaching and learning (M Ed); applied behavior analysis (Graduate Certificate); autism studies (Graduate Certificate); early childhood education (MAT, MS, Ed D); elementary education (MAT); instruction and curriculum (MS, Ed D); instruction design and technology (MS, Ed D); instructional design and technology (Graduate Certificate); literacy, leadership, and coaching (Graduate Certificate); reading (MS, Ed D); school library information specialist (Graduate Certificate); secondary education (MAT); special education (MAT, MS, Ed D); STEM teacher leadership (Graduate Certificate); urban education (Graduate Certificate). *Accreditation:* NCATE (one or more programs are accredited). *Program availability:* Part-time. *Faculty:* 24 full-time (14 women), 17 part-time/adjunct (12 women). *Students:* 66 full-time (52 women), 315 part-time (243 women); includes 163 minority (132 Black or African American, non-Hispanic/Latino; 1 American Indian or Alaska Native, non-Hispanic/Latino; 6 Asian, non-Hispanic/Latino; 13 Hispanic/Latino; 1 Native Hawaiian or other Pacific Islander, non-Hispanic/Latino; 10 Two or more races, non-Hispanic/Latino), 4 international. Average age 35. 215 applicants, 78% accepted, 120 enrolled. In 2016, 111 master's, 21 doctorates, 8 other advanced degrees awarded. Terminal master's awarded for partial completion of doctoral program. *Degree requirements:* For master's, comprehensive exam, thesis or alternative; for doctorate, comprehensive exam, thesis/dissertation. *Entrance requirements:* For master's, GRE General Test, PRAXIS, minimum GPA of 2.5, letters of reference; for doctorate, GRE General Test, GRE Subject Test, 2 years of teaching experience, letters of reference, statement of purpose, interview. Additional exam requirements/recommendations for international students: Required—TOEFL (minimum score 550 paper-based; 79 iBT). *Application deadline:* For fall admission, 4/1 priority date for domestic students; for spring admission, 10/1 priority date for domestic students; for summer admission, 2/1 priority date for domestic students. Applications are processed on a rolling basis. Application fee: $35 ($60 for international students). Electronic applications accepted. *Expenses:* $5,231.50 per semester full-time in-state, $9,623.50 full-time out-of-state. *Financial support:* In 2016–17, 2 research assistantships with full tuition reimbursements (averaging $10,000 per year), 3 teaching assistantships with full tuition reimbursements (averaging $10,666 per year) were awarded; career-related internships or fieldwork, Federal Work-Study, institutionally sponsored loans, scholarships/grants, traineeships, and unspecified assistantships also available. Support available to part-time students. Financial award application deadline: 2/1; financial award applicants required to submit FAFSA. *Faculty research:* Effective urban teachers, preparation and retention of urban teachers, technology utilization in schools, field-based teacher preparation programs, effective use of online instruction. *Unit head:* Dr. Angiline Powell, Interim Chair, 901-678-3310, E-mail: apowell3@memphis.edu. *Application contact:* Dr. James Meindl, Coordinator of Graduate Studies, 901-678-3310, E-mail: jnmeindl@memphis.edu.
Website: http://www.memphis.edu/icl/

University of Miami, Graduate School, School of Education and Human Development, Department of Teaching and Learning, Program in Teaching and Learning, Coral Gables, FL 33124. Offers language and literacy learning in multilingual settings (PhD); science, technology, engineering and mathematics (PhD); special education (PhD). *Faculty:* 14 full-time (10 women), 9 part-time/adjunct (all women). *Students:* 21 full-time (16 women); includes 6 minority (2 Black or African American, non-Hispanic/Latino; 3 Hispanic/Latino; 1 Two or more races, non-Hispanic/Latino), 7 international. Average age 33. 20 applicants, 30% accepted, 4 enrolled. In 2016, 1 doctorate awarded. *Degree requirements:* For doctorate, thesis/dissertation, qualifying exam, electronic portfolio. *Entrance requirements:* For doctorate, GRE General Test. Additional exam requirements/recommendations for international students: Required—TOEFL (minimum score 550 paper-based; 80 iBT); Recommended—IELTS (minimum score 6.5). *Application deadline:* For fall admission, 2/15 for domestic students, 10/1 for international students. Application fee: $65. Electronic applications accepted. *Financial support:* Fellowships, research assistantships, teaching assistantships, health care benefits, tuition waivers (full and partial), and unspecified assistantships available. Financial award application deadline: 3/1; financial award applicants required to submit FAFSA. *Faculty research:* Teacher education, multicultural education, special education, second language acquisition, math and science education. *Unit head:* Dr. Luciana de Oliveira, Department Chairperson/Associate Professor, 305-284-4961, Fax: 305-284-6998, E-mail: ludeoliveira@miami.edu. *Application contact:* Lois Heffernan, Graduate Admission Coordinator, 305-284-2167, Fax: 305-284-9395, E-mail: lheffernan@miami.edu.
Website: http://www.education.miami.edu

University of Michigan–Dearborn, College of Education, Health, and Human Services, Master of Science Program in Science Education, Dearborn, MI 48126. Offers MS. *Accreditation:* TEAC. *Program availability:* Part-time, evening/weekend. *Faculty:* 6 full-time (3 women), 2 part-time/adjunct (1 woman). *Students:* 7 part-time (6 women); includes 1 minority (Black or African American, non-Hispanic/Latino). Average age 33. 3 applicants, 100% accepted, 3 enrolled. In 2016, 5 master's awarded. *Entrance requirements:* For master's, minimum GPA of 3.0, 3 letters of recommendation from supervisors or university faculty, proof of baccalaureate degree, valid teaching certificate, one-page statement of philosophy of teaching science, one-page statement of educational/career goals. Additional exam requirements/recommendations for international students: Required—TOEFL (minimum score 560 paper-based; 84 iBT), IELTS (minimum score 6.5). *Application deadline:* For fall admission, 8/1 priority date for domestic students, 5/1 priority date for international students; for winter admission, 12/1

priority date for domestic students, 9/1 priority date for international students; for spring admission, 4/1 priority date for domestic students, 1/1 priority date for international students. Applications are processed on a rolling basis. Application fee: $60. Electronic applications accepted. *Expenses:* Contact institution. *Financial support:* In 2016–17, 1 student received support. Scholarships/grants available. Financial award application deadline: 3/1; financial award applicants required to submit FAFSA. *Faculty research:* Inquiry pedagogy. *Unit head:* Dr. Stein Brunvand, Director, Master's Programs, 313-583-6415, E-mail: sbrunvan@umich.edu. *Application contact:* Elizabeth Morden, Graduate Programs Assistant, 313-593-5090, E-mail: emorden@umich.edu.
Website: http://umdearborn.edu/cehhs/cehhs_msse/

University of Minnesota, Twin Cities Campus, Graduate School, College of Education and Human Development, Department of Curriculum and Instruction, Program in Teaching, Minneapolis, MN 55455-0213. Offers teaching (M Ed), including arts in education, elementary education, English education, mathematics, science, second language education, social studies. *Students:* 237 full-time (169 women), 171 part-time (112 women); includes 91 minority (23 Black or African American, non-Hispanic/Latino; 3 American Indian or Alaska Native, non-Hispanic/Latino; 19 Asian, non-Hispanic/Latino; 25 Hispanic/Latino; 21 Two or more races, non-Hispanic/Latino), 10 international. Average age 27. 421 applicants, 72% accepted, 275 enrolled. In 2016, 584 master's awarded. Application fee: $75 ($95 for international students). *Unit head:* Dr. Cynthia Lewis, Chair, 612-625-6313, Fax: 612-624-8277, E-mail: lewis@umn.edu. *Application contact:* Dr. Kendall King, Director of Graduate Studies, 612-625-3692, E-mail: roehr013@umn.edu.
Website: http://www.cehd.umn.edu/ci/

University of Missouri, Office of Research and Graduate Studies, College of Education, Department of Learning, Teaching and Curriculum, Columbia, MO 65211. Offers agricultural education (M Ed, PhD, Ed S); art education (M Ed, PhD, Ed S); business and office education (M Ed, PhD, Ed S); early childhood education (M Ed, PhD, Ed S); elementary education (M Ed, PhD, Ed S); English education (M Ed, PhD, Ed S); foreign language education (M Ed, PhD, Ed S); health education and promotion (M Ed, PhD); learning and instruction (M Ed); marketing education (M Ed, PhD, Ed S); mathematics education (M Ed, PhD, Ed S); music education (M Ed, PhD, Ed S); reading education (M Ed, PhD, Ed S); science education (M Ed, PhD, Ed S); social studies education (M Ed, PhD, Ed S); vocational education (M Ed, PhD, Ed S). *Program availability:* Part-time. *Faculty:* 30 full-time (18 women), 1 (woman) part-time/adjunct. *Students:* 157 full-time (124 women), 157 part-time (125 women). Terminal master's awarded for partial completion of doctoral program. *Degree requirements:* For doctorate, thesis/dissertation. *Entrance requirements:* For master's and Ed S, GRE General Test or MAT, minimum GPA of 3.0; for doctorate, GRE General Test, minimum GPA of 3.0. Additional exam requirements/recommendations for international students: Required—TOEFL (minimum score 600 paper-based; 100 iBT). *Application deadline:* For fall admission, 12/1 priority date for domestic and international students. Applications are processed on a rolling basis. Application fee: $75 ($90 for international students). Electronic applications accepted. *Expenses:* Tuition, state resident: full-time $6347; part-time $352.60 per credit hour. Tuition, nonresident: full-time $17,379; part-time $965.50 per credit hour. *Required fees:* $1035. Tuition and fees vary according to course load, campus/location and program. *Financial support:* Fellowships, research assistantships, teaching assistantships, institutionally sponsored loans, traineeships, health care benefits, and unspecified assistantships available. Support available to part-time students.
Website: http://education.missouri.edu/LTC/index.php

University of Missouri–St. Louis, College of Education, Department of Education Sciences and Professional Programs, St. Louis, MO 63121. Offers adult and higher education (M Ed); educational leadership and policy studies (PhD); educational psychology (M Ed), including character and citizenship education, research and program evaluation; program evaluation (Certificate); school psychology (Ed S). *Faculty:* 36 full-time (25 women), 53 part-time/adjunct (40 women). *Students:* 47 full-time (34 women), 247 part-time (175 women); includes 107 minority (86 Black or African American, non-Hispanic/Latino; 2 American Indian or Alaska Native, non-Hispanic/Latino; 5 Asian, non-Hispanic/Latino; 10 Hispanic/Latino; 4 Two or more races, non-Hispanic/Latino), 7 international. 106 applicants, 92% accepted, 70 enrolled. *Degree requirements:* For other advanced degree, comprehensive exam, thesis or alternative, internship. *Entrance requirements:* For degree, GRE General Test, 2-4 letters of recommendation, personal interview. Additional exam requirements/recommendations for international students: Required—IELTS (minimum score 6.5); Recommended—TOEFL (minimum score 550 paper-based; 79 iBT). *Application deadline:* For fall admission, 2/15 priority date for domestic students, 2/15 for international students. Application fee: $50 ($40 for international students). Electronic applications accepted. *Financial support:* Application deadline: 4/1; applicants required to submit FAFSA. *Faculty research:* Child/adolescent psychology, quantitative and qualitative methodology, evaluation processes, measurement and assessment. *Unit head:* Dr. Donald Gouwens, Chairperson, 314-516-4773, Fax: 314-516-5784, E-mail: gouwensd@umsl.edu. *Application contact:* 314-516-5458, Fax: 314-516-6996, E-mail: gradadm@umsl.edu.
Website: https://coe.umsl.edu/dept/espp.html

University of Nebraska at Kearney, College of Natural and Social Sciences, Department of Biology, Kearney, NE 68849. Offers biology (MS); science/math education (MA Ed). *Program availability:* Part-time, evening/weekend, 100% online. *Faculty:* 17 full-time (6 women). *Students:* 27 full-time (21 women), 222 part-time (153 women); includes 44 minority (11 Black or African American, non-Hispanic/Latino; 2 American Indian or Alaska Native, non-Hispanic/Latino; 5 Asian, non-Hispanic/Latino; 17 Hispanic/Latino; 9 Two or more races, non-Hispanic/Latino), 3 international. Average age 32. 86 applicants, 83% accepted, 49 enrolled. In 2016, 57 master's awarded. *Degree requirements:* For master's, comprehensive exam, thesis optional. *Entrance requirements:* For master's, GRE (for thesis option and for online program applicants if undergraduate GPA is below 2.75), letter of interest. Additional exam requirements/recommendations for international students: Recommended—TOEFL (minimum score 550 paper-based; 79 iBT), IELTS (minimum score 6.5). *Application deadline:* For fall admission, 6/15 for domestic and international students; for spring admission, 10/15 for domestic and international students; for summer admission, 3/15 for domestic and international students. Application fee: $45. Electronic applications accepted. *Expenses:* $285 per hour resident; $507 per hour non-resident. *Financial support:* In 2016–17, 11 students received support, including 3 research assistantships with full tuition reimbursements available (averaging $10,500 per year), 8 teaching assistantships with full tuition reimbursements available (averaging $10,500 per year); career-related internships or fieldwork, scholarships/grants, health care benefits, and unspecified assistantships also available. Support available to part-time students. Financial award application deadline: 2/28; financial award applicants required to submit FAFSA. *Faculty research:* Pollution injury, molecular biology-viral gene expression, prairie range condition modeling, evolution of symbiotic nitrogen fixation, geographic information systems (GIS), molecular genetics of aging. *Unit head:* Dr. Paul Twig, Graduate Program Chair, 308-865-8315, E-mail: twiggp@unk.edu. *Application contact:* Brian Peterson, Coordinator, Online MA Program, 308-865-1589, E-mail: msbiology@unk.edu.
Website: http://unkcms.unk.edu/academics/biology/index.php

University of Nebraska at Omaha, Graduate Studies, College of Arts and Sciences, Department of Biology, Omaha, NE 68182. Offers biology (MS); business for bioscientists (Certificate). *Program availability:* Part-time. *Faculty:* 13 full-time (5 women). *Students:* 13 full-time (6 women), 14 part-time (7 women); includes 2 minority (1 Black or African American, non-Hispanic/Latino; 1 Hispanic/Latino), 2 international. Average age 30. 12 applicants, 42% accepted, 4 enrolled. In 2016, 9 master's awarded. *Degree requirements:* For master's, comprehensive exam (for some programs), thesis (for some programs). *Entrance requirements:* For master's, GRE General Test, minimum GPA of 3.0, transcripts, 24 undergraduate biology hours, 3 letters of recommendation, statement of purpose. Additional exam requirements/recommendations for international students: Required—TOEFL, IELTS, PTE. *Application deadline:* For fall admission, 2/15 priority date for domestic and international students; for spring admission, 10/15 priority date for domestic and international students; for summer admission, 2/15 priority date for domestic and international students. Applications are processed on a rolling basis. Application fee: $45. Electronic applications accepted. *Financial support:* In 2016–17, 19 students received support, including 2 research assistantships with tuition reimbursements available, 17 teaching assistantships with tuition reimbursements available; fellowships, Federal Work-Study, institutionally sponsored loans, scholarships/grants, health care benefits, tuition waivers (partial), and unspecified assistantships also available. Support available to part-time students. Financial award application deadline: 3/1; financial award applicants required to submit FAFSA. *Unit head:* Dr. LaReesa Wolfenbarger, Chairperson, 402-554-2341, E-mail: graduate@unomaha.edu. *Application contact:* Dr. John McCarty, Graduate Program Chair, 402-554-2341, E-mail: graduate@unomaha.edu.

University of New Hampshire, Graduate School, College of Engineering and Physical Sciences, Department of Chemistry, Durham, NH 03824. Offers chemistry (MS, PhD); chemistry education (PhD). Terminal master's awarded for partial completion of doctoral program. *Degree requirements:* For master's, thesis; for doctorate, one foreign language, thesis/dissertation. *Entrance requirements:* Additional exam requirements/recommendations for international students: Required—TOEFL (minimum score 550 paper-based; 80 iBT). *Application deadline:* For fall admission, 4/1 priority date for domestic students, 4/1 for international students; for spring admission, 12/1 for domestic students. Applications are processed on a rolling basis. Application fee: $65. Electronic applications accepted. *Financial support:* Fellowships, research assistantships, teaching assistantships, Federal Work-Study, scholarships/grants, and tuition waivers (full and partial) available. Support available to part-time students. Financial award application deadline: 2/15. *Faculty research:* Analytical, physical, organic, and inorganic chemistry. *Unit head:* Glen P. Miller, Chair, 603-862-2456. *Application contact:* Laura Bicknell, Administrative Assistant, 603-862-1550, E-mail: chem.dept@unh.edu.
Website: http://www.ceps.unh.edu/chemistry

University of New Haven, Graduate School, College of Arts and Sciences, Program in Environmental Science, West Haven, CT 06516. Offers environmental ecology (MS); environmental education (MS); environmental geoscience (MS); environmental health and management (MS); environmental science (MS); geographical information systems (MS, Graduate Certificate). *Program availability:* Part-time, evening/weekend. *Students:* 25 full-time (16 women), 10 part-time (5 women); includes 4 minority (1 Black or African American, non-Hispanic/Latino; 1 Asian, non-Hispanic/Latino; 1 Hispanic/Latino; 1 Two or more races, non-Hispanic/Latino), 8 international. Average age 26. 36 applicants, 83% accepted, 15 enrolled. In 2016, 13 master's awarded. *Degree requirements:* For master's, thesis optional, research project. *Entrance requirements:* Additional exam requirements/recommendations for international students: Required—TOEFL (minimum score 80 iBT), IELTS, PTE. *Application deadline:* Applications are processed on a rolling basis. Application fee: $50. Electronic applications accepted. Application fee is waived when completed online. *Expenses: Tuition:* Full-time $15,660; part-time $870 per credit hour. *Required fees:* $200; $85 per term. Tuition and fees vary according to program. *Financial support:* Research assistantships with partial tuition reimbursements, teaching assistantships with partial tuition reimbursements, career-related internships or fieldwork, Federal Work-Study, scholarships/grants, and unspecified assistantships available. Support available to part-time students. Financial award applicants required to submit FAFSA. *Unit head:* Dr. Roman Zajac, Coordinator, 203-932-7114, E-mail: rzajac@newhaven.edu. *Application contact:* Michelle Mason, Director of Graduate Enrollment, 203-932-7067, E-mail: mmason@newhaven.edu.
Website: http://www.newhaven.edu/4728/

University of New Mexico, School of Medicine, Program in University Science Teaching, Albuquerque, NM 87131-2039. Offers Certificate. In 2016, 1 Certificate awarded. *Unit head:* Dr. Sherry Rogers, Program Director, 505-272-0007, E-mail: srogers@salud.unm.edu. *Application contact:* Dr. Angela Wandinger-Ness, Coordinator, 505-272-1459, Fax: 505-272-8738, E-mail: awandinger@salud.unm.edu.

The University of North Carolina at Chapel Hill, Graduate School, School of Education, Program in Secondary Education, Chapel Hill, NC 27599. Offers English (Grades 9-12) (MAT); English as a second language (MAT); French (Grades K-12) (MAT); German (Grades K-12) (MAT); Japanese (Grades K-12) (MAT); Latin (Grades 9-12) (MAT); mathematics (Grades 9-12) (MAT); music (Grades K-12) (MAT); science (Grades 9-12) (MAT); social studies (Grades 9-12) (MAT); Spanish (Grades K-12) (MAT). *Accreditation:* NCATE. *Degree requirements:* For master's, comprehensive exam. *Entrance requirements:* For master's, GRE General Test, minimum GPA of 3.0 during last 2 years of undergraduate course work. Additional exam requirements/recommendations for international students: Required—TOEFL (minimum score 550 paper-based). Electronic applications accepted.

The University of North Carolina at Greensboro, Graduate School, School of Education, Department of Teacher Education and Higher Education, Greensboro, NC 27412-5001. Offers college teaching and adult learning (Certificate); curriculum and instruction (M Ed), including chemistry education, elementary education, English as a second language, French education, instructional technology, mathematics education, middle grades education, reading education, science education, social studies education, Spanish education; curriculum and teaching (PhD), including higher education, teacher education and development; English as a second language (Certificate); higher education (M Ed); supervision (M Ed). *Accreditation:* NCATE. *Program availability:* Part-time. *Degree requirements:* For doctorate, thesis/dissertation. *Entrance requirements:* For master's and doctorate, GRE General Test. Additional exam requirements/recommendations for international students: Required—TOEFL. Electronic applications accepted. *Faculty research:* Community college literacy program, middle school mathematics/computer mathematics.

The University of North Carolina at Pembroke, The Graduate School, Department of Biology, Pembroke, NC 28372-1510. Offers science education (MA, MAT). *Program availability:* Part-time, evening/weekend. *Degree requirements:* For master's, thesis. *Entrance requirements:* For master's, GRE or MAT, minimum GPA of 3.0 in major or 2.5 overall.

University of Northern Colorado, Graduate School, College of Natural and Health Sciences, Department of Chemistry and Biochemistry, Greeley, CO 80639. Offers

chemical education (MS, PhD); chemistry (MS). *Program availability:* Part-time. *Degree requirements:* For master's, comprehensive exam, thesis or alternative; for doctorate, comprehensive exam, thesis/dissertation. *Entrance requirements:* For master's, 3 letters of reference; for doctorate, GRE General Test, 3 letters of reference. *Application deadline:* Applications are processed on a rolling basis. Application fee: $50 ($60 for international students). Electronic applications accepted. *Financial support:* Fellowships, research assistantships, teaching assistantships, and unspecified assistantships available. Financial award application deadline: 3/1; financial award applicants required to submit FAFSA. *Unit head:* Dr. Richard Hyslop, Program Coordinator, 970-351-2559. *Application contact:* Linda Sisson, Graduate Student Admission Coordinator, 970-351-1807, Fax: 970-351-2371, E-mail: linda.sisson@unco.edu.
Website: http://www.unco.edu/nhs/chemistry/

University of Northern Colorado, Graduate School, College of Natural and Health Sciences, School of Biology, Program in Biology Education, Greeley, CO 80639. Offers PhD. *Program availability:* Part-time. *Degree requirements:* For doctorate, comprehensive exam, thesis/dissertation. *Entrance requirements:* For doctorate, GRE General Test, 3 letters of recommendation. *Application deadline:* Applications are processed on a rolling basis. Application fee: $50 ($60 for international students). Electronic applications accepted. *Financial support:* Teaching assistantships available. Financial award application deadline: 3/1; financial award applicants required to submit FAFSA. *Unit head:* Dr. Susan Keenan, Program Coordinator, 970-351-2921, Fax: 970-951-2335. *Application contact:* Linda Sisson, Graduate Student Admission Coordinator, 970-351-1807, Fax: 970-351-2371, E-mail: linda.sisson@unco.edu.
Website: http://www.unco.edu/nhs/biology/

University of Northern Iowa, Graduate College, College of Humanities, Arts and Sciences, MA Program in Science Education, Cedar Falls, IA 50614. Offers earth science education (MA); physics education (MA); science education (MA). *Degree requirements:* For master's, comprehensive exam (for some programs), thesis or alternative. *Entrance requirements:* For master's, minimum GPA of 3.0. Additional exam requirements/recommendations for international students: Required—TOEFL (minimum score 500 paper-based; 61 iBT). Electronic applications accepted.

University of Oklahoma, Jeannine Rainbolt College of Education, Department of Instructional Leadership and Academic Curriculum, Norman, OK 73019. Offers instructional leadership and academic curriculum (M Ed, PhD), including biomedical education (PhD), early childhood education, elementary education (M Ed), English education, instructional leadership, mathematics education, reading education, science education, social studies education, world languages education (M Ed). *Accreditation:* NCATE. *Program availability:* Part-time. *Faculty:* 19 full-time (15 women), 1 (woman) part-time/adjunct. *Students:* 66 full-time (49 women), 116 part-time (88 women); includes 49 minority (12 Black or African American, non-Hispanic/Latino; 6 American Indian or Alaska Native, non-Hispanic/Latino; 6 Asian, non-Hispanic/Latino; 11 Hispanic/Latino; 1 Native Hawaiian or other Pacific Islander, non-Hispanic/Latino; 13 Two or more races, non-Hispanic/Latino), 13 international. Average age 35. 38 applicants, 97% accepted, 28 enrolled. In 2016, 33 master's, 10 doctorates awarded. Terminal master's awarded for partial completion of doctoral program. *Degree requirements:* For master's, comprehensive exam (for some programs), thesis (for some programs); for doctorate, comprehensive exam (for some programs), thesis/dissertation. *Entrance requirements:* For doctorate, GRE. Additional exam requirements/recommendations for international students: Required—TOEFL (minimum score 79 iBT) or IELTS (minimum score 6.5). Application fee: $50 ($100 for international students). Electronic applications accepted. *Expenses:* Tuition, state resident: full-time $4886; part-time $203.60 per credit hour. Tuition, nonresident: full-time $18,989; part-time $791.20 per credit hour. *Required fees:* $3283; $126.25 per credit hour. $126.50 per semester. *Financial support:* In 2016–17, 112 students received support, including 7 research assistantships with partial tuition reimbursements available (averaging $10,373 per year), 6 teaching assistantships with partial tuition reimbursements available (averaging $11,446 per year); fellowships, scholarships/grants, and unspecified assistantships also available. Financial award application deadline: 6/1; financial award applicants required to submit FAFSA. *Faculty research:* Teacher preparation; instruction; curriculum; learning; constructivist theory. *Total annual research expenditures:* $165,297. *Unit head:* Dr. Stacy Reeder, Chair, 405-325-1498, Fax: 405-325-4061, E-mail: reeder@ou.edu. *Application contact:* Anna Steele, Graduate Programs Officer, 405-325-4525, E-mail: anna.steele@ou.edu.
Website: http://www.ou.edu/education/ilac

University of Pennsylvania, Graduate School of Education, Medical Education Program, Philadelphia, PA 19104. Offers MS Ed, Certificate. Program offered jointly with Perelman School of Medicine and The Children's Hospital of Philadelphia. *Program availability:* Evening/weekend. *Students:* 3 full-time (all women), 30 part-time (17 women); includes 15 minority (2 Black or African American, non-Hispanic/Latino; 11 Asian, non-Hispanic/Latino; 2 Hispanic/Latino), 3 international. Average age 38. 45 applicants, 78% accepted, 33 enrolled. In 2016, 5 master's awarded. *Degree requirements:* For master's, thesis. *Entrance requirements:* For master's, bachelor's degree; professional health care experience. Additional exam requirements/recommendations for international students: Required—TOEFL, IELTS. *Application deadline:* Applications are processed on a rolling basis. Application fee: $75. Electronic applications accepted. *Expenses: Tuition:* Full-time $31,068; part-time $5762 per course. *Required fees:* $3200; $336 per course. Full-time tuition and fees vary according to degree level, program and student level. Part-time tuition and fees vary according to course load, degree level and program. *Faculty research:* Strategic leadership, workplace learning, evidenced-best decision making, technology in the work place. *Unit head:* Elizabeth Ulivella, Associate Director, 215-573-0591, E-mail: ulivella@upenn.edu.
Website: http://www.gse.upenn.edu/med-ed/

University of Phoenix–Online Campus, College of Education, Phoenix, AZ 85034-7209. Offers administration and supervision (MAEd, Certificate); adult education and training (MAEd); curriculum and instruction (MAEd), including computer education, curriculum and instruction, English as a second language, language arts, mathematics, reading; early childhood education (MAEd); educational studies (MAEd); elementary teacher education (MAEd), including early childhood, elementary teacher education, high school middle level, middle level; principal licensure (Certificate); secondary teacher education (MAEd); special education (MAEd, Certificate); teacher education (MAEd), including middle level generalist; teacher education middle level mathematics (MAEd), including middle level mathematics; teacher education middle level science (MAEd), including middle level science; teacher education secondary mathematics (MAEd); teacher education secondary science (MAEd); teacher leadership (MAEd); teachers of English learners (Certificate); transition to teaching (Certificate), including elementary education, secondary education. *Program availability:* Evening/weekend, online learning. *Entrance requirements:* Additional exam requirements/recommendations for international students: Required—TOEFL, TOEIC (Test of English as an International Communication), Berlitz Online English Proficiency Exam, PTE, or IELTS. Electronic applications accepted. *Expenses:* Contact institution.

University of Pittsburgh, School of Education, Department of Instruction and Learning, Program in Secondary Education, Pittsburgh, PA 15260. Offers English and communications education (M Ed, MAT); foreign language education (M Ed, MAT); language, literacy and culture education (Ed D, PhD); mathematics education (M Ed, MAT, Ed D, PhD); science education (M Ed, MAT, Ed D, PhD); secondary education (PhD); social studies education (M Ed, MAT); STEM education (Ed D). *Program availability:* Part-time, evening/weekend. *Degree requirements:* For master's, thesis; for doctorate, thesis/dissertation. *Entrance requirements:* For master's, PRAXIS I; for doctorate, GRE General Test. Additional exam requirements/recommendations for international students: Required—TOEFL. Electronic applications accepted. Tuition and fees vary according to program.

University of Puerto Rico, Río Piedras Campus, College of Education, Program in Curriculum and Teaching, San Juan, PR 00931-3300. Offers biology education (M Ed); chemistry education (M Ed); curriculum and teaching (Ed D); history education (M Ed); mathematics education (M Ed); physics education (M Ed); Spanish education (M Ed). *Program availability:* Part-time. *Degree requirements:* For master's, thesis; for doctorate, thesis/dissertation, internship. *Entrance requirements:* For master's, PAEG or GRE, minimum GPA of 3.0, letter of recommendation; for doctorate, GRE or PAEG, master's degree, minimum GPA of 3.0, letter of recommendation (2), interview. *Faculty research:* Curriculum, math teaching.

University of St. Francis, College of Education, Joliet, IL 60435-6169. Offers educational leadership (MS, Ed D); elementary education (M Ed); reading (MS); secondary education (M Ed), including English education, math education, science education, social studies education, visual arts education; special education (M Ed); teaching and learning (MS); TESOL (Certificate). *Accreditation:* NCATE. *Program availability:* Part-time, evening/weekend, 100% online, blended/hybrid learning. *Faculty:* 11 full-time (8 women), 60 part-time/adjunct (42 women). *Students:* 34 full-time (26 women), 420 part-time (318 women); includes 92 minority (51 Black or African American, non-Hispanic/Latino; 5 Asian, non-Hispanic/Latino; 31 Hispanic/Latino; 5 Two or more races, non-Hispanic/Latino), 4 international. Average age 36. 242 applicants, 48% accepted, 96 enrolled. In 2016, 229 master's, 44 doctorates, 10 other advanced degrees awarded. *Degree requirements:* For master's, comprehensive exam; for doctorate, thesis/dissertation. *Entrance requirements:* Additional exam requirements/recommendations for international students: Required—TOEFL (minimum score 550 paper-based; 79 iBT), IELTS (minimum score 6). *Application deadline:* Applications are processed on a rolling basis. Application fee: $30. Electronic applications accepted. Application fee is waived when completed online. *Expenses:* Contact institution. *Financial support:* In 2016–17, 48 students received support. Career-related internships or fieldwork and unspecified assistantships available. Support available to part-time students. Financial award applicants required to submit FAFSA. *Unit head:* Dr. John Gambro, Dean, 815-740-3829, Fax: 815-740-2264, E-mail: jgambro@stfrancis.edu. *Application contact:* Sandra Sloka, Director of Admissions for Graduate and Degree Completion Programs, 800-735-7500, Fax: 815-740-3431, E-mail: ssloka@stfrancis.edu.
Website: http://www.stfrancis.edu/academics/college-of-education/

University of San Diego, School of Leadership and Education Sciences, Department of Learning and Teaching, San Diego, CA 92110-2492. Offers inclusive learning (M Ed); literacy and digital learning (M Ed); school leadership (M Ed); special education with deaf and hard of hearing (M Ed); STEAM (science, technology, engineering, arts, and mathematics) (M Ed); teaching (MAT); TESOL, literacy and culture (M Ed). *Program availability:* Part-time, evening/weekend. *Faculty:* 9 full-time (7 women), 29 part-time/adjunct (19 women). *Students:* 161 full-time (126 women), 188 part-time (153 women); includes 127 minority (4 Black or African American, non-Hispanic/Latino; 24 Asian, non-Hispanic/Latino; 86 Hispanic/Latino; 1 Native Hawaiian or other Pacific Islander, non-Hispanic/Latino; 12 Two or more races, non-Hispanic/Latino), 20 international. Average age 33. 383 applicants, 83% accepted, 194 enrolled. In 2016, 114 master's awarded. *Degree requirements:* For master's, thesis (for some programs), international experience. *Entrance requirements:* For master's, California Basic Educational Skills Test, California Subject Examination for Teachers, minimum GPA of 2.75. Additional exam requirements/recommendations for international students: Required—TOEFL (minimum score 580 paper-based; 83 iBT), TWE. *Application deadline:* Applications are processed on a rolling basis. Application fee: $45. Electronic applications accepted. *Financial support:* In 2016–17, 46 students received support. Career-related internships or fieldwork, Federal Work-Study, institutionally sponsored loans, and stipends available. Financial award application deadline: 4/1; financial award applicants required to submit FAFSA. *Faculty research:* Action research methodology, cultural studies, instructional theories and practices, second language acquisition, school reform. *Unit head:* Dr. Maya Kalyanpur, Chair, 619-260-7655, E-mail: mkalyanpur@sandiego.edu. *Application contact:* Monica Mahon, Associate Director of Graduate Admissions, 619-260-4524, Fax: 619-260-4158, E-mail: grads@sandiego.edu.
Website: http://www.sandiego.edu/soles/departments/learning-and-teaching/

University of South Africa, College of Human Sciences, Pretoria, South Africa. Offers adult education (M Ed); African languages (MA, PhD); African politics (MA, PhD); Afrikaans (MA, PhD); ancient history (MA, PhD); ancient Near Eastern studies (MA, PhD); anthropology (MA, PhD); applied linguistics (MA); Arabic (MA, PhD); archaeology (MA); art history (MA); Biblical archaeology (MA); Biblical studies (M Th, D Th, PhD); Christian spirituality (M Th, D Th); church history (M Th, D Th); classical studies (MA, PhD); clinical psychology (MA); communication (MA, PhD); comparative education (M Ed, Ed D); consulting psychology (D Admin, D Com, PhD); curriculum studies (M Ed, Ed D); development studies (M Admin, MA, D Admin, PhD); didactics (M Ed, Ed D); education (M Tech); education management (M Ed, Ed D); educational psychology (M Ed); English (MA); environmental education (M Ed); French (MA, PhD); German (MA, PhD); Greek (MA); guidance and counseling (M Ed); health studies (MA, PhD), including health sciences education (MA), health services management (MA), medical and surgical nursing science (critical care general) (MA), midwifery and neonatal nursing science (MA), trauma and emergency care (MA); history (MA, PhD); history of education (Ed D); inclusive education (M Ed, Ed D); information and communications technology policy and regulation (MA); information science (MA, MIS, PhD); international politics (MA, PhD); Islamic studies (MA, PhD); Italian (MA, PhD); Judaica (MA, PhD); linguistics (MA, PhD); mathematical education (M Ed); mathematics education (MA); missiology (M Th, D Th); modern Hebrew (MA, PhD); musicology (MA, MMus, D Mus, PhD); natural science education (M Ed); New Testament (M Th, D Th); Old Testament (D Th); pastoral therapy (M Th, D Th); philosophy (MA); philosophy of education (M Ed, Ed D); politics (MA, PhD); Portuguese (MA, PhD); practical theology (M Th, D Th); psychology (MA, MS, PhD); psychology of education (M Ed, Ed D); public health (MA); religious studies (MA, D Th, PhD); Romance languages (MA); Russian (MA, PhD); Semitic languages (MA, PhD); social behavior studies in HIV/AIDS (MA); social science (mental health) (MA); social science in development studies (MA); social science in psychology (MA); social science in social work (MA); social science in sociology (MA); social work (MSW, DSW, PhD); socio-education (M Ed, Ed D); sociolinguistics (MA); sociology (MA, PhD); Spanish (MA, PhD); systematic theology (M Th, D Th); TESOL (teaching English to speakers of other languages) (MA); theological ethics (M Th, D Th); theory of literature (MA, PhD); urban ministries (D Th); urban ministry (M Th).

University of South Africa, Institute for Science and Technology Education, Pretoria, South Africa. Offers mathematics, science and technology education (M Sc, PhD).

University of South Alabama, College of Education and Professional Studies, Department of Leadership and Teacher Education, Mobile, AL 36688. Offers art education (M Ed); early childhood education (M Ed); educational leadership (M Ed, Ed D); elementary education (M Ed); reading education (M Ed); science education (M Ed); secondary education (M Ed); special education (M Ed). *Accreditation:* NCATE. *Program availability:* Part-time, 100% online, blended/hybrid learning. *Faculty:* 16 full-time (12 women), 6 part time/adjunct (3 women). *Students:* 198 full-time (150 women), 77 part-time (58 women); includes 77 minority (61 Black or African American, non-Hispanic/Latino; 2 American Indian or Alaska Native, non-Hispanic/Latino; 2 Asian, non-Hispanic/Latino; 7 Hispanic/Latino; 1 Native Hawaiian or other Pacific Islander, non-Hispanic/Latino; 4 Two or more races, non-Hispanic/Latino). Average age 34. 153 applicants, 53% accepted, 69 enrolled. In 2016, 80 master's, 1 doctorate awarded. *Degree requirements:* For master's, comprehensive exam, thesis (for some programs); for doctorate, comprehensive exam, thesis/dissertation. *Entrance requirements:* For master's, GRE General Test or MAT, minimum GPA of 3.0; for doctorate, GRE, minimum graduate GPA of 3.25, 3 years of experience in field, 3 letters of recommendation, interview, official transcripts. Additional exam requirements/recommendations for international students: Required—TOEFL. *Application deadline:* For fall admission, 7/15 for domestic students; for spring admission, 11/15 for domestic students; for summer admission, 4/15 for domestic students. Applications are processed on a rolling basis. Application fee: $35. Electronic applications accepted. *Expenses:* Tuition, state resident: full-time $9768; part-time $407 per credit hour. Tuition, nonresident: full-time $19,536; part-time $814 per credit hour. *Financial support:* Fellowships, research assistantships, teaching assistantships, career-related internships or fieldwork, Federal Work-Study, institutionally sponsored loans, scholarships/grants, and unspecified assistantships available. Support available to part-time students. Financial award application deadline: 5/31; financial award applicants required to submit FAFSA. *Unit head:* Dr. Susan Santoli, Department Chair, 251-380-2836, Fax: 251-380-2758, E-mail: ssantoli@southalabama.edu. *Application contact:* Dr. Susan Santoli, Director of Graduate Studies, 251-380-2836, Fax: 251-380-2758, E-mail: ssantoli@southalabama.edu.
Website: http://www.southalabama.edu/colleges/coe/lte/index.html

University of South Carolina, The Graduate School, College of Arts and Sciences, Department of Biological Sciences, Columbia, SC 29208. Offers biology (MS, PhD); biology education (IMA, MAT); ecology, evolution and organismal biology (MS, PhD); molecular, cellular, and developmental biology (MS, PhD). IMA and MAT offered in cooperation with the College of Education. Terminal master's awarded for partial completion of doctoral program. *Degree requirements:* For master's, one foreign language, thesis (for some programs); for doctorate, one foreign language, thesis/dissertation. *Entrance requirements:* For master's and doctorate, GRE General Test, minimum GPA of 3.0 in science. Electronic applications accepted. *Faculty research:* Marine ecology, population and evolutionary biology, molecular biology and genetics, development.

University of South Carolina, The Graduate School, College of Arts and Sciences, Department of Geography, Columbia, SC 29208. Offers geography (MA, MS, PhD); geography education (IMA). IMA and MAT offered in cooperation with the College of Education. *Program availability:* Part-time. *Degree requirements:* For master's, comprehensive exam, thesis (for some programs); for doctorate, comprehensive exam, thesis/dissertation. *Entrance requirements:* For master's, GRE General Test; for doctorate, GRE General Test, master's degree. Electronic applications accepted. *Faculty research:* Geographic information processing; economic, cultural, physical, and environmental geography.

University of South Carolina, The Graduate School, College of Education, Department of Instruction and Teacher Education, Program in Secondary Education, Columbia, SC 29208. Offers art education (IMA, MAT); business education (IMA, MAT); English (MAT); foreign language (MAT); health education (MAT); mathematics (MAT); science (IMA, MAT); secondary (Ed D); secondary education (MT, PhD); social studies (MAT); theatre and speech (MAT). IMA and MT offered jointly with the subject areas. *Accreditation:* NCATE. *Degree requirements:* For master's, comprehensive exam, thesis (for some programs), foreign language (MA); for doctorate, one foreign language, comprehensive exam, thesis/dissertation. *Entrance requirements:* For master's, GRE General Test or MAT, teaching certificate (IMA, M Ed), interview; for doctorate, GRE General Test or MAT, interview. *Faculty research:* Middle school programs, professional development, school collaboration.

University of Southern Mississippi, Graduate School, College of Science and Technology, Center for Science and Mathematics Education, Hattiesburg, MS 39406. Offers MS, PhD. *Program availability:* Part-time. *Degree requirements:* For master's, comprehensive exam, thesis or alternative; for doctorate, comprehensive exam, thesis/dissertation. *Entrance requirements:* For master's, GRE General Test, minimum GPA of 2.75 in last 60 hours; for doctorate, GRE General Test, minimum GPA of 3.5. Additional exam requirements/recommendations for international students: Required—TOEFL, IELTS. *Application deadline:* For fall admission, 3/15 priority date for domestic students, 3/15 for international students; for spring admission, 1/10 priority date for domestic and international students. Applications are processed on a rolling basis. Application fee: $60. *Expenses: Tuition, area resident:* Full-time $15,708; part-time $437 per credit hour. *Financial support:* Fellowships with full tuition reimbursements, research assistantships with full tuition reimbursements, teaching assistantships with full tuition reimbursements, Federal Work-Study, scholarships/grants, health care benefits, and unspecified assistantships available. Financial award application deadline: 3/15; financial award applicants required to submit FAFSA. *Unit head:* Dr. Sherry Herron, Director, 601-266-4739, Fax: 601-266-4741, E-mail: sherry.herron@usm.edu. *Application contact:* Shonna Breland, Manager of Graduate School Admissions, 601-266-6567, Fax: 601-266-5138.
Website: https://www.usm.edu/science-math-education

University of South Florida, St. Petersburg, College of Education, St. Petersburg, FL 33701. Offers educational leadership development (M Ed); elementary education (MA), including math/science; English education (MA); middle grades STEM education (MS); reading education (MA). *Program availability:* Part-time. *Degree requirements:* For master's, comprehensive exam, practicum, internship, comprehensive portfolio. *Entrance requirements:* For master's, State of Florida General Knowledge Test (GKT), Florida Teaching Certificate (for non-initial certification programs), letters of recommendation. Additional exam requirements/recommendations for international students: Required—TOEFL (minimum score 550 paper-based; 79 iBT); Recommended—IELTS. Electronic applications accepted.

The University of Tennessee, Graduate School, College of Education, Health and Human Sciences, Program in Education, Knoxville, TN 37996. Offers art education (MS); counseling education (PhD); cultural studies in education (PhD); curriculum (MS, Ed S); curriculum, educational research and evaluation (Ed D, PhD); early childhood education (PhD); early childhood special education (MS); education of deaf and hard of hearing (MS); educational administration and policy studies (Ed D, PhD); educational administration and supervision (Ed S); educational psychology (Ed D, PhD); elementary education (MS, Ed S); elementary teaching (MS); English education (MS, Ed S); exercise science (PhD); foreign language/ESL education (MS, Ed S); instructional technology (MS, Ed D, PhD, Ed S); literacy, language and ESL education (PhD); literacy, language education, and ESL education (Ed D); mathematics education (MS, Ed S); modified and comprehensive special education (MS); reading education (MS, Ed S); school counseling (Ed S); school psychology (PhD, Ed S); science education (MS, Ed S); secondary teaching (MS); social foundations (MS); social science education (MS, Ed S); socio-cultural foundations of sports and education (PhD); special education (Ed S); teacher education (Ed D, PhD). *Accreditation:* NCATE. *Program availability:* Part-time, evening/weekend. *Degree requirements:* For master's and Ed S, thesis optional; for doctorate, variable foreign language requirement, thesis/dissertation. *Entrance requirements:* For master's, minimum GPA of 2.7; for doctorate and Ed S, GRE General Test, minimum GPA of 2.7. Additional exam requirements/recommendations for international students: Required—TOEFL. Electronic applications accepted.

The University of Texas at Arlington, Graduate School, College of Education, Department of Curriculum and Instruction, Arlington, TX 76019. Offers curriculum and instruction (M Ed), including literacy studies, mathematics education, mind, brain, and education, science education; teaching (with certification) (M Ed T). *Accreditation:* NCATE. *Program availability:* Part-time, evening/weekend, online learning. *Degree requirements:* For master's, comprehensive exam (for some programs), comprehensive activity, research project. *Entrance requirements:* For master's, GRE General Test, minimum undergraduate GPA of 3.0 in last 60 hours of course work, writing sample, 3 letters of recommendation. Additional exam requirements/recommendations for international students: Required—TOEFL (minimum score 550 paper-based). *Application deadline:* For fall admission, 6/1 priority date for domestic students, 4/1 priority date for international students; for spring admission, 10/15 priority date for domestic students, 9/15 priority date for international students. Applications are processed on a rolling basis. Application fee: $50. Electronic applications accepted. *Financial support:* Research assistantships, teaching assistantships, career-related internships or fieldwork, Federal Work-Study, scholarships/grants, and unspecified assistantships available. Financial award application deadline: 6/1; financial award applicants required to submit FAFSA. *Unit head:* Daniel H. Robinson, Chair, 817-272-0116, Fax: 817-272-2618, E-mail: daniel.robinson@uta.edu. *Application contact:* Caitlin Guerrero, Graduate Academic Advisor, 817-272-2956, Fax: 817-272-7624, E-mail: caitling@uta.edu.
Website: http://www.uta.edu/coed/curricandinstruct/index.php

The University of Texas at Dallas, School of Natural Sciences and Mathematics, Department of Science/Mathematics Education, Richardson, TX 75080. Offers mathematics education (MAT); science education (MAT). *Program availability:* Part-time, evening/weekend, online learning. *Faculty:* 4 full-time (1 woman). *Students:* 7 full-time (5 women), 25 part-time (16 women); includes 8 minority (4 Black or African American, non-Hispanic/Latino; 3 Asian, non-Hispanic/Latino; 1 Hispanic/Latino), 3 international. Average age 36. 13 applicants, 77% accepted, 5 enrolled. In 2016, 9 master's awarded. *Degree requirements:* For master's, thesis optional. *Entrance requirements:* For master's, GRE General Test, minimum GPA of 3.0 in upper-level coursework in field. Additional exam requirements/recommendations for international students: Required—TOEFL (minimum score 550 paper-based). *Application deadline:* For fall admission, 7/15 for domestic students, 5/1 priority date for international students; for spring admission, 11/15 for domestic students, 9/1 priority date for international students. Applications are processed on a rolling basis. Application fee: $50 ($100 for international students). Electronic applications accepted. *Expenses:* Tuition, state resident: full-time $12,418; part-time $690 per semester hour. Tuition, nonresident: full-time $24,150; part-time $1342 per semester hour. Tuition and fees vary according to course load. *Financial support:* In 2016–17, 15 students received support, including 1 fellowship (averaging $1,000 per year), 3 teaching assistantships with partial tuition reimbursements available (averaging $17,100 per year); research assistantships with partial tuition reimbursements available, career-related internships or fieldwork, Federal Work-Study, institutionally sponsored loans, scholarships/grants, and unspecified assistantships also available. Support available to part-time students. Financial award application deadline: 4/30; financial award applicants required to submit FAFSA. *Faculty research:* Innovative science/math education programs. *Unit head:* Dr. Mary Urquhart Kelly, Department Head, 972-883-2499, Fax: 972-883-6796, E-mail: scimathed@utdallas.edu. *Application contact:* 972-883-2496, Fax: 972-883-6796, E-mail: barbc@utdallas.edu.
Website: http://www.utdallas.edu/sme/

The University of Texas at El Paso, Graduate School, College of Science, Master of Arts in Teaching Science Program, El Paso, TX 79968-0001. Offers MAT. *Program availability:* Part-time, evening/weekend. *Degree requirements:* For master's, thesis optional. *Entrance requirements:* For master's, minimum GPA of 3.0. Additional exam requirements/recommendations for international students: Required—TOEFL; Recommended—IELTS. Electronic applications accepted.

The University of Toledo, College of Graduate Studies, Judith Herb College of Education, Department of Curriculum and Instruction, Toledo, OH 43606-3390. Offers art education (ME); career and technical education (ME, Ed S); curriculum and instruction (ME, PhD, Ed S); early childhood education (Ed S); education and anthropology (MAE); education and biology (MES); education and chemistry (MES); education and classics (MAE); education and economics (MAE); education and English (MAE); education and French (MAE); education and geology (MES); education and German (MAE); education and history (MAE); education and mathematics (MAE, MES); education and physics (MES); education and political science (MAE); education and sociology (MAE); education and Spanish (MAE); educational media (PhD); educational technology (ME); educational technology: virtual educator (Certificate); elementary education (PhD); English as a second language (MAE); gifted and talented education (PhD); middle childhood education (ME); secondary education (ME, PhD); special education (PhD). *Accreditation:* NCATE. *Program availability:* Part-time, evening/weekend. *Degree requirements:* For master's, comprehensive exam, thesis or alternative; for doctorate, comprehensive exam, thesis/dissertation; for other advanced degree, thesis optional. *Entrance requirements:* For master's, doctorate, and other advanced degree, minimum cumulative GPA of 2.7 for all previous academic work, letters of recommendation. Additional exam requirements/recommendations for international students: Required—TOEFL (minimum score 550 paper-based; 80 iBT). Electronic applications accepted.

The University of Tulsa, Graduate School, Kendall College of Arts and Sciences, School of Urban Education, Program in Mathematics and Science Education, Tulsa, OK 74104-3189. Offers MSMSE. *Program availability:* Part-time. *Students:* 8 full-time (3 women), 2 part-time (0 women); includes 4 minority (2 Black or African American, non-Hispanic/Latino; 1 Asian, non-Hispanic/Latino; 1 Hispanic/Latino). Average age 26. 15 applicants, 73% accepted, 8 enrolled. In 2016, 6 master's awarded. *Entrance requirements:* For master's, GRE General Test. Additional exam requirements/recommendations for international students: Required—TOEFL (minimum score 577 paper-based), IELTS (minimum score 6.5). *Application deadline:* Applications are processed on a rolling basis. Application fee: $55. Electronic applications accepted. *Expenses: Tuition:* Full-time $22,230; part-time $1235 per credit hour. *Required fees:* $990 per semester. Tuition and fees vary according to course load. *Financial support:* In 2016–17, 3 students received support, including 3 teaching assistantships with full tuition reimbursements available (averaging $13,410 per year); fellowships with tuition reimbursements available, research assistantships, career-related internships or fieldwork, Federal Work-Study, scholarships/grants, health care benefits, tuition waivers (full and partial), and unspecified assistantships also available. Support available to part-time students. Financial award application deadline: 2/1; financial award applicants required to submit FAFSA. *Unit head:* Dr. Sharon Baker, Chair, 918-631-2238, Fax: 918-631-3721, E-mail: sharon-baker@utulsa.edu. *Application contact:* Dr. David Brown, Advisor, 918-631-2719, Fax: 918-631-2133, E-mail: david-brown@utulsa.edu.

University of Utah, Graduate School, College of Science, Department of Chemistry, Salt Lake City, UT 84112-0850. Offers chemistry (MS, PhD); science teacher education (MS). *Program availability:* Part-time, online learning. *Faculty:* 32 full-time (9 women), 8 part-time/adjunct (2 women). *Students:* 147 full-time (60 women), 23 part-time (5 women); includes 14 minority (1 Black or African American, non-Hispanic/Latino; 1 American Indian or Alaska Native, non-Hispanic/Latino; 5 Asian, non-Hispanic/Latino; 7 Hispanic/Latino), 44 international. Average age 27. 298 applicants, 34% accepted, 37 enrolled. In 2016, 16 master's, 22 doctorates awarded. Terminal master's awarded for partial completion of doctoral program. *Degree requirements:* For master's, thesis optional, 20 hours of course work, 10 hours of research; for doctorate, thesis/dissertation, 18 hours of course work, 14 hours of research. *Entrance requirements:* For master's and doctorate, GRE General Test, minimum GPA of 3.0. Additional exam requirements/recommendations for international students: Required—TOEFL (minimum score 620 paper-based; 105 iBT). *Application deadline:* For fall admission, 4/1 for domestic students, 2/1 for international students; for spring admission, 11/1 for domestic and international students. Application fee: $55 ($65 for international students). Electronic applications accepted. Application fee is waived when completed online. *Expenses:* Contact institution. *Financial support:* In 2016–17, 1 fellowship with tuition reimbursement (averaging $25,000 per year), 119 research assistantships with tuition reimbursements (averaging $25,500 per year), 55 teaching assistantships with tuition reimbursements (averaging $25,000 per year) were awarded; scholarships/grants and tuition waivers (full) also available. Financial award application deadline: 4/1; financial award applicants required to submit FAFSA. *Faculty research:* Analytical, biological, inorganic, materials, organic, physical and theoretical chemistry. *Unit head:* Dr. Cynthia J. Burrows, Chair, 801-585-7290, Fax: 801-581-8433, E-mail: chair@chemistry.utah.edu. *Application contact:* Jo Vallejo, Graduate Coordinator, 801-581-4393, E-mail: jvallejo@chem.utah.edu.
Website: http://www.chem.utah.edu/

University of Utah, Graduate School, College of Science, Department of Physics and Astronomy, Salt Lake City, UT 84112. Offers chemical physics (PhD); medical physics (MS, PhD); physics (MA, MS, PhD); physics teaching (PhD). *Program availability:* Part-time. *Faculty:* 38 full-time (5 women), 12 part-time/adjunct (1 woman). *Students:* 99 full-time (34 women), 4 part-time (0 women); includes 5 minority (2 Asian, non-Hispanic/Latino; 3 Hispanic/Latino), 52 international. Average age 24. 137 applicants, 31% accepted, 19 enrolled. In 2016, 7 master's, 11 doctorates awarded. Terminal master's awarded for partial completion of doctoral program. *Degree requirements:* For master's, comprehensive exam (for some programs), thesis or alternative, teaching experience, departmental exam; for doctorate, comprehensive exam, thesis/dissertation, departmental qualifying exam. *Entrance requirements:* For master's and doctorate, GRE Subject Test, minimum GPA of 3.0. Additional exam requirements/recommendations for international students: Required—TOEFL (minimum score 550 paper-based; 85 iBT). *Application deadline:* For fall admission, 2/1 priority date for domestic and international students. Applications are processed on a rolling basis. Application fee: $55 ($65 for international students). Electronic applications accepted. *Expenses:* Contact institution. *Financial support:* In 2016–17, 76 students received support, including 23 research assistantships with full tuition reimbursements available (averaging $23,500 per year), 52 teaching assistantships with full tuition reimbursements available (averaging $20,641 per year); unspecified assistantships also available. Financial award application deadline: 2/15; financial award applicants required to submit FAFSA. *Faculty research:* High-energy, cosmic-ray, medical physics, condensed matter, relativity applied physics, biophysics, astronomy and astrophysics. *Total annual research expenditures:* $5.6 million. *Unit head:* Dr. Benjamin Bromley, Chair, 801-581-3538, Fax: 801-581-4801, E-mail: bromley@physics.utah.edu. *Application contact:* Krista Perkins, Academic Coordinator, 801-581-6861, Fax: 801-581-4801, E-mail: krista@physics.utah.edu.
Website: http://www.physics.utah.edu/

University of Vermont, Graduate College, College of Arts and Sciences, Department of Biology, Burlington, VT 05405. Offers biology (MS, PhD); biology education (MST). *Degree requirements:* For master's, thesis; for doctorate, thesis/dissertation. *Entrance requirements:* For master's and doctorate, GRE General Test. Additional exam requirements/recommendations for international students: Required—TOEFL (minimum score 550 paper-based; 80 iBT). Electronic applications accepted. *Expenses:* Tuition, state resident: full-time $5814. Tuition, nonresident: full-time $14,670.

University of Victoria, Faculty of Graduate Studies, Faculty of Education, Department of Curriculum and Instruction, Victoria, BC V8W 2Y2, Canada. Offers art education (M Ed, PhD); curriculum studies (M Ed, MA, PhD); early childhood education (M Ed, PhD); educational studies (PhD); language and literacy (M Ed, MA, PhD); mathematics (M Ed, MA, PhD); music education (M Ed, MA, PhD); science (M Ed, MA, PhD); social studies (M Ed, MA); social, cultural and foundational studies (MA, PhD); technology and environmental education (PhD). *Program availability:* Part-time. *Degree requirements:* For master's, thesis, project (M Ed); for doctorate, comprehensive exam, thesis/dissertation. *Entrance requirements:* For master's, minimum B average. Additional exam requirements/recommendations for international students: Required—TOEFL (minimum score 575 paper-based), IELTS (minimum score 7). Electronic applications accepted. *Faculty research:* Elementary and secondary English, language arts, curriculum theory and practice, educational media and technology, educational administration and leadership, history and philosophy of education.

University of Virginia, College and Graduate School of Arts and Sciences, Department of Physics, Charlottesville, VA 22903. Offers physics (MA, MS, PhD); physics education (MAPE). *Faculty:* 35 full-time (5 women). *Students:* 98 full-time (19 women); includes 9 minority (1 Black or African American, non-Hispanic/Latino; 6 Asian, non-Hispanic/Latino; 1 Hispanic/Latino; 1 Two or more races, non-Hispanic/Latino), 64 international. Average age 26. 181 applicants, 36% accepted, 20 enrolled. In 2016, 8 master's, 14 doctorates awarded. *Degree requirements:* For master's, thesis (for some programs); for doctorate, comprehensive exam, thesis/dissertation. *Entrance requirements:* For master's and doctorate, GRE General Test, GRE Subject Test, 2 or more letters of recommendation. Additional exam requirements/recommendations for international students: Required—TOEFL (minimum score 600 paper-based; 90 iBT), IELTS. *Application deadline:* For fall admission, 1/7 for domestic and international students. Applications are processed on a rolling basis. Application fee: $60. Electronic applications accepted. *Expenses:* Tuition, state resident: full-time $15,026; part-time $834 per credit hour. Tuition, nonresident: full-time $25,168; part-time $1378 per credit hour. *Required fees:* $2654. *Financial support:* Fellowships, research assistantships, and teaching assistantships available. Financial award applicants required to submit FAFSA. *Unit head:* Joe Poon, Chair, 434-924-3781, Fax: 434-924-4576, E-mail: phys-chair@physics.virginia.edu. *Application contact:* Olivier Pfister, Director of Graduate Studies, 434-924-3781, Fax: 434-924-4576, E-mail: grad-info-request@physics.virginia.edu.
Website: http://www.phys.virginia.edu/

University of Virginia, Curry School of Education, Department of Curriculum, Instruction, and Special Education, Program in Curriculum and Instruction, Charlottesville, VA 22903. Offers curriculum and instruction (M Ed, Ed S); elementary education (M Ed, Ed D); English education (M Ed, Ed D); foreign language education (M Ed); mathematics education (M Ed, Ed D); science education (Ed D); social studies education (M Ed); MBA/M Ed. *Students:* 43 full-time (35 women), 24 part-time (16 women); includes 7 minority (1 Black or African American, non-Hispanic/Latino; 1 Asian, non-Hispanic/Latino; 2 Hispanic/Latino; 3 Two or more races, non-Hispanic/Latino), 4 international. Average age 33. 93 applicants, 78% accepted, 54 enrolled. In 2016, 52 master's, 14 other advanced degrees awarded. *Degree requirements:* For master's, comprehensive exam (for some programs); for doctorate, comprehensive exam, thesis/dissertation; for Ed S, comprehensive exam. *Entrance requirements:* For master's, doctorate, and Ed S, GRE General Test, 2 letters of recommendation. Additional exam requirements/recommendations for international students: Required—TOEFL (minimum score 600 paper-based; 90 iBT), IELTS (minimum score 7). *Application deadline:* Applications are processed on a rolling basis. Application fee: $60. Electronic applications accepted. *Expenses:* Tuition, state resident: full-time $15,026; part-time $834 per credit hour. Tuition, nonresident: full-time $25,168; part-time $1378 per credit hour. *Required fees:* $2654. *Financial support:* Fellowships with tuition reimbursements, research assistantships with tuition reimbursements, and teaching assistantships with tuition reimbursements available. Financial award application deadline: 1/5; financial award applicants required to submit FAFSA. *Unit head:* Susan Mintz, Program Area Director, 434-924-3128, E-mail: slm4r@virginia.edu. *Application contact:* Eric Molnar, Assistant Director, Admissions and Enrollment Reporting, 434-243-2085, E-mail: eric.molnar@virginia.edu.
Website: http://curry.virginia.edu/academics/areas-of-study/curriculum-teaching-learning

University of Virginia, Curry School of Education, Program in Education, Charlottesville, VA 22903. Offers administration and supervision (PhD); applied developmental science (PhD); counselor education (PhD); curriculum and instruction (PhD); early childhood special education (MT); education evaluation (PhD); educational psychology (PhD); educational research (PhD); elementary education (MT); English education (MT, PhD); foreign language education (MT); higher education (PhD); instructional technology (PhD); kinesiology (MT, PhD); math education (PhD); reading education (PhD); research, statistics and evaluation (PhD); school psychology (PhD); science education (PhD); social studies education (MT, PhD); special education (PhD); world languages education (MT). *Students:* 452 full-time (357 women), 18 part-time (13 women); includes 100 minority (28 Black or African American, non-Hispanic/Latino; 39 Asian, non-Hispanic/Latino; 18 Hispanic/Latino; 15 Two or more races, non-Hispanic/Latino), 14 international. Average age 25. 309 applicants, 51% accepted, 87 enrolled. In 2016, 144 master's, 31 doctorates awarded. *Degree requirements:* For master's, comprehensive exam (for some programs), field project; for doctorate, comprehensive exam, thesis/dissertation. *Entrance requirements:* For doctorate, GRE General Test. Additional exam requirements/recommendations for international students: Required—TOEFL (minimum score 600 paper-based; 90 iBT), IELTS (minimum score 7). *Application deadline:* Applications are processed on a rolling basis. Application fee: $60. Electronic applications accepted. *Expenses:* Tuition, state resident: full-time $15,026; part-time $834 per credit hour. Tuition, nonresident: full-time $25,168; part-time $1378 per credit hour. *Required fees:* $2654. *Financial support:* Fellowships, research assistantships, and teaching assistantships available. Financial award application deadline: 1/5; financial award applicants required to submit FAFSA. *Unit head:* Robert C. Pianta, Dean, 434-924-3334, E-mail: pianta@virginia.edu. *Application contact:* Eric Molnar, Assistant Director, Admissions and Enrollment Reporting, 434-243-2085, E-mail: eric.molnar@virginia.edu.
Website: http://curry.virginia.edu/teacher-education

University of Washington, Graduate School, College of Education, Seattle, WA 98195. Offers curriculum and instruction (M Ed, Ed D, PhD), including educational technology, general curriculum (Ed D, PhD), language, literacy, and culture, mathematics education, multicultural education, reading and language arts education (Ed D), science education, social studies education, teaching and curriculum (M Ed); educational leadership and policy studies (M Ed, Ed D, PhD), including administration (Ed D), educational policy, organization, and leadership (M Ed, PhD), higher education, leadership for learning (Ed D), social and cultural foundations of education (M Ed, PhD); educational psychology (M Ed, PhD), including educational psychology (PhD), human development and cognition (M Ed), learning sciences, measurement, statistics and research design (M Ed), school psychology (M Ed); instructional leadership (M Ed); intercollegiate athletic leadership (M Ed); special education (M Ed, Ed D, PhD), including early childhood special education (M Ed), emotional and behavioral disabilities (M Ed), learning disabilities (M Ed), low-incidence disabilities (M Ed), severe disabilities (M Ed), special education (Ed D, PhD); teacher education (MIT). *Accreditation:* APA. *Program availability:* Part-time, evening/weekend. *Degree requirements:* For master's, thesis optional; for doctorate, thesis/dissertation. *Entrance requirements:* For master's and doctorate, GRE General Test, minimum GPA of 3.0. Additional exam requirements/recommendations for international students: Required—TOEFL. Electronic applications accepted. *Faculty research:* School restructuring/effective schools, special education interventions, literacy and writing, technology, school partnerships, teacher preparation.

University of Washington, Graduate School, Interdisciplinary Program in Biology for Teachers, Seattle, WA 98195. Offers MS. *Program availability:* Part-time. *Degree requirements:* For master's, research project and oral exam. *Entrance requirements:* For master's, GRE General Test, minimum GPA of 3.0, teaching certificate or professional teaching experience. Electronic applications accepted.

University of Washington, Tacoma, Graduate Programs, Program in Education, Tacoma, WA 98402-3100. Offers education (M Ed); educational administration (principal or program administrator certification) (M Ed); elementary education teacher certification (M Ed); elementary education/special education teacher certification (M Ed); secondary science or math teacher certification (M Ed). *Program availability:* Part-time, evening/weekend. *Degree requirements:* For master's, culminating project. *Entrance requirements:* For master's, WEST-B, WEST-E (teacher certification programs only), official sealed transcript from every college/university attended, personal goal statement, letters of recommendation, copy of valid teaching certificate. Additional exam requirements/recommendations for international students: Required—TOEFL (minimum score 580 paper-based; 92 iBT). Electronic applications accepted. *Faculty research:* Global learning communities for English/Chinese languages, evaluation of mathematics and reading intervention programs, response to intervention, school-wide behavioral and emotional support, mathematics education and culturally responsive mathematics education.

The University of West Alabama, School of Graduate Studies, College of Education, Departments of Instructional Leadership and Support/Curriculum and Instruction, Program in Secondary Education, Livingston, AL 35470. Offers biology (MAT); English language arts (MAT); high school 6-12 (M Ed); history (MAT); mathematics (MAT);

science (MAT); social science (MAT). *Program availability:* Part-time, evening/weekend, 100% online. *Faculty:* 19 full-time (7 women), 7 part-time/adjunct (3 women). *Students:* 236 (159 women); includes 59 minority (53 Black or African American, non-Hispanic/Latino; 2 American Indian or Alaska Native, non-Hispanic/Latino; 1 Asian, non-Hispanic/Latino; 1 Hispanic/Latino; 2 Two or more races, non-Hispanic/Latino). Average age 32. 85 applicants, 88% accepted, 52 enrolled. In 2016, 84 master's awarded. *Degree requirements:* For master's, comprehensive exam, thesis optional. *Entrance requirements:* For master's, GRE General Test, MAT, minimum GPA of 2.75. Additional exam requirements/recommendations for international students: Required—TOEFL (minimum score 500 paper-based; 61 iBT). *Application deadline:* Applications are processed on a rolling basis. Application fee: $40. Electronic applications accepted. *Expenses:* Tuition, state resident: part-time $355 per credit hour. Tuition, nonresident: part-time $710 per credit hour. *Required fees:* $130 per semester. *Financial support:* Teaching assistantships, Federal Work-Study, scholarships/grants, and unspecified assistantships available. Support available to part-time students. Financial award application deadline: 3/1; financial award applicants required to submit FAFSA. *Faculty research:* Integrated arts in the curriculum, moral development of children. *Unit head:* Dr. Jodie Winship, Chair of Curriculum and Instruction, 205-652-5415, Fax: 205-652-3706, E-mail: jwinship@uwa.edu. *Application contact:* Dr. B. J. Kimbrough, Dean of Graduate Studies, 205-652-3647, Fax: 205-652-3706, E-mail: bkimbrough@uwa.edu.
Website: http://www.uwa.edu/highschool612.aspx

University of Wisconsin–Madison, Graduate School, School of Education, Department of Curriculum and Instruction, Madison, WI 53706-1380. Offers art education (MA); curriculum and instruction (MS, PhD); education and mathematics (MA); French education (MA); German education (MA); music education (MS); science education (MS); Spanish education (MA). *Accreditation:* NASM (one or more programs are accredited). *Degree requirements:* For doctorate, thesis/dissertation.

University of Wisconsin–Milwaukee, Graduate School, School of Education, Department of Curriculum and Instruction, Milwaukee, WI 53201-0413. Offers curriculum and instruction (MS), including cross-curricular focus, early childhood education, English education, mathematics education, middle childhood/early adolescence education, reading education, science education, urban social studies education. *Program availability:* Part-time. *Students:* 21 full-time (13 women), 44 part-time (42 women); includes 10 minority (1 Black or African American, non-Hispanic/Latino; 1 Asian, non-Hispanic/Latino; 2 Hispanic/Latino; 6 Two or more races, non-Hispanic/Latino), 2 international. Average age 33. 42 applicants, 71% accepted, 20 enrolled. In 2016, 45 master's awarded. *Degree requirements:* For master's, thesis or alternative. *Entrance requirements:* Additional exam requirements/recommendations for international students: Required—TOEFL (minimum score 550 paper-based; 79 iBT), IELTS (minimum score 6.5). *Application deadline:* For fall admission, 1/1 priority date for domestic students; for spring admission, 9/1 for domestic students. Applications are processed on a rolling basis. Application fee: $56 ($96 for international students). Electronic applications accepted. *Financial support:* In 2016–17, 1 fellowship was awarded; research assistantships, teaching assistantships, career-related internships or fieldwork, health care benefits, unspecified assistantships, and project assistantships also available. Support available to part-time students. Financial award application deadline: 4/15; financial award applicants required to submit FAFSA. *Application contact:* General Information Contact, 414-229-4721, E-mail: soeinfo@uwm.edu.
Website: http://uwm.edu/education/academics/curriculum-instruction-department/

University of Wisconsin–River Falls, Outreach and Graduate Studies, College of Arts and Science, Program in Science, River Falls, WI 54022. Offers science education (MSE). *Program availability:* Part-time. *Degree requirements:* For master's, comprehensive exam, thesis or alternative. *Entrance requirements:* For master's, minimum GPA of 2.75. Additional exam requirements/recommendations for international students: Required—TOEFL (minimum score 500 paper-based; 65 iBT), IELTS (minimum score 5.5). Electronic applications accepted.

University of Wisconsin–Stevens Point, College of Letters and Science, Department of Biology, Stevens Point, WI 54481-3897. Offers MST. *Degree requirements:* For master's, thesis or alternative. *Entrance requirements:* For master's, minimum undergraduate GPA of 2.75 overall, 3.0 in biology; bachelor's degree; teacher's license.

University of Wyoming, College of Education, Science and Mathematics Teaching Center, Laramie, WY 82071. Offers MS, MST. *Degree requirements:* For master's, thesis. *Entrance requirements:* For master's, GRE General Test, minimum GPA of 3.0, writing sample, 3 letters of recommendation. Electronic applications accepted.

Vanderbilt University, Department of Physics and Astronomy, Nashville, TN 37240-1001. Offers astronomy (MS); health physics (MA); physics (MAT, MS, PhD). *Faculty:* 26 full-time (4 women). *Students:* 50 full-time (10 women), 1 part-time (0 women); includes 7 minority (3 Black or African American, non-Hispanic/Latino; 1 Asian, non-Hispanic/Latino; 1 Hispanic/Latino; 2 Two or more races, non-Hispanic/Latino), 17 international. Average age 27. 115 applicants, 21% accepted, 8 enrolled. In 2016, 4 master's, 16 doctorates awarded. *Degree requirements:* For master's, thesis; for doctorate, comprehensive exam, thesis/dissertation, final and qualifying exams. *Entrance requirements:* For master's, GRE General Test; for doctorate, GRE General Test, GRE Subject Test. Additional exam requirements/recommendations for international students: Required—TOEFL (minimum score 570 paper-based; 88 iBT). *Application deadline:* For fall admission, 1/1 for domestic and international students. Electronic applications accepted. *Expenses: Tuition:* Part-time $1854 per credit hour. *Financial support:* Fellowships with tuition reimbursements, research assistantships with full tuition reimbursements, teaching assistantships with full tuition reimbursements, career-related internships or fieldwork, Federal Work-Study, and institutionally sponsored loans available. Financial award application deadline: 1/15; financial award applicants required to submit CSS PROFILE or FAFSA. *Faculty research:* Experimental and theoretical physics, free electron laser, living-state physics, heavy-ion physics, nuclear structure. *Unit head:* Dr. Robert Sherrer, Chair, 615-322-2828, E-mail: robert.scherrer@vanderbilt.edu. *Application contact:* Julia Velkovska, Director of Graduate Studies, 615-322-2828, E-mail: julia.velkovska@vanderbilt.edu.
Website: http://www.vanderbilt.edu/physics/

Wagner College, Division of Graduate Studies, Education Department, Program in Secondary Education/Students with Disabilities, Staten Island, NY 10301-4495. Offers secondary education 7-12 (MS Ed), including language arts, languages other than English, mathematics and technology, science and technology, social studies. *Program availability:* Part-time, evening/weekend. *Degree requirements:* For master's, thesis (for some programs), completion of state certification exams before student teaching. *Entrance requirements:* For master's, minimum GPA of 3.0, interview, recommendations. Electronic applications accepted. Tuition and fees vary according to degree level.

Walden University, Graduate Programs, Richard W. Riley College of Education and Leadership, Minneapolis, MN 55401. Offers adult education (Post-Master's Certificate); adult learning (Graduate Certificate); college teaching and learning (Graduate Certificate); community college leadership (Ed D); curriculum, instruction and assessment (Ed D, Ed S, Graduate Certificate); developmental education (Graduate Certificate); early childhood administration, management, and leadership (Graduate Certificate); early childhood education (Ed D, Ed S); early childhood public policy and advocacy (Graduate Certificate); early childhood studies (MS), including administration, management and leadership, early childhood public policy and advocacy, teaching adults in the early childhood field, teaching and diversity in early childhood education; education (MS, PhD), including adolescent literacy and learning (MS), curriculum, instruction, and assessment (grades K-12) (MS), curriculum, instruction, assessment, and evaluation (PhD), early childhood leadership and advocacy (PhD), early childhood special education (PhD), educational leadership (MS), educational leadership and administration (principal preparation) (MS), educational technology and design (PhD), elementary reading and literacy (PreK-6) (MS), elementary reading and mathematics (grades K-6) (MS), global and comparative education (PhD), higher education leadership management and policy (PhD), integrating technology in the classroom (grades K-12) (MS), learning, instruction and innovation (PhD), mathematics (grades 5-8) (MS), mathematics (grades K-6) (MS), mathematics and science (grades K-8) (MS), organizational research, assessment, and evaluation (PhD), reading and literacy with a reading K-12 endorsement (MS), reading literacy assessment and evaluation (PhD), science (grades K-8) (MS), special education (non-licensure) (grades K-12) (MS), teacher leadership (grades K-12) (MS), teaching English language learners (grades K-12) (MS); educational administration and leadership (Ed D); educational leadership and administration (principal preparation) (Ed S); educational technology (Ed D, Ed S, Post Master's Certificate); elementary reading and literacy (Graduate Certificate); engaging culturally diverse learners (Graduate Certificate); enrollment management and institutional marketing (Graduate Certificate); higher education (MS), including adult learning, college teaching and learning, enrollment management and institutional marketing, global higher education, leadership for student success, online and distance learning; higher education and adult learning (Ed D); higher education leadership and management (Ed D); higher education leadership for student success (Graduate Certificate); instructional design and technology (MS, Postbaccalaureate Certificate), including general program (MS), online learning (MS), training and performance improvement (MS); integrating technology in the classroom (Graduate Certificate); mathematics 5-8 (Graduate Certificate); mathematics K-6 (Graduate Certificate); online teaching for adult educators (Graduate Certificate); reading, literacy, and assessment (Ed D, Ed S); science K-8 (Graduate Certificate); special education (Ed D, Ed S, Graduate Certificate); special education (K-age 21) (MAT); teacher leadership (Graduate Certificate); teaching adults English as a second language (Graduate Certificate); teaching adults in the early childhood field (Graduate Certificate); teaching and diversity in early childhood education (Graduate Certificate); teaching English language learners (grades K-12) (Graduate Certificate); teaching K-12 students online (Graduate Certificate). *Accreditation:* NCATE. *Program availability:* Part-time, evening/weekend, online only, 100% online. *Degree requirements:* For doctorate, thesis/dissertation (for some programs), residency; for other advanced degree, residency (for some programs). *Entrance requirements:* For master's, bachelor's degree or higher; minimum GPA of 2.5; official transcripts; goal statement (for some programs); access to computer and Internet; for doctorate, master's degree or higher; three years of related professional or academic experience (preferred); minimum GPA of 3.0; goal statement and current resume (for select programs); official transcripts; access to computer and Internet; for other advanced degree, relevant work experience; access to computer and Internet. Additional exam requirements/recommendations for international students: Required—TOEFL (minimum score 550 paper-based, 79 iBT), IELTS (minimum score 6.5), Michigan English Language Assessment Battery (minimum score 82), or PTE (minimum score 53). Electronic applications accepted.

Warner University, School of Education, Lake Wales, FL 33859. Offers curriculum and instruction (MAEd); elementary education (MAEd); science, technology, engineering, and mathematics (STEM) (MAEd). *Program availability:* Part-time, evening/weekend, online learning. *Degree requirements:* For master's, thesis, accomplished practices portfolio. *Entrance requirements:* For master's, minimum GPA of 3.0 in last 60 hours of undergraduate coursework; 2 letters of recommendation. Additional exam requirements/recommendations for international students: Required—TOEFL (minimum score 550 paper-based). *Application deadline:* Applications are processed on a rolling basis. Application fee: $50. Electronic applications accepted. *Financial support:* Scholarships/grants available. Financial award applicants required to submit FAFSA. *Unit head:* Dr. Bill Rigel, Dean, 863-638-7207, Fax: 863-638-4907, E-mail: bill.rigel@warner.edu. *Application contact:* Torshanda Howard, Admissions Advisor, 863-638-7501, Fax: 863-638-4907, E-mail: admissons@warner.edu.
Website: http://warner.edu/graduate/degrees-offered/arts-in-education/

Wayland Baptist University, Graduate Programs, Program in Education, Plainview, TX 79072-6998. Offers education administration (M Ed); education diagnostics (M Ed); education literacy (M Ed); elementary certification (M Ed); English (M Ed); English as a second language (M Ed); higher education administration (M Ed); human resources (M Ed); instructional leadership (M Ed); instructional technology (M Ed); leadership training and development (M Ed); science education (M Ed); secondary certification (M Ed); social studies (M Ed); special education (M Ed); sports administration and management (M Ed). *Program availability:* Part-time, evening/weekend, online learning. *Degree requirements:* For master's, comprehensive exam, capstone course. *Entrance requirements:* For master's, GRE, GMAT or MAT. Additional exam requirements/recommendations for international students: Required—TOEFL (minimum score 500 paper-based; 61 iBT). Electronic applications accepted.

Wayland Baptist University, Graduate Programs, Program in Multidisciplinary Science, Plainview, TX 79072-6998. Offers MS. *Program availability:* Part-time, evening/weekend. *Degree requirements:* For master's, comprehensive exam. *Entrance requirements:* For master's, GRE or MAT. Additional exam requirements/recommendations for international students: Required—TOEFL (minimum score 500 paper-based; 61 iBT). Electronic applications accepted.

Wayne State College, School of Education and Counseling, Department of Educational Foundations and Leadership, Program in Curriculum and Instruction, Wayne, NE 68787. Offers alternative education (MSE); business and information technology education (MSE); communication arts education (MSE); early childhood education (MSE); elementary education (MSE); English as a second language (MSE); English education (MSE); family and consumer sciences education (MSE); industrial technology and vocational education (MSE); learning communities (MSE); mathematics education (MSE); music education (MSE); science education (MSE); social science education (MSE). *Accreditation:* NCATE. *Program availability:* Part-time, evening/weekend. *Degree requirements:* For master's, comprehensive exam, thesis optional. *Entrance requirements:* For master's, GRE General Test. Additional exam requirements/recommendations for international students: Required—TOEFL (minimum score 550 paper-based).

Wayne State University, College of Education, Division of Teacher Education, Detroit, MI 48202. Offers art education (M Ed); bilingual/bicultural education (M Ed, Certificate); career and technical education (M Ed); curriculum and instruction (Ed D, PhD, Ed S), including art education (Ed D, PhD), bilingual education (Ed D, Ed S), career and technical education (MAT, Ed D, PhD, Ed S), early childhood education (MAT, Ed D, PhD, Ed S), elementary education, English as a second language (MAT, Ed D, Ed S), English education (MAT, Ed D, PhD, Ed S), foreign language education (MAT, Ed D,

PhD), K-12 curriculum, mathematics education (MAT, Ed D, PhD, Ed S), science education (MAT, Ed D, PhD, Ed S), secondary education, social studies education (MAT, Ed D, PhD, Ed S); early childhood education (M Ed); elementary education (M Ed, MAT), including bilingual/bicultural education (MAT), early childhood education (MAT, Ed D, PhD, Ed S), English as a second language (MAT, Ed D, Ed S), general elementary education (MAT), mathematics education (MAT, Ed D, PhD, Ed S), science education (MAT, Ed D, PhD, Ed S), social studies education (MAT, Ed D, PhD, Ed S); English as a second language (Certificate); English education (M Ed); foreign language education (M Ed); mathematics education (M Ed); reading (M Ed, Ed S); reading, language and literature (Ed D); science education (M Ed); secondary education (MAT), including art education (K-12), bilingual/bicultural education, career and technical education (MAT, Ed D, PhD, Ed S), English as a second language (MAT, Ed D, Ed S), English education (MAT, Ed D, PhD, Ed S), foreign language education (MAT, Ed D, PhD), kinesiology, mathematics education (MAT, Ed D, PhD, Ed S); social studies education (M Ed); special education (M Ed, MAT, Ed D, PhD, Ed S), including autism spectrum disorders (MAT), cognitive development (MAT), emotional impairment (MAT), learning disabilities (MAT). *Program availability:* Part-time, blended/hybrid learning. *Faculty:* 29. *Students:* 106 full-time (73 women), 351 part-time (276 women); includes 115 minority (76 Black or African American, non-Hispanic/Latino; 10 Asian, non-Hispanic/Latino; 20 Hispanic/Latino; 1 Native Hawaiian or other Pacific Islander, non-Hispanic/Latino; 8 Two or more races, non-Hispanic/Latino), 12 international. Average age 37. 242 applicants, 37% accepted, 72 enrolled. In 2016, 178 master's, 19 doctorates, 17 other advanced degrees awarded. *Degree requirements:* For master's, essay or project (for some M Ed programs), professional field experience (for MAT programs); for doctorate, thesis/dissertation. *Entrance requirements:* For master's, Michigan Test for Teacher Certification, verification of participation in group work with children, Michigan State Police criminal background check; for doctorate, minimum undergraduate GPA of 3.0, graduate 3.5; interview; curriculum vitae; references. Additional exam requirements/recommendations for international students: Required—TOEFL (minimum score 550 paper-based; 79 iBT), TWE (minimum score 5.5), Michigan English Language Assessment Battery (minimum score 85); Recommended—IELTS (minimum score 6.5). *Application deadline:* For fall admission, 6/1 priority date for domestic students, 5/1 priority date for international students; for winter admission, 10/1 priority date for domestic students, 9/1 priority date for international students; for spring admission, 2/1 priority date for domestic students, 1/1 priority date for international students. Applications are processed on a rolling basis. Application fee: $50. Electronic applications accepted. *Expenses:* $16,503 per year resident tuition and fees, $33,697 per year non-resident tuition and fees. *Financial support:* In 2016–17, 101 students received support, including 3 fellowships (averaging $11,409 per year); research assistantships with tuition reimbursements available, Federal Work-Study, scholarships/grants, and unspecified assistantships also available. Support available to part-time students. Financial award applicants required to submit FAFSA. *Faculty research:* Improving students' skill achievement in mathematics, improving elementary children's understanding of informational text, teachers' use of their pedagogical and mathematical knowledge in the interactive work of teaching, the intersection of identity construction in teaching and learning, identifying effective methods of literacy instruction and assessments for bilingual students in elementary language arts classrooms. *Unit head:* Dr. Kathleen Crawford-McKinney, Assistant Dean, 313-577-0122. *Application contact:* Janice Green, Assistant Dean, 313-577-1605, E-mail: jwgreen@wayne.edu.
Website: http://coe.wayne.edu/ted/index.php

West Chester University of Pennsylvania, College of the Sciences and Mathematics, Department of Biology, West Chester, PA 19383. Offers MS, Teaching Certificate. *Program availability:* Part-time, evening/weekend. *Faculty:* 11 full-time (6 women). *Students:* 12 full-time (8 women), 14 part-time (10 women); includes 3 minority (2 Black or African American, non-Hispanic/Latino; 1 Hispanic/Latino), 2 international. Average age 28. 28 applicants, 43% accepted, 5 enrolled. In 2016, 8 master's, 1 other advanced degree awarded. *Degree requirements:* For master's, comprehensive exam (for some programs), thesis (for some programs). *Entrance requirements:* For master's, two letters of reference. Additional exam requirements/recommendations for international students: Required—TOEFL or IELTS. *Application deadline:* For fall admission, 5/15 for international students; for spring admission, 10/15 for international students. Applications are processed on a rolling basis. Application fee: $50. Electronic applications accepted. *Expenses:* Tuition, state resident: full-time $8694; part-time $483 per credit. Tuition, nonresident: full-time $13,050; part-time $725 per credit. *Required fees:* $2399; $119.05 per credit. Tuition and fees vary according to campus/location and program. *Financial support:* Scholarships/grants and unspecified assistantships available. Financial award application deadline: 2/15; financial award applicants required to submit FAFSA. *Faculty research:* Medical microbiology, molecular genetics and physiology of living systems, mammalian biomechanics, invertebrate and vertebrate animal systems, aquatic and terrestrial ecology. *Unit head:* Dr. Giovanni Casotti, Department Chair, 610-436-2538, E-mail: gcasotti@wcupa.edu. *Application contact:* Dr. Anne Boettger, Graduate Coordinator, 610-430-4601, E-mail: aboettger@wcupa.edu.
Website: http://bio.wcupa.edu/biology/index.php

West Chester University of Pennsylvania, College of the Sciences and Mathematics, Department of Physics, West Chester, PA 19383. Offers Teaching Certificate. In 2016, 2 Teaching Certificates awarded. *Entrance requirements:* For degree, bachelor's degree or higher, minimum GPA of 3.0. Additional exam requirements/recommendations for international students: Required—TOEFL or IELTS. *Application deadline:* For fall admission, 5/15 for international students; for spring admission, 10/15 for international students. Applications are processed on a rolling basis. Application fee: $50. Electronic applications accepted. *Expenses:* Tuition, state resident: full-time $8694; part-time $483 per credit. Tuition, nonresident: full-time $13,050; part-time $725 per credit. *Required fees:* $2399; $119.05 per credit. Tuition and fees vary according to campus/location and program. *Financial support:* Scholarships/grants and unspecified assistantships available. Financial award application deadline: 2/15; financial award applicants required to submit FAFSA. *Unit head:* Dr. Anthony J. Nicastro, Chairperson, 610-436-2497, Fax: 610-436-3013. *Application contact:* Dr. Jeffrey J. Sudol, Graduate Coordinator, 610-436-2592, Fax: 610-436-3013, E-mail: jsudol@wcupa.edu.
Website: http://www.wcupa.edu/sciences-mathematics/physics/

Western Governors University, Teachers College, Salt Lake City, UT 84107. Offers curriculum and instruction (MS); educational leadership (MS); educational studies (MA); educational studies (5-12) (MA), including mathematics; elementary education (K-8) (MAT, Postbaccalaureate Certificate); elementary education (PreK-8) (MAT); English language learning (K-12) (MA); instructional design (MAT); learning and technology (M Ed, MA); management and innovation (M Ed); mathematics (5-12) (MAT, Postbaccalaureate Certificate); mathematics (5-9) (MAT, Postbaccalaureate Certificate); mathematics education (5-12) (MA); mathematics education (5-9) (MA); mathematics education (K-6) (MA); measurement and evaluation (M Ed); science (5-12) (Postbaccalaureate Certificate); science (5-9) (MAT, Postbaccalaureate Certificate); science education (5-12) (MA), including biology, chemistry, geology, physics; science education (5-9) (MA); social science (5-12) (MAT, Postbaccalaureate Certificate); special education (MAT, MS). *Accreditation:* NCATE. *Program availability:* Evening/weekend, online learning. *Degree requirements:* For master's, capstone project. *Entrance requirements:* For master's and Postbaccalaureate Certificate, Readiness Assessment, transcripts. Additional exam requirements/recommendations for international students: Required—TOEFL (minimum score 450 paper-based; 80 iBT). Electronic applications accepted. *Expenses:* Contact institution.

Western Michigan University, Graduate College, College of Arts and Sciences, Department of Interdisciplinary Arts and Sciences, Kalamazoo, MI 49008. Offers science education (MA, PhD), including biological sciences (PhD), chemistry (PhD), geosciences (PhD), physical geography (PhD), physics (PhD), science education (PhD). *Degree requirements:* For doctorate, thesis/dissertation.

Western Oregon University, Graduate Programs, College of Education, Division of Teacher Education, Program in Secondary Education, Monmouth, OR 97361. Offers bilingual education (MS Ed); health (MS Ed); humanities (MAT, MS Ed); initial licensure (MAT); mathematics (MAT, MS Ed); science (MAT, MS Ed); social science (MAT, MS Ed). *Accreditation:* NCATE. *Program availability:* Part-time, evening/weekend. *Degree requirements:* For master's, thesis optional, written exam. *Entrance requirements:* For master's, minimum GPA of 3.0, teaching license. Additional exam requirements/recommendations for international students: Required—TOEFL (minimum score 550 paper-based; 79 iBT), IELTS (minimum score 6.5). *Faculty research:* Literacy, science in primary grades, geography education, retention, teacher burnout.

Western Washington University, Graduate School, College of Sciences and Technology, Program in Natural Science/Science Education, Bellingham, WA 98225-5996. Offers M Ed. Electronic applications accepted. *Faculty research:* Science education reform.

Westfield State University, College of Graduate and Continuing Education, Department of Education, Westfield, MA 01086. Offers early childhood education (M Ed); elementary education (M Ed); reading specialist (M Ed); secondary education (M Ed), including biology teacher education, chemistry teacher education, general science teacher education, history teacher education, mathematics teacher education, physical education teacher education; special education (M Ed), including moderate disabilities, 5-12, moderate disabilities, preK-8; vocational technical education (M Ed). *Accreditation:* NCATE. *Program availability:* Part-time, evening/weekend. *Faculty:* 16 full-time (7 women), 33 part-time/adjunct (24 women). *Students:* 21 full-time (10 women), 168 part-time (126 women); includes 6 minority (2 Black or African American, non-Hispanic/Latino; 2 Hispanic/Latino; 2 Two or more races, non-Hispanic/Latino), 1 international. Average age 32. 47 applicants, 85% accepted, 30 enrolled. In 2016, 51 master's awarded. *Degree requirements:* For master's, comprehensive exam, practicum. *Entrance requirements:* For master's, GRE General Test or MAT, minimum undergraduate GPA of 2.8. Additional exam requirements/recommendations for international students: Recommended—TOEFL (minimum score 550 paper-based; 79 iBT). *Application deadline:* For fall admission, 6/30 for domestic students; for spring admission, 10/31 for domestic students; for summer admission, 3/31 for domestic students. Applications are processed on a rolling basis. Application fee: $50. Electronic applications accepted. *Expenses:* Tuition, state resident: part-time $318 per semester hour. Tuition, nonresident: part-time $318 per semester hour. *Required fees:* $75 per semester. Tuition and fees vary according to course load and program. *Financial support:* Unspecified assistantships and SOS scholarships for education majors only available. Financial award application deadline: 3/1; financial award applicants required to submit FAFSA. *Faculty research:* Collaborative teacher education, developmental early childhood education. *Unit head:* Dr. Sandra Berkowitz, Department Chair, 413-572-5323, E-mail: sberkowitz@westfield.ma.edu. *Application contact:* Shelly Henrichon, Coordinator of DGCE Admissions, 413-572-8022, Fax: 413-572-5227, E-mail: mhenrichon@westfield.ma.edu.
Website: http://www.westfield.ma.edu/academics/degrees/education-graduate-programs

Westfield State University, College of Graduate and Continuing Education, Department of Education, Programs in Secondary Education, Program in Biology Teacher Education, Westfield, MA 01086. Offers secondary education-biology (M Ed). *Program availability:* Part-time, evening/weekend. *Faculty:* 2 full-time (1 woman). *Students:* 1 full-time (0 women), 4 part-time (3 women). Average age 22. 2 applicants, 50% accepted, 1 enrolled. In 2016, 3 master's awarded. *Degree requirements:* For master's, comprehensive exam, thesis (for some programs). *Entrance requirements:* For master's, GRE General Test or MAT, minimum undergraduate GPA of 2.8. Additional exam requirements/recommendations for international students: Recommended—TOEFL (minimum score 550 paper-based; 79 iBT). *Application deadline:* For fall admission, 6/30 for domestic students; for spring admission, 10/31 for domestic students; for summer admission, 3/31 for domestic students. Applications are processed on a rolling basis. Application fee: $50. *Expenses:* Tuition, state resident: part-time $318 per semester hour. Tuition, nonresident: part-time $318 per semester hour. *Required fees:* $75 per semester. Tuition and fees vary according to course load and program. *Financial support:* Unspecified assistantships and SOS scholarships for education majors only available. Financial award application deadline: 3/1; financial award applicants required to submit FAFSA. *Unit head:* Dr. Sandra Berkowitz, Chair, 413-572-5323. *Application contact:* Shelly Henrichon, Coordinator of DGCE Admissions, 413-572-8022, Fax: 413-572-5227, E-mail: mhenrichon@westfield.ma.edu.

Westfield State University, College of Graduate and Continuing Education, Department of Education, Programs in Secondary Education, Program in Chemistry Teacher Education, Westfield, MA 01086. Offers secondary education-chemistry (M Ed). *Program availability:* Part-time, evening/weekend. *Faculty:* 1 full-time (0 women). *Degree requirements:* For master's, comprehensive exam, thesis (for some programs). *Entrance requirements:* For master's, GRE General Test or MAT, minimum undergraduate GPA of 2.8. Additional exam requirements/recommendations for international students: Recommended—TOEFL (minimum score 550 paper-based; 79 iBT). *Application deadline:* For fall admission, 6/30 for domestic students; for spring admission, 10/31 for domestic students; for summer admission, 3/31 for domestic students. Applications are processed on a rolling basis. Application fee: $50. *Expenses:* Tuition, state resident: part-time $318 per semester hour. Tuition, nonresident: part-time $318 per semester hour. *Required fees:* $75 per semester. Tuition and fees vary according to course load and program. *Financial support:* Unspecified assistantships and SOS scholarships for education majors only available. Financial award application deadline: 3/1; financial award applicants required to submit FAFSA. *Unit head:* Dr. Sandra Berkowitz, Chair, 413-572-5323. *Application contact:* Shelly Henrichon, Coordinator of DGCE Admissions, 413-572-8022, Fax: 413-572-5227, E-mail: mhenrichon@westfield.ma.edu.

Westfield State University, College of Graduate and Continuing Education, Department of Education, Programs in Secondary Education, Program in General Science Teacher Education, Westfield, MA 01086. Offers secondary education-general science (M Ed). *Program availability:* Part-time, evening/weekend. *Faculty:* 1 full-time (0 women). *Students:* 3 part-time (all women). In 2016, 2 master's awarded. *Degree requirements:* For master's, comprehensive exam, thesis (for some programs). *Entrance requirements:* For master's, GRE General Test or MAT, minimum undergraduate GPA of 2.8. Additional exam requirements/recommendations for international students: Recommended—TOEFL (minimum score 550 paper-based; 79 iBT). *Application deadline:* For fall admission, 6/30 for domestic students; for spring admission, 10/31 for domestic students; for summer admission, 3/31 for domestic students. Applications are processed on a rolling basis. Application fee: $50. *Expenses:* Tuition, state resident: part-time $318 per semester hour. Tuition, nonresident: part-time $318 per semester hour. *Required fees:* $75 per semester. Tuition and fees vary according to course load and program. *Financial support:* Unspecified assistantships and SOS scholarships for education majors only available. Financial award application deadline: 3/1; financial award applicants required to submit FAFSA. *Unit head:* Dr. Sandra Berkowitz, Chair, 413-572-5323. *Application contact:* Shelly Henrichon, Coordinator of DGCE Admissions, 413-572-8022, Fax: 413-572-5227, E-mail: mhenrichon@westfield.ma.edu.

Widener University, School of Education, Hospitality, and Continuing Studies, Chester, PA 19013-5792. Offers adult education (M Ed); counseling in higher education (M Ed); counselor education (M Ed); early childhood education (M Ed); educational foundations (M Ed); educational leadership (M Ed); educational psychology (M Ed); elementary education (M Ed); English and language arts (M Ed); health education (M Ed); higher education leadership (Ed D); home and school visitor (M Ed); human sexuality (M Ed, PhD); mathematics education (M Ed); middle school education (M Ed); principalship (M Ed); reading and language arts (Ed D); reading education (M Ed); school administration (Ed D); science education (M Ed); social studies education (M Ed); special education (M Ed); technology education (M Ed). *Accreditation:* NCATE. *Program availability:* Part-time, evening/weekend. *Faculty:* 34 full-time (22 women), 37 part-time/adjunct (14 women). *Students:* 97 full-time (64 women), 201 part-time (143 women); includes 56 minority (44 Black or African American, non-Hispanic/Latino; 1 American Indian or Alaska Native, non-Hispanic/Latino; 2 Asian, non-Hispanic/Latino; 8 Hispanic/Latino; 1 Two or more races, non-Hispanic/Latino), 32 international. Average age 39. 139 applicants, 88% accepted. In 2016, 45 master's, 21 doctorates awarded. Terminal master's awarded for partial completion of doctoral program. *Degree requirements:* For doctorate, thesis/dissertation. *Entrance requirements:* For master's, minimum GPA of 2.5; for doctorate, GRE or MAT, minimum GPA of 2.0 (undergraduate), 3.5 (graduate). *Application deadline:* Applications are processed on a rolling basis. Application fee: $25 ($300 for international students). Electronic applications accepted. *Expenses:* Contact institution. *Financial support:* Career-related internships or fieldwork, tuition waivers (full and partial), and unspecified assistantships available. Support available to part-time students. Financial award application deadline: 5/1. *Faculty research:* Reading and cognition, adult education, technology education, educational leadership, special education. *Unit head:* Dr. Shawn Fitzgerald, Dean, 610-499-4294, Fax: 610-499-4623, E-mail: smfitzgerald@widener.edu. *Application contact:* Dr. Roberta Nolan, Director of Graduate Admissions, 610-499-4125, E-mail: rdnolan@widener.edu.
Website: http://www.widener.edu/academics/schools/eics

Wilkes University, College of Graduate and Professional Studies, School of Education, Wilkes-Barre, PA 18766-0002. Offers 21st century teaching and learning (MS Ed); art and science of teaching (MS Ed); classroom technology (MS Ed); early childhood literacy (MS Ed); educational development and strategies (MS Ed); educational leadership (MS Ed, Ed D); effective teaching (MS Ed); instructional media (MS Ed); instructional technology (MS Ed); international school leadership (MS Ed); international teaching and learning (MS Ed); middle level education (MS Ed); online teaching (MS Ed); reading (MS Ed); school business leadership (MS Ed); special education (MS Ed); teaching English to speakers of other languages (MS Ed). *Program availability:* Part-time, evening/weekend, 100% online, blended/hybrid learning. *Students:* 87 full-time (70 women), 1,496 part-time (1,111 women); includes 77 minority (11 Black or African American, non-Hispanic/Latino; 2 American Indian or Alaska Native, non-Hispanic/Latino; 12 Asian, non-Hispanic/Latino; 28 Hispanic/Latino; 3 Native Hawaiian or other Pacific Islander, non-Hispanic/Latino; 21 Two or more races, non-Hispanic/Latino). Average age 33. In 2016, 524 master's, 21 doctorates awarded. *Entrance requirements:* Additional exam requirements/recommendations for international students: Required—TOEFL (minimum score 550 paper-based; 79 iBT). *Application deadline:* Applications are processed on a rolling basis. Application fee: $45. Electronic applications accepted. *Expenses:* Contact institution. *Financial support:* Unspecified assistantships available. Financial award application deadline: 3/1; financial award applicants required to submit FAFSA. *Unit head:* Dr. Rhonda Rabbitt, Dean, 570-408-4680, Fax: 570-408-7872, E-mail: rhonda.rabbitt@wilkes.edu. *Application contact:* Director of Graduate Education, 570-408-4234, Fax: 570-408-7846.
Website: http://www.wilkes.edu/academics/graduate-programs/masters-programs/graduate-education/index.aspx

Wisconsin Lutheran College, College of Adult and Graduate Studies, Milwaukee, WI 53226-9942. Offers high performance instruction (MA Ed); instructional technology (MA Ed); leadership and innovation (MA Ed); science instruction (MA Ed).

Wright State University, Graduate School, College of Science and Mathematics, Department of Earth and Environmental Sciences, Program in Earth Science Education, Dayton, OH 45435. Offers MST. *Entrance requirements:* For master's, GRE General Test. Additional exam requirements/recommendations for international students: Required—TOEFL. Application fee: $25. *Expenses:* Tuition, state resident: full-time $9952; part-time $622 per credit hour. Tuition, nonresident: full-time $16,960; part-time $1060 per credit hour. *Financial support:* Fellowships, research assistantships, and teaching assistantships available. Support available to part-time students. Financial award application deadline: 3/1; financial award applicants required to submit FAFSA. *Faculty research:* Pedagogy. *Unit head:* Dr. William Slattery, Program Director, 937-775-3441, Fax: 937-775-3462, E-mail: william.slattery@wright.edu. *Application contact:* Deborah L. Cowles, Assistant to Chair, 937-775-3455, Fax: 937-775-3462, E-mail: deborah.cowles@wright.edu.

Wright State University, Graduate School, College of Science and Mathematics, Interdisciplinary Program in Science and Mathematics, Dayton, OH 45435. Offers PhD. *Expenses:* Tuition, state resident: full-time $9952; part-time $622 per credit hour. Tuition, nonresident: full-time $16,960; part-time $1060 per credit hour. *Unit head:* Dr. Beth Basista, Director, 937-775-2954, Fax: 937-775-2571, E-mail: beth.basista@wright.edu. *Application contact:* John Kimble, Associate Director of Graduate Admissions and Records, 937-775-2957, Fax: 937-775-2453, E-mail: john.kimble@wright.edu.

Youngstown State University, Graduate School, College of Science, Technology, Engineering and Mathematics, Department of Chemistry, Youngstown, OH 44555-0001. Offers analytical chemistry (MS); biochemistry (MS); chemistry education (MS); inorganic chemistry (MS); organic chemistry (MS); physical chemistry (MS). *Program availability:* Part-time. *Degree requirements:* For master's, thesis. *Entrance requirements:* For master's, bachelor's degree in chemistry, minimum GPA of 2.7. Additional exam requirements/recommendations for international students: Required—TOEFL. *Faculty research:* Analysis of antioxidants, chromatography, defects and disorder in crystalline oxides, hydrogen bonding, novel organic and organometallic materials.

Social Sciences Education

Acadia University, Faculty of Professional Studies, School of Education, Program in Curriculum Studies, Wolfville, NS B4P 2R6, Canada. Offers cultural and media studies (M Ed); learning and technology (M Ed); science, math and technology (M Ed). *Program availability:* Part-time. *Degree requirements:* For master's, thesis optional. *Entrance requirements:* For master's, B Ed or the equivalent, minimum B average in undergraduate course work, 2 years of teaching experience. Additional exam requirements/recommendations for international students: Required—TOEFL (minimum score 580 paper-based; 93 iBT), IELTS (minimum score 6.5). *Faculty research:* Literacy development, postmodern philosophy and curriculum theory, historiography, philosophy of education, learning and technology.

Alabama Agricultural and Mechanical University, School of Graduate Studies, College of Education, Humanities, and Behavioral Sciences, Department of Educational Leadership and Secondary Education, Huntsville, AL 35811. Offers biology (M Ed); business/marketing education (M Ed, Ed S); chemistry (M Ed); collaborative teacher secondary education (M Ed, Ed S); education (M Ed, Ed S); English language arts (M Ed); family/consumer science education (M Ed, Ed S); general science (M Ed); general social science (M Ed); mathematics (M Ed, Ed S); physics (M Ed, Ed S); technology education (M Ed). *Accreditation:* NCATE. *Program availability:* Evening/weekend. *Degree requirements:* For master's, comprehensive exam; for Ed S, thesis. *Entrance requirements:* For master's, GRE General Test. Additional exam requirements/recommendations for international students: Required—TOEFL (minimum score 500 paper-based; 61 iBT). *Application deadline:* For fall admission, 5/1 for domestic students. Applications are processed on a rolling basis. Application fee: $25. Electronic applications accepted. *Expenses:* Tuition, nonresident: part-time $826 per credit hour. Full-time tuition and fees vary according to course load and program. *Financial support:* Research assistantships, career-related internships or fieldwork, Federal Work-Study, institutionally sponsored loans, and traineeships available. Financial award application deadline: 4/1. *Faculty research:* World peace through education, computer-assisted instruction. *Unit head:* Dr. Derrick Davis, Chair, 256-372-4047, Fax: 256-372-5526.

Alabama State University, College of Education, Department of Curriculum and Instruction, Montgomery, AL 36101-0271. Offers early childhood education (M Ed, Ed S); elementary education (M Ed, Ed S); secondary education (M Ed, Ed S), including biology education, English language arts education (M Ed), history education, math education, music education (M Ed), reading education (M Ed), social science education; special education (M Ed). *Program availability:* Part-time. *Faculty:* 7 full-time (4 women), 7 part-time/adjunct (4 women). *Students:* 37 full-time (30 women), 82 part-time (69 women); includes 117 minority (115 Black or African American, non-Hispanic/Latino; 2 Two or more races, non-Hispanic/Latino). Average age 33. 65 applicants, 55% accepted, 22 enrolled. In 2016, 25 master's, 5 Ed Ss awarded. *Degree requirements:* For master's, comprehensive exam, thesis optional; for Ed S, comprehensive exam, thesis. *Entrance requirements:* For master's, GRE General Test, MAT, writing competency test; for Ed S, writing competency test, GRE, MAT. Additional exam requirements/recommendations for international students: Required—TOEFL (minimum score 500 paper-based). *Application deadline:* For fall admission, 4/15 for domestic and international students; for spring admission, 11/15 for domestic and international students; for summer admission, 3/15 for domestic and international students. Applications are processed on a rolling basis. Application fee: $25. Electronic applications accepted. *Expenses:* Tuition, state resident: full-time $3087; part-time $2744 per credit. Tuition, nonresident: full-time $6174; part-time $5488 per credit. *Required fees:* $2284; $1142 per credit. $571 per semester. Tuition and fees vary according to class time, course level, course load, degree level, program and student level. *Financial support:* Research assistantships available. Financial award application deadline: 6/30; financial award applicants required to submit FAFSA. *Unit head:* Dr. Joyce Johnson, Acting Chairperson, 334-229-4485, Fax: 334-229-5603, E-mail: jjohnson@alasu.edu. *Application contact:* Dr. William Person, Dean of Graduate Studies, 334-229-4274, Fax: 334-229-4928, E-mail: wperson@alasu.edu.
Website: http://www.alasu.edu/academics/colleges—departments/college-of-education/curriculum—instruction/index.aspx

American Public University System, AMU/APU Graduate Programs, Charles Town, WV 25414. Offers accounting (MBA, MS); applied business analytics (MBA, MS); criminal justice (MA), including business administration, emergency and disaster management, general (MA, MS); educational leadership (M Ed); emergency and disaster management (MA); entrepreneurship (MBA); environmental policy and management (MS), including environmental planning, environmental sustainability, fish and wildlife management, general (MA, MS), global environmental management; finance (MBA); general (MBA); government contracting and acquisition (MBA); health care administration (MBA); health information management (MS); history (MA), including American history, ancient and classical history, European history, global history, public history; homeland security (MA), including business administration, counterterrorism studies, criminal justice, cyber, emergency management and public health, intelligence studies, transportation security; homeland security resource allocation (MBA); humanities (MA); information technology (MS), including digital forensics, enterprise software development, information assurance and security, IT project management; information technology management (MBA); intelligence studies (MA), including criminal intelligence, cyber, general (MA, MS), homeland security, intelligence analysis, intelligence collection, intelligence management, intelligence operations, terrorism studies; international relations and conflict resolution (MA), including comparative and security issues, conflict resolution, international and transnational security issues, peacekeeping; legal studies (MA); management (MA), including strategic consulting; marketing (MBA); military history (MA), including American military history, American Revolution, civil war, war since 1945, World War II; military studies (MA), including joint warfare, strategic leadership; national security studies (MA), including cyber, general (MA, MS), homeland security, regional security studies, security and intelligence analysis, terrorism studies; nonprofit management (MBA); political science (MA), including American politics and government, comparative government and development, general (MA, MS), international relations, public policy; psychology (MA); public administration (MPA), including disaster management, environmental policy, health policy, human resources, national security, organizational management, security management; public health (MPH); reverse logistics management (MA); security

management (MA); space studies (MS), including aerospace science, general (MA, MS), planetary science; sports and health sciences (MS); sports management (MBA); teaching (M Ed), including autism spectrum disorder, curriculum and instruction for elementary teachers, elementary reading, English language learners, instructional leadership, online learning, special education, STEAM (STEM plus the arts); transportation and logistics management (MA). *Program availability:* Part-time, evening/weekend, online only, 100% online. *Faculty:* 401 full-time (228 women), 1,678 part-time/adjunct (781 women). *Students:* 378 full-time (184 women), 8,455 part-time (3,484 women); includes 2,972 minority (1,552 Black or African American, non-Hispanic/Latino; 52 American Indian or Alaska Native, non-Hispanic/Latino; 211 Asian, non-Hispanic/Latino; 791 Hispanic/Latino; 70 Native Hawaiian or other Pacific Islander, non-Hispanic/Latino; 296 Two or more races, non-Hispanic/Latino), 109 international. Average age 37. In 2016, 3,185 master's awarded. *Degree requirements:* For master's, comprehensive exam or practicum. *Entrance requirements:* For master's, official transcript showing earned bachelor's degree from institution accredited by recognized accrediting body. Additional exam requirements/recommendations for international students: Required—TOEFL (minimum score 550 paper-based), IELTS (minimum score 6.5). *Application deadline:* Applications are processed on a rolling basis. Application fee: $0. Electronic applications accepted. *Expenses: Tuition:* Part-time $350 per credit hour. *Required fees:* $50 per course. *Financial support:* Scholarships/grants available. Financial award applicants required to submit FAFSA. *Unit head:* Dr. Karan Powell, President, 877-468-6268, Fax: 304-724-3780. *Application contact:* Terry Grant, Vice President of Enrollment Management, 877-468-6268, Fax: 304-724-3780, E-mail: info@apus.edu.
Website: http://www.apus.edu

Andrews University, School of Graduate Studies, School of Education, Department of Teaching, Learning, and Curriculum, Berrien Springs, MI 49104. Offers curriculum and instruction (MA, Ed D, PhD, Ed S); elementary education (MAT); secondary education (MAT), including biology, education, English, English as a second language, French, history, physics; teacher education (MAT). *Faculty:* 7 full-time (5 women). *Students:* 17 full-time (12 women), 10 part-time (all women); includes 11 minority (6 Black or African American, non-Hispanic/Latino; 5 Hispanic/Latino), 7 international. Average age 38. In 2016, 9 master's, 7 doctorates awarded. *Entrance requirements:* For master's, GRE Subject Test. Additional exam requirements/recommendations for international students: Required—TOEFL (minimum score 550 paper-based). *Application deadline:* For fall admission, 8/15 for domestic students. Applications are processed on a rolling basis. Application fee: $40. *Unit head:* Dr. Lee C. Davidson, Chair, 269-471-6364. *Application contact:* Justina Clayburn, Supervisor of Graduate Admission, 800-253-2874, Fax: 269-471-6321, E-mail: graduate@andrews.edu.

Appalachian State University, Cratis D. Williams Graduate School, Department of Curriculum and Instruction, Boone, NC 28608. Offers curriculum specialist (MA); educational media (MA); elementary education (MA); middle grades education (MA), including language arts, mathematics, science, social studies. *Accreditation:* NCATE. *Program availability:* Part-time, evening/weekend, online learning. *Degree requirements:* For master's, comprehensive exam, thesis or alternative. *Entrance requirements:* For master's, GRE General Test or MAT, 3 letters of recommendation. Additional exam requirements/recommendations for international students: Required—TOEFL (minimum score 570 paper-based; 79 iBT), IELTS (minimum score 6.5). *Application deadline:* For fall admission, 3/14 for domestic students, 2/1 for international students; for spring admission, 11/1 for domestic students, 7/1 for international students. Applications are processed on a rolling basis. Application fee: $55. Electronic applications accepted. *Expenses:* Tuition, state resident: full-time $4744. Tuition, nonresident: full-time $17,913. Full-time tuition and fees vary according to program. *Financial support:* Fellowships, research assistantships, teaching assistantships, career-related internships or fieldwork, Federal Work-Study, scholarships/grants, and unspecified assistantships available. Financial award application deadline: 4/1; financial award applicants required to submit FAFSA. *Faculty research:* Media literacy, elementary teaching, curriculum development, online learning environments. *Unit head:* Dr. Michael Jacobson, Chairperson, 828-262-2224. *Application contact:* Dr. Chrystal Dean, Program Director, 828-262-8009, E-mail: deanco@appstate.edu.
Website: http://www.ced.appstate.edu/departments/ci

Arkansas State University, Graduate School, College of Humanities and Social Sciences, Department of Criminology, Sociology, and Geography, State University, AR 72467. Offers criminal justice (MA); sociology (MA); sociology education (SCCT). *Program availability:* Part-time. *Degree requirements:* For master's, one foreign language, comprehensive exam, thesis or alternative; for SCCT, comprehensive exam. *Entrance requirements:* For master's, GRE General Test or MAT, appropriate bachelor's degree, letters of recommendation, official transcripts, immunization records; for SCCT, GRE General Test or MAT, interview, master's degree, official transcript, immunization records. Additional exam requirements/recommendations for international students: Required—TOEFL (minimum score 550 paper-based; 79 iBT), IELTS (minimum score 6), PTE (minimum score 56). Electronic applications accepted.

Arkansas State University, Graduate School, College of Humanities and Social Sciences, Department of History, State University, AR 72467. Offers history (MA); history education (SCCT); social science education (MSE). *Program availability:* Part-time. *Degree requirements:* For master's, comprehensive exam, thesis or alternative; for SCCT, comprehensive exam. *Entrance requirements:* For master's, GRE General Test or MAT, GMAT, appropriate bachelor's degree, letters of reference, official transcript, valid teaching certificate (for MSE), immunization records; for SCCT, GRE General Test or MAT, interview, master's degree, letters of reference, official transcript, immunization records. Additional exam requirements/recommendations for international students: Required—TOEFL (minimum score 550 paper-based; 79 iBT), IELTS (minimum score 6), PTE (minimum score 56). Electronic applications accepted.

Arkansas State University, Graduate School, College of Humanities and Social Sciences, Department of Political Science, State University, AR 72467. Offers political science (MA); political science education (SCCT); public administration (MPA). *Accreditation:* NASPAA (one or more programs are accredited). *Program availability:* Part-time. *Degree requirements:* For master's, comprehensive exam, thesis or alternative; for SCCT, comprehensive exam. *Entrance requirements:* For master's, GRE General Test or MAT, GMAT, appropriate bachelor's degree, letters of recommendation, official transcripts, immunization records, statement of purpose; for SCCT, GRE General Test or MAT, GMAT, interview, master's degree, official transcript, letters of recommendation, immunization records. Additional exam requirements/recommendations for international students: Required—TOEFL (minimum score 550 paper-based; 79 iBT), IELTS (minimum score 6), PTE (minimum score 56). Electronic applications accepted.

Arkansas State University, Graduate School, College of Humanities and Social Sciences, Heritage Studies Program, State University, AR 72467. Offers heritage studies (MA, PhD). *Program availability:* Part-time. *Degree requirements:* For master's, comprehensive exam, thesis or alternative, portfolio; for doctorate, comprehensive exam, thesis/dissertation, portfolio. *Entrance requirements:* For master's, GRE, MAT or GMAT, appropriate bachelor's degree, letters of reference, official transcript, interview, letter of interest, writing sample, immunization records; for doctorate, GRE, MAT, or GMAT, appropriate bachelor's or master's degree, interview, letters of reference, official transcript, letter of interest, writing sample, immunization records. Additional exam requirements/recommendations for international students: Required—TOEFL (minimum score 550 paper-based; 79 iBT), IELTS (minimum score 6), PTE (minimum score 56). Electronic applications accepted.

Asbury University, School of Graduate and Professional Studies, Wilmore, KY 40390-1198. Offers biology: alternative certificate (MA Ed); chemistry: alternative certificate (MA Ed); English (MA Ed); English as a second language (MA Ed); ESL (MA Ed); French (MA Ed); Latin: alternative certificate (MA Ed); mathematics: alternative certificate (MA Ed); reading/writing endorsement (MA Ed); social studies (MA Ed); social work (MSW), including child and family services; Spanish (MA Ed); special education (MA Ed); special education: alternative certificate (MA Ed); teacher as leader endorsement (MA Ed). *Accreditation:* NCATE. *Program availability:* Part-time. *Degree requirements:* For master's, action research project, portfolio. *Entrance requirements:* For master's, PRAXIS/NTE, minimum GPA of 2.75, letters of recommendation. Additional exam requirements/recommendations for international students: Required—TOEFL (minimum score 550 paper-based). Electronic applications accepted.

Binghamton University, State University of New York, Graduate School, Graduate School of Education, Program in Adolescence Education, Binghamton, NY 13902-6000. Offers biology education (MAT, MS Ed); chemistry education (MAT, MS Ed); earth science education (MAT, MS Ed); English education (MAT, MS Ed); French education (MAT, MS Ed); literacy education (MS Ed); mathematical sciences education (MAT, MS Ed); physics (MAT, MS Ed); social studies (MAT, MS Ed); Spanish education (MAT, MS Ed). *Accreditation:* TEAC. *Program availability:* Part-time, evening/weekend. *Students:* 59 full-time (36 women), 7 part-time (2 women); includes 10 minority (2 Black or African American, non-Hispanic/Latino; 1 American Indian or Alaska Native, non-Hispanic/Latino; 1 Asian, non-Hispanic/Latino; 5 Hispanic/Latino; 1 Two or more races, non-Hispanic/Latino). Average age 26. 46 applicants, 76% accepted, 25 enrolled. In 2016, 26 master's awarded. *Degree requirements:* For master's, portfolio. *Entrance requirements:* For master's, GRE General Test, teaching certification. Additional exam requirements/recommendations for international students: Required—TOEFL (minimum score 550 paper-based; 80 iBT). *Application deadline:* For fall admission, 2/1 priority date for domestic and international students; for spring admission, 10/15 priority date for domestic and international students. Application fee: $75. Electronic applications accepted. *Financial support:* In 2016–17, 6 students received support. Research assistantships, teaching assistantships, career-related internships or fieldwork, Federal Work-Study, institutionally sponsored loans, scholarships/grants, health care benefits, tuition waivers (full and partial), and unspecified assistantships available. Financial award applicants required to submit FAFSA. *Unit head:* Dr. Susan Strehle, Dean, 607-777-7329, E-mail: sstrehle@binghamton.edu. *Application contact:* Ben Balkaya, Assistant Dean and Director, 607-777-2151, Fax: 607-777-2501, E-mail: balkaya@binghamton.edu.

Bloomsburg University of Pennsylvania, School of Graduate Studies, College of Education, Department of Teaching and Learning, Program in Middle Level Education Grades 4-8, Bloomsburg, PA 17815-1301. Offers language arts (M Ed); math (M Ed); science (M Ed); social studies (M Ed). *Accreditation:* NCATE. *Faculty:* 6 full-time (1 woman). *Students:* 3 applicants, 67% accepted. In 2016, 2 master's awarded. *Degree requirements:* For master's, thesis optional, practicum, student teaching. *Entrance requirements:* For master's, MAT, GRE, or PRAXIS, minimum QPA of 3.0, teaching certificate, U.S. citizenship, related undergraduate coursework, professional liability insurance, recent TB test. Additional exam requirements/recommendations for international students: Required—TOEFL (minimum score 550 paper-based), IELTS. *Application deadline:* Applications are processed on a rolling basis. Application fee: $35 ($60 for international students). Electronic applications accepted. *Expenses:* Tuition, state resident: full-time $9660; part-time $483 per credit. Tuition, nonresident: full-time $14,500; part-time $725 per credit. *Required fees:* $2410; $107 per credit. $75 per term. Tuition and fees vary according to course load, degree level and program. *Financial support:* Federal Work-Study and unspecified assistantships available. Financial award applicants required to submit FAFSA. *Unit head:* Dr. Ingrid Everett, Program Coordinator, 570-389-5120, Fax: 570-389-3030, E-mail: ieverett@bloomu.edu. *Application contact:* Jennifer Kessler, Administrative Assistant, 570-389-4015, Fax: 570-389-3054, E-mail: jkessler@bloomu.edu.
Website: http://www.bloomu.edu/gradschool/middle-level-education

Bob Jones University, Graduate Programs, Greenville, SC 29614. Offers accountancy (MS); Bible (MA); Bible translation (MA); Biblical studies (Certificate); broadcast management (MS); business administration (MBA); church history (MA, PhD); church ministries (MA); church music (MM); cinema and video production (MA); counseling (MS); curriculum and instruction (Ed D); divinity (M Div); dramatic production (MA); educational leadership (MS, Ed D, Ed S); elementary education (M Ed, MAT); English (M Ed, MA, MAT); fine arts (MA); graphic design (MA); history (M Ed, MA); illustration (MA); interpretative speech (MA); mathematics (M Ed, MAT); medical missions (Certificate); ministry (MM, D Min); multi-categorical special education (M Ed, MAT); music (M Ed); New Testament interpretation (PhD); Old Testament interpretation (PhD); orchestral instrument performance (MM); organ performance (MM); pastoral studies (MA); personnel services (MS, Ed S); piano pedagogy (MM); piano performance (MM); platform arts (MA); radio and television broadcasting (MS); rhetoric and public address (MA); secondary education (M Ed); studio art (MA); teaching Bible (MA); theology (MA, PhD); voice performance (MM); youth ministries (MA); M Div/MM.

Bridgewater State University, College of Graduate Studies, College of Humanities and Social Sciences, Department of History, Bridgewater, MA 02325. Offers MAT. *Program availability:* Part-time, evening/weekend. *Entrance requirements:* For master's, GRE General Test.

Brooklyn College of the City University of New York, School of Education, Program in Adolescence Science Education and Special Subjects, Brooklyn, NY 11210-2889. Offers adolescence science education (MAT); biology teacher (7-12) (MA); chemistry teacher (7-12) (MA); earth science teacher (7-12) (MAT); English teacher (7-12) (MA); French teacher (7-12) (MA); mathematics teacher (7-12) (MA); music teacher (MA); physics teacher (7-12) (MA); social studies teacher (7-12) (MA); Spanish teacher (7-12) (MA). *Program availability:* Part-time, evening/weekend. *Degree requirements:* For master's, comprehensive exam (for some programs), thesis (for some programs). *Entrance requirements:* For master's, LAST, previous course work in education, resume, 2 letters of recommendation, essay. Additional exam requirements/recommendations for international students: Required—TOEFL (minimum score 500 paper-based; 61 iBT). Electronic applications accepted. *Faculty research:* Interdisciplinary education, semiotics, discourse analysis, autobiography, teacher identity.

Brown University, Graduate School, Department of Education, Program in Teaching, Providence, RI 02912. Offers elementary education (MAT); English (MAT); history/social studies (MAT); science (MAT); secondary education (MAT). *Degree requirements:* For master's, student teaching, portfolio. *Entrance requirements:* For master's, GRE General Test, transcript, personal statement, 3 letters of recommendation, interview, writing sample (English applicants only). Additional exam requirements/recommendations for international students: Required—TOEFL (minimum score 577 paper-based). Electronic applications accepted. *Faculty research:* Literacy, English language learners, diversity, special education, biodiversity.

Buffalo State College, State University of New York, The Graduate School, Faculty of Natural and Social Sciences, Department of History and Social Studies, Buffalo, NY 14222-1095. Offers history (MA); secondary education (MS Ed), including social studies. *Program availability:* Part-time, evening/weekend. *Degree requirements:* For master's, one foreign language, thesis (for some programs), project (MS Ed). *Entrance requirements:* For master's, minimum GPA of 2.75, 30 hours in history (MA), 36 hours in history or social sciences (MS Ed). Additional exam requirements/recommendations for international students: Required—TOEFL (minimum score 550 paper-based).

California State University, East Bay, Office of Graduate Studies, College of Letters, Arts, and Social Sciences, Department of History, Hayward, CA 94542-3000. Offers history (MA); public history (MA); teaching (MA). *Program availability:* Part-time, evening/weekend. *Students:* 3 full-time (1 woman), 20 part-time (12 women); includes 7 minority (2 Black or African American, non-Hispanic/Latino; 4 Hispanic/Latino; 1 Two or more races, non-Hispanic/Latino). Average age 37. 28 applicants, 57% accepted, 13 enrolled. In 2016, 8 master's awarded. *Degree requirements:* For master's, one foreign language, comprehensive exam, project, thesis, or exam. *Entrance requirements:* For master's, GRE (strongly recommended), minimum GPA of 3.0 in field, 3.3 in history; 2 letters of recommendation; writing sample. Additional exam requirements/recommendations for international students: Required—TOEFL (minimum score 550 paper-based). *Application deadline:* For fall admission, 5/16 for domestic and international students. Applications are processed on a rolling basis. Application fee: $55. Electronic applications accepted. *Financial support:* Fellowships, teaching assistantships, career-related internships or fieldwork, Federal Work-Study, institutionally sponsored loans, and scholarships/grants available. Support available to part-time students. Financial award application deadline: 3/2; financial award applicants required to submit FAFSA. *Faculty research:* Digital history, American women, early America, Native Americans, medieval colonial India. *Unit head:* Dr. Linda L. Ivey, Chair, 510-885-4015, E-mail: linda.ivey@csueastbay.edu. *Application contact:* Dr. Khal Schneider, Graduate Coordinator, 510-885-3237, Fax: 510-885-4791, E-mail: khal.schneider@csueastbay.edu.
Website: http://www20.csueastbay.edu/class/departments/history/

California State University, Fresno, Division of Research and Graduate Studies, College of Social Sciences, Department of History, Fresno, CA 93740-8027. Offers history (MA); history teaching (MA). *Program availability:* Part-time, evening/weekend. *Degree requirements:* For master's, project; thesis or comprehensive examination. *Entrance requirements:* For master's, GRE General Test, minimum GPA of 3.0. Additional exam requirements/recommendations for international students: Required—TOEFL. *Application deadline:* For fall admission, 6/1 for domestic and international students; for spring admission, 11/1 for domestic and international students. Applications are processed on a rolling basis. Application fee: $55. Electronic applications accepted. *Financial support:* Teaching assistantships, career-related internships or fieldwork, Federal Work-Study, scholarships/grants, and unspecified assistantships available. Support available to part-time students. Financial award application deadline: 3/1; financial award applicants required to submit FAFSA. *Faculty research:* International education, classical art history, improving teacher quality. *Unit head:* Michelle DenBeste, Chair, 559-278-2153, Fax: 559-278-5321, E-mail: michelle_denbeste@csufresno.edu. *Application contact:* Dr. Brad Jones, Graduate Program Coordinator, 559-278-2153, Fax: 559-278-5321, E-mail: brajones@csufresno.edu.
Website: http://www.fresnostate.edu/socialsciences/historydept/

Cambridge College, School of Education, Cambridge, MA 02138-5304. Offers autism specialist (M Ed); autism/behavior analyst (M Ed); behavior analyst (Post-Master's Certificate); behavioral management (M Ed); early childhood teacher (M Ed); education specialist in curriculum and instruction (CAGS); educational leadership (Ed D); elementary teacher (M Ed); English as a second language (M Ed, Certificate); general science (M Ed); health education (Post-Master's Certificate); health/family and consumer sciences (M Ed); history (M Ed); individualized (M Ed); information technology literacy (M Ed); instructional technology (M Ed); interdisciplinary studies (M Ed); library teacher (M Ed); literacy education (M Ed); mathematics (M Ed); mathematics specialist (Certificate); middle school mathematics and science (M Ed); school administration (M Ed, CAGS); school guidance counselor (M Ed); school nurse education (M Ed); school social worker/school adjustment counselor (M Ed); special education administrator (CAGS); special education/moderate disabilities (M Ed); teaching skills and methodologies (M Ed). *Program availability:* Part-time, evening/weekend, online learning. *Degree requirements:* For master's, thesis, internship/practicum (licensure program only); for doctorate, thesis/dissertation; for other advanced degree, thesis. *Entrance requirements:* For master's, interview, resume, documentation of licensure, 2 professional references; for doctorate, official transcripts, interview, resume, documentation of licensure (if any), written personal statement/essay, portfolio of scholarly and professional work, qualifying assessment, 2 professional references, health insurance, immunizations form; for other advanced degree, official transcripts, interview, resume, documentation of licensure (if any), written personal statement/essay, 2 professional references, health insurance, immunizations form. Additional exam requirements/recommendations for international students: Required—TOEFL (minimum score 550 paper-based; 79 iBT), Michigan English Language Assessment Battery (minimum score 85); Recommended—IELTS (minimum score 6). Electronic applications accepted. *Expenses:* Contact institution. *Faculty research:* Adult education, accelerated learning, mathematics education, brain compatible learning, special education and law.

Caribbean University, Graduate School, Bayamón, PR 00960-0493. Offers administration and supervision (MA Ed); criminal justice (MA); curriculum and instruction (MA Ed, PhD), including elementary education (MA Ed), English education (MA Ed), history education (MA Ed), mathematics education (MA Ed), primary education (MA Ed), science education (MA Ed), Spanish education (MA Ed); educational technology in instructional systems (MA Ed); gerontology (MSN); human resources (MBA); museology, archiving and art history (MA Ed); neonatal pediatrics (MSN); physical education (MA Ed); special education (MA Ed). *Entrance requirements:* For master's, interview, minimum GPA of 2.5.

Carthage College, Division of Teacher Education, Kenosha, WI 53140. Offers classroom guidance and counseling (M Ed); creative arts (M Ed); gifted and talented children (M Ed); language arts (M Ed); modern language (M Ed); natural sciences (M Ed); reading (M Ed, Certificate); social sciences (M Ed); teacher leadership (M Ed). *Program availability:* Part-time, evening/weekend. *Degree requirements:* For master's, thesis optional. *Entrance requirements:* For master's, MAT, minimum B average, letters of reference.

Chadron State College, School of Professional and Graduate Studies, Department of Education, Chadron, NE 69337. Offers business (MA Ed); community counseling (MA Ed); educational administration (MS Ed, Sp Ed); elementary education (MS Ed); history (MA Ed); language and literature (MA Ed); secondary administration (MS Ed); secondary education (MS Ed). *Accreditation:* NCATE. *Program availability:* Part-time, evening/weekend, online learning. *Degree requirements:* For master's, thesis optional. *Entrance requirements:* For master's, GRE General Test, GRE Writing Test, minimum GPA of 2.75 or 12 graduate hours at CSC with minimum GPA of 3.25. Additional exam requirements/recommendations for international students: Required—TOEFL. Electronic applications accepted. *Faculty research:* Rural education, technology, mental health.

Chatham University, Program in Education, Pittsburgh, PA 15232-2826. Offers early childhood education (MAT); elementary education (MAT); environmental education (K-12) (MAT); secondary art (MAT); secondary biology education (MAT); secondary chemistry education (MAT); secondary English education (MAT); secondary math education (MAT); secondary physics education (MAT); secondary social studies education (MAT); special education (MAT). *Degree requirements:* For master's, thesis, teaching experience. *Entrance requirements:* For master's, minimum GPA of 3.0, sample of written work, recommendation letters. Additional exam requirements/recommendations for international students: Required—TOEFL (minimum score 600 paper-based; 100 iBT), IELTS (minimum score 7), TWE. Electronic applications accepted. Application fee is waived when completed online. *Expenses: Tuition:* Full-time $16,254; part-time $903 per credit hour. *Required fees:* $468; $26 per credit hour. *Faculty research:* Gifted education, environmental education, technology in education, writing as learning, class size and achievement.

The Citadel, The Military College of South Carolina, Citadel Graduate College, Zucker Family School of Education, Charleston, SC 29409. Offers elementary/secondary school administration and supervision (M Ed); elementary/secondary school counseling (M Ed); interdisciplinary STEM education (M Ed); literacy education (M Ed, Graduate Certificate); middle grades (MAT), including English, mathematics, science, social studies; physical education (grades K-12) (MAT); school superintendency (Ed S); secondary education (MAT), including biology, English, mathematics, social studies; student affairs (Graduate Certificate); student affairs and college counseling (M Ed). *Accreditation:* NCATE. *Program availability:* Part-time, evening/weekend, 100% online, blended/hybrid learning. *Faculty:* 9 full-time (4 women), 9 part-time/adjunct (5 women). *Students:* 70 full-time (58 women), 249 part-time (200 women); includes 87 minority (70 Black or African American, non-Hispanic/Latino; 1 Asian, non-Hispanic/Latino; 9 Hispanic/Latino; 7 Two or more races, non-Hispanic/Latino), 2 international. 146 applicants, 98% accepted, 105 enrolled. In 2016, 85 master's, 7 other advanced degrees awarded. *Degree requirements:* For master's, comprehensive exam (for some programs). *Entrance requirements:* For master's, GRE (minimum combined verbal and quantitative score of 290) or MAT (minimum score 396). Additional exam requirements/recommendations for international students: Required—TOEFL (minimum score 550 paper-based; 79 iBT). *Application deadline:* Applications are processed on a rolling basis. Application fee: $40. Electronic applications accepted. *Expenses:* Tuition, state resident: full-time $5121; part-time $569 per credit hour. Tuition, nonresident: full-time $8613; part-time $957 per credit hour. *Required fees:* $90 per term. *Financial support:* Fellowships and unspecified assistantships available. Support available to part-time students. Financial award application deadline: 7/1; financial award applicants required to submit FAFSA. *Unit head:* Dr. Larry G. Daniel, Dean, 843-953-5097, E-mail: ldaniel@citadel.edu. *Application contact:* Dr. Tammy J. Graham, Associate Professor, 843-953-6854, E-mail: tammy.graham@citadel.edu.
Website: http://www.citadel.edu/root/education-graduate-programs

City College of the City University of New York, Graduate School, School of Education, Department of Secondary Education, New York, NY 10031-9198. Offers adolescent mathematics education (MA, AC); English education (MA); middle school mathematics education (MS); science education (MA); social studies education (AC). *Accreditation:* NCATE. *Entrance requirements:* For master's, Liberal Arts and Sciences Test (LAST), Content Specialty Test (CST). Additional exam requirements/recommendations for international students: Required—TOEFL. Tuition and fees vary according to course load, degree level and program.

The College at Brockport, State University of New York, School of Education, Health, and Human Services, Department of Education and Human Development, Program in Adolescence Education, Brockport, NY 14420-2997. Offers adolescence biology education (MS Ed); adolescence chemistry education (MS Ed); adolescence earth science education (MS Ed); adolescence English education (MS Ed); adolescence mathematics education (MS Ed); adolescence physics education (MS Ed); adolescence social studies education (MS Ed). *Accreditation:* NCATE. *Program availability:* Part-time. *Students:* 4 full-time (1 woman), 35 part-time (23 women); includes 3 minority (2 Black or African American, non-Hispanic/Latino; 1 Two or more races, non-Hispanic/Latino). 21 applicants, 71% accepted, 11 enrolled. In 2016, 18 master's awarded. *Degree requirements:* For master's, thesis or alternative. *Entrance requirements:* For master's, minimum GPA of 3.0, letters of recommendation, statement of objectives, current resume. Additional exam requirements/recommendations for international students: Required—TOEFL (minimum score 550 paper-based; 79 iBT), IELTS (minimum score 6.5). *Application deadline:* For fall admission, 3/15 priority date for domestic and international students; for spring admission, 10/15 priority date for domestic and international students; for summer admission, 3/15 priority date for domestic students, 3/13 priority date for international students. Application fee: $80. Electronic applications accepted. *Expenses:* Contact institution. *Financial support:* Federal Work-Study, scholarships/grants, and unspecified assistantships available. Support available to part-time students. Financial award application deadline: 3/15; financial award applicants required to submit FAFSA. *Unit head:* Dr. Sue Robb, Chairperson, 585-395-5935, Fax: 585-395-2172, E-mail: srobb@brockport.edu. *Application contact:* Anne Walton, Coordinator of Certification and Graduate Advisement, 585-395-2326, Fax: 585-395-2172, E-mail: awalton@brockport.edu.
Website: http://www.brockport.edu/ehd/

The College at Brockport, State University of New York, School of Education, Health, and Human Services, Department of Education and Human Development, Program in Inclusive Generalist Education, Brockport, NY 14420-2997. Offers biology (MS Ed, AGC); chemistry (MS Ed, AGC); English (MS Ed, Advanced Certificate); mathematics (MS Ed, Advanced Certificate); science (MS Ed, Advanced Certificate); social studies (MS Ed, Advanced Certificate). *Students:* 28 full-time (15 women), 19 part-time (10 women); includes 9 minority (2 Black or African American, non-Hispanic/Latino; 3 Asian, non-Hispanic/Latino; 1 Hispanic/Latino; 3 Two or more races, non-Hispanic/Latino). 21 applicants, 52% accepted, 11 enrolled. In 2016, 12 master's, 3 AGCs awarded. *Degree requirements:* For master's, thesis or alternative. *Entrance requirements:* For master's, minimum GPA of 3.0, letters of recommendation, statement of objectives, academic major (or equivalent) in program discipline, current resume. Additional exam requirements/recommendations for international students: Required—TOEFL (minimum score 550 paper-based; 79 iBT), IELTS (minimum score 6.5). *Application deadline:* For fall admission, 3/15 priority date for domestic and international students; for spring admission, 10/15 priority date for domestic and international students; for summer admission, 3/15 for domestic and international students. Application fee: $80. Electronic applications accepted. *Expenses:* Contact institution. *Financial support:* Federal Work-Study, scholarships/grants, and unspecified assistantships available. Support available to part-time students. Financial award application deadline: 3/15; financial award applicants required to submit FAFSA. *Unit head:* Dr. Sue Robb, Chairperson, 585-395-5935, Fax: 585-395-2171, E-mail: awalton@

brockport.edu. *Application contact:* Anne Walton, Coordinator of Certification and Graduate Advisement, 585-395-2326, Fax: 585-395-2172, E-mail: awalton@brockport.edu.
Website: http://www.brockport.edu/ehd/

College of St. Joseph, Graduate Programs, Division of Education, Program in Secondary Education, Rutland, VT 05701-3899. Offers English (M Ed); social studies (M Ed). *Program availability:* Part-time, evening/weekend. *Degree requirements:* For master's, comprehensive exam. *Entrance requirements:* For master's, PRAXIS I, official college transcripts; 2 letters of reference; minimum GPA of 3.0 (initial licensure) or 2.7 (nonlicensure); interview. Additional exam requirements/recommendations for international students: Required—TOEFL (minimum score 550 paper-based). *Application deadline:* Applications are processed on a rolling basis. Application fee: $35. Electronic applications accepted. *Expenses: Tuition:* Full-time $13,800; part-time $560 per credit. *Required fees:* $75 per semester. Full-time tuition and fees vary according to course load. *Financial support:* Career-related internships or fieldwork, Federal Work-Study, and unspecified assistantships available. Support available to part-time students. Financial award application deadline: 3/1. *Unit head:* Dr. Maria Bove, Chair, 802-773-5900 Ext. 3243, Fax: 802-776-5258, E-mail: mbove@csj.edu. *Application contact:* Alan Young, Director of Admissions, 802-773-5900 Ext. 3227, Fax: 802-776-5310, E-mail: alanyoung@csj.edu.

College of Staten Island of the City University of New York, Graduate Programs, School of Education, Program in Adolescence Education, Staten Island, NY 10314-6600. Offers biology (MS Ed); English (MS Ed); mathematics (MS Ed); social studies (MS Ed). *Program availability:* Part-time, evening/weekend. *Faculty:* 18 full-time, 8 part-time/adjunct. *Students:* 4 full-time, 84 part-time. Average age 29. 40 applicants, 88% accepted, 14 enrolled. In 2016, 41 master's awarded. *Degree requirements:* For master's, thesis, educational research project supervised by faculty; minimum of 33-38 credits distributed among 11 courses or minimum of 46-53 credits. *Entrance requirements:* For master's, GRE General Test or an approved equivalent examination, relevant bachelor's degree, minimum overall GPA of 3.0, two letters of recommendation, one- or two-page personal statement. Additional exam requirements/recommendations for international students: Required—TOEFL (minimum score 550 paper-based; 79 iBT), IELTS (minimum score 6.5). *Application deadline:* For fall admission, 4/25 for domestic and international students; for spring admission, 11/25 for domestic and international students. Applications are processed on a rolling basis. Application fee: $125. Electronic applications accepted. *Expenses:* Tuition, state resident: full-time $10,130; part-time $425 per credit. Tuition, nonresident: full-time $18,720; part-time $780 per credit. *Required fees:* $181.10 per semester. Tuition and fees vary according to program. *Faculty research:* Development and assessment of TPACK (technological pedagogical content knowledge), technology and differentiation in stem classrooms, teacher effectiveness and student achievement, teacher knowledge, knowledge transfer from college to classroom. *Unit head:* Dr. Bethany Rogers, Graduate Faculty Advisor, 718-982-4247, E-mail: bethany.rogers@csi.cuny.edu. *Application contact:* Sasha Spence, Associate Director for Graduate Admissions, 718-982-2019, Fax: 718-982-2500, E-mail: sasha.spence@csi.cuny.edu.
Website: http://www.csi.cuny.edu/catalog/graduate/graduate-programs-in-education.htm#o2608

College of Staten Island of the City University of New York, Graduate Programs, School of Education, Program in Childhood Education, Staten Island, NY 10314-6600. Offers learning and development (MS Ed); literacy education (MS Ed); mathematics education (MS Ed); music education (MS Ed); science education (MS Ed); social foundations of education (MS Ed); social studies education (MS Ed). *Program availability:* Part-time, evening/weekend. *Faculty:* 2 full-time, 11 part-time/adjunct. *Students:* 16 full-time, 53 part-time. Average age 30. 40 applicants, 53% accepted, 13 enrolled. In 2016, 20 master's awarded. *Degree requirements:* For master's, educational research project; ten courses and a minimum of 32-38 credits in five required areas of study or minimum of 45-49 credits in six required core courses before selecting from array of advanced courses. *Entrance requirements:* For master's, GRE General Test or an approved equivalent examination, relevant bachelor's degree, letters of recommendation, one- or two-page personal statement. Additional exam requirements/recommendations for international students: Required—TOEFL (minimum score 550 paper-based; 79 iBT), IELTS (minimum score 6.5). *Application deadline:* For fall admission, 4/25 for domestic and international students; for spring admission, 11/25 for domestic and international students. Applications are processed on a rolling basis. Application fee: $125. Electronic applications accepted. *Expenses:* Tuition, state resident: full-time $10,130; part-time $425 per credit. Tuition, nonresident: full-time $18,720; part-time $780 per credit. *Required fees:* $181.10 per semester. Tuition and fees vary according to program. *Faculty research:* Preservice teacher preparation, music integration, music education through children's songs, literacy, emergent bilingual. *Unit head:* Dr. Vivian Shulman, Graduate Faculty Advisor, 718-982-4086, E-mail: vivian.shulman@csi.cuny.edu. *Application contact:* Sasha Spence, Associate Director for Graduate Admissions, 718-982-2019, Fax: 718-982-2500, E-mail: sasha.spence@csi.cuny.edu.
Website: http://www.csi.cuny.edu/admissions/grad/pdf/Education%20Fact%20Sheet.pdf

The Colorado College, Education Department, Program in Secondary Education, Colorado Springs, CO 80903-3294. Offers art teaching (K-12) (MAT); English teaching (MAT); foreign language teaching (MAT); mathematics teaching (MAT); music teaching (MAT); science teaching (MAT); social studies teaching (MAT). *Degree requirements:* For master's, thesis, internship. Electronic applications accepted.

Columbus State University, Graduate Studies, College of Education and Health Professions, Department of Teacher Education, Columbus, GA 31907-5645. Offers curriculum and instruction in accomplished teaching (M Ed); early childhood education (M Ed, MAT, Ed S); middle grades education (M Ed, MAT, Ed S); secondary education (M Ed, MAT, Ed S), including biology (MAT), chemistry (MAT), earth and space science (MAT), English/language arts, general science (M Ed), history (MAT), mathematics, science (Ed S), social science (M Ed, Ed S); special education (M Ed, MAT, Ed S), including general curriculum (M Ed, MAT); teacher leadership (M Ed). *Accreditation:* NCATE. *Program availability:* Part-time, evening/weekend, 100% online, blended/hybrid learning. *Faculty:* 20 full-time (13 women), 19 part-time/adjunct (16 women). *Students:* 92 full-time (66 women), 212 part-time (179 women); includes 113 minority (104 Black or African American, non-Hispanic/Latino; 1 American Indian or Alaska Native, non-Hispanic/Latino; 2 Asian, non-Hispanic/Latino; 4 Hispanic/Latino; 2 Two or more races, non-Hispanic/Latino), 5 international. Average age 34. 209 applicants, 56% accepted, 79 enrolled. In 2016, 111 master's, 18 other advanced degrees awarded. *Degree requirements:* For Ed S, thesis or alternative. *Entrance requirements:* For master's, GRE General Test, minimum undergraduate GPA of 2.75; for Ed S, GRE General Test, minimum undergraduate GPA of 2.75, graduate 3.0. Additional exam requirements/recommendations for international students: Required—TOEFL (minimum score 550 paper-based; 79 iBT). *Application deadline:* For fall admission, 6/30 for domestic students, 5/1 for international students; for spring admission, 11/1 for domestic and international students; for summer admission, 3/1 for domestic and international students. Applications are processed on a rolling basis. Application fee: $50. Electronic applications accepted. *Expenses:* Tuition, state resident: full-time $4804; part-time $2412 per semester hour. Tuition, nonresident: full-time $19,218; part-time $9612 per semester hour. *Required fees:* $1850; $1850 per semester hour. Tuition and fees vary according to program. *Financial support:* In 2016–17, 60 students received support, including 12 research assistantships with partial tuition reimbursements available (averaging $3,000 per year); career-related internships or fieldwork, Federal Work-Study, institutionally sponsored loans, scholarships/grants, tuition waivers (partial), and unspecified assistantships also available. Support available to part-time students. Financial award application deadline: 5/1; financial award applicants required to submit FAFSA. *Unit head:* Dr. Jan Burcham, Department Chair, 706-507-8519, Fax: 706-568-3134, E-mail: burcham_jan@columbusstate.edu. *Application contact:* Kristin Williams, Director of International and Graduate Recruitment, 706-507-8848, Fax: 706-568-5091, E-mail: williams_kristin@columbusstate.edu.
Website: http://te.columbusstate.edu/

Converse College, School of Education and Graduate Studies, Program in Middle Level Education, Spartanburg, SC 29302. Offers language arts/English (MAT); mathematics (MAT); middle level education (M Ed); science (MAT); social studies (MAT). *Expenses: Tuition:* Full-time $3600; part-time $400 per credit hour. *Required fees:* $70 per term. *Application contact:* 864-596-9404, E-mail: graduate@converse.edu.

Converse College, School of Education and Graduate Studies, Program in Secondary Education, Spartanburg, SC 29302. Offers biology (MAT); chemistry (MAT); English (M Ed, MAT); mathematics (M Ed, MAT); natural sciences (M Ed); social sciences (M Ed, MAT). *Program availability:* Part-time. *Degree requirements:* For master's, capstone paper. *Entrance requirements:* For master's, NTE or PRAXIS II (M Ed), minimum GPA of 2.75, 2 recommendations. *Application deadline:* For fall admission, 8/1 for domestic and international students; for winter admission, 11/15 for domestic and international students; for spring admission, 1/15 for domestic and international students. Applications are processed on a rolling basis. Application fee: $40. Electronic applications accepted. *Expenses: Tuition:* Full-time $3600; part-time $400 per credit hour. *Required fees:* $70 per term. *Financial support:* Available to part-time students. Applicants required to submit FAFSA. *Application contact:* 864-596-9404, E-mail: graduate@converse.edu.

Delta State University, Graduate Programs, College of Arts and Sciences, Division of Social Sciences and History, Cleveland, MS 38733-0001. Offers community development (MS); social justice and criminology (MSJC); social science secondary education (M Ed), including history, social sciences. *Program availability:* Part-time, online learning. *Degree requirements:* For master's, thesis or alternative.

Duquesne University, School of Education, Department of Instruction and Leadership, Program in Secondary Education, Pittsburgh, PA 15282-0001. Offers biology (MS Ed); chemistry (MS Ed); English (MS Ed); K-12 education (MS Ed), including Latin; mathematics (MS Ed); physics (MS Ed); social studies (MS Ed). *Program availability:* Part-time, evening/weekend. *Faculty:* 5 full-time (4 women). *Students:* 21 full-time (8 women), 4 part-time (0 women); includes 3 minority (2 Black or African American, non-Hispanic/Latino; 1 Two or more races, non-Hispanic/Latino). Average age 28. 12 applicants, 100% accepted, 7 enrolled. In 2016, 19 master's awarded. *Degree requirements:* For master's, thesis optional. *Entrance requirements:* For master's, letters of recommendation, letter of intent, interview, bachelor's degree. Additional exam requirements/recommendations for international students: Required—TOEFL (minimum score 550 paper-based), IELTS (minimum score 7). *Application deadline:* For fall admission, 9/1 for domestic students; for spring admission, 1/1 for domestic students. Applications are processed on a rolling basis. Application fee: $0. Electronic applications accepted. *Expenses: Tuition:* Full-time $22,212; part-time $1234 per credit. Tuition and fees vary according to program. *Financial support:* Research assistantships and Federal Work-Study available. Support available to part-time students. *Unit head:* Dr. Melissa Boston, Associate Professor and Director, 412-396-6109, E-mail: bostonm@duq.edu. *Application contact:* Michael Dolinger, Director of Student and Academic Services, 412-396-6647, Fax: 412-396-5585, E-mail: dolingerm@duq.edu.
Website: http://www.duq.edu/academics/schools/education/graduate-programs-education/ms-ed-secondary-education

East Carolina University, Graduate School, College of Education, Department of Elementary and Middle Grades Education, Greenville, NC 27858-4353. Offers elementary education (MA Ed, MAT); English education (MAT); family and consumer science (MAT); health education (MAT); Hispanic studies (MAT); history education (MAT); middle grades education (MA Ed, MAT); music education (MAT); science education (MAT); special education (MAT), including general curriculum; vocational education (MAT). *Accreditation:* NCATE. *Program availability:* Part-time, evening/weekend, online learning. *Students:* 5 full-time (4 women), 18 part-time (16 women); includes 4 minority (3 Black or African American, non-Hispanic/Latino; 1 Hispanic/Latino). Average age 31. 19 applicants, 95% accepted, 13 enrolled. In 2016, 8 master's awarded. *Degree requirements:* For master's, comprehensive exam, thesis optional. *Entrance requirements:* For master's, GRE or MAT, minimum GPA of 2.5, bachelor's degree in related field, teaching license (MA Ed). Additional exam requirements/recommendations for international students: Required—TOEFL. *Application deadline:* For fall admission, 6/1 priority date for domestic students. Applications are processed on a rolling basis. Application fee: $70. *Financial support:* Federal Work-Study available. Support available to part-time students. Financial award application deadline: 6/1. *Unit head:* Dr. Ann Bullock, Chair, 252-328-1126, E-mail: bullockv@ecu.edu. *Application contact:* Dean of Graduate School, 252-328-6012, Fax: 252-328-6071, E-mail: gradschool@ecu.edu.
Website: http://www.ecu.edu/cs-educ/elmid/index.cfm

East Carolina University, Graduate School, College of Education, Department of Literacy Studies, English and History Education, Greenville, NC 27858-4353. Offers history education (MA Ed); reading education (MA Ed). *Accreditation:* NCATE. *Program availability:* Part-time, evening/weekend, online learning. *Students:* 3 full-time (2 women), 44 part-time (42 women); includes 5 minority (4 Black or African American, non-Hispanic/Latino; 1 Hispanic/Latino). Average age 31. 23 applicants, 100% accepted, 20 enrolled. In 2016, 20 master's awarded. *Degree requirements:* For master's, comprehensive exam, thesis optional. *Entrance requirements:* For master's, GRE General Test or MAT, interview, minimum GPA of 2.5, bachelor's degree in related field, teaching license (MA Ed). Additional exam requirements/recommendations for international students: Required—TOEFL. *Application deadline:* For fall admission, 6/1 priority date for domestic students. Applications are processed on a rolling basis. Application fee: $50. *Financial support:* Research assistantships, teaching assistantships, and Federal Work-Study available. Support available to part-time students. Financial award application deadline: 6/1. *Unit head:* Katherine Misulis, Chair, 252-328-6128, E-mail: misulisk@ecu.edu. *Application contact:* Dean of Graduate School, 252-328-6012, Fax: 252-328-6071, E-mail: gradschool@ecu.edu.
Website: http://www.ecu.edu/cs-educ/libs/index.cfm

East Carolina University, Graduate School, Thomas Harriot College of Arts and Sciences, Department of History, Greenville, NC 27858-4353. Offers American history (MA); Atlantic world (MA); European history (MA); history education (MA Ed); maritime studies (MA); military history (MA); public history (MA). *Program availability:* Part-time, evening/weekend. *Students:* 44 full-time (21 women), 48 part-time (27 women); includes

8 minority (1 Black or African American, non-Hispanic/Latino; 5 Hispanic/Latino; 2 Two or more races, non-Hispanic/Latino), 2 international. Average age 29. 46 applicants, 80% accepted, 23 enrolled. In 2016, 24 master's awarded. *Degree requirements:* For master's, one foreign language, comprehensive exam, thesis. *Entrance requirements:* For master's, GRE General Test, GRE Subject Test. Additional exam requirements/recommendations for international students: Required—TOEFL. *Application deadline:* For fall admission, 6/1 priority date for domestic students, for spring admission, 10/15 for domestic students. Applications are processed on a rolling basis. Application fee: $50. *Financial support:* Fellowships, research assistantships with partial tuition reimbursements, teaching assistantships with partial tuition reimbursements, and Federal Work-Study available. Support available to part-time students. Financial award application deadline: 6/1. *Unit head:* Dr. Gerry Prokopowicz, Chair, 252-328-6587, E-mail: prokopowiczg@ecu.edu.
Website: http://www.ecu.edu/cs-cas/history/graduatedegrees.cfm

Eastern Kentucky University, The Graduate School, College of Education, Department of Curriculum and Instruction, Program in Secondary and Higher Education, Richmond, KY 40475-3102. Offers secondary education (MA Ed), including agricultural education, art education, biological sciences education, business education, English education, geography education, history education, home economics education, industrial education, mathematical sciences education, physical education, school health education. *Accreditation:* NCATE. *Program availability:* Part-time. *Entrance requirements:* For master's, GRE General Test, minimum GPA of 2.5.

Eastern University, Loeb School of Education, St. Davids, PA 19087-3696. Offers ESL program specialist (K-12) (Certificate); general supervisor (PreK-12) (Certificate); health and physical education (K-12) (Certificate); middle level (4-8) (Certificate); multicultural education (M Ed); organizational leadership with education (PhD); Pre K-4 (Certificate); Pre K-4 with special education (Certificate); reading (M Ed); reading specialist (K-12) (Certificate); reading supervisor (K-12) (Certificate); school health supervisor (Certificate); school nurse (K-12) (Certificate); secondary biology education (7-12) (Certificate); secondary chemistry education (7-12) (Certificate); secondary communication education (7-12) (Certificate); secondary education (7-12) (Certificate); secondary English education (7-12) (Certificate); secondary math education (7-12) (Certificate); secondary social studies education (7-12) (Certificate); special education (M Ed); special education (7-12) (Certificate); special education (Pre K-8) (Certificate); special education supervisor (N-12) (Certificate); TESOL (M Ed); world language (Certificate), including French, Spanish. *Program availability:* Part-time, evening/weekend, online learning. *Students:* 41 full-time (32 women), 89 part-time (68 women); includes 54 minority (38 Black or African American, non-Hispanic/Latino; 3 Asian, non-Hispanic/Latino; 11 Hispanic/Latino; 2 Two or more races, non-Hispanic/Latino), 2 international. Average age 37. In 2016, 64 master's awarded. *Entrance requirements:* Additional exam requirements/recommendations for international students: Required—TOEFL. *Application deadline:* Applications are processed on a rolling basis. Application fee: $35. Electronic applications accepted. Application fee is waived when completed online. *Expenses:* $690 per credit. *Unit head:* Michael Dziedziak, Executive Director of Enrollment, 800-452-0996, E-mail: gpsadmissions@eastern.edu.
Website: http://www.eastern.edu/academics/programs/loeb-school-education-0

Fayetteville State University, Graduate School, Programs in Middle Grades, Secondary, Special and Elementary Education, Fayetteville, NC 28301-4298. Offers middle grades (MA Ed); sociology (MA Ed); special education (MA Ed), including behavioral-emotional handicaps, mentally handicapped, specific training disability. *Accreditation:* NCATE. *Program availability:* Part-time, evening/weekend. *Faculty:* 12 full-time (8 women), 4 part-time/adjunct (3 women). *Students:* 9 full-time (6 women), 11 part-time (10 women); includes 12 minority (11 Black or African American, non-Hispanic/Latino; 1 Asian, non-Hispanic/Latino). Average age 35. 20 applicants, 100% accepted, 1 enrolled. In 2016, 11 master's awarded. *Degree requirements:* For master's, comprehensive exam, internship. *Entrance requirements:* Additional exam requirements/recommendations for international students: Required—TOEFL. *Application deadline:* For fall admission, 4/15 for domestic students; for spring admission, 10/15 for domestic students. Applications are processed on a rolling basis. Application fee: $40. Electronic applications accepted. *Financial support:* Application deadline: 3/1; applicants required to submit FAFSA. *Faculty research:* Students with disabilities and selected leadership behaviors, new vision for professional development, gifted and talented students, emotional and behavioral disabilities, professional development for high school biology teachers. *Unit head:* Dr. Kimberly Smith-Burton, Chairperson, 910-672-1181, Fax: 910-672-1941, E-mail: ksmith@uncfsu.edu. *Application contact:* Debra D. Brown, Administrative Support Associate, 910-672-1181, Fax: 910-672-1596, E-mail: ddbrown@uncfsu.edu.

Fitchburg State University, Division of Graduate and Continuing Education, Programs in History and Teaching History (Secondary Level), Fitchburg, MA 01420-2697. Offers MA, MAT, Certificate. *Accreditation:* NCATE. *Program availability:* Part-time, evening/weekend. *Entrance requirements:* Additional exam requirements/recommendations for international students: Required—TOEFL (minimum score 550 paper-based; 79 iBT). Electronic applications accepted. *Expenses:* Tuition, state resident: full-time $2871; part-time $1914 per year. Tuition, nonresident: full-time $2871; part-time $1914 per year. *Required fees:* $3828. Tuition and fees vary according to program.

Florida Agricultural and Mechanical University, Division of Graduate Studies, Research, and Continuing Education, College of Education, Program in Secondary Education and Foundation, Tallahassee, FL 32307-3200. Offers biology (M Ed); chemistry (MS Ed); English (MS Ed); history (MS Ed); math (MS Ed); physics (MS Ed). *Accreditation:* NCATE. *Degree requirements:* For master's, thesis (for some programs). *Entrance requirements:* For master's, GRE General Test, minimum GPA of 3.0. Additional exam requirements/recommendations for international students: Required—TOEFL.

Florida Atlantic University, College of Education, Department of Teaching and Learning, Boca Raton, FL 33431-0991. Offers curriculum and instruction (M Ed), including art, biology, chemistry, English, French, German, mathematics, music, physics, Pre-K and primary education, reading, social sciences, Spanish; elementary education (M Ed); environmental education (M Ed); reading education (M Ed); social foundations of education (M Ed), including educational psychology, educational technology, multilingual education. *Accreditation:* NCATE. *Program availability:* Part-time, evening/weekend. *Faculty:* 15 full-time (12 women), 2 part-time/adjunct (1 woman). *Students:* 25 full-time (20 women), 41 part-time (37 women); includes 18 minority (9 Black or African American, non-Hispanic/Latino; 2 Asian, non-Hispanic/Latino; 7 Hispanic/Latino), 7 international. Average age 32. 54 applicants, 59% accepted, 18 enrolled. In 2016, 36 master's awarded. *Entrance requirements:* For master's, GRE General Test, minimum GPA of 3.0 in last 2 years of undergraduate course work. Additional exam requirements/recommendations for international students: Required—TOEFL (minimum score 500 paper-based; 61 iBT), IELTS (minimum score 6). *Application deadline:* For fall admission, 7/1 for domestic students, 2/15 for international students; for spring admission, 11/1 for domestic students, 7/15 for international students. Applications are processed on a rolling basis. Application fee: $30. *Expenses:* Tuition, state resident: full-time $7392; part-time $369.82 per credit hour. Tuition, nonresident: full-time $19,432; part-time $1024.81 per credit hour. *Financial support:* Fellowships with partial tuition reimbursements, research assistantships with partial tuition reimbursements, teaching assistantships with partial tuition reimbursements, career-related internships or fieldwork, scholarships/grants, and unspecified assistantships available. *Faculty research:* Technology, teaching English to speakers of other languages, math teaching, electronic portfolio assessment, global perspectives through social studies. *Unit head:* Dr. Barbara Ridener, Chairperson, 561-297-3588, E-mail: bridener@fau.edu. *Application contact:* Dr. Eliah Watlington, Associate Dean, 561-296-8520, Fax: 261-297-2991, E-mail: ewatling@fau.edu.
Website: http://www.coe.fau.edu/academicdepartments/tl/

Florida Gulf Coast University, College of Education, Program in Curriculum and Instruction, Fort Myers, FL 33965-6565. Offers elementary education (M Ed); English education (M Ed); gifted education (M Ed); mathematics education (M Ed); middle school education (M Ed); science education (M Ed); social science education (M Ed). *Program availability:* Part-time, evening/weekend, online learning. *Faculty:* 26 full-time (18 women), 44 part-time/adjunct (32 women). *Students:* 1 (woman) full-time, 22 part-time (20 women); includes 49 minority (19 Black or African American, non-Hispanic/Latino; 4 Asian, non-Hispanic/Latino; 24 Hispanic/Latino; 2 Two or more races, non-Hispanic/Latino), 2 international. Average age 28. 9 applicants, 78% accepted, 2 enrolled. In 2016, 9 master's awarded. *Degree requirements:* For master's, final project or portfolio. *Entrance requirements:* For master's, GRE General Test, MAT, minimum undergraduate GPA of 3.0 in last 2 years. Additional exam requirements/recommendations for international students: Required—TOEFL (minimum score 550 paper-based). *Application deadline:* For fall admission, 7/1 priority date for domestic students; for spring admission, 10/15 for domestic students. Applications are processed on a rolling basis. Application fee: $30. Electronic applications accepted. *Expenses:* Tuition, state resident: full-time $6721. Tuition, nonresident: full-time $28,170. *Required fees:* $1987. Tuition and fees vary according to course load and degree level. *Financial support:* In 2016–17, 1 student received support. Application deadline: 3/1; applicants required to submit FAFSA. *Faculty research:* Internet in schools, technology in pre-service and in-service teacher training. *Unit head:* Dr. Diane Schmidt, Department Chair, 239-590-7741, Fax: 239-590-7801, E-mail: dschmidt@fgcu.edu. *Application contact:* Keiana Desmore, Adviser/Counselor, 239-590-7759, Fax: 239-590-7801, E-mail: kdesmore@fgcu.edu.
Website: http://coe.fgcu.edu/c-imed/

Florida International University, College of Arts, Sciences, and Education, Department of Teaching and Learning, Miami, FL 33199. Offers art education (MA, MS); curriculum and instruction (MS, Ed D, PhD, Ed S), including curriculum development (MS), elementary education (MS), English education (MS), learning technologies (MS), mathematics education (MS), modern language education (MS), physical education (MS), science education (MS), social studies education (MS), special education (MS); early childhood education (MS); exceptional student education (Ed D); foreign language education (MS), including foreign language education, teaching English to speakers of other languages (TESOL); international/intercultural education (MS); language, literacy and culture (PhD); mathematics, science, and learning technologies (PhD); physical education (MS), including sport and fitness; reading education (MS). *Program availability:* Part-time, evening/weekend. *Faculty:* 34 full-time (23 women), 64 part-time/adjunct (48 women). *Students:* 182 full-time (154 women), 231 part-time (190 women); includes 323 minority (69 Black or African American, non-Hispanic/Latino; 10 Asian, non-Hispanic/Latino; 237 Hispanic/Latino; 7 Two or more races, non-Hispanic/Latino), 19 international. Average age 34. 282 applicants, 58% accepted, 113 enrolled. In 2016, 184 master's, 12 doctorates awarded. *Degree requirements:* For doctorate, comprehensive exam, thesis/dissertation. *Entrance requirements:* For master's, GRE General Test, Florida General Knowledge Test or Florida College Level Academic Skills Test; for doctorate and Ed S, GRE General Test. Additional exam requirements/recommendations for international students: Required—TOEFL (minimum score 550 paper-based; 80 iBT), IELTS (minimum score 6.3). *Application deadline:* For fall admission, 6/1 priority date for domestic students, 4/1 for international students; for winter admission, 10/1 priority date for domestic students, 9/1 for international students; for spring admission, 3/1 priority date for domestic students, 2/1 for international students. Applications are processed on a rolling basis. Application fee: $30. Electronic applications accepted. *Expenses:* Tuition, state resident: full-time $8912; part-time $446 per credit hour. Tuition, nonresident: full-time $21,393; part-time $992 per credit hour. *Required fees:* $2185; $195 per semester. Tuition and fees vary according to program. *Financial support:* Research assistantships with tuition reimbursements and teaching assistantships with tuition reimbursements available. *Unit head:* Dr. Lynn Miller, Chair, 305-348-2005, Fax: 305-348-2086, E-mail: lynne.miller@fiu.edu. *Application contact:* Nanett Rojas, Assistant Director, Graduate Admissions, 305-348-7464, Fax: 305-348-7441, E-mail: gradadm@fiu.edu.
Website: http://education.fiu.edu

Florida State University, The Graduate School, College of Education, Program in Curriculum and Instruction, Tallahassee, FL 32306. Offers curriculum and instruction (MS, PhD, Ed S), including early childhood education, elementary education, English education, English teaching (MS), exceptional student education (MS), foreign and second language education, foreign and second language teaching (MS), mathematics education, mathematics teaching (MS), reading education and language arts, science education, social science education, social science teaching (MS), special education, special education studies (MS), visual disabilities (MS, Ed S). *Program availability:* Part-time, evening/weekend. Terminal master's awarded for partial completion of doctoral program. *Degree requirements:* For master's and Ed S, comprehensive exam, thesis optional; for doctorate, comprehensive exam, thesis/dissertation, diagnostic exam, preliminary exam, prospectus defense, dissertation defense. *Entrance requirements:* For master's, doctorate, and Ed S, GRE General Test, minimum upper-division GPA of 3.0. Additional exam requirements/recommendations for international students: Required—TOEFL (minimum score 550 paper-based, 80 iBT), IELTS (minimum score 6.5), Michigan English Language Assessment Battery (minimum score 77), or PTE (minimum score 55). Application fee: $30. Electronic applications accepted. *Expenses:* Tuition, state resident: full-time $7263; part-time $403.51 per credit hour. Tuition, nonresident: full-time $18,087; part time $1004.85 per credit hour. *Required fees:* $1365; $75.81 per credit hour. $20 per semester. Tuition and fees vary according to campus/location. *Financial support:* Fellowships, research assistantships, teaching assistantships, scholarships/grants, tuition waivers (full and partial), and unspecified assistantships available. Financial award application deadline: 1/15; financial award applicants required to submit FAFSA. *Faculty research:* Identifying effective intervention strategies to improve reading skills; improving literacy teaching and learning through technology; understanding of student sense making, problem solving, the history and structure of STEM disciplines, and teacher education to support the development of ambitious instruction that supports the STEM learning of all students; examining practices of international education; identifying ways to support the professional development of teachers. *Unit head:* Dr. Sherry Southerland, Professor/Department Chair, 850-644-4880, Fax: 850-644-7736, E-mail: ssoutherland@admin.fsu.edu. *Application contact:* Libbie Crowley, Academic Support Specialist, 850-644-2122, Fax: 850-644-7736, E-mail: ecrowley@fsu.edu.
Website: http://education.fsu.edu/degrees-and-programs/graduate-programs

Social Sciences Education

Framingham State University, Continuing Education, Program in History, Framingham, MA 01701-9101. Offers M Ed.

George Mason University, College of Education and Human Development, Programs in Curriculum and Instruction, Fairfax, VA 22030. Offers advanced international baccalaureate (M Ed); assistive technology (M Ed); designing digital learning in schools (M Ed); early childhood education (M Ed); early childhood education for diverse learners (M Ed); elementary education (M Ed); English as a second language (M Ed); gifted child education (M Ed); history (M Ed); literacy (M Ed), including PK-12 classroom teachers, reading specialist; literacy leadership for diverse schools (M Ed), including K-12 reading; physical education (M Ed); science K-12 (M Ed); secondary education (M Ed), including biology, chemistry, earth science, English, history/social science, math, physics; special education (M Ed); teacher leadership (M Ed); teaching culturally, linguistically diverse and exceptional learners (M Ed); transformative teaching (M Ed). *Faculty:* 41 full-time (35 women), 53 part-time/adjunct (46 women). *Students:* 155 full-time (127 women), 821 part-time (697 women); includes 267 minority (82 Black or African American, non-Hispanic/Latino; 5 American Indian or Alaska Native, non-Hispanic/Latino; 75 Asian, non-Hispanic/Latino; 88 Hispanic/Latino; 1 Native Hawaiian or other Pacific Islander, non-Hispanic/Latino; 16 Two or more races, non-Hispanic/Latino), 19 international. Average age 33. 513 applicants, 90% accepted, 352 enrolled. In 2016, 347 master's awarded. *Degree requirements:* For master's, comprehensive exam, thesis (for some programs). *Entrance requirements:* For master's, PRAXIS Core (for some programs), minimum GPA of 3.0 in last 60 hours, licensed as teacher or educational administrator, official transcripts, goals statement, 3 recommendation letters, interview or writing sample (depending on program), up to 3 years' teaching experience (depending on program). Additional exam requirements/recommendations for international students: Required—TOEFL (minimum score 575 paper-based; 88 iBT), IELTS (minimum score 6.5), PTE (minimum score 59). *Application deadline:* For spring admission, 11/1 priority date for domestic and international students. Application fee: $75 ($80 for international students). Electronic applications accepted. *Expenses:* Tuition, state resident: full-time $10,628; part-time $443 per credit. Tuition, nonresident: full-time $29,306; part-time $1221 per credit. *Required fees:* $3096; $129 per credit. Tuition and fees vary according to program. *Financial support:* In 2016–17, 1 student received support, including 1 teaching assistantship (averaging $4,060 per year); career-related internships or fieldwork, Federal Work-Study, scholarships/grants, unspecified assistantships, and health care benefits (for full-time research or teaching assistantship recipients) also available. Support available to part-time students. Financial award application deadline: 3/1; financial award applicants required to submit FAFSA. *Faculty research:* Achievement gaps and superintendent decisions, constructivist view of classroom teaching, cost of cheating, creating a critical literacy milieu in kindergarten. *Unit head:* Rebecca Fox, Professor and Academic Program Coordinator, 703-993-4123, E-mail: rfox@gmu.edu.
Website: http://gse.gmu.edu/programs/gsemasters

Georgia State University, College of Education and Human Development, Department of Middle and Secondary Education, Atlanta, GA 30302-3083. Offers curriculum and instruction (Ed D); English education (MAT); mathematics education (M Ed, MAT); middle level education (MAT); reading, language and literacy education (M Ed, MAT), including reading instruction (M Ed); science education (M Ed, MAT), including biology (MAT), broad field science (MAT), chemistry (MAT), earth science (MAT), physics (MAT); social studies education (M Ed, MAT), including economics (MAT), geography (MAT), history (MAT), political science (MAT); teaching and learning (PhD), including language and literacy, mathematics education, music education, science education, social studies education, teaching and teacher education. *Accreditation:* NCATE. *Program availability:* Part-time, evening/weekend, online learning. *Faculty:* 24 full-time (18 women). *Students:* 145 full-time (91 women), 151 part-time (102 women); includes 141 minority (104 Black or African American, non-Hispanic/Latino; 1 American Indian or Alaska Native, non-Hispanic/Latino; 16 Asian, non-Hispanic/Latino; 12 Hispanic/Latino; 8 Two or more races, non-Hispanic/Latino), 10 international. Average age 36. 115 applicants, 50% accepted, 41 enrolled. In 2016, 94 master's, 22 doctorates awarded. *Degree requirements:* For master's, comprehensive exam (for some programs), thesis or alternative, exit portfolio; for doctorate, comprehensive exam, thesis/dissertation. *Entrance requirements:* For master's, GRE; GACE I (for initial teacher preparation programs), baccalaureate degree or equivalent, resume, goals statement, two letters of recommendation, minimum undergraduate GPA of 2.5; proof of initial teacher certification in the content area (for M Ed); for doctorate, GRE, resume, goals statement, writing sample, two letters of recommendation, minimum graduate GPA of 3.3, interview. Additional exam requirements/recommendations for international students: Required—TOEFL (minimum score 550 paper-based; 79 iBT) or IELTS (minimum score 6.5). *Application deadline:* For fall admission, 1/15 priority date for domestic and international students; for spring admission, 10/1 for domestic and international students. Application fee: $50. Electronic applications accepted. *Expenses:* Tuition, state resident: full-time $6876; part-time $382 per credit hour. Tuition, nonresident: full-time $22,374; part-time $1243 per credit hour. *Required fees:* $2128; $1064 per term. Part-time tuition and fees vary according to course load and program. *Financial support:* In 2016–17, fellowships with full tuition reimbursements (averaging $19,667 per year), research assistantships with full tuition reimbursements (averaging $5,436 per year), teaching assistantships with full tuition reimbursements (averaging $2,779 per year) were awarded; career-related internships or fieldwork, Federal Work-Study, scholarships/grants, health care benefits, tuition waivers (full and partial), and unspecified assistantships also available. Financial award application deadline: 3/15. *Faculty research:* Teacher education in language and literacy, mathematics, science, and social studies in urban middle and secondary school settings; learning technologies in school, community, and corporate settings; multicultural education and education for social justice; urban education; international education. *Unit head:* Dr. Dana L. Fox, Chair, 404-413-8060, Fax: 404-413-8063, E-mail: dfox@gsu.edu. *Application contact:* Bobbie Turner, Administrative Coordinator I, 404-413-8405, Fax: 404-413-8063, E-mail: bnturner@gsu.edu.
Website: http://mse.education.gsu.edu/

Grambling State University, School of Graduate Studies and Research, College of Arts and Sciences, Department of History and Geography, Grambling, LA 71245. Offers social sciences (MA). *Program availability:* Part-time. *Degree requirements:* For master's, comprehensive exam (for some programs), thesis optional. *Entrance requirements:* For master's, GRE, minimum GPA of 3.0 on last degree. Additional exam requirements/recommendations for international students: Required—TOEFL (minimum score 500 paper-based; 62 iBT). Electronic applications accepted.

Harding University, Cannon-Clary College of Education, Searcy, AR 72149-0001. Offers advanced studies in teaching and learning (M Ed); art (MSE); behavioral science (MSE); counseling (MS, Ed S); early childhood special education (M Ed, MSE); education (MSE); educational leadership (M Ed, Ed S); elementary education (M Ed); English (MSE); French (MSE); history/social science (MSE); kinesiology (MSE); math (MSE); reading (M Ed); secondary education (M Ed); Spanish (MSE); teaching (MAT); teaching English as a second language (MSE). *Accreditation:* NCATE. *Program availability:* Part-time, evening/weekend. *Faculty:* 22 full-time (9 women), 51 part-time/adjunct (37 women). *Students:* 130 full-time (94 women), 321 part-time (234 women); includes 83 minority (50 Black or African American, non-Hispanic/Latino; 4 American Indian or Alaska Native, non-Hispanic/Latino; 6 Asian, non-Hispanic/Latino; 13 Hispanic/Latino; 10 Two or more races, non-Hispanic/Latino), 11 international. Average age 35. 125 applicants, 88% accepted, 110 enrolled. In 2016, 124 master's, 27 other advanced degrees awarded. *Degree requirements:* For master's, comprehensive exam (for some programs), thesis optional, portfolio(s); for Ed S, comprehensive exam, portfolio, project. *Entrance requirements:* For master's, GRE, MAT, PRAXIS; for Ed S, MAT or GRE. Additional exam requirements/recommendations for international students: Required—TOEFL (minimum score 550 paper-based; 79 iBT). *Application deadline:* For fall admission, 8/1 for domestic and international students; for spring admission, 1/1 for domestic and international students. Applications are processed on a rolling basis. Application fee: $35. Tuition and fees vary according to degree level and program. *Financial support:* In 2016–17, 31 students received support. Unspecified assistantships available. *Faculty research:* Reading, comprehension, school violence, educational technology, behavior, college choice, differentiated instruction, brain-based teaching. *Unit head:* Dr. Clara Carroll, Chair, 501-279-4501, Fax: 501-279-4083, E-mail: ccarroll@harding.edu. *Application contact:* Information Contact, 501-279-4315, E-mail: gradstudiesedu@harding.edu.
Website: http://www.harding.edu/education

Hofstra University, School of Education, Programs in Teacher Education, Hempstead, NY 11549. Offers bilingual education (MA, Advanced Certificate); bilingual extension (Advanced Certificate), including education/speech language pathology; business education (MS Ed); early childhood and childhood education (MS Ed); early childhood education (MA, MS Ed); education technology (Advanced Certificate); elementary education (MA, MS Ed), including science, technology, engineering, and mathematics (STEM) (MA); English education (MS Ed); family and consumer science (MS Ed); fine arts and music education (Advanced Certificate); fine arts education (MS Ed); foreign language and TESOL (MS Ed); foreign language education (MS Ed), including French, German, Russian, Spanish; learning and teaching (Ed D), including applied linguistics, art education, arts and humanities, early childhood education, English education, human development, math education, math, science, and technology, multicultural education, physical education, science education, social studies education, special education; mathematics education (MA, MS Ed); middle school extension (Advanced Certificate), including grades 5-6, grades 7-9; music education (MA, MS Ed); science education (MA, MS Ed), including biology, chemistry, earth science, geology, physics; secondary education (Advanced Certificate); social studies education (MA, MS Ed); teaching languages other than English and TESOL (MS Ed); TESOL (MS Ed, Advanced Certificate). *Program availability:* Part-time, evening/weekend, blended/hybrid learning. *Students:* 139 full-time (97 women), 145 part-time (106 women); includes 60 minority (15 Black or African American, non-Hispanic/Latino; 1 American Indian or Alaska Native, non-Hispanic/Latino; 12 Asian, non-Hispanic/Latino; 31 Hispanic/Latino; 1 Two or more races, non-Hispanic/Latino), 21 international. Average age 29. 255 applicants, 86% accepted, 122 enrolled. In 2016, 101 master's, 4 doctorates, 43 other advanced degrees awarded. *Degree requirements:* For master's, comprehensive exam, thesis (for some programs), exit project, student teaching, fieldwork, electronic portfolio, curriculum project, minimum GPA of 3.0; for doctorate, thesis/dissertation; for Advanced Certificate, 3 foreign languages, comprehensive exam (for some programs), thesis project. *Entrance requirements:* For master's, GRE, MAT, 2 letters of recommendation, portfolio, teacher certification (MA), interview, essay; for doctorate, GMAT, GRE, LSAT, or MAT; for Advanced Certificate, 2 letters of recommendation, essay, interview and/or portfolio, teaching certificate. Additional exam requirements/recommendations for international students: Required—TOEFL (minimum score 550 paper-based; 80 iBT). *Application deadline:* Applications are processed on a rolling basis. Application fee: $75. Electronic applications accepted. *Expenses: Tuition:* Full-time $1240. *Required fees:* $970. Tuition and fees vary according to program. *Financial support:* In 2016–17, 149 students received support, including 58 fellowships with full and partial tuition reimbursements available (averaging $5,309 per year), 5 research assistantships with full and partial tuition reimbursements available (averaging $7,073 per year); career-related internships or fieldwork, Federal Work-Study, institutionally sponsored loans, scholarships/grants, traineeships, tuition waivers (full and partial), and unspecified assistantships also available. Support available to part-time students. Financial award applicants required to submit FAFSA. *Faculty research:* Educational interventions that foster critical-thinking skills; teachers' attitudes about professional development; threats to teacher quality. *Unit head:* Dr. Eustace Thompson, Chairperson, 516-463-5749, Fax: 516-463-6275, E-mail: eustace.g.thompson@hofstra.edu. *Application contact:* Sunil Samuel, Assistant Vice President of Admissions, 516-463-4723, Fax: 516-463-4664, E-mail: graduateadmission@hofstra.edu.
Website: http://www.hofstra.edu/education/

Hunter College of the City University of New York, Graduate School, School of Education, Programs in Secondary Education, Concentration in Social Studies Education, New York, NY 10065-5085. Offers MA. *Accreditation:* NCATE. *Degree requirements:* For master's, thesis, professional teaching portfolio, New York State Teacher Certification Exam, research project. *Entrance requirements:* For master's, minimum GPA of 3.0 in history, 2.8 overall; 2 letters of reference; minimum of 30 credits in social studies areas. Additional exam requirements/recommendations for international students: Required—TOEFL, TWE. *Application deadline:* For fall admission, 4/1 for domestic students, 2/1 for international students; for spring admission, 11/1 for domestic students, 9/1 for international students. Applications are processed on a rolling basis. *Financial support:* Federal Work-Study and tuition waivers (partial) available. Support available to part-time students. *Unit head:* Dr. Debbie Sonu, Education Program Coordinator, 212-772-5445, E-mail: dsonu@hunter.cuny.edu.

Indiana University Bloomington, School of Education, Department of Curriculum and Instruction, Bloomington, IN 47405-7000. Offers art education (MS, Ed D, PhD); curriculum studies (Ed D, PhD); elementary education (MS, Ed D, PhD, Ed S); mathematics education (MS, Ed D, PhD); science education (MS, Ed D, PhD); secondary education (MS, Ed D, PhD); social studies education (MS, PhD); special education (PhD, Ed S). *Accreditation:* NCATE. *Program availability:* Part-time, evening/weekend. Terminal master's awarded for partial completion of doctoral program. *Degree requirements:* For doctorate, thesis/dissertation; for Ed S, comprehensive exam or project. *Entrance requirements:* For master's, doctorate, and Ed S, GRE General Test. Electronic applications accepted.

Instituto Tecnologico de Santo Domingo, Graduate School, Area of Humanities and Social Sciences, Santo Domingo, Dominican Republic. Offers accounting (Certificate); adult education (Certificate); applied linguistics (MA); economics (MA); education (M Ed); educational psychology (MA, Certificate); gender and development (MA, Certificate); humanistic studies (MA); international marketing management (Certificate); international relations in the Caribbean basin (Certificate); intervention systems in family therapy (MA); linguistic and literary communication (Certificate); pedagogical support (MA); social science education (M Ed); sustainable human development (MA); terminal illness and death psychology (Certificate); youth and adult education (M Ed).

Inter American University of Puerto Rico, Arecibo Campus, Programs in Education, Arecibo, PR 00614-4050. Offers administration and educational supervision (MA Ed); counseling and guidance (MA Ed); curriculum and teaching (MA Ed), including biology education, English as a second language, history education, math education, Spanish; elementary education (MA Ed). *Accreditation:* TEAC. *Degree requirements:* For master's, comprehensive exam, thesis optional. *Entrance requirements:* For master's, GRE, EXADEP, bachelor's degree in education or teaching license (administration and supervision) or courses in education and psychology (counseling and guidance), minimum GPA of 2.5 in last 60 credits.

Inter American University of Puerto Rico, Barranquitas Campus, Program in Education, Barranquitas, PR 00794. Offers curriculum and teaching (M Ed), including biology education, English as a second language, history education, mathematics education, Spanish; educational leadership and management (MA); elementary education (M Ed); information and library service technology (M Ed); special education (MA). *Accreditation:* TEAC. *Degree requirements:* For master's, comprehensive exam, thesis optional. *Entrance requirements:* For master's, EXADEP, letter of recommendation. Electronic applications accepted.

Inter American University of Puerto Rico, Metropolitan Campus, Graduate Programs, Program in History Education, San Juan, PR 00919-1293. Offers MA.

Inter American University of Puerto Rico, Ponce Campus, Graduate School, Mercedita, PR 00715-1602. Offers accounting (MBA); biology (M Ed); chemistry (M Ed); criminal justice (MA); elementary education (M Ed); English as a Second Language (M Ed); finance (MBA); history (M Ed); human resources (MBA); marketing (MBA); mathematics (M Ed); Spanish (M Ed). *Entrance requirements:* For master's, minimum GPA of 2.5.

Iona College, School of Arts and Science, Department of Education, New Rochelle, NY 10801-1890. Offers adolescence education: biology (MS Ed, MST); adolescence education: English (MS Ed); adolescence education: mathematics (MST); adolescence education: social studies (MS Ed, MST); adolescence education: Spanish (MS Ed); adolescence special education 5-12 (MST); childhood and special education (MST); early childhood and childhood (MST); educational leadership (MS Ed). *Accreditation:* NCATE. *Program availability:* Part-time, evening/weekend. *Faculty:* 7 full-time (6 women), 4 part-time/adjunct (2 women). *Students:* 27 full-time (19 women), 27 part-time (18 women); includes 18 minority (4 Black or African American, non-Hispanic/Latino; 1 Asian, non-Hispanic/Latino; 12 Hispanic/Latino; 1 Two or more races, non-Hispanic/Latino). Average age 26. 6 applicants, 67% accepted, 3 enrolled. In 2016, 25 master's awarded. *Degree requirements:* For master's, thesis or alternative. *Entrance requirements:* For master's, minimum GPA of 3.0, NY State teaching certificate and bachelor's degree (for MS Ed). Additional exam requirements/recommendations for international students: Required—TOEFL (minimum score 550 paper-based; 80 iBT), IELTS (minimum score 6.5). *Application deadline:* For fall admission, 8/1 priority date for domestic students, 5/1 priority date for international students; for spring admission, 1/1 priority date for domestic students, 9/1 priority date for international students. Applications are processed on a rolling basis. Application fee: $50. Electronic applications accepted. *Expenses: Tuition:* Full-time $19,692; part-time $1094 per credit. *Required fees:* $245 per term. Tuition and fees vary according to program. *Financial support:* In 2016–17, 3 students received support. Unspecified assistantships available. Support available to part-time students. Financial award application deadline: 4/15; financial award applicants required to submit FAFSA. *Faculty research:* Engaging teacher educators in scientific process, cross-national comparisons of mathematics teaching, questioning strategies in the classroom, research methods, literacy development. *Unit head:* Margaret Smith, PhD, Chair, 914-633-2210, Fax: 914-633-2608, E-mail: msmith@iona.edu. *Application contact:* Richard McMahon, Coordinator, Graduate School of Education, 914-633-2552, E-mail: rmcmahon@iona.edu.
Website: http://www.iona.edu/Academics/School-of-Arts-Science/Departments/Education/Graduate-Programs.aspx

Ithaca College, School of Humanities and Sciences, Program in Adolescence Education, Ithaca, NY 14850. Offers biology (MAT); chemistry (MAT); earth science (MAT); English (MAT); French (MAT); mathematics (MAT); physics (MAT); social studies (MAT); Spanish (MAT). *Program availability:* Part-time. *Faculty:* 26 full-time (12 women). *Students:* 11 full-time (4 women). Average age 26. 17 applicants, 94% accepted, 10 enrolled. *Degree requirements:* For master's, thesis or alternative. *Entrance requirements:* Additional exam requirements/recommendations for international students: Required—TOEFL (minimum score 550 paper-based; 80 iBT). *Application deadline:* For fall admission, 2/15 for domestic and international students; for spring admission, 12/1 for domestic and international students. Applications are processed on a rolling basis. Application fee: $40. Electronic applications accepted. *Expenses:* Contact institution. *Financial support:* In 2016–17, 5 students received support, including 5 research assistantships (averaging $13,259 per year); career-related internships or fieldwork, Federal Work-Study, scholarships/grants, and unspecified assistantships also available. Support available to part-time students. Financial award application deadline: 2/15; financial award applicants required to submit CSS PROFILE or FAFSA. *Unit head:* Peter Martin, Chair, 607-274-1076, E-mail: pmartin@ithaca.edu. *Application contact:* Nicole Eversley Bradwell, Director, Office of Admission, 607-274-3124, Fax: 607-274-1263, E-mail: admission@ithaca.edu.
Website: http://www.ithaca.edu/gradprograms/education/programs/aded

Johns Hopkins University, School of Education, Master's Programs in Education, Baltimore, MD 21218. Offers counseling (MS), including clinical mental health counseling, school counseling; education (MS), including educational studies, gifted education, reading, school administration and supervision, technology for educators; elementary education (MAT); health professions (M Ed); intelligence analysis (MS); organizational leadership (MS); secondary education (MAT), including biology, chemistry, earth/space science, English, physics, social studies; special education (MS), including early childhood special education, general special education studies, mild to moderate disabilities, severe disabilities. *Program availability:* Part-time, evening/weekend, 100% online, blended/hybrid learning. *Students:* 345 full-time (265 women), 1,601 part-time (1,245 women); includes 837 minority (392 Black or African American, non-Hispanic/Latino; 7 American Indian or Alaska Native, non-Hispanic/Latino; 141 Asian, non-Hispanic/Latino; 207 Hispanic/Latino; 7 Native Hawaiian or other Pacific Islander, non-Hispanic/Latino; 83 Two or more races, non-Hispanic/Latino), 55 international. Average age 27. 1,352 applicants, 76% accepted, 819 enrolled. In 2016, 642 master's awarded. *Degree requirements:* For master's, comprehensive exam (for some programs), portfolio, capstone project and/or internship; PRAXIS II (subject area assessments) for initial teacher preparation programs that lead to licensure. *Entrance requirements:* For master's, GRE (for full-time programs only); PRAXIS I/core or state-approved alternative (for initial teacher preparation programs that lead to licensure), minimum of bachelor's degree from regionally- or nationally-accredited institution; minimum GPA of 3.0 in all previous programs of study; official transcripts from all post-secondary institutions attended; essay; curriculum vitae/resume; letters of recommendation (3 for full-time programs, 2 for part-time programs); dispositions survey. Additional exam requirements/recommendations for international students: Required—TOEFL (minimum score 600 paper-based; 100 iBT), IELTS (minimum score 7). *Application deadline:* For fall admission, 4/1 priority date for domestic students, 4/1 for international students; for spring admission, 10/1 priority date for domestic students, 10/1 for international students; for summer admission, 2/1 priority date for domestic students, 2/1 for international students. Applications are processed on a rolling basis. Application fee: $80. Electronic applications accepted. *Expenses:* Contact institution. *Financial support:* Application deadline: 4/1; applicants required to submit FAFSA. *Unit head:* Dr. Christopher C. Morphew, Dean. *Application contact:* Elisabeth Woodward, Director of Admissions, 410-516-9796, Fax: 410-516-9817, E-mail: soe.info@jhu.edu.
Website: http://education.jhu.edu

Kutztown University of Pennsylvania, College of Education, Program in Secondary Education, Kutztown, PA 19530-0730. Offers biology (M Ed); curriculum and instruction (M Ed); English (M Ed); mathematics (M Ed); middle level (M Ed); social studies (M Ed); teaching (M Ed). *Accreditation:* NCATE. *Program availability:* Part-time, evening/weekend. *Faculty:* 4 full-time (2 women), 2 part-time/adjunct (0 women). *Students:* 35 full-time (23 women), 58 part-time (37 women); includes 4 minority (2 Black or African American, non-Hispanic/Latino; 2 Hispanic/Latino). Average age 31. 96 applicants, 86% accepted, 43 enrolled. In 2016, 35 master's awarded. *Degree requirements:* For master's, comprehensive exam, thesis optional. *Entrance requirements:* For master's, GRE General Test, minimum undergraduate major GPA of 3.0, 3 letters of recommendation, copy of PRAXIS II or valid instructional I or II teaching certificate. Additional exam requirements/recommendations for international students: Required—TOEFL (minimum score 550 paper-based, 79 iBT) or IELTS (minimum score 6.5). *Application deadline:* For fall admission, 8/1 for domestic and international students; for spring admission, 12/1 for domestic and international students. Application fee: $35. Electronic applications accepted. *Expenses:* Tuition, state resident: full-time $4347; part-time $483 per credit. Tuition, nonresident: full-time $6525; part-time $725 per credit. *Required fees:* $88 per credit. One-time fee: $50 full-time. *Financial support:* Career-related internships or fieldwork, Federal Work-Study, scholarships/grants, and unspecified assistantships available. Financial award application deadline: 3/1; financial award applicants required to submit FAFSA. *Unit head:* Dr. Theresa Stahler, Chairperson, 610-683-4259, Fax: 610-683-1338, E-mail: stahler@kutztown.edu. *Application contact:* Dr. Patricia Walsh Coates, Graduate Coordinator, 610-638-4289, Fax: 610-683-1338, E-mail: coates@kutztown.edu.
Website: https://www.kutztown.edu/academcs/graduate-programs/secondary-education.htm

Lake Forest College, Master of Arts in Teaching Program, Lake Forest, IL 60045. Offers elementary education (MAT); K-12 French (MAT); K-12 music (MAT); K-12 Spanish (MAT); K-12 visual art (MAT); secondary biology (MAT); secondary chemistry (MAT); secondary English (MAT); secondary history (MAT); secondary mathematics (MAT). *Degree requirements:* For master's, comprehensive exam, portfolio. *Entrance requirements:* For master's, GRE.

La Salle University, School of Arts and Sciences, Program in Education, Philadelphia, PA 19141-1199. Offers autism spectrum disorders (MA, Certificate); bilingual/bicultural studies (MA); classroom management (MA); dual early childhood and special education (MA); dual middle-level science and math and special education (MA); education (MA); English (MA); English as a second language (Certificate); history (MA); instructional coach (Certificate); instructional leadership (MA); reading specialist (MA, Certificate); secondary education (MA); special education (MA, Certificate). *Program availability:* Part-time, evening/weekend. *Faculty:* 5 full-time (4 women), 12 part-time/adjunct (8 women). *Students:* 10 full-time (all women), 98 part-time (74 women); includes 28 minority (13 Black or African American, non-Hispanic/Latino; 1 American Indian or Alaska Native, non-Hispanic/Latino; 1 Asian, non-Hispanic/Latino; 10 Hispanic/Latino; 3 Two or more races, non-Hispanic/Latino). Average age 34. 128 applicants, 84% accepted, 69 enrolled. In 2016, 53 master's awarded. *Degree requirements:* For master's, comprehensive exam. *Entrance requirements:* For master's, MAT or GRE, 2 letters of recommendation; for Certificate, GMAT or GRE, 2 letters of recommendation. Additional exam requirements/recommendations for international students: Required—TOEFL. *Application deadline:* For fall admission, 8/15 priority date for domestic students, 7/15 for international students; for spring admission, 12/15 priority date for domestic students, 11/15 for international students; for summer admission, 4/15 priority date for domestic students, 3/15 for international students. Applications are processed on a rolling basis. Application fee: $35. Electronic applications accepted. Application fee is waived when completed online. *Expenses:* Contact institution. *Financial support:* In 2016–17, 27 students received support. Scholarships/grants available. Support available to part-time students. Financial award application deadline: 8/31; financial award applicants required to submit FAFSA. *Unit head:* Dr. Greer Richardson, Director, 215-951-1806, Fax: 215-951-1843, E-mail: graded@lasalle.edu. *Application contact:* Elizabeth Heenan, Director, Graduate and Adult Enrollment, 215-951-1100, Fax: 215-951-1462, E-mail: heenan@lasalle.edu.
Website: http://www.lasalle.edu/grad-education-programs/

La Salle University, School of Arts and Sciences, Program in History, Philadelphia, PA 19141-1199. Offers American history (Certificate); European history (Certificate); history (MA); history for educators (MA); public history (MA); teaching advanced placement history (Certificate); world history (Certificate). *Program availability:* Part-time. *Faculty:* 4 full-time (1 woman), 1 (woman) part-time/adjunct. *Students:* 4 full-time (1 woman), 16 part-time (7 women); includes 2 minority (1 Hispanic/Latino; 1 Two or more races, non-Hispanic/Latino). Average age 33. 8 applicants, 75% accepted, 3 enrolled. In 2016, 11 master's awarded. *Degree requirements:* For master's, thesis or comprehensive exam. *Entrance requirements:* For master's, GRE or MAT, 18 hours of undergraduate coursework in history or a related discipline with minimum GPA of 3.0; two letters of recommendation; brief personal statement (250 to 500 words); writing sample (preferably from an undergraduate research paper). Additional exam requirements/recommendations for international students: Required—TOEFL. *Application deadline:* For fall admission, 8/15 priority date for domestic students, 7/15 for international students; for spring admission, 12/15 priority date for domestic students, 11/15 for international students; for summer admission, 4/15 priority date for domestic students, 3/15 for international students. Applications are processed on a rolling basis. Application fee: $35. Electronic applications accepted. Application fee is waived when completed online. *Expenses:* Contact institution. *Financial support:* In 2016–17, 1 student received support. Scholarships/grants available. Support available to part-time students. Financial award application deadline: 8/31; financial award applicants required to submit FAFSA. *Unit head:* Dr. George B. Stow, Director, 215-951-1097, E-mail: grahis@lasalle.edu. *Application contact:* Elizabeth Heenan, Director, Graduate and Adult Enrollment, 215-951-1100, Fax: 215-951-1462, E-mail: heenan@lasalle.edu.
Website: http://www.lasalle.edu/master-history/

Lebanon Valley College, Program in Science Education, Annville, PA 17003-1400. Offers Integrative STEM Education (Certificate); STEM education (MSE). *Program availability:* Part-time-only, evening/weekend. *Faculty:* 11 part-time/adjunct (6 women). *Students:* 1 full-time (0 women), 14 part-time (9 women). Average age 35. 10 applicants, 70% accepted, 7 enrolled. In 2016, 6 master's awarded. *Degree requirements:* For master's, thesis or capstone project. *Entrance requirements:* For master's, baccalaureate degree, minimum GPA of 3.0, teacher certification, 3 letters of recommendation, transcripts, goal statement. Additional exam requirements/recommendations for international students: Required—TOEFL (minimum score 80 iBT). *Application deadline:* Applications are processed on a rolling basis. Application fee: $0. Electronic applications accepted. *Expenses:* $595 per credit hour. *Financial support:* Scholarships/grants available. Financial award application deadline: 3/1; financial award applicants required to submit FAFSA. *Faculty research:* Teacher quality and student achievement, STEM reform, STEM education. *Unit head:* Carrie Coryer, Director of MSE

and STEM-based programs, 717-867-6190, Fax: 717-867-6018, E-mail: coryer@lvc.edu.
Website: http://www.lvc.edu/academics/graduate-studies/master-of-science-in-stem-education/

Lee University, Program in Education, Cleveland, TN 37320-3450. Offers art (MAT); curriculum and instruction (M Ed, Ed S); early childhood (MAT); educational leadership (M Ed, Ed S); elementary education (MAT); English and math (MAT); English and science (MAT); English and social studies (MAT); higher education administration (MS); history (MAT); history and economics (MAT); math and science (MAT); math and social studies (MAT); middle grades (MAT); science and social studies (MASW); secondary education (MAT); Spanish (MAT); special education (M Ed, MAT); TESOL (MAT). *Accreditation:* NCATE. *Program availability:* Part-time. *Faculty:* 13 full-time (6 women), 9 part-time/adjunct (4 women). *Students:* 35 full-time (27 women), 50 part-time (32 women); includes 12 minority (5 Black or African American, non-Hispanic/Latino; 5 Hispanic/Latino; 2 Two or more races, non-Hispanic/Latino), 4 international. Average age 30. 43 applicants, 79% accepted, 28 enrolled. In 2016, 42 master's, 6 other advanced degrees awarded. *Degree requirements:* For master's, variable foreign language requirement, thesis optional, internship. *Entrance requirements:* For master's, MAT or GRE General Test, minimum undergraduate GPA of 2.75, 3 letters of recommendation, interview, writing sample, official transcripts, background check; for Ed S, minimum undergraduate and master's GPA of 2.75, official transcripts for undergraduate and master's degrees. Additional exam requirements/recommendations for international students: Required—TOEFL (minimum score 61 iBT). *Application deadline:* For fall admission, 6/1 priority date for domestic and international students; for spring admission, 11/1 priority date for domestic and international students; for summer admission, 4/1 priority date for domestic and international students. Applications are processed on a rolling basis. Application fee: $25. Electronic applications accepted. *Expenses: Tuition:* Full-time $11,367; part-time $632 per credit hour. *Required fees:* $35 per term. One-time fee: $25. Tuition and fees vary according to program. *Financial support:* In 2016–17, 42 students received support. Career-related internships or fieldwork, Federal Work-Study, institutionally sponsored loans, scholarships/grants, and unspecified assistantships available. Financial award application deadline: 3/1; financial award applicants required to submit FAFSA. *Unit head:* Dr. William Kamm, Director, 423-614-8544, E-mail: wkamm@leeuniversity.edu. *Application contact:* Crystal Keeter, Graduate Education Secretary, 423-614-8544, E-mail: ckeeter@leeuniversity.edu.
Website: http://www.leeuniversity.edu/academics/graduate/education

Lehman College of the City University of New York, School of Education, Department of Middle and High School Education, Program in Social Studies 7–12, Bronx, NY 10468-1589. Offers MA. *Accreditation:* NCATE. *Entrance requirements:* For master's, minimum GPA of 3.0 in social sciences, 2.7 overall.

Le Moyne College, Department of Education, Syracuse, NY 13214. Offers adolescent education (MS Ed, MST); adolescent education/special education (MS Ed, MST); adolescent English (MST), including grades 7-12; adolescent English/special education (MST), including grades 7-12; adolescent foreign language (MST), including grades 7-12; adolescent history (MST), including grades 7-12; childhood education (MS Ed); childhood education/special education (MS Ed); elementary education (MS Ed); general education (MS Ed); inclusive childhood education (MST); literacy education (MS Ed), including birth to grade 6, grades 5-12; school building leader (MS Ed); school building leadership (CAS); school district business leader (MS Ed, CAS); school district leader (MS Ed); school district leadership (CAS); secondary education (MS Ed); special education (MS Ed); teaching English to speakers of other languages (MS Ed); urban studies (MS Ed). *Accreditation:* TEAC. *Program availability:* Part-time, evening/weekend. *Faculty:* 8 full-time (5 women), 20 part-time/adjunct (12 women). *Students:* 66 full-time (40 women), 155 part-time (117 women); includes 13 minority (4 Black or African American, non-Hispanic/Latino; 2 American Indian or Alaska Native, non-Hispanic/Latino; 2 Asian, non-Hispanic/Latino; 5 Hispanic/Latino), 3 international. Average age 30. 74 applicants, 99% accepted, 66 enrolled. In 2016, 81 master's, 53 CASs awarded. *Degree requirements:* For master's, thesis. *Entrance requirements:* For master's, bachelor's degree with minimum undergraduate GPA of 3.0, 2 letters of recommendation, transcripts. Additional exam requirements/recommendations for international students: Required—TOEFL (minimum score 550 paper-based; 79 iBT); Recommended—IELTS (minimum score 6.5). *Application deadline:* For fall admission, 4/1 priority date for domestic and international students; for spring admission, 10/1 priority date for domestic and international students; for summer admission, 3/1 priority date for domestic and international students. Applications are processed on a rolling basis. Application fee: $50. Electronic applications accepted. *Expenses:* $700 per credit hour. *Financial support:* In 2016–17, 21 students received support. Career-related internships or fieldwork, scholarships/grants, and health care benefits available. Support available to part-time students. Financial award applicants required to submit FAFSA. *Faculty research:* Minority teachers, special education, multiculturalism, literacy, technology, media literacy learning, autism, school district organization, service-learning, higher level problem solving, teacher leadership. *Unit head:* Dr. Stephen C. Fleury, Chair, Department of Education, 315-445-4376, Fax: 315-445-4744, E-mail: fleurysc@lemoyne.edu. *Application contact:* Kristen P. Richards, Senior Director of Enrollment Management, 315-445-5444, Fax: 315-445-6092, E-mail: trapaskp@lemoyne.edu.
Website: http://www.lemoyne.edu/education

Lewis University, College of Education, Program in Secondary Education, Romeoville, IL 60446. Offers biology (MA); chemistry (MA); English (MA); history (MA); math (MA); physics (MA); psychology and social science (MA). *Program availability:* Part-time. *Students:* 12 full-time (7 women), 16 part-time (12 women); includes 6 minority (2 Black or African American, non-Hispanic/Latino; 3 Hispanic/Latino; 1 Two or more races, non-Hispanic/Latino). Average age 27. *Degree requirements:* For master's, departmental qualifying exam. *Entrance requirements:* For master's, writing exam, minimum GPA of 2.75, 2 letters of recommendation, interview. Additional exam requirements/recommendations for international students: Required—TOEFL (minimum score 550 paper-based; 80 iBT). *Application deadline:* For fall admission, 5/1 priority date for international students; for spring admission, 11/15 priority date for international students. Applications are processed on a rolling basis. Application fee: $40. Electronic applications accepted. *Expenses: Tuition:* Full-time $13,860; part-time $770 per credit hour. *Required fees:* $75 per semester. Tuition and fees vary according to degree level and program. *Financial support:* Federal Work-Study, scholarships/grants, and unspecified assistantships available. Financial award application deadline: 5/1; financial award applicants required to submit FAFSA. *Unit head:* Dr. Dorene Huvaere, Program Director, 815-838-0500 Ext. 5885, E-mail: huvaersdo@lewisu.edu. *Application contact:* Linda Campbell, Graduate Admissions Counselor, 815-836-5610, E-mail: campbeld@lewisu.edu.

Long Island University–LIU Brooklyn, Richard L. Conolly College of Liberal Arts and Sciences, Brooklyn, NY 11201-8423. Offers biology (MS); chemistry (MS); clinical psychology (PhD); communication sciences and disorders (MS); creative writing (MFA); English (MA); media arts (MA, MFA); political science (MA); psychology (MA); social science (MS); sociology (MA); speech-language pathology (MS); United Nations (Advanced Certificate); urban studies (MA); writing and production for television (MFA). *Program availability:* Part-time, evening/weekend. *Faculty:* 90 full-time (35 women), 125 part-time/adjunct (67 women). *Students:* 355 full-time (276 women), 220 part-time (161 women); includes 245 minority (119 Black or African American, non-Hispanic/Latino; 32 Asian, non-Hispanic/Latino; 80 Hispanic/Latino; 1 Native Hawaiian or other Pacific Islander, non-Hispanic/Latino; 13 Two or more races, non-Hispanic/Latino), 85 international. 792 applicants, 41% accepted, 141 enrolled. In 2016, 154 master's, 18 doctorates, 4 other advanced degrees awarded. *Degree requirements:* For master's, comprehensive exam (for some programs), thesis (for some programs); for doctorate, comprehensive exam (for some programs), thesis/dissertation (for some programs). *Entrance requirements:* For master's and doctorate, GRE. Additional exam requirements/recommendations for international students: Recommended—TOEFL (minimum score 550 paper-based; 79 iBT). *Application deadline:* Applications are processed on a rolling basis. Application fee: $50. Electronic applications accepted. *Expenses: Tuition:* Full-time $28,272; part-time $1178 per credit. *Required fees:* $451 per term. Tuition and fees vary according to degree level, program and student level. *Financial support:* In 2016–17, 120 fellowships with full and partial tuition reimbursements (averaging $915 per year), 5 research assistantships with full and partial tuition reimbursements (averaging $2,300 per year), 136 teaching assistantships with full and partial tuition reimbursements (averaging $2,300 per year) were awarded; career-related internships or fieldwork, Federal Work-Study, institutionally sponsored loans, scholarships/grants, tuition waivers (full and partial), and unspecified assistantships also available. Support available to part-time students. Financial award application deadline: 2/15; financial award applicants required to submit FAFSA. *Faculty research:* Nanocrystal polymerization of cellulose using electron microscopy. *Unit head:* Dr. Kevin Lauth, Acting Dean, 718-488-1347, E-mail: kevin.lauth@liu.edu. *Application contact:* Gabrielle Gannon, Director of Graduate Admissions, 718-488-1011, Fax: 718-780-6110, E-mail: bkln-admissions@liu.edu.

Manhattanville College, School of Education, Program in Middle Childhood/Adolescence Education (Grades 5-12), Purchase, NY 10577-2132. Offers biology (MAT); biology and special education (MPS); chemistry (MAT); chemistry and special education (MPS); English (MAT); English and special education (MPS); literacy and special education (MPS); literacy specialist (MPS); math and special education (MPS); mathematics (MAT); physics (MAT); social studies (MAT); social studies and special education (MPS); special education generalist (MPS); teaching languages other than English (MAT), including French, Italian, Latin, Spanish. *Program availability:* Part-time, evening/weekend. *Students:* 28 applicants, 86% accepted, 21 enrolled. In 2016, 23 master's awarded. *Degree requirements:* For master's, comprehensive exam (for some programs), thesis (for some programs), student teaching, research seminars, portfolios, internships, writing assessment. *Entrance requirements:* For master's, GRE or MAT, minimum undergraduate GPA of 3.0, 2 letters of recommendation. Additional exam requirements/recommendations for international students: Required—TOEFL (minimum score 85 iBT); Recommended—IELTS. *Application deadline:* For fall admission, 7/1 priority date for domestic and international students; for spring admission, 11/1 priority date for domestic and international students; for summer admission, 4/1 priority date for domestic and international students. Applications are processed on a rolling basis. Application fee: $75. Electronic applications accepted. *Expenses: Tuition:* Full-time $16,470; part-time $915 per credit. *Required fees:* $60 per semester. Part-time tuition and fees vary according to course load and program. *Financial support:* Teaching assistantships, career-related internships or fieldwork, Federal Work-Study, institutionally sponsored loans, scholarships/grants, and unspecified assistantships available. Financial award applicants required to submit FAFSA. *Unit head:* Victoria Fantozzi, Chairperson, Department of Curriculum and Instruction, 914-323-7138, E-mail: victoria.fantozzi@mville.edu. *Application contact:* Jeanine Pardey-Levine, Director of Graduate Enrollment Management, 914-323-3208, Fax: 914-694-1732, E-mail: edschool@mville.edu.
Website: http://www.mville.edu/programs#/search/19

Michigan State University, The Graduate School, College of Social Science, Department of History, East Lansing, MI 48824. Offers history (MA, PhD); history-secondary school teaching (MA). *Entrance requirements:* Additional exam requirements/recommendations for international students: Required—TOEFL. Electronic applications accepted.

Minnesota State University Mankato, College of Graduate Studies and Research, College of Social and Behavioral Sciences, Department of History, Mankato, MN 56001. Offers history (MA, MS); social studies (MAT). *Faculty:* 11. *Students:* 2 full-time (both women), 6 part-time (1 woman). *Degree requirements:* For master's, one foreign language, comprehensive exam, thesis or alternative. *Entrance requirements:* For master's, minimum GPA of 3.0, statement of purpose. Additional exam requirements/recommendations for international students: Required—TOEFL (minimum score 600 paper-based). *Application deadline:* For fall admission, 7/1 priority date for domestic students; for spring admission, 11/1 for domestic students. Applications are processed on a rolling basis. Application fee: $40. Electronic applications accepted. *Financial support:* Research assistantships, teaching assistantships with full tuition reimbursements, career-related internships or fieldwork, Federal Work-Study, institutionally sponsored loans, and unspecified assistantships available. Support available to part-time students. Financial award application deadline: 3/15. *Unit head:* Chris Corley, Graduate Coordinator, 507-389-1618, E-mail: christopher.corley@mnsu.edu.
Website: http://sbs.mnsu.edu/history/

Mississippi College, Graduate School, School of Education, Department of Teacher Education and Leadership, Clinton, MS 39058. Offers art (M Ed); biological science (M Ed); business education (M Ed); computer science (M Ed); dyslexia therapy (M Ed); educational leadership (M Ed, Ed D, Ed S); elementary education (M Ed, Ed S); English (M Ed); higher education administration (MS); mathematics (M Ed); secondary education (M Ed); social studies (history) (M Ed); teaching arts (M Ed). *Program availability:* Part-time, online learning. *Degree requirements:* For master's, comprehensive exam, thesis optional. *Entrance requirements:* For master's, NTE. Additional exam requirements/recommendations for international students: Recommended—TOEFL, IELTS. Electronic applications accepted.

Missouri State University, Graduate College, College of Humanities and Public Affairs, Department of History, Springfield, MO 65897. Offers history (MA); history education (MS Ed); history for teachers (Certificate). *Program availability:* Part-time, 100% online, blended/hybrid learning. *Faculty:* 18 full-time (7 women). *Students:* 6 full-time (1 woman), 33 part-time (11 women); includes 2 minority (1 Black or African American, non-Hispanic/Latino; 1 Asian, non-Hispanic/Latino), 1 international. Average age 34. 20 applicants, 65% accepted, 6 enrolled. In 2016, 8 master's awarded. *Degree requirements:* For master's, comprehensive exam, thesis or alternative. *Entrance requirements:* For master's, minimum GPA of 2.75, 24 hours of undergraduate course work in history (MA), 9-12 teaching certification (MS Ed). Additional exam requirements/recommendations for international students: Required—TOEFL (minimum score 550 paper-based; 79 iBT), IELTS (minimum score 6). *Application deadline:* For fall admission, 7/20 priority date for domestic students, 5/1 for international students; for spring admission, 12/20 priority date for domestic students, 9/1 for international students. Applications are processed on a rolling basis. Application fee: $35 ($50 for

international students). Electronic applications accepted. *Expenses:* Tuition, state resident: full-time $5830. Tuition, nonresident: full-time $10,708. *Required fees:* $1130. Tuition and fees vary according to class time, course level, course load and program. *Financial support:* Federal Work-Study, scholarships/grants, and unspecified assistantships available. Support available to part-time students. Financial award application deadline: 3/31; financial award applicants required to submit FAFSA. *Faculty research:* Early modern France, cultural history of modern Britain, Latin American history, women's history, American Civil War in Missouri. *Unit head:* Dr. Kathleen Kennedy, Department Head, 417-836-5511, Fax: 417-836-5523, E-mail: history@missouristate.edu. *Application contact:* Michael Edwards, Coordinator of Graduate Admissions, 417-836-5330, Fax: 417-836-6200, E-mail: michaeledwards@missouristate.edu.
Website: http://history.missouristate.edu/

Molloy College, Graduate Education Program, Rockville Centre, NY 11571-5002. Offers adolescent education in biology (MS Ed); adolescent special education (Advanced Certificate); bilingual extension (Advanced Certificate); childhood education (MS Ed); childhood special education (Advanced Certificate); early childhood education (MS Ed); educational technology (MS Ed); English (MS Ed); mathematics (MS Ed); social studies (MS Ed); Spanish (MS Ed); special education on both childhood and adolescent levels (MS Ed); teaching English to speakers of other languages (TESOL) in grades Pre-K to 12 (MS Ed); TESOL (Advanced Certificate). *Accreditation:* NCATE. *Program availability:* Part-time, evening/weekend. *Faculty:* 17 full-time (16 women), 23 part-time/adjunct (19 women). *Students:* 95 full-time (75 women), 221 part-time (177 women); includes 59 minority (14 Black or African American, non-Hispanic/Latino; 6 Asian, non-Hispanic/Latino; 38 Hispanic/Latino; 1 Two or more races, non-Hispanic/Latino), 1 international. Average age 42. 214 applicants, 66% accepted, 125 enrolled. In 2016, 95 master's, 4 Advanced Certificates awarded. *Entrance requirements:* Additional exam requirements/recommendations for international students: Required—TOEFL (minimum score 550 paper-based; 79 iBT). *Application deadline:* Applications are processed on a rolling basis. Application fee: $60. Electronic applications accepted. *Expenses: Tuition:* Full-time $19,170; part-time $1065 per credit. *Required fees:* $950; $790 per credit. Tuition and fees vary according to course load. *Financial support:* Applicants required to submit FAFSA. *Faculty research:* ESL - general education teacher collaboration; special education; school desegregation; American intellectual and social history; families and schools. *Unit head:* Joanne O'Brien, Associate Dean/Director, 516-323-3116, E-mail: jobrien@molloy.edu. *Application contact:* Jaclyn Machowicz, Assistant Director for Admissions, 516-323-4010, E-mail: jmachowicz@molloy.edu.

Morehead State University, Graduate Programs, College of Education, Department of Foundational and Graduate Studies in Education, Morehead, KY 40351. Offers adult and higher education (MA, Ed S); certified professional counselor (Ed S); counseling P-12 (MA); curriculum and instruction (Ed S); educational technology (MA Ed); instructional leadership (Ed S); school administration (MA); school counseling (Ed S); teacher leader business and marketing content (MA Ed); teacher leader business and marketing technology (MA Ed); teacher leader educational technology (MA Ed); teacher leader English (MA Ed); teacher leader gifted education (MA Ed); teacher leader IECE certification (MA Ed); teacher leader interdisciplinary education P-5 (MA Ed); teacher leader middle grades (MA Ed); teacher leader non IECE certification (MA Ed); teacher leader reading/writing - non-certification (MA Ed); teacher leader reading/writing certification (MA Ed); teacher leader school communication - certification (MA Ed); teacher leader school communication - non-certification (MA Ed); teacher leader social studies (MA Ed); teacher leader special education (MA Ed). *Accreditation:* NCATE. *Program availability:* Part-time, evening/weekend. *Degree requirements:* For master's, thesis optional, oral and/or written comprehensive exams; for Ed S, thesis, oral exam. *Entrance requirements:* For master's, GRE General Test, minimum overall undergraduate GPA of 2.5; for Ed S, GRE General Test, interview, master's degree, minimum GPA of 3.5, work experience. Additional exam requirements/recommendations for international students: Required—TOEFL (minimum score 500 paper-based). Electronic applications accepted. *Faculty research:* Character education, school accountability, computer applications for school administrators.

Morehead State University, Graduate Programs, College of Education, Department of Middle Grades and Secondary Education, Morehead, KY 40351. Offers business and marketing education (MAT); English/language arts 5-9 (MAT); French (MAT); health P-12 (MAT); mathematics 5-9 (MAT); physical education P-12 (MAT); science 5-9 (MAT); secondary biology (MAT); secondary chemistry (MAT); secondary earth science (MAT); secondary English (MAT); secondary math (MAT); secondary physics (MAT); secondary social studies (MAT); social studies 5-9 (MAT); Spanish (MAT). *Program availability:* Part-time, evening/weekend. *Degree requirements:* For master's, portfolio. *Entrance requirements:* For master's, GRE or PRAXIS II content exam, minimum overall undergraduate GPA of 2.5. Additional exam requirements/recommendations for international students: Required—TOEFL (minimum score 500 paper-based). Electronic applications accepted.

New York University, Steinhardt School of Culture, Education, and Human Development, Department of Art and Art Professions, Program in Art Education, New York, NY 10003-5799. Offers art, education, and community practice (MA); teachers of art, all grades (MA); teaching art/social studies 7-12 (MA), including 5-6 extension. *Accreditation:* TEAC. *Program availability:* Part-time. *Degree requirements:* For master's, thesis (for some programs). *Entrance requirements:* For master's, portfolio. Additional exam requirements/recommendations for international students: Required—TOEFL (minimum score 100 iBT). Electronic applications accepted. *Faculty research:* Multicultural aesthetic inquiry, urban art education, feminism, equity and social justice.

New York University, Steinhardt School of Culture, Education, and Human Development, Department of Music and Performing Arts Professions, Program in Educational Theatre, New York, NY 10012. Offers educational theatre and English 7-12 (MA); educational theatre and social studies 7-12 (MA); educational theatre in colleges and communities (MA, Ed D, PhD); educational theatre, all grades (MA). *Program availability:* Part-time. *Degree requirements:* For master's, thesis (for some programs); for doctorate, thesis/dissertation. *Entrance requirements:* For master's, audition; for doctorate, GRE General Test, interview. Additional exam requirements/recommendations for international students: Required—TOEFL (minimum score 100 iBT). Electronic applications accepted. *Faculty research:* Theatre for young audiences, drama in education, applied theatre, arts education assessment, reflective praxis.

New York University, Steinhardt School of Culture, Education, and Human Development, Department of Teaching and Learning, Program in Social Studies Education, New York, NY 10003. Offers teaching art/social studies 7-12 (MA), including 5-6 extension; teaching social studies 7-12 (MA). *Accreditation:* TEAC. *Program availability:* Part-time, evening/weekend. *Degree requirements:* For master's, thesis (for some programs). *Entrance requirements:* Additional exam requirements/recommendations for international students: Required—TOEFL (minimum score 100 iBT). Electronic applications accepted. *Faculty research:* Social studies education reform, ethnography and oral history, civic education, labor history and social studies curriculum, material culture.

North Carolina State University, Graduate School, College of Education, Department of Curriculum and Instruction, Program in Social Studies Education, Raleigh, NC 27695. Offers M Ed. *Entrance requirements:* For master's, GRE or MAT, 3 letters of reference, interview, minimum GPA of 3.0.

North Dakota State University, College of Graduate and Interdisciplinary Studies, College of Human Development and Education, School of Education, Fargo, ND 58102. Offers agricultural education (M Ed, MS), including agricultural education; counselor education (M Ed, MS, PhD), including clinical mental health counseling (M Ed, MS), counselor education and supervision (PhD), school counseling (M Ed, MS); curriculum and instruction (M Ed, MS); education (PhD); educational leadership (M Ed, MS, Ed S); family and consumer sciences education (M Ed, MS); history education (M Ed, MS); institutional analysis (Ed D); mathematics education (M Ed, MS); music education (M Ed, MS); occupational and adult education (Ed D); science education (M Ed, MS). *Accreditation:* NCATE. *Program availability:* Part-time, evening/weekend, online learning. *Degree requirements:* For master's, comprehensive exam; for doctorate, thesis/dissertation; for Ed S, thesis. *Entrance requirements:* For degree, GRE General Test, master's degree, minimum GPA of 3.25. Additional exam requirements/recommendations for international students: Required—TOEFL.

Northwest Missouri State University, Graduate School, College of Arts and Sciences, Maryville, MO 64468-6001. Offers biology (MS); elementary mathematics specialist (MS Ed); English (MA); English education (MS Ed); English pedagogy (MA); geographic information science (MS, Certificate); history (MS Ed); mathematics (MS); mathematics education (MS Ed); teaching: science (MS Ed). *Program availability:* Part-time. *Students:* 12 full-time (8 women), 69 part-time (31 women). *Degree requirements:* For master's, comprehensive exam. *Entrance requirements:* For master's, GRE General Test, writing sample. Additional exam requirements/recommendations for international students: Required—TOEFL (minimum score 550 paper-based). *Application deadline:* For fall admission, 7/1 for domestic and international students; for spring admission, 11/15 for domestic and international students. Applications are processed on a rolling basis. Application fee: $0 ($50 for international students). Electronic applications accepted. *Expenses:* Tuition, state resident: full-time $3447; part-time $383 per credit hour. Tuition, nonresident: full-time $5724; part-time $636 per credit hour. *Required fees:* $130 per credit hour. *Financial support:* Research assistantships with full tuition reimbursements, teaching assistantships with full tuition reimbursements, and administrative assistantships, tutorial assistantships available. Financial award application deadline: 4/1; financial award applicants required to submit FAFSA. *Unit head:* Dr. Michael Steiner, Dean, 660-562-1197.
Website: http://www.nwmissouri.edu/academics/arts/

Oregon State University, College of Education, Program in Teaching, Corvallis, OR 97331. Offers clinically based elementary education (MAT); elementary education (MAT); language arts (MAT); mathematics (MAT); music education (MAT); science (MAT); social studies (MAT). *Program availability:* Part-time, blended/hybrid learning. *Faculty:* 17 full-time (8 women), 2 part-time/adjunct (both women). *Students:* 57 full-time (39 women), 22 part-time (18 women); includes 11 minority (2 Hispanic/Latino; 1 Native Hawaiian or other Pacific Islander, non-Hispanic/Latino; 8 Two or more races, non-Hispanic/Latino). Average age 29. 131 applicants, 76% accepted, 76 enrolled. In 2016, 92 master's awarded. *Entrance requirements:* For master's, CBEST. Additional exam requirements/recommendations for international students: Required—TOEFL (minimum score 575 paper-based). *Application deadline:* For fall admission, 12/1 for domestic students. Application fee: $60. *Expenses:* Contact institution. *Unit head:* Dr. Larry Flick, Dean. *Application contact:* E-mail: askcoed@oregonstate.edu.
Website: http://education.oregonstate.edu/mat

Oregon State University, Interdisciplinary/Institutional Programs, Program in Environmental Sciences, Corvallis, OR 97331. Offers biogeochemistry (MA, MS, PhD); ecology (MA, MS, PhD); environmental education (MA, MS, PhD); environmental sciences (PSM); natural resources (MA, MS, PhD); quantitative analysis (MA, MS, PhD); social science (MA, MS, PhD); water resources (MA, MS, PhD). *Program availability:* Part-time. *Students:* 22 full-time (16 women), 10 part-time (4 women); includes 5 minority (2 Asian, non-Hispanic/Latino; 1 Hispanic/Latino; 2 Two or more races, non-Hispanic/Latino), 4 international. Average age 33. 51 applicants, 33% accepted, 8 enrolled. In 2016, 4 master's, 6 doctorates awarded. *Degree requirements:* For master's, variable foreign language requirement, thesis; for doctorate, thesis/dissertation. *Entrance requirements:* For master's and doctorate, GRE. Additional exam requirements/recommendations for international students: Required—TOEFL (minimum score 80 iBT), IELTS (minimum score 6.5). *Application deadline:* For fall admission, 1/15 priority date for domestic and international students. Application fee: $75 ($85 for international students). *Expenses:* Tuition, state resident: full-time $12,150; part-time $450 per credit. Tuition, nonresident: full-time $21,789; part-time $807 per credit. *Required fees:* $1651; $1507 per credit. One-time fee: $350. Tuition and fees vary according to course load, campus/location and program. *Unit head:* Dr. Carolyn Fonyo Boggess, Interim Director, 541-760-4196, E-mail: carolyn.fonyo@oregonstate.edu.
Website: http://gradschool.oregonstate.edu/environmental-sciences-graduate-program-esgp

Pace University, School of Education, New York, NY 10038. Offers adolescent education (MST), including biology, business education, chemistry, earth science, English, foreign languages, mathematics, physics, social studies, visual arts; childhood education (MST); early childhood development, learning and intervention (MST); educational technology studies (MS); inclusive adolescent education (MST), including biology, business education, chemistry, earth science, English, foreign languages, mathematics, physics, social studies, visual arts; integrated instruction for educational technology (Certificate); integrated instruction for literacy and technology (Certificate); literacy (MS Ed); special education (MS Ed). *Accreditation:* NCATE. *Program availability:* Part-time, evening/weekend, blended/hybrid learning. *Faculty:* 19 full-time (13 women), 86 part-time/adjunct (49 women). *Students:* 115 full-time (97 women), 543 part-time (381 women); includes 280 minority (137 Black or African American, non-Hispanic/Latino; 1 American Indian or Alaska Native, non-Hispanic/Latino; 40 Asian, non-Hispanic/Latino; 87 Hispanic/Latino; 15 Two or more races, non-Hispanic/Latino), 13 international. Average age 30. 181 applicants, 78% accepted, 72 enrolled. In 2016, 193 master's, 9 other advanced degrees awarded. *Degree requirements:* For master's, certification exams. *Entrance requirements:* For master's, GRE, interview, teaching certificate (except for MST). Additional exam requirements/recommendations for international students: Required—TOEFL (minimum score 88 iBT), IELTS or PTE. *Application deadline:* For fall admission, 8/1 priority date for domestic students, 6/1 for international students; for spring admission, 12/1 priority date for domestic students, 10/1 for international students. Applications are processed on a rolling basis. Application fee: $70. Electronic applications accepted. *Expenses:* Contact institution. *Financial support:* In 2016–17, 17 students received support, including 17 research assistantships with partial tuition reimbursements available (averaging $6,020 per year); career-related internships or fieldwork and Federal Work-Study also available. Financial award application deadline: 9/1; financial award applicants required to submit FAFSA. *Faculty research:* STEM education, TESOL, teacher education, special education, language and literary development. *Total annual research expenditures:* $290,153. *Unit head:* Dr. Xiao-Lei Wang, Dean, School of Education, 914-773-3876, E-mail: xwang@

pace.edu. *Application contact:* Susan Ford-Goldschein, Director of Graduate Admissions, 212-346-1531, Fax: 212-346-1585, E-mail: graduateadmission@pace.edu. Website: http://www.pace.edu/school-of-education

Plymouth State University, College of Graduate Studies, Graduate Studies in Education, Program in Heritage Studies, Plymouth, NH 03264-1595. Offers M Ed. *Program availability:* Part-time, evening/weekend. *Degree requirements:* For master's, internship. *Entrance requirements:* For master's, GRE General Test or MAT, minimum GPA of 3.0, resume.

Plymouth State University, College of Graduate Studies, Graduate Studies in Education, Program in Secondary Education, Plymouth, NH 03264-1595. Offers curriculum and instruction (M Ed); language education (M Ed); library media (M Ed); physical education (M Ed); social studies education (M Ed); special education (M Ed). *Program availability:* Part-time, evening/weekend. *Entrance requirements:* For master's, MAT.

Portland State University, Graduate Studies, College of Liberal Arts and Sciences, Interdisciplinary Programs in General Science, General Social Science, and General Arts and Letters, Portland, OR 97207-0751. Offers general arts and letters education (MAT, MST); general science education (MAT, MST); general social science education (MAT, MST). *Program availability:* Part-time, evening/weekend. *Degree requirements:* For master's, variable foreign language requirement, written exam. *Entrance requirements:* For master's, minimum GPA of 3.0 in upper-division course work or 2.75 overall. Additional exam requirements/recommendations for international students: Required—TOEFL (minimum score 550 paper-based; 80 iBT), IELTS (minimum score 6.5). *Application deadline:* For fall admission, 4/1 priority date for domestic students, 3/1 priority date for international students. *Expenses:* Contact institution. *Financial support:* Federal Work-Study and unspecified assistantships available. Support available to part-time students. Financial award application deadline: 3/1; financial award applicants required to submit FAFSA. *Unit head:* Robert Mercer, Associate Dean, 503-725-5059, Fax: 503-725-3693, E-mail: mercerr@pdx.edu. *Application contact:* 503-725-3511, Fax: 503-725-5525.

Purdue University, Graduate School, College of Education, Department of Curriculum and Instruction, West Lafayette, IN 47907. Offers agricultural and extension education (MS, MS Ed, PhD, Ed S); art education (PhD); career and technical education (MS Ed, PhD, Ed S); curriculum studies (MS Ed, PhD, Ed S); educational technology (MS Ed, PhD, Ed S); elementary education (MS Ed); family and consumer sciences education (MS Ed, PhD, Ed S); foreign language education (MS Ed, PhD, Ed S); industrial technology (PhD, Ed S); language arts (MS Ed, PhD, Ed S); literacy (MS Ed, PhD, Ed S); mathematics education (MS, MS Ed, PhD, Ed S); science education (MS, MS Ed, PhD, Ed S); social studies education (MS Ed, PhD, Ed S). *Accreditation:* NCATE. *Program availability:* Part-time, evening/weekend. *Faculty:* 37 full-time (27 women), 1 (woman) part-time/adjunct. *Students:* 78 full-time (50 women), 286 part-time (195 women); includes 68 minority (25 Black or African American, non-Hispanic/Latino; 3 American Indian or Alaska Native, non-Hispanic/Latino; 10 Asian, non-Hispanic/Latino; 22 Hispanic/Latino; 1 Native Hawaiian or other Pacific Islander, non-Hispanic/Latino; 7 Two or more races, non-Hispanic/Latino), 44 international. Average age 36. 150 applicants, 79% accepted, 73 enrolled. In 2016, 107 master's, 20 doctorates, 2 other advanced degrees awarded. *Degree requirements:* For master's, thesis optional; for doctorate, thesis/dissertation, oral and written exams; for Ed S, oral presentation, project. *Entrance requirements:* For master's, GRE General Test (if undergraduate GPA is below 3.0), minimum undergraduate GPA of 3.0 or equivalent; for doctorate, GRE General Test (minimum combined verbal and quantitative score of 1000, 300 for new scoring), minimum undergraduate GPA of 3.0 or equivalent; master's degree with minimum GPA of 3.0 or equivalent; for Ed S, GRE General Test (minimum combined verbal and quantitative score of 1000, 300 for new scoring), minimum undergraduate GPA of 3.0 or equivalent; master's degree. Additional exam requirements/recommendations for international students: Required—TOEFL (minimum score 550 paper-based; 77 iBT). *Application deadline:* For fall admission, 12/15 for domestic students, 3/1 for international students; for spring admission, 9/15 for domestic students, 8/1 for international students. Application fee: $60 ($75 for international students). Electronic applications accepted. *Financial support:* Fellowships with full tuition reimbursements, research assistantships with full tuition reimbursements, teaching assistantships with full tuition reimbursements, career-related internships or fieldwork, and tuition waivers (full) available. Support available to part-time students. Financial award application deadline: 3/1; financial award applicants required to submit FAFSA. *Faculty research:* Literacy acquisition and development, teacher beliefs and knowledge, recruitment and retention of underrepresented students, economic education, literacy discourse. *Unit head:* Janet M. Alsup, Head, 765-494-9667, E-mail: alsupj@purdue.edu. *Application contact:* Heather Brinkman, Graduate Contact, 765-494-2345, E-mail: hbrinkma@purdue.edu.
Website: http://www.edci.purdue.edu/

Queens College of the City University of New York, Division of Education, Department of Secondary Education and Youth Services, Queens, NY 11367-1597. Offers adolescent biology (MAT); art (MS Ed); biology (MS Ed, AC); chemistry (MS Ed, AC); earth sciences (MS Ed, AC); English (MS Ed, AC); French (MS Ed); Italian (MS Ed, AC); literacy education (MS Ed); mathematics (MS Ed, AC); music (MS Ed, AC); physics (MS Ed, AC); social studies (MS Ed, AC); Spanish (MS Ed, AC). *Program availability:* Part-time, evening/weekend. *Faculty:* 22 full-time (14 women), 40 part-time/adjunct (26 women). *Students:* 31 full-time (21 women), 356 part-time (211 women); includes 164 minority (22 Black or African American, non-Hispanic/Latino; 54 Asian, non-Hispanic/Latino; 81 Hispanic/Latino; 7 Two or more races, non-Hispanic/Latino), 11 international. Average age 29. 236 applicants, 88% accepted, 121 enrolled. In 2016, 119 master's, 51 other advanced degrees awarded. *Degree requirements:* For master's, research project. *Entrance requirements:* For master's, minimum GPA of 3.0. Additional exam requirements/recommendations for international students: Required—TOEFL, IELTS. *Application deadline:* For fall admission, 4/1 for domestic students; for spring admission, 11/1 for domestic students. Applications are processed on a rolling basis. Application fee: $125. Electronic applications accepted. *Expenses:* Tuition, state resident: full-time $5065; part-time $425 per credit. Tuition, nonresident: part-time $780 per credit. *Required fees:* $522; $397 per credit. Part-time tuition and fees vary according to course load and program. *Financial support:* Career-related internships or fieldwork available. Financial award application deadline: 4/1; financial award applicants required to submit FAFSA. *Unit head:* Dr. Eleanor Armour-Thomas, Chairperson, 718-997-5150, E-mail: armourthomas@yahoo.com.

Quinnipiac University, School of Education, Program in Secondary Education, Hamden, CT 06518-1940. Offers biology (MAT); English (MAT); history/social studies (MAT); mathematics (MAT); Spanish (MAT). *Accreditation:* NCATE. *Faculty:* 6 full-time (2 women), 24 part-time/adjunct (16 women). *Students:* 43 full-time (29 women), 1 part-time (0 women); includes 6 minority (1 Asian, non-Hispanic/Latino; 4 Hispanic/Latino; 1 Two or more races, non-Hispanic/Latino). 43 applicants, 98% accepted, 36 enrolled. In 2016, 32 master's awarded. *Entrance requirements:* For master's, PRAXIS I or PRAXIS Core Academic Skills Exam, minimum GPA of 3.0, interview. *Application deadline:* For fall admission, 5/1 priority date for domestic students. Applications are processed on a rolling basis. Application fee: $45. Electronic applications accepted. *Expenses: Tuition:* Part-time $985 per credit. *Required fees:* $40 per credit. $150 per semester. Tuition and fees vary according to program. *Financial support:* Career-related internships or fieldwork, Federal Work-Study, and unspecified assistantships available. Financial award application deadline: 6/1; financial award applicants required to submit FAFSA. *Faculty research:* Multicultural and urban education/leadership, challenges of teaching diverse learners, scholarship of teaching and learning, technology and teaching, humor and education. *Unit head:* Mordechai Gordon, Program Director, 203-582-8442, E-mail: mordechai.gordon@qu.edu. *Application contact:* Office of Graduate Admissions, 203-582-8672, Fax: 203-582-3443, E-mail: graduate@qu.edu.
Website: http://www.qu.edu/gradeducation

Regis College, Program in Heritage Studies for a Global Society, Weston, MA 02493. Offers heritage studies for a global society (MA). *Program availability:* Part-time, blended/hybrid learning. *Degree requirements:* For master's, capstone. *Entrance requirements:* Additional exam requirements/recommendations for international students: Required—TOEFL; Recommended—IELTS. *Application deadline:* Applications are processed on a rolling basis. Application fee: $65. Electronic applications accepted. *Financial support:* Federal Work-Study and unspecified assistantships available. Financial award applicants required to submit FAFSA. *Unit head:* Kathryn Edney, Director, 781-768-7196.

Rhode Island College, School of Graduate Studies, Feinstein School of Education and Human Development, Department of Educational Studies, Providence, RI 02908-1991. Offers advanced studies in teaching and learning (M Ed); English (MAT); French (MAT); history (MAT); math (MAT); secondary education (MAT); Spanish (MAT); teaching English as a second language (M Ed). *Accreditation:* NCATE. *Program availability:* Part-time, evening/weekend. *Faculty:* 6 full-time (5 women), 8 part-time/adjunct (6 women). *Students:* 5 full-time (2 women), 53 part-time (48 women); includes 8 minority (2 Black or African American, non-Hispanic/Latino; 2 Asian, non-Hispanic/Latino; 3 Hispanic/Latino; 1 Two or more races, non-Hispanic/Latino). Average age 39. In 2016, 29 master's awarded. *Degree requirements:* For master's, capstone or comprehensive assessment. *Entrance requirements:* For master's, GRE or MAT (for most programs), minimum undergraduate GPA of 3.0; baccalaureate degree in English, French, history, math or Spanish; 3 letters of recommendation; interview. Additional exam requirements/recommendations for international students: Recommended—TOEFL (minimum score 550 paper-based; 79 iBT). *Application deadline:* For fall admission, 3/1 for domestic students; for spring admission, 11/1 for domestic students. Applications are processed on a rolling basis. Application fee: $50. Electronic applications accepted. *Expenses:* Tuition, state resident: full-time $8928; part-time $372 per credit. Tuition, nonresident: full-time $17,376; part-time $724 per credit. *Required fees:* $604; $22 per credit. One-time fee: $74. *Financial support:* In 2016–17, 1 teaching assistantship with full tuition reimbursement (averaging $3,000 per year) was awarded; career-related internships or fieldwork, Federal Work-Study, scholarships/grants, health care benefits, and unspecified assistantships also available. Support available to part-time students. Financial award application deadline: 5/15; financial award applicants required to submit FAFSA. *Unit head:* Dr. Gerri August, Chair, 401-456-8170. *Application contact:* Graduate Studies, 401-456-8700.
Website: http://www.ric.edu/educationalStudies/

Rider University, Department of Graduate Education, Leadership and Counseling, Teacher Certification Program, Lawrenceville, NJ 08648-3001. Offers business education (Certificate); elementary education (Certificate); English as a second language (Certificate); English education (Certificate); mathematics education (Certificate); preschool to grade 3 (Certificate); science education (Certificate); social studies education (Certificate); world languages (Certificate), including French, German, Spanish. *Program availability:* Part-time. *Degree requirements:* For Certificate, internship, professional portfolio. *Entrance requirements:* For degree, PRAXIS, resume. Additional exam requirements/recommendations for international students: Required—TOEFL (minimum score 550 paper-based). Electronic applications accepted. *Faculty research:* Conceptual foundations for optimal development of creativity; creative theory, cognitive processes in mathematics learning, teacher collaboration.

Rivier University, School of Graduate Studies, Department of History, Law and Government, Nashua, NH 03060. Offers social studies education (MAT).

Rutgers University–New Brunswick, Graduate School of Education, Department of Educational Theory, Policy and Administration, Program in Social Studies Education, Piscataway, NJ 08854-8097. Offers Ed M, Ed D. *Program availability:* Part-time, evening/weekend. Terminal master's awarded for partial completion of doctoral program. *Degree requirements:* For master's, comprehensive exam; for doctorate, thesis/dissertation, qualifying exam. *Entrance requirements:* For master's and doctorate, GRE General Test. Additional exam requirements/recommendations for international students: Required—TOEFL. Electronic applications accepted. *Faculty research:* Academic freedom, equal educational opportunity, social studies curricula.

St. John Fisher College, Ralph C. Wilson Jr. School of Education, Program in Adolescence Education and Special Education, Rochester, NY 14618-3597. Offers adolescence education: biology with special education (MS Ed); adolescence education: chemistry with special education (MS Ed); adolescence education: English with special education (MS Ed); adolescence education: French with special education (MS Ed); adolescence education: math with special education (MS Ed); adolescence education: physics with special education (MS Ed); adolescence education: social studies with special education (MS Ed); adolescence education: Spanish with special education (MS Ed). *Program availability:* Part-time, evening/weekend. *Faculty:* 7 full-time (6 women), 5 part-time/adjunct (all women). *Students:* 15 full-time (6 women), 9 part-time (6 women); includes 3 minority (2 Black or African American, non-Hispanic/Latino; 1 Hispanic/Latino). Average age 28. 16 applicants, 56% accepted, 6 enrolled. In 2016, 8 master's awarded. *Degree requirements:* For master's, field experiences, student teaching, LAST. *Entrance requirements:* For master's, 2 letters of recommendation, personal statement, current resume. Additional exam requirements/recommendations for international students: Required—TOEFL (minimum score 575 paper-based; 80 iBT). *Application deadline:* Applications are processed on a rolling basis. Application fee: $30. Electronic applications accepted. *Expenses:* $885 per credit hour. *Financial support:* Scholarships/grants available. Financial award applicants required to submit FAFSA. *Faculty research:* Arts and humanities, urban schools, constructivist learning, at-risk students, mentoring. *Unit head:* Dr. Susan Hildenbrand, Program Director, 585-385-7297, E-mail: shildenbrand@sjfc.edu. *Application contact:* Michelle Gosier, Associate Director of Transfer and Graduate Admissions, 585-385-8064, E-mail: mgosier@sjfc.edu.

Slippery Rock University of Pennsylvania, Graduate Studies (Recruitment), College of Education, Department of Secondary Education/Foundations of Education, Slippery Rock, PA 16057-1383. Offers secondary education (M Ed), including English, math/science, social studies. *Accreditation:* NCATE. *Program availability:* Part-time, evening/weekend, 100% online. *Faculty:* 7 full-time (2 women), 1 part-time/adjunct (0 women). *Students:* 43 full-time (23 women), 36 part-time (23 women); includes 2 minority (1 Black or African American, non-Hispanic/Latino; 1 Two or more races, non-Hispanic/Latino). Average age 29. 77 applicants, 79% accepted, 35 enrolled. In 2016, 36 master's awarded. *Degree requirements:* For master's, comprehensive exam, thesis (for some programs). *Entrance requirements:* For master's, copy of teaching certification and two

letters of recommendation (for some programs). Additional exam requirements/recommendations for international students: Required—TOEFL (minimum score 550 paper-based; 80 iBT). *Application deadline:* For fall admission, 3/1 priority date for domestic students, 5/1 priority date for international students; for spring admission, 10/1 priority date for domestic students, 9/1 priority date for international students. Applications are processed on a rolling basis. Application fee: $25 ($30 for international students). Electronic applications accepted. *Expenses:* $646.50 per credit in-state, $936.80 per credit out-of-state; $581.45 per online credit in-state, $648.65 per online credit out-of-state. *Financial support:* In 2016–17, 12 students received support. Career-related internships or fieldwork, Federal Work-Study, institutionally sponsored loans, scholarships/grants, tuition waivers (partial), and unspecified assistantships available. Support available to part-time students. Financial award application deadline: 5/1; financial award applicants required to submit FAFSA. *Unit head:* Dr. Jeffrey Lehman, Graduate Coordinator, 724-738-2311, Fax: 724-738-4987, E-mail: jeffrey.lehman@sru.edu. *Application contact:* Brandi Weber-Mortimer, Director of Graduate Studies, 724-738-2051, Fax: 724-738-2146, E-mail: graduate.admissions@sru.edu.
Website: http://www.sru.edu/academics/colleges-and-departments/coe/departments/secondary-education-/-foundations-of-education

Smith College, Graduate and Special Programs, Department of Education and Child Study, Program in Secondary Education, Northampton, MA 01063. Offers secondary education (MAT), including biological sciences education, chemistry education, English education, French education, geology education, government education, history education, mathematics education, physics education, Spanish education. *Program availability:* Part-time. *Students:* 3 full-time (2 women), 3 part-time (2 women). Average age 31. 14 applicants, 79% accepted, 4 enrolled. In 2016, 11 master's awarded. *Entrance requirements:* Additional exam requirements/recommendations for international students: Required—TOEFL (minimum score 595 paper-based; 97 iBT), IELTS. *Application deadline:* For fall admission, 4/1 for domestic students, 1/15 priority date for international students; for spring admission, 12/1 for domestic students. Application fee: $60. *Expenses: Tuition:* Full-time $34,560; part-time $1440 per credit. Tuition and fees vary according to course load and program. *Financial support:* In 2016–17, 5 students received support, including 1 fellowship with full tuition reimbursement available; scholarships/grants also available. Support available to part-time students. Financial award application deadline: 4/1; financial award applicants required to submit CSS PROFILE or FAFSA. *Unit head:* Rosetta Cohen, Graduate Student Advisor, 413-585-3266, E-mail: rcohen@smith.edu. *Application contact:* Ruth Morgan, Program Assistant, 413-585-3050, Fax: 413-585-3054, E-mail: gradstdy@smith.edu.
Website: http://www.smith.edu/educ/

Smith College, Graduate and Special Programs, Department of Government, Northampton, MA 01063. Offers secondary education (MAT), including government education. *Program availability:* Part-time. *Students:* 1 applicant, 100% accepted, 1 enrolled. *Entrance requirements:* Additional exam requirements/recommendations for international students: Required—TOEFL (minimum score 595 paper-based; 97 iBT), IELTS. *Application deadline:* For fall admission, 4/1 for domestic students, 1/15 for international students; for spring admission, 12/1 for domestic students. Application fee: $60. *Expenses: Tuition:* Full-time $34,560; part-time $1440 per credit. Tuition and fees vary according to course load and program. *Financial support:* Scholarships/grants available. Support available to part-time students. Financial award application deadline: 4/1; financial award applicants required to submit CSS PROFILE or FAFSA. *Unit head:* Gregory White, Department Chair, 413-585-3542, E-mail: gwhite@smith.edu. *Application contact:* Ruth Morgan, Program Assistant, 413-585-3050, Fax: 413-585-3054, E-mail: gradstdy@smith.edu.
Website: http://www.smith.edu/gov/

Smith College, Graduate and Special Programs, Department of History, Northampton, MA 01063. Offers secondary education (MAT), including history education. *Program availability:* Part-time. *Students:* 2 full-time (1 woman), 1 part-time (0 women). Average age 28. 6 applicants, 83% accepted, 3 enrolled. In 2016, 2 master's awarded. *Entrance requirements:* Additional exam requirements/recommendations for international students: Required—TOEFL (minimum score 595 paper-based; 97 iBT), IELTS. *Application deadline:* For fall admission, 4/1 for domestic students, 1/15 for international students; for spring admission, 12/1 for domestic students. Application fee: $60. *Expenses: Tuition:* Full-time $34,560; part-time $1440 per credit. Tuition and fees vary according to course load and program. *Financial support:* In 2016–17, 2 students received support. Scholarships/grants available. Support available to part-time students. Financial award application deadline: 4/1; financial award applicants required to submit CSS PROFILE or FAFSA. *Unit head:* Joshua Birk, Graduate Student Adviser, 413-585-3740, E-mail: jbirk@smith.edu. *Application contact:* Ruth Morgan, Program Assistant, 413-585-3050, Fax: 413-585-3054, E-mail: gradstdy@smith.edu.
Website: http://www.smith.edu/history/

South Carolina State University, College of Graduate and Professional Studies, Department of Education, Orangeburg, SC 29117-0001. Offers early childhood education (MAT); education (M Ed); elementary education (M Ed, MAT); English (MAT); general science/biology (MAT); mathematics (MAT); secondary education (M Ed), including biology education, business education, counselor education, English education, home economics education, industrial education, mathematics education, science education, social studies education; special education (M Ed), including emotionally handicapped, learning disabilities, mentally handicapped. *Accreditation:* NCATE. *Program availability:* Part-time, evening/weekend. *Faculty:* 12 full-time (8 women), 3 part-time/adjunct (1 woman). *Students:* 28 full-time (20 women), 20 part-time (17 women); includes 45 minority (44 Black or African American, non-Hispanic/Latino; 1 Two or more races, non-Hispanic/Latino). Average age 31. 22 applicants, 100% accepted, 16 enrolled. In 2016, 9 master's awarded. *Degree requirements:* For master's, thesis optional, departmental qualifying exam. *Entrance requirements:* For master's, GRE General Test, NTE, interview, teaching certificate. *Application deadline:* For fall admission, 6/15 priority date for domestic students, 6/15 for international students; for spring admission, 11/1 for domestic and international students. Application fee: $25. Electronic applications accepted. *Expenses:* Tuition, state resident: full-time $8938; part-time $579 per credit hour. Tuition, nonresident: full-time $19,010; part-time $1139 per credit hour. *Required fees:* $1482; $82 per credit hour. *Financial support:* Fellowships, career-related internships or fieldwork, Federal Work-Study, and scholarships/grants available. Financial award application deadline: 6/1. *Unit head:* Dr. Charlie Spell, Interim Chair, Department of Education, 803-536-8963, Fax: 803-516-4568, E-mail: cspell@scsu.edu. *Application contact:* Curtis Foskey, Coordinator of Graduate Studies, 803-536-8419, Fax: 803-536-8812, E-mail: cfoskey@scsu.edu.

Southwestern Oklahoma State University, College of Arts and Sciences, Department of Social Sciences, Weatherford, OK 73096-3098. Offers M Ed. *Degree requirements:* For master's, exam. *Entrance requirements:* For master's, GRE General Test or minimum undergraduate GPA of 3.0. Additional exam requirements/recommendations for international students: Required—TOEFL.

Spring Hill College, Graduate Programs, Program in Liberal Arts, Mobile, AL 36608-1791. Offers fine arts (MLA); history and social science (MLA); leadership and ethics (MLA, Postbaccalaureate Certificate); literature (MLA); studio art (Postbaccalaureate Certificate). *Program availability:* Part-time, evening/weekend. *Faculty:* 5 full-time (0 women), 2 part-time/adjunct (1 woman). *Students:* 2 full-time (1 woman), 31 part-time (10 women); includes 4 minority (3 Black or African American, non-Hispanic/Latino; 1 Hispanic/Latino), 3 international. Average age 35. In 2016, 7 master's, 1 other advanced degree awarded. *Degree requirements:* For master's, capstone course, completion of program within 6 years of initial admittance. *Entrance requirements:* For master's, bachelor's degree with minimum undergraduate GPA of 3.0 or graduate/professional degree. Additional exam requirements/recommendations for international students: Required—TOEFL (minimum score 550 paper-based; 80 iBT), IELTS (minimum score 6.5), CPE or CAE (minimum score C), Michigan English Language Assessment Battery (minimum score 90). *Application deadline:* For fall admission, 8/1 priority date for domestic and international students; for spring admission, 12/1 priority date for domestic and international students. Applications are processed on a rolling basis. Application fee: $25 ($35 for international students). Electronic applications accepted. *Expenses:* Contact institution. *Financial support:* Applicants required to submit FAFSA. *Unit head:* Dr. Thomas J. Hoffman, Director, 251-380-4184, Fax: 251-460-2115, E-mail: thoffman@shc.edu. *Application contact:* Robert Stewart, Vice President of Enrollment, 251-380-3030, Fax: 251-460-2186, E-mail: rstewart@shc.edu.
Website: http://ug.shc.edu/graduate-degrees/master-liberal-arts/

State University of New York at New Paltz, Graduate School, School of Education, Department of Secondary Education, New Paltz, NY 12561. Offers adolescence education: biology (MAT, MS Ed); adolescence education: chemistry (MAT, MS Ed); adolescence education: earth science (MAT, MS Ed); adolescence education: English (MAT, MS Ed); adolescence education: French (MAT, MS Ed); adolescence education: social studies (MAT, MS Ed); adolescence education: Spanish (MAT, MS Ed); second language education (MS Ed, AC), including second language education (MS Ed), teaching English language learners (AC). *Accreditation:* NCATE. *Program availability:* Part-time, evening/weekend. *Students:* 60 full-time (36 women), 59 part-time (48 women); includes 28 minority (2 Black or African American, non-Hispanic/Latino; 2 Asian, non-Hispanic/Latino; 22 Hispanic/Latino; 2 Two or more races, non-Hispanic/Latino). 96 applicants, 83% accepted, 54 enrolled. In 2016, 56 master's awarded. *Degree requirements:* For master's, comprehensive exam (for some programs), portfolio. *Entrance requirements:* For master's, minimum GPA of 3.0, New York state teaching certificate (MS Ed). Additional exam requirements/recommendations for international students: Required—TOEFL (minimum score 550 paper-based; 80 iBT), IELTS (minimum score 6.5). *Application deadline:* For fall admission, 3/1 priority date for domestic students, 3/1 for international students; for spring admission, 10/1 priority date for domestic students, 10/1 for international students. Application fee: $50. Electronic applications accepted. *Financial support:* Application deadline: 8/1. *Unit head:* Dr. Laura Dull, Chair, 845-257-2849, E-mail: dullj@newpaltz.edu. *Application contact:* Vika Shock, Director of Graduate Admissions, 845-257-3285, Fax: 845-257-3284, E-mail: gradschool@newpaltz.edu.
Website: http://www.newpaltz.edu/secondaryed/

State University of New York at Plattsburgh, School of Education, Health, and Human Services, Program in Teacher Education: Adolescence Education, Plattsburgh, NY 12901-2681. Offers adolescence education (MST); biology 7-12 (MST); chemistry 7-12 (MST); earth science 7-12 (MST); English 7-12 (MST); French 7-12 (MST); mathematics 7-12 (MST); physics 7-12 (MST); social studies 7-12 (MST); Spanish 7-12 (MST). *Accreditation:* TEAC. *Program availability:* Part-time, evening/weekend. *Entrance requirements:* For master's, minimum GPA of 2.75. Additional exam requirements/recommendations for international students: Required—TOEFL.

State University of New York College at Old Westbury, School of Education, Old Westbury, NY 11568-0210. Offers biology (MAT, MS); chemistry (MAT, MS); English language arts (MAT, MS); math (MAT, MS); social studies (MAT, MS); Spanish (MAT, MS). *Program availability:* Part-time, evening/weekend. *Faculty:* 17 full-time (9 women), 5 part-time/adjunct (2 women). *Students:* 46 full-time (19 women), 26 part-time (17 women); includes 20 minority (1 Black or African American, non-Hispanic/Latino; 4 Asian, non-Hispanic/Latino; 15 Hispanic/Latino). Average age 30. 35 applicants, 77% accepted, 23 enrolled. In 2016, 25 master's awarded. *Entrance requirements:* For master's, Liberal Arts and Sciences Test, undergraduate degree with at least 30 semester hours of appropriate coursework as defined by the respective discipline; minimum cumulative undergraduate GPA of 3.0; two letters of recommendation (one from an academic source); essay. Additional exam requirements/recommendations for international students: Required—TOEFL (minimum score 550 paper-based); Recommended—IELTS. Application fee: $50. *Expenses:* Tuition, state resident: full-time $10,870; part-time $453 per credit. Tuition, nonresident: full-time $22,210; part-time $925 per credit. *Required fees:* $24.35 per credit. $76 per semester. Tuition and fees vary according to course load. *Financial support:* Applicants required to submit FAFSA. *Unit head:* Dr. Nancy Brown, Dean, School of Education, 516-876-3275, E-mail: brownn@oldwestbury.edu. *Application contact:* Philip D'Angelo, Graduate Admissions Office, 516-876-3073, E-mail: enroll@oldwestbury.edu.

State University of New York College at Potsdam, School of Education and Professional Studies, Program in Secondary Education, Potsdam, NY 13676. Offers English education (MST); mathematics education (MST); science education (MST), including biology, chemistry, earth science, physics; social studies education (MST). *Accreditation:* NCATE. *Degree requirements:* For master's, culminating experience. *Entrance requirements:* For master's, minimum GPA of 2.75 in last 60 hours of course work (3.0 for English program). Additional exam requirements/recommendations for international students: Required—TOEFL (minimum score 550 paper-based; 80 iBT), IELTS (minimum score 6). Electronic applications accepted.

Stony Brook University, State University of New York, School of Professional Development, Stony Brook, NY 11794-443. Offers biology (MAT); chemistry (MAT); coaching (Graduate Certificate); earth science (MAT); educational computing (Graduate Certificate); educational leadership (Advanced Certificate); English (MAT); environmental management (MPS, Graduate Certificate); French (MAT); German (MAT); higher education administration (MA, Certificate); human resource management (MS, Graduate Certificate); industrial management (Graduate Certificate); information systems management (Graduate Certificate); Italian (MAT); liberal studies (MA); mathematics (MAT); operations research (Graduate Certificate); physics (MAT); school district business leadership (Advanced Certificate); social studies (MAT); Spanish (MAT). *Program availability:* Part-time, evening/weekend, online learning. *Faculty:* 4 full-time (3 women), 77 part-time/adjunct (34 women). *Students:* 197 full-time (125 women), 965 part-time (674 women); includes 222 minority (79 Black or African American, non-Hispanic/Latino; 2 American Indian or Alaska Native, non-Hispanic/Latino; 35 Asian, non-Hispanic/Latino; 87 Hispanic/Latino; 1 Native Hawaiian or other Pacific Islander, non-Hispanic/Latino; 18 Two or more races, non-Hispanic/Latino), 5 international. Average age 33. 462 applicants, 87% accepted, 317 enrolled. In 2016, 348 master's, 159 other advanced degrees awarded. *Degree requirements:* For master's, one foreign language, thesis or alternative. *Entrance requirements:* Additional exam requirements/recommendations for international students: Required—TOEFL (minimum score 85 iBT). *Application deadline:* For fall admission, 1/15 for domestic students, 6/1 for international students; for spring admission, 10/1 for domestic and international students. Applications are processed on a rolling basis. Application fee: $100.

Social Sciences Education

Expenses: Contact institution. *Financial support:* Fellowships, research assistantships, teaching assistantships, and career-related internships or fieldwork available. Support available to part-time students. *Unit head:* Dr. Ken Lindblom, Dean, 631-632-7049, Fax: 631-632-9046, E-mail: kenneth.lindblom@stonybrook.edu. *Application contact:* Melissa Jordan, Assistant Dean, 631-632-7751, E-mail: melissa.jordan@stonybrook.edu.
Website: http://www.stonybrook.edu/spd/

Syracuse University, School of Education, MS Program in Social Studies Education Preparation (Grades 7-12), Syracuse, NY 13244. Offers MS. *Program availability:* Part-time. *Students:* Average age 24. *Degree requirements:* For master's, thesis or alternative. *Entrance requirements:* For master's, GRE, baccalaureate degree from regionally-accredited college/university, experience working with young people, personal statement, recommendations. Additional exam requirements/recommendations for international students: Required—TOEFL (minimum score 100 iBT). *Application deadline:* For fall admission, 1/15 priority date for domestic and international students; for spring admission, 10/15 priority date for domestic and international students; for summer admission, 4/15 priority date for domestic and international students. Applications are processed on a rolling basis. Application fee: $75. Electronic applications accepted. *Expenses: Tuition:* Full-time $25,974; part-time $1443 per credit hour. *Required fees:* $802; $50 per course. Tuition and fees vary according to course load and program. *Financial support:* Fellowships with full tuition reimbursements, research assistantships, teaching assistantships with tuition reimbursements, career-related internships or fieldwork, and scholarships/grants available. Financial award application deadline: 1/15; financial award applicants required to submit FAFSA. *Faculty research:* Teaching youth with diverse backgrounds and abilities, issues in educating English language learners, social studies and democracy, assessment and data driven instruction, literacy across the curriculum. *Unit head:* Dr. Jeffery Mangram, Program Coordinator/Associate Professor, 315-443-3293, E-mail: jamangra@syr.edu. *Application contact:* Speranza Migliore, Graduate Admissions Recruiter, 315-443-2505, E-mail: gradrcrt@syr.edu.
Website: http://soe.syr.edu/academic/teaching_and_leadership/graduate/masters/social_studies/default.aspx

Teachers College, Columbia University, Department of Arts and Humanities, New York, NY 10027. Offers applied linguistics (MA, Ed D); art and art education (Ed M, MA, Ed D, Ed DCT); arts administration (MA); bilingual and bicultural education (MA); global competence (Certificate); history and education (Ed D, PhD); music and music education (Ed DCT); philosophy and education (MA, Ed D, PhD); social studies education (Ed M, PhD); teaching English to speakers of other languages (Ed M); teaching of English and English education (Ed M, MA, Ed D, PhD), including English education (Ed M, Ed D, PhD), teaching of English (MA); teaching of social studies (MA); TESOL (MA, Ed D). *Program availability:* Part-time, evening/weekend. *Students:* 429 full-time (329 women), 467 part-time (332 women); includes 268 minority (62 Black or African American, non-Hispanic/Latino; 1 American Indian or Alaska Native, non-Hispanic/Latino; 108 Asian, non-Hispanic/Latino; 76 Hispanic/Latino; 21 Two or more races, non-Hispanic/Latino), 212 international. 1,068 applicants, 53% accepted, 272 enrolled. Terminal master's awarded for partial completion of doctoral program. *Expenses: Tuition:* Full-time $36,288; part-time $1512 per credit. *Required fees:* $438 per semester. One-time fee: $510 full-time. Full-time tuition and fees vary according to course load. *Financial support:* Fellowships, research assistantships, teaching assistantships, career-related internships or fieldwork, Federal Work-Study, institutionally sponsored loans, tuition waivers (full and partial), and unspecified assistantships available. Support available to part-time students. *Unit head:* Prof. William Gaudelli, Department Chair, 212-678-3150, E-mail: wg74@columbia.edu. *Application contact:* David Estrella, Director of Admissions, 212-678-3305, Fax: 212-678-4171, E-mail: estrella@tc.columbia.edu.
Website: http://www.tc.edu/a%26h/

Temple University, College of Education, Department of Teaching and Learning, Philadelphia, PA 19122-6096. Offers career and technical education (Ed M), including business, computing, and information technology, industrial education, marketing education; middle grades education (Ed M), including math and language arts, math and science, science and language arts; secondary education (Ed M), including English, math, social studies; teaching English to speakers of other languages (MS Ed); urban education (Ed M). *Program availability:* Part-time, evening/weekend. *Faculty:* 26 full-time (16 women), 74 part-time/adjunct (54 women). *Students:* 204 full-time (139 women), 320 part-time (201 women); includes 112 minority (66 Black or African American, non-Hispanic/Latino; 17 Asian, non-Hispanic/Latino; 18 Hispanic/Latino; 11 Two or more races, non-Hispanic/Latino), 18 international. 300 applicants, 55% accepted, 99 enrolled. In 2016, 93 master's awarded. Terminal master's awarded for partial completion of doctoral program. *Degree requirements:* For master's, thesis or alternative. *Entrance requirements:* Additional exam requirements/recommendations for international students: Required—TOEFL (minimum score 550 paper-based; 79 iBT). *Application deadline:* For fall admission, 4/1 for domestic students, 12/15 for international students; for spring admission, 10/1 for domestic students, 8/1 for international students. Application fee: $60. Electronic applications accepted. *Expenses:* Contact institution. *Financial support:* Fellowships, research assistantships, and teaching assistantships available. Financial award application deadline: 1/15; financial award applicants required to submit FAFSA. *Faculty research:* Workforce development, vocational education, technical education, industrial education, professional development, literacy, classroom management, school communities, curriculum development, instruction, applied linguistics, cross linguistic influence, bilingual education, oral proficiency, multilingualism. *Unit head:* Dr. Christine Woyshner, Chairperson, 215-204-6387, E-mail: christine.woyshner@temple.edu. *Application contact:* Sarah Stapleton, Assistant Director, Academic Operations, 215-204-8220, E-mail: sarah.stapleton@temple.edu.
Website: http://education.temple.edu/tl

Trinity Washington University, School of Education, Washington, DC 20017-1094. Offers clinical mental health counseling (MA); early childhood education (MAT); educating for change (M Ed); educational administration (MSA); elementary education (MAT); reading (M Ed); school counseling (MA); secondary education (MAT), including English, social studies; special education (MAT). *Accreditation:* NCATE. *Program availability:* Part-time, evening/weekend. *Degree requirements:* For master's, thesis (for some programs), capstone project(s). *Entrance requirements:* For master's, PRAXIS I, minimum GPA of 2.8. Additional exam requirements/recommendations for international students: Required—TOEFL (minimum score 550 paper-based). *Faculty research:* Technology, literacy, special education, organizations, inclusion models.

University at Buffalo, the State University of New York, Graduate School, Graduate School of Education, Department of Learning and Instruction, Buffalo, NY 14260. Offers biology education (Ed M, Certificate); chemistry education (Ed M, Certificate); childhood education (Ed M); childhood education with bilingual extension (Ed M); college teaching (Advanced Certificate); curriculum, instruction and the science of learning (PhD); early childhood education (Ed M); early childhood education with bilingual extension (Ed M); earth science education (Ed M, Certificate); education and technology (Ed M); education studies (Ed M); educational technology and new literacies (Certificate); educational technology and new literacies (Advanced Certificate); elementary education (Ed D); English education (Ed M, Certificate); English education studies (Ed M); English for speakers of other languages (Ed M); foreign and second language education (PhD); French education (Ed M, Certificate); German education (Ed M, Certificate); gifted education (Certificate); Latin education (Ed M, Certificate); literacy education studies (Ed M); literacy specialist (Ed M); literacy teaching and learning (Certificate); mathematics education (Ed M, Certificate); music education (Ed M, Certificate); music education studies (Ed M); music learning theory (Advanced Certificate); online education (Advanced Certificate); physics education (Ed M, Certificate); science and the public (Ed M); social studies education (Ed M, Certificate); Spanish education (Ed M, Certificate); special education (PhD); teaching English to speakers of other languages (Ed M). *Program availability:* Part-time, evening/weekend, 100% online. *Faculty:* 28 full-time (21 women), 67 part-time/adjunct (49 women). *Students:* 198 full-time (153 women), 312 part-time (220 women); includes 48 minority (28 Black or African American, non-Hispanic/Latino; 4 American Indian or Alaska Native, non-Hispanic/Latino; 15 Asian, non-Hispanic/Latino; 1 Hispanic/Latino), 66 international. Average age 33. 336 applicants, 86% accepted, 178 enrolled. In 2016, 137 master's, 24 doctorates, 25 other advanced degrees awarded. *Degree requirements:* For master's, comprehensive exam; for doctorate, thesis/dissertation, research analysis exam, research experience. *Entrance requirements:* For master's, letters of reference; for doctorate, GRE General Test or MAT, interview, writing sample, letters of recommendation. Additional exam requirements/recommendations for international students: Required—TOEFL (minimum score 600 paper-based; 96 iBT). *Application deadline:* For fall admission, 2/1 priority date for domestic and international students; for spring admission, 11/15 priority date for domestic students, 10/1 for international students. Applications are processed on a rolling basis. Application fee: $50. Electronic applications accepted. *Financial support:* In 2016–17, 44 fellowships (averaging $4,010 per year), 39 research assistantships with tuition reimbursements (averaging $9,897 per year) were awarded; teaching assistantships, career-related internships or fieldwork, Federal Work-Study, institutionally sponsored loans, scholarships/grants, tuition waivers (full and partial), and unspecified assistantships also available. Financial award application deadline: 2/28; financial award applicants required to submit FAFSA. *Faculty research:* Science assessment, foreign language teaching and learning, early learning, new literacies, gender and education. *Total annual research expenditures:* $534,880. *Unit head:* Dr. Deborah Moore-Russo, Chair, 716-645-4069, Fax: 716-645-3161, E-mail: dam29@buffalo.edu. *Application contact:* Luann Zak, Admissions Assistant, 716-645-2110, Fax: 716-645-7937, E-mail: luannzak@buffalo.edu.
Website: http://gse.buffalo.edu/lai

The University of Akron, Graduate School, College of Education, Department of Curricular and Instructional Studies, Program in Adolescent to Young Adult Education, Akron, OH 44325. Offers chemistry (MS); chemistry and physics (MS); earth science (MS); earth science and chemistry (MS); earth science and physics (MS); integrated language arts (MS); integrated mathematics (MS); integrated social studies (MS); life science (MS); life science and chemistry (MS); life science and earth science (MS); life science and physics (MS); physics (MS). *Accreditation:* NCATE. *Degree requirements:* For master's, comprehensive exam, portfolio. *Entrance requirements:* Additional exam requirements/recommendations for international students: Required—TOEFL (minimum score 550 paper-based, 79 iBT) or IELTS (minimum score 6.5). *Application deadline:* For fall admission, 3/1 for domestic and international students; for spring admission, 10/1 for domestic and international students. Applications are processed on a rolling basis. Application fee: $45 ($70 for international students). Electronic applications accepted. *Expenses:* Tuition, state resident: full-time $8618; part-time $359 per credit hour. Tuition, nonresident: full-time $17,149; part-time $715 per credit hour. *Required fees:* $1652. *Unit head:* Dr. Peggy McCann, Interim Chair, 330-972-5742, E-mail: plm@uakron.edu.

The University of Alabama in Huntsville, School of Graduate Studies, College of Education, Huntsville, AL 35899. Offers autism spectrum disorders (M Ed, Graduate Certificate); biology (MAT); chemistry (MAT); differentiated instruction in elementary education (M Ed); English language arts (MAT); English speakers of other languages (M Ed, MAT); history (MAT); mathematics (MAT); physics (MAT); reading education (M Ed); secondary education (M Ed). *Expenses:* Tuition, state resident: full-time $9834; part-time $600 per credit hour. Tuition, nonresident: full-time $21,830; part-time $1325 per credit hour.

University of Arkansas at Pine Bluff, School of Education, Pine Bluff, AR 71601-2799. Offers elementary education (M Ed); secondary education (M Ed), including English education, mathematics education, science education, social studies education; teaching (MAT). *Accreditation:* NCATE. *Program availability:* Part-time, evening/weekend. *Degree requirements:* For master's, comprehensive exam. *Entrance requirements:* For master's, GRE, minimum GPA of 2.75, NTE or Standard Arkansas Teaching Certificate. Application fee: $25. *Expenses:* Tuition, state resident: full-time $4776. Tuition, nonresident: full-time $10,824. *Required fees:* $1612. Tuition and fees vary according to course load. *Financial support:* Research assistantships with full and partial tuition reimbursements, teaching assistantships with full and partial tuition reimbursements, institutionally sponsored loans, and scholarships/grants available. Support available to part-time students. *Faculty research:* Teacher certification, accreditation, assessment, standards, portfolio development, rehabilitation, technology. *Unit head:* Dr. George Herts, Dean, 870-575-8000, E-mail: johnson_c@uapb.edu.
Website: http://www.uapb.edu/academics/school_of_education.aspx

The University of British Columbia, Faculty of Education, Department of Curriculum and Pedagogy, Vancouver, BC V6T 1Z4, Canada. Offers art education (M Ed, MA); curriculum studies (M Ed, MA, PhD); home economics education (M Ed, MA); mathematics education (M Ed, MA); media and technology studies education (M Ed, MA); music education (M Ed, MA); physical education (M Ed, MA); science education (M Ed, MA); social studies education (M Ed, MA). *Program availability:* Part-time, online learning. *Degree requirements:* For master's, thesis (MA); for doctorate, comprehensive exam, thesis/dissertation. *Entrance requirements:* Additional exam requirements/recommendations for international students: Required—TOEFL, IELTS. Application fee: $100 Canadian dollars ($162 Canadian dollars for international students). Electronic applications accepted. *Expenses:* $6,865 per year tuition and fees domestic, $10,938 per year international (for MA and M Ed); $4,802 per year tuition and fees, $8,436 per year international (for PhD). *Financial support:* Fellowships with partial tuition reimbursements, research assistantships with partial tuition reimbursements, teaching assistantships with partial tuition reimbursements, and tuition waivers (partial) available. *Faculty research:* School subjects, teaching and learning. *Application contact:* Alan Jay, Graduate Programs Assistant, 604-822-5367, Fax: 604-822-4714, E-mail: edcp.grad@ubc.ca.
Website: http://www.edcp.educ.ubc.ca/

University of California, Santa Cruz, Division of Graduate Studies, Division of Social Sciences, Program in Social Documentation, Santa Cruz, CA 95064. Offers MA. *Entrance requirements:* For master's, resume or curriculum vitae, sample of documentary production work. Additional exam requirements/recommendations for international students: Required—TOEFL (minimum score 550 paper-based; 83 iBT); Recommended—IELTS (minimum score 8). Electronic applications accepted. *Faculty research:* Documentation of underrepresented areas of community life.

University of Central Florida, College of Education and Human Performance, Education Doctoral Programs, Orlando, FL 32816. Offers communication sciences and disorders (PhD); curriculum and instruction (Ed D); early childhood education (PhD); educational leadership (Ed D); elementary education (PhD); exceptional education (PhD); exercise physiology (PhD); higher education (PhD); instructional technology (PhD); mathematics education (PhD); methodology, measurement and analysis (PhD); reading education (PhD); science education (PhD); social science education (PhD); TESOL (PhD). *Students:* 127 full-time (91 women), 43 part-time (29 women); includes 33 minority (17 Black or African American, non-Hispanic/Latino; 5 Asian, non-Hispanic/Latino; 7 Hispanic/Latino; 4 Two or more races, non-Hispanic/Latino), 26 international. Average age 37. 163 applicants, 40% accepted, 52 enrolled. In 2016, 57 doctorates awarded. Application fee: $30. Electronic applications accepted. *Expenses:* Tuition, state resident: part-time $288.16 per credit hour. Tuition, nonresident: part-time $1071.31 per credit hour. *Financial support:* In 2016–17, 78 students received support, including 41 fellowships with partial tuition reimbursements available (averaging $5,916 per year), 44 research assistantships with partial tuition reimbursements available (averaging $7,637 per year), 48 teaching assistantships with partial tuition reimbursements available (averaging $9,633 per year). Financial award application deadline: 3/1; financial award applicants required to submit FAFSA. *Unit head:* Dr. Edward Robinson, Director of Doctoral Programs, 407-823-6106, E-mail: edward.robinson@ucf.edu. *Application contact:* Assistant Director, Graduate Admissions, 407-823-2766, Fax: 407-823-6442, E-mail: gradadmissions@ucf.edu.
Website: http://education.ucf.edu/programs.cfm?pid=g&cat=2

University of Central Florida, College of Education and Human Performance, School of Teaching, Learning, and Leadership, Program in Teacher Education, Orlando, FL 32816. Offers art education (MAT); English language (MAT); mathematics education (MAT); middle school mathematics (MAT); middle school science (MAT); science education (MAT), including biology, chemistry, physics; social science education (MAT). *Accreditation:* NCATE. *Program availability:* Part-time, evening/weekend. *Students:* 16 full-time (11 women), 28 part-time (23 women); includes 16 minority (6 Black or African American, non-Hispanic/Latino; 1 Asian, non-Hispanic/Latino; 8 Hispanic/Latino; 1 Two or more races, non-Hispanic/Latino), 1 international. Average age 31. 1 applicant, 100% accepted. In 2016, 33 master's awarded. *Entrance requirements:* For master's, GRE General Test. Additional exam requirements/recommendations for international students: Required—TOEFL. *Application deadline:* For spring admission, 12/1 for domestic students; for summer admission, 4/15 for domestic students. Application fee: $30. Electronic applications accepted. *Expenses:* Tuition, state resident: part-time $288.16 per credit hour. Tuition, nonresident: part-time $1071.31 per credit hour. *Financial support:* Fellowships, research assistantships, teaching assistantships, career-related internships or fieldwork, Federal Work-Study, institutionally sponsored loans, tuition waivers (partial), and unspecified assistantships available. Financial award application deadline: 3/1; financial award applicants required to submit FAFSA. *Unit head:* Dr. Michael Hynes, Director, 407-823-2005, E-mail: mychael.hynes@ucf.edu. *Application contact:* Assistant Director, Graduate Admissions, 407-823-2766, Fax: 407-823-6442, E-mail: gradadmissions@ucf.edu.
Website: http://education.ucf.edu/programs.cfm?pid=g&cat=2

University of Cincinnati, Graduate School, College of Education, Criminal Justice, and Human Services, Division of Teacher Education, Cincinnati, OH 45221. Offers curriculum and instruction (M Ed, Ed D); deaf studies (Certificate); early childhood education (M Ed); middle childhood education (M Ed); postsecondary literacy instruction (Certificate); reading/literacy (M Ed, Ed D); secondary education (M Ed); special education (M Ed, Ed D); teaching English as a second language (Ed D, Certificate); teaching science (MS). *Program availability:* Part-time. *Degree requirements:* For doctorate, thesis/dissertation. *Entrance requirements:* For master's, GRE General Test. Additional exam requirements/recommendations for international students: Required—TOEFL (minimum score 550 paper-based). Electronic applications accepted. *Expenses: Tuition, area resident:* Full-time $12,790; part-time $389 per credit hour. Tuition, state resident: full-time $13,290; part-time $419 per credit hour. Tuition, nonresident: full-time $24,532; part-time $976 per credit hour. *International tuition:* $24,832 full-time. *Required fees:* $3958; $140 per credit hour. Tuition and fees vary according to course load, degree level, program and reciprocity agreements.

University of Connecticut, Graduate School, Neag School of Education, Department of Curriculum and Instruction, Program in History and Social Sciences Education, Storrs, CT 06269. Offers MA, PhD. *Accreditation:* NCATE. Terminal master's awarded for partial completion of doctoral program. *Degree requirements:* For master's, comprehensive exam, thesis or alternative; for doctorate, thesis/dissertation. *Entrance requirements:* For doctorate, GRE General Test. Additional exam requirements/recommendations for international students: Required—TOEFL (minimum score 550 paper-based). Electronic applications accepted.

University of Florida, Graduate School, College of Education, School of Teaching and Learning, Gainesville, FL 32611. Offers curriculum and instruction (M Ed, MAE, Ed D, PhD, Ed S); elementary education (M Ed, MAE); English education (M Ed, MAE); mathematics education (M Ed, MAE); reading education (M Ed, MAE); science education (M Ed, MAE); social studies education (M Ed, MAE). *Accreditation:* NCATE. *Program availability:* Part-time, evening/weekend, online learning. Terminal master's awarded for partial completion of doctoral program. *Degree requirements:* For master's, comprehensive exam (for some programs), thesis (for some programs); for doctorate, comprehensive exam (for some programs), thesis/dissertation (for some programs). *Entrance requirements:* For master's and doctorate, GRE General Test, minimum GPA of 3.0; for Ed S, GRE General Test. Additional exam requirements/recommendations for international students: Required—TOEFL (minimum score 550 paper-based; 80 iBT), IELTS (minimum score 6). Electronic applications accepted. *Faculty research:* STEM education; curriculum; teaching and teacher education; languages and literacy; schools, culture, and society; theories and processes of learning.

University of Illinois at Chicago, Program in Learning Sciences, Chicago, IL 60607-7128. Offers PhD.

University of Indianapolis, Graduate Programs, School of Education, Indianapolis, IN 46227-3697. Offers art education (MAT); biology (MAT); chemistry (MAT); curriculum and instruction (MA); earth sciences (MAT); education (MA, MAT); educational leadership (MA); elementary education (MA); English (MAT); French (MAT); math (MAT); physical education (MAT); physics (MAT); secondary education (MA), including art education, education, English education, social studies education; social studies (MAT); Spanish (MAT). *Accreditation:* NCATE. *Program availability:* Part-time, evening/weekend. *Entrance requirements:* For master's, GRE Subject Test, PRAXIS I, minimum GPA of 2.5, 3 letters of recommendation, interview. Additional exam requirements/recommendations for international students: Required—TOEFL (minimum score 550 paper-based). *Faculty research:* Assessment of teacher education, perceptions of prospective teachers by parents.

The University of Iowa, Graduate College, College of Education, Department of Teaching and Learning, Program in Education, Iowa City, IA 52242-1316. Offers art education (MA); developmental reading (MA); elementary education (MA); English education (MA, MAT); foreign and second language education (MAT); foreign language education (MA); foreign language/ESL education (PhD); language, literacy and culture (PhD); mathematics education (MA, MAT, PhD); music education (MM, PhD); science education (MA); secondary education (MA); social studies (MA, PhD). *Degree requirements:* For master's, thesis optional, exam; for doctorate, comprehensive exam, thesis/dissertation. *Entrance requirements:* For master's and doctorate, GRE General Test, minimum GPA of 3.0. Additional exam requirements/recommendations for international students: Required—TOEFL (minimum score 550 paper-based; 81 iBT). Electronic applications accepted.

University of Louisiana at Monroe, Graduate School, College of Arts, Education, and Sciences, School of Education, Program in Curriculum and Instruction, Monroe, LA 71209-0001. Offers art education (M Ed); biology education (M Ed); chemistry education (M Ed); curriculum and instruction (Ed D); early childhood education (M Ed); earth science education (M Ed); educational leadership (M Ed); elementary education (1-5) (M Ed); English as a second language (M Ed); English education (M Ed); family and consumer education (M Ed); French education (M Ed); history education (M Ed); math education (M Ed); middle school education (M Ed); music education (M Ed); reading education (K-12) (M Ed); Spanish education (M Ed); special education - academically gifted (M Ed); special education - early intervention (M Ed); special education - educational diagnostician (M Ed); special education - mild/moderate disabilities (M Ed); speech education (M Ed). *Accreditation:* NCATE. *Faculty:* 8 full-time (4 women), 4 part-time/adjunct (3 women). *Students:* 13 full-time (11 women), 80 part-time (65 women); includes 25 minority (19 Black or African American, non-Hispanic/Latino; 1 Asian, non-Hispanic/Latino; 3 Hispanic/Latino; 2 Two or more races, non-Hispanic/Latino). Average age 37. 118 applicants, 30% accepted, 16 enrolled. In 2016, 23 master's, 4 doctorates awarded. *Degree requirements:* For master's, comprehensive exam (for some programs), thesis; for doctorate, thesis/dissertation, internships. *Entrance requirements:* For master's, GRE General Test; for doctorate, GRE General Test, minimum undergraduate GPA of 2.75, graduate 3.25. Additional exam requirements/recommendations for international students: Required—TOEFL (minimum score 500 paper-based; 61 iBT). *Application deadline:* For fall admission, 8/24 priority date for domestic students, 7/1 for international students; for winter admission, 12/14 priority date for domestic students; for spring admission, 1/19 for domestic students, 11/1 for international students. Applications are processed on a rolling basis. Application fee: $20 ($30 for international students). Electronic applications accepted. *Expenses:* Tuition, state resident: full-time $6489. Tuition, nonresident: full-time $18,589. *Required fees:* $8984. Tuition and fees vary according to course level, course load, degree level and program. *Financial support:* Research assistantships, career-related internships or fieldwork, Federal Work-Study, and unspecified assistantships available. Financial award application deadline: 4/1; financial award applicants required to submit FAFSA. *Unit head:* Dr. Dorothy Schween, Director, 318-342-1268, Fax: 318-342-3131, E-mail: schween@ulm.edu.

University of Maine, Graduate School, College of Education and Human Development, School of Learning and Teaching, Orono, ME 04469. Offers counselor education (M Ed, MA, MS, CAS); early childhood teacher (CGS); education (PhD), including counselor education, literacy education, prevention and intervention studies; elementary education (M Ed, CAS); individualized education (M Ed); literacy education (CAS); response to intervention for behavior (CGS); secondary education (M Ed, CAS); social studies education (M Ed); special education (M Ed, CAS). *Program availability:* Part-time. *Students:* 89 full-time (82 women), 184 part-time (162 women); includes 13 minority (8 American Indian or Alaska Native, non-Hispanic/Latino; 3 Hispanic/Latino; 1 Native Hawaiian or other Pacific Islander, non-Hispanic/Latino; 1 Two or more races, non-Hispanic/Latino), 4 international. Average age 37. 132 applicants, 97% accepted, 100 enrolled. In 2016, 50 master's, 3 doctorates, 19 other advanced degrees awarded. *Degree requirements:* For master's, thesis (for some programs); for doctorate, comprehensive exam, thesis/dissertation. *Entrance requirements:* For master's, GRE General Test, MAT. Additional exam requirements/recommendations for international students: Required—TOEFL. *Application deadline:* For fall admission, 2/1 priority date for domestic students. Applications are processed on a rolling basis. Application fee: $65. Electronic applications accepted. *Expenses:* Tuition, state resident: full-time $7524; part-time $2508 per credit. Tuition, nonresident: full-time $24,498; part-time $8166 per credit. *Required fees:* $1148; $571 per credit. *Financial support:* In 2016–17, 20 students received support, including 12 teaching assistantships (averaging $14,600 per year); Federal Work-Study, scholarships/grants, and unspecified assistantships also available. Financial award application deadline: 3/1. *Unit head:* Dr. Jim Artesani, Associate Dean of Accreditation and Graduate Affairs, 207-581-4061. *Application contact:* Scott G. Delcourt, Assistant Vice President for Graduate Studies and Senior Associate Dean, 207-581-3291, Fax: 207-581-3232, E-mail: graduate@maine.edu.
Website: http://umaine.edu/edhd/

University of Maryland, Baltimore County, The Graduate School, College of Arts, Humanities and Social Sciences, Department of Education, Program in Teaching, Baltimore, MD 21250. Offers early childhood education (MAT); elementary education (MAT); teaching (MAT), including art, biology, chemistry, choral music, classical foreign language, dance, earth/space science, English, instrumental music, mathematics, modern foreign language, physical science, physics, social studies, theatre. *Program availability:* Part-time, evening/weekend. *Faculty:* 24 full-time (18 women), 25 part-time/adjunct (19 women). *Students:* 41 full-time (34 women), 27 part-time (18 women); includes 26 minority (6 Black or African American, non-Hispanic/Latino; 9 Asian, non-Hispanic/Latino; 7 Hispanic/Latino; 1 Native Hawaiian or other Pacific Islander, non-Hispanic/Latino; 3 Two or more races, non-Hispanic/Latino), 2 international. Average age 30. 54 applicants, 83% accepted, 35 enrolled. In 2016, 50 master's awarded. *Degree requirements:* For master's, comprehensive exam (for some programs), thesis (for some programs). *Entrance requirements:* For master's, PRAXIS Core Examination or GRE (minimum score of 1000), minimum GPA of 3.0. Additional exam requirements/recommendations for international students: Required—TOEFL. *Application deadline:* For fall admission, 6/1 for domestic and international students; for spring admission, 11/1 for domestic and international students. Applications are processed on a rolling basis. Application fee: $50. Electronic applications accepted. *Expenses:* Tuition, state resident: full-time $13,294. Tuition, nonresident: full-time $20,286. *Financial support:* In 2016–17, 8 students received support, including teaching assistantships with tuition reimbursements available (averaging $12,000 per year); career-related internships or fieldwork, Federal Work-Study, scholarships/grants, tuition waivers, and unspecified assistantships also available. Financial award application deadline: 3/15. *Faculty research:* STEM teacher education, culturally sensitive pedagogy, ESOL/bilingual education, early childhood education, language, literacy and culture. *Total annual research expenditures:* $100,000. *Unit head:* Dr. Susan M. Blunck, Graduate Program Director, 410-455-2869, Fax: 410-455-3986, E-mail: blunck@umbc.edu. *Application contact:* Cheryl Johnson, MAT Program Specialist, 410-455-3388, E-mail: blackwel@umbc.edu.
Website: http://www.umbc.edu/education/

University of Minnesota, Twin Cities Campus, Graduate School, College of Education and Human Development, Department of Curriculum and Instruction, Program in Teaching, Minneapolis, MN 55455-0213. Offers teaching (M Ed), including arts in education, elementary education, English education, mathematics, science, second language education, social studies. *Students:* 237 full-time (169 women), 171 part-time (112 women); includes 91 minority (23 Black or African American, non-

Hispanic/Latino; 3 American Indian or Alaska Native, non-Hispanic/Latino; 19 Asian, non-Hispanic/Latino; 25 Hispanic/Latino; 21 Two or more races, non-Hispanic/Latino), 10 international. Average age 27. 421 applicants, 72% accepted, 275 enrolled. In 2016, 584 master's awarded. Application fee: $75 ($95 for international students). *Unit head:* Dr. Cynthia Lewis, Chair, 612-625-6313, Fax: 612-624-8277, E-mail: lewis@umn.edu. *Application contact:* Dr. Kendall King, Director of Graduate Studies, 612-625-3692, E-mail: roehr013@umn.edu.
Website: http://www.cehd.umn.edu/ci/

University of Missouri, Office of Research and Graduate Studies, College of Education, Department of Learning, Teaching and Curriculum, Columbia, MO 65211. Offers agricultural education (M Ed, PhD, Ed S); art education (M Ed, PhD, Ed S); business and office education (M Ed, PhD, Ed S); early childhood education (M Ed, PhD, Ed S); elementary education (M Ed, PhD, Ed S); English education (M Ed, PhD, Ed S); foreign language education (M Ed, PhD, Ed S); health education and promotion (M Ed, PhD); learning and instruction (M Ed); marketing education (M Ed, PhD, Ed S); mathematics education (M Ed, PhD, Ed S); music education (M Ed, PhD, Ed S); reading education (M Ed, PhD, Ed S); science education (M Ed, PhD, Ed S); social studies education (M Ed, PhD, Ed S); vocational education (M Ed, PhD, Ed S). *Program availability:* Part-time. *Faculty:* 30 full-time (18 women), 1 (woman) part-time/adjunct. *Students:* 157 full-time (124 women), 157 part-time (125 women). Terminal master's awarded for partial completion of doctoral program. *Degree requirements:* For doctorate, thesis/dissertation. *Entrance requirements:* For master's and Ed S, GRE General Test or MAT, minimum GPA of 3.0; for doctorate, GRE General Test, minimum GPA of 3.0. Additional exam requirements/recommendations for international students: Required—TOEFL (minimum score 600 paper-based; 100 iBT). *Application deadline:* For fall admission, 12/1 priority date for domestic and international students. Applications are processed on a rolling basis. Application fee: $75 ($90 for international students). Electronic applications accepted. *Expenses:* Tuition, state resident: full-time $6347; part-time $352.60 per credit hour. Tuition, nonresident: full-time $17,379; part-time $965.50 per credit hour. *Required fees:* $1035. Tuition and fees vary according to course load, campus/location and program. *Financial support:* Fellowships, research assistantships, teaching assistantships, institutionally sponsored loans, traineeships, health care benefits, and unspecified assistantships available. Support available to part-time students.
Website: http://education.missouri.edu/LTC/index.php

The University of North Carolina at Chapel Hill, Graduate School, School of Education, Program in Secondary Education, Chapel Hill, NC 27599. Offers English (Grades 9-12) (MAT); English as a second language (MAT); French (Grades K-12) (MAT); German (Grades K-12) (MAT); Japanese (Grades K-12) (MAT); Latin (Grades 9-12) (MAT); mathematics (Grades 9-12) (MAT); music (Grades K-12) (MAT); science (Grades 9-12) (MAT); social studies (Grades 9-12) (MAT); Spanish (Grades K-12) (MAT). *Accreditation:* NCATE. *Degree requirements:* For master's, comprehensive exam. *Entrance requirements:* For master's, GRE General Test, minimum GPA of 3.0 during last 2 years of undergraduate course work. Additional exam requirements/recommendations for international students: Required—TOEFL (minimum score 550 paper-based). Electronic applications accepted.

The University of North Carolina at Greensboro, Graduate School, School of Education, Department of Teacher Education and Higher Education, Greensboro, NC 27412-5001. Offers college teaching and adult learning (Certificate); curriculum and instruction (M Ed), including chemistry education, elementary education, English as a second language, French education, instructional technology, mathematics education, middle grades education, reading education, science education, social studies education, Spanish education; curriculum and teaching (PhD), including higher education, teacher education and development; English as a second language (Certificate); higher education (M Ed); supervision (M Ed). *Accreditation:* NCATE. *Program availability:* Part-time. *Degree requirements:* For doctorate, thesis/dissertation. *Entrance requirements:* For master's and doctorate, GRE General Test. Additional exam requirements/recommendations for international students: Required—TOEFL. Electronic applications accepted. *Faculty research:* Community college literacy program, middle school mathematics/computer mathematics.

The University of North Carolina at Pembroke, The Graduate School, Department of History, Pembroke, NC 28372-1510. Offers social studies education (MA, MAT). *Program availability:* Part-time, evening/weekend. *Degree requirements:* For master's, thesis optional. *Entrance requirements:* For master's, GRE General Test or MAT, minimum GPA of 3.0 in major, 2.5 overall. Additional exam requirements/recommendations for international students: Required—TOEFL.

University of North Georgia, College of Education, Dahlonega, GA 30597. Offers early childhood education (M Ed); middle grades education (M Ed, MAT); physical education (MS); school leadership (Ed S); secondary education (M Ed), including English education, history education, mathematics education, physical education. *Accreditation:* NCATE. *Program availability:* Part-time, evening/weekend, online learning. *Faculty:* 16 full-time (12 women), 3 part-time/adjunct (all women). *Students:* 11 full-time (8 women), 146 part-time (107 women); includes 19 minority (10 Black or African American, non-Hispanic/Latino; 2 Asian, non-Hispanic/Latino; 6 Hispanic/Latino; 1 Two or more races, non-Hispanic/Latino). Average age 28. 77 applicants, 83% accepted, 47 enrolled. In 2016, 79 master's awarded. *Degree requirements:* For master's, comprehensive exam, thesis optional. *Entrance requirements:* For master's, GRE or MAT, GACE, minimum GPA of 2.75; for Ed S, GRE General Test or MAT, 3 years of teaching experience, master's degree, minimum graduate GPA of 3.25, leadership position in the school. Additional exam requirements/recommendations for international students: Required—TOEFL (minimum score 550 paper-based; 79 iBT), IELTS (minimum score 6.5). *Application deadline:* For fall admission, 8/1 priority date for domestic students, 7/1 priority date for international students; for spring admission, 12/1 priority date for domestic students, 11/1 priority date for international students. Applications are processed on a rolling basis. Application fee: $40. Electronic applications accepted. *Expenses:* Contact institution. *Financial support:* Teaching assistantships, career-related internships or fieldwork, scholarships/grants, and unspecified assistantships available. Financial award application deadline: 5/1; financial award applicants required to submit CSS PROFILE or FAFSA. *Unit head:* Dr. Susan Ayers, Dean, College of Education, 706-864-1998, E-mail: susan.ayres@ung.edu. *Application contact:* Regina Boling, Teacher Education Graduate Admissions, 706-864-1533, E-mail: regina.boling@ung.edu.
Website: http://ung.edu/college-of-education/

University of Oklahoma, Jeannine Rainbolt College of Education, Department of Instructional Leadership and Academic Curriculum, Norman, OK 73019. Offers instructional leadership and academic curriculum (M Ed, PhD), including biomedical education (PhD), early childhood education, elementary education (M Ed), English education, instructional leadership, mathematics education, reading education, science education, social studies education, world languages education (M Ed). *Accreditation:* NCATE. *Program availability:* Part-time. *Faculty:* 19 full-time (15 women), 1 (woman) part-time/adjunct. *Students:* 66 full-time (49 women), 116 part-time (88 women); includes 49 minority (12 Black or African American, non-Hispanic/Latino; 6 American Indian or Alaska Native, non-Hispanic/Latino; 6 Asian, non-Hispanic/Latino; 11 Hispanic/Latino; 1 Native Hawaiian or other Pacific Islander, non-Hispanic/Latino; 13 Two or more races, non-Hispanic/Latino), 13 international. Average age 35. 38 applicants, 97% accepted, 28 enrolled. In 2016, 33 master's, 10 doctorates awarded. Terminal master's awarded for partial completion of doctoral program. *Degree requirements:* For master's, comprehensive exam (for some programs), thesis (for some programs); for doctorate, comprehensive exam (for some programs), thesis/dissertation. *Entrance requirements:* For doctorate, GRE. Additional exam requirements/recommendations for international students: Required—TOEFL (minimum score 79 iBT) or IELTS (minimum score 6.5). Application fee: $50 ($100 for international students). Electronic applications accepted. *Expenses:* Tuition, state resident: full-time $4886; part-time $203.60 per credit hour. Tuition, nonresident: full-time $18,989; part-time $791.20 per credit hour. *Required fees:* $3283; $126.25 per credit hour. $126.50 per semester. *Financial support:* In 2016–17, 112 students received support, including 7 research assistantships with partial tuition reimbursements available (averaging $10,373 per year), 6 teaching assistantships with partial tuition reimbursements available (averaging $11,446 per year); fellowships, scholarships/grants, and unspecified assistantships also available. Financial award application deadline: 6/1; financial award applicants required to submit FAFSA. *Faculty research:* Teacher preparation; instruction; curriculum; learning; constructivist theory. *Total annual research expenditures:* $165,297. *Unit head:* Dr. Stacy Reeder, Chair, 405-325-1498, Fax: 405-325-4061, E-mail: reeder@ou.edu. *Application contact:* Anna Steele, Graduate Programs Officer, 405-325-4525, E-mail: anna.steele@ou.edu.
Website: http://www.ou.edu/education/ilac

University of Pittsburgh, School of Education, Department of Instruction and Learning, Program in Secondary Education, Pittsburgh, PA 15260. Offers English and communications education (M Ed, MAT); foreign language education (M Ed, MAT); language, literacy and culture education (Ed D, PhD); mathematics education (M Ed, MAT, Ed D, PhD); science education (M Ed, MAT, Ed D, PhD); secondary education (PhD); social studies education (M Ed, MAT); STEM education (Ed D). *Program availability:* Part-time, evening/weekend. *Degree requirements:* For master's, thesis; for doctorate, thesis/dissertation. *Entrance requirements:* For master's, PRAXIS I; for doctorate, GRE General Test. Additional exam requirements/recommendations for international students: Required—TOEFL. Electronic applications accepted. Tuition and fees vary according to program.

University of Puerto Rico, Río Piedras Campus, College of Education, Program in Curriculum and Teaching, San Juan, PR 00931-3300. Offers biology education (M Ed); chemistry education (M Ed); curriculum and teaching (Ed D); history education (M Ed); mathematics education (M Ed); physics education (M Ed); Spanish education (M Ed). *Program availability:* Part-time. *Degree requirements:* For master's, thesis; for doctorate, thesis/dissertation, internship. *Entrance requirements:* For master's, PAEG or GRE, minimum GPA of 3.0, letter of recommendation; for doctorate, GRE or PAEG, master's degree, minimum GPA of 3.0, letter of recommendation (2), interview. *Faculty research:* Curriculum, math teaching.

University of St. Francis, College of Education, Joliet, IL 60435-6169. Offers educational leadership (MS, Ed D); elementary education (M Ed); reading (MS); secondary education (M Ed), including English education, math education, science education, social studies education, visual arts education; special education (M Ed); teaching and learning (MS); TESOL (Certificate). *Accreditation:* NCATE. *Program availability:* Part-time, evening/weekend, 100% online, blended/hybrid learning. *Faculty:* 11 full-time (8 women), 60 part-time/adjunct (42 women). *Students:* 34 full-time (26 women), 420 part-time (318 women); includes 92 minority (51 Black or African American, non-Hispanic/Latino; 5 Asian, non-Hispanic/Latino; 31 Hispanic/Latino; 5 Two or more races, non-Hispanic/Latino), 4 international. Average age 36. 242 applicants, 48% accepted, 96 enrolled. In 2016, 229 master's, 44 doctorates, 10 other advanced degrees awarded. *Degree requirements:* For master's, comprehensive exam; for doctorate, thesis/dissertation. *Entrance requirements:* Additional exam requirements/recommendations for international students: Required—TOEFL (minimum score 550 paper-based; 79 iBT), IELTS (minimum score 6). *Application deadline:* Applications are processed on a rolling basis. Application fee: $30. Electronic applications accepted. Application fee is waived when completed online. *Expenses:* Contact institution. *Financial support:* In 2016–17, 48 students received support. Career-related internships or fieldwork and unspecified assistantships available. Support available to part-time students. Financial award applicants required to submit FAFSA. *Unit head:* Dr. John Gambro, Dean, 815-740-3829, Fax: 815-740-2264, E-mail: jgambro@stfrancis.edu. *Application contact:* Sandra Sloka, Director of Admissions for Graduate and Degree Completion Programs, 800-735-7500, Fax: 815-740-3431, E-mail: ssloka@stfrancis.edu.
Website: http://www.stfrancis.edu/academics/college-of-education/

University of South Carolina, The Graduate School, College of Education, Department of Instruction and Teacher Education, Program in Secondary Education, Columbia, SC 29208. Offers art education (IMA, MAT); business education (IMA, MAT); English (MAT); foreign language (MAT); health education (MAT); mathematics (MAT); science (IMA, MAT); secondary (Ed D); secondary education (MT, PhD); social studies (MAT); theatre and speech (MAT). IMA and MT offered jointly with the subject areas. *Accreditation:* NCATE. *Degree requirements:* For master's, comprehensive exam, thesis (for some programs), foreign language (MA); for doctorate, one foreign language, comprehensive exam, thesis/dissertation. *Entrance requirements:* For master's, GRE General Test or MAT, teaching certificate (IMA, M Ed), interview; for doctorate, GRE General Test or MAT, interview. *Faculty research:* Middle school programs, professional development, school collaboration.

University of South Florida, College of Arts and Sciences, Department of Anthropology, Tampa, FL 33620-9951. Offers applied anthropology (MA, PhD), including archaeological and forensic sciences, biocultural medical anthropology, cultural resource management, heritage studies; medical anthropology (Graduate Certificate). *Program availability:* Part-time. *Faculty:* 23 full-time (14 women). *Students:* 70 full-time (52 women), 41 part-time (28 women); includes 28 minority (6 Black or African American, non-Hispanic/Latino; 2 Asian, non-Hispanic/Latino; 16 Hispanic/Latino; 1 Native Hawaiian or other Pacific Islander, non-Hispanic/Latino; 3 Two or more races, non-Hispanic/Latino), 6 international. Average age 31. 130 applicants, 34% accepted, 18 enrolled. In 2016, 15 master's, 11 doctorates awarded. *Degree requirements:* For master's, one foreign language, comprehensive exam, thesis; for doctorate, one foreign language, comprehensive exam, thesis/dissertation. *Entrance requirements:* For master's and doctorate, GRE, minimum GPA of 3.0, 3 letters of recommendation, statement of purpose, signed research ethics statement, resume or curriculum vitae; for Graduate Certificate, bachelor's degree with minimum GPA of 3.0. Additional exam requirements/recommendations for international students: Required—TOEFL (minimum score 550 paper-based; 79 iBT) or IELTS (minimum score 6.5). *Application deadline:* For fall admission, 12/15 for domestic and international students. Application fee: $30. Electronic applications accepted. *Expenses:* Tuition, state resident: full-time $7766; part-time $431.43 per credit hour. Tuition, nonresident: full-time $15,789; part-time $877.17 per credit hour. *Required fees:* $37 per term. *Financial support:* In 2016–17, 32 students received support, including 14 research assistantships with tuition reimbursements available (averaging $14,475 per year), 52 teaching assistantships with partial tuition reimbursements available (averaging $12,540

per year); scholarships/grants and tuition waivers (partial) also available. Financial award application deadline: 1/15; financial award applicants required to submit FAFSA. *Faculty research:* Biocultural medical anthropology; archaeology and culture resource management in the Americas; community identity and heritage; urban community issues; verbal and nonverbal communications in media and education; global dynamics of sustainable resource management and economic development; social and cultural constructions of race, ethnicity, and gender. *Total annual research expenditures:* $1.1 million. *Unit head:* Dr. David Himmelgreen, Professor/Department Chairperson, 813-974-2138, Fax: 813-974-2668, E-mail: dhimmelg@usf.edu. *Application contact:* Dr. Heide Castaneda, Assistant Professor and Graduate Director, 813-974-2138, Fax: 813-974-2668, E-mail: hcastaneda@usf.edu.
Website: http://anthropology.usf.edu/graduate/

The University of Tennessee, Graduate School, College of Education, Health and Human Sciences, Program in Education, Knoxville, TN 37996. Offers art education (MS); counseling education (PhD); cultural studies in education (PhD); curriculum (MS, Ed S); curriculum, educational research and evaluation (Ed D, PhD); early childhood education (PhD); early childhood special education (MS); education of deaf and hard of hearing (MS); educational administration and policy studies (Ed D, PhD); educational administration and supervision (Ed S); educational psychology (Ed D, PhD); elementary education (MS, Ed S); elementary teaching (MS); English education (MS, Ed S); exercise science (PhD); foreign language/ESL education (MS, Ed S); instructional technology (MS, Ed D, PhD, Ed S); literacy, language and ESL education (PhD); literacy, language education, and ESL education (Ed D); mathematics education (MS, Ed S); modified and comprehensive special education (MS); reading education (MS, Ed S); school counseling (Ed S); school psychology (PhD, Ed S); science education (MS, Ed S); secondary teaching (MS); social foundations (MS); social science education (MS, Ed S); socio-cultural foundations of sports and education (PhD); special education (Ed S); teacher education (Ed D, PhD). *Accreditation:* NCATE. *Program availability:* Part-time, evening/weekend. *Degree requirements:* For master's and Ed S, thesis optional; for doctorate, variable foreign language requirement, thesis/dissertation. *Entrance requirements:* For master's, minimum GPA of 2.7; for doctorate and Ed S, GRE General Test, minimum GPA of 2.7. Additional exam requirements/recommendations for international students: Required—TOEFL. Electronic applications accepted.

University of the District of Columbia, College of Arts and Sciences, Program in Teaching, Washington, DC 20008-1175. Offers elementary education (MAT); middle school mathematics (MAT); secondary English language arts (MAT); secondary social studies (MAT).

The University of Toledo, College of Graduate Studies, Judith Herb College of Education, Department of Curriculum and Instruction, Toledo, OH 43606-3390. Offers art education (ME); career and technical education (ME, Ed S); curriculum and instruction (ME, PhD, Ed S); early childhood education (Ed S); education and anthropology (MAE); education and biology (MES); education and chemistry (MES); education and classics (MAE); education and economics (MAE); education and English (MAE); education and French (MAE); education and geology (MES); education and German (MAE); education and history (MAE); education and mathematics (MAE, MES); education and physics (MES); education and political science (MAE); education and sociology (MAE); education and Spanish (MAE); educational media (PhD); educational technology (ME); educational technology: virtual educator (Certificate); elementary education (PhD); English as a second language (MAE); gifted and talented education (PhD); middle childhood education (ME); secondary education (ME, PhD); special education (PhD). *Accreditation:* NCATE. *Program availability:* Part-time, evening/weekend. *Degree requirements:* For master's, comprehensive exam, thesis or alternative; for doctorate, comprehensive exam, thesis/dissertation; for other advanced degree, thesis optional. *Entrance requirements:* For master's, doctorate, and other advanced degree, minimum cumulative GPA of 2.7 for all previous academic work, letters of recommendation. Additional exam requirements/recommendations for international students: Required—TOEFL (minimum score 550 paper-based; 80 iBT). Electronic applications accepted.

University of Victoria, Faculty of Graduate Studies, Faculty of Education, Department of Curriculum and Instruction, Victoria, BC V8W 2Y2, Canada. Offers art education (M Ed, PhD); curriculum studies (M Ed, MA, PhD); early childhood education (M Ed, PhD); educational studies (PhD); language and literacy (M Ed, MA, PhD); mathematics (M Ed, MA, PhD); music education (M Ed, MA, PhD); science (M Ed, MA, PhD); social studies (M Ed, MA); social, cultural and foundational studies (MA, PhD); technology and environmental education (PhD). *Program availability:* Part-time. *Degree requirements:* For master's, thesis, project (M Ed); for doctorate, comprehensive exam, thesis/dissertation. *Entrance requirements:* For master's, minimum B average. Additional exam requirements/recommendations for international students: Required—TOEFL (minimum score 575 paper-based), IELTS (minimum score 7). Electronic applications accepted. *Faculty research:* Elementary and secondary English, language arts, curriculum theory and practice, educational media and technology, educational administration and leadership, history and philosophy of education.

University of Virginia, Curry School of Education, Department of Curriculum, Instruction, and Special Education, Program in Curriculum and Instruction, Charlottesville, VA 22903. Offers curriculum and instruction (M Ed, Ed S); elementary education (M Ed, Ed D); English education (M Ed, Ed D); foreign language education (M Ed); mathematics education (M Ed, Ed D); science education (Ed D); social studies education (M Ed); MBA/M Ed. *Students:* 43 full-time (35 women), 24 part-time (16 women); includes 7 minority (1 Black or African American, non-Hispanic/Latino; 1 Asian, non-Hispanic/Latino; 2 Hispanic/Latino; 3 Two or more races, non Hispanic/Latino), 4 international. Average age 33. 93 applicants, 78% accepted, 54 enrolled. In 2016, 52 master's, 14 other advanced degrees awarded. *Degree requirements:* For master's, comprehensive exam (for some programs); for doctorate, comprehensive exam, thesis/dissertation; for Ed S, comprehensive exam. *Entrance requirements:* For master's, doctorate, and Ed S, GRE General Test, 2 letters of recommendation. Additional exam requirements/recommendations for international students: Required—TOEFL (minimum score 600 paper-based; 90 iBT), IELTS (minimum score 7). *Application deadline:* Applications are processed on a rolling basis. Application fee: $60. Electronic applications accepted. *Expenses:* Tuition, state resident: full-time $15,026; part-time $834 per credit hour. Tuition, nonresident: full-time $25,168; part-time $1378 per credit hour. *Required fees:* $2654. *Financial support:* Fellowships with tuition reimbursements, research assistantships with tuition reimbursements, and teaching assistantships with tuition reimbursements available. Financial award application deadline: 1/5; financial award applicants required to submit FAFSA. *Unit head:* Susan Mintz, Program Area Director, 434-924-3128, E-mail: slm4r@virginia.edu. *Application contact:* Eric Molnar, Assistant Director, Admissions and Enrollment Reporting, 434-243-2085, E-mail: eric.molnar@virginia.edu.
Website: http://curry.virginia.edu/academics/areas-of-study/curriculum-teaching-learning

University of Virginia, Curry School of Education, Program in Education, Charlottesville, VA 22903. Offers administration and supervision (PhD); applied developmental science (PhD); counselor education (PhD); curriculum and instruction (PhD); early childhood special education (MT); education evaluation (PhD); educational psychology (PhD); educational research (PhD); elementary education (MT); English education (MT, PhD); foreign language education (MT); higher education (PhD); instructional technology (PhD); kinesiology (MT, PhD); math education (PhD); reading education (PhD); research, statistics and evaluation (PhD); school psychology (PhD); science education (PhD); social studies education (MT, PhD); special education (PhD); world languages education (MT). *Students:* 452 full-time (357 women), 18 part-time (13 women); includes 100 minority (28 Black or African American, non-Hispanic/Latino; 39 Asian, non-Hispanic/Latino; 18 Hispanic/Latino; 15 Two or more races, non-Hispanic/Latino), 14 international. Average age 25. 309 applicants, 51% accepted, 87 enrolled. In 2016, 144 master's, 31 doctorates awarded. *Degree requirements:* For master's, comprehensive exam (for some programs), field project; for doctorate, comprehensive exam, thesis/dissertation. *Entrance requirements:* For doctorate, GRE General Test. Additional exam requirements/recommendations for international students: Required—TOEFL (minimum score 600 paper-based; 90 iBT), IELTS (minimum score 7). *Application deadline:* Applications are processed on a rolling basis. Application fee: $60. Electronic applications accepted. *Expenses:* Tuition, state resident: full-time $15,026; part-time $834 per credit hour. Tuition, nonresident: full-time $25,168; part-time $1378 per credit hour. *Required fees:* $2654. *Financial support:* Fellowships, research assistantships, and teaching assistantships available. Financial award application deadline: 1/5; financial award applicants required to submit FAFSA. *Unit head:* Robert C. Pianta, Dean, 434-924-3334, E-mail: pianta@virginia.edu. *Application contact:* Eric Molnar, Assistant Director, Admissions and Enrollment Reporting, 434-243-2085, E-mail: eric.molnar@virginia.edu.
Website: http://curry.virginia.edu/teacher-education

University of Washington, Graduate School, College of Education, Seattle, WA 98195. Offers curriculum and instruction (M Ed, Ed D, PhD), including educational technology, general curriculum (Ed D, PhD), language, literacy, and culture, mathematics education, multicultural education, reading and language arts education (Ed D), science education, social studies education, teaching and curriculum (M Ed); educational leadership and policy studies (M Ed, Ed D, PhD), including administration (Ed D), educational policy, organization, and leadership (M Ed, PhD), higher education, leadership for learning (Ed D), social and cultural foundations of education (M Ed, PhD); educational psychology (M Ed, PhD), including educational psychology (PhD), human development and cognition (M Ed), learning sciences, measurement, statistics and research design (M Ed), school psychology (M Ed); instructional leadership (M Ed); intercollegiate athletic leadership (M Ed); special education (M Ed, Ed D, PhD), including early childhood special education (M Ed), emotional and behavioral disabilities (M Ed), learning disabilities (M Ed), low-incidence disabilities (M Ed), severe disabilities (M Ed), special education (Ed D, PhD); teacher education (MIT). *Accreditation:* APA. *Program availability:* Part-time, evening/weekend. *Degree requirements:* For master's, thesis optional; for doctorate, thesis/dissertation. *Entrance requirements:* For master's and doctorate, GRE General Test, minimum GPA of 3.0. Additional exam requirements/recommendations for international students: Required—TOEFL. Electronic applications accepted. *Faculty research:* School restructuring/effective schools, special education interventions, literacy and writing, technology, school partnerships, teacher preparation.

The University of West Alabama, School of Graduate Studies, College of Education, Departments of Instructional Leadership and Support/Curriculum and Instruction, Program in Secondary Education, Livingston, AL 35470. Offers biology (MAT); English language arts (MAT); high school 6-12 (M Ed); history (MAT); mathematics (MAT); science (MAT); social science (MAT). *Program availability:* Part-time, evening/weekend, 100% online. *Faculty:* 19 full-time (7 women), 7 part-time/adjunct (3 women). *Students:* 236 (159 women); includes 59 minority (53 Black or African American, non-Hispanic/Latino; 2 American Indian or Alaska Native, non-Hispanic/Latino; 1 Asian, non-Hispanic/Latino; 1 Hispanic/Latino; 2 Two or more races, non-Hispanic/Latino). Average age 32. 85 applicants, 88% accepted, 52 enrolled. In 2016, 84 master's awarded. *Degree requirements:* For master's, comprehensive exam, thesis optional. *Entrance requirements:* For master's, GRE General Test, MAT, minimum GPA of 2.75. Additional exam requirements/recommendations for international students: Required—TOEFL (minimum score 500 paper-based; 61 iBT). *Application deadline:* Applications are processed on a rolling basis. Application fee: $40. Electronic applications accepted. *Expenses:* Tuition, state resident: part-time $355 per credit hour. Tuition, nonresident: part-time $710 per credit hour. *Required fees:* $130 per semester. *Financial support:* Teaching assistantships, Federal Work-Study, scholarships/grants, and unspecified assistantships available. Support available to part-time students. Financial award application deadline: 3/1; financial award applicants required to submit FAFSA. *Faculty research:* Integrated arts in the curriculum, moral development of children. *Unit head:* Dr. Jodie Winship, Chair of Curriculum and Instruction, 205-652-5415, Fax: 205-652-3706, E-mail: jwinship@uwa.edu. *Application contact:* Dr. B. J. Kimbrough, Dean of Graduate Studies, 205-652-3647, Fax: 205-652-3706, E-mail: bkimbrough@uwa.edu.
Website: http://www.uwa.edu/highschool612.aspx

University of Wisconsin–Milwaukee, Graduate School, School of Education, Department of Curriculum and Instruction, Milwaukee, WI 53201-0413. Offers curriculum and instruction (MS), including cross-curricular focus, early childhood education, English education, mathematics education, middle childhood/early adolescence education, reading education, science education, urban social studies education. *Program availability:* Part-time. *Students:* 21 full-time (13 women), 44 part-time (42 women); includes 10 minority (1 Black or African American, non-Hispanic/Latino; 1 Asian, non-Hispanic/Latino; 2 Hispanic/Latino; 6 Two or more races, non-Hispanic/Latino), 2 international. Average age 33. 42 applicants, 71% accepted, 20 enrolled. In 2016, 45 master's awarded. *Degree requirements:* For master's, thesis or alternative. *Entrance requirements:* Additional exam requirements/recommendations for international students: Required—TOEFL (minimum score 550 paper-based; 79 iBT), IELTS (minimum score 6.5). *Application deadline:* For fall admission, 1/1 priority date for domestic students; for spring admission, 9/1 for domestic students. Applications are processed on a rolling basis. Application fee: $56 ($96 for international students). Electronic applications accepted. *Financial support:* In 2016–17, 1 fellowship was awarded; research assistantships, teaching assistantships, career-related internships or fieldwork, health care benefits, unspecified assistantships, and project assistantships also available. Support available to part-time students. Financial award application deadline: 4/15; financial award applicants required to submit FAFSA. *Application contact:* General Information Contact, 414-229-4721, E-mail: soeinfo@uwm.edu.
Website: http://uwm.edu/education/academics/curriculum-instruction-department/

University of Wisconsin–River Falls, Outreach and Graduate Studies, College of Arts and Science, Department of History and Philosophy, River Falls, WI 54022. Offers social science education (MSE). *Program availability:* Part-time. *Degree requirements:* For master's, thesis (for some programs). *Entrance requirements:* For master's, minimum GPA of 2.75. Additional exam requirements/recommendations for international students: Required—TOEFL (minimum score 500 paper-based; 65 iBT), IELTS (minimum score 5.5). Electronic applications accepted. *Faculty research:* World War II, Hitler, modern China, women's history, immigration history.

Virginia Polytechnic Institute and State University, Graduate School, College of Liberal Arts and Human Sciences, Blacksburg, VA 24061. Offers career and technical

education (MS Ed, Ed D, PhD, Ed S); communication (MA); counselor education (MA Ed, Ed D, PhD, Ed S); creative writing (MFA); curriculum and instruction (MA Ed, Ed D, PhD, Ed S); educational leadership and policy studies (MA Ed, Ed D, PhD, Ed S); educational research and evaluation (PhD); English (MA); foreign languages, cultures, and literatures (MA); higher education (PhD); higher education and student affairs (MA Ed); history (MA); human development (MS, PhD); material culture and public humanities (MA); philosophy (MA); political science (MA); rhetoric and writing (PhD); science and technology studies (MS, PhD); social, political, ethical, and cultural thought (PhD); sociology (MS, PhD); theater arts (MFA). *Faculty:* 408 full-time (204 women), 3 part-time/adjunct (2 women). *Students:* 657 full-time (446 women), 457 part-time (292 women); includes 213 minority (114 Black or African American, non-Hispanic/Latino; 3 American Indian or Alaska Native, non-Hispanic/Latino; 29 Asian, non-Hispanic/Latino; 44 Hispanic/Latino; 23 Two or more races, non-Hispanic/Latino), 93 international. Average age 33. 805 applicants, 55% accepted, 328 enrolled. In 2016, 270 master's, 91 doctorates awarded. *Degree requirements:* For master's, comprehensive exam (for some programs), thesis (for some programs); for doctorate, comprehensive exam (for some programs), thesis/dissertation (for some programs). *Entrance requirements:* For master's and doctorate, GRE/GMAT. Additional exam requirements/recommendations for international students: Required—TOEFL (minimum score 80 iBT). *Application deadline:* For fall admission, 8/1 for domestic students, 4/1 for international students; for spring admission, 1/1 for domestic students, 9/1 for international students. Applications are processed on a rolling basis. Application fee: $75. Electronic applications accepted. *Expenses:* Tuition, state resident: full-time $12,467; part-time $692.50 per credit hour. Tuition, nonresident: full-time $25,095; part-time $1394.25 per credit hour. *Required fees:* $2669; $491.50 per semester. Tuition and fees vary according to course load, campus/location and program. *Financial support:* In 2016–17, 21 research assistantships with full tuition reimbursements (averaging $19,817 per year), 237 teaching assistantships with full tuition reimbursements (averaging $15,497 per year) were awarded. Financial award application deadline: 3/1; financial award applicants required to submit FAFSA. *Total annual research expenditures:* $6.6 million. *Unit head:* Rosemary Blieszner, Interim Dean, 540-231-6779, Fax: 540-231-7157, E-mail: liberalartsdean@vt.edu. *Application contact:* Chelsea Blanchet, Executive Assistant, 540-231-6779, Fax: 540-231-7157, E-mail: bchels1@vt.edu.
Website: http://www.liberalarts.vt.edu/

Wagner College, Division of Graduate Studies, Education Department, Program in Secondary Education/Students with Disabilities, Staten Island, NY 10301-4495. Offers secondary education 7-12 (MS Ed), including language arts, languages other than English, mathematics and technology, science and technology, social studies. *Program availability:* Part-time, evening/weekend. *Degree requirements:* For master's, thesis (for some programs), completion of state certification exams before student teaching. *Entrance requirements:* For master's, minimum GPA of 3.0, interview, recommendations. Electronic applications accepted. Tuition and fees vary according to degree level.

Wayland Baptist University, Graduate Programs, Program in Education, Plainview, TX 79072-6998. Offers education administration (M Ed); education diagnostics (M Ed); education literacy (M Ed); elementary certification (M Ed); English (M Ed); English as a second language (M Ed); higher education administration (M Ed); human resources (M Ed); instructional leadership (M Ed); instructional technology (M Ed); leadership training and development (M Ed); science education (M Ed); secondary certification (M Ed); social studies (M Ed); special education (M Ed); sports administration and management (M Ed). *Program availability:* Part-time, evening/weekend, online learning. *Degree requirements:* For master's, comprehensive exam, capstone course. *Entrance requirements:* For master's, GRE, GMAT or MAT. Additional exam requirements/recommendations for international students: Required—TOEFL (minimum score 500 paper-based; 61 iBT). Electronic applications accepted.

Wayne State College, School of Education and Counseling, Department of Educational Foundations and Leadership, Program in Curriculum and Instruction, Wayne, NE 68787. Offers alternative education (MSE); business and information technology education (MSE); communication arts education (MSE); early childhood education (MSE); elementary education (MSE); English as a second language (MSE); English education (MSE); family and consumer sciences education (MSE); industrial technology and vocational education (MSE); learning communities (MSE); mathematics education (MSE); music education (MSE); science education (MSE); social science education (MSE). *Accreditation:* NCATE. *Program availability:* Part-time, evening/weekend. *Degree requirements:* For master's, comprehensive exam, thesis optional. *Entrance requirements:* For master's, GRE General Test. Additional exam requirements/recommendations for international students: Required—TOEFL (minimum score 550 paper-based).

Wayne State University, College of Education, Division of Teacher Education, Detroit, MI 48202. Offers art education (M Ed); bilingual/bicultural education (M Ed, Certificate); career and technical education (M Ed); curriculum and instruction (Ed D, PhD, Ed S), including art education (Ed D, PhD), bilingual education (Ed D, Ed S), career and technical education (MAT, Ed D, PhD, Ed S), early childhood education (MAT, Ed D, PhD, Ed S), elementary education, English as a second language (MAT, Ed D, Ed S), English education (MAT, Ed D, PhD, Ed S), foreign language education (MAT, Ed D, PhD), K-12 curriculum, mathematics education (MAT, Ed D, PhD, Ed S), science education (MAT, Ed D, PhD, Ed S), secondary education, social studies education (MAT, Ed D, PhD, Ed S); early childhood education (M Ed); elementary education (M Ed, MAT), including bilingual/bicultural education (MAT), early childhood education (MAT, Ed D, PhD, Ed S), English as a second language (MAT, Ed D, Ed S), general elementary education (MAT), mathematics education (MAT, Ed D, PhD, Ed S), science education (MAT, Ed D, PhD, Ed S), social studies education (MAT, Ed D, PhD, Ed S); English as a second language (Certificate); English education (M Ed); foreign language education (M Ed); mathematics education (M Ed); reading (M Ed, Ed S); reading, language and literature (Ed D); science education (M Ed); secondary education (MAT), including art education (K-12), bilingual/bicultural education, career and technical education (MAT, Ed D, PhD, Ed S), English as a second language (MAT, Ed D, Ed S), English education (MAT, Ed D, PhD, Ed S), foreign language education (MAT, Ed D, PhD), kinesiology, mathematics education (MAT, Ed D, PhD, Ed S); social studies education (M Ed); special education (M Ed, MAT, Ed D, PhD, Ed S), including autism spectrum disorders (MAT), cognitive development (MAT), emotional impairment (MAT), learning disabilities (MAT). *Program availability:* Part-time, blended/hybrid learning. *Faculty:* 29. *Students:* 106 full-time (73 women), 351 part-time (276 women); includes 115 minority (76 Black or African American, non-Hispanic/Latino; 10 Asian, non-Hispanic/Latino; 20 Hispanic/Latino; 1 Native Hawaiian or other Pacific Islander, non-Hispanic/Latino; 8 Two or more races, non-Hispanic/Latino), 12 international. Average age 37. 242 applicants, 37% accepted, 72 enrolled. In 2016, 178 master's, 19 doctorates, 17 other advanced degrees awarded. *Degree requirements:* For master's, essay or project (for some M Ed programs), professional field experience (for MAT programs); for doctorate, thesis/dissertation. *Entrance requirements:* For master's, Michigan Test for Teacher Certification, verification of participation in group work with children, Michigan State Police criminal background check; for doctorate, minimum undergraduate GPA of 3.0, graduate 3.5; interview; curriculum vitae; references. Additional exam requirements/recommendations for international students: Required—TOEFL (minimum score 550 paper-based; 79 iBT), TWE (minimum score 5.5), Michigan English Language Assessment Battery (minimum score 85); Recommended—IELTS (minimum score 6.5). *Application deadline:* For fall admission, 6/1 priority date for domestic students, 5/1 priority date for international students; for winter admission, 10/1 priority date for domestic students, 9/1 priority date for international students; for spring admission, 2/1 priority date for domestic students, 1/1 priority date for international students. Applications are processed on a rolling basis. Application fee: $50. Electronic applications accepted. *Expenses:* $16,503 per year resident tuition and fees, $33,697 per year non-resident tuition and fees. *Financial support:* In 2016–17, 101 students received support, including 3 fellowships (averaging $11,409 per year); research assistantships with tuition reimbursements available, Federal Work-Study, scholarships/grants, and unspecified assistantships also available. Support available to part-time students. Financial award applicants required to submit FAFSA. *Faculty research:* Improving students' skill achievement in mathematics, improving elementary children's understanding of informational text, teachers' use of their pedagogical and mathematical knowledge in the interactive work of teaching, the intersection of identity construction in teaching and learning, identifying effective methods of literacy instruction and assessments for bilingual students in elementary language arts classrooms. *Unit head:* Dr. Kathleen Crawford-McKinney, Assistant Dean, 313-577-0122. *Application contact:* Janice Green, Assistant Dean, 313-577-1605, E-mail: jwgreen@wayne.edu.
Website: http://coe.wayne.edu/ted/index.php

Western Governors University, Teachers College, Salt Lake City, UT 84107. Offers curriculum and instruction (MS); educational leadership (MS); educational studies (MA); educational studies (5-12) (MA), including mathematics; elementary education (K-8) (MAT, Postbaccalaureate Certificate); elementary education (PreK-8) (MAT); English language learning (K-12) (MA); instructional design (MAT); learning and technology (M Ed, MA); management and innovation (M Ed); mathematics (5-12) (MAT, Postbaccalaureate Certificate); mathematics (5-9) (MAT, Postbaccalaureate Certificate); mathematics education (5-12) (MA); mathematics education (5-9) (MA); mathematics education (K-6) (MA); measurement and evaluation (M Ed); science (5-12) (Postbaccalaureate Certificate); science (5-9) (MAT, Postbaccalaureate Certificate); science education (5-12) (MA), including biology, chemistry, geology, physics; science education (5-9) (MA); social science (5-12) (MAT, Postbaccalaureate Certificate); special education (MAT, MS). *Accreditation:* NCATE. *Program availability:* Evening/weekend, online learning. *Degree requirements:* For master's, capstone project. *Entrance requirements:* For master's and Postbaccalaureate Certificate, Readiness Assessment, transcripts. Additional exam requirements/recommendations for international students: Required—TOEFL (minimum score 450 paper-based; 80 iBT). Electronic applications accepted. *Expenses:* Contact institution.

Western Oregon University, Graduate Programs, College of Education, Division of Teacher Education, Program in Secondary Education, Monmouth, OR 97361. Offers bilingual education (MS Ed); health (MS Ed); humanities (MAT, MS Ed); initial licensure (MAT); mathematics (MAT, MS Ed); science (MAT, MS Ed); social science (MAT, MS Ed). *Accreditation:* NCATE. *Program availability:* Part-time, evening/weekend. *Degree requirements:* For master's, thesis optional, written exam. *Entrance requirements:* For master's, minimum GPA of 3.0, teaching license. Additional exam requirements/recommendations for international students: Required—TOEFL (minimum score 550 paper-based; 79 iBT), IELTS (minimum score 6.5). *Faculty research:* Literacy, science in primary grades, geography education, retention, teacher burnout.

Westfield State University, College of Graduate and Continuing Education, Department of Education, Westfield, MA 01086. Offers early childhood education (M Ed); elementary education (M Ed); reading specialist (M Ed); secondary education (M Ed), including biology teacher education, chemistry teacher education, general science teacher education, history teacher education, mathematics teacher education, physical education teacher education; special education (M Ed), including moderate disabilities, 5-12, moderate disabilities, preK-8; vocational technical education (M Ed). *Accreditation:* NCATE. *Program availability:* Part-time, evening/weekend. *Faculty:* 16 full-time (7 women), 33 part-time/adjunct (24 women). *Students:* 21 full-time (10 women), 168 part-time (126 women); includes 6 minority (2 Black or African American, non-Hispanic/Latino; 2 Hispanic/Latino; 2 Two or more races, non-Hispanic/Latino), 1 international. Average age 32. 47 applicants, 85% accepted, 30 enrolled. In 2016, 51 master's awarded. *Degree requirements:* For master's, comprehensive exam, practicum. *Entrance requirements:* For master's, GRE General Test or MAT, minimum undergraduate GPA of 2.8. Additional exam requirements/recommendations for international students: Recommended—TOEFL (minimum score 550 paper-based; 79 iBT). *Application deadline:* For fall admission, 6/30 for domestic students; for spring admission, 10/31 for domestic students; for summer admission, 3/31 for domestic students. Applications are processed on a rolling basis. Application fee: $50. Electronic applications accepted. *Expenses:* Tuition, state resident: part-time $318 per semester hour. Tuition, nonresident: part-time $318 per semester hour. *Required fees:* $75 per semester. Tuition and fees vary according to course load and program. *Financial support:* Unspecified assistantships and SOS scholarships for education majors only available. Financial award application deadline: 3/1; financial award applicants required to submit FAFSA. *Faculty research:* Collaborative teacher education, developmental early childhood education. *Unit head:* Dr. Sandra Berkowitz, Department Chair, 413-572-5323, E-mail: sberkowitz@westfield.ma.edu. *Application contact:* Shelly Henrichon, Coordinator of DGCE Admissions, 413-572-8022, Fax: 413-572-5227, E-mail: mhenrichon@westfield.ma.edu.
Website: http://www.westfield.ma.edu/academics/degrees/education-graduate-programs

Westfield State University, College of Graduate and Continuing Education, Department of Education, Programs in Secondary Education, Program in History Teacher Education, Westfield, MA 01086. Offers secondary education-history (M Ed). *Program availability:* Part-time, evening/weekend. *Faculty:* 1 full-time (0 women). *Students:* 6 full-time (0 women), 15 part-time (5 women). Average age 25. 8 applicants, 88% accepted, 6 enrolled. In 2016, 6 master's awarded. *Degree requirements:* For master's, comprehensive exam, thesis (for some programs). *Entrance requirements:* For master's, GRE General Test or MAT, minimum undergraduate GPA of 2.8. Additional exam requirements/recommendations for international students: Recommended—TOEFL (minimum score 550 paper-based; 79 iBT). *Application deadline:* For fall admission, 6/30 for domestic students; for spring admission, 10/31 for domestic students; for summer admission, 3/31 for domestic students. Applications are processed on a rolling basis. Application fee: $50. *Expenses:* Tuition, state resident: part-time $318 per semester hour. Tuition, nonresident: part-time $318 per semester hour. *Required fees:* $75 per semester. Tuition and fees vary according to course load and program. *Financial support:* Unspecified assistantships and SOS scholarships for education majors only available. Financial award application deadline: 3/1; financial award applicants required to submit FAFSA. *Unit head:* Dr. Sandra Berkowitz, Chair, 413-572-5323. *Application contact:* Shelly Henrichon, Coordinator of DGCE Admissions, 413-572-8022, Fax: 413-572-5227, E-mail: mhenrichon@westfield.ma.edu.

Widener University, School of Education, Hospitality, and Continuing Studies, Chester, PA 19013-5792. Offers adult education (M Ed); counseling in higher education (M Ed); counselor education (M Ed); early childhood education (M Ed); educational foundations

(M Ed); educational leadership (M Ed); educational psychology (M Ed); elementary education (M Ed); English and language arts (M Ed); health education (M Ed); higher education leadership (Ed D); home and school visitor (M Ed); human sexuality (M Ed, PhD); mathematics education (M Ed); middle school education (M Ed); principalship (M Ed); reading and language arts (Ed D); reading education (M Ed); school administration (Ed D); science education (M Ed); social studies education (M Ed); special education (M Ed); technology education (M Ed). *Accreditation:* NCATE. *Program availability:* Part-time, evening/weekend. *Faculty:* 34 full-time (22 women), 37 part-time/adjunct (14 women). *Students:* 97 full-time (64 women), 201 part-time (143 women); includes 56 minority (44 Black or African American, non-Hispanic/Latino; 1 American Indian or Alaska Native, non-Hispanic/Latino; 2 Asian, non-Hispanic/Latino; 8 Hispanic/Latino; 1 Two or more races, non-Hispanic/Latino), 32 international. Average age 39. 139 applicants, 88% accepted. In 2016, 45 master's, 21 doctorates awarded. Terminal master's awarded for partial completion of doctoral program. *Degree requirements:* For doctorate, thesis/dissertation. *Entrance requirements:* For master's, minimum GPA of 2.5; for doctorate, GRE or MAT, minimum GPA of 2.0 (undergraduate), 3.5 (graduate). *Application deadline:* Applications are processed on a rolling basis. Application fee: $25 ($300 for international students). Electronic applications accepted. *Expenses:* Contact institution. *Financial support:* Career-related internships or fieldwork, tuition waivers (full and partial), and unspecified assistantships available. Support available to part-time students. Financial award application deadline: 5/1. *Faculty research:* Reading and cognition, adult education, technology education, educational leadership, special education. *Unit head:* Dr. Shawn Fitzgerald, Dean, 610-499-4294, Fax: 610-499-4623, E-mail: smfitzgerald@widener.edu. *Application contact:* Dr. Roberta Nolan, Director of Graduate Admissions, 610-499-4125, E-mail: rdnolan@widener.edu.
Website: http://www.widener.edu/academics/schools/eics

William Carey University, School of Education, Hattiesburg, MS 39401-5499. Offers art education (M Ed); art of teaching (M Ed); elementary education (M Ed, Ed S); English education (M Ed); gifted education (M Ed); history and social science (M Ed); mild/moderate disabilities (M Ed); secondary education (M Ed). *Accreditation:* NCATE. *Program availability:* Part-time. *Degree requirements:* For master's, comprehensive exam. *Entrance requirements:* For master's, GRE, MAT, minimum GPA of 2.5, Class A teacher's license. Additional exam requirements/recommendations for international students: Required—TOEFL (minimum score 550 paper-based).

Worcester State University, Graduate Studies, Program in History, Worcester, MA 01602-2597. Offers MA. *Program availability:* Part-time. *Faculty:* 6 full-time (4 women), 1 part-time/adjunct (0 women). *Students:* 3 full-time (2 women), 9 part-time (4 women); includes 1 minority (American Indian or Alaska Native, non-Hispanic/Latino). Average age 37. 15 applicants, 73% accepted, 4 enrolled. In 2016, 12 master's awarded. *Degree requirements:* For master's, comprehensive exam (for some programs), thesis (for some programs), portfolio. *Entrance requirements:* For master's, GRE General Test or MAT, 18 undergraduate credits in history, including U.S. history and Western civilizations. Additional exam requirements/recommendations for international students: Required—TOEFL (minimum score 550 paper-based; 79 iBT). *Application deadline:* For fall admission, 6/15 for domestic and international students; for spring admission, 11/1 for domestic and international students; for summer admission, 4/1 for domestic and international students. Applications are processed on a rolling basis. Application fee: $50. Electronic applications accepted. *Expenses:* Tuition, state resident: part-time $150 per credit. Tuition, nonresident: part-time $150 per credit. *Financial support:* Career-related internships or fieldwork, scholarships/grants, and unspecified assistantships available. Financial award application deadline: 3/1; financial award applicants required to submit FAFSA. *Unit head:* Dr. Erika Briesacher, Coordinator, 508-929-8692, Fax: 508-929-8155, E-mail: ebriesacher@worcester.edu. *Application contact:* Sara Grady, Associate Dean, Graduate Studies and Professional Development, 508-929-8787, Fax: 508-929-8100, E-mail: sara.grady@worcester.edu.

Vocational and Technical Education

Alcorn State University, School of Graduate Studies, Department of Advanced Technologies, Lorman, MS 39096-7500. Offers workforce education leadership (MS).

Alcorn State University, School of Graduate Studies, School of Psychology and Education, Lorman, MS 39096-7500. Offers agricultural education (MS Ed); elementary education (MS Ed, Ed S); guidance and counseling (MS Ed); industrial education (MS Ed); secondary education (MS Ed), including health and physical education; special education (MS Ed). *Accreditation:* NCATE. *Degree requirements:* For master's, thesis optional.

Appalachian State University, Cratis D. Williams Graduate School, Department of Sustainable Technology and the Built Environment, Boone, NC 28608. Offers appropriate technology (MS); renewable energy engineering (MS). *Program availability:* Part-time. *Degree requirements:* For master's, comprehensive exam, thesis optional. *Entrance requirements:* For master's, GRE General Test, 3 letters of recommendation. Additional exam requirements/recommendations for international students: Required—TOEFL (minimum score 550 paper-based; 79 iBT), IELTS (minimum score 6.5). *Application deadline:* For fall admission, 3/15 priority date for domestic students, 2/1 for international students; for spring admission, 11/1 for domestic students, 7/1 for international students. Applications are processed on a rolling basis. Application fee: $55. Electronic applications accepted. *Expenses:* Tuition, state resident: full-time $4744. Tuition, nonresident: full-time $17,913. Full-time tuition and fees vary according to program. *Financial support:* Fellowships, research assistantships, teaching assistantships, career-related internships or fieldwork, Federal Work-Study, institutionally sponsored loans, scholarships/grants, and unspecified assistantships available. Financial award application deadline: 4/1; financial award applicants required to submit FAFSA. *Faculty research:* Wind power, biofuels, green construction, solar energy production. *Unit head:* Dr. Jeff Tiller, Chair, 828-262-6351, E-mail: tillerjs@appstate.edu. *Application contact:* Dr. Marie Hoepfl, Graduate Program Director, 828-262-3122, E-mail: hoepflmc@appstate.edu.
Website: http://www.tec.appstate.edu

Bowling Green State University, Graduate College, College of Technology, Program in Career and Technology Education, Bowling Green, OH 43403. Offers career and technology education (M Ed), including technology. *Program availability:* Part-time. *Degree requirements:* For master's, thesis or alternative. *Entrance requirements:* For master's, GRE General Test. Additional exam requirements/recommendations for international students: Required—TOEFL. *Application deadline:* For fall admission, 3/1 for domestic students. Application fee: $30. Electronic applications accepted. *Financial support:* Research assistantships with full tuition reimbursements, teaching assistantships with full tuition reimbursements, career-related internships or fieldwork, Federal Work-Study, tuition waivers (full and partial), and unspecified assistantships available. Financial award applicants required to submit FAFSA. *Faculty research:* Curriculum in technology education. *Unit head:* Dr. James Maxwell, Chair, 419-372-2437. *Application contact:* Dr. Terry Herman, Graduate Coordinator, 419-372-7265.

Buffalo State College, State University of New York, The Graduate School, Faculty of Applied Science and Education, Department of Educational Foundations, Program in Career and Technical Education, Buffalo, NY 14222-1095. Offers MS Ed. *Accreditation:* NCATE. *Program availability:* Part-time, evening/weekend. *Degree requirements:* For master's, thesis or project. *Entrance requirements:* For master's, minimum GPA of 2.5 in last 60 hours, New York teaching certificate. Additional exam requirements/recommendations for international students: Required—TOEFL (minimum score 550 paper-based).

Buffalo State College, State University of New York, The Graduate School, Faculty of Applied Science and Education, Department of Technology, Program in Technology Education, Buffalo, NY 14222-1095. Offers MS Ed. *Accreditation:* NCATE. *Degree requirements:* For master's, thesis or project. *Entrance requirements:* For master's, minimum GPA of 2.5 in last 60 hours, New York teaching certificate. Additional exam requirements/recommendations for international students: Required—TOEFL (minimum score 550 paper-based).

California Baptist University, Program in Education, Riverside, CA 92504-3206. Offers educational leadership (MS); educational leadership for faith-based institutions (MS); educational leadership for public institutions (MS); educational technology (MS); instructional computer applications (MS); international education (MS); leadership and adult learning (MS); leadership and organizational studies (MS); online teaching and learning (MS); reading (MS); science education (MA); special education in mild/moderate disabilities (MS); special education in moderate/severe disabilities (MS); teacher leadership (MS); teaching (MS); teaching and learning (MS). *Program availability:* Part-time, evening/weekend, 100% online, blended/hybrid learning. *Faculty:* 20 full-time (8 women), 11 part-time/adjunct (7 women). *Students:* 191 full-time (148 women), 234 part-time (178 women); includes 194 minority (23 Black or African American, non-Hispanic/Latino; 5 American Indian or Alaska Native, non-Hispanic/Latino; 15 Asian, non-Hispanic/Latino; 131 Hispanic/Latino; 4 Native Hawaiian or other Pacific Islander, non-Hispanic/Latino; 16 Two or more races, non-Hispanic/Latino), 2 international. Average age 31. 277 applicants, 61% accepted, 150 enrolled. In 2016, 280 master's awarded. *Degree requirements:* For master's, comprehensive exam, project, or thesis. *Entrance requirements:* For master's, minimum undergraduate GPA of 2.75; 500-word essay; three letters of recommendation; two prerequisite courses completed with minimum C grade. Additional exam requirements/recommendations for international students: Required—TOEFL (minimum score 80 iBT). *Application deadline:* For fall admission, 8/1 priority date for domestic students, 7/1 for international students; for spring admission, 12/1 priority date for domestic students, 11/1 for international students. Applications are processed on a rolling basis. Application fee: $45. Electronic applications accepted. *Expenses:* Contact institution. *Financial support:* In 2016–17, 162 students received support. Federal Work-Study and scholarships/grants available. Financial award applicants required to submit CSS PROFILE or FAFSA. *Faculty research:* Leadership development, complexity theory, faith and learning, special education, social and philosophical contexts of education. *Unit head:* Dr. John Shoup, Dean, School of Education, 951-343-4516, E-mail: jshoup@calbaptist.edu.
Website: http://www.calbaptist.edu/mastersined/

California University of Pennsylvania, School of Graduate Studies and Research, College of Education and Human Services, Program in Technology Education, California, PA 15419-1394. Offers M Ed. *Accreditation:* NCATE. *Program availability:* Part-time, evening/weekend, online only, 100% online. *Degree requirements:* For master's, comprehensive exam, thesis optional. *Entrance requirements:* For master's, MAT, minimum GPA of 3.0, teaching experience in industrial arts. Additional exam requirements/recommendations for international students: Required—TOEFL (minimum score 550 paper-based; 80 iBT). Electronic applications accepted. *Expenses:* Tuition, state resident: full-time $11,592; part-time $483 per credit. Tuition, nonresident: full-time $17,400; part-time $725 per credit. *Required fees:* $3916. Tuition and fees vary according to course load, degree level, campus/location and reciprocity agreements. *Faculty research:* Curriculum, trends in technology, standards-based assessment.

Capella University, School of Business and Technology, Doctoral Programs in Technology, Minneapolis, MN 55402. Offers general information technology (PhD); global operations and supply chain management (DBA); information assurance and security (PhD); information technology education (PhD); information technology management (DBA, PhD).

Central Connecticut State University, School of Graduate Studies, School of Engineering, Science and Technology, Department of Technology and Engineering Education, New Britain, CT 06050-4010. Offers STEM education (MS). *Program availability:* Part-time, evening/weekend. *Faculty:* 4 full-time (1 woman). *Students:* 4 full-time (1 woman), 50 part-time (24 women); includes 1 minority (Hispanic/Latino). Average age 36. 17 applicants, 82% accepted, 10 enrolled. In 2016, 4 master's awarded. *Degree requirements:* For master's, thesis or alternative, special project. *Entrance requirements:* For master's, minimum undergraduate GPA of 2.7. Additional exam requirements/recommendations for international students: Required—TOEFL (minimum score 550 paper-based; 79 iBT). *Application deadline:* For fall admission, 6/1 for domestic students, 5/1 for international students; for spring admission, 11/1 for domestic and international students. Applications are processed on a rolling basis. Application fee: $50. Electronic applications accepted. *Expenses: Tuition, area resident:* Full-time $6497; part-time $606 per credit. Tuition, state resident: full-time $9748; part-time $622 per credit. Tuition, nonresident: full-time $18,102; part-time $622 per credit. *Required fees:* $4459; $246 per credit. *Financial support:* In 2016–17, 7 students received support. Career-related internships or fieldwork, Federal Work-Study, and scholarships/grants available. Support available to part-time students. Financial award application deadline: 3/1; financial award applicants required to submit FAFSA. *Faculty research:* Instruction, curriculum development, administration, occupational training. *Unit head:* Dr. James DeLaura, Chair, 860-832-1850, E-mail: delaura@ccsu.edu. *Application contact:* Patricia Gardner, Associate Director of Graduate Studies, 860-832-2350, Fax: 860-832-2362.
Website: http://www.ccsu.edu/teched/

Vocational and Technical Education

Central Washington University, Graduate Studies and Research, College of Education and Professional Studies, Department of Family and Consumer Sciences, Ellensburg, WA 98926. Offers career and technical education (MS); family and consumer sciences education (MS); family studies (MS). *Program availability:* Part-time. *Degree requirements:* For master's, thesis or alternative. *Entrance requirements:* For master's, minimum GPA of 3.0. Additional exam requirements/recommendations for international students: Required—TOEFL (minimum score 550 paper-based; 79 iBT). Electronic applications accepted.

Chicago State University, School of Graduate and Professional Studies, College of Education, Department of Technology and Education, Chicago, IL 60628. Offers secondary education (MAT); technology and education (MS Ed). *Program availability:* Online learning. *Degree requirements:* For master's, thesis optional. *Entrance requirements:* For master's, minimum GPA of 2.75.

Clarion University of Pennsylvania, Office of Transfer, Adult and Graduate Admissions, Master of Education Program, Clarion, PA 16214. Offers curriculum and instruction (M Ed); early childhood (M Ed); math education (M Ed); reading (M Ed); science education (M Ed); special education (M Ed); technology (M Ed). *Accreditation:* NCATE. *Program availability:* Part-time, evening/weekend, 100% online, blended/hybrid learning. *Faculty:* 12 full-time (8 women), 5 part-time/adjunct (all women). *Students:* 17 full-time (15 women), 97 part-time (78 women); includes 1 minority (Two or more races, non-Hispanic/Latino). Average age 29. 76 applicants, 99% accepted, 48 enrolled. In 2016, 34 master's awarded. *Degree requirements:* For master's, comprehensive exam, thesis, or portfolio. *Entrance requirements:* For master's, minimum QPA of 3.0. Additional exam requirements/recommendations for international students: Required—TOEFL (minimum score 550 paper-based; 80 iBT), IELTS (minimum score 7). *Application deadline:* For fall admission, 8/1 for domestic students, 4/15 for international students; for spring admission, 8/1 for domestic students, 9/15 for international students. Applications are processed on a rolling basis. Application fee: $40. Electronic applications accepted. *Expenses:* $632.35 per credit. *Financial support:* Career-related internships or fieldwork, Federal Work-Study, scholarships/grants, and unspecified assistantships available. Support available to part-time students. Financial award application deadline: 3/1; financial award applicants required to submit FAFSA. *Unit head:* Dr. John McCullough, Chair, Department of Education, 814-393-2104, Fax: 814-393-2446, E-mail: gradstudies@clarion.edu. *Application contact:* Dana Bearer, Associate Director for Transfer, Adult, and Graduate Programs, 814-393-2337, Fax: 814-393-2722, E-mail: gradstudies@clarion.edu.

Clarkson University, Program in Education, Schenectady, NY 12308. Offers adolescence education 7-12 (MAT); technology education K-12 (MAT). *Accreditation:* TEAC. *Faculty:* 8 full-time (all women), 31 part-time/adjunct (17 women). *Students:* 38 full-time (23 women), 2 part-time (0 women); includes 6 minority (3 Asian, non-Hispanic/Latino; 2 Hispanic/Latino; 1 Two or more races, non-Hispanic/Latino), 7 international. 39 applicants, 79% accepted, 26 enrolled. In 2016, 15 master's awarded. *Degree requirements:* For master's, thesis (for some programs), thesis or project. *Entrance requirements:* For master's, GRE, minimum undergraduate GPA of 3.0. Additional exam requirements/recommendations for international students: Required—TOEFL (minimum score 550 paper-based, 80 iBT) or IELTS (6.5). *Application deadline:* Applications are processed on a rolling basis. Application fee: $50. Electronic applications accepted. *Expenses:* $900 per credit. *Financial support:* Scholarships/grants available. *Unit head:* Dr. Catherine Snyder, Chair of Education, 518-631-9870, E-mail: csnyder@clarkson.edu. *Application contact:* Dan Capogna, Graduate Admissions Contact, 518-631-9910, E-mail: graduate@clarkson.edu.
Website: http://graduate.clarkson.edu

Concordia University, College of Education, Portland, OR 97211-6099. Offers career and technical education (M Ed); curriculum and instruction (M Ed), including adolescent literacy, career and technical education, e-learning/technology education, early childhood education, English for speakers of other languages, English language development, environmental education, mathematics, methods and curriculum, reading, science, teacher leadership, the inclusive classroom; early childhood (MAT); education leadership (Ed D); educational administration (M Ed); elementary education (MAT); secondary education (MAT); special education (M Ed); teacher leadership (Ed D). *Program availability:* Part-time, online learning. *Degree requirements:* For master's, comprehensive exam, work samples/portfolio. *Entrance requirements:* For master's, California Basic Educational Skills Test or PRAXIS I, minimum undergraduate GPA of 2.8, graduate 3.0; 2 letters of recommendation. Additional exam requirements/recommendations for international students: Required—TOEFL (minimum score 525 paper-based). Electronic applications accepted. *Faculty research:* Learner-centered classroom, brain-based learning, future of online learning.

East Carolina University, Graduate School, College of Education, Department of Elementary and Middle Grades Education, Greenville, NC 27858-4353. Offers elementary education (MA Ed, MAT); English education (MAT); family and consumer science (MAT); health education (MAT); Hispanic studies (MAT); history education (MAT); middle grades education (MA Ed, MAT); music education (MAT); science education (MAT); special education (MAT), including general curriculum; vocational education (MAT). *Accreditation:* NCATE. *Program availability:* Part-time, evening/weekend, online learning. *Students:* 5 full-time (4 women), 18 part-time (16 women); includes 4 minority (3 Black or African American, non-Hispanic/Latino; 1 Hispanic/Latino). Average age 31. 19 applicants, 95% accepted, 13 enrolled. In 2016, 8 master's awarded. *Degree requirements:* For master's, comprehensive exam, thesis optional. *Entrance requirements:* For master's, GRE or MAT, minimum GPA of 2.5, bachelor's degree in related field, teaching license (MA Ed). Additional exam requirements/recommendations for international students: Required—TOEFL. *Application deadline:* For fall admission, 6/1 priority date for domestic students. Applications are processed on a rolling basis. Application fee: $70. *Financial support:* Federal Work-Study available. Support available to part-time students. Financial award application deadline: 6/1. *Unit head:* Dr. Ann Bullock, Chair, 252-328-1126, E-mail: bullockv@ecu.edu. *Application contact:* Dean of Graduate School, 252-328-6012, Fax: 252-328-6071, E-mail: gradschool@ecu.edu.
Website: http://www.ecu.edu/cs-educ/elmid/index.cfm

East Carolina University, Graduate School, College of Education, Department of Interdisciplinary Professions, Greenville, NC 27858-4353. Offers adult education (MA Ed); business and marketing education (MA); career and technical education (MA Ed); counselor education (MS); library science (MLS); vocational education (MS). *Accreditation:* ACA; NCATE. *Program availability:* Part-time, evening/weekend. *Students:* 95 full-time (79 women), 427 part-time (374 women); includes 106 minority (68 Black or African American, non-Hispanic/Latino; 13 American Indian or Alaska Native, non-Hispanic/Latino; 4 Asian, non-Hispanic/Latino; 13 Hispanic/Latino; 8 Two or more races, non-Hispanic/Latino). Average age 37. 225 applicants, 93% accepted, 174 enrolled. In 2016, 86 master's awarded. *Degree requirements:* For master's, comprehensive exam, thesis optional. *Entrance requirements:* For master's, GRE General Test or MAT, interview, minimum GPA of 2.5, bachelor's degree in related field, teaching license (MA Ed). Additional exam requirements/recommendations for international students: Required—TOEFL. *Application deadline:* For fall admission, 5/15 priority date for domestic students. Applications are processed on a rolling basis. Application fee: $50. *Financial support:* Research assistantships with partial tuition reimbursements, teaching assistantships with partial tuition reimbursements, and Federal Work-Study available. Support available to part-time students. Financial award application deadline: 6/1. *Unit head:* Dr. Vivian W. Mott, Chair, 252-328-6177, Fax: 252-328-4368, E-mail: mottv@ecu.edu. *Application contact:* Dean of Graduate School, 252-328-6012, Fax: 252-328-6071, E-mail: gradschool@ecu.edu.
Website: http://www.ecu.edu/cs-educ/idp/index.cfm

Eastern Kentucky University, The Graduate School, College of Business and Technology, Department of Technology, Program in Industrial Education, Richmond, KY 40475-3102. Offers occupational training and development (MS); technical administration (MS); technology education (MS). *Accreditation:* NCATE. *Program availability:* Part-time. *Entrance requirements:* For master's, GRE General Test, minimum GPA of 2.5.

Eastern Kentucky University, The Graduate School, College of Education, Department of Curriculum and Instruction, Program in Secondary and Higher Education, Richmond, KY 40475-3102. Offers secondary education (MA Ed), including agricultural education, art education, biological sciences education, business education, English education, geography education, history education, home economics education, industrial education, mathematical sciences education, physical education, school health education. *Accreditation:* NCATE. *Program availability:* Part-time. *Entrance requirements:* For master's, GRE General Test, minimum GPA of 2.5.

Eastern New Mexico University, Graduate School, College of Education and Technology, Department of Curriculum and Instruction, Portales, NM 88130. Offers bilingual education (M Ed); educational technology (M Ed); elementary education (M Ed); English as a second language (M Ed); pedagogy and learning (M Ed); professional technical education (M Ed); reading/literacy (M Ed). *Program availability:* Part-time, online learning. *Degree requirements:* For master's, comprehensive exam, thesis optional. *Entrance requirements:* For master's, minimum GPA of 3.0, photocopy of teaching license, writing assessment, letter of recommendation. Additional exam requirements/recommendations for international students: Required—TOEFL (minimum score 550 paper-based; 79 iBT), IELTS (minimum score 6). Electronic applications accepted.

Fitchburg State University, Division of Graduate and Continuing Education, Program in Occupational Education, Fitchburg, MA 01420-2697. Offers M Ed. *Accreditation:* NCATE. *Program availability:* Part-time, evening/weekend. *Entrance requirements:* Additional exam requirements/recommendations for international students: Required—TOEFL (minimum score 550 paper-based; 79 iBT). Electronic applications accepted. *Expenses:* Tuition, state resident: full-time $2871; part-time $1914 per year. Tuition, nonresident: full-time $2871; part-time $1914 per year. *Required fees:* $3828. Tuition and fees vary according to program.

Fitchburg State University, Division of Graduate and Continuing Education, Program in Technology Education, Fitchburg, MA 01420-2697. Offers M Ed. *Accreditation:* NCATE. *Program availability:* Part-time, evening/weekend. *Entrance requirements:* Additional exam requirements/recommendations for international students: Required—TOEFL (minimum score 550 paper-based; 79 iBT). Electronic applications accepted. *Expenses:* Tuition, state resident: full-time $2871; part-time $1914 per year. Tuition, nonresident: full-time $2871; part-time $1914 per year. *Required fees:* $3828. Tuition and fees vary according to program.

Florida Agricultural and Mechanical University, Division of Graduate Studies, Research, and Continuing Education, College of Education, Department of Vocational Education, Tallahassee, FL 32307-3200. Offers business education (MBE); industrial education (MS Ed); technology education (M Ed). *Accreditation:* NCATE. *Degree requirements:* For master's, thesis (for some programs). *Entrance requirements:* For master's, GRE General Test, minimum GPA of 3.0. Additional exam requirements/recommendations for international students: Required—TOEFL.

The George Washington University, Graduate School of Education and Human Development, Department of Counseling and Human Development, Program in Job Development and Placement, Washington, DC 20052. Offers Graduate Certificate. *Program availability:* Online learning. *Students:* 1 part-time (0 women). Average age 29. 1 applicant, 100% accepted, 1 enrolled. *Financial support:* Fellowships available. *Unit head:* Dr. Kenneth C. Hergenrather, Director, 202-994-1334, E-mail: hergenkc@gwu.edu. *Application contact:* Sarah Lang, Director of Graduate Admissions, 202-994-1447, Fax: 202-994-7207, E-mail: slang@gwu.edu.
Website: http://gsehd.gwu.edu/

Idaho State University, Office of Graduate Studies, College of Technology, Department of Human Resource Training and Development, Pocatello, ID 83209-8380. Offers MTD. *Program availability:* Part-time, evening/weekend. *Degree requirements:* For master's, comprehensive exam, thesis optional, statistical procedures. *Entrance requirements:* For master's, GRE or MAT, minimum GPA of 3.0 in upper-division courses. Additional exam requirements/recommendations for international students: Required—TOEFL (minimum score 550 paper-based; 80 iBT). Electronic applications accepted. *Faculty research:* Learning styles, instructional methodology, leadership administration.

Indiana State University, College of Graduate and Professional Studies, College of Technology, Department of Human Resource Development and Performance Technologies, Terre Haute, IN 47809. Offers career and technical education (MS); human resource development (MS).

Indiana University of Pennsylvania, School of Graduate Studies and Research, College of Education and Educational Technology, Department of Adult and Community Education, Program in Business/Administrative, Indiana, PA 15705. Offers M Ed. *Program availability:* Part-time. *Faculty:* 2 full-time (1 woman). *Students:* 1 full-time (0 women), all international. Average age 24. 2 applicants, 50% accepted, 1 enrolled. In 2016, 1 master's awarded. *Degree requirements:* For master's, thesis optional. *Entrance requirements:* For master's, GMAT or GRE. Additional exam requirements/recommendations for international students: Required—TOEFL (minimum score 540 paper-based). *Application deadline:* Applications are processed on a rolling basis. Application fee: $50. Electronic applications accepted. *Expenses:* Tuition, state resident: full-time $8694; part-time $483 per credit. Tuition, nonresident: full-time $13,050; part-time $725 per credit. *Required fees:* $157 per credit. $50 per term. Tuition and fees vary according to course load and program. *Financial support:* Career-related internships or fieldwork, Federal Work-Study, scholarships/grants, and unspecified assistantships available. Financial award application deadline: 4/15; financial award applicants required to submit FAFSA. *Unit head:* Dr. Lucinda Willis, Graduate Coordinator, 724-357-4585, E-mail: lucinda.willis@iup.edu.
Website: http://www.iup.edu/ace/grad/default.aspx

Inter American University of Puerto Rico, Metropolitan Campus, Graduate Programs, Program in Occupational Education, San Juan, PR 00919-1293. Offers MA. *Degree requirements:* For master's, comprehensive exam. *Entrance requirements:* For master's, GRE or EXADEP, interview. Electronic applications accepted.

Iowa State University of Science and Technology, Program in Industrial Agriculture and Technology, Ames, IA 50011. Offers MS, PhD. *Entrance requirements:* For master's

and doctorate, GRE General Test. Additional exam requirements/recommendations for international students: Required—TOEFL (minimum score 550 paper-based; 79 iBT), IELTS (minimum score 6.5). *Application deadline:* For fall admission, 2/1 priority date for domestic and international students; for spring admission, 7/1 for domestic and international students. Application fee: $60 ($90 for international students). Electronic applications accepted. *Faculty research:* Industrial technology, technology education, training and development, technical education. *Application contact:* Kris Bell, Application Contact, 515-294-1033, E-mail: kabell@iastate.edu.
Website: http://www.abe.iastate.edu

Jackson State University, Graduate School, College of Science, Engineering and Technology, Department of Civil and Environmental Engineering and Industrial Systems and Technology, Jackson, MS 39217. Offers civil engineering (MS, PhD); coastal engineering (MS, PhD); environmental engineering (MS, PhD); hazardous materials management (MS); technology education (MS Ed). *Program availability:* Part-time, evening/weekend. *Degree requirements:* For master's, comprehensive exam, thesis or alternative. *Entrance requirements:* For master's, GRE General Test. Additional exam requirements/recommendations for international students: Required—TOEFL (minimum score 520 paper-based; 67 iBT). *Application deadline:* For fall admission, 3/1 priority date for domestic students, 3/1 for international students; for spring admission, 10/1 for domestic and international students. Applications are processed on a rolling basis. Application fee: $25. *Expenses:* Tuition, state resident: full-time $7141. Tuition, nonresident: full-time $17,494. *Required fees:* $1080. Tuition and fees vary according to class time, course level, course load, degree level, campus/location, program and student level. *Financial support:* Career-related internships or fieldwork, Federal Work-Study, scholarships/grants, and unspecified assistantships available. Support available to part-time students. Financial award application deadline: 3/1; financial award applicants required to submit FAFSA. *Unit head:* Dr. Farshad Amini, Chair, 601-979-3913, Fax: 601-979-3238, E-mail: famini@jsums.edu. *Application contact:* Fatoumatta Sisay, Manager of Graduate Admissions, 601-979-0342, Fax: 601-979-4325, E-mail: fatoumatta.sisay@jsums.edu.
Website: http://www.jsums.edu/ceeist/

James Madison University, The Graduate School, College of Education, Program in Adult Education and Human Resource Development, Harrisonburg, VA 22802. Offers higher education (MS Ed); human resource management (MS Ed); individualized (MS Ed); instructional design (MS Ed); leadership and facilitation (MS Ed); program evaluation and measurement (MS Ed). *Accreditation:* NCATE. *Program availability:* Part-time, evening/weekend. *Students:* 10 full-time (8 women), 11 part-time (10 women); includes 7 minority (4 Black or African American, non-Hispanic/Latino; 1 Hispanic/Latino; 2 Two or more races, non-Hispanic/Latino), 1 international. Average age 30. 23 applicants, 91% accepted, 18 enrolled. In 2016, 17 master's awarded. Application fee: $55. Electronic applications accepted. *Financial support:* In 2016–17, 15 students received support. Teaching assistantships, Federal Work-Study, and 8 assistantships (averaging $7911), 1 athletic assistantship (averaging $9284) available. Financial award application deadline: 3/1; financial award applicants required to submit FAFSA. *Unit head:* Dr. Jane B. Thall, Department Head, 540-568-5531, E-mail: thalljb@jmu.edu. *Application contact:* Lynette D. Michael, Director of Graduate Admissions, 540-568-6131 Ext. 6395, Fax: 540-568-7860, E-mail: michaeld@jmu.edu.

Kent State University, College of Education, Health and Human Services, School of Teaching, Learning and Curriculum Studies, Program in Career Technical Teacher Education, Kent, OH 44242-0001. Offers M Ed. *Program availability:* Part-time, evening/weekend. *Entrance requirements:* For master's, 2 letters of reference, goals statement. Additional exam requirements/recommendations for international students: Required—TOEFL (minimum score 550 paper-based; 80 iBT). Electronic applications accepted. *Expenses:* Tuition, state resident: full-time $10,864; part-time $495 per credit hour. Tuition, nonresident: full-time $18,380; part-time $837 per credit hour. *Faculty research:* Workforce education/development, adult education, training and organizational change.

Louisiana State University and Agricultural & Mechanical College, Graduate School, College of Human Sciences and Education, School of Human Resource Education and Workforce Development, Baton Rouge, LA 70803. Offers agriculture and extension education and youth development (MS, PhD); career and technical education (MS, PhD); comprehensive vocational education (MS, PhD); extension and international education (MS, PhD); human resource and leadership development (MS, PhD); industrial education (MS); vocational agriculture education (MS, PhD); vocational business education (MS); vocational home economics education (MS). *Accreditation:* NCATE.

Marshall University, Academic Affairs Division, College of Education and Professional Development, Programs in Adult and Technical Education, Huntington, WV 25755. Offers MS. *Accreditation:* NCATE. *Program availability:* Evening/weekend. *Degree requirements:* For master's, thesis optional, comprehensive assessment.

Middle Tennessee State University, College of Graduate Studies, College of Basic and Applied Sciences, Department of Engineering Technology and Industrial Studies, Murfreesboro, TN 37132. Offers engineering technology (MS). *Program availability:* Part-time, evening/weekend, online learning. *Degree requirements:* For master's, comprehensive exam. *Entrance requirements:* For master's, GRE. Additional exam requirements/recommendations for international students: Required—TOEFL (minimum score 525 paper-based; 71 iBT) or IELTS (minimum score 6). Electronic applications accepted.

Millersville University of Pennsylvania, College of Graduate Studies and Adult Learning, College of Science and Technology, Department of Applied Engineering, Safety, and Technology, Millersville, PA 17551-0302. Offers technology and innovation (M Ed). *Accreditation:* NCATE. *Program availability:* Part-time, evening/weekend. *Faculty:* 14 full-time (2 women). *Students:* 2 full-time (both women), 17 part-time (7 women); includes 2 minority (1 Asian, non-Hispanic/Latino; 1 Hispanic/Latino), 1 international. Average age 27. 7 applicants, 100% accepted, 6 enrolled. In 2016, 3 master's awarded. *Degree requirements:* For master's, comprehensive exam (for some programs), thesis optional, graded portfolio (educational foundations). *Entrance requirements:* For master's, GRE or MAT (if undergraduate cumulative GPA is 3.0 or lower). Additional exam requirements/recommendations for international students: Required—TOEFL (minimum score 600 paper-based), IELTS (minimum score 6). *Application deadline:* Applications are processed on a rolling basis. Application fee: $40. Electronic applications accepted. *Expenses:* $483 per credit resident tuition; $725 per credit non-resident tuition. *Financial support:* In 2016–17, 2 students received support. Unspecified assistantships available. Financial award application deadline: 3/15; financial award applicants required to submit FAFSA. *Faculty research:* Co-teaching model for clinical experiences, professional development schools. *Unit head:* Dr. Leonard S. Litowitz, Chair, 717-871-7215, Fax: 717-871-7931, E-mail: len.litowitz@millersville.edu. *Application contact:* Dr. Victor S. DeSantis, Dean of College of Graduate Studies and Adult Learning/Associate Provost for Civic and Community Engagement, 717-871-7619, Fax: 717-871-7954, E-mail: victor.desantis@millersville.edu.
Website: http://www.millersville.edu/aest/

Mississippi State University, College of Education, Department of Instructional Systems and Workforce Development, Mississippi State, MS 39762. Offers distance education (MSIT); instructional design (MSIT); instructional systems and workforce development (MST, PhD); multimedia (MSIT); technology (Ed S). *Faculty:* 12 full-time (8 women). *Students:* 14 full-time (10 women), 53 part-time (44 women); includes 41 minority (39 Black or African American, non-Hispanic/Latino; 1 American Indian or Alaska Native, non-Hispanic/Latino; 1 Two or more races, non-Hispanic/Latino). Average age 38. 17 applicants, 47% accepted, 8 enrolled. In 2016, 6 master's, 3 doctorates, 5 other advanced degrees awarded. *Degree requirements:* For master's, thesis optional, comprehensive oral or written exam; for doctorate, thesis/dissertation, comprehensive oral and written exam; for Ed S, thesis, comprehensive written exam. *Entrance requirements:* For master's, GRE, minimum GPA of 2.75 on undergraduate work, 3.0 graduate; for doctorate, GRE, minimum GPA of 3.4 on graduate work; for Ed S, GRE, minimum GPA of 3.2, master's degree. Additional exam requirements/recommendations for international students: Required—TOEFL (minimum score 550 paper-based; 79 iBT); Recommended—IELTS (minimum score 6.5). *Application deadline:* For fall admission, 7/1 for domestic students, 5/1 for international students; for spring admission, 11/1 for domestic students, 9/1 for international students. Applications are processed on a rolling basis. Application fee: $60. Electronic applications accepted. *Expenses:* Tuition, state resident: full-time $7670; part-time $852.50 per credit hour. Tuition, nonresident: full-time $20,790; part-time $2310.50 per credit hour. Part-time tuition and fees vary according to course load. *Financial support:* In 2016–17, 2 research assistantships with full tuition reimbursements (averaging $13,755 per year), 2 teaching assistantships with full tuition reimbursements (averaging $10,800 per year) were awarded; Federal Work-Study, institutionally sponsored loans, scholarships/grants, and unspecified assistantships also available. Financial award application deadline: 4/1; financial award applicants required to submit FAFSA. *Faculty research:* Computer technology, nontraditional students, interactive video, instructional technology, educational leadership. *Unit head:* Dr. Connie Forde, Professor and Department Head, 662-325-2281, Fax: 662-325-7599, E-mail: cforde@colled.msstate.edu. *Application contact:* Linda Bonner, Senior Admissions Assistant, 662-325-3363, E-mail: lbonner@grad.msstate.edu.
Website: http://www.iswd.msstate.edu

Mississippi State University, College of Education, Educational Leadership Program, Mississippi State, MS 39762. Offers community college education (MAT, PhD); elementary, middle and secondary education administration (PhD); school administration (MS, Ed S); workforce education leadership (MS). MS in workforce education leadership held jointly with Alcorn State University. *Faculty:* 16 full-time (10 women). *Students:* 32 full-time (16 women), 158 part-time (101 women); includes 82 minority (80 Black or African American, non-Hispanic/Latino; 1 Hispanic/Latino; 1 Two or more races, non-Hispanic/Latino). Average age 38. 60 applicants, 58% accepted, 34 enrolled. In 2016, 24 master's, 15 doctorates, 5 other advanced degrees awarded. *Degree requirements:* For master's and Ed S, comprehensive exam, thesis; for doctorate, comprehensive exam, thesis/dissertation. *Entrance requirements:* For master's, GRE, minimum GPA of 2.75 in junior and senior courses; for doctorate, GRE, minimum GPA of 3.4 on previous graduate work; for Ed S, GRE, minimum GPA of 3.2, master's degree. Additional exam requirements/recommendations for international students: Required—TOEFL (minimum score 550 paper-based; 79 iBT); Recommended—IELTS (minimum score 6.5). *Application deadline:* For fall admission, 7/1 for domestic students, 5/1 for international students; for spring admission, 11/1 for domestic students, 9/1 for international students. Application fee: $60. Electronic applications accepted. *Expenses:* Tuition, state resident: full-time $7670; part-time $852.50 per credit hour. Tuition, nonresident: full-time $20,790; part-time $2310.50 per credit hour. Part-time tuition and fees vary according to course load. *Financial support:* In 2016–17, 2 research assistantships with full tuition reimbursements (averaging $12,940 per year) were awarded; Federal Work-Study, institutionally sponsored loans, and unspecified assistantships also available. Financial award application deadline: 4/1; financial award applicants required to submit FAFSA. *Unit head:* Dr. Ed Davis, Interim Department Head/Professor, 662-325-0969, Fax: 662-325-0975, E-mail: jed11@colled.msstate.edu. *Application contact:* Linda Bonner, Senior Admissions Assistant, 662-325-3363, E-mail: lbonner@grad.msstate.edu.
Website: http://www.educationalleadership.msstate.edu/

Montana State University, The Graduate School, College of Education, Health, and Human Development, Department of Education, Bozeman, MT 59717. Offers adult and higher education (Ed D); curriculum and instruction (M Ed, Ed D), including professional educator (M Ed), technology education (M Ed); education (M Ed), including adult and higher education, educational leadership, school counseling; educational leadership (Ed D, Ed S). *Accreditation:* TEAC. *Program availability:* Part-time, online learning. *Degree requirements:* For master's, comprehensive exam; for doctorate, comprehensive exam, thesis/dissertation. *Entrance requirements:* For master's, GRE, 3 letters of reference, essays, BA transcripts; for doctorate, GRE, MAT, 3 letters of reference, essay, BA and M Ed transcripts; for Ed S, PRAXIS. Additional exam requirements/recommendations for international students: Required—TOEFL (minimum score 550 paper-based). Electronic applications accepted. *Faculty research:* Critical literacy; standards-based education; school Improvement, organizational change, leadership in rural education, leadership in Indian education; student Learning; multicultural/culturally responsive education for social justice Native American indigenous education, community-centered education teacher preparation.

Morehead State University, Graduate Programs, College of Science and Technology, Department of Industrial and Engineering Technology, Morehead, KY 40351. Offers career and technical education (MS); engineering technology (MS). *Program availability:* Part-time, evening/weekend. *Degree requirements:* For master's, completion and defense of thesis or written and oral comprehensive exit exams. *Entrance requirements:* For master's, GRE, minimum undergraduate GPA of 3.0 in major. Additional exam requirements/recommendations for international students: Required—TOEFL (minimum score 500 paper-based). Electronic applications accepted.

Murray State University, College of Education, Department of Adolescent, Career and Special Education, Program in Industrial and Technical Education, Murray, KY 42071. Offers MS. *Accreditation:* NCATE. *Program availability:* Part time. *Degree requirements:* For master's, thesis (for some programs), portfolio. *Entrance requirements:* For master's, GRE General Test. Additional exam requirements/recommendations for international students: Required—TOEFL.

North Carolina Agricultural and Technical State University, School of Graduate Studies, School of Technology, Department of Graphic Communication Systems and Technological Studies, Greensboro, NC 27411. Offers graphic communication systems (MSTM); technology education (MAT). *Accreditation:* NCATE (one or more programs are accredited). *Program availability:* Part-time, evening/weekend. *Degree requirements:* For master's, comprehensive exam, thesis or alternative, qualifying exam. *Entrance requirements:* For master's, GRE General Test, minimum GPA of 3.0.

North Dakota State University, College of Graduate and Interdisciplinary Studies, College of Human Development and Education, School of Education, Fargo, ND 58102. Offers agricultural education (M Ed, MS), including agricultural education; counselor education (M Ed, MS, PhD), including clinical mental health counseling (M Ed, MS), counselor education and supervision (PhD), school counseling (M Ed, MS); curriculum and instruction (M Ed, MS); education (PhD); educational leadership (M Ed, MS, Ed S);

family and consumer sciences education (M Ed, MS); history education (M Ed, MS); institutional analysis (Ed D); mathematics education (M Ed, MS); music education (M Ed, MS); occupational and adult education (Ed D); science education (M Ed, MS). *Accreditation:* NCATE. *Program availability:* Part-time, evening/weekend, online learning. *Degree requirements:* For master's, comprehensive exam; for doctorate, thesis/dissertation; for Ed S, thesis. *Entrance requirements:* For degree, GRE General Test, master's degree, minimum GPA of 3.25. Additional exam requirements/recommendations for international students: Required—TOEFL.

Northern Arizona University, Graduate College, College of Education, Department of Educational Specialties, Flagstaff, AZ 86011. Offers autism spectrum disorders (Certificate); bilingual/multicultural education (M Ed), including bilingual education, ESL education; career and technical education (M Ed, Certificate); culturally and linguistically diverse special education (Certificate); early childhood special education (M Ed); educational technology (M Ed, Certificate); English as a second language (Certificate); mild/moderate disabilities (M Ed); positive behavior support (Certificate); special education (M Ed). *Degree requirements:* For master's, comprehensive exam (for some programs), thesis (for some programs). *Entrance requirements:* For master's, minimum GPA of 3.0. Additional exam requirements/recommendations for international students: Required—TOEFL (minimum score 550 paper-based; 80 iBT), IELTS (minimum score 7). Electronic applications accepted. *Expenses:* Tuition, state resident: full-time $8971; part-time $444 per credit hour. Tuition, nonresident: full-time $20,958; part-time $1164 per credit hour. *Required fees:* $1018; $644 per credit hour. Tuition and fees vary according to course load, campus/location and program.

Old Dominion University, Darden College of Education, Programs in STEM Education and Professional Studies, Norfolk, VA 23529. Offers community college teaching (MS); human resources training (PhD); technology education (PhD). *Accreditation:* NCATE (one or more programs are accredited). *Program availability:* Part-time, evening/weekend, blended/hybrid learning, mix of synchronous and asynchronous study. *Faculty:* 6 full-time (2 women). *Students:* 12 full-time (7 women), 33 part-time (20 women); includes 16 minority (15 Black or African American, non-Hispanic/Latino; 1 Two or more races, non-Hispanic/Latino), 2 international. Average age 42. 3 applicants, 100% accepted, 3 enrolled. In 2016, 6 master's, 6 doctorates awarded. Terminal master's awarded for partial completion of doctoral program. *Degree requirements:* For master's, comprehensive exam, thesis optional, writing exam, candidacy exam; for doctorate, comprehensive exam, thesis/dissertation, writing exam, candidacy exam. *Entrance requirements:* For master's, GRE General Test or MAT, minimum GPA of 2.8, 2 letters of reference; for doctorate, GRE, minimum GPA of 3.0, 3 letters of reference. Additional exam requirements/recommendations for international students: Required—TOEFL. *Application deadline:* For fall admission, 6/1 priority date for domestic students, 6/1 for international students; for winter admission, 11/1 priority date for domestic students, 11/1 for international students; for spring admission, 3/1 priority date for domestic students, 3/1 for international students. Applications are processed on a rolling basis. Application fee: $50. Electronic applications accepted. *Expenses:* Tuition, state resident: full-time $8604; part-time $478 per credit hour. Tuition, nonresident: full-time $21,510; part-time $1195 per credit hour. *Required fees:* $66 per semester. Tuition and fees vary according to campus/location, program and reciprocity agreements. *Financial support:* In 2016–17, 3 students received support, including 2 teaching assistantships with partial tuition reimbursements available (averaging $15,000 per year). Financial award application deadline: 2/15; financial award applicants required to submit FAFSA. *Faculty research:* Training and development, STEM education, visualization, leadership, technology literacy. *Total annual research expenditures:* $1 million. *Unit head:* Dr. Petros Katsioloudis, Graduate Program Director, 757-683-5323, E-mail: pkatsiol@odu.edu.
Website: http://education.odu.edu/ots/

Penn State University Park, Graduate School, College of Education, Department of Learning and Performance Systems, University Park, PA 16802. Offers adult education (M Ed, D Ed, PhD, Certificate); corporate training (MPS); learning, design, and technology (M Ed, MS, PhD, Certificate); lifelong learning and adult education (M Ed, D Ed, PhD, Certificate); organization development and change (MPS); workforce education and development (M Ed, MS, PhD). *Unit head:* Dr. David H. Monk, Dean, 814-865-2523, Fax: 814-865-0555. *Application contact:* Lori Hawn, Director, Graduate Student Services, 814-865-1795, Fax: 814-863-4627, E-mail: l-gswww@lists.psu.edu.
Website: http://ed.psu.edu/lps/dept-lps

Pittsburg State University, Graduate School, College of Technology, Department of Technology and Workforce Learning, Pittsburg, KS 66762. Offers career and technical education (MS); human resource development (MS); technology (MS), including automotive technology, construction management, graphic design, graphics management, innovation in technology, personnel development, technology management, workforce learning; workforce development and education (Ed S). *Program availability:* Part-time, evening/weekend, 100% online, blended/hybrid learning. *Students:* 171 (79 women); includes 20 minority (4 Black or African American, non-Hispanic/Latino; 5 American Indian or Alaska Native, non-Hispanic/Latino; 2 Asian, non-Hispanic/Latino; 4 Hispanic/Latino; 5 Two or more races, non-Hispanic/Latino), 61 international. In 2016, 62 master's, 2 other advanced degrees awarded. *Degree requirements:* For master's, thesis or alternative; for Ed S, thesis optional. *Entrance requirements:* Additional exam requirements/recommendations for international students: Required—TOEFL (minimum score 520 paper-based; 68 iBT), IELTS (minimum score 6), PTE (minimum score 47). *Application deadline:* For fall admission, 7/15 for domestic students, 6/1 for international students; for spring admission, 12/15 for domestic students, 10/15 for international students; for summer admission, 5/15 for domestic students, 4/1 for international students. Applications are processed on a rolling basis. Application fee: $35 ($60 for international students). Electronic applications accepted. *Expenses:* Contact institution. *Financial support:* In 2016–17, 8 teaching assistantships with full tuition reimbursements (averaging $5,500 per year) were awarded; career-related internships or fieldwork also available. Financial award application deadline: 2/1; financial award applicants required to submit FAFSA. *Unit head:* Dr. John Iley, Chairperson, 620-235-4373, E-mail: jiley@pittstate.edu. *Application contact:* Lisa Allen, Assistant Director of Graduate and Continuing Studies, 620-235-4218, Fax: 620-235-4219, E-mail: lallen@pittstate.edu.

Purdue University, Graduate School, College of Education, Department of Curriculum and Instruction, West Lafayette, IN 47907. Offers agricultural and extension education (MS, MS Ed, PhD, Ed S); art education (PhD); career and technical education (MS Ed, PhD, Ed S); curriculum studies (MS Ed, PhD, Ed S); educational technology (MS Ed, PhD, Ed S); elementary education (MS Ed); family and consumer sciences education (MS Ed, PhD, Ed S); foreign language education (MS Ed, PhD, Ed S); industrial technology (PhD, Ed S); language arts (MS Ed, PhD, Ed S); literacy (MS Ed, PhD, Ed S); mathematics education (MS, MS Ed, PhD, Ed S); science education (MS, MS Ed, PhD, Ed S); social studies education (MS Ed, PhD, Ed S). *Accreditation:* NCATE. *Program availability:* Part-time, evening/weekend. *Faculty:* 37 full-time (27 women), 1 (woman) part-time/adjunct. *Students:* 78 full-time (50 women), 286 part-time (195 women); includes 68 minority (25 Black or African American, non-Hispanic/Latino; 3 American Indian or Alaska Native, non-Hispanic/Latino; 10 Asian, non-Hispanic/Latino; 22 Hispanic/Latino; 1 Native Hawaiian or other Pacific Islander, non-Hispanic/Latino; 7 Two or more races, non-Hispanic/Latino), 44 international. Average age 36. 150 applicants, 79% accepted, 73 enrolled. In 2016, 107 master's, 20 doctorates, 2 other advanced degrees awarded. *Degree requirements:* For master's, thesis optional; for doctorate, thesis/dissertation, oral and written exams; for Ed S, oral presentation, project. *Entrance requirements:* For master's, GRE General Test (if undergraduate GPA is below 3.0), minimum undergraduate GPA of 3.0 or equivalent; for doctorate, GRE General Test (minimum combined verbal and quantitative score of 1000, 300 for new scoring), minimum undergraduate GPA of 3.0 or equivalent; master's degree with minimum GPA of 3.0 or equivalent; for Ed S, GRE General Test (minimum combined verbal and quantitative score of 1000, 300 for new scoring), minimum undergraduate GPA of 3.0 or equivalent; master's degree. Additional exam requirements/recommendations for international students: Required—TOEFL (minimum score 550 paper-based; 77 iBT). *Application deadline:* For fall admission, 12/15 for domestic students, 3/1 for international students; for spring admission, 9/15 for domestic students, 8/1 for international students. Application fee: $60 ($75 for international students). Electronic applications accepted. *Financial support:* Fellowships with full tuition reimbursements, research assistantships with full tuition reimbursements, teaching assistantships with full tuition reimbursements, career-related internships or fieldwork, and tuition waivers (full) available. Support available to part-time students. Financial award application deadline: 3/1; financial award applicants required to submit FAFSA. *Faculty research:* Literacy acquisition and development, teacher beliefs and knowledge, recruitment and retention of underrepresented students, economic education, literacy discourse. *Unit head:* Janet M. Alsup, Head, 765-494-9667, E-mail: alsupj@purdue.edu. *Application contact:* Heather Brinkman, Graduate Contact, 765-494-2345, E-mail: hbrinkma@purdue.edu.
Website: http://www.edci.purdue.edu/

South Carolina State University, College of Graduate and Professional Studies, Department of Education, Orangeburg, SC 29117-0001. Offers early childhood education (MAT); education (M Ed); elementary education (M Ed, MAT); English (MAT); general science/biology (MAT); mathematics (MAT); secondary education (M Ed), including biology education, business education, counselor education, English education, home economics education, industrial education, mathematics education, science education, social studies education; special education (M Ed), including emotionally handicapped, learning disabilities, mentally handicapped. *Accreditation:* NCATE. *Program availability:* Part-time, evening/weekend. *Faculty:* 12 full-time (8 women), 3 part-time/adjunct (1 woman). *Students:* 28 full-time (20 women), 20 part-time (17 women); includes 45 minority (44 Black or African American, non-Hispanic/Latino; 1 Two or more races, non-Hispanic/Latino). Average age 31. 22 applicants, 100% accepted, 16 enrolled. In 2016, 9 master's awarded. *Degree requirements:* For master's, thesis optional, departmental qualifying exam. *Entrance requirements:* For master's, GRE General Test, NTE, interview, teaching certificate. *Application deadline:* For fall admission, 6/15 priority date for domestic students, 6/15 for international students; for spring admission, 11/1 for domestic and international students. Application fee: $25. Electronic applications accepted. *Expenses:* Tuition, state resident: full-time $8938; part-time $579 per credit hour. Tuition, nonresident: full-time $19,018; part-time $1139 per credit hour. *Required fees:* $1482; $82 per credit hour. *Financial support:* Fellowships, career-related internships or fieldwork, Federal Work-Study, and scholarships/grants available. Financial award application deadline: 6/1. *Unit head:* Dr. Charlie Spell, Interim Chair, Department of Education, 803-536-8963, Fax: 803-516-4568, E-mail: cspell@scsu.edu. *Application contact:* Curtis Foskey, Coordinator of Graduate Studies, 803-536-8419, Fax: 803-536-8812, E-mail: cfoskey@scsu.edu.

Southern Illinois University Carbondale, Graduate School, College of Education and Human Services, Department of Workforce Education and Development, Carbondale, IL 62901-4701. Offers MS Ed, PhD. *Accreditation:* NCATE. *Program availability:* Part-time. *Degree requirements:* For master's, thesis; for doctorate, thesis/dissertation. *Entrance requirements:* For master's, minimum GPA of 2.7; for doctorate, GRE General Test, minimum GPA of 3.25. Additional exam requirements/recommendations for international students: Required—TOEFL. *Faculty research:* Career education, technical training, curriculum development, competency-based instruction, impact of technology on workplace and workforce.

State University of New York at Oswego, Graduate Studies, School of Education, Department of Technology, Oswego, NY 13126. Offers MS Ed. *Accreditation:* NCATE. *Program availability:* Part-time. *Degree requirements:* For master's, thesis optional, departmental exam. *Entrance requirements:* For master's, provisional teaching certificate in technology education. Additional exam requirements/recommendations for international students: Required—TOEFL (minimum score 560 paper-based). *Faculty research:* Curriculum development, microcomputer applications.

State University of New York at Oswego, Graduate Studies, School of Education, Department of Vocational Teacher Preparation, Oswego, NY 13126. Offers agriculture (MS Ed); business and marketing (MS Ed); family and consumer sciences (MS Ed); health careers (MS Ed); technical education (MS Ed); trade education (MS Ed). *Accreditation:* NCATE. *Program availability:* Part-time, evening/weekend. *Degree requirements:* For master's, comprehensive exam, thesis or alternative. *Entrance requirements:* Additional exam requirements/recommendations for international students: Required—TOEFL (minimum score 560 paper-based).

Temple University, College of Education, Department of Teaching and Learning, Philadelphia, PA 19122-6096. Offers career and technical education (Ed M), including business, computing, and information technology, industrial education, marketing education; middle grades education (Ed M), including math and language arts, math and science, science and language arts; secondary education (Ed M), including English, math, social studies; teaching English to speakers of other languages (MS Ed); urban education (Ed M). *Program availability:* Part-time, evening/weekend. *Faculty:* 26 full-time (16 women), 74 part-time/adjunct (54 women). *Students:* 204 full-time (139 women), 320 part-time (201 women); includes 112 minority (66 Black or African American, non-Hispanic/Latino; 17 Asian, non-Hispanic/Latino; 18 Hispanic/Latino; 11 Two or more races, non-Hispanic/Latino), 18 international. 300 applicants, 55% accepted, 99 enrolled. In 2016, 93 master's awarded. Terminal master's awarded for partial completion of doctoral program. *Degree requirements:* For master's, thesis or alternative. *Entrance requirements:* Additional exam requirements/recommendations for international students: Required—TOEFL (minimum score 550 paper-based; 79 iBT). *Application deadline:* For fall admission, 4/1 for domestic students, 12/15 for international students; for spring admission, 10/1 for domestic students, 8/1 for international students. Application fee: $60. Electronic applications accepted. *Expenses:* Contact institution. *Financial support:* Fellowships, research assistantships, and teaching assistantships available. Financial award application deadline: 1/15; financial award applicants required to submit FAFSA. *Faculty research:* Workforce development, vocational education, technical education, industrial education, professional development, literacy, classroom management, school communities, curriculum development, instruction, applied linguistics, cross linguistic influence, bilingual education, oral proficiency, multilingualism. *Unit head:* Dr. Christine Woyshner, Chairperson, 215-204-6387, E-mail: christine.woyshner@temple.edu. *Application contact:* Sarah Stapleton, Assistant Director, Academic Operations, 215-204-8220,

E-mail: sarah.stapleton@temple.edu.
Website: http://education.temple.edu/tl

Texas State University, The Graduate College, College of Applied Arts, Interdisciplinary Studies Program in Occupational Education, San Marcos, TX 78666. Offers MAIS, MSIS. *Program availability:* Part-time. *Faculty:* 5 full-time (3 women), 1 part-time/adjunct (0 women). *Students:* 28 full-time (14 women), 34 part-time (20 women); includes 34 minority (15 Black or African American, non-Hispanic/Latino; 2 Asian, non-Hispanic/Latino; 16 Hispanic/Latino; 1 Two or more races, non-Hispanic/Latino), 1 international. Average age 38. 34 applicants, 91% accepted, 20 enrolled. In 2016, 21 master's awarded. *Degree requirements:* For master's, comprehensive exam, thesis optional. *Entrance requirements:* For master's, minimum GPA of 2.75 for last 60 hours of undergraduate work, statement of personal goals. Additional exam requirements/recommendations for international students: Required—TOEFL (minimum score 550 paper-based; 78 iBT). *Application deadline:* For fall admission, 2/15 priority date for domestic and international students; for spring admission, 10/15 priority date for domestic students, 10/1 for international students. Applications are processed on a rolling basis. Application fee: $40 ($90 for international students). Electronic applications accepted. *Expenses:* $9,702 per year. *Financial support:* In 2016–17, 39 students received support, including 1 research assistantship (averaging $15,000 per year); teaching assistantships, Federal Work-Study, institutionally sponsored loans, scholarships/grants, health care benefits, and unspecified assistantships also available. Support available to part-time students. Financial award application deadline: 4/1; financial award applicants required to submit FAFSA. *Unit head:* Dr. Matthew Eichler, Director, 512-245-2115, E-mail: me21@txstate.edu. *Application contact:* Dr. Andrea Golato, Dean of Graduate School, 512-245-2581, Fax: 512-245-8365, E-mail: gradcollege@txstate.edu.
Website: http://www.OCED.txstate.edu/

Texas State University, The Graduate College, College of Applied Arts, Program in Management of Technical Education, San Marcos, TX 78666. Offers M Ed. *Program availability:* Part-time, evening/weekend. *Faculty:* 3 full-time (1 woman), 4 part-time/adjunct (3 women). *Students:* 6 full-time (3 women), 14 part-time (8 women); includes 15 minority (2 Black or African American, non-Hispanic/Latino; 1 American Indian or Alaska Native, non-Hispanic/Latino; 12 Hispanic/Latino). Average age 42. 12 applicants, 100% accepted, 7 enrolled. In 2016, 6 master's awarded. *Degree requirements:* For master's, comprehensive exam. *Entrance requirements:* For master's, baccalaureate degree from regionally-accredited university with minimum GPA of 2.75 in last 60 hours of course work. Additional exam requirements/recommendations for international students: Required—TOEFL (minimum score 550 paper-based; 78 iBT). *Application deadline:* For fall admission, 2/15 priority date for domestic students, 2/1 priority date for international students; for spring admission, 10/15 for domestic students, 10/1 for international students; for summer admission, 4/15 for domestic students, 3/15 for international students. Applications are processed on a rolling basis. Application fee: $40 ($90 for international students). Electronic applications accepted. *Expenses:* $9,702 per year. *Financial support:* In 2016–17, 10 students received support. Research assistantships, teaching assistantships, career-related internships or fieldwork, Federal Work-Study, institutionally sponsored loans, and scholarships/grants available. Support available to part-time students. Financial award application deadline: 4/1; financial award applicants required to submit FAFSA. *Unit head:* Dr. Matthew Eichler, Graduate Advisor, 512-245-2115, E-mail: me21@txstate.edu. *Application contact:* Dr. Andrea Golato, Dean of the Graduate College, 512-245-2581, Fax: 512-245-8365, E-mail: gradcollege@txstate.edu.
Website: http://www.owls.txstate.edu/graduate-degrees/management-technical-education.html

University of Arkansas, Graduate School, College of Education and Health Professions, Department of Rehabilitation, Human Resources and Communication Disorders, Fayetteville, AR 72701. Offers adult and lifelong learning (M Ed, Ed D); communication disorders (MS); counseling (MS, PhD, Ed S); higher education (M Ed, Ed D, Ed S); human resource and workforce development education (M Ed, Ed D); rehabilitation (MS, PhD); vocational education (MAT). *Program availability:* Part-time. In 2016, 92 master's, 17 doctorates awarded. *Degree requirements:* For doctorate, thesis/dissertation. *Application deadline:* For fall admission, 4/1 for international students; for spring admission, 10/1 for international students. Applications are processed on a rolling basis. Application fee: $40 ($50 for international students). Electronic applications accepted. *Financial support:* In 2016–17, 55 research assistantships, 3 teaching assistantships were awarded; fellowships with tuition reimbursements, career-related internships or fieldwork, and Federal Work-Study also available. Support available to part-time students. Financial award application deadline: 4/1; financial award applicants required to submit FAFSA. *Unit head:* Dr. Kate Mamiseishvili, Department Chairperson, 479-575-4258, Fax: 479-575-3319, E-mail: kmamisei@uark.edu. *Application contact:* Dr. Brent Williams, Graduate Coordinator, 479-575-4758, E-mail: btwilli@uark.edu.
Website: http://rhrc.uark.edu/

The University of British Columbia, Faculty of Education, Department of Curriculum and Pedagogy, Vancouver, BC V6T 1Z4, Canada. Offers art education (M Ed, MA); curriculum studies (M Ed, MA, PhD); home economics education (M Ed, MA); mathematics education (M Ed, MA); media and technology studies education (M Ed, MA); music education (M Ed, MA); physical education (M Ed, MA); science education (M Ed, MA); social studies education (M Ed, MA). *Program availability:* Part-time, online learning. *Degree requirements:* For master's, thesis (MA); for doctorate, comprehensive exam, thesis/dissertation. *Entrance requirements:* Additional exam requirements/recommendations for international students: Required—TOEFL, IELTS. Application fee: $100 Canadian dollars ($162 Canadian dollars for international students). Electronic applications accepted. *Expenses:* $6,865 per year tuition and fees domestic, $10,930 per year international (for MA and M Ed); $4,802 per year tuition and fees, $8,436 per year international (for PhD). *Financial support:* Fellowships with partial tuition reimbursements, research assistantships with partial tuition reimbursements, teaching assistantships with partial tuition reimbursements, and tuition waivers (partial) available. *Faculty research:* School subjects, teaching and learning. *Application contact:* Alan Jay, Graduate Programs Assistant, 604-822-5367, Fax: 604-822-4714, E-mail: edcp.grad@ubc.ca.
Website: http://www.edcp.educ.ubc.ca/

University of Central Florida, College of Arts and Humanities, Department of English, Orlando, FL 32816. Offers creative writing (MFA); English (MA, Certificate); texts and technology (PhD). *Program availability:* Part-time, evening/weekend. *Faculty:* 41 full-time (21 women), 12 part-time/adjunct (9 women). *Students:* 76 full-time (53 women), 72 part-time (54 women); includes 23 minority (4 Black or African American, non-Hispanic/Latino; 3 Asian, non-Hispanic/Latino; 14 Hispanic/Latino; 2 Two or more races, non-Hispanic/Latino), 5 international. Average age 33. 142 applicants, 62% accepted, 49 enrolled. In 2016, 31 master's, 7 doctorates, 8 other advanced degrees awarded. *Degree requirements:* For master's, one foreign language, thesis or alternative. *Entrance requirements:* For master's, GRE General Test, minimum GPA of 3.0 in last 60 hours of course work. Additional exam requirements/recommendations for international students: Required—TOEFL. *Application deadline:* For fall admission, 3/30 for domestic students; for spring admission, 11/1 for domestic students. Application fee: $30. Electronic applications accepted. *Expenses:* Tuition, state resident: part-time $288.16 per credit hour. Tuition, nonresident: part-time $1071.31 per credit hour. *Financial support:* In 2016–17, 49 students received support, including 19 fellowships with partial tuition reimbursements available (averaging $5,874 per year), 12 research assistantships with partial tuition reimbursements available (averaging $8,630 per year), 34 teaching assistantships with partial tuition reimbursements available (averaging $9,949 per year); career-related internships or fieldwork, Federal Work-Study, institutionally sponsored loans, tuition waivers (partial), and unspecified assistantships also available. Financial award application deadline: 3/1; financial award applicants required to submit FAFSA. *Unit head:* Dr. Trey Philpotts, Chair, 407-823-1159, E-mail: trey.philpotts@ucf.edu. *Application contact:* Assistant Director, Graduate Admissions, 407-823-2766, Fax: 407-823-6442, E-mail: gradadmissions@ucf.edu.
Website: http://www.english.cah.ucf.edu/

University of Central Florida, College of Education and Human Performance, Department of Educational and Human Sciences, Program in Career and Technical Education, Orlando, FL 32816. Offers MA. *Accreditation:* NCATE. *Program availability:* Part-time, evening/weekend. *Students:* 18 full-time (13 women), 24 part-time (15 women); includes 23 minority (12 Black or African American, non-Hispanic/Latino; 10 Hispanic/Latino; 1 Two or more races, non-Hispanic/Latino). Average age 35. 20 applicants, 90% accepted, 12 enrolled. In 2016, 15 master's awarded. *Degree requirements:* For master's, comprehensive exam. *Entrance requirements:* Additional exam requirements/recommendations for international students: Required—TOEFL. *Application deadline:* For fall admission, 7/15 for domestic students; for spring admission, 12/1 for domestic students. Application fee: $30. Electronic applications accepted. *Expenses:* Tuition, state resident: part-time $288.16 per credit hour. Tuition, nonresident: part-time $1071.31 per credit hour. *Financial support:* Career-related internships or fieldwork, Federal Work-Study, institutionally sponsored loans, and unspecified assistantships available. Financial award application deadline: 3/1; financial award applicants required to submit FAFSA. *Unit head:* Dr. Jo Ann M. Whiteman, Program Coordinator, 407-823-5303, E-mail: joann.whiteman@ucf.edu. *Application contact:* Assistant Director, Graduate Admissions, 407-823-2766, Fax: 407-823-6442, E-mail: gradadmissions@ucf.edu.
Website: http://education.ucf.edu/teched/

University of Central Missouri, The Graduate School, Warrensburg, MO 64093. Offers accountancy (MA); accounting (MBA); applied mathematics (MS); aviation safety (MA); biology (MS); business administration (MBA); career and technical education leadership (MS); college student personnel administration (MS); communication (MA); computer science (MS); counseling (MS); criminal justice (MS); educational leadership (Ed D); educational technology (MS); elementary and early childhood education (MSE); English (MA); environmental studies (MA); finance (MBA); history (MA); human services/educational technology (Ed S); human services/learning resources (Ed S); human services/professional counseling (Ed S); industrial hygiene (MS); industrial management (MS); information systems (MBA); information technology (MS); kinesiology (MS); library science and information services (MS); literacy education (MSE); marketing (MBA); mathematics (MS); music (MA); occupational safety management (MS); psychology (MS); rural family nursing (MS); school administration (MSE); social gerontology (MS); sociology (MA); special education (MSE); speech language pathology (MS); superintendency (Ed S); teaching (MAT); teaching English as a second language (MA); technology (MS); technology management (PhD); theatre (MA). *Program availability:* Part-time, 100% online, blended/hybrid learning. *Degree requirements:* For master's and Ed S, comprehensive exam (for some programs), thesis (for some programs). *Entrance requirements:* Additional exam requirements/recommendations for international students: Required—TOEFL (minimum score 550 paper-based; 79 iBT). Electronic applications accepted.

University of Georgia, College of Education, Department of Career and Information Studies, Athens, GA 30602. Offers learning, design, and technology (M Ed, PhD, Ed S), including instructional design and development (M Ed, Ed S); workforce education (MAT, Ed D), including business education (MAT). *Accreditation:* NCATE. *Faculty:* 14 full-time (7 women). *Students:* 27 full-time (15 women), 70 part-time (46 women); includes 24 minority (23 Black or African American, non-Hispanic/Latino; 1 Native Hawaiian or other Pacific Islander, non-Hispanic/Latino), 5 international. Average age 37. 40 applicants, 63% accepted, 8 enrolled. In 2016, 16 master's, 23 doctorates, 5 other advanced degrees awarded. *Entrance requirements:* For master's, GRE General Test, MAT; for doctorate, GRE General Test; for Ed S, GRE General Test or MAT. *Application deadline:* For fall admission, 7/1 priority date for domestic students; for spring admission, 11/15 for domestic students. Application fee: $50. Electronic applications accepted. *Financial support:* Fellowships, research assistantships, teaching assistantships, and unspecified assistantships available. *Unit head:* Dr. Robert C. Branch, Head, 706-542-4100, Fax: 706-542-4054. *Application contact:* Dr. Robert C. Wicklein, Graduate Coordinator, 706-542-4503, Fax: 706-542-4054, E-mail: wickone@uga.edu.
Website: http://www.coe.uga.edu/cis/

University of Idaho, College of Graduate Studies, College of Education, Department of Curriculum and Instruction, Moscow, ID 83844. Offers career and technology education (M Ed); curriculum and instruction (M Ed, Ed S); special education (M Ed). *Faculty:* 25 full-time, 2 part-time/adjunct. *Students:* 21 full-time (16 women), 35 part-time (29 women). Average age 37. In 2016, 17 master's awarded. *Entrance requirements:* For master's, minimum GPA of 3.0. Additional exam requirements/recommendations for international students: Required—TOEFL. *Application deadline:* For fall admission, 8/1 for domestic students; for spring admission, 12/15 for domestic students. Applications are processed on a rolling basis. Application fee: $60. Electronic applications accepted. *Expenses:* Tuition, state resident: full-time $6460; part-time $414 per credit hour. Tuition, nonresident: full-time $21,268; part-time $1237 per credit hour. *Required fees:* $2070; $60 per credit hour. Full-time tuition and fees vary according to course load and reciprocity agreements. *Financial support:* Research assistantships and teaching assistantships available. Financial award applicants required to submit FAFSA. *Unit head:* Dr. Allen Kitchel, Interim Chair, 208-885-6587, E-mail: teached@uidaho.edu. *Application contact:* Sean Scoggin, Graduate Recruitment Coordinator, 208-885-4001, Fax: 208-885-4406, E-mail: graduateadmissions@uidaho.edu.
Website: http://www.uidaho.edu/ed/ci

University of Maryland Eastern Shore, Graduate Programs, Department of Technology, Princess Anne, MD 21853-1299. Offers career and technology education (M Ed). *Program availability:* Part-time, evening/weekend. *Degree requirements:* For master's, comprehensive exam, seminar paper. *Entrance requirements:* For master's, PRAXIS, writing sample. Additional exam requirements/recommendations for international students: Required—TOEFL (minimum score 80 iBT). Electronic applications accepted. *Faculty research:* Doppler Radar study.

University of Minnesota, Twin Cities Campus, Graduate School, College of Education and Human Development, Department of Organizational Leadership, Policy and Development, Minneapolis, MN 55455-0213. Offers adult education (M Ed, Certificate); adult literacy (Certificate); comparative and international development education (MA, PhD); disability policy and services (Certificate); education policy and leadership (M Ed, MA, Ed D, PhD), including educational policy and leadership (MA, Ed D, PhD), leadership in education (M Ed); evaluation studies (MA, PhD); higher

education (MA, Ed D, PhD), including higher education (MA, PhD), multicultural college teaching and learning (MA); human resource development (M Ed, MA, Ed D, PhD, Certificate); PK-12 administrative licensure (Certificate); private college leadership (Certificate); professional development (Certificate); program evaluation (Certificate); technical education (Certificate); undergraduate multicultural teaching and learning (Certificate); work and human resource education (M Ed). *Faculty:* 33 full-time (15 women). *Students:* 281 full-time (186 women), 240 part-time (147 women); includes 110 minority (43 Black or African American, non-Hispanic/Latino; 3 American Indian or Alaska Native, non-Hispanic/Latino; 23 Asian, non-Hispanic/Latino; 29 Hispanic/Latino; 12 Two or more races, non-Hispanic/Latino), 63 international. Average age 37. 422 applicants, 59% accepted, 225 enrolled. In 2016, 76 master's, 56 doctorates, 37 other advanced degrees awarded. Application fee: $75 ($95 for international students). *Financial support:* In 2016–17, 7 fellowships, 41 research assistantships with full tuition reimbursements (averaging $10,156 per year), 28 teaching assistantships with full tuition reimbursements (averaging $9,170 per year) were awarded. *Faculty research:* Organizational issues in schools, universities, and other organizations; international education and development; program evaluation and research on applied evaluation methods; international human resource development and change; gender and race/ethnicity in relation to learning and leadership. *Total annual research expenditures:* $987,854. *Unit head:* Dr. Heidi Barajas, Chair, 612-625-4823, Fax: 612-624-3377, E-mail: hbarajas@umn.edu. *Application contact:* Dr. Jeremy J. Hernandez, Coordinator of Graduate Studies, 612-626-9377, E-mail: herna220@umn.edu.
Website: http://www.cehd.umn.edu/olpd/

University of Missouri, Office of Research and Graduate Studies, College of Education, Department of Learning, Teaching and Curriculum, Columbia, MO 65211. Offers agricultural education (M Ed, PhD, Ed S); art education (M Ed, PhD, Ed S); business and office education (M Ed, PhD, Ed S); early childhood education (M Ed, PhD, Ed S); elementary education (M Ed, PhD, Ed S); English education (M Ed, PhD, Ed S); foreign language education (M Ed, PhD, Ed S); health education and promotion (M Ed, PhD); learning and instruction (M Ed); marketing education (M Ed, PhD, Ed S); mathematics education (M Ed, PhD, Ed S); music education (M Ed, PhD, Ed S); reading education (M Ed, PhD, Ed S); science education (M Ed, PhD, Ed S); social studies education (M Ed, PhD, Ed S); vocational education (M Ed, PhD, Ed S). *Program availability:* Part-time. *Faculty:* 30 full-time (18 women), 1 (woman) part-time/adjunct. *Students:* 157 full-time (124 women), 157 part-time (125 women). Terminal master's awarded for partial completion of doctoral program. *Degree requirements:* For doctorate, thesis/dissertation. *Entrance requirements:* For master's and Ed S, GRE General Test or MAT, minimum GPA of 3.0; for doctorate, GRE General Test, minimum GPA of 3.0. Additional exam requirements/recommendations for international students: Required—TOEFL (minimum score 600 paper-based; 100 iBT). *Application deadline:* For fall admission, 12/1 priority date for domestic and international students. Applications are processed on a rolling basis. Application fee: $75 ($90 for international students). Electronic applications accepted. *Expenses:* Tuition, state resident: full-time $6347; part-time $352.60 per credit hour. Tuition, nonresident: full-time $17,379; part-time $965.50 per credit hour. *Required fees:* $1035. Tuition and fees vary according to course load, campus/location and program. *Financial support:* Fellowships, research assistantships, teaching assistantships, institutionally sponsored loans, traineeships, health care benefits, and unspecified assistantships available. Support available to part-time students.
Website: http://education.missouri.edu/LTC/index.php

University of Nebraska–Lincoln, Graduate College, College of Education and Human Sciences, Department of Teaching, Learning and Teacher Education, Lincoln, NE 68588. Offers adult and continuing education (MA); educational studies (Ed D, PhD), including special education (Ed D); teaching, learning and teacher education (M Ed, MA, MST, Ed D, PhD); vocational and adult education (M Ed, MA). *Accreditation:* NCATE. *Degree requirements:* For master's, thesis optional. *Entrance requirements:* Additional exam requirements/recommendations for international students: Required—TOEFL (minimum score 550 paper-based). Electronic applications accepted. *Faculty research:* Teacher education, instructional leadership, literacy education, technology, improvement of school curriculum.

University of New England, College of Graduate and Professional Studies, Portland, ME 04103. Offers applied nutrition (MS); career and technical education (MS Ed); curriculum and instruction (MS Ed); education (CAGS, Post-Master's Certificate); education leadership (Ed D); educational leadership (MS Ed); generalist (MS Ed); health informatics (MS, Graduate Certificate); inclusion education (MS Ed); literacy K-12 (MS Ed); medical education leadership (MMEL); public health (Graduate Certificate); reading specialist (MS Ed); social work (MSW). *Program availability:* Part-time, evening/weekend, online only, 100% online. *Faculty:* 67 part-time/adjunct (46 women). *Students:* 891 full-time (667 women), 359 part-time (261 women); includes 309 minority (215 Black or African American, non-Hispanic/Latino; 2 American Indian or Alaska Native, non-Hispanic/Latino; 63 Asian, non-Hispanic/Latino; 18 Hispanic/Latino; 2 Native Hawaiian or other Pacific Islander, non-Hispanic/Latino; 9 Two or more races, non-Hispanic/Latino). Average age 36. 777 applicants, 50% accepted, 316 enrolled. In 2016, 292 master's, 34 doctorates, 130 other advanced degrees awarded. *Application deadline:* Applications are processed on a rolling basis. Electronic applications accepted. Tuition and fees vary according to degree level, program and student level. *Financial support:* Application deadline: 5/1; applicants required to submit FAFSA. *Unit head:* Dr. Martha Wilson, Associate Provost for Online Worldwide Learning/Dean of the College of Graduate and Professional Studies, 207-221-4985, E-mail: mwilson13@une.edu.
Website: http://online.une.edu

University of Northern Iowa, Graduate College, College of Humanities, Arts and Sciences, Department of Technology, Doctor of Industrial Technology Program, Cedar Falls, IA 50614. Offers DIT.

University of Northern Iowa, Graduate College, College of Humanities, Arts and Sciences, Department of Technology, MS Program in Technology, Cedar Falls, IA 50614. Offers MS.

University of North Texas, Robert B. Toulouse School of Graduate Studies, Denton, TX 76203-5459. Offers accounting (MS); applied anthropology (MA, MS); applied behavior analysis (Certificate); applied geography (MA); applied technology and performance improvement (M Ed, MS); art education (MA); art history (MA); art museum education (Certificate); arts leadership (Certificate); audiology (Au D); behavior analysis (MS); behavioral science (PhD); biochemistry and molecular biology (MS); biology (MA, MS); biomedical engineering (MS); business analysis (MS); chemistry (MS); clinical health psychology (PhD); communication studies (MA, MS); computer engineering (MS); computer science (MS); counseling (M Ed, MS, including clinical mental health counseling (MS), college and university counseling, elementary school counseling, secondary school counseling; creative writing (MA); criminal justice (MS); curriculum and instruction (M Ed); decision sciences (MBA); design (MA, MFA), including fashion design (MFA), innovation studies, interior design (MFA); early childhood studies (MS); economics (MS); educational leadership (M Ed, Ed D); educational psychology (MS, PhD), including family studies (MS), gifted and talented (MS), human development (MS), learning and cognition (MS), research, measurement and evaluation (MS); electrical engineering (MS); emergency management (MPA); engineering technology (MS); English (MA); English as a second language (MA); environmental science (MS); finance (MBA, MS); financial management (MPA); French (MA); health services management (MBA); higher education (M Ed, Ed D); history (MA, MS); hospitality management (MS); human resources management (MPA); information science (MS); information systems (PhD); information technologies (MBA); interdisciplinary studies (MA, MS); international studies (MA); international sustainable tourism (MS); jazz studies (MM); journalism (MA, MJ, Graduate Certificate), including interactive and virtual digital communication (Graduate Certificate), narrative journalism (Graduate Certificate), public relations (Graduate Certificate); kinesiology (MS); linguistics (MA); local government management (MPA); logistics (PhD); logistics and supply chain management (MBA); long-term care, senior housing, and aging services (MA); management (PhD); marketing (MBA); mathematics (MA, MS); mechanical and energy engineering (MS, PhD); music (MA), including ethnomusicology, music theory, musicology, performance; music composition (PhD); music education (MM Ed, PhD); nonprofit management (MPA); operations and supply chain management (MBA); performance (MM, DMA); philosophy (MA); political science (MA); professional and technical communication (MA); radio, television and film (MA, MFA); rehabilitation counseling (Certificate); sociology (MA); Spanish (MA); special education (M Ed); speech-language pathology (MA); strategic management (MBA); studio art (MFA); teaching (M Ed); MBA/MS. *Program availability:* Part-time, evening/weekend, online learning. Terminal master's awarded for partial completion of doctoral program. *Degree requirements:* For master's, variable foreign language requirement, comprehensive exam (for some programs), thesis (for some programs); for doctorate, variable foreign language requirement, comprehensive exam (for some programs), thesis/dissertation; for other advanced degree, variable foreign language requirement, comprehensive exam (for some programs). *Entrance requirements:* For master's and doctorate, GRE, GMAT. Additional exam requirements/recommendations for international students: Required—TOEFL (minimum score 550 paper-based; 79 iBT). Electronic applications accepted.

University of Phoenix–Phoenix Campus, College of Education, Tempe, AZ 85282-2371. Offers administration and supervision (MA Ed); adult education and training (MA Ed); curriculum and instruction reading (MA Ed); early childhood education (MA Ed); education studies (MA Ed); elementary teacher education (MA Ed); secondary teacher education (MA Ed); special education (MA Ed); teacher leadership (MA Ed). *Program availability:* Evening/weekend, online learning. *Entrance requirements:* Additional exam requirements/recommendations for international students: Required—TOEFL, TOEIC (Test of English as an International Communication), Berlitz Online English Proficiency Exam, PTE, or IELTS. Electronic applications accepted. *Expenses:* Contact institution.

University of South Africa, Institute for Science and Technology Education, Pretoria, South Africa. Offers mathematics, science and technology education (M Sc, PhD).

University of South Florida, College of Education, Department of Leadership, Counseling, Adult, Career and Higher Education, Tampa, FL 33620-9951. Offers adult education (MA, Ed D, PhD, Ed S); career and technical education (MA); career and workforce education (PhD); higher education/community college teaching (MA, Ed D, PhD); vocational education (Ed S). *Faculty:* 17 full-time (10 women). *Students:* 137 full-time (96 women), 331 part-time (237 women); includes 170 minority (75 Black or African American, non-Hispanic/Latino; 2 American Indian or Alaska Native, non-Hispanic/Latino; 12 Asian, non-Hispanic/Latino; 71 Hispanic/Latino; 2 Native Hawaiian or other Pacific Islander, non-Hispanic/Latino; 8 Two or more races, non-Hispanic/Latino), 18 international. Average age 35. 175 applicants, 66% accepted, 93 enrolled. In 2016, 111 master's, 22 doctorates, 1 other advanced degree awarded. Application fee: $30. *Expenses:* Tuition, state resident: full-time $7766; part-time $431.43 per credit hour. Tuition, nonresident: full-time $15,789; part-time $877.17 per credit hour. *Required fees:* $37 per term. *Total annual research expenditures:* $545,936. *Unit head:* Dr. Judith Ponticell, Chair, 813-974-4897, Fax: 813-974-5423, E-mail: jponticell@usf.edu.
Website: http://www.coedu.usf.edu/main/departments/ache/ache.html

The University of Toledo, College of Graduate Studies, Judith Herb College of Education, Department of Curriculum and Instruction, Toledo, OH 43606-3390. Offers art education (ME); career and technical education (ME, Ed S); curriculum and instruction (ME, PhD, Ed S); early childhood education (Ed S); education and anthropology (MAE); education and biology (MES); education and chemistry (MES); education and classics (MAE); education and economics (MAE); education and English (MAE); education and French (MAE); education and geology (MES); education and German (MAE); education and history (MAE); education and mathematics (MAE, MES); education and physics (MES); education and political science (MAE); education and sociology (MAE); education and Spanish (MAE); educational media (PhD); educational technology (ME); educational technology: virtual educator (Certificate); elementary education (PhD); English as a second language (MAE); gifted and talented education (PhD); middle childhood education (ME); secondary education (ME, PhD); special education (PhD). *Accreditation:* NCATE. *Program availability:* Part-time, evening/weekend. *Degree requirements:* For master's, comprehensive exam, thesis or alternative; for doctorate, comprehensive exam, thesis/dissertation; for other advanced degree, thesis optional. *Entrance requirements:* For master's, doctorate, and other advanced degree, minimum cumulative GPA of 2.7 for all previous academic work, letters of recommendation. Additional exam requirements/recommendations for international students: Required—TOEFL (minimum score 550 paper-based; 80 iBT). Electronic applications accepted.

University of Victoria, Faculty of Graduate Studies, Faculty of Education, Department of Curriculum and Instruction, Victoria, BC V8W 2Y2, Canada. Offers art education (M Ed, PhD); curriculum studies (M Ed, MA, PhD); early childhood education (M Ed, PhD); educational studies (PhD); language and literacy (M Ed, MA, PhD); mathematics (M Ed, MA, PhD); music education (M Ed, MA, PhD); science (M Ed, MA, PhD); social studies (M Ed, MA); social, cultural and foundational studies (MA, PhD); technology and environmental education (PhD). *Program availability:* Part-time. *Degree requirements:* For master's, thesis, project (M Ed); for doctorate, comprehensive exam, thesis/dissertation. *Entrance requirements:* For master's, minimum B average. Additional exam requirements/recommendations for international students: Required—TOEFL (minimum score 575 paper-based), IELTS (minimum score 7). Electronic applications accepted. *Faculty research:* Elementary and secondary English, language arts, curriculum theory and practice, educational media and technology, educational administration and leadership, history and philosophy of education.

University of Wisconsin–Stout, Graduate School, College of Education, Health and Human Sciences, School of Education, Program in Career and Technical Education, Menomonie, WI 54751. Offers MS, Ed D, Ed S. *Program availability:* Part-time, online learning. *Degree requirements:* For master's and Ed S, thesis. *Entrance requirements:* For master's, minimum GPA of 2.75; for Ed S, minimum GPA of 3.25. Additional exam requirements/recommendations for international students: Required—TOEFL (minimum score 500 paper-based; 61 iBT). Electronic applications accepted. *Faculty research:* Needs assessment, task analysis, instructional development, learning technologies.

Utah State University, School of Graduate Studies, College of Engineering, Department of Engineering and Technology Education, Logan, UT 84322. Offers industrial technology (MS). *Program availability:* Part-time, evening/weekend. *Degree requirements:* For master's, thesis optional. *Entrance requirements:* For master's, GRE

General Test, MAT, minimum GPA of 3.0 in last 30 hours of course work. Additional exam requirements/recommendations for international students: Required—TOEFL. *Faculty research:* Computer-aided design drafting, technology and the public school, materials, electronics, aviation.

Valley City State University, Online Master of Education Program, Valley City, ND 58072. Offers elementary education (M Ed); English education (M Ed); library and information technologies (M Ed); teaching (MAT); teaching and technology (M Ed); teaching English language learners (M Ed); technology education (M Ed). *Accreditation:* NCATE. *Program availability:* Part-time, evening/weekend, online only, 100% online. *Faculty:* 21 full-time (12 women), 15 part-time/adjunct (11 women). *Students:* 4 full-time (3 women), 133 part-time (92 women); includes 9 minority (1 American Indian or Alaska Native, non-Hispanic/Latino; 4 Hispanic/Latino; 4 Two or more races, non-Hispanic/Latino), 1 international. Average age 34. 35 applicants, 91% accepted, 28 enrolled. In 2016, 45 master's awarded. *Degree requirements:* For master's, action research report, comprehensive portfolio. *Entrance requirements:* For master's, GRE, MAT, PRAXIS II or National Teaching Board for Professional Standards (if GPA is less than 3.0). Additional exam requirements/recommendations for international students: Required—TOEFL (minimum score 525 paper-based; 71 iBT); Recommended—IELTS (minimum score 5.5). *Application deadline:* For fall admission, 7/21 priority date for domestic and international students; for spring admission, 12/8 priority date for domestic and international students; for summer admission, 5/5 priority date for domestic and international students. Applications are processed on a rolling basis. Application fee: $35. Electronic applications accepted. *Expenses:* $373 per credit. *Financial support:* In 2016–17, 23 students received support. Scholarships/grants, tuition waivers (full and partial), and unspecified assistantships available. Financial award application deadline: 6/14; financial award applicants required to submit FAFSA. *Faculty research:* Universal accessibility, instructional design and technology, gender communication, STEM education in K-12. *Unit head:* Dr. Gary Thompson, Dean, 701-845-7197, E-mail: gary.thompson@vcsu.edu. *Application contact:* Misty Lindgren, Graduate Studies, 701-845-7303, Fax: 701-845-7190, E-mail: misty.lindgren@vcsu.edu.
Website: http://www.vcsu.edu/graduate

Virginia Polytechnic Institute and State University, Graduate School, College of Liberal Arts and Human Sciences, Blacksburg, VA 24061. Offers career and technical education (MS Ed, Ed D, PhD, Ed S); communication (MA); counselor education (MA Ed, Ed D, PhD, Ed S); creative writing (MFA); curriculum and instruction (MA Ed, Ed D, PhD, Ed S); educational leadership and policy studies (MA Ed, Ed D, PhD, Ed S); educational research and evaluation (PhD); English (MA); foreign languages, cultures, and literatures (MA); higher education (PhD); higher education and student affairs (MA Ed); history (MA); human development (MS, PhD); material culture and public humanities (MA); philosophy (MA); political science (MA); rhetoric and writing (PhD); science and technology studies (MS, PhD); social, political, ethical, and cultural thought (PhD); sociology (MS, PhD); theater arts (MFA). *Faculty:* 408 full-time (204 women), 3 part-time/adjunct (2 women). *Students:* 657 full-time (446 women), 457 part-time (292 women); includes 213 minority (114 Black or African American, non-Hispanic/Latino; 3 American Indian or Alaska Native, non-Hispanic/Latino; 29 Asian, non-Hispanic/Latino; 44 Hispanic/Latino; 23 Two or more races, non-Hispanic/Latino), 93 international. Average age 33. 805 applicants, 55% accepted, 328 enrolled. In 2016, 270 master's, 91 doctorates awarded. *Degree requirements:* For master's, comprehensive exam (for some programs), thesis (for some programs); for doctorate, comprehensive exam (for some programs), thesis/dissertation (for some programs). *Entrance requirements:* For master's and doctorate, GRE/GMAT. Additional exam requirements/recommendations for international students: Required—TOEFL (minimum score 80 iBT). *Application deadline:* For fall admission, 8/1 for domestic students, 4/1 for international students; for spring admission, 1/1 for domestic students, 9/1 for international students. Applications are processed on a rolling basis. Application fee: $75. Electronic applications accepted. *Expenses:* Tuition, state resident: full-time $12,467; part-time $692.50 per credit hour. Tuition, nonresident: full-time $25,095; part-time $1394.25 per credit hour. *Required fees:* $2669; $491.50 per semester. Tuition and fees vary according to course load, campus/location and program. *Financial support:* In 2016–17, 21 research assistantships with full tuition reimbursements (averaging $19,817 per year), 237 teaching assistantships with full tuition reimbursements (averaging $15,497 per year) were awarded. Financial award application deadline: 3/1; financial award applicants required to submit FAFSA. *Total annual research expenditures:* $6.6 million. *Unit head:* Rosemary Blieszner, Interim Dean, 540-231-6779, Fax: 540-231-7157, E-mail: liberalartsdean@vt.edu. *Application contact:* Chelsea Blanchet, Executive Assistant, 540-231-6779, Fax: 540-231-7157, E-mail: bchels1@vt.edu.
Website: http://www.liberalarts.vt.edu/

Virginia Polytechnic Institute and State University, VT Online, Blacksburg, VA 24061. Offers advanced transportation systems (Certificate); aerospace engineering (MS); agricultural and life sciences (MSLFS); business information systems (Graduate Certificate); career and technical education (MS); civil engineering (MS); computer engineering (M Eng, MS); decision support systems (Graduate Certificate); eLearning leadership (MA); electrical engineering (M Eng, MS); engineering administration (MEA); environmental engineering (Certificate); environmental politics and policy (Graduate Certificate); environmental sciences and engineering (MS); foundations of political analysis (Graduate Certificate); health product risk management (Graduate Certificate); industrial and systems engineering (MS); information policy and society (Graduate Certificate); information security (Graduate Certificate); information technology (MIT); instructional technology (MA); integrative STEM education (MA Ed); liberal arts (Graduate Certificate); life sciences: health product risk management (MS); natural resources (MNR, Graduate Certificate); networking (Graduate Certificate); nonprofit and nongovernmental organization management (Graduate Certificate); ocean engineering (MS); political science (MA); security studies (Graduate Certificate); software development (Graduate Certificate). *Expenses:* Tuition, state resident: full-time $12,467; part-time $692.50 per credit hour. Tuition, nonresident: full-time $25,095; part-time $1394.25 per credit hour. *Required fees:* $2669; $491.50 per semester. Tuition and fees vary according to course load, campus/location and program.

Washington State University, College of Education, Department of Teaching and Learning, Pullman, WA 99164-2132. Offers cultural studies and social thought in education (PhD); curriculum and instruction (Ed M, MA); English language learners (Ed M, MA); language, literacy and technology (PhD); literacy education (Ed M, MA); mathematics education (PhD); special education (Ed M, MA, PhD); teacher leadership (Ed D); teaching (MIT), including elementary education, secondary education. Programs offered at the Pullman, Spokane, Tri-cities, Vancouver and Global (online) campuses. *Program availability:* Part-time, online learning. *Degree requirements:* For master's, comprehensive exam, thesis, oral or written exam; for doctorate, comprehensive exam, thesis/dissertation, oral and written exam. *Entrance requirements:* For master's, GRE General Test, minimum GPA of 3.0, 3 letters of recommendation, letter of intent, transcripts, resume/curriculum vitae; for doctorate, GRE General Test, minimum GPA of 3.0, 3 letters of recommendation, letter of intent, transcripts, writing sample, resume/curriculum vitae. Additional exam requirements/recommendations for international students: Required—TOEFL (minimum score 550 paper-based; 80 iBT). Electronic applications accepted. *Faculty research:* Intersection of gender, youth cultures and schooling; examination of ideology of power in children's literature; early childhood special education; analyzing pre-service and in-service teacher development; second language acquisition.

Wayne State College, School of Education and Counseling, Department of Educational Foundations and Leadership, Program in Curriculum and Instruction, Wayne, NE 68787. Offers alternative education (MSE); business and information technology education (MSE); communication arts education (MSE); early childhood education (MSE); elementary education (MSE); English as a second language (MSE); English education (MSE); family and consumer sciences education (MSE); industrial technology and vocational education (MSE); learning communities (MSE); mathematics education (MSE); music education (MSE); science education (MSE); social science education (MSE). *Accreditation:* NCATE. *Program availability:* Part-time, evening/weekend. *Degree requirements:* For master's, comprehensive exam, thesis optional. *Entrance requirements:* For master's, GRE General Test. Additional exam requirements/recommendations for international students: Required—TOEFL (minimum score 550 paper-based).

Wayne State University, College of Education, Division of Teacher Education, Detroit, MI 48202. Offers art education (M Ed); bilingual/bicultural education (M Ed, Certificate); career and technical education (M Ed); curriculum and instruction (Ed D, PhD, Ed S), including art education (Ed D, PhD), bilingual education (Ed D, Ed S), career and technical education (MAT, Ed D, PhD, Ed S), early childhood education (MAT, Ed D, PhD, Ed S), elementary education, English as a second language (MAT, Ed D, Ed S), English education (MAT, Ed D, PhD, Ed S), foreign language education (MAT, Ed D, PhD), K-12 curriculum, mathematics education (MAT, Ed D, PhD, Ed S), science education (MAT, Ed D, PhD, Ed S), secondary education, social studies education (MAT, Ed D, PhD, Ed S); early childhood education (M Ed); elementary education (M Ed, MAT), including bilingual/bicultural education (MAT), early childhood education (MAT, Ed D, PhD, Ed S), English as a second language (MAT, Ed D, Ed S), general elementary education (MAT), mathematics education (MAT, Ed D, PhD, Ed S), science education (MAT, Ed D, PhD, Ed S), social studies education (MAT, Ed D, PhD, Ed S); English as a second language (Certificate); English education (M Ed); foreign language education (M Ed); mathematics education (M Ed); reading (M Ed, Ed S); reading, language and literature (Ed D); science education (M Ed); secondary education (MAT), including art education (K-12), bilingual/bicultural education, career and technical education (MAT, Ed D, PhD, Ed S), English as a second language (MAT, Ed D, Ed S), English education (MAT, Ed D, PhD, Ed S), foreign language education (MAT, Ed D, PhD), kinesiology, mathematics education (MAT, Ed D, PhD, Ed S); social studies education (M Ed); special education (M Ed, MAT, Ed D, PhD, Ed S), including autism spectrum disorders (MAT), cognitive development (MAT), emotional impairment (MAT), learning disabilities (MAT). *Program availability:* Part-time, blended/hybrid learning. *Faculty:* 29. *Students:* 106 full-time (73 women), 351 part-time (276 women); includes 115 minority (76 Black or African American, non-Hispanic/Latino; 10 Asian, non-Hispanic/Latino; 20 Hispanic/Latino; 1 Native Hawaiian or other Pacific Islander, non-Hispanic/Latino; 8 Two or more races, non-Hispanic/Latino), 12 international. Average age 37. 242 applicants, 37% accepted, 72 enrolled. In 2016, 178 master's, 19 doctorates, 17 other advanced degrees awarded. *Degree requirements:* For master's, essay or project (for some M Ed programs), professional field experience (for MAT programs); for doctorate, thesis/dissertation. *Entrance requirements:* For master's, Michigan Test for Teacher Certification, verification of participation in group work with children, Michigan State Police criminal background check; for doctorate, minimum undergraduate GPA of 3.0, graduate 3.5; interview; curriculum vitae; references. Additional exam requirements/recommendations for international students: Required—TOEFL (minimum score 550 paper-based; 79 iBT), TWE (minimum score 5.5), Michigan English Language Assessment Battery (minimum score 85); Recommended—IELTS (minimum score 6.5). *Application deadline:* For fall admission, 6/1 priority date for domestic students, 5/1 priority date for international students; for winter admission, 10/1 priority date for domestic students, 9/1 priority date for international students; for spring admission, 2/1 priority date for domestic students, 1/1 priority date for international students. Applications are processed on a rolling basis. Application fee: $50. Electronic applications accepted. *Expenses:* $16,503 per year resident tuition and fees, $33,697 per year non-resident tuition and fees. *Financial support:* In 2016–17, 101 students received support, including 3 fellowships (averaging $11,409 per year); research assistantships with tuition reimbursements available, Federal Work-Study, scholarships/grants, and unspecified assistantships also available. Support available to part-time students. Financial award applicants required to submit FAFSA. *Faculty research:* Improving students' skill achievement in mathematics, improving elementary children's understanding of informational text, teachers' use of their pedagogical and mathematical knowledge in the interactive work of teaching, the intersection of identity construction in teaching and learning, identifying effective methods of literacy instruction and assessments for bilingual students in elementary language arts classrooms. *Unit head:* Dr. Kathleen Crawford-McKinney, Assistant Dean, 313-577-0122. *Application contact:* Janice Green, Assistant Dean, 313-577-1605, E-mail: jwgreen@wayne.edu.
Website: http://coe.wayne.edu/ted/index.php

Western Michigan University, Graduate College, College of Education and Human Development, Department of Family and Consumer Sciences, Kalamazoo, MI 49008. Offers career and technical education (MA); family and consumer sciences (MA).

Westfield State University, College of Graduate and Continuing Education, Department of Education, Program in Vocational Technical Education, Westfield, MA 01086. Offers M Ed. *Accreditation:* NCATE. *Program availability:* Part-time, evening/weekend. *Students:* 4 part-time (all women). Average age 40. 3 applicants, 100% accepted. In 2016, 4 master's awarded. *Degree requirements:* For master's, comprehensive exam. *Entrance requirements:* For master's, GRE General Test or MAT, minimum undergraduate GPA of 2.8. Additional exam requirements/recommendations for international students: Recommended—TOEFL (minimum score 550 paper-based; 79 iBT). *Application deadline:* For fall admission, 6/30 for domestic students; for spring admission, 10/31 for domestic students; for summer admission, 3/31 for domestic students. Applications are processed on a rolling basis. Application fee: $50. Electronic applications accepted. *Expenses:* Tuition, state resident: part-time $318 per semester hour. Tuition, nonresident: part-time $318 per semester hour. *Required fees:* $75 per semester. Tuition and fees vary according to course load and program. *Financial support:* Unspecified assistantships and SOS scholarships for education majors only available. Financial award application deadline: 3/1; financial award applicants required to submit FAFSA. *Unit head:* Dr. Sandra Berkowitz, Department Chair, 413-572-5323, E-mail: sberkowitz@westfield.ma.edu. *Application contact:* Shelly Henrichon, Coordinator of DGCE Admissions, 413-572-8022, Fax: 413-572-5227, E-mail: mhenrichon@westfield.ma.edu.
Website: http://www.westfield.ma.edu/academics/degrees/education-graduate-programs

Wilmington University, College of Education, New Castle, DE 19720-6491. Offers applied technology in education (M Ed); career and technical education (M Ed); educational leadership (Ed D); elementary and secondary school counseling (M Ed); elementary studies (M Ed); ESOL literacy (M Ed); higher education leadership (Ed D); instruction: gifted and talented (M Ed); instruction: teacher of reading (M Ed); instruction: teaching and learning (M Ed); organizational leadership (Ed D); school leadership

(M Ed); secondary education (MAT); special education (M Ed). *Accreditation:* NCATE. *Program availability:* Part-time, evening/weekend. *Faculty:* 19 full-time (11 women), 178 part-time/adjunct (99 women). *Students:* 248 full-time (176 women), 999 part-time (738 women); includes 244 minority (193 Black or African American, non-Hispanic/Latino; 17 American Indian or Alaska Native, non-Hispanic/Latino; 9 Asian, non-Hispanic/Latino; 19 Hispanic/Latino; 2 Native Hawaiian or other Pacific Islander, non-Hispanic/Latino; 4 Two or more races, non-Hispanic/Latino), 7 international. Average age 34. 672 applicants, 96% accepted, 348 enrolled. In 2016, 529 master's, 87 doctorates awarded. *Entrance requirements:* For master's, 2 letters of recommendation, interview. Additional exam requirements/recommendations for international students: Required—TOEFL (minimum score 500 paper-based). *Application deadline:* For fall admission, 4/30 for domestic students. Applications are processed on a rolling basis. Application fee: $35. Electronic applications accepted. *Expenses: Tuition:* Full-time $8388; part-time $466 per credit. *Required fees:* $25 per semester. Tuition and fees vary according to degree level. *Financial support:* Applicants required to submit FAFSA. *Unit head:* Dr. John C. Gray, Dean. *Application contact:* Laura Morris, Director of Admissions, 877-967-5464, E-mail: infocenter@wilmu.edu. Website: http://www.wilmu.edu/education/

ACADEMIC AND PROFESSIONAL PROGRAMS IN LAW

Section 27
Law

This section contains a directory of institutions offering graduate work in law. Additional information about programs listed in the directory may be obtained by writing directly to the dean of a graduate school or chair of a department at the address given in the directory.

For programs offering related work, see also in this book *Business Administration and Management* and *Social Work.* In the other guides in this series:

Graduate Programs in the Humanities, Arts & Social Sciences
See *Criminology and Forensics; Public, Regional, and Industrial Affairs; Economics;* and *Political Science and International Affairs*

Graduate Programs in the Physical Sciences, Mathematics, Agricultural Sciences, the Environment & Natural Resources
See *Environmental Sciences and Management*

Graduate Programs in Engineering & Applied Sciences
See *Management of Engineering and Technology*

CONTENTS

Program Directories

Featured School: Display and Close-Up

See:

Environmental Law

Chapman University, Fowler School of Law, Orange, CA 92866. Offers advocacy and dispute resolution (JD); business law (LL M, JD); criminal law (JD); entertainment and media law (LL M); entertainment law (JD); environmental, land use, and real estate law (JD); international and comparative law (LL M); international law (JD); law (JD); prosecutorial science (LL M); tax law (JD); taxation (LL M); trial advocacy (LL M); JD/MBA; JD/MFA. *Accreditation:* ABA. *Program availability:* Part-time. *Faculty:* 44 full-time (18 women), 22 part-time/adjunct (6 women). *Students:* 471 full-time (252 women), 38 part-time (19 women); includes 208 minority (8 Black or African American, non-Hispanic/Latino; 3 American Indian or Alaska Native, non-Hispanic/Latino; 76 Asian, non-Hispanic/Latino; 92 Hispanic/Latino; 29 Two or more races, non-Hispanic/Latino), 13 international. Average age 26. 1,499 applicants, 50% accepted, 190 enrolled. In 2016, 21 master's, 159 doctorates awarded. *Entrance requirements:* For doctorate, LSAT. Additional exam requirements/recommendations for international students: Required—TOEFL (minimum score 600 paper-based; 100 iBT). *Application deadline:* For fall admission, 4/15 priority date for domestic students. Applications are processed on a rolling basis. Electronic applications accepted. *Expenses:* Contact institution. *Financial support:* Fellowships, Federal Work-Study, and scholarships/grants available. Financial award applicants required to submit FAFSA. *Unit head:* Matthew J. Parlow, Dean, 714-628-2678, E-mail: parlow@chapman.edu. *Application contact:* Grace Alcantara, Assistant Dean of Admissions and Diversity Initiatives, 714-628-2500, E-mail: lawadmission@chapman.edu.
Website: http://www.chapman.edu/law/

Florida State University, College of Law, Tallahassee, FL 32306-1601. Offers American law for foreign lawyers (LL M); business law (LL M); environmental law and policy (LL M); law (JM, JD); JD/MAES; JD/MBA; JD/MPA; JD/MS; JD/MSI; JD/MSP; JD/MSW. *Accreditation:* ABA. *Program availability:* 100% online. *Faculty:* 57 full-time (29 women), 30 part-time/adjunct (7 women). *Students:* 550 full-time (255 women), 52 part-time (24 women); includes 174 minority (42 Black or African American, non-Hispanic/Latino; 1 American Indian or Alaska Native, non-Hispanic/Latino; 15 Asian, non-Hispanic/Latino; 91 Hispanic/Latino; 25 Two or more races, non-Hispanic/Latino), 18 international. Average age 25. 1,929 applicants, 35% accepted, 174 enrolled. In 2016, 11 master's, 195 doctorates awarded. Terminal master's awarded for partial completion of doctoral program. *Degree requirements:* For master's, comprehensive exam (for some programs). *Entrance requirements:* For master's, one graduate-level standardized test (for JM), JD or equivalent degree (for LL M); for doctorate, LSAT (for JD). Additional exam requirements/recommendations for international students: Required—TOEFL (minimum score 600 paper-based; 80 iBT), IELTS (minimum score 6.5). *Application deadline:* For fall admission, 7/15 for domestic students, 5/15 for international students. Applications are processed on a rolling basis. Electronic applications accepted. *Expenses:* $20,683. *Financial support:* In 2016–17, 406 students received support, including 4 fellowships with full tuition reimbursements available (averaging $20,683 per year), 39 research assistantships (averaging $1,557 per year), 13 teaching assistantships (averaging $1,451 per year); career-related internships or fieldwork, scholarships/grants, and unspecified assistantships also available. Financial award application deadline: 3/1; financial award applicants required to submit FAFSA. *Faculty research:* Business law; environmental, energy and land use law; international law; criminal law. *Total annual research expenditures:* $120,000. *Unit head:* Erin O'Hara O'Connor, Dean, 850-644-3400, Fax: 850-644-5487, E-mail: eoconnor@law.fsu.edu. *Application contact:* Jennifer L. Kessinger, Director of Admissions and Records, 850-644-3787, Fax: 850-644-7284, E-mail: jkessing@law.fsu.edu.
Website: http://www.law.fsu.edu/

Georgetown University, Law Center, Washington, DC 20001. Offers environmental law (LL M); global health law (LL M); global health law and international institutions (LL M); individualized study (LL M); international business and economic law (LL M); law (JD, SJD); national security law (LL M); securities and financial regulation (LL M); taxation (LL M); JD/LL M; JD/MA; JD/MBA; JD/MPH; JD/PhD. *Accreditation:* ABA. *Program availability:* Part-time, evening/weekend. *Degree requirements:* For master's, thesis; for doctorate, thesis/dissertation (for some programs). *Entrance requirements:* For master's, JD, LL B, or first law degree earned in country of origin; for doctorate, LSAT (for JD). Additional exam requirements/recommendations for international students: Required—TOEFL. *Expenses:* Contact institution. *Faculty research:* Constitutional law, legal history, jurisprudence.

Golden Gate University, School of Law, San Francisco, CA 94105-2968. Offers environmental law (LL M); estate planning (LL M); intellectual property law (LL M); international legal studies (LL M, SJD); law (JD); taxation (LL M); U.S. legal studies (LL M); JD/MBA; JD/PhD. *Accreditation:* ABA. *Program availability:* Part-time, evening/weekend. *Faculty:* 41 full-time (19 women), 67 part-time/adjunct (27 women). *Students:* 246 full-time (142 women), 228 part-time (133 women); includes 213 minority (28 Black or African American, non-Hispanic/Latino; 2 American Indian or Alaska Native, non-Hispanic/Latino; 68 Asian, non-Hispanic/Latino; 84 Hispanic/Latino; 7 Native Hawaiian or other Pacific Islander, non-Hispanic/Latino; 24 Two or more races, non-Hispanic/Latino), 58 international. Average age 31. 1,473 applicants, 65% accepted, 189 enrolled. In 2016, 54 master's, 117 doctorates awarded. *Degree requirements:* For doctorate, thesis/dissertation (for some programs). *Entrance requirements:* For doctorate, LSAT (for JD). Additional exam requirements/recommendations for international students: Required—TOEFL (minimum score 600 paper-based). *Application deadline:* For fall admission, 8/18 for domestic students, 4/1 for international students; for spring admission, 1/12 for domestic students; for summer admission, 6/4 for domestic students. Applications are processed on a rolling basis. Electronic applications accepted. *Expenses:* Contact institution. *Financial support:* In 2016–17, 315 students received support. Fellowships, research assistantships, teaching assistantships, career-related internships or fieldwork, Federal Work-Study, institutionally sponsored loans, scholarships/grants, tuition waivers (full and partial), and unspecified assistantships available. Support available to part-time students. Financial award applicants required to submit FAFSA. *Faculty research:* International law, intellectual property law, environmental law, real estate, civil rights. *Unit head:* Rachel Van Cleave, Dean, 415-442-6601, Fax: 415-442-6609. *Application contact:* Greg Egertson, Associate Dean and Director of Admissions, 415-442-6636, Fax: 415-442-6609, E-mail: lawadmit@ggu.edu.
Website: http://www.ggu.edu/law/

Lehigh University, College of Arts and Sciences, Environmental Policy Design Program, Bethlehem, PA 18015. Offers environmental policy and law (Graduate Certificate); environmental policy design (MA); sustainable development (Graduate Certificate); urban environmental policy (Graduate Certificate). *Program availability:* Part-time. *Faculty:* 11 full-time (4 women). *Students:* 5 full-time (3 women), 2 part-time (both women); includes 2 minority (1 Black or African American, non-Hispanic/Latino; 1 Hispanic/Latino). Average age 30. 8 applicants, 88% accepted, 3 enrolled. In 2016, 4 master's awarded. *Degree requirements:* For master's, thesis or additional course work. *Entrance requirements:* For master's, GRE, minimum GPA of 2.75, 3.0 for last two undergraduate semesters; essay; 2 letters of recommendation. Additional exam requirements/recommendations for international students: Required—TOEFL (minimum score 85 iBT). *Application deadline:* For fall admission, 1/1 for domestic and international students; for spring admission, 12/1 for domestic and international students. Applications are processed on a rolling basis. Application fee: $75. *Expenses:* $1,240 per credit. *Financial support:* Fellowships, scholarships/grants, tuition waivers (partial), and community fellowship and tuition remission available. Financial award application deadline: 1/1. *Faculty research:* Environmental policy, environmental law, urban policy, urban politics, urban environmental policy, sustainability, sustainable development, international environmental law, international environmental policy, environmental justice, social justice. *Unit head:* Dr. Donald P. Morris, Director, 610-758-5175, E-mail: dpm2@lehigh.edu. *Application contact:* Gary Burgess, Academic Coordinator, 610-758-4281, Fax: 610-758-6232, E-mail: glb215@lehigh.edu.
Website: http://ei.cas2.lehigh.edu/

Lewis & Clark College, Lewis & Clark Law School, Portland, OR 97219. Offers animal law (LL M); environmental, natural resources, and energy law (LL M, MSL); law (JD). *Accreditation:* ABA. *Program availability:* Part-time, evening/weekend. *Entrance requirements:* For doctorate, LSAT. Additional exam requirements/recommendations for international students: Recommended—TOEFL (minimum score 600 paper-based). *Application deadline:* For fall admission, 3/1 for domestic students, 1/15 priority date for international students. Applications are processed on a rolling basis. Application fee: $50. Electronic applications accepted. Application fee is waived when completed online. *Expenses:* Contact institution. *Financial support:* Research assistantships, teaching assistantships, career-related internships or fieldwork, Federal Work-Study, scholarships/grants, and tuition waivers (partial) available. Support available to part-time students. Financial award application deadline: 3/1; financial award applicants required to submit FAFSA. *Unit head:* Jennifer Johnson, Dean, 503-768-6601, Fax: 503-768-6671. *Application contact:* Office of Admissions, 503-768-6613, Fax: 503-768-6793, E-mail: lawadmss@lclark.edu.
Website: http://law.lclark.edu/

Montclair State University, The Graduate School, College of Science and Mathematics, Environmental Forensics Certificate Program, Montclair, NJ 07043-1624. Offers Certificate. *Expenses:* Tuition, state resident: part-time $553 per credit. Tuition, nonresident: part-time $854 per credit. *Required fees:* $91 per credit. Tuition and fees vary according to program.

Pace University, Elisabeth Haub School of Law, White Plains, NY 10603. Offers comparative legal studies (LL M); environmental law (LL M, SJD), including climate change (LL M), land use and sustainability (LL M); law (JD); JD/LL M; JD/MA; JD/MBA; JD/MEM; JD/MPA; JD/MS. JD/MA offered jointly with Sarah Lawrence College; JD/MEM offered jointly with Yale University School of Forestry and Environmental Studies. *Accreditation:* ABA. *Program availability:* Part-time. *Faculty:* 26 full-time (11 women), 52 part-time/adjunct (19 women). *Students:* 516 full-time (274 women), 63 part-time (36 women); includes 150 minority (30 Black or African American, non-Hispanic/Latino; 2 American Indian or Alaska Native, non-Hispanic/Latino; 23 Asian, non-Hispanic/Latino; 58 Hispanic/Latino; 37 Two or more races, non-Hispanic/Latino), 2 international. Average age 26. 1,423 applicants, 56% accepted, 206 enrolled. In 2016, 20 master's, 171 doctorates awarded. *Degree requirements:* For master's, writing sample; for doctorate, thesis/dissertation (for some programs), extensive thesis proposal (for SJD). *Entrance requirements:* For doctorate, LSAT (for JD). Additional exam requirements/recommendations for international students: Required—TOEFL (minimum score 100 iBT); Recommended—TWE. *Application deadline:* For fall admission, 6/1 priority date for domestic students; for winter admission, 11/15 priority date for domestic students. Applications are processed on a rolling basis. Application fee: $65. Electronic applications accepted. *Expenses:* Contact institution. *Financial support:* In 2016–17, 430 students received support. Fellowships, research assistantships, career-related internships or fieldwork, Federal Work-Study, institutionally sponsored loans, scholarships/grants, and unspecified assistantships available. Support available to part-time students. Financial award application deadline: 2/1; financial award applicants required to submit FAFSA. *Faculty research:* Reform of energy regulations, international law, land use law, prosecutorial misconduct, corporation law, international sale of goods. *Total annual research expenditures:* $2.2 million. *Unit head:* David Yassky, Dean, 914-422-4407, E-mail: dyassky@law.pace.edu. *Application contact:* Cathy Alexander, Assistant Dean, 914-422-4210, Fax: 914-989-8714, E-mail: calexander@law.pace.edu.
Website: http://www.law.pace.edu/

Stanford University, Law School, Stanford, CA 94305-8610. Offers corporate governance and practice (LL M); environmental law and policy (LL M); international economic law, business and policy (LL M); international legal studies (JSM); law (JD, JSD); law, science and technology (LL M); legal studies (MLS); JD/MA; JD/MBA; JD/MPP; JD/MS; JD/PhD. *Accreditation:* ABA. *Degree requirements:* For doctorate, thesis/dissertation (for some programs). *Entrance requirements:* For doctorate, LSAT (for JD). Electronic applications accepted. *Expenses:* Contact institution.

University of Calgary, Faculty of Graduate Studies, Faculty of Law, Programs in Natural Resources, Energy and Environmental Law, Calgary, AB T2N 1N4, Canada. Offers LL M, Postbaccalaureate Certificate. *Program availability:* Part-time, evening/weekend. *Degree requirements:* For master's, thesis optional. *Entrance requirements:* For master's, JD or LL B. Additional exam requirements/recommendations for international students: Required—TOEFL (minimum score 100 iBT), IELTS (minimum score 7). Electronic applications accepted. *Faculty research:* Natural resources law and regulations; environmental law, ethics and policies; oil and gas and energy law; water and municipal law; Aboriginal law.

University of Colorado Denver, School of Public Affairs, Program in Public Affairs and Administration, Denver, CO 80127. Offers public administration (MPA), including domestic violence, emergency management and homeland security, environmental policy, management and law, homeland security and defense, local government, nonprofit management, public administration; public affairs (PhD). *Accreditation:* NASPAA. *Program availability:* Part-time, evening/weekend, online learning. *Students:* 241 full-time (146 women), 135 part-time (86 women); includes 61 minority (15 Black or African American, non-Hispanic/Latino; 1 American Indian or Alaska Native, non-Hispanic/Latino; 10 Asian, non-Hispanic/Latino; 26 Hispanic/Latino; 2 Native Hawaiian or other Pacific Islander, non-Hispanic/Latino; 7 Two or more races, non-Hispanic/Latino), 26 international. Average age 36. 240 applicants, 70% accepted, 91 enrolled. In 2016, 158 master's, 8 doctorates awarded. *Degree requirements:* For master's, thesis or alternative, 36-39 credit hours; for doctorate, comprehensive exam, thesis/dissertation, minimum of 66 semester hours, including at least 30 hours of dissertation. *Entrance requirements:* For master's, GRE, GMAT or LSAT, resume, essay, transcripts,

recommendations; for doctorate, GRE, resume, essay, transcripts, recommendations. Additional exam requirements/recommendations for international students: Required—TOEFL (minimum score 550 paper-based; 80 iBT); Recommended—IELTS (minimum score 6.5). *Application deadline:* For fall admission, 2/1 priority date for domestic students, 1/15 priority date for international students; for spring admission, 10/15 priority date for domestic students, 10/1 priority date for international students. Application fee: $50 ($75 for international students). Electronic applications accepted. *Expenses:* Contact institution. *Financial support:* In 2016–17, 92 students received support. Fellowships with partial tuition reimbursements available, research assistantships with partial tuition reimbursements available, teaching assistantships with partial tuition reimbursements available, Federal Work-Study, institutionally sponsored loans, scholarships/grants, traineeships, and unspecified assistantships available. Financial award application deadline: 4/1; financial award applicants required to submit FAFSA. *Faculty research:* Housing, education and the social and economic issues of vulnerable populations; nonprofit governance and management; education finance, effectiveness and reform; P-20 education initiatives; municipal government accountability. *Unit head:* Dr. Christine Martell, Director of MPA Program, 303-315-2716, Fax: 303-315-2229, E-mail: christine.martell@ucdenver.edu. *Application contact:* Dawn Savage, Student Services Coordinator, 303-315-2743, Fax: 303-315-2229, E-mail: dawn.savage@ucdenver.edu.
Website: http://www.ucdenver.edu/academics/colleges/SPA/Academics/programs/PublicAffairsAdmin/Pages/index.aspx

University of Florida, Levin College of Law, Gainesville, FL 32611. Offers comparative law (LL M), including tropical conservation and development; environmental and land use law (LL M); international taxation (LL M); law (JD); taxation (LL M, SJD). *Accreditation:* ABA. *Entrance requirements:* For doctorate, LSAT (for JD). Electronic applications accepted. *Faculty research:* Environmental and land use law, taxation, dispute resolution, family law, Constitutional law.

University of Houston, Law Center, Houston, TX 77204-6060. Offers energy, environment, and natural resources (LL M); health law (LL M); intellectual property and information law (LL M); international law (LL M); law (LL M, JD); tax law (LL M). *Accreditation:* ABA. *Program availability:* Part-time, evening/weekend. *Entrance requirements:* For doctorate, LSAT. Additional exam requirements/recommendations for international students: Required—TOEFL (minimum score 600 paper-based; 100 iBT). Electronic applications accepted. *Expenses:* Contact institution. *Faculty research:* Health law, international, tax, environmental/energy, information law/intellectual property.

University of Idaho, College of Law, Moscow, ID 83844-2321. Offers business law and entrepreneurship (JD); law (JD); litigation and alternative dispute resolution (JD); Native American law (JD); natural resources and environmental law (JD). *Accreditation:* ABA. *Faculty:* 32 full-time, 11 part-time/adjunct. *Students:* Average age 28. *Entrance requirements:* For doctorate, LSAT, Law School Admission Council Credential Assembly Service (CAS) Report. Additional exam requirements/recommendations for international students: Required—TOEFL. *Application deadline:* For fall admission, 3/15 priority date for domestic students. Applications are processed on a rolling basis. Application fee: $50 ($60 for international students). Electronic applications accepted. *Expenses:* Contact institution. *Financial support:* Career-related internships or fieldwork, Federal Work-Study, and institutionally sponsored loans available. Financial award applicants required to submit FAFSA. *Faculty research:* Transboundary river governance, tribal protection and stewardship, regional water issues, environmental law. *Unit head:* Mark Adams, Dean, 208-885-4977, E-mail: uilaw@uidaho.edu. *Application contact:* Carole Wells, Director of Admissions, 208-885-2300, Fax: 208-885-2252, E-mail: lawadmit@uidaho.edu.
Website: http://www.uidaho.edu/law/

University of Pittsburgh, School of Law, Master of Studies in Law Program, Pittsburgh, PA 15260. Offers business law (MSL), including commercial law, corporate law, general business law, international business, tax law; Constitutional law (MSL); criminal law and justice (MSL); disability law (MSL); education law (MSL); elder and estate planning law (MSL); employment and labor law (MSL); energy law (MSL); environmental and real estate law (MSL); family law (MSL); health law (MSL); intellectual property and technology law (MSL); international and human rights law (MSL); jurisprudence (MSL); personal injury and civil litigation (MSL); regulatory law (MSL); self-designed (MSL); sports and entertainment law (MSL). *Program availability:* Part-time. *Faculty:* 48 full-time (21 women), 104 part-time/adjunct (34 women). *Students:* 5 full-time (4 women), 14 part-time (9 women); includes 7 minority (4 Black or African American, non-Hispanic/Latino; 1 Asian, non-Hispanic/Latino; 2 Native Hawaiian or other Pacific Islander, non-Hispanic/Latino). Average age 27. 17 applicants, 53% accepted, 7 enrolled. In 2016, 4 master's awarded. *Entrance requirements:* Additional exam requirements/recommendations for international students: Required—TOEFL (minimum score 600 paper-based; 100 iBT). *Application deadline:* For fall admission, 6/30 for domestic students, 5/1 for international students. Applications are processed on a rolling basis. Application fee: $0. Tuition and fees vary according to program. *Faculty research:* Law, health law, business law, contracts, intellectual property, environmental law. *Unit head:* Prof. Alan Meisel, Director, 412-648-1384, Fax: 412-648-2649, E-mail: meisel@pitt.edu. *Application contact:* Beth Ann Pischke, Administrative Coordinator, 412-648-7120, Fax: 412-648-2649, E-mail: pischke@pitt.edu.
Website: http://www.law.pitt.edu/msl

The University of Tulsa, College of Law, Tulsa, OK 74104. Offers American Indian and indigenous law (LL M); American law for foreign lawyers (LL M); energy and natural resources law (LL M); energy law (MJ); health law (Certificate); Indian law (MJ); law (JD); Native American law (Certificate); natural resources, energy, and environmental law (Certificate); JD/MA; JD/MBA; JD/MS. *Accreditation:* ABA. *Program availability:* Part-time, 100% online. *Faculty:* 23 full-time (13 women), 12 part-time/adjunct (4 women). *Students:* 233 full-time (103 women), 30 part-time (17 women); includes 70 minority (10 Black or African American, non-Hispanic/Latino; 16 American Indian or Alaska Native, non-Hispanic/Latino; 2 Asian, non-Hispanic/Latino; 12 Hispanic/Latino; 30 Two or more races, non-Hispanic/Latino), 5 international. Average age 27. 602 applicants, 40% accepted, 92 enrolled. In 2016, 5 master's, 81 doctorates awarded. *Degree requirements:* For master's, thesis optional. *Entrance requirements:* For master's, JD from an ABA-approved U.S. law school or a JD equivalent from non-U.S. university; for doctorate, LSAT, BS or BA from 4-year regionally-accredited college/university; for Certificate, BS or BA from 4-year regionally-accredited college/university. Additional exam requirements/recommendations for international students: Required—TOEFL (minimum score 570 paper-based; 90 iBT), IELTS (minimum score 6.5). *Application deadline:* For fall admission, 7/31 priority date for domestic and international students; for spring admission, 12/5 priority date for domestic students, 12/5 for international students; for summer admission, 4/13 for domestic and international students. Applications are processed on a rolling basis. Application fee: $30. Electronic applications accepted. *Expenses:* $37,960 per year tuition; $654 fees. *Financial support:* In 2016–17, 255 students received support. Scholarships/grants available. Support available to part-time students. Financial award application deadline: 8/1; financial award applicants required to submit FAFSA. *Faculty research:* Native American law, criminal law, commercial speech, copyright law, international law. *Unit head:* Prof. Lyn Suzanne Entzeroth, Dean, 918-631-2400, Fax: 918-631-3126, E-mail: lyn-entzeroth@utulsa.edu. *Application contact:* April M. Fox, Associate Dean of Admissions and Financial Aid, 918-631-2406, Fax: 918-631-3630, E-mail: april-fox@utulsa.edu.
Website: http://www.utulsa.edu/law/

Vermont Law School, Graduate and Professional Programs, Master's Programs, South Royalton, VT 05068-0096. Offers American legal studies (LL M); energy law (LL M); energy regulation and law (MERL); environmental law (LL M); environmental law and policy (MELP); food and agriculture law (LL M); food and agriculture law and policy (MFALP); JD/MELP; JD/MERL; JD/MFALP. *Program availability:* Part-time, 100% online, blended/hybrid learning. *Entrance requirements:* Additional exam requirements/recommendations for international students: Required—TOEFL. *Application deadline:* For fall admission, 3/1 priority date for domestic students. Applications are processed on a rolling basis. Application fee: $60. *Expenses: Tuition:* Full-time $47,998. *Financial support:* Fellowships with full tuition reimbursements, career-related internships or fieldwork, Federal Work-Study, institutionally sponsored loans, scholarships/grants, and tuition waivers (partial) available. Support available to part-time students. Financial award application deadline: 3/1; financial award applicants required to submit FAFSA. *Faculty research:* Environment and new economy; takings; international environmental law; interaction among science, law, and environmental policy; climate change and the law. *Unit head:* Marc B. Mihaly, President and Dean, 802-831-1237, Fax: 802-763-2490. *Application contact:* John D. Miller, Jr., Vice President for Enrollment Management, Marketing and Communications, 802-831-1239, Fax: 802-831-1174, E-mail: admiss@vermontlaw.edu.
Website: http://www.vermontlaw.edu/Academics/degrees/masters

Western Michigan University Thomas M. Cooley Law School, Graduate Programs, Lansing, MI 48901-3038. Offers administrative law (public law) (JD); business transactions (JD); Canadian law practice (JD); constitutional law/civil rights (public law) (JD); corporate law and finance (LL M); environmental law (public law) (JD); general practice (JD), including solo and small firm; homeland and national security law (LL M); insurance law (LL M); intellectual property (JD); intellectual property law (LL M); international law (JD); litigation (JD); self-directed (LL M, JD); tax law (LL M); taxation (JD); U.S. legal studies for foreign attorneys (LL M); JD/LL M; JD/MBA; JD/MPA; JD/MSW. *Program availability:* Part-time, evening/weekend, 100% online, blended/hybrid learning. *Degree requirements:* For master's, thesis optional; for doctorate, minimum of 3 credits of clinical experience. *Entrance requirements:* For master's, JD or LL B; for doctorate, LSAT. Additional exam requirements/recommendations for international students: Required—TOEFL (for U.S. legal studies for foreign attorneys LL M program); Recommended—TOEFL. Electronic applications accepted. *Faculty research:* Wrongful convictions, civil rights, environmental law, litigation techniques, data mining, intellectual property, practical and skills-based legal education.

Health Law

Case Western Reserve University, School of Law, Cleveland, OH 44106. Offers financial integrity (MA); health law (SJD); intellectual property (LL M); international business law (LL M); international criminal law (LL M); law (JD, SJD); patent practice (MA); U.S. legal studies (LL M); JD/MA; JD/MBA; JD/MD; JD/MNM; JD/MPH; JD/MS; JD/MSSA. *Accreditation:* ABA. *Faculty:* 40 full-time (15 women), 25 part-time/adjunct (4 women). *Students:* 421 full-time (215 women), 1 (woman) part-time; includes 76 minority (37 Black or African American, non-Hispanic/Latino; 17 Asian, non-Hispanic/Latino; 19 Hispanic/Latino, 3 Two or more races, non-Hispanic/Latino), 37 international. Average age 24. 1,645 applicants, 43% accepted, 144 enrolled. In 2016, 72 master's, 99 doctorates awarded. *Entrance requirements:* For doctorate, LSAT, LSDAS. Additional exam requirements/recommendations for international students: Required—TOEFL. *Application deadline:* For fall admission, 4/1 priority date for domestic and international students. Applications are processed on a rolling basis. Application fee: $40. Electronic applications accepted. Application fee is waived when completed online. *Expenses:* Contact institution. *Financial support:* In 2016–17, 345 students received support. Career-related internships or fieldwork, Federal Work-Study, institutionally sponsored loans, and scholarships/grants available. Financial award application deadline: 5/1; financial award applicants required to submit FAFSA. *Unit head:* Jessica Berg, Co-Dean, 216-368-3283. *Application contact:* Kelli Curtis, Associate Dean for Admissions, 216-368 3600, Fax: 216-368-0185, E-mail: lawadmissions@case.edu.
Website: http://law.case.edu/

DePaul University, College of Law, Chicago, IL 60604-2287. Offers health law (LL M); intellectual property law (LL M); international law (LL M); law (JD); taxation (LL M); JD/MA; JD/MBA; JD/MPS; JD/MS. *Accreditation:* ABA. *Program availability:* Part-time, evening/weekend. *Entrance requirements:* For doctorate, LSAT, LSAC applicant evaluation/letter of recommendation, personal statement, resume. Additional exam requirements/recommendations for international students: Required—TOEFL (minimum score 577 paper-based; 90 iBT), IELTS (minimum score 6.5). Electronic applications accepted. *Expenses:* Contact institution.

Georgetown University, Law Center, Washington, DC 20001. Offers environmental law (LL M); global health law (LL M); global health law and international institutions (LL M); individualized study (LL M); international business and economic law (LL M); law (JD, SJD); national security law (LL M); securities and financial regulation (LL M); taxation (LL M); JD/LL M; JD/MA; JD/MBA; JD/MPH; JD/PhD. *Accreditation:* ABA. *Program availability:* Part-time, evening/weekend. *Degree requirements:* For master's, thesis; for doctorate, thesis/dissertation (for some programs). *Entrance requirements:* For master's, JD, LL B, or first law degree earned in country of origin; for doctorate, LSAT (for JD). Additional exam requirements/recommendations for international students. Required—TOEFL. *Expenses:* Contact institution. *Faculty research:* Constitutional law, legal history, jurisprudence.

Hofstra University, Maurice A. Deane School of Law, Hempstead, NY 11549. Offers American legal studies (LL M); family law (LL M); health law and policy (LL M, MA); law

(JD); JD/MBA. *Accreditation:* ABA. *Program availability:* Part-time, 100% online. *Faculty:* 41 full-time (22 women), 47 part-time/adjunct (9 women). *Students:* 692 full-time (377 women), 93 part-time (56 women); includes 216 minority (79 Black or African American, non-Hispanic/Latino; 3 American Indian or Alaska Native, non-Hispanic/Latino; 34 Asian, non-Hispanic/Latino; 87 Hispanic/Latino; 8 Native Hawaiian or other Pacific Islander, non-Hispanic/Latino; 5 Two or more races, non-Hispanic/Latino), 22 international. Average age 27. In 2016, 10 master's, 198 doctorates awarded. *Entrance requirements:* For doctorate, LSAT, letter of recommendation, personal statement, undergraduate transcripts. Additional exam requirements/recommendations for international students: Recommended—TOEFL (minimum score 600 paper-based; 100 iBT). *Application deadline:* For fall admission, 4/15 priority date for domestic and international students. Applications are processed on a rolling basis. Application fee: $75. Electronic applications accepted. *Expenses:* Contact institution. *Financial support:* In 2016–17, 508 students received support, including 491 fellowships with full and partial tuition reimbursements available (averaging $31,765 per year), 3 research assistantships with full and partial tuition reimbursements available (averaging $6,675 per year); career-related internships or fieldwork, Federal Work-Study, institutionally sponsored loans, scholarships/grants, tuition waivers (full and partial), and unspecified assistantships also available. Support available to part-time students. Financial award applicants required to submit FAFSA. *Faculty research:* Family law; international law; constitutional law; legal ethics; health law. *Total annual research expenditures:* $59,468. *Unit head:* Gail Prudenti, Dean, 516-463-4068, E-mail: gail.prudenti@hofstra.edu. *Application contact:* Sunil Samuel, Assistant Vice President of Admissions, 516-463-4723, Fax: 516-463-4664.
Website: http://law.hofstra.edu/

Indiana University–Purdue University Indianapolis, Robert H. McKinney School of Law, Indianapolis, IN 46202. Offers advocacy skills (Certificate); American law for foreign lawyers (LL M); civil and human rights (Certificate); corporate and commercial law (LL M, Certificate); criminal law (Certificate); environmental and natural resources (Certificate); health law (Certificate); health law, policy and bioethics (LL M); intellectual property law (LL M, Certificate); international and comparative law (LL M, Certificate); international human rights law (LL M); law (MJ, JD, SJD); JD/M Phil; JD/MBA; JD/MD; JD/MHA; JD/MLS; JD/MPA; JD/MPH; JD/MSW. *Accreditation:* ABA. *Program availability:* Part-time. *Faculty:* 47 full-time (24 women), 40 part-time/adjunct (17 women). *Students:* 578 full-time (285 women), 328 part-time (154 women); includes 157 minority (71 Black or African American, non-Hispanic/Latino; 1 American Indian or Alaska Native, non-Hispanic/Latino; 17 Asian, non-Hispanic/Latino; 42 Hispanic/Latino; 3 Native Hawaiian or other Pacific Islander, non-Hispanic/Latino; 23 Two or more races, non-Hispanic/Latino), 59 international. Average age 29. 915 applicants, 58% accepted, 253 enrolled. In 2016, 25 master's, 258 doctorates, 100 Certificates awarded. *Entrance requirements:* For doctorate, LSAT. Additional exam requirements/recommendations for international students: Required—TOEFL (minimum score 79 iBT), IELTS (minimum score 6.5). *Application deadline:* For fall admission, 7/31 for domestic students. Applications are processed on a rolling basis. Application fee: $0. Electronic applications accepted. *Expenses:* $843.84 per credit hour resident tuition, $1,472.10 per credit hour non-resident tuition. *Financial support:* In 2016–17, 528 students received support. Fellowships, research assistantships with full and partial tuition reimbursements available, career-related internships or fieldwork, Federal Work-Study, scholarships/grants, and tuition waivers available. Support available to part-time students. Financial award application deadline: 7/31; financial award applicants required to submit FAFSA. *Unit head:* Andrew R. Klein, Dean, 317-274-2099, E-mail: anrklein@iupui.edu. *Application contact:* Patricia Kinney, Assistant Dean of Admissions, 317-274-2459, E-mail: pkkinney@iupui.edu.
Website: http://mckinneylaw.iu.edu/

Nova Southeastern University, Shepard Broad College of Law, Fort Lauderdale, FL 33314. Offers education law (MS), including cybersecurity law, education law advocacy, exceptional education; employment law (MS), including cybersecurity law, employee relations law, human resource managerial law; health law (MS, JD), including clinical research law and regulatory compliance (MS), cybersecurity law (MS), health care administrative law (MS), regulatory compliance (MS), risk management (MS); international law (JD); law and policy (MS), including cybersecurity law; JD/DO; JD/M Acc; JD/M Tax; JD/MBA; JD/MIB; JD/MPA; JD/MS; JD/PhD. *Accreditation:* ABA. *Program availability:* Part-time, evening/weekend, 100% online, blended/hybrid learning. *Faculty:* 42 full-time (23 women), 35 part-time/adjunct (14 women). *Students:* 554 full-time (298 women), 325 part-time (230 women); includes 351 minority (71 Black or African American, non-Hispanic/Latino; 3 American Indian or Alaska Native, non-Hispanic/Latino; 17 Asian, non-Hispanic/Latino; 251 Hispanic/Latino; 2 Native Hawaiian or other Pacific Islander, non-Hispanic/Latino; 7 Two or more races, non-Hispanic/Latino), 36 international. Average age 29. 1,414 applicants, 49% accepted, 256 enrolled. In 2016, 46 master's, 236 doctorates awarded. *Degree requirements:* For master's, thesis optional, capstone research project; for doctorate, rigorous upper-level writing fulfilled through faculty-supervised seminar paper, law journal article, workshop, or other research. *Entrance requirements:* For master's, regionally-accredited undergraduate degree; at least 2 years' experience in related field (for employment law and health law); for doctorate, LSAT. Additional exam requirements/recommendations for international students: Recommended—TOEFL (minimum score 600 paper-based; 100 iBT), IELTS (minimum score 7). *Application deadline:* For fall admission, 5/1 priority date for domestic and international students; for winter admission, 12/12 for domestic and international students; for spring admission, 3/31 for domestic and international students; for summer admission, 4/1 for domestic and international students. Applications are processed on a rolling basis. Application fee: $0. Electronic applications accepted. *Expenses:* Contact institution. *Financial support:* In 2016–17, 231 students received support, including 221 fellowships (averaging $12,680 per year); Federal Work-Study, institutionally sponsored loans, scholarships/grants, and unspecified assistantships also available. Support available to part-time students. Financial award application deadline: 4/15; financial award applicants required to submit FAFSA. *Faculty research:* Legal issues in health law, international law, the legal profession, family law, civil rights. *Unit head:* Jon M. Garon, Dean, 954-262-6101, Fax: 954-262-2862, E-mail: garon@nova.edu. *Application contact:* William Daniel Perez, Assistant Dean of Admissions, 954-262-6121, Fax: 954-262-3844, E-mail: wperez1@nova.edu.
Website: http://www.law.nova.edu/

Seton Hall University, School of Law, Newark, NJ 07102-5210. Offers health law (LL M, JD); intellectual property (LL M, JD); law (MSJ); JD/MADIR; JD/MBA; MD/JD; MD/MSJ. MD/JD, MD/MSJ offered jointly with University of Medicine and Dentistry of New Jersey. *Accreditation:* ABA. *Program availability:* Part-time, evening/weekend. *Degree requirements:* For master's, thesis optional. *Entrance requirements:* For master's, professional experience, letters of recommendation; for doctorate, LSAT, active LSDAS registration, letters of recommendation. Additional exam requirements/recommendations for international students: Recommended—TOEFL. Electronic applications accepted. *Expenses:* Contact institution. *Faculty research:* Health law, intellectual property law, science and the law, international law and employment/labor law.

Southern Illinois University Carbondale, School of Law, Program in Legal Studies, Carbondale, IL 62901-4701. Offers general law (MLS); health law and policy (MLS).

Suffolk University, Law School, Boston, MA 02108. Offers business law and financial services (JD); civil litigation (JD); global law and technology (LL M); health and biomedical law (JD); intellectual property law (JD); international law (JD); JD/MBA; JD/MPA; JD/MSCJ; JD/MSF; JD/MSIE. *Accreditation:* ABA. *Program availability:* Part-time, evening/weekend. *Faculty:* 58 full-time (26 women), 47 part-time/adjunct (17 women). *Students:* 647 full-time (357 women), 380 part-time (197 women); includes 219 minority (61 Black or African American, non-Hispanic/Latino; 1 American Indian or Alaska Native, non-Hispanic/Latino; 50 Asian, non-Hispanic/Latino; 82 Hispanic/Latino; 25 Two or more races, non-Hispanic/Latino), 42 international. Average age 27. 1,924 applicants, 64% accepted, 355 enrolled. In 2016, 21 master's, 416 doctorates awarded. *Degree requirements:* For master's, legal writing. *Entrance requirements:* For master's, 2 letters of recommendation, resume, personal statement; for doctorate, LSAT, LSDAS, dean's certification, recommendation. Additional exam requirements/recommendations for international students: Required—TOEFL (minimum score 600 paper-based; 100 iBT). *Application deadline:* For fall admission, 4/1 for domestic and international students. Applications are processed on a rolling basis. Application fee: $60. Electronic applications accepted. *Expenses:* $45,922 per year full-time tuition, $34,440 per year part-time tuition. *Financial support:* In 2016–17, 572 students received support, including 1 fellowship (averaging $31,390 per year); career-related internships or fieldwork, Federal Work-Study, institutionally sponsored loans, and scholarships/grants also available. Support available to part-time students. Financial award application deadline: 3/1; financial award applicants required to submit FAFSA. *Faculty research:* Civil law, international law, health/biomedical law, business and finance, intellectual property. *Unit head:* Andrew Perlman, Dean, 617-573-8144, Fax: 617-994-6838, E-mail: lawadmin@suffolk.edu. *Application contact:* Matthew Gavin, Assistant Dean for Admissions and Financial Aid, 617-573-8144, Fax: 617-994-6838, E-mail: lawadm@suffolk.edu.
Website: http://www.suffolk.edu/law/

Université de Sherbrooke, Faculty of Law, Sherbrooke, QC J1K 2R1, Canada. Offers alternative dispute resolution (LL M, Diploma); business law (Diploma); common law (JD); criminal and penal law (Diploma); health law (LL M, Diploma); international law (LL M); law (LL D); legal management (Diploma); notarial law (Diploma); transnational law (Diploma). *Program availability:* Part-time, evening/weekend. *Degree requirements:* For master's, thesis; for Diploma, one foreign language. *Entrance requirements:* For master's and Diploma, LL B. Electronic applications accepted.

University of California, San Diego, Graduate Division, Program in Health Policy and Law, La Jolla, CA 92093. Offers MAS. Program offered jointly with School of Medicine and California Western School of Law. *Program availability:* Part-time. *Students:* 2 full-time (both women), 26 part-time (19 women). 21 applicants, 71% accepted, 9 enrolled. In 2016, 9 master's awarded. *Degree requirements:* For master's, capstone project. *Entrance requirements:* For master's, appropriate medical, healthcare, legal or related degree; minimum GPA of 3.0 in final two years of study; minimum 3 years of relevant work experience or equivalent. Additional exam requirements/recommendations for international students: Required—TOEFL (minimum score 550 paper-based; 80 iBT), IELTS (minimum score 7). *Application deadline:* For fall admission, 8/4 for domestic students. Applications are processed on a rolling basis. Application fee: $105 ($125 for international students). Electronic applications accepted. *Expenses:* Contact institution. *Financial support:* Scholarships/grants available. *Unit head:* Gerard Manecke, Program Co-Director, 619-543-3164, E-mail: gmanecke@ucsd.edu. *Application contact:* Jessica Nguyen, Program Coordinator, 858-534-9162, E-mail: healthpolicyandlaw@ucsd.edu.
Website: http://hlaw.ucsd.edu/

University of California, San Francisco, Graduate Division, Program in Health Policy and Law, San Francisco, CA 94143. Offers MS. Program offered in conjunction with University of California, Hastings College of the Law and University of California, Berkeley. *Program availability:* Part-time, online learning. *Degree requirements:* For master's, capstone project, comprehensive written and oral final examination.

University of Houston, Law Center, Houston, TX 77204-6060. Offers energy, environment, and natural resources (LL M); health law (LL M); intellectual property and information law (LL M); international law (LL M); law (LL M, JD); tax law (LL M). *Accreditation:* ABA. *Program availability:* Part-time, evening/weekend. *Entrance requirements:* For doctorate, LSAT. Additional exam requirements/recommendations for international students: Required—TOEFL (minimum score 600 paper-based; 100 iBT). Electronic applications accepted. *Expenses:* Contact institution. *Faculty research:* Health law, international, tax, environmental/energy, information law/intellectual property.

The University of Manchester, School of Law, Manchester, United Kingdom. Offers bioethics and medical jurisprudence (PhD); criminology (M Phil, PhD); law (M Phil, PhD).

University of Pittsburgh, School of Law, Master of Studies in Law Program, Pittsburgh, PA 15260. Offers business law (MSL), including commercial law, corporate law, general business law, international business, tax law; Constitutional law (MSL); criminal law and justice (MSL); disability law (MSL); education law (MSL); elder and estate planning law (MSL); employment and labor law (MSL); energy law (MSL); environmental and real estate law (MSL); family law (MSL); health law (MSL); intellectual property and technology law (MSL); international and human rights law (MSL); jurisprudence (MSL); personal injury and civil litigation (MSL); regulatory law (MSL); self-designed (MSL); sports and entertainment law (MSL). *Program availability:* Part-time. *Faculty:* 48 full-time (21 women), 104 part-time/adjunct (34 women). *Students:* 5 full-time (4 women), 14 part-time (9 women); includes 7 minority (4 Black or African American, non-Hispanic/Latino; 1 Asian, non-Hispanic/Latino; 2 Native Hawaiian or other Pacific Islander, non-Hispanic/Latino). Average age 27. 17 applicants, 53% accepted, 7 enrolled. In 2016, 4 master's awarded. *Entrance requirements:* Additional exam requirements/recommendations for international students: Required—TOEFL (minimum score 600 paper-based; 100 iBT). *Application deadline:* For fall admission, 6/30 for domestic students, 5/1 for international students. Applications are processed on a rolling basis. Application fee: $0. Tuition and fees vary according to program. *Faculty research:* Law, health law, business law, contracts, intellectual property, environmental law. *Unit head:* Prof. Alan Meisel, Director, 412-648-1384, Fax: 412-648-2649, E-mail: meisel@pitt.edu. *Application contact:* Beth Ann Pischke, Administrative Coordinator, 412-648-7120, Fax: 412-648-2649, E-mail: pischke@pitt.edu.
Website: http://www.law.pitt.edu/msl

The University of Tulsa, College of Law, Tulsa, OK 74104. Offers American Indian and indigenous law (LL M); American law for foreign lawyers (LL M); energy and natural resources law (LL M); energy law (MJ); health law (Certificate); Indian law (MJ); law (JD); Native American law (Certificate); natural resources, energy, and environmental law (Certificate); JD/MA; JD/MBA; JD/MS. *Accreditation:* ABA. *Program availability:* Part-time, 100% online. *Faculty:* 23 full-time (13 women), 12 part-time/adjunct (4 women). *Students:* 233 full-time (103 women), 30 part-time (17 women); includes 70 minority (10 Black or African American, non-Hispanic/Latino; 16 American Indian or Alaska Native, non-Hispanic/Latino; 2 Asian, non-Hispanic/Latino; 12 Hispanic/Latino; 30 Two or more races, non-Hispanic/Latino), 5 international. Average age 27. 602 applicants, 40% accepted, 92 enrolled. In 2016, 5 master's, 81 doctorates awarded. *Degree requirements:* For master's, thesis optional. *Entrance requirements:* For

master's, JD from an ABA-approved U.S. law school or a JD equivalent from non-U.S. university; for doctorate, LSAT, BS or BA from 4-year regionally-accredited college/university; for Certificate, BS or BA from 4-year regionally-accredited college/university. Additional exam requirements/recommendations for international students: Required—TOEFL (minimum score 570 paper-based; 90 iBT), IELTS (minimum score 6.5). *Application deadline:* For fall admission, 7/31 priority date for domestic and international students; for spring admission, 12/5 priority date for domestic students, 12/5 for international students; for summer admission, 4/13 for domestic and international students. Applications are processed on a rolling basis. Application fee: $30. Electronic applications accepted. *Expenses:* $37,960 per year tuition; $654 fees. *Financial support:* In 2016–17, 255 students received support. Scholarships/grants available. Support available to part-time students. Financial award application deadline: 8/1; financial award applicants required to submit FAFSA. *Faculty research:* Native American law, criminal law, commercial speech, copyright law, international law. *Unit head:* Prof. Lyn Suzanne Entzeroth, Dean, 918-631-2400, Fax: 918-631-3126, E-mail: lyn-entzeroth@utulsa.edu. *Application contact:* April M. Fox, Associate Dean of Admissions and Financial Aid, 918-631-2406, Fax: 918-631-3630, E-mail: april-fox@utulsa.edu.
Website: http://www.utulsa.edu/law/

Widener University, Delaware Law School, Wilmington, DE 19803-0474. Offers corporate and business law (MJ); corporate law and finance (LL M); health law (LL M, MJ, D Law); higher education compliance (MJ); juridical science (SJD); law (JD). *Accreditation:* ABA. *Program availability:* Part-time, 100% online. *Faculty:* 24 full-time (13 women), 42 part-time/adjunct (15 women). *Students:* 479 full-time (252 women), 38 part-time (29 women); includes 128 minority (70 Black or African American, non-Hispanic/Latino; 12 American Indian or Alaska Native, non-Hispanic/Latino; 14 Asian, non-Hispanic/Latino; 26 Hispanic/Latino; 6 Two or more races, non-Hispanic/Latino), 39 international. Average age 26. 735 applicants, 80% accepted, 126 enrolled. *Degree requirements:* For doctorate, thesis/dissertation (for some programs). *Entrance requirements:* For master's, GMAT. *Application deadline:* For fall admission, 5/15 for domestic students; for spring admission, 12/1 for domestic students. Applications are processed on a rolling basis. Application fee: $60. Tuition and fees vary according to degree level and program. *Financial support:* Career-related internships or fieldwork, Federal Work-Study, institutionally sponsored loans, and scholarships/grants available. Support available to part-time students. Financial award application deadline: 2/15; financial award applicants required to submit FAFSA. *Unit head:* Rod Smolla, Dean, 302-477-2100, Fax: 302-477-2282, E-mail: rasmolla@widener.edu. *Application contact:* Barbara L. Ayars, Assistant Dean of Admissions, 302-477-2210, Fax: 302-477-2224, E-mail: barbara.l.ayars@law.widener.edu.
Website: http://delawarelaw.widener.edu/

Intellectual Property Law

Case Western Reserve University, School of Law, Cleveland, OH 44106. Offers financial integrity (MA); health law (SJD); intellectual property (LL M); international business law (LL M); international criminal law (LL M); law (JD, SJD); patent practice (MA); U.S. legal studies (LL M); JD/MA; JD/MBA; JD/MD; JD/MNM; JD/MPH; JD/MS; JD/MSSA. *Accreditation:* ABA. *Faculty:* 40 full-time (15 women), 25 part-time/adjunct (4 women). *Students:* 421 full-time (215 women), 1 (woman) part-time; includes 76 minority (37 Black or African American, non-Hispanic/Latino; 17 Asian, non-Hispanic/Latino; 19 Hispanic/Latino; 3 Two or more races, non-Hispanic/Latino), 37 international. Average age 24. 1,645 applicants, 43% accepted, 144 enrolled. In 2016, 72 master's, 99 doctorates awarded. *Entrance requirements:* For doctorate, LSAT, LSDAS. Additional exam requirements/recommendations for international students: Required—TOEFL. *Application deadline:* For fall admission, 4/1 priority date for domestic and international students. Applications are processed on a rolling basis. Application fee: $40. Electronic applications accepted. Application fee is waived when completed online. *Expenses:* Contact institution. *Financial support:* In 2016–17, 345 students received support. Career-related internships or fieldwork, Federal Work-Study, institutionally sponsored loans, and scholarships/grants available. Financial award application deadline: 5/1; financial award applicants required to submit FAFSA. *Unit head:* Jessica Berg, Co-Dean, 216-368-3283. *Application contact:* Kelli Curtis, Associate Dean for Admissions, 216-368-3600, Fax: 216-368-0185, E-mail: lawadmissions@case.edu.
Website: http://law.case.edu/

DePaul University, College of Law, Chicago, IL 60604-2287. Offers health law (LL M); intellectual property law (LL M); international law (LL M); law (JD); taxation (LL M); JD/MA; JD/MBA; JD/MPS; JD/MS. *Accreditation:* ABA. *Program availability:* Part-time, evening/weekend. *Entrance requirements:* For doctorate, LSAT, LSAC applicant evaluation/letter of recommendation, personal statement, resume. Additional exam requirements/recommendations for international students: Required—TOEFL (minimum score 577 paper-based; 90 iBT), IELTS (minimum score 6.5). Electronic applications accepted. *Expenses:* Contact institution.

Fordham University, School of Law, New York, NY 10023. Offers banking, corporate and finance law (LL M); corporate compliance (MSL); fashion law (MSL); intellectual property and information law (LL M); international business and trade law (LL M); law (JD); JD/MA; JD/MBA; JD/MSW. *Accreditation:* ABA. *Program availability:* Part-time, evening/weekend. *Entrance requirements:* For doctorate, LSAT. Additional exam requirements/recommendations for international students: Required—TOEFL. Electronic applications accepted. *Expenses:* Contact institution. *Faculty research:* Intellectual property, business law, international law.

Golden Gate University, School of Law, San Francisco, CA 94105-2968. Offers environmental law (LL M); estate planning (LL M); intellectual property law (LL M); international legal studies (LL M, SJD); law (JD); taxation (LL M); U.S. legal studies (LL M); JD/MBA; JD/PhD. *Accreditation:* ABA. *Program availability:* Part-time, evening/weekend. *Faculty:* 41 full-time (19 women), 67 part-time/adjunct (27 women). *Students:* 246 full-time (142 women), 228 part-time (133 women); includes 213 minority (28 Black or African American, non-Hispanic/Latino; 2 American Indian or Alaska Native, non-Hispanic/Latino; 68 Asian, non-Hispanic/Latino; 84 Hispanic/Latino; 7 Native Hawaiian or other Pacific Islander, non-Hispanic/Latino; 24 Two or more races, non-Hispanic/Latino), 58 international. Average age 31. 1,473 applicants, 65% accepted, 189 enrolled. In 2016, 54 master's, 117 doctorates awarded. *Degree requirements:* For doctorate, thesis/dissertation (for some programs). *Entrance requirements:* For doctorate, LSAT (for JD). Additional exam requirements/recommendations for international students: Required—TOEFL (minimum score 600 paper-based). *Application deadline:* For fall admission, 8/18 for domestic students, 4/1 for international students; for spring admission, 1/12 for domestic students; for summer admission, 6/4 for domestic students. Applications are processed on a rolling basis. Electronic applications accepted. *Expenses:* Contact institution. *Financial support:* In 2016–17, 315 students received support. Fellowships, research assistantships, teaching assistantships, career-related internships or fieldwork, Federal Work-Study, institutionally sponsored loans, scholarships/grants, tuition waivers (full and partial), and unspecified assistantships available. Support available to part-time students. Financial award applicants required to submit FAFSA. *Faculty research:* International law, intellectual property law, environmental law, real estate, civil rights. *Unit head:* Rachel Van Cleave, Dean, 415-442-6601, Fax: 415-442-6609. *Application contact:* Greg Egertson, Associate Dean and Director of Admissions, 415-442-6636, Fax: 415-442-6609, E-mail: lawadmit@ggu.edu.
Website: http://www.ggu.edu/law/

Indiana University–Purdue University Indianapolis, Robert H. McKinney School of Law, Indianapolis, IN 46202. Offers advocacy skills (Certificate); American law for foreign lawyers (LL M); civil and human rights (Certificate); corporate and commercial law (LL M, Certificate); criminal law (Certificate); environmental and natural resources (Certificate); health law (Certificate); health law, policy and bioethics (LL M); intellectual property law (LL M, Certificate); international and comparative law (LL M, Certificate); international human rights law (LL M); law (MJ, JD, SJD); JD/M Phil; JD/MBA; JD/MD; JD/MHA; JD/MLS; JD/MPA; JD/MPH; JD/MSW. *Accreditation:* ABA. *Program availability:* Part-time. *Faculty:* 47 full-time (24 women), 40 part-time/adjunct (17 women). *Students:* 578 full-time (285 women), 328 part-time (154 women); includes 157 minority (71 Black or African American, non-Hispanic/Latino; 1 American Indian or Alaska Native, non-Hispanic/Latino; 17 Asian, non-Hispanic/Latino; 42 Hispanic/Latino; 3 Native Hawaiian or other Pacific Islander, non-Hispanic/Latino; 23 Two or more races, non-Hispanic/Latino), 59 international. Average age 29. 915 applicants, 58% accepted, 253 enrolled. In 2016, 25 master's, 258 doctorates, 100 Certificates awarded. *Entrance requirements:* For doctorate, LSAT. Additional exam requirements/recommendations for international students: Required—TOEFL (minimum score 79 iBT), IELTS (minimum score 6.5). *Application deadline:* For fall admission, 7/31 for domestic students. Applications are processed on a rolling basis. Application fee: $0. Electronic applications accepted. *Expenses:* $843.84 per credit hour resident tuition, $1,472.10 per credit hour non-resident tuition. *Financial support:* In 2016–17, 528 students received support. Fellowships, research assistantships with full and partial tuition reimbursements available, career-related internships or fieldwork, Federal Work-Study, scholarships/grants, and tuition waivers available. Support available to part-time students. Financial award application deadline: 7/31; financial award applicants required to submit FAFSA. *Unit head:* Andrew R. Klein, Dean, 317-274-2099, E-mail: anrklein@iupui.edu. *Application contact:* Patricia Kinney, Assistant Dean of Admissions, 317-274-2459, E-mail: pkkinney@iupui.edu.
Website: http://mckinneylaw.iu.edu/

Michigan State University College of Law, Professional Program, East Lansing, MI 48824-1300. Offers American legal system (LL M, MJ); global food law (LL M, MJ); intellectual property (LL M, MJ); law (JD); legal doctrine and analysis (MJ). *Accreditation:* ABA. *Program availability:* Part-time. *Faculty:* 55 full-time (22 women), 85 part-time/adjunct (32 women). *Students:* 723 full-time (362 women), 123 part-time (70 women); includes 173 minority (57 Black or African American, non-Hispanic/Latino; 9 American Indian or Alaska Native, non-Hispanic/Latino; 28 Asian, non-Hispanic/Latino; 40 Hispanic/Latino; 2 Native Hawaiian or other Pacific Islander, non-Hispanic/Latino; 37 Two or more races, non-Hispanic/Latino), 91 international. Average age 24. 2,362 applicants, 45% accepted, 259 enrolled. In 2016, 45 master's, 265 doctorates awarded. *Entrance requirements:* For doctorate, LSAT. Additional exam requirements/recommendations for international students: Required—TOEFL (minimum score 600 paper-based), IELTS. *Application deadline:* For fall admission, 4/30 priority date for domestic students, 7/1 priority date for international students. Applications are processed on a rolling basis. Application fee: $60. Electronic applications accepted. *Expenses:* Contact institution. *Financial support:* In 2016–17, 559 students received support. Career-related internships or fieldwork, Federal Work-Study, scholarships/grants, and tuition waivers (full and partial) available. Support available to part-time students. Financial award application deadline: 4/1; financial award applicants required to submit FAFSA. *Faculty research:* International, constitutional, health, tax and environmental law; intellectual property, trial practice, corporate law. *Unit head:* Lawrence Ponoroff, Dean/Professor of Law, 517-432-6993, Fax: 517-432-6801, E-mail: lponoroff@law.msu.edu. *Application contact:* Charles Roboski, Assistant Dean of Admissions, 517-432-0222, Fax: 517-432-0098, E-mail: roboski@law.msu.edu.
Website: http://www.law.msu.edu/

Montclair State University, The Graduate School, College of Humanities and Social Sciences, MA Program in Law and Governance, Montclair, NJ 07043-1624. Offers conflict management and peace studies (MA); governance, compliance and regulation (MA); intellectual property (MA); law and governance (MA); legal management (MA). *Program availability:* Part-time, evening/weekend. *Degree requirements:* For master's, thesis or comprehensive exam. *Entrance requirements:* For master's, GRE General Test, minimum cumulative GPA of 2.75 for undergraduate work, 2 letters of recommendation, essay. Additional exam requirements/recommendations for international students: Required—TOEFL (minimum score 83 iBT) or IELTS (minimum score 6.5). Electronic applications accepted. *Expenses:* Tuition, state resident: part-time $553 per credit. Tuition, nonresident: part-time $854 per credit. *Required fees:* $91 per credit. Tuition and fees vary according to program.

Santa Clara University, School of Law, Santa Clara, CA 95053. Offers intellectual property (LL M); international and comparative law (LL M); law (JD); United States law (LL M); JD/MBA; JD/MSIS. LL M in United States law track only open to non-U.S. attorneys; JD/MBA, JD/MSIS are joint programs with the Leavey School of Business. *Accreditation:* ABA. *Program availability:* Part-time, evening/weekend. *Faculty:* 56 full-time (30 women), 38 part-time/adjunct (23 women). *Students:* 641 full-time (334 women), 72 part-time (30 women); includes 304 minority (29 Black or African American, non-Hispanic/Latino; 128 Asian, non-Hispanic/Latino; 108 Hispanic/Latino; 2 Native Hawaiian or other Pacific Islander, non-Hispanic/Latino; 37 Two or more races, non-Hispanic/Latino), 81 international. Average age 27. 2,235 applicants, 75% accepted, 305 enrolled. In 2016, 27 master's, 218 doctorates awarded. *Entrance requirements:* For master's and doctorate, LSAT, transcripts, personal statement. Additional exam requirements/recommendations for international students: Required—TOEFL or IELTS. *Application deadline:* Applications are processed on a rolling basis. Application fee: $75. Electronic applications accepted. Application fee is waived when completed online. *Expenses:* $1,747 per unit (for JD); $1,960 per unit (for LL M). *Financial support:*

Intellectual Property Law

Fellowships, research assistantships, teaching assistantships, career-related internships or fieldwork, Federal Work-Study, scholarships/grants, traineeships, health care benefits, tuition waivers, and unspecified assistantships available. Support available to part-time students. Financial award application deadline: 3/1; financial award applicants required to submit FAFSA. *Unit head:* Lisa Kloppenberg, Dean, 408-554-4362. *Application contact:* Nanette Cannon, Director of Admissions, 408-551-1846, E-mail: ncannon@scu.edu.
Website: http://law.scu.edu/

Suffolk University, Law School, Boston, MA 02108. Offers business law and financial services (JD); civil litigation (JD); global law and technology (LL M); health and biomedical law (JD); intellectual property law (JD); international law (JD); JD/MBA; JD/MPA; JD/MSCJ; JD/MSF; JD/MSIE. *Accreditation:* ABA. *Program availability:* Part-time, evening/weekend. *Faculty:* 58 full-time (26 women), 47 part-time/adjunct (17 women). *Students:* 647 full-time (357 women), 380 part-time (197 women); includes 219 minority (61 Black or African American, non-Hispanic/Latino; 1 American Indian or Alaska Native, non-Hispanic/Latino; 50 Asian, non-Hispanic/Latino; 82 Hispanic/Latino; 25 Two or more races, non-Hispanic/Latino), 42 international. Average age 27. 1,924 applicants, 64% accepted, 355 enrolled. In 2016, 21 master's, 416 doctorates awarded. *Degree requirements:* For master's, legal writing. *Entrance requirements:* For master's, 2 letters of recommendation, resume, personal statement; for doctorate, LSAT, LSDAS, dean's certification, recommendation. Additional exam requirements/recommendations for international students: Required—TOEFL (minimum score 600 paper-based; 100 iBT). *Application deadline:* For fall admission, 4/1 for domestic and international students. Applications are processed on a rolling basis. Application fee: $60. Electronic applications accepted. *Expenses:* $45,922 per year full-time tuition, $34,440 per year part-time tuition. *Financial support:* In 2016–17, 572 students received support, including 1 fellowship (averaging $31,390 per year); career-related internships or fieldwork, Federal Work-Study, institutionally sponsored loans, and scholarships/grants also available. Support available to part-time students. Financial award application deadline: 3/1; financial award applicants required to submit FAFSA. *Faculty research:* Civil law, international law, health/biomedical law, business and finance, intellectual property. *Unit head:* Andrew Perlman, Dean, 617-573-8144, Fax: 617-994-6838, E-mail: lawadmin@suffolk.edu. *Application contact:* Matthew Gavin, Assistant Dean for Admissions and Financial Aid, 617-573-8144, Fax: 617-994-6838, E-mail: lawadm@suffolk.edu.
Website: http://www.suffolk.edu/law/

University of Baltimore, School of Law, Baltimore, MD 21201. Offers business law (JD); criminal practice (JD); estate planning (JD); family law (JD); intellectual property (JD); international law (JD); law (JD); law of the United States (LL M); litigation and advocacy (JD); public service (JD); real estate practice (JD); taxation (LL M); JD/LL M; JD/MBA; JD/MPA; JD/MS; JD/PhD. JD/MS offered jointly with Division of Criminology, Criminal Justice, and Social Policy; JD/PhD with University of Maryland, Baltimore. *Accreditation:* ABA. *Program availability:* Part-time, evening/weekend. *Faculty:* 53 full-time (25 women), 61 part-time/adjunct (18 women). *Students:* 464 full-time (233 women), 297 part-time (140 women); includes 243 minority (142 Black or African American, non-Hispanic/Latino; 35 Asian, non-Hispanic/Latino; 38 Hispanic/Latino; 28 Two or more races, non-Hispanic/Latino), 20 international. Average age 27. 1,090 applicants, 58% accepted, 208 enrolled. In 2016, 279 doctorates awarded. *Entrance requirements:* For doctorate, LSAT. Additional exam requirements/recommendations for international students: Required—TOEFL (for LL M in law of the United States). *Application deadline:* For fall admission, 7/30 for domestic students, 4/1 priority date for international students. Applications are processed on a rolling basis. Application fee: $60. Electronic applications accepted. *Expenses:* $30,144 per year full-time in-state; $43,972 per year full-time out-of-state. *Financial support:* In 2016–17, 344 students received support. Research assistantships, teaching assistantships, career-related internships or fieldwork, Federal Work-Study, and scholarships/grants available. Support available to part-time students. Financial award application deadline: 4/1; financial award applicants required to submit FAFSA. *Faculty research:* Plain view doctrine, statute of limitations, bankruptcy, family law, international and comparative law, Constitutional law. *Unit head:* Ronald Weich, Dean, 410-837-4458. *Application contact:* Jeffrey L. Zavrotny, Assistant Dean for Admissions, 410-837-5809, Fax: 410-837-4188, E-mail: jzavrotny@ubalt.edu.
Website: http://law.ubalt.edu/

University of Houston, Law Center, Houston, TX 77204-6060. Offers energy, environment, and natural resources (LL M); health law (LL M); intellectual property and information law (LL M); international law (LL M); law (LL M, JD); tax law (LL M). *Accreditation:* ABA. *Program availability:* Part-time, evening/weekend. *Entrance requirements:* For doctorate, LSAT. Additional exam requirements/recommendations for international students: Required—TOEFL (minimum score 600 paper-based; 100 iBT). Electronic applications accepted. *Expenses:* Contact institution. *Faculty research:* Health law, international, tax, environmental/energy, information law/intellectual property.

University of New Hampshire, School of Law, Concord, NH 03301. Offers business law (JD); commerce and technology (LL M, MCT, Diploma); criminal law (JD); intellectual property (LL M, MIP, JD, Diploma), including patent law (JD), trademarks and copyright (JD); international criminal law and justice (LL M, MICLJ); litigation (JD); public interest and social justice (JD); sports and entertainment law (JD); JD/LL M; JD/MBA; JD/MIP; JD/MPP; JD/MSW. *Accreditation:* ABA. *Program availability:* Part-time, 100% online, limited residential. *Faculty:* 25 full-time (11 women), 29 part-time/adjunct (9 women). *Students:* 252 full-time (107 women), 4 part-time (3 women); includes 30 minority (3 Black or African American, non-Hispanic/Latino; 7 Asian, non-Hispanic/Latino; 11 Hispanic/Latino; 9 Two or more races, non-Hispanic/Latino), 36 international. Average age 36. 564 applicants, 53% accepted, 103 enrolled. In 2016, 27 master's, 69 doctorates awarded. *Degree requirements:* For doctorate, comprehensive exam. *Entrance requirements:* For doctorate, LSAT. Additional exam requirements/recommendations for international students: Required—TOEFL (minimum score 600 paper-based; 100 iBT), minimum TOEFL iBT score of 80 (for master's programs). *Application deadline:* For fall admission, 4/1 priority date for domestic and international students; for spring admission, 1/3 for domestic and international students. Applications are processed on a rolling basis. Application fee: $0. Electronic applications accepted. *Expenses:* Contact institution. *Financial support:* Fellowships, career-related internships or fieldwork, Federal Work-Study, and scholarships/grants available. Financial award applicants required to submit FAFSA. *Faculty research:* Intellectual property, health law and policy, sports and entertainment law, patent law, trademarks and copyright. *Unit head:* Megan Carpenter, Dean, 603-228-1541, Fax: 603-228-1074. *Application contact:* Brenda Brooks, Director of Admissions, 603-513-5300, Fax: 603-513-5234, E-mail: brenda.brooks@law.unh.edu.
Website: http://law.unh.edu/

University of Pittsburgh, School of Law, Master of Studies in Law Program, Pittsburgh, PA 15260. Offers business law (MSL), including commercial law, corporate law, general business law, international business, tax law; Constitutional law (MSL); criminal law and justice (MSL); disability law (MSL); education law (MSL); elder and estate planning law (MSL); employment and labor law (MSL); energy law (MSL); environmental and real estate law (MSL); family law (MSL); health law (MSL); intellectual property and technology law (MSL); international and human rights law (MSL); jurisprudence (MSL); personal injury and civil litigation (MSL); regulatory law (MSL); self-designed (MSL); sports and entertainment law (MSL). *Program availability:* Part-time. *Faculty:* 48 full-time (21 women), 104 part-time/adjunct (34 women). *Students:* 5 full-time (4 women), 14 part-time (9 women); includes 7 minority (4 Black or African American, non-Hispanic/Latino; 1 Asian, non-Hispanic/Latino; 2 Native Hawaiian or other Pacific Islander, non-Hispanic/Latino). Average age 27. 17 applicants, 53% accepted, 7 enrolled. In 2016, 4 master's awarded. *Entrance requirements:* Additional exam requirements/recommendations for international students: Required—TOEFL (minimum score 600 paper-based; 100 iBT). *Application deadline:* For fall admission, 6/30 for domestic students, 5/1 for international students. Applications are processed on a rolling basis. Application fee: $0. Tuition and fees vary according to program. *Faculty research:* Law, health law, business law, contracts, intellectual property, environmental law. *Unit head:* Prof. Alan Meisel, Director, 412-648-1384, Fax: 412-648-2649, E-mail: meisel@pitt.edu. *Application contact:* Beth Ann Pischke, Administrative Coordinator, 412-648-7120, Fax: 412-648-2649, E-mail: pischke@pitt.edu.
Website: http://www.law.pitt.edu/msl

University of San Francisco, School of Law, Master of Law Programs, San Francisco, CA 94117-1080. Offers intellectual property and technology law (LL M); international transactions and comparative law (LL M). *Program availability:* Part-time. *Faculty:* 13 full-time (6 women), 11 part-time/adjunct (2 women). *Students:* 21 full-time (18 women), 65 part-time (31 women); includes 21 minority (3 Black or African American, non-Hispanic/Latino; 13 Asian, non-Hispanic/Latino; 1 Hispanic/Latino; 4 Two or more races, non-Hispanic/Latino), 17 international. Average age 34. 111 applicants, 87% accepted, 46 enrolled. In 2016, 30 master's awarded. *Entrance requirements:* For master's, law degree from U.S. or foreign school (intellectual property and technology law); law degree from foreign school (international transactions and comparative law). Application fee: $60. Electronic applications accepted. *Expenses: Tuition:* Full-time $23,310; part-time $1295 per credit. Tuition and fees vary according to course load, degree level, campus/location and program. *Financial support:* In 2016–17, 28 students received support. Applicants required to submit FAFSA. *Unit head:* Constance De La Vega, Director, 650-728-6658. *Application contact:* Julianne Traylor, Program Assistant, 415-422-6658, E-mail: masterlaws@usfca.edu.
Website: http://www.usfca.edu/law/llm/

University of Washington, Graduate School, School of Law, Seattle, WA 98195-3020. Offers Asian law (LL M, PhD); intellectual property law and policy (LL M); law (JD); law of sustainable international development (LL M); taxation (LL M); JD/LL M; JD/MA; JD/MAIS; JD/MBA; JD/MPA; JD/MS; JD/PhD. *Accreditation:* ABA. *Degree requirements:* For master's, thesis; for doctorate, thesis/dissertation (for some programs). *Entrance requirements:* For master's, language proficiency (LL M in Asian law); for doctorate, LSAT (for JD). Additional exam requirements/recommendations for international students: Required—TOEFL. *Expenses:* Contact institution. *Faculty research:* Asian, international and comparative law, intellectual property law, health law, environmental law, taxation.

Western Michigan University Thomas M. Cooley Law School, Graduate Programs, Lansing, MI 48901-3038. Offers administrative law (public law) (JD); business transactions (JD); Canadian law practice (JD); constitutional law/civil rights (public law) (JD); corporate law and finance (LL M); environmental law (public law) (JD); general practice (JD), including solo and small firm; homeland and national security law (LL M); insurance law (LL M); intellectual property (JD); intellectual property law (LL M); international law (JD); litigation (JD); self-directed (LL M, JD); tax law (LL M); taxation (JD); U.S. legal studies for foreign attorneys (LL M); JD/LL M; JD/MBA; JD/MPA; JD/MSW. *Program availability:* Part-time, evening/weekend, 100% online, blended/hybrid learning. *Degree requirements:* For master's, thesis optional; for doctorate, minimum of 3 credits of clinical experience. *Entrance requirements:* For master's, JD or LL B; for doctorate, LSAT. Additional exam requirements/recommendations for international students: Required—TOEFL (for U.S. legal studies for foreign attorneys LL M program); Recommended—TOEFL. Electronic applications accepted. *Faculty research:* Wrongful convictions, civil rights, environmental law, litigation techniques, data mining, intellectual property, practical and skills-based legal education.

Yeshiva University, Benjamin N. Cardozo School of Law, New York, NY 10003-4301. Offers comparative legal thought (LL M); dispute resolution and advocacy (LL M); general studies (LL M); intellectual property law (LL M); law (JD). *Accreditation:* ABA. *Program availability:* Part-time. *Faculty:* 61 full-time (24 women), 92 part-time/adjunct (38 women). *Students:* 992 full-time (506 women), 85 part-time (48 women); includes 277 minority (65 Black or African American, non-Hispanic/Latino; 88 Asian, non-Hispanic/Latino; 112 Hispanic/Latino; 1 Native Hawaiian or other Pacific Islander, non-Hispanic/Latino; 11 Two or more races, non-Hispanic/Latino), 69 international. Average age 25. 2,475 applicants, 56% accepted, 272 enrolled. In 2016, 70 master's, 391 doctorates awarded. *Entrance requirements:* For doctorate, LSAT, 2 letters of recommendation. Additional exam requirements/recommendations for international students: Required—TOEFL (minimum score 100 iBT); Recommended—IELTS (minimum score 7). *Application deadline:* For fall admission, 4/1 priority date for domestic students; for spring admission, 12/1 for domestic students. Applications are processed on a rolling basis. Application fee: $50. Electronic applications accepted. *Expenses:* Contact institution. *Financial support:* In 2016–17, 745 students received support, including 87 research assistantships (averaging $1,599 per year); career-related internships or fieldwork, Federal Work-Study, institutionally sponsored loans, scholarships/grants, health care benefits, and tuition waivers (full and partial) also available. Support available to part-time students. Financial award application deadline: 3/1; financial award applicants required to submit FAFSA. *Faculty research:* Corporate and commercial law, intellectual property law, criminal law and litigation, Constitutional law, legal theory and jurisprudence. *Unit head:* David G. Martinidez, Dean of Admissions, 212-790-0357, Fax: 212-790-0482, E-mail: lawinfo@yu.edu. *Application contact:* David G. Martinidez, Dean of Admissions, 212-790-0357, Fax: 212-790-0482, E-mail: lawinfo@yu.edu.
Website: http://www.cardozo.yu.edu/

Law

Albany Law School, Professional Program, Albany, NY 12208-3494. Offers LL M, JD, JD/MBA, JD/MPA, JD/MRP, JD/MS, JD/MSW. JD/MBA offered jointly with The College of Saint Rose, The Sage Colleges, Union Graduate College, and University at Albany, State University of New York; JD/MPA, JD/MRP, and JD/MSW offered jointly with University at Albany, State University of New York. *Accreditation:* ABA. *Program availability:* Part-time. *Entrance requirements:* For master's, GRE or LSAT; for doctorate, LSAT. Additional exam requirements/recommendations for international students: Recommended—TOEFL (minimum score 600 paper-based). *Expenses:* Contact institution. *Faculty research:* Federal tax, Constitutional law, secured transactions, international law, American politics.

Alliant International University–San Francisco, San Francisco Law School, JD Program, San Francisco, CA 94133. Offers JD. *Program availability:* Part-time, evening/weekend. *Entrance requirements:* For doctorate, LSAT, personal statement, interview. Electronic applications accepted.

The American University in Cairo, School of Global Affairs and Public Policy, Cairo, Egypt. Offers gender and women's studies (MA); global affairs (MGA); international and comparative law (LL M); international human rights law (MA); journalism and mass communication (MA); Middle East studies (MA); migration and refugee studies (MA, Diploma); public administration (MPA); public policy (MPP); television and digital journalism (MA). *Program availability:* Part-time, evening/weekend. *Faculty:* 27 full-time (13 women), 5 part-time/adjunct (3 women). *Students:* 69 full-time (40 women), 194 part-time (134 women), 33 international. Average age 29. 322 applicants, 51% accepted, 86 enrolled. In 2016, 112 master's awarded. *Degree requirements:* For master's, comprehensive exam (for some programs), thesis (for some programs). *Entrance requirements:* Additional exam requirements/recommendations for international students: Required—TOEFL (minimum score 450 paper-based; 45 iBT), IELTS (minimum score 5). *Application deadline:* For fall admission, 2/1 for domestic and international students; for spring admission, 10/15 for domestic and international students. Applications are processed on a rolling basis. Application fee: $80. Electronic applications accepted. *Expenses:* Contact institution. *Financial support:* Fellowships with partial tuition reimbursements, scholarships/grants, and unspecified assistantships available. Financial award application deadline: 3/10. *Faculty research:* Law, media and journalism; public policy and public administration, gender studies, Middle East Studies, global affairs, refugees studies. *Unit head:* Dr. Nabil Fahmy, Dean, 20-2-2615-2671, E-mail: nfahmy@aucegypt.edu. *Application contact:* Maha Hegazi, Director for Graduate Admissions, 20-2-2615-1462, E-mail: mahahegazi@aucegypt.edu.
Website: http://www.aucegypt.edu/GAPP/Pages/default.aspx

American University of Armenia, Graduate Programs, Yerevan, Armenia. Offers business administration (MBA); computer and information science (MS), including business management, design and manufacturing, energy (ME, MS), industrial engineering and systems management; economics (MS); industrial engineering and systems management (ME), including business, computer aided design/manufacturing, energy (ME, MS), information technology; law (LL M); political science and international affairs (MPSIA); public health (MPH); teaching English as a foreign language (MA). *Program availability:* Part-time, evening/weekend. *Degree requirements:* For master's, thesis (for some programs), capstone/project. *Entrance requirements:* For master's, GRE, GMAT, or LSAT. Additional exam requirements/recommendations for international students: Recommended—TOEFL (minimum score 79 iBT), IELTS (minimum score 6.5). *Faculty research:* Microfinance, finance (rural/development, international, corporate), firm life cycle theory, TESOL, language proficiency testing, public policy, administrative law, economic development, cryptography, artificial intelligence, energy efficiency/renewable energy, computer-aided design/manufacturing, health financing, tuberculosis control, mother/child health, preventive ophthalmology, post-earthquake psychopathological investigations, tobacco control, environmental health risk assessments.

The American University of Paris, Graduate Programs, Paris, France. Offers cross-cultural and sustainable business management (MA); cultural translation (MA); global communications (MA); global communications and civil society (MA); international affairs (MA); international affairs, conflict resolution and civil society development (MA); Middle East and Islamic studies (MA); Middle East and Islamic studies and international affairs (MA); public policy and international affairs (MA); public policy and international law (MA). *Degree requirements:* For master's, thesis (for some programs). *Entrance requirements:* For master's, minimum undergraduate GPA of 3.0. Additional exam requirements/recommendations for international students: Recommended—TOEFL, IELTS. Electronic applications accepted.

Appalachian School of Law, Professional Program in Law, Grundy, VA 24614. Offers JD. *Accreditation:* ABA. *Entrance requirements:* For doctorate, LSAT, bachelor's degree from accredited institution. Electronic applications accepted. *Faculty research:* Natural resources, alternative dispute resolution, Constitutional law, professional ethics, intellectual property.

Arizona State University at the Tempe campus, Sandra Day O'Connor College of Law, Phoenix, AZ 85004-4467. Offers biotechnology and genomics (LL M); law (JD); legal studies (MLS); patent practice (MLS); sports law and business (MSLB); tribal policy, law and government (LL M); JD/MBA; JD/MD; JD/MSW; JD/PhD. *Accreditation:* ABA. *Program availability:* 100% online. *Faculty:* 71 full-time (31 women), 67 part-time/adjunct (16 women). *Students:* 718 full-time (300 women); includes 195 minority (17 Black or African American, non-Hispanic/Latino; 14 American Indian or Alaska Native, non-Hispanic/Latino; 27 Asian, non-Hispanic/Latino; 98 Hispanic/Latino; 3 Native Hawaiian or other Pacific Islander, non-Hispanic/Latino; 36 Two or more races, non-Hispanic/Latino), 13 international. Average age 28. 1,860 applicants, 42% accepted, 228 enrolled. In 2016, 52 master's, 190 doctorates awarded. *Entrance requirements:* For master's, bachelor's degree and JD (for LL M); for doctorate, LSAT, bachelor's degree. Additional exam requirements/recommendations for international students: Required—TOEFL (minimum score 550 paper-based; 80 iBT). *Application deadline:* For fall admission, 3/1 priority date for domestic and international students. Applications are processed on a rolling basis. Application fee: $65. Electronic applications accepted. *Expenses:* Contact institution. *Financial support:* In 2016–17, 432 students received support. Institutionally sponsored loans and scholarships/grants available. Financial award application deadline: 3/15; financial award applicants required to submit FAFSA. *Faculty research:* Emerging technologies and the law, Indian law, international law, intellectual property, health law, sports law and business. *Total annual research expenditures:* $1.9 million. *Unit head:* Douglas Sylvester, Dean/Professor, 480-965-6188, Fax: 480-965-6521, E-mail: douglas.sylvester@asu.edu. *Application contact:* Chitra Damania, Director of Operations, 480-965-1474, Fax: 480-727-7930, E-mail: law.admissions@asu.edu.
Website: http://www.law.asu.edu/

Arizona Summit Law School, JD Program, Phoenix, AZ 85004. Offers JD. *Program availability:* Part-time, evening/weekend. *Faculty:* 17 full-time (13 women), 25 part-time/adjunct (7 women). *Students:* 184 full-time (91 women), 202 part-time (113 women); includes 165 minority (68 Black or African American, non-Hispanic/Latino; 11 American Indian or Alaska Native, non-Hispanic/Latino; 20 Asian, non-Hispanic/Latino; 63 Hispanic/Latino; 2 Native Hawaiian or other Pacific Islander, non-Hispanic/Latino; 1 Two or more races, non-Hispanic/Latino), 5 international. Average age 33. In 2016, 221 doctorates awarded. *Expenses:* $43,306 tuition, $2,048 fees per full-time academic year (2 semesters); $34,644 tuition, $2,048 fees per part-time academic year (2 semesters). *Financial support:* Applicants required to submit FAFSA. *Faculty research:* Civil procedure, alternative dispute resolution, indigenous peoples and natural resources, cultural property, American Indian environmental law. *Application contact:* Rick Jackson, Associate Dean of Admissions, 602-682-6817, E-mail: admissions@azsummitlaw.edu.

Atlanta's John Marshall Law School, JD and LL M Programs, Atlanta, GA 30309. Offers American legal studies (LL M); employment law (LL M); law (JD). *Accreditation:* ABA. *Program availability:* Part-time, evening/weekend, online learning. *Entrance requirements:* For master's, JD from accredited law school or bar admission; for doctorate, LSAT, LSDAS report, personal statement, two letters of reference. Additional exam requirements/recommendations for international students: Required—TOEFL. Electronic applications accepted. *Faculty research:* Tort reform, terrorism and the use of the U.S. military, Title VII's referral and deferral scheme, public utilities, eminent domain and land use regulations, recent films and their visions of law in Western society.

Ave Maria School of Law, Professional Program, Naples, FL 34119. Offers law (JD). *Accreditation:* ABA. *Faculty:* 24 full-time (6 women), 9 part-time/adjunct (3 women). *Students:* 248 full-time (130 women); includes 78 minority (16 Black or African American, non-Hispanic/Latino; 5 American Indian or Alaska Native, non-Hispanic/Latino; 3 Asian, non-Hispanic/Latino; 54 Hispanic/Latino), 5 international. Average age 26. 637 applicants, 54% accepted, 88 enrolled. In 2016, 88 doctorates awarded. *Entrance requirements:* For doctorate, LSAT, 2 letters of recommendation, LSDAS, personal statement. Additional exam requirements/recommendations for international students: Required—TOEFL (minimum score 600 paper-based). *Application deadline:* For fall admission, 7/15 priority date for domestic and international students. Applications are processed on a rolling basis. Application fee: $0. Electronic applications accepted. *Expenses:* Contact institution. *Financial support:* In 2016–17, 158 students received support. Research assistantships, career-related internships or fieldwork, Federal Work-Study, and scholarships/grants available. Financial award application deadline: 6/30; financial award applicants required to submit FAFSA. *Faculty research:* International law, immigration, religious freedom, litigation, military law. *Unit head:* Kevin Cieply, President/Dean, 239-687-5300, E-mail: kcieply@avemarialaw.edu. *Application contact:* Claire T. O'Keefe, Assistant Dean of Admissions, 239-687-5423, Fax: 239-352-2890, E-mail: info@avemarialaw.edu.
Website: http://www.avemarialaw.edu/

Barry University, Dwayne O. Andreas School of Law, Orlando, FL 32807. Offers JD, JD/MS. *Accreditation:* ABA. *Entrance requirements:* For doctorate, LSAT.

Baylor University, School of Law, Waco, TX 76798-7288. Offers JD, JD/M Div, JD/M Tax, JD/MBA, JD/MPPA. *Accreditation:* ABA. *Faculty:* 28 full-time (9 women), 20 part-time/adjunct (2 women). *Students:* 367 full-time (190 women), 2 part-time (1 woman); includes 89 minority (14 Black or African American, non-Hispanic/Latino; 4 American Indian or Alaska Native, non-Hispanic/Latino; 18 Asian, non-Hispanic/Latino; 48 Hispanic/Latino; 2 Native Hawaiian or other Pacific Islander, non-Hispanic/Latino; 3 Two or more races, non-Hispanic/Latino), 4 international. Average age 24. 1,724 applicants, 41% accepted, 72 enrolled. In 2016, 140 doctorates awarded. *Entrance requirements:* For doctorate, LSAT. Additional exam requirements/recommendations for international students: Recommended—TOEFL. *Application deadline:* For fall admission, 3/15 for domestic and international students; for spring admission, 11/15 for domestic and international students; for summer admission, 3/15 for domestic and international students. Applications are processed on a rolling basis. Application fee: $0. Electronic applications accepted. *Expenses:* $19,251 per quarter. *Financial support:* In 2016–17, 259 students received support. Career-related internships or fieldwork, Federal Work-Study, and scholarships/grants available. Financial award application deadline: 2/1; financial award applicants required to submit FAFSA. *Unit head:* Bradley J. B. Toben, Dean, 254-710-1911, Fax: 254-710-2316. *Application contact:* Jenny Branson, Assistant Dean of Admissions and Financial Aid, 254-710-1911, Fax: 254-710-2316, E-mail: jenny_branson@baylor.edu.
Website: http://www.baylor.edu/law

Belmont University, College of Law, Nashville, TN 37212. Offers JD. *Accreditation:* ABA. *Faculty:* 27 full-time (10 women), 8 part-time/adjunct (3 women). *Students:* 261 full-time (139 women); includes 33 minority (9 Black or African American, non-Hispanic/Latino; 18 Asian, non-Hispanic/Latino; 2 Hispanic/Latino; 1 Native Hawaiian or other Pacific Islander, non-Hispanic/Latino; 3 Two or more races, non-Hispanic/Latino). Average age 26. *Entrance requirements:* For doctorate, LSAT. Additional exam requirements/recommendations for international students: Required—TOEFL. *Application deadline:* For fall admission, 7/31 priority date for domestic students, 7/30 priority date for international students. Applications are processed on a rolling basis. Electronic applications accepted. Tuition and fees vary according to program. *Financial support:* Applicants required to submit FAFSA. *Unit head:* Alberto R. Gonzales, Dean, 615-460-8259, E-mail: alberto.gonzales@belmont.edu. *Application contact:* Ehren Green, Director of Admissions, 615-460-8273, Fax: 615-460-5434, E-mail: ehren.green@belmont.edu.
Website: http://www.belmont.edu/law/

Boston College, Law School, Newton, MA 02459. Offers JD, JD/MA, JD/MBA, JD/MSW. *Accreditation:* ABA. *Entrance requirements:* For doctorate, LSAT. Additional exam requirements/recommendations for international students: Required—TOEFL. Electronic applications accepted. *Expenses:* Contact institution. *Faculty research:* Commercial law, labor law, legal history, comparative law, international law, business law, intellectual property law, tax law, environmental law.

Boston University, School of Law, Boston, MA 02215. Offers LL M, JD, JD/LL M, JD/MA, JD/MBA, JD/MPH, JD/MS, JD/MSW, MD/JD. MD/JD offered jointly with the School of Medicine. *Accreditation:* ABA. *Program availability:* 100% online, blended/hybrid learning. *Faculty:* 45 full-time (23 women), 111 part-time/adjunct (34 women). *Students:* 903 full-time (492 women), 150 part-time (76 women); includes 227 minority (43 Black or African American, non-Hispanic/Latino; 2 American Indian or Alaska Native, non-Hispanic/Latino; 61 Asian, non-Hispanic/Latino; 94 Hispanic/Latino; 1 Native Hawaiian or other Pacific Islander, non-Hispanic/Latino; 26 Two or more races, non-Hispanic/Latino), 224 international. Average age 27. 4,800 applicants, 29% accepted, 208 enrolled. In 2016, 258 master's, 224 doctorates awarded. *Degree requirements:* For

master's, thesis (for some programs); for doctorate, thesis/dissertation, research project resulting in a paper. *Entrance requirements:* For master's, JD; for doctorate, LSAT. Additional exam requirements/recommendations for international students: Required—TOEFL (minimum score 100 iBT), IELTS. *Application deadline:* For fall admission, 4/1 for domestic and international students. Applications are processed on a rolling basis. Application fee: $85. Electronic applications accepted. *Expenses:* $51,210. *Financial support:* In 2016–17, 616 students received support. Career-related internships or fieldwork, Federal Work-Study, institutionally sponsored loans, and scholarships/grants available. Financial award application deadline: 3/1; financial award applicants required to submit FAFSA. *Faculty research:* Health law, tax, intellectual property, Constitutional law, corporate law, business organizations and financial law, international law, family law. *Unit head:* Maureen A. O'Rourke, Dean, 617-353-3112, Fax: 617-358-4706, E-mail: lawdean@bu.edu. *Application contact:* Alissa Leonard, Director of Admissions and Financial Aid, 617-353-3100, Fax: 617-353-0578, E-mail: bulawadm@bu.edu.
Website: http://www.bu.edu/law/

Boston University, School of Public Health, Health Law, Policy and Management Department, Boston, MA 02215. Offers health services research (MS). *Accreditation:* CAHME. *Program availability:* Part-time, evening/weekend. *Faculty:* 37 full-time, 31 part-time/adjunct. *Students:* 134 full-time (105 women), 108 part-time (86 women); includes 75 minority (22 Black or African American, non-Hispanic/Latino; 1 American Indian or Alaska Native, non-Hispanic/Latino; 28 Asian, non-Hispanic/Latino; 16 Hispanic/Latino; 8 Two or more races, non-Hispanic/Latino), 23 international. Average age 29. 507 applicants, 44% accepted, 77 enrolled. In 2016, 203 master's, 10 doctorates awarded. *Degree requirements:* For master's, comprehensive exam (for some programs), thesis (for some programs); for doctorate, comprehensive exam, thesis/dissertation. *Entrance requirements:* For master's, GRE, MCAT, GMAT; for doctorate, GRE. Additional exam requirements/recommendations for international students: Required—TOEFL (minimum score 600 paper-based; 100 iBT), IELTS (minimum score 7). *Application deadline:* For fall admission, 12/1 priority date for domestic and international students; for spring admission, 10/15 priority date for domestic students. Applications are processed on a rolling basis. Application fee: $115. Electronic applications accepted. *Financial support:* Career-related internships or fieldwork, Federal Work-Study, institutionally sponsored loans, scholarships/grants, and tuition waivers (partial) available. Support available to part-time students. Financial award application deadline: 3/1; financial award applicants required to submit FAFSA. *Faculty research:* Health policy, health law and ethics, human rights, healthcare management. *Unit head:* Dr. David Rosenbloom, Interim Chair, 617-638-5042. *Application contact:* LePhan Quan, Associate Director of Admissions, 617-638-4640, Fax: 617-638-5299, E-mail: asksph@bu.edu.
Website: http://www.bu.edu/sph/about/departments/health-law-policy-and-management/

Brigham Young University, Graduate Studies, J. Reuben Clark Law School, Provo, UT 84602-8000. Offers LL M, JD, JD/M Ed, JD/MBA, JD/MPA. *Accreditation:* ABA. *Faculty:* 26 full-time (10 women), 35 part-time/adjunct (7 women). *Students:* 397 full-time (146 women), 12 part-time (8 women); includes 65 minority (4 Black or African American, non-Hispanic/Latino; 5 American Indian or Alaska Native, non-Hispanic/Latino; 12 Asian, non-Hispanic/Latino; 20 Hispanic/Latino; 9 Native Hawaiian or other Pacific Islander, non-Hispanic/Latino; 15 Two or more races, non-Hispanic/Latino), 10 international. Average age 27. 436 applicants, 44% accepted, 138 enrolled. In 2016, 4 master's, 143 doctorates awarded. *Entrance requirements:* For doctorate, LSAT. Additional exam requirements/recommendations for international students: Recommended—TOEFL (minimum score 590 paper-based; 96 iBT), IELTS (minimum score 7). *Application deadline:* For fall admission, 3/1 priority date for domestic students, 3/1 for international students. Applications are processed on a rolling basis. Application fee: $50. Electronic applications accepted. *Expenses:* Contact institution. *Financial support:* In 2016–17, 221 students received support, including 12 fellowships (averaging $36,299 per year); career-related internships or fieldwork, institutionally sponsored loans, scholarships/grants, unspecified assistantships, and student employment also available. Financial award application deadline: 6/1; financial award applicants required to submit FAFSA. *Faculty research:* Law, innovation, and entrepreneurship; law and disadvantaged peoples; law and corpus linguistics; law and religion; and international law. *Total annual research expenditures:* $17,068. *Unit head:* D. Gordon Smith, Dean, 801-422-6383, Fax: 801-422-0389, E-mail: smithg@law.byu.edu. *Application contact:* Rebeca Welch, Admissions Coordinator, 801-422-4356, Fax: 801-422-0389, E-mail: welchr@law.byu.edu.
Website: http://www.law2.byu.edu/

Brooklyn Law School, Graduate and Professional Programs, Brooklyn, NY 11201-3798. Offers LL M, JD, JD/MA, JD/MBA, JD/MS, JD/MUP. JD/MBA offered jointly with Bernard M. Baruch College of the City University of New York; JD/MS with Pratt Institute; JD/MUP with Hunter College of the City University of New York; and JD/MA with Brooklyn College of the City University of New York. *Accreditation:* ABA. *Program availability:* Part-time, evening/weekend. *Entrance requirements:* For doctorate, LSAT, dean's certification, 2 faculty letters of evaluation. Additional exam requirements/recommendations for international students: Required—TOEFL and TWE (required for Foreign Trained Lawyers Program); Recommended—TOEFL (minimum score 600 paper-based; 100 iBT), TWE. Electronic applications accepted. *Faculty research:* Civil procedure, securities regulation, family law, corporate finance, international business and law, health law.

California Western School of Law, Graduate and Professional Programs, San Diego, CA 92101-3090. Offers law (JD); Spanish language in trial advocacy (LL M); JD/MBA; JD/MSW; MCL/LL M. JD/MSW and JD/MBA offered jointly with San Diego State University. *Accreditation:* ABA. *Program availability:* Part-time. *Faculty:* 43 full-time (18 women), 48 part-time/adjunct (20 women). *Students:* 568 full-time (339 women), 189 part-time (84 women); includes 267 minority (41 Black or African American, non-Hispanic/Latino; 9 American Indian or Alaska Native, non-Hispanic/Latino; 42 Asian, non-Hispanic/Latino; 123 Hispanic/Latino; 9 Native Hawaiian or other Pacific Islander, non-Hispanic/Latino; 43 Two or more races, non-Hispanic/Latino), 12 international. Average age 27. 1,408 applicants, 70% accepted, 230 enrolled. *Entrance requirements:* For doctorate, LSAT. Additional exam requirements/recommendations for international students: Required—TOEFL. *Application deadline:* For fall admission, 4/1 for domestic students; for spring admission, 11/1 for domestic students. Applications are processed on a rolling basis. Electronic applications accepted. *Expenses: Tuition:* Full-time $48,800; part-time $34,200 per year. *Required fees:* $100; $100 per unit. Tuition and fees vary according to degree level. *Financial support:* Career-related internships or fieldwork, Federal Work-Study, institutionally sponsored loans, and scholarships/grants available. Support available to part-time students. Financial award applicants required to submit FAFSA. *Faculty research:* Biotechnology, health law, international law, labor and employment law, business law. *Unit head:* Niels B. Schaumann, Dean, 619-239-0391, Fax: 619-685-2916. *Application contact:* Traci D. Howard, Assistant Dean for Admissions, 619-525-1404, Fax: 619-615-1404, E-mail: admissions@cwsl.edu.
Website: http://www.californiawestern.edu/

Campbell University, Graduate and Professional Programs, Norman Adrian Wiggins School of Law, Raleigh, NC 27603. Offers JD, JD/MPA. JD/MPA offered in partnership with North Carolina State University. *Accreditation:* ABA. *Entrance requirements:* For doctorate, LSAT, interview. Additional exam requirements/recommendations for international students: Recommended—TOEFL. Electronic applications accepted. *Expenses:* Contact institution. *Faculty research:* Interdisciplinary approaches to legal problems, management and planning for lawyers, church/state constitutional problems, basic research in substantive legal areas.

Capital University, Law School, Columbus, OH 43215-3200. Offers LL M, MT, JD, JD/LL M, JD/MBA, JD/MSA, JD/MSN, JD/MTS. *Accreditation:* ABA. *Program availability:* Part-time, evening/weekend. *Entrance requirements:* For master's, 24 credit hours of business and accounting courses (including a federal taxation course and business law course); 4-year bachelor's degree from regionally-accredited college or university; for doctorate, LSAT, 4-year bachelor's degree from regionally-accredited college or university. Additional exam requirements/recommendations for international students: Required—TOEFL (minimum score 600 paper-based; 100 iBT); Recommended—IELTS (minimum score 7). Electronic applications accepted. *Expenses:* Contact institution.

Case Western Reserve University, School of Law, Cleveland, OH 44106. Offers financial integrity (MA); health law (SJD); intellectual property (LL M); international business law (LL M); international criminal law (LL M); law (JD, SJD); patent practice (MA); U.S. legal studies (LL M); JD/MA; JD/MBA; JD/MD; JD/MNM; JD/MPH; JD/MS; JD/MSSA. *Accreditation:* ABA. *Faculty:* 40 full-time (15 women), 25 part-time/adjunct (4 women). *Students:* 421 full-time (215 women), 1 (woman) part-time; includes 76 minority (37 Black or African American, non-Hispanic/Latino; 17 Asian, non-Hispanic/Latino; 19 Hispanic/Latino; 3 Two or more races, non-Hispanic/Latino), 37 international. Average age 24. 1,645 applicants, 43% accepted, 144 enrolled. In 2016, 72 master's, 99 doctorates awarded. *Entrance requirements:* For doctorate, LSAT, LSDAS. Additional exam requirements/recommendations for international students: Required—TOEFL. *Application deadline:* For fall admission, 4/1 priority date for domestic and international students. Applications are processed on a rolling basis. Application fee: $40. Electronic applications accepted. Application fee is waived when completed online. *Expenses:* Contact institution. *Financial support:* In 2016–17, 345 students received support. Career-related internships or fieldwork, Federal Work-Study, institutionally sponsored loans, and scholarships/grants available. Financial award application deadline: 5/1; financial award applicants required to submit FAFSA. *Unit head:* Jessica Berg, Co-Dean, 216-368-3283. *Application contact:* Kelli Curtis, Associate Dean for Admissions, 216-368-3600, Fax: 216-368-0185, E-mail: lawadmissions@case.edu.
Website: http://law.case.edu/

The Catholic University of America, Columbus School of Law, Washington, DC 20064. Offers MLS, JD, JD/JCL, JD/MA, JD/MLS, JD/MSBA, JD/MSW. *Accreditation:* ABA. *Program availability:* Part-time, evening/weekend. *Faculty:* 43 full-time (21 women), 83 part-time/adjunct (19 women). *Students:* 262 full-time (141 women), 131 part-time (62 women); includes 70 minority (32 Black or African American, non-Hispanic/Latino; 2 American Indian or Alaska Native, non-Hispanic/Latino; 2 Asian, non-Hispanic/Latino; 22 Hispanic/Latino; 12 Two or more races, non-Hispanic/Latino), 3 international. Average age 26. 1,265 applicants, 51% accepted, 123 enrolled. In 2016, 138 doctorates awarded. *Entrance requirements:* For doctorate, LSAT. Additional exam requirements/recommendations for international students: Required—TOEFL (minimum score 600 paper-based; 100 iBT), IELTS (minimum score 7). *Application deadline:* For fall admission, 3/16 priority date for domestic students, 3/16 for international students. Applications are processed on a rolling basis. Application fee: $65. Electronic applications accepted. Application fee is waived when completed online. *Expenses:* Contact institution. *Financial support:* In 2016–17, 330 students received support. Career-related internships or fieldwork, Federal Work-Study, institutionally sponsored loans, and scholarships/grants available. Support available to part-time students. Financial award application deadline: 8/15; financial award applicants required to submit FAFSA. *Unit head:* Daniel F. Attridge, Dean, 202-319-5139, Fax: 202-319-5473. *Application contact:* Shani J. P. Butts, Assistant Dean of Admissions, 202-319-5151, Fax: 202-319-4462, E-mail: butts@law.edu.
Website: http://www.law.edu/

Central European University, Department of Legal Studies, Budapest, Hungary. Offers comparative Constitutional law (LL M); human rights (LL M, MA); international business law (LL M); juridical sciences (SJD); law and economics (LL M, MA). *Faculty:* 10 full-time (5 women), 15 part-time/adjunct (3 women). *Students:* 89 full-time (43 women). Average age 27. 420 applicants, 27% accepted, 66 enrolled. In 2016, 52 master's, 4 doctorates awarded. Terminal master's awarded for partial completion of doctoral program. *Degree requirements:* For master's, one foreign language, thesis; for doctorate, one foreign language, comprehensive exam, thesis/dissertation. *Entrance requirements:* For master's and doctorate, LSAT. Additional exam requirements/recommendations for international students: Required—TOEFL (minimum score 570 paper-based); Recommended—IELTS (minimum score 6.5). *Application deadline:* For fall admission, 2/4 for domestic and international students. Application fee: $30. Electronic applications accepted. *Expenses:* Contact institution. *Financial support:* Fellowships, career-related internships or fieldwork, institutionally sponsored loans, scholarships/grants, and tuition waivers (full and partial) available. Financial award application deadline: 2/4. *Faculty research:* Institutional, Constitutional and human rights in European Union law; biomedical law and reproductive rights; data protection law; comparative and international business law and the regulation of business environments;. *Unit head:* Dr. Karoly Bard, Head of Department, 36 1 327-3294, Fax: 361-327-3198, E-mail: legalst@ceu.edu. *Application contact:* Zsuzsanna Jaszberenyi, Department Coordinator, 361-327-3272, Fax: 361-327-3198, E-mail: admissions@ceu.edu.
Website: http://legal.ceu.edu

Champlain College, Graduate Studies, Burlington, VT 05402-0670. Offers business (MBA); digital forensic science (MS); early childhood education (M Ed); emergent media (MFA, MS); executive leadership (MS); health care administration (MS); information security operations (MS); law (MS); mediation and applied conflict studies (MS). MS in emergent media program held in Shanghai. *Program availability:* Part-time, online learning. *Degree requirements:* For master's, capstone project. *Entrance requirements:* Additional exam requirements/recommendations for international students: Required—TOEFL (minimum score 550 paper-based; 80 iBT). Electronic applications accepted.

Chapman University, Fowler School of Law, Orange, CA 92866. Offers advocacy and dispute resolution (JD); business law (LL M, JD); criminal law (JD); entertainment and media law (LL M); entertainment law (JD); environmental, land use, and real estate law (JD); international and comparative law (LL M); international law (JD); law (JD); prosecutorial science (LL M); tax law (JD); taxation (LL M); trial advocacy (LL M); JD/MBA; JD/MFA. *Accreditation:* ABA. *Program availability:* Part-time. *Faculty:* 44 full-time (18 women), 22 part-time/adjunct (6 women). *Students:* 471 full-time (252 women), 38 part-time (19 women); includes 208 minority (8 Black or African American, non-Hispanic/Latino; 3 American Indian or Alaska Native, non-Hispanic/Latino; 76 Asian, non-Hispanic/Latino; 92 Hispanic/Latino; 29 Two or more races, non-Hispanic/Latino), 13 international. Average age 26. 1,499 applicants, 50% accepted, 190 enrolled. In 2016, 21 master's, 159 doctorates awarded. *Entrance requirements:* For doctorate, LSAT. Additional exam requirements/recommendations for international students: Required—TOEFL (minimum score 600 paper-based; 100 iBT). *Application deadline:* For fall admission, 4/15 priority date for domestic students. Applications are processed on a rolling basis. Electronic applications accepted. *Expenses:* Contact institution. *Financial*

support: Fellowships, Federal Work-Study, and scholarships/grants available. Financial award applicants required to submit FAFSA. *Unit head:* Matthew J. Parlow, Dean, 714-628-2678, E-mail: parlow@chapman.edu. *Application contact:* Grace Alcantara, Assistant Dean of Admissions and Diversity Initiatives, 714-628-2500, E-mail: lawadmission@chapman.edu.
Website: http://www.chapman.edu/law/

Charleston School of Law, Graduate and Professional Programs, Charleston, SC 29403. Offers admiralty and maritime law (LL M); law (JD). *Faculty:* 25 full-time (13 women), 45 part-time/adjunct (18 women). *Students:* 363 full-time (189 women), 53 part-time (34 women). *Entrance requirements:* For doctorate, LSAT, two letters of recommendation, personal statement, current resume, official transcripts. *Application deadline:* For fall admission, 6/1 for domestic students; for spring admission, 11/1 for domestic students. Applications are processed on a rolling basis. Electronic applications accepted. *Expenses: Tuition:* Full-time $40,596; part-time $16,309 per semester. *Required fees:* $120; $60 per semester. *Financial support:* Scholarships/grants available. *Application contact:* Jacqueline B. Bell, Assistant Dean of Admission, 843-377-2143, Fax: 843-329-4091, E-mail: info@charlestonlaw.edu.

City University of New York School of Law, Professional Program, Long Island City, NY 11101-4356. Offers JD, JD/MIA, JD/MPA. *Accreditation:* ABA. *Program availability:* Part-time, evening/weekend. *Faculty:* 47 full-time (30 women), 3 part-time/adjunct (all women). *Students:* 336 full-time (217 women), 88 part-time (50 women); includes 205 minority (55 Black or African American, non-Hispanic/Latino; 3 American Indian or Alaska Native, non-Hispanic/Latino; 50 Asian, non-Hispanic/Latino; 81 Hispanic/Latino; 16 Two or more races, non-Hispanic/Latino), 14 international. Average age 29. 1,427 applicants, 46% accepted, 193 enrolled. In 2016, 104 doctorates awarded. *Entrance requirements:* For doctorate, LSAT, CAS report, bachelor's degree. Additional exam requirements/recommendations for international students: Recommended—TOEFL. *Application deadline:* For fall admission, 6/15 priority date for domestic students. Applications are processed on a rolling basis. Application fee: $60. Electronic applications accepted. *Expenses:* Tuition, state resident: full-time $14,663; part-time $10,028 per year. Tuition, nonresident: full-time $23,983; part-time $16,448 per year. *Required fees:* $563; $173.95 per term. *Financial support:* In 2016–17, 171 students received support, including 37 fellowships (averaging $13,849 per year), 18 research assistantships (averaging $839 per year); Federal Work-Study, scholarships/grants, tuition waivers (full and partial), and unspecified assistantships also available. Support available to part-time students. Financial award application deadline: 5/1; financial award applicants required to submit FAFSA. *Faculty research:* Capital punishment, domestic violence, indigenous land rights, cross cultural lawyering, LGBT issues, aging, ecology, international human rights, pedagogy, environmental justice. *Unit head:* Mary Lu Bilek, Dean/Professor of Law, 718-340-4201, Fax: 718-340-4482. *Application contact:* Degna P. Levister, Assistant Dean of Admissions and Enrollment Management, 718-340-4210, Fax: 718-340-4435, E-mail: admissions@law.cuny.edu.
Website: http://www.law.cuny.edu/

Cleveland State University, Cleveland-Marshall College of Law, Cleveland, OH 44115. Offers LL M, MLS, JD, Certificate, JD/MAES, JD/MBA, JD/MPA, JD/MSES, JD/MUPDD. *Accreditation:* ABA. *Program availability:* Part-time, evening/weekend. *Faculty:* 34 full-time (17 women), 61 part-time/adjunct (16 women). *Students:* 240 full-time (113 women), 140 part-time (83 women); includes 75 minority (40 Black or African American, non-Hispanic/Latino; 10 Asian, non-Hispanic/Latino; 17 Hispanic/Latino; 8 Two or more races, non-Hispanic/Latino), 4 international. Average age 28. 711 applicants, 44% accepted, 118 enrolled. In 2016, 10 master's, 115 doctorates, 2 Certificates awarded. *Degree requirements:* For master's, thesis for graduates of U.S. law schools (for LL M); 30 credits, 6 in required courses (for MLS); for doctorate, 90 credits (41 in required courses). *Entrance requirements:* For master's, JD or LL B (for LL M); bachelor's degree (for MLS); for doctorate, LSAT, bachelor's degree. Additional exam requirements/recommendations for international students: Required—TOEFL (minimum score 550 paper-based; 78 iBT), TOEFL (minimum score 600 paper-based, 100 iBT) or IELTS (minimum score 7) for LL M. *Application deadline:* For fall admission, 5/1 for domestic and international students. Applications are processed on a rolling basis. Application fee: $0. Electronic applications accepted. *Expenses:* Contact institution. *Financial support:* In 2016–17, 198 students received support, including 17 fellowships (averaging $2,500 per year), 34 research assistantships, 7 teaching assistantships with partial tuition reimbursements available (averaging $6,700 per year); career-related internships or fieldwork, Federal Work-Study, scholarships/grants, and unspecified assistantships also available. Support available to part-time students. Financial award application deadline: 5/1; financial award applicants required to submit FAFSA. *Faculty research:* Health law, international law, Constitutional law, criminal law, business law. *Unit head:* Craig M. Boise, Dean, 216-687-2300, Fax: 216-687-6881, E-mail: c.boise@csuohio.edu. *Application contact:* Christopher Lucak, Assistant Dean for Admission and Financial Aid, 216-687-2304, Fax: 216-687-6881, E-mail: law.admissions@csuohio.edu.
Website: http://www.law.csuohio.edu/

The College of William and Mary, William and Mary Law School, Williamsburg, VA 23187-8795. Offers LL M, JD, JD/MA, JD/MBA, JD/MPP. *Accreditation:* ABA. *Faculty:* 44 full-time (19 women), 41 part-time/adjunct (10 women). *Students:* 654 full-time (351 women), 15 part-time (10 women); includes 76 minority (24 Black or African American, non-Hispanic/Latino; 11 Asian, non-Hispanic/Latino; 27 Hispanic/Latino; 14 Two or more races, non-Hispanic/Latino), 49 international. Average age 25. 4,833 applicants, 38% accepted, 238 enrolled. In 2016, 33 master's, 178 doctorates awarded. *Degree requirements:* For doctorate, major paper. *Entrance requirements:* For master's, LL B, references; for doctorate, LSAT, baccalaureate degree, references. Additional exam requirements/recommendations for international students: Required—TOEFL (minimum score 600 paper-based; 100 iBT); Recommended—IELTS (minimum score 7). *Application deadline:* For fall admission, 3/1 priority date for domestic and international students. Application fee: $50. Electronic applications accepted. *Expenses:* Contact institution. *Financial support:* In 2016–17, 604 students received support, including 242 fellowships (averaging $4,000 per year), 62 research assistantships (averaging $2,419 per year), 35 teaching assistantships (averaging $5,391 per year); career-related internships or fieldwork, Federal Work-Study, and scholarships/grants also available. Financial award application deadline: 2/15; financial award applicants required to submit FAFSA. *Faculty research:* Constitutional law, criminal law, corporate law, international law, intellectual property law. *Total annual research expenditures:* $338,733. *Unit head:* Davison M. Douglas, Dean/Professor, 757-221-3790, Fax: 757-221-3261, E-mail: dmdoug@wm.edu. *Application contact:* Faye F. Shealy, Associate Dean for Admission, 757-221-3785, Fax: 757-221-3261, E-mail: ffshea@wm.edu.
Website: http://law.wm.edu/

Columbia University, School of Law, New York, NY 10027. Offers LL M, JD, JSD, JD/M Phil, JD/MA, JD/MBA, JD/MFA, JD/MIA, JD/MPA, JD/MPH, JD/MSW. *Accreditation:* ABA. *Entrance requirements:* For doctorate, LSAT (for JD). Electronic applications accepted. *Expenses:* Contact institution. *Faculty research:* Human rights, law and philosophy, corporate governance, regulation of the workplace, death penalty.

Concord Law School, Program in Law, Los Angeles, CA 90024. Offers EJD, JD. *Program availability:* Part-time, evening/weekend, online learning. *Degree requirements:* For doctorate, comprehensive exam. *Entrance requirements:* For doctorate, online admissions test. Additional exam requirements/recommendations for international students: Required—TOEFL (minimum score 520 paper-based). Electronic applications accepted.

Cornell University, Cornell Law School, Ithaca, NY 14853-4901. Offers LL M, JD, JSD, JD/DESS, JD/LL M, JD/MA, JD/MBA, JD/MILR, JD/MLLP, JD/MLP, JD/MPA, JD/MRP, JD/Maitrise en Droit, JD/PhD. JD/MLLP offered jointly with Humboldt University, Berlin; JD/DESS offered jointly with Institut d'etudes Politiques de Paris ("Sciences Po") and Paris I. *Accreditation:* ABA. *Entrance requirements:* For doctorate, LSAT (for JD). Electronic applications accepted. *Expenses:* Contact institution. *Faculty research:* International law, Constitutional law, corporate laws, public interest law, feminist legal theory.

Cornell University, Graduate School, Graduate Field in the Law School, Ithaca, NY 14853. Offers JSD. *Entrance requirements:* For doctorate, JD, LL M, or equivalent; 2 letters of recommendation. Additional exam requirements/recommendations for international students: Required—TOEFL (minimum score 550 paper-based). Electronic applications accepted. *Expenses:* Contact institution. *Faculty research:* International economic integration (World Trade Organization and European Union), international commercial arbitration, feminist jurisprudence, human rights.

Creighton University, School of Law, Omaha, NE 68178-0001. Offers MS, JD, Certificate, JD/MBA, JD/MS. *Accreditation:* ABA. *Program availability:* Part-time. *Faculty:* 29 full-time (10 women), 16 part-time/adjunct (4 women). *Students:* 299 full-time (130 women), 8 part-time (1 woman); includes 65 minority (8 Black or African American, non-Hispanic/Latino; 1 American Indian or Alaska Native, non-Hispanic/Latino; 11 Asian, non-Hispanic/Latino; 32 Hispanic/Latino; 13 Two or more races, non-Hispanic/Latino), 2 international. Average age 25. 923 applicants, 74% accepted, 107 enrolled. In 2016, 129 doctorates awarded. *Entrance requirements:* For doctorate, LSAT, bachelor's degree. Additional exam requirements/recommendations for international students: Recommended—TOEFL. *Application deadline:* For fall admission, 5/1 priority date for domestic and international students; for summer admission, 4/1 priority date for domestic and international students. Applications are processed on a rolling basis. Electronic applications accepted. Application fee is waived when completed online. *Expenses:* Contact institution. *Financial support:* In 2016–17, 216 students received support. Career-related internships or fieldwork, institutionally sponsored loans, and scholarships/grants available. Support available to part-time students. Financial award application deadline: 7/1; financial award applicants required to submit FAFSA. *Faculty research:* Conflict of laws, international law, evidence, cyber warfare, Constitutional law. *Unit head:* Paul E. McGreal, Dean and Professor of Law, 402-280-2874, Fax: 402-280-3161. *Application contact:* Andrea D. Bashara, Assistant Dean, 402-280-2586, Fax: 402-280-3161, E-mail: bashara@creighton.edu.
Website: http://law.creighton.edu

Dalhousie University, Faculty of Graduate Studies, Dalhousie Law School, Halifax, NS B3H 4H9, Canada. Offers LL M, JSD, LL B/MBA, LL B/MLIS, LL B/MPA. *Program availability:* Part-time. *Degree requirements:* For master's, thesis or alternative; for doctorate, thesis/dissertation. *Entrance requirements:* For master's, LL B; for doctorate, LL M. Additional exam requirements/recommendations for international students: Required—1 of 5 approved tests: TOEFL, IELTS, CANTEST, CAEL, Michigan English Language Assessment Battery. Electronic applications accepted. *Expenses:* Contact institution. *Faculty research:* Marine and environmental law, health law, the family law program.

DePaul University, College of Law, Chicago, IL 60604-2287. Offers health law (LL M); intellectual property law (LL M); international law (LL M); law (JD); taxation (LL M); JD/MA; JD/MBA; JD/MPS; JD/MS. *Accreditation:* ABA. *Program availability:* Part-time, evening/weekend. *Entrance requirements:* For doctorate, LSAT, LSAC applicant evaluation/letter of recommendation, personal statement, resume. Additional exam requirements/recommendations for international students: Required—TOEFL (minimum score 577 paper-based; 90 iBT), IELTS (minimum score 6.5). Electronic applications accepted. *Expenses:* Contact institution.

Drake University, Law School, Des Moines, IA 50311-4505. Offers LL M, MJ, JD, JD/MBA, JD/MPA, JD/Pharm D. *Accreditation:* ABA. *Program availability:* Part-time. *Faculty:* 28 full-time (10 women), 18 part-time/adjunct (5 women). *Students:* 306 full-time (153 women), 23 part-time (16 women); includes 49 minority (17 Black or African American, non-Hispanic/Latino; 1 American Indian or Alaska Native, non-Hispanic/Latino; 5 Asian, non-Hispanic/Latino; 16 Hispanic/Latino; 10 Two or more races, non-Hispanic/Latino), 7 international. Average age 27. 521 applicants, 44% accepted, 117 enrolled. In 2016, 1 master's, 106 doctorates awarded. *Degree requirements:* For doctorate, 2 internships. *Entrance requirements:* For doctorate, LSAT, LSDAS report. Additional exam requirements/recommendations for international students: Required—TOEFL (minimum score 560 paper-based), TWE. *Application deadline:* For fall admission, 4/1 priority date for domestic and international students. Applications are processed on a rolling basis. Application fee: $40. Electronic applications accepted. *Expenses:* Contact institution. *Financial support:* In 2016–17, 20 research assistantships (averaging $757 per year), 6 teaching assistantships (averaging $2,142 per year) were awarded; career-related internships or fieldwork, Federal Work-Study, institutionally sponsored loans, scholarships/grants, and tuition waivers (full and partial) also available. Support available to part-time students. Financial award application deadline: 3/1; financial award applicants required to submit FAFSA. *Faculty research:* Constitutional law, environmental law, agricultural law, computers and the law, bioethics and health law. *Unit head:* Jerry Anderson, Dean, 515-271-2658, Fax: 515-271-4118, E-mail: jerry.anderson@drake.edu. *Application contact:* Kara Blanchard, Director of Admission, 515-271-2953, Fax: 515-271-2530, E-mail: kara.blanchard@drake.edu.
Website: http://www.law.drake.edu/

Duke University, School of Law, Durham, NC 27708. Offers LL M, MJS, JD, SJD, JD/LL M, JD/MA, JD/MBA, JD/MEM, JD/MPP, JD/MS, JD/MTS, JD/PhD, MD/JD. LL M and SJD offered only to international students; MJS offered only to sitting judges. *Accreditation:* ABA. *Faculty:* 83 full-time (39 women), 35 part-time/adjunct (11 women). *Students:* 676 full-time; includes 160 minority (46 Black or African American, non-Hispanic/Latino; 2 American Indian or Alaska Native, non-Hispanic/Latino; 69 Asian, non-Hispanic/Latino; 39 Hispanic/Latino; 1 Native Hawaiian or other Pacific Islander, non-Hispanic/Latino; 3 Two or more races, non-Hispanic/Latino), 44 international. Average age 24. 4,819 applicants, 23% accepted, 225 enrolled. In 2016, 131 master's, 222 doctorates awarded. *Degree requirements:* For doctorate, thesis/dissertation (for some programs). *Entrance requirements:* For doctorate, LSAT (for JD). Additional exam requirements/recommendations for international students: Required—TOEFL (minimum score 600 paper-based). *Application deadline:* For fall admission, 2/15 for domestic and international students. Applications are processed on a rolling basis. Application fee: $70. Electronic applications accepted. *Expenses:* Contact institution. *Financial support:* In 2016–17, 560 students received support. Institutionally sponsored loans, scholarships/grants, and unspecified assistantships available. Financial award application deadline: 3/15; financial award applicants required to submit FAFSA. *Faculty research:* International and comparative law; Constitutional and public law; intellectual property law; science and technology law; business, finance, and corporate law; environmental law and policy; criminal law; health care law and policy. *Unit head:* David F. Levi, Dean/Professor of Law, 919-613-7001, Fax: 919-613-7158. *Application contact:*

Law

William J. Hoye, Associate Dean for Admissions and Student Affairs, 919-613-7020, Fax: 919-613-7257, E-mail: hoye@law.duke.edu.
Website: http://www.law.duke.edu/

Dunlap-Stone University, Graduate Law Center, Phoenix, AZ 85024. Offers regulatory trade compliance (M Sc); U.S. regulatory trade law (LL M).

Duquesne University, Bayer School of Natural and Environmental Sciences, Program in Forensic Science and Law, Pittsburgh, PA 15282-0001. Offers MS. *Faculty:* 5 full-time (3 women), 15 part-time/adjunct (9 women). *Students:* 21 full-time (18 women); includes 2 minority (1 Hispanic/Latino; 1 Two or more races, non-Hispanic/Latino). Average age 22. In 2016, 10 master's awarded. *Degree requirements:* For master's, comprehensive exam. *Entrance requirements:* For master's, SAT or ACT, recommendation form; minimum total QPA of 3.0, 2.5 in math and science. *Application deadline:* For fall admission, 7/1 for domestic and international students. Applications are processed on a rolling basis. Application fee: $0. Electronic applications accepted. *Expenses:* $1,264 per credit. *Financial support:* In 2016–17, 10 students received support. Career-related internships or fieldwork and scholarships/grants available. Financial award application deadline: 5/1. *Faculty research:* Extraction protocols, mass spectrometry, synthetic fiber analysis, synthetic polymer characterization, trace analysis, amplification of DNA, methods for labeling DNA, construction of a genetic profile, experiential exploration of mitochondrial DNA, the Y-chromosome, amelogenin. *Total annual research expenditures:* $50,419. *Unit head:* Dr. Federick W. Fochtman, Director, 412-396-6373, E-mail: fochtman@duq.edu. *Application contact:* Valerie L. Lijewski, Assistant Director/Academic Advisor, 412-396-1084, E-mail: lijewski@duq.edu.
Website: http://www.duq.edu/academics/schools/natural-and-environmental-sciences/academic-programs/forensic-science-and-law

Duquesne University, School of Law, Pittsburgh, PA 15282-0700. Offers American law for foreign lawyers (LL M); law (JD); JD/M Div; JD/MBA; JD/MS; JD/MSEM. JD/M Div offered jointly with Pittsburgh Theological Seminary. *Accreditation:* ABA. *Program availability:* Part-time, evening/weekend. *Faculty:* 28 full-time (13 women), 32 part-time/adjunct (9 women). *Students:* 392 full-time (211 women); includes 30 minority (6 Black or African American, non-Hispanic/Latino; 1 American Indian or Alaska Native, non-Hispanic/Latino; 5 Asian, non-Hispanic/Latino; 8 Hispanic/Latino; 10 Two or more races, non-Hispanic/Latino), 5 international. Average age 26. 825 applicants, 61% accepted, 127 enrolled. In 2016, 1 master's, 124 doctorates awarded. *Entrance requirements:* For doctorate, LSAT. Additional exam requirements/recommendations for international students: Required—TOEFL. *Application deadline:* For fall admission, 3/1 priority date for domestic and international students. Applications are processed on a rolling basis. Application fee: $0. Electronic applications accepted. *Expenses:* $15,538 tuition per semester (JD part-time day and evening); $20,219 tuition per semester (JD day); $11,675 tuition per semester (LL M). *Financial support:* Research assistantships with partial tuition reimbursements, teaching assistantships with partial tuition reimbursements, career-related internships or fieldwork, scholarships/grants, and tuition waivers (partial) available. Support available to part-time students. Financial award application deadline: 5/31; financial award applicants required to submit FAFSA. *Faculty research:* Constitutional law, law and religion, intellectual property and patents, neuroscience and law, civil and criminal law and procedure, feminist perspective on environmental law. *Total annual research expenditures:* $100,000. *Unit head:* Nancy Perkins, Interim Dean, 412-396-6285, Fax: 412-396-6283, E-mail: perkins@duq.edu. *Application contact:* Office of Admissions, 412-396-6296, Fax: 412-396-6659, E-mail: lawadmissions@duq.edu.
Website: http://www.duq.edu/academics/schools/law

Elon University, Program in Law, Elon, NC 27244-2010. Offers JD. *Accreditation:* ABA. *Faculty:* 34 full-time (15 women), 55 part-time/adjunct (20 women). *Students:* 335 full-time (195 women); includes 75 minority (53 Black or African American, non-Hispanic/Latino; 4 American Indian or Alaska Native, non-Hispanic/Latino; 2 Asian, non-Hispanic/Latino; 16 Hispanic/Latino), 1 international. Average age 26. 744 applicants, 45% accepted, 128 enrolled. In 2016, 89 doctorates awarded. *Entrance requirements:* For doctorate, LSAT, LSDAS. Additional exam requirements/recommendations for international students: Required—TOEFL (minimum score 550 paper-based; 79 iBT). *Application deadline:* For fall admission, 7/30 for domestic students; for spring admission, 4/1 priority date for domestic students. Applications are processed on a rolling basis. Application fee: $50. Electronic applications accepted. *Financial support:* Scholarships/grants available. Financial award applicants required to submit FAFSA. *Faculty research:* Quality of life and job satisfaction, civil procedure, damages, assessment for development of instruments, psychological types. *Unit head:* Dr. Luke Bierman, Dean, 336-279-9201, E-mail: lbierman@elon.edu. *Application contact:* Alan Woodlief, Associate Dean of School of Law/Director of Law School Admissions, 336-279-9203, E-mail: awoodlief@elon.edu.
Website: http://www.elon.edu/law

Emory University, School of Law, Atlanta, GA 30322-2770. Offers LL M, JD, Certificate, JD/Certificate, JD/LL M, JD/M Div, JD/MA, JD/MBA, JD/MPH, JD/MTS, JD/PhD. *Accreditation:* ABA. *Entrance requirements:* For doctorate, LSAT, 2 letters of recommendation. Additional exam requirements/recommendations for international students: Required—TOEFL (minimum score 600 paper-based). Electronic applications accepted. *Expenses:* Contact institution. *Faculty research:* Law and economics, law and religion, international law, human rights, feminism and legal theory.

Empire College, School of Law, Santa Rosa, CA 95403. Offers MLS, JD.

Faulkner University, Thomas Goode Jones School of Law, Montgomery, AL 36109-3398. Offers JD. *Accreditation:* ABA. *Entrance requirements:* For doctorate, LSAT. Additional exam requirements/recommendations for international students: Recommended—TOEFL. Electronic applications accepted.

Florida Agricultural and Mechanical University, College of Law, Tallahassee, FL 32307-3200. Offers JD. *Accreditation:* ABA. *Program availability:* Part-time, evening/weekend. *Entrance requirements:* For doctorate, LSAT, LSDAS, 2 letters of recommendation. Additional exam requirements/recommendations for international students: Required—TOEFL. *Expenses:* Contact institution.

Florida Coastal School of Law, Professional Program, Jacksonville, FL 32256. Offers JD. *Accreditation:* ABA. *Program availability:* Part-time. *Entrance requirements:* For doctorate, LSAT. Additional exam requirements/recommendations for international students: Recommended—TOEFL (minimum score 600 paper-based). Electronic applications accepted. *Expenses:* Contact institution. *Faculty research:* Law and business, law technology and intellectual property, juvenile justice and family law, constitutional law, labor law.

Florida International University, College of Law, Miami, FL 33199. Offers American law for foreign lawyers (LL M); law (JD); JD/MA; JD/MIB. *Accreditation:* ABA. *Program availability:* Part-time, evening/weekend. *Faculty:* 30 full-time (14 women), 42 part-time/adjunct (11 women). *Students:* 494 full-time (262 women), 22 part-time (14 women); includes 319 minority (24 Black or African American, non-Hispanic/Latino; 1 American Indian or Alaska Native, non-Hispanic/Latino; 11 Asian, non-Hispanic/Latino; 278 Hispanic/Latino; 5 Two or more races, non-Hispanic/Latino), 18 international. Average age 27. 2,019 applicants, 30% accepted, 204 enrolled. In 2016, 20 master's, 157 doctorates awarded. *Entrance requirements:* For doctorate, LSAT, 3 letters of recommendation. Additional exam requirements/recommendations for international students: Recommended—TOEFL. *Application deadline:* For fall admission, 5/1 for domestic and international students. Applications are processed on a rolling basis. Application fee: $20. Electronic applications accepted. *Expenses:* Contact institution. *Financial support:* Application deadline: 3/1; applicants required to submit FAFSA. *Unit head:* Chris Carbot, Assistant Dean for Administration, 305-348-1118, Fax: 305-348-1159, E-mail: christopher.carbot1@fiu.edu. *Application contact:* Chris Carbot, Assistant Dean for Administration, 305-348-1118, Fax: 305-348-1159, E-mail: christopher.carbot1@fiu.edu.
Website: http://law.fiu.edu

Florida State University, College of Law, Tallahassee, FL 32306-1601. Offers American law for foreign lawyers (LL M); business law (LL M); environmental law and policy (LL M); law (JM, JD); JD/MAES; JD/MBA; JD/MPA; JD/MS; JD/MSI; JD/MSP; JD/MSW. *Accreditation:* ABA. *Program availability:* 100% online. *Faculty:* 57 full-time (29 women), 30 part-time/adjunct (7 women). *Students:* 550 full-time (255 women), 52 part-time (24 women); includes 174 minority (42 Black or African American, non-Hispanic/Latino; 1 American Indian or Alaska Native, non-Hispanic/Latino; 15 Asian, non-Hispanic/Latino; 91 Hispanic/Latino; 25 Two or more races, non-Hispanic/Latino), 18 international. Average age 25. 1,929 applicants, 35% accepted, 174 enrolled. In 2016, 11 master's, 195 doctorates awarded. Terminal master's awarded for partial completion of doctoral program. *Degree requirements:* For master's, comprehensive exam (for some programs). *Entrance requirements:* For master's, one graduate-level standardized test (for JM), JD or equivalent degree (for LL M); for doctorate, LSAT (for JD). Additional exam requirements/recommendations for international students: Required—TOEFL (minimum score 600 paper-based; 80 iBT), IELTS (minimum score 6.5). *Application deadline:* For fall admission, 7/15 for domestic students, 5/15 for international students. Applications are processed on a rolling basis. Electronic applications accepted. *Expenses:* $20,683. *Financial support:* In 2016–17, 406 students received support, including 4 fellowships with full tuition reimbursements available (averaging $20,683 per year), 39 research assistantships (averaging $1,557 per year), 13 teaching assistantships (averaging $1,451 per year); career-related internships or fieldwork, scholarships/grants, and unspecified assistantships also available. Financial award application deadline: 3/1; financial award applicants required to submit FAFSA. *Faculty research:* Business law; environmental, energy and land use law; international law; criminal law. *Total annual research expenditures:* $120,000. *Unit head:* Erin O'Hara O'Connor, Dean, 850-644-3400, Fax: 850-644-5487, E-mail: eoconnor@law.fsu.edu. *Application contact:* Jennifer L. Kessinger, Director of Admissions and Records, 850-644-3787, Fax: 850-644-7284, E-mail: jkessing@law.fsu.edu.
Website: http://www.law.fsu.edu/

Fordham University, School of Law, New York, NY 10023. Offers banking, corporate and finance law (LL M); corporate compliance (MSL); fashion law (MSL); intellectual property and information law (LL M); international business and trade law (LL M); law (JD); JD/MA; JD/MBA; JD/MSW. *Accreditation:* ABA. *Program availability:* Part-time, evening/weekend. *Entrance requirements:* For doctorate, LSAT. Additional exam requirements/recommendations for international students: Required—TOEFL. Electronic applications accepted. *Expenses:* Contact institution. *Faculty research:* Intellectual property, business law, international law.

Friends University, Graduate School, Wichita, KS 67213. Offers family therapy (MSFT); global business administration (MBA), including accounting, business law, change management, health care leadership, management information systems, supply chain management and logistics; health care leadership (MHCL); management information systems (MMIS); professional business administration (MBA), including accounting, business law, change management, health care leadership, management information systems, supply chain management and logistics. *Program availability:* Part-time, evening/weekend, online learning. *Degree requirements:* For master's, research project. *Entrance requirements:* For master's, bachelor's degree from accredited institution, official transcripts, interview with program director, letter(s) of recommendation. Additional exam requirements/recommendations for international students: Required—TOEFL (minimum score 560 paper-based). Electronic applications accepted.

George Mason University, Antonin Scalia Law School, Arlington, VA 22201. Offers global antitrust law and economics (LL M); intellectual property (LL M); law (JD); law and economics (LL M); U.S. law (LL M); JD/MA; JD/MPP; JD/PhD. *Accreditation:* ABA. *Program availability:* Part-time, evening/weekend. *Faculty:* 41 full-time (9 women), 84 part-time/adjunct (20 women). *Students:* 382 full-time (172 women), 159 part-time (83 women). 2,587 applicants, 24% accepted, 179 enrolled. *Entrance requirements:* For master's, JD or international equivalent; for doctorate, LSAT, baccalaureate degree or international equivalent. Additional exam requirements/recommendations for international students: Required—TOEFL or IELTS (for LL M applicants only). *Application deadline:* For fall admission, 4/1 for domestic and international students. Applications are processed on a rolling basis. Application fee: $0. Electronic applications accepted. *Expenses:* Contact institution. *Financial support:* Fellowships, research assistantships, career-related internships or fieldwork, scholarships/grants, and tuition waivers (full and partial) available. Support available to part-time students. *Faculty research:* Law and economics; infrastructure protection, including homeland and national security; intellectual property. *Unit head:* Henry N. Butler, Dean, 703-993-8644, Fax: 703-993-8088. *Application contact:* Alison H. Price, Associate Dean for Admissions and Enrollment Management, 703-993-8010, Fax: 703-993-8088, E-mail: lawadmit@gmu.edu.
Website: http://www.law.gmu.edu/

Georgetown University, Law Center, Washington, DC 20001. Offers environmental law (LL M); global health law (LL M); global health law and international institutions (LL M); individualized study (LL M); international business and economic law (LL M); law (JD, SJD); national security law (LL M); securities and financial regulation (LL M); taxation (LL M); JD/LL M; JD/MA; JD/MBA; JD/MPH; JD/PhD. *Accreditation:* ABA. *Program availability:* Part-time, evening/weekend. *Degree requirements:* For master's, thesis; for doctorate, thesis/dissertation (for some programs). *Entrance requirements:* For master's, JD, LL B, or first law degree earned in country of origin; for doctorate, LSAT (for JD). Additional exam requirements/recommendations for international students: Required—TOEFL. *Expenses:* Contact institution. *Faculty research:* Constitutional law, legal history, jurisprudence.

The George Washington University, Law School, Washington, DC 20052. Offers law (SJD); national security and U.S. foreign relations (LL M). *Accreditation:* ABA. *Program availability:* Part-time, evening/weekend. *Faculty:* 84 full-time (33 women). *Students:* 1,622 full-time (867 women), 315 part-time (150 women); includes 482 minority (164 Black or African American, non-Hispanic/Latino; 15 American Indian or Alaska Native, non-Hispanic/Latino; 234 Asian, non-Hispanic/Latino; 55 Hispanic/Latino; 4 Native Hawaiian or other Pacific Islander, non-Hispanic/Latino; 10 Two or more races, non-Hispanic/Latino), 222 international. Average age 27. 223 applicants, 100% accepted, 133 enrolled. In 2016, 166 master's, 1 doctorate awarded. *Degree requirements:* For doctorate, thesis/dissertation (for some programs). *Entrance requirements:* For master's, JD or equivalent; for doctorate, LSAT (for JD), LL M or equivalent (for SJD). *Application deadline:* For fall admission, 3/1 for domestic students. Applications are

processed on a rolling basis. Application fee: $75. *Expenses:* Contact institution. *Financial support:* Research assistantships, career-related internships or fieldwork, Federal Work-Study, institutionally sponsored loans, scholarships/grants, and tuition waivers (full and partial) available. Support available to part-time students. Financial award application deadline: 3/1; financial award applicants required to submit CSS PROFILE or FAFSA. *Unit head:* Blake D. Morant, Dean, E-mail: bmorant@law.gwu.edu. *Application contact:* Sophia Sim, Assistant Dean of Admissions and Financial Aid, 202-994-7235, Fax: 202-739-0624, E-mail: ssim@law.gwu.edu.
Website: http://www.law.gwu.edu/

Georgia State University, College of Law, Atlanta, GA 30302-4037. Offers JD, JD/MA, JD/MBA, JD/MCRP, JD/MHA, JD/MPA, JD/MSHA. *Accreditation:* ABA. *Program availability:* Part-time, evening/weekend. *Faculty:* 56 full-time (32 women). *Students:* 647 full-time (321 women), 23 part-time (16 women); includes 195 minority (89 Black or African American, non-Hispanic/Latino; 1 American Indian or Alaska Native, non-Hispanic/Latino; 47 Asian, non-Hispanic/Latino; 46 Hispanic/Latino; 12 Two or more races, non-Hispanic/Latino), 15 international. Average age 29. 2,053 applicants, 30% accepted, 245 enrolled. In 2016, 203 doctorates awarded. *Entrance requirements:* For doctorate, LSAT. Additional exam requirements/recommendations for international students: Recommended—TOEFL. *Application deadline:* For fall admission, 3/15 for domestic students, 3/15 priority date for international students. Applications are processed on a rolling basis. Application fee: $50. Electronic applications accepted. *Expenses:* Contact institution. *Financial support:* In 2016–17, research assistantships with tuition reimbursements (averaging $2,500 per year), teaching assistantships (averaging $2,500 per year) were awarded; scholarships/grants, tuition waivers, and unspecified assistantships also available. Financial award application deadline: 4/1; financial award applicants required to submit FAFSA. *Faculty research:* Health law; land use, urban planning and environmental law; intellectual property; criminal law and procedure; Constitutional law. *Unit head:* Dr. Steven J. Kaminshine, Dean, College of Law, 404-413-9035, Fax: 404-413-9227, E-mail: skaminshine@gsu.edu. *Application contact:* Dr. Cheryl Jester-George, Senior Director of Admissions, 404-413-9004, Fax: 404-413-9203, E-mail: cjgeorge@gsu.edu.
Website: http://law.gsu.edu/

Golden Gate University, School of Law, San Francisco, CA 94105-2968. Offers environmental law (LL M); estate planning (LL M); intellectual property law (LL M); international legal studies (LL M, SJD); law (JD); taxation (LL M); U.S. legal studies (LL M); JD/MBA; JD/PhD. *Accreditation:* ABA. *Program availability:* Part-time, evening/weekend. *Faculty:* 41 full-time (19 women), 67 part-time/adjunct (27 women). *Students:* 246 full-time (142 women), 228 part-time (133 women); includes 213 minority (28 Black or African American, non-Hispanic/Latino; 2 American Indian or Alaska Native, non-Hispanic/Latino; 68 Asian, non-Hispanic/Latino; 84 Hispanic/Latino; 7 Native Hawaiian or other Pacific Islander, non-Hispanic/Latino; 24 Two or more races, non-Hispanic/Latino), 58 international. Average age 31. 1,473 applicants, 65% accepted, 189 enrolled. In 2016, 54 master's, 117 doctorates awarded. *Degree requirements:* For doctorate, thesis/dissertation (for some programs). *Entrance requirements:* For doctorate, LSAT (for JD). Additional exam requirements/recommendations for international students: Required—TOEFL (minimum score 600 paper-based). *Application deadline:* For fall admission, 8/18 for domestic students, 4/1 for international students; for spring admission, 1/12 for domestic students; for summer admission, 6/4 for domestic students. Applications are processed on a rolling basis. Electronic applications accepted. *Expenses:* Contact institution. *Financial support:* In 2016–17, 315 students received support. Fellowships, research assistantships, teaching assistantships, career-related internships or fieldwork, Federal Work-Study, institutionally sponsored loans, scholarships/grants, tuition waivers (full and partial), and unspecified assistantships available. Support available to part-time students. Financial award applicants required to submit FAFSA. *Faculty research:* International law, intellectual property law, environmental law, real estate, civil rights. *Unit head:* Rachel Van Cleave, Dean, 415-442-6601, Fax: 415-442-6609. *Application contact:* Greg Egertson, Associate Dean and Director of Admissions, 415-442-6636, Fax: 415-442-6609, E-mail: lawadmit@ggu.edu.
Website: http://www.ggu.edu/law/

Gonzaga University, School of Law, Spokane, WA 99220-3528. Offers JD. *Accreditation:* ABA. *Program availability:* Part-time. *Faculty:* 17 full-time (11 women), 15 part-time/adjunct (3 women). *Students:* 306 full-time (138 women), 2 part-time (1 woman); includes 49 minority (7 Black or African American, non-Hispanic/Latino; 2 American Indian or Alaska Native, non-Hispanic/Latino; 4 Asian, non-Hispanic/Latino; 20 Hispanic/Latino; 16 Two or more races, non-Hispanic/Latino), 5 international. Average age 27. 859 applicants, 57% accepted, 103 enrolled. In 2016, 113 doctorates awarded. *Degree requirements:* For doctorate, experiential learning. *Entrance requirements:* For doctorate, LSAT, bachelor's degree, all academic transcripts, 2-4 letters of recommendation, resume, personal statement. *Application deadline:* For fall admission, 4/15 priority date for domestic students. Application fee: $50. Electronic applications accepted. *Expenses:* $1,236 per credit. *Financial support:* In 2016–17, 279 students received support. Federal Work-Study and scholarships/grants available. Support available to part-time students. Financial award applicants required to submit FAFSA. *Faculty research:* Environmental law, business law, public interest law, tax law. *Unit head:* Jane Korn, Dean, 509-313-3700. *Application contact:* Susan Lee, Director of Admissions, 509-313-3734, E-mail: slee@lawschool.gonzaga.edu.
Website: http://www.law.gonzaga.edu

Harvard University, Law School, Graduate Programs in Law, Cambridge, MA 02138. Offers LL M, SJD. *Accreditation:* ABA. *Degree requirements:* For master's, thesis optional; for doctorate, thesis/dissertation. *Entrance requirements:* Additional exam requirements/recommendations for international students: Required—TOEFL. *Faculty research:* Corporation finance, national and international law, legal ethics, family law, criminal law, administrative law, constitutional law.

Harvard University, Law School, Professional Programs in Law, Cambridge, MA 02138. Offers international and comparative law (JD); law and business (JD); law and government (JD); law and social change (JD); law, science and technology (JD); JD/MALD; JD/MBA; JD/MPH; JD/MPP; JD/PhD. *Accreditation:* ABA. *Degree requirements:* For doctorate, 3rd-year paper. *Entrance requirements:* For doctorate, LSAT. *Faculty research:* Constitutional law, voting rights law, cyber law.

Hofstra University, Maurice A. Deane School of Law, Hempstead, NY 11549. Offers American legal studies (LL M); family law (LL M); health law and policy (LL M, MA); law (JD); JD/MBA. *Accreditation:* ABA. *Program availability:* Part-time, 100% online. *Faculty:* 41 full-time (22 women), 47 part-time/adjunct (9 women). *Students:* 692 full-time (377 women), 93 part-time (56 women); includes 216 minority (79 Black or African American, non-Hispanic/Latino; 3 American Indian or Alaska Native, non-Hispanic/Latino; 34 Asian, non-Hispanic/Latino; 87 Hispanic/Latino; 8 Native Hawaiian or other Pacific Islander, non-Hispanic/Latino; 5 Two or more races, non-Hispanic/Latino), 22 international. Average age 27. In 2016, 10 master's, 198 doctorates awarded. *Entrance requirements:* For doctorate, LSAT, letter of recommendation, personal statement, undergraduate transcripts. Additional exam requirements/recommendations for international students: Recommended—TOEFL (minimum score 600 paper-based; 100 iBT). *Application deadline:* For fall admission, 4/15 priority date for domestic and international students. Applications are processed on a rolling basis. Application fee: $75. Electronic applications accepted. *Expenses:* Contact institution. *Financial support:* In 2016–17, 508 students received support, including 491 fellowships with full and partial tuition reimbursements available (averaging $31,765 per year), 3 research assistantships with full and partial tuition reimbursements available (averaging $6,675 per year); career-related internships or fieldwork, Federal Work Study, institutionally sponsored loans, scholarships/grants, tuition waivers (full and partial), and unspecified assistantships also available. Support available to part-time students. Financial award applicants required to submit FAFSA. *Faculty research:* Family law; international law; constitutional law; legal ethics; health law. *Total annual research expenditures:* $59,468. *Unit head:* Gail Prudenti, Dean, 516-463-4068, E-mail: gail.prudenti@hofstra.edu. *Application contact:* Sunil Samuel, Assistant Vice President of Admissions, 516-463-4723, Fax: 516-463-4664.
Website: http://law.hofstra.edu/

Howard University, School of Law, Washington, DC 20008. Offers LL M, JD, JD/MBA. *Accreditation:* ABA. *Degree requirements:* For master's, one foreign language, thesis; for doctorate, thesis/dissertation (for some programs). *Entrance requirements:* For doctorate, LSAT. Additional exam requirements/recommendations for international students: Required—TOEFL. Electronic applications accepted. *Expenses:* Contact institution. *Faculty research:* Criminal law, family law, telecommunications, religion, antitrust.

Humphreys University, Drivon School of Law, Stockton, CA 95207-3896. Offers JD. *Program availability:* Part-time, evening/weekend. *Faculty:* 3 full-time (0 women), 20 part-time/adjunct (6 women). *Students:* 79 part-time (49 women); includes 34 minority (7 Black or African American, non-Hispanic/Latino; 7 Asian, non-Hispanic/Latino; 15 Hispanic/Latino; 5 Native Hawaiian or other Pacific Islander, non-Hispanic/Latino). Average age 36. 26 applicants, 81% accepted, 15 enrolled. In 2016, 30 doctorates awarded. *Entrance requirements:* For doctorate, LSAT, minimum GPA of 2.5. *Application deadline:* For fall admission, 9/3 priority date for domestic students; for winter admission, 12/3 priority date for domestic students; for summer admission, 6/3 priority date for domestic students. Applications are processed on a rolling basis. Application fee: $40. Electronic applications accepted. Application fee is waived when completed online. *Expenses:* Contact institution. *Financial support:* In 2016–17, 63 students received support. Federal Work-Study available. Support available to part-time students. Financial award application deadline: 9/1; financial award applicants required to submit FAFSA. *Unit head:* Leo Patrick Piggott, Dean, 209-235-2905, E-mail: ppiggott@humphreys.edu. *Application contact:* Santa Lopez-Minatre, Admission Counselor, 209-478-0800 Ext. 202, Fax: 209-478-8721, E-mail: slopez@humphreys.edu.
Website: http://www.humphreys.edu/academics/drivon-school-of-law/

Illinois Institute of Technology, Chicago-Kent College of Law, Chicago, IL 60661-3691. Offers family law (LL M); financial services law (LL M); international intellectual property law (LL M); law (JD); legal studies (JSD); taxation (LL M); U.S., international, and transnational law (LL M); JD/LL M; JD/MBA; JD/MPA; JD/MPH; JD/MS. *Accreditation:* ABA. *Program availability:* Part-time, evening/weekend. Terminal master's awarded for partial completion of doctoral program. *Entrance requirements:* For master's, 1st degree in law or certified license to practice law; for doctorate, LSAT. Additional exam requirements/recommendations for international students: Required—TOEFL (minimum score 600 paper-based; 100 iBT); Recommended—IELTS (minimum score 7). Electronic applications accepted. *Expenses:* Contact institution. *Faculty research:* Constitutional law, bioethics, environmental law, intellectual property.

Indiana University Bloomington, Maurer School of Law, Bloomington, IN 47405-7000. Offers comparative law (MCL); juridical science (SJD); law (LL M, JD); law and social sciences (PhD); legal studies (Certificate); JD/MA; JD/MBA; JD/MLS; JD/MPA; JD/MS; JD/MSES. PhD offered through University Graduate School. *Accreditation:* ABA. *Degree requirements:* For master's, thesis or practicum; for doctorate, thesis/dissertation (for some programs), research seminar (for JD). *Entrance requirements:* For master's, LSAT, 3 letters of recommendation, law degree or license to practice; for doctorate, LSAT. Additional exam requirements/recommendations for international students: Required—TOEFL (minimum score 560 paper-based; 80 iBT). Electronic applications accepted. *Faculty research:* Environmental risk assessment and policy analysis, information privacy and security, judicial independence, accountability, ethics.

Indiana University–Purdue University Indianapolis, Robert H. McKinney School of Law, Indianapolis, IN 46202. Offers advocacy skills (Certificate); American law for foreign lawyers (LL M); civil and human rights (Certificate); corporate and commercial law (LL M, Certificate); criminal law (Certificate); environmental and natural resources (Certificate); health law (Certificate); health law, policy and bioethics (LL M); intellectual property law (LL M, Certificate); international and comparative law (LL M, Certificate); international human rights law (LL M); law (MJ, JD, SJD); JD/M Phil; JD/MBA; JD/MD; JD/MHA; JD/MLS; JD/MPA; JD/MPH; JD/MSW. *Accreditation:* ABA. *Program availability:* Part-time. *Faculty:* 47 full-time (24 women), 40 part-time/adjunct (17 women). *Students:* 578 full-time (285 women), 328 part-time (154 women); includes 157 minority (71 Black or African American, non-Hispanic/Latino; 1 American Indian or Alaska Native, non-Hispanic/Latino; 17 Asian, non-Hispanic/Latino; 42 Hispanic/Latino; 3 Native Hawaiian or other Pacific Islander, non-Hispanic/Latino; 23 Two or more races, non-Hispanic/Latino), 59 international. Average age 29. 915 applicants, 58% accepted, 253 enrolled. In 2016, 25 master's, 258 doctorates, 100 Certificates awarded. *Entrance requirements:* For doctorate, LSAT. Additional exam requirements/recommendations for international students: Required—TOEFL (minimum score 79 iBT), IELTS (minimum score 6.5). *Application deadline:* For fall admission, 7/31 for domestic students. Applications are processed on a rolling basis. Application fee: $0. Electronic applications accepted. *Expenses:* $843.84 per credit hour resident tuition, $1,472.10 per credit hour non-resident tuition. *Financial support:* In 2016–17, 528 students received support. Fellowships, research assistantships with full and partial tuition reimbursements available, career-related internships or fieldwork, Federal Work-Study, scholarships/grants, and tuition waivers available. Support available to part-time students. Financial award application deadline: 7/31; financial award applicants required to submit FAFSA. *Unit head:* Andrew R. Klein, Dean, 317-274-2099, E-mail: anrklein@iupui.edu. *Application contact:* Patricia Kinney, Assistant Dean of Admissions, 317-274-2459, E-mail: pkkinney@iupui.edu.
Website: http://mckinneylaw.iu.edu/

Instituto Tecnológico y de Estudios Superiores de Monterrey, Campus Ciudad de México, School of Humanities and Social Sciences, Ciudad de Mexico, Mexico. Offers LL B. *Program availability:* Part-time, evening/weekend. *Entrance requirements:* For degree, Instituto entrance exam. Additional exam requirements/recommendations for international students: Required—TOEFL. *Faculty research:* Law; politics; international relations.

Inter American University of Puerto Rico School of Law, Professional Program, San Juan, PR 00936-8351. Offers JD. *Accreditation:* ABA. *Program availability:* Part time, evening/weekend. *Entrance requirements:* For doctorate, LSAT, PAEG, minimum GPA of 2.5. *Expenses:* Contact institution.

John F. Kennedy University, School of Law, Pleasant Hill, CA 94523-4817. Offers JD. *Program availability:* Part-time, evening/weekend. *Entrance requirements:* For doctorate, LSAT, interview. Additional exam requirements/recommendations for international students: Required—TOEFL. *Expenses:* Contact institution.

The John Marshall Law School, Graduate and Professional Programs, Chicago, IL 60604-3968. Offers LL M, MJ, JD, JD/LL M, JD/MA, JD/MBA, JD/MPA. *Accreditation:* ABA. *Program availability:* Part-time, evening/weekend, 100% online, blended/hybrid learning. *Faculty:* 55 full-time (23 women), 226 part-time/adjunct (79 women). *Students:* 839 full-time (415 women), 365 part-time (170 women); includes 380 minority (104 Black or African American, non-Hispanic/Latino; 24 American Indian or Alaska Native, non-Hispanic/Latino; 107 Asian, non-Hispanic/Latino; 117 Hispanic/Latino; 28 Two or more races, non-Hispanic/Latino), 63 international. Average age 27. 1,764 applicants, 73% accepted, 334 enrolled. In 2016, 66 master's, 296 doctorates awarded. *Degree requirements:* For master's, 24 credits; for doctorate, 90 credits. *Entrance requirements:* For master's, JD; for doctorate, LSAT. Additional exam requirements/recommendations for international students: Required—TOEFL (minimum score 90 iBT), IELTS (minimum score 7). *Application deadline:* For fall admission, 3/1 priority date for domestic and international students; for spring admission, 10/15 priority date for domestic and international students. Applications are processed on a rolling basis. Application fee: $0. Electronic applications accepted. *Expenses:* $1,540 per credit; $385 fees (for LL M and MJ); $2,548 fees (for JD). *Financial support:* In 2016–17, 798 students received support. Research assistantships, Federal Work-Study, scholarships/grants, and tuition waivers (full and partial) available. Support available to part-time students. Financial award application deadline: 4/1; financial award applicants required to submit FAFSA. *Unit head:* Darby Dickerson, Dean, 312-427-2737 Ext. 828, E-mail: ddickerson@jmls.edu. *Application contact:* Chante Spann, Interim Assistant Dean for Admissions, 800-537-4280, Fax: 312-427-5136, E-mail: admissions@jmls.edu.

The Judge Advocate General's School, U.S. Army, Graduate Programs, Charlottesville, VA 22903-1781. Offers LL M. Program available only to active duty military lawyers. *Accreditation:* ABA. *Degree requirements:* For master's, thesis optional. *Entrance requirements:* For master's, active duty military lawyer, international military officer, or DOD civilian attorney; JD or LL B. *Faculty research:* Criminal law, administrative and civil law, contract law, international law, legal research and writing.

Kaplan University, Davenport Campus, School of Criminal Justice, Davenport, IA 52807. Offers corrections (MSCJ); global issues in criminal justice (MSCJ); law (MSCJ); leadership and executive management (MSCJ); policing (MSCJ). *Program availability:* Part-time, evening/weekend, online learning. *Entrance requirements:* Additional exam requirements/recommendations for international students: Required—TOEFL (minimum score 550 paper-based; 80 iBT). Electronic applications accepted.

Lewis & Clark College, Lewis & Clark Law School, Portland, OR 97219. Offers animal law (LL M); environmental, natural resources, and energy law (LL M, MSL); law (JD). *Accreditation:* ABA. *Program availability:* Part-time, evening/weekend. *Entrance requirements:* For doctorate, LSAT. Additional exam requirements/recommendations for international students: Recommended—TOEFL (minimum score 600 paper-based). *Application deadline:* For fall admission, 3/1 for domestic students, 1/15 priority date for international students. Applications are processed on a rolling basis. Application fee: $50. Electronic applications accepted. Application fee is waived when completed online. *Expenses:* Contact institution. *Financial support:* Research assistantships, teaching assistantships, career-related internships or fieldwork, Federal Work-Study, scholarships/grants, and tuition waivers (partial) available. Support available to part-time students. Financial award application deadline: 3/1; financial award applicants required to submit FAFSA. *Unit head:* Jennifer Johnson, Dean, 503-768-6601, Fax: 503-768-6671. *Application contact:* Office of Admissions, 503-768-6613, Fax: 503-768-6793, E-mail: lawadmss@lclark.edu.
Website: http://law.lclark.edu/

Liberty University, School of Law, Lynchburg, VA 24515. Offers JD. *Program availability:* Online learning. *Students:* 209 full-time (91 women), 61 part-time (30 women); includes 51 minority (27 Black or African American, non-Hispanic/Latino; 3 American Indian or Alaska Native, non-Hispanic/Latino; 7 Asian, non-Hispanic/Latino; 8 Hispanic/Latino; 6 Two or more races, non-Hispanic/Latino), 4 international. Average age 31. 305 applicants, 55% accepted, 113 enrolled. In 2016, 58 doctorates awarded. *Entrance requirements:* For doctorate, LSAT, 2 letters of recommendation, interview, subscription to LSDAS. Additional exam requirements/recommendations for international students: Required—TOEFL (minimum score 600 paper-based; 100 iBT). *Application deadline:* For fall admission, 6/1 for domestic students. *Expenses:* Contact institution. *Financial support:* Applicants required to submit FAFSA. *Unit head:* B. Keith Faulkner, Dean, 434-592-5300, Fax: 434-592-5400, E-mail: law@liberty.edu. *Application contact:* Joleen Thaxton, Assistant Director of Admissions, 434-592-5300, Fax: 434-592-5400, E-mail: lawadmissions@liberty.edu.

Lincoln Memorial University, Duncan School of Law, Harrogate, TN 37752-1901. Offers JD. *Program availability:* Part-time. *Entrance requirements:* For doctorate, LSAT. Additional exam requirements/recommendations for international students: Required—TOEFL (minimum score 500 paper-based). Electronic applications accepted. *Expenses:* Contact institution.

London Metropolitan University, Graduate Programs, London, United Kingdom. Offers applied psychology (M Sc); architecture (MA); biomedical science (M Sc); blood science (M Sc); cancer pharmacology (M Sc); computer networking and cyber security (M Sc); computing and information systems (M Sc); conference interpreting (MA); counter-terrorism studies (M Sc); creative, digital and professional writing (MA); crime, violence and prevention (M Sc); criminology (M Sc); curating contemporary art (MA); data analytics (M Sc); digital media (MA); early childhood studies (MA); education (MA, Ed D); financial services law, regulation and compliance (LL M); food science (M Sc); forensic psychology (M Sc); health and social care management and policy (M Sc); human nutrition (M Sc); human resource management (MA); human rights and international conflict (MA); information technology (M Sc); intelligence and security studies (M Sc); international oil, gas and energy law (LL M); international relations (MA); interpreting (MA); learning and teaching in higher education (MA); legal practice (LL M); media and entertainment law (LL M); organizational and consumer psychology (M Sc); psychological therapy (M Sc); psychology of mental health (M Sc); public health (M Sc); public policy and management (MPA); security studies (M Sc); social work (M Sc); spatial planning and urban design (MA); sports therapy (M Sc); supporting older children and young people with dyslexia (MA); teaching languages (MA), including Arabic, English; translation (MA); woman and child abuse (MA).

Louisiana State University and Agricultural & Mechanical College, Paul M. Hebert Law Center, Baton Rouge, LA 70803. Offers LL M, JD. *Accreditation:* ABA. *Faculty:* 36 full-time (12 women), 20 part-time/adjunct (2 women). *Students:* 544 full-time (247 women), 11 part-time (5 women); includes 78 minority (28 Black or African American, non-Hispanic/Latino; 1 American Indian or Alaska Native, non-Hispanic/Latino; 8 Asian, non-Hispanic/Latino; 25 Hispanic/Latino; 16 Two or more races, non-Hispanic/Latino), 10 international. Average age 26. 847 applicants, 60% accepted, 198 enrolled. In 2016, 4 master's awarded. *Degree requirements:* For master's, thesis. *Entrance requirements:* For doctorate, LSAT. Additional exam requirements/recommendations for international students: Required—TOEFL (minimum score 600 paper-based; 100 iBT). *Application deadline:* For fall admission, 3/1 priority date for domestic and international students. Applications are processed on a rolling basis. Application fee: $50. Electronic applications accepted. Application fee is waived when completed online. *Expenses:* $22,520 per year full-time resident; $37,960 per year full-time non-resident. *Financial support:* In 2016–17, 454 students received support. Scholarships/grants and tuition waivers (full and partial) available. Financial award application deadline: 7/1; financial award applicants required to submit FAFSA. *Unit head:* Thomas Galligan, Dean, 225-578-8491, Fax: 225-578-8202, E-mail: thomas.galligan@law.lsu.edu. *Application contact:* Jake T. Henry, III, Director of Admissions, 225-578-8646, Fax: 225-578-8647, E-mail: jake.henry@law.lsu.edu.
Website: http://www.law.lsu.edu/

Loyola Marymount University, College of Business Administration, MBA/JD Program, Los Angeles, CA 90045-2659. Offers MBA/JD. *Program availability:* Part-time. *Students:* 1 full-time (0 women), 3 part-time (2 women); includes 2 minority (1 Hispanic/Latino; 1 Two or more races, non-Hispanic/Latino), 1 international. Average age 26. *Entrance requirements:* Additional exam requirements/recommendations for international students: Required—TOEFL (minimum score 600 paper-based; 100 iBT). *Application deadline:* For fall admission, 7/1 for domestic students. Application fee: $75. Electronic applications accepted. *Expenses:* Contact institution. *Financial support:* In 2016–17, 2 students received support. Scholarships/grants and unspecified assistantships available. Financial award application deadline: 6/30; financial award applicants required to submit FAFSA. *Unit head:* Dr. Dennis Draper, Dean, 310-338-7504, E-mail: ddraper@lmu.edu. *Application contact:* Chake H. Kouyoumjian, Associate Dean of Graduate Studies, 310-338-2721, E-mail: ckouyoum@lmu.edu.
Website: http://www.lls.edu/academics/degreesoffered/jdmbaprogram/

Loyola Marymount University, Loyola Law School Los Angeles, Los Angeles, CA 90015. Offers law (LL M, MLS, JD, JSD); tax (LL M in Tax, MT); JD/LL M; JD/MBA. *Accreditation:* ABA. *Program availability:* Part-time, evening/weekend. *Faculty:* 57 full-time (27 women), 60 part-time/adjunct (21 women). *Students:* 771 full-time (439 women), 167 part-time (82 women); includes 387 minority (46 Black or African American, non-Hispanic/Latino; 6 American Indian or Alaska Native, non-Hispanic/Latino; 112 Asian, non-Hispanic/Latino; 183 Hispanic/Latino; 40 Two or more races, non-Hispanic/Latino), 45 international. Average age 25. 4,048 applicants, 37% accepted, 306 enrolled. In 2016, 36 master's, 355 doctorates awarded. *Degree requirements:* For master's and doctorate, comprehensive exam. *Entrance requirements:* For master's, JD; for doctorate, LSAT. Additional exam requirements/recommendations for international students: Required—TOEFL (minimum score 600 paper-based; 100 iBT). *Application deadline:* For fall admission, 2/23 priority date for domestic students, 2/1 for international students. Applications are processed on a rolling basis. Application fee: $0. Electronic applications accepted. *Financial support:* Research assistantships, Federal Work-Study, and scholarships/grants available. Financial award application deadline: 3/15; financial award applicants required to submit FAFSA. *Unit head:* Michael Waterstone, Dean, 213-736-2243, Fax: 213-487-6736, E-mail: michael.waterstone@lls.edu. *Application contact:* Jannell Lundy Roberts, Assistant Dean, Admissions, 213-736-1074, Fax: 213-736-6523, E-mail: admissions@lls.edu.
Website: http://www.lls.edu/

Loyola University Chicago, School of Law, Chicago, IL 60611. Offers LL M, MJ, JD, SJD, JD/MA, JD/MBA, JD/MPP, JD/MSW, MJ/MSW, MS/MJ. *Accreditation:* ABA. *Program availability:* Part-time, evening/weekend, 100% online, blended/hybrid learning. *Faculty:* 54 full-time (27 women), 178 part-time/adjunct (82 women). *Students:* 788 full-time (432 women), 283 part-time (217 women); includes 328 minority (139 Black or African American, non-Hispanic/Latino; 3 American Indian or Alaska Native, non-Hispanic/Latino; 53 Asian, non-Hispanic/Latino; 94 Hispanic/Latino; 2 Native Hawaiian or other Pacific Islander, non-Hispanic/Latino; 37 Two or more races, non-Hispanic/Latino), 39 international. Average age 31. 2,581 applicants, 53% accepted, 377 enrolled. In 2016, 152 master's, 212 doctorates awarded. *Degree requirements:* For master's, thesis (for some programs); for doctorate, thesis/dissertation (for some programs). *Entrance requirements:* For doctorate, LSAT. Additional exam requirements/recommendations for international students: Required—TOEFL (minimum score 650 paper-based; 114 iBT); Recommended—IELTS (minimum score 6.5). *Application deadline:* For fall admission, 4/1 for domestic and international students. Applications are processed on a rolling basis. Application fee: $0. Electronic applications accepted. *Expenses:* Contact institution. *Financial support:* In 2016–17, 549 students received support, including 72 fellowships; Federal Work-Study and scholarships/grants also available. Financial award application deadline: 3/1; financial award applicants required to submit FAFSA. *Faculty research:* Health disparities and effects of lead paint, constitutional law including hate speech and supreme court advocacy, early childhood education including law policy and pedagogy, income inequality of markets and homelessness, hedonic psychology - legal and social determinants of happiness. *Unit head:* James Faught, JD, Associate Dean for Administration, Law School, 312-915-7131, Fax: 312-915-6911, E-mail: law-admissions@luc.edu. *Application contact:* Ron Martin, Associate Director, Graduate and Professional Enrollment Management Operations, 312-915-8951, E-mail: rmarti7@luc.edu.
Website: http://www.luc.edu/law/

Loyola University New Orleans, College of Law, New Orleans, LA 70118. Offers LL M, JD, JD/MBA, JD/MPA, JD/MURP. *Accreditation:* ABA. *Program availability:* Part-time, evening/weekend, online learning. *Faculty:* 40 full-time (22 women), 19 part-time/adjunct (5 women). *Students:* 466 full-time (246 women), 13 part-time (9 women); includes 140 minority (64 Black or African American, non-Hispanic/Latino; 8 American Indian or Alaska Native, non-Hispanic/Latino; 9 Asian, non-Hispanic/Latino; 49 Hispanic/Latino; 10 Two or more races, non-Hispanic/Latino), 9 international. Average age 28. 729 applicants, 82% accepted, 173 enrolled. In 2016, 217 doctorates awarded. *Entrance requirements:* For doctorate, LSAT, 2 letters of recommendation, interview, resume, personal statement, bachelor's degree from accredited college/university. Additional exam requirements/recommendations for international students: Required—TOEFL (minimum score 550 paper-based; 89 iBT). *Application deadline:* For fall admission, 8/1 priority date for domestic and international students. Applications are processed on a rolling basis. Application fee: $0. Electronic applications accepted. *Expenses:* $42,000 per year full-time, $31,500 per year part-time. *Financial support:* Fellowships, research assistantships, teaching assistantships, career-related internships or fieldwork, institutionally sponsored loans, scholarships/grants, traineeships, health care benefits, tuition waivers, and unspecified assistantships available. Support available to part-time students. Financial award applicants required to submit FAFSA. *Faculty research:* Louisiana civil code, international law, commercial law, comparative law. *Unit head:* Dr. Lawrence W. Moore, Interim Dean, 504-861-5575, Fax: 504-861-5677, E-mail: lmoore@loyno.edu. *Application contact:* Kimberly Jones, Director of Law Admissions, 504-861-5575, Fax: 504-861-5772, E-mail: ladmit@loyno.edu.
Website: http://www.loyno.edu/law/

Marquette University, Law School, Milwaukee, WI 53201-1881. Offers JD, JD/Certificate, JD/MA, JD/MBA. *Accreditation:* ABA. *Program availability:* Part-time, evening/weekend. *Faculty:* 32 full-time (13 women), 36 part-time/adjunct (19 women). *Students:* 520 full-time (207 women), 55 part-time (32 women); includes 105 minority (22 Black or African American, non-Hispanic/Latino; 1 American Indian or Alaska Native,

non-Hispanic/Latino; 16 Asian, non-Hispanic/Latino; 51 Hispanic/Latino; 15 Two or more races, non-Hispanic/Latino), 2 international. Average age 26. 2,259 applicants, 100% accepted, 810 enrolled. In 2016, 573 doctorates awarded. *Entrance requirements:* For doctorate, LSAT, subscription to LSAC's Credential Assembly Service. Additional exam requirements/recommendations for international students: Required—TOEFL. *Application deadline:* For fall admission, 4/1 for domestic students. Applications are processed on a rolling basis. Application fee: $50. Electronic applications accepted. *Expenses:* Contact institution. *Financial support:* Career-related internships or fieldwork, Federal Work-Study, and scholarships/grants available. Support available to part-time students. Financial award application deadline: 3/1; financial award applicants required to submit FAFSA. *Faculty research:* Constitutional law, sports law, dispute resolution, intellectual property, legal ethics. *Total annual research expenditures:* $8,960. *Unit head:* Joseph D. Kearney, Dean, 414-288-7090, Fax: 414-288-6403.
Website: http://law.marquette.edu/

Massachusetts School of Law at Andover, Professional Program, Andover, MA 01810. Offers JD. *Program availability:* Part-time, evening/weekend. *Entrance requirements:* For doctorate, Massachusetts School of Law Aptitude Test (MSLAT), interview. Additional exam requirements/recommendations for international students: Recommended—TOEFL. Electronic applications accepted.

McGill University, Faculty of Graduate and Postdoctoral Studies, Faculty of Law, Department of Law, Montréal, QC H3A 2T5, Canada. Offers LL M, DCL.

McGill University, Faculty of Graduate and Postdoctoral Studies, Faculty of Law, Institute of Air and Space Law, Montréal, QC H3A 2T5, Canada. Offers LL M, DCL, Graduate Certificate.

McGill University, Faculty of Graduate and Postdoctoral Studies, Faculty of Law, Institute of Comparative Law, Montréal, QC H3A 2T5, Canada. Offers LL M, DCL, Graduate Certificate.

Mercer University, Walter F. George School of Law, Macon, GA 31207. Offers JD, JD/MBA. *Accreditation:* ABA. *Program availability:* Part-time. *Entrance requirements:* For doctorate, LSAT. Electronic applications accepted. *Expenses:* Contact institution. *Faculty research:* Legal ethics, environmental law, employment discrimination, statutory law, legal writing.

Michigan State University College of Law, Professional Program, East Lansing, MI 48824-1300. Offers American legal system (LL M, MJ); global food law (LL M, MJ); intellectual property (LL M, MJ); law (JD); legal doctrine and analysis (MJ). *Accreditation:* ABA. *Program availability:* Part-time. *Faculty:* 55 full-time (22 women), 85 part-time/adjunct (32 women). *Students:* 723 full-time (362 women), 123 part-time (70 women); includes 173 minority (57 Black or African American, non-Hispanic/Latino; 9 American Indian or Alaska Native, non-Hispanic/Latino; 28 Asian, non-Hispanic/Latino; 40 Hispanic/Latino; 2 Native Hawaiian or other Pacific Islander, non-Hispanic/Latino; 37 Two or more races, non-Hispanic/Latino), 91 international. Average age 24. 2,362 applicants, 45% accepted, 259 enrolled. In 2016, 45 master's, 265 doctorates awarded. *Entrance requirements:* For doctorate, LSAT. Additional exam requirements/recommendations for international students: Required—TOEFL (minimum score 600 paper-based), IELTS. *Application deadline:* For fall admission, 4/30 priority date for domestic students, 7/1 priority date for international students. Applications are processed on a rolling basis. Application fee: $60. Electronic applications accepted. *Expenses:* Contact institution. *Financial support:* In 2016–17, 559 students received support. Career-related internships or fieldwork, Federal Work-Study, scholarships/grants, and tuition waivers (full and partial) available. Support available to part-time students. Financial award application deadline: 4/1; financial award applicants required to submit FAFSA. *Faculty research:* International, constitutional, health, tax and environmental law; intellectual property, trial practice, corporate law. *Unit head:* Lawrence Ponoroff, Dean/Professor of Law, 517-432-6993, Fax: 517-432-6801, E-mail: lponoroff@law.msu.edu. *Application contact:* Charles Roboski, Assistant Dean of Admissions, 517-432-0222, Fax: 517-432-0098, E-mail: roboski@law.msu.edu.
Website: http://www.law.msu.edu/

Mississippi College, School of Law, Jackson, MS 39201. Offers civil law studies (Certificate); law (JD); JD/MBA. *Accreditation:* ABA. *Degree requirements:* For doctorate, thesis/dissertation. *Entrance requirements:* For doctorate, LSAT, LDAS report. Additional exam requirements/recommendations for international students: Recommended—TOEFL, IELTS. Electronic applications accepted. *Expenses:* Contact institution.

Mitchell Hamline School of Law, Graduate and Professional Programs, Saint Paul, MN 55105-3076. Offers LL M, JD. *Program availability:* Part-time, evening/weekend, blended/hybrid learning. *Faculty:* 44 full-time (20 women), 215 part-time/adjunct (129 women). *Students:* 477 full-time (243 women), 510 part-time (264 women); includes 93 minority (22 Black or African American, non-Hispanic/Latino; 6 American Indian or Alaska Native, non-Hispanic/Latino; 19 Asian, non-Hispanic/Latino; 20 Hispanic/Latino; 1 Native Hawaiian or other Pacific Islander, non-Hispanic/Latino; 25 Two or more races, non-Hispanic/Latino), 12 international. Average age 28. *Entrance requirements:* For master's, any law degree from the U.S. or foreign country; for doctorate, LSAT. Additional exam requirements/recommendations for international students: Required—TOEFL. *Application deadline:* For fall admission, 8/1 for domestic and international students; for spring admission, 11/1 for domestic and international students. Applications are processed on a rolling basis. Application fee: $0. Electronic applications accepted. *Expenses: Tuition:* Full-time $40,570. *Financial support:* Research assistantships, Federal Work-Study, and scholarships/grants available. Financial award application deadline: 4/15; financial award applicants required to submit FAFSA. *Faculty research:* Child protection, domestic violence, elder law, intellectual property law, preventive detention and post release civil commitment. *Unit head:* Mark C. Gordon, President/Dean, 651-290-6310, Fax: 651-290-6426. *Application contact:* Emily Dunsworth, Dean of Admissions, 651-290-6434, E-mail: admissions@mitchellhamline.edu.

Montclair State University, The Graduate School, College of Humanities and Social Sciences, MA Program in Law and Governance, Montclair, NJ 07043-1624. Offers conflict management and peace studies (MA); governance, compliance and regulation (MA); intellectual property (MA); law and governance (MA), legal management (MA). *Program availability:* Part-time, evening/weekend. *Degree requirements:* For master's, thesis or comprehensive exam. *Entrance requirements:* For master's, GRE General Test, minimum cumulative GPA of 2.75 for undergraduate work, 2 letters of recommendation, essay. Additional exam requirements/recommendations for international students: Required—TOEFL (minimum score 83 iBT) or IELTS (minimum score 6.5). Electronic applications accepted. *Expenses:* Tuition, state resident: part-time $553 per credit. Tuition, nonresident: part-time $854 per credit. *Required fees:* $91 per credit. Tuition and fees vary according to program.

New York Law School, Graduate Programs, New York, NY 10013. Offers LL M, JD, JD/MA, JD/MBA. JD/MBA offered jointly with Baruch College of the City University of New York; JD/MA in forensic psychology offered jointly with John Jay College of Criminal Justice of the City University of New York. *Accreditation:* ABA. *Program availability:* Part-time, evening/weekend. *Faculty:* 59 full-time (27 women), 63 part-time/adjunct (16 women). *Students:* 633 full-time (379 women), 257 part-time (127 women); includes 308 minority (69 Black or African American, non-Hispanic/Latino; 66 Asian, non-Hispanic/Latino; 143 Hispanic/Latino; 30 Two or more races, non-Hispanic/Latino), 35 international. Average age 27. 2,694 applicants, 56% accepted, 326 enrolled. In 2016, 20 master's, 304 doctorates awarded. *Entrance requirements:* For master's, JD (for LL M); for doctorate, LSAT, undergraduate degree, letter of recommendation, resume, essay/personal statement. Additional exam requirements/recommendations for international students: Required—TOEFL (minimum score 600 paper-based; 100 iBT). *Application deadline:* For fall admission, 7/1 priority date for domestic and international students; for winter admission, 11/15 priority date for domestic and international students. Applications are processed on a rolling basis. Application fee: $0. Electronic applications accepted. *Expenses:* $49,240 per year (for full-time JD); $37,880 per year (for part-time JD); $1,500 per credit (for LL M). *Financial support:* In 2016–17, 698 students received support, including 100 fellowships (averaging $3,010 per year), 22 research assistantships (averaging $4,663 per year), 19 teaching assistantships (averaging $4,661 per year); career-related internships or fieldwork, Federal Work-Study, and scholarships/grants also available. Support available to part-time students. Financial award application deadline: 7/1; financial award applicants required to submit FAFSA. *Faculty research:* Immigration law, intellectual property, civil rights, family law, international law. *Unit head:* Anthony W. Crowell, Dean and President, 212-431-2840, Fax: 212-219-3752, E-mail: acrowell@nyls.edu. *Application contact:* Ella Mae Estrada, Associate Dean for Enrollment Management, Financial Aid and Diversity Initiatives, 212-431-2888, Fax: 212-966-1522, E-mail: admissions@nyls.edu.
Website: http://www.nyls.edu

New York University, School of Law, New York, NY 10012-1019. Offers law (LL M, JD, JSD); law and business (Advanced Certificate); taxation (MSL, Advanced Certificate); JD/JD; JD/LL B; JD/LL M; JD/MA; JD/MBA; JD/MPA; JD/MPP; JD/MSW; JD/MUP; JD/PhD. *Accreditation:* ABA. *Program availability:* Part-time, online learning. *Entrance requirements:* For doctorate, LSAT (for JD). Electronic applications accepted. *Expenses:* Contact institution. *Faculty research:* International law, environmental law, corporate law, globalization of law, philosophy of law.

North Carolina Central University, School of Law, Durham, NC 27707. Offers JD, JD/MLS, MBA/JD. *Accreditation:* ABA. *Program availability:* Part-time, evening/weekend. *Entrance requirements:* For doctorate, LSAT, LSDAS. Additional exam requirements/recommendations for international students: Required—TOEFL. *Expenses:* Contact institution.

Northeastern University, School of Law, Boston, MA 02115-5005. Offers LL M, MLS, JD, JD/MA, JD/MBA, JD/MELP, JD/MPH, JD/MS, JD/MSA/MBA, LL M/MA, LL M/MBA. JD/MPH offered jointly with Tufts University; JD/MSA/MBA with Graduate School of Professional Accounting; JD/MS with Program in Law and Public Policy; JD/MELP with Vermont Law School; and JD/MA with Brandeis University. *Accreditation:* ABA. *Program availability:* Online learning. *Faculty:* 46 full-time (30 women), 26 part-time/adjunct (16 women). *Students:* 564 full-time (359 women), 4 part-time (all women). In 2016, 32 master's, 175 doctorates awarded. *Application deadline:* Applications are processed on a rolling basis. Application fee: $75. Electronic applications accepted. *Expenses:* $47,790 per year. *Financial support:* Scholarships/grants available. Financial award applicants required to submit FAFSA. *Faculty research:* Human rights, health, criminal, corporate/finance, international. *Unit head:* Jeremy R. Paul, Dean, 617-373-3307, Fax: 617-373-8793, E-mail: j.paul@northeastern.edu. *Application contact:* Information Contact, 617-373-2395, Fax: 617-373-8865, E-mail: lawadmissions@northeastern.edu.
Website: http://www.northeastern.edu/law/

Northern Illinois University, College of Law, De Kalb, IL 60115-2854. Offers JD. *Accreditation:* ABA. *Program availability:* Part-time. *Faculty:* 22 full-time (11 women). *Students:* 229 full-time (110 women), 35 part-time (17 women); includes 66 minority (26 Black or African American, non-Hispanic/Latino; 12 Asian, non-Hispanic/Latino; 23 Hispanic/Latino; 2 Native Hawaiian or other Pacific Islander, non-Hispanic/Latino; 3 Two or more races, non-Hispanic/Latino), 1 international. Average age 28. 564 applicants, 63% accepted, 106 enrolled. In 2016, 88 doctorates awarded. *Entrance requirements:* For doctorate, LSAT. Additional exam requirements/recommendations for international students: Required—TOEFL. *Application deadline:* For fall admission, 4/1 priority date for domestic and international students. Applications are processed on a rolling basis. Electronic applications accepted. *Expenses:* Contact institution. *Financial support:* In 2016–17, 8 teaching assistantships were awarded; research assistantships, career-related internships or fieldwork, Federal Work-Study, tuition waivers (full and partial), and unspecified assistantships also available. Support available to part-time students. Financial award application deadline: 3/1; financial award applicants required to submit FAFSA. *Faculty research:* Criminal practice, intellectual property, environmental law, taxation. *Unit head:* Eric Dannenmaier, Dean, 815-753-5300, Fax: 815-753-8552, E-mail: edan@niu.edu. *Application contact:* Amanda Noascono, Director of Admissions and Financial Aid, 815-753-8595, Fax: 815-753-5680, E-mail: law-admit@niu.edu.
Website: http://law.niu.edu/

Northern Kentucky University, Chase College of Law, Highland Heights, KY 41099. Offers JD, JD/MBA, JD/MBI, JD/MHI. *Accreditation:* ABA. *Program availability:* Part-time, evening/weekend. *Entrance requirements:* For doctorate, LSAT. Additional exam requirements/recommendations for international students: Required—TOEFL. Electronic applications accepted. *Expenses:* Contact institution. *Faculty research:* Business law, Constitutional law, criminal law, environmental law, law and technology.

Northwestern University, Pritzker School of Law, Chicago, IL 60611-3069. Offers international human rights (LL M); law (JD); law and business (LL M); science law (MSL); tax (LL M in Tax); JD/LL M; JD/MBA; JD/PhD; LL M/Certificate. Executive LL M programs offered in Madrid (Spain), Seoul (South Korea), and Tel Aviv (Israel). *Accreditation:* ABA. *Entrance requirements:* For master's, law degree or equivalent, letter of recommendation, resume; for doctorate, LSAT, 1 letter of recommendation, resume. Additional exam requirements/recommendations for international students: Required—TOEFL. Electronic applications accepted. *Expenses:* Contact institution. *Faculty research:* Constitutional law, corporate law, international law, law and social policy, ethical studies.

Nova Southeastern University, Shepard Broad College of Law, Fort Lauderdale, FL 33314. Offers education law (MS), including cybersecurity law, education law advocacy, exceptional education; employment law (MS), including cybersecurity law, employee relations law, human resource managerial law; health law (MS, JD), including clinical research law and regulatory compliance (MS), cybersecurity law (MS), health care administrative law (MS), regulatory compliance (MS), risk management (MS); international law (JD); law and policy (MS), including cybersecurity law; JD/DO; JD/M Acc; JD/M Tax; JD/MBA; JD/MIB; JD/MPA; JD/MS; JD/PhD. *Accreditation:* ABA. *Program availability:* Part-time, evening/weekend, 100% online, blended/hybrid learning. *Faculty:* 42 full-time (23 women), 35 part-time/adjunct (14 women). *Students:* 554 full-time (298 women), 325 part-time (230 women); includes 351 minority (71 Black or African American, non-Hispanic/Latino; 3 American Indian or Alaska Native, non-Hispanic/Latino; 17 Asian, non-Hispanic/Latino; 251 Hispanic/Latino; 2 Native Hawaiian or other Pacific Islander, non-Hispanic/Latino; 7 Two or more races, non-Hispanic/Latino), 36 international. Average age 29. 1,414 applicants, 49% accepted, 256 enrolled. In 2016, 46 master's, 236 doctorates awarded. *Degree requirements:* For master's, thesis optional, capstone research project; for doctorate, rigorous upper-level writing

fulfilled through faculty-supervised seminar paper, law journal article, workshop, or other research. *Entrance requirements:* For master's, regionally-accredited undergraduate degree; at least 2 years' experience in related field (for employment law and health law); for doctorate, LSAT. Additional exam requirements/recommendations for international students: Recommended—TOEFL (minimum score 600 paper-based; 100 iBT), IELTS (minimum score 7). *Application deadline:* For fall admission, 5/1 priority date for domestic and international students; for winter admission, 12/12 for domestic and international students; for spring admission, 3/31 for domestic and international students; for summer admission, 4/1 for domestic and international students. Applications are processed on a rolling basis. Application fee: $0. Electronic applications accepted. *Expenses:* Contact institution. *Financial support:* In 2016–17, 231 students received support, including 221 fellowships (averaging $12,680 per year); Federal Work-Study, institutionally sponsored loans, scholarships/grants, and unspecified assistantships also available. Support available to part-time students. Financial award application deadline: 4/15; financial award applicants required to submit FAFSA. *Faculty research:* Legal issues in health law, international law, the legal profession, family law, civil rights. *Unit head:* Jon M. Garon, Dean, 954-262-6101, Fax: 954-262-2862, E-mail: garon@nova.edu. *Application contact:* William Daniel Perez, Assistant Dean of Admissions, 954-262-6121, Fax: 954-262-3844, E-mail: wperez1@nova.edu.
Website: http://www.law.nova.edu/

Ohio Northern University, Claude W. Pettit College of Law, Ada, OH 45810-1599. Offers LL M, JD. *Accreditation:* ABA. *Entrance requirements:* For doctorate, LSAT. Additional exam requirements/recommendations for international students: Required—TOEFL. Electronic applications accepted. *Expenses:* Contact institution. *Faculty research:* Constitutional law, environmental law, business law and taxation, criminal law, public interest law, death penalty for women and juveniles, international human rights, sports violence.

The Ohio State University, Moritz College of Law, Columbus, OH 43210. Offers LL M, MSL, JD, JD/MA, JD/MBA, JD/MD, JD/MHA, JD/MPH. *Accreditation:* ABA. *Faculty:* 48 full-time (21 women). *Students:* 546 full-time (267 women); includes 100 minority (36 Black or African American, non-Hispanic/Latino; 1 American Indian or Alaska Native, non-Hispanic/Latino; 22 Asian, non-Hispanic/Latino; 28 Hispanic/Latino; 1 Native Hawaiian or other Pacific Islander, non-Hispanic/Latino; 12 Two or more races, non-Hispanic/Latino), 7 international. Average age 25. 1,574 applicants, 49% accepted, 166 enrolled. In 2016, 179 doctorates awarded. *Entrance requirements:* Additional exam requirements/recommendations for international students: Required—TOEFL (minimum score 650 paper-based; 100 iBT). *Application deadline:* For fall admission, 4/1 priority date for domestic students. Applications are processed on a rolling basis. Application fee: $60 ($70 for international students). Electronic applications accepted. *Expenses:* Contact institution. *Financial support:* In 2016–17, 516 students received support. Career-related internships or fieldwork, institutionally sponsored loans, and scholarships/grants available. Financial award application deadline: 4/1; financial award applicants required to submit FAFSA. *Faculty research:* Alternative dispute resolution, law and policy, criminal law, intellectual property, big data and governance. *Unit head:* Alan Michaels, Dean, 614-292-0574, Fax: 614-292-1492. *Application contact:* Moritz College of Law Admissions, 614-292-8810, Fax: 614-292-3895, E-mail: lawadmit@osu.edu.
Website: http://moritzlaw.osu.edu/

Oklahoma City University, School of Law, Oklahoma City, OK 73106-1402. Offers LL M, JD, JD/MBA. *Accreditation:* ABA. *Program availability:* Part-time, evening/weekend. *Faculty:* 20 full-time (6 women), 31 part-time/adjunct (8 women). *Students:* 385 full-time (189 women), 28 part-time (12 women); includes 141 minority (25 Black or African American, non-Hispanic/Latino; 28 American Indian or Alaska Native, non-Hispanic/Latino; 18 Asian, non-Hispanic/Latino; 42 Hispanic/Latino; 2 Native Hawaiian or other Pacific Islander, non-Hispanic/Latino; 26 Two or more races, non-Hispanic/Latino), 4 international. Average age 28. In 2016, 139 doctorates awarded. *Entrance requirements:* For doctorate, LSAT, bachelor's degree from accredited undergraduate institution (except for OCU students admitted through the Oxford plan). Additional exam requirements/recommendations for international students: Required—TOEFL (minimum score 100 iBT). *Application deadline:* For fall admission, 8/1 for domestic and international students. Application fee: $50. Electronic applications accepted. *Expenses:* Contact institution. *Financial support:* In 2016–17, 304 students received support. Career-related internships or fieldwork, Federal Work-Study, institutionally sponsored loans, scholarships/grants, and tuition waivers (full and partial) available. Support available to part-time students. Financial award application deadline: 2/1; financial award applicants required to submit FAFSA. *Faculty research:* Family law, environmental law, consumer law, alternative dispute resolution, criminal law and procedure. *Unit head:* Dr. Valerie K. Couch, Dean, 405-208-5440, Fax: 405-208-6041, E-mail: vcouch@okcu.edu. *Application contact:* Dr. Laurie W. Jones, Associate Dean of Admissions, Law School, 405-208-5354, Fax: 405-208-5814, E-mail: ljones@okcu.edu.
Website: http://law.okcu.edu/

Pace University, Elisabeth Haub School of Law, White Plains, NY 10603. Offers comparative legal studies (LL M); environmental law (LL M, SJD), including climate change (LL M), land use and sustainability (LL M); law (JD); JD/LL M; JD/MA; JD/MBA; JD/MEM; JD/MPA; JD/MS. JD/MA offered jointly with Sarah Lawrence College; JD/MEM offered jointly with Yale University School of Forestry and Environmental Studies. *Accreditation:* ABA. *Program availability:* Part-time. *Faculty:* 26 full-time (11 women), 52 part-time/adjunct (19 women). *Students:* 516 full-time (274 women), 63 part-time (36 women); includes 150 minority (30 Black or African American, non-Hispanic/Latino; 2 American Indian or Alaska Native, non-Hispanic/Latino; 23 Asian, non-Hispanic/Latino; 58 Hispanic/Latino; 37 Two or more races, non-Hispanic/Latino), 2 international. Average age 26. 1,423 applicants, 56% accepted, 206 enrolled. In 2016, 20 master's, 171 doctorates awarded. *Degree requirements:* For master's, writing sample; for doctorate, thesis/dissertation (for some programs), extensive thesis proposal (for SJD). *Entrance requirements:* For doctorate, LSAT (for JD). Additional exam requirements/recommendations for international students: Required—TOEFL (minimum score 100 iBT); Recommended—TWE. *Application deadline:* For fall admission, 6/1 priority date for domestic students; for winter admission, 11/15 priority date for domestic students. Applications are processed on a rolling basis. Application fee: $65. Electronic applications accepted. *Expenses:* Contact institution. *Financial support:* In 2016–17, 430 students received support. Fellowships, research assistantships, career-related internships or fieldwork, Federal Work-Study, institutionally sponsored loans, scholarships/grants, and unspecified assistantships available. Support available to part-time students. Financial award application deadline: 2/1; financial award applicants required to submit FAFSA. *Faculty research:* Reform of energy regulations, international law, land use law, prosecutorial misconduct, corporation law, international sale of goods. *Total annual research expenditures:* $2.2 million. *Unit head:* David Yassky, Dean, 914-422-4407, E-mail: dyassky@law.pace.edu. *Application contact:* Cathy Alexander, Assistant Dean, 914-422-4210, Fax: 914-989-8714, E-mail: calexander@law.pace.edu.
Website: http://www.law.pace.edu/

Penn State University–Dickinson Law, Graduate and Professional Programs, Carlisle, PA 17013. Offers LL M, JD. *Accreditation:* ABA. *Faculty:* 24 full-time (15 women), 15 part-time/adjunct (4 women). *Students:* 186 full-time (84 women). *Entrance requirements:* For doctorate, LSAT. *Application deadline:* Applications are processed on a rolling basis. Electronic applications accepted. *Expenses:* Tuition, state resident: full-time $46,176. Tuition, nonresident: full-time $46,176. *Required fees:* $678. *Financial support:* Research assistantships, Federal Work-Study, and scholarships/grants available. Financial award application deadline: 4/15; financial award applicants required to submit FAFSA. *Unit head:* Gary S. Gildin, Dean, 717-240-5238, Fax: 717-240-5213, E-mail: gsg2@psu.edu. *Application contact:* Bekah A. Saidman-Krauss, Assistant Dean of Admissions and Financial Aid, 717-240-5207, E-mail: ras1075@psu.edu.
Website: https://dickinsonlaw.psu.edu/

Penn State University Park, Penn State Law, University Park, PA 16802. Offers LL M, JD, SJD. *Accreditation:* ABA. *Faculty:* 42 full-time (18 women), 7 part-time/adjunct (3 women). *Students:* 533 full-time (247 women). 2,214 applicants, 42% accepted, 242 enrolled. *Entrance requirements:* For master's, BA or LL B in law; for doctorate, LSAT. Additional exam requirements/recommendations for international students: Required—TOEFL, IELTS. *Application deadline:* For fall admission, 3/31 for domestic students. Applications are processed on a rolling basis. Application fee: $60. Electronic applications accepted. *Unit head:* Hari M. Osofsky, Dean, 814-863-1521. *Application contact:* Amanda DiPolvere, Assistant Dean, Admissions and Financial Aid, 800-840-1122, E-mail: admissions@pennstatelaw.psu.edu.
Website: http://pennstatelaw.psu.edu/

Pepperdine University, School of Law, Juris Doctor Program, Malibu, CA 90263. Offers JD, JD/M Div, JD/MBA, JD/MDR, JD/MPP. *Accreditation:* ABA. *Students:* 593 full-time (319 women), 5 part-time (0 women); includes 200 minority (28 Black or African American, non-Hispanic/Latino; 3 American Indian or Alaska Native, non-Hispanic/Latino; 52 Asian, non-Hispanic/Latino; 78 Hispanic/Latino; 39 Two or more races, non-Hispanic/Latino), 16 international. Average age 25. 2,372 applicants, 47% accepted, 207 enrolled. In 2016, 179 doctorates awarded. *Entrance requirements:* For doctorate, LSAT, 2 letters of recommendation, resume, personal statement, registration with the Credential Assembly Service (CAS). Additional exam requirements/recommendations for international students: Required—TOEFL. *Application deadline:* For fall admission, 2/1 priority date for domestic students, 6/1 priority date for international students. Applications are processed on a rolling basis. Application fee: $60. *Expenses:* $52,140 per academic year. *Financial support:* Federal Work-Study, institutionally sponsored loans, and scholarships/grants available. Financial award application deadline: 4/1; financial award applicants required to submit FAFSA. *Unit head:* Dr. Deanell Tacha, Dean/Professor of Law, 310-506-4621, E-mail: deanell.tacha@pepperdine.edu. *Application contact:* Shannon Phillips, Director of Admissions and Records, 310-506-4631, Fax: 310-506-4266, E-mail: shannon.phillips@pepperdine.edu.
Website: http://law.pepperdine.edu/degrees-programs/juris-doctor/

Pontifical Catholic University of Puerto Rico, School of Law, Ponce, PR 00717-0777. Offers JD. *Accreditation:* ABA. *Program availability:* Part-time, evening/weekend. *Entrance requirements:* For doctorate, LSAT, PAEG, 3 letters of recommendation.

Pontificia Universidad Catolica Madre y Maestra, Graduate School, Faculty of Social and Administrative Sciences, Santiago, Dominican Republic. Offers business administration (MBA), including business development, finance, international business, management skills (M Mgmt, MBA), marketing, operations, strategic cost management, strategy, tourist destination planning and management; law (LL M), including civil law, corporate business law, criminal law, international relations, real estate law; management (M Mgmt), including higher financial management, insurance program administration, management skills (M Mgmt, MBA); psychology (MA), including clinical child and adolescent psychology, forensic psychology; strategic human resources (EMBA).

Queen's University at Kingston, Faculty of Law, Kingston, ON K7L 3N6, Canada. Offers LL M, JD, JD/MBA, JD/MIR, JD/MPA. *Program availability:* Part-time. *Degree requirements:* For master's, thesis. *Entrance requirements:* For doctorate, LSAT, minimum 2 years of college. Additional exam requirements/recommendations for international students: Required—TOEFL, TWE. *Faculty research:* Labor relations law, tax law and policy, criminal law and policy, critical legal theories, international legal relations.

Quinnipiac University, School of Law, Hamden, CT 06518-1940. Offers LL M, JD, JD/MBA, JD/MELP. *Accreditation:* ABA. *Program availability:* Part-time, evening/weekend. *Entrance requirements:* For doctorate, LSAT. Additional exam requirements/recommendations for international students: Recommended—TOEFL. Electronic applications accepted. Application fee is waived when completed online. *Expenses:* Contact institution. *Faculty research:* Sentencing, death penalty, public health law, tax law, legal history.

Regent University, Graduate School, Robertson School of Government, Virginia Beach, VA 23464-9800. Offers government (MA), including American government, healthcare policy and ethics (MA, MPA), international relations, law and public policy, national security studies, political communication, political theory, religion and politics; public administration (MPA), including emergency management and homeland security, federal government, general public administration, healthcare policy and ethics (MA, MPA), law, nonprofit administration and faith-based organizations, public leadership and management, servant leadership. *Program availability:* Part-time, evening/weekend, 100% online, blended/hybrid learning. *Faculty:* 8 full-time (1 woman), 19 part-time/adjunct (3 women). *Students:* 40 full-time (27 women), 119 part-time (69 women); includes 73 minority (47 Black or African American, non-Hispanic/Latino; 3 Asian, non-Hispanic/Latino; 15 Hispanic/Latino; 8 Two or more races, non-Hispanic/Latino), 6 international. Average age 35. 253 applicants, 41% accepted, 70 enrolled. In 2016, 34 master's awarded. *Degree requirements:* For master's, thesis optional, internship. *Entrance requirements:* For master's, GRE General Test or LSAT, personal essay, writing sample, resume, college transcripts. Additional exam requirements/recommendations for international students: Required—TOEFL (minimum score 577 paper-based). *Application deadline:* For fall admission, 5/1 priority date for domestic students; for spring admission, 11/1 priority date for domestic students. Applications are processed on a rolling basis. Application fee: $50. Electronic applications accepted. *Expenses:* $650 per credit (MA/MPA); $250 per semester technology fee. *Financial support:* In 2016–17, 78 students received support. Career-related internships or fieldwork, scholarships/grants, and unspecified assistantships available. Support available to part-time students. *Faculty research:* International relations and politics, public administration, leadership and ethics, Biblical law, Constitutional law and Supreme Court. *Unit head:* Dr. Eric Patterson, Dean, 757-352-4616, Fax: 757-352-4735, E-mail: epatterson@regent.edu. *Application contact:* Heidi Cece, Assistant Vice President of Enrollment Management, 800-373-5504, Fax: 757-352-4381, E-mail: admissions@regent.edu.
Website: http://www.regent.edu/rsg/

Regent University, Graduate School, School of Law, Virginia Beach, VA 23464-9800. Offers American legal studies (LL M); human rights (LL M); law (MA, JD), including business (MA), criminal justice (MA), general legal studies (MA), human resources management (MA), human rights (MA), mediation (MA), national security (MA), non-profit management (MA), regulatory compliance (MA), wealth management and financial planning (MA); JD/MA; JD/MBA. *Accreditation:* ABA. *Program availability:* Part-time,

100% online, blended/hybrid learning. *Faculty:* 20 full-time (6 women), 67 part-time/adjunct (19 women). *Students:* 364 full-time (219 women), 170 part-time (118 women); includes 213 minority (150 Black or African American, non-Hispanic/Latino; 1 American Indian or Alaska Native, non-Hispanic/Latino; 10 Asian, non-Hispanic/Latino; 34 Hispanic/Latino; 1 Native Hawaiian or other Pacific Islander, non-Hispanic/Latino; 17 Two or more races, non-Hispanic/Latino), 87 international. Average age 34. 834 applicants, 45% accepted, 174 enrolled. In 2016, 48 master's, 85 doctorates awarded. *Entrance requirements:* For master's, college transcripts, resume, personal statement; for doctorate, LSAT, minimum undergraduate GPA of 3.0, official transcripts, 2 letters of recommendation, resume, personal statement. Additional exam requirements/recommendations for international students: Required—TOEFL (minimum score 600 paper-based). *Application deadline:* For fall admission, 3/1 for domestic students. Applications are processed on a rolling basis. Application fee: $50. Electronic applications accepted. *Expenses:* $1,140 per credit (for JD); $650 per credit (for MA); $833 per credit (for LL M); $250 technology fee. *Financial support:* In 2016–17, 319 students received support. Career-related internships or fieldwork, scholarships/grants, and unspecified assistantships available. Support available to part-time students. *Faculty research:* Family law, Constitutional law, law and culture, evidence and practice, intellectual property. *Unit head:* Michael Hernandez, Dean, 757-352-4040, Fax: 757-352-4595, E-mail: michher@regent.edu. *Application contact:* Katie Kerley, Director of Law Admissions, 877-267-5072, Fax: 757-352-4139, E-mail: lawschool@regent.edu.
Website: http://www.regent.edu/law/

Roger Williams University, School of Law, Bristol, RI 02809-5171. Offers MSL, JD, JD/MLRHR, JD/MMA, JD/MS, JD/MSCJ. JD/MMA and JD/MLRHR offered jointly with University of Rhode Island. *Accreditation:* ABA. *Program availability:* Part-time. *Faculty:* 25 full-time (15 women), 52 part-time/adjunct (20 women). *Students:* 420 full-time (217 women), 5 part-time (4 women); includes 105 minority (32 Black or African American, non-Hispanic/Latino; 2 American Indian or Alaska Native, non-Hispanic/Latino; 14 Asian, non-Hispanic/Latino; 40 Hispanic/Latino; 2 Native Hawaiian or other Pacific Islander, non-Hispanic/Latino; 15 Two or more races, non-Hispanic/Latino), 1 international. Average age 26. 856 applicants, 69% accepted, 158 enrolled. In 2016, 86 doctorates awarded. *Entrance requirements:* For master's, GRE, GMAT; for doctorate, LSAT. Additional exam requirements/recommendations for international students: Required—TOEFL (minimum score 600 paper-based; 100 iBT). *Application deadline:* For fall admission, 4/1 priority date for domestic and international students. Applications are processed on a rolling basis. Application fee: $60. Electronic applications accepted. *Expenses: Tuition:* Part-time $809 per credit hour. Tuition and fees vary according to program. *Financial support:* In 2016–17, 289 students received support, including 12 fellowships (averaging $623 per year), 37 research assistantships (averaging $695 per year); Federal Work-Study also available. Financial award application deadline: 3/31; financial award applicants required to submit FAFSA. *Faculty research:* Civil rights, constitutional, contract, intellectual property, conflicts of law, national security, and international law. *Unit head:* Michael Yelnosky, Dean, 401-254-4500, Fax: 401-254-3525, E-mail: myelnosky@rwu.edu. *Application contact:* Michael W. Donnelly-Boylen, Assistant Dean of Admissions, 401-254-4555, Fax: 401-254-4516, E-mail: mdonnelly-boylen@rwu.edu.
Website: http://law.rwu.edu

Rutgers University–Camden, School of Law, Camden, NJ 08102. Offers JD, JD/DO, JD/MA, JD/MBA, JD/MCRP, JD/MD, JD/MPA, JD/MPH, JD/MS, JD/MSW. JD/MCRP, JD/MA, JD/MPA, JD/MSW, JD/MS offered jointly with Rutgers, The State University of New Jersey, New Brunswick; JD/MPA, JD/MD, JD/DO with University of Medicine and Dentistry of New Jersey. *Accreditation:* ABA. *Program availability:* Part-time, evening/weekend. *Entrance requirements:* For doctorate, LSAT. Additional exam requirements/recommendations for international students: Recommended—TOEFL. Electronic applications accepted. *Expenses:* Contact institution. *Faculty research:* International law, commercial law, public law, health law, constitutional law, jurisprudence.

Rutgers University–Newark, School of Law, Newark, NJ 07102-3094. Offers JD, JD/MA, JD/MBA, JD/MCRP, JD/MD, JD/MSW, JD/PhD. JD/MCRP, JD/PhD offered jointly with Rutgers, The State University of New Jersey, New Brunswick. *Accreditation:* ABA. *Program availability:* Part-time, evening/weekend. *Entrance requirements:* For doctorate, LSAT. *Expenses:* Contact institution. *Faculty research:* Civil rights and liberties, women and the law, international human rights and world order, corporate law, employment law.

St. John's University, School of Law, Program in International and Comparative Sports Law, Queens, NY 11439. Offers LL M. *Degree requirements:* For master's, thesis, practicum, seminar. *Entrance requirements:* For master's, resume, 2 letters of recommendation, writing sample, personal statement, interview, transcript, proficiency in English. Additional exam requirements/recommendations for international students: Required—TOEFL (minimum score 600 paper-based), IELTS (minimum score 7), TWE (minimum score 5). *Expenses:* Contact institution.

St. John's University, School of Law, Program in Law, Queens, NY 11439. Offers JD, JD/LL M, MA/JD, MBA/JD. *Accreditation:* ABA. *Program availability:* Part-time, evening/weekend. *Entrance requirements:* For doctorate, LSAT, personal statement, CAS Report, 2 letters of recommendation, bachelor's degree. Additional exam requirements/recommendations for international students: Required—TOEFL (minimum score 600 paper-based; 100 iBT), IELTS (minimum score 7). Electronic applications accepted. *Expenses:* Contact institution.

Saint Joseph's University, College of Arts and Sciences, Department of Criminal Justice, Philadelphia, PA 19131-1395. Offers behavior analysis (MS, Post-Master's Certificate); behavior management (MS); criminal justice (MS); federal law (MS); intelligence and crime (MS). *Program availability:* Part-time, evening/weekend, 100% online, blended/hybrid learning. *Faculty:* 4 full-time (3 women), 43 part-time/adjunct (18 women). *Students:* 23 full-time (13 women), 380 part-time (269 women); includes 116 minority (91 Black or African American, non-Hispanic/Latino; 2 American Indian or Alaska Native, non-Hispanic/Latino; 5 Asian, non-Hispanic/Latino; 16 Hispanic/Latino; 2 Native Hawaiian or other Pacific Islander, non-Hispanic/Latino), 7 international. Average age 31. 214 applicants, 73% accepted, 110 enrolled. In 2016, 141 master's, 34 other advanced degrees awarded. *Degree requirements:* For master's, thesis. *Entrance requirements:* For master's, 2 letters of recommendation, personal statement, resume, official transcripts, minimum GPA of 3.0. Additional exam requirements/recommendations for international students: Required—TOEFL (minimum score 550 paper-based; 80 iBT). *Application deadline:* For fall admission, 7/15 for international students; for spring admission, 11/1 for international students. Applications are processed on a rolling basis. Application fee: $35. Electronic applications accepted. *Expenses:* $853 per credit. *Financial support:* In 2016–17, 5 students received support. Federal Work-Study and unspecified assistantships available. Financial award application deadline: 5/1; financial award applicants required to submit FAFSA. *Faculty research:* Ethics in policing, multiculturalism, behavior analysis. *Total annual research expenditures:* $17,309. *Unit head:* Sylvia DeSantis, Director, 610-660-3131, E-mail: gradcas@sju.edu. *Application contact:* Graduate Admissions, College of Arts and Sciences, 610-660-3131, E-mail: gradcas@sju.edu.
Website: http://www.sju.edu/majors-programs/graduate-arts-sciences/masters/criminal-justice-ms

Saint Louis University, School of Law, St. Louis, MO 63108. Offers LL M, JD. *Accreditation:* ABA. *Program availability:* Part-time, evening/weekend. *Degree requirements:* For master's, thesis (for some programs). *Entrance requirements:* For master's, JD or equivalent; for doctorate, LSAT, letters of recommendation, resume, personal statement, LSDAS. Additional exam requirements/recommendations for international students: Required—TOEFL (minimum score 590 paper-based). Electronic applications accepted. *Expenses:* Contact institution. *Faculty research:* Health law, employment law, international comparative law, lawyering skills (clinical).

St. Mary's University, School of Law, JD Program, San Antonio, TX 78228-8507. Offers JD. *Program availability:* Part-time, evening/weekend. *Students:* 557 full-time (257 women), 170 part-time (71 women). Average age 29. In 2016, 216 doctorates awarded. *Degree requirements:* For doctorate, 90 credit hours, minimum cumulative GPA of 2.0. *Entrance requirements:* For doctorate, LSAT, personal statement, letters of recommendation. Additional exam requirements/recommendations for international students: Required—TOEFL (minimum score 550 paper-based; 80 iBT), IELTS (minimum score 6). *Application deadline:* For spring admission, 3/1 priority date for domestic students. *Expenses: Tuition:* Full-time $15,600; part-time $865 per credit hour. *Required fees:* $148 per semester. *Unit head:* Stephen Sheppard, Dean, 210-436-3684, E-mail: sheppard@stmarytx.edu. *Application contact:* Kim Thornton, Director, Graduate and Adult Enrollment Services, 210-436-3101, E-mail: akthornton@stmarytx.edu.
Website: https://law.stmarytx.edu/academics/jd-programs/

St. Mary's University, School of Law, LL M Program, San Antonio, TX 78228-8507. Offers American legal studies (LL M); international and comparative law (LL M); international criminal law (LL M). *Program availability:* Part-time, evening/weekend. *Students:* 31 full-time (8 women); includes 10 minority (1 Black or African American, non-Hispanic/Latino; 2 Asian, non-Hispanic/Latino; 7 Hispanic/Latino). Average age 36. In 2016, 26 master's awarded. *Degree requirements:* For master's, thesis, 24 hours of academic credit. *Entrance requirements:* For master's, official transcripts, personal statement, resume, 2 letters of recommendation. Additional exam requirements/recommendations for international students: Required—TOEFL (minimum score 550 paper-based; 80 iBT), IELTS (minimum score 6). *Application deadline:* Applications are processed on a rolling basis. Electronic applications accepted. *Expenses: Tuition:* Full-time $15,600; part-time $865 per credit hour. *Required fees:* $148 per semester. *Unit head:* Robert Lee Summers, Jr., Professor of Law/Co-Director of LL M Programs/Co-Director of International Legal Studies, 210-618-5014, E-mail: rsummers@stmarytx.edu. *Application contact:* Gary Liu, Professor of Law/Co-Director of LL M Programs, 210-431-2145, E-mail: cliu@stmarytx.edu.
Website: https://law.stmarytx.edu/academics/ll-m-programs/

St. Mary's University, School of Law, Master of Jurisprudence Program, San Antonio, TX 78228-8507. Offers MJ. *Accreditation:* ABA. *Program availability:* Part-time, evening/weekend. *Students:* 9 full-time (7 women), 13 part-time (9 women); includes 17 minority (2 American Indian or Alaska Native, non-Hispanic/Latino; 2 Asian, non-Hispanic/Latino; 13 Hispanic/Latino). Average age 38. *Degree requirements:* For master's, 30 credits, minimum GPA of 2.0. *Entrance requirements:* For master's, official transcripts, personal statement, resume, 2 letters of recommendation, proof of four-year undergraduate degree from accredited U.S. college/university or foreign institution approved by government or accrediting authority. Additional exam requirements/recommendations for international students: Required—TOEFL (minimum score 550 paper-based; 80 iBT), IELTS (minimum score 6). *Application deadline:* Applications are processed on a rolling basis. *Expenses:* Contact institution. *Unit head:* Stephen Sheppard, Dean, 210-436-3684, E-mail: sheppard@stmarytx.edu. *Application contact:* Kim Thornton, Director, Graduate and Adult Enrollment Services, 210-436-3101, E-mail: akthornton@stmarytx.edu.
Website: https://law.stmarytx.edu/law-admission/applying-to-the-m-jur/#304300

St. Thomas University, School of Law, Miami Gardens, FL 33054-6459. Offers international human rights (LL M); international taxation (LL M); law (JD); JD/MBA; JD/MS. *Accreditation:* ABA. *Program availability:* Online learning. *Degree requirements:* For master's, thesis (international taxation). *Entrance requirements:* For doctorate, LSAT. Electronic applications accepted. *Expenses:* Contact institution.

Samford University, Cumberland School of Law, Birmingham, AL 35229. Offers MCL, JD, JD/M Acc, JD/M Div, JD/MATS, JD/MBA, JD/MPA, JD/MPH, JD/MS, JD/MSEM. JD/MPH, JD/MPA offered jointly with The University of Alabama at Birmingham; JD/MS offered with Albany Medical College. *Accreditation:* ABA. *Faculty:* 22 full-time (7 women), 20 part-time/adjunct (8 women). *Students:* 456 full-time (221 women), 9 part-time (7 women); includes 78 minority (40 Black or African American, non-Hispanic/Latino; 5 American Indian or Alaska Native, non-Hispanic/Latino; 6 Asian, non-Hispanic/Latino; 18 Hispanic/Latino; 1 Native Hawaiian or other Pacific Islander, non-Hispanic/Latino; 8 Two or more races, non-Hispanic/Latino), 7 international. Average age 26. 579 applicants, 68% accepted, 149 enrolled. In 2016, 158 doctorates awarded. *Degree requirements:* For master's, thesis. *Entrance requirements:* For doctorate, LSAT. Additional exam requirements/recommendations for international students: Required—TOEFL (minimum score 550 paper-based). *Application deadline:* For fall admission, 6/1 for domestic students, 6/1 priority date for international students. Applications are processed on a rolling basis. Electronic applications accepted. *Expenses:* $55,900 per year. *Financial support:* In 2016–17, 345 students received support. Career-related internships or fieldwork, Federal Work-Study, institutionally sponsored loans, and scholarships/grants available. Financial award application deadline: 3/1; financial award applicants required to submit FAFSA. *Unit head:* Henry C. Strickland, Dean/Professor of Law, 205-726-2704, Fax: 205-726-4457, E-mail: hcstrick@samford.edu. *Application contact:* Jen Hartzog, Director of Admissions, 205-726-2701, Fax: 205-726-2057, E-mail: jhartzog@samford.edu.
Website: http://cumberland.samford.edu/

San Joaquin College of Law, Law Program, Clovis, CA 93612-1312. Offers JD. *Program availability:* Part-time, evening/weekend. *Entrance requirements:* For doctorate, LSAT.

The Santa Barbara and Ventura Colleges of Law–Santa Barbara, Graduate and Professional Programs, Santa Barbara, CA 93101. Offers MLS, JD.

The Santa Barbara and Ventura Colleges of Law–Ventura, Graduate and Professional Programs, Ventura, CA 93003. Offers MLS, JD.

Santa Clara University, School of Law, Santa Clara, CA 95053. Offers intellectual property (LL M); international and comparative law (LL M); law (JD); United States law (LL M); JD/MBA; JD/MSIS. LL M in United States law track only open to non-U.S. attorneys; JD/MBA, JD/MSIS are joint programs with the Leavey School of Business. *Accreditation:* ABA. *Program availability:* Part-time, evening/weekend. *Faculty:* 56 full-time (30 women), 38 part-time/adjunct (23 women). *Students:* 641 full-time (334 women), 72 part-time (30 women); includes 304 minority (29 Black or African American, non-Hispanic/Latino; 128 Asian, non-Hispanic/Latino; 108 Hispanic/Latino; 2 Native Hawaiian or other Pacific Islander, non-Hispanic/Latino; 37 Two or more races, non-Hispanic/Latino), 81 international. Average age 27. 2,235 applicants, 75% accepted, 305 enrolled. In 2016, 27 master's, 218 doctorates awarded. *Entrance requirements:* For master's and doctorate, LSAT, transcripts, personal statement. Additional exam requirements/recommendations for international students: Required—TOEFL or IELTS.

Law

Application deadline: Applications are processed on a rolling basis. Application fee: $75. Electronic applications accepted. Application fee is waived when completed online. *Expenses:* $1,747 per unit (for JD); $1,960 per unit (for LL M). *Financial support:* Fellowships, research assistantships, teaching assistantships, career-related internships or fieldwork, Federal Work-Study, scholarships/grants, traineeships, health care benefits, tuition waivers, and unspecified assistantships available. Support available to part-time students. Financial award application deadline: 3/1; financial award applicants required to submit FAFSA. *Unit head:* Lisa Kloppenberg, Dean, 408-554-4362. *Application contact:* Nanette Cannon, Director of Admissions, 408-551-1846, E-mail: ncannon@scu.edu.
Website: http://law.scu.edu/

Savannah Law School, JD Program, Savannah, GA 31401. Offers JD. *Program availability:* Part-time. *Entrance requirements:* For doctorate, LSAT, 2-3 page personal statement, resume, two letters of recommendation. Electronic applications accepted. *Expenses:* $20,686 per semester full-time tuition, $12,411 part-time. *Financial support:* Fellowships and scholarships/grants available. Financial award application deadline: 6/1; financial award applicants required to submit FAFSA. *Unit head:* Malcolm L. Morris, Dean, 912-525-3910, E-mail: mmorris@savannahlawschool.org. *Application contact:* Rebecca Milter, Director of Admissions, E-mail: rmilter@savannahlawschool.org.

Seattle University, School of Law, Seattle, WA 98122-4340. Offers JD, JD/MATL, JD/MBA, JD/MCJ, JD/MIB, JD/MPA, JD/MSAL, JD/MSF, JD/MSL. *Accreditation:* ABA. *Program availability:* Part-time. *Entrance requirements:* For doctorate, LSAT. Additional exam requirements/recommendations for international students: Required—TOEFL (minimum score 600 paper-based; 100 iBT). Electronic applications accepted. Application fee is waived when completed online. *Expenses:* Contact institution. *Faculty research:* Race, postcolonial theory, and U.S. civil rights; secrecy and democratic decisions; linguistic features of police culture and the coercive impact of police officer swearing in police-citizen interaction; the imprisoned parent: differential power in same-sex families based on legal and cultural understandings of parentage; theology in public reason and legal discourse: a case for the preferential option for the poor.

Seton Hall University, School of Law, Newark, NJ 07102-5210. Offers health law (LL M, JD); intellectual property (LL M, JD); law (MSJ); JD/MADIR; JD/MBA; MD/JD; MD/MSJ. MD/JD, MD/MSJ offered jointly with University of Medicine and Dentistry of New Jersey. *Accreditation:* ABA. *Program availability:* Part-time, evening/weekend. *Degree requirements:* For master's, thesis optional. *Entrance requirements:* For master's, professional experience, letters of recommendation; for doctorate, LSAT, active LSDAS registration, letters of recommendation. Additional exam requirements/recommendations for international students: Recommended—TOEFL. Electronic applications accepted. *Expenses:* Contact institution. *Faculty research:* Health law, intellectual property law, science and the law, international law and employment/labor law.

Southern Illinois University Carbondale, School of Law, Carbondale, IL 62901-6804. Offers general law (LL M); health law and policy (LL M); law (JD); legal studies (MLS), including general law, health law and policy; JD/M Acc; JD/MBA; JD/MD; JD/MPA; JD/MSW; JD/PhD. *Accreditation:* ABA. *Program availability:* Part-time. *Entrance requirements:* For doctorate, LSAT. Additional exam requirements/recommendations for international students: Required—TOEFL (minimum score 600 paper-based). Electronic applications accepted. *Expenses:* Contact institution. *Faculty research:* Health care, criminal, environmental, and international law; tort reform.

Southern Methodist University, Dedman College of Humanities and Sciences, Department of Economics, Dallas, TX 75205. Offers applied economics (MA); applied economics and predictive analytics (MS); economics (PhD); law and economics (MA). *Program availability:* Part-time, evening/weekend. Terminal master's awarded for partial completion of doctoral program. *Degree requirements:* For master's, thesis, oral qualifying exam; for doctorate, thesis/dissertation, written exams. *Entrance requirements:* For master's, GRE General Test or GMAT, 12 hours of course work in economics, minimum GPA of 3.0, previous course work in calculus and statistics; for doctorate, GRE General Test, minimum GPA of 3.0; 3 semesters of course work in calculus; 1 semester each of course work in statistics and linear algebra. Additional exam requirements/recommendations for international students: Required—TOEFL (minimum score 550 paper-based). Electronic applications accepted. *Faculty research:* Economic theory, game theory, econometrics, international trade, labor.

Southern Methodist University, Dedman School of Law, Dallas, TX 75275-0110. Offers law (JD, SJD); law (for foreign law school graduates) (LL M); law (general) (LL M); taxation (LL M); JD/MA; JD/MBA. *Accreditation:* ABA. *Program availability:* Part-time, evening/weekend. *Degree requirements:* For master's, thesis optional; for doctorate, thesis/dissertation (for some programs), 30 hours of public service (for JD). *Entrance requirements:* For master's, JD; for doctorate, LSAT (for JD). Additional exam requirements/recommendations for international students: Required—TOEFL (minimum score 575 paper-based; 91 iBT). Electronic applications accepted. *Expenses:* Contact institution. *Faculty research:* Corporate law, intellectual property, international law, commercial law, dispute resolution.

Southern University and Agricultural and Mechanical College, Southern University Law Center, Baton Rouge, LA 70813. Offers JD. *Accreditation:* ABA; SACS/CC. *Program availability:* Part-time, evening/weekend. *Entrance requirements:* For doctorate, LSAT. Additional exam requirements/recommendations for international students: Recommended—TOEFL. Electronic applications accepted. *Expenses:* Contact institution. *Faculty research:* Civil law, comparative law, constitutional law, civil rights law.

South Texas College of Law Houston, Professional Program, Houston, TX 77002-7000. Offers JD. *Accreditation:* ABA. *Program availability:* Part-time, evening/weekend. *Degree requirements:* For doctorate, completion of 90 hours within 7 years of enrollment. *Entrance requirements:* For doctorate, LSAT (taken within last 4 years), degree from accredited 4-year institution. Electronic applications accepted.

Southwestern Law School, Graduate and Professional Programs, Los Angeles, CA 90010. Offers individualized studies (LL M); law (JD). *Accreditation:* ABA. *Program availability:* Part-time, evening/weekend. *Faculty:* 60 full-time (30 women), 85 part-time/adjunct (33 women). *Students:* 659 full-time (393 women), 318 part-time (173 women); includes 418 minority (64 Black or African American, non-Hispanic/Latino; 1 American Indian or Alaska Native, non-Hispanic/Latino; 86 Asian, non-Hispanic/Latino; 202 Hispanic/Latino; 5 Native Hawaiian or other Pacific Islander, non-Hispanic/Latino; 60 Two or more races, non-Hispanic/Latino), 16 international. Average age 27. 1,806 applicants, 52% accepted, 278 enrolled. *Median time to degree:* Of those who began their doctoral program in fall 2008, 100% received their degree in 8 years or less. *Entrance requirements:* For master's, JD; for doctorate, LSAT, CAS. Additional exam requirements/recommendations for international students: Required—TOEFL. *Application deadline:* For fall admission, 3/1 priority date for domestic students, 4/1 priority date for international students. Applications are processed on a rolling basis. Application fee: $60. Electronic applications accepted. *Expenses:* Contact institution. *Financial support:* Federal Work-Study, institutionally sponsored loans, and scholarships/grants available. Support available to part-time students. Financial award application deadline: 4/1; financial award applicants required to submit FAFSA. *Faculty research:* International trade and law, mediation/arbitration, land use and urban planning, antitrust law, entertainment and media law. *Unit head:* Susan Westerberg Prager, Dean, 213-738-6710, Fax: 213-383-1688. *Application contact:* Lisa Gear, Assistant Dean of Admissions, 213-738-6834, Fax: 213-383-1688, E-mail: admissions@swlaw.edu.
Website: http://www.swlaw.edu

Stanford University, Law School, Stanford, CA 94305-8610. Offers corporate governance and practice (LL M); environmental law and policy (LL M); international economic law, business and policy (LL M); international legal studies (JSM); law (JD, JSD); law, science and technology (LL M); legal studies (MLS); JD/MA; JD/MBA; JD/MPP; JD/MS; JD/PhD. *Accreditation:* ABA. *Degree requirements:* For doctorate, thesis/dissertation (for some programs). *Entrance requirements:* For doctorate, LSAT (for JD). Electronic applications accepted. *Expenses:* Contact institution.

Stetson University, College of Law, Gulfport, FL 33707-3299. Offers advocacy (LL M); elder law (LL M); international law (LL M); law (JD); JD/LL M; JD/MBA. *Accreditation:* ABA. *Program availability:* Part-time, evening/weekend, 100% online. *Faculty:* 46 full-time (26 women), 61 part-time/adjunct (21 women). *Students:* 769 full-time (390 women), 110 part-time (51 women); includes 234 minority (53 Black or African American, non-Hispanic/Latino; 3 American Indian or Alaska Native, non-Hispanic/Latino; 23 Asian, non-Hispanic/Latino; 128 Hispanic/Latino; 27 Two or more races, non-Hispanic/Latino), 30 international. Average age 28. 1,812 applicants, 51% accepted, 271 enrolled. In 2016, 31 master's, 345 doctorates awarded. *Entrance requirements:* For doctorate, LSAT. Additional exam requirements/recommendations for international students: Required—TOEFL (minimum score 600 paper-based, 100 iBT) or IELTS (minimum score 7). *Application deadline:* For fall admission, 5/15 for domestic and international students. Applications are processed on a rolling basis. Application fee: $55. Electronic applications accepted. *Expenses:* $41,134 tuition; $320 fees. *Financial support:* In 2016–17, 510 students received support, including 86 research assistantships (averaging $911 per year), 42 teaching assistantships (averaging $933 per year); career-related internships or fieldwork, Federal Work-Study, and scholarships/grants also available. Support available to part-time students. Financial award application deadline: 8/15; financial award applicants required to submit FAFSA. *Faculty research:* Advocacy and legal communication, law and higher education, elder law, international law including biodiversity and Caribbean law, veterans law and policy. *Total annual research expenditures:* $401,410. *Unit head:* Christopher M. Pietruszkiewicz, Dean/Professor of Law, 727-562-7809, Fax: 727-562-6428, E-mail: cmp@law.stetson.edu. *Application contact:* Darren Kettles, Director of Admissions, 727-562-7802, Fax: 727-343-0136, E-mail: lawadmit@law.stetson.edu.
Website: http://www.law.stetson.edu/

Suffolk University, Law School, Boston, MA 02108. Offers business law and financial services (JD); civil litigation (JD); global law and technology (LL M); health and biomedical law (JD); intellectual property law (JD); international law (JD); JD/MBA; JD/MPA; JD/MSCJ; JD/MSF; JD/MSIE. *Accreditation:* ABA. *Program availability:* Part-time, evening/weekend. *Faculty:* 58 full-time (26 women), 47 part-time/adjunct (17 women). *Students:* 647 full-time (357 women), 380 part-time (197 women); includes 219 minority (61 Black or African American, non-Hispanic/Latino; 1 American Indian or Alaska Native, non-Hispanic/Latino; 50 Asian, non-Hispanic/Latino; 82 Hispanic/Latino; 25 Two or more races, non-Hispanic/Latino), 42 international. Average age 27. 1,924 applicants, 64% accepted, 355 enrolled. In 2016, 21 master's, 416 doctorates awarded. *Degree requirements:* For master's, legal writing. *Entrance requirements:* For master's, 2 letters of recommendation, resume, personal statement; for doctorate, LSAT, LSDAS, dean's certification, recommendation. Additional exam requirements/recommendations for international students: Required—TOEFL (minimum score 600 paper-based; 100 iBT). *Application deadline:* For fall admission, 4/1 for domestic and international students. Applications are processed on a rolling basis. Application fee: $60. Electronic applications accepted. *Expenses:* $45,922 per year full-time tuition, $34,440 per year part-time tuition. *Financial support:* In 2016–17, 572 students received support, including 1 fellowship (averaging $31,390 per year); career-related internships or fieldwork, Federal Work-Study, institutionally sponsored loans, and scholarships/grants also available. Support available to part-time students. Financial award application deadline: 3/1; financial award applicants required to submit FAFSA. *Faculty research:* Civil law, international law, health/biomedical law, business and finance, intellectual property. *Unit head:* Andrew Perlman, Dean, 617-573-8144, Fax: 617-994-6838, E-mail: lawadmin@suffolk.edu. *Application contact:* Matthew Gavin, Assistant Dean for Admissions and Financial Aid, 617-573-8144, Fax: 617-994-6838, E-mail: lawadm@suffolk.edu.
Website: http://www.suffolk.edu/law/

Syracuse University, College of Law, JD Program, Syracuse, NY 13244. Offers JD. *Expenses: Tuition:* Full-time $25,974; part-time $1443 per credit hour. *Required fees:* $802; $50 per course. Tuition and fees vary according to course load and program. *Unit head:* Craig M. Boise, Dean and Professor of Law, 315-443-9580, E-mail: cmboise@law.syr.edu. *Application contact:* Nolana McKinstry, Associate Director of Admissions, 315-443-1962, Fax: 315-443-9568, E-mail: nrmckins@law.syr.edu.
Website: http://law.syr.edu/academics/j.d.-degree

Syracuse University, College of Law, Master of Laws Program in American Law, Syracuse, NY 13244. Offers LL M. *Expenses: Tuition:* Full-time $25,974; part-time $1443 per credit hour. *Required fees:* $802; $50 per course. Tuition and fees vary according to course load and program. *Unit head:* Craig M. Boise, Dean and Professor of Law, 315-443-9580, E-mail: cmboise@law.syr.edu. *Application contact:* Andrew Horsfall, Executive Director of International Programs and Initiatives, 315-443-1962, Fax: 315-443-9568, E-mail: ashorsfa@law.syr.edu.
Website: http://law.syr.edu/academics/llm-degree

Taft University System, Taft Law School, Denver, CO 80246. Offers American jurisprudence (LL M); law (JD); taxation (LL M).

Temple University, Beasley School of Law, Philadelphia, PA 19122. Offers law (JD); legal education (SJD); taxation (LL M); transnational law (LL M); trial advocacy (LL M); JD/LL M; JD/MBA; JD/MPH. *Accreditation:* ABA. *Program availability:* Part-time, evening/weekend. *Faculty:* 64 full-time (30 women), 102 part-time/adjunct (37 women). *Students:* 534 full-time (282 women), 153 part-time (66 women); includes 191 minority (59 Black or African American, non-Hispanic/Latino; 2 American Indian or Alaska Native, non-Hispanic/Latino; 60 Asian, non-Hispanic/Latino; 62 Hispanic/Latino; 8 Two or more races, non-Hispanic/Latino), 9 international. Average age 26. 2,046 applicants, 42% accepted, 218 enrolled. In 2016, 202 doctorates awarded. *Entrance requirements:* For doctorate, LSAT (for JD). Additional exam requirements/recommendations for international students: Recommended—TOEFL. *Application deadline:* For fall admission, 3/1 for domestic and international students. Applications are processed on a rolling basis. Application fee: $60. Electronic applications accepted. *Expenses:* $24,786 per year full-time resident tuition; $37,500 per year full-time non-resident tuition; $20,018 per year part-time resident tuition; $30,196 per year part-time non-resident tuition. *Financial support:* In 2016–17, 469 students received support, including research assistantships (averaging $5,500 per year), teaching assistantships (averaging $5,500 per year); fellowships, Federal Work-Study, scholarships/grants, tuition waivers (full and partial), and unspecified assistantships also available. Support available to part-time

students. Financial award application deadline: 3/1; financial award applicants required to submit FAFSA. *Faculty research:* Cybersecurity, gender issues, health care law, immigration law, intellectual property law. *Unit head:* Gregory N. Mandel, Dean, 215-204-7863, Fax: 215-204-1185, E-mail: law@temple.edu. *Application contact:* Johanne L. Johnston, Assistant Dean for Admissions and Financial Aid, 800-560-1428, Fax: 215-204-9319, E-mail: lawadmis@temple.edu.
Website: http://www.law.temple.edu

Texas A&M University, School of Law, College Station, TX 77843. Offers JM, LL M, M Jur, JD. *Accreditation:* ABA. *Faculty:* 88. *Students:* 466 full-time (234 women), 17 part-time (6 women); includes 115 minority (29 Black or African American, non-Hispanic/Latino; 2 American Indian or Alaska Native, non-Hispanic/Latino; 12 Asian, non-Hispanic/Latino; 65 Hispanic/Latino; 7 Two or more races, non-Hispanic/Latino), 6 international. Average age 28. 1,893 applicants, 24% accepted, 133 enrolled. *Entrance requirements:* For doctorate, LSAT, personal statement, resume, all post-secondary transcripts, 2-4 letters of recommendation and up to 2 LSAC evaluations, CAS Report. *Application deadline:* For fall admission, 7/1 for domestic students. Applications are processed on a rolling basis. Application fee: $55. *Expenses:* Contact institution. *Financial support:* In 2016–17, 359 students received support, including 4 fellowships with tuition reimbursements available (averaging $13,649 per year); career-related internships or fieldwork, institutionally sponsored loans, scholarships/grants, traineeships, health care benefits, and tuition waivers (full and partial) also available. Support available to part-time students. Financial award applicants required to submit FAFSA. *Unit head:* Dr. Andrew P. Morriss, Dean, 817-212-4139, Fax: 817-212-4139, E-mail: amorriss@law.tamu.edu. *Application contact:* Law School Admissions, 817-212-4040, E-mail: law-admissions@law.tamu.edu.
Website: http://law.tamu.edu/

Texas Southern University, Thurgood Marshall School of Law, Houston, TX 77004-4584. Offers JD. *Accreditation:* ABA. *Entrance requirements:* For doctorate, LSAT. Electronic applications accepted. *Expenses:* Contact institution. *Faculty research:* Sports law, civil rights and minors, international economics regulation, contracts principle, standards of judicial review.

Texas Tech University, School of Law, Lubbock, TX 79409-0004. Offers law (JD); United States legal studies (LL M); JD/M Engr; JD/MBA; JD/MD; JD/MPA; JD/MS; JD/MSA. *Accreditation:* ABA. *Faculty:* 37 full-time (11 women), 2 part-time/adjunct (1 woman). *Students:* 524 full-time (233 women), 1 (woman) part-time; includes 131 minority (9 Black or African American, non-Hispanic/Latino; 16 Asian, non-Hispanic/Latino; 83 Hispanic/Latino; 23 Two or more races, non-Hispanic/Latino), 18 international. Average age 26. 1,236 applicants, 52% accepted, 167 enrolled. In 2016, 9 master's, 182 doctorates awarded. *Entrance requirements:* For master's, first/basic degree in law from non-U.S. law school approved by LL M admissions committee; for doctorate, LSAT. Additional exam requirements/recommendations for international students: Required—TOEFL (minimum score 600 paper-based; 100 iBT), IELTS (minimum score 7). *Application deadline:* For fall admission, 3/1 priority date for domestic and international students. Applications are processed on a rolling basis. Application fee: $50. Electronic applications accepted. *Expenses:* $620 per credit hour full-time resident tuition, $998 per credit hour full-time non-resident tuition; $98 per credit hour fee plus $608 per term fee. *Financial support:* In 2016–17, 402 students received support, including 31 research assistantships, 31 teaching assistantships; Federal Work-Study, tuition waivers, and tutorships also available. Financial award application deadline: 5/1; financial award applicants required to submit FAFSA. *Faculty research:* Advocacy/legal practice, energy law, criminal law/innocence, business/estate planning, law and science. *Total annual research expenditures:* $81,099. *Unit head:* Richard Rosen, Interim Dean and Professor, 806-834-7585, Fax: 806-742-4014, E-mail: richard.rosen@ttu.edu. *Application contact:* Wendy A. Humphrey, Associate Dean for Admissions and Financial Aid, 806-834-4446, E-mail: admissions.law@ttu.edu.
Website: http://www.law.ttu.edu/

Thomas Jefferson School of Law, Graduate and Professional Programs, San Diego, CA 92110-2905. Offers JD. JD/MBA offered in partnership with San Diego State University. *Accreditation:* ABA. *Program availability:* Part-time, evening/weekend. *Entrance requirements:* For doctorate, LSAT. Additional exam requirements/recommendations for international students: Required—TOEFL. Electronic applications accepted. *Faculty research:* Tenant's rights, fetal rights/medical ethics, bilateral treaties/international law, sexual harassment and gender treatment.

Touro College, Jacob D. Fuchsberg Law Center, Central Islip, NY 11743. Offers general law (LL M); law (JD); U.S. legal studies (LL M); JD/MBA; JD/MPA; JD/MSW. JD/MBA and JD/MPA offered with Long Island University-LIU Post; JD/MSW offered with Stony Brook University, State University of New York. *Accreditation:* ABA. *Program availability:* Part-time, evening/weekend. *Faculty:* 35 full-time (17 women), 30 part-time/adjunct (7 women). *Students:* 445 full-time (245 women), 22 part-time (15 women); includes 166 minority (47 Black or African American, non-Hispanic/Latino; 2 American Indian or Alaska Native, non-Hispanic/Latino; 41 Asian, non-Hispanic/Latino; 72 Hispanic/Latino; 4 Two or more races, non-Hispanic/Latino), 9 international. Average age 30. *Entrance requirements:* For doctorate, LSAT. *Application deadline:* Applications are processed on a rolling basis. Application fee: $60. *Expenses:* Contact institution. *Financial support:* Fellowships, career-related internships or fieldwork, and Federal Work-Study available. Support available to part-time students. Financial award application deadline: 5/1. *Faculty research:* Business law, civil rights, international law, criminal justice. *Unit head:* Dr. Harry Ballan, Dean, 631-761-7100. *Application contact:* Dr. Susan Thompson, Office of Admissions, 631-761-7010, E-mail: admissions@tourolaw.edu.
Website: http://www.tourolaw.edu/

Trine University, Program in Criminal Justice, Angola, IN 46703-1764. Offers emergency management (MS); forensic psychology (MS); law (MS); public administration (MS). *Program availability:* Part-time, evening/weekend. *Entrance requirements:* Additional exam requirements/recommendations for international students: Required—TOEFL. *Expenses: Tuition:* Full-time $13,320. *Required fees:* $460. Tuition and fees vary according to degree level, campus/location, program and student level. *Financial support:* Application deadline: 3/1; applicants required to submit FAFSA. *Unit head:* Craig Laker, Dean, College of Graduate and Professional Studies/Associate Professor, 260-665-4862, E-mail: lakerc@trine.edu.
Website: http://www.trine.edu/academics/majors-and-minors/graduate/criminal-justice/index.aspx

Trinity International University, Trinity Law School, Santa Ana, CA 92705. Offers bioethics (MLS); church and ministry management (MLS); general legal studies (MLS); human resources management (MLS); human rights (MLS); law (JD); nonprofit organizations (MLS). *Program availability:* Part-time, evening/weekend. *Entrance requirements:* For doctorate, LSAT. Additional exam requirements/recommendations for international students: Required—TOEFL (minimum score 580 paper-based). *Application deadline:* For fall admission, 5/1 priority date for domestic and international students; for spring admission, 12/1 priority date for domestic and international students. Applications are processed on a rolling basis. Application fee: $35. *Expenses:* Contact institution. *Financial support:* Scholarships/grants available. Financial award application deadline: 8/15; financial award applicants required to submit FAFSA. *Unit head:* Kevin P. Holsclaw, Academic Dean, 714-836-7160, Fax: 714-796-7190, E-mail: kholscla@tiu.edu. *Application contact:* Doug Eaton, Director of Admissions, 714-796-7103, Fax: 714-796-7190, E-mail: deaton@tiu.edu.
Website: http://www.tls.edu/

Tufts University, The Fletcher School of Law and Diplomacy, Medford, MA 02155. Offers LL M, MA, MALD, MIB, PhD, DVM/MA, JD/MALD, MALD/MA, MALD/MBA, MALD/MS, MD/MA. *Program availability:* Online learning. *Degree requirements:* For master's, one foreign language, thesis; for doctorate, one foreign language, comprehensive exam, thesis/dissertation, dissertation defense. *Entrance requirements:* For master's and doctorate, GMAT or GRE General Test. Additional exam requirements/recommendations for international students: Required—TOEFL (minimum score 600 paper-based; 100 iBT), IELTS (minimum score 7). Electronic applications accepted. *Expenses:* Contact institution. *Faculty research:* Negotiation and conflict resolution, international organizations, international business and economic law, security studies, development economics.

Tulane University, School of Law, New Orleans, LA 70118. Offers American business law (LL M); international development (MS, PhD), including international development; law (JD, SJD). *Accreditation:* ABA. *Degree requirements:* For doctorate, thesis/dissertation (for some programs). *Entrance requirements:* For doctorate, LSAT (for JD). Additional exam requirements/recommendations for international students: Required—TOEFL (minimum score 575 paper-based). Electronic applications accepted. *Expenses:* Contact institution. *Faculty research:* Civil law.

Universidad Autonoma de Guadalajara, Graduate Programs, Guadalajara, Mexico. Offers administrative law and justice (LL M); advertising and corporate communications (MA); architecture (M Arch); business (MBA); computational science (MCC); education (Ed M, Ed D); English-Spanish translation (MA); entrepreneurship and management (MBA); integrated management of digital animation (MA); international business (MIB); international corporate law (LL M); internet technologies (MS); manufacturing systems (MMS); occupational health (MS); philosophy (MA, PhD); power electronics (MS); quality systems (MQS); renewable energy (MS); social evaluation of projects (MBA); strategic market research (MBA); tax law (MA); teaching mathematics (MA).

Universidad Central del Este, Law School, San Pedro de Macoris, Dominican Republic. Offers JD.

Universidad Iberoamericana, Graduate School, Santo Domingo D.N., Dominican Republic. Offers business administration (MBA, PMBA); constitutional law (LL M); dentistry (DMD); educational management (MA); integrated marketing communication (MA); psychopedagogical intervention (M Ed); real estate law (LL M); strategic management of human talent (MM).

Université de Montréal, Faculty of Law, Montréal, QC H3C 3J7, Canada. Offers business law (DESS); common law (North America) (JD); international law (DESS); law (LL M, LL D, DDN, DESS, LL B); tax law (LL M). *Program availability:* Part-time. *Degree requirements:* For master's, thesis; for doctorate, thesis/dissertation, project; for other advanced degree, thesis (for some programs). Electronic applications accepted. *Faculty research:* Legal theory; constitutional, private, and public law.

Université de Sherbrooke, Faculty of Law, Sherbrooke, QC J1K 2R1, Canada. Offers alternative dispute resolution (LL M, Diploma); business law (Diploma); common law (JD); criminal and penal law (Diploma); health law (LL M, Diploma); international law (LL M); law (LL D); legal management (Diploma); notarial law (Diploma); transnational law (Diploma). *Program availability:* Part-time, evening/weekend. *Degree requirements:* For master's, thesis; for Diploma, one foreign language. *Entrance requirements:* For master's and Diploma, LL B. Electronic applications accepted.

Université du Québec à Montréal, Graduate Programs, Program in Social and Labor Law, Montréal, QC H3C 3P8, Canada. Offers Certificate.

Université Laval, Faculty of Law, Programs in Law, Québec, QC G1K 7P4, Canada. Offers environment, sustainable development and food safety (LL M); international and transnational law (LL M, Diploma); law (LL M, LL D); law of business (LL M, Diploma). *Program availability:* Part-time. Terminal master's awarded for partial completion of doctoral program. *Degree requirements:* For master's, thesis (for some programs); for doctorate, thesis/dissertation. *Entrance requirements:* For master's, doctorate, and Diploma, knowledge of French and English. Electronic applications accepted.

University at Albany, State University of New York, School of Business, Department of Accounting and Law, Albany, NY 12222-0001. Offers accounting (MS); forensic accounting (MS); professional accounting (MS); tax practice (MS); taxation (MS). *Accreditation:* AACSB. *Faculty:* 9 full-time (2 women), 8 part-time/adjunct (3 women). *Students:* 137 full-time (62 women), 9 part-time (4 women); includes 31 minority (7 Black or African American, non-Hispanic/Latino; 11 Asian, non-Hispanic/Latino; 9 Hispanic/Latino; 4 Two or more races, non-Hispanic/Latino), 22 international. 257 applicants, 67% accepted, 117 enrolled. In 2016, 110 master's awarded. *Degree requirements:* For master's, research project. *Entrance requirements:* For master's, GMAT. Additional exam requirements/recommendations for international students: Required—TOEFL (minimum score 550 paper-based). *Application deadline:* For fall admission, 3/1 priority date for domestic students, 4/1 for international students. Applications are processed on a rolling basis. Application fee: $75. Electronic applications accepted. *Expenses:* Tuition, state resident: full-time $10,870; part-time $453 per credit hour. Tuition, nonresident: full-time $22,210; part-time $925 per credit hour. *International tuition:* $21,550 full-time. *Required fees:* $1864; $96 per credit hour. *Financial support:* Application deadline: 4/1. *Faculty research:* Professional ethics, statistical analysis, cost management systems, accounting theory. *Unit head:* Ingrid Fisher, Chair, 518-956-8365, E-mail: ifisher@albany.edu. *Application contact:* Michael DeRensis, Director, Graduate Admissions, 518-442-3980, Fax: 518-442-3922, E-mail: graduate@albany.edu.
Website: http://www.albany.edu/business/accounting_index.shtml

University at Buffalo, the State University of New York, Graduate School, School of Law, Buffalo, NY 14260. Offers criminal law (LL M); general law (LL M); law (JD); JD/MA; JD/MBA; JD/MLS; JD/MSW; JD/MUP; JD/PhD; LL M/LL M. *Accreditation:* ABA. *Faculty:* 42 full-time (23 women), 60 part-time/adjunct (21 women). *Students:* 455 full-time (228 women), 4 part-time (3 women); includes 79 minority (20 Black or African American, non-Hispanic/Latino; 15 Asian, non-Hispanic/Latino; 30 Hispanic/Latino; 14 Two or more races, non-Hispanic/Latino), 19 international. Average age 26. 1,202 applicants, 48% accepted, 151 enrolled. In 2016, 189 doctorates awarded. *Entrance requirements:* For master's, JD; for doctorate, LSAT. Additional exam requirements/recommendations for international students: Required—TOEFL (minimum score 85 iBT), IELTS (minimum score 6.5). *Application deadline:* For fall admission, 3/1 priority date for domestic and international students. Applications are processed on a rolling basis. Application fee: $85. Electronic applications accepted. *Expenses:* $27,979 per year resident, full-time; $45,249 per year non-resident, full-time. *Financial support:* In 2016–17, 325 students received support. Federal Work-Study, institutionally sponsored loans, scholarships/grants, tuition waivers (full and partial), and unspecified assistantships available. Financial award application deadline: 3/1; financial award applicants required to submit FAFSA. *Faculty research:* Criminal law, environmental law, international law and human rights, law and finance, cross-border legal studies.

Total annual research expenditures: $184,009. *Unit head:* James A. Gardner, Interim Dean, 716-645-2052, Fax: 716-645-2064, E-mail: jgard@buffalo.edu. *Application contact:* Lindsay J. Gladney, Vice Dean for Admissions, 716-645-2907, Fax: 716-645-6676, E-mail: law-admissions@buffalo.edu.
Website: http://www.law.buffalo.edu/

The University of Akron, School of Law, Akron, OH 44325. Offers LL M, JD, JD/LL M, JD/M Tax, JD/MAP, JD/MBA, JD/MPA. *Accreditation:* ABA. *Program availability:* Part-time, evening/weekend. *Faculty:* 38 full-time (16 women), 16 part-time/adjunct (2 women). *Students:* 270 full-time (115 women), 114 part-time (65 women); includes 61 minority (23 Black or African American, non-Hispanic/Latino; 14 Asian, non-Hispanic/Latino; 15 Hispanic/Latino; 9 Two or more races, non-Hispanic/Latino), 5 international. Average age 28. 885 applicants, 51% accepted, 159 enrolled. In 2016, 6 master's, 125 doctorates awarded. *Entrance requirements:* For doctorate, LSAT, LSDAS. Additional exam requirements/recommendations for international students: Required—TOEFL (minimum score 650 paper-based; 115 iBT). *Application deadline:* For fall admission, 3/1 priority date for domestic and international students. Applications are processed on a rolling basis. Application fee: $45 ($70 for international students). Electronic applications accepted. *Expenses:* Contact institution. *Financial support:* In 2016–17, 264 students received support. Career-related internships or fieldwork, scholarships/grants, and tuition waivers (full and partial) available. Support available to part-time students. Financial award applicants required to submit FAFSA. *Faculty research:* Intellectual property; law and science; trust and elder law, including taxation and retirement benefits; professional responsibility and judicial ethics; Constitutional law, theory, and process. *Unit head:* Martin H. Belsky, Dean, 330-972-6359, Fax: 330-258-2343, E-mail: belsky@uakron.edu. *Application contact:* Lauri S. File, Assistant Dean of Admission and Financial Aid, 330-972-7331, Fax: 330-258-2343, E-mail: lfile@uakron.edu.
Website: http://www.uakron.edu/law/index.dot

The University of Alabama, School of Law, Tuscaloosa, AL 35487. Offers business transactions (LL M); comparative law (LL M, JSD); law (JD, JSD); taxation (LL M); JD/MBA. *Accreditation:* ABA. *Faculty:* 40 full-time (16 women), 38 part-time/adjunct (10 women). *Students:* 417 full-time (185 women), 74 part-time (27 women); includes 98 minority (51 Black or African American, non-Hispanic/Latino; 5 American Indian or Alaska Native, non-Hispanic/Latino; 14 Asian, non-Hispanic/Latino; 20 Hispanic/Latino; 8 Two or more races, non-Hispanic/Latino), 7 international. Average age 27. 1,634 applicants, 21% accepted, 172 enrolled. In 2016, 60 master's, 144 doctorates awarded. *Degree requirements:* For master's, 24 hours, exams; for doctorate, 90 hours, including 6 hours of experiential learning, 1 seminar, and 34 required hours. *Entrance requirements:* For master's, LSAT, JD (for business transactions and taxation); undergraduate degree in law, letters of recommendation, personal statement, resume, and official transcripts (for comparative law); for doctorate, LSAT (for JD), undergraduate degree, letter of recommendation, resume, personal statement, and CAS report (for JD). Additional exam requirements/recommendations for international students: Required—TOEFL, IELTS. *Application deadline:* Applications are processed on a rolling basis. Application fee: $40. Electronic applications accepted. *Expenses:* Contact institution. *Financial support:* Applicants required to submit FAFSA. *Faculty research:* Public interest law, Constitutional law, civil rights, international law, tax law. *Total annual research expenditures:* $90,932. *Unit head:* Claude R. Arrington, Associate Dean for Admissions, 205-348-6557, Fax: 205-348-3077, E-mail: carrington@law.ua.edu. *Application contact:* Martha Griffith, Assistant Director for Admissions, 205-348-7945, Fax: 205-348-3917, E-mail: mgriffith@law.ua.edu.
Website: http://www.law.ua.edu/

University of Alberta, Faculty of Law, Edmonton, AB T6G 2E1, Canada. Offers LL M, PhD. *Program availability:* Part-time. *Degree requirements:* For master's, thesis. *Entrance requirements:* For master's, minimum GPA of 3.0, curriculum vitae, 3 letters of recommendation; for doctorate, LSAT. Additional exam requirements/recommendations for international students: Required—TOEFL (minimum score 600 paper-based). Electronic applications accepted. *Faculty research:* Health law, environmental law, native law issues, constitutional law, human rights.

The University of Arizona, James E. Rogers College of Law, Tucson, AZ 85721-0176. Offers indigenous peoples law and policy (LL M); international trade and business law (LL M); law (JD); JD/MA; JD/MBA; JD/MPA; JD/PhD. *Accreditation:* ABA. *Degree requirements:* For doctorate, publishable paper. *Entrance requirements:* For doctorate, LSAT, LSDAS, resume, 2 letters of recommendation. Additional exam requirements/recommendations for international students: Required—TOEFL. Electronic applications accepted. *Expenses:* Contact institution. *Faculty research:* Tax law, employment law, corporate law, torts, trial practice and skills, constitutional law, Indian law, family law, estates and trusts.

University of Arkansas, School of Law, Fayetteville, AR 72701. Offers agricultural law (LL M); law (JD). *Accreditation:* ABA. In 2016, 104 doctorates awarded. *Entrance requirements:* For doctorate, LSAT. *Application deadline:* For fall admission, 4/1 for domestic students. Applications are processed on a rolling basis. Application fee: $0. *Expenses:* Contact institution. *Financial support:* In 2016–17, fellowships with full tuition reimbursements (averaging $6,000 per year), 8 research assistantships (averaging $2,500 per year) were awarded; teaching assistantships, career-related internships or fieldwork, Federal Work-Study, and scholarships/grants also available. Support available to part-time students. Financial award application deadline: 4/1; financial award applicants required to submit FAFSA. *Unit head:* Stacy L. Leeds, Dean, 479-575-5601, Fax: 479-575-3320, E-mail: sleeds@uark.edu.
Website: http://www.law.uark.edu/

University of Arkansas at Little Rock, William H. Bowen School of Law, Little Rock, AR 72202-5142. Offers JD, JD/MPS. *Accreditation:* ABA. *Program availability:* Part-time, evening/weekend. *Entrance requirements:* For doctorate, LSAT. Electronic applications accepted. *Expenses:* Contact institution. *Faculty research:* Employment discrimination, uniform commercial code, Arkansas legal history, scientific evidence, mediation.

University of Baltimore, School of Law, Baltimore, MD 21201. Offers business law (JD); criminal practice (JD); estate planning (JD); family law (JD); intellectual property (JD); international law (JD); law (JD); law of the United States (LL M); litigation and advocacy (JD); public service (JD); real estate practice (JD); taxation (LL M); JD/LL M; JD/MBA; JD/MPA; JD/MS; JD/PhD. JD/MS offered jointly with Division of Criminology, Criminal Justice, and Social Policy; JD/PhD with University of Maryland, Baltimore. *Accreditation:* ABA. *Program availability:* Part-time, evening/weekend. *Faculty:* 53 full-time (25 women), 61 part-time/adjunct (18 women). *Students:* 464 full-time (233 women), 297 part-time (140 women); includes 243 minority (142 Black or African American, non-Hispanic/Latino; 35 Asian, non-Hispanic/Latino; 38 Hispanic/Latino; 28 Two or more races, non-Hispanic/Latino), 20 international. Average age 27. 1,090 applicants, 58% accepted, 208 enrolled. In 2016, 279 doctorates awarded. *Entrance requirements:* For doctorate, LSAT. Additional exam requirements/recommendations for international students: Required—TOEFL (for LL M in law of the United States). *Application deadline:* For fall admission, 7/30 for domestic students, 4/1 priority date for international students. Applications are processed on a rolling basis. Application fee: $60. Electronic applications accepted. *Expenses:* $30,144 per year full-time in-state; $43,972 per year full-time out-of-state. *Financial support:* In 2016–17, 344 students received support. Research assistantships, teaching assistantships, career-related internships or fieldwork, Federal Work-Study, and scholarships/grants available. Support available to part-time students. Financial award application deadline: 4/1; financial award applicants required to submit FAFSA. *Faculty research:* Plain view doctrine, statute of limitations, bankruptcy, family law, international and comparative law, Constitutional law. *Unit head:* Ronald Weich, Dean, 410-837-4458. *Application contact:* Jeffrey L. Zavrotny, Assistant Dean for Admissions, 410-837-5809, Fax: 410-837-4188, E-mail: jzavrotny@ubalt.edu.
Website: http://law.ubalt.edu/

The University of British Columbia, Peter A. Allard School of Law, Vancouver, BC V6T 1Z1, Canada. Offers common law (LL M CL); law (LL M, PhD); taxation (LL M). *Program availability:* Part-time. *Degree requirements:* For master's, variable foreign language requirement, thesis, seminar; for doctorate, variable foreign language requirement, comprehensive exam, thesis/dissertation, seminar. *Entrance requirements:* For master's, LL B or JD, thesis proposal, 3 letters of reference; for doctorate, LL B or JD, LL M, thesis proposal, 3 letters of reference. Additional exam requirements/recommendations for international students: Required—TOEFL, IELTS. *Application deadline:* Applications are processed on a rolling basis. Application fee: $100 ($162 for international students). Electronic applications accepted. *Expenses:* Contact institution. *Financial support:* Fellowships, research assistantships, teaching assistantships, Federal Work-Study, scholarships/grants, and unspecified assistantships available. Financial award application deadline: 9/1. *Faculty research:* Aboriginal rights/native law, Asian legal studies, criminal law, environmental law, international law, corporate, human rights, intellectual property, dispute resolution, entertainment. *Application contact:* Joanne Chung, Graduate Administrator, 604-822-6449, Fax: 604-822-4781, E-mail: graduates@law.ubc.ca.
Website: http://www.allard.ubc.ca/

University of Calgary, Faculty of Graduate Studies, Faculty of Law, Calgary, AB T2N 1N4, Canada. Offers LL M, JD, Postbaccalaureate Certificate, JD/MBA. *Entrance requirements:* For doctorate, LSAT. Additional exam requirements/recommendations for international students: Required—TOEFL (minimum score 600 paper-based; 100 iBT). *Expenses:* Contact institution.

University of California, Berkeley, Graduate Division, Haas School of Business and School of Law, Concurrent JD/MBA Program, Berkeley, CA 94720-1500. Offers JD/MBA. *Accreditation:* AACSB; ABA. *Students:* 1 full-time (0 women). Average age 29. *Entrance requirements:* Additional exam requirements/recommendations for international students: Required—TOEFL (minimum score 570 paper-based; 90 iBT). *Application deadline:* For fall admission, 10/1 for domestic and international students; for winter admission, 1/7 for domestic and international students; for spring admission, 3/31 for domestic and international students. Application fee: $200. Electronic applications accepted. *Expenses:* Contact institution. *Financial support:* Fellowships, research assistantships with partial tuition reimbursements, teaching assistantships with partial tuition reimbursements, career-related internships or fieldwork, institutionally sponsored loans, scholarships/grants, and non-resident tuition waivers for some students, such as veterans available. Financial award application deadline: 5/18; financial award applicants required to submit FAFSA. *Faculty research:* Accounting, business and public policy, economic analysis and public policy, entrepreneurship, finance, management of organizations, marketing, operations and information technology management, real estate. *Application contact:* Morgan Bernstein, Executive Director, Full-time MBA Admissions, 510-642-1405, Fax: 510-643-6659, E-mail: mbernstein@haas.berkeley.edu.
Website: http://mba.haas.berkeley.edu/academics/concurrentdegrees.html

University of California, Berkeley, School of Law, Berkeley, CA 94720-7200. Offers jurisprudence and social policy (PhD); law (LL M, JD, JSD); JD/MA; JD/MBA; JD/MCP; JD/MJ; JD/MPP; JD/MSW. *Accreditation:* ABA. *Faculty:* 70 full-time (27 women), 52 part-time/adjunct (17 women). *Students:* 1,185 full-time (671 women); includes 390 minority (66 Black or African American, non-Hispanic/Latino; 9 American Indian or Alaska Native, non-Hispanic/Latino; 192 Asian, non-Hispanic/Latino; 123 Hispanic/Latino), 229 international. Average age 25. 7,316 applicants, 547 enrolled. In 2016, 194 master's, 350 doctorates awarded. Terminal master's awarded for partial completion of doctoral program. *Degree requirements:* For master's, thesis; for doctorate, variable foreign language requirement, thesis/dissertation (for some programs). *Entrance requirements:* For master's and doctorate, letters of recommendation. Additional exam requirements/recommendations for international students: Required—TOEFL. *Application deadline:* For fall admission, 2/1 for domestic students. Applications are processed on a rolling basis. Application fee: $75. *Expenses:* Contact institution. *Financial support:* In 2016–17, 718 students received support, including 44 fellowships with partial tuition reimbursements available (averaging $13,541 per year), 162 research assistantships with partial tuition reimbursements available (averaging $4,393 per year), 23 teaching assistantships (averaging $10,440 per year); career-related internships or fieldwork, Federal Work-Study, institutionally sponsored loans, scholarships/grants, health care benefits, tuition waivers (partial), and unspecified assistantships also available. Financial award application deadline: 3/2; financial award applicants required to submit FAFSA. *Faculty research:* Law and technology; social justice; environmental law; business, law and economics; international/comparative law. *Unit head:* Prof. Melissa Murray, Dean, 510-642-6483. *Application contact:* Edward Tom, Director of Admissions, 510-642-2273, Fax: 510-643-6222, E-mail: admissions@law.berkeley.edu.
Website: http://www.law.berkeley.edu/

University of California, Davis, School of Law, Davis, CA 95616-5201. Offers LL M, JD, JD/MA, JD/MBA. *Accreditation:* ABA. *Faculty:* 54 full-time (28 women), 27 part-time/adjunct (7 women). *Students:* 505 full-time (270 women); includes 210 minority (7 Black or African American, non-Hispanic/Latino; 1 American Indian or Alaska Native, non-Hispanic/Latino; 87 Asian, non-Hispanic/Latino; 76 Hispanic/Latino; 1 Native Hawaiian or other Pacific Islander, non-Hispanic/Latino; 38 Two or more races, non-Hispanic/Latino), 22 international. Average age 24. 2,852 applicants, 33% accepted, 156 enrolled. In 2016, 138 doctorates awarded. *Degree requirements:* For doctorate, 88 semester units, including skills courses (6 units), Professional Responsibility and upper-division writing requirement. *Entrance requirements:* For doctorate, LSAT. Additional exam requirements/recommendations for international students: Required—TOEFL. *Application deadline:* For fall admission, 3/15 priority date for domestic students, 3/15 for international students. Applications are processed on a rolling basis. Application fee: $0. Electronic applications accepted. *Expenses:* $47,409 resident tuition and fees, $56,660 non-resident. *Financial support:* In 2016–17, 431 students received support, including 35 research assistantships, 27 teaching assistantships with partial tuition reimbursements available; Federal Work-Study, institutionally sponsored loans, scholarships/grants, and health care benefits also available. Financial award application deadline: 3/2; financial award applicants required to submit FAFSA. *Faculty research:* International law, intellectual property, immigration, environmental law, public interest law. *Unit head:* Kevin R. Johnson, Dean, 530-752-0243, Fax: 530-752-7279, E-mail: krjohnson@ucdavis.edu. *Application contact:* Kristen Mercado, JD, Director, Admissions, 530-752-6477, Fax: 530-754-8371, E-mail: admissions@law.ucdavis.edu.
Website: http://www.law.ucdavis.edu/

University of California, Hastings College of the Law, Graduate Programs, San Francisco, CA 94102-4978. Offers LL M, MS, MSL, JD. MSL and MS offered jointly with

University of California, San Francisco. *Accreditation:* ABA. *Students:* 977 full-time (550 women), 30 part-time (25 women); includes 382 minority (36 Black or African American, non-Hispanic/Latino; 14 American Indian or Alaska Native, non-Hispanic/Latino; 159 Asian, non-Hispanic/Latino; 159 Hispanic/Latino; 3 Native Hawaiian or other Pacific Islander, non-Hispanic/Latino; 11 Two or more races, non-Hispanic/Latino), 76 international. Average age 24. 3,416 applicants, 47% accepted, 348 enrolled. In 2016, 31 master's, 301 doctorates awarded. *Entrance requirements:* For doctorate, LSAT. *Application deadline:* For fall admission, 3/1 for domestic students, 5/1 for international students. Applications are processed on a rolling basis. Application fee: $75. Electronic applications accepted. *Financial support:* Fellowships, research assistantships, teaching assistantships, career-related internships or fieldwork, Federal Work-Study, institutionally sponsored loans, scholarships/grants, traineeships, health care benefits, and unspecified assistantships available. Support available to part-time students. Financial award application deadline: 3/1; financial award applicants required to submit FAFSA. *Unit head:* Bryan Zerbe, Admissions Office, 415-565-4623, Fax: 415-581-8946, E-mail: admiss@uchastings.edu. *Application contact:* Admissions Office, 415-565-4623, Fax: 415-565-4863, E-mail: admiss@uchastings.edu.
Website: http://www.uchastings.edu/

University of California, Irvine, School of Law, Irvine, CA 92697-8000. Offers JD. *Accreditation:* ABA. *Degree requirements:* For doctorate, project. *Entrance requirements:* For doctorate, LSAT, bachelor's degree, official transcripts, two letters of recommendation, personal statement, current resume. *Application deadline:* For fall admission, 3/1 for domestic students. Application fee: $0. Electronic applications accepted. *Expenses:* $48,740 in-state tuition and fees; $55,234 out-of-state tuition and fees. *Unit head:* Erwin Chemerinsky, Dean, 949-824-7722, E-mail: echemerinsky@law.uci.edu.
Website: http://www.law.uci.edu/

University of California, Los Angeles, School of Law, Los Angeles, CA 90095. Offers LL M, JD, SJD, JD/MA, JD/MBA, JD/MPH, JD/MPP, JD/MSW, JD/MURP, JD/PhD. *Accreditation:* ABA. *Entrance requirements:* For doctorate, LSAT (for JD). Additional exam requirements/recommendations for international students: Required—TOEFL for LL M. Electronic applications accepted. *Expenses:* Contact institution. *Faculty research:* Business law and policy; critical race studies, entertainment; media, and intellectual property law; law and philosophy; public interest law and policy.

University of California, San Diego, Graduate Division, Program in Health Policy and Law, La Jolla, CA 92093. Offers MAS. Program offered jointly with School of Medicine and California Western School of Law. *Program availability:* Part-time. *Students:* 2 full-time (both women), 26 part-time (19 women). 21 applicants, 71% accepted, 9 enrolled. In 2016, 9 master's awarded. *Degree requirements:* For master's, capstone project. *Entrance requirements:* For master's, appropriate medical, healthcare, legal or related degree; minimum GPA of 3.0 in final two years of study; minimum 3 years of relevant work experience or equivalent. Additional exam requirements/recommendations for international students: Required—TOEFL (minimum score 550 paper-based; 80 iBT), IELTS (minimum score 7). *Application deadline:* For fall admission, 8/4 for domestic students. Applications are processed on a rolling basis. Application fee: $105 ($125 for international students). Electronic applications accepted. *Expenses:* Contact institution. *Financial support:* Scholarships/grants available. *Unit head:* Gerard Manecke, Program Co-Director, 619-543-3164, E-mail: gmanecke@ucsd.edu. *Application contact:* Jessica Nguyen, Program Coordinator, 858-534-9162, E-mail: healthpolicyandlaw@ucsd.edu.
Website: http://hlaw.ucsd.edu/

University of Chicago, The Law School, Chicago, IL 60637. Offers LL M, MCL, DCL, JD, JSD, JD/AM, JD/MBA, JD/MPP. *Accreditation:* ABA. *Entrance requirements:* For doctorate, LSAT (for JD). Additional exam requirements/recommendations for international students: Required—TOEFL (minimum score 104 iBT). Electronic applications accepted. *Expenses:* Contact institution. *Faculty research:* Law.

University of Cincinnati, College of Law, Cincinnati, OH 45221-0040. Offers LL M, JD, JD/MA, JD/MBA, JD/MCP, JD/MWS. *Accreditation:* ABA. *Faculty:* 31 full-time (15 women), 58 part-time/adjunct (21 women). *Students:* 286 full-time (130 women), 3 part-time (all women); includes 51 minority (23 Black or African American, non-Hispanic/Latino; 1 American Indian or Alaska Native, non-Hispanic/Latino; 8 Asian, non-Hispanic/Latino; 17 Hispanic/Latino; 2 Two or more races, non-Hispanic/Latino), 5 international. Average age 25. 829 applicants, 52% accepted, 126 enrolled. In 2016, 8 master's, 109 doctorates awarded. *Entrance requirements:* For master's, Credential evaluation report, diploma for law degree, curriculum vitae, personal statement, two letters of recommendation; for doctorate, LSAT. Additional exam requirements/recommendations for international students: Required—TOEFL (minimum iBT score of 85), IELTS (7), or PTE (65). *Application deadline:* For fall admission, 3/15 priority date for domestic and international students. Applications are processed on a rolling basis. Application fee: $35. Electronic applications accepted. *Expenses:* Contact institution. *Financial support:* In 2016–17, 235 students received support. Fellowships, research assistantships, career-related internships or fieldwork, Federal Work-Study, scholarships/grants, tuition waivers (full and partial), and unspecified assistantships available. Financial award application deadline: 3/15; financial award applicants required to submit FAFSA. *Faculty research:* Constitutional law; business law; international law; employment law; civil procedure. *Unit head:* Verna L. Williams, Interim Dean, 513-556-0080, Fax: 513-556-2391, E-mail: verna.williams@uc.edu. *Application contact:* Al Watson, Senior Assistant Dean and Director of Admissions, 513-556-0077, Fax: 513-556-2391, E-mail: alfred.watson@uc.edu.
Website: http://www.law.uc.edu/

University of Colorado Boulder, School of Law, Boulder, CO 80309-0401. Offers JD, JD/MBA, JD/MPA, JD/MS, JD/PhD. *Accreditation:* ABA. *Faculty:* 41 full-time (16 women). *Students:* 529 full-time (262 women), 9 part-time (3 women); includes 100 minority (10 Black or African American, non-Hispanic/Latino; 14 American Indian or Alaska Native, non-Hispanic/Latino; 25 Asian, non-Hispanic/Latino; 48 Hispanic/Latino; 3 Two or more races, non-Hispanic/Latino), 6 international. Average age 27. 1,118 applicants, 100% accepted, 178 enrolled. In 2016, 184 doctorates awarded. *Entrance requirements:* For doctorate, LSAT, minimum undergraduate GPA of 2.75. *Application deadline:* For fall admission, 2/15 for domestic students. Applications are processed on a rolling basis. Application fee: $60 ($80 for international students). Electronic applications accepted. Application fee is waived when completed online. *Expenses:* Contact institution. *Financial support:* In 2016–17, 1,078 students received support, including 817 fellowships (averaging $7,178 per year); institutionally sponsored loans, scholarships/grants, health care benefits, and unspecified assistantships also available. Financial award applicants required to submit FAFSA. *Faculty research:* Law and society, law, Constitutional law, business/corporate law, contracts. *Total annual research expenditures:* $1.4 million. *Application contact:* E-mail: lawadmin@colorado.edu.
Website: http://www.colorado.edu/law/

University of Connecticut, School of Law, Hartford, CT 06105. Offers JD, JD/LL M, JD/MBA, JD/MLS, JD/MPA, JD/MPH, JD/MSW. *Accreditation:* ABA. *Program availability:* Part-time. *Degree requirements:* For doctorate, extensive research paper. *Entrance requirements:* For doctorate, LSAT, undergraduate degree. Additional exam requirements/recommendations for international students: Required—TOEFL. Electronic applications accepted. *Expenses:* Contact institution. *Faculty research:* International law, intellectual property, human rights, taxation, energy and environmental law.

University of Dayton, School of Law, Dayton, OH 45469-2772. Offers intellectual property and technology (LL M, MSL); law (JD); JD/MBA; JD/MPA; JD/MS Ed. *Accreditation:* ABA. *Faculty:* 24 full-time (12 women), 25 part-time/adjunct (10 women). *Students:* 263 full-time (128 women), 16 part-time (5 women); includes 48 minority (24 Black or African American, non-Hispanic/Latino; 1 American Indian or Alaska Native, non-Hispanic/Latino; 4 Asian, non-Hispanic/Latino; 19 Hispanic/Latino), 13 international. Average age 27. 545 applicants, 21% accepted. In 2016, 9 master's, 93 doctorates awarded. *Degree requirements:* For master's, variable foreign language requirement, comprehensive exam (for some programs), thesis optional. *Entrance requirements:* For master's, JD (for LL M); for doctorate, LSAT, bachelor's degree. Additional exam requirements/recommendations for international students: Required—TOEFL (minimum score 600 paper-based; 100 iBT); Recommended—IELTS (minimum score 7). *Application deadline:* For fall admission, 8/1 priority date for domestic students; for summer admission, 4/15 for domestic students. Applications are processed on a rolling basis. Application fee: $0. Electronic applications accepted. *Expenses:* $35,247 tuition; $418 fees (healthcare, graduation). *Financial support:* In 2016–17, 12 research assistantships (averaging $400 per year) were awarded; fellowships, teaching assistantships, Federal Work-Study, and scholarships/grants also available. Financial award application deadline: 3/1; financial award applicants required to submit FAFSA. *Faculty research:* Trademark and unfair competition law, cyber and cybersecurity law, patent law, trade secret law, copyright law. *Unit head:* Andrew Strauss, Dean, 937-229-3795, Fax: 937-229-2469, E-mail: astrauss1@udayton.edu. *Application contact:* Claire Schrader, Assistant Dean/Executive Director of Enrollment Management and Marketing, 937-229-3555, Fax: 937-229-4194, E-mail: lawinfo@udayton.edu.
Website: http://www.udayton.edu/law

University of Denver, Sturm College of Law, JD Program, Denver, CO 80208. Offers JD. *Accreditation:* ABA. *Program availability:* Part-time, evening/weekend. *Faculty:* 72 full-time (37 women), 62 part-time/adjunct (28 women). *Students:* 755 full-time (397 women), 19 part-time (9 women); includes 165 minority (18 Black or African American, non-Hispanic/Latino; 4 American Indian or Alaska Native, non-Hispanic/Latino; 19 Asian, non-Hispanic/Latino; 94 Hispanic/Latino; 30 Two or more races, non-Hispanic/Latino), 7 international. Average age 28. 2,217 applicants, 53% accepted, 260 enrolled. In 2016, 267 doctorates awarded. *Entrance requirements:* For doctorate, LSAT. Additional exam requirements/recommendations for international students: Required—TOEFL (minimum score 587 paper-based; 95 iBT). *Application deadline:* For fall admission, 3/1 for domestic and international students. Applications are processed on a rolling basis. Application fee: $65. Electronic applications accepted. *Expenses:* $44,530 per year full-time. *Financial support:* In 2016–17, 427 students received support, including 2 teaching assistantships (averaging $8,268 per year); career-related internships or fieldwork, Federal Work-Study, institutionally sponsored loans, scholarships/grants, unspecified assistantships, and tutorships also available. Support available to part-time students. Financial award application deadline: 2/15; financial award applicants required to submit FAFSA. *Faculty research:* Lawyering skills, international and legal studies, natural resources law (domestic and international), transportation law, public interest law, business and commercial law. *Unit head:* Dr. Bruce Smith, Dean, 303-871-6103. *Application contact:* Yvonne Cherena-Pacheco, Associate Director of Admissions, 303-871-6151, Fax: 303-871-6992, E-mail: admissions@law.du.edu.
Website: http://www.law.du.edu

University of Denver, Sturm College of Law, Programs in Environmental and Natural Resources Law and Policy, Denver, CO 80208. Offers environmental and natural resources law and policy (LL M, MLS); natural resources law and policy (Certificate). *Faculty:* 12 full-time (4 women), 13 part-time/adjunct (1 woman). *Students:* 13 full-time (7 women), 4 part-time (all women); includes 2 minority (both Hispanic/Latino), 4 international. Average age 30. 27 applicants, 78% accepted, 9 enrolled. In 2016, 20 master's awarded. *Degree requirements:* For master's, internship. *Entrance requirements:* For master's, bachelor's degree (for MRLS), JD (for LL M), transcripts, two letters of recommendation. Additional exam requirements/recommendations for international students: Required—TOEFL (minimum score 550 paper-based; 80 iBT). *Application deadline:* For fall admission, 7/27 for domestic students, 6/15 for international students; for spring admission, 12/12 for domestic students, 11/7 for international students. Applications are processed on a rolling basis. Application fee: $65. Electronic applications accepted. *Expenses:* $44,530 per year full-time. *Financial support:* In 2016–17, 3 students received support. Federal Work-Study, institutionally sponsored loans, scholarships/grants, and unspecified assistantships available. Support available to part-time students. Financial award application deadline: 2/15; financial award applicants required to submit FAFSA. *Unit head:* Don Smith, Director, 303-871-6052, E-mail: dcsmith@law.du.edu. *Application contact:* E-mail: gradlegalstudies@law.du.edu.
Website: http://www.law.du.edu/index.php/graduate-legal-studies/masters-programs/mls-enrlp

University of Detroit Mercy, School of Law, Detroit, MI 48226. Offers JD, JD/MBA. *Accreditation:* ABA. *Program availability:* Part-time. *Entrance requirements:* For doctorate, LSAT. *Expenses:* Contact institution.

University of Florida, Levin College of Law, Gainesville, FL 32611. Offers comparative law (LL M), including tropical conservation and development; environmental and land use law (LL M); international taxation (LL M), law (JD); taxation (LL M, SJD). *Accreditation:* ABA. *Entrance requirements:* For doctorate, LSAT (for JD). Electronic applications accepted. *Faculty research:* Environmental and land use law, taxation, dispute resolution, family law, Constitutional law.

University of Georgia, School of Law, Athens, GA 30602. Offers LL M, MSL, JD. *Accreditation:* ABA. *Degree requirements:* For master's, thesis. *Entrance requirements:* For doctorate, LSAT. Additional exam requirements/recommendations for international students: Required—TOEFL. *Application deadline:* For fall admission, 7/1 priority date for domestic students; for spring admission, 11/15 for domestic students. Application fee: $50. Electronic applications accepted. *Expenses:* Contact institution. *Financial support:* Fellowships, research assistantships, teaching assistantships, Federal Work-Study, institutionally sponsored loans, tuition waivers (partial), and unspecified assistantships available. Financial award application deadline: 1/31. *Unit head:* Rebecca H. White, Dean, 706-542-7140, Fax: 706-542-5283, E-mail: rhwhite@uga.edu. *Application contact:* Laura Tate Kagel, Graduate Coordinator, 706-542-7875, E-mail: lkagel@uga.edu.
Website: http://www.law.uga.edu/

University of Hawaii at Manoa, William S. Richardson School of Law, Honolulu, HI 96822-2328. Offers LL M, JD, Graduate Certificate, JD/Certificate, JD/MA, JD/MBA, JD/MLI Sc, JD/MS, JD/MURP, JD/PhD. *Accreditation:* ABA. *Degree requirements:* For doctorate, 6 semesters of full-time residency. *Entrance requirements:* For doctorate, LSAT. Additional exam requirements/recommendations for international students: Required—TOEFL. *Expenses:* Contact institution. *Faculty research:* Law of the sea, Asian and Pacific comparative law, native Hawaiian rights, environmental law.

Law

University of Houston, Law Center, Houston, TX 77204-6060. Offers energy, environment, and natural resources (LL M); health law (LL M); intellectual property and information law (LL M); international law (LL M); law (LL M, JD); tax law (LL M). *Accreditation:* ABA. *Program availability:* Part-time, evening/weekend. *Entrance requirements:* For doctorate, LSAT. Additional exam requirements/recommendations for international students: Required—TOEFL (minimum score 600 paper-based; 100 iBT). Electronic applications accepted. *Expenses:* Contact institution. *Faculty research:* Health law, international, tax, environmental/energy, information law/intellectual property.

University of Idaho, College of Law, Moscow, ID 83844-2321. Offers business law and entrepreneurship (JD); law (JD); litigation and alternative dispute resolution (JD); Native American law (JD); natural resources and environmental law (JD). *Accreditation:* ABA. *Faculty:* 32 full-time, 11 part-time/adjunct. *Students:* Average age 28. *Entrance requirements:* For doctorate, LSAT, Law School Admission Council Credential Assembly Service (CAS) Report. Additional exam requirements/recommendations for international students: Required—TOEFL. *Application deadline:* For fall admission, 3/15 priority date for domestic students. Applications are processed on a rolling basis. Application fee: $50 ($60 for international students). Electronic applications accepted. *Expenses:* Contact institution. *Financial support:* Career-related internships or fieldwork, Federal Work-Study, and institutionally sponsored loans available. Financial award applicants required to submit FAFSA. *Faculty research:* Transboundary river governance, tribal protection and stewardship, regional water issues, environmental law. *Unit head:* Mark Adams, Dean, 208-885-4977, E-mail: uilaw@uidaho.edu. *Application contact:* Carole Wells, Director of Admissions, 208-885-2300, Fax: 208-885-2252, E-mail: lawadmit@uidaho.edu.
Website: http://www.uidaho.edu/law/

University of Illinois at Urbana–Champaign, College of Law, Champaign, IL 61820. Offers LL M, MCL, JD, JSD, JD/DVM, JD/MBA, JD/MCS, JD/MHRIR, JD/MS, JD/MUP, MAS/JD, MD/JD. *Accreditation:* ABA. *Expenses:* Contact institution.

The University of Iowa, College of Law, Iowa City, IA 52242. Offers LL M, MSL, JD, SJD, JD/MA, JD/MBA, JD/MD, JD/MHA, JD/MPH, JD/MS, JD/PhD. *Accreditation:* ABA. *Faculty:* 37 full-time (13 women), 14 part-time/adjunct (4 women). *Students:* 439 full-time (188 women), 4 part-time (3 women); includes 88 minority (16 Black or African American, non-Hispanic/Latino; 2 American Indian or Alaska Native, non-Hispanic/Latino; 19 Asian, non-Hispanic/Latino; 36 Hispanic/Latino; 15 Two or more races, non-Hispanic/Latino), 28 international. Average age 25. 1,406 applicants, 44% accepted, 154 enrolled. In 2016, 4 master's, 100 doctorates awarded. *Degree requirements:* For master's, thesis (for some programs); for doctorate, thesis/dissertation. *Entrance requirements:* For doctorate, LSAT. Additional exam requirements/recommendations for international students: Required—TOEFL. *Application deadline:* For fall admission, 5/1 priority date for domestic and international students. Applications are processed on a rolling basis. Application fee: $0. Electronic applications accepted. *Expenses:* $24,930 per year resident, $43,214 per year non-resident (for JD); $22,894 per year resident, $27,142 per year non-resident (for LL M and SJD); $14,741 per year resident, $25,641 per year non-resident (for MSL). *Financial support:* In 2016–17, 340 students received support, including 338 fellowships with partial tuition reimbursements available (averaging $19,195 per year), 109 research assistantships with partial tuition reimbursements available (averaging $2,175 per year); career-related internships or fieldwork, Federal Work-Study, scholarships/grants, and health care benefits also available. Financial award applicants required to submit FAFSA. *Faculty research:* International and comparative law, business law, intellectual property law, competition law, and constitutional law. *Total annual research expenditures:* $247,219. *Unit head:* Gail Agrawal, Dean, 319-335-9034, Fax: 319-335-9019, E-mail: gail-agrawal@uiowa.edu. *Application contact:* Collins Byrd, Assistant Dean of Enrollment Management, 319-335-9095, Fax: 319-335-9646, E-mail: law-admissions@uiowa.edu.
Website: https://law.uiowa.edu/

The University of Kansas, School of Law, Lawrence, KS 66045-7608. Offers JD, JD/MA, JD/MBA, JD/MHSA, JD/MPA, JD/MS, JD/MSW, JD/MUP. *Accreditation:* ABA. *Faculty:* 32 full-time (17 women), 22 part-time/adjunct (10 women). *Students:* 351 full-time (146 women), 19 part-time (1 woman); includes 52 minority (11 Black or African American, non-Hispanic/Latino; 4 American Indian or Alaska Native, non-Hispanic/Latino; 8 Asian, non-Hispanic/Latino; 22 Hispanic/Latino; 7 Two or more races, non-Hispanic/Latino), 22 international. Average age 25. 644 applicants, 57% accepted, 107 enrolled. In 2016, 109 doctorates awarded. *Entrance requirements:* For doctorate, LSAT, 2 letters of recommendation. Additional exam requirements/recommendations for international students: Required—TOEFL. *Application deadline:* For fall admission, 5/1 for domestic and international students. Applications are processed on a rolling basis. Application fee: $55. Electronic applications accepted. *Expenses:* $714 per credit hour residents; $1,243 per credit hour non-residents. *Financial support:* In 2016–17, 8 fellowships (averaging $1,350 per year), 62 research assistantships (averaging $1,358 per year), 8 teaching assistantships (averaging $2,000 per year) were awarded; career-related internships or fieldwork, Federal Work-Study, institutionally sponsored loans, and scholarships/grants also available. Financial award application deadline: 2/15; financial award applicants required to submit FAFSA. *Faculty research:* International law, business law, criminal law, tribal law, law and public policy. *Unit head:* Stephen W. Mazza, Dean, 785-864-4550, Fax: 785-864-5054. *Application contact:* Steven Freedman, Assistant Dean for Admissions, 866-220-3654, E-mail: admitlaw@ku.edu.
Website: http://www.law.ku.edu/

University of Kentucky, College of Law, Lexington, KY 40506-0048. Offers JD, JD/MA, JD/MBA, JD/MPA. *Accreditation:* ABA. *Entrance requirements:* For doctorate, LSAT, LSDAS. Additional exam requirements/recommendations for international students: Required—TOEFL. Electronic applications accepted. *Expenses:* Contact institution. *Faculty research:* Health law, education law, advocacy, business law, white collar crime, international trade law, corporate mergers, taxation of Internet transactions.

University of La Verne, College of Law, Ontario, CA 91764. Offers JD. *Accreditation:* ABA. *Program availability:* Part-time, evening/weekend. *Entrance requirements:* For doctorate, LSAT. Additional exam requirements/recommendations for international students: Recommended—TOEFL. Electronic applications accepted. *Expenses:* Contact institution.

University of Louisville, Louis D. Brandeis School of Law, Louisville, KY 40208. Offers JD, JD/M Div, JD/MAH, JD/MAPS, JD/MBA, JD/MSSW, JD/MUP. *Accreditation:* ABA. *Program availability:* Part-time. *Degree requirements:* For doctorate, 30 work hours of pro bono service. *Entrance requirements:* For doctorate, LSAT. Additional exam requirements/recommendations for international students: Required—TOEFL (minimum score 550 paper-based). Electronic applications accepted. *Expenses:* Contact institution. *Faculty research:* Intellectual property, environmental law, corporate law, taxation, health law, disability law.

University of Maine, University of Maine School of Law, Portland, ME 04102. Offers JD, JD/MBA, JD/MPH, JD/MPPM. JD/MBA offered in conjunction with the University of Southern Maine; JD/MPH and JD/MPPM offered with the Muskie School of Public Service. *Accreditation:* ABA. *Program availability:* Part-time. *Faculty:* 19 full-time (8 women), 21 part-time/adjunct (14 women). *Students:* 219 full-time (109 women), 15 part-time (9 women); includes 21 minority (7 Black or African American, non-Hispanic/Latino; 4 American Indian or Alaska Native, non-Hispanic/Latino; 4 Asian, non-Hispanic/Latino; 6 Hispanic/Latino), 2 international. Average age 27. 486 applicants, 66% accepted, 76 enrolled. In 2016, 82 doctorates awarded. *Entrance requirements:* For doctorate, LSAT. Additional exam requirements/recommendations for international students: Required—TOEFL. *Application deadline:* For fall admission, 4/15 for domestic and international students. Applications are processed on a rolling basis. Application fee: $0. Electronic applications accepted. *Expenses:* $23,560 per year in-state full-time, $743 per credit part-time; $34,630 per year out-of-state full-time, $1,112 per credit part-time (for JD); $36,270 per year full-time, $1,459 per credit part-time (for LL M). *Financial support:* In 2016–17, 168 students received support, including 28 fellowships (averaging $3,300 per year), 6 research assistantships (averaging $2,000 per year); teaching assistantships, Federal Work-Study, and scholarships/grants also available. Financial award application deadline: 2/15; financial award applicants required to submit FAFSA. *Faculty research:* Commercial law aspects of intellectual property; domestic violence; race, gender, and law; environmental and land use law; bankruptcy and predatory lending; international investment law; community development law; law governing use and development of the arctic. *Unit head:* Danielle Conway, Dean, 207-780-4344, Fax: 207-780-4239. *Application contact:* Caroline Wilshusen, Director of Admissions, 207-780-4341, Fax: 207-780-4239, E-mail: lawadmissions@maine.edu.
Website: http://mainelaw.maine.edu/

The University of Manchester, School of Law, Manchester, United Kingdom. Offers bioethics and medical jurisprudence (PhD); criminology (M Phil, PhD); law (M Phil, PhD).

University of Manitoba, Faculty of Graduate Studies, Faculty of Law, Winnipeg, MB R3T 2N2, Canada. Offers LL M. *Degree requirements:* For master's, thesis. *Entrance requirements:* For master's, LL B, minimum GPA of 3.0. Additional exam requirements/recommendations for international students: Required—TOEFL (minimum score 600 paper-based). Electronic applications accepted. *Faculty research:* Constitutional law, alternative dispute resolution, human rights law, international trade law, corporate law.

University of Maryland, Baltimore, Francis King Carey School of Law, Baltimore, MD 21201. Offers LL M, JD, JD/MA, JD/MBA, JD/MCP, JD/MPH, JD/MPM, JD/MPP, JD/MS, JD/MSN, JD/MSW, JD/PhD, JD/Pharm D. *Accreditation:* ABA. *Program availability:* Part-time, evening/weekend, 100% online. *Faculty:* 54 full-time (29 women), 52 part-time/adjunct (17 women). *Students:* 530 full-time (275 women), 204 part-time (112 women); includes 263 minority (114 Black or African American, non-Hispanic/Latino; 2 American Indian or Alaska Native, non-Hispanic/Latino; 68 Asian, non-Hispanic/Latino; 53 Hispanic/Latino; 26 Two or more races, non-Hispanic/Latino), 41 international. Average age 27. 1,911 applicants, 55% accepted, 280 enrolled. In 2016, 19 master's, 215 doctorates awarded. *Degree requirements:* For master's, thesis optional. *Entrance requirements:* For doctorate, LSAT, CAS (transcripts, transcript analysis, letters of recommendation). Additional exam requirements/recommendations for international students: Required—TOEFL (minimum score 600 paper-based; 90 iBT), IELTS (minimum score 7). *Application deadline:* For fall admission, 4/1 priority date for domestic and international students. Applications are processed on a rolling basis. Application fee: $70. Electronic applications accepted. *Expenses:* Contact institution. *Financial support:* In 2016–17, 529 students received support, including 28 fellowships (averaging $4,000 per year), 90 research assistantships (averaging $1,500 per year); Federal Work-Study, institutionally sponsored loans, and scholarships/grants also available. Support available to part-time students. Financial award application deadline: 3/1; financial award applicants required to submit FAFSA. *Faculty research:* Environmental regulation, health care policy, intellectual property, civil rights and race history and policy, international and comparative law. *Total annual research expenditures:* $4.4 million. *Unit head:* Donald B. Tobin, Dean/Professor, 410-706-7214, Fax: 410-706-4045, E-mail: dtobin@law.umaryland.edu. *Application contact:* Susan Krinsky, Associate Dean for Student Affairs and Communications, 410-706-3492, Fax: 410-706-1793, E-mail: admissions@law.umaryland.edu.
Website: http://www.law.umaryland.edu/

University of Maryland, College Park, Academic Affairs, Robert H. Smith School of Business, Program in Business Management/Law, College Park, MD 20742. Offers JD/MBA. *Accreditation:* AACSB. *Entrance requirements:* Additional exam requirements/recommendations for international students: Required—TOEFL.

University of Maryland, College Park, Academic Affairs, School of Public Policy, Joint Program in Public Policy/Law, College Park, MD 20742. Offers JD/MPM. Electronic applications accepted.

University of Massachusetts Dartmouth, Graduate School, University of Massachusetts School of Law –Dartmouth, Dartmouth, MA 02747. Offers JD. *Accreditation:* ABA. *Program availability:* Part-time, evening/weekend. *Faculty:* 17 full-time (8 women), 11 part-time/adjunct (2 women). *Students:* 124 full-time (65 women), 61 part-time (36 women); includes 49 minority (16 Black or African American, non-Hispanic/Latino; 9 Asian, non-Hispanic/Latino; 18 Hispanic/Latino; 1 Native Hawaiian or other Pacific Islander, non-Hispanic/Latino; 5 Two or more races, non-Hispanic/Latino), 1 international. Average age 30. 800 applicants, 60% accepted, 66 enrolled. In 2016, 53 doctorates awarded. *Degree requirements:* For doctorate, thesis/dissertation, bar exam. *Entrance requirements:* For doctorate, LSAT, LSAS report, 2 letters of recommendation, resume, personal statement of intent, offical transcripts. Additional exam requirements/recommendations for international students: Recommended—TOEFL (minimum score 533 paper-based). *Application deadline:* For fall admission, 6/30 priority date for domestic students, 5/30 priority date for international students. Application fee: $50. Electronic applications accepted. *Expenses:* Contact institution. *Financial support:* Fellowships, institutionally sponsored loans, and scholarships/grants available. Support available to part-time students. Financial award application deadline: 3/1; financial award applicants required to submit FAFSA. *Faculty research:* Constitutionality of design patents, legal history, legal philosophy, criminal law, criminal procedure issues, privacy law and the empirical analysis of legal writing. *Unit head:* Daniel Fitzpatrick, Assistant Dean, University of Massachusetts School of Law - Dartmouth, 508-985-1110, Fax: 508-985-1175, E-mail: lawadmissions@umassd.edu. *Application contact:* Nancy Fitzsimmons-Hebert, Assistant Director of Marketing and Recruitment, 508-985-1110, Fax: 508-985-1175, E-mail: lawadmissions@umassd.edu.
Website: http://www.umassd.edu/law

University of Memphis, Cecil C. Humphreys School of Law, Memphis, TN 38103-2189. Offers JD, JD/MA, JD/MBA, JD/MPH. *Accreditation:* ABA. *Program availability:* Part-time. *Faculty:* 25 full-time (11 women), 23 part-time/adjunct (7 women). *Students:* 308 full-time (135 women), 17 part-time (12 women); includes 80 minority (52 Black or African American, non-Hispanic/Latino; 4 American Indian or Alaska Native, non-Hispanic/Latino; 8 Asian, non-Hispanic/Latino; 16 Hispanic/Latino). Average age 25. 583 applicants, 55% accepted, 106 enrolled. In 2016, 1 doctorate awarded. *Entrance requirements:* For doctorate, LSAT, CAS report, letters of recommendation, or evaluations. Additional exam requirements/recommendations for international students: Required—TOEFL. *Application deadline:* For fall admission, 3/15 priority date for domestic and international students. Applications are processed on a rolling basis. Application fee: $0 ($40 for international students). Electronic applications accepted. *Expenses:* $18,763 full-time resident tuition and fees, $25,968 full-time non-resident

tuition and fees. *Financial support:* In 2016–17, 138 students received support, including 26 fellowships (averaging $12,118 per year), 20 research assistantships (averaging $5,000 per year); teaching assistantships, career-related internships or fieldwork, Federal Work-Study, scholarships/grants, and tuition waivers (partial) also available. Support available to part-time students. Financial award application deadline: 5/1; financial award applicants required to submit FAFSA. *Faculty research:* Tort law gun violence, privacy law, legal education, elders' rights, shareholder rights, evidence law, employment law. *Total annual research expenditures:* $37,000. *Unit head:* Peter V. Letsou, Dean, 901-678-2421, Fax: 901-678-5210, E-mail: pvletsou@memphis.edu. *Application contact:* Dr. Sue Ann McClellan, Assistant Dean for Law Admissions, Recruiting and Scholarships, 901-678-5403, Fax: 901-678-0741, E-mail: smcclell@memphis.edu.
Website: http://www.memphis.edu/law/

University of Miami, Graduate School, University of Miami School of Law, Coral Gables, FL 33124-8087. Offers entertainment, arts, and sports law (LL M); estate planning (LL M); international arbitration (LL M); international law (LL M), including general international law, inter-American law, U.S. and transnational law for foreign lawyers; law (JD); maritime law (LL M); real estate/property development (LL M); taxation (LL M); taxation of cross-border investment (LL M); JD/LL M; JD/MA; JD/MBA; JD/MBA/LL M; JD/MD; JD/MM; JD/MPA; JD/MPH; JD/MPS; JD/MS Ed; JD/PhD. *Accreditation:* ABA. *Program availability:* Part-time. *Faculty:* 78 full-time (35 women), 98 part-time/adjunct (22 women). *Students:* 995 full-time (464 women), 74 part-time (33 women); includes 457 minority (69 Black or African American, non-Hispanic/Latino; 3 American Indian or Alaska Native, non-Hispanic/Latino; 31 Asian, non-Hispanic/Latino; 323 Hispanic/Latino; 1 Native Hawaiian or other Pacific Islander, non-Hispanic/Latino; 30 Two or more races, non-Hispanic/Latino), 82 international. 2,443 applicants, 55% accepted, 300 enrolled. *Entrance requirements:* For doctorate, LSAT, 2 letters of recommendation. Additional exam requirements/recommendations for international students: Required—TOEFL (minimum score 580 paper-based; 92 iBT), IELTS (minimum score 7). *Application deadline:* For fall admission, 7/31 for domestic and international students. Applications are processed on a rolling basis. Application fee: $60. Electronic applications accepted. *Expenses:* Contact institution. *Financial support:* Fellowships, research assistantships, career-related internships or fieldwork, Federal Work-Study, institutionally sponsored loans, scholarships/grants, and unspecified assistantships available. Financial award application deadline: 3/1; financial award applicants required to submit FAFSA. *Faculty research:* Energy/climate change, international finance, Internet law/law of electronic commerce, race/social justice, art law/cultural heritage law. *Unit head:* Michael Goodnight, Associate Dean of Admissions and Enrollment Management, 305-284-2527, Fax: 305-284-3084, E-mail: mgoodnig@law.miami.edu. *Application contact:* Therese Lambert, Director of Student Recruitment, 305-284-6746, Fax: 305-284-3084, E-mail: tlambert@law.miami.edu.
Website: http://www.law.miami.edu/

University of Michigan, Law School, Ann Arbor, MI 48109-1215. Offers comparative law (MCL); international tax (LL M); law (LL M, JD, SJD); JD/MA; JD/MBA; JD/MHSA; JD/MPH; JD/MPP; JD/MS; JD/MSI; JD/MSW; JD/MUP; JD/PhD. *Accreditation:* ABA. *Faculty:* 107 full-time (36 women), 36 part-time/adjunct (8 women). *Students:* 933 full-time (438 women); includes 205 minority (35 Black or African American, non-Hispanic/Latino; 8 American Indian or Alaska Native, non-Hispanic/Latino; 78 Asian, non-Hispanic/Latino; 42 Hispanic/Latino; 42 Two or more races, non-Hispanic/Latino), 59 international. 5,076 applicants, 24% accepted, 305 enrolled. In 2016, 36 master's, 328 doctorates awarded. *Entrance requirements:* For doctorate, LSAT. *Application deadline:* For fall admission, 2/15 for domestic students. Applications are processed on a rolling basis. Application fee: $75. Electronic applications accepted. *Expenses:* Contact institution. *Financial support:* In 2016–17, 779 students received support. Career-related internships or fieldwork, Federal Work-Study, institutionally sponsored loans, and scholarships/grants available. Financial award applicants required to submit FAFSA. *Unit head:* Mark D. West, Dean, 734-764-1358. *Application contact:* Sarah C. Zearfoss, Assistant Dean and Director of Admissions, 734-764-0537, Fax: 734-647-3218, E-mail: law.jd.admissions@umich.edu.
Website: http://www.law.umich.edu/

University of Minnesota, Twin Cities Campus, Law School, Minneapolis, MN 55455. Offers LL M, MS, JD, SJD, JD/MA, JD/MBA, JD/MBS, JD/MD, JD/MHA, JD/MPA, JD/MPH, JD/MPP, JD/MS, JD/MSST, JD/MURP, JD/PhD. *Accreditation:* ABA. *Faculty:* 54 full-time (22 women), 102 part-time/adjunct (31 women). *Students:* 721 full-time (307 women), 12 part-time (8 women); includes 102 minority (14 Black or African American, non-Hispanic/Latino; 3 American Indian or Alaska Native, non-Hispanic/Latino; 43 Asian, non-Hispanic/Latino; 12 Hispanic/Latino; 30 Two or more races, non-Hispanic/Latino), 55 international. Average age 25. 1,960 applicants, 45% accepted, 176 enrolled. In 2016, 73 master's, 246 doctorates awarded. *Entrance requirements:* For doctorate, LSAT. Additional exam requirements/recommendations for international students: Required—TOEFL. *Application deadline:* For fall admission, 5/2 for domestic students. Applications are processed on a rolling basis. Application fee: $60. Electronic applications accepted. *Expenses:* Contact institution. *Financial support:* In 2016–17, 514 students received support. Fellowships, research assistantships, career-related internships or fieldwork, Federal Work-Study, institutionally sponsored loans, and scholarships/grants available. Financial award application deadline: 7/15; financial award applicants required to submit FAFSA. *Faculty research:* International and comparative law; law, science, and technology; criminal justice; environmental and energy law; business law. *Unit head:* Garry Jenkins, Dean, 612-625-4841. *Application contact:* Robin Ingli, Director of Admissions, 612-625-3487, Fax: 612-625-2011, E-mail: jdadmissions@umn.edu.
Website: http://www.law.umn.edu/

University of Mississippi, School of Law, University, MS 38677. Offers LL M, JD, JD/MBA. *Accreditation:* ABA. *Faculty:* 32 full-time (19 women), 8 part-time/adjunct (6 women). *Students:* 364 full-time (161 women), 3 part-time (1 woman); includes 83 minority (53 Black or African American, non-Hispanic/Latino; 1 American Indian or Alaska Native, non-Hispanic/Latino; 2 Asian, non-Hispanic/Latino; 12 Hispanic/Latino; 15 Two or more races, non-Hispanic/Latino), 1 international. Average age 24. In 2016, 179 doctorates awarded. *Entrance requirements:* For doctorate, LSAT, LSDAS. Additional exam requirements/recommendations for international students: Required—TOEFL. *Application deadline:* For fall admission, 4/1 for domestic students. Application fee: $40. *Expenses:* Contact institution. *Financial support:* Fellowships, research assistantships, teaching assistantships, career-related internships or fieldwork, Federal Work-Study, institutionally sponsored loans, and scholarships/grants available. Support available to part-time students. Financial award application deadline: 3/1; financial award applicants required to submit FAFSA. *Unit head:* Dr. Deborah Bell, Dean, 662-915-6900, Fax: 662-915-6895, E-mail: lawadmin@olemiss.edu. *Application contact:* Macey Edmondson, Assistant Dean for Admissions and Scholarships, 662-915-6819, Fax: 662-915-7577, E-mail: clee@olemiss.edu.

University of Missouri, School of Law, Columbia, MO 65211. Offers dispute resolution (LL M); law (JD); JD/MA; JD/MBA; JD/MPA. *Accreditation:* ABA. *Faculty:* 34 full-time (14 women), 5 part-time/adjunct (2 women). *Students:* 304 full-time (123 women), 15 part-time (10 women); includes 54 minority (35 Black or African American, non-Hispanic/Latino; 5 Asian, non-Hispanic/Latino; 5 Hispanic/Latino; 1 Native Hawaiian or other Pacific Islander, non-Hispanic/Latino; 8 Two or more races, non-Hispanic/Latino), 6 international. Average age 26. *Entrance requirements:* For doctorate, LSAT. Additional exam requirements/recommendations for international students: Required—TOEFL (minimum score 600 paper-based; 100 iBT), IELTS (minimum score 7). *Application deadline:* For fall admission, 3/1 priority date for domestic students. Applications are processed on a rolling basis. *Expenses:* Contact institution. *Financial support:* Fellowships, Federal Work-Study, and institutionally sponsored loans available. Financial award application deadline: 3/1; financial award applicants required to submit FAFSA.
Website: http://www.law.missouri.edu/

University of Missouri–Kansas City, School of Law, Kansas City, MO 64110-2499. Offers LL M, JD, JD/LL M, JD/MBA, JD/MPA, LL M/MPA. *Accreditation:* ABA. *Program availability:* Part-time. *Faculty:* 36 full-time (17 women), 9 part-time/adjunct (2 women). *Students:* 403 full-time (171 women), 43 part-time (25 women); includes 72 minority (22 Black or African American, non-Hispanic/Latino; 1 American Indian or Alaska Native, non-Hispanic/Latino; 7 Asian, non-Hispanic/Latino; 36 Hispanic/Latino; 6 Two or more races, non-Hispanic/Latino), 24 international. Average age 27. 588 applicants, 25% accepted, 154 enrolled. In 2016, 25 master's, 159 doctorates awarded. *Degree requirements:* For master's, thesis (for general). *Entrance requirements:* For master's, LSAT, minimum GPA of 3.0 (for general), 2.7 (for taxation); for doctorate, LSAT. Additional exam requirements/recommendations for international students: Required—TOEFL (minimum score 550 paper-based; 80 iBT). *Application deadline:* For fall admission, 3/1 priority date for domestic and international students. Applications are processed on a rolling basis. Application fee: $50. Electronic applications accepted. *Expenses:* Contact institution. *Financial support:* In 2016–17, 21 teaching assistantships with partial tuition reimbursements (averaging $2,350 per year) were awarded; career-related internships or fieldwork, Federal Work-Study, institutionally sponsored loans, scholarships/grants, and tuition waivers (full and partial) also available. Support available to part-time students. Financial award application deadline: 3/1; financial award applicants required to submit FAFSA. *Faculty research:* Family and children's issues, litigation, estate planning, urban law, business, tax entrepreneurial law. *Unit head:* Barbara Glesner Fines, Acting Dean, 816-235-2380, Fax: 816-235-5276, E-mail: glesnerb@umkc.edu. *Application contact:* Lydia Dagenais, Director of Law School Admissions, 816-235-1677, Fax: 816-235-5276, E-mail: dagenaisl@umkc.edu.
Website: http://www.law.umkc.edu/

University of Montana, School of Law, Missoula, MT 59812. Offers JD, JD/MBA, JD/MPA. *Accreditation:* ABA. *Degree requirements:* For doctorate, oral presentation, paper. *Entrance requirements:* For doctorate, LSAT. *Expenses:* Contact institution. *Faculty research:* Legal education curriculum, business and probate law reform, rules of civil procedure reform, tribal courts, women's issues.

University of Nebraska–Lincoln, College of Law, Lincoln, NE 68583-0902. Offers law (JD); legal studies (MLS); space and telecommunications law (LL M); JD/MA; JD/MBA; JD/MCRP; JD/MPA; JD/PhD. *Accreditation:* ABA. *Entrance requirements:* For doctorate, LSAT. Electronic applications accepted. *Expenses:* Contact institution. *Faculty research:* Law and medicine, constitutional law, criminal procedure, international trade.

University of Nevada, Las Vegas, William S. Boyd School of Law, Las Vegas, NV 89154-1003. Offers gaming law and regulation (LL M); law (JD); JD/MBA; JD/MSW; JD/PhD. *Accreditation:* ABA. *Program availability:* Part-time, evening/weekend. *Faculty:* 39 full-time (25 women), 22 part-time/adjunct (5 women). *Students:* 294 full-time (137 women), 102 part-time (47 women); includes 135 minority (24 Black or African American, non-Hispanic/Latino; 3 American Indian or Alaska Native, non-Hispanic/Latino; 18 Asian, non-Hispanic/Latino; 69 Hispanic/Latino; 1 Native Hawaiian or other Pacific Islander, non-Hispanic/Latino; 20 Two or more races, non-Hispanic/Latino), 9 international. Average age 30. 669 applicants, 35% accepted, 116 enrolled. In 2016, 9 master's, 116 doctorates awarded. *Degree requirements:* For doctorate, scholarly paper, community service, drafting project or externship. *Entrance requirements:* For doctorate, LSAT. Additional exam requirements/recommendations for international students: Required—TOEFL (minimum score 61 iBT), IELTS (minimum score 6), PTE (minimum score 44). *Application deadline:* For fall admission, 6/1 for domestic and international students. Applications are processed on a rolling basis. Application fee: $50. Electronic applications accepted. *Expenses:* $12,950 per semester full-time resident tuition, $18,900 per semester full-time non-resident tuition; $926 per credit hour part-time resident tuition, $1,350 per credit hour part-time non-resident tuition. *Financial support:* In 2016–17, 249 students received support, including 13 fellowships (averaging $12,950 per year), 61 research assistantships (averaging $1,000 per year); career-related internships or fieldwork and scholarships/grants also available. Support available to part-time students. Financial award application deadline: 6/1; financial award applicants required to submit FAFSA. *Faculty research:* Health law, intellectual property, immigration, dispute resolution. *Total annual research expenditures:* $171,920. *Unit head:* Daniel W. Hamilton, Dean, 702-895-3671, Fax: 702-895-1095, E-mail: christine.smith@unlv.edu. *Application contact:* Christina Prendergast, Admission and Records Assistant, 702-895-2424, Fax: 702-895-2414, E-mail: christina.prendergast@unlv.edu.
Website: http://law.unlv.edu

University of New Hampshire, School of Law, Concord, NH 03301. Offers business law (JD); commerce and technology (LL M, MCT, Diploma); criminal law (JD); intellectual property (LL M, MIP, JD, Diploma), including patent law (JD), trademarks and copyright (JD); international criminal law and justice (LL M, MICLJ); litigation (JD), public interest and social justice (JD); sports and entertainment law (JD); JD/LL M; JD/MBA; JD/MIP; JD/MPP; JD/MSW. *Accreditation:* ABA. *Program availability:* Part-time, 100% online, limited residential. *Faculty:* 25 full-time (11 women), 29 part-time/adjunct (9 women). *Students:* 252 full-time (107 women), 4 part-time (3 women); includes 30 minority (3 Black or African American, non-Hispanic/Latino; 7 Asian, non-Hispanic/Latino; 11 Hispanic/Latino; 9 Two or more races, non-Hispanic/Latino), 36 international. Average age 36. 564 applicants, 53% accepted, 103 enrolled. In 2016, 27 master's, 69 doctorates awarded. *Degree requirements:* For doctorate, comprehensive exam. *Entrance requirements:* For doctorate, LSAT. Additional exam requirements/recommendations for international students: Required—TOEFL (minimum score 600 paper-based; 100 iBT), minimum TOEFL iBT score of 80 (for master's programs). *Application deadline:* For fall admission, 4/1 priority date for domestic and international students; for spring admission, 1/3 for domestic and international students. Applications are processed on a rolling basis. Application fee: $0. Electronic applications accepted. *Expenses:* Contact institution. *Financial support:* Fellowships, career-related internships or fieldwork, Federal Work-Study, and scholarships/grants available. Financial award applicants required to submit FAFSA. *Faculty research:* Intellectual property, health law and policy, sports and entertainment law, patent law, trademarks and copyright. *Unit head:* Megan Carpenter, Dean, 603-228-1541, Fax: 603-228-1074. *Application contact:* Brenda Brooks, Director of Admissions, 603-513-5300, Fax: 603-513-5234, E-mail: brenda.brooks@law.unh.edu.
Website: http://law.unh.edu/

University of New Mexico, School of Law, Albuquerque, NM 87131-0001. Offers JD, JD/M Acct, JD/MA, JD/MBA, JD/MPA. *Degree requirements:* For doctorate, ethics class,

2 writing classes, clinic. *Entrance requirements:* For doctorate, LSAT, bachelor's degree. Additional exam requirements/recommendations for international students: Required—TOEFL (minimum score 600 paper-based; 100 iBT). Electronic applications accepted. *Expenses:* Contact institution. *Faculty research:* Clinical legal education, international law, Indian law, natural resources and environmental law, Constitutional law, business and tax law, legal writing.

University of North Alabama, College of Arts and Sciences, Department of Politics, Justice, and Law, Florence, AL 35632-0001. Offers criminal justice (MSCJ). *Program availability:* Part-time, 100% online. *Faculty:* 3 full-time (0 women), 2 part-time/adjunct (1 woman). *Students:* 4 full-time (2 women), 21 part-time (9 women); includes 4 minority (3 Black or African American, non-Hispanic/Latino; 1 Hispanic/Latino), 4 international. Average age 30. 13 applicants, 77% accepted, 10 enrolled. In 2016, 3 master's awarded. *Degree requirements:* For master's, comprehensive exam. *Entrance requirements:* For master's, GRE General Test, MAT. Additional exam requirements/recommendations for international students: Required—TOEFL (minimum score 79 iBT), IELTS (minimum score 6), PTE (minimum score 54). *Application deadline:* Applications are processed on a rolling basis. Application fee: $50 ($100 for international students). Electronic applications accepted. *Expenses:* Tuition, state resident: full-time $2799; part-time $1866 per semester. Tuition, nonresident: full-time $5598; part-time $3732 per semester. *Required fees:* $915; $642 per semester. Tuition and fees vary according to course load. *Financial support:* In 2016–17, 2 students received support. Scholarships/grants and unspecified assistantships available. Financial award application deadline: 2/1; financial award applicants required to submit FAFSA. *Unit head:* Dr. Tim Collins, Chair, 256-765-5045, E-mail: jtcollins@una.edu. *Application contact:* Hillary N. Coats, Graduate Admissions Coordinator, 256-765-4447, E-mail: graduate@una.edu.
Website: http://www.una.edu/criminaljustice/

The University of North Carolina at Chapel Hill, School of Law, Chapel Hill, NC 27599-3380. Offers JD, JD/MAMC, JD/MAPPS, JD/MASA, JD/MBA, JD/MPA, JD/MPH, JD/MRP, JD/MSIS, JD/MSLS, JD/MSW. JD/MAPPS offered jointly with Duke University. *Accreditation:* ABA. *Entrance requirements:* For doctorate, LSAT, bachelor's degree from accredited college or university, two letters of recommendation, essays, resume. Additional exam requirements/recommendations for international students: Required—TOEFL (minimum score 650 paper-based; 100 iBT). Electronic applications accepted. *Expenses:* Contact institution. *Faculty research:* Corporate and banking law, environmental policy, state and U.S. Constitutional law, health law policy, immigration law and civil rights.

University of Notre Dame, Law School, Notre Dame, IN 46556-0780. Offers human rights (LL M, JSD); international and comparative law (LL M); law (JD). *Accreditation:* ABA. *Faculty:* 56 full-time (17 women), 60 part-time/adjunct (24 women). *Students:* 645 full-time (291 women), 1 part-time (0 women); includes 158 minority (28 Black or African American, non-Hispanic/Latino; 3 American Indian or Alaska Native, non-Hispanic/Latino; 44 Asian, non-Hispanic/Latino; 60 Hispanic/Latino; 23 Two or more races, non-Hispanic/Latino), 51 international. 2,797 applicants, 32% accepted, 223 enrolled. In 2016, 26 master's, 173 doctorates awarded. *Degree requirements:* For master's, thesis, 1-year residency; for doctorate, thesis/dissertation, 2-year residency (for JSD). *Entrance requirements:* For doctorate, LSAT (for JD), LL M (for JSD). Additional exam requirements/recommendations for international students: Required—TOEFL. *Application deadline:* For fall admission, 3/15 for domestic and international students. Applications are processed on a rolling basis. Application fee: $75. Electronic applications accepted. *Expenses:* Contact institution. *Financial support:* In 2016–17, 503 students received support, including 503 fellowships with tuition reimbursements available (averaging $28,332 per year); research assistantships, teaching assistantships, career-related internships or fieldwork, Federal Work-Study, institutionally sponsored loans, scholarships/grants, health care benefits, unspecified assistantships, and university dormitory rector assistantships also available. Financial award application deadline: 2/28; financial award applicants required to submit FAFSA. *Faculty research:* Constitutional structure; international law (public and private); law and religion; land, energy, and environmental law; intellectual property, including patent, copyright, and trademark law. *Unit head:* Nell Jessup Newton, Dean, 574-631-6789, Fax: 574-631-8400, E-mail: nell.newton@nd.edu. *Application contact:* Jacob Baska, Director of Admissions, 574-631-6626, Fax: 574-631-5474, E-mail: lawadmit@nd.edu.
Website: http://www.law.nd.edu/

University of Oklahoma, College of Law, Norman, OK 73019. Offers LL M, JD, JD/MA, JD/MBA, JD/MPH, JD/MS. *Accreditation:* ABA. *Program availability:* Part-time, 100% online. *Faculty:* 38 full-time (18 women), 14 part-time/adjunct (5 women). *Students:* 544 full-time (239 women), 58 part-time (30 women); includes 169 minority (22 Black or African American, non-Hispanic/Latino; 59 American Indian or Alaska Native, non-Hispanic/Latino; 16 Asian, non-Hispanic/Latino; 24 Hispanic/Latino; 48 Two or more races, non-Hispanic/Latino), 3 international. Average age 28. 853 applicants, 50% accepted, 176 enrolled. In 2016, 25 master's, 143 doctorates awarded. *Entrance requirements:* For master's, JD or equivalent; for doctorate, LSAT. Additional exam requirements/recommendations for international students: Required—TOEFL, TOEFL (minimum score 550 paper-based, 79 iBT for LL M; 600 paper-based, 100 iBT for JD). *Application deadline:* For fall admission, 3/15 for domestic and international students. Applications are processed on a rolling basis. Application fee: $50. Electronic applications accepted. *Expenses:* Contact institution. *Financial support:* In 2016–17, 401 students received support. Career-related internships or fieldwork, Federal Work-Study, scholarships/grants, and tuition waivers (full and partial) available. Financial award application deadline: 6/1; financial award applicants required to submit FAFSA. *Faculty research:* Energy and natural resources; indigenous peoples law; business and commercial; litigation and procedure; tax, pensions and retirement. *Total annual research expenditures:* $25,000. *Unit head:* Joseph Harroz, Jr., Dean, 405-325-4884, Fax: 405-325-7712, E-mail: jharroz@ou.edu. *Application contact:* Vicki Ferguson, Admissions Coordinator, 405-325-4728, Fax: 405-325-0502, E-mail: admissions@law.ou.edu.
Website: http://www.law.ou.edu/

University of Oregon, School of Law, Eugene, OR 97403. Offers MA, MS, JD, JD/MBA, JD/MS. *Accreditation:* ABA. *Entrance requirements:* For doctorate, LSAT. *Expenses:* Contact institution.

University of Ottawa, Faculty of Graduate and Postdoctoral Studies, Faculty of Law, Ottawa, ON K1N 6N5, Canada. Offers LL M, LL D. *Program availability:* Part-time, evening/weekend. *Degree requirements:* For master's, thesis or alternative; for doctorate, thesis/dissertation. *Entrance requirements:* For master's, minimum B average, LL B; for doctorate, LL M, minimum B+ average. Electronic applications accepted. *Faculty research:* International law, human rights law, family law.

University of Pennsylvania, Law School, Philadelphia, PA 19104. Offers LL CM, LL M, ML, JD, SJD, JD/DMD, JD/Ed D, JD/LL M, JD/MA, JD/MBA, JD/MBE, JD/MCIT, JD/MCP, JD/MD, JD/MES, JD/MPA, JD/MPH, JD/MS, JD/MS Ed, JD/MSE, JD/MSSP, JD/MSW, JD/PhD. JD/LL M offered jointly with Hong Kong University. *Accreditation:* ABA. *Faculty:* 75 full-time (26 women), 75 part-time/adjunct (24 women). *Students:* 749 full-time (346 women); includes 216 minority (51 Black or African American, non-Hispanic/Latino; 2 American Indian or Alaska Native, non-Hispanic/Latino; 95 Asian, non-Hispanic/Latino; 46 Hispanic/Latino; 22 Two or more races, non-Hispanic/Latino), 42 international. Average age 27. 5,593 applicants, 17% accepted, 242 enrolled. In 2016, 117 master's, 258 doctorates awarded. *Degree requirements:* For master's, thesis optional; for doctorate, thesis/dissertation. *Entrance requirements:* For master's, prior law degree (for LL M); for doctorate, LSAT (for JD), LL M (for SJD). Additional exam requirements/recommendations for international students: Recommended—TOEFL (minimum score 600 paper-based; 100 iBT), IELTS (minimum score 7). *Application deadline:* For fall admission, 3/1 for domestic students, 12/15 for international students. Applications are processed on a rolling basis. Application fee: $80. Electronic applications accepted. *Expenses:* Contact institution. *Financial support:* In 2016–17, 366 students received support, including 1 fellowship (averaging $3,500 per year), 119 research assistantships (averaging $3,255 per year), 11 teaching assistantships (averaging $2,782 per year); career-related internships or fieldwork, Federal Work-Study, institutionally sponsored loans, and scholarships/grants also available. Financial award application deadline: 3/1; financial award applicants required to submit FAFSA. *Faculty research:* Administrative law and regulation, business and corporate law, civil procedure, Constitutional law, criminal law, environmental law, health law, intellectual property and technology law, international and comparative law, law and economics, legal history, philosophy, tax law and policy. *Total annual research expenditures:* $697,292. *Unit head:* Theodore W. Ruger, Dean, 215-898-7463, Fax: 215-573-2025. *Application contact:* Renee Post, Associate Dean of Admissions and Financial Aid, 215-898-7400, Fax: 215-898-9606, E-mail: contactadmissions@law.upenn.edu.
Website: http://www.law.upenn.edu/

University of Pittsburgh, Katz Graduate School of Business, MBA/Juris Doctor Program, Pittsburgh, PA 15260. Offers MBA/JD. *Program availability:* Evening/weekend. *Faculty:* 88 full-time (27 women), 42 part-time/adjunct (15 women). *Students:* 8 full-time (2 women); includes 1 minority (Black or African American, non-Hispanic/Latino), 1 international. Average age 28. 5 applicants, 80% accepted, 2 enrolled. *Entrance requirements:* Additional exam requirements/recommendations for international students: Required—TOEFL (minimum score 100 iBT) or IELTS (minimum score 7.0). *Application deadline:* For fall admission, 4/1 priority date for domestic students, 2/1 priority date for international students. Application fee: $50. Electronic applications accepted. *Expenses:* Contact institution. *Financial support:* Scholarships/grants available. Financial award application deadline: 6/1; financial award applicants required to submit FAFSA. *Faculty research:* Accounting systems/financial reporting, corporate finance, shopper marketing/consumer behavior, management information systems, organizational behavior and entrepreneurship. *Total annual research expenditures:* $493,036. *Unit head:* Dr. Arjang A. Assad, Dean, 412-648-1556, Fax: 412-648-1552, E-mail: aassad@katz.pitt.edu. *Application contact:* Thomas Keller, Director of MBA Admissions, 412-648-1700, Fax: 412-648-1659, E-mail: mba@katz.pitt.edu.
Website: http://www.business.pitt.edu/katz/mba/academics/programs/mba-jd.php

See Display on page 160 and Close-Up on page 189.

University of Pittsburgh, School of Law, LL M Program for Foreign-Trained Lawyers, Pittsburgh, PA 15260. Offers LL M. Program offered to international students only. *Accreditation:* ABA. *Program availability:* Part-time. *Faculty:* 48 full-time (21 women), 104 part-time/adjunct (34 women). *Students:* 19 full-time (12 women), 4 part-time (2 women); includes 6 minority (2 Black or African American, non-Hispanic/Latino; 2 Asian, non-Hispanic/Latino; 2 Hispanic/Latino). Average age 25. 55 applicants, 73% accepted, 16 enrolled. In 2016, 23 master's awarded. *Entrance requirements:* For master's, law degree from foreign university. Additional exam requirements/recommendations for international students: Required—TOEFL (minimum score 577 paper-based; 90 iBT), IELTS (minimum score 6.5). *Application deadline:* Applications are processed on a rolling basis. Application fee: $0 ($55 for international students). Electronic applications accepted. *Expenses:* $37,500 tuition; $870 fees. *Financial support:* In 2016–17, 10 students received support, including 9 fellowships with partial tuition reimbursements available (averaging $14,000 per year). *Faculty research:* International arbitration, private international law, Islamic law, environmental criminal and comparative law. *Unit head:* Prof. Ronald A. Brand, Academic Director, 412-648-1307, Fax: 412-648-2648, E-mail: rbrand@pitt.edu. *Application contact:* Austin A. Lebo, Program Administrator, 412-648-7023, Fax: 412-648-2648, E-mail: aal37@pitt.edu.
Website: http://www.law.pitt.edu/llm

University of Puerto Rico, Río Piedras Campus, School of Law, San Juan, PR 00931-3349. Offers LL M, JD. *Accreditation:* ABA. *Program availability:* Part-time, evening/weekend. *Entrance requirements:* For master's, LSAT, minimum GPA of 3.0, letter of recommendation; for doctorate, GMAT, GRE, LSAT, EXADEP, minimum GPA of 3.0. Additional exam requirements/recommendations for international students: Required—TOEFL. *Faculty research:* Civil code; Puerto Rico constitutional law; professional behavior, rules and regulations; international law; expert testimony.

University of Richmond, School of Law, University of Richmond, VA 23173. Offers JD, JD/MA, JD/MBA, JD/MHA, JD/MPA, JD/MS, JD/MSW, JD/MURP. JD/MSW, JD/MHA, JD/MPA offered jointly with Virginia Commonwealth University; JD/MURP with Virginia Commonwealth University; JD/MA with Department of History; JD/MS with Department of Biology. *Accreditation:* ABA. *Entrance requirements:* For doctorate, LSAT. Electronic applications accepted. *Expenses:* Contact institution.

University of St. Thomas, Graduate Studies, School of Law, Minneapolis, MN 55403-2015. Offers law (JD); organizational ethics and compliance (LL M, MSL); U.S. law (LL M); JD/LL M; JD/MA; JD/MBA; JD/MSW. *Accreditation:* ABA. *Degree requirements:* For doctorate, mentor externship, public service. *Entrance requirements:* For doctorate, LSAT, 2 letters of recommendation. Additional exam requirements/recommendations for international students: Required—TOEFL (minimum score 550 paper-based), IELTS (minimum score 6.5), or Michigan English Language Assessment Battery (minimum score 80). *Application deadline:* For fall admission, 7/1 priority date for domestic and international students. Applications are processed on a rolling basis. Application fee: $0. Electronic applications accepted. *Expenses: Tuition:* Full-time $19,354; part-time $1320 per credit. One-time fee: $214. Tuition and fees vary according to course load, degree level, program and reciprocity agreements. *Financial support:* Scholarships/grants available. Financial award application deadline: 7/1; financial award applicants required to submit FAFSA. *Faculty research:* Constitutional law (executive powers and First Amendment); banking, securities, and financial markets; law, religion, and jurisprudence; international law, development and dispute resolution; formation of professional identity, values, and skills. *Unit head:* Robert K. Vischer, Dean, 651-962-4838, Fax: 651-962-4881, E-mail: rkvischer@stthomas.edu. *Application contact:* Cari Haaland, Assistant Dean for Admissions, 651-962-4872, Fax: 651-962-4876, E-mail: lawschool@stthomas.edu.
Website: http://www.stthomas.edu/law/

University of San Diego, School of Law, San Diego, CA 92110-2492. Offers business and corporate law (LL M); comparative law (LL M); general studies (LL M); international law (LL M); law (JD); taxation (LL M, Diploma); JD/IMBA; JD/MA; JD/MBA. *Accreditation:* ABA. *Program availability:* Part-time, evening/weekend. *Faculty:* 46 full-time (14 women), 71 part-time/adjunct (21 women). *Students:* 644 full-time (320 women), 118 part-time (46 women); includes 250 minority (24 Black or African American, non-Hispanic/Latino; 11 American Indian or Alaska Native, non-Hispanic/

Latino; 96 Asian, non-Hispanic/Latino; 106 Hispanic/Latino; 3 Native Hawaiian or other Pacific Islander, non-Hispanic/Latino; 10 Two or more races, non-Hispanic/Latino), 26 international. Average age 27. 3,106 applicants, 192 enrolled. In 2016, 65 master's, 216 doctorates awarded. *Entrance requirements:* For master's, JD, LL B or equivalent from an ABA-accredited law school; for doctorate, LSAT (less than 5 years old), bachelor's degree, registration with the Credential Assemble Service (CAS). Additional exam requirements/recommendations for international students: Required—TOEFL (minimum score 600 paper-based; 100 IBT). *Application deadline:* For fall admission, 2/1 priority date for domestic students. Applications are processed on a rolling basis. Electronic applications accepted. *Expenses:* Contact institution. *Financial support:* In 2016–17, 567 students received support. Career-related internships or fieldwork, Federal Work-Study, institutionally sponsored loans, and scholarships/grants available. Support available to part-time students. Financial award application deadline: 3/1; financial award applicants required to submit FAFSA. *Faculty research:* Corporate law, children's advocacy, Constitutional and criminal law, international and comparative law, public interest law, intellectual property and tax law. *Unit head:* Dr. Stephen C. Ferruolo, Dean, 619-260-4527, E-mail: lawdean@sandiego.edu. *Application contact:* Jorge Garcia, Assistant Dean, JD Admissions, 619-260-4528, Fax: 619-260-2218, E-mail: jdinfo@sandiego.edu.
Website: http://www.sandiego.edu/law/

University of San Francisco, School of Law, JD Program, San Francisco, CA 94117-1080. Offers JD. *Program availability:* Part-time. *Faculty:* 34 full-time (18 women), 35 part-time/adjunct (12 women). *Students:* 425 full-time (234 women), 95 part-time (53 women); includes 287 minority (39 Black or African American, non-Hispanic/Latino; 93 Asian, non-Hispanic/Latino; 126 Hispanic/Latino; 2 Native Hawaiian or other Pacific Islander, non-Hispanic/Latino; 27 Two or more races, non-Hispanic/Latino), 11 international. Average age 28. 1,929 applicants, 63% accepted, 169 enrolled. In 2016, 140 doctorates awarded. *Expenses: Tuition:* Full-time $23,310; part-time $1295 per credit. Tuition and fees vary according to course load, degree level, campus/location and program. *Financial support:* In 2016–17, 249 students received support. *Unit head:* John Trasvina. *Application contact:* Alan P. Guerrero, Director of Admissions, 415-422-2975, E-mail: lawadmissions@usfca.edu.
Website: http://www.usfca.edu/law/academics/jd

University of Saskatchewan, College of Graduate Studies and Research, College of Law, Saskatoon, SK S7N 5A2, Canada. Offers LL M, JD. *Program availability:* Part-time. *Degree requirements:* For master's, thesis. *Entrance requirements:* For master's, LL B; for doctorate, LSAT. Additional exam requirements/recommendations for international students: Required—TOEFL. *Faculty research:* Cooperative, native/aboriginal, constitutional, commercial, consumer, and natural resource law; criminal justice; human rights.

University of South Africa, College of Law, Pretoria, South Africa. Offers correctional services management (M Tech); criminology (MA, PhD); law (LL M, LL D); penology (MA, PhD); police science (MA, PhD); policing (M Tech); security risk management (M Tech); social science in criminology (MA).

University of South Carolina, School of Law, Columbia, SC 29208. Offers JD, JD/IMBA, JD/M Acc, JD/MCJ, JD/MEERM, JD/MHA, JD/MHR, JD/MIBS, JD/MPA, JD/MSEL, JD/MSW. *Accreditation:* ABA. *Degree requirements:* For doctorate, thesis/dissertation. *Entrance requirements:* For doctorate, LSAT. *Expenses:* Contact institution.

The University of South Dakota, Graduate School, School of Law, Vermillion, SD 57069. Offers JD, JD/MA, JD/MBA, JD/MP Acc, JD/MPA, JD/MS. *Accreditation:* ABA. *Program availability:* Part-time. *Entrance requirements:* For doctorate, LSAT. Additional exam requirements/recommendations for international students: Required—TOEFL (minimum score 600 paper-based). Electronic applications accepted. *Expenses:* Contact institution. *Faculty research:* Indian law, skills training, international law, family law, evidence.

University of Southern California, Graduate School, Gould School of Law, Los Angeles, CA 90089. Offers comparative law for foreign attorneys (MCL); law (JD); law for foreign-educated attorneys (LL M); JD/MA; JD/MBA; JD/MBT; JD/MPA; JD/MPP; JD/MRED; JD/MS; JD/MSW; JD/PhD; JD/Pharm D. *Accreditation:* ABA. *Entrance requirements:* For doctorate, LSAT. Additional exam requirements/recommendations for international students: Required—TOEFL. *Faculty research:* Intellectual property law, tax law, criminal law, law and philosophy, law and history.

The University of Tennessee, College of Law, Knoxville, TN 37996-1810. Offers business transactions (JD); law (JD); trial advocacy and dispute resolution (JD); JD/MA; JD/MBA; JD/MPH; JD/MPPA. *Accreditation:* ABA. *Faculty:* 43 full-time (23 women), 63 part-time/adjunct (25 women). *Students:* 333 full-time (145 women); includes 57 minority (26 Black or African American, non-Hispanic/Latino; 1 American Indian or Alaska Native, non-Hispanic/Latino; 5 Asian, non-Hispanic/Latino; 9 Hispanic/Latino; 16 Two or more races, non-Hispanic/Latino), 1 international. Average age 24. 1,003 applicants, 36% accepted, 113 enrolled. In 2016, 158 doctorates awarded. *Entrance requirements:* For doctorate, LSAT. Additional exam requirements/recommendations for international students: Recommended—TOEFL. *Application deadline:* For fall admission, 3/1 priority date for domestic and international students. Applications are processed on a rolling basis. Application fee: $15. Electronic applications accepted. Application fee is waived when completed online. *Expenses:* $19,308 in-state, $37,982 out-of-state. *Financial support:* In 2016–17, 248 students received support, including 12 research assistantships with full tuition reimbursements available (averaging $23,763 per year); career-related internships or fieldwork, Federal Work-Study, institutionally sponsored loans, scholarships/grants, and unspecified assistantships also available. Support available to part-time students. Financial award application deadline: 3/1; financial award applicants required to submit FAFSA. *Faculty research:* Legal expert systems, medical malpractice remedies, professional ethics, insanity defense. *Unit head:* Janet S. Hatcher, Associate Director of Admissions and Financial Aid, 865-974-4131, Fax: 865-974-1572, E-mail: lawadmit@utk.edu. *Application contact:* Janet S. Hatcher, Associate Director of Admissions and Financial Aid, 865-974-4131, Fax: 865-974-1572, E-mail: hatcher@utk.edu.
Website: http://www.law.utk.edu/

The University of Texas at Austin, Graduate School, College of Liberal Arts, Teresa Lozano Long Institute of Latin American Studies, Austin, TX 78712-1111. Offers cultural politics of Afro-Latin and indigenous peoples (MA); development studies (MA); environmental studies (MA); human rights (MA); Latin American and international law (LL M); JD/MA; MA/MA; MBA/MA; MP Aff/MA; MSCRP/MA. LL M offered jointly with The University of Texas School of Law. *Entrance requirements:* For master's, GRE General Test.

The University of Texas at Austin, School of Law, Austin, TX 78705-3224. Offers LL M, JD, JD/MA, JD/MBA, JD/MGPS, JD/MP Aff, JD/MSCRP. *Accreditation:* ABA. *Faculty:* 90 full-time (34 women), 115 part-time/adjunct (33 women). *Students:* 951 full-time (426 women); includes 280 minority (50 Black or African American, non-Hispanic/Latino; 3 American Indian or Alaska Native, non-Hispanic/Latino; 56 Asian, non-Hispanic/Latino; 126 Hispanic/Latino; 1 Native Hawaiian or other Pacific Islander, non-Hispanic/Latino; 44 Two or more races, non-Hispanic/Latino), 21 international. Average age 24. 4,424 applicants, 27% accepted, 295 enrolled. In 2016, 34 master's, 361 doctorates awarded. *Entrance requirements:* For doctorate, LSAT, minimum GPA of 2.2. *Application deadline:* For fall admission, 11/1 for domestic students; for spring admission, 3/1 for domestic students. Application fee: $70. Electronic applications accepted. *Expenses:* Contact institution. *Financial support:* In 2016–17, 871 students received support, including 4 fellowships (averaging $55,000 per year), 175 research assistantships (averaging $4,000 per year), 30 teaching assistantships with partial tuition reimbursements available (averaging $3,000 per year); career-related internships or fieldwork, scholarships/grants, and tuition waivers (full) also available. Financial award application deadline: 12/1; financial award applicants required to submit FAFSA. *Faculty research:* Constitutional law, corporate law, environmental law, employment and labor law, intellectual property law. *Unit head:* Ward Farnsworth, Dean, 512-232-1120, Fax: 512-471-6987, E-mail: wfarnsworth@law.utexas.edu. *Application contact:* School of Law Admissions, 512-232-1200, Fax: 512-471-2765, E-mail: admissions@law.utexas.edu.
Website: http://law.utexas.edu/

The University of Texas at Dallas, School of Economic, Political and Policy Sciences, Program in Political Science, Richardson, TX 75080. Offers Constitutional law (MA); legislative studies (MA); political science (MA, PhD). *Program availability:* Part-time, evening/weekend. *Faculty:* 12 full-time (2 women). *Students:* 27 full-time (7 women), 15 part-time (10 women); includes 11 minority (7 Black or African American, non-Hispanic/Latino; 1 Asian, non-Hispanic/Latino; 3 Hispanic/Latino), 9 international. Average age 35. 27 applicants, 59% accepted, 11 enrolled. In 2016, 9 master's, 4 doctorates awarded. Terminal master's awarded for partial completion of doctoral program. *Degree requirements:* For master's, thesis optional, independent study; for doctorate, thesis/dissertation, practicum research. *Entrance requirements:* For master's, GRE (minimum combined verbal and quantitative score of 1100), minimum undergraduate GPA of 3.0; for doctorate, GRE (minimum combined verbal and quantitative score of 1200, writing 4.5), minimum undergraduate GPA of 3.2. Additional exam requirements/recommendations for international students: Required—TOEFL (minimum score 550 paper-based). *Application deadline:* For fall admission, 7/15 for domestic students, 5/1 priority date for international students; for spring admission, 11/15 for domestic students, 9/1 priority date for international students. Applications are processed on a rolling basis. Application fee: $50 ($100 for international students). Electronic applications accepted. *Expenses:* Tuition, state resident: full-time $12,418; part-time $690 per semester hour. Tuition, nonresident: full-time $24,150; part-time $1342 per semester hour. Tuition and fees vary according to course load. *Financial support:* In 2016–17, 25 students received support, including 1 research assistantship with partial tuition reimbursement available (averaging $20,000 per year), 16 teaching assistantships with partial tuition reimbursements available (averaging $13,100 per year); career-related internships or fieldwork, Federal Work-Study, institutionally sponsored loans, and scholarships/grants also available. Support available to part-time students. Financial award application deadline: 4/30; financial award applicants required to submit FAFSA. *Faculty research:* Terrorism and democratic stability, redistricting and representation, trust and social exchange, how economic ideas impact political thought and public policy. *Unit head:* Dr. Jennifer Holmes, Program Head, 972-883-6843, Fax: 972-883-2735, E-mail: jholmes@utdallas.edu. *Application contact:* Cheryl Berry, Graduate Program Administrator, 972-883-2932, Fax: 972-883-2735, E-mail: politicalscience@utdallas.edu.
Website: http://www.utdallas.edu/epps/political-science/

University of the District of Columbia, David A. Clarke School of Law, Washington, DC 20008. Offers clinical teaching and social justice (LL M); law (JD). *Accreditation:* ABA. *Program availability:* Part-time, evening/weekend. *Degree requirements:* For doctorate, 90 credits, advanced legal writing. *Entrance requirements:* For doctorate, LSAT. Additional exam requirements/recommendations for international students: Recommended—TOEFL. Electronic applications accepted. *Expenses:* Contact institution. *Faculty research:* HIV law, juvenile law, legislative law, community development, small business, immigration and human rights.

University of the Pacific, McGeorge School of Law, Sacramento, CA 95817. Offers advocacy (JD); international water resources law (JSD); public policy and law (LL M); JD/MBA; JD/MPPA. *Accreditation:* ABA. *Program availability:* Part-time, evening/weekend. *Faculty:* 38 full-time (17 women), 40 part-time/adjunct (11 women). *Students:* 365 full-time (195 women), 188 part-time (105 women); includes 187 minority (24 Black or African American, non-Hispanic/Latino; 3 American Indian or Alaska Native, non-Hispanic/Latino; 43 Asian, non-Hispanic/Latino; 114 Hispanic/Latino; 1 Native Hawaiian or other Pacific Islander, non-Hispanic/Latino; 2 Two or more races, non-Hispanic/Latino), 1 international. Average age 28. In 2016, 4 master's, 158 doctorates awarded. *Degree requirements:* For master's, thesis (for some programs); for doctorate, thesis/dissertation (for some programs). *Entrance requirements:* For master's, JD; for doctorate, LSAT (for JD), LL M (for JSD). Additional exam requirements/recommendations for international students: Required—TOEFL (minimum score 600 paper-based; 100 iBT). *Application deadline:* For fall admission, 3/15 priority date for domestic students. Applications are processed on a rolling basis. Application fee: $50. Electronic applications accepted. *Expenses:* Contact institution. *Financial support:* Fellowships, research assistantships, teaching assistantships, career-related internships or fieldwork, Federal Work-Study, institutionally sponsored loans, and scholarships/grants available. Support available to part-time students. Financial award applicants required to submit FAFSA. *Faculty research:* International legal studies, public policy and law, advocacy, intellectual property law, taxation, criminal law. *Unit head:* Francis Jay Mootz, III, Dean, 916-739-7151, E-mail: jmootz@pacific.edu. *Application contact:* 916-739-7105, Fax: 916-739-7301, E-mail: mcgeorge@pacific.edu.
Website: http://www.mcgeorge.edu/

The University of Toledo, College of Law, Toledo, OH 43606. Offers compliance (Certificate); health care compliance (Certificate); higher education compliance (Certificate); law (MLW, JD); JD/MACJ; JD/MBA; JD/MD; JD/MPH; JD/MSE. *Accreditation:* ABA. *Program availability:* Part-time-only, evening/weekend, online only, 100% online. *Faculty:* 27 full-time (13 women), 12 part-time/adjunct (4 women). *Students:* 179 full-time (81 women), 62 part-time (37 women); includes 38 minority (22 Black or African American, non-Hispanic/Latino; 4 Asian, non-Hispanic/Latino; 9 Hispanic/Latino; 1 Native Hawaiian or other Pacific Islander, non-Hispanic/Latino; 2 Two or more races, non-Hispanic/Latino), 1 international. Average age 29. 428 applicants, 57% accepted, 85 enrolled. In 2016, 3 master's, 88 doctorates awarded. *Degree requirements:* For master's, thesis or alternative, 30 credits (mix of required and elective courses); for doctorate, 89 credits (mix of required and elective courses); for Certificate, 16-17 credits. *Entrance requirements:* For master's, LSAT, GRE, GMAT or MCAT (if undergraduate GPA below 2.7), bachelor's degree, undergraduate and graduate transcripts, letters of recommendation, personal statement; for doctorate, LSAT, bachelor's degree. Additional exam requirements/recommendations for international students: Recommended—TOEFL (minimum score 600 paper-based; 100 iBT). *Application deadline:* For fall admission, 8/1 priority date for domestic students, 7/31 for international students; for winter admission, 11/15 for domestic students; for summer admission, 4/15 priority date for domestic students. Applications are processed on a rolling basis. Application fee: $0. Electronic applications accepted. *Expenses:* $19,612 full-time resident, $31,161 full-time non-resident; $14,713 part-time resident, $23,374 part-time non-resident. *Financial support:* In 2016–17, 195 students received support,

including 13 research assistantships (averaging $372 per year), 7 teaching assistantships; career-related internships or fieldwork, Federal Work-Study, and scholarships/grants also available. Support available to part-time students. Financial award application deadline: 8/1; financial award applicants required to submit FAFSA. *Faculty research:* Interlocutory appeals in Federal court; sentencing, punishment, and judging; bankruptcy abuse; state constitutional restrictions on statutes that target named individuals; undue hardship defense to an employer's obligation to provide reasonable accommodations when more than one employee has requested the same accommodation; revising of securities regulation in cyberspace; Federal health law waiver programs; feminist theory. *Total annual research expenditures:* $100,595. *Unit head:* D. Benjamin Barros, Dean, 419-530-2379, Fax: 419-530-4526, E-mail: ben.barros@utoledo.edu. *Application contact:* Jessica Mehl, Assistant Dean of Law Admissions, 419-530-4131, Fax: 419-530-4345, E-mail: law.admissions@utoledo.edu.
Website: http://www.utoledo.edu/law/

University of Toronto, School of Graduate Studies, Faculty of Law and School of Graduate Studies, Graduate Programs in Law, Toronto, ON M5S 1A1, Canada. Offers LL M, MSL, SJD. *Degree requirements:* For master's, thesis (for some programs); for doctorate, thesis/dissertation. *Entrance requirements:* Additional exam requirements/recommendations for international students: Required—TOEFL (minimum score 600 paper-based; 100 iBT), TWE (minimum score 5). Electronic applications accepted.

University of Toronto, School of Graduate Studies, Faculty of Law, Professional Program in Law, Toronto, ON M5S 1A1, Canada. Offers JD, JD/Certificate, JD/MA, JD/MBA, JD/MI, JD/MSW, JD/PhD. *Entrance requirements:* For doctorate, LSAT. *Expenses:* Contact institution.

The University of Tulsa, College of Law, Tulsa, OK 74104. Offers American Indian and indigenous law (LL M); American law for foreign lawyers (LL M); energy and natural resources law (LL M); energy law (MJ); health law (Certificate); Indian law (MJ); law (JD); Native American law (Certificate); natural resources, energy, and environmental law (Certificate); JD/MA; JD/MBA; JD/MS. *Accreditation:* ABA. *Program availability:* Part-time, 100% online. *Faculty:* 23 full-time (13 women), 12 part-time/adjunct (4 women). *Students:* 233 full-time (103 women), 30 part-time (17 women); includes 70 minority (10 Black or African American, non-Hispanic/Latino; 16 American Indian or Alaska Native, non-Hispanic/Latino; 2 Asian, non-Hispanic/Latino; 12 Hispanic/Latino; 30 Two or more races, non-Hispanic/Latino), 5 international. Average age 27. 602 applicants, 40% accepted, 92 enrolled. In 2016, 5 master's, 81 doctorates awarded. *Degree requirements:* For master's, thesis optional. *Entrance requirements:* For master's, JD from an ABA-approved U.S. law school or a JD equivalent from non-U.S. university; for doctorate, LSAT, BS or BA from 4-year regionally-accredited college/university; for Certificate, BS or BA from 4-year regionally-accredited college/university. Additional exam requirements/recommendations for international students: Required—TOEFL (minimum score 570 paper-based; 90 iBT), IELTS (minimum score 6.5). *Application deadline:* For fall admission, 7/31 priority date for domestic and international students; for spring admission, 12/5 priority date for domestic students, 12/5 for international students; for summer admission, 4/13 for domestic and international students. Applications are processed on a rolling basis. Application fee: $30. Electronic applications accepted. *Expenses:* $37,960 per year tuition; $654 fees. *Financial support:* In 2016–17, 255 students received support. Scholarships/grants available. Support available to part-time students. Financial award application deadline: 8/1; financial award applicants required to submit FAFSA. *Faculty research:* Native American law, criminal law, commercial speech, copyright law, international law. *Unit head:* Prof. Lyn Suzanne Entzeroth, Dean, 918-631-2400, Fax: 918-631-3126, E-mail: lyn-entzeroth@utulsa.edu. *Application contact:* April M. Fox, Associate Dean of Admissions and Financial Aid, 918-631-2406, Fax: 918-631-3630, E-mail: april-fox@utulsa.edu.
Website: http://www.utulsa.edu/law/

University of Utah, S. J. Quinney College of Law, Salt Lake City, UT 84112-0730. Offers LL M, JD, JD/MBA, JD/MCMP, JD/MPA, JD/MPP, JD/MRED, JD/MSW. *Accreditation:* ABA. *Faculty:* 32 full-time (13 women), 18 part-time/adjunct (7 women). *Students:* 294 full-time (127 women), 12 part-time (4 women); includes 36 minority (2 Black or African American, non-Hispanic/Latino; 2 American Indian or Alaska Native, non-Hispanic/Latino; 10 Asian, non-Hispanic/Latino; 21 Hispanic/Latino; 1 Native Hawaiian or other Pacific Islander, non-Hispanic/Latino). Average age 28. 612 applicants, 49% accepted, 93 enrolled. In 2016, 124 doctorates awarded. *Entrance requirements:* For doctorate, LSAT, bachelor's degree from college or university whose accreditation is recognized by the U.S. Department of Education. Additional exam requirements/recommendations for international students: Required—TOEFL (minimum score 100 iBT). *Application deadline:* For fall admission, 1/15 priority date for domestic students, 2/15 priority date for international students; for winter admission, 3/10 for domestic and international students. Applications are processed on a rolling basis. Application fee: $60. Electronic applications accepted. *Expenses:* Contact institution. *Financial support:* In 2016–17, 174 students received support, including 165 fellowships with partial tuition reimbursements available (averaging $6,013 per year), 47 research assistantships with partial tuition reimbursements available (averaging $6,721 per year); career-related internships or fieldwork, Federal Work-Study, institutionally sponsored loans, scholarships/grants, and unspecified assistantships also available. Financial award application deadline: 4/7; financial award applicants required to submit FAFSA. *Faculty research:* Environmental law, intellectual property, international law, criminal law, business law. *Total annual research expenditures:* $403,800. *Unit head:* Reyes Aguilar, Jr., Associate Dean for Admissions and Financial Aid, 801-581-6833, Fax: 801-581-6897, E-mail: reyes.aguilar@utah.edu. *Application contact:* Susan Baca, Operations Manager for Admissions and Financial Aid, 801-581-7479, Fax: 801-581-6897, E-mail: susan.baca@law.utah.edu.
Website: http://www.law.utah.edu

University of Victoria, Faculty of Law, Victoria, BC V8W 2Y2, Canada. Offers LL M, JD, PhD, MBA/JD, MPA/JD. *Program availability:* Part-time. *Degree requirements:* For master's, thesis; for doctorate, thesis/dissertation (for some programs), major research paper (for JD). *Entrance requirements:* For master's, LL B or JD; for doctorate, LSAT (for JD), LL B or JD (for PhD); minimum 3 years of full-time study or part-time equivalent leading toward a bachelor's degree (for JD). Additional exam requirements/recommendations for international students: Required—TOEFL (minimum score 600 paper-based; 100 iBT). Electronic applications accepted. *Expenses:* Contact institution. *Faculty research:* Environmental law and policy, international law, alternative dispute resolution, intellectual property law, Aboriginal law.

University of Virginia, School of Law, Charlottesville, VA 22903-1789. Offers LL M, JD, SJD, JD/MA, JD/MBA, JD/MP, JD/MPH, JD/MS, JD/MUEP. JD/MA in international relations offered jointly with The Johns Hopkins University. *Accreditation:* ABA. *Faculty:* 83 full-time (22 women), 5 part-time/adjunct (2 women). *Students:* 952 full-time (402 women); includes 190 minority (43 Black or African American, non-Hispanic/Latino; 69 Asian, non-Hispanic/Latino; 36 Hispanic/Latino; 1 Native Hawaiian or other Pacific Islander, non-Hispanic/Latino; 41 Two or more races, non-Hispanic/Latino), 61 international. Average age 25. 5,345 applicants, 21% accepted, 338 enrolled. In 2016, 49 master's, 330 doctorates awarded. *Degree requirements:* For doctorate, thesis/dissertation (for some programs), oral exam (for SJD). *Entrance requirements:* For master's, 2 letters of recommendation; personal statement; for doctorate, LSAT (for JD). Additional exam requirements/recommendations for international students: Required—TOEFL. *Application deadline:* For fall admission, 3/1 priority date for domestic students, 3/2 for international students. Applications are processed on a rolling basis. Application fee: $75. Electronic applications accepted. *Expenses:* $53,606 tuition, $2,694 fees in-state; $55,924 tuition, $3,376 fees out-of-state. *Financial support:* Fellowships, career-related internships or fieldwork, Federal Work-Study, and institutionally sponsored loans available. Financial award application deadline: 3/1; financial award applicants required to submit FAFSA. *Unit head:* Risa Goluboff, Dean, 434-924-7343, Fax: 434-982-2128, E-mail: goluboff@virginia.edu. *Application contact:* Grace Applefeld Cleveland, Director of Admissions, 434-243-1456, Fax: 434-982-2128, E-mail: lawadmit@virginia.edu.
Website: http://www.law.virginia.edu/

University of Washington, Graduate School, School of Law, Seattle, WA 98195-3020. Offers Asian law (LL M, PhD); intellectual property law and policy (LL M); law (JD); law of sustainable international development (LL M); taxation (LL M); JD/LL M; JD/MA; JD/MAIS; JD/MBA; JD/MPA; JD/MS; JD/PhD. *Accreditation:* ABA. *Degree requirements:* For master's, thesis; for doctorate, thesis/dissertation (for some programs). *Entrance requirements:* For master's, language proficiency (LL M in Asian law); for doctorate, LSAT (for JD). Additional exam requirements/recommendations for international students: Required—TOEFL. *Expenses:* Contact institution. *Faculty research:* Asian, international and comparative law, intellectual property law, health law, environmental law, taxation.

The University of Western Ontario, Faculty of Law, London, ON N6A 5B8, Canada. Offers LL M, MLS, JD, Diploma. *Entrance requirements:* For master's, B+ average in BA, sample of legal academic writing; for doctorate, LSAT. Additional exam requirements/recommendations for international students: Required—TOEFL. *Expenses:* Contact institution. *Faculty research:* Taxation, administrative law, torts, drug and alcohol law and policy, property.

University of Wisconsin–Madison, Law School, Madison, WI 53706-1399. Offers LL M, JD, SJD. *Accreditation:* ABA. *Program availability:* Part-time, evening/weekend. *Faculty:* 60 full-time (40 women), 44 part-time/adjunct (17 women). *Students:* 544 full-time (268 women), 26 part-time (17 women); includes 114 minority (32 Black or African American, non-Hispanic/Latino; 1 American Indian or Alaska Native, non-Hispanic/Latino; 13 Asian, non-Hispanic/Latino; 47 Hispanic/Latino; 21 Two or more races, non-Hispanic/Latino), 69 international. Average age 26. 1,406 applicants, 46% accepted, 149 enrolled. In 2016, 42 master's, 190 doctorates awarded. *Degree requirements:* For master's, thesis (for some programs); for doctorate, thesis/dissertation (for some programs). *Entrance requirements:* For doctorate, LSAT (for JD). Additional exam requirements/recommendations for international students: Required—TOEFL. *Application deadline:* For fall admission, 4/1 for domestic students, 3/1 for international students. Applications are processed on a rolling basis. Application fee: $60. Electronic applications accepted. *Expenses:* $21,450 resident full-time; $40,147 non-resident full-time. *Financial support:* In 2016–17, 353 students received support. Fellowships, research assistantships, career-related internships or fieldwork, scholarships/grants, health care benefits, tuition waivers (full and partial), and unspecified assistantships available. Support available to part-time students. Financial award application deadline: 4/1; financial award applicants required to submit FAFSA. *Unit head:* Margaret Raymond, Dean, 608-262-0618, Fax: 608-262-5485. *Application contact:* Rebecca L. Scheller, Assistant Dean for Admissions and Financial Aid, 608-262-5914, Fax: 608-263-3190, E-mail: admissions@law.wisc.edu.
Website: https://www.law.wisc.edu/

University of Wyoming, College of Law, Laramie, WY 82071. Offers JD, JD/MPA. *Accreditation:* ABA. *Entrance requirements:* For doctorate, LSAT. Additional exam requirements/recommendations for international students: Required—TOEFL. Electronic applications accepted. *Expenses:* Contact institution. *Faculty research:* Environmental, public land, constitutional, securities law, criminal law.

Valparaiso University, School of Law, Valparaiso, IN 46383-4945. Offers LL M, JD, JD/MA, JD/MALS, JD/MBA, JD/MS, JD/MSSA. *Accreditation:* ABA. *Program availability:* Part-time. *Degree requirements:* For doctorate, 60 hours of pro bono service. *Entrance requirements:* For doctorate, LSAT. Additional exam requirements/recommendations for international students: Required—TOEFL (minimum score 600 paper-based; 95 iBT), IELTS (minimum score 7), or LSAT. Electronic applications accepted. *Expenses:* Contact institution. *Faculty research:* Animal law, food law, national security law, immigration law, tax law.

Vanderbilt University, Vanderbilt Law School, Nashville, TN 37203. Offers law (LL M, JD); law and economics (PhD); JD/M Div; JD/MA; JD/MBA; JD/MD; JD/MPP; JD/MTS; JD/PhD; LL M/MA. *Accreditation:* ABA. *Faculty:* 37 full-time (14 women), 51 part-time/adjunct (21 women). *Students:* 572 full-time (292 women); includes 128 minority (60 Black or African American, non-Hispanic/Latino; 3 American Indian or Alaska Native, non-Hispanic/Latino; 25 Asian, non-Hispanic/Latino; 34 Hispanic/Latino; 6 Two or more races, non-Hispanic/Latino), 17 international. Average age 23. 4,380 applicants, 32% accepted, 204 enrolled. In 2016, 35 master's, 195 doctorates awarded. *Degree requirements:* For doctorate, comprehensive exam (for some programs), thesis/dissertation (for some programs), 72 hours of coursework and research (for PhD). *Entrance requirements:* For master's, foreign law degree; for doctorate, GRE (for PhD), LSAT, advanced undergraduate economics (for PhD). Additional exam requirements/recommendations for international students: Required—TOEFL. *Application deadline:* For fall admission, 4/1 for domestic and international students. Applications are processed on a rolling basis. Application fee: $50. Electronic applications accepted. *Expenses:* Contact institution. *Financial support:* In 2016–17, 486 students received support. Career-related internships or fieldwork, Federal Work-Study, institutionally sponsored loans, scholarships/grants, and health care benefits available. Financial award application deadline: 2/15; financial award applicants required to submit FAFSA. *Unit head:* G. Todd Morton, Assistant Dean of Admissions, 615-322-6452, Fax: 615-322-1531, E-mail: admissions@law.vanderbilt.edu. *Application contact:* Admissions Office, 615-322-6452, Fax: 615-322-1531, E-mail: admissions@law.vanderbilt.edu.
Website: http://law.vanderbilt.edu/

Vermont Law School, Graduate and Professional Programs, Professional Program, South Royalton, VT 05068-0096. Offers JD, JD/LL M, JD/MELP, JD/MERL, JD/MFALP. *Accreditation:* ABA. *Faculty:* 48 full-time (26 women), 22 part-time/adjunct (7 women). *Students:* 383 full-time (218 women); includes 81 minority (26 Black or African American, non-Hispanic/Latino; 4 American Indian or Alaska Native, non-Hispanic/Latino; 13 Asian, non-Hispanic/Latino; 27 Hispanic/Latino; 11 Two or more races, non-Hispanic/Latino), 10 international. Average age 27. 647 applicants, 81% accepted, 139 enrolled. In 2016, 116 doctorates awarded. *Entrance requirements:* For doctorate, LSAT, LSDAS/registration, resume. Additional exam requirements/recommendations for international students: Required—TOEFL (minimum score 600 paper-based). *Application deadline:* For fall admission, 3/1 priority date for domestic students; for spring admission, 11/15 priority date for domestic students. Applications are processed on a rolling basis. Application fee: $60. Electronic applications accepted. *Expenses:* Contact institution. *Financial support:* Career-related internships or fieldwork, Federal Work-Study, institutionally sponsored loans, scholarships/grants, and tuition waivers (partial) available. Financial award application deadline: 3/1; financial award applicants required to submit FAFSA. *Faculty research:* Environmental law, energy regulation and law, food and agriculture law, international law, water and justice. *Unit head:* Marc B. Mihaly, President and Dean, 802-831-1225, Fax: 802-831-1163, E-mail: kevans@vermontlaw.edu. *Application contact:* John D. Miller, Jr., Vice President for Enrollment Management, Marketing and Communications, 802-831-1239, Fax: 802-831-1174, E-mail: admiss@vermontlaw.edu. Website: http://www.vermontlaw.edu/

Villanova University, School of Law, Program in Law, Villanova, PA 19085. Offers JD, JD/LL M, JD/MBA. *Accreditation:* ABA. *Entrance requirements:* For doctorate, LSAT. Electronic applications accepted. *Expenses:* Contact institution. *Faculty research:* Business law; international law (public and private); tax law; criminal law, procedure, and sentencing; law and religion.

Wake Forest University, School of Law, Winston-Salem, NC 27109. Offers LL M, MSL, JD, SJD, JD/M Div, JD/MA, JD/MBA. LL M program is designed for foreign law graduates in American law. *Accreditation:* ABA. *Entrance requirements:* For doctorate, LSAT (for JD). Additional exam requirements/recommendations for international students: Required—TOEFL (minimum score 600 paper-based, 100 iBT) or IELTS (minimum score 7). Electronic applications accepted. *Expenses:* Contact institution. *Faculty research:* Constitutional law, family law, land use planning, torts, taxation.

Walden University, Graduate Programs, School of Public Policy and Administration, Minneapolis, MN 55401. Offers criminal justice (MPA, MPP, MS, Graduate Certificate), including emergency management (MS, PhD), general program (MS), global leadership (MS, PhD), homeland security and policy coordination (MS, PhD), law and public policy (MS, PhD), policy analysis (MS, PhD), public management and leadership (MS, PhD), self-designed (MS), terrorism, mediation, and peace (MS, PhD); criminal justice and executive management (MS), including global leadership (MS, PhD); criminal justice leadership and executive management (MS), including emergency management (MS, PhD), general program, homeland security and policy coordination (MS, PhD), law and public policy (MS, PhD), policy analysis (MS, PhD), public management and leadership (MS, PhD), self-designed, terrorism, mediation, and peace (MS, PhD); emergency management (MPA, MPP, MS), including criminal justice (MS, PhD), general program (MS), homeland security (MS), public management and leadership (MS, PhD), terrorism and emergency management (MS); general program (MPA, MPP); global leadership (MPA, MPP); government management (Graduate Certificate); health policy (MPA, MPP); homeland security (Graduate Certificate); homeland security and policy coordination (MPA, MPP); international nongovernmental organizations (MPA, MPP); law and public policy (MPA, MPP); local government management for sustainable communities (MPA, MPP); nonprofit management (Graduate Certificate); nonprofit management and leadership (MPA, MPP, MS), including global leadership (MS, PhD), international nongovernmental organization (MS), local government for sustainable communities (MS), self designed (MS); online teaching in higher education (Post-Master's Certificate); policy analysis (MPA); public management and leadership (MPA, MPP, Graduate Certificate); public policy (Graduate Certificate); public policy and administration (PhD), including criminal justice (MS, PhD), emergency management (MS, PhD), global leadership (MS, PhD), health policy, homeland security and policy coordination (MS, PhD), international nongovernmental organizations, law and public policy (MS, PhD), local government management for sustainable communities, nonprofit management and leadership, policy analysis (MS, PhD), public management and leadership (MS, PhD), terrorism, mediation, and peace (MS, PhD); strategic planning and public policy (Graduate Certificate); terrorism, mediation, and peace (MPA, MPP). *Program availability:* Part-time, evening/weekend, online only, 100% online. *Degree requirements:* For doctorate, thesis/dissertation, residency. *Entrance requirements:* For master's, bachelor's degree or higher; minimum GPA of 2.5; official transcripts; goal statement (for some programs); access to computer and Internet; for doctorate, master's degree or higher; three years of related professional or academic experience (preferred); minimum GPA of 3.0; goal statement and current resume (for select programs); official transcripts; access to computer and Internet; for other advanced degree, relevant work experience; access to computer and Internet. Additional exam requirements/recommendations for international students: Required—TOEFL (minimum score 550 paper-based, 79 iBT), IELTS (minimum score 6.5), Michigan English Language Assessment Battery (minimum score 82), or PTE (minimum score 53). Electronic applications accepted.

Washburn University, School of Law, Topeka, KS 66621. Offers global legal studies (LL M); law (MSL, JD). *Accreditation:* ABA. *Entrance requirements:* For doctorate, LSAT. Additional exam requirements/recommendations for international students: Recommended—TOEFL (minimum score 550 paper-based). Electronic applications accepted. Application fee is waived when completed online. *Expenses:* Contact institution. *Faculty research:* Constitutional law, family law, energy law, banking and securities law, oil and gas.

Washington and Lee University, School of Law, Lexington, VA 24450. Offers law (JD). *Accreditation:* ABA. *Faculty:* 34 full-time (13 women), 33 part-time/adjunct (5 women). *Students:* 329 full-time (148 women); includes 65 minority (16 Black or African American, non-Hispanic/Latino; 2 American Indian or Alaska Native, non-Hispanic/Latino; 9 Asian, non-Hispanic/Latino; 27 Hispanic/Latino; 11 Two or more races, non-Hispanic/Latino), 9 international. Average age 23. 1,911 applicants, 47% accepted, 117 enrolled. *Entrance requirements:* For doctorate, LSAT. *Application deadline:* For fall admission, 3/1 priority date for domestic and international students. Applications are processed on a rolling basis. Application fee: $0. Electronic applications accepted. *Expenses:* $45,330 per year. *Financial support:* In 2016–17, 310 students received support. Fellowships, research assistantships, career-related internships or fieldwork, Federal Work-Study, institutionally sponsored loans, and scholarships/grants available. Financial award application deadline: 2/15; financial award applicants required to submit FAFSA. *Faculty research:* Criminal law, corporate law, experiential education, international and comparative law, public interest law. *Unit head:* Brant Hellwig, Dean, 540-458-8502, Fax: 540-458-8488, E-mail: hellwigb@wlu.edu. *Application contact:* Lisa Rodocker, Director of Admissions, 540-458-8503, Fax: 540-458-8586, E-mail: rodockerl@wlu.edu.
Website: http://law.wlu.edu/

Washington University in St. Louis, School of Law, St. Louis, MO 63130-4899. Offers LL M, MJS, JD, JSD, JD/MA, JD/MBA, JD/MHA, JD/MS, JD/MSW, JD/PhD. *Accreditation:* ABA. *Entrance requirements:* For doctorate, LSAT (for JD). Electronic applications accepted. *Expenses:* Contact institution. *Faculty research:* International law, environmental law, employment discrimination, reproductive rights, bankruptcy and white-collar crime.

Wayne State University, Law School, Detroit, MI 48202. Offers corporate and finance law (LL M); labor and employment law (LL M); law (JD); taxation (LL M); United States law (LL M); JD/MA; JD/MADR; JD/MBA; JD/MS. *Accreditation:* ABA. *Faculty:* 40 full-time (15 women), 27 part-time/adjunct (12 women). *Students:* 379 full-time (162 women), 58 part-time (26 women); includes 63 minority (35 Black or African American, non-Hispanic/Latino; 1 American Indian or Alaska Native, non-Hispanic/Latino; 9 Asian, non-Hispanic/Latino; 3 Hispanic/Latino; 15 Two or more races, non-Hispanic/Latino), 13 international. Average age 27. 684 applicants, 53% accepted, 138 enrolled. In 2016, 16 master's, 133 doctorates awarded. *Degree requirements:* For master's, thesis (for some programs). *Entrance requirements:* For master's, JD from ABA-accredited institution and member institution of the AALS; for doctorate, LSAT, LDAS report, bachelor's degree from accredited institution, personal statement, transcripts from all U.S. undergraduate schools attended and an analysis and summary of the transcripts; letter of recommendation (up to two are accepted). Additional exam requirements/recommendations for international students: Required—TOEFL (minimum score 600 paper-based; 100 iBT), Michigan English Language Assessment Battery (minimum score 85); Recommended—IELTS (minimum score 7). *Application deadline:* For fall admission, 7/1 for domestic students, 5/1 priority date for international students. Applications are processed on a rolling basis. Application fee: $0. Electronic applications accepted. *Expenses:* Contact institution. *Financial support:* In 2016–17, 353 students received support. Fellowships, Federal Work-Study, and scholarships/grants available. Support available to part-time students. Financial award application deadline: 6/30; financial award applicants required to submit FAFSA. *Faculty research:* Public interest law, tax law, international law, environmental law, health law. *Unit head:* Lance Gable, Interim Dean, 313-577-3933, E-mail: jbenson@wayne.edu. *Application contact:* Kathy Fox, Assistant Dean of Admissions, 313-577-3937, Fax: 313-993-8129, E-mail: lawinquire@wayne.edu.
Website: http://law.wayne.edu/

Western Michigan University Thomas M. Cooley Law School, Graduate Programs, Lansing, MI 48901-3038. Offers administrative law (public law) (JD); business transactions (JD); Canadian law practice (JD); constitutional law/civil rights (public law) (JD); corporate law and finance (LL M); environmental law (public law) (JD); general practice (JD), including solo and small firm; homeland and national security law (LL M); insurance law (LL M); intellectual property (JD); intellectual property law (LL M); international law (JD); litigation (JD); self-directed (LL M, JD); tax law (LL M); taxation (JD); U.S. legal studies for foreign attorneys (LL M); JD/LL M; JD/MBA; JD/MPA; JD/MSW. *Program availability:* Part-time, evening/weekend, 100% online, blended/hybrid learning. *Degree requirements:* For master's, thesis optional; for doctorate, minimum of 3 credits of clinical experience. *Entrance requirements:* For master's, JD or LL B; for doctorate, LSAT. Additional exam requirements/recommendations for international students: Required—TOEFL (for U.S. legal studies for foreign attorneys LL M program); Recommended—TOEFL. Electronic applications accepted. *Faculty research:* Wrongful convictions, civil rights, environmental law, litigation techniques, data mining, intellectual property, practical and skills-based legal education.

Western New England University, School of Law, Springfield, MA 01119. Offers estate planning and elder law (LL M, MS); law (JD). *Accreditation:* ABA. *Program availability:* Part-time, evening/weekend. *Faculty:* 21 full-time (12 women), 30 part-time/adjunct (8 women). *Students:* 174 full-time (93 women), 133 part-time (82 women); includes 80 minority (41 Black or African American, non-Hispanic/Latino; 4 American Indian or Alaska Native, non-Hispanic/Latino; 12 Asian, non-Hispanic/Latino; 23 Hispanic/Latino). Average age 32. 645 applicants, 55% accepted, 72 enrolled. In 2016, 15 master's, 105 doctorates awarded. *Entrance requirements:* For master's, official law school transcript, resume; for doctorate, LSAT, two letters of recommendation, personal statement. *Application deadline:* For fall admission, 3/15 priority date for domestic students. Applications are processed on a rolling basis. Application fee: $0. Electronic applications accepted. *Expenses:* $40,954 (for full-time JD); $30,928 (for part-time JD); $1,458 per credit (for LL M and MS programs). *Financial support:* Career-related internships or fieldwork, Federal Work-Study, and scholarships/grants available. Support available to part-time students. Financial award application deadline: 4/15; financial award applicants required to submit FAFSA. *Unit head:* Eric Gouvin, Dean/Professor, 413-796-2031, E-mail: eric.gouvin@law.wne.edu. *Application contact:* Amy Mangione, Assistant Dean of Law/Director of Law Admissions, 413-782-1286, Fax: 413-796-2067, E-mail: admissions@law.wne.edu.
Website: http://www.law.wne.edu/

Western State College of Law at Argosy University, Professional Program, Irvine, CA 92618-3601. Offers JD. *Accreditation:* ABA. *Program availability:* Part-time, evening/weekend. *Entrance requirements:* For doctorate, LSAT, 2 letters of recommendation. Additional exam requirements/recommendations for international students: Required—TOEFL (minimum score 550 paper-based; 80 iBT). Electronic applications accepted. *Faculty research:* Criminal law and practice, entrepreneurship, teaching effectiveness and student success, learning theory and legal education.

West Virginia University, College of Law, Morgantown, WV 26506-6130. Offers LL M, JD, JD/MBA, JD/MPA. *Accreditation:* ABA. *Program availability:* Part-time. *Entrance requirements:* For doctorate, LSAT. Additional exam requirements/recommendations for international students: Required—TOEFL (minimum score 600 paper-based; 100 iBT). Electronic applications accepted. *Expenses:* Contact institution. *Faculty research:* Constitutional law, public interest law, corporate law, environment and natural resources innocence project, professional skills, leadership, intellectual property, entrepreneurship, labor, sustainable development, family law, IR human rights, immigration.

Widener University, Commonwealth Law School, Harrisburg, PA 17106-9381. Offers JD. *Accreditation:* ABA. *Program availability:* Part-time. *Faculty:* 17 full-time (8 women), 18 part-time/adjunct (6 women). *Students:* 236 full-time (112 women), 50 part-time (44 women); includes 51 minority (22 Black or African American, non-Hispanic/Latino; 3 American Indian or Alaska Native, non-Hispanic/Latino; 13 Asian, non-Hispanic/Latino; 13 Hispanic/Latino). Average age 25. 506 applicants, 67% accepted, 66 enrolled. *Entrance requirements:* For doctorate, LSAT. *Application deadline:* For fall admission, 5/15 for domestic students. Applications are processed on a rolling basis. Application fee: $60. Electronic applications accepted. *Expenses:* Contact institution. *Financial support:* Fellowships, research assistantships, career-related internships or fieldwork, Federal Work-Study, institutionally sponsored loans, and scholarships/grants available. Support available to part-time students. Financial award application deadline: 2/15; financial award applicants required to submit FAFSA. *Faculty research:* Health law, toxic torts, Constitutional law, intellectual property, corporate law. *Unit head:* Christian Johnson, Dean, 302-477-2100, Fax: 302-477-2282, E-mail: cajohnson2@widener.edu. *Application contact:* John Benfield, Associate Dean for Admissions and Administration, 302-477-2210, Fax: 302-477-2224, E-mail: jsbenfield@widener.edu.
Website: http://www.law.widener.edu/

Widener University, Delaware Law School, Wilmington, DE 19803-0474. Offers corporate and business law (MJ); corporate law and finance (LL M); health law (LL M, MJ, D Law); higher education compliance (MJ); juridical science (SJD); law (JD). *Accreditation:* ABA. *Program availability:* Part-time, 100% online. *Faculty:* 24 full-time (13 women), 42 part-time/adjunct (15 women). *Students:* 479 full-time (252 women), 38 part-time (29 women); includes 128 minority (70 Black or African American, non-Hispanic/Latino; 12 American Indian or Alaska Native, non-Hispanic/Latino; 14 Asian, non-Hispanic/Latino; 26 Hispanic/Latino; 6 Two or more races, non-Hispanic/Latino), 39 international. Average age 26. 735 applicants, 80% accepted, 126 enrolled. *Degree requirements:* For doctorate, thesis/dissertation (for some programs). *Entrance requirements:* For master's, GMAT. *Application deadline:* For fall admission, 5/15 for domestic students; for spring admission, 12/1 for domestic students. Applications are processed on a rolling basis. Application fee: $60. Tuition and fees vary according to degree level and program. *Financial support:* Career-related internships or fieldwork, Federal Work-Study, institutionally sponsored loans, and scholarships/grants available. Support available to part-time students. Financial award application deadline: 2/15; financial award applicants required to submit FAFSA. *Unit head:* Rod Smolla, Dean,

302-477-2100, Fax: 302-477-2282, E-mail: rasmolla@widener.edu. *Application contact:* Barbara L. Ayars, Assistant Dean of Admissions, 302-477-2210, Fax: 302-477-2224, E-mail: barbara.l.ayars@law.widener.edu.
Website: http://delawarelaw.widener.edu/

Widener University, School of Human Service Professions, Institute for Graduate Clinical Psychology, Law-Psychology Program, Chester, PA 19013-5792. Offers JD/Psy D. *Faculty:* 15 full-time (6 women), 18 part-time/adjunct (10 women). *Students:* 1 full-time (0 women), 1 (woman) part-time. Average age 23. 21 applicants, 19% accepted. *Application deadline:* For fall admission, 2/1 for domestic students. Applications are processed on a rolling basis. Application fee: $60. Electronic applications accepted. Tuition and fees vary according to degree level and program. *Financial support:* Research assistantships, career-related internships or fieldwork, Federal Work-Study, institutionally sponsored loans, and scholarships/grants available. Financial award application deadline: 5/31. *Unit head:* Dr. Amiram Elwork, Director, 610-499-1206, Fax: 610-499-4625, E-mail: amiram.elwork@widener.edu. *Application contact:* Maureen A. Brennan, Admissions Coordinator, 610-499-1206, Fax: 610-499-4625, E-mail: maureen.a.brennan@widener.edu.

Willamette University, College of Law, Salem, OR 97301-3922. Offers dispute resolution (LL M); law (MLS, JD); transnational law (LL M); JD/MBA. *Accreditation:* ABA. *Program availability:* Part-time. *Degree requirements:* For master's, thesis, 25 credit hours (for LL M); 26 credit hours (for MLS); for doctorate, thesis/dissertation, 90 credit hours. *Entrance requirements:* For master's, bachelor's degree (for MLS); domestic or foreign JD (for LL M); for doctorate, LSAT. Additional exam requirements/recommendations for international students: Required—TOEFL (minimum score 480 paper-based; 45 iBT); Recommended—IELTS (minimum score 5). Electronic applications accepted. Application fee is waived when completed online. *Expenses:* Contact institution. *Faculty research:* Dispute resolution, international law, business law, law and government, sustainability.

Yale University, Yale Law School, New Haven, CT 06520-8215. Offers LL M, MSL, JD, JSD, PhD, JD/MA, JD/MAR, JD/MBA, JD/MD, JD/MES, JD/PhD. *Accreditation:* ABA. *Faculty:* 66 full-time, 103 part-time/adjunct. *Students:* 632 full-time (301 women). Average age 26. 2,735 applicants, 9% accepted, 210 enrolled. *Entrance requirements:* For doctorate, LSAT (for JD). Additional exam requirements/recommendations for international students: Required—TOEFL (minimum score 600 paper-based). *Application deadline:* For fall admission, 2/28 for domestic students. Applications are processed on a rolling basis. Application fee: $60. Electronic applications accepted. *Expenses:* Contact institution. *Financial support:* Application deadline: 3/15; applicants required to submit FAFSA. *Unit head:* Robert Post, Dean, 203-432-1660. *Application contact:* Asha Rangappa, Associate Dean, 203-432-4995, E-mail: admissions.law@yale.edu.
Website: http://www.law.yale.edu/

Yeshiva University, Benjamin N. Cardozo School of Law, New York, NY 10003-4301. Offers comparative legal thought (LL M); dispute resolution and advocacy (LL M); general studies (LL M); intellectual property law (LL M); law (JD). *Accreditation:* ABA. *Program availability:* Part-time. *Faculty:* 61 full-time (24 women), 92 part-time/adjunct (38 women). *Students:* 992 full-time (506 women), 85 part-time (48 women); includes 277 minority (65 Black or African American, non-Hispanic/Latino; 88 Asian, non-Hispanic/Latino; 112 Hispanic/Latino; 1 Native Hawaiian or other Pacific Islander, non-Hispanic/Latino; 11 Two or more races, non-Hispanic/Latino), 69 international. Average age 25. 2,475 applicants, 56% accepted, 272 enrolled. In 2016, 70 master's, 391 doctorates awarded. *Entrance requirements:* For doctorate, LSAT, 2 letters of recommendation. Additional exam requirements/recommendations for international students: Required—TOEFL (minimum score 100 iBT); Recommended—IELTS (minimum score 7). *Application deadline:* For fall admission, 4/1 priority date for domestic students; for spring admission, 12/1 for domestic students. Applications are processed on a rolling basis. Application fee: $50. Electronic applications accepted. *Expenses:* Contact institution. *Financial support:* In 2016–17, 745 students received support, including 87 research assistantships (averaging $1,599 per year); career-related internships or fieldwork, Federal Work-Study, institutionally sponsored loans, scholarships/grants, health care benefits, and tuition waivers (full and partial) also available. Support available to part-time students. Financial award application deadline: 3/1; financial award applicants required to submit FAFSA. *Faculty research:* Corporate and commercial law, intellectual property law, criminal law and litigation, Constitutional law, legal theory and jurisprudence. *Unit head:* David G. Martinidez, Dean of Admissions, 212-790-0357, Fax: 212-790-0482, E-mail: lawinfo@yu.edu. *Application contact:* David G. Martinidez, Dean of Admissions, 212-790-0357, Fax: 212-790-0482, E-mail: lawinfo@yu.edu.
Website: http://www.cardozo.yu.edu/

York University, Faculty of Graduate Studies, Faculty of Liberal Arts and Professional Studies, Program in Public Policy, Administration and Law, Toronto, ON M3J 1P3, Canada. Offers MPPAL.

York University, Faculty of Graduate Studies, Osgoode Hall Law School, Toronto, ON M3J 1P3, Canada. Offers LL M, JD, PhD. *Program availability:* Part-time, evening/weekend. *Degree requirements:* For master's, thesis; for doctorate, comprehensive exam, thesis/dissertation. *Entrance requirements:* For doctorate, LSAT. Electronic applications accepted.

Legal and Justice Studies

American Public University System, AMU/APU Graduate Programs, Charles Town, WV 25414. Offers accounting (MBA, MS); applied business analytics (MBA, MS); criminal justice (MA), including business administration, emergency and disaster management, general (MA, MS); educational leadership (M Ed); emergency and disaster management (MA); entrepreneurship (MBA); environmental policy and management (MS), including environmental planning, environmental sustainability, fish and wildlife management, general (MA, MS), global environmental management; finance (MBA); general (MBA); government contracting and acquisition (MBA); health care administration (MBA); health information management (MS); history (MA), including American history, ancient and classical history, European history, global history, public history; homeland security (MA), including business administration, counterterrorism studies, criminal justice, cyber, emergency management and public health, intelligence studies, transportation security; homeland security resource allocation (MBA); humanities (MA); information technology (MS), including digital forensics, enterprise software development, information assurance and security, IT project management; information technology management (MBA); intelligence studies (MA), including criminal intelligence, cyber, general (MA, MS), homeland security, intelligence analysis, intelligence collection, intelligence management, intelligence operations, terrorism studies; international relations and conflict resolution (MA), including comparative and security issues, conflict resolution, international and transnational security issues, peacekeeping; legal studies (MA); management (MA), including strategic consulting; marketing (MBA); military history (MA), including American military history, American Revolution, civil war, war since 1945, World War II; military studies (MA), including joint warfare, strategic leadership; national security studies (MA), including cyber, general (MA, MS), homeland security, regional security studies, security and intelligence analysis, terrorism studies; nonprofit management (MBA); political science (MA), including American politics and government, comparative government and development, general (MA, MS), international relations, public policy; psychology (MA); public administration (MPA), including disaster management, environmental policy, health policy, human resources, national security, organizational management, security management; public health (MPH); reverse logistics management (MA); security management (MA); space studies (MS), including aerospace science, general (MA, MS), planetary science; sports and health sciences (MS); sports management (MBA); teaching (M Ed), including autism spectrum disorder, curriculum and instruction for elementary teachers, elementary reading, English language learners, instructional leadership, online learning, special education, STEAM (STEM plus the arts); transportation and logistics management (MA). *Program availability:* Part-time, evening/weekend, online only, 100% online. *Faculty:* 401 full-time (228 women), 1,678 part-time/adjunct (781 women). *Students:* 378 full-time (184 women), 8,455 part-time (3,484 women); includes 2,972 minority (1,552 Black or African American, non-Hispanic/Latino; 52 American Indian or Alaska Native, non-Hispanic/Latino; 211 Asian, non-Hispanic/Latino; 791 Hispanic/Latino; 70 Native Hawaiian or other Pacific Islander, non-Hispanic/Latino; 296 Two or more races, non-Hispanic/Latino), 109 international. Average age 37. In 2016, 3,185 master's awarded. *Degree requirements:* For master's, comprehensive exam or practicum. *Entrance requirements:* For master's, official transcript showing earned bachelor's degree from institution accredited by recognized accrediting body. Additional exam requirements/recommendations for international students: Required—TOEFL (minimum score 550 paper-based), IELTS (minimum score 6.5). *Application deadline:* Applications are processed on a rolling basis. Application fee: $0. Electronic applications accepted. *Expenses: Tuition:* Part-time $350 per credit hour. *Required fees:* $50 per course. *Financial support:* Scholarships/grants available. Financial award applicants required to submit FAFSA. *Unit head:* Dr. Karan Powell, President, 877-468-6268, Fax: 304-724-3780. *Application contact:* Terry Grant, Vice President of Enrollment Management, 877-468-6268, Fax: 304-724-3780, E-mail: info@apus.edu.
Website: http://www.apus.edu

Arizona State University at the Tempe campus, College of Liberal Arts and Sciences, School of Social Transformation, Tempe, AZ 85287-4902. Offers African studies (Graduate Certificate); gender studies (PhD, Graduate Certificate); justice studies (MS, PhD); social and cultural pedagogy (MA); socio-economic justice (Graduate Certificate); PhD/JD. *Program availability:* Part-time. Terminal master's awarded for partial completion of doctoral program. *Degree requirements:* For master's, thesis or alternative, interactive Program of Study (iPOS) submitted before completing 50 percent of required credit hours; for doctorate, comprehensive exam, thesis/dissertation, interactive Program of Study (iPOS) submitted before completing 50 percent of required credit hours. *Entrance requirements:* For master's, GRE or LSAT, minimum GPA of 3.0 or equivalent in last 2 years of work leading to bachelor's degree; for doctorate, GRE or LSAT (for justice studies program), minimum GPA of 3.0 or equivalent in last 2 years of work leading to bachelor's degree. Additional exam requirements/recommendations for international students: Required—TOEFL, IELTS, or PTE. Electronic applications accepted.

Arizona State University at the Tempe campus, New College of Interdisciplinary Arts and Sciences, Program in Social Justice and Human Rights, Phoenix, AZ 85069-7100. Offers MA. Fall admission only. *Program availability:* Part-time, evening/weekend. *Degree requirements:* For master's, thesis or applied project, interactive Program of Study (iPOS) submitted before completing 50 percent of required credit hours. *Entrance requirements:* For master's, GRE, minimum GPA of 3.0 or equivalent in last 2 years of work leading to bachelor's degree, 2 letters of recommendation, official transcripts, writing sample, personal statement, resume. Additional exam requirements/recommendations for international students: Required—TOEFL, IELTS, or PTE. Electronic applications accepted. *Faculty research:* Social movements, violence against women, globalization, innovative uses of human rights law, environmental ethics, social justice and art, women and international development, slavery, genocide, metropolitan studies, urban culture and social space, fair trade, citizenship; immigration.

Arizona State University at the Tempe campus, Sandra Day O'Connor College of Law, Phoenix, AZ 85004-4467. Offers biotechnology and genomics (LL M); law (JD); legal studies (MLS); patent practice (MLS); sports law and business (MSLB); tribal policy, law and government (LL M); JD/MBA; JD/MD; JD/MSW; JD/PhD. *Accreditation:* ABA. *Program availability:* 100% online. *Faculty:* 71 full-time (31 women), 67 part-time/adjunct (16 women). *Students:* 718 full-time (300 women); includes 195 minority (17 Black or African American, non-Hispanic/Latino; 14 American Indian or Alaska Native, non-Hispanic/Latino; 27 Asian, non-Hispanic/Latino; 98 Hispanic/Latino; 3 Native Hawaiian or other Pacific Islander, non-Hispanic/Latino; 36 Two or more races, non-Hispanic/Latino), 13 international. Average age 28. 1,860 applicants, 42% accepted, 228 enrolled. In 2016, 52 master's, 190 doctorates awarded. *Entrance requirements:* For master's, bachelor's degree and JD (for LL M); for doctorate, LSAT, bachelor's degree. Additional exam requirements/recommendations for international students: Required—TOEFL (minimum score 550 paper-based; 80 iBT). *Application deadline:* For fall admission, 3/1 priority date for domestic and international students. Applications are processed on a rolling basis. Application fee: $65. Electronic applications accepted. *Expenses:* Contact institution. *Financial support:* In 2016–17, 432 students received support. Institutionally sponsored loans and scholarships/grants available. Financial award application deadline: 3/15; financial award applicants required to submit FAFSA. *Faculty research:* Emerging technologies and the law, Indian law, international law, intellectual property, health law, sports law and business. *Total annual research expenditures:* $1.9 million. *Unit head:* Douglas Sylvester, Dean/Professor, 480-965-6188, Fax: 480-965-6521, E-mail: douglas.sylvester@asu.edu. *Application contact:* Chitra Damania, Director of Operations, 480-965-1474, Fax: 480-727-7930, E-mail: law.admissions@asu.edu.
Website: http://www.law.asu.edu/

Auburn University at Montgomery, College of Public Policy and Justice, Department of Justice and Public Safety, Montgomery, AL 36124-4023. Offers criminal studies (MSJPS); homeland security (MSJPS); homeland security and emergency management (MS); legal studies (MSJPS); organizational leadership (MSJPS). *Program availability:* Part-time, evening/weekend. *Students:* 13 full-time (8 women), 44 part-time (27 women); includes 21 minority (20 Black or African American, non-Hispanic/Latino; 1 Two or more races, non-Hispanic/Latino), 3 international. Average age 32. *Degree requirements:* For master's, comprehensive exam, thesis optional. *Entrance requirements:* For master's, GRE General Test or MAT. *Application deadline:* Applications are processed on a rolling basis. Electronic applications accepted. *Expenses:* Tuition, state resident: full-time $6462; part-time $359 per credit hour. Tuition, nonresident: full-time $14,526; part-time $807 per credit hour. *Required fees:* $554. *Financial support:* Career-related internships or fieldwork and scholarships/grants available. Support available to part-time students. Financial award application deadline: 3/1; financial award applicants required to submit FAFSA. *Faculty research:* Law enforcement, corrections, juvenile justice. *Unit head:* Dr. Ralph Ioimo, Head, 334-244-3691, Fax: 334-244-3244, E-mail: rioimo@aum.edu. *Application contact:* Dr. Ralph Ioimo, Head, 334-244-3691, Fax: 334-244-3244, E-mail: rioimo@aum.edu.
Website: http://cppj.aum.edu/departments/justice-and-public-safety

Binghamton University, State University of New York, Graduate School, Harpur College of Arts and Sciences, Program in Social, Political, Ethical and Legal Philosophy, Binghamton, NY 13902-6000. Offers MA, PhD. *Program availability:* Part-time. *Faculty:* 14 full-time (6 women), 2 part-time/adjunct (0 women). *Students:* 15 full-time (3 women), 23 part-time (9 women); includes 7 minority (1 Black or African American, non-Hispanic/Latino; 1 Asian, non-Hispanic/Latino; 5 Hispanic/Latino), 7 international. Average age 32. 53 applicants, 40% accepted, 8 enrolled. In 2016, 4 master's, 4 doctorates awarded. Terminal master's awarded for partial completion of doctoral program. *Degree requirements:* For master's, comprehensive exam, thesis or alternative; for doctorate, one foreign language, thesis/dissertation. *Entrance requirements:* For master's and doctorate, GRE General Test, writing sample. Additional exam requirements/recommendations for international students: Required—TOEFL (minimum score 550 paper-based; 80 iBT). *Application deadline:* For fall admission, 2/1 for domestic and international students; for spring admission, 10/15 for domestic and international students. Application fee: $75. Electronic applications accepted. *Financial support:* In 2016–17, 22 students received support, including 23 teaching assistantships with full tuition reimbursements available (averaging $15,000 per year); career-related internships or fieldwork, Federal Work-Study, institutionally sponsored loans, scholarships/grants, health care benefits, tuition waivers (full and partial), and unspecified assistantships also available. Financial award applicants required to submit FAFSA. *Unit head:* Dr. Christopher M. Knapp, Chairperson, 607-777-4163, E-mail: c.morgan-knapp@binghamton.edu. *Application contact:* Ben Balkaya, Assistant Dean and Director, 607-777-2151, Fax: 607-777-2501, E-mail: balkaya@binghamton.edu.
Website: http://philosophy.binghamton.edu

Brock University, Faculty of Graduate Studies, Faculty of Social Sciences, Program in Social Justice and Equity Studies, St. Catharines, ON L2S 3A1, Canada. Offers MA. *Program availability:* Part-time. *Degree requirements:* For master's, thesis optional. *Entrance requirements:* For master's, honors degree. Additional exam requirements/recommendations for international students: Required—TOEFL (minimum score 550 paper-based; 80 iBT), IELTS (minimum score 6.5), TWE (minimum score 4). Electronic applications accepted. *Faculty research:* Social inequality, social movements, gender, racism, environmental justice.

California University of Pennsylvania, School of Graduate Studies and Research, Eberly College of Science and Technology, Department of Professional Studies, California, PA 15419-1394. Offers legal studies (MS), including criminal justice, homeland security, law and public policy. *Program availability:* Part-time, evening/weekend, online learning. *Degree requirements:* For master's, thesis optional. *Entrance requirements:* For master's, interview, minimum GPA of 3.0. Additional exam requirements/recommendations for international students: Required—TOEFL (minimum score 550 paper-based; 80 iBT). Electronic applications accepted. *Expenses:* Tuition, state resident: full-time $11,592; part-time $483 per credit. Tuition, nonresident: full-time $17,400; part-time $725 per credit. *Required fees:* $3916. Tuition and fees vary according to course load, degree level, campus/location and reciprocity agreements. *Faculty research:* Ethics in political practice, ethics and law, law and morality, St. Thomas Aquinas and crime, police policy.

Capital University, School of Nursing, Columbus, OH 43209-2394. Offers administration (MSN); legal studies (MSN); theological studies (MSN); JD/MSN; MBA/MSN; MSN/MTS. *Accreditation:* AACN. *Program availability:* Part-time, evening/weekend. *Degree requirements:* For master's, thesis or alternative. *Entrance requirements:* For master's, BSN, current RN license, minimum GPA of 3.0, undergraduate courses in statistics and research. Additional exam requirements/recommendations for international students: Required—TOEFL (minimum score 550 paper-based). *Expenses:* Contact institution. *Faculty research:* Bereavement, wellness/health promotion, emergency cardiac care, critical thinking, complementary and alternative healthcare.

Carleton University, Faculty of Graduate Studies, Faculty of Public Affairs and Management, Department of Law, Ottawa, ON K1S 5B6, Canada. Offers conflict resolution (Certificate); legal studies (MA). *Degree requirements:* For master's, thesis. *Entrance requirements:* For master's, honors degree. Additional exam requirements/recommendations for international students: Required—TOEFL. *Faculty research:* Legal and social theory; women, law, and gender relations; law, crime, and social order; political economy of law; international law.

Case Western Reserve University, School of Law, Cleveland, OH 44106. Offers financial integrity (MA); health law (SJD); intellectual property (LL M); international business law (LL M); international criminal law (LL M); law (JD, SJD); patent practice (MA); U.S. legal studies (LL M); JD/MA; JD/MBA; JD/MD; JD/MNM; JD/MPH; JD/MS; JD/MSSA. *Accreditation:* ABA. *Faculty:* 40 full-time (15 women), 25 part-time/adjunct (4 women). *Students:* 421 full-time (215 women), 1 (woman) part-time; includes 76 minority (37 Black or African American, non-Hispanic/Latino; 17 Asian, non-Hispanic/Latino; 19 Hispanic/Latino; 3 Two or more races, non-Hispanic/Latino), 37 international. Average age 24. 1,645 applicants, 43% accepted, 144 enrolled. In 2016, 72 master's, 99 doctorates awarded. *Entrance requirements:* For doctorate, LSAT, LSDAS. Additional exam requirements/recommendations for international students: Required—TOEFL. *Application deadline:* For fall admission, 4/1 priority date for domestic and international students. Applications are processed on a rolling basis. Application fee: $40. Electronic applications accepted. Application fee is waived when completed online. *Expenses:* Contact institution. *Financial support:* In 2016–17, 345 students received support. Career-related internships or fieldwork, Federal Work-Study, institutionally sponsored loans, and scholarships/grants available. Financial award application deadline: 5/1; financial award applicants required to submit FAFSA. *Unit head:* Jessica Berg, Co-Dean, 216-368-3283. *Application contact:* Kelli Curtis, Associate Dean for Admissions, 216-368-3600, Fax: 216-368-0185, E-mail: lawadmissions@case.edu.
Website: http://law.case.edu/

The Catholic University of America, School of Canon Law, Washington, DC 20064. Offers Canon law (JCD, JCL); church administration (MCA); JD/JCL. JD/JCL offered jointly with Columbus School of Law. *Program availability:* Part-time. *Faculty:* 8 full-time (1 woman), 2 part-time/adjunct (0 women). *Students:* 25 full-time (2 women), 49 part-time (7 women); includes 9 minority (1 Black or African American, non-Hispanic/Latino; 2 Asian, non-Hispanic/Latino; 5 Hispanic/Latino; 1 Two or more races, non-Hispanic/Latino), 11 international. Average age 38. 26 applicants, 88% accepted, 21 enrolled. In 2016, 25 master's, 2 doctorates awarded. *Degree requirements:* For master's, one foreign language, comprehensive exam, thesis, fluency in canonical Latin; for doctorate, 2 foreign languages, thesis/dissertation, fluency in canonical Latin. *Entrance requirements:* For master's, GRE General Test, statement of purpose, official copies of academic transcripts, two letters of recommendation; for doctorate, GRE General Test, minimum A- average, JCL. Additional exam requirements/recommendations for international students: Required—TOEFL (minimum score 550 paper-based; 80 iBT). *Application deadline:* For fall admission, 7/15 priority date for domestic students, 7/1 for international students; for spring admission, 11/15 priority date for domestic students, 11/1 for international students. Applications are processed on a rolling basis. Application fee: $55. Electronic applications accepted. *Expenses:* $1,650 per credit hour. *Financial support:* Fellowships, research assistantships, teaching assistantships, Federal Work-Study, scholarships/grants, tuition waivers (full and partial), and unspecified assistantships available. Financial award application deadline: 2/1; financial award applicants required to submit FAFSA. *Faculty research:* Ecclesiology and the Sacrament of Orders, procedural law, temporal goods, matrimonial jurisprudence, sacramental and liturgical law. *Unit head:* Msgr. Ronny Jenkins, Dean, 202-319-5492, Fax: 202-319-4187, E-mail: cua-canonlaw@cua.edu. *Application contact:* Director of Graduate Admissions, 202-319-5057, Fax: 202-319-6533, E-mail: cua-admissions@cua.edu.
Website: http://canonlaw.cua.edu

Central European University, Department of Legal Studies, Budapest, Hungary. Offers comparative Constitutional law (LL M); human rights (LL M, MA); international business law (LL M); juridical sciences (SJD); law and economics (LL M, MA). *Faculty:* 10 full-time (5 women), 15 part-time/adjunct (3 women). *Students:* 89 full-time (43 women). Average age 27. 420 applicants, 27% accepted, 66 enrolled. In 2016, 52 master's, 4 doctorates awarded. Terminal master's awarded for partial completion of doctoral program. *Degree requirements:* For master's, one foreign language, thesis; for doctorate, one foreign language, comprehensive exam, thesis/dissertation. *Entrance requirements:* For master's and doctorate, LSAT. Additional exam requirements/recommendations for international students: Required—TOEFL (minimum score 570 paper-based); Recommended—IELTS (minimum score 6.5). *Application deadline:* For fall admission, 2/4 for domestic and international students. Application fee: $30. Electronic applications accepted. *Expenses:* Contact institution. *Financial support:* Fellowships, career-related internships or fieldwork, institutionally sponsored loans, scholarships/grants, and tuition waivers (full and partial) available. Financial award application deadline: 2/4. *Faculty research:* Institutional, Constitutional and human rights in European Union law; biomedical law and reproductive rights; data protection law; comparative and international business law and the regulation of business environments;. *Unit head:* Dr. Karoly Bard, Head of Department, 36 1 327-3294, Fax: 361-327-3198, E-mail: legalst@ceu.edu. *Application contact:* Zsuzsanna Jaszberenyi, Department Coordinator, 361-327-3272, Fax: 361-327-3198, E-mail: admissions@ceu.edu.
Website: http://legal.ceu.edu

Columbia University, Graduate School of Arts and Sciences, New York, NY 10027. Offers African-American studies (MA); American studies (MA); anthropology (MA, PhD); art history and archaeology (MA, PhD); astronomy (PhD); biological sciences (PhD); biotechnology (MA); chemical physics (PhD); chemistry (PhD); classical studies (MA, PhD); classics (MA, PhD); climate and society (MA); conservation biology (MA); earth and environmental sciences (PhD); East Asia: regional studies (MA); East Asian languages and cultures (MA, PhD); ecology, evolution and environmental biology (MA), including conservation biology; ecology, evolution, and environmental biology (PhD), including ecology and evolutionary biology, evolutionary primatology; economics (MA, PhD); English and comparative literature (MA, PhD); French and Romance philology (MA, PhD); Germanic languages (MA, PhD); global French studies (MA); global thought (MA); Hispanic cultural studies (MA); history (PhD); history and literature (MA); human rights studies (MA); Islamic studies (MA); Italian (MA, PhD); Japanese pedagogy (MA); Jewish studies (MA); Latin America and the Caribbean: regional studies (MA); Latin American and Iberian cultures (PhD); mathematics (MA, PhD), including finance (MA); medieval and Renaissance studies (MA); Middle Eastern, South Asian, and African studies (MA, PhD); modern art: critical and curatorial studies (MA); modern European studies (MA); museum anthropology (MA); music (DMA, PhD); oral history (MA); philosophical foundations of physics (MA); philosophy (MA, PhD); physics (PhD); political science (MA, PhD); psychology (PhD); quantitative methods in the social sciences (MA); religion (MA, PhD); Russia, Eurasia and East Europe: regional studies (MA); Russian translation (MA); Slavic cultures (MA); Slavic languages (MA, PhD); sociology (MA, PhD); South Asian studies (MA); statistics (MA, PhD); theatre (PhD). Dual-degree programs require admission to both Graduate School of Arts and Sciences and another Columbia school. *Program availability:* Part-time. Terminal master's awarded for partial completion of doctoral program. *Degree requirements:* For master's, variable foreign language requirement, comprehensive exam (for some programs), thesis (for some programs); for doctorate, variable foreign language requirement, comprehensive exam (for some programs), thesis/dissertation. *Entrance requirements:* For master's and doctorate, GRE General Test, GRE Subject Test (for some programs). Additional exam requirements/recommendations for international students: Required—TOEFL, IELTS. Electronic applications accepted.

The George Washington University, College of Professional Studies, Paralegal Studies Programs, Washington, DC 20037. Offers MPS, Graduate Certificate. *Students:* 24 full-time (22 women), 96 part-time (83 women); includes 54 minority (30 Black or African American, non-Hispanic/Latino; 4 Asian, non-Hispanic/Latino; 14 Hispanic/Latino; 6 Two or more races, non-Hispanic/Latino). Average age 38. 104 applicants, 79% accepted, 48 enrolled. In 2016, 47 master's, 39 other advanced degrees awarded. *Application deadline:* For fall admission, 7/15 for domestic and international students; for spring admission, 10/1 for domestic and international students. Electronic applications accepted. *Unit head:* Toni Marsh, Director, 202-994-2844, E-mail: marsht01@gwu.edu. *Application contact:* Analisa Encinas, Paralegal Studies Program Representative, 703-248-6011, E-mail: aencinas@gwu.edu.
Website: http://nearyou.gwu.edu/plx/

The George Washington University, College of Professional Studies, Program in Law Firm Management, Washington, DC 20052. Offers MPS, Graduate Certificate. Program offered in partnership with The Hildebrandt Institute and held in Alexandria, VA. *Program availability:* Online learning. *Students:* 11 part-time (4 women); includes 1 minority (Asian, non-Hispanic/Latino). Average age 40. 16 applicants, 75% accepted, 7 enrolled. In 2016, 4 master's, 1 other advanced degree awarded. *Entrance requirements:* For master's, resume, 2 references. Additional exam requirements/recommendations for international students: Required—TOEFL. *Application deadline:* For fall admission, 4/1 for domestic and international students. Electronic applications accepted. *Unit head:* Kathleen M. Burke, Dean, 202-994-9711. *Application contact:* Kristin Williams, Assistant

Legal and Justice Studies

Vice President for Graduate and Special Enrollment Management, 202-994-0467, Fax: 202-994-0371, E-mail: ksw@gwu.edu.
Website: http://nearyou.gwu.edu/lawfirm/

The George Washington University, Columbian College of Arts and Sciences, Department of Political Science, Washington, DC 20052. Offers legal institutions and theory (MA); political science (MA). *Program availability:* Part-time, evening/weekend. *Faculty:* 29 full-time (9 women). *Students:* 34 full-time (10 women), 50 part-time (22 women); includes 13 minority (2 Black or African American, non-Hispanic/Latino; 5 Asian, non-Hispanic/Latino; 5 Hispanic/Latino; 1 Two or more races, non-Hispanic/Latino), 19 international. Average age 31. 317 applicants, 15% accepted, 13 enrolled. In 2016, 12 master's, 12 doctorates awarded. Terminal master's awarded for partial completion of doctoral program. *Degree requirements:* For master's, one foreign language, comprehensive exam, thesis or alternative; for doctorate, 2 foreign languages, thesis/dissertation, general exam. *Entrance requirements:* For master's and doctorate, GRE General Test, minimum GPA of 3.0. Additional exam requirements/recommendations for international students: Required—TOEFL (minimum score 550 paper-based; 80 iBT). *Application deadline:* For fall admission, 1/15 priority date for domestic students; for spring admission, 10/1 priority date for domestic students. Applications are processed on a rolling basis. Application fee: $75. Electronic applications accepted. *Financial support:* In 2016–17, 43 students received support. Fellowships with tuition reimbursements available, teaching assistantships with tuition reimbursements available, Federal Work-Study, and tuition waivers available. *Unit head:* Christopher J. Deering, Chair, 202-994-6564, E-mail: rocket@gwu.edu. *Application contact:* 202-994-6210, Fax: 202-994-6213, E-mail: askccas@gwu.edu.
Website: http://politicalscience.columbian.gwu.edu/

The George Washington University, Law School, Washington, DC 20052. Offers law (SJD); national security and U.S. foreign relations (LL M). *Accreditation:* ABA. *Program availability:* Part-time, evening/weekend. *Faculty:* 84 full-time (33 women). *Students:* 1,622 full-time (867 women), 315 part-time (150 women); includes 482 minority (164 Black or African American, non-Hispanic/Latino; 15 American Indian or Alaska Native, non-Hispanic/Latino; 234 Asian, non-Hispanic/Latino; 55 Hispanic/Latino; 4 Native Hawaiian or other Pacific Islander, non-Hispanic/Latino; 10 Two or more races, non-Hispanic/Latino), 222 international. Average age 27. 223 applicants, 100% accepted, 133 enrolled. In 2016, 166 master's, 1 doctorate awarded. *Degree requirements:* For doctorate, thesis/dissertation (for some programs). *Entrance requirements:* For master's, JD or equivalent; for doctorate, LSAT (for JD), LL M or equivalent (for SJD). *Application deadline:* For fall admission, 3/1 for domestic students. Applications are processed on a rolling basis. Application fee: $75. *Expenses:* Contact institution. *Financial support:* Research assistantships, career-related internships or fieldwork, Federal Work-Study, institutionally sponsored loans, scholarships/grants, and tuition waivers (full and partial) available. Support available to part-time students. Financial award application deadline: 3/1; financial award applicants required to submit CSS PROFILE or FAFSA. *Unit head:* Blake D. Morant, Dean, E-mail: bmorant@law.gwu.edu. *Application contact:* Sophia Sim, Assistant Dean of Admissions and Financial Aid, 202-994-7235, Fax: 202-739-0624, E-mail: ssim@law.gwu.edu.
Website: http://www.law.gwu.edu/

Golden Gate University, School of Law, San Francisco, CA 94105-2968. Offers environmental law (LL M); estate planning (LL M); intellectual property law (LL M); international legal studies (LL M, SJD); law (JD); taxation (LL M); U.S. legal studies (LL M); JD/MBA; JD/PhD. *Accreditation:* ABA. *Program availability:* Part-time, evening/weekend. *Faculty:* 41 full-time (19 women), 67 part-time/adjunct (27 women). *Students:* 246 full-time (142 women), 228 part-time (133 women); includes 213 minority (28 Black or African American, non-Hispanic/Latino; 2 American Indian or Alaska Native, non-Hispanic/Latino; 68 Asian, non-Hispanic/Latino; 84 Hispanic/Latino; 7 Native Hawaiian or other Pacific Islander, non-Hispanic/Latino; 24 Two or more races, non-Hispanic/Latino), 58 international. Average age 31. 1,473 applicants, 65% accepted, 189 enrolled. In 2016, 54 master's, 117 doctorates awarded. *Degree requirements:* For doctorate, thesis/dissertation (for some programs). *Entrance requirements:* For doctorate, LSAT (for JD). Additional exam requirements/recommendations for international students: Required—TOEFL (minimum score 600 paper-based). *Application deadline:* For fall admission, 8/18 for domestic students, 4/1 for international students; for spring admission, 1/12 for domestic students; for summer admission, 6/4 for domestic students. Applications are processed on a rolling basis. Electronic applications accepted. *Expenses:* Contact institution. *Financial support:* In 2016–17, 315 students received support. Fellowships, research assistantships, teaching assistantships, career-related internships or fieldwork, Federal Work-Study, institutionally sponsored loans, scholarships/grants, tuition waivers (full and partial), and unspecified assistantships available. Support available to part-time students. Financial award applicants required to submit FAFSA. *Faculty research:* International law, intellectual property law, environmental law, real estate, civil rights. *Unit head:* Rachel Van Cleave, Dean, 415-442-6601, Fax: 415-442-6609. *Application contact:* Greg Egertson, Associate Dean and Director of Admissions, 415-442-6636, Fax: 415-442-6609, E-mail: lawadmit@ggu.edu.
Website: http://www.ggu.edu/law/

Governors State University, College of Arts and Sciences, Program in Political and Justice Studies, University Park, IL 60484. Offers MA. *Program availability:* Part-time. *Faculty:* 91 full-time (43 women), 125 part-time/adjunct (64 women). *Students:* 6 full-time (4 women), 21 part-time (11 women); includes 16 minority (all Black or African American, non-Hispanic/Latino), 1 international. Average age 37. 29 applicants, 66% accepted, 16 enrolled. In 2016, 13 master's awarded. *Entrance requirements:* Additional exam requirements/recommendations for international students: Required—TOEFL (minimum score 550 paper-based; 80 iBT), IELTS. *Application deadline:* For fall admission, 4/1 for domestic students. Application fee: $50. Electronic applications accepted. *Expenses:* $307 per credit hour; $38 per term or $76 per credit hour fees. *Financial support:* Application deadline: 5/1; applicants required to submit FAFSA. *Unit head:* Lori Montalbano, Chair, Division of Humanities and Social Science, 708-235-2802, E-mail: lmontalbano@govst.edu. *Application contact:* Yakeea Daniels, Assistant Vice President for Enrollment Services/Director of Admission, 708-534-4510, E-mail: ydaniels@govst.edu.

Harrison Middleton University, Graduate Program, Tempe, AZ 85282. Offers education (MA, Ed D); humanities (MA); imaginative literature (MA); interdisciplinary studies (DA); jurisprudence (MA); natural science (MA); philosophy and religion (MA); social science (MA). *Program availability:* Part-time, evening/weekend, online learning. *Degree requirements:* For master's and doctorate, capstone project. *Entrance requirements:* For master's, interview; for doctorate, 2 academic letters of reference, interview, essay. Additional exam requirements/recommendations for international students: Required—TOEFL (minimum score 550 paper-based; 80 iBT). Electronic applications accepted. *Faculty research:* Japanese animation, educational leadership, war art, John Muir's wilderness.

Harvard University, Law School, Professional Programs in Law, Cambridge, MA 02138. Offers international and comparative law (JD); law and business (JD); law and government (JD); law and social change (JD); law, science and technology (JD); JD/MALD; JD/MBA; JD/MPH; JD/MPP; JD/PhD. *Accreditation:* ABA. *Degree requirements:* For doctorate, 3rd-year paper. *Entrance requirements:* For doctorate, LSAT. *Faculty research:* Constitutional law, voting rights law, cyber law.

Hodges University, Graduate Programs, Naples, FL 34119. Offers accounting (M Acc); business administration (MBA); clinical mental health counseling (MS); health services administration (MS); information systems management (MIS); legal studies (MS); management (MSM). *Program availability:* Part-time, evening/weekend, 100% online, blended/hybrid learning. *Degree requirements:* For master's, comprehensive exam (for some programs), thesis (for some programs). *Entrance requirements:* For master's, essay. Additional exam requirements/recommendations for international students: Recommended—TOEFL. Electronic applications accepted.

Hofstra University, Maurice A. Deane School of Law, Hempstead, NY 11549. Offers American legal studies (LL M); family law (LL M); health law and policy (LL M, MA); law (JD); JD/MBA. *Accreditation:* ABA. *Program availability:* Part-time, 100% online. *Faculty:* 41 full-time (22 women), 47 part-time/adjunct (9 women). *Students:* 692 full-time (377 women), 93 part-time (56 women); includes 216 minority (79 Black or African American, non-Hispanic/Latino; 3 American Indian or Alaska Native, non-Hispanic/Latino; 34 Asian, non-Hispanic/Latino; 87 Hispanic/Latino; 8 Native Hawaiian or other Pacific Islander, non-Hispanic/Latino; 5 Two or more races, non-Hispanic/Latino), 22 international. Average age 27. In 2016, 10 master's, 198 doctorates awarded. *Entrance requirements:* For doctorate, LSAT, letter of recommendation, personal statement, undergraduate transcripts. Additional exam requirements/recommendations for international students: Recommended—TOEFL (minimum score 600 paper-based; 100 iBT). *Application deadline:* For fall admission, 4/15 priority date for domestic and international students. Applications are processed on a rolling basis. Application fee: $75. Electronic applications accepted. *Expenses:* Contact institution. *Financial support:* In 2016–17, 508 students received support, including 491 fellowships with full and partial tuition reimbursements available (averaging $31,765 per year), 3 research assistantships with full and partial tuition reimbursements available (averaging $6,675 per year); career-related internships or fieldwork, Federal Work-Study, institutionally sponsored loans, scholarships/grants, tuition waivers (full and partial), and unspecified assistantships also available. Support available to part-time students. Financial award applicants required to submit FAFSA. *Faculty research:* Family law; international law; constitutional law; legal ethics; health law. *Total annual research expenditures:* $59,468. *Unit head:* Gail Prudenti, Dean, 516-463-4068, E-mail: gail.prudenti@hofstra.edu. *Application contact:* Sunil Samuel, Assistant Vice President of Admissions, 516-463-4723, Fax: 516-463-4664.
Website: http://law.hofstra.edu/

Illinois Institute of Technology, Chicago-Kent College of Law, Chicago, IL 60661-3691. Offers family law (LL M); financial services law (LL M); international intellectual property law (LL M); law (JD); legal studies (JSD); taxation (LL M); U.S., international, and transnational law (LL M); JD/LL M; JD/MBA; JD/MPA; JD/MPH; JD/MS. *Accreditation:* ABA. *Program availability:* Part-time, evening/weekend. Terminal master's awarded for partial completion of doctoral program. *Entrance requirements:* For master's, 1st degree in law or certified license to practice law; for doctorate, LSAT. Additional exam requirements/recommendations for international students: Required—TOEFL (minimum score 600 paper-based; 100 iBT); Recommended—IELTS (minimum score 7). Electronic applications accepted. *Expenses:* Contact institution. *Faculty research:* Constitutional law, bioethics, environmental law, intellectual property.

Indiana University South Bend, College of Liberal Arts and Sciences, South Bend, IN 46634-7111. Offers advanced computer programming (Graduate Certificate); applied informatics (Graduate Certificate); applied mathematics and computer science (MS); behavior modification (Graduate Certificate); computer applications (Graduate Certificate); computer programming (Graduate Certificate); correctional management and supervision (Graduate Certificate); English (MA); health systems management (Graduate Certificate); international studies (Graduate Certificate); liberal studies (MLS); nonprofit management (Graduate Certificate); paralegal studies (Graduate Certificate); professional writing (Graduate Certificate); public affairs (MPA); public management (Graduate Certificate); social and cultural diversity (Graduate Certificate); strategic sustainability leadership (Graduate Certificate); technology for administration (Graduate Certificate). *Program availability:* Part-time, evening/weekend. *Faculty:* 79 full-time (33 women). *Students:* 31 full-time (11 women), 92 part-time (53 women); includes 28 minority (9 Black or African American, non-Hispanic/Latino; 8 Asian, non-Hispanic/Latino; 5 Hispanic/Latino; 6 Two or more races, non-Hispanic/Latino), 19 international. Average age 38. 51 applicants, 84% accepted, 31 enrolled. In 2016, 30 master's, 6 other advanced degrees awarded. *Degree requirements:* For master's, variable foreign language requirement, thesis (for some programs). *Entrance requirements:* For master's, minimum GPA of 3.0. Additional exam requirements/recommendations for international students: Required—TOEFL (minimum score 550 paper-based; 80 iBT). *Application deadline:* For fall admission, 7/31 priority date for domestic students, 7/1 priority date for international students; for spring admission, 3/31 priority date for domestic students, 11/1 priority date for international students. Applications are processed on a rolling basis. Application fee: $40 ($60 for international students). *Expenses:* $276.98 per credit hour in-state; $652.54 per credit hour out-of-state. *Financial support:* In 2016–17, 5 teaching assistantships were awarded; Federal Work-Study also available. Support available to part-time students. Financial award application deadline: 3/10. *Faculty research:* Artificial intelligence, bioinformatics, English language and literature, creative writing, computer networks. *Total annual research expenditures:* $127,000. *Unit head:* Dr. Elizabeth E. Dunn, Dean, 574-520-4290, E-mail: elizdunn@iusb.edu. *Application contact:* Admissions Counselor, 574-520-4839, Fax: 574-520-4834, E-mail: graduate@iusb.edu.
Website: https://www.iusb.edu/clas/

John Jay College of Criminal Justice of the City University of New York, Graduate Studies, Programs in Criminal Justice, New York, NY 10019. Offers criminal justice (MA, PhD); criminology and deviance (PhD); forensic psychology (PhD); forensic science (PhD); international crime and justice (MA); law and philosophy (PhD); organizational behavior (PhD); public policy (PhD). *Program availability:* Part-time, evening/weekend. Terminal master's awarded for partial completion of doctoral program. *Degree requirements:* For master's, thesis or alternative; for doctorate, one foreign language, thesis/dissertation. *Entrance requirements:* For master's, GRE General Test, minimum B average; for doctorate, GRE General Test. Additional exam requirements/recommendations for international students: Required—TOEFL (minimum score 500 paper-based).

Kaplan University, Davenport Campus, School of Legal Studies, Davenport, IA 52807. Offers health care delivery (MS); pathway to paralegal (Postbaccalaureate Certificate); state and local government (MS). *Program availability:* Part-time, evening/weekend, online learning. *Entrance requirements:* Additional exam requirements/recommendations for international students: Required—TOEFL (minimum score 550 paper-based; 80 iBT).

Loyola University Chicago, Institute of Pastoral Studies, Chicago, IL 60611. Offers Christian spirituality (MA), including spiritual direction; church management (Certificate); counseling for ministry (MA); health care ministry leadership (Certificate); health care mission leadership (MA); pastoral counseling (MA, Certificate); pastoral studies (M Div, MA); religious education (Certificate); social justice (MA, Certificate); spiritual direction

(Certificate); M Div/MA; M Div/MSW; MSW/MA. MSW/MA offered with School of Social Work. *Accreditation:* ACIPE. *Program availability:* Part-time, evening/weekend, 100% online, blended/hybrid learning. *Faculty:* 11 full-time (4 women), 25 part-time/adjunct (11 women). *Students:* 79 full-time (58 women), 120 part-time (76 women); includes 54 minority (22 Black or African American, non-Hispanic/Latino; 1 American Indian or Alaska Native, non-Hispanic/Latino; 6 Asian, non-Hispanic/Latino; 23 Hispanic/Latino; 2 Two or more races, non-Hispanic/Latino), 23 international. Average age 42. 116 applicants, 83% accepted, 71 enrolled. In 2016, 63 master's, 4 other advanced degrees awarded. *Degree requirements:* For master's, thesis optional, project. *Entrance requirements:* Additional exam requirements/recommendations for international students: Required—TOEFL (minimum score 550 paper-based; 79 iBT), IELTS (minimum score 6.5). *Application deadline:* Applications are processed on a rolling basis. Application fee: $50. Electronic applications accepted. Application fee is waived when completed online. *Expenses:* Contact institution. *Financial support:* In 2016–17, 84 students received support. Career-related internships or fieldwork, Federal Work-Study, institutionally sponsored loans, scholarships/grants, tuition waivers (partial), and unspecified assistantships available. Support available to part-time students. Financial award application deadline: 3/1; financial award applicants required to submit FAFSA. *Faculty research:* Catholic theology, skills of religious ministry, family ministries, spirituality and divorced men. *Unit head:* Dr. Brian J. Schmisek, Dean, 312-915-7400, Fax: 312-915-7410, E-mail: bschmisek@luc.edu. *Application contact:* Dr. M. Therese Lysaught, Associate Dean, 312-915-7485, Fax: 312-915-7410, E-mail: mlysaught@luc.edu.
Website: http://www.luc.edu/ips/

Marlboro College, Graduate and Professional Studies, Program in Teaching for Social Justice, Marlboro, VT 05344. Offers MAT. *Program availability:* Evening/weekend. *Faculty:* 5 part-time/adjunct (all women). *Students:* 9 full-time (5 women); includes 3 minority (1 Asian, non-Hispanic/Latino; 1 Hispanic/Latino; 1 Two or more races, non-Hispanic/Latino). Average age 31. 15 applicants, 73% accepted, 8 enrolled. In 2016, 4 master's awarded. *Degree requirements:* For master's, 36 credits including teaching internship and portfolio. *Entrance requirements:* For master's, statement of intent, 2 letters of recommendation, transcripts, interview. Additional exam requirements/recommendations for international students: Required—TOEFL (minimum scores 577 paper-based, 90 iBT) or IELTS (minimum score 7). *Application deadline:* For fall admission, 7/1 priority date for domestic and international students; for winter admission, 11/1 priority date for domestic and international students. Applications are processed on a rolling basis. Electronic applications accepted. *Expenses:* $765 per credit. *Financial support:* In 2016–17, 2 students received support. Scholarships/grants available. Financial award application deadline: 8/5; financial award applicants required to submit FAFSA. *Unit head:* Janaki Natarajan, Degree Chair, 802-451-7506, Fax: 802-258-9201, E-mail: graduateadmissions@marlboro.edu. *Application contact:* Don Parker, Admissions Assistant, 802-451-7505, Fax: 802-258-9201, E-mail: graduateadmissions@marlboro.edu.
Website: https://www.marlboro.edu/academics/graduate/teach

Marygrove College, Graduate Division, Program in Social Justice, Detroit, MI 48221-2599. Offers MA.

Michigan State University College of Law, Professional Program, East Lansing, MI 48824-1300. Offers American legal system (LL M, MJ); global food law (LL M, MJ); intellectual property (LL M, MJ); law (JD); legal doctrine and analysis (MJ). *Accreditation:* ABA. *Program availability:* Part-time. *Faculty:* 55 full-time (22 women), 85 part-time/adjunct (32 women). *Students:* 723 full-time (362 women), 123 part-time (70 women); includes 173 minority (57 Black or African American, non-Hispanic/Latino; 9 American Indian or Alaska Native, non-Hispanic/Latino; 28 Asian, non-Hispanic/Latino; 40 Hispanic/Latino; 2 Native Hawaiian or other Pacific Islander, non-Hispanic/Latino; 37 Two or more races, non-Hispanic/Latino), 91 international. Average age 24. 2,362 applicants, 45% accepted, 259 enrolled. In 2016, 45 master's, 265 doctorates awarded. *Entrance requirements:* For doctorate, LSAT. Additional exam requirements/recommendations for international students: Required—TOEFL (minimum score 600 paper-based), IELTS. *Application deadline:* For fall admission, 4/30 priority date for domestic students, 7/1 priority date for international students. Applications are processed on a rolling basis. Application fee: $60. Electronic applications accepted. *Expenses:* Contact institution. *Financial support:* In 2016–17, 559 students received support. Career-related internships or fieldwork, Federal Work-Study, scholarships/grants, and tuition waivers (full and partial) available. Support available to part-time students. Financial award application deadline: 4/1; financial award applicants required to submit FAFSA. *Faculty research:* International, constitutional, health, tax and environmental law; intellectual property, trial practice, corporate law. *Unit head:* Lawrence Ponoroff, Dean/Professor of Law, 517-432-6993, Fax: 517-432-6801, E-mail: lponoroff@law.msu.edu. *Application contact:* Charles Roboski, Assistant Dean of Admissions, 517-432-0222, Fax: 517-432-0098, E-mail: roboski@law.msu.edu.
Website: http://www.law.msu.edu/

Mississippi College, Graduate School, College of Arts and Sciences, School of Humanities and Social Sciences, Department of History, Political Science, Administration of Justice, and Paralegal Studies, Clinton, MS 39058. Offers administration of justice (MSS); history (M Ed, MA, MSS); paralegal studies (Certificate); political science (MSS); social sciences (M Ed, MSS). *Program availability:* Part-time. *Degree requirements:* For master's, one foreign language, comprehensive exam, thesis (for some programs). *Entrance requirements:* For master's, GRE or NTE, minimum GPA of 2.5. Additional exam requirements/recommendations for international students: Recommended—TOEFL, IELTS. Electronic applications accepted.

Montclair State University, The Graduate School, College of Humanities and Social Sciences, Paralegal Studies Certificate Program, Montclair, NJ 07043-1624. Offers Certificate. *Program availability:* Part-time, evening/weekend. *Entrance requirements:* For degree, 2 letters of recommendation, essay. Additional exam requirements/recommendations for international students: Required—TOEFL (minimum score 83 iBT) or IELTS. Electronic applications accepted. *Expenses:* Tuition, state resident: part-time $553 per credit. Tuition, nonresident: part-time $854 per credit. *Required fees:* $91 per credit. Tuition and fees vary according to program.

National Paralegal College, Graduate Programs, Phoenix, AZ 85014. Offers compliance law (MS); legal studies (MS); taxation (MS). *Program availability:* Part-time. Electronic applications accepted.

National University, Academic Affairs, School of Professional Studies, La Jolla, CA 92037-1011. Offers criminal justice (MCJ); digital cinema (MFA); digital journalism (MA); juvenile justice (MS); public administration (MPA), including human resource management. *Program availability:* Part-time, evening/weekend, 100% online, blended/hybrid learning. *Faculty:* 21 full-time (8 women), 35 part-time/adjunct (9 women). *Students:* 280 full-time (155 women), 100 part-time (54 women); includes 226 minority (76 Black or African American, non-Hispanic/Latino; 1 American Indian or Alaska Native, non-Hispanic/Latino; 27 Asian, non-Hispanic/Latino; 102 Hispanic/Latino; 3 Native Hawaiian or other Pacific Islander, non-Hispanic/Latino; 17 Two or more races, non-Hispanic/Latino), 3 international. Average age 37. In 2016, 21 master's awarded. *Degree requirements:* For master's, thesis (for some programs). *Entrance requirements:* For master's, interview, minimum GPA of 2.5. Additional exam requirements/recommendations for international students: Required—TOEFL (minimum score 550 paper-based; 79 iBT), IELTS (minimum score 6). *Application deadline:* Applications are processed on a rolling basis. Application fee: $60 ($65 for international students). Electronic applications accepted. *Financial support:* Career-related internships or fieldwork, institutionally sponsored loans, scholarships/grants, and tuition waivers (partial) available. Support available to part-time students. Financial award application deadline: 6/30; financial award applicants required to submit FAFSA. *Unit head:* School of Professional Studies, 800-628-8648, E-mail: sops@nu.edu. *Application contact:* Brandon Jouganatos, Vice President for Enrollment Services, 800-628-8648, E-mail: advisor@nu.edu.
Website: http://www.nu.edu/OurPrograms/School-of-Professional-Studies.html

New York University, Graduate School of Arts and Science and School of Law, Institute for Law and Society, New York, NY 10012-1019. Offers MA, PhD, JD/MA, JD/PhD. *Degree requirements:* For doctorate, one foreign language, thesis/dissertation. *Entrance requirements:* Additional exam requirements/recommendations for international students: Required—TOEFL. *Faculty research:* Politics of law, law and social policy, law in comparative global perspective, rights and social movements.

New York University, School of Continuing and Professional Studies, Tisch Institute for Sports Management, Media, and Business, New York, NY 10012-1019. Offers global sports media (MS); professional and collegiate sports operations (MS); sports business (Advanced Certificate); sports law (MS); sports marketing and sales (MS). *Program availability:* Part-time, evening/weekend. *Degree requirements:* For master's, thesis. *Entrance requirements:* For master's, GRE or GMAT (only upon request), bachelor's degree, resume with relevant professional work, internship or volunteer experience, two letters of recommendation, statement of purpose. Additional exam requirements/recommendations for international students: Required—TOEFL (minimum score 600 paper-based; 100 iBT), IELTS (minimum score 7). Electronic applications accepted. *Faculty research:* Implications of college football's bowl coalition series from a legal, economic, and academic perspective; social history of sports.

Northeastern University, College of Social Sciences and Humanities, Boston, MA 02115. Offers criminology and criminal justice (MSCJ); criminology and justice policy (PhD); economics (MA, PhD); English (MA, PhD); international affairs (MA); law and public policy (PhD); political science (MA, PhD); public administration (MPA); public history (MA); public policy (MPP); security and resilience studies (MS); sociology (MA, PhD); urban and regional policy (MS); urban informatics (MS); world history (MA, PhD); JD/MS. *Program availability:* Online learning. *Faculty:* 234 full-time (114 women), 55 part-time/adjunct (34 women). *Students:* 427 full-time (239 women), 77 part-time (42 women). In 2016, 143 master's, 38 doctorates awarded. *Degree requirements:* For doctorate, variable foreign language requirement, comprehensive exam, thesis/dissertation. *Entrance requirements:* For master's and doctorate, GRE. Additional exam requirements/recommendations for international students: Required—TOEFL, IELTS. Application fee: $75. Electronic applications accepted. *Expenses:* $1,295 per credit. *Financial support:* Teaching assistantships, career-related internships or fieldwork, scholarships/grants, health care benefits, tuition waivers (full and partial), and unspecified assistantships available. Support available to part-time students. Financial award applicants required to submit FAFSA. *Unit head:* Dr. Uta Poiger, Dean, 617-373-5173. *Application contact:* Amber Crowe, Administrative Coordinator, 617-373-5990, Fax: 617-373-7281, E-mail: gradcssh@northeastern.edu.
Website: http://www.northeastern.edu/cssh/graduate

Nova Southeastern University, Shepard Broad College of Law, Fort Lauderdale, FL 33314. Offers education law (MS), including cybersecurity law, education law advocacy, exceptional education; employment law (MS), including cybersecurity law, employee relations law, human resource managerial law; health law (MS, JD), including clinical research law and regulatory compliance (MS), cybersecurity law (MS), health care administrative law (MS), regulatory compliance (MS), risk management (MS); international law (JD); law and policy (MS), including cybersecurity law; JD/DO; JD/M Acc; JD/M Tax; JD/MBA; JD/MIB; JD/MPA; JD/MS; JD/PhD. *Accreditation:* ABA. *Program availability:* Part-time, evening/weekend, 100% online, blended/hybrid learning. *Faculty:* 42 full-time (23 women), 35 part-time/adjunct (14 women). *Students:* 554 full-time (298 women), 325 part-time (230 women); includes 351 minority (71 Black or African American, non-Hispanic/Latino; 3 American Indian or Alaska Native, non-Hispanic/Latino; 17 Asian, non-Hispanic/Latino; 251 Hispanic/Latino; 2 Native Hawaiian or other Pacific Islander, non-Hispanic/Latino; 7 Two or more races, non-Hispanic/Latino), 36 international. Average age 29. 1,414 applicants, 49% accepted, 256 enrolled. In 2016, 46 master's, 236 doctorates awarded. *Degree requirements:* For master's, thesis optional, capstone research project; for doctorate, rigorous upper-level writing fulfilled through faculty-supervised seminar paper, law journal article, workshop, or other research. *Entrance requirements:* For master's, regionally-accredited undergraduate degree; at least 2 years' experience in related field (for employment law and health law); for doctorate, LSAT. Additional exam requirements/recommendations for international students: Recommended—TOEFL (minimum score 600 paper-based; 100 iBT), IELTS (minimum score 7). *Application deadline:* For fall admission, 5/1 priority date for domestic and international students; for winter admission, 12/12 for domestic and international students; for spring admission, 3/31 for domestic and international students; for summer admission, 4/1 for domestic and international students. Applications are processed on a rolling basis. Application fee: $0. Electronic applications accepted. *Expenses:* Contact institution. *Financial support:* In 2016–17, 231 students received support, including 221 fellowships (averaging $12,680 per year); Federal Work-Study, institutionally sponsored loans, scholarships/grants, and unspecified assistantships also available. Support available to part-time students. Financial award application deadline: 4/15; financial award applicants required to submit FAFSA. *Faculty research:* Legal issues in health law, international law, the legal profession, family law, civil rights. *Unit head:* Jon M. Garon, Dean, 954-262-6101, Fax: 954-262-2862, E-mail: garon@nova.edu. *Application contact:* William Daniel Perez, Assistant Dean of Admissions, 954-262-6121, Fax: 954-262-3844, E-mail: wperez1@nova.edu.
Website: http://www.law.nova.edu/

Oregon State University, College of Education, Program in Education, Corvallis, OR 97331. Offers advanced science and mathematics education (Ed M); agricultural education (PhD); education (Ed D); free-choice learning (Ed M); language equity and educational policy (PhD); mathematics education (MS); pre-K-12 English to speakers of other languages (ESOL) (Ed M); science education (MS); science/mathematics education (PhD); social justice in education (Ed M). *Program availability:* Part-time, 100% online, blended/hybrid learning. *Faculty:* 9 full-time (8 women), 6 part-time/adjunct (2 women). *Students:* 14 full-time (8 women), 76 part-time (53 women); includes 25 minority (6 Black or African American, non-Hispanic/Latino; 2 American Indian or Alaska Native, non-Hispanic/Latino; 5 Asian, non-Hispanic/Latino; 10 Hispanic/Latino; 2 Two or more races, non-Hispanic/Latino), 3 international. Average age 38. 72 applicants, 69% accepted, 40 enrolled. In 2016, 14 master's, 21 doctorates awarded. Terminal master's awarded for partial completion of doctoral program. *Degree requirements:* For master's, variable foreign language requirement, thesis (for some programs); for doctorate, variable foreign language requirement, thesis/dissertation. *Entrance requirements:* Additional exam requirements/recommendations for international students: Required—TOEFL (minimum score 575 paper-based). Application fee: $75 ($85 for international students). *Expenses:* Tuition, state resident: full-time $12,150; part-time $450 per credit. Tuition, nonresident: full-time $21,789; part-time $807 per credit. *Required fees:* $1651; $1507 per credit. One-time fee: $350. Tuition and fees vary according to course load, campus/location and program. *Financial support:* Fellowships, research assistantships, teaching assistantships, career-related internships or fieldwork, Federal Work-Study, and institutionally sponsored loans available. Support available to part-time students. *Faculty research:* School administration, educational foundations, research methodology, education policy development, higher education administration. *Unit head:* Dr. Larry Flick, Dean. *Application contact:* E-mail: askcoed@oregonstate.edu.

Oregon State University, College of Liberal Arts, Program in Applied Ethics, Corvallis, OR 97331. Offers biomedical ethics (MA); environmental ethics (MA); ethics and religion (MA); global justice, peace, and war (MA); social justice (MA). *Program availability:* Part-time. *Faculty:* 12 full-time (4 women), 1 (woman) part-time/adjunct. *Students:* 10 full-time (7 women), 1 part-time (0 women); includes 3 minority (1 American Indian or Alaska Native, non-Hispanic/Latino; 2 Hispanic/Latino), 1 international. Average age 29. 9 applicants, 67% accepted, 6 enrolled. In 2016, 1 master's awarded. *Entrance requirements:* For master's, writing sample of 5-7 pages. Additional exam requirements/recommendations for international students: Required—TOEFL (minimum score 80 iBT), IELTS (minimum score 6.5). *Application deadline:* For fall admission, 1/15 priority date for domestic and international students. Application fee: $75 ($85 for international students). *Expenses:* Tuition, state resident: full-time $12,150; part-time $450 per credit. Tuition, nonresident: full-time $21,789; part-time $807 per credit. *Required fees:* $1651; $1507 per credit. One-time fee: $350. Tuition and fees vary according to course load, campus/location and program. *Unit head:* Dr. Ben Mutschler, Director. *Application contact:* Dr. Allen Thompson, Director of Graduate Studies, 541-737-5654, E-mail: allen.thompson@oregonstate.edu.
Website: http://liberalarts.oregonstate.edu/shpr/philosophy

Pace University, Elisabeth Haub School of Law, White Plains, NY 10603. Offers comparative legal studies (LL M); environmental law (LL M, SJD), including climate change (LL M), land use and sustainability (LL M); law (JD); JD/LL M; JD/MA; JD/MBA; JD/MEM; JD/MPA; JD/MS. JD/MA offered jointly with Sarah Lawrence College; JD/MEM offered jointly with Yale University School of Forestry and Environmental Studies. *Accreditation:* ABA. *Program availability:* Part-time. *Faculty:* 26 full-time (11 women), 52 part-time/adjunct (19 women). *Students:* 516 full-time (274 women), 63 part-time (36 women); includes 150 minority (30 Black or African American, non-Hispanic/Latino; 2 American Indian or Alaska Native, non-Hispanic/Latino; 23 Asian, non-Hispanic/Latino; 58 Hispanic/Latino; 37 Two or more races, non-Hispanic/Latino), 2 international. Average age 26. 1,423 applicants, 56% accepted, 206 enrolled. In 2016, 20 master's, 171 doctorates awarded. *Degree requirements:* For master's, writing sample; for doctorate, thesis/dissertation (for some programs), extensive thesis proposal (for SJD). *Entrance requirements:* For doctorate, LSAT (for JD). Additional exam requirements/recommendations for international students: Required—TOEFL (minimum score 100 iBT); Recommended—TWE. *Application deadline:* For fall admission, 6/1 priority date for domestic students; for winter admission, 11/15 priority date for domestic students. Applications are processed on a rolling basis. Application fee: $65. Electronic applications accepted. *Expenses:* Contact institution. *Financial support:* In 2016–17, 430 students received support. Fellowships, research assistantships, career-related internships or fieldwork, Federal Work-Study, institutionally sponsored loans, scholarships/grants, and unspecified assistantships available. Support available to part-time students. Financial award application deadline: 2/1; financial award applicants required to submit FAFSA. *Faculty research:* Reform of energy regulations, international law, land use law, prosecutorial misconduct, corporation law, international sale of goods. *Total annual research expenditures:* $2.2 million. *Unit head:* David Yassky, Dean, 914-422-4407, E-mail: dyassky@law.pace.edu. *Application contact:* Cathy Alexander, Assistant Dean, 914-422-4210, Fax: 914-989-8714, E-mail: calexander@law.pace.edu.
Website: http://www.law.pace.edu/

Prairie View A&M University, College of Juvenile Justice and Psychology, Prairie View, TX 77446. Offers clinical adolescent psychology (PhD); juvenile forensic psychology (MSJFP); juvenile justice (MSJJ, PhD). *Program availability:* Part-time, evening/weekend, online only, 100% online. *Faculty:* 6 full-time (2 women), 6 part-time/adjunct (3 women). *Students:* 29 full-time (24 women), 31 part-time (22 women); includes 53 minority (49 Black or African American, non-Hispanic/Latino; 3 Hispanic/Latino; 1 Two or more races, non-Hispanic/Latino), 5 international. Average age 30. 37 applicants, 92% accepted, 25 enrolled. In 2016, 16 master's, 2 doctorates awarded. *Degree requirements:* For master's, comprehensive exam; for doctorate, thesis/dissertation. *Entrance requirements:* For master's, GRE, minimum GPA of 2.75; for doctorate, GRE, previous course work in clinical adolescent psychology, minimum GPA of 3.5. Additional exam requirements/recommendations for international students: Required—TOEFL (minimum score 550 paper-based; 79 iBT). *Application deadline:* For fall admission, 5/1 priority date for domestic and international students; for spring admission, 10/1 priority date for domestic students, 9/1 priority date for international students; for summer admission, 3/1 priority date for domestic students, 2/1 priority date for international students. Applications are processed on a rolling basis. Application fee: $50. Electronic applications accepted. *Expenses:* Tuition, state resident: full-time $4362; part-time $273.48 per credit hour. Tuition, nonresident: full-time $12,390; part-time $534.10 per credit hour. *Required fees:* $2782; $178.26 per credit hour. *Financial support:* In 2016–17, 20 students received support, including 20 research assistantships; teaching assistantships, scholarships/grants, and unspecified assistantships also available. Financial award application deadline: 4/1; financial award applicants required to submit FAFSA. *Faculty research:* Juvenile justice, community policing, adolescent substance use, reducing mental illness stigma and promoting positive psychological well-being in diverse communities, promoting prosocial behavior among at-risk youth. *Unit head:* Dr. Tamara L. Brown, Dean, 936-261-5206, Fax: 936-261-5253, E-mail: tlbrown@pvamu.edu. *Application contact:* Pauline Walker, Executive Secretary, Graduate Program, 936-261-3521, Fax: 936-261-3529, E-mail: gradadmissions@pvamu.edu.

Prescott College, Graduate Programs, Program in Arts and Humanities, Prescott, AZ 86301. Offers humanities (MA); social justice and human rights (MA); student-directed independent study (MA). *Program availability:* Part-time, online learning. *Faculty:* 3 full-time (0 women). *Students:* 3 full-time (1 woman), 13 part-time (10 women); includes 1 minority (Hispanic/Latino). Average age 42. 28 applicants, 79% accepted, 17 enrolled. In 2016, 20 master's awarded. *Degree requirements:* For master's, thesis, fieldwork or internship, practicum. *Entrance requirements:* For master's, 2 letters of recommendation, resume, essay. Additional exam requirements/recommendations for international students: Required—TOEFL (minimum score 500 paper-based). *Application deadline:* For fall admission, 4/15 priority date for domestic and international students; for spring admission, 9/15 priority date for domestic and international students. Applications are processed on a rolling basis. Application fee: $40. Electronic applications accepted. *Expenses: Tuition:* Full-time $19,680. One-time fee: $260 part-time. *Financial support:* Fellowships, research assistantships, teaching assistantships, career-related internships or fieldwork, Federal Work-Study, institutionally sponsored loans, scholarships/grants, traineeships, health care benefits, tuition waivers, and unspecified assistantships available. Support available to part-time students. Financial award applicants required to submit FAFSA. *Unit head:* Ellen Greenblum, 928-350-3209, E-mail: egreenblum@prescott.edu. *Application contact:* Amber Harris, Assistant Director, Graduate Admissions, 928-615-8446, Fax: 928-776-5242, E-mail: amber.harris@prescott.edu.

Queen's University at Kingston, School of Graduate Studies, Faculty of Arts and Sciences, Department of Sociology, Kingston, ON K7L 3N6, Canada. Offers communication and Information technology (MA, PhD); feminist sociology (MA, PhD); socio-legal studies (MA, PhD); sociological theory (MA, PhD). *Program availability:* Part-time. *Degree requirements:* For master's, thesis; for doctorate, comprehensive exam, thesis/dissertation. *Entrance requirements:* For master's, honors bachelors degree in sociology; for doctorate, honors bachelors degree, masters degree in sociology. Additional exam requirements/recommendations for international students: Required—TOEFL. *Faculty research:* Social change and modernization, social control, deviance and criminology, surveillance.

Regent University, Graduate School, School of Law, Virginia Beach, VA 23464-9800. Offers American legal studies (LL M); human rights (LL M); law (MA, JD), including business (MA), criminal justice (MA), general legal studies (MA), human resources management (MA), human rights (MA), mediation (MA), national security (MA), non-profit management (MA), regulatory compliance (MA), wealth management and financial planning (MA); JD/MA; JD/MBA. *Accreditation:* ABA. *Program availability:* Part-time, 100% online, blended/hybrid learning. *Faculty:* 20 full-time (6 women), 67 part-time/adjunct (19 women). *Students:* 364 full-time (219 women), 170 part-time (118 women); includes 213 minority (150 Black or African American, non-Hispanic/Latino; 1 American Indian or Alaska Native, non-Hispanic/Latino; 10 Asian, non-Hispanic/Latino; 34 Hispanic/Latino; 1 Native Hawaiian or other Pacific Islander, non-Hispanic/Latino; 17 Two or more races, non-Hispanic/Latino), 87 international. Average age 34. 834 applicants, 45% accepted, 174 enrolled. In 2016, 48 master's, 85 doctorates awarded. *Entrance requirements:* For master's, college transcripts, resume, personal statement; for doctorate, LSAT, minimum undergraduate GPA of 3.0, official transcripts, 2 letters of recommendation, resume, personal statement. Additional exam requirements/recommendations for international students: Required—TOEFL (minimum score 600 paper-based). *Application deadline:* For fall admission, 3/1 for domestic students. Applications are processed on a rolling basis. Application fee: $50. Electronic applications accepted. *Expenses:* $1,140 per credit (for JD); $650 per credit (for MA); $833 per credit (for LL M); $250 technology fee. *Financial support:* In 2016–17, 319 students received support. Career-related internships or fieldwork, scholarships/grants, and unspecified assistantships available. Support available to part-time students. *Faculty research:* Family law, Constitutional law, law and culture, evidence and practice, intellectual property. *Unit head:* Michael Hernandez, Dean, 757-352-4040, Fax: 757-352-4595, E-mail: michher@regent.edu. *Application contact:* Katie Kerley, Director of Law Admissions, 877-267-5072, Fax: 757-352-4139, E-mail: lawschool@regent.edu.
Website: http://www.regent.edu/law/

Rutgers University–New Brunswick, Graduate School-New Brunswick, Department of Political Science, Piscataway, NJ 08854-8097. Offers American politics (PhD); comparative politics (PhD); international relations (PhD); political theory (PhD); public law (PhD); United Nations and global policy studies (MA); women and politics (PhD). *Degree requirements:* For doctorate, one foreign language, comprehensive exam, thesis/dissertation. *Entrance requirements:* For master's, bachelor's degree from accredited U.S. college or university or a comparable institution in another country; for doctorate, GRE General Test. Additional exam requirements/recommendations for international students: Required—TOEFL.

St. John's University, College of Professional Studies, Department of Criminal Justice and Legal Studies, Queens, NY 11439. Offers criminal justice leadership (MPS). *Program availability:* Part-time, evening/weekend, online learning. *Degree requirements:* For master's, comprehensive exam, thesis optional, capstone project. *Entrance requirements:* For master's, bachelor's degree from regionally-accredited college or university, minimum overall GPA of 3.0, 2 letters of recommendation, 300-word essay. Additional exam requirements/recommendations for international students: Required—TOEFL (minimum score 600 paper-based; 100 iBT), IELTS (minimum score 7). Electronic applications accepted. *Faculty research:* Fire litigation, forensic psychology, organized crime, probation and parole, leadership studies, criminal justice ethics and integration control.

St. John's University, St. John's College of Liberal Arts and Sciences, Program in Global Development and Social Justice, Queens, NY 11439. Offers MA. Program offered jointly with Unicaritas. *Program availability:* Part-time, evening/weekend, online learning. *Degree requirements:* For master's, capstone project. *Entrance requirements:* For master's, 2 letters of recommendation, personal essay, proficiency in English. Additional exam requirements/recommendations for international students: Required—TOEFL (minimum score 600 paper-based; 100 iBT), IELTS (minimum score 7). Electronic applications accepted.

St. John's University, School of Law, Program in Bankruptcy, Queens, NY 11439. Offers LL M. *Program availability:* Part-time. *Degree requirements:* For master's, thesis. *Entrance requirements:* For master's, LSAT, personal statement, 2 letters of recommendation, official transcript including class rank, resume. Additional exam requirements/recommendations for international students: Required—TOEFL (minimum score 600 paper-based; 100 iBT), IELTS (minimum score 7). Electronic applications accepted. *Expenses:* Contact institution.

St. John's University, School of Law, Program in Transnational Legal Practice, Queens, NY 11439. Offers LL M. *Entrance requirements:* For master's, resume, 2 letters of recommendation, writing sample, interview, transcript, personal statement. Additional exam requirements/recommendations for international students: Required—TOEFL (minimum score 600 paper-based), IELTS (minimum score 7), TWE (minimum score 5). Electronic applications accepted. *Expenses:* Contact institution.

St. John's University, School of Law, Program in U.S. Legal Studies for Foreign Law School Graduates, Queens, NY 11439. Offers LL M. *Program availability:* Part-time. *Entrance requirements:* For master's, law degree from non-U.S. law school, resume, 2 letters of recommendation, writing sample, interview, personal statement. Additional exam requirements/recommendations for international students: Required—TWE, TOEFL (minimum score 600 paper-based, 100 iBT) or IELTS (minimum score 7). Electronic applications accepted. *Expenses:* Contact institution.

Saint Leo University, Graduate Studies in Public Safety Administration, Saint Leo, FL 33574-6665. Offers criminal justice (MS), including corrections, criminal investigation, emergency and disaster management, forensic science, legal studies; emergency and disaster management (MS). *Program availability:* Part-time, evening/weekend, 100% online, blended/hybrid learning. *Faculty:* 7 full-time (2 women), 32 part-time/adjunct (8 women). *Students:* 3 full-time (1 woman), 667 part-time (446 women); includes 355 minority (275 Black or African American, non-Hispanic/Latino; 6 American Indian or Alaska Native, non-Hispanic/Latino; 4 Asian, non-Hispanic/Latino; 56 Hispanic/Latino; 3 Native Hawaiian or other Pacific Islander, non-Hispanic/Latino; 11 Two or more races, non-Hispanic/Latino). Average age 37. 361 applicants, 87% accepted, 177 enrolled. In 2016, 265 master's awarded. *Degree requirements:* For master's, comprehensive project. *Entrance requirements:* For master's, official transcripts, bachelor's degree from regionally-accredited university with minimum GPA of 3.0. Additional exam

requirements/recommendations for international students: Required—TOEFL (minimum score 550 paper-based; 80 iBT). *Application deadline:* For fall admission, 7/1 priority date for domestic and international students; for spring admission, 11/1 priority date for domestic and international students. Applications are processed on a rolling basis. Application fee: $80. Electronic applications accepted. *Expenses:* $535 per semester hour (for MS in emergency/disaster management); $555 per semester hour (for MS in criminal justice). *Financial support:* In 2016–17, 14 students received support. Scholarships/grants and health care benefits available. Financial award application deadline: 3/1; financial award applicants required to submit FAFSA. *Unit head:* Dr. Robert Diemer, Director of Graduate Studies in Safety Administration, 352-588-8974, Fax: 352-588-8289, E-mail: graduatepublicsafety@saintleo.edu. *Application contact:* Jennifer Shelley, Senior Associate Director of Graduate Admissions, 800-707-8846, Fax: 352-588-7873, E-mail: grad.admissions@saintleo.edu.
Website: http://www.saintleo.edu/academics/graduate

St. Mary's University, School of Law, LL M Program, San Antonio, TX 78228-8507. Offers American legal studies (LL M); international and comparative law (LL M); international criminal law (LL M). *Program availability:* Part-time, evening/weekend. *Students:* 31 full-time (8 women); includes 10 minority (1 Black or African American, non-Hispanic/Latino; 2 Asian, non-Hispanic/Latino; 7 Hispanic/Latino). Average age 36. In 2016, 26 master's awarded. *Degree requirements:* For master's, thesis, 24 hours of academic credit. *Entrance requirements:* For master's, official transcripts, personal statement, resume, 2 letters of recommendation. Additional exam requirements/recommendations for international students: Required—TOEFL (minimum score 550 paper-based; 80 iBT), IELTS (minimum score 6). *Application deadline:* Applications are processed on a rolling basis. Electronic applications accepted. *Expenses: Tuition:* Full-time $15,600; part-time $865 per credit hour. *Required fees:* $148 per semester. *Unit head:* Robert Lee Summers, Jr., Professor of Law/Co-Director of LL M Programs/Co-Director of International Legal Studies, 210-618-5014, E-mail: rsummers@stmarytx.edu. *Application contact:* Gary Liu, Professor of Law/Co-Director of LL M Programs, 210-431-2145, E-mail: cliu@stmarytx.edu.
Website: https://law.stmarytx.edu/academics/ll-m-programs/

San Francisco State University, Division of Graduate Studies, College of Education, Department of Equity, Leadership Studies, and Instructional Technologies, Program in Equity and Social Justice, San Francisco, CA 94132-1722. Offers MA. *Expenses:* Tuition, state resident: full-time $6738. Tuition, nonresident: full-time $15,666. *Required fees:* $1012. Tuition and fees vary according to degree level and program. *Unit head:* Dr. Doris Flowers, Chair, 415-338-2614, Fax: 415-338-0568, E-mail: dflowers@sfsu.edu. *Application contact:* Dr. Ming-yeh Lee, Graduate Coordinator, 415-338-1061, Fax: 415-338-0568, E-mail: mylee@sfsu.edu.
Website: http://gcoe.sfsu.edu/

San Jose State University, Graduate Studies and Research, College of Applied Sciences and Arts, San Jose, CA 95192-0001. Offers big data (Certificate); California library media teacher services (Credential); collaborative response to family violence (Certificate); justice studies (MS); kinesiology (MA), including applied sciences and arts (MA, MS), athletic training, exercise physiology, sport management, sport studies; library and information science (MLIS, Certificate); mass communication (MA); nutritional science (MS); occupational therapy (MS); public health (MPH); pupil personnel services (Credential); recreation (MS), including applied sciences and arts (MA, MS), international tourism; social work (MSW); Spanish language counseling (Certificate); strategic management of digital assets and services (Certificate). *Program availability:* Part-time, evening/weekend. Electronic applications accepted.

The Santa Barbara and Ventura Colleges of Law–Santa Barbara, Graduate and Professional Programs, Santa Barbara, CA 93101. Offers MLS, JD.

The Santa Barbara and Ventura Colleges of Law–Ventura, Graduate and Professional Programs, Ventura, CA 93003. Offers MLS, JD.

Simon Fraser University, Office of Graduate Studies and Postdoctoral Fellows, Faculty of Arts and Social Sciences, School of Criminology, Burnaby, BC V5A 1S6, Canada. Offers applied legal studies (MA); criminology (MA, PhD). *Faculty:* 29 full-time (10 women). *Students:* 154 full-time (97 women), 7 part-time (3 women). 131 applicants, 54% accepted, 56 enrolled. In 2016, 38 master's, 6 doctorates awarded. *Degree requirements:* For master's, thesis or alternative, practicum; for doctorate, thesis/dissertation. *Entrance requirements:* For master's, minimum GPA of 3.0 (on scale of 4.33) or 3.33 based on last 60 credits of undergraduate courses; for doctorate, minimum GPA of 3.5 (on scale of 4.33). Additional exam requirements/recommendations for international students: Recommended—TOEFL (minimum score 580 paper-based; 93 iBT), IELTS (minimum score 7), TWE (minimum score 5). *Application deadline:* For fall admission, 2/1 for domestic and international students; for spring admission, 2/1 for domestic students. Application fee: $90 ($125 for international students). Electronic applications accepted. *Financial support:* In 2016–17, 51 students received support, including 28 fellowships (averaging $6,500 per year), teaching assistantships (averaging $5,608 per year); research assistantships, career-related internships or fieldwork, Federal Work-Study, and scholarships/grants also available. *Faculty research:* Media and crime, feminist jurisprudence, policy evaluation, forensic entomology, restorative justice. *Unit head:* Dr. Martin Andresen, Associate Director, Graduate Programs, 778-782-7628, Fax: 778-782-4140, E-mail: crim-grad-chair@sfu.ca. *Application contact:* Shaneza Bacchus, Graduate Secretary, 778-782-4762, Fax: 778-782-4140, E-mail: crimgrad@sfu.ca.
Website: http://www.sfu.ca/criminology/

Southern Illinois University Carbondale, School of Law, Program in Legal Studies, Carbondale, IL 62901-4701. Offers general law (MLS); health law and policy (MLS).

Southern New Hampshire University, School of Business, Manchester, NH 03106-1045. Offers accounting (MBA, MS, Graduate Certificate); accounting finance (MS); accounting/auditing (MS); accounting/forensic accounting (MS); accounting/taxation (MS); athletic administration (MBA, Graduate Certificate); business administration (IMBA, MBA, Certificate, Graduate Certificate), including accounting (Certificate), business administration (MBA), business information systems (Graduate Certificate), human resource management (Certificate); corporate social responsibility (MBA); entrepreneurship (MBA); finance (MBA, MS, Graduate Certificate); finance/corporate finance (MS); finance/investments and securities (MS); forensic accounting (MBA); healthcare informatics (MBA); healthcare management (MBA); human resource management (Graduate Certificate); information technology (MS, Graduate Certificate); information technology management (MBA); international business (Graduate Certificate); international business and information technology (Graduate Certificate); international finance (Graduate Certificate); international sport management (Graduate Certificate); justice studies (MBA); leadership of nonprofit organizations (Graduate Certificate); management (MS); marketing (MBA, MS, Graduate Certificate); operations and project management (MS); operations and supply chain management (MBA, Graduate Certificate); organizational leadership (MS); project management (MBA, Graduate Certificate); Six Sigma (MBA); Six Sigma quality (Graduate Certificate); social media marketing (MBA); sport management (MBA, MS, Graduate Certificate); sustainability and environmental compliance (MBA); workplace conflict management (MBA); MBA/Certificate. *Accreditation:* ACBSP. *Program availability:* Part-time, evening/weekend, online learning. Terminal master's awarded for partial completion of doctoral program. *Degree requirements:* For master's, one foreign language, comprehensive exam (for some programs), thesis or alternative. *Entrance requirements:* For master's, minimum GPA of 2.5. Additional exam requirements/recommendations for international students: Required—TOEFL (minimum score 500 paper-based). Electronic applications accepted.

Stanford University, Law School, Stanford, CA 94305-8610. Offers corporate governance and practice (LL M); environmental law and policy (LL M); international economic law, business and policy (LL M); international legal studies (JSM); law (JD, JSD); law, science and technology (LL M); legal studies (MLS); JD/MA; JD/MBA; JD/MPP; JD/MS; JD/PhD. *Accreditation:* ABA. *Degree requirements:* For doctorate, thesis/dissertation (for some programs). *Entrance requirements:* For doctorate, LSAT (for JD). Electronic applications accepted. *Expenses:* Contact institution.

Stetson University, College of Arts and Sciences, Division of Education, DeLand, FL 32723. Offers counselor education (MS), including marriage, couple and family counseling, mental health counseling, school counseling; teacher education (M Ed), including educating for social justice, educational leadership. *Accreditation:* NCATE (one or more programs are accredited). *Program availability:* Part-time, evening/weekend. *Faculty:* 12 full-time (8 women), 8 part-time/adjunct (7 women). *Students:* 190 full-time (160 women), 17 part-time (13 women); includes 56 minority (20 Black or African American, non-Hispanic/Latino; 1 Asian, non-Hispanic/Latino; 30 Hispanic/Latino; 5 Two or more races, non-Hispanic/Latino), 3 international. Average age 32. 145 applicants, 81% accepted, 98 enrolled. In 2016, 47 master's awarded. *Entrance requirements:* For master's, GRE or MAT. *Application deadline:* For fall admission, 8/1 priority date for domestic students; for spring admission, 1/1 priority date for domestic students; for summer admission, 5/1 priority date for domestic students. Applications are processed on a rolling basis. Application fee: $50. Electronic applications accepted. *Expenses:* $886 per credit hour. *Financial support:* In 2016–17, 119 students received support. Career-related internships or fieldwork, Federal Work-Study, institutionally sponsored loans, scholarships/grants, unspecified assistantships, and tuition waivers for staff and dependents available. Support available to part-time students. *Faculty research:* School leadership succession planning; restorative practices in schools; literacy and art teacher evaluation and support in place of personnel appraisal; mission-driven leadership. *Unit head:* Dr. Karen Ryan, Dean, 386-822-7515. *Application contact:* Jamie Vanderlip, Senior Associate Director of Graduate Admissions, 386-822-7100, Fax: 386-822-7112, E-mail: jlvander@stetson.edu.

Taft University System, Taft Law School, Denver, CO 80246. Offers American jurisprudence (LL M); law (JD); taxation (LL M).

Temple University, Beasley School of Law, Philadelphia, PA 19122. Offers law (JD); legal education (SJD); taxation (LL M); transnational law (LL M); trial advocacy (LL M); JD/LL M; JD/MBA; JD/MPH. *Accreditation:* ABA. *Program availability:* Part-time, evening/weekend. *Faculty:* 64 full-time (30 women), 102 part-time/adjunct (37 women). *Students:* 534 full-time (282 women), 153 part-time (66 women); includes 191 minority (59 Black or African American, non-Hispanic/Latino; 2 American Indian or Alaska Native, non-Hispanic/Latino; 60 Asian, non-Hispanic/Latino; 62 Hispanic/Latino; 8 Two or more races, non-Hispanic/Latino), 9 international. Average age 26. 2,046 applicants, 42% accepted, 218 enrolled. In 2016, 202 doctorates awarded. *Entrance requirements:* For doctorate, LSAT (for JD). Additional exam requirements/recommendations for international students: Recommended—TOEFL. *Application deadline:* For fall admission, 3/1 for domestic and international students. Applications are processed on a rolling basis. Application fee: $60. Electronic applications accepted. *Expenses:* $24,786 per year full-time resident tuition; $37,500 per year full-time non-resident tuition; $20,018 per year part-time resident tuition; $30,196 per year part-time non-resident tuition. *Financial support:* In 2016–17, 469 students received support, including research assistantships (averaging $5,500 per year), teaching assistantships (averaging $5,500 per year); fellowships, Federal Work-Study, scholarships/grants, tuition waivers (full and partial), and unspecified assistantships also available. Support available to part-time students. Financial award application deadline: 3/1; financial award applicants required to submit FAFSA. *Faculty research:* Cybersecurity, gender issues, health care law, immigration law, intellectual property law. *Unit head:* Gregory N. Mandel, Dean, 215-204-7863, Fax: 215-204-1185, E-mail: law@temple.edu. *Application contact:* Johanne L. Johnston, Assistant Dean for Admissions and Financial Aid, 800-560-1428, Fax: 215-204-9319, E-mail: lawadmis@temple.edu.
Website: http://www.law.temple.edu

Texas State University, The Graduate College, College of Liberal Arts, Program in Legal Studies, San Marcos, TX 78666. Offers MA. *Program availability:* Part-time. *Faculty:* 5 full-time (1 woman), 2 part-time/adjunct (1 woman). *Students:* 42 full-time (32 women), 26 part-time (16 women); includes 39 minority (6 Black or African American, non-Hispanic/Latino; 2 Asian, non-Hispanic/Latino; 29 Hispanic/Latino; 2 Two or more races, non-Hispanic/Latino), 1 international. Average age 29. 56 applicants, 84% accepted, 26 enrolled. In 2016, 29 master's awarded. *Degree requirements:* For master's, comprehensive exam. *Entrance requirements:* For master's, baccalaureate degree from regionally-accredited university with minimum GPA of 3.0 on last 60 undergraduate semester hours. Additional exam requirements/recommendations for international students: Required—TOEFL (minimum score 550 paper-based; 78 iBT), IELTS (minimum score 6.5). *Application deadline:* For fall admission, 2/15 priority date for domestic and international students; for spring admission, 10/15 priority date for domestic students, 10/1 priority date for international students; for summer admission, 4/15 for domestic students, 3/15 for international students. Applications are processed on a rolling basis. Application fee: $90 ($110 for international students). Electronic applications accepted. *Expenses:* $4,851 per semester. *Financial support:* In 2016–17, 44 students received support, including 3 research assistantships (averaging $13,284 per year), 2 teaching assistantships (averaging $13,676 per year); Federal Work-Study, institutionally sponsored loans, scholarships/grants, health care benefits, and unspecified assistantships also available. Financial award application deadline: 3/1; financial award applicants required to submit FAFSA. *Unit head:* Dr. Lynn Crossett, Graduate Advisor, 512-245-2233, Fax: 512-245-7815, E-mail: lc25@txstate.edu. *Application contact:* Dr. Andrea Golato, Dean of Graduate School, 512-245-2581, Fax: 512-245-8365, E-mail: gradcollege@txstate.edu.
Website: http://www.polisci.txstate.edu/

Texas Tech University, School of Law, Lubbock, TX 79409-0004. Offers law (JD); United States legal studies (LL M); JD/M Engr; JD/MBA; JD/MD; JD/MPA; JD/MS; JD/MSA. *Accreditation:* ABA. *Faculty:* 37 full-time (11 women), 2 part-time/adjunct (1 woman). *Students:* 524 full-time (233 women), 1 (woman) part-time; includes 131 minority (9 Black or African American, non-Hispanic/Latino; 16 Asian, non-Hispanic/Latino; 83 Hispanic/Latino; 23 Two or more races, non-Hispanic/Latino), 18 international. Average age 26. 1,236 applicants, 52% accepted, 167 enrolled. In 2016, 9 master's, 182 doctorates awarded. *Entrance requirements:* For master's, first/basic degree in law from non-U.S. law school approved by LL M admissions committee; for doctorate, LSAT. Additional exam requirements/recommendations for international students: Required—TOEFL (minimum score 600 paper-based; 100 iBT), IELTS (minimum score 7). *Application deadline:* For fall admission, 3/1 priority date for domestic and international students. Applications are processed on a rolling basis.

Application fee: $50. Electronic applications accepted. *Expenses:* $620 per credit hour full-time resident tuition, $998 per credit hour full-time non-resident tuition; $98 per credit hour fee plus $608 per term fee. *Financial support:* In 2016–17, 402 students received support, including 31 research assistantships, 31 teaching assistantships; Federal Work-Study, tuition waivers, and tutorships also available. Financial award application deadline: 5/1; financial award applicants required to submit FAFSA. *Faculty research:* Advocacy/legal practice, energy law, criminal law/innocence, business/estate planning, law and science. *Total annual research expenditures:* $81,099. *Unit head:* Richard Rosen, Interim Dean and Professor, 806-834-7585, Fax: 806-742-4014, E-mail: richard.rosen@ttu.edu. *Application contact:* Wendy A. Humphrey, Associate Dean for Admissions and Financial Aid, 806-834-4446, E-mail: admissions.law@ttu.edu.
Website: http://www.law.ttu.edu/

Touro College, Jacob D. Fuchsberg Law Center, Central Islip, NY 11743. Offers general law (LL M); law (JD); U.S. legal studies (LL M); JD/MBA; JD/MPA; JD/MSW. JD/MBA and JD/MPA offered with Long Island University-LIU Post; JD/MSW offered with Stony Brook University, State University of New York. *Accreditation:* ABA. *Program availability:* Part-time, evening/weekend. *Faculty:* 35 full-time (17 women), 30 part-time/adjunct (7 women). *Students:* 445 full-time (245 women), 22 part-time (15 women); includes 166 minority (47 Black or African American, non-Hispanic/Latino; 2 American Indian or Alaska Native, non-Hispanic/Latino; 41 Asian, non-Hispanic/Latino; 72 Hispanic/Latino; 4 Two or more races, non-Hispanic/Latino), 9 international. Average age 30. *Entrance requirements:* For doctorate, LSAT. *Application deadline:* Applications are processed on a rolling basis. Application fee: $60. *Expenses:* Contact institution. *Financial support:* Fellowships, career-related internships or fieldwork, and Federal Work-Study available. Support available to part-time students. Financial award application deadline: 5/1. *Faculty research:* Business law, civil rights, international law, criminal justice. *Unit head:* Dr. Harry Ballan, Dean, 631-761-7100. *Application contact:* Dr. Susan Thompson, Office of Admissions, 631-761-7010, E-mail: admissions@tourolaw.edu.
Website: http://www.tourolaw.edu/

Trident University International, College of Health Sciences, Program in Health Sciences, Cypress, CA 90630. Offers clinical research administration (MS, Certificate); emergency and disaster management (MS, Certificate); environmental health science (Certificate); health care administration (PhD); health care management (MS), including health informatics; health education (MS, Certificate); health informatics (Certificate); health sciences (PhD); international health (MS); international health: educator or researcher option (PhD); international health: practitioner option (PhD); law and expert witness studies (MS, Certificate); public health (MS); quality assurance (Certificate). *Program availability:* Part-time, evening/weekend, online learning. *Degree requirements:* For doctorate, comprehensive exam, thesis/dissertation, defense of dissertation. *Entrance requirements:* For master's, minimum GPA of 2.5 (students with GPA 3.0 or greater may transfer up to 30% of graduate level credits); for doctorate, minimum GPA of 3.4, curriculum vitae, course work in research methods or statistics. Additional exam requirements/recommendations for international students: Required—TOEFL. Electronic applications accepted.

Universidad Autonoma de Guadalajara, Graduate Programs, Guadalajara, Mexico. Offers administrative law and justice (LL M); advertising and corporate communications (MA); architecture (M Arch); business (MBA); computational science (MCC); education (Ed M, Ed D); English-Spanish translation (MA); entrepreneurship and management (MBA); integrated management of digital animation (MA); international business (MIB); international corporate law (LL M); internet technologies (MS); manufacturing systems (MMS); occupational health (MS); philosophy (MA, PhD); power electronics (MS); quality systems (MQS); renewable energy (MS); social evaluation of projects (MBA); strategic market research (MBA); tax law (MA); teaching mathematics (MA).

Université Laval, Faculty of Law, Program in Notarial Law, Québec, QC G1K 7P4, Canada. Offers Diploma. *Program availability:* Part-time. *Entrance requirements:* For degree, knowledge of French. Electronic applications accepted.

University of Baltimore, Graduate School, Yale Gordon College of Arts and Sciences, Program in Legal and Ethical Studies, Baltimore, MD 21201-5779. Offers MA. *Program availability:* Part-time, evening/weekend. *Degree requirements:* For master's, thesis optional. *Entrance requirements:* For master's, minimum GPA of 3.0. Additional exam requirements/recommendations for international students: Required—TOEFL (minimum score 550 paper-based). Electronic applications accepted. *Faculty research:* Morality in law and economics, religion in lawmaking, comparative legal history, law and social change, critical issues in Constitutional law, theories of justice.

University of Calgary, Faculty of Graduate Studies, Faculty of Law, Programs in Natural Resources, Energy and Environmental Law, Calgary, AB T2N 1N4, Canada. Offers LL M, Postbaccalaureate Certificate. *Program availability:* Part-time, evening/weekend. *Degree requirements:* For master's, thesis optional. *Entrance requirements:* For master's, JD or LL B. Additional exam requirements/recommendations for international students: Required—TOEFL (minimum score 100 iBT), IELTS (minimum score 7). Electronic applications accepted. *Faculty research:* Natural resources law and regulations; environmental law, ethics and policies; oil and gas and energy law; water and municipal law; Aboriginal law.

University of California, Berkeley, School of Law, Program in Jurisprudence and Social Policy, Berkeley, CA 94720-1500. Offers PhD. *Faculty:* 11 full-time (3 women), 4 part-time/adjunct (0 women). *Students:* 47 full-time (21 women); includes 11 minority (1 Black or African American, non-Hispanic/Latino; 5 Asian, non-Hispanic/Latino; 5 Hispanic/Latino), 8 international. Average age 25. 68 applicants, 6 enrolled. In 2016, 8 doctorates awarded. *Degree requirements:* For doctorate, one foreign language, thesis/dissertation, oral qualifying exam. *Entrance requirements:* For doctorate, GRE General Test, sample of written work, letters of recommendation. *Application deadline:* For fall admission, 1/5 for domestic students. Application fee: $105 ($125 for international students). Electronic applications accepted. *Expenses:* Contact institution. *Financial support:* In 2016–17, 25 students received support, including fellowships with full and partial tuition reimbursements available (averaging $19,500 per year), research assistantships with full and partial tuition reimbursements available (averaging $3,000 per year), teaching assistantships with full and partial tuition reimbursements available (averaging $7,286 per year); Federal Work-Study, institutionally sponsored loans, scholarships/grants, tuition waivers (full and partial), and unspecified assistantships also available. Support available to part-time students. Financial award application deadline: 1/5; financial award applicants required to submit FAFSA. *Faculty research:* Law and philosophy, legal history, law and economics, law and political science, law and sociology. *Unit head:* Calvin Morrill, Associate Dean/Chair, 510-642-4038, Fax: 510-642-2951. *Application contact:* Margo Rodriguez, Graduate Assistant for Admission, 510-642-3771, Fax: 510-642-2951, E-mail: calbiston@law.berkeley.edu.
Website: https://www.law.berkeley.edu/academics/doctoral-programs/jsp/

University of California, San Diego, Graduate Division, Program in Health Policy and Law, La Jolla, CA 92093. Offers MAS. Program offered jointly with School of Medicine and California Western School of Law. *Program availability:* Part-time. *Students:* 2 full-time (both women), 26 part-time (19 women). 21 applicants, 71% accepted, 9 enrolled. In 2016, 9 master's awarded. *Degree requirements:* For master's, capstone project. *Entrance requirements:* For master's, appropriate medical, healthcare, legal or related degree; minimum GPA of 3.0 in final two years of study; minimum 3 years of relevant work experience or equivalent. Additional exam requirements/recommendations for international students: Required—TOEFL (minimum score 550 paper-based; 80 iBT), IELTS (minimum score 7). *Application deadline:* For fall admission, 8/4 for domestic students. Applications are processed on a rolling basis. Application fee: $105 ($125 for international students). Electronic applications accepted. *Expenses:* Contact institution. *Financial support:* Scholarships/grants available. *Unit head:* Gerard Manecke, Program Co-Director, 619-543-3164, E-mail: gmanecke@ucsd.edu. *Application contact:* Jessica Nguyen, Program Coordinator, 858-534-9162, E-mail: healthpolicyandlaw@ucsd.edu.
Website: http://hlaw.ucsd.edu/

University of Charleston, Master of Forensic Accounting Program, Charleston, WV 25304-1099. Offers EMFA. *Program availability:* Part-time, blended/hybrid learning. *Students:* 23 full-time (16 women); includes 4 minority (2 Black or African American, non-Hispanic/Latino; 1 Hispanic/Latino; 1 Native Hawaiian or other Pacific Islander, non-Hispanic/Latino), 1 international. Average age 36. *Entrance requirements:* Additional exam requirements/recommendations for international students: Required—TOEFL. *Application deadline:* Applications are processed on a rolling basis. Application fee: $50. Electronic applications accepted. *Expenses: Tuition:* Full-time $20,602; part-time $425 per credit. *Required fees:* $200. Tuition and fees vary according to course load, campus/location, program and student level. *Financial support:* Applicants required to submit FAFSA. *Unit head:* Christina Chard, Program Director, 304-352-0033, E-mail: christinachard@ucwv.edu. *Application contact:* Bobby Redd, Admissions Representative, 304-860-5621, E-mail: bobbyredd@ucwv.edu.
Website: http://www.ucwv.edu/Forensic-Accounting/

University of Denver, Sturm College of Law, Program in Legal Administration, Denver, CO 80208. Offers MSLA, Certificate. *Program availability:* Part-time, evening/weekend. *Faculty:* 10 full-time (3 women), 5 part-time/adjunct (3 women). *Students:* 7 full-time (5 women), 12 part-time (10 women); includes 9 minority (2 Black or African American, non-Hispanic/Latino; 1 American Indian or Alaska Native, non-Hispanic/Latino; 4 Hispanic/Latino; 2 Two or more races, non-Hispanic/Latino). Average age 36. 9 applicants, 100% accepted, 3 enrolled. In 2016, 8 master's awarded. *Degree requirements:* For master's, internship. *Entrance requirements:* For master's, GRE General Test, GMAT, or LSAT. Additional exam requirements/recommendations for international students: Required—TOEFL (minimum score 570 paper-based; 88 iBT). *Application deadline:* For fall admission, 8/15 priority date for domestic and international students; for spring admission, 1/11 priority date for domestic and international students; for summer admission, 5/31 priority date for domestic and international students. Applications are processed on a rolling basis. Application fee: $65. Electronic applications accepted. *Expenses:* $44,530 per year full-time. *Financial support:* In 2016–17, 7 students received support. Career-related internships or fieldwork, Federal Work-Study, scholarships/grants, and unspecified assistantships available. Support available to part-time students. Financial award application deadline: 2/15; financial award applicants required to submit FAFSA. *Unit head:* Carol Larkin, Interim Director, 303-871-6249, E-mail: gradlegalstudies@law.du.edu. *Application contact:* E-mail: gradlegalstudies@law.du.edu.
Website: http://www.law.du.edu/index.php/msla

University of Illinois at Springfield, Graduate Programs, College of Public Affairs and Administration, Program in Legal Studies, Springfield, IL 62703-5407. Offers MA. *Program availability:* Part-time, evening/weekend, 100% online. *Faculty:* 2 full-time (1 woman). *Students:* 6 full-time (5 women), 38 part-time (27 women); includes 11 minority (6 Black or African American, non-Hispanic/Latino; 1 Asian, non-Hispanic/Latino; 2 Hispanic/Latino; 2 Two or more races, non-Hispanic/Latino). Average age 39. 28 applicants, 43% accepted, 8 enrolled. In 2016, 19 master's awarded. *Degree requirements:* For master's, thesis or seminar. *Entrance requirements:* For master's, minimum undergraduate GPA of 3.0; demonstration of writing ability. Additional exam requirements/recommendations for international students: Required—TOEFL (minimum score 570 paper-based; 100 iBT). *Application deadline:* Applications are processed on a rolling basis. Application fee: $60 ($75 for international students). Electronic applications accepted. *Expenses:* Tuition, state resident: part-time $329 per credit hour. Tuition, nonresident: part-time $675 per credit hour. *Financial support:* In 2016–17, fellowships with full tuition reimbursements (averaging $9,900 per year), research assistantships with full tuition reimbursements (averaging $9,991 per year), teaching assistantships with full tuition reimbursements (averaging $10,059 per year) were awarded; career-related internships or fieldwork, Federal Work-Study, scholarships/grants, health care benefits, and unspecified assistantships also available. Support available to part-time students. Financial award application deadline: 11/15; financial award applicants required to submit FAFSA. *Unit head:* Dr. Gwen Jordan, JD, Program Administrator, 217-206-8520, Fax: 217-206-7807, E-mail: gjorda2@uis.edu. *Application contact:* Dr. Cecelia Cornell, Associate Vice Chancellor for Graduate Education, 217-206-7230, E-mail: ccorn1@uis.edu.
Website: http://www.uis.edu/legalstudies/

University of Massachusetts Lowell, College of Fine Arts, Humanities and Social Sciences, School of Criminology and Justice Studies, Lowell, MA 01854. Offers criminal justice (MA). *Program availability:* Part-time, evening/weekend. *Degree requirements:* For master's, thesis optional. *Entrance requirements:* For master's, GRE General Test or MAT. Electronic applications accepted. *Faculty research:* Family violence, criminal justice management, corrections, policing, delinquency.

University of Montana, Graduate School, College of Humanities and Sciences, Department of Sociology, Missoula, MT 59812-0002. Offers criminology (MA); inequality and social justice (MA); rural and environmental change (MA); sociology (MA). *Entrance requirements:* For master's, GRE General Test. Additional exam requirements/recommendations for international students: Required—TOEFL. *Faculty research:* Housing, homelessness, hunger, infant mortality, work safety.

University of Nebraska–Lincoln, College of Law, Program in Legal Studies, Lincoln, NE 68588. Offers MLS. *Entrance requirements:* For master's, GRE or LSAT. Additional exam requirements/recommendations for international students: Required—TOEFL (minimum score 600 paper-based). Electronic applications accepted.

University of Nevada, Reno, Graduate School, College of Liberal Arts, School of Social Research and Justice Studies, Program in Judicial Studies, Reno, NV 89557. Offers MJS, PhD. Offered jointly with the National Judicial College and the National Council of Juvenile and Family Court Judges. *Program availability:* Part-time. Terminal master's awarded for partial completion of doctoral program. *Degree requirements:* For master's, thesis; for doctorate, thesis/dissertation. *Entrance requirements:* For master's and doctorate, sitting judge, law degree from an accredited school. Additional exam requirements/recommendations for international students: Required—TOEFL (minimum score 500 paper-based; 61 iBT), IELTS (minimum score 6). Electronic applications accepted. *Expenses:* Contact institution. *Faculty research:* Jury research, capital punishment, expert testimony, environmental law, medical issues.

University of New Hampshire, Graduate School, College of Liberal Arts, Program in Justice Studies, Durham, NH 03824. Offers MA. Program offered in summer only. *Program availability:* Part-time. *Degree requirements:* For master's, thesis optional.

Entrance requirements: For master's, GRE. Additional exam requirements/recommendations for international students: Required—TOEFL (minimum score 550 paper-based; 80 iBT); Recommended—TWE. *Application deadline:* For fall admission, 3/1 for domestic students, 3/1 priority date for international students. Applications are processed on a rolling basis. Application fee: $65. Electronic applications accepted. *Financial support:* Fellowships, research assistantships, teaching assistantships, career-related internships or fieldwork, Federal Work-Study, scholarships/grants, and tuition waivers (full and partial) available. Support available to part-time students. Financial award application deadline: 3/1. *Unit head:* Todd DeMitchell, Chair, 603-862-5043. *Application contact:* Deborah Briand, Administrative Assistant, 603-862-1716, E-mail: justice.studies@unh.edu.
Website: http://www.cola.unh.edu/justice-studies

University of New Hampshire, School of Law, Concord, NH 03301. Offers business law (JD); commerce and technology (LL M, MCT, Diploma); criminal law (JD); intellectual property (LL M, MIP, JD, Diploma), including patent law (JD), trademarks and copyright (JD); international criminal law and justice (LL M, MICLJ); litigation (JD); public interest and social justice (JD); sports and entertainment law (JD); JD/LL M; JD/MBA; JD/MIP; JD/MPP; JD/MSW. *Accreditation:* ABA. *Program availability:* Part-time, 100% online, limited residential. *Faculty:* 25 full-time (11 women), 29 part-time/adjunct (9 women). *Students:* 252 full-time (107 women), 4 part-time (3 women); includes 30 minority (3 Black or African American, non-Hispanic/Latino; 7 Asian, non-Hispanic/Latino; 11 Hispanic/Latino; 9 Two or more races, non-Hispanic/Latino), 36 international. Average age 36. 564 applicants, 53% accepted, 103 enrolled. In 2016, 27 master's, 69 doctorates awarded. *Degree requirements:* For doctorate, comprehensive exam. *Entrance requirements:* For doctorate, LSAT. Additional exam requirements/recommendations for international students: Required—TOEFL (minimum score 600 paper-based; 100 iBT), minimum TOEFL iBT score of 80 (for master's programs). *Application deadline:* For fall admission, 4/1 priority date for domestic and international students; for spring admission, 1/3 for domestic and international students. Applications are processed on a rolling basis. Application fee: $0. Electronic applications accepted. *Expenses:* Contact institution. *Financial support:* Fellowships, career-related internships or fieldwork, Federal Work-Study, and scholarships/grants available. Financial award applicants required to submit FAFSA. *Faculty research:* Intellectual property, health law and policy, sports and entertainment law, patent law, trademarks and copyright. *Unit head:* Megan Carpenter, Dean, 603-228-1541, Fax: 603-228-1074. *Application contact:* Brenda Brooks, Director of Admissions, 603-513-5300, Fax: 603-513-5234, E-mail: brenda.brooks@law.unh.edu.
Website: http://law.unh.edu/

University of Pennsylvania, Wharton School, Legal Studies and Business Ethics Department, Philadelphia, PA 19104. Offers MBA, PhD. *Expenses: Tuition:* Full-time $31,068; part-time $5762 per course. *Required fees:* $3200; $336 per course. Full-time tuition and fees vary according to degree level, program and student level. Part-time tuition and fees vary according to course load, degree level and program.

University of Pittsburgh, School of Law, Master of Studies in Law Program, Pittsburgh, PA 15260. Offers business law (MSL), including commercial law, corporate law, general business law, international business, tax law; Constitutional law (MSL); criminal law and justice (MSL); disability law (MSL); education law (MSL); elder and estate planning law (MSL); employment and labor law (MSL); energy law (MSL); environmental and real estate law (MSL); family law (MSL); health law (MSL); intellectual property and technology law (MSL); international and human rights law (MSL); jurisprudence (MSL); personal injury and civil litigation (MSL); regulatory law (MSL); self-designed (MSL); sports and entertainment law (MSL). *Program availability:* Part-time. *Faculty:* 48 full-time (21 women), 104 part-time/adjunct (34 women). *Students:* 5 full-time (4 women), 14 part-time (9 women); includes 7 minority (4 Black or African American, non-Hispanic/Latino; 1 Asian, non-Hispanic/Latino; 2 Native Hawaiian or other Pacific Islander, non-Hispanic/Latino). Average age 27. 17 applicants, 53% accepted, 7 enrolled. In 2016, 4 master's awarded. *Entrance requirements:* Additional exam requirements/recommendations for international students: Required—TOEFL (minimum score 600 paper-based; 100 iBT). *Application deadline:* For fall admission, 6/30 for domestic students, 5/1 for international students. Applications are processed on a rolling basis. Application fee: $0. Tuition and fees vary according to program. *Faculty research:* Law, health law, business law, contracts, intellectual property, environmental law. *Unit head:* Prof. Alan Meisel, Director, 412-648-1384, Fax: 412-648-2649, E-mail: meisel@pitt.edu. *Application contact:* Beth Ann Pischke, Administrative Coordinator, 412-648-7120, Fax: 412-648-2649, E-mail: pischke@pitt.edu.
Website: http://www.law.pitt.edu/msl

University of San Diego, School of Law, San Diego, CA 92110-2492. Offers business and corporate law (LL M); comparative law (LL M); general studies (LL M); international law (LL M); law (JD); taxation (LL M, Diploma); JD/IMBA; JD/MA; JD/MBA. *Accreditation:* ABA. *Program availability:* Part-time, evening/weekend. *Faculty:* 46 full-time (14 women), 71 part-time/adjunct (21 women). *Students:* 644 full-time (320 women), 118 part-time (46 women); includes 250 minority (24 Black or African American, non-Hispanic/Latino; 11 American Indian or Alaska Native, non-Hispanic/Latino; 96 Asian, non-Hispanic/Latino; 106 Hispanic/Latino; 3 Native Hawaiian or other Pacific Islander, non-Hispanic/Latino; 10 Two or more races, non-Hispanic/Latino), 26 international. Average age 27. 3,106 applicants, 192 enrolled. In 2016, 65 master's, 216 doctorates awarded. *Entrance requirements:* For master's, JD, LL B or equivalent from an ABA-accredited law school; for doctorate, LSAT (less than 5 years old), bachelor's degree, registration with the Credential Assemble Service (CAS). Additional exam requirements/recommendations for international students: Required—TOEFL (minimum score 600 paper-based; 100 iBT). *Application deadline:* For fall admission, 2/1 priority date for domestic students. Applications are processed on a rolling basis. Electronic applications accepted. *Expenses:* Contact institution. *Financial support:* In 2016–17, 567 students received support. Career-related internships or fieldwork, Federal Work-Study, institutionally sponsored loans, and scholarships/grants available. Support available to part-time students. Financial award application deadline: 3/1; financial award applicants required to submit FAFSA. *Faculty research:* Corporate law, children's advocacy, Constitutional and criminal law, international and comparative law, public interest law, intellectual property and tax law. *Unit head:* Dr. Stephen C. Ferruolo, Dean, 619-260-4527, E-mail: lawdean@sandiego.edu. *Application contact:* Jorge Garcia, Assistant Dean, JD Admissions, 619-260-4528, Fax: 619-260-2218, E-mail: jdinfo@sandiego.edu.
Website: http://www.sandiego.edu/law/

University of South Florida, Innovative Education, Tampa, FL 33620-9951. Offers adult, career and higher education (Graduate Certificate), including college teaching, leadership in developing human resources, leadership in higher education; Africana studies (Graduate Certificate), including diasporas and health disparities, genocide and human rights; aging studies (Graduate Certificate), including gerontology; art research (Graduate Certificate), including museum studies; business foundations (Graduate Certificate); chemical and biomedical engineering (Graduate Certificate), including materials science and engineering, water, health and sustainability; child and family studies (Graduate Certificate), including positive behavior support; civil and industrial engineering (Graduate Certificate), including transportation systems analysis; community and family health (Graduate Certificate), including maternal and child health, social marketing and public health, violence and injury: prevention and intervention, women's health; criminology (Graduate Certificate), including criminal justice administration; educational measurement and research (Graduate Certificate), including evaluation; English (Graduate Certificate), including comparative literary studies, creative writing, professional and technical communication; entrepreneurship (Graduate Certificate); environmental health (Graduate Certificate), including safety management; epidemiology and biostatistics (Graduate Certificate), including applied biostatistics, biostatistics, concepts and tools of epidemiology, epidemiology, epidemiology of infectious diseases; geography, environment and planning (Graduate Certificate); including community development, environmental policy and management, geographical information systems; geology (Graduate Certificate), including hydrogeology; global health (Graduate Certificate), including disaster management, global health and Latin American and Caribbean studies, global health practice, humanitarian assistance, infection control; government and international affairs (Graduate Certificate), including Cuban studies, globalization studies; health policy and management (Graduate Certificate), including health management and leadership, public health policy and programs; hearing specialist: early intervention (Graduate Certificate); industrial and management systems engineering (Graduate Certificate), including systems engineering, technology management; information studies (Graduate Certificate), including school library media specialist; information systems/decision sciences (Graduate Certificate), including analytics and business intelligence; instructional technology (Graduate Certificate), including distance education, Florida digital/virtual educator, instructional design, multimedia design, Web design; internal medicine, bioethics and medical humanities (Graduate Certificate), including biomedical ethics; Latin American and Caribbean studies (Graduate Certificate); mass communications (Graduate Certificate), including multimedia journalism; mathematics and statistics (Graduate Certificate), including mathematics; medicine (Graduate Certificate), including aging and neuroscience, bioinformatics, biotechnology, brain fitness and memory management, clinical investigation, health informatics, health sciences, integrative weight management, intellectual property, medicine and gender, metabolic and nutritional medicine, metabolic cardiology, pharmacy sciences; national and competitive intelligence (Graduate Certificate); psychological and social foundations (Graduate Certificate), including career counseling, college teaching, diversity in education, mental health counseling, school counseling; public affairs (Graduate Certificate), including nonprofit management, public management, research administration; public health (Graduate Certificate), including environmental health, health equity, public health generalist, translational research in adolescent behavioral health; public health practices (Graduate Certificate), including planning for healthy communities; rehabilitation and mental health counseling (Graduate Certificate), including integrative mental health care, marriage and family therapy, rehabilitation technology; secondary education (Graduate Certificate), including ESOL, foreign language education: culture and content, foreign language education: professional; social work (Graduate Certificate), including geriatric social work/clinical gerontology; special education (Graduate Certificate), including autism spectrum disorder, disabilities education: severe/profound; world languages (Graduate Certificate), including teaching English as a second language (TESL) or foreign language. *Expenses:* Tuition, state resident: full-time $7766; part-time $431.43 per credit hour. Tuition, nonresident: full-time $15,789; part-time $877.17 per credit hour. *Required fees:* $37 per term. *Unit head:* Kathy Barnes, Interdisciplinary Programs Coordinator, 813-974-8031, Fax: 813-974-7061, E-mail: barnesk@usf.edu. *Application contact:* Karen Tylinski, Metro Initiatives, 813-974-9943, Fax: 813-974-7061, E-mail: ktylinsk@usf.edu.
Website: http://www.usf.edu/innovative-education/

University of the District of Columbia, David A. Clarke School of Law, Washington, DC 20008. Offers clinical teaching and social justice (LL M); law (JD). *Accreditation:* ABA. *Program availability:* Part-time, evening/weekend. *Degree requirements:* For doctorate, 90 credits, advanced legal writing. *Entrance requirements:* For doctorate, LSAT. Additional exam requirements/recommendations for international students: Recommended—TOEFL. Electronic applications accepted. *Expenses:* Contact institution. *Faculty research:* HIV law, juvenile law, legislative law, community development, small business, immigration and human rights.

University of the Sacred Heart, Graduate Programs, Program in Systems of Justice, San Juan, PR 00914-0383. Offers human rights and anti-discriminatory processes (MASJ); mediation and transformation of conflicts (MASJ).

University of Washington, Graduate School, School of Law, Seattle, WA 98195-3020. Offers Asian law (LL M, PhD); intellectual property law and policy (LL M); law (JD); law of sustainable international development (LL M); taxation (LL M); JD/LL M; JD/MA; JD/MAIS; JD/MBA; JD/MPA; JD/MS; JD/PhD. *Accreditation:* ABA. *Degree requirements:* For master's, thesis; for doctorate, thesis/dissertation (for some programs). *Entrance requirements:* For master's, language proficiency (LL M in Asian law); for doctorate, LSAT (for JD). Additional exam requirements/recommendations for international students: Required—TOEFL. *Expenses:* Contact institution. *Faculty research:* Asian, international and comparative law, intellectual property law, health law, environmental law, taxation.

University of Windsor, Faculty of Graduate Studies, Faculty of Arts and Social Sciences, Department of Communication Studies, Windsor, ON N9B 3P4, Canada. Offers communication and social justice (MA). *Degree requirements:* For master's, thesis. *Entrance requirements:* For master's, writing sample/media production or multimedia portfolio. Additional exam requirements/recommendations for international students: Required—TOEFL (minimum score 600 paper-based). Electronic applications accepted. *Faculty research:* Sociology of news, media ownership and control, communication networks and social movements, issues of media representation.

Valparaiso University, Graduate School and Continuing Education, Program in Legal Studies and Principles, Valparaiso, IN 46383. Offers Certificate. *Program availability:* Part-time, evening/weekend. *Entrance requirements:* Additional exam requirements/recommendations for international students: Required—TOEFL (minimum score 550 paper-based; 80 iBT), IELTS (minimum score 6). Electronic applications accepted. *Expenses: Tuition:* Full-time $11,070; part-time $615 per credit hour. *Required fees:* $116 per semester. Tuition and fees vary according to course load, degree level and program.

Vermont Law School, Graduate and Professional Programs, Master's Programs, South Royalton, VT 05068-0096. Offers American legal studies (LL M); energy law (LL M); energy regulation and law (MERL); environmental law (LL M); environmental law and policy (MELP); food and agriculture law (LL M); food and agriculture law and policy (MFALP); JD/MELP; JD/MERL; JD/MFALP. *Program availability:* Part-time, 100% online, blended/hybrid learning. *Entrance requirements:* Additional exam requirements/recommendations for international students: Required—TOEFL. *Application deadline:* For fall admission, 3/1 priority date for domestic students. Applications are processed on a rolling basis. Application fee: $60. *Expenses: Tuition:* Full-time $47,998. *Financial support:* Fellowships with full tuition reimbursements, career-related internships or fieldwork, Federal Work-Study, institutionally sponsored loans, scholarships/grants, and tuition waivers (partial) available. Support available to part-time students. Financial award application deadline: 3/1; financial award applicants required to submit FAFSA.

Faculty research: Environment and new economy; takings; international environmental law; interaction among science, law, and environmental policy; climate change and the law. *Unit head:* Marc B. Mihaly, President and Dean, 802-831-1237, Fax: 802-763-2490. *Application contact:* John D. Miller, Jr., Vice President for Enrollment Management, Marketing and Communications, 802-831-1239, Fax: 802-831-1174,
E-mail: admiss@vermontlaw.edu.
Website: http://www.vermontlaw.edu/Academics/degrees/masters

Washburn University, School of Law, Topeka, KS 66621. Offers global legal studies (LL M); law (MSL, JD). *Accreditation:* ABA. *Entrance requirements:* For doctorate, LSAT. Additional exam requirements/recommendations for international students: Recommended—TOEFL (minimum score 550 paper-based). Electronic applications accepted. Application fee is waived when completed online. *Expenses:* Contact institution. *Faculty research:* Constitutional law, family law, energy law, banking and securities law, oil and gas.

Weber State University, College of Social and Behavioral Sciences, Program in Criminal Justice, Ogden, UT 84408-1001. Offers MCJ. *Program availability:* Part-time, evening/weekend, 100% online. *Faculty:* 6 full-time (0 women), 1 part-time/adjunct (0 women). *Students:* 5 full-time (2 women), 23 part-time (9 women); includes 7 minority (3 Black or African American, non-Hispanic/Latino; 1 American Indian or Alaska Native, non-Hispanic/Latino; 2 Hispanic/Latino; 1 Two or more races, non-Hispanic/Latino). Average age 35. In 2016, 12 master's awarded. *Entrance requirements:* Additional exam requirements/recommendations for international students: Required—TOEFL (minimum score 550 paper-based). *Application deadline:* For fall admission, 7/29 for domestic students; for spring admission, 12/11 for domestic students; for summer admission, 4/1 for domestic students. Applications are processed on a rolling basis. Application fee: $60 ($90 for international students). Electronic applications accepted. *Expenses:* Contact institution. *Financial support:* In 2016–17, 1 student received support. Scholarships/grants available. Financial award application deadline: 2/1; financial award applicants required to submit FAFSA. *Unit head:* Dr. Bruce Bayley, Graduate Director/Associate Professor, 801-626-8134, Fax: 801-626-6145, E-mail: bbayley@weber.edu. *Application contact:* Faye Medd, Secretary, 801-626-6146, Fax: 801-626-6146, E-mail: fmedd@weber.edu.
Website: http://www.weber.edu/cj/CJMastersDegree/CJMastersDegree.html

Webster University, College of Arts and Sciences, Department of Legal Studies, St. Louis, MO 63119-3194. Offers MA, Graduate Certificate. *Program availability:* Part-time, evening/weekend. *Degree requirements:* For master's, thesis optional. *Entrance requirements:* Additional exam requirements/recommendations for international students: Required—TOEFL. *Application deadline:* Applications are processed on a rolling basis. Application fee: $25 ($50 for international students). *Expenses: Tuition:* Full-time $21,900; part-time $730 per credit hour. Tuition and fees vary according to campus/location and program. *Financial support:* Career-related internships or fieldwork and Federal Work-Study available. Support available to part-time students. Financial award application deadline: 4/1; financial award applicants required to submit FAFSA. *Faculty research:* Intellectual property rights, emerging torts, death penalty, juvenile justice, confidentiality issues in banking. *Unit head:* Robin Jefferson Higgins, Director, 314-968-7068, E-mail: robinjefferson85@webster.edu. *Application contact:* Linda C. Wynn, Department Manager, 314-246-7068, Fax: 314-246-6094, E-mail: wynnslc@webster.edu.

Western Michigan University Thomas M. Cooley Law School, Graduate Programs, Lansing, MI 48901-3038. Offers administrative law (public law) (JD); business transactions (JD); Canadian law practice (JD); constitutional law/civil rights (public law) (JD); corporate law and finance (LL M); environmental law (public law) (JD); general practice (JD), including solo and small firm; homeland and national security law (LL M); insurance law (LL M); intellectual property (JD); intellectual property law (LL M); international law (JD); litigation (JD); self-directed (LL M, JD); tax law (LL M); taxation (JD); U.S. legal studies for foreign attorneys (LL M); JD/LL M; JD/MBA; JD/MPA; JD/MSW. *Program availability:* Part-time, evening/weekend, 100% online, blended/hybrid learning. *Degree requirements:* For master's, thesis optional; for doctorate, minimum of 3 credits of clinical experience. *Entrance requirements:* For master's, JD or LL B; for doctorate, LSAT. Additional exam requirements/recommendations for international students: Required—TOEFL (for U.S. legal studies for foreign attorneys LL M program); Recommended—TOEFL. Electronic applications accepted. *Faculty research:* Wrongful convictions, civil rights, environmental law, litigation techniques, data mining, intellectual property, practical and skills-based legal education.

West Virginia University, Eberly College of Arts and Sciences, Department of Public Administration, Morgantown, WV 26506. Offers legal studies (MLS); public administration (MPA); JD/MPA; MSW/MPA. *Accreditation:* NASPAA. *Program availability:* Part-time. *Degree requirements:* For master's, internship. *Entrance requirements:* For master's, GRE General Test, minimum GPA of 2.75. Additional exam requirements/recommendations for international students: Required—TOEFL. Electronic applications accepted. *Faculty research:* Public management and organization, conflict resolution, work satisfaction, health administration, social policy and welfare.

Wilfrid Laurier University, Faculty of Graduate and Postdoctoral Studies, School of International Policy and Governance, Global Governance Program, Waterloo, ON N2L 3C5, Canada. Offers conflict and security (PhD); global environment (PhD); global justice and human rights (PhD); global political economy (PhD); global social governance (PhD); multilateral institutions and diplomacy (PhD). Offered jointly with University of Waterloo. *Degree requirements:* For doctorate, thesis/dissertation. *Entrance requirements:* For doctorate, MA in political science, history, economics, international development studies, international peace studies, globalization studies, environmental studies or related field with minimum A-. Additional exam requirements/recommendations for international students: Required—TOEFL (minimum score 89 iBT). Electronic applications accepted. *Faculty research:* Global political economy, global environment, conflict and security, global justice and human rights, multilateral institutions and diplomacy.

ACADEMIC AND PROFESSIONAL PROGRAMS IN LIBRARY AND INFORMATION STUDIES

Section 28
Library and Information Studies

This section contains a directory of institutions offering graduate work in library and information studies, followed by in-depth entries submitted by institutions that chose to prepare detailed program descriptions. Additional information about programs listed in the directory but not augmented by an in-depth entry may be obtained by writing directly to the dean of a graduate school or chair of a department at the address given in the directory.

For programs offering related work, see also in this book *Education.* In another guide in this series:

Graduate Programs in Engineering & Applied Sciences
See *Computer Science and Information Technology*

CONTENTS

Program Directories

Featured Schools: Displays and Close-Ups

Archives/Archival Administration

Claremont Graduate University, Graduate Programs, School of Arts and Humanities, Department of History, Claremont, CA 91711-6160. Offers Africana history (Certificate); American studies and U.S. history (MA, PhD); archival studies (MA); early modern studies (MA, PhD); European studies (MA, PhD); oral history (MA, PhD); MBA/MA; MBA/PhD. *Faculty:* 5 full-time (3 women), 2 part-time/adjunct (0 women). *Students:* 45 full-time (23 women), 24 part-time (14 women); includes 21 minority (2 Black or African American, non-Hispanic/Latino; 1 American Indian or Alaska Native, non-Hispanic/Latino; 5 Asian, non-Hispanic/Latino; 6 Hispanic/Latino; 1 Native Hawaiian or other Pacific Islander, non-Hispanic/Latino; 6 Two or more races, non-Hispanic/Latino). Average age 38. In 2016, 5 master's, 2 doctorates awarded. Terminal master's awarded for partial completion of doctoral program. *Entrance requirements:* For master's and doctorate, GRE General Test. Additional exam requirements/recommendations for international students: Required—TOEFL (minimum score 75 iBT). *Application deadline:* For fall admission, 2/1 priority date for domestic and international students. Applications are processed on a rolling basis. Application fee: $80. Electronic applications accepted. *Expenses: Tuition:* Full-time $44,328; part-time $1847 per unit. *Required fees:* $600; $300 per semester. Tuition and fees vary according to course load and program. *Financial support:* Fellowships, research assistantships, Federal Work-Study, institutionally sponsored loans, and scholarships/grants available. Support available to part-time students. Financial award application deadline: 2/15; financial award applicants required to submit FAFSA. *Faculty research:* Intellectual and social history, cultural studies, gender studies, Western history, Chicano history. *Unit head:* Joshua Goode, Chair, 909-607-7430, E-mail: joshua.goode@cgu.edu. *Application contact:* Amy Sandefur, Assistant Director of Admissions, 909-607-9101, E-mail: amy.sandefur@cgu.edu.
Website: https://www.cgu.edu/departments/history/

Clayton State University, School of Graduate Studies, College of Information and Mathematical Sciences, Program in Archival Studies, Morrow, GA 30260-0285. Offers MAS. *Program availability:* Online learning. *Entrance requirements:* For master's, GRE, 2 official transcripts; 3 letters of recommendation; statement of purpose; essay. Additional exam requirements/recommendations for international students: Required—TOEFL (minimum score 550 paper-based). Electronic applications accepted. *Expenses:* Tuition, state resident: full-time $3528; part-time $196 per credit hour. Tuition, nonresident: full-time $13,176; part-time $732 per credit hour. *Required fees:* $1454; $1454 per credit hour. $727 per semester. Tuition and fees vary according to campus/location and program.

Columbia University, School of Continuing Education, Program in Information and Archive Management, New York, NY 10027. Offers MS. *Program availability:* Part-time. *Entrance requirements:* For master's, minimum undergraduate GPA of 3.0. Additional exam requirements/recommendations for international students: Required—American Language Program placement test. Electronic applications accepted. *Faculty research:* Library science technology, information systems.

Drexel University, Westphal College of Media Arts and Design, Program in Museum Leadership, Philadelphia, PA 19104-2875. Offers MS. Offered in partnership with the Academy of Natural Sciences of Drexel University. *Program availability:* Part-time, online learning. *Students:* 11 full-time (9 women), 2 part-time (both women); includes 4 minority (2 Black or African American, non-Hispanic/Latino; 1 Hispanic/Latino; 1 Two or more races, non-Hispanic/Latino), 2 international. Average age 26. In 2016, 6 master's awarded. *Degree requirements:* For master's, practicum. *Expenses: Tuition:* Full-time $32,184; part-time $1192 per credit hour. *Required fees:* $280. Tuition and fees vary according to campus/location and program. *Unit head:* College Recruitment Office, 215-895-1675, Fax: 215-895-5838. *Application contact:* Graduate Admissions Office, 215-895-6700, E-mail: enroll@drexel.edu.
Website: http://www.drexel.edu/westphal/graduate/MUSL/

Middle Tennessee State University, College of Graduate Studies, College of Liberal Arts, Department of History, Murfreesboro, TN 37132. Offers archival management (Graduate Certificate); history (MA); public history (PhD). *Program availability:* Part-time, evening/weekend, online learning. *Degree requirements:* For master's, one foreign language, comprehensive exam, thesis optional; for doctorate, one foreign language, comprehensive exam, thesis/dissertation. *Entrance requirements:* For master's and doctorate, GRE. Additional exam requirements/recommendations for international students: Required—TOEFL (minimum score 525 paper-based; 71 iBT) or IELTS (minimum score 6). Electronic applications accepted.

Montclair State University, The Graduate School, College of the Arts, Program in Fine Art, Montclair, NJ 07043-1624. Offers museum management (MA); studio (MA). *Accreditation:* NASAD. *Program availability:* Part-time, evening/weekend. *Degree requirements:* For master's, project. *Entrance requirements:* For master's, GRE or MAT, 2 letters of recommendation, essay. Electronic applications accepted. *Expenses:* Tuition, state resident: part-time $553 per credit. Tuition, nonresident: part-time $854 per credit. *Required fees:* $91 per credit. Tuition and fees vary according to program.

New York University, Graduate School of Arts and Science, Department of History, New York, NY 10012-1019. Offers African diaspora (PhD); African history (PhD); archival management (Advanced Certificate); Atlantic history (PhD); French studies/history (PhD); Hebrew and Judaic studies/history (PhD); history (MA, PhD), including Europe (PhD), Latin America and the Caribbean (PhD), United States (PhD), women's history (MA); Middle Eastern history (MA); Middle Eastern studies/history (PhD); public history (Advanced Certificate); world history (MA); JD/MA; MA/Advanced Certificate. *Program availability:* Part-time. Terminal master's awarded for partial completion of doctoral program. *Degree requirements:* For master's, seminar paper; for doctorate, one foreign language, thesis/dissertation, oral and written exams; for Advanced Certificate, internship. *Entrance requirements:* For master's, GRE General Test, minimum GPA of 3.0, writing sample; for doctorate, GRE. Additional exam requirements/recommendations for international students: Required—TOEFL. *Faculty research:* African, East Asian, medieval, early modern, and modern European history; U.S. history; African and African diaspora; Latin American history; Atlantic world.

New York University, Tisch School of the Arts, Program in Moving Image Archiving and Preservation, New York, NY 10012-1019. Offers MA. *Degree requirements:* For master's, internship. *Entrance requirements:* For master's, GRE. Additional exam requirements/recommendations for international students: Required—TOEFL or IELTS. Electronic applications accepted.

The University of British Columbia, Faculty of Arts, School of Library, Archival and Information Studies, Master of Archival Studies Program, Vancouver, BC V6T 1Z1, Canada. Offers MAS. *Degree requirements:* For master's, thesis optional. *Entrance requirements:* For master's, minimum B+ average or minimum GPA of 3.3 in undergraduate upper-division courses. Additional exam requirements/recommendations for international students: Required—TOEFL. Application fee: $100 Canadian dollars ($162 Canadian dollars for international students). Electronic applications accepted. *Expenses:* $4,911 per year tuition and fees, $8,774 per year international. *Financial support:* Fellowships, research assistantships, career-related internships or fieldwork, Federal Work-Study, institutionally sponsored loans, scholarships/grants, health care benefits, tuition waivers (partial), and unspecified assistantships available. *Faculty research:* Diplomatic, electronic record, appraisal, descriptive standards, preservation. *Application contact:* Alynne Pols, Graduate Program Staff, 604-822-3459, Fax: 604-822-6006, E-mail: ischool.program@ubc.ca.
Website: http://slais.ubc.ca/

The University of British Columbia, Faculty of Arts, School of Library, Archival and Information Studies, PhD Program in Library, Archival and Information Studies, Vancouver, BC V6T 1Z1, Canada. Offers PhD. *Degree requirements:* For doctorate, thesis/dissertation. *Entrance requirements:* For doctorate, GRE, minimum GPA of 3.3 in MAS or MLIS. Additional exam requirements/recommendations for international students: Required—TOEFL. Application fee: $100 Canadian dollars ($162 Canadian dollars for international students). Electronic applications accepted. *Expenses:* $4,802 per year tuition and fees, $8,436 per year international. *Financial support:* Fellowships, research assistantships, teaching assistantships, Federal Work-Study, institutionally sponsored loans, scholarships/grants, health care benefits, tuition waivers (partial), and unspecified assistantships available. *Faculty research:* Computer systems/database design; library and archival management; archival description and organization; children's literature and youth services; interactive information retrieval. *Application contact:* Alynne Pols, Graduate Program Staff, 604-822-3459, Fax: 604-822-6006, E-mail: ischool.program@ubc.ca.
Website: http://slais.ubc.ca/

University of California, Los Angeles, Graduate Division, Graduate School of Education and Information Studies, Department of Information Studies, Los Angeles, CA 90095-1521. Offers archival studies (MLIS); informatics (MLIS); information studies (PhD); library and information science (Certificate); library studies (MLIS); moving image archive studies (MA); rare books, print and visual culture (MLIS); MBA/MLIS; MLIS/MA. *Accreditation:* ALA (one or more programs are accredited). Terminal master's awarded for partial completion of doctoral program. *Degree requirements:* For master's, thesis or alternative, professional portfolio; for doctorate, thesis/dissertation, oral and written qualifying exams. *Entrance requirements:* For master's, GRE General Test, previous course work in statistics; for doctorate, GRE General Test, previous course work in statistics, 2 samples of research writing in English. Additional exam requirements/recommendations for international students: Required—TOEFL (minimum score 560 paper-based; 87 iBT), IELTS (minimum score 7). Electronic applications accepted. *Faculty research:* Digital libraries, archives and electronic records, interface design, cultural informatics, preservation/conservation, access.

University of California, Los Angeles, Graduate Division, School of Theater, Film and Television, Interdepartmental Program in Moving Image Archive Studies, Los Angeles, CA 90095. Offers MA. *Degree requirements:* For master's, comprehensive exam, thesis. *Entrance requirements:* For master's, bachelor's degree; minimum undergraduate GPA of 3.0 (or its equivalent if letter grade system not used); writing sample. Additional exam requirements/recommendations for international students: Required—TOEFL. Electronic applications accepted.

University of California, Riverside, Graduate Division, Department of History, Riverside, CA 92521-0102. Offers archival management (MA); history (PhD). *Program availability:* Part-time. Terminal master's awarded for partial completion of doctoral program. *Degree requirements:* For master's, one foreign language, comprehensive exam, internship report and oral exams, or thesis; for doctorate, 2 foreign languages, thesis/dissertation, qualifying exams. *Entrance requirements:* For master's and doctorate, GRE General Test, minimum GPA of 3.2. Additional exam requirements/recommendations for international students: Required—TOEFL (minimum score 550 paper-based; 80 iBT). Electronic applications accepted. *Expenses:* Tuition, state resident: full-time $16,666. Tuition, nonresident: full-time $31,768. *Required fees:* $11,055.54 per quarter. $3685.18 per quarter. Tuition and fees vary according to campus/location and program. *Faculty research:* Native American history, United States, public history, Europe, Latin America.

University of Manitoba, Faculty of Graduate Studies, Faculty of Arts, Department of History, Winnipeg, MB R3T 2N2, Canada. Offers archival studies (MA); history (MA, PhD). MA offered jointly with The University of Winnipeg. *Degree requirements:* For master's, thesis; for doctorate, one foreign language, thesis/dissertation.

University of Massachusetts Boston, College of Liberal Arts, Program in History, Boston, MA 02125-3393. Offers archival methods (MA). *Program availability:* Part-time, evening/weekend. *Faculty:* 17 full-time (10 women), 11 part-time/adjunct (6 women). *Students:* 9 full-time (6 women), 63 part-time (34 women); includes 9 minority (3 Black or African American, non-Hispanic/Latino; 2 Asian, non-Hispanic/Latino; 3 Hispanic/Latino; 1 Two or more races, non-Hispanic/Latino). Average age 35. 40 applicants, 88% accepted, 25 enrolled. In 2016, 22 master's awarded. *Degree requirements:* For master's, thesis, oral exam. *Entrance requirements:* For master's, minimum GPA of 2.75. *Application deadline:* For fall admission, 3/1 for domestic students; for spring admission, 11/1 for domestic students. *Expenses:* Tuition, state resident: full-time $16,863. Tuition, nonresident: full-time $32,913. *Required fees:* $177. *Financial support:* Research assistantships with full tuition reimbursements, teaching assistantships with full tuition reimbursements, career-related internships or fieldwork, Federal Work-Study, and unspecified assistantships available. Support available to part-time students. Financial award application deadline: 3/1; financial award applicants required to submit FAFSA. *Faculty research:* European intellectual history, American labor and social history in nineteenth century, colonial American Revolution, Afro-American Cold War. *Unit head:* Dr. Spencer DiScala, Director, 617-287-6860, E-mail: spencer.discala@umb.edu. *Application contact:* Peggy Roldan Patel, Graduate Admissions Coordinator, 617-287-6400, Fax: 617-287-6236, E-mail: bos.gadm@dpc.umassp.edu.

University of Rochester, School of Arts and Sciences, Program in Photographic Preservation and Collections Management, Rochester, NY 14627. Offers MA. Program offered jointly with George Eastman House. *Program availability:* Part-time. *Students:* 15 full-time (10 women). Average age 29. 18 applicants, 78% accepted, 5 enrolled. In 2016, 2 master's awarded. *Degree requirements:* For master's, thesis (for some programs). *Entrance requirements:* Additional exam requirements/recommendations for international students: Required—TOEFL (minimum score 600 paper-based; 100 iBT). *Application deadline:* For fall admission, 3/3 for domestic students. Application fee: $60. Electronic applications accepted. *Expenses:* $1,583 per credit. *Faculty research:* Photographic preservation, collections management, photography. *Unit head:* Joan Saab, Co-Director, 585-275-4287, E-mail: joan.saab@rochester.edu. *Application*

contact: Lorna Maier, Administrative Assistant, 585-275-9249, E-mail: lmaier@ ur.rochester.edu.
Website: http://www.rochester.edu/college/ppcm

University of South Carolina, The Graduate School, College of Arts and Sciences, Department of History, Program in Public History, Columbia, SC 29208. Offers archive management (MA); historic preservation (MA); museum administration (MA); museum management (Certificate); MLIS/MA. *Degree requirements:* For master's, one foreign language, thesis, internship. *Entrance requirements:* For master's, GRE General Test, writing sample. Additional exam requirements/recommendations for international students: Required—TOEFL. Electronic applications accepted. *Faculty research:* Museum studies, historic preservation, archives administration.

Wayne State University, School of Library and Information Science, Detroit, MI 48202. Offers archival administration (Graduate Certificate); information management (Graduate Certificate); library and information science (MLIS, Spec); public library services to children and young adults (Graduate Certificate); MLIS/MA. *Accreditation:* ALA (one or more programs are accredited). *Program availability:* Part-time, evening/ weekend, 100% online, blended/hybrid learning. *Faculty:* 11 full-time (7 women), 30 part-time/adjunct (20 women). *Students:* 90 full-time (69 women), 376 part-time (312 women); includes 74 minority (38 Black or African American, non-Hispanic/Latino; 2 American Indian or Alaska Native, non-Hispanic/Latino; 4 Asian, non-Hispanic/Latino; 17 Hispanic/Latino; 2 Native Hawaiian or other Pacific Islander, non-Hispanic/Latino; 11 Two or more races, non-Hispanic/Latino), 3 international. Average age 32. 265 applicants, 73% accepted, 120 enrolled. In 2016, 145 master's, 34 other advanced degrees awarded. *Degree requirements:* For master's and other advanced degree, e-portfolio. *Entrance requirements:* For master's, GRE or MAT (if undergraduate GPA is between 2.5 and 2.99), minimum undergraduate GPA of 3.0 or graduate degree, personal statement, resume or curriculum vitae; for other advanced degree, GRE or MAT (if undergraduate GPA is between 2.5 and 2.99), minimum undergraduate GPA of 3.0 or graduate degree, personal statement, resume or curriculum vitae, MLIS (for specialist certificate). Additional exam requirements/recommendations for international students: Required—TOEFL (minimum score 550 paper-based; 79 iBT); Recommended—IELTS (minimum score 6.5), TWE (minimum score 5.5). *Application deadline:* For fall admission, 7/1 for domestic students, 5/1 priority date for international students; for winter admission, 10/1 priority date for domestic students, 9/1 priority date for international students; for spring admission, 2/1 priority date for domestic students, 1/1 priority date for international students. Applications are processed on a rolling basis. Application fee: $50. Electronic applications accepted. *Expenses:* $18,871 per year resident tuition and fees, $36,065 per year non-resident tuition and fees. *Financial support:* In 2016–17, 107 students received support. Fellowships with tuition reimbursements available, scholarships/grants, health care benefits, and unspecified assistantships available. Support available to part-time students. Financial award applicants required to submit FAFSA. *Faculty research:* Library services, information management issues, digital content management, library/community engagement, archives and preservation. *Unit head:* Dr. Sandra Yee, Dean, 313-577-4059, E-mail: aj0533@wayne.edu. *Application contact:* Academic Services Officer II, 313-577-1825, E-mail: asklis@wayne.edu.
Website: http://slis.wayne.edu/

Information Studies

The Catholic University of America, School of Arts and Sciences, Department of Library and Information Science, Washington, DC 20064. Offers MSLS, Certificate, JD/ MSLS, MSLS/MA, MSLS/MS. *Accreditation:* ALA (one or more programs are accredited). *Program availability:* Part-time. *Faculty:* 7 full-time (6 women), 2 part-time/ adjunct (0 women). *Students:* 22 full-time (11 women), 59 part-time (48 women); includes 24 minority (14 Black or African American, non-Hispanic/Latino; 3 Asian, non-Hispanic/Latino; 3 Hispanic/Latino; 4 Two or more races, non-Hispanic/Latino), 4 international. Average age 32. 65 applicants, 91% accepted, 31 enrolled. In 2016, 43 master's awarded. *Degree requirements:* For master's, comprehensive exam. *Entrance requirements:* For master's, statement of purpose, official copies of academic transcripts, three letters of recommendation, interview. Additional exam requirements/ recommendations for international students: Required—TOEFL (minimum score 550 paper-based; 80 iBT). *Application deadline:* For fall admission, 7/15 priority date for domestic students, 7/1 for international students; for spring admission, 11/15 priority date for domestic students, 11/1 for international students. Applications are processed on a rolling basis. Application fee: $55. Electronic applications accepted. *Expenses:* $42,850 per year; $1,170 per credit; $200 per semester part-time fees. *Financial support:* Fellowships, research assistantships, teaching assistantships, Federal Work-Study, scholarships/grants, tuition waivers (full and partial), and unspecified assistantships available. Financial award application deadline: 2/1; financial award applicants required to submit FAFSA. *Faculty research:* Digital collections, library and information science education, information design and architecture, information system design and evaluation. *Unit head:* Dr. Youngok Choi, Chair, 202-319-5877, E-mail: choiy@cua.edu. *Application contact:* Director of Graduate Admissions, 202-319-5057, Fax: 202-319-6533, E-mail: cua-admissions@cua.edu.
Website: http://lis.cua.edu/

Central Connecticut State University, School of Graduate Studies, College of Liberal Arts and Social Sciences, Department of Design, New Britain, CT 06050-4010. Offers information design (MA). *Program availability:* Part-time, evening/weekend. *Faculty:* 2 full-time (1 woman), 1 (woman) part-time/adjunct. *Students:* 8 full-time (4 women), 4 part-time (all women); includes 2 minority (1 Black or African American, non-Hispanic/ Latino; 1 Asian, non-Hispanic/Latino). Average age 31. 11 applicants, 82% accepted, 5 enrolled. In 2016, 4 master's awarded. *Degree requirements:* For master's, thesis or alternative, research project. *Entrance requirements:* For master's, portfolio, minimum undergraduate GPA of 3.0, essay. Additional exam requirements/recommendations for international students: Required—TOEFL (minimum score 550 paper-based; 79 iBT). *Application deadline:* For fall admission, 6/1 for domestic students, 5/1 for international students; for spring admission, 11/1 for domestic and international students. Applications are processed on a rolling basis. Application fee: $50. Electronic applications accepted. *Expenses: Tuition, area resident:* Full-time $6497; part-time $606 per credit. Tuition, state resident: full-time $9748; part-time $622 per credit. Tuition, nonresident: full-time $18,102; part-time $622 per credit. *Required fees:* $4459; $246 per credit. *Financial support:* In 2016–17, 2 students received support. Career-related internships or fieldwork, Federal Work-Study, scholarships/grants, and unspecified assistantships available. Support available to part-time students. Financial award application deadline: 3/1; financial award applicants required to submit FAFSA. *Unit head:* Dr. Eleanor Thornton, Chair, 860-832-2564, E-mail: thorntone@ccsu.edu. *Application contact:* Patricia Gardner, Associate Director of Graduate Studies, 860-832-2350, Fax: 860-832-2362.
Website: http://www.design.ccsu.edu/

Columbia University, School of Continuing Education, Program in Information and Archive Management, New York, NY 10027. Offers MS. *Program availability:* Part-time. *Entrance requirements:* For master's, minimum undergraduate GPA of 3.0. Additional exam requirements/recommendations for international students: Required—American Language Program placement test. Electronic applications accepted. *Faculty research:* Library science technology, information systems.

Cornell University, Graduate School, Graduate Fields of Arts and Sciences, Field of Information Science, Ithaca, NY 14853. Offers cognition (PhD); human computer interaction (PhD); information science (PhD); information systems (PhD); social aspects of information (PhD). *Degree requirements:* For doctorate, comprehensive exam, thesis/ dissertation. *Entrance requirements:* For doctorate, GRE General Test, 3 letters of recommendation. Additional exam requirements/recommendations for international students: Required—TOEFL (minimum score 550 paper-based; 77 iBT). Electronic applications accepted. *Faculty research:* Digital libraries, game theory, data mining, human-computer interaction, computational linguistics.

Dalhousie University, Faculty of Management, School of Information Management, Halifax, NS B3H 3J5, Canada. Offers MIM, MLIS, LL B/MLIS, MBA/MLIS, MLIS/MPA, MLIS/MREM. *Accreditation:* ALA (one or more programs are accredited). *Program availability:* Part-time. *Degree requirements:* For master's, one foreign language, thesis optional. *Entrance requirements:* For master's, resume, interview. Additional exam requirements/recommendations for international students: Required—TOEFL, IELTS, CANTEST, CAEL, or Michigan English Language Assessment Battery. Electronic applications accepted. *Faculty research:* Information-seeking behavior, electronic text design, browsing in digital environments, information diffusion among scientists.

Dominican University, School of Information Studies, River Forest, IL 60305-1099. Offers information management (MSIM); knowledge management (Certificate); library and information science (MLIS, MPS, PhD); special studies (CSS); MBA/MLIS; MLIS/ MA. MLIS/M Div offered jointly with McCormick Theological Seminary, MLIS/MA with Loyola University Chicago, MLIS/MM with Northwestern University. *Accreditation:* ALA (one or more programs are accredited). *Program availability:* Part-time, evening/ weekend, 100% online, blended/hybrid learning. *Faculty:* 11 full-time (7 women), 8 part-time/adjunct (6 women). *Students:* 79 full-time (66 women), 170 part-time (133 women); includes 46 minority (21 Black or African American, non-Hispanic/Latino; 2 Asian, non-Hispanic/Latino; 20 Hispanic/Latino; 1 Native Hawaiian or other Pacific Islander, non-Hispanic/Latino; 2 Two or more races, non-Hispanic/Latino), 3 international. Average age 33. 121 applicants, 82% accepted, 74 enrolled. In 2016, 113 master's, 3 doctorates awarded. *Degree requirements:* For doctorate, thesis/dissertation. *Entrance requirements:* For master's, minimum GPA of 3.0, GRE General Test, or MAT; for doctorate, MLIS or related MA, minimum GPA of 3.0, GRE General Test, or MAT. Additional exam requirements/recommendations for international students: Required—TOEFL. *Application deadline:* For fall admission, 6/1 priority date for domestic students; for winter admission, 3/1 priority date for domestic students; for spring admission, 10/1 priority date for domestic students. Applications are processed on a rolling basis. Application fee: $25. *Expenses:* $830 per credit hour. *Financial support:* Fellowships, research assistantships, career-related internships or fieldwork, scholarships/grants, and unspecified assistantships available. Support available to part-time students. Financial award application deadline: 4/15; financial award applicants required to submit FAFSA. *Faculty research:* Productivity and the information environment, bibliometrics, library history, subject access, library materials and services for children. *Unit head:* Dr. Kate Marek, Dean and Professor, 708-524-6648, Fax: 708-524-6657, E-mail: kmarek@ dom.edu. *Application contact:* Catherine Galarza-Espino, Coordinator of Graduate Marketing and Recruiting, 708-524-6983, E-mail: cgalarza@dom.edu.
Website: http://sois.dom.edu/

Emporia State University, Program in Informatics, Emporia, KS 66801-5415. Offers nursing (MS). *Program availability:* Part-time, 100% online. *Faculty:* 9 full-time (6 women). *Students:* 6 part-time (5 women); includes 2 minority (both Black or African American, non-Hispanic/Latino). 5 applicants, 100% accepted. *Degree requirements:* For master's, practicum. *Entrance requirements:* Additional exam requirements/ recommendations for international students: Required—TOEFL. *Application deadline:* Applications are processed on a rolling basis. Application fee: $40. Electronic applications accepted. *Expenses:* Tuition, state resident: full-time $5922; part-time $246.75 per credit hour. Tuition, nonresident: full-time $18,414; part-time $767.25 per credit hour. *Required fees:* $1884; $78.50 per credit hour. *Unit head:* Dr. Mirah Dow, Interim Dean, 620-341-5203, E-mail: mdow@emporia.edu. *Application contact:* April Huddleston, Recruitment and Development Specialist, 800-950-GRAD, Fax: 620-341-5909, E-mail: ahuddles@emporia.edu.

Florida State University, The Graduate School, College of Communication and Information, School of Information, Tallahassee, FL 32306-2100. Offers information (MA, MS, PhD, Specialist); information studies (MA, MS, PhD, Specialist); information technology (MS). *Accreditation:* ALA (one or more programs are accredited). *Program availability:* Part-time, evening/weekend, 100% online, blended/hybrid learning. *Faculty:* 27 full-time (13 women), 8 part-time/adjunct (5 women). *Students:* 74 full-time (51 women), 244 part-time (182 women); includes 89 minority (30 Black or African American, non-Hispanic/Latino; 10 Asian, non-Hispanic/Latino; 44 Hispanic/Latino; 5 Two or more races, non-Hispanic/Latino), 10 international. Average age 35. 183 applicants, 70% accepted, 97 enrolled. In 2016, 132 master's, 12 doctorates, 1 other advanced degree awarded. Terminal master's awarded for partial completion of doctoral program. *Degree requirements:* For master's, thesis optional, minimum GPA of 3.0, 36 hours (MSI); 32 hours (MSIT); for doctorate, comprehensive exam, thesis/dissertation, dissertation defense, manuscript clearance, minimum GPA of 3.0; for Specialist, minimum GPA of 3.0; 30 hours. *Entrance requirements:* For master's, GRE (recommended minimum percentile of 50 on each of the verbal and quantitative portions and writing score of 4.0), minimum GPA of 3.0 on last 2 years of baccalaureate degree, resume, statement of goals, two letters of recommendation, official transcripts from every college-level institution attended; for doctorate, GRE (recommended minimum percentile of 50 on each of the verbal and quantitative portions and writing score of 4.0), minimum GPA of 3.0 on last degree program, resume, 3 letters of recommendation, personal/goals statement, writing sample, brief digital video, official transcripts from all

college-level institutions attended; for Specialist, GRE (recommended minimum percentile of 50 on each of the verbal and quantitative portions and writing score of 4.0), minimum graduate GPA of 3.2, resume, statement of goals, 2 letters of recommendation, writing sample, official transcripts from every college-level institution attended. Additional exam requirements/recommendations for international students: Required—TOEFL (minimum score 585 paper-based; 94 iBT), IELTS (minimum score 6.5). *Application deadline:* For fall admission, 7/1 for domestic and international students; for spring admission, 11/1 for domestic and international students. Applications are processed on a rolling basis. Application fee: $30. Electronic applications accepted. *Expenses:* Contact institution. *Financial support:* In 2016–17, 192 students received support, including 1 research assistantship with full tuition reimbursement available (averaging $18,578 per year), 18 teaching assistantships with full tuition reimbursements available (averaging $18,578 per year); career-related internships or fieldwork, Federal Work-Study, health care benefits, tuition waivers (full), and 13 assistantships (averaging $17,200); 26 scholarships (averaging $1000) also available. Financial award application deadline: 3/1; financial award applicants required to submit FAFSA. *Faculty research:* Information technology, social informatics, health information, human information behavior, youth services. *Total annual research expenditures:* $3.8 million. *Unit head:* Dr. Lorri Mon, Director/Associate Professor, 850-644-5776, Fax: 850-644-9763, E-mail: lmon@fsu.edu. *Application contact:* Student Services, 850-645-3280, Fax: 850-644-9763, E-mail: ischooladvising@admin.fsu.edu.
Website: http://ischool.cci.fsu.edu

Lock Haven University of Pennsylvania, The Stephen Poorman College of Business, Information Systems, and Human Services, Lock Haven, PA 17745-2390. Offers clinical mental health counseling (MS); sport science (MS). *Program availability:* Online learning. *Degree requirements:* For master's, thesis. *Entrance requirements:* For master's, minimum undergraduate GPA of 3.0. Additional exam requirements/recommendations for international students: Required—TOEFL. Electronic applications accepted.

Louisiana State University and Agricultural & Mechanical College, Graduate School, College of Human Sciences and Education, School of Library and Information Science, Baton Rouge, LA 70803. Offers MLIS. *Accreditation:* ALA.

Loyola University Chicago, Quinlan School of Business, Department of Information Systems and Supply Chain Management, Chicago, IL 60611. Offers data warehousing (Certificate); information systems and supply chain management (MSSCM). *Program availability:* Part-time, evening/weekend. *Faculty:* 12 full-time (1 woman), 8 part-time/adjunct (4 women). *Students:* 9 full-time (3 women), 9 part-time (2 women); includes 3 minority (1 Black or African American, non-Hispanic/Latino; 2 Asian, non-Hispanic/Latino), 5 international. Average age 31. 50 applicants, 30% accepted, 7 enrolled. In 2016, 9 master's, 28 Certificates awarded. *Entrance requirements:* For master's, GMAT or GRE, official transcripts, two letters of recommendation, statement of purpose, resume. Additional exam requirements/recommendations for international students: Required—TOEFL (minimum score 90 iBT) or IELTS (minimum score 6.5). *Application deadline:* For fall admission, 7/15 for domestic and international students; for winter admission, 10/1 for domestic and international students; for spring admission, 1/15 for domestic students, 1/14 for international students; for summer admission, 4/1 for domestic and international students. Applications are processed on a rolling basis. Application fee: $50. Electronic applications accepted. Application fee is waived when completed online. *Expenses:* Contact institution. *Financial support:* In 2016–17, 11 students received support. Federal Work-Study, scholarships/grants, health care benefits, and unspecified assistantships available. Support available to part-time students. *Faculty research:* Consistent vehicle routing policies, logistics, operations management. *Unit head:* Dr. Mary Malliaris, Chair, 312-915-7064, E-mail: mmallia@luc.edu. *Application contact:* Lauren Griffin, Enrollment Advisor, Quinlan School of Business Graduate Programs, 312-915-6124, Fax: 312-915-7202,
E-mail: lgriffin3@luc.edu.
Website: http://www.luc.edu/quinlan/mba/supply-chain-management-degrees/index.shtml

Mansfield University of Pennsylvania, Graduate Studies, Program in School Library and Information Technologies, Mansfield, PA 16933. Offers library science (M Ed). *Program availability:* Part-time, evening/weekend, online learning. *Degree requirements:* For master's, comprehensive exam, thesis optional. *Entrance requirements:* For master's, minimum GPA of 3.0. Additional exam requirements/recommendations for international students: Required—TOEFL (minimum score 550 paper-based). Electronic applications accepted. *Expenses:* Contact institution.

McGill University, Faculty of Graduate and Postdoctoral Studies, Faculty of Education, School of Information Studies, Montréal, QC H3A 2T5, Canada. Offers MLIS, PhD, Certificate, Diploma. *Accreditation:* ALA (one or more programs are accredited).

Metropolitan State University, College of Management, St. Paul, MN 55106-5000. Offers business administration (MBA, DBA); database administration (Graduate Certificate); healthcare information technology management (Graduate Certificate); information assurance security (Graduate Certificate); management information systems (MMIS); MIS generalist (Graduate Certificate); MIS systems analysis and design (Graduate Certificate); project management (Graduate Certificate); public and nonprofit administration (MPNA). *Program availability:* Part-time, evening/weekend. *Degree requirements:* For master's, thesis optional, computer language (MMIS). *Entrance requirements:* For master's, GMAT (for MBA), resume. Additional exam requirements/recommendations for international students: Required—TOEFL (minimum score 550 paper-based). Electronic applications accepted. *Faculty research:* Yugoslav economic system, workers' cooperatives, participative management and job enrichment, global business systems.

Missouri Western State University, Program in Information Management, St. Joseph, MO 64507-2294. Offers enterprise resource planning (MIM). *Program availability:* Part-time. *Students:* 21 full-time (8 women), 18 part-time (9 women); includes 3 minority (1 Black or African American, non-Hispanic/Latino; 1 Asian, non-Hispanic/Latino; 1 Two or more races, non-Hispanic/Latino), 25 international. Average age 30. 10 applicants, 80% accepted, 5 enrolled. In 2016, 2 master's awarded. *Entrance requirements:* Additional exam requirements/recommendations for international students: Recommended—TOEFL (minimum score 79 iBT), IELTS (minimum score 6). *Application deadline:* For fall admission, 7/15 for domestic and international students; for spring admission, 10/1 for domestic and international students; for summer admission, 3/15 for domestic students. Applications are processed on a rolling basis. Application fee: $50. Electronic applications accepted. *Expenses:* Tuition, state resident: full-time $6548; part-time $327.39 per credit hour. Tuition, nonresident: full-time $11,848; part-time $592.39 per credit hour. *Required fees:* $542; $99 per credit hour. $176 per semester. One-time fee: $50. Tuition and fees vary according to course load and program. *Financial support:* Scholarships/grants and unspecified assistantships available. Support available to part-time students. *Unit head:* Dr. Peggy Lane, Professor, 816-271-5832, E-mail: plane3@missouriwestern.edu. *Application contact:* Dr. Benjamin D. Caldwell, Dean of the Graduate School, 816-271-4394, Fax: 816-271-4525, E-mail: graduate@missouriwestern.edu.
Website: https://www.missouriwestern.edu/mim/

Neumann University, Graduate Programs in Business and Information Management, Aston, PA 19014-1298. Offers accounting (MS), including forensic and fraud detection; sport business (MS). *Program availability:* Part-time, evening/weekend. *Faculty:* 3 full-time (2 women), 4 part-time/adjunct (1 woman). *Students:* 9 full-time (2 women), 33 part-time (12 women); includes 14 minority (11 Black or African American, non-Hispanic/Latino; 1 Asian, non-Hispanic/Latino; 2 Hispanic/Latino). Average age 31. 58 applicants, 50% accepted, 26 enrolled. In 2016, 16 master's awarded. *Degree requirements:* For master's, thesis (for some programs). *Entrance requirements:* For master's, official transcripts from all institutions attended, resume, letter of intent, 2-3 official letters of recommendation. Additional exam requirements/recommendations for international students: Required—TOEFL (minimum score 70 iBT). *Application deadline:* Applications are processed on a rolling basis. Application fee: $0. Electronic applications accepted. *Expenses:* $600 per credit (for MS in accounting); $495 per credit (MS in sport business). *Financial support:* Scholarships/grants and health care benefits available. Support available to part-time students. Financial award application deadline: 3/15; financial award applicants required to submit FAFSA. *Unit head:* Dr. Eric Wellington, Dean of Business and Information Management, 610-558-5596, Fax: 610-558-5574, E-mail: wellinge@neumann.edu. *Application contact:* Dr. Erika Davis, Director of Adult and Graduate Admissions, 800-9-NEUMANN Ext. 5208, Fax: 610-361-2548, E-mail: GradAdultAdmiss@neumann.edu.

North Carolina Central University, School of Library and Information Sciences, Durham, NC 27707-3129. Offers MIS, MLS. *Accreditation:* ALA (one or more programs are accredited). *Program availability:* Part-time, evening/weekend. *Degree requirements:* For master's, one foreign language, thesis, research paper, or project. *Entrance requirements:* For master's, GRE, 90 hours in liberal arts. Additional exam requirements/recommendations for international students: Required—TOEFL.

Pratt Institute, School of Information, New York, NY 10011. Offers MS, Adv C, JD/MS, MS/MFA. *Accreditation:* ALA. *Program availability:* Part-time. *Faculty:* 9 full-time (4 women), 26 part-time/adjunct (13 women). *Students:* 95 full-time (77 women), 62 part-time (50 women); includes 43 minority (11 Black or African American, non-Hispanic/Latino; 12 Asian, non-Hispanic/Latino; 17 Hispanic/Latino; 3 Two or more races, non-Hispanic/Latino), 11 international. Average age 31. 129 applicants, 88% accepted, 59 enrolled. In 2016, 64 master's, 1 other advanced degree awarded. *Degree requirements:* For master's, thesis. *Entrance requirements:* For degree, master's degree in library and information science. Additional exam requirements/recommendations for international students: Required—TOEFL (minimum score 600 paper-based; 100 iBT). *Application deadline:* For fall admission, 1/5 for domestic and international students; for spring admission, 10/1 for domestic and international students. Applications are processed on a rolling basis. Application fee: $50 ($90 for international students). Electronic applications accepted. *Expenses:* $23,814 full-time tuition, $1,938 fees. *Financial support:* Career-related internships or fieldwork, Federal Work-Study, institutionally sponsored loans, scholarships/grants, health care benefits, and unspecified assistantships available. Support available to part-time students. Financial award application deadline: 2/1; financial award applicants required to submit FAFSA. *Faculty research:* Development of urban libraries and information centers, medical and law librarianship, information management. *Unit head:* Dr. Tula Giannini, Dean, 212-647-7682, Fax: 212-367-2492, E-mail: giannini@pratt.edu. *Application contact:* Natalie Capannelli, Director of Graduate Admissions, 718-636-3551, Fax: 718-399-4242, E-mail: ncapanne@pratt.edu.
Website: https://www.pratt.edu/academics/information/

See Display on next page and Close-Up on page 1563.

Queens College of the City University of New York, Division of Social Sciences, Graduate School of Library and Information Studies, Queens, NY 11367-1597. Offers archives, records management and preservation (AC); children's and young adult services in the public library (AC); library media specialist (MLS, AC); library science (MLS, AC); school media specialist (MLS). *Accreditation:* ALA (one or more programs are accredited). *Program availability:* Part-time, evening/weekend. *Faculty:* 12 full-time (7 women), 15 part-time/adjunct (11 women). *Students:* 28 full-time (22 women), 230 part-time (153 women); includes 106 minority (35 Black or African American, non-Hispanic/Latino; 21 Asian, non-Hispanic/Latino; 38 Hispanic/Latino; 12 Two or more races, non-Hispanic/Latino), 5 international. Average age 33. 163 applicants, 82% accepted, 92 enrolled. In 2016, 74 master's, 4 other advanced degrees awarded. *Degree requirements:* For master's, thesis; for AC, thesis optional. *Entrance requirements:* For master's, minimum GPA of 3.0; for AC, master's degree or equivalent. Additional exam requirements/recommendations for international students: Required—TOEFL, IELTS. *Application deadline:* For fall admission, 4/1 for domestic students; for spring admission, 11/1 for domestic students. Applications are processed on a rolling basis. Application fee: $125. Electronic applications accepted. *Expenses:* Tuition, state resident: full-time $5065; part-time $425 per credit. Tuition, nonresident: part-time $780 per credit. *Required fees:* $522; $397 per credit. Part-time tuition and fees vary according to course load and program. *Financial support:* Career-related internships or fieldwork and unspecified assistantships available. Financial award application deadline: 4/1; financial award applicants required to submit FAFSA. *Unit head:* Dr. Roberta Brody, Director/Chair, 718-997-3790, E-mail: roberta.brody@qc.cuny.edu.

Queen's University at Kingston, School of Graduate Studies, Faculty of Arts and Sciences, Department of Sociology, Kingston, ON K7L 3N6, Canada. Offers communication and information technology (MA, PhD); feminist sociology (MA, PhD); socio-legal studies (MA, PhD); sociological theory (MA, PhD). *Program availability:* Part-time. *Degree requirements:* For master's, thesis; for doctorate, comprehensive exam, thesis/dissertation. *Entrance requirements:* For master's, honors bachelors degree in sociology; for doctorate, honors bachelors degree, masters degree in sociology. Additional exam requirements/recommendations for international students: Required—TOEFL. *Faculty research:* Social change and modernization, social control, deviance and criminology, surveillance.

Rutgers University–New Brunswick, School of Communication and Information, Program in Communication and Information Studies, Piscataway, NJ 08854-8097. Offers MCIS. *Program availability:* Part-time. *Entrance requirements:* For master's, GRE General Test. Additional exam requirements/recommendations for international students: Required—TOEFL. Electronic applications accepted. *Faculty research:* Communication processes and systems, information process and systems, human information and communication behavior.

Rutgers University–New Brunswick, School of Communication and Information, Program in Communication, Information and Library Studies, Piscataway, NJ 08854-8097. Offers PhD. *Program availability:* Part-time. *Degree requirements:* For doctorate, comprehensive exam, thesis/dissertation, qualifying exams. *Entrance requirements:* For doctorate, GRE General Test, proficiency in statistics. Additional exam requirements/recommendations for international students: Required—TOEFL (minimum score 600 paper-based). Electronic applications accepted. *Faculty research:* Information science, media studies.

St. Catherine University, Graduate Programs, Program in Library and Information Science, St. Paul, MN 55105. Offers MLIS. *Accreditation:* ALA. *Program availability:*

Part-time, evening/weekend. *Degree requirements:* For master's, microcomputer competency. *Entrance requirements:* For master's, GRE or MAT, minimum GPA of 3.2 or GRE. Additional exam requirements/recommendations for international students: Required—Michigan English Language Assessment Battery or TOEFL (minimum score 600 paper-based; 100 iBT). *Expenses:* Contact institution.

St. John's University, St. John's College of Liberal Arts and Sciences, Division of Library and Information Science, Queens, NY 11439. Offers MS, Adv C, MA/MS, MS/MS. *Accreditation:* ALA (one or more programs are accredited). *Program availability:* Part-time, evening/weekend, online learning. *Degree requirements:* For master's, comprehensive exam, portfolio. *Entrance requirements:* For master's, interview, minimum GPA of 3.0, 2 letters of recommendation, bachelor's degree, personal statement, transcript. Additional exam requirements/recommendations for international students: Required—TOEFL (minimum score 600 paper-based; 100 iBT), IELTS (minimum score 7). Electronic applications accepted. *Expenses:* Contact institution. *Faculty research:* Indexes and metatags, information use and users, competitive intelligence, knowledge management, database theory, young adult and children services, school media services, archives, oral history.

Southern Connecticut State University, School of Graduate Studies, School of Education, Department of Information and Library Science, New Haven, CT 06515-1355. Offers information studies (Diploma); library science (MLS). *Program availability:* Part-time, evening/weekend. *Faculty:* 4 full-time (2 women). *Students:* 2 full-time (1 woman), 8 part-time (7 women). Average age 39. 27 applicants, 52% accepted, 12 enrolled. In 2016, 30 master's, 1 other advanced degree awarded. *Degree requirements:* For master's and Diploma, thesis or alternative. *Entrance requirements:* For master's, GRE General Test, interview, minimum QPA of 2.7, introductory computer science course; for Diploma, master's degree in library science or information science. *Application deadline:* For fall admission, 7/15 priority date for domestic students. Applications are processed on a rolling basis. Application fee: $50. Electronic applications accepted. *Expenses:* Tuition, state resident: full-time $6497; part-time $519 per credit hour. Tuition, nonresident: full-time $18,102; part-time $535 per credit hour. *Required fees:* $4722; $55 per semester. Tuition and fees vary according to program. *Financial support:* Career-related internships or fieldwork, scholarships/grants, and unspecified assistantships available. Financial award application deadline: 4/15; financial award applicants required to submit FAFSA. *Unit head:* Dr. Hak Joon Kim, Chairperson, 203-392-5703, Fax: 203-392-5780, E-mail: kimh1@southernct.edu. *Application contact:* Lisa Galvin, Director of Graduate Admissions, 203-392-5240, Fax: 203-392-5235, E-mail: galvinl1@southernct.edu.

Syracuse University, School of Information Studies, MS Program in Information Management, Syracuse, NY 13244. Offers MS. *Program availability:* Part-time, evening/weekend, online learning. *Entrance requirements:* For master's, GRE General Test, personal statement, two letters of recommendation, resume. Additional exam requirements/recommendations for international students: Required—TOEFL (minimum score 100 iBT). *Application deadline:* For fall admission, 2/1 priority date for domestic and international students; for spring admission, 10/15 priority date for domestic and international students. Applications are processed on a rolling basis. Application fee: $75. Electronic applications accepted. *Expenses: Tuition:* Full-time $25,974; part-time $1443 per credit hour. *Required fees:* $802; $50 per course. Tuition and fees vary according to course load and program. *Financial support:* Fellowships with full tuition reimbursements, research assistantships with partial tuition reimbursements, teaching assistantships with partial tuition reimbursements, and scholarships/grants available. Financial award application deadline: 1/1; financial award applicants required to submit FAFSA. *Faculty research:* Increasing the effectiveness of managers and executives who work with information resources, designing and managing mission-critical information technologies within organizations, developing corporate and government policies to maximize the benefits resulting from the widespread use of these technologies. *Unit head:* Carsten Oesterlund, Program Director, 315-443-2911, Fax: 315-443-6886, E-mail: igrad@syr.edu. *Application contact:* Susan Corieri, Director of Enrollment Management, 315-443-2575, E-mail: ischool@syr.edu.
Website: http://ischool.syr.edu/

Universidad del Turabo, Graduate Programs, Programs in Education, Program in Library Service and Information Technology, Gurabo, PR 00778-3030. Offers M Ed. *Program availability:* Part-time, evening/weekend. *Students:* 1 part-time (0 women); minority (Hispanic/Latino). Average age 60. 1 applicant, 100% accepted, 1 enrolled. In 2016, 3 master's awarded. *Entrance requirements:* For master's, GRE, EXADEP, GMAT, interview, official transcript, essay, recommendation letters. *Application deadline:* Applications are processed on a rolling basis. Application fee: $25. Electronic applications accepted. *Financial support:* Institutionally sponsored loans available. Financial award applicants required to submit FAFSA. *Unit head:* Israel Rodríguez, Dean, 787-743-7979 Ext. 4627. *Application contact:* Diriee Rodríguez, Admissions Director, 787-743-7979 Ext. 4453, E-mail: admisiones-ut@suagm.edu.
Website: http://ut.suagm.edu/es/educacion

Université de Montréal, Faculty of Arts and Sciences, School of Library and Information Sciences, Montréal, QC H3C 3J7, Canada. Offers information sciences (MIS, PhD). *Accreditation:* ALA (one or more programs are accredited). *Degree requirements:* For master's, thesis optional. *Entrance requirements:* For master's, interview, master's degree in library and information science or equivalent. Electronic applications accepted.

University at Albany, State University of New York, College of Engineering and Applied Sciences, MS Program in Information Science, Albany, NY 12222-0001. Offers information science (MS); library and information science (CAS). *Faculty:* 8 full-time (5 women), 6 part-time/adjunct (3 women). *Students:* 50 full-time (30 women), 41 part-time (32 women); includes 17 minority (8 Black or African American, non-Hispanic/Latino; 2 Asian, non-Hispanic/Latino; 6 Hispanic/Latino; 1 Two or more races, non-Hispanic/Latino), 5 international. Average age 33. 90 applicants, 61% accepted, 23 enrolled. In 2016, 54 master's awarded. Application fee: $75. *Expenses:* Tuition, state resident: full-time $10,870; part-time $453 per credit hour. Tuition, nonresident: full-time $22,210; part-time $925 per credit hour. *International tuition:* $21,550 full time. *Required fees:* $1004; $90 per credit hour. *Financial support:* Research assistantships and teaching assistantships available. Financial award applicants required to submit FAFSA. *Faculty research:* Electronic information across technologies system dynamics modeling archives, records administration. *Total annual research expenditures:* $357,256. *Unit head:* Philip B. Eppard, Chair, 518-442-5119, E-mail: peppard@albany.edu.
Website: http://www.albany.edu/informationstudies/

University at Buffalo, the State University of New York, Graduate School, Graduate School of Education, Department of Library and Information Studies, Buffalo, NY 14260. Offers information and library science (MS); library and information studies (Certificate); school librarianship (MS). *Accreditation:* ALA (one or more programs are accredited). *Program availability:* Part-time, 100% online. *Faculty:* 10 full-time (6 women), 9 part-time/adjunct (6 women). *Students:* 35 full-time (28 women), 144 part-time (112 women); includes 9 minority (4 Black or African American, non-Hispanic/Latino; 1 American Indian or Alaska Native, non-Hispanic/Latino; 4 Asian, non-Hispanic/Latino), 6 international. Average age 33. 93 applicants, 91% accepted, 63 enrolled. In 2016, 81 master's awarded. *Degree requirements:* For master's, thesis optional; for Certificate,

thesis. *Entrance requirements:* For master's, letters of recommendation. Additional exam requirements/recommendations for international students: Required—TOEFL (minimum score 550 paper-based; 79 iBT). *Application deadline:* For fall admission, 4/1 priority date for domestic and international students; for spring admission, 10/15 priority date for domestic students, 10/15 for international students. Applications are processed on a rolling basis. Application fee: $50. Electronic applications accepted. *Financial support:* In 2016–17, 19 fellowships (averaging $2,816 per year), 6 research assistantships with tuition reimbursements (averaging $10,128 per year) were awarded; teaching assistantships, Federal Work-Study, scholarships/grants, tuition waivers (full and partial), and unspecified assistantships also available. Support available to part-time students. Financial award application deadline: 3/1; financial award applicants required to submit FAFSA. *Faculty research:* Information-seeking behavior, thesauri, impact of technology, questioning behaviors, educational informatics. *Total annual research expenditures:* $91,973. *Unit head:* Dr. Heidi Julien, Chair, 716-645-1474, Fax: 716-645-3775, E-mail: heidijul@buffalo.edu. *Application contact:* Pat Glinski, Admissions Assistant, 716-645-2110, Fax: 716-645-7937, E-mail: gse-info@buffalo.edu.
Website: http://www.gse.buffalo.edu/lis/

The University of Alabama, Graduate School, College of Communication and Information Sciences, School of Library and Information Studies, Tuscaloosa, AL 35487. Offers book arts (MFA); library and information studies (MLIS, PhD). *Accreditation:* ALA (one or more programs are accredited). *Program availability:* Part-time, evening/weekend, online learning. *Faculty:* 10 full-time (5 women), 1 (woman) part-time/adjunct. *Students:* 46 full-time (31 women), 154 part-time (128 women); includes 27 minority (15 Black or African American, non-Hispanic/Latino; 2 Asian, non-Hispanic/Latino; 5 Hispanic/Latino; 5 Two or more races, non-Hispanic/Latino), 3 international. Average age 34. 126 applicants, 75% accepted, 83 enrolled. In 2016, 98 master's awarded. *Degree requirements:* For master's, comprehensive exam (for some programs), thesis optional; for doctorate, comprehensive exam, thesis/dissertation. *Entrance requirements:* For master's, GRE General Test or MAT, minimum GPA of 3.0; for doctorate, GRE. Additional exam requirements/recommendations for international students: Required—TOEFL. *Application deadline:* For fall admission, 7/1 priority date for domestic and international students; for spring admission, 11/1 priority date for domestic and international students. Applications are processed on a rolling basis. Application fee: $50 ($60 for international students). Electronic applications accepted. *Expenses:* Tuition, state resident: full-time $10,470. Tuition, nonresident: full-time $26,950. *Financial support:* In 2016–17, 64 students received support, including 3 fellowships with full tuition reimbursements available (averaging $15,000 per year), 18 research assistantships with tuition reimbursements available (averaging $6,183 per year), 12 teaching assistantships with tuition reimbursements available (averaging $6,183 per year); career-related internships or fieldwork, scholarships/grants, health care benefits, tuition waivers (full), unspecified assistantships, and 15 grant-funded fellowships also available. Support available to part-time students. Financial award application deadline: 3/15. *Faculty research:* Library administration, user services, digital libraries, book arts, evaluation. *Unit head:* Dr. Ann Ethelynd Prentice, Director and Professor, 205-348-4610, Fax: 205-348-3746, E-mail: aeprentice@ua.edu. *Application contact:* Dr. Ann Bourne, Assistant Director, 205-348-1524, Fax: 205-348-3746, E-mail: abourne@ua.edu.
Website: http://www.slis.ua.edu/

University of Alberta, Faculty of Graduate Studies and Research, School of Library and Information Studies, Edmonton, AB T6G 2E1, Canada. Offers MLIS. *Accreditation:* ALA. *Entrance requirements:* Additional exam requirements/recommendations for international students: Required—TOEFL, Canadian Academic English Language Assessment. Electronic applications accepted. *Faculty research:* Intellectual freedom, materials for children and young adults, library classification, multi-media literacy.

The University of Arizona, College of Social and Behavioral Sciences, School of Information Resources and Library Science, Tucson, AZ 85721. Offers MA, PhD. *Accreditation:* ALA (one or more programs are accredited). *Program availability:* Part-time. *Degree requirements:* For master's, proficiency in disk operating system (DOS); for doctorate, thesis/dissertation. *Entrance requirements:* For master's and doctorate, GRE General Test, 3 letters of recommendation, resume. Additional exam requirements/recommendations for international students: Required—TOEFL (minimum score 550 paper-based; 79 iBT). Electronic applications accepted. *Faculty research:* Microcomputer applications; quantitative methods systems; information transfer, planning, evaluation, and technology.

The University of British Columbia, Faculty of Arts, School of Library, Archival and Information Studies, Dual Master of Archival Studies/Master of Library and Information Studies Program, Vancouver, BC V6T 1Z1, Canada. Offers MLIS/MAS. *Entrance requirements:* Additional exam requirements/recommendations for international students: Required—TOEFL. *Application deadline:* Applications are processed on a rolling basis. Application fee: $100 Canadian dollars ($162 Canadian dollars for international students). Electronic applications accepted. *Expenses:* $4,911 per year tuition and fees, $8,774 per year international. *Financial support:* Fellowships, research assistantships, Federal Work-Study, institutionally sponsored loans, scholarships/grants, health care benefits, tuition waivers (partial), and unspecified assistantships available. *Faculty research:* Computer systems/database design, information-seeking behavior, archives and records management, children's literature and services, digital libraries and archives. *Application contact:* Alynne Pols, Graduate Program Staff, 604-822-3459, Fax: 604-822-6006, E-mail: ischool.program@ubc.ca.
Website: http://slais.ubc.ca/

The University of British Columbia, Faculty of Arts, School of Library, Archival and Information Studies, Master of Library and Information Studies Program, Vancouver, BC V6T 1Z1, Canada. Offers MLIS. *Accreditation:* ALA. *Program availability:* Part-time. *Degree requirements:* For master's, thesis optional. *Entrance requirements:* For master's, minimum GPA of 3.3 in undergraduate upper-division courses. Additional exam requirements/recommendations for international students: Required—TOEFL. Application fee: $100 ($162 for international students). Electronic applications accepted. *Expenses:* $4,911 per year tuition and fees, $8,774 per year international. *Financial support:* Fellowships, research assistantships, career-related internships or fieldwork, Federal Work-Study, institutionally sponsored loans, scholarships/grants, health care benefits, tuition waivers, and unspecified assistantships available. *Faculty research:* Computer systems/database design; digital libraries; metadata/classification; human-computer interaction; children's literature and services. *Application contact:* Alynne Pols, Graduate Program Staff, 604-822-3459, Fax: 604-822-6006, E-mail: ischool.program@ubc.ca.
Website: http://slais.ubc.ca/

The University of British Columbia, Faculty of Arts, School of Library, Archival and Information Studies, PhD Program in Library, Archival and Information Studies, Vancouver, BC V6T 1Z1, Canada. Offers PhD. *Degree requirements:* For doctorate, thesis/dissertation. *Entrance requirements:* For doctorate, GRE, minimum GPA of 3.3 in MAS or MLIS. Additional exam requirements/recommendations for international students: Required—TOEFL. Application fee: $100 Canadian dollars ($162 Canadian dollars for international students). Electronic applications accepted. *Expenses:* $4,802 per year tuition and fees, $8,436 per year international. *Financial support:* Fellowships, research assistantships, teaching assistantships, Federal Work-Study, institutionally sponsored loans, scholarships/grants, health care benefits, tuition waivers (partial), and unspecified assistantships available. *Faculty research:* Computer systems/database design; library and archival management; archival description and organization; children's literature and youth services; interactive information retrieval. *Application contact:* Alynne Pols, Graduate Program Staff, 604-822-3459, Fax: 604-822-6006, E-mail: ischool.program@ubc.ca.
Website: http://slais.ubc.ca/

University of California, Berkeley, Graduate Division, School of Information, Berkeley, CA 94720-1500. Offers MIDS, MIMS, PhD. *Students:* 448 full-time (141 women); includes 117 minority (2 Black or African American, non-Hispanic/Latino; 1 American Indian or Alaska Native, non-Hispanic/Latino; 99 Asian, non-Hispanic/Latino; 15 Hispanic/Latino), 133 international. Average age 31. 1,434 applicants, 227 enrolled. In 2016, 146 master's, 1 doctorate awarded. *Degree requirements:* For doctorate, thesis/dissertation, qualifying exam. *Entrance requirements:* For master's, GRE General Test, minimum GPA of 3.0, previous course work in java or C programming, 3 letters of recommendation; for doctorate, GRE General Test, minimum GPA of 3.0. Additional exam requirements/recommendations for international students: Required—TOEFL. *Application deadline:* For fall admission, 12/1 for domestic students. Application fee: $105 ($125 for international students). Electronic applications accepted. *Financial support:* Fellowships, research assistantships, teaching assistantships, institutionally sponsored loans, health care benefits, and unspecified assistantships available. *Faculty research:* Information retrieval research, design and evaluation of information systems, work practice-based design of information systems, economics of information, intellectual property law. *Unit head:* Prof. AnnaLee Saxenian, Dean, 510-642-1464, E-mail: admissions@ischool.berkeley.edu. *Application contact:* 510-642-1464, Fax: 510-642-5814, E-mail: admissions@ischool.berkeley.edu.
Website: http://www.ischool.berkeley.edu/

University of California, Los Angeles, Graduate Division, Graduate School of Education and Information Studies, Department of Information Studies, Los Angeles, CA 90095-1521. Offers archival studies (MLIS); informatics (MLIS); information studies (PhD); library and information science (Certificate); library studies (MLIS); moving image archive studies (MA); rare books, print and visual culture (MLIS); MBA/MLIS; MLIS/MA. *Accreditation:* ALA (one or more programs are accredited). Terminal master's awarded for partial completion of doctoral program. *Degree requirements:* For master's, thesis or alternative, professional portfolio; for doctorate, thesis/dissertation, oral and written qualifying exams. *Entrance requirements:* For master's, GRE General Test, previous course work in statistics; for doctorate, GRE General Test, previous course work in statistics, 2 samples of research writing in English. Additional exam requirements/recommendations for international students: Required—TOEFL (minimum score 560 paper-based; 87 iBT), IELTS (minimum score 7). Electronic applications accepted. *Faculty research:* Digital libraries, archives and electronic records, interface design, cultural informatics, preservation/conservation, access.

University of Hawaii at Manoa, Graduate Division, College of Natural Sciences, Department of Information and Computer Sciences, Library and Information Science Program, Honolulu, HI 96822-2233. Offers advanced library and information science (Graduate Certificate); library and information science (MLI Sc). *Accreditation:* ALA (one or more programs are accredited). *Program availability:* Part-time. *Degree requirements:* For master's, comprehensive exam, thesis optional. *Entrance requirements:* For master's, GRE General Test. Additional exam requirements/recommendations for international students: Required—TOEFL (minimum score 600 paper-based). Electronic applications accepted. *Faculty research:* Information behavior, evaluation of electronic information sources, online learning, history of libraries, information literacy.

University of Illinois at Urbana–Champaign, Graduate College, School of Information Sciences, Champaign, IL 61820. Offers bioinformatics (MS); digital libraries (CAS); information management (MS); library and information science (MS, PhD, CAS). *Accreditation:* ALA (one or more programs are accredited). *Program availability:* Part-time, online learning. *Entrance requirements:* For degree, master's degree in library and information science or related field with minimum GPA of 3.0.

The University of Iowa, Graduate College, School of Library and Information Science, Iowa City, IA 52242-1316. Offers MA, PhD, MA/Certificate, PhD/Certificate. *Accreditation:* ALA (one or more programs are accredited). *Degree requirements:* For master's, thesis optional, exam, portfolio. *Entrance requirements:* For master's, GRE General Test, minimum GPA of 3.0. Additional exam requirements/recommendations for international students: Required—TOEFL (minimum score 550 paper-based; 81 iBT). Electronic applications accepted.

University of Maryland, College Park, Academic Affairs, College of Information Studies, College Park, MD 20742. Offers MIM, MLS, PhD, MA/MLS. *Accreditation:* ALA (one or more programs are accredited). *Program availability:* Part-time, evening/weekend. Terminal master's awarded for partial completion of doctoral program. *Degree requirements:* For master's, thesis optional; for doctorate, comprehensive exam, thesis/dissertation, 1-year residency. *Entrance requirements:* For master's and doctorate, GRE General Test, minimum GPA of 3.0, 3 letters of recommendation. Additional exam requirements/recommendations for international students: Required—TOEFL. Electronic applications accepted.

University of Michigan, Rackham Graduate School, School of Information, Ann Arbor, MI 48109-1285. Offers health informatics (MHI); information (MSI, PhD). *Accreditation:* ALA (one or more programs are accredited). *Program availability:* Part-time. *Students:* 453 full-time (270 women), 32 part-time (20 women); includes 99 minority (16 Black or African American, non-Hispanic/Latino; 49 Asian, non-Hispanic/Latino; 21 Hispanic/Latino; 13 Two or more races, non-Hispanic/Latino), 212 international. Average age 27. 829 applicants, 53% accepted, 199 enrolled. In 2016, 179 master's, 7 doctorates awarded. Terminal master's awarded for partial completion of doctoral program. *Degree requirements:* For master's, thesis optional, internship; for doctorate, thesis/dissertation. *Entrance requirements:* For master's and doctorate, GRE General Test. Additional exam requirements/recommendations for international students: Required—TOEFL (minimum score 100 iBT). *Application deadline:* Applications are processed on a rolling basis. Application fee: $75 ($90 for international students). Electronic applications accepted. *Expenses:* Contact institution. *Financial support:* In 2016–17, 122 students received support, including 2 fellowships (averaging $28,200 per year), 33 research assistantships (averaging $28,200 per year), 41 teaching assistantships (averaging $28,200 per year); scholarships/grants and tuition waivers (full and partial) also available. *Unit head:* Dr. Thomas A. Finholt, Dean, School of Information, 734-647-3576. *Application contact:* School of Information Admissions, 734-763-2285, Fax: 734-615-3587, E-mail: umsi.admissions@umich.edu.
Website: http://www.si.umich.edu/

University of Missouri, Office of Research and Graduate Studies, College of Education, School of Information Science and Learning Technologies, Columbia, MO 65211. Offers educational technology (M Ed, Ed S); information science and learning technology (PhD, Certificate); library science (MA). *Accreditation:* ALA (one or more programs are accredited). *Program availability:* Part-time, evening/weekend. *Faculty:* 13 full-time (11 women), 1 part-time/adjunct (0 women). *Students:* 99 full-time (75 women),

187 part-time (126 women). *Entrance requirements:* For master's, GRE General Test or MAT, minimum GPA of 3.0. Additional exam requirements/recommendations for international students: Required—TOEFL (minimum score 540 paper-based; 76 iBT). *Application deadline:* For fall admission, 2/15 priority date for domestic and international students; for winter admission, 9/15 priority date for domestic and international students; for spring admission, 3/1 priority date for domestic students. Applications are processed on a rolling basis. Application fee: $75 ($90 for international students). Electronic applications accepted. *Expenses:* Tuition, state resident: full-time $6347; part-time $352.60 per credit hour. Tuition, nonresident: full-time $17,379; part-time $965.50 per credit hour. *Required fees:* $1035. Tuition and fees vary according to course load, campus/location and program. *Financial support:* Fellowships, teaching assistantships, scholarships/grants, health care benefits, and unspecified assistantships available. Support available to part-time students.
Website: http://education.missouri.edu/information-science-learning-technologies/

The University of North Carolina at Chapel Hill, Graduate School, School of Information and Library Science, Chapel Hill, NC 27599. Offers data curation (PMC); information and library science (PhD); information science (MSIS); library science (MSLS). *Accreditation:* ALA (one or more programs are accredited). *Program availability:* Part-time. *Faculty:* 26 full-time (11 women), 46 part-time/adjunct (23 women). *Students:* 190 full-time (140 women), 26 part-time (15 women); includes 35 minority (7 Black or African American, non-Hispanic/Latino; 7 Asian, non-Hispanic/Latino; 6 Hispanic/Latino; 15 Two or more races, non-Hispanic/Latino), 36 international. Average age 28. 258 applicants, 68% accepted, 83 enrolled. In 2016, 69 master's, 4 doctorates awarded. Terminal master's awarded for partial completion of doctoral program. *Degree requirements:* For master's, comprehensive exam, paper or project; for doctorate, comprehensive exam, thesis/dissertation. *Entrance requirements:* For master's and doctorate, GRE General Test. Additional exam requirements/recommendations for international students: Required—TOEFL (minimum score 550 paper-based; 79 iBT). *Application deadline:* For fall admission, 12/13 priority date for domestic and international students; for spring admission, 10/11 for domestic and international students. Applications are processed on a rolling basis. Application fee: $85. Electronic applications accepted. *Expenses:* $7,000 full-time resident, $16,000 non-resident (for master's); $7,000 full-time resident, $15,000 non-resident (for PMC); $5,800 full-time resident, $14,400 non-resident (for PhD). *Financial support:* In 2016–17, 59 fellowships with full tuition reimbursements (averaging $2,565 per year), 46 research assistantships with full tuition reimbursements (averaging $25,120 per year), 15 teaching assistantships with full tuition reimbursements (averaging $11,628 per year) were awarded; career-related internships or fieldwork, Federal Work-Study, scholarships/grants, health care benefits, and unspecified assistantships also available. Financial award application deadline: 12/13. *Faculty research:* Information retrieval and management, digital libraries, management of information resources, archives and records management, health informatics. *Unit head:* Dr. Gary Marchionini, Dean, 919-962-8363, Fax: 919-962-8071, E-mail: gary@ils.unc.edu. *Application contact:* Lara Bailey, Student Services Coordinator, 919-962-7601, Fax: 919-962-8071, E-mail: bailey@email.unc.edu.
Website: http://sils.unc.edu

The University of North Carolina at Greensboro, Graduate School, School of Education, Department of Library and Information Studies, Greensboro, NC 27412-5001. Offers MLIS. *Accreditation:* ALA. *Program availability:* Part-time, evening/weekend, online learning. *Degree requirements:* For master's, portfolio. *Entrance requirements:* For master's, GRE General Test. Additional exam requirements/recommendations for international students: Required—TOEFL (minimum score 550 paper-based), IELTS (minimum score 6.5). Electronic applications accepted. *Faculty research:* Library history, gender studies, children's literature, web design, homeless, technical services.

University of Oklahoma, College of Arts and Sciences, School of Library and Information Studies, Norman, OK 73019. Offers MLIS, M Ed/MLIS, MBA/MLIS. *Accreditation:* ALA (one or more programs are accredited). *Program availability:* Part-time, evening/weekend, online learning. *Faculty:* 11 full-time (8 women). *Students:* 49 full-time (43 women), 97 part-time (76 women); includes 30 minority (3 Black or African American, non-Hispanic/Latino; 5 American Indian or Alaska Native, non-Hispanic/Latino; 2 Asian, non-Hispanic/Latino; 8 Hispanic/Latino; 1 Native Hawaiian or other Pacific Islander, non-Hispanic/Latino; 11 Two or more races, non-Hispanic/Latino), 1 international. Average age 32. 40 applicants, 85% accepted, 27 enrolled. In 2016, 45 master's awarded. *Degree requirements:* For master's, comprehensive exam (for some programs), thesis optional. *Entrance requirements:* For master's, three letters of recommendation, personal statement, resume. Additional exam requirements/recommendations for international students: Required—TOEFL (minimum score 79 iBT) or IELTS (minimum score 6.5). *Application deadline:* Applications are processed on a rolling basis. Application fee: $50 ($100 for international students). Electronic applications accepted. *Expenses:* Tuition, state resident: full-time $4886; part-time $203.60 per credit hour. Tuition, nonresident: full-time $18,989; part-time $791.20 per credit hour. *Required fees:* $3283; $126.25 per credit hour. $126.50 per semester. *Financial support:* In 2016–17, 81 students received support, including 4 research assistantships with full tuition reimbursements available (averaging $12,801 per year), 5 teaching assistantships (averaging $10,579 per year); scholarships/grants, health care benefits, and unspecified assistantships also available. Financial award application deadline: 6/1; financial award applicants required to submit FAFSA. *Faculty research:* Teen services, health information, big data analytics. *Total annual research expenditures:* $131,980. *Unit head:* Dr. Susan Burke, Interim Director, 405-325-3921, Fax: 405-325-7648, E-mail: sburke@ou.edu. *Application contact:* Sarah Connelly, Admissions and Student Services Coordinator, 405-325-3921, Fax: 405-325-7648, E-mail: sarahee@ou.edu.
Website: http://slis.ou.edu/

University of Pittsburgh, School of Information Sciences, Library and Information Science Program, Pittsburgh, PA 15260. Offers MLIS, PhD. *Accreditation:* ALA (one or more programs are accredited). *Program availability:* Part-time, evening/weekend, 100% online. *Faculty:* 8 full-time (5 women), 5 part-time/adjunct (4 women). *Students:* 62 full-time (50 women), 57 part-time (44 women); includes 6 minority (2 Black or African American, non-Hispanic/Latino; 1 Asian, non-Hispanic/Latino; 3 Hispanic/Latino), 11 international. Average age 32. 148 applicants, 80% accepted, 68 enrolled. In 2016, 59 master's, 1 doctorate awarded. *Degree requirements:* For master's, thesis optional; for doctorate, comprehensive exam, thesis/dissertation. *Entrance requirements:* For master's, GRE, GMAT, MAT, MCAT, LSAT, bachelor's degree from accredited university; minimum GPA of 3.0; for doctorate, GRE, minimum GPA of 3.5. Additional exam requirements/recommendations for international students: Required—TOEFL (minimum score 550 paper-based; 80 iBT). *Application deadline:* For fall admission, 1/15 priority date for domestic and international students. Applications are processed on a rolling basis. Application fee: $50. Electronic applications accepted. *Expenses:* $22,628 per year in-state, $37,754 per year out-of-state (fall and spring); $931 per credit in-state, $1,553 per credit out-of-state (summer). *Financial support:* Fellowships with full and partial tuition reimbursements, research assistantships with full and partial tuition reimbursements, teaching assistantships with full and partial tuition reimbursements, career-related internships or fieldwork, institutionally sponsored loans, scholarships/grants, traineeships, health care benefits, and unspecified assistantships available. Financial award application deadline: 1/15; financial award applicants required to submit FAFSA. *Faculty research:* Archives, children's resources and services, digital libraries, cyber scholarship and citizen science, learning technology. *Unit head:* Dr. Leanne Bowler, Co-Chair, 412-624-7679, Fax: 412-624-5231, E-mail: lbowler@sis.pitt.edu. *Application contact:* Shabana Reza, Enrollment Manager, 412-624-3988, Fax: 412-624-5231, E-mail: sreza@sis.pitt.edu.
Website: http://www.ischool.pitt.edu/lis

University of Puerto Rico, Río Piedras Campus, Graduate School of Information Sciences and Technologies, San Juan, PR 00931-3300. Offers administration of academic libraries (PMC); administration of public libraries (PMC); administration of special libraries (PMC); consultant in information services (PMC); documents and files administration (Post-Graduate Certificate); electronic information resources analyst (Post-Graduate Certificate); information science (MIS); librarianship and information services (MLS); school librarian (Post-Graduate Certificate); school librarian distance education mode (Post-Graduate Certificate); specialist in legal information (PMC). *Accreditation:* ALA. *Program availability:* Part-time. *Degree requirements:* For master's, comprehensive exam, thesis, portfolio. *Entrance requirements:* For master's, PAEG, GRE, interview, minimum GPA of 3.0, 3 letters of recommendation; for other advanced degree, PAEG, GRE, minimum GPA of 3.0, IST master's degree. *Faculty research:* Investigating the users needs and preferences for a specialized environmental library.

University of Rhode Island, Graduate School, College of Arts and Sciences, Graduate School of Library and Information Studies, Kingston, RI 02881. Offers libraries, leadership and transforming communities (MLIS); organization of digital media (MLIS); school library media (MLIS); MLIS/MA; MLIS/MPA. *Accreditation:* ALA (one or more programs are accredited). *Program availability:* Part-time. *Faculty:* 4 full-time (all women). *Students:* 31 full-time (23 women), 71 part-time (61 women); includes 3 minority (1 Black or African American, non-Hispanic/Latino; 2 Asian, non-Hispanic/Latino). In 2016, 31 master's awarded. *Degree requirements:* For master's, comprehensive exam. *Entrance requirements:* For master's, GRE or MAT if undergraduate GPA below 3.3, 2 letters of recommendation. Additional exam requirements/recommendations for international students: Required—TOEFL. *Application deadline:* For fall admission, 6/15 for domestic students, 2/1 for international students; for spring admission, 10/15 for domestic students, 7/15 for international students; for summer admission, 3/15 for domestic students. Application fee: $65. Electronic applications accepted. *Expenses:* Tuition, state resident: full-time $11,796; part-time $655 per credit. Tuition, nonresident: full-time $24,206; part-time $1345 per credit. *Required fees:* $1546; $44 per credit. One-time fee: $155 full-time; $35 part-time. *Financial support:* In 2016–17, 1 teaching assistantship (averaging $17,184 per year) was awarded; research assistantships also available. Financial award application deadline: 1/15; financial award applicants required to submit FAFSA. *Unit head:* Dr. Valerie Karno, Director, Graduate School of Library and Information Studies, 401-874-4682, Fax: 401-874-4127, E-mail: karno@uri.edu. *Application contact:* GSLIS Student Services Office, 401-874-2872, Fax: 401-874-5787, E-mail: stefaniemetko@mail.uri.edu.
Website: http://www.uri.edu/artsci/lsc/

University of South Carolina, The Graduate School, College of Mass Communications and Information Studies, School of Library and Information Science, Columbia, SC 29208. Offers MLIS, PhD, Certificate, Specialist, MLIS/MA. *Accreditation:* ALA (one or more programs are accredited). *Program availability:* Part-time, online learning. *Degree requirements:* For master's, end of program portfolio; for doctorate, comprehensive exam, thesis/dissertation. *Entrance requirements:* For master's and other advanced degree, GRE General Test or MAT; for doctorate, GTE, writing sample. Additional exam requirements/recommendations for international students: Required—TOEFL (minimum score 570 paper-based; 75 iBT). Electronic applications accepted. *Faculty research:* Information technology management, distance education, library services for children and young adults, special libraries.

University of South Florida, College of Arts and Sciences, School of Information, Tampa, FL 33620-9951. Offers intelligence studies (MS), including cyber intelligence, strategic intelligence; library and information science (MA). *Accreditation:* ALA (one or more programs are accredited). *Program availability:* Part-time, evening/weekend, online learning. *Faculty:* 17 full-time (8 women). *Students:* 112 full-time (73 women), 163 part-time (127 women); includes 80 minority (28 Black or African American, non-Hispanic/Latino; 11 Asian, non-Hispanic/Latino; 32 Hispanic/Latino; 1 Native Hawaiian or other Pacific Islander, non-Hispanic/Latino; 8 Two or more races, non-Hispanic/Latino), 1 international. Average age 33. 167 applicants, 84% accepted, 90 enrolled. In 2016, 61 master's awarded. *Degree requirements:* For master's, comprehensive exam, thesis (for some programs). *Entrance requirements:* For master's, GRE General Test (for some programs). Additional exam requirements/recommendations for international students: Required—TOEFL (minimum score 550 paper-based; 79 iBT) or IELTS (minimum score 6.5). *Application deadline:* For fall admission, 6/1 for domestic students, 2/15 for international students; for spring admission, 10/15 for domestic students, 9/15 for international students. Applications are processed on a rolling basis. Application fee: $30. Electronic applications accepted. *Expenses:* Tuition, state resident: full-time $7766; part-time $431.43 per credit hour. Tuition, nonresident: full-time $15,789; part-time $877.17 per credit hour. *Required fees:* $37 per term. *Financial support:* In 2016–17, 47 students received support. Unspecified assistantships available. Financial award application deadline: 6/30. *Faculty research:* Youth services in libraries, community engagement and libraries, information architecture, biomedical informatics, health informatics. *Total annual research expenditures:* $378,531. *Unit head:* Dr. Jim Andrews, Director and Associate Professor, 813-974-2108, Fax: 813-974-6840, E-mail: jimandrews@usf.edu. *Application contact:* Dr. Diane Austin, Assistant Director, 813-974-6364, Fax: 813-974-6840, E-mail: dianeaustin@usf.edu.
Website: http://si.usf.edu/

University of South Florida, Innovative Education, Tampa, FL 33620-9951. Offers adult, career and higher education (Graduate Certificate), including college teaching, leadership in developing human resources, leadership in higher education; Africana studies (Graduate Certificate), including diasporas and health disparities, genocide and human rights; aging studies (Graduate Certificate), including gerontology; art research (Graduate Certificate), including museum studies; business foundations (Graduate Certificate); chemical and biomedical engineering (Graduate Certificate), including materials science and engineering, water, health and sustainability; child and family studies (Graduate Certificate), including positive behavior support; civil and industrial engineering (Graduate Certificate), including transportation systems analysis; community and family health (Graduate Certificate), including maternal and child health, social marketing and public health, violence and injury: prevention and intervention, women's health; criminology (Graduate Certificate), including criminal justice administration; educational measurement and research (Graduate Certificate), including evaluation; English (Graduate Certificate), including comparative literary studies, creative writing, professional and technical communication; entrepreneurship (Graduate Certificate); environmental health (Graduate Certificate), including safety management; epidemiology and biostatistics (Graduate Certificate), including applied biostatistics, biostatistics, concepts and tools of epidemiology, epidemiology, epidemiology of

infectious diseases; geography, environment and planning (Graduate Certificate), including community development, environmental policy and management, geographical information systems; geology (Graduate Certificate), including hydrogeology; global health (Graduate Certificate), including disaster management, global health and Latin American and Caribbean studies, global health practice, humanitarian assistance, infection control; government and international affairs (Graduate Certificate), including Cuban studies, globalization studies; health policy and management (Graduate Certificate), including health management and leadership, public health policy and programs; hearing specialist: early intervention (Graduate Certificate); industrial and management systems engineering (Graduate Certificate), including systems engineering, technology management; information studies (Graduate Certificate), including school library media specialist; information systems/decision sciences (Graduate Certificate), including analytics and business intelligence; instructional technology (Graduate Certificate), including distance education, Florida digital/virtual educator, instructional design, multimedia design, Web design; internal medicine, bioethics and medical humanities (Graduate Certificate), including biomedical ethics; Latin American and Caribbean studies (Graduate Certificate); mass communications (Graduate Certificate), including multimedia journalism; mathematics and statistics (Graduate Certificate), including mathematics; medicine (Graduate Certificate), including aging and neuroscience, bioinformatics, biotechnology, brain fitness and memory management, clinical investigation, health informatics, health sciences, integrative weight management, intellectual property, medicine and gender, metabolic and nutritional medicine, metabolic cardiology, pharmacy sciences; national and competitive intelligence (Graduate Certificate); psychological and social foundations (Graduate Certificate), including career counseling, college teaching, diversity in education, mental health counseling, school counseling; public affairs (Graduate Certificate), including nonprofit management, public management, research administration; public health (Graduate Certificate), including environmental health, health equity, public health generalist, translational research in adolescent behavioral health; public health practices (Graduate Certificate), including planning for healthy communities; rehabilitation and mental health counseling (Graduate Certificate), including integrative mental health care, marriage and family therapy, rehabilitation technology; secondary education (Graduate Certificate), including ESOL, foreign language education: culture and content, foreign language education: professional; social work (Graduate Certificate), including geriatric social work/clinical gerontology; special education (Graduate Certificate), including autism spectrum disorder, disabilities education: severe/profound; world languages (Graduate Certificate), including teaching English as a second language (TESL) or foreign language. *Expenses:* Tuition, state resident: full-time $7766; part-time $431.43 per credit hour. Tuition, nonresident: full-time $15,789; part-time $877.17 per credit hour. *Required fees:* $37 per term. *Unit head:* Kathy Barnes, Interdisciplinary Programs Coordinator, 813-974-8031, Fax: 813-974-7061, E-mail: barnesk@usf.edu. *Application contact:* Karen Tylinski, Metro Initiatives, 813-974-9943, Fax: 813-974-7061, E-mail: ktylinsk@usf.edu.
Website: http://www.usf.edu/innovative-education/

The University of Texas at Austin, Graduate School, School of Information, Austin, TX 78712-1111. Offers identity management and security (MSIMS); information (PhD); information studies (MSIS); MSIS/MA. MSIMS program offered in conjunction with the Center for Identity. *Accreditation:* ALA (one or more programs are accredited). *Program availability:* Part-time. *Degree requirements:* For doctorate, 2 foreign languages, thesis/dissertation. *Entrance requirements:* For master's and doctorate, GRE General Test. Electronic applications accepted. *Faculty research:* Information retrieval and artificial intelligence, library history and administration, classification and cataloguing.

University of Toronto, School of Graduate Studies, Faculty of Information, Toronto, ON M5S 1A1, Canada. Offers information (MI, PhD); museum studies (MM St); JD/MI. *Accreditation:* ALA (one or more programs are accredited). *Program availability:* Part-time. *Degree requirements:* For master's, thesis optional; for doctorate, thesis/dissertation, oral exam/thesis defense. *Entrance requirements:* For master's, 2 letters of reference; for doctorate, 3 letters of reference, minimum B+ average. Additional exam requirements/recommendations for international students: Required—TOEFL (minimum score 600 paper-based; 100 iBT), IELTS (minimum score 8), TWE (minimum score 5.5), or Michigan English Language Assessment Battery (minimum score 95). Electronic applications accepted. *Expenses:* Contact institution.

The University of Western Ontario, Faculty of Graduate Studies, Faculty of Information and Media Studies, Programs in Library and Information Science, London, ON N6A 5B8, Canada. Offers MLIS, PhD. Program conducted on a trimester basis. *Accreditation:* ALA (one or more programs are accredited). *Program availability:* Part-time, evening/weekend. *Degree requirements:* For doctorate, comprehensive exam, thesis/dissertation. *Entrance requirements:* For master's, honors degree, minimum B average during previous 2 years of course work; for doctorate, MLIS or equivalent. Additional exam requirements/recommendations for international students: Required—TOEFL (minimum score 625 paper-based), TWE (minimum score 5). Electronic applications accepted. *Faculty research:* Information, individuals, and society; information systems, policy, power, and institutions.

University of Wisconsin–Madison, Graduate School, College of Letters and Science, School of Library and Information Studies, Madison, WI 53706-1380. Offers MA, PhD. *Accreditation:* ALA (one or more programs are accredited). *Program availability:* Part-time. *Degree requirements:* For doctorate, comprehensive exam, thesis/dissertation. Electronic applications accepted. *Faculty research:* Intellectual freedom, children's literature, print culture history, information systems design and evaluation, school library media centers.

University of Wisconsin–Milwaukee, Graduate School, School of Information Studies, Milwaukee, WI 53201-0413. Offers MLIS, MS, PhD, CAS. *Accreditation:* ALA (one or more programs are accredited). *Program availability:* Part-time. *Students:* 119 full-time (82 women), 250 part-time (194 women); includes 55 minority (13 Black or African American, non-Hispanic/Latino; 12 Asian, non-Hispanic/Latino; 2 Hispanic/Latino; 1 Native Hawaiian or other Pacific Islander, non-Hispanic/Latino; 27 Two or more races, non-Hispanic/Latino), 15 international. Average age 35. 203 applicants, 75% accepted, 81 enrolled. In 2016, 116 master's, 2 doctorates, 5 other advanced degrees awarded. *Entrance requirements:* For master's, GRE General Test or MAT; for doctorate, GRE. Additional exam requirements/recommendations for international students: Required—TOEFL (minimum score 550 paper-based), IELTS (minimum score 6.5). *Application deadline:* For fall admission, 1/1 priority date for domestic students; for spring admission, 9/1 for domestic students. Applications are processed on a rolling basis. Application fee: $56 ($96 for international students). Electronic applications accepted. *Financial support:* In 2016–17, 4 teaching assistantships were awarded; fellowships, research assistantships, career-related internships or fieldwork, Federal Work-Study, health care benefits, unspecified assistantships, and project assistantships also available. Support available to part-time students. Financial award application deadline: 4/15; financial award applicants required to submit FAFSA. *Unit head:* Tomas A. Lipinski, Dean/Professor, 414-229-4707, E-mail: tlipinsk@uwm.edu. *Application contact:* Linda Barajas, Admissions Coordinator, 414-229-3316, E-mail: barajas@uwm.edu.
Website: http://uwm.edu/informationstudies

Valdosta State University, Program in Library and Information Science, Valdosta, GA 31698. Offers MLIS. *Accreditation:* ALA. *Program availability:* 100% online. *Degree requirements:* For master's, comprehensive exam. *Entrance requirements:* For master's, two essays, resume, three recommendations. Additional exam requirements/recommendations for international students: Required—TOEFL (minimum score 523 paper-based); Recommended—IELTS. *Expenses:* Contact institution.

Wayne State University, School of Library and Information Science, Detroit, MI 48202. Offers archival administration (Graduate Certificate); information management (Graduate Certificate); library and information science (MLIS, Spec); public library services to children and young adults (Graduate Certificate); MLIS/MA. *Accreditation:* ALA (one or more programs are accredited). *Program availability:* Part-time, evening/weekend, 100% online, blended/hybrid learning. *Faculty:* 11 full-time (7 women), 30 part-time/adjunct (20 women). *Students:* 90 full-time (69 women), 376 part-time (312 women); includes 74 minority (38 Black or African American, non-Hispanic/Latino; 2 American Indian or Alaska Native, non-Hispanic/Latino; 4 Asian, non-Hispanic/Latino; 17 Hispanic/Latino; 2 Native Hawaiian or other Pacific Islander, non-Hispanic/Latino; 11 Two or more races, non-Hispanic/Latino), 3 international. Average age 32. 265 applicants, 73% accepted, 120 enrolled. In 2016, 145 master's, 34 other advanced degrees awarded. *Degree requirements:* For master's and other advanced degree, e-portfolio. *Entrance requirements:* For master's, GRE or MAT (if undergraduate GPA is between 2.5 and 2.99), minimum undergraduate GPA of 3.0 or graduate degree, personal statement, resume or curriculum vitae; for other advanced degree, GRE or MAT (if undergraduate GPA is between 2.5 and 2.99), minimum undergraduate GPA of 3.0 or graduate degree, personal statement, resume or curriculum vitae, MLIS (for specialist certificate). Additional exam requirements/recommendations for international students: Required—TOEFL (minimum score 550 paper-based; 79 iBT); Recommended—IELTS (minimum score 6.5), TWE (minimum score 5.5). *Application deadline:* For fall admission, 7/1 for domestic students, 5/1 priority date for international students; for winter admission, 10/1 priority date for domestic students, 9/1 priority date for international students; for spring admission, 2/1 priority date for domestic students, 1/1 priority date for international students. Applications are processed on a rolling basis. Application fee: $50. Electronic applications accepted. *Expenses:* $18,871 per year resident tuition and fees, $36,065 per year non-resident tuition and fees. *Financial support:* In 2016–17, 107 students received support. Fellowships with tuition reimbursements available, scholarships/grants, health care benefits, and unspecified assistantships available. Support available to part-time students. Financial award applicants required to submit FAFSA. *Faculty research:* Library services, information management issues, digital content management, library/community engagement, archives and preservation. *Unit head:* Dr. Sandra Yee, Dean, 313-577-4059, E-mail: aj0533@wayne.edu. *Application contact:* Academic Services Officer II, 313-577-1825, E-mail: asklis@wayne.edu.
Website: http://slis.wayne.edu/

Library Science

Appalachian State University, Cratis D. Williams Graduate School, Department of Leadership and Educational Studies, Boone, NC 28608. Offers educational administration (Ed S); educational media (MA); higher education (MA, Ed S); library science (MLS); school administration (MSA). *Program availability:* Part-time, evening/weekend, online learning. *Degree requirements:* For master's and Ed S, comprehensive exam, thesis optional. *Entrance requirements:* For master's and Ed S, GRE or MAT, 3 letters of recommendation. Additional exam requirements/recommendations for international students: Required—TOEFL (minimum score 570 paper-based; 79 iBT), IELTS (minimum score 6.5). *Application deadline:* For fall admission, 3/14 priority date for domestic students, 2/1 for international students; for spring admission, 11/1 for domestic students, 7/1 for international students. Applications are processed on a rolling basis. Application fee: $55. Electronic applications accepted. *Expenses:* Tuition, state resident: full-time $4744. Tuition, nonresident: full-time $17,913. Full-time tuition and fees vary according to program. *Financial support:* Research assistantships, career-related internships or fieldwork, scholarships/grants, and unspecified assistantships available. Financial award application deadline: 4/1; financial award applicants required to submit FAFSA. *Faculty research:* Brain, learning and meditation; leadership of teaching and learning. *Unit head:* Dr. Robert Sanders, Interim Director, 828-262-3112, E-mail: sandersrl@appstate.edu. *Application contact:* Dr. Vachel Miller, Program Director, 828-262-2287, E-mail: millervw@appstate.edu.
Website: http://www.les.appstate.edu

Azusa Pacific University, School of Education, Department of Advanced Studies, Program in School Librarianship, Azusa, CA 91702-7000. Offers MA.

Azusa Pacific University, School of Education, Department of Advanced Studies, Program in Teacher Librarian Services, Azusa, CA 91702-7000. Offers Credential. *Program availability:* Online learning.

The Catholic University of America, School of Arts and Sciences, Department of Library and Information Science, Washington, DC 20064. Offers MSLS, Certificate, JD/MSLS, MSLS/MA, MSLS/MS. *Accreditation:* ALA (one or more programs are accredited). *Program availability:* Part-time. *Faculty:* 7 full-time (6 women), 2 part-time/adjunct (0 women). *Students:* 22 full-time (11 women), 59 part-time (48 women); includes 24 minority (14 Black or African American, non-Hispanic/Latino; 3 Asian, non-Hispanic/Latino; 3 Hispanic/Latino; 4 Two or more races, non-Hispanic/Latino), 4 international. Average age 32. 65 applicants, 91% accepted, 31 enrolled. In 2016, 43 master's awarded. *Degree requirements:* For master's, comprehensive exam. *Entrance requirements:* For master's, statement of purpose, official copies of academic transcripts, three letters of recommendation, interview. Additional exam requirements/recommendations for international students: Required—TOEFL (minimum score 550 paper-based; 80 iBT). *Application deadline:* For fall admission, 7/15 priority date for domestic students, 7/1 for international students; for spring admission, 11/15 priority date for domestic students, 11/1 for international students. Applications are processed

on a rolling basis. Application fee: $55. Electronic applications accepted. *Expenses:* $42,850 per year; $1,170 per credit; $200 per semester part-time fees. *Financial support:* Fellowships, research assistantships, teaching assistantships, Federal Work-Study, scholarships/grants, tuition waivers (full and partial), and unspecified assistantships available. Financial award application deadline: 2/1; financial award applicants required to submit FAFSA. *Faculty research:* Digital collections, library and information science education, information design and architecture, information system design and evaluation. *Unit head:* Dr. Youngok Choi, Chair, 202-319-5877, E-mail: choiy@cua.edu. *Application contact:* Director of Graduate Admissions, 202-319-5057, Fax: 202-319-6533, E-mail: cua-admissions@cua.edu.
Website: http://lis.cua.edu/

Chicago State University, School of Graduate and Professional Studies, College of Education, Department of Reading, Elementary Education, Library Information and Media Studies, Program in Library Information and Media Studies, Chicago, IL 60628. Offers MS Ed. *Entrance requirements:* For master's, minimum GPA of 2.75.

Clarion University of Pennsylvania, Office of Transfer, Adult and Graduate Admissions, Online Certificate Programs, Clarion, PA 16214. Offers family nurse practitioner (Post-Master's Certificate); library science (CAS); nurse educator (Post-Master's Certificate); public relations (Certificate). *Accreditation:* ALA (one or more programs are accredited at the [master's] level). *Program availability:* Part-time, 100% online. *Faculty:* 19 full-time (15 women), 5 part-time/adjunct (all women). *Students:* 6 part-time (5 women); includes 3 minority (1 Black or African American, non-Hispanic/Latino; 1 Asian, non-Hispanic/Latino; 1 Two or more races, non-Hispanic/Latino). Average age 43. 7 applicants, 100% accepted, 1 enrolled. In 2016, 12 CASs awarded. *Entrance requirements:* Additional exam requirements/recommendations for international students: Required—TOEFL (minimum score 550 paper-based; 80 iBT), IELTS (minimum score 7). *Application deadline:* For fall admission, 8/1 priority date for domestic students, 4/15 priority date for international students; for spring admission, 12/1 priority date for domestic students, 9/15 priority date for international students. Applications are processed on a rolling basis. Application fee: $40. Electronic applications accepted. *Expenses:* $687.55 per credit. *Financial support:* Career-related internships or fieldwork, Federal Work-Study, scholarships/grants, and unspecified assistantships available. Support available to part-time students. Financial award application deadline: 3/1. *Unit head:* E-mail: gradstudies@clarion.edu. *Application contact:* Dana Bearer, Associate Director, Transfer, Adult, and Graduate Programs, 814-393-2337, Fax: 814-393-2722, E-mail: gradstudies@clarion.edu.
Website: http://www.clarion.edu/admissions/graduate/index.html

Clarion University of Pennsylvania, Office of Transfer, Adult and Graduate Admissions, Online Master of Science Programs, Clarion, PA 16214. Offers accounting (MS); applied data analytics (MS); clinical mental health counseling (MS); library science (MSLS); mass media arts and journalism (MS). *Program availability:* Part-time, 100% online. *Faculty:* 15 full-time (7 women), 3 part-time/adjunct (2 women). *Students:* 84 full-time (69 women), 304 part-time (246 women); includes 36 minority (19 Black or African American, non-Hispanic/Latino; 3 Asian, non-Hispanic/Latino; 10 Hispanic/Latino; 4 Two or more races, non-Hispanic/Latino), 1 international. Average age 34. 179 applicants, 93% accepted, 131 enrolled. In 2016, 146 master's awarded. *Degree requirements:* For master's, comprehensive exam, thesis or alternative. *Entrance requirements:* For master's, minimum QPA of 3.0. Additional exam requirements/recommendations for international students: Required—TOEFL (minimum score 600 paper-based; 100 iBT), IELTS (minimum score 7.5). *Application deadline:* For fall admission, 8/1 priority date for domestic students, 4/15 priority date for international students; for spring admission, 12/1 priority date for domestic students, 9/15 priority date for international students. Applications are processed on a rolling basis. Application fee: $40. Electronic applications accepted. *Expenses:* $632.35 per credit. *Financial support:* Career-related internships or fieldwork, Federal Work-Study, scholarships/grants, and unspecified assistantships available. Support available to part-time students. Financial award application deadline: 3/1. *Application contact:* Dana Bearer, Associate Director, Transfer, Adult, and Graduate Programs, 814-393-2337, Fax: 814-393-2772, E-mail: gradstudies@clarion.edu.
Website: http://www.clarion.edu/admissions/graduate/index.html

Dalhousie University, Faculty of Management, School of Information Management, Halifax, NS B3H 3J5, Canada. Offers MIM, MLIS, LL B/MLIS, MBA/MLIS, MLIS/MPA, MLIS/MREM. *Accreditation:* ALA (one or more programs are accredited). *Program availability:* Part-time. *Degree requirements:* For master's, one foreign language, thesis optional. *Entrance requirements:* For master's, resume, interview. Additional exam requirements/recommendations for international students: Required—TOEFL, IELTS, CANTEST, CAEL, or Michigan English Language Assessment Battery. Electronic applications accepted. *Faculty research:* Information-seeking behavior, electronic text design, browsing in digital environments, information diffusion among scientists.

Drexel University, College of Computing and Informatics, Philadelphia, PA 19104-2875. Offers MS, PhD, Post-Master's Certificate, Postbaccalaureate Certificate. *Accreditation:* ALA (one or more programs are accredited). *Program availability:* Part-time, evening/weekend, 100% online. *Faculty:* 64 full-time (23 women), 9 part-time/adjunct (3 women). *Students:* 172 full-time (76 women), 344 part-time (190 women); includes 88 minority (30 Black or African American, non-Hispanic/Latino; 20 Asian, non-Hispanic/Latino; 29 Hispanic/Latino; 9 Two or more races, non-Hispanic/Latino), 105 international. Average age 33. 871 applicants, 35% accepted, 137 enrolled. In 2016, 270 master's, 11 doctorates, 28 other advanced degrees awarded. *Degree requirements:* For doctorate, thesis/dissertation. *Entrance requirements:* For master's and doctorate, GRE General Test. Additional exam requirements/recommendations for international students: Required—TOEFL (minimum score 600 paper-based; 100 iBT), IELTS (minimum score 6.5). *Application deadline:* For fall admission, 8/15 for domestic students, 7/15 for international students; for spring admission, 3/1 for domestic students, 2/1 for international students. Applications are processed on a rolling basis. Application fee: $65. Electronic applications accepted. Application fee is waived when completed online. *Expenses: Tuition:* Full-time $32,184; part-time $1192 per credit hour. *Required fees:* $280. Tuition and fees vary according to campus/location and program. *Financial support:* In 2016–17, 97 students received support, including 1 fellowship with full tuition reimbursement available (averaging $35,000 per year), 31 research assistantships with full tuition reimbursements available (averaging $27,290 per year), 20 teaching assistantships with full tuition reimbursements available (averaging $26,750 per year); career-related internships or fieldwork, institutionally sponsored loans, scholarships/grants, health care benefits, and tuition waivers (partial) also available. Support available to part-time students. Financial award application deadline: 3/1; financial award applicants required to submit FAFSA. *Faculty research:* Computer science: theory of algorithms, graph theory, combinatorial optimization, computer vision; human-centered computing: social computing, human-computer interaction, computer-supported cooperative work, computer-supported collaborative learning, information literacy; systems and software engineering: formal software design modeling and analysis, software economics, software evolution and modularity. *Total annual research expenditures:* $3.9 million. *Unit head:* Dr. Yi Deng, Dean/Professor, 215-895-2475, Fax: 215-895-2494, E-mail: yd362@drexel.edu. *Application contact:* Matthew Lechtenberg, Director, Recruitment, 215-895-2474, Fax: 215-895-2303, E-mail: cciinfo@drexel.edu.
Website: http://cci.drexel.edu/

East Carolina University, Graduate School, College of Education, Department of Interdisciplinary Professions, Greenville, NC 27858-4353. Offers adult education (MA Ed); business and marketing education (MA); career and technical education (MA Ed); counselor education (MS); library science (MLS); vocational education (MS). *Accreditation:* ACA; NCATE. *Program availability:* Part-time, evening/weekend. *Students:* 95 full-time (79 women), 427 part-time (374 women); includes 106 minority (68 Black or African American, non-Hispanic/Latino; 13 American Indian or Alaska Native, non-Hispanic/Latino; 4 Asian, non-Hispanic/Latino; 13 Hispanic/Latino; 8 Two or more races, non-Hispanic/Latino). Average age 37. 225 applicants, 93% accepted, 174 enrolled. In 2016, 86 master's awarded. *Degree requirements:* For master's, comprehensive exam, thesis optional. *Entrance requirements:* For master's, GRE General Test or MAT, interview, minimum GPA of 2.5, bachelor's degree in related field, teaching license (MA Ed). Additional exam requirements/recommendations for international students: Required—TOEFL. *Application deadline:* For fall admission, 5/15 priority date for domestic students. Applications are processed on a rolling basis. Application fee: $50. *Financial support:* Research assistantships with partial tuition reimbursements, teaching assistantships with partial tuition reimbursements, and Federal Work-Study available. Support available to part-time students. Financial award application deadline: 6/1. *Unit head:* Dr. Vivian W. Mott, Chair, 252-328-6177, Fax: 252-328-4368, E-mail: mottv@ecu.edu. *Application contact:* Dean of Graduate School, 252-328-6012, Fax: 252-328-6071, E-mail: gradschool@ecu.edu.
Website: http://www.ecu.edu/cs-educ/idp/index.cfm

Eastern Kentucky University, The Graduate School, College of Education, Department of Curriculum and Instruction, Richmond, KY 40475-3102. Offers elementary education (MA Ed), including early elementary education, reading; library science (MA Ed); music education (MA Ed); secondary and higher education (MA Ed), including secondary education; teaching (MAT). *Accreditation:* NCATE. *Program availability:* Part-time. *Degree requirements:* For master's, portfolio is part of exam. *Entrance requirements:* For master's, GRE General Test, PRAXIS II (KY), minimum GPA of 2.5. *Faculty research:* Technology in education, reading instruction, e-portfolios, induction to teacher education, dispositions of teachers.

East Tennessee State University, School of Graduate Studies, College of Education, Department of Curriculum and Instruction, Johnson City, TN 37614. Offers educational technology (M Ed), including educational communications and technology, school library media; elementary education (M Ed); reading (MA), including reading education; school library professional (Post-Master's Certificate); secondary education (M Ed), including classroom technology; teacher education with multiple levels (MAT), including elementary education, middle grades education, secondary education. *Accreditation:* NCATE. *Program availability:* Part-time, evening/weekend, online learning. *Degree requirements:* For master's, comprehensive exam, thesis optional, student teaching, practicum; for Post-Master's Certificate, field work (school library); culminating experience (storytelling). *Entrance requirements:* For master's, GRE, SAT, ACT, PRAXIS, minimum GPA of 3.0; for Post-Master's Certificate, master's degree, TN teaching license. Additional exam requirements/recommendations for international students: Required—TOEFL (minimum score 550 paper-based; 79 iBT). Electronic applications accepted. *Faculty research:* Critical thinking; curriculum development in reading, math, and science education; cultural diversity; cognitive processes; effective teaching strategies.

Emporia State University, School of Library and Information Management, Emporia, KS 66801-5415. Offers archives studies (Certificate); library and information management (MLS, PhD). *Accreditation:* ALA (one or more programs are accredited). *Program availability:* Part-time, evening/weekend, online learning. *Faculty:* 9 full-time (6 women). *Students:* 24 full-time (18 women), 281 part-time (218 women); includes 23 minority (3 Black or African American, non-Hispanic/Latino; 1 American Indian or Alaska Native, non-Hispanic/Latino; 1 Asian, non-Hispanic/Latino; 14 Hispanic/Latino; 1 Native Hawaiian or other Pacific Islander, non-Hispanic/Latino; 3 Two or more races, non-Hispanic/Latino), 5 international. 118 applicants, 97% accepted, 71 enrolled. In 2016, 140 master's, 1 doctorate, 8 other advanced degrees awarded. *Degree requirements:* For master's, comprehensive exam, thesis optional; for doctorate, thesis/dissertation. *Entrance requirements:* For master's, GRE General Test, interview, minimum undergraduate GPA of 3.0, letters of recommendation; for doctorate, GRE General Test, interview, minimum graduate GPA of 3.5. Additional exam requirements/recommendations for international students: Required—TOEFL (minimum score 520 paper-based; 68 iBT). *Application deadline:* For fall admission, 8/15 priority date for domestic students. Applications are processed on a rolling basis. Application fee: $30 ($75 for international students). Electronic applications accepted. *Expenses:* Tuition, state resident: full-time $5922; part-time $246.75 per credit hour. Tuition, nonresident: full-time $18,414; part-time $767.25 per credit hour. *Required fees:* $1884; $78.50 per credit hour. *Financial support:* In 2016–17, 10 research assistantships with full tuition reimbursements (averaging $7,500 per year), 5 teaching assistantships (averaging $7,500 per year) were awarded; Federal Work-Study, institutionally sponsored loans, and unspecified assistantships also available. Financial award application deadline: 3/15; financial award applicants required to submit FAFSA. *Unit head:* Dr. Wooseob Jeong, Dean, 620-341-5203, Fax: 620-341-5203, E-mail: wjeong1@emporia.edu. *Application contact:* Candace Boardman, Director, Kansas MLS Program, 620-341-6159, E-mail: cboardma@emporia.edu.
Website: http://www.emporia.edu/slim/

Florida State University, The Graduate School, College of Communication and Information, School of Information, Tallahassee, FL 32306-2100. Offers information (MA, MS, PhD, Specialist); information studies (MA, MS, PhD, Specialist); information technology (MS). *Accreditation:* ALA (one or more programs are accredited). *Program availability:* Part-time, evening/weekend, 100% online, blended/hybrid learning. *Faculty:* 27 full-time (13 women), 8 part-time/adjunct (5 women). *Students:* 74 full-time (51 women), 244 part-time (182 women); includes 89 minority (30 Black or African American, non-Hispanic/Latino; 10 Asian, non-Hispanic/Latino; 44 Hispanic/Latino; 5 Two or more races, non-Hispanic/Latino), 10 international. Average age 35. 183 applicants, 70% accepted, 97 enrolled. In 2016, 132 master's, 12 doctorates, 1 other advanced degree awarded. Terminal master's awarded for partial completion of doctoral program. *Degree requirements:* For master's, thesis optional, minimum GPA of 3.0, 36 hours (MSI); 32 hours (MSIT); for doctorate, comprehensive exam, thesis/dissertation, dissertation defense, manuscript clearance, minimum GPA of 3.0; for Specialist, minimum GPA of 3.0; 30 hours. *Entrance requirements:* For master's, GRE (recommended minimum percentile of 50 on each of the verbal and quantitative portions and writing score of 4.0), minimum GPA of 3.0 on last 2 years of baccalaureate degree, resume, statement of goals, two letters of recommendation, official transcripts from every college-level institution attended; for doctorate, GRE (recommended minimum percentile of 50 on each of the verbal and quantitative portions and writing score of 4.0), minimum GPA of 3.0 on last degree program, resume, 3 letters of recommendation, personal/goals statement, writing sample, brief digital video, official transcripts from all college-level institutions attended; for Specialist, GRE (recommended minimum percentile of 50 on each of the verbal and quantitative portions and writing score of 4.0),

minimum graduate GPA of 3.2, resume, statement of goals, 2 letters of recommendation, writing sample, official transcripts from every college-level institution attended. Additional exam requirements/recommendations for international students: Required—TOEFL (minimum score 585 paper-based; 94 iBT), IELTS (minimum score 6.5). *Application deadline:* For fall admission, 7/1 for domestic and international students; for spring admission, 11/1 for domestic and international students. Applications are processed on a rolling basis. Application fee: $30. Electronic applications accepted. *Expenses:* Contact institution. *Financial support:* In 2016–17, 192 students received support, including 1 research assistantship with full tuition reimbursement available (averaging $18,578 per year), 18 teaching assistantships with full tuition reimbursements available (averaging $18,578 per year); career-related internships or fieldwork, Federal Work-Study, health care benefits, tuition waivers (full), and 13 assistantships (averaging $17,200); 26 scholarships (averaging $1000) also available. Financial award application deadline: 3/1; financial award applicants required to submit FAFSA. *Faculty research:* Information technology, social informatics, health information, human information behavior, youth services. *Total annual research expenditures:* $3.8 million. *Unit head:* Dr. Lorri Mon, Director/Associate Professor, 850-644-5776, Fax: 850-644-9763, E-mail: lmon@fsu.edu. *Application contact:* Student Services, 850-645-3280, Fax: 850-644-9763, E-mail: ischooladvising@admin.fsu.edu.
Website: http://ischool.cci.fsu.edu

Indiana University Bloomington, School of Informatics and Computing, Department of Information and Library Science, Bloomington, IN 47405-3907. Offers information architecture (Graduate Certificate); information science (MIS, PhD); library and information science (Sp LIS); library science (MLS); JD/MLS; MIS/MA; MLS/MA; MPA/MIS; MPA/MLS. *Accreditation:* ALA (one or more programs are accredited). *Program availability:* Part-time. *Faculty:* 12 full-time (6 women), 19 part-time/adjunct (11 women). *Students:* 151 full-time (109 women), 52 part-time (36 women); includes 23 minority (2 Black or African American, non-Hispanic/Latino; 5 Asian, non-Hispanic/Latino; 8 Hispanic/Latino; 8 Two or more races, non-Hispanic/Latino), 42 international. Average age 28. 943 applicants, 62% accepted, 73 enrolled. In 2016, 87 master's, 4 doctorates, 9 other advanced degrees awarded. Terminal master's awarded for partial completion of doctoral program. *Degree requirements:* For master's, internship; for doctorate, comprehensive exam, thesis/dissertation. *Entrance requirements:* For master's, GRE General Test (for applicants whose previous undergraduate degree GPA was below 3.0 or previous graduate degree GPA was below 3.2), 3 letters of reference, resume, personal statement (500 words minimum), transcripts; for doctorate, GRE General Test, resume, personal statement (800-1000 words), writing sample, transcripts, 3 letters of reference. Additional exam requirements/recommendations for international students: Required—TOEFL (minimum score 600 paper-based; 100 iBT), IELTS. *Application deadline:* For fall admission, 5/15 priority date for domestic students, 12/1 priority date for international students; for spring admission, 11/1 priority date for domestic students, 9/1 priority date for international students. Applications are processed on a rolling basis. Application fee: $55 ($65 for international students). Electronic applications accepted. *Expenses:* Contact institution. *Financial support:* In 2016–17, 55 students received support, including 20 fellowships; research assistantships with full and partial tuition reimbursements available, teaching assistantships, career-related internships or fieldwork, scholarships/grants, health care benefits, tuition waivers (partial), and unspecified assistantships also available. Financial award application deadline: 1/15. *Faculty research:* Scholarly communication, interface design, library and management policy, computer-mediated communication, information retrieval, documentation, web analysis, e-business, information architecture, social informatics, virtual groups and online communities, online deviant behaviors, knowledge sharing, indexing, philosophy of information, information policy, resource management, research methods digital humanities, digital libraries, semantic web, digital preservation, natural language processing. *Unit head:* Dr. John Walsh, Interim Director of Graduate Programs, 812-856-0707, E-mail: jawalsh@indiana.edu. *Application contact:* Corbet Tarbell, Director of Graduate Student Services, 812-856-7214, Fax: 812-855-6166, E-mail: ilsmain@indiana.edu.
Website: http://ils.indiana.edu/

Indiana University–Purdue University Indianapolis, School of Informatics and Computing, Department of Information and Library Science, Indianapolis, IN 46202. Offers MLS. *Program availability:* Part-time, evening/weekend. *Entrance requirements:* For master's, GRE General Test. Additional exam requirements/recommendations for international students: Required—TOEFL (minimum score 600 paper-based).

Indiana University–Purdue University Indianapolis, School of Public and Environmental Affairs, Indianapolis, IN 46202. Offers criminal justice and public safety (MS); homeland security and emergency management (Graduate Certificate); library management (Graduate Certificate); nonprofit management (Graduate Certificate); public affairs (MPA); public management (Graduate Certificate); social entrepreneurship: nonprofit and public benefit organizations (Graduate Certificate); JD/MPA; MLS/NMC; MLS/PMC; MPA/MA. *Accreditation:* CAHME (one or more programs are accredited); NASPAA. *Program availability:* Part-time, evening/weekend, online learning. *Entrance requirements:* For master's, GRE General Test, GMAT or LSAT, minimum GPA of 3.0 (preferred). Additional exam requirements/recommendations for international students: Required—TOEFL (minimum score 93 iBT), IELTS (minimum score 6.5). Electronic applications accepted. *Faculty research:* Nonprofit and public management, public policy, urban policy, sustainability policy, disaster preparedness and recovery, vehicular safety, homicide, offender rehabilitation and re-entry.

Instituto Tecnológico y de Estudios Superiores de Monterrey, Campus Irapuato, Graduate Programs, Irapuato, Mexico. Offers administration (MBA); administration of information technology (MAIT); administration of telecommunications (MAT); architecture (M Arch); computer science (MCS); education (M Ed); educational administration (MEA); educational innovation and technology (DEIT); educational technology (MET); electronic commerce (MBA); environmental administration and planning (MEAP); environmental systems (MES); finances (MBA); humanistic studies (MHS); international management for Latin American executives (MIMLAE); library and information science (MLIS); manufacturing quality management (MMQM); marketing research (MBA).

Inter American University of Puerto Rico, Barranquitas Campus, Program in Education, Barranquitas, PR 00794. Offers curriculum and teaching (M Ed), including biology education, English as a second language, history education, mathematics education, Spanish; educational leadership and management (MA); elementary education (M Ed); information and library service technology (M Ed); special education (MA). *Accreditation:* TEAC. *Degree requirements:* For master's, comprehensive exam, thesis optional. *Entrance requirements:* For master's, EXADEP, letter of recommendation. Electronic applications accepted.

Inter American University of Puerto Rico, San Germán Campus, Graduate Studies Center, Program in Library Sciences, San Germán, PR 00683-5008. Offers MLS. *Program availability:* Part-time, evening/weekend. *Degree requirements:* For master's, comprehensive exam. *Entrance requirements:* For master's, GRE General Test or EXADEP, minimum GPA of 3.0.

Kent State University, College of Communication and Information, School of Library and Information Science, Kent, OH 44242-0001. Offers information architecture and knowledge management (MS), including health informatics, knowledge management, user experience design; library and information science (MLIS), including school library media; M Ed/MLIS; MBA/MLIS. *Accreditation:* ALA (one or more programs are accredited). *Program availability:* Part-time, online learning. *Faculty:* 19 full-time (16 women). *Students:* 208 full-time (163 women), 633 part-time (459 women); includes 112 minority (41 Black or African American, non-Hispanic/Latino; 2 American Indian or Alaska Native, non-Hispanic/Latino; 12 Asian, non-Hispanic/Latino; 36 Hispanic/Latino; 1 Native Hawaiian or other Pacific Islander, non-Hispanic/Latino; 20 Two or more races, non-Hispanic/Latino), 10 international. Average age 33. 269 applicants, 80% accepted, 175 enrolled. In 2016, 294 master's awarded. *Degree requirements:* For master's, thesis optional. *Entrance requirements:* For master's, GRE, minimum GPA of 3.0, statement of purpose, 3 letters of recommendation, curriculum vitae/resume, transcripts, writing sample, personal interview. Additional exam requirements/recommendations for international students: Required—TOEFL (minimum score of 600 paper-based, 100 iBT), IELTS (minimum score of 7.0), Michigan English Language Assessment Battery (minimum score of 85), or PTE (minimum score of 68). *Application deadline:* For fall admission, 3/15 for domestic and international students; for spring admission, 9/15 for domestic and international students; for summer admission, 1/15 for domestic and international students. Applications are processed on a rolling basis. Application fee: $45 ($70 for international students). Electronic applications accepted. *Expenses:* Tuition, state resident: full-time $10,864; part-time $495 per credit hour. Tuition, nonresident: full-time $18,380; part-time $837 per credit hour. *Financial support:* Fellowships with full tuition reimbursements, research assistantships with full tuition reimbursements, teaching assistantships with full tuition reimbursements, scholarships/grants, and unspecified assistantships available. Financial award application deadline: 3/1. *Unit head:* Dr. Kendra Albright, Director and Professor, 330-672-8535, E-mail: kalbrig7@kent.edu. *Application contact:* Dr. Karen Gracy, Graduate Co-Coordinator/Associate Professor, 330-672-2782, E-mail: kgracy@kent.edu.
Website: http://www.kent.edu/slis/

Kutztown University of Pennsylvania, College of Education, Program in Library Science, Kutztown, PA 19530-0730. Offers MLS. *Program availability:* Part-time, evening/weekend. *Faculty:* 1 (woman) full-time, 1 (woman) part-time/adjunct. *Students:* 3 full-time (all women), 28 part-time (24 women). Average age 35. 29 applicants, 93% accepted, 16 enrolled. In 2016, 4 master's awarded. *Degree requirements:* For master's, comprehensive exam. *Entrance requirements:* For master's, GRE General Test or valid PA teaching certificate, 3 letters of recommendation. Additional exam requirements/recommendations for international students: Required—TOEFL (minimum score 550 paper-based, 79 iBT) or IELTS (minimum score 6.5). *Application deadline:* For fall admission, 8/1 for domestic and international students; for spring admission, 12/1 for domestic and international students. Application fee: $35. Electronic applications accepted. *Expenses:* Tuition, state resident: full-time $4347; part-time $483 per credit. Tuition, nonresident: full-time $6525; part-time $725 per credit. *Required fees:* $88 per credit. One-time fee: $50 full-time. *Financial support:* Career-related internships or fieldwork, Federal Work-Study, scholarships/grants, and unspecified assistantships available. Financial award application deadline: 3/1; financial award applicants required to submit FAFSA. *Unit head:* Dr. Andrea Harmer, Chairperson, 610-683-4301, Fax: 610-683-1326, E-mail: harmer@kutztown.edu.
Website: https://www.kutztown.edu/academics/graduate-programs/library-science.htm

Louisiana State University and Agricultural & Mechanical College, Graduate School, College of Human Sciences and Education, School of Library and Information Science, Baton Rouge, LA 70803. Offers MLIS. *Accreditation:* ALA.

Mansfield University of Pennsylvania, Graduate Studies, Program in School Library and Information Technologies, Mansfield, PA 16933. Offers library science (M Ed). *Program availability:* Part-time, evening/weekend, online learning. *Degree requirements:* For master's, comprehensive exam, thesis optional. *Entrance requirements:* For master's, minimum GPA of 3.0. Additional exam requirements/recommendations for international students: Required—TOEFL (minimum score 550 paper-based). Electronic applications accepted. *Expenses:* Contact institution.

McDaniel College, Graduate and Professional Studies, Program in School Librarianship, Westminster, MD 21157-4390. Offers MS. *Program availability:* Part-time, evening/weekend, online only, 100% online. *Faculty:* 1 (woman) full-time, 5 part-time/adjunct (all women). *Students:* 3 full-time (all women), 51 part-time (47 women); includes 3 minority (1 Black or African American, non-Hispanic/Latino; 2 Asian, non-Hispanic/Latino). Average age 37. 15 applicants, 80% accepted. In 2016, 6 master's awarded. *Degree requirements:* For master's, comprehensive exam, thesis optional. *Entrance requirements:* For master's, PRAXIS, 3 recommendations, essay. Additional exam requirements/recommendations for international students: Required—TOEFL (minimum score 79 iBT), IELTS (minimum score 6). *Application deadline:* For fall admission, 6/1 priority date for domestic students; for spring admission, 11/1 priority date for domestic students; for summer admission, 3/1 priority date for domestic students. Applications are processed on a rolling basis. Application fee: $75. Electronic applications accepted. *Expenses: Tuition:* Full-time $8370; part-time $465 per credit. *Required fees:* $75 per semester. Tuition and fees vary according to course load, program and reciprocity agreements. *Financial support:* Career-related internships or fieldwork available. Financial award application deadline: 3/1; financial award applicants required to submit FAFSA. *Unit head:* Fax: 410-857-2515, E-mail: gradadms@mcdaniel.edu. *Application contact:* Crystal L. Perry, Assistant Director, Graduate Enrollment Management, 410-857-2516, Fax: 410-857-2515, E-mail: cperry@mcdaniel.edu.

McGill University, Faculty of Graduate and Postdoctoral Studies, Faculty of Education, School of Information Studies, Montréal, QC H3A 2T5, Canada. Offers MLIS, PhD, Certificate, Diploma. *Accreditation:* ALA (one or more programs are accredited).

McNeese State University, Doré School of Graduate Studies, Burton College of Education, Office of Student Teaching and Professional Education Services, Program in School Librarian, Lake Charles, LA 70609. Offers Postbaccalaureate Certificate. *Entrance requirements:* For degree, PRAXIS, 2 letters of recommendation, autobiography.

North Carolina Central University, School of Library and Information Sciences, Durham, NC 27707-3129. Offers MIS, MLS. *Accreditation:* ALA (one or more programs are accredited). *Program availability:* Part-time, evening/weekend. *Degree requirements:* For master's, one foreign language, thesis, research paper, or project. *Entrance requirements:* For master's, GRE, 90 hours in liberal arts. Additional exam requirements/recommendations for international students: Required—TOEFL.

Old Dominion University, Darden College of Education, Program in Elementary/Middle Education, Norfolk, VA 23529. Offers elementary education (Postbaccalaureate Certificate); instructional technology (MS Ed); library science (MS Ed). *Accreditation:* NCATE. *Program availability:* Part-time, evening/weekend, 100% online, blended/hybrid learning. *Faculty:* 21 full-time (19 women), 24 part-time/adjunct (22 women). *Students:* 120 full-time (112 women), 138 part-time (125 women); includes 60 minority (36 Black or African American, non-Hispanic/Latino; 1 American Indian or Alaska Native, non-Hispanic/Latino; 5 Asian, non-Hispanic/Latino; 12 Hispanic/Latino; 6 Two or more races, non-Hispanic/Latino). Average age 33. 213 applicants, 88% accepted, 172 enrolled. In

2016, 127 master's awarded. *Degree requirements:* For master's, comprehensive exam. *Entrance requirements:* For master's, GRE General Test or MAT; PRAXIS I, SAT or ACT, minimum GPA of 2.8. Additional exam requirements/recommendations for international students: Required—TOEFL (minimum score 600 paper-based). *Application deadline:* For fall admission, 6/1 priority date for domestic students; for winter admission, 11/1 priority date for domestic students; for spring admission, 3/1 priority date for domestic students. Applications are processed on a rolling basis. Application fee: $50. Electronic applications accepted. *Expenses:* $478 per credit hour in-state; $1,195 per credit hour out-of-state. *Financial support:* In 2016–17, 180 students received support. Unspecified assistantships available. Financial award application deadline: 2/15; financial award applicants required to submit FAFSA. *Faculty research:* Education pre-K to 6, school librarianship, reading, TESOL, literacy. *Unit head:* Dr. KaaVonia Hinton, Chair, Department of Teaching and Learning, 757-683-3284, Fax: 757-683-5862, E-mail: khintonj@odu.edu. *Application contact:* William Heffelfinger, Director of Graduate Admissions, 757-683-5554, Fax: 757-683-3255, E-mail: gradadmit@odu.edu.
Website: http://education.odu.edu/eci/

Olivet Nazarene University, Graduate School, Division of Education, Program in Library Information Specialist, Bourbonnais, IL 60914. Offers MAE.

Pratt Institute, School of Information, New York, NY 10011. Offers MS, Adv C, JD/MS, MS/MFA. *Accreditation:* ALA. *Program availability:* Part-time. *Faculty:* 9 full-time (4 women), 26 part-time/adjunct (13 women). *Students:* 95 full-time (77 women), 62 part-time (50 women); includes 43 minority (11 Black or African American, non-Hispanic/Latino; 12 Asian, non-Hispanic/Latino; 17 Hispanic/Latino; 3 Two or more races, non-Hispanic/Latino), 11 international. Average age 31. 129 applicants, 88% accepted, 59 enrolled. In 2016, 64 master's, 1 other advanced degree awarded. *Degree requirements:* For master's, thesis. *Entrance requirements:* For degree, master's degree in library and information science. Additional exam requirements/recommendations for international students: Required—TOEFL (minimum score 600 paper-based; 100 iBT). *Application deadline:* For fall admission, 1/5 for domestic and international students; for spring admission, 10/1 for domestic and international students. Applications are processed on a rolling basis. Application fee: $50 ($90 for international students). Electronic applications accepted. *Expenses:* $23,814 full-time tuition, $1,938 fees. *Financial support:* Career-related internships or fieldwork, Federal Work-Study, institutionally sponsored loans, scholarships/grants, health care benefits, and unspecified assistantships available. Support available to part-time students. Financial award application deadline: 2/1; financial award applicants required to submit FAFSA. *Faculty research:* Development of urban libraries and information centers, medical and law librarianship, information management. *Unit head:* Dr. Tula Giannini, Dean, 212-647-7682, Fax: 212-367-2492, E-mail: giannini@pratt.edu. *Application contact:* Natalie Capannelli, Director of Graduate Admissions, 718-636-3551, Fax: 718-399-4242, E-mail: ncapanne@pratt.edu.
Website: https://www.pratt.edu/academics/information/

See Display on page 1551 and Close-Up on page 1563.

Queens College of the City University of New York, Division of Social Sciences, Graduate School of Library and Information Studies, Queens, NY 11367-1597. Offers archives, records management and preservation (AC); children's and young adult services in the public library (AC); library media specialist (MLS, AC); library science (MLS, AC); school media specialist (MLS). *Accreditation:* ALA (one or more programs are accredited). *Program availability:* Part-time, evening/weekend. *Faculty:* 12 full-time (7 women), 15 part-time/adjunct (11 women). *Students:* 28 full-time (22 women), 230 part-time (153 women); includes 106 minority (35 Black or African American, non-Hispanic/Latino; 21 Asian, non-Hispanic/Latino; 38 Hispanic/Latino; 12 Two or more races, non-Hispanic/Latino), 5 international. Average age 33. 163 applicants, 82% accepted, 92 enrolled. In 2016, 74 master's, 4 other advanced degrees awarded. *Degree requirements:* For master's, thesis; for AC, thesis optional. *Entrance requirements:* For master's, minimum GPA of 3.0; for AC, master's degree or equivalent. Additional exam requirements/recommendations for international students: Required—TOEFL, IELTS. *Application deadline:* For fall admission, 4/1 for domestic students; for spring admission, 11/1 for domestic students. Applications are processed on a rolling basis. Application fee: $125. Electronic applications accepted. *Expenses:* Tuition, state resident: full-time $5065; part-time $425 per credit. Tuition, nonresident: part-time $780 per credit. *Required fees:* $522; $397 per credit. Part-time tuition and fees vary according to course load and program. *Financial support:* Career-related internships or fieldwork and unspecified assistantships available. Financial award application deadline: 4/1; financial award applicants required to submit FAFSA. *Unit head:* Dr. Roberta Brody, Director/Chair, 718-997-3790, E-mail: roberta.brody@qc.cuny.edu.

Rowan University, Graduate School, College of Education, Department of Educational Services and Leadership, Glassboro, NJ 08028-1701. Offers counseling in educational settings (MA); educational leadership (Ed D, CAGS); higher education administration (MA); principal preparation (CAGS); school administration (MA); school and public librarianship (MA); school nursing (Postbaccalaureate Certificate); school psychology (MA, Ed S); supervisor (CAGS). *Accreditation:* NCATE. *Program availability:* Part-time, evening/weekend. *Degree requirements:* For master's, comprehensive exam, thesis; for other advanced degree, thesis or alternative. *Entrance requirements:* For master's and other advanced degree, GRE General Test. Additional exam requirements/recommendations for international students: Required—TOEFL. Electronic applications accepted.

Rutgers University–New Brunswick, School of Communication and Information, Program in Communication, Information and Library Studies, Piscataway, NJ 08854-8097. Offers PhD. *Program availability:* Part-time. *Degree requirements:* For doctorate, comprehensive exam, thesis/dissertation, qualifying exams. *Entrance requirements:* For doctorate, GRE General Test, proficiency in statistics. Additional exam requirements/recommendations for international students: Required—TOEFL (minimum score 600 paper-based). Electronic applications accepted. *Faculty research:* Information science, media studies.

St. Catherine University, Graduate Programs, Program in Library and Information Science, St. Paul, MN 55105. Offers MLIS. *Accreditation:* ALA. *Program availability:* Part-time, evening/weekend. *Degree requirements:* For master's, microcomputer competency. *Entrance requirements:* For master's, GRE or MAT, minimum GPA of 3.2 or GRE. Additional exam requirements/recommendations for international students: Required—Michigan English Language Assessment Battery or TOEFL (minimum score 600 paper-based; 100 iBT). *Expenses:* Contact institution.

St. John's University, St. John's College of Liberal Arts and Sciences, Department of Government and Politics and Division of Library and Information Science, Program in Government and Library and Information Science, Queens, NY 11439. Offers MA/MS. *Program availability:* Part-time, evening/weekend. *Entrance requirements:* Additional exam requirements/recommendations for international students: Required—TOEFL (minimum score 600 paper-based; 100 iBT), IELTS (minimum score 7). Electronic applications accepted.

St. John's University, St. John's College of Liberal Arts and Sciences, Division of Library and Information Science, Queens, NY 11439. Offers MS, Adv C, MA/MS, MS/MS. *Accreditation:* ALA (one or more programs are accredited). *Program availability:* Part-time, evening/weekend, online learning. *Degree requirements:* For master's, comprehensive exam, portfolio. *Entrance requirements:* For master's, interview, minimum GPA of 3.0, 2 letters of recommendation, bachelor's degree, personal statement, transcript. Additional exam requirements/recommendations for international students: Required—TOEFL (minimum score 600 paper-based; 100 iBT), IELTS (minimum score 7). Electronic applications accepted. *Expenses:* Contact institution. *Faculty research:* Indexes and metatags, information use and users, competitive intelligence, knowledge management, database theory, young adult and children services, school media services, archives, oral history.

Sam Houston State University, College of Education, Department of Library Science, Huntsville, TX 77341. Offers MLS. *Program availability:* Part-time, evening/weekend. *Degree requirements:* For master's, portfolio, intership. *Entrance requirements:* For master's, GRE General Test. Additional exam requirements/recommendations for international students: Required—TOEFL (minimum score 550 paper-based; 79 iBT), IELTS (minimum score 6.5). Electronic applications accepted.

San Jose State University, Graduate Studies and Research, College of Applied Sciences and Arts, San Jose, CA 95192-0001. Offers big data (Certificate); California library media teacher services (Credential); collaborative response to family violence (Certificate); justice studies (MS); kinesiology (MA), including applied sciences and arts (MA, MS), athletic training, exercise physiology, sport management, sport studies; library and information science (MLIS, Certificate); mass communication (MA); nutritional science (MS); occupational therapy (MS); public health (MPH); pupil personnel services (Credential); recreation (MS), including applied sciences and arts (MA, MS), international tourism; social work (MSW); Spanish language counseling (Certificate); strategic management of digital assets and services (Certificate). *Program availability:* Part-time, evening/weekend. Electronic applications accepted.

Simmons College, School of Library and Information Science, Boston, MA 02115. Offers children's literature (MA); library and information science (MS, PhD, Certificate), including archives management (MS), cultural heritage (MS), information science and technology (MS), school library teacher (MS); writing for children (MFA); MA/MA; MA/MAT; MA/MFA; MS/MA. *Accreditation:* ALA (one or more programs are accredited). *Program availability:* Part-time, evening/weekend, 100% online, blended/hybrid learning. *Faculty:* 23 full-time (17 women), 23 part-time/adjunct (16 women). *Students:* 313 full-time (262 women), 511 part-time (420 women); includes 88 minority (13 Black or African American, non-Hispanic/Latino; 10 Asian, non-Hispanic/Latino; 41 Hispanic/Latino; 24 Two or more races, non-Hispanic/Latino), 19 international. Average age 30. 568 applicants, 98% accepted, 319 enrolled. In 2016, 245 master's, 3 doctorates, 4 other advanced degrees awarded. *Degree requirements:* For master's, thesis optional, capstone project experience; for doctorate, comprehensive exam, thesis/dissertation, 36 credit hours. *Entrance requirements:* For doctorate, GRE, transcripts, personal statement, resume, recommendations, master's degree. Additional exam requirements/recommendations for international students: Required—TOEFL (minimum score 550 paper-based; 79 iBT), IELTS (minimum score 7). *Application deadline:* For fall admission, 3/1 for domestic and international students; for spring admission, 9/1 for domestic and international students; for summer admission, 2/1 for domestic and international students. Applications are processed on a rolling basis. Application fee: $65. Electronic applications accepted. *Expenses:* $1,210 per credit, $3,630 per course, $52 activity fee per semester. *Financial support:* In 2016–17, 10 fellowships with partial tuition reimbursements were awarded; scholarships/grants, tuition waivers, and unspecified assistantships also available. Support available to part-time students. Financial award application deadline: 2/1; financial award applicants required to submit FAFSA. *Faculty research:* Archives and social justice, information-seeking behavior, information retrieval, organization of information, cultural heritage informatics. *Unit head:* Dr. Eileen G. Abels, Dean, 617-521-2869. *Application contact:* Sarah Petrakos, Assistant Dean for Admission and Recruitment, 617-521-2868, Fax: 617-521-3192, E-mail: gslisadm@simmons.edu.
Website: http://www.simmons.edu/slis/

Southern Arkansas University–Magnolia, School of Graduate Studies, Magnolia, AR 71753. Offers agriculture (MS); business administration (MBA), including agri-business, social entrepreneurship, supply chain management; clinical and mental health counseling (MS); computer and information sciences (MS), including cyber security and privacy, data science, information technology; gifted and talented (M Ed), including curriculum and instruction, educational administration and supervision, gifted and talented P-8/7-12, instructional specialist P-4; higher, adult and lifelong education (M Ed); kinesiology (M Ed), including coaching; library media and information specialist (M Ed); public administration (MPA); school counseling K-12 (M Ed); student affairs and college counseling (M Ed); teaching (MAT). *Accreditation:* NCATE. *Program availability:* Part-time, 100% online, blended/hybrid learning. *Faculty:* 36 full-time (19 women), 33 part-time/adjunct (14 women). *Students:* 605 full-time (143 women), 879 part-time (352 women); includes 130 minority (113 Black or African American, non-Hispanic/Latino; 7 American Indian or Alaska Native, non-Hispanic/Latino; 2 Asian, non-Hispanic/Latino; 2 Hispanic/Latino; 6 Two or more races, non-Hispanic/Latino), 1,048 international. Average age 28. 904 applicants, 81% accepted, 262 enrolled. In 2016, 278 master's awarded. *Degree requirements:* For master's, comprehensive exam (for some programs), thesis optional. *Entrance requirements:* For master's, GRE, MAT or GMAT, minimum GPA of 2.5. Additional exam requirements/recommendations for international students: Required—TOEFL (minimum score 550 paper-based), IELTS (minimum score 6). *Application deadline:* For fall admission, 7/20 for domestic students, 7/10 for international students; for spring admission, 12/1 for domestic students, 11/15 for international students; for summer admission, 4/1 for domestic students, 5/1 for international students. Applications are processed on a rolling basis. Application fee: $25 ($50 for international students). Electronic applications accepted. *Expenses:* Tuition, state resident: full-time $2511; part-time $279 per credit hour. Tuition, nonresident: full-time $3726; part-time $414 per credit hour. *Required fees:* $307 per semester. Tuition and fees vary according to course load and program. *Financial support:* Career-related internships or fieldwork, Federal Work-Study, scholarships/grants, tuition waivers (full), and unspecified assistantships available. Financial award applicants required to submit FAFSA. *Faculty research:* Alternative certification for teachers, supervision of instruction, instructional leadership, counseling. *Unit head:* Dr. Kim Bloss, Dean, School of Graduate Studies, 870-235-4150, Fax: 870-235-5227, E-mail: kkbloss@saumag.edu. *Application contact:* Shrijana Malakar, Admissions Specialist, 870-235-4150, Fax: 870-235-5227, E-mail: smalakar@saumag.edu.
Website: http://www.saumag.edu/graduate

Southern Connecticut State University, School of Graduate Studies, School of Education, Department of Information and Library Science, New Haven, CT 06515-1355. Offers information studies (Diploma); library science (MLS). *Program availability:* Part-time, evening/weekend. *Faculty:* 4 full-time (2 women). *Students:* 2 full-time (1 woman), 8 part-time (7 women). Average age 39. 27 applicants, 52% accepted, 12 enrolled. In 2016, 30 master's, 1 other advanced degree awarded. *Degree requirements:* For master's and Diploma, thesis or alternative. *Entrance requirements:* For master's, GRE General Test, interview, minimum QPA of 2.7, introductory computer science course; for Diploma, master's degree in library science or information science.

Library Science

Application deadline: For fall admission, 7/15 priority date for domestic students. Applications are processed on a rolling basis. Application fee: $50. Electronic applications accepted. *Expenses:* Tuition, state resident: full-time $6497; part-time $519 per credit hour. Tuition, nonresident: full-time $18,102; part-time $535 per credit hour. *Required fees:* $4722; $55 per semester. Tuition and fees vary according to program. *Financial support:* Career-related internships or fieldwork, scholarships/grants, and unspecified assistantships available. Financial award application deadline: 4/15; financial award applicants required to submit FAFSA. *Unit head:* Dr. Hak Joon Kim, Chairperson, 203-392-5703, Fax: 203-392-5780, E-mail: kimh1@southernct.edu. *Application contact:* Lisa Galvin, Director of Graduate Admissions, 203-392-5240, Fax: 203-392-5235, E-mail: galvinl1@southernct.edu.

Syracuse University, School of Information Studies, MS Program in Library and Information Science, Syracuse, NY 13244. Offers MS. *Accreditation:* ALA. *Program availability:* Part-time, evening/weekend, online learning. *Students:* Average age 30. *Degree requirements:* For master's, fieldwork or research paper. *Entrance requirements:* For master's, GRE General Test, two letters of recommendation, personal statement, resume. Additional exam requirements/recommendations for international students: Required—TOEFL (minimum score 100 iBT). *Application deadline:* For fall admission, 2/1 priority date for domestic and international students; for spring admission, 10/15 priority date for domestic and international students. Applications are processed on a rolling basis. Application fee: $75. Electronic applications accepted. *Expenses: Tuition:* Full-time $25,974; part-time $1443 per credit hour. *Required fees:* $802; $50 per course. Tuition and fees vary according to course load and program. *Financial support:* Fellowships with full tuition reimbursements and teaching assistantships available. Financial award application deadline: 1/1; financial award applicants required to submit FAFSA. *Faculty research:* Information environments, library planning and marketing, management principles, information policy. *Unit head:* Prof. Jill Hurst-Wahl, Program Director, 315-443-2911, E-mail: igrad@syr.edu. *Application contact:* Susan Corieri, Director of Enrollment Management, 315-443-1070, E-mail: ischool@syr.edu. Website: http://ischool.syr.edu/

See Display below and Close-Up on page 1565.

Tennessee Technological University, College of Graduate Studies, College of Education, Department of Curriculum and Instruction, Program in Library Science, Cookeville, TN 38505. Offers MA, Ed S. *Program availability:* Part-time, evening/weekend. *Students:* 2 full-time (both women), 9 part-time (7 women). 5 applicants, 60% accepted, 3 enrolled. In 2016, 2 master's, 1 other advanced degree awarded. *Degree requirements:* For master's, comprehensive exam, thesis or alternative. *Entrance requirements:* For master's, MAT or GRE. Additional exam requirements/recommendations for international students: Required—TOEFL (minimum score 527 paper-based; 71 iBT), IELTS (minimum score 5.5), PTE (minimum score 48), or TOEIC (Test of English as an International Communication). *Application deadline:* For fall admission, 8/1 for domestic students, 5/1 for international students; for spring admission, 12/1 for domestic students, 10/1 for international students; for summer admission, 5/1 for domestic students, 2/1 for international students. Applications are processed on a rolling basis. Application fee: $35 ($40 for international students). Electronic applications accepted. *Expenses:* Tuition, state resident: full-time $9375; part-time $534 per credit hour. Tuition, nonresident: full-time $22,443; part-time $1260 per credit hour. *Financial support:* Research assistantships and teaching assistantships available. Financial award application deadline: 4/1. *Unit head:* Dr. Jeremy Wendt, Interim Chairperson, 931-372-3181, Fax: 931-372-6270, E-mail: jwendt@tntech.edu. *Application contact:* Shelia K. Kendrick, Coordinator of Graduate Studies, 931-372-3808, Fax: 931-372-3497, E-mail: skendrick@tntech.edu.

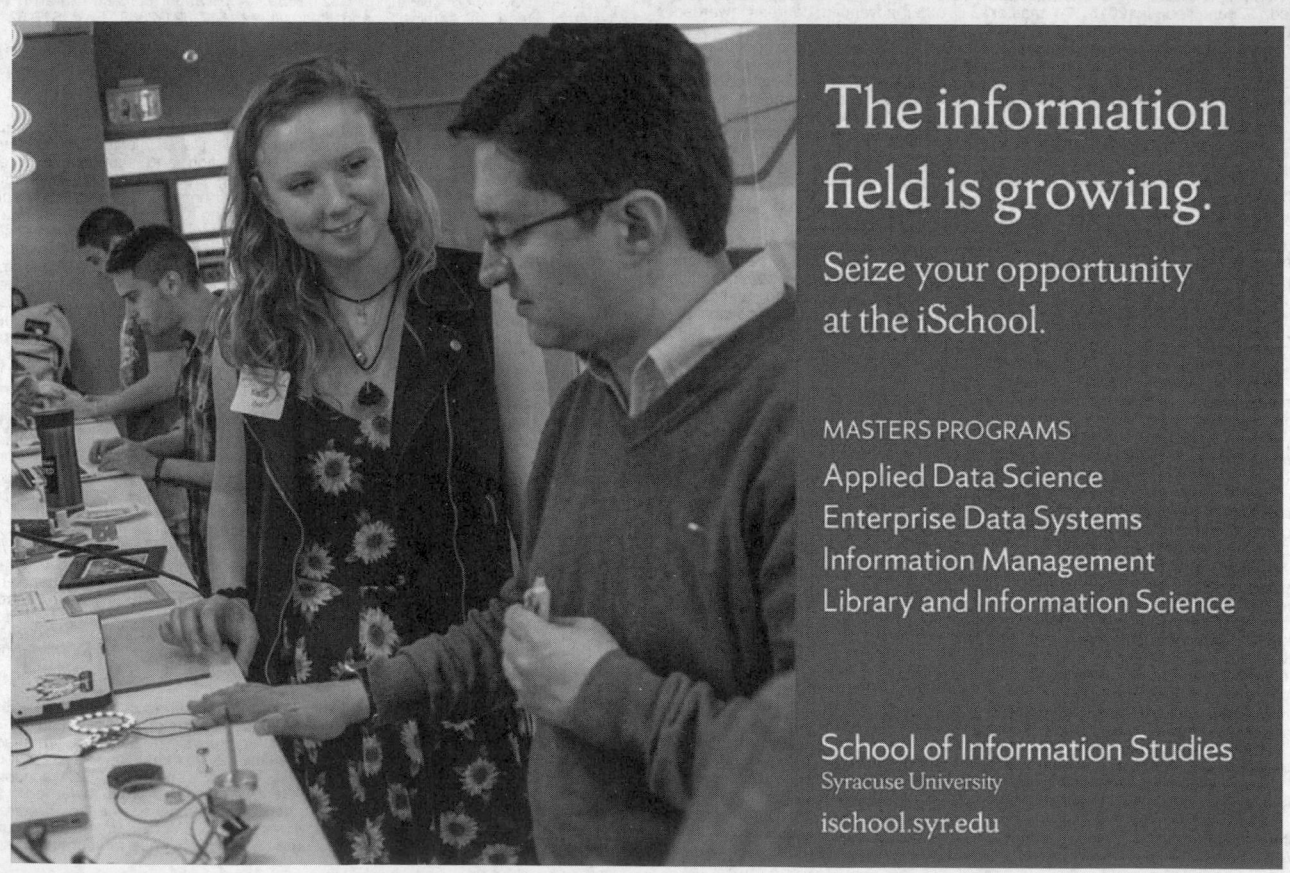

Texas A&M University–Commerce, College of Education and Human Services, Commerce, TX 75429-3011. Offers counseling (MS); curriculum and instruction (M Ed, MS); early childhood education (M Ed, MS); educational administration (M Ed, Ed D); educational psychology (PhD); educational technology leadership (MS); educational technology library science (MS); health, kinesiology and sports studies (MS); higher education (MS, Ed D); organization, learning, and technology (MS); psychology (MS); reading (M Ed, MS); school psychology (SSP); secondary education (M Ed, MS); social work (MSW); special education (M Ed); supervision, curriculum and instruction-elementary education (Ed D). *Program availability:* Part-time, 100% online, blended/hybrid learning. *Faculty:* 88 full-time (52 women), 31 part-time/adjunct (24 women). *Students:* 341 full-time (276 women), 1,495 part-time (1,156 women); includes 762 minority (429 Black or African American, non-Hispanic/Latino; 4 American Indian or Alaska Native, non-Hispanic/Latino; 27 Asian, non-Hispanic/Latino; 247 Hispanic/Latino; 1 Native Hawaiian or other Pacific Islander, non-Hispanic/Latino; 54 Two or more races, non-Hispanic/Latino), 18 international. Average age 37. 1,070 applicants, 54% accepted, 452 enrolled. In 2016, 579 master's, 31 doctorates awarded. *Degree requirements:* For master's, one foreign language, comprehensive exam, thesis optional, departmental qualifying exams (for some programs); for doctorate, comprehensive exam, thesis/dissertation, departmental qualifying exam; for SSP, comprehensive exam, thesis optional. *Entrance requirements:* For master's and doctorate, GRE General Test. Additional exam requirements/recommendations for international students: Required—TOEFL (minimum score 550 paper-based; 79 iBT), IELTS (minimum score 6). *Application deadline:* For fall admission, 6/1 priority date for international students; for spring admission, 10/15 priority date for international students; for summer admission, 3/15 priority date for international students. Applications are processed on a rolling basis. Application fee: $50. Electronic applications accepted. *Expenses:* $2,254 resident; $4,744 non-resident. *Financial support:* In 2016–17, 301 students received support, including 39 research assistantships with partial tuition reimbursements available (averaging $9,000 per year), 17 teaching assistantships with partial tuition reimbursements available (averaging $9,000 per year); career-related internships or fieldwork, Federal Work-Study, institutionally sponsored loans, scholarships/grants, health care benefits, and unspecified assistantships also available. Financial award application deadline: 5/1; financial award applicants required to submit FAFSA. *Faculty research:* Cognitive and bilingual education, positive behavioral intervention, literacy, math readiness. *Total annual research expenditures:* $470,963. *Unit head:* Dr. Timothy Letzring, Dean, 903-886-5181, Fax: 903-886-5905, E-mail: tim.letzring@tamuc.edu. *Application contact:* Jennifer Faunce, Graduate Recruiter, 903-886-5030, Fax: 903-886-5905, E-mail: jennifer.faunce@tamuc.edu.
Website: http://www.tamuc.edu/academics/graduateSchool/programs/education/default.aspx

Texas Woman's University, Graduate School, College of Professional Education, School of Library and Information Studies, Denton, TX 76204-5438. Offers library science (MA, MLS, PhD). *Accreditation:* ALA (one or more programs are accredited). *Program availability:* Part-time, evening/weekend, online only, 100% online. *Students:* 93 full-time (91 women), 398 part-time (384 women); includes 158 minority (35 Black or African American, non-Hispanic/Latino; 3 American Indian or Alaska Native, non-Hispanic/Latino; 6 Asian, non-Hispanic/Latino; 106 Hispanic/Latino; 8 Two or more races, non-Hispanic/Latino). Average age 36. In 2016, 167 master's, 2 doctorates awarded. *Degree requirements:* For master's, comprehensive exam, thesis or alternative. *Entrance requirements:* For master's, GRE (preferred), GMAT, MCAT, MAT, 3 letters of recommendation, 2-page statement of intent, resume. Additional exam requirements/recommendations for international students: Required—TOEFL (minimum score 550 paper-based; 79 iBT). *Application deadline:* For fall admission, 2/15 priority date for domestic students, 2/15 for international students. Applications are processed

on a rolling basis. Application fee: $50 ($75 for international students). Electronic applications accepted. *Expenses:* Tuition, state resident: full-time $9046; part-time $251 per credit hour. Tuition, nonresident: full-time $22,922; part-time $614 per credit hour. *International tuition:* $23,046 full-time. *Required fees:* $2690; $1285 per credit hour. One-time fee: $50. Tuition and fees vary according to course level, course load, program and reciprocity agreements. *Financial support:* Research assistantships, teaching assistantships, career-related internships or fieldwork, Federal Work-Study, institutionally sponsored loans, scholarships/grants, traineeships, health care benefits, and unspecified assistantships available. Support available to part-time students. Financial award application deadline: 3/1; financial award applicants required to submit FAFSA. *Faculty research:* Children's literature, health information, information needs analysis, school library leadership, library management and assessment. *Unit head:* Dr. Ling Hwey Jeng, Director, 940-898-2602, Fax: 940-898-2611, E-mail: slis@twu.edu. *Application contact:* Dr. Samuel Wheeler, Assistant Director of Admissions, 940-898-3188, Fax: 940-898-3081, E-mail: wheelersr@twu.edu.
Website: http://www.twu.edu/slis/

Trevecca Nazarene University, Graduate Education Program, Nashville, TN 37210-2877. Offers accountability and instructional leadership (Ed S); curriculum and instruction for Christian school educators (M Ed); curriculum and instruction K-12 (M Ed); educational leadership (M Ed); English second language (M Ed); library and information science (MLI Sc); special education: visual impairments (M Ed); teaching (MAT), including teaching 6-12, teaching K-5. *Accreditation:* NCATE. *Program availability:* Part-time, evening/weekend, online learning. *Faculty:* 5 full-time (3 women), 18 part-time/adjunct (12 women). *Students:* 80 full-time (64 women), 16 part-time (13 women); includes 19 minority (17 Black or African American, non-Hispanic/Latino; 2 Hispanic/Latino). Average age 35. In 2016, 68 master's, 7 other advanced degrees awarded. *Degree requirements:* For master's, comprehensive exam, exit assessment/e-portfolio. *Entrance requirements:* For master's, GRE (minimum score of 290) or MAT (minimum score of 378); PRAXIS (for MAT), minimum GPA of 3.0, official transcript from regionally-accredited institution, at least 3 years' successful teaching experience (for M Ed in educational leadership major). Additional exam requirements/recommendations for international students: Required—TOEFL (minimum score 550 paper-based). *Application deadline:* Applications are processed on a rolling basis. Electronic applications accepted. *Expenses:* Contact institution. *Financial support:* Applicants required to submit FAFSA. *Unit head:* Dr. Suzie Harris, Dean, School of Education/Director of Graduate Education Programs, 615-248-1201, Fax: 615-248-1597, E-mail: admissions_ged@trevecca.edu. *Application contact:* 844-TNU-GRAD,
E-mail: sgcsadmissions@trevecca.edu. Website: http://www.trevecca.edu/soe

Universidad del Turabo, Graduate Programs, Programs in Education, Program in Library Service and Information Technology, Gurabo, PR 00778-3030. Offers M Ed. *Program availability:* Part-time, evening/weekend. *Students:* 1 part-time (0 women); minority (Hispanic/Latino). Average age 60. 1 applicant, 100% accepted, 1 enrolled. In 2016, 3 master's awarded. *Entrance requirements:* For master's, GRE, EXADEP, GMAT, interview, official transcript, essay, recommendation letters. *Application deadline:* Applications are processed on a rolling basis. Application fee: $25. Electronic applications accepted. *Financial support:* Institutionally sponsored loans available. Financial award applicants required to submit FAFSA. *Unit head:* Israel Rodríguez, Dean, 787-743-7979 Ext. 4627. *Application contact:* Diriee Rodríguez, Admissions Director, 787-743-7979 Ext. 4453, E-mail: admisiones-ut@suagm.edu.
Website: http://ut.suagm.edu/es/educacion

Université de Montréal, Faculty of Arts and Sciences, School of Library and Information Sciences, Montréal, QC H3C 3J7, Canada. Offers information sciences (MIS, PhD). *Accreditation:* ALA (one or more programs are accredited). *Degree requirements:* For master's, thesis optional. *Entrance requirements:* For master's, interview, master's degree in library and information science or equivalent. Electronic applications accepted.

University at Albany, State University of New York, College of Engineering and Applied Sciences, MS Program in Information Science, Albany, NY 12222-0001. Offers information science (MS); library and information science (CAS). *Faculty:* 8 full-time (5 women), 6 part-time/adjunct (3 women). *Students:* 50 full-time (30 women), 41 part-time (32 women); includes 17 minority (8 Black or African American, non-Hispanic/Latino; 2 Asian, non-Hispanic/Latino; 6 Hispanic/Latino; 1 Two or more races, non-Hispanic/Latino), 5 international. Average age 33. 90 applicants, 61% accepted, 23 enrolled. In 2016, 54 master's awarded. Application fee: $75. *Expenses:* Tuition, state resident: full-time $10,870; part-time $453 per credit hour. Tuition, nonresident: full-time $22,210; part-time $925 per credit hour. *International tuition:* $21,550 full-time. *Required fees:* $1864; $96 per credit hour. *Financial support:* Research assistantships and teaching assistantships available. Financial award applicants required to submit FAFSA. *Faculty research:* Electronic information across technologies system dynamics modeling archives, records administration. *Total annual research expenditures:* $357,256. *Unit head:* Philip B. Eppard, Chair, 518-442-5119, E-mail: peppard@albany.edu.
Website: http://www.albany.edu/informationstudies/

University at Buffalo, the State University of New York, Graduate School, Graduate School of Education, Department of Library and Information Studies, Buffalo, NY 14260. Offers information and library science (MS); library and information studies (Certificate); school librarianship (MS). *Accreditation:* ALA (one or more programs are accredited). *Program availability:* Part-time, 100% online. *Faculty:* 10 full-time (6 women), 9 part-time/adjunct (6 women). *Students:* 35 full-time (28 women), 144 part-time (112 women); includes 9 minority (4 Black or African American, non-Hispanic/Latino; 1 American Indian or Alaska Native, non-Hispanic/Latino; 4 Asian, non-Hispanic/Latino), 6 international. Average age 33. 93 applicants, 91% accepted, 63 enrolled. In 2016, 81 master's awarded. *Degree requirements:* For master's, thesis optional; for Certificate, thesis. *Entrance requirements:* For master's, letters of recommendation. Additional exam requirements/recommendations for international students: Required—TOEFL (minimum score 550 paper-based; 79 iBT). *Application deadline:* For fall admission, 4/1 priority date for domestic and international students; for spring admission, 10/15 priority date for domestic students, 10/15 for international students. Applications are processed on a rolling basis. Application fee: $50. Electronic applications accepted. *Financial support:* In 2016–17, 19 fellowships (averaging $2,816 per year), 6 research assistantships with tuition reimbursements (averaging $10,128 per year) were awarded; teaching assistantships, Federal Work-Study, scholarships/grants, tuition waivers (full and partial), and unspecified assistantships also available. Support available to part-time students. Financial award application deadline: 3/1; financial award applicants required to submit FAFSA. *Faculty research:* Information-seeking behavior, thesauri, impact of technology, questioning behaviors, educational informatics. *Total annual research expenditures:* $91,973. *Unit head:* Dr. Heidi Julien, Chair, 716-645-1474, Fax: 716-645-3775, E-mail: heidijul@buffalo.edu. *Application contact:* Pat Glinski, Admissions Assistant, 716-645-2110, Fax: 716-645-7937, E-mail: gse-info@buffalo.edu.
Website: http://www.gse.buffalo.edu/lis/

The University of Alabama, Graduate School, College of Communication and Information Sciences, School of Library and Information Studies, Tuscaloosa, AL 35487. Offers book arts (MFA); library and information studies (MLIS, PhD). *Accreditation:* ALA (one or more programs are accredited). *Program availability:* Part-time, evening/weekend, online learning. *Faculty:* 10 full-time (5 women), 1 (woman) part-time/adjunct. *Students:* 46 full-time (31 women), 154 part-time (128 women); includes 27 minority (15 Black or African American, non-Hispanic/Latino; 2 Asian, non-Hispanic/Latino; 5 Hispanic/Latino; 5 Two or more races, non-Hispanic/Latino), 3 international. Average age 34. 126 applicants, 75% accepted, 83 enrolled. In 2016, 98 master's awarded. *Degree requirements:* For master's, comprehensive exam (for some programs), thesis optional; for doctorate, comprehensive exam, thesis/dissertation. *Entrance requirements:* For master's, GRE General Test or MAT, minimum GPA of 3.0; for doctorate, GRE. Additional exam requirements/recommendations for international students: Required—TOEFL. *Application deadline:* For fall admission, 7/1 priority date for domestic and international students; for spring admission, 11/1 priority date for domestic and international students. Applications are processed on a rolling basis. Application fee: $50 ($60 for international students). Electronic applications accepted. *Expenses:* Tuition, state resident: full-time $10,470. Tuition, nonresident: full-time $26,950. *Financial support:* In 2016–17, 64 students received support, including 3 fellowships with full tuition reimbursements available (averaging $15,000 per year), 18 research assistantships with tuition reimbursements available (averaging $6,183 per year), 12 teaching assistantships with tuition reimbursements available (averaging $6,183 per year); career-related internships or fieldwork, scholarships/grants, health care benefits, tuition waivers (full), unspecified assistantships, and 15 grant-funded fellowships also available. Support available to part-time students. Financial award application deadline: 3/15. *Faculty research:* Library administration, user services, digital libraries, book arts, evaluation. *Unit head:* Dr. Ann Ethelynd Prentice, Director and Professor, 205-348-4610, Fax: 205-348-3746, E-mail: aeprentice@ua.edu. *Application contact:* Dr. Ann Bourne, Assistant Director, 205-348-1524, Fax: 205-348-3746,
E-mail: abourne@ua.edu. Website: http://www.slis.ua.edu/

University of Alberta, Faculty of Graduate Studies and Research, School of Library and Information Studies, Edmonton, AB T6G 2E1, Canada. Offers MLIS. *Accreditation:* ALA. *Entrance requirements:* Additional exam requirements/recommendations for international students: Required—TOEFL, Canadian Academic English Language Assessment. Electronic applications accepted. *Faculty research:* Intellectual freedom, materials for children and young adults, library classification, multi-media literacy.

The University of Arizona, College of Social and Behavioral Sciences, School of Information Resources and Library Science, Tucson, AZ 85721. Offers MA, PhD. *Accreditation:* ALA (one or more programs are accredited). *Program availability:* Part-time. *Degree requirements:* For master's, proficiency in disk operating system (DOS); for doctorate, thesis/dissertation. *Entrance requirements:* For master's and doctorate, GRE General Test, 3 letters of recommendation, resume. Additional exam requirements/recommendations for international students: Required—TOEFL (minimum score 550 paper-based; 79 iBT). Electronic applications accepted. *Faculty research:* Microcomputer applications; quantitative methods systems; information transfer, planning, evaluation, and technology.

The University of British Columbia, Faculty of Arts, School of Library, Archival and Information Studies, Dual Master of Archival Studies/Master of Library and Information Studies Program, Vancouver, BC V6T 1Z1, Canada. Offers MLIS/MAS. *Entrance requirements:* Additional exam requirements/recommendations for international students: Required—TOEFL. *Application deadline:* Applications are processed on a rolling basis. Application fee: $100 Canadian dollars ($162 Canadian dollars for international students). Electronic applications accepted. *Expenses:* $4,911 per year tuition and fees, $8,774 per year international. *Financial support:* Fellowships, research assistantships, Federal Work-Study, institutionally sponsored loans, scholarships/grants, health care benefits, tuition waivers (partial), and unspecified assistantships available. *Faculty research:* Computer systems/database design, information-seeking behavior, archives and records management, children's literature and services, digital libraries and archives. *Application contact:* Alynne Pols, Graduate Program Staff, 604-822-3459, Fax: 604-822-6006, E-mail: ischool.program@ubc.ca.
Website: http://slais.ubc.ca/

The University of British Columbia, Faculty of Arts, School of Library, Archival and Information Studies, Master of Library and Information Studies Program, Vancouver, BC V6T 1Z1, Canada. Offers MLIS. *Accreditation:* ALA. *Program availability:* Part-time. *Degree requirements:* For master's, thesis optional. *Entrance requirements:* For master's, minimum GPA of 3.3 in undergraduate upper-division courses. Additional exam requirements/recommendations for international students: Required—TOEFL. Application fee: $100 ($162 for international students). Electronic applications accepted. *Expenses:* $4,911 per year tuition and fees, $8,774 per year international. *Financial support:* Fellowships, research assistantships, career-related internships or fieldwork, Federal Work-Study, institutionally sponsored loans, scholarships/grants, health care benefits, tuition waivers, and unspecified assistantships available. *Faculty research:* Computer systems/database design; digital libraries; metadata/classification; human-computer interaction; children's literature and services. *Application contact:* Alynne Pols, Graduate Program Staff, 604-822-3459, Fax: 604-822-6006, E-mail: ischool.program@ubc.ca.
Website: http://slais.ubc.ca/

The University of British Columbia, Faculty of Arts, School of Library, Archival and Information Studies, PhD Program in Library, Archival and Information Studies, Vancouver, BC V6T 1Z1, Canada. Offers PhD. *Degree requirements:* For doctorate, thesis/dissertation. *Entrance requirements:* For doctorate, GRE, minimum GPA of 3.3 in MAS or MLIS. Additional exam requirements/recommendations for international students: Required—TOEFL. Application fee: $100 Canadian dollars ($162 Canadian dollars for international students). Electronic applications accepted. *Expenses:* $4,802 per year tuition and fees, $8,436 per year international. *Financial support:* Fellowships, research assistantships, teaching assistantships, Federal Work-Study, institutionally sponsored loans, scholarships/grants, health care benefits, tuition waivers (partial), and unspecified assistantships available. *Faculty research:* Computer systems/database design; library and archival management; archival description and organization; children's literature and youth services; interactive information retrieval. *Application contact:* Alynne Pols, Graduate Program Staff, 604-822-3459, Fax: 604-822-6006, E-mail: ischool.program@ubc.ca.
Website: http://slais.ubc.ca/

University of California, Los Angeles, Graduate Division, Graduate School of Education and Information Studies, Department of Information Studies, Los Angeles, CA 90095-1521. Offers archival studies (MLIS); informatics (MLIS); information studies (PhD); library and information science (Certificate); library studies (MLIS); moving image archive studies (MA); rare books, print and visual culture (MLIS); MBA/MLIS; MLIS/MA. *Accreditation:* ALA (one or more programs are accredited). Terminal master's awarded for partial completion of doctoral program. *Degree requirements:* For master's, thesis or alternative, professional portfolio; for doctorate, thesis/dissertation, oral and written qualifying exams. *Entrance requirements:* For master's, GRE General Test, previous course work in statistics; for doctorate, GRE General Test, previous course work in statistics, 2 samples of research writing in English. Additional exam requirements/recommendations for international students: Required—TOEFL (minimum score 560 paper-based; 87 iBT), IELTS (minimum score 7). Electronic applications accepted.

Library Science

Faculty research: Digital libraries, archives and electronic records, interface design, cultural informatics, preservation/conservation, access.

University of Central Arkansas, Graduate School, College of Education, Department of Leadership Studies, Program in Library Media and Information Technology, Conway, AR 72035-0001. Offers MS. *Program availability:* Part-time, evening/weekend, online learning. *Degree requirements:* For master's, comprehensive exam. *Entrance requirements:* For master's, GRE General Test, minimum GPA of 2.7. Additional exam requirements/recommendations for international students: Required—TOEFL (minimum score 550 paper-based). Electronic applications accepted.

University of Central Missouri, The Graduate School, Warrensburg, MO 64093. Offers accountancy (MA); accounting (MBA); applied mathematics (MS); aviation safety (MA); biology (MS); business administration (MBA); career and technical education leadership (MS); college student personnel administration (MS); communication (MA); computer science (MS); counseling (MS); criminal justice (MS); educational leadership (Ed D); educational technology (MS); elementary and early childhood education (MSE); English (MA); environmental studies (MA); finance (MBA); history (MA); human services/educational technology (Ed S); human services/learning resources (Ed S); human services/professional counseling (Ed S); industrial hygiene (MS); industrial management (MS); information systems (MBA); information technology (MS); kinesiology (MS); library science and information services (MS); literacy education (MSE); marketing (MBA); mathematics (MS); music (MA); occupational safety management (MS); psychology (MS); rural family nursing (MS); school administration (MSE); social gerontology (MS); sociology (MA); special education (MSE); speech language pathology (MS); superintendency (Ed S); teaching (MAT); teaching English as a second language (MA); technology (MS); technology management (PhD); theatre (MA). *Program availability:* Part-time, 100% online, blended/hybrid learning. *Degree requirements:* For master's and Ed S, comprehensive exam (for some programs), thesis (for some programs). *Entrance requirements:* Additional exam requirements/recommendations for international students: Required—TOEFL (minimum score 550 paper-based; 79 iBT). Electronic applications accepted.

University of Central Oklahoma, The Jackson College of Graduate Studies, College of Education and Professional Studies, Department of Advanced Professional and Special Services, Edmond, OK 73034-5209. Offers educational leadership (M Ed); library media education (M Ed); reading (M Ed); school counseling (M Ed); special education (M Ed), including mild/moderate disabilities, severe-profound/multiple disabilities, special education; speech-language pathology (MS). *Accreditation:* ASHA. *Program availability:* Part-time. *Degree requirements:* For master's, comprehensive exam (for some programs), thesis (for some programs). *Entrance requirements:* For master's, GRE. Additional exam requirements/recommendations for international students: Required—TOEFL (minimum score 550 paper-based; 79 iBT), IELTS (minimum score 6.5). Electronic applications accepted. *Faculty research:* Intellectual freedom, fair use copyright, technology integration, young adult literature, distance learning.

University of Denver, Morgridge College of Education, Denver, CO 80208. Offers child, family and school psychology (MA, PhD, Ed S); counseling psychology (MA, PhD); curriculum and instruction (MA, Ed D, PhD); curriculum instruction and teaching (Certificate); early childhood special education (MA, Certificate); educational leadership and policy studies (MA, Ed D, PhD, Certificate); higher education (Ed D, PhD); library and information science (MLIS); research methods and statistics (MA, PhD). *Accreditation:* ALA; APA (one or more programs are accredited). *Program availability:* Part-time, evening/weekend, online learning. *Faculty:* 39 full-time (29 women), 60 part-time/adjunct (42 women). *Students:* 498 full-time (392 women), 362 part-time (282 women); includes 223 minority (63 Black or African American, non-Hispanic/Latino; 6 American Indian or Alaska Native, non-Hispanic/Latino; 20 Asian, non-Hispanic/Latino; 102 Hispanic/Latino; 1 Native Hawaiian or other Pacific Islander, non-Hispanic/Latino; 31 Two or more races, non-Hispanic/Latino), 40 international. Average age 32. 1,027 applicants, 69% accepted, 386 enrolled. In 2016, 252 master's, 36 doctorates, 141 other advanced degrees awarded. Terminal master's awarded for partial completion of doctoral program. *Degree requirements:* For master's, comprehensive exam; for doctorate, 2 foreign languages, comprehensive exam, thesis/dissertation. *Entrance requirements:* For master's and doctorate, GRE General Test or GMAT. Additional exam requirements/recommendations for international students: Required—TOEFL (minimum score 550 paper-based; 80 iBT). *Application deadline:* Applications are processed on a rolling basis. Application fee: $65. Electronic applications accepted. *Expenses:* $29,022 per year full-time. *Financial support:* In 2016–17, 697 students received support, including 37 research assistantships with tuition reimbursements available (averaging $11,209 per year), 66 teaching assistantships with tuition reimbursements available (averaging $3,742 per year); career-related internships or fieldwork, Federal Work-Study, institutionally sponsored loans, scholarships/grants, and unspecified assistantships also available. Support available to part-time students. Financial award application deadline: 2/15; financial award applicants required to submit FAFSA. *Faculty research:* Early childhood education, access and equity, educational leadership, family and school partnerships, neurodevelopmental disorders. *Total annual research expenditures:* $3.3 million. *Unit head:* Dr. Karen Riley, Dean, 303-871-3665, Fax: 303-871-4456, E-mail: karen.riley@du.edu. *Application contact:* Jodi Dye, Director of Admissions, 303-871-2510, Fax: 303-871-4456, E-mail: jodi.dye@du.edu.
Website: http://morgridge.du.edu

University of Hawaii at Manoa, Graduate Division, College of Natural Sciences, Department of Information and Computer Sciences, Library and Information Science Program, Honolulu, HI 96822-2233. Offers advanced library and information science (Graduate Certificate); library and information science (MLI Sc). *Accreditation:* ALA (one or more programs are accredited). *Program availability:* Part-time. *Degree requirements:* For master's, comprehensive exam, thesis optional. *Entrance requirements:* For master's, GRE General Test. Additional exam requirements/recommendations for international students: Required—TOEFL (minimum score 600 paper-based). Electronic applications accepted. *Faculty research:* Information behavior, evaluation of electronic information sources, online learning, history of libraries, information literacy.

University of Houston–Clear Lake, School of Education, Program in Curriculum and Instruction, Houston, TX 77058-1002. Offers curriculum and instruction (MS); early childhood education (MS); reading (MS); school library and information science (MS). *Program availability:* Part-time, evening/weekend. *Degree requirements:* For master's, thesis (for some programs). *Entrance requirements:* For master's, GRE or minimum GPA of 3.0 in last 60 hours. Additional exam requirements/recommendations for international students: Required—TOEFL (minimum score 550 paper-based). Electronic applications accepted.

University of Illinois at Urbana–Champaign, Graduate College, School of Information Sciences, Champaign, IL 61820. Offers bioinformatics (MS); digital libraries (CAS); information management (MS); library and information science (MS, PhD, CAS). *Accreditation:* ALA (one or more programs are accredited). *Program availability:* Part-time, online learning. *Entrance requirements:* For degree, master's degree in library and information science or related field with minimum GPA of 3.0.

The University of Iowa, Graduate College, School of Library and Information Science, Iowa City, IA 52242-1316. Offers MA, PhD, MA/Certificate, PhD/Certificate. *Accreditation:* ALA (one or more programs are accredited). *Degree requirements:* For master's, thesis optional, exam, portfolio. *Entrance requirements:* For master's, GRE General Test, minimum GPA of 3.0. Additional exam requirements/recommendations for international students: Required—TOEFL (minimum score 550 paper-based; 81 iBT). Electronic applications accepted.

University of Kentucky, Graduate School, College of Communication and Information, Program in Library and Information Science, Lexington, KY 40506-0032. Offers MA, MSLS. *Accreditation:* ALA (one or more programs are accredited). *Program availability:* Part-time. *Degree requirements:* For master's, variable foreign language requirement, comprehensive exam. *Entrance requirements:* For master's, GRE General Test, minimum undergraduate GPA of 2.75. Additional exam requirements/recommendations for international students: Required—TOEFL (minimum score 550 paper-based). *Faculty research:* Information retrieval systems, information-seeking behavior, organizational behavior, computer cataloging, library resource sharing.

University of Maryland, College Park, Academic Affairs, Program in History, Library, and Information Services, College Park, MD 20742. Offers MA/MLS. *Entrance requirements:* Additional exam requirements/recommendations for international students: Required—TOEFL. Electronic applications accepted.

University of Missouri, Office of Research and Graduate Studies, College of Education, School of Information Science and Learning Technologies, Columbia, MO 65211. Offers educational technology (M Ed, Ed S); information science and learning technology (PhD, Certificate); library science (MA). *Accreditation:* ALA (one or more programs are accredited). *Program availability:* Part-time, evening/weekend. *Faculty:* 13 full-time (11 women), 1 part-time/adjunct (0 women). *Students:* 99 full-time (75 women), 187 part-time (126 women). *Entrance requirements:* For master's, GRE General Test or MAT, minimum GPA of 3.0. Additional exam requirements/recommendations for international students: Required—TOEFL (minimum score 540 paper-based; 76 iBT). *Application deadline:* For fall admission, 2/15 priority date for domestic and international students; for winter admission, 9/15 priority date for domestic and international students; for spring admission, 3/1 priority date for domestic students. Applications are processed on a rolling basis. Application fee: $75 ($90 for international students). Electronic applications accepted. *Expenses:* Tuition, state resident: full-time $6347; part-time $352.60 per credit hour. Tuition, nonresident: full-time $17,379; part-time $965.50 per credit hour. *Required fees:* $1035. Tuition and fees vary according to course load, campus/location and program. *Financial support:* Fellowships, teaching assistantships, scholarships/grants, health care benefits, and unspecified assistantships available. Support available to part-time students.
Website: http://education.missouri.edu/information-science-learning-technologies/

University of Nebraska at Kearney, College of Education, Department of Teacher Education, Kearney, NE 68849-0001. Offers curriculum and instruction (MA Ed), including early childhood education, elementary education, English as a second language, instructional effectiveness, reading/special education, secondary education; instructional technology (MS Ed), including information technology, instructional technology, school librarian; reading PK-12 (MA Ed); special education (MA Ed), including advanced practitioner: assistive technology specialist, advanced practitioner: behavioral interventionist, advanced practitioner: inclusive collaboration specialist, gifted, teacher education. *Program availability:* Part-time, evening/weekend, online only, 100% online. *Faculty:* 18 full-time (13 women). *Students:* 21 full-time (15 women), 296 part-time (240 women); includes 21 minority (3 Black or African American, non-Hispanic/Latino; 1 Asian, non-Hispanic/Latino; 14 Hispanic/Latino; 1 Native Hawaiian or other Pacific Islander, non-Hispanic/Latino; 2 Two or more races, non-Hispanic/Latino), 1 international. Average age 32. 81 applicants, 100% accepted, 61 enrolled. In 2016, 129 master's awarded. *Degree requirements:* For master's, comprehensive exam, thesis optional. *Entrance requirements:* For master's, portfolio or GRE. Additional exam requirements/recommendations for international students: Recommended—TOEFL (minimum score 550 paper-based; 79 iBT), IELTS (minimum score 6.5). *Application deadline:* For fall admission, 6/15 for domestic students, 5/15 for international students; for spring admission, 10/15 for domestic and international students; for summer admission, 3/15 for domestic and international students. Application fee: $45. Electronic applications accepted. *Expenses:* $285 per credit hour resident tuition, $415 per credit hour non-resident tuition (online). *Financial support:* In 2016–17, 6 students received support, including 6 research assistantships with full tuition reimbursements available (averaging $10,500 per year); career-related internships or fieldwork, scholarships/grants, health care benefits, and unspecified assistantships also available. Support available to part-time students. Financial award application deadline: 2/28; financial award applicants required to submit FAFSA. *Unit head:* Sarah Bartling, Administrative Assistant, 308-865-8513, E-mail: bartlingseg@unk.edu. *Application contact:* Linda Johnson, Director, Graduate Admissions and Programs, 308-865-8841, Fax: 308-865-8837, E-mail: johnsonli@unk.edu.
Website: http://www.unk.edu/academics/ted/index.php

The University of North Carolina at Chapel Hill, Graduate School, School of Information and Library Science, Chapel Hill, NC 27599. Offers data curation (PMC); information and library science (PhD); information science (MSIS); library science (MSLS). *Accreditation:* ALA (one or more programs are accredited). *Program availability:* Part-time. *Faculty:* 26 full-time (11 women), 46 part-time/adjunct (23 women). *Students:* 190 full-time (140 women), 26 part-time (15 women); includes 35 minority (7 Black or African American, non-Hispanic/Latino; 7 Asian, non-Hispanic/Latino; 6 Hispanic/Latino; 15 Two or more races, non-Hispanic/Latino), 36 international. Average age 28. 258 applicants, 68% accepted, 83 enrolled. In 2016, 69 master's, 4 doctorates awarded. Terminal master's awarded for partial completion of doctoral program. *Degree requirements:* For master's, comprehensive exam, paper or project; for doctorate, comprehensive exam, thesis/dissertation. *Entrance requirements:* For master's and doctorate, GRE General Test. Additional exam requirements/recommendations for international students: Required—TOEFL (minimum score 550 paper-based; 79 iBT). *Application deadline:* For fall admission, 12/13 priority date for domestic and international students; for spring admission, 10/11 for domestic and international students. Applications are processed on a rolling basis. Application fee: $85. Electronic applications accepted. *Expenses:* $7,000 full-time resident, $16,000 non-resident (for master's); $7,000 full-time resident, $15,000 non-resident (for PMC); $5,800 full-time resident, $14,400 non-resident (for PhD). *Financial support:* In 2016–17, 59 fellowships with full tuition reimbursements (averaging $2,565 per year), 46 research assistantships with full tuition reimbursements (averaging $25,120 per year), 15 teaching assistantships with full tuition reimbursements (averaging $11,628 per year) were awarded; career-related internships or fieldwork, Federal Work-Study, scholarships/grants, health care benefits, and unspecified assistantships also available. Financial award application deadline: 12/13. *Faculty research:* Information retrieval and management, digital libraries, management of information resources, archives and records management, health informatics. *Unit head:* Dr. Gary Marchionini, Dean, 919-962-8363, Fax: 919-962-8071, E-mail: gary@ils.unc.edu. *Application contact:* Lara Bailey, Student Services Coordinator, 919-962-7601, Fax: 919-962-8071, E-mail: bailey@email.unc.edu.
Website: http://sils.unc.edu

The University of North Carolina at Greensboro, Graduate School, School of Education, Department of Library and Information Studies, Greensboro, NC 27412-5001. Offers MLIS. *Accreditation:* ALA. *Program availability:* Part-time, evening/weekend, online learning. *Degree requirements:* For master's, portfolio. *Entrance requirements:* For master's, GRE General Test. Additional exam requirements/recommendations for international students: Required—TOEFL (minimum score 550 paper-based), IELTS (minimum score 6.5). Electronic applications accepted. *Faculty research:* Library history, gender studies, children's literature, web design, homeless, technical services.

University of Oklahoma, College of Arts and Sciences, School of Library and Information Studies, Norman, OK 73019. Offers MLIS, M Ed/MLIS, MBA/MLIS. *Accreditation:* ALA (one or more programs are accredited). *Program availability:* Part-time, evening/weekend, online learning. *Faculty:* 11 full-time (8 women). *Students:* 49 full-time (43 women), 97 part-time (76 women); includes 30 minority (3 Black or African American, non-Hispanic/Latino; 5 American Indian or Alaska Native, non-Hispanic/Latino; 2 Asian, non-Hispanic/Latino; 8 Hispanic/Latino; 1 Native Hawaiian or other Pacific Islander, non-Hispanic/Latino; 11 Two or more races, non-Hispanic/Latino), 1 international. Average age 32. 40 applicants, 85% accepted, 27 enrolled. In 2016, 45 master's awarded. *Degree requirements:* For master's, comprehensive exam (for some programs), thesis optional. *Entrance requirements:* For master's, three letters of recommendation, personal statement, resume. Additional exam requirements/recommendations for international students: Required—TOEFL (minimum score 79 iBT) or IELTS (minimum score 6.5). *Application deadline:* Applications are processed on a rolling basis. Application fee: $50 ($100 for international students). Electronic applications accepted. *Expenses:* Tuition, state resident: full-time $4886; part-time $203.60 per credit hour. Tuition, nonresident: full-time $18,989; part-time $791.20 per credit hour. *Required fees:* $3283; $126.25 per credit hour. $126.50 per semester. *Financial support:* In 2016–17, 81 students received support, including 4 research assistantships with full tuition reimbursements available (averaging $12,801 per year), 5 teaching assistantships (averaging $10,579 per year); scholarships/grants, health care benefits, and unspecified assistantships also available. Financial award application deadline: 6/1; financial award applicants required to submit FAFSA. *Faculty research:* Teen services, health information, big data analytics. *Total annual research expenditures:* $131,980. *Unit head:* Dr. Susan Burke, Interim Director, 405-325-3921, Fax: 405-325-7648, E-mail: sburke@ou.edu. *Application contact:* Sarah Connelly, Admissions and Student Services Coordinator, 405-325-3921, Fax: 405-325-7648, E-mail: sarahee@ou.edu. Website: http://slis.ou.edu/

University of Pittsburgh, School of Information Sciences, Library and Information Science Program, Pittsburgh, PA 15260. Offers MLIS, PhD. *Accreditation:* ALA (one or more programs are accredited). *Program availability:* Part-time, evening/weekend, 100% online. *Faculty:* 8 full-time (5 women), 5 part-time/adjunct (4 women). *Students:* 62 full-time (50 women), 57 part-time (44 women); includes 6 minority (2 Black or African American, non-Hispanic/Latino; 1 Asian, non-Hispanic/Latino; 3 Hispanic/Latino), 11 international. Average age 32. 148 applicants, 80% accepted, 68 enrolled. In 2016, 59 master's, 1 doctorate awarded. *Degree requirements:* For master's, thesis optional; for doctorate, comprehensive exam, thesis/dissertation. *Entrance requirements:* For master's, GRE, GMAT, MAT, MCAT, LSAT, bachelor's degree from accredited university; minimum GPA of 3.0; for doctorate, GRE, minimum GPA of 3.5. Additional exam requirements/recommendations for international students: Required—TOEFL (minimum score 550 paper-based; 80 iBT). *Application deadline:* For fall admission, 1/15 priority date for domestic and international students. Applications are processed on a rolling basis. Application fee: $50. Electronic applications accepted. *Expenses:* $22,628 per year in-state, $37,754 per year out-of-state (fall and spring); $931 per credit in-state, $1,553 per credit out-of-state (summer). *Financial support:* Fellowships with full and partial tuition reimbursements, research assistantships with full and partial tuition reimbursements, teaching assistantships with full and partial tuition reimbursements, career-related internships or fieldwork, institutionally sponsored loans, scholarships/grants, traineeships, health care benefits, and unspecified assistantships available. Financial award application deadline: 1/15; financial award applicants required to submit FAFSA. *Faculty research:* Archives, children's resources and services, digital libraries, cyber scholarship and citizen science, learning technology. *Unit head:* Dr. Leanne Bowler, Co-Chair, 412-624-7679, Fax: 412-624-5231, E-mail: lbowler@sis.pitt.edu. *Application contact:* Shabana Reza, Enrollment Manager, 412-624-3988, Fax: 412-624-5231, E-mail: sreza@sis.pitt.edu. Website: http://www.ischool.pitt.edu/lis

University of Puerto Rico, Río Piedras Campus, Graduate School of Information Sciences and Technologies, San Juan, PR 00931-3300. Offers administration of academic libraries (PMC); administration of public libraries (PMC); administration of special libraries (PMC); consultant in information services (PMC); documents and files administration (Post-Graduate Certificate); electronic information resources analyst (Post-Graduate Certificate); information science (MIS); librarianship and information services (MLS); school librarian (Post-Graduate Certificate); school librarian distance education mode (Post-Graduate Certificate); specialist in legal information (PMC). *Accreditation:* ALA. *Program availability:* Part-time. *Degree requirements:* For master's, comprehensive exam, thesis, portfolio. *Entrance requirements:* For master's, PAEG, GRE, interview, minimum GPA of 3.0, 3 letters of recommendation; for other advanced degree, PAEG, GRE, minimum GPA of 3.0, IST master's degree. *Faculty research:* Investigating the users needs and preferences for a specialized environmental library.

University of Rhode Island, Graduate School, College of Arts and Sciences, Graduate School of Library and Information Studies, Kingston, RI 02881. Offers libraries, leadership and transforming communities (MLIS); organization of digital media (MLIS); school library media (MLIS); MLIS/MA; MLIS/MPA. *Accreditation:* ALA (one or more programs are accredited). *Program availability:* Part-time. *Faculty:* 4 full-time (all women). *Students:* 31 full-time (23 women), 71 part-time (61 women); includes 3 minority (1 Black or African American, non-Hispanic/Latino; 2 Asian, non-Hispanic/Latino). In 2016, 31 master's awarded. *Degree requirements:* For master's, comprehensive exam. *Entrance requirements:* For master's, GRE or MAT if undergraduate GPA below 3.3, 2 letters of recommendation. Additional exam requirements/recommendations for international students: Required—TOEFL. *Application deadline:* For fall admission, 6/15 for domestic students, 2/1 for international students; for spring admission, 10/15 for domestic students, 7/15 for international students; for summer admission, 3/15 for domestic students. Application fee: $65. Electronic applications accepted. *Expenses:* Tuition, state resident: full-time $11,796; part-time $655 per credit. Tuition, nonresident: full-time $24,206; part-time $1345 per credit. *Required fees:* $1546; $44 per credit. One-time fee: $155 full-time; $35 part-time. *Financial support:* In 2016–17, 1 teaching assistantship (averaging $17,184 per year) was awarded; research assistantships also available. Financial award application deadline: 1/15; financial award applicants required to submit FAFSA. *Unit head:* Dr. Valerie Karno, Director, Graduate School of Library and Information Studies, 401-874-4682, Fax: 401-874-4127, E-mail: karno@uri.edu. *Application contact:* GSLIS Student Services Office, 401-874-2872, Fax: 401-874-5787, E-mail: stefaniemetko@mail.uri.edu. Website: http://www.uri.edu/artsci/lsc/

University of South Carolina, The Graduate School, College of Mass Communications and Information Studies, School of Library and Information Science, Columbia, SC 29208. Offers MLIS, PhD, Certificate, Specialist, MLIS/MA. *Accreditation:* ALA (one or more programs are accredited). *Program availability:* Part-time, online learning. *Degree requirements:* For master's, end of program portfolio; for doctorate, comprehensive exam, thesis/dissertation. *Entrance requirements:* For master's and other advanced degree, GRE General Test or MAT; for doctorate, GTE, writing sample. Additional exam requirements/recommendations for international students: Required—TOEFL (minimum score 570 paper-based; 75 iBT). Electronic applications accepted. *Faculty research:* Information technology management, distance education, library services for children and young adults, special libraries.

University of Southern Mississippi, Graduate School, College of Education and Psychology, School of Library and Information Science, Hattiesburg, MS 39406. Offers archives and special collections (Graduate Certificate); library and information science (MLIS); youth services and literature (Graduate Certificate). *Accreditation:* ALA (one or more programs are accredited). *Program availability:* Part-time, evening/weekend, online learning. *Degree requirements:* For master's, comprehensive exam, thesis. *Entrance requirements:* For master's, GRE General Test, minimum GPA of 3.0. Additional exam requirements/recommendations for international students: Required—TOEFL, IELTS. *Application deadline:* For fall admission, 3/15 priority date for domestic students, 3/15 for international students; for spring admission, 1/10 priority date for domestic and international students. Applications are processed on a rolling basis. Application fee: $60. Electronic applications accepted. *Expenses: Tuition, area resident:* Full-time $15,708; part-time $437 per credit hour. *Financial support:* Fellowships with tuition reimbursements, research assistantships with full tuition reimbursements, teaching assistantships with full tuition reimbursements, career-related internships or fieldwork, Federal Work-Study, institutionally sponsored loans, scholarships/grants, health care benefits, and unspecified assistantships available. Financial award application deadline: 3/15; financial award applicants required to submit FAFSA. *Faculty research:* Printing, library history, children's literature, telecommunications, management. *Unit head:* Dr. Melanie J. Norton, Director, 601-266-4236, Fax: 601-266-5774. *Application contact:* Shonna Breland, Manager of Graduate Admissions, 601-266-6563, Fax: 601-266-5138.
Website: https://www.usm.edu/library-information-science

University of South Florida, College of Arts and Sciences, School of Information, Tampa, FL 33620-9951. Offers intelligence studies (MS), including cyber intelligence, strategic intelligence; library and information science (MA). *Accreditation:* ALA (one or more programs are accredited). *Program availability:* Part-time, evening/weekend, online learning. *Faculty:* 17 full-time (8 women). *Students:* 112 full-time (73 women), 163 part-time (127 women); includes 80 minority (28 Black or African American, non-Hispanic/Latino; 11 Asian, non-Hispanic/Latino; 32 Hispanic/Latino; 1 Native Hawaiian or other Pacific Islander, non-Hispanic/Latino; 8 Two or more races, non-Hispanic/Latino), 1 international. Average age 33. 167 applicants, 84% accepted, 90 enrolled. In 2016, 61 master's awarded. *Degree requirements:* For master's, comprehensive exam, thesis (for some programs). *Entrance requirements:* For master's, GRE General Test (for some programs). Additional exam requirements/recommendations for international students: Required—TOEFL (minimum score 550 paper-based; 79 iBT) or IELTS (minimum score 6.5). *Application deadline:* For fall admission, 6/1 for domestic students, 2/15 for international students; for spring admission, 10/15 for domestic students, 9/15 for international students. Applications are processed on a rolling basis. Application fee: $30. Electronic applications accepted. *Expenses:* Tuition, state resident: full-time $7766; part-time $431.43 per credit hour. Tuition, nonresident: full-time $15,789; part-time $877.17 per credit hour. *Required fees:* $37 per term. *Financial support:* In 2016–17, 47 students received support. Unspecified assistantships available. Financial award application deadline: 6/30. *Faculty research:* Youth services in libraries, community engagement and libraries, information architecture, biomedical informatics, health informatics. *Total annual research expenditures:* $378,531. *Unit head:* Dr. Jim Andrews, Director and Associate Professor, 813-974-2108, Fax: 813-974-6840, E-mail: jimandrews@usf.edu. *Application contact:* Dr. Diane Austin, Assistant Director, 813-974-6364, Fax: 813-974-6840, E-mail: dianeaustin@usf.edu.
Website: http://si.usf.edu/

University of Washington, Graduate School, Information School, Seattle, WA 98195. Offers information management (MSIM), including business intelligence, data science, information architecture, information consulting, information security, user experience; information science (PhD); library and information science (MLIS). *Accreditation:* ALA (one or more programs are accredited). *Program availability:* Part-time, 100% online coursework with required attendance at on-campus orientation at start of program. *Faculty:* 35 full-time (19 women), 22 part-time/adjunct (12 women). *Students:* 367 full-time (233 women), 237 part-time (170 women); includes 132 minority (20 Black or African American, non-Hispanic/Latino; 9 American Indian or Alaska Native, non-Hispanic/Latino; 59 Asian, non-Hispanic/Latino; 41 Hispanic/Latino; 3 Native Hawaiian or other Pacific Islander, non-Hispanic/Latino), 151 international. Average age 32. 1,208 applicants, 39% accepted, 254 enrolled. In 2016, 237 master's, 2 doctorates awarded. Terminal master's awarded for partial completion of doctoral program. *Degree requirements:* For master's, comprehensive exam (for some programs), thesis or alternative, capstone project; for doctorate, comprehensive exam, thesis/dissertation. *Entrance requirements:* For master's, GRE General Test, GMAT; for doctorate, GRE General Test. Additional exam requirements/recommendations for international students: Required—TOEFL (minimum score 590 paper-based; 100 iBT). *Application deadline:* For fall admission, 12/1 priority date for domestic and international students. Application fee: $85. Electronic applications accepted. *Expenses:* $785 per quarter credit hour, $23,550 per year full-time, $1,000 university fees per quarter. *Financial support:* In 2016–17, 69 students received support, including 1 fellowship with full tuition reimbursement available (averaging $6,651 per year), 27 research assistantships with full tuition reimbursements available (averaging $19,418 per year), 27 teaching assistantships with full tuition reimbursements available (averaging $19,521 per year); Federal Work-Study, institutionally sponsored loans, scholarships/grants, health care benefits, tuition waivers (full and partial), and unspecified assistantships also available. Support available to part-time students. Financial award application deadline: 10/1; financial award applicants required to submit FAFSA. *Faculty research:* Human/computer interaction, information policy and ethics, knowledge organization, information literacy and access, data science, information assurance and cyber security, digital youth, information architecture, project management, systems analyst, user experience design. *Total annual research expenditures:* $3.6 million. *Unit head:* Dr. Harry Bruce, Dean, 206-616-0985, E-mail: harryb@uw.edu. *Application contact:* Kari Brothers, Admissions Counselor, 206-616-5541, Fax: 206-616-3152, E-mail: kari683@uw.edu.
Website: http://ischool.uw.edu/

The University of Western Ontario, Faculty of Graduate Studies, Faculty of Information and Media Studies, Programs in Library and Information Science, London, ON N6A 5B8, Canada. Offers MLIS, PhD. Program conducted on a trimester basis. *Accreditation:* ALA (one or more programs are accredited). *Program availability:* Part-time, evening/weekend. *Degree requirements:* For doctorate, comprehensive exam, thesis/dissertation. *Entrance requirements:* For master's, honors degree, minimum B average during previous 2 years of course work; for doctorate, MLIS or equivalent. Additional exam requirements/recommendations for international students: Required—TOEFL (minimum score 625 paper-based), TWE (minimum score 5). Electronic applications accepted. *Faculty research:* Information, individuals, and society; information systems, policy, power, and institutions.

University of Wisconsin–Eau Claire, College of Education and Human Sciences, Program in Secondary Education, Eau Claire, WI 54702-4004. Offers professional development (ME-PD), including library science, professional development. *Program availability:* Part-time, online learning. *Degree requirements:* For master's, comprehensive exam, thesis, research paper, portfolio or written exam; oral exam. *Entrance requirements:* For master's, certification to teach, minimum GPA of 2.75. Additional exam requirements/recommendations for international students: Required—TOEFL (minimum score 79 iBT).

University of Wisconsin–Madison, Graduate School, College of Letters and Science, School of Library and Information Studies, Madison, WI 53706-1380. Offers MA, PhD. *Accreditation:* ALA (one or more programs are accredited). *Program availability:* Part-time. *Degree requirements:* For doctorate, comprehensive exam, thesis/dissertation. Electronic applications accepted. *Faculty research:* Intellectual freedom, children's literature, print culture history, information systems design and evaluation, school library media centers.

University of Wisconsin–Milwaukee, Graduate School, School of Information Studies, Milwaukee, WI 53201-0413. Offers MLIS, MS, PhD, CAS. *Accreditation:* ALA (one or more programs are accredited). *Program availability:* Part-time. *Students:* 119 full-time (82 women), 250 part-time (194 women); includes 55 minority (13 Black or African American, non-Hispanic/Latino; 12 Asian, non-Hispanic/Latino; 2 Hispanic/Latino; 1 Native Hawaiian or other Pacific Islander, non-Hispanic/Latino; 27 Two or more races, non-Hispanic/Latino), 15 international. Average age 35. 203 applicants, 75% accepted, 81 enrolled. In 2016, 116 master's, 2 doctorates, 5 other advanced degrees awarded. *Entrance requirements:* For master's, GRE General Test or MAT; for doctorate, GRE. Additional exam requirements/recommendations for international students: Required—TOEFL (minimum score 550 paper-based), IELTS (minimum score 6.5). *Application deadline:* For fall admission, 1/1 priority date for domestic students; for spring admission, 9/1 for domestic students. Applications are processed on a rolling basis. Application fee: $56 ($96 for international students). Electronic applications accepted. *Financial support:* In 2016–17, 4 teaching assistantships were awarded; fellowships, research assistantships, career-related internships or fieldwork, Federal Work-Study, health care benefits, unspecified assistantships, and project assistantships also available. Support available to part-time students. Financial award application deadline: 4/15; financial award applicants required to submit FAFSA. *Unit head:* Tomas A. Lipinski, Dean/Professor, 414-229-4707, E-mail: tlipinsk@uwm.edu. *Application contact:* Linda Barajas, Admissions Coordinator, 414-229-3316, E-mail: barajas@uwm.edu.
Website: http://uwm.edu/informationstudies

Valdosta State University, Program in Library and Information Science, Valdosta, GA 31698. Offers MLIS. *Accreditation:* ALA. *Program availability:* 100% online. *Degree requirements:* For master's, comprehensive exam. *Entrance requirements:* For master's, two essays, resume, three recommendations. Additional exam requirements/recommendations for international students: Required—TOEFL (minimum score 523 paper-based); Recommended—IELTS. *Expenses:* Contact institution.

Valley City State University, Online Master of Education Program, Valley City, ND 58072. Offers elementary education (M Ed); English education (M Ed); library and information technologies (M Ed); teaching (MAT); teaching and technology (M Ed); teaching English language learners (M Ed); technology education (M Ed). *Accreditation:* NCATE. *Program availability:* Part-time, evening/weekend, online only, 100% online. *Faculty:* 21 full-time (12 women), 15 part-time/adjunct (11 women). *Students:* 4 full-time (3 women), 133 part-time (92 women); includes 9 minority (1 American Indian or Alaska Native, non-Hispanic/Latino; 4 Hispanic/Latino; 4 Two or more races, non-Hispanic/Latino), 1 international. Average age 34. 35 applicants, 91% accepted, 28 enrolled. In 2016, 45 master's awarded. *Degree requirements:* For master's, action research report, comprehensive portfolio. *Entrance requirements:* For master's, GRE, MAT, PRAXIS II or National Teaching Board for Professional Standards (if GPA is less than 3.0). Additional exam requirements/recommendations for international students: Required—TOEFL (minimum score 525 paper-based; 71 iBT); Recommended—IELTS (minimum score 5.5). *Application deadline:* For fall admission, 7/21 priority date for domestic and international students; for spring admission, 12/8 priority date for domestic and international students; for summer admission, 5/5 priority date for domestic and international students. Applications are processed on a rolling basis. Application fee: $35. Electronic applications accepted. *Expenses:* $373 per credit. *Financial support:* In 2016–17, 23 students received support. Scholarships/grants, tuition waivers (full and partial), and unspecified assistantships available. Financial award application deadline: 6/14; financial award applicants required to submit FAFSA. *Faculty research:* Universal accessibility, instructional design and technology, gender communication, STEM education in K-12. *Unit head:* Dr. Gary Thompson, Dean, 701-845-7197, E-mail: gary.thompson@vcsu.edu. *Application contact:* Misty Lindgren, Graduate Studies, 701-845-7303, Fax: 701-845-7190, E-mail: misty.lindgren@vcsu.edu.
Website: http://www.vcsu.edu/graduate

Wayne State University, School of Library and Information Science, Detroit, MI 48202. Offers archival administration (Graduate Certificate); information management (Graduate Certificate); library and information science (MLIS, Spec); public library services to children and young adults (Graduate Certificate); MLIS/MA. *Accreditation:* ALA (one or more programs are accredited). *Program availability:* Part-time, evening/weekend, 100% online, blended/hybrid learning. *Faculty:* 11 full-time (7 women), 30 part-time/adjunct (20 women). *Students:* 90 full-time (69 women), 376 part-time (312 women); includes 74 minority (38 Black or African American, non-Hispanic/Latino; 2 American Indian or Alaska Native, non-Hispanic/Latino; 4 Asian, non-Hispanic/Latino; 17 Hispanic/Latino; 2 Native Hawaiian or other Pacific Islander, non-Hispanic/Latino; 11 Two or more races, non-Hispanic/Latino), 3 international. Average age 32. 265 applicants, 73% accepted, 120 enrolled. In 2016, 145 master's, 34 other advanced degrees awarded. *Degree requirements:* For master's and other advanced degree, e-portfolio. *Entrance requirements:* For master's, GRE or MAT (if undergraduate GPA is between 2.5 and 2.99), minimum undergraduate GPA of 3.0 or graduate degree, personal statement, resume or curriculum vitae; for other advanced degree, GRE or MAT (if undergraduate GPA is between 2.5 and 2.99), minimum undergraduate GPA of 3.0 or graduate degree, personal statement, resume or curriculum vitae, MLIS (for specialist certificate). Additional exam requirements/recommendations for international students: Required—TOEFL (minimum score 550 paper-based; 79 iBT); Recommended—IELTS (minimum score 6.5), TWE (minimum score 5.5). *Application deadline:* For fall admission, 7/1 for domestic students, 5/1 priority date for international students; for winter admission, 10/1 priority date for domestic students, 9/1 priority date for international students; for spring admission, 2/1 priority date for domestic students, 1/1 priority date for international students. Applications are processed on a rolling basis. Application fee: $50. Electronic applications accepted. *Expenses:* $18,871 per year resident tuition and fees, $36,065 per year non-resident tuition and fees. *Financial support:* In 2016–17, 107 students received support. Fellowships with tuition reimbursements available, scholarships/grants, health care benefits, and unspecified assistantships available. Support available to part-time students. Financial award applicants required to submit FAFSA. *Faculty research:* Library services, information management issues, digital content management, library/community engagement, archives and preservation. *Unit head:* Dr. Sandra Yee, Dean, 313-577-4059, E-mail: aj0533@wayne.edu. *Application contact:* Academic Services Officer II, 313-577-1825, E-mail: asklis@wayne.edu.
Website: http://slis.wayne.edu/

PRATT INSTITUTE

School of Information

 For more information, visit http://petersons.to/prattlibraryscience

Programs of Study

Distinguished as the only ALA-accredited graduate library and information science (LIS) program based in Manhattan and the oldest library and information science school in North America, Pratt's School of Information, established in 1890 and renamed in 2015, has been continuously accredited since 1923, when accreditation was first introduced to the field. The Archives program was ranked 11th in the country by *U.S. News & World Report.*

Building upon Pratt's national reputation as a leading school in art and design, Pratt brings creativity and innovation to library science education to offer students exciting and cutting-edge programs and courses from archives and digital libraries, to special libraries and school library media.

Pratt's School of Information offers five 36-credit Master of Science degrees: M.S. in Library and Information Science (M.S.L.I.S.), M.S. in Museums and Digital Culture, M.S. in Data Analytics and Visualization, and M.S. in Information Experience Design. Pratt offers three joint-degree programs, one with Pratt's History of Art Department (M.S.L.I.S./M.S. in history of art, 60 credits), one with Pratt's Digital Arts M.F.A. (M.S.L.I.S./M.F.A. in digital arts, 75 credits), and one with the Brooklyn Law School (M.S.L.I.S./J.D., 86 credits). The School of Information also offers advanced certificate programs in Archives Conservation and Digital Curation, Digital Humanities, Library and Information Studies, Museum Libraries, and User Experience (UX).

The School of Information prepares students for leadership positions in the information professions, including special opportunities in arts and humanities librarianship for students pursuing careers in academic and research libraries, art and museum libraries, and archives and special collections. The program combines a core curriculum (information professions, information services and sources, information technologies, and knowledge organization) with elective courses, such as advanced Web design, digital libraries, human information behavior, information architecture, information policy, and projects in digital archives. Some courses are taught on location in museums and libraries, such as the New York Public Library, the Watson Library, and the Metropolitan Museum of Art. Other courses are held on the Brooklyn Campus in the Pratt Library, and students in the library and media specialist (LMS) studies program take courses in the Art and Design Education Department. The School of Information maintains a dean's office in North Hall. Students carry out practicum internships at many of New York's leading cultural institutions. Students may choose from a number of program concentrations, depending on their interests and career goals, including business, cultural informatics, digital technology and knowledge organization, legal and health information, library media specialist studies, management and leadership, public urban libraries, and reference and information literacy.

The master's program may be completed in as little as two semesters and one summer and must be completed within four years of enrollment. Courses are offered in the evening, during the day, and on Saturday and Sunday to accommodate students who work.

Research Facilities

The program's teaching and research facilities occupy the entire sixth floor of a seven-story facility in its home at 144 West 14th Street, Manhattan, in a beautifully restored landmark building, designated the Pratt Manhattan Center (PMC). Here, students find faculty and staff offices, smart classrooms, large computer labs, an elegant conference room, and the student cyber place. The fifth-floor computer lab adds to the School of Information's resources, and a separate scanning lab supports digital library projects. The fourth floor is home to the PMC library, containing extensive LIS collections of books, journals, and full-text online databases. Special School of Information events and lectures are held in a 150-person lecture hall adjoining the second-floor gallery space. This rich complex of facilities, all with wireless access and convenient to students and faculty members, adds greatly to effective operations and enhances the learning environment.

Financial Aid

Financial aid awards are offered through a variety of institutional, state, and federally funded programs. These include Graduate Scholarships awarded to incoming students on the basis of merit, endowed and restricted scholarships for continuing students, and student employment. Assistantships are awarded on a competitive basis to continuing students in all departments. Special alumni-sponsored fellowships are also available.

Cost of Study

In 2017–18, tuition is $1,376 per credit for the M.S.L.I.S. degree, and student fees are approximately $1,974 per year. The cost of books and supplies varies widely among the different programs.

Living and Housing Costs

Limited graduate housing is available for single students on the Brooklyn Campus. The cost averages $18,880 (room and board $22,500) per year. The Office of Residential Life maintains extensive listings of off-campus housing to help students find suitable accommodations.

Student Group

Graduate students at Pratt are drawn from all parts of the United States (45 states) and fifty-six other countries. The SILS graduate program average age is 31, with most students working full-time while taking M.S.L.I.S. courses. The employment outlook for Pratt graduates is bright. At present, more than 95 percent of the graduates obtain positions in a broad range of work environments from academic libraries and museums, to special libraries, including those in the corporate, business, and medical fields. The growth potential of the job market is seemingly unlimited. Job opportunities have been increasing for graduates of the information and library science program.

Location

Pratt's School of Information is headquartered in the heart of Manhattan. Here, most School of Information courses are offered at times convenient to those students who wish to work as well as those who wish to pursue full-time study. The main campus of Pratt Institute is located in the Clinton Hill section of Brooklyn. Some courses are offered there to support programs such as the joint degree with Brooklyn Law School and program courses in urban librarianship at Brooklyn Public Library. In Manhattan, courses are taught at Cornell Medical Center for health sciences specialization and the New York Public Library/ Research Libraries for special collections.

School of Information students enjoy the advantages of New York's position as a world center for the information professions. Students also benefit from the wealth of professional experience and expertise that complements their formal study. A vast variety of cultural and recreational activities are available in the neighborhood, in Brooklyn, in the city, and in the region. Pratt has a park-like campus in a quiet neighborhood of Victorian buildings set in the midst of one of the most vibrant cities in the world.

The Institute

A private, nonsectarian institute of higher education, Pratt was founded in 1887 by industrialist and philanthropist Charles Pratt. Changing with the requirements of the professions for which it educates, Pratt today prepares a student body of more than 4,600 undergraduate and graduate students for a wide range of careers in architecture and planning, design and fine arts, and information science.

Applying

The deadline for applications and all supporting materials, including portfolio, is January 5. Applicants should complete the application process online. Early submission of applications with all necessary credentials is highly desirable. Applications received after these dates are considered if openings exist in a particular program. For applicants who intend to file for financial aid, the FAFSA should be filed by March 1 for fall entrance and by October 1 for spring entrance

Correspondence and Information

Graduate Admissions Office
Pratt Institute
200 Willoughby Avenue
Brooklyn, New York 11205
Phone: 718-636-3514
800-331-0834 (toll-free)
Fax: 718-399-4242
Website: http://www.pratt.edu/admissions

School of Information
Pratt Institute
144 West 14th Street, 6th Floor
New York, New York 10011
Phone: 212-647-7682
E-mail: infosils@pratt.edu
Website: http://www.pratt.edu/academics/information

THE FACULTY

Anthony Cocciolo, Acting Chair, Associate Professor; Ed.D., Columbia.
Johanna Bauman, Visiting Assistant Professor; M.L.S., CUNY, Queens.
Jason Baumann, Visiting Assistant Professor; M.L.S., CUNY, Queens.
Amber Billey, Visiting Assistant Professor; M.S.L.I.S., Pratt.
Anthony M. Cucchiara, Visiting Assistant Professor; M.L.S., Pratt.
Sara Devine, Visiting Assistant Professor; M.A., George Washington.
Deirdre Donohue, Visiting Assistant Professor; M.L.S., Pratt.
Emily Drabinski, Visiting Assistant Professor; M.L.S., Syracuse.
Nancy Friedland, Visiting Associate Professor; M.L.S., Rutgers.
Barbara Genco, Visiting Associate Professor; M.L.S., Pratt.
Tula Giannini, Professor; Ph.D., Bryn Mawr.
Joshua Hadro, Visiting Instructor; M.L.S., Pratt.
Alexis Hagadorn, Visiting Assistant Professor; M.L.S., Columbia.
Jessica Lee Hochman, Assistant Professor; Ph.D., Columbia.
Emily Holmes, Visiting Assistant Professor; M.L.S., Simmons.
Jennifer Hubert-Swan, Visiting Assistant Professor; M.L.S., Wayne State (Michigan).
Matthew Knutzen, Assistant Professor; M.F.A., Pratt.
Lisa Kropp, Visiting Assistant Professor; M.L.S., CUNY, Queens
Irene Lopatovska, Associate Professor; Ph.D., Rutgers.
Laura Lutz, Visiting Assistant Professor; M.L.S., Arizona.
Craig MacDonald, Assistant Professor; Ph.D., Information Studies, Drexel.
Monica Maceli, Assistant Professor; M.S.I.S., Drexel.
Susan L. Malbin, Visiting Instructor; Ph.D., Brandeis.
David Marcinkowski, Visiting Associate Professor; M.A., New School.
Seoud M. Matta, Dean Emeritus; D.L.S., Columbia.
Matthew Miller, Visiting Assistant Professor; M.S.L.I.S., Pratt.
Jacob Nadal, Visiting Assistant Professor; M.L.S., Indiana Bloomington.
Maria Cristina Pattuelli, Associate Professor; Ph.D., North Carolina at Chapel Hill.
Slava Polishchuk, Visiting Assistant Professor; M.F.A., CUNY, Brooklyn.
Deborah Rabina, Professor; Ph.D., Rutgers.
Charles Rubenstein, Professor; Ph.D., Polytechnic of NYU.
Kenneth Soehner, Visiting Associate Professor; M.L.S., Columbia.
Chris Alen Sula, Assistant Professor; Ph.D., CUNY Graduate Center.
Cynthia Tobar, Visiting Assistant Professor; M.S.L.I.S., Pratt.
Jeremiah Trinidad-Christensen, Visiting Assistant Professor; M.L.S., LIU.
Kyle Triplett, Visiting Instructor; M.S.L.I.S., Pratt.
Kevin B. Winkler, Visiting Assistant Professor; M.L.S., Columbia.
William Ying, Visiting Associate Professor; Ph.D., Columbia.

© 2017 Bob Handelman

© 2017 Bob Handelman

SYRACUSE UNIVERSITY

School of Information Studies
Master of Science in Applied Data Science
Master of Science in Enterprise Data Systems
Master of Science in Information Management
Master of Science in Library and Information Science

School of Information Studies
Syracuse University

Programs of Study

The Syracuse University School of Information Studies (iSchool), ranked number two in Information Systems in Library and Information Studies by *U.S. News & World Report*, offers M.S. degree programs to prepare students for a growing number of dynamic careers that involve the management and use of information. Master's students in the iSchool obtain specialized skills in areas such as cloud management, digital enterprises, data science, global enterprise technologies, library science, virtual environments, databases, information security, IT governance, information and communication technologies, school media librarianship, wireless networks, and mobile and web applications. Students can earn M.S. degrees on campus or online with limited residency requirements. *Note:* The Enterprise Data Systems program is offered only on campus.

The M.S. in applied data science (ADS) prepares students with the practical analytical and technical skills to apply analytical concepts to gain insight from small and large datasets. The program requires completion of 36 credit hours and the curriculum combines a primary core, analytics application core, and electives to give students a strong data science and analytics foundation with a secondary focus of their choosing. The M.S. in ADS is a fully interdisciplinary degree and is offered in collaboration with Syracuse University's Whitman School of Management.

The M.S. in enterprise data systems (EDS) requires completion of 36 credit hours and is designed for students who want to prepare professionally to manage, design, support and optimize the infrastructure that supports the digital enterprise. The EDS curriculum is built around the core concepts and procedures required to understand the technical, security, policy, and management principles of current and future information network infrastructures and systems. Students can choose from focus areas that include cloud and virtualized information systems, and infrastructure and applications related to data science, enterprise IT infrastructure management, information security, and mobile services and applications.

The iSchool's M.S. in information management (IM) requires the completion of 42 credit hours. Each student completes course work in management approaches and strategies, user information needs, technological infrastructures, and elective subjects to prepare for a wide range of positions in the information field. The program's interdisciplinary philosophy means that students from any academic or professional background have the opportunity to thrive in the program. Many IM students concurrently pursue a Certificate of Advanced Study in information security management or data science Graduates have become consultants and analysts, worked for technology giants and the U.S. government, and worked for startup companies—or founded their own..

The iSchool also offers a 30-credit executive track for the M.S. in information management, geared toward midcareer professionals looking to advance their organizations and their job prospects. This track can be completed online or on campus.

Accredited by the American Library Association (ALA), the M.S. in library and information science (LIS) program requires the completion of 36 credit hours. The program is dedicated to educating students to become leaders in the evolution of the library and information profession. LIS students work with interdisciplinary faculty advisers to plan their programs of study, which may include course work in other academic areas. The program offers a specialization in school media (ranked fourth in the 2018 *U.S. News & World Report* rankings) and certificates of advanced study in digital libraries and school media, as well as a certificate in cultural heritage preservation and data science.

All four degree programs focus on employing technology and digital tools to find, evaluate, organize, and use information for the betterment of people. Graduates of the iSchool at Syracuse work in a broad range of managerial and technical positions in business, government, education, health care, and other fields.

The iSchool also offers a research-oriented Ph.D. in information science and technology for those individuals interested in becoming researchers, professors, and consultants.

The iSchool's Certificates of Advanced Study have broad appeal and attract students across disciplines. Options include information security management, e-government management and leadership, school media, and data science. These certificates can be earned on campus or online, and provide a valuable development opportunity both for emerging and experienced professionals in the information field.

Research Facilities

Research at the iSchool is characterized by the faculty's diverse interests in information, its uses by people, and the increasing opportunities and issues provided by digital and computational resources. iSchool researchers are trained in a range of disciplines and pursue independent and collaborative work with colleagues across campus and across the world.

Many of the faculty conduct their research individually and in small, flexible, interdisciplinary teams. For certain specialized areas and cross-unit collaborations, however, research centers and laboratories provide a venue that supports long-term commitment to a particular research area. These research and development centers, which have achieved national and international distinction, allow students to apply classroom lessons to authentic problems, sometimes using technologies that have not yet made it to market. These centers include the Behavior, Information, Technology, and Society Lab; the Center for Computational and Data Sciences; the Center for Convergence and Emerging Network Technologies; the Center for Digital Literacy; the Smart Grid Project Center; and the Social Computing Systems Lab.

The University's library system includes collections of 3.1 million volumes, more than 24,000 online and print journals, and extensive collections of microforms, maps, images, music scores, videos, rare books, and manuscripts. Many of these resources can be accessed from academic and residence hall computer clusters. Among its special collections is the Belfer Audio Laboratory and Archive, which contains more than 340,000 historical sound recordings in all formats, including a collection of 22,000 cylinder records, the largest held by any private institution in North America.

Financial Aid

Fellowships, scholarships, and assistantships are available to full-time students on campus. The most prestigious and competitive are Syracuse University graduate fellowships, which include a scholarship and a stipend for the academic year. University scholarships provide 24 credit hours of tuition, and graduate assistantships provide tuition and a stipend for the academic year. Syracuse also offers fellowships through the McNair Scholars program and Graduate Education for Minorities (GEM) program. Tuition scholarships and other small scholarships are available to part-time students.

Loans are available through the University financial aid office. For Federal Work-Study Program contracts, students work through the University student employment office. Financial aid is awarded according to federal financial need guidelines.

Cost of Study

Tuition for 2017–18 is $1,500 per graduate credit hour.

Living and Housing Costs

Academic-year living expenses are about $19,000 for single students. The University has residence hall rooms and on-campus apartments for single and married graduate students. Many graduate students choose to live off campus.

Student Group

Syracuse University has about 20,000 students, including about 5,000 graduate students. Approximately 750 graduate students are enrolled in the School of Information Studies. Fifty percent are international students, with the remainder coming from all parts of the United States. Students have diverse backgrounds, with undergraduate majors in the liberal arts, natural sciences, fine arts, business administration, computer science, and engineering. They participate in more than 300 student groups and extracurricular activities, including Women in Information Technology, Information Studies Graduate Organization, Black and Latino Information Studies Support, the Association for Computing Machinery, and chapters of national information and library associations.

Student Outcomes

Career opportunities for graduates of the programs are excellent. Graduates of the iSchool's master's programs find lucrative professional positions in a wide variety of organizations, with responsibilities ranging from cloud architecture, information systems analysis, information security, and database design to risk assessment and systems management. Library and information science graduates not only work in library settings, but they also hold professional positions in corporations, media and communications outlets, museums, government agencies, and universities. Placements rates are 95 percent from 2014–17. (Placement rates do not apply to the ADS and EDS degrees, which are new in 2017.)

Location

The Syracuse metropolitan area is home to more than a half million people and is the commercial, industrial, medical, and cultural center of central New York State. The 200-acre Main Campus is spacious and attractive, and new University facilities extend the campus into the heart of downtown Syracuse, which is only a 20-minute walk from the University. Winters are snowy and summers are pleasant. Lake Ontario, the Finger Lakes, and the Adirondack and Catskill Mountains are nearby. Boston, Toronto, New York, and Philadelphia are within a 5-hour drive.

The School

The School of Information Studies is a leading center for innovative graduate programs in information fields. The school's focus on information users and understanding user information needs sets it apart from other institutions that offer computer science, management, and related programs. The interdisciplinary faculty combines expertise in information science, telecommunications, public administration, education, school media, business management and management information systems, social science, design, linguistics, computer science, library science, and communications. The iSchool also offers an undergraduate degree program in information management and technology.

Applying

Applicants for the master's degree programs must have a bachelor's degree from an accredited undergraduate institution and an academic record that is satisfactory for admission to the graduate school. Two letters of recommendation, a resume, and an essay on academic plans and professional goals are also required. Applicants for the master's degree and doctoral programs are required to submit scores from the Graduate Record Examinations (GRE). Whenever possible, an interview is recommended. International students should plan to take the Test of English as a Foreign Language (TOEFL); a score of at least 90 on the internet-based test is expected. Students interested in University fellowships must apply by January 8. Other financial aid applicants must submit all materials by February 1.

For additional information, please visit the School of Information Studies website, http://ischool.syr.edu or e-mail iGrad@syr.edu. Follow the School on Facebook or Twitter at http://facebook.com/su.ischool and http://twitter.com/ischoolsu. Videos about the School can be found at http://www.youtube.com/user/syracuseischool.

Correspondence and Information

School of Information Studies
343 Hinds Hall
Syracuse University
Syracuse, New York 13244-4100
United States
Phone: 315-443-2911
E-mail: iGrad@syr.edu
Websites: http://ischool.syr.edu
http://facebook.com/su.ischool (Facebook)
http://twitter.com/ischoolsu (Twitter)

THE FACULTY AND THEIR RESEARCH

Daniel E. Acuna, Assistant Professor; Ph.D. (computer science), Minnesota, Twin Cities. Scientific innovation, artificial intelligence, machine learning.

Marilyn Arnone, Research Associate Professor; Ph.D. (instructional design, development, and evaluation), Syracuse. Information literacy education, children's learning and curiosity in interactive multimedia environments.

Bahram Attaie, Assistant Professor of Practice. Microsoft and Cisco certification, business information technology, networking and database programming for the corporate world.

Carlos E. Caicedo, Assistant Professor; Ph.D. (telecommunications), Pittsburgh. Security in future data environments, spectrum trading markets and technology, security management, telecommunication and network systems management.

Kevin Crowston, Professor; Ph.D. (information technologies), MIT. Organizational implications of technology, free/libre open source software development, coordination in distributed teams, ICT in real estate.

Rachel Ivy Clarke, Assistant Professor; Ph.D. (information sciences), Washington. Application of design methodologies and epistemologies to librarianship.

Jason Dedrick, Associate Professor; Ph.D. (management information systems), California, Irvine. Globalization of information technology, national technology policy, offshoring of knowledge work, personal computing industry, green information technologies.

Michael D'Eredita, Assistant Professor of Practice; Ph.D. (experimental/cognitive psychology), Syracuse. Enterprise skill acquisition, collective expertise, virtual apprenticeship, organizational behavior, collaboration.

Ingrid Erickson, Assistant Professor; Ph.D. (management science and engineering), Stanford. Work and technology, organizational studies, human-centered computing.

Michael Fudge, Assistant Professor of Practice; M.S. (information management), Syracuse. Database management systems; systems analysis and design; programming, scripting, and web/mobile development; big data; data lakes; warehousing and business intelligence; cloud services and technologies.

Paul Gandel, Professor; Ph.D. (information studies), Syracuse. Digital libraries; digital services; information organization and retrieval; information technology and development; information, organizations, and society knowledge.

Martha A. Garcia-Murillo, Associate Professor; Ph.D. (international political economy and telecommunications), USC. Digital divide, economics of the information industry, information and communications policy and regulations.

Caroline Haythornthwaite, Professor; Ph.D. (information science), Toronto. ICT support of work, learning and social interaction.

Jeff Hemsley, Assistant Professor: Ph.D. (information sciences), Washington. Power as it relates to information asymmetries, computer-medicated social networks in the context of politics or social movements.

Yun Huang, Assistant Professor; Ph.D. (information and computer science), California, Irvine. Crowdsourcing systems, mobile applications, human-computer interaction, social media.

Jill Hurst-Wahl, Assistant Professor of Practice; M.L.S., Maryland. Digitization, digital libraries, copyright, online social networking, web 2.0, virtual worlds.

Michelle Lynn Kaarst-Brown, Associate Professor; Ph.D. (organizational theory and management information systems), York. Information technology culture, strategic alignment of information technology with business strategy, perceptions of risk and opportunity in IT adoption, influences on IT governance, Internet-based business.

Bruce Kingma, Professor of Entrepreneurship; Ph.D. (economics), Rochester. Economics of online education, digital libraries, scholarly publishing, library and nonprofit management.

Barbara Kwasnik, Professor; Ph.D. (library and information studies), Rutgers. Classification research, knowledge representation and organization, research methods, information-related behavior.

Elizabeth D. Liddy, Dean and Trustee Professor; Ph.D. (information transfer), Syracuse. Indexing, data mining, natural-language processing, information retrieval.

Ian MacInnes, Associate Dean for Academic Affairs; Ph.D. (political economy and public policy), USC. Electronic commerce, competition policy, information technology and globalization, public policy, standardization, network economics, microeconomics.

Nancy McCracken, Research Associate Professor; Ph.D. (computer and information science), Syracuse. Computational linguistics, natural language processing, data mining, information extraction and retrieval, question answering, knowledge representation.

Lee McKnight, Associate Professor; Ph.D. (political science, communication, and international relations), MIT. Wireless grids, nomadicity, social networking of devices, Internet economics and policy, national and international technology policy.

David Molta, Assistant Dean, Technology Integration; M.P.A., North Texas. Mobile and wireless information systems; interoperability and performance testing; impact of mobile communications technologies on individuals, organizations, and society.

Deborah Nosky, Assistant Professor of Practice; M.S., Syracuse. Technology, project and time management, presentation delivery.

Megan Oakleaf, Assistant Professor; Ph.D. (information and library science), North Carolina at Chapel Hill. Evolution and assessment of information services, outcomes-based assessment, evidence-based decision making, digital reference, digital libraries, information services.

Carsten Osterlund, Associate Professor; Ph.D. (organization studies and behavioral policy science), MIT. Medical informatics, documenting work, distributed work, organizational implications of information technology, indoor tracking systems, qualitative research techniques.

Joon S. Park, Professor; Ph.D. (information technology and information security), George Mason. Information and systems security; security policies, models, mechanisms, evaluation, survivability, and applications.

Jian Qin, Associate Professor; Ph.D. (library and information science), Illinois at Urbana-Champaign. Knowledge organization, information organization, information technology applications in managing knowledge and information.

Jeffrey Rubin, Assistant Professor of Practice; M.S. (telecommunications and network management), Syracuse. Managing websites, e-business, content management systems, information architecture, designing Internet services, web analytics.

Jeff Saltz, Associate Professor; Ph.D. (information systems), NJIT. Analyzing and visualizing large datasets, experiential learning and teaching, investigating startup ecosystems.

Steven B. Sawyer, Associate Professor; D.B.A. (management information systems), Boston. Social informatics, design and development of information systems, project management, role of information and communication technologies relative to organizational and social change.

Carl Schramm, Professor; Ph.D. (labor economics and industrial relations), Wisconsin. Entrepreneurship, innovation and economic growth.

Bryan Semaan, Assistant Professor; Ph.D. (information and computer science), California, Irvine. How people appropriate and are shaped by interactive and collaborative technologies.

Ruth V. Small, Meredith Professor; Ph.D. (instructional design, development, and evaluation), Syracuse. Motivational aspects of information literacy, design and use of information and information technologies in education, role of school media specialist, information components of inventive thinking.

Marcene Sonneborn, Assistant Professor of Practice; M.B.A., Syracuse. Strategic planning, business development, organizational leadership, entrepreneurship.

Jeffrey Stanton, Associate Provost, Professor; Ph.D. (information studies), Connecticut. Organizational psychology and data collection; behavioral information security; statistical models to predict attitudes, motivation, and behavior; interactions between people and technology.

Barbara Stripling, Senior Associate Dean, Associate Professor of Practice; D.P.S., Syracuse. Library leadership, school library programs.

Jennifer Stromer-Galley, Professor, Ph.D. (communication), Pennsylvania. Social media, presidential campaigns, online political participation, social dynamics in online groups.

Arthur Thomas, Assistant Professor of Practice; Ph.D. (research and evaluation/instructional systems design and management), SUNY at Buffalo. Performance improvement, project management, data networking engineering, instructional design, information systems management.

Murali Venkatesh, Associate Professor; Ph.D. (management), Indiana. Civic network design, group-based decision support systems, sociological analyses of administrative documents, human-computer interaction, telecommunications.

Jun Wang, Assistant Research Professor; Ph.D. (library and information science), Illinois at Urbana-Champaign. Human computation, machine learning, computational neuroscience, computational language evolution.

Yang Wang, Assistant Professor; Ph.D. (information and computer science), California, Irvine. Privacy and security, social media, crowdsourcing, online communities, persuasive computing.

Bei Yu, Assistant Professor; Ph.D. (library and information science), Illinois at Urbana-Champaign. Text classification and analysis, natural language processing, political linguistics, language and social behavior, automated language extraction and classification development.

Ping Zhang, Professor; Ph.D. (information systems), Texas at Austin. Human computer interaction, information management, intellectual development of information-related fields.

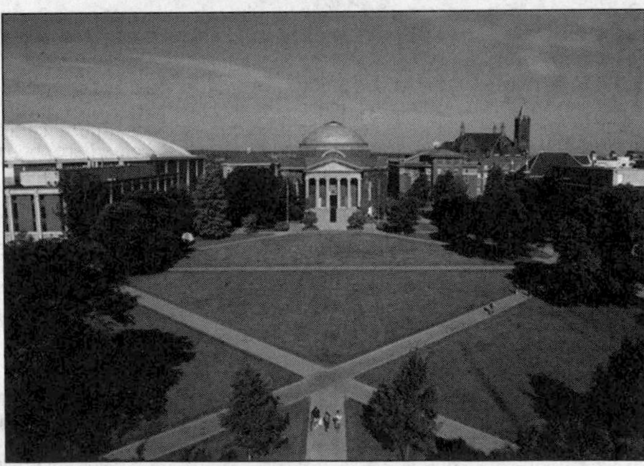

The iSchool is located on the Main Campus Quad in the heart of the Syracuse University campus.

ACADEMIC AND PROFESSIONAL PROGRAMS IN PHYSICAL EDUCATION, SPORTS, AND RECREATION

Section 29
Leisure Studies and Recreation

This section contains a directory of institutions offering graduate work in leisure studies and recreation. Additional information about programs listed in the directory may be obtained by writing directly to the dean of a graduate school or chair of a department at the address given in the directory.

In the other guides in this series:

Graduate Programs in the Humanities, Arts & Social Sciences
See *Performing Arts*

Graduate Programs in the Physical Sciences, Mathematics, Agricultural Sciences, the Environment & Natural Resources
See *Natural Resources*

CONTENTS

Program Directories

Featured School: Display and Close-Up

See:

Leisure Studies

Bowling Green State University, Graduate College, College of Education and Human Development, School of Human Movement, Sport, and Leisure Studies, Bowling Green, OH 43403. Offers developmental kinesiology (M Ed); recreation and leisure (M Ed); sport administration (M Ed). *Program availability:* Part-time. *Degree requirements:* For master's, thesis or alternative. *Entrance requirements:* For master's, GRE General Test, minimum GPA of 2.7. Additional exam requirements/recommendations for international students: Required—TOEFL. *Application deadline:* For fall admission, 1/15 priority date for domestic students. Applications are processed on a rolling basis. Application fee: $30. Electronic applications accepted. *Financial support:* Research assistantships with full tuition reimbursements, teaching assistantships with full tuition reimbursements, career-related internships or fieldwork, Federal Work-Study, and unspecified assistantships available. Financial award applicants required to submit FAFSA. *Faculty research:* Teacher-learning process, travel and tourism, sport marketing and management, exercise physiology and sport psychology, life-span motor development. *Unit head:* Dr. Bonnie Berger, Director, 419-372-2334. *Application contact:* Dr. Geoff Meek, Graduate Coordinator, 419-372-0501.

California State University, Long Beach, Graduate Studies, College of Health and Human Services, Department of Recreation and Leisure Studies, Long Beach, CA 90840. Offers recreation administration (MS). *Program availability:* Part-time. *Degree requirements:* For master's, comprehensive exam or thesis. *Entrance requirements:* For master's, GRE General Test. *Application deadline:* For fall admission, 7/1 for domestic students. Applications are processed on a rolling basis. Application fee: $55. Electronic applications accepted. *Financial support:* Federal Work-Study, institutionally sponsored loans, and scholarships/grants available. Financial award application deadline: 3/2. *Unit head:* Monica Lounsbery, Dean, College of Health and Human Services.

Dalhousie University, Faculty of Health Professions, School of Health and Human Performance, Program in Leisure Studies, Halifax, NS B3H 1T8, Canada. Offers MA. *Program availability:* Part-time. *Degree requirements:* For master's, thesis. *Entrance requirements:* For master's, minimum GPA of 3.3. Additional exam requirements/recommendations for international students: Required—TOEFL, IELTS, CANTEST, CAEL, or Michigan English Language Assessment Battery. Electronic applications accepted. *Faculty research:* Leisure and lifestyles of social groups such as older adults, women, and persons with health problems or disabilities; historical analysis of leisure; sport and leisure administration.

East Carolina University, Graduate School, College of Health and Human Performance, Department of Recreation and Leisure Studies, Greenville, NC 27858-4353. Offers aquatic therapy (Certificate); biofeedback (Certificate); recreation and park administration (MS), including generalist, recreational sports management. *Program availability:* Part-time, evening/weekend, online learning. *Students:* 25 full-time (17 women), 4 part-time (2 women); includes 6 minority (3 Black or African American, non-Hispanic/Latino; 1 Hispanic/Latino; 2 Two or more races, non-Hispanic/Latino). Average age 25. 11 applicants, 100% accepted, 9 enrolled. In 2016, 4 master's awarded. *Degree requirements:* For master's, comprehensive exam, thesis optional. *Entrance requirements:* For master's, GRE General Test or MAT. Additional exam requirements/recommendations for international students: Required—TOEFL. *Application deadline:* For fall admission, 6/1 priority date for domestic students. Applications are processed on a rolling basis. Application fee: $50. *Financial support:* Research assistantships and teaching assistantships with partial tuition reimbursements available. Financial award application deadline: 6/1. *Faculty research:* Therapeutic recreation, stress and coping behavior, medicine carrying capacity, choice behavior, tourism preferences. *Unit head:* Dr. Matthew Mahar, Interim Chair, 252-328-0008, E-mail: maharm@ecu.edu.
Website: http://www.ecu.edu/rcls/

Howard University, Graduate School, Department of Health, Human Performance and Leisure Studies, Washington, DC 20059-0002. Offers exercise physiology (MS); health education (MS); sports studies (MS), including sociology of sports, sports management; urban recreation (MS), including leisure studies. *Program availability:* Part-time, evening/weekend. *Degree requirements:* For master's, comprehensive exam, thesis. *Entrance requirements:* For master's, BS in human performance or related field. Additional exam requirements/recommendations for international students: Recommended—TOEFL. Electronic applications accepted. *Faculty research:* Health promotion, cardiovascular hypertension, physical activity, sport and human rights issues.

Indiana University Bloomington, School of Public Health, Department of Recreation, Park, and Tourism Studies, Bloomington, IN 47405-7000. Offers leisure behavior (PhD); outdoor recreation (MS); park and public lands management (MS); recreation administration (MS); recreational sports administration (MS); recreational therapy (MS); tourism management (MS). Terminal master's awarded for partial completion of doctoral program. *Degree requirements:* For master's, thesis optional; for doctorate, comprehensive exam, thesis/dissertation. *Entrance requirements:* For master's, GRE General Test, minimum GPA of 2.8; for doctorate, GRE General Test, minimum GPA of 3.0 (undergraduate), 3.5 (graduate). Additional exam requirements/recommendations for international students: Required—TOEFL (minimum score 550 paper-based; 80 iBT). Electronic applications accepted. *Faculty research:* Leisure counseling, gerontology, special populations, planning and development.

Murray State University, College of Health Sciences and Human Services, Department of Wellness and Therapeutic Sciences, Program in Exercise and Leisure Studies, Murray, KY 42071. Offers MS. *Program availability:* Part-time. *Degree requirements:* For master's, thesis optional. *Entrance requirements:* For master's, GRE General Test or MAT. Additional exam requirements/recommendations for international students: Required—TOEFL. *Faculty research:* Exercise and cancer recovery.

Penn State University Park, Graduate School, College of Health and Human Development, Department of Recreation, Park and Tourism Management, University Park, PA 16802. Offers MS, PhD. *Unit head:* Dr. Ann C. Crouter, Dean, 814-865-1420, Fax: 814-865-3282. *Application contact:* Lori Hawn, Director, Graduate Student Services, 814-865-1795, Fax: 814-863-4627, E-mail: l-gswww@lists.psu.edu.
Website: http://hhd.psu.edu/rptm

Prescott College, Graduate Programs, Program in Adventure Education, Prescott, AZ 86301. Offers adventure education (MA); adventure-based environmental education (MA); student-directed concentration (MA). *Program availability:* Part-time, online learning. *Faculty:* 1 (woman) full-time, 1 (woman) part-time/adjunct. *Students:* 18 part-time (10 women); includes 1 minority (Two or more races, non-Hispanic/Latino), 1 international. Average age 33. 16 applicants, 75% accepted, 5 enrolled. In 2016, 8 master's awarded. *Degree requirements:* For master's, thesis, fieldwork or internship, practicum. *Entrance requirements:* For master's, 2 letters of recommendation, resume. Additional exam requirements/recommendations for international students: Required—TOEFL (minimum score 500 paper-based). *Application deadline:* For fall admission, 4/15 priority date for domestic and international students; for spring admission, 9/15 priority date for domestic and international students. Applications are processed on a rolling basis. Application fee: $0. Electronic applications accepted. *Expenses: Tuition:* Full-time $19,680. One-time fee: $260 part-time. *Financial support:* Career-related internships or fieldwork, Federal Work-Study, and scholarships/grants available. Financial award applicants required to submit FAFSA. *Unit head:* Denise Mitten, Chair, 303-350-1004, E-mail: dmitten@prescott.edu. *Application contact:* Amber Harris, Assistant Director, Graduate Admissions, 928-615-8446, Fax: 928-776-5242, E-mail: amber.harris@prescott.edu.

San Francisco State University, Division of Graduate Studies, College of Health and Social Sciences, Department of Recreation, Parks, and Tourism, San Francisco, CA 94132-1722. Offers MS. *Program availability:* Part-time. *Application deadline:* Applications are processed on a rolling basis. *Expenses:* Tuition, state resident: full-time $6738. Tuition, nonresident: full-time $15,666. *Required fees:* $1012. Tuition and fees vary according to degree level and program. *Financial support:* Career-related internships or fieldwork available. *Unit head:* Dr. Erik Rosegard, Chair, 415-338-7529, Fax: 415-338-0543, E-mail: rosegard@sfsu.edu. *Application contact:* Dr. Jackson Wilson, Graduate Coordinator, 415-338-1487, Fax: 415-338-0543, E-mail: wilsonj@sfsu.edu.
Website: http://recdept.sfsu.edu/graduate

Southeast Missouri State University, School of Graduate Studies, Department of Health, Human Performance and Recreation, Cape Girardeau, MO 63701-4799. Offers MS. *Program availability:* Part-time. *Faculty:* 8 full-time (2 women), 2 part-time/adjunct (1 woman). *Students:* 20 full-time (12 women), 19 part-time (10 women), 17 international. Average age 25. 39 applicants, 62% accepted, 11 enrolled. In 2016, 8 master's awarded. *Degree requirements:* For master's, comprehensive exam, thesis optional. *Entrance requirements:* For master's, GRE General Test (minimum combined score of 950). Additional exam requirements/recommendations for international students: Required—TOEFL (minimum score 550 paper-based; 79 iBT), IELTS (minimum score 6), PTE (minimum score 53). *Application deadline:* For fall admission, 8/1 for domestic students, 5/1 for international students; for spring admission, 11/21 for domestic students, 10/1 for international students; for summer admission, 5/15 for domestic students. Applications are processed on a rolling basis. Application fee: $30 ($40 for international students). Electronic applications accepted. *Expenses:* Tuition, state resident: full-time $3130; part-time $260.80 per credit hour. Tuition, nonresident: full-time $5842; part-time $486.80 per credit hour. *Required fees:* $33.70 per credit hour. *Financial support:* In 2016–17, 19 students received support. Teaching assistantships with full tuition reimbursements available, career-related internships or fieldwork, Federal Work-Study, scholarships/grants, traineeships, tuition waivers (full), and unspecified assistantships available. Financial award application deadline: 6/30; financial award applicants required to submit FAFSA. *Faculty research:* Body composition assessment techniques, serum lipid adaptations with physical activity in smokers, professional attitudes of pre-service teachers, high intensity training with clinical populations. *Unit head:* Dr. Joe Pujol, Professor and Chairperson, 573-651-2664, Fax: 573-651-5150, E-mail: jpujol@semo.edu. *Application contact:* Dr. Jeremy Barnes, Professor/Graduate Coordinator, 573-651-2197, Fax: 573-651-5150, E-mail: jbarnes@semo.edu.
Website: http://www.semo.edu/health/

Southern Connecticut State University, School of Graduate Studies, School of Health and Human Services, Department of Recreation and Leisure Studies, New Haven, CT 06515-1355. Offers MS. *Program availability:* Part-time, evening/weekend. *Faculty:* 4 full-time (1 woman), 5 part-time/adjunct (3 women). *Students:* 26 full-time (16 women), 32 part-time (15 women); includes 16 minority (12 Black or African American, non-Hispanic/Latino; 4 Hispanic/Latino). Average age 28. 43 applicants, 72% accepted, 23 enrolled. In 2016, 16 master's awarded. *Degree requirements:* For master's, thesis or alternative. *Entrance requirements:* For master's, interview, minimum undergraduate QPA of 3.0 in graduate major field or 2.5 overall. *Application deadline:* For fall admission, 7/15 priority date for domestic students. Applications are processed on a rolling basis. Application fee: $50. Electronic applications accepted. *Expenses:* Tuition, state resident: full-time $6497; part-time $519 per credit hour. Tuition, nonresident: full-time $18,102; part-time $535 per credit hour. *Required fees:* $4722; $55 per semester. Tuition and fees vary according to program. *Financial support:* Career-related internships or fieldwork, scholarships/grants, and unspecified assistantships available. Financial award application deadline: 4/15; financial award applicants required to submit FAFSA. *Unit head:* Dr. James MacGregor, Chairperson, 203-392-6385, Fax: 203-392-6965, E-mail: macgregorj1@southernct.edu. *Application contact:* Lisa Galvin, Director of Graduate Admissions, 203-392-5240, Fax: 203-392-5235, E-mail: galvinl1@southernct.edu.

Texas State University, The Graduate College, College of Education, Recreation Management, San Marcos, TX 78666. Offers recreation management (MSRLS). *Program availability:* Part-time. *Faculty:* 5 full-time (3 women), 1 (woman) part-time/adjunct. *Students:* 15 full-time (5 women), 6 part-time (3 women); includes 8 minority (3 Black or African American, non-Hispanic/Latino; 1 Asian, non-Hispanic/Latino; 4 Hispanic/Latino). Average age 25. 28 applicants, 71% accepted, 8 enrolled. In 2016, 10 master's awarded. *Degree requirements:* For master's, comprehensive exam, thesis optional. *Entrance requirements:* For master's, GRE (preferred), baccalaureate degree from regionally-accredited institution with minimum GPA of 2.75 in last 60 hours of course work. Additional exam requirements/recommendations for international students: Required—TOEFL (minimum score 550 paper-based; 78 iBT), IELTS (minimum score 6.5). *Application deadline:* For fall admission, 2/15 priority date for domestic students, 2/15 for international students; for spring admission, 10/15 priority date for domestic students, 10/1 for international students; for summer admission, 4/15 for domestic students, 3/15 for international students. Applications are processed on a rolling basis. Application fee: $40 ($90 for international students). Electronic applications accepted. *Expenses:* $4,851 per semester. *Financial support:* In 2016–17, 12 students received support, including 2 teaching assistantships (averaging $13,522 per year); research assistantships, scholarships/grants, and unspecified assistantships also available. Financial award application deadline: 3/1; financial award applicants required to submit FAFSA. *Faculty research:* Effects of neuromuscular electrical stimulation frequency on metabolic markers, effects of focal knee join cooling on different modes of the quadriceps strength. *Unit head:* Dr. Jan Hodges, Graduate Advisor, 512-245-7482, Fax: 512-245-8678, E-mail: jh223@txstate.edu. *Application contact:* Dr. Andrea Golato, Dean of the Graduate College, 512-245-2581, Fax: 512-245-8365, E-mail: gradcollege@txstate.edu.
Website: http://www.hhp.txstate.edu/Degree-Plans/Graduate.html

Universidad Metropolitana, School of Education, Program in Managing Recreation and Sports Services, San Juan, PR 00928-1150. Offers M Ed. *Program availability:* Part-time. *Degree requirements:* For master's, thesis or alternative. *Entrance requirements:* For master's, EXADEP, interview. Electronic applications accepted.

Université du Québec à Trois-Rivières, Graduate Programs, Program in Leisure, Culture and Tourism Sciences, Trois-Rivières, QC G9A 5H7, Canada. Offers MA, DESS. *Program availability:* Part-time. *Degree requirements:* For master's, thesis optional. *Entrance requirements:* For master's, appropriate bachelor's degree, proficiency in French.

University of Illinois at Urbana–Champaign, Graduate College, College of Applied Health Sciences, Department of Recreation, Sport and Tourism, Champaign, IL 61820. Offers MS, PhD. *Program availability:* Part-time, online learning.

The University of Iowa, Graduate College, College of Liberal Arts and Sciences, Department of Health and Human Physiology, Iowa City, IA 52242-1316. Offers athletic training (MS); clinical exercise physiology (MS); health and human physiology (PhD); leisure studies (MA, PhD), including recreational sport management (PhD), therapeutic recreation (MA). *Degree requirements:* For master's, thesis optional, exam; for doctorate, comprehensive exam, thesis/dissertation. *Entrance requirements:* For master's and doctorate, GRE General Test, minimum GPA of 3.0. Additional exam requirements/ recommendations for international students: Required—TOEFL (minimum score 600 paper-based; 100 iBT). Electronic applications accepted.

University of Nebraska at Kearney, College of Education, Kinesiology and Sport Sciences Department, Kearney, NE 68849-0001. Offers general physical education (MA Ed), including recreation and leisure, sports administration; physical education exercise science (MA Ed); physical education master teacher (MA Ed), including pedagogy, special populations. *Program availability:* Part-time, evening/weekend, 100% online. *Faculty:* 17 full-time (5 women). *Students:* 4 full-time (2 women), 39 part-time (16 women); includes 3 minority (2 Black or African American, non-Hispanic/Latino; 1 Hispanic/Latino). Average age 28. 20 applicants, 100% accepted, 14 enrolled. In 2016, 25 master's awarded. *Degree requirements:* For master's, comprehensive exam, thesis optional. *Entrance requirements:* For master's, GRE General Test (for some programs), personal statement. Additional exam requirements/recommendations for international students: Recommended—TOEFL (minimum score 550 paper-based; 79 iBT), IELTS (minimum score 6.5). *Application deadline:* For fall admission, 6/15 for domestic and international students; for spring admission, 10/15 for domestic and international students; for summer admission, 3/15 for domestic and international students. Application fee: $45. Electronic applications accepted. *Expenses:* Tuition, state resident: full-time $4064; part-time $225.75 per credit hour. Tuition, nonresident: full-time $8915; part-time $495.25 per credit hour. *Required fees:* $772; $23 per credit hour. Part-time tuition and fees vary according to course load, campus/ location, program and reciprocity agreements. *Financial support:* In 2016–17, 9 students received support, including 3 research assistantships with full tuition reimbursements available (averaging $10,500 per year), 6 teaching assistantships with full tuition reimbursements available (averaging $10,500 per year); career-related internships or fieldwork, scholarships/grants, health care benefits, and unspecified assistantships also available. Support available to part-time students. Financial award application deadline: 2/ 28; financial award applicants required to submit FAFSA. *Faculty research:* Ergonomic aids, nutrition, motor development, sports pedagogy, applied behavior analysis, physical activity and wellness, athletic training, therapeutic interventions, exercise physiology, endocrinology and metabolism. *Unit head:* Dr. Nita Unruh, Chair, 308-865-8335, E-mail: unruhnc@ unk.edu. *Application contact:* Linda Johnson, Director, Graduate Admissions and Programs, 308-865-8841, Fax: 308-865-8837, E-mail: johnsonli@unk.edu.
Website: http://www.unk.edu/academics/hperls/index.php

The University of Tennessee, Graduate School, College of Education, Health and Human Sciences, Department of Exercise, Sport, and Leisure Studies, Knoxville, TN 37996. Offers exercise science (MS, PhD), including biomechanics/sports medicine, exercise physiology; recreation and leisure studies (MS); sport management (MS); sport studies (MS, PhD); therapeutic recreation (MS). *Program availability:* Part-time, evening/weekend. *Degree requirements:* For master's, thesis optional. *Entrance requirements:* For master's, minimum GPA of 2.7. Additional exam requirements/recommendations for international students: Required—TOEFL. Electronic applications accepted.

The University of Toledo, College of Graduate Studies, College of Health and Human Services, Department of Health and Recreation Professions, Toledo, OH 43606-3390. Offers health education (PhD); recreation and leisure studies (MA). *Program availability:* Part-time. *Degree requirements:* For master's, comprehensive exam, thesis; for doctorate, thesis/dissertation. *Entrance requirements:* For master's and doctorate, minimum cumulative GPA of 2.7 for all previous academic work, letters of recommendation. Additional exam requirements/recommendations for international students: Required—TOEFL (minimum score 550 paper-based; 80 iBT). Electronic applications accepted.

University of Utah, Graduate School, College of Health, Department of Parks, Recreation, and Tourism, Salt Lake City, UT 84112. Offers M Phil, MS, PhD. *Program availability:* Part-time. *Faculty:* 8 full-time (4 women), 8 part-time/adjunct (3 women). *Students:* 26 full-time (16 women), 10 part-time (8 women), 2 international. Average age 29. 30 applicants, 37% accepted, 9 enrolled. In 2016, 11 master's awarded. Terminal master's awarded for partial completion of doctoral program. *Degree requirements:* For master's, comprehensive exam, thesis or alternative; for doctorate, comprehensive exam, thesis/dissertation. *Entrance requirements:* For master's and doctorate, GRE General Test, minimum GPA of 3.0. Additional exam requirements/recommendations for international students: Required—TOEFL (minimum score 500 paper-based). *Application deadline:* For fall admission, 1/15 priority date for domestic and international students. Application fee: $55 ($65 for international students). Electronic applications accepted. *Expenses:* Contact institution. *Financial support:* In 2016–17, 15 students received support, including 3 research assistantships with full tuition reimbursements available, 8 teaching assistantships with full tuition reimbursements available; career-related internships or fieldwork, scholarships/ grants, health care benefits, and unspecified assistantships also available. Financial award application deadline: 1/15; financial award applicants required to submit FAFSA. *Faculty research:* Therapeutic recreation, community and sport, outdoor recreation, protected area management, sustainable tourism and youth development. *Total annual research expenditures:* $39,469. *Unit head:* Dr. Kelly S. Bricker, Chair, 801-585-6503, E-mail: kelly.bricker@health.utah.edu. *Application contact:* Dr. Jim Sibthorp, Director of Graduate Studies, 801-581-5940, Fax: 801-581-4930, E-mail: jim.sibthorp@health.utah.edu.
Website: http://www.health.utah.edu/prt/

University of Victoria, Faculty of Graduate Studies, Faculty of Education, School of Exercise Science, Physical, and Health Education, Victoria, BC V8W 2Y2, Canada. Offers coaching studies (co-operative education) (M Ed); kinesiology (M Sc, MA); leisure service administration (MA); physical education (MA). *Program availability:* Part-time. *Degree requirements:* For master's, comprehensive exam (for some programs), thesis (for some programs). *Entrance requirements:* For master's, minimum B average. Additional exam requirements/recommendations for international students: Required—TOEFL (minimum score 575 paper-based), IELTS (minimum score 7). Electronic applications accepted. *Faculty research:* Children and exercise, mental skills in sports, teaching effectiveness, neural control of human movement, physical performance and health.

University of Waterloo, Graduate Studies, Faculty of Applied Health Sciences, Department of Recreation and Leisure Studies, Waterloo, ON N2L 3G1, Canada. Offers MA, PhD. *Program availability:* Part-time. *Degree requirements:* For master's, thesis; for doctorate, comprehensive exam, thesis/dissertation. *Entrance requirements:* For master's, honors degree, minimum B average, writing sample, resume; for doctorate, GRE (recommended), master's degree, minimum B average, writing sample, resume. Additional exam requirements/recommendations for international students: Required—TOEFL, IELTS, PTE. Electronic applications accepted. *Faculty research:* Tourism, leisure behavior, special populations, leisure service management, outdoor resources, aging, health and well-being, work and health.

University of West Florida, Usha Kundu, MD College of Health, Department of Exercise Science and Community Health, Pensacola, FL 32514-5750. Offers health promotion (MS); health, leisure, and exercise science (MS), including exercise science, physical education. *Program availability:* Part-time, evening/weekend. *Degree requirements:* For master's, thesis or alternative. *Entrance requirements:* For master's, GRE or MAT, official transcripts; minimum GPA of 3.0; letter of intent; three personal references; work experience as reflected in resume. Additional exam requirements/recommendations for international students: Required—TOEFL (minimum score 550 paper-based). *Application deadline:* For fall admission, 6/1 for domestic and international students; for spring admission, 10/1 for domestic and international students. Applications are processed on a rolling basis. Application fee: $30. *Expenses:* Tuition, state resident: full-time $5316.12. Tuition, nonresident: full-time $11,308. *Required fees:* $583.92. Tuition and fees vary according to course load and program. *Financial support:* Fellowships, research assistantships with partial tuition reimbursements, teaching assistantships with partial tuition reimbursements, tuition waivers (partial), and unspecified assistantships available. Financial award application deadline: 4/15; financial award applicants required to submit FAFSA. *Unit head:* Dr. John Todorovich, Chairperson, 850-473-7248, Fax: 850-474-2106. *Application contact:* Terry McCray, Assistant Director of Graduate Admissions, 850-473-7718, Fax: 850-473-7714, E-mail: gradadmissions@uwf.edu.
Website: http://uwf.edu/coh/departments/exercise-science-and-community-health/

Recreation and Park Management

Acadia University, Faculty of Professional Studies, School of Recreation Management and Community Development, Wolfville, NS B4P 2R6, Canada. Offers MR. *Degree requirements:* For master's, thesis. *Entrance requirements:* Additional exam requirements/ recommendations for international students: Required—TOEFL (minimum score 630 paper-based; 93 iBT), IELTS (minimum score 6.5).

Bowling Green State University, Graduate College, College of Education and Human Development, School of Human Movement, Sport, and Leisure Studies, Bowling Green, OH 43403. Offers developmental kinesiology (M Ed); recreation and leisure (M Ed); sport administration (M Ed). *Program availability:* Part-time. *Degree requirements:* For master's, thesis or alternative. *Entrance requirements:* For master's, GRE General Test, minimum GPA of 2.7. Additional exam requirements/recommendations for international students: Required—TOEFL. *Application deadline:* For fall admission, 1/15 priority date for domestic students. Applications are processed on a rolling basis. Application fee: $30. Electronic applications accepted. *Financial support:* Research assistantships with full tuition reimbursements, teaching assistantships with full tuition reimbursements, career-related internships or fieldwork, Federal Work-Study, and unspecified assistantships available. Financial award applicants required to submit FAFSA. *Faculty research:* Teacher-learning process, travel and tourism, sport marketing and management, exercise physiology and sport psychology, life-span motor development. *Unit head:* Dr. Bonnie Berger, Director, 419-372-2334. *Application contact:* Dr. Geoff Meek, Graduate Coordinator, 419-372-0501.

California State University, Chico, Office of Graduate Studies, College of Communication and Education, Recreation, Hospitality and Parks Management Department, Chico, CA 95929-0722. Offers recreation, parks, and tourism (MS). *Program availability:* Part-time. *Faculty:* 9 full-time (3 women), 9 part-time/adjunct (5 women). *Students:* 6 part-time (3 women). 4 applicants, 100% accepted, 3 enrolled. In 2016, 3 master's awarded. *Degree requirements:* For master's, thesis or project. *Entrance requirements:* For master's, GRE General Test, 3 letters of recommendation, statement of purpose, resume. Additional exam requirements/recommendations for international students: Required—TOEFL (minimum score 550 paper-based; 80 iBT), IELTS (minimum score 6.5), PTE. *Application deadline:* For fall admission, 3/1 priority date for domestic students, 3/1 for international students; for spring admission, 9/15 priority date for domestic students, 9/15 for international students. Application fee: $55. Electronic applications accepted. *Financial support:* Fellowships, career-related internships or fieldwork, scholarships/grants, and traineeships available. Financial award application deadline: 3/1; financial award applicants required to submit FAFSA. *Unit head:* Dr. Morgan Geddie, Chair, 530-898-6408, Fax: 530-898-6557, E-mail: recr@csuchico.edu. *Application contact:* Judy L. Morris, Graduate Admissions Coordinator, 530-898-5416, Fax: 530-898-3342, E-mail: jlmorris@csuchico.edu.
Website: http://www.csuchico.edu/recr/

California State University, East Bay, Office of Graduate Studies, College of Education and Allied Studies, Department of Hospitality, Recreation and Tourism, Hayward, CA 94542-3000. Offers recreation and tourism (MS). *Program availability:* Part-time, evening/weekend, online learning. *Students:* 19 full-time (12 women), 12 part-time (9 women); includes 26 minority (6 Black or African American, non-Hispanic/Latino; 6 Asian, non-Hispanic/Latino; 11 Hispanic/Latino; 1 Native Hawaiian or other Pacific Islander, non-Hispanic/Latino; 2 Two or more races, non-Hispanic/Latino). Average age 34. 15 applicants, 47% accepted, 6 enrolled. In 2016, 11 master's awarded. *Degree requirements:* For master's, thesis optional. *Entrance requirements:* For master's, minimum GPA of 2.75; 2 years' related work experience; 3 letters of recommendation; resume; baccalaureate degree. Additional exam requirements/ recommendations for international students: Required—TOEFL (minimum score 550 paper-based). *Application deadline:* For fall admission, 6/30 for domestic and international students. Applications are processed on a rolling basis. Application fee: $55. Electronic applications accepted. *Financial support:* Federal Work-Study, institutionally sponsored loans, and scholarships/grants available. Support available to part-time students. Financial award application deadline: 3/2; financial award applicants required to submit FAFSA. *Faculty research:* Leisure, online vs. face-to-face (F2F) learning, risk management, leadership, tourism consumer behavior. *Unit head:* Dr. Chris Chamberlain, Chair, 510-885-2101, E-mail: chris.chamberlain@csueastbay.edu. *Application contact:* Dr. Donna Wiley, Interim Associate Vice President for Academic Programs and Graduate Studies, 510-885-3716, Fax: 510-885-4777, E-mail: donna.wiley@csueastbay.edu.

California State University, Long Beach, Graduate Studies, College of Health and Human Services, Department of Recreation and Leisure Studies, Long Beach, CA 90840. Offers recreation administration (MS). *Program availability:* Part-time. *Degree requirements:* For master's, comprehensive exam or thesis. *Entrance requirements:* For master's, GRE General Test. *Application deadline:* For fall admission, 7/1 for domestic students. Applications are processed on a rolling basis. Application fee: $55. Electronic applications accepted. *Financial support:* Federal Work-Study, institutionally sponsored loans, and scholarships/grants available. Financial award application deadline: 3/2. *Unit head:* Monica Lounsbery, Dean, College of Health and Human Services.

California State University, Northridge, Graduate Studies, College of Health and Human Development, Department of Recreation and Tourism Management, Northridge, CA 91330. Offers hospitality and tourism (MS); recreational sport management/campus recreation (MS). *Faculty:* 7 full-time (4 women), 19 part-time/adjunct (8 women). *Students:* 22 full-time (10 women), 13 part-time (10 women); includes 12 minority (1 Black or African American, non-Hispanic/Latino; 7 Hispanic/Latino; 1 Native Hawaiian or other Pacific Islander, non-Hispanic/Latino; 3 Two or more races, non-Hispanic/Latino), 7 international. Average age 29. 57 applicants, 49% accepted, 18 enrolled. *Degree requirements:* For master's, thesis (for some programs). *Entrance requirements:* For master's, GRE (if cumulative undergraduate GPA less than 3.0). Additional exam requirements/recommendations for international students: Required—TOEFL. *Application deadline:* For fall admission, 11/30 for domestic students. Application fee: $55. *Expenses:* Tuition, state resident: full-time $4152. *Financial support:* Application deadline: 3/1. *Unit head:* Dr. Mechelle Best, Chair, 818-677-3202. Website: http://www.csun.edu/hhd/rtm/

California State University, Northridge, Graduate Studies, The Tseng College of Extended Learning, Northridge, CA 91330. Offers business administration (Graduate Certificate); health administration (MPA); health education (MPH); knowledge management (MKM); music industry administration (MA); nonprofit-sector management (Graduate Certificate); public administration (MPA); public sector management and leadership (MPA); social work (MSW); taxation (MS); tourism, hospitality and recreation management (MS). *Faculty:* 55 part-time/adjunct (28 women). *Students:* 1 (woman) full-time, 1 (woman) part-time. Average age 40. *Entrance requirements:* For master's, GRE (if cumulative undergraduate GPA less than 3.0). *Expenses:* Tuition, state resident: full-time $4152. *Unit head:* Joyce Feucht-Haviar, Dean, 866-873-6439.

See Display on page 1665 and Close-Up on page 1687.

California State University, Sacramento, Office of Graduate Studies, College of Health and Human Services, Department of Recreation, Parks and Tourism Administration, Sacramento, CA 95819. Offers MS. *Program availability:* Part-time. *Students:* 2 full-time (both women), 17 part-time (12 women); includes 5 minority (1 Black or African American, non-Hispanic/Latino; 1 Asian, non-Hispanic/Latino; 3 Hispanic/Latino). Average age 30. 16 applicants, 94% accepted, 11 enrolled. *Degree requirements:* For master's, thesis or project; writing proficiency exam. *Entrance requirements:* For master's, minimum overall GPA of 2.75, 3.0 in the major. Additional exam requirements/recommendations for international students: Required—TOEFL (minimum score 550 paper-based; 80 iBT). *Application deadline:* For fall admission, 3/1 for domestic and international students; for spring admission, 9/30 for international students. Applications are processed on a rolling basis. Application fee: $55. Electronic applications accepted. *Expenses:* $4,302 full-time tuition and fees per semester, $2,796 part-time. *Financial support:* Research assistantships, teaching assistantships, career-related internships or fieldwork, and Federal Work-Study available. Support available to part-time students. Financial award application deadline: 3/1; financial award applicants required to submit FAFSA. *Unit head:* Dr. Greg Shaw, Chair, 916-278-6752, E-mail: shaw@csus.edu. *Application contact:* Jose Martinez, Graduate Admissions Supervisor, 916-278-7871, E-mail: martinj@skymail.csus.edu. Website: http://www.csus.edu/hhs/rpta

Central Michigan University, Central Michigan University Global Campus, Program in Administration, Mount Pleasant, MI 48859. Offers acquisitions administration (MSA, Certificate); engineering management administration (MSA, Certificate); general administration (MSA, Certificate); health services administration (MSA, Certificate); human resources administration (MSA, Certificate); information resource management (MSA); information resource management administration (Certificate); international administration (MSA, Certificate); leadership (MSA, Certificate); philanthropy and fundraising administration (MSA, Certificate); public administration (MSA, Certificate); recreation and park administration (MSA); research administration (MSA, Certificate). *Program availability:* Part-time, evening/weekend, online learning. *Faculty:* 21 full-time (5 women), 168 part-time/adjunct (43 women). *Students:* 3,059 (1,741 women); includes 1,392 minority (1,003 Black or African American, non-Hispanic/Latino; 27 American Indian or Alaska Native, non-Hispanic/Latino; 93 Asian, non-Hispanic/Latino; 49 Hispanic/Latino; 10 Native Hawaiian or other Pacific Islander, non-Hispanic/Latino; 210 Two or more races, non-Hispanic/Latino). Average age 38. In 2016, 289 master's awarded. *Entrance requirements:* For master's, minimum GPA of 2.7 in major. *Application deadline:* Applications are processed on a rolling basis. Application fee: $50. Electronic applications accepted. *Financial support:* Scholarships/grants available. Support available to part-time students. Financial award applicants required to submit FAFSA. *Unit head:* Dr. Patricia Chase, Director, 989-774-6525, E-mail: chase1pb@cmich.edu. *Application contact:* 877-268-4636, E-mail: cmuglobal@cmich.edu.

Clemson University, Graduate School, College of Behavioral, Social and Health Sciences, Department of Parks, Recreation, and Tourism Management, Clemson, SC 29634. Offers international parks and tourism (Certificate); parks, recreation and tourism management (MS, PhD), including recreational therapy (PhD); public administration (MPA); recreational therapy (MS); youth development leadership (MS); youth leadership development (Certificate). *Program availability:* Part-time, evening/weekend, 100% online. *Faculty:* 36 full-time (14 women), 2 part-time/adjunct (0 women). *Students:* 79 full-time (52 women), 159 part-time (100 women); includes 50 minority (36 Black or African American, non-Hispanic/Latino; 2 Asian, non-Hispanic/Latino; 6 Hispanic/Latino; 6 Two or more races, non-Hispanic/Latino), 14 international. Average age 32. 143 applicants, 62% accepted, 71 enrolled. In 2016, 37 master's, 4 doctorates, 38 other advanced degrees awarded. *Degree requirements:* For master's, comprehensive exam (for some programs), thesis (for some programs); for doctorate, comprehensive exam, thesis/dissertation; for Certificate, portfolio. *Entrance requirements:* For master's and doctorate, GRE General Test, unofficial transcripts, letter of intent, letters of reference; for Certificate, letter of recommendation, unofficial transcripts, personal statement, resume. Additional exam requirements/recommendations for international students: Required—TOEFL (minimum score 610 paper-based; 80 iBT), IELTS (minimum score 6.5). *Application deadline:* For fall admission, 1/15 priority date for domestic and international students; for spring admission, 11/15 priority date for domestic and international students. Applications are processed on a rolling basis. Application fee: $80 ($90 for international students). Electronic applications accepted. *Expenses:* $4,264 per semester full-time resident, $8,485 per semester full-time non-resident, $471 per credit hour part-time resident, $942 per credit hour part-time non-resident. *Financial support:* In 2016–17, 83 students received support, including 2 fellowships with partial tuition reimbursements available (averaging $1,750 per year), 4 research assistantships with partial tuition reimbursements available (averaging $9,219 per year), 69 teaching assistantships with partial tuition reimbursements available (averaging $10,425 per year); unspecified assistantships also available. Financial award application deadline: 1/15. *Faculty research:* Human behavior, land use, recreational therapy, sustainability, tourism. *Total annual research expenditures:* $97,805. *Unit head:* Dr. Fran McGuire, Chair, 864-656-3036, Fax: 864-656-2226, E-mail: lefty@clemson.edu. *Application contact:* Dr. Bill Norman, Graduate Coordinator, 864-656-2060, Fax: 864-656-2226, E-mail: wnorman@clemson.edu. Website: http://www.clemson.edu/hehd/departments/prtm/

Colorado State University, Warner College of Natural Resources, Department of Human Dimensions of Natural Resources, Fort Collins, CO 80523-1480. Offers conservation leadership (MS); human dimensions of natural resources (MS, PhD); tourism management (MTM). *Program availability:* Part-time, 100% online. *Faculty:* 14 full-time (7 women), 1 (woman) part-time/adjunct. *Students:* 63 full-time (42 women), 99 part-time (49 women); includes 19 minority (6 Black or African American, non-Hispanic/Latino; 1 American Indian or Alaska Native, non-Hispanic/Latino; 1 Asian, non-Hispanic/Latino; 8 Hispanic/Latino; 3 Two or more races, non-Hispanic/Latino), 25 international. Average age 29. 125 applicants, 88% accepted, 91 enrolled. In 2016, 55 master's, 4 doctorates awarded. *Degree requirements:* For master's, thesis or alternative; for doctorate, comprehensive exam, thesis/dissertation. *Entrance requirements:* For master's, GRE General Test (minimum combined score of 300), minimum GPA of 3.0, 3 letters of recommendation, statement of interest, official transcripts; for doctorate, GRE General Test (minimum combined score of 300), minimum GPA of 3.0, 3 letters of recommendation, copy of master's thesis or professional paper, interview, statement of interest, official transcripts. Additional exam requirements/recommendations for international students: Required—TOEFL (minimum score 550 paper-based; 80 iBT). *Application deadline:* For fall admission, 2/15 priority date for domestic students, 2/15 for international students. Application fee: $60 ($70 for international students). Electronic applications accepted. *Expenses:* Contact institution. *Financial support:* In 2016–17, 15 students received support, including 4 fellowships (averaging $39,500 per year), 8 research assistantships with full and partial tuition reimbursements available (averaging $22,854 per year), 9 teaching assistantships with full and partial tuition reimbursements available (averaging $13,932 per year); career-related internships or fieldwork, scholarships/grants, and unspecified assistantships also available. Financial award application deadline: 2/15. *Faculty research:* Conservation and sustainable development, environmental communication and governance, human dimensions of wildlife conservation, protected areas, social aspects of wildfire. *Total annual research expenditures:* $1.4 million. *Unit head:* Dr. Michael J. Manfredo, Professor and Department Head, 970-491-6591, Fax: 970-491-2255, E-mail: michael.manfredo@colostate.edu. *Application contact:* Graduate Contact, 970-491-6591, Fax: 970-491-2255, E-mail: wcrnhdnr_info@mail.colostate.edu. Website: http://warnercnr.colostate.edu/hdnr-home

Delta State University, Graduate Programs, College of Education, Division of Health, Physical Education, and Recreation, Cleveland, MS 38733-0001. Offers health, physical education, and recreation (M Ed); sport and human performance (MS). *Program availability:* Part-time, evening/weekend. *Degree requirements:* For master's, thesis optional. *Entrance requirements:* For master's, GRE General Test or MAT, Class A teaching certificate. *Faculty research:* Blood pressure, body fat, power and reaction time, learning disorders of athletes, effects of walking.

East Carolina University, Graduate School, College of Health and Human Performance, Department of Recreation and Leisure Studies, Greenville, NC 27858-4353. Offers aquatic therapy (Certificate); biofeedback (Certificate); recreation and park administration (MS), including generalist, recreational sports management. *Program availability:* Part-time, evening/weekend, online learning. *Students:* 25 full-time (17 women), 4 part-time (2 women); includes 6 minority (3 Black or African American, non-Hispanic/Latino; 1 Hispanic/Latino; 2 Two or more races, non-Hispanic/Latino). Average age 25. 11 applicants, 100% accepted, 9 enrolled. In 2016, 4 master's awarded. *Degree requirements:* For master's, comprehensive exam, thesis optional. *Entrance requirements:* For master's, GRE General Test or MAT. Additional exam requirements/recommendations for international students: Required—TOEFL. *Application deadline:* For fall admission, 6/1 priority date for domestic students. Applications are processed on a rolling basis. Application fee: $50. *Financial support:* Research assistantships and teaching assistantships with partial tuition reimbursements available. Financial award application deadline: 6/1. *Faculty research:* Therapeutic recreation, stress and coping behavior, medicine carrying capacity, choice behavior, tourism preferences. *Unit head:* Dr. Matthew Mahar, Interim Chair, 252-328-0008, E-mail: maharm@ecu.edu. Website: http://www.ecu.edu/rcls/

Eastern Kentucky University, The Graduate School, College of Health Sciences, Department of Recreation and Park Administration, Richmond, KY 40475-3102. Offers MS. *Program availability:* Part-time. *Degree requirements:* For master's, comprehensive exam, thesis optional. *Entrance requirements:* For master's, GRE General Test, MAT, minimum GPA of 2.5. *Faculty research:* Marketing, at risk youth, outdoor education, event planning, TR in schools.

Eastern Washington University, Graduate Studies, College of Arts, Letters and Education, Department of Physical Education, Health and Recreation, Cheney, WA 99004-2431. Offers exercise science (MS); sports and recreation administration (MS). *Faculty:* 17 full-time (7 women), 5 part-time/adjunct (2 women). *Students:* 26 full-time (10 women), 8 part-time (3 women); includes 7 minority (3 Black or African American, non-Hispanic/Latino; 1 American Indian or Alaska Native, non-Hispanic/Latino; 2 Asian, non-Hispanic/Latino; 1 Hispanic/Latino). Average age 29. 64 applicants, 38% accepted, 21 enrolled. In 2016, 14 master's awarded. *Degree requirements:* For master's, comprehensive exam, thesis or alternative. *Entrance requirements:* For master's, minimum GPA of 3.0. Additional exam requirements/recommendations for international students: Required—TOEFL (minimum score 580 paper-based; 92 iBT), IELTS (minimum score 7), PTE (minimum score 63). *Application deadline:* For fall admission, 4/1 priority date for domestic students; for spring admission, 1/15 for domestic students. Applications are processed on a rolling basis. Application fee: $50. Electronic applications accepted. *Expenses:* Tuition, state resident: full-time $11,000; part-time $5500 per credit. Tuition, nonresident: full-time $24,000; part-time $12,000 per credit. *Required fees:* $1300. One-time fee: $50 full-time. Part-time tuition and fees vary according to course load, campus/location and program. *Financial support:* In 2016–17, 10 teaching assistantships with partial tuition reimbursements (averaging $6,624 per year) were awarded; career-related internships or fieldwork, Federal Work-Study, institutionally sponsored loans, and scholarships/grants also available. Support available to part-time students. Financial award application deadline: 2/1; financial award applicants required to submit FAFSA. *Unit head:* Dr. Chadron Hazelbaker, Graduate Program Director, 509-359-2486, Fax: 509-359-4833, E-mail: chazelbaker@ewu.edu.

Florida International University, College of Arts, Sciences, and Education, Department of Leadership and Professional Studies, Miami, FL 33199. Offers adult education and human resource development (MS, Ed D); counseling (MS), including rehabilitation counseling, school counseling; counselor education (MS), including clinical mental health counseling; educational administration and supervision (Ed D); educational leadership (MS, Certificate, Ed S); higher education (Ed D); higher education administration (MS); international and comparative education (MS); recreation and sport management (MS), including recreation and sport management, recreational therapy; school psychology (Ed S); urban education (MS), including instruction in urban settings, learning technologies, multicultural/bilingual, multicultural/TESOL, urban education. *Program availability:* Part-time, evening/weekend. *Faculty:* 27 full-time (19 women), 38 part-time/adjunct (25 women). *Students:* 253 full-time (191 women), 306 part-time (241 women); includes 444 minority (129 Black or African American, non-Hispanic/Latino; 3 Asian, non-Hispanic/Latino; 304 Hispanic/Latino; 8 Two or more races, non-Hispanic/Latino), 18 international. Average age 31. 366 applicants, 60% accepted, 115 enrolled. In 2016, 193 master's, 8 doctorates awarded. *Degree requirements:* For doctorate, thesis/dissertation. *Entrance requirements:* For master's, minimum GPA of 3.0; for doctorate and other advanced degree, GRE General Test. Additional exam requirements/recommendations for international students: Required—TOEFL (minimum score 550 paper-based; 80 iBT), IELTS (minimum score 6.3). *Application deadline:* For fall admission, 6/1 priority date for domestic students, 4/1 for international students; for winter

admission, 10/1 priority date for domestic students, 9/1 for international students; for spring admission, 3/1 priority date for domestic students, 2/1 for international students. Applications are processed on a rolling basis. Application fee: $30. Electronic applications accepted. *Expenses:* Tuition, state resident: full-time $8912; part-time $446 per credit hour. Tuition, nonresident: full-time $21,393; part-time $992 per credit hour. *Required fees:* $2185; $195 per semester. Tuition and fees vary according to program. *Financial support:* Fellowships, research assistantships with tuition reimbursements, teaching assistantships with tuition reimbursements, Federal Work-Study, and tuition waivers (full and partial) available. Support available to part-time students. Financial award applicants required to submit FAFSA. *Unit head:* Dr. Benjamin Baez, Chair, 305-348-3214, Fax: 305-348-1515, E-mail: benjamin.baez@fiu.edu. *Application contact:* Nanett Rojas, Assistant Director, Graduate Admissions, 305-348-7464, Fax: 305-348-7441, E-mail: gradadm@fiu.edu.
Website: http://education.fiu.edu

Frostburg State University, Graduate School, College of Education, Program in Parks and Recreational Management, Frostburg, MD 21532-1099. Offers MS. *Program availability:* Part-time, evening/weekend. *Degree requirements:* For master's, thesis. *Entrance requirements:* For master's, resume. Additional exam requirements/recommendations for international students: Required—TOEFL. Electronic applications accepted.

Hardin-Simmons University, Graduate School, Irvin School of Education, Department of Fitness and Sport Sciences, Program in Kinesiology, Sport, and Recreation, Abilene, TX 79698-0001. Offers M Ed. *Program availability:* Part-time. *Faculty:* 5 full-time (2 women). *Students:* 9 full-time (6 women), 18 part-time (9 women); includes 10 minority (5 Black or African American, non-Hispanic/Latino; 4 Hispanic/Latino; 1 Two or more races, non-Hispanic/Latino), 1 international. Average age 25. In 2016, 14 master's awarded. *Degree requirements:* For master's, comprehensive exam, thesis optional, internship, project. *Entrance requirements:* For master's, minimum undergraduate GPA of 3.0 in major, 2.7 overall; interview; writing sample; letters of recommendation; resume. Additional exam requirements/recommendations for international students: Required—TOEFL (minimum score 550 paper-based; 75 iBT). *Application deadline:* For fall admission, 8/15 priority date for domestic students, 4/1 for international students; for spring admission, 1/5 priority date for domestic students, 9/1 for international students. Applications are processed on a rolling basis. Application fee: $50. Electronic applications accepted. *Expenses: Tuition:* Full-time $12,510; part-time $695 per credit hour. *Required fees:* $325; $110 per semester. *Financial support:* In 2016–17, 12 students received support, including 8 fellowships (averaging $2,500 per year); career-related internships or fieldwork, scholarships/grants, and recreation assistantships also available. Support available to part-time students. Financial award application deadline: 6/30; financial award applicants required to submit FAFSA. *Unit head:* Dr. Lindsay Edwards, Program Director, 325-670-5893, Fax: 325-670-1218, E-mail: ledwards@hsutx.edu. *Application contact:* Dr. Nancy Kucinski, Dean of Graduate Studies, 325-670-1298, Fax: 325-670-1564, E-mail: gradoff@hsutx.edu.
Website: http://www.hsutx.edu/academics/irvin/graduate/kinesiology

Indiana State University, College of Graduate and Professional Studies, College of Nursing, Health, and Human Services, Department of Kinesiology, Recreation, and Sport, Terre Haute, IN 47809. Offers physical education (MS); recreation and sport management (MS); sport management (PhD). *Degree requirements:* For master's, comprehensive exam (for some programs), thesis (for some programs). *Entrance requirements:* For master's, GRE General Test, undergraduate major in related field. Electronic applications accepted.

Indiana University Bloomington, School of Public Health, Department of Recreation, Park, and Tourism Studies, Bloomington, IN 47405-7000. Offers leisure behavior (PhD); outdoor recreation (MS); park and public lands management (MS); recreation administration (MS); recreational sports administration (MS); recreational therapy (MS); tourism management (MS). Terminal master's awarded for partial completion of doctoral program. *Degree requirements:* For master's, thesis optional; for doctorate, comprehensive exam, thesis/dissertation. *Entrance requirements:* For master's, GRE General Test, minimum GPA of 2.8; for doctorate, GRE General Test, minimum GPA of 3.0 (undergraduate), 3.5 (graduate). Additional exam requirements/recommendations for international students: Required—TOEFL (minimum score 550 paper-based; 80 iBT). Electronic applications accepted. *Faculty research:* Leisure counseling, gerontology, special populations, planning and development.

Iona College, Hagan School of Business, Department of Marketing and International Business, New Rochelle, NY 10801-1890. Offers international business (AC, PMC); marketing (MBA); sports and entertainment management (AC). *Program availability:* Part-time, evening/weekend. *Faculty:* 2 full-time (1 woman), 3 part-time/adjunct (all women). *Students:* 11 full-time (1 woman), 22 part-time (11 women); includes 9 minority (4 Black or African American, non-Hispanic/Latino; 2 Asian, non-Hispanic/Latino; 3 Hispanic/Latino), 5 international. Average age 25. 19 applicants, 100% accepted, 9 enrolled. In 2016, 22 master's awarded. *Entrance requirements:* For master's, GMAT, 2 letters of recommendation, minimum GPA of 3.0; for other advanced degree, GMAT, minimum GPA of 3.0. Additional exam requirements/recommendations for international students: Required—TOEFL (minimum score 550 paper-based; 80 iBT), IELTS (minimum score 6.5). *Application deadline:* For fall admission, 8/15 priority date for domestic students, 8/1 priority date for international students; for winter admission, 11/15 priority date for domestic students, 11/1 priority date for international students; for spring admission, 2/15 priority date for domestic students, 2/1 priority date for international students; for summer admission, 5/15 for domestic students, 5/1 priority date for international students. Applications are processed on a rolling basis. Application fee: $50. Electronic applications accepted. *Expenses:* Contact institution. *Financial support:* In 2016–17, 13 students received support. Scholarships/grants, tuition waivers (partial), and unspecified assistantships available. Support available to part-time students. Financial award application deadline: 4/15; financial award applicants required to submit FAFSA. *Faculty research:* Business ethics, international retailing, mega-marketing, consumer behavior and consumer confidence. *Unit head:* Dr. Susan G. Rozensher, Department Chair, 914-637-2748, E-mail: srozensher@iona.edu. *Application contact:* Katelyn Brunck, Director of MBA Admissions, 914-633-2451, Fax: 914-633-2277, E-mail: kbrunck@iona.edu.
Website: http://www.iona.edu/Academics/Hagan-School-of-Business/Departments/Marketing/Graduate-Programs.aspx

Kent State University, College of Education, Health and Human Services, School of Foundations, Leadership and Administration, Sports Recreation and Management Program, Kent, OH 44242-0001. Offers sport and recreation management (MA); sports studies (MA). *Degree requirements:* For master's, thesis optional. *Entrance requirements:* For master's, GRE if undergraduate GPA below 3.0, goals statement, 2 letters of recommendation. Additional exam requirements/recommendations for international students: Required—TOEFL (minimum score 550 paper-based; 80 iBT). *Expenses:* Tuition, state resident: full-time $10,864; part-time $495 per credit hour. Tuition, nonresident: full-time $18,380; part-time $837 per credit hour.

Lehman College of the City University of New York, School of Health Sciences, Human Services and Nursing, Department of Health Sciences, Program in Recreation, Bronx, NY 10468-1589. Offers recreation education (MA, MS Ed). *Program availability:* Part-time, evening/weekend. *Degree requirements:* For master's, comprehensive exam, thesis or alternative. *Entrance requirements:* For master's, minimum GPA of 2.7. *Faculty research:* Therapeutic recreation philosophy, curriculum, current approaches to treatment, impact of societal trends, ethical issues.

Liberty University, School of Education, Lynchburg, VA 24515. Offers educational leadership (Ed D); gifted education (Certificate); math specialist (M Ed); middle grades (MAT, Certificate); reading specialist (M Ed); school leadership (Certificate); secondary education (MAT); sport management (MS), including administration, outdoor recreation, sport management, tourism. *Accreditation:* NCATE. *Program availability:* Part-time, online learning. *Students:* 1,910 full-time (1,427 women), 4,420 part-time (3,311 women); includes 1,451 minority (1,182 Black or African American, non-Hispanic/Latino; 33 American Indian or Alaska Native, non-Hispanic/Latino; 44 Asian, non-Hispanic/Latino; 46 Hispanic/Latino; 11 Native Hawaiian or other Pacific Islander, non-Hispanic/Latino; 135 Two or more races, non-Hispanic/Latino), 87 international. Average age 37. 5,120 applicants, 44% accepted, 1193 enrolled. In 2016, 1,378 master's, 151 doctorates, 497 other advanced degrees awarded. *Degree requirements:* For doctorate, comprehensive exam, thesis/dissertation. *Entrance requirements:* For master's, GRE General Test or MAT (if taken in or before 1999), 2 letters of recommendation, minimum undergraduate GPA of 3.0, curriculum vitae; for doctorate and Certificate, GRE General Test or MAT (if taken before 1999), minimum master's GPA of 3.0, 3 years of teaching experience. Additional exam requirements/recommendations for international students: Required—TOEFL (minimum score 600 paper-based; 100 iBT). *Application deadline:* For fall admission, 6/1 for domestic students; for spring admission, 11/1 for domestic students. Applications are processed on a rolling basis. Application fee: $50. Electronic applications accepted. *Expenses:* Contact institution. *Financial support:* Federal Work-Study and tuition waivers (partial) available. *Faculty research:* Self-determination, character education, bibliotherapy, learning styles, distance education. *Unit head:* Dr. Heather Schoffstall, Dean, 434-582-2445, Fax: 434-582-2468, E-mail: awgunter@liberty.edu. *Application contact:* Jay Bridge, Director of Graduate Admissions, 800-424-9595, Fax: 800-628-7977, E-mail: gradadmissions@liberty.edu.
Website: http://www.liberty.edu/academics/education/graduate/

Loyola Marymount University, College of Liberal Arts, Program in Yoga Studies, Los Angeles, CA 90045. Offers MA. *Students:* 27 full-time (21 women), 1 (woman) part-time; includes 12 minority (4 Asian, non-Hispanic/Latino; 6 Hispanic/Latino; 2 Two or more races, non-Hispanic/Latino), 3 international. Average age 33. 30 applicants, 93% accepted, 14 enrolled. In 2016, 19 master's awarded. *Degree requirements:* For master's, comprehensive exam, thesis. *Entrance requirements:* For master's, bachelor's degree, official transcripts, two-page letter of intent, two letters of recommendation. Additional exam requirements/recommendations for international students: Required—TOEFL (minimum score 600 paper-based; 100 iBT). *Application deadline:* Applications are processed on a rolling basis. Application fee: $50. Electronic applications accepted. *Financial support:* In 2016–17, 27 students received support, including 3 teaching assistantships. Financial award application deadline: 6/30; financial award applicants required to submit FAFSA. *Unit head:* Dr. Christopher Key Chapple, Director, 310-338-2846, E-mail: cchapple@lmu.edu. *Application contact:* Chake H. Kouyoumjian, Associate Dean of Graduate Studies, 310-338-2721, E-mail: ckouyoum@lmu.edu.
Website: http://bellarmine.lmu.edu/yoga/

Michigan State University, The Graduate School, College of Agriculture and Natural Resources, Department of Community, Agriculture, Recreation, and Resource Studies, East Lansing, MI 48824. Offers MS, PhD. *Entrance requirements:* Additional exam requirements/recommendations for international students: Required—TOEFL. Electronic applications accepted.

Middle Tennessee State University, College of Graduate Studies, College of Behavioral and Health Sciences, Department of Health and Human Performance, Program in Health, Physical Education and Recreation, Murfreesboro, TN 37132. Offers health and human performance (MS); leisure and sport management (MS). *Program availability:* Part-time, evening/weekend, online learning. *Degree requirements:* For master's, comprehensive exam, thesis optional. *Entrance requirements:* For master's, GRE. Additional exam requirements/recommendations for international students: Required—TOEFL (minimum score 525 paper-based; 71 iBT) or IELTS (minimum score 6). *Faculty research:* Kinesiometrics, leisure behavior, health, lifestyles.

Naropa University, Graduate Programs, Program in Clinical Mental Health Counseling, Concentration in Transpersonal Wilderness Therapy, Boulder, CO 80302-6697. Offers MA. *Faculty:* 10 full-time (7 women), 23 part-time/adjunct (17 women). *Students:* 29 full-time (25 women), 15 part-time (9 women); includes 8 minority (5 Hispanic/Latino; 3 Two or more races, non-Hispanic/Latino). Average age 27. 36 applicants, 83% accepted, 16 enrolled. In 2016, 9 master's awarded. *Degree requirements:* For master's, internship, counseling practicum. *Entrance requirements:* For master's, interview; 2 letters of recommendation; transcripts; curriculum vitae/resume with pertinent academic, employment and volunteer activities; statement of interest essay; 10 consecutive days of wilderness experience in the backcountry; wilderness/outdoor skills. Additional exam requirements/recommendations for international students: Required—TOEFL (minimum score 550 paper-based; 80 iBT). *Application deadline:* For fall admission, 1/15 priority date for domestic and international students. Applications are processed on a rolling basis. Application fee: $60. Electronic applications accepted. *Expenses:* $27,140 for first year. *Financial support:* In 2016–17, 22 students received support. Career-related internships or fieldwork, Federal Work-Study, scholarships/grants, tuition waivers (partial), and unspecified assistantships available. Support available to part-time students. Financial award application deadline: 3/1; financial award applicants required to submit FAFSA. *Unit head:* Dr. Deborah Bowman, Dean, Graduate School of Counseling and Psychology, 303-546-3559, E-mail: bowman@naropa.edu. *Application contact:* Office of Admissions, 303-546-3572, Fax: 303-546-3583, E-mail: admissions@naropa.edu.
Website: http://www.naropa.edu/academics/masters/clinical-mental-health-counseling/wilderness-therapy/index.php

New England College, Program in Sports and Recreation Management: Coaching, Henniker, NH 03242-3293. Offers MS. *Entrance requirements:* For master's, resume, 2 letters of reference.

North Carolina Central University, College of Behavioral and Social Sciences, Department of Physical Education and Recreation, Durham, NC 27707-3129. Offers athletic administration (MS); physical education (MS); recreation administration (MS); therapeutic recreation (MS). *Program availability:* Part-time, evening/weekend. *Degree requirements:* For master's, one foreign language, comprehensive exam, thesis. *Entrance requirements:* For master's, GRE, minimum GPA of 3.0 in major, 2.5 overall. Additional exam requirements/recommendations for international students: Required—TOEFL.

North Carolina State University, Graduate School, College of Natural Resources, Department of Parks, Recreation and Tourism Management, Raleigh, NC 27695. Offers natural resource management (MPRTM, MS); park and recreation management (MPRTM, MS); parks, recreation and tourism management (PhD); recreational sport management (MPRTM, MS); spatial information science (MPRTM, MS); tourism policy and development (MPRTM, MS). *Degree requirements:* For master's, thesis (for some programs); for doctorate, thesis/dissertation. *Entrance requirements:* For master's and doctorate, GRE General Test. Additional exam requirements/recommendations for international students: Required—TOEFL. Electronic applications accepted. *Faculty research:* Tourism policy and development, spatial information systems, natural resource management, recreational sports management, park and recreation management.

Northwest Missouri State University, Graduate School, School of Health Science and Wellness, Maryville, MO 64468-6001. Offers applied health and sport sciences (MS);

recreation (MS). *Accreditation:* NCATE. *Program availability:* Part-time. *Students:* 68 full-time (38 women), 27 part-time (19 women). *Degree requirements:* For master's, comprehensive exam. *Entrance requirements:* For master's, GRE General Test, minimum undergraduate GPA of 2.75, teaching certificate, writing sample. Additional exam requirements/recommendations for international students: Required—TOEFL (minimum score 550 paper-based). *Application deadline:* For fall admission, 7/1 for domestic and international students; for spring admission, 11/15 for domestic and international students. Applications are processed on a rolling basis. Application fee: $0 ($50 for international students). *Expenses:* Tuition, state resident: full-time $3447; part-time $383 per credit hour. Tuition, nonresident: full-time $5724; part-time $636 per credit hour. *Required fees:* $130 per credit hour. *Financial support:* Teaching assistantships with full tuition reimbursements and unspecified assistantships available. Financial award application deadline: 4/1; financial award applicants required to submit FAFSA. *Unit head:* Dr. Terry Long, Director, School of Health Science and Wellness, 660-562-1706, E-mail: tlong@nwmissouri.edu. *Application contact:* Cathie Hannigan, Office Manager, 660-562-1297, Fax: 660-562-1483, E-mail: channig@nwmissouri.edu.
Website: http://www.nwmissouri.edu/health/

Ohio University, Graduate College, Gladys W. and David H. Patton College of Education and Human Services, Department of Recreation and Sport Pedagogy, Program in Recreation Studies, Athens, OH 45701-2979. Offers MS. *Program availability:* Part-time. *Degree requirements:* For master's, thesis or alternative. *Entrance requirements:* For master's, GRE. Additional exam requirements/recommendations for international students: Required—TOEFL (minimum score 550 paper-based; 80 iBT) or IELTS (minimum score 6.5). *Application deadline:* For fall admission, 3/1 priority date for domestic and international students; for winter admission, 11/1 priority date for domestic and international students; for spring admission, 1/1 priority date for domestic and international students. Application fee: $50 ($55 for international students). Electronic applications accepted. *Financial support:* Teaching assistantships with full tuition reimbursements, Federal Work-Study, scholarships/grants, tuition waivers (full), and unspecified assistantships available. Financial award application deadline: 3/15. *Faculty research:* Recreation, leisure studies, physical education, national parks. *Unit head:* Dr. Beth VanDerveer, Chair, 740-593-4656, Fax: 740-593-0284, E-mail: vanderve@ohio.edu. *Application contact:* Dr. Bruce Martin, Assistant Professor, 740-593-4647, E-mail: martinc2@ohio.edu.
Website: http://www.ohio.edu/graduate/programinfo/RecStudies-Info.cfm

Penn State University Park, Graduate School, College of Health and Human Development, Department of Recreation, Park and Tourism Management, University Park, PA 16802. Offers MS, PhD. *Unit head:* Dr. Ann C. Crouter, Dean, 814-865-1420, Fax: 814-865-3282. *Application contact:* Lori Hawn, Director, Graduate Student Services, 814-865-1795, Fax: 814-863-4627, E-mail: l-gswww@lists.psu.edu.
Website: http://hhd.psu.edu/rptm

Purdue University, Graduate School, College of Health and Human Sciences, Department of Health and Kinesiology, West Lafayette, IN 47907. Offers athletic training education administration (MS, PhD); biomechanics (MS, PhD); exercise physiology (MS, PhD); health education (MS, PhD); history/philosophy of sport (MS, PhD); motor control and development (MS, PhD); physical education pedagogy (PhD); physical education teacher education (MS); recreation and sport management (MS, PhD); sport and exercise psychology (MS, PhD). *Program availability:* Part-time. *Faculty:* 19 full-time (7 women). *Students:* 30 full-time (13 women), 10 part-time (5 women); includes 2 minority (1 Asian, non-Hispanic/Latino; 1 Two or more races, non-Hispanic/Latino), 6 international. Average age 26. 77 applicants, 29% accepted, 18 enrolled. In 2016, 18 master's, 9 doctorates awarded. *Degree requirements:* For master's, thesis optional; for doctorate, comprehensive exam, thesis/dissertation, qualifying examination, preliminary examination. *Entrance requirements:* For master's, GRE General Test (minimum score 1000 combined verbal and quantitative), minimum undergraduate GPA of 3.0 or equivalent; for doctorate, GRE General Test (minimum score 1100 combined verbal and quantitative), minimum undergraduate GPA of 3.0 or equivalent; master's degree with minimum GPA of 3.25 (recommended). Additional exam requirements/recommendations for international students: Required—TOEFL (minimum score 77 iBT); Recommended—TWE. *Application deadline:* For fall admission, 4/30 for domestic and international students; for spring admission, 10/15 for domestic and international students. Applications are processed on a rolling basis. Application fee: $60 ($75 for international students). Electronic applications accepted. *Financial support:* Fellowships with partial tuition reimbursements, research assistantships with partial tuition reimbursements, teaching assistantships with partial tuition reimbursements, and Federal Work-Study available. Support available to part-time students. Financial award applicants required to submit FAFSA. *Faculty research:* Wellness, motivation, teaching effectiveness, learning and development. *Unit head:* Dr. Timothy P. Gavin, Head of the Graduate Program, 765-494-3178, Fax: 765-494-1239, E-mail: gavin1@purdue.edu. *Application contact:* Christy F. Daugherty, Graduate Contact, 765-494-3162, E-mail: daugher2@purdue.edu.
Website: http://www.purdue.edu/hhs/hk/

San Francisco State University, Division of Graduate Studies, College of Health and Social Sciences, Department of Recreation, Parks, and Tourism, San Francisco, CA 94132-1722. Offers MS. *Program availability:* Part-time. *Application deadline:* Applications are processed on a rolling basis. *Expenses:* Tuition, state resident: full-time $6738. Tuition, nonresident: full-time $15,666. *Required fees:* $1012. Tuition and fees vary according to degree level and program. *Financial support:* Career-related internships or fieldwork available. *Unit head:* Dr. Erik Rosegard, Chair, 415-338-7529, Fax: 415-338-0543, E-mail: rosegard@sfsu.edu. *Application contact:* Dr. Jackson Wilson, Graduate Coordinator, 415-338-1487, Fax: 415-338-0543, E-mail: wilsonj@sfsu.edu.
Website: http://recdept.sfsu.edu/graduate

San Jose State University, Graduate Studies and Research, College of Applied Sciences and Arts, San Jose, CA 95192-0001. Offers big data (Certificate); California library media teacher services (Credential); collaborative response to family violence (Certificate); justice studies (MS); kinesiology (MA), including applied sciences and arts (MA, MS), athletic training, exercise physiology, sport management, sport studies; library and information science (MLIS, Certificate); mass communication (MA); nutritional science (MS); occupational therapy (MS); public health (MPH); pupil personnel services (Credential); recreation (MS), including applied sciences and arts (MA, MS), international tourism; social work (MSW); Spanish language counseling (Certificate); strategic management of digital assets and services (Certificate). *Program availability:* Part-time, evening/weekend. Electronic applications accepted.

Slippery Rock University of Pennsylvania, Graduate Studies (Recruitment), College of Health, Environment, and Science, Department of Parks and Recreation, Slippery Rock, PA 16057-1383. Offers environmental education (M Ed); park and resource management (MS). *Program availability:* Part-time, evening/weekend, online only, 100% online. *Faculty:* 2 full-time (1 woman), 1 (woman) part-time/adjunct. *Students:* 8 full-time (4 women), 86 part-time (59 women); includes 7 minority (4 Black or African American, non-Hispanic/Latino; 1 Asian, non-Hispanic/Latino; 1 Hispanic/Latino; 1 Two or more races, non-Hispanic/Latino), 1 international. Average age 31. 66 applicants, 74% accepted, 31 enrolled. In 2016, 42 master's awarded. *Degree requirements:* For master's, comprehensive exam (for some programs), thesis (for some programs), internship. *Entrance requirements:* For master's, official transcripts, minimum GPA of 2.75, personal statement. Additional exam requirements/recommendations for international students: Required—TOEFL (minimum score 550 paper-based; 80 iBT). *Application deadline:* For fall admission, 3/1 priority date for domestic students, 5/1 priority date for international students; for spring admission, 10/1 priority date for domestic students, 9/1 priority date for international students. Applications are processed on a rolling basis. Application fee: $25 ($30 for international students). Electronic applications accepted. *Expenses:* $646.50 per credit in-state, $936.80 per credit out-of-state; $581.45 per online credit in-state, $648.65 per online credit out-of-state. *Financial support:* In 2016–17, 5 students received support. Career-related internships or fieldwork, Federal Work-Study, institutionally sponsored loans, scholarships/grants, tuition waivers (partial), and unspecified assistantships available. Support available to part-time students. Financial award application deadline: 5/1; financial award applicants required to submit FAFSA. *Unit head:* Dr. John Lisco, Graduate Coordinator, 724-738-2596, Fax: 724-738-2938, E-mail: john.lisco@sru.edu. *Application contact:* Brandi Weber-Mortimer, Director of Graduate Admissions, 724-738-2051, Fax: 724-738-2146, E-mail: graduate.admissions@sru.edu.
Website: http://www.sru.edu/academics/colleges-and-departments/ches/departments/parks-and-recreation

South Dakota State University, Graduate School, College of Education and Human Sciences, Department of Health and Nutritional Sciences, Brookings, SD 57007. Offers athletic training (MS); dietetics (MS); nutrition and exercise sciences (MS, PhD); sport and recreation studies (MS). *Program availability:* Part-time. *Degree requirements:* For master's, comprehensive exam (for some programs), thesis (for some programs), oral exam. *Entrance requirements:* Additional exam requirements/recommendations for international students: Required—TOEFL (minimum score 525 paper-based). *Faculty research:* Food chemistry, bone density, functional food, nutrition education, nutrition biochemistry.

Southern Adventist University, School of Business and Management, Collegedale, TN 37315-0370. Offers accounting (MBA); church administration (MSA); church and nonprofit leadership (MBA); financial management (MFM); healthcare administration (MBA); management (MBA); marketing management (MBA); outdoor education (MSA). *Program availability:* Part-time, evening/weekend, online learning. *Entrance requirements:* For master's, GMAT. Additional exam requirements/recommendations for international students: Required—TOEFL (minimum score 600 paper-based; 100 iBT). Electronic applications accepted.

Southern Connecticut State University, School of Graduate Studies, School of Health and Human Services, Department of Recreation and Leisure Studies, New Haven, CT 06515-1355. Offers MS. *Program availability:* Part-time, evening/weekend. *Faculty:* 4 full-time (1 woman), 5 part-time/adjunct (3 women). *Students:* 26 full-time (16 women), 32 part-time (15 women); includes 16 minority (12 Black or African American, non-Hispanic/Latino; 4 Hispanic/Latino). Average age 28. 43 applicants, 72% accepted, 23 enrolled. In 2016, 16 master's awarded. *Degree requirements:* For master's, thesis or alternative. *Entrance requirements:* For master's, interview, minimum undergraduate QPA of 3.0 in graduate major field or 2.5 overall. *Application deadline:* For fall admission, 7/15 priority date for domestic students. Applications are processed on a rolling basis. Application fee: $50. Electronic applications accepted. *Expenses:* Tuition, state resident: full-time $6497; part-time $519 per credit hour. Tuition, nonresident: full-time $18,102; part-time $535 per credit hour. *Required fees:* $4722; $55 per semester. Tuition and fees vary according to program. *Financial support:* Career-related internships or fieldwork, scholarships/grants, and unspecified assistantships available. Financial award application deadline: 4/15; financial award applicants required to submit FAFSA. *Unit head:* Dr. James MacGregor, Chairperson, 203-392-6385, Fax: 203-392-6965, E-mail: macgregorj1@southernct.edu. *Application contact:* Lisa Galvin, Director of Graduate Admissions, 203-392-5240, Fax: 203-392-5235, E-mail: galvinl1@southernct.edu.

Southern Illinois University Carbondale, Graduate School, College of Education and Human Services, Department of Health Education and Recreation, Program in Recreation, Carbondale, IL 62901-4701. Offers MS Ed. *Program availability:* Part-time. *Degree requirements:* For master's, thesis. *Entrance requirements:* For master's, minimum GPA of 2.7. Additional exam requirements/recommendations for international students: Required—TOEFL. *Faculty research:* Leisure across the life span, outdoor recreation, recreation therapy, leisure service administration.

Southern University and Agricultural and Mechanical College, College of Nursing and Allied Health, Department of Therapeutic Recreation and Leisure Studies, Baton Rouge, LA 70813. Offers therapeutic recreation (MS). *Degree requirements:* For master's, comprehensive exam, thesis optional. *Entrance requirements:* For master's, GMAT or GRE General Test. Additional exam requirements/recommendations for international students: Required—TOEFL (minimum score 525 paper-based).

Southwestern Oklahoma State University, College of Professional and Graduate Studies, School of Behavioral Sciences and Education, Specialization in Parks and Recreation Management, Weatherford, OK 73096-3098. Offers M Ed.

Springfield College, Graduate Programs, Programs in Sport Management and Recreation, Springfield, MA 01109-3797. Offers recreation management (M Ed); sport management (M Ed, MS). *Program availability:* Part-time. *Degree requirements:* For master's, comprehensive exam, research project. *Entrance requirements:* Additional exam requirements/recommendations for international students: Required—TOEFL (minimum score 550 paper-based); Recommended—IELTS (minimum score 6). Electronic applications accepted. *Expenses: Tuition:* Full-time $29,640; part-time $988 per credit. *Required fees:* $195.

State University of New York College at Cortland, Graduate Studies, School of Professional Studies, Department of Recreation, Parks and Leisure Studies, Cortland, NY 13045. Offers outdoor education (MS, MS Ed); recreation management (MS, MS Ed); therapeutic recreation (MS, MS Ed). *Program availability:* Part-time, evening/weekend. *Degree requirements:* For master's, comprehensive exam, thesis (for some programs). *Entrance requirements:* Additional exam requirements/recommendations for international students: Required—TOEFL.

Temple University, College of Public Health, Department of Rehabilitation Sciences, Philadelphia, PA 19122-6096. Offers occupational therapy (MOT, DOT); therapeutic recreation (MS), including recreation therapy. *Program availability:* Part-time. *Faculty:* 15 full-time (14 women), 10 part-time/adjunct (8 women). *Students:* 96 full-time (85 women), 33 part-time (30 women); includes 22 minority (6 Black or African American, non-Hispanic/Latino; 6 Asian, non-Hispanic/Latino; 5 Hispanic/Latino; 5 Two or more races, non-Hispanic/Latino). 22 applicants, 77% accepted, 11 enrolled. In 2016, 46 master's, 6 doctorates awarded. *Degree requirements:* For doctorate, comprehensive exam (for some programs), thesis/dissertation (for some programs). *Entrance requirements:* For master's and doctorate, GRE General Test, minimum GPA of 3.0. Additional exam requirements/recommendations for international students: Required—TOEFL (minimum score 550 paper-based; 79 iBT). *Application deadline:* For fall admission, 2/1 for domestic students, 1/1 for international students; for spring admission, 11/1 for domestic students, 10/1 for international students. Applications are processed on a rolling basis. Application fee: $60. Electronic applications accepted. *Expenses:* Contact institution. *Financial support:* Career-related internships or fieldwork and Federal Work-Study available. *Faculty research:* Participation, community inclusion, disability issues, leisure/recreation, occupation, quality of life, adaptive equipment and technology. *Unit head:* Dr. Mark Salzer, Chair, 215-204-7879, E-mail: mark.salzer@temple.edu. *Application contact:* Dr. Mark Salzer, Chair, 215-204-7879, E-mail: mark.salzer@temple.edu.
Website: http://cph.temple.edu/rs/home

Texas A&M University, College of Agriculture and Life Sciences, Department of Recreation, Park and Tourism Sciences, College Station, TX 77843. Offers recreation and resources development (MRRD); recreation, park, and tourism sciences (MS, PhD). *Faculty:* 18. *Students:* 57 full-time (26 women), 19 part-time (7 women); includes 18 minority (8 Black or African American, non-Hispanic/Latino; 4 Asian, non-Hispanic/Latino; 4 Hispanic/Latino; 2 Two or more races, non-Hispanic/Latino), 26 international. Average age 32. 14 applicants, 93% accepted, 11 enrolled. In 2016, 18 master's, 6 doctorates awarded. *Degree requirements:* For master's, thesis (for some programs), internship and professional paper (M Agr); for doctorate, thesis/dissertation. *Entrance requirements:* For master's and doctorate, GRE General Test. Additional exam requirements/recommendations for international students: Required—TOEFL (minimum score 550 paper-based; 80 iBT), IELTS (minimum score 6), PTE (minimum score 53). *Application deadline:* For fall admission, 3/1 for domestic and international students; for spring admission, 8/1 for domestic and international students; for summer admission, 11/1 for domestic and international students. Applications are processed on a rolling basis. Application fee: $50 ($90 for international students). Electronic applications accepted. *Expenses:* Contact institution. *Financial support:* In 2016–17, 64 students received support, including 8 fellowships with tuition reimbursements available (averaging $10,696 per year), 13 research assistantships with tuition reimbursements available (averaging $4,735 per year), 26 teaching assistantships with tuition reimbursements available (averaging $9,148 per year); career-related internships or fieldwork, institutionally sponsored loans, scholarships/grants, traineeships, health care benefits, tuition waivers (full and partial), and unspecified assistantships also available. Support available to part-time students. Financial award application deadline: 3/15; financial award applicants required to submit FAFSA. *Faculty research:* Administration and tourism, outdoor recreation, commercial recreation, environmental law, system planning. *Unit head:* Dr. Gary Ellis, Department Head, 979-845-7324, E-mail: gellis@ag.tamu.edu. *Application contact:* Irina Shatruk, Graduate Program Coordinator, 979-845-5412, E-mail: jshatruk@tamu.edu.
Website: http://rpts.tamu.edu/

Texas State University, The Graduate College, College of Education, Recreation Management, San Marcos, TX 78666. Offers recreation management (MSRLS). *Program availability:* Part-time. *Faculty:* 5 full-time (3 women), 1 (woman) part-time/adjunct. *Students:* 15 full-time (5 women), 6 part-time (3 women); includes 8 minority (3 Black or African American, non-Hispanic/Latino; 1 Asian, non-Hispanic/Latino; 4 Hispanic/Latino). Average age 25. 28 applicants, 71% accepted, 8 enrolled. In 2016, 10 master's awarded. *Degree requirements:* For master's, comprehensive exam, thesis optional. *Entrance requirements:* For master's, GRE (preferred), baccalaureate degree from regionally-accredited institution with minimum GPA of 2.75 in last 60 hours of course work. Additional exam requirements/recommendations for international students: Required—TOEFL (minimum score 550 paper-based; 78 iBT), IELTS (minimum score 6.5). *Application deadline:* For fall admission, 2/15 priority date for domestic students, 2/15 for international students; for spring admission, 10/15 priority date for domestic students, 10/1 for international students; for summer admission, 4/15 for domestic students, 3/15 for international students. Applications are processed on a rolling basis. Application fee: $40 ($90 for international students). Electronic applications accepted. *Expenses:* $4,851 per semester. *Financial support:* In 2016–17, 12 students received support, including 2 teaching assistantships (averaging $13,522 per year); research assistantships, scholarships/grants, and unspecified assistantships also available. Financial award application deadline: 3/1; financial award applicants required to submit FAFSA. *Faculty research:* Effects of neuromuscular electrical stimulation frequency on metabolic markers, effects of focal knee join cooling on different modes of the quadriceps strength. *Unit head:* Dr. Jan Hodges, Graduate Advisor, 512-245-7482, Fax: 512-245-8678, E-mail: jh223@txstate.edu. *Application contact:* Dr. Andrea Golato, Dean of the Graduate College, 512-245-2581, Fax: 512-245-8365, E-mail: gradcollege@txstate.edu.
Website: http://www.hhp.txstate.edu/Degree-Plans/Graduate.html

Universidad Metropolitana, School of Education, Program in Managing Recreation and Sports Services, San Juan, PR 00928-1150. Offers M Ed. *Program availability:* Part-time. *Degree requirements:* For master's, thesis or alternative. *Entrance requirements:* For master's, EXADEP, interview. Electronic applications accepted.

University of Alberta, Faculty of Graduate Studies and Research, Department of Physical Education and Recreation, Edmonton, AB T6G 2E1, Canada. Offers physical education (M Sc); recreation and physical education (MA, PhD). *Program availability:* Part-time. Terminal master's awarded for partial completion of doctoral program. *Degree requirements:* For master's, thesis (for some programs); for doctorate, thesis/dissertation. *Entrance requirements:* For master's, bachelor's degree in related field; for doctorate, master's degree in related field with thesis. Additional exam requirements/recommendations for international students: Required—TOEFL. *Faculty research:* Motivation and adherence to physical ability, performance enhancement, adapted physical activity, exercise physiology, sport administration, tourism.

University of Arkansas, Graduate School, College of Education and Health Professions, Department of Health, Human Performance and Recreation, Program in Recreation and Sports Management, Fayetteville, AR 72701. Offers M Ed, Ed D. In 2016, 31 master's, 2 doctorates awarded. *Degree requirements:* For master's, thesis optional; for doctorate, thesis/dissertation. *Entrance requirements:* For doctorate, GRE General Test. *Application deadline:* For fall admission, 4/1 for international students; for spring admission, 10/1 for international students. Applications are processed on a rolling basis. Application fee: $40 ($50 for international students). Electronic applications accepted. *Financial support:* In 2016–17, 8 research assistantships, 10 teaching assistantships were awarded; fellowships with tuition reimbursements, career-related internships or fieldwork, and Federal Work-Study also available. Support available to part-time students. Financial award application deadline: 4/1; financial award applicants required to submit FAFSA. *Unit head:* Dr. Bart Hammig, Department Chairperson, 479-575-2857, Fax: 479-575-5728, E-mail: bhammig@uark.edu. *Application contact:* Dr. Stephen Dittmore, Coordinator of Graduate Studies, 479-575-6625, E-mail: dittmore@uark.edu.
Website: http://recr.uark.edu/

University of Florida, Graduate School, College of Health and Human Performance, Department of Tourism, Recreation and Sport Management, Gainesville, FL 32611. Offers health and human performance (PhD), including historic preservation (MS, PhD), recreation, parks and tourism (MS, PhD), sport management; recreation, parks and tourism (MS), including historic preservation (MS, PhD), natural resource recreation, recreation, parks and tourism (MS, PhD), therapeutic recreation, tourism, tropical conservation and development; sport management (MS), including historic preservation (MS, PhD), tropical conservation and development; JD/MS; MSM/MS. *Degree requirements:* For master's, comprehensive exam (for some programs), thesis (for some programs); for doctorate, comprehensive exam, thesis/dissertation. *Entrance requirements:* For master's and doctorate, GRE General Test, minimum GPA of 3.0. Additional exam requirements/recommendations for international students: Required—TOEFL (minimum score 550 paper-based; 80 iBT), IELTS (minimum score 6). Electronic applications accepted. *Faculty research:* Hospitality, natural resource management, sport management, tourism.

University of Idaho, College of Graduate Studies, College of Education, Department of Movement Sciences, Moscow, ID 83844. Offers athletic training (MSAT, DAT); movement and leisure sciences (MS); physical education (M Ed). *Faculty:* 14 full-time, 5 part-time/adjunct. *Students:* 79 full-time (41 women), 24 part-time (12 women). Average age 30. In 2016, 24 master's awarded. *Degree requirements:* For doctorate, thesis/dissertation. *Entrance requirements:* For master's and doctorate, minimum GPA of 3.0. Additional exam requirements/recommendations for international students: Required—TOEFL. *Application deadline:* For fall admission, 8/1 for domestic students; for spring admission, 12/15 for domestic students. Applications are processed on a rolling basis. Application fee: $60. Electronic applications accepted. *Expenses:* Tuition, state resident: full-time $6460; part-time $414 per credit hour. Tuition, nonresident: full-time $21,268; part-time $1237 per credit hour. *Required fees:* $2070; $60 per credit hour. Full-time tuition and fees vary according to course load and reciprocity agreements. *Financial support:* Research assistantships and teaching assistantships available. Financial award applicants required to submit FAFSA. *Unit head:* Dr. Philip W. Scruggs, Chair, 208-885-7921, E-mail: movementsciences@uidaho.edu. *Application contact:* Sean Scoggin, Graduate Recruitment Coordinator, 208-885-4001, Fax: 208-885-4406, E-mail: graduateadmissions@uidaho.edu.
Website: https://www.uidaho.edu/ed/mvsc

The University of Iowa, Graduate College, College of Liberal Arts and Sciences, Department of Health and Human Physiology, Iowa City, IA 52242-1316. Offers athletic training (MS); clinical exercise physiology (MS); health and human physiology (PhD); leisure studies (MA, PhD), including recreational sport management (PhD), therapeutic recreation (MA). *Degree requirements:* For master's, thesis optional, exam; for doctorate, comprehensive exam, thesis/dissertation. *Entrance requirements:* For master's and doctorate, GRE General Test, minimum GPA of 3.0. Additional exam requirements/recommendations for international students: Required—TOEFL (minimum score 600 paper-based; 100 iBT). Electronic applications accepted.

University of Louisiana at Monroe, Graduate School, College of Health and Pharmaceutical Sciences, Department of Kinesiology, Monroe, LA 71209-0001. Offers applied exercise science (MS); clinical exercise physiology (MS); sports, fitness and recreation management (MS). *Program availability:* Part-time, evening/weekend, online learning. *Faculty:* 4 full-time (1 woman), 1 part-time/adjunct (0 women). *Students:* 31 full-time (12 women), 9 part-time (4 women); includes 11 minority (7 Black or African American, non-Hispanic/Latino; 4 Hispanic/Latino), 3 international. Average age 24. 96 applicants, 34% accepted, 14 enrolled. In 2016, 17 master's awarded. *Degree requirements:* For master's, comprehensive exam, thesis, 6-hour internship. *Entrance requirements:* For master's, GRE General Test. Additional exam requirements/recommendations for international students: Required—TOEFL (minimum score 500 paper-based; 61 iBT). *Application deadline:* For fall admission, 8/24 priority date for domestic students, 7/1 for international students; for winter admission, 12/14 priority date for domestic students; for spring admission, 1/19 for domestic students, 11/1 for international students. Applications are processed on a rolling basis. Application fee: $20 ($30 for international students). Electronic applications accepted. *Expenses:* Tuition, state resident: full-time $6489. Tuition, nonresident: full-time $18,589. *Required fees:* $8984. Tuition and fees vary according to course level, course load, degree level and program. *Financial support:* Research assistantships, career-related internships or fieldwork, Federal Work-Study, and unspecified assistantships available. Financial award application deadline: 4/1; financial award applicants required to submit FAFSA. *Faculty research:* Cardiovascular disease risk factors; exercise and immunological system; attitude, exercise, and the aged. *Unit head:* Dr. Ken Alford, Director, 318-342-1306, E-mail: alford@ulm.edu. *Application contact:* Dr. Tommie Church, Director of Graduate Studies, 318-342-1321, E-mail: church@ulm.edu.
Website: http://www.ulm.edu/kinesiology/

University of Manitoba, Faculty of Graduate Studies, Faculty of Kinesiology and Recreation Management, Winnipeg, MB R3T 2N2, Canada. Offers kinesiology and recreation (M Sc, MA).

University of Mississippi, Graduate School, School of Applied Sciences, University, MS 38677. Offers communicative disorders (MS); exercise science (MS); food and nutrition services (MS); health and kinesiology (PhD); health promotion (MS); park and recreation management (MA); social work (MSW). *Faculty:* 68 full-time (29 women), 29 part-time/adjunct (17 women). *Students:* 176 full-time (137 women), 36 part-time (21 women); includes 45 minority (40 Black or African American, non-Hispanic/Latino; 4 Hispanic/Latino; 1 Two or more races, non-Hispanic/Latino), 9 international. Average age 24. *Entrance requirements:* For master's, GRE General Test, minimum GPA of 3.0. Additional exam requirements/recommendations for international students: Required—TOEFL. *Application deadline:* For fall admission, 4/1 for domestic students; for spring admission, 10/1 for domestic students. Applications are processed on a rolling basis. Application fee: $40. Electronic applications accepted. *Financial support:* Scholarships/grants available. Financial award application deadline: 3/1; financial award applicants required to submit FAFSA. *Unit head:* Dr. Velmer Stanley Burton, Dean, 662-915-1081, Fax: 662-915-5717, E-mail: applsci@olemiss.edu. *Application contact:* Dr. Christy M. Wyandt, Associate Dean of Graduate School, 662-915-7474, Fax: 662-915-7577, E-mail: cwyandt@olemiss.edu.
Website: https://www.olemiss.edu

University of Montana, Graduate School, College of Forestry and Conservation, Missoula, MT 59812-0002. Offers fish and wildlife biology (PhD); forest and conservation sciences (PhD); forestry (MS); recreation management (MS); resource conservation (MS); systems ecology (MS, PhD); wildlife biology (MS). *Degree requirements:* For doctorate, thesis/dissertation. *Entrance requirements:* For master's and doctorate, GRE General Test. Additional exam requirements/recommendations for international students: Required—TOEFL (minimum score 575 paper-based).

University of Nebraska at Kearney, College of Education, Kinesiology and Sport Sciences Department, Kearney, NE 68849-0001. Offers general physical education (MA Ed), including recreation and leisure, sports administration; physical education exercise science (MA Ed); physical education master teacher (MA Ed), including pedagogy, special populations. *Program availability:* Part-time, evening/weekend, 100% online. *Faculty:* 17 full-time (5 women). *Students:* 4 full-time (2 women), 39 part-time (16 women); includes 3 minority (2 Black or African American, non-Hispanic/Latino; 1 Hispanic/Latino). Average age 28. 20 applicants, 100% accepted, 14 enrolled. In 2016, 25 master's awarded. *Degree requirements:* For master's, comprehensive exam, thesis optional. *Entrance requirements:* For master's, GRE General Test (for some programs), personal statement. Additional exam requirements/recommendations for international students: Recommended—TOEFL (minimum score 550 paper-based; 79 iBT), IELTS (minimum score 6.5). *Application deadline:* For fall admission, 6/15 for domestic and international students; for spring admission, 10/15 for domestic and international students; for summer admission, 3/15 for domestic and international students. Application fee: $45. Electronic applications accepted. *Expenses:* Tuition, state resident: full-time $4064; part-time $225.75 per credit hour. Tuition, nonresident: full-time $8915; part-time $495.25 per credit hour. *Required fees:* $772; $23 per credit hour. Part-time tuition and fees vary according to course load, campus/location, program and reciprocity agreements. *Financial support:* In 2016–17, 9 students received support, including 3 research assistantships with full tuition reimbursements available (averaging $10,500 per year), 6 teaching assistantships with full tuition reimbursements available (averaging $10,500 per year); career-related internships or fieldwork, scholarships/grants, health care benefits, and unspecified assistantships also available. Support available to part-time students. Financial award application deadline: 2/28; financial award applicants required to submit FAFSA. *Faculty research:* Ergonomic aids, nutrition, motor development, sports pedagogy, applied behavior analysis, physical activity and wellness, athletic training, therapeutic interventions, exercise physiology, endocrinology and metabolism. *Unit head:* Dr. Nita Unruh, Chair, 308-865-8335, E-mail: unruhnc@unk.edu. *Application contact:* Linda Johnson, Director, Graduate Admissions and Programs

Section 30
Physical Education and Kinesiology

This section contains a directory of institutions offering graduate work in physical education and kinesiology. Additional information about programs listed in the directory may be obtained by writing directly to the dean of a graduate school or chair of a department at the address given in the directory.

For programs offering related work, see also in this book *Business Administration and Management, Education,* and *Sports Management.* In another guide in this series:

Graduate Programs in the Humanities, Arts & Social Sciences
See *Performing Arts*

CONTENTS

Program Directories

Athletic Training and Sports Medicine

Adrian College, Graduate Programs, Adrian, MI 49221-2575. Offers accounting (MS); athletic training (MS); criminal justice (MA). *Degree requirements:* For master's, comprehensive exam (for some programs), thesis (for some programs), thesis, internship or practicum with corresponding in-depth paper and/or presentation. *Entrance requirements:* For master's, appropriate undergraduate degree, minimum cumulative and major GPA of 3.0, personal statement.

Armstrong State University, School of Graduate Studies, Program in Sports Medicine, Savannah, GA 31419-1997. Offers sports health sciences (MSSM); strength and conditioning (Certificate). *Program availability:* Part-time. *Faculty:* 3 full-time (0 women). *Students:* 20 full-time (11 women), 9 part-time (4 women); includes 10 minority (7 Black or African American, non-Hispanic/Latino; 1 Asian, non-Hispanic/Latino; 2 Hispanic/Latino). Average age 25. 40 applicants, 45% accepted, 15 enrolled. In 2016, 7 master's awarded. *Degree requirements:* For master's, comprehensive exam, thesis optional, project. *Entrance requirements:* For master's, GRE General Test, MAT, GMAT, minimum GPA of 2.7, letter of intent. Additional exam requirements/recommendations for international students: Required—TOEFL (minimum score 523 paper-based; 70 iBT). *Application deadline:* For fall admission, 6/1 priority date for domestic students, 5/1 priority date for international students; for spring admission, 11/15 priority date for domestic students, 9/15 priority date for international students; for summer admission, 4/15 for domestic students, 9/15 for international students. Applications are processed on a rolling basis. Application fee: $30. Electronic applications accepted. *Expenses:* Tuition, state resident: full-time $1781; part-time $161.93 per credit hour. Tuition, nonresident: full-time $6482; part-time $589.27 per credit hour. *Required fees:* $1224 per unit. $612 per semester. Tuition and fees vary according to course load, campus/location and program. *Financial support:* In 2016–17, research assistantships with full tuition reimbursements (averaging $5,000 per year) were awarded; scholarships/grants, tuition waivers (full), and unspecified assistantships also available. Financial award application deadline: 3/15; financial award applicants required to submit FAFSA. *Unit head:* Dr. Robert LeFavi, Department Head, 912-921-3208, Fax: 912-344-3490, E-mail: robert.lefavi@armstrong.edu. *Application contact:* McKenzie Peterman, Assistant Director of Graduate Admissions, 912-344-2503, Fax: 912-344-3417, E-mail: graduate@armstrong.edu.
Website: http://www.armstrong.edu/Majors/degree/sports_medicine1

A.T. Still University, Arizona School of Health Sciences, Mesa, AZ 85206. Offers advanced occupational therapy (MS); advanced physician assistant studies (MS); athletic training (MS, DAT); audiology (Au D); clinical decision making in athletic training (Graduate Certificate); occupational therapy (MS, OTD); orthopedic rehabilitation (Graduate Certificate); physical therapy (DPT); physician assistant studies (MS); transitional audiology (Au D); transitional physical therapy (DPT). *Accreditation:* AOTA (one or more programs are accredited); ASHA. *Program availability:* Part-time, 100% online. *Faculty:* 54 full-time (31 women), 188 part-time/adjunct (132 women). *Students:* 555 full-time (370 women), 411 part-time (297 women); includes 243 minority (49 Black or African American, non-Hispanic/Latino; 6 American Indian or Alaska Native, non-Hispanic/Latino; 90 Asian, non-Hispanic/Latino; 79 Hispanic/Latino; 19 Two or more races, non-Hispanic/Latino), 64 international. Average age 33. 4,529 applicants, 9% accepted, 271 enrolled. In 2016, 139 master's, 253 doctorates, 1 other advanced degree awarded. *Degree requirements:* For master's, thesis (for some programs); for doctorate, thesis/dissertation (for some programs). *Entrance requirements:* For master's, GRE General Test; for doctorate, GRE, Physical Therapist Evaluation Tool (for DPT), current state licensure. Additional exam requirements/recommendations for international students: Required—TOEFL (minimum score 80 iBT). *Application deadline:* For fall admission, 7/7 for domestic and international students; for winter admission, 10/3 for domestic and international students; for spring admission, 1/16 for domestic and international students; for summer admission, 4/17 for domestic and international students. Applications are processed on a rolling basis. Application fee: $70. Electronic applications accepted. Application fee is waived when completed online. *Expenses:* Contact institution. *Financial support:* In 2016–17, 140 students received support. Federal Work-Study and scholarships/grants available. Financial award application deadline: 6/1; financial award applicants required to submit FAFSA. *Faculty research:* Pediatric sport-related concussion, adolescent athlete health-related quality of life; geriatric and pediatric well-being, pain management for participation, practice-based research network, BMI and dental caries. *Total annual research expenditures:* $86,113. *Unit head:* Dr. Randy Danielsen, Dean, 480-219-6000, Fax: 480-219-6110, E-mail: rdanielsen@atsu.edu. *Application contact:* Donna Sparks, Associate Director, Admissions Processing, 660-626-2117, Fax: 660-626-2969, E-mail: admissions@atsu.edu.
Website: http://www.atsu.edu/ashs

Azusa Pacific University, School of Behavioral and Applied Sciences, Department of Exercise and Sport Science, Azusa, CA 91702-7000. Offers athletic training (MS); physical education (MA, MS).

Barry University, School of Human Performance and Leisure Sciences, Programs in Movement Science, Specialization in Athletic Training, Miami Shores, FL 33161-6695. Offers MS. *Program availability:* Part-time, evening/weekend. *Degree requirements:* For master's, comprehensive exam, project or thesis. *Entrance requirements:* For master's, GRE General Test, minimum GPA of 3.0. Electronic applications accepted. *Faculty research:* Pain management, prevention and injury analysis, low energy static magnetic field therapy, upper extremity biomechanics.

Bloomsburg University of Pennsylvania, School of Graduate Studies, College of Science and Technology, Department of Exercise Science and Athletics, Bloomsburg, PA 17815-1301. Offers clinical athletic training (MS); exercise science (MS). *Faculty:* 5 full-time (1 woman). *Students:* 40 full-time (24 women); includes 4 minority (1 Asian, non-Hispanic/Latino; 1 Hispanic/Latino; 2 Two or more races, non-Hispanic/Latino), 1 international. Average age 24. 62 applicants, 55% accepted, 19 enrolled. In 2016, 22 master's awarded. *Degree requirements:* For master's, thesis optional, practical clinical experience. *Entrance requirements:* For master's, GRE, minimum QPA of 3.0, related undergraduate coursework, interview. Additional exam requirements/recommendations for international students: Required—TOEFL (minimum score 550 paper-based; 79 iBT), IELTS. *Application deadline:* Applications are processed on a rolling basis. Application fee: $35 ($60 for international students). Electronic applications accepted. *Expenses:* Tuition, state resident: full-time $9660; part-time $483 per credit. Tuition, nonresident: full-time $14,500; part-time $725 per credit. *Required fees:* $2410; $107 per credit. $75 per term. Tuition and fees vary according to course load, degree level and program. *Financial support:* Federal Work-Study and unspecified assistantships available. Financial award applicants required to submit FAFSA. *Unit head:* Dr. Joseph Andreacci, MS Program Coordinator, 570-389-3959, Fax: 570-389-5047, E-mail: jandreac@bloomu.edu. *Application contact:* Jennifer Kessler, Administrative Assistant, 570-389-4015, Fax: 570-389-3054, E-mail: jkessler@bloomu.edu.
Website: http://www.bloomu.edu/exercise_science

Boston University, College of Health and Rehabilitation Sciences: Sargent College, Department of Physical Therapy and Athletic Training, Boston, MA 02215. Offers athletic training (PhD); physical therapy (DPT); rehabilitation sciences (PhD). *Accreditation:* APTA (one or more programs are accredited). *Faculty:* 13 full-time (10 women), 26 part-time/adjunct (12 women). *Students:* 191 full-time (137 women), 4 part-time (1 woman); includes 37 minority (2 Black or African American, non-Hispanic/Latino; 18 Asian, non-Hispanic/Latino; 7 Hispanic/Latino; 10 Two or more races, non-Hispanic/Latino), 3 international. Average age 24. 668 applicants, 13% accepted, 39 enrolled. In 2016, 109 doctorates awarded. *Degree requirements:* For doctorate, comprehensive exam and thesis (for PhD). *Entrance requirements:* For doctorate, GRE General Test, master's degree (for PhD), bachelor's degree (for DPT). Additional exam requirements/recommendations for international students: Required—TOEFL (minimum score 550 paper-based; 84 iBT). *Application deadline:* For fall admission, 12/15 priority date for domestic and international students. Applications are processed on a rolling basis. Application fee: $120. Electronic applications accepted. *Expenses:* $6,372 total ($1,593 per year in Spring semester of first two years, $3,186 in final semester of program). *Financial support:* In 2016–17, 120 students received support, including 4 research assistantships with full tuition reimbursements available (averaging $21,500 per year), 6 teaching assistantships (averaging $2,500 per year); fellowships, career-related internships or fieldwork, Federal Work-Study, institutionally sponsored loans, scholarships/grants, and tuition waivers (full and partial) also available. Financial award application deadline: 12/15; financial award applicants required to submit FAFSA. *Faculty research:* Gait, balance, motor control, dynamic systems analysis, spinal cord injury. *Total annual research expenditures:* $651,000. *Unit head:* Dr. LaDora Thompson, Department Chair, 617-353-2724, E-mail: pt@bu.edu. *Application contact:* Sharon Sankey, Assistant Dean, Student Services, 617-353-2713, Fax: 617-353-7500, E-mail: ssankey@bu.edu.

Bridgewater College, Program in Athletic Training, Bridgewater, VA 22812-1599. Offers MS. Electronic applications accepted.

Brigham Young University, Graduate Studies, College of Life Sciences, Department of Exercise Sciences, Provo, UT 84602. Offers athletic training (MS); exercise physiology (MS, PhD); exercise sciences (MS); health promotion (MS, PhD); physical medicine and rehabilitation (PhD). *Faculty:* 20 full-time (2 women). *Students:* 14 full-time (6 women), 17 part-time (11 women); includes 4 minority (3 Asian, non-Hispanic/Latino; 1 Hispanic/Latino). Average age 30. 21 applicants, 38% accepted, 4 enrolled. In 2016, 11 master's awarded. *Degree requirements:* For master's, thesis, oral defense; for doctorate, comprehensive exam, thesis/dissertation, oral defense, oral and written exams. *Entrance requirements:* For master's, GRE General Test (minimum score of 300, 4.0 on analytic writing portion), minimum GPA of 3.2 in last 60 hours of course work; for doctorate, GRE General Test (minimum score of 300, 4.0 on analytic writing portion), minimum GPA of 3.5 in last 60 hours of course work. Additional exam requirements/recommendations for international students: Required—TOEFL (minimum score 580 paper-based; 85 iBT), IELTS (minimum score 7). *Application deadline:* For fall admission, 2/1 for domestic and international students. Application fee: $50. Electronic applications accepted. *Expenses:* Contact institution. *Financial support:* In 2016–17, 168 students received support, including 32 research assistantships (averaging $7,330 per year), 42 teaching assistantships (averaging $2,772 per year); career-related internships or fieldwork, institutionally sponsored loans, scholarships/grants, unspecified assistantships, and 7 PhD full-tuition scholarships also available. Financial award application deadline: 4/15. *Faculty research:* Injury prevention and rehabilitation, human skeletal muscle adaptation, cardiovascular health and fitness, lifestyle modification and health promotion. *Total annual research expenditures:* $158,655. *Unit head:* Dr. Allen Parcell, Chair, 801-422-4450, Fax: 801-422-0555, E-mail: allenparcell@gmail.com. *Application contact:* Dr. J. William Myrer, Graduate Coordinator, 801-422-2690, Fax: 801-422-0555, E-mail: bill_myrer@byu.edu.
Website: http://exsc.byu.edu/

California Baptist University, Program in Athletic Training, Riverside, CA 92504-3206. Offers MS. *Program availability:* Part-time. *Faculty:* 4 full-time (3 women). *Students:* 37 full-time (22 women); includes 17 minority (3 Black or African American, non-Hispanic/Latino; 4 Asian, non-Hispanic/Latino; 10 Hispanic/Latino). Average age 25. In 2016, 20 master's awarded. *Degree requirements:* For master's, 53-56 units of core courses; at least 900 cumulative hours of athletic training clinical education courses. *Entrance requirements:* For master's, minimum GPA of 2.75; three recommendations; comprehensive essay; current resume; CPR Professional Rescuer Certification; 150 hours of clinical observation; interview. Additional exam requirements/recommendations for international students: Required—TOEFL (minimum score 80 iBT). *Application deadline:* For fall admission, 8/1 priority date for domestic students, 7/1 for international students; for spring admission, 12/1 priority date for domestic students, 11/1 for international students. Applications are processed on a rolling basis. Application fee: $45. Electronic applications accepted. *Expenses:* Contact institution. *Financial support:* In 2016–17, 3 students received support. Research assistantships, Federal Work-Study, and scholarships/grants available. Financial award applicants required to submit CSS PROFILE or FAFSA. *Faculty research:* Nutrition, weight management, public health, stress, athletic training. *Unit head:* Dr. David Pearson, Dean of the College of Health Science, 951-343-4298, E-mail: dpearson@calbaptist.edu. *Application contact:* Dr. Nicole MacDonald, Director, Athletic Training Program, 951-343-4379, E-mail: nmacdona@calbaptist.edu.
Website: http://www.calbaptist.edu/at/

California State University, Long Beach, Graduate Studies, College of Health and Human Services, Department of Kinesiology, Long Beach, CA 90840. Offers adapted physical education (MA); coaching and student athlete development (MA); exercise physiology and nutrition (MS); exercise science (MS); individualized studies (MA); kinesiology (MA); pedagogical studies (MA); sport and exercise psychology (MS); sport management (MA); sports medicine and injury studies (MS). *Program availability:* Part-time. *Degree requirements:* For master's, oral and written comprehensive exams or thesis. *Entrance requirements:* For master's, GRE General Test, minimum GPA of 2.75 during previous 2 years of course work. *Application deadline:* For fall admission, 6/1 for domestic students. Applications are processed on a rolling basis. Application fee: $55. Electronic applications accepted. *Financial support:* Federal Work-Study, institutionally sponsored loans, and scholarships/grants available. Financial award application deadline: 3/2. *Faculty research:* Pulmonary functioning, feedback and practice structure, strength training, history and politics of sports, special population research issues. *Unit head:* Jan Schroeder, Chair, 562-985-4051.

California University of Pennsylvania, School of Graduate Studies and Research, College of Education and Human Services, Department of Health Science, California, PA 15419-1394. Offers athletic training (MS). *Degree requirements:* For master's, comprehensive exam, thesis. *Entrance requirements:* For master's, minimum GPA of 3.0. Additional exam requirements/recommendations for international students: Required—TOEFL (minimum score 550 paper-based; 80 iBT). *Expenses:* Tuition, state resident: full-time $11,592; part-time $483 per credit. Tuition, nonresident: full-time $17,400; part-time $725 per credit. *Required fees:* $3916. Tuition and fees vary according to course load, degree level, campus/location and reciprocity agreements. *Faculty research:* Exercise physiology, pedagogy, athletic training, biomechanical engineering, case studies in injury and athletic medicine.

Chapman University, Crean College of Health and Behavioral Sciences, Athletic Training Program, Orange, CA 92866. Offers MS. *Faculty:* 4 full-time (2 women). *Students:* 14 full-time (10 women), 7 part-time (5 women); includes 8 minority (1 Black or African American, non-Hispanic/Latino; 1 Asian, non-Hispanic/Latino; 5 Hispanic/Latino; 1 Two or more races, non-Hispanic/Latino). Average age 23. *Degree requirements:* For master's, 1200 hours of clinical fieldwork. *Entrance requirements:* For master's, GRE. Additional exam requirements/recommendations for international students: Required—TOEFL (minimum score 550 paper-based, 80 iBT), IELTS (6.5), PTE Academic (53), or CAE. *Application deadline:* For summer admission, 12/1 priority date for domestic students. Application fee: $60. Electronic applications accepted. *Expenses:* Contact institution. *Financial support:* Fellowships, scholarships/grants, and unspecified assistantships available. Financial award applicants required to submit FAFSA. *Unit head:* Dr. Jason Bennett, Director, 714-997-6567, E-mail: jbennett@chapman.edu. *Application contact:* Monica Chen, Graduate Admission Counselor, 714-289-3590, E-mail: mchen@chapman.edu.

The College of St. Scholastica, Graduate Studies, Department of Athletic Training, Duluth, MN 55811-4199. Offers MS. *Program availability:* Part-time, online learning. *Entrance requirements:* Additional exam requirements/recommendations for international students: Required—TOEFL. Electronic applications accepted.

Eastern Michigan University, Graduate School, College of Health and Human Services, School of Health Promotion and Human Performance, Programs in Exercise Physiology, Ypsilanti, MI 48197. Offers exercise physiology (MS); sports medicine-biomechanics (MS); sports medicine-corporate adult fitness (MS); sports medicine-exercise physiology (MS). *Program availability:* Part-time, evening/weekend. *Students:* 13 full-time (5 women), 19 part-time (9 women); includes 3 minority (1 Black or African American, non-Hispanic/Latino; 1 Asian, non-Hispanic/Latino; 1 Hispanic/Latino), 2 international. Average age 31. 29 applicants, 69% accepted, 10 enrolled. In 2016, 12 master's awarded. *Degree requirements:* For master's, comprehensive exam, thesis or 450-hour internship. *Entrance requirements:* Additional exam requirements/recommendations for international students: Required—TOEFL. *Application deadline:* For fall admission, 8/1 for domestic students, 5/1 for international students; for winter admission, 12/1 for domestic students, 10/1 for international students; for spring admission, 3/15 for domestic students, 3/1 for international students. Application fee: $45. *Application contact:* Dr. Stephen McGregor, Program Coordinator, 734-487-0090, Fax: 734-487-2024, E-mail: smcgregor@emich.edu.

Eastern Michigan University, Graduate School, College of Health and Human Services, School of Health Promotion and Human Performance, Programs in Orthotics and Prosthetics, Ypsilanti, MI 48197. Offers orthotics (Graduate Certificate); orthotics/prosthetics (MS); prosthetics (Graduate Certificate). *Students:* 37 full-time (22 women); includes 4 minority (1 Black or African American, non-Hispanic/Latino; 2 Hispanic/Latino; 1 Two or more races, non-Hispanic/Latino), 1 international. Average age 25. 86 applicants, 36% accepted, 20 enrolled. In 2016, 18 master's awarded. *Degree requirements:* For master's, comprehensive exam, thesis or project, 500 hours of clinicals. *Entrance requirements:* For master's, MAT. Additional exam requirements/recommendations for international students: Required—TOEFL. *Application deadline:* For fall admission, 5/1 for domestic students. Applications are processed on a rolling basis. Application fee: $45. *Financial support:* Fellowships, research assistantships with full tuition reimbursements, teaching assistantships with full tuition reimbursements, career-related internships or fieldwork, Federal Work-Study, institutionally sponsored loans, scholarships/grants, tuition waivers (partial), and unspecified assistantships available. Support available to part-time students. Financial award applicants required to submit FAFSA. *Application contact:* Wendy Beattie, Clinical and Program Director, 734-487-2814, Fax: 734-487-2024, E-mail: wbeattie@emich.edu.

East Stroudsburg University of Pennsylvania, Graduate and Extended Studies, College of Health Sciences, Department of Athletic Training, East Stroudsburg, PA 18301-2999. Offers MS. *Program availability:* Part-time, evening/weekend, online learning. *Students:* 48 full-time (30 women), 1 part-time (0 women); includes 9 minority (5 Black or African American, non-Hispanic/Latino; 2 Hispanic/Latino; 2 Two or more races, non-Hispanic/Latino). *Entrance requirements:* For master's, GRE. Additional exam requirements/recommendations for international students: Recommended—TOEFL (minimum score 560 paper-based; 83 iBT), IELTS. *Application deadline:* For fall admission, 7/31 for domestic students, 6/30 for international students; for spring admission, 10/30 for domestic students, 10/31 for international students. Applications are processed on a rolling basis. Application fee: $50. Electronic applications accepted. *Expenses:* Tuition, state resident: full-time $8694; part-time $5796 per year. Tuition, nonresident: full-time $13,050; part time $8700 per year. *Required fees:* $2550; $1690 per unit. $845 per semester. Tuition and fees vary according to course load, campus/location and program. *Financial support:* Research assistantships with tuition reimbursements, career-related internships or fieldwork, Federal Work-Study, and unspecified assistantships available. Support available to part-time students. *Unit head:* Keith Vanic, Graduate Coordinator, 570-422-3314, E-mail: kvanic@esu.edu. *Application contact:* Kevin Quintero, Associate Director, Graduate and Extended Studies, 570-422-3890, Fax: 570-422-2711, E-mail: kquintero@esu.edu.

Florida International University, Nicole Wertheim College of Nursing and Health Sciences, Department of Athletic Training, Miami, FL 33199. Offers MS. *Faculty:* 4 full-time (3 women), 4 part-time/adjunct (2 women). *Students:* 44 full-time (33 women); includes 35 minority (17 Black or African American, non-Hispanic/Latino; 1 Asian, non-Hispanic/Latino; 17 Hispanic/Latino), 1 international. Average age 24. 3 applicants. In 2016, 26 master's awarded. *Degree requirements:* For master's, 800 clinical education hours. *Entrance requirements:* For master's, bachelor's degree from accredited institution; minimum GPA of 3.0 overall and in last 60 credits of upper-division courses of the bachelor's degree; three letters of recommendation; resume; personal statement of professional/educational goals. Additional exam requirements/recommendations for international students: Required—TOEFL (minimum score 550 paper-based; 80 iBT). *Application deadline:* For fall admission, 2/15 for domestic and international students. Application fee: $30. Electronic applications accepted. *Expenses:* Contact institution. *Financial support:* Institutionally sponsored loans and scholarships/grants available. Financial award application deadline: 3/1; financial award applicants required to submit FAFSA. *Faculty research:* Continuing professional education, leadership styles and outcomes, professionalism and professional image. *Unit head:* Dr. Jennifer Doherty-Restrepo, Director, 305-348-3398, Fax: 305-348-2125, E-mail: jennifer.doherty@fiu.edu. *Application contact:* Nanett Rojas, Manager, Admissions Operations, 305-348-7464, Fax: 305-348-7441, E-mail: gradadm@fiu.edu.

Franklin College, Program in Athletic Training, Franklin, IN 46131. Offers MSAT.

Gannon University, School of Graduate Studies, Morosky College of Health Professions and Sciences, School of Health Professions, Program in Athletic Training, Erie, PA 16541-0001. Offers MAT. *Program availability:* Part-time, evening/weekend. *Students:* 14 full-time (12 women). Average age 23. In 2016, 6 master's awarded. *Entrance requirements:* For master's, undergraduate degree in exercise science, kinesiology, human performance, sports medicine or related field; minimum GPA of 2.75; 3 letters of recommendation. Additional exam requirements/recommendations for international students: Required—TOEFL (minimum score 79 iBT). *Application deadline:* Applications are processed on a rolling basis. Application fee: $25. Electronic applications accepted. Application fee is waived when completed online. *Expenses:* *Tuition:* Full-time $17,370. *Required fees:* $550. Tuition and fees vary according to course load and program. *Financial support:* Federal Work-Study and unspecified assistantships available. Financial award application deadline: 7/1; financial award applicants required to submit FAFSA. *Unit head:* Dr. Jason Willow, Chairperson, 814-871-7788, E-mail: willow001@gannon.edu. *Application contact:* Bridget Philip, Director of Graduate Admissions, 814-871-7412, E-mail: graduate@gannon.edu.

Georgia State University, College of Education and Human Development, Department of Kinesiology and Health, Program in Sports Medicine, Atlanta, GA 30302-3083. Offers MS. *Degree requirements:* For master's, comprehensive exam. *Entrance requirements:* For master's, GRE General Test, minimum GPA of 2.5. *Application deadline:* For fall admission, 5/1 for domestic students; for spring admission, 10/1 for domestic students. Application fee: $50. *Expenses:* Tuition, state resident: full-time $6876; part-time $382 per credit hour. Tuition, nonresident: full-time $22,374; part-time $1243 per credit hour. *Required fees:* $2128; $1064 per term. Part-time tuition and fees vary according to course load and program. *Financial support:* Research assistantships available. *Faculty research:* Athletic training. *Unit head:* Dr. Jacalyn Lea Lund, Chair, 404-413-8051, E-mail: jlund@gsu.edu. *Application contact:* Dr. Shelley Linens, Program Coordinator, 404-413-8366, E-mail: slinens@gsu.edu.
Website: http://education.gsu.edu/KIN/kh_sportsMed_MS.html

Grand View University, Graduate Studies, Des Moines, IA 50316-1599. Offers athletic training (MS); clinical nurse leader (MSN, Post Master's Certificate); nursing education (MSN, Post Master's Certificate); organizational leadership (MS); sport management (MS); teacher leadership (M Ed); urban education (M Ed). *Program availability:* Part-time, evening/weekend. *Degree requirements:* For master's, completion of all required coursework in common core and selected track with minimum cumulative GPA of 3.0 and no more than two grades of C. *Entrance requirements:* For master's, GRE, GMAT, or essay, minimum undergraduate GPA of 3.0, professional resume, 3 letters of recommendation, interview. Additional exam requirements/recommendations for international students: Required—TOEFL (minimum score 550 paper-based). Electronic applications accepted.

Indiana State University, College of Graduate and Professional Studies, College of Nursing, Health, and Human Services, Department of Applied Medicine and Rehabilitation, Terre Haute, IN 47809. Offers athletic training (MS, DAT); occupational therapy (MS); physical therapy (DPT); physician assistant (MS). *Degree requirements:* For master's, thesis or alternative. *Entrance requirements:* For master's, GRE General Test. Electronic applications accepted.

Indiana University Bloomington, School of Public Health, Department of Kinesiology, Bloomington, IN 47405. Offers applied sport science (MS); athletic administration/sport management (MS); athletic training (MS); biomechanics (MS); ergonomics (MS); exercise physiology (MS); human performance (PhD), including biomechanics, exercise physiology, motor learning/control, sport management; motor learning/control (MS); physical activity (MPH); physical activity, fitness and wellness (MS). *Program availability:* Part-time. Terminal master's awarded for partial completion of doctoral program. *Degree requirements:* For master's, thesis optional; for doctorate, variable foreign language requirement, comprehensive exam, thesis/dissertation. *Entrance requirements:* For master's, GRE General Test, minimum GPA of 2.8; for doctorate, GRE General Test, minimum graduate GPA of 3.5, undergraduate 3.0. Additional exam requirements/recommendations for international students: Required—TOEFL (minimum score 80 iBT). *Faculty research:* Exercise physiology and biochemistry, sports biomechanics, human motor control, adaptation of fitness and exercise to special populations.

Inter American University of Puerto Rico, Metropolitan Campus, Graduate Programs, Program in Physical Education, San Juan, PR 00919-1293. Offers teaching of physical education (MA); training and sport performance (MA). *Degree requirements:* For master's, comprehensive exam. *Entrance requirements:* For master's, GRE or EXADEP, interview. Electronic applications accepted.

Kent State University, College of Education, Health and Human Services, School of Health Sciences, Program in Exercise Physiology, Kent, OH 44242-0001. Offers athletic training (MS); exercise physiology (PhD). *Degree requirements:* For doctorate, comprehensive exam, thesis/dissertation. *Entrance requirements:* For master's, GRE, 2 letters of reference, goals statement; for doctorate, GRE, 2 letters of reference, goals statement, minimum master's-level GPA of 3.0. Additional exam requirements/recommendations for international students: Required—TOEFL (minimum score 550 paper-based; 80 iBT). *Expenses:* Tuition, state resident: full-time $10,864; part-time $495 per credit hour. Tuition, nonresident: full-time $18,380; part-time $837 per credit hour.

Lebanon Valley College, Program in Athletic Training, Annville, PA 17003. Offers MAT. *Faculty:* 4 full-time (2 women), 4 part-time/adjunct (2 women). *Students:* 65 applicants, 85% accepted, 13 enrolled. *Degree requirements:* For master's, research project. *Entrance requirements:* For master's, GRE. Additional exam requirements/recommendations for international students: Required—TOEFL (minimum score 80 iBT). *Application deadline:* Applications are processed on a rolling basis. Electronic applications accepted. *Expenses:* Contact institution. *Financial support:* Career-related internships or fieldwork, Federal Work-Study, and scholarships/grants available. Financial award applicants required to submit FAFSA. *Faculty research:* Epidemiology, clinical education, clinical decision making. *Unit head:* Dr. Joseph M. Murphy, Assistant Professor/Director of Athletic Training, 717-867-6845, Fax: 717-867-6849, E-mail: jmurphy@lvc.edu. *Application contact:* Dr. Joseph M. Murphy, Assistant Professor/Director of Athletic Training, 717-867-6845, Fax: 717-867-6849, E-mail: jmurphy@lvc.edu.
Website: http://www.lvc.edu/academics/programs-of-study/athletic-training

Lenoir-Rhyne University, Graduate Programs, School of Health, Exercise and Sport Science, Program in Athletic Training, Hickory, NC 28601. Offers MS. *Program availability:* Part-time. *Entrance requirements:* For master's, GRE or MAT, official transcripts, 75 observational hours with certified athletic trainer, essay, resume. Additional exam requirements/recommendations for international students: Required—TOEFL (minimum score 600 paper-based). Electronic applications accepted. *Expenses:* Contact institution.

Athletic Training and Sports Medicine

Life University, Graduate Programs, Marietta, GA 30060-2903. Offers athletic training (MAT); chiropractic sport science (MS); clinical nutrition (MS); nutrition and sport science (MS), including chiropractic sport science; sport coaching (MS), including exercise sport science; sport injury management (MS), including nutrition and sport science; sports health science (MS). *Program availability:* Part-time, 100% online, blended/hybrid learning. *Degree requirements:* For master's, comprehensive exam (for some programs), thesis optional. *Entrance requirements:* For master's, GRE General Test, minimum GPA of 3.0, 3 letters of recommendation, curriculum vitae. Additional exam requirements/recommendations for international students: Required—TOEFL (minimum score 500 paper-based). Electronic applications accepted. *Expenses:* Contact institution.

Lock Haven University of Pennsylvania, College of Natural, Behavioral and Health Sciences, Lock Haven, PA 17745-2390. Offers actuarial science (PSM); athletic training (MS); health promotion/education (MHS); healthcare management (MHS); physician assistant (MHS). Program also offered at the Clearfield, Coudersport, and Harrisburg campuses. *Accreditation:* ARC-PA. *Entrance requirements:* For master's, minimum undergraduate GPA of 3.0. Additional exam requirements/recommendations for international students: Required—TOEFL. Electronic applications accepted.

London Metropolitan University, Graduate Programs, London, United Kingdom. Offers applied psychology (M Sc); architecture (MA); biomedical science (M Sc); blood science (M Sc); cancer pharmacology (M Sc); computer networking and cyber security (M Sc); computing and information systems (M Sc); conference interpreting (MA); counter-terrorism studies (M Sc); creative, digital and professional writing (MA); crime, violence and prevention (M Sc); criminology (M Sc); curating contemporary art (MA); data analytics (M Sc); digital media (MA); early childhood studies (MA); education (MA, Ed D); financial services law, regulation and compliance (LL M); food science (M Sc); forensic psychology (M Sc); health and social care management and policy (M Sc); human nutrition (M Sc); human resource management (MA); human rights and international conflict (MA); information technology (M Sc); intelligence and security studies (M Sc); international oil, gas and energy law (LL M); international relations (MA); interpreting (MA); learning and teaching in higher education (MA); legal practice (LL M); media and entertainment law (LL M); organizational and consumer psychology (M Sc); psychological therapy (M Sc); psychology of mental health (M Sc); public health (M Sc); public policy and management (MPA); security studies (M Sc); social work (M Sc); spatial planning and urban design (MA); sports therapy (M Sc); supporting older children and young people with dyslexia (MA); teaching languages (MA), including Arabic, English; translation (MA); woman and child abuse (MA).

Long Island University–LIU Brooklyn, School of Health Professions, Brooklyn, NY 11201-8423. Offers athletic training and sport sciences (MS); community health (MS Ed); exercise science (MS); forensic social work (Advanced Certificate); occupational therapy (MS); physical therapy (DPT); physician assistant (MS); public health (MPH); social work (MSW). *Faculty:* 60 full-time (42 women), 109 part-time/adjunct (62 women). *Students:* 603 full-time (405 women), 69 part-time (52 women); includes 219 minority (117 Black or African American, non-Hispanic/Latino; 1 American Indian or Alaska Native, non-Hispanic/Latino; 38 Asian, non-Hispanic/Latino; 48 Hispanic/Latino; 15 Two or more races, non-Hispanic/Latino), 68 international. 1,127 applicants, 43% accepted, 213 enrolled. In 2016, 192 master's, 42 doctorates awarded. *Degree requirements:* For master's, comprehensive exam (for some programs), thesis (for some programs), research capstone; for doctorate, comprehensive exam, research capstone. *Entrance requirements:* For master's, doctorate, and Advanced Certificate, GRE. Additional exam requirements/recommendations for international students: Required—TOEFL (minimum score 550 paper-based; 79 iBT). *Application deadline:* Applications are processed on a rolling basis. Application fee: $50. Electronic applications accepted. *Expenses: Tuition:* Full-time $28,272; part-time $1178 per credit. *Required fees:* $451 per term. Tuition and fees vary according to degree level, program and student level. *Financial support:* Research assistantships, teaching assistantships, career-related internships or fieldwork, Federal Work-Study, institutionally sponsored loans, scholarships/grants, tuition waivers (partial), and unspecified assistantships available. Support available to part-time students. Financial award application deadline: 2/15; financial award applicants required to submit FAFSA. *Faculty research:* Kinesiology, gender disparities, exercise physiology, gait analysis, social justice. *Unit head:* Dr. Barry S. Eckert, Dean, 718-780-6578, Fax: 718-780-4561, E-mail: barry.eckert@liu.edu. *Application contact:* Dr. Dominick Fortugno, Dean of Admissions, 718-780-6578, Fax: 718-780-4561, E-mail: dominick.fortugno@liu.edu.
Website: http://liu.edu/brooklyn/academics/school-of-health-professions

Manchester University, Master of Athletic Training Program, North Manchester, IN 46962-1225. Offers MAT. *Faculty:* 6 full-time (2 women), 1 part-time/adjunct (0 women). *Students:* 21 full-time (16 women); includes 4 minority (3 Black or African American, non-Hispanic/Latino; 1 Hispanic/Latino). Average age 23. 31 applicants, 74% accepted, 15 enrolled. In 2016, 7 master's awarded. *Degree requirements:* For master's, 51 semester hours; minimum cumulative GPA of 3.0, 2.0 in each required course; completion of all required didactic and clinical courses. *Entrance requirements:* For master's, baccalaureate degree from regionally-accredited institution; minimum cumulative undergraduate GPA of 3.0; certification in first aid and CPR; letters of recommendation. Additional exam requirements/recommendations for international students: Required—TOEFL (minimum score 550 paper-based; 79 iBT). *Application deadline:* For fall admission, 1/1 priority date for domestic students. Applications are processed on a rolling basis. Application fee: $60. Electronic applications accepted. *Expenses:* $24,050. *Financial support:* In 2016–17, 21 students received support, including 21 fellowships (averaging $7,850 per year). Financial award application deadline: 5/1; financial award applicants required to submit FAFSA. *Unit head:* Mark Huntington, Program Director, Graduate Athletic Training Education, 260-982-5033, E-mail: mwhuntington@manchester.edu.
Website: https://www.manchester.edu/academics/colleges/college-of-pharmacy-natural-health-sciences/academic-programs/exercise-science-athletic-training/exercis

Marshall University, Academic Affairs Division, College of Health Professions, School of Kinesiology, Program in Athletic Training, Huntington, WV 25755. Offers MS. *Entrance requirements:* For master's, GRE.

Merrimack College, School of Science and Engineering, North Andover, MA 01845-5800. Offers athletic training (MS); civil engineering (MS); community health education (MS); computer science (MS); data science (MS); exercise and sport science (MS); health and wellness management (MS); mechanical engineering (MS), including engineering management. *Program availability:* Part-time, evening/weekend, 100% online. *Faculty:* 16 full-time, 2 part-time/adjunct. *Students:* 88 full-time (32 women), 13 part-time (6 women); includes 6 minority (4 Hispanic/Latino; 2 Two or more races, non-Hispanic/Latino), 39 international. Average age 25. 156 applicants, 67% accepted, 59 enrolled. In 2016, 46 master's awarded. *Degree requirements:* For master's, comprehensive exam, thesis optional, internship or capstone (for some programs). *Entrance requirements:* For master's, official college transcripts, resume, personal statement, 2 recommendations. Additional exam requirements/recommendations for international students: Required—TOEFL (minimum score 84 iBT), IELTS (minimum score 6.5), PTE (minimum score 56). *Application deadline:* For fall admission, 8/14 for domestic students, 7/14 for international students; for spring admission, 1/10 for domestic students, 12/10 for international students; for summer admission, 5/10 for domestic students, 4/10 for international students. Applications are processed on a rolling basis. Application fee: $0. Electronic applications accepted. *Expenses:* Contact institution. *Financial support:* Fellowships with full tuition reimbursements, career-related internships or fieldwork, scholarships/grants, and health care benefits available. Support available to part-time students. Financial award application deadline: 5/1; financial award applicants required to submit FAFSA. *Faculty research:* Viral genomics and evolution (biology), robotics (mechanical engineering), knot theory (mathematics), computer graphics and network security (computer science), water management (civil engineering). *Application contact:* Allison Pena, Graduate Admissions Counselor, 978-837-3563, E-mail: penaa@merrimack.edu.
Website: http://www.merrimack.edu/academics/graduate/

Missouri State University, Graduate College, College of Health and Human Services, Department of Sports Medicine and Athletic Training, Springfield, MO 65897. Offers athletic training (MS); occupational therapy (MOT). *Program availability:* Part-time. *Faculty:* 7 full-time (4 women), 5 part-time/adjunct (3 women). *Students:* 26 full-time (13 women), 1 (woman) part-time; includes 1 minority (Two or more races, non-Hispanic/Latino), 2 international. Average age 24. 46 applicants, 78% accepted, 36 enrolled. In 2016, 7 master's awarded. *Degree requirements:* For master's, comprehensive exam, thesis or alternative. *Entrance requirements:* For master's, GRE, current Professional Rescuer and AED certification, BOC certification, licensure as an athletic trainer, minimum undergraduate GPA of 3.0 (for MS); OTCAS application (for MOT). Additional exam requirements/recommendations for international students: Required—TOEFL (minimum score 550 paper-based; 79 iBT), IELTS (minimum score 6). *Application deadline:* For fall admission, 1/15 for domestic and international students. Application fee: $35 ($50 for international students). Electronic applications accepted. *Expenses:* Tuition, state resident: full-time $5830. Tuition, nonresident: full-time $10,708. *Required fees:* $1130. Tuition and fees vary according to class time, course level, course load and program. *Financial support:* In 2016–17, 5 teaching assistantships with partial tuition reimbursements (averaging $8,772 per year) were awarded; Federal Work-Study, institutionally sponsored loans, and unspecified assistantships also available. Financial award application deadline: 3/31; financial award applicants required to submit FAFSA. *Unit head:* Dr. Tona Hetzler, Head, 417-836-8924, Fax: 417-836-8554, E-mail: tonahetzler@missouristate.edu. *Application contact:* Michael Edwards, Coordinator of Graduate Admissions, 417-836-5330, Fax: 417-836-6200, E-mail: michaeledwards@missouristate.edu.
Website: http://sportsmed.missouristate.edu/

Montana State University Billings, College of Allied Health Professions, Program in Athletic Training, Billings, MT 59101. Offers MS. *Program availability:* Part-time. *Faculty:* 4 full-time (2 women), 1 part-time/adjunct (0 women). *Students:* 19. *Degree requirements:* For master's, thesis optional. *Entrance requirements:* For master's, GRE, minimum GPA of 3.0, letters of recommendation, letter of intent. Additional exam requirements/recommendations for international students: Required—TOEFL (minimum score 79 iBT), IELTS (minimum score 6.5). *Application deadline:* Applications are processed on a rolling basis. Electronic applications accepted. *Expenses:* Tuition, state resident: full-time $5265; part-time $3436 per year. Tuition, nonresident: full-time $14,030; part-time $9280 per year. *International tuition:* $19,295 full-time. Tuition and fees vary according to degree level, campus/location and program. *Financial support:* Research assistantships with partial tuition reimbursements, teaching assistantships with partial tuition reimbursements, institutionally sponsored loans, scholarships/grants, and unspecified assistantships available. Support available to part-time students. Financial award application deadline: 5/1; financial award applicants required to submit FAFSA. *Unit head:* Dr. Suzette Nynas, Director, 406-657-2351, E-mail: snynas@msubillings.edu. *Application contact:* David M. Sullivan, Graduate Studies Counselor, 406-657-2053, Fax: 406-657-2299, E-mail: dsullivan@msubillings.edu.

Moravian College, Graduate and Continuing Studies, Rehabilitation Science Programs, Bethlehem, PA 18018-6650. Offers athletic training (MS). *Faculty:* 2 full-time (1 woman). *Students:* 7 full-time (4 women); includes 1 minority (Hispanic/Latino). Average age 22. 9 applicants, 100% accepted, 7 enrolled. *Entrance requirements:* For master's, GRE, official transcripts, bachelor's degree from accredited institution, minimum undergraduate GPA of 3.0, documentation of clinical observation with supervision of certified/licensed athletic trainer, interview, essay. *Application deadline:* For fall admission, 8/1 priority date for domestic and international students; for spring admission, 1/1 priority date for domestic and international students; for summer admission, 5/1 priority date for domestic and international students. Applications are processed on a rolling basis. Electronic applications accepted. *Expenses:* Contact institution. *Financial support:* In 2016–17, 2 students received support, including 1 teaching assistantship with full tuition reimbursement available. Financial award applicants required to submit FAFSA. *Faculty research:* Shortwave diathermy, cryotherapy, iontophoresis, immersion clinical education, sacroiliac joint. *Unit head:* Dr. James Scifers, Chair, 610-625-7210, E-mail: scifersj@moravian.edu. *Application contact:* Kristy Sullivan, Director of Student Recruitment Operations, 610-861-1400, Fax: 610-861-1466, E-mail: graduate@moravian.edu.

North Dakota State University, College of Graduate and Interdisciplinary Studies, College of Human Development and Education, Department of Health, Nutrition, and Exercise Sciences, Fargo, ND 58102. Offers athletic training (MAT, MS); dietetics (MS); exercise science and nutrition (PhD); exercise/nutrition science (MS); health promotion (MPH); leadership in physical education and sport (MS). *Program availability:* Part-time, evening/weekend, online learning. *Degree requirements:* For master's, thesis (for some programs). *Entrance requirements:* For master's, minimum GPA of 3.0. Additional exam requirements/recommendations for international students: Required—TOEFL (minimum score 525 paper-based; 71 iBT). Electronic applications accepted. *Faculty research:* Biomechanics, sport specialization, recreation, nutrition, athletic training.

Ohio University, Graduate College, College of Health Sciences and Professions, School of Applied Health Sciences and Wellness, Program in Athletic Training, Athens, OH 45701-2979. Offers MS. *Entrance requirements:* For master's, GRE. Additional exam requirements/recommendations for international students: Required—TOEFL (minimum score 550 paper-based; 80 iBT) or IELTS (minimum score 7.5). Application fee: $50 ($55 for international students). *Financial support:* Teaching assistantships with full tuition reimbursements, Federal Work-Study, and unspecified assistantships available. Financial award application deadline: 2/15. *Faculty research:* Athletic training, heart, injuries, health, muscles, exercise, sport. *Unit head:* Dr. Chad Starkey, Coordinator, 740-593-1217, Fax: 740-593-0284, E-mail: starkeyc@ohio.edu. *Application contact:* Marnie Miller, Graduate Admissions, 740-593-2800, Fax: 740-593-4625, E-mail: graduate@ohio.edu.
Website: http://www.ohio.edu/chsp/ahsw/academics/atg.cfm

Old Dominion University, College of Health Sciences, School of Physical Therapy and Athletic Training, Program in Athletic Training, Norfolk, VA 23529. Offers MSAT. *Faculty:* 4 full-time (3 women). *Students:* 19 full-time (10 women); includes 2 minority (both Hispanic/Latino). Average age 23. 55 applicants, 18% accepted, 10 enrolled. In 2016, 10 master's awarded. *Degree requirements:* For master's, variable foreign language requirement, comprehensive exam, thesis or alternative. *Entrance requirements:* For master's, GRE, bachelor's degree, minimum undergraduate GPA of 3.0 overall and in all

science/athletic training prerequisite course work, three letters of recommendation, two-page statement of career goals, current copy of resume, transcripts. Additional exam requirements/recommendations for international students: Required—TOEFL (minimum score 550 paper-based; 79 iBT). *Application deadline:* For fall admission, 1/1 for domestic students. Applications are processed on a rolling basis. Application fee: $50. Electronic applications accepted. *Expenses:* Contact institution. *Financial support:* In 2016–17, 10 students received support, including 10 research assistantships with partial tuition reimbursements available (averaging $15,000 per year). Financial award application deadline: 4/15. *Faculty research:* Patient outcomes, chronic ankle instability, standardized patients, student learning outcomes, lower extremity injuries. *Total annual research expenditures:* $11,040. *Unit head:* Dr. Bonnie L. Van Lunen, Director, 757-683-4519, Fax: 757-683-4410, E-mail: bvanlune@odu.edu. *Application contact:* William Heffelfinger, Director of Graduate Admissions, 757-683-5554, Fax: 757-683-3255, E-mail: gradadmit@odu.edu.
Website: http://www.odu.edu/ptat

Oregon State University, College of Public Health and Human Sciences, Program in Athletic Training, Corvallis, OR 97331. Offers MATRN. *Faculty:* 3 full-time (1 woman). *Students:* 9 full-time (6 women). 10 applicants, 90% accepted, 8 enrolled. *Entrance requirements:* For master's, GRE, baccalaureate degree; two letters of recommendation; personal statement; minimum of 50 hours of work, volunteering and/or observation under a certified athletic trainer. *Application deadline:* For fall admission, 1/1 priority date for domestic and international students. Application fee: $75 ($85 for international students). Electronic applications accepted. *Expenses:* Tuition, state resident: full-time $12,150; part-time $450 per credit. Tuition, nonresident: full-time $21,789; part-time $807 per credit. *Required fees:* $1651; $1507 per credit. One-time fee: $350. Tuition and fees vary according to course load, campus/location and program. *Unit head:* Kim Hannigan, Director and Associate Professor, 541-737-5314, E-mail: kim.hannigan-downs@oregonstate.edu.
Website: http://health.oregonstate.edu/degrees/athletic-training

Pacific University, School of Physical Therapy, Forest Grove, OR 97116-1797. Offers athletic training (MSAT); physical therapy (DPT). *Accreditation:* APTA. *Degree requirements:* For doctorate, evidence-based capstone project thesis. *Entrance requirements:* For doctorate, 100 hours of volunteer/observational hours, minimum cumulative GPA of 3.0, prerequisite courses with a C grade or better, minimum GPA of 2.5 in science/statistics. Additional exam requirements/recommendations for international students: Required—TOEFL (minimum score 600 paper-based). Electronic applications accepted. *Expenses:* Contact institution. *Faculty research:* Balance disorders, geriatrics, orthopedic treatment outcomes, obesity, women's health.

Philadelphia University, College of Science, Health and the Liberal Arts, Program in Athletic Training, Philadelphia, PA 19144. Offers MS.

Plymouth State University, College of Graduate Studies, Graduate Studies in Education, Program in Athletic Training, Plymouth, NH 03264-1595. Offers MS. *Program availability:* Part-time, evening/weekend. *Entrance requirements:* For master's, MAT, GRE General Test.

Saint Louis University, Graduate Education, Doisy College of Health Sciences, Department of Physical Therapy, St. Louis, MO 63103. Offers athletic training (MAT); physical therapy (DPT). *Accreditation:* APTA. *Program availability:* Part-time. *Entrance requirements:* Additional exam requirements/recommendations for international students: Required—TOEFL (minimum score 525 paper-based; 55 iBT). Electronic applications accepted. *Faculty research:* Patellofemoral pain and associated risk factors; prevalence of disordered eating in physical therapy students; effects of selected interventions for children with cerebral palsy on gait and posture: hippotherapy, ankle strengthening, supported treadmill training, spirituality in physical therapy/patient care, risk factors for exercise-related leg pain in running athletes.

Salisbury University, Program in Athletic Training, Salisbury, MD 21801-6837. Offers MSAT. *Faculty:* 2 full-time (both women). *Students:* 5 full-time (4 women); includes 1 minority (Hispanic/Latino). Average age 22. 1 applicant, 100% accepted. *Entrance requirements:* Additional exam requirements/recommendations for international students: Required—TOEFL (minimum score 550 paper-based, 79 iBT) or IELTS (6.5). *Application deadline:* For summer admission, 3/15 priority date for domestic and international students. Applications are processed on a rolling basis. Application fee: $65. Electronic applications accepted. *Expenses:* $600 per credit hour resident tuition, $750 per credit hour non-resident tuition; $84 per credit hour fees. *Financial support:* Career-related internships or fieldwork and scholarships/grants available. Support available to part-time students. Financial award application deadline: 3/1; financial award applicants required to submit FAFSA. *Faculty research:* Concussion; student learning; rehabilitation outcomes; knee injuries; problem based learning. *Unit head:* Dr. Jenny Toonstra, Graduate Program Director, Athletic Training, 410-677-5493, E-mail: jltoonstra@salisbury.edu.
Website: http://www.salisbury.edu/gsr/gradstudies/MSATpage.html

Samford University, School of Health Professions, Birmingham, AL 35229. Offers athletic training (MAT); physical therapy (DPT); respiratory care (MS); speech language pathology (MS). *Faculty:* 19 full-time (12 women). *Students:* 102 full-time (74 women); includes 5 minority (1 Asian, non-Hispanic/Latino; 2 Hispanic/Latino; 2 Two or more races, non-Hispanic/Latino). Average age 24. 244 applicants, 44% accepted, 58 enrolled. *Degree requirements:* For master's, thesis or alternative; for doctorate, thesis/dissertation or alternative. *Entrance requirements:* For master's and doctorate, GRE, recommendations, resume, on-campus interview, personal statement. Additional exam requirements/recommendations for international students: Required—TOEFL (minimum score 550 paper-based). *Application deadline:* For fall admission, 6/1 for domestic students; for spring admission, 10/1 for domestic students. Application fee: $120. Electronic applications accepted. *Expenses:* Contact institution. *Financial support:* In 2016–17, 7 students received support. Application deadline: 3/1; applicants required to submit FAFSA. *Faculty research:* Parkinson's disease. *Unit head:* Dr. Alan P. Jung, Dean, School of Health Professions, 205-726-2716, E-mail: apjung@samford.edu. *Application contact:* Dr. Marian Carter, Assistant Dean of Enrollment Management and Student Services, 205-726-2611, E-mail: mwcarter@samford.edu.
Website: http://www.samford.edu/healthprofessions/

San Jose State University, Graduate Studies and Research, College of Applied Sciences and Arts, San Jose, CA 95192-0001. Offers big data (Certificate); California library media teacher services (Credential); collaborative response to family violence (Certificate); justice studies (MS); kinesiology (MA), including applied sciences and arts (MA, MS), athletic training, exercise physiology, sport management, sport studies; library and information science (MLIS, Certificate); mass communication (MA); nutritional science (MS); occupational therapy (MS); public health (MPH); pupil personnel services (Credential); recreation (MS), including applied sciences and arts (MA, MS), international tourism; social work (MSW); Spanish language counseling (Certificate); strategic management of digital assets and services (Certificate). *Program availability:* Part-time, evening/weekend. Electronic applications accepted.

Seton Hall University, School of Health and Medical Sciences, Program in Athletic Training, South Orange, NJ 07079-2697. Offers MS. *Degree requirements:* For master's, research project. *Entrance requirements:* Additional exam requirements/recommendations for international students: Required—TOEFL. Electronic applications accepted. *Faculty research:* Electrotherapy

Shenandoah University, School of Health Professions, Winchester, VA 22601-5195. Offers athletic training (MS); occupational therapy (MS); performing arts medicine (Certificate); physical therapy (DPT); physician assistant studies (MS). *Program availability:* Online learning. *Faculty:* 34 full-time (27 women), 28 part-time/adjunct (16 women). *Students:* 420 full-time (334 women), 131 part-time (104 women); includes 90 minority (16 Black or African American, non-Hispanic/Latino; 36 Asian, non-Hispanic/Latino; 26 Hispanic/Latino; 1 Native Hawaiian or other Pacific Islander, non-Hispanic/Latino; 11 Two or more races, non-Hispanic/Latino), 17 international. Average age 28. 1,511 applicants, 27% accepted, 227 enrolled. In 2016, 91 master's, 77 doctorates awarded. *Degree requirements:* For master's, comprehensive exam, thesis (for some programs), evidence-based practice research or quality improvement project; for doctorate, comprehensive exam, thesis/dissertation, evidence-based practice research project. *Entrance requirements:* For master's, GRE, interview on campus with athletic training faculty; athletic experience documentation listing all sports; interview, shadowing/volunteer experience, and recommendation letters (for most programs); for doctorate, GRE, PCAT; for Certificate, GRE (minimum recommended combined score of 297), minimum overall GPA of 2.8 for undergraduate prerequisite courses (3.0 recommended in science/math courses); interview on campus with Division of Athletic Training faculty; athletic experience documentation listing all sports. Additional exam requirements/recommendations for international students: Required—TOEFL (minimum score 558 paper-based; 83 iBT). *Application deadline:* For fall admission, 7/1 for domestic and international students; for summer admission, 4/1 for domestic and international students. Application fee: $30. Electronic applications accepted. *Expenses:* Contact institution. *Financial support:* In 2016–17, 51 students received support. Scholarships/grants and unspecified assistantships available. Financial award applicants required to submit FAFSA. *Faculty research:* 3D motion analysis of running mechanics; quality improvement in clinical practice; functional movement screen to predict injury in professional athletes and dancer; sensory integration for children with autism; chronic ankle instability. *Total annual research expenditures:* $10,000. *Unit head:* Karen Abraham, PhD, Interim Dean of Health Professions, 540-545-6209, Fax: 540-665.5564, E-mail: kabraham@su.edu. *Application contact:* Andrew Woodall, Executive Director of Recruitment and Admissions, 540-665-4581, Fax: 540-665-4627, E-mail: admit@su.edu.
Website: http://www.health.su.edu/

South Dakota State University, Graduate School, College of Education and Human Sciences, Department of Health and Nutritional Sciences, Brookings, SD 57007. Offers athletic training (MS); dietetics (MS); nutrition and exercise sciences (MS, PhD); sport and recreation studies (MS). *Program availability:* Part-time. *Degree requirements:* For master's, comprehensive exam (for some programs), thesis (for some programs), oral exam. *Entrance requirements:* Additional exam requirements/recommendations for international students: Required—TOEFL (minimum score 525 paper-based). *Faculty research:* Food chemistry, bone density, functional food, nutrition education, nutrition biochemistry.

Spalding University, Graduate Studies, Kosair College of Health and Natural Sciences, Program in Athletic Training, Louisville, KY 40203-2188. Offers MS. *Faculty:* 8 full-time (6 women), 1 (woman) part-time/adjunct. *Students:* 23 full-time (14 women); includes 7 minority (6 Black or African American, non-Hispanic/Latino; 1 Native Hawaiian or other Pacific Islander, non-Hispanic/Latino). Average age 27. 11 applicants, 73% accepted, 8 enrolled. In 2016, 5 master's awarded. *Entrance requirements:* For master's, transcripts, letter of recommendation, 20 observation hours, interview, writing sample. Additional exam requirements/recommendations for international students: Required—TOEFL (minimum score 535 paper-based). *Application deadline:* Applications are processed on a rolling basis. Application fee: $30. Application fee is waived when completed online. *Expenses: Tuition:* Full-time $15,300. *Financial support:* In 2016–17, 3 research assistantships (averaging $3,140 per year) were awarded; career-related internships or fieldwork, scholarships/grants, and unspecified assistantships also available. Financial award applicants required to submit FAFSA. *Unit head:* Dr. John Nyland, Director, 502-873-4224, E-mail: jnyland@spalding.edu. *Application contact:* Admissions Office, 502-585-7111, E-mail: admissions@spalding.edu.
Website: https://spalding.edu/academics/athletic-training/

Springfield College, Graduate Programs, Programs in Exercise Science and Sport Studies, Springfield, MA 01109-3797. Offers athletic training (MS); exercise physiology (MS); health promotion and disease prevention (MS); sport and exercise psychology (MS). *Program availability:* Part-time. Terminal master's awarded for partial completion of doctoral program. *Degree requirements:* For master's, comprehensive exam, research project or thesis; for doctorate, comprehensive exam, thesis/dissertation. *Entrance requirements:* For master's and doctorate, GRE General Test. Additional exam requirements/recommendations for international students: Required—TOEFL (minimum score 550 paper-based); Recommended—IELTS (minimum score 6). Electronic applications accepted. *Expenses: Tuition:* Full-time $29,640; part-time $988 per credit. *Required fees:* $195.

Stephen F. Austin State University, Graduate School, College of Education, Department of Kinesiology and Health Science, Nacogdoches, TX 75962. Offers athletic training (MS); kinesiology (M Ed). *Degree requirements:* For master's, comprehensive exam. *Entrance requirements:* For master's, GRE General Test. Additional exam requirements/recommendations for international students: Required—TOEFL.

Tarleton State University, College of Graduate Studies, College of Education, Department of Kinesiology, Stephenville, TX 76402. Offers athletic training (MS); kinesiology (MS). *Program availability:* Part-time, evening/weekend. *Faculty:* 8 full-time (2 women), 1 (woman) part-time/adjunct. *Students:* 25 full-time (11 women), 43 part-time (25 women); includes 19 minority (13 Black or African American, non-Hispanic/Latino; 5 Hispanic/Latino; 1 Two or more races, non-Hispanic/Latino), 1 international. 28 applicants, 96% accepted, 22 enrolled. In 2016, 32 master's awarded. *Degree requirements:* For master's, comprehensive exam, thesis optional. *Entrance requirements:* For master's, GRE General Test, minimum GPA of 3.0. Additional exam requirements/recommendations for international students: Required—TOEFL (minimum score 550 paper-based; 80 iBT). *Application deadline:* For fall admission, 8/15 priority date for domestic students; for spring admission, 1/7 for domestic students. Applications are processed on a rolling basis. Application fee: $45 ($145 for international students). Electronic applications accepted. *Expenses:* $3,672 tuition; $2,437 fees. *Financial support:* Research assistantships, teaching assistantships with partial tuition reimbursements, career-related internships or fieldwork, Federal Work-Study, and institutionally sponsored loans available. Support available to part-time students. Financial award application deadline: 5/1; financial award applicants required to submit FAFSA. *Unit head:* Dr. Steve Simpson, Department Head, 254-968-9756, E-mail: simpson@tarleton.edu. *Application contact:* Information Contact, 254-968-9104, Fax: 254-968-9670, E-mail: gradoffice@tarleton.edu.
Website: http://www.tarleton.edu/kinesiology/

Temple University, College of Public Health, Department of Kinesiology, Philadelphia, PA 19122. Offers athletic training (MSAT, DAT); kinesiology (MS, PhD); neuromotor science (MS, PhD). *Program availability:* Part-time. *Faculty:* 16 full-time (6 women), 6

part-time/adjunct (2 women). *Students:* 38 full-time (28 women), 23 part-time (9 women); includes 15 minority (4 Black or African American, non-Hispanic/Latino; 1 Asian, non-Hispanic/Latino; 8 Hispanic/Latino; 2 Two or more races, non-Hispanic/Latino), 6 international. 74 applicants, 66% accepted, 35 enrolled. In 2016, 26 master's, 5 doctorates awarded. Terminal master's awarded for partial completion of doctoral program. *Degree requirements:* For master's, thesis, final project; for doctorate, comprehensive exam, thesis/dissertation. *Entrance requirements:* For master's, GRE General Test or MAT, minimum undergraduate GPA of 3.0, 3 letters of reference, statement of goals, interview, resume; for doctorate, GRE General Test, minimum undergraduate GPA of 3.0, 3 letters of reference, statement of goals, interview, resume. Additional exam requirements/recommendations for international students: Required—TOEFL (minimum score 550 paper-based; 79 iBT). *Application deadline:* For fall admission, 1/15 for domestic students, 12/15 for international students; for spring admission, 10/1 for domestic students, 8/1 for international students. Applications are processed on a rolling basis. Application fee: $60. Electronic applications accepted. *Expenses:* Contact institution. *Financial support:* Fellowships, research assistantships with tuition reimbursements, teaching assistantships with tuition reimbursements, career-related internships or fieldwork, Federal Work-Study, scholarships/grants, tuition waivers, and unspecified assistantships available. Financial award application deadline: 1/15. *Faculty research:* Exercise physiology, athletic training, motor neuroscience, exercise and sports psychology. *Unit head:* John Jeka, Chair, 214-204-4405, Fax: 215-204-4414, E-mail: jjeka@temple.edu. *Application contact:* Rosalind Robinson, Department Coordinator, E-mail: rosalind.robinson@temple.edu.
Website: http://cph.temple.edu/kinesiology/home

Texas A&M University, College of Education and Human Development, Department of Health and Kinesiology, College Station, TX 77843. Offers athletic training (MS); health education (M Ed, MS, Ed D, PhD); kinesiology (MS, PhD); sports management (MS). *Program availability:* Part-time. *Faculty:* 56. *Students:* 216 full-time (119 women), 116 part-time (55 women); includes 100 minority (37 Black or African American, non-Hispanic/Latino; 9 Asian, non-Hispanic/Latino; 49 Hispanic/Latino; 5 Two or more races, non-Hispanic/Latino), 28 international. Average age 29. 169 applicants, 72% accepted, 77 enrolled. In 2016, 104 master's, 24 doctorates awarded. *Degree requirements:* For master's, thesis (for some programs); for doctorate, comprehensive exam, thesis/dissertation. *Entrance requirements:* For master's and doctorate, GRE General Test. Additional exam requirements/recommendations for international students: Required—TOEFL (minimum score 550 paper-based; 80 iBT), IELTS (minimum score 6), PTE (minimum score 53). *Application deadline:* For fall admission, 1/15 for domestic students; for spring admission, 10/1 for domestic students. Applications are processed on a rolling basis. Application fee: $50 ($90 for international students). Electronic applications accepted. *Expenses:* Contact institution. *Financial support:* In 2016–17, 172 students received support, including 3 fellowships with tuition reimbursements available (averaging $18,412 per year), 43 research assistantships with tuition reimbursements available (averaging $5,089 per year), 76 teaching assistantships with tuition reimbursements available (averaging $8,295 per year); career-related internships or fieldwork, institutionally sponsored loans, scholarships/grants, traineeships, health care benefits, tuition waivers (full and partial), and unspecified assistantships also available. Support available to part-time students. Financial award application deadline: 3/15; financial award applicants required to submit FAFSA. *Unit head:* Dr. Richard Kreider, Head, 979-845-1333, Fax: 979-847-8987, E-mail: rkreider@hlkn.tamu.edu. *Application contact:* Jenny Bilski, Academic Advisor, 979-862-4052, E-mail: jenny.bilski@tamu.edu.
Website: http://hlknweb.tamu.edu/

Texas State University, The Graduate College, College of Education, Program in Athletic Training, San Marcos, TX 78666. Offers MS. *Faculty:* 3 full-time (1 woman), 2 part-time/adjunct (1 woman). *Students:* 32 full-time (15 women); includes 12 minority (3 Black or African American, non-Hispanic/Latino; 1 Asian, non-Hispanic/Latino; 8 Hispanic/Latino), 1 international. Average age 24. 63 applicants, 48% accepted, 19 enrolled. In 2016, 13 master's awarded. *Degree requirements:* For master's, comprehensive exam, thesis optional. *Entrance requirements:* For master's, baccalaureate degree from regionally-accredited institution with minimum GPA of 3.0 in last 60 hours of undergraduate work, statement of purpose, resume, Athletic Trainer Certification or eligible to sit for the exam, 3 recommendation forms. Additional exam requirements/recommendations for international students: Required—TOEFL (minimum score 550 paper-based; 78 iBT), IELTS (minimum score 6.5). *Application deadline:* For fall admission, 1/15 priority date for domestic and international students; for spring admission, 10/15 for domestic students, 10/1 for international students; for summer admission, 4/15 for domestic students, 3/15 for international students. Applications are processed on a rolling basis. Application fee: $40 ($90 for international students). Electronic applications accepted. *Expenses:* $4,851 per semester. *Financial support:* In 2016–17, 5 students received support, including 31 teaching assistantships (averaging $13,969 per year); research assistantships, Federal Work-Study, scholarships/grants, and unspecified assistantships also available. Financial award application deadline: 3/1; financial award applicants required to submit FAFSA. *Faculty research:* Effects of magnitude and number of head impacts on vestibular function. *Unit head:* Dr. Rod Harter, Graduate Advisor, 512-245-2972, E-mail: rh56@txstate.edu. *Application contact:* Dr. Andrea Golato, Dean of the Graduate College, 512-245-2581, Fax: 512-245-8365, E-mail: gradcollege@txstate.edu.
Website: http://www.hhp.txstate.edu/Degree-Plans/Graduate.html

Texas Tech University Health Sciences Center, School of Health Professions, Program in Athletic Training, Lubbock, TX 79430. Offers MAT. *Faculty:* 4 full-time (2 women). *Students:* 46 full-time (29 women), 2 part-time (1 woman); includes 18 minority (7 Black or African American, non-Hispanic/Latino; 2 Asian, non-Hispanic/Latino; 9 Hispanic/Latino). Average age 24. 88 applicants, 25% accepted, 22 enrolled. In 2016, 26 master's awarded. *Entrance requirements:* Additional exam requirements/recommendations for international students: Required—TOEFL (minimum score 550 paper-based; 79 iBT), IELTS. *Application deadline:* For summer admission, 2/1 for domestic students. Applications are processed on a rolling basis. Application fee: $40. Electronic applications accepted. *Expenses:* Contact institution. *Financial support:* Career-related internships or fieldwork, institutionally sponsored loans, and scholarships/grants available. Financial award application deadline: 9/1; financial award applicants required to submit FAFSA. *Unit head:* Dr. LesLee Taylor, Program Director, 806-743-1032, Fax: 806-743-2189, E-mail: leslee.taylor@ttuhsc.edu. *Application contact:* Lindsay Johnson, Associate Dean for Admissions and Student Affairs, 806-743-3220, Fax: 806-743-2994, E-mail: lindsay.johnson@ttuhsc.edu.
Website: http://www.ttuhsc.edu/health-professions/master-athletic-training/

Trinity International University, Trinity Graduate School, Deerfield, IL 60015-1284. Offers athletic training (MA); bioethics (MA); counseling psychology (MA); diverse learning (M Ed); leadership (MA); teaching (MA). *Program availability:* Part-time, evening/weekend, online learning. *Degree requirements:* For master's, comprehensive exam. *Entrance requirements:* For master's, GRE General Test or MAT, minimum undergraduate GPA of 3.0. Additional exam requirements/recommendations for international students: Required—TOEFL (minimum score 580 paper-based), TWE (minimum score 4). *Application deadline:* For fall admission, 8/1 priority date for domestic students, 5/1 for international students; for spring admission, 12/1 priority date for domestic students, 12/1 for international students. Applications are processed on a rolling basis. Application fee: $25. Electronic applications accepted. *Expenses: Tuition:* Full-time $19,898. *Required fees:* $200. *Financial support:* Career-related internships or fieldwork, Federal Work-Study, institutionally sponsored loans, and tuition waivers (partial) available. Support available to part-time students. Financial award application deadline: 4/1; financial award applicants required to submit FAFSA. *Unit head:* Dr. Thomas Cornman, Dean, 847-317-7001, Fax: 847-317-4786. *Application contact:* Blaise Brankatelli, Director of Graduate Admissions, 847-317-8000, Fax: 847-317-8097, E-mail: gradadmissions@tiu.edu.
Website: https://graduate.tiu.edu/

United States Sports Academy, Graduate Programs, Program in Sports Medicine, Daphne, AL 36526-7055. Offers MSS. *Program availability:* Part-time, online learning. *Degree requirements:* For master's, comprehensive exam, thesis optional. *Entrance requirements:* For master's, GRE General Test, GMAT, or MAT, minimum GPA of 2.5, 3 letters of recommendation, resume. Additional exam requirements/recommendations for international students: Required—TOEFL (minimum score 500 paper-based). Electronic applications accepted. *Faculty research:* Psychiatric aspects of injury rehabilitation, geriatric exercises and mobility.

Universidad del Turabo, Graduate Programs, Programs in Education, Program in Athletic Therapeutic, Gurabo, PR 00778-3030. Offers MPHE. *Program availability:* Part-time, evening/weekend. *Students:* 26 full-time (10 women), 3 part-time (0 women); all minorities (all Hispanic/Latino). Average age 27. 23 applicants, 74% accepted, 15 enrolled. In 2016, 9 master's awarded. *Entrance requirements:* For master's, GRE, EXADEP, GMAT, interview, official transcript, essay, recommendation letters. *Application deadline:* For fall admission, 8/5 for domestic students. Applications are processed on a rolling basis. Application fee: $25. Electronic applications accepted. *Financial support:* Institutionally sponsored loans available. Financial award applicants required to submit FAFSA. *Unit head:* Jorge Garofalo, Dean, 787-743-7979. *Application contact:* Diriee Rodríguez, Admission's Director, 787-743-7979 Ext. 4453, E-mail: admisiones-ut@suagm.edu.
Website: http://ut.suagm.edu/es/educacion

University of Arkansas, Graduate School, College of Education and Health Professions, Department of Health, Human Performance and Recreation, Program in Athletic Training, Fayetteville, AR 72701. Offers MAT. In 2016, 15 master's awarded. *Application deadline:* For fall admission, 4/1 for international students; for spring admission, 10/1 for international students. Applications are processed on a rolling basis. Electronic applications accepted. *Financial support:* In 2016–17, 2 research assistantships were awarded; teaching assistantships also available. *Unit head:* Dr. Bart Hammig, Department Head, 479-575-2858, Fax: 479-575-5778, E-mail: bhammig@uark.edu. *Application contact:* Dr. Stephen Dittmore, Coordinator of Graduate Studies, 479-575-6625, Fax: 479-575-5778, E-mail: dittmore@uark.edu.
Website: http://kins.uark.edu/

University of Central Oklahoma, The Jackson College of Graduate Studies, College of Education and Professional Studies, Department of Kinesiology and Health Studies, Edmond, OK 73034-5209. Offers athletic training (MS); wellness management (MS), including exercise science, health studies. *Degree requirements:* For master's, comprehensive exam (for some programs), thesis (for some programs). *Entrance requirements:* For master's, GRE. Additional exam requirements/recommendations for international students: Required—TOEFL (minimum score 550 paper-based; 79 iBT), IELTS (minimum score 6.5). Electronic applications accepted.

University of Evansville, College of Education and Health Sciences, School of Health Sciences, Evansville, IN 47722. Offers athletic training (MSAT); health policy (MPH); health services administration (MS). *Program availability:* Part-time, evening/weekend. *Entrance requirements:* Additional exam requirements/recommendations for international students: Required—TOEFL, IELTS (minimum score 6.5). *Application deadline:* For fall admission, 7/1 for domestic and international students; for spring admission, 10/1 for domestic students. Application fee: $35. *Expenses:* Contact institution. *Financial support:* Unspecified assistantships available. Financial award application deadline: 6/1; financial award applicants required to submit FAFSA. *Unit head:* Dr. William Stroube, Chair, 812-488-2870, Fax: 812-488-2087, E-mail: bs52@evansville.edu.
Website: https://www.evansville.edu/schools/healthsciences/

The University of Findlay, Office of Graduate Admissions, Findlay, OH 45840-3653. Offers applied security and analytics (MSAS); athletic training (MAT); business (MBA), including certified management accountant, certified public accountant, health care management, hospitality management; education (MA Ed, Ed D), including children's literature (MA Ed), curriculum and teaching (MA Ed), education (MA Ed), educational administration (MA Ed), human resource development (MA Ed), reading (MA Ed), science education (MA Ed), superintendent (Ed D), teaching (Ed D), technology (MA Ed); environmental, safety and health management (MSEM); health informatics (MS); occupational therapy (MOT); pharmacy (Pharm D); physical therapy (DPT); physician assistant (MPA); rhetoric and writing (MA); teaching English to speakers of other languages (TESOL) and bilingual education (MA). *Program availability:* Part-time, evening/weekend, 100% online, blended/hybrid learning. *Faculty:* 114 full-time (63 women), 44 part-time/adjunct (18 women). *Students:* 751 full-time (452 women), 573 part-time (323 women); includes 164 minority (82 Black or African American, non-Hispanic/Latino; 1 American Indian or Alaska Native, non-Hispanic/Latino; 27 Asian, non-Hispanic/Latino; 37 Hispanic/Latino; 17 Two or more races, non-Hispanic/Latino), 280 international. Average age 28. 661 applicants, 52% accepted, 288 enrolled. In 2016, 366 master's, 137 doctorates awarded. *Degree requirements:* For master's, comprehensive exam (for some programs), thesis, cumulative project, capstone project; for doctorate, thesis/dissertation. *Entrance requirements:* For master's, GRE (for some programs), bachelor's degree from accredited institution, minimum undergraduate GPA of 3.0 in last 64 hours of course work; for doctorate, MAT, minimum cumulative GPA of 3.0, master's degree. Additional exam requirements/recommendations for international students: Recommended—TOEFL (minimum score 79 iBT), IELTS (minimum score 7). *Application deadline:* For fall admission, 6/15 for international students; for spring admission, 12/1 for international students; for summer admission, 4/1 for international students. Applications are processed on a rolling basis. Electronic applications accepted. *Expenses:* Contact institution. *Financial support:* In 2016–17, 139 students received support, including 15 research assistantships with partial tuition reimbursements available (averaging $7,200 per year), 25 teaching assistantships with partial tuition reimbursements available (averaging $7,200 per year); Federal Work-Study, institutionally sponsored loans, and unspecified assistantships also available. Financial award application deadline: 4/1; financial award applicants required to submit FAFSA. *Unit head:* Christopher M. Harris, Director of Admissions, 419-434-4347, E-mail: harrisc1@findlay.edu. *Application contact:* Madeline Fauser Brennan, Graduate Admissions Counselor, 419-434-4636, Fax: 419-434-4898, E-mail: fauserbrennan@findlay.edu.
Website: http://www.findlay.edu/admissions/graduate/Pages/default.aspx

University of Florida, Graduate School, College of Health and Human Performance, Department of Applied Physiology and Kinesiology, Gainesville, FL 32611. Offers applied physiology and kinesiology (MS); athletic training/sports medicine (MS);

biobehavioral science (MS); clinical exercise physiology (MS); exercise physiology (MS); health and human performance (PhD), including applied physiology and kinesiology, biobehavioral science, exercise physiology; human performance (MS). *Degree requirements:* For master's, comprehensive exam, thesis (for some programs); for doctorate, comprehensive exam, thesis/dissertation. *Entrance requirements:* For master's and doctorate, GRE General Test, minimum GPA of 3.0. Additional exam requirements/recommendations for international students: Required—TOEFL (minimum score 550 paper-based; 80 iBT), IELTS (minimum score 6). Electronic applications accepted. *Faculty research:* Cardiovascular disease; basic mechanisms that underlie exercise-induced changes in the body at the organ, tissue, cellular and molecular level; development of rehabilitation techniques for regaining motor control after stroke or as a consequence of Parkinson's disease; maintaining optimal health and delaying age-related declines in physiological function; psychomotor mechanisms impacting health and performance across the life span.

University of Idaho, College of Graduate Studies, College of Education, Department of Movement Sciences, Moscow, ID 83844. Offers athletic training (MSAT, DAT); movement and leisure sciences (MS); physical education (M Ed). *Faculty:* 14 full-time, 5 part-time/adjunct. *Students:* 79 full-time (41 women), 24 part-time (12 women). Average age 30. In 2016, 24 master's awarded. *Degree requirements:* For doctorate, thesis/dissertation. *Entrance requirements:* For master's and doctorate, minimum GPA of 3.0. Additional exam requirements/recommendations for international students: Required—TOEFL. *Application deadline:* For fall admission, 8/1 for domestic students; for spring admission, 12/15 for domestic students. Applications are processed on a rolling basis. Application fee: $60. Electronic applications accepted. *Expenses:* Tuition, state resident: full-time $6460; part-time $414 per credit hour. Tuition, nonresident: full-time $21,268; part-time $1237 per credit hour. *Required fees:* $2070; $60 per credit hour. Full-time tuition and fees vary according to course load and reciprocity agreements. *Financial support:* Research assistantships and teaching assistantships available. Financial award applicants required to submit FAFSA. *Unit head:* Dr. Philip W. Scruggs, Chair, 208-885-7921, E-mail: movementsciences@uidaho.edu. *Application contact:* Sean Scoggin, Graduate Recruitment Coordinator, 208-885-4001, Fax: 208-885-4406, E-mail: graduateadmissions@uidaho.edu.
Website: https://www.uidaho.edu/ed/mvsc

The University of Iowa, Graduate College, College of Liberal Arts and Sciences, Department of Health and Human Physiology, Iowa City, IA 52242-1316. Offers athletic training (MS); clinical exercise physiology (MS); health and human physiology (PhD); leisure studies (MA, PhD), including recreational sport management (PhD), therapeutic recreation (MA). *Degree requirements:* For master's, thesis optional, exam; for doctorate, comprehensive exam, thesis/dissertation. *Entrance requirements:* For master's and doctorate, GRE General Test, minimum GPA of 3.0. Additional exam requirements/recommendations for international students: Required—TOEFL (minimum score 600 paper-based; 100 iBT). Electronic applications accepted.

University of Kentucky, Graduate School, College of Health Sciences, Division of Athletic Training, Lexington, KY 40506-0032. Offers MS.

University of Miami, Graduate School, School of Education and Human Development, Department of Kinesiology and Sport Sciences, Program in Exercise Physiology, Coral Gables, FL 33124. Offers exercise physiology (MS Ed, PhD); strength and conditioning (MS Ed). *Program availability:* Part-time, evening/weekend. *Faculty:* 4 full-time (1 woman). *Students:* 46 full-time (16 women), 5 part-time (2 women); includes 20 minority (2 Black or African American, non-Hispanic/Latino; 3 Asian, non-Hispanic/Latino; 10 Hispanic/Latino; 5 Two or more races, non-Hispanic/Latino), 4 international. Average age 28. 75 applicants, 49% accepted, 21 enrolled. In 2016, 16 master's, 5 doctorates awarded. Terminal master's awarded for partial completion of doctoral program. *Degree requirements:* For master's, comprehensive exam (for some programs), thesis optional, special project; for doctorate, thesis/dissertation, qualifying exam. *Entrance requirements:* For master's and doctorate, GRE General Test. Additional exam requirements/recommendations for international students: Required—TOEFL (minimum score 550 paper-based; 80 iBT); Recommended—IELTS (minimum score 6.5). *Application deadline:* For fall admission, 10/1 for international students; for spring admission, 10/1 for international students. Applications are processed on a rolling basis. Application fee: $65. Electronic applications accepted. *Financial support:* Fellowships, research assistantships, teaching assistantships, health care benefits, tuition waivers (full and partial), and unspecified assistantships available. Support available to part-time students. Financial award application deadline: 3/1; financial award applicants required to submit FAFSA. *Faculty research:* Women's health, cardiovascular health, aging, metabolism, obesity. *Unit head:* Dr. Kevin Jacobs, Associate Professor and Program Director, 305-284-5873, E-mail: k.jacobs@miami.edu. *Application contact:* Lois Heffernan, Graduate Admissions Coordinator, 305-284-2167, Fax: 305-284-9395, E-mail: lheffernan@miami.edu.
Website: http://www.education.miami.edu

University of Miami, Graduate School, School of Education and Human Development, Department of Kinesiology and Sport Sciences, Program in Sports Medicine, Coral Gables, FL 33124. Offers athletic training (MS Ed). *Program availability:* Part-time, evening/weekend. *Degree requirements:* For master's, comprehensive exam, thesis optional, special project. *Entrance requirements:* For master's, GRE General Test. Additional exam requirements/recommendations for international students: Required—TOEFL (minimum score 550 paper-based; 80 iBT); Recommended—IELTS (minimum score 6.5). *Application deadline:* Applications are processed on a rolling basis. Application fee: $65. Electronic applications accepted. *Financial support:* Available to part-time students. Application deadline: 3/1; applicants required to submit FAFSA. *Faculty research:* Care, prevention, and treatment of athletic injuries. *Unit head:* Dr. Kysha Harriell, Associate Professor of Professional Practice, 305-284-3201, Fax: 305-284-5168, E-mail: kharriell@miami.edu. *Application contact:* Lois Heffernan, Graduate Admissions Coordinator, 305-284-2167, Fax: 305-284-9395, E-mail: lheffernan@miami.edu.
Website: http://www.education.miami.edu

University of Nebraska at Omaha, Graduate Studies, College of Education, School of Health and Kinesiology, Omaha, NE 68182. Offers athletic training (MA); exercise science (PhD); health, physical education, and recreation (MA, MS). *Program availability:* Part-time, evening/weekend. *Faculty:* 7 full-time (2 women). *Students:* 79 full-time (31 women), 28 part-time (13 women); includes 8 minority (2 Black or African American, non-Hispanic/Latino; 1 Asian, non-Hispanic/Latino; 2 Hispanic/Latino; 3 Two or more races, non-Hispanic/Latino), 18 international. Average age 26. 65 applicants, 74% accepted, 34 enrolled. In 2016, 38 master's, 1 doctorate awarded. *Degree requirements:* For master's, comprehensive exam, thesis (for some programs). *Entrance requirements:* For master's, GRE; entrance exam, minimum GPA of 3.0, official transcripts, statement of purpose, 2 letters of recommendation; for doctorate, GRE, minimum GPA of 3.2, official transcripts, statement of purpose, 3 letters of recommendation, resume, writing sample. Additional exam requirements/recommendations for international students: Required—TOEFL, IELTS, PTE. *Application deadline:* For fall admission, 7/1 priority date for domestic and international students; for spring admission, 11/1 priority date for domestic and international students; for summer admission, 1/15 for domestic and international students. Applications are processed on a rolling basis. Application fee: $45. Electronic applications accepted. *Financial support:* In 2016–17, 47 students received support, including 34 research assistantships with tuition reimbursements available, 13 teaching assistantships with tuition reimbursements available; fellowships, Federal Work-Study, institutionally sponsored loans, scholarships/grants, health care benefits, tuition waivers (full), and unspecified assistantships also available. Support available to part-time students. Financial award application deadline: 3/1; financial award applicants required to submit FAFSA. *Unit head:* Dr. Roland Bulbulian, Director, 402-554-2341, E-mail: graduate@unomaha.edu. *Application contact:* Dr. Dustin Slivka, Graduate Program Chair, 402-554-2341, E-mail: graduate@unomaha.edu.

The University of North Carolina at Chapel Hill, Graduate School, College of Arts and Sciences, Department of Exercise and Sport Science, Chapel Hill, NC 27599. Offers athletic training (MA); exercise physiology (MA); sport administration (MA). *Degree requirements:* For master's, comprehensive exam, thesis. *Entrance requirements:* For master's, GRE General Test, minimum GPA of 3.0. Additional exam requirements/recommendations for international students: Required—TOEFL (minimum score 550 paper-based). Electronic applications accepted. *Faculty research:* Mild head injury in sport, endocrine system's response to exercise, obesity and children, effect of aerobic exercise on cerebral bloodflow in elderly population.

The University of North Carolina at Greensboro, Graduate School, School of Health and Human Sciences, Department of Kinesiology, Greensboro, NC 27412-5001. Offers athletic training (MSAT); kinesiology (MS, Ed D, PhD). *Program availability:* Online learning. *Degree requirements:* For master's, thesis (for some programs); for doctorate, thesis/dissertation. *Entrance requirements:* For master's and doctorate, GRE General Test. Additional exam requirements/recommendations for international students: Required—TOEFL. Electronic applications accepted.

University of Northern Iowa, Graduate College, College of Education, School of Kinesiology, Allied Health and Human Services, MS Program in Athletic Training, Cedar Falls, IA 50614. Offers MS. *Program availability:* Part-time, evening/weekend. *Degree requirements:* For master's, comprehensive exam. *Entrance requirements:* Additional exam requirements/recommendations for international students: Required—TOEFL (minimum score 550 paper-based; 79 iBT). Electronic applications accepted.

University of Pittsburgh, School of Health and Rehabilitation Sciences, Master's Programs in Health and Rehabilitation Sciences, Pittsburgh, PA 15260. Offers health and rehabilitation sciences (MS), including health information systems, healthcare supervision and management, occupational therapy, physical therapy, rehabilitation counseling, rehabilitation science and technology, sports medicine, wellness and human performance. *Accreditation:* APTA. *Program availability:* Part-time, evening/weekend. *Faculty:* 30 full-time (19 women). *Students:* 93 full-time (65 women), 32 part-time (26 women); includes 15 minority (3 Black or African American, non-Hispanic/Latino; 1 American Indian or Alaska Native, non-Hispanic/Latino; 4 Asian, non-Hispanic/Latino; 4 Hispanic/Latino; 3 Two or more races, non-Hispanic/Latino), 58 international. Average age 29. 247 applicants, 64% accepted, 70 enrolled. In 2016, 37 master's awarded. *Degree requirements:* For master's, comprehensive exam (for some programs), thesis optional. *Entrance requirements:* For master's, minimum GPA of 3.0. Additional exam requirements/recommendations for international students: Required—TOEFL (minimum score 550 paper-based; 80 iBT), IELTS (minimum score 6.5). *Application deadline:* For fall admission, 3/1 for international students; for spring admission, 9/1 for international students; for summer admission, 2/1 for international students. Applications are processed on a rolling basis. Application fee: $50. Electronic applications accepted. Tuition and fees vary according to program. *Financial support:* In 2016–17, 6 fellowships with full tuition reimbursements (averaging $17,550 per year), 4 research assistantships with full tuition reimbursements (averaging $21,900 per year) were awarded; traineeships also available. *Faculty research:* Assistive technology, seating and wheelchair mobility, cellular neurophysiology, low back syndrome, augmentative communication. *Total annual research expenditures:* $2.7 million. *Unit head:* Dr. Anthony Delitto, Dean, 412-383-6560, Fax: 412-383-6535, E-mail: delitto@pitt.edu. *Application contact:* Jessica Maguire, Director of Admissions, 412-383-6557, Fax: 412-383-6535, E-mail: maguire@pitt.edu.

University of St. Augustine for Health Sciences, Graduate Programs, Master of Health Science Program, San Marcos, CA 92069. Offers athletic training (MHS); executive leadership (MHS); informatics (MHS); teaching and learning (MHS). *Program availability:* Online learning. *Degree requirements:* For master's, comprehensive project.

University of South Florida, Morsani College of Medicine and College of Graduate Studies, Graduate Programs in Medical Sciences, Tampa, FL 33620-9951. Offers advanced athletic training (MS); athletic training (MS); bioinformatics and computational biology (MSBCB); biotechnology (MSB); health informatics (MSHI); medical sciences (MSMS, PhD), including aging and neuroscience (MSMS), allergy, immunology and infectious disease (PhD), anatomy, biochemistry and molecular biology, clinical and translational research, health science (MSMS), interdisciplinary medical sciences (MSMS), medical microbiology and immunology (MSMS), metabolic and nutritional medicine (MSMS), microbiology and immunology (PhD), molecular medicine, molecular pharmacology and physiology (PhD), neuroscience (PhD), pathology and cell biology (PhD), women's health (MSMS). *Students:* 454 full-time (239 women), 273 part-time (173 women); includes 347 minority (110 Black or African American, non-Hispanic/Latino; 1 American Indian or Alaska Native, non-Hispanic/Latino; 99 Asian, non-Hispanic/Latino; 113 Hispanic/Latino; 1 Native Hawaiian or other Pacific Islander, non-Hispanic/Latino; 23 Two or more races, non-Hispanic/Latino), 61 international. Average age 27. 7,242 applicants, 8% accepted, 395 enrolled. In 2016, 374 master's, 13 doctorates awarded. Terminal master's awarded for partial completion of doctoral program. *Degree requirements:* For master's, comprehensive exam, thesis; for doctorate, comprehensive exam, thesis/dissertation. *Entrance requirements:* For master's, GRE General Test or GMAT, bachelor's degree or equivalent from regionally-accredited university with minimum GPA of 3.0 in upper-division sciences coursework; prerequisites in general biology, general chemistry, general physics, organic chemistry, quantitative analysis, and integral and differential calculus; for doctorate, GRE General Test, bachelor's degree from regionally-accredited university with minimum GPA of 3.0 in upper-division sciences coursework; 3 letters of recommendation; personal interview; 1-2 page personal statement; prerequisites in biology, chemistry, physics, organic chemistry, quantitative analysis, and integral/differential calculus. Additional exam requirements/recommendations for international students: Required—TOEFL (minimum score 550 paper-based; 79 iBT) or IELTS (minimum score 6.5). *Application deadline:* For fall admission, 2/1 for domestic and international students. Application fee: $30. Electronic applications accepted. *Expenses:* Contact institution. *Financial support:* In 2016–17, 116 students received support. *Faculty research:* Anatomy, biochemistry, cancer biology, cardiovascular disease, cell biology, immunology, microbiology, molecular biology, neuroscience, pharmacology, physiology. *Total annual research expenditures:* $42.3 million. *Unit head:* Dr. Michael Barber, Professor/Associate Dean for Graduate and Postdoctoral Affairs, 813-974-9908, Fax: 813-974-4317, E-mail: mbarber@health.usf.edu. *Application contact:* Dr. Eric Bennett, Graduate Director, PhD Program in Medical Sciences, 813-974-1545, Fax: 813-974-4317, E-mail: esbennet@health.usf.edu.
Website: http://health.usf.edu/nocms/medicine/graduatestudies/

The University of Tennessee, Graduate School, College of Education, Health and Human Sciences, Department of Exercise, Sport, and Leisure Studies, Program in Exercise Science, Knoxville, TN 37996. Offers biomechanics/sports medicine (MS, PhD); exercise physiology (MS, PhD). *Accreditation:* CEPH (one or more programs are accredited). *Program availability:* Part-time. *Degree requirements:* For master's, thesis optional. *Entrance requirements:* For master's, minimum GPA of 2.7. Additional exam requirements/recommendations for international students: Required—TOEFL. Electronic applications accepted.

The University of Tennessee at Chattanooga, Department of Health and Human Performance, Chattanooga, TN 37403. Offers athletic training (MSAT); health and human performance (MS). *Faculty:* 4 full-time (1 woman). *Students:* 43 full-time (32 women); includes 7 minority (2 Black or African American, non-Hispanic/Latino; 3 Hispanic/Latino; 2 Two or more races, non-Hispanic/Latino). Average age 23. 25 applicants, 92% accepted, 21 enrolled. In 2016, 21 master's awarded. *Degree requirements:* For master's, thesis or alternative, clinical rotations. *Entrance requirements:* For master's, GRE General Test, minimum GPA of 2.75 overall or 3.0 in last 60 hours; CPR and First Aid certification. Additional exam requirements/recommendations for international students: Required—TOEFL (minimum score 550 paper-based; 79 iBT), IELTS (minimum score 6). *Application deadline:* For fall admission, 6/15 priority date for domestic students, 7/1 for international students; for spring admission, 11/1 priority date for domestic students, 11/1 for international students. Applications are processed on a rolling basis. Application fee: $35 ($40 for international students). Electronic applications accepted. *Expenses:* $9,876 full-time in-state; $25,994 full-time out-of-state; $450 per credit part-time in-state; $1,345 per credit part-time out-of-state. *Financial support:* In 2016–17, 5 research assistantships with tuition reimbursements, 4 teaching assistantships with tuition reimbursements were awarded; career-related internships or fieldwork, scholarships/grants, and unspecified assistantships also available. Support available to part-time students. Financial award application deadline: 7/1; financial award applicants required to submit FAFSA. *Faculty research:* Therapeutic exercise, lumbar spine biomechanics, physical activity epidemiology, functional rehabilitation outcomes, metabolic health. *Unit head:* Dr. Marisa Colston, Interim Department Head, 423-425-4743, E-mail: marisa-colston@utc.edu. *Application contact:* Dr. Joanne Romagni, Dean of the Graduate School, 423-425-4478, Fax: 423-425-5223, E-mail: joanne-romagni@utc.edu.
Website: https://www.utc.edu/health-human-performance/

University of Utah, Graduate School, College of Health, Department of Physical Therapy and Athletic Training, Salt Lake City, UT 84112-1290. Offers physical therapy (DPT); rehabilitation science (PhD). *Accreditation:* APTA. *Faculty:* 13 full-time (5 women), 14 part-time/adjunct (7 women). *Students:* 158 full-time (86 women), 2 part-time (1 woman); includes 21 minority (3 Black or African American, non-Hispanic/Latino; 2 Asian, non-Hispanic/Latino; 9 Hispanic/Latino; 7 Two or more races, non-Hispanic/Latino), 1 international. Average age 28. 437 applicants, 11% accepted, 48 enrolled. In 2016, 50 doctorates awarded. *Degree requirements:* For doctorate, thesis/dissertation. *Entrance requirements:* For doctorate, GRE, minimum GPA of 3.0, volunteer work, bachelor's degree. Additional exam requirements/recommendations for international students: Required—TOEFL (minimum score 90 iBT); Recommended—IELTS (minimum score 7). *Application deadline:* For fall admission, 10/3 priority date for domestic students, 10/3 for international students. Application fee: $55 ($65 for international students). Electronic applications accepted. *Expenses:* Contact institution. *Financial support:* In 2016–17, 29 students received support. Research assistantships with full tuition reimbursements available, teaching assistantships with full tuition reimbursements available, Federal Work-Study, scholarships/grants, tuition waivers (full), and unspecified assistantships available. Financial award application deadline: 10/1; financial award applicants required to submit FAFSA. *Faculty research:* Rehabilitation and Parkinson's disease, motor control and musculoskeletal dysfunction, burns/wound care, rehabilitation and multiple sclerosis, cancer. *Total annual research expenditures:* $600,129. *Unit head:* Dr. R. Scott Ward, Chair, 801-581-4895, E-mail: scott.ward@hsc.utah.edu. *Application contact:* Dee-Dee Darby-Duffin, Academic Advisor, 801-585-9510, E-mail: d.darby-duffin@hsc.utah.edu.
Website: http://www.health.utah.edu/pt

University of Wisconsin–La Crosse, College of Science and Health, Department of Exercise and Sport Science, Program in Human Performance, La Crosse, WI 54601-3742. Offers applied sport science (MS); strength and conditioning (MS). *Program availability:* Part-time. *Students:* 13 full-time (5 women), 8 part-time (5 women). Average age 24. 21 applicants, 81% accepted, 9 enrolled. In 2016, 8 master's awarded. *Degree requirements:* For master's, comprehensive exam (for some programs), thesis optional. *Entrance requirements:* For master's, GRE, course work in anatomy, physiology, biomechanics, and exercise physiology. Additional exam requirements/recommendations for international students: Required—TOEFL (minimum score 550 paper-based; 79 iBT). *Application deadline:* For fall admission, 2/1 priority date for domestic and international students. Electronic applications accepted. *Financial support:* Federal Work-Study, scholarships/grants, health care benefits, and tuition waivers (partial) available. Support available to part-time students. Financial award application deadline: 3/15; financial award applicants required to submit FAFSA. *Faculty research:* Anaerobic metabolism, power development, strength training, biomechanics, athletic performance. *Unit head:* Dr. Glenn Wright, Director, 608-785-8689, Fax: 608-785-8172, E-mail: wright.glen@uwlax.edu. *Application contact:* Brandon Schaller, Senior Graduate Student Status Examiner, 608-785-8941, E-mail: admissions@uwlax.edu.
Website: https://www.uwlax.edu/human-performance-ms/

University of Wisconsin–Milwaukee, Graduate School, College of Health Sciences, Department of Kinesiology, Milwaukee, WI 53201-0413. Offers athletic training (MS); kinesiology (MS, PhD), including exercise and nutrition in health and disease (MS), integrative human performance (MS), neuromechanics (MS); physical therapy (DPT). *Program availability:* Part-time. *Students:* 104 full-time (54 women), 6 part-time (3 women); includes 11 minority (1 Black or African American, non-Hispanic/Latino; 10 Two or more races, non-Hispanic/Latino), 3 international. Average age 27. 34 applicants, 47% accepted, 12 enrolled. In 2016, 9 master's, 24 doctorates awarded. *Degree requirements:* For master's, comprehensive exam, thesis optional. *Entrance requirements:* For master's, GRE General Test. Additional exam requirements/recommendations for international students: Required—TOEFL (minimum score 550 paper-based; 79 iBT), IELTS (minimum score 6.5). *Application deadline:* For fall admission, 1/1 priority date for domestic students; for spring admission, 9/1 for domestic students. Applications are processed on a rolling basis. Application fee: $56 ($96 for international students). *Financial support:* In 2016–17, 2 fellowships, 7 teaching assistantships were awarded; research assistantships, career-related internships or fieldwork, unspecified assistantships, and project assistantships also available. Support available to part-time students. Financial award application deadline: 4/15. *Unit head:* Dr. Kyle T. Ebersole, Department Chair, 414-229-6717, Fax: 414-229-3366, E-mail: ebersole@uwm.edu. *Application contact:* Stephen C. Cobb, Graduate Program Coordinator, 414-229-3369, Fax: 414-229-3366, E-mail: cobbsc@uwm.edu.
Website: http://uwm.edu/healthsciences/academics/kinesiology/

Weber State University, Jerry and Vickie Moyes College of Education, Program in Athletic Training, Ogden, UT 84408-1001. Offers MSAT. *Program availability:* Part-time. *Faculty:* 10 full-time (3 women). *Students:* 34 full-time (17 women), 2 part-time (both women); includes 3 minority (1 Hispanic/Latino; 2 Two or more races, non-Hispanic/Latino), 4 international. Average age 25. In 2016, 15 master's awarded. *Degree requirements:* For master's, thesis. *Entrance requirements:* For master's, GRE (if GPA less than 3.0), physical, immunizations. Additional exam requirements/recommendations for international students: Required—TOEFL (minimum score 525 paper-based). *Application deadline:* For fall admission, 1/15 priority date for domestic and international students. Applications are processed on a rolling basis. Application fee: $60 ($90 for international students). Electronic applications accepted. *Expenses:* Contact institution. *Financial support:* In 2016–17, 26 students received support. Scholarships/grants available. Financial award application deadline: 4/1; financial award applicants required to submit FAFSA. *Unit head:* Dr. Valerie W. Herzog, Program Director, 801-626-7675, Fax: 801-626-6228, E-mail: valerieherzog@weber.edu.
Website: http://www.weber.edu/athletictraining/graduateprograms.html

West Chester University of Pennsylvania, College of Health Sciences, Department of Kinesiology, West Chester, PA 19383. Offers adapted physical education (Certificate); exercise and sport physiology (MS), including athletic training, exercise and sport physiology; general physical education (MS); sport management and athletics (MPA), including administration. *Program availability:* Part-time, evening/weekend. *Faculty:* 9 full-time (6 women). *Students:* 34 full-time (22 women), 21 part-time (7 women); includes 5 minority (4 Black or African American, non-Hispanic/Latino; 1 Hispanic/Latino), 1 international. Average age 26. 68 applicants, 85% accepted, 30 enrolled. In 2016, 23 master's, 1 other advanced degree awarded. *Degree requirements:* For master's, thesis or research report (for MS); two internships and capstone course that includes a research project or thesis (for MPA). *Entrance requirements:* For master's, GRE (for MS), 2 letters of recommendation, statement of goals; transcripts (for MS); resume (for MPA). Additional exam requirements/recommendations for international students: Required—TOEFL or IELTS. *Application deadline:* For fall admission, 5/15 for international students; for spring admission, 10/15 for international students. Applications are processed on a rolling basis. Application fee: $50. Electronic applications accepted. *Expenses:* Tuition, state resident: full-time $8694; part-time $483 per credit. Tuition, nonresident: full-time $13,050; part-time $725 per credit. *Required fees:* $2399; $119.05 per credit. Tuition and fees vary according to campus/location and program. *Financial support:* Scholarships/grants and unspecified assistantships available. Financial award application deadline: 2/15; financial award applicants required to submit FAFSA. *Faculty research:* Metabolism during exercise, biomechanics, rating of perceived exertion, motor learning, environmental physiology. *Unit head:* Dr. Frank Fry, Chair/Graduate Coordinator for the MS in General Physical Education Program, 610-436-2610, Fax: 610-436-2860, E-mail: ffry@wcupa.edu. *Application contact:* Office of Graduate Studies and Extended Education, 610-436-2943, Fax: 610-436-2763, E-mail: gradstudy@wcupa.edu.
Website: http://www.wcupa.edu/healthsciences/kinesiology/

Western Michigan University, Graduate College, College of Education and Human Development, Department of Health, Physical Education and Recreation, Kalamazoo, MI 49008. Offers athletic training (MS), including exercise physiology; sport management (MA), including pedagogy, special physical education.

West Virginia University, College of Physical Activity and Sport Sciences, Morgantown, WV 26506-6116. Offers athletic training (MS); coaching and sport education (MS); coaching and teaching studies (Ed D); physical education/teacher education (MS, PhD), including curriculum and instruction (PhD), physical education supervision (PhD); sport and exercise psychology (MS, PhD); sport coaching (MS); sport management (MS). *Degree requirements:* For doctorate, comprehensive exam, thesis/dissertation, oral exam. *Entrance requirements:* For master's, GRE or MAT, minimum GPA of 3.0; for doctorate, GRE General Test or MAT, minimum GPA of 3.5. Additional exam requirements/recommendations for international students: Required—TOEFL (minimum score 550 paper-based). Electronic applications accepted. *Faculty research:* Sport psychosociology, teacher education, exercise psychology, counseling.

West Virginia Wesleyan College, Department of Exercise Science, Buckhannon, WV 26201. Offers athletic training (MS).

Xavier University, College of Social Sciences, Health and Education, Department of Sports Studies, Cincinnati, OH 45207. Offers coaching education and athlete development (M Ed); sport administration (M Ed). *Program availability:* Part-time, evening/weekend, online learning. *Degree requirements:* For master's, thesis optional, internship or research project. *Entrance requirements:* For master's, GRE or MAT, official transcript; resume; one-page statement of career goals; 2 letters of recommendation. Additional exam requirements/recommendations for international students: Required—TOEFL (minimum score 550 paper-based; 79 iBT). Electronic applications accepted. Application fee is waived when completed online. *Expenses:* Contact institution. *Faculty research:* Coaching education, brand equity, strategic management, economic impact, place marketing.

Exercise and Sports Science

American International College, School of Health Sciences, Springfield, MA 01109-3189. Offers exercise science (MS); family nurse practitioner (MSN); nursing administrator (MSN); nursing educator (MSN); occupational therapy (MSOT, OTD); physical therapy (DPT). *Program availability:* Part-time, 100% online. *Faculty:* 25 full-time (22 women), 14 part-time/adjunct (13 women). *Students:* 160 full-time (136 women), 4 part-time (all women); includes 57 minority (24 Black or African American, non-Hispanic/Latino; 13 Asian, non-Hispanic/Latino; 14 Hispanic/Latino; 6 Two or more races, non-Hispanic/Latino), 1 international. Average age 30. 673 applicants, 41% accepted, 100 enrolled. In 2016, 41 master's, 35 doctorates awarded. *Degree requirements:* For master's, practicum; for doctorate, thesis/dissertation, practicum. *Entrance requirements:* For master's, BS or BA; minimum GPA of 3.0 (MSOT and MSN); 2 letters of recommendation; 2 clinical OT observations (MSOT); personal goal

statement; for doctorate, minimum GPA of 3.2, interview, BS or BA, 3 letters of recommendation, 2 clinical PT observations, personal goal statement. Additional exam requirements/recommendations for international students: Required—TOEFL, IELTS. *Application deadline:* For fall admission, 12/1 priority date for domestic and international students. Applications are processed on a rolling basis. Application fee: $50. Electronic applications accepted. *Expenses:* $49,000 per year (for DPT), $20,355 per year (for MSOT), $23,625 per program (for MSN). *Financial support:* Application deadline: 4/1; applicants required to submit FAFSA. *Faculty research:* Teaching simulation, ergonomics, orthopedics, use of social media in health care. *Unit head:* Dr. Cesarina Thompson, Dean, 413-205-3056, Fax: 413-654-1430, E-mail: cesarina.thompson@aic.edu. *Application contact:* Kerry Barnes, Director of Graduate Admissions, 413-205-3703, Fax: 413-205-3051, E-mail: kerry.barnes@aic.edu.
Website: http://www.aic.edu/academics/hs

American Public University System, AMU/APU Graduate Programs, Charles Town, WV 25414. Offers accounting (MBA, MS); applied business analytics (MBA, MS); criminal justice (MA), including business administration, emergency and disaster management, general (MA, MS); educational leadership (M Ed); emergency and disaster management (MA); entrepreneurship (MBA); environmental policy and management (MS), including environmental planning, environmental sustainability, fish and wildlife management, general (MA, MS), global environmental management; finance (MBA); general (MBA); government contracting and acquisition (MBA); health care administration (MBA); health information management (MS); history (MA), including American history, ancient and classical history, European history, global history, public history; homeland security (MA), including business administration, counterterrorism studies, criminal justice, cyber, emergency management and public health, intelligence studies, transportation security; homeland security resource allocation (MBA); humanities (MA); information technology (MS), including digital forensics, enterprise software development, information assurance and security, IT project management; information technology management (MBA); intelligence studies (MA), including criminal intelligence, cyber, general (MA, MS), homeland security, intelligence analysis, intelligence collection, intelligence management, intelligence operations, terrorism studies; international relations and conflict resolution (MA), including comparative and security issues, conflict resolution, international and transnational security issues, peacekeeping; legal studies (MA); management (MA), including strategic consulting; marketing (MBA); military history (MA), including American military history, American Revolution, civil war, war since 1945, World War II; military studies (MA), including joint warfare, strategic leadership; national security studies (MA), including cyber, general (MA, MS), homeland security, regional security studies, security and intelligence analysis, terrorism studies; nonprofit management (MBA); political science (MA), including American politics and government, comparative government and development, general (MA, MS), international relations, public policy; psychology (MA); public administration (MPA), including disaster management, environmental policy, health policy, human resources, national security, organizational management, security management; public health (MPH); reverse logistics management (MA); security management (MA); space studies (MS), including aerospace science, general (MA, MS), planetary science; sports and health sciences (MS); sports management (MBA); teaching (M Ed), including autism spectrum disorder, curriculum and instruction for elementary teachers, elementary reading, English language learners, instructional leadership, online learning, special education, STEAM (STEM plus the arts); transportation and logistics management (MA). *Program availability:* Part-time, evening/weekend, online only, 100% online. *Faculty:* 401 full-time (228 women), 1,678 part-time/adjunct (781 women). *Students:* 378 full-time (184 women), 8,455 part-time (3,484 women); includes 2,972 minority (1,552 Black or African American, non-Hispanic/Latino; 52 American Indian or Alaska Native, non-Hispanic/Latino; 211 Asian, non-Hispanic/Latino; 791 Hispanic/Latino; 70 Native Hawaiian or other Pacific Islander, non-Hispanic/Latino; 296 Two or more races, non-Hispanic/Latino), 109 international. Average age 37. In 2016, 3,185 master's awarded. *Degree requirements:* For master's, comprehensive exam or practicum. *Entrance requirements:* For master's, official transcript showing earned bachelor's degree from institution accredited by recognized accrediting body. Additional exam requirements/recommendations for international students: Required—TOEFL (minimum score 550 paper-based), IELTS (minimum score 6.5). *Application deadline:* Applications are processed on a rolling basis. Application fee: $0. Electronic applications accepted. *Expenses: Tuition:* Part-time $350 per credit hour. *Required fees:* $50 per course. *Financial support:* Scholarships/grants available. Financial award applicants required to submit FAFSA. *Unit head:* Dr. Karan Powell, President, 877-468-6268, Fax: 304-724-3780. *Application contact:* Terry Grant, Vice President of Enrollment Management, 877-468-6268, Fax: 304-724-3780, E-mail: info@apus.edu.
Website: http://www.apus.edu

Appalachian State University, Cratis D. Williams Graduate School, Department of Health and Exercise Science, Boone, NC 28608. Offers exercise science (MS), including clinical exercise physiology, strength and conditioning. *Degree requirements:* For master's, comprehensive exam, thesis optional. *Entrance requirements:* For master's, GRE General Test, 3 letters of recommendation. Additional exam requirements/recommendations for international students: Required—TOEFL (minimum score 570 paper-based; 79 iBT), IELTS (minimum score 6.5). *Application deadline:* For fall admission, 3/1 priority date for domestic students, 2/1 for international students; for spring admission, 11/1 for domestic students, 7/1 for international students. Applications are processed on a rolling basis. Application fee: $55. Electronic applications accepted. *Expenses:* Tuition, state resident: full-time $4744. Tuition, nonresident: full-time $17,913. Full-time tuition and fees vary according to program. *Financial support:* Research assistantships, career-related internships or fieldwork, Federal Work-Study, scholarships/grants, and unspecified assistantships available. Financial award application deadline: 4/1; financial award applicants required to submit FAFSA. *Faculty research:* Exercise immunology, biomechanics, exercise and chronic disease, muscle damage, strength and conditioning. *Unit head:* Dr. Paul Gaskill, Head, 828-262-6336, E-mail: gaskillpl@appstate.edu. *Application contact:* Dr. Andrew Shanely, Program Director, 828-262-6319, E-mail: esgrad@appstate.edu.
Website: https://hes.appstate.edu/

Arizona State University at the Tempe campus, College of Health Solutions, School of Nutrition and Health Promotion, Tempe, AZ 85287. Offers clinical exercise physiology (MS); exercise and wellness (MS); nutrition (MS), including dietetics, human nutrition; obesity prevention and management (MS); physical activity, nutrition and wellness (PhD).

Arkansas State University, Graduate School, College of Education and Behavioral Science, Department of Health, Physical Education, and Sport Sciences, State University, AR 72467. Offers exercise science (MS); physical education (MSE, SCCT); sports administration (MS). *Program availability:* Part-time. *Degree requirements:* For master's, comprehensive exam, thesis or alternative; for SCCT, comprehensive exam. *Entrance requirements:* For master's, GRE General Test or MAT, appropriate bachelor's degree, official transcripts, immunization records, statement of goals, letters of recommendation; for SCCT, GRE General Test or MAT, interview, master's degree, official transcript, immunization records. Additional exam requirements/recommendations for international students: Required—TOEFL (minimum score 550 paper-based; 79 iBT), IELTS (minimum score 6), PTE (minimum score 56). Electronic applications accepted.

Armstrong State University, School of Graduate Studies, Program in Sports Medicine, Savannah, GA 31419-1997. Offers sports health sciences (MSSM); strength and conditioning (Certificate). *Program availability:* Part-time. *Faculty:* 3 full-time (0 women). *Students:* 20 full-time (11 women), 9 part-time (4 women); includes 10 minority (7 Black or African American, non-Hispanic/Latino; 1 Asian, non-Hispanic/Latino; 2 Hispanic/Latino). Average age 25. 40 applicants, 45% accepted, 15 enrolled. In 2016, 7 master's awarded. *Degree requirements:* For master's, comprehensive exam, thesis optional, project. *Entrance requirements:* For master's, GRE General Test, MAT, GMAT, minimum GPA of 2.7, letter of intent. Additional exam requirements/recommendations for international students: Required—TOEFL (minimum score 523 paper-based; 70 iBT). *Application deadline:* For fall admission, 6/1 priority date for domestic students, 5/1 priority date for international students; for spring admission, 11/15 priority date for domestic students, 9/15 priority date for international students; for summer admission, 4/15 for domestic students, 9/15 for international students. Applications are processed on a rolling basis. Application fee: $30. Electronic applications accepted. *Expenses:* Tuition, state resident: full-time $1781; part-time $161.93 per credit hour. Tuition, nonresident: full-time $6482; part-time $589.27 per credit hour. *Required fees:* $1224 per unit. $612 per semester. Tuition and fees vary according to course load, campus/location and program. *Financial support:* In 2016–17, research assistantships with full tuition reimbursements (averaging $5,000 per year) were awarded; scholarships/grants, tuition waivers (full), and unspecified assistantships also available. Financial award application deadline: 3/15; financial award applicants required to submit FAFSA. *Unit head:* Dr. Robert LeFavi, Department Head, 912-921-3208, Fax: 912-344-3490, E-mail: robert.lefavi@armstrong.edu. *Application contact:* McKenzie Peterman, Assistant Director of Graduate Admissions, 912-344-2503, Fax: 912-344-3417, E-mail: graduate@armstrong.edu.
Website: http://www.armstrong.edu/Majors/degree/sports_medicine1

Ashland University, Dwight Schar College of Nursing and Health Sciences, Department of Health Sciences, Ashland, OH 44805-3702. Offers applied exercise science (MS). *Program availability:* Part-time. *Degree requirements:* For master's, practicum, inquiry seminar, thesis, or internship. *Entrance requirements:* For master's, teaching certificate or license, bachelor's degree, minimum cumulative GPA of 2.75. Additional exam requirements/recommendations for international students: Required—TOEFL. *Application deadline:* For fall admission, 8/27 for domestic students; for spring admission, 1/15 for domestic students. Applications are processed on a rolling basis. Application fee: $30. *Financial support:* Teaching assistantships, institutionally sponsored loans, and scholarships/grants available. Financial award application deadline: 4/15. *Faculty research:* Coaching, legal issues, strength and conditioning, sport management rating of perceived exertion, youth fitness, geriatric exercise science. *Unit head:* Dr. Randall F. Gearhart, Chair, 419-289-6198, E-mail: rgearhar@ashland.edu. *Application contact:* Dr. Linda Billman, Director and Chair, Graduate Studies in Education/Associate Dean, 419-289-5369, Fax: 419-289-5331, E-mail: lbillman@ashland.edu.

Auburn University, Graduate School, College of Education, Department of Kinesiology, Auburn University, AL 36849. Offers exercise science (M Ed). *Accreditation:* NCATE. *Program availability:* Part-time. *Faculty:* 18 full-time (9 women), 1 part-time/adjunct (0 women). *Students:* 96 full-time (57 women), 28 part-time (11 women); includes 132 minority (114 Black or African American, non-Hispanic/Latino; 2 American Indian or Alaska Native, non-Hispanic/Latino; 4 Asian, non-Hispanic/Latino; 6 Hispanic/Latino; 1 Native Hawaiian or other Pacific Islander, non-Hispanic/Latino; 5 Two or more races, non-Hispanic/Latino), 14 international. Average age 26. 127 applicants, 66% accepted, 53 enrolled. In 2016, 63 master's, 4 doctorates, 1 other advanced degree awarded. *Degree requirements:* For master's, thesis (for some programs); for doctorate, thesis/dissertation; for Ed S, exam, field project. *Entrance requirements:* For master's, GRE General Test; for doctorate and Ed S, GRE General Test, interview, master's degree. *Application deadline:* Applications are processed on a rolling basis. Application fee: $50 ($60 for international students). Electronic applications accepted. *Expenses:* Tuition, state resident: full-time $9072; part-time $504 per credit hour. Tuition, nonresident: full-time $27,216; part-time $1512 per credit hour. *Required fees:* $812 per semester. Tuition and fees vary according to degree level and program. *Financial support:* Research assistantships, teaching assistantships, and Federal Work-Study available. Support available to part-time students. Financial award application deadline: 3/15; financial award applicants required to submit FAFSA. *Faculty research:* Biomechanics, exercise physiology, motor skill learning, school health, curriculum development. *Unit head:* Dr. Mary E. Rudisill, Director, 334-844-1458. *Application contact:* Dr. George Flowers, Dean of the Graduate School, 334-844-2125.

Auburn University at Montgomery, College of Education, Department of Kinesiology, Montgomery, AL 36124-4023. Offers exercise science (M Ed); physical education (Ed S); sport management (M Ed). *Faculty:* 6 full-time (2 women), 2 part-time/adjunct (both women). *Students:* 23 full-time (14 women), 19 part-time (9 women); includes 10 minority (9 Black or African American, non-Hispanic/Latino; 1 Hispanic/Latino), 2 international. Average age 28. *Entrance requirements:* Additional exam requirements/recommendations for international students: Recommended—TOEFL (minimum score 500 paper-based; 61 iBT), IELTS (minimum score 5.5), TSE (minimum score 44). *Expenses:* Tuition, state resident: full-time $6462; part-time $359 per credit hour. Tuition, nonresident: full-time $14,526; part-time $807 per credit hour. *Required fees:* $554. *Financial support:* Teaching assistantships available. Financial award application deadline: 3/1; financial award applicants required to submit FAFSA. *Unit head:* Dr. George Schaefer, Head, 334-244-3887, Fax: 334-244-3835, E-mail: gschaefe@aum.edu. *Application contact:* Janis Bigelow, Graduate Advisor, 334-244-3135, E-mail: jbigelo1@aum.edu.
Website: http://www.education.aum.edu/academic-programs/academic-programs/kinesiology

Austin Peay State University, College of Graduate Studies, College of Behavioral and Health Sciences, Department of Health and Human Performance, Clarksville, TN 37044. Offers public health education (MS); sports and wellness leadership (MS). *Program availability:* Part-time, evening/weekend, online learning. *Faculty:* 7 full-time (4 women). *Students:* 22 full-time (8 women), 36 part-time (26 women); includes 16 minority (10 Black or African American, non-Hispanic/Latino; 1 Asian, non-Hispanic/Latino; 2 Hispanic/Latino; 3 Two or more races, non-Hispanic/Latino), 2 international. Average age 29. 79 applicants, 70% accepted, 43 enrolled. In 2016, 27 master's awarded. *Degree requirements:* For master's, comprehensive exam, thesis optional. *Entrance requirements:* For master's, GRE General Test, 3 letters of recommendation, minimum undergraduate GPA of 2.5. Additional exam requirements/recommendations for international students: Required—TOEFL (minimum score 500 paper-based). *Application deadline:* For fall admission, 8/9 priority date for domestic students. Applications are processed on a rolling basis. Application fee: $45 ($50 for international students). Electronic applications accepted. *Expenses:* Tuition, state resident: full-time $8300; part-time $415 per credit hour. Tuition, nonresident: full-time $22,280; part-time $1114 per credit hour. *Required fees:* $1473; $73.65 per credit hour. *Financial support:* Research assistantships with full tuition reimbursements, career-related internships or

fieldwork, Federal Work-Study, institutionally sponsored loans, scholarships/grants, and unspecified assistantships available. Support available to part-time students. Financial award application deadline: 4/1; financial award applicants required to submit FAFSA. *Unit head:* Dr. Marcy Maurer, Chair, 931-221-6105, Fax: 931-221-7040, E-mail: maurerm@apsu.edu. *Application contact:* Brad Averitt, Coordinator of Graduate Admissions, 800-859-4723, Fax: 931-221-7641, E-mail: gradadmissions@apsu.edu.
Website: http://www.apsu.edu/hhp/

Ball State University, Graduate School, College of Applied Sciences and Technology, School of Kinesiology, Program in Exercise Science, Muncie, IN 47306. Offers exercise science (MA, MS), including biomechanics (MS), clinical exercise physiology, exercise physiology (MS), sports performance. *Program availability:* Part-time. *Entrance requirements:* For master's, GRE General Test, minimum baccalaureate GPA of 2.75 or 3.0 in latter half of baccalaureate, curriculum vitae, three letters of recommendation, transcripts of all prior course work; campus visit to meet faculty and see facilities (strongly encouraged). Additional exam requirements/recommendations for international students: Required—TOEFL (minimum score 550 paper-based; 79 iBT), IELTS (minimum score 6.5). Electronic applications accepted.

Ball State University, Graduate School, College of Applied Sciences and Technology, School of Kinesiology, Program in Human Bioenergetics, Muncie, IN 47306. Offers PhD. *Program availability:* Part-time. *Degree requirements:* For doctorate, comprehensive exam, thesis/dissertation. *Entrance requirements:* For doctorate, GRE General Test, curriculum vitae, three letters of recommendation, electronic transcripts of all prior college work, minimum graduate GPA of 3.2, approval of Human Performance Lab selection committee; campus visit to meet faculty and see facilities (strongly encouraged). Additional exam requirements/recommendations for international students: Required—TOEFL (minimum score 550 paper-based; 79 iBT), IELTS (minimum score 6.5). Electronic applications accepted.

Barry University, School of Human Performance and Leisure Sciences, Programs in Movement Science, Specialization in Exercise Science, Miami Shores, FL 33161-6695. Offers MS. *Degree requirements:* For master's, comprehensive exam, thesis. *Entrance requirements:* For master's, GRE, minimum GPA of 3.0. Electronic applications accepted. *Faculty research:* Physiological adaptations to exercise.

Benedictine University, Graduate Programs, Program in Clinical Exercise Physiology, Lisle, IL 60532. Offers MS. *Program availability:* Part-time. *Students:* 12 full-time (9 women), 13 part-time (8 women); includes 5 minority (1 Black or African American, non-Hispanic/Latino; 4 Hispanic/Latino). 24 applicants, 75% accepted, 11 enrolled. In 2016, 14 master's awarded. *Entrance requirements:* Additional exam requirements/recommendations for international students: Required—TOEFL (minimum score 550 paper-based). *Application deadline:* For fall admission, 9/1 for domestic students; for winter admission, 12/1 for domestic students; for spring admission, 2/15 for domestic students. Applications are processed on a rolling basis. Application fee: $40. Electronic applications accepted. *Expenses: Tuition:* Full-time $15,600; part-time $650 per hour. *Required fees:* $300. One-time fee: $125 part-time. Tuition and fees vary according to class time, course load, campus/location and program. *Financial support:* Career-related internships or fieldwork and health care benefits available. Support available to part-time students. *Faculty research:* Protein synthesis cell signaling control, aging. *Unit head:* Dr. Allison Wilson, Director of New Faculty Mentoring Program, 630-829-6520, E-mail: awilson@ben.edu. *Application contact:* Kari Gibbons, Associate Vice President, Enrollment Center, 630-829-6200, Fax: 630-829-6584, E-mail: kgibbons@ben.edu.

Bloomsburg University of Pennsylvania, School of Graduate Studies, College of Science and Technology, Department of Exercise Science and Athletics, Bloomsburg, PA 17815-1301. Offers clinical athletic training (MS); exercise science (MS). *Faculty:* 5 full-time (1 woman). *Students:* 40 full-time (24 women); includes 4 minority (1 Asian, non-Hispanic/Latino; 1 Hispanic/Latino; 2 Two or more races, non-Hispanic/Latino), 1 international. Average age 24. 62 applicants, 55% accepted, 19 enrolled. In 2016, 22 master's awarded. *Degree requirements:* For master's, thesis optional, practical clinical experience. *Entrance requirements:* For master's, GRE, minimum QPA of 3.0, related undergraduate coursework, interview. Additional exam requirements/recommendations for international students: Required—TOEFL (minimum score 550 paper-based; 79 iBT), IELTS. *Application deadline:* Applications are processed on a rolling basis. Application fee: $35 ($60 for international students). Electronic applications accepted. *Expenses:* Tuition, state resident: full-time $9660; part-time $483 per credit. Tuition, nonresident: full-time $14,500; part-time $725 per credit. *Required fees:* $2410; $107 per credit. $75 per term. Tuition and fees vary according to course load, degree level and program. *Financial support:* Federal Work-Study and unspecified assistantships available. Financial award applicants required to submit FAFSA. *Unit head:* Dr. Joseph Andreacci, MS Program Coordinator, 570-389-3959, Fax: 570-389-5047, E-mail: jandreac@bloomu.edu. *Application contact:* Jennifer Kessler, Administrative Assistant, 570-389-4015, Fax: 570-389-3054, E-mail: jkessler@bloomu.edu.
Website: http://www.bloomu.edu/exercise_science

Brigham Young University, Graduate Studies, College of Life Sciences, Department of Exercise Sciences, Provo, UT 84602. Offers athletic training (MS); exercise physiology (MS, PhD); exercise sciences (MS); health promotion (MS, PhD); physical medicine and rehabilitation (PhD). *Faculty:* 20 full-time (2 women). *Students:* 14 full-time (6 women), 17 part-time (11 women); includes 4 minority (3 Asian, non-Hispanic/Latino; 1 Hispanic/Latino). Average age 30. 21 applicants, 38% accepted, 4 enrolled. In 2016, 11 master's awarded. *Degree requirements:* For master's, thesis, oral defense; for doctorate, comprehensive exam, thesis/dissertation, oral defense, oral and written exams. *Entrance requirements:* For master's, GRE General Test (minimum score of 300, 4.0 on analytic writing portion), minimum GPA of 3.2 in last 60 hours of course work; for doctorate, GRE General Test (minimum score of 300, 4.0 on analytic writing portion), minimum GPA of 3.5 in last 60 hours of course work. Additional exam requirements/recommendations for international students: Required—TOEFL (minimum score 580 paper-based; 85 iBT), IELTS (minimum score 7). *Application deadline:* For fall admission, 2/1 for domestic and international students. Application fee: $50. Electronic applications accepted. *Expenses:* Contact institution. *Financial support:* In 2016–17, 168 students received support, including 32 research assistantships (averaging $7,330 per year), 42 teaching assistantships (averaging $2,772 per year); career-related internships or fieldwork, institutionally sponsored loans, scholarships/grants, unspecified assistantships, and 7 PhD full-tuition scholarships also available. Financial award application deadline: 4/15. *Faculty research:* Injury prevention and rehabilitation, human skeletal muscle adaptation, cardiovascular health and fitness, lifestyle modification and health promotion. *Total annual research expenditures:* $158,655. *Unit head:* Dr. Allen Parcell, Chair, 801-422-4450, Fax: 801-422-0555, E-mail: allenparcell@gmail.com. *Application contact:* Dr. J. William Myrer, Graduate Coordinator, 801-422-2690, Fax: 801-422-0555, E-mail: bill_myrer@byu.edu.
Website: http://exsc.byu.edu/

Brooklyn College of the City University of New York, School of Natural and Behavioral Sciences, Department of Kinesiology, Brooklyn, NY 11210-2889. Offers exercise and sports science (MS); physical education teacher (MS); sport management (MS). *Program availability:* Part-time. *Degree requirements:* For master's, comprehensive exam or thesis. *Entrance requirements:* For master's, previous course work in physical education and education, minimum GPA of 3.0, 2 letters of recommendation, essay. Additional exam requirements/recommendations for international students: Required—TOEFL (minimum score 500 paper-based; 61 iBT). Electronic applications accepted. *Faculty research:* Exercise physiology, motor learning, sports psychology, women in athletics.

California Baptist University, Program in Kinesiology, Riverside, CA 92504-3206. Offers exercise science (MS); physical education (MS); sport management (MS). *Program availability:* Part-time, 100% online, blended/hybrid learning. *Faculty:* 10 full-time (3 women), 3 part-time/adjunct (0 women). *Students:* 77 full-time (43 women), 37 part-time (16 women); includes 48 minority (16 Black or African American, non-Hispanic/Latino; 9 Asian, non-Hispanic/Latino; 20 Hispanic/Latino; 1 Native Hawaiian or other Pacific Islander, non-Hispanic/Latino; 2 Two or more races, non-Hispanic/Latino), 26 international. Average age 28. 71 applicants, 76% accepted, 47 enrolled. In 2016, 43 master's awarded. *Degree requirements:* For master's, comprehensive exam or research thesis. *Entrance requirements:* For master's, minimum undergraduate GPA of 2.75; completion of course prerequisites with minimum C grade; three recommendations; 500-word essay; resume; interview. Additional exam requirements/recommendations for international students: Required—TOEFL (minimum score 80 iBT). *Application deadline:* For fall admission, 8/1 priority date for domestic students, 7/1 for international students; for spring admission, 12/1 priority date for domestic students, 11/1 for international students. Applications are processed on a rolling basis. Application fee: $45. Electronic applications accepted. *Expenses:* Contact institution. *Financial support:* In 2016–17, 11 students received support. Federal Work-Study, scholarships/grants, and unspecified assistantships available. Financial award applicants required to submit CSS PROFILE or FAFSA. *Faculty research:* Physical education pedagogy, exercise management and prevention of cardiovascular and metabolic diseases, sport management, immune function, carbohydrate oxidation. *Unit head:* Dr. David Pearson, Dean, College of Allied Health, 951-343-4298, E-mail: dpearson@calbaptist.edu. *Application contact:* Dr. Sean Sullivan, Chair, Department of Kinesiology, 951-343-4528, Fax: 951-343-5095, E-mail: ssullivan@calbaptist.edu.
Website: http://www.calbaptist.edu/mskin/

California State University, Fresno, Division of Research and Graduate Studies, College of Health and Human Services, Department of Kinesiology, Fresno, CA 93740-8027. Offers exercise science (MA); general kinesiology (MA); sport administration (MA); sport psychology (MA). *Program availability:* Part-time, evening/weekend. *Degree requirements:* For master's, thesis or alternative. *Entrance requirements:* For master's, GRE General Test, minimum GPA of 2.7. Additional exam requirements/recommendations for international students: Required—TOEFL. *Application deadline:* For fall admission, 5/1 for domestic and international students; for spring admission, 10/1 for domestic and international students. Applications are processed on a rolling basis. Application fee: $55. Electronic applications accepted. *Financial support:* Teaching assistantships, career-related internships or fieldwork, Federal Work-Study, and scholarships/grants available. Support available to part-time students. Financial award application deadline: 3/1; financial award applicants required to submit FAFSA. *Faculty research:* Refugee education, homeless, geriatrics, fitness. *Unit head:* Dr. Tim Anderson, Chair, 559-278-2203, Fax: 559-278-7010, E-mail: tima@csufresno.edu. *Application contact:* Dr. Jenelle Gilbert, Coordinator, 559-278-8902, Fax: 559-278-7010, E-mail: jgilbert@csufresno.edu.
Website: http://www.fresnostate.edu/chhs/kinesiology/

California State University, Long Beach, Graduate Studies, College of Health and Human Services, Department of Kinesiology, Long Beach, CA 90840. Offers adapted physical education (MA); coaching and student athlete development (MA); exercise physiology and nutrition (MS); exercise science (MS); individualized studies (MA); kinesiology (MA); pedagogical studies (MA); sport and exercise psychology (MS); sport management (MA); sports medicine and injury studies (MS). *Program availability:* Part-time. *Degree requirements:* For master's, oral and written comprehensive exams or thesis. *Entrance requirements:* For master's, GRE General Test, minimum GPA of 2.75 during previous 2 years of course work. *Application deadline:* For fall admission, 6/1 for domestic students. Applications are processed on a rolling basis. Application fee: $55. Electronic applications accepted. *Financial support:* Federal Work-Study, institutionally sponsored loans, and scholarships/grants available. Financial award application deadline: 3/2. *Faculty research:* Pulmonary functioning, feedback and practice structure, strength training, history and politics of sports, special population research issues. *Unit head:* Jan Schroeder, Chair, 562-985-4051.

California University of Pennsylvania, School of Graduate Studies and Research, College of Education and Human Services, Program in Exercise Science and Health Promotion, California, PA 15419-1394. Offers performance enhancement and injury prevention (MS); rehabilitation science (MS); sport psychology (MS); wellness and fitness (MS). *Program availability:* Part-time, evening/weekend, online learning. *Degree requirements:* For master's, comprehensive exam, thesis optional. *Entrance requirements:* For master's, minimum GPA of 3.0. Additional exam requirements/recommendations for international students: Required—TOEFL (minimum score 550 paper-based; 80 iBT). Electronic applications accepted. *Expenses:* Contact institution. *Faculty research:* Reducing obesity in children, sport performance, creating unique biomechanical assessment techniques, web-based training for fitness professionals, webcams.

Central Connecticut State University, School of Graduate Studies, School of Education and Professional Studies, Department of Physical Education and Human Performance, New Britain, CT 06050-4010. Offers physical education (MS). *Program availability:* Part-time, evening/weekend. *Faculty:* 6 full-time (2 women), 1 (woman) part-time/adjunct. *Students:* 19 full-time (11 women), 31 part-time (14 women); includes 6 minority (1 Black or African American, non-Hispanic/Latino; 1 Asian, non-Hispanic/Latino; 3 Hispanic/Latino; 1 Two or more races, non-Hispanic/Latino), 1 international. Average age 27. 28 applicants, 89% accepted, 15 enrolled. In 2016, 20 master's, 4 other advanced degrees awarded. *Degree requirements:* For master's, comprehensive exam, thesis or alternative; for Certificate, qualifying exam. *Entrance requirements:* For master's, minimum GPA of 2.7, bachelor's degree in physical education (preferred), essay, interview, letters of recommendation. Additional exam requirements/recommendations for international students: Required—TOEFL (minimum score 550 paper-based; 79 iBT). *Application deadline:* For fall admission, 5/1 for domestic and international students; for spring admission, 11/1 for domestic and international students. Applications are processed on a rolling basis. Application fee: $50. Electronic applications accepted. *Expenses: Tuition, area resident:* Full-time $6497; part-time $606 per credit. Tuition, state resident: full-time $9748; part-time $622 per credit. Tuition, nonresident: full-time $18,102; part-time $622 per credit. *Required fees:* $4459; $246 per credit. *Financial support:* In 2016–17, 8 students received support. Career-related internships or fieldwork, Federal Work-Study, scholarships/grants, and unspecified assistantships available. Support available to part-time students. Financial award application deadline: 3/1; financial award applicants required to submit FAFSA. *Faculty research:* Exercise science, athletic training, preparation of physical education for schools. *Unit head:* Dr. Kimberly Kostelis, Chair, 860-832-2155, E-mail: kostelisk@ccsu.edu. *Application contact:* Patricia Gardner, Associate Director of Graduate Studies, 860-832-2350, Fax: 860-832-2362.
Website: http://www.ccsu.edu/pehp/

Central Michigan University, College of Graduate Studies, The Herbert H. and Grace A. Dow College of Health Professions, Department of Physical Education and Sport, Mount Pleasant, MI 48859. Offers sport administration (MA). *Program availability:* Part-time, evening/weekend. *Degree requirements:* For master's, thesis or alternative. *Entrance requirements:* For master's, GRE (recommended). Electronic applications accepted. *Faculty research:* Athletic administration and sport management, performance enhancing substance use in sport, computer applications for sport managers, mental skill development for ultimate performance, teaching methods.

Central Michigan University, College of Graduate Studies, The Herbert H. and Grace A. Dow College of Health Professions, School of Health Sciences, Mount Pleasant, MI 48859. Offers exercise science (MA); health administration (DHA). *Program availability:* Part-time, evening/weekend, online learning. *Degree requirements:* For doctorate, comprehensive exam, thesis/dissertation. *Entrance requirements:* For doctorate, accredited master's or doctoral degree, 5 years of related work experience. Electronic applications accepted. *Faculty research:* Exercise science.

Central Washington University, Graduate Studies and Research, College of Education and Professional Studies, Department of Nutrition, Exercise and Health Services, Ellensburg, WA 98926. Offers exercise science (MS); nutrition (MS). *Program availability:* Part-time. *Degree requirements:* For master's, thesis or alternative. *Entrance requirements:* For master's, GRE, minimum GPA of 3.0; writing sample (for exercise students). Additional exam requirements/recommendations for international students: Required—TOEFL (minimum score 550 paper-based; 79 iBT). Electronic applications accepted.

College of Saint Elizabeth, Department of Foods and Nutrition, Morristown, NJ 07960-6989. Offers dietetic internship (Certificate); dietetics verification (Certificate); nutrition (MS); sports nutrition and wellness (Certificate). *Program availability:* Part-time, blended/hybrid learning. *Degree requirements:* For master's, thesis. *Entrance requirements:* For master's, GRE, GMAT, minimum cumulative undergraduate GPA of 3.0. Additional exam requirements/recommendations for international students: Required—TOEFL (minimum score 550 paper-based; 79 iBT), IELTS (minimum score 6.5). Electronic applications accepted. Application fee is waived when completed online. *Expenses:* Contact institution. *Faculty research:* Medical nutrition intervention, public policy, obesity, hunger and food security, osteoporosis, nutrition and exercise.

The College of St. Scholastica, Graduate Studies, Department of Exercise Physiology, Duluth, MN 55811-4199. Offers MA. *Program availability:* Part-time. *Degree requirements:* For master's, thesis (for some programs). *Entrance requirements:* Additional exam requirements/recommendations for international students: Required—TOEFL (minimum score 550 paper-based; 79 iBT). Electronic applications accepted. *Faculty research:* Cardiovascular and metabolic responses, cardiorespiratory effects, orthostatic intolerance, lower extremity asymmetry.

Colorado State University, College of Health and Human Sciences, Department of Food Science and Human Nutrition, Fort Collins, CO 80523-1571. Offers dietetics (MS); food science and human nutrition (PhD); food science and nutrition (MS); nutrition and exercise science (MS). *Accreditation:* AND. *Program availability:* Part-time, 100% online, blended/hybrid learning. *Faculty:* 19 full-time (12 women), 1 (woman) part-time/adjunct. *Students:* 54 full-time (43 women), 52 part-time (46 women); includes 7 minority (1 Asian, non-Hispanic/Latino; 4 Hispanic/Latino; 2 Two or more races, non-Hispanic/Latino), 2 international. Average age 31. 115 applicants, 42% accepted, 34 enrolled. In 2016, 16 master's, 4 doctorates awarded. Terminal master's awarded for partial completion of doctoral program. *Degree requirements:* For master's, thesis; for doctorate, thesis/dissertation. *Entrance requirements:* For master's and doctorate, GRE (minimum 50th percentile), minimum GPA of 3.0. Additional exam requirements/recommendations for international students: Required—TOEFL (minimum score 550 paper-based; 80 iBT), IELTS (minimum score 6.5). *Application deadline:* For fall admission, 2/1 priority date for domestic and international students. Application fee: $60 ($70 for international students). Electronic applications accepted. *Expenses:* $545 per credit hour (online). *Financial support:* In 2016–17, 29 students received support, including 2 fellowships with full and partial tuition reimbursements available (averaging $43,424 per year), 10 research assistantships with partial tuition reimbursements available (averaging $15,789 per year), 12 teaching assistantships with partial tuition reimbursements available (averaging $11,030 per year); Federal Work-Study and scholarships/grants also available. Financial award application deadline: 2/1; financial award applicants required to submit FAFSA. *Faculty research:* Community nutrition, bioactive compounds, nutrition and health disparities, fatty acids and pregnancy, nutrition and obesity related disorders. *Total annual research expenditures:* $1.9 million. *Unit head:* Dr. Michael Pagliassotti, Department Head, 970-491-1390, E-mail: michael.pagliassotti@colostate.edu. *Application contact:* Paula Coleman, Administrative Assistant, 970-491-3819, Fax: 970-491-3875, E-mail: paula.coleman@colostate.edu. Website: http://www.fshn.chhs.colostate.edu/

Colorado State University, College of Health and Human Sciences, Department of Health and Exercise Science, Fort Collins, CO 80523-1582. Offers exercise science and nutrition (MS); health and exercise science (MS); human bioenergetics (PhD). *Faculty:* 8 full-time (3 women). *Students:* 25 full-time (10 women), 10 part-time (4 women); includes 3 minority (2 Hispanic/Latino; 1 Two or more races, non-Hispanic/Latino), 1 international. Average age 28. 40 applicants, 45% accepted, 12 enrolled. In 2016, 10 master's, 1 doctorate awarded. Terminal master's awarded for partial completion of doctoral program. *Degree requirements:* For master's, thesis; for doctorate, comprehensive exam, thesis/dissertation. *Entrance requirements:* For master's and doctorate, GRE, minimum overall GPA of 3.0. Additional exam requirements/recommendations for international students: Required—TOEFL (minimum score 550 paper-based; 80 iBT), IELTS (minimum score 6.5). *Application deadline:* For fall admission, 1/31 for domestic and international students; for spring admission, 9/30 for domestic and international students. Application fee: $60 ($70 for international students). Electronic applications accepted. *Expenses:* Tuition, state resident: full-time $9628. Tuition, nonresident: full-time $20,000. *Required fees:* $2253; $528.14 per credit hour. $264.07 per semester. Tuition and fees vary according to course load and program. *Financial support:* In 2016–17, 20 students received support, including 1 fellowship (averaging $51,120 per year), 5 research assistantships (averaging $18,527 per year), 16 teaching assistantships (averaging $15,253 per year). *Faculty research:* Gerontology, chronic disease, human physiology, neurophysiology. *Total annual research expenditures:* $1.4 million. *Unit head:* Dr. Barry Braun, Professor and Department Head, 970-491-7875, Fax: 970-491-0445, E-mail: barry.braun@colostate.edu. *Application contact:* Dr. Matt Hickey, Professor, 970-491-5727, Fax: 970-491-0445, E-mail: matthew.hickey@colostate.edu.
Website: http://www.hes.chhs.colostate.edu/

Columbus State University, Graduate Studies, College of Education and Health Professions, Department of Health, Physical Education and Exercise Science, Columbus, GA 31907-5645. Offers exercise science (MS); health and physical education (M Ed, MAT). *Program availability:* Part-time, evening/weekend. *Faculty:* 5 full-time (3 women). *Students:* 21 full-time (11 women), 8 part-time (2 women); includes 17 minority (12 Black or African American, non-Hispanic/Latino; 1 Asian, non-Hispanic/Latino; 3 Hispanic/Latino; 1 Two or more races, non-Hispanic/Latino). Average age 28. 19 applicants, 37% accepted, 3 enrolled. In 2016, 12 master's awarded. *Degree requirements:* For master's, thesis optional. *Entrance requirements:* For master's, GRE, minimum undergraduate GPA of 2.75. Additional exam requirements/recommendations for international students: Required—TOEFL (minimum score 550 paper-based; 79 iBT). *Application deadline:* For fall admission, 5/1 for domestic students, 4/1 for international students; for spring admission, 11/1 for domestic and international students; for summer admission, 2/1 for domestic students, 3/1 for international students. Applications are processed on a rolling basis. Application fee: $50. Electronic applications accepted. *Expenses:* Tuition, state resident: full-time $4804; part-time $2412 per semester hour. Tuition, nonresident: full-time $19,218; part-time $9612 per semester hour. *Required fees:* $1850; $1850 per semester hour. Tuition and fees vary according to program. *Financial support:* In 2016–17, 3 students received support, including 4 research assistantships (averaging $3,000 per year). Financial award application deadline: 5/15; financial award applicants required to submit FAFSA. *Unit head:* Dr. Tara Underwood, Chair, 706-568-2485, E-mail: underwood_tara@columbusstate.edu. *Application contact:* Kristin Williams, Director of International and Graduate Admissions, 706-507-8848, Fax: 706-568-5091, E-mail: williams_kristin@columbusstate.edu.
Website: http://hpex.columbusstate.edu/

Concordia University, School of Graduate Studies, Faculty of Arts and Science, Department of Exercise Science, Montréal, QC H3G 1M8, Canada. Offers M Sc.

Concordia University Chicago, College of Graduate and Innovative Programs, Program in Human Services, River Forest, IL 60305-1499. Offers human services (MA), including administration, exercise science. *Program availability:* Part-time, evening/weekend. *Degree requirements:* For master's, comprehensive exam, thesis. *Entrance requirements:* For master's, minimum GPA of 2.9. Additional exam requirements/recommendations for international students: Required—TOEFL (minimum score 550 paper-based). Electronic applications accepted.

Concordia University, St. Paul, College of Health and Science, St. Paul, MN 55104-5494. Offers criminal justice leadership (MA); exercise science (MS); family science (MA); human services (MA); orthotics and prosthetics (MS); physical therapy (DPT); sports management (MA). *Program availability:* Part-time, evening/weekend, 100% online, blended/hybrid learning. *Faculty:* 7 full-time (2 women), 27 part-time/adjunct (9 women). *Students:* 337 full-time (194 women), 18 part-time (7 women); includes 65 minority (35 Black or African American, non-Hispanic/Latino; 7 Asian, non-Hispanic/Latino; 8 Hispanic/Latino; 4 Native Hawaiian or other Pacific Islander, non-Hispanic/Latino; 11 Two or more races, non-Hispanic/Latino), 3 international. Average age 30. 388 applicants, 40% accepted, 117 enrolled. In 2016, 92 master's awarded. *Degree requirements:* For master's, comprehensive exam (for some programs), thesis (for some programs); for doctorate, at least one 8-12 week clinical rotation outside the St. Paul area. *Entrance requirements:* For master's, official transcripts from regionally-accredited institution stating the conferral of a bachelor's degree with minimum cumulative GPA of 3.0; personal statement; undergraduate degree at accredited college or university in the U.S., English-speaking Canada, the United Kingdom, Ireland, Australia, or New Zealand; for doctorate, undergraduate or graduate degree at accredited college or university in the U.S., English-speaking Canada, the United Kingdom, Ireland, Australia, or New Zealand. Additional exam requirements/recommendations for international students: Recommended—TOEFL (minimum score 547 paper-based; 78 iBT), IELTS (minimum score 6), TSE (minimum score 52). *Application deadline:* For fall admission, 4/1 for domestic students. Applications are processed on a rolling basis. Application fee: $50. Electronic applications accepted. *Expenses:* Contact institution. *Financial support:* In 2016–17, 114 students received support. Scholarships/grants and unspecified assistantships available. Financial award applicants required to submit FAFSA. *Faculty research:* Developmental screening in early childhood, cardiovascular responses to aerobic exercise. *Unit head:* Dr. Katie Fischer, Interim Dean, 651-641-8735, E-mail: fischer@csp.edu. *Application contact:* Kimberly Craig, Associate Vice President, Cohort Enrollment Management, 651-603-6223, Fax: 651-603-6320, E-mail: craig@csp.edu.

Delaware State University, Graduate Programs, College of Education, Health and Public Policy, Department of Sport Sciences, Dover, DE 19901-2277. Offers sport administration (MS). *Entrance requirements:* Additional exam requirements/recommendations for international students: Required—TOEFL (minimum score 550 paper-based). Electronic applications accepted.

Delta State University, Graduate Programs, College of Education, Division of Health, Physical Education, and Recreation, Cleveland, MS 38733-0001. Offers health, physical education, and recreation (M Ed); sport and human performance (MS). *Program availability:* Part-time, evening/weekend. *Degree requirements:* For master's, thesis optional. *Entrance requirements:* For master's, GRE General Test or MAT, Class A teaching certificate. *Faculty research:* Blood pressure, body fat, power and reaction time, learning disorders of athletes, effects of walking.

East Carolina University, Graduate School, College of Health and Human Performance, Department of Kinesiology, Greenville, NC 27858-4353. Offers adapted physical education (MS); bioenergetics and exercise science (PhD); biomechanics (MS); exercise physiology (MS); physical activity promotion (MS); physical education (MA Ed, MAT); physical education pedagogy (MS); sport and exercise psychology (MS); sport management (MS, Certificate). *Students:* 90 full-time (33 women), 23 part-time (9 women); includes 16 minority (8 Black or African American, non-Hispanic/Latino; 3 Asian, non-Hispanic/Latino; 3 Hispanic/Latino; 2 Two or more races, non-Hispanic/Latino), 7 international. Average age 26. 98 applicants, 53% accepted, 38 enrolled. In 2016, 28 master's, 2 doctorates awarded. *Degree requirements:* For master's, comprehensive exam, thesis optional; for doctorate, comprehensive exam, thesis/dissertation. *Entrance requirements:* For master's, GRE General Test or MAT; for doctorate, GRE. Additional exam requirements/recommendations for international students: Required—TOEFL. *Application deadline:* For fall admission, 2/1 priority date for domestic students, 2/1 for international students. Applications are processed on a rolling basis. Application fee: $50. *Financial support:* Research assistantships with tuition reimbursements and teaching assistantships available. Support available to part-time students. Financial award application deadline: 2/1. *Faculty research:* Diabetes metabolism, pediatric obesity, biomechanics of arthritis, physical activity measurement. *Total annual research expenditures:* $26. *Unit head:* Dr. Stacey Altman, Chair, 252-328-2973, E-mail: altmans@ecu.edu.

Eastern Illinois University, Graduate School, College of Education and Professional Studies, Department of Kinesiology and Sports Studies, Charleston, IL 61920. Offers MS. *Program availability:* Part-time, evening/weekend. *Degree requirements:* For master's, comprehensive exam (for some programs), thesis (for some programs). *Entrance requirements:* For master's, minimum GPA of 3.0 with kinesiology focus, three letters of recommendation, resume, personal statement. Additional exam requirements/recommendations for international students: Required—TOEFL (minimum score 500 paper-based; 61 iBT), IELTS (minimum score 6). Electronic applications accepted.

Eastern Michigan University, Graduate School, College of Health and Human Services, School of Health Promotion and Human Performance, Programs in Exercise Physiology, Ypsilanti, MI 48197. Offers exercise physiology (MS); sports medicine-biomechanics (MS); sports medicine-corporate adult fitness (MS); sports medicine-exercise physiology (MS). *Program availability:* Part-time, evening/weekend. *Students:* 13 full-time (5 women), 19 part-time (9 women); includes 3 minority (1 Black or African

American, non-Hispanic/Latino; 1 Asian, non-Hispanic/Latino; 1 Hispanic/Latino), 2 international. Average age 31. 29 applicants, 69% accepted, 10 enrolled. In 2016, 12 master's awarded. *Degree requirements:* For master's, comprehensive exam, thesis or 450-hour internship. *Entrance requirements:* Additional exam requirements/recommendations for international students: Required—TOEFL. *Application deadline:* For fall admission, 8/1 for domestic students, 5/1 for international students; for winter admission, 12/1 for domestic students, 10/1 for international students; for spring admission, 3/15 for domestic students, 3/1 for international students. Application fee: $45. *Application contact:* Dr. Stephen McGregor, Program Coordinator, 734-487-0090, Fax: 734-487-2024, E-mail: smcgregor@emich.edu.

Eastern New Mexico University, Graduate School, College of Education and Technology, Department of Health and Physical Education, Portales, NM 88130. Offers physical education (MS), including sport administration, sport science. *Program availability:* Part-time. *Degree requirements:* For master's, comprehensive exam, thesis optional. *Entrance requirements:* For master's, minimum GPA of 3.0, 15 hours of leveling courses without bachelor's degree in physical education, two references. Additional exam requirements/recommendations for international students: Required—TOEFL (minimum score 550 paper-based; 79 iBT), IELTS (minimum score 6). Electronic applications accepted.

Eastern Washington University, Graduate Studies, College of Arts, Letters and Education, Department of Physical Education, Health and Recreation, Cheney, WA 99004-2431. Offers exercise science (MS); sports and recreation administration (MS). *Faculty:* 17 full-time (7 women), 5 part-time/adjunct (2 women). *Students:* 26 full-time (10 women), 8 part-time (3 women); includes 7 minority (3 Black or African American, non-Hispanic/Latino; 1 American Indian or Alaska Native, non-Hispanic/Latino; 2 Asian, non-Hispanic/Latino; 1 Hispanic/Latino). Average age 29. 64 applicants, 38% accepted, 21 enrolled. In 2016, 14 master's awarded. *Degree requirements:* For master's, comprehensive exam, thesis or alternative. *Entrance requirements:* For master's, minimum GPA of 3.0. Additional exam requirements/recommendations for international students: Required—TOEFL (minimum score 580 paper-based; 92 iBT), IELTS (minimum score 7), PTE (minimum score 63). *Application deadline:* For fall admission, 4/1 priority date for domestic students; for spring admission, 1/15 for domestic students. Applications are processed on a rolling basis. Application fee: $50. Electronic applications accepted. *Expenses:* Tuition, state resident: full-time $11,000; part-time $5500 per credit. Tuition, nonresident: full-time $24,000; part-time $12,000 per credit. *Required fees:* $1300. One-time fee: $50 full-time. Part-time tuition and fees vary according to course load, campus/location and program. *Financial support:* In 2016–17, 10 teaching assistantships with partial tuition reimbursements (averaging $6,624 per year) were awarded; career-related internships or fieldwork, Federal Work-Study, institutionally sponsored loans, and scholarships/grants also available. Support available to part-time students. Financial award application deadline: 2/1; financial award applicants required to submit FAFSA. *Unit head:* Dr. Chadron Hazelbaker, Graduate Program Director, 509-359-2486, Fax: 509-359-4833, E-mail: chazelbaker@ewu.edu.

East Tennessee State University, School of Graduate Studies, College of Education, Department of Exercise and Sport Science, Johnson City, TN 37614. Offers exercise physiology and performance (MA), including coaching and sports performance, research; sport physiology and performance (PhD), including sport performance, sport physiology. *Program availability:* Part-time, evening/weekend. *Degree requirements:* For master's, comprehensive exam, thesis or internship; for doctorate, comprehensive exam, thesis/dissertation, two semesters of full-time residency. *Entrance requirements:* For master's, GRE General Test, undergraduate degree in related field; minimum GPA of 2.7; resume; three references; essay explaining goals and reasons for pursuing degree; for doctorate, GRE General Test, curriculum vitae or resume; four letters of recommendation (minimum of two from previous college professors); interview. Additional exam requirements/recommendations for international students: Required—TOEFL (minimum score 550 paper-based; 79 iBT). Electronic applications accepted.

Fairmont State University, Programs in Education, Fairmont, WV 26554. Offers digital media, new literacies and learning (M Ed); education (MAT); exercise science, fitness and wellness (M Ed); professional studies (M Ed); reading (M Ed); special education (M Ed). *Accreditation:* NCATE. *Program availability:* Part-time, evening/weekend, 100% online. *Faculty:* 18 full-time (11 women), 5 part-time/adjunct (3 women). *Students:* 62 full-time (52 women), 102 part-time (82 women); includes 6 minority (2 Black or African American, non-Hispanic/Latino; 1 American Indian or Alaska Native, non-Hispanic/Latino; 1 Hispanic/Latino; 2 Two or more races, non-Hispanic/Latino). Average age 33. 68 applicants, 84% accepted, 47 enrolled. In 2016, 44 degrees awarded. *Entrance requirements:* For master's, GRE. Additional exam requirements/recommendations for international students: Required—TOEFL (minimum score 80 iBT), IELTS (minimum score 6.5). *Application deadline:* For fall admission, 5/1 for domestic and international students. Applications are processed on a rolling basis. Application fee: $40. Electronic applications accepted. *Expenses:* Tuition, state resident: full-time $7504; part-time $405 per credit hour. Tuition, nonresident: full-time $16,060; part-time $880 per credit hour. Part-time tuition and fees vary according to course load. *Financial support:* In 2016–17, 20 students received support. Research assistantships, teaching assistantships, scholarships/grants, and unspecified assistantships available. Financial award applicants required to submit FAFSA. *Unit head:* Dr. Carolyn Crislip-Tacy, Interim Dean, School of Education, 304-367-4143, Fax: 304-367-4599, E-mail: carolyn.crislip-tacy@fairmontstate.edu. *Application contact:* Jack Kirby, Director of Graduate Studies, 304-367-4101, E-mail: jack.kirby@fairmontstate.edu.
Website: http://www.fairmontstate.edu/graduatestudies/

Florida Atlantic University, College of Education, Department of Exercise Science and Health Promotion, Boca Raton, FL 33431-0991. Offers MS. *Program availability:* Part-time, evening/weekend. *Faculty:* 7 full-time (3 women). *Students:* 41 full-time (16 women), 21 part-time (8 women); includes 19 minority (9 Black or African American, non-Hispanic/Latino; 1 Asian, non-Hispanic/Latino; 6 Hispanic/Latino; 3 Two or more races, non-Hispanic/Latino), 2 international. Average age 27. 79 applicants, 54% accepted, 26 enrolled. In 2016, 23 master's awarded. *Degree requirements:* For master's, comprehensive exam, thesis optional. *Entrance requirements:* For master's, GRE General Test, minimum GPA of 3.0 during last 60 hours of course work. Additional exam requirements/recommendations for international students: Required—TOEFL (minimum score 500 paper-based; 61 iBT), IELTS (minimum score 6). *Application deadline:* For fall admission, 7/1 priority date for domestic students, 2/15 for international students; for spring admission, 11/1 priority date for domestic students, 7/15 for international students. Applications are processed on a rolling basis. Application fee: $30. *Expenses:* Tuition, state resident: full-time $7392; part-time $369.82 per credit hour. Tuition, nonresident: full-time $19,432; part-time $1024.81 per credit hour. *Financial support:* Research assistantships with partial tuition reimbursements, teaching assistantships with partial tuition reimbursements, and career-related internships or fieldwork available. *Faculty research:* Pulmonary limitations during exercise, metabolism regulation, determinants of performance, age-related change in functional mobility and geriatric exercise, behavioral change aimed at promoting active lifestyles. *Unit head:* Dr. Robert Zoeller, 561-297-2549, E-mail: rzoeller@fau.edu.
Website: http://www.coe.fau.edu/academicdepartments/eshp/

Florida State University, The Graduate School, College of Human Sciences, Department of Nutrition, Food and Exercise Sciences, Tallahassee, FL 32306-1493. Offers exercise physiology (MS, PhD); nutrition and food science (MS, PhD), including clinical nutrition (MS), food science, human nutrition (PhD), nutrition education and health promotion (MS), nutrition science (MS); sports nutrition (MS); sports sciences (MS). *Program availability:* Part-time. *Faculty:* 20 full-time (8 women). *Students:* 84 full-time (49 women), 12 part-time (8 women); includes 17 minority (3 Black or African American, non-Hispanic/Latino; 1 Asian, non-Hispanic/Latino; 6 Hispanic/Latino; 7 Two or more races, non-Hispanic/Latino), 16 international. 125 applicants, 50% accepted, 37 enrolled. In 2016, 30 master's, 2 doctorates awarded. *Degree requirements:* For master's, thesis optional; for doctorate, thesis/dissertation. *Entrance requirements:* For master's and doctorate, GRE General Test, minimum upper-division GPA of 3.0. Additional exam requirements/recommendations for international students: Required—TOEFL (minimum score 550 paper-based; 80 iBT). *Application deadline:* For fall admission, 4/1 for domestic and international students; for spring admission, 10/1 for domestic and international students. Applications are processed on a rolling basis. Application fee: $30. Electronic applications accepted. *Expenses:* Tuition, state resident: full-time $7263; part-time $403.51 per credit hour. Tuition, nonresident: full-time $18,087; part-time $1004.85 per credit hour. *Required fees:* $1365; $75.81 per credit hour. $20 per semester. Tuition and fees vary according to campus/location. *Financial support:* In 2016–17, 50 students received support, including 22 research assistantships with full tuition reimbursements available (averaging $7,026 per year), 47 teaching assistantships with full tuition reimbursements available (averaging $8,508 per year); career-related internships or fieldwork, Federal Work-Study, institutionally sponsored loans, scholarships/grants, and unspecified assistantships also available. Financial award application deadline: 2/1; financial award applicants required to submit FAFSA. *Faculty research:* Body composition, functional food, chronic disease and aging response; food safety, food allergy, and safety/quality detection methods; sports nutrition, energy and human performance; strength training, functional performance, cardiovascular physiology, sarcopenia. *Total annual research expenditures:* $712,777. *Unit head:* Dr. Chester Ray, Department Chair, 850-644-1850, Fax: 850-645-5000, E-mail: caray@fsu.edu. *Application contact:* Ann R. Smith, Office Administrator, 850-644-1828, Fax: 850-645-5000, E-mail: asmith@fsu.edu.
Website: http://www.chs.fsu.edu/Departments/Nutrition-Food-Exercise-Sciences

Gannon University, School of Graduate Studies, Morosky College of Health Professions and Sciences, School of Health Professions, Program in Sport and Exercise Science, Erie, PA 16541-0001. Offers human performance (MS). *Program availability:* Part-time, evening/weekend. *Students:* 9 full-time (4 women), 1 international. Average age 23. 2 applicants, 50% accepted, 1 enrolled. In 2016, 12 master's awarded. *Degree requirements:* For master's, thesis (for some programs), internship (for some programs). *Entrance requirements:* For master's, undergraduate degree in exercise science, kinesiology, human performance, sports medicine, or related field with minimum GPA of 2.75; 3 letters of recommendation. Additional exam requirements/recommendations for international students: Required—TOEFL (minimum score 79 iBT). *Application deadline:* Applications are processed on a rolling basis. Application fee: $25. Electronic applications accepted. Application fee is waived when completed online. *Expenses: Tuition:* Full-time $17,370. *Required fees:* $550. Tuition and fees vary according to course load and program. *Financial support:* Federal Work-Study and unspecified assistantships available. Financial award application deadline: 7/1; financial award applicants required to submit FAFSA. *Unit head:* Dr. Kory Stauffer, Program Director, 814-871-7515, E-mail: stauffer005@gannon.edu. *Application contact:* Bridget Philip, Director of Graduate Admissions, 814-871-7412, E-mail: graduate@gannon.edu.

Gardner-Webb University, Graduate School, Department of Physical Education, Wellness, and Sport Studies, Boiling Springs, NC 28017. Offers sport science and pedagogy (MA). *Program availability:* Part-time, evening/weekend. *Faculty:* 2 full-time (1 woman). *Students:* 1 (woman) full-time, 9 part-time (2 women); includes 1 minority (Asian, non-Hispanic/Latino). Average age 24. 27 applicants, 48% accepted, 7 enrolled. In 2016, 5 master's awarded. *Degree requirements:* For master's, comprehensive exam. *Entrance requirements:* For master's, GRE General Test or NTE, PRAXIS, minimum GPA of 2.5. *Application deadline:* For fall admission, 8/1 priority date for domestic students. Applications are processed on a rolling basis. Application fee: $0. Electronic applications accepted. *Expenses:* Contact institution. *Financial support:* Unspecified assistantships available. *Unit head:* Dr. Ken Baker, Chair, 704-406-4481, Fax: 704-406-4739. *Application contact:* Office of Graduate Admissions, 877-498-4723, Fax: 704-406-3895, E-mail: gradinfo@gardner-webb.edu.

George Mason University, College of Education and Human Development, School of Recreation, Health and Tourism, Manassas, VA 20110. Offers exercise, fitness, and health promotion (MS), including advanced practitioner; recreation, health and tourism (Certificate). *Faculty:* 30 full-time (12 women), 74 part-time/adjunct (37 women). *Students:* 45 full-time (27 women), 23 part-time (11 women); includes 15 minority (9 Black or African American, non-Hispanic/Latino; 3 Asian, non-Hispanic/Latino; 1 Hispanic/Latino; 2 Two or more races, non-Hispanic/Latino), 3 international. Average age 26. 69 applicants, 99% accepted, 33 enrolled. In 2016, 14 master's awarded. *Degree requirements:* For master's, thesis (for some programs). *Entrance requirements:* For master's, GRE General Test or MAT, 3 letters of recommendation; official transcripts; expanded goals statement; undergraduate course in statistics and minimum GPA of 3.0 in last 60 credit hours and overall (for MS in sport and recreation studies); baccalaureate degree related to kinesiology, exercise science or athletic training (for MS in exercise, fitness and health promotion). Additional exam requirements/recommendations for international students: Required—TOEFL (minimum score 575 paper-based; 88 iBT), IELTS (minimum score 6.5), PTE (minimum score 59). *Application deadline:* For spring admission, 11/1 priority date for domestic and international students. Application fee: $75 ($80 for international students). Electronic applications accepted. *Expenses:* Tuition, state resident: full-time $10,628; part-time $443 per credit. Tuition, nonresident: full-time $29,306; part-time $1221 per credit. *Required fees:* $3096; $129 per credit. Tuition and fees vary according to program. *Financial support:* In 2016–17, 10 students received support, including 3 fellowships (averaging $13,575 per year), 3 research assistantships with tuition reimbursements available (averaging $9,467 per year); career-related internships or fieldwork, Federal Work-Study, scholarships/grants, unspecified assistantships, and health care benefits (for full-time research or teaching assistantship recipients) also available. Support available to part-time students. Financial award application deadline: 3/1; financial award applicants required to submit FAFSA. *Faculty research:* Informing policy; promoting economic development; advocating stewardship of natural resources; improving the quality of life of individuals, families, and communities at the local, national and international levels. *Total annual research expenditures:* $1.1 million. *Unit head:* Martin Ford, Senior Associate Dean, 703-993-2004, E-mail: mford@gmu.edu. *Application contact:* Lindsey Olson, Office Assistant, 703-993-2098, Fax: 703-993-2025, E-mail: lolson7@gmu.edu.
Website: http://rht.gmu.edu/

The George Washington University, Milken Institute School of Public Health, Department of Exercise and Nutrition Sciences, Washington, DC 20052. Offers MS. *Faculty:* 11 full-time (8 women). *Students:* 12 full-time (6 women), 3 part-time (0 women); includes 5 minority (2 Black or African American, non-Hispanic/Latino; 2 Asian, non-Hispanic/Latino; 1 Hispanic/Latino). Average age 27. 25 applicants, 56% accepted, 7 enrolled. In 2016, 12 master's awarded. *Degree requirements:* For master's, comprehensive exam, thesis. *Entrance requirements:* For master's, GRE General Test or MAT. Additional exam requirements/recommendations for international students: Required—TOEFL. *Application deadline:* For fall admission, 4/15 priority date for domestic students, 4/15 for international students; for spring admission, 11/1 for domestic and international students. Applications are processed on a rolling basis. Application fee: $75. *Financial support:* In 2016–17, 12 students received support. Tuition waivers available. Financial award application deadline: 2/15. *Faculty research:* Fitness and cardiac rehabilitation, exercise testing, women in exercise. *Unit head:* Dr. Loretta DiPietro, Chair, 202-994-4910, Fax: 202-994-1420, E-mail: ldp1@gwu.edu. *Application contact:* Jane Smith, Director of Admissions, 202-994-0248, Fax: 202-994-1860, E-mail: sphhsinfo@gwumc.edu.

Georgia College & State University, Graduate School, College of Health Sciences, School of Health and Human Performance, Milledgeville, GA 31061. Offers health and human performance (MS), including health performance, health promotion; kinesiology/health education (MAT). *Accreditation:* NCATE (one or more programs are accredited). *Program availability:* Part-time, evening/weekend, 100% online. *Students:* 43 full-time (25 women), 17 part-time (15 women); includes 6 minority (4 Black or African American, non-Hispanic/Latino; 1 Asian, non-Hispanic/Latino; 1 Hispanic/Latino), 1 international. Average age 28. 33 applicants, 100% accepted, 28 enrolled. In 2016, 23 master's awarded. *Degree requirements:* For master's, completed in 6 years with minimum GPA of 3.0, thesis or project (for MS); minimum GPA of 3.0, GACE Exam and Assessment, and electronic teaching portfolio (for MAT). *Entrance requirements:* For master's, GRE with minimum score of 297 or MAT with minimum score of 385 (for MS); SAT (minimum score of 1000), ACT (minimum score of 43), GRE (minimum score of 297), MAT (minimum score of 385), or GACE Program Admission Assessment (for MAT), resume, 3 professional references; minimum GPA of 2.75 in upper-level undergraduate courses and undergraduate statistics course (for MS); minimum GPA of 2.75 on upper-division major courses (for MAT). *Application deadline:* For fall admission, 7/15 priority date for domestic students, 4/1 for international students; for spring admission, 11/15 priority date for domestic students, 9/1 for international students; for summer admission, 4/15 priority date for domestic students. Applications are processed on a rolling basis. Application fee: $40. Electronic applications accepted. *Expenses:* $228 per credit hour in-state tuition, $1,027 per credit hour out-of-state tuition, $1,990 per year fees (for MAT); $338 per credit hour (for MS). *Financial support:* In 2016–17, 24 students received support. Unspecified assistantships available. Support available to part-time students. Financial award application deadline: 3/1; financial award applicants required to submit FAFSA. *Unit head:* Dr. Lisa Griffin, Director, School of Health and Human Performance, 478-445-4072, Fax: 478-445-4074, E-mail: lisa.griffin@gcsu.edu.
Website: http://www.gcsu.edu/health/shhp

Georgia State University, College of Education and Human Development, Department of Kinesiology and Health, Program in Exercise Science, Atlanta, GA 30302-3083. Offers MS. *Degree requirements:* For master's, comprehensive exam. *Entrance requirements:* For master's, GRE General Test, minimum GPA of 2.5. *Application deadline:* For fall admission, 5/1 for domestic students; for spring admission, 10/1 for domestic students. Application fee: $50. *Expenses:* Tuition, state resident: full-time $6876; part-time $382 per credit hour. Tuition, nonresident: full-time $22,374; part-time $1243 per credit hour. *Required fees:* $2128; $1064 per term. Part-time tuition and fees vary according to course load and program. *Financial support:* Research assistantships available. *Faculty research:* Aging, exercise metabolism, biomechanics and ergonomics, blood pressure regulation, exercise performance. *Unit head:* Dr. Jacalyn Lea Lund, Chair, 404-413-8051, E-mail: jlund@gsu.edu. *Application contact:* Dr. Christopher Ingalls, Program Coordinator, 404-413-8377, E-mail: cingalls@gsu.edu.
Website: http://kh.education.gsu.edu/academics-admissions/exercise-science/exercise-science-b-s/

Howard University, Graduate School, Department of Health, Human Performance and Leisure Studies, Washington, DC 20059-0002. Offers exercise physiology (MS); health education (MS); sports studies (MS), including sociology of sports, sports management; urban recreation (MS), including leisure studies. *Program availability:* Part-time, evening/weekend. *Degree requirements:* For master's, comprehensive exam, thesis. *Entrance requirements:* For master's, BS in human performance or related field. Additional exam requirements/recommendations for international students: Recommended—TOEFL. Electronic applications accepted. *Faculty research:* Health promotion, cardiovascular hypertension, physical activity, sport and human rights issues.

Indiana University Bloomington, School of Public Health, Department of Kinesiology, Bloomington, IN 47405. Offers applied sport science (MS); athletic administration/sport management (MS); athletic training (MS); biomechanics (MS); ergonomics (MS); exercise physiology (MS); human performance (PhD), including biomechanics, exercise physiology, motor learning/control, sport management; motor learning/control (MS); physical activity (MPH); physical activity, fitness and wellness (MS). *Program availability:* Part-time. Terminal master's awarded for partial completion of doctoral program. *Degree requirements:* For master's, thesis optional; for doctorate, variable foreign language requirement, comprehensive exam, thesis/dissertation. *Entrance requirements:* For master's, GRE General Test, minimum GPA of 2.8; for doctorate, GRE General Test, minimum graduate GPA of 3.5, undergraduate 3.0. Additional exam requirements/recommendations for international students: Required—TOEFL (minimum score 80 iBT). *Faculty research:* Exercise physiology and biochemistry, sports biomechanics, human motor control, adaptation of fitness and exercise to special populations.

Indiana University of Pennsylvania, School of Graduate Studies and Research, College of Health and Human Services, Department of Kinesiology, Health, and Sport Science, MS Program in Sport Science/Exercise Science, Indiana, PA 15705. Offers MS. *Program availability:* Part-time. *Faculty:* 10 full-time (3 women). *Students:* 16 full-time (7 women), 2 part-time (0 women); includes 2 minority (both Black or African American, non-Hispanic/Latino). Average age 23. 37 applicants, 70% accepted, 18 enrolled. In 2016, 14 master's awarded. *Degree requirements:* For master's, thesis optional. *Entrance requirements:* For master's, 2 letters of recommendation. Additional exam requirements/recommendations for international students: Required—TOEFL (minimum score 540 paper-based). *Application deadline:* Applications are processed on a rolling basis. Application fee: $50. Electronic applications accepted. *Expenses:* Tuition, state resident: full-time $8694; part-time $483 per credit. Tuition, nonresident: full-time $13,050; part-time $725 per credit. *Required fees:* $157 per credit. $50 per term. Tuition and fees vary according to course load and program. *Financial support:* In 2016–17, 5 research assistantships with tuition reimbursements (averaging $4,208 per year) were awarded; fellowships with partial tuition reimbursements, career-related internships or fieldwork, scholarships/grants, and unspecified assistantships also available. Support available to part-time students. Financial award application deadline: 4/15; financial award applicants required to submit FAFSA. *Unit head:* Dr. Madeline Bayles, Coordinator, 724-357-7835, E-mail: mpbayles@iup.edu.
Website: http://www.iup.edu/kines/grad/sport-science-exercise-science-ms/default.aspx

Indiana University of Pennsylvania, School of Graduate Studies and Research, College of Health and Human Services, Department of Kinesiology, Health, and Sport Science, Program in Sport Science/Sport Studies, Indiana, PA 15705. Offers MS. *Program availability:* Part-time. *Faculty:* 10 full-time (3 women). *Students:* 5 full-time (2 women); includes 1 minority (Black or African American, non-Hispanic/Latino). Average age 22. 8 applicants, 88% accepted, 4 enrolled. In 2016, 9 master's awarded. *Degree requirements:* For master's, thesis optional. *Entrance requirements:* Additional exam requirements/recommendations for international students: Required—TOEFL (minimum score 540 paper-based). *Application deadline:* Applications are processed on a rolling basis. Application fee: $50. Electronic applications accepted. *Expenses:* Contact institution. *Financial support:* In 2016–17, 2 research assistantships with tuition reimbursements (averaging $2,720 per year) were awarded; career-related internships or fieldwork, Federal Work-Study, scholarships/grants, and unspecified assistantships also available. Support available to part-time students. Financial award application deadline: 4/15; financial award applicants required to submit FAFSA. *Unit head:* Dr. Robert Kostelnik, Graduate Coordinator, 724-357-7645, E-mail: bkostel@iup.edu.
Website: http://www.iup.edu/grad/sportscience/default.aspx

Inter American University of Puerto Rico, Metropolitan Campus, Graduate Programs, Program in Physical Education, San Juan, PR 00919-1293. Offers teaching of physical education (MA); training and sport performance (MA). *Degree requirements:* For master's, comprehensive exam. *Entrance requirements:* For master's, GRE or EXADEP, interview. Electronic applications accepted.

Iowa State University of Science and Technology, Program in Diet and Exercise, Ames, IA 50011. Offers MS. *Entrance requirements:* For master's, GRE, minimum GPA of 3.5, 3 letters of recommendation. Additional exam requirements/recommendations for international students: Required—TOEFL (minimum score 550 paper-based; 79 iBT), IELTS (minimum score 6.5). Application fee: $60 ($90 for international students). Electronic applications accepted. *Financial support:* Unspecified assistantships available. *Application contact:* Lorraine Lanningham-Foster, Application Contact, 515-294-4684, Fax: 515-294-6193, E-mail: lmlf@iastate.edu.
Website: http://www.hs.iastate.edu/dietandexercise/

Ithaca College, School of Health Sciences and Human Performance, Program in Exercise and Sport Sciences, Ithaca, NY 14850. Offers MS. *Program availability:* Part-time. *Faculty:* 11 full-time (4 women). *Students:* 26 full-time (10 women), 14 part-time (11 women); includes 1 minority (Hispanic/Latino), 5 international. Average age 23. 104 applicants, 63% accepted, 23 enrolled. In 2016, 19 master's awarded. *Degree requirements:* For master's, comprehensive exam (for some programs), thesis optional. *Entrance requirements:* For master's, GRE General Test. Additional exam requirements/recommendations for international students: Required—TOEFL (minimum score 550 paper-based; 80 iBT). *Application deadline:* For fall admission, 3/1 priority date for domestic students, 3/1 for international students. Applications are processed on a rolling basis. Application fee: $40. Electronic applications accepted. *Expenses:* Contact institution. *Financial support:* In 2016–17, 25 students received support, including 25 research assistantships (averaging $14,714 per year); career-related internships or fieldwork, Federal Work-Study, scholarships/grants, and unspecified assistantships also available. Support available to part-time students. Financial award application deadline: 3/1; financial award applicants required to submit CSS PROFILE or FAFSA. *Unit head:* Dr. Jeff Ives, Chair, 607-274-1751, Fax: 607-274-1263, E-mail: jives@ithaca.edu. *Application contact:* Nicole Eversley Bradwell, Director, Office of Admission, 607-274-3124, Fax: 607-274-1263, E-mail: admission@ithaca.edu.
Website: http://www.ithaca.edu/gradprograms/ess

James Madison University, The Graduate School, College of Health and Behavioral Sciences, Program in Kinesiology, Harrisonburg, VA 22802. Offers clinical exercise physiology (MS); exercise physiology (MS); kinesiology (MAT, MS); nutrition and exercise (MS); physical and health education (MAT); sport and recreation leadership (MS). *Program availability:* Part-time, evening/weekend. *Faculty:* 9 full-time (3 women), 2 part-time/adjunct (1 woman). *Students:* 64 full-time (27 women), 8 part-time (5 women); includes 6 minority (1 Black or African American, non-Hispanic/Latino; 1 Asian, non-Hispanic/Latino; 2 Hispanic/Latino; 2 Two or more races, non-Hispanic/Latino). Average age 30. 140 applicants, 70% accepted, 44 enrolled. In 2016, 42 master's awarded. Application fee: $55. Electronic applications accepted. *Financial support:* In 2016–17, 45 students received support, including 14 teaching assistantships with full tuition reimbursements available (averaging $8,837 per year); Federal Work-Study and 25 assistantships (averaging $7911), 20 athletic assistantships (averaging $9284) also available. Financial award application deadline: 3/1; financial award applicants required to submit FAFSA. *Unit head:* Dr. Christopher J. Womack, Department Head, 540-568-6145, E-mail: womackcx@jmu.edu. *Application contact:* Lynette D. Michael, Director of Graduate Admissions, 540-568-6131 Ext. 6395, Fax: 540-568-7860, E-mail: michaeld@jmu.edu.
Website: http://www.jmu.edu/kinesiology/

Kean University, College of Education, Program in Exercise Science, Union, NJ 07083. Offers MS. *Program availability:* Part-time. *Faculty:* 16 full-time (9 women). *Students:* 13 full-time (5 women), 10 part-time (3 women); includes 11 minority (4 Black or African American, non-Hispanic/Latino; 1 Asian, non-Hispanic/Latino; 6 Hispanic/Latino). Average age 26. 20 applicants, 45% accepted, 12 enrolled. In 2016, 1 master's awarded. *Degree requirements:* For master's, comprehensive exam, thesis, research component. *Entrance requirements:* For master's, GRE General Test, minimum B average in undergraduate prerequisites; minimum cumulative GPA of 3.0; official transcripts from all institutions attended; two letters of recommendation; personal statement; professional resume/curriculum vitae. Additional exam requirements/recommendations for international students: Required—TOEFL (minimum score 550 paper-based; 79 iBT), IELTS (minimum score 6.5). *Application deadline:* For fall admission, 6/1 for domestic and international students; for spring admission, 12/1 for domestic and international students. Applications are processed on a rolling basis. Application fee: $75. Electronic applications accepted. *Expenses:* Tuition, state resident: full-time $13,156; part-time $640 per credit. Tuition, nonresident: full-time $17,831; part-time $785 per credit. *Required fees:* $3316; $151 per credit. Tuition and fees vary according to course level, course load, degree level and program. *Financial support:* Scholarships/grants and unspecified assistantships available. Financial award applicants required to submit FAFSA. *Unit head:* Dr. Walter D. Andzel, Program Coordinator, 908-737-0662, E-mail: wandzel@kean.edu. *Application contact:* Brittany Gerstenhaber, Admissions Counselor, 908-737-7100, E-mail: grad-adm@kean.edu.
Website: http://grad.kean.edu/masters-programs/exercise-science

Kennesaw State University, WellStar College of Health and Human Services, Program in Applied Exercise and Health Science, Kennesaw, GA 30144. Offers MS. *Program availability:* Part-time, evening/weekend. *Entrance requirements:* For master's, GRE, resume. Additional exam requirements/recommendations for international students: Required—TOEFL (minimum score 550 paper-based; 80 iBT), IELTS (minimum score 6.5). Electronic applications accepted.

Kent State University, College of Education, Health and Human Services, School of Foundations, Leadership and Administration, Sports Recreation and Management Program, Kent, OH 44242-0001. Offers sport and recreation management (MA); sports studies (MA). *Degree requirements:* For master's, thesis optional. *Entrance* *requirements:* For master's, GRE if undergraduate GPA below 3.0, goals statement, 2 letters of recommendation. Additional exam requirements/recommendations for international students: Required—TOEFL (minimum score 550 paper-based; 80 iBT). *Expenses:* Tuition, state resident: full-time $10,864; part-time $495 per credit hour. Tuition, nonresident: full-time $18,380; part-time $837 per credit hour.

Kent State University, College of Education, Health and Human Services, School of Health Sciences, Program in Exercise Physiology, Kent, OH 44242-0001. Offers athletic training (MS); exercise physiology (PhD). *Degree requirements:* For doctorate, comprehensive exam, thesis/dissertation. *Entrance requirements:* For master's, GRE, 2 letters of reference, goals statement; for doctorate, GRE, 2 letters of reference, goals statement, minimum master's-level GPA of 3.0. Additional exam requirements/ recommendations for international students: Required—TOEFL (minimum score 550 paper-based; 80 iBT). *Expenses:* Tuition, state resident: full-time $10,864; part-time $495 per credit hour. Tuition, nonresident: full-time $18,380; part-time $837 per credit hour.

Lakehead University, Graduate Studies, School of Kinesiology, Thunder Bay, ON P7B 5E1, Canada. Offers kinesiology (M Sc); kinesiology and gerontology (M Sc). *Program availability:* Part-time. *Degree requirements:* For master's, thesis. *Entrance requirements:* For master's, minimum B average. Additional exam requirements/ recommendations for international students: Required—TOEFL. *Faculty research:* Social psychology and physical education, sport history, sports medicine, exercise physiology, gerontology.

Life University, Graduate Programs, Marietta, GA 30060-2903. Offers athletic training (MAT); chiropractic sport science (MS); clinical nutrition (MS); nutrition and sport science (MS), including chiropractic sport science; sport coaching (MS), including exercise sport science; sport injury management (MS), including nutrition and sport science; sports health science (MS). *Program availability:* Part-time, 100% online, blended/hybrid learning. *Degree requirements:* For master's, comprehensive exam (for some programs), thesis optional. *Entrance requirements:* For master's, GRE General Test, minimum GPA of 3.0, 3 letters of recommendation, curriculum vitae. Additional exam requirements/recommendations for international students: Required—TOEFL (minimum score 500 paper-based). Electronic applications accepted. *Expenses:* Contact institution.

Lipscomb University, Program in Exercise and Nutrition Science, Nashville, TN 37204-3951. Offers MS. *Program availability:* Part-time, evening/weekend. *Faculty:* 7 full-time (4 women). *Students:* 25 full-time (16 women), 15 part-time (12 women); includes 7 minority (4 Black or African American, non-Hispanic/Latino; 3 Hispanic/Latino). Average age 27. In 2016, 31 master's awarded. *Degree requirements:* For master's, comprehensive exam (for some programs), thesis optional. *Entrance requirements:* For master's, GRE (minimum score of 800), minimum GPA of 2.75 on all undergraduate work; 2 letters of recommendation; resume. Additional exam requirements/ recommendations for international students: Required—TOEFL (minimum score 570 paper-based; 80 iBT). *Application deadline:* For fall admission, 6/1 for domestic students; for spring admission, 12/1 for domestic students. Applications are processed on a rolling basis. Application fee: $50 ($75 for international students). Electronic applications accepted. *Expenses:* $930 per hour. *Financial support:* Unspecified assistantships available. Financial award applicants required to submit FAFSA. *Unit head:* Dr. Karen Robichaud, Director, 615-966-5602, E-mail: karen.robichaud@lipscomb.edu. *Application contact:* Julie Lillicrap, Administrative Assistant, 615-966-5700, E-mail: julie.lillicrap@lipscomb.edu.
Website: http://www.lipscomb.edu/kinesiology/graduate-programs

Logan University, College of Health Sciences, Chesterfield, MO 63017. Offers health informatics (MS); health professionals education (DHPE); nutrition and human performance (MS); sports science and rehabilitation (MS). *Program availability:* Part-time, online only, 100% online. *Faculty:* 2 full-time (1 woman), 14 part-time/adjunct (6 women). *Students:* 54 full-time (40 women), 255 part-time (182 women); includes 38 minority (16 Black or African American, non-Hispanic/Latino; 4 Asian, non-Hispanic/ Latino; 10 Hispanic/Latino; 8 Two or more races, non-Hispanic/Latino), 14 international. Average age 35. 229 applicants, 88% accepted, 164 enrolled. In 2016, 89 master's awarded. *Entrance requirements:* For master's, minimum GPA of 2.5; 6 hours of biology and physical science; bachelor's degree and 9 hours of business health administration (for health informatics). Additional exam requirements/recommendations for international students: Required—TOEFL (minimum score 500 paper-based; 79 iBT); Recommended—IELTS (minimum score 6.5). *Application deadline:* Applications are processed on a rolling basis. Application fee: $50. Electronic applications accepted. *Expenses:* $650 tuition per credit hour (for DHPE), $450 tuition per credit hour (for MS); $80 fees per trimester. *Financial support:* In 2016–17, 4 students received support. Federal Work-Study and scholarships/grants available. Support available to part-time students. Financial award applicants required to submit FAFSA. *Faculty research:* Ankle injury prevention in high school athletes, low back pain in college football players, short arc banding and low back pain, the effects of enzymes on inflammatory blood markers, gait analysis in high school and college athletes. *Unit head:* Dr. Sherri Cole, Dean, College of Health Sciences, 636-227-2100 Ext. 2702, Fax: 636-207-2418, E-mail: sherri.cole@logan.edu. *Application contact:* Jordan LaMarca, Assistant Director of Admissions, 636-227-2100 Ext. 1973, Fax: 636-207-2425, E-mail: admissions@logan.edu.

Long Island University–LIU Brooklyn, School of Health Professions, Brooklyn, NY 11201-8423. Offers athletic training and sport sciences (MS); community health (MS Ed); exercise science (MS); forensic social work (Advanced Certificate); occupational therapy (MS); physical therapy (DPT); physician assistant (MS); public health (MPH); social work (MSW). *Faculty:* 60 full-time (42 women), 109 part-time/ adjunct (62 women). *Students:* 603 full-time (405 women), 69 part-time (52 women); includes 219 minority (117 Black or African American, non-Hispanic/Latino; 1 American Indian or Alaska Native, non-Hispanic/Latino; 38 Asian, non-Hispanic/Latino; 48 Hispanic/Latino; 15 Two or more races, non-Hispanic/Latino), 68 international. 1,127 applicants, 43% accepted, 213 enrolled. In 2016, 192 master's, 42 doctorates awarded. *Degree requirements:* For master's, comprehensive exam (for some programs), thesis (for some programs), research capstone; for doctorate, comprehensive exam, research capstone. *Entrance requirements:* For master's, doctorate, and Advanced Certificate, GRE. Additional exam requirements/recommendations for international students: Required—TOEFL (minimum score 550 paper-based; 79 iBT). *Application deadline:* Applications are processed on a rolling basis. Application fee: $50. Electronic applications accepted. *Expenses: Tuition:* Full-time $28,272; part-time $1178 per credit. *Required fees:* $451 per term. Tuition and fees vary according to degree level, program and student level. *Financial support:* Research assistantships, teaching assistantships, career-related internships or fieldwork, Federal Work-Study, institutionally sponsored loans, scholarships/grants, tuition waivers (partial), and unspecified assistantships available. Support available to part-time students. Financial award application deadline: 2/15; financial award applicants required to submit FAFSA. *Faculty research:* Kinesiology, gender disparities, exercise physiology, gait analysis, social justice. *Unit head:* Dr. Barry S. Eckert, Dean, 718-780-6578, Fax: 718-780-4561, E-mail: barry.eckert@liu.edu. *Application contact:* Dr. Dominick Fortugno, Dean of Admissions, 718-780-6578, Fax: 718-780-4561, E-mail: dominick.fortugno@liu.edu.
Website: http://liu.edu/brooklyn/academics/school-of-health-professions

Louisiana Tech University, Graduate School, College of Education, Department of Kinesiology, Ruston, LA 71272. Offers administration of sport and physical activity (MS); sports performance (MS). *Accreditation:* NCATE. *Program availability:* Part-time. *Degree requirements:* For master's, thesis or alternative. *Entrance requirements:* For master's, GRE General Test. *Application deadline:* For fall admission, 7/29 for domestic students; for spring admission, 2/3 for domestic students. Application fee: $20 ($30 for international students). *Financial support:* Fellowships and research assistantships available. Financial award application deadline: 2/1. *Unit head:* Dr. David Szymanski, Interim Chair, 318-257-4432, Fax: 318-257-2379, E-mail: dszyman@latech.edu. *Application contact:* Dr. Cathy Stockton, Associate Dean of Graduate Studies, 318-257-3229, Fax: 318-257-2379, E-mail: cstock@latech.edu.
Website: http://education.latech.edu/departments/kinesiology/

Manhattanville College, School of Education, Program in Physical Education and Sport Pedagogy, Purchase, NY 10577-2132. Offers health and wellness specialist (Advanced Certificate); physical education and sport pedagogy (MAT). *Program availability:* Part-time, evening/weekend. *Students:* 32 applicants, 69% accepted, 19 enrolled. In 2016, 31 master's awarded. *Degree requirements:* For master's, comprehensive exam (for some programs), thesis (for some programs), student teaching, research seminars, portfolios, internships, writing assessment; for Advanced Certificate, comprehensive exam (for some programs). *Entrance requirements:* For master's, GRE or MAT, minimum undergraduate GPA of 3.0, 2 letters of recommendation. Additional exam requirements/ recommendations for international students: Required—TOEFL (minimum score 85 iBT); Recommended—IELTS. *Application deadline:* For fall admission, 7/1 priority date for domestic and international students; for spring admission, 11/1 priority date for domestic and international students; for summer admission, 4/1 priority date for domestic and international students. Applications are processed on a rolling basis. Application fee: $75. Electronic applications accepted. *Expenses: Tuition:* Full-time $16,470; part-time $915 per credit. *Required fees:* $60 per semester. Part-time tuition and fees vary according to course load and program. *Financial support:* Teaching assistantships, career-related internships or fieldwork, Federal Work-Study, institutionally sponsored loans, scholarships/grants, and unspecified assistantships available. Financial award applicants required to submit FAFSA. *Unit head:* Rhonda Clements, Director of Physical Education, 914-323-5327, Fax: 914-694-2386, E-mail: rhonda.clements@mville.edu. *Application contact:* Jeanine Pardey-Levine, Director of Graduate Enrollment Management, 914-373-3208, Fax: 914-694-1732, E-mail: edschool@mville.edu.
Website: http://www.mville.edu/programs/physical-education-and-sports-pedagogy

Marshall University, Academic Affairs Division, College of Health Professions, School of Kinesiology, Program in Exercise Science, Huntington, WV 25755. Offers MS. *Degree requirements:* For master's, thesis optional, comprehensive assessment. *Entrance requirements:* For master's, GRE General Test.

Marywood University, Academic Affairs, College of Health and Human Services, Department of Nutrition and Dietetics, Program in Sports Nutrition and Exercise Science, Scranton, PA 18509-1598. Offers MS. *Program availability:* Part-time. Electronic applications accepted.

McDaniel College, Graduate and Professional Studies, Program in Exercise Science and Physical Education, Westminster, MD 21157-4390. Offers MS. *Program availability:* Part-time, evening/weekend. *Faculty:* 2 full-time (both women), 5 part-time/adjunct (1 woman). *Students:* 17 full-time (4 women), 28 part-time (13 women); includes 7 minority (all Black or African American, non-Hispanic/Latino). Average age 28. 19 applicants, 100% accepted. In 2016, 45 master's awarded. *Degree requirements:* For master's, comprehensive exam, thesis optional. *Entrance requirements:* For master's, 3 references. Additional exam requirements/recommendations for international students: Required—TOEFL (minimum score 79 iBT), IELTS (minimum score 6). *Application deadline:* For fall admission, 6/1 priority date for domestic students; for spring admission, 11/1 priority date for domestic students; for summer admission, 3/1 priority date for domestic students. Applications are processed on a rolling basis. Application fee: $75. Electronic applications accepted. *Expenses: Tuition:* Full-time $8370; part-time $465 per credit. *Required fees:* $75 per semester. Tuition and fees vary according to course load, program and reciprocity agreements. *Financial support:* Unspecified assistantships available. Financial award application deadline: 3/1; financial award applicants required to submit FAFSA. *Unit head:* Fax: 410-857-2515, E-mail: gradadms@mcdaniel.edu. *Application contact:* Penny Pfeiffer, Senior Graduate Enrollment Management Specialist, 410-857-2516, Fax: 410-857-2515, E-mail: cperry@mcdaniel.edu.

McNeese State University, Doré School of Graduate Studies, Burton College of Education, Department of Health and Human Performance, Lake Charles, LA 70609. Offers exercise physiology (MS); health promotion (MS); nutrition and wellness (MS). *Accreditation:* NCATE. *Program availability:* Evening/weekend. *Entrance requirements:* For master's, GRE, undergraduate major or minor in health and human performance or related field of study.

Memorial University of Newfoundland, School of Graduate Studies, School of Human Kinetics and Recreation, St. John's, NL A1C 5S7, Canada. Offers administration, curriculum and supervision (MPE); biomechanics/ergonomics (MS Kin); exercise and work physiology (MS Kin); psychology of sport, exercise and recreation (MS Kin); socio-cultural studies of physical activity and health (MS Kin). *Program availability:* Part-time. *Degree requirements:* For master's, thesis optional, seminars, thesis presentations. *Entrance requirements:* For master's, bachelor's degree in a related field, minimum B average. Electronic applications accepted. *Faculty research:* Administration, sociology of sports, kinesiology, physiology/recreation.

Merrimack College, School of Science and Engineering, North Andover, MA 01845-5800. Offers athletic training (MS); civil engineering (MS); community health education (MS); computer science (MS); data science (MS); exercise and sport science (MS); health and wellness management (MS); mechanical engineering (MS), including engineering management. *Program availability:* Part-time, evening/weekend, 100% online. *Faculty:* 16 full-time, 2 part-time/adjunct. *Students:* 88 full-time (32 women), 13 part-time (6 women); includes 6 minority (4 Hispanic/Latino; 2 Two or more races, non-Hispanic/Latino), 39 international. Average age 25. 156 applicants, 67% accepted, 59 enrolled. In 2016, 46 master's awarded. *Degree requirements:* For master's, comprehensive exam, thesis optional, internship or capstone (for some programs). *Entrance requirements:* For master's, official college transcripts, resume, personal statement, 2 recommendations. Additional exam requirements/recommendations for international students: Required—TOEFL (minimum score 84 iBT), IELTS (minimum score 6.5), PTE (minimum score 56). *Application deadline:* For fall admission, 8/14 for domestic students, 7/14 for international students; for spring admission, 1/10 for domestic students, 12/10 for international students; for summer admission, 5/10 for domestic students, 4/10 for international students. Applications are processed on a rolling basis. Application fee: $0. Electronic applications accepted. *Expenses:* Contact institution. *Financial support:* Fellowships with full tuition reimbursements, career-related internships or fieldwork, scholarships/grants, and health care benefits available.

Support available to part-time students. Financial award application deadline: 5/1; financial award applicants required to submit FAFSA. *Faculty research:* Viral genomics and evolution (biology), robotics (mechanical engineering), knot theory (mathematics), computer graphics and network security (computer science), water management (civil engineering). *Application contact:* Allison Pena, Graduate Admissions Counselor, 978-837-3563, E-mail: penaa@merrimack.edu.
Website: http://www.merrimack.edu/academics/graduate/

Miami University, College of Education, Health and Society, Department of Kinesiology and Health, Oxford, OH 45056. Offers MS. *Students:* 50 full-time (28 women), 6 part-time (4 women); includes 10 minority (3 Black or African American, non-Hispanic/Latino; 2 Asian, non-Hispanic/Latino; 1 Hispanic/Latino; 4 Two or more races, non-Hispanic/Latino), 2 international. Average age 24. In 2016, 29 master's awarded. *Expenses:* Tuition, state resident: full-time $12,890; part-time $564 per credit hour. Tuition, nonresident: full-time $29,604; part-time $1260 per credit hour. *Required fees:* $638. Part-time tuition and fees vary according to course load and program. *Unit head:* Dr. Helaine Alessio, Professor and Chair, 513-529-2700, E-mail: alessih@miamioh.edu. *Application contact:* 513-529-2700, E-mail: knhdept@miamioh.edu.
Website: http://www.MiamiOH.edu/KNH

Middle Tennessee State University, College of Graduate Studies, College of Behavioral and Health Sciences, Department of Health and Human Performance, Program in Exercise Science, Murfreesboro, TN 37132. Offers MS. *Program availability:* Part-time, evening/weekend, online learning. *Degree requirements:* For master's, comprehensive exam, thesis optional. *Entrance requirements:* For master's, GRE. Additional exam requirements/recommendations for international students: Required—TOEFL (minimum score 525 paper-based; 71 iBT) or IELTS (minimum score 6). *Faculty research:* Kinesiometrics, leisure behavior, health, lifestyles.

Middle Tennessee State University, College of Graduate Studies, College of Behavioral and Health Sciences, Department of Health and Human Performance, Program in Human Performance, Murfreesboro, TN 37132. Offers PhD. *Program availability:* Part-time, evening/weekend, online learning. *Degree requirements:* For doctorate, comprehensive exam, thesis/dissertation. *Entrance requirements:* For doctorate, GRE. Additional exam requirements/recommendations for international students: Required—TOEFL (minimum score 525 paper-based; 71 iBT) or IELTS (minimum score 6). *Faculty research:* Kinesiometrics, leisure behavior, health/lifestyles.

Midwestern State University, Billie Doris McAda Graduate School, Robert D. and Carol Gunn College of Health Sciences and Human Services, Department of Athletic Training and Exercise Physiology, Wichita Falls, TX 76308. Offers exercise physiology (MS). *Program availability:* Part-time. *Degree requirements:* For master's, comprehensive exam, thesis optional. *Entrance requirements:* For master's, GRE General Test or MAT. Additional exam requirements/recommendations for international students: Required—TOEFL (minimum score 550 paper-based). Electronic applications accepted. *Faculty research:* Exercise adherence, muscular tissue remodeling during hypertrophy, student engagement and success, operational paradigms of the exercise sciences.

Mississippi State University, College of Education, Department of Kinesiology, Mississippi State, MS 39762. Offers exercise physiology (MS); exercise science (PhD); sport administration (MS); sport pedagogy (MS); sport studies (PhD). *Program availability:* Part-time, blended/hybrid learning. *Faculty:* 14 full-time (2 women). *Students:* 57 full-time (17 women), 6 part-time (0 women); includes 11 minority (5 Black or African American, non-Hispanic/Latino; 2 Asian, non-Hispanic/Latino; 2 Hispanic/Latino; 2 Two or more races, non-Hispanic/Latino), 6 international. Average age 26. 75 applicants, 56% accepted, 30 enrolled. In 2016, 32 master's awarded. *Degree requirements:* For master's, comprehensive exam, thesis optional; for doctorate, comprehensive exam. *Entrance requirements:* For master's, GRE General Test, minimum GPA of 2.75 on undergraduate work from four-year accredited institution, 3.0 graduate; for doctorate, GRE, minimum GPA of 3.4 on previous graduate degree(s) earned from accredited institutions. Additional exam requirements/recommendations for international students: Required—TOEFL (minimum score 550 paper-based; 79 iBT); Recommended—IELTS (minimum score 6.5). *Application deadline:* For fall admission, 7/1 for domestic students, 5/1 for international students; for spring admission, 11/1 for domestic students, 9/1 for international students. Applications are processed on a rolling basis. Application fee: $60. Electronic applications accepted. *Expenses:* Tuition, state resident: full-time $7670; part-time $852.50 per credit hour. Tuition, nonresident: full-time $20,790; part-time $2310.50 per credit hour. Part-time tuition and fees vary according to course load. *Financial support:* In 2016–17, 16 teaching assistantships with partial tuition reimbursements (averaging $10,227 per year) were awarded; career-related internships or fieldwork, Federal Work-Study, institutionally sponsored loans, and unspecified assistantships also available. Financial award application deadline: 4/1; financial award applicants required to submit FAFSA. *Faculty research:* Static balance and stepping performance of older adults, organizational justice, public health, strength training and recovery drinks, high risk drinking perceptions and behaviors. *Unit head:* Dr. Stanley P. Brown, Professor and Department Head, 662-325-2963, Fax: 662-325-4525, E-mail: spb107@msstate.edu. *Application contact:* Linda Bonner, Senior Admissions Assistant, 662-325-3363, E-mail: lbonner@grad.msstate.edu.
Website: http://www.kinesiology.msstate.edu/

Montclair State University, The Graduate School, College of Education and Human Services, Nutrition and Exercise Science Certificate Program, Montclair, NJ 07043-1624. Offers Certificate. Electronic applications accepted. *Expenses:* Tuition, state resident: part-time $553 per credit. Tuition, nonresident: part-time $854 per credit. *Required fees:* $91 per credit. Tuition and fees vary according to program.

Montclair State University, The Graduate School, College of Education and Human Services, Program in Exercise Science and Physical Education, Montclair, NJ 07043-1624. Offers exercise science (MA); sports administration and coaching (MA); teaching and supervision in physical education (MA). *Program availability:* Part-time, evening/weekend. *Degree requirements:* For master's, comprehensive exam, thesis or alternative. *Entrance requirements:* For master's, GRE General Test, essay, 2 letters of recommendation. Additional exam requirements/recommendations for international students: Required—TOEFL (minimum score 83 iBT), IELTS (minimum score 6.5). Electronic applications accepted. *Expenses:* Tuition, state resident: part-time $553 per credit. Tuition, nonresident: part-time $854 per credit. *Required fees:* $91 per credit. Tuition and fees vary according to program.

Morehead State University, Graduate Programs, College of Science and Technology, Department of Health, Wellness and Human Performance, Morehead, KY 40351. Offers health/physical education (MA). *Accreditation:* NCATE. *Program availability:* Part-time, evening/weekend. *Degree requirements:* For master's, comprehensive exam, thesis, oral exam, written core exam. *Entrance requirements:* For master's, GRE General Test or MAT, minimum GPA of 2.5; undergraduate major/minor in health, physical education, or recreation. Additional exam requirements/recommendations for international students: Required—TOEFL (minimum score 500 paper-based). Electronic applications accepted. *Faculty research:* Child growth and performance, instructional strategies, outdoor leadership qualities, exercise science, athletic training.

Murray State University, College of Health Sciences and Human Services, Department of Wellness and Therapeutic Sciences, Program in Exercise and Leisure Studies, Murray, KY 42071. Offers MS. *Program availability:* Part-time. *Degree requirements:* For master's, thesis optional. *Entrance requirements:* For master's, GRE General Test or MAT. Additional exam requirements/recommendations for international students: Required—TOEFL. *Faculty research:* Exercise and cancer recovery.

New Mexico Highlands University, Graduate Studies, College of Arts and Sciences, Department of Exercise and Sport Sciences, Las Vegas, NM 87701. Offers human performance and sport (MA), including human performance and sport sciences, sports administration, teacher education. *Program availability:* Part-time. *Degree requirements:* For master's, comprehensive exam, thesis or alternative. *Entrance requirements:* For master's, minimum undergraduate GPA of 3.0. Additional exam requirements/recommendations for international students: Required—TOEFL (minimum score 540 paper-based). *Faculty research:* Child obesity and physical inactivity, body composition and fitness assessment, motor development, sport marketing, sport finance.

North Dakota State University, College of Graduate and Interdisciplinary Studies, College of Human Development and Education, Department of Health, Nutrition, and Exercise Sciences, Fargo, ND 58102. Offers athletic training (MAT, MS); dietetics (MS); exercise science and nutrition (PhD); exercise/nutrition science (MS); health promotion (MPH); leadership in physical education and sport (MS). *Program availability:* Part-time, evening/weekend, online learning. *Degree requirements:* For master's, thesis (for some programs). *Entrance requirements:* For master's, minimum GPA of 3.0. Additional exam requirements/recommendations for international students: Required—TOEFL (minimum score 525 paper-based; 71 iBT). Electronic applications accepted. *Faculty research:* Biomechanics, sport specialization, recreation, nutrition, athletic training.

Northeastern Illinois University, College of Graduate Studies and Research, College of Education, Program in Exercise Science, Chicago, IL 60625-4699. Offers MS. *Degree requirements:* For master's, thesis optional, internship. *Entrance requirements:* For master's, 21 hours of undergraduate course work in science, minimum GPA of 2.75.

Northeastern University, Bouvé College of Health Sciences, Boston, MA 02115-5096. Offers applied behavior analysis (MS); audiology (Au D); counseling psychology (MS, PhD, CAGS); exercise science (MS); nursing (MS, PhD, CAGS), including administration (MS), adult-gerontology acute care nurse practitioner (MS, CAGS), adult-gerontology primary care nurse practitioner (MS, CAGS), anesthesia (MS), family nurse practitioner (MS, CAGS), neonatal nurse practitioner (MS, CAGS), pediatric nurse practitioner (MS, CAGS), psychiatric mental health nurse practitioner (MS, CAGS); nursing practice (DNP); pharmaceutical sciences (MS, PhD), including interdisciplinary concentration, pharmaceutics and drug delivery systems; pharmacology (MS); pharmacy (Pharm D); school psychology (PhD); urban health (MPH); MS/MBA. *Accreditation:* ACPE (one or more programs are accredited). *Program availability:* Part-time, evening/weekend, online learning. *Faculty:* 192 full-time (119 women), 194 part-time/adjunct (156 women). *Students:* 1,371 full-time (1,009 women), 262 part-time (219 women). In 2016, 352 master's, 312 doctorates, 25 other advanced degrees awarded. *Degree requirements:* For doctorate, thesis/dissertation (for some programs); for CAGS, comprehensive exam. Application fee: $75. Electronic applications accepted. *Expenses:* Contact institution. *Financial support:* Fellowships, research assistantships, teaching assistantships, career-related internships or fieldwork, scholarships/grants, health care benefits, tuition waivers, and unspecified assistantships available. Support available to part-time students. Financial award applicants required to submit FAFSA. *Unit head:* Susan L. Parish, Dean, Bouve College of Health Sciences, 617-373-3323, Fax: 617-373-3030. *Application contact:* E-mail: bouvegrad@northeastern.edu.
Website: http://www.northeastern.edu/bouve/

Northern Michigan University, Office of Graduate Education and Research, College of Health Sciences and Professional Studies, School of Health and Human Performance, Marquette, MI 49855-5301. Offers exercise science (MS). *Program availability:* Part-time. *Degree requirements:* For master's, thesis (for some programs), two scholarly papers or thesis. *Entrance requirements:* For master's, minimum GPA of 3.0 plus relevant major or 9 semester hours of course work in human anatomy/physiology, exercise physiology, physics, biomechanics, kinesiology. Additional exam requirements/recommendations for international students: Required—TOEFL (minimum score 550 paper-based; 79 iBT), IELTS (minimum score 6.6). Electronic applications accepted. *Faculty research:* Physiology of rock climbing and cross country ski racing, physical activity behaviors of children, exercise training and cancer treatment, normobaric hypoxia, concussion.

Northwest Missouri State University, Graduate School, School of Health Science and Wellness, Maryville, MO 64468-6001. Offers applied health and sport sciences (MS); recreation (MS). *Accreditation:* NCATE. *Program availability:* Part-time. *Students:* 68 full-time (38 women), 27 part-time (19 women). *Degree requirements:* For master's, comprehensive exam. *Entrance requirements:* For master's, GRE General Test, minimum undergraduate GPA of 2.75, teaching certificate, writing sample. Additional exam requirements/recommendations for international students: Required—TOEFL (minimum score 550 paper-based). *Application deadline:* For fall admission, 7/1 for domestic and international students; for spring admission, 11/15 for domestic and international students. Applications are processed on a rolling basis. Application fee: $0 ($50 for international students). *Expenses:* Tuition, state resident: full-time $3447; part-time $383 per credit hour. Tuition, nonresident: full-time $5724; part-time $636 per credit hour. *Required fees:* $130 per credit hour. *Financial support:* Teaching assistantships with full tuition reimbursements and unspecified assistantships available. Financial award application deadline: 4/1; financial award applicants required to submit FAFSA. *Unit head:* Dr. Terry Long, Director, School of Health Science and Wellness, 660-562-1706, E-mail: tlong@nwmissouri.edu. *Application contact:* Cathie Hannigan, Office Manager, 660-562-1297, Fax: 660-562-1483, E-mail: channig@nwmissouri.edu.
Website: http://www.nwmissouri.edu/health/

Oakland University, Graduate Study and Lifelong Learning, School of Health Sciences, Program in Exercise Science, Rochester, MI 48309-4401. Offers MS, Graduate Certificate. *Degree requirements:* For master's, thesis (for some programs). *Entrance requirements:* For master's, minimum GPA of 3.0. Additional exam requirements/recommendations for international students: Required—TOEFL (minimum score 550 paper-based). Electronic applications accepted. *Expenses:* Contact institution.

Oakland University, Graduate Study and Lifelong Learning, School of Health Sciences, Program in Physical Therapy, Rochester, MI 48309-4401. Offers clinical exercise science (Dr Sc PT); complementary medicine and wellness (Dr Sc PT); corporate worksite wellness (Dr Sc PT); exercise science (Dr Sc PT); neurological rehabilitation (Dr Sc PT, TDPT); orthopedic manual physical therapy (Dr Sc PT, TDPT, Graduate Certificate); orthopedic physical therapy (Graduate Certificate); orthopedics (Dr Sc PT, TDPT); pediatric rehabilitation (Dr Sc PT, TDPT); physical therapy (DPT); teaching and learning for rehabilitation professionals (Dr Sc PT, TDPT). *Accreditation:* APTA. *Entrance requirements:* For doctorate, GRE General Test. Additional exam requirements/recommendations for international students: Required—TOEFL (minimum score 550 paper-based). *Expenses:* Contact institution.

Ohio University, Graduate College, College of Arts and Sciences, Department of Biological Sciences, Athens, OH 45701-2979. Offers biological sciences (MS, PhD); cell

biology and physiology (MS, PhD); ecology and evolutionary biology (MS, PhD); exercise physiology and muscle biology (MS, PhD); microbiology (MS, PhD); neuroscience (MS, PhD). Terminal master's awarded for partial completion of doctoral program. *Degree requirements:* For master's, comprehensive exam, thesis, 1 quarter of teaching experience; for doctorate, comprehensive exam, thesis/dissertation, 2 quarters of teaching experience. *Entrance requirements:* For master's, GRE General Test, names of three faculty members whose research interests most closely match the applicant's interest; for doctorate, GRE General Test, essay concerning prior training, research interest and career goals, plus names of three faculty members whose research interests most closely match the applicant's interest. Additional exam requirements/recommendations for international students: Required—TOEFL (minimum score 620 paper-based; 105 iBT) or IELTS (minimum score 7.5). *Application deadline:* For fall admission, 1/15 for domestic and international students. Application fee: $50 ($55 for international students). Electronic applications accepted. *Financial support:* Fellowships with full tuition reimbursements, research assistantships with full tuition reimbursements, teaching assistantships with full tuition reimbursements, Federal Work-Study, and institutionally sponsored loans available. Financial award application deadline: 1/15. *Faculty research:* Ecology and evolutionary biology, exercise physiology and muscle biology, neurobiology, cell biology, physiology. *Unit head:* Dr. Ralph DiCaprio, Chair, 740-593-2220, E-mail: dicaprir@ohio.edu. *Application contact:* Dr. Patrick Hassett, Graduate Chair, 740-593-4793, Fax: 740-593-0300, E-mail: hassett@ohio.edu.
Website: http://www.biosci.ohiou.edu/

Ohio University, Graduate College, College of Health Sciences and Professions, School of Applied Health Sciences and Wellness, Program in Physiology of Exercise, Athens, OH 45701-2979. Offers MS. *Degree requirements:* For master's, thesis or alternative. *Entrance requirements:* For master's, GRE, minimum GPA of 3.0. Additional exam requirements/recommendations for international students: Required—TOEFL (minimum score 550 paper-based; 80 iBT) or IELTS (minimum score 6.5). *Application deadline:* For fall admission, 3/1 priority date for domestic and international students. Application fee: $50 ($55 for international students). Electronic applications accepted. *Financial support:* Research assistantships with tuition reimbursements, teaching assistantships with full tuition reimbursements, Federal Work-Study, institutionally sponsored loans, and scholarships/grants available. Financial award application deadline: 3/15. *Faculty research:* Blood pressure, heart rate, health skeleton, muscles, training. *Unit head:* Dr. Roger Gilders, Coordinator, 740-593-0101, Fax: 740-593-0285, E-mail: gilders@ohio.edu.
Website: http://bios.ohio.edu/graduate/integrative-physiology-and-neuroscience/comparative-exercise-physiology

Old Dominion University, Darden College of Education, Program in Physical Education, Exercise and Wellness Emphasis, Norfolk, VA 23529. Offers physical education (MS Ed), including exercise science and wellness. *Program availability:* Part-time, evening/weekend. *Faculty:* 6 full-time (2 women). *Students:* 17 full-time (12 women), 4 part-time (2 women); includes 8 minority (3 Black or African American, non-Hispanic/Latino; 1 Asian, non-Hispanic/Latino; 3 Hispanic/Latino; 1 Two or more races, non-Hispanic/Latino). Average age 25. 19 applicants, 68% accepted, 11 enrolled. In 2016, 11 master's awarded. *Degree requirements:* For master's, comprehensive exam, thesis or alternative, internship, research project. *Entrance requirements:* For master's, GRE, minimum GPA of 2.8 overall, 3.0 in major. Additional exam requirements/recommendations for international students: Required—TOEFL (minimum score 550 paper-based; 79 iBT). *Application deadline:* For fall admission, 3/1 for domestic and international students. Applications are processed on a rolling basis. Application fee: $50. Electronic applications accepted. *Expenses:* Tuition, state resident: full-time $8604; part-time $478 per credit hour. Tuition, nonresident: full-time $21,510; part-time $1195 per credit hour. *Required fees:* $66 per semester. Tuition and fees vary according to campus/location, program and reciprocity agreements. *Financial support:* In 2016–17, 7 students received support, including 4 research assistantships (averaging $10,000 per year), 3 teaching assistantships (averaging $10,000 per year); unspecified assistantships also available. Financial award application deadline: 3/1. *Faculty research:* Cardiovascular response to exercise, exercise prescription, nutrition, lower extremity biomechanics, exercise in special populations. *Total annual research expenditures:* $613,790. *Unit head:* Dr. Lynn Ridinger, Chair, 757-683-4353, E-mail: lridinge@odu.edu. *Application contact:* William Heffelfinger, Director of Graduate Admissions, 757-683-5554, Fax: 757-683-3255, E-mail: gradadmit@odu.edu.
Website: https://www.odu.edu/academics/programs/masters/exercise-science-wellness

Pittsburg State University, Graduate School, College of Education, Department of Health, Physical Education and Recreation, Pittsburg, KS 66762. Offers health, human performance, and recreation (MS), including human performance and wellness, sport and leisure service management. *Program availability:* Part-time, online only, 100% online. *Students:* 65 (25 women); includes 16 minority (8 Black or African American, non-Hispanic/Latino; 1 American Indian or Alaska Native, non-Hispanic/Latino; 5 Hispanic/Latino; 2 Two or more races, non-Hispanic/Latino). In 2016, 33 master's awarded. *Degree requirements:* For master's, thesis or alternative. *Entrance requirements:* For master's, letter of intent. Additional exam requirements/recommendations for international students: Required—TOEFL (minimum score 520 paper-based; 68 iBT), IELTS (minimum score 6), PTE (minimum score 47). *Application deadline:* For fall admission, 6/1 for international students; for spring admission, 10/15 for international students; for summer admission, 4/1 for international students. Applications are processed on a rolling basis. Application fee: $35 ($60 for international students). Electronic applications accepted. *Expenses:* Contact institution. *Financial support:* In 2016–17, 9 teaching assistantships with full tuition reimbursements (averaging $5,500 per year) were awarded; career-related internships or fieldwork, Federal Work-Study, and unspecified assistantships also available. Financial award application deadline: 2/1; financial award applicants required to submit FAFSA. *Faculty research:* Personality of athletes, fitness activities for children, aerobic conditioning, fitness evaluation. *Unit head:* Dr. John Oppliger, Chairperson, 620-235-4668, E-mail: joppliger@pittstate.edu. *Application contact:* Lisa Allen, Assistant Director of Graduate and Continuing Studies, 620-235-4223, Fax: 620-235-4219, E-mail: lallen@pittstate.edu.

Point Loma Nazarene University, Department of Kinesiology, San Diego, CA 92106-2899. Offers integrative wellness (MS); sport performance (MS), including exercise science, sport management, sport performance. *Program availability:* Part-time, online learning. *Faculty:* 3 full-time (1 woman), 6 part-time/adjunct (1 woman). *Students:* 48 full-time (21 women), 4 part-time (1 woman); includes 21 minority (3 Black or African American, non-Hispanic/Latino; 2 Asian, non-Hispanic/Latino; 13 Hispanic/Latino; 3 Two or more races, non-Hispanic/Latino), 4 international. Average age 26. 84 applicants, 80% accepted, 49 enrolled. *Entrance requirements:* For master's, baccalaureate degree, minimum undergraduate cumulative GPA of 3.0. Application fee: $50. *Expenses:* $685 per credit. *Financial support:* Teaching assistantships, scholarships/grants, and unspecified assistantships available. *Unit head:* Jeff Sullivan, Chair, 619-849-2629, E-mail: jeffsullivan@pointloma.edu. *Application contact:* Claire Buckley, Director, Graduate Admissions, 866-563-2846, E-mail: gradinfo@pointloma.edu.

Purdue University, Graduate School, College of Health and Human Sciences, Department of Health and Kinesiology, West Lafayette, IN 47907. Offers athletic training education administration (MS, PhD); biomechanics (MS, PhD); exercise physiology (MS, PhD); health education (MS, PhD); history/philosophy of sport (MS, PhD); motor control and development (MS, PhD); physical education pedagogy (PhD); physical education teacher education (MS); recreation and sport management (MS, PhD); sport and exercise psychology (MS, PhD). *Program availability:* Part-time. *Faculty:* 19 full-time (7 women). *Students:* 30 full-time (13 women), 10 part-time (5 women); includes 2 minority (1 Asian, non-Hispanic/Latino; 1 Two or more races, non-Hispanic/Latino), 6 international. Average age 26. 77 applicants, 29% accepted, 18 enrolled. In 2016, 18 master's, 9 doctorates awarded. *Degree requirements:* For master's, thesis optional; for doctorate, comprehensive exam, thesis/dissertation, qualifying examination, preliminary examination. *Entrance requirements:* For master's, GRE General Test (minimum score 1000 combined verbal and quantitative), minimum undergraduate GPA of 3.0 or equivalent; for doctorate, GRE General Test (minimum score 1100 combined verbal and quantitative), minimum undergraduate GPA of 3.0 or equivalent; master's degree with minimum GPA of 3.25 (recommended). Additional exam requirements/recommendations for international students: Required—TOEFL (minimum score 77 iBT); Recommended—TWE. *Application deadline:* For fall admission, 4/30 for domestic and international students; for spring admission, 10/15 for domestic and international students. Applications are processed on a rolling basis. Application fee: $60 ($75 for international students). Electronic applications accepted. *Financial support:* Fellowships with partial tuition reimbursements, research assistantships with partial tuition reimbursements, teaching assistantships with partial tuition reimbursements, and Federal Work-Study available. Support available to part-time students. Financial award applicants required to submit FAFSA. *Faculty research:* Wellness, motivation, teaching effectiveness, learning and development. *Unit head:* Dr. Timothy P. Gavin, Head of the Graduate Program, 765-494-3178, Fax: 765-494-1239, E-mail: gavin1@purdue.edu. *Application contact:* Christy F. Daugherty, Graduate Contact, 765-494-3162, E-mail: daugher2@purdue.edu.
Website: http://www.purdue.edu/hhs/hk/

Queens College of the City University of New York, Mathematics and Natural Sciences Division, Department of Family, Nutrition and Exercise Sciences, Queens, NY 11367-1597. Offers exercise science specialist (MS); family and consumer science (K-12) (AC); family and consumer science/teaching curriculum (K-12) (MS Ed); nutrition and exercise science (MS); nutrition specialist (MS); physical education (K-12) (AC); physical education/teaching curriculum (pre K-12) (MS Ed). *Program availability:* Part-time, evening/weekend. *Faculty:* 16 full-time (14 women), 46 part-time/adjunct (32 women). *Students:* 16 full-time (6 women), 157 part-time (86 women); includes 67 minority (19 Black or African American, non-Hispanic/Latino; 1 American Indian or Alaska Native, non-Hispanic/Latino; 18 Asian, non-Hispanic/Latino; 27 Hispanic/Latino; 2 Two or more races, non-Hispanic/Latino), 9 international. Average age 30. 95 applicants, 76% accepted, 45 enrolled. In 2016, 34 master's, 14 other advanced degrees awarded. *Degree requirements:* For master's, research project. *Entrance requirements:* For master's, minimum GPA of 3.0. Additional exam requirements/recommendations for international students: Required—TOEFL, IELTS. *Application deadline:* For fall admission, 4/1 for domestic students; for spring admission, 11/1 for domestic students. Applications are processed on a rolling basis. Application fee: $125. Electronic applications accepted. *Expenses:* Tuition, state resident: full-time $5065; part-time $425 per credit. Tuition, nonresident: part-time $780 per credit. *Required fees:* $522; $397 per credit. Part-time tuition and fees vary according to course load and program. *Financial support:* Career-related internships or fieldwork and unspecified assistantships available. Financial award application deadline: 4/1; financial award applicants required to submit FAFSA. *Unit head:* Dr. Michael Toner, Chairperson, 718-997-4168, E-mail: michael.toner@qc.cuny.edu.

Queen's University at Kingston, School of Graduate Studies, School of Kinesiology and Health Studies, Kingston, ON K7L 3N6, Canada. Offers applied exercise science (PhD); biomechanics/ergonomics (M Sc); exercise physiology (M Sc); social psychology of sport and exercise rehabilitation (MA); sociology of sport (MA). *Program availability:* Part-time. *Degree requirements:* For master's, thesis (for some programs); for doctorate, comprehensive exam, thesis/dissertation. *Entrance requirements:* For master's and doctorate, minimum B+ average. Additional exam requirements/recommendations for international students: Required—TOEFL. Electronic applications accepted. *Faculty research:* Expert performance ergonomics, obesity research, pregnancy and exercise, gender and sport participation.

Rowan University, Graduate School, School of Biomedical Science and Health Professions, Department of Health and Exercise Science, Glassboro, NJ 08028-1701. Offers wellness and lifestyle management (MA). *Degree requirements:* For master's, comprehensive exam, thesis. *Entrance requirements:* For master's, GRE General Test, GRE Subject Test, interview, minimum GPA of 2.8. Additional exam requirements/recommendations for international students: Required—TOEFL. Electronic applications accepted.

Sacred Heart University, Graduate Programs, College of Health Professions, Department of Exercise Science, Fairfield, CT 06825. Offers exercise science and nutrition (MS). *Program availability:* Part-time, evening/weekend. *Faculty:* 6 full-time (2 women). *Students:* 28 full-time (13 women), 1 part-time (0 women); includes 5 minority (1 Black or African American, non-Hispanic/Latino; 4 Hispanic/Latino). Average age 23. 62 applicants, 71% accepted, 16 enrolled. In 2016, 16 master's awarded. *Entrance requirements:* For master's, bachelor's degree in related major, minimum GPA of 3.0, anatomy and physiology (with labs), exercise physiology, nutrition, statistics or health/exercise-specific research methods course, kinesiology (preferred). Additional exam requirements/recommendations for international students: Required—TOEFL (minimum score 570 paper-based, 80 iBT), TWE, or IELTS (6.5); Recommended—TSE. *Application deadline:* Applications are processed on a rolling basis. Application fee: $75. Electronic applications accepted. *Expenses:* $940 per credit. *Financial support:* Unspecified assistantships available. Financial award applicants required to submit FAFSA. *Unit head:* Beau Greer, Director of Graduate Exercise Science and Nutrition, 203-396-8064, E-mail: greerb@sacredheart.edu. *Application contact:* William Sweeney, Director of Graduate Admissions Operations, 203-396-4827, E-mail: sweeneyw@sacredheart.edu.
Website: http://www.sacredheart.edu/academics/collegeofhealthprofessions/academicprograms/exercisescience/masterofscienceinexercisesciencenutrition/

St. Cloud State University, School of Graduate Studies, School of Health and Human Services, Department of Kinesiology, St. Cloud, MN 56301-4498. Offers exercise science (MS); sports management (MS). *Degree requirements:* For master's, thesis or alternative. *Entrance requirements:* For master's, GRE General Test, minimum overall GPA of 2.75 in previous undergraduate and graduate records or in last half of undergraduate work. Additional exam requirements/recommendations for international students: Required—Michigan English Language Assessment Battery; Recommended—TOEFL (minimum score 550 paper-based; 79 iBT), IELTS (minimum score 6.5). Electronic applications accepted.

Saint Mary's College of California, School of Liberal Arts, Department of Kinesiology, Moraga, CA 94575. Offers fitness management (MA); sport management (MA); sport studies (MA). *Program availability:* Part-time. *Degree requirements:* For master's, thesis or special project. *Entrance requirements:* For master's, minimum GPA of 2.75, BA in physical education or related field, or professional experience. Electronic applications accepted. *Expenses:* Contact institution. *Faculty research:* Moral development in sport, applied motor learning, achievement motivation, sport history.

San Diego State University, Graduate and Research Affairs, College of Health and Human Services, School of Exercise and Nutritional Sciences, Program in Exercise Physiology, San Diego, CA 92182. Offers MS, MS/MS. *Degree requirements:* For master's, thesis. *Entrance requirements:* For master's, GRE General Test, 2 letters of reference. Additional exam requirements/recommendations for international students: Required—TOEFL. Electronic applications accepted.

San Jose State University, Graduate Studies and Research, College of Applied Sciences and Arts, San Jose, CA 95192-0001. Offers big data (Certificate); California library media teacher services (Credential); collaborative response to family violence (Certificate); justice studies (MS); kinesiology (MA), including applied sciences and arts (MA, MS), athletic training, exercise physiology, sport management, sport studies; library and information science (MLIS, Certificate); mass communication (MA); nutritional science (MS); occupational therapy (MS); public health (MPH); pupil personnel services (Credential); recreation (MS), including applied sciences and arts (MA, MS), international tourism; social work (MSW); Spanish language counseling (Certificate); strategic management of digital assets and services (Certificate). *Program availability:* Part-time, evening/weekend. Electronic applications accepted.

Smith College, Graduate and Special Programs, Department of Exercise and Sport Studies, Northampton, MA 01063. Offers MS. *Program availability:* Part-time. *Students:* 18 full-time (16 women), 1 (woman) part-time; includes 4 minority (2 Asian, non-Hispanic/Latino; 2 Hispanic/Latino), 2 international. Average age 26. 69 applicants, 25% accepted, 10 enrolled. In 2016, 15 master's awarded. *Entrance requirements:* Additional exam requirements/recommendations for international students: Required—TOEFL (minimum score 595 paper-based; 97 iBT), IELTS. *Application deadline:* For fall admission, 4/1 for domestic students, 1/15 for international students; for spring admission, 12/1 for domestic students. Application fee: $60. *Expenses: Tuition:* Full-time $34,560; part-time $1440 per credit. Tuition and fees vary according to course load and program. *Financial support:* In 2016–17, 19 students received support, including 2 fellowships with full tuition reimbursements available (averaging $13,850 per year), 9 teaching assistantships with full tuition reimbursements available (averaging $13,850 per year); scholarships/grants also available. Support available to part-time students. Financial award application deadline: 1/15; financial award applicants required to submit CSS PROFILE or FAFSA. *Faculty research:* Women in sport, perceived exertion, motor programming, race in sport, stress management. *Unit head:* Lynn Oberbillig, Graduate Student Adviser, 413-585-2701, E-mail: loberbil@smith.edu. *Application contact:* Ruth Morgan, Program Assistant, 413-585-3050, Fax: 413-585-3054, E-mail: rmorgan@smith.edu.
Website: http://www.smith.edu/ess/

South Dakota State University, Graduate School, College of Education and Human Sciences, Department of Health and Nutritional Sciences, Brookings, SD 57007. Offers athletic training (MS); dietetics (MS); nutrition and exercise sciences (MS, PhD); sport and recreation studies (MS). *Program availability:* Part-time. *Degree requirements:* For master's, comprehensive exam (for some programs), thesis (for some programs), oral exam. *Entrance requirements:* Additional exam requirements/recommendations for international students: Required—TOEFL (minimum score 525 paper-based). *Faculty research:* Food chemistry, bone density, functional food, nutrition education, nutrition biochemistry.

Southeastern Louisiana University, College of Nursing and Health Sciences, Department of Kinesiology and Health Studies, Hammond, LA 70402. Offers health and kinesiology (MS), including exercise science, health promotion and exercise science, health studies, kinesiology. *Accreditation:* NCATE. *Program availability:* Part-time. *Faculty:* 7 full-time (3 women), 2 part-time/adjunct (1 woman). *Students:* 24 full-time (8 women), 14 part-time (11 women); includes 14 minority (8 Black or African American, non-Hispanic/Latino; 3 Hispanic/Latino; 3 Two or more races, non-Hispanic/Latino), 1 international. Average age 25. 32 applicants, 59% accepted, 9 enrolled. In 2016, 19 master's awarded. *Degree requirements:* For master's, comprehensive exam (for some programs), thesis (for some programs). *Entrance requirements:* Additional exam requirements/recommendations for international students: Required—TOEFL (minimum score 500 paper-based; 61 iBT). *Application deadline:* For fall admission, 7/15 priority date for domestic students, 6/1 priority date for international students; for spring admission, 12/1 priority date for domestic students, 10/1 priority date for international students. Applications are processed on a rolling basis. Application fee: $20 ($30 for international students). Electronic applications accepted. *Expenses:* Tuition, state resident: full-time $6540; part-time $465 per credit hour. Tuition, nonresident: full-time $19,017; part-time $1158 per credit hour. *Required fees:* $1829. *Financial support:* In 2016–17, 27 students received support, including 8 research assistantships (averaging $9,413 per year), 4 teaching assistantships (averaging $9,275 per year); career-related internships or fieldwork, Federal Work-Study, institutionally sponsored loans, scholarships/grants, and unspecified assistantships also available. Support available to part-time students. Financial award application deadline: 5/1; financial award applicants required to submit FAFSA. *Faculty research:* Exercise physiology, motor learning, sport and exercise psychology, school health, health and aging. *Unit head:* Dr. Eddie Hebert, Department Head, 985-549-2129, Fax: 985-549-5119, E-mail: ehebert@southeastern.edu. *Application contact:* Amanda Harper, Graduate Admissions Analyst, 985-549-5620, Fax: 985-549-5632, E-mail: admissions@southeastern.edu.
Website: http://www.southeastern.edu/acad_research/depts/kin_hs/index.html

Southeast Missouri State University, School of Graduate Studies, Department of Health, Human Performance and Recreation, Cape Girardeau, MO 63701-4799. Offers MS. *Program availability:* Part-time. *Faculty:* 8 full-time (2 women), 2 part-time/adjunct (1 woman). *Students:* 20 full-time (12 women), 19 part-time (10 women), 17 international. Average age 25. 39 applicants, 62% accepted, 11 enrolled. In 2016, 8 master's awarded. *Degree requirements:* For master's, comprehensive exam, thesis optional. *Entrance requirements:* For master's, GRE General Test (minimum combined score of 950). Additional exam requirements/recommendations for international students: Required—TOEFL (minimum score 550 paper-based; 79 iBT), IELTS (minimum score 6), PTE (minimum score 53). *Application deadline:* For fall admission, 8/1 for domestic students, 5/1 for international students; for spring admission, 11/21 for domestic students, 10/1 for international students; for summer admission, 5/15 for domestic students. Applications are processed on a rolling basis. Application fee: $30 ($40 for international students). Electronic applications accepted. *Expenses:* Tuition, state resident: full-time $3130; part-time $260.80 per credit hour. Tuition, nonresident: full-time $5842; part-time $486.80 per credit hour. *Required fees:* $33.70 per credit hour. *Financial support:* In 2016–17, 19 students received support. Teaching assistantships with full tuition reimbursements available, career-related internships or fieldwork, Federal Work-Study, scholarships/grants, traineeships, tuition waivers (full), and unspecified assistantships available. Financial award application deadline: 6/30; financial award applicants required to submit FAFSA. *Faculty research:* Body composition assessment techniques, serum lipid adaptations with physical activity in smokers, professional attitudes of pre-service teachers, high intensity training with clinical populations. *Unit head:* Dr. Joe Pujol, Professor and Chairperson, 573-651-2664, Fax: 573-651-5150, E-mail: jpujol@semo.edu. *Application contact:* Dr. Jeremy Barnes, Professor/Graduate Coordinator, 573-651-2197, Fax: 573-651-5150, E-mail: jbarnes@semo.edu.
Website: http://www.semo.edu/health/

Southern Connecticut State University, School of Graduate Studies, School of Health and Human Services, Department of Exercise Science, New Haven, CT 06515-1355. Offers human performance (MS); physical education (MS); school health education (MS). *Program availability:* Part-time, evening/weekend. *Faculty:* 5 full-time (0 women). *Students:* 11 full-time (8 women), 16 part-time (9 women); includes 4 minority (3 Hispanic/Latino; 1 Two or more races, non-Hispanic/Latino), 2 international. Average age 26. 8 applicants, 38% accepted, 3 enrolled. In 2016, 12 master's awarded. *Degree requirements:* For master's, thesis or alternative. *Entrance requirements:* For master's, interview. *Application deadline:* For fall admission, 7/15 priority date for domestic students. Applications are processed on a rolling basis. Application fee: $50. Electronic applications accepted. *Expenses:* Tuition, state resident: full-time $6497; part-time $519 per credit hour. Tuition, nonresident: full-time $18,102; part-time $535 per credit hour. *Required fees:* $4722; $55 per semester. Tuition and fees vary according to program. *Financial support:* Career-related internships or fieldwork, scholarships/grants, and unspecified assistantships available. Financial award application deadline: 4/15; financial award applicants required to submit FAFSA. *Unit head:* Dr. Daniel Swartz, Chairperson, 203-392-8721, Fax: 203-392-6911, E-mail: swartzd1@southernct.edu. *Application contact:* Lisa Galvin, Director of Graduate Admissions, 203-392-5240, Fax: 203-392-5235, E-mail: galvinl1@southernct.edu.

Southern Illinois University Edwardsville, Graduate School, School of Education, Health, and Human Behavior, Department of Kinesiology and Health Education, Program in Exercise Physiology, Edwardsville, IL 62026. Offers MS. *Program availability:* Part-time, evening/weekend. *Degree requirements:* For master's, thesis (for some programs), internship. *Entrance requirements:* Additional exam requirements/recommendations for international students: Required—TOEFL (minimum score 550 paper-based, 79 iBT), IELTS (minimum score 6.5), Michigan Test of English Language Proficiency or PTE. Electronic applications accepted.

Southern Utah University, Program in Sports Conditioning, Cedar City, UT 84720-2498. Offers MS. *Program availability:* Part-time, online only, three intensive summer courses/clinical workshops on campus for 1-2 weeks. *Faculty:* 7 full-time (3 women). *Students:* 15 full-time (6 women), 37 part-time (9 women); includes 5 minority (3 Black or African American, non-Hispanic/Latino; 1 American Indian or Alaska Native, non-Hispanic/Latino; 1 Hispanic/Latino). Average age 28. 26 applicants, 77% accepted, 18 enrolled. In 2016, 9 master's awarded. *Entrance requirements:* For master's, GRE or MAT (if GPA is lower than 3.25). Additional exam requirements/recommendations for international students: Required—TOEFL (minimum score 550 paper-based, 79 iBT) or IELTS (minimum score 6). *Application deadline:* For fall admission, 7/15 for domestic and international students; for spring admission, 10/15 for domestic and international students; for summer admission, 2/15 for domestic and international students. Applications are processed on a rolling basis. Application fee: $60 ($65 for international students). Electronic applications accepted. *Expenses:* $6,792 per year residents or online full-time; $20,420 per year on-campus non-resident full-time. *Unit head:* Dr. Camille Thomas, Department Chair, 435-586-7815, Fax: 435-865-8057, E-mail: camillethomas1@suu.edu. *Application contact:* Joan Anderson, Administrative Assistant, 435-586-7816, Fax: 435-865-8057, E-mail: stephanie-smith@leavitt.com.
Website: https://www.suu.edu/ed/pe/master.html

Springfield College, Graduate Programs, Programs in Exercise Science and Sport Studies, Springfield, MA 01109-3797. Offers athletic training (MS); exercise physiology (MS); health promotion and disease prevention (MS); sport and exercise psychology (MS). *Program availability:* Part-time. Terminal master's awarded for partial completion of doctoral program. *Degree requirements:* For master's, comprehensive exam, research project or thesis; for doctorate, comprehensive exam, thesis/dissertation. *Entrance requirements:* For master's and doctorate, GRE General Test. Additional exam requirements/recommendations for international students: Required—TOEFL (minimum score 550 paper-based); Recommended—IELTS (minimum score 6). Electronic applications accepted. *Expenses: Tuition:* Full-time $29,640; part-time $988 per credit. *Required fees:* $195.

Syracuse University, School of Education, MS Program in Exercise Science, Syracuse, NY 13244. Offers MS. *Program availability:* Part-time. *Degree requirements:* For master's, thesis or alternative. *Entrance requirements:* For master's, GRE, baccalaureate degree from regionally-accredited college/university; 8 hours each in general biology and human anatomy and physiology; 6 hours of exercise science (including physiology of exercise and general science); three letters of recommendation; personal statement; resume; transcripts. Additional exam requirements/recommendations for international students: Required—TOEFL. *Application deadline:* For fall admission, 1/15 priority date for domestic and international students; for spring admission, 10/15 priority date for domestic and international students; for summer admission, 1/15 priority date for domestic and international students. Applications are processed on a rolling basis. Application fee: $75. Electronic applications accepted. *Expenses: Tuition:* Full-time $25,974; part-time $1443 per credit hour. *Required fees:* $802; $50 per course. Tuition and fees vary according to course load and program. *Financial support:* Fellowships, research assistantships with tuition reimbursements, teaching assistantships with tuition reimbursements, career-related internships or fieldwork, and scholarships/grants available. Financial award application deadline: 1/15. *Faculty research:* Bone density, obesity in females, cardiovascular functioning, attitudes toward physical education, sports management and psychology. *Unit head:* Dr. Tom Brutsaert, Chair, 315-443-9697, E-mail: tdbrutsa@syr.edu. *Application contact:* Speranza Migliore, Graduate Admissions Recruiter, 315-443-2505, E-mail: gradrcrt@syr.edu.
Website: http://soe.syr.edu/academic/exercise_science/graduate/masters/default.aspx

Tennessee State University, The School of Graduate Studies and Research, College of Health Sciences, Department of Human Performance and Sports Sciences, Nashville, TN 37209-1561. Offers exercise science (MA Ed); sports administration (MA Ed). *Degree requirements:* For master's, thesis optional. *Entrance requirements:* For master's, GRE General Test or MAT.

Texas A&M University–Commerce, College of Education and Human Services, Commerce, TX 75429-3011. Offers counseling (MS); curriculum and instruction (M Ed, MS); early childhood education (M Ed, MS); educational administration (M Ed, Ed D); educational psychology (PhD); educational technology leadership (MS); educational technology library science (MS); health, kinesiology and sports studies (MS); higher education (MS, Ed D); organization, learning, and technology (MS); psychology (MS); reading (M Ed, MS); school psychology (SSP); secondary education (M Ed, MS); social work (MSW); special education (M Ed); supervision, curriculum and instruction-elementary education (Ed D). *Program availability:* Part-time, 100% online, blended/hybrid learning. *Faculty:* 88 full-time (52 women), 31 part-time/adjunct (24 women). *Students:* 341 full-time (276 women), 1,495 part-time (1,156 women); includes 762 minority (429 Black or African American, non-Hispanic/Latino; 4 American Indian or

Alaska Native, non-Hispanic/Latino; 27 Asian, non-Hispanic/Latino; 247 Hispanic/Latino; 1 Native Hawaiian or other Pacific Islander, non-Hispanic/Latino; 54 Two or more races, non-Hispanic/Latino), 18 international. Average age 37. 1,070 applicants, 54% accepted, 452 enrolled. In 2016, 579 master's, 31 doctorates awarded. *Degree requirements:* For master's, one foreign language, comprehensive exam, thesis optional, departmental qualifying exams (for some programs); for doctorate, comprehensive exam, thesis/dissertation, departmental qualifying exam; for SSP, comprehensive exam, thesis optional. *Entrance requirements:* For master's and doctorate, GRE General Test. Additional exam requirements/recommendations for international students: Required—TOEFL (minimum score 550 paper-based; 79 iBT), IELTS (minimum score 6). *Application deadline:* For fall admission, 6/1 priority date for international students; for spring admission, 10/15 priority date for international students; for summer admission, 3/15 priority date for international students. Applications are processed on a rolling basis. Application fee: $50. Electronic applications accepted. *Expenses:* $2,254 resident; $4,744 non-resident. *Financial support:* In 2016–17, 301 students received support, including 39 research assistantships with partial tuition reimbursements available (averaging $9,000 per year), 17 teaching assistantships with partial tuition reimbursements available (averaging $9,000 per year); career-related internships or fieldwork, Federal Work-Study, institutionally sponsored loans, scholarships/grants, health care benefits, and unspecified assistantships also available. Financial award application deadline: 5/1; financial award applicants required to submit FAFSA. *Faculty research:* Cognitive and bilingual education, positive behavioral intervention, literacy, math readiness. *Total annual research expenditures:* $470,963. *Unit head:* Dr. Timothy Letzring, Dean, 903-886-5181, Fax: 903-886-5905, E-mail: tim.letzring@tamuc.edu. *Application contact:* Jennifer Faunce, Graduate Recruiter, 903-886-5030, Fax: 903-886-5905, E-mail: jennifer.faunce@tamuc.edu.
Website: http://www.tamuc.edu/academics/graduateSchool/programs/education/default.aspx

Texas Tech University, Graduate School, College of Arts and Sciences, Department of Kinesiology and Sport Management, Lubbock, TX 79409. Offers kinesiology (MS); sport management (MS). *Program availability:* Part-time. *Faculty:* 23 full-time (11 women), 10 part-time/adjunct (5 women). *Students:* 50 full-time (25 women), 12 part-time (3 women); includes 20 minority (6 Black or African American, non-Hispanic/Latino; 11 Hispanic/Latino; 3 Two or more races, non-Hispanic/Latino), 7 international. Average age 24. 88 applicants, 39% accepted, 23 enrolled. In 2016, 41 master's awarded. *Degree requirements:* For master's, comprehensive exam (for some programs), thesis (for some programs). *Entrance requirements:* For master's, GRE for those whose GPA on last 60 hours of undergraduate coursework is 3.49 and lower (for kinesiology only), letter of intent, 3 letters of recommendation (preferably from academic professors), minimum GPA of 2.8 in the last 60 hours. Additional exam requirements/recommendations for international students: Required—TOEFL (minimum score 550 paper-based; 79 iBT). *Application deadline:* For fall admission, 6/1 priority date for domestic students, 1/15 priority date for international students; for spring admission, 9/1 priority date for domestic students, 6/15 priority date for international students. Applications are processed on a rolling basis. Application fee: $75. Electronic applications accepted. *Expenses:* $300 per credit hour full-time resident tuition, $708 per credit hour full-time non-resident tuition; $50.50 per credit hour fee plus $608 per term fee. *Financial support:* In 2016–17, 58 students received support, including 30 fellowships (averaging $4,699 per year), 47 teaching assistantships (averaging $10,579 per year); research assistantships, career-related internships or fieldwork, scholarships/grants, health care benefits, and unspecified assistantships also available. Financial award application deadline: 8/1; financial award applicants required to submit FAFSA. *Faculty research:* Sport management, exercise physiology, human performance, motor behavior, exercise and sport psychology. *Total annual research expenditures:* $234,707. *Unit head:* Dr. Angela Lumpkin, Professor/Chair, 806-834-6935, Fax: 806-742-1688, E-mail: angela.lumpkin@ttu.edu. *Application contact:* Dr. Donna Torres, Graduate Coordinator, 806-834-7968, Fax: 806-742-1688, E-mail: donna.torres@ttu.edu.
Website: http://www.depts.ttu.edu/ksm/

Texas Woman's University, Graduate School, College of Health Sciences, Department of Kinesiology, Denton, TX 76201. Offers adapted physical activity (MS, PhD); biomechanics (MS, PhD); coaching (MS); exercise physiology (MS, PhD); sport management (MS, PhD). *Program availability:* Part-time, evening/weekend. Terminal master's awarded for partial completion of doctoral program. *Degree requirements:* For master's, comprehensive exam, thesis or alternative; for doctorate, comprehensive exam, thesis/dissertation, qualifying exam. *Entrance requirements:* For master's, GRE General Test (biomechanics emphasis only), 2 letters of reference, curriculum vitae, interview (adapted physical education emphasis only); for doctorate, GRE General Test (biomechanics emphasis only), interview, 3 letters of reference, curriculum vitae. Additional exam requirements/recommendations for international students: Required—TOEFL (minimum score 550 paper-based; 79 iBT). *Application deadline:* For fall admission, 7/1 priority date for domestic students, 3/1 for international students; for spring admission, 11/1 priority date for domestic students, 7/1 for international students. Applications are processed on a rolling basis. Application fee: $50 ($75 for international students). Electronic applications accepted. *Expenses:* Tuition, state resident: full-time $9046; part-time $251 per credit hour. Tuition, nonresident: full-time $22,922; part-time $614 per credit hour. *International tuition:* $23,046 full-time. *Required fees:* $2690; $1285 per credit hour. One-time fee: $50. Tuition and fees vary according to course level, course load, program and reciprocity agreements. *Financial support:* Research assistantships, teaching assistantships, career-related internships or fieldwork, Federal Work-Study, institutionally sponsored loans, scholarships/grants, traineeships, health care benefits, and unspecified assistantships available. Support available to part-time students. Financial award application deadline: 3/1; financial award applicants required to submit FAFSA. *Faculty research:* Exercise and Type 2 diabetes risk, bone mineral density and exercise in special populations, obesity in children, factors influencing sport consumer behavior and loyalty, roles and responsibilities of Para educators in adapted physical education. *Unit head:* Dr. David Nichols, Interim Chair, 940-898-2576, Fax: 940-898-2581, E-mail: dnichols@twu.edu. *Application contact:* Dr. Samuel Wheeler, Assistant Director of Admissions, 940-898-3188, Fax: 940-898-3081, E-mail: wheelersr@twu.edu.
Website: http://www.twu.edu/kinesiology/

United States Sports Academy, Graduate Programs, Program in Sports Fitness and Health, Daphne, AL 36526-7055. Offers MSS. *Program availability:* Part-time, online learning. *Degree requirements:* For master's, comprehensive exam, thesis optional. *Entrance requirements:* For master's, GRE General Test, GMAT, or MAT, minimum GPA of 2.5, 3 letters of recommendation, resume. Additional exam requirements/recommendations for international students: Required—TOEFL (minimum score 500 paper-based). Electronic applications accepted. *Faculty research:* Exercise physiology, conditioning.

United States Sports Academy, Graduate Programs, Program in Sport Studies, Daphne, AL 36526-7055. Offers MSS. *Program availability:* Part-time, online learning. *Degree requirements:* For master's, comprehensive exam, thesis optional. *Entrance requirements:* For master's, GRE General Test, GMAT, or MAT, minimum GPA of 2.5, 3 letters of recommendation, resume. Additional exam requirements/recommendations for international students: Required—TOEFL (minimum score 500 paper-based). Electronic applications accepted.

University at Buffalo, the State University of New York, Graduate School, School of Public Health and Health Professions, Department of Exercise and Nutrition Sciences, Buffalo, NY 14260. Offers exercise science (MS, PhD); nutrition (MS, Advanced Certificate). *Program availability:* Part-time. *Degree requirements:* For master's, comprehensive exam or thesis; for doctorate, comprehensive exam, thesis/dissertation. *Entrance requirements:* For master's, doctorate, and Advanced Certificate, GRE General Test, minimum GPA of 3.0. Additional exam requirements/recommendations for international students: Required—TOEFL (minimum score 550 paper-based; 79 iBT), IELTS (minimum score 6.5). Electronic applications accepted. *Faculty research:* Cardiovascular disease-diet and exercise, respiratory control and muscle function, plasticity of connective and neural tissue, exercise nutrition, diet and cancer.

The University of Akron, Graduate School, College of Health Professions, School of Sport Science and Wellness Education, Program in Exercise Physiology/Adult Fitness, Akron, OH 44325. Offers MA, MS. *Students:* 50 full-time (26 women), 11 part-time (4 women); includes 9 minority (3 Black or African American, non-Hispanic/Latino; 3 Asian, non-Hispanic/Latino; 2 Hispanic/Latino; 1 Two or more races, non-Hispanic/Latino), 5 international. Average age 26. 40 applicants, 88% accepted, 27 enrolled. In 2016, 28 master's awarded. *Degree requirements:* For master's, comprehensive exam, thesis optional. *Entrance requirements:* For master's, minimum GPA of 2.75, three letters of recommendation, statement of purpose. Additional exam requirements/recommendations for international students: Required—TOEFL (minimum score 550 paper-based; 79 iBT), IELTS (minimum score 6.5). *Application deadline:* Applications are processed on a rolling basis. Application fee: $45 ($70 for international students). Electronic applications accepted. *Expenses:* Tuition, state resident: full-time $8618; part-time $359 per credit hour. Tuition, nonresident: full-time $17,149; part-time $715 per credit hour. *Required fees:* $1652. *Unit head:* Dr. Victor Pinheiro, Department Chair, 330-972-6055, E-mail: victor@uakron.edu. *Application contact:* Dr. Ron Otterstetter, Program Contact, 330-972-7738.
Website: http://www.uakron.edu/sswe/

The University of Akron, Graduate School, College of Health Professions, School of Sport Science and Wellness Education, Program in Sport Science/Coaching, Akron, OH 44325. Offers MA, MS. *Students:* 49 full-time (15 women), 9 part-time (5 women); includes 17 minority (16 Black or African American, non-Hispanic/Latino; 1 Two or more races, non-Hispanic/Latino), 2 international. Average age 27. 33 applicants, 67% accepted, 12 enrolled. In 2016, 38 master's awarded. *Degree requirements:* For master's, comprehensive exam, thesis optional. *Entrance requirements:* For master's, minimum GPA of 2.75, three letters of recommendation, statement of purpose. Additional exam requirements/recommendations for international students: Required—TOEFL (minimum score 550 paper-based; 79 iBT), IELTS (minimum score 6.5). *Application deadline:* Applications are processed on a rolling basis. Application fee: $45 ($70 for international students). Electronic applications accepted. *Expenses:* Tuition, state resident: full-time $8618; part-time $359 per credit hour. Tuition, nonresident: full-time $17,149; part-time $715 per credit hour. *Required fees:* $1652. *Unit head:* Dr. Victor Pinheiro, Department Chair, 330-972-6055, E-mail: victor@uakron.edu. *Application contact:* Dr. Alan Kornspan, Program Contact, 330-972-8145.
Website: http://www.uakron.edu/sswe/programs/sport-science-coaching/index.dot

The University of Alabama, Graduate School, College of Education, Department of Kinesiology, Tuscaloosa, AL 35487. Offers alternative sport pedagogy (MA); exercise science (PhD). *Program availability:* Part-time. *Faculty:* 12 full-time (2 women). *Students:* 70 full-time (35 women), 22 part-time (6 women); includes 16 minority (9 Black or African American, non-Hispanic/Latino; 4 Hispanic/Latino; 3 Two or more races, non-Hispanic/Latino), 7 international. Average age 29. 71 applicants, 76% accepted, 38 enrolled. In 2016, 39 master's, 8 doctorates awarded. *Degree requirements:* For master's, comprehensive exam, thesis optional; for doctorate, comprehensive exam, thesis/dissertation. *Entrance requirements:* For master's and doctorate, GRE, minimum GPA of 3.0. Additional exam requirements/recommendations for international students: Required—TOEFL. *Application deadline:* Applications are processed on a rolling basis. Electronic applications accepted. *Expenses:* Tuition, state resident: full-time $10,470. Tuition, nonresident: full-time $26,950. *Financial support:* Application deadline: 3/1. *Total annual research expenditures:* $39,044. *Unit head:* Dr. Jonathan Wingo, Associate Professor and Head, 205-348-4699, Fax: 205-348-0867, E-mail: jwingo@ua.edu.
Website: http://education.ua.edu/academics/kine/

University of Alberta, Faculty of Graduate Studies and Research, Department of Physical Education and Recreation, Edmonton, AB T6G 2E1, Canada. Offers physical education (M Sc); recreation and physical education (MA, PhD). *Program availability:* Part-time. Terminal master's awarded for partial completion of doctoral program. *Degree requirements:* For master's, thesis (for some programs); for doctorate, thesis/dissertation. *Entrance requirements:* For master's, bachelor's degree in related field; for doctorate, master's degree in related field with thesis. Additional exam requirements/recommendations for international students: Required—TOEFL. *Faculty research:* Motivation and adherence to physical ability, performance enhancement, adapted physical activity, exercise physiology, sport administration, tourism.

University of Arkansas at Little Rock, Graduate School, College of Education and Health Professions, Department of Health, Human Performance and Sport Management, Little Rock, AR 72204-1099. Offers exercise science (MS); health education and promotion (MS); sport management (MS). *Program availability:* Part-time, evening/weekend. *Degree requirements:* For master's, directed study or residency. *Entrance requirements:* For master's, GRE General Test, minimum GPA of 3.0, 3 reference letters.

University of California, Davis, Graduate Studies, Graduate Group in Exercise Science, Davis, CA 95616. Offers MS. *Degree requirements:* For master's, thesis. *Entrance requirements:* For master's, GRE, minimum GPA of 3.25. Additional exam requirements/recommendations for international students: Required—TOEFL (minimum score 550 paper-based). Electronic applications accepted.

University of Central Florida, College of Education and Human Performance, Department of Educational and Human Sciences, Program in Sport and Exercise Science, Orlando, FL 32816. Offers applied exercise physiology (MS). *Program availability:* Part-time, evening/weekend. *Students:* 42 full-time (17 women), 22 part-time (8 women); includes 19 minority (4 Black or African American, non-Hispanic/Latino; 3 Asian, non-Hispanic/Latino; 11 Hispanic/Latino; 1 Two or more races, non-Hispanic/Latino), 3 international. Average age 27. 81 applicants, 47% accepted, 15 enrolled. In 2016, 46 master's awarded. *Degree requirements:* For master's, thesis or alternative. *Entrance requirements:* For master's, GRE General Test. Additional exam requirements/recommendations for international students: Required—TOEFL. *Application deadline:* For fall admission, 7/15 for domestic students; for spring admission, 12/1 for domestic students. Application fee: $30. Electronic applications accepted. *Expenses:* Tuition, state resident: part-time $288.16 per credit hour. Tuition, nonresident: part-time $1071.31 per credit hour. *Financial support:* In 2016–17, 5 students received support, including 6 research assistantships with partial tuition reimbursements available (averaging $5,881 per year), 2 teaching assistantships with partial tuition

reimbursements available (averaging $9,252 per year); fellowships, career-related internships or fieldwork, Federal Work-Study, institutionally sponsored loans, tuition waivers (partial), and unspecified assistantships also available. Financial award application deadline: 3/1; financial award applicants required to submit FAFSA. *Unit head:* Dr. Jeffrey Stout, Coordinator, 407-823-0211, E-mail: jeffrey.stout@ucf.edu. *Application contact:* Assistant Director, Graduate Admissions, 407-823-2766, Fax: 407-823-6442, E-mail: gradadmissions@ucf.edu.
Website: http://education.ucf.edu/sportexscience/

University of Central Florida, College of Education and Human Performance, Education Doctoral Programs, Orlando, FL 32816. Offers communication sciences and disorders (PhD); curriculum and instruction (Ed D); early childhood education (PhD); educational leadership (Ed D); elementary education (PhD); exceptional education (PhD); exercise physiology (PhD); higher education (PhD); instructional technology (PhD); mathematics education (PhD); methodology, measurement and analysis (PhD); reading education (PhD); science education (PhD); social science education (PhD); TESOL (PhD). *Students:* 127 full-time (91 women), 43 part-time (29 women); includes 33 minority (17 Black or African American, non-Hispanic/Latino; 5 Asian, non-Hispanic/Latino; 7 Hispanic/Latino; 4 Two or more races, non-Hispanic/Latino), 26 international. Average age 37. 163 applicants, 40% accepted, 52 enrolled. In 2016, 57 doctorates awarded. Application fee: $30. Electronic applications accepted. *Expenses:* Tuition, state resident: part-time $288.16 per credit hour. Tuition, nonresident: part-time $1071.31 per credit hour. *Financial support:* In 2016–17, 78 students received support, including 41 fellowships with partial tuition reimbursements available (averaging $5,916 per year), 44 research assistantships with partial tuition reimbursements available (averaging $7,637 per year), 48 teaching assistantships with partial tuition reimbursements available (averaging $9,633 per year). Financial award application deadline: 3/1; financial award applicants required to submit FAFSA. *Unit head:* Dr. Edward Robinson, Director of Doctoral Programs, 407-823-6106, E-mail: edward.robinson@ucf.edu. *Application contact:* Assistant Director, Graduate Admissions, 407-823-2766, Fax: 407-823-6442, E-mail: gradadmissions@ucf.edu.
Website: http://education.ucf.edu/programs.cfm?pid=g&cat=2

University of Central Oklahoma, The Jackson College of Graduate Studies, College of Education and Professional Studies, Department of Kinesiology and Health Studies, Edmond, OK 73034-5209. Offers athletic training (MS); wellness management (MS), including exercise science, health studies. *Degree requirements:* For master's, comprehensive exam (for some programs), thesis (for some programs). *Entrance requirements:* For master's, GRE. Additional exam requirements/recommendations for international students: Required—TOEFL (minimum score 550 paper-based; 79 iBT), IELTS (minimum score 6.5). Electronic applications accepted.

University of Connecticut, Graduate School, College of Agriculture, Health and Natural Resources, Department of Kinesiology, Program in Exercise Science, Storrs, CT 06269. Offers MS, PhD. Terminal master's awarded for partial completion of doctoral program. *Degree requirements:* For master's, comprehensive exam, thesis or alternative; for doctorate, thesis/dissertation. *Entrance requirements:* For doctorate, GRE General Test. Additional exam requirements/recommendations for international students: Required—TOEFL (minimum score 550 paper-based). Electronic applications accepted.

University of Dayton, Department of Health and Sport Science, Dayton, OH 45469. Offers exercise science (MS Ed). *Faculty:* 7 full-time (3 women). *Students:* 12 full-time (3 women), 1 (woman) part-time; includes 5 minority (3 Black or African American, non-Hispanic/Latino; 1 Asian, non-Hispanic/Latino; 1 Two or more races, non-Hispanic/Latino), 2 international. Average age 23. 37 applicants, 30% accepted. In 2016, 5 master's awarded. *Degree requirements:* For master's, thesis optional. *Entrance requirements:* For master's, GRE General Test or MAT if undergraduate GPA was 2.75 or below, minimum GPA of 2.75; official academic records of all previously-attended colleges or universities; three letters of recommendation from professors or employers; personal statement or resume. Additional exam requirements/recommendations for international students: Required—TOEFL (minimum score 550 paper-based; 80 iBT). *Application deadline:* Applications are processed on a rolling basis. Application fee: $0 ($50 for international students). Electronic applications accepted. *Expenses:* $620 per credit hour, $25 registration fee per term. *Financial support:* In 2016–17, 2 research assistantships with partial tuition reimbursements (averaging $9,390 per year), 2 teaching assistantships with partial tuition reimbursements (averaging $9,390 per year) were awarded; career-related internships or fieldwork, institutionally sponsored loans, health care benefits, and unspecified assistantships also available. Financial award application deadline: 3/1; financial award applicants required to submit FAFSA. *Faculty research:* Energy expenditure, strength, training, teaching nutrition and calcium intake for children and families in Head Start; motion analysis of human gait, pediatric physical therapy, arm function of breast cancer survivors, predicting injury in athletes, neurological rehabilitation in persons with multiple sclerosis. *Unit head:* Dr. Lloyd Laubach, Chair, 937-229-4240, Fax: 937-229-4244, E-mail: llaubach1@udayton.edu. *Application contact:* Laura Greger, Administrative Assistant, 937-229-4225, E-mail: lgreger1@udayton.edu.
Website: https://www.udayton.edu/education/departments_and_programs/hss

University of Florida, Graduate School, College of Health and Human Performance, Department of Applied Physiology and Kinesiology, Gainesville, FL 32611. Offers applied physiology and kinesiology (MS); athletic training/sports medicine (MS), biobehavioral science (MS); clinical exercise physiology (MS); exercise physiology (MS); health and human performance (PhD), including applied physiology and kinesiology, biobehavioral science, exercise physiology; human performance (MS). *Degree requirements:* For master's, comprehensive exam, thesis (for some programs); for doctorate, comprehensive exam, thesis/dissertation. *Entrance requirements:* For master's and doctorate, GRE General Test, minimum GPA of 3.0. Additional exam requirements/recommendations for international students: Required—TOEFL (minimum score 550 paper-based; 80 iBT), IELTS (minimum score 6). Electronic applications accepted. *Faculty research:* Cardiovascular disease; basic mechanisms that underlie exercise-induced changes in the body at the organ, tissue, cellular and molecular level; development of rehabilitation techniques for regaining motor control after stroke or as a consequence of Parkinson's disease; maintaining optimal health and delaying age-related declines in physiological function; psychomotor mechanisms impacting health and performance across the life span.

University of Houston, College of Liberal Arts and Social Sciences, Department of Health and Human Performance, Houston, TX 77204. Offers exercise science (MS); human nutrition (MS); human space exploration sciences (MS); kinesiology (PhD); physical education (M Ed). *Accreditation:* NCATE (one or more programs are accredited). *Program availability:* Part-time, evening/weekend. *Degree requirements:* For master's, comprehensive exam (for some programs), thesis (for some programs); for doctorate, comprehensive exam, thesis/dissertation, qualifying exam, candidacy paper. *Entrance requirements:* For master's, GRE (minimum 35th percentile on each section), minimum cumulative GPA of 3.0; for doctorate, GRE (minimum 35th percentile on each section), minimum cumulative GPA of 3.3. Additional exam requirements/recommendations for international students: Required—TOEFL (minimum score 550 paper-based; 79 iBT). Electronic applications accepted. *Faculty research:* Biomechanics, exercise physiology, obesity, nutrition, space exploration science.

University of Houston–Clear Lake, School of Human Sciences and Humanities, Programs in Human Sciences, Houston, TX 77058-1002. Offers behavioral sciences (MA), including criminology, cross cultural studies, general psychology, sociology; clinical psychology (MA); criminology (MA); cross cultural studies (MA); family therapy (MA); fitness and human performance (MA); school psychology (MA). *Accreditation:* AAMFT/COAMFTE. *Program availability:* Part-time, evening/weekend, online learning. *Degree requirements:* For master's, thesis or alternative. *Entrance requirements:* For master's, GRE General Test. Additional exam requirements/recommendations for international students: Required—TOEFL (minimum score 550 paper-based). Electronic applications accepted. *Faculty research:* Smoking cessation, adolescent sexuality, white collar crime, serial murder, human factors/human computer interaction.

The University of Iowa, Graduate College, College of Liberal Arts and Sciences, Department of Health and Human Physiology, Iowa City, IA 52242-1316. Offers athletic training (MS); clinical exercise physiology (MS); health and human physiology (PhD); leisure studies (MA, PhD), including recreational sport management (PhD), therapeutic recreation (MA). *Degree requirements:* For master's, thesis optional, exam; for doctorate, comprehensive exam, thesis/dissertation. *Entrance requirements:* For master's and doctorate, GRE General Test, minimum GPA of 3.0. Additional exam requirements/recommendations for international students: Required—TOEFL (minimum score 600 paper-based; 100 iBT). Electronic applications accepted.

The University of Kansas, Graduate Studies, School of Education, Department of Health, Sport, and Exercise Sciences, Lawrence, KS 66045. Offers exercise science (MS Ed); health and physical education (MS Ed, PhD); sport management (MS Ed). *Accreditation:* NCATE. *Program availability:* Part-time, evening/weekend. *Students:* 53 full-time (21 women), 12 part-time (5 women); includes 5 minority (1 Black or African American, non-Hispanic/Latino; 1 American Indian or Alaska Native, non-Hispanic/Latino; 3 Two or more races, non-Hispanic/Latino), 3 international. Average age 27. 70 applicants, 64% accepted, 25 enrolled. In 2016, 19 master's, 6 doctorates awarded. *Entrance requirements:* For master's, GRE General Test (minimum score 1000, 450 verbal, 450 quantitative, 4.0 analytical), minimum GPA of 3.0, three letters of recommendation, personal statement, resume, writing sample; for doctorate, GRE General Test (minimum score 1100, verbal 500, quantitative 500, analytical 4.5), minimum graduate GPA of 3.5, undergraduate 3.0; three letters of recommendation; personal statement; resume; writing sample; interview with an advisor. Additional exam requirements/recommendations for international students: Required—TOEFL or IELTS. *Application deadline:* For fall admission, 3/15 for domestic and international students; for spring admission, 10/1 for domestic and international students; for summer admission, 3/15 for domestic and international students. Application fee: $65 ($85 for international students). Electronic applications accepted. *Financial support:* Research assistantships, teaching assistantships, Federal Work-Study, scholarships/grants, and unspecified assistantships available. Financial award application deadline: 2/21. *Faculty research:* Exercise and sport psychology, obesity prevention, sexuality health, sport ethics, skeletal muscle cell signaling and performance. *Unit head:* Dr. Joseph Weir, Chair, 785-864-0784, E-mail: joseph.weir@ku.edu. *Application contact:* Sarah Clopton, Graduate Admissions Coordinator, 785-864-7268, E-mail: sclopton@ku.edu.
Website: http://hses.soe.ku.edu/

University of Kentucky, Graduate School, College of Education, Program in Kinesiology and Health Promotion, Lexington, KY 40506-0032. Offers biomechanics (MS); exercise physiology (MS, PhD); exercise science (PhD); health promotion (MS, Ed D); physical education training (Ed D); sport leadership (MS); teaching and coaching (MS). Terminal master's awarded for partial completion of doctoral program. *Degree requirements:* For master's, comprehensive exam, thesis optional; for doctorate, comprehensive exam, thesis/dissertation. *Entrance requirements:* For master's, GRE General Test, minimum undergraduate GPA of 2.75; for doctorate, GRE General Test, minimum graduate GPA of 3.0. Additional exam requirements/recommendations for international students: Required—TOEFL (minimum score 550 paper-based). Electronic applications accepted.

University of Lethbridge, School of Graduate Studies, Lethbridge, AB T1K 3M4, Canada. Offers addictions counseling (M Sc); agricultural biotechnology (M Sc); agricultural studies (M Sc, MA); anthropology (MA); archaeology (M Sc, MA); art (MA, MFA); biochemistry (M Sc); biological sciences (M Sc); biomolecular science (PhD); biosystems and biodiversity (PhD); Canadian studies (MA); chemistry (M Sc); computer science (M Sc); computer science and geographical information science (M Sc); counseling (MC); counseling psychology (M Ed); dramatic arts (MA); earth, space, and physical science (PhD); economics (MA); education (MA, PhD); educational leadership (M Ed); English (MA); environmental science (M Sc); evolution and behavior (PhD); exercise science (M Sc); French (MA); French/German (MA); French/Spanish (MA); general education (M Ed); geography (M Sc, MA); German (MA); health sciences (M Sc); individualized multidisciplinary (M Sc, MA); kinesiology (M Sc, MA); management (M Sc), including accounting, finance, human resource management and labor relations, information systems, international management, marketing, policy and strategy; mathematics (M Sc); music (M Mus, MA); Native American studies (MA); neuroscience (M Sc, PhD); new media (MA, MFA); nursing (M Sc, MN); philosophy (MA); physics (M Sc); political science (MA); psychology (M Sc, MA); religious studies (MA); sociology (MA); theatre and dramatic arts (MFA); theoretical and computational science (PhD); urban and regional studies (MA); women and gender studies (MA). *Program availability:* Part-time, evening/weekend. *Degree requirements:* For master's, thesis (for some programs); for doctorate, comprehensive exam, thesis/dissertation. *Entrance requirements:* For master's, GMAT (for M Sc in management), bachelor's degree in related field, minimum GPA of 3.0 during previous 20 graded semester courses, 2 years' teaching or related experience (M Ed); for doctorate, master's degree, minimum graduate GPA of 3.5. Additional exam requirements/recommendations for international students: Required—TOEFL (minimum score 580 paper-based; 93 iBT). Electronic applications accepted. *Faculty research:* Movement and brain plasticity, gibberellin physiology, photosynthesis, carbon cycling, molecular properties of main-group ring components.

University of Louisiana at Monroe, Graduate School, College of Health and Pharmaceutical Sciences, Department of Kinesiology, Monroe, LA 71209-0001. Offers applied exercise science (MS); clinical exercise physiology (MS); sports, fitness and recreation management (MS). *Program availability:* Part-time, evening/weekend, online learning. *Faculty:* 4 full-time (1 woman), 1 part-time/adjunct (0 women). *Students:* 31 full-time (12 women), 9 part-time (4 women); includes 11 minority (7 Black or African American, non-Hispanic/Latino; 4 Hispanic/Latino), 3 international. Average age 24. 96 applicants, 34% accepted, 14 enrolled. In 2016, 17 master's awarded. *Degree requirements:* For master's, comprehensive exam, thesis, 6-hour internship. *Entrance requirements:* For master's, GRE General Test. Additional exam requirements/recommendations for international students: Required—TOEFL (minimum score 500 paper-based; 61 iBT). *Application deadline:* For fall admission, 8/24 priority date for domestic students, 7/1 for international students; for winter admission, 12/14 priority date for domestic students; for spring admission, 1/19 for domestic students, 11/1 for international students. Applications are processed on a rolling basis. Application fee:

$20 ($30 for international students). Electronic applications accepted. *Expenses:* Tuition, state resident: full-time $6489. Tuition, nonresident: full-time $18,589. *Required fees:* $8984. Tuition and fees vary according to course level, course load, degree level and program. *Financial support:* Research assistantships, career-related internships or fieldwork, Federal Work-Study, and unspecified assistantships available. Financial award application deadline: 4/1; financial award applicants required to submit FAFSA. *Faculty research:* Cardiovascular disease risk factors; exercise and immunological system; attitude, exercise, and the aged. *Unit head:* Dr. Ken Alford, Director, 318-342-1306, E-mail: alford@ulm.edu. *Application contact:* Dr. Tommie Church, Director of Graduate Studies, 318-342-1321, E-mail: church@ulm.edu.
Website: http://www.ulm.edu/kinesiology/

University of Louisville, Graduate School, College of Education and Human Development, Department of Health and Sport Sciences, Louisville, KY 40292-0001. Offers community health education (M Ed); exercise physiology (MS), including health and sport sciences, strength and conditioning; health and physical education (MAT); sport administration (MS). *Program availability:* Part-time, evening/weekend. *Students:* 39 full-time (18 women), 10 part-time (8 women); includes 7 minority (4 Black or African American, non-Hispanic/Latino; 2 Hispanic/Latino; 1 Two or more races, non-Hispanic/Latino), 1 international. Average age 27. 73 applicants, 63% accepted, 23 enrolled. In 2016, 25 master's awarded. Application fee: $60. *Expenses:* Tuition, state resident: full-time $12,246; part-time $681 per credit hour. Tuition, nonresident: full-time $25,486; part-time $1417 per credit hour. *Required fees:* $196. Tuition and fees vary according to program and reciprocity agreements. *Financial support:* Applicants required to submit FAFSA. *Faculty research:* Sport administration; exercise physiology; exercise science; physical education; health education. *Total annual research expenditures:* $91,688. *Unit head:* Dr. Margaret Hancock, Interim Chair/Assistant Professor, 502-852-6645, E-mail: meg.hancock@louisville.edu. *Application contact:* Betty Hampton, Director of Graduate Student Services, 502-852-5597, Fax: 502-852-1465, E-mail: edadvise@louisville.edu.
Website: http://www.louisville.edu/education/departments/hss

University of Louisville, Graduate School, College of Education and Human Development, Department of Teaching and Learning, Louisville, KY 40292-0001. Offers art education (MAT); autism and applied behavior analysis (Certificate); curriculum and instruction (PhD); early elementary education (MAT); exercise physiology (MS); health and physical education (MAT); health professions education (Certificate); higher education (MA); human resources and organization development (MS); instructional technology (M Ed); interdisciplinary early childhood education (MAT); middle school education (MAT); music education (MAT); secondary education (MAT); special education (MAT); sport administration (MS); teacher leadership (M Ed). *Program availability:* Part-time, evening/weekend. *Students:* 116 full-time (68 women), 158 part-time (112 women); includes 46 minority (24 Black or African American, non-Hispanic/Latino; 8 Asian, non-Hispanic/Latino; 5 Hispanic/Latino; 9 Two or more races, non-Hispanic/Latino), 6 international. Average age 30. 114 applicants, 71% accepted, 57 enrolled. In 2016, 59 master's, 3 doctorates awarded. *Application deadline:* For spring admission, 1/1 priority date for international students. Application fee: $60. *Expenses:* Tuition, state resident: full-time $12,246; part-time $681 per credit hour. Tuition, nonresident: full-time $25,486; part-time $1417 per credit hour. *Required fees:* $196. Tuition and fees vary according to program and reciprocity agreements. *Financial support:* Application deadline: 6/1; applicants required to submit FAFSA. *Faculty research:* STEM teaching and learning; content literacy for English language learners; social justice in teacher education; adolescent literacy; mathematics teacher development. *Total annual research expenditures:* $1.7 million. *Unit head:* Dr. Ann E. Larson, Dean, College of Education and Human Development, 502-852-6411, Fax: 502-852-1464, E-mail: ann@louisville.edu. *Application contact:* Betty Hampton, Director of Graduate Student Services, 502-852-5597, Fax: 502-852-1465, E-mail: edadvise@louisville.edu.
Website: http://louisville.edu/delphi

University of Maine, Graduate School, College of Education and Human Development, School of Kinesiology, Physical Education and Athletic Training, Orono, ME 04469. Offers classroom technology integrationist (CGS); education data specialist (CGS); educational technology coordinator (CGS); kinesiology and physical education (M Ed, MS); science education (M Ed, MS); STEM education (PhD). *Program availability:* Part-time, evening/weekend. *Students:* 13 full-time (4 women), 1 (woman) part-time; includes 1 minority (Hispanic/Latino), 1 international. Average age 24. 15 applicants, 100% accepted, 7 enrolled. In 2016, 16 master's, 10 other advanced degrees awarded. *Degree requirements:* For master's, thesis (for some programs); for doctorate, comprehensive exam, thesis/dissertation. *Entrance requirements:* For master's, GRE General Test, MAT; for doctorate, GRE General Test. Additional exam requirements/recommendations for international students: Required—TOEFL. *Application deadline:* For fall admission, 1/15 for domestic students. Applications are processed on a rolling basis. Application fee: $65. Electronic applications accepted. *Expenses:* Tuition, state resident: full-time $7524; part-time $2508 per credit. Tuition, nonresident: full-time $24,498; part-time $8166 per credit. *Required fees:* $1148; $571 per credit. *Financial support:* In 2016–17, 9 students received support, including 1 research assistantship with full tuition reimbursement available (averaging $14,600 per year), 6 teaching assistantships (averaging $14,600 per year); Federal Work-Study, scholarships/grants, and unspecified assistantships also available. Financial award application deadline: 3/1. *Faculty research:* Integration of technology in K-12 classrooms, instructional theory and practice in science, inquiry-based teaching, professional development, exercise science, adaptive physical education, neuromuscular function/dysfunction. *Unit head:* Dr. Jim Artesani, Associate Dean of Accreditation and Graduate Affairs, 207-581-4061, Fax: 207-581-2423. *Application contact:* Scott G. Delcourt, Assistant Vice President for Graduate Studies and Senior Associate Dean, 207-581-3291, Fax: 207-581-3232, E-mail: graduate@maine.edu.
Website: http://umaine.edu/edhd/

University of Mary, School of Health Sciences, Program in Clinical Exercise Physiology, Bismarck, ND 58504-9652. Offers MS. *Program availability:* Online learning.

University of Mary Hardin-Baylor, Graduate Studies in Exercise Science, Belton, TX 76513. Offers exercise physiology (MS Ed); sport administration (MS Ed). *Program availability:* Part-time, evening/weekend, 100% online. *Faculty:* 6 full-time (1 woman). *Students:* 9 full-time (2 women), 29 part-time (12 women); includes 21 minority (8 Black or African American, non-Hispanic/Latino; 1 Asian, non-Hispanic/Latino; 12 Hispanic/Latino). Average age 27. 19 applicants, 84% accepted, 13 enrolled. In 2016, 18 master's awarded. *Degree requirements:* For master's, comprehensive exam, thesis optional. *Entrance requirements:* For master's, bachelor's degree in exercise science or related field; minimum GPA of 3.0; interview with program director. Additional exam requirements/recommendations for international students: Required—TOEFL (minimum score 60 iBT), IELTS (minimum score 4.5). *Application deadline:* For fall admission, 6/1 for domestic students, 4/30 priority date for international students; for spring admission, 11/1 for domestic students, 9/30 priority date for international students. Applications are processed on a rolling basis. Application fee: $35 ($135 for international students). Electronic applications accepted. *Expenses: Tuition:* Full-time $14,940; part-time $830 per credit hour. *Required fees:* $1350; $75 per credit hour. $50 per term. Tuition and fees vary according to course load and degree level. *Financial support:* In 2016–17, 31 students received support. Federal Work-Study, unspecified assistantships, and scholarships for some active duty military personnel available. Support available to part-time students. Financial award application deadline: 6/1; financial award applicants required to submit FAFSA. *Unit head:* Dr. Lem Taylor, Director, MS Ed in Exercise Physiology Program, 254-295-4895, E-mail: ltaylor@umhb.edu. *Application contact:* Sharon Aguilera, Assistant Director, Graduate Admissions, 254-295-4835, Fax: 254-295-5038, E-mail: saguilera@umhb.edu.
Website: http://www.graduate.umhb.edu/exss

University of Massachusetts Boston, College of Nursing and Health Sciences, Program in Exercise and Health Sciences, Boston, MA 02125-3393. Offers MS, PhD. *Faculty:* 15 full-time (9 women), 4 part-time/adjunct (1 woman). *Students:* 16 full-time (13 women), 3 part-time (2 women); includes 4 minority (1 Black or African American, non-Hispanic/Latino; 2 Hispanic/Latino; 1 Two or more races, non-Hispanic/Latino), 3 international. Average age 26. 28 applicants, 61% accepted, 9 enrolled. In 2016, 9 master's awarded. *Expenses:* Tuition, state resident: full-time $16,863. Tuition, nonresident: full-time $32,913. *Required fees:* $177. *Application contact:* Peggy Roldan Patel, Graduate Admissions Coordinator, 617-287-6400, Fax: 617-287-6236, E-mail: bos.gadm@dpc.umassp.edu.

University of Memphis, Graduate School, School of Health Studies, Memphis, TN 38152. Offers faith and health (Graduate Certificate); health studies (MS), including exercise and sports science, health promotion, physical education teacher education; nutrition (MS), including clinical nutrition, environmental nutrition, nutrition science. *Program availability:* 100% online. *Faculty:* 19 full-time (10 women), 2 part-time/adjunct (both women). *Students:* 73 full-time (58 women), 39 part-time (24 women); includes 31 minority (22 Black or African American, non-Hispanic/Latino; 1 American Indian or Alaska Native, non-Hispanic/Latino; 6 Asian, non-Hispanic/Latino; 2 Hispanic/Latino), 4 international. Average age 27. 62 applicants, 89% accepted, 45 enrolled. In 2016, 42 master's awarded. *Degree requirements:* For master's, comprehensive exam, thesis or alternative, culminating experience; for Graduate Certificate, practicum. *Entrance requirements:* For master's, GRE or PRAXIS II, letters of recommendation, statement of goals, minimum undergraduate GPA of 2.5; for Graduate Certificate, minimum undergraduate GPA of 2.5. Additional exam requirements/recommendations for international students: Required—TOEFL (minimum score 550 paper-based; 79 iBT). *Application deadline:* For fall admission, 4/15 priority date for domestic students; for spring admission, 10/15 priority date for domestic students; for summer admission, 4/15 priority date for domestic students. Application fee: $35 ($60 for international students). *Expenses:* $5,231.50 per semester full-time in-state, $9,623.50 full-time out-of-state. *Financial support:* In 2016–17, 20 research assistantships (averaging $11,360 per year), 8 teaching assistantships (averaging $10,062 per year) were awarded; career-related internships or fieldwork, Federal Work-Study, scholarships/grants, and unspecified assistantships also available. Financial award application deadline: 2/1; financial award applicants required to submit FAFSA. *Unit head:* Dr. Richard J. Bloomer, Director, 901-678-4316, Fax: 901-678-3591, E-mail: rbloomer@memphis.edu. *Application contact:* Dr. Lawrence Weiss, Director of Graduate Programs, 901-678-5037, E-mail: lweiss@memphis.edu.
Website: http://www.memphis.edu/shs/programs

University of Miami, Graduate School, School of Education and Human Development, Department of Kinesiology and Sport Sciences, Program in Exercise Physiology, Coral Gables, FL 33124. Offers exercise physiology (MS Ed, PhD); strength and conditioning (MS Ed). *Program availability:* Part-time, evening/weekend. *Faculty:* 4 full-time (1 woman). *Students:* 46 full-time (16 women), 5 part-time (2 women); includes 20 minority (2 Black or African American, non-Hispanic/Latino; 3 Asian, non-Hispanic/Latino; 10 Hispanic/Latino; 5 Two or more races, non-Hispanic/Latino), 4 international. Average age 28. 75 applicants, 49% accepted, 21 enrolled. In 2016, 16 master's, 5 doctorates awarded. Terminal master's awarded for partial completion of doctoral program. *Degree requirements:* For master's, comprehensive exam (for some programs), thesis optional, special project; for doctorate, thesis/dissertation, qualifying exam. *Entrance requirements:* For master's and doctorate, GRE General Test. Additional exam requirements/recommendations for international students: Required—TOEFL (minimum score 550 paper-based; 80 iBT); Recommended—IELTS (minimum score 6.5). *Application deadline:* For fall admission, 10/1 for international students; for spring admission, 10/1 for international students. Applications are processed on a rolling basis. Application fee: $65. Electronic applications accepted. *Financial support:* Fellowships, research assistantships, teaching assistantships, health care benefits, tuition waivers (full and partial), and unspecified assistantships available. Support available to part-time students. Financial award application deadline: 3/1; financial award applicants required to submit FAFSA. *Faculty research:* Women's health, cardiovascular health, aging, metabolism, obesity. *Unit head:* Dr. Kevin Jacobs, Associate Professor and Program Director, 305-284-5873, E-mail: k.jacobs@miami.edu. *Application contact:* Lois Heffernan, Graduate Admissions Coordinator, 305-284-2167, Fax: 305-284-9395, E-mail: lheffernan@miami.edu.
Website: http://www.education.miami.edu

University of Minnesota, Twin Cities Campus, Graduate School, College of Education and Human Development, School of Kinesiology, Minneapolis, MN 55455-0213. Offers kinesiology (MS, PhD), including behavioral aspects of physical activity, biomechanics and neuromotor control, exercise physiology, perceptual-motor control and learning, sport and exercise psychology, sport management (PhD), sport sociology; sport and exercise science (M Ed); sport management (M Ed, MA). *Program availability:* Part-time. *Faculty:* 15 full-time (6 women). *Students:* 117 full-time (54 women), 32 part-time (17 women); includes 21 minority (5 Black or African American, non-Hispanic/Latino; 1 American Indian or Alaska Native, non-Hispanic/Latino; 5 Asian, non-Hispanic/Latino; 7 Hispanic/Latino; 3 Two or more races, non-Hispanic/Latino), 20 international. Average age 27. 170 applicants, 45% accepted, 66 enrolled. In 2016, 85 master's, 5 doctorates awarded. Terminal master's awarded for partial completion of doctoral program. *Degree requirements:* For master's, final oral exam; for doctorate, thesis/dissertation, preliminary written/oral exam, final oral exam. *Entrance requirements:* For master's, GRE or MAT, minimum GPA of 3.0; for doctorate, GRE or MAT, minimum GPA of 3.0, writing sample. Application fee: $75 ($95 for international students). *Financial support:* In 2016–17, 3 fellowships, 11 research assistantships with full tuition reimbursements (averaging $11,857 per year), 42 teaching assistantships with full tuition reimbursements (averaging $14,262 per year) were awarded; career-related internships or fieldwork, Federal Work-Study, institutionally sponsored loans, and tuition waivers (full and partial) also available. Support available to part-time students. *Faculty research:* Role of physical activity in preventing health related problems; mechanism of age-related disorders, diseases and mental problems, and the ways to ameliorate them; role of sports in society and social justice; sports among populations with low income and racial diversity; fundamental functions of the body and the mechanism controlling the mechanisms; psychological issues related to physical activity and sports. *Total annual research expenditures:* $939,073. *Unit head:* Dr. Li Li Ji, Director, 612-624-9809, E-mail: llji@umn.edu. *Application contact:* Dr. Michael Wade, Director of Graduate Studies, 612-626-2094, E-mail: mwade@umn.edu.
Website: http://www.cehd.umn.edu/kin/

University of Mississippi, Graduate School, School of Applied Sciences, University, MS 38677. Offers communicative disorders (MS); exercise science (MS); food and nutrition services (MS); health and kinesiology (PhD); health promotion (MS); park and recreation management (MA); social work (MSW). *Faculty:* 68 full-time (29 women), 29 part-time/adjunct (17 women). *Students:* 176 full-time (137 women), 36 part-time (21 women); includes 45 minority (40 Black or African American, non-Hispanic/Latino; 4 Hispanic/Latino; 1 Two or more races, non-Hispanic/Latino), 9 international. Average age 24. *Entrance requirements:* For master's, GRE General Test, minimum GPA of 3.0. Additional exam requirements/recommendations for international students: Required—TOEFL. *Application deadline:* For fall admission, 4/1 for domestic students; for spring admission, 10/1 for domestic students. Applications are processed on a rolling basis. Application fee: $40. Electronic applications accepted. *Financial support:* Scholarships/grants available. Financial award application deadline: 3/1; financial award applicants required to submit FAFSA. *Unit head:* Dr. Velmer Stanley Burton, Dean, 662-915-1081, Fax: 662-915-5717, E-mail: applsci@olemiss.edu. *Application contact:* Dr. Christy M. Wyandt, Associate Dean of Graduate School, 662-915-7474, Fax: 662-915-7577, E-mail: cwyandt@olemiss.edu.
Website: https://www.olemiss.edu

University of Montana, Graduate School, Phyllis J. Washington College of Education and Human Sciences, Department of Health and Human Performance, Missoula, MT 59812-0002. Offers community health (MS); exercise science (MS); health and human performance generalist (MS). *Program availability:* Part-time. *Entrance requirements:* For master's, GRE General Test. Additional exam requirements/recommendations for international students: Required—TOEFL. *Faculty research:* Exercise physiology, performance psychology, nutrition, pre-employment physical screening, program evaluation.

University of Nebraska at Kearney, College of Education, Kinesiology and Sport Sciences Department, Kearney, NE 68849-0001. Offers general physical education (MA Ed), including recreation and leisure, sports administration; physical education exercise science (MA Ed); physical education master teacher (MA Ed), including pedagogy, special populations. *Program availability:* Part-time, evening/weekend, 100% online. *Faculty:* 17 full-time (5 women). *Students:* 4 full-time (2 women), 39 part-time (16 women); includes 3 minority (2 Black or African American, non-Hispanic/Latino; 1 Hispanic/Latino). Average age 28. 20 applicants, 100% accepted, 14 enrolled. In 2016, 25 master's awarded. *Degree requirements:* For master's, comprehensive exam, thesis optional. *Entrance requirements:* For master's, GRE General Test (for some programs), personal statement. Additional exam requirements/recommendations for international students: Recommended—TOEFL (minimum score 550 paper-based; 79 iBT), IELTS (minimum score 6.5). *Application deadline:* For fall admission, 6/15 for domestic and international students; for spring admission, 10/15 for domestic and international students; for summer admission, 3/15 for domestic and international students. Application fee: $45. Electronic applications accepted. *Expenses:* Tuition, state resident: full-time $4064; part-time $225.75 per credit hour. Tuition, nonresident: full-time $8915; part-time $495.25 per credit hour. *Required fees:* $772; $23 per credit hour. Part-time tuition and fees vary according to course load, campus/location, program and reciprocity agreements. *Financial support:* In 2016–17, 9 students received support, including 3 research assistantships with full tuition reimbursements available (averaging $10,500 per year), 6 teaching assistantships with full tuition reimbursements available (averaging $10,500 per year); career-related internships or fieldwork, scholarships/grants, health care benefits, and unspecified assistantships also available. Support available to part-time students. Financial award application deadline: 2/28; financial award applicants required to submit FAFSA. *Faculty research:* Ergonomic aids, nutrition, motor development, sports pedagogy, applied behavior analysis, physical activity and wellness, athletic training, therapeutic Interventions, exercise physiology, endocrinology and metabolism. *Unit head:* Dr. Nita Unruh, Chair, 308-865-8335, E-mail: unruhnc@unk.edu. *Application contact:* Linda Johnson, Director, Graduate Admissions and Programs, 308-865-8841, Fax: 308-865-8837, E-mail: johnsonli@unk.edu.
Website: http://www.unk.edu/academics/hperls/index.php

University of Nebraska at Omaha, Graduate Studies, College of Education, School of Health and Kinesiology, Omaha, NE 68182. Offers athletic training (MA); exercise science (PhD); health, physical education, and recreation (MA, MS). *Program availability:* Part-time, evening/weekend. *Faculty:* 7 full-time (2 women). *Students:* 79 full-time (31 women), 28 part-time (13 women); includes 8 minority (2 Black or African American, non-Hispanic/Latino; 1 Asian, non-Hispanic/Latino; 2 Hispanic/Latino; 3 Two or more races, non-Hispanic/Latino), 18 international. Average age 26. 65 applicants, 74% accepted, 34 enrolled. In 2016, 38 master's, 1 doctorate awarded. *Degree requirements:* For master's, comprehensive exam, thesis (for some programs). *Entrance requirements:* For master's, GRE; entrance exam, minimum GPA of 3.0, official transcripts, statement of purpose, 2 letters of recommendation; for doctorate, GRE, minimum GPA of 3.2, official transcripts, statement of purpose, 3 letters of recommendation, resume, writing sample. Additional exam requirements/recommendations for international students: Required—TOEFL, IELTS, PTE. *Application deadline:* For fall admission, 7/1 priority date for domestic and international students; for spring admission, 11/1 priority date for domestic and international students; for summer admission, 1/15 for domestic and international students. Applications are processed on a rolling basis. Application fee: $45. Electronic applications accepted. *Financial support:* In 2016–17, 47 students received support, including 34 research assistantships with tuition reimbursements available, 13 teaching assistantships with tuition reimbursements available; fellowships, Federal Work-Study, institutionally sponsored loans, scholarships/grants, health care benefits, tuition waivers (full), and unspecified assistantships also available. Support available to part-time students. Financial award application deadline: 3/1; financial award applicants required to submit FAFSA. *Unit head:* Dr. Roland Bulbulian, Director, 402-554-2341, E-mail: graduate@unomaha.edu. *Application contact:* Dr. Dustin Slivka, Graduate Program Chair, 402-554-2341, E-mail: graduate@unomaha.edu.

University of Nebraska–Lincoln, Graduate College, College of Education and Human Sciences, Department of Nutrition and Health Sciences, Lincoln, NE 68588. Offers community nutrition and health promotion (MS); nutrition (MS, PhD); nutrition and exercise (MS); nutrition and health sciences (MS, PhD). *Degree requirements:* For master's, thesis optional. *Entrance requirements:* For master's, GRE General Test. Additional exam requirements/recommendations for international students: Required—TOEFL (minimum score 550 paper-based). Electronic applications accepted. *Faculty research:* Foods/food service administration, community nutrition science, diet-health relationships.

University of Nevada, Las Vegas, Graduate College, School of Allied Health Sciences, Department of Kinesiology and Nutrition Sciences, Las Vegas, NV 89154-3034. Offers exercise physiology (MS); kinesiology (PhD); nutrition sciences (MS). *Program availability:* Part-time. *Faculty:* 12 full-time (6 women). *Students:* 35 full-time (20 women), 12 part-time (3 women); includes 8 minority (1 Black or African American, non-Hispanic/Latino; 1 American Indian or Alaska Native, non-Hispanic/Latino; 2 Asian, non-Hispanic/Latino; 2 Hispanic/Latino; 2 Two or more races, non-Hispanic/Latino), 3 international. Average age 28. 49 applicants, 59% accepted, 18 enrolled. In 2016, 11 master's awarded. *Degree requirements:* For master's, thesis (for some programs), professional paper; for doctorate, comprehensive exam, thesis/dissertation. *Entrance requirements:* For master's, GRE General Test, bachelor's degree; statement of purpose; 2 letters of recommendation; for doctorate, GRE General Test (minimum 70th percentile on the Verbal section), master's degree/bachelor's degree with minimum GPA of 3.25; 3 letters of recommendation; statement of purpose; personal interview. Additional exam requirements/recommendations for international students: Required—TOEFL (minimum score 550 paper-based; 80 iBT), IELTS (minimum score 7). *Application deadline:* For fall admission, 6/15 for domestic students, 5/1 for international students; for spring admission, 11/15 for domestic students, 10/1 for international students. Application fee: $60 ($95 for international students). Electronic applications accepted. *Expenses:* $269.25 per credit, $792 per 3-credit course; $9,634 per year resident; $23,274 per year non-resident; $7,094 fees non-resident (7 credits or more); $1,307 annual health insurance fee. *Financial support:* In 2016–17, 13 research assistantships with partial tuition reimbursements (averaging $13,808 per year), 13 teaching assistantships with partial tuition reimbursements (averaging $12,269 per year) were awarded; institutionally sponsored loans, scholarships/grants, health care benefits, and unspecified assistantships also available. Financial award application deadline: 3/15. *Faculty research:* Biomechanics of gait, factors in motor skill acquisition and performance, nutritional supplements and performance, lipoprotein biochemistry, transcranial direct current stimulation. *Total annual research expenditures:* $45,437. *Unit head:* Dr. Brian Schilling, Chair/Professor, 702-895-1130, Fax: 702-895-1500, E-mail: brian.schilling@unlv.edu. *Application contact:* Dr. Janet Dufek, Graduate Coordinator, 702-895-0702, Fax: 702-895-1500, E-mail: janet.dufek@unlv.edu.

University of New Brunswick Fredericton, School of Graduate Studies, Faculty of Kinesiology, Fredericton, NB E3B 5A3, Canada. Offers exercise and sport science (M Sc); sport and recreation management (MBA); sport and recreation studies (MA). *Program availability:* Part-time. *Degree requirements:* For master's, thesis (for some programs). *Entrance requirements:* For master's, GMAT (minimum score of 550 for sport and recreation management program), minimum GPA of 3.0, written statement of research goals and interests. Additional exam requirements/recommendations for international students: Required—TOEFL (minimum score 92 iBT), IELTS (minimum score 7). Electronic applications accepted.

University of New Mexico, Graduate Studies, College of Education, Program in Physical Education, Sports and Exercise Science, Albuquerque, NM 87131-2039. Offers curriculum and instruction (PhD); exercise science (PhD); sports administration (PhD). *Program availability:* Part-time. *Faculty:* 13 full-time (6 women), 2 part-time/adjunct (1 woman). *Students:* 83 full-time (28 women), 48 part-time (21 women); includes 51 minority (12 Black or African American, non-Hispanic/Latino; 2 American Indian or Alaska Native, non-Hispanic/Latino; 1 Asian, non-Hispanic/Latino; 32 Hispanic/Latino; 4 Two or more races, non-Hispanic/Latino), 15 international. Average age 30. 67 applicants, 75% accepted, 35 enrolled. In 2016, 13 doctorates awarded. *Degree requirements:* For doctorate, comprehensive exam, thesis/dissertation, inquiry skills, 24 credits in supporting area. *Entrance requirements:* For doctorate, GRE, letter of intent, 3 letters of reference, minimum cumulative GPA of 3.0 in last 2 years of bachelor's degree. Additional exam requirements/recommendations for international students: Required—TOEFL (minimum score 550 paper-based). *Application deadline:* For fall admission, 3/1 priority date for domestic students; for spring admission, 11/1 priority date for domestic students. Application fee: $50. Electronic applications accepted. *Financial support:* Fellowships, teaching assistantships with full tuition reimbursements, career-related internships or fieldwork, Federal Work-Study, institutionally sponsored loans, scholarships/grants, health care benefits, tuition waivers, and unspecified assistantships available. Financial award application deadline: 3/1; financial award applicants required to submit FAFSA. *Faculty research:* Facility risk management, physical education pedagogy practices, physiological adaptations to exercise, physiological adaptations to heat, sport leadership. *Unit head:* Dr. Todd Seidler, Chair, 505-277-2783, Fax: 505-277-6227, E-mail: tseidler@unm.edu. *Application contact:* Monica Lopez, Program Office, 505-277-5151, Fax: 505-277-6227, E-mail: mllopez@unm.edu.
Website: https://coe.unm.edu/departments-programs/hess/physical-education/physical-education-phd/index.html

University of North Alabama, College of Education, Department of Health, Physical Education, and Recreation, Florence, AL 35632-0001. Offers health and human performance (MS), including exercise science, kinesiology, wellness and health promotion. *Program availability:* Part-time. *Faculty:* 7 full-time (2 women). *Students:* 10 full-time (5 women), 11 part-time (4 women); includes 2 minority (both Black or African American, non-Hispanic/Latino), 2 international. Average age 24. 19 applicants, 68% accepted, 11 enrolled. In 2016, 14 master's awarded. *Degree requirements:* For master's, comprehensive exam (for some programs), thesis optional. *Entrance requirements:* For master's, MAT or GRE, 3 letters of recommendation, essay. Additional exam requirements/recommendations for international students: Required—TOEFL (minimum score 79 iBT), IELTS (minimum score 6), PTE (minimum score 54). *Application deadline:* Applications are processed on a rolling basis. Application fee: $50 ($100 for international students). Electronic applications accepted. *Expenses:* Tuition, state resident: full-time $2799; part-time $1866 per semester. Tuition, nonresident: full-time $5598; part-time $3732 per semester. *Required fees:* $915; $642 per semester. Tuition and fees vary according to course load. *Financial support:* In 2016–17, 19 students received support. Scholarships/grants and unspecified assistantships available. Financial award application deadline: 2/1; financial award applicants required to submit FAFSA. *Unit head:* Dr. Thomas E. Coates, Chair, 256-765-4377. *Application contact:* Hillary N. Coats, Graduate Admissions Coordinator, 256-765-4447, E-mail: graduate@una.edu.
Website: https://www.una.edu/hper/index.html

The University of North Carolina at Chapel Hill, Graduate School, College of Arts and Sciences, Department of Exercise and Sport Science, Chapel Hill, NC 27599. Offers athletic training (MA); exercise physiology (MA); sport administration (MA). *Degree requirements:* For master's, comprehensive exam, thesis. *Entrance requirements:* For master's, GRE General Test, minimum GPA of 3.0. Additional exam requirements/recommendations for international students: Required—TOEFL (minimum score 550 paper-based). Electronic applications accepted. *Faculty research:* Mild head injury in sport, endocrine system's response to exercise, obesity and children, effect of aerobic exercise on cerebral bloodflow in elderly population.

The University of North Carolina at Pembroke, The Graduate School, School of Education, Department of Health and Human Performance, Pembroke, NC 28372-1510. Offers physical education (MA). *Program availability:* Part-time, evening/weekend. *Degree requirements:* For master's, comprehensive exam, thesis optional. *Entrance requirements:* For master's, MAT or GRE, minimum GPA of 3.0 in major, 2.5 overall. Additional exam requirements/recommendations for international students: Required—TOEFL.

University of Northern Colorado, Graduate School, College of Natural and Health Sciences, School of Sport and Exercise Science, Greeley, CO 80639. Offers exercise science (MS, PhD); physical education and physical activity leadership (MAT); sport administration (MS, PhD); sport pedagogy (MS, PhD); sports coaching (MA). *Program availability:* Part-time, evening/weekend. *Degree requirements:* For master's,

comprehensive exam; for doctorate, comprehensive exam, thesis/dissertation. *Entrance requirements:* For master's, 2 letters of recommendation, resume; for doctorate, GRE General Test, 3 letters of recommendation, resume. *Application deadline:* Applications are processed on a rolling basis. Application fee: $50 ($60 for international students). Electronic applications accepted. *Financial support:* Fellowships, research assistantships, teaching assistantships, and unspecified assistantships available. Financial award application deadline: 3/1; financial award applicants required to submit FAFSA. *Unit head:* Dr. David Stotlar, Director, 970-351-2535, Fax: 970-351-1762. *Application contact:* Linda Sisson, Graduate Student Admission Coordinator, 970-351-1807, Fax: 970-351-2371, E-mail: linda.sisson@unco.edu.
Website: http://www.unco.edu/nhs/sport-exercise-science/

University of North Florida, Brooks College of Health, Department of Clinical and Applied Movement Sciences, Jacksonville, FL 32224. Offers MSH, DPT. *Accreditation:* APTA. *Program availability:* Part-time, evening/weekend. *Faculty:* 12 full-time (7 women), 5 part-time/adjunct (4 women). *Students:* 92 full-time (47 women); includes 24 minority (2 Black or African American, non-Hispanic/Latino; 3 Asian, non-Hispanic/Latino; 12 Hispanic/Latino; 7 Two or more races, non-Hispanic/Latino). Average age 25. 484 applicants, 11% accepted, 29 enrolled. In 2016, 26 doctorates awarded. *Entrance requirements:* For master's, GRE General Test, minimum GPA of 3.0 in last 60 hours, volunteer/observation experience. Additional exam requirements/recommendations for international students: Required—TOEFL (minimum score 500 paper-based). *Application deadline:* For fall admission, 7/15 for domestic students, 1/15 for international students. Application fee: $30. Electronic applications accepted. Tuition and fees vary according to course load, campus/location and program. *Financial support:* In 2016–17, 10 students received support, including 6 research assistantships (averaging $2,500 per year); career-related internships or fieldwork, Federal Work-Study, scholarships/grants, and tuition waivers (partial) also available. Support available to part-time students. Financial award application deadline: 4/1; financial award applicants required to submit FAFSA. *Faculty research:* Clinical outcomes related to orthopedic physical therapy interventions, instructional multimedia in physical therapy education, effect of functional electrical stimulation orthostatic hypotension in acute complete spinal cord injury individuals. *Total annual research expenditures:* $12,679. *Unit head:* Dr. Joel Beam, Chair, 904-620-2841, E-mail: jbeam@unf.edu. *Application contact:* Amanda Lovins, Assistant Director, 904-620-2841, E-mail: ptadmissions@unf.edu.
Website: http://www.unf.edu/brooks/movement_science/

University of Oklahoma, College of Arts and Sciences, Department of Health and Exercise Science, Norman, OK 73019. Offers exercise physiology (MS, PhD); health and exercise science (MS); health promotion (MS, PhD). *Faculty:* 11 full-time (5 women), 1 part-time/adjunct (0 women). *Students:* 42 full-time (16 women), 19 part-time (14 women); includes 14 minority (3 Black or African American, non-Hispanic/Latino; 1 American Indian or Alaska Native, non-Hispanic/Latino; 1 Asian, non-Hispanic/Latino; 3 Hispanic/Latino; 6 Two or more races, non-Hispanic/Latino), 10 international. Average age 26. 43 applicants, 56% accepted, 22 enrolled. In 2016, 7 master's, 4 doctorates awarded. *Degree requirements:* For master's, comprehensive exam (for some programs), thesis; for doctorate, comprehensive exam, thesis/dissertation. *Entrance requirements:* For master's and doctorate, GRE. Additional exam requirements/recommendations for international students: Required—TOEFL (minimum score 79 iBT) or IELTS (minimum score 6.5). *Application deadline:* For fall admission, 2/1 priority date for domestic and international students. Applications are processed on a rolling basis. Application fee: $50 ($100 for international students). Electronic applications accepted. *Expenses:* Tuition, state resident: full-time $4886; part-time $203.60 per credit hour. Tuition, nonresident: full-time $18,989; part-time $791.20 per credit hour. *Required fees:* $3283; $126.25 per credit hour. $126.50 per semester. *Financial support:* In 2016–17, 55 students received support, including 53 teaching assistantships with full tuition reimbursements available (averaging $12,593 per year); health care benefits, tuition waivers (full), and unspecified assistantships also available. Financial award application deadline: 6/1; financial award applicants required to submit FAFSA. *Faculty research:* Health promotion, neuromuscular exercise physiology, aging, endocrine and bone metabolism, behavioral science. *Total annual research expenditures:* $6,404. *Unit head:* Dr. Michael G. Bemben, Professor/Chair, 405-325-2717, Fax: 405-325-0594, E-mail: mgbemben@ou.edu. *Application contact:* Dr. Paul Branscum, Assistant Professor/Graduate Liaison, 405-325-9028, Fax: 405-325-0594, E-mail: pbranscum@ou.edu.
Website: http://cas.ou.edu/hes

University of Pittsburgh, School of Education, Department of Health and Physical Activity, Program in Developmental Movement, Pittsburgh, PA 15260. Offers MS. *Degree requirements:* For master's, thesis. *Entrance requirements:* Additional exam requirements/recommendations for international students: Required—TOEFL. Electronic applications accepted. Tuition and fees vary according to program.

University of Pittsburgh, School of Education, Department of Health and Physical Activity, Program in Exercise Physiology, Pittsburgh, PA 15260. Offers MS, PhD. *Entrance requirements:* Additional exam requirements/recommendations for international students: Required—TOEFL (minimum score 550 paper-based; 80 iBT). Electronic applications accepted. Tuition and fees vary according to program.

University of Pittsburgh, School of Health and Rehabilitation Sciences, Master's Programs in Health and Rehabilitation Sciences, Pittsburgh, PA 15260. Offers health and rehabilitation sciences (MS), including health information systems, healthcare supervision and management, occupational therapy, physical therapy, rehabilitation counseling, rehabilitation science and technology, sports medicine, wellness and human performance. *Accreditation:* APTA. *Program availability:* Part-time, evening/weekend. *Faculty:* 30 full-time (19 women). *Students:* 93 full-time (65 women), 32 part-time (26 women); includes 15 minority (3 Black or African American, non-Hispanic/Latino; 1 American Indian or Alaska Native, non-Hispanic/Latino; 4 Asian, non-Hispanic/Latino; 4 Hispanic/Latino; 3 Two or more races, non-Hispanic/Latino), 58 international. Average age 29. 247 applicants, 64% accepted, 70 enrolled. In 2016, 37 master's awarded. *Degree requirements:* For master's, comprehensive exam (for some programs), thesis optional. *Entrance requirements:* For master's, minimum GPA of 3.0. Additional exam requirements/recommendations for international students: Required—TOEFL (minimum score 550 paper-based; 80 iBT), IELTS (minimum score 6.5). *Application deadline:* For fall admission, 3/1 for international students; for spring admission, 9/1 for international students; for summer admission, 2/1 for international students. Applications are processed on a rolling basis. Application fee: $50. Electronic applications accepted. Tuition and fees vary according to program. *Financial support:* In 2016–17, 6 fellowships with full tuition reimbursements (averaging $17,550 per year), 4 research assistantships with full tuition reimbursements (averaging $21,900 per year) were awarded; traineeships also available. *Faculty research:* Assistive technology, seating and wheelchair mobility, cellular neurophysiology, low back syndrome, augmentative communication. *Total annual research expenditures:* $2.7 million. *Unit head:* Dr. Anthony Delitto, Dean, 412-383-6560, Fax: 412-383-6535, E-mail: delitto@pitt.edu. *Application contact:* Jessica Maguire, Director of Admissions, 412-383-6557, Fax: 412-383-6535, E-mail: maguire@pitt.edu.

University of Puerto Rico, Mayagüez Campus, Graduate Studies, College of Arts and Sciences, Department of Kinesiology, Mayagüez, PR 00681-9000. Offers kinesiology (MA), including biomechanics, education, exercise physiology, sports training. *Program availability:* Part-time. *Faculty:* 12 full-time (4 women). *Students:* 8 full-time (2 women), 6 part-time (1 woman); includes 12 minority (all Hispanic/Latino), 2 international. Average age 25. 9 applicants, 33% accepted, 3 enrolled. In 2016, 2 master's awarded. *Degree requirements:* For master's, thesis. *Entrance requirements:* For master's, EXADEP or GRE, minimum GPA of 2.5. *Application deadline:* For fall admission, 2/15 for domestic and international students; for spring admission, 9/15 for domestic and international students. Applications are processed on a rolling basis. Application fee: $25. Electronic applications accepted. *Expenses: Tuition, area resident:* Full-time $2466. *International tuition:* $7166 full-time. *Required fees:* $210. Tuition and fees vary according to course level, campus/location, program and student level. *Financial support:* In 2016–17, 6 students received support, including 6 teaching assistantships with full and partial tuition reimbursements available (averaging $2,885 per year). *Unit head:* Luis Del Río Pérez, PhD, Director, 787-832-4040 Ext. 3564, Fax: 787-833-4825, E-mail: luiso.delrio@upr.edu. *Application contact:* Aracelys Gonzlez, Administrative Secretary V, 787-832-4040 Ext. 3841, Fax: 787-833-4825, E-mail: aracelis.gonzalez3@upr.edu.
Website: http://edfi.uprm.edu/

University of Puerto Rico, Río Piedras Campus, College of Education, Program in Exercise Sciences, San Juan, PR 00931-3300. Offers MS. *Entrance requirements:* For master's, PAEG or GRE, minimum GPA of 3.0.

University of Rhode Island, Graduate School, College of Health Sciences, Department of Kinesiology, Kingston, RI 02881. Offers cultural studies of sport and physical culture (MS); exercise science (MS); psychosocial/behavioral aspects of physical activity (MS). *Accreditation:* NCATE. *Program availability:* Part-time. *Faculty:* 15 full-time (9 women). *Students:* 16 full-time (9 women), 8 part-time (5 women); includes 4 minority (1 Black or African American, non-Hispanic/Latino; 1 Asian, non-Hispanic/Latino; 2 Hispanic/Latino). In 2016, 8 master's awarded. *Degree requirements:* For master's, thesis optional. *Entrance requirements:* For master's, GRE, 2 letters of recommendation. Additional exam requirements/recommendations for international students: Required—TOEFL. *Application deadline:* For fall admission, 7/15 for domestic students, 2/1 for international students; for spring admission, 11/15 for domestic students, 7/15 for international students. Application fee: $65. Electronic applications accepted. *Expenses:* Tuition, state resident: full-time $11,796; part-time $655 per credit. Tuition, nonresident: full-time $24,206; part-time $1345 per credit. *Required fees:* $1546; $44 per credit. One-time fee: $155 full-time; $35 part-time. *Financial support:* In 2016–17, 5 teaching assistantships with tuition reimbursements (averaging $10,740 per year) were awarded; research assistantships also available. Financial award application deadline: 7/15; financial award applicants required to submit FAFSA. *Unit head:* Dr. Disa Hatfield, Interim Chair, 401-874-5183, E-mail: doch@uri.edu. *Application contact:* Dr. Matthew Delmonico, Graduate Program Director, 401-874-5440, E-mail: delmonico@uri.edu.
Website: http://web.uri.edu/kinesiology/

University of South Alabama, College of Education and Professional Studies, Department of Health, Kinesiology, and Sport, Mobile, AL 36688. Offers exercise science (MS); health education (M Ed); physical education (M Ed); sport management (MS). *Accreditation:* NCATE (one or more programs are accredited). *Program availability:* Part-time. *Faculty:* 7 full-time (2 women). *Students:* 50 full-time (15 women), 4 part-time (2 women); includes 21 minority (17 Black or African American, non-Hispanic/Latino; 1 Asian, non-Hispanic/Latino; 1 Hispanic/Latino; 2 Two or more races, non-Hispanic/Latino), 3 international. Average age 27. 53 applicants, 57% accepted, 28 enrolled. In 2016, 16 master's awarded. *Degree requirements:* For master's, comprehensive exam, thesis optional. *Entrance requirements:* For master's, GRE General Test or MAT, Alabama Class B certificate or the equivalent (for students seeking the master's-level/Class A certification). Additional exam requirements/recommendations for international students: Required—TOEFL. *Application deadline:* For fall admission, 7/15 priority date for domestic students, 6/15 priority date for international students; for spring admission, 11/15 priority date for domestic students, 10/15 priority date for international students; for summer admission, 4/15 for domestic students. Applications are processed on a rolling basis. Application fee: $35. Electronic applications accepted. *Expenses:* Tuition, state resident: full-time $9768; part-time $407 per credit hour. Tuition, nonresident: full-time $19,536; part-time $814 per credit hour. *Financial support:* Fellowships, research assistantships, teaching assistantships with partial tuition reimbursements, career-related internships or fieldwork, Federal Work-Study, institutionally sponsored loans, scholarships/grants, and unspecified assistantships available. Support available to part-time students. Financial award application deadline: 5/31; financial award applicants required to submit FAFSA. *Unit head:* Dr. John Kovaleski, Department Chair, 251-461-1622, Fax: 251-460-7252, E-mail: jkovales@southalabama.edu. *Application contact:* Dr. Susan Santoli, Director of Graduate Studies, 251-380-2738, Fax: 251-380-2758, E-mail: ssantoli@southalabama.edu.
Website: http://www.southalabama.edu/colleges/coe/hks/index.html

University of South Carolina, The Graduate School, Arnold School of Public Health, Department of Exercise Science, Columbia, SC 29208. Offers MS, DPT, PhD. *Program availability:* Part-time. *Degree requirements:* For master's, comprehensive exam, thesis (for some programs), project; for doctorate, comprehensive exam, thesis/dissertation. *Entrance requirements:* For master's and doctorate, GRE General Test. Additional exam requirements/recommendations for international students: Required—TOEFL (minimum score 570 paper-based). Electronic applications accepted. *Faculty research:* Effects of acute and chronic exercise on human function and health, motor control.

The University of South Dakota, Graduate School, School of Education, Division of Kinesiology and Sport Management, Vermillion, SD 57069. Offers MA. *Accreditation:* NCATE. *Program availability:* Part-time. *Degree requirements:* For master's, comprehensive exam, thesis or alternative. *Entrance requirements:* For master's, GRE General Test, MAT, minimum GPA of 3.0. Additional exam requirements/recommendations for international students: Required—TOEFL (minimum score 550 paper-based; 79 iBT). Electronic applications accepted.

University of Southern Mississippi, Graduate School, College of Health, School of Kinesiology, Hattiesburg, MS 39406. Offers kinesiology (MS, PhD), including biomechanics (PhD), exercise physiology (PhD), exercise science (MS), physical education (MS), sport pedagogy (PhD); sport coaching education (MS). *Program availability:* Part-time, evening/weekend. *Degree requirements:* For master's, comprehensive exam, thesis optional; for doctorate, comprehensive exam, thesis/dissertation. *Entrance requirements:* For master's, GRE General Test, minimum GPA of 2.75 in last 60 hours; for doctorate, GRE General Test, minimum GPA of 3.5. Additional exam requirements/recommendations for international students: Required—TOEFL, IELTS. *Application deadline:* For fall admission, 3/1 priority date for domestic students, 3/1 for international students; for spring admission, 1/10 priority date for domestic and international students. Applications are processed on a rolling basis. Application fee: $60. Electronic applications accepted. *Expenses: Tuition, area resident:* Full-time $15,708; part-time $437 per credit hour. *Financial support:* Fellowships, research assistantships with full tuition reimbursements, teaching assistantships with full tuition reimbursements, career-related internships or fieldwork, Federal Work-Study, institutionally sponsored loans, scholarships/grants, health care benefits, and unspecified assistantships available. Financial award application deadline: 3/15;

financial award applicants required to submit FAFSA. *Faculty research:* Exercise physiology, health behaviors, resource management, activity interaction, site development. *Unit head:* Dr. Scott Piland, Director, 601-266-5386, Fax: 601-266-4445, E-mail: scott.piland@usm.edu. *Application contact:* Dr. Trenton Gould, Dean, College of Health, 601-266-6339, Fax: 601-266-4445.
Website: https://www.usm.edu/kinesiology

The University of Tampa, Program in Exercise and Nutrition Science, Tampa, FL 33606-1490. Offers MS. *Program availability:* Part-time, evening/weekend. *Faculty:* 4 full-time (2 women), 1 (woman) part-time/adjunct. *Students:* 46 full-time (20 women), 3 part-time (1 woman); includes 8 minority (4 Black or African American, non-Hispanic/ Latino; 1 Asian, non-Hispanic/Latino; 3 Two or more races, non-Hispanic/Latino), 2 international. Average age 25. 207 applicants, 52% accepted, 33 enrolled. In 2016, 48 master's awarded. *Degree requirements:* For master's, comprehensive exam, practicum. *Entrance requirements:* For master's, GMAT or GRE, official transcripts from all colleges and/or universities previously attended, resume, personal statement, letters of recommendation, bachelor's degree in related field. Additional exam requirements/ recommendations for international students: Required—TOEFL (minimum score 577 paper-based; 90 iBT), IELTS (minimum score 7.5). *Application deadline:* Applications are processed on a rolling basis. Application fee: $40. Electronic applications accepted. *Expenses:* $588 per credit tuition, $40 per term fees. *Financial support:* In 2016–17, 1 student received support. Career-related internships or fieldwork, scholarships/grants, and unspecified assistantships available. Financial award applicants required to submit FAFSA. *Unit head:* Dr. Ronda C. Sturgill, Associate Professor, Health Sciences and Human Performance, 813-257-3445, E-mail: rsturgill@ut.edu. *Application contact:* Chanelle Cox, Staff Assistant, Admissions for Graduate and Continuing Studies, 813-253-6249, E-mail: ccox@ut.edu.
Website: http://www.ut.edu/msexercisenutrition/

The University of Tennessee, Graduate School, College of Education, Health and Human Sciences, Department of Exercise, Sport, and Leisure Studies, Program in Exercise Science, Knoxville, TN 37996. Offers biomechanics/sports medicine (MS, PhD); exercise physiology (MS, PhD). *Accreditation:* CEPH (one or more programs are accredited). *Program availability:* Part-time. *Degree requirements:* For master's, thesis optional. *Entrance requirements:* For master's, minimum GPA of 2.7. Additional exam requirements/recommendations for international students: Required—TOEFL. Electronic applications accepted.

The University of Tennessee, Graduate School, College of Education, Health and Human Sciences, Program in Education, Knoxville, TN 37996. Offers art education (MS); counseling education (PhD); cultural studies in education (PhD); curriculum (MS, Ed S); curriculum, educational research and evaluation (Ed D, PhD); early childhood education (PhD); early childhood special education (MS); education of deaf and hard of hearing (MS); educational administration and policy studies (Ed D, PhD); educational administration and supervision (Ed S); educational psychology (Ed D, PhD); elementary education (MS, Ed S); elementary teaching (MS); English education (MS, Ed S); exercise science (PhD); foreign language/ESL education (MS, Ed S); instructional technology (MS, Ed D, PhD, Ed S); literacy, language and ESL education (PhD); literacy, language education, and ESL education (Ed D); mathematics education (MS, Ed S); modified and comprehensive special education (MS); reading education (MS, Ed S); school counseling (Ed S); school psychology (PhD, Ed S); science education (MS, Ed S); secondary teaching (MS); social foundations (MS); social science education (MS, Ed S); socio-cultural foundations of sports and education (PhD); special education (Ed S); teacher education (Ed D, PhD). *Accreditation:* NCATE. *Program availability:* Part-time, evening/weekend. *Degree requirements:* For master's and Ed S, thesis optional; for doctorate, variable foreign language requirement, thesis/dissertation. *Entrance requirements:* For master's, minimum GPA of 2.7; for doctorate and Ed S, GRE General Test, minimum GPA of 2.7. Additional exam requirements/ recommendations for international students: Required—TOEFL. Electronic applications accepted.

The University of Texas at Austin, Graduate School, College of Education, Department of Kinesiology and Health Education, Austin, TX 78712-1111. Offers behavioral health (PhD); exercise and sport psychology (M Ed, MA); exercise science (M Ed, MS, PhD); health education (M Ed, MS, Ed D, PhD). *Program availability:* Part-time. Terminal master's awarded for partial completion of doctoral program. *Degree requirements:* For master's, thesis (for some programs); for doctorate, thesis/ dissertation. *Entrance requirements:* For master's and doctorate, GRE General Test. Additional exam requirements/recommendations for international students: Required—TOEFL. Electronic applications accepted. *Faculty research:* Health promotion, human performance and exercise biochemistry, motor behavior and biomechanics, sport management, aging and pediatric development.

The University of Texas Rio Grande Valley, College of Health Affairs, Department of Health and Human Performance, Edinburg, TX 78539. Offers exercise science (MS); kinesiology (MS). *Program availability:* Part-time, evening/weekend, online learning. *Degree requirements:* For master's, comprehensive exam, thesis optional, oral exam. *Entrance requirements:* For master's, minimum GPA of 3.0 in last 60 hours. Tuition and fees vary according to course load and program. *Faculty research:* History, physiology of exercise, fitness levels, Mexican American children, winter tourist profiles, sports psychology.

University of the Pacific, College of the Pacific, Department of Health, Exercise and Sport Science, Stockton, CA 95211-0197. Offers MA. *Students:* 20 part-time (11 women); includes 6 minority (1 Black or African American, non-Hispanic/Latino; 1 Asian, non-Hispanic/Latino; 3 Hispanic/Latino; 1 Two or more races, non-Hispanic/Latino). Average age 25. 20 applicants, 65% accepted, 10 enrolled. In 2016, 10 master's awarded. *Degree requirements:* For master's, comprehensive exam (for some programs), thesis (for some programs). *Entrance requirements:* For master's, GRE General Test. Additional exam requirements/recommendations for international students: Required—TOEFL. *Application deadline:* For fall admission, 3/1 priority date for domestic students; for spring admission, 10/1 for domestic students. Applications are processed on a rolling basis. Application fee: $75. *Financial support:* Teaching assistantships and institutionally sponsored loans available. Support available to part-time students. Financial award application deadline: 3/1; financial award applicants required to submit FAFSA. *Unit head:* Dr. Margaret J. Ciccolella, Chairperson, 209-946-2473, E-mail: mciccolella@pacific.edu. *Application contact:* Miguel Medrano, Information Contact, 209-946-2209, E-mail: mmedrano@pacific.edu.

The University of Toledo, College of Graduate Studies, College of Health and Human Services, Department of Kinesiology, Toledo, OH 43606-3390. Offers exercise science (MSES, PhD). *Program availability:* Part-time. *Degree requirements:* For master's, comprehensive exam, thesis; for doctorate, comprehensive exam, thesis/dissertation. *Entrance requirements:* For master's and doctorate, minimum cumulative GPA of 2.7 for all previous academic work, letters of recommendation. Additional exam requirements/ recommendations for international students: Required—TOEFL (minimum score 550 paper-based; 80 iBT). Electronic applications accepted.

University of West Florida, Usha Kundu, MD College of Health, Department of Exercise Science and Community Health, Pensacola, FL 32514-5750. Offers health promotion (MS); health, leisure, and exercise science (MS), including exercise science, physical education. *Program availability:* Part-time, evening/weekend. *Degree requirements:* For master's, thesis or alternative. *Entrance requirements:* For master's, GRE or MAT, official transcripts; minimum GPA of 3.0; letter of intent; three personal references; work experience as reflected in resume. Additional exam requirements/ recommendations for international students: Required—TOEFL (minimum score 550 paper-based). *Application deadline:* For fall admission, 6/1 for domestic and international students; for spring admission, 10/1 for domestic and international students. Applications are processed on a rolling basis. Application fee: $30. *Expenses:* Tuition, state resident: full-time $5316.12. Tuition, nonresident: full-time $11,308. *Required fees:* $583.92. Tuition and fees vary according to course load and program. *Financial support:* Fellowships, research assistantships with partial tuition reimbursements, teaching assistantships with partial tuition reimbursements, tuition waivers (partial), and unspecified assistantships available. Financial award application deadline: 4/15; financial award applicants required to submit FAFSA. *Unit head:* Dr. John Todorovich, Chairperson, 850-473-7248, Fax: 850-474-2106. *Application contact:* Terry McCray, Assistant Director of Graduate Admissions, 850-473-7718, Fax: 850-473-7714, E-mail: gradadmissions@uwf.edu.
Website: http://uwf.edu/coh/departments/exercise-science-and-community-health/

University of Wisconsin–La Crosse, College of Science and Health, Department of Exercise and Sport Science, Program in Clinical Exercise Physiology, La Crosse, WI 54601-3742. Offers MS. *Students:* 16 full-time (11 women), 2 part-time (both women). Average age 24. 31 applicants, 52% accepted, 16 enrolled. In 2016, 15 master's awarded. *Degree requirements:* For master's, thesis optional. *Entrance requirements:* Additional exam requirements/recommendations for international students: Required—TOEFL (minimum score 550 paper-based; 79 iBT). *Application deadline:* For fall admission, 2/1 priority date for domestic and international students. Electronic applications accepted. *Financial support:* Federal Work-Study, scholarships/grants, health care benefits, and tuition waivers (partial) available. Support available to part-time students. Financial award application deadline: 3/15; financial award applicants required to submit FAFSA. *Unit head:* Dr. John Porcari, Director, 608-785-8684, Fax: 608-785-8686, E-mail: porcari.john@uwlax.edu. *Application contact:* Brandon Schaller, Senior Graduate Student Status Examiner, 608-785-8941, E-mail: admissions@uwlax.edu.
Website: http://www.uwlax.edu/sah/ess/cep/

University of Wisconsin–La Crosse, College of Science and Health, Department of Exercise and Sport Science, Program in Human Performance, La Crosse, WI 54601-3742. Offers applied sport science (MS); strength and conditioning (MS). *Program availability:* Part-time. *Students:* 13 full-time (5 women), 8 part-time (5 women). Average age 24. 21 applicants, 81% accepted, 9 enrolled. In 2016, 8 master's awarded. *Degree requirements:* For master's, comprehensive exam (for some programs), thesis optional. *Entrance requirements:* For master's, GRE, course work in anatomy, physiology, biomechanics, and exercise physiology. Additional exam requirements/ recommendations for international students: Required—TOEFL (minimum score 550 paper-based; 79 iBT). *Application deadline:* For fall admission, 2/1 priority date for domestic and international students. Electronic applications accepted. *Financial support:* Federal Work-Study, scholarships/grants, health care benefits, and tuition waivers (partial) available. Support available to part-time students. Financial award application deadline: 3/15; financial award applicants required to submit FAFSA. *Faculty research:* Anaerobic metabolism, power development, strength training, biomechanics, athletic performance. *Unit head:* Dr. Glenn Wright, Director, 608-785-8689, Fax: 608-785-8172, E-mail: wright.glen@uwlax.edu. *Application contact:* Brandon Schaller, Senior Graduate Student Status Examiner, 608-785-8941, E-mail: admissions@uwlax.edu.
Website: https://www.uwlax.edu/human-performance-ms/

University of Wisconsin–Milwaukee, Graduate School, College of Health Sciences, Department of Kinesiology, Milwaukee, WI 53201-0413. Offers athletic training (MS); kinesiology (MS, PhD), including exercise and nutrition in health and disease (MS), integrative human performance (MS), neuromechanics (MS); physical therapy (DPT). *Program availability:* Part-time. *Students:* 104 full-time (54 women), 6 part-time (3 women); includes 11 minority (1 Black or African American, non-Hispanic/Latino; 10 Two or more races, non-Hispanic/Latino), 3 international. Average age 27. 34 applicants, 47% accepted, 12 enrolled. In 2016, 9 master's, 24 doctorates awarded. *Degree requirements:* For master's, comprehensive exam, thesis optional. *Entrance requirements:* For master's, GRE General Test. Additional exam requirements/ recommendations for international students: Required—TOEFL (minimum score 550 paper-based; 79 iBT), IELTS (minimum score 6.5). *Application deadline:* For fall admission, 1/1 priority date for domestic students; for spring admission, 9/1 for domestic students. Applications are processed on a rolling basis. Application fee: $56 ($96 for international students). *Financial support:* In 2016–17, 2 fellowships, 7 teaching assistantships were awarded; research assistantships, career-related internships or fieldwork, unspecified assistantships, and project assistantships also available. Support available to part-time students. Financial award application deadline: 4/15. *Unit head:* Dr. Kyle T. Ebersole, Department Chair, 414-229-6717, Fax: 414-229-3366, E-mail: ebersole@uwm.edu. *Application contact:* Stephen C. Cobb, Graduate Program Coordinator, 414-229-3369, Fax: 414-229-3366, E-mail: cobbsc@uwm.edu.
Website: http://uwm.edu/healthsciences/academics/kinesiology/

University of Wyoming, College of Health Sciences, Division of Kinesiology and Health, Laramie, WY 82071. Offers MS. *Accreditation:* NCATE. *Program availability:* Part-time, online learning. *Degree requirements:* For master's, comprehensive exam (for some programs), thesis (for some programs). *Entrance requirements:* For master's, GRE General Test, minimum GPA of 3.0. Additional exam requirements/ recommendations for international students: Required—TOEFL. Electronic applications accepted. *Faculty research:* Teacher effectiveness, effects of exercising on heart function, physiological responses of overtraining, psychological benefits of physical activity, health behavior.

Virginia Commonwealth University, Graduate School, College of Humanities and Sciences, Department of Kinesiology and Health Sciences, Program in Health and Movement Sciences, Richmond, VA 23284-9005. Offers MS. *Entrance requirements:* For master's, GRE or MAT. Additional exam requirements/recommendations for international students: Required—TOEFL (minimum score 600 paper-based; 100 iBT). *Application deadline:* For fall admission, 3/15 for domestic students; for spring admission, 11/1 for domestic students. Applications are processed on a rolling basis. Application fee: $50. Electronic applications accepted. *Financial support:* Applicants required to submit FAFSA. *Unit head:* Dr. Edmund O. Acevedo, Chair, Department of Health and Human Performance, 804-828-1948, E-mail: eoacevedo@vcu.edu. *Application contact:* Dr. Ronald K. Evans, Graduate Program Director, 804-828-1948, E-mail: rkevans@vcu.edu.

Virginia Polytechnic Institute and State University, Graduate School, College of Agriculture and Life Sciences, Blacksburg, VA 24061. Offers agricultural and applied economics (MS); agricultural and life sciences (MS); animal and poultry science (MS, PhD); crop and soil environmental sciences (MS, PhD); dairy science (MS); entomology (PhD); horticulture (MS, PhD); human nutrition, foods and exercise (MS, PhD); life sciences (MS, PhD); plant pathology, physiology and weed science (PhD). *Faculty:* 235 full-time (69 women). *Students:* 360 full-time (193 women), 150 part-time (89 women);

includes 73 minority (30 Black or African American, non-Hispanic/Latino; 15 Asian, non-Hispanic/Latino; 15 Hispanic/Latino; 13 Two or more races, non-Hispanic/Latino), 113 international. Average age 29. 311 applicants, 45% accepted, 106 enrolled. In 2016, 111 master's, 50 doctorates awarded. *Degree requirements:* For master's, comprehensive exam (for some programs), thesis (for some programs); for doctorate, comprehensive exam (for some programs), thesis/dissertation (for some programs). *Entrance requirements:* For master's and doctorate, GRE/GMAT. Additional exam requirements/recommendations for international students: Required—TOEFL (minimum score 80 iBT). *Application deadline:* For fall admission, 8/1 for domestic students, 4/1 for international students; for spring admission, 1/1 for domestic students, 9/1 for international students. Applications are processed on a rolling basis. Application fee: $75. Electronic applications accepted. *Expenses:* Tuition, state resident: full-time $12,467; part-time $692.50 per credit hour. Tuition, nonresident: full-time $25,095; part-time $1394.25 per credit hour. *Required fees:* $2669; $491.50 per semester. Tuition and fees vary according to course load, campus/location and program. *Financial support:* In 2016–17, 258 research assistantships with full tuition reimbursements (averaging $20,636 per year), 107 teaching assistantships with full tuition reimbursements (averaging $20,004 per year) were awarded. Financial award application deadline: 3/1; financial award applicants required to submit FAFSA. *Total annual research expenditures:* $46.9 million. *Unit head:* Dr. Alan L. Grant, Dean, 540-231-4152, Fax: 540-231-4163, E-mail: algrant@vt.edu. *Application contact:* Crystal Tawney, Administrative Assistant, 540-231-4152, Fax: 540-231-4163, E-mail: cdtawney@vt.edu.
Website: http://www.cals.vt.edu/

Wake Forest University, Graduate School of Arts and Sciences, Department of Health and Exercise Science, Winston-Salem, NC 27106. Offers MS. *Degree requirements:* For master's, one foreign language, thesis. *Entrance requirements:* For master's, GRE General Test, resume. Additional exam requirements/recommendations for international students: Required—TOEFL (minimum score 79 iBT). Electronic applications accepted. *Faculty research:* Cardiac rehabilitation, biomechanics, health psychology, exercise physiology.

Washington State University, College of Pharmacy, Nutrition and Exercise Physiology Program, Pullman, WA 99164. Offers MS. Programs offered at the Spokane campus. *Accreditation:* AND. *Degree requirements:* For master's, internship. *Entrance requirements:* For master's, BS in nutrition and exercise physiology, exercise science, human nutrition, or related degree; interview.

Wayne State College, Department of Health, Human Performance and Sport, Wayne, NE 68787. Offers exercise science (MSE); organizational management (MS), including sport management. *Program availability:* Part-time, evening/weekend. *Degree requirements:* For master's, comprehensive exam, thesis optional. *Entrance requirements:* For master's, GRE General Test, minimum GPA of 3.0. Additional exam requirements/recommendations for international students: Required—TOEFL (minimum score 550 paper-based). Electronic applications accepted.

Wayne State University, College of Education, Division of Kinesiology, Health and Sports Studies, Detroit, MI 48202. Offers health education (M Ed); kinesiology (M Ed, PhD), including exercise and sport science (PhD), physical education and physical activity leadership (PhD); sports administration (MA). *Program availability:* Part-time, 100% online. *Faculty:* 10. *Students:* 57 full-time (30 women), 131 part-time (68 women); includes 72 minority (63 Black or African American, non-Hispanic/Latino; 1 American Indian or Alaska Native, non-Hispanic/Latino; 1 Asian, non-Hispanic/Latino; 3 Hispanic/Latino; 4 Two or more races, non-Hispanic/Latino), 10 international. Average age 29. 160 applicants, 56% accepted, 51 enrolled. In 2016, 66 master's awarded. *Degree requirements:* For master's, thesis (for some programs); for doctorate, thesis/dissertation. *Entrance requirements:* For master's, minimum undergraduate GPA of 3.0; undergraduate degree directly relating to the field of specialization being applied for or one accompanied by extensive educational background in closely-related field; teaching certificates in specific areas (for some programs); for doctorate, minimum undergraduate GPA of 3.0; undergraduate degree directly relating to the field of specialization being applied for or one accompanied by extensive educational background in closely-related field. Additional exam requirements/recommendations for international students: Required—TOEFL (minimum score 79 iBT), TWE (minimum score 5.5), Michigan English Language Assessment Battery (minimum score 85); Recommended—IELTS (minimum score 6.5). *Application deadline:* For fall admission, 6/1 priority date for domestic students, 5/1 priority date for international students; for winter admission, 10/1 priority date for domestic students, 9/1 priority date for international students; for spring admission, 2/1 priority date for domestic students, 1/1 priority date for international students. Application fee: $50. Electronic applications accepted. *Expenses:* $18,522 per year resident tuition and fees, $35,715 per year non-resident tuition and fees. *Financial support:* In 2016–17, 49 students received support, including 6 research assistantships with tuition reimbursements available (averaging $17,994 per year); fellowships with tuition reimbursements available, scholarships/grants, health care benefits, and unspecified assistantships also available. Support available to part-time students. Financial award applicants required to submit FAFSA. *Faculty research:* Exercise and sport science, nutrition and physical activity interventions, school and community health, obesity prevention. *Total annual research expenditures:* $974,985. *Unit head:* Dr. Nate McCaughtry, Assistant Dean, Division of Kinesiology, Health and Sport Studies/Director, Center for School Health, 313-577-0014, Fax: 313-577-5002, E-mail: aj4391@wayne.edu. *Application contact:* Janice Green, Assistant Dean, 313-577-1605, E-mail: jwgreen@wayne.edu.
Website: http://coe.wayne.edu/kinesiology/index.php

West Chester University of Pennsylvania, College of Health Sciences, Department of Kinesiology, West Chester, PA 19383. Offers adapted physical education (Certificate); exercise and sport physiology (MS), including athletic training, exercise and sport physiology; general physical education (MS); sport management and athletics (MPA), including administration. *Program availability:* Part-time, evening/weekend. *Faculty:* 9 full-time (6 women). *Students:* 34 full-time (22 women), 21 part-time (7 women); includes 5 minority (4 Black or African American, non-Hispanic/Latino; 1 Hispanic/Latino), 1 international. Average age 26. 68 applicants, 85% accepted, 30 enrolled. In 2016, 23 master's, 1 other advanced degree awarded. *Degree requirements:* For master's, thesis or research report (for MS); two internships and capstone course that includes a research project or thesis (for MPA). *Entrance requirements:* For master's, GRE (for MS), 2 letters of recommendation, statement of goals; transcripts (for MS); resume (for MPA). Additional exam requirements/recommendations for international students: Required—TOEFL or IELTS. *Application deadline:* For fall admission, 5/15 for international students; for spring admission, 10/15 for international students. Applications are processed on a rolling basis. Application fee: $50. Electronic applications accepted. *Expenses:* Tuition, state resident: full-time $8694; part-time $483 per credit. Tuition, nonresident: full-time $13,050; part-time $725 per credit. *Required fees:* $2399; $119.05 per credit. Tuition and fees vary according to campus/location and program. *Financial support:* Scholarships/grants and unspecified assistantships available. Financial award application deadline: 2/15; financial award applicants required to submit FAFSA. *Faculty research:* Metabolism during exercise, biomechanics, rating of perceived exertion, motor learning, environmental physiology. *Unit head:* Dr. Frank Fry, Chair/Graduate Coordinator for the MS in General Physical Education Program, 610-436-2610, Fax: 610-436-2860, E-mail: ffry@wcupa.edu. *Application contact:* Office of Graduate Studies and Extended Education, 610-436-2943, Fax: 610-436-2763, E-mail: gradstudy@wcupa.edu.
Website: http://www.wcupa.edu/healthsciences/kinesiology/

Western Michigan University, Graduate College, College of Education and Human Development, Department of Health, Physical Education and Recreation, Kalamazoo, MI 49008. Offers athletic training (MS), including exercise physiology; sport management (MA), including pedagogy, special physical education.

Western Washington University, Graduate School, College of Humanities and Social Sciences, Department of Physical Education, Health, and Recreation, Bellingham, WA 98225-5996. Offers exercise science (MS); sport psychology (MS). *Program availability:* Part-time. *Degree requirements:* For master's, thesis. *Entrance requirements:* For master's, GRE General Test, minimum GPA of 3.0 in last 60 semester hours or last 90 quarter hours. Additional exam requirements/recommendations for international students: Required—TOEFL (minimum score 567 paper-based). Electronic applications accepted. *Faculty research:* Spinal motor control, biomechanics/kinesiology, biomechanics of aging, mobility of older adults, fall prevention, exercise interventions and function, magnesium and inspiratory muscle training (IMT).

West Texas A&M University, College of Nursing and Health Sciences, Department of Sports and Exercise Sciences, Canyon, TX 79016-0001. Offers sport management (MS); sports and exercise sciences (MS). *Program availability:* Part-time, evening/weekend. *Degree requirements:* For master's, comprehensive exam, thesis optional. *Entrance requirements:* For master's, GRE General Test. Additional exam requirements/recommendations for international students: Required—TOEFL. *Application deadline:* For fall admission, 8/1 for domestic students, 6/1 for international students; for spring admission, 12/1 for domestic students, 11/1 for international students; for summer admission, 5/1 for domestic students. Applications are processed on a rolling basis. Application fee: $40 ($75 for international students). Electronic applications accepted. *Financial support:* Application deadline: 2/1; applicants required to submit FAFSA. *Unit head:* Lorna Strong, Department Head, 806-651-2382. *Application contact:* Dr. Vanessa Fiaud, Assistant Professor, 806-651-2677.

West Virginia University, College of Physical Activity and Sport Sciences, Morgantown, WV 26506-6116. Offers athletic training (MS); coaching and sport education (MS); coaching and teaching studies (Ed D); physical education/teacher education (MS, PhD), including curriculum and instruction (PhD), physical education supervision (PhD); sport and exercise psychology (MS, PhD); sport coaching (MS); sport management (MS). *Degree requirements:* For doctorate, comprehensive exam, thesis/dissertation, oral exam. *Entrance requirements:* For master's, GRE or MAT, minimum GPA of 3.0; for doctorate, GRE General Test or MAT, minimum GPA of 3.5. Additional exam requirements/recommendations for international students: Required—TOEFL (minimum score 550 paper-based). Electronic applications accepted. *Faculty research:* Sport psychosociology, teacher education, exercise psychology, counseling.

West Virginia University, School of Medicine, Graduate Programs at the Health Sciences Center, Interdisciplinary Graduate Programs in Biomedical Sciences, Exercise Physiology Program, Morgantown, WV 26506. Offers MS, PhD, MD/PhD. *Degree requirements:* For doctorate, comprehensive exam, thesis/dissertation. *Entrance requirements:* For doctorate, GRE General Test, minimum GPA of 3.0. Additional exam requirements/recommendations for international students: Required—TOEFL. Electronic applications accepted. *Faculty research:* Cardiovascular function in health and disease, circulatory adaptations to exercise training, aging, microgravity, muscle adaptation and injury.

Wichita State University, Graduate School, College of Education, Department of Human Performance Studies, Wichita, KS 67260. Offers exercise science (M Ed). *Program availability:* Part-time. *Unit head:* Dr. Michael Rogers, Chairperson, 316-978-3340, Fax: 316-978-3302, E-mail: michael.rogers@wichita.edu. *Application contact:* Jordan Oleson, Admissions Coordinator, 316-978-3095, Fax: 316-978-3253, E-mail: jordan.oleson@wichita.edu.
Website: http://www.wichita.edu/hps

William Paterson University of New Jersey, College of Science and Health, Wayne, NJ 07470-8420. Offers biology (MS); biotechnology (MS); communication disorders (MS); exercise and sport studies (MS); nursing (MSN); nursing practice (DNP). *Program availability:* Part-time, evening/weekend. *Faculty:* 30 full-time (19 women), 26 part-time/adjunct (24 women). *Students:* 63 full-time (53 women), 199 part-time (171 women); includes 110 minority (14 Black or African American, non-Hispanic/Latino; 45 Asian, non-Hispanic/Latino; 44 Hispanic/Latino; 7 Two or more races, non-Hispanic/Latino), 2 international. Average age 33. 118 applicants, 98% accepted, 83 enrolled. In 2016, 51 master's, 2 doctorates awarded. *Degree requirements:* For master's, comprehensive exam (for some programs), thesis (for some programs), non-thesis internship/practicum (for some programs). *Entrance requirements:* For master's, GRE/MAT, minimum GPA of 3.0; 2-3 letters of recommendation; personal statement; work experience (for some programs); for doctorate, GRE/MAT, minimum GPA of 3.3; work experience; 3 letters of recommendation; interview; master's degree in nursing. Additional exam requirements/recommendations for international students: Required—TOEFL (minimum score 550 paper-based; 79 iBT), IELTS (minimum score 6). *Application deadline:* For fall admission, 8/1 for domestic students, 4/1 for international students; for spring admission, 12/1 for domestic students, 11/1 for international students; for summer admission, 5/1 for domestic students, 2/1 for international students. Applications are processed on a rolling basis. Application fee: $50. Electronic applications accepted. *Expenses:* Tuition, state resident: full-time $12,480; part-time $611 per credit. Tuition, nonresident: full-time $20,263; part-time $992 per credit. *Required fees:* $1573; $77 per credit. Tuition and fees vary according to course load, degree level and program. *Financial support:* Career-related internships or fieldwork, Federal Work-Study, scholarships/grants, and unspecified assistantships available. Support available to part-time students. Financial award applicants required to submit FAFSA. *Faculty research:* Alcohol prevention in Passaic county, plant genome and gene expression, human and animal genomes, predicting molecular motion in certain situations, traumatic brain injury. *Total annual research expenditures:* $177,820. *Unit head:* Dr. Kenneth Wolf, Dean, 973-720-2194, Fax: 973-720-3414, E-mail: wolfk@wpunj.edu. *Application contact:* Christina Aiello, Assistant Director, Graduate Admissions, 973-720-2506, Fax: 973-720-2035, E-mail: aielloc@wpunj.edu.
Website: http://www.wpunj.edu/cosh

Kinesiology and Movement Studies

Alabama Agricultural and Mechanical University, School of Graduate Studies, College of Education, Humanities, and Behavioral Sciences, Department of Health Sciences, Human Performance, and Communicative Disorders, Huntsville, AL 35811. Offers kinesiology (MS); physical education (MS); speech-language pathology (MS). *Program availability:* Part-time, evening/weekend. *Degree requirements:* For master's, comprehensive exam. *Entrance requirements:* For master's, GRE General Test. Additional exam requirements/recommendations for international students: Required—TOEFL (minimum score 500 paper-based; 61 iBT). *Application deadline:* For fall admission, 5/1 for domestic students. Applications are processed on a rolling basis. Application fee: $25. Electronic applications accepted. *Expenses:* Tuition, nonresident: part-time $826 per credit hour. Full-time tuition and fees vary according to course load and program. *Financial support:* Career-related internships or fieldwork available. Financial award application deadline: 4/1. *Faculty research:* Cardiorespiratory assessment. *Unit head:* Dr. Rodney Whittle, Chair, 256-372-8268, E-mail: rodney.whittle@aamu.edu.

A.T. Still University, College of Graduate Health Studies, Kirksville, MO 63501. Offers dental public health (MPH); exercise and sport psychology (Certificate); fundamentals of education (Certificate); geriatric exercise science (Certificate); global health (Certificate); health administration (MHA, DHA); health professions (Ed D); health sciences (DH Sc); kinesiology (MS); leadership and organizational behavior (Certificate); public health (MPH); sports conditioning (Certificate). *Program availability:* Part-time, online only, 100% online, blended/hybrid learning. *Faculty:* 29 full-time (18 women), 89 part-time/adjunct (46 women). *Students:* 505 full-time (319 women), 461 part-time (276 women); includes 337 minority (151 Black or African American, non-Hispanic/Latino; 19 American Indian or Alaska Native, non-Hispanic/Latino; 70 Asian, non-Hispanic/Latino; 89 Hispanic/Latino; 1 Native Hawaiian or other Pacific Islander, non-Hispanic/Latino; 7 Two or more races, non-Hispanic/Latino), 29 international. Average age 37. 366 applicants, 98% accepted, 370 enrolled. In 2016, 113 master's, 94 doctorates, 110 other advanced degrees awarded. *Degree requirements:* For master's, thesis, integrated terminal project, practicum; for doctorate, thesis/dissertation. *Entrance requirements:* For master's, minimum GPA of 2.5, bachelor's degree or equivalent, background check, essay, three references; for doctorate, minimum GPA of 2.5, master's or terminal degree, background check, essay, three references, past experience in relevant field. Additional exam requirements/recommendations for international students: Required—TOEFL (minimum score 550 paper-based; 80 iBT). *Application deadline:* For fall admission, 5/20 for domestic and international students; for winter admission, 9/12 for domestic and international students; for spring admission, 12/12 for domestic and international students; for summer admission, 3/6 for domestic and international students. Applications are processed on a rolling basis. Application fee: $70. Electronic applications accepted. Application fee is waived when completed online. *Expenses:* Contact institution. *Financial support:* Scholarships/grants available. Financial award applicants required to submit FAFSA. *Faculty research:* Public health: influence of availability of comprehensive wellness resources online, student wellness, oral health care needs assessment of community, oral health knowledge and behaviors of Medicaid-eligible pregnant women and mothers of young children in relations to early childhood caries and tooth decay, alcohol use and alcohol related problems among college students. *Unit head:* Dr. Donald Altman, Dean, 660-626-2820, Fax: 660-626-2826, E-mail: daltman@atsu.edu. *Application contact:* Amie Waldemer, Associate Director, Online Admissions, 480-219-6146, E-mail: awaldemer@atsu.edu.
Website: http://www.atsu.edu/college-of-graduate-health-studies

Ball State University, Graduate School, College of Applied Sciences and Technology, School of Kinesiology, Muncie, IN 47306. Offers athletic coaching education (Certificate); exercise science (MA, MS), including exercise science; human bioenergetics (PhD), including human bioenergetics; physical education (MS); physical education and sport (MA, MS), including physical education and sport; wellness management (MA, MS). *Program availability:* Part-time, 100% online. *Degree requirements:* For doctorate, thesis/dissertation. *Entrance requirements:* For master's, minimum baccalaureate GPA of 2.75 or 3.0 in latter half of baccalaureate; for doctorate, GRE General Test, minimum graduate GPA of 3.2. Additional exam requirements/recommendations for international students: Required—TOEFL (minimum score 550 paper-based; 79 iBT), IELTS (minimum score 6.5). Electronic applications accepted.

Barry University, School of Human Performance and Leisure Sciences, Programs in Movement Science, General Movement Science Program, Miami Shores, FL 33161-6695. Offers MS.

Barry University, School of Human Performance and Leisure Sciences, Programs in Movement Science, Specialization in Biomechanics, Miami Shores, FL 33161-6695. Offers MS. *Entrance requirements:* For master's, GRE General Test, minimum GPA of 3.0. Electronic applications accepted. *Faculty research:* Upper extremity biomechanics, orthopedic biomechanics.

Boise State University, College of Health Sciences, Department of Kinesiology, Boise, ID 83725-1710. Offers athletic leadership (MAL); kinesiology (MK, MS). *Program availability:* Part-time. *Faculty:* 11. *Students:* 23 full-time (9 women), 31 part-time (10 women); includes 11 minority (4 Black or African American, non-Hispanic/Latino; 6 Hispanic/Latino; 1 Two or more races, non-Hispanic/Latino). Average age 25. 37 applicants, 65% accepted, 15 enrolled. In 2016, 22 master's awarded. *Degree requirements:* For master's, thesis (for some programs). *Entrance requirements:* For master's, minimum GPA of 3.0. Additional exam requirements/recommendations for international students: Required—TOEFL (minimum score 550 paper-based; 80 iBT), IELTS (minimum score 6). *Application deadline:* For fall admission, 5/1 for domestic and international students. Application fee: $65 ($95 for international students). Electronic applications accepted. *Expenses:* Tuition, state resident: full-time $6058; part-time $358 per credit hour. Tuition, nonresident: full-time $20,108; part-time $608 per credit hour. *Required fees:* $2108. Tuition and fees vary according to program. *Financial support:* In 2016–17, 31 students received support. Scholarships/grants and unspecified assistantships available. Financial award application deadline: 1/15; financial award applicants required to submit FAFSA. *Unit head:* Dr. John McChesney, Department Chair, 208-426-4270, E-mail: johnmcchesney@boisestate.edu. *Application contact:* Dr. Laura Patranek, Graduate Program Coordinator, 208-426-4366, E-mail: laurajonespetranek@boisestate.edu.
Website: http://kinesiology.boisestate.edu/graduate-programs/

Bowling Green State University, Graduate College, College of Education and Human Development, School of Human Movement, Sport, and Leisure Studies, Bowling Green, OH 43403. Offers developmental kinesiology (M Ed); recreation and leisure (M Ed); sport administration (M Ed). *Program availability:* Part-time. *Degree requirements:* For master's, thesis or alternative. *Entrance requirements:* For master's, GRE General Test, minimum GPA of 2.7. Additional exam requirements/recommendations for international students: Required—TOEFL. *Application deadline:* For fall admission, 1/15 priority date for domestic students. Applications are processed on a rolling basis. Application fee: $30. Electronic applications accepted. *Financial support:* Research assistantships with full tuition reimbursements, teaching assistantships with full tuition reimbursements, career-related internships or fieldwork, Federal Work-Study, and unspecified assistantships available. Financial award applicants required to submit FAFSA. *Faculty research:* Teacher-learning process, travel and tourism, sport marketing and management, exercise physiology and sport psychology, life-span motor development. *Unit head:* Dr. Bonnie Berger, Director, 419-372-2334. *Application contact:* Dr. Geoff Meek, Graduate Coordinator, 419-372-0501.

Brooklyn College of the City University of New York, School of Natural and Behavioral Sciences, Department of Kinesiology, Brooklyn, NY 11210-2889. Offers exercise and sports science (MS); physical education teacher (MS); sport management (MS). *Program availability:* Part-time. *Degree requirements:* For master's, comprehensive exam or thesis. *Entrance requirements:* For master's, previous course work in physical education and education, minimum GPA of 3.0, 2 letters of recommendation, essay. Additional exam requirements/recommendations for international students: Required—TOEFL (minimum score 500 paper-based; 61 iBT). Electronic applications accepted. *Faculty research:* Exercise physiology, motor learning, sports psychology, women in athletics.

California Polytechnic State University, San Luis Obispo, College of Science and Mathematics, Department of Kinesiology, San Luis Obispo, CA 93407. Offers MS. *Program availability:* Part-time. *Faculty:* 5 full-time (2 women), 1 (woman) part-time/adjunct. *Students:* 9 full-time (4 women), 9 part-time (4 women); includes 8 minority (2 Asian, non-Hispanic/Latino; 5 Hispanic/Latino; 1 Two or more races, non-Hispanic/Latino). Average age 25. 18 applicants, 44% accepted, 5 enrolled. In 2016, 5 master's awarded. *Degree requirements:* For master's, comprehensive exam (for some programs), thesis (for some programs). *Entrance requirements:* For master's, GRE. Additional exam requirements/recommendations for international students: Required—TOEFL (minimum score 80 iBT). *Application deadline:* For fall admission, 3/1 for domestic and international students. Applications are processed on a rolling basis. Application fee: $55. Electronic applications accepted. *Expenses:* Tuition, state resident: full-time $6738; part-time $3906 per year. Tuition, nonresident: full-time $15,666; part-time $8370 per year. *Required fees:* $3603; $3141 per unit. $1047 per term. *Financial support:* Fellowships, research assistantships, teaching assistantships, career-related internships or fieldwork, Federal Work-Study, and scholarships/grants available. Support available to part-time students. Financial award application deadline: 3/2; financial award applicants required to submit FAFSA. *Faculty research:* Biomechanics, motor learning and control, physiology of exercise, commercial fitness, cardiac rehabilitation. *Unit head:* Dr. Kris Jankovitz, E-mail: kjankovi@calpoly.edu. *Application contact:* Dr. Alison Ventura, Graduate Coordinator, E-mail: akventur@calpoly.edu.
Website: http://www.kinesiology.calpoly.edu/

California State Polytechnic University, Pomona, Program in Kinesiology, Pomona, CA 91768-2557. Offers MS. *Program availability:* Part-time, evening/weekend. *Students:* 7 full-time (3 women), 10 part-time (6 women); includes 10 minority (6 Asian, non-Hispanic/Latino; 3 Hispanic/Latino; 1 Two or more races, non-Hispanic/Latino). Average age 26. 6 applicants, 100% accepted, 5 enrolled. In 2016, 2 master's awarded. *Degree requirements:* For master's, thesis or alternative. *Entrance requirements:* Additional exam requirements/recommendations for international students: Required—TOEFL. *Application deadline:* Applications are processed on a rolling basis. Application fee: $55. Electronic applications accepted. *Expenses:* Contact institution. *Financial support:* Application deadline: 3/2; applicants required to submit FAFSA. *Unit head:* Dr. Ken Hansen, Graduate Coordinator, 909-869-4638, Fax: 909-869-4797, E-mail: kahansen@cpp.edu. *Application contact:* Andrew M. Wright, Director of Admissions, 909-869-3130, Fax: 909-869-4529, E-mail: awright@cpp.edu.
Website: http://www.cpp.edu/~sci/kinesiology-health-promotion/academic-programs/graduate-program.shtml

California State University, Chico, Office of Graduate Studies, College of Communication and Education, Department of Kinesiology, Chico, CA 95929-0722. Offers MA. *Program availability:* Part-time. *Faculty:* 18 full-time (7 women), 27 part-time/adjunct (14 women). *Students:* 20 full-time (10 women), 10 part-time (5 women); includes 11 minority (1 Asian, non-Hispanic/Latino; 6 Hispanic/Latino; 4 Two or more races, non-Hispanic/Latino). 25 applicants, 68% accepted, 13 enrolled. In 2016, 18 master's awarded. *Degree requirements:* For master's, thesis, project, or comprehensive examination. *Entrance requirements:* For master's, GRE General Test, 2 letters of recommendation, statement of purpose. Additional exam requirements/recommendations for international students: Required—TOEFL (minimum score 550 paper-based; 80 iBT), IELTS (minimum score 6.5), PTE (minimum score 59). *Application deadline:* For fall admission, 3/1 priority date for domestic students, 3/1 for international students; for spring admission, 9/15 priority date for domestic students, 9/15 for international students. Application fee: $55. Electronic applications accepted. *Financial support:* Fellowships, teaching assistantships, career-related internships or fieldwork, scholarships/grants, and unspecified assistantships available. Financial award application deadline: 3/1; financial award applicants required to submit FAFSA. *Unit head:* Dr. Josh Trout, Chair, 530-898-6373, Fax: 530-898-4932, E-mail: kinestudent@csuchico.edu. *Application contact:* Judy L. Morrice, Graduate Admissions Coordinator, 530-898-6116, Fax: 530-898-3342, E-mail: jlmorris@csuchico.edu.
Website: http://www.csuchico.edu/kine/

California State University, Fresno, Division of Research and Graduate Studies, College of Health and Human Services, Department of Kinesiology, Fresno, CA 93740-8027. Offers exercise science (MA); general kinesiology (MA); sport administration (MA); sport psychology (MA). *Program availability:* Part-time, evening/weekend. *Degree requirements:* For master's, thesis or alternative. *Entrance requirements:* For master's, GRE General Test, minimum GPA of 2.7. Additional exam requirements/recommendations for international students: Required—TOEFL. *Application deadline:* For fall admission, 5/1 for domestic and international students; for spring admission, 10/1 for domestic and international students. Applications are processed on a rolling basis. Application fee: $55. Electronic applications accepted. *Financial support:* Teaching assistantships, career-related internships or fieldwork, Federal Work-Study, and scholarships/grants available. Support available to part-time students. Financial award application deadline: 3/1; financial award applicants required to submit FAFSA. *Faculty research:* Refugee education, homeless, geriatrics, fitness. *Unit head:* Dr. Tim Anderson, Chair, 559-278-2203, Fax: 559-278-7010, E-mail: tima@csufresno.edu. *Application contact:* Dr. Jenelle Gilbert, Coordinator, 559-278-8902, Fax: 559-278-7010,

E-mail: jgilbert@csufresno.edu.
Website: http://www.fresnostate.edu/chhs/kinesiology/

California State University, Long Beach, Graduate Studies, College of Health and Human Services, Department of Kinesiology, Long Beach, CA 90840. Offers adapted physical education (MA); coaching and student athlete development (MA); exercise physiology and nutrition (MS); exercise science (MS); individualized studies (MA); kinesiology (MA); pedagogical studies (MA); sport and exercise psychology (MS); sport management (MA); sports medicine and injury studies (MS). *Program availability:* Part-time. *Degree requirements:* For master's, oral and written comprehensive exams or thesis. *Entrance requirements:* For master's, GRE General Test, minimum GPA of 2.75 during previous 2 years of course work. *Application deadline:* For fall admission, 6/1 for domestic students. Applications are processed on a rolling basis. Application fee: $55. Electronic applications accepted. *Financial support:* Federal Work-Study, institutionally sponsored loans, and scholarships/grants available. Financial award application deadline: 3/2. *Faculty research:* Pulmonary functioning, feedback and practice structure, strength training, history and politics of sports, special population research issues. *Unit head:* Jan Schroeder, Chair, 562-985-4051.

California State University, Los Angeles, Graduate Studies, College of Health and Human Services, Department of Kinesiology and Nutritional Sciences, Los Angeles, CA 90032-8530. Offers nutritional science (MS); physical education and kinesiology (MA). *Accreditation:* AND. *Program availability:* Part-time, evening/weekend. *Degree requirements:* For master's, comprehensive exam, project or thesis. *Entrance requirements:* For master's, minimum GPA of 2.75. Additional exam requirements/recommendations for international students: Required—TOEFL (minimum score 500 paper-based).

California State University, Northridge, Graduate Studies, College of Health and Human Development, Department of Kinesiology, Northridge, CA 91330. Offers MS. *Program availability:* Part-time, evening/weekend. *Faculty:* 22 full-time (13 women), 65 part-time/adjunct (35 women). *Students:* 31 full-time (13 women), 41 part-time (21 women); includes 40 minority (3 Black or African American, non-Hispanic/Latino; 1 American Indian or Alaska Native, non-Hispanic/Latino; 10 Asian, non-Hispanic/Latino; 23 Hispanic/Latino; 3 Two or more races, non-Hispanic/Latino), 8 international. Average age 28. 72 applicants, 54% accepted, 22 enrolled. *Degree requirements:* For master's, thesis or alternative. *Entrance requirements:* For master's, GRE General Test or minimum GPA of 3.0, 3 letters of recommendation. Additional exam requirements/recommendations for international students: Required—TOEFL. *Application deadline:* For fall admission, 11/30 for domestic students. Application fee: $55. *Expenses:* Tuition, state resident: full-time $4152. *Financial support:* Teaching assistantships and unspecified assistantships available. Financial award application deadline: 3/1. *Unit head:* Dr. K. Dino Vrongistinos, Chair, 818-677-3205.
Website: http://www.csun.edu/hhd/kin/

Canisius College, Graduate Division, School of Education and Human Services, Department of Kinesiology, Buffalo, NY 14208-1098. Offers physical education (MS Ed); physical education birth - 12 (MS Ed). *Program availability:* Part-time, evening/weekend, 100% online, blended/hybrid learning. *Faculty:* 5 full-time (1 woman), 5 part-time/adjunct (3 women). *Students:* 16 full-time (5 women), 41 part-time (12 women); includes 2 minority (both Black or African American, non-Hispanic/Latino), 1 international. Average age 28. 33 applicants, 82% accepted, 22 enrolled. In 2016, 41 master's awarded. *Degree requirements:* For master's, research project. *Entrance requirements:* For master's, official college and/or university transcript(s) showing completion of bachelor's degree from accredited institution with evidence of teaching certification (not for initial certification candidates); two letters of recommendation; minimum cumulative undergraduate GPA of 2.7. Additional exam requirements/recommendations for international students: Required—TOEFL (minimum score 550 paper-based, 79 iBT), IELTS (minimum score 6.5), or CAEL (minimum score 70). *Application deadline:* Applications are processed on a rolling basis. Application fee: $25. Electronic applications accepted. Application fee is waived when completed online. *Expenses:* Contact institution. *Financial support:* Career-related internships or fieldwork, Federal Work-Study, scholarships/grants, tuition waivers (partial), and unspecified assistantships available. Support available to part-time students. Financial award application deadline: 4/30; financial award applicants required to submit FAFSA. *Faculty research:* Culturally congruent pedagogy in physical education, information processing and perceptual styles of athletes, qualities of effective coaches. *Unit head:* Dr. Peter M. Koehneke, Chair/Professor of Kinesiology, 716-888-2954, Fax: 716-888-8445, E-mail: koehneke@canisius.edu. *Application contact:* Kathleen B. Davis, Vice President of Enrollment Management, 716-888-2500, Fax: 716-888-3195, E-mail: daviskb@canisius.edu.
Website: http://www.canisius.edu/graduate/

Columbia University, College of Physicians and Surgeons, Programs in Occupational Therapy, New York, NY 10032. Offers movement science (Ed D), including occupational therapy; occupational therapy (MS); occupational therapy and cognition (OTD); MPH/MS. EdD offered in tandem with Teachers College, Columbia University. *Accreditation:* AOTA. *Faculty:* 11 full-time (8 women), 6 part-time/adjunct (4 women). *Students:* 111 full-time (97 women), 5 part-time (4 women); includes 35 minority (8 Black or African American, non-Hispanic/Latino; 13 Asian, non-Hispanic/Latino; 14 Hispanic/Latino). In 2016, 51 master's, 2 doctorates awarded. *Degree requirements:* For master's, project, 6 months of fieldwork, thesis (for post-professional students); for doctorate, comprehensive exam, thesis/dissertation. *Entrance requirements:* For master's, undergraduate course work in anatomy, physiology, statistics, psychology, social sciences, humanities, and English composition; for doctorate, master's degree in occupational therapy (for OTD). Additional exam requirements/recommendations for international students: Required—TOEFL (minimum score 100 iBT) or IELTS (minimum score 8). *Application deadline:* For fall admission, 12/2 for domestic and international students. Application fee: $85. Electronic applications accepted. *Expenses:* Contact institution. *Financial support:* Career-related internships or fieldwork, Federal Work-Study, institutionally sponsored loans, and scholarships/grants available. Financial award application deadline: 4/15; financial award applicants required to submit FAFSA. *Faculty research:* Community mental health, motor learning, cognition, literacy, LGBTQ. *Total annual research expenditures:* $75,000. *Unit head:* Dr. Janet Falk-Kessler, Director, 212-305-5267, Fax: 212-305-4569, E-mail: jf6@columbia.edu. *Application contact:* Marilyn Harper, Administrative Assistant, 212-305-5267, Fax: 212-305-4569, E-mail: mh15@columbia.edu.

Dalhousie University, Faculty of Health Professions, School of Health and Human Performance, Program in Kinesiology, Halifax, NS B3H 3J5, Canada. Offers M Sc. *Program availability:* Part-time. *Degree requirements:* For master's, thesis. *Entrance requirements:* Additional exam requirements/recommendations for international students: Required—TOEFL, IELTS, CANTEST, CAEL, or Michigan English Language Assessment Battery. Electronic applications accepted. *Faculty research:* Sport science, fitness, neuromuscular physiology, biomechanics, ergonomics, sport psychology.

Dallas Baptist University, Dorothy M. Bush College of Education, Program in Kinesiology, Dallas, TX 75211-9299. Offers M Ed. *Program availability:* Part-time, evening/weekend, 100% online, blended/hybrid learning. *Application deadline:* Applications are processed on a rolling basis. Application fee: $25. Electronic applications accepted. Application fee is waived when completed online. *Expenses: Tuition:* Full-time $15,408; part-time $856 per credit hour. *Required fees:* $400 per semester. Tuition and fees vary according to course load and degree level. *Unit head:* Dr. Ray Galloway, Director, 214-333-5414, E-mail: rayg@dbu.edu. *Application contact:* Bobby Soto, Director of Admissions, 214-333-5242, E-mail: graduate@dbu.edu.
Website: http://www3.dbu.edu/graduate/kinesiology.asp

East Carolina University, Graduate School, College of Health and Human Performance, Department of Kinesiology, Greenville, NC 27858-4353. Offers adapted physical education (MS); bioenergetics and exercise science (PhD); biomechanics (MS); exercise physiology (MS); physical activity promotion (MS); physical education (MA Ed, MAT); physical education pedagogy (MS); sport and exercise psychology (MS); sport management (MS, Certificate). *Students:* 90 full-time (33 women), 23 part-time (9 women); includes 16 minority (8 Black or African American, non-Hispanic/Latino; 3 Asian, non-Hispanic/Latino; 3 Hispanic/Latino; 2 Two or more races, non-Hispanic/Latino), 7 international. Average age 26. 98 applicants, 53% accepted, 38 enrolled. In 2016, 28 master's, 2 doctorates awarded. *Degree requirements:* For master's, comprehensive exam, thesis optional; for doctorate, comprehensive exam, thesis/dissertation. *Entrance requirements:* For master's, GRE General Test or MAT; for doctorate, GRE. Additional exam requirements/recommendations for international students: Required—TOEFL. *Application deadline:* For fall admission, 2/1 priority date for domestic students, 2/1 for international students. Applications are processed on a rolling basis. Application fee: $50. *Financial support:* Research assistantships with tuition reimbursements and teaching assistantships available. Support available to part-time students. Financial award application deadline: 2/1. *Faculty research:* Diabetes metabolism, pediatric obesity, biomechanics of arthritis, physical activity measurement. *Total annual research expenditures:* $26. *Unit head:* Dr. Stacey Altman, Chair, 252-328-2973, E-mail: altmans@ecu.edu.

Eastern Illinois University, Graduate School, College of Education and Professional Studies, Department of Kinesiology and Sports Studies, Charleston, IL 61920. Offers MS. *Program availability:* Part-time, evening/weekend. *Degree requirements:* For master's, comprehensive exam (for some programs), thesis (for some programs). *Entrance requirements:* For master's, minimum GPA of 3.0 with kinesiology focus, three letters of recommendation, resume, personal statement. Additional exam requirements/recommendations for international students: Required—TOEFL (minimum score 500 paper-based; 61 iBT), IELTS (minimum score 6). Electronic applications accepted.

Eastern Michigan University, Graduate School, College of Health and Human Services, School of Health Promotion and Human Performance, Programs in Exercise Physiology, Ypsilanti, MI 48197. Offers exercise physiology (MS); sports medicine-biomechanics (MS); sports medicine-corporate adult fitness (MS); sports medicine-exercise physiology (MS). *Program availability:* Part-time, evening/weekend. *Students:* 13 full-time (5 women), 19 part-time (9 women); includes 3 minority (1 Black or African American, non-Hispanic/Latino; 1 Asian, non-Hispanic/Latino; 1 Hispanic/Latino), 2 international. Average age 31. 29 applicants, 69% accepted, 10 enrolled. In 2016, 12 master's awarded. *Degree requirements:* For master's, comprehensive exam, thesis or 450-hour internship. *Entrance requirements:* Additional exam requirements/recommendations for international students: Required—TOEFL. *Application deadline:* For fall admission, 8/1 for domestic students, 5/1 for international students; for winter admission, 12/1 for domestic students, 10/1 for international students; for spring admission, 3/15 for domestic students, 3/1 for international students. Application fee: $45. *Application contact:* Dr. Stephen McGregor, Program Coordinator, 734-487-0090, Fax: 734-487-2024, E-mail: smcgregor@emich.edu.

East Tennessee State University, School of Graduate Studies, College of Education, Department of Kinesiology, Sport and Recreation Management, Johnson City, TN 37614. Offers kinesiology, sport and recreation management (Post-Master's Certificate); sport management (MA). *Program availability:* Part-time, evening/weekend. Terminal master's awarded for partial completion of doctoral program. *Degree requirements:* For master's, comprehensive exam, thesis or internship. *Entrance requirements:* For master's, GRE General Test or GMAT, undergraduate degree in related field; minimum GPA of 2.7; resume; three references; essay explaining goals and reasons for pursuing degree; for Post-Master's Certificate, three letters of recommendation. Additional exam requirements/recommendations for international students: Required—TOEFL (minimum score 550 paper-based; 79 iBT). Electronic applications accepted. *Faculty research:* Methods of training for individual and team sports, enhancing acute sport performance, fatigue management in athletes, risk management, facilities management, motorsport.

East Texas Baptist University, Master of Science in Kinesiology Program, Marshall, TX 75670-1498. Offers MS. *Program availability:* Part-time, evening/weekend. *Faculty:* 2 full-time (0 women). *Students:* 3 part-time (0 women); includes 1 minority (Black or African American, non-Hispanic/Latino). Average age 29. 2 applicants, 100% accepted, 2 enrolled. *Entrance requirements:* Additional exam requirements/recommendations for international students: Recommended—TOEFL (minimum score 550 paper-based; 79 iBT). *Application deadline:* For fall admission, 8/17 for domestic students; for spring admission, 1/10 for domestic students; for summer admission, 5/2 for domestic students. Applications are processed on a rolling basis. Application fee: $50. Electronic applications accepted. *Expenses:* $700 per credit hour tuition; $150 per semester fees (6 or more hours enrolled); $75 per semester fees (1-5 hours enrolled). *Financial support:* In 2016–17, 3 students received support. Federal Work-Study, scholarships/grants, unspecified assistantships, and staff grants available. Financial award applicants required to submit FAFSA. *Unit head:* Dr. Joseph D. Brown, Dean, Frank S. Groner School of Professional Studies, 903-923-2270, Fax: 903-935-4318, E-mail: jbrown@etbu.edu. *Application contact:* Den Murley, Director of Graduate Admissions, 903-923-2079, Fax: 903-934-8115, E-mail: dmurley@etbu.edu.
Website: https://www.etbu.edu/school-professional-studies/kinesiology/ms-kinesiology/

Fresno Pacific University, Graduate Programs, Program in Kinesiology, Fresno, CA 93702-4709. Offers MA. *Entrance requirements:* Additional exam requirements/recommendations for international students: Required—TOEFL (minimum score 550 paper-based).

Georgia College & State University, Graduate School, College of Health Sciences, School of Health and Human Performance, Milledgeville, GA 31061. Offers health and human performance (MS), including health performance, health promotion; kinesiology/health education (MAT). *Accreditation:* NCATE (one or more programs are accredited). *Program availability:* Part-time, evening/weekend, 100% online. *Students:* 43 full-time (25 women), 17 part-time (15 women); includes 6 minority (4 Black or African American, non-Hispanic/Latino; 1 Asian, non-Hispanic/Latino; 1 Hispanic/Latino), 1 international. Average age 28. 33 applicants, 100% accepted, 28 enrolled. In 2016, 23 master's awarded. *Degree requirements:* For master's, completed in 6 years with minimum GPA of 3.0, thesis or project (for MS); minimum GPA of 3.0, GACE Exam and Assessment, and electronic teaching portfolio (for MAT). *Entrance requirements:* For master's, GRE with minimum score of 297 or MAT with minimum score of 385 (for MS); SAT (minimum score of 1000), ACT (minimum score of 43), GRE (minimum score of 297), MAT (minimum score of 385), or GACE Program Admission Assessment (for MAT), resume, 3 professional references; minimum GPA of 2.75 in upper-level undergraduate courses and undergraduate statistics course (for MS); minimum GPA of 2.75 on upper-division major courses (for MAT). *Application deadline:* For fall admission, 7/15 priority date for

domestic students, 4/1 for international students; for spring admission, 11/15 priority date for domestic students, 9/1 for international students; for summer admission, 4/15 priority date for domestic students. Applications are processed on a rolling basis. Application fee: $40. Electronic applications accepted. *Expenses:* $228 per credit hour in-state tuition, $1,027 per credit hour out-of-state tuition, $1,990 per year fees (for MAT); $338 per credit hour (for MS). *Financial support:* In 2016–17, 24 students received support. Unspecified assistantships available. Support available to part-time students. Financial award application deadline: 3/1; financial award applicants required to submit FAFSA. *Unit head:* Dr. Lisa Griffin, Director, School of Health and Human Performance, 478-445-4072, Fax: 478-445-4074, E-mail: lisa.griffin@gcsu.edu.
Website: http://www.gcsu.edu/health/shhp

Georgia Southern University, Jack N. Averitt College of Graduate Studies, College of Health and Human Sciences, School of Health and Kinesiology, Program in Kinesiology, Statesboro, GA 30458. Offers MS. *Program availability:* Part-time. *Students:* 68 full-time (41 women), 28 part-time (8 women); includes 14 minority (7 Black or African American, non-Hispanic/Latino; 6 Hispanic/Latino; 1 Two or more races, non-Hispanic/Latino), 3 international. Average age 26. 105 applicants, 34% accepted, 21 enrolled. In 2016, 46 master's awarded. *Entrance requirements:* For master's, minimum GPA of 2.75. Additional exam requirements/recommendations for international students: Required—TOEFL (minimum score 550 paper-based; 80 iBT), IELTS (minimum score 6). *Application deadline:* For fall admission, 2/1 for domestic students. Application fee: $50. Electronic applications accepted. *Expenses:* Contact institution. *Financial support:* In 2016–17, 21 students received support, including 12 fellowships with full tuition reimbursements available (averaging $7,750 per year), 1 research assistantship with full tuition reimbursement available (averaging $7,750 per year), 33 teaching assistantships with full tuition reimbursements available (averaging $7,750 per year). Financial award application deadline: 4/20; financial award applicants required to submit FAFSA. *Faculty research:* Athletic training, coaching, exercise science, nutrition and food science, sport psychology, sport management, physical education. *Unit head:* Dr. Kathi Thomas, Chair, 912-478-0200, Fax: 912-478-0381, E-mail: kthomas@georgiasouthern.edu.

Georgia State University, College of Education and Human Development, Department of Kinesiology and Health, Program in Kinesiology, Atlanta, GA 30302-3083. Offers PhD. *Degree requirements:* For doctorate, comprehensive exam, thesis/dissertation. *Entrance requirements:* For doctorate, GRE General Test or MAT, minimum GPA of 3.3. *Application deadline:* For fall admission, 3/1 for domestic students; for spring admission, 10/1 for domestic students. Application fee: $50. *Expenses:* Tuition, state resident: full-time $6876; part-time $382 per credit hour. Tuition, nonresident: full-time $22,374; part-time $1243 per credit hour. *Required fees:* $2128; $1064 per term. Part-time tuition and fees vary according to course load and program. *Financial support:* Research assistantships and teaching assistantships available. *Faculty research:* Aging, exercise metabolism, biomechanics and ergonomics, blood pressure regulation, exercise performance. *Unit head:* Dr. Jacalyn Lea Lund, Chair, 404-413-8051, E-mail: jlund@gsu.edu. *Application contact:* Dr. Christopher Ingalls, Program Coordinator, 404-413-8377, E-mail: cingalls@gsu.edu.
Website: http://kh.education.gsu.edu/

Hardin-Simmons University, Graduate School, Irvin School of Education, Department of Fitness and Sport Sciences, Program in Kinesiology, Sport, and Recreation, Abilene, TX 79698-0001. Offers M Ed. *Program availability:* Part-time. *Faculty:* 5 full-time (2 women). *Students:* 9 full-time (6 women), 18 part-time (9 women); includes 10 minority (5 Black or African American, non-Hispanic/Latino; 4 Hispanic/Latino; 1 Two or more races, non-Hispanic/Latino), 1 international. Average age 25. In 2016, 14 master's awarded. *Degree requirements:* For master's, comprehensive exam, thesis optional, internship, project. *Entrance requirements:* For master's, minimum undergraduate GPA of 3.0 in major, 2.7 overall; interview; writing sample; letters of recommendation; resume. Additional exam requirements/recommendations for international students: Required—TOEFL (minimum score 550 paper-based; 75 iBT). *Application deadline:* For fall admission, 8/15 priority date for domestic students, 4/1 for international students; for spring admission, 1/5 priority date for domestic students, 9/1 for international students. Applications are processed on a rolling basis. Application fee: $50. Electronic applications accepted. *Expenses: Tuition:* Full-time $12,510; part-time $695 per credit hour. *Required fees:* $325; $110 per semester. *Financial support:* In 2016–17, 12 students received support, including 8 fellowships (averaging $2,500 per year); career-related internships or fieldwork, scholarships/grants, and recreation assistantships also available. Support available to part-time students. Financial award application deadline: 6/30; financial award applicants required to submit FAFSA. *Unit head:* Dr. Lindsay Edwards, Program Director, 325-670-5893, Fax: 325-670-1218, E-mail: ledwards@hsutx.edu. *Application contact:* Dr. Nancy Kucinski, Dean of Graduate Studies, 325-670-1298, Fax: 325-670-1564, E-mail: gradoff@hsutx.edu.
Website: http://www.hsutx.edu/academics/irvin/graduate/kinesiology

Humboldt State University, Academic Programs, College of Professional Studies, Department of Kinesiology and Recreation Administration, Arcata, CA 95521-8299. Offers kinesiology (MS). *Degree requirements:* For master's, thesis or alternative. *Entrance requirements:* For master's, GMAT, minimum GPA of 2.5. Additional exam requirements/recommendations for international students: Required—TOEFL. *Expenses:* Tuition, state resident: full-time $6738; part-time $1953 per semester. Tuition, nonresident: full-time $13,434; part-time $3813 per semester. *Required fees:* $1738; $653 per semester. Tuition and fees vary according to program. *Faculty research:* Human performance, adapted physical education, physical therapy.

Indiana University Bloomington, School of Public Health, Department of Kinesiology, Bloomington, IN 47405. Offers applied sport science (MS); athletic administration/sport management (MS); athletic training (MS); biomechanics (MS); ergonomics (MS); exercise physiology (MS); human performance (PhD), including biomechanics, exercise physiology, motor learning/control, sport management; motor learning/control (MS); physical activity (MPH); physical activity, fitness and wellness (MS). *Program availability:* Part-time. Terminal master's awarded for partial completion of doctoral program. *Degree requirements:* For master's, thesis optional; for doctorate, variable foreign language requirement, comprehensive exam, thesis/dissertation. *Entrance requirements:* For master's, GRE General Test, minimum GPA of 2.8; for doctorate, GRE General Test, minimum graduate GPA of 3.5, undergraduate 3.0. Additional exam requirements/recommendations for international students: Required—TOEFL (minimum score 80 iBT). *Faculty research:* Exercise physiology and biochemistry, sports biomechanics, human motor control, adaptation of fitness and exercise to special populations.

Indiana University–Purdue University Indianapolis, School of Physical Education and Tourism Management, Indianapolis, IN 46202-5193. Offers event tourism (MS), including sport event tourism; kinesiology (MS), including clinical exercise science; public health (Graduate Certificate). *Faculty:* 15 full-time (4 women). *Students:* 18 full-time (9 women), 16 part-time (8 women); includes 4 minority (3 Black or African American, non-Hispanic/Latino; 1 Hispanic/Latino), 1 international. Average age 26. 22 applicants, 86% accepted, 13 enrolled. In 2016, 11 master's awarded. *Degree requirements:* For master's, comprehensive exam (for some programs), thesis (for some programs). *Entrance requirements:* For master's, GRE. Additional exam requirements/recommendations for international students: Required—TOEFL. Application fee: $60 ($65 for international students). Electronic applications accepted. *Expenses:* Contact institution. *Financial support:* In 2016–17, 15 students received support. Teaching assistantships, unspecified assistantships, and assistantships with community partners available. Financial award application deadline: 3/15; financial award applicants required to submit FAFSA. *Faculty research:* Physical activity, exercise and diseases; human movement science; sport performance; sport event tourism; destination marketing and event management;. *Unit head:* Dr. Zachary Riley, Assistant Professor and Director of Graduate Program, 317-274-0600, Fax: 317-278-2041, E-mail: zariley@iupui.edu.
Website: http://petm.iupui.edu/

Inter American University of Puerto Rico, San Germán Campus, Graduate Studies Center, Program in Health and Physical Education, San Germán, PR 00683-5008. Offers MA. *Program availability:* Part-time, evening/weekend. *Degree requirements:* For master's, comprehensive exam. *Entrance requirements:* For master's, GRE General Test or EXADEP, minimum GPA of 3.0.

Iowa State University of Science and Technology, Department of Kinesiology, Ames, IA 50011. Offers MS, PhD. *Entrance requirements:* For master's and doctorate, GRE General Test. Additional exam requirements/recommendations for international students: Required—TOEFL (minimum score 560 paper-based; 79 iBT), IELTS (minimum score 6.5). *Application deadline:* For fall admission, 1/1 priority date for domestic students, 1/1 for international students. Application fee: $60 ($90 for international students). Electronic applications accepted. *Application contact:* Dr. Jason Gillette, Application Contact, 515-294-8009, Fax: 515-294-8740, E-mail: gillette@iastate.edu.
Website: http://www.kin.hs.iastate.edu/graduate/

Jacksonville University, Brooks Rehabilitation College of Healthcare Sciences, School of Applied Health Sciences, Program in Kinesiological Sciences, Jacksonville, FL 32211. Offers MS. *Degree requirements:* For master's, thesis, internship. *Expenses: Tuition:* Full-time $13,320. One-time fee: $50 part-time. Tuition and fees vary according to course load, degree level, campus/location and program.

James Madison University, The Graduate School, College of Health and Behavioral Sciences, Program in Health Sciences, Harrisonburg, VA 22807. Offers nutrition and physical activity (MS). *Program availability:* Part-time. *Students:* 6 full-time (2 women), 1 (woman) part-time; includes 2 minority (1 Black or African American, non-Hispanic/Latino; 1 Hispanic/Latino), 1 international. Average age 30. 9 applicants, 78% accepted, 5 enrolled. In 2016, 5 master's awarded. Application fee: $55. Electronic applications accepted. *Financial support:* Federal Work-Study and 1 assistantship (averaging $7911) available. Financial award application deadline: 3/1; financial award applicants required to submit FAFSA. *Unit head:* Dr. Allen Lewis, Department Head, 540-568-6510, E-mail: amatohk@jmu.edu. *Application contact:* Lynette D. Michael, Director of Graduate Admissions and Student Records, 540-568-6131 Ext. 6395, Fax: 540-568-7860, E-mail: michaeld@jmu.edu.
Website: http://www.healthsci.jmu.edu/index.html

James Madison University, The Graduate School, College of Health and Behavioral Sciences, Program in Kinesiology, Harrisonburg, VA 22802. Offers clinical exercise physiology (MS); exercise physiology (MS); kinesiology (MAT, MS); nutrition and exercise (MS); physical and health education (MAT); sport and recreation leadership (MS). *Program availability:* Part-time, evening/weekend. *Faculty:* 9 full-time (3 women), 2 part-time/adjunct (1 woman). *Students:* 64 full-time (27 women), 8 part-time (5 women); includes 6 minority (1 Black or African American, non-Hispanic/Latino; 1 Asian, non-Hispanic/Latino; 2 Hispanic/Latino; 2 Two or more races, non-Hispanic/Latino). Average age 30. 140 applicants, 70% accepted, 44 enrolled. In 2016, 42 master's awarded. Application fee: $55. Electronic applications accepted. *Financial support:* In 2016–17, 45 students received support, including 14 teaching assistantships with full tuition reimbursements available (averaging $8,837 per year); Federal Work-Study and 25 assistantships (averaging $7911), 20 athletic assistantships (averaging $9284) also available. Financial award application deadline: 3/1; financial award applicants required to submit FAFSA. *Unit head:* Dr. Christopher J. Womack, Department Head, 540-568-6145, E-mail: womackcx@jmu.edu. *Application contact:* Lynette D. Michael, Director of Graduate Admissions, 540-568-6131 Ext. 6395, Fax: 540-568-7860, E-mail: michaeld@jmu.edu.
Website: http://www.jmu.edu/kinesiology/

Kansas State University, Graduate School, College of Human Ecology, Department of Food, Nutrition, Dietetics and Health, Manhattan, KS 66506. Offers dietetics (MS); human nutrition (PhD); nutrition, dietetics and sensory sciences (MS); nutritional sciences (PhD); public health nutrition (PhD); public health physical activity (PhD); sensory analysis and consumer behavior (PhD). *Program availability:* Part-time. *Faculty:* 17 full-time (11 women), 11 part-time/adjunct (3 women). *Students:* 27 full-time (20 women), 32 part-time (26 women); includes 5 minority (2 Black or African American, non-Hispanic/Latino; 1 Asian, non-Hispanic/Latino; 2 Hispanic/Latino), 17 international. Average age 31. 18 applicants, 50% accepted, 5 enrolled. In 2016, 15 master's, 5 doctorates awarded. *Degree requirements:* For master's, thesis or alternative, residency; for doctorate, thesis/dissertation, residency. *Entrance requirements:* For master's, GRE General Test, minimum undergraduate GPA of 3.0; for doctorate, GRE General Test, minimum graduate GPA of 3.0. Additional exam requirements/recommendations for international students: Required—TOEFL (minimum score 550 paper-based; 79 iBT), IELTS (minimum score 6.5). *Application deadline:* For fall admission, 2/1 priority date for domestic and international students; for spring admission, 8/1 priority date for domestic and international students. Applications are processed on a rolling basis. Application fee: $50 ($75 for international students). Electronic applications accepted. *Expenses:* Tuition, state resident: full-time $9670. Tuition, nonresident: full-time $21,828. *Required fees:* $862. *Financial support:* In 2016–17, 29 students received support, including 16 research assistantships with full and partial tuition reimbursements available (averaging $15,711 per year), 6 teaching assistantships with full and partial tuition reimbursements available (averaging $10,107 per year); career-related internships or fieldwork, Federal Work-Study, institutionally sponsored loans, scholarships/grants, health care benefits, and tuition waivers (full and partial) also available. Support available to part-time students. Financial award application deadline: 3/1; financial award applicants required to submit FAFSA. *Faculty research:* Cancer and immunology, obesity, sensory analysis and consumer behavior, nutrient metabolism, clinical and community interventions. *Total annual research expenditures:* $1.1 million. *Unit head:* Dr. Mark Haub, Head, 785-532-5508, Fax: 785-532-3132, E-mail: haub@ksu.edu. *Application contact:* Karen Rogers, Administrative Assistant, 785-532-0124, E-mail: karen39@k-state.edu.
Website: http://www.he.k-state.edu/fndh/

Kansas State University, Graduate School, College of Human Ecology, Department of Kinesiology, Manhattan, KS 66506. Offers MS, PhD. *Program availability:* Part-time. *Faculty:* 10 full-time (3 women), 1 part-time/adjunct (0 women). *Students:* 13 full-time (8 women), 6 part-time (0 women); includes 2 minority (both Hispanic/Latino). Average age 25. 19 applicants, 58% accepted, 5 enrolled. In 2016, 12 master's awarded. *Degree requirements:* For master's, thesis or final comprehensive exam; for doctorate, comprehensive exam, thesis/dissertation. *Entrance requirements:* For master's, GRE General Test, bachelor's degree in kinesiology or exercise science, minimum GPA of 3.0; for doctorate, GRE General Test. Additional exam requirements/recommendations

for international students: Required—TOEFL. *Application deadline:* For fall admission, 2/1 priority date for domestic and international students; for spring admission, 8/1 priority date for domestic and international students. Applications are processed on a rolling basis. Application fee: $50 ($75 for international students). Electronic applications accepted. *Expenses:* Contact institution. *Financial support:* In 2016–17, 15 teaching assistantships with full tuition reimbursements (averaging $14,167 per year) were awarded. Financial award application deadline: 3/1; financial award applicants required to submit FAFSA. *Faculty research:* Exercise physiology, vascular function, cardiorespiratory disease, microgravity, cancer, physical inactivity, exercise adherence and compliance, public health/physical activity. *Total annual research expenditures:* $82,627. *Unit head:* Dr. Craig Harms, Head, 785-532-6765, Fax: 785-532-6486, E-mail: caharms@ksu.edu. *Application contact:* Prof. Thomas J. Barstow, Graduate Program Coordinator, 785-532-0712, Fax: 785-532-6486, E-mail: tbarsto@ksu.edu.
Website: http://www.k-state.edu/kines/

Kansas State University, Graduate School, College of Human Ecology, Doctorate in Human Ecology Program, Manhattan, KS 66506-1407. Offers apparel and textiles (PhD); applied family sciences (PhD); couple and family therapy (PhD); hospitality administration (PhD); kinesiology (PhD); life-span human development (PhD). *Program availability:* Part-time. *Faculty:* 36 full-time (23 women). *Students:* 44 full-time (26 women), 16 part-time (10 women); includes 9 minority (3 Black or African American, non-Hispanic/Latino; 2 Asian, non-Hispanic/Latino; 2 Hispanic/Latino; 2 Two or more races, non-Hispanic/Latino), 18 international. Average age 30. 43 applicants, 35% accepted, 8 enrolled. In 2016, 13 doctorates awarded. *Degree requirements:* For doctorate, thesis/dissertation. *Entrance requirements:* Additional exam requirements/recommendations for international students: Required—TOEFL. *Application deadline:* For fall admission, 2/1 priority date for domestic and international students; for spring admission, 8/1 priority date for domestic and international students. Applications are processed on a rolling basis. Application fee: $50 ($75 for international students). Electronic applications accepted. *Expenses:* Tuition, state resident: full-time $9670. Tuition, nonresident: full-time $21,828. *Required fees:* $862. *Financial support:* In 2016–17, research assistantships with partial tuition reimbursements (averaging $12,000 per year), teaching assistantships with partial tuition reimbursements (averaging $12,000 per year) were awarded. Financial award application deadline: 3/1. *Total annual research expenditures:* $1.8 million. *Unit head:* Dr. John Buckwalter, Dean, 785-532-5500, Fax: 785-532-5504, E-mail: jbb3@ksu.edu. *Application contact:* Dr. Bronwyn Fees, Associate Dean for Academic Affairs, 785-532-5500, Fax: 785-532-5504, E-mail: fees@ksu.edu.

Lakehead University, Graduate Studies, School of Kinesiology, Thunder Bay, ON P7B 5E1, Canada. Offers kinesiology (M Sc); kinesiology and gerontology (M Sc). *Program availability:* Part-time. *Degree requirements:* For master's, thesis. *Entrance requirements:* For master's, minimum B average. Additional exam requirements/recommendations for international students: Required—TOEFL. *Faculty research:* Social psychology and physical education, sport history, sports medicine, exercise physiology, gerontology.

Lamar University, College of Graduate Studies, College of Education and Human Development, Department of Health and Kinesiology, Beaumont, TX 77710. Offers public health (MS); science of kinesiology promotion (MS). *Faculty:* 9 full-time (4 women). *Students:* 49 full-time (29 women), 19 part-time (12 women); includes 42 minority (32 Black or African American, non-Hispanic/Latino; 6 Hispanic/Latino; 1 Native Hawaiian or other Pacific Islander, non-Hispanic/Latino; 3 Two or more races, non-Hispanic/Latino), 4 international. Average age 28. 42 applicants, 100% accepted, 31 enrolled. In 2016, 13 master's awarded. *Degree requirements:* For master's, comprehensive exam (for some programs), thesis optional. *Entrance requirements:* For master's, GRE General Test, minimum GPA of 2.5. Additional exam requirements/recommendations for international students: Required—TOEFL (minimum score 550 paper-based; 79 iBT), IELTS (minimum score 6.5). *Application deadline:* For fall admission, 8/10 for domestic students, 7/1 for international students; for spring admission, 1/5 for domestic students, 12/1 for international students. Applications are processed on a rolling basis. Application fee: $25. Electronic applications accepted. *Expenses:* $8,134 in-state full-time, $5,574 in-state part-time; $15,604 out-of-state full-time, $10,554 out-of-state part-time per year. *Financial support:* Teaching assistantships available. Financial award application deadline: 4/1; financial award applicants required to submit FAFSA. *Faculty research:* Motor learning, exercise physiology, pedagogy. *Unit head:* Dr. Bill Holmes, Interim Chair, 409-880-8724, Fax: 409-880-1761. *Application contact:* Deidre Mayer, Interim Director, Admissions and Academic Services, 409-880-8888, Fax: 409-880-7419, E-mail: gradmissions@lamar.edu.
Website: http://education.lamar.edu/health-and-kinesiology

Louisiana State University and Agricultural & Mechanical College, Graduate School, College of Human Sciences and Education, Department of Kinesiology, Baton Rouge, LA 70803. Offers MS, PhD.

McGill University, Faculty of Graduate and Postdoctoral Studies, Faculty of Education, Department of Kinesiology and Physical Education, Montréal, QC H3A 2T5, Canada. Offers M Sc, MA, PhD, Certificate, Diploma.

McMaster University, School of Graduate Studies, Faculty of Social Sciences, Department of Kinesiology, Hamilton, ON L8S 4M2, Canada. Offers human biodynamics (M Sc, PhD). *Degree requirements:* For master's, thesis. *Entrance requirements:* For master's, minimum B+ average in undergraduate course work. Additional exam requirements/recommendations for international students: Required—TOEFL (minimum score 580 paper-based). *Faculty research:* Motor learning and control, neuromuscular physiology, exercise rehabilitation, cellular responses to exercise, management.

Memorial University of Newfoundland, School of Graduate Studies, School of Human Kinetics and Recreation, St. John's, NL A1C 5S7, Canada. Offers administration, curriculum and supervision (MPE); biomechanics/ergonomics (MS Kin); exercise and work physiology (MS Kin); psychology of sport, exercise and recreation (MS Kin); socio-cultural studies of physical activity and health (MS Kin). *Program availability:* Part-time. *Degree requirements:* For master's, thesis optional, seminars, thesis presentations. *Entrance requirements:* For master's, bachelor's degree in a related field, minimum B average. Electronic applications accepted. *Faculty research:* Administration, sociology of sports, kinesiology, physiology/recreation.

Michigan State University, The Graduate School, College of Education, Department of Kinesiology, East Lansing, MI 48824. Offers MS, PhD. *Entrance requirements:* Additional exam requirements/recommendations for international students: Required—TOEFL. Electronic applications accepted.

Michigan Technological University, Graduate School, College of Sciences and Arts, Department of Kinesiology and Integrative Physiology, Houghton, MI 49931. Offers kinesiology (MS). *Program availability:* Part-time. *Faculty:* 9 full-time, 2 part-time/adjunct. *Students:* 3 full-time, 3 part-time. Average age 24. 10 applicants, 40% accepted, 3 enrolled. In 2016, 7 master's awarded. *Degree requirements:* For master's, thesis (for some programs). *Entrance requirements:* For master's, GRE (Michigan Tech students with a GPA of 3.5 or above exempt), statement of purpose, personal statement, official transcripts, 2-3 letters of recommendation, resume/curriculum vitae. Additional exam requirements/recommendations for international students: Required—TOEFL (recommended minimum score 79 iBT) or IELTS (minimum score 6.5). *Application deadline:* Applications are processed on a rolling basis. Electronic applications accepted. *Expenses:* Tuition, state resident: full-time $16,290; part-time $905 per credit. Tuition, nonresident: full-time $16,290; part-time $905 per credit. *Required fees:* $248; $124 per term. Tuition and fees vary according to course load and program. *Financial support:* In 2016–17, 4 students received support, including 2 fellowships (averaging $15,242 per year), research assistantships (averaging $15,242 per year), teaching assistantships (averaging $15,242 per year); career-related internships or fieldwork, Federal Work-Study, health care benefits, and unspecified assistantships also available. Financial award applicants required to submit FAFSA. *Faculty research:* Electrophysiology and hypertension, neural control of circulation, molecular physiology and hypertension, human aeromechanics, musculoskeletal control of movement. *Total annual research expenditures:* $371,761. *Unit head:* Dr. Jason R. Carter, Chair, 906-487-2994, Fax: 906-487-0985, E-mail: jcarter@mtu.edu. *Application contact:* Carol T. Wingerson, Administrative Aide, 906-487-2328, Fax: 906-487-2284, E-mail: gradadms@mtu.edu.
Website: http://www.mtu.edu/kip/

Mississippi College, Graduate School, School of Education, Department of Kinesiology, Clinton, MS 39058. Offers athletic administration (MS). *Degree requirements:* For master's, comprehensive exam, thesis optional. *Entrance requirements:* For master's, GRE, GMAT, or PRAXIS, minimum GPA of 2.5. Additional exam requirements/recommendations for international students: Recommended—TOEFL, IELTS. Electronic applications accepted.

Mississippi State University, College of Education, Department of Kinesiology, Mississippi State, MS 39762. Offers exercise physiology (MS); exercise science (PhD); sport administration (MS); sport pedagogy (MS); sport studies (PhD). *Program availability:* Part-time, blended/hybrid learning. *Faculty:* 14 full-time (2 women). *Students:* 57 full-time (17 women), 6 part-time (0 women); includes 11 minority (5 Black or African American, non-Hispanic/Latino; 2 Asian, non-Hispanic/Latino; 2 Hispanic/Latino; 2 Two or more races, non-Hispanic/Latino), 6 international. Average age 26. 75 applicants, 56% accepted, 30 enrolled. In 2016, 32 master's awarded. *Degree requirements:* For master's, comprehensive exam, thesis optional; for doctorate, comprehensive exam. *Entrance requirements:* For master's, GRE General Test, minimum GPA of 2.75 on undergraduate work from four-year accredited institution, 3.0 graduate; for doctorate, GRE, minimum GPA of 3.4 on previous graduate degree(s) earned from accredited institutions. Additional exam requirements/recommendations for international students: Required—TOEFL (minimum score 550 paper-based; 79 iBT); Recommended—IELTS (minimum score 6.5). *Application deadline:* For fall admission, 7/1 for domestic students, 5/1 for international students; for spring admission, 11/1 for domestic students, 9/1 for international students. Applications are processed on a rolling basis. Application fee: $60. Electronic applications accepted. *Expenses:* Tuition, state resident: full-time $7670; part-time $852.50 per credit hour. Tuition, nonresident: full-time $20,790; part-time $2310.50 per credit hour. Part-time tuition and fees vary according to course load. *Financial support:* In 2016–17, 16 teaching assistantships with partial tuition reimbursements (averaging $10,227 per year) were awarded; career-related internships or fieldwork, Federal Work-Study, institutionally sponsored loans, and unspecified assistantships also available. Financial award application deadline: 4/1; financial award applicants required to submit FAFSA. *Faculty research:* Static balance and stepping performance of older adults, organizational justice, public health, strength training and recovery drinks, high risk drinking perceptions and behaviors. *Unit head:* Dr. Stanley P. Brown, Professor and Department Head, 662-325-2963, Fax: 662-325-4525, E-mail: spb107@msstate.edu. *Application contact:* Linda Bonner, Senior Admissions Assistant, 662-325-3363, E-mail: lbonner@grad.msstate.edu.
Website: http://www.kinesiology.msstate.edu/

Missouri State University, Graduate College, College of Health and Human Services, Department of Kinesiology, Springfield, MO 65897. Offers health promotion and wellness management (MS); secondary education (MS Ed), including physical education. *Program availability:* Part-time. *Faculty:* 14 full-time (6 women). *Students:* 19 full-time (7 women), 8 part-time (4 women); includes 3 minority (1 Black or African American, non-Hispanic/Latino; 1 Asian, non-Hispanic/Latino; 1 Hispanic/Latino), 1 international. Average age 26. 19 applicants, 63% accepted, 7 enrolled. In 2016, 14 master's awarded. *Degree requirements:* For master's, comprehensive exam, thesis or alternative. *Entrance requirements:* For master's, GRE (for MS), minimum GPA of 2.8 (MS); 9-12 teaching certification (MS Ed). Additional exam requirements/recommendations for international students: Required—TOEFL (minimum score 550 paper-based; 79 iBT), IELTS (minimum score 6). *Application deadline:* For fall admission, 7/20 priority date for domestic students, 5/1 for international students; for spring admission, 12/20 priority date for domestic students, 9/1 for international students. Applications are processed on a rolling basis. Application fee: $35 ($50 for international students). Electronic applications accepted. *Expenses:* Tuition, state resident: full-time $5830. Tuition, nonresident: full-time $10,708. *Required fees:* $1130. Tuition and fees vary according to class time, course level, course load and program. *Financial support:* In 2016–17, 7 teaching assistantships with partial tuition reimbursements (averaging $8,772 per year) were awarded; Federal Work-Study, institutionally sponsored loans, scholarships/grants, and unspecified assistantships also available. Financial award application deadline: 3/31; financial award applicants required to submit FAFSA. *Unit head:* Dr. Sarah McCallister, Head, 417-836-6582, Fax: 417-836-5371, E-mail: sarahmccallister@missouristate.edu. *Application contact:* Michael Edwards, Coordinator of Graduate Admissions, 417-836-5330, Fax: 417-836-6200, E-mail: michaeledwards@missouristate.edu.
Website: http://www.missouristate.edu/kinesiology/

New Mexico State University, College of Education, Department of Kinesiology and Dance, Las Cruces, NM 88003. Offers kinesiology (PhD). *Program availability:* Part-time. *Faculty:* 10 full-time (3 women). *Students:* 1 full-time, 1 (woman) part-time; includes 1 minority (Two or more races, non-Hispanic/Latino), 1 international. Average age 29. 2 applicants, 100% accepted, 1 enrolled. *Degree requirements:* For doctorate, comprehensive exam, thesis/dissertation, qualifying exam. *Entrance requirements:* For doctorate, GRE General Test, bachelor's and master's degrees in related field; minimum cumulative GPA of 3.0; 3 letters of recommendation; curriculum vitae or resume. Additional exam requirements/recommendations for international students: Required—TOEFL (minimum score 550 paper-based; 79 iBT), IELTS (minimum score 6.5). *Application deadline:* For fall admission, 1/15 for domestic and international students. Application fee: $40 ($50 for international students). Electronic applications accepted. *Expenses:* Tuition, state resident: full-time $4086. Tuition, nonresident: full-time $14,254. *Required fees:* $853. Tuition and fees vary according to course load. *Financial support:* In 2016–17, 1 student received support, including 4 research assistantships (averaging $13,228 per year), 7 teaching assistantships (averaging $13,551 per year); career-related internships or fieldwork, Federal Work-Study, scholarships/grants, traineeships, health care benefits, and unspecified assistantships also available. Support available to part-time students. Financial award application deadline: 3/1. *Faculty research:* Biomechanics of muscle injury; fighting youth inactivity and obesity; aging and falls prevention. *Total annual research expenditures:* $5,965. *Unit head:* Dr. Robert Wood, Department Head, 575-646-2441, Fax: 575-646-4065, E-mail:

bobwood@nmsu.edu. *Application contact:* 575-646-4067, Fax: 575-646-4065.
Website: http://kind.nmsu.edu

New York University, Steinhardt School of Culture, Education, and Human Development, Department of Physical Therapy, New York, NY 10010-5615. Offers orthopedic physical therapy (Advanced Certificate); physical therapy (MA, DPT, PhD), including pathokinesiology (MA). *Accreditation:* APTA (one or more programs are accredited). *Program availability:* Part-time. *Degree requirements:* For master's, thesis (for some programs); for doctorate, thesis/dissertation. *Entrance requirements:* For master's, physical therapy certificate; for doctorate, GRE General Test, interview, physical therapy certificate. Additional exam requirements/recommendations for international students: Required—TOEFL (minimum score 100 iBT). Electronic applications accepted. *Faculty research:* Motor learning and control, neuromuscular disorders, biomechanics and ergonomics, movement analysis, pathomechanics.

Northeastern State University, College of Education, Department of Health and Kinesiology, Tahlequah, OK 74464-2399. Offers MS. *Program availability:* Part-time, evening/weekend. *Faculty:* 3 full-time (all women). *Students:* 11 full-time (4 women), 22 part-time (11 women); includes 14 minority (2 Black or African American, non-Hispanic/Latino; 8 American Indian or Alaska Native, non-Hispanic/Latino; 1 Hispanic/Latino; 3 Two or more races, non-Hispanic/Latino), 3 international. Average age 27. In 2016, 14 master's awarded. *Entrance requirements:* For master's, MAT or GRE, minimum GPA of 2.5. Additional exam requirements/recommendations for international students: Required—TOEFL. *Application deadline:* For fall admission, 6/1 for domestic and international students; for winter admission, 11/1 for domestic and international students; for spring admission, 3/1 for domestic students, 2/1 for international students. Applications are processed on a rolling basis. Application fee: $25. Electronic applications accepted. *Expenses:* Tuition, state resident: full-time $2816; part-time $216.60 per credit hour. Tuition, nonresident: full-time $6365; part-time $489.60 per credit hour. *Required fees:* $37.40 per credit hour. *Unit head:* Dr. Sonia Tinsley, Department Chair, 918-444-3915, E-mail: tinsleys@nsuok.edu. *Application contact:* Josh McCollum, Graduate Coordinator, 918-444-2093, E-mail: mccolluj@nsuok.edu.
Website: http://academics.nsuok.edu/education/DegreePrograms/GraduatePrograms/HealthandKinesiology.aspx

Northwestern University, Feinberg School of Medicine, Department of Physical Therapy and Human Movement Sciences, Chicago, IL 60611-2814. Offers neuroscience (PhD), including movement and rehabilitation science; physical therapy (DPT); DPT/PhD. *Accreditation:* APTA. *Faculty:* 32 full-time, 26 part-time/adjunct. *Students:* 281 full-time (208 women); includes 56 minority (8 Black or African American, non-Hispanic/Latino; 1 American Indian or Alaska Native, non-Hispanic/Latino; 32 Asian, non-Hispanic/Latino; 12 Hispanic/Latino; 1 Native Hawaiian or other Pacific Islander, non-Hispanic/Latino; 2 Two or more races, non-Hispanic/Latino). Average age 25. 581 applicants, 32% accepted, 93 enrolled. *Degree requirements:* For doctorate, research project. *Entrance requirements:* For doctorate, GRE General Test (for DPT), baccalaureate degree with minimum GPA of 3.0 in required course work (DPT). Additional exam requirements/recommendations for international students: Required—TOEFL (minimum score 600 paper-based; 100 iBT). *Application deadline:* For fall admission, 10/2 for domestic and international students. Applications are processed on a rolling basis. Application fee: $50. Electronic applications accepted. *Expenses:* Contact institution. *Financial support:* Institutionally sponsored loans and scholarships/grants available. Financial award application deadline: 3/1; financial award applicants required to submit FAFSA. *Faculty research:* Motor control, robotics, neuromuscular imaging, student performance (academic/professional), clinical outcomes. *Unit head:* Dr. Julius P. A. Dewald, Professor and Chair, 312-908-8160, Fax: 312-908-0741. *Application contact:* Dr. Jane Sullivan, Associate Professor/Assistant Chair for Recruitment and Admissions, 312-908-8160, Fax: 312-908-0741, E-mail: dpt-admissions@northwestern.edu.
Website: http://www.feinberg.northwestern.edu/sites/pthms/

The Ohio State University, Graduate School, College of Education and Human Ecology, Department of Human Sciences, Columbus, OH 43210. Offers consumer sciences (MS, PhD); human development and family science (PhD); human nutrition (MS, PhD); kinesiology (MA, PhD). *Program availability:* Part-time. *Faculty:* 54. *Students:* 128 full-time (77 women), 8 part-time (6 women); includes 21 minority (7 Black or African American, non-Hispanic/Latino; 8 Hispanic/Latino; 6 Two or more races, non-Hispanic/Latino), 30 international. Average age 27. In 2016, 27 master's, 17 doctorates awarded. *Degree requirements:* For master's, thesis optional; for doctorate, thesis/dissertation. *Entrance requirements:* For master's and doctorate, GRE. Additional exam requirements/recommendations for international students: Required—TOEFL (minimum score 550 paper-based; 79 iBT), Michigan English Language Assessment Battery (minimum score 82); Recommended—IELTS (minimum score 7). *Application deadline:* For fall admission, 12/1 priority date for domestic and international students. Applications are processed on a rolling basis. Application fee: $60 ($70 for international students). Electronic applications accepted. *Financial support:* Fellowships with tuition reimbursements, research assistantships with tuition reimbursements, teaching assistantships with tuition reimbursements, Federal Work-Study, and institutionally sponsored loans available. Support available to part-time students. *Unit head:* Dr. Joe Wheaton, Interim Chair, E-mail: wheaton.3@osu.edu. *Application contact:* Graduate and Professional Admissions, 614-292-9444, Fax: 614-292-3895, E-mail: gpadmissions@osu.edu.
Website: http://ehe.osu.edu/human-sciences/

Old Dominion University, College of Health Sciences, School of Physical Therapy and Athletic Training, Doctor of Kinesiology and Rehabilitation Program, Norfolk, VA 23529. Offers PhD. *Faculty:* 3 full-time (1 woman), 7 part-time/adjunct (3 women). *Students:* 7 full-time (5 women), 2 part-time (both women); includes 1 minority (Hispanic/Latino). Average age 29. 11 applicants, 82% accepted, 9 enrolled. *Degree requirements:* For doctorate, comprehensive exam, thesis/dissertation. *Entrance requirements:* For doctorate, master's degree or higher in an associated area of basic science, such as kinesiology, exercise science, or biomechanics, or in a health profession such as athletic training, nursing, occupational therapy, physical therapy, or speech/language pathology. Additional exam requirements/recommendations for international students: Recommended—TOEFL (minimum score 550 paper-based; 79 iBT), IELTS (minimum score 6.5). *Application deadline:* For fall admission, 2/1 for domestic and international students. Application fee: $50. Electronic applications accepted. *Expenses:* Tuition, state resident: full-time $8604; part-time $478 per credit hour. Tuition, nonresident: full-time $21,510; part-time $1195 per credit hour. *Required fees:* $66 per semester. Tuition and fees vary according to campus/location, program and reciprocity agreements. *Financial support:* In 2016–17, 5 students received support, including 5 research assistantships with full tuition reimbursements available (averaging $15,000 per year); unspecified assistantships also available. *Faculty research:* Balance and falls, gait, perceptual information in action and virtual reality, sensorimotor compromise following joint injury, evidence-based practice and patient-centered care. *Unit head:* Daniel Russell, Director, 757-683-6016, E-mail: dmrussel@odu.edu. *Application contact:* William Heffelfinger, Director of Graduate Admissions, 757-683-5554, Fax: 757-683-3255, E-mail: gradadmit@odu.edu.
Website: http://www.odu.edu/ptat/phd-kinesiology-rehabilitation

Old Dominion University, Darden College of Education, Program in Human Movement Science, Norfolk, VA 23529. Offers PhD. *Faculty:* 8 full-time (3 women). *Students:* 6 full-time (4 women), 3 part-time (1 woman); includes 2 minority (1 Black or African American, non-Hispanic/Latino; 1 Hispanic/Latino). Average age 33. 5 applicants, 20% accepted, 1 enrolled. In 2016, 2 doctorates awarded. *Degree requirements:* For doctorate, comprehensive exam, thesis/dissertation. *Entrance requirements:* For doctorate, GRE, minimum GPA of 3.0. Additional exam requirements/recommendations for international students: Required—TOEFL. *Application deadline:* For fall admission, 1/15 for domestic students. Application fee: $50. Electronic applications accepted. *Expenses:* Tuition, state resident: full-time $8604; part-time $478 per credit hour. Tuition, nonresident: full-time $21,510; part-time $1195 per credit hour. *Required fees:* $66 per semester. Tuition and fees vary according to campus/location, program and reciprocity agreements. *Financial support:* In 2016–17, 6 students received support, including 2 fellowships with full tuition reimbursements available (averaging $15,000 per year), 3 teaching assistantships with full tuition reimbursements available (averaging $15,000 per year); career-related internships or fieldwork, scholarships/grants, and unspecified assistantships also available. Financial award application deadline: 5/1. *Faculty research:* Biomechanics, exercise physiology, sport management, recreation management. *Total annual research expenditures:* $10,000. *Unit head:* Dr. Lynn Ridinger, Chair, 757-683-4353, Fax: 757-683-4270, E-mail: lridinge@odu.edu. *Application contact:* William Heffelfinger, Director of Graduate Admissions, 757-683-5554, Fax: 757-683-3255, E-mail: gradadmit@odu.edu.
Website: http://www.odu.edu/academics/programs/doctoral/human-movement-science

Old Dominion University, Darden College of Education, Program in Physical Education, Curriculum and Instruction Emphasis, Norfolk, VA 23529. Offers human movement sciences (PhD), including health and sport pedagogy; physical education (MS Ed), including adapted physical education, coaching education, curriculum and instruction. *Program availability:* Part-time, evening/weekend. *Faculty:* 2 full-time (0 women), 1 (woman) part-time/adjunct. *Students:* 5 full-time (2 women), 2 part-time (1 woman); includes 1 minority (Hispanic/Latino). Average age 29. 8 applicants, 75% accepted, 4 enrolled. In 2016, 4 master's awarded. *Degree requirements:* For master's, comprehensive exam (for some programs), thesis or alternative, internship, research project. *Entrance requirements:* For master's, GRE, PRAXIS Core (for licensure only), minimum GPA of 2.8 overall, 3.0 in major. Additional exam requirements/recommendations for international students: Required—TOEFL (minimum score 500 paper-based; 97 iBT). *Application deadline:* For fall admission, 3/1 priority date for domestic students; for spring admission, 11/1 for domestic students. Applications are processed on a rolling basis. Application fee: $50. Electronic applications accepted. *Expenses:* Tuition, state resident: full-time $8604; part-time $478 per credit hour. Tuition, nonresident: full-time $21,510; part-time $1195 per credit hour. *Required fees:* $66 per semester. Tuition and fees vary according to campus/location, program and reciprocity agreements. *Financial support:* In 2016–17, 2 students received support, including 1 teaching assistantship (averaging $10,000 per year); unspecified assistantships also available. Financial award application deadline: 4/15. *Faculty research:* Motor development, physical activity and fitness, motivation and learning in physical education, curriculum and instruction. *Unit head:* Dr. Lynn Ridinger, Chair, 757-683-4995, E-mail: lridinge@odu.edu. *Application contact:* William Heffelfinger, Director of Graduate Admissions, 757-683-5554, Fax: 757-683-3255, E-mail: gradadmit@odu.edu.
Website: http://education.odu.edu/eci/ciphd/

Oregon State University, College of Public Health and Human Sciences, Program in Kinesiology, Corvallis, OR 97331. Offers biophysical kinesiology (MS, PhD); psychosocial kinesiology (MS, PhD). *Program availability:* Part-time. *Faculty:* 14 full-time (6 women), 2 part-time/adjunct (1 woman). *Students:* 32 full-time (20 women), 1 (woman) part-time; includes 9 minority (1 Black or African American, non-Hispanic/Latino; 3 Asian, non-Hispanic/Latino; 3 Hispanic/Latino; 2 Two or more races, non-Hispanic/Latino), 3 international. Average age 29. 62 applicants, 39% accepted, 19 enrolled. In 2016, 13 master's, 5 doctorates awarded. Terminal master's awarded for partial completion of doctoral program. *Degree requirements:* For doctorate, thesis/dissertation. *Entrance requirements:* For master's and doctorate, GRE, minimum GPA of 3.0 in last 90 hours. Additional exam requirements/recommendations for international students: Required—TOEFL (minimum score 80 iBT), IELTS (minimum score 6.5). *Application deadline:* For fall admission, 12/1 for domestic and international students. Electronic applications accepted. *Expenses:* Tuition, state resident: full-time $12,150; part-time $450 per credit. Tuition, nonresident: full-time $21,789; part-time $807 per credit. *Required fees:* $1651; $1507 per credit. One-time fee: $350. Tuition and fees vary according to course load, campus/location and program. *Financial support:* Research assistantships, teaching assistantships, career-related internships or fieldwork, Federal Work-Study, and institutionally sponsored loans available. Support available to part-time students. Financial award application deadline: 12/1. *Faculty research:* Motor control, sports medicine, exercise physiology, sport psychology, biomechanics. *Unit head:* Dr. Marc Norcross, Professor. *Application contact:* Debi Rothermund, Administrative Program Specialist, 541-737-3324, E-mail: debi.rothermund@oregonstate.edu.
Website: http://health.oregonstate.edu/degrees/graduate/kinesiology

Penn State University Park, Graduate School, College of Health and Human Development, Department of Kinesiology, University Park, PA 16802. Offers MS, PhD, Certificate. *Unit head:* Dr. Ann C. Crouter, Dean, 814-865-1420, Fax: 814-865-3282. *Application contact:* Lori Hawn, Director, Graduate Student Services, 814-865-1795, Fax: 814-863-4627, E-mail: l-gswww@lists.psu.edu.
Website: http://hhd.psu.edu/kines

Point Loma Nazarene University, Department of Kinesiology, San Diego, CA 92106-2899. Offers integrative wellness (MS); sport performance (MS), including exercise science, sport management, sport performance. *Program availability:* Part-time, online learning. *Faculty:* 3 full-time (1 woman), 6 part-time/adjunct (1 woman). *Students:* 48 full-time (21 women), 4 part-time (1 woman); includes 21 minority (3 Black or African American, non-Hispanic/Latino; 2 Asian, non-Hispanic/Latino; 13 Hispanic/Latino; 3 Two or more races, non-Hispanic/Latino), 4 international. Average age 26. 84 applicants, 80% accepted, 49 enrolled. *Entrance requirements:* For master's, baccalaureate degree, minimum undergraduate cumulative GPA of 3.0. Application fee: $50. *Expenses:* $685 per credit. *Financial support:* Teaching assistantships, scholarships/grants, and unspecified assistantships available. *Unit head:* Jeff Sullivan, Chair, 619-849-2629, E-mail: jeffsullivan@pointloma.edu. *Application contact:* Claire Buckley, Director, Graduate Admissions, 866-563-2846, E-mail: gradinfo@pointloma.edu.

Prairie View A&M University, College of Education, Department of Health and Kinesiology, Prairie View, TX 77446. Offers M Ed, MS. *Accreditation:* NCATE. *Program availability:* Part-time, evening/weekend. *Faculty:* 4 full-time (all women). *Students:* 23 full-time (14 women), 11 part-time (4 women); includes 33 minority (31 Black or African American, non-Hispanic/Latino; 2 Hispanic/Latino). Average age 26. 24 applicants, 96% accepted, 16 enrolled. In 2016, 7 master's awarded. *Degree requirements:* For master's, thesis. *Entrance requirements:* For master's, GRE General Test. Additional exam requirements/recommendations for international students: Required—TOEFL (minimum score 550 paper-based; 79 iBT). *Application deadline:* For fall admission, 5/1 priority date for domestic and international students; for spring admission, 10/1 priority date for domestic students, 9/1 priority date for international students; for summer admission, 3/1 priority date for domestic students, 2/1 priority date for international students. Applications are processed on a rolling basis. Application fee: $50. Electronic applications accepted. *Expenses:* Tuition, state resident: full-time $4362; part-time $273.48 per credit hour. Tuition, nonresident: full-time $12,390; part-time $534.10 per credit hour. *Required fees:* $2782; $178.26 per credit hour. *Financial support:* Career-related internships or fieldwork available. Support available to part-time students. Financial award application deadline: 4/1; financial award applicants required to submit FAFSA. *Unit head:* Dr. Angela Branch-Vital, Department Head, 936-261-3900, Fax: 936-261-3905, E-mail: abranch-vital@pvamu.edu. *Application contact:* Pauline Walker, Administrative Assistant II, Research and Graduate Studies, 936-261-3521, Fax: 936-261-3529, E-mail: gradadmissions@pvamu.edu.

Purdue University, Graduate School, College of Health and Human Sciences, Department of Health and Kinesiology, West Lafayette, IN 47907. Offers athletic training education administration (MS, PhD); biomechanics (MS, PhD); exercise physiology (MS, PhD); health education (MS, PhD); history/philosophy of sport (MS, PhD); motor control and development (MS, PhD); physical education pedagogy (PhD); physical education teacher education (MS); recreation and sport management (MS, PhD); sport and exercise psychology (MS, PhD). *Program availability:* Part-time. *Faculty:* 19 full-time (7 women). *Students:* 30 full-time (13 women), 10 part-time (5 women); includes 2 minority (1 Asian, non-Hispanic/Latino; 1 Two or more races, non-Hispanic/Latino), 6 international. Average age 26. 77 applicants, 29% accepted, 18 enrolled. In 2016, 18 master's, 9 doctorates awarded. *Degree requirements:* For master's, thesis optional; for doctorate, comprehensive exam, thesis/dissertation, qualifying examination, preliminary examination. *Entrance requirements:* For master's, GRE General Test (minimum score 1000 combined verbal and quantitative), minimum undergraduate GPA of 3.0 or equivalent; for doctorate, GRE General Test (minimum score 1100 combined verbal and quantitative), minimum undergraduate GPA of 3.0 or equivalent; master's degree with minimum GPA of 3.25 (recommended). Additional exam requirements/recommendations for international students: Required—TOEFL (minimum score 77 iBT); Recommended—TWE. *Application deadline:* For fall admission, 4/30 for domestic and international students; for spring admission, 10/15 for domestic and international students. Applications are processed on a rolling basis. Application fee: $60 ($75 for international students). Electronic applications accepted. *Financial support:* Fellowships with partial tuition reimbursements, research assistantships with partial tuition reimbursements, teaching assistantships with partial tuition reimbursements, and Federal Work-Study available. Support available to part-time students. Financial award applicants required to submit FAFSA. *Faculty research:* Wellness, motivation, teaching effectiveness, learning and development. *Unit head:* Dr. Timothy P. Gavin, Head of the Graduate Program, 765-494-3178, Fax: 765-494-1239, E-mail: gavin1@purdue.edu. *Application contact:* Christy F. Daugherty, Graduate Contact, 765-494-3162, E-mail: daugher2@purdue.edu.
Website: http://www.purdue.edu/hhs/hk/

Saint Mary's College of California, School of Liberal Arts, Department of Kinesiology, Moraga, CA 94575. Offers fitness management (MA); sport management (MA); sport studies (MA). *Program availability:* Part-time. *Degree requirements:* For master's, thesis or special project. *Entrance requirements:* For master's, minimum GPA of 2.75, BA in physical education or related field, or professional experience. Electronic applications accepted. *Expenses:* Contact institution. *Faculty research:* Moral development in sport, applied motor learning, achievement motivation, sport history.

Sam Houston State University, College of Health Sciences, Department of Kinesiology, Huntsville, TX 77341. Offers sport and human performance (MA); sport management (MA). *Program availability:* Part-time. *Degree requirements:* For master's, comprehensive exam, thesis optional. *Entrance requirements:* For master's, GRE, letters of recommendation, statement of interest/intent. Additional exam requirements/recommendations for international students: Required—TOEFL (minimum score 550 paper-based; 79 iBT), IELTS (minimum score 6.5). Electronic applications accepted.

San Diego State University, Graduate and Research Affairs, College of Health and Human Services, School of Exercise and Nutritional Sciences, Program in Kinesiology, San Diego, CA 92182. Offers MA. *Degree requirements:* For master's, thesis. *Entrance requirements:* For master's, GRE General Test, 2 letters of reference. Additional exam requirements/recommendations for international students: Required—TOEFL. Electronic applications accepted.

San Francisco State University, Division of Graduate Studies, College of Health and Social Sciences, Department of Kinesiology, San Francisco, CA 94132-1722. Offers MS. *Application deadline:* Applications are processed on a rolling basis. *Expenses:* Tuition, state resident: full-time $6738. Tuition, nonresident: full-time $15,666. *Required fees:* $1012. Tuition and fees vary according to degree level and program. *Unit head:* Dr. Marialice Kern, Chair, 415-338-2244, Fax: 415-338-7566, E-mail: mkern@sfsu.edu. *Application contact:* Prof. Kate Hamel, Graduate Coordinator, 415-338-2186, Fax: 415-338-7566, E-mail: hamelk@sfsu.edu.
Website: http://kin.sfsu.edu/

San Jose State University, Graduate Studies and Research, College of Applied Sciences and Arts, San Jose, CA 95192-0001. Offers big data (Certificate); California library media teacher services (Credential); collaborative response to family violence (Certificate); justice studies (MS); kinesiology (MA), including applied sciences and arts (MA, MS), athletic training, exercise physiology, sport management, sport studies; library and information science (MLIS, Certificate); mass communication (MA); nutritional science (MS); occupational therapy (MS); public health (MPH); pupil personnel services (Credential); recreation (MS), including applied sciences and arts (MA, MS), international tourism; social work (MSW); Spanish language counseling (Certificate); strategic management of digital assets and services (Certificate). *Program availability:* Part-time, evening/weekend. Electronic applications accepted.

Sarah Lawrence College, Graduate Studies, Program in Dance/Movement Therapy, Bronxville, NY 10708-5999. Offers MS. *Degree requirements:* For master's, thesis, practicum.

Simon Fraser University, Office of Graduate Studies and Postdoctoral Fellows, Faculty of Science, Department of Biomedical Physiology and Kinesiology, Burnaby, BC V5A 1S6, Canada. Offers M Sc, PhD. *Faculty:* 29 full-time (8 women). *Students:* 54 full-time (30 women). 23 applicants, 43% accepted, 9 enrolled. In 2016, 8 master's, 7 doctorates awarded. *Degree requirements:* For master's, thesis, thesis proposal; for doctorate, comprehensive exam, thesis/dissertation, dissertation proposal, seminar presentations. *Entrance requirements:* For master's, minimum GPA of 3.0 (on scale of 4.33) or 3.33 based on last 60 credits of undergraduate courses; for doctorate, minimum GPA of 3.5 (on scale of 4.33). Additional exam requirements/recommendations for international students: Recommended—TOEFL (minimum score 580 paper-based; 93 iBT), IELTS (minimum score 7), TWE (minimum score 5). *Application deadline:* For fall admission, 1/15 for domestic and international students; for winter admission, 8/31 for domestic and international students; for spring admission, 1/15 for domestic and international students. Applications are processed on a rolling basis. Application fee: $90 ($125 for international students). Electronic applications accepted. *Financial support:* In 2016–17, 32 students received support, including 18 fellowships (averaging $6,319 per year), teaching assistantships (averaging $5,608 per year); research assistantships and scholarships/grants also available. *Faculty research:* Cardiovascular physiology, chronic disease, environmental physiology, neuromechanics, neuroscience. *Unit head:* Dr. Thomas Claydon, Graduate Chair, 778-782-8514, Fax: 778-782-3040, E-mail: bpk-grad-chair@sfu.ca. *Application contact:* Clare Zheng, Graduate Secretary, 778-782-4061, Fax: 778-782-3040, E-mail: bpk-grad-sec@sfu.ca.
Website: http://www.sfu.ca/bpk.html

Sonoma State University, School of Science and Technology, Department of Kinesiology, Rohnert Park, CA 94928. Offers adapted physical education (MA); interdisciplinary (MA); interdisciplinary pre-occupational therapy (MA); lifetime physical activity (MA), including coach education, fitness and wellness; physical education (MA); pre-physical therapy (MA). *Program availability:* Part-time. *Degree requirements:* For master's, thesis, oral exam. *Entrance requirements:* For master's, minimum GPA of 2.8. Additional exam requirements/recommendations for international students: Required—TOEFL (minimum score 500 paper-based). *Application deadline:* For fall admission, 11/30 for domestic students; for spring admission, 9/1 for domestic students. Applications are processed on a rolling basis. Application fee: $55. *Expenses:* Tuition, state resident: full-time $6738; part-time $3906 per unit. *Required fees:* $1916; $1916 per year. Tuition and fees vary according to course load, degree level and program. *Financial support:* Career-related internships or fieldwork available. Financial award application deadline: 3/2; financial award applicants required to submit FAFSA. *Unit head:* Dr. Steven Winter, Chair, 707-664-2188, E-mail: steven.winter@sonoma.edu. *Application contact:* Dr. Bulent Sokmen, Graduate Coordinator, 707-664-2789, E-mail: sokmen@sonoma.edu.
Website: http://www.sonoma.edu/kinesiology/

Southeastern Louisiana University, College of Nursing and Health Sciences, Department of Kinesiology and Health Studies, Hammond, LA 70402. Offers health and kinesiology (MS), including exercise science, health promotion and exercise science, health studies, kinesiology. *Accreditation:* NCATE. *Program availability:* Part-time. *Faculty:* 7 full-time (3 women), 2 part-time/adjunct (1 woman). *Students:* 24 full-time (8 women), 14 part-time (11 women); includes 14 minority (8 Black or African American, non-Hispanic/Latino; 3 Hispanic/Latino; 3 Two or more races, non-Hispanic/Latino), 1 international. Average age 25. 32 applicants, 59% accepted, 9 enrolled. In 2016, 19 master's awarded. *Degree requirements:* For master's, comprehensive exam (for some programs), thesis (for some programs). *Entrance requirements:* Additional exam requirements/recommendations for international students: Required—TOEFL (minimum score 500 paper-based; 61 iBT). *Application deadline:* For fall admission, 7/15 priority date for domestic students, 6/1 priority date for international students; for spring admission, 12/1 priority date for domestic students, 10/1 priority date for international students. Applications are processed on a rolling basis. Application fee: $20 ($30 for international students). Electronic applications accepted. *Expenses:* Tuition, state resident: full-time $6540; part-time $465 per credit hour. Tuition, nonresident: full-time $19,017; part-time $1158 per credit hour. *Required fees:* $1829. *Financial support:* In 2016–17, 27 students received support, including 8 research assistantships (averaging $9,413 per year), 4 teaching assistantships (averaging $9,275 per year); career-related internships or fieldwork, Federal Work-Study, institutionally sponsored loans, scholarships/grants, and unspecified assistantships also available. Support available to part-time students. Financial award application deadline: 5/1; financial award applicants required to submit FAFSA. *Faculty research:* Exercise physiology, motor learning, sport and exercise psychology. school health, health and aging. *Unit head:* Dr. Eddie Hebert, Department Head, 985-549-2129, Fax: 985-549-5119, E-mail: ehebert@southeastern.edu. *Application contact:* Amanda Harper, Graduate Admissions Analyst, 985-549-5620, Fax: 985-549-5632, E-mail: admissions@southeastern.edu.
Website: http://www.southeastern.edu/acad_research/depts/kin_hs/index.html

Southern Arkansas University–Magnolia, School of Graduate Studies, Magnolia, AR 71753. Offers agriculture (MS); business administration (MBA), including agri-business, social entrepreneurship, supply chain management; clinical and mental health counseling (MS); computer and information sciences (MS), including cyber security and privacy, data science, information technology; gifted and talented (M Ed), including curriculum and instruction, educational administration and supervision, gifted and talented P-8/7-12, instructional specialist P-4; higher, adult and lifelong education (M Ed); kinesiology (M Ed), including coaching; library media and information specialist (M Ed); public administration (MPA); school counseling K-12 (M Ed); student affairs and college counseling (M Ed); teaching (MAT). *Accreditation:* NCATE. *Program availability:* Part-time, 100% online, blended/hybrid learning. *Faculty:* 36 full-time (19 women), 33 part-time/adjunct (14 women). *Students:* 605 full-time (143 women), 879 part-time (352 women); includes 130 minority (113 Black or African American, non-Hispanic/Latino; 7 American Indian or Alaska Native, non-Hispanic/Latino; 2 Asian, non-Hispanic/Latino; 2 Hispanic/Latino; 6 Two or more races, non-Hispanic/Latino), 1,048 international. Average age 28. 904 applicants, 81% accepted, 262 enrolled. In 2016, 278 master's awarded. *Degree requirements:* For master's, comprehensive exam (for some programs), thesis optional. *Entrance requirements:* For master's, GRE, MAT or GMAT, minimum GPA of 2.5. Additional exam requirements/recommendations for international students: Required—TOEFL (minimum score 550 paper-based), IELTS (minimum score 6). *Application deadline:* For fall admission, 7/20 for domestic students, 7/10 for international students; for spring admission, 12/1 for domestic students, 11/15 for international students; for summer admission, 4/1 for domestic students, 5/1 for international students. Applications are processed on a rolling basis. Application fee: $25 ($50 for international students). Electronic applications accepted. *Expenses:* Tuition, state resident: full-time $2511; part-time $279 per credit hour. Tuition, nonresident: full-time $3726; part-time $414 per credit hour. *Required fees:* $307 per semester. Tuition and fees vary according to course load and program. *Financial support:* Career-related internships or fieldwork, Federal Work-Study, scholarships/grants, tuition waivers (full), and unspecified assistantships available. Financial award applicants required to submit FAFSA. *Faculty research:* Alternative certification for teachers, supervision of instruction, instructional leadership, counseling. *Unit head:* Dr. Kim Bloss, Dean, School of Graduate Studies, 870-235-4150, Fax: 870-235-5227, E-mail: kkbloss@saumag.edu. *Application contact:* Shrijana Malakar, Admissions Specialist, 870-235-4150, Fax: 870-235-5227, E-mail: smalakar@saumag.edu.
Website: http://www.saumag.edu/graduate

Southern Illinois University Carbondale, Graduate School, College of Education and Human Services, Department of Kinesiology, Carbondale, IL 62901-4701. Offers MS Ed. *Program availability:* Part-time. *Degree requirements:* For master's, thesis. *Entrance requirements:* For master's, GRE, minimum GPA of 2.7. Additional exam requirements/recommendations for international students: Required—TOEFL. *Faculty research:* Caffeine and exercise effects, ground reaction forces in walking and running, social psychology of sports.

Southern Illinois University Edwardsville, Graduate School, School of Education, Health, and Human Behavior, Department of Kinesiology and Health Education, Program in Physical Education and Coaching Pedagogy, Edwardsville, IL 62026. Offers MS Ed. *Program availability:* Part-time, evening/weekend. *Degree requirements:* For master's, comprehensive exam (for some programs), thesis (for some programs). *Entrance requirements:* Additional exam requirements/recommendations for international students: Required—TOEFL (minimum score 550 paper-based, 79 iBT), IELTS (minimum score 6.5), Michigan Test of English Language Proficiency or PTE. Electronic applications accepted.

Southwestern Oklahoma State University, College of Professional and Graduate Studies, School of Behavioral Sciences and Education, Specialization in Kinesiology, Weatherford, OK 73096-3098. Offers M Ed. *Program availability:* Part-time. *Degree requirements:* For master's, exam. *Entrance requirements:* For master's, GRE General Test or minimum undergraduate GPA of 3.0. Additional exam requirements/recommendations for international students: Required—TOEFL.

Stephen F. Austin State University, Graduate School, College of Education, Department of Kinesiology and Health Science, Nacogdoches, TX 75962. Offers athletic training (MS); kinesiology (M Ed). *Degree requirements:* For master's, comprehensive exam. *Entrance requirements:* For master's, GRE General Test. Additional exam requirements/recommendations for international students: Required—TOEFL.

Syracuse University, David B. Falk College of Sport and Human Dynamics, Syracuse, NY 13244. Offers MA, MS, MSW, PhD, CAS, MSW/MA. *Accreditation:* AAMFT/COAMFTE (one or more programs are accredited). *Program availability:* Part-time, evening/weekend. *Faculty:* 71 full-time (42 women), 25 part-time/adjunct (18 women). *Students:* 222 full-time (180 women), 105 part-time (79 women); includes 69 minority (35 Black or African American, non-Hispanic/Latino; 2 American Indian or Alaska Native, non-Hispanic/Latino; 5 Asian, non-Hispanic/Latino; 16 Hispanic/Latino; 1 Native Hawaiian or other Pacific Islander, non-Hispanic/Latino; 10 Two or more races, non-Hispanic/Latino), 30 international. Average age 29. 474 applicants, 74% accepted, 172 enrolled. In 2016, 147 master's, 27 other advanced degrees awarded. *Degree requirements:* For master's, comprehensive exam (for some programs), thesis (for some programs); for doctorate, comprehensive exam, thesis/dissertation. *Entrance requirements:* For master's, GRE (for most programs), resume, official transcripts, personal statement, three letters of recommendation; for doctorate, GRE, resume, official transcripts, personal statement, three letters of recommendation. Additional exam requirements/recommendations for international students: Required—TOEFL. *Application deadline:* For fall admission, 2/15 priority date for domestic and international students; for spring admission, 11/15 priority date for domestic students, 11/15 for international students; for summer admission, 3/15 priority date for domestic students, 3/15 for international students. Applications are processed on a rolling basis. Application fee: $75. Electronic applications accepted. *Expenses: Tuition:* Full-time $25,974; part-time $1443 per credit hour. *Required fees:* $802; $50 per course. Tuition and fees vary according to course load and program. *Financial support:* Fellowships with full tuition reimbursements, research assistantships with tuition reimbursements, teaching assistantships with tuition reimbursements, and tuition waivers available. Financial award application deadline: 1/1; financial award applicants required to submit FAFSA. *Faculty research:* Child and family studies, marriage and family therapy, public health, food studies and nutrition, social work, sport management. *Unit head:* Dr. Diane Lyden Murphy, Dean, 315-443-5582, Fax: 315-443-2562. *Application contact:* Felicia Otero, Director of College Admissions, 315-443-5555, Fax: 315-443-2562, E-mail: falk@syr.edu.
Website: http://falk.syr.edu/

Tarleton State University, College of Graduate Studies, College of Education, Department of Kinesiology, Stephenville, TX 76402. Offers athletic training (MS); kinesiology (MS). *Program availability:* Part-time, evening/weekend. *Faculty:* 8 full-time (2 women), 1 (woman) part-time/adjunct. *Students:* 25 full-time (11 women), 43 part-time (25 women); includes 19 minority (13 Black or African American, non-Hispanic/Latino; 5 Hispanic/Latino; 1 Two or more races, non-Hispanic/Latino), 1 international. 28 applicants, 96% accepted, 22 enrolled. In 2016, 32 master's awarded. *Degree requirements:* For master's, comprehensive exam, thesis optional. *Entrance requirements:* For master's, GRE General Test, minimum GPA of 3.0. Additional exam requirements/recommendations for international students: Required—TOEFL (minimum score 550 paper-based; 80 iBT). *Application deadline:* For fall admission, 8/15 priority date for domestic students; for spring admission, 1/7 for domestic students. Applications are processed on a rolling basis. Application fee: $45 ($145 for international students). Electronic applications accepted. *Expenses:* $3,672 tuition; $2,437 fees. *Financial support:* Research assistantships, teaching assistantships with partial tuition reimbursements, career-related internships or fieldwork, Federal Work-Study, and institutionally sponsored loans available. Support available to part-time students. Financial award application deadline: 5/1; financial award applicants required to submit FAFSA. *Unit head:* Dr. Steve Simpson, Department Head, 254-968-9756, E-mail: simpson@tarleton.edu. *Application contact:* Information Contact, 254-968-9104, Fax: 254-968-9670, E-mail: gradoffice@tarleton.edu.
Website: http://www.tarleton.edu/kinesiology/

Teachers College, Columbia University, Department of Biobehavioral Sciences, New York, NY 10027-6696. Offers applied exercise physiology (Ed M, MA, Ed D); communication sciences and disorders (MS, Ed D, PhD); kinesiology (PhD); motor learning and control (Ed M, MA); motor learning/movement science (Ed D); neuroscience and education (MS); physical education (MA, Ed D). *Accreditation:* ASHA. *Program availability:* Part-time, evening/weekend. *Students:* 162 full-time (133 women), 158 part-time (116 women); includes 119 minority (20 Black or African American, non-Hispanic/Latino; 38 Asian, non-Hispanic/Latino; 54 Hispanic/Latino; 7 Two or more races, non-Hispanic/Latino), 28 international. 821 applicants, 33% accepted, 125 enrolled. *Expenses: Tuition:* Full-time $36,288; part-time $1512 per credit. *Required fees:* $438 per semester. One-time fee: $510 full-time. Full-time tuition and fees vary according to course load. *Financial support:* Fellowships, teaching assistantships, career-related internships or fieldwork, Federal Work-Study, institutionally sponsored loans, traineeships, and tuition waivers (full and partial) available. Support available to part-time students. *Unit head:* Prof. Carol Garber, Chair, 212-678-3891, E-mail: garber@tc.columbia.edu. *Application contact:* David Estrella, Director of Admissions, 212-678-3305, E-mail: estrella@tc.columbia.edu.
Website: http://www.tc.columbia.edu/biobehavioral-sciences/

Temple University, College of Public Health, Department of Kinesiology, Philadelphia, PA 19122. Offers athletic training (MSAT, DAT); kinesiology (MS, PhD); neuromotor science (MS, PhD). *Program availability:* Part-time. *Faculty:* 16 full-time (6 women), 6 part-time/adjunct (2 women). *Students:* 38 full-time (28 women), 23 part-time (9 women); includes 15 minority (4 Black or African American, non-Hispanic/Latino; 1 Asian, non-Hispanic/Latino; 8 Hispanic/Latino; 2 Two or more races, non-Hispanic/Latino), 6 international. 74 applicants, 66% accepted, 35 enrolled. In 2016, 26 master's, 5 doctorates awarded. Terminal master's awarded for partial completion of doctoral program. *Degree requirements:* For master's, thesis, final project; for doctorate, comprehensive exam, thesis/dissertation. *Entrance requirements:* For master's, GRE General Test or MAT, minimum undergraduate GPA of 3.0, 3 letters of reference, statement of goals, interview, resume; for doctorate, GRE General Test, minimum undergraduate GPA of 3.0, 3 letters of reference, statement of goals, interview, resume. Additional exam requirements/recommendations for international students: Required—TOEFL (minimum score 550 paper-based; 79 iBT). *Application deadline:* For fall admission, 1/15 for domestic students, 12/15 for international students; for spring admission, 10/1 for domestic students, 8/1 for international students. Applications are processed on a rolling basis. Application fee: $60. Electronic applications accepted. *Expenses:* Contact institution. *Financial support:* Fellowships, research assistantships with tuition reimbursements, teaching assistantships with tuition reimbursements, career-related internships or fieldwork, Federal Work-Study, scholarships/grants, tuition waivers, and unspecified assistantships available. Financial award application deadline: 1/15. *Faculty research:* Exercise physiology, athletic training, motor neuroscience, exercise and sports psychology. *Unit head:* John Jeka, Chair, 214-204-4405, Fax: 215-204-4414, E-mail: jjeka@temple.edu. *Application contact:* Rosalind Robinson, Department Coordinator, E-mail: rosalind.robinson@temple.edu.
Website: http://cph.temple.edu/kinesiology/home

Tennessee Technological University, College of Graduate Studies, College of Education, Department of Exercise Science, Physical Education and Wellness, Cookeville, TN 38505. Offers adapted physical education (MA); elementary/middle school physical education (MA); lifetime wellness (MA); sport management (MA). *Accreditation:* NCATE. *Program availability:* Part-time, online learning. *Faculty:* 7 full-time (0 women). *Students:* 17 full-time (5 women), 32 part-time (17 women); includes 6 minority (4 Black or African American, non-Hispanic/Latino; 1 Hispanic/Latino; 1 Two or more races, non-Hispanic/Latino). Average age 27. 29 applicants, 59% accepted, 15 enrolled. In 2016, 24 master's awarded. *Degree requirements:* For master's, comprehensive exam, thesis or alternative. *Entrance requirements:* For master's, MAT or GRE. Additional exam requirements/recommendations for international students: Required—TOEFL (minimum score 527 paper-based; 71 iBT), IELTS (minimum score 5.5), PTE (minimum score 48), or TOEIC (Test of English as an International Communication). *Application deadline:* For fall admission, 8/1 for domestic students, 5/1 for international students; for spring admission, 12/1 for domestic students, 10/1 for international students; for summer admission, 5/1 for domestic students, 2/1 for international students. Applications are processed on a rolling basis. Application fee: $35 ($40 for international students). Electronic applications accepted. *Expenses:* Tuition, state resident: full-time $9375; part-time $534 per credit hour. Tuition, nonresident: full-time $22,443; part-time $1260 per credit hour. *Financial support:* In 2016–17, 2 research assistantships (averaging $4,400 per year), 9 teaching assistantships (averaging $4,400 per year) were awarded; fellowships and career-related internships or fieldwork also available. Financial award application deadline: 4/1. *Unit head:* Dr. Christy Killman, Chairperson, 931-372-3467, Fax: 931-372-6319, E-mail: ckillman@tntech.edu. *Application contact:* Shelia K. Kendrick, Coordinator of Graduate Studies, 931-372-3808, Fax: 931-372-3497, E-mail: skendrick@tntech.edu.

Texas A&M University, College of Education and Human Development, Department of Health and Kinesiology, College Station, TX 77843. Offers athletic training (MS); health education (M Ed, MS, Ed D, PhD); kinesiology (MS, PhD); sports management (MS). *Program availability:* Part-time. *Faculty:* 56. *Students:* 216 full-time (119 women), 116 part-time (55 women); includes 100 minority (37 Black or African American, non-Hispanic/Latino; 9 Asian, non-Hispanic/Latino; 49 Hispanic/Latino; 5 Two or more races, non-Hispanic/Latino), 28 international. Average age 29. 169 applicants, 72% accepted, 77 enrolled. In 2016, 104 master's, 24 doctorates awarded. *Degree requirements:* For master's, thesis (for some programs); for doctorate, comprehensive exam, thesis/dissertation. *Entrance requirements:* For master's and doctorate, GRE General Test. Additional exam requirements/recommendations for international students: Required—TOEFL (minimum score 550 paper-based; 80 iBT), IELTS (minimum score 6), PTE (minimum score 53). *Application deadline:* For fall admission, 1/15 for domestic students; for spring admission, 10/1 for domestic students. Applications are processed on a rolling basis. Application fee: $50 ($90 for international students). Electronic applications accepted. *Expenses:* Contact institution. *Financial support:* In 2016–17, 172 students received support, including 3 fellowships with tuition reimbursements available (averaging $18,412 per year), 43 research assistantships with tuition reimbursements available (averaging $5,089 per year), 76 teaching assistantships with tuition reimbursements available (averaging $8,295 per year); career-related internships or fieldwork, institutionally sponsored loans, scholarships/grants, traineeships, health care benefits, tuition waivers (full and partial), and unspecified assistantships also available. Support available to part-time students. Financial award application deadline: 3/15; financial award applicants required to submit FAFSA. *Unit head:* Dr. Richard Kreider, Head, 979-845-1333, Fax: 979-847-8987, E-mail: rkreider@hlkn.tamu.edu. *Application contact:* Jenny Bilski, Academic Advisor, 979-862-4052, E-mail: jenny.bilski@tamu.edu.
Website: http://hlknweb.tamu.edu/

Texas A&M University–Commerce, College of Education and Human Services, Commerce, TX 75429-3011. Offers counseling (MS); curriculum and instruction (M Ed, MS); early childhood education (M Ed, MS); educational administration (M Ed, Ed D); educational psychology (PhD); educational technology leadership (MS); educational technology library science (MS); health, kinesiology and sports studies (MS); higher education (MS, Ed D); organization, learning, and technology (MS); psychology (MS); reading (M Ed, MS); school psychology (SSP); secondary education (M Ed, MS); social work (MSW); special education (M Ed); supervision, curriculum and instruction-elementary education (Ed D). *Program availability:* Part-time, 100% online, blended/hybrid learning. *Faculty:* 88 full-time (52 women), 31 part-time/adjunct (24 women). *Students:* 341 full-time (276 women), 1,495 part-time (1,156 women); includes 762 minority (429 Black or African American, non-Hispanic/Latino; 4 American Indian or Alaska Native, non-Hispanic/Latino; 27 Asian, non-Hispanic/Latino; 247 Hispanic/Latino; 1 Native Hawaiian or other Pacific Islander, non-Hispanic/Latino; 54 Two or more races, non-Hispanic/Latino), 18 international. Average age 37. 1,070 applicants, 54% accepted, 452 enrolled. In 2016, 579 master's, 31 doctorates awarded. *Degree requirements:* For master's, one foreign language, comprehensive exam, thesis optional, departmental qualifying exams (for some programs); for doctorate, comprehensive exam, thesis/dissertation, departmental qualifying exam; for SSP, comprehensive exam, thesis optional. *Entrance requirements:* For master's and doctorate, GRE General Test. Additional exam requirements/recommendations for international students: Required—TOEFL (minimum score 550 paper-based; 79 iBT), IELTS (minimum score 6). *Application deadline:* For fall admission, 6/1 priority date for international students; for spring admission, 10/15 priority date for international students; for summer admission, 3/15 priority date for international students. Applications are processed on a rolling basis. Application fee: $50. Electronic applications accepted. *Expenses:* $2,254 resident; $4,744 non-resident. *Financial support:* In 2016–17, 301 students received support, including 39 research assistantships with partial tuition reimbursements available (averaging $9,000 per year), 17 teaching assistantships with partial tuition reimbursements available (averaging $9,000 per year); career-related internships or fieldwork, Federal Work-Study, institutionally sponsored loans, scholarships/grants, health care benefits, and unspecified assistantships also available. Financial award application deadline: 5/1; financial award applicants required to submit FAFSA. *Faculty research:* Cognitive and bilingual education, positive behavioral intervention, literacy, math readiness. *Total annual research expenditures:* $470,963. *Unit head:* Dr. Timothy Letzring, Dean, 903-886-5181, Fax: 903-886-5905, E-mail: tim.letzring@tamuc.edu. *Application contact:* Jennifer Faunce, Graduate Recruiter, 903-886-5030, Fax: 903-886-5905, E-mail: jennifer.faunce@tamuc.edu.
Website: http://www.tamuc.edu/academics/graduateSchool/programs/education/default.aspx

Kinesiology and Movement Studies

Texas A&M University–Corpus Christi, College of Graduate Studies, College of Education, Corpus Christi, TX 78412-5503. Offers counseling (MS), including counseling; counselor education (PhD); curriculum and instruction (MS, PhD); early childhood education (MS); educational administration (MS); educational leadership (Ed D); elementary education (MS); instructional design and educational technology (MS); kinesiology (MS); reading (MS); secondary education (MS); special education (MS). *Program availability:* Part-time, evening/weekend, online learning. *Faculty:* 50 full-time (29 women), 29 part-time/adjunct (18 women). *Students:* 158 full-time (130 women), 344 part-time (281 women); includes 288 minority (28 Black or African American, non-Hispanic/Latino; 2 American Indian or Alaska Native, non-Hispanic/Latino; 8 Asian, non-Hispanic/Latino; 246 Hispanic/Latino; 4 Two or more races, non-Hispanic/Latino), 22 international. Average age 35. 273 applicants, 60% accepted, 142 enrolled. In 2016, 67 master's, 13 doctorates awarded. *Degree requirements:* For master's, comprehensive exam, capstone; for doctorate, thesis/dissertation. *Entrance requirements:* For master's, GRE General Test, essay (300 words); for doctorate, GRE, essay, resume, 3-4 reference forms. *Application deadline:* For fall admission, 7/15 priority date for domestic students, 5/1 priority date for international students; for spring admission, 11/15 priority date for domestic students, 9/1 priority date for international students. Applications are processed on a rolling basis. Application fee: $50 ($70 for international students). Electronic applications accepted. *Financial support:* Research assistantships, teaching assistantships, career-related internships or fieldwork, Federal Work-Study, institutionally sponsored loans, scholarships/grants, health care benefits, and unspecified assistantships available. Support available to part-time students. Financial award application deadline: 3/15; financial award applicants required to submit FAFSA. *Unit head:* Dr. Arthur Hernandez, Dean, 361-825-2660, E-mail: art.hernandez@tamucc.edu. *Application contact:* Graduate Admissions Coordinator, 361-825-2177, Fax: 361-825-2755, E-mail: gradweb@tamucc.edu.
Website: http://education.tamucc.edu/

Texas A&M University–Kingsville, College of Graduate Studies, College of Education and Human Performance, Department of Health and Kinesiology, Kingsville, TX 78363. Offers MA, MS. *Degree requirements:* For master's, variable foreign language requirement, comprehensive exam, thesis (for some programs). *Entrance requirements:* For master's, GRE, MAT, GMAT, essay. Additional exam requirements/recommendations for international students: Required—TOEFL (minimum score 550 paper-based; 79 iBT). Electronic applications accepted.

Texas A&M University–San Antonio, Department of Curriculum and Kinesiology, San Antonio, TX 78224. Offers bilingual education (MA); early childhood education (M Ed); kinesiology (MS); reading (MS); special education (M Ed), including educational diagnostician, instructional specialist. *Program availability:* Part-time, evening/weekend. *Degree requirements:* For master's, comprehensive exam, thesis or alternative. *Entrance requirements:* For master's, MAT. Additional exam requirements/recommendations for international students: Required—TOEFL (minimum score 550 paper-based; 80 iBT), IELTS (minimum score 6). Electronic applications accepted.

Texas Christian University, Harris College of Nursing and Health Sciences, Department of Kinesiology, Fort Worth, TX 76129. Offers MS. *Program availability:* Part-time. *Faculty:* 8 full-time (4 women). *Students:* 26 full-time (16 women); includes 7 minority (all Hispanic/Latino), 3 international. Average age 25. 36 applicants, 72% accepted, 12 enrolled. In 2016, 3 master's awarded. *Degree requirements:* For master's, thesis. *Entrance requirements:* For master's, GRE General Test. Additional exam requirements/recommendations for international students: Recommended—TOEFL (minimum score 600 paper-based; 100 iBT). *Application deadline:* For fall admission, 3/1 for domestic and international students; for spring admission, 12/1 for domestic and international students. Applications are processed on a rolling basis. Application fee: $50. Electronic applications accepted. *Expenses: Tuition:* Full-time $26,640; part-time $1480 per credit hour. *Required fees:* $48. Tuition and fees vary according to program. *Financial support:* In 2016–17, 16 students received support, including 16 research assistantships with full and partial tuition reimbursements available (averaging $6,300 per year); tuition waivers (full and partial) also available. Financial award application deadline: 3/1. *Faculty research:* Meal composition and gut hormones, exercise and reduction of inflammation, mental toughness, risk factors for disease in special populations, eating behavior and caloric intake, concussion risk in impact sports, physical activity in elementary school children. *Total annual research expenditures:* $150,000. *Unit head:* Dr. Joel Mitchell, Professor/Chair, 817-257-7665, Fax: 817-257-7702, E-mail: j.mitchell@tcu.edu.
Website: http://www.kinesiology.tcu.edu

Texas Tech University, Graduate School, College of Arts and Sciences, Department of Kinesiology and Sport Management, Lubbock, TX 79409. Offers kinesiology (MS); sport management (MS). *Program availability:* Part-time. *Faculty:* 23 full-time (11 women), 10 part-time/adjunct (5 women). *Students:* 50 full-time (25 women), 12 part-time (3 women); includes 20 minority (6 Black or African American, non-Hispanic/Latino; 11 Hispanic/Latino; 3 Two or more races, non-Hispanic/Latino), 7 international. Average age 24. 88 applicants, 39% accepted, 23 enrolled. In 2016, 41 master's awarded. *Degree requirements:* For master's, comprehensive exam (for some programs), thesis (for some programs). *Entrance requirements:* For master's, GRE for those whose GPA on last 60 hours of undergraduate coursework is 3.49 and lower (for kinesiology only), letter of intent, 3 letters of recommendation (preferably from academic professors), minimum GPA of 2.8 in the last 60 hours. Additional exam requirements/recommendations for international students: Required—TOEFL (minimum score 550 paper-based; 79 iBT). *Application deadline:* For fall admission, 6/1 priority date for domestic students, 1/15 priority date for international students; for spring admission, 9/1 priority date for domestic students, 6/15 priority date for international students. Applications are processed on a rolling basis. Application fee: $75. Electronic applications accepted. *Expenses:* $300 per credit hour full-time resident tuition, $708 per credit hour full-time non-resident tuition; $50.50 per credit hour fee plus $608 per term fee. *Financial support:* In 2016–17, 58 students received support, including 30 fellowships (averaging $4,699 per year), 47 teaching assistantships (averaging $10,579 per year); research assistantships, career-related internships or fieldwork, scholarships/grants, health care benefits, and unspecified assistantships also available. Financial award application deadline: 8/1; financial award applicants required to submit FAFSA. *Faculty research:* Sport management, exercise physiology, human performance, motor behavior, exercise and sport psychology. *Total annual research expenditures:* $234,707. *Unit head:* Dr. Angela Lumpkin, Professor/Chair, 806-834-6935, Fax: 806-742-1688, E-mail: angela.lumpkin@ttu.edu. *Application contact:* Dr. Donna Torres, Graduate Coordinator, 806-834-7968, Fax: 806-742-1688, E-mail: donna.torres@ttu.edu.
Website: http://www.depts.ttu.edu/ksm/

Texas Woman's University, Graduate School, College of Health Sciences, Department of Kinesiology, Denton, TX 76201. Offers adapted physical activity (MS, PhD); biomechanics (MS, PhD); coaching (MS); exercise physiology (MS, PhD); sport management (MS, PhD). *Program availability:* Part-time, evening/weekend. Terminal master's awarded for partial completion of doctoral program. *Degree requirements:* For master's, comprehensive exam, thesis or alternative; for doctorate, comprehensive exam, thesis/dissertation, qualifying exam. *Entrance requirements:* For master's, GRE General Test (biomechanics emphasis only), 2 letters of reference, curriculum vitae, interview (adapted physical education emphasis only); for doctorate, GRE General Test (biomechanics emphasis only), interview, 3 letters of reference, curriculum vitae. Additional exam requirements/recommendations for international students: Required—TOEFL (minimum score 550 paper-based; 79 iBT). *Application deadline:* For fall admission, 7/1 priority date for domestic students, 3/1 for international students; for spring admission, 11/1 priority date for domestic students, 7/1 for international students. Applications are processed on a rolling basis. Application fee: $50 ($75 for international students). Electronic applications accepted. *Expenses:* Tuition, state resident: full-time $9046; part-time $251 per credit hour. Tuition, nonresident: full-time $22,922; part-time $614 per credit hour. *International tuition:* $23,046 full-time. *Required fees:* $2690; $1285 per credit hour. One-time fee: $50. Tuition and fees vary according to course level, course load, program and reciprocity agreements. *Financial support:* Research assistantships, teaching assistantships, career-related internships or fieldwork, Federal Work-Study, institutionally sponsored loans, scholarships/grants, traineeships, health care benefits, and unspecified assistantships available. Support available to part-time students. Financial award application deadline: 3/1; financial award applicants required to submit FAFSA. *Faculty research:* Exercise and Type 2 diabetes risk, bone mineral density and exercise in special populations, obesity in children, factors influencing sport consumer behavior and loyalty, roles and responsibilities of Para educators in adapted physical education. *Unit head:* Dr. David Nichols, Interim Chair, 940-898-2576, Fax: 940-898-2581, E-mail: dnichols@twu.edu. *Application contact:* Dr. Samuel Wheeler, Assistant Director of Admissions, 940-898-3188, Fax: 940-898-3081, E-mail: wheelersr@twu.edu.
Website: http://www.twu.edu/kinesiology/

Université de Montréal, Department of Kinesiology, Montréal, QC H3C 3J7, Canada. Offers kinesiology (M Sc, DESS); physical activity (M Sc, PhD). *Degree requirements:* For master's, one foreign language, thesis (for some programs); for doctorate, one foreign language, thesis/dissertation, general exam. Electronic applications accepted. *Faculty research:* Physiology of exercise, psychology of sports, biomechanics, dance, sociology of sports.

Université de Sherbrooke, Faculty of Physical Education and Sports, Program in Physical Education, Sherbrooke, QC J1K 2R1, Canada. Offers kinanthropology (M Sc); physical activity (Diploma). *Degree requirements:* For master's, thesis. *Entrance requirements:* For master's, minimum GPA of 2.7; for Diploma, bachelor's degree in physical education. *Faculty research:* Physical fitness, nutrition, human factors, sociology, teaching.

Université du Québec à Montréal, Graduate Programs, Program in Human Movement Studies, Montréal, QC H3C 3P8, Canada. Offers M Sc. *Program availability:* Part-time. *Degree requirements:* For master's, thesis optional. *Entrance requirements:* For master's, appropriate bachelor's degree or equivalent and proficiency in French.

Université Laval, Faculty of Medicine, Graduate Programs in Medicine, Programs in Kinesiology, Québec, QC G1K 7P4, Canada. Offers M Sc, PhD. Terminal master's awarded for partial completion of doctoral program. *Degree requirements:* For master's, thesis; for doctorate, comprehensive exam, thesis/dissertation. *Entrance requirements:* For master's and doctorate, French exam, knowledge of French, comprehension of written English. Electronic applications accepted.

The University of Alabama, Graduate School, College of Education, Department of Kinesiology, Tuscaloosa, AL 35487. Offers alternative sport pedagogy (MA); exercise science (PhD). *Program availability:* Part-time. *Faculty:* 12 full-time (2 women). *Students:* 70 full-time (35 women), 22 part-time (6 women); includes 16 minority (9 Black or African American, non-Hispanic/Latino; 4 Hispanic/Latino; 3 Two or more races, non-Hispanic/Latino), 7 international. Average age 29. 71 applicants, 76% accepted, 38 enrolled. In 2016, 39 master's, 8 doctorates awarded. *Degree requirements:* For master's, comprehensive exam, thesis optional; for doctorate, comprehensive exam, thesis/dissertation. *Entrance requirements:* For master's and doctorate, GRE, minimum GPA of 3.0. Additional exam requirements/recommendations for international students: Required—TOEFL. *Application deadline:* Applications are processed on a rolling basis. Electronic applications accepted. *Expenses:* Tuition, state resident: full-time $10,470. Tuition, nonresident: full-time $26,950. *Financial support:* Application deadline: 3/1. *Total annual research expenditures:* $39,044. *Unit head:* Dr. Jonathan Wingo, Associate Professor and Head, 205-348-4699, Fax: 205-348-0867, E-mail: jwingo@ua.edu.
Website: http://education.ua.edu/academics/kine/

University of Arkansas, Graduate School, College of Education and Health Professions, Department of Health, Human Performance and Recreation, Program in Kinesiology, Fayetteville, AR 72701. Offers MS, PhD. In 2016, 20 master's, 1 doctorate awarded. *Degree requirements:* For doctorate, thesis/dissertation. *Entrance requirements:* For doctorate, GRE General Test. *Application deadline:* For fall admission, 4/1 for international students; for spring admission, 10/1 for international students. Applications are processed on a rolling basis. Application fee: $40 ($50 for international students). Electronic applications accepted. *Financial support:* Fellowships with tuition reimbursements, research assistantships, teaching assistantships, career-related internships or fieldwork, and Federal Work-Study available. Support available to part-time students. Financial award application deadline: 4/1; financial award applicants required to submit FAFSA. *Unit head:* Dr. Bart Hammig, Departmental Chairperson, 479-575-2857, Fax: 479-575-5778, E-mail: bhammig@uark.edu. *Application contact:* Dr. Stephen Dittmore, Coordinator of Graduate Studies, 479-575-6625, E-mail: dittmore@uark.edu.
Website: http://kins.uark.edu/

The University of British Columbia, Faculty of Education, School of Kinesiology, Vancouver, BC V6T 1Z1, Canada. Offers high performance coaching and technical leadership (MHPCTL); kinesiology (M Kin, M Sc, MA, PhD). *Program availability:* Part-time. *Degree requirements:* For master's, thesis (for some programs); for doctorate, comprehensive exam, thesis/dissertation. *Entrance requirements:* For doctorate, thesis-based master's degree. Additional exam requirements/recommendations for international students: Required—TOEFL, IELTS. *Application deadline:* Applications are processed on a rolling basis. Application fee: $100 Canadian dollars ($162 Canadian dollars for international students). Electronic applications accepted. *Expenses:* Contact institution. *Financial support:* Fellowships, research assistantships, teaching assistantships, career-related internships or fieldwork, Federal Work-Study, institutionally sponsored loans, scholarships/grants, and tuition waivers (full and partial) available. Financial award application deadline: 3/1. *Faculty research:* Exercise physiology, biomechanics, motor learning, natural sciences, socio-managerial. *Application contact:* Helen Luk, Graduate Program Staff, 604-822-4641, Fax: 604-822-6842, E-mail: kin.gradsec@ubc.ca.

University of Calgary, Faculty of Graduate Studies, Faculty of Kinesiology, Calgary, AB T2N 1N4, Canada. Offers M Kin, M Sc, PhD. *Degree requirements:* For master's, thesis (M Sc); for doctorate, thesis/dissertation. *Entrance requirements:* Additional exam requirements/recommendations for international students: Required—TOEFL. Electronic applications accepted. *Faculty research:* Load acting on the human body, muscle mechanics and physiology, optimizing high performance athlete performance, eye movement in sports, analysis of body composition.

University of Central Arkansas, Graduate School, College of Health and Behavioral Sciences, Department of Kinesiology, Conway, AR 72035-0001. Offers MS. *Program availability:* Part-time. *Degree requirements:* For master's, comprehensive exam, thesis optional. *Entrance requirements:* For master's, GRE General Test, minimum GPA of 2.7. Additional exam requirements/recommendations for international students: Required—TOEFL (minimum score 550 paper-based; 80 iBT). Electronic applications accepted.

University of Central Missouri, The Graduate School, Warrensburg, MO 64093. Offers accountancy (MA); accounting (MBA); applied mathematics (MS); aviation safety (MA); biology (MS); business administration (MBA); career and technical education leadership (MS); college student personnel administration (MS); communication (MA); computer science (MS); counseling (MS); criminal justice (MS); educational leadership (Ed D); educational technology (MS); elementary and early childhood education (MSE); English (MA); environmental studies (MA); finance (MBA); history (MA); human services/educational technology (Ed S); human services/learning resources (Ed S); human services/professional counseling (Ed S); industrial hygiene (MS); industrial management (MS); information systems (MBA); information technology (MS); kinesiology (MS); library science and information services (MS); literacy education (MSE); marketing (MBA); mathematics (MS); music (MA); occupational safety management (MS); psychology (MS); rural family nursing (MS); school administration (MSE); social gerontology (MS); sociology (MA); special education (MSE); speech language pathology (MS); superintendency (Ed S); teaching (MAT); teaching English as a second language (MA); technology (MS); technology management (PhD); theatre (MA). *Program availability:* Part-time, 100% online, blended/hybrid learning. *Degree requirements:* For master's and Ed S, comprehensive exam (for some programs), thesis (for some programs). *Entrance requirements:* Additional exam requirements/recommendations for international students: Required—TOEFL (minimum score 550 paper-based; 79 iBT). Electronic applications accepted.

University of Colorado Boulder, Graduate School, College of Arts and Sciences, Department of Integrative Physiology, Boulder, CO 80309. Offers MS, PhD. *Faculty:* 23 full-time (7 women). *Students:* 61 full-time (30 women), 3 part-time (1 woman); includes 7 minority (1 Black or African American, non-Hispanic/Latino; 1 Asian, non-Hispanic/Latino; 4 Hispanic/Latino; 1 Two or more races, non-Hispanic/Latino), 2 international. Average age 27. 94 applicants, 22% accepted, 18 enrolled. In 2016, 16 master's, 4 doctorates awarded. Terminal master's awarded for partial completion of doctoral program. *Degree requirements:* For master's, comprehensive exam, thesis or alternative; for doctorate, thesis/dissertation. *Entrance requirements:* For master's, GRE General Test, minimum undergraduate GPA of 2.75. *Application deadline:* For fall admission, 1/15 for domestic students, 12/15 for international students. Applications are processed on a rolling basis. Application fee: $60 ($80 for international students). Electronic applications accepted. Application fee is waived when completed online. *Financial support:* In 2016–17, 191 students received support, including 51 fellowships (averaging $4,560 per year), 27 research assistantships with full and partial tuition reimbursements available (averaging $21,483 per year), 41 teaching assistantships with full and partial tuition reimbursements available (averaging $32,627 per year); institutionally sponsored loans, scholarships/grants, health care benefits, and unspecified assistantships also available. Financial award application deadline: 2/1; financial award applicants required to submit FAFSA. *Faculty research:* Aging/gerontology, human physiology, nervous system, neurophysiology, neuroscience. *Total annual research expenditures:* $6.3 million. *Application contact:* E-mail: iphygrad@colorado.edu.
Website: http://www.colorado.edu/intphys/

University of Delaware, College of Arts and Sciences, Interdisciplinary Program in Biomechanics and Movement Science, Newark, DE 19716. Offers MS, PhD. *Program availability:* Part-time. Terminal master's awarded for partial completion of doctoral program. *Degree requirements:* For master's, thesis; for doctorate, thesis/dissertation. *Entrance requirements:* For master's and doctorate, GRE General Test, minimum undergraduate GPA of 3.0. Additional exam requirements/recommendations for international students: Required—TOEFL (minimum score 550 paper-based). Electronic applications accepted. *Faculty research:* Muscle modeling, gait, motor control, human movement.

University of Delaware, College of Health Sciences, Department of Kinesiology and Applied Physiology, Newark, DE 19716. Offers MS, PhD.

University of Florida, Graduate School, College of Health and Human Performance, Department of Applied Physiology and Kinesiology, Gainesville, FL 32611. Offers applied physiology and kinesiology (MS); athletic training/sports medicine (MS); biobehavioral science (MS); clinical exercise physiology (MS); exercise physiology (MS); health and human performance (PhD), including applied physiology and kinesiology, biobehavioral science, exercise physiology; human performance (MS). *Degree requirements:* For master's, comprehensive exam, thesis (for some programs); for doctorate, comprehensive exam, thesis/dissertation. *Entrance requirements:* For master's and doctorate, GRE General Test, minimum GPA of 3.0. Additional exam requirements/recommendations for international students: Required—TOEFL (minimum score 550 paper-based; 80 iBT), IELTS (minimum score 6). Electronic applications accepted. *Faculty research:* Cardiovascular disease; basic mechanisms that underlie exercise-induced changes in the body at the organ, tissue, cellular and molecular level; development of rehabilitation techniques for regaining motor control after stroke or as a consequence of Parkinson's disease; maintaining optimal health and delaying age-related declines in physiological function; psychomotor mechanisms impacting health and performance across the life span.

University of Georgia, College of Education, Department of Kinesiology, Athens, GA 30602. Offers MS, PhD. *Entrance requirements:* For master's, GRE General Test or MAT; for doctorate, GRE General Test. Additional exam requirements/recommendations for international students: Required—TOEFL. *Application deadline:* For fall admission, 7/1 priority date for domestic students; for spring admission, 11/15 for domestic students. Application fee: $50. Electronic applications accepted. *Unit head:* Dr. Kirk J. Cureton, Head, 706-542-4387, Fax: 706-542-3148, E-mail: kcureton@uga.edu. *Application contact:* Ellen M. Evans, Graduate Coordinator, 706-542-9257, E-mail: emevans@uga.edu.
Website: http://www.coe.uga.edu/kinesiology

University of Hawaii at Manoa, Graduate Division, College of Education, Department of Kinesiology and Rehabilitation Science, Honolulu, HI 96822. Offers kinesiology (MS). *Program availability:* Part-time. *Degree requirements:* For master's, thesis optional. *Entrance requirements:* For master's, GRE General Test. Additional exam requirements/recommendations for international students: Required—TOEFL (minimum score 540 paper-based; 76 iBT), IELTS (minimum score 5).

University of Hawaii at Manoa, Graduate Division, College of Education, PhD in Education Program, Honolulu, HI 96822. Offers curriculum and instruction (PhD); educational administration (PhD); educational foundations (PhD); educational policy studies (PhD); educational psychology (PhD); exceptionalities (PhD); kinesiology (PhD); learning design and technology (PhD). *Program availability:* Part-time, evening/weekend. *Degree requirements:* For doctorate, thesis/dissertation. *Entrance requirements:* For doctorate, GRE General Test, sample of written work. Additional exam requirements/recommendations for international students: Required—TOEFL (minimum score 600 paper-based; 100 iBT), IELTS (minimum score 7).

University of Houston, College of Liberal Arts and Social Sciences, Department of Health and Human Performance, Houston, TX 77204. Offers exercise science (MS); human nutrition (MS); human space exploration sciences (MS); kinesiology (PhD); physical education (M Ed). *Accreditation:* NCATE (one or more programs are accredited). *Program availability:* Part-time, evening/weekend. *Degree requirements:* For master's, comprehensive exam (for some programs), thesis (for some programs); for doctorate, comprehensive exam, thesis/dissertation, qualifying exam, candidacy paper. *Entrance requirements:* For master's, GRE (minimum 35th percentile on each section), minimum cumulative GPA of 3.0; for doctorate, GRE (minimum 35th percentile on each section), minimum cumulative GPA of 3.3. Additional exam requirements/recommendations for international students: Required—TOEFL (minimum score 550 paper-based; 79 iBT). Electronic applications accepted. *Faculty research:* Biomechanics, exercise physiology, obesity, nutrition, space exploration science.

University of Illinois at Chicago, College of Applied Health Sciences, Program in Kinesiology, Chicago, IL 60607-7128. Offers MS, PhD. *Program availability:* Part-time. *Degree requirements:* For master's, thesis. *Entrance requirements:* For master's, GRE General Test, minimum GPA of 2.75. Additional exam requirements/recommendations for international students: Required—TOEFL. Electronic applications accepted. *Expenses:* Contact institution. *Faculty research:* Mitochondrial biogenesis, glucocorticoid lipid metabolism, at-risk youth, motor control.

University of Illinois at Urbana–Champaign, Graduate College, College of Applied Health Sciences, Department of Kinesiology and Community Health, Champaign, IL 61820. Offers community health (MS, MSPH, PhD); kinesiology (MS, PhD); public health (MPH); rehabilitation (MS); PhD/MPH.

University of Kentucky, Graduate School, College of Education, Program in Kinesiology and Health Promotion, Lexington, KY 40506-0032. Offers biomechanics (MS); exercise physiology (MS, PhD); exercise science (PhD); health promotion (MS, Ed D); physical education training (Ed D); sport leadership (MS); teaching and coaching (MS). Terminal master's awarded for partial completion of doctoral program. *Degree requirements:* For master's, comprehensive exam, thesis optional; for doctorate, comprehensive exam, thesis/dissertation. *Entrance requirements:* For master's, GRE General Test, minimum undergraduate GPA of 2.75; for doctorate, GRE General Test, minimum graduate GPA of 3.0. Additional exam requirements/recommendations for international students: Required—TOEFL (minimum score 550 paper-based). Electronic applications accepted.

University of Lethbridge, School of Graduate Studies, Lethbridge, AB T1K 3M4, Canada. Offers addictions counseling (M Sc); agricultural biotechnology (M Sc); agricultural studies (M Sc, MA); anthropology (MA); archaeology (M Sc, MA); art (MA, MFA); biochemistry (M Sc); biological sciences (M Sc); biomolecular science (PhD); biosystems and biodiversity (PhD); Canadian studies (MA); chemistry (M Sc); computer science (M Sc); computer science and geographical information science (M Sc); counseling (MC); counseling psychology (M Ed); dramatic arts (MA); earth, space, and physical science (PhD); economics (MA); education (MA, PhD); educational leadership (M Ed); English (MA); environmental science (M Sc); evolution and behavior (PhD); exercise science (M Sc); French (MA); French/German (MA); French/Spanish (MA); general education (M Ed); geography (M Sc, MA); German (MA); health sciences (M Sc); individualized multidisciplinary (M Sc, MA); kinesiology (M Sc, MA); management (M Sc), including accounting, finance, human resource management and labor relations, information systems, international management, marketing, policy and strategy, mathematics (M Sc); music (M Mus, MA); Native American studies (MA); neuroscience (M Sc, PhD); new media (MA, MFA); nursing (M Sc, MN); philosophy (MA); physics (M Sc); political science (MA); psychology (M Sc, MA); religious studies (MA); sociology (MA); theatre and dramatic arts (MFA); theoretical and computational science (PhD); urban and regional studies (MA); women and gender studies (MA). *Program availability:* Part-time, evening/weekend. *Degree requirements:* For master's, thesis (for some programs); for doctorate, comprehensive exam, thesis/dissertation. *Entrance requirements:* For master's, GMAT (for M Sc in management), bachelor's degree in related field, minimum GPA of 3.0 during previous 20 graded semester courses, 2 years' teaching or related experience (M Ed); for doctorate, master's degree, minimum graduate GPA of 3.5. Additional exam requirements/recommendations for international students: Required—TOEFL (minimum score 580 paper-based; 93 iBT). Electronic applications accepted. *Faculty research:* Movement and brain plasticity, gibberellin physiology, photosynthesis, carbon cycling, molecular properties of main-group ring components.

University of Maine, Graduate School, College of Education and Human Development, School of Kinesiology, Physical Education and Athletic Training, Orono, ME 04469. Offers classroom technology integrationist (CGS); education data specialist (CGS); educational technology coordinator (CGS); kinesiology and physical education (M Ed, MS); science education (M Ed, MS); STEM education (PhD). *Program availability:* Part-time, evening/weekend. *Students:* 13 full-time (4 women), 1 (woman) part-time; includes 1 minority (Hispanic/Latino), 1 international. Average age 24. 15 applicants, 100% accepted, 7 enrolled. In 2016, 16 master's, 10 other advanced degrees awarded. *Degree requirements:* For master's, thesis (for some programs); for doctorate, comprehensive exam, thesis/dissertation. *Entrance requirements:* For master's, GRE General Test, MAT; for doctorate, GRE General Test. Additional exam requirements/recommendations for international students: Required—TOEFL. *Application deadline:* For fall admission, 1/15 for domestic students. Applications are processed on a rolling basis. Application fee: $65. Electronic applications accepted. *Expenses:* Tuition, state resident: full-time $7524; part-time $2508 per credit. Tuition, nonresident: full-time $24,498; part-time $8166 per credit. *Required fees:* $1148; $571 per credit. *Financial support:* In 2016–17, 9 students received support, including 1 research assistantship with full tuition reimbursement available (averaging $14,600 per year), 6 teaching assistantships (averaging $14,600 per year); Federal Work-Study, scholarships/grants, and unspecified assistantships also available. Financial award application deadline: 3/1. *Faculty research:* Integration of technology in K-12 classrooms, instructional theory and practice in science, inquiry-based teaching, professional development, exercise science, adaptive physical education, neuromuscular function/dysfunction. *Unit head:* Dr. Jim Artesani, Associate Dean of Accreditation and Graduate Affairs, 207-581-4061, Fax: 207-581-2423. *Application contact:* Scott G. Delcourt, Assistant Vice President for Graduate Studies and Senior Associate Dean, 207-581-3291, Fax: 207-581-3232, E-mail: graduate@maine.edu.
Website: http://umaine.edu/edhd/

University of Manitoba, Faculty of Graduate Studies, Faculty of Kinesiology and Recreation Management, Winnipeg, MB R3T 2N2, Canada. Offers kinesiology and recreation (M Sc, MA).

University of Mary, School of Health Sciences, Program in Kinesiology, Bismarck, ND 58504-9652. Offers MS. *Program availability:* Part-time, online learning.

University of Maryland, College Park, Academic Affairs, School of Public Health, Department of Kinesiology, College Park, MD 20742. Offers MA, PhD. *Program availability:* Part-time, evening/weekend. *Degree requirements:* For master's, thesis optional; for doctorate, thesis/dissertation. *Entrance requirements:* For master's, GRE General Test, minimum GPA of 3.0, 3 letters of recommendation; for doctorate, GRE General Test, minimum GPA of 3.5, 3 letters of recommendation. Electronic applications accepted. *Faculty research:* Sports, biophysical and professional studies, cognitive motor behavior, exercise physiology.

University of Massachusetts Amherst, Graduate School, School of Public Health and Health Sciences, Department of Kinesiology, Amherst, MA 01003. Offers MS, PhD. *Program availability:* Part-time. Terminal master's awarded for partial completion of doctoral program. *Degree requirements:* For master's, comprehensive exam (for some programs), thesis optional; for doctorate, comprehensive exam, thesis/dissertation. *Entrance requirements:* For master's and doctorate, GRE General Test. Additional exam requirements/recommendations for international students: Required—TOEFL (minimum score 550 paper-based; 80 iBT), IELTS (minimum score 6.5). Electronic applications accepted.

University of Michigan, Rackham Graduate School, School of Kinesiology, Ann Arbor, MI 48109. Offers movement science (MS, PhD); sport management (MS, PhD). *Faculty:* 31 full-time (16 women). *Students:* 87 full-time (32 women); includes 39 minority (5 Black or African American, non-Hispanic/Latino; 1 American Indian or Alaska Native, non-Hispanic/Latino; 23 Asian, non-Hispanic/Latino; 6 Hispanic/Latino; 4 Two or more races, non-Hispanic/Latino). 229 applicants, 45% accepted, 49 enrolled. In 2016, 30 master's, 6 doctorates awarded. Terminal master's awarded for partial completion of doctoral program. *Degree requirements:* For master's, thesis optional; for doctorate, comprehensive exam, thesis/dissertation, oral defense of dissertation. *Entrance requirements:* For master's and doctorate, GRE General Test. Additional exam requirements/recommendations for international students: Required—TOEFL (minimum score 84 iBT). *Application deadline:* For fall admission, 1/15 priority date for domestic students, 1/15 for international students. Applications are processed on a rolling basis. Application fee: $75 ($90 for international students). Electronic applications accepted. *Expenses:* Tuition, state resident: full-time $21,466; part-time $1152 per credit hour. Tuition, nonresident: full-time $43,346; part-time $2367 per credit hour. Part-time tuition and fees vary according to course load, degree level and program. *Financial support:* In 2016–17, 3 fellowships, 18 research assistantships, 12 teaching assistantships were awarded; Federal Work-Study, scholarships/grants, traineeships, health care benefits, and unspecified assistantships also available. Financial award application deadline: 1/15. *Faculty research:* Motor development, exercise physiology, biomechanics, sport medicine, sport management. *Unit head:* Dr. Ketra L. Armstrong, Associate Dean for Graduate Programs and Faculty Affairs, 734-647-3027, Fax: 734-647-2808, E-mail: ketra@umich.edu. *Application contact:* Charlene F. Ruloff, Graduate Program Coordinator, 734-764-1343, Fax: 734-647-2808, E-mail: cruloff@umich.edu.
Website: http://www.kines.umich.edu/

University of Minnesota, Twin Cities Campus, Graduate School, College of Education and Human Development, School of Kinesiology, Minneapolis, MN 55455-0213. Offers kinesiology (MS, PhD), including behavioral aspects of physical activity, biomechanics and neuromotor control, exercise physiology, perceptual-motor control and learning, sport and exercise psychology, sport management (PhD), sport sociology; sport and exercise science (M Ed); sport management (M Ed, MA). *Program availability:* Part-time. *Faculty:* 15 full-time (6 women). *Students:* 117 full-time (54 women), 32 part-time (17 women); includes 21 minority (5 Black or African American, non-Hispanic/Latino; 1 American Indian or Alaska Native, non-Hispanic/Latino; 5 Asian, non-Hispanic/Latino; 7 Hispanic/Latino; 3 Two or more races, non-Hispanic/Latino), 20 international. Average age 27. 170 applicants, 45% accepted, 66 enrolled. In 2016, 85 master's, 5 doctorates awarded. Terminal master's awarded for partial completion of doctoral program. *Degree requirements:* For master's, final oral exam; for doctorate, thesis/dissertation, preliminary written/oral exam, final oral exam. *Entrance requirements:* For master's, GRE or MAT, minimum GPA of 3.0; for doctorate, GRE or MAT, minimum GPA of 3.0, writing sample. Application fee: $75 ($95 for international students). *Financial support:* In 2016–17, 3 fellowships, 11 research assistantships with full tuition reimbursements (averaging $11,857 per year), 42 teaching assistantships with full tuition reimbursements (averaging $14,262 per year) were awarded; career-related internships or fieldwork, Federal Work-Study, institutionally sponsored loans, and tuition waivers (full and partial) also available. Support available to part-time students. *Faculty research:* Role of physical activity in preventing health related problems; mechanism of age-related disorders, diseases and mental problems, and the ways to ameliorate them; role of sports in society and social justice; sports among populations with low income and racial diversity; fundamental functions of the body and the mechanism controlling the mechanisms; psychological issues related to physical activity and sports. *Total annual research expenditures:* $939,073. *Unit head:* Dr. Li Li Ji, Director, 612-624-9809, E-mail: llji@umn.edu. *Application contact:* Dr. Michael Wade, Director of Graduate Studies, 612-626-2094, E-mail: mwade@umn.edu.
Website: http://www.cehd.umn.edu/kin/

University of Mississippi, Graduate School, School of Applied Sciences, University, MS 38677. Offers communicative disorders (MS); exercise science (MS); food and nutrition services (MS); health and kinesiology (PhD); health promotion (MS); park and recreation management (MA); social work (MSW). *Faculty:* 68 full-time (29 women), 29 part-time/adjunct (17 women). *Students:* 176 full-time (137 women), 36 part-time (21 women); includes 45 minority (40 Black or African American, non-Hispanic/Latino; 4 Hispanic/Latino; 1 Two or more races, non-Hispanic/Latino), 9 international. Average age 24. *Entrance requirements:* For master's, GRE General Test, minimum GPA of 3.0. Additional exam requirements/recommendations for international students: Required—TOEFL. *Application deadline:* For fall admission, 4/1 for domestic students; for spring admission, 10/1 for domestic students. Applications are processed on a rolling basis. Application fee: $40. Electronic applications accepted. *Financial support:* Scholarships/grants available. Financial award application deadline: 3/1; financial award applicants required to submit FAFSA. *Unit head:* Dr. Velmer Stanley Burton, Dean, 662-915-1081, Fax: 662-915-5717, E-mail: applsci@olemiss.edu. *Application contact:* Dr. Christy M. Wyandt, Associate Dean of Graduate School, 662-915-7474, Fax: 662-915-7577, E-mail: cwyandt@olemiss.edu.
Website: https://www.olemiss.edu

University of Nebraska at Omaha, Graduate Studies, College of Education, School of Health and Kinesiology, Omaha, NE 68182. Offers athletic training (MA); exercise science (PhD); health, physical education, and recreation (MA, MS). *Program availability:* Part-time, evening/weekend. *Faculty:* 7 full-time (2 women). *Students:* 79 full-time (31 women), 28 part-time (13 women); includes 8 minority (2 Black or African American, non-Hispanic/Latino; 1 Asian, non-Hispanic/Latino; 2 Hispanic/Latino; 3 Two or more races, non-Hispanic/Latino), 18 international. Average age 26. 65 applicants, 74% accepted, 34 enrolled. In 2016, 38 master's, 1 doctorate awarded. *Degree requirements:* For master's, comprehensive exam, thesis (for some programs). *Entrance requirements:* For master's, GRE; entrance exam, minimum GPA of 3.0, official transcripts, statement of purpose, 2 letters of recommendation; for doctorate, GRE, minimum GPA of 3.2, official transcripts, statement of purpose, 3 letters of recommendation, resume, writing sample. Additional exam requirements/recommendations for international students: Required—TOEFL, IELTS, PTE. *Application deadline:* For fall admission, 7/1 priority date for domestic and international students; for spring admission, 11/1 priority date for domestic and international students; for summer admission, 1/15 for domestic and international students. Applications are processed on a rolling basis. Application fee: $45. Electronic applications accepted. *Financial support:* In 2016–17, 47 students received support, including 34 research assistantships with tuition reimbursements available, 13 teaching assistantships with tuition reimbursements available; fellowships, Federal Work-Study, institutionally sponsored loans, scholarships/grants, health care benefits, tuition waivers (full), and unspecified assistantships also available. Support available to part-time students. Financial award application deadline: 3/1; financial award applicants required to submit FAFSA. *Unit head:* Dr. Roland Bulbulian, Director, 402-554-2341, E-mail: graduate@unomaha.edu. *Application contact:* Dr. Dustin Slivka, Graduate Program Chair, 402-554-2341, E-mail: graduate@unomaha.edu.

University of Nevada, Las Vegas, Graduate College, School of Allied Health Sciences, Department of Kinesiology and Nutrition Sciences, Las Vegas, NV 89154-3034. Offers exercise physiology (MS); kinesiology (PhD); nutrition sciences (MS). *Program availability:* Part-time. *Faculty:* 12 full-time (6 women). *Students:* 35 full-time (20 women), 12 part-time (3 women); includes 8 minority (1 Black or African American, non-Hispanic/Latino; 1 American Indian or Alaska Native, non-Hispanic/Latino; 2 Asian, non-Hispanic/Latino; 2 Hispanic/Latino; 2 Two or more races, non-Hispanic/Latino), 3 international. Average age 28. 49 applicants, 59% accepted, 18 enrolled. In 2016, 11 master's awarded. *Degree requirements:* For master's, thesis (for some programs), professional paper; for doctorate, comprehensive exam, thesis/dissertation. *Entrance requirements:* For master's, GRE General Test, bachelor's degree; statement of purpose; 2 letters of recommendation; for doctorate, GRE General Test (minimum 70th percentile on the Verbal section), master's degree/bachelor's degree with minimum GPA of 3.25; 3 letters of recommendation; statement of purpose; personal interview. Additional exam requirements/recommendations for international students: Required—TOEFL (minimum score 550 paper-based; 80 iBT), IELTS (minimum score 7). *Application deadline:* For fall admission, 6/15 for domestic students, 5/1 for international students; for spring admission, 11/15 for domestic students, 10/1 for international students. Application fee: $60 ($95 for international students). Electronic applications accepted. *Expenses:* $269.25 per credit, $792 per 3-credit course; $9,634 per year resident; $23,274 per year non-resident; $7,094 fees non-resident (7 credits or more); $1,307 annual health insurance fee. *Financial support:* In 2016–17, 13 research assistantships with partial tuition reimbursements (averaging $13,808 per year), 13 teaching assistantships with partial tuition reimbursements (averaging $12,269 per year) were awarded; institutionally sponsored loans, scholarships/grants, health care benefits, and unspecified assistantships also available. Financial award application deadline: 3/15. *Faculty research:* Biomechanics of gait, factors in motor skill acquisition and performance, nutritional supplements and performance, lipoprotein biochemistry, transcranial direct current stimulation. *Total annual research expenditures:* $45,437. *Unit head:* Dr. Brian Schilling, Chair/Professor, 702-895-1130, Fax: 702-895-1500, E-mail: brian.schilling@unlv.edu. *Application contact:* Dr. Janet Dufek, Graduate Coordinator, 702-895-0702, Fax: 702-895-1500, E-mail: janet.dufek@unlv.edu.

University of New Hampshire, Graduate School, College of Health and Human Services, Department of Kinesiology, Durham, NH 03824. Offers adapted physical education (Postbaccalaureate Certificate); kinesiology (MS); kinesiology and social work (MS). *Program availability:* Part-time. *Degree requirements:* For master's, thesis or alternative. *Entrance requirements:* For master's, GRE General Test. Additional exam requirements/recommendations for international students: Required—TOEFL (minimum score 550 paper-based; 80 iBT). *Application deadline:* For fall admission, 6/1 priority date for domestic students, 4/1 for international students; for spring admission, 12/1 for domestic students. Applications are processed on a rolling basis. Application fee: $65. *Financial support:* Fellowships, research assistantships, teaching assistantships, career-related internships or fieldwork, Federal Work-Study, scholarships/grants, and tuition waivers (full and partial) available. Support available to part-time students. Financial award application deadline: 2/15. *Faculty research:* Exercise specialist, sports studies, special physical education, pediatric exercises and motor behavior. *Unit head:* Karen Collins, Chair, 603-862-0361. *Application contact:* Tarah Beaupre, Administrative Assistant, 603-862-2071, E-mail: kinesiology.dept@unh.edu.
Website: http://chhs.unh.edu/kin

University of New Hampshire, Graduate School, College of Health and Human Services, Department of Social Work, Durham, NH 03824. Offers child welfare (Postbaccalaureate Certificate); intellectual and development disabilities (Postbaccalaureate Certificate); social work (MSW); social work and kinesiology (MSW); substance use disorders (Postbaccalaureate Certificate); MSW/JD. *Accreditation:* CSWE. *Program availability:* Part-time. *Entrance requirements:* Additional exam requirements/recommendations for international students: Required—TOEFL (minimum score 550 paper-based; 80 iBT). *Application deadline:* For fall admission, 2/1 for domestic and international students. Applications are processed on a rolling basis. Application fee: $65. Electronic applications accepted. *Financial support:* Fellowships, research assistantships, teaching assistantships, career-related internships or fieldwork, Federal Work-Study, and scholarships/grants available. Support available to part-time students. Financial award application deadline: 2/15. *Unit head:* Vernon Carter, Chair, 603-862-0199. *Application contact:* Emilie Cilley, Administrative Assistant, 603-862-0215, E-mail: emilie.cilley@unh.edu.
Website: http://www.chhs.unh.edu/sw

University of North Alabama, College of Education, Department of Health, Physical Education, and Recreation, Florence, AL 35632-0001. Offers health and human performance (MS), including exercise science, kinesiology, wellness and health promotion. *Program availability:* Part-time. *Faculty:* 7 full-time (2 women). *Students:* 10 full-time (5 women), 11 part-time (4 women); includes 2 minority (both Black or African American, non-Hispanic/Latino), 2 international. Average age 24. 19 applicants, 68% accepted, 11 enrolled. In 2016, 14 master's awarded. *Degree requirements:* For master's, comprehensive exam (for some programs), thesis optional. *Entrance requirements:* For master's, MAT or GRE, 3 letters of recommendation, essay. Additional exam requirements/recommendations for international students: Required—TOEFL (minimum score 79 iBT), IELTS (minimum score 6), PTE (minimum score 54). *Application deadline:* Applications are processed on a rolling basis. Application fee: $50 ($100 for international students). Electronic applications accepted. *Expenses:* Tuition, state resident: full-time $2799; part-time $1866 per semester. Tuition, nonresident: full-time $5598; part-time $3732 per semester. *Required fees:* $915; $642 per semester. Tuition and fees vary according to course load. *Financial support:* In 2016–17, 19 students received support. Scholarships/grants and unspecified assistantships available. Financial award application deadline: 2/1; financial award applicants required to submit FAFSA. *Unit head:* Dr. Thomas E. Coates, Chair, 256-765-4377. *Application contact:* Hillary N. Coats, Graduate Admissions Coordinator, 256-765-4447, E-mail: graduate@una.edu.
Website: https://www.una.edu/hper/index.html

The University of North Carolina at Chapel Hill, School of Medicine and Graduate School, Graduate Programs in Medicine, Chapel Hill, NC 27599. Offers allied health sciences (MPT, MS, Au D, DPT, PhD), including human movement science (MS, PhD), occupational science (MS, PhD), physical therapy (MPT, MS, DPT), rehabilitation counseling and psychology (MS), speech and hearing sciences (MS, Au D, PhD); biochemistry and biophysics (MS, PhD); bioinformatics and computational biology (PhD); biomedical engineering (MS, PhD); cell and developmental biology (PhD); cell and molecular physiology (PhD); genetics and molecular biology (PhD); microbiology and immunology (MS, PhD), including immunology, microbiology; neurobiology (PhD); pathology and laboratory medicine (PhD), including experimental pathology; pharmacology (PhD); MD/PhD. *Program availability:* Online learning. Terminal master's awarded for partial completion of doctoral program. *Degree requirements:* For master's, comprehensive exam; for doctorate, thesis/dissertation. Electronic applications accepted. *Expenses:* Contact institution.

The University of North Carolina at Chapel Hill, School of Medicine and Graduate School, Graduate Programs in Medicine, Department of Allied Health Sciences, Curriculum in Human Movement Science, Chapel Hill, NC 27599. Offers PhD. *Degree requirements:* For doctorate, comprehensive exam, thesis/dissertation or alternative. *Entrance requirements:* For doctorate, GRE General Test, curriculum vitae, minimum GPA of 3.0. Additional exam requirements/recommendations for international students: Required—TOEFL (minimum score 550 paper-based). Electronic applications accepted. *Faculty research:* Orthopaedics, neuromuscular, biomedical endocrinology, postural control developmental disabilities.

The University of North Carolina at Chapel Hill, School of Medicine and Graduate School, Graduate Programs in Medicine, Department of Allied Health Sciences, Program in Human Movement Science, Chapel Hill, NC 27599. Offers PhD. *Entrance requirements:* Additional exam requirements/recommendations for international students: Required—TOEFL (minimum score 550 paper-based). Electronic applications accepted.

The University of North Carolina at Charlotte, College of Health and Human Services, Department of Kinesiology, Charlotte, NC 28223-0001. Offers kinesiology (MS); respiratory care (MS). *Program availability:* Part-time. *Faculty:* 14 full-time (6 women). *Students:* 23 full-time (12 women), 16 part-time (10 women); includes 13 minority (9 Black or African American, non-Hispanic/Latino; 3 Hispanic/Latino; 1 Two or more races, non-Hispanic/Latino), 1 international. Average age 25. 36 applicants, 81% accepted, 18 enrolled. In 2016, 20 master's awarded. *Degree requirements:* For master's, comprehensive exam, thesis (for some programs), thesis or practicum. *Entrance requirements:* For master's, GRE, minimum overall cumulative GPA of 3.0 in all college coursework, upper-division 3.25; demonstrated evidence of sufficient interest, ability, and preparation to adequately profit from graduate study. Additional exam requirements/recommendations for international students: Required—TOEFL (minimum score 523 paper-based, 70 iBT) or IELTS (6.5). *Application deadline:* For fall admission, 2/1 priority date for domestic and international students; for spring admission, 10/1 priority date for domestic and international students; for summer admission, 2/1 priority date for domestic and international students. Applications are processed on a rolling basis. Application fee: $75. Electronic applications accepted. *Expenses:* Tuition, state resident: full-time $4252. Tuition, nonresident: full-time $17,423. *Required fees:* $3026. Tuition and fees vary according to course load and program. *Financial support:* In 2016–17, 25 students received support, including 9 research assistantships (averaging $6,069 per year), 16 teaching assistantships (averaging $11,062 per year); career-related internships or fieldwork, institutionally sponsored loans, scholarships/grants, traineeships, and unspecified assistantships also available. Support available to part-time students. Financial award application deadline: 3/1; financial award applicants required to submit FAFSA. *Total annual research expenditures:* $106,445. *Unit head:* Dr. Scott E. Gordon, Chair, 704-687-0855, E-mail: scott.gordon@uncc.edu. *Application contact:* Kathy B. Giddings, Director of Graduate Admissions, 704-687-5503, Fax: 704-687-1668, E-mail: gradadm@uncc.edu.
Website: http://kinesiology.uncc.edu/

The University of North Carolina at Greensboro, Graduate School, School of Health and Human Sciences, Department of Kinesiology, Greensboro, NC 27412-5001. Offers athletic training (MSAT); kinesiology (MS, Ed D, PhD). *Program availability:* Online learning. *Degree requirements:* For master's, thesis (for some programs); for doctorate, thesis/dissertation. *Entrance requirements:* For master's and doctorate, GRE General Test. Additional exam requirements/recommendations for international students: Required—TOEFL. Electronic applications accepted.

University of North Dakota, Graduate School, College of Education and Human Development, Department of Kinesiology and Public Health Education, Grand Forks, ND 58202. Offers kinesiology (MS). *Program availability:* Part-time. *Degree requirements:* For master's, thesis or alternative, final or comprehensive examination. *Entrance requirements:* For master's, GRE General Test, minimum GPA of 3.0. Additional exam requirements/recommendations for international students: Required—TOEFL (minimum score 550 paper-based; 79 iBT), IELTS (minimum score 6.5). *Application deadline:* For fall admission, 8/1 priority date for domestic and international students; for spring admission, 12/1 priority date for domestic and international students. Applications are processed on a rolling basis. Application fee: $35. Electronic applications accepted. *Financial support:* Fellowships, research assistantships, teaching assistantships with full tuition reimbursements, Federal Work-Study, institutionally sponsored loans, scholarships/grants, health care benefits, tuition waivers (full and partial), and unspecified assistantships available. Support available to part-time students. Financial award application deadline: 3/15; financial award applicants required to submit FAFSA. *Faculty research:* Exercise physiology, exercise biomechanics, anatomy and physiology, exercise psychology. *Unit head:* Dr. James Whitehead, Graduate Director, 701-777-4325, Fax: 701-777-3619, E-mail: jameswhitehead@und.edu. *Application contact:* Staci Wells, Admissions Specialist, 701-777-0748, Fax: 701-777-3619, E-mail: staci.wells@gradschool.und.edu.
Website: http://www.und.edu/dept/pexs/

University of Northern Iowa, Graduate College, College of Education, School of Kinesiology, Allied Health and Human Services, MA Program in Physical Education, Cedar Falls, IA 50614. Offers kinesiology (MA); teaching/coaching (MA). *Program availability:* Part-time, evening/weekend. *Degree requirements:* For master's, comprehensive exam, thesis or alternative. *Entrance requirements:* For master's, minimum GPA of 3.0. Additional exam requirements/recommendations for international students: Required—TOEFL (minimum score 500 paper-based; 61 iBT). Electronic applications accepted.

University of North Texas, Robert B. Toulouse School of Graduate Studies, Denton, TX 76203-5459. Offers accounting (MS); applied anthropology (MA, MS); applied behavior analysis (Certificate); applied geography (MA); applied technology and performance improvement (M Ed, MS); art education (MA); art history (MA); art museum education (Certificate); arts leadership (Certificate); audiology (Au D); behavior analysis (MS); behavioral science (PhD); biochemistry and molecular biology (MS); biology (MA, MS); biomedical engineering (MS); business analysis (MS); chemistry (MS); clinical health psychology (PhD); communication studies (MA, MS); computer engineering (MS); computer science (MS); counseling (M Ed, MS), including clinical mental health counseling (MS), college and university counseling, elementary school counseling, secondary school counseling; creative writing (MA); criminal justice (MS); curriculum and instruction (M Ed); decision sciences (MBA); design (MA, MFA), including fashion design (MFA), innovation studies, interior design (MFA); early childhood studies (MS); economics (MS); educational leadership (M Ed, Ed D); educational psychology (MS, PhD), including family studies (MS), gifted and talented (MS), human development (MS), learning and cognition (MS), research, measurement and evaluation (MS); electrical engineering (MS); emergency management (MPA); engineering technology (MS); English (MA); English as a second language (MA); environmental science (MS); finance (MBA, MS); financial management (MPA); French (MA); health services management (MBA); higher education (M Ed, Ed D); history (MA, MS); hospitality management (MS); human resources management (MPA); information science (MS); information systems (PhD); information technologies (MBA); interdisciplinary studies (MA, MS); international studies (MA); international sustainable tourism (MS); jazz studies (MM); journalism (MA, MJ, Graduate Certificate), including interactive and virtual digital communication (Graduate Certificate), narrative journalism (Graduate Certificate), public relations (Graduate Certificate); kinesiology (MS); linguistics (MA); local government management (MPA); logistics (PhD); logistics and supply chain management (MBA); long-term care, senior housing, and aging services (MA); management (PhD); marketing (MBA); mathematics (MA, MS); mechanical and energy engineering (MS, PhD); music (MA), including ethnomusicology, music theory, musicology, performance; music composition (PhD); music education (MM Ed, PhD); nonprofit management (MPA); operations and supply chain management (MBA); performance (MM, DMA); philosophy (MA); political science (MA); professional and technical communication (MA); radio, television and film (MA, MFA); rehabilitation counseling (Certificate); sociology (MA); Spanish (MA); special education (M Ed); speech-language pathology (MA); strategic management (MBA); studio art (MFA); teaching (M Ed); MBA/MS. *Program availability:* Part-time, evening/weekend, online learning. Terminal master's awarded for partial completion of doctoral program. *Degree requirements:* For master's, variable foreign language requirement, comprehensive exam (for some programs), thesis (for some programs); for doctorate, variable foreign language requirement, comprehensive exam (for some programs), thesis/dissertation; for other advanced degree, variable foreign language requirement, comprehensive exam (for some programs). *Entrance requirements:* For master's and doctorate, GRE, GMAT. Additional exam requirements/recommendations for international students: Required—TOEFL (minimum score 550 paper-based; 79 iBT). Electronic applications accepted.

University of Ottawa, Faculty of Graduate and Postdoctoral Studies, Faculty of Health Sciences, School of Human Kinetics, Ottawa, ON K1N 6N5, Canada. Offers MA. *Degree requirements:* For master's, thesis or alternative. *Entrance requirements:* For master's, honors degree or equivalent, minimum B average. Electronic applications accepted. *Faculty research:* Psychosocial sciences, physical and health administration of sport and physical activity, intervention and consultation in sport, physical activity and health.

University of Puerto Rico, Mayagüez Campus, Graduate Studies, College of Arts and Sciences, Department of Kinesiology, Mayagüez, PR 00681-9000. Offers kinesiology (MA), including biomechanics, education, exercise physiology, sports training. *Program availability:* Part-time. *Faculty:* 12 full-time (4 women). *Students:* 8 full-time (2 women), 6 part-time (1 woman); includes 12 minority (all Hispanic/Latino), 2 international. Average age 25. 9 applicants, 33% accepted, 3 enrolled. In 2016, 2 master's awarded. *Degree requirements:* For master's, thesis. *Entrance requirements:* For master's, EXADEP or GRE, minimum GPA of 2.5. *Application deadline:* For fall admission, 2/15 for domestic and international students; for spring admission, 9/15 for domestic and international students. Applications are processed on a rolling basis. Application fee: $25. Electronic applications accepted. *Expenses: Tuition, area resident:* Full-time $2466. *International tuition:* $7166 full-time. *Required fees:* $210. Tuition and fees vary according to course level, campus/location, program and student level. *Financial support:* In 2016–17, 6 students received support, including 6 teaching assistantships with full and partial tuition reimbursements available (averaging $2,885 per year). *Unit head:* Luis Del Río Pérez, PhD, Director, 787-832-4040 Ext. 3564, Fax: 787-833-4825, E-mail: luiso.delrio@upr.edu. *Application contact:* Aracelys Gonzlez, Administrative Secretary V, 787-832-4040 Ext. 3841, Fax: 787-833-4825, E-mail: aracelis.gonzalez3@upr.edu.
Website: http://edfi.uprm.edu/

University of Regina, Faculty of Graduate Studies and Research, Faculty of Kinesiology and Health Studies, Regina, SK S4S 0A2, Canada. Offers M Sc, PhD. *Faculty:* 17 full-time (8 women), 26 part-time/adjunct (14 women). *Students:* 28 full-time (14 women), 7 part-time (5 women). 15 applicants, 47% accepted. In 2016, 3 master's, 1 doctorate awarded. *Degree requirements:* For master's, thesis; for doctorate, thesis/dissertation. *Entrance requirements:* For doctorate, writing sample. Additional exam requirements/recommendations for international students: Required—TOEFL (minimum score 580 paper-based; 80 iBT), IELTS (minimum score 6.5), PTE (minimum score 59). *Application deadline:* Applications are processed on a rolling basis. Application fee: $100. Electronic applications accepted. *Financial support:* In 2016–17, 8 fellowships (averaging $6,750 per year), 7 teaching assistantships (averaging $2,518 per year) were awarded; scholarships/grants also available. Financial award application deadline: 6/15. *Faculty research:* Social psychology of physical activity and health, social science of physical activity and recreation, recreation and leisure, sport management, exercise science. *Unit head:* Dr. Harold Riemer, Dean, 306-585-4535, Fax: 306-585-4854, E-mail: khs.dean@uregina.ca. *Application contact:* Dr. Darren Candow, Associate Dean, Graduate Studies and Research, 306-585-4906, Fax: 306-585-4854, E-mail: darren.candow@uregina.ca.
Website: http://www.uregina.ca/kinesiology/

University of Saskatchewan, College of Graduate Studies and Research, College of Kinesiology, Saskatoon, SK S7N 5A2, Canada. Offers M Sc, PhD, Diploma. *Degree requirements:* For master's, thesis; for doctorate, thesis/dissertation. *Entrance requirements:* Additional exam requirements/recommendations for international students: Required—TOEFL.

University of South Alabama, College of Education and Professional Studies, Department of Health, Kinesiology, and Sport, Mobile, AL 36688. Offers exercise science (MS); health education (M Ed); physical education (M Ed); sport management (MS). *Accreditation;* NCATE (one or more programs are accredited). *Program availability:* Part-time. *Faculty:* 7 full-time (2 women). *Students:* 50 full-time (15 women), 4 part-time (2 women); includes 21 minority (17 Black or African American, non-Hispanic/Latino; 1 Asian, non-Hispanic/Latino; 1 Hispanic/Latino; 2 Two or more races, non-Hispanic/Latino), 3 international. Average age 27. 53 applicants, 57% accepted, 28 enrolled. In 2016, 16 master's awarded. *Degree requirements:* For master's, comprehensive exam, thesis optional. *Entrance requirements:* For master's, GRE General Test or MAT, Alabama Class B certificate or the equivalent (for students seeking the master's-level/Class A certification). Additional exam requirements/recommendations for international students: Required—TOEFL. *Application deadline:* For fall admission, 7/15 priority date for domestic students, 6/15 priority date for international students; for spring admission, 11/15 priority date for domestic students, 10/15 priority date for international students; for summer admission, 4/15 for domestic students. Applications are processed on a rolling basis. Application fee: $35. Electronic applications accepted. *Expenses:* Tuition, state resident: full-time $9768; part-time $407 per credit hour. Tuition, nonresident: full-time $19,536; part-time $814 per credit hour. *Financial support:* Fellowships, research assistantships, teaching assistantships with partial tuition reimbursements, career-related internships or fieldwork, Federal Work-Study, institutionally sponsored loans, scholarships/grants, and unspecified

assistantships available. Support available to part-time students. Financial award application deadline: 5/31; financial award applicants required to submit FAFSA. *Unit head:* Dr. John Kovaleski, Department Chair, 251-461-1622, Fax: 251-460-7252, E-mail: jkovales@southalabama.edu. *Application contact:* Dr. Susan Santoli, Director of Graduate Studies, 251-380-2738, Fax: 251-380-2758, E-mail: ssantoli@southalabama.edu.
Website: http://www.southalabama.edu/colleges/coe/hks/index.html

The University of South Dakota, Graduate School, School of Education, Division of Kinesiology and Sport Management, Vermillion, SD 57069. Offers MA. *Accreditation:* NCATE. *Program availability:* Part-time. *Degree requirements:* For master's, comprehensive exam, thesis or alternative. *Entrance requirements:* For master's, GRE General Test, MAT, minimum GPA of 3.0. Additional exam requirements/recommendations for international students: Required—TOEFL (minimum score 550 paper-based; 79 iBT). Electronic applications accepted.

University of Southern California, Graduate School, Herman Ostrow School of Dentistry, Division of Biokinesiology and Physical Therapy, Los Angeles, CA 90089. Offers biokinesiology (MS, PhD); physical therapy (DPT). *Accreditation:* APTA (one or more programs are accredited). *Degree requirements:* For master's, comprehensive exam; for doctorate, thesis/dissertation. *Entrance requirements:* For master's and doctorate, GRE (minimum combined score 1200, verbal 600, quantitative 600). Additional exam requirements/recommendations for international students: Required—TOEFL. Electronic applications accepted. *Expenses:* Contact institution. *Faculty research:* Exercise and aging biomechanics, musculoskeletal biomechanics, exercise and hormones related to muscle wasting, computational neurorehabilitation, motor behavior and neurorehabilitation, motor development, infant motor performance.

The University of Tennessee, Graduate School, College of Education, Health and Human Sciences, Department of Exercise, Sport, and Leisure Studies, Program in Exercise Science, Knoxville, TN 37996. Offers biomechanics/sports medicine (MS, PhD); exercise physiology (MS, PhD). *Accreditation:* CEPH (one or more programs are accredited). *Program availability:* Part-time. *Degree requirements:* For master's, thesis optional. *Entrance requirements:* For master's, minimum GPA of 2.7. Additional exam requirements/recommendations for international students: Required—TOEFL. Electronic applications accepted.

The University of Texas at Austin, Graduate School, College of Education, Department of Kinesiology and Health Education, Austin, TX 78712-1111. Offers behavioral health (PhD); exercise and sport psychology (M Ed, MA); exercise science (M Ed, MS, PhD); health education (M Ed, MS, Ed D, PhD). *Program availability:* Part-time. Terminal master's awarded for partial completion of doctoral program. *Degree requirements:* For master's, thesis (for some programs); for doctorate, thesis/dissertation. *Entrance requirements:* For master's and doctorate, GRE General Test. Additional exam requirements/recommendations for international students: Required—TOEFL. Electronic applications accepted. *Faculty research:* Health promotion, human performance and exercise biochemistry, motor behavior and biomechanics, sport management, aging and pediatric development.

The University of Texas at El Paso, Graduate School, College of Health Sciences, Department of Kinesiology, El Paso, TX 79968-0001. Offers MS. *Program availability:* Part-time, evening/weekend, online learning. *Degree requirements:* For master's, thesis optional. *Entrance requirements:* For master's, GRE. Additional exam requirements/recommendations for international students: Required—TOEFL; Recommended—IELTS. Electronic applications accepted.

The University of Texas at San Antonio, College of Education and Human Development, Department of Kinesiology, Health, and Nutrition, San Antonio, TX 78249-0617. Offers health and kinesiology (MS). *Program availability:* Part-time, evening/weekend. *Faculty:* 13 full-time (6 women). *Students:* 76 full-time (41 women), 61 part-time (35 women); includes 97 minority (16 Black or African American, non-Hispanic/Latino; 7 Asian, non-Hispanic/Latino; 70 Hispanic/Latino; 4 Two or more races, non-Hispanic/Latino), 2 international. Average age 27. 70 applicants, 80% accepted, 37 enrolled. In 2016, 54 master's awarded. *Degree requirements:* For master's, comprehensive exam, thesis optional. *Entrance requirements:* For master's, bachelor's degree with minimum GPA of 3.0 in last 60 hours of coursework; resume; statement of purpose; two letters of recommendation. Additional exam requirements/recommendations for international students: Required—TOEFL (minimum score 550 paper-based; 79 iBT), IELTS (minimum score 6.5). *Application deadline:* For fall admission, 7/1 for domestic students, 4/1 for international students; for spring admission, 11/1 for domestic students, 9/1 for international students; for summer admission, 4/1 for domestic students, 3/1 for international students. Applications are processed on a rolling basis. Application fee: $45 ($80 for international students). Electronic applications accepted. *Expenses:* Contact institution. *Financial support:* In 2016–17, 10 students received support. Unspecified assistantships available. Financial award application deadline: 3/31; financial award applicants required to submit FAFSA. *Faculty research:* Childhood obesity, health disparities, community health, exercise physiology, sport psychology. *Total annual research expenditures:* $169,815. *Unit head:* Dr. William Cooke, Chair, 210-458-5642, E-mail: william.cooke@utsa.edu.
Website: http://education.utsa.edu/health_and_kinesiology

The University of Texas at Tyler, College of Nursing and Health Sciences, Department of Health and Kinesiology, Tyler, TX 75799-0001. Offers health and kinesiology (M Ed, MA); health sciences (MS); kinesiology (MS). *Accreditation:* TEAC. *Program availability:* Part-time, online learning. *Degree requirements:* For master's, comprehensive exam (for some programs), thesis (for some programs). *Entrance requirements:* Additional exam requirements/recommendations for international students: Required—TOEFL. Electronic applications accepted. *Faculty research:* Osteoporosis, muscle soreness, economy of locomotion, adoption of rehabilitation programs, effect of inactivity and aging on muscle blood vessels, territoriality.

The University of Texas of the Permian Basin, Office of Graduate Studies, College of Arts and Sciences, Department of Kinesiology, Odessa, TX 79762-0001. Offers MS. *Program availability:* Part-time, evening/weekend, online learning. *Degree requirements:* For master's, comprehensive exam (for some programs), thesis (for some programs). *Entrance requirements:* For master's, GRE General Test, minimum GPA of 2.5. Additional exam requirements/recommendations for international students: Required—TOEFL (minimum score 550 paper-based).

The University of Texas Rio Grande Valley, College of Health Affairs, Department of Health and Human Performance, Edinburg, TX 78539. Offers exercise science (MS); kinesiology (MS). *Program availability:* Part-time, evening/weekend, online learning. *Degree requirements:* For master's, comprehensive exam, thesis optional, oral exam. *Entrance requirements:* For master's, minimum GPA of 3.0 in last 60 hours. Tuition and fees vary according to course load and program. *Faculty research:* History, physiology of exercise, fitness levels, Mexican American children, winter tourist profiles, sports psychology.

University of Toronto, School of Graduate Studies, Faculty of Kinesiology and Physical Education, Toronto, ON M5S 1A1, Canada. Offers M Sc, PhD. *Degree requirements:* For master's, thesis, oral defense of thesis; for doctorate, comprehensive exam, defense of thesis. *Entrance requirements:* For master's, background in physical education and health, minimum B+ average in final year of undergraduate study, 2 letters of reference, resume, 2 writing samples; for doctorate, master's degree with successful defense of thesis, background in exercise sciences, minimum A- average, 2 letters of reference. Additional exam requirements/recommendations for international students: Required—TOEFL (minimum score 580 paper-based; 93 iBT), TWE (minimum score 5). Electronic applications accepted.

The University of Tulsa, Graduate School, Oxley College of Health Sciences, Department of Kinesiology and Rehabilitative Sciences, Tulsa, OK 74104-3189. Offers MAT. *Faculty:* 9 full-time (4 women), 10 part-time/adjunct (3 women). *Students:* 2 full-time (1 woman). Average age 26. 4 applicants, 100% accepted, 2 enrolled. *Entrance requirements:* For master's, GRE General Test. Additional exam requirements/recommendations for international students: Required—TOEFL (minimum score 577 paper-based; 90 iBT), IELTS (minimum score 6.5). Application fee: $55. *Expenses: Tuition:* Full-time $22,230; part-time $1235 per credit hour. *Required fees:* $990 per semester. Tuition and fees vary according to course load. *Financial support:* Applicants required to submit FAFSA. *Unit head:* Robin Ploeger, Interim Dean, 918-631-3170, E-mail: robin-ploeger@utulsa.edu. *Application contact:* Dr. Ron Walker, Program Advisor, 918-631-3240, Fax: 918-631-2156, E-mail: ron-walker@utulsa.edu.
Website: https://healthsciences.utulsa.edu/departments-schools/athletic-training/graduate-program/

University of Utah, Graduate School, College of Health, Kinesiology Program, Salt Lake City, UT 84112. Offers MS, PhD. *Faculty:* 9 full-time (5 women), 3 part-time/adjunct (2 women). *Students:* 73 full-time (36 women), 2 part-time (0 women); includes 5 minority (2 Black or African American, non-Hispanic/Latino; 2 Asian, non-Hispanic/Latino; 1 Native Hawaiian or other Pacific Islander, non-Hispanic/Latino), 5 international. Average age 25. 173 applicants, 27% accepted, 41 enrolled. In 2016, 22 master's, 6 doctorates awarded. Terminal master's awarded for partial completion of doctoral program. *Degree requirements:* For master's, comprehensive exam, thesis (for some programs); for doctorate, comprehensive exam, thesis/dissertation. *Entrance requirements:* For master's, GRE, curriculum vitae, 2 letters of recommendation, 500-word statement of intent, minimum GPA of 3.0; for doctorate, GRE, curriculum vitae, 3 letters of recommendation, 800-word statement of intent, minimum GPA of 3.0. Additional exam requirements/recommendations for international students: Required—TOEFL (minimum score 500 paper-based; 61 iBT). *Application deadline:* For fall admission, 12/1 for domestic and international students. Application fee: $55 ($65 for international students). Electronic applications accepted. *Expenses:* Contact institution. *Financial support:* In 2016–17, 62 students received support, including 3 fellowships with full tuition reimbursements available (averaging $17,000 per year), 25 research assistantships with full tuition reimbursements available (averaging $13,500 per year), 32 teaching assistantships with full tuition reimbursements available (averaging $13,500 per year); career-related internships or fieldwork, Federal Work-Study, scholarships/grants, traineeships, health care benefits, and unspecified assistantships also available. Financial award application deadline: 4/15; financial award applicants required to submit FAFSA. *Faculty research:* Exercise physiology, psychosocial aspects of sports and physical education, special physical education, elementary/secondary physical education. *Unit head:* Dr. Tim Brusseau, Chair, 801-587-7900, Fax: 801-585-3992, E-mail: tim.brusseau@utah.edu. *Application contact:* Dr. Maria Newton, Director of Graduate Studies, 801-581-4729, Fax: 801-585-3992, E-mail: maria.newton@health.utah.edu.
Website: http://www.health.utah.edu/ess/

University of Victoria, Faculty of Graduate Studies, Faculty of Education, School of Exercise Science, Physical, and Health Education, Victoria, BC V8W 2Y2, Canada. Offers coaching studies (co-operative education) (M Ed); kinesiology (M Sc, MA); leisure service administration (MA); physical education (MA). *Program availability:* Part-time. *Degree requirements:* For master's, comprehensive exam (for some programs), thesis (for some programs). *Entrance requirements:* For master's, minimum B average. Additional exam requirements/recommendations for international students: Required—TOEFL (minimum score 575 paper-based), IELTS (minimum score 7). Electronic applications accepted. *Faculty research:* Children and exercise, mental skills in sports, teaching effectiveness, neural control of human movement, physical performance and health.

University of Virginia, Curry School of Education, Department of Kinesiology, Charlottesville, VA 22903. Offers M Ed, PhD. *Faculty:* 12 full-time (3 women). *Students:* 54 full-time (30 women), 8 part-time (5 women); includes 10 minority (1 Black or African American, non-Hispanic/Latino; 2 Asian, non-Hispanic/Latino; 5 Hispanic/Latino; 2 Two or more races, non-Hispanic/Latino), 1 international. Average age 25. 46 applicants, 61% accepted, 21 enrolled. In 2016, 42 master's awarded. *Entrance requirements:* For master's and doctorate, GRE General Test, 2 letters of recommendation. Additional exam requirements/recommendations for international students: Required—TOEFL (minimum score 600 paper-based; 90 iBT), IELTS (minimum score 7). *Application deadline:* Applications are processed on a rolling basis. Application fee: $60. Electronic applications accepted. *Expenses:* Tuition, state resident: full-time $15,026; part-time $834 per credit hour. Tuition, nonresident: full-time $25,168; part-time $1378 per credit hour. *Required fees:* $2654. *Financial support:* Applicants required to submit FAFSA. *Unit head:* Arthur L. Weltman, Chair, Kinesiology, 434-924-6191, E-mail: alw2v@virginia.edu. *Application contact:* Eric Molnar, Assistant Director, Admissions and Enrollment Reporting, 434-243-2085, E-mail: eric.molnar@virginia.edu.
Website: http://curry.virginia.edu/academics/department/kinesiology

University of Virginia, Curry School of Education, Program in Education, Charlottesville, VA 22903. Offers administration and supervision (PhD); applied developmental science (PhD); counselor education (PhD); curriculum and instruction (PhD); early childhood special education (MT); education evaluation (PhD); educational psychology (PhD); educational research (PhD); elementary education (MT); English education (MT, PhD); foreign language education (MT); higher education (PhD); instructional technology (PhD); kinesiology (MT, PhD); math education (PhD); reading education (PhD); research, statistics and evaluation (PhD); school psychology (PhD); science education (PhD); social studies education (MT, PhD); special education (PhD); world languages education (MT). *Students:* 452 full-time (357 women), 18 part-time (13 women); includes 100 minority (28 Black or African American, non-Hispanic/Latino; 39 Asian, non-Hispanic/Latino; 18 Hispanic/Latino; 15 Two or more races, non-Hispanic/Latino), 14 international. Average age 25. 309 applicants, 51% accepted, 87 enrolled. In 2016, 144 master's, 31 doctorates awarded. *Degree requirements:* For master's, comprehensive exam (for some programs), field project; for doctorate, comprehensive exam, thesis/dissertation. *Entrance requirements:* For doctorate, GRE General Test. Additional exam requirements/recommendations for international students: Required—TOEFL (minimum score 600 paper-based; 90 iBT), IELTS (minimum score 7). *Application deadline:* Applications are processed on a rolling basis. Application fee: $60. Electronic applications accepted. *Expenses:* Tuition, state resident: full-time $15,026; part-time $834 per credit hour. Tuition, nonresident: full-time $25,168; part-time $1378 per credit hour. *Required fees:* $2654. *Financial support:* Fellowships, research assistantships, and teaching assistantships available. Financial award application deadline: 1/5; financial award applicants required to submit FAFSA. *Unit head:* Robert C. Pianta, Dean, 434-924-3334, E-mail: pianta@virginia.edu. *Application contact:* Eric

Molnar, Assistant Director, Admissions and Enrollment Reporting, 434-243-2085, E-mail: eric.molnar@virginia.edu.
Website: http://curry.virginia.edu/teacher-education

University of Waterloo, Graduate Studies, Faculty of Applied Health Sciences, Department of Kinesiology, Waterloo, ON N2L 3G1, Canada. Offers M Sc, PhD. *Program availability:* Part-time. *Degree requirements:* For master's, thesis; for doctorate, comprehensive exam, thesis/dissertation. *Entrance requirements:* For master's, honors degree, minimum B average, writing sample; for doctorate, GRE (recommended), master's degree, minimum B average, writing sample. Additional exam requirements/recommendations for international students: Required—TOEFL, IELTS, PTE. Electronic applications accepted. *Faculty research:* Work physiology, biomechanics and neural control of human movement, psychomotor learning and performance, aging, health and well-being, work and health.

The University of Western Ontario, Faculty of Graduate Studies, Health Sciences Division, School of Kinesiology, London, ON N6A 5B8, Canada. Offers M Sc, MA, PhD. *Degree requirements:* For master's, thesis optional; for doctorate, comprehensive exam, thesis/dissertation. *Entrance requirements:* For doctorate, MA in physical education or kinesiology. Additional exam requirements/recommendations for international students: Required—Michigan English Language Assessment Battery, TOEFL or IELTS. *Faculty research:* Exercise physiology/biochemistry, sports injuries, sport psychology, sport history, sport philosophy.

University of Windsor, Faculty of Graduate Studies, Faculty of Human Kinetics, Windsor, ON N9B 3P4, Canada. Offers MHK. *Program availability:* Part-time. *Degree requirements:* For master's, thesis optional. *Entrance requirements:* For master's, minimum B average. Additional exam requirements/recommendations for international students: Required—TOEFL (minimum score 600 paper-based). Electronic applications accepted. *Faculty research:* Movement sciences, sport and lifestyle management, historical and sociological studies of sport.

University of Wisconsin–Madison, Graduate School, School of Education, Department of Kinesiology, Madison, WI 53706-1380. Offers kinesiology (MS, PhD); occupational therapy (MS, PhD). *Accreditation:* AOTA. *Degree requirements:* For doctorate, thesis/dissertation. *Entrance requirements:* For master's and doctorate, GRE General Test. Electronic applications accepted.

University of Wisconsin–Milwaukee, Graduate School, College of Health Sciences, Department of Kinesiology, Milwaukee, WI 53201-0413. Offers athletic training (MS); kinesiology (MS, PhD), including exercise and nutrition in health and disease (MS), integrative human performance (MS), neuromechanics (MS); physical therapy (DPT). *Program availability:* Part-time. *Students:* 104 full-time (54 women), 6 part-time (3 women); includes 11 minority (1 Black or African American, non-Hispanic/Latino; 10 Two or more races, non-Hispanic/Latino), 3 international. Average age 27. 34 applicants, 47% accepted, 12 enrolled. In 2016, 9 master's, 24 doctorates awarded. *Degree requirements:* For master's, comprehensive exam, thesis optional. *Entrance requirements:* For master's, GRE General Test. Additional exam requirements/recommendations for international students: Required—TOEFL (minimum score 550 paper-based; 79 iBT), IELTS (minimum score 6.5). *Application deadline:* For fall admission, 1/1 priority date for domestic students; for spring admission, 9/1 for domestic students. Applications are processed on a rolling basis. Application fee: $56 ($96 for international students). *Financial support:* In 2016–17, 2 fellowships, 7 teaching assistantships were awarded; research assistantships, career-related internships or fieldwork, unspecified assistantships, and project assistantships also available. Support available to part-time students. Financial award application deadline: 4/15. *Unit head:* Dr. Kyle T. Ebersole, Department Chair, 414-229-6717, Fax: 414-229-3366, E-mail: ebersole@uwm.edu. *Application contact:* Stephen C. Cobb, Graduate Program Coordinator, 414-229-3369, Fax: 414-229-3366, E-mail: cobbsc@uwm.edu.
Website: http://uwm.edu/healthsciences/academics/kinesiology/

University of Wisconsin–Milwaukee, Graduate School, College of Health Sciences, Program in Health Sciences, Milwaukee, WI 53201-0413. Offers health sciences (PhD), including diagnostic and biomedical sciences, disability and rehabilitation, health administration and policy, human movement sciences, population health. *Students:* 16 full-time (12 women), 8 part-time (5 women); includes 5 minority (1 Black or African American, non-Hispanic/Latino; 3 Asian, non-Hispanic/Latino; 1 Two or more races, non-Hispanic/Latino), 10 international. Average age 35. 7 applicants, 57% accepted, 2 enrolled. In 2016, 5 doctorates awarded. *Degree requirements:* For doctorate, comprehensive exam, thesis/dissertation. *Entrance requirements:* For doctorate, GRE. Additional exam requirements/recommendations for international students: Required—TOEFL (minimum score 600 paper-based), IELTS (minimum score 6.5). Application fee: $56 ($96 for international students). *Financial support:* Fellowships, research assistantships, teaching assistantships, and project assistantships available. *Application contact:* Susan Cashin, PhD, Assistant Dean, 414-229-3303, E-mail: scashin@uwm.edu.
Website: http://uwm.edu/healthsciences/academics/phd-health-sciences/

University of Wyoming, College of Health Sciences, Division of Kinesiology and Health, Laramie, WY 82071. Offers MS. *Accreditation:* NCATE. *Program availability:* Part-time, online learning. *Degree requirements:* For master's, comprehensive exam (for some programs), thesis (for some programs). *Entrance requirements:* For master's, GRE General Test, minimum GPA of 3.0. Additional exam requirements/recommendations for international students: Required—TOEFL. Electronic applications accepted. *Faculty research:* Teacher effectiveness, effects of exercising on heart function, physiological responses of overtraining, psychological benefits of physical activity, health behavior.

Washington University in St. Louis, School of Medicine, Interdisciplinary Program in Movement Science, St. Louis, MO 63130-4899. Offers PhD. *Degree requirements:* For doctorate, thesis/dissertation. *Entrance requirements:* For doctorate, GRE General Test. Electronic applications accepted.

Wayne State University, College of Education, Division of Kinesiology, Health and Sports Studies, Detroit, MI 48202. Offers health education (M Ed); kinesiology (M Ed, PhD), including exercise and sport science (PhD), physical education and physical activity leadership (PhD); sports administration (MA). *Program availability:* Part-time, 100% online. *Faculty:* 10. *Students:* 57 full-time (30 women), 131 part-time (68 women); includes 72 minority (63 Black or African American, non-Hispanic/Latino; 1 American Indian or Alaska Native, non-Hispanic/Latino; 1 Asian, non-Hispanic/Latino; 3 Hispanic/Latino; 4 Two or more races, non-Hispanic/Latino), 10 international. Average age 29. 160 applicants, 56% accepted, 51 enrolled. In 2016, 66 master's awarded. *Degree requirements:* For master's, thesis (for some programs); for doctorate, thesis/dissertation. *Entrance requirements:* For master's, minimum undergraduate GPA of 3.0; undergraduate degree directly relating to the field of specialization being applied for or one accompanied by extensive educational background in closely-related field; teaching certificates in specific areas (for some programs); for doctorate, minimum undergraduate GPA of 3.0; undergraduate degree directly relating to the field of specialization being applied for or one accompanied by extensive educational background in closely-related field. Additional exam requirements/recommendations for international students: Required—TOEFL (minimum score 79 iBT), TWE (minimum score 5.5), Michigan English Language Assessment Battery (minimum score 85); Recommended—IELTS (minimum score 6.5). *Application deadline:* For fall admission, 6/1 priority date for domestic students, 5/1 priority date for international students; for winter admission, 10/1 priority date for domestic students, 9/1 priority date for international students; for spring admission, 2/1 priority date for domestic students, 1/1 priority date for international students. Application fee: $50. Electronic applications accepted. *Expenses:* $18,522 per year resident tuition and fees, $35,715 per year non-resident tuition and fees. *Financial support:* In 2016–17, 49 students received support, including 6 research assistantships with tuition reimbursements available (averaging $17,994 per year); fellowships with tuition reimbursements available, scholarships/grants, health care benefits, and unspecified assistantships also available. Support available to part-time students. Financial award applicants required to submit FAFSA. *Faculty research:* Exercise and sport science, nutrition and physical activity interventions, school and community health, obesity prevention. *Total annual research expenditures:* $974,985. *Unit head:* Dr. Nate McCaughtry, Assistant Dean, Division of Kinesiology, Health and Sport Studies/Director, Center for School Health, 313-577-0014, Fax: 313-577-5002, E-mail: aj4391@wayne.edu. *Application contact:* Janice Green, Assistant Dean, 313-577-1605, E-mail: jwgreen@wayne.edu.
Website: http://coe.wayne.edu/kinesiology/index.php

Wayne State University, College of Education, Division of Teacher Education, Detroit, MI 48202. Offers art education (M Ed); bilingual/bicultural education (M Ed, Certificate); career and technical education (M Ed); curriculum and instruction (Ed D, PhD, Ed S), including art education (Ed D, PhD), bilingual education (Ed D, Ed S), career and technical education (MAT, Ed D, PhD, Ed S), early childhood education (MAT, Ed D, PhD, Ed S), elementary education, English as a second language (MAT, Ed D, Ed S), English education (MAT, Ed D, PhD, Ed S), foreign language education (MAT, Ed D, PhD), K-12 curriculum, mathematics education (MAT, Ed D, PhD, Ed S), science education (MAT, Ed D, PhD, Ed S), secondary education, social studies education (MAT, Ed D, PhD, Ed S); early childhood education (M Ed); elementary education (M Ed, MAT), including bilingual/bicultural education (MAT), early childhood education (MAT, Ed D, PhD, Ed S), English as a second language (MAT, Ed D, Ed S), general elementary education (MAT), mathematics education (MAT, Ed D, PhD, Ed S), science education (MAT, Ed D, PhD, Ed S), social studies education (MAT, Ed D, PhD, Ed S); English as a second language (Certificate); English education (M Ed); foreign language education (M Ed); mathematics education (M Ed); reading (M Ed, Ed S); reading, language and literature (Ed D); science education (M Ed); secondary education (MAT), including art education (K-12), bilingual/bicultural education, career and technical education (MAT, Ed D, PhD, Ed S), English as a second language (MAT, Ed D, Ed S), English education (MAT, Ed D, PhD, Ed S), foreign language education (MAT, Ed D, PhD), kinesiology, mathematics education (MAT, Ed D, PhD, Ed S); social studies education (M Ed); special education (M Ed, MAT, Ed D, PhD, Ed S), including autism spectrum disorders (MAT), cognitive development (MAT), emotional impairment (MAT), learning disabilities (MAT). *Program availability:* Part-time, blended/hybrid learning. *Faculty:* 29. *Students:* 106 full-time (73 women), 351 part-time (276 women); includes 115 minority (76 Black or African American, non-Hispanic/Latino; 10 Asian, non-Hispanic/Latino; 20 Hispanic/Latino; 1 Native Hawaiian or other Pacific Islander, non-Hispanic/Latino; 8 Two or more races, non-Hispanic/Latino), 12 international. Average age 37. 242 applicants, 37% accepted, 72 enrolled. In 2016, 178 master's, 19 doctorates, 17 other advanced degrees awarded. *Degree requirements:* For master's, essay or project (for some M Ed programs), professional field experience (for MAT programs); for doctorate, thesis/dissertation. *Entrance requirements:* For master's, Michigan Test for Teacher Certification, verification of participation in group work with children, Michigan State Police criminal background check; for doctorate, minimum undergraduate GPA of 3.0, graduate 3.5; interview; curriculum vitae; references. Additional exam requirements/recommendations for international students: Required—TOEFL (minimum score 550 paper-based; 79 iBT), TWE (minimum score 5.5), Michigan English Language Assessment Battery (minimum score 85); Recommended—IELTS (minimum score 6.5). *Application deadline:* For fall admission, 6/1 priority date for domestic students, 5/1 priority date for international students; for winter admission, 10/1 priority date for domestic students, 9/1 priority date for international students; for spring admission, 2/1 priority date for domestic students, 1/1 priority date for international students. Applications are processed on a rolling basis. Application fee: $50. Electronic applications accepted. *Expenses:* $16,503 per year resident tuition and fees, $33,697 per year non-resident tuition and fees. *Financial support:* In 2016–17, 101 students received support, including 3 fellowships (averaging $11,409 per year); research assistantships with tuition reimbursements available, Federal Work-Study, scholarships/grants, and unspecified assistantships also available. Support available to part-time students. Financial award applicants required to submit FAFSA. *Faculty research:* Improving students' skill achievement in mathematics, improving elementary children's understanding of informational text, teachers' use of their pedagogical and mathematical knowledge in the interactive work of teaching, the intersection of identity construction in teaching and learning, identifying effective methods of literacy instruction and assessments for bilingual students in elementary language arts classrooms. *Unit head:* Dr. Kathleen Crawford-McKinney, Assistant Dean, 313-577-0122. *Application contact:* Janice Green, Assistant Dean, 313-577-1605, E-mail: jwgreen@wayne.edu.
Website: http://coe.wayne.edu/ted/index.php

West Chester University of Pennsylvania, College of Health Sciences, Department of Kinesiology, West Chester, PA 19383. Offers adapted physical education (Certificate); exercise and sport physiology (MS), including athletic training, exercise and sport physiology; general physical education (MS); sport management and athletics (MPA), including administration. *Program availability:* Part-time, evening/weekend. *Faculty:* 9 full-time (6 women). *Students:* 34 full-time (22 women), 21 part-time (7 women); includes 5 minority (4 Black or African American, non-Hispanic/Latino; 1 Hispanic/Latino), 1 international. Average age 26. 68 applicants, 85% accepted, 30 enrolled. In 2016, 23 master's, 1 other advanced degree awarded. *Degree requirements:* For master's, thesis or research report (for MS); two internships and capstone course that includes a research project or thesis (for MPA). *Entrance requirements:* For master's, GRE (for MS), 2 letters of recommendation, statement of goals; transcripts (for MS); resume (for MPA). Additional exam requirements/recommendations for international students: Required—TOEFL or IELTS. *Application deadline:* For fall admission, 5/15 for international students; for spring admission, 10/15 for international students. Applications are processed on a rolling basis. Application fee: $50. Electronic applications accepted. *Expenses:* Tuition, state resident: full-time $8694; part-time $483 per credit. Tuition, nonresident: full-time $13,050; part-time $725 per credit. *Required fees:* $2399; $119.05 per credit. Tuition and fees vary according to campus/location and program. *Financial support:* Scholarships/grants and unspecified assistantships available. Financial award application deadline: 2/15; financial award applicants required to submit FAFSA. *Faculty research:* Metabolism during exercise, biomechanics, rating of perceived exertion, motor learning, environmental physiology. *Unit head:* Dr. Frank Fry, Chair/Graduate Coordinator for the MS in General Physical Education Program, 610-436-2610, Fax: 610-436-2860, E-mail: ffry@wcupa.edu. *Application contact:* Office of Graduate Studies and Extended Education, 610-436-2943, Fax: 610-436-2763, E-mail: gradstudy@wcupa.edu.
Website: http://www.wcupa.edu/healthsciences/kinesiology/

Kinesiology and Movement Studies

Western Illinois University, School of Graduate Studies, College of Education and Human Services, Department of Kinesiology, Program in Kinesiology, Macomb, IL 61455-1390. Offers MS. *Program availability:* Part-time. *Students:* 38 full-time (18 women), 9 part-time (5 women); includes 7 minority (2 Black or African American, non-Hispanic/Latino; 5 Hispanic/Latino), 4 international. Average age 25. 46 applicants, 76% accepted, 24 enrolled. In 2016, 15 master's awarded. *Entrance requirements:* For master's, minimum GPA of 3.0. Additional exam requirements/recommendations for international students: Required—TOEFL (minimum score 550 paper-based; 80 iBT). *Application deadline:* Applications are processed on a rolling basis. Application fee: $30. Electronic applications accepted. *Financial support:* In 2016–17, 29 students received support, including 6 teaching assistantships with full tuition reimbursements available (averaging $8,688 per year); unspecified assistantships also available. Financial award applicants required to submit FAFSA. *Unit head:* Dr. Janet Wigglesworth, Chairperson, 309-298-1981. *Application contact:* Dr. Nancy Parsons, Associate Provost and Director of Graduate Studies, 309-298-1806, Fax: 309-298-2345, E-mail: grad-office@wiu.edu. Website: http://wiu.edu/kinesiology

Wilfrid Laurier University, Faculty of Graduate and Postdoctoral Studies, Faculty of Science, Department of Kinesiology and Physical Education, Waterloo, ON N2L 3C5, Canada. Offers physical activity and health (M Sc). *Degree requirements:* For master's, thesis. *Entrance requirements:* For master's, honours degree in kinesiology, health, physical education with a minimum B+ in kinesiology and health-related courses. Additional exam requirements/recommendations for international students: Required—TOEFL (minimum score 89 iBT). Electronic applications accepted. *Faculty research:* Biomechanics, health, exercise physiology, motor control, sport psychology.

York University, Faculty of Graduate Studies, Faculty of Health, Program in Kinesiology and Health Science, Toronto, ON M3J 1P3, Canada. Offers M Sc, MA, PhD. *Program availability:* Part-time. *Degree requirements:* For master's, thesis or alternative; for doctorate, comprehensive exam, thesis/dissertation. Electronic applications accepted.

Physical Education

Adams State University, The Graduate School, Department of Human Performance and Physical Education, Alamosa, CO 81101. Offers MA. *Program availability:* Part-time. *Degree requirements:* For master's, comprehensive exam. *Entrance requirements:* For master's, GRE General Test or MAT, minimum undergraduate GPA of 2.75.

Adelphi University, Ruth S. Ammon School of Education, Program in Physical Education and Human Performance Science, Garden City, NY 11530-0701. Offers aging (Certificate); physical/educational human performance science (MA). *Program availability:* Part-time, evening/weekend. *Students:* 67 full-time (31 women), 95 part-time (33 women); includes 56 minority (22 Black or African American, non-Hispanic/Latino; 2 Asian, non-Hispanic/Latino; 29 Hispanic/Latino; 3 Two or more races, non-Hispanic/Latino), 3 international. Average age 27. 140 applicants, 84% accepted, 69 enrolled. In 2016, 40 master's awarded. *Degree requirements:* For master's, internship. *Entrance requirements:* For master's, 3 letters of recommendation, resume. Additional exam requirements/recommendations for international students: Required—TOEFL (minimum score 550 paper-based; 80 iBT), IELTS (minimum score 6.5). *Application deadline:* For fall admission, 4/1 for international students; for spring admission, 11/1 for international students. Applications are processed on a rolling basis. Application fee: $50. Electronic applications accepted. *Expenses:* Contact institution. *Financial support:* Research assistantships, teaching assistantships, career-related internships or fieldwork, institutionally sponsored loans, scholarships/grants, traineeships, and unspecified assistantships available. Support available to part-time students. Financial award application deadline: 2/15; financial award applicants required to submit FAFSA. *Faculty research:* Physical education for the handicapped, sport sociology, sport pedagogy. *Unit head:* Dr. Ronald Feingold, Chair, 516-877-4764, E-mail: feingold@adelphi.edu. *Application contact:* Christine Murphy, Director of Admissions, 516-877-3050, Fax: 516-877-3039, E-mail: graduateadmissions@adelphi.edu.

Alabama Agricultural and Mechanical University, School of Graduate Studies, College of Education, Humanities, and Behavioral Sciences, Department of Health Sciences, Human Performance, and Communicative Disorders, Huntsville, AL 35811. Offers kinesiology (MS); physical education (MS); speech-language pathology (MS). *Program availability:* Part-time, evening/weekend. *Degree requirements:* For master's, comprehensive exam. *Entrance requirements:* For master's, GRE General Test. Additional exam requirements/recommendations for international students: Required—TOEFL (minimum score 500 paper-based; 61 iBT). *Application deadline:* For fall admission, 5/1 for domestic students. Applications are processed on a rolling basis. Application fee: $25. Electronic applications accepted. *Expenses:* Tuition, nonresident: part-time $826 per credit hour. Full-time tuition and fees vary according to course load and program. *Financial support:* Career-related internships or fieldwork available. Financial award application deadline: 4/1. *Faculty research:* Cardiorespiratory assessment. *Unit head:* Dr. Rodney Whittle, Chair, 256-372-8268, E-mail: rodney.whittle@aamu.edu.

Alabama State University, College of Education, Department of Health, Physical Education, and Recreation, Montgomery, AL 36101-0271. Offers health education (M Ed); physical education (M Ed). *Program availability:* Part-time. *Students:* 6 full-time (3 women), 11 part-time (4 women); includes 16 minority (all Black or African American, non-Hispanic/Latino). Average age 29. 7 applicants, 71% accepted, 5 enrolled. In 2016, 3 master's awarded. *Degree requirements:* For master's, comprehensive exam. *Entrance requirements:* For master's, GRE General Test, MAT, writing competency test, bachelor's degree or its equivalent from accredited college or university with minimum GPA of 2.5. Additional exam requirements/recommendations for international students: Required—TOEFL (minimum score 500 paper-based). *Application deadline:* For fall admission, 4/15 for domestic and international students; for spring admission, 11/15 for domestic and international students; for summer admission, 3/15 for domestic and international students. Applications are processed on a rolling basis. Application fee: $25. Electronic applications accepted. *Expenses:* Tuition, state resident: full-time $3087; part-time $2744 per credit. Tuition, nonresident: full-time $6174; part-time $5488 per credit. *Required fees:* $2284; $1142 per credit. $571 per semester. Tuition and fees vary according to class time, course level, course load, degree level, program and student level. *Financial support:* Research assistantships available. Financial award application deadline: 6/30; financial award applicants required to submit FAFSA. *Faculty research:* Risk factors for heart disease in the college-age population, cardiovascular reactivity for the Cold Pressor Test. *Unit head:* Dr. Charlie Gibbons, Interim Chair, 334-229-4504, Fax: 334-229-4928, E-mail: cgibbons@alasu.edu. *Application contact:* Dr. William Person, Dean of Graduate Studies, 334-229-4274, Fax: 334-229-4928, E-mail: wperson@alasu.edu.
Website: http://www.alasu.edu/academics/colleges—departments/college-of-education/health-physical-education—recreation/index.aspx

Albany State University, College of Education, Albany, GA 31705-2717. Offers early childhood education (M Ed); educational leadership (Ed S); health and physical education (M Ed); middle grades education (M Ed); school counseling (M Ed); special education (M Ed). *Accreditation:* NCATE. *Program availability:* Part-time, evening/weekend, online learning. *Degree requirements:* For master's, comprehensive exam, internship, GACE Content Exam. *Entrance requirements:* For master's, GRE or MAT. *Application deadline:* For fall admission, 6/1 for domestic students, 5/1 for international students; for spring admission, 11/1 for domestic students, 10/1 for international students. Applications are processed on a rolling basis. Application fee: $20. Electronic applications accepted. *Financial support:* Scholarships/grants available. Financial award application deadline: 4/15; financial award applicants required to submit FAFSA. *Faculty research:* GACE preparation, STEM (science, technology, engineering, and mathematics), technology education, special education, professional teacher development, health implications liberation philosophy, NET-Q, learning community, disabled or at-risk students. *Unit head:* Dr. Rhonda C. Porter, Interim Dean, 229-430-1718, Fax: 229-430-4993. *Application contact:* Jeffrey Pierce, II, Graduate Admissions Counselor, 229-430-4646, Fax: 229-430-4105, E-mail: jeffrey.pierce@asurams.edu.
Website: https://www.asurams.edu/Academics/collegeofeducation/

Alcorn State University, School of Graduate Studies, School of Psychology and Education, Lorman, MS 39096-7500. Offers agricultural education (MS Ed); elementary education (MS Ed, Ed S); guidance and counseling (MS Ed); industrial education (MS Ed); secondary education (MS Ed), including health and physical education; special education (MS Ed). *Accreditation:* NCATE. *Degree requirements:* For master's, thesis optional.

American University of Puerto Rico, Program in Education, Bayamon, PR 00960-2037. Offers art education (M Ed); elementary education 4-6 (M Ed); elementary education K-3 (M Ed); general science education (M Ed); physical education (M Ed); special education (M Ed). *Program availability:* Part-time, evening/weekend. *Faculty:* 17 part-time/adjunct (7 women). *Students:* 22 full-time (18 women), 54 part-time (42 women); all minorities (all Hispanic/Latino). Average age 33. 22 applicants, 86% accepted, 19 enrolled. In 2016, 53 master's awarded. *Entrance requirements:* For master's, EXADEP, GRE, or MAT, 2 letters of recommendation, minimum GPA of 2.5. *Application deadline:* For fall admission, 8/1 for domestic students; for winter admission, 10/18 for domestic students; for spring admission, 3/15 for domestic students. Applications are processed on a rolling basis. Application fee: $25. *Financial support:* In 2016–17, 79 students received support, including 76 fellowships (averaging $400 per year), 55 teaching assistantships (averaging $1,741 per year). Financial award applicants required to submit FAFSA. *Unit head:* Prof. Bolivar Ramirez-Carlo, III, Dean of Faculty, 787-620-2040 Ext. 2010, Fax: 787-620-2958, E-mail: bramirez@aupr.edu. *Application contact:* Keren I. Llanos-Figueroa, Information Contact, 787-620-2040 Ext. 2021, Fax: 787-785-7377, E-mail: oficnaadmisiones@aupr.edu.

Arizona State University at the Tempe campus, Mary Lou Fulton Teachers College, Program in Curriculum and Instruction, Phoenix, AZ 85069. Offers curriculum and instruction (M Ed, MA); elementary education (M Ed); physical education (MPE); secondary education (M Ed). *Program availability:* Part-time, evening/weekend, online learning. Terminal master's awarded for partial completion of doctoral program. *Degree requirements:* For master's, thesis or alternative, applied project, interactive Program of Study (iPOS) submitted before completing 50 percent of required credit hours. *Entrance requirements:* For master's, GRE or GMAT (for some programs), minimum GPA of 3.0 or equivalent in last 2 years of work leading to bachelor's degree, 3 letters of recommendation, personal statement describing research and career goals, curriculum vitae or resume, IVP fingerprint clearance card (for those seeking Arizona certification). Additional exam requirements/recommendations for international students: Required—TOEFL, IELTS, or PTE. Electronic applications accepted. *Expenses:* Contact institution. *Faculty research:* Early childhood, media and computers, elementary education, secondary education, English education, bilingual education, language and literacy, science education, engineering education, exercise and wellness education.

Arkansas State University, Graduate School, College of Education and Behavioral Science, Department of Health, Physical Education, and Sport Sciences, State University, AR 72467. Offers exercise science (MS); physical education (MSE, SCCT); sports administration (MS). *Program availability:* Part-time. *Degree requirements:* For master's, comprehensive exam, thesis or alternative; for SCCT, comprehensive exam. *Entrance requirements:* For master's, GRE General Test or MAT, appropriate bachelor's degree, official transcripts, immunization records, statement of goals, letters of recommendation; for SCCT, GRE General Test or MAT, interview, master's degree, official transcript, immunization records. Additional exam requirements/recommendations for international students: Required—TOEFL (minimum score 550 paper-based; 79 iBT), IELTS (minimum score 6), PTE (minimum score 56). Electronic applications accepted.

Armstrong State University, School of Graduate Studies, Department of Secondary, Adult, and Physical Education, Savannah, GA 31419-1997. Offers adolescent and adult education (Certificate); adult education and community leadership (M Ed); curriculum and instruction (M Ed); secondary education (MAT). *Program availability:* Part-time, evening/weekend, online learning. *Faculty:* 9 full-time (all women), 3 part-time/adjunct (all women). *Students:* 23 full-time (16 women), 103 part-time (68 women); includes 47 minority (40 Black or African American, non-Hispanic/Latino; 1 Asian, non-Hispanic/Latino; 2 Hispanic/Latino; 4 Two or more races, non-Hispanic/Latino), 1 international. Average age 32. 77 applicants, 52% accepted, 28 enrolled. In 2016, 36 master's, 1 other advanced degree awarded. *Degree requirements:* For master's, comprehensive exam (for some programs), thesis (for some programs), capstone project (for M Ed). *Entrance requirements:* For master's, edTPA (for MAT). Additional exam requirements/recommendations for international students: Required—TOEFL (minimum score 523 paper-based). *Application deadline:* For fall admission, 6/30 priority date for domestic students, 5/1 priority date for international students; for spring admission, 11/15 priority date for domestic students, 9/15 priority date for international students; for summer admission, 4/15 priority date for domestic students, 9/15 for international students. Applications are processed on a rolling basis. Application fee: $30. Electronic applications accepted. *Expenses:* Tuition, state resident: full-time $1781; part-time

$161.93 per credit hour. Tuition, nonresident: full-time $6482; part-time $589.27 per credit hour. *Required fees:* $1224 per unit. $612 per semester. Tuition and fees vary according to course load, campus/location and program. *Financial support:* In 2016–17, research assistantships with full tuition reimbursements (averaging $5,000 per year) were awarded; career-related internships or fieldwork, Federal Work-Study, scholarships/grants, and unspecified assistantships also available. Support available to part-time students. Financial award application deadline: 3/15; financial award applicants required to submit FAFSA. *Faculty research:* Quality of teacher leadership, classroom management and first year teachers; edTPA preparation and success of candidates; social justice issues related to educational preparation; recruitment of STEM teachers. *Unit head:* Dr. Regina Rahimi, Interim Department Head, 912-344-2562, E-mail: regina.rahimi@armstrong.edu. *Application contact:* McKenzie Peterman, Assistant Director of Graduate Admissions, 912-344-2503, Fax: 912-344-3417, E-mail: graduate@armstrong.edu.
Website: http://www.armstrong.edu/Education/adolescent_adult_education2/aaed_welcome

Auburn University, Graduate School, College of Education, Department of Kinesiology, Auburn University, AL 36849. Offers exercise science (M Ed). *Accreditation:* NCATE. *Program availability:* Part-time. *Faculty:* 18 full-time (9 women), 1 part-time/adjunct (0 women). *Students:* 96 full-time (57 women), 28 part-time (11 women); includes 132 minority (114 Black or African American, non-Hispanic/Latino; 2 American Indian or Alaska Native, non-Hispanic/Latino; 4 Asian, non-Hispanic/Latino; 6 Hispanic/Latino; 1 Native Hawaiian or other Pacific Islander, non-Hispanic/Latino; 5 Two or more races, non-Hispanic/Latino), 14 international. Average age 26. 127 applicants, 66% accepted, 53 enrolled. In 2016, 63 master's, 4 doctorates, 1 other advanced degree awarded. *Degree requirements:* For master's, thesis (for some programs); for doctorate, thesis/dissertation; for Ed S, exam, field project. *Entrance requirements:* For master's, GRE General Test; for doctorate and Ed S, GRE General Test, interview, master's degree. *Application deadline:* Applications are processed on a rolling basis. Application fee: $50 ($60 for international students). Electronic applications accepted. *Expenses:* Tuition, state resident: full-time $9072; part-time $504 per credit hour. Tuition, nonresident: full-time $27,216; part-time $1512 per credit hour. *Required fees:* $812 per semester. Tuition and fees vary according to degree level and program. *Financial support:* Research assistantships, teaching assistantships, and Federal Work-Study available. Support available to part-time students. Financial award application deadline: 3/15; financial award applicants required to submit FAFSA. *Faculty research:* Biomechanics, exercise physiology, motor skill learning, school health, curriculum development. *Unit head:* Dr. Mary E. Rudisill, Director, 334-844-1458. *Application contact:* Dr. George Flowers, Dean of the Graduate School, 334-844-2125.

Auburn University at Montgomery, College of Education, Department of Kinesiology, Montgomery, AL 36124-4023. Offers exercise science (M Ed); physical education (Ed S); sport management (M Ed). *Faculty:* 6 full-time (2 women), 2 part-time/adjunct (both women). *Students:* 23 full-time (14 women), 19 part-time (9 women); includes 10 minority (9 Black or African American, non-Hispanic/Latino; 1 Hispanic/Latino), 2 international. Average age 28. *Entrance requirements:* Additional exam requirements/recommendations for international students: Recommended—TOEFL (minimum score 500 paper-based; 61 iBT), IELTS (minimum score 5.5), TSE (minimum score 44). *Expenses:* Tuition, state resident: full-time $6462; part-time $359 per credit hour. Tuition, nonresident: full-time $14,526; part-time $807 per credit hour. *Required fees:* $554. *Financial support:* Teaching assistantships available. Financial award application deadline: 3/1; financial award applicants required to submit FAFSA. *Unit head:* Dr. George Schaefer, Head, 334-244-3887, Fax: 334-244-3835, E-mail: gschaefe@aum.edu. *Application contact:* Janis Bigelow, Graduate Advisor, 334-244-3135, E-mail: jbigelo1@aum.edu.
Website: http://www.education.aum.edu/academic-programs/academic-programs/kinesiology

Azusa Pacific University, School of Behavioral and Applied Sciences, Department of Exercise and Sport Science, Azusa, CA 91702-7000. Offers athletic training (MS); physical education (MA, MS).

Azusa Pacific University, School of Education, Department of Advanced Studies, Program in Physical Education, Azusa, CA 91702-7000. Offers M Ed. *Program availability:* Evening/weekend. *Degree requirements:* For master's, core exams, oral exam, oral presentation. *Entrance requirements:* For master's, BA in physical education or 12 units of course work in education, minimum GPA of 3.0.

Ball State University, Graduate School, College of Applied Sciences and Technology, School of Kinesiology, Program in Physical Education and Sport, Muncie, IN 47306. Offers physical education and sport (MA, MS), including athletic coaching education, sport administration, sport and exercise psychology. *Program availability:* Part-time, 100% online. *Entrance requirements:* For master's, GRE General Test, minimum baccalaureate GPA of 2.75 or 3.0 in latter half of baccalauareate, curriculum vitae, three letters of recommendation; campus visit to meet faculty and see facilities (strongly encouraged). Additional exam requirements/recommendations for international students: Required—TOEFL (minimum score 550 paper-based; 79 iBT), IELTS (minimum score 6.5). Electronic applications accepted.

Baylor University, Graduate School, Robbins College of Health and Human Sciences, Department of Health, Human Performance and Recreation, Waco, TX 76798. Offers MPH, MS, PhD. *Accreditation:* NCATE. *Program availability:* Part-time. *Faculty:* 13 full-time (5 women), 3 part-time/adjunct (1 woman). *Students:* 71 full-time (43 women), 10 part-time (7 women); includes 18 minority (5 Black or African American, non-Hispanic/Latino; 3 Asian, non-Hispanic/Latino; 6 Hispanic/Latino; 4 Two or more races, non-Hispanic/Latino), 7 international. 109 applicants, 59% accepted, 44 enrolled. In 2016, 31 master's, 1 doctorate awarded. *Degree requirements:* For master's, comprehensive exam, thesis optional; for doctorate, comprehensive exam, thesis/dissertation. *Entrance requirements:* For master's and doctorate, GRE General Test. Additional exam requirements/recommendations for international students: Required—TOEFL (minimum score 550 paper-based; 80 iBT). *Application deadline:* For fall admission, 2/1 priority date for domestic students, 2/1 for international students; for spring admission, 10/1 for domestic and international students. Applications are processed on a rolling basis. Application fee: $25. Electronic applications accepted. *Expenses: Tuition:* Full-time $28,494; part-time $1583 per credit hour. *Required fees:* $167 per credit hour. Tuition and fees vary according to course load and program. *Financial support:* In 2016–17, 60 students received support, including 1 research assistantship with full tuition reimbursement available (averaging $12,700 per year), 33 teaching assistantships with full tuition reimbursements available (averaging $7,650 per year); career-related internships or fieldwork, Federal Work-Study, institutionally sponsored loans, scholarships/grants, tuition waivers (full), and unspecified assistantships also available. Financial award application deadline: 2/1. *Faculty research:* Behavior change theory, nutrition and enzyme therapy, exercise testing, health planning. *Unit head:* Dr. Jaeho Shim, Graduate Program Director, 254-710-4009, Fax: 254-710-3527, E-mail: joe_shim@baylor.edu. *Application contact:* Kathy Mirick, Administrative Assistant, 254-710-3526, Fax: 254-710-3527, E-mail: kathy_mirick@baylor.edu.
Website: http://www.baylor.edu/HHPR/

Bridgewater State University, College of Graduate Studies, College of Education and Allied Studies, Department of Movement Arts, Health Promotion, and Leisure Studies, Program in Physical Education, Bridgewater, MA 02325. Offers MS. *Program availability:* Part-time, evening/weekend. *Degree requirements:* For master's, thesis or alternative. *Entrance requirements:* For master's, GRE General Test.

Brigham Young University, Graduate Studies, David O. McKay School of Education, Department of Teacher Education, Provo, UT 84602. Offers integrative science-technology-engineering-mathematics (STEM) (MA); literacy education (MA); physical education teacher education (MA); teacher education (MA). *Program availability:* Part-time-only, evening/weekend. *Faculty:* 28 full-time (15 women). *Students:* 22 part-time (19 women); includes 2 minority (both Native Hawaiian or other Pacific Islander, non-Hispanic/Latino). Average age 34. 24 applicants, 79% accepted, 17 enrolled. In 2016, 6 master's awarded. *Degree requirements:* For master's, thesis. *Entrance requirements:* For master's, GRE General Test, minimum 1 year of teaching experience (preferred), minimum cumulative GPA of 3.25. Additional exam requirements/recommendations for international students: Required—TOEFL. *Application deadline:* For fall admission, 2/1 for international students; for winter admission, 2/1 for international students; for summer admission, 2/1 priority date for domestic students, 2/1 for international students. Application fee: $50. Electronic applications accepted. *Expenses:* Contact institution. *Financial support:* In 2016–17, 20 students received support. Tuition waivers (full and partial) available. *Faculty research:* Multicultural education, physical education teacher education, curriculum and instructional education, teacher education, teaching English language learners. *Unit head:* Ramona Cutri, Graduate Coordinator, 801-422-4982, Fax: 801-422-0652, E-mail: ramona_cutri@byu.edu. *Application contact:* Hannah Nelson, Graduate Program Manager, 801-422-2089, Fax: 801-422-0652, E-mail: hannah_nelson@byu.edu.
Website: http://education.byu.edu/ted/

Brooklyn College of the City University of New York, School of Natural and Behavioral Sciences, Department of Kinesiology, Brooklyn, NY 11210-2889. Offers exercise and sports science (MS); physical education teacher (MS); sport management (MS). *Program availability:* Part-time. *Degree requirements:* For master's, comprehensive exam or thesis. *Entrance requirements:* For master's, previous course work in physical education and education, minimum GPA of 3.0, 2 letters of recommendation, essay. Additional exam requirements/recommendations for international students: Required—TOEFL (minimum score 500 paper-based; 61 iBT). Electronic applications accepted. *Faculty research:* Exercise physiology, motor learning, sports psychology, women in athletics.

California Baptist University, Program in Kinesiology, Riverside, CA 92504-3206. Offers exercise science (MS); physical education (MS); sport management (MS). *Program availability:* Part-time, 100% online, blended/hybrid learning. *Faculty:* 10 full-time (3 women), 3 part-time/adjunct (0 women). *Students:* 77 full-time (43 women), 37 part-time (16 women); includes 48 minority (16 Black or African American, non-Hispanic/Latino; 9 Asian, non-Hispanic/Latino; 20 Hispanic/Latino; 1 Native Hawaiian or other Pacific Islander, non-Hispanic/Latino; 2 Two or more races, non-Hispanic/Latino), 26 international. Average age 28. 71 applicants, 76% accepted, 47 enrolled. In 2016, 43 master's awarded. *Degree requirements:* For master's, comprehensive exam or research thesis. *Entrance requirements:* For master's, minimum undergraduate GPA of 2.75; completion of course prerequisites with minimum C grade; three recommendations; 500-word essay; resume; interview. Additional exam requirements/recommendations for international students: Required—TOEFL (minimum score 80 iBT). *Application deadline:* For fall admission, 8/1 priority date for domestic students, 7/1 for international students; for spring admission, 12/1 priority date for domestic students, 11/1 for international students. Applications are processed on a rolling basis. Application fee: $45. Electronic applications accepted. *Expenses:* Contact institution. *Financial support:* In 2016–17, 11 students received support. Federal Work-Study, scholarships/grants, and unspecified assistantships available. Financial award applicants required to submit CSS PROFILE or FAFSA. *Faculty research:* Physical education pedagogy, exercise management and prevention of cardiovascular and metabolic diseases, sport management, immune function, carbohydrate oxidation. *Unit head:* Dr. David Pearson, Dean, College of Allied Health, 951-343-4298, E-mail: dpearson@calbaptist.edu. *Application contact:* Dr. Sean Sullivan, Chair, Department of Kinesiology, 951-343-4528, Fax: 951-343-5095, E-mail: ssullivan@calbaptist.edu.
Website: http://www.calbaptist.edu/mskin/

California State University, Dominguez Hills, College of Health, Human Services and Nursing, Program in Physical Education Administration, Carson, CA 90747-0001. Offers MA. *Program availability:* Part-time. *Degree requirements:* For master's, comprehensive exam. *Entrance requirements:* For master's, minimum GPA of 2.75. Additional exam requirements/recommendations for international students: Required—TOEFL, IELTS. *Faculty research:* Teaching pedagogy, physical activity.

California State University, East Bay, Office of Graduate Studies, College of Education and Allied Studies, Department of Kinesiology, Hayward, CA 94542-3000. Offers MS. *Students:* 10 full-time (2 women), 18 part-time (6 women); includes 20 minority (4 Black or African American, non-Hispanic/Latino; 4 Asian, non-Hispanic/Latino; 5 Hispanic/Latino; 1 Native Hawaiian or other Pacific Islander, non-Hispanic/Latino; 6 Two or more races, non-Hispanic/Latino), 1 international. Average age 30. 20 applicants, 60% accepted, 4 enrolled. In 2016, 4 master's awarded. *Degree requirements:* For master's, exam or thesis. *Entrance requirements:* For master's, BA in kinesiology or related discipline, minimum major course work GPA of 3.0. Additional exam requirements/recommendations for international students: Required—TOEFL (minimum score 550 paper-based). *Application deadline:* For fall admission, 6/30 for domestic and international students. Applications are processed on a rolling basis. Application fee: $55. Electronic applications accepted. *Financial support:* Fellowships, Federal Work-Study, institutionally sponsored loans, and scholarships/grants available. Support available to part-time students. Financial award application deadline: 3/2; financial award applicants required to submit FAFSA. *Faculty research:* Physiology, psychology of sport/movement, skill acquisition, cultural influence on physical activity. *Unit head:* Dr. Paul Carpenter, Chair, 510-885-3061, E-mail: paul.carpenter@csueastbay.edu. *Application contact:* Prof. Cathy Inouye, Kinesiology Graduate Advisor, 510-885-3048, Fax: 510-885-2423, E-mail: cathy.inouye@csueastbay.edu.
Website: http://www20.csueastbay.edu/ecat/graduate-chapters/g-kin.html

California State University, Fullerton, Graduate Studies, College of Health and Human Development, Department of Kinesiology, Fullerton, CA 92834-9480. Offers MS. *Program availability:* Part-time. *Degree requirements:* For master's, project or thesis. *Entrance requirements:* For master's, minimum GPA of 3.0 in field, 2.5 overall. Application fee: $55. *Expenses:* Tuition, state resident: full-time $3369; part-time $1953 per unit. Tuition, nonresident: full-time $3915; part-time $2499 per unit. Tuition and fees vary according to course load, degree level and program. *Financial support:* Career-related internships or fieldwork, Federal Work-Study, institutionally sponsored loans, and scholarships/grants available. Support available to part-time students. Financial award application deadline: 3/1; financial award applicants required to submit FAFSA. *Unit head:* Dr. Stephen Walk, Head, 657-278-3320. *Application contact:* Admissions/Applications, 657-278-2371.

Physical Education

California State University, Long Beach, Graduate Studies, College of Health and Human Services, Department of Kinesiology, Long Beach, CA 90840. Offers adapted physical education (MA); coaching and student athlete development (MA); exercise physiology and nutrition (MS); exercise science (MS); individualized studies (MA); kinesiology (MA); pedagogical studies (MA); sport and exercise psychology (MS); sport management (MA); sports medicine and injury studies (MS). *Program availability:* Part-time. *Degree requirements:* For master's, oral and written comprehensive exams or thesis. *Entrance requirements:* For master's, GRE General Test, minimum GPA of 2.75 during previous 2 years of course work. *Application deadline:* For fall admission, 6/1 for domestic students. Applications are processed on a rolling basis. Application fee: $55. Electronic applications accepted. *Financial support:* Federal Work-Study, institutionally sponsored loans, and scholarships/grants available. Financial award application deadline: 3/2. *Faculty research:* Pulmonary functioning, feedback and practice structure, strength training, history and politics of sports, special population research issues. *Unit head:* Jan Schroeder, Chair, 562-985-4051.

California State University, Los Angeles, Graduate Studies, College of Health and Human Services, Department of Kinesiology and Nutritional Sciences, Los Angeles, CA 90032-8530. Offers nutritional science (MS); physical education and kinesiology (MA). *Accreditation:* AND. *Program availability:* Part-time, evening/weekend. *Degree requirements:* For master's, comprehensive exam, project or thesis. *Entrance requirements:* For master's, minimum GPA of 2.75. Additional exam requirements/recommendations for international students: Required—TOEFL (minimum score 500 paper-based).

California State University, Sacramento, Office of Graduate Studies, College of Health and Human Services, Department of Kinesiology and Health Science, Sacramento, CA 95819. Offers MS. *Accreditation:* APTA. *Program availability:* Part-time. *Students:* 14 full-time (9 women), 24 part-time (13 women); includes 9 minority (1 Black or African American, non-Hispanic/Latino; 3 Asian, non-Hispanic/Latino; 5 Hispanic/Latino). Average age 29. 47 applicants, 64% accepted, 17 enrolled. In 2016, 7 master's awarded. *Degree requirements:* For master's, thesis or project; writing proficiency exam. *Entrance requirements:* For master's, minimum overall GPA of 2.8, 3.0 in last 60 semester units; upper-division statistics course. Additional exam requirements/recommendations for international students: Required—TOEFL (minimum score 550 paper-based; 80 iBT). *Application deadline:* For fall admission, 1/28 for domestic students, 3/1 for international students; for spring admission, 9/30 for international students. Applications are processed on a rolling basis. Application fee: $55. Electronic applications accepted. *Expenses:* $4,302 full-time tuition and fees per semester, $2,796 part-time. *Financial support:* Research assistantships, teaching assistantships, career-related internships or fieldwork, and Federal Work-Study available. Support available to part-time students. Financial award application deadline: 3/1; financial award applicants required to submit FAFSA. *Unit head:* Katherine Jamieson, Chair, 916-278-6441, E-mail: katherine.jamieson@csus.edu. *Application contact:* Jose Martinez, Graduate Admissions Supervisor, 916-278-7871, E-mail: martinj@skymail.csus.edu.
Website: http://www.csus.edu/hhs/khs

California State University, Stanislaus, College of Education, Program in Education (MA), Turlock, CA 95382. Offers curriculum and instruction (MA), including education technology, elementary education, multilingual education, physical education, reading, secondary education, special education; school administration (MA); school counseling (MA). *Program availability:* Part-time, evening/weekend. *Degree requirements:* For master's, comprehensive exam (for some programs), thesis (for some programs). *Entrance requirements:* For master's, MAT, GRE, or CBEST (varies by concentration), 3 letters of recommendation, personal statement. Additional exam requirements/recommendations for international students: Required—TOEFL (minimum score 550 paper-based). Electronic applications accepted. *Faculty research:* Children's perspectives on historical events, method elementary schools dual language education, K-12 reading programs.

Campbell University, Graduate and Professional Programs, School of Education, Buies Creek, NC 27506. Offers elementary education (M Ed); interdisciplinary studies (M Ed); middle grades education (M Ed); physical education (M Ed); school administration (MSA); school counseling (M Ed); secondary education (M Ed). *Accreditation:* NCATE. *Program availability:* Part-time, evening/weekend. *Degree requirements:* For master's, comprehensive exam. *Entrance requirements:* For master's, GRE General Test, minimum GPA of 2.7. *Faculty research:* Spiritual values and wellness issues in counseling, stress and professional burnout among counselors, thinking strategies, leadership, adaptive technology.

Canisius College, Graduate Division, School of Education and Human Services, Department of Kinesiology, Buffalo, NY 14208-1098. Offers physical education (MS Ed); physical education birth - 12 (MS Ed). *Program availability:* Part-time, evening/weekend, 100% online, blended/hybrid learning. *Faculty:* 5 full-time (1 woman), 5 part-time/adjunct (3 women). *Students:* 16 full-time (5 women), 41 part-time (12 women); includes 2 minority (both Black or African American, non-Hispanic/Latino), 1 international. Average age 28. 33 applicants, 82% accepted, 22 enrolled. In 2016, 41 master's awarded. *Degree requirements:* For master's, research project. *Entrance requirements:* For master's, official college and/or university transcript(s) showing completion of bachelor's degree from accredited institution with evidence of teaching certification (not for initial certification candidates); two letters of recommendation; minimum cumulative undergraduate GPA of 2.7. Additional exam requirements/recommendations for international students: Required—TOEFL (minimum score 550 paper-based, 79 iBT), IELTS (minimum score 6.5), or CAEL (minimum score 70). *Application deadline:* Applications are processed on a rolling basis. Application fee: $25. Electronic applications accepted. Application fee is waived when completed online. *Expenses:* Contact institution. *Financial support:* Career-related internships or fieldwork, Federal Work-Study, scholarships/grants, tuition waivers (partial), and unspecified assistantships available. Support available to part-time students. Financial award application deadline: 4/30; financial award applicants required to submit FAFSA. *Faculty research:* Culturally congruent pedagogy in physical education, information processing and perceptual styles of athletes, qualities of effective coaches. *Unit head:* Dr. Peter M. Koehneke, Chair/Professor of Kinesiology, 716-888-2954, Fax: 716-888-8445, E-mail: koehneke@canisius.edu. *Application contact:* Kathleen B. Davis, Vice President of Enrollment Management, 716-888-2500, Fax: 716-888-3195, E-mail: daviskb@canisius.edu.
Website: http://www.canisius.edu/graduate/

Canisius College, Graduate Division, School of Education and Human Services, Office of Professional Studies, Buffalo, NY 14208-1098. Offers applied nutrition (MS, Certificate); community and school health (MS); health and human performance (MS); health information technology (MS); respiratory care (MS). *Program availability:* Part-time, evening/weekend, 100% online, blended/hybrid learning. *Faculty:* 2 full-time (0 women), 6 part-time/adjunct (3 women). *Students:* 18 full-time (13 women), 59 part-time (43 women); includes 11 minority (5 Black or African American, non-Hispanic/Latino; 2 Asian, non-Hispanic/Latino; 3 Hispanic/Latino; 1 Two or more races, non-Hispanic/Latino), 2 international. Average age 36. 48 applicants, 85% accepted, 25 enrolled. In 2016, 42 master's awarded. *Entrance requirements:* For master's, GRE (recommended), bachelor's degree transcript, two letters of recommendation, current licensure (for applied nutrition), minimum GPA of 2.7, current resume. Additional exam requirements/recommendations for international students: Required—TOEFL (minimum score 550 paper-based, 79 iBT), IELTS (minimum score 6.5), or CAEL (minimum score 70). *Application deadline:* Applications are processed on a rolling basis. Application fee: $25. Electronic applications accepted. Application fee is waived when completed online. *Expenses: Tuition:* Full-time $14,742. *Required fees:* $724. *Financial support:* Career-related internships or fieldwork, Federal Work-Study, scholarships/grants, tuition waivers (partial), and unspecified assistantships available. Support available to part-time students. Financial award application deadline: 4/30; financial award applicants required to submit FAFSA. *Faculty research:* Nutrition, community and school health; community and health; health and human performance applied; nutrition and respiratory care. *Unit head:* Sandy McKenna, Director, Professional Studies, 716-888-8296, E-mail: mckekkas@canisius.edu. *Application contact:* Kathleen B. Davis, Vice President of Enrollment Management, 716-888-2500, Fax: 716-888-3195, E-mail: daviskb@canisius.edu.
Website: http://www.canisius.edu/graduate/

Caribbean University, Graduate School, Bayamón, PR 00960-0493. Offers administration and supervision (MA Ed); criminal justice (MA); curriculum and instruction (MA Ed, PhD), including elementary education (MA Ed), English education (MA Ed), history education (MA Ed), mathematics education (MA Ed), primary education (MA Ed), science education (MA Ed), Spanish education (MA Ed); educational technology in instructional systems (MA Ed); gerontology (MSN); human resources (MBA); museology, archiving and art history (MA Ed); neonatal pediatrics (MSN); physical education (MA Ed); special education (MA Ed). *Entrance requirements:* For master's, interview, minimum GPA of 2.5.

Central Connecticut State University, School of Graduate Studies, School of Education and Professional Studies, Department of Physical Education and Human Performance, New Britain, CT 06050-4010. Offers physical education (MS). *Program availability:* Part-time, evening/weekend. *Faculty:* 6 full-time (2 women), 1 (woman) part-time/adjunct. *Students:* 19 full-time (11 women), 31 part-time (14 women); includes 6 minority (1 Black or African American, non-Hispanic/Latino; 1 Asian, non-Hispanic/Latino; 3 Hispanic/Latino; 1 Two or more races, non-Hispanic/Latino), 1 international. Average age 27. 28 applicants, 89% accepted, 15 enrolled. In 2016, 20 master's, 4 other advanced degrees awarded. *Degree requirements:* For master's, comprehensive exam, thesis or alternative; for Certificate, qualifying exam. *Entrance requirements:* For master's, minimum GPA of 2.7, bachelor's degree in physical education (preferred), essay, interview, letters of recommendation. Additional exam requirements/recommendations for international students: Required—TOEFL (minimum score 550 paper-based; 79 iBT). *Application deadline:* For fall admission, 5/1 for domestic and international students; for spring admission, 11/1 for domestic and international students. Applications are processed on a rolling basis. Application fee: $50. Electronic applications accepted. *Expenses: Tuition, area resident:* Full-time $6497; part-time $606 per credit. Tuition, state resident: full-time $9748; part-time $622 per credit. Tuition, nonresident: full-time $18,102; part-time $622 per credit. *Required fees:* $4459; $246 per credit. *Financial support:* In 2016–17, 8 students received support. Career-related internships or fieldwork, Federal Work-Study, scholarships/grants, and unspecified assistantships available. Support available to part-time students. Financial award application deadline: 3/1; financial award applicants required to submit FAFSA. *Faculty research:* Exercise science, athletic training, preparation of physical education for schools. *Unit head:* Dr. Kimberly Kostelis, Chair, 860-832-2155, E-mail: kostelisk@ccsu.edu. *Application contact:* Patricia Gardner, Associate Director of Graduate Studies, 860-832-2350, Fax: 860-832-2362.
Website: http://www.ccsu.edu/pehp/

Central Washington University, Graduate Studies and Research, College of Education and Professional Studies, Department of Physical Education, School and Public Health, Ellensburg, WA 98926. Offers athletic administration (MS); health and physical education (MS). *Program availability:* Part-time. *Degree requirements:* For master's, comprehensive exam, thesis or alternative. *Entrance requirements:* For master's, minimum GPA of 3.0. Additional exam requirements/recommendations for international students: Required—TOEFL (minimum score 550 paper-based; 79 iBT), IELTS. Electronic applications accepted.

Chicago State University, School of Graduate and Professional Studies, College of Education, Department of Health, Physical Education and Recreation, Chicago, IL 60628. Offers physical education (MS Ed). *Program availability:* Part-time, evening/weekend, online learning. *Degree requirements:* For master's, thesis optional. *Entrance requirements:* For master's, minimum GPA of 2.75. *Faculty research:* Sports psychology, recreation and leisure studies administration.

The Citadel, The Military College of South Carolina, Citadel Graduate College, School of Science and Mathematics, Department of Health, Exercise, and Sport Science, Charleston, SC 29409. Offers health, exercise, and sport science (MS); sport management (MA, Graduate Certificate). *Accreditation:* NCATE. *Program availability:* Part-time, evening/weekend. *Faculty:* 4 full-time (2 women), 1 (woman) part-time/adjunct. *Students:* 13 full-time (5 women), 17 part-time (9 women); includes 6 minority (4 Black or African American, non-Hispanic/Latino; 1 Hispanic/Latino; 1 Native Hawaiian or other Pacific Islander, non-Hispanic/Latino), 1 international. 11 applicants, 82% accepted, 8 enrolled. In 2016, 24 master's, 3 other advanced degrees awarded. *Degree requirements:* For master's, comprehensive exam (for some programs), internship and professional portfolio (for some programs). *Entrance requirements:* For master's, GRE (minimum combined verbal and quantitative score 290) or MAT (minimum score 396), official transcript reflecting highest degree earned from regionally-accredited college or university, minimum undergraduate GPA of 2.5, 3 letters of recommendation, resume detailing previous work experience. Additional exam requirements/recommendations for international students: Required—TOEFL (minimum score 550 paper-based; 79 iBT). *Application deadline:* Applications are processed on a rolling basis. Application fee: $40. Electronic applications accepted. *Expenses:* Tuition, state resident: full-time $5121; part-time $569 per credit hour. Tuition, nonresident: full-time $8613; part-time $957 per credit hour. *Required fees:* $90 per term. *Financial support:* Fellowships and unspecified assistantships available. Support available to part-time students. Financial award application deadline: 7/1; financial award applicants required to submit FAFSA. *Unit head:* Dr. Harry D. Davakos, Department Head, 843-953-5060, E-mail: harry.davakos@citadel.edu. *Application contact:* Dr. Dena P. Garner, Program Director, 843-953-6323, E-mail: garnerd1@citadel.edu.
Website: http://www.citadel.edu/root/hess

The Citadel, The Military College of South Carolina, Citadel Graduate College, Zucker Family School of Education, Charleston, SC 29409. Offers elementary/secondary school administration and supervision (M Ed); elementary/secondary school counseling (M Ed); interdisciplinary STEM education (M Ed); literacy education (M Ed, Graduate Certificate); middle grades (MAT), including English, mathematics, science, social studies; physical education (grades K-12) (MAT); school superintendency (Ed S); secondary education (MAT), including biology, English, mathematics, social studies; student affairs (Graduate Certificate); student affairs and college counseling (M Ed). *Accreditation:* NCATE. *Program availability:* Part-time, evening/weekend, 100% online,

blended/hybrid learning. *Faculty:* 9 full-time (4 women), 9 part-time/adjunct (5 women). *Students:* 70 full-time (58 women), 249 part-time (200 women); includes 87 minority (70 Black or African American, non-Hispanic/Latino; 1 Asian, non-Hispanic/Latino; 9 Hispanic/Latino; 7 Two or more races, non-Hispanic/Latino), 2 international. 146 applicants, 98% accepted, 105 enrolled. In 2016, 85 master's, 7 other advanced degrees awarded. *Degree requirements:* For master's, comprehensive exam (for some programs). *Entrance requirements:* For master's, GRE (minimum combined verbal and quantitative score of 290) or MAT (minimum score 396). Additional exam requirements/recommendations for international students: Required—TOEFL (minimum score 550 paper-based; 79 iBT). *Application deadline:* Applications are processed on a rolling basis. Application fee: $40. Electronic applications accepted. *Expenses:* Tuition, state resident: full-time $5121; part-time $569 per credit hour. Tuition, nonresident: full-time $8613; part-time $957 per credit hour. *Required fees:* $90 per term. *Financial support:* Fellowships and unspecified assistantships available. Support available to part-time students. Financial award application deadline: 7/1; financial award applicants required to submit FAFSA. *Unit head:* Dr. Larry G. Daniel, Dean, 843-953-5097, E-mail: ldaniel@citadel.edu. *Application contact:* Dr. Tammy J. Graham, Associate Professor, 843-953-6854, E-mail: tammy.graham@citadel.edu.
Website: http://www.citadel.edu/root/education-graduate-programs

Clemson University, Graduate School, College of Education, Department of Educational and Organizational Leadership Development, Program in Human Resource Development, Greenville, SC 29607. Offers human resource development (MHRD), including intercollegiate athletic leadership. *Program availability:* Part-time, evening/weekend, online only, 100% online. *Faculty:* 3 full-time (2 women), 1 (woman) part-time/adjunct. *Students:* 58 part-time (30 women); includes 22 minority (15 Black or African American, non-Hispanic/Latino; 2 Asian, non-Hispanic/Latino; 4 Hispanic/Latino; 1 Two or more races, non-Hispanic/Latino). Average age 36. 37 applicants, 62% accepted, 20 enrolled. In 2016, 58 master's awarded. *Degree requirements:* For master's, comprehensive exam. *Entrance requirements:* For master's, GRE General Test, unofficial transcripts, personal statement, resume, 2 letters of recommendation. Additional exam requirements/recommendations for international students: Required—TOEFL (minimum score 80 iBT), IELTS (minimum score 7). *Application deadline:* For fall admission, 7/1 priority date for domestic students. Application fee: $80 ($90 for international students). Electronic applications accepted. *Expenses:* $695 per credit hour, $10 per credit hour IT fee, $39 per semester miscellaneous fees. *Financial support:* Application deadline: 7/1. *Faculty research:* Organizational development, human performance improvement, attachment theory, social constructivism, technology-mediated teaching and learning, corporate universities. *Unit head:* Dr. Phillip McGee, Program Coordinator, 864-474-2459, E-mail: pmcgee@clemson.edu. *Application contact:* Alison Search, Student Services Program Coordinator, 864-656-8370, E-mail: alisonp@clemson.edu.
Website: http://www.clemson.edu/education/academics/masters-specialist-programs/masters-education-human-resource-development/index.html

Cleveland State University, College of Graduate Studies, College of Education and Human Services, Department of Health and Human Performance, Cleveland, OH 44115. Offers physical education pedagogy (M Ed); public health (MPH). *Program availability:* Part-time. *Faculty:* 7 full-time (4 women), 3 part-time/adjunct (2 women). *Students:* 39 full-time (20 women), 63 part-time (38 women); includes 37 minority (26 Black or African American, non-Hispanic/Latino; 2 Asian, non-Hispanic/Latino; 5 Hispanic/Latino; 1 Native Hawaiian or other Pacific Islander, non-Hispanic/Latino; 3 Two or more races, non-Hispanic/Latino), 15 international. Average age 27. 103 applicants, 72% accepted, 43 enrolled. In 2016, 33 master's awarded. *Degree requirements:* For master's, comprehensive exam, thesis optional. *Entrance requirements:* For master's, GRE General Test or MAT (if undergraduate GPA less than 2.75), minimum undergraduate GPA of 2.75. Additional exam requirements/recommendations for international students: Required—TOEFL (minimum score 550 paper-based; 78 iBT), IELTS (minimum score 6). *Application deadline:* For fall admission, 7/15 priority date for domestic students; for spring admission, 12/15 priority date for domestic students. Applications are processed on a rolling basis. Application fee: $30. Electronic applications accepted. *Expenses:* Tuition, state resident: full-time $9565. Tuition, nonresident: full-time $17,980. Tuition and fees vary according to program. *Financial support:* In 2016–17, 6 research assistantships with tuition reimbursements (averaging $3,480 per year), 1 teaching assistantship with tuition reimbursement (averaging $3,480 per year) were awarded; career-related internships or fieldwork, tuition waivers (full), and unspecified assistantships also available. Financial award application deadline: 3/15; financial award applicants required to submit FAFSA. *Faculty research:* Bone density, marketing fitness centers, motor development of disabled, online learning and survey research. *Unit head:* Dr. Sheila M. Patterson, Chairperson, 216-687-4870, Fax: 216-687-5410, E-mail: s.m.patterson@csuohio.edu. *Application contact:* Deborah L. Brown, Interim Assistant Director, Graduate Admissions, 216-523-7572, Fax: 216-687-5400, E-mail: d.l.brown@csuohio.edu.
Website: http://www.csuohio.edu/cehs/departments/HPERD/hperd_dept.html

The College at Brockport, State University of New York, School of Education, Health, and Human Services, Department of Kinesiology, Sports Studies and Physical Education, Brockport, NY 14420-2997. Offers adapted physical education (AGC); physical education (MS Ed), including adapted physical education, athletic administration, physical education/pedagogy. *Program availability:* Part-time. *Faculty:* 11 full-time (4 women), 1 part-time/adjunct (0 women). *Students:* 29 full-time (16 women), 28 part-time (7 women); includes 12 minority (2 Black or African American, non-Hispanic/Latino; 2 Asian, non-Hispanic/Latino; 5 Hispanic/Latino; 3 Two or more races, non-Hispanic/Latino), 1 international. 35 applicants, 91% accepted, 22 enrolled. In 2016, 43 master's awarded. *Degree requirements:* For master's, thesis or alternative. *Entrance requirements:* For master's, minimum GPA of 3.0; statement of objectives. Additional exam requirements/recommendations for international students: Required—TOEFL (minimum score 550 paper-based; 79 iBT), IELTS (minimum score 6.5). *Application deadline:* For fall admission, 4/15 priority date for domestic and international students; for spring admission, 11/15 priority date for domestic and international students; for summer admission, 4/15 priority date for domestic students, 4/15 for international students. Application fee: $80. Electronic applications accepted. *Expenses:* Contact institution. *Financial support:* In 2016–17, 11 teaching assistantships with full tuition reimbursements (averaging $7,000 per year) were awarded; Federal Work-Study, scholarships/grants, and unspecified assistantships also available. Support available to part-time students. Financial award application deadline: 3/15; financial award applicants required to submit FAFSA. *Faculty research:* Athletic administration, adapted physical education, physical education curriculum, physical education teaching/coaching, children's physical activity. *Unit head:* Dr. Cathy Houston-Wilson, Chairperson, 585-395-5352, Fax: 585-395-2771, E-mail: chouston@brockport.edu. *Application contact:* Dr. Francis Kozub, Graduate Program Director, 585-395-5946, Fax: 585-395-2771, E-mail: fkozub@brockport.edu.

The College of New Jersey, Office of Graduate and Advancing Education, School of Nursing, Health and Exercise Science, Department of Health and Exercise Science, Program in Health Education, Ewing, NJ 08628. Offers health (MAT); physical education (M Ed). *Accreditation:* NCATE. *Program availability:* Part-time. *Degree requirements:* For master's, comprehensive exam. *Entrance requirements:* For master's, GRE, minimum GPA of 3.0 in field or 2.75 overall. Additional exam requirements/recommendations for international students: Required—TOEFL. Electronic applications accepted.

The College of New Jersey, Office of Graduate and Advancing Education, School of Nursing, Health and Exercise Science, Department of Health and Exercise Science, Program in Physical Education, Ewing, NJ 08628. Offers M Ed, MAT. *Program availability:* Part-time. *Degree requirements:* For master's, comprehensive exam. *Entrance requirements:* For master's, GRE, minimum GPA of 2.75 overall or 3.0 in field. Additional exam requirements/recommendations for international students: Required—TOEFL. Electronic applications accepted.

Colorado State University–Pueblo, College of Education, Engineering and Professional Studies, Education Program, Pueblo, CO 81001-4901. Offers art education (M Ed); foreign language education (M Ed); health and physical education (M Ed); instructional technology (M Ed); linguistically diverse education (M Ed); music education (M Ed); special education (M Ed). *Accreditation:* TEAC. *Program availability:* Part-time. *Degree requirements:* For master's, portfolio. *Entrance requirements:* For master's, 3 recommendations, teaching license. Additional exam requirements/recommendations for international students: Required—TOEFL (minimum score 500 paper-based). Electronic applications accepted. *Faculty research:* Portfolio assessment, math education, science education.

Columbus State University, Graduate Studies, College of Education and Health Professions, Department of Health, Physical Education and Exercise Science, Columbus, GA 31907-5645. Offers exercise science (MS); health and physical education (M Ed, MAT). *Program availability:* Part-time, evening/weekend. *Faculty:* 5 full-time (3 women). *Students:* 21 full-time (11 women), 8 part-time (2 women); includes 17 minority (12 Black or African American, non-Hispanic/Latino; 1 Asian, non-Hispanic/Latino; 3 Hispanic/Latino; 1 Two or more races, non-Hispanic/Latino). Average age 28. 19 applicants, 37% accepted, 3 enrolled. In 2016, 12 master's awarded. *Degree requirements:* For master's, thesis optional. *Entrance requirements:* For master's, GRE, minimum undergraduate GPA of 2.75. Additional exam requirements/recommendations for international students: Required—TOEFL (minimum score 550 paper-based; 79 iBT). *Application deadline:* For fall admission, 5/1 for domestic students, 4/1 for international students; for spring admission, 11/1 for domestic and international students; for summer admission, 2/1 for domestic students, 3/1 for international students. Applications are processed on a rolling basis. Application fee: $50. Electronic applications accepted. *Expenses:* Tuition, state resident: full-time $4804; part-time $2412 per semester hour. Tuition, nonresident: full-time $19,218; part-time $9612 per semester hour. *Required fees:* $1850; $1850 per semester hour. Tuition and fees vary according to program. *Financial support:* In 2016–17, 3 students received support, including 4 research assistantships (averaging $3,000 per year). Financial award application deadline: 5/15; financial award applicants required to submit FAFSA. *Unit head:* Dr. Tara Underwood, Chair, 706-568-2485, E-mail: underwood_tara@columbusstate.edu. *Application contact:* Kristin Williams, Director of International and Graduate Admissions, 706-507-8848, Fax: 706-568-5091, E-mail: williams_kristin@columbusstate.edu.
Website: http://hpex.columbusstate.edu/

Concordia University Irvine, School of Arts and Sciences, Irvine, CA 92612-3299. Offers coaching and athletic administration (MA). *Program availability:* Part-time, evening/weekend, online learning. *Degree requirements:* For master's, culminating project. *Entrance requirements:* For master's, official college/university transcript(s); signed statement of intent. Additional exam requirements/recommendations for international students: Required—TOEFL (minimum score 550 paper-based; 79 iBT). Electronic applications accepted. *Expenses:* Contact institution.

Delta State University, Graduate Programs, College of Education, Division of Health, Physical Education, and Recreation, Cleveland, MS 38733-0001. Offers health, physical education, and recreation (M Ed); sport and human performance (MS). *Program availability:* Part-time, evening/weekend. *Degree requirements:* For master's, thesis optional. *Entrance requirements:* For master's, GRE General Test or MAT, Class A teaching certificate. *Faculty research:* Blood pressure, body fat, power and reaction time, learning disorders of athletes, effects of walking.

East Carolina University, Graduate School, College of Health and Human Performance, Department of Kinesiology, Greenville, NC 27858-4353. Offers adapted physical education (MS); bioenergetics and exercise science (PhD); biomechanics (MS); exercise physiology (MS); physical activity promotion (MS); physical education (MA Ed, MAT); physical education pedagogy (MS); sport and exercise psychology (MS); sport management (MS, Certificate). *Students:* 90 full-time (33 women), 23 part-time (9 women); includes 16 minority (8 Black or African American, non-Hispanic/Latino; 3 Asian, non-Hispanic/Latino; 3 Hispanic/Latino; 2 Two or more races, non-Hispanic/Latino), 7 international. Average age 26. 98 applicants, 53% accepted, 38 enrolled. In 2016, 28 master's, 2 doctorates awarded. *Degree requirements:* For master's, comprehensive exam, thesis optional; for doctorate, comprehensive exam, thesis/dissertation. *Entrance requirements:* For master's, GRE General Test or MAT; for doctorate, GRE. Additional exam requirements/recommendations for international students: Required—TOEFL. *Application deadline:* For fall admission, 2/1 priority date for domestic students, 2/1 for international students. Applications are processed on a rolling basis. Application fee: $50. *Financial support:* Research assistantships with tuition reimbursements and teaching assistantships available. Support available to part-time students. Financial award application deadline: 2/1. *Faculty research:* Diabetes metabolism, pediatric obesity, biomechanics of arthritis, physical activity measurement. *Total annual research expenditures:* $26. *Unit head:* Dr. Stacey Altman, Chair, 252-328-2973, E-mail: altmans@ecu.edu.

Eastern Kentucky University, The Graduate School, College of Education, Department of Curriculum and Instruction, Program in Secondary and Higher Education, Richmond, KY 40475-3102. Offers secondary education (MA Ed), including agricultural education, art education, biological sciences education, business education, English education, geography education, history education, home economics education, industrial education, mathematical sciences education, physical education, school health education. *Accreditation:* NCATE. *Program availability:* Part-time. *Entrance requirements:* For master's, GRE General Test, minimum GPA of 2.5.

Eastern Kentucky University, The Graduate School, College of Health Sciences, Department of Exercise and Sport Science, Richmond, KY 40475-3102. Offers exercise and sport science (MS); exercise and wellness (MS); sports administration (MS). *Program availability:* Part-time. *Entrance requirements:* For master's, GRE General Test (minimum score 700 verbal and quantitative), minimum GPA of 2.5 (for most), minimum GPA of 3.0 (analytical writing). *Faculty research:* Nutrition and exercise.

Eastern Michigan University, Graduate School, College of Health and Human Services, School of Health Promotion and Human Performance, Programs in Physical Education Pedagogy, Ypsilanti, MI 48197. Offers adapted physical education (MS); physical education pedagogy (MS). *Program availability:* Part-time, evening/weekend, online learning. *Students:* 4 part-time (1 woman); includes 1 minority (Hispanic/Latino). Average age 31. 1 applicant. In 2016, 2 master's awarded. *Degree requirements:* For master's, thesis or independent study project and comprehensive exams. *Entrance requirements:* Additional exam requirements/recommendations for international students: Required—TOEFL. *Application deadline:* For fall admission, 8/1 for domestic students, 5/1 for international students; for winter admission, 12/1 for domestic students, 10/1 for international students; for spring admission, 4/15 for domestic students, 3/1 for international students. Applications are processed on a rolling basis. Application fee: $45. *Financial support:* Fellowships, research assistantships with full tuition reimbursements, teaching assistantships with full tuition reimbursements, career-related internships or fieldwork, Federal Work-Study, institutionally sponsored loans, scholarships/grants, tuition waivers (partial), and unspecified assistantships available. Support available to part-time students. Financial award applicants required to submit FAFSA. *Application contact:* Dr. Roberta Faust, Program Coordinator, 734-487-7120 Ext. 2745, Fax: 734-487-2024, E-mail: rfaust@emich.edu.

Eastern New Mexico University, Graduate School, College of Education and Technology, Department of Health and Physical Education, Portales, NM 88130. Offers physical education (MS), including sport administration, sport science. *Program availability:* Part-time. *Degree requirements:* For master's, comprehensive exam, thesis optional. *Entrance requirements:* For master's, minimum GPA of 3.0, 15 hours of leveling courses without bachelor's degree in physical education, two references. Additional exam requirements/recommendations for international students: Required—TOEFL (minimum score 550 paper-based; 79 iBT), IELTS (minimum score 6). Electronic applications accepted.

Eastern University, Loeb School of Education, St. Davids, PA 19087-3696. Offers ESL program specialist (K-12) (Certificate); general supervisor (PreK-12) (Certificate); health and physical education (K-12) (Certificate); middle level (4-8) (Certificate); multicultural education (M Ed); organizational leadership with education (PhD); Pre K-4 (Certificate); Pre K-4 with special education (Certificate); reading (M Ed); reading specialist (K-12) (Certificate); reading supervisor (K-12) (Certificate); school health supervisor (Certificate); school nurse (K-12) (Certificate); secondary biology education (7-12) (Certificate); secondary chemistry education (7-12) (Certificate); secondary communication education (7-12) (Certificate); secondary education (7-12) (Certificate); secondary English education (7-12) (Certificate); secondary math education (7-12) (Certificate); secondary social studies education (7-12) (Certificate); special education (M Ed); special education (7-12) (Certificate); special education (Pre K-8) (Certificate); special education supervisor (N-12) (Certificate); TESOL (M Ed); world language (Certificate), including French, Spanish. *Program availability:* Part-time, evening/weekend, online learning. *Students:* 41 full-time (32 women), 89 part-time (68 women); includes 54 minority (38 Black or African American, non-Hispanic/Latino; 3 Asian, non-Hispanic/Latino; 11 Hispanic/Latino; 2 Two or more races, non-Hispanic/Latino), 2 international. Average age 37. In 2016, 64 master's awarded. *Entrance requirements:* Additional exam requirements/recommendations for international students: Required—TOEFL. *Application deadline:* Applications are processed on a rolling basis. Application fee: $35. Electronic applications accepted. Application fee is waived when completed online. *Expenses:* $690 per credit. *Unit head:* Michael Dziedziak, Executive Director of Enrollment, 800-452-0996, E-mail: gpsadmissions@eastern.edu.
Website: http://www.eastern.edu/academics/programs/loeb-school-education-0

Eastern Washington University, Graduate Studies, College of Arts, Letters and Education, Department of Physical Education, Health and Recreation, Cheney, WA 99004-2431. Offers exercise science (MS); sports and recreation administration (MS). *Faculty:* 17 full-time (7 women), 5 part-time/adjunct (2 women). *Students:* 26 full-time (10 women), 8 part-time (3 women); includes 7 minority (3 Black or African American, non-Hispanic/Latino; 1 American Indian or Alaska Native, non-Hispanic/Latino; 2 Asian, non-Hispanic/Latino; 1 Hispanic/Latino). Average age 29. 64 applicants, 38% accepted, 21 enrolled. In 2016, 14 master's awarded. *Degree requirements:* For master's, comprehensive exam, thesis or alternative. *Entrance requirements:* For master's, minimum GPA of 3.0. Additional exam requirements/recommendations for international students: Required—TOEFL (minimum score 580 paper-based; 92 iBT), IELTS (minimum score 7), PTE (minimum score 63). *Application deadline:* For fall admission, 4/1 priority date for domestic students; for spring admission, 1/15 for domestic students. Applications are processed on a rolling basis. Application fee: $50. Electronic applications accepted. *Expenses:* Tuition, state resident: full-time $11,000; part-time $5500 per credit. Tuition, nonresident: full-time $24,000; part-time $12,000 per credit. *Required fees:* $1300. One-time fee: $50 full-time. Part-time tuition and fees vary according to course load, campus/location and program. *Financial support:* In 2016–17, 10 teaching assistantships with partial tuition reimbursements (averaging $6,624 per year) were awarded; career-related internships or fieldwork, Federal Work-Study, institutionally sponsored loans, and scholarships/grants also available. Support available to part-time students. Financial award application deadline: 2/1; financial award applicants required to submit FAFSA. *Unit head:* Dr. Chadron Hazelbaker, Graduate Program Director, 509-359-2486, Fax: 509-359-4833, E-mail: chazelbaker@ewu.edu.

East Stroudsburg University of Pennsylvania, Graduate and Extended Studies, College of Health Sciences, Department of Exercise Science, East Stroudsburg, PA 18301-2999. Offers MS. *Program availability:* Part-time, evening/weekend, online learning. *Faculty:* 2 full-time, 5 part-time/adjunct. *Students:* 54 full-time (25 women), 2 part-time (0 women); includes 10 minority (3 Black or African American, non-Hispanic/Latino; 5 Hispanic/Latino; 1 Native Hawaiian or other Pacific Islander, non-Hispanic/Latino; 1 Two or more races, non-Hispanic/Latino), 2 international. *Degree requirements:* For master's, comprehensive exam, thesis or alternative, computer literacy. *Entrance requirements:* Additional exam requirements/recommendations for international students: Recommended—TOEFL (minimum score 560 paper-based; 83 iBT), IELTS. *Application deadline:* For fall admission, 3/1 priority date for domestic and international students; for spring admission, 11/30 for domestic students, 10/31 for international students. Applications are processed on a rolling basis. Application fee: $50. Electronic applications accepted. *Expenses:* Tuition, state resident: full-time $8694; part-time $5796 per year. Tuition, nonresident: full-time $13,050; part-time $8700 per year. *Required fees:* $2550; $1690 per unit. $845 per semester. Tuition and fees vary according to course load, campus/location and program. *Financial support:* Research assistantships with tuition reimbursements, Federal Work-Study, and unspecified assistantships available. Support available to part-time students. Financial award application deadline: 3/1. *Unit head:* Dr. Chad Witmer, Graduate Coordinator, 570-422-3362, E-mail: cwitmer@esu.edu. *Application contact:* Kevin Quintero, Associate Director, Graduate and Extended Studies, 570-422-3890, Fax: 570-422-2711, E-mail: kquintero@esu.edu.

East Texas Baptist University, Master of Education Program, Marshall, TX 75670-1498. Offers college and university leadership (M Ed); curriculum and instruction (M Ed); principal certification (M Ed); sports and exercise leadership (M Ed); teacher certification (M Ed). *Program availability:* Part-time, evening/weekend. *Faculty:* 3 full-time (1 woman), 3 part-time/adjunct (all women). *Students:* 33 part-time (19 women); includes 14 minority (10 Black or African American, non-Hispanic/Latino; 4 Hispanic/Latino), 1 international. Average age 29. 53 applicants, 51% accepted, 25 enrolled. In 2016, 20 master's awarded. *Entrance requirements:* Additional exam requirements/recommendations for international students: Recommended—TOEFL (minimum score 550 paper-based; 79 iBT). *Application deadline:* For fall admission, 8/17 for domestic students; for spring admission, 1/10 for domestic students; for summer admission, 5/2 for domestic students. Applications are processed on a rolling basis. Application fee: $50. Electronic applications accepted. *Expenses:* $700 per credit hour tuition; $150 per semester fees (6 or more hours enrolled); $75 per semester fees (1-5 hours enrolled). *Financial support:* In 2016–17, 14 students received support. Federal Work-Study, unspecified assistantships, and staff grants available. Financial award applicants required to submit FAFSA. *Unit head:* Dr. PJ Winters, Director, 903-923-2276, Fax: 903-935-4318, E-mail: med@etbu.edu. *Application contact:* Den Murley, Director of Graduate Admissions, 903-923-2079, Fax: 903-934-8115, E-mail: dmurley@etbu.edu.
Website: https://www.etbu.edu/education/master-education/

Emporia State University, Department of Health, Physical Education and Recreation, Emporia, KS 66801-5415. Offers MS. *Program availability:* Part-time, 100% online. *Faculty:* 17 full-time (10 women), 2 part-time/adjunct (both women). *Students:* 25 full-time (9 women), 168 part-time (69 women); includes 11 minority (6 Black or African American, non-Hispanic/Latino; 1 Asian, non-Hispanic/Latino; 3 Hispanic/Latino; 1 Two or more races, non-Hispanic/Latino). 54 applicants, 33 enrolled. In 2016, 110 master's awarded. *Degree requirements:* For master's, comprehensive exam or thesis. *Entrance requirements:* For master's, bachelor's degree in physical education, health, and recreation; letters of recommendation. Additional exam requirements/recommendations for international students: Required—TOEFL (minimum score 520 paper-based; 68 iBT). *Application deadline:* For fall admission, 8/15 priority date for domestic students. Applications are processed on a rolling basis. Application fee: $30 ($75 for international students). Electronic applications accepted. *Expenses:* Tuition, state resident: full-time $5922; part-time $246.75 per credit hour. Tuition, nonresident: full-time $18,414; part-time $767.25 per credit hour. *Required fees:* $1884; $78.50 per credit hour. *Financial support:* In 2016–17, 3 research assistantships with full tuition reimbursements (averaging $7,353 per year), 10 teaching assistantships with full tuition reimbursements (averaging $7,353 per year) were awarded; career-related internships or fieldwork, Federal Work-Study, institutionally sponsored loans, health care benefits, and unspecified assistantships also available. Financial award application deadline: 3/15; financial award applicants required to submit FAFSA. *Unit head:* Dr. Shawna Shane, Chair, 620-341-5848, E-mail: sshane@emporia.edu. *Application contact:* Mary Sewell, Admissions Coordinator, 800-950-GRAD, Fax: 620-341-5909, E-mail: msewell@emporia.edu.
Website: http://www.emporia.edu/hper/

Florida Agricultural and Mechanical University, Division of Graduate Studies, Research, and Continuing Education, College of Education, Department of Health, Physical Education, and Recreation, Tallahassee, FL 32307-3200. Offers sport management (MS). *Accreditation:* NCATE. *Program availability:* Part-time, evening/weekend. *Degree requirements:* For master's, thesis optional. *Entrance requirements:* For master's, GRE General Test, minimum GPA of 3.0. Additional exam requirements/recommendations for international students: Required—TOEFL. *Faculty research:* Administration/curriculum, work behavior, psychology.

Florida International University, College of Arts, Sciences, and Education, Department of Teaching and Learning, Miami, FL 33199. Offers art education (MA, MS); curriculum and instruction (MS, Ed D, PhD, Ed S), including curriculum development (MS), elementary education (MS), English education (MS), learning technologies (MS), mathematics education (MS), modern language education (MS), physical education (MS), science education (MS), social studies education (MS), special education (MS); early childhood education (MS); exceptional student education (Ed D); foreign language education (MS), including foreign language education, teaching English to speakers of other languages (TESOL); international/intercultural education (MS); language, literacy and culture (PhD); mathematics, science, and learning technologies (PhD); physical education (MS), including sport and fitness; reading education (MS). *Program availability:* Part-time, evening/weekend. *Faculty:* 34 full-time (23 women), 64 part-time/adjunct (48 women). *Students:* 182 full-time (154 women), 231 part-time (190 women); includes 323 minority (69 Black or African American, non-Hispanic/Latino; 10 Asian, non-Hispanic/Latino; 237 Hispanic/Latino; 7 Two or more races, non-Hispanic/Latino), 19 international. Average age 34. 282 applicants, 58% accepted, 113 enrolled. In 2016, 184 master's, 12 doctorates awarded. *Degree requirements:* For doctorate, comprehensive exam, thesis/dissertation. *Entrance requirements:* For master's, GRE General Test, Florida General Knowledge Test or Florida College Level Academic Skills Test; for doctorate and Ed S, GRE General Test. Additional exam requirements/recommendations for international students: Required—TOEFL (minimum score 550 paper-based; 80 iBT), IELTS (minimum score 6.3). *Application deadline:* For fall admission, 6/1 priority date for domestic students, 4/1 for international students; for winter admission, 10/1 priority date for domestic students, 9/1 for international students; for spring admission, 3/1 priority date for domestic students, 2/1 for international students. Applications are processed on a rolling basis. Application fee: $30. Electronic applications accepted. *Expenses:* Tuition, state resident: full-time $8912; part-time $446 per credit hour. Tuition, nonresident: full-time $21,393; part-time $992 per credit hour. *Required fees:* $2185; $195 per semester. Tuition and fees vary according to program. *Financial support:* Research assistantships with tuition reimbursements and teaching assistantships with tuition reimbursements available. *Unit head:* Dr. Lynn Miller, Chair, 305-348-2005, Fax: 305-348-2086, E-mail: lynne.miller@fiu.edu. *Application contact:* Nanett Rojas, Assistant Director, Graduate Admissions, 305-348-7464, Fax: 305-348-7441, E-mail: gradadm@fiu.edu.
Website: http://education.fiu.edu

Fort Hays State University, Graduate School, College of Health and Life Sciences, Department of Health and Human Performance, Hays, KS 67601-4099. Offers MS. *Program availability:* Part-time. *Degree requirements:* For master's, comprehensive exam, thesis optional. *Entrance requirements:* For master's, GRE General Test or MAT. Additional exam requirements/recommendations for international students: Required—TOEFL (minimum score 550 paper-based). Electronic applications accepted. *Faculty research:* Isoproterenol hydrochloride and exercise, dehydrogenase and high-density lipoprotein levels in athletics, venous blood parameters to adipose fat.

Gardner-Webb University, Graduate School, Department of Physical Education, Wellness, and Sport Studies, Boiling Springs, NC 28017. Offers sport science and pedagogy (MA). *Program availability:* Part-time, evening/weekend. *Faculty:* 2 full-time (1 woman). *Students:* 1 (woman) full-time, 9 part-time (2 women); includes 1 minority (Asian, non-Hispanic/Latino). Average age 24. 27 applicants, 48% accepted, 7 enrolled. In 2016, 5 master's awarded. *Degree requirements:* For master's, comprehensive exam. *Entrance requirements:* For master's, GRE General Test or NTE, PRAXIS, minimum GPA of 2.5. *Application deadline:* For fall admission, 8/1 priority date for domestic students. Applications are processed on a rolling basis. Application fee: $0. Electronic applications accepted. *Expenses:* Contact institution. *Financial support:* Unspecified assistantships available. *Unit head:* Dr. Ken Baker, Chair, 704-406-4481, Fax: 704-406-4739. *Application contact:* Office of Graduate Admissions, 877-498-4723, Fax: 704-406-3895, E-mail: gradinfo@gardner-webb.edu.

George Mason University, College of Education and Human Development, Programs in Curriculum and Instruction, Fairfax, VA 22030. Offers advanced international baccalaureate (M Ed); assistive technology (M Ed); designing digital learning in schools (M Ed); early childhood education (M Ed); early childhood education for diverse learners (M Ed); elementary education (M Ed); English as a second language (M Ed); gifted child

education (M Ed); history (M Ed); literacy (M Ed), including PK-12 classroom teachers, reading specialist; literacy leadership for diverse schools (M Ed), including K-12 reading; physical education (M Ed); science K-12 (M Ed); secondary education (M Ed), including biology, chemistry, earth science, English, history/social science, math, physics; special education (M Ed); teacher leadership (M Ed); teaching culturally, linguistically diverse and exceptional learners (M Ed); transformative teaching (M Ed). *Faculty:* 41 full-time (35 women), 53 part-time/adjunct (46 women). *Students:* 155 full-time (127 women), 821 part-time (697 women); includes 267 minority (82 Black or African American, non-Hispanic/Latino; 5 American Indian or Alaska Native, non-Hispanic/Latino; 75 Asian, non-Hispanic/Latino; 88 Hispanic/Latino; 1 Native Hawaiian or other Pacific Islander, non-Hispanic/Latino; 16 Two or more races, non-Hispanic/Latino), 19 international. Average age 33. 513 applicants, 90% accepted, 352 enrolled. In 2016, 347 master's awarded. *Degree requirements:* For master's, comprehensive exam, thesis (for some programs). *Entrance requirements:* For master's, PRAXIS Core (for some programs), minimum GPA of 3.0 in last 60 hours, licensed as teacher or educational administrator, official transcripts, goals statement, 3 recommendation letters, interview or writing sample (depending on program), up to 3 years' teaching experience (depending on program). Additional exam requirements/recommendations for international students: Required—TOEFL (minimum score 575 paper-based; 88 iBT), IELTS (minimum score 6.5), PTE (minimum score 59). *Application deadline:* For spring admission, 11/1 priority date for domestic and international students. Application fee: $75 ($80 for international students). Electronic applications accepted. *Expenses:* Tuition, state resident: full-time $10,628; part-time $443 per credit. Tuition, nonresident: full-time $29,306; part-time $1221 per credit. *Required fees:* $3096; $129 per credit. Tuition and fees vary according to program. *Financial support:* In 2016–17, 1 student received support, including 1 teaching assistantship (averaging $4,060 per year); career-related internships or fieldwork, Federal Work-Study, scholarships/grants, unspecified assistantships, and health care benefits (for full-time research or teaching assistantship recipients) also available. Support available to part-time students. Financial award application deadline: 3/1; financial award applicants required to submit FAFSA. *Faculty research:* Achievement gaps and superintendent decisions, constructivist view of classroom teaching, cost of cheating, creating a critical literacy milieu in kindergarten. *Unit head:* Rebecca Fox, Professor and Academic Program Coordinator, 703-993-4123, E-mail: rfox@gmu.edu.
Website: http://gse.gmu.edu/programs/gsemasters

Georgia College & State University, Graduate School, College of Health Sciences, School of Health and Human Performance, Milledgeville, GA 31061. Offers health and human performance (MS), including health performance, health promotion; kinesiology/health education (MAT). *Accreditation:* NCATE (one or more programs are accredited). *Program availability:* Part-time, evening/weekend, 100% online. *Students:* 43 full-time (25 women), 17 part-time (15 women); includes 6 minority (4 Black or African American, non-Hispanic/Latino; 1 Asian, non-Hispanic/Latino; 1 Hispanic/Latino), 1 international. Average age 28. 33 applicants, 100% accepted, 28 enrolled. In 2016, 23 master's awarded. *Degree requirements:* For master's, completed in 6 years with minimum GPA of 3.0, thesis or project (for MS); minimum GPA of 3.0, GACE Exam and Assessment, and electronic teaching portfolio (for MAT). *Entrance requirements:* For master's, GRE with minimum score of 297 or MAT with minimum score of 385 (for MS); SAT (minimum score of 1000), ACT (minimum score of 43), GRE (minimum score of 297), MAT (minimum score of 385), or GACE Program Admission Assessment (for MAT), resume, 3 professional references; minimum GPA of 2.75 in upper-level undergraduate courses and undergraduate statistics course (for MS); minimum GPA of 2.75 on upper-division major courses (for MAT). *Application deadline:* For fall admission, 7/15 priority date for domestic students, 4/1 for international students; for spring admission, 11/15 priority date for domestic students, 9/1 for international students; for summer admission, 4/15 priority date for domestic students. Applications are processed on a rolling basis. Application fee: $40. Electronic applications accepted. *Expenses:* $228 per credit hour in-state tuition, $1,027 per credit hour out-of-state tuition, $1,990 per year fees (for MAT); $338 per credit hour (for MS). *Financial support:* In 2016–17, 24 students received support. Unspecified assistantships available. Support available to part-time students. Financial award application deadline: 3/1; financial award applicants required to submit FAFSA. *Unit head:* Dr. Lisa Griffin, Director, School of Health and Human Performance, 478-445-4072, Fax: 478-445-4074, E-mail: lisa.griffin@gcsu.edu.
Website: http://www.gcsu.edu/health/shhp

Georgia State University, College of Education and Human Development, Department of Kinesiology and Health, Program in Health and Physical Education, Atlanta, GA 30302-3083. Offers M Ed. *Program availability:* Part-time, evening/weekend. *Degree requirements:* For master's, comprehensive exam. *Entrance requirements:* For master's, GRE General Test, minimum GPA of 2.5. *Application deadline:* For fall admission, 5/1 for domestic students; for spring admission, 10/1 for domestic students. Application fee: $50. *Expenses:* Tuition, state resident: full-time $6876; part-time $382 per credit hour. Tuition, nonresident: full-time $22,374; part-time $1243 per credit hour. *Required fees:* $2128; $1064 per term. Part-time tuition and fees vary according to course load and program. *Financial support:* Teaching assistantships and career-related internships or fieldwork available. *Faculty research:* Exercise science, teacher behavior. *Unit head:* Dr. Jacalyn Lea Lund, Chair, 404-413-8051, E-mail: jlund@gsu.edu. *Application contact:* Dr. Rachel Gurvitch, Program Coordinator, 404-413-8374, E-mail: rgurvitch@gsu.edu.
Website: http://education.gsu.edu/KIN/kh_programs.htm

Goucher College, Graduate Programs in Education, Baltimore, MD 21204-2794. Offers at-risk and diverse learners (M Ed, Certificate); athletic program leadership and administration (M Ed, Certificate); elementary and special education (MAT); elementary education (MAT); literacy strategies for content learning (M Ed, Certificate); middle school (M Ed, Certificate); Montessori studies (M Ed); reading instruction (M Ed, Certificate); school improvement leadership (M Ed, Certificate); school mediation (M Ed, Certificate); secondary and special education (MAT); secondary education (MAT); special education (MAT), including elementary education, secondary education; special education for certified teachers (M Ed, Certificate), teacher as leader in technology (M Ed, Certificate). *Program availability:* Part-time, evening/weekend. *Faculty:* 3 full-time (all women), 52 part-time/adjunct (40 women). *Students:* 29 full-time (20 women), 285 part-time (217 women); includes 54 minority (41 Black or African American, non-Hispanic/Latino; 3 Asian, non-Hispanic/Latino; 7 Hispanic/Latino; 3 Two or more races, non-Hispanic/Latino), 1 international. Average age 34. 85 applicants, 100% accepted, 61 enrolled. In 2016, 207 master's awarded. *Degree requirements:* For master's, thesis (M Ed), final presentation (MAT). *Entrance requirements:* For master's, minimum GPA of 3.0. Additional exam requirements/recommendations for international students: Required—TOEFL (minimum score 560 paper-based). *Application deadline:* For fall admission, 9/1 for domestic students; for spring admission, 1/15 for domestic students. Applications are processed on a rolling basis. Application fee: $75. Electronic applications accepted. *Expenses:* Contact institution. *Financial support:* Career-related internships or fieldwork and unspecified assistantships available. Support available to part-time students. Financial award application deadline: 4/15; financial award applicants required to submit FAFSA. *Faculty research:* Urban education, middle school, school improvement, teacher education, at-risk student achievement. *Unit head:* Dr. Phyllis Sunshine, Assistant Provost, 410-337-6047, Fax: 410-337-6394, E-mail: psunshin@goucher.edu. *Application contact:* Shelby Hillers, Admissions Coordinator, 410-337-6200, Fax: 410-337-6085, E-mail: shelby.hillers@goucher.edu.
Website: http://www.goucher.edu/graduate-programs/graduate-programs-in-education

Henderson State University, Graduate Studies, Teachers College, Department of Health, Physical Education, Recreation and Athletic Training, Arkadelphia, AR 71999-0001. Offers sports administration (MS). *Program availability:* Part-time. *Faculty:* 2 full-time (0 women), 1 part-time/adjunct (0 women). *Students:* 3 full-time (1 woman), 52 part-time (15 women); includes 23 minority (22 Black or African American, non-Hispanic/Latino; 1 Hispanic/Latino), 7 international. Average age 25. 23 applicants, 91% accepted, 21 enrolled. In 2016, 20 master's awarded. *Entrance requirements:* For master's, GRE General Test or MAT, minimum GPA of 2.7 as an undergraduate student. Additional exam requirements/recommendations for international students: Required—TOEFL (minimum score 600 paper-based); Recommended—IELTS (minimum score 6.5). *Application deadline:* For fall admission, 8/1 priority date for domestic students, 6/30 priority date for international students; for spring admission, 1/1 priority date for domestic students, 11/30 priority date for international students. Applications are processed on a rolling basis. Application fee: $25 ($75 for international students). *Expenses:* Tuition, state resident: full-time $6288; part-time $3144 per credit hour. Tuition, nonresident: full-time $12,888; part-time $6444 per credit hour. *Required fees:* $1429; $1024 per credit hour. Tuition and fees vary according to course load and student level. *Financial support:* In 2016–17, 10 teaching assistantships with partial tuition reimbursements (averaging $4,000 per year) were awarded; scholarships/grants and unspecified assistantships also available. Financial award application deadline: 4/15; financial award applicants required to submit FAFSA. *Unit head:* Dr. Lynn Glover-Stanley, Chair, 870-230-5200, E-mail: stanlel@hsu.edu. *Application contact:* Dr. Ken Taylor, Graduate Dean, 870-230-5126, Fax: 870-230-5479, E-mail: taylorke@hsu.edu.
Website: http://www.hsu.edu/hper/

Hofstra University, School of Education, Programs in Teacher Education, Hempstead, NY 11549. Offers bilingual education (MA, Advanced Certificate); bilingual extension (Advanced Certificate), including education/speech language pathology; business education (MS Ed); early childhood and childhood education (MS Ed); early childhood education (MA, MS Ed); education technology (Advanced Certificate); elementary education (MA, MS Ed), including science, technology, engineering, and mathematics (STEM) (MA); English education (MS Ed); family and consumer science (MS Ed); fine arts and music education (Advanced Certificate); fine arts education (MS Ed); foreign language and TESOL (MS Ed); foreign language education (MS Ed), including French, German, Russian, Spanish; learning and teaching (Ed D), including applied linguistics, art education, arts and humanities, early childhood education, English education, human development, math education, math, science, and technology, multicultural education, physical education, science education, social studies education, special education; mathematics education (MA, MS Ed); middle school extension (Advanced Certificate), including grades 5-6, grades 7-9; music education (MA, MS Ed); science education (MA, MS Ed), including biology, chemistry, earth science, geology, physics; secondary education (Advanced Certificate); social studies education (MA, MS Ed); teaching languages other than English and TESOL (MS Ed); TESOL (MS Ed, Advanced Certificate). *Program availability:* Part-time, evening/weekend, blended/hybrid learning. *Students:* 139 full-time (97 women), 145 part-time (106 women); includes 60 minority (15 Black or African American, non-Hispanic/Latino; 1 American Indian or Alaska Native, non-Hispanic/Latino; 12 Asian, non-Hispanic/Latino; 31 Hispanic/Latino; 1 Two or more races, non-Hispanic/Latino), 21 international. Average age 29. 255 applicants, 86% accepted, 122 enrolled. In 2016, 101 master's, 4 doctorates, 43 other advanced degrees awarded. *Degree requirements:* For master's, comprehensive exam, thesis (for some programs), exit project, student teaching, fieldwork, electronic portfolio, curriculum project, minimum GPA of 3.0; for doctorate, thesis/dissertation; for Advanced Certificate, 3 foreign languages, comprehensive exam (for some programs), thesis project. *Entrance requirements:* For master's, GRE, MAT, 2 letters of recommendation, portfolio, teacher certification (MA), interview, essay; for doctorate, GMAT, GRE, LSAT, or MAT; for Advanced Certificate, 2 letters of recommendation, essay, interview and/or portfolio, teaching certificate. Additional exam requirements/recommendations for international students: Required—TOEFL (minimum score 550 paper-based; 80 iBT). *Application deadline:* Applications are processed on a rolling basis. Application fee: $75. Electronic applications accepted. *Expenses: Tuition:* Full-time $1240. *Required fees:* $970. Tuition and fees vary according to program. *Financial support:* In 2016–17, 149 students received support, including 58 fellowships with full and partial tuition reimbursements available (averaging $5,309 per year), 5 research assistantships with full and partial tuition reimbursements available (averaging $7,073 per year); career-related internships or fieldwork, Federal Work-Study, institutionally sponsored loans, scholarships/grants, traineeships, tuition waivers (full and partial), and unspecified assistantships also available. Support available to part-time students. Financial award applicants required to submit FAFSA. *Faculty research:* Educational interventions that foster critical-thinking skills; teachers' attitudes about professional development; threats to teacher quality. *Unit head:* Dr. Eustace Thompson, Chairperson, 516-463-5749, Fax: 516-463-6275, E-mail: eustace.g.thompson@hofstra.edu. *Application contact:* Sunil Samuel, Assistant Vice President of Admissions, 516-463-4723, Fax: 516-463-4664, E-mail: graduateadmission@hofstra.edu.
Website: http://www.hofstra.edu/education/

Hofstra University, School of Education, Specialized Programs in Education, Hempstead, NY 11549. Offers applied behavior analysis (Advanced Certificate); early childhood special education (MS Ed, Advanced Certificate); educational and policy leadership (Ed D); educational leadership (Advanced Certificate), including school building leader/school district business leader; educational leadership and policy studies (MS Ed), including K-12; gifted education (Advanced Certificate), including school building leader/school district business leader; health education PK-12 teaching certification (MS); inclusive early childhood special education (MS Ed); inclusive elementary special education (MS Ed); inclusive secondary special education (MS Ed); literacy studies (MS Ed, Ed D, PhD, Advanced Certificate), including birth-grade 6 (MS Ed, Advanced Certificate), birth-grade 6 and special education (birth-grade2) (MS Ed), grades 5-12 (MS Ed, Advanced Certificate); physical education (MS); secondary education generalist (MS Ed), including students with disabilities 7-12; special education (MS Ed, Advanced Certificate); special education assessment and diagnosis (Advanced Certificate); special education generalist (MS Ed), including extension in secondary education; sport science (MS), including strength and conditioning; teaching students with severe or multiple disabilities (Advanced Certificate). *Program availability:* Part-time, evening/weekend, 100% online, blended/hybrid learning. *Students:* 149 full-time (115 women), 258 part-time (187 women); includes 97 minority (50 Black or African American, non-Hispanic/Latino; 1 American Indian or Alaska Native, non-Hispanic/Latino; 11 Asian, non-Hispanic/Latino; 34 Hispanic/Latino; 1 Native Hawaiian or other Pacific Islander, non-Hispanic/Latino), 5 international. Average age 32. 250 applicants, 88% accepted, 146 enrolled. In 2016, 85 master's, 13 doctorates, 35 other advanced degrees awarded. *Degree requirements:* For master's, one foreign language, comprehensive exam (for some programs), thesis (for some programs), electronic portfolio, capstone course, internship, practicum, student teaching, seminars, minimum GPA of 3.0; for doctorate, one foreign language, comprehensive exam, thesis/dissertation, qualifying hearing. *Entrance requirements:*

Physical Education

For master's, GRE, interview, letters of recommendation, portfolio, essay, certification; for doctorate, GRE or MAT, interview, resume, essay, master's degree, 3 letters of recommendation, writing sample; for Advanced Certificate, GRE, interview, letters of recommendation, essay, professional experience, resume, master's degree. Additional exam requirements/recommendations for international students: Required—TOEFL (minimum score 550 paper-based; 80 iBT). *Application deadline:* Applications are processed on a rolling basis. Application fee: $75. Electronic applications accepted. *Expenses: Tuition:* Full-time $1240. *Required fees:* $970. Tuition and fees vary according to program. *Financial support:* In 2016–17, 244 students received support, including 117 fellowships with full and partial tuition reimbursements available (averaging $3,705 per year), 12 research assistantships with full and partial tuition reimbursements available (averaging $6,490 per year); career-related internships or fieldwork, Federal Work-Study, institutionally sponsored loans, scholarships/grants, traineeships, tuition waivers (full and partial), and unspecified assistantships also available. Support available to part-time students. Financial award applicants required to submit FAFSA. *Faculty research:* Collaborative teaching and learning; language and culture; new media literacies; applied behavior analysis; K-12 leadership development. *Unit head:* Dr. Elfreda Blue, Chairperson, 516-463-5762, Fax: 516-463-6184, E-mail: elfreda.blue@hofstra.edu. *Application contact:* Sunil Samuel, Assistant Vice President of Admissions, 516-463-4723, Fax: 516-463-4664, E-mail: graduateadmission@hofstra.edu.
Website: http://www.hofstra.edu/education/

Howard University, Graduate School, Department of Health, Human Performance and Leisure Studies, Washington, DC 20059-0002. Offers exercise physiology (MS); health education (MS); sports studies (MS), including sociology of sports, sports management; urban recreation (MS), including leisure studies. *Program availability:* Part-time, evening/weekend. *Degree requirements:* For master's, comprehensive exam, thesis. *Entrance requirements:* For master's, BS in human performance or related field. Additional exam requirements/recommendations for international students: Recommended—TOEFL. Electronic applications accepted. *Faculty research:* Health promotion, cardiovascular hypertension, physical activity, sport and human rights issues.

Idaho State University, Office of Graduate Studies, College of Education, Department of Sports Science and Physical Education, Pocatello, ID 83209-8105. Offers physical education (MPE). *Program availability:* Part-time. *Degree requirements:* For master's, comprehensive exam (for some programs), thesis optional, internship, oral defense of dissertation, or written exams. *Entrance requirements:* For master's, MAT or GRE General Test, minimum GPA of 3.0 in upper division classes. Additional exam requirements/recommendations for international students: Required—TOEFL (minimum score 550 paper-based; 80 iBT). Electronic applications accepted. *Faculty research:* Gender and diversity; concussion awareness/sports medicine; legal aspects of athletic health care; sports psychology; exercise physiology; sports management and leadership; adapted activities; fitness, wellness, and nutrition; coaching perspectives; critical features of athletic activities.

Illinois State University, Graduate School, College of Applied Science and Technology, School of Kinesiology and Recreation, Normal, IL 61790-2200. Offers health education (MS). *Degree requirements:* For master's, thesis or alternative. *Entrance requirements:* For master's, GRE General Test, minimum GPA of 2.6 in last 60 hours of course work. *Faculty research:* Influences on positive youth development through sport, country-wide health fitness project, graduate practicum in athletic training, perceived exertion and self-selected intensity during resistance exercise in younger and older.

Indiana State University, College of Graduate and Professional Studies, College of Nursing, Health, and Human Services, Department of Kinesiology, Recreation, and Sport, Terre Haute, IN 47809. Offers physical education (MS); recreation and sport management (MS); sport management (PhD). *Degree requirements:* For master's, comprehensive exam (for some programs), thesis (for some programs). *Entrance requirements:* For master's, GRE General Test, undergraduate major in related field. Electronic applications accepted.

Indiana University Bloomington, School of Public Health, Department of Kinesiology, Bloomington, IN 47405. Offers applied sport science (MS); athletic administration/sport management (MS); athletic training (MS); biomechanics (MS); ergonomics (MS); exercise physiology (MS); human performance (PhD), including biomechanics, exercise physiology, motor learning/control, sport management; motor learning/control (MS); physical activity (MPH); physical activity, fitness and wellness (MS). *Program availability:* Part-time. Terminal master's awarded for partial completion of doctoral program. *Degree requirements:* For master's, thesis optional; for doctorate, variable foreign language requirement, comprehensive exam, thesis/dissertation. *Entrance requirements:* For master's, GRE General Test, minimum GPA of 2.8; for doctorate, GRE General Test, minimum graduate GPA of 3.5, undergraduate 3.0. Additional exam requirements/recommendations for international students: Required—TOEFL (minimum score 80 iBT). *Faculty research:* Exercise physiology and biochemistry, sports biomechanics, human motor control, adaptation of fitness and exercise to special populations.

Indiana University of Pennsylvania, School of Graduate Studies and Research, College of Health and Human Services, Department of Kinesiology, Health, and Sport Science, Program in Health and Physical Education, Indiana, PA 15705. Offers M Ed. *Program availability:* Part-time. *Faculty:* 10 full-time (3 women). *Students:* 23 full-time (12 women), 3 part-time (1 woman). Average age 25. 6 applicants, 100% accepted, 5 enrolled. In 2016, 12 master's awarded. *Entrance requirements:* Additional exam requirements/recommendations for international students: Required—TOEFL (minimum score 540 paper-based). *Application deadline:* Applications are processed on a rolling basis. Application fee: $50. Electronic applications accepted. *Expenses:* Tuition, state resident: full-time $8694; part-time $483 per credit. Tuition, nonresident: full-time $13,050; part-time $725 per credit. *Required fees:* $157 per credit. $50 per term. Tuition and fees vary according to course load and program. *Financial support:* In 2016–17, 7 research assistantships with tuition reimbursements (averaging $3,303 per year) were awarded; career-related internships or fieldwork, Federal Work-Study, scholarships/grants, and unspecified assistantships also available. Support available to part-time students. Financial award application deadline: 4/15; financial award applicants required to submit FAFSA. *Unit head:* Dr. Keri Kulik, Coordinator, 724-357-5656, E-mail: kskulik@iup.edu.
Website: http://www.iup.edu/grad/healthphysed/default.aspx

Indiana University–Purdue University Indianapolis, School of Physical Education and Tourism Management, Indianapolis, IN 46202-5193. Offers event tourism (MS), including sport event tourism; kinesiology (MS), including clinical exercise science; public health (Graduate Certificate). *Faculty:* 15 full-time (4 women). *Students:* 18 full-time (9 women), 16 part-time (8 women); includes 4 minority (3 Black or African American, non-Hispanic/Latino; 1 Hispanic/Latino), 1 international. Average age 26. 22 applicants, 86% accepted, 13 enrolled. In 2016, 11 master's awarded. *Degree requirements:* For master's, comprehensive exam (for some programs), thesis (for some programs). *Entrance requirements:* For master's, GRE. Additional exam requirements/recommendations for international students: Required—TOEFL. Application fee: $60 ($65 for international students). Electronic applications accepted. *Expenses:* Contact institution. *Financial support:* In 2016–17, 15 students received support. Teaching assistantships, unspecified assistantships, and assistantships with community partners available. Financial award application deadline: 3/15; financial award applicants required to submit FAFSA. *Faculty research:* Physical activity, exercise and diseases; human movement science; sport performance; sport event tourism; destination marketing and event management;. *Unit head:* Dr. Zachary Riley, Assistant Professor and Director of Graduate Program, 317-274-0600, Fax: 317-278-2041, E-mail: zariley@iupui.edu.
Website: http://petm.iupui.edu/

Inter American University of Puerto Rico, Metropolitan Campus, Graduate Programs, Program in Physical Education, San Juan, PR 00919-1293. Offers teaching of physical education (MA); training and sport performance (MA). *Degree requirements:* For master's, comprehensive exam. *Entrance requirements:* For master's, GRE or EXADEP, interview. Electronic applications accepted.

Inter American University of Puerto Rico, San Germán Campus, Graduate Studies Center, Program in Health and Physical Education, San Germán, PR 00683-5008. Offers MA. *Program availability:* Part-time, evening/weekend. *Degree requirements:* For master's, comprehensive exam. *Entrance requirements:* For master's, GRE General Test or EXADEP, minimum GPA of 3.0.

Ithaca College, School of Health Sciences and Human Performance, Program in Physical Education, Ithaca, NY 14850. Offers MS. *Program availability:* Part-time. *Faculty:* 9 full-time (6 women). *Students:* 1 part-time. Average age 51. 2 applicants, 1 enrolled. *Degree requirements:* For master's, thesis optional, student teaching. *Entrance requirements:* Additional exam requirements/recommendations for international students: Required—TOEFL (minimum score 550 paper-based; 80 iBT). *Application deadline:* For fall admission, 3/1 priority date for domestic and international students; for spring admission, 12/1 for domestic and international students. Applications are processed on a rolling basis. Application fee: $40. Electronic applications accepted. Tuition and fees vary according to program. *Financial support:* Research assistantships, career-related internships or fieldwork, Federal Work-Study, scholarships/grants, and unspecified assistantships available. Support available to part-time students. Financial award application deadline: 3/1; financial award applicants required to submit CSS PROFILE or FAFSA. *Unit head:* Dr. Stewart Auyash, Chair, 607-274-1312, E-mail: auyash@ithaca.edu. *Application contact:* Nicole Eversley Bradwell, Director, Office of Admission, 607-274-3124, Fax: 607-274-1263, E-mail: admission@ithaca.edu.
Website: http://www.ithaca.edu/gradprograms/hppe/programs/physed

Jackson State University, Graduate School, College of Education and Human Development, Department of Health, Physical Education and Recreation, Jackson, MS 39217. Offers physical education (MS Ed); sport science (MS). *Accreditation:* NCATE. *Program availability:* Part-time, evening/weekend, 100% online, blended/hybrid learning. *Faculty:* 4 full-time (1 woman). *Students:* 37 full-time (21 women), 66 part-time (37 women); includes 99 minority (98 Black or African American, non-Hispanic/Latino; 1 Two or more races, non-Hispanic/Latino), 2 international. Average age 32. 74 applicants, 70% accepted, 30 enrolled. In 2016, 21 master's awarded. *Degree requirements:* For master's, comprehensive exam, thesis or alternative. *Entrance requirements:* For master's, GRE General Test. Additional exam requirements/recommendations for international students: Required—TOEFL (minimum score 520 paper-based; 67 iBT). *Application deadline:* For fall admission, 3/1 priority date for domestic students, 3/1 for international students; for spring admission, 10/1 for domestic and international students. Applications are processed on a rolling basis. Application fee: $25. Electronic applications accepted. *Expenses:* Contact institution. *Financial support:* Career-related internships or fieldwork, Federal Work-Study, scholarships/grants, and unspecified assistantships available. Support available to part-time students. Financial award application deadline: 3/1; financial award applicants required to submit FAFSA. *Unit head:* Dr. Patricia Kennedy, Interim Chair, 601-979-2765, Fax: 601-979-2766, E-mail: patricia.r.kennedy@jsums.edu. *Application contact:* Dr. Hill Williams, Interim Director of Sport Science, 601-979-0275, Fax: 601-979-2766, E-mail: hill.williams@jsums.edu.
Website: http://www.jsums.edu/healthedu/

Jacksonville State University, College of Graduate Studies and Continuing Education, College of Education and Professional Studies, Program in Physical Education, Jacksonville, AL 36265-1602. Offers MS Ed, Ed S. *Accreditation:* NCATE. *Program availability:* Part-time, evening/weekend. *Faculty:* 4 full-time (0 women), 1 (woman) part-time/adjunct. *Students:* 13 full-time (6 women), 26 part-time (11 women); includes 9 minority (all Black or African American, non-Hispanic/Latino). Average age 30. 25 applicants, 84% accepted, 15 enrolled. In 2016, 15 master's awarded. *Degree requirements:* For master's, comprehensive exam, thesis (for some programs). *Entrance requirements:* For master's, GRE General Test or MAT. Additional exam requirements/recommendations for international students: Required—TOEFL (minimum score 500 paper-based; 61 iBT). *Application deadline:* Applications are processed on a rolling basis. Application fee: $35. Electronic applications accepted. *Financial support:* In 2016–17, 9 students received support. Available to part-time students. Application deadline: 4/1; applicants required to submit FAFSA. *Unit head:* Dr. Gina Mabrey, Interim Head, 256-782-8059, E-mail: gmabrey@jsu.edu. *Application contact:* Dr. Jean Pugliese, Associate Dean, 256-782-8278, Fax: 256-782-5321, E-mail: pugliese@jsu.edu.

James Madison University, The Graduate School, College of Health and Behavioral Sciences, Program in Kinesiology, Harrisonburg, VA 22802. Offers clinical exercise physiology (MS); exercise physiology (MS); kinesiology (MAT, MS); nutrition and exercise (MS); physical and health education (MAT); sport and recreation leadership (MS). *Program availability:* Part-time, evening/weekend. *Faculty:* 9 full-time (3 women), 2 part-time/adjunct (1 woman). *Students:* 64 full-time (27 women), 8 part-time (5 women); includes 6 minority (1 Black or African American, non-Hispanic/Latino; 1 Asian, non-Hispanic/Latino; 2 Hispanic/Latino; 2 Two or more races, non-Hispanic/Latino). Average age 30. 140 applicants, 70% accepted, 44 enrolled. In 2016, 42 master's awarded. Application fee: $55. Electronic applications accepted. *Financial support:* In 2016–17, 45 students received support, including 14 teaching assistantships with full tuition reimbursements available (averaging $8,837 per year); Federal Work-Study and 25 assistantships (averaging $7911), 20 athletic assistantships (averaging $9284) also available. Financial award application deadline: 3/1; financial award applicants required to submit FAFSA. *Unit head:* Dr. Christopher J. Womack, Department Head, 540-568-6145, E-mail: womackcx@jmu.edu. *Application contact:* Lynette D. Michael, Director of Graduate Admissions, 540-568-6131 Ext. 6395, Fax: 540-568-7860, E-mail: michaeld@jmu.edu.
Website: http://www.jmu.edu/kinesiology/

Longwood University, College of Graduate and Professional Studies, College of Education and Human Services, Farmville, VA 23909. Offers education (MS), including algebra and middle school mathematics, counselor education, elementary and middle school mathematics, elementary education, elementary education initial licensure, health and physical education, special education general curriculum, special education initial licensure; reading, literacy and learning (M Ed); school librarianship (M Ed); social work and communication sciences and disorders (MS), including communication sciences and disorders. *Accreditation:* NCATE. *Program availability:* Part-time, evening/weekend. *Degree requirements:* For master's, comprehensive exam (for some programs), thesis optional, professional portfolio, internship, clinical experience, or practicum. *Entrance requirements:* For master's, PRAXIS I (for initial teaching licensure programs); GRE (for some programs), bachelor's degree from regionally-accredited institution, 2 recommendations (3 for some programs), minimum 500-word personal essay, official transcripts, minimum GPA of 2.75, valid teaching license (for some programs). Additional exam requirements/recommendations for international students: Required—TOEFL (minimum score 570 paper-based), IELTS (minimum score 6.5). Electronic applications accepted. *Expenses:* Contact institution.

Louisiana Tech University, Graduate School, College of Education, Department of Kinesiology, Ruston, LA 71272. Offers administration of sport and physical activity (MS); sports performance (MS). *Accreditation:* NCATE. *Program availability:* Part-time. *Degree requirements:* For master's, thesis or alternative. *Entrance requirements:* For master's, GRE General Test. *Application deadline:* For fall admission, 7/29 for domestic students; for spring admission, 2/3 for domestic students. Application fee: $20 ($30 for international students). *Financial support:* Fellowships and research assistantships available. Financial award application deadline: 2/1. *Unit head:* Dr. David Szymanski, Interim Chair, 318-257-4432, Fax: 318-257-2379, E-mail: dszyman@latech.edu. *Application contact:* Dr. Cathy Stockton, Associate Dean of Graduate Studies, 318-257-3229, Fax: 318-257-2379, E-mail: cstock@latech.edu.
Website: http://education.latech.edu/departments/kinesiology/

Massachusetts College of Liberal Arts, Graduate Programs, North Adams, MA 01247-4100. Offers business (MBA); educational administration (M Ed); educational leadership (CAGS); instruction and curriculum (M Ed); instructional technology (M Ed); physical education and health (M Ed); reading (M Ed); special education (M Ed). *Program availability:* Part-time, evening/weekend. *Degree requirements:* For master's, thesis. *Entrance requirements:* For master's, writing sample.

McDaniel College, Graduate and Professional Studies, Program in Exercise Science and Physical Education, Westminster, MD 21157-4390. Offers MS. *Program availability:* Part-time, evening/weekend. *Faculty:* 2 full-time (both women), 5 part-time/adjunct (1 woman). *Students:* 17 full-time (4 women), 28 part-time (13 women); includes 7 minority (all Black or African American, non-Hispanic/Latino). Average age 28. 19 applicants, 100% accepted. In 2016, 45 master's awarded. *Degree requirements:* For master's, comprehensive exam, thesis optional. *Entrance requirements:* For master's, 3 references. Additional exam requirements/recommendations for international students: Required—TOEFL (minimum score 79 iBT), IELTS (minimum score 6). *Application deadline:* For fall admission, 6/1 priority date for domestic students; for spring admission, 11/1 priority date for domestic students; for summer admission, 3/1 priority date for domestic students. Applications are processed on a rolling basis. Application fee: $75. Electronic applications accepted. *Expenses: Tuition:* Full-time $8370; part-time $465 per credit. *Required fees:* $75 per semester. Tuition and fees vary according to course load, program and reciprocity agreements. *Financial support:* Unspecified assistantships available. Financial award application deadline: 3/1; financial award applicants required to submit FAFSA. *Unit head:* Fax: 410-857-2515, E-mail: gradadms@mcdaniel.edu. *Application contact:* Penny Pfeiffer, Senior Graduate Enrollment Management Specialist, 410-857-2516, Fax: 410-857-2515, E-mail: cperry@mcdaniel.edu.

McGill University, Faculty of Graduate and Postdoctoral Studies, Faculty of Education, Department of Kinesiology and Physical Education, Montréal, QC H3A 2T5, Canada. Offers M Sc, MA, PhD, Certificate, Diploma.

Memorial University of Newfoundland, School of Graduate Studies, School of Human Kinetics and Recreation, St. John's, NL A1C 5S7, Canada. Offers administration, curriculum and supervision (MPE); biomechanics/ergonomics (MS Kin); exercise and work physiology (MS Kin); psychology of sport, exercise and recreation (MS Kin); socio-cultural studies of physical activity and health (MS Kin). *Program availability:* Part-time. *Degree requirements:* For master's, thesis optional, seminars, thesis presentations. *Entrance requirements:* For master's, bachelor's degree in a related field, minimum B average. Electronic applications accepted. *Faculty research:* Administration, sociology of sports, kinesiology, physiology/recreation.

Meredith College, School of Education, Health and Human Sciences, Raleigh, NC 27607-5298. Offers academically and intellectually gifted (M Ed); curriculum instruction specialist (M Ed); elementary education (M Ed, MAT); English as a second language (M Ed, MAT); health and physical education (MAT); nutrition, health and human performance (MS, Postbaccalaureate Certificate), including dietetic internship (Postbaccalaureate Certificate), nutrition (MS); reading (M Ed); special education (MAT). *Accreditation:* NCATE. *Program availability:* Part-time, evening/weekend. *Degree requirements:* For master's, thesis optional. *Entrance requirements:* For master's, GRE General Test or MAT, minimum GPA of 2.5, teaching license, recommendations. Additional exam requirements/recommendations for international students: Required—TOEFL. Electronic applications accepted. *Expenses:* Contact institution.

Middle Tennessee State University, College of Graduate Studies, College of Behavioral and Health Sciences, Department of Health and Human Performance, Program in Health, Physical Education and Recreation, Murfreesboro, TN 37132. Offers health and human performance (MS); leisure and sport management (MS). *Program availability:* Part-time, evening/weekend, online learning. *Degree requirements:* For master's, comprehensive exam, thesis optional. *Entrance requirements:* For master's, GRE. Additional exam requirements/recommendations for international students: Required—TOEFL (minimum score 525 paper-based; 71 iBT) or IELTS (minimum score 6). *Faculty research:* Kinesiometrics, leisure behavior, health, lifestyles.

Millersville University of Pennsylvania, College of Graduate Studies and Adult Learning, College of Education and Human Services, Department of Wellness and Sport Sciences, Program in Sport Management: Athletic Coaching Option, Millersville, PA 17551-0302. Offers coaching education (Post-Master's Certificate); sport management: athletic coaching (M Ed). *Program availability:* Part-time, evening/weekend. *Faculty:* 7 full-time (3 women). *Students:* 6 part-time (2 women). Average age 27. 3 applicants, 67% accepted. In 2016, 4 master's awarded. Terminal master's awarded for partial completion of doctoral program. *Degree requirements:* For master's, thesis optional, internship. *Entrance requirements:* For master's, GRE, MAT, GMAT, or interview with writing assignment if undergraduate cumulative GPA lower than 3.0, all transcripts, at least 1 academic reference, sport management goal statement. Additional exam requirements/recommendations for international students: Required—TOEFL (minimum score 600 paper-based), IELTS (minimum score 6). *Application deadline:* Applications are processed on a rolling basis. Application fee: $40. Electronic applications accepted. *Expenses:* $483 per credit resident tuition; $725 per credit non-resident tuition. *Financial support:* In 2016–17, 2 students received support. Unspecified assistantships available. Financial award application deadline: 3/15; financial award applicants required to submit FAFSA. *Faculty research:* Applied sport management; leadership and sport; marketing and sport; gender and sport; leadership development; ADR, restorative justice and hazing; legal issues applied to sport management; women and fitness/sport. *Unit head:* Dr. Rebecca J. Mowrey, Coordinator, 717-871-4214, Fax: 717-871-7987, E-mail: rebecca.mowrey@millersville.edu. *Application contact:* Dr. Victor S. DeSantis, Dean of College of Graduate Studies and Adult Learning/Associate Provost for Civic and Community Engagement, 717-871-7619, Fax: 717-871-7954, E-mail: victor.desantis@millersville.edu.
Website: http://www.millersville.edu/wssd/graduate/index.php

Minnesota State University Mankato, College of Graduate Studies and Research, College of Allied Health and Nursing, Department of Human Performance, Mankato, MN 56001. Offers physical education (MA, MS). *Program availability:* Part-time. *Students:* 67 full-time (30 women), 30 part-time (13 women). *Degree requirements:* For master's, comprehensive exam, thesis. *Entrance requirements:* For master's, minimum GPA of 3.0 during previous 2 years. Additional exam requirements/recommendations for international students: Required—TOEFL. *Application deadline:* For fall admission, 3/1 priority date for domestic and international students. Applications are processed on a rolling basis. Application fee: $40. *Financial support:* Research assistantships with full tuition reimbursements, teaching assistantships with full tuition reimbursements, career-related internships or fieldwork, Federal Work-Study, institutionally sponsored loans, and unspecified assistantships available. Support available to part-time students. Financial award application deadline: 3/15; financial award applicants required to submit FAFSA. *Unit head:* Dr. Lynnette M. Engeswick, Chair, 507-389-2768, E-mail: lynnette.engeswick@mnsu.edu.
Website: http://ahn.mnsu.edu/hp/

Mississippi State University, College of Education, Department of Kinesiology, Mississippi State, MS 39762. Offers exercise physiology (MS); exercise science (PhD); sport administration (MS); sport pedagogy (MS); sport studies (PhD). *Program availability:* Part-time, blended/hybrid learning. *Faculty:* 14 full-time (2 women). *Students:* 57 full-time (17 women), 6 part-time (0 women); includes 11 minority (5 Black or African American, non-Hispanic/Latino; 2 Asian, non-Hispanic/Latino; 2 Hispanic/Latino; 2 Two or more races, non-Hispanic/Latino), 6 international. Average age 26. 75 applicants, 56% accepted, 30 enrolled. In 2016, 32 master's awarded. *Degree requirements:* For master's, comprehensive exam, thesis optional; for doctorate, comprehensive exam. *Entrance requirements:* For master's, GRE General Test, minimum GPA of 2.75 on undergraduate work from four-year accredited institution, 3.0 graduate; for doctorate, GRE, minimum GPA of 3.4 on previous graduate degree(s) earned from accredited institutions. Additional exam requirements/recommendations for international students: Required—TOEFL (minimum score 550 paper-based; 79 iBT); Recommended—IELTS (minimum score 6.5). *Application deadline:* For fall admission, 7/1 for domestic students, 5/1 for international students; for spring admission, 11/1 for domestic students, 9/1 for international students. Applications are processed on a rolling basis. Application fee: $60. Electronic applications accepted. *Expenses:* Tuition, state resident: full-time $7670; part-time $852.50 per credit hour. Tuition, nonresident: full-time $20,790; part-time $2310.50 per credit hour. Part-time tuition and fees vary according to course load. *Financial support:* In 2016–17, 16 teaching assistantships with partial tuition reimbursements (averaging $10,227 per year) were awarded; career-related internships or fieldwork, Federal Work-Study, institutionally sponsored loans, and unspecified assistantships also available. Financial award application deadline: 4/1; financial award applicants required to submit FAFSA. *Faculty research:* Static balance and stepping performance of older adults, organizational justice, public health, strength training and recovery drinks, high risk drinking perceptions and behaviors. *Unit head:* Dr. Stanley P. Brown, Professor and Department Head, 662-325-2963, Fax: 662-325-4525, E-mail: spb107@msstate.edu. *Application contact:* Linda Bonner, Senior Admissions Assistant, 662-325-3363, E-mail: lbonner@grad.msstate.edu.
Website: http://www.kinesiology.msstate.edu/

Missouri State University, Graduate College, College of Health and Human Services, Department of Kinesiology, Springfield, MO 65897. Offers health promotion and wellness management (MS); secondary education (MS Ed), including physical education. *Program availability:* Part-time. *Faculty:* 14 full-time (6 women). *Students:* 19 full-time (7 women), 8 part-time (4 women); includes 3 minority (1 Black or African American, non-Hispanic/Latino; 1 Asian, non-Hispanic/Latino; 1 Hispanic/Latino), 1 international. Average age 26. 19 applicants, 63% accepted, 7 enrolled. In 2016, 14 master's awarded. *Degree requirements:* For master's, comprehensive exam, thesis or alternative. *Entrance requirements:* For master's, GRE (for MS), minimum GPA of 2.8 (MS); 9-12 teaching certification (MS Ed). Additional exam requirements/recommendations for international students: Required—TOEFL (minimum score 550 paper-based; 79 iBT), IELTS (minimum score 6). *Application deadline:* For fall admission, 7/20 priority date for domestic students, 5/1 for international students; for spring admission, 12/20 priority date for domestic students, 9/1 for international students. Applications are processed on a rolling basis. Application fee: $35 ($50 for international students). Electronic applications accepted. *Expenses:* Tuition, state resident: full-time $5830. Tuition, nonresident: full-time $10,708. *Required fees:* $1130. Tuition and fees vary according to class time, course level, course load and program. *Financial support:* In 2016–17, 7 teaching assistantships with partial tuition reimbursements (averaging $8,772 per year) were awarded; Federal Work-Study, institutionally sponsored loans, scholarships/grants, and unspecified assistantships also available. Financial award application deadline: 3/31; financial award applicants required to submit FAFSA. *Unit head:* Dr. Sarah McCallister, Head, 417-836-6582, Fax: 417-836-5371, E-mail: sarahmccallister@missouristate.edu. *Application contact:* Michael Edwards, Coordinator of Graduate Admissions, 417-836-5330, Fax: 417-836-6200, E-mail: michaeledwards@missouristate.edu.
Website: http://www.missouristate.edu/kinesiology/

Montclair State University, The Graduate School, College of Education and Human Services, MAT Program in Teaching, Montclair, NJ 07043-1624. Offers art (MAT); biology (MAT); chemistry (MAT); earth science (MAT); English (MAT); French (MAT); health and physical education (MAT); health education (MAT); mathematics (MAT); music (MAT); physical education (MAT); physical science (MAT); social studies (MAT); Spanish (MAT); teacher of English as a second language (MAT). *Degree requirements:* For master's, comprehensive exam, thesis or alternative. *Entrance requirements:* For master's, interview, 2 letters of recommendation. Additional exam requirements/recommendations for international students: Required—TOEFL (minimum score 83 iBT), IELTS (minimum score 6.5). Electronic applications accepted. *Expenses:* Tuition, state resident: part-time $553 per credit. Tuition, nonresident: part-time $854 per credit. *Required fees:* $91 per credit. Tuition and fees vary according to program.

Montclair State University, The Graduate School, College of Education and Human Services, Program in Exercise Science and Physical Education, Montclair, NJ 07043-1624. Offers exercise science (MA); sports administration and coaching (MA); teaching and supervision in physical education (MA). *Program availability:* Part-time, evening/weekend. *Degree requirements:* For master's, comprehensive exam, thesis or alternative. *Entrance requirements:* For master's, GRE General Test, essay, 2 letters of recommendation. Additional exam requirements/recommendations for international students: Required—TOEFL (minimum score 83 iBT), IELTS (minimum score 6.5). Electronic applications accepted. *Expenses:* Tuition, state resident: part-time $553 per credit. Tuition, nonresident: part-time $854 per credit. *Required fees:* $91 per credit. Tuition and fees vary according to program.

Montclair State University, The Graduate School, College of Science and Mathematics, Program in Teaching Physical Education, Montclair, NJ 07043-1624. Offers MAT. *Degree requirements:* For master's, comprehensive exam. *Entrance requirements:* For master's, GRE General Test, interview, 2 letters of recommendation, essay. Additional exam requirements/recommendations for international students: Required—TOEFL (minimum score 83 iBT), IELTS (minimum score 6.5). Electronic applications accepted. *Expenses:* Tuition, state resident: part-time $553 per credit. Tuition, nonresident: part-time $854 per credit. *Required fees:* $91 per credit. Tuition and fees vary according to program. *Faculty research:* Teaching physics.

Morehead State University, Graduate Programs, College of Education, Department of Middle Grades and Secondary Education, Morehead, KY 40351. Offers business and marketing education (MAT); English/language arts 5-9 (MAT); French (MAT); health P-12 (MAT); mathematics 5-9 (MAT); physical education P-12 (MAT); science 5-9 (MAT); secondary biology (MAT); secondary chemistry (MAT); secondary earth science (MAT); secondary English (MAT); secondary math (MAT); secondary physics (MAT); secondary social studies (MAT); social studies 5-9 (MAT); Spanish (MAT). *Program availability:* Part-time, evening/weekend. *Degree requirements:* For master's, portfolio. *Entrance requirements:* For master's, GRE or PRAXIS II content exam, minimum overall undergraduate GPA of 2.5. Additional exam requirements/recommendations for international students: Required—TOEFL (minimum score 500 paper-based). Electronic applications accepted.

Morehead State University, Graduate Programs, College of Science and Technology, Department of Health, Wellness and Human Performance, Morehead, KY 40351. Offers health/physical education (MA). *Accreditation:* NCATE. *Program availability:* Part-time, evening/weekend. *Degree requirements:* For master's, comprehensive exam, thesis, oral exam, written core exam. *Entrance requirements:* For master's, GRE General Test or MAT, minimum GPA of 2.5; undergraduate major/minor in health, physical education, or recreation. Additional exam requirements/recommendations for international students: Required—TOEFL (minimum score 500 paper-based). Electronic applications accepted. *Faculty research:* Child growth and performance, instructional strategies, outdoor leadership qualities, exercise science, athletic training.

Murray State University, College of Education, Department of Adolescent, Career and Special Education, Murray, KY 42071. Offers health, physical education, and recreation (MA), including physical education; industrial and technical education (MS); middle school education (MA Ed, Ed S); secondary education (MA Ed, Ed S); special education (MA Ed), including advanced learning behavior disorders, learning disabilities, moderate/severe disorders. *Accreditation:* NCATE. *Program availability:* Part-time. *Entrance requirements:* Additional exam requirements/recommendations for international students: Required—TOEFL.

North Carolina Agricultural and Technical State University, School of Graduate Studies, School of Education, Department of Human Performance and Leisure Studies, Greensboro, NC 27411. Offers physical education (MAT, MS). *Accreditation:* NCATE. *Program availability:* Part-time, evening/weekend. *Degree requirements:* For master's, comprehensive exam, thesis or alternative, qualifying exam. *Entrance requirements:* For master's, GRE General Test or MAT.

North Carolina Central University, College of Behavioral and Social Sciences, Department of Physical Education and Recreation, Durham, NC 27707-3129. Offers athletic administration (MS); physical education (MS); recreation administration (MS); therapeutic recreation (MS). *Program availability:* Part-time, evening/weekend. *Degree requirements:* For master's, one foreign language, comprehensive exam, thesis. *Entrance requirements:* For master's, GRE, minimum GPA of 3.0 in major, 2.5 overall. Additional exam requirements/recommendations for international students: Required—TOEFL.

Northern Illinois University, Graduate School, College of Education, Department of Kinesiology and Physical Education, De Kalb, IL 60115-2854. Offers MS, MS Ed. *Program availability:* Part-time, evening/weekend. *Faculty:* 21 full-time (12 women). *Students:* 81 full-time (31 women), 45 part-time (20 women); includes 31 minority (14 Black or African American, non-Hispanic/Latino; 3 Asian, non-Hispanic/Latino; 6 Hispanic/Latino; 8 Two or more races, non-Hispanic/Latino), 5 international. Average age 26. 98 applicants, 70% accepted, 51 enrolled. In 2016, 71 master's awarded. *Degree requirements:* For master's, comprehensive exam, thesis optional. *Entrance requirements:* For master's, GRE General Test, minimum GPA of 2.75, undergraduate major in related area. Additional exam requirements/recommendations for international students: Required—TOEFL (minimum score 550 paper-based). *Application deadline:* For fall admission, 6/1 for domestic students, 5/1 for international students; for spring admission, 11/1 for domestic students, 10/1 for international students. Applications are processed on a rolling basis. Application fee: $40. Electronic applications accepted. *Financial support:* In 2016–17, 9 research assistantships with full tuition reimbursements, 25 teaching assistantships with full tuition reimbursements were awarded; fellowships with full tuition reimbursements, career-related internships or fieldwork, Federal Work-Study, scholarships/grants, tuition waivers (full), and unspecified assistantships also available. Support available to part-time students. Financial award applicants required to submit FAFSA. *Faculty research:* Leadership in athletic training, motor development, dance education, gait analysis, fat phobia. *Unit head:* Dr. Chad D. McEvoy, Chair, 815-753-8284, Fax: 815-753-1413, E-mail: knpe@niu.edu. *Application contact:* Dr. Laurie Zittel, Director, Graduate Studies, 815-753-1425, E-mail: lzape@niu.edu.
Website: http://cedu.niu.edu/knpe/

Northwest Missouri State University, Graduate School, School of Health Science and Wellness, Maryville, MO 64468-6001. Offers applied health and sport sciences (MS); recreation (MS). *Accreditation:* NCATE. *Program availability:* Part-time. *Students:* 68 full-time (38 women), 27 part-time (19 women). *Degree requirements:* For master's, comprehensive exam. *Entrance requirements:* For master's, GRE General Test, minimum undergraduate GPA of 2.75, teaching certificate, writing sample. Additional exam requirements/recommendations for international students: Required—TOEFL (minimum score 550 paper-based). *Application deadline:* For fall admission, 7/1 for domestic and international students; for spring admission, 11/15 for domestic and international students. Applications are processed on a rolling basis. Application fee: $0 ($50 for international students). *Expenses:* Tuition, state resident: full-time $3447; part-time $383 per credit hour. Tuition, nonresident: full-time $5724; part-time $636 per credit hour. *Required fees:* $130 per credit hour. *Financial support:* Teaching assistantships with full tuition reimbursements and unspecified assistantships available. Financial award application deadline: 4/1; financial award applicants required to submit FAFSA. *Unit head:* Dr. Terry Long, Director, School of Health Science and Wellness, 660-562-1706, E-mail: tlong@nwmissouri.edu. *Application contact:* Cathie Hannigan, Office Manager, 660-562-1297, Fax: 660-562-1483, E-mail: channig@nwmissouri.edu.
Website: http://www.nwmissouri.edu/health/

The Ohio State University, Graduate School, College of Education and Human Ecology, Department of Human Sciences, Columbus, OH 43210. Offers consumer sciences (MS, PhD); human development and family science (PhD); human nutrition (MS, PhD); kinesiology (MA, PhD). *Program availability:* Part-time. *Faculty:* 54. *Students:* 128 full-time (77 women), 8 part-time (6 women); includes 21 minority (7 Black or African American, non-Hispanic/Latino; 8 Hispanic/Latino; 6 Two or more races, non-Hispanic/Latino), 30 international. Average age 27. In 2016, 27 master's, 17 doctorates awarded. *Degree requirements:* For master's, thesis optional; for doctorate, thesis/dissertation. *Entrance requirements:* For master's and doctorate, GRE. Additional exam requirements/recommendations for international students: Required—TOEFL (minimum score 550 paper-based; 79 iBT), Michigan English Language Assessment Battery (minimum score 82); Recommended—IELTS (minimum score 7). *Application deadline:* For fall admission, 12/1 priority date for domestic and international students. Applications are processed on a rolling basis. Application fee: $60 ($70 for international students). Electronic applications accepted. *Financial support:* Fellowships with tuition reimbursements, research assistantships with tuition reimbursements, teaching assistantships with tuition reimbursements, Federal Work-Study, and institutionally sponsored loans available. Support available to part-time students. *Unit head:* Dr. Joe Wheaton, Interim Chair, E-mail: wheaton.3@osu.edu. *Application contact:* Graduate and Professional Admissions, 614-292-9444, Fax: 614-292-3895, E-mail: gpadmissions@osu.edu.
Website: http://ehe.osu.edu/human-sciences/

Ohio University, Graduate College, Gladys W. and David H. Patton College of Education and Human Services, Department of Recreation and Sport Pedagogy, Program in Coaching Education, Athens, OH 45701-2979. Offers MS. *Entrance requirements:* For master's, GRE. Additional exam requirements/recommendations for international students: Required—TOEFL (minimum score 550 paper-based; 80 iBT) or IELTS (minimum score 6.5). *Application deadline:* For fall admission, 3/1 priority date for domestic and international students. Applications are processed on a rolling basis. Application fee: $50 ($55 for international students). Electronic applications accepted. *Financial support:* Research assistantships with full tuition reimbursements, teaching assistantships with full tuition reimbursements, scholarships/grants, and stipends available. Financial award application deadline: 3/1. *Faculty research:* Sports, physical activity, athletes. *Unit head:* Dr. Beth VanDerveer, Assistant Professor and Coordinator, 740-593-4656, Fax: 740-593-0284, E-mail: vanderve@ohio.edu. *Application contact:* Dr. David Carr, Assistant Professor and Coordinator, 740-593-4651, Fax: 740-593-0284, E-mail: carrd@ohio.edu.
Website: https://www.ohio.edu/education/academic-programs/recreation-and-sport-pedagogy/graduate/

Old Dominion University, Darden College of Education, Program in Physical Education, Adapted Physical Education Emphasis, Norfolk, VA 23529. Offers MS Ed. *Program availability:* Part-time. *Faculty:* 1 full-time. *Students:* 1 (woman) full-time. Average age 29. *Degree requirements:* For master's, comprehensive exam (for some programs), thesis (for some programs). *Entrance requirements:* Additional exam requirements/recommendations for international students: Required—TOEFL (minimum score 550 paper-based; 79 iBT). *Expenses:* Tuition, state resident: full-time $8604; part-time $478 per credit hour. Tuition, nonresident: full-time $21,510; part-time $1195 per credit hour. *Required fees:* $66 per semester. Tuition and fees vary according to campus/location, program and reciprocity agreements. *Financial support:* Application deadline: 3/1; applicants required to submit FAFSA. *Faculty research:* Adapted physical education/activity, inclusion, individuals with disabilities. *Unit head:* Dr. Lynn Ridinger, Chair, 757-683-3351. *Application contact:* Justin Haegele, Coordinator, 757-683-4353, E-mail: jhaegele@odu.edu.

Old Dominion University, Darden College of Education, Program in Physical Education, Coaching Education Emphasis, Norfolk, VA 23529. Offers MS Ed. *Faculty:* 1 full-time. *Students:* 3 full-time (0 women), 1 (woman) part-time; includes 2 minority (both Black or African American, non-Hispanic/Latino). Average age 26. *Degree requirements:* For master's, internship, research project, or thesis. *Entrance requirements:* For master's, GRE, bachelor's degree with minimum cumulative undergraduate GPA of 2.8, 3.0 in undergraduate major courses. Additional exam requirements/recommendations for international students: Required—TOEFL (minimum score 550 paper-based; 79 iBT). *Application deadline:* Applications are processed on a rolling basis. *Expenses:* Tuition, state resident: full-time $8604; part-time $478 per credit hour. Tuition, nonresident: full-time $21,510; part-time $1195 per credit hour. *Required fees:* $66 per semester. Tuition and fees vary according to campus/location, program and reciprocity agreements. *Financial support:* Application deadline: 3/1. *Faculty research:* Curriculum development, coaching theory, planning and administration in physical education and sports. *Unit head:* Dr. Lynn Ridinger, Chair, 757-683-4995. *Application contact:* Dr. Xihe Zhu, Coordinator, 757-683-3545.

Old Dominion University, Darden College of Education, Program in Physical Education, Curriculum and Instruction Emphasis, Norfolk, VA 23529. Offers human movement sciences (PhD), including health and sport pedagogy; physical education (MS Ed), including adapted physical education, coaching education, curriculum and instruction. *Program availability:* Part-time, evening/weekend. *Faculty:* 2 full-time (0 women), 1 (woman) part-time/adjunct. *Students:* 5 full-time (2 women), 2 part-time (1 woman); includes 1 minority (Hispanic/Latino). Average age 29. 8 applicants, 75% accepted, 4 enrolled. In 2016, 4 master's awarded. *Degree requirements:* For master's, comprehensive exam (for some programs), thesis or alternative, internship, research project. *Entrance requirements:* For master's, GRE, PRAXIS Core (for licensure only), minimum GPA of 2.8 overall, 3.0 in major. Additional exam requirements/recommendations for international students: Required—TOEFL (minimum score 500 paper-based; 97 iBT). *Application deadline:* For fall admission, 3/1 priority date for domestic students; for spring admission, 11/1 for domestic students. Applications are processed on a rolling basis. Application fee: $50. Electronic applications accepted. *Expenses:* Tuition, state resident: full-time $8604; part-time $478 per credit hour. Tuition, nonresident: full-time $21,510; part-time $1195 per credit hour. *Required fees:* $66 per semester. Tuition and fees vary according to campus/location, program and reciprocity agreements. *Financial support:* In 2016–17, 2 students received support, including 1 teaching assistantship (averaging $10,000 per year); unspecified assistantships also available. Financial award application deadline: 4/15. *Faculty research:* Motor development, physical activity and fitness, motivation and learning in physical education, curriculum and instruction. *Unit head:* Dr. Lynn Ridinger, Chair, 757-683-4995, E-mail: lridinge@odu.edu. *Application contact:* William Heffelfinger, Director of Graduate Admissions, 757-683-5554, Fax: 757-683-3255, E-mail: gradadmit@odu.edu.
Website: http://education.odu.edu/eci/ciphd/

Old Dominion University, Darden College of Education, Program in Physical Education, Exercise and Wellness Emphasis, Norfolk, VA 23529. Offers physical education (MS Ed), including exercise science and wellness. *Program availability:* Part-time, evening/weekend. *Faculty:* 6 full-time (2 women). *Students:* 17 full-time (12 women), 4 part-time (2 women); includes 8 minority (3 Black or African American, non-Hispanic/Latino; 1 Asian, non-Hispanic/Latino; 3 Hispanic/Latino; 1 Two or more races, non-Hispanic/Latino). Average age 25. 19 applicants, 68% accepted, 11 enrolled. In 2016, 11 master's awarded. *Degree requirements:* For master's, comprehensive exam, thesis or alternative, internship, research project. *Entrance requirements:* For master's, GRE, minimum GPA of 2.8 overall, 3.0 in major. Additional exam requirements/recommendations for international students: Required—TOEFL (minimum score 550 paper-based; 79 iBT). *Application deadline:* For fall admission, 3/1 for domestic and international students. Applications are processed on a rolling basis. Application fee: $50. Electronic applications accepted. *Expenses:* Tuition, state resident: full-time $8604; part-time $478 per credit hour. Tuition, nonresident: full-time $21,510; part-time $1195 per credit hour. *Required fees:* $66 per semester. Tuition and fees vary according

to campus/location, program and reciprocity agreements. *Financial support:* In 2016–17, 7 students received support, including 4 research assistantships (averaging $10,000 per year), 3 teaching assistantships (averaging $10,000 per year); unspecified assistantships also available. Financial award application deadline: 3/1. *Faculty research:* Cardiovascular response to exercise, exercise prescription, nutrition, lower extremity biomechanics, exercise in special populations. *Total annual research expenditures:* $613,790. *Unit head:* Dr. Lynn Ridinger, Chair, 757-683-4353, E-mail: lridinge@odu.edu. *Application contact:* William Heffelfinger, Director of Graduate Admissions, 757-683-5554, Fax: 757-683-3255, E-mail: gradadmit@odu.edu.
Website: https://www.odu.edu/academics/programs/masters/exercise-science-wellness

Pittsburg State University, Graduate School, College of Education, Department of Health, Physical Education and Recreation, Pittsburg, KS 66762. Offers health, human performance, and recreation (MS), including human performance and wellness, sport and leisure service management. *Program availability:* Part-time, online only, 100% online. *Students:* 65 (25 women); includes 16 minority (8 Black or African American, non-Hispanic/Latino; 1 American Indian or Alaska Native, non-Hispanic/Latino; 5 Hispanic/Latino; 2 Two or more races, non-Hispanic/Latino). In 2016, 33 master's awarded. *Degree requirements:* For master's, thesis or alternative. *Entrance requirements:* For master's, letter of intent. Additional exam requirements/recommendations for international students: Required—TOEFL (minimum score 520 paper-based; 68 iBT), IELTS (minimum score 6), PTE (minimum score 47). *Application deadline:* For fall admission, 6/1 for international students; for spring admission, 10/15 for international students; for summer admission, 4/1 for international students. Applications are processed on a rolling basis. Application fee: $35 ($60 for international students). Electronic applications accepted. *Expenses:* Contact institution. *Financial support:* In 2016–17, 9 teaching assistantships with full tuition reimbursements (averaging $5,500 per year) were awarded; career-related internships or fieldwork, Federal Work-Study, and unspecified assistantships also available. Financial award application deadline: 2/1; financial award applicants required to submit FAFSA. *Faculty research:* Personality of athletes, fitness activities for children, aerobic conditioning, fitness evaluation. *Unit head:* Dr. John Oppliger, Chairperson, 620-235-4668, E-mail: joppliger@pittstate.edu. *Application contact:* Lisa Allen, Assistant Director of Graduate and Continuing Studies, 620-235-4223, Fax: 620-235-4219, E-mail: lallen@pittstate.edu.

Plymouth State University, College of Graduate Studies, Graduate Studies in Education, Program in Secondary Education, Plymouth, NH 03264-1595. Offers curriculum and instruction (M Ed); language education (M Ed); library media (M Ed); physical education (M Ed); social studies education (M Ed); special education (M Ed). *Program availability:* Part-time, evening/weekend. *Entrance requirements:* For master's, MAT.

Purdue University, Graduate School, College of Health and Human Sciences, Department of Health and Kinesiology, West Lafayette, IN 47907. Offers athletic training education administration (MS, PhD); biomechanics (MS, PhD); exercise physiology (MS, PhD); health education (MS, PhD); history/philosophy of sport (MS, PhD); motor control and development (MS, PhD); physical education pedagogy (PhD); physical education teacher education (MS); recreation and sport management (MS, PhD); sport and exercise psychology (MS, PhD). *Program availability:* Part-time. *Faculty:* 19 full-time (7 women). *Students:* 30 full-time (13 women), 10 part-time (5 women); includes 2 minority (1 Asian, non-Hispanic/Latino; 1 Two or more races, non-Hispanic/Latino), 6 international. Average age 26. 77 applicants, 29% accepted, 18 enrolled. In 2016, 18 master's, 9 doctorates awarded. *Degree requirements:* For master's, thesis optional; for doctorate, comprehensive exam, thesis/dissertation, qualifying examination, preliminary examination. *Entrance requirements:* For master's, GRE General Test (minimum score 1000 combined verbal and quantitative), minimum undergraduate GPA of 3.0 or equivalent; for doctorate, GRE General Test (minimum score 1100 combined verbal and quantitative), minimum undergraduate GPA of 3.0 or equivalent; master's degree with minimum GPA of 3.25 (recommended). Additional exam requirements/recommendations for international students: Required—TOEFL (minimum score 77 iBT); Recommended—TWE. *Application deadline:* For fall admission, 4/30 for domestic and international students; for spring admission, 10/15 for domestic and international students. Applications are processed on a rolling basis. Application fee: $60 ($75 for international students). Electronic applications accepted. *Financial support:* Fellowships with partial tuition reimbursements, research assistantships with partial tuition reimbursements, teaching assistantships with partial tuition reimbursements, and Federal Work-Study available. Support available to part-time students. Financial award applicants required to submit FAFSA. *Faculty research:* Wellness, motivation, teaching effectiveness, learning and development. *Unit head:* Dr. Timothy P. Gavin, Head of the Graduate Program, 765-494-3178, Fax: 765-494-1239, E-mail: gavin1@purdue.edu. *Application contact:* Christy F. Daugherty, Graduate Contact, 765-494-3162, E-mail: daugher2@purdue.edu.
Website: http://www.purdue.edu/hhs/hk/

Queens College of the City University of New York, Mathematics and Natural Sciences Division, Department of Family, Nutrition and Exercise Sciences, Queens, NY 11367-1597. Offers exercise science specialist (MS); family and consumer science (K-12) (AC); family and consumer science/teaching curriculum (K-12) (MS Ed); nutrition and exercise science (MS); nutrition specialist (MS); physical education (K-12) (AC); physical education/teaching curriculum (pre K-12) (MS Ed). *Program availability:* Part-time, evening/weekend. *Faculty:* 16 full-time (14 women), 46 part-time/adjunct (32 women). *Students:* 16 full-time (6 women), 157 part-time (86 women); includes 67 minority (19 Black or African American, non-Hispanic/Latino; 1 American Indian or Alaska Native, non-Hispanic/Latino; 18 Asian, non-Hispanic/Latino; 27 Hispanic/Latino; 2 Two or more races, non-Hispanic/Latino), 9 international. Average age 30. 95 applicants, 76% accepted, 45 enrolled. In 2016, 34 master's, 14 other advanced degrees awarded. *Degree requirements:* For master's, research project. *Entrance requirements:* For master's, minimum GPA of 3.0. Additional exam requirements/recommendations for international students: Required—TOEFL, IELTS. *Application deadline:* For fall admission, 4/1 for domestic students; for spring admission, 11/1 for domestic students. Applications are processed on a rolling basis. Application fee: $125. Electronic applications accepted. *Expenses:* Tuition, state resident: full-time $5065; part-time $425 per credit. Tuition, nonresident: part-time $780 per credit. *Required fees:* $522; $397 per credit. Part-time tuition and fees vary according to course load and program. *Financial support:* Career-related internships or fieldwork and unspecified assistantships available. Financial award application deadline: 4/1; financial award applicants required to submit FAFSA. *Unit head:* Dr. Michael Toner, Chairperson, 718-997-4168, E-mail: michael.toner@qc.cuny.edu.

Rhode Island College, School of Graduate Studies, Feinstein School of Education and Human Development, Department of Health and Physical Education, Providence, RI 02908-1991. Offers health education (M Ed); physical education (CGS). *Accreditation:* NCATE. *Program availability:* Part-time, evening/weekend. *Faculty:* 2 part-time/adjunct (1 woman). *Students:* 1 (woman) full-time, 5 part-time (all women). Average age 45. In 2016, 6 master's awarded. *Degree requirements:* For master's, comprehensive assessment. *Entrance requirements:* For master's, GRE General Test or MAT, undergraduate transcripts; minimum undergraduate GPA of 3.0; 3 letters of recommendation; for CGS, GRE or MAT (for most programs), undergraduate transcripts; minimum undergraduate GPA of 3.0; 3 letters of recommendation. Additional exam requirements/recommendations for international students: Recommended—TOEFL (minimum score 550 paper-based; 79 iBT). *Application deadline:* For fall admission, 3/1 for domestic students; for spring admission, 11/1 for domestic students. Applications are processed on a rolling basis. Application fee: $50. Electronic applications accepted. *Expenses:* Tuition, state resident: full-time $8928; part-time $372 per credit. Tuition, nonresident: full-time $17,376; part-time $724 per credit. *Required fees:* $604; $22 per credit. One-time fee: $74. *Financial support:* In 2016–17, 1 teaching assistantship with full tuition reimbursement (averaging $1,500 per year) was awarded; Federal Work-Study, scholarships/grants, health care benefits, and unspecified assistantships also available. Support available to part-time students. Financial award application deadline: 5/15; financial award applicants required to submit FAFSA. *Unit head:* Dr. Robin Auld, Chair, 401-456-8046. *Application contact:* Graduate Studies, 401-456-8700.
Website: http://www.ric.edu/healthPhysicalEducation/

Salem State University, School of Graduate Studies, Program in Physical Education, Salem, MA 01970-5353. Offers M Ed. *Program availability:* Part-time, evening/weekend. *Entrance requirements:* For master's, GRE or MAT. Additional exam requirements/recommendations for international students: Required—TOEFL (minimum score 550 paper-based; 80 iBT) or IELTS (minimum score 5.5).

Shenandoah University, School of Education and Human Development, Winchester, VA 22601-5195. Offers administrative leadership (D Ed); educational administration (MSE); emphasis in teaching (MSE); health and physical education (Certificate); individual focus (MSE); literacy education (MS); middle school teacher education (Certificate); organizational leadership (MS, D Prof); secondary school teacher education (Certificate); special education (MSE). *Accreditation:* TEAC. *Program availability:* Part-time, evening/weekend. *Faculty:* 9 full-time (7 women), 43 part-time/adjunct (33 women). *Students:* 31 full-time (25 women), 236 part-time (160 women); includes 39 minority (19 Black or African American, non-Hispanic/Latino; 1 American Indian or Alaska Native, non-Hispanic/Latino; 10 Asian, non-Hispanic/Latino; 7 Hispanic/Latino; 1 Native Hawaiian or other Pacific Islander, non-Hispanic/Latino; 1 Two or more races, non-Hispanic/Latino), 4 international. Average age 37. 90 applicants, 97% accepted, 56 enrolled. In 2016, 113 master's, 13 doctorates, 38 other advanced degrees awarded. *Degree requirements:* For master's, comprehensive exam (for some programs), thesis (for some programs); for doctorate, comprehensive exam, thesis/dissertation. *Entrance requirements:* For degree, PRAXIS Academic Core, SAT/ACT, PRAXIS Academic Core Math, or VCLA, three letters of recommendation, writing sample, undergraduate degree. Additional exam requirements/recommendations for international students: Required—TOEFL (minimum score 550 paper-based; 79 iBT), IELTS (minimum score 6.5). *Application deadline:* For fall admission, 5/1 priority date for domestic students, 5/1 for international students; for spring admission, 10/15 priority date for domestic students, 10/15 for international students; for summer admission, 3/15 priority date for domestic students, 3/15 for international students. Application fee: $30. Electronic applications accepted. *Expenses:* Contact institution. *Financial support:* In 2016–17, 18 students received support. Scholarships/grants and unspecified assistantships available. Financial award applicants required to submit FAFSA. *Faculty research:* Exploring helplessness and anxiety in learning statistics, facilitating effective classroom group work, expert-novice dynamics in teaching, K-12 policy implementation and change, adult education, family-school-community relations, mentoring of first-year school principals. *Total annual research expenditures:* $2,000. *Unit head:* Dennis William Kellison, PhD, Director, 540-535-7324, Fax: 540-665-4726, E-mail: dkelliso@su.edu. *Application contact:* Andrew Woodall, Executive Director of Recruitment and Admissions, 540-665-4581, Fax: 540-665-4627, E-mail: admit@su.edu.
Website: http://www.su.edu/education/

Slippery Rock University of Pennsylvania, Graduate Studies (Recruitment), College of Education, Department of Physical and Health Education, Slippery Rock, PA 16057-1383. Offers adapted physical activity (MS). *Faculty:* 3 full-time (2 women). *Students:* 21 full-time (17 women), 1 (woman) part-time; includes 3 minority (2 Black or African American, non-Hispanic/Latino; 1 Hispanic/Latino). Average age 24. 37 applicants, 62% accepted, 17 enrolled. In 2016, 25 master's awarded. *Degree requirements:* For master's, internship. *Entrance requirements:* For master's, official transcripts, minimum GPA of 2.75, two letters of recommendation, essay. Additional exam requirements/recommendations for international students: Required—TOEFL (minimum score 550 paper-based; 80 iBT). *Application deadline:* For fall admission, 3/1 priority date for domestic students, 5/1 priority date for international students; for spring admission, 10/1 priority date for domestic students. Applications are processed on a rolling basis. Application fee: $25 ($30 for international students). Electronic applications accepted. *Expenses:* $646.50 per credit in-state, $936.80 per credit out-of-state; $581.45 per online credit in-state, $648.65 per online credit out-of-state. *Financial support:* In 2016–17, 4 students received support. Career-related internships or fieldwork, Federal Work-Study, institutionally sponsored loans, scholarships/grants, tuition waivers (partial), and unspecified assistantships available. Support available to part-time students. Financial award application deadline: 5/1; financial award applicants required to submit FAFSA. *Unit head:* Dr. Randall Nichols, Graduate Coordinator, 724-738-2818, Fax: 724-738-2921, E-mail: randall.nichols@sru.edu. *Application contact:* Brandi Weber-Mortimer, Director of Graduate Admissions, 724-738-2051, Fax: 724-738-2146, E-mail: graduate.admissions@sru.edu.
Website: http://www.sru.edu/academics/colleges-and-departments/coe/departments/physical-and-health-education

Sonoma State University, School of Science and Technology, Department of Kinesiology, Rohnert Park, CA 94928. Offers adapted physical education (MA); interdisciplinary (MA); interdisciplinary pre-occupational therapy (MA); lifetime physical activity (MA), including coach education, fitness and wellness; physical education (MA); pre-physical therapy (MA). *Program availability:* Part-time. *Degree requirements:* For master's, thesis, oral exam. *Entrance requirements:* For master's, minimum GPA of 2.8. Additional exam requirements/recommendations for international students: Required—TOEFL (minimum score 500 paper-based). *Application deadline:* For fall admission, 11/30 for domestic students; for spring admission, 9/1 for domestic students. Applications are processed on a rolling basis. Application fee: $55. *Expenses:* Tuition, state resident: full-time $6738; part-time $3906 per unit. *Required fees:* $1916; $1916 per year. Tuition and fees vary according to course load, degree level and program. *Financial support:* Career-related internships or fieldwork available. Financial award application deadline: 3/2; financial award applicants required to submit FAFSA. *Unit head:* Dr. Steven Winter, Chair, 707-664-2188, E-mail: steven.winter@sonoma.edu. *Application contact:* Dr. Bulent Sokmen, Graduate Coordinator, 707-664-2789, E-mail: sokmen@sonoma.edu.
Website: http://www.sonoma.edu/kinesiology/

Southern Connecticut State University, School of Graduate Studies, School of Health and Human Services, Department of Exercise Science, New Haven, CT 06515-1355. Offers human performance (MS); physical education (MS); school health education (MS). *Program availability:* Part-time, evening/weekend. *Faculty:* 5 full-time (0 women). *Students:* 11 full-time (8 women), 16 part-time (9 women); includes 4 minority (3 Hispanic/Latino; 1 Two or more races, non-Hispanic/Latino), 2 international. Average

age 26. 8 applicants, 38% accepted, 3 enrolled. In 2016, 12 master's awarded. *Degree requirements:* For master's, thesis or alternative. *Entrance requirements:* For master's, interview. *Application deadline:* For fall admission, 7/15 priority date for domestic students. Applications are processed on a rolling basis. Application fee: $50. Electronic applications accepted. *Expenses:* Tuition, state resident: full-time $6497; part-time $519 per credit hour. Tuition, nonresident: full-time $18,102; part-time $535 per credit hour. *Required fees:* $4722; $55 per semester. Tuition and fees vary according to program. *Financial support:* Career-related internships or fieldwork, scholarships/grants, and unspecified assistantships available. Financial award application deadline: 4/15; financial award applicants required to submit FAFSA. *Unit head:* Dr. Daniel Swartz, Chairperson, 203-392-8721, Fax: 203-392-6911, E-mail: swartzd1@southernct.edu. *Application contact:* Lisa Galvin, Director of Graduate Admissions, 203-392-5240, Fax: 203-392-5235, E-mail: galvinl1@southernct.edu.

Southern Illinois University Carbondale, Graduate School, College of Education and Human Services, Department of Kinesiology, Carbondale, IL 62901-4701. Offers MS Ed. *Program availability:* Part-time. *Degree requirements:* For master's, thesis. *Entrance requirements:* For master's, GRE, minimum GPA of 2.7. Additional exam requirements/recommendations for international students: Required—TOEFL. *Faculty research:* Caffeine and exercise effects, ground reaction forces in walking and running, social psychology of sports.

Southern Illinois University Edwardsville, Graduate School, School of Education, Health, and Human Behavior, Department of Kinesiology and Health Education, Program in Physical Education and Coaching Pedagogy, Edwardsville, IL 62026. Offers MS Ed. *Program availability:* Part-time, evening/weekend. *Degree requirements:* For master's, comprehensive exam (for some programs), thesis (for some programs). *Entrance requirements:* Additional exam requirements/recommendations for international students: Required—TOEFL (minimum score 550 paper-based, 79 iBT), IELTS (minimum score 6.5), Michigan Test of English Language Proficiency or PTE. Electronic applications accepted.

Springfield College, Graduate Programs, Programs in Physical Education, Springfield, MA 01109-3797. Offers adapted physical education (MS); advanced-level coaching (M Ed); athletic administration (MS). *Program availability:* Part-time. *Degree requirements:* For master's, comprehensive exam, thesis (for some programs). *Entrance requirements:* For master's and doctorate, GRE General Test. Additional exam requirements/recommendations for international students: Required—TOEFL (minimum score 550 paper-based); Recommended—IELTS (minimum score 6). Electronic applications accepted. *Expenses: Tuition:* Full-time $29,640; part-time $988 per credit. *Required fees:* $195.

State University of New York College at Cortland, Graduate Studies, School of Professional Studies, Department of Physical Education, Cortland, NY 13045. Offers adapted physical education (MS Ed); coaching pedagogy (MS Ed); physical education leadership (MS Ed). *Program availability:* Part-time, evening/weekend. *Entrance requirements:* Additional exam requirements/recommendations for international students: Required—TOEFL.

Stony Brook University, State University of New York, School of Professional Development, Stony Brook, NY 11794-443. Offers biology (MAT); chemistry (MAT); coaching (Graduate Certificate); earth science (MAT); educational computing (Graduate Certificate); educational leadership (Advanced Certificate); English (MAT); environmental management (MPS, Graduate Certificate); French (MAT); German (MAT); higher education administration (MA, Certificate); human resource management (MS, Graduate Certificate); industrial management (Graduate Certificate); information systems management (Graduate Certificate); Italian (MAT); liberal studies (MA); mathematics (MAT); operations research (Graduate Certificate); physics (MAT); school district business leadership (Advanced Certificate); social studies (MAT); Spanish (MAT). *Program availability:* Part-time, evening/weekend, online learning. *Faculty:* 4 full-time (3 women), 77 part-time/adjunct (34 women). *Students:* 197 full-time (125 women), 965 part-time (674 women); includes 222 minority (79 Black or African American, non-Hispanic/Latino; 2 American Indian or Alaska Native, non-Hispanic/Latino; 35 Asian, non-Hispanic/Latino; 87 Hispanic/Latino; 1 Native Hawaiian or other Pacific Islander, non-Hispanic/Latino; 18 Two or more races, non-Hispanic/Latino), 5 international. Average age 33. 462 applicants, 87% accepted, 317 enrolled. In 2016, 348 master's, 159 other advanced degrees awarded. *Degree requirements:* For master's, one foreign language, thesis or alternative. *Entrance requirements:* Additional exam requirements/recommendations for international students: Required—TOEFL (minimum score 85 iBT). *Application deadline:* For fall admission, 1/15 for domestic students, 6/1 for international students; for spring admission, 10/1 for domestic and international students. Applications are processed on a rolling basis. Application fee: $100. *Expenses:* Contact institution. *Financial support:* Fellowships, research assistantships, teaching assistantships, and career-related internships or fieldwork available. Support available to part-time students. *Unit head:* Dr. Ken Lindblom, Dean, 631-632-7049, Fax: 631-632-9046, E-mail: kenneth.lindblom@stonybrook.edu. *Application contact:* Melissa Jordan, Assistant Dean, 631-632-7751, E-mail: melissa.jordan@stonybrook.edu.
Website: http://www.stonybrook.edu/spd/

Sul Ross State University, College of Professional Studies, Department of Physical Education, Alpine, TX 79832. Offers M Ed. *Program availability:* Part-time. *Entrance requirements:* For master's, GMAT or GRE General Test, minimum GPA of 2.5 in last 60 hours of undergraduate work.

Teachers College, Columbia University, Department of Biobehavioral Sciences, New York, NY 10027-6696. Offers applied exercise physiology (Ed M, MA, Ed D); communication sciences and disorders (MS, Ed D, PhD); kinesiology (PhD); motor learning and control (Ed M, MA); motor learning/movement science (Ed D); neuroscience and education (MS); physical education (MA, Ed D). *Accreditation:* ASHA. *Program availability:* Part-time, evening/weekend. *Students:* 162 full-time (133 women), 158 part-time (116 women); includes 119 minority (20 Black or African American, non-Hispanic/Latino; 38 Asian, non-Hispanic/Latino; 54 Hispanic/Latino; 7 Two or more races, non-Hispanic/Latino), 28 international. 821 applicants, 33% accepted, 125 enrolled. *Expenses: Tuition:* Full-time $36,288; part-time $1512 per credit. *Required fees:* $438 per semester. One-time fee: $510 full-time. Full-time tuition and fees vary according to course load. *Financial support:* Fellowships, teaching assistantships, career-related internships or fieldwork, Federal Work-Study, institutionally sponsored loans, traineeships, and tuition waivers (full and partial) available. Support available to part-time students. *Unit head:* Prof. Carol Garber, Chair, 212-678-3891, E-mail: garber@tc.columbia.edu. *Application contact:* David Estrella, Director of Admissions, 212-678-3305, E-mail: estrella@tc.columbia.edu.
Website: http://www.tc.columbia.edu/biobehavioral-sciences/

Temple University, College of Public Health, Department of Kinesiology, Philadelphia, PA 19122. Offers athletic training (MSAT, DAT); kinesiology (MS, PhD); neuromotor science (MS, PhD). *Program availability:* Part-time. *Faculty:* 16 full-time (6 women), 6 part-time/adjunct (2 women). *Students:* 38 full-time (28 women), 23 part-time (9 women); includes 15 minority (4 Black or African American, non-Hispanic/Latino; 1 Asian, non-Hispanic/Latino; 8 Hispanic/Latino; 2 Two or more races, non-Hispanic/Latino), 6 international. 74 applicants, 66% accepted, 35 enrolled. In 2016, 26 master's, 5 doctorates awarded. Terminal master's awarded for partial completion of doctoral program. *Degree requirements:* For master's, thesis, final project; for doctorate, comprehensive exam, thesis/dissertation. *Entrance requirements:* For master's, GRE General Test or MAT, minimum undergraduate GPA of 3.0, 3 letters of reference, statement of goals, interview, resume; for doctorate, GRE General Test, minimum undergraduate GPA of 3.0, 3 letters of reference, statement of goals, interview, resume. Additional exam requirements/recommendations for international students: Required—TOEFL (minimum score 550 paper-based; 79 iBT). *Application deadline:* For fall admission, 1/15 for domestic students, 12/15 for international students; for spring admission, 10/1 for domestic students, 8/1 for international students. Applications are processed on a rolling basis. Application fee: $60. Electronic applications accepted. *Expenses:* Contact institution. *Financial support:* Fellowships, research assistantships with tuition reimbursements, teaching assistantships with tuition reimbursements, career-related internships or fieldwork, Federal Work-Study, scholarships/grants, tuition waivers, and unspecified assistantships available. Financial award application deadline: 1/15. *Faculty research:* Exercise physiology, athletic training, motor neuroscience, exercise and sports psychology. *Unit head:* John Jeka, Chair, 214-204-4405, Fax: 215-204-4414, E-mail: jjeka@temple.edu. *Application contact:* Rosalind Robinson, Department Coordinator, E-mail: rosalind.robinson@temple.edu.
Website: http://cph.temple.edu/kinesiology/home

Tennessee State University, The School of Graduate Studies and Research, College of Health Sciences, Department of Human Performance and Sports Sciences, Nashville, TN 37209-1561. Offers exercise science (MA Ed); sports administration (MA Ed). *Degree requirements:* For master's, thesis optional. *Entrance requirements:* For master's, GRE General Test or MAT.

Tennessee Technological University, College of Graduate Studies, College of Education, Department of Exercise Science, Physical Education and Wellness, Cookeville, TN 38505. Offers adapted physical education (MA); elementary/middle school physical education (MA); lifetime wellness (MA); sport management (MA). *Accreditation:* NCATE. *Program availability:* Part-time, online learning. *Faculty:* 7 full-time (0 women). *Students:* 17 full-time (5 women), 32 part-time (17 women); includes 6 minority (4 Black or African American, non-Hispanic/Latino; 1 Hispanic/Latino; 1 Two or more races, non-Hispanic/Latino). Average age 27. 29 applicants, 59% accepted, 15 enrolled. In 2016, 24 master's awarded. *Degree requirements:* For master's, comprehensive exam, thesis or alternative. *Entrance requirements:* For master's, MAT or GRE. Additional exam requirements/recommendations for international students: Required—TOEFL (minimum score 527 paper-based; 71 iBT), IELTS (minimum score 5.5), PTE (minimum score 48), or TOEIC (Test of English as an International Communication). *Application deadline:* For fall admission, 8/1 for domestic students, 5/1 for international students; for spring admission, 12/1 for domestic students, 10/1 for international students; for summer admission, 5/1 for domestic students, 2/1 for international students. Applications are processed on a rolling basis. Application fee: $35 ($40 for international students). Electronic applications accepted. *Expenses:* Tuition, state resident: full-time $9375; part-time $534 per credit hour. Tuition, nonresident: full-time $22,443; part-time $1260 per credit hour. *Financial support:* In 2016–17, 2 research assistantships (averaging $4,400 per year), 9 teaching assistantships (averaging $4,400 per year) were awarded; fellowships and career-related internships or fieldwork also available. Financial award application deadline: 4/1. *Unit head:* Dr. Christy Killman, Chairperson, 931-372-3467, Fax: 931-372-6319, E-mail: ckillman@tntech.edu. *Application contact:* Shelia K. Kendrick, Coordinator of Graduate Studies, 931-372-3808, Fax: 931-372-3497, E-mail: skendrick@tntech.edu.

Texas Southern University, College of Education, Department of Health and Kinesiology, Houston, TX 77004-4584. Offers health education (MS); human performance (MS). *Program availability:* Part-time, evening/weekend. *Degree requirements:* For master's, comprehensive exam, thesis optional. *Entrance requirements:* For master's, GRE General Test, minimum GPA of 2.5. Additional exam requirements/recommendations for international students: Required—TOEFL. Electronic applications accepted.

Texas State University, The Graduate College, College of Education, Program in Physical Education, San Marcos, TX 78666. Offers M Ed. *Program availability:* Part-time, evening/weekend. *Faculty:* 4 full-time (2 women). *Students:* 1 full-time (0 women), 5 part-time (2 women); includes 4 minority (all Hispanic/Latino). Average age 27. 5 applicants, 60% accepted, 1 enrolled. In 2016, 7 master's awarded. *Degree requirements:* For master's, comprehensive exam, thesis optional. *Entrance requirements:* For master's, GRE General Test (minimum preferred score of 291 verbal and quantitative combined) or minimum GPA of 3.0 on last 60 undergraduate hours, baccalaureate degree from regionally-accredited institution with minimum GPA of 2.75 in last 60 hours of course work; 3 letters of recommendation; resume; statement of aspiration addressing professional goals, motivation, strengths and weaknesses to be evaluated for content, style and quality. Additional exam requirements/recommendations for international students: Required—TOEFL (minimum score 550 paper-based; 78 iBT), IELTS (minimum score 6.5). *Application deadline:* For fall admission, 3/1 priority date for domestic and international students; for spring admission, 11/1 for domestic students, 10/1 for international students; for summer admission, 1/15 for domestic and international students. Applications are processed on a rolling basis. Application fee: $40 ($90 for international students). Electronic applications accepted. *Expenses:* $4,851 per semester. *Financial support:* In 2016–17, 3 students received support. Research assistantships, teaching assistantships, career-related internships or fieldwork, Federal Work-Study, institutionally sponsored loans, and scholarships/grants available. Support available to part-time students. Financial award application deadline: 3/1; financial award applicants required to submit FAFSA. *Faculty research:* Employee wellness, isometric strength evaluation. *Unit head:* Dr. Karen Meaney, Graduate Advisor, 512-245-2952, Fax: 512-245-8678, E-mail: km66@txstate.edu. *Application contact:* Dr. Andrea Golato, Head, 512-245-2581, Fax: 512-245-8365, E-mail: gradcollege@txstate.edu.
Website: http://www.hhp.txstate.edu/Degree-Plans/Graduate.html

Texas Woman's University, Graduate School, College of Health Sciences, Department of Kinesiology, Denton, TX 76201. Offers adapted physical activity (MS, PhD); biomechanics (MS, PhD); coaching (MS); exercise physiology (MS, PhD); sport management (MS, PhD). *Program availability:* Part-time, evening/weekend. Terminal master's awarded for partial completion of doctoral program. *Degree requirements:* For master's, comprehensive exam, thesis or alternative; for doctorate, comprehensive exam, thesis/dissertation, qualifying exam. *Entrance requirements:* For master's, GRE General Test (biomechanics emphasis only), 2 letters of reference, curriculum vitae, interview (adapted physical education emphasis only); for doctorate, GRE General Test (biomechanics emphasis only), interview, 3 letters of reference, curriculum vitae. Additional exam requirements/recommendations for international students: Required—TOEFL (minimum score 550 paper-based; 79 iBT). *Application deadline:* For fall admission, 7/1 priority date for domestic students, 3/1 for international students; for spring admission, 11/1 priority date for domestic students, 7/1 for international students. Applications are processed on a rolling basis. Application fee: $50 ($75 for international students). Electronic applications accepted. *Expenses:* Tuition, state resident: full-time $9046; part-time $251 per credit hour. Tuition, nonresident: full-time $22,922; part-time

$614 per credit hour. *International tuition:* $23,046 full-time. *Required fees:* $2690; $1285 per credit hour. One-time fee: $50. Tuition and fees vary according to course level, course load, program and reciprocity agreements. *Financial support:* Research assistantships, teaching assistantships, career-related internships or fieldwork, Federal Work-Study, institutionally sponsored loans, scholarships/grants, traineeships, health care benefits, and unspecified assistantships available. Support available to part-time students. Financial award application deadline: 3/1; financial award applicants required to submit FAFSA. *Faculty research:* Exercise and Type 2 diabetes risk, bone mineral density and exercise in special populations, obesity in children, factors influencing sport consumer behavior and loyalty, roles and responsibilities of Para educators in adapted physical education. *Unit head:* Dr. David Nichols, Interim Chair, 940-898-2576, Fax: 940-898-2581, E-mail: dnichols@twu.edu. *Application contact:* Dr. Samuel Wheeler, Assistant Director of Admissions, 940-898-3188, Fax: 940-898-3081, E-mail: wheelersr@twu.edu.
Website: http://www.twu.edu/kinesiology/

Union College, Graduate Programs, Department of Education, Barbourville, KY 40906-1499. Offers elementary education (MA); health and physical education (MA); middle grades (MA); music education (MA); principalship (MA); reading specialist (MA); secondary education (MA); special education (MA). *Degree requirements:* For master's, thesis optional. *Entrance requirements:* For master's, GRE General Test, NTE.

United States Sports Academy, Graduate Programs, Program in Sports Coaching, Daphne, AL 36526-7055. Offers MSS. *Program availability:* Part-time, online learning. *Degree requirements:* For master's, comprehensive exam, thesis optional. *Entrance requirements:* For master's, GRE General Test, GMAT, or MAT, minimum GPA of 2.5, 3 letters of recommendation, resume. Additional exam requirements/recommendations for international students: Required—TOEFL (minimum score 500 paper-based). Electronic applications accepted. *Faculty research:* Effect of attentional skill on sports performance, survey of coaching qualifications, coaching certification.

Universidad del Turabo, Graduate Programs, Programs in Education, Program in Coaching, Gurabo, PR 00778-3030. Offers MPHE. *Students:* 12 full-time (3 women), 4 part-time (0 women); all minorities (all Hispanic/Latino). Average age 31. 15 applicants, 47% accepted, 6 enrolled. In 2016, 1 master's awarded. *Entrance requirements:* For master's, GRE, EXADEP, GMAT, interview, official transcript, essay, recommendation letters. *Application deadline:* Applications are processed on a rolling basis. Application fee: $25. Electronic applications accepted. *Financial support:* Institutionally sponsored loans available. Financial award applicants required to submit FAFSA. *Unit head:* Israel Rodríguez, Dean, 787-743-7979 Ext. 4627. *Application contact:* Diriee Rodríguez, Admissions Director, 787-743-7979 Ext. 4453, E-mail: admisiones-ut@suagm.edu.
Website: http://ut.suagm.edu/es/educacion

Universidad Metropolitana, School of Education, Program in Teaching of Physical Education, San Juan, PR 00928-1150. Offers teaching of adult physical education (M Ed); teaching of elementary physical education (M Ed); teaching of secondary physical education (M Ed). *Degree requirements:* For master's, thesis or alternative. *Entrance requirements:* For master's, EXADEP, interview. Electronic applications accepted.

Université de Montréal, Department of Kinesiology, Montréal, QC H3C 3J7, Canada. Offers kinesiology (M Sc, DESS); physical activity (M Sc, PhD). *Degree requirements:* For master's, one foreign language, thesis (for some programs); for doctorate, one foreign language, thesis/dissertation, general exam. Electronic applications accepted. *Faculty research:* Physiology of exercise, psychology of sports, biomechanics, dance, sociology of sports.

Université de Sherbrooke, Faculty of Physical Education and Sports, Program in Physical Education, Sherbrooke, QC J1K 2R1, Canada. Offers kinanthropology (M Sc); physical activity (Diploma). *Degree requirements:* For master's, thesis. *Entrance requirements:* For master's, minimum GPA of 2.7; for Diploma, bachelor's degree in physical education. *Faculty research:* Physical fitness, nutrition, human factors, sociology, teaching.

Université du Québec à Trois-Rivières, Graduate Programs, Program in Physical Education, Trois-Rivières, QC G9A 5H7, Canada. Offers M Sc. *Program availability:* Part-time. *Degree requirements:* For master's, thesis. *Entrance requirements:* For master's, appropriate bachelor's degree, proficiency in French.

The University of Akron, Graduate School, College of Health Professions, School of Sport Science and Wellness Education, Program in Sport Science/Coaching, Akron, OH 44325. Offers MA, MS. *Students:* 49 full-time (15 women), 9 part-time (5 women); includes 17 minority (16 Black or African American, non-Hispanic/Latino; 1 Two or more races, non-Hispanic/Latino), 2 international. Average age 27. 33 applicants, 67% accepted, 12 enrolled. In 2016, 38 master's awarded. *Degree requirements:* For master's, comprehensive exam, thesis optional. *Entrance requirements:* For master's, minimum GPA of 2.75, three letters of recommendation, statement of purpose. Additional exam requirements/recommendations for international students: Required—TOEFL (minimum score 550 paper-based; 79 iBT), IELTS (minimum score 6.5). *Application deadline:* Applications are processed on a rolling basis. Application fee: $45 ($70 for international students). Electronic applications accepted. *Expenses:* Tuition, state resident: full-time $8618; part-time $359 per credit hour. Tuition, nonresident: full-time $17,149; part-time $715 per credit hour. *Required fees:* $1652. *Unit head:* Dr. Victor Pinheiro, Department Chair, 330-972-6055, E-mail: victor@uakron.edu. *Application contact:* Dr. Alan Kornspan, Program Contact, 330-972-8145.
Website: http://www.uakron.edu/sswe/programs/sport-science-coaching/index.dot

The University of Alabama, Graduate School, College of Education, Department of Kinesiology, Tuscaloosa, AL 35487. Offers alternative sport pedagogy (MA); exercise science (PhD). *Program availability:* Part-time. *Faculty:* 12 full-time (2 women). *Students:* 70 full-time (35 women), 22 part-time (6 women); includes 16 minority (9 Black or African American, non-Hispanic/Latino; 4 Hispanic/Latino; 3 Two or more races, non-Hispanic/Latino), 7 international. Average age 29. 71 applicants, 76% accepted, 38 enrolled. In 2016, 39 master's, 8 doctorates awarded. *Degree requirements:* For master's, comprehensive exam, thesis optional; for doctorate, comprehensive exam, thesis/dissertation. *Entrance requirements:* For master's and doctorate, GRE, minimum GPA of 3.0. Additional exam requirements/recommendations for international students: Required—TOEFL. *Application deadline:* Applications are processed on a rolling basis. Electronic applications accepted. *Expenses:* Tuition, state resident: full-time $10,470. Tuition, nonresident: full-time $26,950. *Financial support:* Application deadline: 3/1. *Total annual research expenditures:* $39,044. *Unit head:* Dr. Jonathan Wingo, Associate Professor and Head, 205-348-4699, Fax: 205-348-0867, E-mail: jwingo@ua.edu.
Website: http://education.ua.edu/academics/kine/

University of Alberta, Faculty of Graduate Studies and Research, Department of Physical Education and Recreation, Edmonton, AB T6G 2E1, Canada. Offers physical education (M Sc); recreation and physical education (MA, PhD). *Program availability:* Part-time. Terminal master's awarded for partial completion of doctoral program. *Degree requirements:* For master's, thesis (for some programs); for doctorate, thesis/dissertation. *Entrance requirements:* For master's, bachelor's degree in related field; for doctorate, master's degree in related field with thesis. Additional exam requirements/recommendations for international students: Required—TOEFL. *Faculty research:* Motivation and adherence to physical ability, performance enhancement, adapted physical activity, exercise physiology, sport administration, tourism.

University of Arkansas, Graduate School, College of Education and Health Professions, Department of Health, Human Performance and Recreation, Program in Physical Education, Fayetteville, AR 72701. Offers M Ed, MAT. In 2016, 9 master's awarded. *Degree requirements:* For master's, thesis optional. *Application deadline:* For fall admission, 4/1 for international students; for spring admission, 10/1 for international students. Applications are processed on a rolling basis. Application fee: $40 ($50 for international students). Electronic applications accepted. *Financial support:* Fellowships with tuition reimbursements, research assistantships, teaching assistantships, career-related internships or fieldwork, and Federal Work-Study available. Support available to part-time students. Financial award application deadline: 4/1; financial award applicants required to submit FAFSA. *Unit head:* Dr. Bart Hammig, Department Chairperson, 479-575-2890, Fax: 479-575-5778, E-mail: bhammig@uark.edu. *Application contact:* Dr. Stephen Dittmore, Coordinator of Graduate Studies, 479-575-6625, E-mail: dittmore@uark.edu.
Website: http://hkrd.uark.edu/

The University of British Columbia, Faculty of Education, Department of Curriculum and Pedagogy, Vancouver, BC V6T 1Z4, Canada. Offers art education (M Ed, MA); curriculum studies (M Ed, MA, PhD); home economics education (M Ed, MA); mathematics education (M Ed, MA); media and technology studies education (M Ed, MA); music education (M Ed, MA); physical education (M Ed, MA); science education (M Ed, MA); social studies education (M Ed, MA). *Program availability:* Part-time, online learning. *Degree requirements:* For master's, thesis (MA); for doctorate, comprehensive exam, thesis/dissertation. *Entrance requirements:* Additional exam requirements/recommendations for international students: Required—TOEFL, IELTS. Application fee: $100 Canadian dollars ($162 Canadian dollars for international students). Electronic applications accepted. *Expenses:* $6,865 per year tuition and fees domestic, $10,938 per year international (for MA and M Ed); $4,802 per year tuition and fees, $8,436 per year international (for PhD). *Financial support:* Fellowships with partial tuition reimbursements, research assistantships with partial tuition reimbursements, teaching assistantships with partial tuition reimbursements, and tuition waivers (partial) available. *Faculty research:* School subjects, teaching and learning. *Application contact:* Alan Jay, Graduate Programs Assistant, 604-822-5367, Fax: 604-822-4714, E-mail: edcp.grad@ubc.ca.
Website: http://www.edcp.educ.ubc.ca/

University of Dayton, Department of Health and Sport Science, Dayton, OH 45469. Offers exercise science (MS Ed). *Faculty:* 7 full-time (3 women). *Students:* 12 full-time (3 women), 1 (woman) part-time; includes 5 minority (3 Black or African American, non-Hispanic/Latino; 1 Asian, non-Hispanic/Latino; 1 Two or more races, non-Hispanic/Latino), 2 international. Average age 23. 37 applicants, 30% accepted. In 2016, 5 master's awarded. *Degree requirements:* For master's, thesis optional. *Entrance requirements:* For master's, GRE General Test or MAT if undergraduate GPA was 2.75 or below, minimum GPA of 2.75; official academic records of all previously-attended colleges or universities; three letters of recommendation from professors or employers; personal statement or resume. Additional exam requirements/recommendations for international students: Required—TOEFL (minimum score 550 paper-based; 80 iBT). *Application deadline:* Applications are processed on a rolling basis. Application fee: $0 ($50 for international students). Electronic applications accepted. *Expenses:* $620 per credit hour, $25 registration fee per term. *Financial support:* In 2016–17, 2 research assistantships with partial tuition reimbursements (averaging $9,390 per year), 2 teaching assistantships with partial tuition reimbursements (averaging $9,390 per year) were awarded; career-related internships or fieldwork, institutionally sponsored loans, health care benefits, and unspecified assistantships also available. Financial award application deadline: 3/1; financial award applicants required to submit FAFSA. *Faculty research:* Energy expenditure, strength, training, teaching nutrition and calcium intake for children and families in Head Start; motion analysis of human gait, pediatric physical therapy, arm function of breast cancer survivors, predicting injury in athletes, neurological rehabilitation in persons with multiple sclerosis. *Unit head:* Dr. Lloyd Laubach, Chair, 937-229-4240, Fax: 937-229-4244, E-mail: llaubach1@udayton.edu. *Application contact:* Laura Greger, Administrative Assistant, 937-229-4225, E-mail: lgreger1@udayton.edu.
Website: https://www.udayton.edu/education/departments_and_programs/hss

University of Florida, Graduate School, College of Health and Human Performance, Department of Applied Physiology and Kinesiology, Gainesville, FL 32611. Offers applied physiology and kinesiology (MS); athletic training/sports medicine (MS); biobehavioral science (MS); clinical exercise physiology (MS); exercise physiology (MS); health and human performance (PhD), including applied physiology and kinesiology, biobehavioral science, exercise physiology; human performance (MS). *Degree requirements:* For master's, comprehensive exam, thesis (for some programs); for doctorate, comprehensive exam, thesis/dissertation. *Entrance requirements:* For master's and doctorate, GRE General Test, minimum GPA of 3.0. Additional exam requirements/recommendations for international students: Required—TOEFL (minimum score 550 paper-based; 80 iBT), IELTS (minimum score 6). Electronic applications accepted. *Faculty research:* Cardiovascular disease; basic mechanisms that underlie exercise-induced changes in the body at the organ, tissue, cellular and molecular level; development of rehabilitation techniques for regaining motor control after stroke or as a consequence of Parkinson's disease; maintaining optimal health and delaying age-related declines in physiological function; psychomotor mechanisms impacting health and performance across the life span.

University of Georgia, College of Education, Department of Kinesiology, Athens, GA 30602. Offers MS, PhD. *Entrance requirements:* For master's, GRE General Test or MAT; for doctorate, GRE General Test. Additional exam requirements/recommendations for international students: Required—TOEFL. *Application deadline:* For fall admission, 7/1 priority date for domestic students; for spring admission, 11/15 for domestic students. Application fee: $50. Electronic applications accepted. *Unit head:* Dr. Kirk J. Cureton, Head, 706-542-4387, Fax: 706-542-3148, E-mail: kcureton@uga.edu. *Application contact:* Ellen M. Evans, Graduate Coordinator, 706-542-9257, E-mail: emevans@uga.edu.
Website: http://www.coe.uga.edu/kinesiology

University of Houston, College of Liberal Arts and Social Sciences, Department of Health and Human Performance, Houston, TX 77204. Offers exercise science (MS); human nutrition (MS); human space exploration sciences (MS); kinesiology (PhD); physical education (M Ed). *Accreditation:* NCATE (one or more programs are accredited). *Program availability:* Part-time, evening/weekend. *Degree requirements:* For master's, comprehensive exam (for some programs), thesis (for some programs); for doctorate, comprehensive exam, thesis/dissertation, qualifying exam, candidacy paper. *Entrance requirements:* For master's, GRE (minimum 35th percentile on each section), minimum cumulative GPA of 3.0; for doctorate, GRE (minimum 35th percentile on each section), minimum cumulative GPA of 3.3. Additional exam requirements/recommendations for international students: Required—TOEFL (minimum score 550 paper-based; 79 iBT). Electronic applications accepted. *Faculty research:* Biomechanics, exercise physiology, obesity, nutrition, space exploration science.

Physical Education

University of Idaho, College of Graduate Studies, College of Education, Department of Movement Sciences, Moscow, ID 83844. Offers athletic training (MSAT, DAT); movement and leisure sciences (MS); physical education (M Ed). *Faculty:* 14 full-time, 5 part-time/adjunct. *Students:* 79 full-time (41 women), 24 part-time (12 women). Average age 30. In 2016, 24 master's awarded. *Degree requirements:* For doctorate, thesis/dissertation. *Entrance requirements:* For master's and doctorate, minimum GPA of 3.0. Additional exam requirements/recommendations for international students: Required—TOEFL. *Application deadline:* For fall admission, 8/1 for domestic students; for spring admission, 12/15 for domestic students. Applications are processed on a rolling basis. Application fee: $60. Electronic applications accepted. *Expenses:* Tuition, state resident: full-time $6460; part-time $414 per credit hour. Tuition, nonresident: full-time $21,268; part-time $1237 per credit hour. *Required fees:* $2070; $60 per credit hour. Full-time tuition and fees vary according to course load and reciprocity agreements. *Financial support:* Research assistantships and teaching assistantships available. Financial award applicants required to submit FAFSA. *Unit head:* Dr. Philip W. Scruggs, Chair, 208-885-7921, E-mail: movementsciences@uidaho.edu. *Application contact:* Sean Scoggin, Graduate Recruitment Coordinator, 208-885-4001, Fax: 208-885-4406, E-mail: graduateadmissions@uidaho.edu.
Website: https://www.uidaho.edu/ed/mvsc

University of Indianapolis, Graduate Programs, School of Education, Indianapolis, IN 46227-3697. Offers art education (MAT); biology (MAT); chemistry (MAT); curriculum and instruction (MA); earth sciences (MAT); education (MA, MAT); educational leadership (MA); elementary education (MA); English (MAT); French (MAT); math (MAT); physical education (MAT); physics (MAT); secondary education (MA), including art education, education, English education, social studies education; social studies (MAT); Spanish (MAT). *Accreditation:* NCATE. *Program availability:* Part-time, evening/weekend. *Entrance requirements:* For master's, GRE Subject Test, PRAXIS I, minimum GPA of 2.5, 3 letters of recommendation, interview. Additional exam requirements/recommendations for international students: Required—TOEFL (minimum score 550 paper-based). *Faculty research:* Assessment of teacher education, perceptions of prospective teachers by parents.

The University of Kansas, Graduate Studies, School of Education, Department of Health, Sport, and Exercise Sciences, Lawrence, KS 66045. Offers exercise science (MS Ed); health and physical education (MS Ed, PhD); sport management (MS Ed). *Accreditation:* NCATE. *Program availability:* Part-time, evening/weekend. *Students:* 53 full-time (21 women), 12 part-time (5 women); includes 5 minority (1 Black or African American, non-Hispanic/Latino; 1 American Indian or Alaska Native, non-Hispanic/Latino; 3 Two or more races, non-Hispanic/Latino), 3 international. Average age 27. 70 applicants, 64% accepted, 25 enrolled. In 2016, 19 master's, 6 doctorates awarded. *Entrance requirements:* For master's, GRE General Test (minimum score 1000, 450 verbal, 450 quantitative, 4.0 analytical), minimum GPA of 3.0, three letters of recommendation, personal statement, resume, writing sample; for doctorate, GRE General Test (minimum score 1100, verbal 500, quantitative 500, analytical 4.5), minimum graduate GPA of 3.5, undergraduate 3.0; three letters of recommendation; personal statement; resume; writing sample; interview with an advisor. Additional exam requirements/recommendations for international students: Required—TOEFL or IELTS. *Application deadline:* For fall admission, 3/15 for domestic and international students; for spring admission, 10/1 for domestic and international students; for summer admission, 3/15 for domestic and international students. Application fee: $65 ($85 for international students). Electronic applications accepted. *Financial support:* Research assistantships, teaching assistantships, Federal Work-Study, scholarships/grants, and unspecified assistantships available. Financial award application deadline: 2/21. *Faculty research:* Exercise and sport psychology, obesity prevention, sexuality health, sport ethics, skeletal muscle cell signaling and performance. *Unit head:* Dr. Joseph Weir, Chair, 785-864-0784, E-mail: joseph.weir@ku.edu. *Application contact:* Sarah Clopton, Graduate Admissions Coordinator, 785-864-7268, E-mail: sclopton@ku.edu.
Website: http://hses.soe.ku.edu/

University of Kentucky, Graduate School, College of Education, Program in Kinesiology and Health Promotion, Lexington, KY 40506-0032. Offers biomechanics (MS); exercise physiology (MS, PhD); exercise science (PhD); health promotion (MS, Ed D); physical education training (Ed D); sport leadership (MS); teaching and coaching (MS). Terminal master's awarded for partial completion of doctoral program. *Degree requirements:* For master's, comprehensive exam, thesis optional; for doctorate, comprehensive exam, thesis/dissertation. *Entrance requirements:* For master's, GRE General Test, minimum undergraduate GPA of 2.75; for doctorate, GRE General Test, minimum graduate GPA of 3.0. Additional exam requirements/recommendations for international students: Required—TOEFL (minimum score 550 paper-based). Electronic applications accepted.

University of Louisville, Graduate School, College of Education and Human Development, Department of Health and Sport Sciences, Louisville, KY 40292-0001. Offers community health education (M Ed); exercise physiology (MS), including health and sport sciences, strength and conditioning; health and physical education (MAT); sport administration (MS). *Program availability:* Part-time, evening/weekend. *Students:* 39 full-time (18 women), 10 part-time (8 women); includes 7 minority (4 Black or African American, non-Hispanic/Latino; 2 Hispanic/Latino; 1 Two or more races, non-Hispanic/Latino), 1 international. Average age 27. 73 applicants, 63% accepted, 23 enrolled. In 2016, 25 master's awarded. Application fee: $60. *Expenses:* Tuition, state resident: full-time $12,246; part-time $681 per credit hour. Tuition, nonresident: full-time $25,486; part-time $1417 per credit hour. *Required fees:* $196. Tuition and fees vary according to program and reciprocity agreements. *Financial support:* Applicants required to submit FAFSA. *Faculty research:* Sport administration; exercise physiology; exercise science; physical education; health education. *Total annual research expenditures:* $91,688. *Unit head:* Dr. Margaret Hancock, Interim Chair/Assistant Professor, 502-852-6645, E-mail: meg.hancock@louisville.edu. *Application contact:* Betty Hampton, Director of Graduate Student Services, 502-852-5597, Fax: 502-852-1465, E-mail: edadvise@louisville.edu.
Website: http://www.louisville.edu/education/departments/hss

University of Louisville, Graduate School, College of Education and Human Development, Department of Teaching and Learning, Louisville, KY 40292-0001. Offers art education (MAT); autism and applied behavior analysis (Certificate); curriculum and instruction (PhD); early elementary education (MAT); exercise physiology (MS); health and physical education (MAT); health professions education (Certificate); higher education (MA); human resources and organization development (MS); instructional technology (M Ed); interdisciplinary early childhood education (MAT); middle school education (MAT); music education (MAT); secondary education (MAT); special education (MAT); sport administration (MS); teacher leadership (M Ed). *Program availability:* Part-time, evening/weekend. *Students:* 116 full-time (68 women), 158 part-time (112 women); includes 46 minority (24 Black or African American, non-Hispanic/Latino; 8 Asian, non-Hispanic/Latino; 5 Hispanic/Latino; 9 Two or more races, non-Hispanic/Latino), 6 international. Average age 30. 114 applicants, 71% accepted, 57 enrolled. In 2016, 59 master's, 3 doctorates awarded. *Application deadline:* For spring admission, 1/1 priority date for international students. Application fee: $60. *Expenses:* Tuition, state resident: full-time $12,246; part-time $681 per credit hour. Tuition, nonresident: full-time $25,486; part-time $1417 per credit hour. *Required fees:* $196. Tuition and fees vary according to program and reciprocity agreements. *Financial support:* Application deadline: 6/1; applicants required to submit FAFSA. *Faculty research:* STEM teaching and learning; content literacy for English language learners; social justice in teacher education; adolescent literacy; mathematics teacher development. *Total annual research expenditures:* $1.7 million. *Unit head:* Dr. Ann E. Larson, Dean, College of Education and Human Development, 502-852-6411, Fax: 502-852-1464, E-mail: ann@louisville.edu. *Application contact:* Betty Hampton, Director of Graduate Student Services, 502-852-5597, Fax: 502-852-1465, E-mail: edadvise@louisville.edu.
Website: http://louisville.edu/delphi

University of Maine, Graduate School, College of Education and Human Development, School of Kinesiology, Physical Education and Athletic Training, Orono, ME 04469. Offers classroom technology integrationist (CGS); education data specialist (CGS); educational technology coordinator (CGS); kinesiology and physical education (M Ed, MS); science education (M Ed, MS); STEM education (PhD). *Program availability:* Part-time, evening/weekend. *Students:* 13 full-time (4 women), 1 (woman) part-time; includes 1 minority (Hispanic/Latino), 1 international. Average age 24. 15 applicants, 100% accepted, 7 enrolled. In 2016, 16 master's, 10 other advanced degrees awarded. *Degree requirements:* For master's, thesis (for some programs); for doctorate, comprehensive exam, thesis/dissertation. *Entrance requirements:* For master's, GRE General Test, MAT; for doctorate, GRE General Test. Additional exam requirements/recommendations for international students: Required—TOEFL. *Application deadline:* For fall admission, 1/15 for domestic students. Applications are processed on a rolling basis. Application fee: $65. Electronic applications accepted. *Expenses:* Tuition, state resident: full-time $7524; part-time $2508 per credit. Tuition, nonresident: full-time $24,498; part-time $8166 per credit. *Required fees:* $1148; $571 per credit. *Financial support:* In 2016–17, 9 students received support, including 1 research assistantship with full tuition reimbursement available (averaging $14,600 per year), 6 teaching assistantships (averaging $14,600 per year); Federal Work-Study, scholarships/grants, and unspecified assistantships also available. Financial award application deadline: 3/1. *Faculty research:* Integration of technology in K-12 classrooms, instructional theory and practice in science, inquiry-based teaching, professional development, exercise science, adaptive physical education, neuromuscular function/dysfunction. *Unit head:* Dr. Jim Artesani, Associate Dean of Accreditation and Graduate Affairs, 207-581-4061, Fax: 207-581-2423. *Application contact:* Scott G. Delcourt, Assistant Vice President for Graduate Studies and Senior Associate Dean, 207-581-3291, Fax: 207-581-3232, E-mail: graduate@maine.edu.
Website: http://umaine.edu/edhd/

University of Manitoba, Faculty of Graduate Studies, Faculty of Kinesiology and Recreation Management, Winnipeg, MB R3T 2N2, Canada. Offers kinesiology and recreation (M Sc, MA).

University of Mary, School of Health Sciences, Program in Sports and Physical Education Administration, Bismarck, ND 58504-9652. Offers MS. *Program availability:* Online learning. *Entrance requirements:* For master's, bachelors degree in athletic training, exercise science, physical education, or a related field; minimum undergraduate GPA of 2.5.

University of Memphis, Graduate School, School of Health Studies, Memphis, TN 38152. Offers faith and health (Graduate Certificate); health studies (MS), including exercise and sports science, health promotion, physical education teacher education; nutrition (MS), including clinical nutrition, environmental nutrition, nutrition science. *Program availability:* 100% online. *Faculty:* 19 full-time (10 women), 2 part-time/adjunct (both women). *Students:* 73 full-time (58 women), 39 part-time (24 women); includes 31 minority (22 Black or African American, non-Hispanic/Latino; 1 American Indian or Alaska Native, non-Hispanic/Latino; 6 Asian, non-Hispanic/Latino; 2 Hispanic/Latino), 4 international. Average age 27. 62 applicants, 89% accepted, 45 enrolled. In 2016, 42 master's awarded. *Degree requirements:* For master's, comprehensive exam, thesis or alternative, culminating experience; for Graduate Certificate, practicum. *Entrance requirements:* For master's, GRE or PRAXIS II, letters of recommendation, statement of goals, minimum undergraduate GPA of 2.5; for Graduate Certificate, minimum undergraduate GPA of 2.5. Additional exam requirements/recommendations for international students: Required—TOEFL (minimum score 550 paper-based; 79 iBT). *Application deadline:* For fall admission, 4/15 priority date for domestic students; for spring admission, 10/15 priority date for domestic students; for summer admission, 4/15 priority date for domestic students. Application fee: $35 ($60 for international students). *Expenses:* $5,231.50 per semester full-time in-state, $9,623.50 full-time out-of-state. *Financial support:* In 2016–17, 20 research assistantships (averaging $11,360 per year), 8 teaching assistantships (averaging $10,062 per year) were awarded; career-related internships or fieldwork, Federal Work-Study, scholarships/grants, and unspecified assistantships also available. Financial award application deadline: 2/1; financial award applicants required to submit FAFSA. *Unit head:* Dr. Richard J. Bloomer, Director, 901-678-4316, Fax: 901-678-3591, E-mail: rbloomer@memphis.edu. *Application contact:* Dr. Lawrence Weiss, Director of Graduate Programs, 901-678-5037, E-mail: lweiss@memphis.edu.
Website: http://www.memphis.edu/shs/programs

University of Montana, Graduate School, Phyllis J. Washington College of Education and Human Sciences, Department of Health and Human Performance, Missoula, MT 59812-0002. Offers community health (MS); exercise science (MS); health and human performance generalist (MS). *Program availability:* Part-time. *Entrance requirements:* For master's, GRE General Test. Additional exam requirements/recommendations for international students: Required—TOEFL. *Faculty research:* Exercise physiology, performance psychology, nutrition, pre-employment physical screening, program evaluation.

University of Nebraska at Kearney, College of Education, Kinesiology and Sport Sciences Department, Kearney, NE 68849-0001. Offers general physical education (MA Ed), including recreation and leisure, sports administration; physical education exercise science (MA Ed); physical education master teacher (MA Ed), including pedagogy, special populations. *Program availability:* Part-time, evening/weekend, 100% online. *Faculty:* 17 full-time (5 women). *Students:* 4 full-time (2 women), 39 part-time (16 women); includes 3 minority (2 Black or African American, non-Hispanic/Latino; 1 Hispanic/Latino). Average age 28. 20 applicants, 100% accepted, 14 enrolled. In 2016, 25 master's awarded. *Degree requirements:* For master's, comprehensive exam, thesis optional. *Entrance requirements:* For master's, GRE General Test (for some programs), personal statement. Additional exam requirements/recommendations for international students: Recommended—TOEFL (minimum score 550 paper-based; 79 iBT), IELTS (minimum score 6.5). *Application deadline:* For fall admission, 6/15 for domestic and international students; for spring admission, 10/15 for domestic and international students; for summer admission, 3/15 for domestic and international students. Application fee: $45. Electronic applications accepted. *Expenses:* Tuition, state resident: full-time $4064; part-time $225.75 per credit hour. Tuition, nonresident: full-time $8915; part-time $495.25 per credit hour. *Required fees:* $772; $23 per credit hour. Part-time tuition and fees vary according to course load, campus/location, program and reciprocity agreements. *Financial support:* In 2016–17, 9 students received support, including 3 research assistantships with full tuition reimbursements available (averaging

$10,500 per year), 6 teaching assistantships with full tuition reimbursements available (averaging $10,500 per year); career-related internships or fieldwork, scholarships/grants, health care benefits, and unspecified assistantships also available. Support available to part-time students. Financial award application deadline: 2/28; financial award applicants required to submit FAFSA. *Faculty research:* Ergonomic aids, nutrition, motor development, sports pedagogy, applied behavior analysis, physical activity and wellness, athletic training, therapeutic interventions, exercise physiology, endocrinology and metabolism. *Unit head:* Dr. Nita Unruh, Chair, 308-865-8335, E-mail: unruhnc@unk.edu. *Application contact:* Linda Johnson, Director, Graduate Admissions and Programs, 308-865-8841, Fax: 308-865-8837, E-mail: johnsonli@unk.edu.
Website: http://www.unk.edu/academics/hperls/index.php

University of New Brunswick Fredericton, School of Graduate Studies, Faculty of Kinesiology, Fredericton, NB E3B 5A3, Canada. Offers exercise and sport science (M Sc); sport and recreation management (MBA); sport and recreation studies (MA). *Program availability:* Part-time. *Degree requirements:* For master's, thesis (for some programs). *Entrance requirements:* For master's, GMAT (minimum score of 550 for sport and recreation management program), minimum GPA of 3.0, written statement of research goals and interests. Additional exam requirements/recommendations for international students: Required—TOEFL (minimum score 92 iBT), IELTS (minimum score 7). Electronic applications accepted.

University of New Hampshire, Graduate School, College of Health and Human Services, Department of Kinesiology, Durham, NH 03824. Offers adapted physical education (Postbaccalaureate Certificate); kinesiology (MS); kinesiology and social work (MS). *Program availability:* Part-time. *Degree requirements:* For master's, thesis or alternative. *Entrance requirements:* For master's, GRE General Test. Additional exam requirements/recommendations for international students: Required—TOEFL (minimum score 550 paper-based; 80 iBT). *Application deadline:* For fall admission, 6/1 priority date for domestic students, 4/1 for international students; for spring admission, 12/1 for domestic students. Applications are processed on a rolling basis. Application fee: $65. *Financial support:* Fellowships, research assistantships, teaching assistantships, career-related internships or fieldwork, Federal Work-Study, scholarships/grants, and tuition waivers (full and partial) available. Support available to part-time students. Financial award application deadline: 2/15. *Faculty research:* Exercise specialist, sports studies, special physical education, pediatric exercises and motor behavior. *Unit head:* Karen Collins, Chair, 603-862-0361. *Application contact:* Tarah Beaupre, Administrative Assistant, 603-862-2071, E-mail: kinesiology.dept@unh.edu.
Website: http://chhs.unh.edu/kin

University of New Mexico, Graduate Studies, College of Education, Program in Physical Education, Sports and Exercise Science, Albuquerque, NM 87131-2039. Offers curriculum and instruction (PhD); exercise science (PhD); sports administration (PhD). *Program availability:* Part-time. *Faculty:* 13 full-time (6 women), 2 part-time/adjunct (1 woman). *Students:* 83 full-time (28 women), 48 part-time (21 women); includes 51 minority (12 Black or African American, non-Hispanic/Latino; 2 American Indian or Alaska Native, non-Hispanic/Latino; 1 Asian, non-Hispanic/Latino; 32 Hispanic/Latino; 4 Two or more races, non-Hispanic/Latino), 15 international. Average age 30. 67 applicants, 75% accepted, 35 enrolled. In 2016, 13 doctorates awarded. *Degree requirements:* For doctorate, comprehensive exam, thesis/dissertation, inquiry skills, 24 credits in supporting area. *Entrance requirements:* For doctorate, GRE, letter of intent, 3 letters of reference, minimum cumulative GPA of 3.0 in last 2 years of bachelor's degree. Additional exam requirements/recommendations for international students: Required—TOEFL (minimum score 550 paper-based). *Application deadline:* For fall admission, 3/1 priority date for domestic students; for spring admission, 11/1 priority date for domestic students. Application fee: $50. Electronic applications accepted. *Financial support:* Fellowships, teaching assistantships with full tuition reimbursements, career-related internships or fieldwork, Federal Work-Study, institutionally sponsored loans, scholarships/grants, health care benefits, tuition waivers, and unspecified assistantships available. Financial award application deadline: 3/1; financial award applicants required to submit FAFSA. *Faculty research:* Facility risk management, physical education pedagogy practices, physiological adaptations to exercise, physiological adaptations to heat, sport leadership. *Unit head:* Dr. Todd Seidler, Chair, 505-277-2783, Fax: 505-277-6227, E-mail: tseidler@unm.edu. *Application contact:* Monica Lopez, Program Office, 505-277-5151, Fax: 505-277-6227, E-mail: mllopez@unm.edu.
Website: https://coe.unm.edu/departments-programs/hess/physical-education/physical-education-phd/index.html

University of North Alabama, College of Education, Department of Health, Physical Education, and Recreation, Florence, AL 35632-0001. Offers health and human performance (MS), including exercise science, kinesiology, wellness and health promotion. *Program availability:* Part-time. *Faculty:* 7 full-time (2 women). *Students:* 10 full-time (5 women), 11 part-time (4 women); includes 2 minority (both Black or African American, non-Hispanic/Latino), 2 international. Average age 24. 19 applicants, 68% accepted, 11 enrolled. In 2016, 14 master's awarded. *Degree requirements:* For master's, comprehensive exam (for some programs), thesis optional. *Entrance requirements:* For master's, MAT or GRE, 3 letters of recommendation, essay. Additional exam requirements/recommendations for international students: Required—TOEFL (minimum score 79 iBT), IELTS (minimum score 6), PTE (minimum score 54). *Application deadline:* Applications are processed on a rolling basis. Application fee: $50 ($100 for international students). Electronic applications accepted. *Expenses:* Tuition, state resident: full-time $2799; part-time $1866 per semester. Tuition, nonresident: full-time $5598; part-time $3732 per semester. *Required fees:* $915; $642 per semester. Tuition and fees vary according to course load. *Financial support:* In 2016–17, 19 students received support. Scholarships/grants and unspecified assistantships available. Financial award application deadline: 2/1; financial award applicants required to submit FAFSA. *Unit head:* Dr. Thomas E. Coates, Chair, 256-765-4377. *Application contact:* Hillary N. Coats, Graduate Admissions Coordinator, 256-765-4447, E-mail: graduate@una.edu.
Website: https://www.una.edu/hper/index.html

The University of North Carolina at Chapel Hill, Graduate School, College of Arts and Sciences, Department of Exercise and Sport Science, Chapel Hill, NC 27599. Offers athletic training (MA); exercise physiology (MA); sport administration (MA). *Degree requirements:* For master's, comprehensive exam, thesis. *Entrance requirements:* For master's, GRE General Test, minimum GPA of 3.0. Additional exam requirements/recommendations for international students: Required—TOEFL (minimum score 550 paper-based). Electronic applications accepted. *Faculty research:* Mild head injury in sport, endocrine system's response to exercise, obesity and children, effect of aerobic exercise on cerebral bloodflow in elderly population.

The University of North Carolina at Pembroke, The Graduate School, School of Education, Department of Health and Human Performance, Pembroke, NC 28372-1510. Offers physical education (MA). *Program availability:* Part-time, evening/weekend. *Degree requirements:* For master's, comprehensive exam, thesis optional. *Entrance requirements:* For master's, MAT or GRE, minimum GPA of 3.0 in major, 2.5 overall. Additional exam requirements/recommendations for international students: Required—TOEFL.

The University of North Carolina Wilmington, Watson College of Education, Department of Instructional Technology, Foundations and Secondary Education, Wilmington, NC 28403-3297. Offers academically or intellectually gifted (M Ed); English as a second language (M Ed, MAT); instructional technology (MS); physical education and health (M Ed, MAT); secondary education (M Ed, MAT); Spanish (MAT); Spanish education (MASS). *Program availability:* Part-time. *Faculty:* 17 full-time (11 women). *Students:* 36 full-time (22 women), 62 part-time (49 women); includes 17 minority (12 Black or African American, non-Hispanic/Latino; 3 Hispanic/Latino; 2 Two or more races, non-Hispanic/Latino), 5 international. Average age 34. 89 applicants, 89% accepted, 59 enrolled. In 2016, 36 master's awarded. *Degree requirements:* For master's, comprehensive exam (for some programs), thesis (for some programs), thesis or research project. *Entrance requirements:* For master's, GRE or MAT, statement of interest, 3 letters of recommendation, minimum GPA of 3.0 in undergraduate work. Additional exam requirements/recommendations for international students: Required—TOEFL (minimum score 79 iBT), IELTS (minimum score 6.5). *Application deadline:* For fall admission, 5/15 for domestic students; for spring admission, 10/15 for domestic students; for summer admission, 3/15 for domestic students. Applications are processed on a rolling basis. Application fee: $60. Electronic applications accepted. *Expenses:* Contact institution. *Financial support:* Scholarships/grants and unspecified assistantships available. Financial award application deadline: 3/15; financial award applicants required to submit FAFSA. *Unit head:* Dr. Donyell Roseboro, Chair, 910-962-2289, Fax: 910-962-3609, E-mail: roseborod@uncw.edu. *Application contact:* Dr. Mahnaz Moallem, Graduate Coordinator, 910-962-4183, E-mail: moallemm@uncw.edu.
Website: http://www.uncw.edu/ed/itfse/

University of Northern Colorado, Graduate School, College of Natural and Health Sciences, School of Sport and Exercise Science, Greeley, CO 80639. Offers exercise science (MS, PhD); physical education and physical activity leadership (MAT); sport administration (MS, PhD); sport pedagogy (MS, PhD); sports coaching (MA). *Program availability:* Part-time, evening/weekend. *Degree requirements:* For master's, comprehensive exam; for doctorate, comprehensive exam, thesis/dissertation. *Entrance requirements:* For master's, 2 letters of recommendation, resume; for doctorate, GRE General Test, 3 letters of recommendation, resume. *Application deadline:* Applications are processed on a rolling basis. Application fee: $50 ($60 for international students). Electronic applications accepted. *Financial support:* Fellowships, research assistantships, teaching assistantships, and unspecified assistantships available. Financial award application deadline: 3/1; financial award applicants required to submit FAFSA. *Unit head:* Dr. David Stotlar, Director, 970-351-2535, Fax: 970-351-1762. *Application contact:* Linda Sisson, Graduate Student Admission Coordinator, 970-351-1807, Fax: 970-351-2371, E-mail: linda.sisson@unco.edu.
Website: http://www.unco.edu/nhs/sport-exercise-science/

University of Northern Iowa, Graduate College, College of Education, School of Kinesiology, Allied Health and Human Services, MA Program in Physical Education, Cedar Falls, IA 50614. Offers kinesiology (MA); teaching/coaching (MA). *Program availability:* Part-time, evening/weekend. *Degree requirements:* For master's, comprehensive exam, thesis or alternative. *Entrance requirements:* For master's, minimum GPA of 3.0. Additional exam requirements/recommendations for international students: Required—TOEFL (minimum score 500 paper-based; 61 iBT). Electronic applications accepted.

University of North Georgia, College of Education, Dahlonega, GA 30597. Offers early childhood education (M Ed); middle grades education (M Ed, MAT); physical education (MS); school leadership (Ed S); secondary education (M Ed), including English education, history education, mathematics education, physical education. *Accreditation:* NCATE. *Program availability:* Part-time, evening/weekend, online learning. *Faculty:* 16 full-time (12 women), 3 part-time/adjunct (all women). *Students:* 11 full-time (8 women), 146 part-time (107 women); includes 19 minority (10 Black or African American, non-Hispanic/Latino; 2 Asian, non-Hispanic/Latino; 6 Hispanic/Latino; 1 Two or more races, non-Hispanic/Latino). Average age 28. 77 applicants, 83% accepted, 47 enrolled. In 2016, 79 master's awarded. *Degree requirements:* For master's, comprehensive exam, thesis optional. *Entrance requirements:* For master's, GRE or MAT, GACE, minimum GPA of 2.75; for Ed S, GRE General Test or MAT, 3 years of teaching experience, master's degree, minimum graduate GPA of 3.25, leadership position in the school. Additional exam requirements/recommendations for international students: Required—TOEFL (minimum score 550 paper-based; 79 iBT), IELTS (minimum score 6.5). *Application deadline:* For fall admission, 8/1 priority date for domestic students, 7/1 priority date for international students; for spring admission, 12/1 priority date for domestic students, 11/1 priority date for international students. Applications are processed on a rolling basis. Application fee: $40. Electronic applications accepted. *Expenses:* Contact institution. *Financial support:* Teaching assistantships, career-related internships or fieldwork, scholarships/grants, and unspecified assistantships available. Financial award application deadline: 5/1; financial award applicants required to submit CSS PROFILE or FAFSA. *Unit head:* Dr. Susan Ayers, Dean, College of Education, 706-864-1998, E-mail: susan.ayres@ung.edu. *Application contact:* Regina Boling, Teacher Education Graduate Admissions, 706-864-1533, E-mail: regina.boling@ung.edu.
Website: http://ung.edu/college-of-education/

University of Rhode Island, Graduate School, College of Health Sciences, Department of Kinesiology, Kingston, RI 02881. Offers cultural studies of sport and physical culture (MS); exercise science (MS), psychosocial/behavioral aspects of physical activity (MS). *Accreditation:* NCATE. *Program availability:* Part-time. *Faculty:* 15 full-time (9 women). *Students:* 16 full-time (9 women), 8 part-time (5 women); includes 4 minority (1 Black or African American, non-Hispanic/Latino; 1 Asian, non-Hispanic/Latino; 2 Hispanic/Latino). In 2016, 8 master's awarded. *Degree requirements:* For master's, thesis optional. *Entrance requirements:* For master's, GRE, 2 letters of recommendation. Additional exam requirements/recommendations for international students: Required—TOEFL. *Application deadline:* For fall admission, 7/15 for domestic students, 2/1 for international students; for spring admission, 11/15 for domestic students, 7/15 for international students. Application fee: $65. Electronic applications accepted. *Expenses:* Tuition, state resident: full-time $11,796; part-time $655 per credit. Tuition, nonresident: full-time $24,206; part-time $1345 per credit. *Required fees:* $1546; $44 per credit. One-time fee: $155 full-time; $35 part-time. *Financial support:* In 2016–17, 5 teaching assistantships with tuition reimbursements (averaging $10,740 per year) were awarded; research assistantships also available. Financial award application deadline: 7/15; financial award applicants required to submit FAFSA. *Unit head:* Dr. Disa Hatfield, Interim Chair, 401-874-5183, E-mail: doch@uri.edu. *Application contact:* Dr. Matthew Delmonico, Graduate Program Director, 401-874-5440, E-mail: delmonico@uri.edu.
Website: http://web.uri.edu/kinesiology/

University of Rio Grande, Graduate School, Rio Grande, OH 45674. Offers athletic coaching leadership (M Ed); educational leadership (M Ed); integrated arts (M Ed); intervention specialist in early childhood (M Ed); intervention specialist in mild/moderate (M Ed). *Accreditation:* NCATE. *Program availability:* Part-time. *Degree requirements:* For master's, final research project, portfolio. *Entrance requirements:* For master's, minimum GPA of 2.7 in major, 2.5 overall. Additional exam requirements/recommendations for international students: Required—TOEFL. *Application deadline:*

Physical Education

Applications are processed on a rolling basis. Application fee: $20. *Financial support:* Career-related internships or fieldwork available. Support available to part-time students. Financial award application deadline: 7/1; financial award applicants required to submit FAFSA. *Faculty research:* Interagency collaboration, reading and mathematics, learning styles, college access, literacy. *Unit head:* Dr. Greg Miller, Director, 740-245-7030, E-mail: gmiller@rio.edu. *Application contact:* Nancy Downs, Secretary, 740-245-7328, Fax: 740-245-7175, E-mail: ndowns@rio.edu.

University of South Alabama, College of Education and Professional Studies, Department of Health, Kinesiology, and Sport, Mobile, AL 36688. Offers exercise science (MS); health education (M Ed); physical education (M Ed); sport management (MS). *Accreditation:* NCATE (one or more programs are accredited). *Program availability:* Part-time. *Faculty:* 7 full-time (2 women). *Students:* 50 full-time (15 women), 4 part-time (2 women); includes 21 minority (17 Black or African American, non-Hispanic/Latino; 1 Asian, non-Hispanic/Latino; 1 Hispanic/Latino; 2 Two or more races, non-Hispanic/Latino), 3 international. Average age 27. 53 applicants, 57% accepted, 28 enrolled. In 2016, 16 master's awarded. *Degree requirements:* For master's, comprehensive exam, thesis optional. *Entrance requirements:* For master's, GRE General Test or MAT, Alabama Class B certificate or the equivalent (for students seeking the master's-level/Class A certification). Additional exam requirements/recommendations for international students: Required—TOEFL. *Application deadline:* For fall admission, 7/15 priority date for domestic students, 6/15 priority date for international students; for spring admission, 11/15 priority date for domestic students, 10/15 priority date for international students; for summer admission, 4/15 for domestic students. Applications are processed on a rolling basis. Application fee: $35. Electronic applications accepted. *Expenses:* Tuition, state resident: full-time $9768; part-time $407 per credit hour. Tuition, nonresident: full-time $19,536; part-time $814 per credit hour. *Financial support:* Fellowships, research assistantships, teaching assistantships with partial tuition reimbursements, career-related internships or fieldwork, Federal Work-Study, institutionally sponsored loans, scholarships/grants, and unspecified assistantships available. Support available to part-time students. Financial award application deadline: 5/31; financial award applicants required to submit FAFSA. *Unit head:* Dr. John Kovaleski, Department Chair, 251-461-1622, Fax: 251-460-7252, E-mail: jkovales@southalabama.edu. *Application contact:* Dr. Susan Santoli, Director of Graduate Studies, 251-380-2738, Fax: 251-380-2758, E-mail: ssantoli@southalabama.edu.
Website: http://www.southalabama.edu/colleges/coe/hks/index.html

University of South Carolina, The Graduate School, College of Education, Department of Physical Education, Columbia, SC 29208. Offers IMA, MAT, MS, PhD. *Program availability:* Part-time. *Degree requirements:* For master's, comprehensive exam, thesis (for some programs); for doctorate, comprehensive exam, thesis/dissertation. *Entrance requirements:* For master's, GRE General Test, or Miller Analogies Test, writing sample, letter of intent, letters of recommendation; for doctorate, GRE General Test or Miller Analogies Test, writing sample, interview, letter of intent, letters of recommendation. *Faculty research:* Teaching/learning processes, anthropometric measurement, growth and development, motor development.

University of Southern Mississippi, Graduate School, College of Health, School of Kinesiology, Hattiesburg, MS 39406. Offers kinesiology (MS, PhD), including biomechanics (PhD), exercise physiology (PhD), exercise science (MS), physical education (MS), sport pedagogy (PhD); sport coaching education (MS). *Program availability:* Part-time, evening/weekend. *Degree requirements:* For master's, comprehensive exam, thesis optional; for doctorate, comprehensive exam, thesis/dissertation. *Entrance requirements:* For master's, GRE General Test, minimum GPA of 2.75 in last 60 hours; for doctorate, GRE General Test, minimum GPA of 3.5. Additional exam requirements/recommendations for international students: Required—TOEFL, IELTS. *Application deadline:* For fall admission, 3/1 priority date for domestic students, 3/1 for international students; for spring admission, 1/10 priority date for domestic and international students. Applications are processed on a rolling basis. Application fee: $60. Electronic applications accepted. *Expenses: Tuition, area resident:* Full-time $15,708; part-time $437 per credit hour. *Financial support:* Fellowships, research assistantships with full tuition reimbursements, teaching assistantships with full tuition reimbursements, career-related internships or fieldwork, Federal Work-Study, institutionally sponsored loans, scholarships/grants, health care benefits, and unspecified assistantships available. Financial award application deadline: 3/15; financial award applicants required to submit FAFSA. *Faculty research:* Exercise physiology, health behaviors, resource management, activity interaction, site development. *Unit head:* Dr. Scott Piland, Director, 601-266-5386, Fax: 601-266-4445, E-mail: scott.piland@usm.edu. *Application contact:* Dr. Trenton Gould, Dean, College of Health, 601-266-6339, Fax: 601-266-4445.
Website: https://www.usm.edu/kinesiology

The University of Tennessee at Chattanooga, Department of Health and Human Performance, Chattanooga, TN 37403. Offers athletic training (MSAT); health and human performance (MS). *Faculty:* 4 full-time (1 woman). *Students:* 43 full-time (32 women); includes 7 minority (2 Black or African American, non-Hispanic/Latino; 3 Hispanic/Latino; 2 Two or more races, non-Hispanic/Latino). Average age 23. 25 applicants, 92% accepted, 21 enrolled. In 2016, 21 master's awarded. *Degree requirements:* For master's, thesis or alternative, clinical rotations. *Entrance requirements:* For master's, GRE General Test, minimum GPA of 2.75 overall or 3.0 in last 60 hours; CPR and First Aid certification. Additional exam requirements/recommendations for international students: Required—TOEFL (minimum score 550 paper-based; 79 iBT), IELTS (minimum score 6). *Application deadline:* For fall admission, 6/15 priority date for domestic students, 7/1 for international students; for spring admission, 11/1 priority date for domestic students, 11/1 for international students. Applications are processed on a rolling basis. Application fee: $35 ($40 for international students). Electronic applications accepted. *Expenses:* $9,876 full-time in-state; $25,994 full-time out-of-state; $450 per credit part-time in-state; $1,345 per credit part-time out-of-state. *Financial support:* In 2016–17, 5 research assistantships with tuition reimbursements, 4 teaching assistantships with tuition reimbursements were awarded; career-related internships or fieldwork, scholarships/grants, and unspecified assistantships also available. Support available to part-time students. Financial award application deadline: 7/1; financial award applicants required to submit FAFSA. *Faculty research:* Therapeutic exercise, lumbar spine biomechanics, physical activity epidemiology, functional rehabilitation outcomes, metabolic health. *Unit head:* Dr. Marisa Colston, Interim Department Head, 423-425-4743, E-mail: marisa-colston@utc.edu. *Application contact:* Dr. Joanne Romagni, Dean of the Graduate School, 423-425-4478, Fax: 423-425-5223, E-mail: joanne-romagni@utc.edu.
Website: https://www.utc.edu/health-human-performance/

The University of Tennessee at Martin, Graduate Programs, College of Education, Health and Behavioral Sciences, Program in Teaching, Martin, TN 38238. Offers curriculum and instruction (MS Ed), including 7-12, K-6; initial licensure (MS Ed), including elementary education, secondary education; initial licensure K-12 (MS Ed), including physical education, special education; interdisciplinary (MS Ed). *Students:* 21 full-time (14 women), 125 part-time (87 women); includes 22 minority (18 Black or African American, non-Hispanic/Latino; 3 Hispanic/Latino; 1 Two or more races, non-Hispanic/Latino). 115 applicants, 81% accepted, 51 enrolled. In 2016, 26 master's awarded. *Expenses:* Tuition, state resident: full-time $8254; part-time $459 per credit hour. Tuition, nonresident: full-time $22,198; part-time $1234 per credit hour. *Required fees:* $79 per credit hour. Part-time tuition and fees vary according to course load and campus/location. *Faculty research:* Special education, science/math/technology, school reform, reading. *Unit head:* Cynthia West, Dean, 731-881-7125, Fax: 731-881-7975, E-mail: cwest@utm.edu. *Application contact:* Jolene L. Cunningham, Student Services Specialist, 731-881-7012, Fax: 731-881-7499, E-mail: jcunningham@utm.edu.

The University of Texas at Austin, Graduate School, College of Education, Department of Curriculum and Instruction, Austin, TX 78712-1111. Offers bilingual/bicultural education (M Ed, MA, PhD); cultural studies in education (M Ed, MA, PhD); early childhood education (M Ed, MA, PhD); language and literacy studies (M Ed, PhD); learning technologies (M Ed, MA, PhD); physical education (M Ed, MA, PhD). Terminal master's awarded for partial completion of doctoral program. *Degree requirements:* For doctorate, thesis/dissertation. *Entrance requirements:* For master's and doctorate, GRE General Test. Electronic applications accepted.

The University of Toledo, College of Graduate Studies, Judith Herb College of Education, Department of Early Childhood, Physical and Special Education, Toledo, OH 43606-3390. Offers early childhood education (ME); physical education (ME); special education (ME). *Program availability:* Part-time. *Degree requirements:* For master's, thesis. *Entrance requirements:* For master's, minimum cumulative GPA of 2.7 for all previous academic work, letters of recommendation. Additional exam requirements/recommendations for international students: Required—TOEFL (minimum score 550 paper-based; 80 iBT). Electronic applications accepted.

University of Toronto, School of Graduate Studies, Faculty of Kinesiology and Physical Education, Toronto, ON M5S 1A1, Canada. Offers M Sc, PhD. *Degree requirements:* For master's, thesis, oral defense of thesis; for doctorate, comprehensive exam, defense of thesis. *Entrance requirements:* For master's, background in physical education and health, minimum B+ average in final year of undergraduate study, 2 letters of reference, resume, 2 writing samples; for doctorate, master's degree with successful defense of thesis, background in exercise sciences, minimum A- average, 2 letters of reference. Additional exam requirements/recommendations for international students: Required—TOEFL (minimum score 580 paper-based; 93 iBT), TWE (minimum score 5). Electronic applications accepted.

University of Victoria, Faculty of Graduate Studies, Faculty of Education, School of Exercise Science, Physical, and Health Education, Victoria, BC V8W 2Y2, Canada. Offers coaching studies (co-operative education) (M Ed); kinesiology (M Sc, MA); leisure service administration (MA); physical education (MA). *Program availability:* Part-time. *Degree requirements:* For master's, comprehensive exam (for some programs), thesis (for some programs). *Entrance requirements:* For master's, minimum B average. Additional exam requirements/recommendations for international students: Required—TOEFL (minimum score 575 paper-based), IELTS (minimum score 7). Electronic applications accepted. *Faculty research:* Children and exercise, mental skills in sports, teaching effectiveness, neural control of human movement, physical performance and health.

University of Virginia, Curry School of Education, Department of Kinesiology, Charlottesville, VA 22903. Offers M Ed, PhD. *Faculty:* 12 full-time (3 women). *Students:* 54 full-time (30 women), 8 part-time (5 women); includes 10 minority (1 Black or African American, non-Hispanic/Latino; 2 Asian, non-Hispanic/Latino; 5 Hispanic/Latino; 2 Two or more races, non-Hispanic/Latino), 1 international. Average age 25. 46 applicants, 61% accepted, 21 enrolled. In 2016, 42 master's awarded. *Entrance requirements:* For master's and doctorate, GRE General Test, 2 letters of recommendation. Additional exam requirements/recommendations for international students: Required—TOEFL (minimum score 600 paper-based; 90 iBT), IELTS (minimum score 7). *Application deadline:* Applications are processed on a rolling basis. Application fee: $60. Electronic applications accepted. *Expenses:* Tuition, state resident: full-time $15,026; part-time $834 per credit hour. Tuition, nonresident: full-time $25,168; part-time $1378 per credit hour. *Required fees:* $2654. *Financial support:* Applicants required to submit FAFSA. *Unit head:* Arthur L. Weltman, Chair, Kinesiology, 434-924-6191, E-mail: alw2v@virginia.edu. *Application contact:* Eric Molnar, Assistant Director, Admissions and Enrollment Reporting, 434-243-2085, E-mail: eric.molnar@virginia.edu.
Website: http://curry.virginia.edu/academics/department/kinesiology

University of Washington, Graduate School, College of Education, Seattle, WA 98195. Offers curriculum and instruction (M Ed, Ed D, PhD), including educational technology, general curriculum (Ed D, PhD), language, literacy, and culture, mathematics education, multicultural education, reading and language arts education (Ed D), science education, social studies education, teaching and curriculum (M Ed); educational leadership and policy studies (M Ed, Ed D, PhD), including administration (Ed D), educational policy, organization, and leadership (M Ed, PhD), higher education, leadership for learning (Ed D), social and cultural foundations of education (M Ed, PhD); educational psychology (M Ed, PhD), including educational psychology (PhD), human development and cognition (M Ed), learning sciences, measurement, statistics and research design (M Ed), school psychology (M Ed); instructional leadership (M Ed); intercollegiate athletic leadership (M Ed); special education (M Ed, Ed D, PhD), including early childhood special education (M Ed), emotional and behavioral disabilities (M Ed), learning disabilities (M Ed), low-incidence disabilities (M Ed), severe disabilities (M Ed), special education (Ed D, PhD); teacher education (MIT). *Accreditation:* APA. *Program availability:* Part-time, evening/weekend. *Degree requirements:* For master's, thesis optional; for doctorate, thesis/dissertation. *Entrance requirements:* For master's and doctorate, GRE General Test, minimum GPA of 3.0. Additional exam requirements/recommendations for international students: Required—TOEFL. Electronic applications accepted. *Faculty research:* School restructuring/effective schools, special education interventions, literacy and writing, technology, school partnerships, teacher preparation.

The University of West Alabama, School of Graduate Studies, College of Education, Department of Physical Education and Athletic Training, Livingston, AL 35470. Offers physical education (M Ed, MAT). *Program availability:* Part-time, evening/weekend. *Faculty:* 5 full-time (1 woman), 1 part-time/adjunct (0 women). *Students:* 77 (22 women); includes 34 minority (32 Black or African American, non-Hispanic/Latino; 1 American Indian or Alaska Native, non-Hispanic/Latino; 1 Hispanic/Latino). Average age 30. 33 applicants, 85% accepted, 24 enrolled. In 2016, 25 master's awarded. *Degree requirements:* For master's, comprehensive exam, thesis optional, field experience, internship. *Entrance requirements:* For master's, GRE General Test, MAT, minimum GPA of 2.75. Additional exam requirements/recommendations for international students: Required—TOEFL (minimum score 500 paper-based; 61 iBT). *Application deadline:* Applications are processed on a rolling basis. Application fee: $40. Electronic applications accepted. *Expenses:* Tuition, state resident: part-time $355 per credit hour. Tuition, nonresident: part-time $710 per credit hour. *Required fees:* $130 per semester. *Financial support:* Teaching assistantships, Federal Work-Study, scholarships/grants, and unspecified assistantships available. Support available to part-time students. Financial award applicants required to submit FAFSA. *Unit head:* Dr. R. T. Floyd, Chairperson, 205-652-3714, Fax: 205-652-3706, E-mail: rtf@uwa.edu. *Application*

contact: Dr. B. J. Kimbrough, Dean of Graduate Studies, 205-652-3647, Fax: 205-652-3670, E-mail: bkimbrough@uwa.edu.
Website: http://www.uwa.edu/peat/

University of West Florida, College of Education and Professional Studies, Ed D Programs, Specialization in Physical Education and Health, Pensacola, FL 32514-5750. Offers Ed D. *Program availability:* Part-time, evening/weekend. *Degree requirements:* For doctorate, comprehensive exam, thesis/dissertation. *Entrance requirements:* For doctorate, GRE, MAT, or GMAT, letter of intent; writing sample; three letters of recommendation; two completed disposition assessment forms; written statement of goals; interview with admissions committee. Additional exam requirements/recommendations for international students: Required—TOEFL (minimum score 550 paper-based). *Application deadline:* For fall admission, 6/1 for domestic and international students; for spring admission, 10/1 for domestic students. Applications are processed on a rolling basis. Application fee: $30. *Expenses:* Tuition, state resident: full-time $5316.12. Tuition, nonresident: full-time $11,308. *Required fees:* $583.92. Tuition and fees vary according to course load and program. *Unit head:* Dr. Pam Northrup, Interim Dean, 850-474-2769, Fax: 850-474-3205. *Application contact:* Terry McCray, Assistant Director of Graduate Admissions, 850-473-7718, Fax: 850-473-7714, E-mail: gradadmissions@uwf.edu.
Website: http://uwf.edu/edd/physicaled_health.cfm

University of West Florida, Usha Kundu, MD College of Health, Department of Exercise Science and Community Health, Pensacola, FL 32514-5750. Offers health promotion (MS); health, leisure, and exercise science (MS), including exercise science, physical education. *Program availability:* Part-time, evening/weekend. *Degree requirements:* For master's, thesis or alternative. *Entrance requirements:* For master's, GRE or MAT, official transcripts; minimum GPA of 3.0; letter of intent; three personal references; work experience as reflected in resume. Additional exam requirements/recommendations for international students: Required—TOEFL (minimum score 550 paper-based). *Application deadline:* For fall admission, 6/1 for domestic and international students; for spring admission, 10/1 for domestic and international students. Applications are processed on a rolling basis. Application fee: $30. *Expenses:* Tuition, state resident: full-time $5316.12. Tuition, nonresident: full-time $11,308. *Required fees:* $583.92. Tuition and fees vary according to course load and program. *Financial support:* Fellowships, research assistantships with partial tuition reimbursements, teaching assistantships with partial tuition reimbursements, tuition waivers (partial), and unspecified assistantships available. Financial award application deadline: 4/15; financial award applicants required to submit FAFSA. *Unit head:* Dr. John Todorovich, Chairperson, 850-473-7248, Fax: 850-474-2106. *Application contact:* Terry McCray, Assistant Director of Graduate Admissions, 850-473-7718, Fax: 850-473-7714, E-mail: gradadmissions@uwf.edu.
Website: http://uwf.edu/coh/departments/exercise-science-and-community-health/

University of Wisconsin–La Crosse, College of Science and Health, Department of Exercise and Sport Science, Program in Physical Education Teaching, La Crosse, WI 54601-3742. Offers adapted physical education (MS); adventure education (MS). *Program availability:* Part-time, evening/weekend. *Students:* 7 full-time (1 woman), 3 part-time (0 women). Average age 25. 8 applicants, 88% accepted. In 2016, 10 master's awarded. *Degree requirements:* For master's, thesis optional. *Entrance requirements:* For master's, minimum GPA of 3.0 during previous 2 years, 2.85 overall; BA in physical education. Additional exam requirements/recommendations for international students: Required—TOEFL (minimum score 550 paper-based; 79 iBT). *Application deadline:* Applications are processed on a rolling basis. Electronic applications accepted. *Financial support:* Federal Work-Study, scholarships/grants, health care benefits, and tuition waivers (partial) available. Support available to part-time students. Financial award application deadline: 3/15; financial award applicants required to submit FAFSA. *Unit head:* Dr. Jooyeon Jin, Program Director, 608-785-8182, E-mail: jjin@uwlax.edu. *Application contact:* Brandon Schaller, Senior Graduate Student Status Examiner, 608-785-8941, E-mail: admissions@uwlax.edu.
Website: http://www.uwlax.edu/sah/ess/pe/

University of Wyoming, College of Health Sciences, Division of Kinesiology and Health, Laramie, WY 82071. Offers MS. *Accreditation:* NCATE. *Program availability:* Part-time, online learning. *Degree requirements:* For master's, comprehensive exam (for some programs), thesis (for some programs). *Entrance requirements:* For master's, GRE General Test, minimum GPA of 3.0. Additional exam requirements/recommendations for international students: Required—TOEFL. Electronic applications accepted. *Faculty research:* Teacher effectiveness, effects of exercising on heart function, physiological responses of overtraining, psychological benefits of physical activity, health behavior.

Utah State University, School of Graduate Studies, Emma Eccles Jones College of Education and Human Services, Department of Health, Physical Education and Recreation, Logan, UT 84322. Offers M Ed, MS. *Program availability:* Part-time, evening/weekend, online learning. *Degree requirements:* For master's, thesis (for some programs). *Entrance requirements:* For master's, GRE General Test or MAT, minimum GPA of 3.0. Additional exam requirements/recommendations for international students: Required—TOEFL. *Faculty research:* Sport psychology intervention, motor learning biomechanics, pedagogy, physiology.

Wayne State College, Department of Health, Human Performance and Sport, Wayne, NE 68787. Offers exercise science (MSE); organizational management (MS), including sport management. *Program availability:* Part-time, evening/weekend. *Degree requirements:* For master's, comprehensive exam, thesis optional. *Entrance requirements:* For master's, GRE General Test, minimum GPA of 3.0. Additional exam requirements/recommendations for international students: Required—TOEFL (minimum score 550 paper-based). Electronic applications accepted.

Wayne State University, College of Education, Division of Kinesiology, Health and Sports Studies, Detroit, MI 48202. Offers health education (M Ed); kinesiology (M Ed, PhD), including exercise and sport science (PhD), physical education and physical activity leadership (PhD); sports administration (MA). *Program availability:* Part-time, 100% online. *Faculty:* 10. *Students:* 57 full-time (30 women), 131 part-time (68 women); includes 72 minority (63 Black or African American, non-Hispanic/Latino; 1 American Indian or Alaska Native, non-Hispanic/Latino; 1 Asian, non-Hispanic/Latino; 3 Hispanic/Latino; 4 Two or more races, non-Hispanic/Latino), 10 international. Average age 29. 160 applicants, 56% accepted, 51 enrolled. In 2016, 66 master's awarded. *Degree requirements:* For master's, thesis (for some programs); for doctorate, thesis/dissertation. *Entrance requirements:* For master's, minimum undergraduate GPA of 3.0; undergraduate degree directly relating to the field of specialization being applied for or one accompanied by extensive educational background in closely-related field; teaching certificates in specific areas (for some programs); for doctorate, minimum undergraduate GPA of 3.0; undergraduate degree directly relating to the field of specialization being applied for or one accompanied by extensive educational background in closely-related field. Additional exam requirements/recommendations for international students: Required—TOEFL (minimum score 79 iBT), TWE (minimum score 5.5), Michigan English Language Assessment Battery (minimum score 85); Recommended—IELTS (minimum score 6.5). *Application deadline:* For fall admission, 6/1 priority date for domestic students, 5/1 priority date for international students; for winter admission, 10/1 priority date for domestic students, 9/1 priority date for international students; for spring admission, 2/1 priority date for domestic students, 1/1 priority date for international students. Application fee: $50. Electronic applications accepted. *Expenses:* $18,522 per year resident tuition and fees, $35,715 per year non-resident tuition and fees. *Financial support:* In 2016–17, 49 students received support, including 6 research assistantships with tuition reimbursements available (averaging $17,994 per year); fellowships with tuition reimbursements available, scholarships/grants, health care benefits, and unspecified assistantships also available. Support available to part-time students. Financial award applicants required to submit FAFSA. *Faculty research:* Exercise and sport science, nutrition and physical activity interventions, school and community health, obesity prevention. *Total annual research expenditures:* $974,985. *Unit head:* Dr. Nate McCaughtry, Assistant Dean, Division of Kinesiology, Health and Sport Studies/Director, Center for School Health, 313-577-0014, Fax: 313-577-5002, E-mail: aj4391@wayne.edu. *Application contact:* Janice Green, Assistant Dean, 313-577-1605, E-mail: jwgreen@wayne.edu.
Website: http://coe.wayne.edu/kinesiology/index.php

West Chester University of Pennsylvania, College of Health Sciences, Department of Kinesiology, West Chester, PA 19383. Offers adapted physical education (Certificate); exercise and sport physiology (MS), including athletic training, exercise and sport physiology; general physical education (MS); sport management and athletics (MPA), including administration. *Program availability:* Part-time, evening/weekend. *Faculty:* 9 full-time (6 women). *Students:* 34 full-time (22 women), 21 part-time (7 women); includes 5 minority (4 Black or African American, non-Hispanic/Latino; 1 Hispanic/Latino), 1 international. Average age 26. 68 applicants, 85% accepted, 30 enrolled. In 2016, 23 master's, 1 other advanced degree awarded. *Degree requirements:* For master's, thesis or research report (for MS); two internships and capstone course that includes a research project or thesis (for MPA). *Entrance requirements:* For master's, GRE (for MS), 2 letters of recommendation, statement of goals; transcripts (for MS); resume (for MPA). Additional exam requirements/recommendations for international students: Required—TOEFL or IELTS. *Application deadline:* For fall admission, 5/15 for international students; for spring admission, 10/15 for international students. Applications are processed on a rolling basis. Application fee: $50. Electronic applications accepted. *Expenses:* Tuition, state resident: full-time $8694; part-time $483 per credit. Tuition, nonresident: full-time $13,050; part-time $725 per credit. *Required fees:* $2399; $119.05 per credit. Tuition and fees vary according to campus/location and program. *Financial support:* Scholarships/grants and unspecified assistantships available. Financial award application deadline: 2/15; financial award applicants required to submit FAFSA. *Faculty research:* Metabolism during exercise, biomechanics, rating of perceived exertion, motor learning, environmental physiology. *Unit head:* Dr. Frank Fry, Chair/Graduate Coordinator for the MS in General Physical Education Program, 610-436-2610, Fax: 610-436-2860, E-mail: ffry@wcupa.edu. *Application contact:* Office of Graduate Studies and Extended Education, 610-436-2943, Fax: 610-436-2763, E-mail: gradstudy@wcupa.edu.
Website: http://www.wcupa.edu/healthsciences/kinesiology/

Western Kentucky University, Graduate Studies, College of Health and Human Services, Department of Kinesiology, Recreation and Sport, Bowling Green, KY 42101. Offers athletic administration and coaching (MS); physical education (MS); recreation and sport administration (MS). *Program availability:* Part-time, evening/weekend, online learning. *Degree requirements:* For master's, comprehensive exam, thesis optional. *Entrance requirements:* For master's, GRE General Test, minimum GPA of 2.75. Additional exam requirements/recommendations for international students: Required—TOEFL (minimum score 555 paper-based; 79 iBT). *Faculty research:* Orthopedic rehabilitation, fitness center coordination, heat acclimation, biomechanical and physiological parameters.

Western Michigan University, Graduate College, College of Education and Human Development, Department of Health, Physical Education and Recreation, Kalamazoo, MI 49008. Offers athletic training (MS), including exercise physiology; sport management (MA), including pedagogy, special physical education.

Western Washington University, Graduate School, College of Humanities and Social Sciences, Department of Physical Education, Health, and Recreation, Bellingham, WA 98225-5996. Offers exercise science (MS); sport psychology (MS). *Program availability:* Part-time. *Degree requirements:* For master's, thesis. *Entrance requirements:* For master's, GRE General Test, minimum GPA of 3.0 in last 60 semester hours or last 90 quarter hours. Additional exam requirements/recommendations for international students: Required—TOEFL (minimum score 567 paper-based). Electronic applications accepted. *Faculty research:* Spinal motor control, biomechanics/kinesiology, biomechanics of aging, mobility of older adults, fall prevention, exercise interventions and function, magnesium and inspiratory muscle training (IMT).

Westfield State University, College of Graduate and Continuing Education, Department of Education, Westfield, MA 01086. Offers early childhood education (M Ed); elementary education (M Ed); reading specialist (M Ed); secondary education (M Ed), including biology teacher education, chemistry teacher education, general science teacher education, history teacher education, mathematics teacher education, physical education teacher education; special education (M Ed), including moderate disabilities, 5-12, moderate disabilities, preK-8; vocational technical education (M Ed). *Accreditation:* NCATE. *Program availability:* Part-time, evening/weekend. *Faculty:* 16 full-time (7 women), 33 part-time/adjunct (24 women). *Students:* 21 full-time (10 women), 168 part-time (126 women); includes 6 minority (2 Black or African American, non-Hispanic/Latino; 2 Hispanic/Latino; 2 Two or more races, non-Hispanic/Latino), 1 international. Average age 32. 47 applicants, 85% accepted, 30 enrolled. In 2016, 51 master's awarded. *Degree requirements:* For master's, comprehensive exam, practicum. *Entrance requirements:* For master's, GRE General Test or MAT, minimum undergraduate GPA of 2.8. Additional exam requirements/recommendations for international students: Recommended—TOEFL (minimum score 550 paper-based; 70 iBT). *Application deadline:* For fall admission, 6/30 for domestic students; for spring admission, 10/31 for domestic students; for summer admission, 3/31 for domestic students. Applications are processed on a rolling basis. Application fee: $50. Electronic applications accepted. *Expenses:* Tuition, state resident: part-time $318 per semester hour. Tuition, nonresident: part-time $318 per semester hour. *Required fees:* $75 per semester. Tuition and fees vary according to course load and program. *Financial support:* Unspecified assistantships and SOS scholarships for education majors only available. Financial award application deadline: 3/1; financial award applicants required to submit FAFSA. *Faculty research:* Collaborative teacher education, developmental early childhood education. *Unit head:* Dr. Sandra Berkowitz, Department Chair, 413-572-5323, E-mail: sberkowitz@westfield.ma.edu. *Application contact:* Shelly Henrichon, Coordinator of DGCE Admissions, 413-572-8022, Fax: 413-572-5227, E-mail: mhenrichon@westfield.ma.edu.
Website: http://www.westfield.ma.edu/academics/degrees/education-graduate-programs

Westfield State University, College of Graduate and Continuing Education, Department of Education, Programs in Secondary Education, Program in Physical Education Teacher Education, Westfield, MA 01086. Offers secondary education-physical education (M Ed). *Program availability:* Part-time, evening/weekend. *Faculty:* 2

part-time/adjunct (0 women). *Students:* 4 full-time (1 woman), 13 part-time (7 women). Average age 23. 4 applicants, 100% accepted, 3 enrolled. In 2016, 4 master's awarded. *Degree requirements:* For master's, comprehensive exam, thesis (for some programs). *Entrance requirements:* For master's, GRE General Test or MAT, minimum undergraduate GPA of 2.8. Additional exam requirements/recommendations for international students: Recommended—TOEFL (minimum score 550 paper-based; 79 iBT). *Application deadline:* For fall admission, 6/30 for domestic students; for spring admission, 10/31 for domestic students; for summer admission, 3/31 for domestic students. Applications are processed on a rolling basis. Application fee: $50. *Expenses:* Tuition, state resident: part-time $318 per semester hour. Tuition, nonresident: part-time $318 per semester hour. *Required fees:* $75 per semester. Tuition and fees vary according to course load and program. *Financial support:* Unspecified assistantships and SOS scholarships for education majors only available. Financial award application deadline: 3/1; financial award applicants required to submit FAFSA. *Unit head:* Dr. Sandra Berkowitz, Chair, 413-572-5323. *Application contact:* Shelly Henrichon, Coordinator of DGCE Admissions, 413-572-8022, Fax: 413-572-5227, E-mail: mhenrichon@westfield.ma.edu.

West Virginia University, College of Physical Activity and Sport Sciences, Morgantown, WV 26506-6116. Offers athletic training (MS); coaching and sport education (MS); coaching and teaching studies (Ed D); physical education/teacher education (MS, PhD), including curriculum and instruction (PhD), physical education supervision (PhD); sport and exercise psychology (MS, PhD); sport coaching (MS); sport management (MS). *Degree requirements:* For doctorate, comprehensive exam, thesis/dissertation, oral exam. *Entrance requirements:* For master's, GRE or MAT, minimum GPA of 3.0; for doctorate, GRE General Test or MAT, minimum GPA of 3.5. Additional exam requirements/recommendations for international students: Required—TOEFL (minimum score 550 paper-based). Electronic applications accepted. *Faculty research:* Sport psychosociology, teacher education, exercise psychology, counseling.

Wilfrid Laurier University, Faculty of Graduate and Postdoctoral Studies, Faculty of Science, Department of Kinesiology and Physical Education, Waterloo, ON N2L 3C5, Canada. Offers physical activity and health (M Sc). *Degree requirements:* For master's, thesis. *Entrance requirements:* For master's, honours degree in kinesiology, health, physical education with a minimum B+ in kinesiology and health-related courses. Additional exam requirements/recommendations for international students: Required—TOEFL (minimum score 89 iBT). Electronic applications accepted. *Faculty research:* Biomechanics, health, exercise physiology, motor control, sport psychology.

William Woods University, Graduate and Adult Studies, Fulton, MO 65251-1098. Offers administration (M Ed, Ed S); athletic/activities administration (M Ed); curriculum and instruction (M Ed, Ed S); educational leadership (Ed D); equestrian education (M Ed); health management (MBA); human resources (MBA); leadership (MBA); marketing, advertising, and public relations (MBA); teaching and technology (M Ed). *Program availability:* Part-time, evening/weekend. *Degree requirements:* For master's, capstone course (MBA), action research (M Ed); for Ed S, field experience. *Entrance requirements:* Additional exam requirements/recommendations for international students: Required—TOEFL (minimum score 550 paper-based). Electronic applications accepted. *Expenses:* Contact institution.

Winthrop University, College of Education, Program in Physical Education, Rock Hill, SC 29733. Offers MAT. *Program availability:* Part-time. *Degree requirements:* For master's, comprehensive exam, thesis optional. *Entrance requirements:* For master's, GRE General Test or PRAXIS. Additional exam requirements/recommendations for international students: Required—TOEFL (minimum score 550 paper-based; 79 iBT), IELTS (minimum score 6). Electronic applications accepted. *Expenses:* Tuition, state resident: full-time $14,312; part-time $599 per credit hour. Tuition, nonresident: full-time $27,570; part-time $1153 per credit hour.

Section 31
Sports Management

This section contains a directory of institutions offering graduate work in sports management. Additional information about programs listed in the directory may be obtained by writing directly to the dean of a graduate school or chair of a department at the address given in the directory.

For programs offering related work, see also in this book *Business Administration and Management, Education,* and *Physical Education and Kinesiology.*

CONTENTS

Sports Management

Adelphi University, Robert B. Willumstad School of Business, MBA Program, Garden City, NY 11530-0701. Offers accounting (MBA); finance (MBA); health services administration (MBA); human resource management (MBA); management (MBA); management information systems (MBA); marketing (MBA); sport management (MBA). *Accreditation:* AACSB. *Program availability:* Part-time, evening/weekend. *Students:* 172 full-time (74 women), 129 part-time (66 women); includes 30 minority (9 Black or African American, non-Hispanic/Latino; 11 Asian, non-Hispanic/Latino; 9 Hispanic/Latino; 1 Two or more races, non-Hispanic/Latino), 29 international. Average age 32. 4 applicants. In 2016, 130 master's awarded. *Degree requirements:* For master's, capstone course. *Entrance requirements:* For master's, GMAT, 2 letters of recommendation. Additional exam requirements/recommendations for international students: Required—TOEFL (minimum score 550 paper-based; 80 iBT), IELTS (minimum score 6.5). *Application deadline:* For fall admission, 4/1 for international students; for spring admission, 11/1 for international students. Applications are processed on a rolling basis. Application fee: $50. Electronic applications accepted. *Expenses:* Contact institution. *Financial support:* Research assistantships with partial tuition reimbursements, career-related internships or fieldwork, Federal Work-Study, institutionally sponsored loans, scholarships/grants, tuition waivers (partial), and unspecified assistantships available. Financial award application deadline: 3/1; financial award applicants required to submit FAFSA. *Faculty research:* Supply chain management, distribution channels, productivity benchmark analysis, data envelopment analysis, financial portfolio analysis. *Unit head:* Dr. Rakesh Gupta, Associate Dean, 516-877-4629. *Application contact:* Christine Murphy, Director of Admissions, 516-877-3050, Fax: 516-877-3039, E-mail: graduateadmissions@adelphi.edu.
Website: http://business.adelphi.edu/degree-programs/graduate-degree-programs/m-b-a/

American Public University System, AMU/APU Graduate Programs, Charles Town, WV 25414. Offers accounting (MBA, MS); applied business analytics (MBA, MS); criminal justice (MA), including business administration, emergency and disaster management, general (MA, MS); educational leadership (M Ed); emergency and disaster management (MA); entrepreneurship (MBA); environmental policy and management (MS), including environmental planning, environmental sustainability, fish and wildlife management, general (MA, MS), global environmental management; finance (MBA); general (MBA); government contracting and acquisition (MBA); health care administration (MBA); health information management (MS); history (MA), including American history, ancient and classical history, European history, global history, public history; homeland security (MA), including business administration, counterterrorism studies, criminal justice, cyber, emergency management and public health, intelligence studies, transportation security; homeland security resource allocation (MBA); humanities (MA); information technology (MS), including digital forensics, enterprise software development, information assurance and security, IT project management; information technology management (MBA); intelligence studies (MA), including criminal intelligence, cyber, general (MA, MS), homeland security, intelligence analysis, intelligence collection, intelligence management, intelligence operations, terrorism studies; international relations and conflict resolution (MA), including comparative and security issues, conflict resolution, international and transnational security issues, peacekeeping; legal studies (MA); management (MA), including strategic consulting; marketing (MBA); military history (MA), including American military history, American Revolution, civil war, war since 1945, World War II; military studies (MA), including joint warfare, strategic leadership; national security studies (MA), including cyber, general (MA, MS), homeland security, regional security studies, security and intelligence analysis, terrorism studies; nonprofit management (MBA); political science (MA), including American politics and government, comparative government and development, general (MA, MS), international relations, public policy; psychology (MA); public administration (MPA), including disaster management, environmental policy, health policy, human resources, national security, organizational management, security management; public health (MPH); reverse logistics management (MA); security management (MA); space studies (MS), including aerospace science, general (MA, MS), planetary science; sports and health sciences (MS); sports management (MBA); teaching (M Ed), including autism spectrum disorder, curriculum and instruction for elementary teachers, elementary reading, English language learners, instructional leadership, online learning, special education, STEAM (STEM plus the arts); transportation and logistics management (MA). *Program availability:* Part-time, evening/weekend, online only, 100% online. *Faculty:* 401 full-time (228 women), 1,678 part-time/adjunct (781 women). *Students:* 378 full-time (184 women), 8,455 part-time (3,484 women); includes 2,972 minority (1,552 Black or African American, non-Hispanic/Latino; 52 American Indian or Alaska Native, non-Hispanic/Latino; 211 Asian, non-Hispanic/Latino; 791 Hispanic/Latino; 70 Native Hawaiian or other Pacific Islander, non-Hispanic/Latino; 296 Two or more races, non-Hispanic/Latino), 109 international. Average age 37. In 2016, 3,185 master's awarded. *Degree requirements:* For master's, comprehensive exam or practicum. *Entrance requirements:* For master's, official transcript showing earned bachelor's degree from institution accredited by recognized accrediting body. Additional exam requirements/recommendations for international students: Required—TOEFL (minimum score 550 paper-based), IELTS (minimum score 6.5). *Application deadline:* Applications are processed on a rolling basis. Application fee: $0. Electronic applications accepted. *Expenses: Tuition:* Part-time $350 per credit hour. *Required fees:* $50 per course. *Financial support:* Scholarships/grants available. Financial award applicants required to submit FAFSA. *Unit head:* Dr. Karan Powell, President, 877-468-6268, Fax: 304-724-3780. *Application contact:* Terry Grant, Vice President of Enrollment Management, 877-468-6268, Fax: 304-724-3780, E-mail: info@apus.edu.
Website: http://www.apus.edu

American University, School of Professional and Extended Studies, Washington, DC 20016. Offers healthcare management (MS, Graduate Certificate); human resource analytics and management (Graduate Certificate); measurement and evaluation (MS); project monitoring and evaluation (Graduate Certificate); sports analytics and management (MS, Graduate Certificate). *Program availability:* 100% online. *Faculty:* 28 full-time (12 women), 8 part-time/adjunct (4 women). *Students:* 26 part-time (22 women); includes 1 minority (American Indian or Alaska Native, non-Hispanic/Latino), 2 international. Average age 38. 37 applicants, 100% accepted, 22 enrolled. *Entrance requirements:* For master's, statement of purpose, current resume/curriculum vitae, official transcripts from all academic institutions, letters of recommendation. Additional exam requirements/recommendations for international students: Required—TOEFL or IELTS. *Application deadline:* Applications are processed on a rolling basis. Application fee: $55. Electronic applications accepted. *Expenses:* $1,579 per credit; $690 mandatory fees; some programs charge different fee for spring enrollment. *Financial support:* Applicants required to submit FAFSA. *Unit head:* Carola Weil, Dean, 202-885-5990, Fax: 202-895-4960, E-mail: weil@american.edu. *Application contact:* Heather Broberg, Assistant Director for Recruitment and Admission, 202-895-4953, E-mail: broberg@american.edu.
Website: http://www.american.edu/spexs/

Angelo State University, College of Graduate Studies and Research, Archer College of Health and Human Services, Department of Kinesiology, San Angelo, TX 76909. Offers coaching, sport, recreation and fitness administration (M Ed). *Program availability:* Part-time, evening/weekend. *Students:* 9 full-time (4 women), 43 part-time (18 women); includes 18 minority (9 Black or African American, non-Hispanic/Latino; 9 Hispanic/Latino), 3 international. Average age 27. *Degree requirements:* For master's, comprehensive exam. *Entrance requirements:* Additional exam requirements/recommendations for international students: Required—TOEFL or IELTS. *Application deadline:* For fall admission, 7/15 priority date for domestic students, 6/10 for international students; for spring admission, 12/1 priority date for domestic students, 11/1 for international students. Applications are processed on a rolling basis. Application fee: $40 ($50 for international students). Electronic applications accepted. *Expenses:* Tuition, state resident: full-time $3726; part-time $2484 per year. Tuition, nonresident: full-time $10,746; part-time $7164 per year. *Required fees:* $2538; $1702 per unit. *Financial support:* Career-related internships or fieldwork, Federal Work-Study, scholarships/grants, and unspecified assistantships available. Support available to part-time students. Financial award application deadline: 3/1; financial award applicants required to submit FAFSA. *Unit head:* Dr. Steven Snowden, Chair, 325-486-6178, Fax: 325-942-2129, E-mail: steven.snowden@angelo.edu. *Application contact:* Dr. Warren Simpson, Graduate Advisor, 325-942-2173 Ext. 224, Fax: 325-942-2129, E-mail: warren.simpson@angelo.edu.
Website: http://www.angelo.edu/dept/kinesiology/

Arkansas State University, Graduate School, College of Education and Behavioral Science, Department of Health, Physical Education, and Sport Sciences, State University, AR 72467. Offers exercise science (MS); physical education (MSE, SCCT); sports administration (MS). *Program availability:* Part-time. *Degree requirements:* For master's, comprehensive exam, thesis or alternative; for SCCT, comprehensive exam. *Entrance requirements:* For master's, GRE General Test or MAT, appropriate bachelor's degree, official transcripts, immunization records, statement of goals, letters of recommendation; for SCCT, GRE General Test or MAT, interview, master's degree, official transcript, immunization records. Additional exam requirements/recommendations for international students: Required—TOEFL (minimum score 550 paper-based; 79 iBT), IELTS (minimum score 6), PTE (minimum score 56). Electronic applications accepted.

Auburn University at Montgomery, College of Education, Department of Kinesiology, Montgomery, AL 36124-4023. Offers exercise science (M Ed); physical education (Ed S); sport management (M Ed). *Faculty:* 6 full-time (2 women), 2 part-time/adjunct (both women). *Students:* 23 full-time (14 women), 19 part-time (9 women); includes 10 minority (9 Black or African American, non-Hispanic/Latino; 1 Hispanic/Latino), 2 international. Average age 28. *Entrance requirements:* Additional exam requirements/recommendations for international students: Recommended—TOEFL (minimum score 500 paper-based; 61 iBT), IELTS (minimum score 5.5), TSE (minimum score 44). *Expenses:* Tuition, state resident: full-time $6462; part-time $359 per credit hour. Tuition, nonresident: full-time $14,526; part-time $807 per credit hour. *Required fees:* $554. *Financial support:* Teaching assistantships available. Financial award application deadline: 3/1; financial award applicants required to submit FAFSA. *Unit head:* Dr. George Schaefer, Head, 334-244-3887, Fax: 334-244-3835, E-mail: gschaefe@aum.edu. *Application contact:* Janis Bigelow, Graduate Advisor, 334-244-3135, E-mail: jbigelo1@aum.edu.
Website: http://www.education.aum.edu/academic-programs/academic-programs/kinesiology

Augustana University, Sports Administration and Leadership Program, Sioux Falls, SD 57197. Offers MA. *Program availability:* Part-time. *Degree requirements:* For master's, thesis or alternative. *Entrance requirements:* For master's, minimum cumulative undergraduate GPA of 3.0 for last 60 semester hours; appropriate bachelor's degree; 2-3 page essay discussing academic interests, education goals, and plans for graduate study. Additional exam requirements/recommendations for international students: Required—TOEFL (minimum score 550 paper-based). *Application deadline:* For fall admission, 6/1 priority date for domestic and international students. Applications are processed on a rolling basis. Application fee: $50. Electronic applications accepted. *Expenses:* Contact institution. *Financial support:* Unspecified assistantships available. Financial award application deadline: 3/1; financial award applicants required to submit FAFSA. *Unit head:* Dr. Sherry Barkley, Director, 605-274-4312, E-mail: sherry.barkley@augie.edu. *Application contact:* Jody Nitz, Graduate Education Assistant, 605-274-4043, Fax: 605-274-4450, E-mail: graduate@augie.edu.
Website: http://www.augie.edu/academics/graduate-education/sal

Austin Peay State University, College of Graduate Studies, College of Behavioral and Health Sciences, Department of Health and Human Performance, Clarksville, TN 37044. Offers public health education (MS); sports and wellness leadership (MS). *Program availability:* Part-time, evening/weekend, online learning. *Faculty:* 7 full-time (4 women). *Students:* 22 full-time (8 women), 36 part-time (26 women); includes 16 minority (10 Black or African American, non-Hispanic/Latino; 1 Asian, non-Hispanic/Latino; 2 Hispanic/Latino; 3 Two or more races, non-Hispanic/Latino), 2 international. Average age 29. 79 applicants, 70% accepted, 43 enrolled. In 2016, 27 master's awarded. *Degree requirements:* For master's, comprehensive exam, thesis optional. *Entrance requirements:* For master's, GRE General Test, 3 letters of recommendation, minimum undergraduate GPA of 2.5. Additional exam requirements/recommendations for international students: Required—TOEFL (minimum score 500 paper-based). *Application deadline:* For fall admission, 8/9 priority date for domestic students. Applications are processed on a rolling basis. Application fee: $45 ($50 for international students). Electronic applications accepted. *Expenses:* Tuition, state resident: full-time $8300; part-time $415 per credit hour. Tuition, nonresident: full-time $22,280; part-time $1114 per credit hour. *Required fees:* $1473; $73.65 per credit hour. *Financial support:* Research assistantships with full tuition reimbursements, career-related internships or fieldwork, Federal Work-Study, institutionally sponsored loans, scholarships/grants, and unspecified assistantships available. Support available to part-time students. Financial award application deadline: 4/1; financial award applicants required to submit FAFSA. *Unit head:* Dr. Marcy Maurer, Chair, 931-221-6105, Fax: 931-221-7040, E-mail: maurerm@apsu.edu. *Application contact:* Brad Averitt, Coordinator of Graduate Admissions, 800-859-4723, Fax: 931-221-7641, E-mail: gradadmissions@apsu.edu.
Website: http://www.apsu.edu/hhp/

Ball State University, Graduate School, College of Applied Sciences and Technology, School of Kinesiology, Program in Physical Education and Sport, Muncie, IN 47306. Offers physical education and sport (MA, MS), including athletic coaching education, sport administration, sport and exercise psychology. *Program availability:* Part-time, 100% online. *Entrance requirements:* For master's, GRE General Test, minimum baccalaureate GPA of 2.75 or 3.0 in latter half of baccalauareate, curriculum vitae, three letters of recommendation; campus visit to meet faculty and see facilities (strongly encouraged). Additional exam requirements/recommendations for international students: Required—TOEFL (minimum score 550 paper-based; 79 iBT), IELTS (minimum score 6.5). Electronic applications accepted.

Barry University, School of Human Performance and Leisure Sciences, Program in Sport Management, Miami Shores, FL 33161-6695. Offers MS. *Program availability:* Part-time, evening/weekend. *Degree requirements:* For master's, comprehensive exam, project or thesis. *Entrance requirements:* For master's, GMAT or GRE General Test, minimum GPA of 3.0. Electronic applications accepted. *Faculty research:* Economic impact of professional sports, sport marketing.

Barry University, School of Human Performance and Leisure Sciences and Andreas School of Business, Program in Sport Management and Business Administration, Miami Shores, FL 33161-6695. Offers MS/MBA. *Program availability:* Part-time, evening/weekend. Electronic applications accepted. *Faculty research:* Economic impact of professional sports, sport marketing.

Belhaven University, School of Business, Jackson, MS 39202-1789. Offers business administration (MBA); health administration (MBA, MHA); human resources (MBA, MSL); leadership (MBA); public administration (MPA); sports administration (MBA, MSA). *Program availability:* Part-time, evening/weekend, 100% online. *Faculty:* 16 full-time (3 women), 82 part-time/adjunct (32 women). *Students:* 953 full-time (677 women), 392 part-time (292 women); includes 1,082 minority (1,027 Black or African American, non-Hispanic/Latino; 14 American Indian or Alaska Native, non-Hispanic/Latino; 4 Asian, non-Hispanic/Latino; 20 Hispanic/Latino; 2 Native Hawaiian or other Pacific Islander, non-Hispanic/Latino; 15 Two or more races, non-Hispanic/Latino), 11 international. Average age 35. In 2016, 235 master's awarded. *Degree requirements:* For master's, comprehensive exam (for some programs), thesis (for some programs). *Application deadline:* Applications are processed on a rolling basis. Application fee: $25. Electronic applications accepted. *Expenses:* $535 per credit hour tuition, $75 per course technology fee. *Financial support:* Applicants required to submit FAFSA. *Unit head:* Dr. Ralph Mason, Dean, 601-968-8949, Fax: 601-968-8951, E-mail: cmason@belhaven.edu. *Application contact:* Dr. Audrey Kelleher, Vice President of Adult and Graduate Marketing and Development, 407-804-1424, Fax: 407-620-5210, E-mail: akelleher@belhaven.edu.
Website: http://www.belhaven.edu/campuses/index.htm

Boise State University, College of Health Sciences, Department of Kinesiology, Boise, ID 83725-1710. Offers athletic leadership (MAL); kinesiology (MK, MS). *Program availability:* Part-time. *Faculty:* 11. *Students:* 23 full-time (9 women), 31 part-time (10 women); includes 11 minority (4 Black or African American, non-Hispanic/Latino; 6 Hispanic/Latino; 1 Two or more races, non-Hispanic/Latino). Average age 25. 37 applicants, 65% accepted, 15 enrolled. In 2016, 22 master's awarded. *Degree requirements:* For master's, thesis (for some programs). *Entrance requirements:* For master's, minimum GPA of 3.0. Additional exam requirements/recommendations for international students: Required—TOEFL (minimum score 550 paper-based; 80 iBT), IELTS (minimum score 6). *Application deadline:* For fall admission, 5/1 for domestic and international students. Application fee: $65 ($95 for international students). Electronic applications accepted. *Expenses:* Tuition, state resident: full-time $6058; part-time $358 per credit hour. Tuition, nonresident: full-time $20,108; part-time $608 per credit hour. *Required fees:* $2108. Tuition and fees vary according to program. *Financial support:* In 2016–17, 31 students received support. Scholarships/grants and unspecified assistantships available. Financial award application deadline: 1/15; financial award applicants required to submit FAFSA. *Unit head:* Dr. John McChesney, Department Chair, 208-426-4270, E-mail: johnmcchesney@boisestate.edu. *Application contact:* Dr. Laura Patranek, Graduate Program Coordinator, 208-426-4366, E-mail: laurajonespetranek@boisestate.edu.
Website: http://kinesiology.boisestate.edu/graduate-programs/

Bowling Green State University, Graduate College, College of Education and Human Development, School of Human Movement, Sport, and Leisure Studies, Bowling Green, OH 43403. Offers developmental kinesiology (M Ed); recreation and leisure (M Ed); sport administration (M Ed). *Program availability:* Part-time. *Degree requirements:* For master's, thesis or alternative. *Entrance requirements:* For master's, GRE General Test, minimum GPA of 2.7. Additional exam requirements/recommendations for international students: Required—TOEFL. *Application deadline:* For fall admission, 1/15 priority date for domestic students. Applications are processed on a rolling basis. Application fee: $30. Electronic applications accepted. *Financial support:* Research assistantships with full tuition reimbursements, teaching assistantships with full tuition reimbursements, career-related internships or fieldwork, Federal Work-Study, and unspecified assistantships available. Financial award applicants required to submit FAFSA. *Faculty research:* Teacher-learning process, travel and tourism, sport marketing and management, exercise physiology and sport psychology, life-span motor development. *Unit head:* Dr. Bonnie Berger, Director, 419-372-2334. *Application contact:* Dr. Geoff Meek, Graduate Coordinator, 419-372-0501.

Bristol University, Program in Business Administration, Anaheim, CA 92806. Offers business administration (MBA); international business (MBA); marketing (MBA); sports management (MBA). *Degree requirements:* For master's, capstone.

Brooklyn College of the City University of New York, School of Natural and Behavioral Sciences, Department of Kinesiology, Brooklyn, NY 11210-2889. Offers exercise and sports science (MS); physical education teacher (MS); sport management (MS). *Program availability:* Part-time. *Degree requirements:* For master's, comprehensive exam or thesis. *Entrance requirements:* For master's, previous course work in physical education and education, minimum GPA of 3.0, 2 letters of recommendation, essay. Additional exam requirements/recommendations for international students: Required—TOEFL (minimum score 500 paper-based; 61 iBT). Electronic applications accepted. *Faculty research:* Exercise physiology, motor learning, sports psychology, women in athletics.

California Baptist University, Program in Kinesiology, Riverside, CA 92504-3206. Offers exercise science (MS); physical education (MS); sport management (MS). *Program availability:* Part-time, 100% online, blended/hybrid learning. *Faculty:* 10 full-time (3 women), 3 part-time/adjunct (0 women). *Students:* 77 full-time (43 women), 37 part-time (16 women); includes 48 minority (16 Black or African American, non-Hispanic/Latino; 9 Asian, non-Hispanic/Latino; 20 Hispanic/Latino; 1 Native Hawaiian or other Pacific Islander, non-Hispanic/Latino; 2 Two or more races, non-Hispanic/Latino), 26 international. Average age 28. 71 applicants, 76% accepted, 47 enrolled. In 2016, 43 master's awarded. *Degree requirements:* For master's, comprehensive exam or research thesis. *Entrance requirements:* For master's, minimum undergraduate GPA of 2.75; completion of course prerequisites with minimum C grade; three recommendations; 500-word essay; resume; interview. Additional exam requirements/recommendations for international students: Required—TOEFL (minimum score 80 iBT). *Application deadline:* For fall admission, 8/1 priority date for domestic students, 7/1 for international students; for spring admission, 12/1 priority date for domestic students, 11/1 for international students. Applications are processed on a rolling basis. Application fee: $45. Electronic applications accepted. *Expenses:* Contact institution. *Financial support:* In 2016–17, 11 students received support. Federal Work-Study, scholarships/grants, and unspecified assistantships available. Financial award applicants required to submit CSS PROFILE or FAFSA. *Faculty research:* Physical education pedagogy, exercise management and prevention of cardiovascular and metabolic diseases, sport management, immune function, carbohydrate oxidation. *Unit head:* Dr. David Pearson, Dean, College of Allied Health, 951-343-4298, E-mail: dpearson@calbaptist.edu. *Application contact:* Dr. Sean Sullivan, Chair, Department of Kinesiology, 951-343-4528, Fax: 951-343-5095, E-mail: ssullivan@calbaptist.edu.
Website: http://www.calbaptist.edu/mskin/

California State University, Fresno, Division of Research and Graduate Studies, College of Health and Human Services, Department of Kinesiology, Fresno, CA 93740-8027. Offers exercise science (MA); general kinesiology (MA); sport administration (MA); sport psychology (MA). *Program availability:* Part-time, evening/weekend. *Degree requirements:* For master's, thesis or alternative. *Entrance requirements:* For master's, GRE General Test, minimum GPA of 2.7. Additional exam requirements/recommendations for international students: Required—TOEFL. *Application deadline:* For fall admission, 5/1 for domestic and international students; for spring admission, 10/1 for domestic and international students. Applications are processed on a rolling basis. Application fee: $55. Electronic applications accepted. *Financial support:* Teaching assistantships, career-related internships or fieldwork, Federal Work-Study, and scholarships/grants available. Support available to part-time students. Financial award application deadline: 3/1; financial award applicants required to submit FAFSA. *Faculty research:* Refugee education, homeless, geriatrics, fitness. *Unit head:* Dr. Tim Anderson, Chair, 559-278-2203, Fax: 559-278-7010, E-mail: tima@csufresno.edu. *Application contact:* Dr. Jenelle Gilbert, Coordinator, 559-278-8902, Fax: 559-278-7010, E-mail: jgilbert@csufresno.edu.
Website: http://www.fresnostate.edu/chhs/kinesiology/

California State University, Long Beach, Graduate Studies, College of Health and Human Services, Department of Kinesiology, Long Beach, CA 90840. Offers adapted physical education (MA); coaching and student athlete development (MA); exercise physiology and nutrition (MS); exercise science (MS); individualized studies (MA); kinesiology (MA); pedagogical studies (MA); sport and exercise psychology (MS); sport management (MA); sports medicine and injury studies (MS). *Program availability:* Part-time. *Degree requirements:* For master's, oral and written comprehensive exams or thesis. *Entrance requirements:* For master's, GRE General Test, minimum GPA of 2.75 during previous 2 years of course work. *Application deadline:* For fall admission, 6/1 for domestic students. Applications are processed on a rolling basis. Application fee: $55. Electronic applications accepted. *Financial support:* Federal Work-Study, institutionally sponsored loans, and scholarships/grants available. Financial award application deadline: 3/2. *Faculty research:* Pulmonary functioning, feedback and practice structure, strength training, history and politics of sports, special population research issues. *Unit head:* Jan Schroeder, Chair, 562-985-4051.

California University of Management and Sciences, Graduate Programs, Anaheim, CA 92801. Offers business administration (MBA, DBA); computer information systems (MS); economics (MS); international business (MS); sports management (MS).

California University of Pennsylvania, School of Graduate Studies and Research, College of Education and Human Services, Program in Sport Management Studies, California, PA 15419-1394. Offers intercollegiate athletic administration (MS); sport management (MS); sports counseling (MS). *Program availability:* Part-time, 100% online. *Expenses:* Tuition, state resident: full-time $11,592; part-time $483 per credit. Tuition, nonresident: full-time $17,400; part-time $725 per credit. *Required fees:* $3916. Tuition and fees vary according to course load, degree level, campus/location and reciprocity agreements.

Canisius College, Graduate Division, School of Education and Human Services, Program in Sport Administration, Buffalo, NY 14208-1098. Offers MSA. *Program availability:* Part-time, evening/weekend, 100% online. *Faculty:* 9 part-time/adjunct (1 woman). *Students:* 56 full-time (21 women), 58 part-time (16 women); includes 27 minority (19 Black or African American, non-Hispanic/Latino; 5 Hispanic/Latino; 3 Two or more races, non-Hispanic/Latino), 4 international. Average age 27. 64 applicants, 94% accepted, 53 enrolled. In 2016, 93 master's awarded. *Entrance requirements:* For master's, transcripts, essay, minimum GPA of 2.7, resume, BA. Additional exam requirements/recommendations for international students: Required—TOEFL (minimum score 550 paper-based, 79 iBT), IELTS (minimum score 6.5), or CAEL (minimum score 70). *Application deadline:* Applications are processed on a rolling basis. Application fee: $25. Electronic applications accepted. Application fee is waived when completed online. *Expenses: Tuition:* Full-time $14,742. *Required fees:* $724. *Financial support:* Career-related internships or fieldwork, Federal Work-Study, scholarships/grants, tuition waivers (partial), and unspecified assistantships available. Support available to part-time students. Financial award application deadline: 4/30; financial award applicants required to submit FAFSA. *Unit head:* Dr. Shawn O'Rourke, Associate Dean, 716-888-3179, E-mail: orourke1@canisius.edu. *Application contact:* Kathleen B. Davis, Vice President of Enrollment Management, 716-888-2500, Fax: 716-888-3195, E-mail: daviskb@canisius.edu.
Website: http://www.canisius.edu/graduate/

Cardinal Stritch University, College of Arts and Sciences, Department of Sport Science and Management, Milwaukee, WI 53217-3985. Offers sport management (MS). *Program availability:* Part-time, evening/weekend. *Students:* 19 part-time (7 women); includes 3 minority (2 Black or African American, non-Hispanic/Latino; 1 American Indian or Alaska Native, non-Hispanic/Latino). Average age 30. 28 applicants, 100% accepted, 3 enrolled. In 2016, 20 master's awarded. *Entrance requirements:* Additional exam requirements/recommendations for international students: Required—TOEFL (minimum score 79 iBT), IELTS (minimum score 6.5) *Application deadline:* Applications are processed on a rolling basis. Electronic applications accepted. *Expenses: Tuition:* Full-time $11,890; part-time $765 per credit hour. Tuition and fees vary according to class time, course load, degree level, program and student's religious affiliation. *Financial support:* Career-related internships or fieldwork, Federal Work-Study, scholarships/grants, and unspecified assistantships available. Financial award applicants required to submit FAFSA. *Unit head:* Alexandra Fairchild, Chair, 414-410-4494, E-mail: anfairchild1@stritch.edu. *Application contact:* Graduate Admissions, 800-347-8822 Ext. 4042, E-mail: admissions@stritch.edu.

Central Michigan University, College of Graduate Studies, The Herbert H. and Grace A. Dow College of Health Professions, Department of Physical Education and Sport, Mount Pleasant, MI 48859. Offers sport administration (MA). *Program availability:* Part-time, evening/weekend. *Degree requirements:* For master's, thesis or alternative. *Entrance requirements:* For master's, GRE (recommended). Electronic applications accepted. *Faculty research:* Athletic administration and sport management, performance enhancing substance use in sport, computer applications for sport managers, mental skill development for ultimate performance, teaching methods.

Central Michigan University, College of Graduate Studies, Interdisciplinary Administration Programs, Mount Pleasant, MI 48859. Offers acquisitions administration

(MSA, Graduate Certificate); general administration (MSA, Graduate Certificate); health services administration (MSA, Graduate Certificate); human resource administration (Graduate Certificate); human resources administration (MSA); information resource management (MSA, Graduate Certificate); international administration (MSA, Graduate Certificate); leadership (MSA, Graduate Certificate); public administration (MSA, Graduate Certificate); research administration (Graduate Certificate); sport administration (MSA). *Accreditation:* AACSB. *Program availability:* Part-time, evening/weekend, online learning. *Degree requirements:* For master's, thesis or alternative. *Entrance requirements:* For master's, bachelor's degree with minimum GPA of 2.7. Electronic applications accepted. *Faculty research:* Interdisciplinary studies in acquisitions administration, health services administration, sport administration, recreation and park administration, and international administration.

Central Washington University, Graduate Studies and Research, College of Education and Professional Studies, Department of Physical Education, School and Public Health, Ellensburg, WA 98926. Offers athletic administration (MS); health and physical education (MS). *Program availability:* Part-time. *Degree requirements:* For master's, comprehensive exam, thesis or alternative. *Entrance requirements:* For master's, minimum GPA of 3.0. Additional exam requirements/recommendations for international students: Required—TOEFL (minimum score 550 paper-based; 79 iBT), IELTS. Electronic applications accepted.

The Citadel, The Military College of South Carolina, Citadel Graduate College, School of Science and Mathematics, Department of Health, Exercise, and Sport Science, Charleston, SC 29409. Offers health, exercise, and sport science (MS); sport management (MA, Graduate Certificate). *Accreditation:* NCATE. *Program availability:* Part-time, evening/weekend. *Faculty:* 4 full-time (2 women), 1 (woman) part-time/adjunct. *Students:* 13 full-time (5 women), 17 part-time (9 women); includes 6 minority (4 Black or African American, non-Hispanic/Latino; 1 Hispanic/Latino; 1 Native Hawaiian or other Pacific Islander, non-Hispanic/Latino), 1 international. 11 applicants, 82% accepted, 8 enrolled. In 2016, 24 master's, 3 other advanced degrees awarded. *Degree requirements:* For master's, comprehensive exam (for some programs), internship and professional portfolio (for some programs). *Entrance requirements:* For master's, GRE (minimum combined verbal and quantitative score 290) or MAT (minimum score 396), official transcript reflecting highest degree earned from regionally-accredited college or university, minimum undergraduate GPA of 2.5, 3 letters of recommendation, resume detailing previous work experience. Additional exam requirements/recommendations for international students: Required—TOEFL (minimum score 550 paper-based; 79 iBT). *Application deadline:* Applications are processed on a rolling basis. Application fee: $40. Electronic applications accepted. *Expenses:* Tuition, state resident: full-time $5121; part-time $569 per credit hour. Tuition, nonresident: full-time $8613; part-time $957 per credit hour. *Required fees:* $90 per term. *Financial support:* Fellowships and unspecified assistantships available. Support available to part-time students. Financial award application deadline: 7/1; financial award applicants required to submit FAFSA. *Unit head:* Dr. Harry D. Davakos, Department Head, 843-953-5060, E-mail: harry.davakos@citadel.edu. *Application contact:* Dr. Dena P. Garner, Program Director, 843-953-6323, E-mail: garnerd1@citadel.edu.
Website: http://www.citadel.edu/root/hess

Clayton State University, School of Graduate Studies, College of Business, Program in Business Administration, Morrow, GA 30260-0285. Offers accounting (MBA); human resource leadership (MBA); international business (MBA); sports and entertainment management (MBA); supply chain management (MBA). *Accreditation:* AACSB. *Program availability:* Part-time, evening/weekend. *Degree requirements:* For master's, thesis. *Entrance requirements:* For master's, GMAT, 3 letters of recommendation; statement of purpose; 2 official transcripts. Additional exam requirements/recommendations for international students: Required—TOEFL (minimum score 550 paper-based; 80 iBT). Electronic applications accepted. *Expenses:* Contact institution.

Clemson University, Graduate School, College of Education, Clemson, SC 29634-0702. Offers administration and supervision (K-12) (M Ed, Ed S); education and organizational leadership (MS), including athletic leadership; educational leadership (PhD), including P-12; human resource development (MHRD); middle-level education (MAT). *Program availability:* Part-time, evening/weekend, 100% online. *Faculty:* 75 full-time (54 women), 1 part-time/adjunct (0 women). *Students:* 120 full-time (84 women), 309 part-time (206 women); includes 96 minority (68 Black or African American, non-Hispanic/Latino; 1 American Indian or Alaska Native, non-Hispanic/Latino; 3 Asian, non-Hispanic/Latino; 19 Hispanic/Latino; 5 Two or more races, non-Hispanic/Latino), 11 international. Average age 34. 417 applicants, 50% accepted, 133 enrolled. In 2016, 239 master's, 21 doctorates, 59 other advanced degrees awarded. *Degree requirements:* For master's, comprehensive exam (for some programs), thesis (for some programs); for doctorate, comprehensive exam, thesis/dissertation. *Entrance requirements:* For master's, doctorate, and other advanced degree, GRE General Test, unofficial transcripts, letters of recommendation. Additional exam requirements/recommendations for international students: Required—TOEFL (minimum score 80 iBT), IELTS (minimum score 7). *Application deadline:* Applications are processed on a rolling basis. Application fee: $80 ($90 for international students). Electronic applications accepted. *Expenses:* Contact institution. *Financial support:* In 2016–17, 75 students received support, including 22 fellowships with partial tuition reimbursements available (averaging $6,316 per year), 28 research assistantships with partial tuition reimbursements available (averaging $15,399 per year), 5 teaching assistantships with partial tuition reimbursements available (averaging $30,000 per year); unspecified assistantships also available. *Faculty research:* Early literacy and motivation, STEAM education, legal/policy issues in education, leadership, special education interventions/assessment/policy. *Total annual research expenditures:* $2.8 million. *Unit head:* Dr. George Petersen, Dean, 864-656-4444, Fax: 864-656-0311, E-mail: soedean@clemson.edu. *Application contact:* Dr. David Fleming, Graduate Programs Coordinator, 864-656-1881, Fax: 864-656-0311, E-mail: dflemin@clemson.edu.
Website: http://www.clemson.edu/education/

Clemson University, Graduate School, College of Education, Department of Educational and Organizational Leadership Development, Program in Athletic Leadership, Clemson, SC 29634. Offers MS, Certificate. *Program availability:* Part-time, evening/weekend, online only, 100% online. *Faculty:* 2 full-time (1 woman). *Students:* 7 full-time (1 woman), 33 part-time (15 women); includes 9 minority (6 Black or African American, non-Hispanic/Latino; 1 American Indian or Alaska Native, non-Hispanic/Latino; 1 Hispanic/Latino; 1 Two or more races, non-Hispanic/Latino). Average age 25. 28 applicants, 86% accepted, 22 enrolled. *Entrance requirements:* For master's, GRE General Test, unofficial transcripts, letters of recommendation. Additional exam requirements/recommendations for international students: Required—TOEFL (minimum score 80 iBT), IELTS (minimum score 6.5). *Application deadline:* For fall admission, 7/1 for domestic and international students. Applications are processed on a rolling basis. Application fee: $80 ($90 for international students). Electronic applications accepted. *Expenses:* $4,264 per semester full-time resident, $8,485 per semester full-time non-resident, $471 per credit hour part-time resident, $942 per credit hour part-time non-resident. *Financial support:* Career-related internships or fieldwork available. Financial award application deadline: 7/1. *Unit head:* Dr. Michael Godfrey, Program Coordinator, 864-656-3650, E-mail: mgodfe@clemson.edu. *Application contact:* Dr. David Fleming, Graduate Coordinator, 864-656-1881, Fax: 864-656-0311, E-mail: dflemin@clemson.edu.
Website: http://www.clemson.edu/education/academics/masters-specialist-programs/masters-science-athletic-leadership/index.html

Coastal Carolina University, College of Science, Conway, SC 29528-6054. Offers applied computing and information systems (Certificate); coastal marine and wetland studies (MS); information systems technology (MS); marine science (PhD); sports management (MS). *Program availability:* Part-time, evening/weekend. *Faculty:* 23 full-time (5 women), 1 part-time/adjunct (0 women). *Students:* 41 full-time (14 women), 29 part-time (15 women); includes 7 minority (4 Black or African American, non-Hispanic/Latino; 1 American Indian or Alaska Native, non-Hispanic/Latino; 1 Hispanic/Latino; 1 Two or more races, non-Hispanic/Latino), 6 international. Average age 27. 72 applicants, 57% accepted, 35 enrolled. In 2016, 13 master's awarded. *Degree requirements:* For master's, thesis or internship; for doctorate, comprehensive exam, thesis/dissertation. *Entrance requirements:* For master's, GRE, 3 letters of recommendation, resume, official transcripts, written statement of educational and career goals, baccalaureate degree; for doctorate, GRE, official transcripts; baccalaureate or master's degree; minimum GPA of 3.0 for all collegiate coursework; successful completion of at least two semesters of college-level calculus, physics, and chemistry; 3 letters of recommendation; written statement of educational and career goals; resume; for Certificate, 2 letters of reference, official transcripts, minimum GPA of 3.0 in all computing and information systems courses, documentation of graduation from accredited four-year college or university. Additional exam requirements/recommendations for international students: Required—TOEFL (minimum score 550 paper-based; 79 iBT), IELTS (minimum score 6.5). *Application deadline:* For fall admission, 1/15 priority date for domestic and international students; for spring admission, 11/1 priority date for domestic and international students. Applications are processed on a rolling basis. Application fee: $45. Electronic applications accepted. *Expenses:* Tuition, state resident: full-time $9990; part-time $555 per credit hour. Tuition, nonresident: full-time $18,108; part-time $1006 per credit hour. *Required fees:* $90; $5 per credit hour. *Financial support:* Fellowships, research assistantships, and unspecified assistantships available. Support available to part-time students. Financial award application deadline: 3/1; financial award applicants required to submit FAFSA. *Unit head:* Dr. Michael H. Roberts, Dean, 843-349-2282, Fax: 843-349-2545, E-mail: mroberts@coastal.edu. *Application contact:* Dr. James O. Luken, Associate Provost/Vice-Dean of the Coastal Environment, 843-349-2235, Fax: 843-349-6444, E-mail: joluken@coastal.edu.
Website: http://www.coastal.edu/academics/colleges/science/

Coker College, Graduate Programs, Hartsville, SC 29550. Offers athletic administration (MS); literacy studies (M Ed). *Program availability:* Part-time, 100% online. *Degree requirements:* For master's, comprehensive exam, portfolio. *Entrance requirements:* For master's, GRE or GMAT, minimum overall GPA of 2.85 in bachelor's program, official transcripts, resume, three letters of recommendation, teacher licensure. Electronic applications accepted.

The College at Brockport, State University of New York, School of Education, Health, and Human Services, Department of Kinesiology, Sports Studies and Physical Education, Brockport, NY 14420-2997. Offers adapted physical education (AGC); physical education (MS Ed), including adapted physical education, athletic administration, physical education/pedagogy. *Program availability:* Part-time. *Faculty:* 11 full-time (4 women), 1 part-time/adjunct (0 women). *Students:* 29 full-time (16 women), 28 part-time (7 women); includes 12 minority (2 Black or African American, non-Hispanic/Latino; 2 Asian, non-Hispanic/Latino; 5 Hispanic/Latino; 3 Two or more races, non-Hispanic/Latino), 1 international. 35 applicants, 91% accepted, 22 enrolled. In 2016, 43 master's awarded. *Degree requirements:* For master's, thesis or alternative. *Entrance requirements:* For master's, minimum GPA of 3.0; statement of objectives. Additional exam requirements/recommendations for international students: Required—TOEFL (minimum score 550 paper-based; 79 iBT), IELTS (minimum score 6.5). *Application deadline:* For fall admission, 4/15 priority date for domestic and international students; for spring admission, 11/15 priority date for domestic and international students; for summer admission, 4/15 priority date for domestic students, 4/15 for international students. Application fee: $80. Electronic applications accepted. *Expenses:* Contact institution. *Financial support:* In 2016–17, 11 teaching assistantships with full tuition reimbursements (averaging $7,000 per year) were awarded; Federal Work-Study, scholarships/grants, and unspecified assistantships also available. Support available to part-time students. Financial award application deadline: 3/15; financial award applicants required to submit FAFSA. *Faculty research:* Athletic administration, adapted physical education, physical education curriculum, physical education teaching/coaching, children's physical activity. *Unit head:* Dr. Cathy Houston-Wilson, Chairperson, 585-395-5352, Fax: 585-395-2771, E-mail: chouston@brockport.edu. *Application contact:* Dr. Francis Kozub, Graduate Program Director, 585-395-5946, Fax: 585-395-2771, E-mail: fkozub@brockport.edu.

Columbia University, School of Continuing Education, Program in Global Sports Law and Sports Management, New York, NY 10027. Offers MS/MGSL. Program offered in collaboration with Instituto Superior de Derecho y Economia (ISDE) in Madrid.

Columbia University, School of Continuing Education, Program in Sports Management, New York, NY 10027. Offers MS. *Program availability:* Part-time. *Entrance requirements:* For master's, minimum GPA of 3.0, 2 letters of recommendation, professional resume. Electronic applications accepted.

Concordia University Irvine, School of Arts and Sciences, Irvine, CA 92612-3299. Offers coaching and athletic administration (MA). *Program availability:* Part-time, evening/weekend, online learning. *Degree requirements:* For master's, culminating project. *Entrance requirements:* For master's, official college/university transcript(s); signed statement of intent. Additional exam requirements/recommendations for international students: Required—TOEFL (minimum score 550 paper-based; 79 iBT). Electronic applications accepted. *Expenses:* Contact institution.

Concordia University, St. Paul, College of Health and Science, St. Paul, MN 55104-5494. Offers criminal justice leadership (MA); exercise science (MS); family science (MA); human services (MA); orthotics and prosthetics (MS); physical therapy (DPT); sports management (MA). *Program availability:* Part-time, evening/weekend, 100% online, blended/hybrid learning. *Faculty:* 7 full-time (2 women), 27 part-time/adjunct (9 women). *Students:* 337 full-time (194 women), 18 part-time (7 women); includes 65 minority (35 Black or African American, non-Hispanic/Latino; 7 Asian, non-Hispanic/Latino; 8 Hispanic/Latino; 4 Native Hawaiian or other Pacific Islander, non-Hispanic/Latino; 11 Two or more races, non-Hispanic/Latino), 3 international. Average age 30. 388 applicants, 40% accepted, 117 enrolled. In 2016, 92 master's awarded. *Degree requirements:* For master's, comprehensive exam (for some programs), thesis (for some programs); for doctorate, at least one 8-12 week clinical rotation outside the St. Paul area. *Entrance requirements:* For master's, official transcripts from regionally-accredited institution stating the conferral of a bachelor's degree with minimum cumulative GPA of 3.0; personal statement; undergraduate degree at accredited college or university in the U.S., English-speaking Canada, the United Kingdom, Ireland, Australia, or New Zealand; for doctorate, undergraduate or graduate degree at accredited college or university in the U.S., English-speaking Canada, the United Kingdom, Ireland, Australia, or New Zealand. Additional exam requirements/recommendations for international students: Recommended—TOEFL (minimum score 547 paper-based; 78 iBT), IELTS (minimum score 6), TSE (minimum score 52). *Application deadline:* For fall admission, 4/1 for domestic students. Applications are processed on a rolling basis. Application fee: $50. Electronic applications accepted. *Expenses:* Contact institution. *Financial support:* In 2016–17, 114 students received support. Scholarships/grants and unspecified assistantships available. Financial award applicants required to submit FAFSA. *Faculty research:* Developmental screening in early childhood, cardiovascular responses to aerobic exercise. *Unit head:* Dr. Katie Fischer, Interim Dean, 651-641-8735, E-mail: fischer@csp.edu. *Application contact:* Kimberly Craig, Associate Vice President, Cohort Enrollment Management, 651-603-6223, Fax: 651-603-6320, E-mail: craig@csp.edu.

Dallas Baptist University, Dorothy M. Bush College of Education, Sport Management Program, Dallas, TX 75211-9299. Offers MA. *Program availability:* Part-time, evening/weekend. *Application deadline:* Applications are processed on a rolling basis. Application fee: $25. Electronic applications accepted. Application fee is waived when completed online. *Expenses: Tuition:* Full-time $15,408; part-time $856 per credit hour. *Required fees:* $400 per semester. Tuition and fees vary according to course load and degree level. *Unit head:* Dr. Jim Tennison, Director, 214-333-5253, E-mail: jimt@dbu.edu. *Application contact:* Bobby Soto, Director of Admissions, 214-333-5242, E-mail: graduate@dbu.edu.
Website: http://www3.dbu.edu/graduate/sport_management.asp

DePaul University, Kellstadt Graduate School of Business, Chicago, IL 60604. Offers accountancy (M Acc, MS, MSA); applied economics (MBA); banking (MBA); behavioral finance (MBA); brand and product management (MBA); business development (MBA); business information technology (MS); business strategy and decision-making (MBA); computational finance (MS); consumer insights (MBA); corporate finance (MBA); economic policy analysis (MS); entrepreneurship (MBA, MS); finance (MBA, MS); financial analysis (MBA); general business (MBA); health sector management (MBA); hospitality leadership (MBA); hospitality leadership and operational performance (MS); human resource management (MBA); human resources (MS); investment management (MBA); leadership and change management (MBA); management accounting (MBA); marketing (MBA, MS); marketing analysis (MS); marketing strategy and planning (MBA); operations management (MBA); organizational diversity (MBA); real estate (MS); real estate finance and investment (MBA); revenue management (MBA); sports management (MBA); strategic global marketing (MBA); strategy, execution and valuation (MBA); sustainable management (MBA, MS); taxation (MS); wealth management (MS); JD/MBA. *Accreditation:* AACSB. *Program availability:* Part-time, evening/weekend, online learning. *Entrance requirements:* For master's, GMAT, 2 letters of recommendation, resume, essay, official transcripts. Additional exam requirements/recommendations for international students: Required—TOEFL (minimum score 550 paper-based; 80 iBT). Electronic applications accepted. *Expenses:* Contact institution.

Drexel University, Goodwin College of Professional Studies, School of Technology and Professional Studies, Philadelphia, PA 19104-2875. Offers construction management (MS); creativity and innovation (MS); engineering technology (MS); food science (MS); hospitality management (MS); professional studies: creativity studies (MS); professional studies: e-learning leadership (MS); professional studies: homeland security management (MS); project management (MS); property management (MS); sport management (MS). *Program availability:* Part-time, evening/weekend. *Faculty:* 37 full-time (14 women). *Students:* 13 full-time, 462 part-time; includes 133 minority (86 Black or African American, non-Hispanic/Latino; 24 Asian, non-Hispanic/Latino; 23 Hispanic/Latino). In 2016, 88 master's awarded. *Entrance requirements:* Additional exam requirements/recommendations for international students: Required—TOEFL, IELTS. *Application deadline:* For fall admission, 9/1 for domestic students; for winter admission, 12/1 for domestic students; for spring admission, 3/1 for domestic students. Applications are processed on a rolling basis. Application fee: $75. Electronic applications accepted. Application fee is waived when completed online. *Expenses: Tuition:* Full-time $32,184; part-time $1192 per credit hour. *Required fees:* $280. Tuition and fees vary according to campus/location and program. *Financial support:* Applicants required to submit FAFSA. *Unit head:* Dr. William F. Lynch, Dean, 215-895-2159, E-mail: goodwin@drexel.edu. *Application contact:* Matthew Gray, Manager, Recruitment and Enrollment, 215-895-6255, Fax: 215-895-2153, E-mail: mdg67@drexel.edu.
Website: http://drexel.edu/grad/programs/goodwin/

Duquesne University, Palumbo-Donahue School of Business, Pittsburgh, PA 15282-0001. Offers accounting (M Acc); finance (MBA); information systems management (MSISM); management (MBA, MS); marketing (MBA); sports business (MS); sustainability (MBA); JD/MBA; MBA/M Acc; MBA/MA; MBA/MES; MBA/MHMS; MSISM/MBA; Pharm D/MBA. *Accreditation:* AACSB. *Program availability:* Part-time, evening/weekend, 100% online, minimal on-campus study. *Faculty:* 59 full-time (23 women), 25 part-time/adjunct (6 women). *Students:* 92 full-time (43 women), 176 part-time (71 women); includes 20 minority (9 Black or African American, non-Hispanic/Latino; 8 Asian, non-Hispanic/Latino; 2 Hispanic/Latino; 1 Two or more races, non-Hispanic/Latino), 35 international. Average age 28. 272 applicants, 86% accepted, 137 enrolled. In 2016, 137 master's awarded. *Entrance requirements:* For master's, GMAT or GRE, undergraduate transcripts, 2 letters of recommendation, current resume, personal statement. Additional exam requirements/recommendations for international students: Required—TOEFL (minimum score 577 paper-based; 90 iBT), IELTS (minimum score 7). *Application deadline:* For fall admission, 7/1 priority date for domestic and international students; for spring admission, 12/1 for domestic and international students; for summer admission, 4/1 for domestic and international students. Applications are processed on a rolling basis. Application fee: $0. Electronic applications accepted. *Expenses:* Contact institution. *Financial support:* In 2016–17, 211 students received support, including 12 fellowships with partial tuition reimbursements available (averaging $14,200 per year), 20 research assistantships with partial tuition reimbursements available (averaging $22,212 per year); career-related internships or fieldwork, scholarships/grants, and unspecified assistantships also available. Support available to part-time students. Financial award application deadline: 7/1; financial award applicants required to submit FAFSA. *Faculty research:* Investment management, business ethics, technology management, supply chain management, entrepreneurship. *Unit head:* Dr. Karen Donovan, Associate Dean of Graduate Programs and Executive Education, 412-396-6276, Fax: 412-396-1726, E-mail: donovan6@duq.edu. *Application contact:* Jeff Jewett, Director of Admissions and Enrollment Management, 412-396-6244, Fax: 412-396-1726, E-mail: decrostam@duq.edu.
Website: http://www.duq.edu/business/grad

East Carolina University, Graduate School, College of Health and Human Performance, Department of Kinesiology, Greenville, NC 27858-4353. Offers adapted physical education (MS); bioenergetics and exercise science (PhD); biomechanics (MS); exercise physiology (MS); physical activity promotion (MS); physical education (MA Ed, MAT); physical education pedagogy (MS); sport and exercise psychology (MS); sport management (MS, Certificate). *Students:* 90 full-time (33 women), 23 part-time (9 women); includes 16 minority (8 Black or African American, non-Hispanic/Latino; 3 Asian, non-Hispanic/Latino; 3 Hispanic/Latino; 2 Two or more races, non-Hispanic/Latino), 7 international. Average age 26. 98 applicants, 53% accepted, 38 enrolled. In 2016, 28 master's, 2 doctorates awarded. *Degree requirements:* For master's, comprehensive exam, thesis optional; for doctorate, comprehensive exam, thesis/dissertation. *Entrance requirements:* For master's, GRE General Test or MAT; for doctorate, GRE. Additional exam requirements/recommendations for international students: Required—TOEFL. *Application deadline:* For fall admission, 2/1 priority date for domestic students, 2/1 for international students. Applications are processed on a rolling basis. Application fee: $50. *Financial support:* Research assistantships with tuition reimbursements and teaching assistantships available. Support available to part-time students. Financial award application deadline: 2/1. *Faculty research:* Diabetes metabolism, pediatric obesity, biomechanics of arthritis, physical activity measurement. *Total annual research expenditures:* $26. *Unit head:* Dr. Stacey Altman, Chair, 252-328-2973, E-mail: altmans@ecu.edu.

East Carolina University, Graduate School, College of Health and Human Performance, Department of Recreation and Leisure Studies, Greenville, NC 27858-4353. Offers aquatic therapy (Certificate); biofeedback (Certificate); recreation and park administration (MS), including generalist, recreational sports management. *Program availability:* Part-time, evening/weekend, online learning. *Students:* 25 full-time (17 women), 4 part-time (2 women); includes 6 minority (3 Black or African American, non-Hispanic/Latino; 1 Hispanic/Latino; 2 Two or more races, non-Hispanic/Latino). Average age 25. 11 applicants, 100% accepted, 9 enrolled. In 2016, 4 master's awarded. *Degree requirements:* For master's, comprehensive exam, thesis optional. *Entrance requirements:* For master's, GRE General Test or MAT. Additional exam requirements/recommendations for international students: Required—TOEFL. *Application deadline:* For fall admission, 6/1 priority date for domestic students. Applications are processed on a rolling basis. Application fee: $50. *Financial support:* Research assistantships and teaching assistantships with partial tuition reimbursements available. Financial award application deadline: 6/1. *Faculty research:* Therapeutic recreation, stress and coping behavior, medicine carrying capacity, choice behavior, tourism preferences. *Unit head:* Dr. Matthew Mahar, Interim Chair, 252-328-0008, E-mail: maharm@ecu.edu.
Website: http://www.ecu.edu/rcls/

Eastern Kentucky University, The Graduate School, College of Health Sciences, Department of Exercise and Sport Science, Richmond, KY 40475-3102. Offers exercise and sport science (MS); exercise and wellness (MS); sports administration (MS). *Program availability:* Part-time. *Entrance requirements:* For master's, GRE General Test (minimum score 700 verbal and quantitative), minimum GPA of 2.5 (for most), minimum GPA of 3.0 (analytical writing). *Faculty research:* Nutrition and exercise.

Eastern Michigan University, Graduate School, College of Health and Human Services, School of Health Promotion and Human Performance, Program in Sports Management, Ypsilanti, MI 48197. Offers MS. *Program availability:* Part-time, evening/weekend. *Students:* 20 full-time (10 women), 28 part-time (6 women); includes 7 minority (4 Black or African American, non-Hispanic/Latino; 2 Hispanic/Latino; 1 Two or more races, non-Hispanic/Latino), 3 international. Average age 27. 46 applicants, 67% accepted, 17 enrolled. In 2016, 15 master's awarded. *Degree requirements:* For master's, comprehensive exams or thesis. *Entrance requirements:* For master's, minimum GPA of 2.75. Additional exam requirements/recommendations for international students: Required—TOEFL. *Application deadline:* For fall admission, 8/1 for domestic students, 5/1 for international students; for winter admission, 12/1 for domestic students, 10/1 for international students; for spring admission, 4/15 for domestic students, 3/1 for international students. Applications are processed on a rolling basis. Application fee: $45. *Financial support:* Fellowships, research assistantships with full tuition reimbursements, teaching assistantships with full tuition reimbursements, career-related internships or fieldwork, Federal Work-Study, institutionally sponsored loans, scholarships/grants, tuition waivers (partial), and unspecified assistantships available. Support available to part-time students. Financial award applicants required to submit FAFSA. *Application contact:* Dr. Brenda Riemer, Advisor, 734-487-0090 Ext. 2745, Fax: 734-487-2024, E-mail: briemer@emich.edu.

Eastern New Mexico University, Graduate School, College of Education and Technology, Department of Health and Physical Education, Portales, NM 88130. Offers physical education (MS), including sport administration, sport science. *Program availability:* Part-time. *Degree requirements:* For master's, comprehensive exam, thesis optional. *Entrance requirements:* For master's, minimum GPA of 3.0, 15 hours of leveling courses without bachelor's degree in physical education, two references. Additional exam requirements/recommendations for international students: Required—TOEFL (minimum score 550 paper-based; 79 iBT), IELTS (minimum score 6). Electronic applications accepted.

Eastern Washington University, Graduate Studies, College of Arts, Letters and Education, Department of Physical Education, Health and Recreation, Cheney, WA 99004-2431. Offers exercise science (MS); sports and recreation administration (MS). *Faculty:* 17 full-time (7 women), 5 part-time/adjunct (2 women). *Students:* 26 full-time (10 women), 8 part-time (3 women); includes 7 minority (3 Black or African American, non-Hispanic/Latino; 1 American Indian or Alaska Native, non-Hispanic/Latino; 2 Asian, non-Hispanic/Latino; 1 Hispanic/Latino). Average age 29. 64 applicants, 38% accepted, 21 enrolled. In 2016, 14 master's awarded. *Degree requirements:* For master's, comprehensive exam, thesis or alternative. *Entrance requirements:* For master's, minimum GPA of 3.0. Additional exam requirements/recommendations for international students: Required—TOEFL (minimum score 580 paper-based; 92 iBT), IELTS (minimum score 7), PTE (minimum score 63). *Application deadline:* For fall admission, 4/1 priority date for domestic students; for spring admission, 1/15 for domestic students. Applications are processed on a rolling basis. Application fee: $50. Electronic applications accepted. *Expenses:* Tuition, state resident: full-time $11,000; part-time $5500 per credit. Tuition, nonresident: full-time $24,000; part-time $12,000 per credit. *Required fees:* $1300. One-time fee: $50 full-time. Part-time tuition and fees vary according to course load, campus/location and program. *Financial support:* In 2016–17, 10 teaching assistantships with partial tuition reimbursements (averaging $6,624 per year) were awarded; career-related internships or fieldwork, Federal Work-Study, institutionally sponsored loans, and scholarships/grants also available. Support available to part-time students. Financial award application deadline: 2/1; financial award applicants required to submit FAFSA. *Unit head:* Dr. Chadron Hazelbaker, Graduate Program Director, 509-359-2486, Fax: 509-359-4833, E-mail: chazelbaker@ewu.edu.

East Stroudsburg University of Pennsylvania, Graduate and Extended Studies, College of Business and Management, Department of Sport Management, East Stroudsburg, PA 18301-2999. Offers MS. *Program availability:* Part-time, evening/weekend, online learning. *Students:* 21 full-time (7 women), 8 part-time (2 women); includes 7 minority (all Black or African American, non-Hispanic/Latino), 3 international. *Degree requirements:* For master's, comprehensive exam. *Entrance requirements:* For master's, GRE and/or GMAT. Additional exam requirements/recommendations for international students: Recommended—TOEFL (minimum score 560 paper-based; 83 iBT), IELTS. *Application deadline:* For fall admission, 7/31 priority date for domestic students, 6/30 priority date for international students; for spring admission, 11/30 for domestic students, 10/31 for international students. Applications are processed on a rolling basis. Application fee: $50. Electronic applications accepted. *Expenses:* Tuition, state resident: full-time $8694; part-time $5796 per year. Tuition, nonresident: full-time

$13,050; part-time $8700 per year. *Required fees:* $2550; $1690 per unit. $845 per semester. Tuition and fees vary according to course load, campus/location and program. *Financial support:* Research assistantships, Federal Work-Study, and unspecified assistantships available. Support available to part-time students. Financial award application deadline: 3/1; financial award applicants required to submit FAFSA. *Unit head:* Dr. Jaedock Lee, Chair, 570-422-3874, Fax: 570-422-3340, E-mail: jaedeock@esu.edu. *Application contact:* Kevin Quintero, Associate Director, Graduate and Extended Studies, 570-422-3890, Fax: 570-422-2711, E-mail: kquintero@esu.edu.

East Tennessee State University, School of Graduate Studies, College of Education, Department of Kinesiology, Sport and Recreation Management, Johnson City, TN 37614. Offers kinesiology, sport and recreation management (Post-Master's Certificate); sport management (MA). *Program availability:* Part-time, evening/weekend. Terminal master's awarded for partial completion of doctoral program. *Degree requirements:* For master's, comprehensive exam, thesis or internship. *Entrance requirements:* For master's, GRE General Test or GMAT, undergraduate degree in related field; minimum GPA of 2.7; resume; three references; essay explaining goals and reasons for pursuing degree; for Post-Master's Certificate, three letters of recommendation. Additional exam requirements/recommendations for international students: Required—TOEFL (minimum score 550 paper-based; 79 iBT). Electronic applications accepted. *Faculty research:* Methods of training for individual and team sports, enhancing acute sport performance, fatigue management in athletes, risk management, facilities management, motorsport.

Endicott College, Van Loan School of Graduate and Professional Studies, Program in Athletic Administration, Beverly, MA 01915-2096. Offers M Ed. *Program availability:* Part-time, evening/weekend. *Faculty:* 5 full-time (4 women), 4 part-time/adjunct (0 women). *Students:* 29 full-time (5 women), 28 part-time (6 women); includes 5 minority (4 Black or African American, non-Hispanic/Latino; 1 Two or more races, non-Hispanic/Latino). Average age 31. 15 applicants, 100% accepted, 13 enrolled. In 2016, 20 master's awarded. *Degree requirements:* For master's, thesis, practicum. *Entrance requirements:* For master's, GRE or MAT, undergraduate transcript, personal statement, interview, two letters of recommendation. Additional exam requirements/recommendations for international students: Required—TOEFL. *Application deadline:* Applications are processed on a rolling basis. Application fee: $50. Electronic applications accepted. *Expenses:* Contact institution. *Financial support:* Scholarships/grants available. Financial award applicants required to submit FAFSA. *Unit head:* Anthony D'Onofrio, Associate Director, Graduate Athletic Administration, 978-998-7791, Fax: 978-232-3000, E-mail: adonofri@endicott.edu. *Application contact:* Ian Menchini, Director, Graduate Enrollment and Advising, 978-232-2744, Fax: 978-232-5292, E-mail: imenchin@endicott.edu.
Website: http://www.endicott.edu/VanLoan/Graduate-Studies/Master-Education/Athletic-Administration.aspx

Fairleigh Dickinson University, College at Florham, Anthony J. Petrocelli College of Continuing Studies, Program in Sports Administration, Madison, NJ 07940-1099. Offers MSA.

Fairleigh Dickinson University, Metropolitan Campus, Anthony J. Petrocelli College of Continuing Studies, Department of Sports Administration, Program in Sports Administration, Teaneck, NJ 07666-1914. Offers MSA.

Florida Agricultural and Mechanical University, Division of Graduate Studies, Research, and Continuing Education, College of Education, Department of Health, Physical Education, and Recreation, Tallahassee, FL 32307-3200. Offers sport management (MS). *Accreditation:* NCATE. *Program availability:* Part-time, evening/weekend. *Degree requirements:* For master's, thesis optional. *Entrance requirements:* For master's, GRE General Test, minimum GPA of 3.0. Additional exam requirements/recommendations for international students: Required—TOEFL. *Faculty research:* Administration/curriculum, work behavior, psychology.

Florida International University, College of Arts, Sciences, and Education, Department of Leadership and Professional Studies, Miami, FL 33199. Offers adult education and human resource development (MS, Ed D); counseling (MS), including rehabilitation counseling, school counseling; counselor education (MS), including clinical mental health counseling; educational administration and supervision (Ed D); educational leadership (MS, Certificate, Ed S); higher education (Ed D); higher education administration (MS); international and comparative education (MS); recreation and sport management (MS), including recreation and sport management, recreational therapy; school psychology (Ed S); urban education (MS), including instruction in urban settings, learning technologies, multicultural/bilingual, multicultural/TESOL, urban education. *Program availability:* Part-time, evening/weekend. *Faculty:* 27 full-time (19 women), 38 part-time/adjunct (25 women). *Students:* 253 full-time (191 women), 306 part-time (241 women); includes 444 minority (129 Black or African American, non-Hispanic/Latino; 3 Asian, non-Hispanic/Latino; 304 Hispanic/Latino; 8 Two or more races, non-Hispanic/Latino), 18 international. Average age 31. 366 applicants, 60% accepted, 115 enrolled. In 2016, 193 master's, 8 doctorates awarded. *Degree requirements:* For doctorate, thesis/dissertation. *Entrance requirements:* For master's, minimum GPA of 3.0; for doctorate and other advanced degree, GRE General Test. Additional exam requirements/recommendations for international students: Required—TOEFL (minimum score 550 paper-based; 80 iBT), IELTS (minimum score 6.3). *Application deadline:* For fall admission, 6/1 priority date for domestic students, 4/1 for international students; for winter admission, 10/1 priority date for domestic students, 9/1 for international students; for spring admission, 3/1 priority date for domestic students, 2/1 for international students. Applications are processed on a rolling basis. Application fee: $30. Electronic applications accepted. *Expenses:* Tuition, state resident: full-time $8912; part-time $446 per credit hour. Tuition, nonresident: full-time $21,393; part-time $992 per credit hour. *Required fees:* $2185; $195 per semester. Tuition and fees vary according to program. *Financial support:* Fellowships, research assistantships with tuition reimbursements, teaching assistantships with tuition reimbursements, Federal Work-Study, and tuition waivers (full and partial) available. Support available to part-time students. Financial award applicants required to submit FAFSA. *Unit head:* Dr. Benjamin Baez, Chair, 305-348-3214, Fax: 305-348-1515, E-mail: benjamin.baez@fiu.edu. *Application contact:* Nanett Rojas, Assistant Director, Graduate Admissions, 305-348-7464, Fax: 305-348-7441, E-mail: gradadm@fiu.edu.
Website: http://education.fiu.edu

Florida International University, College of Arts, Sciences, and Education, Department of Teaching and Learning, Miami, FL 33199. Offers art education (MA, MS); curriculum and instruction (MS, Ed D, PhD, Ed S), including curriculum development (MS), elementary education (MS), English education (MS), learning technologies (MS), mathematics education (MS), modern language education (MS), physical education (MS), science education (MS), social studies education (MS), special education (MS); early childhood education (MS); exceptional student education (Ed D); foreign language education (MS), including foreign language education, teaching English to speakers of other languages (TESOL); international/intercultural education (MS); language, literacy and culture (PhD); mathematics, science, and learning technologies (PhD); physical education (MS), including sport and fitness; reading education (MS). *Program availability:* Part-time, evening/weekend. *Faculty:* 34 full-time (23 women), 64 part-time/adjunct (48 women). *Students:* 182 full-time (154 women), 231 part-time (190 women); includes 323 minority (69 Black or African American, non-Hispanic/Latino; 10 Asian, non-Hispanic/Latino; 237 Hispanic/Latino; 7 Two or more races, non-Hispanic/Latino), 19 international. Average age 34. 282 applicants, 58% accepted, 113 enrolled. In 2016, 184 master's, 12 doctorates awarded. *Degree requirements:* For doctorate, comprehensive exam, thesis/dissertation. *Entrance requirements:* For master's, GRE General Test, Florida General Knowledge Test or Florida College Level Academic Skills Test; for doctorate and Ed S, GRE General Test. Additional exam requirements/recommendations for international students: Required—TOEFL (minimum score 550 paper-based; 80 iBT), IELTS (minimum score 6.3). *Application deadline:* For fall admission, 6/1 priority date for domestic students, 4/1 for international students; for winter admission, 10/1 priority date for domestic students, 9/1 for international students; for spring admission, 3/1 priority date for domestic students, 2/1 for international students. Applications are processed on a rolling basis. Application fee: $30. Electronic applications accepted. *Expenses:* Tuition, state resident: full-time $8912; part-time $446 per credit hour. Tuition, nonresident: full-time $21,393; part-time $992 per credit hour. *Required fees:* $2185; $195 per semester. Tuition and fees vary according to program. *Financial support:* Research assistantships with tuition reimbursements and teaching assistantships with tuition reimbursements available. *Unit head:* Dr. Lynn Miller, Chair, 305-348-2005, Fax: 305-348-2086, E-mail: lynne.miller@fiu.edu. *Application contact:* Nanett Rojas, Assistant Director, Graduate Admissions, 305-348-7464, Fax: 305-348-7441, E-mail: gradadm@fiu.edu.
Website: http://education.fiu.edu

Florida State University, The Graduate School, College of Education, Program in Sport Management, Tallahassee, FL 32306. Offers coaching (Certificate); sport management (MS, PhD). *Degree requirements:* For master's, comprehensive exam, thesis optional; for doctorate, comprehensive exam, thesis/dissertation, diagnostic exam, preliminary exam, prospectus defense, dissertation defense. *Entrance requirements:* For master's, doctorate, and Certificate, GRE General Test, minimum upper-division GPA of 3.0. Additional exam requirements/recommendations for international students: Required—TOEFL (minimum score 550 paper-based, 80 iBT), IELTS (minimum score 6.5), Michigan English Language Assessment Battery (minimum score 77), or PTE (minimum score 55). Application fee: $30. Electronic applications accepted. *Expenses:* Tuition, state resident: full-time $7263; part-time $403.51 per credit hour. Tuition, nonresident: full-time $18,087; part-time $1004.85 per credit hour. *Required fees:* $1365; $75.81 per credit hour. $20 per semester. Tuition and fees vary according to campus/location. *Financial support:* Fellowships, research assistantships, teaching assistantships, scholarships/grants, tuition waivers (full and partial), and unspecified assistantships available. Financial award application deadline: 1/15; financial award applicants required to submit FAFSA. *Faculty research:* Sociology of sport; media and culture studies in sport; sport marketing and sport consumer behavior; legal and policy studies in sport; sports gambling; sport management; social network analysis. *Unit head:* Dr. Jeffrey D. James, Professor/Department Chair, 850-644-4813, Fax: 850-644-0975, E-mail: jdjames@fsu.edu. *Application contact:* Dr. Thomas F. McMorrow, Academic Program Specialist, 850-644-0577, Fax: 850-644-0975, E-mail: tmcmorrow@fsu.edu.
Website: http://education.fsu.edu/degrees-and-programs/graduate-programs

Franklin Pierce University, Graduate and Professional Studies, Rindge, NH 03461-0060. Offers curriculum and instruction (M Ed); elementary education (MS Ed); emerging network technologies (Graduate Certificate); energy and sustainability studies (MBA, Graduate Certificate); health administration (MBA, Graduate Certificate); human resource management (MBA, Graduate Certificate); information technology (MBA); leadership (MBA); nursing education (MS); nursing leadership (MS); physical therapy (DPT); physician assistant studies (MPAS); special education (M Ed); sports management (MBA). *Accreditation:* APTA. *Program availability:* Part-time, 100% online, blended/hybrid learning. *Faculty:* 47 full-time (36 women), 165 part-time/adjunct (108 women). *Students:* 380 full-time (226 women), 245 part-time (158 women); includes 52 minority (13 Black or African American, non-Hispanic/Latino; 2 American Indian or Alaska Native, non-Hispanic/Latino; 14 Asian, non-Hispanic/Latino; 22 Hispanic/Latino; 1 Native Hawaiian or other Pacific Islander, non-Hispanic/Latino), 13 international. Average age 29. 1,995 applicants, 28% accepted, 267 enrolled. In 2016, 120 master's, 86 doctorates awarded. *Degree requirements:* For master's, concentrated original research projects; student teaching; fieldwork and/or internship; leadership project; PRAXIS I and II (for M Ed); for doctorate, concentrated original research projects, clinical fieldwork and/or internship, leadership project. *Entrance requirements:* For master's, minimum GPA of 2.5, 3 letters of recommendation; competencies in accounting, economics, statistics, and computer skills through life experience or undergraduate coursework (for MBA); certification/e-portfolio, minimum C grade in all education courses (for M Ed); license to practice as RN (for MS); for doctorate, GRE, 80 hours of observation/work in PT settings; completion of anatomy, chemistry, physics, and statistics; minimum GPA of 3.0. Additional exam requirements/recommendations for international students: Required—TOEFL (minimum score 550 paper-based; 61 iBT). *Application deadline:* Applications are processed on a rolling basis. Application fee: $0. Electronic applications accepted. *Expenses: Tuition:* Full-time $15,960; part-time $665 per credit hour. Tuition and fees vary according to program. *Financial support:* Teaching assistantships with tuition reimbursements, career-related internships or fieldwork, and unspecified assistantships available. Support available to part-time students. Financial award applicants required to submit FAFSA. *Faculty research:* Evidence-based practice in sports physical therapy, human resource management in economic crisis, leadership in nursing, innovation in sports facility management, differentiated learning and understanding by design. *Unit head:* Dr. Maria Altobello, Dean, 603-647-3509, Fax: 603-229-4580, E-mail: altobellom@franklinpierce.edu. *Application contact:* Graduate Studies, 800-325-1090, Fax: 603-626-4815, E-mail: cgps@franklinpierce.edu.
Website: http://www.franklinpierce.edu/academics/gradstudies/index.htm

Georgetown University, Graduate School of Arts and Sciences, School of Continuing Studies, Washington, DC 20057. Offers American studies (MALS); Catholic studies (MALS); classical civilizations (MALS); emergency and disaster management (MPS); ethics and the professions (MALS); global strategic communications (MPS); hospitality management (MPS); human resources management (MPS); humanities (MALS); individualized study (MALS); integrated marketing communications (MPS); international affairs (MALS); Islam and Muslim-Christian relations (MALS); journalism (MPS); liberal studies (DLS); literature and society (MALS); medieval and early modern European studies (MALS); public relations and corporate communications (MPS); real estate (MPS); religious studies (MALS); social and public policy (MALS); sports industry management (MPS); systems engineering management (MPS); technology management (MPS); the theory and practice of American democracy (MALS); urban and regional planning (MPS); visual culture (MALS). MPS in systems engineering management offered jointly with Stevens Institute of Technology. *Entrance requirements:* Additional exam requirements/recommendations for international students: Required—TOEFL.

The George Washington University, School of Business, Department of Tourism and Hospitality Management, Washington, DC 20052. Offers destination management (Professional Certificate); event and meeting management (MTA); event management (Professional Certificate); hospitality management (MTA); individualized studies (MTA); sport management (MTA); sustainable tourism destination management (MTA); tourism and hospitality management (MBA). *Program availability:* Part-time, online learning. *Students:* 66 full-time (46 women), 38 part-time (30 women); includes 27 minority (16

Black or African American, non-Hispanic/Latino; 6 Asian, non-Hispanic/Latino; 3 Hispanic/Latino; 2 Two or more races, non-Hispanic/Latino), 44 international. Average age 28. 113 applicants, 76% accepted, 40 enrolled. In 2016, 45 master's awarded. *Degree requirements:* For master's, comprehensive exam, thesis. *Entrance requirements:* For master's, GRE General Test. Additional exam requirements/recommendations for international students: Required—TOEFL. *Application deadline:* For fall admission, 4/1 priority date for domestic students; for spring admission, 10/1 for domestic students. Applications are processed on a rolling basis. Application fee: $75. *Financial support:* In 2016–17, 32 students received support. Fellowships, teaching assistantships, career-related internships or fieldwork, Federal Work-Study, institutionally sponsored loans, and tuition waivers (partial) available. Financial award application deadline: 4/1. *Faculty research:* Tourism policy, tourism impact forecasting, geotourism. *Unit head:* Prof. Lisa Delpy Neirotti, Faculty Director, 202-994-6623, E-mail: delpy@gwu.edu. *Application contact:* Christopher Storer, Executive Director, Graduate Admissions, 202-994-1212, E-mail: gwmba@gwu.edu.
Website: http://business.gwu.edu/tourism/

Georgia Southern University, Jack N. Averitt College of Graduate Studies, College of Health and Human Sciences, School of Health and Kinesiology, Program in Sport Management, Statesboro, GA 30460. Offers MS. *Program availability:* Part-time. *Students:* 11 full-time (2 women), 19 part-time (10 women); includes 9 minority (7 Black or African American, non-Hispanic/Latino; 1 Hispanic/Latino; 1 Two or more races, non-Hispanic/Latino), 1 international. Average age 28. 52 applicants, 58% accepted, 16 enrolled. In 2016, 19 master's awarded. *Degree requirements:* For master's, terminal exam. *Entrance requirements:* For master's, GMAT, GRE, resume. Additional exam requirements/recommendations for international students: Required—TOEFL (minimum score 550 paper-based; 80 iBT), IELTS (minimum score 6). *Application deadline:* For fall admission, 3/1 priority date for domestic and international students; for spring admission, 10/15 priority date for domestic students, 10/15 for international students. Applications are processed on a rolling basis. Application fee: $50. Electronic applications accepted. *Expenses:* Tuition, state resident: full-time $7236; part-time $277 per semester hour. Tuition, nonresident: full-time $27,118; part-time $1105 per semester hour. *Required fees:* $2092. *Financial support:* In 2016–17, 5 students received support, including 12 fellowships with full tuition reimbursements available (averaging $7,750 per year), 9 research assistantships with full tuition reimbursements available (averaging $7,750 per year), 33 teaching assistantships with full tuition reimbursements available (averaging $7,750 per year); career-related internships or fieldwork, Federal Work-Study, scholarships/grants, and tuition waivers (full) also available. Support available to part-time students. Financial award application deadline: 4/15; financial award applicants required to submit FAFSA. *Faculty research:* Outsourcing sport marketing, international integration of North American sports, sport law, sport financing, sport economics. *Unit head:* Dr. Kathi Thomas, Chair, 912-478-0200, Fax: 912-478-0386, E-mail: kthomas@georgiasouthern.edu.

Georgia State University, College of Education and Human Development, Department of Kinesiology and Health, Program in Sports Administration, Atlanta, GA 30302-3083. Offers MS. *Degree requirements:* For master's, comprehensive exam. *Entrance requirements:* For master's, GRE General Test, minimum GPA of 2.5. *Application deadline:* For fall admission, 5/1 for domestic students; for spring admission, 10/1 for domestic students. Application fee: $50. *Expenses:* Tuition, state resident: full-time $6876; part-time $382 per credit hour. Tuition, nonresident: full-time $22,374; part-time $1243 per credit hour. *Required fees:* $2128; $1064 per term. Part-time tuition and fees vary according to course load and program. *Financial support:* Research assistantships available. *Faculty research:* Sports marketing. *Unit head:* Dr. Jacalyn Lea Lund, Chair, 404-413-8051, E-mail: jlund@gsu.edu. *Application contact:* Kaila Muecke, Academic Ambassador, 404-413-8360, E-mail: khambassador@gsu.edu.
Website: http://kh.education.gsu.edu/academics-admissions/sports-administration/

Gonzaga University, School of Education, Spokane, WA 99258. Offers clinical mental health counseling (MA); elementary education (MIT); leadership and administration (MA); marriage and family counseling (MA); school counseling (MA); secondary education (MIT); special education (M Ed, MIT); sport and athletic administration (MA). *Accreditation:* NCATE. *Program availability:* Part-time, evening/weekend, 100% online. *Faculty:* 22 full-time (17 women), 38 part-time/adjunct (22 women). *Students:* 104 full-time (73 women), 275 part-time (184 women); includes 31 minority (5 Black or African American, non-Hispanic/Latino; 1 American Indian or Alaska Native, non-Hispanic/Latino; 3 Asian, non-Hispanic/Latino; 18 Hispanic/Latino; 4 Two or more races, non-Hispanic/Latino), 163 international. Average age 32. 419 applicants, 67% accepted, 165 enrolled. In 2016, 39 master's awarded. *Degree requirements:* For master's, comprehensive exam. *Entrance requirements:* For master's, GRE, MAT, and/or Washington Educators Skills Test-Basic (WEST-B), official transcripts from all colleges or universities attended, interview, two letters of recommendation, resume, essay, minimum GPA of 3.0. Additional exam requirements/recommendations for international students: Required—TOEFL (minimum score 580 paper-based, 88 iBT) or IELTS (minimum score 6.5). *Application deadline:* Applications are processed on a rolling basis. Application fee: $50. Electronic applications accepted. *Expenses:* Contact institution. *Financial support:* In 2016–17, 28 students received support. Scholarships/grants and tuition waivers available. Support available to part-time students. Financial award applicants required to submit FAFSA. *Unit head:* Dr. Vincent Alfonso, Dean, 509-313-3594, Fax: 509-313-5821, E-mail: alfonso@gonzaga.edu. *Application contact:* Luke Cairney, Graduate Admissions Program Specialist, 509-313-3821, E-mail: cairney@gonzaga.edu.
Website: http://www.gonzaga.edu/Academics/Colleges-and-Schools/School-of-Education

Grambling State University, School of Graduate Studies and Research, College of Education, Department of Kinesiology, Sport and Leisure Studies, Grambling, LA 71245. Offers sports administration (MS). *Program availability:* Part-time. *Degree requirements:* For master's, comprehensive exam. *Entrance requirements:* For master's, GRE General Test, minimum GPA of 2.5 on last degree. Additional exam requirements/recommendations for international students: Required—TOEFL (minimum score 500 paper-based; 62 iBT). Electronic applications accepted. *Faculty research:* Administrative relations and organization, measuring human performance, sport history from ancient times through current date, learning dynamics of personality and sports selection.

Grand Canyon University, Colangelo College of Business, Phoenix, AZ 85017-1097. Offers accounting (MBA, MS); business analytics (MS); disaster preparedness and executive fire service leadership (MS); finance (MBA); general management (MBA); health systems management (MBA); information technology management (MS); leadership (MBA, MS); marketing (MBA); organizational leadership and entrepreneurship (MS); project management (MBA); sports business (MBA); strategic human resource management (MBA). *Accreditation:* ACBSP. *Program availability:* Part-time, evening/weekend, online learning. *Faculty:* 8 full-time (3 women), 147 part-time/adjunct (49 women). *Students:* 1 full-time (0 women), 2,121 part-time (1,165 women); includes 341 minority (249 Black or African American, non-Hispanic/Latino; 17 American Indian or Alaska Native, non-Hispanic/Latino; 15 Asian, non-Hispanic/Latino; 29 Hispanic/Latino; 4 Native Hawaiian or other Pacific Islander, non-Hispanic/Latino; 27 Two or more races, non-Hispanic/Latino), 20 international. Average age 38. In 2016, 569 master's awarded. *Entrance requirements:* For master's, equivalent of two years' full-time professional work experience. Additional exam requirements/recommendations for international students: Required—TOEFL (minimum score 575 paper-based; 90 iBT), IELTS (minimum score 7). *Application deadline:* For fall admission, 8/21 for domestic students, 7/2 for international students; for spring admission, 12/24 for domestic students, 11/1 for international students. Applications are processed on a rolling basis. Application fee: $0. Electronic applications accepted. *Financial support:* Federal Work-Study available. Support available to part-time students. Financial award applicants required to submit FAFSA. *Unit head:* Kim Donaldson, Dean, 602-639-6597, E-mail: kdonaldson@gcu.edu. *Application contact:* Matt Tidwell, Enrollment Manager, 602-639-6020, E-mail: mtidwell@gcu.edu.
Website: https://www.gcu.edu/colangelo-college-of-business.php

Grand View University, Graduate Studies, Des Moines, IA 50316-1599. Offers athletic training (MS); clinical nurse leader (MSN, Post Master's Certificate); nursing education (MSN, Post Master's Certificate); organizational leadership (MS); sport management (MS); teacher leadership (M Ed); urban education (M Ed). *Program availability:* Part-time, evening/weekend. *Degree requirements:* For master's, completion of all required coursework in common core and selected track with minimum cumulative GPA of 3.0 and no more than two grades of C. *Entrance requirements:* For master's, GRE, GMAT, or essay, minimum undergraduate GPA of 3.0, professional resume, 3 letters of recommendation, interview. Additional exam requirements/recommendations for international students: Required—TOEFL (minimum score 550 paper-based). Electronic applications accepted.

Hampton University, School of Education and Human Development, Program in Sport Administration, Hampton, VA 23668. Offers MS. *Program availability:* Part-time, evening/weekend. *Faculty:* 4 full-time (1 woman). *Students:* 19 full-time (7 women), 22 part-time (1 woman); includes 37 minority (all Black or African American, non-Hispanic/Latino), 1 international. Average age 24. 34 applicants, 79% accepted, 25 enrolled. In 2016, 20 master's awarded. *Degree requirements:* For master's, thesis (for some programs). *Entrance requirements:* For master's, GRE. Additional exam requirements/recommendations for international students: Required—TOEFL (minimum score 525 paper-based) or IELTS (6.5). *Application deadline:* For fall admission, 6/1 priority date for domestic students, 4/1 priority date for international students; for spring admission, 11/1 priority date for domestic students, 9/1 priority date for international students; for summer admission, 4/1 priority date for domestic students, 2/1 priority date for international students. Applications are processed on a rolling basis. Application fee: $35. Electronic applications accepted. *Expenses:* Contact institution. *Financial support:* Fellowships, research assistantships, teaching assistantships, and career-related internships or fieldwork available. Financial award application deadline: 6/30; financial award applicants required to submit FAFSA. *Faculty research:* International sport, intercollegiate sport, sport leadership, professional sport, event management. *Unit head:* Dr. Aaron Livingston, Program Coordinator, 757-637-2278, E-mail: aaron.livingston@hamptonu.edu.

Hardin-Simmons University, Graduate School, Kelley College of Business, Abilene, TX 79698-0001. Offers business administration (MBA); sports management (MBA). *Accreditation:* ACBSP. *Program availability:* Part-time. *Faculty:* 7 full-time (2 women), 1 part-time/adjunct (0 women). *Students:* 16 full-time (7 women), 11 part-time (3 women); includes 2 minority (1 Hispanic/Latino; 1 Two or more races, non-Hispanic/Latino), 4 international. Average age 23. In 2016, 11 master's awarded. *Degree requirements:* For master's, thesis or alternative. *Entrance requirements:* For master's, GMAT, minimum GPA of 3.0 in upper-level course work, resume, interview. Additional exam requirements/recommendations for international students: Required—TOEFL (minimum score 600 paper-based; 75 iBT). *Application deadline:* For fall admission, 8/15 priority date for domestic students, 4/1 for international students; for spring admission, 1/5 priority date for domestic students, 9/1 for international students. Applications are processed on a rolling basis. Application fee: $50. Electronic applications accepted. *Expenses: Tuition:* Full-time $12,510; part-time $695 per credit hour. *Required fees:* $325; $110 per semester. *Financial support:* In 2016–17, 18 students received support. Fellowships and scholarships/grants available. Support available to part-time students. Financial award application deadline: 6/30; financial award applicants required to submit FAFSA. *Unit head:* Dr. Jennifer Plantier, Program Director, 325-671-2166, Fax: 325-670-1523, E-mail: jplantier@hsutx.edu. *Application contact:* Dr. Nancy Kucinski, Dean of Graduate Studies, 325-670-1298, Fax: 325-670-1564, E-mail: gradoff@hsutx.edu.
Website: http://www.hsutx.edu/academics/kelley/graduate/

Henderson State University, Graduate Studies, Teachers College, Department of Health, Physical Education, Recreation and Athletic Training, Arkadelphia, AR 71999-0001. Offers sports administration (MS). *Program availability:* Part-time. *Faculty:* 2 full-time (0 women), 1 part-time/adjunct (0 women). *Students:* 3 full-time (1 woman), 52 part-time (15 women); includes 23 minority (22 Black or African American, non-Hispanic/Latino; 1 Hispanic/Latino), 7 international. Average age 25. 23 applicants, 91% accepted, 21 enrolled. In 2016, 20 master's awarded. *Entrance requirements:* For master's, GRE General Test or MAT, minimum GPA of 2.7 as an undergraduate student. Additional exam requirements/recommendations for international students: Required—TOEFL (minimum score 600 paper-based); Recommended—IELTS (minimum score 6.5). *Application deadline:* For fall admission, 8/1 priority date for domestic students, 6/30 priority date for international students; for spring admission, 1/1 priority date for domestic students, 11/30 priority date for international students. Applications are processed on a rolling basis. Application fee: $25 ($75 for international students). *Expenses:* Tuition, state resident: full-time $6288; part-time $3144 per credit hour. Tuition, nonresident: full-time $12,888; part-time $6444 per credit hour. *Required fees:* $1429; $1024 per credit hour. Tuition and fees vary according to course load and student level. *Financial support:* In 2016–17, 10 teaching assistantships with partial tuition reimbursements (averaging $4,000 per year) were awarded; scholarships/grants and unspecified assistantships also available. Financial award application deadline: 4/15; financial award applicants required to submit FAFSA. *Unit head:* Dr. Lynn Glover-Stanley, Chair, 870-230-5200, E-mail: stanlel@hsu.edu. *Application contact:* Dr. Ken Taylor, Graduate Dean, 870-230-5126, Fax: 870-230-5479, E-mail: taylorke@hsu.edu.
Website: http://www.hsu.edu/hper/

Hofstra University, Frank G. Zarb School of Business, Programs in Management and General Business, Hempstead, NY 11549. Offers business administration (MBA), including health services management, management, sports and entertainment management, strategic business management, strategic healthcare management; general management (Advanced Certificate); human resource management (MS, Advanced Certificate). *Program availability:* Part-time, evening/weekend, blended/hybrid learning. *Students:* 140 full-time (67 women), 159 part-time (70 women); includes 100 minority (24 Black or African American, non-Hispanic/Latino; 41 Asian, non-Hispanic/Latino; 32 Hispanic/Latino; 1 Native Hawaiian or other Pacific Islander, non-Hispanic/Latino; 2 Two or more races, non-Hispanic/Latino), 26 international. Average age 33. 354 applicants, 58% accepted, 94 enrolled. In 2016, 84 master's awarded. *Degree requirements:* For master's, thesis optional, capstone course (for MBA), thesis (for MS), minimum GPA of 3.0. *Entrance requirements:* For master's, GMAT/GRE, 2 letters of recommendation, resume, essay. Additional exam requirements/recommendations for international students: Required—TOEFL (minimum score 550 paper-based; 80 iBT);

Sports Management

Recommended—IELTS (minimum score 6). *Application deadline:* Applications are processed on a rolling basis. Application fee: $75. Electronic applications accepted. *Expenses:* $1,170 per credit. *Financial support:* In 2016–17, 65 students received support, including 43 fellowships with full and partial tuition reimbursements available (averaging $4,813 per year); research assistantships with full and partial tuition reimbursements available, career-related internships or fieldwork, Federal Work-Study, institutionally sponsored loans, scholarships/grants, tuition waivers (full and partial), and unspecified assistantships also available. Support available to part-time students. Financial award applicants required to submit FAFSA. *Faculty research:* Organizational change; sustainability; entrepreneurial spawning; family business; global supply chain strategies. *Unit head:* Dr. Kaushik Sengupta, Chairperson, 516-463-7825, Fax: 516-463-4834, E-mail: kaushik.sengupta@hofstra.edu. *Application contact:* Sunil Samuel, Assistant Vice President of Admissions, 516-463-4723, Fax: 516-463-4664, E-mail: graduateadmission@hofstra.edu.
Website: http://www.hofstra.edu/business/

Hofstra University, School of Education, Specialized Programs in Education, Hempstead, NY 11549. Offers applied behavior analysis (Advanced Certificate); early childhood special education (MS Ed, Advanced Certificate); educational and policy leadership (Ed D); educational leadership (Advanced Certificate), including school building leader/school district business leader; educational leadership and policy studies (MS Ed), including K-12; gifted education (Advanced Certificate), including school building leader/school district business leader; health education PK-12 teaching certification (MS); inclusive early childhood special education (MS Ed); inclusive elementary special education (MS Ed); inclusive secondary special education (MS Ed); literacy studies (MS Ed, Ed D, PhD, Advanced Certificate), including birth-grade 6 (MS Ed, Advanced Certificate), birth-grade 6 and special education (birth-grade2) (MS Ed), grades 5-12 (MS Ed, Advanced Certificate); physical education (MS); secondary education generalist (MS Ed), including students with disabilities 7-12; special education (MS Ed, Advanced Certificate); special education assessment and diagnosis (Advanced Certificate); special education generalist (MS Ed), including extension in secondary education; sport science (MS), including strength and conditioning; teaching students with severe or multiple disabilities (Advanced Certificate). *Program availability:* Part-time, evening/weekend, 100% online, blended/hybrid learning. *Students:* 149 full-time (115 women), 258 part-time (187 women); includes 97 minority (50 Black or African American, non-Hispanic/Latino; 1 American Indian or Alaska Native, non-Hispanic/Latino; 11 Asian, non-Hispanic/Latino; 34 Hispanic/Latino; 1 Native Hawaiian or other Pacific Islander, non-Hispanic/Latino), 5 international. Average age 32. 250 applicants, 88% accepted, 146 enrolled. In 2016, 85 master's, 13 doctorates, 35 other advanced degrees awarded. *Degree requirements:* For master's, one foreign language, comprehensive exam (for some programs), thesis (for some programs), electronic portfolio, capstone course, internship, practicum, student teaching, seminars, minimum GPA of 3.0; for doctorate, one foreign language, comprehensive exam, thesis/dissertation, qualifying hearing. *Entrance requirements:* For master's, GRE, interview, letters of recommendation, portfolio, essay, certification; for doctorate, GRE or MAT, interview, resume, essay, master's degree, 3 letters of recommendation, writing sample; for Advanced Certificate, GRE, interview, letters of recommendation, essay, professional experience, resume, master's degree. Additional exam requirements/recommendations for international students: Required—TOEFL (minimum score 550 paper-based; 80 iBT). *Application deadline:* Applications are processed on a rolling basis. Application fee: $75. Electronic applications accepted. *Expenses: Tuition:* Full-time $1240. *Required fees:* $970. Tuition and fees vary according to program. *Financial support:* In 2016–17, 244 students received support, including 117 fellowships with full and partial tuition reimbursements available (averaging $3,705 per year), 12 research assistantships with full and partial tuition reimbursements available (averaging $6,490 per year); career-related internships or fieldwork, Federal Work-Study, institutionally sponsored loans, scholarships/grants, traineeships, tuition waivers (full and partial), and unspecified assistantships also available. Support available to part-time students. Financial award applicants required to submit FAFSA. *Faculty research:* Collaborative teaching and learning; language and culture; new media literacies; applied behavior analysis; K-12 leadership development. *Unit head:* Dr. Elfreda Blue, Chairperson, 516-463-5762, Fax: 516-463-6184, E-mail: elfreda.blue@hofstra.edu. *Application contact:* Sunil Samuel, Assistant Vice President of Admissions, 516-463-4723, Fax: 516-463-4664, E-mail: graduateadmission@hofstra.edu.
Website: http://www.hofstra.edu/education/

Hofstra University, School of Health Professions and Human Services, Programs in Health, Hempstead, NY 11549. Offers health administration (MHA); health informatics (MS); occupational therapy (MS); public health (MPH); sport science (MS), including strength and conditioning. *Program availability:* Part-time, evening/weekend. *Students:* 213 full-time (133 women), 96 part-time (65 women); includes 155 minority (54 Black or African American, non-Hispanic/Latino; 1 American Indian or Alaska Native, non-Hispanic/Latino; 63 Asian, non-Hispanic/Latino; 32 Hispanic/Latino; 4 Native Hawaiian or other Pacific Islander, non-Hispanic/Latino; 1 Two or more races, non-Hispanic/Latino), 25 international. Average age 27. 582 applicants, 47% accepted, 140 enrolled. In 2016, 116 master's awarded. *Degree requirements:* For master's, internship, minimum GPA of 3.0. *Entrance requirements:* For master's, interview, 2 letters of recommendation, essay, resume. Additional exam requirements/recommendations for international students: Required—TOEFL (minimum score 550 paper-based; 80 iBT). *Application deadline:* Applications are processed on a rolling basis. Application fee: $75. Electronic applications accepted. *Expenses: Tuition:* Full-time $1240. *Required fees:* $970. Tuition and fees vary according to program. *Financial support:* In 2016–17, 127 students received support, including 74 fellowships with full and partial tuition reimbursements available (averaging $3,271 per year), 5 research assistantships with full and partial tuition reimbursements available (averaging $7,505 per year); career-related internships or fieldwork, Federal Work-Study, institutionally sponsored loans, scholarships/grants, traineeships, tuition waivers (full and partial), and unspecified assistantships also available. Support available to part-time students. Financial award applicants required to submit FAFSA. *Faculty research:* HIV/AIDS, LGBTQ health, correctional health, dental public health, fitness assessment and injury risk in collegiate athletes, fitness assessment and screening in wild land firefighters. *Unit head:* Dr. Jayne Ellinger, Chairperson, 516-463-6952, Fax: 516-463-6275, E-mail: jayne.ellinger@hofstra.edu. *Application contact:* Sunil Samuel, Assistant Vice President of Admissions, 516-463-4723, Fax: 516-463-4664, E-mail: graduateadmission@hofstra.edu.
Website: http://www.hofstra.edu/academics/colleges/healthscienceshumanservices/

Howard Payne University, Program in Sport and Wellness Leadership, Brownwood, TX 76801-2715. Offers M Ed. *Program availability:* Part-time. *Faculty:* 2 full-time (0 women). *Students:* 19 part-time (4 women); includes 4 minority (1 Black or African American, non-Hispanic/Latino; 3 Hispanic/Latino). Average age 30. *Entrance requirements:* For master's, baccalaureate degree and major or minor in exercise and sport science, kinesiology, sport administration, wellness or a related field; minimum undergraduate GPA of 3.0; official transcripts; 500-word statement of professional goals; two letters of recommendation. Additional exam requirements/recommendations for international students: Required—TOEFL. Electronic applications accepted. *Financial support:* Unspecified assistantships available. Financial award applicants required to submit FAFSA. *Unit head:* Dr. Graham Hatcher, Professor and Chair, Exercise and Sport Science/Director, Graduate Program in Sport and Recreation Leadership, 325-649-8966, E-mail: ghatcher@hputx.edu.

Howard University, Graduate School, Department of Health, Human Performance and Leisure Studies, Washington, DC 20059-0002. Offers exercise physiology (MS); health education (MS); sports studies (MS), including sociology of sports, sports management; urban recreation (MS), including leisure studies. *Program availability:* Part-time, evening/weekend. *Degree requirements:* For master's, comprehensive exam, thesis. *Entrance requirements:* For master's, BS in human performance or related field. Additional exam requirements/recommendations for international students: Recommended—TOEFL. Electronic applications accepted. *Faculty research:* Health promotion, cardiovascular hypertension, physical activity, sport and human rights issues.

Husson University, Master of Business Administration Program, Bangor, ME 04401-2999. Offers athletic administration (MBA); biotechnology and innovation (MBA); general business administration (MBA); healthcare management (MBA); hospitality and tourism management (MBA); organizational management (MBA); risk management (MBA). *Program availability:* Part-time, evening/weekend, 100% online, blended/hybrid learning. *Faculty:* 8 full-time (4 women), 20 part-time/adjunct (5 women). *Students:* 81 full-time (47 women), 249 part-time (142 women); includes 32 minority (9 Black or African American, non-Hispanic/Latino; 2 American Indian or Alaska Native, non-Hispanic/Latino; 17 Asian, non-Hispanic/Latino; 3 Hispanic/Latino; 1 Two or more races, non-Hispanic/Latino), 11 international. Average age 34. 199 applicants, 78% accepted, 119 enrolled. In 2016, 109 master's awarded. *Degree requirements:* For master's, comprehensive exam (for some programs), thesis optional. *Entrance requirements:* For master's, minimum GPA of 3.0, letter of recommendation. Additional exam requirements/recommendations for international students: Required—TOEFL (minimum score 550 paper-based; 80 iBT), IELTS (minimum score 6.5). *Application deadline:* Applications are processed on a rolling basis. Application fee: $50. Electronic applications accepted. *Expenses:* $450 per credit; $450 fees per full-time year or $220 part-time. *Financial support:* Career-related internships or fieldwork, Federal Work-Study, scholarships/grants, and unspecified assistantships available. Financial award application deadline: 4/15; financial award applicants required to submit FAFSA. *Unit head:* Prof. Stephanie Shayne, Director, Graduate and Online Programs, 207-404-5632, Fax: 207-992-4987, E-mail: shaynes@husson.edu. *Application contact:* Kristen Card, Director of Graduate Admissions, 207-404-5660, Fax: 207-941-7935, E-mail: cardk@husson.edu.
Website: http://www.husson.edu/college-of-business/school-of-business-and-management/master-of-business-administration-mba/

Indiana State University, College of Graduate and Professional Studies, College of Nursing, Health, and Human Services, Department of Kinesiology, Recreation, and Sport, Terre Haute, IN 47809. Offers physical education (MS); recreation and sport management (MS); sport management (PhD). *Degree requirements:* For master's, comprehensive exam (for some programs), thesis (for some programs). *Entrance requirements:* For master's, GRE General Test, undergraduate major in related field. Electronic applications accepted.

Indiana University Bloomington, School of Public Health, Department of Kinesiology, Bloomington, IN 47405. Offers applied sport science (MS); athletic administration/sport management (MS); athletic training (MS); biomechanics (MS); ergonomics (MS); exercise physiology (MS); human performance (PhD), including biomechanics, exercise physiology, motor learning/control, sport management; motor learning/control (MS); physical activity (MPH); physical activity, fitness and wellness (MS). *Program availability:* Part-time. Terminal master's awarded for partial completion of doctoral program. *Degree requirements:* For master's, thesis optional; for doctorate, variable foreign language requirement, comprehensive exam, thesis/dissertation. *Entrance requirements:* For master's, GRE General Test, minimum GPA of 2.8; for doctorate, GRE General Test, minimum graduate GPA of 3.5, undergraduate 3.0. Additional exam requirements/recommendations for international students: Required—TOEFL (minimum score 80 iBT). *Faculty research:* Exercise physiology and biochemistry, sports biomechanics, human motor control, adaptation of fitness and exercise to special populations.

Indiana University Bloomington, School of Public Health, Department of Recreation, Park, and Tourism Studies, Bloomington, IN 47405-7000. Offers leisure behavior (PhD); outdoor recreation (MS); park and public lands management (MS); recreation administration (MS); recreational sports administration (MS); recreational therapy (MS); tourism management (MS). Terminal master's awarded for partial completion of doctoral program. *Degree requirements:* For master's, thesis optional; for doctorate, comprehensive exam, thesis/dissertation. *Entrance requirements:* For master's, GRE General Test, minimum GPA of 2.8; for doctorate, GRE General Test, minimum GPA of 3.0 (undergraduate), 3.5 (graduate). Additional exam requirements/recommendations for international students: Required—TOEFL (minimum score 550 paper-based; 80 iBT). Electronic applications accepted. *Faculty research:* Leisure counseling, gerontology, special populations, planning and development.

Indiana University of Pennsylvania, School of Graduate Studies and Research, College of Health and Human Services, Department of Kinesiology, Health, and Sport Science, Program in Sport Science/Sport Management, Indiana, PA 15705. Offers MS. *Faculty:* 10 full-time (3 women). *Students:* 16 full-time (8 women), 1 part-time (0 women); includes 4 minority (2 Black or African American, non-Hispanic/Latino; 2 Two or more races, non-Hispanic/Latino), 1 international. Average age 25. 29 applicants, 79% accepted, 14 enrolled. In 2016, 10 master's awarded. *Degree requirements:* For master's, thesis or internship. *Entrance requirements:* Additional exam requirements/recommendations for international students: Required—TOEFL (minimum score 540 paper-based). Application fee: $50. *Expenses:* Contact institution. *Financial support:* In 2016–17, 7 research assistantships with tuition reimbursements (averaging $4,417 per year) were awarded. Financial award application deadline: 4/15; financial award applicants required to submit FAFSA. *Unit head:* Dr. Richard Hsaio, Graduate Coordinator, 724-357-0123, E-mail: hsaio@iup.edu.
Website: http://www.iup.edu/grad/sportscience/default.aspx

Iona College, Hagan School of Business, Department of Marketing and International Business, New Rochelle, NY 10801-1890. Offers international business (AC, PMC); marketing (MBA); sports and entertainment management (AC). *Program availability:* Part-time, evening/weekend. *Faculty:* 2 full-time (1 woman), 3 part-time/adjunct (all women). *Students:* 11 full-time (1 woman), 22 part-time (11 women); includes 9 minority (4 Black or African American, non-Hispanic/Latino; 2 Asian, non-Hispanic/Latino; 3 Hispanic/Latino), 5 international. Average age 25. 19 applicants, 100% accepted, 9 enrolled. In 2016, 22 master's awarded. *Entrance requirements:* For master's, GMAT, 2 letters of recommendation, minimum GPA of 3.0; for other advanced degree, GMAT, minimum GPA of 3.0. Additional exam requirements/recommendations for international students: Required—TOEFL (minimum score 550 paper-based; 80 iBT), IELTS (minimum score 6.5). *Application deadline:* For fall admission, 8/15 priority date for domestic students, 8/1 priority date for international students; for winter admission, 11/15 priority date for domestic students, 11/1 priority date for international students; for spring admission, 2/15 priority date for domestic students, 2/1 priority date for

international students; for summer admission, 5/15 for domestic students, 5/1 priority date for international students. Applications are processed on a rolling basis. Application fee: $50. Electronic applications accepted. *Expenses:* Contact institution. *Financial support:* In 2016–17, 13 students received support. Scholarships/grants, tuition waivers (partial), and unspecified assistantships available. Support available to part-time students. Financial award application deadline: 4/15; financial award applicants required to submit FAFSA. *Faculty research:* Business ethics, international retailing, mega-marketing, consumer behavior and consumer confidence. *Unit head:* Dr. Susan G. Rozensher, Department Chair, 914-637-2748, E-mail: srozensher@iona.edu. *Application contact:* Katelyn Brunck, Director of MBA Admissions, 914-633-2451, Fax: 914-633-2277, E-mail: kbrunck@iona.edu.
Website: http://www.iona.edu/Academics/Hagan-School-of-Business/Departments/Marketing/Graduate-Programs.aspx

Ithaca College, School of Business, Program in Business Administration, Ithaca, NY 14850. Offers sport management (MBA). *Accreditation:* AACSB. *Faculty:* 15 full-time (6 women), 2 part-time/adjunct (0 women). *Students:* 7 full-time (3 women), 1 part-time (0 women); includes 1 minority (Black or African American, non-Hispanic/Latino), 1 international. Average age 24. 8 applicants, 75% accepted, 4 enrolled. In 2016, 4 master's awarded. *Degree requirements:* For master's, thesis optional. *Entrance requirements:* For master's, GMAT. Additional exam requirements/recommendations for international students: Required—TOEFL (minimum score 550 paper-based; 80 iBT). *Application deadline:* For fall admission, 5/15 for domestic and international students; for spring admission, 11/1 for domestic and international students. Applications are processed on a rolling basis. Application fee: $40. Electronic applications accepted. *Expenses:* Contact institution. *Financial support:* In 2016–17, 6 students received support, including 5 fellowships (averaging $7,700 per year); career-related internships or fieldwork, Federal Work-Study, and scholarships/grants also available. Support available to part-time students. Financial award application deadline: 3/1; financial award applicants required to submit CSS PROFILE or FAFSA. *Unit head:* Rasoul Resvanian, Associate Dean and Director, MBA Programs, 607-274-1762, Fax: 607-274-1263, E-mail: rrezvanian@ithaca.edu. *Application contact:* Nicole Eversley Bradwell, Director, Office of Admission, 607-274-3124, Fax: 607-274-1263, E-mail: admission@ithaca.edu.
Website: http://www.ithaca.edu/business/mba

Jackson State University, Graduate School, College of Education and Human Development, Department of Health, Physical Education and Recreation, Jackson, MS 39217. Offers physical education (MS Ed); sport science (MS). *Accreditation:* NCATE. *Program availability:* Part-time, evening/weekend, 100% online, blended/hybrid learning. *Faculty:* 4 full-time (1 woman). *Students:* 37 full-time (21 women), 66 part-time (37 women); includes 99 minority (98 Black or African American, non-Hispanic/Latino; 1 Two or more races, non-Hispanic/Latino), 2 international. Average age 32. 74 applicants, 70% accepted, 30 enrolled. In 2016, 21 master's awarded. *Degree requirements:* For master's, comprehensive exam, thesis or alternative. *Entrance requirements:* For master's, GRE General Test. Additional exam requirements/recommendations for international students: Required—TOEFL (minimum score 520 paper-based; 67 iBT). *Application deadline:* For fall admission, 3/1 priority date for domestic students, 3/1 for international students; for spring admission, 10/1 for domestic and international students. Applications are processed on a rolling basis. Application fee: $25. Electronic applications accepted. *Expenses:* Contact institution. *Financial support:* Career-related internships or fieldwork, Federal Work-Study, scholarships/grants, and unspecified assistantships available. Support available to part-time students. Financial award application deadline: 3/1; financial award applicants required to submit FAFSA. *Unit head:* Dr. Patricia Kennedy, Interim Chair, 601-979-2765, Fax: 601-979-2766, E-mail: patricia.r.kennedy@jsums.edu. *Application contact:* Dr. Hill Williams, Interim Director of Sport Science, 601-979-0275, Fax: 601-979-2766, E-mail: hill.williams@jsums.edu.
Website: http://www.jsums.edu/healthedu/

Jacksonville University, Brooks Rehabilitation College of Healthcare Sciences, School of Applied Health Sciences, Program in Sport Management, Jacksonville, FL 32211. Offers MS. Program offered in conjunction with the Davis College of Business. *Program availability:* Online learning. *Expenses: Tuition:* Full-time $13,320. One-time fee: $50 part-time. Tuition and fees vary according to course load, degree level, campus/location and program.

Kansas Wesleyan University, Program in Business Administration, Salina, KS 67401-6196. Offers business administration (MBA); sports management (MBA). *Program availability:* Part-time, evening/weekend. *Entrance requirements:* For master's, GMAT, minimum graduate GPA of 3.0 or undergraduate GPA of 3.25.

Kent State University, College of Education, Health and Human Services, School of Foundations, Leadership and Administration, Sports Recreation and Management Program, Kent, OH 44242-0001. Offers sport and recreation management (MA); sports studies (MA). *Degree requirements:* For master's, thesis optional. *Entrance requirements:* For master's, GRE if undergraduate GPA below 3.0, goals statement, 2 letters of recommendation. Additional exam requirements/recommendations for international students: Required—TOEFL (minimum score 550 paper-based; 80 iBT). *Expenses:* Tuition, state resident: full-time $10,864; part-time $495 per credit hour. Tuition, nonresident: full-time $18,380; part-time $837 per credit hour.

Keystone College, Program in Sport Leadership and Management, La Plume, PA 18440. Offers MS. *Program availability:* Part-time, online only, 100% online. *Faculty:* 2 full-time (1 woman), 3 part-time/adjunct (2 women). *Students:* 8 applicants, 88% accepted, 4 enrolled. *Degree requirements:* For master's, internship or research project. *Entrance requirements:* For master's, college transcripts, resume or curriculum vitae. Additional exam requirements/recommendations for international students: Required—TOEFL (minimum score 80 iBT) or IELTS (minimum score 6.5). *Application deadline:* For fall admission, 8/1 for domestic students; for spring admission, 12/1 for domestic students; for summer admission, 5/1 for domestic students. Applications are processed on a rolling basis. Application fee: $50. Electronic applications accepted. *Expenses:* Contact institution. *Financial support:* In 2016–17, 1 student received support. Unspecified assistantships available. Financial award application deadline: 5/1; financial award applicants required to submit FAFSA. *Unit head:* Mac Ross, PhD, Assistant Professor, 570-945-8434, E-mail: mac.ross@keystone.edu. *Application contact:* Jennifer Sekol, Director of Admissions, 570-945-8117, Fax: 570-945-7916, E-mail: jennifer.sekol@keystone.edu.

Lasell College, Graduate and Professional Studies in Sport Management, Newton, MA 02466. Offers sport hospitality management (MS, Graduate Certificate); sport leadership (MS, Graduate Certificate); sport non-profit management (MS, Graduate Certificate). *Program availability:* Part-time, evening/weekend, online only, 100% online. *Faculty:* 4 full-time (0 women), 3 part-time/adjunct (1 woman). *Students:* 14 full-time (4 women), 30 part-time (10 women); includes 10 minority (9 Black or African American, non-Hispanic/Latino; 1 Hispanic/Latino). Average age 30. 40 applicants, 43% accepted, 9 enrolled. In 2016, 21 master's, 2 other advanced degrees awarded. *Degree requirements:* For master's, minimum GPA of 3.0; internship or thesis. *Entrance requirements:* For master's, one-page personal statement, 2 letters of recommendation, resume, bachelor's degree transcript; for Graduate Certificate, bachelor's degree transcript, 2 letters of recommendation, 1-page personal statement, resume. Additional exam requirements/recommendations for international students: Required—TOEFL (minimum score 550 paper-based, 79 iBT) or IELTS (minimum score 6). *Application deadline:* For fall admission, 8/31 priority date for domestic students, 6/30 priority date for international students; for spring admission, 12/31 priority date for domestic students, 10/31 priority date for international students. Applications are processed on a rolling basis. Electronic applications accepted. *Expenses:* $600 per credit. *Financial support:* In 2016–17, 4 students received support. Federal Work-Study, scholarships/grants, and tuition discounts available. Support available to part-time students. Financial award application deadline: 8/31; financial award applicants required to submit FAFSA. *Faculty research:* How do fans attribute team failure, investigating cross-cultural difference in attribution; sense of ownership as a key predictor of fan loyalty; fans' normative beliefs about sponsorship and sponsors, investigation of new attitudinal variables in sponsorship. *Unit head:* Dr. Joan Dolamore, Dean of Graduate and Professional Studies, 617-243-2485, Fax: 617-243-2450, E-mail: gradinfo@lasell.edu. *Application contact:* Adrienne Franciosi, Director of Graduate Enrollment, 617-243-2214, Fax: 617-243-2450, E-mail: gradinfo@lasell.edu.
Website: http://www.lasell.edu/academics/graduate-and-professional-studies/programs-of-study/master-of-science-in-sport-management.html

Lewis University, College of Arts and Sciences, Program in Organizational Leadership, Romeoville, IL 60446. Offers higher education/student services (MA); non-profit management (MA); organizational management (MA); professional and executive coaching (MA); training and development (MA). *Program availability:* Part-time, evening/weekend, 100% online. *Students:* 15 full-time (12 women), 176 part-time (130 women); includes 75 minority (51 Black or African American, non-Hispanic/Latino; 2 American Indian or Alaska Native, non-Hispanic/Latino; 2 Asian, non-Hispanic/Latino; 16 Hispanic/Latino; 4 Two or more races, non-Hispanic/Latino), 2 international. Average age 36. *Entrance requirements:* For master's, bachelor's degree, at least 24 years of age, minimum of 3 years of work experience, minimum GPA of 3.0, letter of recommendation. Additional exam requirements/recommendations for international students: Required—TOEFL (minimum score 550 paper-based; 80 iBT). *Application deadline:* For fall admission, 5/1 priority date for international students; for spring admission, 11/15 priority date for international students. Applications are processed on a rolling basis. Application fee: $40. Electronic applications accepted. *Expenses: Tuition:* Full-time $13,860; part-time $770 per credit hour. *Required fees:* $75 per semester. Tuition and fees vary according to degree level and program. *Financial support:* Tuition waivers and unspecified assistantships available. Financial award application deadline: 5/1; financial award applicants required to submit FAFSA. *Unit head:* Dr. Keith Lavine, Chair of Organizational Leadership, 815-838-0500, E-mail: lavineke@lewisu.edu. *Application contact:* Nancy Wiksten, Graduate Admission Counselor, 815-836-5628, Fax: 815-836-5578, E-mail: grad@lewisu.edu.

Liberty University, School of Education, Lynchburg, VA 24515. Offers educational leadership (Ed D); gifted education (Certificate); math specialist (M Ed); middle grades (MAT, Certificate); reading specialist (M Ed); school leadership (Certificate); secondary education (MAT); sport management (MS), including administration, outdoor recreation, sport management, tourism. *Accreditation:* NCATE. *Program availability:* Part-time, online learning. *Students:* 1,910 full-time (1,427 women), 4,420 part-time (3,311 women); includes 1,451 minority (1,182 Black or African American, non-Hispanic/Latino; 33 American Indian or Alaska Native, non-Hispanic/Latino; 44 Asian, non-Hispanic/Latino; 46 Hispanic/Latino; 11 Native Hawaiian or other Pacific Islander, non-Hispanic/Latino; 135 Two or more races, non-Hispanic/Latino), 87 international. Average age 37. 5,120 applicants, 44% accepted, 1193 enrolled. In 2016, 1,378 master's, 151 doctorates, 497 other advanced degrees awarded. *Degree requirements:* For doctorate, comprehensive exam, thesis/dissertation. *Entrance requirements:* For master's, GRE General Test or MAT (if taken in or before 1999), 2 letters of recommendation, minimum undergraduate GPA of 3.0, curriculum vitae; for doctorate and Certificate, GRE General Test or MAT (if taken before 1999), minimum master's GPA of 3.0, 3 years of teaching experience. Additional exam requirements/recommendations for international students: Required—TOEFL (minimum score 600 paper-based; 100 iBT). *Application deadline:* For fall admission, 6/1 for domestic students; for spring admission, 11/1 for domestic students. Applications are processed on a rolling basis. Application fee: $50. Electronic applications accepted. *Expenses:* Contact institution. *Financial support:* Federal Work-Study and tuition waivers (partial) available. *Faculty research:* Self-determination, character education, bibliotherapy, learning styles, distance education. *Unit head:* Dr. Heather Schoffstall, Dean, 434-582-2445, Fax: 434-582-2468, E-mail: awgunter@liberty.edu. *Application contact:* Jay Bridge, Director of Graduate Admissions, 800-424-9595, Fax: 800-628-7977, E-mail: gradadmissions@liberty.edu.
Website: http://www.liberty.edu/academics/education/graduate/

Lindenwood University, Graduate Programs, Plaster School of Business and Entrepreneurship, St. Charles, MO 63301-1695. Offers accountancy (M Acc); accounting (MBA); business administration (MBA); entrepreneurial studies (MBA); finance (MBA, MS); human resource management (MBA); international business (MBA); leadership (MA); management (MBA); marketing (MBA, MS); nonprofit administration (MA); public administration (MBA); sport management (MA); supply chain management (MBA). *Accreditation:* ACBSP. *Program availability:* Part-time, evening/weekend, 100% online. *Faculty:* 15 full-time (6 women), 25 part-time/adjunct (7 women). *Students:* 197 full-time (97 women), 213 part-time (132 women); includes 81 minority (62 Black or African American, non-Hispanic/Latino; 1 American Indian or Alaska Native, non-Hispanic/Latino; 4 Asian, non-Hispanic/Latino; 9 Hispanic/Latino; 5 Two or more races, non-Hispanic/Latino), 83 international. Average age 31. 279 applicants, 54% accepted, 133 enrolled. In 2016, 269 master's awarded. *Degree requirements:* For master's, comprehensive exam (for some programs), thesis (for some programs), minimum GPA of 3.0. *Entrance requirements:* For master's, interview, minimum undergraduate cumulative GPA of 3.0, letter of recommendation. Additional exam requirements/recommendations for international students: Required—TOEFL (minimum score 550 paper-based; 80 iBT); Recommended—IELTS (minimum score 6.5). *Application deadline:* For fall admission, 8/28 priority date for domestic and international students; for winter admission, 1/8 priority date for domestic and international students; for spring admission, 3/5 for domestic students, 3/5 priority date for international students; for summer admission, 6/4 priority date for domestic and international students. Applications are processed on a rolling basis. Application fee: $30 ($100 for international students). Electronic applications accepted. *Expenses:* Contact institution. *Financial support:* In 2016–17, 256 students received support. Career-related internships or fieldwork, Federal Work-Study, institutionally sponsored loans, scholarships/grants, tuition waivers (partial), and unspecified assistantships available. Financial award application deadline: 6/30; financial award applicants required to submit FAFSA. *Unit head:* Roger Ellis, Dean, School of Business and Entrepreneurship, 636-949-4839, E-mail: rellis@lindenwood.edu. *Application contact:* Tylor Kostich, Director, Evening and Graduate Admissions, 636-949-4138, Fax: 636-949-4109, E-mail: adultadmissions@lindenwood.edu.
Website: http://www.lindenwood.edu/academics/academic-schools/robert-w-plaster-school-of-business-entrepreneurship/

Lipscomb University, College of Business, Nashville, TN 37204-3951. Offers accountancy (M Acc); accounting (MBA); business administration (MM); conflict management (MBA); financial services (MBA); health care informatics (MBA);

healthcare management (MBA); information security (MBA); leadership (MBA); nonprofit management (MBA); professional accountancy (Certificate); sports management (MBA); strategic human resources (MBA); sustainability (MBA); MBA/MS; Pharm D/MM. *Accreditation:* ACBSP. *Program availability:* Part-time, evening/weekend. *Faculty:* 22 full-time (4 women), 12 part-time/adjunct (4 women). *Students:* 112 full-time (51 women), 69 part-time (34 women); includes 30 minority (17 Black or African American, non-Hispanic/Latino; 3 Asian, non-Hispanic/Latino; 8 Hispanic/Latino; 2 Two or more races, non-Hispanic/Latino), 5 international. Average age 32. 244 applicants, 55% accepted, 54 enrolled. In 2016, 164 master's awarded. *Entrance requirements:* For master's, GMAT, transcripts, interview, 2 references, resume. Additional exam requirements/recommendations for international students: Required—TOEFL (minimum score 570 paper-based). *Application deadline:* For fall admission, 6/15 for domestic students, 2/1 for international students; for winter admission, 6/1 for international students; for spring admission, 11/15 for domestic students. Applications are processed on a rolling basis. Application fee: $50 ($75 for international students). Electronic applications accepted. *Expenses:* $1,150-$1,290 per hour, depending on program. *Financial support:* Career-related internships or fieldwork, scholarships/grants, tuition waivers (partial), and unspecified assistantships available. Support available to part-time students. Financial award application deadline: 7/1; financial award applicants required to submit FAFSA. *Faculty research:* Impact of spirituality on organization commitment, women in corporate leadership, psychological empowerment, training. *Unit head:* Allison Duke, Associate Dean of Graduate Business Programs, 615-966-5732, Fax: 615-966-1818, E-mail: allison.duke@lipscomb.edu. *Application contact:* Karen Risley, Manager, Graduate Business Recruiting, 615-966-5145, E-mail: karen.risley@lipscomb.edu.
Website: http://www.lipscomb.edu/business/Graduate-Programs

Lock Haven University of Pennsylvania, The Stephen Poorman College of Business, Information Systems, and Human Services, Lock Haven, PA 17745-2390. Offers clinical mental health counseling (MS); sport science (MS). *Program availability:* Online learning. *Degree requirements:* For master's, thesis. *Entrance requirements:* For master's, minimum undergraduate GPA of 3.0. Additional exam requirements/recommendations for international students: Required—TOEFL. Electronic applications accepted.

Lynn University, College of Business and Management, Boca Raton, FL 33431-5598. Offers business administration (MBA), including aviation management, financial valuation and investment management, hospitality management, human resource management, international business management, marketing, media management, sports management. *Program availability:* Part-time, evening/weekend, 100% online, blended/hybrid learning. *Faculty:* 24 full-time (9 women), 24 part-time/adjunct (4 women). *Students:* 265 full-time (125 women), 182 part-time (96 women); includes 100 minority (41 Black or African American, non-Hispanic/Latino; 11 Asian, non-Hispanic/Latino; 42 Hispanic/Latino; 6 Two or more races, non-Hispanic/Latino), 119 international. Average age 28. 280 applicants, 94% accepted, 181 enrolled. In 2016, 219 master's awarded. *Degree requirements:* For master's, strategic management seminar, simulation capstone. *Entrance requirements:* For master's, bachelor's degree from accredited institution, resume, letter of recommendation, official transcripts, essay/personal statement. Additional exam requirements/recommendations for international students: Required—TOEFL (minimum score 550 paper-based; 80 iBT), IELTS (minimum score 6.5). *Application deadline:* For fall admission, 8/18 for domestic students, 8/4 for international students; for spring admission, 12/15 for domestic students, 12/1 for international students; for summer admission, 4/17 for domestic students, 4/3 for international students. Applications are processed on a rolling basis. Application fee: $45. Electronic applications accepted. *Expenses:* $725 per credit. *Financial support:* In 2016–17, 115 students received support. Career-related internships or fieldwork, Federal Work-Study, scholarships/grants, tuition waivers (full and partial), and unspecified assistantships available. Support available to part-time students. Financial award application deadline: 3/1; financial award applicants required to submit FAFSA. *Faculty research:* Market volatility investing, biometric research, sports legal history, organizational leadership, urban economic development and productivity. *Unit head:* Dr. RT Good, Dean of the College of Business and Management, 561-237-7458, E-mail: rgood@lynn.edu. *Application contact:* Steven Pruitt, Director of Graduate and Undergraduate Evening Admission, 561-237-7834, Fax: 561-237-7100, E-mail: spruitt@lynn.edu.
Website: http://www.lynn.edu/academics/colleges/business-and-management

Manhattanville College, School of Business, Master of Science in Sport Business Management Program, Purchase, NY 10577-2132. Offers MS. *Program availability:* Part-time, evening/weekend. *Students:* 46 (28 women); includes 12 minority (8 Black or African American, non-Hispanic/Latino; 1 Asian, non-Hispanic/Latino; 3 Hispanic/Latino). Average age 25. 54 applicants, 54% accepted, 18 enrolled. In 2016, 23 master's awarded. *Degree requirements:* For master's, thesis (for some programs), internship, portfolio. *Entrance requirements:* For master's, transcripts, 2 letters of recommendation, resume. Additional exam requirements/recommendations for international students: Required—TOEFL (minimum score 563 paper-based; 85 iBT). *Application deadline:* Applications are processed on a rolling basis. Application fee: $75. Electronic applications accepted. *Expenses: Tuition:* Full-time $16,470; part-time $915 per credit. *Required fees:* $60 per semester. Part-time tuition and fees vary according to course load and program. *Financial support:* Federal Work-Study, institutionally sponsored loans, scholarships/grants, and unspecified assistantships available. Financial award applicants required to submit FAFSA. *Faculty research:* Use of analytics by teams, leagues, and corporations; technology for athletes and for marketing; fan experience; quantitative methods; sports marketing. *Unit head:* Dave Torromeo, Executive Director of Sport Business Management Program, 914-323-5301, Fax: 914-694-3488, E-mail: david.torromeo@mville.edu. *Application contact:* Monika Pottgen, Assistant Director, Recruitment and Admissions, 914-323-5150, E-mail: business@mville.edu.
Website: https://www.mville.edu/programs/ms-sport-business-management

Marquette University, Graduate School of Management, Executive MBA Program, Milwaukee, WI 53201-1881. Offers economics (MBA); finance (MBA); human resources (MBA); international business (MBA); management information systems (MBA); marketing (MBA); operations and supply chain management (MBA); sports business (MBA). *Accreditation:* AACSB. *Students:* 39 full-time (12 women); includes 7 minority (4 Black or African American, non-Hispanic/Latino; 2 Asian, non-Hispanic/Latino; 1 Hispanic/Latino). Average age 38. 25 applicants, 96% accepted, 29 enrolled. In 2016, 14 master's awarded. *Degree requirements:* For master's, international trip. *Entrance requirements:* For master's, GMAT or GRE, two letters of recommendation, official transcripts from current and previous colleges/universities. Additional exam requirements/recommendations for international students: Required—TOEFL (minimum score 550 paper-based; 88 iBT), IELTS (minimum score 6.5), PTE. *Application deadline:* For fall admission, 2/15 for domestic and international students. Application fee: $50. Electronic applications accepted. *Expenses:* Contact institution. *Financial support:* Application deadline: 2/15. *Faculty research:* International trade and finance, customer relationship management, consumer satisfaction, customer service. *Unit head:* Dr. Brian Till, Dean, 414-288-5724. *Application contact:* Dr. Jeanne Simmons, Associate Dean, 414-288-7145.
Website: http://www.busadm.mu.edu/emba/

Marquette University, Graduate School of Management, Program in Business Administration, Milwaukee, WI 53201-1881. Offers business administration (MBA); economics (MBA); entrepreneurship (Certificate); finance (MBA); human resources (MBA); international business (MBA); management information systems (MBA); marketing (MBA); operations and supply chain management (MBA); sports business (MBA); JD/MBA; MBA/MA; MBA/MSN. *Accreditation:* AACSB. *Program availability:* Part-time, evening/weekend. *Students:* 25 full-time (12 women), 202 part-time (57 women); includes 17 minority (5 Black or African American, non-Hispanic/Latino; 6 Asian, non-Hispanic/Latino; 2 Hispanic/Latino; 1 Native Hawaiian or other Pacific Islander, non-Hispanic/Latino; 3 Two or more races, non-Hispanic/Latino), 7 international. Average age 31. 107 applicants, 87% accepted, 113 enrolled. In 2016, 107 master's, 5 other advanced degrees awarded. *Degree requirements:* For Certificate, business plan. *Entrance requirements:* For master's, GMAT or GRE, letters of recommendation. Additional exam requirements/recommendations for international students: Required—TOEFL (minimum score 550 paper-based; 88 iBT), IELTS (minimum score 6.5), PTE. *Application deadline:* For fall admission, 2/15 for domestic and international students. Applications are processed on a rolling basis. Application fee: $50. Electronic applications accepted. *Financial support:* Fellowships, research assistantships, teaching assistantships, Federal Work-Study, institutionally sponsored loans, scholarships/grants, and tuition waivers (full and partial) available. Support available to part-time students. Financial award application deadline: 2/15. *Faculty research:* Ethics in the professions, services marketing, technology impact on decision-making, mentoring. *Unit head:* Dr. Brian Till, Dean, 414-288-5724. *Application contact:* Dr. Jeanne Simmons, Associate Dean, 414-288-7145.
Website: http://business.marquette.edu/academics/mba

Marshall University, Academic Affairs Division, College of Health Professions, School of Kinesiology, Program in Sport Administration, Huntington, WV 25755. Offers MS. *Degree requirements:* For master's, thesis optional, comprehensive assessment. *Entrance requirements:* For master's, GRE General Test.

Maryville University of Saint Louis, The John E. Simon School of Business, St. Louis, MO 63141-7299. Offers accounting (MBA, Certificate); business studies (Certificate); cyber security (MBA); cybersecurity (Certificate); financial services (MBA, Certificate); healthcare practice management (MBA, Certificate); human resource management (MBA); information technology (MBA, Certificate); management (MBA, Certificate); management and leadership (MA); marketing (MBA, Certificate); project management (MBA); sport business management (MBA); supply chain management/logistics (MBA). *Accreditation:* ACBSP. *Program availability:* Part-time, evening/weekend, 100% online, blended/hybrid learning. *Faculty:* 7 full-time (3 women), 34 part-time/adjunct (9 women). *Students:* 84 full-time (40 women), 223 part-time (118 women); includes 67 minority (40 Black or African American, non-Hispanic/Latino; 2 American Indian or Alaska Native, non-Hispanic/Latino; 8 Asian, non-Hispanic/Latino; 12 Hispanic/Latino; 1 Native Hawaiian or other Pacific Islander, non-Hispanic/Latino; 4 Two or more races, non-Hispanic/Latino), 15 international. Average age 32. In 2016, 67 master's awarded. *Entrance requirements:* Additional exam requirements/recommendations for international students: Required—TOEFL (minimum score 563 paper-based; 85 iBT). *Application deadline:* Applications are processed on a rolling basis. Electronic applications accepted. *Expenses:* $650 per credit hour. *Financial support:* Career-related internships or fieldwork, Federal Work-Study, tuition waivers (partial), and campus employment available. Financial award application deadline: 3/1; financial award applicants required to submit FAFSA. *Faculty research:* Global business, e-marketing, strategic planning, interpersonal management skills, financial analysis. *Unit head:* Pam Horwitz, Interim Dean, 314-529-9680, Fax: 314-529-9975. *Application contact:* Dustin Loeffler, Director for Graduate Studies in Business, 314-529-9571, Fax: 314-529-9975, E-mail: dloeffler@maryville.edu.
Website: http://www.maryville.edu/bu/business-administration-masters/

Mercyhurst University, Graduate Studies, Program in Organizational Leadership, Erie, PA 16546. Offers accounting (MS); higher education administration (MS); human resources (MS); organizational leadership (MS, Certificate); sports leadership (MS); strategy and innovation (MS). *Program availability:* Part-time, evening/weekend. *Degree requirements:* For master's, thesis. *Entrance requirements:* For master's, GRE General Test or MAT, interview, resume, essay, three professional references, transcripts. Additional exam requirements/recommendations for international students: Required—TOEFL (minimum score 80 iBT), IELTS (minimum score 6.5). Electronic applications accepted. *Faculty research:* Leadership training, organizational communication, leadership pedagogy.

Messiah College, Program in Higher Education, Mechanicsburg, PA 17055. Offers college athletics management (MA); self-designed concentration (MA); student affairs (MA). *Program availability:* Part-time. Electronic applications accepted. *Faculty research:* College athletics management, assessment and student learning outcomes, the life and legacy of Ernest L. Boyer, common learning, student affairs practice.

Midwestern State University, Billie Doris McAda Graduate School, West College of Education, Program in Sport Administration, Wichita Falls, TX 76308. Offers M Ed.

Millersville University of Pennsylvania, College of Graduate Studies and Adult Learning, College of Education and Human Services, Department of Wellness and Sport Sciences, Program in Sport Management: Athletic Coaching Option, Millersville, PA 17551-0302. Offers coaching education (Post-Master's Certificate); sport management: athletic coaching (M Ed). *Program availability:* Part-time, evening/weekend. *Faculty:* 7 full-time (3 women). *Students:* 6 part-time (2 women). Average age 27. 3 applicants, 67% accepted. In 2016, 4 master's awarded. Terminal master's awarded for partial completion of doctoral program. *Degree requirements:* For master's, thesis optional, internship. *Entrance requirements:* For master's, GRE, MAT, GMAT, or interview with writing assignment if undergraduate cumulative GPA lower than 3.0, all transcripts, at least 1 academic reference, sport management goal statement. Additional exam requirements/recommendations for international students: Required—TOEFL (minimum score 600 paper-based), IELTS (minimum score 6). *Application deadline:* Applications are processed on a rolling basis. Application fee: $40. Electronic applications accepted. *Expenses:* $483 per credit resident tuition; $725 per credit non-resident tuition. *Financial support:* In 2016–17, 2 students received support. Unspecified assistantships available. Financial award application deadline: 3/15; financial award applicants required to submit FAFSA. *Faculty research:* Applied sport management; leadership and sport; marketing and sport; gender and sport; leadership development; ADR, restorative justice and hazing; legal issues applied to sport management; women and fitness/sport. *Unit head:* Dr. Rebecca J. Mowrey, Coordinator, 717-871-4214, Fax: 717-871-7987, E-mail: rebecca.mowrey@millersville.edu. *Application contact:* Dr. Victor S. DeSantis, Dean of College of Graduate Studies and Adult Learning/Associate Provost for Civic and Community Engagement, 717-871-7619, Fax: 717-871-7954, E-mail: victor.desantis@millersville.edu.
Website: http://www.millersville.edu/wssd/graduate/index.php

Millersville University of Pennsylvania, College of Graduate Studies and Adult Learning, College of Education and Human Services, Department of Wellness and Sport Sciences, Program in Sport Management: Athletic Management Option, Millersville, PA 17551-0302. Offers M Ed. *Program availability:* Part-time, evening/weekend. *Faculty:* 7 full-time (3 women). *Students:* 3 full-time (1 woman), 18 part-time (7 women); includes 6

minority (4 Black or African American, non-Hispanic/Latino; 1 Hispanic/Latino; 1 Two or more races, non-Hispanic/Latino). Average age 25. 17 applicants, 88% accepted, 6 enrolled. In 2016, 11 master's awarded. *Degree requirements:* For master's, thesis optional, internship. *Entrance requirements:* For master's, GRE, MAT, GMAT, or interview with writing assignment if undergraduate cumulative GPA lower than 3.0, all transcripts, at least 1 academic reference, sport management goal statement. Additional exam requirements/recommendations for international students: Required—TOEFL (minimum score 600 paper-based), IELTS (minimum score 6). *Application deadline:* Applications are processed on a rolling basis. Application fee: $40. Electronic applications accepted. *Expenses:* $483 per credit resident tuition; $725 per credit non-resident tuition. *Financial support:* In 2016–17, 11 students received support. Unspecified assistantships available. Financial award application deadline: 3/15; financial award applicants required to submit FAFSA. *Faculty research:* Applied sport management; leadership and sport; marketing and sport; gender and sport; leadership development; ADR, restorative justice and hazing; legal issues applied to sport management; women and fitness/sport; growth and physical activity. *Unit head:* Dr. Rebecca J. Mowrey, Coordinator, 717-871-4214, Fax: 717-871-7987, E-mail: rebecca.mowrey@millersville.edu. *Application contact:* Dr. Victor S. DeSantis, Dean of College of Graduate Studies and Adult Learning/Associate Provost for Civic and Community Engagement, 717-871-7619, Fax: 717-871-7954, E-mail: victor.desantis@millersville.edu.
Website: http://www.millersville.edu/wssd/

Misericordia University, College of Business, Master of Business Administration Program, Dallas, PA 18612-1098. Offers accounting (MBA); healthcare management (MBA); human resources (MBA); management (MBA); sport management (MBA). *Program availability:* Part-time, evening/weekend, online learning. *Entrance requirements:* For master's, GMAT, MAT, GRE (50th percentile or higher), or minimum undergraduate GPA of 3.0, interview. Additional exam requirements/recommendations for international students: Required—TOEFL. Electronic applications accepted. Application fee is waived when completed online.

Mississippi State University, College of Education, Department of Kinesiology, Mississippi State, MS 39762. Offers exercise physiology (MS); exercise science (PhD); sport administration (MS); sport pedagogy (MS); sport studies (PhD). *Program availability:* Part-time, blended/hybrid learning. *Faculty:* 14 full-time (2 women). *Students:* 57 full-time (17 women), 6 part-time (0 women); includes 11 minority (5 Black or African American, non-Hispanic/Latino; 2 Asian, non-Hispanic/Latino; 2 Hispanic/Latino; 2 Two or more races, non-Hispanic/Latino), 6 international. Average age 26. 75 applicants, 56% accepted, 30 enrolled. In 2016, 32 master's awarded. *Degree requirements:* For master's, comprehensive exam, thesis optional; for doctorate, comprehensive exam. *Entrance requirements:* For master's, GRE General Test, minimum GPA of 2.75 on undergraduate work from four-year accredited institution, 3.0 graduate; for doctorate, GRE, minimum GPA of 3.4 on previous graduate degree(s) earned from accredited institutions. Additional exam requirements/recommendations for international students: Required—TOEFL (minimum score 550 paper-based; 79 iBT); Recommended—IELTS (minimum score 6.5). *Application deadline:* For fall admission, 7/1 for domestic students, 5/1 for international students; for spring admission, 11/1 for domestic students, 9/1 for international students. Applications are processed on a rolling basis. Application fee: $60. Electronic applications accepted. *Expenses:* Tuition, state resident: full-time $7670; part-time $852.50 per credit hour. Tuition, nonresident: full-time $20,790; part-time $2310.50 per credit hour. Part-time tuition and fees vary according to course load. *Financial support:* In 2016–17, 16 teaching assistantships with partial tuition reimbursements (averaging $10,227 per year) were awarded; career-related internships or fieldwork, Federal Work-Study, institutionally sponsored loans, and unspecified assistantships also available. Financial award application deadline: 4/1; financial award applicants required to submit FAFSA. *Faculty research:* Static balance and stepping performance of older adults, organizational justice, public health, strength training and recovery drinks, high risk drinking perceptions and behaviors. *Unit head:* Dr. Stanley P. Brown, Professor and Department Head, 662-325-2963, Fax: 662-325-4525, E-mail: spb107@msstate.edu. *Application contact:* Linda Bonner, Senior Admissions Assistant, 662-325-3363, E-mail: lbonner@grad.msstate.edu.
Website: http://www.kinesiology.msstate.edu/

Missouri State University, Graduate College, Interdisciplinary Program in Professional Studies, Springfield, MO 65897. Offers administrative studies (Certificate); applied communication (MS); criminal justice (MS); environmental management (MS); homeland security (MS); individualized (MS); screenwriting and producing (MS); sports management (MS). *Program availability:* Part-time, evening/weekend, 100% online, blended/hybrid learning. *Students:* 60 full-time (34 women), 66 part-time (29 women); includes 17 minority (7 Black or African American, non-Hispanic/Latino; 1 Asian, non-Hispanic/Latino; 5 Hispanic/Latino; 4 Two or more races, non-Hispanic/Latino), 43 international. Average age 33. 76 applicants, 58% accepted, 38 enrolled. In 2016, 48 master's awarded. *Degree requirements:* For master's, comprehensive exam, thesis or alternative. *Entrance requirements:* For master's, GRE, GMAT (if GPA less than 3.0). Additional exam requirements/recommendations for international students: Required—TOEFL (minimum score 550 paper-based; 79 iBT), IELTS (minimum score 6). *Application deadline:* For fall admission, 7/15 priority date for domestic students; for spring admission, 12/1 priority date for domestic students; for summer admission, 5/1 for domestic students. Applications are processed on a rolling basis. Application fee: $35 ($50 for international students). Electronic applications accepted. *Expenses:* Tuition, state resident: full-time $5830. Tuition, nonresident: full-time $10,708. *Required fees:* $1130. Tuition and fees vary according to class time, course level, course load and program. *Financial support:* Career-related internships or fieldwork, Federal Work-Study, institutionally sponsored loans, scholarships/grants, and unspecified assistantships available. Support available to part-time students. Financial award application deadline: 3/31; financial award applicants required to submit FAFSA. *Unit head:* Dr. Gerald Masterson, Program Director, 417-836-5251, Fax: 417-836-6888, E-mail: mps@missouristate.edu. *Application contact:* Michael Edwards, Coordinator of Graduate Admissions, 417-836-5330, Fax: 417-836-6200, E-mail: michaeledwards@missouristate.edu.
Website: http://mps.missouristate.edu

Missouri Western State University, Program in Applied Science, St. Joseph, MO 64507-2294. Offers chemistry (MAS); engineering technology management (MAS); human factors and usability testing (MAS); industrial life science (MAS); sport and fitness management (MAS). *Accreditation:* AACSB. *Program availability:* Part-time. *Students:* 41 full-time (18 women), 27 part-time (11 women); includes 7 minority (6 Black or African American, non-Hispanic/Latino; 1 Two or more races, non-Hispanic/Latino), 15 international. Average age 29. 43 applicants, 88% accepted, 30 enrolled. In 2016, 34 master's awarded. *Entrance requirements:* Additional exam requirements/recommendations for international students: Recommended—TOEFL (minimum score 79 iBT), IELTS (minimum score 6). *Application deadline:* For fall admission, 7/15 for domestic and international students; for spring admission, 10/1 for domestic and international students; for summer admission, 3/15 for domestic students. Applications are processed on a rolling basis. Application fee: $50. Electronic applications accepted. *Expenses:* Tuition, state resident: full-time $6548; part-time $327.39 per credit hour. Tuition, nonresident: full-time $11,848; part-time $592.39 per credit hour. *Required fees:* $542; $99 per credit hour. $176 per semester. One-time fee: $50. Tuition and fees vary according to course load and program. *Financial support:* Scholarships/grants and unspecified assistantships available. Support available to part-time students. *Unit head:* Dr. Benjamin D. Caldwell, Dean of the Graduate School, 816-271-4394, Fax: 816-271-4525, E-mail: graduate@missouriwestern.edu.

Montclair State University, The Graduate School, College of Education and Human Services, Program in Exercise Science and Physical Education, Montclair, NJ 07043-1624. Offers exercise science (MA); sports administration and coaching (MA); teaching and supervision in physical education (MA). *Program availability:* Part-time, evening/weekend. *Degree requirements:* For master's, comprehensive exam, thesis or alternative. *Entrance requirements:* For master's, GRE General Test, essay, 2 letters of recommendation. Additional exam requirements/recommendations for international students: Required—TOEFL (minimum score 83 iBT), IELTS (minimum score 6.5). Electronic applications accepted. *Expenses:* Tuition, state resident: part-time $553 per credit. Tuition, nonresident: part-time $854 per credit. *Required fees:* $91 per credit. Tuition and fees vary according to program.

Morehead State University, Graduate Programs, College of Business and Public Affairs, School of Business Administration, Morehead, KY 40351. Offers business administration (MBA); information systems (MSIS); sport management (MA). *Program availability:* Part-time, evening/weekend. *Entrance requirements:* For master's, GRE or GMAT. Additional exam requirements/recommendations for international students: Required—TOEFL (minimum score 500 paper-based). Electronic applications accepted.

Mount Ida College, Program in Management, Newton, MA 02459-3310. Offers healthcare management (MSM); human resource management (MSM); interior architecture (MSM); leadership in sport (MSM); management (MSM). *Program availability:* Part-time, evening/weekend, online learning. *Entrance requirements:* For master's, resume, undergraduate transcripts, letters of reference, personal essay. Additional exam requirements/recommendations for international students: Required—TOEFL (minimum score 550 paper-based; 79 iBT); Recommended—IELTS (minimum score 5.5). Electronic applications accepted. *Expenses:* Contact institution.

Mount St. Mary's University, Program in Sport Management, Emmitsburg, MD 21727-7799. Offers MS. *Program availability:* Part-time, evening/weekend. *Faculty:* 2 full-time (1 woman). *Students:* 8 full-time (5 women), 8 part-time (2 women); includes 3 minority (2 Black or African American, non-Hispanic/Latino; 1 Hispanic/Latino), 1 international. Average age 25. 15 applicants, 80% accepted, 8 enrolled. *Degree requirements:* For master's, project or internship. *Entrance requirements:* For master's, personal essay; baccalaureate degree; minimum undergraduate GPA of 2.75, two full years of relevant work experience with resume, or GMAT. Additional exam requirements/recommendations for international students: Required—TOEFL (minimum score 550 paper-based; 83 iBT). *Application deadline:* Applications are processed on a rolling basis. Electronic applications accepted. *Expenses:* $610 per credit hour. *Financial support:* Unspecified assistantships available. Financial award applicants required to submit FAFSA. *Unit head:* Carol Rinkoff, Director of Graduate Business Program, 301-447-5840, E-mail: rinkoff@msmary.edu. *Application contact:* Melissa Flohr, Assistant Director of Graduate Programs, Business, 301-447-5451, E-mail: mflohr@msmary.edu.
Website: http://msmary.edu/School_of_business/graduate-programs/Sport-Management.html

Neumann University, Graduate Programs in Business and Information Management, Aston, PA 19014-1298. Offers accounting (MS), including forensic and fraud detection; sport business (MS). *Program availability:* Part-time, evening/weekend. *Faculty:* 3 full-time (2 women), 4 part-time/adjunct (1 woman). *Students:* 9 full-time (2 women), 33 part-time (12 women); includes 14 minority (11 Black or African American, non-Hispanic/Latino; 1 Asian, non-Hispanic/Latino; 2 Hispanic/Latino). Average age 31. 58 applicants, 50% accepted, 26 enrolled. In 2016, 16 master's awarded. *Degree requirements:* For master's, thesis (for some programs). *Entrance requirements:* For master's, official transcripts from all institutions attended, resume, letter of intent, 2-3 official letters of recommendation. Additional exam requirements/recommendations for international students: Required—TOEFL (minimum score 70 iBT). *Application deadline:* Applications are processed on a rolling basis. Application fee: $0. Electronic applications accepted. *Expenses:* $600 per credit (for MS in accounting); $495 per credit (MS in sport business). *Financial support:* Scholarships/grants and health care benefits available. Support available to part-time students. Financial award application deadline: 3/15; financial award applicants required to submit FAFSA. *Unit head:* Dr. Eric Wellington, Dean of Business and Information Management, 610-558-5596, Fax: 610-558-5574, E-mail: wellinge@neumann.edu. *Application contact:* Dr. Erika Davis, Director of Adult and Graduate Admissions, 800-9-NEUMANN Ext. 5208, Fax: 610-361-2548, E-mail: GradAdultAdmiss@neumann.edu.

New England College, Program in Sports and Recreation Management: Coaching, Henniker, NH 03242-3293. Offers MS. *Entrance requirements:* For master's, resume, 2 letters of reference.

New Mexico Highlands University, Graduate Studies, College of Arts and Sciences, Department of Exercise and Sport Sciences, Las Vegas, NM 87701. Offers human performance and sport (MA), including human performance and sport sciences, sports administration, teacher education. *Program availability:* Part-time. *Degree requirements:* For master's, comprehensive exam, thesis or alternative. *Entrance requirements:* For master's, minimum undergraduate GPA of 3.0. Additional exam requirements/recommendations for international students: Required—TOEFL (minimum score 540 paper-based). *Faculty research:* Child obesity and physical inactivity, body composition and fitness assessment, motor development, sport marketing, sport finance.

New York University, School of Continuing and Professional Studies, Tisch Institute for Sports Management, Media, and Business, New York, NY 10012-1019. Offers global sports media (MS); professional and collegiate sports operations (MS); sports business (Advanced Certificate); sports law (MS); sports marketing and sales (MS). *Program availability:* Part-time, evening/weekend. *Degree requirements:* For master's, thesis. *Entrance requirements:* For master's, GRE or GMAT (only upon request), bachelor's degree, resume with relevant professional work, internship or volunteer experience, two letters of recommendation, statement of purpose. Additional exam requirements/recommendations for international students: Required—TOEFL (minimum score 600 paper-based; 100 iBT), IELTS (minimum score 7). Electronic applications accepted. *Faculty research:* Implications of college football's bowl coalition series from a legal, economic, and academic perspective; social history of sports.

North Carolina Central University, College of Behavioral and Social Sciences, Department of Physical Education and Recreation, Durham, NC 27707-3129. Offers athletic administration (MS); physical education (MS); recreation administration (MS); therapeutic recreation (MS). *Program availability:* Part-time, evening/weekend. *Degree requirements:* For master's, one foreign language, comprehensive exam, thesis. *Entrance requirements:* For master's, GRE, minimum GPA of 3.0 in major, 2.5 overall. Additional exam requirements/recommendations for international students: Required—TOEFL.

North Carolina State University, Graduate School, College of Natural Resources, Department of Parks, Recreation and Tourism Management, Raleigh, NC 27695. Offers natural resource management (MPRTM, MS); park and recreation management

(MPRTM, MS); parks, recreation and tourism management (PhD); recreational sport management (MPRTM, MS); spatial information science (MPRTM, MS); tourism policy and development (MPRTM, MS). *Degree requirements:* For master's, thesis (for some programs); for doctorate, thesis/dissertation. *Entrance requirements:* For master's and doctorate, GRE General Test. Additional exam requirements/recommendations for international students: Required—TOEFL. Electronic applications accepted. *Faculty research:* Tourism policy and development, spatial information systems, natural resource management, recreational sports management, park and recreation management.

Northeastern University, College of Professional Studies, Boston, MA 02115-5096. Offers applied nutrition (MS); college athletics administration (MSL); commerce and economic development (MS); corporate and organizational communication (MS); criminal justice (MS); digital media (MPS); elearning and instructional design (M Ed); elementary education (MAT); geographic information technology (MPS); global studies and international relations (MS); higher education administration (M Ed); homeland security (MA); human services (MS); informatics (MPS); leadership (MS); learning analytics (M Ed); learning and instruction (M Ed); nonprofit management (MS); professional sports administration (MSL); project management (MS); regulatory affairs for drugs, biologics, and medical devices (MS); respiratory care leadership (MS); special education (M Ed); technical communication (MS). *Program availability:* Part-time, evening/weekend, 100% online, blended/hybrid learning. *Faculty:* 82 full-time (51 women), 853 part-time/adjunct (366 women). *Students:* 4,947 part-time (3,076 women). In 2016, 1,456 master's awarded. *Application deadline:* Applications are processed on a rolling basis. Application fee: $0. Electronic applications accepted. *Expenses:* Contact institution. *Financial support:* Applicants required to submit FAFSA. *Unit head:* Dr. Mary Loeffelholz, Interim Dean of the College of Professional Studies.
Website: http://www.cps.neu.edu/

Northern State University, MS Ed Program in Sport Performance and Leadership, Aberdeen, SD 57401-7198. Offers MS Ed. *Program availability:* Part-time. *Degree requirements:* For master's, comprehensive exam, thesis optional. *Entrance requirements:* For master's, minimum GPA of 2.75. Additional exam requirements/recommendations for international students: Required—TOEFL (minimum score 550 paper-based; 78 iBT), IELTS (minimum score 6). Electronic applications accepted.

Northwestern University, School of Professional Studies, Program in Sports Administration, Evanston, IL 60208. Offers MA.

Ohio Dominican University, Division of Business, Program in Business Administration, Columbus, OH 43219-2099. Offers accounting (MBA); data analytics (MBA); finance (MBA); leadership (MBA); risk management (MBA); sport management (MBA). *Program availability:* Part-time, evening/weekend, 100% online, blended/hybrid learning. *Faculty:* 8 full-time (4 women), 17 part-time/adjunct (3 women). *Students:* 63 full-time (26 women), 112 part-time (59 women); includes 50 minority (29 Black or African American, non-Hispanic/Latino; 2 American Indian or Alaska Native, non-Hispanic/Latino; 6 Asian, non-Hispanic/Latino; 6 Hispanic/Latino; 1 Native Hawaiian or other Pacific Islander, non-Hispanic/Latino; 6 Two or more races, non-Hispanic/Latino), 7 international. Average age 31. 65 applicants, 51% accepted, 26 enrolled. In 2016, 120 master's awarded. *Entrance requirements:* For master's, minimum overall GPA of 3.0 in undergraduate degree from regionally-accredited institution or 2.75 in last 60 semester hours of bachelor's degree. Additional exam requirements/recommendations for international students: Required—TOEFL (minimum score 550 paper-based), IELTS (minimum score 6.5). *Application deadline:* For fall admission, 8/15 for domestic students, 6/10 for international students; for spring admission, 1/4 for domestic students, 11/2 for international students; for summer admission, 5/30 for domestic students. Applications are processed on a rolling basis. Application fee: $25. Electronic applications accepted. *Expenses:* $590 per credit hour; $225 fees per semester. *Financial support:* Applicants required to submit FAFSA. *Unit head:* Dr. Steve Vickner, Director of Master of Business Administration Program, 614-251-4569, E-mail: vickners@ohiodominican.edu. *Application contact:* John W. Naughton, Director for Graduate Admissions, 614-251-4721, Fax: 614-251-6654, E-mail: grad@ohiodominican.edu.
Website: http://www.ohiodominican.edu/academics/graduate/mba

Ohio Dominican University, Division of Business, Program in Sport Management, Columbus, OH 43219-2099. Offers MS. *Program availability:* Part-time, evening/weekend. *Faculty:* 2 full-time, 3 part-time/adjunct (all women). *Students:* 9 full-time (3 women), 8 part-time (4 women); includes 6 minority (5 Black or African American, non-Hispanic/Latino; 1 Native Hawaiian or other Pacific Islander, non-Hispanic/Latino). Average age 26. 12 applicants, 58% accepted, 4 enrolled. In 2016, 3 master's awarded. *Degree requirements:* For master's, thesis or alternative. *Entrance requirements:* For master's, GRE, bachelor's degree from regionally-accredited institution; minimum undergraduate cumulative GPA of 3.0. Additional exam requirements/recommendations for international students: Required—TOEFL (minimum score 550 paper-based), IELTS (minimum score 6.5). *Application deadline:* For fall admission, 8/15 for domestic students, 6/10 for international students; for spring admission, 1/4 for domestic students, 11/2 for international students; for summer admission, 5/30 for domestic students. Applications are processed on a rolling basis. Application fee: $25. Electronic applications accepted. *Expenses:* $590 per credit hour; $225 fees per semester. *Financial support:* Applicants required to submit FAFSA. *Unit head:* Dr. James Strode, Associate Professor, Sport Management, 614-251-4669, E-mail: strodej@ohiodominican.edu. *Application contact:* John W. Naughton, Director for Graduate Admissions, 614-251-4721, Fax: 614-251-6654, E-mail: grad@ohiodominican.edu.
Website: http://www.ohiodominican.edu/academics/graduate/mssm

Ohio University, Graduate College, College of Business, Department of Sports Administration, Athens, OH 45701-2979. Offers athletic administration (MS). *Program availability:* Part-time, evening/weekend, online learning. *Degree requirements:* For master's, 11-week internship. *Entrance requirements:* For master's, interview. Additional exam requirements/recommendations for international students: Required—TOEFL (minimum score 600 paper-based; 100 iBT) or IELTS (minimum score 7.5). *Application deadline:* For fall admission, 2/1 for domestic and international students. Application fee: $50 ($55 for international students). Electronic applications accepted. *Financial support:* Fellowships with full tuition reimbursements, research assistantships with full and partial tuition reimbursements, Federal Work-Study, institutionally sponsored loans, scholarships/grants, tuition waivers (partial), and stipends available. Financial award application deadline: 2/1. *Faculty research:* Sport management, sport marketing, sports and technology, career development. *Unit head:* Dr. Ken Cutright, Interim Director, 740-593-4666, Fax: 740-593-0284, E-mail: sportsad@ohio.edu. *Application contact:* Teresa Tedrow, Administrative Coordinator, 740-593-4666, Fax: 740-593-0539, E-mail: sportsad@ohio.edu.
Website: http://ohiou.edu/sportadmin/

Old Dominion University, Darden College of Education, Program in Physical Education, Sport Management Emphasis, Norfolk, VA 23529. Offers MS Ed. *Program availability:* Part-time, evening/weekend, 100% online, blended/hybrid learning. *Faculty:* 5 full-time (2 women), 8 part-time/adjunct (4 women). *Students:* 21 full-time (7 women), 23 part-time (7 women); includes 10 minority (7 Black or African American, non-Hispanic/Latino; 1 Hispanic/Latino; 2 Two or more races, non-Hispanic/Latino), 1 international. Average age 28. 44 applicants, 68% accepted, 23 enrolled. In 2016, 18 master's awarded. *Degree requirements:* For master's, comprehensive exam, thesis or alternative, internship, research project. *Entrance requirements:* For master's, GRE, GMAT, or MAT, minimum GPA of 2.8 overall, 3.0 in major. Additional exam requirements/recommendations for international students: Required—TOEFL (minimum score 500 paper-based). *Application deadline:* For fall admission, 3/1 for domestic students. Application fee: $50. Electronic applications accepted. *Expenses:* Tuition, state resident: full-time $8604; part-time $478 per credit hour. Tuition, nonresident: full-time $21,510; part-time $1195 per credit hour. *Required fees:* $66 per semester. Tuition and fees vary according to campus/location, program and reciprocity agreements. *Financial support:* In 2016–17, 3 students received support. Unspecified assistantships available. Financial award application deadline: 4/15; financial award applicants required to submit FAFSA. *Faculty research:* Leadership, consumer behavior in sport, sport finance, sport marketing, sport involvement. *Total annual research expenditures:* $10,000. *Unit head:* Dr. Lynn Ridinger, Chair, 757-683-4353, Fax: 757-683-4270, E-mail: lridinge@odu.edu. *Application contact:* William Heffelfinger, Director of Graduate Admissions, 757-683-5554, Fax: 757-683-3255, E-mail: gradadmit@odu.edu.
Website: http://www.odu.edu/academics/programs/masters/sports-management

Pittsburg State University, Graduate School, College of Education, Department of Health, Physical Education and Recreation, Pittsburg, KS 66762. Offers health, human performance, and recreation (MS), including human performance and wellness, sport and leisure service management. *Program availability:* Part-time, online only, 100% online. *Students:* 65 (25 women); includes 16 minority (8 Black or African American, non-Hispanic/Latino; 1 American Indian or Alaska Native, non-Hispanic/Latino; 5 Hispanic/Latino; 2 Two or more races, non-Hispanic/Latino). In 2016, 33 master's awarded. *Degree requirements:* For master's, thesis or alternative. *Entrance requirements:* For master's, letter of intent. Additional exam requirements/recommendations for international students: Required—TOEFL (minimum score 520 paper-based; 68 iBT), IELTS (minimum score 6), PTE (minimum score 47). *Application deadline:* For fall admission, 6/1 for international students; for spring admission, 10/15 for international students; for summer admission, 4/1 for international students. Applications are processed on a rolling basis. Application fee: $35 ($60 for international students). Electronic applications accepted. *Expenses:* Contact institution. *Financial support:* In 2016–17, 9 teaching assistantships with full tuition reimbursements (averaging $5,500 per year) were awarded; career-related internships or fieldwork, Federal Work-Study, and unspecified assistantships also available. Financial award application deadline: 2/1; financial award applicants required to submit FAFSA. *Faculty research:* Personality of athletes, fitness activities for children, aerobic conditioning, fitness evaluation. *Unit head:* Dr. John Oppliger, Chairperson, 620-235-4668, E-mail: joppliger@pittstate.edu. *Application contact:* Lisa Allen, Assistant Director of Graduate and Continuing Studies, 620-235-4223, Fax: 620-235-4219, E-mail: lallen@pittstate.edu.

Point Loma Nazarene University, Department of Kinesiology, San Diego, CA 92106-2899. Offers integrative wellness (MS); sport performance (MS), including exercise science, sport management, sport performance. *Program availability:* Part-time, online learning. *Faculty:* 3 full-time (1 woman), 6 part-time/adjunct (1 woman). *Students:* 48 full-time (21 women), 4 part-time (1 woman); includes 21 minority (3 Black or African American, non-Hispanic/Latino; 2 Asian, non-Hispanic/Latino; 13 Hispanic/Latino; 3 Two or more races, non-Hispanic/Latino), 4 international. Average age 26. 84 applicants, 80% accepted, 49 enrolled. *Entrance requirements:* For master's, baccalaureate degree, minimum undergraduate cumulative GPA of 3.0. Application fee: $50. *Expenses:* $685 per credit. *Financial support:* Teaching assistantships, scholarships/grants, and unspecified assistantships available. *Unit head:* Jeff Sullivan, Chair, 619-849-2629, E-mail: jeffsullivan@pointloma.edu. *Application contact:* Claire Buckley, Director, Graduate Admissions, 866-563-2846, E-mail: gradinfo@pointloma.edu.

Point Park University, School of Business, Department of Business, Pittsburgh, PA 15222-1984. Offers business analytics (MBA); health systems management (MBA); international business (MBA); management (MBA); management information systems (MBA); sports, arts and entertainment management (MBA). *Program availability:* Evening/weekend, online learning.

Purdue University, Graduate School, College of Health and Human Sciences, Department of Health and Kinesiology, West Lafayette, IN 47907. Offers athletic training education administration (MS, PhD); biomechanics (MS, PhD); exercise physiology (MS, PhD); health education (MS, PhD); history/philosophy of sport (MS, PhD); motor control and development (MS, PhD); physical education pedagogy (PhD); physical education teacher education (MS); recreation and sport management (MS, PhD); sport and exercise psychology (MS, PhD). *Program availability:* Part-time. *Faculty:* 19 full-time (7 women). *Students:* 30 full-time (13 women), 10 part-time (5 women); includes 2 minority (1 Asian, non-Hispanic/Latino; 1 Two or more races, non-Hispanic/Latino), 6 international. Average age 26. 77 applicants, 29% accepted, 18 enrolled. In 2016, 18 master's, 9 doctorates awarded. *Degree requirements:* For master's, thesis optional; for doctorate, comprehensive exam, thesis/dissertation, qualifying examination, preliminary examination. *Entrance requirements:* For master's, GRE General Test (minimum score 1000 combined verbal and quantitative), minimum undergraduate GPA of 3.0 or equivalent; for doctorate, GRE General Test (minimum score 1100 combined verbal and quantitative), minimum undergraduate GPA of 3.0 or equivalent; master's degree with minimum GPA of 3.25 (recommended). Additional exam requirements/recommendations for international students: Required—TOEFL (minimum score 77 iBT); Recommended—TWE. *Application deadline:* For fall admission, 4/30 for domestic and international students; for spring admission, 10/15 for domestic and international students. Applications are processed on a rolling basis. Application fee: $60 ($75 for international students). Electronic applications accepted. *Financial support:* Fellowships with partial tuition reimbursements, research assistantships with partial tuition reimbursements, teaching assistantships with partial tuition reimbursements, and Federal Work-Study available. Support available to part-time students. Financial award applicants required to submit FAFSA. *Faculty research:* Wellness, motivation, teaching effectiveness, learning and development. *Unit head:* Dr. Timothy P. Gavin, Head of the Graduate Program, 765-494-3178, Fax: 765-494-1239, E-mail: gavin1@purdue.edu. *Application contact:* Christy F. Daugherty, Graduate Contact, 765-494-3162, E-mail: daugher2@purdue.edu.
Website: http://www.purdue.edu/hhs/hk/

Robert Morris University Illinois, Morris Graduate School of Management, Chicago, IL 60605. Offers accounting (MBA); accounting/finance (MBA); business analytics (MIS); design and media (MM); design management (MM); educational technology (MM); health care administration (MM); higher education administration (MM); human resource management (MBA); information security (MIS); information systems (MBA, MIS); law enforcement administration (MM); management (MBA); management/finance (MBA); management/human resource management (MBA); mobile computing (MIS); sports administration (MM). *Program availability:* Part-time, evening/weekend. *Faculty:* 4 full-time (1 woman), 25 part-time/adjunct (5 women). *Students:* 196 full-time (98 women), 151 part-time (85 women); includes 200 minority (114 Black or African American, non-Hispanic/Latino; 17 Asian, non-Hispanic/Latino; 67 Hispanic/Latino; 2 Two or more races, non-Hispanic/Latino), 23 international. Average age 33. 174 applicants, 61% accepted, 97 enrolled. In 2016, 190 master's awarded. *Entrance requirements:* For master's, official transcripts and letters of recommendation (for some programs); written personal statement. Additional exam requirements/recommendations for international students: Required—TOEFL (minimum score 550 paper-based). *Application deadline:* Applications are processed on a rolling basis. Application fee: $20 ($100 for international students). Electronic applications accepted. *Expenses: Tuition:* Full-time $16,500; part-time $2750 per course. *Financial support:* In 2016–17, 444 students received support. Federal Work-Study, scholarships/grants, and unspecified assistantships available. Support available to part-time students. Financial award applicants required to submit FAFSA. *Unit head:* Kayed Akkawi, Dean, 312-935-6050, Fax: 312-935-6020, E-mail: kakkawi@robertmorris.edu. *Application contact:* Danielle Naffziger, Vice President of Marketing and Enrollment, 312-935-4812, Fax: 312-935-6020, E-mail: dnaffziger@robertmorris.edu.

St. Cloud State University, School of Graduate Studies, School of Health and Human Services, Department of Kinesiology, St. Cloud, MN 56301-4498. Offers exercise science (MS); sports management (MS). *Degree requirements:* For master's, thesis or alternative. *Entrance requirements:* For master's, GRE General Test, minimum overall GPA of 2.75 in previous undergraduate and graduate records or in last half of undergraduate work. Additional exam requirements/recommendations for international students: Required—Michigan English Language Assessment Battery; Recommended—TOEFL (minimum score 550 paper-based; 79 iBT), IELTS (minimum score 6.5). Electronic applications accepted.

St. John's University, College of Professional Studies, Department of Sport Management, Queens, NY 11439. Offers MPS. *Program availability:* Part-time, evening/weekend. *Degree requirements:* For master's, comprehensive exam, thesis optional, capstone project, internship. *Entrance requirements:* For master's, bachelor's degree from regionally-accredited college or university, minimum GPA of 3.0, 2 letters of recommendation, 300-word essay. Additional exam requirements/recommendations for international students: Required—TOEFL (minimum score 600 paper-based; 100 iBT), IELTS (minimum score 7). Electronic applications accepted. *Faculty research:* The Olympic Movement, sports economics, administration of intercollegiate athletics, sport management education.

Saint Mary's College of California, School of Liberal Arts, Department of Kinesiology, Moraga, CA 94575. Offers fitness management (MA); sport management (MA); sport studies (MA). *Program availability:* Part-time. *Degree requirements:* For master's, thesis or special project. *Entrance requirements:* For master's, minimum GPA of 2.75, BA in physical education or related field, or professional experience. Electronic applications accepted. *Expenses:* Contact institution. *Faculty research:* Moral development in sport, applied motor learning, achievement motivation, sport history.

St. Thomas University, School of Business, Department of Management, Miami Gardens, FL 33054-6459. Offers accounting (MBA); general management (MSM, Certificate); health management (MBA, MSM, Certificate); human resource management (MBA, MSM, Certificate); international business (MBA, MIB, MSM, Certificate); justice administration (MSM, Certificate); management accounting (MSM, Certificate); public management (MSM, Certificate); sports administration (MS). *Program availability:* Part-time, evening/weekend. *Degree requirements:* For master's, comprehensive exam. *Entrance requirements:* For master's, interview, minimum GPA of 3.0 or GMAT. Additional exam requirements/recommendations for international students: Required—TOEFL (minimum score 550 paper-based; 79 iBT). Electronic applications accepted.

Sam Houston State University, College of Health Sciences, Department of Kinesiology, Huntsville, TX 77341. Offers sport and human performance (MA); sport management (MA). *Program availability:* Part-time. *Degree requirements:* For master's, comprehensive exam, thesis optional. *Entrance requirements:* For master's, GRE, letters of recommendation, statement of interest/intent. Additional exam requirements/recommendations for international students: Required—TOEFL (minimum score 550 paper-based; 79 iBT), IELTS (minimum score 6.5). Electronic applications accepted.

San Diego State University, Graduate and Research Affairs, College of Business Administration, Sports Business Management Program, San Diego, CA 92182. Offers MBA.

San Jose State University, Graduate Studies and Research, College of Applied Sciences and Arts, San Jose, CA 95192-0001. Offers big data (Certificate); California library media teacher services (Credential); collaborative response to family violence (Certificate); justice studies (MS); kinesiology (MA), including applied sciences and arts (MA, MS), athletic training, exercise physiology, sport management, sport studies; library and information science (MLIS, Certificate); mass communication (MA); nutritional science (MS); occupational therapy (MS); public health (MPH); pupil personnel services (Credential); recreation (MS), including applied sciences and arts (MA, MS), international tourism; social work (MSW); Spanish language counseling (Certificate); strategic management of digital assets and services (Certificate). *Program availability:* Part-time, evening/weekend. Electronic applications accepted.

Seattle University, College of Arts and Sciences, Center for the Study of Sport and Exercise, Seattle, WA 98122-1090. Offers MSAL, JD/MSAL. *Program availability:* Part-time, evening/weekend. *Faculty:* 2 full-time (1 woman). *Students:* 7 full-time (4 women), 35 part-time (12 women); includes 9 minority (3 Black or African American, non-Hispanic/Latino; 4 Asian, non-Hispanic/Latino; 1 Hispanic/Latino; 1 Two or more races, non-Hispanic/Latino), 6 international. Average age 26. 5 applicants, 100% accepted, 5 enrolled. In 2016, 14 master's awarded. *Degree requirements:* For master's, thesis or applied inquiry. *Entrance requirements:* For master's, GRE (Verbal, Quantitative, and Analytical), minimum GPA of 3.0, three letters of recommendation, essay, resume. Additional exam requirements/recommendations for international students: Required—TOEFL, IELTS. *Application deadline:* For fall admission, 2/15 for domestic and international students. Application fee: $55. Electronic applications accepted. *Financial support:* In 2016–17, 24 students received support. Research assistantships and scholarships/grants available. Financial award applicants required to submit FAFSA. *Faculty research:* Sport consumer behavior, strategic management of sport organizations, leadership in sport, organizational behavior, lifestyle sports. *Total annual research expenditures:* $1,000. *Unit head:* Dr. Dan Tripps, Director, 206-398-4605, E-mail: trippsd@seattleu.edu. *Application contact:* Janet Shandley, Associate Dean of Graduate Admissions, 206-296-5900, Fax: 206-298-5656, E-mail: grad_admissions@seattleu.edu.
Website: https://www.seattleu.edu/artsci/departments/sport-exercise/

Seton Hall University, Stillman School of Business, Programs in Business Administration, South Orange, NJ 07079-2697. Offers accounting (MBA); entrepreneurship (Certificate); finance (MBA, Certificate); information technology management (MBA); international business (MBA); management (MBA); marketing (MBA); sport management (MBA); supply chain management (MBA, Certificate). *Program availability:* Part-time, evening/weekend. *Degree requirements:* For master's, 20 hours of community service (Social Responsibility Project). *Entrance requirements:* For master's, GMAT or CPA, GRE (waived based on work experience or advanced degree from AACSB institution), MS in business discipline, professional degree (MD, JD, PhD, DVM, DDS, CPA, etc.), minimum undergraduate GPA of 3.0. Additional exam requirements/recommendations for international students: Required—TOEFL (minimum score 607 paper-based; 102 iBT), IELTS (minimum score 6), PTE. Electronic applications accepted. *Expenses:* Contact institution. *Faculty research:* Sport, hedge funds, executive compensation, social media, legal studies.

Sonoma State University, School of Science and Technology, Department of Kinesiology, Rohnert Park, CA 94928. Offers adapted physical education (MA); interdisciplinary (MA); interdisciplinary pre-occupational therapy (MA); lifetime physical activity (MA), including coach education, fitness and wellness; physical education (MA); pre-physical therapy (MA). *Program availability:* Part-time. *Degree requirements:* For master's, thesis, oral exam. *Entrance requirements:* For master's, minimum GPA of 2.8. Additional exam requirements/recommendations for international students: Required—TOEFL (minimum score 500 paper-based). *Application deadline:* For fall admission, 11/30 for domestic students; for spring admission, 9/1 for domestic students. Applications are processed on a rolling basis. Application fee: $55. *Expenses:* Tuition, state resident: full-time $6738; part-time $3906 per unit. *Required fees:* $1916; $1916 per year. Tuition and fees vary according to course load, degree level and program. *Financial support:* Career-related internships or fieldwork available. Financial award application deadline: 3/2; financial award applicants required to submit FAFSA. *Unit head:* Dr. Steven Winter, Chair, 707-664-2188, E-mail: steven.winter@sonoma.edu. *Application contact:* Dr. Bulent Sokmen, Graduate Coordinator, 707-664-2789, E-mail: sokmen@sonoma.edu.
Website: http://www.sonoma.edu/kinesiology/

Southeastern University, Jannetides College of Business and Entrepreneurial Leadership, Lakeland, FL 33801-6099. Offers executive leadership (MBA); missional leadership (MBA); sport management (MBA). *Accreditation:* ACBSP. *Program availability:* Evening/weekend, online learning. *Entrance requirements:* For master's, GMAT, minimum cumulative GPA of 3.0, writing sample. Electronic applications accepted. *Expenses: Tuition:* Full-time $9450; part-time $6300 per credit. *Required fees:* $500; $250 per semester. One-time fee: $150. Tuition and fees vary according to degree level, campus/location and program. *Unit head:* Lyle L. Bowlin, Dean, 863-667-5118, E-mail: llbowlin@seu.edu.
Website: http://www.seu.edu/business/

Southeast Missouri State University, School of Graduate Studies, Harrison College of Business, Cape Girardeau, MO 63701-4799. Offers accounting (MBA); entrepreneurship (MBA); financial management (MBA); sport management (MBA). *Accreditation:* AACSB. *Program availability:* Part-time, evening/weekend, 100% online. *Faculty:* 27 full-time (7 women), 1 (woman) part-time/adjunct. *Students:* 72 full-time (39 women), 112 part-time (41 women); includes 20 minority (10 Black or African American, non-Hispanic/Latino; 6 Asian, non-Hispanic/Latino; 4 Hispanic/Latino), 64 international. Average age 29. 106 applicants, 70% accepted, 55 enrolled. In 2016, 65 master's awarded. *Degree requirements:* For master's, variable foreign language requirement, comprehensive exam (for some programs), thesis or alternative. *Entrance requirements:* For master's, GMAT or GRE, minimum undergraduate GPA of 2.5, minimum grade of C in prerequisite courses. Additional exam requirements/recommendations for international students: Required—TOEFL (minimum score 550 paper-based; 79 iBT), IELTS (minimum score 6), PTE (minimum score 53). *Application deadline:* For fall admission, 8/1 for domestic students, 6/1 for international students; for spring admission, 11/21 for domestic students, 10/1 for international students; for summer admission, 5/15 for domestic students. Applications are processed on a rolling basis. Application fee: $30 ($40 for international students). Electronic applications accepted. *Expenses:* Tuition, state resident: full-time $3130; part-time $260.80 per credit hour. Tuition, nonresident: full-time $5842; part-time $486.80 per credit hour. *Required fees:* $33.70 per credit hour. *Financial support:* In 2016–17, 61 students received support. Career-related internships or fieldwork, Federal Work-Study, scholarships/grants, traineeships, tuition waivers (full), and unspecified assistantships available. Financial award application deadline: 6/30; financial award applicants required to submit FAFSA. *Faculty research:* Organizational justice, ethics, leadership, corporate finance, generational differences. *Unit head:* Dr. James L. Caldwell, Director, Graduate Business Studies, 573-651-2851, Fax: 573-651-5032, E-mail: jcaldwell@semo.edu. *Application contact:* Gail Amick, Admissions Specialist, 573-651-2590, Fax: 573-651-5936, E-mail: gamick@semo.edu.
Website: http://www.semo.edu/mba

Southern Methodist University, Annette Caldwell Simmons School of Education and Human Development, Department of Allied Physiology and Wellness, Dallas, TX 75275. Offers sport management (MS). Program offered jointly with Cox School of Business. *Entrance requirements:* For master's, GMAT, resume, essays, transcripts from all colleges and universities attended, two references. Additional exam requirements/recommendations for international students: Required—TOEFL or PTE.

Southern Nazarene University, College of Professional and Graduate Studies, School of Kinesiology, Bethany, OK 73008. Offers sports management and administration (MA). *Entrance requirements:* For master's, baccalaureate degree from regionally-accredited college or university, official transcripts from each institution attended, three letters of recommendation, essay.

Southern New Hampshire University, School of Business, Manchester, NH 03106-1045. Offers accounting (MBA, MS, Graduate Certificate); accounting finance (MS); accounting/auditing (MS); accounting/forensic accounting (MS); accounting/taxation (MS); athletic administration (MBA, Graduate Certificate); business administration (IMBA, MBA, Certificate, Graduate Certificate), including accounting (Certificate), business administration (MBA), business information systems (Graduate Certificate), human resource management (Certificate); corporate social responsibility (MBA); entrepreneurship (MBA); finance (MBA, MS, Graduate Certificate); finance/corporate finance (MS); finance/investments and securities (MS); forensic accounting (MBA); healthcare informatics (MBA); healthcare management (MBA); human resource management (Graduate Certificate); information technology (MS, Graduate Certificate); information technology management (MBA); international business (Graduate Certificate); international business and information technology (Graduate Certificate); international finance (Graduate Certificate); international sport management (Graduate Certificate); justice studies (MBA); leadership of nonprofit organizations (Graduate Certificate); management (MS); marketing (MBA, MS, Graduate Certificate); operations and project management (MS); operations and supply chain management (MBA, Graduate Certificate); organizational leadership (MS); project management (MBA, Graduate Certificate); Six Sigma (MBA); Six Sigma quality (Graduate Certificate); social media marketing (MBA); sport management (MBA, MS, Graduate Certificate); sustainability and environmental compliance (MBA); workplace conflict management (MBA); MBA/Certificate. *Accreditation:* ACBSP. *Program availability:* Part-time, evening/weekend, online learning. Terminal master's awarded for partial completion of doctoral program. *Degree requirements:* For master's, one foreign language, comprehensive exam (for some programs), thesis or alternative. *Entrance requirements:* For master's, minimum GPA of 2.5. Additional exam requirements/recommendations for international students: Required—TOEFL (minimum score 500 paper-based). Electronic applications accepted.

Springfield College, Graduate Programs, Programs in Physical Education, Springfield, MA 01109-3797. Offers adapted physical education (MS); advanced-level coaching (M Ed); athletic administration (MS). *Program availability:* Part-time. *Degree requirements:* For master's, comprehensive exam, thesis (for some programs). *Entrance* *requirements:* For master's and doctorate, GRE General Test. Additional exam requirements/recommendations for international students: Required—TOEFL (minimum score 550 paper-based); Recommended—IELTS (minimum score 6). Electronic applications accepted. *Expenses: Tuition:* Full-time $29,640; part-time $988 per credit. *Required fees:* $195.

Springfield College, Graduate Programs, Programs in Sport Management and Recreation, Springfield, MA 01109-3797. Offers recreation management (M Ed); sport management (M Ed, MS). *Program availability:* Part-time. *Degree requirements:* For master's, comprehensive exam, research project. *Entrance requirements:* Additional exam requirements/recommendations for international students: Required—TOEFL (minimum score 550 paper-based); Recommended—IELTS (minimum score 6). Electronic applications accepted. *Expenses: Tuition:* Full-time $29,640; part-time $988 per credit. *Required fees:* $195.

State University of New York College at Cortland, Graduate Studies, School of Professional Studies, Department of Sport Management, Cortland, NY 13045. Offers international sport management (MS); sport management (MS). *Entrance requirements:* For master's, GMAT or GRE, 2 letters of recommendation.

Syracuse University, David B. Falk College of Sport and Human Dynamics, MS Program in Sport Venue and Event Management, Syracuse, NY 13244. Offers MS. *Entrance requirements:* For master's, GRE, undergraduate transcripts, three recommendations, resume, personal statement. Additional exam requirements/recommendations for international students: Required—TOEFL (minimum score 100 iBT). *Application deadline:* For fall admission, 2/15 for domestic students; for spring admission, 11/1 priority date for domestic and international students. Application fee: $75. Electronic applications accepted. *Expenses: Tuition:* Full-time $25,974; part-time $1443 per credit hour. *Required fees:* $802; $50 per course. Tuition and fees vary according to course load and program. *Financial support:* Fellowships, research assistantships, teaching assistantships, and career-related internships or fieldwork available. Financial award application deadline: 1/1; financial award applicants required to submit FAFSA. *Faculty research:* Managing and operating sport and entertainment facilities and events, sociology of sport, psychological and social issues in sport. *Unit head:* Jeff Pauline, Graduate Program Director, 315-443-0364, Fax: 315-443-9811, E-mail: jspaulin@syr.edu. *Application contact:* Felicia Otero, Director of Admissions, 315-443-5555, E-mail: falk@syr.edu.
Website: http://falk.syr.edu/SportManagement/Default.aspx

Temple University, Fox School of Business, Doctoral Programs in Business, Philadelphia, PA 19122-6096. Offers accounting (PhD); entrepreneurship (PhD); finance (PhD); international business (PhD); management information systems (PhD); marketing (PhD); risk management and insurance (PhD); statistics (PhD); strategic management (PhD); tourism and sport (PhD). *Accreditation:* AACSB. *Degree requirements:* For doctorate, thesis/dissertation. *Entrance requirements:* For doctorate, GRE General Test, GMAT, minimum GPA of 3.0, master's degree. Additional exam requirements/recommendations for international students: Required—TOEFL (minimum score 600 paper-based; 100 iBT), IELTS (minimum score 7.5). Electronic applications accepted.

★ **Temple University,** School of Sport, Tourism and Hospitality Management, Philadelphia, PA 19122-6096. Offers sport business (MS); tourism and hospitality management (MTHM); tourism and sport (PhD); travel and tourism (MS). *Program availability:* Part-time, evening/weekend. *Faculty:* 21 full-time (7 women), 10 part-time/adjunct (3 women). *Students:* 95 full-time (47 women), 32 part-time (16 women); includes 37 minority (27 Black or African American, non-Hispanic/Latino; 6 Hispanic/Latino; 4 Two or more races, non-Hispanic/Latino), 22 international. 152 applicants, 70% accepted, 66 enrolled. In 2016, 31 master's awarded. *Degree requirements:* For master's, thesis optional, internship/project; for doctorate, thesis/dissertation. *Entrance requirements:* For master's, GRE General Test, GMAT, or MAT, bachelor's degree or equivalent with minimum GPA of 3.0, 500-word essay, 2 letters of recommendation, resume; for doctorate, GMAT or GRE. Additional exam requirements/recommendations for international students: Required—TOEFL (minimum score 550 paper-based; 79 iBT), IELTS (minimum score 6.5). *Application deadline:* For fall admission, 3/1 priority date for domestic students, 1/15 priority date for international students; for spring admission, 8/15 priority date for domestic students, 6/30 priority date for international students. Applications are processed on a rolling basis. Application fee: $60. Electronic applications accepted. *Expenses:* Contact institution. *Financial support:* Fellowships with full tuition reimbursements, research assistantships with full tuition reimbursements, and teaching assistantships with full tuition reimbursements available. Financial award application deadline: 3/1; financial award applicants required to submit FAFSA. *Unit head:* Dr. M. Moshe Porat, Dean, 215-204-1836, Fax: 215-204-8705, E-mail: porat@temple.edu. *Application contact:* James Alton, Manager of Graduate Student Services, 215-204-7140, Fax: 215-204-8705, E-mail: jim.alton@temple.edu.
Website: http://sthm.temple.edu/

See Display below and Close-Ups on pages 349 and 1651.

Tennessee State University, The School of Graduate Studies and Research, College of Health Sciences, Department of Human Performance and Sports Sciences, Nashville, TN 37209-1561. Offers exercise science (MA Ed); sports administration (MA Ed). *Degree requirements:* For master's, thesis optional. *Entrance requirements:* For master's, GRE General Test or MAT.

Tennessee Technological University, College of Graduate Studies, College of Education, Department of Exercise Science, Physical Education and Wellness, Cookeville, TN 38505. Offers adapted physical education (MA); elementary/middle school physical education (MA); lifetime wellness (MA); sport management (MA). *Accreditation:* NCATE. *Program availability:* Part-time, online learning. *Faculty:* 7 full-time (0 women). *Students:* 17 full-time (5 women), 32 part-time (17 women); includes 6 minority (4 Black or African American, non-Hispanic/Latino; 1 Hispanic/Latino; 1 Two or more races, non-Hispanic/Latino). Average age 27. 29 applicants, 59% accepted, 15 enrolled. In 2016, 24 master's awarded. *Degree requirements:* For master's, comprehensive exam, thesis or alternative. *Entrance requirements:* For master's, MAT or GRE. Additional exam requirements/recommendations for international students: Required—TOEFL (minimum score 527 paper-based; 71 iBT), IELTS (minimum score 5.5), PTE (minimum score 48), or TOEIC (Test of English as an International Communication). *Application deadline:* For fall admission, 8/1 for domestic students, 5/1 for international students; for spring admission, 12/1 for domestic students, 10/1 for international students; for summer admission, 5/1 for domestic students, 2/1 for international students. Applications are processed on a rolling basis. Application fee: $35 ($40 for international students). Electronic applications accepted. *Expenses:* Tuition, state resident: full-time $9375; part-time $534 per credit hour. Tuition, nonresident: full-time $22,443; part-time $1260 per credit hour. *Financial support:* In 2016–17, 2 research assistantships (averaging $4,400 per year), 9 teaching assistantships (averaging $4,400 per year) were awarded; fellowships and career-related internships or fieldwork also available. Financial award application deadline: 4/1. *Unit head:* Dr. Christy Killman, Chairperson, 931-372-3467, Fax: 931-372-6319, E-mail: ckillman@tntech.edu. *Application contact:* Shelia K. Kendrick, Coordinator of Graduate Studies, 931-372-3808, Fax: 931-372-3497, E-mail: skendrick@tntech.edu.

Texas A&M University, College of Education and Human Development, Department of Health and Kinesiology, College Station, TX 77843. Offers athletic training (MS); health education (M Ed, MS, Ed D, PhD); kinesiology (MS, PhD); sports management (MS). *Program availability:* Part-time. *Faculty:* 56. *Students:* 216 full-time (119 women), 116

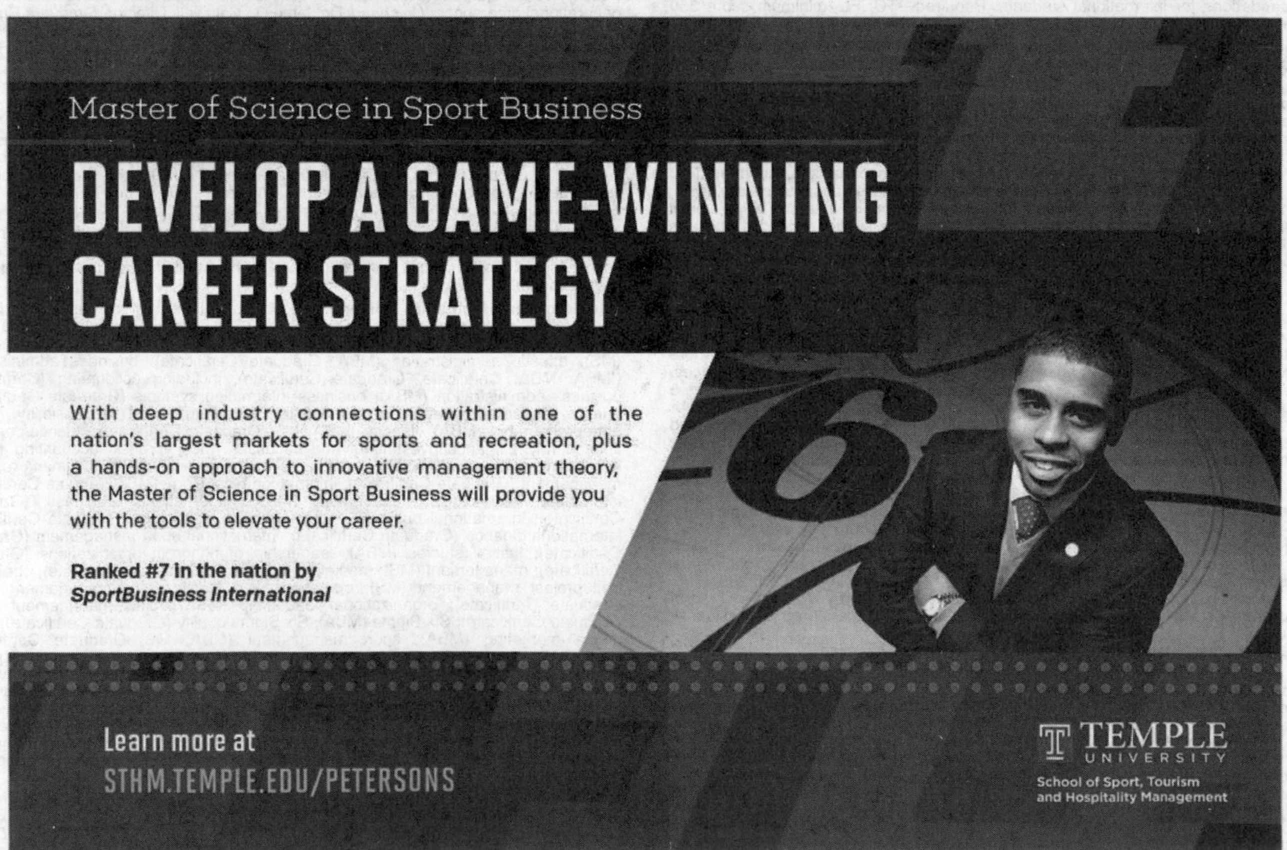

part-time (55 women); includes 100 minority (37 Black or African American, non-Hispanic/Latino; 9 Asian, non-Hispanic/Latino; 49 Hispanic/Latino; 5 Two or more races, non-Hispanic/Latino), 28 international. Average age 29. 169 applicants, 72% accepted, 77 enrolled. In 2016, 104 master's, 24 doctorates awarded. *Degree requirements:* For master's, thesis (for some programs); for doctorate, comprehensive exam, thesis/dissertation. *Entrance requirements:* For master's and doctorate, GRE General Test. Additional exam requirements/recommendations for international students: Required—TOEFL (minimum score 550 paper-based; 80 iBT), IELTS (minimum score 6), PTE (minimum score 53). *Application deadline:* For fall admission, 1/15 for domestic students; for spring admission, 10/1 for domestic students. Applications are processed on a rolling basis. Application fee: $50 ($90 for international students). Electronic applications accepted. *Expenses:* Contact institution. *Financial support:* In 2016–17, 172 students received support, including 3 fellowships with tuition reimbursements available (averaging $18,412 per year), 43 research assistantships with tuition reimbursements available (averaging $5,089 per year), 76 teaching assistantships with tuition reimbursements available (averaging $8,295 per year); career-related internships or fieldwork, institutionally sponsored loans, scholarships/grants, traineeships, health care benefits, tuition waivers (full and partial), and unspecified assistantships also available. Support available to part-time students. Financial award application deadline: 3/15; financial award applicants required to submit FAFSA. *Unit head:* Dr. Richard Kreider, Head, 979-845-1333, Fax: 979-847-8987, E-mail: rkreider@hlkn.tamu.edu. *Application contact:* Jenny Bilski, Academic Advisor, 979-862-4052, E-mail: jenny.bilski@tamu.edu.
Website: http://hlknweb.tamu.edu/

Texas Tech University, Graduate School, College of Arts and Sciences, Department of Kinesiology and Sport Management, Lubbock, TX 79409. Offers kinesiology (MS); sport management (MS). *Program availability:* Part-time. *Faculty:* 23 full-time (11 women), 10 part-time/adjunct (5 women). *Students:* 50 full-time (25 women), 12 part-time (3 women); includes 20 minority (6 Black or African American, non-Hispanic/Latino; 11 Hispanic/Latino; 3 Two or more races, non-Hispanic/Latino), 7 international. Average age 24. 88 applicants, 39% accepted, 23 enrolled. In 2016, 41 master's awarded. *Degree requirements:* For master's, comprehensive exam (for some programs), thesis (for some programs). *Entrance requirements:* For master's, GRE for those whose GPA on last 60 hours of undergraduate coursework is 3.49 and lower (for kinesiology only), letter of intent, 3 letters of recommendation (preferably from academic professors), minimum GPA of 2.8 in the last 60 hours. Additional exam requirements/recommendations for international students: Required—TOEFL (minimum score 550 paper-based; 79 iBT). *Application deadline:* For fall admission, 6/1 priority date for domestic students, 1/15 priority date for international students; for spring admission, 9/1 priority date for domestic students, 6/15 priority date for international students. Applications are processed on a rolling basis. Application fee: $75. Electronic applications accepted. *Expenses:* $300 per credit hour full-time resident tuition, $708 per credit hour full-time non-resident tuition; $50.50 per credit hour fee plus $608 per term fee. *Financial support:* In 2016–17, 58 students received support, including 30 fellowships (averaging $4,699 per year), 47 teaching assistantships (averaging $10,579 per year); research assistantships, career-related internships or fieldwork, scholarships/grants, health care benefits, and unspecified assistantships also available. Financial award application deadline: 8/1; financial award applicants required to submit FAFSA. *Faculty research:* Sport management, exercise physiology, human performance, motor behavior, exercise and sport psychology. *Total annual research expenditures:* $234,707. *Unit head:* Dr. Angela Lumpkin, Professor/Chair, 806-834-6935, Fax: 806-742-1688, E-mail: angela.lumpkin@ttu.edu. *Application contact:* Dr. Donna Torres, Graduate Coordinator, 806-834-7968, Fax: 806-742-1688, E-mail: donna.torres@ttu.edu.
Website: http://www.depts.ttu.edu/ksm/

Texas Woman's University, Graduate School, College of Health Sciences, Department of Kinesiology, Denton, TX 76201. Offers adapted physical activity (MS, PhD); biomechanics (MS, PhD); coaching (MS); exercise physiology (MS, PhD); sport management (MS, PhD). *Program availability:* Part-time, evening/weekend. Terminal master's awarded for partial completion of doctoral program. *Degree requirements:* For master's, comprehensive exam, thesis or alternative; for doctorate, comprehensive exam, thesis/dissertation, qualifying exam. *Entrance requirements:* For master's, GRE General Test (biomechanics emphasis only), 2 letters of reference, curriculum vitae, interview (adapted physical education emphasis only); for doctorate, GRE General Test (biomechanics emphasis only), interview, 3 letters of reference, curriculum vitae. Additional exam requirements/recommendations for international students: Required—TOEFL (minimum score 550 paper-based; 79 iBT). *Application deadline:* For fall admission, 7/1 priority date for domestic students, 3/1 for international students; for spring admission, 11/1 priority date for domestic students, 7/1 for international students. Applications are processed on a rolling basis. Application fee: $50 ($75 for international students). Electronic applications accepted. *Expenses:* Tuition, state resident: full-time $9046; part-time $251 per credit hour. Tuition, nonresident: full-time $22,922; part-time $614 per credit hour. *International tuition:* $23,046 full-time. *Required fees:* $2690; $1285 per credit hour. One-time fee: $50. Tuition and fees vary according to course level, course load, program and reciprocity agreements. *Financial support:* Research assistantships, teaching assistantships, career-related internships or fieldwork, Federal Work-Study, institutionally sponsored loans, scholarships/grants, traineeships, health care benefits, and unspecified assistantships available. Support available to part-time students. Financial award application deadline: 3/1; financial award applicants required to submit FAFSA. *Faculty research:* Exercise and Type 2 diabetes risk, bone mineral density and exercise in special populations, obesity in children, factors influencing sport consumer behavior and loyalty, roles and responsibilities of Para educators in adapted physical education. *Unit head:* Dr. David Nichols, Interim Chair, 940-898-2576, Fax: 940-898-2581, E-mail: dnichols@twu.edu. *Application contact:* Dr. Samuel Wheeler, Assistant Director of Admissions, 940-898-3188, Fax: 940-898-3081, E-mail: wheelersr@twu.edu.
Website: http://www.twu.edu/kinesiology/

Tiffin University, Program in Business Administration, Tiffin, OH 44883-2161. Offers finance (MBA); general management (MBA); healthcare administration (MBA); human resource management (MBA); international business (MBA); leadership (MBA); marketing (MBA); non-profit management (MBA); sports management (MBA). *Accreditation:* ACBSP. *Program availability:* Part-time, evening/weekend, online learning. *Students:* 10 full-time (4 women), 497 part-time (240 women); includes 91 minority (67 Black or African American, non-Hispanic/Latino; 1 American Indian or Alaska Native, non-Hispanic/Latino; 5 Asian, non-Hispanic/Latino; 15 Hispanic/Latino; 3 Two or more races, non-Hispanic/Latino), 102 international. Average age 31. 214 applicants, 86% accepted, 146 enrolled. In 2016, 183 master's awarded. *Entrance requirements:* For master's, minimum undergraduate GPA of 2.5, work experience. Additional exam requirements/recommendations for international students: Required—TOEFL (minimum score 550 paper-based; 79 iBT), IELTS. *Application deadline:* For fall admission, 8/15 for domestic students, 8/1 for international students; for spring admission, 1/9 for domestic students, 12/1 for international students. Applications are processed on a rolling basis. Application fee: $50. Electronic applications accepted. Application fee is waived when completed online. *Expenses: Tuition:* Full-time $21,000; part-time $700 per credit hour. *Required fees:* $150. Tuition and fees vary according to program. *Financial support:* Unspecified assistantships available. Support available to part-time students. Financial award application deadline: 7/31; financial award applicants required to submit FAFSA. *Faculty research:* Small business, executive development operations, research and statistical analysis, market research, management information systems. *Unit head:* Dr. Bonnie Tiell, Dean of Graduate Studies, 419-448-3261, Fax: 419-443-5002, E-mail: btiell@tiffin.edu. *Application contact:* Nikki Hintze, Director of Graduate and Distance Education Academic Advising, 800-968-6446 Ext. 3596, Fax: 419-443-5002, E-mail: hintzenm@tiffin.edu.
Website: http://www.tiffin.edu/graduateprograms/

Troy University, Graduate School, College of Health and Human Services, Program in Sport and Fitness Management, Troy, AL 36082. Offers MS. *Program availability:* Part-time, evening/weekend. *Faculty:* 12 full-time (2 women), 2 part-time/adjunct (0 women). *Students:* 51 full-time (22 women), 74 part-time (26 women); includes 51 minority (23 Black or African American, non-Hispanic/Latino; 1 American Indian or Alaska Native, non-Hispanic/Latino; 2 Asian, non-Hispanic/Latino; 3 Hispanic/Latino; 22 Two or more races, non-Hispanic/Latino). Average age 27. 70 applicants, 94% accepted, 17 enrolled. In 2016, 35 master's awarded. *Degree requirements:* For master's, comprehensive exam, minimum GPA of 3.0, candidacy, research course. *Entrance requirements:* For master's, GRE (minimum score of 850 on old exam or 290 on new exam), GMAT (minimum score of 380), or MAT (minimum score of 385), bachelor's degree; minimum undergraduate GPA of 2.5 or 3.0 on last 30 semester hours, letter of recommendation. Additional exam requirements/recommendations for international students: Required—TOEFL (minimum score 523 paper-based; 70 iBT), IELTS (minimum score 6). *Application deadline:* Applications are processed on a rolling basis. Application fee: $50. Electronic applications accepted. *Expenses:* Tuition, state resident: full-time $7146; part-time $397 per credit hour. Tuition, nonresident: full-time $14,292; part-time $794 per credit hour. *Required fees:* $802; $50 per semester. Tuition and fees vary according to campus/location and program. *Financial support:* Fellowships, career-related internships or fieldwork, scholarships/grants, and unspecified assistantships available. Support available to part-time students. *Faculty research:* Sport marketing, fitness, sport law. *Unit head:* Dr. John Miller, Associate Dean, College of Health and Human Services, 334-670-6712, Fax: 334-670-3743, E-mail: johnm@troy.edu. *Application contact:* Jessica A. Kimbro, Director of Graduate Admissions, 334-670-3178, E-mail: jacord@troy.edu.

United States Sports Academy, Graduate Programs, Program in Sport Management, Daphne, AL 36526-7055. Offers MSS, Ed D. *Program availability:* Part-time, online learning. *Degree requirements:* For master's, comprehensive exam, thesis optional; for doctorate, comprehensive exam, thesis/dissertation. *Entrance requirements:* For master's, GRE General Test, GMAT, or MAT, minimum GPA of 2.5, 3 letters of recommendation, resume; for doctorate, GRE General Test, GMAT, or MAT, master's degree, 3 letters of recommendation, resume. Additional exam requirements/recommendations for international students: Required—TOEFL (minimum score 500 paper-based). Electronic applications accepted. *Faculty research:* Sport law, leadership behavior, personnel evaluation.

The University of Alabama, Graduate School, College of Human Environmental Sciences, Program in Human Environmental Science, Tuscaloosa, AL 35487. Offers interactive technology (MS); quality management (MS); restaurant and meeting management (MS); rural community health (MS); sport management (MS). *Program availability:* Part-time, evening/weekend, online learning. *Faculty:* 52 full-time (38 women), 3 part-time/adjunct (2 women). *Students:* 213 full-time (138 women), 392 part-time (278 women); includes 142 minority (105 Black or African American, non-Hispanic/Latino; 3 American Indian or Alaska Native, non-Hispanic/Latino; 4 Asian, non-Hispanic/Latino; 17 Hispanic/Latino; 2 Native Hawaiian or other Pacific Islander, non-Hispanic/Latino; 11 Two or more races, non-Hispanic/Latino), 5 international. Average age 33. 400 applicants, 74% accepted, 232 enrolled. In 2016, 230 master's awarded. *Degree requirements:* For master's, comprehensive exam. *Entrance requirements:* For master's, GRE (for some specializations), minimum GPA of 3.0. Additional exam requirements/recommendations for international students: Required—TOEFL. *Application deadline:* For fall admission, 7/1 for domestic students; for spring admission, 11/1 for domestic students; for summer admission, 4/15 for domestic students. Applications are processed on a rolling basis. Application fee: $50 ($60 for international students). Electronic applications accepted. *Expenses:* Tuition, state resident: full-time $10,470. Tuition, nonresident: full-time $26,950. *Financial support:* In 2016–17, 2 teaching assistantships with full tuition reimbursements were awarded. Financial award application deadline: 7/1. *Faculty research:* Rural health, hospitality management, sport management, interactive technology, consumer quality management, environmental health and safety. *Unit head:* Dr. Milla D. Boschung, Dean, 205-348-6250, Fax: 205-348-1786, E-mail: mboschun@ches.ua.edu. *Application contact:* Dr. Stuart Usdan, Associate Dean, 205-348-6150, Fax: 205-348-3789, E-mail: susdan@ches.ua.edu.
Website: http://www.ches.ua.edu/programs-of-study.html

University of Alberta, Faculty of Graduate Studies and Research, Program in Business Administration, Edmonton, AB T6G 2E1, Canada. Offers international business (MBA); leisure and sport management (MBA); natural resources and energy (MBA); technology commercialization (MBA); MBA/LL B; MBA/M Ag; MBA/M Eng; MBA/MF; MBA/PhD. *Accreditation:* AACSB. *Program availability:* Part-time, evening/weekend. *Degree requirements:* For master's, thesis or alternative. *Entrance requirements:* For master's, GMAT. Additional exam requirements/recommendations for international students: Required—TOEFL (minimum score 600 paper-based). Electronic applications accepted. *Faculty research:* Natural resources and energy/management and policy/family enterprise/international business/healthcare research management.

University of Arkansas, Graduate School, College of Education and Health Professions, Department of Health, Human Performance and Recreation, Program in Recreation and Sports Management, Fayetteville, AR 72701. Offers M Ed, Ed D. In 2016, 31 master's, 2 doctorates awarded. *Degree requirements:* For master's, thesis optional; for doctorate, thesis/dissertation. *Entrance requirements:* For doctorate, GRE General Test. *Application deadline:* For fall admission, 4/1 for international students; for spring admission, 10/1 for international students. Applications are processed on a rolling basis. Application fee: $40 ($50 for international students). Electronic applications accepted. *Financial support:* In 2016–17, 8 research assistantships, 10 teaching assistantships were awarded; fellowships with tuition reimbursements, career-related internships or fieldwork, and Federal Work-Study also available. Support available to part-time students. Financial award application deadline: 4/1; financial award applicants required to submit FAFSA. *Unit head:* Dr. Bart Hammig, Department Chairperson, 479-575-2857, Fax: 479-575-5728, E-mail: bhammig@uark.edu. *Application contact:* Dr. Stephen Dittmore, Coordinator of Graduate Studies, 479-575-6625, E-mail: dittmore@uark.edu.
Website: http://recr.uark.edu/

University of Arkansas at Little Rock, Graduate School, College of Education and Health Professions, Department of Health, Human Performance and Sport Management, Little Rock, AR 72204-1099. Offers exercise science (MS); health education and promotion (MS); sport management (MS). *Program availability:* Part-time, evening/weekend. *Degree requirements:* For master's, directed study or residency.

Sports Management

Entrance requirements: For master's, GRE General Test, minimum GPA of 3.0, 3 reference letters.

University of Central Florida, College of Business Administration, Program in Sport Business Management, Orlando, FL 32816. Offers MSBM. *Faculty:* 5 full-time (0 women), 3 part-time/adjunct (0 women). *Students:* 70 full-time (28 women), 3 part-time (1 woman); includes 25 minority (15 Black or African American, non-Hispanic/Latino; 2 Asian, non-Hispanic/Latino; 8 Hispanic/Latino), 9 international. Average age 25. 74 applicants, 55% accepted, 33 enrolled. In 2016, 38 master's awarded. *Degree requirements:* For master's, thesis or alternative, internship. *Entrance requirements:* For master's, GMAT, minimum GPA of 3.0, letters of recommendation. Additional exam requirements/recommendations for international students: Required—TOEFL. *Application deadline:* For fall admission, 1/15 for domestic students. Application fee: $30. Electronic applications accepted. *Expenses:* Tuition, state resident: part-time $288.16 per credit hour. Tuition, nonresident: part-time $1071.31 per credit hour. *Financial support:* In 2016–17, 54 students received support, including 10 fellowships with partial tuition reimbursements available (averaging $2,600 per year), 41 research assistantships with partial tuition reimbursements available (averaging $8,292 per year), 4 teaching assistantships (averaging $9,996 per year). Financial award application deadline: 11/1; financial award applicants required to submit FAFSA. *Unit head:* Dr. Richard Lapchick, Director, 407-823-4887, E-mail: rlapchick@ucf.edu. *Application contact:* Assistant Director, Graduate Admissions, 407-823-2766, Fax: 407-823-6442, E-mail: gradadmissions@ucf.edu.
Website: http://business.ucf.edu/devos/

University of Cincinnati, Graduate School, College of Education, Criminal Justice, and Human Services, School of Human Services, Program in Sport Administration, Cincinnati, OH 45221. Offers MS. *Program availability:* 100% online. *Degree requirements:* For master's, thesis or alternative, capstone internship. *Entrance requirements:* Additional exam requirements/recommendations for international students: Required—TOEFL. *Application deadline:* For fall admission, 2/1 for domestic and international students; for spring admission, 12/1 for domestic and international students; for summer admission, 4/1 for domestic and international students. Applications are processed on a rolling basis. Application fee: $65 ($70 for international students). Electronic applications accepted. *Expenses: Tuition, area resident:* Full-time $12,790; part-time $389 per credit hour. Tuition, state resident: full-time $13,290; part-time $419 per credit hour. Tuition, nonresident: full-time $24,532; part-time $976 per credit hour. *International tuition:* $24,832 full-time. *Required fees:* $3958; $140 per credit hour. Tuition and fees vary according to course load, degree level, program and reciprocity agreements. *Financial support:* Unspecified assistantships available. Financial award application deadline: 4/1. *Unit head:* Dr. Thomas Aicher, Program Director, 513-556-1331, Fax: 513-556-3898, E-mail: thomas.aicher@uc.edu. *Application contact:* Amanda Carlisle, Program Coordinator, 513-556-3335, Fax: 513-556-3898, E-mail: amanda.carlisle@uc.edu.
Website: http://cech.uc.edu/human-services/graduate-programs/sadmin.html

University of Colorado Denver, Business School, Master of Business Administration Program, Denver, CO 80217. Offers bioinnovation and entrepreneurship (MBA); business intelligence (MBA); business strategy (MBA); business to business marketing (MBA); business to consumer marketing (MBA); change management (MBA); corporate financial management (MBA); enterprise technology management (MBA); entrepreneurship (MBA); health administration (MBA), including financial management, health administration, health information technologies, international health management and policy; human resources management (MBA); international business (MBA); investment management (MBA); managing for sustainability (MBA); sports and entertainment management (MBA). *Accreditation:* AACSB. *Program availability:* Part-time, evening/weekend, 100% online, blended/hybrid learning. *Students:* 544 full-time (210 women), 112 part-time (22 women); includes 99 minority (15 Black or African American, non-Hispanic/Latino; 4 American Indian or Alaska Native, non-Hispanic/Latino; 38 Asian, non-Hispanic/Latino; 36 Hispanic/Latino; 6 Two or more races, non-Hispanic/Latino), 22 international. Average age 32. 335 applicants, 73% accepted, 179 enrolled. In 2016, 251 master's awarded. *Degree requirements:* For master's, 48 semester hours, including 30 of core courses, 3 in international business, and 15 in electives from over 50 other business courses. *Entrance requirements:* For master's, GMAT, resume, official transcripts, essay, two letters of recommendation, financial statements (for international applicants). Additional exam requirements/recommendations for international students: Required—TOEFL (minimum score 560 paper-based; 83 iBT); Recommended—IELTS (minimum score 6.5). *Application deadline:* For fall admission, 4/15 priority date for domestic students, 3/15 priority date for international students; for spring admission, 10/15 priority date for domestic students, 9/15 priority date for international students; for summer admission, 2/15 priority date for domestic students, 1/15 priority date for international students. Applications are processed on a rolling basis. Application fee: $50 ($75 for international students). Electronic applications accepted. *Expenses:* Contact institution. *Financial support:* In 2016–17, 171 students received support. Fellowships, research assistantships, teaching assistantships, Federal Work-Study, institutionally sponsored loans, scholarships/grants, traineeships, and unspecified assistantships available. Financial award application deadline: 4/1; financial award applicants required to submit FAFSA. *Faculty research:* Marketing, management, entrepreneurship, finance, health administration. *Unit head:* Woodrow Eckard, MBA Director, 303-315-8470, E-mail: woody.eckard@ucdenver.edu. *Application contact:* Shelly Townley, Admissions Director, Graduate Programs, 303-315-8202, E-mail: shelly.townley@ucdenver.edu.
Website: http://www.ucdenver.edu/academics/colleges/business/degrees/mba/Pages/MBA.aspx

University of Colorado Denver, Business School, Program in Management and Organization, Denver, CO 80217. Offers business strategy (MS); change and innovation (MS); enterprise technology management (MS); entrepreneurship and innovation (MS); global management (MS); leadership (MS); managing for sustainability (MS); managing human resources (MS); sports and entertainment management (MS). *Accreditation:* AACSB. *Program availability:* Part-time, evening/weekend, online learning. *Students:* 20 full-time (13 women), 17 part-time (10 women); includes 6 minority (3 Black or African American, non-Hispanic/Latino; 1 American Indian or Alaska Native, non-Hispanic/Latino; 1 Hispanic/Latino; 1 Two or more races, non-Hispanic/Latino), 6 international. Average age 33. 24 applicants, 58% accepted, 6 enrolled. In 2016, 19 master's awarded. *Degree requirements:* For master's, 30 semester hours (12 of required courses, 12 of management electives, and 6 of free electives). *Entrance requirements:* For master's, GMAT, resume, two letters of recommendation, essay, financial statements (for international applicants). Additional exam requirements/recommendations for international students: Required—TOEFL (minimum score 525 paper-based; 71 iBT); Recommended—IELTS (minimum score 6.5). *Application deadline:* For fall admission, 4/15 priority date for domestic students, 3/15 priority date for international students; for spring admission, 10/15 priority date for domestic students, 9/15 priority date for international students; for summer admission, 2/15 priority date for domestic students, 1/15 priority date for international students. Applications are processed on a rolling basis. Application fee: $50 ($75 for international students). Electronic applications accepted. *Expenses:* Contact institution. *Financial support:* In 2016–17, 7 students received support. Fellowships, research assistantships, teaching assistantships, Federal Work-Study, institutionally sponsored loans, scholarships/grants, and traineeships available. Financial award application deadline: 4/1; financial award applicants required to submit FAFSA. *Faculty research:* Human resource management, management of catastrophe, turnaround strategies. *Unit head:* Dr. Kenneth Bettenhausen, Associate Professor/Director of MS in Management, 303-315-8425, E-mail: kenneth.bettenhausen@ucdenver.edu. *Application contact:* 303-315-8200, E-mail: bschool.admissions@ucdenver.edu.
Website: http://www.ucdenver.edu/academics/colleges/business/degrees/ms/management/Pages/Management.aspx

University of Connecticut, Graduate School, College of Agriculture, Health and Natural Resources, Department of Kinesiology, Sport Management Program, Storrs, CT 06269. Offers MS. Terminal master's awarded for partial completion of doctoral program. *Degree requirements:* For master's, comprehensive exam, thesis or alternative. *Entrance requirements:* Additional exam requirements/recommendations for international students: Required—TOEFL (minimum score 550 paper-based). Electronic applications accepted.

University of Dallas, Satish and Yasmin Gupta College of Business, Irving, TX 75062-4736. Offers accounting (MBA, MS); business administration (DBA); business analytics (MS); business management (MBA); corporate finance (MBA); cybersecurity (MS); finance (MS); financial services (MBA); global business (MBA, MS); health services management (MBA); human resource management (MBA); information and technology management (MS); information assurance (MBA); information technology (MBA); information technology service management (MBA); marketing management (MBA); organization development (MBA); project management (MBA); sports and entertainment management (MBA); strategic leadership (MBA); supply chain management (MBA). *Accreditation:* AACSB. *Program availability:* Part-time, evening/weekend, online learning. *Entrance requirements:* Additional exam requirements/recommendations for international students: Required—TOEFL. Electronic applications accepted. *Expenses:* Contact institution.

University of Florida, Graduate School, College of Health and Human Performance, Department of Tourism, Recreation and Sport Management, Gainesville, FL 32611. Offers health and human performance (PhD), including historic preservation (MS, PhD), recreation, parks and tourism (MS, PhD), sport management; recreation, parks and tourism (MS), including historic preservation (MS, PhD), natural resource recreation, recreation, parks and tourism (MS, PhD), therapeutic recreation, tourism, tropical conservation and development; sport management (MS), including historic preservation (MS, PhD), tropical conservation and development; JD/MS; MSM/MS. *Degree requirements:* For master's, comprehensive exam (for some programs), thesis (for some programs); for doctorate, comprehensive exam, thesis/dissertation. *Entrance requirements:* For master's and doctorate, GRE General Test, minimum GPA of 3.0. Additional exam requirements/recommendations for international students: Required—TOEFL (minimum score 550 paper-based; 80 iBT), IELTS (minimum score 6). Electronic applications accepted. *Faculty research:* Hospitality, natural resource management, sport management, tourism.

University of Indianapolis, Graduate Programs, College of Health Sciences, Department of Kinesiology, Indianapolis, IN 46227-3697. Offers sport management (MS). *Program availability:* Evening/weekend.

The University of Iowa, Graduate College, College of Liberal Arts and Sciences, Department of Health and Human Physiology, Iowa City, IA 52242-1316. Offers athletic training (MS); clinical exercise physiology (MS); health and human physiology (PhD); leisure studies (MA, PhD), including recreational sport management (PhD), therapeutic recreation (MA). *Degree requirements:* For master's, thesis optional, exam; for doctorate, comprehensive exam, thesis/dissertation. *Entrance requirements:* For master's and doctorate, GRE General Test, minimum GPA of 3.0. Additional exam requirements/recommendations for international students: Required—TOEFL (minimum score 600 paper-based; 100 iBT). Electronic applications accepted.

The University of Kansas, Graduate Studies, School of Education, Department of Health, Sport, and Exercise Sciences, Lawrence, KS 66045. Offers exercise science (MS Ed); health and physical education (MS Ed, PhD); sport management (MS Ed). *Accreditation:* NCATE. *Program availability:* Part-time, evening/weekend. *Students:* 53 full-time (21 women), 12 part-time (5 women); includes 5 minority (1 Black or African American, non-Hispanic/Latino; 1 American Indian or Alaska Native, non-Hispanic/Latino; 3 Two or more races, non-Hispanic/Latino), 3 international. Average age 27. 70 applicants, 64% accepted, 25 enrolled. In 2016, 19 master's, 6 doctorates awarded. *Entrance requirements:* For master's, GRE General Test (minimum score 1000, 450 verbal, 450 quantitative, 4.0 analytical), minimum GPA of 3.0, three letters of recommendation, personal statement, resume, writing sample; for doctorate, GRE General Test (minimum score 1100, verbal 500, quantitative 500, analytical 4.5), minimum graduate GPA of 3.5, undergraduate 3.0; three letters of recommendation; personal statement; resume; writing sample; interview with an advisor. Additional exam requirements/recommendations for international students: Required—TOEFL or IELTS. *Application deadline:* For fall admission, 3/15 for domestic and international students; for spring admission, 10/1 for domestic and international students; for summer admission, 3/15 for domestic and international students. Application fee: $65 ($85 for international students). Electronic applications accepted. *Financial support:* Research assistantships, teaching assistantships, Federal Work-Study, scholarships/grants, and unspecified assistantships available. Financial award application deadline: 2/21. *Faculty research:* Exercise and sport psychology, obesity prevention, sexuality health, sport ethics, skeletal muscle cell signaling and performance. *Unit head:* Dr. Joseph Weir, Chair, 785-864-0784, E-mail: joseph.weir@ku.edu. *Application contact:* Sarah Clopton, Graduate Admissions Coordinator, 785-864-7268, E-mail: sclopton@ku.edu.
Website: http://hses.soe.ku.edu/

University of Louisiana at Monroe, Graduate School, College of Health and Pharmaceutical Sciences, Department of Kinesiology, Monroe, LA 71209-0001. Offers applied exercise science (MS); clinical exercise physiology (MS); sports, fitness and recreation management (MS). *Program availability:* Part-time, evening/weekend, online learning. *Faculty:* 4 full-time (1 woman), 1 part-time/adjunct (0 women). *Students:* 31 full-time (12 women), 9 part-time (4 women); includes 11 minority (7 Black or African American, non-Hispanic/Latino; 4 Hispanic/Latino), 3 international. Average age 24. 96 applicants, 34% accepted, 14 enrolled. In 2016, 17 master's awarded. *Degree requirements:* For master's, comprehensive exam, thesis, 6-hour internship. *Entrance requirements:* For master's, GRE General Test. Additional exam requirements/recommendations for international students: Required—TOEFL (minimum score 500 paper-based; 61 iBT). *Application deadline:* For fall admission, 8/24 priority date for domestic students, 7/1 for international students; for winter admission, 12/14 priority date for domestic students; for spring admission, 1/19 for domestic students, 11/1 for international students. Applications are processed on a rolling basis. Application fee: $20 ($30 for international students). Electronic applications accepted. *Expenses:* Tuition, state resident: full-time $6489. Tuition, nonresident: full-time $18,589. *Required fees:* $8984. Tuition and fees vary according to course level, course load, degree level and program. *Financial support:* Research assistantships, career-related internships or fieldwork, Federal Work-Study, and unspecified assistantships available. Financial award application deadline: 4/1; financial award applicants required to submit FAFSA.

Faculty research: Cardiovascular disease risk factors; exercise and immunological system; attitude, exercise, and the aged. *Unit head:* Dr. Ken Alford, Director, 318-342-1306, E-mail: alford@ulm.edu. *Application contact:* Dr. Tommie Church, Director of Graduate Studies, 318-342-1321, E-mail: church@ulm.edu.
Website: http://www.ulm.edu/kinesiology/

University of Louisville, Graduate School, College of Education and Human Development, Department of Health and Sport Sciences, Louisville, KY 40292-0001. Offers community health education (M Ed); exercise physiology (MS), including health and sport sciences, strength and conditioning; health and physical education (MAT); sport administration (MS). *Program availability:* Part-time, evening/weekend. *Students:* 39 full-time (18 women), 10 part-time (8 women); includes 7 minority (4 Black or African American, non-Hispanic/Latino; 2 Hispanic/Latino; 1 Two or more races, non-Hispanic/Latino), 1 international. Average age 27. 73 applicants, 63% accepted, 23 enrolled. In 2016, 25 master's awarded. Application fee: $60. *Expenses:* Tuition, state resident: full-time $12,246; part-time $681 per credit hour. Tuition, nonresident: full-time $25,486; part-time $1417 per credit hour. *Required fees:* $196. Tuition and fees vary according to program and reciprocity agreements. *Financial support:* Applicants required to submit FAFSA. *Faculty research:* Sport administration; exercise physiology; exercise science; physical education; health education. *Total annual research expenditures:* $91,688. *Unit head:* Dr. Margaret Hancock, Interim Chair/Assistant Professor, 502-852-6645, E-mail: meg.hancock@louisville.edu. *Application contact:* Betty Hampton, Director of Graduate Student Services, 502-852-5597, Fax: 502-852-1465, E-mail: edadvise@louisville.edu.
Website: http://www.louisville.edu/education/departments/hss

University of Louisville, Graduate School, College of Education and Human Development, Department of Teaching and Learning, Louisville, KY 40292-0001. Offers art education (MAT); autism and applied behavior analysis (Certificate); curriculum and instruction (PhD); early elementary education (MAT); exercise physiology (MS); health and physical education (MAT); health professions education (Certificate); higher education (MA); human resources and organization development (MS); instructional technology (M Ed); interdisciplinary early childhood education (MAT); middle school education (MAT); music education (MAT); secondary education (MAT); special education (MAT); sport administration (MS); teacher leadership (M Ed). *Program availability:* Part-time, evening/weekend. *Students:* 116 full-time (68 women), 158 part-time (112 women); includes 46 minority (24 Black or African American, non-Hispanic/Latino; 8 Asian, non-Hispanic/Latino; 5 Hispanic/Latino; 9 Two or more races, non-Hispanic/Latino), 6 international. Average age 30. 114 applicants, 71% accepted, 57 enrolled. In 2016, 59 master's, 3 doctorates awarded. *Application deadline:* For spring admission, 1/1 priority date for international students. Application fee: $60. *Expenses:* Tuition, state resident: full-time $12,246; part-time $681 per credit hour. Tuition, nonresident: full-time $25,486; part-time $1417 per credit hour. *Required fees:* $196. Tuition and fees vary according to program and reciprocity agreements. *Financial support:* Application deadline: 6/1; applicants required to submit FAFSA. *Faculty research:* STEM teaching and learning; content literacy for English language learners; social justice in teacher education; adolescent literacy; mathematics teacher development. *Total annual research expenditures:* $1.7 million. *Unit head:* Dr. Ann E. Larson, Dean, College of Education and Human Development, 502-852-6411, Fax: 502-852-1464, E-mail: ann@louisville.edu. *Application contact:* Betty Hampton, Director of Graduate Student Services, 502-852-5597, Fax: 502-852-1465, E-mail: edadvise@louisville.edu.
Website: http://louisville.edu/delphi

University of Mary, School of Health Sciences, Program in Sports and Physical Education Administration, Bismarck, ND 58504-9652. Offers MS. *Program availability:* Online learning. *Entrance requirements:* For master's, bachelors degree in athletic training, exercise science, physical education, or a related field; minimum undergraduate GPA of 2.5.

University of Mary Hardin-Baylor, Graduate Studies in Exercise Science, Belton, TX 76513. Offers exercise physiology (MS Ed); sport administration (MS Ed). *Program availability:* Part-time, evening/weekend, 100% online. *Faculty:* 6 full-time (1 woman). *Students:* 9 full-time (2 women), 29 part-time (12 women); includes 21 minority (8 Black or African American, non-Hispanic/Latino; 1 Asian, non-Hispanic/Latino; 12 Hispanic/Latino). Average age 27. 19 applicants, 84% accepted, 13 enrolled. In 2016, 18 master's awarded. *Degree requirements:* For master's, comprehensive exam, thesis optional. *Entrance requirements:* For master's, bachelor's degree in exercise science or related field; minimum GPA of 3.0; interview with program director. Additional exam requirements/recommendations for international students: Required—TOEFL (minimum score 60 iBT), IELTS (minimum score 4.5). *Application deadline:* For fall admission, 6/1 for domestic students, 4/30 priority date for international students; for spring admission, 11/1 for domestic students, 9/30 priority date for international students. Applications are processed on a rolling basis. Application fee: $35 ($135 for international students). Electronic applications accepted. *Expenses: Tuition:* Full-time $14,940; part-time $830 per credit hour. *Required fees:* $1350; $75 per credit hour. $50 per term. Tuition and fees vary according to course load and degree level. *Financial support:* In 2016–17, 31 students received support. Federal Work-Study, unspecified assistantships, and scholarships for some active duty military personnel available. Support available to part-time students. Financial award application deadline: 6/1; financial award applicants required to submit FAFSA. *Unit head:* Dr. Lem Taylor, Director, MS Ed in Exercise Physiology Program, 254-295-4895, E-mail: ltaylor@umhb.edu. *Application contact:* Sharon Aguilera, Assistant Director, Graduate Admissions, 254-295-4835, Fax: 254-295-5038, E-mail: saguilera@umhb.edu.
Website: http://www.graduate.umhb.edu/exss

University of Massachusetts Amherst, Graduate School, Interdisciplinary Programs, Dual Degree Program in Management and Sport Management, Amherst, MA 01003. Offers MBA/MS. *Program availability:* Part-time. *Entrance requirements:* Additional exam requirements/recommendations for international students: Required—TOEFL (minimum score 600 paper-based; 100 iBT), IELTS (minimum score 7). Electronic applications accepted.

University of Massachusetts Amherst, Graduate School, Isenberg School of Management, Department of Sport Management, Amherst, MA 01003. Offers MBA, MS, MBA/MS. *Program availability:* Part-time. Terminal master's awarded for partial completion of doctoral program. *Degree requirements:* For master's, thesis or alternative. *Entrance requirements:* For master's, GMAT or GRE General Test. Additional exam requirements/recommendations for international students: Required—TOEFL (minimum score 550 paper-based; 80 iBT), IELTS (minimum score 6.5). Electronic applications accepted.

University of Massachusetts Amherst, Graduate School, Isenberg School of Management, Program in Management, Amherst, MA 01003. Offers accounting (PhD); business administration (MBA); entrepreneurship (MBA); finance (MBA, PhD); healthcare administration (MBA); hospitality and tourism management (PhD); management science (PhD); marketing (MBA, PhD); organization studies (PhD); sport management (PhD); strategic management (PhD); MBA/MS. *Accreditation:* AACSB. *Program availability:* Part-time, evening/weekend, online learning. Terminal master's awarded for partial completion of doctoral program. *Degree requirements:* For doctorate, comprehensive exam, thesis/dissertation. *Entrance requirements:* For master's and doctorate, GMAT or GRE General Test. Additional exam requirements/recommendations for international students: Required—TOEFL (minimum score 550 paper-based; 80 iBT), IELTS (minimum score 6.5). Electronic applications accepted.

University of Miami, Graduate School, School of Education and Human Development, Department of Kinesiology and Sport Sciences, Program in Sport Administration, Coral Gables, FL 33124. Offers MS Ed. *Program availability:* Part-time, evening/weekend, 100% online. *Faculty:* 6 full-time (3 women). *Students:* 160 full-time (48 women), 12 part-time (3 women); includes 67 minority (44 Black or African American, non-Hispanic/Latino; 16 Hispanic/Latino; 1 Native Hawaiian or other Pacific Islander, non-Hispanic/Latino; 6 Two or more races, non-Hispanic/Latino), 3 international. Average age 28. 223 applicants, 42% accepted, 46 enrolled. In 2016, 17 master's awarded. *Degree requirements:* For master's, thesis optional, special project. *Entrance requirements:* For master's, GRE General Test. Additional exam requirements/recommendations for international students: Required—TOEFL (minimum score 550 paper-based; 80 iBT); Recommended—IELTS (minimum score 6.5). *Application deadline:* For fall admission, 10/1 for international students; for spring admission, 10/1 for international students. Applications are processed on a rolling basis. Application fee: $65. Electronic applications accepted. *Financial support:* Institutionally sponsored loans and scholarships/grants available. Financial award application deadline: 3/1; financial award applicants required to submit FAFSA. *Faculty research:* Constitutional procedural due process, legal liability, tort law, moral development in sports administration, ethics intervention. *Unit head:* Dr. Warren Whisenant, Professor and Program Director, 305-284-5622, E-mail: wwhisenant@miami.edu. *Application contact:* Lois Heffernan, Graduate Admissions Coordinator, 305-284-2167, Fax: 305-284-9395, E-mail: lheffernan@miami.edu.
Website: http://www.education.miami.edu

University of Michigan, Rackham Graduate School, School of Kinesiology, Ann Arbor, MI 48109. Offers movement science (MS, PhD); sport management (MS, PhD). *Faculty:* 31 full-time (16 women). *Students:* 87 full-time (32 women); includes 39 minority (5 Black or African American, non-Hispanic/Latino; 1 American Indian or Alaska Native, non-Hispanic/Latino; 23 Asian, non-Hispanic/Latino; 6 Hispanic/Latino; 4 Two or more races, non-Hispanic/Latino). 229 applicants, 45% accepted, 49 enrolled. In 2016, 30 master's, 6 doctorates awarded. Terminal master's awarded for partial completion of doctoral program. *Degree requirements:* For master's, thesis optional; for doctorate, comprehensive exam, thesis/dissertation, oral defense of dissertation. *Entrance requirements:* For master's and doctorate, GRE General Test. Additional exam requirements/recommendations for international students: Required—TOEFL (minimum score 84 iBT). *Application deadline:* For fall admission, 1/15 priority date for domestic students, 1/15 for international students. Applications are processed on a rolling basis. Application fee: $75 ($90 for international students). Electronic applications accepted. *Expenses:* Tuition, state resident: full-time $21,466; part-time $1152 per credit hour. Tuition, nonresident: full-time $43,346; part-time $2367 per credit hour. Part-time tuition and fees vary according to course load, degree level and program. *Financial support:* In 2016–17, 3 fellowships, 18 research assistantships, 12 teaching assistantships were awarded; Federal Work-Study, scholarships/grants, traineeships, health care benefits, and unspecified assistantships also available. Financial award application deadline: 1/15. *Faculty research:* Motor development, exercise physiology, biomechanics, sport medicine, sport management. *Unit head:* Dr. Ketra L. Armstrong, Associate Dean for Graduate Programs and Faculty Affairs, 734-647-3027, Fax: 734-647-2808, E-mail: ketra@umich.edu. *Application contact:* Charlene F. Ruloff, Graduate Program Coordinator, 734-764-1343, Fax: 734-647-2808, E-mail: cruloff@umich.edu.
Website: http://www.kines.umich.edu/

University of Minnesota, Twin Cities Campus, Graduate School, College of Education and Human Development, School of Kinesiology, Minneapolis, MN 55455-0213. Offers kinesiology (MS, PhD), including behavioral aspects of physical activity, biomechanics and neuromotor control, exercise physiology, perceptual-motor control and learning, sport and exercise psychology, sport management (PhD), sport sociology; sport and exercise science (M Ed); sport management (M Ed, MA). *Program availability:* Part-time. *Faculty:* 15 full-time (6 women). *Students:* 117 full-time (54 women), 32 part-time (17 women); includes 21 minority (5 Black or African American, non-Hispanic/Latino; 1 American Indian or Alaska Native, non-Hispanic/Latino; 5 Asian, non-Hispanic/Latino; 7 Hispanic/Latino; 3 Two or more races, non-Hispanic/Latino), 20 international. Average age 27. 170 applicants, 45% accepted, 66 enrolled. In 2016, 85 master's, 5 doctorates awarded. Terminal master's awarded for partial completion of doctoral program. *Degree requirements:* For master's, final oral exam; for doctorate, thesis/dissertation, preliminary written/oral exam, final oral exam. *Entrance requirements:* For master's, GRE or MAT, minimum GPA of 3.0; for doctorate, GRE or MAT, minimum GPA of 3.0, writing sample. Application fee: $75 ($95 for international students). *Financial support:* In 2016–17, 3 fellowships, 11 research assistantships with full tuition reimbursements (averaging $11,857 per year), 42 teaching assistantships with full tuition reimbursements (averaging $14,262 per year) were awarded; career-related internships or fieldwork, Federal Work-Study, institutionally sponsored loans, and tuition waivers (full and partial) also available. Support available to part-time students. *Faculty research:* Role of physical activity in preventing health related problems; mechanism of age-related disorders, diseases and mental problems, and the ways to ameliorate them; role of sports in society and social justice; sports among populations with low income and racial diversity; fundamental functions of the body and the mechanism controlling the mechanisms; psychological issues related to physical activity and sports. *Total annual research expenditures:* $939,073. *Unit head:* Dr. Li Li Ji, Director, 612-624-9809, E-mail: llji@umn.edu. *Application contact:* Dr. Michael Wade, Director of Graduate Studies, 612-626-2094, E-mail: mwade@umn.edu.
Website: http://www.cehd.umn.edu/kin/

University of Nebraska at Kearney, College of Education, Kinesiology and Sport Sciences Department, Kearney, NE 68849-0001. Offers general physical education (MA Ed), including recreation and leisure, sports administration; physical education exercise science (MA Ed); physical education master teacher (MA Ed), including pedagogy, special populations. *Program availability:* Part-time, evening/weekend, 100% online. *Faculty:* 17 full-time (5 women). *Students:* 4 full-time (2 women), 39 part-time (16 women); includes 3 minority (2 Black or African American, non-Hispanic/Latino; 1 Hispanic/Latino). Average age 28. 20 applicants, 100% accepted, 14 enrolled. In 2016, 25 master's awarded. *Degree requirements:* For master's, comprehensive exam, thesis optional. *Entrance requirements:* For master's, GRE General Test (for some programs), personal statement. Additional exam requirements/recommendations for international students: Recommended—TOEFL (minimum score 550 paper-based; 79 iBT), IELTS (minimum score 6.5). *Application deadline:* For fall admission, 6/15 for domestic and international students; for spring admission, 10/15 for domestic and international students; for summer admission, 3/15 for domestic and international students. Application fee: $45. Electronic applications accepted. *Expenses:* Tuition, state resident: full-time $4064; part-time $225.75 per credit hour. Tuition, nonresident: full-time $8915; part-time $495.25 per credit hour. *Required fees:* $772; $23 per credit hour. Part-time tuition and fees vary according to course load, campus/location, program and reciprocity agreements. *Financial support:* In 2016–17, 9 students received support, including 3 research assistantships with full tuition reimbursements available (averaging $10,500 per year), 6 teaching assistantships with full tuition reimbursements available

(averaging $10,500 per year); career-related internships or fieldwork, scholarships/grants, health care benefits, and unspecified assistantships also available. Support available to part-time students. Financial award application deadline: 2/28; financial award applicants required to submit FAFSA. *Faculty research:* Ergonomic aids, nutrition, motor development, sports pedagogy, applied behavior analysis, physical activity and wellness, athletic training, therapeutic Interventions, exercise physiology, endocrinology and metabolism. *Unit head:* Dr. Nita Unruh, Chair, 308-865-8335, E-mail: unruhnc@unk.edu. *Application contact:* Linda Johnson, Director, Graduate Admissions and Programs, 308-865-8841, Fax: 308-865-8837, E-mail: johnsonli@unk.edu.
Website: http://www.unk.edu/academics/hperls/index.php

University of New Brunswick Fredericton, School of Graduate Studies, Faculty of Business Administration, Fredericton, NB E3B 5A3, Canada. Offers business administration (MBA); engineering management (MBA); entrepreneurship (MBA); sports and recreation management (MBA); MBA/LL B. *Program availability:* Part-time. *Degree requirements:* For master's, thesis optional. *Entrance requirements:* For master's, GMAT (minimum score 550), minimum GPA of 3.0; 3-5 years of work experience; 3 letters of reference with at least one academic reference. Additional exam requirements/recommendations for international students: Required—TOEFL (minimum score 580 paper-based; 92 iBT) or IELTS (minimum score 7). Electronic applications accepted. *Faculty research:* Entrepreneurship, finance, law, sport and recreation management, engineering management.

University of New Brunswick Fredericton, School of Graduate Studies, Faculty of Kinesiology, Fredericton, NB E3B 5A3, Canada. Offers exercise and sport science (M Sc); sport and recreation management (MBA); sport and recreation studies (MA). *Program availability:* Part-time. *Degree requirements:* For master's, thesis (for some programs). *Entrance requirements:* For master's, GMAT (minimum score of 550 for sport and recreation management program), minimum GPA of 3.0, written statement of research goals and interests. Additional exam requirements/recommendations for international students: Required—TOEFL (minimum score 92 iBT), IELTS (minimum score 7). Electronic applications accepted.

University of New Haven, Graduate School, College of Business, Program in Business Administration, West Haven, CT 06516. Offers accounting (MBA), including CPA; business administration (MBA); business intelligence (MBA); business management (Graduate Certificate); business policy and strategic leadership (MBA); finance (MBA), including CFA; global marketing (MBA); human resources management (MBA, Graduate Certificate); sport management (MBA). *Accreditation:* AACSB. *Program availability:* Part-time, evening/weekend. *Students:* 123 full-time (56 women), 74 part-time (29 women); includes 46 minority (24 Black or African American, non-Hispanic/Latino; 8 Asian, non-Hispanic/Latino; 10 Hispanic/Latino; 4 Two or more races, non-Hispanic/Latino), 57 international. Average age 27. In 2016, 100 master's awarded. *Entrance requirements:* For master's, GMAT. Additional exam requirements/recommendations for international students: Required—TOEFL (minimum score 80 iBT), IELTS, PTE. *Application deadline:* Applications are processed on a rolling basis. Application fee: $50. Electronic applications accepted. Application fee is waived when completed online. *Expenses: Tuition:* Full-time $15,660; part-time $870 per credit hour. *Required fees:* $200; $85 per term. Tuition and fees vary according to program. *Financial support:* Research assistantships with partial tuition reimbursements, teaching assistantships with partial tuition reimbursements, career-related internships or fieldwork, Federal Work-Study, scholarships/grants, and unspecified assistantships available. Support available to part-time students. Financial award applicants required to submit FAFSA. *Unit head:* Darell Singleterry, Director, 203-932-1085, E-mail: dsingleterry@newhaven.edu. *Application contact:* Michelle Mason, Director of Graduate Enrollment, 203-932-7067, E-mail: mmason@newhaven.edu.
Website: http://www.newhaven.edu/business/programs/EMBA/

University of New Haven, Graduate School, College of Business, Program in Sport Management, West Haven, CT 06516. Offers collegiate athletic administration (MS); facility management (MS); sport analytics (MS); sport management (Graduate Certificate). *Program availability:* Part-time, evening/weekend. *Students:* 15 full-time (7 women), 9 part-time (2 women); includes 5 minority (3 Black or African American, non-Hispanic/Latino; 1 Hispanic/Latino; 1 Two or more races, non-Hispanic/Latino), 6 international. Average age 25. 26 applicants, 96% accepted, 13 enrolled. In 2016, 12 master's awarded. *Entrance requirements:* For master's, GMAT. Additional exam requirements/recommendations for international students: Required—TOEFL (minimum score 80 iBT), IELTS, PTE. *Application deadline:* Applications are processed on a rolling basis. Application fee: $50. Electronic applications accepted. Application fee is waived when completed online. *Expenses: Tuition:* Full-time $15,660; part-time $870 per credit hour. *Required fees:* $200; $85 per term. Tuition and fees vary according to program. *Financial support:* Research assistantships with partial tuition reimbursements, teaching assistantships with partial tuition reimbursements, career-related internships or fieldwork, Federal Work-Study, scholarships/grants, and unspecified assistantships available. Support available to part-time students. Financial award applicants required to submit FAFSA. *Unit head:* Gil B. Fried, Professor, 203-932-7081, E-mail: gfried@newhaven.edu.
Website: http://www.newhaven.edu/6851/

University of New Mexico, Graduate Studies, College of Education, Program in Physical Education, Sports and Exercise Science, Albuquerque, NM 87131-2039. Offers curriculum and instruction (PhD); exercise science (PhD); sports administration (PhD). *Program availability:* Part-time. *Faculty:* 13 full-time (6 women), 2 part-time/adjunct (1 woman). *Students:* 83 full-time (28 women), 48 part-time (21 women); includes 51 minority (12 Black or African American, non-Hispanic/Latino; 2 American Indian or Alaska Native, non-Hispanic/Latino; 1 Asian, non-Hispanic/Latino; 32 Hispanic/Latino; 4 Two or more races, non-Hispanic/Latino), 15 international. Average age 30. 67 applicants, 75% accepted, 35 enrolled. In 2016, 13 doctorates awarded. *Degree requirements:* For doctorate, comprehensive exam, thesis/dissertation, inquiry skills, 24 credits in supporting area. *Entrance requirements:* For doctorate, GRE, letter of intent, 3 letters of reference, minimum cumulative GPA of 3.0 in last 2 years of bachelor's degree. Additional exam requirements/recommendations for international students: Required—TOEFL (minimum score 550 paper-based). *Application deadline:* For fall admission, 3/1 priority date for domestic students; for spring admission, 11/1 priority date for domestic students. Application fee: $50. Electronic applications accepted. *Financial support:* Fellowships, teaching assistantships with full tuition reimbursements, career-related internships or fieldwork, Federal Work-Study, institutionally sponsored loans, scholarships/grants, health care benefits, tuition waivers, and unspecified assistantships available. Financial award application deadline: 3/1; financial award applicants required to submit FAFSA. *Faculty research:* Facility risk management, physical education pedagogy practices, physiological adaptations to exercise, physiological adaptations to heat, sport leadership. *Unit head:* Dr. Todd Seidler, Chair, 505-277-2783, Fax: 505-277-6227, E-mail: tseidler@unm.edu. *Application contact:* Monica Lopez, Program Office, 505-277-5151, Fax: 505-277-6227, E-mail: mllopez@unm.edu.
Website: https://coe.unm.edu/departments-programs/hess/physical-education/physical-education-phd/index.html

The University of North Carolina at Chapel Hill, Graduate School, College of Arts and Sciences, Department of Exercise and Sport Science, Chapel Hill, NC 27599. Offers athletic training (MA); exercise physiology (MA); sport administration (MA). *Degree requirements:* For master's, comprehensive exam, thesis. *Entrance requirements:* For master's, GRE General Test, minimum GPA of 3.0. Additional exam requirements/recommendations for international students: Required—TOEFL (minimum score 550 paper-based). Electronic applications accepted. *Faculty research:* Mild head injury in sport, endocrine system's response to exercise, obesity and children, effect of aerobic exercise on cerebral bloodflow in elderly population.

University of Northern Colorado, Graduate School, College of Natural and Health Sciences, School of Sport and Exercise Science, Greeley, CO 80639. Offers exercise science (MS, PhD); physical education and physical activity leadership (MAT); sport administration (MS, PhD); sport pedagogy (MS, PhD); sports coaching (MA). *Program availability:* Part-time, evening/weekend. *Degree requirements:* For master's, comprehensive exam; for doctorate, comprehensive exam, thesis/dissertation. *Entrance requirements:* For master's, 2 letters of recommendation, resume; for doctorate, GRE General Test, 3 letters of recommendation, resume. *Application deadline:* Applications are processed on a rolling basis. Application fee: $50 ($60 for international students). Electronic applications accepted. *Financial support:* Fellowships, research assistantships, teaching assistantships, and unspecified assistantships available. Financial award application deadline: 3/1; financial award applicants required to submit FAFSA. *Unit head:* Dr. David Stotlar, Director, 970-351-2535, Fax: 970-351-1762. *Application contact:* Linda Sisson, Graduate Student Admission Coordinator, 970-351-1807, Fax: 970-351-2371, E-mail: linda.sisson@unco.edu.
Website: http://www.unco.edu/nhs/sport-exercise-science/

University of Northern Iowa, Graduate College, College of Education, School of Kinesiology, Allied Health and Human Services, MA Program in Physical Education, Cedar Falls, IA 50614. Offers kinesiology (MA); teaching/coaching (MA). *Program availability:* Part-time, evening/weekend. *Degree requirements:* For master's, comprehensive exam, thesis or alternative. *Entrance requirements:* For master's, minimum GPA of 3.0. Additional exam requirements/recommendations for international students: Required—TOEFL (minimum score 500 paper-based; 61 iBT). Electronic applications accepted.

University of North Florida, College of Education and Human Services, Department of Leadership, School Counseling and Sport Management, Jacksonville, FL 32224. Offers counselor education (M Ed), including school counseling; educational leadership (M Ed, Ed D), including athletic administration (M Ed), educational leadership, educational technology (M Ed), instructional leadership (M Ed). *Program availability:* Part-time, evening/weekend. *Faculty:* 18 full-time (10 women), 1 (woman) part-time/adjunct. *Students:* 74 full-time (61 women), 219 part-time (149 women); includes 93 minority (65 Black or African American, non-Hispanic/Latino; 1 American Indian or Alaska Native, non-Hispanic/Latino; 3 Asian, non-Hispanic/Latino; 15 Hispanic/Latino; 1 Native Hawaiian or other Pacific Islander, non-Hispanic/Latino; 8 Two or more races, non-Hispanic/Latino), 14 international. Average age 34. 128 applicants, 57% accepted, 55 enrolled. In 2016, 94 master's, 7 doctorates awarded. *Degree requirements:* For doctorate, thesis/dissertation. *Entrance requirements:* For master's, GRE General Test, minimum GPA of 3.0 in last 60 hours, interview, 3 letters of recommendation; for doctorate, GRE General Test, master's degree, interview, 3 letters of recommendation, writing sample. Additional exam requirements/recommendations for international students: Required—TOEFL (minimum score 500 paper-based). *Application deadline:* For fall admission, 5/1 priority date for domestic students, 5/1 for international students. Application fee: $30. Electronic applications accepted. Tuition and fees vary according to course load, campus/location and program. *Financial support:* In 2016–17, 48 students received support, including 1 research assistantship (averaging $4,445 per year), 1 teaching assistantship (averaging $5,378 per year); career-related internships or fieldwork, Federal Work-Study, scholarships/grants, tuition waivers (partial), and unspecified assistantships also available. Support available to part-time students. Financial award application deadline: 4/1; financial award applicants required to submit FAFSA. *Faculty research:* Counseling: ethics; lesbian, bisexual and transgender issues; educational leadership: school culture and climate; educational assessment and accountability; school safety and student discipline. *Total annual research expenditures:* $45,589. *Unit head:* Dr. Liz Gregg, Chair, 904-620-5199, E-mail: liz.gregg@unf.edu. *Application contact:* Dr. Amanda Pascale, Director, The Graduate School, 904-620-1360, Fax: 904-620-1362, E-mail: graduateschool@unf.edu.
Website: http://www.unf.edu/coehs/lscsm/

University of Oregon, Graduate School, Charles H. Lundquist College of Business, Program in Sports Product Management, Portland, OR 97209. Offers MS.

University of San Francisco, College of Arts and Sciences, Sport Management Program, San Francisco, CA 94117-1080. Offers MA. *Program availability:* Evening/weekend. *Faculty:* 5 full-time (1 woman), 9 part-time/adjunct (1 woman). *Students:* 193 full-time (87 women), 8 part-time (3 women); includes 92 minority (22 Black or African American, non-Hispanic/Latino; 16 Asian, non-Hispanic/Latino; 38 Hispanic/Latino; 16 Two or more races, non-Hispanic/Latino), 11 international. Average age 25. 218 applicants, 49% accepted, 73 enrolled. In 2016, 94 master's awarded. *Degree requirements:* For master's, thesis or alternative. *Entrance requirements:* For master's, interview, minimum GPA of 2.75. Additional exam requirements/recommendations for international students: Required—TOEFL, IELTS, PTE. *Application deadline:* For spring admission, 9/1 for domestic and international students; for summer admission, 2/1 for domestic and international students. Applications are processed on a rolling basis. Application fee: $55 ($65 for international students). *Expenses: Tuition:* Full-time $23,310; part-time $1295 per credit. Tuition and fees vary according to course load, degree level, campus/location and program. *Financial support:* In 2016–17, 68 students received support. Career-related internships or fieldwork, Federal Work-Study, and institutionally sponsored loans available. Financial award application deadline: 3/2; financial award applicants required to submit FAFSA. *Faculty research:* Media and sports, sports marketing, sports law, management and organization. *Unit head:* Andrew Roberts, Director of Administration, 415-422-2678, Fax: 415-422-6267, E-mail: sminfo@usfca.edu. *Application contact:* Mark Landerghini, Information Contact, 415-422-5101, Fax: 415-422-2217, E-mail: asgraduate@usfca.edu.
Website: https://www.usfca.edu/arts-sciences/graduate-programs/sport-management

University of South Alabama, College of Education and Professional Studies, Department of Health, Kinesiology, and Sport, Mobile, AL 36688. Offers exercise science (MS); health education (M Ed); physical education (M Ed); sport management (MS). *Accreditation:* NCATE (one or more programs are accredited). *Program availability:* Part-time. *Faculty:* 7 full-time (2 women). *Students:* 50 full-time (15 women), 4 part-time (2 women); includes 21 minority (17 Black or African American, non-Hispanic/Latino; 1 Asian, non-Hispanic/Latino; 1 Hispanic/Latino; 2 Two or more races, non-Hispanic/Latino), 3 international. Average age 27. 53 applicants, 57% accepted, 28 enrolled. In 2016, 16 master's awarded. *Degree requirements:* For master's, comprehensive exam, thesis optional. *Entrance requirements:* For master's, GRE General Test or MAT, Alabama Class B certificate or the equivalent (for students seeking the master's-level/Class A certification). Additional exam requirements/recommendations for international students: Required—TOEFL. *Application deadline:*

For fall admission, 7/15 priority date for domestic students, 6/15 priority date for international students; for spring admission, 11/15 priority date for domestic students, 10/15 priority date for international students; for summer admission, 4/15 for domestic students. Applications are processed on a rolling basis. Application fee: $35. Electronic applications accepted. *Expenses:* Tuition, state resident: full-time $9768; part-time $407 per credit hour. Tuition, nonresident: full-time $19,536; part-time $814 per credit hour. *Financial support:* Fellowships, research assistantships, teaching assistantships with partial tuition reimbursements, career-related internships or fieldwork, Federal Work-Study, institutionally sponsored loans, scholarships/grants, and unspecified assistantships available. Support available to part-time students. Financial award application deadline: 5/31; financial award applicants required to submit FAFSA. *Unit head:* Dr. John Kovaleski, Department Chair, 251-461-1622, Fax: 251-460-7252, E-mail: jkovales@southalabama.edu. *Application contact:* Dr. Susan Santoli, Director of Graduate Studies, 251-380-2738, Fax: 251-380-2758, E-mail: ssantoli@southalabama.edu.
Website: http://www.southalabama.edu/colleges/coe/hks/index.html

University of South Carolina, The Graduate School, College of Hospitality, Retail, and Sport Management, Department of Sport and Entertainment Management, Columbia, SC 29208. Offers live sport and entertainment events (MS); public assembly facilities management (MS). *Program availability:* Part-time. *Degree requirements:* For master's, comprehensive exam, thesis optional. *Entrance requirements:* For master's, GRE General Test or GMAT (preferred), minimum GPA of 3.0. Additional exam requirements/recommendations for international students: Required—TOEFL (minimum score 570 paper-based; 70 iBT). Electronic applications accepted. *Expenses:* Contact institution. *Faculty research:* Public assembly marketing, operations, box office, booking and scheduling, law/economic impacts.

University of Southern Indiana, Graduate Studies, Pott College of Science, Engineering, and Education, Program in Sport Management, Evansville, IN 47712-3590. Offers MSSM. *Program availability:* Part-time, evening/weekend. *Faculty:* 3 full-time (2 women), 1 (woman) part-time/adjunct. *Students:* 25 full-time (7 women), 1 (woman) part-time; includes 2 minority (1 Black or African American, non-Hispanic/Latino; 1 Hispanic/Latino), 1 international. Average age 25. *Entrance requirements:* For master's, personal statement, three letters of recommendation. Additional exam requirements/recommendations for international students: Required—TOEFL (minimum score 550 paper-based; 79 iBT), IELTS (minimum score 6). *Application deadline:* Applications are processed on a rolling basis. Application fee: $40. Electronic applications accepted. *Expenses:* Tuition, state resident: full-time $8497. Tuition, nonresident: full-time $16,691. *Required fees:* $500. *Financial support:* In 2016–17, 11 students received support. Federal Work-Study, scholarships/grants, tuition waivers (full and partial), and unspecified assistantships available. Financial award application deadline: 3/1; financial award applicants required to submit FAFSA. *Unit head:* Dr. Glenna G. Bower, Department Chair, 812-464-1709, E-mail: gbower@usi.edu. *Application contact:* Dr. Mayola Rowser, Director, Graduate Studies, 812-465-7015, Fax: 812-464-1956, E-mail: mrowser@usi.edu.
Website: https://www.usi.edu/science/kinesiology-and-sport/programs/master-of-science-in-sport-management

University of Southern Mississippi, Graduate School, College of Health, School of Kinesiology, Hattiesburg, MS 39406. Offers kinesiology (MS, PhD), including biomechanics (PhD), exercise physiology (PhD), exercise science (MS), physical education (MS), sport pedagogy (PhD); sport coaching education (MS). *Program availability:* Part-time, evening/weekend. *Degree requirements:* For master's, comprehensive exam, thesis optional; for doctorate, comprehensive exam, thesis/dissertation. *Entrance requirements:* For master's, GRE General Test, minimum GPA of 2.75 in last 60 hours; for doctorate, GRE General Test, minimum GPA of 3.5. Additional exam requirements/recommendations for international students: Required—TOEFL, IELTS. *Application deadline:* For fall admission, 3/1 priority date for domestic students, 3/1 for international students; for spring admission, 1/10 priority date for domestic and international students. Applications are processed on a rolling basis. Application fee: $60. Electronic applications accepted. *Expenses: Tuition, area resident:* Full-time $15,708; part-time $437 per credit hour. *Financial support:* Fellowships, research assistantships with full tuition reimbursements, teaching assistantships with full tuition reimbursements, career-related internships or fieldwork, Federal Work-Study, institutionally sponsored loans, scholarships/grants, health care benefits, and unspecified assistantships available. Financial award application deadline: 3/15; financial award applicants required to submit FAFSA. *Faculty research:* Exercise physiology, health behaviors, resource management, activity interaction, site development. *Unit head:* Dr. Scott Piland, Director, 601-266-5386, Fax: 601-266-4445, E-mail: scott.piland@usm.edu. *Application contact:* Dr. Trenton Gould, Dean, College of Health, 601-266-6339, Fax: 601-266-4445.
Website: https://www.usm.edu/kinesiology

The University of Tennessee, Graduate School, College of Education, Health and Human Sciences, Department of Exercise, Sport, and Leisure Studies, Knoxville, TN 37996. Offers exercise science (MS, PhD), including biomechanics/sports medicine, exercise physiology; recreation and leisure studies (MS); sport management (MS); sport studies (MS, PhD); therapeutic recreation (MS). *Program availability:* Part-time, evening/weekend. *Degree requirements:* For master's, thesis optional. *Entrance requirements:* For master's, minimum GPA of 2.7. Additional exam requirements/recommendations for international students: Required—TOEFL. Electronic applications accepted.

University of the Southwest, Graduate Programs, Hobbs, NM 88240-9129. Offers business administration (MBA); curriculum and instruction (MSE); curriculum and instruction: bilingual (MSE); curriculum and instruction: TESOL (MSE); early childhood education (MSE); educational administration (MSE); mental health counseling (MSE); school counseling (MSE); special education (MSE); sports management (MBA). *Program availability:* Part-time, evening/weekend, online learning. *Degree requirements:* For master's, comprehensive exam, thesis (for some programs). *Entrance requirements:* Additional exam requirements/recommendations for international students: Recommended—TOEFL. Electronic applications accepted.

Upper Iowa University, Online Master's Programs, Fayette, IA 52142-1857. Offers accounting (MBA); corporate financial management (MBA); emergency management and homeland security (MPA); general management (MBA); general studies (MPA); government administration (MPA); health and human services (MPA); human resources management (MBA); nonprofit organizational management (MPA); organizational development (MBA); public management (MPA); sport administration (MSA). MBA also available at Madison, WI campus. *Program availability:* Part-time, online learning. *Degree requirements:* For master's, research project. *Entrance requirements:* For master's, GMAT, GRE, or minimum GPA of 2.7 during last 60 hours. Additional exam requirements/recommendations for international students: Required—TOEFL (minimum score 570 paper-based). Electronic applications accepted. *Faculty research:* Total quality management, teams, organization culture and climate, management.

Valparaiso University, Graduate School and Continuing Education, Program in Sports Administration, Valparaiso, IN 46383. Offers MS, JD/MS. *Program availability:* Part-time, evening/weekend. *Entrance requirements:* For master's, minimum GPA of 3.0. Additional exam requirements/recommendations for international students: Required—TOEFL (minimum score 550 paper-based; 80 iBT), IELTS (minimum score 6). Electronic applications accepted. *Expenses: Tuition:* Full-time $11,070; part-time $615 per credit hour. *Required fees:* $116 per semester. Tuition and fees vary according to course load, degree level and program.

Waldorf University, Program in Organizational Leadership, Forest City, IA 50436. Offers criminal justice leadership (MA); emergency management leadership (MA); fire/rescue executive leadership (MA); human resource development (MA); public administration (MA); sport management (MA); teacher leader (MA).

Washington State University, College of Education, Department of Educational Leadership, Sports Studies, and Educational/Counseling Psychology, Pullman, WA 99164-2136. Offers counseling psychology (PhD); educational leadership (Ed M, MA, Ed D, PhD); educational psychology (MA, PhD); sport management (MA). Programs also offered at the Spokane, Tri-Cities, Vancouver and Global (online) campuses. *Program availability:* Part-time, online learning. *Degree requirements:* For master's, comprehensive exam (for some programs), thesis (for some programs), oral or written exam; for doctorate, comprehensive exam, thesis/dissertation, oral and written exam, internship. *Entrance requirements:* For master's and doctorate, GRE General Test, minimum GPA of 3.0, 3 letters of recommendation, transcripts showing all college or university course work, statement of professional objectives, current curriculum vitae/resume. Additional exam requirements/recommendations for international students: Required—TOEFL (minimum score 550 paper-based; 80 iBT). Electronic applications accepted. *Faculty research:* Multicultural counseling and career development, educational and psychological measurement issues, business decision-making process and power relationships, leadership practices and processes as suffused with and constituted by emotion work.

Wayland Baptist University, Graduate Programs, Program in Education, Plainview, TX 79072-6998. Offers education administration (M Ed); education diagnostics (M Ed); education literacy (M Ed); elementary certification (M Ed); English (M Ed); English as a second language (M Ed); higher education administration (M Ed); human resources (M Ed); instructional leadership (M Ed); instructional technology (M Ed); leadership training and development (M Ed); science education (M Ed); secondary certification (M Ed); social studies (M Ed); special education (M Ed); sports administration and management (M Ed). *Program availability:* Part-time, evening/weekend, online learning. *Degree requirements:* For master's, comprehensive exam, capstone course. *Entrance requirements:* For master's, GRE, GMAT or MAT. Additional exam requirements/recommendations for international students: Required—TOEFL (minimum score 500 paper-based; 61 iBT). Electronic applications accepted.

Wayne State College, Department of Health, Human Performance and Sport, Wayne, NE 68787. Offers exercise science (MSE); organizational management (MS), including sport management. *Program availability:* Part-time, evening/weekend. *Degree requirements:* For master's, comprehensive exam, thesis optional. *Entrance requirements:* For master's, GRE General Test, minimum GPA of 3.0. Additional exam requirements/recommendations for international students: Required—TOEFL (minimum score 550 paper-based). Electronic applications accepted.

Wayne State University, College of Education, Division of Kinesiology, Health and Sports Studies, Detroit, MI 48202. Offers health education (M Ed); kinesiology (M Ed, PhD), including exercise and sport science (PhD), physical education and physical activity leadership (PhD); sports administration (MA). *Program availability:* Part-time, 100% online. *Faculty:* 10. *Students:* 57 full-time (30 women), 131 part-time (68 women); includes 72 minority (63 Black or African American, non-Hispanic/Latino; 1 American Indian or Alaska Native, non-Hispanic/Latino; 1 Asian, non-Hispanic/Latino; 3 Hispanic/Latino; 4 Two or more races, non-Hispanic/Latino), 10 international. Average age 29. 160 applicants, 56% accepted, 51 enrolled. In 2016, 66 master's awarded. *Degree requirements:* For master's, thesis (for some programs); for doctorate, thesis/dissertation. *Entrance requirements:* For master's, minimum undergraduate GPA of 3.0; undergraduate degree directly relating to the field of specialization being applied for or one accompanied by extensive educational background in closely-related field; teaching certificates in specific areas (for some programs); for doctorate, minimum undergraduate GPA of 3.0; undergraduate degree directly relating to the field of specialization being applied for or one accompanied by extensive educational background in closely-related field. Additional exam requirements/recommendations for international students: Required—TOEFL (minimum score 79 iBT), TWE (minimum score 5.5), Michigan English Language Assessment Battery (minimum score 85); Recommended—IELTS (minimum score 6.5). *Application deadline:* For fall admission, 6/1 priority date for domestic students, 5/1 priority date for international students; for winter admission, 10/1 priority date for domestic students, 9/1 priority date for international students; for spring admission, 2/1 priority date for domestic students, 1/1 priority date for international students. Application fee: $50. Electronic applications accepted. *Expenses:* $18,522 per year resident tuition and fees, $35,715 per year non-resident tuition and fees. *Financial support:* In 2016–17, 49 students received support, including 6 research assistantships with tuition reimbursements available (averaging $17,994 per year); fellowships with tuition reimbursements available, scholarships/grants, health care benefits, and unspecified assistantships also available. Support available to part-time students. Financial award applicants required to submit FAFSA. *Faculty research:* Exercise and sport science, nutrition and physical activity interventions, school and community health, obesity prevention. *Total annual research expenditures:* $974,985. *Unit head:* Dr. Nate McCaughtry, Assistant Dean, Division of Kinesiology, Health and Sport Studies/Director, Center for School Health, 313-577-0014, Fax: 313-577-5002, E-mail: aj4391@wayne.edu. *Application contact:* Janice Green, Assistant Dean, 313-577-1605, E-mail: jwgreen@wayne.edu.
Website: http://coe.wayne.edu/kinesiology/index.php

Webber International University, Graduate School of Business, Babson Park, FL 33827-0096. Offers accounting (MBA); business (MBA); criminal justice management (MBA); international business (MBA); sport business management (MBA). *Program availability:* Part-time, evening/weekend, 100% online. *Faculty:* 11 full-time (3 women), 1 part-time/adjunct (0 women). *Students:* 44 full-time (21 women), 6 part-time (2 women); includes 11 minority (5 Black or African American, non-Hispanic/Latino; 5 Hispanic/Latino; 1 Two or more races, non-Hispanic/Latino), 11 international. Average age 27. 32 applicants, 69% accepted, 18 enrolled. In 2016, 16 master's awarded. *Degree requirements:* For master's, class trip (for international business); practicum (for criminal justice management). *Entrance requirements:* For master's, three recommendation letters, résumé, essay, official transcripts from all colleges and universities attended. Additional exam requirements/recommendations for international students: Recommended—TOEFL (minimum score 500 paper-based; 61 iBT), IELTS (minimum score 6). *Application deadline:* For fall admission, 7/1 for international students. Applications are processed on a rolling basis. Application fee: $50 ($75 for international students). Electronic applications accepted. *Expenses:* $2,013 tuition per course; $207 technology fee per course (for online courses only). *Financial support:* In 2016–17, 11 students received support. Scholarships/grants and unspecified assistantships available. Financial award application deadline: 8/16; financial award applicants required to submit FAFSA. *Unit head:* Dr. Nikos Orphanoudakis, Dean, 863-638-2910, Fax: 863-638-1591, E-mail: orphanoudakisn@webber.edu. *Application contact:* Lacy Edwards,

Admissions Counselor and MBA Coordinator, 863-638-2910, Fax: 863-638-1591, E-mail: admissions@webber.edu.

West Chester University of Pennsylvania, College of Health Sciences, Department of Kinesiology, West Chester, PA 19383. Offers adapted physical education (Certificate); exercise and sport physiology (MS), including athletic training, exercise and sport physiology; general physical education (MS); sport management and athletics (MPA), including administration. *Program availability:* Part-time, evening/weekend. *Faculty:* 9 full-time (6 women). *Students:* 34 full-time (22 women), 21 part-time (7 women); includes 5 minority (4 Black or African American, non-Hispanic/Latino; 1 Hispanic/Latino), 1 international. Average age 26. 68 applicants, 85% accepted, 30 enrolled. In 2016, 23 master's, 1 other advanced degree awarded. *Degree requirements:* For master's, thesis or research report (for MS); two internships and capstone course that includes a research project or thesis (for MPA). *Entrance requirements:* For master's, GRE (for MS), 2 letters of recommendation, statement of goals; transcripts (for MS); resume (for MPA). Additional exam requirements/recommendations for international students: Required—TOEFL or IELTS. *Application deadline:* For fall admission, 5/15 for international students; for spring admission, 10/15 for international students. Applications are processed on a rolling basis. Application fee: $50. Electronic applications accepted. *Expenses:* Tuition, state resident: full-time $8694; part-time $483 per credit. Tuition, nonresident: full-time $13,050; part-time $725 per credit. *Required fees:* $2399; $119.05 per credit. Tuition and fees vary according to campus/location and program. *Financial support:* Scholarships/grants and unspecified assistantships available. Financial award application deadline: 2/15; financial award applicants required to submit FAFSA. *Faculty research:* Metabolism during exercise, biomechanics, rating of perceived exertion, motor learning, environmental physiology. *Unit head:* Dr. Frank Fry, Chair/Graduate Coordinator for the MS in General Physical Education Program, 610-436-2610, Fax: 610-436-2860, E-mail: ffry@wcupa.edu. *Application contact:* Office of Graduate Studies and Extended Education, 610-436-2943, Fax: 610-436-2763, E-mail: gradstudy@wcupa.edu.
Website: http://www.wcupa.edu/healthsciences/kinesiology/

Western Illinois University, School of Graduate Studies, College of Education and Human Services, Department of Kinesiology, Program in Sport Management, Macomb, IL 61455-1390. Offers MS. *Program availability:* Part-time. *Students:* 45 full-time (11 women), 2 part-time (0 women); includes 18 minority (14 Black or African American, non-Hispanic/Latino; 2 Hispanic/Latino; 2 Two or more races, non-Hispanic/Latino), 2 international. Average age 25. 42 applicants, 88% accepted, 26 enrolled. In 2016, 30 master's awarded. *Entrance requirements:* For master's, minimum GPA of 3.0. Additional exam requirements/recommendations for international students: Required—TOEFL (minimum score 550 paper-based; 80 iBT). *Application deadline:* Applications are processed on a rolling basis. Application fee: $30. Electronic applications accepted. *Financial support:* In 2016–17, 28 students received support. Unspecified assistantships available. *Unit head:* Dr. Janet Wigglesworth, Chairperson, 309-298-1981. *Application contact:* Dr. Nancy Parsons, Associate Provost and Director of Graduate Studies, 309-298-1806, Fax: 309-298-2345, E-mail: grad-office@wiu.edu.
Website: http://wiu.edu/kinesiology

Western Kentucky University, Graduate Studies, College of Health and Human Services, Department of Kinesiology, Recreation and Sport, Bowling Green, KY 42101. Offers athletic administration and coaching (MS); physical education (MS); recreation and sport administration (MS). *Program availability:* Part-time, evening/weekend, online learning. *Degree requirements:* For master's, comprehensive exam, thesis optional. *Entrance requirements:* For master's, GRE General Test, minimum GPA of 2.75. Additional exam requirements/recommendations for international students: Required—TOEFL (minimum score 555 paper-based; 79 iBT). *Faculty research:* Orthopedic rehabilitation, fitness center coordination, heat acclimation, biomechanical and physiological parameters.

Western Michigan University, Graduate College, College of Education and Human Development, Department of Health, Physical Education and Recreation, Kalamazoo, MI 49008. Offers athletic training (MS), including exercise physiology; sport management (MA), including pedagogy, special physical education.

Western New England University, College of Business, Program in Business Administration, Springfield, MA 01119. Offers general business (MBA); sport management (MBA); JD/MBA; Pharm D/MBA. *Accreditation:* AACSB. *Program availability:* Part-time, evening/weekend, online learning. *Faculty:* 7 full-time (5 women). *Students:* 85 part-time (35 women); includes 11 minority (6 Black or African American, non-Hispanic/Latino; 3 Asian, non-Hispanic/Latino; 2 Hispanic/Latino), 4 international. Average age 31. 73 applicants, 27% accepted, 18 enrolled. In 2016, 66 master's awarded. *Entrance requirements:* For master's, GMAT or GRE, official transcript, two letters of recommendation, essay, resume. Additional exam requirements/recommendations for international students: Required—TOEFL (minimum score 79 iBT). *Application deadline:* Applications are processed on a rolling basis. Application fee: $30. Electronic applications accepted. *Expenses:* Contact institution. *Financial support:* Application deadline: 4/15; applicants required to submit FAFSA. *Unit head:* Dr. Rob Kleine, Dean, 413-782-1395, E-mail: rob.kleine@wne.edu. *Application contact:* Matthew Fox, Director of Admissions for Graduate Students and Adult Learners, 413-782-1410, Fax: 413-782-1777, E-mail: study@wne.edu.
Website: http://www1.wne.edu/academics/graduate/mba.cfm

West Texas A&M University, College of Nursing and Health Sciences, Department of Sports and Exercise Sciences, Canyon, TX 79016-0001. Offers sport management (MS); sports and exercise sciences (MS). *Program availability:* Part-time, evening/weekend. *Degree requirements:* For master's, comprehensive exam, thesis optional. *Entrance requirements:* For master's, GRE General Test. Additional exam requirements/recommendations for international students: Required—TOEFL. *Application deadline:* For fall admission, 8/1 for domestic students, 6/1 for international students; for spring admission, 12/1 for domestic students, 11/1 for international students; for summer admission, 5/1 for domestic students. Applications are processed on a rolling basis. Application fee: $40 ($75 for international students). Electronic applications accepted. *Financial support:* Application deadline: 2/1; applicants required to submit FAFSA. *Unit head:* Lorna Strong, Department Head, 806-651-2382. *Application contact:* Dr. Vanessa Fiaud, Assistant Professor, 806-651-2677.

West Virginia University, College of Physical Activity and Sport Sciences, Morgantown, WV 26506-6116. Offers athletic training (MS); coaching and sport education (MS); coaching and teaching studies (Ed D); physical education/teacher education (MS, PhD), including curriculum and instruction (PhD), physical education supervision (PhD); sport and exercise psychology (MS, PhD); sport coaching (MS); sport management (MS). *Degree requirements:* For doctorate, comprehensive exam, thesis/dissertation, oral exam. *Entrance requirements:* For master's, GRE or MAT, minimum GPA of 3.0; for doctorate, GRE General Test or MAT, minimum GPA of 3.5. Additional exam requirements/recommendations for international students: Required—TOEFL (minimum score 550 paper-based). Electronic applications accepted. *Faculty research:* Sport psychosociology, teacher education, exercise psychology, counseling.

Wichita State University, Graduate School, College of Education, Department of Sport Management, Wichita, KS 67260. Offers M Ed. *Unit head:* Dr. Mark Vermillion, Chair, 316-978-5444, Fax: 316-978-5451, E-mail: mark.vermillion@wichita.edu. *Application contact:* Jordan Oleson, Admissions Coordinator, 316-978-3095, Fax: 316-978-3253, E-mail: jordan.oleson@wichita.edu.
Website: http://www.wichita.edu/sportmanagement

Wingate University, School of Sport Sciences, Wingate, NC 28174. Offers sport management (MA). *Entrance requirements:* For master's, MAT, GRE, or GMAT, bachelor's degree, minimum GPA of 2.75, two recommendation forms, official transcripts. *Application deadline:* For fall admission, 7/1 for domestic students; for spring admission, 12/1 for domestic students. Electronic applications accepted. *Unit head:* Dr. Travis L. Teague, Dean, 704-233-8297, E-mail: t.teague@wingate.edu. *Application contact:* Dr. Dawn Norwood, Program Director, 980-359-1036, E-mail: masm@wingate.edu.

Winona State University, College of Education, Department of Education Leadership, Winona, MN 55987. Offers educational leadership (Ed S), including general superintendency, K-12 principalship; general school leadership (MS); K-12 principalship (MS); outdoor education/adventure-based leadership (MS); sports management (MS); teacher leadership (MS). *Accreditation:* NCATE. *Program availability:* Part-time, evening/weekend. *Degree requirements:* For master's, comprehensive exam, thesis optional; for Ed S, thesis optional.

Xavier University, College of Social Sciences, Health and Education, Department of Sports Studies, Cincinnati, OH 45207. Offers coaching education and athlete development (M Ed); sport administration (M Ed). *Program availability:* Part-time, evening/weekend, online learning. *Degree requirements:* For master's, thesis optional, internship or research project. *Entrance requirements:* For master's, GRE or MAT, official transcript; resume; one-page statement of career goals; 2 letters of recommendation. Additional exam requirements/recommendations for international students: Required—TOEFL (minimum score 550 paper-based; 79 iBT). Electronic applications accepted. Application fee is waived when completed online. *Expenses:* Contact institution. *Faculty research:* Coaching education, brand equity, strategic management, economic impact, place marketing.

TEMPLE UNIVERSITY

Master of Science in Sport Business

School of Sport, Tourism and Hospitality Management

 For more information, visit http://petersons.to/templeu_sportsmgmt

Programs of Study

Temple University's School of Sport, Tourism and Hospitality Management (STHM) offers a Master of Science (MS) in Sport Business that prepares graduates for mid- to high-level management, marketing, and planning positions in all sectors of the $200 billion-a-year sport industry. These include professional sports, college athletics, event and venue management, sport analytics, and sales and promotions.

Headed by a distinguished faculty, this 36-credit program at Temple University emphasizes the theoretical foundation of sport business with an industry-specific curriculum that equips students with critical insight, strategic business principles, and practical application techniques.

A typical course load comprises nine credits per semester, enabling most students to complete the degree program in four semesters. Students who elect to take on larger course loads may be able to finish in as few as 12 months. A flexible schedule of courses is available, with all classes held after 5 p.m., allowing students to maintain full-time employment or pursue internships or assistantships during the day.

Several optional concentrations to complement the degree program are available.

The **Athletics Administration concentration** equips graduates with the tools to fulfill management roles in organizations that oversee student athlete programs. With a focus on intercollegiate athletics, the curriculum exposes students to critical issues in governance, policy-making, facility operations, fundraising, development, and compliance. Arizona State University, Florida State University, University of Oregon, Villanova University, and Temple University are among the organizations that have recently provided opportunities for student volunteering, projects, internships, and employment.

The **Recreation and Event Management concentration** prepares graduate to become effective managers and leaders in public and nonprofit sectors of the sport industry. In addition, it allows students to learn and apply critical theory and best practices in the areas of programming, event execution, and fundraising. Among the companies and organizations that have recently provided opportunities for students in this concentration are Back On My Feet, Northern Virginia Regional Park Authority, and YMCA.

The **Sport Analytics concentration** produces managers and future executives who understand the role of data-driven decisions in the sport industry. Capitalizing on the strength of the Fox School of Business' Master of Science in Business Analytics, the Sport Analytics concentration creates a unique interdisciplinary synergy, producing the next generation of analytical leaders in the sport industry. The faculty of these programs collaborated to create a curriculum that is one of the first of its kind in the nation.

The **Sport Marketing and Promotions concentration** gives students the tools and skills to create innovative approaches to spectator and participant sport. They learn to develop and leverage strategies that impact production, pricing, consumer behavior, and distribution to generate sustainable results. Among the organizations providing internships and career opportunities for students in this concentration are Comcast-Spectacor, IMG, LiveNation, Madison Square Garden, and Octagon.

Industry-specific career coaching and advising are housed within STHM, providing a personalized approach to each student's individual needs.

STHM's Center for Student Professional Development (CSPD) coordinates activities supporting students' career growth. The CSPD staff works with students to provide the latest resources that will help them gain greater insight into their career options.

STHM's Center for Student Services encourages a collaborative relationship between advisers and students, empowering them to make sound and responsible decisions concerning their education. Academic advisers assist students with their academic and pre-professional needs, including individualized course sequences, elective options, registration, financial assistance, scheduling, career planning, and academic resources.

Research Facilities and Resources

The Sport Industry Research Center (SIRC) provides opportunities for academics, students, and practitioners to explore the potential of sport to impact the communities within which they exist. Through a series of initiatives, SIRC conducts and disseminates research, educates and trains executives, and functions as a think tank and informational resource for those involved in the sport industry. SIRC initiatives include: executive workshops, doctoral student training, community-based programming, event management and program consulting, and academic dissemination of research and best practices. More information is available at http://sthm.temple.edu/sirc.

Financial Aid

Teaching and research assistantships and graduate externships within the STHM are reserved for students who are capable of teaching undergraduate classes in specialized academic areas or assisting in faculty research. Applications for assistantships and externships are evaluated when a Graduate School application and all appropriate materials are received. Assistantships and externships are available only to admitted students. The evaluation of applicants for these opportunities begins by March and continues until all positions have been filled.

Cost of Study

Temple University is a state-related institution in Pennsylvania. Tuition rates are determined by a student's residency status and program.

The most current information is available online at bursar.temple.edu.

Location

Philadelphia is a living laboratory for the sport, recreation, tourism, and hospitality industries.

Philadelphia is America's Sport Destination. Home to the Phillies, Eagles, 76ers, Flyers, and Union, the city offers students and fans a venue to experience all five major sports. In addition, Philadelphia is home to the Philadelphia Soul and the Philadelphia Freedom, offering a diverse sports scene. The city is also a national destination for college athletics with over 85 NCAA college athletics programs within 25 miles of Temple University's campus.

Temple University

The University and the School

Temple University is a comprehensive public research university located in Philadelphia, Pennsylvania. Nearly 40,000 students from around the globe are enrolled in more than 400 academic degree programs offered at seven campuses in Pennsylvania and three international campuses.

The School of Sport, Tourism and Hospitality Management (STHM) at Temple University is the largest provider of recreation, tourism, and hospitality management programs in the greater Philadelphia region, as well as the area's largest provider of talent for those industries.

Applying

Students with backgrounds from a range of undergraduate majors are welcomed—and encouraged—to apply for admission to the School of Sport, Tourism and Hospitality Management (STHM) at Temple University. The admission process is comprehensive and takes careful consideration of each applicant's goals and academic aptitude.

Complete details about the admission process can be found at sthm.temple.edu/petersons.

Correspondence and Information

School of Sport, Tourism, and Hospitality Management
Speakman Hall 111 (006-68)
1810 North 13th Street
Philadelphia, Pennsylvania 19122
United States
Phone: 215-204-8701
Fax: 215-204-8705
Website: sthm.temple.edu/petersons

The Faculty

Dr. Joris Drayer, Associate Professor, has first-hand knowledge of the sport management industry through his work with the Oakland Athletics. There he served as a marketing and promotions assistant and completed scouting and statistical research on players as a baseball operations assistant. Drayer conducts a variety of research on sport pricing and consumer behavior. Thus far, he has written two book chapters and published more than 30 articles in the *Journal of Sport Management*, *Sport Management Review*, and *Sport Marketing Quarterly*, among others.

Dr. Daniel C. Funk is a world leader in sport consumer behavior and marketing research. Professor, Washburn Senior Research Fellow, and Director of Research and Ph.D. Programs at STHM, Dr. Funk researches the stage-based development of involvement to enhance sport management and health promotion strategies. He has been recognized as a Research Fellow for the Sport Marketing Association and the North American Society for Sport Management, which recognizes scholars who have shown excellence in the area of research and honors the work they have disseminated through its official journal. Funk has participated in over 20 grant-funded projects and published more than 90 research articles in a variety of top academic journals. He has also published three textbooks in the area of sport marketing and contributed numerous book chapters to edited books. His work has been adopted by the industry to understand the stage-based development of involvement and has developed a segmentation framework that is currently being used by a professional sport league to develop marketing and advertising strategy and assess return on investment.

Dr. Jeremy Jordan, Associate Dean, focuses his research on the community benefits of mass participant sport events. Specifically, his research examines consumer expectations and satisfaction, motives for participation, commitment to the event and/or activity, and economic activity, all within the theoretical framework of involvement. As part of the Sport Industry Research Center (SIRC) he has led research projects with numerous industry partners such as: Life Time Athletic Events, Philadelphia Marathon and Half Marathon, National Dog Show, Blue Cross Broad Street Run, Temple Athletics, Tough Mudder, Students Run Philly Style, Black Girls RUN!, Concilio, Philadelphia Hispanic Fiesta, and Welcome America.

Dr. Aubrey Kent, Senior Associate Dean of Faculty Affairs, has focused his sport industry research in the area of industrial/organizational psychology, and more recently in the area of corporate social responsibility. Dr. Kent is a past-president of the North American Society for Sport Management (NASSM) and was inducted in 2006 as a NASSM Research Fellow.

Dr. Joseph Mahan, Associate Professor and Chair of the Department of Sport and Recreation Management, is a nationally recognized researcher in the area of sport consumer psychology. He has authored two book chapters and has been published frequently in the *International Journal of Sport Marketing and Sponsorship*, *Sport Management Review*, and *Sport Management Education Journal*, among others.

A complete listing of STHM faculty and staff can be found at sthm.temple.edu/faculty-and-staff.

ACADEMIC AND PROFESSIONAL PROGRAMS IN SOCIAL WORK

Section 32
Social Work

This section contains a directory of institutions offering graduate work in social work, followed by in-depth entries submitted by institutions that chose to prepare detailed program descriptions. Additional information about programs listed in the directory but not augmented by an in-depth entry may be obtained by writing directly to the dean of a graduate school or chair of a department at the address given in the directory.

For programs offering related work, see also in this book *Allied Health* and *Education*. In another guide in this series:

Graduate Programs in the Humanities, Arts & Social Sciences

See *Criminology and Forensics, Family and Consumer Sciences, Psychology and Counseling,* and *Sociology, Anthropology, and Archaeology*

CONTENTS

Program Directories

Featured Schools: Displays and Close-Ups

Human Services

Abilene Christian University, Graduate Programs, College of Education and Human Services, Abilene, TX 79699. Offers M Ed, MS, Certificate. *Accreditation:* TEAC. *Faculty:* 3 full-time (all women), 26 part-time/adjunct (16 women). *Students:* 137 full-time (124 women), 19 part-time (14 women); includes 39 minority (8 Black or African American, non-Hispanic/Latino; 1 American Indian or Alaska Native, non-Hispanic/Latino; 26 Hispanic/Latino; 4 Two or more races, non-Hispanic/Latino), 2 international. 439 applicants, 38% accepted, 93 enrolled. In 2016, 83 master's, 10 other advanced degrees awarded. *Degree requirements:* For master's, comprehensive exam (for some programs), thesis (for some programs), practicum. *Entrance requirements:* For master's, GRE. Additional exam requirements/recommendations for international students: Required—TOEFL (minimum score 80 iBT), IELTS (minimum score 6), PTE. *Application deadline:* For fall admission, 8/15 priority date for domestic students; for winter admission, 10/1 priority date for domestic students; for spring admission, 12/15 priority date for domestic students; for summer admission, 4/15 for domestic students. Applications are processed on a rolling basis. Application fee: $50. Electronic applications accepted. *Expenses: Tuition:* Full-time $19,890; part-time $1105 per credit hour. Tuition and fees vary according to course load and program. *Financial support:* In 2016–17, 61 students received support. Career-related internships or fieldwork and scholarships/grants available. Financial award application deadline: 4/1; financial award applicants required to submit FAFSA. *Unit head:* Dr. Donnie Snider, Dean, 325-674-2700, Fax: 325-674-3707, E-mail: cehs@acu.edu. *Application contact:* Corey Patterson, Director of Graduate Admission and Recruiting, 325-674-6566, Fax: 325-674-6717, E-mail: gradinfo@acu.edu.
Website: http://www.acu.edu/community/cehs.html

Albertus Magnus College, Master of Science in Human Services Program, New Haven, CT 06511-1189. Offers MS. *Program availability:* Part-time, evening/weekend, blended/hybrid learning. *Faculty:* 3 full-time (1 woman), 6 part-time/adjunct (4 women). *Students:* 49 full-time (41 women), 2 part-time (both women); includes 32 minority (28 Black or African American, non-Hispanic/Latino; 4 Hispanic/Latino), 1 international. Average age 39. In 2016, 32 master's awarded. *Degree requirements:* For master's, thesis, internship, capstone thesis, minimum GPA of 3.0. *Entrance requirements:* For master's, minimum GPA of 2.8; 2 letters of recommendation; official transcripts; minimum of 15 credits in psychology, human services, and/or social work. Additional exam requirements/recommendations for international students: Required—TOEFL (minimum score 550 paper-based; 80 iBT). *Application deadline:* For fall admission, 8/15 for domestic students; for spring admission, 1/15 for domestic students. Applications are processed on a rolling basis. Application fee: $50. Electronic applications accepted. *Expenses:* Contact institution. *Financial support:* Federal Work-Study and unspecified assistantships available. Support available to part-time students. Financial award applicants required to submit FAFSA. *Unit head:* Ragaa Mazen, Director, 203-773-8574, E-mail: rmazen@albertus.edu. *Application contact:* Anthony Reich, Director of Admission, Division of Professional and Graduate Studies, 203-773-5032, E-mail: arreich@albertus.edu.
Website: http://www.albertus.edu/human-services/ms/

Amridge University, Graduate and Professional Programs, Montgomery, AL 36117. Offers Biblical studies (MA, PhD); Christian ministry (MS); family therapy (D Min); human services (MS); leadership and management (MS); marriage and family therapy (M Div, MA, PhD); ministerial leadership (M Div, MS); New Testament studies (MA); Old Testament studies (MA); professional counseling (M Div, MA, PhD); theology (M Div, D Min). *Program availability:* Part-time, evening/weekend, online learning. *Faculty:* 22 full-time (3 women), 10 part-time/adjunct (6 women). *Students:* 81 full-time (49 women), 225 part-time (137 women); includes 81 minority (80 Black or African American, non-Hispanic/Latino; 1 Hispanic/Latino). Average age 41. 122 applicants, 100% accepted, 79 enrolled. *Degree requirements:* For master's, one foreign language, comprehensive exam (for some programs), thesis (for some programs); for doctorate, one foreign language, comprehensive exam (for some programs), thesis/dissertation (for some programs). *Entrance requirements:* For master's, official transcript showing an earned 4-year BA or BS from regionally- or nationally-accredited institution; for doctorate, official transcript showing earned graduate degree from regionally- or nationally-accredited institution; writing sample (e.g. career monograph, published journal article, term paper from master's degree or doctoral dissertation); interview. Additional exam requirements/recommendations for international students: Required—TOEFL (minimum score 79 iBT). *Application deadline:* Applications are processed on a rolling basis. Application fee: $50. Electronic applications accepted. *Expenses: Tuition:* Full-time $12,870; part-time $715 per credit hour. *Required fees:* $1300; $650 per semester. *Financial support:* In 2016–17, 45 students received support. Federal Work-Study and scholarships/grants available. Support available to part-time students. Financial award applicants required to submit FAFSA. *Faculty research:* Technology and mental healthcare, resilience in black families, theology and congregational ministry. *Unit head:* Laina Costanza, Vice President, Student Affairs, 888-790-8080 Ext. 1, Fax: 334-387-3878, E-mail: cc@amridgeuniversity.edu. *Application contact:* Brooks Housley, Student Affairs Coordinator, 888-790-8080 Ext. 1, Fax: 334-387-3878, E-mail: admissions@amridgeuniversity.edu.

Bellevue University, Graduate School, College of Arts and Sciences, Bellevue, NE 68005-3098. Offers clinical counseling (MS); healthcare administration (MHA); human services (MA); international security and intelligence studies (MS); managerial communication (MA). *Program availability:* Online learning.

Boricua College, Program in Human Services, New York, NY 10032-1560. Offers MS. Program offered in Brooklyn and Manhattan. *Program availability:* Evening/weekend. *Degree requirements:* For master's, thesis. *Entrance requirements:* For master's, interview by the faculty. *Application deadline:* Applications are processed on a rolling basis. Application fee: $100. *Expenses: Tuition:* Full-time $13,000. *Required fees:* $100. *Financial support:* Career-related internships or fieldwork and Federal Work-Study available. Financial award applicants required to submit FAFSA. *Unit head:* Victor Garcia, Co-Chairperson, 718-782-2200 Ext. 271. *Application contact:* Miriam Pfeffer, Director of Admissions, 718-782-2200 Ext. 210, E-mail: mpfeffer@boricuacollege.edu.

Brandeis University, The Heller School for Social Policy and Management, Program in Nonprofit Management, Waltham, MA 02454-9110. Offers child, youth, and family management (MBA); health care management (MBA); social impact management (MBA); social policy and management (MBA); sustainable development (MBA); MBA/MA; MBA/MD. MBA/MD program offered in conjunction with Tufts University School of Medicine. *Accreditation:* AACSB. *Program availability:* Part-time. *Degree requirements:* For master's, team consulting project. *Entrance requirements:* For master's, GMAT (preferred) or GRE, 2 letters of recommendation, problem statement analysis, 3-5 years of professional experience. Additional exam requirements/recommendations for international students: Required—TOEFL (minimum score 600 paper-based; 100 iBT). Electronic applications accepted. *Expenses:* Contact institution. *Faculty research:* Health care; children and families; elder and disabled services; social impact management; organizations in the non-profit, for-profit, or public sector.

California State University, Sacramento, Office of Graduate Studies, College of Health and Human Services, Division of Social Work, Sacramento, CA 95819. Offers family and children's services (MSW). *Accreditation:* CSWE. *Students:* 239 full-time (213 women), 18 part-time (14 women); includes 134 minority (25 Black or African American, non-Hispanic/Latino; 4 American Indian or Alaska Native, non-Hispanic/Latino; 30 Asian, non-Hispanic/Latino; 73 Hispanic/Latino; 2 Native Hawaiian or other Pacific Islander, non-Hispanic/Latino). Average age 31. 305 applicants, 47% accepted, 117 enrolled. In 2016, 129 master's awarded. *Degree requirements:* For master's, thesis, research project, or comprehensive exam; writing proficiency exam. *Entrance requirements:* For master's, GRE, minimum GPA of 2.8 during previous 2 years of course work. Additional exam requirements/recommendations for international students: Required—TOEFL (minimum score 550 paper-based; 80 iBT). *Application deadline:* For fall admission, 1/18 for domestic students, 3/1 for international students; for spring admission, 9/30 for international students. Applications are processed on a rolling basis. Application fee: $55. Electronic applications accepted. *Expenses:* $4,302 full-time tuition and fees per semester, $2,796 part-time. *Financial support:* Career-related internships or fieldwork and Federal Work-Study available. Support available to part-time students. Financial award application deadline: 3/1; financial award applicants required to submit FAFSA. *Unit head:* Dr. Dale Russell, Chair, 916-278-6943, E-mail: drussell@csus.edu. *Application contact:* Jose Martinez, Graduate Admissions Supervisor, 916-278-7871, E-mail: martinj@skymail.csus.edu.
Website: http://www.csus.edu/hhs/sw

Capella University, School of Public Service Leadership, Doctoral Programs in Healthcare, Minneapolis, MN 55402. Offers criminal justice (PhD); emergency management (PhD); epidemiology (Dr PH); general health administration (DHA); general public administration (DPA); health advocacy and leadership (Dr PH); health care administration (PhD); health care leadership (DHA); health policy advocacy (DHA); multidisciplinary human services (PhD); nonprofit management and leadership (PhD); public safety leadership (PhD); social and community services (PhD).

Capella University, School of Public Service Leadership, Master's Programs in Healthcare, Minneapolis, MN 55402. Offers criminal justice (MS); emergency management (MS); general public health (MPH); gerontology (MS); health administration (MHA); health care operations (MHA); health management policy (MPH); health policy (MHA); homeland security (MS); multidisciplinary human services (MS); public administration (MPA); public safety leadership (MS); social and community services (MS); social behavioral sciences (MPH); MS/MPA.

Carlos Albizu University, Miami Campus, Graduate Programs, Miami, FL 33172-2209. Offers clinical psychology (PhD, Psy D); entrepreneurship (MBA); exceptional student education (MS); human services (PhD); industrial/organizational psychology (MS); marriage and family therapy (MS); mental health counseling (MS); nonprofit management (MBA); organizational management (MBA); psychology (MS); school counseling (MS); speech and language pathology (MS); teaching English for speakers of other languages (MS). *Accreditation:* APA. *Program availability:* Part-time, evening/weekend, 100% online. *Faculty:* 28 full-time (22 women), 31 part-time/adjunct (19 women). *Students:* 475 full-time (396 women), 191 part-time (161 women); includes 560 minority (56 Black or African American, non-Hispanic/Latino; 1 American Indian or Alaska Native, non-Hispanic/Latino; 4 Asian, non-Hispanic/Latino; 494 Hispanic/Latino; 5 Two or more races, non-Hispanic/Latino), 15 international. Average age 34. 335 applicants, 46% accepted, 122 enrolled. In 2016, 143 master's, 48 doctorates awarded. Terminal master's awarded for partial completion of doctoral program. *Degree requirements:* For master's, comprehensive exam, integrative project (for MBA); research project (for exceptional student education, teaching English as a second language); for doctorate, comprehensive exam, thesis/dissertation, internship, project. *Entrance requirements:* For master's, 3 letters of recommendation, interview, minimum GPA of 3.0, resume, statement of purpose, official transcripts; for doctorate, 3 letters of recommendation, minimum GPA of 3.0, resume, interview, statement of purpose, official transcripts. Additional exam requirements/recommendations for international students: Required—Michigan Test of English Language Proficiency. *Application deadline:* For fall admission, 4/1 priority date for domestic students, 5/1 priority date for international students; for spring admission, 11/1 priority date for domestic students, 9/1 priority date for international students. Applications are processed on a rolling basis. Application fee: $50. Electronic applications accepted. *Expenses:* Contact institution. *Financial support:* In 2016–17, 131 students received support. Federal Work-Study, scholarships/grants, unspecified assistantships, and tuition discounts available. Financial award application deadline: 6/1; financial award applicants required to submit FAFSA. *Faculty research:* Psychotherapy, forensic psychology, neuropsychology, marketing strategy, entrepreneurship, special education, speech-language pathology. *Unit head:* Dr. Etiony Aldarondo, Provost, 305-593-1223 Ext. 3138, Fax: 305-592-7930, E-mail: ealdarondo@albizu.edu. *Application contact:* Sonia Feliciano, Institutional Director of Student Recruitment, 305-593-1223 Ext. 3108, Fax: 305-477-8983, E-mail: sfeliciano@albizu.edu.

Chestnut Hill College, School of Graduate Studies, Program in Administration of Human Services, Philadelphia, PA 19118-2693. Offers administration of human services (MS, CAS), including adult and aging services (CAS), leadership development (CAS). *Program availability:* Part-time, evening/weekend. *Degree requirements:* For master's, special projects or internship. *Entrance requirements:* For master's, GRE General Test or MAT, 100 volunteer hours or 1 year of work-related human services experience, statement of professional goals, writing sample, letters of recommendation. Additional exam requirements/recommendations for international students: Required—TOEFL (minimum score 500 paper-based), IELTS (minimum score 6.0), or TWE (minimum score 22). Electronic applications accepted. *Expenses:* Contact institution. *Faculty research:* Best practices and trends in adult education degree programs, middle and late adulthood development, quality of living issues for older persons.

Concordia University Chicago, College of Graduate and Innovative Programs, Program in Human Services, River Forest, IL 60305-1499. Offers human services (MA), including administration, exercise science. *Program availability:* Part-time, evening/weekend. *Degree requirements:* For master's, comprehensive exam, thesis. *Entrance requirements:* For master's, minimum GPA of 2.9. Additional exam requirements/recommendations for international students: Required—TOEFL (minimum score 550 paper-based). Electronic applications accepted.

Concordia University, St. Paul, College of Health and Science, St. Paul, MN 55104-5494. Offers criminal justice leadership (MA); exercise science (MS); family science (MA); human services (MA); orthotics and prosthetics (MS); physical therapy (DPT); sports management (MA). *Program availability:* Part-time, evening/weekend, 100%

online, blended/hybrid learning. *Faculty:* 7 full-time (2 women), 27 part-time/adjunct (9 women). *Students:* 337 full-time (194 women), 18 part-time (7 women); includes 65 minority (35 Black or African American, non-Hispanic/Latino; 7 Asian, non-Hispanic/ Latino; 8 Hispanic/Latino; 4 Native Hawaiian or other Pacific Islander, non-Hispanic/ Latino; 11 Two or more races, non-Hispanic/Latino), 3 international. Average age 30. 388 applicants, 40% accepted, 117 enrolled. In 2016, 92 master's awarded. *Degree requirements:* For master's, comprehensive exam (for some programs), thesis (for some programs); for doctorate, at least one 8-12 week clinical rotation outside the St. Paul area. *Entrance requirements:* For master's, official transcripts from regionally-accredited institution stating the conferral of a bachelor's degree with minimum cumulative GPA of 3.0; personal statement; undergraduate degree at accredited college or university in the U.S., English-speaking Canada, the United Kingdom, Ireland, Australia, or New Zealand; for doctorate, undergraduate or graduate degree at accredited college or university in the U.S., English-speaking Canada, the United Kingdom, Ireland, Australia, or New Zealand. Additional exam requirements/recommendations for international students: Recommended—TOEFL (minimum score 547 paper-based; 78 iBT), IELTS (minimum score 6), TSE (minimum score 52). *Application deadline:* For fall admission, 4/1 for domestic students. Applications are processed on a rolling basis. Application fee: $50. Electronic applications accepted. *Expenses:* Contact institution. *Financial support:* In 2016–17, 114 students received support. Scholarships/grants and unspecified assistantships available. Financial award applicants required to submit FAFSA. *Faculty research:* Developmental screening in early childhood, cardiovascular responses to aerobic exercise. *Unit head:* Dr. Katie Fischer, Interim Dean, 651-641-8735, E-mail: fischer@csp.edu. *Application contact:* Kimberly Craig, Associate Vice President, Cohort Enrollment Management, 651-603-6223, Fax: 651-603-6320, E-mail: craig@csp.edu.

Coppin State University, Division of Graduate Studies, Division of Arts and Sciences, Department of Social Sciences, Baltimore, MD 21216-3698. Offers human services administration (MS). *Program availability:* Part-time, evening/weekend. *Entrance requirements:* For master's, resume, references, interview.

East Central University, School of Graduate Studies, Department of Human Resources, Ada, OK 74820. Offers administration (MSHR); counseling (MSHR); criminal justice (MSHR); human services (MSHR); rehabilitation counseling (MSHR). *Accreditation:* CORE. *Program availability:* Part-time, evening/weekend. *Degree requirements:* For master's, thesis optional. *Entrance requirements:* For master's, GRE General Test, MAT, minimum GPA of 2.5. Electronic applications accepted.

Eastern Michigan University, Graduate School, College of Health and Human Services, Interdisciplinary Program in Health and Human Services, Ypsilanti, MI 48197. Offers Graduate Certificate. *Program availability:* Part-time, evening/weekend. *Students:* 1 (woman) part-time. Average age 37. 1 applicant. *Entrance requirements:* Additional exam requirements/recommendations for international students: Required—TOEFL. Application fee: $45. *Unit head:* Dr. Marcia Bombyk, Program Coordinator, 734-487-0393, Fax: 734-487-8536, E-mail: mbombyk@emich.edu. *Application contact:* Graduate Admissions, 734-487-2400, Fax: 734-487-6559, E-mail: graduate.admissions@emich.edu.

Eastern New Mexico University, Graduate School, College of Liberal Arts and Sciences, Department of Health and Human Services, Portales, NM 88130. Offers nursing (MSN); speech pathology and audiology (MS). *Accreditation:* ASHA. *Program availability:* Part-time, online learning. *Degree requirements:* For master's, thesis optional, oral and written comprehensive exam, oral presentation of professional portfolio. *Entrance requirements:* For master's, GRE, three letters of recommendation, resume, two essays. Additional exam requirements/recommendations for international students: Required—TOEFL (minimum score 550 paper-based; 79 iBT), IELTS (minimum score 6). Electronic applications accepted.

Ferris State University, College of Education and Human Services, Big Rapids, MI 49307. Offers M Ed, MS, MSCJ, MSCTE. *Program availability:* Part-time, evening/ weekend, blended/hybrid learning. *Faculty:* 15 full-time (6 women), 9 part-time/adjunct (6 women). *Students:* 11 full-time (6 women), 87 part-time (45 women); includes 19 minority (8 Black or African American, non-Hispanic/Latino; 1 American Indian or Alaska Native, non-Hispanic/Latino; 4 Hispanic/Latino; 6 Two or more races, non-Hispanic/ Latino), 9 international. Average age 36. 40 applicants, 78% accepted, 21 enrolled. In 2016, 53 master's awarded. *Degree requirements:* For master's, comprehensive exam or thesis/dissertation, research paper or project. *Entrance requirements:* For master's, minimum GPA of 3.0. Additional exam requirements/recommendations for international students: Required—TOEFL (minimum score 500 paper-based, 79 iBT) or IELTS (minimum score 6.5). *Application deadline:* For fall admission, 7/1 priority date for domestic and international students; for winter admission, 12/15 priority date for domestic and international students; for spring admission, 11/1 priority date for domestic and international students; for summer admission, 3/1 priority date for domestic and international students. Applications are processed on a rolling basis. Application fee: $30. Electronic applications accepted. Application fee is waived when completed online. Tuition and fees vary according to degree level and program. *Financial support:* In 2016–17, 1 research assistantship (averaging $4,850 per year) was awarded; career-related internships or fieldwork, Federal Work-Study, scholarships/grants, and unspecified assistantships also available. Support available to part-time students. Financial award applicants required to submit FAFSA. *Faculty research:* Competency testing, teaching methodologies, assessment of teaching effectiveness, suicide prevention, women in education, special needs. *Unit head:* Arrick L. Jackson, Dean, 231-591-2702, Fax: 231-592-3792, E-mail: arrickjackson@ferris.edu. *Application contact:* Dr. Kristen Salomonson, Dean, Enrollment Services/Director, Admissions and Records, 231-591-2100, Fax: 231-591-3944, E-mail: admissions@ferris.edu.

Georgia State University, Andrew Young School of Policy Studies, School of Social Work, Atlanta, GA 30294. Offers child welfare leadership (Certificate); community partnerships (MSW); forensic social work (Certificate). *Accreditation:* CSWE. *Program availability:* Part-time. *Faculty:* 17 full-time (12 women). *Students:* 123 full-time (111 women), 4 part-time (2 women); includes 83 minority (65 Black or African American, non-Hispanic/Latino; 12 Hispanic/Latino; 6 Two or more races, non-Hispanic/Latino), 1 international. Average age 30. 123 applicants, 70% accepted, 46 enrolled. In 2016, 49 master's awarded. *Entrance requirements:* For master's and Certificate, GRE. Additional exam requirements/recommendations for international students: Required—TOEFL (minimum score 550 paper-based; 100 iBT) or IELTS (minimum score 7). *Application deadline:* For fall admission, 2/1 priority date for domestic and international students. Application fee: $50. Electronic applications accepted. *Expenses:* Tuition, state resident: full-time $6876; part-time $382 per credit hour. Tuition, nonresident: full-time $22,374; part-time $1243 per credit hour. *Required fees:* $2128; $1064 per term. Part-time tuition and fees vary according to course load and program. *Financial support:* In 2016–17, research assistantships with tuition reimbursements (averaging $4,000 per year), teaching assistantships with tuition reimbursements (averaging $4,000 per year) were awarded; career-related internships or fieldwork, institutionally sponsored loans, scholarships/grants, tuition waivers, and unspecified assistantships also available. Financial award application deadline: 2/1; financial award applicants required to submit FAFSA. *Faculty research:* Community partnership, non-profit organizations, child welfare practice and policy, gerontological practice and policy, restorative justice. *Unit head:* Brian Bride, Director of School of Social Work, 404-413-1052, Fax: 404-413-1075, E-mail: bbride@gsu.edu.
Website: http://aysps.gsu.edu/socialwork

Governors State University, College of Health and Human Services, University Park, IL 60484. Offers MHA, MHS, MOT, MSN, MSW, DPT. *Accreditation:* CAHME; CSWE. *Program availability:* Part-time. *Faculty:* 51 full-time (45 women), 60 part-time/adjunct (43 women). *Students:* 382 full-time (294 women), 433 part-time (374 women); includes 424 minority (280 Black or African American, non-Hispanic/Latino; 2 American Indian or Alaska Native, non-Hispanic/Latino; 29 Asian, non-Hispanic/Latino; 96 Hispanic/Latino; 1 Native Hawaiian or other Pacific Islander, non-Hispanic/Latino; 16 Two or more races, non-Hispanic/Latino), 9 international. Average age 34. 1,009 applicants, 53% accepted, 372 enrolled. In 2016, 256 master's, 52 doctorates awarded. *Entrance requirements:* Additional exam requirements/recommendations for international students: Required—TOEFL (minimum score 550 paper-based; 80 iBT), IELTS. *Application deadline:* For fall admission, 4/1 for domestic students. Application fee: $50. Electronic applications accepted. *Expenses:* Contact institution. *Financial support:* Application deadline: 5/1; applicants required to submit FAFSA. *Unit head:* Dr. Elizabeth Cada, Dean, College of Health and Human Services, 708-534-7295, E-mail: bcada@govst.edu. *Application contact:* Yakeea Daniels, Assistant Vice President for Enrollment Services/Director of Admission, 708-534-4510, E-mail: ydaniels@govst.edu.
Website: https://www.govst.edu/chhs/

Judson University, Master of Arts in Human Services Administration Program, Elgin, IL 60123-1498. Offers MA. *Faculty:* 1 (woman) full-time. *Students:* 12 part-time (9 women). *Entrance requirements:* For master's, bachelor's degree, two years of work experience, professional resume, minimum GPA of 2.5, official transcripts, two letters of reference, essay. *Application deadline:* Applications are processed on a rolling basis. Electronic applications accepted. *Faculty research:* Dementia and community services. *Unit head:* Dr. Susan Wesner. *Application contact:* Maria Aguirre, Student Academic Advisor, 847-628-1160, E-mail: maguirre@judsonu.edu.

Kansas State University, Graduate School, College of Human Ecology, School of Family Studies and Human Services, Manhattan, KS 66506-1403. Offers applied family sciences (MS); communication sciences and disorders (MS); conflict resolution (Graduate Certificate); couple and family therapy (MS); early childhood education (MS); family and community service (MS); life-span human development (MS); personal financial planning (MS, PhD, Graduate Certificate); youth development (MS, Graduate Certificate). *Accreditation:* AAMFT/COAMFTE; ASHA. *Program availability:* Part-time, online learning. *Faculty:* 43 full-time (30 women), 4 part-time/adjunct (3 women). *Students:* 55 full-time (45 women), 87 part-time (73 women); includes 30 minority (9 Black or African American, non-Hispanic/Latino; 1 American Indian or Alaska Native, non-Hispanic/Latino; 1 Asian, non-Hispanic/Latino; 14 Hispanic/Latino; 1 Native Hawaiian or other Pacific Islander, non-Hispanic/Latino; 4 Two or more races, non-Hispanic/Latino), 6 international. Average age 29. 182 applicants, 29% accepted, 38 enrolled. In 2016, 39 master's, 17 other advanced degrees awarded. *Degree requirements:* For master's, comprehensive exam (for some programs), thesis optional. *Entrance requirements:* For master's, GRE, minimum GPA of 3.0 in last 2 years (60 semester hours) of undergraduate study; for doctorate, GRE. Additional exam requirements/recommendations for international students: Required—TOEFL (minimum score 600 paper-based). *Application deadline:* For fall admission, 2/1 priority date for domestic students, 1/1 priority date for international students; for spring admission, 10/1 priority date for domestic students, 8/1 priority date for international students; for summer admission, 2/1 priority date for domestic students, 12/1 priority date for international students. Applications are processed on a rolling basis. Application fee: $50 ($75 for international students). Electronic applications accepted. *Expenses:* Tuition, state resident: full-time $9670. Tuition, nonresident: full-time $21,828. *Required fees:* $862. *Financial support:* In 2016–17, 35 students received support, including 25 research assistantships (averaging $10,000 per year), 9 teaching assistantships with full tuition reimbursements available (averaging $10,000 per year); unspecified assistantships also available. Financial award application deadline: 3/1. *Faculty research:* Health and security of military families, training in and evaluation of professional human services (marriage and couple therapy, family life education, treatment of speech and swallowing disorders, financial therapy), disorders of communication and swallowing, family and relationship development and health, financial decision-making. *Total annual research expenditures:* $8.4 million. *Unit head:* Dr. Dottie Durband, Director, 785-532-5510, Fax: 785-532-5505, E-mail: dottie@ksu.edu. *Application contact:* Kristi Hageman, Administrative Specialist, 785-532-5510, Fax: 785-532-5505, E-mail: klsmith@ksu.edu.
Website: http://www.he.k-state.edu/fshs/

Kent State University, College of Education, Health and Human Services, Kent, OH 44242-0001. Offers M Ed, MA, MAT, MS, Au D, PhD, Ed S. *Accreditation:* NCATE. *Program availability:* Part-time, evening/weekend, online learning. *Degree requirements:* For master's, thesis (for some programs); for doctorate, comprehensive exam, thesis/ dissertation. *Entrance requirements:* For doctorate and Ed S, GRE General Test. Additional exam requirements/recommendations for international students: Required—TOEFL (minimum score 550 paper-based; 80 iBT). Electronic applications accepted. *Expenses:* Tuition, state resident: full-time $10,864; part-time $495 per credit hour. Tuition, nonresident: full-time $18,380; part-time $837 per credit hour.

Lehigh University, College of Education, Program in Counseling Psychology, Bethlehem, PA 18015. Offers counseling and human services (M Ed); counseling psychology (PhD); international counseling (M Ed, Certificate); school counseling (M Ed). *Accreditation:* APA (one or more programs are accredited). *Program availability:* Blended/hybrid learning. *Faculty:* 8 full-time (5 women), 6 part-time/adjunct (all women). *Students:* 60 full-time (53 women), 31 part-time (26 women); includes 21 minority (7 Black or African American, non-Hispanic/Latino; 3 Asian, non-Hispanic/Latino; 11 Hispanic/Latino), 15 international. Average age 30. 167 applicants, 31% accepted, 19 enrolled. In 2016, 35 master's, 7 doctorates awarded. *Degree requirements:* For doctorate, comprehensive exam, thesis/dissertation. *Entrance requirements:* For master's, minimum GPA of 3.0, 2 letters of recommendation, essay, transcript; for doctorate, GRE General Test, 2 letters of recommendation, transcript, essay; for Certificate, minimum GPA of 3.0 (undergraduate), 3.5 (graduate). Additional exam requirements/recommendations for international students: Required—TOEFL (minimum score 600 paper-based; 93 iBT). *Application deadline:* For fall admission, 2/1 for domestic and international students. Application fee: $65. Electronic applications accepted. *Expenses:* $565 per credit. *Financial support:* In 2016–17, 23 students received support, including 4 research assistantships with partial tuition reimbursements available (averaging $15,800 per year); fellowships, career-related internships or fieldwork, scholarships/grants, tuition waivers, and unspecified assistantships also available. Financial award application deadline: 2/15; financial award applicants required to submit FAFSA. *Faculty research:* Maternal/infant attachment, multicultural training and counseling, career development and health interventions, intersection of identities, community based participatory research. *Total annual research expenditures:* $729,282. *Unit head:* Dr. Christpher Liang, Director, 610-758-3253, Fax: 610-758-3227, E-mail: ctl212@lehigh.edu. *Application contact:* Lauryn Woodman, Coordinator, Counseling, 610-758-3250, Fax: 610-758-6223, E-mail: laa314@lehigh.edu.
Website: http://coe.lehigh.edu/academics/disciplines/cp

Human Services

Lenoir-Rhyne University, Graduate Programs, School of Counseling and Human Services, Hickory, NC 28601. Offers MA. *Program availability:* Part-time, evening/weekend. *Degree requirements:* For master's, comprehensive exam, thesis optional. *Entrance requirements:* Additional exam requirements/recommendations for international students: Required—TOEFL. Electronic applications accepted. *Expenses:* Contact institution.

Lenoir-Rhyne University, Graduate Programs, School of Education, Program in Human Services, Hickory, NC 28601. Offers management (MA); substance abuse (MA); vocational strategies (MA). *Program availability:* Part-time, online only, 100% online. *Degree requirements:* For master's, comprehensive exam. *Entrance requirements:* For master's, GRE General Test or MAT, essay; minimum GPA of 2.7 undergraduate, 3.0 graduate. Additional exam requirements/recommendations for international students: Required—TOEFL (minimum score 600 paper-based). Electronic applications accepted. *Expenses:* Contact institution.

Liberty University, School of Behavioral Sciences, Lynchburg, VA 24515. Offers clinical mental health counseling (MA); counselor education and supervision (PhD); human services counseling (MA), including addictions and recovery, business, child and family law, Christian ministries, criminal justice, crisis response and trauma, executive leadership, health and wellness, life coaching, marriage and family, military resilience; marriage and family therapy (MA); military resilience (Certificate); professional counseling (MA). *Program availability:* Part-time, online learning. *Students:* 2,041 full-time (1,612 women), 4,970 part-time (3,875 women); includes 1,991 minority (1,678 Black or African American, non-Hispanic/Latino; 33 American Indian or Alaska Native, non-Hispanic/Latino; 48 Asian, non-Hispanic/Latino; 80 Hispanic/Latino; 8 Native Hawaiian or other Pacific Islander, non-Hispanic/Latino; 144 Two or more races, non-Hispanic/Latino), 127 international. Average age 39. 5,496 applicants, 41% accepted, 1257 enrolled. In 2016, 2,813 master's, 11 doctorates, 20 other advanced degrees awarded. *Application deadline:* Applications are processed on a rolling basis. Application fee: $50. Electronic applications accepted. *Financial support:* Applicants required to submit FAFSA. *Unit head:* Dr. Ronald Hawkins, Founding Dean, School of Behavioral Sciences. *Application contact:* Jay Bridge, Director of Admissions, 800-424-9595, Fax: 800-628-7977, E-mail: gradadmissions@liberty.edu.

Lincoln University, Graduate Programs, Philadelphia, PA 19104. Offers counseling (MSC); early childhood education (M Ed), including PreK-4; early childhood education and special education (M Ed); educational leadership (M Ed), including principal certification; finance (MSB); human resources management (MSB); human services (MAHS). *Program availability:* Part-time, evening/weekend. *Faculty:* 11 full-time (5 women), 45 part-time/adjunct (24 women). *Students:* 191 full-time (131 women), 77 part-time (60 women); includes 245 minority (236 Black or African American, non-Hispanic/Latino; 1 American Indian or Alaska Native, non-Hispanic/Latino; 7 Hispanic/Latino; 1 Two or more races, non-Hispanic/Latino), 4 international. Average age 34. 221 applicants, 58% accepted, 55 enrolled. In 2016, 97 master's awarded. *Degree requirements:* For master's, thesis or alternative. *Entrance requirements:* For master's, official academic transcript from accredited institution presenting conferred bachelor's degree. *Application deadline:* For fall admission, 6/1 priority date for domestic and international students. Applications are processed on a rolling basis. Application fee: $50. Electronic applications accepted. *Expenses:* Tuition, state resident: full-time $12,264; part-time $511 per credit hour. Tuition, nonresident: full-time $21,264; part-time $886 per credit hour. *Required fees:* $1344; $56 per credit hour. Tuition and fees vary according to course load. *Financial support:* In 2016–17, 9 students received support. Scholarships/grants available. Financial award application deadline: 8/1; financial award applicants required to submit FAFSA. *Unit head:* Dr. Patricia Joseph, Dean, College of Professional, Graduate and Extended Studies, 484-365-7659, E-mail: joseph@lincoln.edu. *Application contact:* Jernice Lea, Director of Graduate Admissions, 215-590-8231, Fax: 215-387-3859, E-mail: jlea@lincoln.edu.
Website: http://www.lincoln.edu/academics/graduate-programs

Lock Haven University of Pennsylvania, The Stephen Poorman College of Business, Information Systems, and Human Services, Lock Haven, PA 17745-2390. Offers clinical mental health counseling (MS); sport science (MS). *Program availability:* Online learning. *Degree requirements:* For master's, thesis. *Entrance requirements:* For master's, minimum undergraduate GPA of 3.0. Additional exam requirements/recommendations for international students: Required—TOEFL. Electronic applications accepted.

McDaniel College, Graduate and Professional Studies, Program in Human Services Management, Westminster, MD 21157-4390. Offers MS. *Accreditation:* NCATE. *Program availability:* Evening/weekend. *Faculty:* 1 full-time (0 women), 2 part-time/adjunct (1 woman). *Students:* 18 full-time (14 women); includes 4 minority (3 Black or African American, non-Hispanic/Latino; 1 Asian, non-Hispanic/Latino). Average age 26. 4 applicants, 75% accepted. In 2016, 7 master's awarded. *Degree requirements:* For master's, internship. *Entrance requirements:* For master's, 3 recommendations; successful employment interview with Target Community and Educational Services, Inc. Additional exam requirements/recommendations for international students: Required—TOEFL (minimum score 79 iBT), IELTS (minimum score 6). *Application deadline:* Applications are processed on a rolling basis. Application fee: $75. Electronic applications accepted. *Expenses: Tuition:* Full-time $8370; part-time $465 per credit. *Required fees:* $75 per semester. Tuition and fees vary according to course load, program and reciprocity agreements. *Financial support:* Application deadline: 3/1; applicants required to submit FAFSA. *Unit head:* E-mail: gradadms@mcdaniel.edu. *Application contact:* Crystal L. Perry, Assistant Director, Graduate Enrollment Management, 410-857-2516, Fax: 410-857-2515, E-mail: cperry@mcdaniel.edu.

Mercer University, Graduate Studies, Cecil B. Day Campus, Penfield College, Atlanta, GA 30341. Offers certified rehabilitation counseling (MS); clinical mental health (MS); counselor education and supervision (PhD); criminal justice and public safety leadership (MS); health informatics (MS); human services (MS), including child and adolescent services, gerontology services; organizational leadership (MS); school counseling (MS). *Program availability:* Part-time, evening/weekend, 100% online, blended/hybrid learning. *Faculty:* 15 full-time (8 women), 22 part-time/adjunct (18 women). *Students:* 168 full-time (136 women), 242 part-time (201 women); includes 231 minority (192 Black or African American, non-Hispanic/Latino; 1 American Indian or Alaska Native, non-Hispanic/Latino; 15 Asian, non-Hispanic/Latino; 19 Hispanic/Latino; 1 Native Hawaiian or other Pacific Islander, non-Hispanic/Latino; 3 Two or more races, non-Hispanic/Latino), 2 international. Average age 32. 300 applicants, 45% accepted, 114 enrolled. In 2016, 92 master's, 8 doctorates awarded. *Degree requirements:* For master's, comprehensive exam (for some programs), thesis (for some programs); for doctorate, thesis/dissertation. *Entrance requirements:* For master's, GRE or MAT, Georgia Professional Standards Commission (GPSC) Certification at the SC-5 level; for doctorate, GRE or MAT. Additional exam requirements/recommendations for international students: Recommended—TOEFL (minimum score 550 paper-based; 80 iBT), IELTS (minimum score 6.5). *Application deadline:* For fall admission, 7/1 priority date for domestic and international students; for spring admission, 11/1 priority date for domestic and international students; for summer admission, 4/1 priority date for domestic and international students. Application fee: $35. Electronic applications accepted. Application fee is waived when completed online. *Expenses:* $588 per credit hour. *Financial support:* In 2016–17, 32 students received support. Federal Work-Study, scholarships/grants, and unspecified assistantships available. Financial award applicants required to submit FAFSA. *Faculty research:* Marriage and families issues, leadership and ethics, cyber-bullying, trauma, narrative counseling and theory. *Total annual research expenditures:* $85,000. *Unit head:* Dr. Priscilla R. Danheiser, Dean, 678-547-6028, Fax: 678-547-6008, E-mail: danheiser_p@mercer.edu.
Website: http://penfield.mercer.edu/programs/graduate-professional/

Minnesota State University Mankato, College of Graduate Studies and Research, College of Social and Behavioral Sciences, Department of Sociology and Corrections, Mankato, MN 56001. Offers sociology (MA); sociology: college teaching (MA); sociology: corrections (MS); sociology: human services planning and administration (MS). *Program availability:* Part-time. *Students:* 9 full-time (5 women), 19 part-time (16 women). *Degree requirements:* For master's, comprehensive exam, thesis or alternative. *Entrance requirements:* For master's, minimum GPA of 3.0 during previous 2 years, 3 letters of reference, resume. Additional exam requirements/recommendations for international students: Required—TOEFL. *Application deadline:* For fall admission, 7/1 priority date for domestic students; for spring admission, 11/1 for domestic students. Applications are processed on a rolling basis. Application fee: $40. Electronic applications accepted. *Financial support:* Research assistantships with full tuition reimbursements, teaching assistantships with full tuition reimbursements, career-related internships or fieldwork, Federal Work-Study, institutionally sponsored loans, and unspecified assistantships available. Support available to part-time students. Financial award application deadline: 3/15; financial award applicants required to submit FAFSA. *Unit head:* Dr. Luis Posas, Chair, 507-389-2257, E-mail: luis.posas@mnsu.edu. *Application contact:* Donald Ebel, Graduate Studies Coordinator, 507-389-5188, Fax: 507-389-5615, E-mail: donald.ebel@mnsu.edu.
Website: http://sbs.mnsu.edu/soccorr/

Minnesota State University Moorhead, Graduate Studies, College of Education and Human Services, Moorhead, MN 56563. Offers counseling and student affairs (MS); curriculum and instruction (MS); educational leadership (MS, Ed S); special education (MS); speech-language pathology (MS). *Accreditation:* NCATE. *Program availability:* Part-time, 100% online, blended/hybrid learning. *Students:* 133 full-time (116 women), 363 part-time (274 women). Average age 32. 273 applicants, 49% accepted. In 2016, 114 master's awarded. *Degree requirements:* For master's, comprehensive exam (for some programs), thesis. *Entrance requirements:* For master's, GRE, essay, letter of intent, letters of reference, teaching license, teaching verification. Additional exam requirements/recommendations for international students: Required—TOEFL (minimum score 550 paper-based). *Application deadline:* For fall admission, 4/15 priority date for domestic students; for spring admission, 11/1 priority date for domestic students. Applications are processed on a rolling basis. Application fee: $20. Electronic applications accepted. *Expenses:* Tuition, state resident: full-time $9000; part-time $4500 per credit. Tuition, nonresident: full-time $18,000; part-time $9000 per credit. *Required fees:* $942; $39.25 per credit. One-time fee: $90 full-time. Full-time tuition and fees vary according to course load, degree level, program and reciprocity agreements. *Financial support:* Federal Work-Study and unspecified assistantships available. Financial award application deadline: 10/1; financial award applicants required to submit FAFSA. *Unit head:* Dr. Ok-Hee Lee, Dean, 218-477-2095, E-mail: okheelee@mnstate.edu. *Application contact:* Karla Wenger, Office Manager, 218-477-2344, Fax: 218-477-2482, E-mail: wengerk@mnstate.edu.
Website: http://www.mnstate.edu/cehs/

Murray State University, College of Education, Department of Educational Studies, Leadership and Counseling, Program in Human Development and Leadership, Murray, KY 42071. Offers MS. *Program availability:* Part-time. *Degree requirements:* For master's, thesis optional. *Entrance requirements:* Additional exam requirements/recommendations for international students: Required—TOEFL.

National Louis University, College of Arts and Sciences, Chicago, IL 60603. Offers adult education (Ed D); counseling and human services (MS); language and academic development (M Ed, Certificate); psychology (MA, PhD, Certificate); public policy (MA); written communication (MS, Certificate). *Program availability:* Part-time, evening/weekend, online learning. *Degree requirements:* For master's and Certificate, comprehensive exam (for some programs), thesis (for some programs); for doctorate, thesis/dissertation. *Entrance requirements:* For master's, MAT or GRE, 3 professional or academic references, interview, minimum GPA of 3.0; for doctorate, GRE General Test, MAT, or Watson-Glaser Critical Thinking Appraisal, three professional or academic references, statement of academic and professional goals, 3 years of experience in field, interview, master's degree, resume, writing sample; for Certificate, GRE, MAT, or Watson-Glaser Critical Thinking Appraisal, three professional or academic references, statement of academic and professional goals, interview, minimum GPA of 3.0. Additional exam requirements/recommendations for international students: Required—Department of Language Studies Assessment or TOEFL (minimum score 550 paper-based; 79 iBT). Electronic applications accepted.

National University, Academic Affairs, School of Health and Human Services, La Jolla, CA 92037-1011. Offers clinical affairs (MS); healthcare administration (MHA); nursing informatics (Certificate); nursing practice (DNP); public health (MPH), including mental health. *Program availability:* Part-time, evening/weekend, 100% online, blended/hybrid learning. *Faculty:* 30 full-time (20 women), 35 part-time/adjunct (21 women). *Students:* 363 full-time (263 women), 104 part-time (68 women); includes 303 minority (104 Black or African American, non-Hispanic/Latino; 1 American Indian or Alaska Native, non-Hispanic/Latino; 89 Asian, non-Hispanic/Latino; 71 Hispanic/Latino; 5 Native Hawaiian or other Pacific Islander, non-Hispanic/Latino; 33 Two or more races, non-Hispanic/Latino), 29 international. Average age 33. In 2016, 145 master's awarded. *Degree requirements:* For master's, thesis (for some programs). *Entrance requirements:* For master's, interview, minimum GPA of 2.5. Additional exam requirements/recommendations for international students: Required—TOEFL (minimum score 550 paper-based; 79 iBT), IELTS (minimum score 6). *Application deadline:* Applications are processed on a rolling basis. Application fee: $60 ($65 for international students). Electronic applications accepted. *Financial support:* Career-related internships or fieldwork, institutionally sponsored loans, scholarships/grants, and tuition waivers (partial) available. Support available to part-time students. Financial award application deadline: 6/30; financial award applicants required to submit FAFSA. *Faculty research:* Nursing education, obesity prevention, workforce diversity. *Unit head:* School of Health and Human Services, 800-628-8648, E-mail: shhs@nu.edu. *Application contact:* Brandon Jouganatos, Vice President for Enrollment Services, 800-628-8648, E-mail: advisor@nu.edu.
Website: http://www.nu.edu/OurPrograms/SchoolOfHealthAndHumanServices.html

New England College, Program in Community Mental Health Counseling, Henniker, NH 03242-3293. Offers human services (MS); mental health counseling (MS). *Program availability:* Part-time, evening/weekend. *Degree requirements:* For master's, internship.

Northeastern University, College of Professional Studies, Boston, MA 02115-5096. Offers applied nutrition (MS); college athletics administration (MSL); commerce and economic development (MS); corporate and organizational communication (MS); criminal justice (MS); digital media (MPS); elearning and instructional design (M Ed); elementary education (MAT); geographic information technology (MPS); global studies

and international relations (MS); higher education administration (M Ed); homeland security (MA); human services (MS); informatics (MPS); leadership (MS); learning analytics (M Ed); learning and instruction (M Ed); nonprofit management (MS); professional sports administration (MSL); project management (MS); regulatory affairs for drugs, biologics, and medical devices (MS); respiratory care leadership (MS); special education (M Ed); technical communication (MS). *Program availability:* Part-time, evening/weekend, 100% online, blended/hybrid learning. *Faculty:* 82 full-time (51 women), 853 part-time/adjunct (366 women). *Students:* 4,947 part-time (3,076 women). In 2016, 1,456 master's awarded. *Application deadline:* Applications are processed on a rolling basis. Application fee: $0. Electronic applications accepted. *Expenses:* Contact institution. *Financial support:* Applicants required to submit FAFSA. *Unit head:* Dr. Mary Loeffelholz, Interim Dean of the College of Professional Studies.
Website: http://www.cps.neu.edu/

Pontifical Catholic University of Puerto Rico, College of Graduate Studies in Behavioral Science and Community Affairs, Ponce, PR 00717-0777. Offers clinical psychology (PhD, Psy D); clinical social work (MSW); criminology (MA); industrial psychology (PhD); psychology (PhD); public administration (MSS); rehabilitation counseling (MA). *Program availability:* Part-time, evening/weekend. *Degree requirements:* For master's, thesis; for doctorate, comprehensive exam, thesis/dissertation. *Entrance requirements:* For master's, EXADEP, GRE General Test, 3 letters of recommendation, interview, minimum GPA of 2.75.

Post University, Program in Human Services, Waterbury, CT 06723-2540. Offers human services (MS); human services/alcohol and drug counseling (MS); human services/clinical counseling (MS); human services/non-profit management (MS). *Program availability:* Part-time, evening/weekend, online learning.

Purdue University Northwest, Graduate Studies Office, School of Education, Program in Counseling, Hammond, IN 46323-2094. Offers human services (MS Ed); mental health counseling (MS Ed); school counseling (MS Ed). *Accreditation:* ACA. *Entrance requirements:* Additional exam requirements/recommendations for international students: Required—TOEFL.

Roberts Wesleyan College, Department of Social Work, Rochester, NY 14624-1997. Offers child and family practice (MSW); mental health practice (MSW). *Accreditation:* CSWE. *Entrance requirements:* For master's, minimum GPA of 2.75. *Faculty research:* Religion and social work, family studies, values and ethics.

Rosemont College, Schools of Graduate and Professional Studies, Counseling Psychology Program, Rosemont, PA 19010-1699. Offers human services (MA); school counseling (MA). *Program availability:* Part-time, evening/weekend. *Degree requirements:* For master's, thesis or alternative, practicum. *Entrance requirements:* For master's, minimum undergraduate GPA of 3.0, 3 letters of recommendation. Additional exam requirements/recommendations for international students: Required—TOEFL. Electronic applications accepted. Application fee is waived when completed online. *Expenses:* Contact institution. *Faculty research:* Addictions counseling.

St. Joseph's College, Long Island Campus, Programs in Management, Field in Human Services Leadership, Patchogue, NY 11772-2399. Offers MS. *Expenses: Tuition:* Full-time $16,182; part-time $899 per credit. *Required fees:* $440.

St. Joseph's College, New York, Programs in Management, Field in Human Services Management and Leadership, Brooklyn, NY 11205-3688. Offers MS. *Program availability:* Part-time, evening/weekend. *Faculty:* 5 part-time/adjunct (4 women). *Students:* 11 part-time (9 women); includes 9 minority (4 Black or African American, non-Hispanic/Latino; 5 Hispanic/Latino). Average age 43. 8 applicants, 63% accepted, 1 enrolled. In 2016, 5 master's awarded. *Entrance requirements:* For master's, official transcripts, resume, two letters of reference, verification of employment. Additional exam requirements/recommendations for international students: Required—TOEFL (minimum score 80 iBT). *Application deadline:* Applications are processed on a rolling basis. Application fee: $25. Electronic applications accepted. *Expenses:* Contact institution. *Financial support:* In 2016–17, 1 student received support. Federal Work-Study available. *Unit head:* Candis Best, Associate Professor/Associate Chair, 718-940-5849, E-mail: cbest@sjcny.edu.
Website: http://www.sjcny.edu

Saint Leo University, Graduate Studies in Human Services, Saint Leo, FL 33574-6665. Offers MS. *Program availability:* Part-time, evening/weekend. *Faculty:* 2 full-time (both women), 2 part-time/adjunct (both women). *Students:* 20 part-time (19 women); includes 15 minority (14 Black or African American, non-Hispanic/Latino; 1 Two or more races, non-Hispanic/Latino). Average age 42. 12 applicants, 100% accepted, 11 enrolled. *Degree requirements:* For master's, project, field placement. *Entrance requirements:* For master's, official transcripts, bachelor's degree from regionally-accredited university with minimum GPA of 3.0, current resumé, 3 professional recommendations, statement of professional goals. Additional exam requirements/recommendations for international students: Required—TOEFL (minimum score 550 paper-based; 80 iBT). *Application deadline:* For fall admission, 7/1 for domestic and international students; for spring admission, 11/1 for domestic and international students. Application fee: $80. *Expenses:* $520 per semester hour. *Financial support:* Career-related internships or fieldwork, scholarships/grants, and health care benefits available. Financial award applicants required to submit FAFSA. *Faculty research:* Service learning, comparative social policy: U.S. and other countries, social entrepreneurship. *Unit head:* Dr. Susan Kinsella, Dean, School of Education and Social Services, 352-588-8272, Fax: 352-588-8289, E-mail: susan.kinsella@saintleo.edu. *Application contact:* Mary Martinez-Drovie, Graduate Enrollment Counselor, 352-588-5802, Fax: 352-588-8289, E-mail: mary.martinez-drovie@saintleo.edu.
Website: http://www.saintleo.edu/academics/graduate/human-services.aspx

South Carolina State University, College of Graduate and Professional Studies, Department of Human Services, Orangeburg, SC 29117-0001. Offers counselor education (M Ed); rehabilitation counseling (MA). *Accreditation:* CORE. *Program availability:* Part-time, evening/weekend. *Faculty:* 8 full-time (6 women), 1 (woman) part-time/adjunct. *Students:* 81 full-time (65 women), 21 part-time (16 women); includes 97 minority (all Black or African American, non-Hispanic/Latino). Average age 33. 40 applicants, 85% accepted, 32 enrolled. In 2016, 54 master's awarded. *Degree requirements:* For master's, comprehensive exam (for some programs), departmental qualifying exam, internship. *Entrance requirements:* For master's, GRE, MAT, minimum GPA of 2.7. *Application deadline:* For fall admission, 6/15 priority date for domestic students, 6/15 for international students; for spring admission, 11/1 for domestic and international students. Application fee: $25. Electronic applications accepted. *Expenses:* Tuition, state resident: full-time $8938; part-time $579 per credit hour. Tuition, nonresident: full-time $19,018; part-time $1139 per credit hour. *Required fees:* $1482; $82 per credit hour. *Financial support:* Fellowships, career-related internships or fieldwork, scholarships/grants, and unspecified assistantships available. Financial award application deadline: 6/1. *Unit head:* Dr. Michelle Maultsby-Priester, Interim Chair, Department of Human Services, 803-536-7075, Fax: 803-533-3636, E-mail: mmaultsb@scsu.edu. *Application contact:* Curtis Foskey, Coordinator of Graduate Admissions, 803-536-8419, Fax: 803-536-8812, E-mail: cfoskey@scsu.edu.

Southeastern University, College of Behavioral and Social Sciences, Lakeland, FL 33801-6099. Offers human services (MA); international community development (MA); marriage and family counseling (MS); professional counseling (MS); school counseling (MS); social work (MSW). *Program availability:* Evening/weekend. *Expenses: Tuition:* Full-time $9450; part-time $6300 per credit. *Required fees:* $500; $250 per semester. One-time fee: $150. Tuition and fees vary according to degree level, campus/location and program. *Unit head:* Erica H. Sirrine, Dean, 863-667-5341, E-mail: ehsirrine@seu.edu.
Website: http://www.seu.edu/behavior/

Springfield College, Graduate Programs, Program in Human Services, Springfield, MA 01109-3797. Offers MS. *Program availability:* Part-time, evening/weekend. *Degree requirements:* For master's, comprehensive exam, thesis (for some programs), Community Action Research Project. *Entrance requirements:* Additional exam requirements/recommendations for international students: Required—TOEFL (minimum score 550 paper-based). Electronic applications accepted. *Expenses:* Contact institution.

Texas Southern University, College of Liberal Arts and Behavioral Sciences, Department of Human Services and Consumer Sciences, Houston, TX 77004-4584. Offers MS. *Program availability:* Part-time, evening/weekend. *Degree requirements:* For master's, comprehensive exam, thesis (for some programs). *Entrance requirements:* For master's, GRE General Test, minimum GPA of 2.5. Additional exam requirements/recommendations for international students: Required—TOEFL. Electronic applications accepted. *Faculty research:* Food radiation/food for space travel, adolescent parenting, gerontology/grandparenting.

Thomas University, Department of Human Services, Thomasville, GA 31792-7499. Offers community counseling (MSCC); rehabilitation counseling (MRC). *Accreditation:* CORE. *Program availability:* Part-time. *Entrance requirements:* For master's, resume, 3 academic/professional references. Additional exam requirements/recommendations for international students: Required—TOEFL (minimum score 600 paper-based). Electronic applications accepted.

Universidad del Turabo, Graduate Programs, School of Social Sciences and Humanities, Programs in Public Affairs, Program in Human Services Administration, Gurabo, PR 00778-3030. Offers MPA. *Students:* 9 full-time (8 women), 8 part-time (6 women); all minorities (all Hispanic/Latino). Average age 34. 15 applicants, 47% accepted, 5 enrolled. In 2016, 5 master's awarded. *Entrance requirements:* For master's, GRE, EXADEP or GMAT, interview, essay, official transcript, recommendation letters. *Application deadline:* For fall admission, 8/5 for domestic students. Applications are processed on a rolling basis. Application fee: $25. Electronic applications accepted. *Financial support:* Institutionally sponsored loans available. Financial award applicants required to submit FAFSA. *Unit head:* María del Carmen Santos, Dean, 787-743-7979 Ext. 4232. *Application contact:* Diriee Rodríguez, Admissions Director, 787-743-7979 Ext. 4453, E-mail: admisiones-ut@suagm.edu.
Website: http://ut.suagm.edu/es/sociales

Université de Montréal, Faculty of Arts and Sciences, Programs in Applied Human Sciences, Montréal, QC H3C 3J7, Canada. Offers PhD. *Degree requirements:* For doctorate, thesis/dissertation, general exam. Electronic applications accepted.

University of Baltimore, Graduate School, College of Public Affairs, Program in Human Services Administration, Baltimore, MD 21201-5779. Offers MS. *Program availability:* Part-time, evening/weekend. *Entrance requirements:* For master's, interview. Additional exam requirements/recommendations for international students: Required—TOEFL (minimum score 550 paper-based). Electronic applications accepted.

University of Bridgeport, School of Arts and Sciences, Department of Counseling, Bridgeport, CT 06604. Offers clinical mental health counseling (MS); college student personnel (MS); community counseling (MS); human resource development (MS); human service (MS). *Program availability:* Part-time, evening/weekend. *Degree requirements:* For master's, thesis, project. *Entrance requirements:* Additional exam requirements/recommendations for international students: Recommended—TOEFL (minimum score 550 paper-based; 80 iBT), IELTS (minimum score 6.5). Electronic applications accepted. *Expenses:* Contact institution.

University of Central Missouri, The Graduate School, Warrensburg, MO 64093. Offers accountancy (MA); accounting (MBA); applied mathematics (MS); aviation safety (MA); biology (MS); business administration (MBA); career and technical education leadership (MS); college student personnel administration (MS); communication (MA); computer science (MS); counseling (MS); criminal justice (MS); educational leadership (Ed D); educational technology (MS); elementary and early childhood education (MSE); English (MA); environmental studies (MA); finance (MBA); history (MA); human services/educational technology (Ed S); human services/learning resources (Ed S); human services/professional counseling (Ed S); industrial hygiene (MS); industrial management (MS); information systems (MBA); information technology (MS); kinesiology (MS); library science and information services (MS); literacy education (MSE); marketing (MBA); mathematics (MS); music (MA); occupational safety management (MS); psychology (MS); rural family nursing (MS); school administration (MSE); social gerontology (MS); sociology (MA); special education (MSE); speech language pathology (MS); superintendency (Ed S); teaching (MAT); teaching English as a second language (MA); technology (MS); technology management (PhD); theatre (MA). *Program availability:* Part-time, 100% online, blended/hybrid learning. *Degree requirements:* For master's and Ed S, comprehensive exam (for some programs), thesis (for some programs). *Entrance requirements:* Additional exam requirements/recommendations for international students: Required—TOEFL (minimum score 550 paper-based; 79 iBT). Electronic applications accepted.

University of Colorado Colorado Springs, College of Education, Colorado Springs, CO 80918. Offers counseling and human services (MA); curriculum and instruction (MA); educational leadership (MA); educational leadership, research and policy (PhD); special education (MA); teaching English to speakers of other languages (MA). *Accreditation:* ACA; NCATE. *Program availability:* Part-time, evening/weekend, 100% online, blended/hybrid learning. *Faculty:* 26 full-time (18 women), 33 part-time/adjunct (21 women). *Students:* 136 full-time (94 women), 264 part-time (177 women); includes 99 minority (17 Black or African American, non-Hispanic/Latino; 1 American Indian or Alaska Native, non-Hispanic/Latino; 8 Asian, non-Hispanic/Latino; 55 Hispanic/Latino; 18 Two or more races, non-Hispanic/Latino), 9 international. Average age 35. 152 applicants, 89% accepted, 88 enrolled. In 2016, 161 master's, 11 doctorates awarded. *Degree requirements:* For master's, comprehensive exam, thesis or alternative, microcomputer proficiency; for doctorate, comprehensive exam, thesis/dissertation, research lab. *Entrance requirements:* For master's and doctorate, GRE General Test. Additional exam requirements/recommendations for international students: Recommended—TOEFL (minimum score 550 paper-based; 80 iBT), IELTS (minimum score 6). *Application deadline:* For fall admission, 2/1 priority date for domestic students, 2/1 for international students; for spring admission, 10/15 for domestic students, 10/1 for international students. Applications are processed on a rolling basis. Application fee: $60 ($100 for international students). Electronic applications accepted. *Expenses:* Contact institution. *Financial support:* In 2016–17, 108 students received support. Career-related internships or fieldwork, Federal Work-Study, scholarships/grants, and unspecified assistantships available. Support available to part-time students. Financial award application deadline: 3/1; financial award applicants required to submit FAFSA.

Faculty research: Linguistically diverse education (LDE), educational policy, evidence-based reading and writing instruction, relational and social aggression, positive behavior supports, inclusive schooling, K-12 education policy. *Total annual research expenditures:* $272,136. *Unit head:* Dr. Valerie Martin Conley, Dean, 719-255-4133, E-mail: vmconley@uccs.edu. *Application contact:* The College of Education Student Resource Office, 719-255-4996, E-mail: education@uccs.edu.
Website: http://www.uccs.edu/coe

University of Great Falls, Graduate Studies, Program in Organization Management, Great Falls, MT 59405. Offers human development (MSM); management (MSM). *Program availability:* Part-time, evening/weekend, online learning. *Degree requirements:* For master's, thesis optional. *Entrance requirements:* For master's, GRE General Test or MAT, 3 letters of recommendation. Additional exam requirements/recommendations for international students: Required—TOEFL (minimum score 500 paper-based). *Application deadline:* For fall admission, 8/15 priority date for domestic students, 6/15 priority date for international students; for spring admission, 12/15 priority date for domestic students, 10/15 priority date for international students. Applications are processed on a rolling basis. Application fee: $50. Electronic applications accepted. *Expenses: Tuition:* Full-time $14,256; part-time $9504 per semester. *Financial support:* Career-related internships or fieldwork, Federal Work-Study, and institutionally sponsored loans available. Support available to part-time students. Financial award application deadline: 6/1; financial award applicants required to submit FAFSA. *Unit head:* Tami Park, Coordinator, 406-791-5343, E-mail: tami.park@ugf.edu. *Application contact:* Melanie Houge, Director of Admissions, 406-791-5210, Fax: 406-791-5209, E-mail: melanie.houge@ugf.edu.

University of Idaho, College of Graduate Studies, College of Education, Department of Leadership and Counseling, Boise, ID 83702. Offers adult/organizational learning and leadership (MS, Ed S); educational leadership (M Ed, Ed S); rehabilitation counseling and human services (M Ed, MS); school counseling (M Ed, MS); special education (M Ed). *Faculty:* 14 full-time, 7 part-time/adjunct. *Students:* 37 full-time (26 women), 154 part-time (84 women). Average age 39. In 2016, 75 master's, 21 other advanced degrees awarded. *Entrance requirements:* For master's, minimum GPA of 3.0. Additional exam requirements/recommendations for international students: Required—TOEFL. *Application deadline:* Applications are processed on a rolling basis. Application fee: $60. Electronic applications accepted. *Expenses:* Tuition, state resident: full-time $6460; part-time $414 per credit hour. Tuition, nonresident: full-time $21,268; part-time $1237 per credit hour. *Required fees:* $2070; $60 per credit hour. Full-time tuition and fees vary according to course load and reciprocity agreements. *Financial support:* Applicants required to submit FAFSA. *Unit head:* Dr. Kathy Canfield-Davis, Chair, 208-364-4047, E-mail: lead@uidaho.edu. *Application contact:* Sean Scoggin, Graduate Recruitment Coordinator, 208-885-4723, Fax: 208-885-4406, E-mail: graduateadmissions@uidaho.edu.
Website: https://www.uidaho.edu/ed/lc

University of Illinois at Springfield, Graduate Programs, College of Education and Human Services, Program in Human Services, Springfield, IL 62703-5407. Offers alcohol and substance abuse (Graduate Certificate); alcoholism and substance abuse (MA); child and family services (MA); gerontology (MA); social services administration (MA). *Program availability:* Part-time, evening/weekend, 100% online, blended/hybrid learning. *Faculty:* 4 full-time (all women), 2 part-time/adjunct (1 woman). *Students:* 10 full-time (8 women), 62 part-time (53 women); includes 28 minority (23 Black or African American, non-Hispanic/Latino; 3 Hispanic/Latino; 2 Two or more races, non-Hispanic/Latino). Average age 34. 37 applicants, 46% accepted, 16 enrolled. In 2016, 32 master's, 3 other advanced degrees awarded. *Degree requirements:* For master's, internship; capstone project or thesis. *Entrance requirements:* For master's, minimum undergraduate GPA of 3.0, 2 letters of recommendation from professional or academic sources, statement of intent, interview. Additional exam requirements/recommendations for international students: Required—TOEFL (minimum score 500 paper-based; 61 iBT). *Application deadline:* Applications are processed on a rolling basis. Application fee: $60 ($75 for international students). Electronic applications accepted. *Expenses:* Tuition, state resident: part-time $329 per credit hour. Tuition, nonresident: part-time $675 per credit hour. *Financial support:* In 2016–17, fellowships with full tuition reimbursements (averaging $9,900 per year), research assistantships with full tuition reimbursements (averaging $9,991 per year), teaching assistantships with full tuition reimbursements (averaging $10,059 per year) were awarded; career-related internships or fieldwork, Federal Work-Study, scholarships/grants, health care benefits, and unspecified assistantships also available. Support available to part-time students. Financial award application deadline: 11/15; financial award applicants required to submit FAFSA. *Unit head:* Dr. Carolyn Peck, Program Administrator, 217-206-7577, Fax: 217-206-6775, E-mail: peck.carolyn@uis.edu. *Application contact:* Dr. Cecelia Cornell, Associate Vice Chancellor for Graduate Education, 217-206-7230, E-mail: ccorn1@uis.edu.
Website: http://www.uis.edu/humanservices

University of Illinois at Urbana–Champaign, Graduate College, School of Social Work, Champaign, IL 61820. Offers advocacy, leadership, and social change (MSW); children, youth and family services (MSW); health care (MSW); mental health (MSW); school social work (MSW); social work (PhD). *Accreditation:* CSWE (one or more programs are accredited). *Entrance requirements:* For master's and doctorate, minimum GPA of 3.0.

University of Maryland, Baltimore County, The Graduate School, College of Arts, Humanities and Social Sciences, Department of Psychology, Program in Human Services Psychology, Baltimore, MD 21250. Offers applied behavioral analysis (MA); human services psychology (PhD), including behavioral medicine, clinical psychology, community psychology. *Faculty:* 17 full-time (9 women), 11 part-time/adjunct (4 women). *Students:* 82 full-time (65 women), 1 (woman) part-time; includes 26 minority (10 Black or African American, non-Hispanic/Latino; 6 Asian, non-Hispanic/Latino; 9 Hispanic/Latino; 1 Two or more races, non-Hispanic/Latino). Average age 25. 136 applicants, 21% accepted, 18 enrolled. In 2016, 25 master's, 7 doctorates awarded. *Degree requirements:* For master's, thesis; for doctorate, comprehensive exam, thesis/dissertation. *Entrance requirements:* For master's, GRE General Test, minimum GPA of 3.0; for doctorate, GRE General Test, GRE Subject Test, minimum GPA of 3.0. Additional exam requirements/recommendations for international students: Required—TOEFL. *Application deadline:* For fall admission, 12/1 for domestic and international students. Application fee: $50. Electronic applications accepted. *Expenses:* Tuition, state resident: full-time $13,294. Tuition, nonresident: full-time $20,286. *Financial support:* In 2016–17, 43 students received support, including 3 fellowships with full tuition reimbursements available (averaging $26,000 per year), 26 research assistantships with full tuition reimbursements available (averaging $20,400 per year), 9 teaching assistantships with full tuition reimbursements available (averaging $17,250 per year); career-related internships or fieldwork, Federal Work-Study, scholarships/grants, health care benefits, tuition waivers, and unspecified assistantships also available. Financial award application deadline: 3/1; financial award applicants required to submit FAFSA. *Faculty research:* Addictive behaviors, cardiovascular and cerebrovascular disease, family violence, pediatric psychology, community prevention. *Unit head:* Dr. Lynnda Dahlquist, Director, 410-455-2567, Fax: 410-455-1055, E-mail: dahlquis@umbc.edu. *Application contact:* Nicole Mooney, Program Management Specialist, 410-455-2567, Fax: 410-455-1055, E-mail: psycdept@umbc.edu.
Website: http://psychology.umbc.edu/

University of Massachusetts Boston, College of Public and Community Service, Program in Human Services, Boston, MA 02125-3393. Offers MS. *Program availability:* Part-time, evening/weekend. *Faculty:* 3 full-time (2 women), 1 (woman) part-time/adjunct. *Students:* 16 full-time (13 women), 9 part-time (7 women); includes 16 minority (3 Black or African American, non-Hispanic/Latino; 3 Asian, non-Hispanic/Latino; 9 Hispanic/Latino; 1 Two or more races, non-Hispanic/Latino). Average age 36. 14 applicants, 79% accepted. In 2016, 11 master's awarded. *Degree requirements:* For master's, practicum, final project. *Entrance requirements:* For master's, MAT, GRE, minimum GPA of 2.75. Additional exam requirements/recommendations for international students: Recommended—TOEFL. *Application deadline:* For fall admission, 3/1 for domestic students; for spring admission, 11/1 for domestic students. *Expenses:* Tuition, state resident: full-time $16,863. Tuition, nonresident: full-time $32,913. *Required fees:* $177. *Financial support:* Research assistantships with full tuition reimbursements, teaching assistantships with full tuition reimbursements, career-related internships or fieldwork, Federal Work-Study, and unspecified assistantships available. Support available to part-time students. Financial award application deadline: 3/1; financial award applicants required to submit FAFSA. *Faculty research:* Institutional and policy context of human services, ethics and social policy, public law and human services, social welfare, politics and human services. *Unit head:* Dr. Sylvia Mignon, Director, 617-287-7384. *Application contact:* Peggy Roldan Patel, Graduate Admissions Coordinator, 617-287-6400, Fax: 617-287-6236, E-mail: bos.gadm@dpc.umassp.edu.

University of Nebraska at Kearney, College of Business and Technology, Department of Business, Kearney, NE 68849-0001. Offers accounting (MBA); generalist (MBA); human resources (MBA); human services (MBA); marketing (MBA). *Accreditation:* AACSB. *Program availability:* Part-time, evening/weekend. *Faculty:* 32 full-time (13 women). *Students:* 11 full-time (5 women), 30 part-time (14 women), 8 international. Average age 39. 13 applicants, 100% accepted, 10 enrolled. In 2016, 6 master's awarded. *Degree requirements:* For master's, thesis optional, capstone course. *Entrance requirements:* For master's, GRE or GMAT (if no significant managerial experience), letters of recommendation, essay, resume. Additional exam requirements/recommendations for international students: Recommended—TOEFL (minimum score 550 paper-based; 79 iBT), IELTS (minimum score 6.5). *Application deadline:* For fall admission, 6/15 for domestic and international students; for spring admission, 10/15 for domestic and international students; for summer admission, 3/15 for domestic and international students. Application fee: $45. Electronic applications accepted. *Expenses:* Tuition, state resident: full-time $4064; part-time $225.75 per credit hour. Tuition, nonresident: full-time $8915; part-time $495.25 per credit hour. *Required fees:* $772; $23 per credit hour. Part-time tuition and fees vary according to course load, campus/location, program and reciprocity agreements. *Financial support:* In 2016–17, 2 research assistantships with full tuition reimbursements (averaging $10,500 per year), 2 teaching assistantships with full tuition reimbursements (averaging $10,500 per year) were awarded; career-related internships or fieldwork, scholarships/grants, health care benefits, and unspecified assistantships also available. Support available to part-time students. Financial award application deadline: 2/28; financial award applicants required to submit FAFSA. *Faculty research:* Small business financial management, employment law, expert systems, international trade and marketing, environmental economics. *Unit head:* Dr. Sri Seshadri, Director, 308-865-8346, Fax: 308-865-8114. *Application contact:* Linda Johnson, Director, Graduate Admissions and Programs, 800-717-7881, Fax: 308-865-8837, E-mail: gradstudies@unk.edu.

University of Northern Iowa, Graduate College, College of Education, School of Kinesiology, Allied Health and Human Services, MA Program in Leisure, Youth and Human Services, Cedar Falls, IA 50614. Offers MA. *Degree requirements:* For master's, comprehensive exam, thesis or alternative. *Entrance requirements:* For master's, minimum GPA of 3.0. Additional exam requirements/recommendations for international students: Required—TOEFL (minimum score 500 paper-based; 61 iBT). Electronic applications accepted.

University of Northwestern–St. Paul, Master of Arts in Human Services Program, St. Paul, MN 55113-1598. Offers MAHS. *Program availability:* Part-time, evening/weekend, online learning. *Application deadline:* Applications are processed on a rolling basis. Electronic applications accepted. *Application contact:* College of Adult and Graduate Studies Admissions, 651-631-5200, E-mail: gradstudies@unwsp.edu.
Website: https://www.unwsp.edu/web/graduate-studies/master-of-arts-in-human-services

University of Oklahoma, College of Arts and Sciences, Department of Human Relations, Norman, OK 73019. Offers clinical mental health (MHR); helping skills in human relations (Graduate Certificate); human relations (MHR); human resource diversity and development (Graduate Certificate); human resources (MHR); licensed professional counselor (MHR). *Program availability:* Part-time, evening/weekend. *Faculty:* 24 full-time (16 women), 6 part-time/adjunct (3 women). *Students:* 262 full-time (190 women), 397 part-time (260 women); includes 331 minority (161 Black or African American, non-Hispanic/Latino; 23 American Indian or Alaska Native, non-Hispanic/Latino; 25 Asian, non-Hispanic/Latino; 74 Hispanic/Latino; 2 Native Hawaiian or other Pacific Islander, non-Hispanic/Latino; 46 Two or more races, non-Hispanic/Latino), 15 international. Average age 35. 135 applicants, 93% accepted, 89 enrolled. In 2016, 289 master's, 113 other advanced degrees awarded. *Degree requirements:* For master's, comprehensive exam (for some programs), thesis (for some programs), comprehensive exam or thesis; 15 hours in human relations classroom courses. *Entrance requirements:* For degree, minimum GPA of 3.0. Additional exam requirements/recommendations for international students: Required—TOEFL (minimum score 79 iBT) or IELTS (minimum score 6.5). *Application deadline:* For fall admission, 8/21 for domestic and international students; for spring admission, 1/23 for domestic and international students; for summer admission, 6/5 for domestic and international students. Application fee: $50 ($100 for international students). Electronic applications accepted. *Expenses:* Tuition, state resident: full-time $4886; part-time $203.60 per credit hour. Tuition, nonresident: full-time $18,989; part-time $791.20 per credit hour. *Required fees:* $3283; $126.25 per credit hour. $126.50 per semester. *Financial support:* In 2016–17, 148 students received support, including 8 research assistantships with full tuition reimbursements available (averaging $11,124 per year), 5 teaching assistantships with full tuition reimbursements available (averaging $12,199 per year); scholarships/grants also available. Financial award application deadline: 6/1; financial award applicants required to submit FAFSA. *Faculty research:* At-risk youth, strength model, women's health, adolescent addiction and recovery, group psychotherapy. *Unit head:* Dr. Wesley Long, Chair of Department of Human Relations, 405-325-1756, Fax: 405-325-4402, E-mail: wlong@ou.edu. *Application contact:* Lawana Miller, Admissions Coordinator, 405-325-1756, Fax: 405-325-4402, E-mail: lmiller@ou.edu.
Website: http://humanrelations.ou.edu

University of Oklahoma, College of Liberal Studies, Norman, OK 73072. Offers administrative leadership (Graduate Certificate); corrections management (Graduate Certificate); criminal justice (MS); government and military leadership (MA); human and health services administration (MA), including human and health services administration, integrated studies; liberal studies (MPS); organizational leadership (MA);

restorative justice administration (Graduate Certificate); volunteer and non-profit leadership (MA). *Program availability:* Part-time, online only, 100% online, blended/hybrid learning. *Faculty:* 13 full-time (7 women), 1 part-time/adjunct (0 women). *Students:* 74 full-time (48 women), 598 part-time (289 women); includes 175 minority (45 Black or African American, non-Hispanic/Latino; 39 American Indian or Alaska Native, non-Hispanic/Latino; 8 Asian, non-Hispanic/Latino; 46 Hispanic/Latino; 1 Native Hawaiian or other Pacific Islander, non-Hispanic/Latino; 36 Two or more races, non-Hispanic/Latino), 2 international. Average age 35. 191 applicants, 95% accepted, 120 enrolled. In 2016, 192 master's, 6 other advanced degrees awarded. *Degree requirements:* For master's, comprehensive exam, thesis optional, 33 credit hours; project/internship (for museum studies); for Graduate Certificate, 12 credit hours. *Entrance requirements:* For master's and Graduate Certificate, minimum GPA of 3.0 in last 60 undergraduate hours; statement of goals; resume. Additional exam requirements/recommendations for international students: Required—TOEFL (minimum score 79 iBT) or IELTS (minimum score 6.5). *Application deadline:* For fall admission, 7/1 for domestic and international students; for winter admission, 12/1 for domestic and international students; for spring admission, 5/1 for domestic and international students. Applications are processed on a rolling basis. Application fee: $50 ($100 for international students). Electronic applications accepted. *Expenses:* Tuition, state resident: full-time $4886; part-time $203.60 per credit hour. Tuition, nonresident: full-time $18,989; part-time $791.20 per credit hour. *Required fees:* $3283; $126.25 per credit hour. $126.50 per semester. *Financial support:* In 2016–17, 124 students received support. Career-related internships or fieldwork, institutionally sponsored loans, scholarships/grants, health care benefits, and tuition waivers available. Support available to part-time students. Financial award application deadline: 6/1; financial award applicants required to submit FAFSA. *Faculty research:* Management and leadership; policing and corrections management; neuro-psychology of addiction; disproportionate minority contact; ethnic identity and nationalism. *Unit head:* Dr. Martha L. Banz, Associate Provost for Continuing Education/Interim Dean, College of Liberal Studies, 405-325-1061, Fax: 405-325-7132, E-mail: mlbanz@ou.edu. *Application contact:* Michelle Shults, Academic Advisement Services Coordinator, 405-325-2928, Fax: 405-325-7132, E-mail: mshults@ou.edu.
Website: http://www.ou.edu/cls/html

Upper Iowa University, Online Master's Programs, Fayette, IA 52142-1857. Offers accounting (MBA); corporate financial management (MBA); emergency management and homeland security (MPA); general management (MBA); general studies (MPA); government administration (MPA); health and human services (MPA); human resources management (MBA); nonprofit organizational management (MPA); organizational development (MBA); public management (MPA); sport administration (MSA). MBA also available at Madison, WI campus. *Program availability:* Part-time, online learning. *Degree requirements:* For master's, research project. *Entrance requirements:* For master's, GMAT, GRE, or minimum GPA of 2.7 during last 60 hours. Additional exam requirements/recommendations for international students: Required—TOEFL (minimum score 570 paper-based). Electronic applications accepted. *Faculty research:* Total quality management, teams, organization culture and climate, management.

Walden University, Graduate Programs, School of Social Work and Human Services, Minneapolis, MN 55401. Offers addictions and social work (DSW); advanced clinical practice (MSW); clinical expertise (DSW); criminal justice (DSW); disaster, crisis, and intervention (DSW); family studies and interventions (DSW); human and social services (PhD), including advanced research, community and social services, community intervention and leadership, conflict management, criminal justice, disaster crisis and intervention, family studies and intervention, gerontology, global social services, higher education, human services and nonprofit administration, mental health facilitation; medical social work (DSW); military social work (MSW); policy practice (DSW); social work (PhD), including addictions and social work, clinical expertise, criminal justice, disaster, crisis and intervention, family studies and interventions, medical social work, policy practice, social work administration; social work administration (DSW); social work in healthcare (MSW); social work with children and families (MSW). *Accreditation:* CSWE. *Program availability:* Part-time, evening/weekend, online only, 100% online. *Degree requirements:* For master's, residency (for some programs); for doctorate, thesis/dissertation, residency. *Entrance requirements:* For master's, bachelor's degree or higher; minimum GPA of 2.5; official transcripts; goal statement (for some programs); access to computer and Internet; for doctorate, master's degree or higher; three years of related professional or academic experience (preferred); minimum GPA of 3.0; goal statement and current resume (for select programs); official transcripts; access to computer and Internet. Additional exam requirements/recommendations for international students: Required—TOEFL (minimum score 550 paper-based, 79 iBT), IELTS (minimum score 6.5), Michigan English Language Assessment Battery (minimum score 82), or PTE (minimum score 53). Electronic applications accepted.

Warner Pacific College, Graduate Programs, Portland, OR 97215-4099. Offers human services (MA); not-for-profit leadership (MS); organizational leadership (MS); teaching (MAT). *Program availability:* Part-time, evening/weekend. *Degree requirements:* For master's, thesis or alternative, presentation of defense. *Entrance requirements:* For master's, interview, minimum GPA of 2.5, letters of recommendation. *Faculty research:* New Testament studies, nineteenth-century Wesleyan theology, preaching and church growth, Christian ethics.

Washburn University, School of Applied Studies, Department of Human Services, Topeka, KS 66621. Offers addiction counseling (MA). *Program availability:* Evening/weekend. *Entrance requirements:* For master's, minimum GPA of 3.0 in last 60 hours of coursework. Additional exam requirements/recommendations for international students: Required—TOEFL (minimum score 80 iBT). *Faculty research:* Professional identity development in students, expressive therapeutic writing, prevention, community mental health, agency professional development, behavioral analysis, group living among the elderly, ethical identity development, higher education pedagogy, Morita therapy/anxiety disorders, ecological/contextual healing, post-trauma.

Webster University, College of Arts and Sciences, Department of Anthropology and Sociology, St. Louis, MO 63119-3194. Offers human services (MA). *Expenses: Tuition:* Full-time $21,900; part-time $730 per credit hour. Tuition and fees vary according to campus/location and program. *Unit head:* Dr. David Carl Wilson, Dean, 314-968-7160, Fax: 314-963-6043, E-mail: wilson@webster.edu. *Application contact:* Sarah Nandor, Director, Graduate and Transfer Admissions, 314-968-7109, E-mail: gadmit@webster.edu.

Western Michigan University, Graduate College, College of Health and Human Services, Department of Interdisciplinary Health and Human Services, Kalamazoo, MI 49008. Offers interdisciplinary health services (PhD).

West Virginia University, College of Education and Human Services, Morgantown, WV 26506-6122. Offers MA, MS, Au D, Ed D, PhD. *Accreditation:* NCATE. *Program availability:* Part-time, evening/weekend, online learning. *Degree requirements:* For master's, content exams; for doctorate, comprehensive exam, thesis/dissertation. *Entrance requirements:* Additional exam requirements/recommendations for international students: Required—TOEFL (minimum score 500 paper-based; 61 iBT). Electronic applications accepted. *Faculty research:* Internet training and integration for teachers, rural education, teacher preparation, organization of schools, evaluation of personnel.

West Virginia University, Eberly College of Arts and Sciences, School of Social Work, Morgantown, WV 26506. Offers aging and health care (MSW); children and families (MSW); community mental health (MSW); community organization and social administration (MSW); direct (clinical) social work practice (MSW). *Accreditation:* CSWE. *Program availability:* Part-time. *Degree requirements:* For master's, fieldwork. *Entrance requirements:* For master's, GRE, minimum GPA of 2.75, 2 letters of reference. Additional exam requirements/recommendations for international students: Required—TOEFL. *Faculty research:* Rural and small town social work practice, gerontology, health and mental health, welfare reform, child welfare.

Wichita State University, Graduate School, Fairmount College of Liberal Arts and Sciences, School of Community Affairs, Wichita, KS 67260. Offers criminal justice (MA). *Program availability:* Part-time, 100% online, blended/hybrid learning. *Unit head:* Dr. Michael Birzer, Director, 316-978-7200, Fax: 316-978-3626, E-mail: michael.birzer@wichita.edu. *Application contact:* Jordan Oleson, Admissions Coordinator, 316-978-3095, Fax: 316-978-3253, E-mail: jordan.oleson@wichita.edu.
Website: http://www.wichita.edu/cj

Wilmington University, College of Social and Behavioral Sciences, New Castle, DE 19720-6491. Offers administration of human services (MS); administration of justice (MS); clinical mental health counseling (MS); homeland security (MS). *Accreditation:* ACA. *Program availability:* Part-time, evening/weekend. *Faculty:* 8 full-time (5 women), 79 part-time/adjunct (35 women). *Students:* 210 full-time (162 women), 444 part-time (325 women); includes 320 minority (285 Black or African American, non-Hispanic/Latino; 12 American Indian or Alaska Native, non-Hispanic/Latino; 9 Asian, non-Hispanic/Latino; 12 Hispanic/Latino; 1 Native Hawaiian or other Pacific Islander, non-Hispanic/Latino; 1 Two or more races, non-Hispanic/Latino), 4 international. Average age 35. 255 applicants, 100% accepted, 255 enrolled. In 2016, 248 master's awarded. *Entrance requirements:* Additional exam requirements/recommendations for international students: Required—TOEFL (minimum score 500 paper-based). *Application deadline:* Applications are processed on a rolling basis. Application fee: $35. Electronic applications accepted. *Expenses: Tuition:* Full-time $8388; part-time $466 per credit. *Required fees:* $25 per semester. Tuition and fees vary according to degree level. *Financial support:* Applicants required to submit FAFSA. *Unit head:* Dr. Edward L. Guthrie, Dean. *Application contact:* Laura Morris, Director of Admissions, 877-967-5464, E-mail: inquire@wilmcoll.edu.
Website: http://www.wilmu.edu/behavioralscience/

Youngstown State University, Graduate School, Bitonte College of Health and Human Services, Department of Health Professions, Youngstown, OH 44555-0001. Offers health and human services (MHHS); public health (MPH). *Accreditation:* NAACLS. *Program availability:* Part-time, evening/weekend. *Degree requirements:* For master's, thesis optional. *Entrance requirements:* For master's, GRE General Test, minimum GPA of 3.0. Additional exam requirements/recommendations for international students: Required—TOEFL. *Faculty research:* Drug prevention, multiskilling in health care, organizational behavior, health care management, health behaviors, research management.

Social Work

Abilene Christian University, Graduate Programs, College of Education and Human Services, School of Social Work, Abilene, TX 79699. Offers MS. *Accreditation:* CSWE. *Program availability:* Part-time. *Faculty:* 8 part-time/adjunct (4 women). *Students:* 21 full-time (15 women), 8 part-time (7 women); includes 10 minority (3 Black or African American, non-Hispanic/Latino; 5 Hispanic/Latino; 2 Two or more races, non-Hispanic/Latino), 2 international. 36 applicants, 44% accepted, 16 enrolled. In 2016, 15 master's awarded. *Degree requirements:* For master's, thesis. *Entrance requirements:* For master's, GRE (if undergraduate GPA less than 3.0) or MAT. Additional exam requirements/recommendations for international students: Required—TOEFL (minimum score 80 iBT), IELTS (minimum score 6), PTE. *Application deadline:* For fall admission, 2/16 priority date for domestic students; for spring admission, 11/1 for domestic students. Applications are processed on a rolling basis. Application fee: $50. Electronic applications accepted. *Expenses: Tuition:* Full-time $19,890; part-time $1105 per credit hour. Tuition and fees vary according to course load and program. *Financial support:* In 2016–17, 20 students received support, including 2 research assistantships with partial tuition reimbursements available (averaging $5,800 per year); career-related internships or fieldwork, Federal Work-Study, scholarships/grants, and tuition waivers (partial) also available. Financial award application deadline: 4/1; financial award applicants required to submit FAFSA. *Unit head:* Dr. Thomas Winter, Director, 325-674-2072, Fax: 325-674-6525, E-mail: socialwork@acu.edu. *Application contact:* Corey Patterson, Director of Graduate Admission and Recruiting, 325-674-6566, Fax: 325-674-6717, E-mail: gradinfo@acu.edu.
Website: http://www.acu.edu/socialwork

Adelphi University, School of Social Work, MSW Program, Garden City, NY 11530-0701. Offers MSW. *Program availability:* Part-time. *Students:* 369 full-time (316 women), 184 part-time (159 women); includes 280 minority (160 Black or African American, non-Hispanic/Latino; 21 Asian, non-Hispanic/Latino; 91 Hispanic/Latino; 8 Two or more races, non-Hispanic/Latino), 5 international. Average age 33. 493 applicants, 76% accepted, 204 enrolled. In 2016, 253 master's awarded. *Entrance requirements:* For master's, baccalaureate degree, minimum undergraduate cumulative GPA of 3.0, paid or volunteer experience in human services (preferred), interview, two reference letters, official transcripts, personal statement. Additional exam requirements/recommendations for international students: Required—TOEFL (minimum score 585 paper-based; 80 iBT), IELTS (minimum score 6.5). *Application deadline:* Applications are processed on a rolling basis. Application fee: $50. *Expenses: Tuition:* Full-time $37,623; part-time $1179 per credit hour. *Required fees:* $1335; $405 per semester. Tuition and fees vary according to degree level, campus/location and program. *Financial support:* Research assistantships, teaching assistantships, career-related internships or fieldwork, institutionally sponsored loans, scholarships/grants, traineeships, and unspecified assistantships available. Support available to part-time students. *Unit head:* Dr. Andrew Safyer, Dean, 516-877-4300, E-mail: asafyer@adelphi.edu. *Application contact:* Christine Murphy, Director of Admissions, 516-877-3050, Fax: 516-877-3039, E-mail: graduateadmissions@adelphi.edu.

Adelphi University, School of Social Work, PhD in Social Work Program, Garden City, NY 11530-0701. Offers PhD. *Program availability:* Part-time. *Degree requirements:* For doctorate, thesis/dissertation. *Entrance requirements:* For doctorate, four-page essay or personal statement, three letters of recommendation, curriculum vitae, writing sample, official transcripts. Additional exam requirements/recommendations for international students: Required—TOEFL (minimum iBT score of 80) or IELTS (minimum score of 6.5). *Application deadline:* For fall admission, 4/15 for domestic students. *Expenses: Tuition:* Full-time $37,623; part-time $1179 per credit hour. *Required fees:* $1335; $405 per semester. Tuition and fees vary according to degree level, campus/location and program. *Unit head:* Dr. Subadra Panchanadeswaran, Director, 516-877-4310, Fax: 516-877-4392. *Application contact:* Tracy A. Nilsen, Director of Admissions, 516-877-3050, Fax: 516-877-3039, E-mail: graduateadmissions@adelphi.edu.
Website: http://socialwork.adelphi.edu/academics/ph-d-program/

Alabama Agricultural and Mechanical University, School of Graduate Studies, College of Education, Humanities, and Behavioral Sciences, Department of Social Work, Psychology and Counseling, Huntsville, AL 35811. Offers psychology and counseling (MS, Ed S), including clinical psychology (MS), counseling psychology (MS), guidance and counseling, rehabilitation counseling (MS), school counseling (MS), school psychology (MS), school psychometry (MS); social work (MSW). *Accreditation:* CORE; NCATE. *Program availability:* Part-time, evening/weekend. *Degree requirements:* For master's, comprehensive exam. *Entrance requirements:* For master's, GRE General Test. Additional exam requirements/recommendations for international students: Required—TOEFL (minimum score 500 paper-based; 61 iBT). *Application deadline:* For fall admission, 5/1 for domestic students. Application fee: $15 ($20 for international students). *Expenses:* Tuition, nonresident: part-time $826 per credit hour. Full-time tuition and fees vary according to course load and program. *Financial support:* Career-related internships or fieldwork available. Support available to part-time students. Financial award application deadline: 4/1. *Faculty research:* Increasing numbers of minorities in special education and speech-language pathology. *Unit head:* Dr. Shirley King, Chair, 256-372-5520, Fax: 256-372-5526.

Alabama State University, College of Liberal Arts and Social Sciences, Department of Social Work, Montgomery, AL 36101-0271. Offers MSW. *Faculty:* 5 full-time (4 women). *Students:* 26 full-time (23 women), 4 part-time (all women); all minorities (all Black or African American, non-Hispanic/Latino). Average age 28. 42 applicants, 62% accepted, 22 enrolled. *Entrance requirements:* For master's, bachelor's degree or its equivalent from accredited college or university with minimum GPA of 2.5. Additional exam requirements/recommendations for international students: Required—TOEFL (minimum score 500 paper-based). *Application deadline:* For fall admission, 4/15 priority date for domestic and international students; for spring admission, 11/15 priority date for domestic students, 9/15 priority date for international students; for summer admission, 3/15 priority date for domestic and international students. Application fee: $25. Electronic applications accepted. *Expenses:* Tuition, state resident: full-time $3087; part-time $2744 per credit. Tuition, nonresident: full-time $6174; part-time $5488 per credit. *Required fees:* $2284; $1142 per credit. $571 per semester. Tuition and fees vary according to class time, course level, course load, degree level, program and student level. *Financial support:* Fellowships, Federal Work-Study, and tuition waivers (full and partial) available. Support available to part-time students. Financial award applicants required to submit FAFSA. *Unit head:* Dr. Anthony Troy Adams, Dean, 334-229-5176, E-mail: atadams@alasu.edu. *Application contact:* Dr. William Person, Dean of Graduate Studies, 334-229-4274, Fax: 334-229-4928, E-mail: wperson@alasu.edu.

Albany State University, College of Arts and Humanities, Albany, GA 31705-2717. Offers criminal justice (MS); English education (M Ed); public administration (MPA), including community and economic development, criminal justice administration, health administration and policy, human resources management, public management, public policy, water resources management and policy; social work (MSW). *Program availability:* Part-time. *Degree requirements:* For master's, comprehensive exam, professional portfolio (for MPA), internship, capstone report. *Entrance requirements:* For master's, GRE, MAT, minimum GPA of 3.0, official transcript, pre-medical record/certificate of immunization, letters of reference. *Application deadline:* For fall admission, 6/1 for domestic students, 5/1 for international students; for spring admission, 11/1 for domestic students, 10/1 for international students. Applications are processed on a rolling basis. Application fee: $20. Electronic applications accepted. *Financial support:* Application deadline: 4/15; applicants required to submit FAFSA. *Faculty research:* HIV prevention for minority students. *Unit head:* Dr. Rani George, Dean, 229-430-1877, Fax: 229-430-4296. *Application contact:* Jeffrey Pierce, II, Graduate Admissions Counselor, 229-430-4646, Fax: 229-430-4105, E-mail: jeffrey.pierce@asurams.edu.
Website: https://www.asurams.edu/Academics/collegeofarthum/

American Jewish University, Graduate School of Nonprofit Management, Program in Jewish Communal Studies, Bel Air, CA 90077-1599. Offers MAJCS. *Degree requirements:* For master's, thesis. *Entrance requirements:* For master's, GMAT or GRE General Test, interview.

Andrews University, School of Graduate Studies, College of Arts and Sciences, Department of Social Work, Berrien Springs, MI 49104. Offers MSW. *Accreditation:* CSWE. *Faculty:* 7 full-time (6 women). *Students:* 26 full-time (18 women), 21 part-time (18 women); includes 34 minority (18 Black or African American, non-Hispanic/Latino; 6 Asian, non-Hispanic/Latino; 10 Hispanic/Latino), 4 international. Average age 33. In 2016, 14 master's awarded. *Entrance requirements:* For master's, GRE. Additional exam requirements/recommendations for international students: Required—TOEFL (minimum score 550 paper-based). *Application deadline:* Applications are processed on a rolling basis. Application fee: $40. *Unit head:* Dr. Curtis VanderWaal, Chair, 269-471-6196. *Application contact:* Justina Clayburn, Supervisor of Graduate Admission, 800-253-2874, Fax: 269-471-6321, E-mail: graduate@andrews.edu.

Anna Maria College, Graduate Division, Program in Social Work, Paxton, MA 01612. Offers MSW. *Program availability:* Part-time.

Appalachian State University, Cratis D. Williams Graduate School, Department of Social Work, Boone, NC 28608. Offers MSW. *Accreditation:* CSWE. *Program availability:* Part-time, evening/weekend, online learning. *Degree requirements:* For master's, comprehensive exam. *Entrance requirements:* For master's, GRE General Test, 3 letters of recommendation. Additional exam requirements/recommendations for international students: Required—TOEFL (minimum score 550 paper-based; 79 iBT), IELTS (minimum score 6.5). *Application deadline:* For fall admission, 3/1 for domestic students, 2/1 for international students; for spring admission, 7/1 for international students. Applications are processed on a rolling basis. Application fee: $55. Electronic applications accepted. *Expenses:* Tuition, state resident: full-time $4744. Tuition, nonresident: full-time $17,913. Full-time tuition and fees vary according to program. *Financial support:* Research assistantships, career-related internships or fieldwork, Federal Work-Study, scholarships/grants, and unspecified assistantships available. Financial award application deadline: 4/1; financial award applicants required to submit FAFSA. *Faculty research:* Community and organizational practice, individual and family. *Unit head:* Dr. Gail Leedy, Chairperson, 800-355-4084 Ext. 2299, E-mail: leedyg@appstate.edu. *Application contact:* Dr. Kelly Williams, Program Director, 828-262-7942, E-mail: williamska3@appstate.edu.
Website: http://www.socialwork.appstate.edu/

Arizona State University at the Tempe campus, College of Public Programs, School of Social Work, Phoenix, AZ 85004-0689. Offers advanced direct practice (MSW); assessment of integrative health modalities (Graduate Certificate); gerontology (Graduate Certificate); Latino cultural competency (Graduate Certificate); planning, administration and community practice (MSW); social work (PhD); trauma and bereavement (Graduate Certificate); MPA/MSW. *Accreditation:* CSWE (one or more programs are accredited). *Program availability:* Part-time. Terminal master's awarded for partial completion of doctoral program. *Degree requirements:* For master's, thesis or alternative, capstone project, interactive Program of Study (iPOS) submitted before completing 50 percent of required credit hours; for doctorate, comprehensive exam, thesis/dissertation, interactive Program of Study (iPOS) submitted before completing 50 percent of required credit hours. *Entrance requirements:* For master's, GRE or MAT, minimum GPA of 3.2 or equivalent in last 2 years of work leading to bachelor's degree; for doctorate, GRE, minimum GPA of 3.0 or equivalent in last 2 years of work leading to bachelor's degree, 3 letters of recommendation, resume, samples of professional writing, personal statement. Additional exam requirements/recommendations for international students: Required—TOEFL, IELTS, or PTE. Electronic applications accepted. *Expenses:* Contact institution.

Arkansas State University, Graduate School, College of Nursing and Health Professions, Department of Social Work, State University, AR 72467. Offers addiction studies (Graduate Certificate); social work (MSW). *Accreditation:* CSWE. *Program availability:* Part-time. *Degree requirements:* For master's and Graduate Certificate, comprehensive exam, thesis (for some programs). *Entrance requirements:* For master's and Graduate Certificate, GRE or MAT, appropriate bachelor's degree, letters of reference, personal statement, resume, official transcript, immunization records. Additional exam requirements/recommendations for international students: Required—TOEFL (minimum score 550 paper-based; 79 iBT), IELTS (minimum score 6), PTE (minimum score 56). Electronic applications accepted. *Expenses:* Contact institution.

Asbury University, School of Graduate and Professional Studies, Master of Social Work Program, Wilmore, KY 40390-1198. Offers child and family services (MSW). *Accreditation:* CSWE. *Degree requirements:* For master's, comprehensive exam, 954 praticum hours completed in agency. *Entrance requirements:* For master's, prerequisite courses in psychology, sociology, and statistics. Additional exam requirements/recommendations for international students: Required—TOEFL. Electronic applications accepted. *Expenses:* Contact institution. *Faculty research:* Integration of faith and practice, survivors of family violence, program evaluation, cross-cultural counseling.

Augsburg College, Program in Social Work, Minneapolis, MN 55454-1351. Offers MSW. *Accreditation:* CSWE. *Program availability:* Part-time, evening/weekend. *Degree requirements:* For master's, thesis optional. *Entrance requirements:* For master's, previous course work in human biology and statistics.

Aurora University, School of Social Work, Aurora, IL 60506-4892. Offers MSW, DSW. *Accreditation:* CSWE. *Program availability:* Part-time, evening/weekend. *Faculty:* 13 full-time (7 women), 56 part-time/adjunct (48 women). *Students:* 557 full-time (497 women), 242 part-time (207 women); includes 250 minority (105 Black or African American, non-Hispanic/Latino; 1 American Indian or Alaska Native, non-Hispanic/Latino; 16 Asian, non-Hispanic/Latino; 111 Hispanic/Latino; 17 Two or more races, non-Hispanic/Latino), 1 international. Average age 31. 356 applicants, 98% accepted, 205 enrolled. In 2016, 349 master's, 9 doctorates awarded. *Degree requirements:* For master's, thesis optional, field instruction; for doctorate, comprehensive exam, thesis/dissertation. *Entrance requirements:* For master's, minimum GPA of 3.0; for doctorate, GRE, MSW from CSWE-accredited school; minimum GPA of 3.0; at least 3 years of post-MSW social work experience; 3 letters of recommendation; writing sample in the area of clinical social work; personal interview. Additional exam requirements/recommendations for international students: Required—TOEFL (minimum score 550 paper-based; 79 iBT). *Application deadline:* For fall admission, 6/1 for international students; for spring admission, 10/1 for international students. Applications are processed on a rolling basis. Application fee: $0. Electronic applications accepted. *Expenses:* Contact institution. *Financial support:* In 2016–17, 524 students received support. Federal Work-Study, scholarships/grants, and unspecified assistantships available. Support available to part-time students. Financial award applicants required to submit FAFSA. *Unit head:* Dr. Fred McKenzie, Executive Director, 630-947-8930, E-mail: mckenzie@aurora.edu. *Application contact:* Debbie Enlow, Senior Recruiter/Advisor for Adult and Graduate Studies, 630-947-8904, E-mail: denlow@aurora.edu.
Website: http://aurora.edu/socialwork

Austin Peay State University, College of Graduate Studies, College of Behavioral and Health Sciences, Department of Social Work, Clarksville, TN 37044. Offers MSW. *Program availability:* Part-time, evening/weekend. *Faculty:* 4 full-time (1 woman), 1 (woman) part-time/adjunct. *Students:* 36 full-time (28 women), 13 part-time (12 women); includes 23 minority (16 Black or African American, non-Hispanic/Latino; 4 Hispanic/Latino; 3 Two or more races, non-Hispanic/Latino). Average age 31. 45 applicants, 71% accepted, 30 enrolled. In 2016, 22 master's awarded. *Degree requirements:* For master's, internship of 400-500 hours. *Entrance requirements:* For master's, GRE General Test, 3 letters of recommendation, minimum GPA of 2.75. Additional exam requirements/recommendations for international students: Required—TOEFL (minimum score 500 paper-based). *Application deadline:* For fall admission, 8/9 priority date for domestic students. Applications are processed on a rolling basis. Application fee: $45 ($50 for international students). Electronic applications accepted. *Expenses:* Tuition, state resident: full-time $8300; part-time $415 per credit hour. Tuition, nonresident: full-time $22,280; part-time $1114 per credit hour. *Required fees:* $1473; $73.65 per credit hour. *Financial support:* Research assistantships with full tuition reimbursements, career-related internships or fieldwork, Federal Work-Study, institutionally sponsored loans, scholarships/grants, and unspecified assistantships available. Support available to part-time students. Financial award application deadline: 4/1; financial award applicants required to submit FAFSA. *Unit head:* Michelle Blake, Interim Chair, 931-221-7227, Fax: 931-221-6440, E-mail: blakem@apsu.edu. *Application contact:* Brad Averitt, Coordinator of Graduate Admissions, 800-859-4723, Fax: 931-221-7641, E-mail: gradadmissions@apsu.edu.
Website: http://www.apsu.edu/socialwork/

Azusa Pacific University, School of Behavioral and Applied Sciences, Department of Social Work, Azusa, CA 91702-7000. Offers MSW. *Accreditation:* CSWE.

Barry University, School of Social Work, Doctoral Program in Social Work, Miami Shores, FL 33161-6695. Offers PhD. *Program availability:* Part-time, evening/weekend. *Degree requirements:* For doctorate, thesis/dissertation. *Entrance requirements:* For doctorate, GRE, MSW from an accredited school of social work, 2 years of professional experience. Electronic applications accepted. *Faculty research:* Family and children services, homelessness, gerontology, school social work.

Barry University, School of Social Work, Master's Program in Social Work, Miami Shores, FL 33161-6695. Offers MSW. *Accreditation:* CSWE. *Program availability:* Part-time, evening/weekend. *Degree requirements:* For master's, fieldwork. *Entrance requirements:* For master's, minimum GPA of 3.0, minimum of 30 liberal arts credits. Additional exam requirements/recommendations for international students: Required—TOEFL (minimum score 550 paper-based). Electronic applications accepted. *Faculty research:* Family and children services, homelessness, gerontology, school social work.

Baylor University, Diana R. Garland School of Social Work, Waco, TX 76798-7320. Offers MSW, PhD, M Div/MSW, MSW/MBA, MTS/MSW. *Accreditation:* CSWE. *Program availability:* Part-time, blended/hybrid learning. *Faculty:* 11 full-time (5 women), 13 part-time/adjunct (7 women). *Students:* 106 full-time (90 women), 18 part-time (15 women); includes 39 minority (19 Black or African American, non-Hispanic/Latino; 1 Asian, non-Hispanic/Latino; 16 Hispanic/Latino; 3 Two or more races, non-Hispanic/Latino), 3 international. Average age 27. 190 applicants, 72% accepted, 71 enrolled. In 2016, 64 master's awarded. *Degree requirements:* For master's, research project; for doctorate, comprehensive exam, thesis/dissertation. *Entrance requirements:* For master's, writing sample; for doctorate, GRE, writing sample. Additional exam requirements/recommendations for international students: Required—TOEFL (minimum score 550 paper-based; 80 iBT) or IELTS (minimum score 6.5). *Application deadline:* For spring admission, 3/15 for domestic and international students. Applications are processed on a rolling basis. Application fee: $45. Electronic applications accepted. *Expenses: Tuition:* Full-time $28,494; part-time $1583 per credit hour. *Required fees:* $167 per credit hour. Tuition and fees vary according to course load and program. *Financial support:* In 2016–17, 138 students received support, including 12 research assistantships with tuition reimbursements available (averaging $6,800 per year); career-related internships or fieldwork, Federal Work-Study, institutionally sponsored loans, scholarships/grants, traineeships, tuition waivers (full and partial), and unspecified assistantships also available. Support available to part-time students. Financial award application deadline: 6/1; financial award applicants required to submit FAFSA. *Faculty research:* Healthy marriage, family literacy, Alzheimer's and grief, spirituality, congregational community service, clergy sexual abuse, older volunteers, military family support. *Total annual research expenditures:* $533,412. *Unit head:* Dr. David Pooler, Associate Dean for Academic Affairs, 254-710-3884, Fax: 254-710-7412, E-mail: david_pooler@baylor.edu. *Application contact:* Dr. Crystal Diaz-Espinoza, Director of Recruitment and Career Services, 254-710-4479, Fax: 254-710-6455, E-mail: crystal_diaz-espinoza@baylor.edu.
Website: http://www.baylor.edu/social_work/?_buref-661-48570

Binghamton University, State University of New York, Graduate School, College of Community and Public Affairs, Department of Social Work, Binghamton, NY 13902-6000. Offers MSW. *Accreditation:* CSWE. *Program availability:* Part-time. *Faculty:* 13 full-time (10 women), 5 part-time/adjunct (all women). *Students:* 104 full-time (86 women), 62 part-time (57 women); includes 37 minority (12 Black or African American, non-Hispanic/Latino; 3 Asian, non-Hispanic/Latino; 16 Hispanic/Latino; 1 Native Hawaiian or other Pacific Islander, non-Hispanic/Latino; 5 Two or more races, non-Hispanic/Latino). Average age 30. 148 applicants, 66% accepted, 70 enrolled. In 2016, 47 master's awarded. *Degree requirements:* For master's, thesis. *Entrance requirements:* Additional exam requirements/recommendations for international students: Required—TOEFL (minimum score 550 paper-based; 80 iBT). *Application deadline:* For fall admission, 2/1 priority date for domestic and international students. Application fee: $75. Electronic applications accepted. *Expenses:* Contact institution. *Financial support:* In 2016–17, 32 students received support. Fellowships, career-related internships or fieldwork, Federal Work-Study, institutionally sponsored loans, scholarships/grants, health care benefits, and unspecified assistantships available. Financial award applicants required to submit FAFSA. *Unit head:* Dr. Victoria M. Rizzo, Chairperson, 607-777-9179, Fax: 607-777-5683, E-mail: vrizzo@binghamton.edu. *Application contact:* Ben Balkaya, Assistant Dean and Director, 607-777-2151, Fax: 607-777-2501, E-mail: balkaya@binghamton.edu.

Boise State University, College of Health Sciences, School of Social Work, Boise, ID 83725. Offers MSW. *Accreditation:* CSWE. *Program availability:* Part-time, 100% online. *Faculty:* 33. *Students:* 177 full-time (146 women), 23 part-time (22 women); includes 13 minority (2 Black or African American, non-Hispanic/Latino; 10 Hispanic/Latino; 1 Two or more races, non-Hispanic/Latino). Average age 34. 139 applicants, 46% accepted, 47 enrolled. In 2016, 104 master's awarded. *Entrance requirements:* For master's, GRE General Test, minimum GPA of 3.0. Additional exam requirements/recommendations for international students: Required—TOEFL (minimum score 550 paper-based; 80 iBT), IELTS (minimum score 6). *Application deadline:* For fall admission, 1/10 for domestic and international students. Application fee: $65 ($95 for international students). Electronic applications accepted. *Expenses:* Tuition, state resident: full-time $6058; part-time $358 per credit hour. Tuition, nonresident: full-time $20,108; part-time $608 per credit hour. *Required fees:* $2108. Tuition and fees vary according to program. *Financial support:* In 2016–17, 37 students received support, including 2 research assistantships (averaging $4,083 per year); scholarships/grants and unspecified assistantships also available. Financial award applicants required to submit FAFSA. *Unit head:* Dr. Randy Magen, Director, 208-426-1789, E-mail: randymagen@boisestate.edu. *Application contact:* Dr. Cynthia Sanders, Program Coordinator, 208-426-1780, E-mail: cynthiasanders@boisestate.edu.
Website: http://hs.boisestate.edu/socialwork/graduate/

Boston College, School of Social Work, Chestnut Hill, MA 02467-3800. Offers MSW, PhD, JD/MSW, MSW/MA, MSW/MBA. *Accreditation:* CSWE (one or more programs are accredited). *Program availability:* Part-time. *Degree requirements:* For master's, 2 internships; for doctorate, comprehensive exam, thesis/dissertation. *Entrance requirements:* For doctorate, GRE, master's degree. Additional exam requirements/recommendations for international students: Required—TOEFL (minimum score 550 paper-based; 80 iBT). Electronic applications accepted. *Expenses:* Contact institution. *Faculty research:* Well-being of children and families, health and mental health issues, aging and work, consumer-directed services, international social work practice.

Boston University, School of Social Work, Boston, MA 02118. Offers MSW, PhD, D Min/MSW, M Div/MSW, MSW/Ed D, MSW/Ed M, MSW/MPH, MSW/MTS. *Accreditation:* CSWE (one or more programs are accredited). *Program availability:* Part-time, evening/weekend, 100% online. *Faculty:* 28 full-time (18 women), 39 part-time/adjunct (28 women). *Students:* 244 full-time (221 women), 655 part-time (587 women); includes 234 minority (78 Black or African American, non-Hispanic/Latino; 4 American Indian or Alaska Native, non-Hispanic/Latino; 24 Asian, non-Hispanic/Latino; 103 Hispanic/Latino; 3 Native Hawaiian or other Pacific Islander, non-Hispanic/Latino; 22 Two or more races, non-Hispanic/Latino), 8 international. Average age 31. 937 applicants, 64% accepted, 179 enrolled. In 2016, 241 master's, 5 doctorates awarded. *Degree requirements:* For doctorate, one foreign language, thesis/dissertation, critical essay. *Entrance requirements:* For master's, GRE General Test or MAT (if GPA below 3.0), minimum GPA of 3.0; for doctorate, GRE General Test or MAT, writing sample. Additional exam requirements/recommendations for international students: Required—TOEFL (minimum score 577 paper-based; 100 iBT), IELTS (minimum score 7). *Application deadline:* For fall admission, 1/13 priority date for domestic students, 1/13 for international students. Application fee: $95. Electronic applications accepted. *Expenses:* $34,036. *Financial support:* In 2016–17, 158 students received support. Career-related internships or fieldwork, Federal Work-Study, institutionally sponsored loans, and scholarships/grants available. Support available to part-time students. Financial award application deadline: 3/1; financial award applicants required to submit FAFSA. *Faculty research:* Aging, children and families, substance abuse and HIV, trauma and mental health, public health social work. *Total annual research expenditures:* $4.6 million. *Unit head:* Gail Steketee, Dean, 617-353-3760, Fax: 617-353-5612. *Application contact:* Julie Billings, Admissions and Financial Aid Coordinator, 617-353-3750, Fax: 617-353-5612, E-mail: busswad@bu.edu.
Website: http://www.bu.edu/ssw/

Brescia University, Program in Social Work, Owensboro, KY 42301-3023. Offers MSW. *Program availability:* Online learning. *Entrance requirements:* For master's, bachelor's degree, minimum GPA of 3.0 for last 60 hours earned, personal statement. Electronic applications accepted.

Bridgewater State University, College of Graduate Studies, College of Humanities and Social Sciences, School of Social Work, Bridgewater, MA 02325. Offers MSW. *Accreditation:* CSWE.

Brigham Young University, Graduate Studies, College of Family, Home, and Social Sciences, School of Social Work, Provo, UT 84602. Offers social work (MSW), including clinical practice, research. *Accreditation:* CSWE. *Faculty:* 9 full-time (4 women), 5 part-time/adjunct (3 women). *Students:* 81 full-time (59 women); includes 12 minority (2 Black or African American, non-Hispanic/Latino; 1 American Indian or Alaska Native, non-Hispanic/Latino; 1 Asian, non-Hispanic/Latino; 5 Hispanic/Latino; 1 Native Hawaiian or other Pacific Islander, non-Hispanic/Latino; 2 Two or more races, non-Hispanic/Latino). Average age 26. 127 applicants, 36% accepted, 40 enrolled. In 2016, 36 master's awarded. *Degree requirements:* For master's, thesis optional. *Entrance requirements:* Additional exam requirements/recommendations for international students: Required—TOEFL (minimum score 580 paper-based; 85 iBT), IELTS (minimum score 7). *Application deadline:* For fall admission, 1/15 for domestic and international students. Application fee: $50. Electronic applications accepted. *Expenses:* Contact institution. *Financial support:* In 2016–17, 68 students received support, including 68 fellowships with tuition reimbursements available (averaging $1,866 per year), 18 research assistantships (averaging $2,240 per year), 5 teaching assistantships (averaging $2,400 per year); career-related internships or fieldwork, scholarships/grants, and tuition waivers (partial) also available. Financial award application deadline: 1/15. *Faculty research:* Poverty, adoptions, depression, spirituality, child welfare, marriage and family, American Indian child welfare, health care, mental health, mood disorders, substance abuse, women and gender, step families, refugees. *Total annual research expenditures:* $100,000. *Unit head:* Dr. Gordon E. Limb, Director, 801-422-3282, Fax: 801-422-0624, E-mail: socialwork@byu.edu. *Application contact:* Nanci Shumpert, Program Manager, 801-422-5681, Fax: 801-422-0624, E-mail: msw@byu.edu.
Website: https://socialwork.byu.edu/Pages/Home.aspx

Bryn Mawr College, Graduate School of Social Work and Social Research, Bryn Mawr, PA 19010. Offers MSS, PhD. *Accreditation:* CSWE (one or more programs are accredited). *Program availability:* Part-time, evening/weekend. *Faculty:* 8 full-time (5 women), 11 part-time/adjunct (6 women). *Students:* 137 full-time (118 women), 32 part-time (28 women); includes 36 minority (20 Black or African American, non-Hispanic/Latino; 6 Asian, non-Hispanic/Latino; 6 Hispanic/Latino; 4 Two or more races, non-Hispanic/Latino), 1 international. Average age 33. 164 applicants, 79% accepted, 90 enrolled. In 2016, 81 master's, 5 doctorates awarded. *Degree requirements:* For master's, fieldwork; for doctorate, comprehensive exam, thesis/dissertation. *Entrance requirements:* For master's, bachelor's degree, personal statement, 3 letters of recommendation, official transcripts, interview; for doctorate, GRE General Test (minimum scores 500 on the verbal and quantitative sections and 5.0 on analytic writing test), master's degree; minimum undergraduate GPA of 3.0, graduate 3.5; 2 years of post-MSW work experience (recommended); personal statement; 3 letters of recommendation (2 from academic references); official transcripts. *Application deadline:* For fall admission, 4/15 for domestic and international students. Applications are processed on a rolling basis. Application fee: $50. Electronic applications accepted. *Expenses:* Contact institution. *Financial support:* In 2016–17, 147 students received support. Fellowships, research assistantships, teaching assistantships, career-related internships or fieldwork, Federal Work-Study, institutionally sponsored loans, scholarships/grants, tuition waivers, and dissertation awards (for PhD) available. Support available to part-time students. Financial award application deadline: 4/15; financial award applicants required to submit FAFSA. *Unit head:* Dr. Darlyne Bailey, Dean, 610-520-2610, Fax: 610-520-2613, E-mail: dbailey01@brynmawr.edu. *Application contact:* Sheila Gillin, Director of Graduate Admissions, 610-520-7533, E-mail: sgillin@brynmawr.edu.
Website: http://www.brynmawr.edu/socialwork

California Baptist University, Program in Social Work, Riverside, CA 92504-3206. Offers clinical social work (MSW); community social work practice (MSW). *Program availability:* Part-time. *Faculty:* 3 full-time (2 women). *Entrance requirements:* For master's, bachelor's degree, minimum GPA of 2.75, official transcripts, three recommendations, statistics, essay, interview. Additional exam requirements/recommendations for international students: Required—TOEFL (minimum score 80 iBT). *Application deadline:* For fall admission, 8/1 priority date for domestic students, 7/1 for international students; for spring admission, 12/1 priority date for domestic students, 11/1 for international students. Applications are processed on a rolling basis. Application fee: $45. Electronic applications accepted. *Expenses:* Contact institution. *Financial support:* Federal Work-Study and scholarships/grants available. *Faculty research:* Urban/marginalized communities, healthy marriages and families, community organization/engagement, health disparities, global social work. *Unit head:* Dr. Satara Armstrong, Director, Social Work Program, 951-552-8442, E-mail: sarmstrong@calbaptist.edu. *Application contact:* Taylor Neece, Director of Graduate Admissions, 951-343-4871, Fax: 877-228-8877, E-mail: graduateadmissions@calbaptist.edu.

California State University, Bakersfield, Division of Graduate Studies, School of Social Sciences and Education, Program in Social Work, Bakersfield, CA 93311. Offers MSW. *Accreditation:* CSWE. *Students:* 123 full-time (106 women), 37 part-time (29 women); includes 118 minority (17 Black or African American, non-Hispanic/Latino; 2 American Indian or Alaska Native, non-Hispanic/Latino; 11 Asian, non-Hispanic/Latino; 80 Hispanic/Latino; 8 Two or more races, non-Hispanic/Latino), 5 international. Average age 32. 167 applicants, 65% accepted, 79 enrolled. In 2016, 66 master's awarded. *Application deadline:* For fall admission, 2/1 for domestic students. Applications are processed on a rolling basis. Application fee: $55. *Expenses:* Tuition, state resident: full-time $2246; part-time $1302 per semester. *Financial support:* In 2016–17, fellowships (averaging $1,850 per year) were awarded; Federal Work-Study, scholarships/grants, and tuition waivers (full and partial) also available. Financial award application deadline: 3/2; financial award applicants required to submit FAFSA. *Unit head:* Dr. Jong Choi, Graduate Coordinator, 661-654-2308, Fax: 661-665-6928, E-mail: jchoi6@csub.edu. *Application contact:* Debbie Blowers, Assistant Director of

Admissions and Evaluations, 661-664-3381, E-mail: dblowers@csub.edu.
Website: https://www.csub.edu/socialwork/index.html

California State University, Chico, Office of Graduate Studies, College of Behavioral and Social Sciences, School of Social Work, Chico, CA 95929-0722. Offers MSW. *Accreditation:* CSWE. *Program availability:* Evening/weekend. *Faculty:* 9 full-time (7 women), 16 part-time/adjunct (12 women). *Students:* 98 full-time (83 women), 5 part-time (3 women); includes 42 minority (5 Black or African American, non-Hispanic/Latino; 9 Asian, non-Hispanic/Latino; 25 Hispanic/Latino; 3 Two or more races, non-Hispanic/Latino). 113 applicants, 31% accepted, 23 enrolled. In 2016, 44 master's awarded. *Degree requirements:* For master's, thesis, project, or comprehensive exam. *Entrance requirements:* For master's, 3 letters of recommendation on departmental form, statement of purpose, prerequisites/liberal arts worksheet. Additional exam requirements/recommendations for international students: Required—TOEFL (minimum score 550 paper-based; 80 iBT), IELTS (minimum score 6.5), PTE (minimum score 59). *Application deadline:* For fall admission, 3/1 for domestic and international students. Application fee: $55. Electronic applications accepted. *Financial support:* Application deadline: 3/1; applicants required to submit FAFSA. *Unit head:* J. David Bassett, Director, 530-898-6204, Fax: 530-898-5574, E-mail: jbassett2@csuchico.edu. *Application contact:* Judy L. Rice, Graduate Admissions Coordinator, 530-898-6880, Fax: 530-898-6889, E-mail: jlmorris@csuchico.edu.
Website: http://www.csuchico.edu/swrk/

California State University, Dominguez Hills, College of Health, Human Services and Nursing, Program in Social Work, Carson, CA 90747-0001. Offers MSW. *Accreditation:* CSWE. *Program availability:* Part-time, evening/weekend. *Degree requirements:* For master's, thesis. *Entrance requirements:* For master's, minimum GPA of 2.75 in last 60 units; 3 courses in behavioral science, 2 in humanities, 1 each in English composition, elementary statistics, and human biology. *Faculty research:* HIV/AIDS, community capacity, program evaluation.

California State University, East Bay, Office of Graduate Studies, College of Letters, Arts, and Social Sciences, Department of Social Work, Hayward, CA 94542-3000. Offers children, youth, and family services (MSW); community mental health services (MSW). *Accreditation:* CSWE. *Students:* 129 full-time (106 women), 2 part-time (both women); includes 102 minority (33 Black or African American, non-Hispanic/Latino; 1 American Indian or Alaska Native, non-Hispanic/Latino; 20 Asian, non-Hispanic/Latino; 43 Hispanic/Latino; 5 Two or more races, non-Hispanic/Latino), 1 international. Average age 31. 394 applicants, 21% accepted, 68 enrolled. In 2016, 125 master's awarded. *Degree requirements:* For master's, comprehensive exam. *Entrance requirements:* For master's, minimum GPA of 2.8; courses in statistics and either human biology, physiology, or anatomy; liberal arts or social science baccalaureate degree; 3 letters of recommendation; personal statement; criminal background check; student professional liability insurance. Additional exam requirements/recommendations for international students: Required—TOEFL (minimum score 550 paper-based). *Application deadline:* For fall admission, 3/15 for domestic and international students. Applications are processed on a rolling basis. Application fee: $55. Electronic applications accepted. *Financial support:* Fellowships, career-related internships or fieldwork, Federal Work-Study, institutionally sponsored loans, and scholarships/grants available. Support available to part-time students. Financial award application deadline: 3/2; financial award applicants required to submit FAFSA. *Unit head:* Dr. Holly Vugia, Interim Chair, 510-885-2121, E-mail: holly.vugia@csueastbay.edu. *Application contact:* Dr. Donna Wiley, Interim Associate Vice President for Academic Programs and Graduate Studies, 510-885-3716, Fax: 510-885-4777, E-mail: donna.wiley@csueastbay.edu.
Website: http://www20.csueastbay.edu/class/departments/socialwork/

California State University, Fresno, Division of Research and Graduate Studies, College of Health and Human Services, Department of Social Work Education, Fresno, CA 93740-8027. Offers MSW. *Accreditation:* CSWE. *Program availability:* Part-time, evening/weekend. *Degree requirements:* For master's, thesis or alternative. *Entrance requirements:* For master's, GRE General Test, minimum GPA of 2.5. Additional exam requirements/recommendations for international students: Required—TOEFL. *Application deadline:* For fall admission, 5/1 for domestic and international students; for spring admission, 10/1 for domestic and international students. Applications are processed on a rolling basis. Application fee: $55. Electronic applications accepted. *Financial support:* Teaching assistantships, career-related internships or fieldwork, Federal Work-Study, and scholarships/grants available. Support available to part-time students. Financial award application deadline: 3/1; financial award applicants required to submit FAFSA. *Faculty research:* Children at risk, international cooperation, child welfare training, nutrition. *Unit head:* Dr. Martha Vungkhanching, Chair, 559-278-8741, Fax: 559-278-7191, E-mail: marthavu@csufresno.edu. *Application contact:* Dr. Debra Harris, Program Coordinator, 559-278-2966, Fax: 559-278-7191, E-mail: dharris@csufresno.edu.
Website: http://www.fresnostate.edu/chhs/social-work/

California State University, Fullerton, Graduate Studies, College of Health and Human Development, Department of Social Work, Fullerton, CA 92834-9480. Offers aging (MSW); child welfare (MSW); community mental health (MSW). *Accreditation:* CSWE. *Program availability:* Part-time. *Entrance requirements:* For master's, minimum GPA of 3.0 for last 60 semester or 90 quarter units. Application fee: $55. *Expenses:* Tuition, state resident: full-time $3369; part-time $1953 per unit. Tuition, nonresident: full-time $3915; part-time $2499 per unit. Tuition and fees vary according to course load, degree level and program. *Financial support:* Career-related internships or fieldwork, Federal Work-Study, institutionally sponsored loans, and scholarships/grants available. Support available to part-time students. Financial award application deadline: 3/1; financial award applicants required to submit FAFSA. *Unit head:* Dr. David Chenot, Chair, 657-278-8452, E-mail: dchenot@fullerton.edu. *Application contact:* Admissions/Applications, 657-278-2371.
Website: http://hhd.fullerton.edu/msw

California State University, Long Beach, Graduate Studies, College of Health and Human Services, School of Social Work, Long Beach, CA 90840. Offers MSW. *Accreditation:* CSWE. *Program availability:* Part-time, evening/weekend, online learning. *Degree requirements:* For master's, thesis. *Application deadline:* For fall admission, 3/1 for domestic students. Applications are processed on a rolling basis. Application fee: $55. Electronic applications accepted. *Financial support:* Federal Work-Study, institutionally sponsored loans, and scholarships/grants available. Financial award application deadline: 3/2. *Unit head:* Nancy Meyer-Adams, Director.
Website: http://web.csulb.edu/colleges/chhs/departments/social-work/

California State University, Los Angeles, Graduate Studies, College of Health and Human Services, School of Social Work, Los Angeles, CA 90032-8530. Offers MSW. *Accreditation:* CSWE. *Entrance requirements:* Additional exam requirements/recommendations for international students: Required—TOEFL (minimum score 500 paper-based).

California State University, Monterey Bay, College of Health Sciences and Human Services, Seaside, CA 93955-8001. Offers social work (MSW). *Accreditation:* CSWE. *Program availability:* Part-time. *Degree requirements:* For master's, internship. *Entrance requirements:* For master's, GRE, curriculum vitae, recommendations. Additional exam requirements/recommendations for international students: Required—TOEFL (minimum score 525 paper-based; 71 iBT). Electronic applications accepted. *Faculty research:* Social policy, health policy, politics and government.

California State University, Northridge, Graduate Studies, College of Social and Behavioral Sciences, Department of Social Work, Northridge, CA 91330. Offers MSW. *Accreditation:* CSWE. *Program availability:* Part-time. *Faculty:* 10 full-time (4 women), 17 part-time/adjunct (10 women). *Students:* 220 full-time (186 women), 35 part-time (32 women); includes 179 minority (24 Black or African American, non-Hispanic/Latino; 1 American Indian or Alaska Native, non-Hispanic/Latino; 8 Asian, non-Hispanic/Latino; 136 Hispanic/Latino; 10 Two or more races, non-Hispanic/Latino), 6 international. Average age 30. 563 applicants, 30% accepted, 112 enrolled. *Entrance requirements:* For master's, GRE (if cumulative undergraduate GPA less than 3.0). *Application deadline:* For fall admission, 1/15 for domestic students. *Expenses:* Tuition, state resident: full-time $4152. *Unit head:* Dr. Amy Levin, Chair, 818-677-7630.
Website: http://www.csun.edu/csbs/departments/social_work/index.html

★ **California State University, Northridge,** Graduate Studies, The Tseng College of Extended Learning, Northridge, CA 91330. Offers business administration (Graduate Certificate); health administration (MPA); health education (MPH); knowledge management (MKM); music industry administration (MA); nonprofit-sector management (Graduate Certificate); public administration (MPA); public sector management and leadership (MPA); social work (MSW); taxation (MS); tourism, hospitality and recreation management (MS). *Faculty:* 55 part-time/adjunct (28 women). *Students:* 1 (woman) full-time, 1 (woman) part-time. Average age 40. *Entrance requirements:* For master's, GRE (if cumulative undergraduate GPA less than 3.0). *Expenses:* Tuition, state resident: full-time $4152. *Unit head:* Joyce Feucht-Haviar, Dean, 866-873-6439.

See Display on next page and Close-Up on page 1687.

California State University, Sacramento, Office of Graduate Studies, College of Health and Human Services, Division of Social Work, Sacramento, CA 95819. Offers family and children's services (MSW). *Accreditation:* CSWE. *Students:* 239 full-time (213 women), 18 part-time (14 women); includes 134 minority (25 Black or African American, non-Hispanic/Latino; 4 American Indian or Alaska Native, non-Hispanic/Latino; 30 Asian, non-Hispanic/Latino; 73 Hispanic/Latino; 2 Native Hawaiian or other Pacific Islander, non-Hispanic/Latino). Average age 31. 305 applicants, 47% accepted, 117 enrolled. In 2016, 129 master's awarded. *Degree requirements:* For master's, thesis, research project, or comprehensive exam; writing proficiency exam. *Entrance requirements:* For master's, GRE, minimum GPA of 2.8 during previous 2 years of course work. Additional exam requirements/recommendations for international students: Required—TOEFL (minimum score 550 paper-based; 80 iBT). *Application deadline:* For fall admission, 1/18 for domestic students, 3/1 for international students; for spring admission, 9/30 for international students. Applications are processed on a rolling basis. Application fee: $55. Electronic applications accepted. *Expenses:* $4,302 full-time tuition and fees per semester, $2,796 part-time. *Financial support:* Career-related internships or fieldwork and Federal Work-Study available. Support available to part-time students. Financial award application deadline: 3/1; financial award applicants required to submit FAFSA. *Unit head:* Dr. Dale Russell, Chair, 916-278-6943, E-mail: drussell@csus.edu. *Application contact:* Jose Martinez, Graduate Admissions Supervisor, 916-278-7871, E-mail: martinj@skymail.csus.edu.
Website: http://www.csus.edu/hhs/sw

California State University, San Bernardino, Graduate Studies, College of Social and Behavioral Sciences, Program in Social Work, San Bernardino, CA 92407. Offers MSW. *Accreditation:* CSWE. *Program availability:* Part-time, evening/weekend. *Faculty:* 7 full-time (6 women), 15 part-time/adjunct (12 women). *Students:* 164 full-time (137 women), 28 part-time (24 women); includes 132 minority (19 Black or African American, non-Hispanic/Latino; 2 American Indian or Alaska Native, non-Hispanic/Latino; 6 Asian, non-Hispanic/Latino; 102 Hispanic/Latino; 3 Two or more races, non-Hispanic/Latino), 2 international. 284 applicants, 43% accepted, 85 enrolled. In 2016, 86 master's awarded. *Entrance requirements:* Additional exam requirements/recommendations for international students: Required—TOEFL. *Application deadline:* For fall admission, 7/16 for domestic students. Application fee: $55. *Expenses:* Tuition, state resident: full-time $7843; part-time $5011.20 per year. Tuition and fees vary according to course load, degree level, program and reciprocity agreements. *Financial support:* Institutionally sponsored loans available. Financial award application deadline: 5/1. *Faculty research:* Addiction, computers in social work practice, minority issues, gerontology. *Unit head:* Laurie Smith, Director/Associate Professor/Graduate Coordinator, 909-537-3837, Fax: 909-537-7029, E-mail: lasmith@csusb.edu. *Application contact:* Dr. Francisca Beer, Dean of Graduate Studies, 909-537-5058, E-mail: fbeer@csusb.edu.

California State University, San Marcos, College of Education, Health and Human Services, Department of Social Work, San Marcos, CA 92096-0001. Offers behavioral health (MSW); children, youth and families (MSW). *Accreditation:* CSWE. *Degree requirements:* For master's, thesis, capstone project. *Expenses:* Contact institution.

California State University, Stanislaus, College of Human and Health Sciences, Program in Social Work (MSW), Turlock, CA 95382. Offers MSW. *Accreditation:* CSWE. *Degree requirements:* For master's, thesis. *Entrance requirements:* For master's, minimum GPA of 3.0, 3 letters of reference, personal statement. Electronic applications accepted. *Faculty research:* Mental health supervision, health issues on adulthood and aging, geriatric social work, effects of violence on children, rural mental health.

California University of Pennsylvania, School of Graduate Studies and Research, College of Education and Human Services, Department of Social Work, California, PA 15419-1394. Offers MSW. *Accreditation:* CSWE. *Program availability:* Part-time. *Degree requirements:* For master's, comprehensive exam. *Entrance requirements:* For master's, GRE, letters of reference. Additional exam requirements/recommendations for international students: Required—TOEFL. Electronic applications accepted. *Expenses:* Tuition, state resident: full-time $11,592; part-time $483 per credit. Tuition, nonresident: full-time $17,400; part-time $725 per credit. *Required fees:* $3916. Tuition and fees vary according to course load, degree level, campus/location and reciprocity agreements. *Faculty research:* Social welfare and policy, housing and community development, health and mental health, Black Appalachian, aging.

Campbellsville University, Carver School of Social Work, Campbellsville, KY 42718-2799. Offers MA. *Accreditation:* CSWE. *Program availability:* Part-time, evening/weekend, 100% online, blended/hybrid learning. *Faculty:* 11 full-time (9 women), 7 part-time/adjunct (all women). *Students:* 107 full-time (101 women), 63 part-time (55 women); includes 20 minority (15 Black or African American, non-Hispanic/Latino; 1 American Indian or Alaska Native, non-Hispanic/Latino; 2 Asian, non-Hispanic/Latino; 2 Hispanic/Latino), 3 international. Average age 33. 254 applicants, 71% accepted, 121 enrolled. In 2016, 47 master's awarded. *Degree requirements:* For master's, variable foreign language requirement, comprehensive exam, thesis (for some programs). *Entrance requirements:* For master's, GRE, college transcripts, 3 letters of recommendation. Additional exam requirements/recommendations for international students: Recommended—TOEFL (minimum score 550 paper-based; 79 iBT), IELTS (minimum score 6). *Application deadline:* Applications are processed on a rolling basis. Application fee: $25. Electronic applications accepted. Application fee is waived when

completed online. *Expenses:* $525 per credit hour. *Financial support:* Applicants required to submit FAFSA. *Unit head:* Dr. Helen K. Mudd, Program Director, 270-789-5045, Fax: 270-789-5542, E-mail: hkmudd@campbellsville.edu. *Application contact:* Monica Bamwine, Assistant Director of Graduate Admissions, 270-789-5221, Fax: 270-789-5071, E-mail: mkbamwine@campbellsville.edu.
Website: http://www.campbellsville.edu/carver-school

Capella University, Harold Abel School of Social and Behavioral Science, Doctoral Programs in Counseling, Minneapolis, MN 55402. Offers general counselor education and supervision (PhD); general social work (DSW). *Accreditation:* ACA.

Carleton University, Faculty of Graduate Studies, Faculty of Public Affairs and Management, School of Social Work, Ottawa, ON K1S 5B6, Canada. Offers MSW. *Program availability:* Part-time. *Degree requirements:* For master's, thesis optional. *Entrance requirements:* For master's, basic research methods course. Additional exam requirements/recommendations for international students: Required—TOEFL. *Faculty research:* Social administration, program evaluation, history of Canadian social welfare, women's issues, education in social work.

Case Western Reserve University, Jack, Joseph and Morton Mandel School of Applied Social Sciences, Cleveland, OH 44106. Offers nonprofit management (MNO); social welfare (PhD); social work (MSSA); JD/MSSA; MSSA/MA; MSSA/MBA; MSSA/MNO. *Accreditation:* CSWE (one or more programs are accredited). *Program availability:* Evening/weekend, online learning. *Degree requirements:* For master's, fieldwork; for doctorate, thesis/dissertation. *Entrance requirements:* For master's, GRE General Test, MAT, or minimum GPA of 2.7; for doctorate, GRE General Test. Additional exam requirements/recommendations for international students: Required—TOEFL (minimum score 557 paper-based, 90 iBT) or IELTS (minimum score 7). Electronic applications accepted. *Expenses:* Contact institution. *Faculty research:* Urban poverty, community social development, substance abuse, health, child welfare, aging, mental health.

The Catholic University of America, National Catholic School of Social Service, Washington, DC 20064. Offers clinical (MSW), including clinical health care, clinical military, veterans, and families; combined (clinical and social change) (MSW), including clinical and macro practice; social change (MSW); social work (PhD); MSW/JD. MSW/JD offered with Columbus School of Law. *Accreditation:* CSWE (one or more programs are accredited). *Program availability:* Part-time, 100% online. *Faculty:* 16 full-time (13 women), 21 part-time/adjunct (15 women). *Students:* 121 full-time (98 women), 408 part-time (360 women); includes 238 minority (142 Black or African American, non-Hispanic/Latino; 12 Asian, non-Hispanic/Latino; 50 Hispanic/Latino; 34 Two or more races, non-Hispanic/Latino), 7 international. Average age 35. 414 applicants, 64% accepted, 157 enrolled. In 2016, 84 master's, 5 doctorates awarded. *Degree requirements:* For master's, thesis; for doctorate, comprehensive exam, thesis/dissertation, minimum GPA of 3.0. *Entrance requirements:* For master's, GRE or MAT (if undergraduate GPA less than 3.0), statement of purpose, official copies of academic transcripts, three letters of recommendation, resume; for doctorate, GRE General Test, statement of purpose, official copies of academic transcripts, three letters of recommendation, resume, writing sample. Additional exam requirements/recommendations for international students: Required—TOEFL (minimum score 600 paper-based; 92 iBT). *Application deadline:* For fall admission, 7/15 priority date for domestic students, 7/1 for international students; for spring admission, 11/15 priority date for domestic students, 11/1 for international students. Applications are processed on a rolling basis. Application fee: $60. Electronic applications accepted. *Expenses:* $27,720 per year; $1,065 per credit; $905 per credit (for online program); $200 per semester part-time fees. *Financial support:* Fellowships, research assistantships, teaching assistantships, Federal Work-Study, scholarships/grants, tuition waivers (full and partial), and unspecified assistantships available. Financial award application deadline: 3/15; financial award applicants required to submit FAFSA. *Faculty research:* International social development; advancement of children, youth, and families; global aging; community development and social justice; promotion of health and mental health well-being. *Total annual research expenditures:* $324,851. *Unit head:* Dr. Will Rainford, Dean, 202-319-5454, Fax: 202-319-5093, E-mail: rainford@cua.edu. *Application contact:* Director of Graduate Admissions, 202-319-5057, Fax: 202-319-6533, E-mail: cua-admissions@cua.edu.
Website: http://ncsss.cua.edu

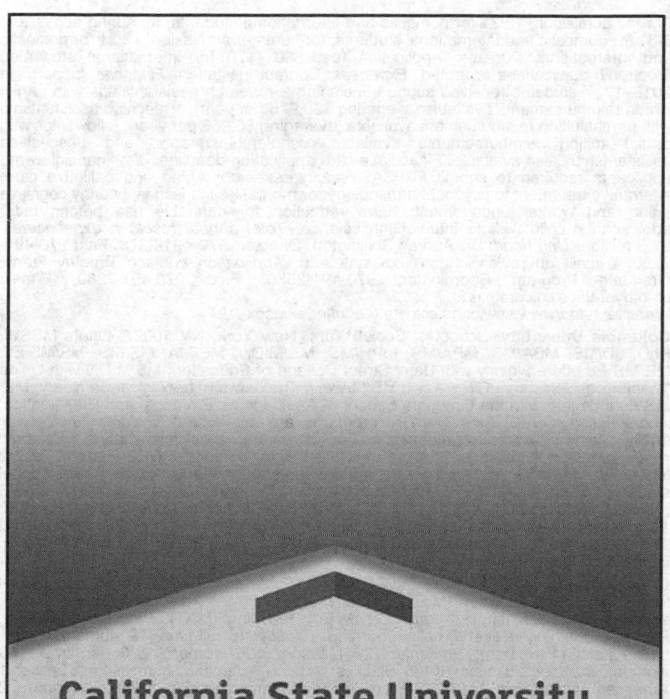

Chicago State University, School of Graduate and Professional Studies, College of Arts and Sciences, Program in Social Work, Chicago, IL 60628. Offers MSW. *Accreditation:* CSWE. Electronic applications accepted.

Clark Atlanta University, School of Social Work, Atlanta, GA 30314. Offers MSW, PhD. *Accreditation:* CSWE (one or more programs are accredited). *Program availability:* Part-time. *Faculty:* 15 full-time (9 women), 4 part-time/adjunct (2 women). *Students:* 238 full-time (201 women), 28 part-time (24 women); includes 209 minority (208 Black or African American, non-Hispanic/Latino; 1 Hispanic/Latino), 12 international. Average age 31. 184 applicants, 74% accepted, 93 enrolled. In 2016, 148 master's, 5 doctorates awarded. Terminal master's awarded for partial completion of doctoral program. *Degree requirements:* For master's, one foreign language; for doctorate, one foreign language, comprehensive exam, thesis/dissertation. *Entrance requirements:* For master's, GRE General Test, minimum undergraduate GPA of 3.0; for doctorate, GRE General Test. Additional exam requirements/recommendations for international students: Required—TOEFL (minimum score 500 paper-based; 61 iBT). *Application deadline:* For fall admission, 4/1 for domestic and international students; for spring admission, 11/1 for domestic and international students. Applications are processed on a rolling basis. Application fee: $40 ($55 for international students). Electronic applications accepted. *Expenses: Tuition:* Full-time $15,498; part-time $861 per credit hour. *Required fees:* $1326; $1326 per credit hour. Tuition and fees vary according to course load. *Financial support:* Career-related internships or fieldwork, Federal Work-Study, scholarships/grants, and unspecified assistantships available. Support available to part-time students. Financial award application deadline: 4/30; financial award applicants required to submit FAFSA. *Unit head:* Dr. Jenny Jones, Dean, 404-880-8549, E-mail: jjones@cau.edu. *Application contact:* Graduate Program Admissions, 404-880-8483, E-mail: graduateadmissions@cau.edu.

Clarke University, Department of Social Work, Dubuque, IA 52001-3198. Offers MSW. *Program availability:* Part-time, evening/weekend. *Faculty:* 7 full-time (all women). *Students:* 16 full-time (13 women), 3 part-time (all women); includes 4 minority (1 Black or African American, non-Hispanic/Latino; 2 Hispanic/Latino; 1 Two or more races, non-Hispanic/Latino). Average age 29. 16 applicants, 94% accepted, 15 enrolled. In 2016, 5 master's awarded. *Entrance requirements:* For master's, prerequisite courses in statistics, biology, psychology, and sociology; minimum major GPA of 3.0; interview. Additional exam requirements/recommendations for international students: Required—TOEFL (minimum score 550 paper-based, 80 iBT) or IELTS (6.5). *Application deadline:* For fall admission, 2/1 priority date for domestic students. Application fee: $35. Electronic applications accepted. *Expenses:* $550 per credit hour. *Financial support:* Applicants required to submit FAFSA. *Unit head:* Regina Boarman, Chair, 888-825-2753 Ext. 6583, E-mail: regina.boarman@clarke.edu. *Application contact:* Kimberly Roush, Director of Admission, Graduate and Adult Programs, 563-588-6539, Fax: 563-552-7994, E-mail: graduate@clarke.edu.

Social Work

Cleveland State University, College of Graduate Studies, College of Liberal Arts and Social Sciences, School of Social Work, Cleveland, OH 44115. Offers MSW. Program offered jointly with The University of Akron. *Accreditation:* CSWE. *Program availability:* Part-time, evening/weekend, online learning. *Faculty:* 10 full-time (2 women), 8 part-time/adjunct (5 women). *Students:* 154 full-time (126 women), 46 part-time (40 women); includes 100 minority (86 Black or African American, non-Hispanic/Latino; 1 Asian, non-Hispanic/Latino; 7 Hispanic/Latino; 6 Two or more races, non-Hispanic/Latino), 1 international. Average age 36. 82 applicants, 78% accepted, 63 enrolled. In 2016, 93 master's awarded. *Entrance requirements:* For master's, 3 letters of reference. Additional exam requirements/recommendations for international students: Required—TOEFL (minimum score 550 paper-based; 78 iBT); Recommended—IELTS (minimum score 6). *Application deadline:* For fall admission, 2/28 for domestic and international students. Application fee: $40. Electronic applications accepted. *Expenses:* Contact institution. *Financial support:* In 2016–17, 15 students received support, including 10 research assistantships with tuition reimbursements available (averaging $3,480 per year); tuition waivers (full) also available. Financial award applicants required to submit FAFSA. *Faculty research:* Mental health, aging. *Total annual research expenditures:* $1.2 million. *Unit head:* Dr. Maggie Jackson, Director, 216-687-4599, Fax: 216-687-5590, E-mail: m.jackson@csuohio.edu. *Application contact:* Deborah L. Brown, Interim Assistant Director, Graduate Admissions, 216-523-7572, Fax: 216-687-5400, E-mail: d.l.brown@csuohio.edu.
Website: http://www.csuohio.edu/class/social-work/social-work

The College at Brockport, State University of New York, School of Education, Health, and Human Services, Greater Rochester Collaborative Master of Social Work Program, Brockport, NY 14420-2997. Offers family and community practice (MSW); gerontology (AGC); interdisciplinary health practice (MSW). Program offered jointly with Nazareth College of Rochester. *Accreditation:* CSWE. *Program availability:* Part-time. *Faculty:* 6 full-time (4 women), 6 part-time/adjunct (4 women). *Students:* 46 full-time (41 women), 142 part-time (121 women); includes 39 minority (20 Black or African American, non-Hispanic/Latino; 2 American Indian or Alaska Native, non-Hispanic/Latino; 3 Asian, non-Hispanic/Latino; 6 Hispanic/Latino; 1 Native Hawaiian or other Pacific Islander, non-Hispanic/Latino; 7 Two or more races, non-Hispanic/Latino), 1 international. 158 applicants, 79% accepted, 81 enrolled. In 2016, 90 master's, 10 other advanced degrees awarded. *Degree requirements:* For master's, thesis or alternative. *Entrance requirements:* For master's, minimum GPA of 3.0, letters of recommendation, statement of objectives. Additional exam requirements/recommendations for international students: Required—TOEFL (minimum score 550 paper-based; 79 iBT), IELTS (minimum score 6.5). *Application deadline:* For fall admission, 1/15 priority date for domestic and international students; for summer admission, 1/15 priority date for domestic and international students. Application fee: $50. Electronic applications accepted. *Expenses:* Contact institution. *Financial support:* Federal Work-Study, scholarships/grants, and unspecified assistantships available. Support available to part-time students. Financial award application deadline: 3/15; financial award applicants required to submit FAFSA. *Faculty research:* Care giving, child welfare, gerontological social work, home-school-community partnerships, domestic violence. *Unit head:* Debra Fromm Faria, Co-Director, 585-395-8455, Fax: 585-395-8603, E-mail: grcmsw@brockport.edu. *Application contact:* Brad Snyder, Coordinator of Admissions, 585-395-3845, Fax: 585-395-8603, E-mail: bsynder@brockport.edu.
Website: http://www.brockport.edu/grcmsw

The College of Saint Rose, Graduate Studies, School of Mathematics and Sciences, Program in Social Work, Albany, NY 12203-1419. Offers MSSW. *Program availability:* Part-time, evening/weekend. *Entrance requirements:* Additional exam requirements/recommendations for international students: Required—TOEFL (minimum score 550 paper-based; 80 iBT), IELTS (minimum score 6), PTE (minimum score 56). *Application deadline:* For fall admission, 4/1 priority date for domestic and international students; for spring admission, 10/15 priority date for domestic and international students; for summer admission, 3/15 priority date for domestic and international students. Applications are processed on a rolling basis. Application fee: $40. Electronic applications accepted. *Expenses: Tuition:* Full-time $14,382; part-time $799 per credit. *Required fees:* $814; $32 per credit. $88 per semester. Tuition and fees vary according to course load. *Financial support:* Career-related internships or fieldwork, scholarships/grants, tuition waivers (partial), and unspecified assistantships available. Support available to part-time students. Financial award application deadline: 4/15. *Unit head:* Maureen Rotondi, Department Chair, 518-454-2003, E-mail: rotondim@strose.edu. *Application contact:* Cris Murray, Assistant Vice President for Graduate Recruitment and Enrollment, 518-485-3390, Fax: 518-458-5479, E-mail: grad@strose.edu.

The College of St. Scholastica, Graduate Studies, Department of Social Work, Duluth, MN 55811-4199. Offers MSW. *Accreditation:* CSWE. *Program availability:* Part-time.

College of Staten Island of the City University of New York, Graduate Programs, School of Health Sciences, Program in Social Work, Staten Island, NY 10314-6600. Offers MSW. *Program availability:* Part-time, evening/weekend. *Faculty:* 6 full-time, 9 part-time/adjunct. *Students:* 40 full-time, 32 part-time. Average age 33. 135 applicants, 30% accepted, 33 enrolled. In 2016, 28 master's awarded. *Degree requirements:* For master's, 12 required courses, 4 internships, 4 integrative seminars, 1 social work elective. *Entrance requirements:* For master's, bachelor's degree from regionally-accredited college, statistics course, 3 letters of recommendation, personal statement, résumé. Additional exam requirements/recommendations for international students: Required—TOEFL (minimum score 600 paper-based; 100 iBT), IELTS (minimum score 7). *Application deadline:* For fall admission, 2/15 for domestic and international students. Application fee: $125. *Expenses:* $6,685 full-time in-state; $560 per equated credit part-time in-state; $910 per equated credit out-of-state. *Faculty research:* Children and adults with disabilities, social work theories and methods, alcohol and drug problems, child welfare, gender and sexuality studies. *Unit head:* Dr. Christine Flynn Saulnier, Program Director, 718-982-2020, E-mail: christine.flynnsaulnier@csi.cuny.edu. *Application contact:* Sasha Spence, Associate Director for Graduate Admissions, 718-982-2019, Fax: 718-982-2500, E-mail: sasha.spence@csi.cuny.edu.
Website: http://www.csi.cuny.edu/departments/socialwork/MSW_welcome.html

Colorado State University, College of Health and Human Sciences, School of Social Work, Fort Collins, CO 80523-1586. Offers MSW, PhD, MSW/MPH. *Accreditation:* CSWE. *Program availability:* Part-time, evening/weekend, 100% online, blended/hybrid learning. *Faculty:* 6 full-time (5 women), 12 part-time/adjunct (10 women). *Students:* 77 full-time (64 women), 75 part-time (64 women); includes 32 minority (8 Black or African American, non-Hispanic/Latino; 1 American Indian or Alaska Native, non-Hispanic/Latino; 21 Hispanic/Latino; 2 Two or more races, non-Hispanic/Latino), 4 international. Average age 32. 64 applicants, 98% accepted, 31 enrolled. In 2016, 54 master's, 8 doctorates awarded. *Degree requirements:* For master's, thesis (for some programs), thesis or program evaluation; for doctorate, thesis/dissertation. *Entrance requirements:* For master's, GRE (for some programs), minimum undergraduate GPA of 3.0, minimum of 400 human service hours; for doctorate, master's degree in social work from accredited institution, at least 2 full years of relevant professional practice experience beyond the MSW, completion of statistics course within two years prior to admission. Additional exam requirements/recommendations for international students: Required—TOEFL (minimum score 550 paper-based, 80 iBT) or IELTS (6.5). *Application deadline:* For fall admission, 12/31 for domestic and international students; for spring admission, 5/31 for domestic and international students; for summer admission, 12/31 for domestic and international students. Application fee: $60 ($70 for international students). Electronic applications accepted. *Expenses:* Contact institution. *Financial support:* In 2016–17, 7 students received support, including 2 research assistantships with partial tuition reimbursements available (averaging $20,976 per year), 1 teaching assistantship with partial tuition reimbursement available (averaging $6,966 per year); fellowships with partial tuition reimbursements available, scholarships/grants, and unspecified assistantships also available. Financial award application deadline: 3/1; financial award applicants required to submit FAFSA. *Faculty research:* Aging and palliative care; alternative treatment to psychopharmacology for mental health issues; healthy cognitive aging and worker engagement; harm reduction for cannabis use among older adolescents; child welfare intervention science. *Total annual research expenditures:* $1.3 million. *Unit head:* Dr. Audrey Shillington, Director, 970-491-2378, Fax: 970-491-7280, E-mail: audrey.shillington@colostate.edu. *Application contact:* Timothy Frank, Graduate Program Coordinator, 970-491-2536, Fax: 970-491-7280, E-mail: timothy.frank@colostate.edu.
Website: http://www.ssw.chhs.colostate.edu/index.aspx

Columbia University, School of Social Work, New York, NY 10027. Offers MSSW, PhD, JD/MS, MBA/MS, MPA/MS, MPH/MS, MS/M Div, MS/MA, MS/MS, MS/MS Ed. MS/MS Ed offered jointly with Bank Street College of Education; MS/M Div with Union Theological Seminary in New York; MS/MA with The Jewish Theological Seminary; MS/MS dual degree with the Graduate School of Architecture, Planning, and Preservation. *Accreditation:* CSWE (one or more programs are accredited). *Program availability:* 100% online. *Degree requirements:* For doctorate, thesis/dissertation. *Entrance requirements:* For master's, 3 letters of reference; for doctorate, GRE General Test, 3 letters of reference. Additional exam requirements/recommendations for international students: Required—TOEFL (minimum score 577 paper-based; 98 iBT), IELTS (minimum score 7), TWE (minimum score 4). Electronic applications accepted. *Expenses:* Contact institution. *Faculty research:* Advanced clinical practice; economic, social, and health inequities; diverse populations at risk; health and mental health; international social welfare.

Concord University, Graduate Studies, Athens, WV 24712-1000. Offers educational leadership and supervision (M Ed); health promotion (MA); reading specialist (M Ed); social work (MSW); special education (M Ed); teaching (MAT). *Program availability:* Part-time, evening/weekend, online learning. *Faculty:* 16 full-time (10 women), 7 part-time/adjunct (4 women). *Students:* 129 full-time (105 women), 220 part-time (169 women); includes 28 minority (26 Black or African American, non-Hispanic/Latino; 1 American Indian or Alaska Native, non-Hispanic/Latino; 1 Hispanic/Latino), 2 international. *Degree requirements:* For master's, thesis (for some programs). *Entrance requirements:* For master's, GRE or MAT, baccalaureate degree with minimum GPA of 2.5 from regionally-accredited institution; teaching license; 2 letters of recommendation; completed disposition assessment form. *Application deadline:* Applications are processed on a rolling basis. Application fee: $30. Electronic applications accepted. *Expenses:* Tuition, state resident: full-time $3800; part-time $2539 per semester. Tuition, nonresident: full-time $6627; part-time $4416 per semester. Tuition and fees vary according to course load. *Financial support:* Tuition waivers and unspecified assistantships available. Financial award applicants required to submit FAFSA. *Unit head:* Dr. Cheryl Barnes, Director, 304-384-6306, E-mail: cbarnes@concord.edu. *Application contact:* Debra Moore, Special Events Assistant, 304-384-5113, E-mail: dlm@concord.edu.
Website: http://www.concord.edu/graduate

Cornell University, Graduate School, Graduate Fields of Human Ecology, Field of Policy Analysis and Management, Ithaca, NY 14853. Offers consumer policy (PhD); family and social welfare policy (PhD); health administration (MHA); health management and policy (PhD); public policy (PhD). *Degree requirements:* For master's, thesis; for doctorate, thesis/dissertation. *Entrance requirements:* For master's, GRE General Test or GMAT, 2 letters of recommendation; for doctorate, GRE General Test, 2 letters of recommendation. Additional exam requirements/recommendations for international students: Required—TOEFL (minimum score 550 paper-based; 77 iBT). Electronic applications accepted. *Faculty research:* Health policy, family policy, social welfare policy, program evaluation, consumer policy.

Daemen College, Program in Social Work, Amherst, NY 14226-3592. Offers MSW.

Dalhousie University, Faculty of Health Professions, School of Social Work, Halifax, NS B3H3J5, Canada. Offers MSW. *Program availability:* Part-time, online learning. *Degree requirements:* For master's, thesis optional, field placement. *Entrance requirements:* For master's, bachelor's degree in social work, 2 years work experience in social work, minimum GPA of 3.0. Additional exam requirements/recommendations for international students: Required—TOEFL, IELTS, CANTEST, CAEL, or Michigan English Language Assessment Battery. Electronic applications accepted. *Expenses:* Contact institution. *Faculty research:* Family and child welfare, physical and mental health, public policy, elder abuse, violence against women, community practice.

Delaware State University, Graduate Programs, College of Education, Health and Public Policy, Department of Social Work, Program in Social Work, Dover, DE 19901-2277. Offers MSW. *Accreditation:* CSWE. *Program availability:* Evening/weekend. *Entrance requirements:* For master's, GRE, minimum GPA of 3.0 in major, 2.75 overall. Additional exam requirements/recommendations for international students: Required—TOEFL. Electronic applications accepted. *Faculty research:* Gerontology, human behavior, corrections, child welfare, adolescent behavior policy.

DePaul University, College of Liberal Arts and Social Sciences, Chicago, IL 60614. Offers Arabic (MA); Chinese (MA); English (MA); French (MA); German (MA); history (MA); interdisciplinary studies (MA, MS); international public service (MS); international studies (MA); Italian (MA); Japanese (MA); leadership and policy studies (MS); liberal studies (MA); new media studies (MA); nonprofit management (MNM); public administration (MPA); public health (MPH); public service management (MS); social work (MSW); sociology (MA); Spanish (MA); sustainable urban development (MA); women and gender studies (MA); writing and publishing (MA); writing, rhetoric, and discourse (MA); MA/PhD. *Program availability:* Part-time, evening/weekend, online learning. Terminal master's awarded for partial completion of doctoral program. *Degree requirements:* For master's, variable foreign language requirement, comprehensive exam (for some programs), thesis (for some programs). Electronic applications accepted.

Dominican University, School of Social Work, River Forest, IL 60305. Offers MSW, MSW/MBA. *Accreditation:* CSWE. *Program availability:* Part-time. *Faculty:* 9 full-time (6 women), 18 part-time/adjunct (16 women). *Students:* 162 full-time (139 women), 84 part-time (72 women); includes 94 minority (50 Black or African American, non-Hispanic/Latino; 5 Asian, non-Hispanic/Latino; 37 Hispanic/Latino; 1 Native Hawaiian or other Pacific Islander, non-Hispanic/Latino; 1 Two or more races, non-Hispanic/Latino), 5 international. Average age 32. 130 applicants, 89% accepted, 77 enrolled. In 2016, 87 master's awarded. *Entrance requirements:* For master's, minimum GPA of 2.75. Additional exam requirements/recommendations for international students: Required—TOEFL (minimum score 83 iBT); Recommended—IELTS (minimum score 7).

Application deadline: For fall admission, 7/1 for domestic and international students; for spring admission, 11/1 for domestic and international students. Applications are processed on a rolling basis. Application fee: $25. Electronic applications accepted. *Expenses:* $830 per credit hour. *Financial support:* Research assistantships with partial tuition reimbursements, Federal Work-Study, scholarships/grants, and unspecified assistantships available. Financial award applicants required to submit FAFSA. *Faculty research:* Human trafficking, domestic violence, gerontology, school social work, child welfare. *Unit head:* Dr. Charles Stoops, Dean, 708-366-3316, E-mail: cstoops@dom.edu. *Application contact:* Catherine Galarza-Espino, Coordinator of Graduate Marketing and Recruiting, 708-524-6983, E-mail: cgalarza@dom.edu.
Website: http://socialwork.dom.edu/

East Carolina University, Graduate School, College of Health and Human Performance, School of Social Work, Greenville, NC 27858-4353. Offers gerontology (Certificate); social work (MSW); substance abuse (Certificate). *Accreditation:* CSWE. *Program availability:* Online learning. *Students:* 99 full-time (90 women), 38 part-time (32 women); includes 63 minority (51 Black or African American, non-Hispanic/Latino; 3 Asian, non-Hispanic/Latino; 7 Hispanic/Latino; 2 Two or more races, non-Hispanic/Latino). Average age 31. 129 applicants, 77% accepted, 66 enrolled. In 2016, 82 master's awarded. *Degree requirements:* For master's, comprehensive exam. *Entrance requirements:* For master's, GRE or MAT. Additional exam requirements/recommendations for international students: Required—TOEFL. *Application deadline:* For fall admission, 2/1 priority date for domestic and international students. Application fee: $50. *Financial support:* Fellowships and research assistantships available. Financial award application deadline: 6/1. *Faculty research:* Social research, gerontology, women's issues, social services in schools, human behavior. *Unit head:* Dr. Shelia Bunch, Director, 252-328-4202, E-mail: bunchs@ecu.edu. *Application contact:* Dean of Graduate School, 252-328-6012, Fax: 252-328-6071, E-mail: gradschool@ecu.edu.
Website: http://www.ecu.edu/cs-hhp/socw/

Eastern Michigan University, Graduate School, College of Health and Human Services, School of Social Work, Ypsilanti, MI 48197. Offers MSW. *Accreditation:* CSWE. *Program availability:* Part-time, evening/weekend. *Faculty:* 29 full-time (26 women). *Students:* 16 full-time (13 women), 216 part-time (172 women); includes 77 minority (57 Black or African American, non-Hispanic/Latino; 1 American Indian or Alaska Native, non-Hispanic/Latino; 3 Asian, non-Hispanic/Latino; 13 Hispanic/Latino; 1 Native Hawaiian or other Pacific Islander, non-Hispanic/Latino; 2 Two or more races, non-Hispanic/Latino). Average age 33. 231 applicants, 46% accepted, 78 enrolled. In 2016, 70 master's awarded. *Entrance requirements:* Additional exam requirements/recommendations for international students: Required—TOEFL. *Application deadline:* For fall admission, 1/15 priority date for domestic students. Applications are processed on a rolling basis. Application fee: $45. *Financial support:* Fellowships, research assistantships with full tuition reimbursements, teaching assistantships with full tuition reimbursements, career-related internships or fieldwork, Federal Work-Study, institutionally sponsored loans, scholarships/grants, tuition waivers (partial), and unspecified assistantships available. Support available to part-time students. Financial award applicants required to submit FAFSA. *Unit head:* Dr. Lynn Nybell, Director, 734-487-0393, Fax: 734-487-6832, E-mail: lnybell@emich.edu. *Application contact:* Julie Harkema, Admissions Coordinator, 734-487-0393, Fax: 734-487-6832, E-mail: jharkema@emich.edu.
Website: http://www.emich.edu/sw

Eastern Washington University, Graduate Studies, College of Social Sciences, School of Social Work, Cheney, WA 99004-2431. Offers MSW, MPA/MSW. *Accreditation:* CSWE. *Program availability:* Part-time. *Faculty:* 32 full-time (17 women), 32 part-time/adjunct (21 women). *Students:* 89 full-time (74 women), 79 part-time (61 women); includes 45 minority (7 Black or African American, non-Hispanic/Latino; 9 American Indian or Alaska Native, non-Hispanic/Latino; 7 Asian, non-Hispanic/Latino; 21 Hispanic/Latino; 1 Native Hawaiian or other Pacific Islander, non-Hispanic/Latino). Average age 35. 98 applicants, 68% accepted, 42 enrolled. In 2016, 47 master's awarded. *Degree requirements:* For master's, comprehensive exam. *Entrance requirements:* For master's, minimum GPA of 3.0. Additional exam requirements/recommendations for international students: Required—TOEFL (minimum score 580 paper-based; 32 iBT), IELTS (minimum score 7), PTE (minimum score 63). *Application deadline:* Applications are processed on a rolling basis. Application fee: $75. Electronic applications accepted. *Expenses:* Tuition, state resident: full-time $11,000; part-time $5500 per credit. Tuition, nonresident: full-time $24,000; part-time $12,000 per credit. *Required fees:* $1300. One-time fee: $50 full-time. Part-time tuition and fees vary according to course load, campus/location and program. *Financial support:* In 2016–17, 3 teaching assistantships with partial tuition reimbursements (averaging $10,000 per year) were awarded; career-related internships or fieldwork, Federal Work-Study, institutionally sponsored loans, scholarships/grants, health care benefits, tuition waivers (partial), and unspecified assistantships also available. Support available to part-time students. Financial award application deadline: 2/1; financial award applicants required to submit FAFSA. *Unit head:* Dr. Sharon Bowland, Associate Professor/MSW Director/Aging Studies Director, 509-359-4584.
Website: http://www.ewu.edu/csbssw/programs/social-work/social-work-degrees/msw.xml

East Tennessee State University, School of Graduate Studies, College of Arts and Sciences, Department of Social Work, Johnson City, TN 37614. Offers MSW. *Accreditation:* CSWE. *Degree requirements:* For master's, comprehensive exam, field practicum. *Entrance requirements:* For master's, bachelor's degree; minimum GPA of 2.75, 3.0 for last 60 hours; three letters of recommendation; resume; autobiographical statement. Additional exam requirements/recommendations for international students: Required—TOEFL (minimum score 550 paper-based; 79 iBT). Electronic applications accepted. *Faculty research:* Social work education, domestic violence, factors that contribute to a quality therapeutic relationship, mental illness stigma.

Edinboro University of Pennsylvania, Department of Social Work, Edinboro, PA 16444. Offers MSW. *Accreditation:* CSWE. *Program availability:* Evening/weekend. *Degree requirements:* For master's, competency exam. Electronic applications accepted.

Fayetteville State University, Graduate School, Program in Social Work, Fayetteville, NC 28301-4298. Offers MSW. *Accreditation:* CSWE. *Program availability:* Part-time, evening/weekend. *Faculty:* 12 full-time (7 women), 7 part-time/adjunct (2 women). *Students:* 98 full-time (85 women), 12 part-time (11 women); includes 78 minority (67 Black or African American, non-Hispanic/Latino; 3 American Indian or Alaska Native, non-Hispanic/Latino; 5 Hispanic/Latino; 3 Two or more races, non-Hispanic/Latino). Average age 35. 39 applicants, 100% accepted, 33 enrolled. In 2016, 78 master's awarded. *Entrance requirements:* For master's, GRE. Additional exam requirements/recommendations for international students: Required—TOEFL. *Application deadline:* For fall admission, 1/15 for domestic students. Application fee: $40. *Financial support:* Application deadline: 3/1; applicants required to submit FAFSA. *Unit head:* Dr. Terri Moore-Brown, Department Chair, 910-672-1853, Fax: 910-672-1755, E-mail: tmbrown@uncfsu.edu. *Application contact:* Gregory Perkins, Assistant Department Chair and Graduate Coordinator, 910-672-1021, Fax: 910-672-1755, E-mail: gperkins@uncfsu.edu.

Florida Agricultural and Mechanical University, Division of Graduate Studies, Research, and Continuing Education, College of Social Sciences, Arts and Humanities, Department of History and Political Science, Program in Social Work, Tallahassee, FL 32307-3200. Offers MSW. *Accreditation:* CSWE. *Entrance requirements:* For master's, GRE General Test, minimum GPA of 3.0, 3 letters of recommendation. Additional exam requirements/recommendations for international students: Required—TOEFL.

Florida Atlantic University, College for Design and Social Inquiry, School of Social Work, Boca Raton, FL 33431-0991. Offers MSW, DSW. *Accreditation:* CSWE. *Program availability:* Part-time, evening/weekend. *Faculty:* 13 full-time (8 women), 1 (woman) part-time/adjunct. *Students:* 147 full-time (129 women), 118 part-time (106 women); includes 121 minority (62 Black or African American, non-Hispanic/Latino; 1 American Indian or Alaska Native, non-Hispanic/Latino; 5 Asian, non-Hispanic/Latino; 45 Hispanic/Latino; 8 Two or more races, non-Hispanic/Latino), 2 international. Average age 33. 361 applicants, 52% accepted, 158 enrolled. In 2016, 109 master's awarded. *Entrance requirements:* Additional exam requirements/recommendations for international students: Required—TOEFL (minimum score 500 paper-based; 61 iBT), IELTS (minimum score 6). *Application deadline:* For fall admission, 5/1 priority date for domestic students, 2/15 for international students. Applications are processed on a rolling basis. Application fee: $30. *Expenses:* Tuition, state resident: full-time $7392; part-time $369.82 per credit hour. Tuition, nonresident: full-time $19,432; part-time $1024.81 per credit hour. *Financial support:* Fellowships with tuition reimbursements, research assistantships with tuition reimbursements, career-related internships or fieldwork, Federal Work-Study, institutionally sponsored loans, and tuition waivers (partial) available. Financial award application deadline: 4/1. *Faculty research:* Child welfare, social work education. *Unit head:* Joy McClellan, 561-297-3234, E-mail: jmcclel2@fau.edu.
Website: http://www.fau.edu/ssw/

Florida Gulf Coast University, College of Health Professions and Social Work, Program in Social Work, Fort Myers, FL 33965-6565. Offers MSW. *Accreditation:* CSWE. *Program availability:* Part-time, evening/weekend. *Faculty:* 66 full-time (45 women), 42 part-time/adjunct (21 women). *Students:* 25 full-time (22 women), 12 part-time (8 women); includes 19 minority (11 Black or African American, non-Hispanic/Latino; 2 Asian, non-Hispanic/Latino; 6 Hispanic/Latino). Average age 29. 53 applicants, 60% accepted, 20 enrolled. In 2016, 16 master's awarded. *Entrance requirements:* For master's, GRE General Test, MAT, minimum GPA of 3.0. Additional exam requirements/recommendations for international students: Required—TOEFL (minimum score 550 paper-based). *Application deadline:* For fall admission, 2/15 priority date for domestic students. Applications are processed on a rolling basis. Application fee: $30. Electronic applications accepted. *Expenses:* Tuition, state resident: full-time $6721. Tuition, nonresident: full-time $28,170. *Required fees:* $1987. Tuition and fees vary according to course load and degree level. *Financial support:* In 2016–17, 4 students received support. Research assistantships, career-related internships or fieldwork, and tuition waivers (partial) available. Support available to part-time students. Financial award application deadline: 3/1; financial award applicants required to submit FAFSA. *Faculty research:* Gerontology, clinical case management, domestic violence, homelessness, migrant workers. *Unit head:* Dr. Mary Hart, Director/Assistant Professor, 239-590-7839, Fax: 239-590-7842, E-mail: mhart@fgcu.edu. *Application contact:* Laura Althouse, Executive Secretary, 239-590-7825, Fax: 239-590-7843, E-mail: lalthouse@fgcu.edu.

Florida International University, Robert Stempel College of Public Health and Social Work, School of Social Work, Miami, FL 33199. Offers social welfare (PhD); social work (MSW). *Accreditation:* CSWE (one or more programs are accredited). *Program availability:* Part-time, evening/weekend. *Faculty:* 20 full-time (13 women), 13 part-time/adjunct (8 women). *Students:* 165 full-time (141 women), 75 part-time (59 women); includes 210 minority (66 Black or African American, non-Hispanic/Latino; 137 Hispanic/Latino; 7 Two or more races, non-Hispanic/Latino), 5 international. Average age 31. 149 applicants, 52% accepted, 58 enrolled. In 2016, 86 master's, 2 doctorates awarded. *Degree requirements:* For doctorate, comprehensive exam, thesis/dissertation. *Entrance requirements:* For master's, minimum undergraduate GPA of 3.0 in upper-level coursework; letters of recommendation; undergraduate courses in biology (including human biology), statistics, and social/behavioral science (12 credits); BSW from accredited program; for doctorate, GRE, minimum graduate GPA of 3.5, 3 letters of recommendation, resume, writing samples, 2 examples of scholarly work. Additional exam requirements/recommendations for international students: Required—TOEFL (minimum score 550 paper-based; 80 iBT). *Application deadline:* For fall admission, 6/1 for domestic students, 4/1 for international students; for spring admission, 10/1 for domestic students, 9/1 for international students. Applications are processed on a rolling basis. Application fee: $30. Electronic applications accepted. *Expenses:* Tuition, state resident: full-time $8912; part-time $446 per credit hour. Tuition, nonresident: full-time $21,393; part-time $992 per credit hour. *Required fees:* $2185; $195 per semester. Tuition and fees vary according to program. *Financial support:* Institutionally sponsored loans and scholarships/grants available. Financial award application deadline: 3/1; financial award applicants required to submit FAFSA. *Unit head:* Dr. Mary Helen Hayden, Director, 305-348-1208, E-mail: haydenm@fiu.edu. *Application contact:* Gladys Ramos, Program Assistant, 305-348-5887, E-mail: gladys.ramos@fiu.edu.
Website: http://ssph.fiu.edu/

Florida State University, The Graduate School, College of Social Work, Tallahassee, FL 32306. Offers clinical social work (MSW); social leadership (MSW); social work (PhD); JD/MSW; MPA/MSW; MS/MSW; MSW/MBA. *Accreditation:* CSWE (one or more programs are accredited). *Program availability:* Part-time, evening/weekend, 100% online coursework in specified areas with mandatory in-person internships. *Faculty:* 31 full-time (20 women), 16 part-time/adjunct (11 women). *Students:* 254 full-time (229 women), 187 part-time (165 women); includes 161 minority (92 Black or African American, non-Hispanic/Latino; 10 Asian, non-Hispanic/Latino; 46 Hispanic/Latino; 1 Native Hawaiian or other Pacific Islander, non-Hispanic/Latino; 12 Two or more races, non-Hispanic/Latino). Average age 30. 293 applicants, 74% accepted, 167 enrolled. In 2016, 220 master's, 3 doctorates awarded. *Degree requirements:* For master's, thesis optional; for doctorate, comprehensive exam, thesis/dissertation. *Entrance requirements:* For master's and doctorate, GRE General Test, minimum upper-division GPA of 3.0. Additional exam requirements/recommendations for international students: Required—TOEFL (minimum score 80 iBT). *Application deadline:* For fall admission, 6/1 for domestic and international students; for spring admission, 10/1 for domestic and international students; for summer admission, 3/1 for domestic and international students. Applications are processed on a rolling basis. Application fee: $30. Electronic applications accepted. *Expenses:* Contact institution. *Financial support:* In 2016–17, 132 students received support, including 1 fellowship with full tuition reimbursement available (averaging $22,000 per year), 25 research assistantships with full tuition reimbursements available (averaging $4,000 per year), 7 teaching assistantships with full tuition reimbursements available (averaging $16,000 per year); career-related internships or fieldwork, scholarships/grants, health care benefits, tuition waivers (partial), and unspecified assistantships also available. Financial award application deadline: 5/1; financial award applicants required to submit FAFSA. *Faculty research:*

Family violence, AIDS/HIV, aging, family therapy, child welfare, criminal justice, mental health, suicide prevention. *Unit head:* Dr. James Clark, Dean, 850-644-4752, Fax: 850-644-9750, E-mail: jclark5@fsu.edu. *Application contact:* Dana DeBoer, Coordinator of MSW Admissions, 800-378-9550, Fax: 850-644-9591, E-mail: ddeboer2@admin.fsu.edu.
Website: http://csw.fsu.edu/

Fordham University, Graduate School of Social Service, New York, NY 10023. Offers nonprofit leadership (MS); social work (MSW, PhD); JD/MSW. MS jointly sponsored with Graduate School of Business and conducted through the Fordham Center for Nonprofit Leaders. *Accreditation:* CSWE (one or more programs are accredited). *Program availability:* Part-time, evening/weekend, 100% online, blended/hybrid learning. *Faculty:* 48 full-time (36 women), 78 part-time/adjunct (61 women). *Students:* 884 full-time (787 women), 366 part-time (327 women); includes 355 minority (198 Black or African American, non-Hispanic/Latino; 1 American Indian or Alaska Native, non-Hispanic/Latino; 19 Asian, non-Hispanic/Latino; 137 Hispanic/Latino). Average age 32. In 2016, 539 master's, 4 doctorates awarded. *Degree requirements:* For master's, 1200 hours of field placement; for doctorate, comprehensive exam, thesis/dissertation. *Entrance requirements:* For master's, BA in liberal arts; for doctorate, GRE, master's degree in social work or related field. Additional exam requirements/recommendations for international students: Required—TOEFL (minimum score 600 paper-based; 100 iBT), IELTS. *Application deadline:* For fall admission, 2/1 priority date for domestic students; for spring admission, 11/1 priority date for domestic students. Applications are processed on a rolling basis. Application fee: $60. Electronic applications accepted. *Expenses:* Contact institution. *Financial support:* In 2016–17, 838 students received support, including 39 research assistantships with partial tuition reimbursements available (averaging $1,980 per year); fellowships with partial tuition reimbursements available, career-related internships or fieldwork, Federal Work-Study, scholarships/grants, tuition waivers (partial), and unspecified assistantships also available. Support available to part-time students. Financial award application deadline: 2/1. *Faculty research:* Aging, children and family, healthcare, domestic violence, substance abuse. *Unit head:* Dr. Debra McPhee, Dean, 212-636-6616. *Application contact:* Melba Remice, Assistant Dean of Admissions, 212-636-6600, Fax: 212-636-6613, E-mail: gssadmission@fordham.edu.
Website: http://www.fordham.edu/gss/

Gallaudet University, The Graduate School, Washington, DC 20002-3625. Offers American Sign Language/English bilingual early childhood deaf education: birth to 5 (Certificate); audiology (Au D); clinical psychology (PhD); deaf and hard of hearing infants, toddlers, and their families (Certificate); deaf education (MA, Ed S); deaf history (Certificate); deaf studies (Certificate); educating deaf students with disabilities (Certificate); education: teacher preparation (MA), including deaf education, early childhood education and deaf education, elementary education and deaf education, secondary education and deaf education; educational neuroscience (PhD); hearing, speech and language sciences (MS, PhD); international development (MA); interpretation (MA, PhD), including combined interpreting practice and research (MA), interpreting research (MA); linguistics (MA, PhD); mental health counseling (MA); peer mentoring (Certificate); public administration (MPA); school counseling (MA); school psychology (Psy S); sign language teaching (MA); social work (MSW); speech-language pathology (MS). *Program availability:* Part-time. *Students:* 297 full-time (231 women), 129 part-time (97 women); includes 105 minority (35 Black or African American, non-Hispanic/Latino; 20 Asian, non-Hispanic/Latino; 39 Hispanic/Latino; 11 Two or more races, non-Hispanic/Latino), 22 international. Average age 30. 471 applicants, 52% accepted, 147 enrolled. In 2016, 138 master's, 25 doctorates, 14 other advanced degrees awarded. Terminal master's awarded for partial completion of doctoral program. *Degree requirements:* For master's, comprehensive exam (for some programs), thesis optional; for doctorate, comprehensive exam, thesis/dissertation. *Entrance requirements:* For master's and doctorate, GRE General Test or MAT, letters of recommendation, interviews, goals statement, American Sign Language proficiency interview, written English competency. Additional exam requirements/recommendations for international students: Required—TOEFL. *Application deadline:* For fall admission, 2/15 for domestic students. Applications are processed on a rolling basis. Application fee: $75. Electronic applications accepted. *Expenses: Tuition:* Full-time $17,100; part-time $950 per credit hour. *Required fees:* $3725; $276 per semester. *Financial support:* Fellowships, research assistantships, teaching assistantships, career-related internships or fieldwork, Federal Work-Study, scholarships/grants, tuition waivers (partial), and unspecified assistantships available. Support available to part-time students. Financial award application deadline: 7/1; financial award applicants required to submit FAFSA. *Faculty research:* Signing math dictionaries, telecommunications access, cancer genetics, linguistics, visual language and visual learning, integrated quantum materials, deaf legal discourse, advance recruitment and retention in geosciences. *Unit head:* Dr. Gaurav Mathur, Dean, Graduate School and Continuing Studies, 202-250-2380, Fax: 202-651-5027, E-mail: gaurav.mathur@gallaudet.edu. *Application contact:* Wednesday Luria, Coordinator of Prospective Graduate Student Services, 202-651-5400, Fax: 202-651-5295, E-mail: graduate.school@gallaudet.edu.

George Fox University, School of Social Work, Newberg, OR 97132-2697. Offers MSW.

George Mason University, College of Health and Human Services, Department of Social Work, Fairfax, VA 22030. Offers MSW. *Accreditation:* CSWE. *Faculty:* 15 full-time (12 women), 29 part-time/adjunct (25 women). *Students:* 143 full-time (129 women), 27 part-time (24 women); includes 87 minority (38 Black or African American, non-Hispanic/Latino; 10 Asian, non-Hispanic/Latino; 33 Hispanic/Latino; 1 Native Hawaiian or other Pacific Islander, non-Hispanic/Latino; 5 Two or more races, non-Hispanic/Latino), 1 international. Average age 30. 291 applicants, 83% accepted, 95 enrolled. In 2016, 98 master's awarded. *Entrance requirements:* For master's, 2 official transcripts; expanded goals statement; resume; bachelor's degree with minimum GPA of 3.0; 30 undergraduate credits in liberal arts with English composition, history or government, social sciences and statistics; 3 letters of recommendation. Additional exam requirements/recommendations for international students: Required—TOEFL (minimum score 570 paper-based; 88 iBT), IELTS (minimum score 6.5), PTE (minimum score 59). *Application deadline:* For fall admission, 1/15 for domestic and international students. Application fee: $75 ($80 for international students). Electronic applications accepted. *Expenses:* Contact institution. *Financial support:* In 2016–17, 15 students received support, including 14 research assistantships with tuition reimbursements available (averaging $8,643 per year), 1 teaching assistantship (averaging $12,900 per year); career-related internships or fieldwork, Federal Work-Study, scholarships/grants, unspecified assistantships, and health care benefits (for full-time research or teaching assistantship recipients) also available. Financial award application deadline: 3/1; financial award applicants required to submit FAFSA. *Faculty research:* Social work methods, child welfare, social work ethics, field education, supervision. *Total annual research expenditures:* $36,700. *Unit head:* Michael Wolf-Branigin, Chair, 703-993-4229, Fax: 703-994-2193, E-mail: mwolfbra@gmu.edu. *Application contact:* Vannary Khov, Administrative Program Specialist, 703-993-2030, Fax: 703-993-2193, E-mail: vkhov@gmu.edu.
Website: http://chhs.gmu.edu/socialwork/

Georgia State University, Andrew Young School of Policy Studies, School of Social Work, Atlanta, GA 30294. Offers child welfare leadership (Certificate); community partnerships (MSW); forensic social work (Certificate). *Accreditation:* CSWE. *Program availability:* Part-time. *Faculty:* 17 full-time (12 women). *Students:* 123 full-time (111 women), 4 part-time (2 women); includes 83 minority (65 Black or African American, non-Hispanic/Latino; 12 Hispanic/Latino; 6 Two or more races, non-Hispanic/Latino), 1 international. Average age 30. 123 applicants, 70% accepted, 46 enrolled. In 2016, 49 master's awarded. *Entrance requirements:* For master's and Certificate, GRE. Additional exam requirements/recommendations for international students: Required—TOEFL (minimum score 550 paper-based; 100 iBT) or IELTS (minimum score 7). *Application deadline:* For fall admission, 2/1 priority date for domestic and international students. Application fee: $50. Electronic applications accepted. *Expenses:* Tuition, state resident: full-time $6876; part-time $382 per credit hour. Tuition, nonresident: full-time $22,374; part-time $1243 per credit hour. *Required fees:* $2128; $1064 per term. Part-time tuition and fees vary according to course load and program. *Financial support:* In 2016–17, research assistantships with tuition reimbursements (averaging $4,000 per year), teaching assistantships with tuition reimbursements (averaging $4,000 per year) were awarded; career-related internships or fieldwork, institutionally sponsored loans, scholarships/grants, tuition waivers, and unspecified assistantships also available. Financial award application deadline: 2/1; financial award applicants required to submit FAFSA. *Faculty research:* Community partnership, non-profit organizations, child welfare practice and policy, gerontological practice and policy, restorative justice. *Unit head:* Brian Bride, Director of School of Social Work, 404-413-1052, Fax: 404-413-1075, E-mail: bbride@gsu.edu.
Website: http://aysps.gsu.edu/socialwork

Governors State University, College of Health and Human Services, Program in Social Work, University Park, IL 60484. Offers MSW. *Accreditation:* CSWE. *Program availability:* Part-time. *Faculty:* 51 full-time (45 women), 60 part-time/adjunct (43 women). *Students:* 91 full-time (80 women), 48 part-time (41 women); includes 89 minority (76 Black or African American, non-Hispanic/Latino; 11 Hispanic/Latino; 2 Two or more races, non-Hispanic/Latino), 2 international. Average age 34. 161 applicants, 39% accepted, 55 enrolled. In 2016, 59 master's awarded. *Entrance requirements:* Additional exam requirements/recommendations for international students: Required—TOEFL (minimum score 550 paper-based; 80 iBT), IELTS. *Application deadline:* For fall admission, 4/1 for domestic students. Application fee: $50. Electronic applications accepted. *Expenses:* $307 per credit hour; $38 per term or $76 per credit hour fees. *Financial support:* Application deadline: 5/1; applicants required to submit FAFSA. *Unit head:* Gerri Outlaw, Chair, Department of Social Work, 708-235-2178, E-mail: goutlaw@govst.edu. *Application contact:* Yakeea Daniels, Assistant Vice President for Enrollment Services/Director of Admission, 708-534-4510, E-mail: ydaniels@govst.edu.

The Graduate Center, City University of New York, Graduate Studies, Program in Social Welfare, New York, NY 10016-4039. Offers DSW, PhD. *Degree requirements:* For doctorate, thesis/dissertation, project, qualifying exam. *Entrance requirements:* For doctorate, MSW or equivalent, 3 years of post-master's work experience. Additional exam requirements/recommendations for international students: Required—TOEFL. Electronic applications accepted.

Grambling State University, School of Graduate Studies and Research, College of Professional Studies, School of Social Work, Grambling, LA 71245. Offers MSW. *Accreditation:* CSWE. *Program availability:* Part-time. *Degree requirements:* For master's, comprehensive exam, research project or thesis. *Entrance requirements:* For master's, GRE, minimum GPA of 3.0 on last degree, 36 hours in liberal arts, autobiography, interview. Additional exam requirements/recommendations for international students: Required—TOEFL (minimum score 500 paper-based; 62 iBT). Electronic applications accepted.

Grand Valley State University, College of Community and Public Service, School of Social Work, Allendale, MI 49401-9403. Offers MSW. *Accreditation:* CSWE. *Program availability:* Part-time. *Faculty:* 15 full-time (11 women), 25 part-time/adjunct (17 women). *Students:* 188 full-time (167 women), 138 part-time (116 women); includes 61 minority (31 Black or African American, non-Hispanic/Latino; 5 Asian, non-Hispanic/Latino; 13 Hispanic/Latino; 12 Two or more races, non-Hispanic/Latino), 1 international. Average age 28. 198 applicants, 91% accepted, 114 enrolled. In 2016, 165 master's awarded. *Entrance requirements:* For master's, three letters of recommendation, current resume, 2- to 3-page essay about life experiences that have led to interest in administrative practice in social agency, 2-page essay on how pursuing MSW will help achieve educational and professional career goals. Additional exam requirements/recommendations for international students: Required—TOEFL. *Application deadline:* For fall admission, 5/1 priority date for domestic students; for winter admission, 10/1 priority date for domestic students; for spring admission, 3/15 priority date for domestic students. Applications are processed on a rolling basis. Application fee: $30. Electronic applications accepted. *Expenses:* $604 per credit hour. *Financial support:* In 2016–17, 40 students received support, including 22 fellowships, 23 research assistantships with full and partial tuition reimbursements available (averaging $8,000 per year); career-related internships or fieldwork, Federal Work-Study, institutionally sponsored loans, and unspecified assistantships also available. *Faculty research:* Drug addiction, aging, management, effectiveness of therapy. *Unit head:* Dr. Dianne Green-Smith, Chair, 616-331-6565, Fax: 616-331-6550, E-mail: greensmd@gvsu.edu. *Application contact:* Dr. Cray Mulder, Graduate Program Director/Recruiting Contact, 616-331-6596, E-mail: muldercra@gvsu.edu.

Gratz College, Graduate Programs, Program in Jewish Communal Service, Melrose Park, PA 19027. Offers MA, Certificate, MA/MSW. MA/MSW offered jointly with University of Pennsylvania. *Program availability:* Part-time, evening/weekend, online learning. *Degree requirements:* For master's, one foreign language, internship. *Application deadline:* Applications are processed on a rolling basis. Application fee: $50. *Financial support:* Fellowships, career-related internships or fieldwork, Federal Work-Study, and unspecified assistantships available. Support available to part-time students. Financial award application deadline: 4/15. *Unit head:* Dr. Jerome Kutnick, Dean for Academic Affairs, 215-635-7300 Ext. 137, Fax: 215-635-7320, E-mail: jkutnick@gratz.edu. *Application contact:* Joanna Boeing Bratton, Director of Admissions, 215-635-7300 Ext. 140, Fax: 215-635-7399, E-mail: admissions@gratz.edu.

Hawai`i Pacific University, College of Health and Society, Program in Social Work, Honolulu, HI 96813. Offers MSW. *Accreditation:* CSWE. *Program availability:* Part-time, evening/weekend. *Faculty:* 4 full-time (2 women), 2 part-time/adjunct (1 woman). *Students:* 54 full-time (40 women), 10 part-time (9 women); includes 41 minority (3 Black or African American, non-Hispanic/Latino; 7 Asian, non-Hispanic/Latino; 9 Hispanic/Latino; 3 Native Hawaiian or other Pacific Islander, non-Hispanic/Latino; 19 Two or more races, non-Hispanic/Latino), 4 international. Average age 31. 53 applicants, 85% accepted, 31 enrolled. In 2016, 41 master's awarded. *Entrance requirements:* For master's, minimum undergraduate GPA of 3.25, interview. Additional exam requirements/recommendations for international students: Recommended—TOEFL (minimum score 550 paper-based; 80 iBT), IELTS (minimum score 6), TWE (minimum score 5). *Application deadline:* For fall admission, 2/15 priority date for domestic students; for spring admission, 10/15 priority date for domestic students. Applications are processed on a rolling basis. Application fee: $50. Electronic applications accepted.

Expenses: Tuition: Full-time $17,190; part-time $955 per credit. *Required fees:* $150; $26 per credit. Tuition and fees vary according to course load and program. *Financial support:* In 2016–17, 11 students received support. Career-related internships or fieldwork, Federal Work-Study, scholarships/grants, tuition waivers, and unspecified assistantships available. Financial award application deadline: 3/1; financial award applicants required to submit FAFSA. *Unit head:* Dr. Howard Karger, Director, School of Social Work, 808-544-1482, E-mail: hkarger@hpu.edu. *Application contact:* Danny Lam, Assistant Director of Graduate Admissions, 808-544-1135, E-mail: graduate@hpu.edu.
Website: https://www.hpu.edu/CHS/Social_Work/index.html

Howard University, School of Social Work, Washington, DC 20059. Offers MSW, PhD. *Accreditation:* CSWE (one or more programs are accredited). *Program availability:* Part-time. *Degree requirements:* For doctorate, comprehensive exam, thesis/dissertation, qualifying exam. *Entrance requirements:* For master's, minimum GPA of 2.5; for doctorate, GRE General Test, minimum GPA of 3.3, MSW or master's in related field. Additional exam requirements/recommendations for international students: Required—TOEFL. *Faculty research:* Infant mortality, child and family services, displaced populations, social work practice, domestic violence, black males, mental health.

Humboldt State University, Academic Programs, College of Professional Studies, Department of Social Work, Arcata, CA 95521-8299. Offers MSW. *Accreditation:* CSWE. *Entrance requirements:* For master's, 3 letters of recommendation. Additional exam requirements/recommendations for international students: Required—TOEFL (minimum score 500 paper-based). *Expenses:* Tuition, state resident: full-time $6738; part-time $1953 per semester. Tuition, nonresident: full-time $13,434; part-time $3813 per semester. *Required fees:* $1738; $653 per semester. Tuition and fees vary according to program.

Hunter College of the City University of New York, Graduate School, Silberman School of Social Work, New York, NY 10065-5085. Offers MSW. *Accreditation:* CSWE. *Students:* 857 full-time (701 women), 231 part-time (178 women); includes 575 minority (242 Black or African American, non-Hispanic/Latino; 67 Asian, non-Hispanic/Latino; 266 Hispanic/Latino), 22 international. Average age 30. 1,488 applicants, 58% accepted, 569 enrolled. In 2016, 523 master's awarded. *Degree requirements:* For master's, major paper. *Entrance requirements:* Additional exam requirements/recommendations for international students: Required—TOEFL. *Application deadline:* For fall admission, 1/15 for domestic and international students. Applications are processed on a rolling basis. *Financial support:* Fellowships, career-related internships or fieldwork, Federal Work-Study, and tuition waivers (partial) available. Support available to part-time students. *Faculty research:* Child welfare, AIDS, homeless, aging, mental health. *Unit head:* Dr. Mary Cavanaugh, Acting Dean, 212-452-7085, Fax: 212-452-7150, E-mail: mary.cavanaugh@hunter.cuny.edu. *Application contact:* Raymond Montero, Coordinator of Admissions, 212-452-7005, E-mail: grad.socworkadvisor@hunter.cuny.edu.
Website: http://sssw.hunter.cuny.edu/

Illinois State University, Graduate School, College of Arts and Sciences, School of Social Work, Normal, IL 61790-2200. Offers MSW. *Accreditation:* CSWE. *Faculty research:* Developing professional careers in child welfare, research and policy work for the Evan B. Donaldson Adoption Institute, evidence-based practice training pilot evaluation.

Indiana State University, College of Graduate and Professional Studies, College of Nursing, Health, and Human Services, Department of Social Work, Terre Haute, IN 47809. Offers MSW. *Accreditation:* CSWE.

Indiana University East, School of Social Work, Richmond, IN 47374-1289. Offers MSW.

Indiana University Northwest, School of Social Work, Gary, IN 46408-1197. Offers health (MSW); mental health and addictions (MSW). *Program availability:* Part-time, evening/weekend. *Faculty:* 3 full-time (all women), 4 part-time/adjunct (3 women). *Students:* 26 full-time (24 women), 64 part-time (56 women); includes 36 minority (21 Black or African American, non-Hispanic/Latino; 13 Hispanic/Latino; 2 Two or more races, non-Hispanic/Latino). Average age 33. 65 applicants, 52% accepted, 24 enrolled. In 2016, 27 master's awarded. *Degree requirements:* For master's, practicum. *Entrance requirements:* For master's, minimum GPA of 3.0; bachelor's degree from accredited university including the successful completion of 6 courses in social or behavioral sciences and 1 course in statistics; 3 professional references. *Application deadline:* For fall admission, 7/14 for domestic students; for spring admission, 2/1 priority date for domestic students. Application fee: $40 ($60 for international students). Electronic applications accepted. *Expenses:* $395.98 per credit hour in-state; $942.42 per credit hour out-of-state. *Financial support:* Career-related internships or fieldwork, Federal Work-Study, and tuition waivers (partial) available. Support available to part-time students. Financial award application deadline: 6/1; financial award applicants required to submit FAFSA. *Faculty research:* Educational outcomes, generalist practice, homelessness. *Unit head:* Dr. Darlene Lynch, Director, 219-980-7111, E-mail: darlynch@iun.edu. *Application contact:* Elena Mrozinske, Clinical Assistant Professor, 219-980-6727, E-mail: emrozins@iun.edu.
Website: http://www.iun.edu/social-work/msw-dgree/index.htm

Indiana University–Purdue University Indianapolis, School of Social Work, Indianapolis, IN 46202. Offers MSW, PhD, Certificate. *Accreditation:* CSWE (one or more programs are accredited). *Program availability:* Part-time, evening/weekend. *Faculty:* 40 full-time. *Students:* 366 full-time (306 women), 290 part-time (240 women); includes 134 minority (71 Black or African American, non-Hispanic/Latino; 9 Asian, non-Hispanic/Latino; 35 Hispanic/Latino; 19 Two or more races, non-Hispanic/Latino), 13 international. Average age 34. 343 applicants, 60% accepted, 167 enrolled. In 2016, 226 master's, 7 doctorates awarded. Terminal master's awarded for partial completion of doctoral program. *Degree requirements:* For master's, field practicum; for doctorate, thesis/dissertation, residential internship. *Entrance requirements:* For master's, minimum GPA of 2.5; course work in social behavior, statistics, research methodology, and human biology; for doctorate, GRE General Test. Additional exam requirements/recommendations for international students: Required—TOEFL. Application fee: $55 ($65 for international students). *Expenses:* Contact institution. *Financial support:* Fellowships with full tuition reimbursements, research assistantships with partial tuition reimbursements, teaching assistantships, Federal Work-Study, institutionally sponsored loans, scholarships/grants, and tuition waivers (partial) available. Support available to part-time students. Financial award applicants required to submit FAFSA. *Faculty research:* Social justice, institutional child welfare, mental health, aging, AIDS/HIV. *Total annual research expenditures:* $145,580. *Unit head:* Dr. Margaret Adamek, Dean, 317-274-6730, Fax: 317-274-8630. *Application contact:* Marlo Dale, Information Contact for MSW, 317-274-6966.
Website: http://socialwork.iu.edu/

Indiana University South Bend, School of Social Work, South Bend, IN 46634-7111. Offers MSW. *Program availability:* Part-time, evening/weekend. *Faculty:* 4 full-time (2 women). *Students:* 49 full-time (43 women), 74 part-time (62 women); includes 27 minority (19 Black or African American, non-Hispanic/Latino; 5 Hispanic/Latino; 3 Two or more races, non-Hispanic/Latino), 1 international. Average age 33. 68 applicants, 81% accepted, 49 enrolled. In 2016, 22 master's awarded. *Application deadline:* For fall admission, 2/1 priority date for domestic students. Applications are processed on a rolling basis. Application fee: $40 ($60 for international students). *Expenses:* $332.04 per credit hour in-state; $856.85 per credit hour out-of-state. *Financial support:* Career-related internships or fieldwork and Federal Work-Study available. Support available to part-time students. Financial award application deadline: 3/1; financial award applicants required to submit FAFSA. *Unit head:* Dr. Michael A Patchner, Dean, 574-520-4880, Fax: 574-520-4876. *Application contact:* Diane Banic, Administrative Assistant, 574-520-4880, E-mail: dbanic@iusb.edu.
Website: https://www.iusb.edu/social-work/msw/index.php

Institute for Clinical Social Work, Graduate Programs, Chicago, IL 60601. Offers PhD. *Program availability:* Part-time. *Degree requirements:* For doctorate, thesis/dissertation, supervised practicum. *Entrance requirements:* For doctorate, 2 years of experience. *Faculty research:* Impact of AIDS on partners, effects of learning disabilities on children and families, clinical social work issues.

Inter American University of Puerto Rico, Metropolitan Campus, Graduate Programs, Program in Social Work, San Juan, PR 00919-1293. Offers advanced clinical services (MSW); advanced social work administration (MSW); clinical services (MSW); social work administration (MSW). *Accreditation:* CSWE. *Program availability:* Evening/weekend. *Degree requirements:* For master's, comprehensive exam. *Entrance requirements:* For master's, GRE or EXADEP, interview. Electronic applications accepted.

Jackson State University, Graduate School, College of Public Service, School of Social Work, Jackson, MS 39217. Offers MSW, PhD. *Accreditation:* CSWE (one or more programs are accredited). *Program availability:* Evening/weekend. *Degree requirements:* For master's, comprehensive exam; for doctorate, comprehensive exam, thesis/dissertation. *Entrance requirements:* For master's, GRE General Test; for doctorate, MAT. Additional exam requirements/recommendations for international students: Required—TOEFL (minimum score 520 paper-based; 67 iBT). *Application deadline:* For fall admission, 3/1 for domestic and international students. Application fee: $25. *Expenses:* Tuition, state resident: full-time $7141. Tuition, nonresident: full-time $17,494. *Required fees:* $1080. Tuition and fees vary according to class time, course level, course load, degree level, campus/location, program and student level. *Financial support:* Career-related internships or fieldwork, Federal Work-Study, scholarships/grants, tuition waivers, and unspecified assistantships available. Support available to part-time students. Financial award application deadline: 3/1; financial award applicants required to submit FAFSA. *Unit head:* Dr. Isiah Marshall, Jr., Associate Dean, 601-979-8896, Fax: 601-979-6812, E-mail: schoolofsw@jsums.edu. *Application contact:* Fatoumatta Sisay, Manager of Graduate Admissions, 601-979-0342, Fax: 601-979-4325, E-mail: fatoumatta.sisay@jsums.edu.
Website: http://www.jsums.edu/socialwork/

Johnson C. Smith University, Program in Social Work, Charlotte, NC 28216-5398. Offers MSW. *Accreditation:* CSWE. *Program availability:* Part-time, evening/weekend. *Faculty:* 6 full-time (2 women), 5 part-time/adjunct (all women). *Students:* 84 full-time (77 women), 18 part-time (16 women); includes 97 minority (93 Black or African American, non-Hispanic/Latino; 1 Asian, non-Hispanic/Latino; 2 Hispanic/Latino; 1 Two or more races, non-Hispanic/Latino). Average age 33. 104 applicants, 98% accepted, 102 enrolled. In 2016, 34 master's awarded. *Degree requirements:* For master's, 60 credit hours (39 for advanced standing) and 900 clock hours of field (500 for advanced standing). *Entrance requirements:* For master's, official transcripts for all colleges attended; 3 references on forms provided; personal statement. Additional exam requirements/recommendations for international students: Required—TOEFL. Application fee: $40. *Expenses: Tuition:* Full-time $8640; part-time $576 per credit hour. *Financial support:* In 2016–17, 17 students received support. Federal Work-Study, scholarships/grants, and unspecified assistantships available. Financial award applicants required to submit FAFSA. *Unit head:* Dr. Jeanne F. Cook, Director of MSW Program, 704-378-1029, E-mail: jfcook@jcsu.edu.
Website: http://www.jcsu.edu/academics/master-of-social-work/

Kean University, Nathan Weiss Graduate College, Program in Social Work, Union, NJ 07083. Offers MSW. *Accreditation:* CSWE. *Program availability:* Part-time. *Faculty:* 6 full-time (all women). *Students:* 130 full-time (105 women), 22 part-time (19 women); includes 105 minority (59 Black or African American, non-Hispanic/Latino; 2 Asian, non-Hispanic/Latino; 42 Hispanic/Latino; 2 Two or more races, non-Hispanic/Latino), 1 international. Average age 30. 208 applicants, 41% accepted, 79 enrolled. In 2016, 47 master's awarded. *Degree requirements:* For master's, field work. *Entrance requirements:* For master's, baccalaureate degree, official transcripts, three letters of recommendation, professional resume/curriculum vitae, personal statement. Additional exam requirements/recommendations for international students: Required—TOEFL (minimum score 550 paper-based; 79 iBT), IELTS (minimum score 6.5). *Application deadline:* For fall admission, 3/1 priority date for domestic students, 5/1 priority date for international students. Applications are processed on a rolling basis. Application fee: $75. Electronic applications accepted. *Expenses:* Contact institution. *Financial support:* Scholarships/grants and unspecified assistantships available. Financial award applicants required to submit FAFSA. *Unit head:* Dr. Josephine Norward, Program Coordinator, 908-737-4033, E-mail: jnorward@kean.edu. *Application contact:* Brittany Gerstenhaber, Admissions Counselor, 908-737-7100, E-mail: grad-adm@kean.edu.
Website: http://grad.kean.edu/msw

Kennesaw State University, WellStar College of Health and Human Services, Program in Social Work, Kennesaw, GA 30144. Offers MSW. *Accreditation:* CSWE. *Entrance requirements:* For master's, GRE, criminal history check, minimum GPA of 2.75, 3 letters of recommendation, resume. Additional exam requirements/recommendations for international students: Required—TOEFL (minimum score 550 paper-based; 80 iBT), IELTS (minimum score 6.5). Electronic applications accepted.

Keuka College, Program in Social Work, Keuka Park, NY 14478. Offers MSW. *Faculty:* 5 full-time (4 women), 6 part-time/adjunct (5 women). *Students:* 50 full-time (43 women); includes 13 minority (6 Black or African American, non-Hispanic/Latino; 3 Hispanic/Latino; 4 Two or more races, non-Hispanic/Latino). Average age 33. 125 applicants, 53% accepted, 27 enrolled. In 2016, 6 master's awarded. *Degree requirements:* For master's, field practicum. *Entrance requirements:* For master's, BS in social work. Additional exam requirements/recommendations for international students: Required—TOEFL (minimum score 550 paper-based). *Application deadline:* For fall admission, 8/15 for domestic students; for winter admission, 12/15 for domestic students; for spring admission, 4/15 for domestic students. Applications are processed on a rolling basis. Application fee: $50. Electronic applications accepted. *Expenses:* Contact institution. *Financial support:* Scholarships/grants and tuition waivers (full and partial) available. Financial award applicants required to submit FAFSA. *Faculty research:* Foster care; maternal health; trauma; family. *Unit head:* Dr. Ed Silverman, Division Chair, 315-279-5120, E-mail: esilverman@keuka.edu. *Application contact:* Jennifer Nielsen, Admissions, 315-279-5203, Fax: 315-279-5386, E-mail: admissions@keuka.edu.
Website: http://www.keuka.edu/academics/programs/master-social-work

Kutztown University of Pennsylvania, College of Liberal Arts and Sciences, Program in Social Work, Kutztown, PA 19530-0730. Offers MSW, DSW. *Accreditation:* CSWE. *Program availability:* Part-time, evening/weekend. *Faculty:* 12 full-time (9 women), 1

part-time/adjunct (0 women). *Students:* 47 full-time (39 women), 48 part-time (38 women); includes 19 minority (10 Black or African American, non-Hispanic/Latino; 1 Asian, non-Hispanic/Latino; 8 Hispanic/Latino). Average age 31. 122 applicants, 85% accepted, 51 enrolled. In 2016, 34 master's awarded. *Degree requirements:* For master's, comprehensive exam; for doctorate, thesis/dissertation. *Entrance requirements:* For master's, GRE (except for BSW and other master's degree holders), 3 letters of recommendation, personal and social issues essay (waived for Kutztown University BSW holders); for doctorate, MSW from CSWE-accredited program, 3 letters of recommendation, knowledge statement, personal statement, curriculum vitae. Additional exam requirements/recommendations for international students: Required—TOEFL (minimum score 550 paper-based, 79 iBT) or IELTS (minimum score 6.5). *Application deadline:* For fall admission, 8/1 for domestic and international students; for spring admission, 12/1 for domestic and international students. Application fee: $35. Electronic applications accepted. *Expenses:* Tuition, state resident: full-time $4347; part-time $483 per credit. Tuition, nonresident: full-time $6525; part-time $725 per credit. *Required fees:* $88 per credit. One-time fee: $50 full-time. *Financial support:* Career-related internships or fieldwork, Federal Work-Study, scholarships/grants, and unspecified assistantships available. Financial award application deadline: 3/1; financial award applicants required to submit FAFSA. *Unit head:* Dr. John Vafeas, Chairperson, 610-683-4235, E-mail: vafeas@kutztown.edu. *Application contact:* Noemi Rivera, Academic Department Secretary, 610-683-4235, E-mail: nrivera@kutztown.edu.
Website: https://www.kutztown.edu/socialwork

Lakehead University, Graduate Studies, Gerontology Collaborative Program-Northern Educational Center for Aging and Health, Thunder Bay, ON P7B 5E1, Canada. Offers gerontology (M Ed, M Sc, MA, MSW). *Program availability:* Part-time. *Degree requirements:* For master's, thesis (for some programs). *Entrance requirements:* Additional exam requirements/recommendations for international students: Required—TOEFL. *Faculty research:* Integrated health information systems.

Lakehead University, Graduate Studies, School of Social Work, Thunder Bay, ON P7B 5E1, Canada. Offers gerontology (MSW); social work (MSW); women's studies (MSW). *Program availability:* Part-time. *Degree requirements:* For master's, thesis or project. *Entrance requirements:* For master's, minimum B average. Additional exam requirements/recommendations for international students: Required—TOEFL. *Faculty research:* Clinical psychology, social work and practice theory, long-term care, health care for frail elderly, women's studies.

Laurentian University, School of Graduate Studies and Research, School of Social Work, Sudbury, ON P3E 2C6, Canada. Offers MSW. Open only to French-speaking students. *Program availability:* Part-time. *Degree requirements:* For master's, thesis. *Faculty research:* Income security, poverty, violence against women, child poverty, effects of economic crisis on families.

Loma Linda University, School of Behavioral Health, Department of Social Work and Social Ecology, Loma Linda, CA 92350. Offers criminal justice (MS); gerontology (MS); social policy and social research (PhD); social work (MSW). *Accreditation:* CSWE. *Degree requirements:* For master's, comprehensive exam, thesis optional; for doctorate, comprehensive exam, thesis/dissertation. *Entrance requirements:* For master's and doctorate, GRE General Test. Additional exam requirements/recommendations for international students: Required—TOEFL, Michigan English Language Assessment Battery. Electronic applications accepted.

London Metropolitan University, Graduate Programs, London, United Kingdom. Offers applied psychology (M Sc); architecture (MA); biomedical science (M Sc); blood science (M Sc); cancer pharmacology (M Sc); computer networking and cyber security (M Sc); computing and information systems (M Sc); conference interpreting (MA); counter-terrorism studies (M Sc); creative, digital and professional writing (MA); crime, violence and prevention (M Sc); criminology (M Sc); curating contemporary art (MA); data analytics (M Sc); digital media (MA); early childhood studies (MA); education (MA, Ed D); financial services law, regulation and compliance (LL M); food science (M Sc); forensic psychology (M Sc); health and social care management and policy (M Sc); human nutrition (M Sc); human resource management (MA); human rights and international conflict (MA); information technology (M Sc); intelligence and security studies (M Sc); international oil, gas and energy law (LL M); international relations (MA); interpreting (MA); learning and teaching in higher education (MA); legal practice (LL M); media and entertainment law (LL M); organizational and consumer psychology (M Sc); psychological therapy (M Sc); psychology of mental health (M Sc); public health (M Sc); public policy and management (MPA); security studies (M Sc); social work (M Sc); spatial planning and urban design (MA); sports therapy (M Sc); supporting older children and young people with dyslexia (MA); teaching languages (MA), including Arabic, English; translation (MA); woman and child abuse (MA).

Long Island University–LIU Brooklyn, School of Health Professions, Brooklyn, NY 11201-8423. Offers athletic training and sport sciences (MS); community health (MS Ed); exercise science (MS); forensic social work (Advanced Certificate); occupational therapy (MS); physical therapy (DPT); physician assistant (MS); public health (MPH); social work (MSW). *Faculty:* 60 full-time (42 women), 109 part-time/adjunct (62 women). *Students:* 603 full-time (405 women), 69 part-time (52 women); includes 219 minority (117 Black or African American, non-Hispanic/Latino; 1 American Indian or Alaska Native, non-Hispanic/Latino; 38 Asian, non-Hispanic/Latino; 48 Hispanic/Latino; 15 Two or more races, non-Hispanic/Latino), 68 international. 1,127 applicants, 43% accepted, 213 enrolled. In 2016, 192 master's, 42 doctorates awarded. *Degree requirements:* For master's, comprehensive exam (for some programs), thesis (for some programs), research capstone; for doctorate, comprehensive exam, research capstone. *Entrance requirements:* For master's, doctorate, and Advanced Certificate, GRE. Additional exam requirements/recommendations for international students: Required—TOEFL (minimum score 550 paper-based; 79 iBT). *Application deadline:* Applications are processed on a rolling basis. Application fee: $50. Electronic applications accepted. *Expenses: Tuition:* Full-time $28,272; part-time $1178 per credit. *Required fees:* $451 per term. Tuition and fees vary according to degree level, program and student level. *Financial support:* Research assistantships, teaching assistantships, career-related internships or fieldwork, Federal Work-Study, institutionally sponsored loans, scholarships/grants, tuition waivers (partial), and unspecified assistantships available. Support available to part-time students. Financial award application deadline: 2/15; financial award applicants required to submit FAFSA. *Faculty research:* Kinesiology, gender disparities, exercise physiology, gait analysis, social justice. *Unit head:* Dr. Barry S. Eckert, Dean, 718-780-6578, Fax: 718-780-4561, E-mail: barry.eckert@liu.edu. *Application contact:* Dr. Dominick Fortugno, Dean of Admissions, 718-780-6578, Fax: 718-780-4561, E-mail: dominick.fortugno@liu.edu.
Website: http://liu.edu/brooklyn/academics/school-of-health-professions

Long Island University–LIU Post, School of Health Professions and Nursing, Brookville, NY 11548-1300. Offers cardiovascular perfusion (MS); clinical lab sciences (MS); clinical laboratory management (MS); dietetic internship (Advanced Certificate); family nurse practitioner (MS, Advanced Certificate); forensic social work (Advanced Certificate); gerontology (Advanced Certificate); health administration (MPA); medical biology (MS); non-profit management (Advanced Certificate); nursing education (MS); nutrition (MS); public administration (MPA); social work (MSW). *Program availability:* Part-time, evening/weekend, blended/hybrid learning. *Faculty:* 27 full-time (20 women), 43 part-time/adjunct (32 women). *Students:* 251 full-time (184 women), 243 part-time (197 women); includes 179 minority (76 Black or African American, non-Hispanic/Latino; 55 Asian, non-Hispanic/Latino; 42 Hispanic/Latino; 1 Native Hawaiian or other Pacific Islander, non-Hispanic/Latino; 5 Two or more races, non-Hispanic/Latino), 79 international. 581 applicants, 67% accepted, 168 enrolled. In 2016, 185 master's, 29 other advanced degrees awarded. *Degree requirements:* For master's, comprehensive exam (for some programs), thesis (for some programs); for Advanced Certificate, comprehensive exam (for some programs). *Entrance requirements:* Additional exam requirements/recommendations for international students: Required—TOEFL (minimum score 550 paper-based, 75 iBT) or IELTS. *Application deadline:* Applications are processed on a rolling basis. Application fee: $50. Electronic applications accepted. *Expenses: Tuition:* Full-time $28,272; part-time $1178 per credit. *Required fees:* $451 per term. Tuition and fees vary according to degree level and program. *Financial support:* In 2016–17, 5 research assistantships with partial tuition reimbursements (averaging $725 per year), 3 teaching assistantships with partial tuition reimbursements (averaging $800 per year) were awarded; career-related internships or fieldwork, Federal Work-Study, institutionally sponsored loans, scholarships/grants, and unspecified assistantships also available. Support available to part-time students. Financial award application deadline: 2/15; financial award applicants required to submit FAFSA. *Faculty research:* Cancer gene regulation, childhood obesity, host-pathogen interaction, interprofessional simulation, interstitial cystitis. *Total annual research expenditures:* $35,000. *Unit head:* Dr. Stacy Gropack, Dean, 516-299-2485, Fax: 516-299-2527, E-mail: post-shpn@liu.edu. *Application contact:* Carol Zerah, Director of Graduate Admissions, 516-299-2900, Fax: 516-299-2137, E-mail: post-enroll@liu.edu.
Website: http://liu.edu/post/health

Louisiana State University and Agricultural & Mechanical College, Graduate School, College of Human Sciences and Education, School of Social Work, Baton Rouge, LA 70803. Offers MSW, PhD. *Accreditation:* CSWE (one or more programs are accredited).

Loyola University Chicago, School of Social Work, Chicago, IL 60660. Offers MSW, PhD, PGC, JD/MSW, M Div/MSW, MJ/MSW, MSW/MA. *Accreditation:* CSWE (one or more programs are accredited). *Program availability:* Part-time. *Degree requirements:* For doctorate, comprehensive exam, thesis/dissertation. *Entrance requirements:* For master's, GRE; for doctorate, GRE or MAT. Additional exam requirements/recommendations for international students: Required—TOEFL (minimum score 550 paper-based; 79 iBT). *Expenses: Tuition:* Full-time $18,594. *Required fees:* $848. Part-time tuition and fees vary according to course load, degree level and program. *Faculty research:* Aging, trauma, migration, poverty, substance abuse.

Marshall University, Academic Affairs Division, College of Health Professions, Department of Social Work, Huntington, WV 25755. Offers MSW. *Program availability:* Part-time, online learning.

Marywood University, Academic Affairs, Center for Interdisciplinary Studies, Scranton, PA 18509-1598. Offers human development (PhD), including educational administration, health promotion, higher education administration, instructional leadership, social work. *Program availability:* Part-time. Electronic applications accepted. *Expenses:* Contact institution.

Marywood University, Academic Affairs, College of Health and Human Services, School of Social Work, Program in Social Work, Scranton, PA 18509-1598. Offers MSW. *Accreditation:* CSWE. *Program availability:* Part-time. *Entrance requirements:* For master's, minimum GPA of 3.0. Electronic applications accepted.

McGill University, Faculty of Graduate and Postdoctoral Studies, Faculty of Arts, School of Social Work, Montréal, QC H3A 2T5, Canada. Offers MSW, PhD, Diploma, MSW/LL B. PhD offered jointly with Université de Montréal.

McMaster University, School of Graduate Studies, Faculty of Social Sciences, School of Social Work, Hamilton, ON L8S 4M2, Canada. Offers analysis of social welfare policy (MSW); analysis of social work practice (MSW). *Program availability:* Part-time. *Entrance requirements:* For master's, minimum B+ average in final year, BSW from accredited program, half course each in introductory statistics and introductory social research methods. Additional exam requirements/recommendations for international students: Required—TOEFL (minimum score 580 paper-based). *Faculty research:* Health policy, income maintenance, child welfare, native issues, immigration policies, racism.

Memorial University of Newfoundland, School of Graduate Studies, School of Social Work, St. John's, NL A1C 5S7, Canada. Offers MSW, PhD. *Degree requirements:* For master's, thesis optional, internship; for doctorate, comprehensive exam, thesis/dissertation, internship, oral thesis defense. *Entrance requirements:* For master's, BSW with a minimum of 2nd-class standing or equivalent; for doctorate, MSW or equivalent, 3 years of post-BSW practice experience. Electronic applications accepted. *Faculty research:* Violence, child abuse, sexual abuse, social policy, gerontology.

Metropolitan State University of Denver, College of Letters, Arts and Sciences, Denver, CO 80204. Offers individual and families (MSW); macro practice (MSW); social work (MSW). *Accreditation:* CSWE. *Faculty:* 17 full-time (15 women), 20 part-time/adjunct (18 women). *Students:* 255 full-time (215 women), 13 part-time (12 women); includes 69 minority (13 Black or African American, non-Hispanic/Latino; 2 American Indian or Alaska Native, non-Hispanic/Latino; 8 Asian, non-Hispanic/Latino; 37 Hispanic/Latino; 2 Native Hawaiian or other Pacific Islander, non-Hispanic/Latino; 7 Two or more races, non-Hispanic/Latino). Average age 33. In 2016, 85 master's awarded. *Degree requirements:* For master's, field work. *Application deadline:* For fall admission, 1/23 for domestic students. Application fee: $50. *Expenses:* $7,658.10 full-time residents; $425.45 per credit hour part-time residents; $595.60 per credit hour part-time non-residents; $10,720.80 full-time non-residents. *Unit head:* Dr. Joan Laura Foster, Dean, 303-556-4453. *Application contact:* Bailee Bannon, Assistant Director, Graduate Program, 303-556-3474, E-mail: bbannon1@msudenver.edu.
Website: http://www.msudenver.edu/las/

Michigan State University, The Graduate School, College of Social Science, School of Social Work, East Lansing, MI 48824. Offers clinical social work (MSW); organizational and community practice (MSW); social work (PhD). *Accreditation:* CSWE. *Program availability:* Part-time, online learning. *Entrance requirements:* Additional exam requirements/recommendations for international students: Required—TOEFL. Electronic applications accepted.

Middle Tennessee State University, College of Graduate Studies, College of Behavioral and Health Sciences, Department of Social Work, Murfreesboro, TN 37132. Offers MSW. *Accreditation:* CSWE. *Entrance requirements:* Additional exam requirements/recommendations for international students: Required—TOEFL (minimum score 525 paper-based; 71 iBT), IELTS (minimum score 6). Electronic applications accepted.

Millersville University of Pennsylvania, College of Graduate Studies and Adult Learning, College of Education and Human Services, School of Social Work, Doctor of Social Work Program, Millersville, PA 17551-0302. Offers DSW. Program offered in partnership with Kutztown University of Pennsylvania. *Program availability:* Part-time, evening/weekend, primarily online, with a weekend residency once a semester. *Faculty:*

11 full-time (8 women), 1 (woman) part-time/adjunct. *Students:* 16 part-time (14 women); includes 4 minority (2 Black or African American, non-Hispanic/Latino; 1 Asian, non-Hispanic/Latino; 1 Hispanic/Latino). Average age 42. *Degree requirements:* For doctorate, thesis/dissertation, weekend residency. *Entrance requirements:* For doctorate, resume; writing sample; MSW. Additional exam requirements/recommendations for international students: Required—TOEFL (minimum score 600 paper-based), IELTS (minimum score 6). *Application deadline:* Applications are processed on a rolling basis. Application fee: $40. Electronic applications accepted. *Expenses:* $628 per credit resident tuition; $943 per credit non-resident tuition. *Financial support:* Unspecified assistantships available. Financial award application deadline: 3/15; financial award applicants required to submit FAFSA. *Unit head:* Dr. Karen M. Rice, Chair, 717-871-5279, Fax: 717-871-7941, E-mail: karen.rice@millersville.edu. *Application contact:* Dr. Victor S. DeSantis, Dean of College of Graduate Studies and Adult Learning/Associate Provost for Civic and Community Engagement, 717-871-7619, Fax: 717-871-7954, E-mail: victor.desantis@millersville.edu.
Website: http://www.millersville.edu/socialwork/dsw/index.php

Millersville University of Pennsylvania, College of Graduate Studies and Adult Learning, College of Education and Human Services, School of Social Work, Master of Social Work Program, Millersville, PA 17551-0302. Offers MSW. Program offered in partnership with Shippensburg University of Pennsylvania. *Accreditation:* CSWE. *Program availability:* Part-time, evening/weekend. *Faculty:* 11 full-time (8 women), 1 (woman) part-time/adjunct. *Students:* 50 full-time (46 women), 86 part-time (77 women); includes 26 minority (11 Black or African American, non-Hispanic/Latino; 1 American Indian or Alaska Native, non-Hispanic/Latino; 1 Asian, non-Hispanic/Latino; 13 Hispanic/Latino). Average age 28. 99 applicants, 87% accepted, 65 enrolled. In 2016, 65 master's awarded. *Degree requirements:* For master's, field practicum. *Entrance requirements:* For master's, GRE or MAT if GPA from all coursework is lower than 2.8, resume, all transcripts, at least 1 academic and 1 supervisory reference (specialized recommendation form). Additional exam requirements/recommendations for international students: Required—TOEFL (minimum score 600 paper-based), IELTS (minimum score 6). *Application deadline:* For summer admission, 2/1 for domestic students. Application fee: $40. Electronic applications accepted. *Expenses:* $483 per credit resident tuition; $725 per credit non-resident tuition. *Financial support:* In 2016–17, 22 students received support. Unspecified assistantships available. Financial award application deadline: 3/15; financial award applicants required to submit FAFSA. *Unit head:* Dr. Karen M. Rice, Chair, 717-871-5279, Fax: 717-871-7941, E-mail: karen.rice@millersville.edu. *Application contact:* Dr. Victor S. DeSantis, Dean of College of Graduate Studies and Adult Learning/Associate Provost for Civic and Community Engagement, 717-871-7619, Fax: 717-871-7954, E-mail: victor.desantis@millersville.edu.
Website: http://www.millersville.edu/socialwork/msw/index.php

Minnesota State University Mankato, College of Graduate Studies and Research, College of Social and Behavioral Sciences, Department of Social Work, Mankato, MN 56001. Offers MSW. *Accreditation:* CSWE. *Students:* 42 full-time (40 women). *Entrance requirements:* Additional exam requirements/recommendations for international students: Required—TOEFL. *Application deadline:* For fall admission, 1/15 priority date for domestic students. *Unit head:* David Beimers, Chair, 507-389-6190, Fax: 507-389-6769, E-mail: david.beimers@mnsu.edu. *Application contact:* Kimberly Zammitt, Program Director, 507-389-1219, E-mail: kimberly.zammitt@mnsu.edu.
Website: http://sbs.mnsu.edu/socialwork/graduate/

Missouri State University, Graduate College, College of Health and Human Services, School of Social Work, Springfield, MO 65897. Offers MSW. *Accreditation:* CSWE. *Program availability:* Part-time. *Faculty:* 10 full-time (9 women), 10 part-time/adjunct (7 women). *Students:* 17 full-time (13 women), 53 part-time (43 women); includes 5 minority (1 Black or African American, non-Hispanic/Latino; 1 Asian, non-Hispanic/Latino; 3 Two or more races, non-Hispanic/Latino). Average age 31. 71 applicants, 42% accepted, 24 enrolled. In 2016, 43 master's awarded. *Degree requirements:* For master's, comprehensive exam, thesis or alternative. *Entrance requirements:* For master's, GRE, minimum GPA of 3.0. Additional exam requirements/recommendations for international students: Required—TOEFL (minimum score 550 paper-based; 79 iBT), IELTS (minimum score 6). *Application deadline:* For fall admission, 1/31 priority date for domestic and international students. Application fee: $35 ($50 for international students). Electronic applications accepted. *Expenses:* Tuition, state resident: full-time $5830. Tuition, nonresident: full-time $10,708. *Required fees:* $1130. Tuition and fees vary according to class time, course level, course load and program. *Financial support:* Federal Work-Study, institutionally sponsored loans, scholarships/grants, and unspecified assistantships available. Financial award application deadline: 3/31; financial award applicants required to submit FAFSA. *Faculty research:* Child and family therapy, rural social work, adolescent social issues, domestic violence. *Unit head:* Michele Day, Department Head, 417-836-6967, Fax: 417-836-7688, E-mail: swk@missouristate.edu. *Application contact:* Michael Edwards, Coordinator of Graduate Admissions, 417-836-5330, Fax: 417-836-6200, E-mail: michaeledwards@missouristate.edu.
Website: http://www.missouristate.edu/swk/

Morgan State University, School of Graduate Studies, School of Social Work, Baltimore, MD 21251. Offers MSW, PhD. *Accreditation:* CSWE. *Entrance requirements:* For doctorate, GRE.

Nazareth College of Rochester, Graduate Studies, Department of Social Work, Rochester, NY 14618. Offers MSW. Program offered jointly with The College at Brockport, State University of New York. *Accreditation:* CSWE. *Program availability:* Part-time, evening/weekend. *Students:* 106 full-time (92 women), 70 part-time (59 women); includes 24 minority (14 Black or African American, non-Hispanic/Latino; 2 American Indian or Alaska Native, non-Hispanic/Latino; 3 Asian, non-Hispanic/Latino; 1 Hispanic/Latino; 4 Two or more races, non-Hispanic/Latino). Average age 30. 183 applicants, 70% accepted, 91 enrolled. *Entrance requirements:* For master's, minimum GPA of 3.0. Additional exam requirements/recommendations for international students: Required—TOEFL (minimum score 550 paper-based; 79 iBT) or IELTS (6.5). *Application deadline:* For fall admission, 3/15 for domestic students; for summer admission, 1/15 for domestic students. Electronic applications accepted. *Expenses:* Contact institution. *Financial support:* Unspecified assistantships available. Financial award application deadline: 3/1; financial award applicants required to submit FAFSA. *Unit head:* Dr. Carol Brownstein-Evans, Director, 585-395-8459, E-mail: cbrown3@naz.edu. *Application contact:* Judith Baker, Director, Transfer and Graduate Admissions, 585-531-1154, Fax: 585-389-2826, E-mail: gradadmissions@naz.edu.

Newman University, School of Social Work, Wichita, KS 67213-2097. Offers MSW. *Accreditation:* CSWE. *Program availability:* Online learning. *Degree requirements:* For master's, comprehensive exam (for some programs), thesis optional, fieldwork. *Entrance requirements:* For master's, minimum GPA of 3.0, 3 letters of reference. Additional exam requirements/recommendations for international students: Required—TOEFL (minimum score 600 paper-based; 100 iBT). *Expenses:* Contact institution.

New Mexico Highlands University, Graduate Studies, School of Social Work, Las Vegas, NM 87701. Offers bilingual/bicultural clinical practice (MSW); clinical practice (MSW). *Accreditation:* CSWE. *Program availability:* Part-time. *Degree requirements:* For master's, comprehensive exam, thesis or alternative. *Entrance requirements:* For master's, minimum undergraduate GPA of 3.0. Additional exam requirements/recommendations for international students: Required—TOEFL (minimum score 540 paper-based). *Faculty research:* Treatment attrition among domestic violence batterers, children's health and mental health, Dejando Huellas: meeting the bilingual/bicultural needs of the Latino mental health patient, impact of culture on the therapeutic process, effects of generational gang involvement on adolescents' future.

New Mexico State University, College of Health and Social Services, School of Social Work, Las Cruces, NM 88003. Offers MSW. *Accreditation:* CSWE. *Program availability:* Part-time. *Faculty:* 12 full-time (10 women), 6 part-time/adjunct (4 women). *Students:* 111 full-time (101 women), 19 part-time (11 women); includes 94 minority (6 Black or African American, non-Hispanic/Latino; 3 American Indian or Alaska Native, non-Hispanic/Latino; 2 Asian, non-Hispanic/Latino; 80 Hispanic/Latino; 3 Two or more races, non-Hispanic/Latino), 2 international. Average age 32. 82 applicants, 72% accepted, 49 enrolled. In 2016, 64 master's awarded. *Degree requirements:* For master's, comprehensive exam, thesis optional, written exam. *Entrance requirements:* For master's, minimum cumulative GPA of 3.0. Additional exam requirements/recommendations for international students: Required—TOEFL (minimum score 550 paper-based; 79 iBT), IELTS (minimum score 6.5). *Application deadline:* For fall admission, 1/16 priority date for domestic students, 2/16 priority date for international students. Applications are processed on a rolling basis. Application fee: $40 ($50 for international students). Electronic applications accepted. *Expenses:* Tuition, state resident: full-time $4086. Tuition, nonresident: full-time $14,254. *Required fees:* $853. Tuition and fees vary according to course load. *Financial support:* In 2016–17, 42 students received support, including 9 teaching assistantships (averaging $8,455 per year); career-related internships or fieldwork, Federal Work-Study, scholarships/grants, traineeships, health care benefits, and unspecified assistantships also available. Support available to part-time students. Financial award application deadline: 3/1. *Faculty research:* Mental health, gerontology, community-based social work, domestic violence, immigration, child welfare. *Total annual research expenditures:* $86,466. *Unit head:* Dr. Stephen Anderson, Interim Department Head, 575-646-3043, Fax: 575-646-4116, E-mail: stephean@nmsu.edu. *Application contact:* Dr. Wanda Whittlesey-Jerome, Coordinator, MSW Program Coordinator, 575-646-0322, Fax: 575-646-4116, E-mail: wkjerome@nmsu.edu.
Website: http://socialwork.nmsu.edu/

New York University, Silver School of Social Work, New York, NY 10003. Offers MSW, PhD, MSW/JD, MSW/MA, MSW/MPA, MSW/MPH. *Accreditation:* CSWE (one or more programs are accredited). *Program availability:* Part-time, evening/weekend. *Degree requirements:* For doctorate, comprehensive exam, thesis/dissertation. *Entrance requirements:* For master's, bachelor's degree; for doctorate, GRE, MSW. Additional exam requirements/recommendations for international students: Required—TOEFL, IELTS, TWE. Electronic applications accepted. *Expenses:* Contact institution. *Faculty research:* Social welfare policies, public health, aging, mental health, substance abuse.

Norfolk State University, School of Graduate Studies, Ethelyn R. Strong School of Social Work, Norfolk, VA 23504. Offers MSW, PhD. *Accreditation:* CSWE (one or more programs are accredited). *Program availability:* Part-time. *Degree requirements:* For doctorate, thesis/dissertation. *Entrance requirements:* For master's, minimum GPA of 2.7. Additional exam requirements/recommendations for international students: Required—TOEFL.

North Carolina Agricultural and Technical State University, School of Graduate Studies, College of Arts and Sciences, Department of Sociology and Social Work, Greensboro, NC 27411. Offers MSW. Joint program with The University of North Carolina at Greensboro. *Accreditation:* CSWE. *Program availability:* Part-time, evening/weekend. *Degree requirements:* For master's, comprehensive exam, qualifying exam. *Entrance requirements:* For master's, GRE General Test.

North Carolina State University, Graduate School, College of Humanities and Social Sciences, Department of Social Work, Raleigh, NC 27695. Offers MSW. *Accreditation:* CSWE.

Northern Kentucky University, Office of Graduate Programs, College of Education and Human Services, Program in Social Work, Highland Heights, KY 41099. Offers MSW. *Accreditation:* CSWE. *Program availability:* Part-time, evening/weekend. *Entrance requirements:* For master's, GRE (minimum score of 1000), minimum GPA of 3.0; undergraduate courses in psychology, sociology, and statistics with minimum C average; 3 letters of recommendation; essay; letter of intent; resume; interview. Additional exam requirements/recommendations for international students: Required—TOEFL (minimum score 79 iBT); Recommended—IELTS (minimum score 6.5). Electronic applications accepted. *Faculty research:* Children and families experiencing homelessness, team-based learning and diversity, impact of mentoring, photovoice and barriers to college, family directed structural therapy.

Northwest Nazarene University, Program in Social Work, Nampa, ID 83686. Offers clinical mental health and addictions practice (MSW). *Accreditation:* CSWE. *Program availability:* Part-time-only, evening/weekend. *Faculty:* 7 full-time (4 women), 9 part-time/adjunct (5 women). *Students:* 123 full-time (85 women), 24 part-time (13 women); includes 23 minority (3 Black or African American, non-Hispanic/Latino; 1 American Indian or Alaska Native, non-Hispanic/Latino; 12 Hispanic/Latino; 7 Two or more races, non-Hispanic/Latino). Average age 27. 152 applicants, 54% accepted, 73 enrolled. In 2016, 54 master's awarded. *Degree requirements:* For master's, comprehensive exam, thesis or alternative. *Entrance requirements:* For master's, interview, letters of reference, degree from regionally-accredited college/university, written personal statement. *Application deadline:* Applications are processed on a rolling basis. Application fee: $50. Electronic applications accepted. *Expenses: Tuition:* Full-time $9315; part-time $4658 per credit hour. *Required fees:* $120. *Faculty research:* Test anxiety, trauma, statistics. *Unit head:* Dr. Lawanna Lancaster, Director/Department Chair, 208-467-8372, Fax: 208-467-8879, E-mail: mswinfo@nnu.edu. *Application contact:* Jodie Rodriguez-Engel, Program Coordinator, 208-467-8679, Fax: 208-467-8879, E-mail: jrodriguez-engel@nnu.edu.
Website: http://msw.nnu.edu

Nyack College, School of Social Work, Nyack, NY 10960. Offers clinical social work practice (MSW); leadership in organizations and communities (MSW). *Program availability:* Part-time, evening/weekend. *Students:* 40 full-time (35 women), 29 part-time (27 women); includes 58 minority (32 Black or African American, non-Hispanic/Latino; 1 American Indian or Alaska Native, non-Hispanic/Latino; 5 Asian, non-Hispanic/Latino; 18 Hispanic/Latino; 2 Two or more races, non-Hispanic/Latino), 1 international. Average age 35. In 2016, 8 master's awarded. *Degree requirements:* For master's, field work. *Entrance requirements:* For master's, official transcripts, academic and professional references, personal statement, essay or case reflection. Additional exam requirements/recommendations for international students: Required—TOEFL (minimum score 550 paper-based; 80 iBT). *Application deadline:* Applications are processed on a rolling basis. Application fee: $45. Electronic applications accepted. *Expenses:* $775 per credit. *Financial support:* Institutionally sponsored loans available. Financial award applicants required to submit FAFSA. *Unit head:* Dr. Janet Furness, Director of MSW Program,

646-378-6169, E-mail: janet.furness@nyack.edu. *Application contact:* Apryll Campbell, Admissions Associate, 646-378-6195, E-mail: admissions.grad@nyack.edu.
Website: https://www.nyack.edu/msw

The Ohio State University, Graduate School, College of Social Work, Columbus, OH 43210. Offers MSW, PhD. *Accreditation:* CSWE (one or more programs are accredited). *Program availability:* Part-time. *Faculty:* 32. *Students:* 413 full-time (353 women), 95 part-time (79 women); includes 97 minority (55 Black or African American, non-Hispanic/Latino; 7 Asian, non-Hispanic/Latino; 17 Hispanic/Latino; 18 Two or more races, non-Hispanic/Latino), 14 international. Average age 29. In 2016, 215 master's, 3 doctorates awarded. *Degree requirements:* For master's, thesis optional; for doctorate, thesis/dissertation. *Entrance requirements:* For master's and doctorate, GRE. Additional exam requirements/recommendations for international students: Required—TOEFL (minimum score 550 paper-based; 79 iBT), Michigan English Language Assessment Battery (minimum score 82); Recommended—IELTS (minimum score 7). *Application deadline:* For fall admission, 12/13 priority date for domestic students, 11/30 priority date for international students; for summer admission, 4/1 for domestic students, 3/1 for international students. Applications are processed on a rolling basis. Application fee: $60 ($70 for international students). Electronic applications accepted. *Financial support:* Fellowships, research assistantships, teaching assistantships, Federal Work-Study, institutionally sponsored loans, and unspecified assistantships available. Support available to part-time students. *Unit head:* Dr. Tom Gregoire, Dean, 614-292-9426, E-mail: gregoire.5@osu.edu. *Application contact:* Graduate and Professional Admissions, 614-292-6031, Fax: 614-292-3656, E-mail: gpadmissions@osu.edu.
Website: http://csw.osu.edu/

The Ohio State University at Lima, Graduate Programs, Lima, OH 45804. Offers social work (MSW). *Program availability:* Part-time. *Faculty:* 36. *Students:* 6 (all women); includes 1 minority (Black or African American, non-Hispanic/Latino). Average age 32. Terminal master's awarded for partial completion of doctoral program. *Degree requirements:* For master's, comprehensive exam (for some programs), thesis (for some programs). *Entrance requirements:* For master's, GRE (in some cases), minimum GPA of 3.0. Additional exam requirements/recommendations for international students: Required—TOEFL (minimum score 550 paper-based, 79 iBT), IELTS (minimum score 7), or Michigan English Language Assessment Battery (minimum score 82). *Application deadline:* For fall admission, 4/1 for domestic students, 3/1 for international students; for spring admission, 10/15 for domestic and international students; for summer admission, 4/10 for domestic students, 3/1 for international students. Applications are processed on a rolling basis. Application fee: $60 ($70 for international students). Electronic applications accepted. *Financial support:* Application deadline: 2/15. *Unit head:* Dr. Charlene Gilbert, Dean and Director, 419-995-8481, E-mail: gilbert.583@osu.edu. *Application contact:* Graduate and Professional Admissions, 614-292-9444, Fax: 614-292-3895, E-mail: gpadmissions@osu.edu.

The Ohio State University–Mansfield Campus, Graduate Programs, Mansfield, OH 44906-1599. Offers education (MA); social work (MSW). *Program availability:* Part-time. *Faculty:* 40. *Students:* 3 (all women). *Degree requirements:* For master's, comprehensive exam (for some programs), thesis (for some programs). *Entrance requirements:* For master's, GRE, minimum GPA of 3.0. Additional exam requirements/recommendations for international students: Required—TOEFL (minimum 550 paper-based, 79 iBT), IELTS (minimum score 7) or Michigan English Language Assessment Battery (minimum score 82). *Application deadline:* For fall admission, 4/1 for domestic students, 3/1 for international students; for spring admission, 10/15 for domestic and international students. Applications are processed on a rolling basis. Application fee: $60 ($70 for international students). Electronic applications accepted. *Financial support:* Teaching assistantships with full tuition reimbursements, Federal Work-Study, and scholarships/grants available. Support available to part-time students. Financial award application deadline: 2/15; financial award applicants required to submit FAFSA. *Application contact:* Graduate and Professional Admissions, 614-292-9444, Fax: 614-292-3895, E-mail: gpadmissions@osu.edu.

The Ohio State University–Newark Campus, Graduate Programs, Newark, OH 43055-1797. Offers education - teaching and learning (MA); social work (MSW). *Program availability:* Part-time. *Faculty:* 51. *Students:* 15 (all women); includes 2 minority (1 Black or African American, non-Hispanic/Latino; 1 Hispanic/Latino). Average age 32. Terminal master's awarded for partial completion of doctoral program. *Degree requirements:* For master's, comprehensive exam (for some programs), thesis (for some programs). *Entrance requirements:* For master's, GRE, minimum GPA of 3.0. Additional exam requirements/recommendations for international students: Required—TOEFL (minimum score 550 paper-based; 79 iBT), IELTS (minimum score 7), or Michigan English Language Assessment Battery (minimum score 82). *Application deadline:* For fall admission, 3/1 for domestic and international students. Applications are processed on a rolling basis. Application fee: $60 ($70 for international students). Electronic applications accepted. *Financial support:* Application deadline: 2/15. *Unit head:* Dr. William L. MacDonald, Dean/Director, 740-366-9333 Ext. 330, E-mail: macdonald.24@osu.edu. *Application contact:* Graduate and Professional Admissions, 614-292-9444, Fax: 614-292-3985, E-mail: gpadmissions@osu.edu.

Ohio University, Graduate College, College of Health Sciences and Professions, Department of Social and Public Health, Program in Social Work, Athens, OH 45701-2979. Offers MSW. *Accreditation:* CSWE. *Program availability:* Part-time. *Degree requirements:* For master's, fieldwork. *Entrance requirements:* For master's, GRE General Test or minimum GPA of 3.0, liberal arts background with coursework in human biology, statistics, and three social science areas; paid or volunteer work in human services. Additional exam requirements/recommendations for international students: Required—TOEFL (minimum score 620 paper-based; 105 iBT) or IELTS (minimum score 7.5). *Application deadline:* For fall admission, 2/1 for domestic students, 8/15 for international students. Application fee: $50 ($55 for international students). Electronic applications accepted. *Financial support:* Research assistantships with full tuition reimbursements, teaching assistantships with full tuition reimbursements, career-related internships or fieldwork, Federal Work-Study, tuition waivers (partial), and unspecified assistantships available. Financial award application deadline: 2/1; financial award applicants required to submit FAFSA. *Faculty research:* Violence, families, rural life. *Unit head:* Dr. Susan Kiss Sarnoff, Chair, 740-593-1301, Fax: 740-593-0427, E-mail: sarnoff@ohio.edu. *Application contact:* Dr. Freve Pace, Graduate Chair, 740-593-1321, E-mail: pace@ohio.edu.
Website: http://www.socialwork.ohiou.edu/

Our Lady of the Lake University, School of Professional Studies, San Antonio, TX 78207-4689. Offers communication and learning disorders (MA), including communication disorders; counseling psychology (Psy D); curriculum and instruction (M Ed), including integrated science teaching; psychology (MS), including family, couple, and individual psychotherapy, school psychology; school counseling (M Ed); social work (MSW); sociology (MA). *Program availability:* Part-time, evening/weekend, 100% online, blended/hybrid learning. *Faculty:* 36 full-time (30 women), 73 part-time/adjunct (54 women). *Students:* 1,059 full-time (950 women), 59 part-time (51 women); includes 713 minority (253 Black or African American, non-Hispanic/Latino; 8 American Indian or Alaska Native, non-Hispanic/Latino; 9 Asian, non-Hispanic/Latino; 426 Hispanic/Latino; 3 Native Hawaiian or other Pacific Islander, non-Hispanic/Latino; 14 Two or more races, non-Hispanic/Latino), 1 international. Average age 34. 565 applicants, 66% accepted, 226 enrolled. In 2016, 251 master's, 9 doctorates awarded. *Degree requirements:* For master's, comprehensive exam (for some programs); for doctorate, comprehensive exam, thesis/dissertation, internship, qualifying exam. *Entrance requirements:* For doctorate, GRE General Test, GRE Subject Test (psychology), master's degree in psychology or closely-related discipline of at least 45 hours from regionally-accredited institution; minimum cumulative GPA of 3.5 in the master's program; criminal background check; 3 letters of recommendation; pertinent professional experience; personal statement. Additional exam requirements/recommendations for international students: Required—TOEFL. Application fee: $40 ($50 for international students). Electronic applications accepted. Application fee is waived when completed online. *Expenses: Tuition:* Full-time $14,796. Tuition and fees vary according to course load, degree level, campus/location and program. *Financial support:* In 2016–17, 111 students received support. Research assistantships, teaching assistantships, Federal Work-Study, scholarships/grants, unspecified assistantships, and tuition discounts available. Support available to part-time students. Financial award application deadline: 5/1; financial award applicants required to submit FAFSA. *Faculty research:* Culturally and linguistically diverse persons within various professional contexts, research, service-learning, student-centeredness, clinical experiences. *Unit head:* Dr. Marcheta Evans, Dean, 210-431-4140, E-mail: sps@ollusa.edu. *Application contact:* Graduate Admissions, 210-431-3995 Ext. 2314, Fax: 210-431-3945, E-mail: gradadm@lake.ollusa.edu.
Website: http://www.ollusa.edu/s/1190/hybrid/hw-hybrid-ollu.aspx?sid-1190&gid-1&pgid-7761

Our Lady of the Lake University, Worden School of Social Service, San Antonio, TX 78207-4689. Offers social work (MSW). *Accreditation:* CSWE. *Program availability:* Part-time, evening/weekend, 100% online, blended/hybrid learning. *Faculty:* 9 full-time (all women), 45 part-time/adjunct (34 women). *Students:* 776 full-time (694 women), 8 part-time (7 women); includes 490 minority (220 Black or African American, non-Hispanic/Latino; 8 American Indian or Alaska Native, non-Hispanic/Latino; 5 Asian, non-Hispanic/Latino; 241 Hispanic/Latino; 3 Native Hawaiian or other Pacific Islander, non-Hispanic/Latino; 13 Two or more races, non-Hispanic/Latino). Average age 34. 248 applicants, 93% accepted, 121 enrolled. In 2016, 185 master's awarded. *Entrance requirements:* For master's, official transcripts demonstrating minimum cumulative GPA of 2.5, 3 letters of recommendation, personal statement, current resume. Additional exam requirements/recommendations for international students: Required—TOEFL. *Application deadline:* For fall admission, 6/15 for domestic and international students; for spring admission, 11/15 for domestic and international students; for summer admission, 4/15 for domestic and international students. Applications are processed on a rolling basis. Application fee: $40 ($50 for international students). Electronic applications accepted. *Expenses: Tuition:* Full-time $14,796. Tuition and fees vary according to course load, degree level, campus/location and program. *Financial support:* In 2016–17, 35 students received support, including 1 research assistantship (averaging $15,300 per year); teaching assistantships, Federal Work-Study, scholarships/grants, unspecified assistantships, and tuition discounts also available. Support available to part-time students. Financial award application deadline: 5/1; financial award applicants required to submit FAFSA. *Faculty research:* Acculturation, mindfulness, pedagogy, spirituality, child welfare. *Unit head:* Rebecca Gomez, Program Director, 210-434-6711 Ext. 5578, E-mail: rjgomez@ollusa.edu. *Application contact:* Office of Graduate Admissions, 210-431-3995, Fax: 210-431-3945, E-mail: gradadm@lake.ollusa.edu.
Website: http://www.ollusa.edu/s/1190/hybrid/default-hybrid-ollu.aspx?sid-1190&gid-1&pgid-7916

Pacific University, Program in Social Work, Forest Grove, OR 97116-1797. Offers MSW.

Park University, School of Graduate and Professional Studies, Kansas City, MO 54105. Offers adult education (M Ed); business and government leadership (Graduate Certificate); business, government, and global society (MPA); communication and leadership (MA); creative and life writing (Graduate Certificate); disaster and emergency management (MPA, Graduate Certificate); educational leadership (M Ed); finance (MBA, Graduate Certificate); general business (MBA); global business (Graduate Certificate); healthcare administration (MHA); healthcare services management and leadership (Graduate Certificate); international business (MBA); language and literacy (M Ed), including English for speakers of other languages, special reading teacher/literacy coach; leadership of international healthcare organizations (Graduate Certificate); management information systems (MBA, Graduate Certificate); music performance (ADP, Graduate Certificate), including cello (MM, ADP), piano (MM, ADP), viola (MM, ADP), violin (MM, ADP); nonprofit and community services management (MPA); nonprofit leadership (Graduate Certificate); performance (MM), including cello (MM, ADP), piano (MM, ADP), viola (MM, ADP), violin (MM, ADP); public management (MPA); social work (MSW); teacher leadership (M Ed), including curriculum and assessment, instructional leader. *Program availability:* Part-time, evening/weekend, online learning. *Degree requirements:* For master's, comprehensive exam (for some programs), thesis (for some programs), internship (for some programs); exam (for some programs). *Entrance requirements:* For master's, GRE or GMAT (for some programs), teacher certification (for some M Ed programs), letters of recommendation, essay, resume (for some programs). Additional exam requirements/recommendations for international students: Required—TOEFL (minimum score 550 paper-based; 79 iBT), IELTS (minimum score 6). Electronic applications accepted.

Phillips Theological Seminary, Programs in Theology, Tulsa, OK 74116. Offers administration of church agencies (M Div); campus ministry (M Div); church-related social work (M Div); college and seminary teaching (M Div); global mission work (M Div); institutional chaplaincy (M Div); ministerial vocations in Christian education (M Div); ministry (D Min), including parish ministry, pastoral counseling, practices of ministry; ministry and culture (MAMC), including Christian education, congregational leadership, history and practice of Christian spirituality, theology, ethics, and culture; ministry of music (M Div); pastoral care and counseling (M Div); pastoral ministry (M Div); theological studies (MTS). *Accreditation:* ATS. *Program availability:* Part-time, online learning. *Degree requirements:* For master's, thesis (for some programs); for doctorate, thesis/dissertation. *Entrance requirements:* For master's, minimum GPA of 2.5; for doctorate, M Div, minimum GPA of 3.0. *Faculty research:* Biblical studies, historical studies, theology and culture, practical theology, theology and film.

Pontifical Catholic University of Puerto Rico, College of Graduate Studies in Behavioral Science and Community Affairs, Program in Clinical Social Work, Ponce, PR 00717-0777. Offers MSW. *Accreditation:* CSWE. *Program availability:* Part-time, evening/weekend. *Entrance requirements:* For master's, EXADEP, 3 letters of recommendation, interview, minimum GPA of 2.75.

Portland State University, Graduate Studies, School of Social Work, Portland, OR 97207-0751. Offers social work (MSW); social work and social research (PhD). *Accreditation:* CSWE (one or more programs are accredited). *Program availability:* Part-time. *Faculty:* 35 full-time (26 women), 41 part-time/adjunct (32 women). *Students:* 358 full-time (284 women), 270 part-time (222 women); includes 188 minority (33 Black or African American, non-Hispanic/Latino; 22 American Indian or Alaska Native, non-Hispanic/Latino; 20 Asian, non-Hispanic/Latino; 75 Hispanic/Latino; 1 Native Hawaiian

or other Pacific Islander, non-Hispanic/Latino; 37 Two or more races, non-Hispanic/ Latino), 2 international. Average age 35. 794 applicants, 33% accepted, 239 enrolled. In 2016, 221 master's, 6 doctorates awarded. *Degree requirements:* For doctorate, comprehensive exam, thesis/dissertation, residency. *Entrance requirements:* For master's, minimum GPA of 3.0 in upper-division course work or 2.75 overall; for doctorate, GRE General Test, 4 references. Additional exam requirements/ recommendations for international students: Required—TOEFL (minimum score 550 paper-based; 80 iBT). *Application deadline:* For fall admission, 2/1 for domestic and international students. Application fee: $65. *Expenses:* Contact institution. *Financial support:* In 2016–17, 6 research assistantships with tuition reimbursements (averaging $7,366 per year), 5 teaching assistantships with tuition reimbursements (averaging $5,621 per year) were awarded; career-related internships or fieldwork, Federal Work-Study, scholarships/grants, tuition waivers (partial), and unspecified assistantships also available. Support available to part-time students. Financial award application deadline: 3/1; financial award applicants required to submit FAFSA. *Faculty research:* Child welfare; child mental health; social welfare policies and services; work, family, and dependent care; adult mental health. *Total annual research expenditures:* $14.7 million. *Unit head:* Dr. Laura B. Nissen, Dean, 503-725-3997, Fax: 503-725-5545, E-mail: nissen@pdx.edu. *Application contact:* Prof. Sarah Bradley, Director of MSW Program, 503-725-8028, Fax: 503-725-5545, E-mail: bradles@pdx.edu.
Website: https://www.pdx.edu/ssw/

Quinnipiac University, School of Health Sciences, Program in Social Work, Hamden, CT 06518-1940. Offers MSW. *Accreditation:* CSWE. *Faculty:* 4 full-time (all women), 5 part-time/adjunct (2 women). *Students:* 54 full-time (43 women), 14 part-time (11 women); includes 20 minority (11 Black or African American, non-Hispanic/Latino; 1 Asian, non-Hispanic/Latino; 6 Hispanic/Latino; 2 Two or more races, non-Hispanic/ Latino). 72 applicants, 90% accepted, 25 enrolled. In 2016, 27 master's awarded. *Entrance requirements:* For master's, bachelor's degree with at least 20 semester credits in liberal arts and a course in statistics with minimum C grade; minimum GPA of 3.0. *Application deadline:* For fall admission, 3/15 for domestic students; for spring admission, 11/15 for domestic students. Applications are processed on a rolling basis. Application fee: $45. Electronic applications accepted. *Expenses: Tuition:* Part-time $985 per credit. *Required fees:* $40 per credit. $150 per semester. Tuition and fees vary according to program. *Financial support:* Federal Work-Study, scholarships/grants, and unspecified assistantships available. Financial award application deadline: 6/1; financial award applicants required to submit FAFSA. *Faculty research:* Older adult sexuality, social work practice in health settings, gerontology and social work, adolescent sexuality, prevention programs in social work practice, international social work, evidence-based treatments for children and families, organizational practice, inter-professional education, curriculum development in social work education and inter-professional practice, stress reduction approaches in clinical practice and professional education. *Unit head:* Deborah Rejent, MSW Program Director, E-mail: graduate@qu.edu. *Application contact:* Office of Graduate Admissions, 800-462-1944, Fax: 203-582-3443, E-mail: graduate@qu.edu.
Website: http://www.qu.edu/msw

Radford University, College of Graduate Studies and Research, Program in Social Work, Radford, VA 24142. Offers MSW. *Accreditation:* CSWE. *Program availability:* Part-time. *Faculty:* 10 full-time (8 women), 10 part-time/adjunct (8 women). *Students:* 54 full-time (42 women), 58 part-time (48 women); includes 26 minority (20 Black or African American, non-Hispanic/Latino; 1 American Indian or Alaska Native, non-Hispanic/ Latino; 4 Hispanic/Latino; 1 Two or more races, non-Hispanic/Latino). Average age 29. 93 applicants, 69% accepted, 41 enrolled. In 2016, 41 master's awarded. *Degree requirements:* For master's, comprehensive exam. *Entrance requirements:* For master's, minimum GPA of 2.75, 3.0 in last 60 hours of upper-division coursework; 3 letters of reference; personal essay; case study; previous experience in the field of human services; legal/military history form; resume; official transcripts. Additional exam requirements/recommendations for international students: Required—TOEFL (minimum score 550 paper-based; 79 iBT), IELTS (minimum score 6.5). *Application deadline:* For fall admission, 2/15 priority date for domestic students, 12/1 for international students; for spring admission, 7/1 for international students. Applications are processed on a rolling basis. Application fee: $50. Electronic applications accepted. *Expenses:* Tuition, state resident: full-time $7868; part-time $328 per credit hour. Tuition, nonresident: full-time $16,394; part-time $683 per credit hour. *Required fees:* $3090; $130 per credit hour. Tuition and fees vary according to course load and program. *Financial support:* In 2016–17, 23 students received support, including 1 research assistantship (averaging $5,000 per year), 2 teaching assistantships (averaging $10,500 per year); career-related internships or fieldwork, scholarships/grants, and unspecified assistantships also available. Support available to part-time students. Financial award application deadline: 3/1; financial award applicants required to submit FAFSA. *Unit head:* Diana Joyce, Admissions Coordinator, 540-831-7682, E-mail: dsjoyce@radford.edu.
Website: http://www.radford.edu/content/wchs/home/social-work.html

Ramapo College of New Jersey, Master of Social Work Program, Mahwah, NJ 07430-1680. Offers MSW. *Program availability:* Part-time. *Faculty:* 4 full-time (all women), 5 part-time/adjunct (4 women). *Students:* 70 full-time (59 women), 14 part-time (all women); includes 24 minority (10 Black or African American, non-Hispanic/Latino; 13 Hispanic/Latino; 1 Two or more races, non-Hispanic/Latino). Average age 31. 167 applicants, 59% accepted, 51 enrolled. *Entrance requirements:* For master's, official transcript of baccalaureate degree from accredited institution with minimum recommended GPA of 3.0; personal statement; 2 letters of recommendation; resume; 3-5 page narrative highlighting personal and professional accomplishments, values, and strengths. Additional exam requirements/recommendations for international students: Required—TOEFL (minimum score 550 paper-based; 79 iBT); Recommended—IELTS (minimum score 6). *Application deadline:* For fall admission, 3/1 for domestic and international students. Applications are processed on a rolling basis. Application fee: $60. Electronic applications accepted. *Expenses:* $606.05 per credit tuition, $130.45 per credit fees. *Financial support:* Scholarships/grants available. Financial award application deadline: 3/1; financial award applicants required to submit FAFSA. *Unit head:* Ann Marie Moreno, Assistant Dean/Director, 201-684-7191, E-mail: amoreno@ramapo.edu.
Website: http://www.ramapo.edu/msw/

Rhode Island College, School of Graduate Studies, School of Social Work, Providence, RI 02908-1991. Offers MSW. *Accreditation:* CSWE. *Program availability:* Part-time. *Faculty:* 9 full-time (6 women), 17 part-time/adjunct (14 women). *Students:* 75 full-time (62 women), 126 part-time (106 women); includes 39 minority (12 Black or African American, non-Hispanic/Latino; 2 American Indian or Alaska Native, non-Hispanic/ Latino; 1 Asian, non-Hispanic/Latino; 23 Hispanic/Latino; 1 Two or more races, non-Hispanic/Latino). Average age 32. In 2016, 73 master's awarded. *Entrance requirements:* For master's, official transcripts, personal statement, 3 letters of recommendation. Additional exam requirements/recommendations for international students: Recommended—TOEFL (minimum score 550 paper-based; 79 iBT). *Application deadline:* For fall admission, 2/1 for domestic students. Applications are processed on a rolling basis. Application fee: $50. Electronic applications accepted. *Expenses:* Contact institution. *Financial support:* Career-related internships or fieldwork, Federal Work-Study, scholarships/grants, health care benefits, and unspecified assistantships available. Support available to part-time students. Financial award application deadline: 5/15; financial award applicants required to submit FAFSA. *Unit head:* Dr. Sue Pearlmutter, Dean, 401-456-8042, E-mail: spearlmutter@ric.edu. *Application contact:* Graduate Studies, 401-456-8700.
Website: http://www.ric.edu/socialWork/

Roberts Wesleyan College, Department of Social Work, Rochester, NY 14624-1997. Offers child and family practice (MSW); mental health practice (MSW). *Accreditation:* CSWE. *Entrance requirements:* For master's, minimum GPA of 2.75. *Faculty research:* Religion and social work, family studies, values and ethics.

★ **Rutgers University–New Brunswick,** School of Social Work, New Brunswick, NJ 08901. Offers MSW, PhD, JD/MSW, M Div/MSW. *Accreditation:* CSWE (one or more programs are accredited). *Program availability:* Part-time. *Degree requirements:* For doctorate, comprehensive exam, thesis/dissertation. *Entrance requirements:* For doctorate, GRE General Test. Additional exam requirements/recommendations for international students: Required—TOEFL. Electronic applications accepted. *Faculty research:* Family theory, adolescent development, child and adolescent mental health delivery systems, poverty and employment policy.

See Display on next page and Close-Up on page 1689.

Sacred Heart University, Graduate Programs, College of Arts and Sciences, Department of Social Work, Fairfield, CT 06825. Offers MSW. *Entrance requirements:* Additional exam requirements/recommendations for international students: Required—TOEFL, TWE, or IELTS; Recommended—TSE. Application fee: $75. *Expenses: Tuition:* Part-time $654 per credit hour. *Unit head:* Dr. Bronwyn Cross-Denny, Chair, 203-371-7941, Fax: 203-365-4892, E-mail: cross-dennyb@sacredheart.edu. *Application contact:* William Sweeney, Director of Graduate Admissions Operations, 203-365-4827, E-mail: gradstudies@sacredheart.edu.

St. Ambrose University, College of Education and Health Sciences, Program in Social Work, Davenport, IA 52803-2898. Offers MSW. *Accreditation:* CSWE. *Program availability:* Part-time, evening/weekend. *Degree requirements:* For master's, comprehensive exam (for some programs), thesis or alternative, integration projects. *Entrance requirements:* For master's, minimum GPA of 3.0, course work in statistics, bachelor's degree in liberal arts. Additional exam requirements/recommendations for international students: Required—TOEFL. Electronic applications accepted. *Faculty research:* Social work practice, cults/sects, family therapy, developmental disabilities.

St. Catherine University, Graduate Programs, Program in Social Work, St. Paul, MN 55105. Offers MSW, DSW. Program offered jointly with University of St. Thomas. *Accreditation:* CSWE. *Program availability:* Part-time, evening/weekend. *Degree requirements:* For master's, clinical research paper. *Entrance requirements:* For master's, minimum GPA of 3.0. Additional exam requirements/recommendations for international students: Required—Michigan English Language Assessment Battery or TOEFL (minimum score 600 paper-based; 100 iBT). *Expenses:* Contact institution.

St. Cloud State University, School of Graduate Studies, School of Health and Human Services, Department of Social Work, St. Cloud, MN 56301-4498. Offers MSW. *Accreditation:* CSWE. *Program availability:* Part-time. *Entrance requirements:* For master's, minimum GPA of 3.0.

Saint Leo University, Graduate Studies in Social Work, Saint Leo, FL 33574-6665. Offers advanced clinical practice (MSW). *Accreditation:* CSWE. *Program availability:* Online only, blended/hybrid learning. *Faculty:* 8 full-time (6 women), 21 part-time/adjunct (17 women). *Students:* 143 full-time (123 women), 83 part-time (68 women); includes 94 minority (67 Black or African American, non-Hispanic/Latino; 1 Asian, non-Hispanic/ Latino; 22 Hispanic/Latino; 4 Two or more races, non-Hispanic/Latino). Average age 36. 275 applicants, 73% accepted, 126 enrolled. In 2016, 73 master's awarded. *Entrance requirements:* For master's, official transcripts, current resumé, 3 professional recommendations, personal statement. Additional exam requirements/ recommendations for international students: Required—TOEFL (minimum score 550 paper-based; 80 iBT). *Application deadline:* For fall admission, 6/1 for domestic and international students. Application fee: $80. Electronic applications accepted. *Expenses:* $465 per semester hour. *Financial support:* In 2016–17, 2 students received support. Career-related internships or fieldwork and health care benefits available. Financial award application deadline: 3/1. *Faculty research:* Juvenile crime and violence, trauma, distance education, animal-assisted therapy, sibling caregivers of families with persons with developmental disabilities. *Unit head:* Dr. Cindy Lee, Director of Graduate Studies in Social Work, 352-588-8869, Fax: 352-588-8289, E-mail: cindy.lee@saintleo.edu. *Application contact:* Jennifer Shelley, Senior Associate Director of Graduate Admissions, 800-707-8846, Fax: 352-588-7873, E-mail: grad.admissions@saintleo.edu.
Website: http://www.saintleo.edu/academics/graduate/social-work.aspx

Saint Louis University, Graduate Education, College of Education and Public Service, School of Social Work, St. Louis, MO 63103. Offers MSW. *Accreditation:* CSWE. *Program availability:* Part-time. *Entrance requirements:* For master's, minimum GPA of 3.0, letters of recommendation. Additional exam requirements/recommendations for international students: Required—TOEFL (minimum score 550 paper-based). *Expenses:* Contact institution. *Faculty research:* Gerontology, mental health issues, child welfare (especially abuse and neglect), social justice, and peace making, homelessness.

Salem State University, School of Graduate Studies, Program in Social Work, Salem, MA 01970-5353. Offers MSW. *Accreditation:* CSWE. *Program availability:* Part-time, evening/weekend. *Entrance requirements:* For master's, GRE, MAT. Additional exam requirements/recommendations for international students: Required—TOEFL (minimum score 550 paper-based; 80 iBT) or IELTS (minimum score 5.5).

Salisbury University, Department of Social Work, Salisbury, MD 21801-6837. Offers MSW. *Accreditation:* CSWE. *Program availability:* Part-time, 100% online, blended/ hybrid learning. *Faculty:* 19 full-time (16 women), 28 part-time/adjunct (24 women). *Students:* 281 full-time (251 women), 55 part-time (49 women); includes 59 minority (32 Black or African American, non-Hispanic/Latino; 15 Hispanic/Latino; 12 Two or more races, non-Hispanic/Latino). Average age 31. 242 applicants, 70% accepted, 144 enrolled. In 2016, 119 master's awarded. *Entrance requirements:* Additional exam requirements/recommendations for international students: Required—TOEFL (minimum score 550 paper-based, 79 iBT) or IELTS (6.5). *Application deadline:* For fall admission, 2/3 for domestic and international students. Application fee: $65. Electronic applications accepted. *Expenses:* $381 per credit hour resident, $670 per credit hour non-resident; $84 per credit hour fees; $750 per credit hour (online). *Financial support:* In 2016–17, 18 students received support, including 6 teaching assistantships with full tuition reimbursements available (averaging $8,042 per year); career-related internships or fieldwork and scholarships/grants also available. Support available to part-time students. Financial award application deadline: 3/1; financial award applicants required to submit FAFSA. *Faculty research:* Aging; mass incarceration; professional identity development. *Unit head:* Dr. Vicki Root, Graduate Program Director, Social Work, 410-543-6307, E-mail: vbroot@salisbury.edu. *Application contact:* Susan Mareski, Administrative Assistant, 410-677-5363, E-mail: smmareski@salisbury.edu.
Website: http://www.salisbury.edu/gsr/gradstudies/MSWpage.html

Social Work

Samford University, School of Public Health, Birmingham, AL 35229. Offers clinical social work (MSW); global community development (MSW); public health (MPH). *Program availability:* Part-time, evening/weekend, 100% online, blended/hybrid learning. *Faculty:* 14 full-time (10 women). *Students:* 83 full-time (77 women), 2 part-time (1 woman); includes 7 minority (1 American Indian or Alaska Native, non-Hispanic/Latino; 2 Asian, non-Hispanic/Latino; 2 Hispanic/Latino; 2 Two or more races, non-Hispanic/Latino). Average age 27. 47 applicants, 100% accepted, 37 enrolled. In 2016, 3 master's awarded. *Entrance requirements:* Additional exam requirements/recommendations for international students: Required—TOEFL (minimum score 550 paper-based). *Application deadline:* For fall admission, 6/1 for domestic and international students; for spring admission, 10/1 for domestic and international students. Application fee: $75. Electronic applications accepted. *Expenses:* Contact institution. *Financial support:* In 2016–17, 28 students received support. Scholarships/grants available. Financial award application deadline: 3/1; financial award applicants required to submit FAFSA. *Unit head:* Dr. Keith Elder, Dean, School of Public Health, 205-726-4655, E-mail: kelder@samford.edu. *Application contact:* Dr. Marian Carter, Assistant Dean of Enrollment Management and Student Services, 205-726-2611, E-mail: mwcarter@samford.edu.
Website: http://www.samford.edu/publichealth/

San Diego State University, Graduate and Research Affairs, College of Health and Human Services, School of Social Work, San Diego, CA 92182. Offers MSW, JD/MSW, MSW/MPH. JD/MSW offered jointly with California Western School of Law. *Accreditation:* CSWE. *Program availability:* Part-time. *Degree requirements:* For master's, comprehensive exam, thesis optional. *Entrance requirements:* For master's, GRE General Test. Additional exam requirements/recommendations for international students: Required—TOEFL. Electronic applications accepted. *Faculty research:* Child maltreatment, substance abuse, neighborhood studies, child welfare.

San Francisco State University, Division of Graduate Studies, College of Health and Social Sciences, School of Social Work, San Francisco, CA 94132-1722. Offers MSW. *Accreditation:* CSWE. *Program availability:* Part-time. *Degree requirements:* For master's, thesis optional. *Application deadline:* Applications are processed on a rolling basis. *Expenses:* Tuition, state resident: full-time $6738. Tuition, nonresident: full-time $15,666. *Required fees:* $1012. Tuition and fees vary according to degree level and program. *Financial support:* Career-related internships or fieldwork and Federal Work-Study available. *Unit head:* Dr. Susanna Jones, Director, 415-405-4084, Fax: 415-338-0591, E-mail: susjones@sfsu.edu. *Application contact:* Rebecca Sanchez, Office Manager, 415-338-7538, Fax: 415-338-0591, E-mail: bex@sfsu.edu.
Website: http://socwork.sfsu.edu/

San Jose State University, Graduate Studies and Research, College of Applied Sciences and Arts, San Jose, CA 95192-0001. Offers big data (Certificate); California library media teacher services (Credential); collaborative response to family violence (Certificate); justice studies (MS); kinesiology (MA), including applied sciences and arts (MA, MS), athletic training, exercise physiology, sport management, sport studies; library and information science (MLIS, Certificate); mass communication (MA); nutritional science (MS); occupational therapy (MS); public health (MPH); pupil personnel services (Credential); recreation (MS), including applied sciences and arts (MA, MS), international tourism; social work (MSW); Spanish language counseling (Certificate); strategic management of digital assets and services (Certificate). *Program availability:* Part-time, evening/weekend. Electronic applications accepted.

Savannah State University, Master of Social Work Program, Savannah, GA 31404. Offers MSW. *Accreditation:* CSWE. *Degree requirements:* For master's, 1000-hour field practicum, seminar course for each semester in field placement. *Entrance requirements:* For master's, GRE General Test (minimum score of 3.0 in analytical writing portion), minimum GPA of 2.8, degree from accredited institution with liberal arts courses, official transcripts, directed essay, 3 letters of recommendation. Additional exam requirements/recommendations for international students: Required—TOEFL. *Expenses:* Contact institution. *Faculty research:* Clinical and administrative social work.

Seattle University, College of Arts and Sciences, Program in Social Work, Seattle, WA 98122-1090. Offers MSW. *Faculty:* 5 full-time (3 women), 3 part-time/adjunct (all women). *Students:* 20 full-time (16 women); includes 7 minority (1 Black or African American, non-Hispanic/Latino; 1 Asian, non-Hispanic/Latino; 2 Hispanic/Latino; 1 Native Hawaiian or other Pacific Islander, non-Hispanic/Latino; 2 Two or more races, non-Hispanic/Latino). Average age 27. 73 applicants, 44% accepted, 20 enrolled. *Application deadline:* For fall admission, 1/20 priority date for domestic students. *Financial support:* In 2016–17, 17 students received support. *Unit head:* Dr. Hye-Kyung Kang, Director, 206-296-5558, E-mail: kangh@seattleu.edu. *Application contact:* Janet Shandley, Director of Graduate Admissions, 206-296-5900, Fax: 206-298-5656, E-mail: grad_admissions@seattleu.edu.
Website: http://www.seattleu.edu/artsci/msw/

Seton Hall University, College of Arts and Sciences, Department of Sociology, Anthropology and Social Work, South Orange, NJ 07079-2697. Offers social work (MSW).

Shippensburg University of Pennsylvania, School of Graduate Studies, College of Education and Human Services, Department of Social Work and Gerontology, Shippensburg, PA 17257-2299. Offers social work (MSW). *Accreditation:* CSWE. *Program availability:* Part-time, evening/weekend, blended/hybrid learning. *Faculty:* 6 full-time (4 women), 5 part-time/adjunct (2 women). *Students:* 43 full-time (39 women), 33 part-time (27 women); includes 9 minority (6 Black or African American, non-Hispanic/Latino; 1 Asian, non-Hispanic/Latino; 1 Hispanic/Latino; 1 Two or more races, non-Hispanic/Latino). Average age 30. 89 applicants, 66% accepted, 45 enrolled. In 2016, 27 master's awarded. *Degree requirements:* For master's, thesis, field practicum. *Entrance requirements:* For master's, GRE or MAT (if GPA is below 2.8), 3 professional references with minimum of one from faculty and one from current or recent agency employer or supervisor; current resume; written personal statement; course work in human biology, economics, government/political science, psychology, sociology/anthropology and statistics. Additional exam requirements/recommendations for international students: Required—TOEFL (minimum score 550 paper-based, 68 iBT) or IELTS (minimum score 6). *Application deadline:* For fall admission, 4/30 for international students; for spring admission, 9/30 for international students. Applications are processed on a rolling basis. Application fee: $45. Electronic applications accepted. *Expenses:* Tuition, state resident: part-time $483 per credit. Tuition, nonresident: part-time $725 per credit. *Required fees:* $141 per credit. *Financial support:* In 2016–17, 8 students received support. Career-related internships or fieldwork, scholarships/grants, unspecified assistantships, and resident hall director and student payroll positions available. Support available to part-time students. Financial award application deadline: 3/1; financial award applicants required to submit FAFSA. *Unit head:* Dr. Deborah F. Jacobs, Co-Director, MU-SU Master of Social Work Program, 717-477-1276, Fax: 717-477-4051, E-mail: dfjaco@ship.edu. *Application contact:* Megan N. Luft, Assistant Dean of Graduate Admissions, 717-477-1231, Fax: 717-477-4016, E-mail: mnluft@ship.edu.
Website: http://www.ship.edu/social_work/

Simmons College, School of Social Work, Boston, MA 02115. Offers behavior analysis (MS, PhD, Ed S); education (MS Ed); social work (MSW, PhD); special education (MS Ed), including moderate and severe disabilities; teaching (MAT), including elementary education; MSW/MBA. *Accreditation:* CSWE (one or more programs are accredited). *Program availability:* Part-time, 100% online. *Faculty:* 37 full-time (28 women), 62 part-time/adjunct (44 women). *Students:* 797 full-time (705 women), 951 part-time (829 women); includes 420 minority (200 Black or African American, non-

Hispanic/Latino; 5 American Indian or Alaska Native, non-Hispanic/Latino; 46 Asian, non-Hispanic/Latino; 122 Hispanic/Latino; 4 Native Hawaiian or other Pacific Islander, non-Hispanic/Latino; 43 Two or more races, non-Hispanic/Latino), 13 international. Average age 31. 1,356 applicants, 78% accepted, 592 enrolled. In 2016, 342 master's, 2 doctorates, 1 other advanced degree awarded. Terminal master's awarded for partial completion of doctoral program. *Degree requirements:* For master's, thesis (for some programs); for doctorate, comprehensive exam (for some programs), thesis/dissertation (for some programs). *Entrance requirements:* For master's, GRE, MAT, Massachusetts Tests for Education Licensure (for different programs); for doctorate, GRE, BCBA Analyst Exam. Additional exam requirements/recommendations for international students: Required—TOEFL (minimum score 600 paper-based; 100 iBT). *Application deadline:* For fall admission, 8/1 for domestic students; for spring admission, 12/15 for domestic students; for summer admission, 5/1 for domestic students. Applications are processed on a rolling basis. Application fee: $35. Electronic applications accepted. *Expenses:* $1,010 per credit; $52 activity fee per semester. *Financial support:* In 2016–17, 12 fellowships with partial tuition reimbursements were awarded; scholarships/grants and unspecified assistantships also available. Support available to part-time students. *Unit head:* Dr. Cheryl Parks, Dean, 617-521-3293, E-mail: cheryl.parks@simmons.edu. *Application contact:* Carlos D. Frontado, Director of Admissions, 617-521-3920, Fax: 617-521-3980, E-mail: ssw@simmons.edu.
Website: http://www.simmons.edu/ssw/

Smith College, School for Social Work, Northampton, MA 01063. Offers clinical social work (MSW, PhD). *Accreditation:* CSWE (one or more programs are accredited). *Faculty:* 14 full-time (11 women), 98 part-time/adjunct (79 women). *Students:* 260 full-time (222 women), 45 part-time (35 women); includes 82 minority (24 Black or African American, non-Hispanic/Latino; 4 American Indian or Alaska Native, non-Hispanic/Latino; 18 Asian, non-Hispanic/Latino; 22 Hispanic/Latino; 1 Native Hawaiian or other Pacific Islander, non-Hispanic/Latino; 13 Two or more races, non-Hispanic/Latino), 9 international. Average age 33. 490 applicants, 53% accepted, 147 enrolled. In 2016, 118 master's, 13 doctorates awarded. *Degree requirements:* For master's, thesis; for doctorate, thesis/dissertation. *Entrance requirements:* For doctorate, MAT. Additional exam requirements/recommendations for international students: Required—TOEFL (minimum score 94 iBT) or IELTS (70). *Application deadline:* For fall admission, 2/21 for domestic students, 2/15 for international students. Applications are processed on a rolling basis. Application fee: $60. Electronic applications accepted. Application fee is waived when completed online. *Expenses:* Contact institution. *Financial support:* In 2016–17, 246 students received support. Career-related internships or fieldwork and scholarships/grants available. Financial award application deadline: 3/1; financial award applicants required to submit FAFSA. *Faculty research:* Social work practice, human behavior in the social environment, social welfare policy, social work research. *Unit head:* Dr. Marianne Yoshioka, Dean/Professor, 413-585-7977, E-mail: myoshioka@smith.edu. *Application contact:* Irene Rodriguez Martin, Associate Dean, Graduate Enrollment and Student Services, 413-585-7960, Fax: 413-585-7994, E-mail: imartin@smith.edu.
Website: http://www.smith.edu/ssw/

Southeastern University, College of Behavioral and Social Sciences, Lakeland, FL 33801-6099. Offers human services (MA); international community development (MA); marriage and family counseling (MS); professional counseling (MS); school counseling (MS); social work (MSW). *Program availability:* Evening/weekend. *Expenses: Tuition:* Full-time $9450; part-time $6300 per credit. *Required fees:* $500; $250 per semester. One-time fee: $150. Tuition and fees vary according to degree level, campus/location and program. *Unit head:* Erica H. Sirrine, Dean, 863-667-5341, E-mail: ehsirrine@seu.edu.
Website: http://www.seu.edu/behavior/

Southern Adventist University, School of Social Work, Collegedale, TN 37315-0370. Offers MSW. *Accreditation:* CSWE. *Program availability:* Online learning.

Southern Connecticut State University, School of Graduate Studies, School of Health and Human Services, Department of Social Work, New Haven, CT 06515-1355. Offers MSW. *Accreditation:* CSWE. *Program availability:* Part-time, evening/weekend. *Faculty:* 14 full-time (8 women), 14 part-time/adjunct (9 women). *Students:* 168 full-time (148 women), 33 part-time (29 women); includes 40 minority (22 Black or African American, non-Hispanic/Latino; 2 Asian, non-Hispanic/Latino; 15 Hispanic/Latino; 1 Two or more races, non-Hispanic/Latino), 2 international. Average age 31. 365 applicants, 69% accepted, 83 enrolled. In 2016, 63 master's awarded. *Degree requirements:* For master's, thesis. *Entrance requirements:* For master's, minimum undergraduate QPA of 3.0 in graduate major field, interview. *Application deadline:* For fall admission, 3/1 for domestic students; for spring admission, 12/1 for domestic students. Application fee: $50. Electronic applications accepted. *Expenses:* Tuition, state resident: full-time $6497; part-time $519 per credit hour. Tuition, nonresident: full-time $18,102; part-time $535 per credit hour. *Required fees:* $4722; $55 per semester. Tuition and fees vary according to program. *Financial support:* Career-related internships or fieldwork, scholarships/grants, and unspecified assistantships available. Financial award application deadline: 4/15; financial award applicants required to submit FAFSA. *Faculty research:* Social work practice; social service development; services for women, the aging, children, and families in educational and health care systems. *Unit head:* Dr. Elizabeth Keenan, Chairperson, 203-392-5108, Fax: 203-392-6580, E-mail: keenane1@southernct.edu. *Application contact:* Lisa Galvin, Director of Graduate Admissions, 203-392-5240, Fax: 203-392-5235, E-mail: galvinl1@southernct.edu.

Southern Illinois University Carbondale, Graduate School, College of Education and Human Services, School of Social Work, Carbondale, IL 62901-4701. Offers MSW, JD/MSW. *Accreditation:* CSWE. *Entrance requirements:* For master's, GRE General Test, minimum GPA of 2.7. Additional exam requirements/recommendations for international students: Required—TOEFL. *Faculty research:* Service delivery systems, comparative race relations, advocacy research, gerontology, child welfare and health.

Southern Illinois University Edwardsville, Graduate School, College of Arts and Sciences, Department of Social Work, Edwardsville, IL 62026. Offers school social work (MSW); social work (MSW). *Accreditation:* CSWE. *Program availability:* Part-time, evening/weekend. *Degree requirements:* For master's, final exam, capstone course. *Entrance requirements:* Additional exam requirements/recommendations for international students: Required—TOEFL (minimum score 550 paper-based; 79 iBT), IELTS (minimum score 6.5). Electronic applications accepted.

Southern University at New Orleans, School of Graduate Studies, New Orleans, LA 70126-1009. Offers criminal justice (MA); management information systems (MS); museum studies (MA); social work (MSW). *Accreditation:* CSWE. *Program availability:* Part-time, evening/weekend. *Degree requirements:* For master's, thesis. *Entrance requirements:* For master's, GRE/GMAT. Additional exam requirements/recommendations for international students: Required—TOEFL.

Spalding University, Graduate Studies, Kosair College of Health and Natural Sciences, School of Social Work, Louisville, KY 40203-2188. Offers MSW. *Accreditation:* CSWE. *Program availability:* Evening/weekend. *Faculty:* 14 full-time (13 women), 4 part-time/adjunct (all women). *Students:* 31 full-time (30 women), 15 part-time (14 women); includes 22 minority (19 Black or African American, non-Hispanic/Latino; 1 Asian, non-Hispanic/Latino; 1 Hispanic/Latino; 1 Two or more races, non-Hispanic/Latino). Average age 36. 46 applicants, 50% accepted, 22 enrolled. In 2016, 17 master's awarded. *Degree requirements:* For master's, thesis or alternative. *Entrance requirements:* For master's, transcripts, letters of recommendation, personal essay, personal interview. Additional exam requirements/recommendations for international students: Required—TOEFL (minimum score 535 paper-based). *Application deadline:* For fall admission, 6/15 priority date for domestic students. Applications are processed on a rolling basis. Application fee: $30. Electronic applications accepted. *Expenses: Tuition:* Full-time $15,300. *Financial support:* Research assistantships, career-related internships or fieldwork, scholarships/grants, and unspecified assistantships available. Financial award applicants required to submit FAFSA. *Faculty research:* Addictions, spirituality, feminist studies, mental retardation, action research. *Unit head:* Dr. Kevin Borders, Chair/MSW Director, 502-873-4482, E-mail: kborders@spalding.edu. *Application contact:* Aundrea Howard, Administrative Assistant, 502-588-7183, E-mail: ahoward02@spalding.edu.
Website: http://spalding.edu/academics/social-work/

Springfield College, Graduate Programs, School of Social Work, Springfield, MA 01109-3797. Offers advanced practice with children and adolescents (Post-Master's Certificate); social work (MSW); JD/MSW. *Accreditation:* CSWE. *Program availability:* Part-time, evening/weekend. *Degree requirements:* For master's, comprehensive exam. *Entrance requirements:* Additional exam requirements/recommendations for international students: Required—TOEFL (minimum score 550 paper-based); Recommended—IELTS (minimum score 6). Electronic applications accepted. *Expenses: Tuition:* Full-time $29,640; part-time $988 per credit. *Required fees:* $195. *Faculty research:* Children and families, health and mental health, school social work, gerontology, international social work.

Stephen F. Austin State University, Graduate School, College of Applied Arts and Science, School of Social Work, Nacogdoches, TX 75962. Offers MSW. *Accreditation:* CSWE. *Degree requirements:* For master's, comprehensive exam, thesis optional. *Entrance requirements:* For master's, GRE General Test, interview. Additional exam requirements/recommendations for international students: Required—TOEFL (minimum score 550 paper-based).

Stockton University, Office of Graduate Studies, Program in Social Work, Galloway, NJ 08205-9441. Offers MSW. *Accreditation:* CSWE. *Program availability:* Evening/weekend. *Faculty:* 8 full-time (6 women), 6 part-time/adjunct (5 women). *Students:* 85 full-time (78 women), 11 part-time (9 women); includes 39 minority (21 Black or African American, non-Hispanic/Latino; 2 Asian, non-Hispanic/Latino; 15 Hispanic/Latino; 1 Two or more races, non-Hispanic/Latino). Average age 31. 150 applicants, 66% accepted, 71 enrolled. In 2016, 61 master's awarded. *Degree requirements:* For master's, thesis optional, field work. *Entrance requirements:* Additional exam requirements/recommendations for international students: Required—TOEFL. *Application deadline:* For fall admission, 2/1 for domestic and international students. Applications are processed on a rolling basis. Application fee: $50. Electronic applications accepted. *Expenses:* $772 per credit in-state. *Financial support:* Fellowships, research assistantships, career-related internships or fieldwork, Federal Work-Study, scholarships/grants, and unspecified assistantships available. Financial award application deadline: 3/1; financial award applicants required to submit FAFSA. *Unit head:* Dr. Diane Falk, Program Director, 609-626-3640, E-mail: gradschool@stockton.edu. *Application contact:* Tara Williams, Assistant Director of Graduate Enrollment Management, 609-626-3640, Fax: 609-626-6050, E-mail: gradschool@stockton.edu.
Website: http://www.stockton.edu/grad

Stony Brook University, State University of New York, Stony Brook Medicine, School of Social Welfare, Doctoral Program in Social Welfare, Stony Brook, NY 11794. Offers PhD. *Faculty:* 18 full-time (12 women), 44 part-time/adjunct (32 women). *Students:* 17 full-time (15 women), 8 part-time (5 women); includes 7 minority (5 Black or African American, non-Hispanic/Latino; 2 Asian, non-Hispanic/Latino). Average age 41. 16 applicants, 31% accepted, 2 enrolled. In 2016, 3 doctorates awarded. *Degree requirements:* For doctorate, thesis/dissertation. *Entrance requirements:* For doctorate, GRE, three letters of reference, personal statement, writing sample. Additional exam requirements/recommendations for international students: Required—TOEFL. *Application deadline:* For fall admission, 1/15 for domestic students; for spring admission, 10/1 for domestic students. Application fee: $100. *Expenses:* Contact institution. *Financial support:* Fellowships and teaching assistantships available. Financial award application deadline: 2/1. *Faculty research:* Social welfare, social work, rape or sexual abuse, child welfare, social justice. *Unit head:* Dr. Jacqueline B. Mondros, Dean and Assistant Vice President for Social Determinants of Health, 631-444-2139, E-mail: jacqueline.mondros@stonybrook.edu. *Application contact:* Mamie Gladden, Staff Assistant, 631-444-3142, Fax: 631-444-7565, E-mail: mamie.gladden@stonybrook.edu.
Website: http://socialwelfare.stonybrookmedicine.edu/

Stony Brook University, State University of New York, Stony Brook Medicine, School of Social Welfare, Master's Program in Social Work, Stony Brook, NY 11794. Offers MSW. *Accreditation:* CSWE. *Faculty:* 18 full-time (12 women), 44 part-time/adjunct (32 women). *Students:* 349 full-time (283 women), 9 part-time (8 women); includes 117 minority (47 Black or African American, non-Hispanic/Latino; 11 Asian, non-Hispanic/Latino; 53 Hispanic/Latino; 6 Two or more races, non-Hispanic/Latino), 1 international. Average age 31. 509 applicants, 78% accepted, 268 enrolled. In 2016, 165 master's awarded. *Degree requirements:* For master's, project or thesis. *Entrance requirements:* For master's, interview, minimum cumulative GPA of 2.5. Additional exam requirements/recommendations for international students: Required—TOEFL. *Application deadline:* For fall admission, 3/1 for domestic students. Application fee: $100. *Expenses:* Contact institution. *Financial support:* Teaching assistantships available. Financial award application deadline: 3/1. *Faculty research:* Social welfare, social work, rape or sexual abuse, child welfare, social justice. *Unit head:* Dr. Jacqueline B. Mondros, Dean and Assistant Vice President for Social Determinants of Health, 631-444-2139, E-mail: jacqueline.mondros@stonybrook.edu. *Application contact:* Kathy Albin, Director of Admission and Student Services, 631-444-3141, Fax: 631-444-7565, E-mail: kathleen.albin@stonybrook.edu.
Website: http://socialwelfare.stonybrookmedicine.edu/

Syracuse University, David B. Falk College of Sport and Human Dynamics, Dual Master's Program in Social Work and Marriage and Family Therapy (MSW/MA), Syracuse, NY 13244. Offers MSW/MA. *Accreditation:* AAMFT/COAMFTE. *Entrance requirements:* Additional exam requirements/recommendations for international students: Required—TOEFL or IELTS. *Application deadline:* For fall admission, 2/15 priority date for domestic and international students; for summer admission, 1/15 priority date for domestic students, 1/15 for international students. Application fee: $75. Electronic applications accepted. *Expenses: Tuition:* Full-time $25,974; part-time $1443 per credit hour. *Required fees:* $802; $50 per course. Tuition and fees vary according to course load and program. *Financial support:* Fellowships, research assistantships, teaching assistantships, career-related internships or fieldwork, and scholarships/grants available. Financial award application deadline: 1/1. *Faculty research:* Human diversity in social context, foundations of social work practice, policy and services in child welfare, child and family policy, social welfare policy and services. *Unit head:* Prof. Keith Alford,

Director, School of Social Work, 315-443-5562, Fax: 315-443-2562, E-mail: kalford@syr.edu. *Application contact:* Felicia Otero, Director of College Admissions, 315-443-5555, Fax: 315-443-2562, E-mail: falk@syr.edu.

Syracuse University, David B. Falk College of Sport and Human Dynamics, MSW Program in Social Work, Syracuse, NY 13244. Offers MSW. *Accreditation:* CSWE. *Program availability:* Part-time, evening/weekend. *Degree requirements:* For master's, thesis or alternative, field placement. *Entrance requirements:* For master's, personal statement, official transcripts, three letters of recommendation, resume. Additional exam requirements/recommendations for international students: Required—TOEFL (minimum score 100 iBT). *Application deadline:* For fall admission, 2/15 priority date for domestic and international students; for spring admission, 11/1 for domestic students, 11/1 priority date for international students. Applications are processed on a rolling basis. Application fee: $75. Electronic applications accepted. *Expenses: Tuition:* Full-time $25,974; part-time $1443 per credit hour. *Required fees:* $802; $50 per course. Tuition and fees vary according to course load and program. *Financial support:* Fellowships with full tuition reimbursements, research assistantships with tuition reimbursements, teaching assistantships with tuition reimbursements, career-related internships or fieldwork, and tuition waivers available. Financial award application deadline: 1/1; financial award applicants required to submit FAFSA. *Faculty research:* Child welfare, substance abuse counseling, health care, public policy, industry and business, school social work, gerontology, and mental health services. *Unit head:* Prof. Keith Alford, Director, School of Social Work, 315-443-5562, E-mail: kalford@syr.edu. *Application contact:* Felicia Otero, Director of College Admissions, 315-443-5555, E-mail: falk@syr.edu.
Website: http://falk.syr.edu/SocialWork/Default.aspx

Tarleton State University, College of Graduate Studies, College of Health Sciences and Human Services, Master of Social Work Program, Stephenville, TX 76402. Offers MSW. *Program availability:* Part-time, evening/weekend. *Faculty:* 6 full-time (5 women). *Students:* 27 full-time (21 women), 6 part-time (5 women); includes 13 minority (9 Black or African American, non-Hispanic/Latino; 3 Hispanic/Latino; 1 Two or more races, non-Hispanic/Latino). 12 applicants, 100% accepted, 11 enrolled. *Entrance requirements:* For master's, GRE, minimum GPA of 2.5. Additional exam requirements/recommendations for international students: Required—TOEFL (minimum score 550 paper-based; 80 iBT). *Application deadline:* Applications are processed on a rolling basis. Application fee: $45 ($145 for international students). Electronic applications accepted. *Expenses:* $3,672 tuition; $2,437 fees. *Financial support:* Applicants required to submit FAFSA. *Unit head:* Dr. Melody Loya, Department Head, 254-968-1696, E-mail: loya@tarleton.edu. *Application contact:* Information Contact, 254-968-9104, Fax: 254-968-9670, E-mail: gradoffice@tarleton.edu.

Temple University, College of Public Health, School of Social Work, Philadelphia, PA 19122. Offers MSW. *Accreditation:* CSWE. *Program availability:* Part-time, evening/weekend. *Faculty:* 28 full-time (15 women), 10 part-time/adjunct (8 women). *Students:* 258 full-time (224 women), 167 part-time (139 women); includes 178 minority (119 Black or African American, non-Hispanic/Latino; 9 Asian, non-Hispanic/Latino; 35 Hispanic/Latino; 15 Two or more races, non-Hispanic/Latino), 3 international. 362 applicants, 63% accepted, 100 enrolled. In 2016, 221 master's awarded. *Degree requirements:* For master's, internship, field practicum. *Entrance requirements:* For master's, minimum GPA of 3.0, 3 letters of recommendation, statement of goals, resume. Additional exam requirements/recommendations for international students: Required—TOEFL (minimum score 550 paper-based; 79 iBT). *Application deadline:* For fall admission, 3/15 priority date for domestic students, 2/15 for international students; for spring admission, 11/1 priority date for domestic students, 10/15 for international students; for summer admission, 3/15 for domestic students, 2/15 for international students. Applications are processed on a rolling basis. Application fee: $60. Electronic applications accepted. *Expenses:* Contact institution. *Financial support:* Research assistantships with tuition reimbursements, career-related internships or fieldwork, Federal Work-Study, scholarships/grants, traineeships, tuition waivers (partial), unspecified assistantships, and field assistantships available. Support available to part-time students. Financial award application deadline: 1/1. *Faculty research:* Child welfare, alcoholism, social work practice, developmental disabilities, human sexuality, mental health services, health and corrections. *Unit head:* Bernie Newman, Chairperson, 215-204-1205, Fax: 215-204-9606, E-mail: bernie.newman@temple.edu. *Application contact:* Cheryl A. Hyde, Associate Professor/MSW Program Director, 215-204-7112, E-mail: chyde@temple.edu.
Website: https://cph.temple.edu/ssa

Tennessee State University, The School of Graduate Studies and Research, College of Public Service, Nashville, TN 37209-1561. Offers human resource management (MPS); public administration (MPA, PhD); social work (MSW); strategic leadership (MPS); training and development (MPS). *Accreditation:* NASPAA (one or more programs are accredited). *Program availability:* Part-time, evening/weekend. *Degree requirements:* For master's, comprehensive exam, thesis optional; for doctorate, comprehensive exam, thesis/dissertation. *Entrance requirements:* For master's, GRE General Test, minimum GPA of 2.5, writing sample; for doctorate, GRE General Test, minimum GPA of 3.25, writing sample. *Faculty research:* Total quality management and process improvement, national health care policy and administration, starting non-profit ventures, public service ethics, state education financing across the U.S. public.

Texas A&M University–Commerce, College of Education and Human Services, Commerce, TX 75429-3011. Offers counseling (MS); curriculum and instruction (M Ed, MS); early childhood education (M Ed, MS); educational administration (M Ed, Ed D); educational psychology (PhD); educational technology leadership (MS); educational technology library science (MS); health, kinesiology and sports studies (MS); higher education (MS, Ed D); organization, learning, and technology (MS); psychology (MS); reading (M Ed, MS); school psychology (SSP); secondary education (M Ed, MS); social work (MSW); special education (M Ed); supervision, curriculum and instruction-elementary education (Ed D). *Program availability:* Part-time, 100% online, blended/hybrid learning. *Faculty:* 88 full-time (52 women), 31 part-time/adjunct (24 women). *Students:* 341 full-time (276 women), 1,495 part-time (1,156 women); includes 762 minority (429 Black or African American, non-Hispanic/Latino; 4 American Indian or Alaska Native, non-Hispanic/Latino; 27 Asian, non-Hispanic/Latino; 247 Hispanic/Latino; 1 Native Hawaiian or other Pacific Islander, non-Hispanic/Latino; 54 Two or more races, non-Hispanic/Latino), 18 international. Average age 37. 1,070 applicants, 54% accepted, 452 enrolled. In 2016, 579 master's, 31 doctorates awarded. *Degree requirements:* For master's, one foreign language, comprehensive exam, thesis optional, departmental qualifying exams (for some programs); for doctorate, comprehensive exam, thesis/dissertation, departmental qualifying exam; for SSP, comprehensive exam, thesis optional. *Entrance requirements:* For master's and doctorate, GRE General Test. Additional exam requirements/recommendations for international students: Required—TOEFL (minimum score 550 paper-based; 79 iBT), IELTS (minimum score 6). *Application deadline:* For fall admission, 6/1 priority date for international students; for spring admission, 10/15 priority date for international students; for summer admission, 3/15 priority date for international students. Applications are processed on a rolling basis. Application fee: $50. Electronic applications accepted. *Expenses:* $2,254 resident; $4,744 non-resident. *Financial support:* In 2016–17, 301 students received support, including 39 research assistantships with partial tuition reimbursements available (averaging $9,000 per year), 17 teaching assistantships with partial tuition reimbursements available (averaging $9,000 per year); career-related internships or fieldwork, Federal Work-Study, institutionally sponsored loans, scholarships/grants, health care benefits, and unspecified assistantships also available. Financial award application deadline: 5/1; financial award applicants required to submit FAFSA. *Faculty research:* Cognitive and bilingual education, positive behavioral intervention, literacy, math readiness. *Total annual research expenditures:* $470,963. *Unit head:* Dr. Timothy Letzring, Dean, 903-886-5181, Fax: 903-886-5905, E-mail: tim.letzring@tamuc.edu. *Application contact:* Jennifer Faunce, Graduate Recruiter, 903-886-5030, Fax: 903-886-5905, E-mail: jennifer.faunce@tamuc.edu.
Website: http://www.tamuc.edu/academics/graduateSchool/programs/education/default.aspx

Texas Christian University, Harris College of Nursing and Health Sciences, Department of Social Work, Fort Worth, TX 76129. Offers advanced generalist (MSW), including health and mental health/children and families. Evening-only part-time option offered every odd-numbered year. *Accreditation:* CSWE. *Program availability:* Part-time, evening/weekend. *Faculty:* 5 full-time (3 women), 5 part-time/adjunct (3 women). *Students:* 40 full-time (31 women); includes 13 minority (4 Black or African American, non-Hispanic/Latino; 2 Asian, non-Hispanic/Latino; 5 Hispanic/Latino; 2 Two or more races, non-Hispanic/Latino), 2 international. Average age 27. 48 applicants, 77% accepted, 25 enrolled. In 2016, 15 master's awarded. *Degree requirements:* For master's, research project in field agency. *Entrance requirements:* Additional exam requirements/recommendations for international students: Required—TOEFL (minimum score 550 paper-based; 80 iBT), IELTS (minimum score 6.5). *Application deadline:* For fall admission, 4/3 for domestic and international students. Application fee: $60. Electronic applications accepted. *Expenses:* Contact institution. *Financial support:* In 2016–17, 39 students received support. Tuition waivers (partial) available. Financial award application deadline: 4/3. *Faculty research:* Homelessness, trans elders, sexual violence prevention, developmental disabilities, gay and lesbian families. *Total annual research expenditures:* $140,000. *Unit head:* Dr. Joel Mitchell, Chair, 817-257-6157, Fax: 817-257-7665, E-mail: j.mitchell@tcu.edu. *Application contact:* Crystal Ledet, Academic Program Specialist, 817-257-7612, Fax: 817-257-5784, E-mail: crystal.ledet@tcu.edu.
Website: http://www.socialwork.tcu.edu/msw.asp

Texas State University, The Graduate College, College of Applied Arts, Program in Social Work, San Marcos, TX 78666. Offers MSW. *Accreditation:* CSWE. *Program availability:* Part-time, 100% online, blended/hybrid learning. *Faculty:* 23 full-time (17 women), 15 part-time/adjunct (12 women). *Students:* 146 full-time (127 women), 154 part-time (140 women); includes 161 minority (50 Black or African American, non-Hispanic/Latino; 2 American Indian or Alaska Native, non-Hispanic/Latino; 1 Asian, non-Hispanic/Latino; 96 Hispanic/Latino; 12 Two or more races, non-Hispanic/Latino), 1 international. Average age 31. 416 applicants, 45% accepted, 126 enrolled. In 2016, 85 master's awarded. *Degree requirements:* For master's, comprehensive exam, field practicum/internship under the supervision of a licensed master social worker within a social service agency. *Entrance requirements:* For master's, baccalaureate degree from regionally-accredited institution with minimum GPA of 3.0 in last 60 hours of course work, resume, statement of purpose. Additional exam requirements/recommendations for international students: Required—TOEFL (minimum score 550 paper-based; 78 iBT). *Application deadline:* For fall admission, 3/15 for domestic and international students; for spring admission, 10/15 for domestic students, 10/1 for international students. Applications are processed on a rolling basis. Application fee: $40 ($90 for international students). Electronic applications accepted. *Expenses:* $9,702 per year. *Financial support:* In 2016–17, 192 students received support, including 11 research assistantships (averaging $12,140 per year), 3 teaching assistantships (averaging $13,500 per year); career-related internships or fieldwork, Federal Work-Study, institutionally sponsored loans, scholarships/grants, and unspecified assistantships also available. Support available to part-time students. Financial award application deadline: 4/1; financial award applicants required to submit FAFSA. *Faculty research:* Community-based HIV education research program for diverse racial and ethnic groups. *Total annual research expenditures:* $4,156. *Unit head:* Dr. Angela Ausbrooks, Graduate Advisor, 512-245-9067, E-mail: aa16@txstate.edu. *Application contact:* Dr. Andrea Golato, Dean of the Graduate College, 512-245-2581, Fax: 512-245-8365, E-mail: gradcollege@txstate.edu.
Website: http://www.socialwork.txstate.edu

Texas Tech University, Graduate School, College of Arts and Sciences, Department of Sociology, Anthropology and Social Work, Lubbock, TX 79409. Offers anthropology (MA); social work (MSW); sociology (MA). *Program availability:* Part-time. *Faculty:* 28 full-time (16 women), 8 part-time/adjunct (4 women). *Students:* 49 full-time (38 women), 11 part-time (6 women); includes 20 minority (4 Black or African American, non-Hispanic/Latino; 14 Hispanic/Latino; 2 Two or more races, non-Hispanic/Latino), 5 international. Average age 27. 63 applicants, 52% accepted, 24 enrolled. In 2016, 19 master's awarded. *Degree requirements:* For master's, one foreign language, comprehensive exam (for some programs), thesis (for some programs). *Entrance requirements:* For master's, GRE (for MA in anthropology), two letters of recommendation, statement of purpose, writing sample, curriculum vitae; minimum GPA of 3.0 and coursework in sociology or closely-related fields (for MA in sociology); coursework in anthropology (for MA in anthropology). Additional exam requirements/recommendations for international students: Required—TOEFL (minimum score 550 paper-based; 79 iBT). *Application deadline:* For fall admission, 6/1 priority date for domestic students, 1/15 priority date for international students; for spring admission, 9/1 priority date for domestic students, 6/15 priority date for international students. Applications are processed on a rolling basis. Application fee: $75. Electronic applications accepted. *Expenses:* $300 per credit hour full-time resident tuition, $708 per credit hour full-time non-resident tuition; $50.50 per credit hour fee plus $608 per term fee. *Financial support:* In 2016–17, 53 students received support, including 42 fellowships (averaging $4,678 per year), 33 teaching assistantships (averaging $12,439 per year); research assistantships, Federal Work-Study, scholarships/grants, tuition waivers (partial), and unspecified assistantships also available. Financial award application deadline: 2/1; financial award applicants required to submit FAFSA. *Faculty research:* Sociology of criminology/deviance, population/migration, forensic anthropology, archaeology, social work (advanced generalist). *Total annual research expenditures:* $122,652. *Unit head:* Dr. Brett A. Houk, Chair and Associate Professor, 806-834-8107, Fax: 806-742-1088, E-mail: brett.houk@ttu.edu. *Application contact:* Dr. Cristina Bradatan, Associate Professor/Sociology Graduate Program Director, 806-834-1796, E-mail: cristina.bradatan@ttu.edu.
Website: http://www.depts.ttu.edu/sasw/

Thompson Rivers University, Program in Social Work, Kamloops, BC V2C 0C8, Canada. Offers MSW.

Touro College, Graduate School of Social Work, New York, NY 10010. Offers MSW. *Accreditation:* CSWE. *Faculty:* 9 full-time (6 women), 54 part-time/adjunct (32 women). *Students:* 226 full-time (194 women), 85 part-time (66 women); includes 165 minority (100 Black or African American, non-Hispanic/Latino; 6 Asian, non-Hispanic/Latino; 56 Hispanic/Latino; 3 Two or more races, non-Hispanic/Latino), 4 international. Average

age 34. *Entrance requirements:* Additional exam requirements/recommendations for international students: Required—TOEFL (minimum score 83 iBT), IELTS (minimum score 6.5), PTE (minimum score 58). *Unit head:* Dr. Steven Huberman, Dean, 212-463-0400 Ext. 5269, E-mail: msw@touro.edu. *Application contact:* Peter Stewart, Director of Recruitment, Admissions and Enrollment Management, 212-463-0400 Ext. 5630, Fax: 212-627-3693, E-mail: peter.stewart@touro.edu.
Website: http://gssw.touro.edu/

Troy University, Graduate School, College of Health and Human Services, Program in Social Work, Troy, AL 36082. Offers MSW. *Program availability:* Part-time, evening/weekend. *Faculty:* 12 full-time (8 women), 3 part-time/adjunct (all women). *Students:* 152 full-time (139 women), 25 part-time (all women); includes 93 minority (89 Black or African American, non-Hispanic/Latino; 1 Asian, non-Hispanic/Latino; 1 Hispanic/Latino; 1 Native Hawaiian or other Pacific Islander, non-Hispanic/Latino; 1 Two or more races, non-Hispanic/Latino). Average age 32. 179 applicants, 94% accepted, 118 enrolled. In 2016, 42 master's awarded. *Degree requirements:* For master's, practicum. *Entrance requirements:* For master's, GRE (minimum score of 850 on old exam or 290 on new exam), GMAT (minimum score of 380) or MAT (minimum score of 385), minimum GPA of 2.5 on last 30 semester hours taken, criminal background check. Additional exam requirements/recommendations for international students: Required—TOEFL (minimum score 523 paper-based; 70 iBT), IELTS (minimum score 6). *Application deadline:* Applications are processed on a rolling basis. Application fee: $50. Electronic applications accepted. *Expenses:* Tuition, state resident: full-time $7146; part-time $397 per credit hour. Tuition, nonresident: full-time $14,292; part-time $794 per credit hour. *Required fees:* $802; $50 per semester. Tuition and fees vary according to campus/location and program. *Financial support:* Fellowships, career-related internships or fieldwork, and scholarships/grants available. Support available to part-time students. *Unit head:* Dr. Denise Green, Chairman, 334-670-5767, E-mail: dmgreen@troy.edu. *Application contact:* Jessica A. Kimbro, Director of Graduate Admissions, 334-670-3178, Fax: 334-670-3733, E-mail: jacord@troy.edu.

Tulane University, School of Social Work, New Orleans, LA 70118-5669. Offers city, culture and community (PhD); disaster resilience leadership (MS); social work (MSW, DSW). *Accreditation:* CSWE (one or more programs are accredited). *Program availability:* Part-time. *Degree requirements:* For master's, thesis. *Entrance requirements:* Additional exam requirements/recommendations for international students: Required—TOEFL. Electronic applications accepted. *Expenses: Tuition:* Full-time $50,920; part-time $2829 per credit hour. *Required fees:* $2040; $44.50 per credit hour. $580 per term. Tuition and fees vary according to course load, degree level and program.

Union University, School of Social Work, Jackson, TN 38305-3697. Offers MSW. *Accreditation:* CSWE. *Expenses: Tuition:* Full-time $10,300. *Required fees:* $20.

Universidad del Este, Graduate School, Carolina, PR 00984. Offers accounting (MBA); adult education (M Ed); agribusiness (MBA); criminal justice and criminology (MA); curriculum and instruction - early education (M Ed); curriculum and instruction - elementary (M Ed); curriculum and instruction - English (M Ed); curriculum and instruction - Spanish (M Ed); human resources (MBA); information security management (MBA); information technology and Web business development (MBA); management (MBA); public policy (MPA); social work (MA), including clinical social work; special education (M Ed); strategic leadership (MBA).

Université de Moncton, Faculty of Arts and Social Sciences, School of Social Work, Moncton, NB E1A 3E9, Canada. Offers MSW. *Degree requirements:* For master's, one foreign language, major paper. *Entrance requirements:* For master's, minimum GPA of 3.0. *Faculty research:* Burnout and education, mental health (institutionalization), unemployment's effect on youth, women and health services.

Université de Montréal, Faculty of Arts and Sciences, School of Social Service, Program in Social Administration, Montréal, QC H3C 3J7, Canada. Offers DESS. Electronic applications accepted.

Université de Sherbrooke, Faculty of Letters and Human Sciences, Department of Social Service, Sherbrooke, QC J1K 2R1, Canada. Offers MSS.

Université du Québec à Montréal, Graduate Programs, Program in Social Intervention, Montréal, QC H3C 3P8, Canada. Offers MA. *Program availability:* Part-time. *Degree requirements:* For master's, thesis. *Entrance requirements:* For master's, appropriate bachelor's degree or equivalent, proficiency in French.

Université du Québec en Abitibi-Témiscamingue, Graduate Programs, Program in Social Work, Rouyn-Noranda, QC J9X 5E4, Canada. Offers MSW.

Université du Québec en Outaouais, Graduate Programs, Program in Social Work, Gatineau, QC J8X 3X7, Canada. Offers MA. *Degree requirements:* For master's, thesis (for some programs).

Université Laval, Faculty of Social Sciences, School of Social Work, Programs in Social Work, Québec, QC G1K 7P4, Canada. Offers M Serv Soc, PhD. Terminal master's awarded for partial completion of doctoral program. *Degree requirements:* For master's, thesis (for some programs); for doctorate, comprehensive exam, thesis/dissertation. *Entrance requirements:* For master's and doctorate, knowledge of French, comprehension of written English. Electronic applications accepted.

University at Albany, State University of New York, School of Social Welfare, Albany, NY 12222-0001. Offers MSW, PhD, MSW/MA. *Accreditation:* CSWE (one or more programs are accredited). *Program availability:* Part-time, evening/weekend. *Faculty:* 18 full-time (8 women), 27 part-time/adjunct (22 women). *Students:* 283 full-time (242 women), 146 part-time (120 women); includes 111 minority (53 Black or African American, non-Hispanic/Latino; 1 American Indian or Alaska Native, non-Hispanic/Latino; 11 Asian, non-Hispanic/Latino; 36 Hispanic/Latino; 10 Two or more races, non-Hispanic/Latino), 15 international. 405 applicants, 66% accepted, 190 enrolled. In 2016, 173 master's, 9 doctorates awarded. *Degree requirements:* For doctorate, thesis/dissertation. *Entrance requirements:* For doctorate, GRE General Test. Additional exam requirements/recommendations for international students: Required—TOEFL (minimum score 550 paper-based). *Application deadline:* For fall admission, 2/15 for domestic and international students. Application fee: $75. Electronic applications accepted. *Expenses:* Tuition, state resident: full-time $10,870; part-time $453 per credit hour. Tuition, nonresident: full-time $22,210; part-time $925 per credit hour. *International tuition:* $21,550 full-time. *Required fees:* $1864; $96 per credit hour. *Financial support:* Fellowships, career-related internships or fieldwork, and Federal Work-Study available. Financial award application deadline: 2/15. *Faculty research:* Welfare reform, homelessness, children and families, mental health, substance abuse. *Total annual research expenditures:* $10.3 million. *Unit head:* Katharine Briar-Lawson, Dean, 518-442-5324.

University at Buffalo, the State University of New York, Graduate School, School of Social Work, Buffalo, NY 14260. Offers social welfare (PhD); social work (MSW); JD/MSW; MBA/MSW; MPH/MSW; MSW/PhD. *Accreditation:* CSWE (one or more programs are accredited). *Program availability:* Part-time, 100% online, blended/hybrid learning. *Faculty:* 29 full-time (23 women), 58 part-time/adjunct (48 women). *Students:* 309 full-time (270 women), 227 part-time (182 women); includes 83 minority (62 Black or African American, non-Hispanic/Latino; 21 Asian, non-Hispanic/Latino). Average age 28. 413 applicants, 70% accepted, 197 enrolled. In 2016, 205 master's, 2 doctorates awarded. *Degree requirements:* For master's, 900 hours of field work; for doctorate, comprehensive exam, thesis/dissertation. *Entrance requirements:* For master's, 24 credits of course work in liberal arts; for doctorate, GRE General Test, MSW or equivalent. Additional exam requirements/recommendations for international students: Required—TOEFL (minimum score 600 paper-based; 100 iBT). *Application deadline:* For fall admission, 3/1 priority date for domestic and international students; for spring admission, 9/15 for domestic and international students; for summer admission, 2/1 for domestic and international students. Application fee: $75. Electronic applications accepted. *Expenses:* Contact institution. *Financial support:* In 2016–17, 6 fellowships with full tuition reimbursements (averaging $12,400 per year), 3 research assistantships with full tuition reimbursements (averaging $16,000 per year), 6 teaching assistantships with full tuition reimbursements (averaging $5,000 per year) were awarded; Federal Work-Study, scholarships/grants, health care benefits, tuition waivers (full and partial), unspecified assistantships, and instructorships and research grants (for PhD students) also available. Financial award application deadline: 4/30; financial award applicants required to submit FAFSA. *Faculty research:* Violence and victimization; trauma and trauma-informed care; health, behavioral health and addictions; children and adolescents; aging. *Total annual research expenditures:* $1.1 million. *Unit head:* Dr. Nancy J. Smyth, Dean, 716-645-3381, Fax: 716-645-3883, E-mail: sw-dean@buffalo.edu. *Application contact:* Maria Carey, Admissions Processor, 716-645-3381, Fax: 716-645-3456, E-mail: sw-info@buffalo.edu.
Website: http://www.socialwork.buffalo.edu

The University of Akron, Graduate School, College of Health Professions, School of Social Work, Akron, OH 44325. Offers MSW. *Accreditation:* CSWE. *Faculty:* 4 full-time (2 women), 55 part-time/adjunct (41 women). *Students:* 120 full-time (102 women), 19 part-time (15 women); includes 28 minority (20 Black or African American, non-Hispanic/Latino; 1 American Indian or Alaska Native, non-Hispanic/Latino; 1 Asian, non-Hispanic/Latino; 3 Hispanic/Latino; 3 Two or more races, non-Hispanic/Latino). Average age 34. 110 applicants, 80% accepted, 65 enrolled. In 2016, 59 master's awarded. *Entrance requirements:* For master's, undergraduate major in social work or related field, three letters of recommendation, essay, resume. Additional exam requirements/recommendations for international students: Required—TOEFL (minimum score 550 paper-based; 79 iBT), IELTS (minimum score 6.5). *Application deadline:* For fall admission, 2/15 for domestic and international students. Application fee: $45 ($70 for international students). Electronic applications accepted. *Expenses:* Tuition, state resident: full-time $8618; part-time $359 per credit hour. Tuition, nonresident: full-time $17,149; part-time $715 per credit hour. *Required fees:* $1652. *Financial support:* Unspecified assistantships and instructional support assistantships available. *Faculty research:* Spirituality and alternative healing, child welfare education and training, ethics and social work practice, evidence-based social work practice, social work continuing education. *Total annual research expenditures:* $45,599. *Unit head:* Dr. Timothy McCarragher, Director, 330-972-5976, E-mail: mccarra@uakron.edu.
Website: http://www.uakron.edu/socialwork/

The University of Alabama, Graduate School, School of Social Work, Tuscaloosa, AL 35487-0314. Offers MSW, PhD. *Accreditation:* CSWE (one or more programs are accredited). *Program availability:* Part-time, blended/hybrid learning. *Faculty:* 29 full-time (22 women), 1 (woman) part-time/adjunct. *Students:* 292 full-time (260 women), 43 part-time (37 women); includes 120 minority (97 Black or African American, non-Hispanic/Latino; 1 American Indian or Alaska Native, non-Hispanic/Latino; 3 Asian, non-Hispanic/Latino; 10 Hispanic/Latino; 9 Two or more races, non-Hispanic/Latino), 8 international. Average age 30. 492 applicants, 43% accepted, 142 enrolled. In 2016, 207 master's, 9 doctorates awarded. *Degree requirements:* For master's, professional internship; for doctorate, comprehensive exam, thesis/dissertation. *Entrance requirements:* For master's, GRE or MAT (if GPA less than 3.0), minimum GPA of 2.5; for doctorate, GRE, minimum GPA of 3.0. Additional exam requirements/recommendations for international students: Required—TOEFL (minimum score 79 iBT), IELTS, PTE. *Application deadline:* For fall admission, 2/1 priority date for domestic and international students; for spring admission, 9/1 priority date for domestic and international students; for summer admission, 2/1 priority date for domestic and international students. Application fee: $50 ($60 for international students). Electronic applications accepted. *Expenses:* Tuition, state resident: full-time $10,470. Tuition, nonresident: full-time $26,950. *Financial support:* In 2016–17, 113 students received support, including 6 research assistantships with full tuition reimbursements available (averaging $12,744 per year), 5 teaching assistantships with full tuition reimbursements available (averaging $12,744 per year); career-related internships or fieldwork, scholarships/grants, traineeships, health care benefits, and unspecified assistantships also available. Financial award application deadline: 2/1; financial award applicants required to submit FAFSA. *Faculty research:* Children and adolescents at risk, trauma, gerontology, child welfare policy, health. *Total annual research expenditures:* $752,961. *Unit head:* Dr. Vikki L. Vandiver, Professor and Dean, 205-348-3924, Fax: 205-348-9419, E-mail: vlvandiver@sw.ua.edu. *Application contact:* Amanda Moore, Coordinator of Student Services, 205-348-5272, Fax: 205-348-9419, E-mail: almoore2@ua.edu.
Website: http://www.socialwork.ua.edu/

University of Alaska Anchorage, College of Health, School of Social Work, Anchorage, AK 99508. Offers clinical social work practice (Certificate); social work (MSW); social work management (Certificate). *Accreditation:* CSWE. *Program availability:* Part-time, evening/weekend, online learning. *Degree requirements:* For master's, comprehensive exam (for some programs), thesis or alternative, research project. *Entrance requirements:* For master's, GRE General Test, writing sample. Additional exam requirements/recommendations for international students: Required—TOEFL (minimum score 550 paper-based). Electronic applications accepted. *Expenses:* Contact institution.

University of Arkansas, Graduate School, J. William Fulbright College of Arts and Sciences, School of Social Work, Fayetteville, AR 72701. Offers MSW. *Accreditation:* CSWE. In 2016, 22 master's awarded. *Entrance requirements:* For master's, GRE General Test. *Application deadline:* For fall admission, 4/1 for international students; for spring admission, 10/1 for international students. Applications are processed on a rolling basis. Application fee: $40 ($50 for international students). Electronic applications accepted. *Financial support:* In 2016–17, 4 research assistantships were awarded; fellowships with tuition reimbursements and teaching assistantships also available. *Unit head:* Dr. Yvette Murphy-Erby, Departmental Chairperson, 479-575-5039, Fax: 479-575-4145, E-mail: ymurphy@uark.edu. *Application contact:* Dr. Glenda House, Graduate Coordinator, 479-575-3783, E-mail: ghouse@uark.edu.
Website: http://socialwork.uark.edu/

University of Arkansas at Little Rock, Graduate School, College of Education and Health Professions, School of Social Work, Program in Social Work, Little Rock, AR 72204-1099. Offers clinical social work (MSW); management and community practice (MSW). *Accreditation:* CSWE. *Entrance requirements:* For master's, GRE General Test or MAT, three letters of reference.

The University of British Columbia, Faculty of Arts and Faculty of Graduate Studies, School of Social Work, Vancouver, BC V6T 1Z2, Canada. Offers MSW, PhD. *Degree requirements:* For master's, thesis or essay; for doctorate, comprehensive exam, thesis/

dissertation. *Entrance requirements:* For master's, BSW; for doctorate, MSW. Additional exam requirements/recommendations for international students: Required—TOEFL. Application fee: $100 Canadian dollars ($162 Canadian dollars for international students). Electronic applications accepted. *Expenses:* $4,802 per year tuition and fees, $8,436 per year international. *Financial support:* Fellowships, research assistantships, teaching assistantships, career-related internships or fieldwork, Federal Work-Study, institutionally sponsored loans, scholarships/grants, and unspecified assistantships available. Financial award application deadline: 4/1. *Faculty research:* Gerontology, family resources, diversity, social inequality. *Application contact:* Christine Graham, Program Advisor, 604-822-4119, Fax: 604-822-8656, E-mail: sowk.advisor@ubc.ca.
Website: http://socialwork.ubc.ca/

University of Calgary, Faculty of Graduate Studies, Faculty of Social Work, Calgary, AB T2N 1N4, Canada. Offers MSW, PhD, Postgraduate Diploma. *Degree requirements:* For master's, thesis (for some programs); for doctorate, thesis/dissertation, candidacy exam. *Entrance requirements:* For master's, BSW, minimum undergraduate GPA of 3.4 (1 year program), minimum GPA of 3.5 (2 year program); for doctorate, minimum graduate GPA of 3.5, MSW (preferred); for Postgraduate Diploma, MSW, minimum graduate GPA of 3.5. Additional exam requirements/recommendations for international students: Required—TOEFL (paper-based 550) or IELTS (7). Electronic applications accepted. *Faculty research:* Family violence, direct practice, gerontology, child welfare, community development.

University of California, Berkeley, Graduate Division, School of Social Welfare, Berkeley, CA 94720-1500. Offers MSW, PhD, MSW/PhD. *Accreditation:* CSWE (one or more programs are accredited). *Students:* 209 full-time (173 women); includes 94 minority (16 Black or African American, non-Hispanic/Latino; 5 American Indian or Alaska Native, non-Hispanic/Latino; 29 Asian, non-Hispanic/Latino; 44 Hispanic/Latino), 3 international. Average age 31. 390 applicants, 87 enrolled. In 2016, 94 master's, 4 doctorates awarded. Terminal master's awarded for partial completion of doctoral program. *Degree requirements:* For master's, thesis optional; for doctorate, thesis/dissertation, qualifying exam. *Entrance requirements:* For master's and doctorate, GRE General Test, minimum GPA of 3.0, 3 letters of recommendation. Additional exam requirements/recommendations for international students: Required—TOEFL (minimum score 570 paper-based; 90 iBT), TWE. *Application deadline:* For fall admission, 12/1 for domestic students. Application fee: $105 ($125 for international students). Electronic applications accepted. *Financial support:* Fellowships, research assistantships with partial tuition reimbursements, teaching assistantships with partial tuition reimbursements, career-related internships or fieldwork, Federal Work-Study, scholarships/grants, traineeships, health care benefits, and unspecified assistantships available. Financial award applicants required to submit FAFSA. *Faculty research:* Child welfare, law and social welfare, minority mental health, social welfare policy analysis, health services. *Unit head:* Prof. Lorraine Midanik, Dean, 510-642-4341, E-mail: swdean@berkeley.edu. *Application contact:* 510-642-9042, E-mail: socwelf@berkeley.edu.
Website: http://socialwelfare.berkeley.edu/

University of California, Los Angeles, Graduate Division, School of Public Affairs, Program in Social Welfare, Los Angeles, CA 90095. Offers MSW, PhD, JD/MSW. *Accreditation:* CSWE (one or more programs are accredited). *Degree requirements:* For master's, comprehensive exam, research project; for doctorate, thesis/dissertation, oral and written qualifying exams. *Entrance requirements:* For master's, GRE General Test, minimum GPA of 3.0; for doctorate, GRE General Test, minimum undergraduate GPA of 3.0. Additional exam requirements/recommendations for international students: Required—TOEFL. Electronic applications accepted.

University of Central Florida, College of Health and Public Affairs, School of Social Work, Orlando, FL 32816. Offers military social work (Certificate); social work (MSW). *Accreditation:* CSWE. *Program availability:* Part-time, evening/weekend. *Faculty:* 28 full-time (24 women), 23 part-time/adjunct (15 women). *Students:* 171 full-time (155 women), 160 part-time (141 women); includes 148 minority (70 Black or African American, non-Hispanic/Latino; 4 Asian, non-Hispanic/Latino; 61 Hispanic/Latino; 2 Native Hawaiian or other Pacific Islander, non-Hispanic/Latino; 11 Two or more races, non-Hispanic/Latino), 1 international. Average age 30. 289 applicants, 60% accepted, 119 enrolled. In 2016, 127 master's, 15 other advanced degrees awarded. *Degree requirements:* For master's, thesis or alternative, field education. *Entrance requirements:* For master's, resume. Additional exam requirements/recommendations for international students: Required—TOEFL. *Application deadline:* For fall admission, 4/1 for domestic students. Application fee: $30. Electronic applications accepted. *Expenses:* Tuition, state resident: part-time $288.16 per credit hour. Tuition, nonresident: part-time $1071.31 per credit hour. *Financial support:* In 2016–17, 3 students received support, including 1 fellowship with partial tuition reimbursement available (averaging $1,000 per year), 2 research assistantships with partial tuition reimbursements available (averaging $4,536 per year); career-related internships or fieldwork, institutionally sponsored loans, and unspecified assistantships also available. Financial award application deadline: 3/1; financial award applicants required to submit FAFSA. *Unit head:* Dr. Bonnie Yegidis, Director, 407-823-2114, E-mail: bonnie.yegidis@ucf.edu. *Application contact:* Assistant Director, Graduate Admissions, 407-823-2766, Fax: 407-823-6442, E-mail: gradadmissions@ucf.edu.
Website: https://www.cohpa.ucf.edu/socialwork/

University of Chicago, School of Social Service Administration, Doctoral Program, Chicago, IL 60637. Offers PhD, AM/PhD. *Students:* 60 full-time (38 women); includes 24 minority (12 Black or African American, non-Hispanic/Latino; 1 American Indian or Alaska Native, non-Hispanic/Latino; 5 Asian, non-Hispanic/Latino; 5 Hispanic/Latino; 1 Two or more races, non-Hispanic/Latino), 8 international. 85 applicants, 14% accepted, 8 enrolled. *Degree requirements:* For doctorate, comprehensive exam, thesis/dissertation. *Entrance requirements:* For doctorate, GRE General Test. Additional exam requirements/recommendations for international students: Required—TOEFL (minimum score 600 paper-based; 104 iBT), IELTS (minimum score 7). *Application deadline:* For fall admission, 12/15 for domestic and international students. Application fee: $75. Electronic applications accepted. *Financial support:* In 2016–17, 10 research assistantships with full tuition reimbursements (averaging $23,000 per year) were awarded; fellowships, teaching assistantships, Federal Work-Study, scholarships/grants, and health care benefits also available. Financial award application deadline: 12/15; financial award applicants required to submit FAFSA. *Faculty research:* Health administration, youth violence prevention, family well-being, social policy, crime, college success, urban education. *Unit head:* Dr. Neil Guterman, Dean, 773-702-1250. *Application contact:* Laura Chavez Hardy, Director of Admissions, 773-702-1250, Fax: 773-834-4751, E-mail: admissions@ssa.uchicago.edu.
Website: http://www.ssa.uchicago.edu/doctoral-program

University of Chicago, School of Social Service Administration, Master's Program, Chicago, IL 60637. Offers MA, AM/M Div, MBA/AM, MPP/AM. *Accreditation:* CSWE. *Program availability:* Part-time, evening/weekend. *Students:* 391 full-time (335 women), 20 part-time (16 women); includes 119 minority (38 Black or African American, non-Hispanic/Latino; 4 American Indian or Alaska Native, non-Hispanic/Latino; 32 Asian, non-Hispanic/Latino; 41 Hispanic/Latino; 1 Native Hawaiian or other Pacific Islander, non-Hispanic/Latino; 3 Two or more races, non-Hispanic/Latino), 21 international. 631 applicants, 62% accepted, 189 enrolled. *Degree requirements:* For master's, field education. *Entrance requirements:* Additional exam requirements/recommendations for international students: Required—TOEFL (minimum score 600 paper-based; 104 iBT), IELTS (minimum score 7). *Application deadline:* For fall admission, 4/1 for domestic students, 1/15 priority date for international students; for spring admission, 10/15 for domestic students. Applications are processed on a rolling basis. Application fee: $75. Electronic applications accepted. *Financial support:* In 2016–17, 13 research assistantships (averaging $5,000 per year) were awarded; Federal Work-Study, institutionally sponsored loans, and scholarships/grants also available. Financial award application deadline: 4/1; financial award applicants required to submit FAFSA. *Unit head:* Dr. Neil Guterman, Dean, 773-702-1250. *Application contact:* Laura Chavez Hardy, Director of Admissions, 773-702-1250, Fax: 773-834-4751, E-mail: admissions@ssa.uchicago.edu.
Website: http://www.ssa.uchicago.edu/masters-program

University of Cincinnati, Graduate School, College of Allied Health Sciences, School of Social Work, Cincinnati, OH 45221. Offers MSW. *Accreditation:* CSWE. *Program availability:* Part-time. *Faculty:* 11 full-time (6 women). *Students:* 153 full-time (128 women), 52 part-time (44 women); includes 46 minority (33 Black or African American, non-Hispanic/Latino; 2 Asian, non-Hispanic/Latino; 7 Hispanic/Latino; 4 Two or more races, non-Hispanic/Latino), 3 international. Average age 35. 218 applicants, 67% accepted, 123 enrolled. In 2016, 94 master's awarded. *Entrance requirements:* Additional exam requirements/recommendations for international students: Required—TOEFL. *Application deadline:* For fall admission, 2/1 priority date for domestic students. Application fee: $30. Electronic applications accepted. *Expenses: Tuition, area resident:* Full-time $12,790; part-time $389 per credit hour. Tuition, state resident: full-time $13,290; part-time $419 per credit hour. Tuition, nonresident: full-time $24,532; part-time $976 per credit hour. *International tuition:* $24,832 full-time. *Required fees:* $3958; $140 per credit hour. Tuition and fees vary according to course load, degree level, program and reciprocity agreements. *Financial support:* In 2016–17, 72 students received support, including 3 research assistantships with full tuition reimbursements available (averaging $17,346 per year); fellowships, career-related internships or fieldwork, tuition waivers (partial), and unspecified assistantships also available. Financial award application deadline: 4/1. *Faculty research:* Fatherhood, mediation, mental illness, child welfare, elderly. *Unit head:* Dr. Ruth Anne Van Loon, Director, 513-556-4628, E-mail: vanloora@ucmail.uc.edu. *Application contact:* Johnny Arguedas, Program Coordinator, 513-556-4615, Fax: 513-556-2077, E-mail: socialworkweb@uc.edu.
Website: http://www.cahs.uc.edu/SocialWork

University of Denver, Graduate School of Social Work, Denver, CO 80208. Offers animal-assisted social work (Certificate); couples and family therapy (Certificate); social work (MSW, PhD); social work with Latinos/as (Certificate). *Accreditation:* CSWE (one or more programs are accredited). *Program availability:* Part-time, evening/weekend. *Faculty:* 40 full-time (27 women), 103 part-time/adjunct (88 women). *Students:* 483 full-time (428 women), 13 part-time (11 women); includes 110 minority (16 Black or African American, non-Hispanic/Latino; 5 American Indian or Alaska Native, non-Hispanic/Latino; 9 Asian, non-Hispanic/Latino; 56 Hispanic/Latino; 24 Two or more races, non-Hispanic/Latino), 2 international. Average age 28. 868 applicants, 78% accepted, 277 enrolled. In 2016, 265 master's, 6 doctorates, 70 other advanced degrees awarded. *Degree requirements:* For doctorate, comprehensive exam, thesis/dissertation. *Entrance requirements:* For master's, 20 undergraduate semester hours in the arts and humanities, social/behavioral sciences, and biological sciences; for doctorate, master's degree in social work or in one of the social sciences with substantial professional experience in the social work field; two years of post-master's practice experience (preferred). Additional exam requirements/recommendations for international students: Required—TOEFL (minimum score 587 paper-based; 95 iBT). *Application deadline:* For fall admission, 1/15 priority date for domestic and international students. Applications are processed on a rolling basis. Application fee: $65. Electronic applications accepted. *Expenses:* $43,458 per year full-time. *Financial support:* In 2016–17, 462 students received support, including 8 teaching assistantships with tuition reimbursements available (averaging $12,559 per year); Federal Work-Study, scholarships/grants, and unspecified assistantships also available. Support available to part-time students. Financial award application deadline: 2/15; financial award applicants required to submit FAFSA. *Faculty research:* Aging, youth, community, mental health, families. *Unit head:* Dr. Amanda Moore McBride, Dean, 303-871-2203, Fax: 303-871-2845. *Application contact:* Colin Schneider, Director of Enrollment Management, 303-871-3634, Fax: 303-871-2845, E-mail: gssw-admission@du.edu.
Website: http://www.du.edu/socialwork

University of Georgia, School of Social Work, Athens, GA 30602. Offers MA, MSW, PhD, Certificate, MSW/JD. *Accreditation:* CSWE (one or more programs are accredited). *Program availability:* Part-time, evening/weekend. *Degree requirements:* For master's, thesis or alternative; for doctorate, one foreign language, thesis/dissertation. *Entrance requirements:* For master's and doctorate, GRE General Test. *Application deadline:* For fall admission, 7/1 priority date for domestic students, 7/1 for international students; for spring admission, 11/15 for domestic and international students. Applications are processed on a rolling basis. Application fee: $50. Electronic applications accepted. *Financial support:* Fellowships, research assistantships, teaching assistantships, career-related internships or fieldwork, Federal Work-Study, scholarships/grants, tuition waivers (full and partial), and unspecified assistantships available. Support available to part-time students. Financial award application deadline: 2/10; financial award applicants required to submit FAFSA. *Faculty research:* Juvenile justice, substance abuse, civil rights and social justice, gerontology, social policy. *Unit head:* Dr. Maurice C. Daniels, Dean, 706-542-5424, Fax: 706-542-3282, E-mail: daniels@uga.edu. *Application contact:* Shari Miller, Graduate Coordinator, 706-542-2328, E-mail: semiller@uga.edu.
Website: http://www.ssw.uga.edu/

University of Guam, Office of Graduate Studies, College of Natural and Applied Sciences, Program in Social Work, Mangilao, GU 96923. Offers MSW.

University of Hawaii at Manoa, Graduate Division, School of Social Work, Honolulu, HI 96822. Offers social welfare (PhD); social work (MSW). *Accreditation:* CSWE (one or more programs are accredited). *Program availability:* Part-time. *Degree requirements:* For doctorate, comprehensive exam, thesis/dissertation. *Entrance requirements:* For doctorate, master's degree (MSW preferred), minimum GPA of 3.0. Additional exam requirements/recommendations for international students: Required—TOEFL (minimum score 560 paper-based; 83 iBT), IELTS (minimum score 5). *Faculty research:* Health, mental health, AIDS, substance abuse, rural health, community-based research, social policy.

University of Houston, Graduate College of Social Work, Houston, TX 77204. Offers MSW, PhD. *Accreditation:* CSWE (one or more programs are accredited). *Program availability:* Part-time. *Degree requirements:* For master's, 900 clock hours of field experience, integrative paper. *Entrance requirements:* For master's, GRE, minimum GPA of 3.0 in last 60 hours, bachelor's degree. Additional exam requirements/recommendations for international students: Required—TOEFL (minimum score 550 paper-based; 79 iBT). *Faculty research:* Health care, gerontology, political social work, mental health, children and families.

University of Houston–Downtown, College of Public Service, Department of Criminal Justice and Social Work, Houston, TX 77002. Offers MS. *Program availability:* Part-time, evening/weekend, 100% online. *Faculty:* 9 full-time (4 women). *Students:* 15 full-time (10 women), 50 part-time (35 women); includes 43 minority (24 Black or African American, non-Hispanic/Latino; 2 Asian, non-Hispanic/Latino; 17 Hispanic/Latino). Average age 33. 31 applicants, 71% accepted, 17 enrolled. In 2016, 26 master's awarded. *Degree requirements:* For master's, thesis or project. *Entrance requirements:* For master's, personal statement, 3 letters of recommendation, minimum GPA of 3.0 on last 60 hours. Additional exam requirements/recommendations for international students: Required—TOEFL (minimum score 550 paper-based; 80 iBT). *Application deadline:* For fall admission, 8/1 for domestic students, 5/1 for international students; for spring admission, 11/15 for domestic students, 10/1 for international students. Application fee: $35 ($60 for international students). Electronic applications accepted. *Expenses:* $305.50 in-state, per credit; $663.50 out-of-state, per credit. *Financial support:* Federal Work-Study and scholarships/grants available. Financial award application deadline: 4/1; financial award applicants required to submit FAFSA. *Faculty research:* Policing issues, issues in security, community supervision, legal and other issues in prisons, juvenile justice. *Unit head:* Dr. Barbara Belbot, Chair, 713-221-8983, Fax: 713-221-2726, E-mail: belbotb@uhd.edu. *Application contact:* Ceshia Love, Director of Graduate and International Admissions, 713-221-8093, Fax: 713-223-7408, E-mail: gradadmissions@uhd.edu.
Website: http://www.uhd.edu/mscj/

University of Illinois at Chicago, Jane Addams College of Social Work, Chicago, IL 60607-7128. Offers MSW, PhD, Certificate. *Accreditation:* CSWE (one or more programs are accredited). *Program availability:* Part-time. Terminal master's awarded for partial completion of doctoral program. *Degree requirements:* For doctorate, thesis/dissertation. *Entrance requirements:* For master's, GMAT, minimum GPA of 2.75; for doctorate, GRE General Test or MAT, minimum GPA of 2.75. Additional exam requirements/recommendations for international students: Required—TOEFL. Electronic applications accepted. *Expenses:* Contact institution. *Faculty research:* Children, youth, and family; criminal justice; health; gerontology; international.

University of Illinois at Urbana–Champaign, Graduate College, School of Social Work, Champaign, IL 61820. Offers advocacy, leadership, and social change (MSW); children, youth and family services (MSW); health care (MSW); mental health (MSW); school social work (MSW); social work (PhD). *Accreditation:* CSWE (one or more programs are accredited). *Entrance requirements:* For master's and doctorate, minimum GPA of 3.0.

The University of Iowa, Graduate College, College of Liberal Arts and Sciences, School of Social Work, Iowa City, IA 52242-1316. Offers MSW, PhD, JD/MSW, MSW/MA, MSW/MS, MSW/PhD. *Accreditation:* CSWE. *Degree requirements:* For master's, thesis optional; for doctorate, comprehensive exam, thesis/dissertation. *Entrance requirements:* For master's, minimum GPA of 3.0; for doctorate, GRE General Test, minimum GPA of 3.0. Additional exam requirements/recommendations for international students: Required—TOEFL (minimum score 600 paper-based; 100 iBT). Electronic applications accepted.

The University of Kansas, Graduate Studies, School of Social Welfare, Lawrence, KS 66045. Offers social work (MSW, PhD); JD/MSW. *Accreditation:* CSWE (one or more programs are accredited). *Program availability:* Part-time, online learning. *Students:* 328 full-time (283 women), 73 part-time (63 women); includes 89 minority (33 Black or African American, non-Hispanic/Latino; 8 American Indian or Alaska Native, non-Hispanic/Latino; 8 Asian, non-Hispanic/Latino; 20 Hispanic/Latino; 20 Two or more races, non-Hispanic/Latino), 4 international. Average age 31. 370 applicants, 88% accepted, 212 enrolled. In 2016, 171 master's, 7 doctorates awarded. *Entrance requirements:* For master's, minimum GPA of 3.0, social work related experience, 3 letters of recommendation, student-issued transcripts from all previously attended schools regardless of degree status; for doctorate, GRE (Quantitative and Verbal), master's degree in social work or related field, minimum GPA of 3.5, personal statement, 3 letters of recommendation, completion of a statistics course with minimum B grade. Additional exam requirements/recommendations for international students: Required—TOEFL, IELTS accepted for MSW. *Application deadline:* For fall admission, 1/17 for domestic and international students. Application fee: $65 ($85 for international students). Electronic applications accepted. *Financial support:* Fellowships, research assistantships, teaching assistantships, Federal Work-Study, scholarships/grants, and tuition waivers (partial) available. Support available to part-time students. Financial award application deadline: 1/17; financial award applicants required to submit FAFSA. *Faculty research:* Poverty, child welfare, children's mental health, aging and long-term care, families and connections. *Unit head:* Steve Kapp, Interim Dean, 785-864-2269, E-mail: stevek@ku.edu. *Application contact:* Becky Hofer, Director of Graduate Admissions, 785-864-8956, E-mail: bhofer@ku.edu.
Website: http://socwel.ku.edu/

University of Kentucky, Graduate School, College of Social Work, Lexington, KY 40506-0032. Offers MSW, PhD. *Accreditation:* CSWE. *Degree requirements:* For master's, comprehensive exam; for doctorate, comprehensive exam, thesis/dissertation. *Entrance requirements:* For master's, GRE General Test, minimum undergraduate GPA of 2.75; for doctorate, GRE General Test, minimum undergraduate GPA of 3.0. Additional exam requirements/recommendations for international students: Required—TOEFL (minimum score 550 paper-based). Electronic applications accepted.

University of Louisville, Graduate School, Raymond A. Kent School of Social Work, Louisville, KY 40292-0001. Offers marriage and family therapy (PMC), including mental health; social work (MSSW, PhD), including alcohol and drug counseling (MSSW), gerontology (MSSW), marriage and family (PhD), school social work (MSSW). *Accreditation:* AAMFT/COAMFTE; CSWE (one or more programs are accredited). *Program availability:* Part-time, evening/weekend, 100% online, blended/hybrid learning. *Faculty:* 29 full-time (19 women), 51 part-time/adjunct (42 women). *Students:* 384 full-time (324 women), 81 part-time (65 women); includes 116 minority (65 Black or African American, non-Hispanic/Latino; 7 Asian, non-Hispanic/Latino; 18 Hispanic/Latino; 1 Native Hawaiian or other Pacific Islander, non-Hispanic/Latino; 25 Two or more races, non-Hispanic/Latino), 7 international. Average age 31. 419 applicants, 63% accepted, 184 enrolled. In 2016, 191 master's, 2 doctorates awarded. *Degree requirements:* For doctorate, comprehensive exam, thesis/dissertation. *Entrance requirements:* For master's, GRE or minimum GPA of 2.75; for doctorate, GRE General Test, interview, writing sample. Additional exam requirements/recommendations for international students: Required—TOEFL (minimum score 550 paper-based; 79 iBT), IELTS (minimum score 6.5). *Application deadline:* For fall admission, 5/30 for domestic and international students; for spring admission, 9/30 for domestic and international students; for summer admission, 2/28 for domestic and international students. Applications are processed on a rolling basis. Application fee: $60. Electronic applications accepted. *Expenses:* Contact institution. *Financial support:* In 2016–17, 12 research assistantships with full tuition reimbursements (averaging $21,500 per year) were awarded; health care benefits and unspecified assistantships also available. Financial award application deadline: 5/15; financial award applicants required to submit FAFSA. *Faculty research:* Equipping young children with skills, assisting abused or neglected children, helping juveniles with sexual behavioral problems, illuminating the contributions that men and women make to their families, managing chronic conditions, enhance trauma-informed services, address social and health issues of older adults, palliative and end-of-life care. *Total annual research expenditures:* $4.8 million. *Unit head:* Dr. David Jenkins, Dean, 502-852-3944, Fax: 502-852-0422, E-mail: dajenk03@exchange.louisville.edu. *Application contact:* Misty Kupka, Program Manager for Admissions and Recruitment, 502-852-0414, Fax: 502-852-0422, E-mail: misty.kupka@louisville.edu.
Website: http://www.louisville.edu/kent

University of Maine, Graduate School, College of Natural Sciences, Forestry, and Agriculture, School of Social Work, Orono, ME 04469. Offers MSW, CGS. *Accreditation:* CSWE. *Program availability:* Part-time, evening/weekend. *Faculty:* 9 full-time (8 women), 10 part-time/adjunct (7 women). *Students:* 110 full-time (90 women), 3 part-time (all women); includes 8 minority (2 Black or African American, non-Hispanic/Latino; 2 American Indian or Alaska Native, non-Hispanic/Latino; 1 Asian, non-Hispanic/Latino; 2 Hispanic/Latino; 1 Two or more races, non-Hispanic/Latino), 4 international. Average age 35. 114 applicants, 72% accepted, 56 enrolled. In 2016, 41 master's, 2 other advanced degrees awarded. *Entrance requirements:* For master's, GRE General Test, MAT. Additional exam requirements/recommendations for international students: Required—TOEFL (minimum score 577 paper-based). *Application deadline:* For fall admission, 2/1 priority date for domestic and international students; for summer admission, 2/1 for domestic and international students. Applications are processed on a rolling basis. Application fee: $65. Electronic applications accepted. *Expenses:* Tuition, state resident: full-time $7524; part-time $2508 per credit. Tuition, nonresident: full-time $24,498; part-time $8166 per credit. *Required fees:* $1148; $571 per credit. *Financial support:* In 2016–17, 16 students received support. Federal Work-Study, scholarships/grants, health care benefits, and unspecified assistantships available. Financial award application deadline: 3/1. *Faculty research:* Aging, poverty, child mental health, disabilities studies, spirituality. *Total annual research expenditures:* $1 million. *Unit head:* Dr. Gail Werrbach, Director, 207-581-2397, Fax: 207-581-2396. *Application contact:* Scott G. Delcourt, Assistant Vice President for Graduate Studies and Senior Associate Dean, 207-581-3291, Fax: 207-581-3232, E-mail: graduate@maine.edu.
Website: https://www.umaine.edu/socialwork/

The University of Manchester, School of Nursing, Midwifery and Social Work, Manchester, United Kingdom. Offers nursing (M Phil, PhD); social work (M Phil, PhD).

University of Manitoba, Faculty of Graduate Studies, Faculty of Social Work, Winnipeg, MB R3T 2N2, Canada. Offers MSW, PhD. *Degree requirements:* For master's, thesis or alternative.

University of Maryland, Baltimore, Graduate School, School of Social Work, Doctoral Program in Social Work, Baltimore, MD 21201. Offers PhD. *Program availability:* Part-time. *Degree requirements:* For doctorate, thesis/dissertation. *Entrance requirements:* For doctorate, GRE General Test, minimum GPA of 3.5, MSW. Tuition and fees vary according to program. *Faculty research:* Social work research, social work teaching.

University of Maryland, Baltimore, Graduate School, School of Social Work, Master's Program in Social Work, Baltimore, MD 21201. Offers MSW, MBA/MSW, MSW/JD, MSW/MA, MSW/MPH. MSW/MA offered jointly with Baltimore Hebrew University; MBA/MSU with University of Maryland, College Park; MSW/MPH with The Johns Hopkins University. *Accreditation:* CSWE. *Entrance requirements:* For master's, minimum GPA of 3.0. Additional exam requirements/recommendations for international students: Required—TOEFL. Electronic applications accepted. Tuition and fees vary according to program. *Faculty research:* Aging, families and children, health, mental health, social action and community development.

University of Maryland, College Park, Academic Affairs, Robert H. Smith School of Business, Combined MSW/MBA Program, College Park, MD 20742. Offers MSW/MBA. *Accreditation:* AACSB. *Entrance requirements:* Additional exam requirements/recommendations for international students: Required—TOEFL.

University of Memphis, Graduate School, College of Arts and Sciences, Department of Social Work, Memphis, TN 38152. Offers adults and families (MSW); children, youth, and families (MSW). *Program availability:* Part-time, online learning. *Faculty:* 7 full-time (5 women), 12 part-time/adjunct (11 women). *Students:* 89 full-time (76 women), 46 part-time (43 women); includes 90 minority (86 Black or African American, non-Hispanic/Latino; 4 Hispanic/Latino). Average age 33. 83 applicants, 88% accepted, 55 enrolled. In 2016, 71 master's awarded. *Expenses:* Tuition, state resident: full-time $10,463; part-time $9483 per year. Tuition, nonresident: full-time $19,247; part-time $17,291 per year. *Required fees:* $821.50 per semester. Tuition and fees vary according to course load and program. *Financial support:* In 2016–17, 11 research assistantships (averaging $7,682 per year) were awarded. *Unit head:* Dr. Susan Neely-Barnes, Chair, 901-678-3438, Fax: 901-678-2981, E-mail: snlybrns@memphis.edu.
Website: http://www.memphis.edu/socialwork/

University of Michigan, School of Social Work, Ann Arbor, MI 48170. Offers MSW, PhD, MSW/JD, MSW/MBA, MSW/MPH, MSW/MPP, MSW/MSI, MSW/MUP. PhD offered through the Rackham Graduate School. *Accreditation:* CSWE (one or more programs are accredited). *Faculty:* 50 full-time (29 women), 62 part-time/adjunct (48 women). *Students:* 709 full-time (607 women); includes 214 minority (82 Black or African American, non-Hispanic/Latino; 1 American Indian or Alaska Native, non-Hispanic/Latino; 27 Asian, non-Hispanic/Latino; 74 Hispanic/Latino; 2 Native Hawaiian or other Pacific Islander, non-Hispanic/Latino; 28 Two or more races, non-Hispanic/Latino), 30 international. Average age 24. 1,396 applicants, 65% accepted, 397 enrolled. In 2016, 350 master's awarded. *Degree requirements:* For doctorate, oral defense of dissertation, preliminary exam. *Entrance requirements:* For master's, minimum of 20 academic semester credits in psychology, sociology, anthropology, economics, history, political science, government, and/or languages; for doctorate, GRE General Test. Additional exam requirements/recommendations for international students: Required—TOEFL (minimum score 600 paper-based; 100 iBT), IELTS (minimum score 7), Michigan English Language Assessment Battery (minimum score 85). *Application deadline:* For fall admission, 3/1 priority date for domestic students, 2/1 priority date for international students. Applications are processed on a rolling basis. Application fee: $75. Electronic applications accepted. *Expenses:* $12,878 per term resident, $20,636 per term non-resident. *Financial support:* In 2016–17, 560 students received support. Career-related internships or fieldwork, Federal Work-Study, scholarships/grants, traineeships, and unspecified assistantships available. Financial award application deadline: 3/15; financial award applicants required to submit FAFSA. *Faculty research:* Children and families, aging, community organization, health and mental health, policy and evaluation. *Total annual research expenditures:* $3.8 million. *Unit head:* Lynn Videka, Dean, 734-764-5347, Fax: 734-615-5403, E-mail: lvideka@umich.edu. *Application contact:* Timothy Colenback, Assistant Dean for Student Services, 734-936-0961, Fax: 734-936-1961, E-mail: timot@umich.edu.
Website: http://www.ssw.umich.edu/

University of Minnesota, Duluth, Graduate School, College of Education and Human Service Professions, Department of Social Work, Duluth, MN 55812-2496. Offers MSW. *Accreditation:* CSWE. *Program availability:* Part-time, evening/weekend, online learning.

Entrance requirements: For master's, minimum GPA of 3.0. Additional exam requirements/recommendations for international students: Required—TOEFL (minimum score 550 paper-based). *Faculty research:* Domestic abuse, substance abuse, minority health, child welfare, gerontology.

University of Minnesota, Twin Cities Campus, Graduate School, College of Education and Human Development, School of Social Work, Minneapolis, MN 55455-0213. Offers social work (MSW, PhD); youth development leadership (M Ed). *Accreditation:* CSWE (one or more programs are accredited). *Program availability:* Part-time, evening/weekend, online learning. *Faculty:* 21 full-time (14 women). *Students:* 280 full-time (231 women), 66 part-time (46 women); includes 114 minority (37 Black or African American, non-Hispanic/Latino; 6 American Indian or Alaska Native, non-Hispanic/Latino; 29 Asian, non-Hispanic/Latino; 23 Hispanic/Latino; 19 Two or more races, non-Hispanic/Latino), 6 international. Average age 30. 379 applicants, 45% accepted, 161 enrolled. In 2016, 128 master's, 5 doctorates awarded. *Degree requirements:* For doctorate, thesis/dissertation. *Entrance requirements:* For master's, minimum GPA of 3.0, 1 year of work experience; for doctorate, GRE, minimum GPA of 3.0, MSW. *Application deadline:* For fall admission, 1/15 for domestic students. Application fee: $75 ($95 for international students). *Financial support:* In 2016–17, 142 students received support, including 42 fellowships, 41 research assistantships (averaging $11,569 per year), 2 teaching assistantships (averaging $7,636 per year); career-related internships or fieldwork, Federal Work-Study, institutionally sponsored loans, and tuition waivers (full and partial) also available. Support available to part-time students. Financial award applicants required to submit FAFSA. *Faculty research:* Behavioral health, clinical mental health, aging and disability, work with youth, family and community violence prevention, new American and immigrant populations, child welfare, youth leadership, community engagement, mediation and restitution, social justice. *Total annual research expenditures:* $4.8 million. *Unit head:* Dr. James Reinardy, Director, 612-624-3673, E-mail: jreinard@umn.edu. *Application contact:* Dr. Joseph Merighi, Director of Graduate Studies, 612-625-1220, E-mail: jmerighi@umn.edu.
Website: http://www.cehd.umn.edu/ssw/

University of Mississippi, Graduate School, School of Applied Sciences, University, MS 38677. Offers communicative disorders (MS); exercise science (MS); food and nutrition services (MS); health and kinesiology (PhD); health promotion (MS); park and recreation management (MA); social work (MSW). *Faculty:* 68 full-time (29 women), 29 part-time/adjunct (17 women). *Students:* 176 full-time (137 women), 36 part-time (21 women); includes 45 minority (40 Black or African American, non-Hispanic/Latino; 4 Hispanic/Latino; 1 Two or more races, non-Hispanic/Latino), 9 international. Average age 24. *Entrance requirements:* For master's, GRE General Test, minimum GPA of 3.0. Additional exam requirements/recommendations for international students: Required—TOEFL. *Application deadline:* For fall admission, 4/1 for domestic students; for spring admission, 10/1 for domestic students. Applications are processed on a rolling basis. Application fee: $40. Electronic applications accepted. *Financial support:* Scholarships/grants available. Financial award application deadline: 3/1; financial award applicants required to submit FAFSA. *Unit head:* Dr. Velmer Stanley Burton, Dean, 662-915-1081, Fax: 662-915-5717, E-mail: applsci@olemiss.edu. *Application contact:* Dr. Christy M. Wyandt, Associate Dean of Graduate School, 662-915-7474, Fax: 662-915-7577, E-mail: cwyandt@olemiss.edu.
Website: https://www.olemiss.edu

University of Missouri, Office of Research and Graduate Studies, School of Social Work, Columbia, MO 65211. Offers gerontological social work (Certificate); military social work (Certificate); social work (MSW, PhD). *Accreditation:* CSWE. *Program availability:* Part-time. *Faculty:* 15 full-time (10 women). *Students:* 84 full-time (77 women), 138 part-time (127 women); includes 21 minority (11 Black or African American, non-Hispanic/Latino; 6 Hispanic/Latino; 4 Two or more races, non-Hispanic/Latino), 2 international. Average age 29. *Entrance requirements:* For master's, GRE General Test, minimum GPA of 3.0. Additional exam requirements/recommendations for international students: Required—TOEFL (minimum score 90 iBT), IELTS (minimum score 7). *Application deadline:* For fall admission, 1/15 priority date for domestic and international students. Applications are processed on a rolling basis. Application fee: $75 ($90 for international students). Electronic applications accepted. *Expenses:* Tuition, state resident: full-time $6347; part-time $352.60 per credit hour. Tuition, nonresident: full-time $17,379; part-time $965.50 per credit hour. *Required fees:* $1035. Tuition and fees vary according to course load, campus/location and program. *Financial support:* Fellowships with tuition reimbursements, research assistantships with tuition reimbursements, teaching assistantships with tuition reimbursements, institutionally sponsored loans, scholarships/grants, health care benefits, and unspecified assistantships available. Support available to part-time students.
Website: http://ssw.missouri.edu/

University of Missouri–Kansas City, College of Arts and Sciences, School of Social Work, Kansas City, MO 64110-2499. Offers MSW. *Accreditation:* CSWE. *Program availability:* Part-time, evening/weekend. *Faculty:* 8 full-time (6 women), 19 part-time/adjunct (12 women). *Students:* 109 full-time (94 women), 42 part-time (33 women); includes 38 minority (23 Black or African American, non-Hispanic/Latino; 2 American Indian or Alaska Native, non-Hispanic/Latino; 1 Asian, non-Hispanic/Latino; 6 Hispanic/Latino; 6 Two or more races, non-Hispanic/Latino), 1 international. Average age 32. 127 applicants, 68% accepted, 71 enrolled. In 2016, 59 master's awarded. *Entrance requirements:* For master's, minimum GPA of 3.0, 3 letters of reference. Additional exam requirements/recommendations for international students: Recommended—TOEFL (minimum score 550 paper-based; 80 iBT). *Application deadline:* For fall admission, 4/30 for domestic and international students; for spring admission, 12/1 for domestic and international students. Applications are processed on a rolling basis. Application fee: $45 ($50 for international students). *Financial support:* In 2016–17, 4 teaching assistantships (averaging $11,760 per year) were awarded; research assistantships with partial tuition reimbursements, career-related internships or fieldwork, and institutionally sponsored loans also available. Financial award application deadline: 3/1; financial award applicants required to submit FAFSA. *Faculty research:* Social justice, LGBT issues, deinstitutionalization, community collaboration and partnerships, evaluation of strengths model with addiction model. *Unit head:* Dr. Bob Prue, Department Chair, 816-235-6308, E-mail: pruer@umkc.edu. *Application contact:* Tamara Byland, Director of Admissions, 816-235-1111, Fax: 816-235-5544, E-mail: admit@umkc.edu.
Website: http://cas.umkc.edu/socialwork/

University of Missouri–St. Louis, School of Social Work, St. Louis, MO 63121. Offers MSW. *Accreditation:* CSWE. *Program availability:* Part-time. *Faculty:* 11 full-time (9 women), 2 part-time/adjunct (both women). *Students:* 80 full-time (68 women), 65 part-time (54 women); includes 35 minority (29 Black or African American, non-Hispanic/Latino; 1 Asian, non-Hispanic/Latino; 3 Hispanic/Latino; 1 Native Hawaiian or other Pacific Islander, non-Hispanic/Latino; 1 Two or more races, non-Hispanic/Latino), 1 international. 101 applicants, 52% accepted, 33 enrolled. *Entrance requirements:* For master's, 3 letters of recommendation, minimum GPA of 2.75. Additional exam requirements/recommendations for international students: Required—TOEFL (minimum score 550 paper-based; 79 iBT), IELTS (minimum score 6.5). *Application deadline:* For fall admission, 3/1 for domestic and international students; for spring admission, 10/15 for domestic and international students. Application fee: $50 ($40 for international students). Electronic applications accepted. *Financial support:* Research assistantships with tuition reimbursements, teaching assistantships with tuition reimbursements, and scholarships/grants available. Financial award applicants required to submit FAFSA. *Faculty research:* Family violence, child abuse/neglect, immigration, community economic development. *Unit head:* Sharon Johnson, Dean, 314-516-6385, Fax: 314-516-5816, E-mail: socialwork@umsl.edu. *Application contact:* 314-516-5458, Fax: 314-516-6996, E-mail: gradadm@umsl.edu.
Website: http://www.umsl.edu/~socialwk/

University of Montana, Graduate School, College of Health Professions and Biomedical Sciences, School of Social Work, Missoula, MT 59812-0002. Offers MSW. *Accreditation:* CSWE.

University of Nebraska at Omaha, Graduate Studies, College of Public Affairs and Community Service, Grace Abbott School of Social Work, Omaha, NE 68182. Offers social work (MSW). *Accreditation:* CSWE. *Faculty:* 9 full-time (8 women). *Students:* 158 full-time (138 women), 120 part-time (112 women); includes 55 minority (13 Black or African American, non-Hispanic/Latino; 1 American Indian or Alaska Native, non-Hispanic/Latino; 2 Asian, non-Hispanic/Latino; 24 Hispanic/Latino; 15 Two or more races, non-Hispanic/Latino). Average age 30. 216 applicants, 75% accepted, 146 enrolled. In 2016, 72 master's awarded. *Degree requirements:* For master's, comprehensive exam, thesis (for some programs). *Entrance requirements:* For master's, minimum GPA of 3.0, 3 letters of recommendation, resume, statement of purpose. Additional exam requirements/recommendations for international students: Required—TOEFL (minimum score 550 paper-based; 61 iBT), IELTS (minimum score 5.5), PTE (minimum score 44). *Application deadline:* For fall admission, 1/15 for domestic and international students. Applications are processed on a rolling basis. Application fee: $45. Electronic applications accepted. *Financial support:* In 2016–17, 8 students received support, including 5 research assistantships with tuition reimbursements available, 3 teaching assistantships with tuition reimbursements available; fellowships, career-related internships or fieldwork, Federal Work-Study, institutionally sponsored loans, scholarships/grants, health care benefits, tuition waivers (partial), and unspecified assistantships also available. Support available to part-time students. Financial award application deadline: 3/1; financial award applicants required to submit FAFSA. *Unit head:* Dr. Amanda Randall, Director, 402-554-2341, E-mail: graduate@unomaha.edu. *Application contact:* Dr. Peter Szto, Graduate Program Chair, 402-554-2341, E-mail: graduate@unomaha.edu.

University of Nevada, Las Vegas, Graduate College, Greenspun College of Urban Affairs, School of Social Work, Las Vegas, NV 89154-5032. Offers MSW, MSW/JD. *Accreditation:* CSWE. *Faculty:* 10 full-time (9 women), 9 part-time/adjunct (7 women). *Students:* 152 full-time (135 women), 50 part-time (38 women); includes 113 minority (38 Black or African American, non-Hispanic/Latino; 1 American Indian or Alaska Native, non-Hispanic/Latino; 15 Asian, non-Hispanic/Latino; 47 Hispanic/Latino; 1 Native Hawaiian or other Pacific Islander, non-Hispanic/Latino; 11 Two or more races, non-Hispanic/Latino), 5 international. Average age 33. 188 applicants, 54% accepted, 79 enrolled. In 2016, 86 master's awarded. *Degree requirements:* For master's, thesis (for some programs). *Entrance requirements:* For master's, bachelor's degree with minimum GPA 2.75; 3 letters of recommendation; completion of some liberal arts courses. Additional exam requirements/recommendations for international students: Required—TOEFL (minimum score 550 paper-based; 80 iBT), IELTS (minimum score 7). *Application deadline:* For fall admission, 11/1 for domestic students. Application fee: $60 ($95 for international students). Electronic applications accepted. *Expenses:* $269.25 per credit, $792 per 3-credit course; $9,634 per year resident; $23,274 per year non-resident; $7,094 fees non-resident (7 credits or more); $1,307 annual health insurance fee. *Financial support:* In 2016–17, 9 research assistantships with partial tuition reimbursements (averaging $10,767 per year), 10 teaching assistantships with partial tuition reimbursements (averaging $10,600 per year) were awarded; institutionally sponsored loans, scholarships/grants, health care benefits, and unspecified assistantships also available. Financial award application deadline: 3/15. *Faculty research:* Child welfare and juvenile justice, health and mental health, poverty and social justice, substance abuse, public policy. *Total annual research expenditures:* $939,393. *Unit head:* Dr. Carlton Craig, Director/Professor, 702-895-0521, Fax: 702-895-4079, E-mail: carlton.craig@unlv.edu. *Application contact:* Dr. Maryann Overcamp-Martini, Graduate Coordinator, 702-895-4603, Fax: 702-895-4079, E-mail: mao.martini@unlv.edu.
Website: http://socialwork.unlv.edu/

University of Nevada, Reno, Graduate School, Division of Health Sciences, School of Social Work, Reno, NV 89557. Offers MSW. *Accreditation:* CSWE. *Degree requirements:* For master's, thesis optional. *Entrance requirements:* For master's, GRE General Test, minimum GPA of 2.75, statistics course. Additional exam requirements/recommendations for international students: Required—TOEFL (minimum score 500 paper-based; 61 iBT), IELTS (minimum score 6). Electronic applications accepted. *Faculty research:* Policy practice, poverty, women's issues, race and diversity, vulnerable family, social justice, social change, diversity.

University of New England, College of Graduate and Professional Studies, Portland, ME 04103. Offers applied nutrition (MS); career and technical education (MS Ed); curriculum and instruction (MS Ed); education (CAGS, Post-Master's Certificate); education leadership (Ed D); educational leadership (MS Ed); generalist (MS Ed); health informatics (MS, Graduate Certificate); inclusion education (MS Ed); literacy K-12 (MS Ed); medical education leadership (MMEL); public health (Graduate Certificate); reading specialist (MS Ed); social work (MSW). *Program availability:* Part-time, evening/weekend, online only, 100% online. *Faculty:* 67 part-time/adjunct (46 women). *Students:* 891 full-time (667 women), 359 part-time (261 women); includes 309 minority (215 Black or African American, non-Hispanic/Latino; 2 American Indian or Alaska Native, non-Hispanic/Latino; 63 Asian, non-Hispanic/Latino; 18 Hispanic/Latino; 2 Native Hawaiian or other Pacific Islander, non-Hispanic/Latino; 9 Two or more races, non-Hispanic/Latino). Average age 36. 777 applicants, 50% accepted, 316 enrolled. In 2016, 292 master's, 34 doctorates, 130 other advanced degrees awarded. *Application deadline:* Applications are processed on a rolling basis. Electronic applications accepted. Tuition and fees vary according to degree level, program and student level. *Financial support:* Application deadline: 5/1; applicants required to submit FAFSA. *Unit head:* Dr. Martha Wilson, Associate Provost for Online Worldwide Learning/Dean of the College of Graduate and Professional Studies, 207-221-4985, E-mail: mwilson13@une.edu.
Website: http://online.une.edu

University of New England, Westbrook College of Health Professions, Biddeford, ME 04005-9526. Offers nurse anesthesia (MSNA); occupational therapy (MS); physical therapy (DPT); physician assistant (MS); social work (MSW). *Program availability:* Part-time, online learning. *Faculty:* 42 full-time (31 women), 81 part-time/adjunct (63 women). *Students:* 1,116 full-time (936 women), 288 part-time (257 women); includes 261 minority (168 Black or African American, non-Hispanic/Latino; 6 American Indian or Alaska Native, non-Hispanic/Latino; 41 Asian, non-Hispanic/Latino; 20 Hispanic/Latino; 9 Native Hawaiian or other Pacific Islander, non-Hispanic/Latino; 17 Two or more races, non-Hispanic/Latino), 2 international. Average age 32. 3,327 applicants, 22% accepted, 453 enrolled. In 2016, 472 master's, 71 doctorates awarded. *Application deadline:*

Applications are processed on a rolling basis. Electronic applications accepted. Tuition and fees vary according to degree level, program and student level. *Financial support:* Application deadline: 5/1; applicants required to submit FAFSA. *Unit head:* Dr. Elizabeth Francis- Connolly, Dean, Westbrook College of Health Professions, 207-221-4523, E-mail: efrancisconnolly@une.edu. *Application contact:* Scott Steinberg, Dean of University Admission, 207-221-4225, Fax: 207-523-1925, E-mail: ssteinberg@une.edu. Website: http://www.une.edu/wchp/index.cfm

University of New Hampshire, Graduate School, College of Health and Human Services, Department of Kinesiology, Durham, NH 03824. Offers adapted physical education (Postbaccalaureate Certificate); kinesiology (MS); kinesiology and social work (MS). *Program availability:* Part-time. *Degree requirements:* For master's, thesis or alternative. *Entrance requirements:* For master's, GRE General Test. Additional exam requirements/recommendations for international students: Required—TOEFL (minimum score 550 paper-based; 80 iBT). *Application deadline:* For fall admission, 6/1 priority date for domestic students, 4/1 for international students; for spring admission, 12/1 for domestic students. Applications are processed on a rolling basis. Application fee: $65. *Financial support:* Fellowships, research assistantships, teaching assistantships, career-related internships or fieldwork, Federal Work-Study, scholarships/grants, and tuition waivers (full and partial) available. Support available to part-time students. Financial award application deadline: 2/15. *Faculty research:* Exercise specialist, sports studies, special physical education, pediatric exercises and motor behavior. *Unit head:* Karen Collins, Chair, 603-862-0361. *Application contact:* Tarah Beaupre, Administrative Assistant, 603-862-2071, E-mail: kinesiology.dept@unh.edu.
Website: http://chhs.unh.edu/kin

University of New Hampshire, Graduate School Manchester Campus, Manchester, NH 03101. Offers business administration (MBA); educational administration and supervision (Ed S); educational studies (M Ed); elementary teacher education (M Ed); information technology (MS); public administration (MPA); public health (MPH, Certificate); secondary teacher education (M Ed, MAT); social work (MSW); substance use disorders (Certificate). *Program availability:* Part-time, evening/weekend. *Degree requirements:* For master's, thesis or alternative. *Entrance requirements:* Additional exam requirements/recommendations for international students: Required—TOEFL (minimum score 550 paper-based; 80 iBT). Electronic applications accepted.

The University of North Carolina at Chapel Hill, Graduate School, School of Social Work, Chapel Hill, NC 27599. Offers MSW, PhD, JD/MSW, MHA/MCRP, MPA/MSW, MSPH/MSW. *Accreditation:* CSWE (one or more programs are accredited). *Program availability:* Part-time. Terminal master's awarded for partial completion of doctoral program. *Degree requirements:* For doctorate, thesis/dissertation, qualifying exam. *Entrance requirements:* For master's and doctorate, GRE General Test, minimum GPA of 3.0. Electronic applications accepted. *Faculty research:* School success, risk and resiliency, welfare reform, aging, substance abuse.

The University of North Carolina at Charlotte, College of Health and Human Services, School of Social Work, Charlotte, NC 28223-0001. Offers MSW. *Accreditation:* CSWE. *Program availability:* Part-time. *Faculty:* 16 full-time (12 women), 10 part-time/adjunct (9 women). *Students:* 148 full-time (136 women), 1 (woman) part-time; includes 43 minority (29 Black or African American, non-Hispanic/Latino; 3 Asian, non-Hispanic/Latino; 8 Hispanic/Latino; 3 Two or more races, non-Hispanic/Latino). Average age 28. 200 applicants, 70% accepted, 98 enrolled. In 2016, 79 master's awarded. *Degree requirements:* For master's, thesis or alternative, capstone. *Entrance requirements:* For master's, GRE, minimum GPA of 3.0, statement of purpose, liberal arts foundation, resume, 3 letters of recommendation, interview, relevant volunteer and/or paid experience. Additional exam requirements/recommendations for international students: Required—TOEFL (minimum score 523 paper-based, 70 iBT) or IELTS (6.5). *Application deadline:* For fall admission, 2/1 for domestic and international students. Applications are processed on a rolling basis. Application fee: $75. Electronic applications accepted. *Expenses:* Tuition, state resident: full-time $4252. Tuition, nonresident: full-time $17,423. *Required fees:* $3026. Tuition and fees vary according to course load and program. *Financial support:* In 2016–17, 16 students received support, including 15 research assistantships (averaging $3,720 per year), 1 teaching assistantship (averaging $2,400 per year); career-related internships or fieldwork, Federal Work-Study, institutionally sponsored loans, scholarships/grants, and unspecified assistantships also available. Support available to part-time students. Financial award application deadline: 3/1; financial award applicants required to submit FAFSA. *Total annual research expenditures:* $284,095. *Unit head:* Dr. Robert Herman-Smith, Associate Professor and MSW Program Director, 704-687-7180, Fax: 704-687-1658, E-mail: bherman@uncc.edu. *Application contact:* Kathy B. Giddings, Director of Graduate Admissions, 704-687-5503, Fax: 704-687-1668, E-mail: gradadm@uncc.edu.
Website: http://socialwork.uncc.edu/

The University of North Carolina at Greensboro, Graduate School, School of Health and Human Sciences, Department of Social Work, Greensboro, NC 27412-5001. Offers MSW. Program offered jointly with North Carolina Agricultural and Technical State University. *Accreditation:* CSWE. *Entrance requirements:* For master's, GRE General Test. Additional exam requirements/recommendations for international students: Required—TOEFL. Electronic applications accepted.

The University of North Carolina at Pembroke, The Graduate School, Department of Social Work, Pembroke, NC 28372-1510. Offers MSW. *Accreditation:* CSWE. *Program availability:* Part-time.

The University of North Carolina Wilmington, School of Social Work, Wilmington, NC 28403-3297. Offers MSW. *Accreditation:* CSWE. *Program availability:* Part-time. *Faculty:* 14 full-time (9 women). *Students:* 75 full-time (68 women), 29 part-time (27 women); includes 20 minority (4 Black or African American, non-Hispanic/Latino; 1 Asian, non-Hispanic/Latino; 13 Hispanic/Latino; 2 Two or more races, non-Hispanic/Latino). Average age 31. 110 applicants, 53% accepted, 44 enrolled. In 2016, 20 master's awarded. *Degree requirements:* For master's, comprehensive exam, thesis or alternative, field experience. *Entrance requirements:* For master's, GRE General Test, 3 letters of recommendation; resume; statement of interest; completion of introduction to sociology, introduction to psychology, basic statistics and either human biology or human development courses at the undergraduate level. Additional exam requirements/recommendations for international students: Required—TOEFL (minimum score 79 iBT), IELTS (minimum score 6.5). *Application deadline:* For fall admission, 2/1 for domestic students. Applications are processed on a rolling basis. Application fee: $60. Electronic applications accepted. *Expenses:* Contact institution. *Financial support:* Teaching assistantships, scholarships/grants, and out-of-state tuition remission available. Financial award application deadline: 3/15; financial award applicants required to submit FAFSA. *Unit head:* Dr. Stacey Kolomer, Director, 910-962-2853, Fax: 910-962-7283, E-mail: kolomers@uncw.edu. *Application contact:* Dr. Peter Nguyen, Graduate Coordinator, 910-962-7642, Fax: 910-962-7283, E-mail: nguyenp@uncw.edu.
Website: http://www.uncw.edu/swk/

University of North Dakota, Graduate School, College of Nursing and Professional Disciplines, Department of Social Work, Grand Forks, ND 58202. Offers MSW. *Accreditation:* CSWE. *Degree requirements:* For master's, comprehensive exam, thesis or alternative. *Entrance requirements:* For master's, minimum GPA of 3.0. Additional exam requirements/recommendations for international students: Required—TOEFL (minimum score 550 paper-based; 79 iBT), IELTS (minimum score 6.5). *Application deadline:* For fall admission, 1/15 for domestic and international students; for spring admission, 6/15 for domestic and international students. Application fee: $35. Electronic applications accepted. *Financial support:* Fellowships with full and partial tuition reimbursements, research assistantships with full and partial tuition reimbursements, teaching assistantships with full and partial tuition reimbursements, Federal Work-Study, institutionally sponsored loans, scholarships/grants, health care benefits, tuition waivers (full and partial), and unspecified assistantships available. Support available to part-time students. Financial award application deadline: 3/15; financial award applicants required to submit FAFSA. *Faculty research:* Mental health, gerontology, chemical abuse, children and families. *Unit head:* Dr. Carenlee Barkdull, Graduate Director, 701-777-2947, Fax: 701-777-3619. *Application contact:* Staci Wells, Admissions Associate, 701-777-2945, Fax: 701-777-3619, E-mail: staci.wells@gradschool.und.edu.
Website: http://www.nursing.und.edu/departments/social-work/

University of Northern British Columbia, Office of Graduate Studies, Prince George, BC V2N 4Z9, Canada. Offers business administration (Diploma); community health science (M Sc); disability management (MA); education (M Ed); first nations studies (MA); gender studies (MA); history (MA); interdisciplinary studies (MA); international studies (MA); mathematical, computer and physical sciences (M Sc); natural resources and environmental studies (M Sc, MA, MNRES, PhD); political science (MA); psychology (M Sc, PhD); social work (MSW). *Program availability:* Part-time, evening/weekend, online learning. *Degree requirements:* For master's, thesis; for doctorate, thesis/dissertation. *Entrance requirements:* For master's, GRE, minimum B average in undergraduate course work; for doctorate, candidacy exam, minimum A average in graduate course work.

University of Northern Iowa, Graduate College, College of Social and Behavioral Sciences, Department of Social Work, Cedar Falls, IA 50614. Offers MSW. *Accreditation:* CSWE. *Entrance requirements:* For master's, minimum GPA of 3.0; 3 letters of recommendation; personal autobiographical statement. Additional exam requirements/recommendations for international students: Required—TOEFL (minimum score 500 paper-based; 61 iBT). Electronic applications accepted.

University of Oklahoma, College of Arts and Sciences, Anne and Henry Zarrow School of Social Work, Norman, OK 73019. Offers direct practice (MSW), including administrative and community practice, direct practice. *Accreditation:* CSWE. *Program availability:* Part-time, evening/weekend. *Faculty:* 24 full-time (17 women), 12 part-time/adjunct (11 women). *Students:* 210 full-time (178 women), 190 part-time (157 women); includes 166 minority (64 Black or African American, non-Hispanic/Latino; 34 American Indian or Alaska Native, non-Hispanic/Latino; 3 Asian, non-Hispanic/Latino; 25 Hispanic/Latino; 1 Native Hawaiian or other Pacific Islander, non-Hispanic/Latino; 39 Two or more races, non-Hispanic/Latino), 1 international. Average age 32. 214 applicants, 90% accepted, 152 enrolled. In 2016, 134 master's awarded. *Degree requirements:* For master's, comprehensive exam, thesis or alternative. *Entrance requirements:* Additional exam requirements/recommendations for international students: Required—TOEFL (minimum score 79 iBT) or IELTS (minimum score 6.5). *Application deadline:* For fall admission, 2/1 priority date for domestic and international students; for summer admission, 2/1 priority date for domestic and international students. Application fee: $50 ($100 for international students). Electronic applications accepted. *Expenses:* Tuition, state resident: full-time $4886; part-time $203.60 per credit hour. Tuition, nonresident: full-time $18,989; part-time $791.20 per credit hour. *Required fees:* $3283; $126.25 per credit hour. $126.50 per semester. *Financial support:* In 2016–17, 119 students received support, including 20 research assistantships with partial tuition reimbursements available (averaging $10,491 per year); career-related internships or fieldwork, scholarships/grants, and unspecified assistantships also available. Support available to part-time students. Financial award application deadline: 6/1; financial award applicants required to submit FAFSA. *Faculty research:* Poverty, health, child welfare, mental health, interpersonal violence, community development. *Total annual research expenditures:* $128,215. *Unit head:* Dr. Julie Miller-Cribbs, Director, 918-660-3378, Fax: 918-660-3383, E-mail: jmcribbs@ou.edu. *Application contact:* Amy Ann Arnold, Admissions and Enrollment Coordinator, 918-660-3385, Fax: 918-660-3383, E-mail: aarnold@ou.edu.
Website: http://socialwork.ou.edu

University of Ottawa, Faculty of Graduate and Postdoctoral Studies, Faculty of Social Sciences, School of Social Work, Ottawa, ON K1N 6N5, Canada. Offers MSS. Program offered in French. *Degree requirements:* For master's, thesis or alternative. *Entrance requirements:* For master's, honors bachelor's degree or equivalent, minimum B average. Electronic applications accepted. *Faculty research:* Family-children, health.

University of Pennsylvania, School of Social Policy and Practice, Graduate Group on Social Welfare, Philadelphia, PA 19104. Offers PhD. *Degree requirements:* For doctorate, thesis/dissertation. *Entrance requirements:* For doctorate, GRE General Test, MSW or master's degree in related field. Additional exam requirements/recommendations for international students: Required—TOEFL (minimum score 600 paper-based; 100 iBT). Electronic applications accepted. *Expenses: Tuition:* Full-time $31,068; part-time $5762 per course. *Required fees:* $3200; $336 per course. Full-time tuition and fees vary according to degree level, program and student level. Part-time tuition and fees vary according to course load, degree level and program. *Faculty research:* Mental health, child welfare, organizational behavior, urban poverty, comparative social welfare.

University of Pennsylvania, School of Social Policy and Practice, Program in Social Work, Philadelphia, PA 19104. Offers MNPL, MSSP, MSW, DSW, JD/MSW, MSW/Certificate, MSW/MBA, MSW/MBE, MSW/MCP, MSW/MGA, MSW/MPH, MSW/MS Ed, MSW/MSC, MSW/PhD. *Accreditation:* CSWE. *Program availability:* Part-time. Terminal master's awarded for partial completion of doctoral program. *Degree requirements:* For master's, fieldwork; for doctorate, thesis/dissertation. *Entrance requirements:* For master's, GRE, GMAT, or LSAT (for MSSP or MNPL); for doctorate, GRE, MSW or master's degree in related field. Additional exam requirements/recommendations for international students: Required—TOEFL (minimum score 600 paper-based; 100 iBT). Electronic applications accepted. *Expenses: Tuition:* Full-time $31,068; part-time $5762 per course. *Required fees:* $3200; $336 per course. Full-time tuition and fees vary according to degree level, program and student level. Part-time tuition and fees vary according to course load, degree level and program. *Faculty research:* Homelessness, juvenile justice, mental health/children's mental health, child welfare, domestic and family violence.

University of Pittsburgh, School of Social Work, Pittsburgh, PA 15260. Offers MSW, PhD, Certificate, M Div/MSW, MPA/MSW, MPH/PhD, MPIA/MSW, MSW/JD, MSW/MBA, MSW/MPH. *Accreditation:* CSWE (one or more programs are accredited). *Program availability:* Part-time. *Faculty:* 24 full-time (14 women), 40 part-time/adjunct (26 women). *Students:* 431 full-time (367 women), 57 part-time (48 women); includes 120 minority (61 Black or African American, non-Hispanic/Latino; 1 American Indian or Alaska Native, non-Hispanic/Latino; 21 Asian, non-Hispanic/Latino; 24 Hispanic/Latino; 13 Two or more races, non-Hispanic/Latino). Average age 28. 597 applicants, 79% accepted, 202 enrolled. In 2016, 261 master's, 6 doctorates awarded. *Degree requirements:* For master's, practicum; for doctorate, comprehensive exam, thesis/

dissertation; for Certificate, thesis. *Entrance requirements:* For master's, minimum GPA of 3.0, course work in statistics; for doctorate, GRE, MSW or related degree, course work in statistics. Additional exam requirements/recommendations for international students: Required—TOEFL (minimum score 600 paper-based; 100 iBT). *Application deadline:* For fall admission, 12/31 priority date for domestic and international students. Applications are processed on a rolling basis. Application fee: $40 ($50 for international students). Electronic applications accepted. *Expenses:* $10,874 state resident full-time per term tuition, $877 per credit part-time; $14,826 non-resident full-time per term tuition, $1,211 per credit part-time; $415 full-time fees per term; $265 part-time fees per term. *Financial support:* In 2016–17, 40 fellowships (averaging $10,000 per year), 11 teaching assistantships with full tuition reimbursements (averaging $17,910 per year) were awarded; research assistantships with full tuition reimbursements, career-related internships or fieldwork, institutionally sponsored loans, scholarships/grants, traineeships, tuition waivers (full), and unspecified assistantships also available. Financial award application deadline: 3/31; financial award applicants required to submit FAFSA. *Faculty research:* Mental health services research, child abuse and neglect, geriatrics, criminal justice, race issues. *Unit head:* Dr. Larry E. Davis, Dean, 412-624-6304, Fax: 412-624-6323, E-mail: ledavis@pitt.edu. *Application contact:* Philip Mack, Director of Admissions, 412-624-6346, Fax: 412-624-6323, E-mail: psm8@pitt.edu.
Website: http://www.socialwork.pitt.edu

University of Puerto Rico, Río Piedras Campus, College of Social Sciences, Graduate School of Social Work, San Juan, PR 00931-3300. Offers MSW, PhD. *Accreditation:* CSWE. *Program availability:* Part-time. *Degree requirements:* For master's, comprehensive exam, thesis; for doctorate, comprehensive exam, thesis/dissertation. *Entrance requirements:* For master's, PAEG or GRE, interview, minimum GPA of 3.0, letter of recommendation; for doctorate, PAEG or GRE, interview, minimum GPA of 3.0, 3 letters of recommendation, social work experience. *Faculty research:* Social work in Puerto Rico, Cuba, and the Dominican Republic; migration; poverty in Puerto Rico.

University of Regina, Faculty of Graduate Studies and Research, Faculty of Social Work, Regina, SK S4S 0A2, Canada. Offers indigenous social work (MISW); social work (MSW, PhD). PhD offered as a special case program. *Program availability:* Part-time. *Faculty:* 22 full-time (15 women), 5 part-time/adjunct (3 women). *Students:* 35 full-time (34 women), 65 part-time (54 women). 72 applicants, 54% accepted. In 2016, 15 master's awarded. *Degree requirements:* For master's, thesis (for some programs), report, internship; for doctorate, thesis/dissertation. *Entrance requirements:* For master's, BSW. Additional exam requirements/recommendations for international students: Required—TOEFL (minimum score 580 paper-based; 80 iBT), IELTS (minimum score 6.5), PTE (minimum score 59). *Application deadline:* For fall admission, 1/31 for domestic and international students. Application fee: $100. Electronic applications accepted. *Financial support:* In 2016–17, 6 fellowships (averaging $6,000 per year), 3 teaching assistantships (averaging $2,501 per year) were awarded; career-related internships or fieldwork and scholarships/grants also available. Financial award application deadline: 6/15. *Faculty research:* Social policy analysis; social justice, human rights, and social work; family and child policies and programs; aging, society, and human service work; work, welfare, and social justice. *Unit head:* Dr. Judy White, Dean, 306-585-4037, Fax: 306-585-5691, E-mail: sw.dean@uregina.ca. *Application contact:* Dr. Nuelle Novik, Graduate Program Coordinator, 306-585-4573, Fax: 306-585-4872, E-mail: nuelle.novik@uregina.ca.
Website: http://www.uregina.ca/socialwork/

University of St. Francis, College of Arts and Sciences, Joliet, IL 60435-6169. Offers forensic social work (Post-Master's Certificate); physician assistant practice (MS); social work (MSW). *Faculty:* 9 full-time (7 women). *Students:* 114 full-time (92 women), 26 part-time (24 women); includes 49 minority (17 Black or African American, non-Hispanic/Latino; 1 American Indian or Alaska Native, non-Hispanic/Latino; 7 Asian, non-Hispanic/Latino; 20 Hispanic/Latino; 1 Native Hawaiian or other Pacific Islander, non-Hispanic/Latino; 3 Two or more races, non-Hispanic/Latino), 1 international. Average age 29. 101 applicants, 38% accepted, 24 enrolled. In 2016, 58 master's awarded. *Entrance requirements:* For master's, GRE (for MS). Additional exam requirements/recommendations for international students: Required—TOEFL (minimum score 550 paper-based; 79 iBT), IELTS (minimum score 6). *Application deadline:* Applications are processed on a rolling basis. Application fee: $30. Electronic applications accepted. Application fee is waived when completed online. *Expenses: Tuition:* Part-time $739 per credit hour. *Required fees:* $125 per semester. Part-time tuition and fees vary according to degree level and program. *Financial support:* In 2016–17, 15 students received support. Career-related internships or fieldwork, scholarships/grants, and unspecified assistantships available. Support available to part-time students. Financial award applicants required to submit FAFSA. *Unit head:* Dr. Robert Kase, Dean, 815-740-3367, Fax: 815-740-6366. *Application contact:* Sandra Sloka, Director of Admissions for Graduate and Degree Completion Programs, 800-735-7500, Fax: 815-740-3431, E-mail: ssloka@stfrancis.edu.
Website: http://www.stfrancis.edu/academics/cas

University of St. Thomas, Graduate Studies, School of Social Work, St. Paul, MN 55105-1096. Offers MSW. Programs offered in collaboration with St. Catherine University. *Accreditation:* CSWE. *Program availability:* Part-time, evening/weekend, blended/hybrid learning. *Degree requirements:* For master's, thesis, fieldwork. *Entrance requirements:* For master's, previous course work in lifespan developmental psychology, human biology, and statistics or research methods. Additional exam requirements/recommendations for international students: Required—TOEFL (minimum score 80 iBT). *Application deadline:* For fall admission, 1/10 for domestic students. Application fee: $35. Electronic applications accepted. *Expenses:* Contact institution. *Financial support:* Fellowships, research assistantships, career-related internships or fieldwork, Federal Work-Study, institutionally sponsored loans, scholarships/grants, and unspecified assistantships available. Support available to part-time students. Financial award application deadline: 7/1; financial award applicants required to submit FAFSA. *Faculty research:* Clinical supervision and practice, group work, child welfare and social work. *Unit head:* Dr. Barbara W. Shank, Dean and Professor, 651-962-5801, Fax: 651-962-5819, E-mail: bwshank@stthomas.edu. *Application contact:* Mary Palin, Graduate Admissions Counselor, 651-690-6185, Fax: 651-690-6549, E-mail: mbpalin@stkate.edu.
Website: http://www.stthomas.edu/socialwork/

University of South Africa, College of Human Sciences, Pretoria, South Africa. Offers adult education (M Ed); African languages (MA, PhD); African politics (MA, PhD); Afrikaans (MA, PhD); ancient history (MA, PhD); ancient Near Eastern studies (MA, PhD); anthropology (MA, PhD); applied linguistics (MA); Arabic (MA, PhD); archaeology (MA); art history (MA); Biblical archaeology (MA); Biblical studies (M Th, D Th, PhD); Christian spirituality (M Th, D Th); church history (M Th, D Th); classical studies (MA, PhD); clinical psychology (MA); communication (MA, PhD); comparative education (M Ed, Ed D); consulting psychology (D Admin, D Com, PhD); curriculum studies (M Ed, Ed D); development studies (M Admin, MA, D Admin, PhD); didactics (M Ed, Ed D); education (M Tech); education management (M Ed, Ed D); educational psychology (M Ed); English (MA); environmental education (M Ed); French (MA, PhD); German (MA, PhD); Greek (MA); guidance and counseling (M Ed); health studies (MA, PhD), including health sciences education (MA), health services management (MA), medical and surgical nursing science (critical care general) (MA), midwifery and neonatal nursing science (MA), trauma and emergency care (MA); history (MA, PhD); history of education (Ed D); inclusive education (M Ed, Ed D); information and communications technology policy and regulation (MA); information science (MA, MIS, PhD); international politics (MA, PhD); Islamic studies (MA, PhD); Italian (MA, PhD); Judaica (MA, PhD); linguistics (MA, PhD); mathematical education (M Ed); mathematics education (MA); missiology (M Th, D Th); modern Hebrew (MA, PhD); musicology (MA, MMus, D Mus, PhD); natural science education (M Ed); New Testament (M Th, D Th); Old Testament (D Th); pastoral therapy (M Th, D Th); philosophy (MA); philosophy of education (M Ed, Ed D); politics (MA, PhD); Portuguese (MA, PhD); practical theology (M Th, D Th); psychology (MA, MS, PhD); psychology of education (M Ed, Ed D); public health (MA); religious studies (MA, D Th, PhD); Romance languages (MA); Russian (MA, PhD); Semitic languages (MA, PhD); social behavior studies in HIV/AIDS (MA); social science (mental health) (MA); social science in development studies (MA); social science in psychology (MA); social science in social work (MA); social science in sociology (MA); social work (MSW, DSW, PhD); socio-education (M Ed, Ed D); sociolinguistics (MA); sociology (MA, PhD); Spanish (MA, PhD); systematic theology (M Th, D Th); TESOL (teaching English to speakers of other languages) (MA); theological ethics (M Th, D Th); theory of literature (MA, PhD); urban ministries (D Th); urban ministry (M Th).

University of South Carolina, The Graduate School, College of Social Work, Columbia, SC 29208. Offers MSW, PhD, JD/MSW, MSW/MPA, MSW/MPH. *Accreditation:* CSWE (one or more programs are accredited). *Program availability:* Part-time. *Degree requirements:* For master's, comprehensive exam; for doctorate, thesis/dissertation. *Entrance requirements:* For master's, GRE (minimum combined score 800), minimum undergraduate GPA of 3.0. Additional exam requirements/recommendations for international students: Required—TOEFL (minimum score 570 paper-based). Electronic applications accepted. *Expenses:* Contact institution. *Faculty research:* Victimization, child abuse and neglect, families.

The University of South Dakota, Graduate School, School of Health Sciences, Department of Social Work, Vermillion, SD 57069. Offers MSW. *Program availability:* Part-time, online learning. *Entrance requirements:* For master's, baccalaureate degree, minimum cumulative undergraduate GPA of 3.0. Additional exam requirements/recommendations for international students: Required—TOEFL (minimum score 550 paper-based; 79 iBT), IELTS (minimum score 6).

University of Southern California, Graduate School, School of Social Work, Los Angeles, CA 90089. Offers community organization, planning and administration (MSW); families and children (MSW); health (MSW); mental health (MSW); military social work and veterans services (MSW); older adults (MSW); public child welfare (MSW); school settings (MSW); social work (MSW, PhD); systems of mental illness recovery (MSW); work and life (MSW); JD/MSW; M Pl/MSW; MPA/MSW; MSW/MBA; MSW/MJCS; MSW/MS. *Accreditation:* CSWE (one or more programs are accredited). *Degree requirements:* For doctorate, comprehensive exam, thesis/dissertation, qualifying exam/publishable paper. *Entrance requirements:* For doctorate, GRE General Test. Additional exam requirements/recommendations for international students: Required—TOEFL (minimum score 600 paper-based; 100 iBT), ESL exam. Electronic applications accepted. *Faculty research:* Department of Defense Educational Activity, detection/treatment of depression among older adults, health/aging, psychosocial adaptation to extreme environments/man made disasters; mental health needs of older adults.

University of Southern Indiana, Graduate Studies, College of Liberal Arts, Program in Social Work, Evansville, IN 47712-3590. Offers MSW. *Accreditation:* CSWE. *Faculty:* 9 full-time (5 women), 2 part-time/adjunct (1 woman). *Students:* 106 full-time (93 women); includes 11 minority (5 Black or African American, non-Hispanic/Latino; 3 Hispanic/Latino; 3 Two or more races, non-Hispanic/Latino), 1 international. Average age 27. In 2016, 41 master's awarded. *Entrance requirements:* For master's, minimum GPA of 3.0, evidence of writing skills, personal interview or video, minimum of 24 hours of social/behavioral science. Additional exam requirements/recommendations for international students: Required—TOEFL (minimum score 550 paper-based; 79 iBT), IELTS (minimum score 6). *Application deadline:* For fall admission, 2/1 for domestic and international students. Application fee: $40. Electronic applications accepted. *Expenses:* Tuition, state resident: full-time $8497. Tuition, nonresident: full-time $16,691. *Required fees:* $500. *Financial support:* In 2016–17, 12 students received support. Federal Work-Study, scholarships/grants, tuition waivers (full and partial), and unspecified assistantships available. Financial award application deadline: 3/1; financial award applicants required to submit FAFSA. *Unit head:* Dr. James G. Dickerson, Director, 812-461-5243, E-mail: jgdickerso1@usi.edu. *Application contact:* Dr. Mayola Rowser, Director, Graduate Studies, 812-465-7015, Fax: 812-464-1956, E-mail: mrowser@usi.edu.
Website: http://www.usi.edu/liberal-arts/master-of-social-work

University of Southern Maine, College of Management and Human Service, School of Social Work, Portland, ME 04103. Offers MSW. *Accreditation:* CSWE. *Program availability:* Part-time, evening/weekend. *Entrance requirements:* For master's, GRE or MAT. Electronic applications accepted. *Faculty research:* Poverty and discrimination, aging, interpersonal violence, evaluation of interventions and effectiveness, child and adult mental health, social welfare history, diversity issues.

University of Southern Mississippi, Graduate School, College of Health, School of Social Work, Hattiesburg, MS 39406. Offers MSW. *Accreditation:* CSWE. *Program availability:* Part-time. *Degree requirements:* For master's, comprehensive exam, thesis or alternative, practicum. *Entrance requirements:* For master's, GRE General Test, minimum GPA of 2.75 in last 60 hours. Additional exam requirements/recommendations for international students: Required—TOEFL, IELTS. *Application deadline:* For fall admission, 4/1 priority date for domestic and international students; for spring admission, 1/10 priority date for domestic and international students. Applications are processed on a rolling basis. Application fee: $60. Electronic applications accepted. *Expenses: Tuition, area resident:* Full-time $15,708; part-time $437 per credit hour. *Financial support:* Research assistantships with tuition reimbursements, teaching assistantships with tuition reimbursements, career-related internships or fieldwork, Federal Work-Study, scholarships/grants, health care benefits, and unspecified assistantships available. Financial award application deadline: 3/15; financial award applicants required to submit FAFSA. *Faculty research:* Delinquency prevention, risk and resiliency in youth, successful aging, women in social service management, social work and the law. *Unit head:* Dr. Tim Rehner, Director, 601-266-4171, Fax: 601-266-4165, E-mail: tim.rehner@usm.edu.
Website: https://www.usm.edu/social-work

University of South Florida, College of Behavioral and Community Sciences, School of Social Work, Tampa, FL 33620. Offers MSW, PhD, MSW/MPH. *Accreditation:* CSWE. *Program availability:* Part-time, evening/weekend. *Faculty:* 11 full-time (10 women). *Students:* 166 full-time (147 women), 25 part-time (22 women); includes 71 minority (33 Black or African American, non-Hispanic/Latino; 1 American Indian or Alaska Native, non-Hispanic/Latino; 2 Asian, non-Hispanic/Latino; 32 Hispanic/Latino; 3 Two or more races, non-Hispanic/Latino), 1 international. Average age 30. 213 applicants, 62% accepted, 88 enrolled. In 2016, 62 master's awarded. *Degree requirements:* For

master's, comprehensive exam, thesis; for doctorate, comprehensive exam, thesis/dissertation. *Entrance requirements:* For master's, GRE General Test, three letters of recommendation; 750-word biographical sketch; interview; field experience (preferred); for doctorate, GRE General Test, minimum GPA of 3.0 in last two years of undergraduate work; master's degree in social work program with minimum GPA of 3.5; three letters of recommendation; statement of purpose, career goals, and research interests; professional/academic writing sample; interview. Additional exam requirements/recommendations for international students: Required—TOEFL (minimum score 550 paper-based; 79 iBT). *Application deadline:* For fall admission, 2/15 priority date for domestic students, 2/15 for international students. Applications are processed on a rolling basis. Application fee: $30. Electronic applications accepted. *Expenses:* Tuition, state resident: full-time $7766; part-time $431.43 per credit hour. Tuition, nonresident: full-time $15,789; part-time $877.17 per credit hour. *Required fees:* $37 per term. *Financial support:* In 2016–17, 50 students received support, including 1 research assistantship with tuition reimbursement available (averaging $9,001 per year); unspecified assistantships also available. Financial award application deadline: 3/15; financial award applicants required to submit FAFSA. *Faculty research:* Kinship care, child trauma, juvenile delinquency, end-of-life issues, aging issues, child welfare, health and mental health disparities among various populations, HIV/AIDS and sexual violence in Haiti, integrated behavioral health care, international social work practice. *Total annual research expenditures:* $636,386. *Unit head:* Dr. Nan Sook Park, PhD Program Chair/Assistant Professor, 813-974-4194, Fax: 813-974-4675, E-mail: nanpark@usf.edu. *Application contact:* Dr. Marion Becker, MSW Chair/Professor, 813-974-7188, Fax: 813-974-4675, E-mail: mbecker2@usf.edu.
Website: http://www.cas.usf.edu/social_work/

University of South Florida, Innovative Education, Tampa, FL 33620-9951. Offers adult, career and higher education (Graduate Certificate), including college teaching, leadership in developing human resources, leadership in higher education; Africana studies (Graduate Certificate), including diasporas and health disparities, genocide and human rights; aging studies (Graduate Certificate), including gerontology; art research (Graduate Certificate), including museum studies; business foundations (Graduate Certificate); chemical and biomedical engineering (Graduate Certificate), including materials science and engineering, water, health and sustainability; child and family studies (Graduate Certificate), including positive behavior support; civil and industrial engineering (Graduate Certificate), including transportation systems analysis; community and family health (Graduate Certificate), including maternal and child health, social marketing and public health, violence and injury: prevention and intervention, women's health; criminology (Graduate Certificate), including criminal justice administration; educational measurement and research (Graduate Certificate), including evaluation; English (Graduate Certificate), including comparative literary studies, creative writing, professional and technical communication; entrepreneurship (Graduate Certificate); environmental health (Graduate Certificate), including safety management; epidemiology and biostatistics (Graduate Certificate), including applied biostatistics, biostatistics, concepts and tools of epidemiology, epidemiology, epidemiology of infectious diseases; geography, environment and planning (Graduate Certificate), including community development, environmental policy and management, geographical information systems; geology (Graduate Certificate), including hydrogeology; global health (Graduate Certificate), including disaster management, global health and Latin American and Caribbean studies, global health practice, humanitarian assistance, infection control; government and international affairs (Graduate Certificate), including Cuban studies, globalization studies; health policy and management (Graduate Certificate), including health management and leadership, public health policy and programs; hearing specialist: early intervention (Graduate Certificate); industrial and management systems engineering (Graduate Certificate), including systems engineering, technology management; information studies (Graduate Certificate), including school library media specialist; information systems/decision sciences (Graduate Certificate), including analytics and business intelligence; instructional technology (Graduate Certificate), including distance education, Florida digital/virtual educator, instructional design, multimedia design, Web design; internal medicine, bioethics and medical humanities (Graduate Certificate), including biomedical ethics; Latin American and Caribbean studies (Graduate Certificate); mass communications (Graduate Certificate), including multimedia journalism; mathematics and statistics (Graduate Certificate), including mathematics; medicine (Graduate Certificate), including aging and neuroscience, bioinformatics, biotechnology, brain fitness and memory management, clinical investigation, health informatics, health sciences, integrative weight management, intellectual property, medicine and gender, metabolic and nutritional medicine, metabolic cardiology, pharmacy sciences; national and competitive intelligence (Graduate Certificate); psychological and social foundations (Graduate Certificate), including career counseling, college teaching, diversity in education, mental health counseling, school counseling; public affairs (Graduate Certificate), including nonprofit management, public management, research administration; public health (Graduate Certificate), including environmental health, health equity, public health generalist, translational research in adolescent behavioral health; public health practices (Graduate Certificate), including planning for healthy communities; rehabilitation and mental health counseling (Graduate Certificate), including integrative mental health care, marriage and family therapy, rehabilitation technology; secondary education (Graduate Certificate), including ESOL, foreign language education: culture and content, foreign language education: professional; social work (Graduate Certificate), including geriatric social work/clinical gerontology; special education (Graduate Certificate), including autism spectrum disorder, disabilities education: severe/profound; world languages (Graduate Certificate), including teaching English as a second language (TESL) or foreign language. *Expenses:* Tuition, state resident: full-time $7766; part-time $431.43 per credit hour. Tuition, nonresident: full-time $15,789; part-time $877.17 per credit hour. *Required fees:* $37 per term. *Unit head:* Kathy Barnes, Interdisciplinary Programs Coordinator, 813-974-8031, Fax: 813-974-7061, E-mail: barnesk@usf.edu. *Application contact:* Karen Tylinski, Metro Initiatives, 813-974-9940, Fax: 813-974-7061, E-mail: ktylinsk@usf.edu.
Website: http://www.usf.edu/innovative-education/

University of South Florida Sarasota-Manatee, College of Liberal Arts and Social Sciences, Sarasota, FL 34243. Offers criminal justice (MA); education (MA); educational leadership (M Ed), including curriculum leadership, K-12 public school leadership, non-public/charter school leadership; elementary education (MAT); English education (MA); social work (MSW). *Program availability:* Part-time, 100% online, blended/hybrid learning. *Faculty:* 11 full-time (9 women), 7 part-time/adjunct (5 women). *Students:* 11 full-time (all women), 55 part-time (41 women); includes 18 minority (5 Black or African American, non-Hispanic/Latino; 1 American Indian or Alaska Native, non-Hispanic/Latino; 2 Asian, non-Hispanic/Latino; 10 Hispanic/Latino). Average age 36. 40 applicants, 43% accepted, 17 enrolled. In 2016, 28 master's awarded. *Degree requirements:* For master's, comprehensive exam (for some programs). *Entrance requirements:* Additional exam requirements/recommendations for international students: Required—TOEFL (minimum score 550 paper-based; 79 iBT), IELTS (minimum score 6.5). *Application deadline:* For fall admission, 3/1 priority date for domestic students, 3/1 for international students; for spring admission, 10/1 priority date for domestic students, 10/1 for international students. Applications are processed on a rolling basis. Application fee: $30. Electronic applications accepted. *Expenses:* Contact institution. *Financial support:* In 2016–17, 9 students received support. Career-related internships or fieldwork, institutionally sponsored loans, scholarships/grants, health care benefits, and unspecified assistantships available. Support available to part-time students. Financial award application deadline: 3/1; financial award applicants required to submit FAFSA. *Faculty research:* Educational leadership, secondary education, elementary education, criminal justice, social work. *Unit head:* Dr. Jane Rose, Dean, 941-359-4469, Fax: 941-359-4778, E-mail: jane.rose@sar.usf.edu. *Application contact:* Brandon Avery, Assistant Director, Admissions, 941-359-4331, E-mail: bavery@sar.usf.edu.
Website: http://usfsm.edu/college-of-liberal-arts-sciences/

The University of Tennessee, Graduate School, College of Social Work, Doctor of Social Work Program, Knoxville, TN 37996. Offers clinical practice and leadership (DSW).

The University of Tennessee, Graduate School, College of Social Work, Master of Science in Social Work Program, Knoxville, TN 37996. Offers evidenced-based interpersonal practice (MSSW); management leadership and community practice (MSSW). *Accreditation:* CSWE. *Program availability:* Part-time, online learning.

The University of Tennessee, Graduate School, College of Social Work, PhD in Social Work Program, Knoxville, TN 37996. Offers PhD.

The University of Texas at Arlington, Graduate School, School of Social Work, Arlington, TX 76019. Offers MSW, PhD. *Accreditation:* CSWE (one or more programs are accredited). *Program availability:* Part-time, evening/weekend, online learning. *Degree requirements:* For master's, thesis optional; for doctorate, comprehensive exam, thesis/dissertation. *Entrance requirements:* For master's, GRE General Test (if GPA less than 3.0), 3 letters of recommendation; for doctorate, GRE General Test (if GPA is below 3.4), minimum graduate GPA of 3.4. Additional exam requirements/recommendations for international students: Required—TOEFL (minimum score 550 paper-based). *Application deadline:* For fall admission, 6/5 for domestic students; for winter admission, 10/15 for domestic students. Applications are processed on a rolling basis. Application fee: $35 ($50 for international students). Electronic applications accepted. *Financial support:* Fellowships with full tuition reimbursements, research assistantships, teaching assistantships, career-related internships or fieldwork, Federal Work-Study, institutionally sponsored loans, scholarships/grants, and unspecified assistantships available. Support available to part-time students. Financial award application deadline: 6/1. *Faculty research:* Community practice, administrative practice, mental health and children and families. *Unit head:* Dr. Scott D. Ryan, Dean, 817-272-1491, Fax: 817-272-5229, E-mail: sdryan@uta.edu. *Application contact:* Darlene Santee, Director of Admissions, 817-272-3613, Fax: 817-272-5229.
Website: http://www.uta.edu/ssw/

The University of Texas at Austin, Graduate School, School of Social Work, Austin, TX 78712-1111. Offers MSSW, PhD. *Accreditation:* CSWE (one or more programs are accredited). *Program availability:* Part-time. *Degree requirements:* For doctorate, thesis/dissertation. *Entrance requirements:* For master's and doctorate, GRE General Test. Additional exam requirements/recommendations for international students: Required—TOEFL. *Faculty research:* Substance abuse, child welfare, gerontology, mental health, public policy.

The University of Texas at El Paso, Graduate School, College of Health Sciences, Social Work Program, El Paso, TX 79968-0001. Offers social work in the border region (MSW). *Accreditation:* CSWE. *Program availability:* Part-time. *Entrance requirements:* For master's, statistics and biology, undergraduate degree from accredited university. Additional exam requirements/recommendations for international students: Required—TOEFL (minimum score 550 paper-based; 80 iBT). Electronic applications accepted. *Faculty research:* Immigration, trauma, health, farm workers, child welfare, mental health.

The University of Texas at San Antonio, College of Public Policy, Department of Social Work, San Antonio, TX 78249-0617. Offers MSW. *Accreditation:* CSWE. *Faculty:* 10 full-time (6 women), 9 part-time/adjunct (6 women). *Students:* 90 full-time (74 women), 119 part-time (98 women); includes 136 minority (37 Black or African American, non-Hispanic/Latino; 1 Asian, non-Hispanic/Latino; 92 Hispanic/Latino; 6 Two or more races, non-Hispanic/Latino), 1 international. Average age 33. 80 applicants, 83% accepted, 57 enrolled. In 2016, 75 master's awarded. *Entrance requirements:* For master's, GRE, bachelor's degree, three letters of recommendation, statement of purpose. Additional exam requirements/recommendations for international students: Required—TOEFL (minimum score 550 paper-based; 79 iBT), IELTS (minimum score 6.5). *Application deadline:* For fall admission, 7/1 for domestic students, 4/1 for international students; for spring admission, 11/1 for domestic students, 9/1 for international students. Application fee: $45 ($80 for international students). *Total annual research expenditures:* $266,582. *Unit head:* Dr. Martell Teasley, Department Chair, 210-458-3004, Fax: 210-458-3001, E-mail: martell.teasley@utsa.edu. *Application contact:* Derek Plantenga, Graduate Advisor of Record, 210-458-2026, Fax: 210-458-2026, E-mail: derek.plantenga@utsa.edu.
Website: http://copp.utsa.edu/social-work/

The University of Texas Rio Grande Valley, College of Health Affairs, Department of Social Work, Edinburg, TX 78539. Offers MSSW. *Accreditation:* CSWE. *Program availability:* Part-time. *Entrance requirements:* For master's, minimum GPA of 3.0, basic statistics course completed within 5 years of admission. Additional exam requirements/recommendations for international students: Recommended—TOEFL (minimum score 500 paper-based). Tuition and fees vary according to course load and program. *Faculty research:* Child welfare, family violence, social justice, Hispanic traditional healing (curanderismo and spirituality), community development.

University of the Fraser Valley, Graduate Studies, Abbotsford, BC V2S 7M8, Canada. Offers criminal justice (MA); social work (MSW). *Program availability:* Evening/weekend. *Faculty:* 23 full-time (10 women). *Students:* 47 full-time (20 women), 2 part-time (1 woman); includes 3 minority (all American Indian or Alaska Native, non-Hispanic/Latino). Average age 37. 79 applicants, 42% accepted, 32 enrolled. In 2016, 19 master's awarded. *Degree requirements:* For master's, thesis optional, major research paper. *Entrance requirements:* For master's, bachelor's degree, work experience in related field. Additional exam requirements/recommendations for international students: Recommended—TOEFL (minimum score 88 iBT), IELTS (minimum score 6.5), TWE. *Application deadline:* For fall admission, 1/31 priority date for domestic students, 4/1 priority date for international students; for winter admission, 9/30 priority date for domestic students, 10/1 priority date for international students; for spring admission, 12/31 priority date for domestic students, 2/1 priority date for international students. Application fee: $45 ($150 for international students). Electronic applications accepted. *Expenses:* Contact institution. *Financial support:* Research assistantships, scholarships/grants, health care benefits, and bursaries available. Financial award application deadline: 5/10. *Faculty research:* Criminal justice, criminology, social work, child welfare. *Unit head:* Dr. Adrienne Chan, Associate Vice President for Research, Engagement and Graduate Studies, 604-504-4074, Fax: 778-880-0356, E-mail: adrienne.chan@ufv.ca. *Application contact:* Educational Advisors, 604-854-4528, Fax:

604-855-7614, E-mail: advising@ufv.ca.
Website: http://www.ufv.ca/Graduate_Studies.htm

The University of Toledo, College of Graduate Studies, College of Social Justice and Human Service, Department of Criminal Justice and Social Work, Toledo, OH 43606-3390. Offers child advocacy (Certificate); criminal justice (MA); elder law (Certificate); juvenile justice (Certificate); patient advocacy (Certificate); social work (MSW); JD/MA. *Accreditation:* CSWE. *Program availability:* Part-time. *Degree requirements:* For master's, comprehensive exam, thesis. *Entrance requirements:* For master's and Certificate, minimum cumulative GPA of 2.7 for all previous academic work, letters of recommendation. Additional exam requirements/recommendations for international students: Required—TOEFL (minimum score 550 paper-based; 80 iBT). Electronic applications accepted.

University of Toronto, School of Graduate Studies, Faculty of Social Work, Toronto, ON M5S 1A1, Canada. Offers MSW, PhD, MH Sc/MSW. *Program availability:* Part-time. *Degree requirements:* For doctorate, thesis/dissertation, oral exam/thesis defense. *Entrance requirements:* For master's, minimum mid-B average in final year of full-time study, 3 full courses in social sciences, experience in social services (recommended), 3 letters of reference, resume; for doctorate, MSW or equivalent, minimum B+ average, competency in basic statistical methods. Additional exam requirements/recommendations for international students: Required—TOEFL (minimum score 580 paper-based; 93 iBT), IELTS (minimum score 7), TWE (minimum score 5), or Michigan English Language Assessment Battery (minimum score 85). Electronic applications accepted. *Expenses:* Contact institution.

University of Utah, Graduate School, College of Social Work, Salt Lake City, UT 84112. Offers MSW, PhD, MSW/JD, MSW/MPA, MSW/MPH. *Accreditation:* CSWE (one or more programs are accredited). *Program availability:* Part-time, evening/weekend. *Faculty:* 18 full-time (10 women), 38 part-time/adjunct (26 women). *Students:* 304 full-time (232 women), 31 part-time (27 women); includes 82 minority (5 Black or African American, non-Hispanic/Latino; 4 American Indian or Alaska Native, non-Hispanic/Latino; 9 Asian, non-Hispanic/Latino; 43 Hispanic/Latino; 1 Native Hawaiian or other Pacific Islander, non-Hispanic/Latino; 20 Two or more races, non-Hispanic/Latino), 4 international. Average age 33. 254 applicants, 71% accepted, 135 enrolled. In 2016, 176 master's, 5 doctorates awarded. *Degree requirements:* For master's, thesis or alternative; for doctorate, comprehensive exam, thesis/dissertation. *Entrance requirements:* For master's, GRE General Test or MAT (if cumulative GPA is below 3.0), minimum GPA of 3.0; for doctorate, GRE General Test. Additional exam requirements/recommendations for international students: Required—TOEFL (minimum score 600 paper-based; 100 iBT). *Application deadline:* For fall admission, 11/1 for domestic and international students. Application fee: $55 ($65 for international students). Electronic applications accepted. *Expenses:* Contact institution. *Financial support:* In 2016–17, 55 students received support, including 19 fellowships with tuition reimbursements available (averaging $8,505 per year), 14 research assistantships with tuition reimbursements available (averaging $14,250 per year), 8 teaching assistantships with partial tuition reimbursements available (averaging $3,250 per year); career-related internships or fieldwork, scholarships/grants, and unspecified assistantships also available. Financial award application deadline: 3/15; financial award applicants required to submit FAFSA. *Faculty research:* Health, mental health, gerontology, child welfare, forensic social work, instructional social work. *Total annual research expenditures:* $265,538. *Unit head:* Dr. Hank Liese, Interim Dean, 801-581-6192, Fax: 801-585-3219, E-mail: hank.liese@socwk.utah.edu. *Application contact:* Dr. Mary Jane Taylor, Associate Dean, 801-581-6192, Fax: 801-585-3219, E-mail: hank.liese@socwk.utah.edu.
Website: http://www.socwk.utah.edu/

University of Vermont, Graduate College, College of Education and Social Services, Department of Social Work, Burlington, VT 05405. Offers MSW. *Accreditation:* CSWE. *Entrance requirements:* For master's, GRE General Test, resume. Additional exam requirements/recommendations for international students: Required—TOEFL (minimum score 550 paper-based; 80 iBT). Electronic applications accepted. *Expenses:* Tuition, state resident: full-time $5814. Tuition, nonresident: full-time $14,670.

University of Victoria, Faculty of Graduate Studies, Faculty of Human and Social Development, School of Social Work, Victoria, BC V8W 2Y2, Canada. Offers MSW. *Entrance requirements:* For master's, BSW. Additional exam requirements/recommendations for international students: Required—TOEFL (minimum score 575 paper-based), IELTS (minimum score 7). Electronic applications accepted. *Faculty research:* Women's issues, public policy formation and implementation, child welfare, First Nations, community development.

University of Victoria, Faculty of Graduate Studies, Faculty of Human and Social Development, Studies in Policy and Practice Program, Victoria, BC V8W 2Y2, Canada. Offers MA. *Program availability:* Part-time. *Degree requirements:* For master's, thesis. *Entrance requirements:* For master's, resume. Additional exam requirements/recommendations for international students: Required—TOEFL (minimum score 575 paper-based), IELTS (minimum score 7). Electronic applications accepted. *Faculty research:* Women's issues, public policy formation and implementation, health promotion and education, children, youth and families.

University of Washington, Graduate School, School of Social Work, Seattle, WA 98195. Offers MSW, PhD, MPH/MSW. *Accreditation:* CSWE (one or more programs are accredited). *Program availability:* Evening/weekend, online learning. *Degree requirements:* For master's, thesis optional; for doctorate, thesis/dissertation. *Entrance requirements:* For master's, GRE General Test, minimum GPA of 3.0; for doctorate, master's degree, sample of scholarly work, minimum GPA of 3.0. Additional exam requirements/recommendations for international students: Required—TOEFL. *Faculty research:* Health and mental health; children, youth, and families; multicultural issues; reducing risk and enhancing protective factors in children; etrology of substance use.

University of Washington, Tacoma, Graduate Programs, Program in Social Work, Tacoma, WA 98402-3100. Offers advanced integrative practice (MSW); social work (MSW). *Program availability:* Part-time, evening/weekend. *Degree requirements:* For master's, completion of all 75 required credits with minimum cumulative GPA of 3.0, 2.7 in each course; degree completion within 6 years. *Entrance requirements:* For master's, baccalaureate degree from regionally-accredited institution, minimum GPA of 3.0 on most recent 90 quarter credit hours or 60 semester hours, resume, social service experience form, two essay question responses, criminal/conviction history and background check clearance, three letters of reference. Additional exam requirements/recommendations for international students: Required—TOEFL (minimum score 580 paper-based; 70 iBT). Electronic applications accepted. *Faculty research:* Domestic violence and prevention, LGBT issues, gerontological social work, transnational social work, child welfare-mental health.

University of West Florida, College of Education and Professional Studies, Department of Social Work, Pensacola, FL 32514-5750. Offers MSW. *Accreditation:* CSWE. *Program availability:* Part-time, evening/weekend. *Entrance requirements:* For master's, GRE or MAT, official transcripts; minimum undergraduate cumulative GPA of 3.0; academic preparation as demonstrated by quality and relevance of undergraduate degree major; letter of intent; 3 letters of recommendation; work experience as documented on the Social Work Supplemental Application. Additional exam requirements/recommendations for international students: Required—TOEFL (minimum score 550 paper-based). *Application deadline:* For fall admission, 6/1 for domestic and international students; for spring admission, 10/1 for domestic and international students. Applications are processed on a rolling basis. Electronic applications accepted. *Expenses:* Tuition, state resident: full-time $5316.12. Tuition, nonresident: full-time $11,308. *Required fees:* $583.92. Tuition and fees vary according to course load and program. *Financial support:* Fellowships, research assistantships with partial tuition reimbursements, and unspecified assistantships available. *Unit head:* Dr. Glenn Rohrer, Chair, 850-474-2154, E-mail: grohrer@uwf.edu. *Application contact:* Terry McCray, Assistant Director of Graduate Admissions, 850-473-7718, Fax: 850-473-7714, E-mail: gradadmissions@uwf.edu.
Website: http://uwf.edu/ceps/departments/social-work/

University of Windsor, Faculty of Graduate Studies, Faculty of Arts and Social Sciences, School of Social Work, Windsor, ON N9B 3P4, Canada. Offers MSW. *Program availability:* Part-time. *Degree requirements:* For master's, thesis or alternative. *Entrance requirements:* For master's, minimum B+ average in last year of undergraduate study. Additional exam requirements/recommendations for international students: Required—TOEFL (minimum score 600 paper-based). Electronic applications accepted. *Faculty research:* Addiction, social policy analysis, gerontology and health care.

University of Wisconsin–Green Bay, Graduate Studies, Program in Social Work, Green Bay, WI 54311-7001. Offers MSW. *Accreditation:* CSWE. *Program availability:* Part-time. *Faculty:* 8 full-time (7 women). *Students:* 35 full-time (31 women), 28 part-time (25 women); includes 10 minority (2 Black or African American, non-Hispanic/Latino; 2 American Indian or Alaska Native, non-Hispanic/Latino; 2 Asian, non-Hispanic/Latino; 1 Hispanic/Latino; 3 Two or more races, non-Hispanic/Latino). Average age 29. 49 applicants, 69% accepted, 25 enrolled. In 2016, 46 master's awarded. *Degree requirements:* For master's, thesis or alternative. *Entrance requirements:* For master's, GRE, minimum GPA of 2.75. *Application deadline:* For fall admission, 8/1 priority date for domestic students; for spring admission, 11/1 priority date for domestic students. Applications are processed on a rolling basis. Application fee: $56. Electronic applications accepted. *Expenses:* Tuition, state resident: full-time $7640; part-time $424 per credit hour. Tuition, nonresident: full-time $16,771; part-time $932 per credit hour. *Required fees:* $1580; $88 per credit hour. Tuition and fees vary according to program and reciprocity agreements. *Financial support:* In 2016–17, 28 students received support. Scholarships/grants available. *Faculty research:* Child welfare. *Unit head:* Dr. Doreen Higgins, Coordinator, 920-465-2567, E-mail: higginsd@uwgb.edu. *Application contact:* Mary Valitchka, Graduate Studies Coordinator, 920-465-2143, Fax: 920-465-2043, E-mail: valitchm@uwgb.edu.
Website: http://www.uwgb.edu/graduate

University of Wisconsin–Madison, Graduate School, College of Letters and Science, School of Social Work, Madison, WI 53706-1380. Offers social welfare (PhD); social work (MSW). *Accreditation:* CSWE (one or more programs are accredited). Terminal master's awarded for partial completion of doctoral program. *Degree requirements:* For doctorate, thesis/dissertation. *Entrance requirements:* For master's, minimum GPA of 3.0 on last 60 credits; for doctorate, GRE General Test, minimum GPA of 3.0 on last 60 credits. Electronic applications accepted. *Expenses:* Contact institution. *Faculty research:* Poverty, caregiving, child welfare, developmental disabilities, mental health, severe mental illnesses, adolescence, family, social policy, child support.

University of Wisconsin–Milwaukee, Graduate School, Helen Bader School of Social Welfare, Department of Social Work, Milwaukee, WI 53201-0413. Offers applied gerontology (Graduate Certificate); nonprofit management (Graduate Certificate); social welfare (PhD); social work (MSW, PhD). *Accreditation:* CSWE. *Program availability:* Part-time. *Students:* 232 full-time (194 women), 84 part-time (69 women); includes 79 minority (43 Black or African American, non-Hispanic/Latino; 1 American Indian or Alaska Native, non-Hispanic/Latino; 6 Asian, non-Hispanic/Latino; 2 Hispanic/Latino; 27 Two or more races, non-Hispanic/Latino), 2 international. Average age 30. 383 applicants, 57% accepted, 129 enrolled. In 2016, 126 master's, 2 doctorates, 6 other advanced degrees awarded. *Degree requirements:* For master's, thesis or alternative. *Entrance requirements:* For doctorate, GRE, bachelor's degree. Additional exam requirements/recommendations for international students: Required—TOEFL (minimum score 550 paper-based; 79 iBT), IELTS (minimum score 6.5). *Application deadline:* For fall admission, 1/1 priority date for domestic students; for spring admission, 9/1 for domestic students. Applications are processed on a rolling basis. Application fee: $56 ($96 for international students). Electronic applications accepted. *Financial support:* Fellowships, research assistantships, teaching assistantships, career-related internships or fieldwork, health care benefits, unspecified assistantships, and project assistantships available. Support available to part-time students. Financial award application deadline: 4/15; financial award applicants required to submit FAFSA. *Application contact:* Deb Padgett, Associate Professor, Social Work, 414-229-6452, E-mail: dpadgett@uwm.edu.
Website: http://uwm.edu/socialwelfare/academics/

University of Wisconsin–Oshkosh, Graduate Studies, Department of Social Work, Oshkosh, WI 54901. Offers MSW. Program offered jointly with University of Wisconsin–Green Bay. *Accreditation:* CSWE. *Program availability:* Part-time. *Entrance requirements:* For master's, GRE, letters of recommendation, previous courses in statistics and human biology, work experience. Additional exam requirements/recommendations for international students: Required—TOEFL (minimum score 550 paper-based; 79 iBT).

University of Wyoming, College of Health Sciences, Division of Social Work, Laramie, WY 82071. Offers MSW. *Accreditation:* CSWE. *Degree requirements:* For master's, comprehensive exam, thesis or alternative. *Entrance requirements:* For master's, minimum GPA of 3.0. Additional exam requirements/recommendations for international students: Required—TOEFL. *Expenses:* Contact institution. *Faculty research:* Social work education, child welfare, mental health, diversity, school social work.

Valdosta State University, Department of Social Work, Valdosta, GA 31698. Offers MSW. *Accreditation:* CSWE. *Program availability:* Part-time, evening/weekend, online learning. *Degree requirements:* For master's, comprehensive exam, 5 practica. *Entrance requirements:* For master's, GRE General Test, MAT, minimum GPA of 3.0 in last 2 years of course work. Additional exam requirements/recommendations for international students: Required—TOEFL (minimum score 523 paper-based); Recommended—IELTS. *Expenses:* Contact institution.

Virginia Commonwealth University, Graduate School, School of Social Work, Doctoral Program in Social Work, Richmond, VA 23284-9005. Offers PhD. *Degree requirements:* For doctorate, comprehensive exam, thesis/dissertation. *Entrance requirements:* For doctorate, GRE General Test, MSW or related degree. Additional exam requirements/recommendations for international students: Required—TOEFL (minimum score 600 paper-based; 100 iBT). *Application deadline:* For fall admission, 2/15 priority date for domestic students. Application fee: $50. Electronic applications accepted. *Financial support:* Fellowships, research assistantships, teaching assistantships, career-related internships or fieldwork, Federal Work-Study,

institutionally sponsored loans, and tuition waivers (full and partial) available. Support available to part-time students. Financial award application deadline: 5/1; financial award applicants required to submit FAFSA. *Unit head:* Dr. Kia J. Bentley, Director, 804-828-0453, E-mail: kbentley@vcu.edu. *Application contact:* Dr. Denise Bernett, Graduate Program Director, 804-828-2859, E-mail: jdburnette@vcu.edu.
Website: http://www.socialwork.vcu.edu/

Virginia Commonwealth University, Graduate School, School of Social Work, Master's Program in Social Work, Richmond, VA 23284-9005. Offers MSW, JD/MSW, MSW/M Div, MSW/MPH. *Accreditation:* CSWE. *Entrance requirements:* Additional exam requirements/recommendations for international students: Required—TOEFL (minimum score 600 paper-based; 100 iBT). *Application deadline:* For fall admission, 2/1 for domestic students. Application fee: $50. Electronic applications accepted. *Financial support:* Fellowships, research assistantships, teaching assistantships, career-related internships or fieldwork, Federal Work-Study, institutionally sponsored loans, and tuition waivers (full and partial) available. Support available to part-time students. Financial award application deadline: 3/1; financial award applicants required to submit FAFSA. *Unit head:* Dr. E. Delores Dungee-Anderson, Director, 804-828-1043, E-mail: eddungee@vcu.edu. *Application contact:* Dr. Melissa L. Abell, Graduate Program Director, 804-828-2007, E-mail: mlabell@vcu.edu.
Website: https://www.socialwork.vcu.edu/programs/msw/

Walden University, Graduate Programs, School of Social Work and Human Services, Minneapolis, MN 55401. Offers addictions and social work (DSW); advanced clinical practice (MSW); clinical expertise (DSW); criminal justice (DSW); disaster, crisis, and intervention (DSW); family studies and interventions (DSW); human and social services (PhD), including advanced research, community and social services, community intervention and leadership, conflict management, criminal justice, disaster crisis and intervention, family studies and intervention, gerontology, global social services, higher education, human services and nonprofit administration, mental health facilitation; medical social work (DSW); military social work (MSW); policy practice (DSW); social work (PhD), including addictions and social work, clinical expertise, criminal justice, disaster, crisis and intervention, family studies and interventions, medical social work, policy practice, social work administration; social work administration (DSW); social work in healthcare (MSW); social work with children and families (MSW). *Accreditation:* CSWE. *Program availability:* Part-time, evening/weekend, online only, 100% online. *Degree requirements:* For master's, residency (for some programs); for doctorate, thesis/dissertation, residency. *Entrance requirements:* For master's, bachelor's degree or higher; minimum GPA of 2.5; official transcripts; goal statement (for some programs); access to computer and Internet; for doctorate, master's degree or higher; three years of related professional or academic experience (preferred); minimum GPA of 3.0; goal statement and current resume (for select programs); official transcripts; access to computer and Internet. Additional exam requirements/recommendations for international students: Required—TOEFL (minimum score 550 paper-based, 79 iBT), IELTS (minimum score 6.5), Michigan English Language Assessment Battery (minimum score 82), or PTE (minimum score 53). Electronic applications accepted.

Walla Walla University, Graduate Studies, Wilma Hepker School of Social Work and Sociology, College Place, WA 99324. Offers social work (MSW). *Accreditation:* CSWE. *Program availability:* Part-time. *Entrance requirements:* For master's, minimum GPA of 2.75, essay. Additional exam requirements/recommendations for international students: Required—TOEFL (minimum score 550 paper-based; 79 iBT). *Application deadline:* For fall admission, 7/15 priority date for domestic students. Applications are processed on a rolling basis. Application fee: $50. Electronic applications accepted. *Expenses: Tuition:* Part-time $592 per quarter hour. *Financial support:* Career-related internships or fieldwork, Federal Work-Study, and scholarships/grants available. Support available to part-time students. Financial award application deadline: 4/30; financial award applicants required to submit FAFSA. *Unit head:* Dr. Susan B. Smith, Dean, 509-527-2443, Fax: 509-527-2270, E-mail: susan.smith@wallawalla.edu. *Application contact:* Dr. Heather Vonderfecht, Program Director, 509-527-2584, Fax: 509-527-2237, E-mail: heather.vonderfecht@wallawalla.edu.
Website: https://wallawalla.edu/academics/areas-of-study/undergraduate-programs/school-of-social-work-and-sociology/

Washburn University, School of Applied Studies, Department of Social Work, Topeka, KS 66621. Offers clinical social work (MSW); JD/MSW. *Accreditation:* CSWE. *Program availability:* Part-time, evening/weekend. *Degree requirements:* For master's, practicum. *Entrance requirements:* For master's, coursework in human biology and cultural anthropology, multiculturalism, or human diversity. Additional exam requirements/recommendations for international students: Required—TOEFL (minimum score 80 iBT). *Faculty research:* Trauma, multicultural issues, school social work, emotional intelligence, animal-assisted therapy.

Washington University in St. Louis, Brown School, St. Louis, MO 63110. Offers American Indian/Alaska native (MSW); children, youth and families (MSW); epidemiology/biostatistics (MPH); health (MSW); health policy analysis (MPH); individualized (MSW), including health; mental health (MSW); older adults and aging societies (MSW); public health sciences (PhD); social and economic development (MSW); social work (PhD); violence and injury prevention (MSW); JD/MSW; M Arch/MSW; MPH/MBA; MSW/M Div; MSW/M Ed; MSW/MAPS; MSW/MBA; MSW/MPH; MUD/MSW. MSW/M Div and MSW/MAPS offered in partnership with Eden Theological Seminary. *Accreditation:* CSWE (one or more programs are accredited). *Faculty:* 54 full-time (31 women), 87 part-time/adjunct (61 women). *Students:* 281 full-time (235 women); includes 105 minority (37 Black or African American, non-Hispanic/Latino; 14 American Indian or Alaska Native, non-Hispanic/Latino; 20 Asian, non-Hispanic/Latino; 15 Hispanic/Latino; 1 Native Hawaiian or other Pacific Islander, non-Hispanic/Latino; 18 Two or more races, non-Hispanic/Latino), 47 international. Average age 25. 1,003 applicants, 281 enrolled. In 2016, 239 master's, 5 doctorates awarded. *Degree requirements:* For master's, 60 credit hours (for MSW); 52 credit hours (for MPH); practicum; for doctorate, comprehensive exam, thesis/dissertation. *Entrance requirements:* For master's, GRE (preferred), GMAT, LSAT, MCAT, PCAT, or United States Medical Licensing Exam (for MPH); for doctorate, GRE. Additional exam requirements/recommendations for international students: Required—TOEFL (minimum score 100 iBT) or IELTS. *Application deadline:* For fall admission, 12/15 priority date for domestic and international students; for winter admission, 3/1 priority date for domestic and international students. Applications are processed on a rolling basis. Electronic applications accepted. *Expenses:* Contact institution. *Financial support:* In 2016–17, 267 students received support, including 35 fellowships, 48 research assistantships; Federal Work-Study, scholarships/grants, and unspecified assistantships also available. Support available to part-time students. Financial award applicants required to submit FAFSA. *Faculty research:* Mental health, social policy, health policy, epidemiology, social and economic development. *Unit head:* Jamie L. Adkisson, Director of Admissions and Recruitment, 314-935-3524, Fax: 314-935-4859, E-mail: jadkisson@wustl.edu. *Application contact:* Office of Admissions and Recruitment, 314-935-6676, Fax: 314-935-4859, E-mail: brownadmissions@wustl.edu.
Website: http://brownschool.wustl.edu

Wayne State University, College of Liberal Arts and Sciences, Department of Anthropology, Detroit, MI 48202. Offers anthropology (MA, PhD); social work (PhD). Doctoral program admits for fall only. *Program availability:* Part-time. *Faculty:* 12. *Students:* 41 full-time (30 women), 22 part-time (13 women); includes 10 minority (4 Black or African American, non-Hispanic/Latino; 3 Hispanic/Latino; 3 Two or more races, non-Hispanic/Latino), 2 international. Average age 35. 48 applicants, 46% accepted, 17 enrolled. In 2016, 7 master's, 2 doctorates awarded. *Degree requirements:* For master's, thesis (for some programs); for doctorate, one foreign language, thesis/dissertation. *Entrance requirements:* For master's, three letters of recommendation, completion of introduction to anthropology, letter of intent, writing sample, minimum undergraduate GPA of 3.2; for doctorate, GRE, bachelor's degree in anthropology or a related field, three letters of recommendation, completion of introduction to anthropology, letter of intent, writing sample, minimum undergraduate GPA of 3.2. Additional exam requirements/recommendations for international students: Required—TOEFL (minimum score 550 paper-based; 79 iBT), TWE (minimum score 5.5), Michigan English Language Assessment Battery (minimum score 85); Recommended—IELTS (minimum score 6.5). *Application deadline:* For fall admission, 1/10 for domestic and international students; for winter admission, 10/1 for domestic and international students. Application fee: $50. Electronic applications accepted. *Expenses:* $16,503 per year resident tuition and fees, $33,697 per year non-resident tuition and fees. *Financial support:* In 2016–17, 28 students received support, including 2 fellowships with tuition reimbursements available (averaging $13,500 per year), 5 teaching assistantships with tuition reimbursements available (averaging $18,394 per year); research assistantships, scholarships/grants, and unspecified assistantships also available. Financial award applicants required to submit FAFSA. *Faculty research:* Business anthropology and organizational culture, African and African-American religions, medical anthropology, Latin American anthropology and archaeology, urban anthropology and historical archaeology. *Unit head:* Dr. Andrea Sankar, Professor and Chair, E-mail: asankar@wayne.edu. *Application contact:* Dr. Stephen Chrisomalis, Director of Graduate Studies, 313-577-9922, E-mail: chrisomalis@wayne.edu.
Website: http://clas.wayne.edu/anthropology/

Wayne State University, School of Social Work, Detroit, MI 48202. Offers alcohol and drug abuse studies (Certificate); clinical social work theory and practice (Certificate); disabilities (Certificate); gerontology (Certificate); social welfare research and evaluation (Certificate); social work (MSW, PhD); social work and anthropology (PhD); social work and gerontology (PhD); social work and infant mental health (MSW, PhD); social work practice with families and couples (Certificate). Application deadlines: April 1 for MSW, December 19 for PhD. *Accreditation:* CSWE (one or more programs are accredited). *Program availability:* Part-time, evening/weekend. *Faculty:* 24. *Students:* 515 full-time (442 women), 150 part-time (128 women); includes 251 minority (179 Black or African American, non-Hispanic/Latino; 4 American Indian or Alaska Native, non-Hispanic/Latino; 11 Asian, non-Hispanic/Latino; 29 Hispanic/Latino; 1 Native Hawaiian or other Pacific Islander, non-Hispanic/Latino; 27 Two or more races, non-Hispanic/Latino), 17 international. Average age 31. 809 applicants, 36% accepted, 200 enrolled. In 2016, 356 master's, 2 doctorates, 20 other advanced degrees awarded. *Degree requirements:* For master's, filed work; for doctorate, variable foreign language requirement, comprehensive exam, thesis/dissertation. *Entrance requirements:* For master's, personal interest statement, resume, 3 references; for doctorate, GRE (minimum combined score of 1000 on Verbal and Quantitative components), minimum undergraduate GPA of 3.5, MSW from CSWE-accredited institution (or working towards one), resume, three letters of reference, personal statement, summary of relevant research and professional experience, writing sample, interview; for Certificate, MSW or actively enrolled in advanced portion of MSW program. Additional exam requirements/recommendations for international students: Required—TOEFL (minimum score 550 paper-based; 79 iBT), TWE (minimum score 5.5), Michigan English Language Assessment Battery (minimum score 85); Recommended—IELTS (minimum score 6.5). *Application deadline:* Applications are processed on a rolling basis. Application fee: $50. Electronic applications accepted. *Expenses:* $16,503 per year resident tuition and fees, $33,697 per year non-resident tuition and fees. *Financial support:* In 2016–17, 119 students received support, including 5 fellowships with tuition reimbursements available (averaging $18,800 per year), 2 research assistantships with tuition reimbursements available (averaging $21,593 per year), 2 teaching assistantships with tuition reimbursements available (averaging $17,994 per year); scholarships/grants and unspecified assistantships also available. Financial award applicants required to submit FAFSA. *Faculty research:* Aging, child welfare, health and behavioral health, interpersonal violence, community development, policy and program development. *Unit head:* Dr. Jerrold Brandell, Interim Dean, 313-577-4409, E-mail: aa4537@wayne.edu. *Application contact:* Shantalea Johns, Interim Director of Admissions, 313-577-4409, E-mail: shantalea@wayne.edu.
Website: http://socialwork.wayne.edu/

West Chester University of Pennsylvania, College of Education and Social Work, Department of Social Work, West Chester, PA 19383. Offers MSW. *Accreditation:* CSWE. *Program availability:* Part-time, evening/weekend. *Faculty:* 12 full-time (10 women), 11 part-time/adjunct (10 women). *Students:* 188 full-time (161 women), 85 part-time (69 women); includes 128 minority (103 Black or African American, non-Hispanic/Latino; 2 Asian, non-Hispanic/Latino; 12 Hispanic/Latino; 11 Two or more races, non-Hispanic/Latino). Average age 31. 273 applicants, 73% accepted, 116 enrolled. In 2016, 80 master's awarded. *Degree requirements:* For master's, completion of foundation courses and field practicums. *Entrance requirements:* For master's, minimum GPA of 3.0, personal statement of 3 to 5 pages clearly articulating professional goals, two letters of recommendation. Additional exam requirements/recommendations for international students: Required—TOEFL or IELTS. *Application deadline:* For fall admission, 5/15 for international students; for spring admission, 10/15 for international students. Applications are processed on a rolling basis. Application fee: $50. Electronic applications accepted. *Expenses:* Contact institution. *Financial support:* Scholarships/grants and unspecified assistantships available. Financial award application deadline: 2/15; financial award applicants required to submit FAFSA. *Faculty research:* Recovery in mental health and substance abuse disorders, integrated health and interprofessional education, trauma and disaster intervention, multicultural resources, human rights including LGBTQA rights. *Unit head:* Dr. Stacie Metz, Chair and Graduate Coordinator, 610-436-2101, E-mail: smetz@wcupa.edu. *Application contact:* Dr. Terrence O. Lewis, Philadelphia Campus Graduate Coordinator, 610-430-4191, Fax: 610-436-2763, E-mail: tlewis@wcupa.edu.
Website: http://www.wcupa.edu/education-socialWork/gradSocialWork/

Western Carolina University, Graduate School, College of Health and Human Sciences, Department of Social Work, Cullowhee, NC 28723. Offers MSW. *Accreditation:* CSWE. *Program availability:* Part-time. *Entrance requirements:* For master's, appropriate undergraduate major with minimum GPA of 3.0, 3 recommendations, resume. Additional exam requirements/recommendations for international students: Required—TOEFL (minimum score 550 paper-based; 79 iBT). *Expenses:* Tuition, state resident: full-time $2174. Tuition, nonresident: full-time $7377. *Required fees:* $1442. Part-time tuition and fees vary according to course load.

Western Kentucky University, Graduate Studies, College of Health and Human Services, Department of Social Work, Bowling Green, KY 42101. Offers MSW. *Accreditation:* CSWE. *Entrance requirements:* Additional exam requirements/

recommendations for international students: Required—TOEFL (minimum score 555 paper-based; 79 iBT).

Western Michigan University, Graduate College, College of Health and Human Services, School of Social Work, Kalamazoo, MI 49008. Offers MSW. *Accreditation:* CSWE. *Program availability:* Part-time.

Western New Mexico University, Graduate Division, Department of Social Work, Silver City, NM 88062-0680. Offers MSW. *Accreditation:* CSWE. *Program availability:* Part-time, evening/weekend, online learning. Electronic applications accepted.

Westfield State University, College of Graduate and Continuing Education, Department of Social Work, Westfield, MA 01086. Offers MSW. *Program availability:* Part-time, evening/weekend. *Faculty:* 7 full-time (3 women), 12 part-time/adjunct (10 women). *Students:* 150 full-time (124 women), 38 part-time (29 women); includes 52 minority (18 Black or African American, non-Hispanic/Latino; 3 Asian, non-Hispanic/Latino; 27 Hispanic/Latino; 4 Two or more races, non-Hispanic/Latino). Average age 32. 118 applicants, 70% accepted, 55 enrolled. In 2016, 58 master's awarded. *Degree requirements:* For master's, comprehensive exam, thesis (for some programs). *Entrance requirements:* For master's, GRE General Test or MAT, minimum undergraduate GPA of 2.8. Additional exam requirements/recommendations for international students: Recommended—TOEFL (minimum score 550 paper-based; 79 iBT). *Application deadline:* For fall admission, 2/1 for domestic students. Applications are processed on a rolling basis. Application fee: $50. *Expenses:* $424 per credit. *Financial support:* Unspecified assistantships available. Financial award application deadline: 3/1; financial award applicants required to submit FAFSA. *Unit head:* Dr. Robert Kersting, Chair, 413-572-5536, Fax: 413-579-3122, E-mail: rkersting@westfield.ma.edu. *Application contact:* Shelly Henrichon, Admissions Coordinator, 413-572-8022, Fax: 413-572-5227, E-mail: mhenrichon@westfield.ma.edu.

West Texas A&M University, College of Education and Social Sciences, Department of Psychology, Sociology and Social Work, Canyon, TX 79016-0001. Offers psychology (MA); social work (MS). *Program availability:* Part-time, evening/weekend. *Degree requirements:* For master's, comprehensive exam, thesis optional. *Entrance requirements:* For master's, GRE General Test, 3 letters of recommendation; interview; minimum GPA of 3.25 in psychology, 3.0 overall. Additional exam requirements/recommendations for international students: Required—TOEFL. *Application deadline:* For fall admission, 8/1 for domestic students, 6/1 for international students; for spring admission, 12/1 for domestic students, 11/1 for international students; for summer admission, 5/1 for domestic students. Applications are processed on a rolling basis. Application fee: $40 ($75 for international students). Electronic applications accepted. *Financial support:* Application deadline: 2/1; applicants required to submit FAFSA. *Unit head:* Dr. Keith Price, Department Head, 806-651-2418.

West Virginia University, Eberly College of Arts and Sciences, School of Social Work, Morgantown, WV 26506. Offers aging and health care (MSW); children and families (MSW); community mental health (MSW); community organization and social administration (MSW); direct (clinical) social work practice (MSW). *Accreditation:* CSWE. *Program availability:* Part-time. *Degree requirements:* For master's, fieldwork. *Entrance requirements:* For master's, GRE, minimum GPA of 2.75, 2 letters of reference. Additional exam requirements/recommendations for international students: Required—TOEFL. *Faculty research:* Rural and small town social work practice, gerontology, health and mental health, welfare reform, child welfare.

Wheelock College, Graduate Programs, Division of Social Work, Boston, MA 02215. Offers MSW. *Accreditation:* CSWE. *Degree requirements:* For master's, comprehensive exam, thesis. *Entrance requirements:* For master's, minimum GPA of 3.0; undergraduate course work in human biology, statistics. Additional exam requirements/recommendations for international students: Required—TOEFL. Electronic applications accepted.

Wichita State University, Graduate School, Fairmount College of Liberal Arts and Sciences, School of Social Work, Wichita, KS 67260. Offers MSW. *Accreditation:* CSWE. *Unit head:* Dr. Brien Bolin, Director, 316-978-7250, Fax: 316-978-3328, E-mail: brien.bolin@wichita.edu. *Application contact:* Jordan Oleson, Admissions Coordinator, 316-978-3095, Fax: 316-978-3253, E-mail: jordan.oleson@wichita.edu.
Website: http://www.wichita.edu/sw

Widener University, School of Human Service Professions, Center for Social Work Education, Chester, PA 19013-5792. Offers MSW, PhD. *Accreditation:* CSWE. *Program availability:* Part-time, 100% online, blended/hybrid learning. *Faculty:* 15 full-time (9 women), 16 part-time/adjunct (9 women). *Students:* 74 full-time (63 women), 676 part-time (606 women); includes 375 minority (287 Black or African American, non-Hispanic/Latino; 2 American Indian or Alaska Native, non-Hispanic/Latino; 12 Asian, non-Hispanic/Latino; 56 Hispanic/Latino; 1 Native Hawaiian or other Pacific Islander, non-Hispanic/Latino; 17 Two or more races, non-Hispanic/Latino). Average age 33. 307 applicants, 60% accepted, 156 enrolled. In 2016, 138 master's, 7 doctorates awarded. *Degree requirements:* For master's, field practica. *Entrance requirements:* For master's, minimum GPA of 3.0. *Application deadline:* For fall admission, 3/1 for domestic students. Applications are processed on a rolling basis. Application fee: $25 ($300 for international students). Electronic applications accepted. *Expenses:* Contact institution. *Financial support:* In 2016–17, 11 students received support, including 6 fellowships; career-related internships or fieldwork, Federal Work-Study, institutionally sponsored loans, and unspecified assistantships also available. Support available to part-time students. Financial award applicants required to submit FAFSA. *Faculty research:* Clinical practice, clinical supervision, gerontology, child welfare, self-psychology. *Total annual research expenditures:* $85,000. *Unit head:* Dr. Paula T. Silver, Associate Dean and Director, 610-499-1150, Fax: 610-499-4617, E-mail: socialwork@widener.edu. *Application contact:* Jill L. Brinker, Secretary, 610-499-1513, Fax: 610-499-4617, E-mail: socialwork@widener.edu.

Wilfrid Laurier University, Faculty of Graduate and Postdoctoral Studies, Lyle S. Hallman Faculty of Social Work, Waterloo, ON N2L 3C5, Canada. Offers Aboriginal studies (MSW); community, policy, planning and organizations (MSW); critical social policy and organizational studies (PhD); individuals, families and groups (MSW); social work practice (individuals, families, groups and communities) (PhD); social work practice: individuals, families, groups and communities (PhD). *Program availability:* Part-time. *Degree requirements:* For master's, thesis optional; for doctorate, thesis/dissertation. *Entrance requirements:* For master's, course work in social science, research methodology, and statistics; honors BA with a minimum B average; for doctorate, master's degree in social work, minimum A- average. Additional exam requirements/recommendations for international students: Required—TOEFL (minimum score 89 iBT). Electronic applications accepted. *Expenses:* Contact institution.

Winthrop University, College of Arts and Sciences, Program in Social Work, Rock Hill, SC 29733. Offers MSW. *Accreditation:* CSWE. *Entrance requirements:* For master's, GRE or MAT, minimum GPA of 3.0, 3 letters of recommendation, resume. Additional exam requirements/recommendations for international students: Required—TOEFL (minimum score 550 paper-based; 79 iBT), IELTS (minimum score 6). Electronic applications accepted. *Expenses:* Tuition, state resident: full-time $14,312; part-time $599 per credit hour. Tuition, nonresident: full-time $27,570; part-time $1153 per credit hour. *Faculty research:* Field study placement opportunities.

Yeshiva University, Wurzweiler School of Social Work, New York, NY 10033-3201. Offers MSW, PhD, MSW/Certificate. *Accreditation:* CSWE (one or more programs are accredited). *Program availability:* Part-time, evening/weekend. Terminal master's awarded for partial completion of doctoral program. *Degree requirements:* For master's, thesis, integrative essay; for doctorate, comprehensive exam, thesis/dissertation. *Entrance requirements:* For master's, interview, minimum GPA of 3.0, letters of reference; for doctorate, GRE, interview, letters of reference, writing sample, MSW, minimum of 2 years of professional social work experience. Additional exam requirements/recommendations for international students: Required—TOEFL (minimum score 577 paper-based). *Expenses:* Contact institution. *Faculty research:* Child abuse, AIDS, day care, non profits, gerontology.

York University, Faculty of Graduate Studies, Faculty of Liberal Arts and Professional Studies, Program in Social Work, Toronto, ON M3J 1P3, Canada. Offers MSW, PhD. *Program availability:* Part-time, evening/weekend. *Degree requirements:* For master's, thesis or alternative. Electronic applications accepted.

CALIFORNIA STATE UNIVERSITY, NORTHRIDGE

The Tseng College of Extended Learning, Social Work

 For more information, visit http://petersons.to/csunmsw

Programs of Study

Master of Social Work Program at California State University, Northridge

The urban setting of California State University, Northridge (CSUN) provides a unique emphasis for its Master of Social Work (M.S.W.) program. Based in the heart of Los Angeles County's San Fernando Valley, the program focuses on urban family practice, giving students the opportunity to work with vulnerable and at-risk populations, and cultivates an appreciation of the planned-change process.

The program's innovative curriculum, which has accreditation from the Council on Social Work Education, offers a generalist approach to social work, and emphasizes urban family practice. Students gain the expertise and perspective to improve quality of life at all levels: individuals/families (micro level), groups/communities (mezzo level), and systems and policies (macro level). The program is rooted in a community-oriented, strengths-based, urban family practice model. It also promotes social justice, including sensitivity to multicultural populations. It incorporates the field's history, philosophy, and purposes, and emphasizes critical and creative thinking. This allows graduates to develop, adapt, and assess interventions for urban families while remaining cognizant to significant national and global issues.

The CSUN M.S.W. program prepares practitioners to address social services needs in the Greater Los Angeles and Southern California regions and enhance social services for people in urban environments. The program prepares students to work with a variety of client systems and is grounded in a framework to promote the well-being of urban families and communities. The program trains professionals to practice ethically and competently, and to integrate knowledge, process, and values into professional social work practice.

The university provides flexible delivery options (online and off-campus locations) that allow students to earn their degrees in two to three years. It also provides a cohesive environment that includes ongoing support from program managers and distance learning staff members, as well as excellent instruction and personalized attention from distinguished faculty members. The Master of Social Work is a cohort degree program that allows students to progress through the program together, which allows them to build valuable professional relationships. Students also benefit from year-round classes, guaranteed enrollment in classes, and fixed class schedules.

An M.S.W. degree from California State University, Northridge prepares students for careers as administrators, community advocates, counselors, direct service providers, policy makers, researchers, service workers, and supervisors. Graduates secure positions in diverse settings including community organizations, government agencies, healthcare centers, and schools.

Master of Social Work—Online

The M.S.W. online program is a two-year (four-semester), full-time program. Students take two eight-week courses at a time for a total of 20 classes (60 graduate units), plus ongoing 16-week field education classes. Classes, except for a weekly field education class, are offered online and can be accessed at any time, so students can attend class and access course materials according to their schedules.

In addition to completing regular online assignments, the M.S.W. program typically meets weekly for live, online sessions one week night per week, in each class, between 5 and 9 p.m. Pacific time, with a start time no later than 6:30 p.m. All classes (except field classes) are asynchronous, which means students can attend the live class or watch the recording later at a more convenient time. The specific day time for live sessions will be announced no later than one month before the cohort launch. Rare exceptions may apply. Field classes meet weekly for one hour at a time determined by the instructor and seven to eight students, depending on their schedule. Students are always invited but will not be required to come to the CSUN campus or any other affiliate university campus during the four-semester online M.S.W. program.

Field hours will be 16 hours per week during the entire duration of the program. Students must be available for field placement Monday through Friday, from 9 a.m. to 5 p.m. Evening and weekend field placements are unavailable. It is not possible for students to complete a field internship at their place of employment. Field placement days and times are determined by the CSUN M.S.W. Field Education Department, based on agency needs, student schedules, and employer approval. If offered admission to the Online M.S.W. program, students are required to successfully complete a field internship interview. All applicants are advised to review the Field Education Manual and Student Manual for the policies governing the field internship and academic program prior to applying to the Online M.S.W. program.

Master of Social Work—Offsite: Ventura, California or Santa Clarita, California

Students attend classes year round. Classes are taught three at a time, in 16-week semesters. Students complete a total of 21 classes (63 graduate units). While CSUN's M.S.W. is a 60-unit degree, students who participate in off-campus cohorts may be required to complete additional units to meet the specific Council on Social Work Education (CSWE) fieldwork requirements for each cohort/location. Classes are held on one weeknight per week from 4–10 p.m., and occasional Saturdays. Students must be available for field placement Monday through Friday, from 9 a.m. to 5 p.m. Evening and weekend field placements are not available. When field internship hours remain incomplete beyond the first and second years of the program, students are required to complete their remaining field hours in the final year of the program. It is not possible for students to complete a field internship at their place of employment.

Starting in the fall semester of the first year, students are required to complete a minimum of 16 hours of field placement internship per week. Field placement days and times are determined by the M.S.W. Field Education Department, based on agency needs, student schedules, and employer approval. If offered admission to the M.S.W. program, students are required to successfully complete a field internship interview on campus. All applicants are advised to review the Field Education Manual and Student Manual for the policies governing the field internship and academic program prior to applying to the M.S.W. program.

Field Practicum

Field practicum is a keystone in graduate social work education. It is in field education where theory, practice concepts and skills, values, and social policy and research information are applied and internalized. Field education provides the guided practice needed to prepare M.S.W. students to become advanced social work professionals.

The CSUN M.S.W. program makes every attempt to place students at sites that are within a one-hour commute from their location. The placement of a student in a field practicum site involves an evaluation and assessment regarding the student's educational experiences, work experiences, and career goals. This information helps in narrowing and selecting the most appropriate field placement sites for the student.

Students are placed at a different agency (private, nonprofit, or public) for each of their two years of field education. Students must be able to commit to their assigned field placement site for the duration of each academic year (September through May). Selection of placement sites is based on populations served by agency, the agency's ability to meet CSWE Field Instructor qualifications, and various student needs.

Students are not approved to complete their first-year internship at their place of employment. In rare instances, students are granted approval for utilizing their employment as a field site during the second year. The M.S.W. program places a strong emphasis on offering each student at least one placement experience different from their prior experiences and sometimes current interests in order to further expand upon strengths and maximize student learning.

M.S.W. Capstone Project

Offered as the culminating experience of the M.S.W. program, students complete an individual or group research project reflecting the student's interests and needs in working with urban families. Outcomes of this seminar will require students to collect, analyze, and report direct observations; write a research paper that includes a title page, abstract, background, methods, and discussion sections conforming to APA Publication Manual guidelines; and present a poster in an open community-invited forum. This project meets the culminating experience requirements.

Financial Aid

The Department of Social Work does have some small scholarships for students and applications are made available at the end of the first year in the program. Students are encouraged to seek scholarships on their own and review the Funding Your Social Work Education section of the CSUN website (http://www.csun.edu/social-behavioral-sciences/social-work/funding-your-social-work-education).

Additional financial aid information is available at the Financial Aid and Scholarship website at http://www.csun.edu/financialaid. Financial opportunities for CSUN graduate students can also be found on the Graduate Studies website (http://www.csun.edu/research-graduate-studies/funding-sources).

Cost of Study

For the 2017–18 academic year, tuition for the online program is $737 per unit for a total tuition of $44,220 and for the offsite it is $310 per unit for a total tuition of $38,430.

CSUN makes every effort to keep student costs to a minimum. Tuition and fees are subject to change.

The College and the University

The Tseng College at California State University, Northridge meets the educational needs of mid-career professionals, international students, and regional employers. Its graduate and certificate programs allow students to build on their strengths and develop expertise in emerging fields.

Flexibility is a key component of program delivery. Programs are offered on campus, off campus, and online as well as in blended formats. Courses are offered year-round, and classes are generally held evenings and weekends.

Established in 1958, California State University, Northridge offers approximately 40,000 students nearly 180 bachelors, master's, doctoral, and teaching credential programs. One of the nation's largest single-campus universities, CSUN encourages students to combine academic pursuits with hands-on experience. It also serves as the intellectual, economic and cultural heart of the San Fernando Valley and beyond. CSUN cultivates professionals, leaders, and innovators who achieve the highest levels of success. Alumni include prominent public officials, award-winning teachers and health professionals.

Faculty

M.S.W. degree program faculty members, like Judy DeBonis, Ph.D., M.S.W., advance social work education and practice, and contribute to the well-being of individuals, families, schools, and communities. Dr. DeBonis has more than 25 years experience in clinical practice, research, program development, and teaching.

Professor Eli Bartle, Ph.D., M.S.W. is a skilled practitioner with experience as a caseworker and youth counselor. He is also a prolific researcher in several areas including child welfare supervision, hate crimes, public assistance, and workplace policy.

Professor James T. Decker, Ph.D., L.C.S.W. is an accomplished researcher, educator, administrator, and clinician with more than 25 years of experience in private practice. He has published numerous juried articles and book chapters, directed three M.S.W. programs, and served as executive director of a behavioral health organization.

Applying

The Department of Social Work invites applications from those who are interested in making a positive difference in the lives of the residents of San Fernando Valley, and the Greater Los Angeles Region. The Admissions Committee reviews all applications and accepts candidates who demonstrate personal and academic qualifications necessary for success as a graduate student and as an autonomous social work practitioner.

Applicants must have earned a baccalaureate degree from an accredited college. A liberal arts background with some course work in the social, behavioral, and biological sciences is strongly preferred. Applicants must present evidence of the ability to complete graduate study. Applicants should have attained a GPA of 3.0, although an exception might be made in some circumstances. If the applicant has less than a 3.0 overall GPA, the University requires the GRE.

Individuals applying should demonstrate evidence of personal maturity, including the ability to withstand difficult emotional challenges, a commitment to interpersonal processing within the parameters of cultural expectations, respect for others and for their life decisions, a readiness to learn advanced clinical and macro practice and research skills, a commitment to social justice and to the profession's Code of Ethics, and a capacity for flexibility and creativity.

Preference will be given to applicants who have had post-baccalaureate work experience. Academic credit, however, cannot be given for prior life and work experience.

More information and the application form is available at visit: http://tsengcollege.csun.edu/programs/MSW

Correspondence and Information

Rachel Navarro
M.S.W. Online and Offsite Coordinator
The Tseng College
California State University Northridge
18111 Nordhoff Street
Northridge, California 91330
United States
Phone: 818-677-1200
Fax: 818-677-5088
E-mail: Rachel.navarro@csun.edu
Website: http://tsengcollege.csun.edu/programs/MSW

RUTGERS UNIVERSITY

School of Social Work
Master of Social Work Program

 For more information, visit http://petersons.to/rutgersu_socialwork

Programs of Study

Rutgers, The State University of New Jersey (Rutgers) is the largest institution of higher learning in New Jersey and one of the nation's leading public research universities. With campuses in Newark, New Brunswick, and Camden, Rutgers is home to the nation's fourth-largest school of social work.

The School of Social Work at Rutgers University offers a full range of programs leading to the M.S.W. degree. Accredited by the Council on Social Work Education, the Rutgers M.S.W. degree program was developed to address the wide range of knowledge, values, tasks, and skills required to prepare competent and effective social work professionals.

The traditional on-campus M.S.W. program is offered on all three campuses and is available on a two-, three-, or four-year basis. Students select a specialization in either clinical social work or management and policy. The Rutgers School of Social Work also offers the M.S.W. curriculum as an intensive weekend program, 100 percent online, and in a blended online format.

The M.S.W. program prepares graduates for advanced social work practice in a variety of human services, including roles as administrative leaders in the state's social welfare departments, government agencies, and the volunteer sector. The curriculum also equips skilled direct-service providers to function in both public and private sectors of social welfare.

The M.S.W. curriculum is organized into two curriculum levels: the professional foundation and the advanced curriculum. Students must earn 30 credits in each level to complete the 60 credits needed to graduate. The professional foundation must be completed successfully before students may begin the advanced curriculum. Students must select an area of concentration before entering the advanced curriculum.

Professional Foundation Courses: These courses provide a body of knowledge, values, and skills essential to the practice of social work that translates across settings, population groups, and problem areas. The foundation courses combine generalist social work practice with corresponding field instruction, human behavior and the social environment, psychopathology, introductory social work research methods, social welfare policy and services, and diversity and oppression.

The required foundation courses are the following: Social Work Practice I with Individuals, Families, and Groups; Social Work Practice II with Organizations and Communities; Human Behavior and the Social Environment; Social Welfare Policy and Services I; Methods of Social Work Research I; Diversity and Oppression; Psychopathology; and Field Education Practicum I and II.

Advanced Curriculum Specializations: Specializations are designed to focus on advanced methods of social work by size and type of client system. The Clinical Social Work specialization prepares students to conceptualize, provide, and supervise the delivery of social work services to individuals, couples, families, and small groups. Clinical Social Work I and II are required courses for this specialization and must be taken concurrently with a clinical social work field education practicum.

The Management and Policy specialization equips social workers to perform administrative functions or planning, organizing, and policy functions within organizations, communities, and in the larger society. Courses required for the specialization, which must be taken concurrently with a management and policy field education practicum, are Management Practice and Theory and Program and Strategic Planning.

Advanced courses comprise Clinical Social Work I or Management Practice and Theory (depending on specialization); Program and Strategic Planning; Social Welfare Policy and Services II; Methods of Social Work Research II; Field Education Practicum III and IV; Advanced Practicum Distribution Requirement; and Advanced Human Behavior Distribution Requirement.

Advanced standing M.S.W.: The School of Social Work offers an advanced standing M.S.W. degree program to students who hold a bachelor's degree in social work from a program accredited by the Council on Social Work Education. Students are admitted to the program with 21 of their undergraduate credits applied toward their M.S.W. degree at Rutgers. Students complete an abbreviated curriculum comprising a concentration in advanced practice, advanced research, advanced field instruction and electives, and course work in advanced practice and human behavior.

Electives: Three general elective courses are required to complete the M.S.W. program. Typically, students complete one general elective during the Professional Foundation program and two during the Advanced Curriculum. Only after successful completion of the professional foundation courses and the statistics requirement are students eligible to take advanced electives.

Among the foundation electives are: Law and Social Work; Community Organizations; Human Behavior and Social Environment (HBSE): Loss Across the Lifespan; HBSE: Social Work with Immigrants and Refugees; Policy Perspectives on Poverty and Inequality; International Social Work; Emerging Issues in Child Welfare and Policy Practice; LGBTQ Issues; Current Issues in Developmental Disabilities; Group Dynamics; Chronic Illness and Disability; Women's Issues; Violence and Abuse in Adulthood; Violence and Abuse in Childhood; HBSE: Understanding Addictive Behaviors; Aging and Gerontological Services; Spirituality and Social Work; Human Sexuality for the Helping Professions; and Direct Practice: Theory and Models.

Advanced electives include Clinical Social Work: Adolescents; Clinical Social Work: Mental Health; Clinical Social Work: Children; Clinical Social Work: Families; Clinical Social Work: School; Clinical Social Work: Addictive Behaviors; Clinical Social Work: Survivors of Abuse and Trauma; Clinical Social Work: Aging; Human Resource Management; HBSE: Adolescents at Risk; Solution-Focused Therapy; Child Welfare Management; Financial Management; Supervision and Consultation; Fundraising and Marketing; and Play Therapy.

M.S.W. Certificates: As part of the M.S.W. curriculum, Rutgers offers four unique M.S.W. certificate programs, providing the opportunity for students to focus on a particular area of interest. The Addiction Counselor Training (ACT) certificate, Violence Against Women and Children (VAWC) certificate, Promoting Child and Adolescent Well-Being certificate, or the certificate in Aging and Health, can all be embedded in the M.S.W. curriculum and require that students complete a relevant field placement.

Areas of Emphasis: Students may also develop an area of emphasis as part of their M.S.W. curriculum. Areas of emphasis focus on a student-driven, student-identified topic, population, or specialization. Students work closely with their adviser to select relevant courses from both inside and outside the School of Social Work. Some popular areas of emphasis include: mental and behavioral health, Latino initiatives, international social work and children, and youth and families.

Dual-degree Programs: The School of Social Work offers different dual-degree programs to help students who want to enhance their credentials as a social worker.

Rutgers University

Juris Doctor/Master of Social Work (J.D./M.S.W.)—Students who wish to combine a legal career with social service work or social policy work can take advantage of the Juris Doctor/Master of Social Work (J.D./M.S.W.) dual-degree program. This program allows students to graduate with a J.D. and an M.S.W. in four years. Typically, this would take five years of work. Course work is completed in the School of Social Work and in collaboration with Rutgers School of Law. Students can start out in either school. In the final year, students complete work in both schools.

Master of Social Work/Master of Divinity (M.S.W./M.Div.)—Students with a desire to combine a ministry calling with an extended knowledge in social work can choose to earn a Master of Social Work/Master of Divinity (M.S.W./M.Div.) dual degree. The School of Social Work collaborates with the Princeton Theological Seminary. Students begin work in the four-year programs with two years at the Princeton Theological Seminary and complete the program with two years at Rutgers School of Social Work.

Combined M.S.W./Ph.D. Programs—Students can also combine an M.S.W. with a Ph.D. program. The program is highly competitive and only one to two students are selected for the program each year. Students admitted to the program have a rare opportunity to pursue a doctorate, studying for a career in advanced education and research positions, and a chance to combine that with studies in social work policy at a highly ranked social work program.

Research Facilities

The Rutgers School of Social Work is home to several internationally-known centers and programs dedicated to creating positive social change. The faculty-led entities create spaces for conversation, collaboration, hands-on training, and research that leads to real and lasting changes in communities.

The centers include the Institute for Families, Center for Gambling Studies, Center for Global Social Work, Center for Leadership and Management, Center on Violence Against Women and Children, and the Huamin Research Center. Additional details regarding the centers can be found online at https://socialwork.rutgers.edu/centers.

The Faculty

Rutgers faculty members are among the world's most respected and accomplished educators and researchers. As a tier-one research institute, faculty are frequently awarded grant funding for research that is unparalleled in the field. Notable faculty members in the School of Social Work include Dr. Edward Alessi, whose research and scholarly interests include LGBTQ mental health issues and clinical social work practice; Dr. Emily Greenfield, whose research interests encompass aging, life course human development, social relationships and health, and supportive services for older adults and family caregivers; and Charles Chear, an expert on refugee issues, community development and organizing, and cultural responsiveness in social work.

Financial Assistance

Rutgers University offers financial assistance to eligible graduate students in the form of loans, grants, scholarships, assistantships, and fellowships. The application deadline for financial awards is March 1.

Costs

For a full-time enrolled student in the Traditional program, the total cost is around $33,072. This amount varies from other formats, as some are taken part-time and/or have additional online course fees. The most current information on tuition and fees is available at https://socialwork.rutgers.edu/admissions/msw-admissions/tuition-and-financial-support.

Admission Requirements

Eligible candidates for admission to the School of Social Work must have completed a bachelor's degree from an accredited undergraduate institution. Strong candidates will have a minimum 3.0 cumulative GPA. Social work experience is advantageous but not required. Applicants to the Advanced Standing programs must also demonstrate competency in all undergraduate social work courses.

Applying

All M.S.W. applications are submitted online; complete information and details can be found at MSWadmissions.rutgers.edu. Once students have submitted their application, they can check their application status online. It is the applicant's responsibility to ensure that all materials are submitted to the Office of Graduate and Professional Admissions. Transcripts, letters, and other application materials should be submitted as soon as possible to ensure full consideration.

Details on the required application materials and deadlines are available at https://socialwork.rutgers.edu/admissions/msw-admissions-msw-application-requirements.

Correspondence and Information

Laura DiMarcantonio, Director of Admissions
School of Social Work
Rutgers University
536 George Street, Room 202
New Brunswick, New Jersey 08901
United States
Phone: 848-932-7520
E-mail: MSWadmissions@ssw.rutgers.edu
Website: MSWadmissions.rutgers.edu

Rutgers School of Social Work faculty members are a dynamic community of over 200 leaders, tenured professors advancing the field through original published research that has national and global impact and actively working in local communities. To ensure the greatest possible impact, teaching and field professionals maintain partnerships with more than 600 public agencies, local nonprofit organizations, foundations, and socially active corporations.

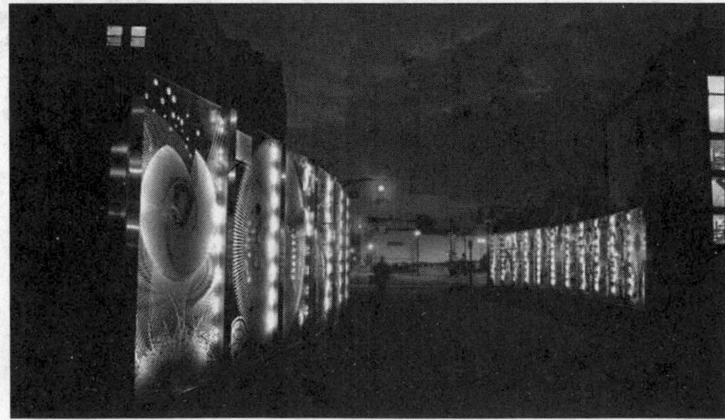

Rutgers flexible M.S.W. program options include an Intensive Weekend M.S.W. for working professionals; a 100 percent online M.S.W.; and full-time, part-time, and evening study options at Rutgers' campuses in Camden, New Brunswick, and Newark, New Jersey.

APPENDIXES

Institutional Changes Since the 2017 Edition

Following is an alphabetical listing of institutions that have recently closed, merged with other institutions, or changed their names or status. In the case of a name change, the former name appears first, followed by the new name.

Alliant International University–México City (Mexico City, Mexico): *closed.*

The American College (Bryn Mawr, PA): *name changed to The American College of Financial Services.*

Andover Newton Theological School (Newton Centre, MA): *now affiliated with Yale Divinity School.*

Argosy University, Washington DC (Arlington, VA): *name changed to Argosy University, Northern Virginia.*

The Art Institute of Dallas, a campus of South University (Dallas, TX): *name changed to The Art Institute of Dallas, a branch of Miami International University of Art & Design.*

Bard Graduate Center: Decorative Arts, Design History, Material Culture (New York, NY): *name changed to Bard Graduate Center.*

Bexley Hall Episcopal Seminary (Columbus, OH): *merged into a single entry for Bexley Seabury Seminary (Chicago, IL).*

Blessing-Rieman College of Nursing (Quincy, IL): *name changed to Blessing-Rieman College of Nursing & Health Sciences.*

California Maritime Academy (Vallejo, CA): *name changed to California State University Maritime Academy.*

California National University for Advanced Studies (Northridge, CA): *closed.*

California School of Podiatric Medicine at Samuel Merritt University (Oakland, CA): *merged as a unit into Samuel Merritt University (Oakland, CA).*

Calvary Bible College and Theological Seminary (Kansas City, MO): *name changed to Calvary University.*

Carolina Graduate School of Divinity (Greensboro, NC): *closed.*

Centenary College (Hackettstown, NJ): *name changed to Centenary University.*

Charlotte School of Law (Charlotte, NC): *will not be enrolling new students for the fall 2017 term.*

Colorado Heights University (Denver, CO): *closed.*

Colorado Technical University Denver South (Aurora, CO): *name changed to Colorado Technical University Aurora.*

The Commonwealth Medical College (Scranton, PA): *name changed to Geisinger Commonwealth School of Medicine.*

Connecticut College (New London, CT): *will not be accepting graduate program applications for the 2017-18 academic year.*

Daniel Webster College (Nashua, NH): *merged into Southern New Hampshire University (Manchester, NH).*

DeVry College of New York (New York, NY): *name changed to DeVry College of New York–Midtown Manhattan Campus.*

DeVry University (Glendale, AZ): *now a DeVry University center and no longer profiled separately.*

DeVry University (Mesa, AZ): *now a DeVry University center and no longer profiled separately.*

DeVry University (Phoenix, AZ): *name changed to DeVry University–Phoenix Campus.*

DeVry University (Alhambra, CA): *closed.*

DeVry University (Anaheim, CA): *now a DeVry University center and no longer profiled separately.*

DeVry University (Fremont, CA): *name changed to DeVry University–Fremont Campus.*

DeVry University (Long Beach, CA): *name changed to DeVry University–Long Beach Campus.*

DeVry University (Oakland, CA): *now a DeVry University center and no longer profiled separately.*

DeVry University (Oxnard, CA): *closed.*

DeVry University (Palmdale, CA): *now a DeVry University center and no longer profiled separately.*

DeVry University (Pomona, CA): *name changed to DeVry University–Pomona Campus.*

DeVry University (San Diego, CA): *name changed to DeVry University–San Diego Campus.*

DeVry University (Colorado Springs, CO): *now a DeVry University center and no longer profiled separately.*

DeVry University (Jacksonville, FL): *name changed to DeVry University–Jacksonville Campus.*

DeVry University (Miramar, FL): *name changed to DeVry University–Miramar Campus.*

DeVry University (Orlando, FL): *name changed to DeVry University–Orlando Campus.*

DeVry University (Alpharetta, GA): *name changed to DeVry University–Alpharetta Campus.*

DeVry University (Decatur, GA): *name changed to DeVry University–Decatur Campus.*

DeVry University (Duluth, GA): *now a DeVry University center and no longer profiled separately.*

DeVry University (Chicago, IL): *name changed to DeVry University–Chicago Campus.*

DeVry University (Downers Grove, IL): *now a DeVry University center and no longer profiled separately.*

DeVry University (Elgin, IL): *now a DeVry University center and no longer profiled separately.*

DeVry University (Gurnee, IL): *now a DeVry University center and no longer profiled separately.*

DeVry University (Naperville, IL): *now a DeVry University center and no longer profiled separately.*

DeVry University (Tinley Park, IL): *name changed to DeVry University–Tinley Park Campus.*

DeVry University (Merrillville, IN): *now a DeVry University center and no longer profiled separately.*

DeVry University (Henderson, NV): *name changed to DeVry University–Henderson Campus.*

DeVry University (North Brunswick, NJ): *name changed to DeVry University–North Brunswick Campus.*

DeVry University (Paramus, NJ): *now a DeVry University center and no longer profiled separately.*

DeVry University (Charlotte, NC): *name changed to DeVry University–Charlotte Campus.*

DeVry University (Columbus, OH): *name changed to DeVry University–Columbus Campus.*

DeVry University (Seven Hills, OH): *name changed to DeVry University–Seven Hills Campus.*

DeVry University (Fort Washington, PA): *name changed to DeVry University–Ft. Washington Campus.*

DeVry University (King of Prussia, PA): *closed.*

DeVry University (Nashville, TN): *name changed to DeVry University–Nashville Campus.*

DeVry University (Irving, TX): *name changed to DeVry University–Irving Campus.*

DeVry University (Arlington, VA): *name changed to DeVry University–Arlington Campus.*

DeVry University (Chesapeake, VA): *name changed to DeVry University–Chesapeake Campus.*

DeVry University (Manassas, VA): *closed.*

Ellis University (Oakbrook Terrace, IL): *closed.*

Everest University (Largo, FL): *closed.*

Everest University (Largo, FL): *closed.*

Everest University (Orlando, FL): *closed.*

Frank Lloyd Wright School of Architecture (Scottsdale, AZ): *name changed to School of Architecture at Taliesin.*

Hillsdale Free Will Baptist College (Moore, OK): *name changed to Randall University.*

Houston College of Law (Houston, TX): *name changed to South Texas College of Law Houston.*

Humphreys College (Stockton, CA): *name changed to Humphreys University.*

ITT Technical Institute (Indianapolis, IN): *closed.*

John Marshall Law School (Chicago, IL): *name changed to The John Marshall Law School.*

Lakehead University–Orillia (Orillia, ON, Canada): *name changed to Lakehead University.*

Long Island University–Hudson at Rockland (Orangeburg, NY): *merged into a single entry for Long Island University–Hudson (Purchase, NY) by request from the institution.*

Mary Baldwin College (Staunton, VA): *name changed to Mary Baldwin University.*

The Master's College and Seminary (Santa Clarita, CA): *name changed to The Master's University.*

Mayo Graduate School (Rochester, MN): *name changed to Mayo Clinic Graduate School of Biomedical Sciences.*

Mayo Medical School (Rochester, MN): *name changed to Mayo Clinic School of Medicine.*

Mayo School of Health Sciences (Rochester, MN): *name changed to Mayo Clinic School of Health Sciences.*

National College of Natural Medicine (Portland, OR): *name changed to National University of Natural Medicine.*

Oregon College of Art & Craft (Portland, OR): *name changed to Oregon College of Art and Craft.*

Our Lady of the Lake University of San Antonio (San Antonio, TX): *name changed to Our Lady of the Lake University.*

Phillips Graduate Institute (Encino, CA): *name changed to Phillips Graduate University.*

Pinchot University (Seattle, WA): *acquired by Presidio Graduate School (San Francisco, CA).*

Purdue University Northwest (Westville, IN): *merged into a single entry for Purdue University Northwest (Hammond, IN).*

Rabbi Isaac Elchanan Theological Seminary (New York, NY): *merged into Yeshiva University (New York, NY).*

Saint Joseph's College (Rensselaer, IN): *closed.*

School of the Museum of Fine Arts, Boston (Boston, MA): *merged as a unit into Tufts University (Medford, MA).*

Seabury-Western Theological Seminary (Evanston, IL): *name changed to Bexley Seabury Seminary.*

Seminary of the Immaculate Conception (Huntington, NY): *no longer degree granting.*

Summit University (Clarks Summit, PA): *name changed to Clarks Summit University.*

Tennessee Wesleyan College (Athens, TN): *name changed to Tennessee Wesleyan University.*

Texas A&M University at Galveston (Galveston, TX): *merged as a unit into Texas A&M University (College Station, TX).*

Waldorf College (Forest City, IA): *name changed to Waldorf University*

Abbreviations Used in the Guides

The following list includes abbreviations of degree names used in the profiles in the 2016 edition of the guides. Because some degrees (e.g., Doctor of Education) can be abbreviated in more than one way (e.g., D.Ed. or Ed.D.), and because the abbreviations used in the guides reflect the preferences of the individual colleges and universities, the list may include two or more abbreviations for a single degree.

DEGREES

A Mus D	Doctor of Musical Arts
AC	Advanced Certificate
AD	Artist's Diploma
	Doctor of Arts
ADP	Artist's Diploma
Adv C	Advanced Certificate
AGC	Advanced Graduate Certificate
AGSC	Advanced Graduate Specialist Certificate
ALM	Master of Liberal Arts
AM	Master of Arts
AMBA	Accelerated Master of Business Administration
AMRS	Master of Arts in Religious Studies
APC	Advanced Professional Certificate
APMPH	Advanced Professional Master of Public Health
App Sc	Applied Scientist
App Sc D	Doctor of Applied Science
AstE	Astronautical Engineer
ATC	Advanced Training Certificate
Au D	Doctor of Audiology
B Th	Bachelor of Theology
BN	Bachelor of Naturopathy
CAES	Certificate of Advanced Educational Specialization
CAGS	Certificate of Advanced Graduate Studies
CAL	Certificate in Applied Linguistics
CAPS	Certificate of Advanced Professional Studies
CAS	Certificate of Advanced Studies
CASPA	Certificate of Advanced Study in Public Administration
CASR	Certificate in Advanced Social Research
CATS	Certificate of Achievement in Theological Studies
CBHS	Certificate in Basic Health Sciences
CCJA	Certificate in Criminal Justice Administration
CCTS	Certificate in Clinical and Translational Science
CE	Civil Engineer
CEM	Certificate of Environmental Management
CET	Certificate in Educational Technologies
CGS	Certificate of Graduate Studies
Ch E	Chemical Engineer
Clin Sc D	Doctor of Clinical Science
CM	Certificate in Management
CMH	Certificate in Medical Humanities
CMM	Master of Church Ministries
CMS	Certificate in Ministerial Studies
CNM	Certificate in Nonprofit Management
CPASF	Certificate Program for Advanced Study in Finance
CPC	Certificate in Professional Counseling
	Certificate in Publication and Communication
CPH	Certificate in Public Health
CPM	Certificate in Public Management
CPS	Certificate of Professional Studies
CScD	Doctor of Clinical Science
CSD	Certificate in Spiritual Direction
CSS	Certificate of Special Studies
CTS	Certificate of Theological Studies
CURP	Certificate in Urban and Regional Planning
D Admin	Doctor of Administration
D Arch	Doctor of Architecture
D Be	Doctor in Bioethics
D Com	Doctor of Commerce
D Couns	Doctor of Counseling
D Des	Doctorate of Design
D Div	Doctor of Divinity
D Ed	Doctor of Education
D Ed Min	Doctor of Educational Ministry
D Eng	Doctor of Engineering
D Engr	Doctor of Engineering
D Ent	Doctor of Enterprise
D Env	Doctor of Environment
D Law	Doctor of Law
D Litt	Doctor of Letters
D Med Sc	Doctor of Medical Science
D Min	Doctor of Ministry
D Miss	Doctor of Missiology
D Mus	Doctor of Music
D Mus A	Doctor of Musical Arts
D Phil	Doctor of Philosophy
D Prof	Doctor of Professional Studies
D Ps	Doctor of Psychology
D Sc	Doctor of Science
D Sc D	Doctor of Science in Dentistry
D Sc IS	Doctor of Science in Information Systems
D Sc PA	Doctor of Science in Physician Assistant Studies
D Th	Doctor of Theology
D Th P	Doctor of Practical Theology
DA	Doctor of Accounting
	Doctor of Arts
DAH	Doctor of Arts in Humanities
DAOM	Doctorate in Acupuncture and Oriental Medicine
DAT	Doctorate of Athletic Training
	Professional Doctor of Art Therapy
DBA	Doctor of Business Administration
DBH	Doctor of Behavioral Health
DBL	Doctor of Business Leadership
DC	Doctor of Chiropractic
DCC	Doctor of Computer Science
DCD	Doctor of Communications Design
DCL	Doctor of Civil Law
	Doctor of Comparative Law
DCM	Doctor of Church Music
DCN	Doctor of Clinical Nutrition
DCS	Doctor of Computer Science
DDN	Diplôme du Droit Notarial
DDS	Doctor of Dental Surgery
DE	Doctor of Education
	Doctor of Engineering
DED	Doctor of Economic Development
DEIT	Doctor of Educational Innovation and Technology
DEL	Doctor of Executive Leadership
DEM	Doctor of Educational Ministry
DEPD	Diplôme Études Spécialisées
DES	Doctor of Engineering Science
DESS	Diplôme Études Supérieures Spécialisées
DET	Doctor of Educational Technology
DFA	Doctor of Fine Arts
DGP	Diploma in Graduate and Professional Studies
DH Ed	Doctor of Health Education

DH Sc	Doctor of Health Sciences
DHA	Doctor of Health Administration
DHCE	Doctor of Health Care Ethics
DHL	Doctor of Hebrew Letters
DHPE	Doctorate of Health Professionals Education
DHS	Doctor of Health Science
DHSc	Doctor of Health Science
Dip CS	Diploma in Christian Studies
DIT	Doctor of Industrial Technology
	Doctor of Information Technology
DJS	Doctor of Jewish Studies
DLS	Doctor of Liberal Studies
DM	Doctor of Management
	Doctor of Music
DMA	Doctor of Musical Arts
DMD	Doctor of Dental Medicine
DME	Doctor of Manufacturing Management
	Doctor of Music Education
DMEd	Doctor of Music Education
DMFT	Doctor of Marital and Family Therapy
DMH	Doctor of Medical Humanities
DML	Doctor of Modern Languages
DMP	Doctorate in Medical Physics
DMPNA	Doctor of Management Practice in Nurse Anesthesia
DN Sc	Doctor of Nursing Science
DNAP	Doctor of Nurse Anesthesia Practice
DNP	Doctor of Nursing Practice
DNP-A	Doctor of Nursing Practice - Anesthesia
DNS	Doctor of Nursing Science
DO	Doctor of Osteopathy
DOT	Doctor of Occupational Therapy
DPA	Doctor of Public Administration
DPDS	Doctor of Planning and Development Studies
DPH	Doctor of Public Health
DPM	Doctor of Plant Medicine
	Doctor of Podiatric Medicine
DPPD	Doctor of Policy, Planning, and Development
DPS	Doctor of Professional Studies
DPT	Doctor of Physical Therapy
DPTSc	Doctor of Physical Therapy Science
Dr DES	Doctor of Design
Dr NP	Doctor of Nursing Practice
Dr OT	Doctor of Occupational Therapy
Dr PH	Doctor of Public Health
Dr Sc PT	Doctor of Science in Physical Therapy
DrAP	Doctor of Anesthesia Practice
DRSc	Doctor of Regulatory Science
DS	Doctor of Science
DS Sc	Doctor of Social Science
DSJS	Doctor of Science in Jewish Studies
DSL	Doctor of Strategic Leadership
DSS	Doctor of Strategic Security
DSW	Doctor of Social Work
DTL	Doctor of Talmudic Law
	Doctor of Transformational Leadership
DV Sc	Doctor of Veterinary Science
DVM	Doctor of Veterinary Medicine
DWS	Doctor of Worship Studies
EAA	Engineer in Aeronautics and Astronautics
EASPh D	Engineering and Applied Science Doctor of Philosophy
ECS	Engineer in Computer Science
Ed D	Doctor of Education
Ed DCT	Doctor of Education in College Teaching
Ed L D	Doctor of Education Leadership
Ed M	Master of Education
Ed S	Specialist in Education
Ed Sp	Specialist in Education
EDB	Executive Doctorate in Business
EDBA	Executive Doctor of Business Administration
EDM	Executive Doctorate in Management
EE	Electrical Engineer
EJD	Executive Juris Doctor
EMBA	Executive Master of Business Administration
EMFA	Executive Master of Forensic Accounting
EMHA	Executive Master of Health Administration
EMIB	Executive Master of International Business
EML	Executive Master of Leadership
EMPA	Executive Master of Public Administration
EMPL	Executive Master in Public Leadership
EMS	Executive Master of Science
EMTM	Executive Master of Technology Management
Eng	Engineer
Eng Sc D	Doctor of Engineering Science
Engr	Engineer
Exec M Tax	Executive Master of Taxation
Exec MAC	Executive Master of Accounting
Exec Ed D	Executive Doctor of Education
Exec MBA	Executive Master of Business Administration
Exec MPA	Executive Master of Public Administration
Exec MPH	Executive Master of Public Health
Exec MS	Executive Master of Science
Executive Fellows MBA	Executive Fellows Master of Business Administration
G Dip	Graduate Diploma
GBC	Graduate Business Certificate
GDM	Graduate Diploma in Management
GDPA	Graduate Diploma in Public Administration
GDRE	Graduate Diploma in Religious Education
GEMBA	Global Executive Master of Business Administration
GMBA	Global Master of Business Administration
GP LL M	Global Professional Master of Laws
GPD	Graduate Performance Diploma
GSS	Graduate Special Certificate for Students in Special Situations
IEMBA	International Executive Master of Business Administration
IMA	Interdisciplinary Master of Arts
IMBA	International Master of Business Administration
IMES	International Master's in Environmental Studies
Ingeniero	Engineer
JCD	Doctor of Canon Law
JCL	Licentiate in Canon Law
JD	Juris Doctor
JM	Juris Master
JSD	Doctor of Juridical Science
	Doctor of Jurisprudence
	Doctor of the Science of Law
JSM	Master of the Science of Law
L Th	Licenciate in Theology
LL B	Bachelor of Laws
LL CM	Master of Comparative Law
LL D	Doctor of Laws
LL M	Master of Laws
LL M in Tax	Master of Laws in Taxation
LL M CL	Master of Laws in Common Law
M Ac	Master of Accountancy
	Master of Accounting
	Master of Acupuncture
M Ac OM	Master of Acupuncture and Oriental Medicine
M Acc	Master of Accountancy
	Master of Accounting
M Acct	Master of Accountancy
	Master of Accounting

M Accy	Master of Accountancy
M Actg	Master of Accounting
M Acy	Master of Accountancy
M Ad	Master of Administration
M Ad Ed	Master of Adult Education
M Adm	Master of Administration
M Adm Mgt	Master of Administrative Management
M Admin	Master of Administration
M ADU	Master of Architectural Design and Urbanism
M Adv	Master of Advertising
M AEST	Master of Applied Environmental Science and Technology
M Ag	Master of Agriculture
M Ag Ed	Master of Agricultural Education
M Agr	Master of Agriculture
M Anesth Ed	Master of Anesthesiology Education
M App Comp Sc	Master of Applied Computer Science
M App St	Master of Applied Statistics
M Appl Stat	Master of Applied Statistics
M Aq	Master of Aquaculture
M Arc	Master of Architecture
M Arch	Master of Architecture
M Arch I	Master of Architecture I
M Arch II	Master of Architecture II
M Arch E	Master of Architectural Engineering
M Arch H	Master of Architectural History
M Bioethics	Master in Bioethics
M Biomath	Master of Biomathematics
M Ch E	Master of Chemical Engineering
M Chem	Master of Chemistry
M Cl D	Master of Clinical Dentistry
M Cl Sc	Master of Clinical Science
M Comp	Master of Computing
M Comp Sc	Master of Computer Science
M Coun	Master of Counseling
M Dent	Master of Dentistry
M Dent Sc	Master of Dental Sciences
M Des	Master of Design
M Des S	Master of Design Studies
M Div	Master of Divinity
M E Sci	Master of Earth Science
M Ec	Master of Economics
M Econ	Master of Economics
M Ed	Master of Education
M Ed T	Master of Education in Teaching
M En	Master of Engineering
M En S	Master of Environmental Sciences
M Eng	Master of Engineering
M Eng Mgt	Master of Engineering Management
M Engr	Master of Engineering
M Ent	Master of Enterprise
M Env	Master of Environment
M Env Des	Master of Environmental Design
M Env E	Master of Environmental Engineering
M Env Sc	Master of Environmental Science
M Fin	Master of Finance
M FSc	Master of Fisheries Science
M Geo E	Master of Geological Engineering
M Geoenv E	Master of Geoenvironmental Engineering
M Geog	Master of Geography
M Hum	Master of Humanities
M IDST	Master's in Interdisciplinary Studies
M Kin	Master of Kinesiology
M Land Arch	Master of Landscape Architecture
M Litt	Master of Letters
M Mat SE	Master of Material Science and Engineering
M Math	Master of Mathematics
M Mech E	Master of Mechanical Engineering
M Med Sc	Master of Medical Science
M Mgmt	Master of Management
M Mgt	Master of Management
M Min	Master of Ministries
M Mtl E	Master of Materials Engineering
M Mu	Master of Music
M Mus	Master of Music
M Mus Ed	Master of Music Education
M Music	Master of Music
M Nat Sci	Master of Natural Science
M Pet E	Master of Petroleum Engineering
M Pharm	Master of Pharmacy
M Phil	Master of Philosophy
M Phil F	Master of Philosophical Foundations
M Pl	Master of Planning
M Plan	Master of Planning
M Pol	Master of Political Science
M Pr Met	Master of Professional Meteorology
M Prob S	Master of Probability and Statistics
M Psych	Master of Psychology
M Pub	Master of Publishing
M Rel	Master of Religion
M Sc	Master of Science
M Sc A	Master of Science (Applied)
M Sc AC	Master of Science in Applied Computing
M Sc AHN	Master of Science in Applied Human Nutrition
M Sc BMC	Master of Science in Biomedical Communications
M Sc CS	Master of Science in Computer Science
M Sc E	Master of Science in Engineering
M Sc Eng	Master of Science in Engineering
M Sc Engr	Master of Science in Engineering
M Sc F	Master of Science in Forestry
M Sc FE	Master of Science in Forest Engineering
M Sc Geogr	Master of Science in Geography
M Sc N	Master of Science in Nursing
M Sc OT	Master of Science in Occupational Therapy
M Sc P	Master of Science in Planning
M Sc Pl	Master of Science in Planning
M Sc PT	Master of Science in Physical Therapy
M Sc T	Master of Science in Teaching
M SEM	Master of Sustainable Environmental Management
M Serv Soc	Master of Social Service
M Soc	Master of Sociology
M Sp Ed	Master of Special Education
M St	Master of Studies
M Stat	Master of Statistics
M Sys E	Master of Systems Engineering
M Sys Sc	Master of Systems Science
M Tax	Master of Taxation
M Tech	Master of Technology
M Th	Master of Theology
M Tox	Master of Toxicology
M Trans E	Master of Transportation Engineering
M U Ed	Master of Urban Education
M Urb	Master of Urban Planning
M Vet Sc	Master of Veterinary Science
MA	Master of Accounting Master of Administration Master of Arts
MA Comm	Master of Arts in Communication
MA Ed	Master of Arts in Education
MA Ed/HD	Master of Arts in Education and Human Development
MA Ext	Master of Agricultural Extension
MA Min	Master of Arts in Ministry
MA Past St	Master of Arts in Pastoral Studies
MA Ph	Master of Arts in Philosophy

MA Psych — Master of Arts in Psychology
MA Sc — Master of Applied Science
MA Sp — Master of Arts (Spirituality)
MA Th — Master of Arts in Theology
MA-R — Master of Arts (Research)
MAA — Master of Administrative Arts
Master of Applied Anthropology
Master of Applied Arts
Master of Arts in Administration
MAAA — Master of Arts in Arts Administration
MAAAP — Master of Arts Administration and Policy
MAAD — Master of Advanced Architectural Design
MAAE — Master of Arts in Art Education
MAAPPS — Master of Arts in Asia Pacific Policy Studies
MAAS — Master of Arts in Aging and Spirituality
MAASJ — Master of Arts in Applied Social Justice
MAAT — Master of Arts in Applied Theology
Master of Arts in Art Therapy
MAB — Master of Agribusiness
MABC — Master of Arts in Biblical Counseling
MABE — Master of Arts in Bible Exposition
MABL — Master of Arts in Biblical Languages
MABM — Master of Agribusiness Management
MABS — Master of Arts in Biblical Studies
MABT — Master of Arts in Bible Teaching
MAC — Master of Accountancy
Master of Accounting
Master of Arts in Communication
Master of Arts in Counseling
MACC — Master of Arts in Christian Counseling
Master of Arts in Clinical Counseling
MACCT — Master of Accounting
MACD — Master of Arts in Christian Doctrine
MACE — Master of Arts in Christian Education
MACH — Master of Arts in Church History
MACI — Master of Arts in Curriculum and Instruction
MACIS — Master of Accounting and Information Systems
MACJ — Master of Arts in Criminal Justice
MACL — Master of Arts in Christian Leadership
Master of Arts in Community Leadership
MACM — Master of Arts in Christian Ministries
Master of Arts in Christian Ministry
Master of Arts in Church Music
Master of Arts in Counseling Ministries
MACN — Master of Arts in Counseling
MACO — Master of Arts in Counseling
MAcOM — Master of Acupuncture and Oriental Medicine
MACP — Master of Arts in Christian Practice
Master of Arts in Church Planting
Master of Arts in Counseling Psychology
MACS — Master of Applied Computer Science
Master of Arts in Catholic Studies
Master of Arts in Christian Studies
MACSE — Master of Arts in Christian School Education
MACT — Master of Arts in Communications and Technology
MAD — Master in Educational Institution Administration
Master of Art and Design
MADR — Master of Arts in Dispute Resolution
MADS — Master of Animal and Dairy Science
Master of Applied Disability Studies
MAE — Master of Aerospace Engineering
Master of Agricultural Economics
Master of Agricultural Education
Master of Applied Economics
Master of Architectural Engineering
Master of Art Education
Master of Arts in Education
Master of Arts in English
MAEd — Master of Arts Education
MAEL — Master of Arts in Educational Leadership
MAEM — Master of Arts in Educational Ministries
MAEP — Master of Arts in Economic Policy
Master of Arts in Educational Psychology
MAES — Master of Arts in Environmental Sciences
MAET — Master of Arts in English Teaching
MAF — Master of Arts in Finance
MAFE — Master of Arts in Financial Economics
MAFLL — Master of Arts in Foreign Language and Literature
MAFM — Master of Accounting and Financial Management
MAFS — Master of Arts in Family Studies
MAG — Master of Applied Geography
MAGS — Master of Arts in Global Service
MAGU — Master of Urban Analysis and Management
MAH — Master of Arts in Humanities
MAHA — Master of Arts in Humanitarian Assistance
MAHCM — Master of Arts in Health Care Mission
MAHG — Master of American History and Government
MAHL — Master of Arts in Hebrew Letters
MAHN — Master of Applied Human Nutrition
MAHR — Master of Applied Historical Research
MAHS — Master of Arts in Human Services
MAHSR — Master in Applied Health Services Research
MAIA — Master of Arts in International Administration
Master of Arts in International Affairs
MAIDM — Master of Arts in Interior Design and Merchandising
MAIH — Master of Arts in Interdisciplinary Humanities
MAIOP — Master of Applied Industrial/Organizational Psychology
MAIPCR — Master of Arts in International Peace and Conflict Management
MAIS — Master of Arts in Intercultural Studies
Master of Arts in Interdisciplinary Studies
Master of Arts in International Studies
MAIT — Master of Administration in Information Technology
MAJ — Master of Arts in Journalism
MAJ Ed — Master of Arts in Jewish Education
MAJCS — Master of Arts in Jewish Communal Service
MAJE — Master of Arts in Jewish Education
MAJPS — Master of Arts in Jewish Professional Studies
MAJS — Master of Arts in Jewish Studies
MAL — Master in Agricultural Leadership
MALA — Master of Arts in Liberal Arts
MALD — Master of Arts in Law and Diplomacy
MALER — Master of Arts in Labor and Employment Relations
MALL — Master of Arts in Language Learning
MALP — Master of Arts in Language Pedagogy
MALS — Master of Arts in Liberal Studies
MAM — Master of Acquisition Management
Master of Agriculture and Management
Master of Applied Mathematics
Master of Arts in Management
Master of Arts in Ministry
Master of Arts Management
Master of Avian Medicine
MAMB — Master of Applied Molecular Biology
MAMC — Master of Arts in Mass Communication
Master of Arts in Ministry and Culture
Master of Arts in Ministry for a Multicultural Church
Master of Arts in Missional Christianity
MAME — Master of Arts in Missions/Evangelism

MAMFC	Master of Arts in Marriage and Family Counseling
MAMFT	Master of Arts in Marriage and Family Therapy
MAMHC	Master of Arts in Mental Health Counseling
MAMS	Master of Applied Mathematical Sciences
	Master of Applied Meditation Studies
	Master of Arts in Ministerial Studies
	Master of Arts in Ministry and Spirituality
MAMT	Master of Arts in Mathematics Teaching
MAN	Master of Applied Nutrition
MANT	Master of Arts in New Testament
MAOL	Master of Arts in Organizational Leadership
MAOM	Master of Acupuncture and Oriental Medicine
MAOT	Master of Arts in Old Testament
MAP	Master of Applied Politics
	Master of Applied Psychology
	Master of Arts in Planning
	Master of Psychology
	Master of Public Administration
MAP Min	Master of Arts in Pastoral Ministry
MAPA	Master of Arts in Public Administration
MAPC	Master of Arts in Pastoral Counseling
MAPE	Master of Arts in Physics Education
	Master of Arts in Political Economy
MAPM	Master of Arts in Pastoral Ministry
	Master of Arts in Pastoral Music
	Master of Arts in Practical Ministry
MAPP	Master of Arts in Public Policy
MAPS	Master of Arts in Pastoral Studies
	Master of Arts in Public Service
MAPT	Master of Practical Theology
MAPW	Master of Arts in Professional Writing
MAR	Master of Arts in Reading
	Master of Arts in Religion
Mar Eng	Marine Engineer
MARC	Master of Arts in Rehabilitation Counseling
MARE	Master of Arts in Religious Education
MARL	Master of Arts in Religious Leadership
MARS	Master of Arts in Religious Studies
MAS	Master of Accounting Science
	Master of Actuarial Science
	Master of Administrative Science
	Master of Advanced Study
	Master of Aeronautical Science
	Master of American Studies
	Master of Animal Science
	Master of Applied Science
	Master of Applied Statistics
	Master of Archival Studies
MASA	Master of Advanced Studies in Architecture
MASD	Master of Arts in Spiritual Direction
MASE	Master of Arts in Special Education
MASF	Master of Arts in Spiritual Formation
MASJ	Master of Arts in Systems of Justice
MASLA	Master of Advanced Studies in Landscape Architecture
MASM	Master of Aging Services Management
	Master of Arts in Specialized Ministries
MASP	Master of Applied Social Psychology
	Master of Arts in School Psychology
MASPAA	Master of Arts in Sports and Athletic Administration
MASS	Master of Applied Social Science
	Master of Arts in Social Science
MAST	Master of Arts in Science Teaching
MAT	Master of Arts in Teaching
	Master of Arts in Theology
	Master of Athletic Training
	Master's in Administration of Telecommunications
Mat E	Materials Engineer
MATCM	Master of Acupuncture and Traditional Chinese Medicine
MATDE	Master of Arts in Theology, Development, and Evangelism
MATDR	Master of Territorial Management and Regional Development
MATE	Master of Arts for the Teaching of English
MATESL	Master of Arts in Teaching English as a Second Language
MATESOL	Master of Arts in Teaching English to Speakers of Other Languages
MATF	Master of Arts in Teaching English as a Foreign Language/Intercultural Studies
MATFL	Master of Arts in Teaching Foreign Language
MATH	Master of Arts in Therapy
MATI	Master of Administration of Information Technology
MATL	Master of Arts in Teacher Leadership
	Master of Arts in Teaching of Languages
	Master of Arts in Transformational Leadership
MATM	Master of Arts in Teaching of Mathematics
MATS	Master of Arts in Theological Studies
	Master of Arts in Transforming Spirituality
MATSL	Master of Arts in Teaching a Second Language
MAUA	Master of Arts in Urban Affairs
MAUD	Master of Arts in Urban Design
MAURP	Master of Arts in Urban and Regional Planning
MAW	Master of Arts in Worship
MAWSHP	Master of Arts in Worship
MAYM	Master of Arts in Youth Ministry
MB	Master of Bioinformatics
MBA	Master of Business Administration
MBA-AM	Master of Business Administration in Aviation Management
MBA-EP	Master of Business Administration–Experienced Professionals
MBAA	Master of Business Administration in Aviation
MBAE	Master of Biological and Agricultural Engineering
	Master of Biosystems and Agricultural Engineering
MBAH	Master of Business Administration in Health
MBAi	Master of Business Administration–International
MBAICT	Master of Business Administration in Information and Communication Technology
MBATM	Master of Business Administration in Technology Management
MBC	Master of Building Construction
MBE	Master of Bilingual Education
	Master of Bioengineering
	Master of Bioethics
	Master of Biomedical Engineering
	Master of Business Economics
	Master of Business Education
MBEE	Master in Biotechnology Enterprise and Entrepreneurship
MBET	Master of Business, Entrepreneurship and Technology
MBID	Master of Biomedical Innovation and Development
MBIOT	Master of Biotechnology
MBiotech	Master of Biotechnology
MBL	Master of Business Law
	Master of Business Leadership
MBLE	Master in Business Logistics Engineering
MBME	Master's in Biomedical Engineering
MBMSE	Master of Business Management and Software Engineering

MBOE Master of Business Operational Excellence
MBS Master of Biblical Studies
Master of Biological Science
Master of Biomedical Sciences
Master of Bioscience
Master of Building Science
Master of Business and Science
MBST Master of Biostatistics
MBT Master of Biomedical Technology
Master of Biotechnology
Master of Business Taxation
MBV Master of Business for Veterans
MC Master of Communication
Master of Counseling
Master of Cybersecurity
MC Ed Master of Continuing Education
MC Sc Master of Computer Science
MCA Master in Collegiate Athletics
Master of Commercial Aviation
Master of Criminology (Applied)
MCAM Master of Computational and Applied Mathematics
MCC Master of Computer Science
MCD Master of Communications Disorders
Master of Community Development
MCE Master in Electronic Commerce
Master of Christian Education
Master of Civil Engineering
Master of Control Engineering
MCEM Master of Construction Engineering Management
MCHE Master of Chemical Engineering
MCIS Master of Communication and Information Studies
Master of Computer and Information Science
Master of Computer Information Systems
MCIT Master of Computer and Information Technology
MCJ Master of Criminal Justice
MCL Master in Communication Leadership
Master of Canon Law
Master of Comparative Law
MCM Master of Christian Ministry
Master of Church Music
Master of City Management
Master of Communication Management
Master of Community Medicine
Master of Construction Management
Master of Contract Management
MCMin Master of Christian Ministry
MCMP Master of City and Metropolitan Planning
MCMS Master of Clinical Medical Science
MCN Master of Clinical Nutrition
MCOL Master of Arts in Community and Organizational Leadership
MCP Master of City Planning
Master of Community Planning
Master of Counseling Psychology
Master of Cytopathology Practice
Master of Science in Quality Systems and Productivity
MCPC Master of Arts in Chaplaincy and Pastoral Care
MCPD Master of Community Planning and Development
MCR Master in Clinical Research
MCRP Master of City and Regional Planning
Master of Community and Regional Planning
MCRS Master of City and Regional Studies
MCS Master of Chemical Sciences
Master of Christian Studies
Master of Clinical Science
Master of Combined Sciences
Master of Communication Studies
Master of Computer Science
Master of Consumer Science
MCSE Master of Computer Science and Engineering
MCSL Master of Catholic School Leadership
MCSM Master of Construction Science and Management
MCTM Master of Clinical Translation Management
MCTP Master of Communication Technology and Policy
MCTS Master of Clinical and Translational Science
MCVS Master of Cardiovascular Science
MD Doctor of Medicine
MDA Master of Dietetic Administration
MDB Master of Design-Build
MDE Master of Developmental Economics
Master of Distance Education
Master of the Education of the Deaf
MDH Master of Dental Hygiene
MDM Master of Design Methods
Master of Digital Media
MDP Master in Sustainable Development Practice
Master of Development Practice
MDR Master of Dispute Resolution
MDS Master of Dental Surgery
Master of Design Studies
Master of Digital Sciences
ME Master of Education
Master of Engineering
Master of Entrepreneurship
ME Sc Master of Engineering Science
ME-PD Master of Education–Professional Development
MEA Master of Educational Administration
Master of Engineering Administration
MEAE Master of Entertainment Arts and Engineering
MEAP Master of Environmental Administration and Planning
MEB Master of Energy Business
MEBD Master in Environmental Building Design
MEBT Master in Electronic Business Technologies
MEC Master of Electronic Commerce
Mech E Mechanical Engineer
MED Master of Education of the Deaf
MEDS Master of Environmental Design Studies
MEE Master in Education
Master of Electrical Engineering
Master of Energy Engineering
Master of Environmental Engineering
MEEM Master of Environmental Engineering and Management
MEENE Master of Engineering in Environmental Engineering
MEEP Master of Environmental and Energy Policy
MEERM Master of Earth and Environmental Resource Management
MEH Master in Humanistic Studies
Master of Environmental Health
Master of Environmental Horticulture
MEHS Master of Environmental Health and Safety
MEIM Master of Entertainment Industry Management
Master of Equine Industry Management
MEL Master of Educational Leadership
Master of English Literature
MELP Master of Environmental Law and Policy
MEM Master of Engineering Management
Master of Environmental Management
Master of Marketing

MEME	Master of Engineering in Manufacturing Engineering
	Master of Engineering in Mechanical Engineering
MENR	Master of Environment and Natural Resources
MENVEGR	Master of Environmental Engineering
MEP	Master of Engineering Physics
MEPC	Master of Environmental Pollution Control
MEPD	Master of Environmental Planning and Design
MER	Master of Employment Relations
MERE	Master of Entrepreneurial Real Estate
MERL	Master of Energy Regulation and Law
MES	Master of Education and Science
	Master of Engineering Science
	Master of Environment and Sustainability
	Master of Environmental Science
	Master of Environmental Studies
	Master of Environmental Systems
	Master of Special Education
MESM	Master of Environmental Science and Management
MET	Master of Educational Technology
	Master of Engineering Technology
	Master of Entertainment Technology
	Master of Environmental Toxicology
METM	Master of Engineering and Technology Management
MEVE	Master of Environmental Engineering
MF	Master of Finance
	Master of Forestry
MFA	Master of Fine Arts
MFALP	Master of Food and Agriculture Law and Policy
MFAM	Master's of Food Animal Medicine
MFAS	Master of Fisheries and Aquatic Science
MFAW	Master of Fine Arts in Writing
MFC	Master of Forest Conservation
MFCS	Master of Family and Consumer Sciences
MFE	Master of Financial Economics
	Master of Financial Engineering
	Master of Forest Engineering
MFES	Master of Fire and Emergency Services
MFG	Master of Functional Genomics
MFHD	Master of Family and Human Development
MFM	Master of Financial Management
	Master of Financial Mathematics
MFPE	Master of Food Process Engineering
MFR	Master of Forest Resources
MFRC	Master of Forest Resources and Conservation
MFRE	Master of Food and Resource Economics
MFS	Master of Food Science
	Master of Forensic Sciences
	Master of Forest Science
	Master of Forest Studies
	Master of French Studies
MFST	Master of Food Safety and Technology
MFT	Master of Family Therapy
	Master of Food Technology
MFWB	Master of Fishery and Wildlife Biology
MFWCB	Master of Fish, Wildlife and Conservation Biology
MFWS	Master of Fisheries and Wildlife Sciences
MFYCS	Master of Family, Youth and Community Sciences
MG	Master of Genetics
MGA	Master of Global Affairs
	Master of Government Administration
	Master of Governmental Administration
MGC	Master of Genetic Counseling
MGD	Master of Graphic Design
MGE	Master of Geotechnical Engineering
MGEM	Master of Global Entrepreneurship and Management
MGIS	Master of Geographic Information Science
	Master of Geographic Information Systems
MGM	Master of Global Management
MGP	Master of Gestion de Projet
MGPS	Master of Global Policy Studies
MGREM	Master of Global Real Estate Management
MGS	Master of Gerontological Studies
	Master of Global Studies
MGsc	Master of Geoscience
MH	Master of Humanities
MH Sc	Master of Health Sciences
MHA	Master of Health Administration
	Master of Healthcare Administration
	Master of Hospital Administration
	Master of Hospitality Administration
MHB	Master of Human Behavior
MHC	Master of Mental Health Counseling
MHCA	Master of Health Care Administration
MHCD	Master of Health Care Design
MHCI	Master of Human-Computer Interaction
MHCL	Master of Health Care Leadership
MHE	Master of Health Education
	Master of Human Ecology
MHE Ed	Master of Home Economics Education
MHEA	Master of Higher Education Administration
MHHS	Master of Health and Human Services
MHI	Master of Health Informatics
	Master of Healthcare Innovation
MHIHIM	Master of Health Informatics and Health Information Management
MHIIM	Master of Health Informatics and Information Management
MHIS	Master of Health Information Systems
MHK	Master of Human Kinetics
MHM	Master of Healthcare Management
MHMS	Master of Health Management Systems
MHP	Master of Health Physics
	Master of Heritage Preservation
	Master of Historic Preservation
MHPA	Master of Heath Policy and Administration
MHPE	Master of Health Professions Education
MHR	Master of Human Resources
MHRD	Master in Human Resource Development
MHRIR	Master of Human Resources and Industrial Relations
MHRLR	Master of Human Resources and Labor Relations
MHRM	Master of Human Resources Management
MHS	Master of Health Science
	Master of Health Sciences
	Master of Health Studies
	Master of Hispanic Studies
	Master of Human Services
	Master of Humanistic Studies
MHSA	Master of Health Services Administration
MHSE	Master of Health Science Education
MHSM	Master of Health Systems Management
MI	Master of Information
	Master of Instruction
MI Arch	Master of Interior Architecture
MIA	Master of Interior Architecture
	Master of International Affairs
MIAA	Master of International Affairs and Administration
MIAM	Master of International Agribusiness Management

MIAPD	Master of Interior Architecture and Product Design
MIB	Master of International Business
MIBA	Master of International Business Administration
MICM	Master of International Construction Management
MID	Master of Industrial Design
	Master of Industrial Distribution
	Master of Interior Design
	Master of International Development
MIDA	Master of International Development Administration
MIDC	Master of Integrated Design and Construction
MIDP	Master of International Development Policy
MIE	Master of Industrial Engineering
MIHTM	Master of International Hospitality and Tourism Management
MIJ	Master of International Journalism
MILR	Master of Industrial and Labor Relations
MIM	Master in Ministry
	Master of Information Management
	Master of International Management
MIMLAE	Master of International Management for Latin American Executives
MIMS	Master of Information Management and Systems
	Master of Integrated Manufacturing Systems
MIP	Master of Infrastructure Planning
	Master of Intellectual Property
	Master of International Policy
MIPA	Master of International Public Affairs
MIPD	Master of Integrated Product Design
MIPM	Master of International Policy Management
MIPP	Master of International Policy and Practice
	Master of International Public Policy
MIPS	Master of International Planning Studies
MIR	Master of Industrial Relations
	Master of International Relations
MIRHR	Master of Industrial Relations and Human Resources
MIS	Master of Imaging Science
	Master of Industrial Statistics
	Master of Information Science
	Master of Information Systems
	Master of Integrated Science
	Master of Interdisciplinary Studies
	Master of International Service
	Master of International Studies
MISE	Master of Industrial and Systems Engineering
MISKM	Master of Information Sciences and Knowledge Management
MISM	Master of Information Systems Management
MISW	Master of Indigenous Social Work
MIT	Master in Teaching
	Master of Industrial Technology
	Master of Information Technology
	Master of Initial Teaching
	Master of International Trade
	Master of Internet Technology
MITA	Master of Information Technology Administration
MITM	Master of Information Technology and Management
MJ	Master of Journalism
	Master of Jurisprudence
MJ Ed	Master of Jewish Education
MJA	Master of Justice Administration
MJM	Master of Justice Management
MJS	Master of Judicial Studies
	Master of Juridical Studies
MK	Master of Kinesiology
MKM	Master of Knowledge Management
ML	Master of Latin
ML Arch	Master of Landscape Architecture
MLA	Master of Landscape Architecture
	Master of Liberal Arts
MLAS	Master of Laboratory Animal Science
	Master of Liberal Arts and Sciences
MLAUD	Master of Landscape Architecture in Urban Development
MLD	Master of Leadership Development
	Master of Leadership Studies
MLE	Master of Applied Linguistics and Exegesis
MLER	Master of Labor and Employment Relations
MLI Sc	Master of Library and Information Science
MLIS	Master of Library and Information Science
	Master of Library and Information Studies
MLM	Master of Leadership in Ministry
MLPD	Master of Land and Property Development
MLRHR	Master of Labor Relations and Human Resources
MLS	Master of Leadership Studies
	Master of Legal Studies
	Master of Liberal Studies
	Master of Library Science
	Master of Life Sciences
MLSCM	Master of Logistics and Supply Chain Management
MLSP	Master of Law and Social Policy
MLT	Master of Language Technologies
MLTCA	Master of Long Term Care Administration
MLW	Master of Studies in Law
MLWS	Master of Land and Water Systems
MM	Master of Management
	Master of Ministry
	Master of Missiology
	Master of Music
MM Ed	Master of Music Education
MM Sc	Master of Medical Science
MM St	Master of Museum Studies
MMA	Master of Marine Affairs
	Master of Media Arts
	Master of Ministry Administration
	Master of Musical Arts
MMAL	Master of Maritime Administration and Logistics
MMAS	Master of Military Art and Science
MMB	Master of Microbial Biotechnology
MMC	Master of Manufacturing Competitiveness
	Master of Mass Communications
	Master of Music Conducting
MMCM	Master of Music in Church Music
MMCSS	Master of Mathematical Computational and Statistical Sciences
MME	Master of Manufacturing Engineering
	Master of Mathematics Education
	Master of Mathematics for Educators
	Master of Mechanical Engineering
	Master of Mining Engineering
	Master of Music Education
MMF	Master of Mathematical Finance
MMFT	Master of Marriage and Family Therapy
MMH	Master of Management in Hospitality
	Master of Medical Humanities
MMI	Master of Management of Innovation
MMIS	Master of Management Information Systems
MML	Master of Managerial Logistics
MMM	Master of Manufacturing Management

	Master of Marine Management
	Master of Medical Management
MMP	Master of Management Practice
	Master of Marine Policy
	Master of Medical Physics
	Master of Music Performance
MMPA	Master of Management and Professional Accounting
MMQM	Master of Manufacturing Quality Management
MMR	Master of Marketing Research
MMRM	Master of Marine Resources Management
MMS	Master of Management Science
	Master of Management Studies
	Master of Manufacturing Systems
	Master of Marine Studies
	Master of Materials Science
	Master of Mathematical Sciences
	Master of Medical Science
	Master of Medieval Studies
MMSE	Master of Manufacturing Systems Engineering
MMSM	Master of Music in Sacred Music
MMT	Master in Marketing
	Master of Music Teaching
	Master of Music Therapy
	Master's in Marketing Technology
MMus	Master of Music
MN	Master of Nursing
	Master of Nutrition
MN NP	Master of Nursing in Nurse Practitioner
MNA	Master of Nonprofit Administration
	Master of Nurse Anesthesia
MNAL	Master of Nonprofit Administration and Leadership
MNAS	Master of Natural and Applied Science
MNCM	Master of Network and Communications Management
MNE	Master of Nuclear Engineering
MNL	Master in International Business for Latin America
MNM	Master of Nonprofit Management
MNO	Master of Nonprofit Organization
MNPL	Master of Not-for-Profit Leadership
MNpS	Master of Nonprofit Studies
MNR	Master of Natural Resources
MNRD	Master of Natural Resources Development
MNRES	Master of Natural Resources and Environmental Studies
MNRM	Master of Natural Resource Management
MNRMG	Master of Natural Resource Management and Geography
MNRS	Master of Natural Resource Stewardship
MNS	Master of Natural Science
MO	Master of Oceanography
MOD	Master of Organizational Development
MOGS	Master of Oil and Gas Studies
MOL	Master of Organizational Leadership
MOM	Master of Organizational Management
	Master of Oriental Medicine
MOR	Master of Operations Research
MOT	Master of Occupational Therapy
MP	Master of Physiology
	Master of Planning
MP Ac	Master of Professional Accountancy
MP Acc	Master of Professional Accountancy
	Master of Professional Accounting
	Master of Public Accounting
MP Aff	Master of Public Affairs
MP Th	Master of Pastoral Theology
MPA	Master of Performing Arts
	Master of Physician Assistant
	Master of Professional Accountancy
	Master of Professional Accounting
	Master of Public Administration
	Master of Public Affairs
MPAC	Master of Professional Accounting
MPAID	Master of Public Administration and International Development
MPAP	Master of Physician Assistant Practice
	Master of Public Administration and Policy
	Master of Public Affairs and Politics
MPAS	Master of Physician Assistant Science
	Master of Physician Assistant Studies
MPC	Master of Professional Communication
	Master of Professional Counseling
MPD	Master of Product Development
	Master of Public Diplomacy
MPDS	Master of Planning and Development Studies
MPE	Master of Physical Education
MPEM	Master of Project Engineering and Management
MPH	Master of Public Health
MPHE	Master of Public Health Education
MPHM	Master in Plant Health Management
MPHS	Master of Population Health Sciences
MPHTM	Master of Public Health and Tropical Medicine
MPI	Master of Product Innovation
MPIA	Master of Public and International Affairs
MPM	Master of Pastoral Ministry
	Master of Pest Management
	Master of Policy Management
	Master of Practical Ministries
	Master of Project Management
	Master of Public Management
MPNA	Master of Public and Nonprofit Administration
MPNL	Master of Philanthropy and Nonprofit Leadership
MPO	Master of Prosthetics and Orthotics
MPOD	Master of Positive Organizational Development
MPP	Master of Public Policy
MPPA	Master of Public Policy Administration
	Master of Public Policy and Administration
MPPAL	Master of Public Policy, Administration and Law
MPPM	Master of Public and Private Management
	Master of Public Policy and Management
MPPPM	Master of Plant Protection and Pest Management
MPRTM	Master of Parks, Recreation, and Tourism Management
MPS	Master of Pastoral Studies
	Master of Perfusion Science
	Master of Planning Studies
	Master of Political Science
	Master of Preservation Studies
	Master of Prevention Science
	Master of Professional Studies
	Master of Public Service
MPSA	Master of Public Service Administration
MPSG	Master of Population and Social Gerontology
MPSIA	Master of Political Science and International Affairs
MPSL	Master of Public Safety Leadership
MPSRE	Master of Professional Studies in Real Estate
MPT	Master of Pastoral Theology
	Master of Physical Therapy
	Master of Practical Theology
MPVM	Master of Preventive Veterinary Medicine
MPW	Master of Professional Writing
	Master of Public Works

MQM	Master of Quality Management
MQS	Master of Quality Systems
MR	Master of Recreation
	Master of Retailing
MRA	Master in Research Administration
MRC	Master of Rehabilitation Counseling
MRCP	Master of Regional and City Planning
	Master of Regional and Community Planning
MRD	Master of Rural Development
MRE	Master of Real Estate
	Master of Religious Education
MRED	Master of Real Estate Development
MREM	Master of Resource and Environmental Management
MRLS	Master of Resources Law Studies
MRM	Master of Resources Management
MRP	Master of Regional Planning
MRRD	Master in Recreation Resource Development
MRS	Master of Religious Studies
MRSc	Master of Rehabilitation Science
MRTP	Master of Rural and Town Planning
MS	Master of Science
MS Cmp E	Master of Science in Computer Engineering
MS Kin	Master of Science in Kinesiology
MS Acct	Master of Science in Accounting
MS Accy	Master of Science in Accountancy
MS Aero E	Master of Science in Aerospace Engineering
MS Ag	Master of Science in Agriculture
MS Arch	Master of Science in Architecture
MS Arch St	Master of Science in Architectural Studies
MS Bio E	Master of Science in Bioengineering
MS Bm E	Master of Science in Biomedical Engineering
MS Ch E	Master of Science in Chemical Engineering
MS Cp E	Master of Science in Computer Engineering
MS Eco	Master of Science in Economics
MS Econ	Master of Science in Economics
MS Ed	Master of Science in Education
MS El	Master of Science in Educational Leadership and Administration
MS En E	Master of Science in Environmental Engineering
MS Eng	Master of Science in Engineering
MS Engr	Master of Science in Engineering
MS Env E	Master of Science in Environmental Engineering
MS Exp Surg	Master of Science in Experimental Surgery
MS Mat E	Master of Science in Materials Engineering
MS Mat SE	Master of Science in Material Science and Engineering
MS Met E	Master of Science in Metallurgical Engineering
MS Mgt	Master of Science in Management
MS Min	Master of Science in Mining
MS Min E	Master of Science in Mining Engineering
MS Mt E	Master of Science in Materials Engineering
MS Otol	Master of Science in Otolaryngology
MS Pet E	Master of Science in Petroleum Engineering
MS Sc	Master of Social Science
MS Sp Ed	Master of Science in Special Education
MS Stat	Master of Science in Statistics
MS Surg	Master of Science in Surgery
MS Tax	Master of Science in Taxation
MS Tc E	Master of Science in Telecommunications Engineering
MS-R	Master of Science (Research)
MSA	Master of School Administration
	Master of Science in Accountancy
	Master of Science in Accounting
	Master of Science in Administration
	Master of Science in Aeronautics
	Master of Science in Agriculture
	Master of Science in Analytics
	Master of Science in Anesthesia
	Master of Science in Architecture
	Master of Science in Aviation
	Master of Sports Administration
	Master of Surgical Assisting
MSAA	Master of Science in Astronautics and Aeronautics
MSAAE	Master of Science in Aeronautical and Astronautical Engineering
MSABE	Master of Science in Agricultural and Biological Engineering
MSAC	Master of Science in Acupuncture
MSACC	Master of Science in Accounting
MSACS	Master of Science in Applied Computer Science
MSAE	Master of Science in Aeronautical Engineering
	Master of Science in Aerospace Engineering
	Master of Science in Applied Economics
	Master of Science in Applied Engineering
	Master of Science in Architectural Engineering
MSAEM	Master of Science in Aerospace Engineering and Mechanics
MSAF	Master of Science in Aviation Finance
MSAG	Master of Science in Applied Geosciences
MSAH	Master of Science in Allied Health
MSAL	Master of Sport Administration and Leadership
MSAM	Master of Science in Applied Mathematics
MSANR	Master of Science in Agriculture and Natural Resources
MSAPM	Master of Security Analysis and Portfolio Management
MSAS	Master of Science in Applied Statistics
	Master of Science in Architectural Studies
MSAT	Master of Science in Accounting and Taxation
	Master of Science in Advanced Technology
	Master of Science in Athletic Training
MSB	Master of Science in Biotechnology
	Master of Sustainable Business
MSBA	Master of Science in Business Administration
	Master of Science in Business Analysis
MSBAE	Master of Science in Biological and Agricultural Engineering
	Master of Science in Biosystems and Agricultural Engineering
MSBC	Master of Science in Building Construction
	Master of Science in Business Communication
MSBCB	Master's in Bioinformatics and Computational Biology
MSBE	Master of Science in Biological Engineering
	Master of Science in Biomedical Engineering
MSBENG	Master of Science in Bioengineering
MSBH	Master of Science in Behavioral Health
MSBIT	Master of Science in Business Information Technology
MSBM	Master of Sport Business Management
MSBME	Master of Science in Biomedical Engineering
MSBMS	Master of Science in Basic Medical Science
MSBS	Master of Science in Biomedical Sciences
MSBTM	Master of Science in Biotechnology and Management
MSC	Master of Science in Commerce
	Master of Science in Communication
	Master of Science in Computers
	Master of Science in Counseling
	Master of Science in Criminology
	Master of Strategic Communication
MSCC	Master of Science in Community Counseling
MSCD	Master of Science in Communication Disorders
	Master of Science in Community Development

MSCE	Master of Science in Civil Engineering
	Master of Science in Clinical Epidemiology
	Master of Science in Computer Engineering
	Master of Science in Continuing Education
MSCEE	Master of Science in Civil and Environmental Engineering
MSCF	Master of Science in Computational Finance
MSCH	Master of Science in Chemical Engineering
MSChE	Master of Science in Chemical Engineering
MSCI	Master of Science in Clinical Investigation
MSCIS	Master of Science in Computer and Information Science
	Master of Science in Computer and Information Systems
	Master of Science in Computer Information Science
	Master of Science in Computer Information Systems
MSCIT	Master of Science in Computer Information Technology
MSCJ	Master of Science in Criminal Justice
MSCJA	Master of Science in Criminal Justice Administration
MSCJS	Master of Science in Crime and Justice Studies
MSCLS	Master of Science in Clinical Laboratory Studies
MSCM	Master of Science in Church Management
	Master of Science in Conflict Management
	Master of Science in Construction Management
	Master of Supply Chain Management
MSCNU	Master of Science in Clinical Nutrition
MSCP	Master of Science in Clinical Psychology
	Master of Science in Community Psychology
	Master of Science in Computer Engineering
	Master of Science in Counseling Psychology
MSCPE	Master of Science in Computer Engineering
MSCPharm	Master of Science in Pharmacy
MSCR	Master of Science in Clinical Research
MSCRP	Master of Science in City and Regional Planning
	Master of Science in Community and Regional Planning
MSCS	Master of Science in Clinical Science
	Master of Science in Computer Science
	Master of Science in Cyber Security
MSCSD	Master of Science in Communication Sciences and Disorders
MSCSE	Master of Science in Computer Science and Engineering
MSCTE	Master of Science in Career and Technical Education
MSD	Master of Science in Dentistry
	Master of Science in Design
	Master of Science in Dietetics
MSE	Master of Science Education
	Master of Science in Economics
	Master of Science in Education
	Master of Science in Engineering
	Master of Science in Engineering Management
	Master of Software Engineering
	Master of Special Education
	Master of Structural Engineering
MSECE	Master of Science in Electrical and Computer Engineering
MSED	Master of Sustainable Economic Development
MSEE	Master of Science in Electrical Engineering
	Master of Science in Environmental Engineering
MSEH	Master of Science in Environmental Health
MSEL	Master of Science in Educational Leadership
MSEM	Master of Science in Engineering Management
	Master of Science in Engineering Mechanics
	Master of Science in Environmental Management
MSENE	Master of Science in Environmental Engineering
MSEO	Master of Science in Electro-Optics
MSEP	Master of Science in Economic Policy
MSES	Master of Science in Embedded Software Engineering
	Master of Science in Engineering Science
	Master of Science in Environmental Science
	Master of Science in Environmental Studies
	Master of Science in Exercise Science
MSET	Master of Science in Educational Technology
	Master of Science in Engineering Technology
MSEV	Master of Science in Environmental Engineering
MSF	Master of Science in Finance
	Master of Science in Forestry
	Master of Spiritual Formation
MSFA	Master of Science in Financial Analysis
MSFCS	Master of Science in Family and Consumer Science
MSFE	Master of Science in Financial Engineering
MSFM	Master of Sustainable Forest Management
MSFOR	Master of Science in Forestry
MSFP	Master of Science in Financial Planning
MSFS	Master of Science in Financial Sciences
	Master of Science in Forensic Science
MSFSB	Master of Science in Financial Services and Banking
MSFT	Master of Science in Family Therapy
MSGC	Master of Science in Genetic Counseling
MSH	Master of Science in Health
	Master of Science in Hospice
MSHA	Master of Science in Health Administration
MSHCA	Master of Science in Health Care Administration
MSHCI	Master of Science in Human Computer Interaction
MSHCPM	Master of Science in Health Care Policy and Management
MSHE	Master of Science in Health Education
MSHES	Master of Science in Human Environmental Sciences
MSHFID	Master of Science in Human Factors in Information Design
MSHFS	Master of Science in Human Factors and Systems
MSHI	Master of Science in Health Informatics
MSHP	Master of Science in Health Professions
	Master of Science in Health Promotion
MSHR	Master of Science in Human Resources
MSHRL	Master of Science in Human Resource Leadership
MSHRM	Master of Science in Human Resource Management
MSHROD	Master of Science in Human Resources and Organizational Development
MSHS	Master of Science in Health Science
	Master of Science in Health Services
	Master of Science in Homeland Security
MSI	Master of Science in Information
	Master of Science in Instruction
	Master of System Integration
MSIA	Master of Science in Industrial Administration
	Master of Science in Information Assurance
MSIB	Master of Science in International Business
MSIDM	Master of Science in Interior Design and Merchandising
MSIE	Master of Science in Industrial Engineering
	Master of Science in International Economics

MSIEM Master of Science in Information Engineering and Management
MSIID Master of Science in Information and Instructional Design
MSIM Master of Science in Information Management
Master of Science in International Management
MSIMC Master of Science in Integrated Marketing Communications
MSIR Master of Science in Industrial Relations
MSIS Master of Science in Information Science
Master of Science in Information Studies
Master of Science in Information Systems
Master of Science in Interdisciplinary Studies
MSISE Master of Science in Infrastructure Systems Engineering
MSISM Master of Science in Information Systems Management
MSISPM Master of Science in Information Security Policy and Management
MSIST Master of Science in Information Systems Technology
MSIT Master of Science in Industrial Technology
Master of Science in Information Technology
Master of Science in Instructional Technology
MSITM Master of Science in Information Technology Management
MSJ Master of Science in Journalism
Master of Science in Jurisprudence
MSJC Master of Social Justice and Criminology
MSJE Master of Science in Jewish Education
MSJFP Master of Science in Juvenile Forensic Psychology
MSJJ Master of Science in Juvenile Justice
MSJPS Master of Science in Justice and Public Safety
MSJS Master of Science in Jewish Studies
MSL Master of School Leadership
Master of Science in Leadership
Master of Science in Limnology
Master of Strategic Leadership
Master of Studies in Law
MSLA Master of Science in Legal Administration
MSLFS Master of Science in Life Sciences
MSLP Master of Speech-Language Pathology
MSLS Master of Science in Library Science
MSLSCM Master of Science in Logistics and Supply Chain Management
MSLT Master of Second Language Teaching
MSM Master of Sacred Ministry
Master of Sacred Music
Master of School Mathematics
Master of Science in Management
Master of Science in Medicine
Master of Science in Organization Management
Master of Security Management
MSMA Master of Science in Marketing Analysis
MSMAE Master of Science in Materials Engineering
MSMC Master of Science in Mass Communications
MSME Master of Science in Mathematics Education
Master of Science in Mechanical Engineering
MSMFT Master of Science in Marriage and Family Therapy
MSMHC Master of Science in Mental Health Counseling
MSMIS Master of Science in Management Information Systems
MSMIT Master of Science in Management and Information Technology
MSMLS Master of Science in Medical Laboratory Science
MSMOT Master of Science in Management of Technology
MSMP Master of Science in Medical Physics
MSMS Master of Science in Management Science
Master of Science in Marine Science
Master of Science in Medical Sciences
MSMSE Master of Science in Manufacturing Systems Engineering
Master of Science in Material Science and Engineering
Master of Science in Mathematics and Science Education
MSMT Master of Science in Management and Technology
MSMus Master of Sacred Music
MSN Master of Science in Nursing
MSNA Master of Science in Nurse Anesthesia
MSNE Master of Science in Nuclear Engineering
MSNED Master of Science in Nurse Education
MSNM Master of Science in Nonprofit Management
MSNS Master of Science in Natural Science
Master of Science in Nutritional Science
MSOD Master of Science in Organization Development
Master of Science in Organizational Development
MSOEE Master of Science in Outdoor and Environmental Education
MSOES Master of Science in Occupational Ergonomics and Safety
MSOH Master of Science in Occupational Health
MSOL Master of Science in Organizational Leadership
MSOM Master of Science in Operations Management
Master of Science in Oriental Medicine
MSOR Master of Science in Operations Research
MSOT Master of Science in Occupational Technology
Master of Science in Occupational Therapy
MSP Master of Science in Pharmacy
Master of Science in Planning
Master of Speech Pathology
MSPA Master of Science in Physician Assistant
Master of Science in Professional Accountancy
MSPAS Master of Science in Physician Assistant Studies
MSPC Master of Science in Professional Communications
MSPE Master of Science in Petroleum Engineering
MSPH Master of Science in Public Health
MSPHR Master of Science in Pharmacy
MSPM Master of Science in Professional Management
Master of Science in Project Management
MSPNGE Master of Science in Petroleum and Natural Gas Engineering
MSPO Master of Science in Prosthetics and Orthotics
MSPPM Master of Science in Public Policy and Management
MSPS Master of Science in Pharmaceutical Science
Master of Science in Political Science
Master of Science in Psychological Services
MSPT Master of Science in Physical Therapy
MSpVM Master of Specialized Veterinary Medicine
MSR Master of Science in Radiology
Master of Science in Reading
MSRA Master of Science in Recreation Administration
MSRE Master of Science in Real Estate
Master of Science in Religious Education
MSRED Master of Science in Real Estate Development
Master of Sustainable Real Estate Development
MSRLS Master of Science in Recreation and Leisure Studies
MSRM Master of Science in Risk Management
MSRMP Master of Science in Radiological Medical Physics
MSRS Master of Science in Radiological Sciences
Master of Science in Rehabilitation Science

MSS	Master of Security Studies
	Master of Social Science
	Master of Social Services
	Master of Software Systems
	Master of Sports Science
	Master of Strategic Studies
	Master's in Statistical Science
MSSA	Master of Science in Social Administration
MSSCM	Master of Science in Supply Chain Management
MSSD	Master of Arts in Software Driven Systems Design
	Master of Science in Sustainable Design
MSSE	Master of Science in Software Engineering
	Master of Science in Special Education
MSSEM	Master of Science in Systems and Engineering Management
MSSI	Master of Science in Security Informatics
	Master of Science in Strategic Intelligence
MSSL	Master of Science in School Leadership
	Master of Science in Strategic Leadership
MSSLP	Master of Science in Speech-Language Pathology
MSSM	Master of Science in Sports Medicine
MSSP	Master of Science in Social Policy
MSSPA	Master of Science in Student Personnel Administration
MSSS	Master of Science in Safety Science
	Master of Science in Systems Science
MSST	Master of Science in Security Technologies
MSSW	Master of Science in Social Work
MSSWE	Master of Science in Software Engineering
MST	Master of Science and Technology
	Master of Science in Taxation
	Master of Science in Teaching
	Master of Science in Technology
	Master of Science in Telecommunications
	Master of Science Teaching
MSTC	Master of Science in Technical Communication
	Master of Science in Telecommunications
MSTCM	Master of Science in Traditional Chinese Medicine
MSTE	Master of Science in Telecommunications Engineering
	Master of Science in Transportation Engineering
MSTL	Master of Science in Teacher Leadership
MSTM	Master of Science in Technology Management
	Master of Science in Transfusion Medicine
MSTOM	Master of Science in Traditional Oriental Medicine
MSUASE	Master of Science in Unmanned and Autonomous Systems Engineering
MSUD	Master of Science in Urban Design
MSUS	Master of Science in Urban Studies
MSW	Master of Social Work
MSWE	Master of Software Engineering
MSWREE	Master of Science in Water Resources and Environmental Engineering
MT	Master of Taxation
	Master of Teaching
	Master of Technology
	Master of Textiles
MTA	Master of Tax Accounting
	Master of Teaching Arts
	Master of Tourism Administration
MTCM	Master of Traditional Chinese Medicine
MTD	Master of Training and Development
MTE	Master in Educational Technology
MTESOL	Master in Teaching English to Speakers of Other Languages

MTHM	Master of Tourism and Hospitality Management
MTI	Master of Information Technology
MTID	Master of Tangible Interaction Design
MTL	Master of Talmudic Law
MTM	Master of Technology Management
	Master of Telecommunications Management
	Master of the Teaching of Mathematics
MTMH	Master of Tropical Medicine and Hygiene
MTMS	Master in Teaching Mathematics and Science
MTOM	Master of Traditional Oriental Medicine
MTPC	Master of Technical and Professional Communication
MTR	Master of Translational Research
MTS	Master of Theatre Studies
	Master of Theological Studies
MTWM	Master of Trust and Wealth Management
MTX	Master of Taxation
MUA	Master of Urban Affairs
MUCD	Master of Urban and Community Design
MUD	Master of Urban Design
MUDS	Master of Urban Design Studies
MUEP	Master of Urban and Environmental Planning
MUP	Master of Urban Planning
MUPDD	Master of Urban Planning, Design, and Development
MUPP	Master of Urban Planning and Policy
MUPRED	Master of Urban Planning and Real Estate Development
MURP	Master of Urban and Regional Planning
	Master of Urban and Rural Planning
MUS	Master of Urban Studies
MUSA	Master of Urban Spatial Analytics
MVP	Master of Voice Pedagogy
MVPH	Master of Veterinary Public Health
MVS	Master of Visual Studies
MWC	Master of Wildlife Conservation
MWM	Master of Water Management
MWPS	Master of Wood and Paper Science
MWR	Master of Water Resources
MWS	Master of Women's Studies
	Master of Worship Studies
MWSc	Master of Wildlife Science
MZS	Master of Zoological Science
Nav Arch	Naval Architecture
Naval E	Naval Engineer
ND	Doctor of Naturopathic Medicine
NE	Nuclear Engineer
Nuc E	Nuclear Engineer
OD	Doctor of Optometry
OTD	Doctor of Occupational Therapy
PBME	Professional Master of Biomedical Engineering
PC	Performer's Certificate
PD	Professional Diploma
PGC	Post-Graduate Certificate
PGD	Postgraduate Diploma
Ph L	Licentiate of Philosophy
Pharm D	Doctor of Pharmacy
PhD	Doctor of Philosophy
PhD Otol	Doctor of Philosophy in Otolaryngology
PhD Surg	Doctor of Philosophy in Surgery
PhDEE	Doctor of Philosophy in Electrical Engineering
PMBA	Professional Master of Business Administration
PMC	Post Master Certificate
PMD	Post-Master's Diploma
PMS	Professional Master of Science
	Professional Master's
Post-Doctoral MS	Post-Doctoral Master of Science
Post-MSN Certificate	Post-Master of Science in Nursing Certificate
PPDPT	Postprofessional Doctor of Physical Therapy

Pro-MS	Professional Science Master's
Professional MA	Professional Master of Arts
Professional MBA	Professional Master of Business Administration
Professional MS	Professional Master of Science
PSM	Professional Master of Science Professional Science Master's
Psy D	Doctor of Psychology
Psy M	Master of Psychology
Psy S	Specialist in Psychology
Psya D	Doctor of Psychoanalysis
S Psy S	Specialist in Psychological Services
Sc D	Doctor of Science
Sc M	Master of Science
SCCT	Specialist in Community College Teaching
ScDPT	Doctor of Physical Therapy Science
SD	Doctor of Science Specialist Degree
SJD	Doctor of Juridical Sciences
SLPD	Doctor of Speech-Language Pathology
SM	Master of Science
SM Arch S	Master of Science in Architectural Studies
SMACT	Master of Science in Art, Culture and Technology
SMBT	Master of Science in Building Technology
SP	Specialist Degree
Sp Ed	Specialist in Education
Sp LIS	Specialist in Library and Information Science
SPA	Specialist in Arts
Spec	Specialist's Certificate
Spec M	Specialist in Music
Spt	Specialist Degree
SSP	Specialist in School Psychology
STB	Bachelor of Sacred Theology
STD	Doctor of Sacred Theology
STL	Licentiate of Sacred Theology
STM	Master of Sacred Theology
TDPT	Transitional Doctor of Physical Therapy
Th D	Doctor of Theology
Th M	Master of Theology
TOTD	Transitional Doctor of Occupational Therapy
VMD	Doctor of Veterinary Medicine
WEMBA	Weekend Executive Master of Business Administration
XMA	Executive Master of Arts

INDEXES

Displays and Close-Ups

Directories and Subject Areas in This Book

Directories and Subject Areas

Following is an alphabetical listing of directories and subject areas. Also listed are cross-references for subject area names not used in the directory structure of the guides, for example, "City and Regional Planning (*see* Urban and Regional Planning).'

Graduate Programs in the Humanities, Arts & Social Sciences

Addictions/Substance Abuse Counseling
Administration (*see* Arts Administration; Public Administration)
African-American Studies
African Languages and Literatures (*see* African Studies)
African Studies
Agribusiness (*see* Agricultural Economics and Agribusiness)
Agricultural Economics and Agribusiness
Alcohol Abuse Counseling (*see* Addictions/Substance Abuse Counseling)
American Indian/Native American Studies
American Studies
Anthropology
Applied Arts and Design—General
Applied Behavior Analysis
Applied Economics
Applied History (*see* Public History)
Applied Psychology
Applied Social Research
Arabic (*see* Near and Middle Eastern Languages)
Arab Studies (*see* Near and Middle Eastern Studies)
Archaeology
Architectural History
Architecture
Archives Administration (*see* Public History)
Area and Cultural Studies (*see* African-American Studies; African Studies; American Indian/Native American Studies; American Studies; Asian-American Studies; Asian Studies; Canadian Studies; Cultural Studies; East European and Russian Studies; Ethnic Studies; Folklore; Gender Studies; Hispanic Studies; Holocaust Studies; Jewish Studies; Latin American Studies; Near and Middle Eastern Studies; Northern Studies; Pacific Area/Pacific Rim Studies; Western European Studies; Women's Studies)
Art/Fine Arts
Art History
Arts Administration
Arts Journalism
Art Therapy
Asian-American Studies
Asian Languages
Asian Studies
Behavioral Sciences (*see* Psychology)
Bible Studies (*see* Religion; Theology)
Biological Anthropology
Black Studies (*see* African-American Studies)
Broadcasting (*see* Communication; Film, Television, and Video Production)
Broadcast Journalism
Building Science
Canadian Studies
Celtic Languages
Ceramics (*see* Art/Fine Arts)
Child and Family Studies
Child Development
Chinese
Chinese Studies (*see* Asian Languages; Asian Studies)
Christian Studies (*see* Missions and Missiology; Religion; Theology)
Cinema (*see* Film, Television, and Video Production)
City and Regional Planning (*see* Urban and Regional Planning)
Classical Languages and Literatures (*see* Classics)
Classics
Clinical Psychology
Clothing and Textiles
Cognitive Psychology (*see* Psychology—General; Cognitive Sciences)
Cognitive Sciences
Communication—General
Community Affairs (*see* Urban and Regional Planning; Urban Studies)
Community Planning (*see* Architecture; Environmental Design; Urban and Regional Planning; Urban Design; Urban Studies)
Community Psychology (*see* Social Psychology)
Comparative and Interdisciplinary Arts
Comparative Literature
Composition (*see* Music)
Computer Art and Design
Conflict Resolution and Mediation/Peace Studies
Consumer Economics
Corporate and Organizational Communication
Corrections (*see* Criminal Justice and Criminology)
Counseling (*see* Counseling Psychology; Pastoral Ministry and Counseling)
Counseling Psychology
Crafts (*see* Art/Fine Arts)
Creative Arts Therapies (*see* Art Therapy; Therapies—Dance, Drama, and Music)
Criminal Justice and Criminology
Cultural Anthropology
Cultural Studies
Dance
Decorative Arts
Demography and Population Studies
Design (*see* Applied Arts and Design; Architecture; Art/Fine Arts; Environmental Design; Graphic Design; Industrial Design; Interior Design; Textile Design; Urban Design)
Developmental Psychology
Diplomacy (*see* International Affairs)
Disability Studies
Drama Therapy (*see* Therapies—Dance, Drama, and Music)
Dramatic Arts (*see* Theater)
Drawing (*see* Art/Fine Arts)
Drug Abuse Counseling (*see* Addictions/Substance Abuse Counseling)
Drug and Alcohol Abuse Counseling (*see* Addictions/Substance Abuse Counseling)
East Asian Studies (*see* Asian Studies)
East European and Russian Studies
Economic Development
Economics
Educational Theater (*see* Theater; Therapies—Dance, Drama, and Music)
Emergency Management
English
Environmental Design
Ethics
Ethnic Studies
Ethnomusicology (*see* Music)
Experimental Psychology
Family and Consumer Sciences—General
Family Studies (*see* Child and Family Studies)
Family Therapy (*see* Child and Family Studies; Clinical Psychology; Counseling Psychology; Marriage and Family Therapy)
Filmmaking (*see* Film, Television, and Video Production)
Film Studies (*see* Film, Television, and Video Production)
Film, Television, and Video Production
Film, Television, and Video Theory and Criticism
Fine Arts (*see* Art/Fine Arts)
Folklore
Foreign Languages (*see* specific language)
Foreign Service (*see* International Affairs; International Development)
Forensic Psychology
Forensic Sciences
Forensics (*see* Speech and Interpersonal Communication)
French
Gender Studies
General Studies (*see* Liberal Studies)
Genetic Counseling
Geographic Information Systems

Geography
German
Gerontology
Graphic Design
Greek (*see* Classics)
Health Communication
Health Psychology
Hebrew (*see* Near and Middle Eastern Languages)
Hebrew Studies (*see* Jewish Studies)
Hispanic and Latin American Languages
Hispanic Studies
Historic Preservation
History
History of Art (*see* Art History)
History of Medicine
History of Science and Technology
Holocaust and Genocide Studies
Home Economics (*see* Family and Consumer Sciences—General)
Homeland Security
Household Economics, Sciences, and Management (*see* Family and Consumer Sciences—General)
Human Development
Humanities
Illustration
Industrial and Labor Relations
Industrial and Organizational Psychology
Industrial Design
Interdisciplinary Studies
Interior Design
International Affairs
International Development
International Economics
International Service (*see* International Affairs; International Development)
International Trade Policy
Internet and Interactive Multimedia
Interpersonal Communication (*see* Speech and Interpersonal Communication)
Interpretation (*see* Translation and Interpretation)
Islamic Studies (*see* Near and Middle Eastern Studies; Religion)
Italian
Japanese
Japanese Studies (*see* Asian Languages; Asian Studies; Japanese)
Jewelry (*see* Art/Fine Arts)
Jewish Studies
Journalism
Judaic Studies (*see* Jewish Studies; Religion)
Labor Relations (*see* Industrial and Labor Relations)
Landscape Architecture
Latin American Studies
Latin (*see* Classics)
Law Enforcement (*see* Criminal Justice and Criminology)
Liberal Studies
Lighting Design
Linguistics
Literature (*see* Classics; Comparative Literature; specific language)
Marriage and Family Therapy
Mass Communication
Media Studies
Medical Illustration
Medieval and Renaissance Studies
Metalsmithing (*see* Art/Fine Arts)
Middle Eastern Studies (*see* Near and Middle Eastern Studies)
Military and Defense Studies
Mineral Economics
Ministry (*see* Pastoral Ministry and Counseling; Theology)
Missions and Missiology
Motion Pictures (*see* Film, Television, and Video Production)
Museum Studies
Music
Musicology (*see* Music)
Music Therapy (*see* Therapies—Dance, Drama, and Music)
National Security
Native American Studies (*see* American Indian/Native American Studies)
Near and Middle Eastern Languages
Near and Middle Eastern Studies
Near Environment (*see* Family and Consumer Sciences)
Northern Studies
Organizational Psychology (*see* Industrial and Organizational Psychology)
Oriental Languages (*see* Asian Languages)
Oriental Studies (*see* Asian Studies)
Pacific Area/Pacific Rim Studies
Painting (*see* Art/Fine Arts)
Pastoral Ministry and Counseling
Philanthropic Studies
Philosophy
Photography
Playwriting (*see* Theater; Writing)
Policy Studies (*see* Public Policy)
Political Science
Population Studies (*see* Demography and Population Studies)
Portuguese
Printmaking (*see* Art/Fine Arts)
Product Design (*see* Industrial Design)
Psychoanalysis and Psychotherapy
Psychology—General
Public Administration
Public Affairs
Public History
Public Policy
Public Speaking (*see* Mass Communication; Rhetoric; Speech and Interpersonal Communication)
Publishing
Regional Planning (*see* Architecture; Urban and Regional Planning; Urban Design; Urban Studies)
Rehabilitation Counseling
Religion
Renaissance Studies (*see* Medieval and Renaissance Studies)
Rhetoric
Romance Languages
Romance Literatures (*see* Romance Languages)
Rural Planning and Studies
Rural Sociology
Russian
Scandinavian Languages
School Psychology
Sculpture (*see* Art/Fine Arts)
Security Administration (*see* Criminal Justice and Criminology)
Slavic Languages
Slavic Studies (*see* East European and Russian Studies; Slavic Languages)
Social Psychology
Social Sciences
Sociology
Southeast Asian Studies (*see* Asian Studies)
Soviet Studies (*see* East European and Russian Studies; Russian)
Spanish
Speech and Interpersonal Communication
Sport Psychology
Studio Art (*see* Art/Fine Arts)
Substance Abuse Counseling (*see* Addictions/Substance Abuse Counseling)
Survey Methodology
Sustainable Development
Technical Communication
Technical Writing
Telecommunications (*see* Film, Television, and Video Production)
Television (*see* Film, Television, and Video Production)
Textile Design
Textiles (*see* Clothing and Textiles; Textile Design)
Thanatology
Theater
Theater Arts (*see* Theater)
Theology
Therapies—Dance, Drama, and Music
Translation and Interpretation
Transpersonal and Humanistic Psychology
Urban and Regional Planning
Urban Design

Urban Planning (*see* Architecture; Urban and Regional Planning; Urban Design; Urban Studies)
Urban Studies
Video (*see* Film, Television, and Video Production)
Visual Arts (*see* Applied Arts and Design; Art/Fine Arts; Film, Television, and Video Production; Graphic Design; Illustration; Photography)
Western European Studies
Women's Studies
World Wide Web (*see* Internet and Interactive Multimedia)
Writing

Graduate Programs in the Biological/ Biomedical Sciences & Health-Related Medical Professions

Acupuncture and Oriental Medicine
Acute Care/Critical Care Nursing Administration (*see* Health Services Management and Hospital Administration; Nursing and Healthcare Administration; Pharmaceutical Administration)
Adult Nursing
Advanced Practice Nursing (*see* Family Nurse Practitioner Studies)
Allied Health—General
Allied Health Professions (*see* Clinical Laboratory Sciences/Medical Technology; Clinical Research; Communication Disorders; Dental Hygiene; Emergency Medical Services; Occupational Therapy; Physical Therapy; Physician Assistant Studies; Rehabilitation Sciences)
Allopathic Medicine
Anatomy
Anesthesiologist Assistant Studies
Animal Behavior
Bacteriology
Behavioral Sciences (*see* Biopsychology; Neuroscience; Zoology)
Biochemistry
Bioethics
Biological and Biomedical Sciences—General Biological Chemistry (*see* Biochemistry)
Biological Oceanography (*see* Marine Biology)
Biophysics
Biopsychology
Botany
Breeding (*see* Botany; Plant Biology; Genetics)
Cancer Biology/Oncology
Cardiovascular Sciences
Cell Biology
Cellular Physiology (*see* Cell Biology; Physiology)
Child-Care Nursing (*see* Maternal and Child/Neonatal Nursing)
Chiropractic
Clinical Laboratory Sciences/Medical Technology
Clinical Research
Community Health
Community Health Nursing
Computational Biology
Conservation (*see* Conservation Biology; Environmental Biology)
Conservation Biology
Crop Sciences (*see* Botany; Plant Biology)
Cytology (*see* Cell Biology)
Dental and Oral Surgery (*see* Oral and Dental Sciences)
Dental Assistant Studies (*see* Dental Hygiene)
Dental Hygiene
Dental Services (*see* Dental Hygiene)
Dentistry
Developmental Biology Dietetics (*see* Nutrition)
Ecology
Embryology (*see* Developmental Biology)
Emergency Medical Services
Endocrinology (*see* Physiology)
Entomology
Environmental Biology
Environmental and Occupational Health
Epidemiology
Evolutionary Biology
Family Nurse Practitioner Studies
Foods (*see* Nutrition)
Forensic Nursing
Genetics
Genomic Sciences
Gerontological Nursing
Health Physics/Radiological Health
Health Promotion
Health-Related Professions (*see* individual allied health professions)
Health Services Management and Hospital Administration
Health Services Research
Histology (*see* Anatomy; Cell Biology)
HIV/AIDS Nursing
Hospice Nursing
Hospital Administration (*see* Health Services Management and Hospital Administration)
Human Genetics
Immunology
Industrial Hygiene
Infectious Diseases
International Health
Laboratory Medicine (*see* Clinical Laboratory Sciences/Medical Technology; Immunology; Microbiology; Pathology)
Life Sciences (*see* Biological and Biomedical Sciences)
Marine Biology
Maternal and Child Health
Maternal and Child/Neonatal Nursing
Medical Imaging
Medical Microbiology
Medical Nursing (*see* Medical/Surgical Nursing)
Medical Physics
Medical/Surgical Nursing
Medical Technology (*see* Clinical Laboratory Sciences/Medical Technology)
Medical Sciences (*see* Biological and Biomedical Sciences)
Medical Science Training Programs (*see* Biological and Biomedical Sciences)
Medicinal and Pharmaceutical Chemistry
Medicinal Chemistry (*see* Medicinal and Pharmaceutical Chemistry)
Medicine (*see* Allopathic Medicine; Naturopathic Medicine; Osteopathic Medicine; Podiatric Medicine)
Microbiology
Midwifery (*see* Nurse Midwifery)
Molecular Biology
Molecular Biophysics
Molecular Genetics
Molecular Medicine
Molecular Pathogenesis
Molecular Pathology
Molecular Pharmacology
Molecular Physiology
Molecular Toxicology
Naturopathic Medicine
Neural Sciences (*see* Biopsychology; Neurobiology; Neuroscience)
Neurobiology
Neuroendocrinology (*see* Biopsychology; Neurobiology; Neuroscience; Physiology)
Neuropharmacology (*see* Biopsychology; Neurobiology; Neuroscience; Pharmacology)
Neurophysiology (*see* Biopsychology; Neurobiology; Neuroscience; Physiology)
Nouroooionoo
Nuclear Medical Technology (*see* Clinical Laboratory Sciences/ Medical Technology)
Nurse Anesthesia
Nurse Midwifery
Nurse Practitioner Studies (*see* Family Nurse Practitioner Studies)
Nursing Administration (*see* Nursing and Healthcare Administration)
Nursing and Healthcare Administration
Nursing Education
Nursing—General
Nursing Informatics
Nutrition
Occupational Health (*see* Environmental and Occupational Health; Occupational Health Nursing)

Occupational Health Nursing
Occupational Therapy
Oncology (*see* Cancer Biology/Oncology)
Oncology Nursing
Optometry
Oral and Dental Sciences
Oral Biology (*see* Oral and Dental Sciences)
Oral Pathology (*see* Oral and Dental Sciences)
Organismal Biology (*see* Biological and Biomedical Sciences; Zoology)
Oriental Medicine and Acupuncture (*see* Acupuncture and Oriental Medicine)
Orthodontics (*see* Oral and Dental Sciences)
Osteopathic Medicine
Parasitology
Pathobiology
Pathology
Pediatric Nursing
Pedontics (*see* Oral and Dental Sciences)
Perfusion
Pharmaceutical Administration
Pharmaceutical Chemistry (*see* Medicinal and Pharmaceutical Chemistry)
Pharmaceutical Sciences
Pharmacology
Pharmacy
Photobiology of Cells and Organelles (*see* Botany; Cell Biology; Plant Biology)
Physical Therapy
Physician Assistant Studies
Physiological Optics (*see* Vision Sciences)
Podiatric Medicine
Preventive Medicine (*see* Community Health and Public Health)
Physiological Optics (*see* Physiology)
Physiology
Plant Biology
Plant Molecular Biology
Plant Pathology
Plant Physiology
Pomology (*see* Botany; Plant Biology)
Psychiatric Nursing
Public Health—General
Public Health Nursing (*see* Community Health Nursing)
Psychiatric Nursing
Psychobiology (*see* Biopsychology)
Psychopharmacology (*see* Biopsychology; Neuroscience; Pharmacology)
Radiation Biology
Radiological Health (*see* Health Physics/Radiological Health)
Rehabilitation Nursing
Rehabilitation Sciences
Rehabilitation Therapy (*see* Physical Therapy)
Reproductive Biology
School Nursing
Sociobiology (*see* Evolutionary Biology)
Structural Biology
Surgical Nursing (*see* Medical/Surgical Nursing)
Systems Biology
Teratology
Therapeutics
Theoretical Biology (*see* Biological and Biomedical Sciences)
Therapeutics (*see* Pharmaceutical Sciences; Pharmacology; Pharmacy)
Toxicology
Transcultural Nursing
Translational Biology
Tropical Medicine (*see* Parasitology)
Veterinary Medicine
Veterinary Sciences
Virology
Vision Sciences
Wildlife Biology (*see* Zoology)
Women's Health Nursing
Zoology

Graduate Programs in the Physical Sciences, Mathematics, Agricultural Sciences, the Environment & Natural Resources

Acoustics
Agricultural Sciences
Agronomy and Soil Sciences
Analytical Chemistry
Animal Sciences
Applied Mathematics
Applied Physics
Applied Statistics
Aquaculture
Astronomy
Astrophysical Sciences (*see* Astrophysics; Atmospheric Sciences; Meteorology; Planetary and Space Sciences)
Astrophysics
Atmospheric Sciences
Biological Oceanography (*see* Marine Affairs; Marine Sciences; Oceanography)
Biomathematics
Biometry
Biostatistics
Chemical Physics
Chemistry
Computational Sciences
Condensed Matter Physics
Dairy Science (*see* Animal Sciences)
Earth Sciences (*see* Geosciences)
Environmental Management and Policy
Environmental Sciences
Environmental Studies (*see* Environmental Management and Policy)
Experimental Statistics (*see* Statistics)
Fish, Game, and Wildlife Management
Food Science and Technology
Forestry
General Science (*see* specific topics)
Geochemistry
Geodetic Sciences
Geological Engineering (*see* Geology)
Geological Sciences (*see* Geology)
Geology
Geophysical Fluid Dynamics (*see* Geophysics)
Geophysics
Geosciences
Horticulture
Hydrogeology
Hydrology
Inorganic Chemistry
Limnology
Marine Affairs
Marine Geology
Marine Sciences
Marine Studies (*see* Marine Affairs; Marine Geology; Marine Sciences; Oceanography)
Mathematical and Computational Finance
Mathematical Physics
Mathematical Statistics (*see* Applied Statistics; Statistics)
Mathematics
Meteorology
Mineralogy
Natural Resource Management (*see* Environmental Management and Policy; Natural Resources)
Natural Resources
Nuclear Physics (*see* Physics)
Ocean Engineering (*see* Marine Affairs; Marine Geology; Marine Sciences; Oceanography)
Oceanography
Optical Sciences
Optical Technologies (*see* Optical Sciences)
Optics (*see* Applied Physics; Optical Sciences; Physics)
Organic Chemistry

Paleontology
Paper Chemistry (*see* Chemistry)
Photonics
Physical Chemistry
Physics
Planetary and Space Sciences
Plant Sciences
Plasma Physics
Poultry Science (*see* Animal Sciences)
Radiological Physics (*see* Physics)
Range Management (*see* Range Science)
Range Science
Resource Management (*see* Environmental Management and Policy; Natural Resources)
Solid-Earth Sciences (*see* Geosciences)
Space Sciences (*see* Planetary and Space Sciences)
Statistics
Theoretical Chemistry
Theoretical Physics
Viticulture and Enology
Water Resources

Graduate Programs in Engineering & Applied Sciences

Aeronautical Engineering (*see* Aerospace/Aeronautical Engineering)
Aerospace/Aeronautical Engineering
Aerospace Studies (*see* Aerospace/Aeronautical Engineering)
Agricultural Engineering
Applied Mechanics (*see* Mechanics)
Applied Science and Technology
Architectural Engineering
Artificial Intelligence/Robotics
Astronautical Engineering (*see* Aerospace/Aeronautical Engineering)
Automotive Engineering
Aviation
Biochemical Engineering
Bioengineering
Bioinformatics
Biological Engineering (*see* Bioengineering)
Biomedical Engineering
Biosystems Engineering
Biotechnology
Ceramic Engineering (*see* Ceramic Sciences and Engineering)
Ceramic Sciences and Engineering
Ceramics (*see* Ceramic Sciences and Engineering)
Chemical Engineering
Civil Engineering
Computer and Information Systems Security
Computer Engineering
Computer Science
Computing Technology (*see* Computer Science)
Construction Engineering
Construction Management
Database Systems
Electrical Engineering
Electronic Materials
Electronics Engineering (*see* Electrical Engineering)
Energy and Power Engineering
Energy Management and Policy
Engineering and Applied Sciences
Engineering and Public Affairs (*see* Technology and Public Policy)
Engineering and Public Policy (*see* Energy Management and Policy; Technology and Public Policy)
Engineering Design
Engineering Management
Engineering Mechanics (*see* Mechanics)
Engineering Metallurgy (*see* Metallurgical Engineering and Metallurgy)
Engineering Physics
Environmental Design (*see* Environmental Engineering)
Environmental Engineering
Ergonomics and Human Factors
Financial Engineering
Fire Protection Engineering
Food Engineering (*see* Agricultural Engineering)
Game Design and Development
Gas Engineering (*see* Petroleum Engineering)
Geological Engineering
Geophysics Engineering (*see* Geological Engineering)
Geotechnical Engineering
Hazardous Materials Management
Health Informatics
Health Systems (*see* Safety Engineering; Systems Engineering)
Highway Engineering (*see* Transportation and Highway Engineering)
Human-Computer Interaction
Human Factors (*see* Ergonomics and Human Factors)
Hydraulics
Hydrology (*see* Water Resources Engineering)
Industrial Engineering (*see* Industrial/Management Engineering)
Industrial/Management Engineering
Information Science
Internet Engineering
Macromolecular Science (*see* Polymer Science and Engineering)
Management Engineering (*see* Engineering Management; Industrial/Management Engineering)
Management of Technology
Manufacturing Engineering
Marine Engineering (*see* Civil Engineering)
Materials Engineering
Materials Sciences
Mechanical Engineering
Mechanics
Medical Informatics
Metallurgical Engineering and Metallurgy
Metallurgy (*see* Metallurgical Engineering and Metallurgy)
Mineral/Mining Engineering
Modeling and Simulation
Nanotechnology
Nuclear Engineering
Ocean Engineering
Operations Research
Paper and Pulp Engineering
Petroleum Engineering
Pharmaceutical Engineering
Plastics Engineering (*see* Polymer Science and Engineering)
Polymer Science and Engineering
Public Policy (*see* Energy Management and Policy; Technology and Public Policy)
Reliability Engineering
Robotics (*see* Artificial Intelligence/Robotics)
Safety Engineering
Software Engineering
Solid-State Sciences (*see* Materials Sciences)
Structural Engineering
Surveying Science and Engineering
Systems Analysis (*see* Systems Engineering)
Systems Engineering
Systems Science
Technology and Public Policy
Telecommunications
Telecommunications Management
Textile Sciences and Engineering
Textiles (*see* Textile Sciences and Engineering)
Transportation and Highway Engineering
Urban Systems Engineering (*see* Systems Engineering)
Waste Management (*see* Hazardous Materials Management)
Water Resources Engineering

Graduate Programs in Business, Education, Information Studies, Law & Social Work

Accounting
Actuarial Science
Adult Education